WHO'S WHO
IN WORLD JEWRY

WHO'S WHO IN WORLD JEWRY

A Biographical Dictionary of Outstanding Jews

I. J. CARMIN KARPMAN

Chief Editor

WHO'S WHO IN WORLD JEWRY, *Incorporated*

Published by PITMAN PUBLISHING CORPORATION, INC.

New York, London, Toronto, Melbourne, Johannesburg, Tel Aviv

CONTENTS

———

INTRODUCTION

WHO'S WHO IN WORLD JEWRY, from its inception, was meant to fill the need for an authoritative record of notable Jews. This need is even greater now as a result of the increased unity between Jews that came about after June 1967. This new edition has been prepared to succeed the first two editions published in 1955 and 1965. But a growing closeness between Diaspora and Israeli Jews is reflected in this new third edition which was edited and printed entirely in the State of Israel, with the help of an editorial office in New York City.

An enormous amount of time and effort went into the compilation of this book. The immense task of contacting people and organizations to recommend nominees started in 1968. The gathering, compiling and processing of the data was painstaking, with constant, time-consuming checking and rechecking. Every effort was made to produce material as up-to-date as possible. Added to other difficulties, this is a record of a dynamic people, prominent in many fields, and constantly on the path of progress and advancement all over the world.

The personalities included were selected on the basis of their influence, positions, and accomplishments, and the data used was supplied by them. Many people who should have been included have not been, simply because in many cases, we received no data from them. Needless to say, the length of the biography is no indication of the relative importance of the subject, but merely depends on the editors' assessment of the relevance of the data submitted.

There are some 14 million Jews in the world today. This work includes some 10,000 biographies. The bulk of the subjects naturally come from the two major free centers of Jewish life today: Israel and the United States. There are also persons included from almost every country where Jews live, with two notable exceptions: the Soviet Union and the Arab countries.

It is the deep regret of the editors, that we could not obtain information about an estimated 3 million Jews living in the Soviet Union, as well as those Jews yet remaining in the once flourishing communities of the Arab countries. This of course is the major tragedy of the Jewish people today.

Especially gratifying to the editors is that this volume includes many more Israelis, often not well known outside their country, but already making their influence felt on World Jewry. We are also happy to welcome a new generation of Jewish leaders who have emerged since 1965.

A brief word on how to read this book: each biography starts with the subject's name, country of residence, occupation, place and date of birth, parents' names, with mother's maiden name in parentheses, followed by the father's last name, if it is different than that of the subject. Length of time in country of residence is indicated in cases of immigration. Higher education, including honorary degrees, and the names of wife and children follow.

The second sentence begins with the subject's present position, followed by his previous positions, usually in chronological order. Then come principal contributions, such as authorship, discoveries, patents or international and communal achievements. Indicated next are military, civic, and social activities. Books and other writings by the subject are recorded. Following is a listing of awards and honors he or she received. Hobbies or special interests follow. Finally, the subject's home and office addresses are given, as authorized by the biographees.

In the transliteration of Hebrew words, the editors tried to make them understandable to an English-reading public. A list of the most commonly used abbreviations is provided.

The editors wish to thank the many people who helped to produce this book. Although a great deal of conscientious and painstaking work has gone into this biographical dictionary, the editors know that, despite their best efforts to produce an accurate and comprehensive work, it may have faults of both omission and commission. At the same time we hope that this book will be a useful tool to the many who, we are sure, will continue to use it.

ACKNOWLEDGMENTS

MR. HARRY J. ALDERMAN, New York, N.Y.
Librarian, American Jewish Committee

MR. JONATHAN BATNITZKY, Johannesburg
Journalist

PROF. IMMANUEL BEN-DOR, Atlanta, Ga.
Professor Archaeology, Emory University

MR. ISRAEL BILECKY, Tel Aviv
Author, poet, lecturer Yiddish literature, Tel Aviv University

MR. BERNARD BROWNSTEIN, New York, N.Y.
President, Congregation Zichron Ephraim

RABBI EMMANUEL BULZ, Luxembourg
Chief Rabbi of Luxembourg

MR. SAADIAH CHERNIAK, New York, N.Y.
Executive Director, American Friends of the Alliance Israelite Universelle

DR. NATHAN ANDRE CHOURAQUI, Jerusalem
Counsellor on resettlement to Prime Minister's Office

RABBI JACK J. COHEN, Jerusalem
Director, B'nai B'rith Hillel Foundation, Hebrew University

MR. NINO COVO, Mexico
Former President, B'nai B'rith

MR. HERSH Z. CYNOWICZ, Bombay
Chairman, Central Jewish Board

MR. JOSEPH EZEKIEL, Singapore
Honorary Secretary, Jewish Welfare Board

DR. ABRAHAM N. FRANZBLAU, New York, N.Y.
Psychiatrist

MR. MOSHE GALLI, Paris
Director for Europe, State of Israel Bonds

MR. HANOCH GIVTON, Jerusalem
Director General, Israel Ministry of Tourism

PROF. MAX GOTTSCHALK, Belgium
Professor Sociology, University of Brussels

MR. YOSEF D. GUR-ARIEH, Tel Aviv,
Deputy Director General, Israel Investment Authority

Acknowledgments

MR. JULES HOROWITZ, Givatayim
President, Israel Skal Club

MISS FLORENCE HUTNER, Toronto
Director, Joint National Committee on Community Services of Canadian Jewish Congress and Canadian Committee of CJFWF

MR. SAMUEL KLIPPEL, New Zealand
Past President, Zionist Council

MR. MARCUS D. KOPNIWSKY, Sweden
Managing Director, Jewish Community of Stockholm

DR. HANS LAMM, Germany
Literary Director, Ner Tamid Verlag, Frankfurt/M.

RABBI DR. CHARLES C. LEHRMANN, Germany
Chief Rabbi of West Berlin

MR. ZVI LEVAVY, New York, N.Y.
C.P.A.

MR. RAPHAEL LEVY, New York, N.Y.
Director, Public Relations, United Jewish Appeal

MR. JULIUS MARGOLINSKY, Denmark
Librarian, Jewish Community, Copenhagen

MR. MAX MAZAR-BARNETT, Argentina
President, Latin American District, B'nai B'rith

MR. MAX MAZIN, Spain
President, Jewish Community of Madrid

MR. OSKAR MENDELSOHN, Norway
Board Member, Jewish Community of Oslo

DR. ASHER MOISSIS, Athens
Hon. Diplomatic Representative of Israel in Greece

MR. JUAN PLAUT, Venezuela
Former President, B'nai B'rith

MR. HILARY H. PRYER, Sydney
Chairman, Australasian Council, B'nai B'rith

MR. EMIL RAAS, Switzerland
President, Jewish Community of Bern

RABBI MOSES DE CASTRO SASSO, Virgin Islands
Rabbi, Hebrew Congregation of St. Thomas

MR. VICTOR B. SEMAH, Athens
Director, Vocational Jewish Institution

DR. ISIDORE SIMON, Paris
Founder, Societe d'Histoire de la Medecine Hebraique

MR. JOACHIM SIMON, New York, N.Y.
Secretary, Encyclopaedia Judaica Research Foundation

Acknowledgments

RABBI DR. JOSEPH P. STERNSTEIN, Roslyn Heights, N.Y.
Rabbi, Temple Beth Sholom

DR. GERHARD TAUSSIG, Amsterdam
Executive Director, Jewish Social Work Foundation

MR. MAURICE WAGNER, Bulawayo
General Secretary, Rhodesian Jewish Board of Deputies

MR. VICTOR J. ZIRINSKY, Hong Kong
Hon. Consul of Israel

Editorial Board

ADVISORY COUNCIL

Advisory Council

DR. WILLIAM HABER, President,
American ORT Federation

MR. CARLOS L. ISRAELS, President,
United HIAS Service

MRS. CHARLOTTE JACOBSON, President,
Hadassah

MR. JOSEPH KARASICK, President,
Union of Orthodox Jewish Congregations of America

MRS. ROSE KAUFMAN, President,
Pioneer Women

DR. ARTHUR J. LELYVELD, President,
American Jewish Congress

JUDGE LOUIS E. LEVINTHAL, Former Chairman,
Board of Governors, Hebrew University, Jerusalem

DR. ISAAC LEWIN, Chairman,
American Section, Agudas Israel World Organization

RABBI ISRAEL MILLER, Chairman,
American Zionist Federation

MR. NEWTON N. MINOW, Former Chairman,
Federal Communications Commission

DR. EMANUEL NEUMANN, Chairman,
Jewish Agency

RABBI MAX NUSSBAUM, Chairman,
American Section, World Jewish Congress

DR. JOACHIM PRINZ, Chairman,
Governing Council, World Jewish Congress

MR. HENRY N. RAPAPORT, President,
United Synagogue of America

DR. NATHAN REICH, Chairman,
Yivo Institute for Jewish Research

RABBI JACOB PHILIP RUDIN, President,
Synagogue Council of America

MR. NATHAN SAPERSTEIN, President,
National Council of Young Israel

MR. DORE SCHARY, National Chairman,
Anti-Defamation League of B'nai B'rith

INTERNATIONAL PUBLICATION COMMITTEE

International Publication Committee

PROF. BENJAMIN MAZAR, Jerusalem, Israel, Former President,
Hebrew University

MR. DARIUS MILHAUD, Paris, France, Oakland, California
Composer

MRS. KADIA MOLODOWSKY-LEW, New York
Poetess

DR. JOSEPH R. NAROT, Miami, Florida, Rabbi,
Temple Israel of Greater Miami

RABBI MORTON H. NARROWE, Stockholm, Sweden,
Rabbi of Stockholm

MR. LAWRENCE D. NATHAN, Auckland, New Zealand, Chairman,
United Synagogues of New Zealand

DR. MOSES ROSEN, Bucharest, Rumania, Chief Rabbi and President,
Federation of Jewish Communities in Rumania

DR. T. SCHNEIDER, Johannesburg, South Africa, President,
South Africa Jewish Board of Deputies

MR. LEONARD N. SIMONS, Detroit, Michigan, Member,
Board of Dirctors, National Conference of Christians and Jews

MR. GILEL STORCH, Stockholm, Sweden, President,
Swedish Section, World Jewish Congress

MR. MELICH TOPIOL, Paris, France, President,
United Israel Appeal

MR. JULIAN B. VENEZKY, Peoria, Illinois, National Chairman
for Regions, State of Israel Bonds

SIR ISAAC WOLFSON, Bt, London, England, Hon. President,
Weizmann Institute of Science Foundation

ISRAEL HONORARY
COMITTEE

LIST OF ABBREVIATIONS

AA, Associate in Arts

AAAS, American Association for the Advancement of Science

AACI, Association of Americans & Canadians in Israel

AAUP, American Association of University Professors

AB/BA, Bachelor of Arts

ABC, American Broadcasting Corporation

ACA, American Contemporary Arts

acad, academy, academic

acct, account

acctnt, accountant, accounting

ACLU, American Civil Liberties Union

ADA, Americans for Democratic Action

adj, adjunct

ADL, Anti-Defamation League of B'nai B'rith

adm, admiral

admn, administration, administrative

admnr, administrator

adv, advisor, advisory

advt, advertising

AEC, Atomic Energy Commission

AFL-CIO, American Federation of Labor-Congress of Industrial Organizations

Afr, Africa, African

AG, Aktien Gesellschaft

agcy, agency

agric, agriculture, agricultural

agron, agronomical, agronomist

agt, agent

AHA, American Heart Association

AJComm, American Jewish Committee

AJCong, American Jewish Congress

Ala, Alabama

AMA, American Medical Association

ambass, ambassador

Amer, America, American

anat, anatomical, anatomist, anatomy

anthol, anthology

AP, Associated Press

appd, appointed

Apr, April

apt, apartment

ARC, American Red Cross

archaeol, archaeological, archaeologist, archaeology

Arg, Argentina, Argentinian

Ariz, Arizona

Ark, Arkansas

AS, Associate in Science

ASCAP, American Society of Composers, Authors, Publishers

assn, association

asso, associate, associated

asst, assistant

att, attended, attending

atty, attorney

Aug, August

Aus, Austria

Austr, Australia

auth, authority

ave, avenue

AZC, American Zionist Council

b. born

B, Bachelor

BA, Bachelor of Arts

BAcc, Bachelor of Accounting

bact, bacteriologist, bacteriology

BAO, Bachelor of Obstetrics

BArch, Bachelor of Architecture

BAS, Bachelor of Agricultural Science

BBA, Bachelor of Business Administration

BBB, Better Business Bureau

BBC, British Broadcasting Corporation

Bc, broadcasting

BC, British Columbia, Companion of the Bath

BCE, Bachelor of Civil Engineering

BCh, Bachelor of Chemistry

BChE, Bachelor of Chemical Engineering

BCL, Bachelor of Civil Law

BCom, Bachelor of Commerce

BCS, Bachelor of Commercial Science

bd, board

BD, Bachelor of Divinity

BDS, Bachelor of Dental Surgery

BE, Bachelor of Education

BEcon, Bachelor of Economics

BEE, Bachelor of Electrical Engineering

BFA, Bachelor of Fine Arts

BHL, Bachelor of Hebrew Literature

bibl, biblical

biol, biological, biologist, biology

BJ, Bachelor of Jurisprudence

BJE, Bachelor of Jewish Education

BJour, Bachelor of Journalism

BJP, Bachelor of Jewish Pedagogy

Bklyn, Brooklyn

BL, Bachelor of Literature

BLA, Bachelor of Landscape Architecture

bldg, building

BLit, Bachelor of Literature

BLL, Bachelor of Law

BLS, Bachelor of Library Science

blvd, boulevard

BMA, British Medical Association

BME, Bachelor of Mechanical Engineering

BMus, Bachelor of Music

BO, Bachelor of Oratory

BP, Bachelor of Painting

BPd, Bachelor of Pedagogy

BPE, Bachelor of Physical Education

br, branch

BRE, Bachelor of Religious Education

brig, brigade, brigadier

Brit, Britain, British

bros, brothers

BS, BSc Bachelor of Science

BSA, Bachelor of Science of Administration

BSE, Bachelor of Science of Engineering

BSL, Bachelor of Science of Law

BSS, Bachelor of Social Science

BTh, Bachelor of Theology

bull, bulletin

bur, bureau

bus, business

BWI, British West Indies

Bx, Bronx

c. child, children

CA, Chartered Accountant

CAA, Civil Aeronautics Administration

CAB, Civil Aeronautics Board

Cal, California

Can, Canada, Canadian

capt, captain

card, cardiology, cardiologist, cardiological

CARE, Cooperative of American Remittances to Europe

CB, Companion of the Bath

CBE, Commander of the Order of the British Empire

CBS, Columbia Broadcasting System

C of C, Chamber of Commerce

CCAR, Central Conference of American Rabbis

CCNY, City College of New York

CD, DS, Doctor of Surgery

cdr, commander

CE, Civil Engineer

cen, center, central

cent, century

cert, certificate, certification, certified, certify

chap, chapter

ChB, Bachelor of Surgery

chem, chemical, chemistry, chemist

comm, committee

commn, commission

commnr, commissioner

conv, convention

coop, cooperative, cooperation

coord, coordinator, coordination, coordinated

corp, corporation

corresp, correspondent, corresponding, correspondence

CPA, Certified Public Accountant

CPH, Certified in Public Health

cpl, corporal

CUNY, City University of New York

CZ, Canal Zone

Czech, Czechoslovakia, Czechoslovakian

d. daughter

D, Doctor (degree)

DAgr, Doctor of Agriculture

DAJA, Delegation of Argentinian Jewish Organizations

DArch, Doctor of Architecture

DC, District of Columbia

DCH, Doctor of Chemistry

DCL, Doctor of Civil Law

DCom, Doctor of Commerce

DCS, Doctor of Commercial Science

DD, Doctor of Divinity

DDS, Doctor of Dental Surgery

DE, Doctor of Education

Dec, December

decd, deceased

DEcon, Doctor of Economics

deg, degree

Del, Delaware

delg, delegate, delegation

dem, democrat, democratic

Den, Denmark

DEng, DEngr, Doctor of Engineering

dent, dentist, dentistry, dental

dep, deputy

dept, department

dermat, dermatological, dermatologist, dermatology

desc, descendant

Des Lettres, Doctor of Letters

devl, develop, developer, development

DFA, Doctor of Fine Arts

DFC, Distinguished Flying Cross

DHC, Doctor Honoris Causa

DHL, Doctor of Hebrew Literature, Hebrew Letters

DHum, Doctor of Humanities

DHumL, Doctor of Humane Letters

dict, dictionary

dipl, diploma, diplomate, diplomat

dir, director

dist, distinguished, district

div, divison, divorced

DJS, Doctor of Juristic Science

DJur, DJ, Doctor of Jurisprudence

DL, DLitt, Doctor of Literature

DLS, Doctor of Library Science

DM, Doctor of Medicine

DMath, Doctor of Mathematics

DMD, Doctor of Medical Dentistry

DMS, Doctor of Medical Science

DMus, Doctor of Music

DNB, Dictionary of National Biography

DO, Doctor of Osteopathy, Doctor of Ophthalmology

DP, Displaced Person

DPed, Doctor of Pedagogy

DPhil, Doctor of Philology

DPM, Diploma in Psychological Medicine

dr, doctor, drive

DRE, Doctor of Religious Education

DRerPol, Doctor Rerum Politicum

DS, DSc, Doctor of Science

DSC, Distinguished Service Cross

DSM, Doctor of Science of Medicine

DSO, Companion of Distinguished Service Order

DSS, Doctor of Social Science

DST, Doctor of Sacred Theology

DTh, Doctor of Theology

DTM, Doctor of Tropical Medicine, Diploma in Tropical Medicine

DVM, Doctor of Veterinary Medicine

DWI, Dutch West Indies

e, east, eastern

ecol, ecological

econ, economic, economical, economist

ECOSOC, United Nations Economic and Social Welfare Council

ed, editor, edition, editorial

EdD, Education Doctor

EdnB, Bachelor of Education

elec, electric, electrical, electronic,

EE, Electrical Engineer

elem, elementary

em, emeritus

Emb, Embassy

EMICA, Section of Jewish Colonization Association

ency, encyclopedia

Eng, England, English

engr, engineer, engineering

Eur, Europe, European

EURATOM, European Atomic Energy Commission

exch, Exchange

exec, executive

exhb, exhibit, exhibition

ext, extension

f, fellow, fellowship

FAA, Federal Aviation Agency

fac, faculty

FACCA, Fellow, Association of Certified and Corporate Accountants

FACP, Fellow, American College of Physicians

FBI, Federal Bureau of Investigation

FCC, Federal Communications Commission

FCDA, Federal Civil Defense Administration

FDA, Food and Drug Administration

Feb, February

Fed, federal, federation, federated

fgn, foreign

FGSM, fellow, Guildhall School of Music

FJP, Federation of Jewish Philanthropies

Fla, Florida

fmr, former, formerly

found, foundation, founder, founding

Fr, France, French

frat, fraternity

FRCP, Fellow, Royal College of Physicians

FRCS, Fellow, Royal College of Surgeons

FRFPS, Fellow, Royal Faculty of Physicians and Surgeons

FRIC, Fellow, Royal Institute of Chemistry

FRSM, Fellow, Royal Society of Medicine

FSA, Federal Security Agency

FSAA, Fellow, Society of Accountants and Auditors

FTC, Federal Trade Commission, Federal Tariff Commission

Ga, Georgia

gal, gallery

gen, general

genet, geneticist, genetics, genetical

geog, geographic, geographical, geography

geophys, geophysical, geophysicist, geophysics

Ger, German, Germany

GM, General Motors

gov, governor

govt, government

grad, graduate

gt, great

Gt Brit, Great Britain

gtr, greater

Guat, Guatemala

gyn, gynecological, gynecologist, gynecology

HC, Honoris Causa

Heb, Hebrew

HEW, US Dept of Health, Education and Welfare

hgts, heights

HI, Hawaiian Islands

HIAS, Hebrew Sheltering and Immigrant Aid Society

HICEM, HIAS and Jewish Colonization Emigration Association

hist, historian, historical, history

HM, Her Majesty, His Majesty

hon, honorable, honorary

hons, honors

hosp, hospital

hqr, headquarters

HS, high school
HUC, Hebrew Union College
hum, humanities, human
Hung, Hungarian, Hungary
hwy, highway

I, Island
Ia, Iowa
IAF, Israel Air Force
IBM, International Business Machines
i/c, in charge
ICA, Jewish Colonization Association
ICC, Interstate Commerce Commission
IDF, Israel Defense Forces
IE, Industrial Engineer
IJFL, Israel-Japan Friendship League
ILGWU, International Ladies' Garment Workers' Union
Ill, Illinois
illus, illustrated, illustration, illustrator
ILO, International Labor Organization
IMA, Israel Medical Association
IMF, International Monetary Fund
inc, incorporated
Ind, Indiana, industry, industrial, industrialist
info, information
Ing, Engineer (Degree)
ins, insurance
insp, inspector
inst, institute
instn, institution
instr, instructor
instrn, instruction
intl, international
inves, investigation, investor, investment
Ir, Ireland, Irish
IRO, International Refugee Organization
IS, Intelligence Service
Isr, Israel
It, Italian, Italy

J, Jew(s), Jewish
JA, Jewish Agency

Jan, January
J App, Jewish Appeal
JBCA, Jewish Book Council of America
JCC, Jewish Community Council
JD, Doctor of Jurisprudence
JDC, American Joint Distribution Committee
JDS, Doctor of Juristic Science
JIAS, Jewish Immigrant Aid Society
JIR, Jewish Institute of Religion
JNF, Jewish National Fund
jour, journal
JP, Justice of the Peace
JPA, Joint Palestine Appeal
jr, junior
jt, joint
JTA, Jewish Telegraph Agency
JTSA, Jewish Theological Seminary of America
jud, judicial
JUD, Juris Utrisque Doctor
JWB, National Jewish Welfare Board
JWF, Jewish Welfare Fund, Federation
JWO, Jewish Welfare Organization
JWV, Jewish War Veternas

Kan, Kansas
KBE, Knight Commander, Order of the British Empire
KCB, Knight Commander of the Bath
KH, Keren Hayesod
KP, Knights of Pythias
Ky, Kentucky

La, Louisiana
LA, Los Angeles
lab, labor, laboratory
lang, language
LDS, Licentiate, Dental Surgery
Leb, Lebanese, Lebanon
lectr, lecturer
leg, legislator, legislature, legislative, legislation
LGSM, Licentiate, Guildhall School of Music
LHD, Doctor of Humane Letters
LI, Long Island

lib, liberal

libr, librarian, library

ling, linguist, linguistic

lit, literature, literary

Lith, Lithuania, Lithuanian

LIU, Long Island University

LLB, Bachelor of Laws

LLD, Doctor of Laws

LLM, Master of Laws

LM, Licentiate, Medicine, Midwifery

LMCC, Licentiate, Medical Council of Canada

LMSSA, Licentiate, Medical and Surgical Society of Apothecaries

L of N, League of Nations

LRCP, Licentiate, Royal College of Physicians

LRCS, Licentiate, Royal College of Surgeons

LRFPS, Licentiate, Royal Faculty of Physicians and Surgeons

LS, Library Science

LSE, London School of Economics

lt, lieutenant

Ltd, limited

LZOA, Labor Zionist Organization of America

m. married

M, Master (Degree)

MA, Master of Arts

mag, magazine

MAgr, Master of Agriculture

maj, major

Man, Manitoba

Mar, March

MArch, Master of Architecture

Mass, Massachusetts

math, mathematical, mathematician, mathematics

MB, Bachelor of Medicine

MBA, Master of Business Administration

MBE, Member of the Order of the British Empire

MBS, Mutual Broadcasting System

MC, Master of Surgery, Military Cross, Medical Corps

MCE, Master of Civil Engineering

MCom, Master of Commerce

Md, Maryland

MCS, Master of Commercial Science

MD, Doctor of Medicine

MDip, Master of Diplomacy

Me, Maine

ME, Mechanical Engineer, Middle East

mech, mechanical, mechanics

med, medical, medicine

MEd, Master of Education

MEE, Master of Electrical Engineering

mem, member, membership

metrop, metropolitan, metropolis

Mex, Mexico

MF, Master of Forestry

MFA, Master of Fine Arts

mfg, manufacturing

mfr, manufacturer

MGM, Metro-Goldwyn-Mayer

mgmt, management

mgn, managing

mgr, manager

Mh, Mental Health

MHA, Master of Hospital Administration

MHL, Master of Hebrew Literature, Hebrew Letters

MHumL Master of Humane Letters

MIA, Master of International Affairs

Mich, Michigan

microbiol, microbiological, microbiologist, microbiology

mil, military

Milw, Milwaukee

min, minister, ministry, ministerial

Minn, Minnesota

Miss, Mississippi

MIT, Massachusetts Institute of Technology

MJ, Master of Jurisprudence

MK, Member of Knesset

ML, Master of Law

MLA, Modern Language Association of America

MLitt, Master of Literature

MLS, Master of Library Science

MME, Master of Mechanical Engineering

MMus, Master of Music

Mo, Missouri

MO, Medical Officer

MOH, Medical Officer of Health

Mont, Montana

MP, Member of Parliament

MPA, Master of Public Administration

MPed, Master of Pedagogy

MPh, Master of Philosophy

MPH, Master of Public Health

MPharm, Master of Pharmacy

MPS, Member, Pharmaceutical Society

MRCP, Member, Royal College of Physicians

MRCS, Member, Royal College of Surgeons

MRE, Master of Religious Education

MS, MSc, Master of Science

MSS, Master of Social Science

MST, Master of Sacred Theology

MSW, Master of Social Work

mt, mount, mountain

MTh, Master of Theology

munic, municipal, municipality

mus, museum

MVD, Master of Veterinary Medicine

N, North, northern

NAACP, National Association for Advancement of Colored People

NACA, National Advisory Council for Aeronautics

NAM, National Association of Manufacturers

NASA, National Aeronautics and Space Administration

natl, national

NATO, North Atlantic Treaty Organization

NB, New Brunswick (Canada)

NBC, National Broadcasting Company

NC, North Carolina

NCCJ, National Conference of Christians and Jews

ND, North Dakota

NDRC, National Defense Research Commission

NE, New England

NEA, National Education Association

Neb, Nebraska

neur, neurological, neurologist, neurology

Nev, Nevada

NF, Newfoundland

NH, New Hampshire

NIH, National Institute of Health

NJ, New Jersey

NLRB, National Labor Relations Board

NM, New Mexico

Nor, Norway, Norwegian

Nov, November

NRC, National Research Council

NS, Nova Scotia

NSC, National Security Council

NSF, National Science Foundation

NSW, New South Wales

NY, New York,

NYC, New York City,

NYU, New York University

NZ, New Zealand

O, Ohio

OBE, Officer of the Order of the British Empire

obstet, obstetrical, obstetrician, obstetrics

Oct, October

OD, Doctor of Optometry

OEO, Office of Economic Opportunity

off, office, officer

Okla, Oklahoma

Ont, Ontario

OPA, Office of Price Administration

ophthal, ophthalmological, ophthalmologist, ophthalmology

opr, operations

orch, orchestra

Ore, Oregon

org, organization, organizer

orl, otorhinolaryngology, otorhinolaryngologist

orthol, orthological, orthologist, orthology

OSE, Oeuvre de Secours aux Enfants

osteo, osteopathic

OTC, Officers Training Corps

OWI, Office of War Information

Pa, Pennsylvania

Pal, Palestine, Palestinian

parl, parliament

path, pathologist, pathological, pathology

PdM, Master of Pedagogy

ped, pediatrician, pediatric

pedg, pedagogue, pedagogy, pedagogical

PEN, Poets, Playwrights, Editors, Essayists and Novelists

penol, penological

perm, permanent

pharm, pharmacology, pharmacy, pharmacist

PharmB, Bachelor of Pharmacy

PharmD, Doctor of Pharmacy

PharmG, Graduate of Pharmacy

PharmM, Master of Pharmacy

PhB, Bachelor of Philosophy

PhC, Pharmaceutical Chemist

PhD, Doctor of Philosophy

phil, philosophical, philosopher, philosophy

Phila, Philadelphia

philol, philologist, philology

phys, physical, physician, physiology, physiological

PJCA, Palestine Jewish Colonization Association

pkwy, parkway

pl, place

plen, plenipotentiary

PM, Prime Minister

PMO, Principal Medical Officer

PO, Post Office

Pol, Poland, Polish

poly, polytechnic

Port, Portugal, Portuguese

Postdoc, postdoctoral, postdoctorate

PR, public relations

prep, preparatory

pres, president, presidential

prin, principal, principle

proc, proceedings

produc, producer, production

prof, professor

profsl, professional

prog, program

prop, proprietor

prot, protestant

pseud, pseudonym

psych, psychological, psychology

psychan, psychoanalyst, psychoanalysis

psychol, psychologist

psycht, psychiatrist, psychiatry

PTA, Parent-Teacher Association

Pty, Proprietary

pub, published, publishing

publ, publication

pvt, private

QC, Queen's Counsel

Que, Quebec

RA, Rabbinical Assembly of America

Rabb, Rabbinical, Rabbinics

RabCA, Rabbinical Council of America

RAF, Royal Air Force

RAM, Royal Academy of Music

RAMC, Royal Army Medical Corps

RASC, Royal Army Service Corps

RCA, Radio Corporation of America

RCAF, Royal Canadian Air Force

rd, road

recd, received

ref, refugee

reg, registered, register

rehab, rehabilitation

rel, religion, religious

rep, republic, republican

repr, representative

res, reserve(s), resident

ret, retired

rev, reverend, revised, revision, review

RGS, Royal Geographic Society

RI, Rhode Island

RKO, Radio Keith Orpheum

RN, Registered Nurse

ROTC, Reserve Officers Training Corps

RR, railroad, railway

RTC, Reserve Training Corps

Rt Hon, Right Honorable
Rum, Rumania, Rumanian
Russ, Russia, Russian

s. son
S, South, southern
SA, Societe Anonyme
SAC, Strategic Air Command
Sask, Saskatchewan
Sc, Societe Cooperative
SC, South Carolina
sch, school
sci, science, scientific, scientist
SD, South Dakota
SEATO, South East Asia Treaty Organization
SEC, Securities and Exchange Commission
sect, section
secy, secretary
sem, seminary, seminar
sen, senate
Sep, September
SF, San Francisco
sgt, sergeant
SMO, Surgical Medical Officer
soc, society
social, sociological, sociologist, sociology
Span, Spanish
spec, special
sq, square
sr, senior
st, saint, street
Sta, station
stat, statistical, statistician, statistics
STD, Doctor of Sacred Theology
SUNY, State University of New York
sup, supervisor
supr, supreme
supt, superintendant
surg, surgeon, surgery, surgical
Swed, Sweden, Swedish
Switz, Switzerland
sym, symphony
syn, synagogue

sys, system

TA, Telegraphic Address
TB, Tuberculosis
tchr, teacher
TD, Territorial Decoration
tech, technical, technological, technology
temp, temporary
Tenn, Tennessee
Terr, Terrace
Tex, Texas
ThB, Bachelor of Theology
theol, theological, theology
trans, translation, translator
transp, transport, transportation
treas, treasurer
TV, televison
TVA, Tennessee Valley Authority

U, University
UA, United Appeal
UAHC, Union of American Hebrew Congregations
UCLA, University of Cal, Los Angeles
UIA, United Israel Appeal
UJA, United Jewish Appeal
UK, United Kingdom
UN, United Nations
UNESCO, United Nations Educational and Scientific Commission
UNICEF, United Nations International Childrens' Emergency Fund
UNRRA, United Nations Relief and Rehabilitation Administration
UPI, United Press International
urol, urological, urologist, urology
US, United States
USA, United States of America
USAAF, United States Army Air Force
USAC, United States Air Corps
USAF, United States Air Force
USCG, United States Coast Guard
USIA, United States Information Agency
USIS, United States Information Service
USMC, United States Marine Corps

USMCR, United States Marine Corps Reserve
USN, United States Navy
USNG, United States National Guard
USNR, United States Naval Reserve
USO, United Service Organizations
USPHS, United States Public Health Service

Va, Virginia
VA, Veterans Administration
Vet, Veteran
vetr, veterinarian, veterinary
VFW, Veterans of Foreign Wars
VI, Virgin Islands
Vic, Victoria
VOA, Voice of America
vol, volume
vs, versus
Vt, Vermont

W, West, western
WAC, Women's Air Corps, in US, Women's Army Corps
Wash, Washington

wfr, welfare
WHO, World Health Organization
Wis, Wisconsin
WIZO, Women's International Zionist Organization
WJC, World Jewish Congress
W Va, West Virginia
WW, World War
Wyo, Wyoming
WZC, World Zionist Congress
WZO, World Zionist Organization

YIVO, Yiddish Scientific Institute
YMCA, Young Men's Christian Association
YMHA, Young Men's Hebrew Association
YWHA, Young Women's Hebrew Association
Yugo, Yugoslavia

ZC, Zionist Council, Zionist Congress
ZF, Zionist Federation
ZOA, Zionist Organization of America
ZOC, Zionist Organization of Canada
zool, zoological, zoologist, zoology

BIOGRAPHIES

A

AARON, Charles, US, attorney; b. NYC, Dec 28, 1890; s. Abraham and Fannie (Charness); LLB, John Marshall Law Sch, 1911; m. Geraldine Weisfeldt, Feb 2, 1964. Sr partner, Aaron, Aaron, Schimberg & Hess and predecessor firms, since 1922; dir: Drovers Natl Bank; Mangood Corp; Agar Packing Co. Dir, fmr pres: J Fed of Metrop Chgo; JWB; J Comty Cens, Chgo; USO, Chgo; fmr dir, exec comm, Chgo chap, ARC; f, Brandeis U; mem: Citizens Bd, U Chgo and Northwestern U Assos; Chgo, Amer, Ill Bar Assns; Assn Bar, NYC; clubs: Bankers; Commercial; Mid-Day; Standard; Tavern; Lake Shore; Northmoor Country. Home: 1300 Lake Shore Dr, Chicago, Ill. Office: 38 S Dearborn St, Chicago, Ill.

AARON, Ely M, US, attorney; b. Chgo, Ill, Apr 29, 1896; s. Abraham and Fannie (Charness); att U Chgo, 1914-15; LLB, Northwestern U, 1918; m. Helen Strauss, Aug 14, 1928; c: Elizabeth, William. Pvt practice since 1919; mem, Aaron, Aaron, Schimberg & Hess and predecessor firms. US Army, WW I. Natl vice-chmn, AJComm, chmn, comm on comty affairs, hon chmn, Chgo chap; pres, J Vocational Service and Employment Cen, 1941-46; hon dir, chmn exec comm, Chgo Jt Defense Appeal campaign, 1957; natl vice-pres, chmn, Chgo Commn on Human Relations, 1960-67; chmn, Mayor's Comm on New Residents; delg, AJComm, London Conf of Hope, 1955; mem: Amer, Ill, Chgo Bar Assns; clubs: City; Mid-Day; Standard; Lake Shore Country; Harmonie. Office: 38 S Dearborn St, Chicago, Ill.

AARON, Herbert Samuel, US, research chemist; b. Minneapolis, Minn, Jan 12, 1929; s. Theodore and Marian (Bassin); BCh, U Minn, 1949; PhD, UCLA, 1953; m. Betty Levey, Mar 29, 1959; c: Marla, Rachel. Research chem: US Army Chem Research and Devl Labs, since 1956; Du Pont Co, 1953-54. US Army, 1954-56. Mem: Amer Chem Soc; Sigma Xi. Contbr to tech chem jours. Home: 7412 Kathydale Rd, Baltimore, Md.

AARON, Reuben, Austr, communal leader; b. Calcutta, India, Sep 27, 1928; s. Moses and Mozelle (Israel); in Austr since 1947; att St Josephs Coll, Calcutta; m. Cornelia Swaab, Sep 12, 1954; c: Debbie, Mandy. Clerk since 1958; clerk, Sheriff's office, 1947-50. Pres: N S Wales Assn of Sepharadim, treas, 1954-65; Sephardi Syn; mem, Masonic lodge Frank Mossong. Hobby: stamp collecting. Home: 23 Gilgandra Rd, N Bondi, NSW, Austr. Office: 179 Pitt St, Sydney, Austr.

AARONS, George, US, sculptor; b. St. Petersburg, Russ, Apr 6, 1896; s. Manuel and Marie (Diamanto); in US since 1906; att: Boston Mus Sch of Fine Arts, 1915-16; NY Beaux Arts Inst of Design, 1916-17; m. Gertrude Band, May 10, 1937. Exhbs: Inst Contemporary Art, Boston; Boston Mus Fine Arts; Busch-Reisinger Mus, Cambridge; Germanic Mus, Cambridge; Addison Gal of Amer Art, Andover, Mass; Whitney Mus Amer Art, NYC; Pa Acad and Art Alliance, Phila; 2nd and 3rd Intl Exhb Sculpture, Phila Mus; Dallas Mus Fine Arts; Cleveland Mus Art; Albright Gal, Buffalo; Corcoran Gal of Art, Wash, DC. One man shows: Guild of Boston Artist, 1948; Stuart Art Gal, Boston, 1949; Cambridge Art Assn, Mass, 1953; Collectors Corner Gal, Wash, DC, 1958; Fitchburg Art Mus, Fitchburg, Mass, 1965; Pluribus Gal, Boston, 1967; Cayuga Mus of Hist and Art, Auburn, NY, 1969; prin works: Five Heroic Figures; Old Harbor Village, S Boston; reliefs: Cincinnati Telephone Bldg; Statuette of Thomas Jefferson, Off of Secy of Treas, Wash, DC; PO, Ripley, Miss; Seifer Hall, Brandeis U; Hillel House, U Conn; facade, Baltimore Heb Cong bldg; perpetual light and memorial candle holder, Temple Shalom, Newton, Mass; portrait reliefs, Brandeis U; metal relief, Hillel House, Boston U; relief for Combined J Philanthropies Bldg, Boston; memorials: to Lincoln Kirstein, Boston Common; to Dorothy Adlow, Hilles Libr, Radcliff Coll, Cambridge; repr works: Brandeis U; Mus of Art: Ein Harod, Isr; Fitchburg; St Denis, Paris. Mem: Natl Sculpture Soc; Sculpture Cen. Home and studio: Eagle Road, Gloucester, Mass.

AARONS, Stuart Harry, US, attorney, business exec; b. Yonkers, NY, Sep 15, 1910; Marvin and Lillian (Geller); AB, cum laude, CCNY, 1929; LLB, cum laude, Harvard Law Sch, 1932; m. Florence Josephson, Feb 26, 1950; c: Barry, Philip. Secy, Glen Alden Corp, since 1958; fmr: vice pres, Stanley Warner Theatres Inc; house counsel, Warner Bros Pictures Inc. Lt, US Army, WW II. Vice pres, Riverdale J Cen; mem: Harvard Club of NYC; Assn Bar, NYC; Phi Beta Kappa; club, Harvard, NYC. Recipient: Bronze Star. Home: 4425 Henry Hudson Pkwy, New York, NY. Office: 1740 Broadway, New York, NY.

AARONSOHN, Michael, US, rabbi; b. Baltimore, Md, July 5, 1896; s. Nathan and Hannah (Bass); att Johns Hopkins U, 1920; AB, Cincinnati, 1923; ordained rabbi, HUC, 1923; att U Chgo, 1924; m. Rachel Zemon, June 4, 1930; c: Miriam, Elizabeth, Jonathan. Spec duty, HUC, since 1931; natl field repr, UAHC, 1923-31; natl chaplain, Disabled Amer Vet, 1921-27; 37th Div Assn, WW I, 1935; VFW, 1942-43; dept chaplain, O Amer Legion, 1948. Sgt to maj, WW I, 1917-18. Co-found, life mem, exec bd, J Braille Inst; mem: Hamilton Co Council Retarded Children, pres, 1948, 1952, 1953, 1954; War Blind Comm; B'nai B'rith; CCAR; adv council, div mental hygiene, O Dept Public Wfr; Amer Legion; club: Hamilton Co Rep. Author: Broken Lights, 1946; Red Pottage, 1956. Recipient: Purple Heart, 1918. Home: 7637 Greenland Pl, Cincinnati, O.

AARONSOHN, Yedidya, Isr, engineer; b. Zichron Yaakov, Isr, Aug 5, 1912; s. Samuel and Miryam (Sternberg); elec-mech engr, Ecole Breguet, Paris, 1934; mech engr, Nancy U, Nancy, Fr, 1935; m. Yehosheva Gross, Apr 13, 1948; c: Samuel, Amazia. Chief insp, div, dir, lab inspection, Min of Lab, Jerusalem, since 1949; engr, Pal Elec Co, 1937-43; insp, lab, Pal Govt, 1943-48. Capt, IAF, 1948-49. Contbr to profsl jours. Home: 6 Alkalay St, Jerusalem. Isr. Office: Min of Lab, Hakirya, Jerusalem, Isr.

AARONSON, Alfred E, US, business exec; b. NYC, Oct 31, 1893; s. Lionel and Cynthia (Rabinowitz); att Columbia Coll; m. Millicent Lubetkin, Oct 5, 1915; c: Grace Goldin, Alice Zlotnick. Pres, fmr vice-pres, Court Arcade Bldg Co, since 1924; dir: Fourth Natl Bank, since 1961; Rassco Isr Corp, Isr, since 1961; fmr pres, Commonwealth Co; vice-pres, Leavell Coal Co. Fmr chmn, City Co Libr Commn, 1960-67; dir, Gilcrease Inst Amer Hist and Art, frm pres, chmn bd; fmr pres: Tulsa JCC; Tulsa Bldg Owners and Mgrs Assn; mem, exec comm, SW Cen Human Relations Studies, U Okla, since 1961; mem: ZOA, life; B'nai B'rith; B'nai Emunah Cong; Masons; Shriners; fmr: mem, Tulsa Human Relations Commn; hon mem: Will Rogers Rotary; Okla Human Rights Comm; Downtown Lions. Recipient, awards: Tulsa JCC, 1955; Urban League, 1963; NCCJ, 1964; hon alumnus, Langston U, Okla, 1966; U Okla, 1966; Tulsa Co Hist Soc, 1966; Tulsa Co Commn, 1967; City of Tulsa, 1967. Hobbies: art, fishing. Home: 1782 E 30 St, Tulsa, Okla. Office: Court Arcade Bldg, Tulsa, Okla.

ABBELL, Fannie E, US, business exec, communal worker; b. Chgo, Ill, Feb 21, 1902; d. Michael and Rachel (Levy) Edelman; m. Maxwell Abbell, Aug 23, 1923, (decd); c: Samuel, Nahami, Miriam Rosenblum, Ruth Ben-Jehuda, Michael. Chmn bd: Abbell Mgmt Co, since 1957; bd pres, Willard Hotel Operating Co, Wash, since 1957; partner: Russ Bldg, SF, since 1955; Sutter Bldg, Shell Towers, Montreal. Bd trustees, Chgo women's div, Amer Friends Heb U; bd dirs: Chgo div, JNF, JTSA; chmn bd, pres, Abbell Family Found. Recipient: Louis Marshall award, JTSA, 1958; woman of valor award, Isr Bonds, 1960; dist service award, JNF, 1961; Ben Gurion award, 1961; natl benefactors award, JTSA; bronze medal, Isr Bonds, 1968. Home and office: 1040 Lake Shore Dr, Chicago, Ill.

ABEL, Elie, US, journalist; b. Montreal, Can, Oct 17, 1920; s. Jacob and Rose (Spitchinetzky); in US since 1947; BA, McGill U, 1941; MS, Columbia U, 1942; m. Corinne Prevost,

Jan 28, 1946; c: Mark, Suzanne. Dean, Grad Sch Journalism, Columbia U, since 1970; corresp: UN Overseas News Agcy, 1947-49; natl and fgn, NY Times, 1949-59; Wash bur chief, The Detroit News, 1959-61; reporter, commentator, NBC News, 1961-70. Royal Can Air Force, 1942-45. Mem: Overseas Writers; Sigma Delta Chi; clubs: Garrick, London; Fed City, Wash; Natl Press. Author: The Missile Crisis, 1966; co-author, The Kennedy Circle, 1961; contbr to: The Reporter; NY Times Mag; The New Leader. Recipient: Pulitzer Traveling scholarship, 1942; George Foster Peabody award, 1968. Office: Columbia U, New York, NY.

ABEL, Reuben, US, educator, business exec; b. NYC, Nov 25, 1911; s. Louis and Dora (Friedsell); BA, Columbia U, 1929; JD, NYU, 1934, MSSc, 1941, PhD, Grad Fac, New Sch for Social Research, 1952; m. Marion Buchman, July 30, 1937; c: Richard, Elizabeth. Adj prof, phil, Grad Fac, New Sch for Social Research, since 1967; chmn, hum div, since 1965, on fac since 1950; pres, Atlas Bedspread Co Inc, 1948-61; regional unit chief, OPA, 1944-46. Mem: Amer Philosophic Assn; Phil of Sci Assn; Intl Assn for Phil of Law; Conf on Methods in Phil and Scis; AAUP; Amer Soc for Aesthetics. Author: The Pragmatic Humanism of FCS Schiller, 1955; ed, Humanistic Pragmatism, 1966. Home: 17 Monroe Ave, Larchmont, NY. Office: New Sch for Social Research, New York, NY.

ABELOFF, Abram Joseph, US, surgeon; b. NYC, Mar 19, 1900; s. Samuel and Rebecca (Rogow); BA, Columbia U, 1922, MD, 1926; m. Gertrude Kopsch, May 15, 1953; c: Tobias. Att surg, Lenox Hill Hosp, since 1954, on staff since 1930; surg, Lexington Sch for Deaf, since 1947; asso clinical prof, NYU, 1948; research asst, Inst of Path, U Freiburg, Ger, 1929; surg service: Frankfurt U, Ger; U Vienna, 1930; adj surg, Beth Isr Hosp, NY, 1930-37; asso surg, Neur Hosp, 1930-33. US Army MC, 1942-46, ret as col. Trustee: Columbia U; Assn Alumni, Coll Phys and Surgs, Columbia U, pres, 1956-57; mem: exec comm, chmn, med adv bd, JDC, 1947; adv bd, Paul Baerwald Sch Social Work, 1947; fmr pres and trustee, Phys Home, NY; dipl, Amer Bd Surg; mem: NY Surg Soc; AMA; NY Acad Med; f: Amer Coll Surgs; Brazilian Coll of Surgs; clubs: Columbia U; Grolier. Contbr to med publs. Recipient: Legion of Merit. Home: 70 E 77 St, New York, NY; summer, Warner Rd, Bridgewater, Conn. Office: 850 Park Ave, New York, NY.

ABELSON, Harold H, US, educator, author; b. NYC, Sep 25, 1904; s. Max and Jennie (Bernstein); BS, CCNY, 1924; MA, Columbia U, 1925, PhD, 1927; m. Lucie Bernard, Aug 24, 1926; c: Jane, Robert. Prof, dean, tchr educ, CUNY, since 1967, acting dean, 1966-67, dean, sch of educ, CUNY, 1952-66, asso psychol educ clinic, 1924-26, dir, 1941-52, fac mem since 1924; visiting prof: U Colo, summer, 1938; New Sch for Social Research, 1948-60; Cornell U, summers, 1949-50; Hunter Coll, summers, 1952-58; cons, Adjutant Gen Off, War Dept, 1944. Author: Improvement of Intelligence Testing, 1927; The Art of Educational Research, 1933; contbr to educ jours. F: Amer Psych Assn; AAAS; mem: Amer Educ Research Assn; AAUP; NEA; Phi Beta Kappa; Kappa Delta Pi. Recipient: Harris Medalist, City College Assn Alumni, 1962. Home: 495 Odell Ave, Yonkers, NY. Office: CUNY Grad Cen, 33 W 42 St, New York, NY.

ABELSON, Louis I, US, dentist; b. NYC, Aug 5, 1895; s. Meyer and Sara (Brainson); att: CCNY, 1916; Columbia U Dent Sch, 1918; m. Lilian Kamsly, July 14, 1932; c: Roger. Pvt practice since 1918; mem staff, Beth Isr Hosp, NYC, 1920-28. Pres: E Dent Soc, 1932-33; Allied Dent Council, 1934-36; Columbia U Dent Alumni Assn, 1945; LI Chrysanthemum Soc; gen chmn: Dent Div for UJA and FJP; prosthodontia sect, First Dist Dent Soc, 1923; comm on dent educ, 1955-59; Henry Spenadel Award comm, 1956-58; dir, Alumni Fed, Columbia U, 1947-49; treas: Amer J Dents Comm for Heb U, Isr, 1930-55; First Dist Dent Soc, 1950-59; f: Intl Coll of Dents; Omicron Kappa Upsilon; Sigma Epsilon Delta; mem: Fed Dentaire Intl; NY Acad of Sci; Amer Dent Assn; NY State Dent; E Dent Socs; Masons; NY Horticultural Soc; clubs: Men's Garden, NY; Camera, NY. Contbr: lectures, courses and papers on dent techniques. Recipient: scroll for meritorious service, Allied Dent Council, 1944; plaque, E Dental Soc, 1957. Hobbies: photography, gardening; spec interest, silver jewelry. Home: 357 Island Ave, Woodmere, NY. Office: 30 Central Park S, New York, NY.

ABILEAH, Joseph William, Isr, musician; b. Mödling, Aus, Apr 25, 1915; s. Ephraim and Miriam (Mosabowsky); in Isr since 1926; att College des Frères, Jaffa, 1930-33; m. Dinah Yarmus, July 8, 1941; c: Adiel, Daniel, Ephrath. Musician, Haifa Sym Orch, since 1950; tchr, Rubin Conservatory of Music, Haifa, since 1950; peace worker, engaged in propagating ME Fed, since 1967; govt off, Survey Dept, 1934-36; bank official, Holland Bank Union, 1936-41. Found mem, Haifa Sym Orch; bd dir, Rubin Conservatory; co-dir, Music-Universum, trustee, Abileah Fund for Culture and Arts; mem: Vegetarian Soc; Haifa br, Music Tchrs Assn; Menorah Masonic lodge; Civil Service Intl; council mem, War Registers Intl. Author: Programme Notes of Symphony Concerts, 1965-68. Recipient: Silver Medal, Ligue d'Union Latine. Spec interests: phil, theol, sociol, geog, langs. Home and office: 55A Hillel St, Haifa, Isr.

ABIR, David, Isr, engineer, educator; b. Kaunas, Lith, Apr 6, 1922; s. Zvi and Yena (Lipschitz) Abramovitz; in Isr since 1934; BSc, U London, 1949; MS, Poly Inst, Bklyn, NY, 1953, PhD, 1958. Head, dept aeronautical engr, Technion, Haifa, 1962-64, head, dept mech, 1959-61; dir, advanced aircraft studies, Isr Aircraft Ind Ltd, since 1968; chief instr, Aero Club of Pal, 1943-46; head, engr dept, IAF, 1954-55. IAF, 1949-55. Prin contrib: designer aircraft components and equipment; research aircraft structural elements at buckling high temperature and speeds. Mem: Natl Council for Civil Aviation, since 1961; pres: Isr Soc for Advancement Sci, since 1969; Isr Astronautical Soc, 1961-62; chmn, Isr Soc Aeronautical Sci, 1955-56, 1959-61, 1965-67; mem: Royal Aeronautical Soc, London; Inst AeroSpace Sci, US; Inst Mechanical Engrs, Eng; Brit Interplanetary Soc. Author: Flight Training, 1950; Aerodynamics, 1958, 1961; ed, contbr, Sky High, 1961; co-ed: Proceedings of Intl Symposium on Second Order Effects in Elasticity, Plasticity and Fluid Dynamics, 1962; Topics in Applied Mechanics, 1965; ed, Contributions to Mechanics, 1969. Recipient: Dov Hoz prize for pioneering work in aviation in Isr, 1944; Ruppin prize, 1959. Hobby: lit. Home: 113 Hagalil St, Haifa, Isr. Office: Technion, Haifa, Isr.

ABOULAFIA, Raphael, Isr, hospital admnr; b. Rishon le Zion, Isr, Mar 28, 1893; s. Shlomo and Rifka (Freiman); desc of Aboulafia family of Spain; m. Shoshana Shimonovitz, Mar 28, 1937; c: Shulamith Zifrony, Ora Joelson, Shlomo. Dir, Migdal Ladach Hosp, Jerusalem, since 1942. Sgt maj, Zion Mule Corps. Grand master, Masons, since 1969; fmr, dist gov, Lions. Recipient: Yakir Yerushalaim, 1968; Itur Lohamei Hamedinah, Min of Defense. Hobbies: numismatics; philately. Home: 7 Gan Rehavia, Jerusalem, Isr.

ABRAHAM, Alexandru Simion, Rum, physician, educator; b. Reghin, Rum, Oct 21, 1923; s. Simon and Clara (Hermann); DM, U Tirgu-Mures, Rum, 1951; m. Blima Sabau, Apr 2, 1949; c: Gheorghe, Anna. Prof, microbiol stomatology, U Tirgu-Mures, since 1965. Author: Coxsackie Viruses, 1958; Rheumatic Fever (Viral Ethiology), 1968; contbr numerous articles to profsl jours. Mem: Internationale Gesellschaft für Allgemeine Medizin; Soc of Med Sci, Rum. Home: 14 Trandafirilor St, Tirgu-Mures, Rum. Office: Institutul de Medicina, Tirgu-Mures, Rum.

ABRAHAM, Claude Kurt, US, educator; b. Lorsch Hessen, Ger, Dec 13, 1931; s. Sigmund and Johanna (Wachenheimer); in US since 1946; BA, U Cincinnati, 1953, AM, 1956; PhD, Ind U, 1959; m. Marcia Phillips, June 3, 1956; c: Susan, Stephen, Catherine, Linda. Asso prof Fr, U Fla, since 1964. US Army, 1953-55. Chmn, Fr sect, S Atlantic MLA; mem: adv council, Amer Council Teaching Fgn Langs; Amer Assn Tchrs Fr; MLA; hon frats: Pi Sigma Phi; Phi Sigma Iota; fmr: chmn, Fr sect, Midwest MLA; mem, biography comm, MLA. Author: Gaston D'Orléans et sa Cour, 2nd ed, 1964; The Strangers, 1966; ed of Molière's Le Bourgeois Gentilhomme, 1966; trans with Marcia Abraham, Pascal by J Mesnard; contbr numerous articles to profsl jours. Recipient: various research grants, U's: Ill; Fla; Natl Endowment for Hum, US Govt, 1969. Home: 1820 NW 46 St, Gainesville, Fla. Office: U of Fla, Gainesville, Fla.

ABRAHAM, Henry J, US, political scientist, author; b. Offenbach, Ger, Aug 25, 1921; s. Fred and Louise (Kullmann); desc, Rabbi Jakob Weil, 15th cent sci; in US since 1937; BA, summa cum laude, Kenyon Coll, 1948; MA, Columbia U, 1949; PhD, U of Pa, 1952; m. Mildred Kosches, Apr 13, 1954; c: Philip, Peter. Prof, U of Pa, since 1962, on fac since 1949, mem, adv comm, fac sen, 1958-61, chmn, grad group, 1962-63; visiting lectr: Swarthmore Coll, 1955, 1956, 1962; Us of Copenhagen, Amsterdam, Nijmegen, Stockholm,

Göteborg, 1960; visiting asso prof, Phila Museum Coll of Art, 1958-59; lectr, civic affairs, Smith Kline & French Labs, 1961; visiting prof: U Aarhus, Denmark, 1959-60; City Coll, CUNY, 1967, 1968; Columbia U, 1969; mem adv bd, Wharton Sch Finance and Commerce, 1950-60. US Army Intelligence, 1943-46, 1950-51. Author: Compulsory Voting, 1955; Government as Entrepreneur and Social Servant, 1956; Courts and Judges: An Introduction to the Judicial Process, 1959; The Judicial Process: An Introductory Analysis of the Courts of the United States, England and France, 1962, 2nd rev ed, 1968; The Judiciary, 1965, 2nd rev ed, 1969; Freedom and the Court, 1967; co-author: Elements of Democratic Government, 1958, 4th rev ed, 1963; Elements of American National Government, 1965, 3rd ed, 1969; ed adv, political sci list, Oxford U Press, since 1958; asso ed, Social Science, 1951-58; mem adv bd, Social Educ, 1956-61; contbr to profsl jours. Natl Scholarship chmn, Phi Epsilon Pi, 1955-57; fac adv, Eta chap, 1953-59; fac adv, Houston Hall, bd dirs, U of Pa, 1951-58; Pa Players, 1955-57; comm mem: adult educ, Cong Rodeph Shalom, 1962, bd trustees since 1963; rel and free soc, NCCJ, 1958-59; mem: AAUP; Amer Acad Political and Social Sci; Amer Political Sci Assn; Pa Political Sci and Public Admn Assn; Pa Speech Assn; Phi Beta Kappa; Pi Gamma Mu; Pi Sigma Alpha; Fellows in Amer Studies. Recipient: award, excellence in undergraduate teaching, U of Pa, 1959; f: grad Amer studies, Dalton, 1948-49; Fulbright, 1959-60; Social Sci Research Council, U Wis, 1958. Spec interests: opera, theatre, philately. Home: 1243 Wyngate Rd, Wynnewood, Pa. Office: U of Pa, Philadelphia, Pa.

ABRAHAMOWICZ, Uriel, Isr, communal leader; b. Vienna, Aus, Sep 29, 1915; s. Reuben and Friedericke (Butschowitz); in Isr since 1934; att U Vienna; m. Kaete Swoboda, 1938; c: Daniel, Jael Zvick. Dep and acting mayor, Ramat Gan, since 1967; secy-gen, Labour Council, Givatayim, 1945-63; vice-chmn, trade union, Histadrut, 1963-65; dir, head of manpower, Solel Boneh, 1965-67. Served Hagana, IDF. Office: Bialik St, Ramat Gan, Isr.

ABRAHAMS, Benjamin, Austr, accountant, communal worker; b. Melbourne, Jan 25, 1894; s. Moss and Rachel (Isaacs); grad, Austr Soc of Acctnts. Public acctnt since 1938; auditor: JNF, Vic; Friends Heb U. Secy, E Melbourne Heb Cong, since 1943; delg, Vic J Bd Deps; trustee, Judean League of Vic; life exec mem, JNF, Vic; mem: exec, United Isr Appeal, Vic; comm, State Zionist Council, Vic, since 1940; J Wfr Soc; Melbourne J Philanthropic Soc; Mogen David Adom; YMHA; club, Mt Trails, pres. Home: 3 Maryville St, Ripponlea, Victoria, Austr. Office: 488 Albert St, E Melbourne, Austr.

ABRAHAMS, Gerald, Eng, author; b. Liverpool, Eng, Apr 15, 1907; s. Harry and Leah (Rabinowitz); desc, Tosefoth Yom Tov; MA, 1st class hons, phil, politics, econs, Wadaam Coll, Oxford, 1928; called to Bar, Hon Soc, Gray's Inn, 1931. Author, barrister, lectr; fmr amateur intl chess player, known for Abrahams Defenses. Author: numerous books; those in print: The Legal Mind, 1954; Police Questioning: The Judges' Rules, 1964; Trade Unions and The Law, 1969; The Jewish Mind, 1961, 1962; Teach Yourself Chess, 1948; The Chess Mind, 1951, 1960; Technique in Chess, 1961, 1965; Test Your Chess, 1963; La Technica en Ajedrez, 1965; Pan Book of Chess, 1965; Handbook of Chess, 1965; Brains in Bridge, 1962; Let's Look at Israel, 1966. Active in Zionist Orgs; club, Author's, London. Hobbies: chess, bridge, lit and cultural lectures, Heb and Talmudic studies. Home: 51 Prince Alfred Rd, Liverpool, Eng. Office: 27 Dale St, Liverpool, Eng; 3 King's Bench Walk, London, Eng.

ABRAHAMS, Israel, Isr, rabbi; b. Vilna, Russ, May 30, 1903; s. Zechariah and Rachel (Sherman); in Isr since 1968; educated: J Coll, U Coll, both Eng; ordained rabbi; m. Ethel Levy, June 4, 1930; c: Rosalind. Official trans of Judaica into Eng for Heb U, Jerusalem; chief rabbi em, United Council Orthodox Heb Congs, Cape Province, SW Afr, Salisbury; prof em, Heb, U Cape Town; rabbi: Shepherd's Bush Syn, London, 1928-32; Gt Syn, Manchester, 1933-37. Author: Pathways in Judaism, essays; Living Waters, sermons and addresses; Hagiga; Birth of a Community; Eng trans of Cassuto's Heb works: Documentary Hypothesis; From Adam to Noah; From Noah to Abraham; Exodus; The Goddess Anath; cons ed, Ency Judaica; Eng ed, Isr Natl Acad of Sci and Hum; author of brochures. Home: 16 Ahad Ha'am St, Jerusalem, Isr.

ABRAHAMS, Robert David, US, lawyer, author; b. Phila, Sep 24, 1905; s. William and Anne (David); JD, Dickinson Law Sch, Carlisle, Pa, 1925; m. Florence Kohn, Nov 21, 1929; c: Roger, Richard, Marjorie Slavin. Sr partner, Abrahams & Loewenstein, since 1953; chief counsel, Legal Aid Soc, Phila, since 1959; lectr, law, Temple U Law Sch, since 1953; exec dir, comty legal service, 1961; asst city solicitor, Phila, 1926-32; hon consul, Dominican Rep, 1931-62; Sec to Consul Gen to Eur, Sesqui-Centenary. Intl Exposition. Phila, 1925. Restored, with wife, Morning Star Plantation and Ancient J Burial Ground, Nevis and maintains free Adm Nelson Mus, Nevis, BWI. Author: Come Forward, 1928; New Tavern Tales, 1930; The Pot-Bellied Gods, 1932; Death after Lunch, 1941; Death in 1-2-3, pub 1942; Three Dozen, 1945; Mr Benjamin's Sword, 1948; The Commodore, 1954; The Uncommon Soldier, 1958; Room for A Son, 1951; Sound of Bow Bells, 1962; Humphrey's Ride, 1964; The Bonus of Redonda, 1967; co-author, Handbook of Pennsylvania Collection Practice, 1931; contbr to natl mags. Pres, Penn Prison Soc; trustee, Dickinson Sch of Law; dir, Comty Legal Service, Phila; fmr: pres, J Family Service, Comm Health Service until merger with J Albert Einstein Med Cen; found chmn: Phila Bar Assn, Neighborhood Law Off Plan, Commn Public Services; trustee, B & F Wolf Scholarship Trust; mem: Phila, Amer and Intl Bar Assns. Recipient: Reginald Heber Smith Medal, Natl Legal Aid and Defender Assn; Order Christopher Columbus, Order of Duarte, both Dominican Repub. Homes: 8204 Cedar Rd, Elkins Park, Pa; Morning Star, Fig Tree, Nevis, BWI. Office: 1730 Land Title Bldg, Philadelphia, Pa.

ABRAHAMS, Samuel, US, attorney; b. NYC, Dec 3, 1923; s. Isaac and Ida (Ehrman); BA, Bklyn Coll, NY, 1945; MA, Columbia U, 1946, cert race relations, Fisk U, 1947; JD, Bklyn Law Sch, 1956; LLM, NYU Sch of Law, 1961. Pvt practice since 1957; investigator, Dept Hosps, NY, 1952; instr, social studies, Jacob Joseph HS, 1953-54; staff, Bklyn Supr Court, 1958-62; Rep candidate, State Sen, Bklyn, 1956. Mem: exec bd, Stephen Wise Young Adult Zionists, ZOA, 1951-60, chmn, educ, 1951-52, chmn, PR, 1952-59, pres, 1957-58; fund raiser, UJA, 1957; chmn, Atlantic Union Comm, Bklyn, 1952-53; mem, exec comm, Bklyn Libr Council, 1958-61; mem: Young Isr, Flatbush; Amer J League Against Communism; NAACP; Civic Cen Council; Rel Zionists of Amer, Kfar Etzion chap; Bklyn Bar Assn; secy, 2nd Assembly Dist Rep Club, Bklyn, 1949-54. Author: Law of the American Family; Law in Family Conflict; contbr to Anglo-J jours and gen mags; lectr, law, politics to J comtys throughout world. Hobbies: travel, writing. Home: 1252 E 8 St, Brooklyn, NY. Office: 66 Court St, Brooklyn, NY.

ABRAHAMSEN, David, US, psychiatrist, author; b. Trondheim, Nor, June 23, 1903; s. Salomon and Marie (Fischer); in US since 1940; MD, Royal Frederick U, Oslo, Nor, 1929; att U clinics of: Oslo; Nor; Den; Eng; MD, NYU, 1943; m. Lova Katz, May 5, 1932; c: Inger McCabe, Anne-Marie Foltz. Research cons psycht, Inst for Social Change, dept psycht, Roosevelt Hosp, NY, since 1969; cons, research dept, mental hygiene, State of NY, since 1955, dir, 1948-52; pvt practice, Nor, 1929-31; res, asst, neur and psycht, Psycht Clinic, Oslo, 1932-36; dir, sup, Children's Home, Oslo, 1934-36; psycht, Dept of Justice, Nor, 1938-40; psycht, research asso, dept psycht, Columbia U, 1944-53, research dir, child guidance and mental hygiene, 1950-53; res psycht: St Elizabeth's Hosp, Wash, DC, 1940-41; diagnostic depot, Ill State Penitentiary, 1941-42; research asso, psycht, Menninger Clinic and Southard Sch, Topeka, Kan, 1942-43; psycht, Bellevue Hosp, NYC, 1943-44; dir, research and treatment, behavior disorders in children, Psycht Inst, NYC, 1944-48. Nor Army, 1940. F: AMA; Amer Psycht Assn; Amer Orthopsycht Assn; Amer Psychopath Assn; NY Acad Med; dipl, Amer Bd Psycht and Neur, 1947; org, dir, Psycht Forum, Inc, since 1946; delg, pre-conf, White House Conf on Educ, 1955; mem: adv bd, Musical Therapy Assn, since 1954; Gov NY Comm to Propose New Leg on Definition of Legal Sanity, Amer Psycht Assn; bd overseers, Lemberg Cen for Study of Violence, Brandeis U, Mass, since 1968; Nor Med Assn; NY Soc Clinical Psycht; NY Co Med Soc; Amer Med Writers Assn; Authors League; fmr, chmn, US comm on juvenile delinquency, Intl Comm Mental Hygiene, London, 1948; club, PEN. Author: I Am a Jew, in Nor, 1935; Crime and the Human Mind, 1944; Mem, Mind and Power, 1945; The Mind and the Death of a Genius, 1946; Who Are the Guilty? A Study of Education and Crime, 1952; The Road to Emotional Maturity, 1958; The Psychology of Crime, 1960; The Emotional Care of Your Child, 1969; Our Violent Society, 1970; contbr of numerous articles to sci jours. Home and office: 1035 Fifth Ave, New York, NY.

ABRAHAMSEN, Samuel, US, educator; b. Trondheim, Nor, Oct 28, 1917; s. Solomon and Miriam (Fischer); in US since 1946; BA, Royal Frederick's U, Nor, 1937; MA, U Oslo, 1939; PhD, New Sch for Social Research, NY, 1955; prin's cert, cert in adult educ, HUC, NYC, 1957; m. Minuha Passman, Aug 6, 1947; c: Joy, Judy. Asst prof, depts educ and modern langs, Bklyn Coll, since 1963; research asso, UNESCO Inst for Educ; cons, Cen for Urban Educ, NYC; mem fac, adult acad, Cong Beth Elohim, 1955-62; tchr, Nor, Bay Ridge HS, Bklyn, 1951-63; educ cons, J Educ Comm of NY, 1956-69. Royal Nor Free Forces, 1942-45. Adv, academic council, Amer Coll, Jerusalem; chmn, libr and info comm, Amer-Scandinavian Found; secy, Tribute to Danes, Inc, NYC; mem: Natl Council for J Educ; MLA; AAUP; Comparative Educ Soc; Nor-Amer Hist Assn; fmr: dir, travel sem to Eng, Netherlands, Scandinavia, CUNY; mem: bd, Norsemen's Fed, steering comm on inter-faith activities, UAHC. Author: Sweden's Foreign Policy, 1957; Say it in Norwegian, 1957; ed: Teacher Education News and Notes; Lux et Veritas, 1958-62; contbr to educ and J publs. Recipient: Agnes Brown Leach F, 1949-55; Royal Nor St Olav Medal, 1968; Scandinavian of the Month, Scandinavian-Amer Bus Assn, 1968; Comty Leader of Amer, 1969. Hobbies: skiing, reading, music. Home: 100 Bleecker St, New York, NY. Office: Bklyn Coll, Brooklyn, NY.

ABRAHAMSON, Abraham E, Rhodesia, legislator; b. Bulawayo, Oct 13, 1922; s. Morris and Leah (Beirachowitz); BA, U Cape Town, 1942; m. Anita Rabinowitz, 1946; c: Irene, Lawrence, Martin. Bus exec and industrialist; Mp for Bulawayo E, 1953-65; Min of Lab, Social Wfr and Housing, S Rhodesia Govt, 1958-62; ret from Parl as Min of Treas, Local Govt and Housing. S Rhodesian Forces, WW II. Prin contrib: introduced ind coalition act, apprenticeship act, workmen's compensation act for all races, 1959; S Rhodesia housing act, 1960; amended children's protection and adoption act, 1960. Pres, J Bd Deps, 1956-58, and since 1963; vice-chmn, J Guild; fmr: pres: Bulawayo Chamber of Inds; Fed Rhodesian Inds; Assn Rhodesian and Nyasaland Inds; chmn: Select Comm on Unemployment Benefits; Chovevei Zionist Soc; mem: Natl Native Lab Bd; Rhodesian ZC; Study Conf on Hum Relations, Oxford; comm, Heb Cong; clubs: New; Parkview Sports. Hobbies: tennis, philately. Home: 2 Hall Rd, Kumalo, Bulawayo, Rhodesia. Office: POB 791, Bulawayo, Rhodesia.

ABRAHAMSON, Albert, US, economist, educator; b. Portland, Me, Nov 4, 1905; s. Lazarus and Rosa (Robinson); BA, Bowdoin Coll, 1926; MA, Columbia U, 1927. Prof, Bowdoin Coll, since 1947, mem fac since 1928, dept econ, 1956-61; cons, NSF, since 1965, sr staff asso, 1964-65; econ, Cabinet Commn on Price Policy, Wash, DC, 1934-35; Works Progress Admn, Me, 1935-37; exec dir, J Occupational Council, NYC, 1939-40; exec dir, Natl Ref Service, NYC, 1943-44; asst dir, War Ref Bd, Wash, DC, 1944-45; spec asst to Secy of Lab, 1945-46; spec cons to chmn, Natl Security Resources bd, 1950; cons, Pres Materials Policy Commn, 1951; econ, UJA, mem, panel mediators, Me, 1957-63; chmn, Me adv commn, US Commn on Civil Rights, 1958-60; cons to Natl Manpower Commn, NYC, 1955-62. US Army, WW II. Bd dirs, Amer Cancer Soc; mem: Amer Econ Assn; Amer Stat Assn; Ind Relations Research Assn; Phi Beta Kappa; Zeta Psi. Co-author: Price and Price Policies, 1935; contbr to periodicals and jours. Home: 234 Maine St. Brunswick, Me.

ABRAHAMSON, Brian, Austr, educator; b. Cape Town, S Afr, Sep 14, 1928; s. Isaac and Rose (Solomon); BSc, U Cape Town, 1948, MSc, 1949; SM, U Chgo, 1951, PhD, 1957; m. Valerie Topham, Oct 24, 1958; c: Isobel, John. Prof math, Flinders U, S Austr, since 1965; lectr, U Cape Town, 1954-57; prof, head, dept math, Rhodes U, 1958-61; asso prof math, U Toronto, 1962-65, mem fac since 1961. Mem: Amer Math Soc; Austr Math Soc; Math Assn of S Austr; fmr Hillel dir, Rhodes U. Contbr to math jours. Home: 79 Malcolm St, Bedford Park, Austr. Office: Flinders U, S Austr.

ABRAHAMSON, Ira A, US, physician; b. St Paul, Minn, Jan 19, 1893; s. Louis and Minna (Goodman); BS, MD, Marquette Sch of Med, 1916; att U's: Vienna; Budapest; Prague; Basle; London; m. Fay Levy, July 6, 1919; c: Margaret Halle, Jean, Ira. Asst clinical prof, ophthal, U Cincinnati, since 1946; dir, eye dept, J Hosp, Cincinnati, 1952-56, vice-pres, staff, 1947-48; ophthal cons: Cincinnati Gen Hosp, 1958; Children's Hosp, Cincinnati, 1960; Good Samaritan Hosp, 1958. US Army, 1917-19, col, 1940-46. Dipl, sr f, Amer Bd Ophthal, 1926; mem: Cincinnati Ophthal Soc; Amer Coll

Surgs; Cincinnati Acad of Med; O State Med Soc; Rockdale Temple; clubs: Losantiville Country; Buckeye. Author: Colored Atlas of Anterior Segment Eye Diseases, 1964; Know Your Eyes; contbr to numerous articles to med jours. Recipient: meritorius award, Legion of Merit, 1945; Ill Ignatio Barraquer Award, 1967. Hobbies: golf, sailing, bridge. Home: 2324 Madison Rd, Cincinnati, O. Office: 925 5/3 Bank Bldg, Cincinnati, O.

ABRAHAMSON, Mervyn L, Ir, physician, educator; b. Dublin, Apr 24, 1921; s. Leonard and Tillie (Nurock); BA, MB, BCh, BAO, MD, FRCPI, Dublin U; m. Marcia Epson, July 22, 1945; c: David, Leonard, Lesley. Phys i/c card dept, Richmond Hosp, Dublin, since 1951, visiting phys since 1962, asst visiting phys, 1948-62; prof, pharm and therapeutics, Royal Coll Surg, Ir, since 1961, fmr: examiner in biol, clinical tutor in med, asst to prof of med, acting prof med, 1961-62; examiner in pharm, Primary FFA; DA. Pres: Biol Soc, Royal Coll Surgs, Ir, since 1962; Friends Heb U, Dublin group; Dublin J Progressive Cong; vice-pres, Royal Coll Phys, Ir; f, Royal Acad Med in Ir; found, mem comm, J Med Soc of Ir, since 1950, fmr chmn; mem, comm Irish Card Soc, since 1962; fmr vice chmn, ZC, Ir; clubs: Clinical; Corrigan; U of Dublin. Hobbies: theatre, golf, rugby. Home: 40 Fitzwilliam Pl, Dublin, Ir.

ABRAM, Morris B, US, attorney, civic leader; b. Fitzgerald, Ga, June 19, 1918; s. Sam and Irene (Jacobeth); BA, U of Ga, 1938; JD, U Chgo, 1940; BA, Oxford U, 1948, MA, 1953; m. Jane Maguire, Dec 23, 1943; c: Ruth, Ann, Morris, Adam, Joshua. Pres, Brandeis U, 1968-70; partner, law firm, Paul, Weiss, Goldberg, Rifkind, Wharton and Garrison, 1962-68; counsel, Heyman, Abram, Young, Hicks and Maloof; regional counsel, Wage Stabilization Bd, Region V, since 1951; counsel, prosecution staff, Intl Mil Tribunal, Nuremberg, Ger,1946; asst to the dir, Marshall Plan, 1948. Maj, USAF, 1941-45. Pres: AJComm, 1964-68; Field Found, Inc, since 1965; Family Service Soc, Fulton, DeKalb and Cobb Cos, 1957-59; chmn, Citizens' Crime Comm, Atlanta, 1958-60; counsel, S Regional Bd, ADL, 1955; mem, bd trustees: Twentieth Century Fund, since 1958; Weizmann Inst of Sci, since 1966; mem, bd dirs: Morehouse Coll, since 1966; JTSA, since 1966; mem: Fgn Policy Assn; jt social action commn, UAHC and CCAR; UN Subcommn on Prevention of Discrimination and Protection of Minorities; UN Commn on Hum Rights; Afro-Amer Inst; Citizens' Comm for Children, NY; Natl Urban League; Amer, Ga, Atlanta, and NY State Bar Assns; Bar, NYC; Phi Beta Kappa; Phi Kappa Phi; Omicron Delta Kappa; club, Lawyers, Atlanta. Co-author: How to Stop Violence in Your Community, 1950. Recipient: Legion of Merit, 1946. Home: Themis House, Weston, Mass. Office: Brandeis U, Waltham, Mass.

ABRAMI, Leo Michel, Curaçao, rabbi; b. Paris, Fr, Nov 10, 1931; s. David and Anna (Slote) Zacharin; in Curaçao since 1967; BS, U Geneva, Switz, 1958; MHL, HUC, Cincinnati, O, ordained rabbi, 1963; m. Susan Rothmann; c: Arianne, Dan. Rabbi, Cong Mikve Isr-Emanuel, since 1967; Heb tchr, cantor, Hillel dir, J Comty, Geneva, Switz 1953-60; rabbi, Cong Bet El, Guatemala City, 1964-65. Prin contrib: pioneer work for World Union for Progressive Judaism in Guat and Mex. Bd mem, comm for trans Bible into Papiamento, Antillan dialect; fmr pres, Hillel Assn J Students, Geneva; mem: CCAR; Reconstructionist Found, NY; B'nai B'rith. Home: POB 380, Curaçao, Netherlands Antilles. Study: Mikve Isr-Emanuel Syn, Curaçao, Netherlands Antilles.

ABRAMOFF, Arie Leon, Isr, physician; b. Sofia, Bulgaria, Sep 24, 1922; s. Chaim and Klara; in Isr since 1949; att fac of med, Sofia, 1944-49; MD, Heb U, Jerusalem, 1951; m. Alisa Achbert, Sep 23, 1952; c: Liora, Irith. Chief phys, dept med B, Ichilov Hosp, Tel Aviv, since 1962; clinical lectr, Tel Aviv U, since 1967; lectr, lab techs, ORT, 1956. Maj, IDF MC. Mem: IMA, since 1952. Hobby: music, violinist, Tel Aviv Sym Orch. Home: 29 Hovevei Zion St, Tel Aviv, Isr. Office: Ichilov Hosp, Weizmann St, Tel Aviv, Isr.

ABRAMOFF, Asya N, Isr, pianist; b. Harbin, China, Apr 11, 1926; d. Nisan and Sofla (Kachanovsky) Shifrin; in Isr since 1950; MMus, Music Sch, Harbin; m. Alex Abramoff; c: Theodor. Pianist, piano tchr, poet; piano recitals and solos in sym orch, mainly in China. Mem: Igud Yotzei Sin and club. Author: poems in Russ, trans into Heb by I Zmora. Hobby: ivory art collections. Home and office: 31 Smilansky St, Netanya, Isr.

ABRAMOV, Jacob, Isr, business exec; b. Bucovina, Aus, Oct, 1904; s. Michael and Golda (Groper); in Isr since 1924; att LSE, 1929-31; m. Betty Haller, 1942; c: Yael Babad, Yaron. Adv, dir, cos, Min of Devl since 1966; land valuer since 1939; mgr, partner, Land Devl Co, 1933-37; dir, secy, Ata Textile Co Ltd, 1934-64. Exec comm: Isr Maritime League; Heb U Assn; mem: Isr Land Valuer Assn; Isr Mgmt Cen. Hobbies: photography, archeol, hist. Home: 118 Hatishbi, Haifa, Isr.

ABRAMOV, Zalman, Isr, attorney; b. Minsk, Russ, May 6, 1908; s. Shabtai and Henia (Roginsky); in Isr since 1920; BA, W Reserve U, 1931, MA, 1933; LLB, 1934; DJur, 1968; m. Hilda Snowman, c: Carmela Kimelfeld, Edna Dollar, Hillel. Pvt practice since 1939, MK since 1959. Knesset repr, Council of Eur, Strasbourg, 1963-69, mem: Law and Constitution Comm, Knesset, 1959-69, House Rules Comm, 1965-69. Contbr to Haaretz, Commentary, Midstream, Ency of Zionism. Chmn, Isr Amer Friendship League, 1950-64. Home: 1 Bar Kochba St, Tel Aviv, Isr. Office: 13 Achad Haam St, Tel Aviv, Isr.

ABRAMOVIC, Pinchas, Isr, painter; b. Mojeik, Lith, Apr 7, 1909; s. Joel and Rachel; in Isr since 1929; att: Art Sch, Lith; Ecole des Beaux Arts, Paris, Fr; m. Emma Olech, Feb 8, 1944; c: Elit. Painter, Art tchr, Folks U and Tchr Sem, since 1952; one-man shows: Katz Gal, Tel Aviv, 1944; London, 1946; Mikra Studio Gal, Tel Aviv, 1948; Artists House, Haifa, 1953; Jerusalem, 1954, 1968; Gal 101, S Afr, 1956, 1966; Tel Aviv Mus, 1958; Yad Lebanim, Petah Tikva, 1969; group shows: Sao Paulo Biennale; Tokyo; Holland; Paris; Art Festival, Tel Aviv; US; Charpentier, Paris; Monaco; Yares Gal, Arizona. Mem: comm, Isr Artists Assn; New Horizons Artists Group. Recipient: Monaco Prize, Intl, Monaco State, 1966; Dizengoff Prize, City of Tel Aviv,1967. Home and studio: 12 Karni St, Ramat Aviv, Isr.

ABRAMOVITCH, Rudolph Abraham, US, educator; b. Alexandria, Egypt, July 19, 1930; s. Lazare and Elise (Litinsky); in US since 1967; BSc, hons, U Alexandria, 1950; PhD, hons, U London, 1953, DSc; m. Liliane Guetta, July 8, 1952; c: Michael, Daniel. Prof, chem, U Ala since 1967; prof, U Sask, 1957-67; ICI F, U London, 1955-57; research chem, Weizmann Inst, 1954-55; Med Research Council F, U Exeter, 1953-54. Pres, Org Div Chem Inst, Can; chmn, Sask sec, Chem Inst, Can; mem: bd local chap, B'nai B'rith; Chem Soc, London; Chem Inst, Can; AAAS; Amer Chem Soc. Ed, Pyridine and its Derivatives, 4 vols; contbr to sci jours. Recipient: Kedder Fletcher Warr Student, U London, 1952; f, Chem Inst, Can, 1963. Hobbies: music, reading, travel. Home: 480 Woodland Hills, Tuscaloosa, Ala. Office: Dept of Chem, U of Ala, University, Ala.

ABRAMOVITCH, Zeev, Isr, author; b. Marinpol, Ukraine, July 16, 1891; s. Moisei and Maria; att: U Odessa; Brussels; m. Lidya. Ret; fmr lectr econ, Tel Aviv Sch Law and Econ. Author: Borokhov and His Theory, 1924; Lectures on Political Economy, 1940; Economics of Arabs in Palestine and Middle East, 1944; The National Problem and Jews of Our Times, 1957; In Service of Movement, memoirs, 1966. Home: 39 Laguardia St, Tel Aviv, Isr.

ABRAMOVITZ, Max, US, architect; b. Chgo, Ill, May 23, 1908; s. Benjamin and Sophia (Maimon); BS, U of Ill, 1929; MS, Columbia U, 1931; att Ecole des Beaux Arts, Paris, 1932-34; hon DFA, U Pittsburgh, 1961; m. Anne Causey, Sep 4, 1937 (div); c: Michael, Katherine Coleman; m. 2nd, Anita Zeltner Brooks, Feb 29, 1964; Mem, firm, Harrison & Abramovitz, NYC, since 1945; partner, Harrison, Fouilhoux & Abramovitz, 1941-45; asso prof, Sch Fine Arts, Yale, 1939-42; dep dir, UN Hqr Planning Off, 1947-52. Prin works in: Corning Glass Center, NY; Alcoa Bldg, Pittsburgh; Mellon Natl Bank, US Steel Bldg, Pittsburgh, US Emb Bldg, Havana, Cuba; Philharmonic Hall, Lincoln Cen for Performing Arts, NYC; Time and Life Bldg, NY; U of Ill, Assembly Hall, Champaign, Ill; US Rubber Bldg, Rockefeller Cen, NYC. Lt col, US Engrs Corps, 1942-45; col, USAF, 1950-52. Dir: Krannert Cen for Performing Arts, U of Ill; Columbia U Law Sch; Phoenix Mutual Life Ins Co, Hartford, Conn; Beth Zion Temple Buffalo,NY; trustee, Mt Sinai Hosp,NYC,since 1947; chmn, bd, Regional Plan Assn, 1966-68; f: Amer Inst Architects; Brandeis U, 1963; club, Cent Assn. Recipient: award of merit: Amer I nst Architects; Amer Assn Sch Admnrs; silver medal, Architectural League, NY; Legion of merit medal; award of achievement, U of Ill Alumni Assn, 1963. Home: 418 E 50 St, New York, NY. Office: 630 Fifth Ave, New York, NY.

ABRAMOVITZ, Moses, US, educator; b. Bklyn, NY, Jan 1, 1912; s. Nathan and Betty (Goldenberg); AB, Harvard, 1932; PhD, Columbia, 1935; m. Carrie Glasser, June 23, 1937; c: Joel. Prof, econ, Stanford U, since 1948; instr, Harvard, 1936-38; lectr, Columbia U, 1940-46; mem, rseearch staff, Natl Bur Econ Research, 1938-68; econ adv: US repr to Allied Commn on Reparations, 1944-46; secy gen, Org for Econ Coop and Devl, 1962-63. Lt, US Army, 1943-46. F: Amer Stat Assn; Amer Acad Arts and Scis; fmr: vice-pres, Amer Econ Assn. Author: Inventories and Business Cycles, 1950; Trend of Public Employment in Great Britain, 1956. Home: 543 W Crescent Dr, Palo Alto, Cal. Office: Dept of Econ, Stanford U, Stanford, Cal.

ABRAMOWITZ, Abraham, US, engineer, educator; b. NYC, Nov 5, 1914; s. Hyman and Frieda (Rashbaum); BS, CCNY, 1936, MEE, 1937; prof engr, license, NY State, 1943; m. Lee Weiner, Dec 23, 1943; c: Ellen (decd), Harvey. Prof, elec engr, CCNY, since 1961, on fac since 1943; engr, pvt ind, 1937-38; elec insp, Dept Water Supply, Gas and Elec, NYC, 1938-40; elec engr, Bd of Transp, NYC, 1940-42; spec examiner, Civil Service Commn, 1946-49, 1960-62, 1967. Mem: Amer Inst of Elec Engrs; Illuminating Engr Soc; Precision Measurements Assn; Amer Soc for Engr Educ; Amer Physics Tchrs; Eta Kappa Nu; Tau Beta Pi. Hobbies: swimming, bicycling. Home: 955 Walton Ave, Bronx, NY. Office: CCNY, Convent Ave at 139 St, New York, NY.

ABRAMOWITZ, Benjamin, US, artist, teacher; b. NYC, July 4, 1917; s. Isadore and Minnie (Paskun); m. Ruth Rosen, 1940; c: Susan, Jonathan. Tchr: grad sch, Dept of Agric, since 1960; League for Arts and Crafts, since 1960; J Comty Cen since 1959; own sch, 1941-59. Exhb: Corcoran Gal Art, 1963; Phila Mus Art, 1965; Southampton Coll, LIU, 1967; i2 one-man shows since 1941. Recipient: Ford Found F to lecture and exhibit in southwest US, 1965. Home and studio: 31 Eastway Rd, Greenbelt, Md.

ABRAMOWITZ, Meyer M, US, rabbi; b. Rochester, NY, Sep 22, 1918; s. Abraham and Fannie (Hersh); BJP, JTSA, 1943; BS, Columbia U, 1943; ordained rabbi, HUC-JIR, 1946; MAHL, 1969; m. Doris Rosenberg, Nov 25, 1943; c: Ann Ballon, Ira, Joel. Rabbi, Temple B'rith Sholom, Springfield, Ill, since 1957, life tenure since 1967; chaplain: Jacksonville State Hosp: Ill Sch for Deaf; Ill Sight Saving Sch, all since 1957; mem, rel fac, Lincoln Acad, Ill; dir, J educ, J Cen, Forest Hills, NY, 1940-44, student rabbi, 1944-46, rabbi, 1946-48; rabbi: Temple Beth Isr, Sharon, Pa, 1948-56; Temple Judea, Reseda, Cal, 1956-57. Mem: bd dirs: exec bd: CCAR; Ill Bd Mh Commn; Springfield NAACP; Ill Heart Assn; Sr Citizen's Cen, Sangamon Co; Consumer's Credit Counseling Service, Interfaith Clergy f, Springfield; Springfield Mh Assn; vice-pres, United World Federalists; chmn, Shenango Valley Amer J Tercentenary Comm, 1954-55; United Negro Coll Fund, 1955; mem: Rabb Council of Combined Campaign, UAHC, HUC, JIR, 1958; mem, ed bd, Union Songster; comm mem, Syn Music, CCAR; mem: B'nai B'rith; Alumni Assn, HUC-JIR; club, Kiwanis. Home: 211 S Park Ave, Springfield, Ill. Study: 1004-1008 S4 St, Springfield, Ill.

ABRAMOWITZ, William Lewis, US, business exec; b. NYC, Nov 9, 1914; s. Mendell and Dora (Smith); SB, MIT, Mass, 1935; m. Lee Epstein, June 4, 1944; c: Susan Slosberg, Gail Duncan, Ava, Kenneth. Chmn bd, Medicon Inc, since 1968; pres, Amer Resinous Chemicals Corp, 1939-55; vice-pres, chem div, Borden, 1955-57; pres: Carlon Products, 1957-60; Muskin Mfg, 1960-62, chmn bd, 1962-68. Bd Govs, Weizmann Inst Sci; trustee, JA; chmn, bldg fund, Temple Sinai, Marblehead-Swampscott, since 1964; vice-pres, J Comty Fed, Lynn, since 1964; mem, Pres's Devl Comm, MIT; chmn, Isr Bonds of N Shore, 1956-58; bd dir, Mass Bay United Fund, 1966-68; mem: Amer Chem Soc; Soc of Plastic Engrs; Soc of Plastic Ind; club, Tech, NY. Home: 93 Atlantic Ave, Swampscott, Mass. Office: 524 Statler Off Bldg, 20 Providence, Boston, Mass.

ABRAMS, Abram Bernard, US, physician; b. Newark, NJ, July 24, 1893; s. Isaac and Rachel (Cohen); MD, U of Pa, 1916; m. Flora Kauder, July 2, 1921; c: Joan Hersh. Sr att surg, Beth Isr Hosp, Newark, NJ, since 1937, pres, chief of staff, 1948-50; cons, Hosps: Irvington Gen; Presbyterian; St Barnabas, all in NJ. Capt, US MC, 1917-19. F: Northern NJ Acad Med; Amer Coll Surgs; dipl: Intl Coll Surgs; Amer Bd Abdominal Surgs; trustee: Essex Co Council, UJA, since 1951; mem: AMA; Essex Co Med Soc; Anat and Path Soc; NJ Soc

Surgs; Phi Delta Epsilon; club, Mountain Ridge Country. Contbr to profsl jours. Hobby: oil painting. Home: 335 Wyoming Ave, Millburn, NJ. Office: 2130 Millburn Ave, Maplewood, NJ.

ABRAMS, Archie A, US, physician, educator; b. Cleveland, O, Apr 10, 1906; s. Joseph and Lena (Richard); BA, W Reserve U, 1927, MD, 1931; m. Ruth Dreyfus, Apr 18, 1932; c: Ruth Brebner, Edwin. Pvt obset and gyn practice since 1935; sr mem, Med Assos of Mass Memorial Hosp, since 1951; cons obstet, gyn, Boston City Hosp; visiting gyn, U Hosp; asso prof, obstet, gyn, Boston U Med Sch, since 1953. USNR, 1942-45. Mem: Phi Beta Kappa; Zeta Beta Tau; AMA; Amer Bd Gyn and Obstet. Contbr to med jours. Home: 15 Fairgreen Pl, Brookline, Mass. Office: 1180 Beacon St, Brookline, Mass.

ABRAMS, Eugene Bernard, Switz, business exec; b. Trenton, NJ, Oct 10, 1919; s. Herman and Sarah (Hirschson); in Switz since 1968; att U of S Cal, 1946-47; dipl, U Paris, 1947; BA, U of Md, 1957; m. Monique Leiba, Apr 28, 1950; c: Monique Jacobson, Jacqueline Dockery. Dir, tech assistance, Worl ORT Union and Amer ORT Fed, since 1968; dir: US Agcy for Intl Devl, Guinea, Œ961-63, Ivory Coast, 1963-65; head, Econ Devl Div, OEC, 1965-67. Pres, Comm on Econ and Social Devl; vice-pres, Intl Council Voluntary Agcys; Swiss chap, Soc for Intl Devl; mem: Soc for Intl Devl, Switz. Author, Coordination of Technical Assistance, 1964. Hobbies: sailing, fishing. Home: 6 Chemin Htg Belotte, Vesenaz, Switz. Office: 1 Rue de Varembé, Geneva, Switz.

ABRAMS, Harry N, US, publisher; b. London, Eng, Dec 8, 1904; s. Morris and Millie (Rosenberg); in US since 1913; m. Nina Bolotoff, Mar 5, 1932; c: Michael, Robert. Pres, chmn bd, Harry N Abrams, Inc, art publisher, since 1950; asso, art dir, produc mgr, Schwab & Beatty, advt agcy, NYC, 1926-36; asso, Book of the Month Club, 1936-50, mem, bd dirs, 1947-50. Hobby: art collecting. Home: 33 E 70 St, New York, NY. Office: 110 E 59 St, New York, NY.

ABRAMS, Herbert, US, lawyer; b. Plainfield, NJ, July 12, 1927; s. Hyman and Leah (Canter); att U of Va, 1945-47; JL, Rutgers Law Sch, 1949; ML, Northeastern Law Sch, Boston, 1956; m. Joan Miller, Oct 28, 1951; c: Richard. Sr partner, Berman, Lewenber and Abrams, counsellors at law; fmr: asst dist atty, Norfolk Co; spec asst atty gen, Commonwealth of Mass; spec town counsel, Brookline; mem, fac, Northeastern U Sch of Law Enforcement and Security. Seaman, USCG, 1944-45. Pres, Amer J Hist Soc, Boston; selectman, Town of Brookline; trustee, Combined J Philanthropies Inc; fmr: pres: J Vocational Services; Rehab Services; chmn, United Fund and Cerebral Palsy Cajpaigns, Brookline; mem: Amer Bar Assn; Boston and Norfolk Co Bar Assns; Natl Assn Dist Attys; Shawmut Lodge, Masons; Aleppo Temple, Shriners; Lodge 886, Elks; clubs: Variety Intl; Brandeis U. Author: Mass Lawyers Diary and Manual, 1960. Home: 65 Chatham St, Brookline, Mass. Office: 2240 Prudential Tower, Boston, Mass.

ABRAMS, Joseph B, US, attorney; b. Boston, Mass, Aug 15, 1897; s. Harris and Rebecca (Cadish); AB, Harvard Coll, 1918; LLB, Harvard Law Sch, 1927; m. Anna Thurman, July 25, 1926; c: Robert, Joan Rosoff. Pvt practice since 1926; spec counsel, Bank Commns of Mass, 1935-38. Org and first secy, NE Zionist Region, 1920; pres: Amos Lodge, B'nai B'rith, 1941-43; Mass Trial Lawyers Assn, 1953-55; treas, NE JNF; hon life trustee, Temple Kehillath Isr, Brookline; bd govs, Shriners' Burns Inst; trustee, Aleppo Temple; mem, Masons, 32 deg. Contbr to legal and lit jours. Hobbies: philately, numismatics. Home: 18 Dean Rd, Brookline, Mass. Office: 40 Court St, Boston, Mass.

ABRAMS, Manuel, US, government official; b. Phila, Pa, Jan 18, 1919; s. Morris and Bessie (Monas); BS, cum laude, CCNY, 1939; att Amer U, Dept Agric Grad Sch, Wash, 1941-44; m. Sylvia Shapiro, Aug 6, 1940; c: Mona, Gaby. Dep chief, US Mission to Eur Comty, Brussels, since 1969, Rome, 1967-69; econ, commercial min, Amer Emb, Rome, It, 1967-69; sr sem fgn policy, 1966-67; econ counselor, Amer emb, Hague, 1962-66; fgn service off since 1959; in US State Dept since 1950; various govt positions, 1940-47; intl econ, US Dept of Commerce, 1947-50. Mem, Phi Beta Kappa. Spec interest, bridge. Home: 1840 NE 186 St, N Miami Beach, Fla. Office: USEC, Brussels, Belgium.

ABRAMS, Max A, US, lawyer; b. Chgo, Ill, Dec 26, 1920; s. Samuel and Rose (Lipsitz) Abramowitz; JD, DePaul U, 1946; m. Goldie Schayer, Apr 2, 1942; c: Ronald, Rosalyn.

Pvt practice since 1947. Bd mem, cong div, J United Fund; mem speakers bur: Isr Bond Org; Heb Theol Coll; mem: Ill State Bar Assn; pres, Cong Beth Itzchok, Chgo, 1955-58; co-found, Tepper-Shub Post JWV, 1947, cdr, 1949-51; co-found, Council Traditional Syns, 1952, vice pres, 1953-58; secy, Maos Chitim Comm, 1950-58; atty, chmn legal comm, Arie Crown Heb Day Sch, 1954-58. Home: 6124 N Central Park, Chicago, Ill. Office: 3322 Peterson, Chicago, Ill.

ABRAMS, Norman, US, educator, attorney; b. Chgo, Ill, July 7, 1933; s. Harry and Gertrude (Dick); BA, U Chgo, 1952, JD, 1955; m; c: Marshall, Julie. Prof, law, UCLA, since 1964, fac mem since 1959; research asso, secy, Harvard-Brandeis Coop Research for Isr Legal Devl, Harvard Law Sch, 1957-58, dir, 1959; cons: Gov Commn on LA Riots, 1965; Pres Comm on Law Enforcement and Admn of Justice, 1966-67; Natl Comm on Reform Fed Crime Laws, 1967-68; spec asst, US Atty Gen, Crime Div, US Dept of Justice, 1966-67. Bd dirs, Comty Justice Cen, LA; mem: Ill, Amer Bar Assns; Soc on Criminal Law; Phi Beta Kappa. Contbr to profsl jours. Office: 405 Hilgard Ave, Los Angeles, Cal.

ABRAMS, Roberta Nathanson, US, communal leader; b. Bklyn, NY, Aug 5, 1933; d. Louis and Minnie (Mazer) Nathanson; BA, Sarah Lawrence Coll, 1954; m. Warren Abrams, Aug 26, 1952; c: Alan, Michael, Carolyn. Chmn, womens div, UJA Gtr NY, since 1967; mem bd dirs: UJA; HIAS; JDC; FJP, N Shore, NY; mem exec comm, womens div, Albert Einstein Coll Med; fmr: pres, Salem Sch PTA, Port Wash, NY; vice-pres, Manhasset chap, ORT. Home: 126 Hemlock Rd, Manhasset, NY.

ABRAMS, Samuel Louis, US, business exec; b. Cleveland, O, July 28, 1912; s. Harry and Rose (Tepper); BA, W Reserve U, 1933; LLB, Cleveland Marshall Law Sch, 1939; m. Anne Roth, Oct 14, 1934; c: Arnold, Susan. Partner, Bellamy and Abrams, since 1965; pres: O Advt Agcy, 1933-56; Mutual Advt Agcy Network, 1952; Suburbia Savings Assn, 1961-65; exec vice-pres, Gerst, Sylvester & Walsh, 1956-65. Chmn: Cleveland chap, Amer Assn of Advt Agcys, 1953; U Hgts Comty Council, since 1961; secy: Cleveland Tobacco Table, since 1938; O Festivals and Events Assn, since 1961; mem exec comm: Bonds for Isr, since 1956; Mayor's Traffic Safety Educ Comm; mem: U Hgts City Council and Zoning Bd; O Dem Finance Comm; bd trustees: Park Syn; pres, U Lodge, B'nai B'rith, 1951-52; mem: Masons; clubs: Hawthorne Valley Country; Cleveland Advt; City. Home: 2420 S Belvoir Blvd, University Heights, O. Office: 3113 Prospect Ave, Cleveland, O.

ABRAMS, Solomon, US, educator, lawyer; b. Baltimore, Md, Aug 16, 1913; s. Israel and Bessie (Sacks); BA, U Pittsburgh, 1935, LLB, JD, 1938, MEd, 1948, DEd, 1952; m. Esther Safyan, Aug 8, 1938; c: Ivan. Exec dir, Heb Inst of Pittsburgh, since 1966, dir activities, 1944-47, educ dir, 1947-66. Prin contrib: helped devl sci of educ admn in J educ. Pres: Midwest region, Natl Council for J Educ; Rel Educ Assn of Pittsburgh, 1964-66; vice-pres: Tri-State Zionist Region; Natl Council for J Educ; Pittsburgh Zionist Dist, 1965-67; mem: Tau Epsilon Rho; ZOA; AJComm; club, Kiwanis. Author: Principles of Human Relations in Curriculum Development, 1952; dir, Heb TV Progs; contbr to profsl jours. Spec interests: J hist, contemporary J life, travel. Recipient: man of year, Heb Inst, 1951; honor citation, Pittsburgh Zionist Dist, 1968. Home: 5446 Plainfield Ave, Pittsburgh, Pa. Office: 6401-07 Forbes Ave, Pittsburgh, Pa.

ABRAMSKY, Chimen, Eng, historian; b. Minsk, Russ, Sep 12, 1916; s. Yecheskel and Genia (Yerusalimsky); in Eng since 1939; BA, with distinction, Heb U, Jerusalem; MA, Oxford U; m. Miriam Nirenstein; c: Yakov, Jennifer. Reader in J hist, U Coll, London, since 1969; sr research F, St Anthony's Coll, Oxford U, since 1967. Co-author: Karl Marx and the English Movement, 1965; contbr to profsl publs. Recipient: Humanitarian Trust Award. Hobbies: rare books, politics, music. Home: 5 Hillway St, London N6, Eng.

ABRAMSKY, Yechezkel, Isr, author, rabbi; b. Russ, 1885; in Isr since 1949; m; four c. Rabbi: Russ, 1912-30; Machzikei Hadath, London, Eng, 1932-35; sr assessor, London Beth Din, 1936-49. Imprisoned in USSR, later expelled. Pres, Va'ad Hayeshnoth in Isr. Author: Chazon Yehezkel on the Tosephta, 23 vols; Eretz-Israel Nachlath Am Israel. Recipient: nominee for Chief Rabbinate of Isr by Va'ad Leumi, 1936; Isr Prize for Rabbinic Lit, 1956; Rabbi Kook Prize, City of Tel Aviv, 1963. Spec interest, Torah. Home: 5 Brever St, Jerusalem, Isr.

ABRAMSON, Arthur S, US, physician, educator; b. Montreal, Can, June 4, 1912; s. Jacob and Dora (Rosenthal); in US since 1937; BS, McGill U, 1933; MD, CM, Fac of Med, 1937; m. Ruth Rumsey, Aug 1, 1956; c: Daniel. Prof, chmn, dept rehab med, Albert Einstein Coll of Med, Yeshiva U, since 1955; dir, dept phys med and rehab, Bx Munic Hosp Cen, since 1955; visiting prof, med dir, div phys therapy, Ithaca Coll, since 1959; chief, phys med, rehab service, Bx VA Hosp, 1950-55; mem, Pres Truman's Comm on Vets Med Services, 1950; visiting chief pro tem, Atlantic City Hosp, 1951; clinical prof, NY Med Coll, 1952-55; cons: Kessler Inst for Rehab since 1951; hosps: Beth Abraham; Montefiore; J Chronic Disease; Misericordia; VA, Bx; E Orange; NJ; VA, Montrose, NY; visiting phys: hosps: Flower and Fifth Ave; Metrop and Bird S Coler; research f, Montefiore Hosp, 1953; spec lectr, Columbia U, 1950; memorial lectures: Gross; Gaffny; Albee; Coulter. Maj, US Army, MC, 1942-46. Pres, NY Soc of Phys Med and Rehab, 1957; chmn, phys council, Amer Red Mogen David, Isr; bd dirs: Amer Acad of Phys Med and Rehab; hon pres, Isr Phys Therapy Assn, since 1953; f: Amer Coll of Phys, 1950; NY Acad of Med, 1950; dipl, Amer Bd Phys Med and Rehab; bd dirs: Amer Bd of Phys Med and Rehab; NY Soc Amer Cong; Amer Acad of Phys Med and Rehab; NY State Med Soc; Bx Co Med Soc; mem: Commn on Educ in Phys Med and Rehab; expert med comm, Amer Rehab Found; Alpha Omega Alpha; AMA; NY Acad of Scis; Intl Soc for Rehab of the Disabled; life, JWV; Gov Rockefeller's Council on Rehab, 1959; natl adv council, Vocational Rehab Admn, 1962; hon mem: Peruvian Urol Assn; Peruvian Psycht Assn. Contbr to med jours. Recipient: Purple Heart, 1944; service cross, NY State, 1948; disabled man of year award, Wfr Council, NY, 1948; annual rehab award, Assn for Phys and Mental Rehab, 1952; cert of merit, JWV, 1953; Amer Red Mogen Dovid for Isr, 1953; pres trophy, handicapped man of year, 1956; award in med, NY Philanthropic League, 1956; dist service key, Amer Cong of Rehab Med, 1966. Home: Hawthorne Way, Hartsdale, NY. Office: Albert Einstein Coll of Med, New York, NY.

ABRAMSON, David I, US, physician; b. NYC, Oct 14, 1905; s. Aaron and Anna (Oschrin); MD, LI Coll Med, 1929; m. Louise Felson, Sep, 1940; c: Julie Syril, M Beth. Att phys: Hines VA Hosp; Michael Reese Hosp; Mt Sinai Hosp, all since 1946; cons, peripheral vascular disease, regional off, VA; Chgo and Oak Pk Hosp, both since 1946; prof med and head dept physical med and rehab, U Ill Coll of Med, since 1955; chief, phys med and rehabilitation, Research and Educ Hosps, since 1955; research asst, physiology and pharm, LI Coll of Med, 1928, instr, 1930-36; dir: cardiovascular research, May Inst for Med Research, Cincinnati, 1937-42; electrocardiography, J Hosp, 1938-42; instr, pharm, U Cincinnati, 1940-42. US Army MC, 1942-46. Mem: sci council, AHA, f, sect on peripheral vascular diseases; low environmental protection comm, NRC; Amer Cong of Med Rehab; Cen Soc for Clinical Research; Amer Phys Soc; Soc for Experimental Biol and Med; Chgo Soc for Internal Med; Chgo Med Soc; AMA; Intl Cardiovascular Soc; Inter-Amer Card Cong; Sigma Xi; FACP. Author: Vascular Responses of the Extremities of Man in Health and in Disease, 1944; Diagnosis and Treatment of Peripheral Vascular Disorders, 1956; Circulation in the Extremities, 1967; ed: Blood Vessels and Lymphatics, 1962; Treatment of Arterial Disorders of the Extremities, 1967; contbr to profsl jours. Recipient: f, cardiovascular research, Michael Reese Hosp, 1935-36; Sutro F, Mt Sinai Hosp, NY, 1936-37; Alumni Medallion for Dist Service to Amer Med, NY State U, 1959. Home: 916 N Oak Park Ave, Oak Park, Ill. Offices: 840 S Wood St, Chicago, Ill; 8 S Michigan Ave, Chicago, Ill.

ABRAMSON, Debora Rose, US, librarian; b. Baton Rouge, La, Dec 20, 1902; d. Abraham and Mathilde (Mendelsohn); BA, La State U, 1924; BS, Columbia U, 1929. Ret; asst libr, La State Libr, 1930-69; instr, Tulane U, summers 1930-31. Mem: Amer, Southwestern, La Libr Assns; club, Mortar Bd. Contbr to profsl jours. Home: 833 N 11 St, Baton Rouge, La.

ABRAMSON, Joseph L, US, psychiatrist; b. New York, NY, Sep 24, 1898; s. Aaron and Annie (Oshrin); att U Mich, 1917-19, MD, 1923; m. Rose Lichter, Sep 15, 1929; c: Donald, William. Cons neuropsycht: J Hosp, pres, med bd, 1959; Kingsbrook Med Cen, pres, med bd, 1962-63; Swed Hosps; att neuropsycht, J Hosp for Chronic Diseases, since 1929; dir, Rehab Clinic for Vets, since 1946; clinical asst prof, neur, Downstate Med Cen, since 1957; asst phys, Kings Park State Hosp, 1924-25; psycht, United Family Wfr Org, 1925-28; instr, neur, State U Med Sch, NY, 1935-51; asso att neur:

Greenpoint Hosp, 1928-35; Kings Co Hosp, 1935-51. Cons psycht, induction cen, US Army, WW II. Dipl, neur, psycht, since 1934; pres: Bklyn Neur Soc, 1959-60; Bklyn Psychiatric Soc, 1955-57; f, Amer Psychiatric Soc; mem: NY Neurologic Soc; AMA; Phi Lambda Kappa, pres, 1959. Contbr to profls jours. Home and office: 20 Plaza St, Brooklyn, NY.

ABRAMSON, Julius, US, physician; b. New Bedford, Mass, July 28, 1903; s. Isaac and Mamie (Zeitz); MD, Tufts Coll Med Sch, 1927; postgrad studies, card, U Vienna, 1929-30; m. Gertrude Kerner, Nov 30, 1930; c: Mark, Jessica. Pvt practice since 1930; dir, Prenatal Clinic, card cons, obstet service, Boston City Hosp; fmr: sr phys, Booth Memorial Hosp, Brookline; asso, Beth Isr Hosp, Boston; chief, med service, Saugus Gen Hosp. Lt col, US Army, WW II. Mem: NE Cardiovascular Soc; Mass Heart Assn; Mass Med Soc; AMA; Phi Delta Epsilon; club, New Century. Contbr to med jours. Home: 393 Lee St, Brookline, Mass. Office: 127 Bay State Rd, Boston, Mass.

ABRAMSON, Lewis, US, pediatrician; b. Woonsocket, RI, Mar 31, 1910; s. Max and Annie (Berman); PhB, Brown U, 1933; MD, Tufts Med Sch, 1937; m. Ruth Hodosh, Aug 7, 1941; c: Stewart, Martha. Chief, ped, Newport Hosp since 1946, pres, staff, 1956-57; pvt practice since 1941; bd mgrs, Old Stone Bank, RI. Dir, Newport Comty Chest since 1959; bd trustees, Temple Shalom; mem: Newport Co and RI Med Socs; AMA; NE Ped Soc; Aquidneck Island Regional Disposal Auth; Masons; Shriners. Home and office: 280 Broadway, Newport, RI.

ABRAMSON, Marcus, US, attorney; b. Latvia, June 30, 1901; s. Samuel and Leah (Elishewitz); in US since 1904; grad, Talmudical Acad, NYC, 1919; BSS, CCNY, 1923; LLB, Harvard Law Sch, 1926; m. Pnina Shankman, Aug 24, 1930; c: Lee, Roselle. Ret since 1967; counsel, Amer Ins Assn, 1926-67. Hon bd dirs, Mosholu J Cen; exec comm, ZOA, 1951-56; pres, Bx Zionist region ZOA, 1963-67; chmn, Bx Zionist Youth Commn, 1951-57; mem: Lakeland J Cen; Amer and State Bar Assns; Intl Assn Ins Counsel. Home: Shrub Oak, NY.

ABRAMSON, Milton, US, physician; b. Floodwood, Minn, Mar 30, 1905; s. Frank and Sophia (Schochet); PhD, U Minn, 1932; m. Ruth Bank, Oct 25, 1929; c: Michael, Burton, Leslie. Pvt practice since 1932; clinical instr, dept obstet, gyn, U Minn; prof, sociol, Hamline U, St Paul, Minn. Mem: AMA; Minn State Med Soc; Cen Assn Obstet and Gyn; Alpha Omega Alpha; Sigma Xi; Phi Delta Epsilon. Contbr to med jours. Home: 3804 Ewing Ave S, Minneapolis, Minn. Office: 4225 Golden Valley Rd, Minneapolis, Minn.

ABRAMSON, Ted, US, certified public acctnt; b. Aurora, Minn, Aug 15, 1906; s. Frank and Sophia (Schochet); BBA, U Minn, 1931; m. Beatrice Mark, June 21, 1934; c: Abby Brown, David, Frank. Gen partner, Alexander Grant & Co, since 1949; Calmenson Abramson & Co, since 1930; lectr: Princeton U Grad Sch, US Army Exch Sch, 1943; U Minn, 1946. Lt col, US Army, 1942-46. Bd dirs: Mt Zion Heb Cong; Sholom Res; St Paul Talmud Torah; pres, St Paul United J Fund and Council, 1958-61, chmn, budget adv comm, CJFWF 1954-56; mem: Minn Soc of CPAs; Amer Inst CPAs. Hobbies: collecting Judaica; philately; bibliophile. Home: 597 Mt Curve Blvd, St Paul, Minn. Office: First Natl Bank Bldg, St Paul, Minn.

ABRAVANEL, Edgar, Fr, engineer, business exec; b. Cairo, Egypt, Sép 1905; s. Salvator and Victoria (Levy); grad, Ecole Supérieure d'Electricité, 1926; m. Berthe Ades, Dec 15, 1937; c: Chantal, Nicole. Mgn dir, Ets Edgar Abravanel, since 1930; elec engr, Singer Sewing Machine Co, 1927-32; gen Eur repr, Diehl Mfg Co, US. Pres, Sephardic Comty, Paris, since 1951; secy gen, United J Social Fund, since 1950; mem: Consistoire Israélite de Paris; B'nai B'rith, fmr secy gen and vice-pres. Home: 88 rue Michel-Ange, Paris 16e, Fr. Office: 22 rue Rennequen, Paris 17e, Fr.

ABSE, Leo, UK, solicitor; b. Cardiff, Wales, Apr 22, 1917; s. Rudolph and Kate; m. Marjorie; c: Tobias, Bathsheba. MP. Prin contribs: sponsor, co-sponsor, bills, divorces, sexual offences, family planning, illegitimacy. Mem: Home Off, Advisory Council on Penal Sys; Council of Inst for Study and Treatment of Delinquency; Natl Council for Unmarried Mother and her Child. Office: 40 Churchill Way C, Cardiff, Wales.

ABT, Harry, S Afr, minister; b. Weener, Ger, Oct 31, 1900; s. Lassar and Rosa (Loewenthal); in S Afr since 1940; PhD, U Frankfurt/M, 1924; m. Frieda Nussbaum, July 1, 1928; c: Eli, Ruth, Raphael. Min: Sydenham Highlands N, since 1969; Oxford Syn, Johannesburg, 1956-64; Etz Hayim, 1944-67; headmaster, J HS, Breslau, 1935. Mem exec, S Afr Natl Youth Council, since 1950; chmn: Council for Adult Educ; Inst for Adult Studies; mem exec council: S Afr J Hist and Sociol Soc, since 1948; found, J Mus, Johannesburg; fmr: cultural off, S Afr Bd J Deps; registrar, People's Coll; mem exec council: S Afr Bd J Educ; S Afr Mins Assn; chmn: J Youth Movement, Ezra; Union Orthodox J Academicians, both Ger. Author: Dorothea Schlegel born Mendelsohn: A Contribution to the History of Jewish Emancipation, 1925; The Jewish Youth Movement in Middle Europe, 1933; mem ed bd, Jewish Affairs, since 1945. Home: 82 Fifth Ave, Highlands N, Johannesburg, S Afr.

ABULAFIA, Bustenai, Isr, engineer; b. Jaffa, Isr, Sep 15, 1899; s. Shlomo and Rivkah (Fryman); BCE, Carnegie Inst of Tech, Pittsburgh, 1928; m. Zipora Rigler, Aug 30, 1927; c: Dalia Aviel, Ziva Paz, Gideon. Engr, Public Works dept, Isr Min of Lab; road engr, Transjordan, 1929; sanitary engr, Pal govt, 1931; engr, Jaffa port, 1936; Tel Aviv, port, 1937. Mem: Tel Aviv Commn, Maccabi; co-found, Young Maccabi, 1919. Author, manuals on construction works; contbr to profsl jours. Home: 9 Macdonald St, Ramat Gan, Isr. Office: Min of Housing, Hakirya, Tel Aviv, Isr.

ABULAFIA, Ziporah, Isr, educator, communal worker; b. Kosov, Pol, July 8, 1903; d. Meir and Ethel (Shapira) Rigler; in Isr since 1928; att Tchrs Sem, Pol, 1921; m. Bustenai Abulafia, Aug 30, 1927; c: Daliah Aviel, Ziva Paz, Gideon. Found, first Golden Age Club, Isr; mem: exec bd, chmn several comms, Grand Lodge, B'nai B'rith, Isr; exec, Assn for Blind; bd: Consumers Assn; Agbal; Brith Ivrit Olamit; found, fmr mem, Commn for Aged, Ramat Gan Munic; fmr: mem: exec bd, WIZO; bd, Soldiers Welfare Comm; Ilan; Akim; Anti-Tuberculosis League; Orphanage Assn. Home: 9 MacDonald St, Ramat Gan, Isr.

ACHENBAUM, Alvin A, US, business exec; b. NYC, Dec 11, 1925; s. Benjamin and Dora (Dvorin); BS, UCLA, 1950; MS, Columbia U, NY, 1951; m. Barbara Greenwald, June 24, 1951; c: Jonathan, Lisa, Martha. Exec vice-pres, dir, secy, Grey Advt Inc, since 1969; mr, mgr, market research, McCann Erickson, 1951-57. Cpl, USAAC, 1944-46. Mem: Amer Econ Assn; Market Research Council, both NY; Beta Gamma Sigma. Home: 34 Mallard Rise, Irvington, NY. Office: 777 Third Ave, New York, NY.

ACKERMAN, Nathan W, US, psychiatrist, educator; b. Bessarabia, Russ, Nov 22, 1908; s. David and Bertha (Frankel); in US since 1912; BA, Columbia U, 1929, MD, Coll Phys and Surgs, 1933; m. Gwendolyn Hills, 1937; c: Jeannie Curhan, Deborah. Clinical prof, psycht, Columbia U, since 1955, lectr, Sch Social Work, 1946-65; att, psychan, psycht clinic for training and research; dir, profsl prog, Family Inst; visiting lectr, Albert Einstein Med Sch; dir, Child Devl Cen, 1946-51; chief psycht, child guidance clinic, J Bd Guardians, 1941-51; cons, sci dept, AJComm; fmr: asst med dir, Southard Sch, Topeka; psycht, asst med dir, Stony Lodge, Ossining, NY; sup, res psycht, Family Mh Clinic, J Family Services, 1956-65. F: Amer Psychiatric and Orthopsychiatric Assns; NY Acad Med; dipl, Amer Bd Psycht and Neur; mem: Amer Group Therapy Assn; Amer Psychoanalytic Assn; Assn for Psychoanalytic Med, fmr pres; Amer Psychopathological Assn; NY Council Child Psycht, fmr vice-pres; Acad of Psychan; hon mem: Assn for Applied Psychan; Mexican Psychoanalytic Soc. Author: Psychodynamics of Family Life, 1958; Treating the Troubled Family, 1966; co-author: Personality and Arterial Hypertension, 1945; Antisemitism and Emotional Disorder, 1950; ed, Exploring the Base for Family Therapy, chmn, bd eds, Family Process; contbr to books, profsl jours, periodicals. Recipient: Adolf Meyer Award, 1958. Home: 124 E 84 St, New York, NY. Office: 149 E 78 St, New York, NY.

ACKERMAN, Norman Bernard, US, surgeon; b. NYC, Nov 27, 1930; s. Louis and Anne (Mukasie); AB, Harvard U, 1952; MD, U of Pa, 1956; PhD, U Minn, 1964; m. Anne Gross, June 14, 1953; c: Sara, Beth, Amy, Jane. Chmn, dept surg, sr att surg, Menorah Med Cen, since 1969; asst, asso prof, surg, Boston U, 1965-69. Capt, US Army, 1964-65. Prin contribs: research in: cancer diagnosis and theapy with radioisotopes; tumor circulation dynamics; carcinogenesis; hyperbaric med. Mem: Amer Coll Surgs; Soc U Surgs; Soc Nuclear Med; Amer Fed for Clinical Research; Amer Assn for Cancer Research; Amer Fed for Experimental Path; Assn for Advancement Med Instrumentation; AAAS; NY Acad of Scis. Contbr: sects in books; numerous articles to sci jours. Recipient: postdoc research f, Natl Cancer Inst, 1960-63; fac research award, Amer Cancer Soc, 1966-69. Home: 5300 W 84 St, Prairie Village, Kan. Office: 4949 Rockhill Rd, Kansas City, Mo.

ACKERMAN, Walter Isidore, US, educator; b. Somerville, Mass, Oct 25, 1925; s. David and Rae (Kushner); BA, cum laude, Harvard Coll, 1950, Harvard Grad Sch Educ, EdM, 1954, EdD, 1956; BJEd, MHL, Heb Tchrs Coll, 1953; att Heb U, Jerusalem, 1950-51; m. Frances Myers, June 8, 1948; c: Shira, David, Miriam, Naomi. Dean, prof educ, Heb Tchrs Coll, U Judaism, since 1964; dir, Camp Yavneh, 1953-69; headmaster, Beth-El Day Sch, 1955-60; dir, United Syn Commn on Educ, 1962-64. S/sgt, US Army, 1943-46. Exec bd: Natl Council for J Educ; Educs Assembly; adv bd, dept J communal affairs, AJComm; mem: NEA; Amer Camping Assn. Ed: Synagogue School, 1962-64; Old Age, 1962-64; asso ed, Jewish Education, since 1962; contbr to educ and J publs. Home: 117 N Gardner, Los Angeles, Cal. Office: 6525 Sunset Blvd, Los Angeles, Cal.

ACKERMANN, Wolfgang, US, surgeon; b. Lisowice, Aus, Oct 23, 1895; s. Gotthold and Sabine (Gruenfeld); desc of Joseph Caro, author of rel code Shulchan Aruch; in US since 1924; grad: with high hons, Sch for Res Offs, Aus Army, 1916, Machine Gun Sch for Offs, 1917; MD, med sch, U Vienna, Aus, 1923. Asso visiting surg, Francis Delafield Hosp, since 1953; instr, anat, surg, Columbia U, 1928-46; res surg, Sea View Hosp, NY, 1925-28; asst, att surg, Vanderbilt Clinic, NY, 1928-46; surg, City Hosp, NY, 1932-36. Lt, Aus Army. Prin contribs: patentee, inventor, instruments for early detection of cancer in bones and soft tissue, 1960. Mem: AMA; NY State Med Soc; NY Co Med Soc; NY Acad Sci. Author: And We are Civilized, 1936; At Last Hitler's End, play, 1940; TV drama, The Chosen One, 1965; contbr to med jours. Recipient: cert award, US Off Sci Research and Devl, 1946; bronze medallion for wartime service, Columbia U, 1946; citations: Amer Acad Orthopedic Surgs, 1958; Amer Coll Surgs, 1960; hon mention, AMA, 1961; three decorations WWI, Aus Govt. Home and office: 240 Central Park S, New York, NY.

ACZEL, Eliezer Ladislas, Isr, master mariner; b. Budapest, Hung, June 2, 1911; s. Joseph and Rachel (Bruenn) Abeles; in Isr since 1934; Merchant Navy Off, Nautical Acad, Fiume, It, 1933; m. Miriam Bloomin, Feb 7, 1941; c: Amir, Ilana. Capt, cdr, ss Theodor Herzl, since 1959; in command of Isr ships since 1938; dir Haifa Nautical Sch, 1943-44; pioneer of J shipping since 1934; tchr Isr seamen for 25 yrs; participated maritime projects, Afr nations. Capt, Royal Naval Armament Supplies, 1940-46. Hon mem, Rotary, 1957-64; mem, Hon Order Ky Cols. Recipient: Hon Aide to Gov, Ky, 1957; Hon Citizen, Baltimore, 1965; Adm, Chesapeake Bay; decorations: Afr Star, It Star, Atlantic Star, 1939-45 Star, Victory Medal, Knight cdr, Order Star of Afr, Liberia. Home: 42A Margalit St, Haifa, Isr. Office: Zim Lines, 7-9 Ha'atzmaut St, Haifa, Isr.

ADAM, Robert, Fr, business exec, builder; b. Botosani, Rum, May 1, 1908; s. Max and Flora (Stolper) Abramovici; in Fr since 1946; deg, econs, U Bucharest, Rum, 1931; div. Pres, ISCPMG, Menton, Fr, since 1967; dir, Ets Socomex, Vaduz, Lichtenstein, since 1951; mgn dir: Société Franco-Australienne, 1948-51; Ameropa, 1951-57; Société Commerciale Financière, 1953-60. Prin contribs: bldg, The Big Marina (1000 boats), Menton, Fr. Mem: Cercle Interallié; Racing club, both Paris. Hobbies: horseback riding, sailing. Home and office: 1 Paul Doumer Ave, Paris, Fr.

ADAMS, Arlin M, US, attorney; b. Phila, Pa, Apr 16, 1921; s. Aaron and Matilda (Landau); BS, Temple U, 1941, MA, 1950; LLB, U of Pa, 1947; hon degs: LLD; DHL; DSc; m. Neysa Cristol, Nov 10, 1942; c: Carol, Judith, Jane. Judge, US Court of Appeal, 3rd circuit, since 1969; partner, Schnader, Harrison, Segal & Lewis, 1952-69; secy, Dept Public Wfr, Pa, 1963-66; fac mem: Amer Inst of Banking, 1948-52; U of Pa Law Sch, 1955-59. Lt, USNR, 1942-46. Hon pres, Keneseth Isr, 1957; chmn, bd dirs, Moss Rehab Hosp, 1961-63; chmn, Phila chap, AJComm, 1962; mem, bd dirs: HUC; U of Pa Law Sch; Fels Inst State and Local Govt, chmn; Bryn Mawr Coll; Sch of Social Work; Jewish Exponent, 1962; Fed of JAs, 1957-62, vice-pres, since 1968; mem, bd govs, Phila Bar Assn, 1960-62, chmn: judiciary comm, 1958, profsl educ, 1958-59, spec services, since 1962; chmn, trade assn comm,

Amer Bar Assn, 1960-62; mem: Amer Law Inst; Judicature Soc; clubs: Locust; Midday; Union League. Home: Kennworth Arts, Phila, Pa. Office: US Courthouse, 9 and Chestnut Sts, Philadelphia, Pa.

ADAMS, Edward, US, business exec; b. Rozwadow, Pol, July 26, 1890; s. Moses and Sarah (Abrahams); m. Ilona Schildkraut, Budapest, Sep 4, 1917; c: Walter. Pres, Champlain Advt Co, since 1960; asso, Leon Tempelsman and Son, since 1949; fmr held various exec positions. Chmn: spec events, UJA Council of Orgs, NY; fund raising, United Galician J of Amer; mem, bd overseers, Bar Ilan U. Home: 155 E 76 St, New York, NY. Office: 60 E 42 St, New York, NY.

ADAMS, Joey, US, entertainer, author; b. NYC, Jan 6, 1911; s. Nathan and Ida (Chonin) Abramowitz; hon D Comedy: CCNY, 1950; Columbia U, 1950; NYU, 1959; m. Cindy Heller, 1952. Actor, comedian, since 1927; appeared in motion pictures: Ringside, 1945; Singing in the Dark, produc, 1956; radio progs: Rate Your Mate, CBS, 1952; Spend a Million, NBC, 1954; Joey Adams Show, 1957; Says Who, 1958; TV progs: Back that Fact, 1955; Gags to Riches, 1958; Person to Person, 1959; recordings for Choral and MGM records; US State Dept repr to entertain GI's around the world, 1958; ambass of good will, President's Cultural Ecxh Tour to SE Asia, State Dept and USIS, 1961. Pres: Amer Guild Variety Artists, since 1959; AGVA Found, since 1959; Youth Fund, 1959; bd dirs, Theater Auth, since 1959; delg, Allied Entertainment Unions, 1959; Commn, Youth, NYC, 1959; mem: Screen Actors Guild; Amer Fed TV and Radio Artists; Actors Equity; J Theatrical Guild; Authors League. Author: From Gags to Riches, 1946; The Curtain Never Falls, 1949; Joey Adams Joke Book, 1952; Strictly for Laughs, 1955; Cindy and I, 1957; It Takes One to Know One, 1959; The Return of Madelaine, 1959; Hamlet's Pratfall, 1960; Joey Adams Joke Dictionary, 1961; A Show Business Vignette, 1961; On the Road for Uncle Sam, 1963; You Could Die Laughing; Joey Adams Encyclopedia of Humor; album, Jewish Folk Songs. Recipient: citations: Damon Runyon Fund, 1955; Heart Fund, 1955; Catholic Youth Org, 1955; Boys Town of It, 1956; Cerebral Palsy Assn, 1957; Muscular Dystrophy Assn, 1958; Disabled Amer Vets, 1958; Boy Scouts of Amer, 1959, 1960, 1961; spec citation for fight against juvenile delinquency: from Mayor Robert F Wagner and Youth Bd, NYC, 1960; NY State, Gov Nelson Rockefeller, 1961; Isr Govt award: for UJA and Isr Bond Drives, 1952; man of year award: March of Dimes, 1958; NYC Police Dept, 1960; City of Hope Torch award, 1959; humanitarian awards: Amer Cancer Soc, 1952; Crusade for Freedom, 1956; Yiddish Theatrical Alliance, 1960; decorations for promoting intl goodwill: Queen of Cambodia, 1961; Roval Thai Army, 1961; AGVA Joey awards for talent and variety field, created in his honor, 1960. Hobby: collector of paintings. Home: 1050 Fifth Ave, New York, NY. Office: 160 W 46 St, New York, NY.

ADAMS, Stanley, US, author, musician, organization exec; b. NYC, Aug 14, 1907; s. Henry and Nan (Josephs); BLL, NYU Law Sch, 1929; m. Berenice Halperin; c: Barbara Hammel. Pres, ASCAP, 1953-56 and since 1959, mem bd of dirs, since 1944, mem since 1934; hon mem, Amer Guild Authors and Composers, vice-pres, 1943-44; 2nd vice-pres, Natl Music Council; adv vd, Amer Fed Musicians. Author, many songs, including: What a Diff'rence a Day Made; Little Old Lady; There Are Such Things; My Shawl. Dir, Country Music Assn; mem, exec bd, President's Music Comm Natl Cultural Cen, Wash, DC; mem: adv bd, Musicians Aid Soc, Inc; bd dirs, Music for Blind; Music Comm, NYC; Natl Comm for Intl Cultural Exch. Recipient: Pres Citation, Natl Fed Music Clubs, 1961; gold medal award, Phila Club of Printing House Craftsmen, 1961; Radio and TV Guide award, Vets Hosp, 1964; medal of hon, Natl Arts Club, 1965; hon citizen, State of Tenn, 1966. Home: 3 Woodland Pl, Great Neck, NY. Office: ASCAP, 575 Madison Ave, New York, NY.

ADAMS, Theodore L, US, rabbi; b. Bangor, Me, Feb 23, 1915; s. Raphael and Ida (Tomchin); BA, Yeshiva U, 1936; ordained rabbi, Rabbi Isaac Elchanan Theol Sem, 1937; grad work, sociol, Columbia U, 1944-47; MS, Yeshiva U, 1960, PhD, 1962; m. Bernice Nemetski, Jan 11, 1938; c: Lawrence, Howard, Sivia, Myril. Rabbi: Cong Ohab Zedek, NY, since 1953; Cong Mt Sinai, Jersey City, NJ, 1938-53; fmr chaplain, Hudson Co. Pres: RabCA, 1952-54; Rabb Council, NJ, 1939-52, hon pres since 1952; mem: exec comm, Jersey City Zionist Dist, Amer Zionist Policy Comm, 1944-46; exec bd Syn Council of Amer; exec bd, Union Orthodox J Cong of Amer;

rel activities div, JWB; delg, Mid Cent White House Conf on Children and Youth, Wash DC, 1950; Pres Eisenhower's People to People Comm, 1957, 1960; Pres Eisenhower's Comm for Intl Econ Growth, 1957-61; rel and wfr comm, NY Comm on Atomic Info, 1956-58; US Mission to UN; exec comm, Conf on Material Claims Against Ger, 1960-61; Amer Sociol Soc; f, Amer Acad Political and Social Sci. Ed, Sermon Manual, 1948; mem, faiths adv comm, Collier's Ency; contbr to jours. Home: 680 West End Ave, New York, NY. Study: 118 W 95 St, New York, NY.

ADAR, Joseph, Isr, engineer; b. Haifa, Feb 22, 1925; s. Elias and Dolla-Debora (Smolisansky) Rabinowitz; desc of Yaakov-Zeev Smolisansky, one of first Zionist settlers in Isr; Licencie-es-Sciences, Fr U, Beirut, 1945; deg, civil engr, Ecole Fr d'Ingenieurs, Beirut, 1946; MSc, elec engr, Ecole Superieure d'Electricite, Paris; m. Chaya Vronsky, Paris, Dec 2, 1959; c: Ori, Yael. Coord for water and power, Isr AEC, since 1966; reactor project mgr, 1957-61; water cons, Natl Council for Research and Devl, since 1967; water research coord, Natl Council for Research and Devl, 1966-67; reactor project engr, Jt US-Isr Desalinization Project, 1965-67; devl projects. Dead Sea Works, Ltd, 1961-65; head, network maintenance, Isr Elec Corp, 1950-57; asst city engr, Rishon le Zion Munic, 1946-47. Capt, IDF. Prin contribs: design and erection of Isr's first large nuclear reactor; devl work, Dead Sea Works, enclosing southern part of Dead Sea by dikes; promoting desalinization and research projects. Mem: Inst Architects and Engrs in Isr; Fed of Engrs, Histadrut. Author: Choice and Optimization of Eventual Heat Sources, 1967; Preliminary Study of a Desalting Power Industry Complex in Israel, 1968; contbr to encys, jours. Home: 13 Nahum St, Ramat Chen, Isr. Office: 26 University Rd, Ramat Aviv, Isr.

ADAR, Ozer, Isr, attorney; b. Lodz, Pol, Dec 12, 1912; s. Abraham and Rebecca (Danielewski) Goldberg; in Isr since 1925; licence en droit et sci econ, U Toulouse, Fr, 1936; licenced atty, Jerusalem, 1940; m. Esther Katz, Feb 3, 1942; c: Naavah, Orna. Dep legal adv, Min of Defense, since 1962; fmr in pvt practice, 1940-48. Chief counsellor, judge, advocate gen, chief defense counsel, lt col, IDF, 1948-55. Mem: council, Academicians Assn; secretariat, Supr Court of Isr Lab Party. Home: 48 Amishav St, Tel Aviv, Isr. Office: Hakiriya, Tel Aviv, Isr.

ADAR, Zvi, Isr, educator; b. Petah Tikva, Isr; MA, PhD, Heb U, Jerusalem; m. Prof, educ, Heb U. Pvt, Brit Army, 1941-46; capt, IDF, 1948-49. Author: The Educational Values of the Bible; The Foundations of Education; other books on the Bible and educ. Home: 6 Harlap St, Jerusalem, Isr. Office: Heb U, Jerusalem, Isr.

ADDLESON, Abraham, S Afr, attorney; b. London, Eng, Oct 10, 1899; s. Samuel and Jessie (Inyol); in S Afr since 1903; att Queen's Coll, Queenstown, S Afr, 1910-16; m. Fanny Shapiro, Oct 29, 1924; c: Norman. Practicing atty and notary public since 1920; city councillor, E London, since 1950, mayor, 1957-59. Fmr pres, E London Heb Cong; mem: Zionist Assn border regional council; Eng Acad of S Afr; club, Alexander Country, fmr first pres. Author: Epic of a People, 1942, 2nd ed, 1944; contbr to Saron & Hotz' History of the Jews of S Africa, 1955. Hobby: golf. Home: 6 Hardy Rd, East London, S Afr. Office: 29 Terminus St, East London, S Afr.

ADELMAN, Albert B, US, business exec; b. Milw, Wis, Sep 5, 1915; s. Benjamin and Regina (Lazoris); BSS, Northwestern U, 1937; m. Edith Margoles, Dec 17, 1938; c: Gary, Craig, Lynn. Pres, Adelman Laundry and Cleaners Inc, since 1947; mem, bd dirs: Pfister Hotel Corp, Milw; Monarch Laundry Co, Chgo. Bd dirs: Mt Sinai Hosp, since 1961; Milwauke JWF, since 1960, fmr pres; exec comm, natl off, UJA; mem: Chief Execs Forum; Wis Laundry and Dry Cleaners Assn; Roundtable Launderers and Drycleaners; Northwestern U Alumni Assn; Cong Emanu-El; Delta Sigma Rho; J Comty Cen; Athletic Hall of Fame; trustee, B'nai B'rith; fmr: mem: Wis Small Bus Assn; exec comm, Milw Co Boy Scouts of Amer; bd dirs: Pops; Shorewood Sch Bd; Young Pres' Org; clubs: Rotary; Brynwood Country, fmr pres. Co-author: Fox Point-Bay Side Curriculum Comm, 1959, Home: 7111 N Barnett La, Fox Point, Wis. Office: 709 E Capitol Dr, Milwaukee, Wis.

ADELMAN, Morris Albert, US, economist, educator; b. NYC, May 31, 1917; s. David and Leah (Albert); BSS, CCNY, 1938; PhD, Harvard U, 1948; m. Millicent Linsen, 1949; c: Lawrence, Barbara. Prof, econ, MIT since 1948; econ, War Production Bd, 1941-42; Fed Res Bd, 1946. USN, 1942-45. F, Social Sci Research Council, 1947-48; mem: Amer Econ Assn; Royal Econ Soc, London. Contbr to econ and law jours. Home: 83 Nehoiden Rd, Waban, Mass. Office: MIT, 354A, Cambridge, Mass.

ADELMAN, William, US, hospital admnr; b. NYC, Apr 22, 1908; s. Samuel and Lena (Saltzman); att: CCNY; Queen's Coll; JTSA; m. Doris Mensch, Feb 14, 1946; c: Mark, Robert. Exec dir, Beth Abraham Home, since 1950; lectr, chronic illness, aging, nursing home admn, Columbia Sch of Public Health and Admn Med; dir, Cen Bur for supr, Fed Works Agcy, 1933-40; asst to pres, Intl Mutoscope Corp, 1940-49; lab relations cons and arbitrator, 1940-50; cons, exec recruitment, US Civil Service Commn, 1940-42. Served, US Mil Police. F: Amer Public Health Assn; Gerontological Soc; licentiate mem, Royal Soc of Health; dir, Cen Bur for J Aged; delg, Hosp Assn of NY State; mem: Gov's Comm on Aged; Citizen's Comm on Aging, Comty Council of Gtr NY; comm on rev of nursing home code, NYC Dept of Hosps; functional comms on care of aged, hosp and med services, comm on social leg, FJP, NY; Amer Arbitration Assn; Commerce and Ind Assn of NY; Queensboro C of C; Natl Conf J Communal Services; Natl Council Aging; Natl Social Wfr Assembly; Natl Assn J Homes for Aged; Amer Assn Homes for Aged. Home: 166 Kneeland Ave, Yonkers, NY. Office: 612 Allerton Ave, Bronx, NY.

ADELSON, Edward, US, physician, educator; b. Boston, Mass, Sep 14, 1923; s. Abraham and Rebecca (Freidman); BS, magna cum laude, Tufts U, Sch of Liberal Arts, Medford, Mass, 1943, MD, magna cum laude, Med Sch, Boston, 1947; m. Lois Potts, Apr 7, 1954; c: Andrew, Nancy, Stephen. Asso clinical prof, med, George Washington U Med Sch, since 1960; cons, hematology, Walter Reed Army Med Cen, since 1955. Prin contribs: research in hematology and med. Capt, US Army, 1953-55. Pres, Jacobi Soc, Wash, DC; mem: bd, Wash Hosp Cen, Wash, DC; Phi Beta Kappa; Alpha Omega Alpha. Contbr numerous articles in hematology to profsl jours. Home: 7020 Richard Dr, Bethesda, Md. Office: 1100 22 St, NW, Washington, DC.

ADELSON, Howard Laurence, US, educator; b. Bklyn, NY, July 16, 1925; s. Moses and Esther (Finkelstein); BA, NYU, 1945; MA, Columbia U, 1948; MA, Princeton U, 1950, PhD, 1952; m. Helen Gottesman, 1958, (div); c: Mark, Sarah. Chmn, dept hist, prof medieval hist, CCNY, since 1967, exec off, PhD prog in hist, 1966-69; dir studies, summer sem, Amer Numismatic Soc, 1964-67. Capt, USAF, 1952-68. Mem: publ comm, J Publ Soc of Amer; academic council, Amer Friends Heb U; ZOA; Amer Hist Assn; Amer Philol Assn; club, Princeton of NY. Author: Light Weight Solidi and Byzantine Trade in the Sixth and Seventh Centuries, 1957; Medieval Commerce, 1962. Recipient: Newell F, Amer Numismatic Soc, 1949, f, 1954. Home: 645 Eastern Pkwy, Brooklyn, NY. Office: City Coll, CUNY, Convent Ave at 137 St, New York, NY.

ADELSON, Judah, US, historian, author; b. Bklyn, NY, Nov 23, 1922; s. Moses and Esther (Finkelstein); BS, NYU, 1943; AM, Columbia U, 1944; PhD, NYU, 1961. Prof, hist, SUNY, New Paltz, since 1968, visiting asso prof, 1967-68; instr, CCNY, 1958-59, lectr, social studies, 1952-58; asst prof, hist, NYU, 1961-67, instr, 1957-61; asst dean, freshman program, grad cen, CUNY, 1967-69; visiting prof, Tobe Coburn Sch, 1957-63. Author: The Reaction of the Vermont Newspapers to the French Revolution, 1961; History of Western Civilization, 1968; contbr to hist jours. Bd govs, Bklyn J Cen; mem: Masons; Amer Hist Assn; Econ Hist Soc; Eng Econ Hist Soc; Amer Numismatic Soc; Natl Educ Assn for Social Studies; Fr Hist Soc; Acad of Political Sci; club, NYU, bd govs. Recipient: Founds Day Award, NYU. Home: 645 Eastern Parkway, Brooklyn, NY. Office: SUNY, New Paltz, NY.

ADELSTEIN, Howard, US, social work exec; b. Montreal, Can, May 14, 1911; s. Louis and Ida (Cohen); in US since 1940; BS, McGill U, 1932; grad study in social work: Montreal Sch of Social Work; U Chgo; m. Clarice Goldner, May 20, 1947; c: Laura. Exec dir: YM & YWHA, Phila, since 1954; Akron J Comty Cen, 1940-44; Bridgeport J Comty Cen, 1944-54. Secy, Natl Assn Social Workers, 1968-70, mem exec comm, 1967-69, chmn, Phila area chap, 1962-64; natl pres: Natl Assn J Cen Workers, 1952-54; Assn of JA Execs, 1957-58; mem: Natl Conf J Communal Service; ACLU; Amer Acad Political and Social Sci; Intl Conf on Social Welfare. Hobby: sculpturing. Home:

7716 Mill Rd, Elkins Park, Pa. Office: YM & YWHA, 401 S Broad St, Philadelphia, Pa.

ADERET, Avraham, Isr, educator; b. Jerusalem; s. Nehemya and Shlomit Peltz; att Agric Sch, Ben Shemen; m. Rifka Samborsky; c: Yair, Jonathan, Joel, Miriam. Tchr: Sem Hakibbutzim, Oranim, since 1963; HS, Mevo Galil, Ayelet HaShachar, since 1952. Served: Haganah; IDF. Mem: Histadrut; Isr Lab Party; Ihud Hakvutzot vehaKibbutzim, fmr with youth dept; leader, youth movements. Author: What are the Men, 1965; The Pioneer Youth Movement, 1964; Sexual Education in the Israel Youth Movement, 1965; The Youth on Itself, 1949; with Petachim, bi-monthly publ of J thought. Spec interest: lit. Home: Kibbutz Ayelet HaShachar, Isr. Office: Oranim, Kiryat Tivon, Isr.

ADINI, Uziel, US, educator; b. Tel Aviv, Isr; s. Israel and Lea (Lichtenberg); in US since 1964; BA, Heb U, 1957; dipl, Mizrachi Sem, 1956; MA, Heb U, 1962; Ed D, Dropsie Coll, Phila, 1967; m. Tamar Low, July 16, 1962; c: Ronit, Tal. Asst prof, Temple U, since 1964; secondary educ cons, asst prof, Gratz Coll, since 1965; instr: Talpiot Sem, Tel Aviv, 1962-64; Mizrachi Sem, Jerusalem, 1957-62. Sgt, IDF. Prin contrib: created audio prog for teaching Heb in elem grades. Cons, Off Secondary J Educ, Phila, Pa; mem: Natl Council J Educ; Amer Assn for J Educ; B'nai B'rith. Recipient: f, Dropsie Coll, 1964; Manstein Award, Beth Sholom, Pa, 1969. Home: 1621 Borbeck Ave, Philadelphia, Pa. Office: Broad and Montgomery Sts, Philadelphia, Pa.

ADLER, Charles, US, inventor; b. Baltimore, Md, June 20, 1899; s. Harry and Carol (Frank); att Johns Hopkins U, 1917-20; m. Alene Steiger, June 10, 1925; c: Amalie, Harry. Inventions: rotating stop-sign; RR hwy crossing signal; Adler double filament incandescent lamps for RR signals, traffic signals, airplane navigation lights; Adler flasher relay, traffic sound detector; aircraft flashing position-light sys; studded reflector tail light, reflector lamp for aircraft, aircraft anti-collision light; aircraft proximity indicator; spaceometer; SATC, 1918; Fmr bd mem, Friendship Intl Airport; mem: Inst of Traffic Engrs; Soc of Automotive Engrs; Md Traffic Safety Commn; Natl Aeronautics Assn; State Aviation Commn, Md. Contbr to mags. Recipient: awards: USAAF, 1945; Natl Aeronautics Assn, 1951; CAA, 1953; USN, 1953; Aircraft Owners and Pilots Assn, 1958. Home and office: 1506 Sutton Place Apts, Baltimore, Md.

ADLER, Erich, Swed, chemist; b. Frankenreuth, Ger, Oct 24, 1905; s. Max and Elfriede (Putzker); in Swed since 1933; DEng, Tech U, Munich, 1931; m. Annemaria Pawel, Aug 10, 1935; c: Eva, Rolf. Prof, organic chem, Chalmers Tekniska Högskola (Tech U), Göteborg, since 1952; docent, Royal Inst of Tech, Stockholm, 1946-52. Contbr of numeorus publs to sci jours. Home: Raketgaten 11, Göteborg, Swed. Office: Chalmers Tekniska Högskola, Göteborg, Swed.

ADLER, H G, Eng, author; b. Prague, Czech, July 2, 1910; s. Emil and Alice (Fraenkel); in Eng since 1947; PhD, U Prague, 1935; m. Gertrud Klepetar (decd); m. 2nd, Bettina Gross; c: Jeremy. Free lance writer, scholar, since 1947; secy, Evening Classes Sch, Prague, 1935-38; sci collaborator, J Mus, Prague, 1945-47. Author: Theresienstadt 1941-1945, 1955, 2nd ed, 1960; Die Verheimlichte Wahrheit, documents on Theresienstadt, 1958; Der Kampf Gegen die "Endlösung der Judenfrage", 1958; Die Juden in Deutschland, 1960, Amer version, 1969; Unser Georg, 1961; Eine Reise, 1962; Der Fürst des Segens, 1964; Die Erfahrung der Ohnmacht, 1964; Sodoms Untergang, 1965; Panorama, 1968; Kontraste und Variationen, 1969; Ereignisse, 1969; contbr papers and articles on J under Nazis, J hist, sociology. Recipient: Leo Baeck Prize, Zentralrat der Juden in Deutschland, 1958; Prix Charles Veillon, Lausanne, 1969. Hobbies: photography, music, hiking. Home and office: 47 Wetherby Mansions, London SW5, Eng.

ADLER, Hans, US, organization exec; b. Vienna, Aus, Feb 16, 1910; s. Siegmund and Therese (Redlich); in US since 1938; MA: U Vienna; Acad of Commerce, Vienna. Dir, comty service dept, ADL, Chgo, since 1945; lectr, phil, logic, Ind U, since 1945; journalist, tutor; officer, Schenker and Co, Vienna, until 1938; ed in chief, Radio Frankfurt, US War Dept, 1945. US Army, 1941-45. Fmr bd mem: B'nai B'rith; UN Org, Gtr Chgo; Amer Vets of WW II. Author: Travel the Rainbow; contbr to mags; weekly column, Pittsburgh Courier, 1951-52. Recipient: 2 battle stars, 1945; medal, Grand Order of Oak Crown, Luxembourg. Home: 5242 S Hyde Park Blvd, Chgo, Ill. Office: 315 Lexington Ave, New York, NY.

ADLER, Helmut E, US, psychologist; b. Nuremberg, Ger, Nov 25, 1920; s. Paul and Lola (Offenbacher); in US since 1940; BS, Columbia U, 1948, AM, 1949, PhD, 1952; m. Leonore Loeb, May 22, 1943; c: Barry, Beverly, Evelyn. Prof, Yeshiva U, since 1964, asso prof, 1957-64, fac mem since 1950; research asso, Amer Mus Natural Hist since 1969, research f, 1955-69; scistaff, Columbia U, 1952-55, lectr, 1955-60. F, Amer Psych Assn; mem: E Psych Assn; Animal Behavior Soc; NY Acad Sci; Ecol Soc of Amer; Amer Meteorological Soc; AAUP; Sigma Xi; Psi Chi. Co-author: Bird Behavior, 1962; Bird Life, 1969; trans, Fechner's Elements of Psychophysics, 1966; contbr to profsl jours. Hobbies: breeding miniature Dachshunds, raising tropical fish. Home: 162-1486 Ave, Jamaica, NY. Office: Yeshiva U, New York, NY.

ADLER, Hermann, Switz, journalist, author; b. Nemet-Diosek, Bratislava, Czech, Oct 2, 1911; s. Simon and Mimi (Lichtig); in Switz since 1954; grad, Jüdisches Lehrerseminar, Würzburg. Mem staff: Radio Basel; Süddeutscher Rundfunk, Stuttgart; Südwestfunk, Baden-Baden; Norddeutscher Rundfunk, Hamburg; Saarländischer Rundfunk, Saarbrücken; Radio Bremen; Westdeutscher Rundfunk, Köln; Zweites Deutsches Fernsehen, Mainz; fmr: tchr for defective children, Landeshut, Ger; journalist: Bratislava; Praha. Served: Czech Legion, Pol, 1939; J Resistance, Budapest; concentration Camp, Bergen-Belsen, 1939-45. Author: Gesange aus der Stadt des Todes, 1945; Ostra Brama, 1946; Balladen der Gekreuzigten, der Auferstandenen, Verachteten, 1947; Fieberworte von Verdammnis und Erlösung, 1948; Bilder nach dem Buche der Verheissung, 1950; Vater, vergib, 1951; Jitzhak Katznelsons Lied vom letzten Juden, 1952; stage dramas; radio, TV plays; contbr to press. Mem: Schutzverband deutschsprachiger Schriftsteller, Switz; PEN Club, Ger group, London; Nordschweizerischer PEN, Club, Basel; Assn de la Presse Etrangère de la Suisse; Psychologische Gesellschaft, Basel; Philosophische Gesellschaft, Basel; hon mem, Psychotherapie-Seminar, Munich, Freudenstadt. Recipient: hon citation of Commn for Lit, from Pres of City of Zurich, 1947; citation, Zweites Deutsches Fernsehen, Mainz. Home: Breisacherstr 95, Basel, Switz.

ADLER, Israel, Isr, librarian, musicologist; b. Berlin, Ger, Jan 17, 1925; s. Hermann and Fanny Friedmann; in Isr since 1937; att: Conservatoire National de Musique, Paris, 1949-53; Docteur du III cycle, Institut de Musicologie, 1963; Eleve diplome, Ecole Pratique des Hautes Etudes, Sorbonne, Paris, 1960; Licence d'Harmonie, Ecole Normale de Musique, Paris, 1953; m. Claire Thiessard, c: Eliezer. Dir, J Natl and U Libr, since 1969, head, music dept, 1963-69; head, Hebraica Judaica Dept, Bibliothèque Nationale, Fr, 1950-63; dir, J music research dept, Heb U, 1964-69. Haganah, 1943-48, Palmach, 1948-49. Pres: Intl Fed of Sound Archives; mem: Repertoire Intl de Literature Musicale; chmn, Isr Musicological Soc, 1967-69. Author: Les Incunables Hebraiques de la Bibliothèque Nationale, 1962; La pratique musicale savante dans quelques communautes juives en Europe aux 17e-18e siecles; contbr of numerous articles to Judaic and musicological periodicals. Home: 14 Antigonos St, Jerusalem, Isr. Office: J Natl and U Libr, Jerusalem, Isr.

ADLER, Jack Franklin, US, business exec; b. Norfolk, Va, Nov 13, 1911; s. Isaac and Jennie (Selig); BS, U of Va, 1931; m. Jean Anathan, Nov 28, 1935; c: Jack, Judy Elitzky. Partner: Touche Ross & Co, since 1967; Goldsmiths' Acctnts, 1936-52; Adler, Faunce & Co, 1953-57; Adler, Faunce & Leonard, 1957-67. Mem, Local Coast Guard, WW II. Trade council chmn, advance gift chmn, gen chmn, Allied J Appeal of Phila; mem: Pa, Amer Insts of CPA; cabinet, exec comm, bd, Fed of JA, chmn, planning comm, past treas, vice-pres; exec comm, bd, Albert Einstein Med Cen, chmn, finance comm; exec comm, bd, United Fund of Phila; bd: Abington YMCA; Assn for J Children; mem bd: Willowcrest Convalescent Home; J Family Service; J Exponent; F Comm; B'nai B'rith; clubs: Midcity, pres; Locust, chmn bd; Philmont Country, fmr pres. Hobbies: golf, reading, traveling. Home: 406 B Elkins Pk House, Elkins Park, Pa. Office: 1770 Market St, Philadelphia, Pa.

ADLER, Kurt Herbert, US, musician; b. Vienna, Aus, Apr 2, 1905; s. Ernst and Ida (Bauer); in US since 1938; att: Vienna St Acad of Music, 1922-26; U Vienna, 1923-27; m. Diantha Warfel, July 7, 1940 (div); c: Kristin, Ronald; m. 2nd, Nancy Miller, Aug, 1965. Gen dir, SF Opera; producer: Spring Opera; Western Opera Theater; conductor, Annual Midsummer Music Festival, SF Opera and Sym, since 1944; fmr: conductor: Chgo Opera Co; Max Reinhardt Theaters: Vienna,

1925-28; opera houses, Ger, It, 1928-34; Volksoper, Vienna, 1934-36; Vienna Concert Orch, 1934-36; asst to Toscanini, Salzburg Festivals, 1936; opera, radio, Czech, 1936-38; Grant Park Concerts, Chgo, 1941-42; guest conductor: Ill Symphony Orch, 1942; New Opera Co, NYC, 1945; San Carlo Opera House, Naples; Hollywood Bowl; NBC Symphony. Dir, Merola Memorial Fund. Recipient: Star of Solidarity, 1957; Knight Order of Merit, Rep of It; Officer's Cross Medal of Honor, 1959; Gt Order of Merit for Services for Rep of Aus, 1961; Cdrs Cross of Medal of Honor, Ger, 1968. Office: War Memorial Opera House, San Francisco, Cal.

ADLER, Matityahu, Isr, administrator; b. Prague, Czech, June 18, 1920; s. Shimon and Rose (Schiffer); in Isr since 1939; MA, Heb U, Jerusalem, 1945; m. Yehudit Friedman, Nov 1, 1946; c: Shimon, Shoshana, Aaron. Dir gen, Bar Ilan U, since 1963; commn, local govt, Min of Interior, 1950-62; mayor, Beersheva, 1962. Home: 26 Yahalom St, Ramat Gan, Isr. Office: Bar Ilan U, Ramat Gan, Isr.

ADLER, Robert, US, business exec; b. NYC, Dec 25, 1906; s. Hyman and Freida (Beyer); att O State U, 1925-27; m. Rose Schuman, Dec 23, 1933; c: Michael. Chmn bd: Progressive Ind Corp, since 1968; Tru-Foto Inc, since 1960; Natl Photo, since 1967; Foto-Fair Intl Inc, since 1968; Intl Acad Inc; publisher: Springfield Shopper, 1933-41; Springfield Jour, 1939-41; pres: Robert Adler Advt Agcy, 1941-45; Rapid Photo Service Inc, 1953-58. Chmn, UJA, 1945, 1956; vice-pres, Temple Sholom, 1943-44, 1954-55; pres, B'nai B'rith lodge, 1943; chmn, Isr Bonds, 1955; bd dirs: C of C, 1953-56; Tecumseh Council, Boy Scouts, since 1956; Jr Achievement, 1956-59; mem, JDC; clubs: Rotary; Meadowbrook Country. Home: 3050 Valerie Arms Dr, Dayton, O. Office: 2030 Kuntz Rd, Dayton, O.

ADLER, Robert Louis, US, business exec; b. Chgo, Ill, July 30, 1918; s. Simon and Mayme (Loeb); BS, U of Ill, 1940; m. Jean Schrayer, Dec 27, 1949; c: Ruth, Steven, Sandi. Vice-pres, Associated Agcys Inc, since 1951; vice-pres, treas, King Korn Enterprises, since 1960; vice-pres: Peal Mfg Co, 1948-49; Fireside Marshmallow Co, 1949-51. US Army, 1940-45. Vice-pres: Chgo chap, AJComm; Better Boys Found; treas: Phi Epsilon Pi Found; Harvard St George Sch; chmn: Chgo J Comty on Scouting; cong div, J United Fund; secy: Amer J Hist Soc; Syn Council of Amer; exec comm, natl bd, UAHC; bd mem: JWF of Chgo; Jackson Wark Hosp; Dreyel Home for the Aged; exec bd mem: Chgo Council Boy Scouts of Amer; fmr pres: Beth Am The Peoples Syn; UAHC, Chgo Fed; Chgo Conf of Men's Clubs; Phi Epsilon Pi Natl Frat; mem, Rabbinic Pension Bd; clubs: Ravisloe Country, bd trustees; Brandeis; Standard, Chgo. Recipient: Bronze Star, Air Medal. Home: 6737 S Bennett Ave, Chicago, Ill. Office: 174 W Jackson Blvd, Chicago, Ill.

ADLER, Ruth G, US, stockbroker; b. NYC, Aug 27, 1921; d. Eugene and Bertha (Friedman); Gratt; BA, Hunter Coll, NY, 1941; att: NY Inst Finance, NY; Inves Bankers Inst, Phila; Wharton Sch Finance; m. Alexander Adler; c: Alison, Linda. Stockbroker, bd mgr, A G Edwards and Sons Inc; fmr: stockbroker, gen partner, Jones, Kreeger and Co; financial lectr. Mem: bd dirs: Wash Soc Inves Analysts; Bethesda-Chevy Chase C of C; club, Natl Econ. Columnist, financial sect, Bethesda-Chevy Chase Tribune; contbr to: Investment Sales Monthly; other inves jours. Home: 8003 Whittier Blvd, Bethesda, Md. Office: 7140 Wisconsin Ave, Bethesda, Md.

ADLER, Samuel Hans, US, educator, composer; b. Mannheim, Ger, May 4, 1928; s. Hugo and Selma (Rothschild); in US since 1939; BMus, Boston U, 1948; MA, Harvard U, 1950; hon DMus, S Methodist U, Tex, 1969; studied with: Aaron Copeland; Serge Koussevitsky; Karl Geiringer; others; m. Carol Stalker, Feb 14, 1960; c: Deborah, Naomi. Prof, composition: Eastman Sch of Music, U Rochester, since 1966; N Tex State U, 1958-66; dir music, Temple Emanu-El, Dallas, Tex, 1953-66; org, conductor, Dallas Chorale, 1954-56; conductor, Dallas Lyric Theatre, 1955-57. Composer: opera; chamber music; songs with piano; large chorale works with accompaniment; secular pieces; sacred pieces; works for children; arrangements; music for: orch, wind ensemble or band; large chamber combinations; received numerous commns. Cpl, US Army, 1950-52; org, 7th Army Sym Orch, toured Ger and Aus; led orch for Royal Dutch Ballet, 1952. Mem: ASCAP; Natl Assn Amer Composers and Conductors; Amer Music Cen; MENC; MTNA; Amer Choral Conductors; Amer Choral Found; hon mem: Phi Mu Alpha; Kappa Kappi Phi. Contbr articles to profsl publs. Recipient: Army Medal of Hon; Dallas Sym Prize, U Tex, 1953; 1st prize, Tex Composers Guild, 1955, 1957-63; First Saminsky Memorial Award, 1959; conductor, lectr, ME tour, selected by State Dept, 1958; Charles Ives Memorial Award, U Houston, 1963; SW Coll Band Masters Award, 1964; Rockefeller Grant, 1965; Ford Grant, 1965; Spec ASCAP Award, annually since 1960. Home: 54 R R Mills Rd, Pittsford, NY. Office: 26 Gibbs St, Rochester, NY.

ADLER, Samuel M, US, artist, educator; b, NYC, July 30, 1898; s. Harris and Rose (Levy); att Natl Acad of Design, New York, NY; m. Sarah Fox, (decd). Prof of art, NYU, since 1948; pvt tchr, 1935-48; visiting prof: U of Ill, Urbana, 1959-60; Notre Dame U, 1965; U of Ga, Athens, 1967-68. One-man exhbs: Joseph Luyber Gal, NYC, 1948; U Ind, 1950; Louisville Art Cen, 1950; Mint Mus, NC, 1951; Grace Borgenicht Gal, NYC, 1952, 1954; Phila Art Alliance, 1954; U of Ill, 1959, 1960; Grand Central Moderns, NYC, 1960; Babcock Gal, NYC, 1962; Krannert Art Mus, Urbana, 1964; Notre Dame U, 1965; Rose Fried Gal, NYC, 1965; U of Ia, 1966; U of Ga, 1967; Rippon Coll, 1968; represented in: natl and regional exhbs throughout US; fgn exhbs: Can; Japan; Den; Ger; Ir; Switz; Swed; Fr; Belgium; It; Eng; Monaco; Greece; perm collections: Butler Inst, Youngstown, O; Clearwater Mus, Fla; Glicenstein Mus, Safad, Isr; Joseph H Hirshhorn; Loeb Collection, NYU; Norfolk Mus, Va; Mus, William Proctor Inst, Utica, NY; S C Johnson & Son; Staten I Inst of Arts and Sci; Whitney Mus of Amer Art; Georgia Mus, Athens; Bklyn Mus, NY; Slater Memorial Mus, Norwich; Smithsonian Inst Mus, Wash, DC; U Syracuse; St Lawrence U; lectr, to Us, mus, colls, art assns, throughout US. Contbr publs on art to various jours. Recipient: J Henry Schiedt Memorial Prize, Pa Acad of Fine Arts, 1951; Purchase Award: U of Ill, 1952; Whitney Mus of Amer Art, 1952, 1963; Staten Island Inst of Art and Sci, 1962; Bayonne Art Assn, 1968; Patrons' Award, Audubon Artists, 1956; Medal of Hon, Audubon Artists, 1960; Ford Found Grant, artist in residence, Notre Dame U, 1965; 2nd prize, Amer Soc of Contemporary Artists, 1967; 1st Prize, 1968. Hobby: chamber music. Home: 45 Christopher St, New York, NY. Studio: 27 E 22 St, New York, NY.

ADLER, Samuel M, US, attorney; b. NYC, Feb 16, 1902; s. Simon and Olga (Melnick); att NYU, 1924; m. Ethel Fineberg, Jan 19, 1927; c: Doris. Pvt practice since 1926; partner, Adler, Mezey & Pressler, 1948-66. USAC, 1942-45. Dir, J Comty Cen; judge advocate: JWV; VFW; pres: J Fed of Raritan Valley, 1966, Urban League, 1956, life delg; Zionist dist, 1949-52; Optimist Club, 1954; Bomb Group Enlisted Men's Club, 1944-45; New Brunswick Bar Assn, 1959-60; vice-pres, NJ region ZOA, 1952; mem: natl scope and planning comm, 1953; Middlesex Co Bar Assn; Elks; Masons; Shriners. Recipient: citation, USAF, 1944-45. Home and office: 25 Perry Rd, Edison, NJ.

ADLER, Selig, US, journalist, editor; b. NYC, June 7, 1908; s. Moses and Anna (Hazelkorn); BA, Columbia U, 1929; m. Henrietta Hoffman, Aug 24, 1932. Chief articles ed, Natl Enquirer, since 1968; city ed, NY Mirror, 1937-58, mgn ed, 1958-63; fmr war corresp; contbr to publs on social and political conditions. Mem: Amer Polar Soc; Silurians. Hobbies: photography, hunting, world travel. Home: 150 Water Hole Rd, East Hampton, NY. Office: 120 Sylvon Ave, Englewood Cliffs, NJ.

ADLER, Selig, US, historian, educator; b. Baltimore, Md, Jan 22, 1909; s. Joseph and Della (Rubenstein); BA, summa cum laude, U Buffalo, 1931; MA, U of Ill, 1932, PhD, 1934; m. Janet Sukernek, Aug 26, 1936; c: Ellen Kantz, Joseph. Samuel Paul Capen prof, Amer hist, SUNY, Buffalo, since 1959; visiting prof, Cornell U, 1951, 1959; U Rochester, 1952-53. Exec council, Amer J Hist Soc; mem: NY Stat e Kosher Law Advisory Bd; Amer Hist Assn; Phi Beta Kappa. Author: The Isolationist Impulse, 1957; The Uncertain Giant, 1965; co-author, From Ararat to Suburbia, 1960; contbr to popular and profsl jours. Home: 123 Frontenac Ave, Buffalo, NY. Office: 115 Crosby Hall, SUNY, Buffalo, NY.

ADLER, Shmuel Steve, Isr, economist; b. Bx, NY, Feb 18, 1940; s. Charles and Mary (Wincelberg); in Isr since 1960; att CCNY, 1957-60; BA, Bar Ilan U, 1963; MA, Heb U, Jerusalem, 1969; m. Shifrah Kavior, 1963; c: Yaakov, Sarah. Dir, off munic research, Min of Interior, since 1964; tchr asst, Bar Ilan U, since 1963. Head, Betar Youth Org, NY, 1957-58; repr, 1959-60. Author: Local Authorities in Israel, 1964-68; Misim B'rashuyot Mekomiot, 1968. Hobbies: stamps, politics.

Home: 25 Reines St, Jerusalem, Isr. Office: Min of Interior, Jerusalem, Isr.

ADLER, Stephen Louis, US, theoretical physicist; b. NYC, Nov 30, 1939; s. Irving and Ruth (Relis); AB, Harvard Coll, 1961; PhD, Princeton U, 1964; m. Judith Curtis, Oct 27, 1962; c: Jessica, Victoria. Prof, Inst for Advanced Study, Princeton, since 1969, mem, since 1966, visiting lectr, with rank of prof, Princeton U, since 1969. Mem: Sigma Xi; Amer Phys Soc; jr F, Soc of Fellows, Harvard U, 1964-66. Co-author: Current Algebras, 1968; contbr to profsl jours. Hobby: figure skating. Home: Veblen Circle, Princeton, NJ. Office: Inst for Advanced Studies, Olden Lane, Princeton, NJ.

ADLER, Walter, US, attorney; b. Vienna, Aus, Nov 9, 1896; s. Joseph and Rose (Pulver), in US since 1900; BA, MA, Brown U, 1918; LLB, Harvard U, 1923; m. Celia Ernstof, Nov 15, 1928; c: Joan Gevertz, Nancy Lewis, Susan Kaplan. Pvt practice since 1923; mem, law firm, Adler Pollock and Sheehan. US Army, WW I, II; lt col, ret. Dir, Narragansett Council, Boy Scouts Amer, since 1937, mem, natl council since 1954; trustee, Temple Beth-El, since 1933, pres, 1961; Repub candidate, atty gen, State of RI, 1946; hon pres, dir, fmr pres, RI Camps, Inc, 1938-61; pres, dir, RI Ref Service, 1941-53; pres: Big Bros, RI, 1954-55; Class Secys Assn, Brown U, 1952-55; RI Alpha Phi Beta Kappa, 1959, 1961; chmn: Harvard Bus Sch Fund, RI, 1959-61; RI mem comm, Amer Bar Assn; asso chmn, RI Housing and Development Campaign, 194ʳ 47; mem, exec comm, Brown U Alumni Assn, 1950-55; cnief staff, Brown Commencement Procession, 1955-60; mem, found comm, Pembroke Coll, 1957-58; fmr dir: J Family Wfr Soc; J Comty Cen; ARC; B'nai B'rith; mem: Amer and RI Bar Assns; Amer Legion; Phi Beta Kappa; Delta Sigma Rho; Phi Epsilon Pi; clubs: Repub; Brown, RI; Harvard, RI. Recipient: silver beaver award, Boy Scouts of Amer, 1953; brotherhood award, JWV, 1956. Home: 33 Stadium Rd, Providence, RI. Office: 530 Hospital Trust Bldg, Providence, RI.

ADLERBLUM, Nima H, US, author, lecturer; b. Jerusalem, Aug 4, 1891; d. Hayyim and Eva (HaCohen) Hirschensohn; father was auth on Talmudic lit; ancestry related to Gaon of Vilna; in US since 1904; PhD, Columbia U, 1926; m. Israel Adlerblum, Apr 9, 1914; c: Ivria Sackton. Author, essays and books: A Study of Gersonides in His Proper Perspective, 1926; A Perspective of Jewish Life Through Its Festivals, 1930; The Elan Vital of the Jewish Woman in Jewish Library Series, 1934; Gersonides in Jewish Thinking of Tomorrow, in J Libr Series, 1946; Bachya Ibn Pakudah in Relation to the Arabic Philosophy of His Time, 1950; A Perspective of Bachya, Author of the Duties of the Heart, in J Book Annual, 1950-51; Sara Bayla and Her Times, in J Libr Series, 1953; Memoirs of Childhood—An Approach to Jewish Philosophy, 1958; The Collective Jewish Spirit: An Interpretation of Jewish Philosophy, in Tradition Mag, 1960; chaps in: Men of the Spirit, J Libr Series, 1964; Translations and Collections in Jewish Studies, 1968; contbr to phil mags, encys. Found, hon secy: Comm for Dissemination and Trans of Amer Works on Phil of Educ, since 1952; Amer Comm for Dissemination and Trans of John Dewey's Phil in Latin Amer, since 1945; chmn, intl comm for celebration of John Dewey's 90th birthday; found, exch of thought movement between Amer and Eur scholars, 1923; research work throughout Eur, Near East and USSR on problems of minorities; study tours to Latin Amer for inter-cultural relationships; lectured on phil of Amer democracy at request of Natl Resources Planning Bd; lectr on Amer phil, phil of rels; granted audience by Pope, 1927; life F, Intl Inst Arts and Letters; mem: Amer Phil Assn; League for Ind Democracy; ZOA; Hadassah, fmr mem, natl bd, chmn, cultural activities; fmr, delg to: Mexico on behalf of Eur refugees; ZC; WJC. Spec interests and hobbies: mountain climbing, swimming, intl affairs. Home: 220 Ocean Ave, Long Branch, NJ.

ADLER-RUDEL, Salomon, Isr, organization exec; b. Czernowitz, June 23, 1894; s. Nathan and Jetti (Adler) Rudel; in Isr since 1936; m. Fanny Hermann, 1920; c: Rahel Myers. Dir, Leo Baeck Inst, Jerusalem, since 1958; secy, J Natl Council, Vienna, 1918-1919; dir: Wfr Org for E Jews, Berlin, 1919-30; dept of J Cmty, Berlin, 1930-34; gen secy, Reichsvertretung der Juden, 1934-36; adv, Cen Brit Fund, JA, London, 1936-45, dir, dept for intl relations, Jerusalem, 1949-55. Mem: Council for J's from Ger; fmr: gen secy, Poalei Zion, Aus; mem exec, ZF, Ger; vice-pres, ZF, Gr Brit; mem actions comm, WZO; delg to WJC's. Author: Ostjuden in Deutschland, 1880-1940, pub, 1959; contbr to: Juedisches Lexikon;

Ency Judaica; Whilo Lexikon, all in Berlin; ed, Juedisch Arbeits-und Wanderfuersorge, 1926-29. Home: 1 Saadya Gaon St, Jerusalem, Isr. Office: 33 Bustanai St, Jerusalem.

ADMON, Jedidiah, Isr, composer; b. Jerusalem, Dec 5, 1894; s. Abraham and Haya; att: Tchrs Sem, Jerusalem; Johns Hopkins U; Ecole Normale de Musique, Paris; m. Esther Izhaki, 1928; c: Yael, Deborah Frumerman, Avraham, Miriam Weisel. Pres: Variview Reader Corp, since 1965; Isr Authors and Composers Assn, 1940-47, dir gen, 1950-55; Brit Army, 1915-18. Composer: Opera, Moses and the Pharoah's Daughter, NY; symphonic poems for choir and soloist; songs and choral works; music for several plays, Tel Aviv. Home: Shdema, Emek Sorek, Isr.

AELION, Joseph, Isr, journalist; b. Thessaloniki, Greece; s. Jacques and Gracia (Hassid); in Isr since 1935; att HS of Journalism, Paris; m. Valentine Chayo, Tel Aviv, July 18, 1943; c: Nava Marmur. Journalist, econ ed, L'information d'Israel, since 1958; found, ed-in-chief, L'Echo d'Israel, 1948-58. Mem: B'nai B'rith; Rotary; Journalist Assn. Recipient: L'Ordre National de Merite; Le Medaille de la Reconnaissance; Les Palmes Academiques. Home: 32 Yehuda Hamaccabi St, Tel Aviv, Isr.

AGADATI, Baruch, Isr, painter; b. Bender, Bessarabia, 1895; s. Aryeh and Batia (Abrahamowitz) Kraushanski; att Sch of Basic Dance, Russ; Bezalel Art Sch, Jerusalem. Painter, dancer, film maker. Full length film: This is the Land, 1934; dir, film, Tomorrow's Yesterday, 1961; Oasis in the Desert, (Documentary), 1960, Stockholm Festival Award; originator, watercolors on silk. Author: Artists of the Hebrew Dance, 1925. Home: 13A Yitzchak Elchanan, Tel Aviv, Isr.

AGEN, Myer, US, journalist, editor; b. Bklyn, NY, June 15, 1895; s. Hyman and Rebecca (Schnitt); att Cooper Union, NYC, 1913-14; m. Helene Siegel, 1919; c: Francine Bossard, Felicia Davidson. Ret since 1965; sr ed, Armed Forces Press Service, info spec, US Govt, 1950-65; ed work: Local Advertiser, Bklyn, NY, 1916; US Army Med Dept, 1917-18; Stars and Stripes, 1918-19; NY Herald, Paris ed, 1919-23; London Daily Mail, continental ed, 1923-35; Jersey Leader, St Helier, Jersey, Channel Islands, 1935; London Daily Sketch, 1936; Market Analysts, NY, 1940; Army Times, 1941; Fgn Broadcast IS, Wash DC, 1941; OWI, NY, 1943; London Daily Mirror, NY, 1944; UJA, Newark, NJ, 1944; VA, Buffalo, NY, 1946; Foods Plus, NYC, 1947-50; Telecommunication Conf, Atlantic City, NJ, 1947. Mem: Amer Legion, Paris; VFW; Natl Union of Journalists, London; Anglo-Amer Press Assn, Paris, both until 1940; clubs: Natl Press, Wash, DC; Overseas Press, NY. Contbr articles, poems to Fr, Eng, Amer publs. Recipient: Silver Star, 1918; Victory Medal with five battle bars, 1919; Chevalier de la Legion d'Honneur, Fr, 1937; Medaille de la Liberation, 1953; Verdun, St Mihiek Medals. Home: 324 W 83 St, NYC.

AGHASSI, Eliyahu Hayim, (Ben Shimon), Isr, communal leader, editor; b. Baghdad, Iraq, Dec 29, 1909; s. Shimon and Chahla (Bahar); in Isr since 1928; att Heb U, Jerusalem, 1930-32; Bet Berl Inst, Tzofit, 1958; m. Ada Varadi, May 15, 1940; c: Roni Luria, Shimon, Raphael. Dir, gen ed, Arabic Pub House, since 1962; found, org, Arab Workers Org, Haifa, Jaffa, Tel Aviv; asst ed, Haqiqat al Amr, Arabic weekly; head, Arab Lab Dep; adv; all in Histadrut, 1932-61. Prin contribs: org, Arab trade unions, later known as Isr Lab League, with local brs, lab exchs, cultural cens, coop socs, in Nazareth, main Arab villages. Author: Husham miBaghdad, 1959; Autobiography, 1963; Colloquial Arabic for Hebrew Speaking Student, 1968. Fmr secy, Arab Affairs Comm, Isr Lab Party; mem: cen comm, Yeda 'Am, Isr Folklore Soc; public council, Culture and Arts, Min of Educ. Contbr numerous articles, pamphlets, on Arabic problems; Arabic folk, nursery tales and melodies; lectures, researches. Hobbies: folklore, poetry, swimming. Home: 11 Liessin St, Tel Aviv, Isr. Office: 17 Hagra St, Tel Aviv, Isr.

AGMON, Avraham, Isr, government official; b. Bialystok, Pol, Sep 11, 1928; s. Tzvi and Tova (Rudy) Wagman; in Isr since 1947; BA, Heb U, Jerusalem, 1955; m. Devorah Efrati, Jan 19, 1954; c: Tzvi, Gil. Dir, bur budget, Min of Finance, Jerusalem, since 1968; second secy, Isr Emb, Moscow, 1956-58; first secy: Isr Emb, Warsaw, 1961-62; Moscow, 1962-64. IDF, 1948-50. Home: 10 Brachiyahu St, Jerusalem. Office: Min of Finance, Jerusalem.

AGNON, Samuel Emil, Isr, mechanical engr; b. Warsaw, Pol, Aug 10, 1905; s. Benjamin and Liuba (Burowik) Snipischki; in Isr since 1932; ME, engr sch, Mannheim; att U Frankfurt; m. Idah Seidelman, Jan 20, 1935; c: Reuben, Dinah. Sr partner, S Argon and Partners, cons engrs, Haifa, since 1950; design engr, heating and air conditioning contracting firms, Ger, 1930-32; contractor, caloria, 1933-39; leader, mech devl engr sect, Haifa main off, Iraq Petroleum Co, 1943-49; parttime engr cons, Isr AEC, 1958-61; designer, Sorek Research Inst. Prin contribs: devl number of technical innovations for which holds US Patents; active in building Haifa Oil Refinery. Mem: Assn Engrs and Architects in Isr; Amer Soc of Heating, Air Conditioning and Refrigeration Engr. Contbr to profsl jours. Home: 15 Vitkin St, Haifa, Isr. Office: 118 Haatzmauth Rd, Haifa, Isr.

AGRANAT, Simon, Isr, judge; b. Louisville, Ky, Sep 5, 1906; in Isr since 1930; JD, U Chgo, Ill, 1929; m. Carmela Friedland; four c. Supr Court Judge since 1965; pvt practice, 1931-40; magistrate, 1940-48; pres, Dist Court, Haifa, 1948-50. Mem comm, Haifa Bar Assn; fmr chmn, Avuka Zionist Students Assn, Chgo. Recipient: Isr Prize, 1968. Home: 62b American-Canadian Quarter, Jerusalem, Isr. Office: Supr Court of Isr, Jerusalem, Isr.

AGUS, Irving Abraham, US, educator, author; b. Swislocz Pol, Feb 20, 1910; s. Judah and Beila (Bereznicki) Agushewitz; in US since 1927; att Heb U, Jerusalem, 1926-27; BS, NYU, 1932; PhD, Dropsie Coll, 1937; m. Tema Gerber, 1939; c: Rachel, Aaron. Prof, J hist, Yeshiva U, since 1951; educ dir, Baron Hirsch Cong, Memphis, 1939-45; prin: Yeshiva, LI, 1945-47; Akiba Acad, Phila, 1949-51; dean, Harry Fischel Inst for Research in Talmud, Jerusalem, 1947-49. Author: Rabbi Meir of Rothenburg, 2 vols, 1947; Responsa of the Tosaphists, 1954; Dibre Yemei Yisrael, 2 vols, 1957-67; Urban Civilization in Pre-Crusade Europe, 2 vols, 1965; The Heroic Age of Franco-German Jewry, 1969; ed, Shainberg Library, 5 vols, 1945. Recipient: La Med Prize for book, Rabbi Meir of Rothenburg. Home: 208 W 179 St, Bronx, NY. Office: Yeshiva U, Amsterdam Ave at 186 St, New York, NY.

AGUS, Jacob Bernard, US, rabbi, author; b. Swislocz, Pol, Nov 8, 1911; s. Judah and Beila (Bereznitzki) Agushewitz; desc, Yom Tov Lipman Heller; Katzenellenbogen dynasty of rabbis in Brest-Litovsk; in US since 1927; AB, Yeshiva Coll, 1933; ordained rabbi, Rabbi Isaac Elchanan Theol Sem, 1935; AM, Harvard U, 1938, PhD, 1939; m. Miriam Shore, June 16, 1940; c: Zalaman, Edna, Robert, Deborah. Rabbi, Cong Beth El, Baltimore, since 1950; prof, Rabb J, Reconstructionist Coll, Phila, since 1969; visiting prof, Rel, Temple U; Cong Beth Abraham, Norfolk, Va, 1943-46; Temple Ashkenazi, Cambridge, Mass, 1936-40; N Shore Cong, Chgo, 1940-42; Beth Abraham United Syn, Dayton, O, 1942-50. Chmn, comm on ideology, RA; fac, B'nai B'rith Adult Insts. Author: Modern Philosophies of Judaism, 1940; Banner of Jerusalem, 1946; Studies in Philosophy of Kabala; Guideposts in Modern Judaism, 1955; The Evolution of Jewish Thought, 1959; The Meaning of Jewish History, 1963; The Vision and the Way, 1963; mem: bd eds, Judaism, since 1951; bd cons, Ency Britannica, 1956-68; contbr to: Current Movements in Jewish Thought, Vol IV; Americana Yiddish Encys. Home: 7906 Winterset Ave, Baltimore, Md. Study: 8101 Park Heights Ave, Baltimore, Md.

AHARONI, Amikam, Isr, physicist; b. Safad, Isr, Aug 5, 1929; s. Arie and Miriam (Cohen); MSc, Heb U, 1953, PhD, 1957; m. Henia Roza, Jan 4, 1955; c: Abraham, Gad, Dan. Asso prof, electronics, Weizmann Inst Sci, since 1953; research asso, elec engr, U of Ill, 1958-59; sr research physicist, Natl Cash Register Co, 1964-65; visiting prof, elec engr, Purdue U, 1965-66. Pvt, IDF, 1948-49. Sr mem, Inst Elec and Electronics Engrs; mem: Isr Physical Soc; Amer Physical Soc. Contbr of numerous articles to sci jours. Hobby: collecting coins. Home: 12 Neveh Weizmann, Rehovot, Isr. Office: Weizmann Inst of Sci, Rehovot, Isr.

AHARONI, Arie, Isr, author; b. Odessa, Russ, Oct 27, 1923; s. Shmuel and Malka (Lisiansky); in Isr since 1931; att Hebrew U, Jerusalem: m. Rachel Tenebaum, June 22, 1951; c: Yael, Yoram, Michal. Mem, Kibbutz Beit Alfa, since 1943; cofound, Moshav Beit Yosef, Beit Shean, 1939. Lt, educ off, Palmach, IDF, 1942-49. Trans into Heb: Mayakovsky; Pushkin; young Russ poets; Aeschylus; Dylan Thomas, Yesenin

Voznesensky, Rachel Fishman, Shalom Alechem,; contr various transs to jours, anthols. Home: Kibbutz Beit Alfa, Isr.

AHARONI, Chaim, Isr, educator; b. Cairo, Egypt, Feb 3, 1927; s. Leon and Lea (Cherezli); in Isr since 1950; MSc, Technion, Haifa, 1958; PhD, Imperial Coll, London, 1967; m. Andree Yadid, Mar 26, 1951; c: Ariel, Lea. Sr lectr, Technion, Haifa, since 1968; sr research chem, Chem and Phosphates, 1959-68. Prin contrib: research, devl in chemisorption and catalysis. Conthr to profsl jours. Home: 5 Horev St, Haifa, Isr. Office: Technion, Haifa, Isr.

AHARONI, Yair, Isr, educator; b. Zichron Yaakov, Isr, Sep 5, 1931; s. Arie and Miriam (Cohen); MA, U Tel Aviv, 1957; PhD, Harvard U, 1961; m. Mira Zauberman, Dec 12, 1953; c: Orna. Dean, grad sch bus admn, Tel Aviv U, since 1966, chmn, research comm fac social sci; fmr: academic adv, Kibbutz Ind Mgrs Sch; cons: IBM, El Al Airlines; Tahal Cons Engrs, Min of Transp, all Isr; cons, spec adv, Isr Govt Corp Auth on Strategic Problems; visiting prof, NYU, 1965-66; asst prof, Columbia U, 1964-65; lectr, Heb U, Jerusalem, 1961-66. Mem: Natl Assn of Acctnts, US; Amer Acctnt Assn; Isr Assn Social and Econ Scis; Amer Marketing Assn; Intl U Contact for Mgmt Educ. Author: Analysis of Financial Statements, 1959; The Functions of Roles of Directors, 1964; Accounting Practices in Israel, 1964, all in Heb; The Foreign Investment Decision Process, 1966; contr to sci jours. Home: 5 Harav Kook St, Neve Magen, Ramat HaSharon, Isr. Office: Tel Aviv U, Ramat Aviv, Isr.

AHARONI, Yohanan, Isr, archaeologist; b. June 7, 1919; s. Heinrich and Eugenie (Simon) Aronheim; in Isr since 1933; MA, Heb U, 1950, PhD, 1955; m. Miriam Gross, 1946; c: Hayim, Yoav, Eyal, Yuval. Prof, archaeol, chmn, dept Ancient Near E Studies, head, Inst of Archaeoi, Tel Aviv U, since 1968; asso prof, archaeol, Heb U, 1959-68; agric laborer, Kibbutz Alonim, 1938-48; insp, Dept of Antiquities, 1950-55; archaeol, Hazor Expedition, 1955-58. IDF, 1948-50. Mem, exec comm, Isr Exploration Soc, since 1954, asso ed, Isr Exploration Jour, since 1959. Author: in Heb: This is My Country, 1953, 2nd ed, 1960; The Setttlement of the Israelite Tribes in Upper Galilee, 1957; The Land of Israel in Biblical Times, Historical Geography, 1962; in Eng: Excavations at Ramat Rahel, 1962; The Land of the Bible, Historical Geography, 1967; Macmillan Bible, 1968; co-author: In the Steps of Kings and Rebels, in Heb, 1960; Hazor I-IV, in Eng, 1958-60; contbr to profsl publs. Recipient: Zippora Klausner Prize, 1955; Warburg Award, 1957-59. Home: 79 Lamerhav St, Ramat Hasharon. Office: Tel Aviv U, Tel Aviv, Isr.

AHREND, Herbert G, US, advertising exec; b. NYC, Sep 16, 1913; s. David and Martha (Herschmann); BA, Columbia U, 1935, grad studies, 1937-39; div; c: Marcia. Head, Ahrend Asso, sales promotion and direct advt agcy, since 1951; mem, expedition to Iran, Amer Inst for Iranian Art and Archeol, 1936. Chmn, N Amer Mensa, since 1967, NYC chmn, 1965-67; bd dirs, NY chap, Assn Ind Advertisers; fmr bd dirs, Assn Advt Men and Women; mem: Direct Mail Advt Assn; Sales Promotion Execs Assn; Advt Fed of Amer; Phi Beta Kappa; Zeta Beta Tau. Author: Sell Your Way To Success, 1969; contr to bus jours. Recipient: numerous awards for advt campaigns, including many best of ind; 2 Dartell Gold medals for excellence in bus letters. Home: 11 W 8 St, New York, NY. Office: 601 Madison Ave, New York, NY.

AIDLIN, Samuel S, US, engineer, educator; b. Newark, NJ, Aug 29, 1913; s. Isidore and Mollie (Horowitz); BME, CCNY, 1937; MME, Bklyn Poly Inst, Stevens Inst, and CCNY, 1945; m. Ruth Baker, Oct 27, 1935; c: Stephen. Cons engr, pres, Aidlin Automation Inc, since 1949; adj prof, mech engr: Poly Inst, Bklyn; Pratt Inst; Baruch Sch, CCNY; engr, draftsman, NY Navy Yard, 1937-39; engr, Raritan Arsenal, NJ, 1939-40; mech engr, Gibbs and Cox, NYC, 1940-44; devl engr, Bendix Aviation, 1944-45; chief, engr, Specialty Engr, 1945-47; off, Aidlin Associates and Pelex Publishers Inc; cons: Gen Elec Co; Western Elec Co; Ford Instrument Div, Sperry-Rand; US Rubber Co; Paragon Oil Co; Kay Mfg Corp; Local Home Service; Walter Balfour & Co. Dir: NYC Tech Inst; Kings Co chap, Profsl Engrs; Pythian TB Found; Pythian Camp; civil defense leader, Public Works Emergency Div; mem: Amer Soc for Engr Educ; Amer Soc Metals; Utopians; KP; Lambda Rho; Bklyn Engrs, dir. Author: Engineering Economics, 1950; Basic Engineering Mechanics and Machine Design, 1951; Professional Engineering, Economics and Practice, 1951. Home: 214 Beaumont St, Brooklyn, NY. Office: 1613 E New York Ave, Brooklyn, NY.

AISICOVITCH, Efraim, Isr, physician, author; b. Bessarabia, Nov 15, 1901; in Isr since 1957; MD, U Bucharest, 1927; m. Pnina Alter; c: Ruth, Arie. Phys since 1927; dir: Bacter Lab, 1927-28; hosp, Russ, 1945-49; chief phys, Polyclinic, Bnei Brak, 1957-69. Mem: Writers Assns, Russ, Rum; Phys Assn in Isr; fmr: vice-pres, cultural sect, J Comty, Bucharest; mem, cen comm, Ahdut Avodah, Poalei Zion. Author: Tinkel in licht, 1948; Oifen Veig, 1950; Shpirn, 1958; Oisgivalte, 1962; Seiz Mir Bashert, 1969, all poems; Vi Imdorf, 1967, prose. Home: 55 Jerusalem St, Bnei Brak, Isr.

AJL, Samuel Jacob, US, research dir; b. Hrubieszow, Pol, Nov 15, 1923; s. Joseph and Celia (Hertz); in US since 1939; BA, Bklyn Coll, 1945; PhD, Ia State Coll, 1949; hon DHL, Dropsie U, 1968; m. Adele Davis, Nov 5, 1924; c: Stephen, Diane, Leslie. Dir, research, Walter Reed Army Inst of Research, since 1960, asst chief, dept bact, 1952-58; dir, metabolic div, NSF, 1958-60. Vice-pres, J Publ Soc Amer; fmr: acting pres, Dropsie U, chmn, exec bd; vice-pres, Lower Merion Syn; bd dirs, AJComm, Phila chap; educ comm, Fed JAs, Phila. Contbr to sci jours on subjects of biomedical research; ed, multi-volume treatise on microbial toxins. Recipient: dist alumnus award, Bklyn Coll, 1964. Home: 2296 Bryn Mawr Ave, Philadelphia, Pa. Office: Albert Einstein Med Cen, Philadelphia, Pa.

AKABAS, Eliezer Shachna, Isr, executive; b. Lith, Feb 1, 1911; s. Yona and Mina (Malach) Mordechai; in Isr since 1935; deg, econ, Kaunas U, Lith, 1935; LLD, U Strasbourg, 1931, U Paris, 1930; m. Amalia Berger; c: Amina. Asst treas, JA, since 1968; dep dir, econ dept, 1955-68; co-owner, Inst for Fine Mech; secy to Mfrs Assn, Haifa, 1944-48; chief clerk, recruiting dept, Defense Min, Haifa, 1948-49; secy gen, Zionist Party, 1949-55; Pal Voluntary Forces, 1940-44; IDF res. Mem: council, Lib Party. Contbr numerous articles, essays to lit jours. Hobbies: journalism, theater, music. Home: 12 Masaryk Sq, Tel Aviv, Isr. Office: 17 Kaplan St, Tel Aviv, Isr.

AKAVIA, Abraham, Isr, certified public acctnt; b. Kolno, Pol, Dec 15, 1916; in Isr since 1925; BSc, Technion, Haifa, 1938; m. Ruth Milioni, Mar 27, 1942; c: Gideon, Eliahu, Uri. Pvt practice since 1964; treas, Amer Isr Paper Mills, Hadera, 1961-64; ed, Hagana mil publs, 1936-40; dist off, Haifa, 1947-48; property tax commn, and head, devl auth, 1949-55; dep dir gen, Isr Min of Devl, 1955-57; head, budget dept and secy gen, Isr Elec Corp, 1957-61. Brit Army, personal asst to Gen Orde Charles Wingate, Ethiopia campaign, 1940-41; maj, J Brig, 1941-46; chief oprs off, Haifa dist, IDF, 1948-49. Mem, Intl Fiscal Assn; Anglo-Ethiopian Soc, Eng; club, Rotary, Haifa. Author: Misshakim Nivharim, 1940; Im Wingate be-Habash, 1944; English-Hebrew Military Dictionary, 1951; ed, Orde Wingate–In Memoriam, 1968; contbr to local press. Recipient: mention in dispatches, 1941; Order of Menelick II, Ethiopia, 1966. Home: 9 Hazvi St, Haifa. Offices: 65 Haazmaouth Rd, Haifa, Isr; 15 Carlebach St, Tel Aviv, Isr.

AKAVIA, Uriel, Isr, psychologist; b. Warsaw, Dec 19, 1911; s. Abraham and Bathia (Cipkus); in Isr since 1929; MA, NYU, 1953; MA, Heb U, 1933; m. Margalith Sapir, 1940; c: Roni Bilev, Naaman, Eden. Asst dean, Levinsky Tchrs Training Coll, since 1968, lectr, sch psych, since 1954; fmr tchr: elementary, secondary schs, tchrs colls; counselor and sch psych, all since 1934. Mem: Gen Tchrs Assn; Isr Assn Psychols; Intl Rorschach Assn; Milloh Writers and Artists Club; Isr Numismatic Soc. Author: The Laughing Dog (Diogenes), 1966; Izreel, 1968; contbr to numerous publs; anthols; poetry (Japanese). Home: 41 Shlomo Hamelech St, Tel Aviv, Isr. Office: 195 Ben Yehuda St, Tel Aviv, Isr.

AKERBERG, Albert D, Fr, organization exec; b. Paris, Nov 10, 1914; s. Jacob and Marcelle (Levy); grad, Faculté de Droit, Paris U; m. Micheline Weil, Jan 19, 1951. Dir, L'Action Sociale par l'Habitat and dir gen, l'Action Sociale Immobiliere SA, since 1956; dir, Social Service for Youth, 1944-56; Seine Childrens Court, 1950; treas, Assn J Social Workers. Off, J Combat Org, 1943-44; leader underground activities, J Youth Movement, N Fr. Recipient: Chevalier du Devourement Social, 1946; Medaille du Combattant Volontaire de la Resistance, 1953; Croix du Combattant, 1953; Croix du Combattant Volontaire, 1957. Home: 87 rue du Ranelagh, Paris 16, Fr. Office: 9 rue Danielle Casanova, Paris 1, Fr.

AKST, Paul, US, attorney, military off; b. NYC, July 6, 1911: s. George and Fanny (Weinreb); LLB, Bklyn Law Coll, 1934: hon DHum, Philathea Coll, 1958; m. Paula Brown, Sep 24,

1947; c: Mark, George. NYC dir, Selective Service, since 1955; atty, pvt practice, 1936-42; staff judge, advocate, Tactical Command, 1945-46; col, USAF, Selective Service, 1948-55. US Army, 1942-46. Bd trustees: Brookdale Hosp Cen; Bklyn Coll Pharm; bd dirs, United Hosp Service; mil comm, JWB; vice-pres: Men's Club, Temple Emanuel; J Day Cen; mem, Masons. Home: 135 E 74 St, New York, NY. Office: 26 Federal Plaza, New York, NY.

AKZIN, Benjamin, Isr, jurist, educator; b. Riga, Latvia, May 6, 1904; s. Meir and Zelda (Garnitz); in Isr since 1949; D Rer Pol, U Vienna; LLD, U Paris; SJD, Harvard U; m. Ilse Lowenthal, 1941. President, Haifa U, since 1969; Herbert Samuel prof prof of political sci and constitutional law, Heb U, Jerusalem, 1949-69; dean, law sch, 1951-54, 1956-58, 1961-63; asst, Paris U, 1930-32, Rockefeller F, 1932-34; asst, Harvard U, 1934-36; lectr, govt, intl relations, CCNY, 1940-41; sr specialist, intl and fgn law: Libr of Cong, Wash, DC, 1941-44; US War Ref Bd, 1944-45; dir, political secy, Amer Zionist Emergency Council, Wash, DC, 1945-47; visiting prof: U Mich, 1953; NYU, 1954-55; Heidelberg U, 1963; U Paris, 1968; Harvard U, 1969. Mem exec, head political dept, New Zionist Org; hon pres, Isr Political Sci Assn; pres, Isr Assn for UN. Author: Problemes Fondamentaux du Droit International Public, 1929; Reflexions sur la Science et l'Education Politiques aux Etats Unis, 1938; Principles of Public Administration, Heb, 1952; New States and International Organizations, 1955; Theory of Government, Heb, 1963; State and Nation, 1964; Law and Politics, Heb, 1966; ed, Political Problems of Poly-Ethnic Studies, 1963; co-ed, Annuaire Interparlamentaire, 1931-40; contbr to legal and political periodicals. Homes: 7 Telmane St, Haifa, Isr; 5 Bartenura Rd, Jersalem, Isr. Office: Haifa U, Haifa, Isr.

ALBAHARI, Nisim, Yugo, public official; b. Tesanj, Jan 28, 1916; s. Abraham and Rehela (Danon); m. Ankica Pavlović, 1945. Active in workers movement in Bosnia and Herzegovina, trade unionist; active in Matatja, J lab youth org and J Soc, Sloboda (Sarajevo); secy and lab min, Govt of Bosnia and Herzegovina; mem exec, Socialist Alliance of Working People of Bosnia Herzegovina; assembly mem, Fed Peoples Assembly of Yugo and Peoples Rep of Bosnia and Herzegovina; mem adv comm, Fed of Govt of Yugo. Participated in org of natl liberation against fascist occupation forces in Bosnia and Herzegovina. Recipient: Order of Natl Hero; Order of Frat and Unity with gold wreath; Order of Merit for the People with gold star; Order of the Rep with gold wreath; Order of the Partisan Star with silver wreath; Order of Valor. Home: Mehmed-pase Sokolovica, Sarajavo, Yugo.

ALBECK, Michael, Isr, chemist; b. Berlin, Ger, Oct 15, 1934; s. Chanoch and Hendel; MS, Heb U, Jerusalem, 1959, PhD, 1962; m. Shulamith Firanko, 1955; c: Amnon, Dan, Yael. Sr lectr, Bar Ilan U, since 1965; sr investigator, Inst for Fiber and Forest Products, 1961-63; dir, chem lab, Mekoroth Water Co, 1961-65. IDF. Mem: Isr Chem Soc. Contbr of numerous articles to sci jours. Home: 8 Harel St, Ramat Gan, Isr. Office: Bar Ilan U, Ramat Gan, Isr.

ALBECK, Plea Sarah, Isr, lawyer; b. Jerusalem, Oct 28, 1937; d. Itzhak and Hildegard (Hollander) Nebenzahl; MJ, Heb U, Jerusalem, 1958; m. Shalom Albeck, Oct 23, 1957; c: Yehudah, Rachel, Rivkah. Dep state atty, Isr, since 1965, chief asst, 1963-65; lawyer, S Horowitz & Co, 1962; ed, Inst for Multiplication. Fmr: member directorate, leader, Ezra, Jerusalem; mem, Hadassah, Hosp Volunteers; mem, Isr Bar. Home: 3 Ben Labrat St, Jerusalem, Isr. Office: Ministry of Justice, Jerusalem, Isr.

ALBECK, Shalom, Isr, educator; b. Berlin, Ger, Sep 4, 1931; s. Chanoch and Hendel (Weiss); in Isr since 1931; BA, Heb U, Jerusalem, 1952, MA, 1955, MJur, 1956, PhD, 1959; m. Plea Nebenzahl, Oct 23, 1958; c: Jehuda, Rachel, Rivkah. Asso prof, Talmudic Law, Bar Ilan U, since 1968, sr lectr, 1963-68; lectr, JTSA, 1960-63. IDF, 1948-50. Mem, Isr Bar. Author: General Principles in the Law of Tort in the Talmud, Heb, 1965; contbr to profsl jours. Home: 3 Ben Labrat St, Jerusalem, Isr. Office: Bar Ilan U, Ramat Gan, Isr.

ALBERSHEIM, Walter J, US, engineering cons; b. Cologne, Ger, Apr 22, 1897; s. Joseph and Anna (Reifenberg); in US since 1924; DEng, Inst of Tech, Aachen, Ger, 1924; Profsl Engr, U State of NY, 1937; m. Alberta Greenberger, June 19, 1929; c: Peter, Anne Andrews. Cons: Riverside Research Inst, since 1959; Sanders Asso Inc, Nashua, NH, 1965; research engr: Elec Research Products Inc, 1929-41; Bell

Telephone Labs Inc, 1941-59; chief engr, vice pres, Spencer Kennedy Labs Inc, 1959-62. Ger Army, 1914-18. Holder of 46 US patents in acoustics, rheology, sound recording, radar, communications. F: Inst Elec and Electronic Engrs; Rosicrucian Order AMORC, NRC; mem: NY Acad of Scis; Soc Motion Picture and TV Engrs. Recipient: Iron Cross, WW I; jour award, Soc Motion Picture and TV Engrs, 1941. Hobbies: sports, travel. Home and office: 15 Waban Ave, Waban, Mass.

ALBERT, A Adrian, US, educator; b. Chgo, Ill, Nov 9, 1905; s. Elias and Fannie (Fradkin); desc of Gaon of Vilna; SB, U Chgo, 1926, SM, 1927, PhD, 1928; hon: LLD, Notre Dame, 1965; DSc, Yeshiva U, 1968; m. Frieda Davis, Dec 18, 1927; c: Alan, Roy (decd), Nancy Goldberg. Dean, div phys scis, U Chgo, since 1962, prof, since 1941, E H Moore Dist Service Prof, since 1960, chmn, dept math, 1958-62; trustee, Inst for Defense Analyses, since 1966, cons since 1959; f, NRC, 1928-29; instr, math, Columbia U, 1929-31; worker, Inst for Advanced Study, 1933-34; asso dir, Applied Math Group, Northwestern U, 1944-45; visiting prof: U Brazil, U Buenos Aires, both 1947; Inst for Defense Analyses, 1961-62; U of S Cal, 1950; Yale U, 1956-57; UCLA, 1958; research math: Rand Corp, 1951; project SCAMP, U Cal, 1953, 1954, 1955, chmn, 1958, 1959; chmn, div math, NRC, 1952-55; cons: Natl Security Agcy, since 1953; off sci, Dir, Defense for Research and Engr; Mitre Corp; dir, communications research div, Inst for Defense Analyses, 1961-62. Mem: Amer Math Soc, fmr pres; Arg and Brazilian Acads of Sci; AAAS; Arg and Mexican Math Socs; Math Assn of Amer; Natl Acad Sci, fmr chmn, math sect; club, Quadrangle. Author: Modern Higher Algebra, 1936; Structure of Algebras, 1939; Introduction to Algebraic Theories, 1940; College Algebra, 1946; Solid Analytic Geometry, 1949; Fundamental Concepts of Higher Algebra, 1956; co-author, Introduction to Finite Proj Planes; ed: Bull of Amer Math Soc; Transaction, Amer Math Soc, 1939-43; Colloquium Publs, 1951-57; Mathematical Surveys, 1941-45; contbr research papers to profsl jours. Recipient: Cole Prize in Algebra, Amer Math Soc, 1939. Home: 1359 E Park Pl, Chicago, Ill. Office: Eckhart Hall, U Chgo, Chicago, Ill.

ALBERT, Sidney P, US, educator; b. Syracuse, NY, Apr 11, 1914; s. Simon and Gertrude (Siskin); AB, Syracuse U, 1934; PhD, Yale U, 1939; m. Lucy Schroeder, 1955; c: Vivian, Alan, Laurence. Prof, phil, Cal State Coll, LA, since 1964, chmn dept, 1960-63, fac mem since 1956; instr, phil: U Conn, 1946; Syracuse U, 1946; asst prof: Triple Cities Coll, 1946-50; Harpur Coll, SUNY, 1950-53. US Army, 1941-46. Fmr pres: Cal div, Amer Soc Aesthetics, LA State Coll chap, AAUP; Triple Cities Coll chap, fmr vice-pres, LA State Coll chap, Assn Cal State Coll Profs; fmr mem: state cen comm, Dem Party, Cal; LA Co Dem Cen Comm; mem: Amer Phil Assn; Amer Soc for Aesthetics; Amer Educ Theater Assn; Phi Beta Kappa; Shaw Soc, London; NY Shavians. Ed bd, Shaw Review, since 1968; contbr to scholarly jours. Home: 847 Eaton Dr, Pasadena, Cal. Office: Cal State Coll, Los Angeles, Cal.

ALBERT, Solomon Naphtali, US, anesthesiologist; b. Beirut, Leb, May 3, 1916; s. Moses and Leah (Elstein); in US since 1951. BA, med, Amer U, Beirut, 1936, MD, 1940; m. Pnina Ben Basset, Apr, 1949; c: Abey, Tilda. Sr staff mem, Wash Hosp Cen, since 1959; dir, anesthesiology research lab, since 1959, vice-chmn, research comm, since 1962; cons neurophysiology, Walter Reed Army Inst of Research, since 1961; cons anesthesiologist: St Elizabeth's Hosp, Wash, DC; Natl Inst Health, Bethesda, Md; Lebanese Army, 1949-51; Glen Dale Sanatorium, Glen Dale, Md, 1955-59; Freedmans Hosp, Wash DC, 1956-60; sr cons, anesthesiology, DC Gen Hosp, 1959-61, chief, 1954-59. Lt, MC, Free Fr Army, 1941-43. Mem: DC Med Soc; AMA; Amer Soc Anesthesiologists; Amer Coll Chest Phys; Soc Nuclear Med; life mem, Masons; dipl: Bio Analytical Nuclear Phsyics Bd; anesthesia, Royal Coll Surgs and Phys; Amer Bd Anesthesiology; f, corresp, Soc of Anesthetists, Gt Brit and Ir; f: Intl Soc of Anesthesiology; FRSM; FFARCS; Amer Coll Anesthesiology. Author: Blood Volume, 1963; Hematocrit in Clinical Practice, 1965; contbr numerous articles to profsl jours. Recipient: Chevalier, Legion of Honor with Croix de Guerre and Palmes, 1950; f, George Wash U Hosp, 1951-53. Home: 828 S Wakefield St, Arlington, Va. Office: Wash Hosp Center, Washington, DC.

ALBERTS, Harold, US, attorney, civic worker; b. San Antonio, Tex, Apr 3, 1920; s. Bernard and Rose (Cassell); LLB, U Tex, 1942; m. Rose Gaskin, Mar 25, 1945; c: Linda Tenant, Barry. Pvt practice; instr, U Tex, 1942. Lt, USN, 1942-45.

Mem: round table, NCCJ, fmr chmn; Costal Bend Mh Assn, vice-pres; Tex State, Amer Bar Assns; Masons; fmr: pres: JWF; ZOA, both Corpus Christi, Tex; vice-pres: Henry Cohen Lodge, B'nai B'rith, secy, pres; Tex State Assn B'nai B'rith, mem exec; vice cdr, Amer Legion Post; mem: bd dirs, Bnai Isr Syn; SW J Cmty Relations Adv Council; Temple Beth El; Hum Relations Comm, City of Corpus Christi; chmn, Nueces Co chap, ARC; vice-chmn, SW region, ADL; club, Kiwanis, fmr bd dirs, pres. Home: 618 Dolphin Pl, Corpus Christi, Tex. Office: 702 Wilson Tower, Corpus Christi, Tex.

ALBU, Austen, UK, engineer, legislator; b. London, Eng, Sep 21, 1903; s. Ferdinand and Beatrice (Lyons); BSc, FCGI, Imperial Coll Sci and Tech, 1923; m. Rose Marks, Apr 14, 1929; c: Martin, Colin. MK, House of Commons for Edmonton, since 1948; Min of State, Dept of Econ Affairs, 1965-67; works mgr, Aladdin Ind Ltd, Greenford, 1930-46; dep pres, govt sub comm, Control Comm for Ger, 1946-47; dep dir, Brit Inst of Mgmt, 1947-48. F, Imperial Coll Sci and Tech; mem: Inst of MEs; fmr exec comm, Fabian Soc. Author: Management in Transition, 1941; pamphlets: The Anatomy of Private Industry, 1951; A Young Man's Guide to Mechanical Engineering, 1962; chap, The Organization of Industry in New Fabian Essays. Office: House of Commons, London SW1, Eng.

ALBUKREK, Ovadiya Marco, Turkey, physician; b. Ankara, Dec 9, 1891; s. Hayim and Simha; MD, Fac Med, Paris, 1924; m. Resine Asseo; c: Simha Plauga, Hayim, Nenette Aseeo, Musa, Yilmaz. Phys, ext consultation, Pasteur, Fr hosp, since 1928; head phys: Union of Paris; Ittihadi-Milli, ins co's, att phys, since 1926; found, dir, Halc Dispanseri; fmr, head phys, Or Hahayim Hosp. Served WW I, reserves, 1941-42. Corresp, Union Mondiale des Ecrivains Medecins, 1969; mem: Fairleri Koruma Cemiyeti; Groupement des Ecrivains-Medecins, Turkey, since 1965; Free Masons, 1918; B'nai B'rith, 1934; Turkish Soc of Med, 1924. Author: Mes Amis les Malades, 1956; bibliographical studies on Heb and other publs; contbr articles under columns: Propos d'un Flâneur; Flâneries; confs on med and social work. Hobbies: painting, music. Home and office: Beyoglu, Yemenici Sokak 1, Istanbul, Turkey.

ALBUM, Manuel M, US, pedodontist, educator; b. Phila, Pa, Nov 20, 1919; s. Leon and Mollie (Sobel); DDS, Temple U, 1943; att: NYU Dent Sch, 1946; U of Pa Dent Sch, 1949; Temple U Dent Sch, 1953-54; U Mich, 1957; m. Shirley Israel, Jan 14, 1951; c: Michael, Fredlyn. Asst prof, Sch of Dent Med, U of Pa, lectr, grad, undergrad depts, since 1954, dir, postgrad prog on handicapped, since 1954, dir, spec patient clinic, since 1961; chief, dent service, Phila Soc of Crippled Children and Adults, since 1946; sr dent, Children's Hosp of Phila, since 1950; asst visiting dent, Abington Hosp, since 1954; dent cons: Natl Soc for Crippled Children and Adults, since 1958; Pa Soc for Cripped Children and Adults, since 1946; Vineland Training Sch, NJ; Elwyn Training Sch, Media, Pa; Home of Merciful Saviour, Phila, Pa; Devereaux Schs, Devon, Pa; instr, ped, Grad Sch of Med, U of Pa, since 1961. F: Amer Acad Dent for Handicapped; Intl Coll Dents; AAAS; Amer Public Health Assn; Intl Assn Dent Research; Amer Assn for Cleft Palate Rehab; Amer Dent Assn; dipl, Amer Bd Pedodontics; mem, exec council, Amer Soc Dent for Children, fmr pres; life mem: Amer Acad Pedodontics; Mil Order of WW's; fmr: pres: and found mem, Acad Dent for Handicapped; Pa unit, Amer Soc Dent for Children, 1958, Phila sect, 1957; dir, Off Vocational Rehab Workshop on Handicapped, U of Pa. Contbr to Textbook on Pediatrics, 1958. Home: 5 Develon Rd, Melrose Park, Pa. Office: Medical Arts Bldg, Jenkintown, Pa.

ALCALAY, Aron Avram, Yugo, business exec; b. Belgrade, Yugo, Mar 21, 1880; s. Avram and Buena (Hasson); att State Commercial Acad, Belgrade; m. Finy Nachman, Sep 19, 1919, (decd). Ret; fmr, gen secy, State Mortgage Bank. Admn capt, Yugo Army, before WW II. Pres, rel sect, J Comty, Belgrade; fmr: pres: J Libr, Belgrade; B'nai B'rith, lodge Serbia; secy, Gt Lodge B'nai B'rith, Yugo. Author: Moses in History and Mythology, 1932; Moses, essay, 1938; A Trip to Israel; Life and Manners in Jewish Mahala of Belgrade; Josephus Flavius and the Fall of Judea; Old Turks and Young Turks in Belgrade; standing collaborator: Jevrejski Pregled; Jewish Almanac, both Belgrade. Spec interest, J hist. Home: 2a Majke Jevrosime, Belgrade, Yugo.

ALCALAY, Moscu, Isr, actor; b. Bucharest, Rum, Sep 10,

1931; s. Lazar and Madeleine (Herscovitz); in Isr since 1962; att Acad Drama, Bucharest, 1948-53; m. Rodica Pascal, June 8, 1958. With Cameri Theater, Tel Aviv, since 1968; Natl Theater, Giulesti Theater, Bucharest, 1949-59; Zavit Theater, Tel Aviv, 1963-68. Mem: Intl Theater Inst; club, Variety. Home: 1 Galinit St, Bat Yam, Isr. Office: Cameri Theater, 101 Dizengoff St, Tel Aviv, Isr.

ALCALAY, Reuben, Isr, lexicographer, govt official, journalist; b. Jerusalem, June 20, 1907; s. Abraham and Rachel (Saporta); grad, Heb Tchrs Coll, Jerusalem, 1926; m. Sara Pardess, May 20, 1947; c: Yaffa, Abraham. Ed, Govt Yearbook, PM off, since 1950; ed, adv on official publs, since 1950; info off, chief press trans, pal Govt, 1930-48; dep dir, Isr Off of Info, 1948-51. Compiled: complete Heb-Eng dict, 4 vols, 1958; Eng-Heb dict, 4 vols, 1963; Heb lexicon of fgn words; Complete Heb Dict, 3 vols; Words of the Wise, dict of Heb-Eng proverbs; trans Eng books to Heb; contbr to local press. Mem: Israel Journalists Assn. Home: 8 Keren Hayesod St, Jerusalem, Isr. Office: Prime Minister's Office, Jerusalem, Isr.

ALDAAG, Hillel, Isr, business exec; b. Bialystok, Pol, Feb 5, 1919; s. Chajkel and Malka; deg, engr architect, Technion, 1941; m. Sarah Cohen, Nov 3, 1925; c: Yoav, Chaim, Amos. Mgn dir, Isr Tractors and Equipment Corp, since 1967; sci counselor, Isr Emb, Wash DC, 1964-67; chief engr, IDF, 1958-64; exec dir, Matzada Oil Drilling, 1955-58. Lt, engr corps, Brit Army; chief engr, IDF. Treas, Bet Shitrit Youth Org; mem: Isr Architects and Engrs; Natl Fire Protection Assn Mil Engrs, US. Recipient: War of Independence, Sinai, Parachute decorations. Hobbies: woodwork, photography. Home: 18 Hamaapil St, Rehovot, Irs. Office: Kiriat Matalon, Petach Tikva, Isr.

ALDERMAN, Harry J, US, librarian, archivist; b. Yonkers, NY, July 10, 1911; s. Solomon and Sarah (Berman); BA, NYU, 1931; BLS, Columbia U, 1937; postgrad studies: Columbia U, Amer U, 1945-49; m. Alice Ross, Nov 10, 1946. Libr dir, AJComm, since 1939; libr asst, NYU, 1931-39. US Army, 1942-45. Mem: Spec Librs Assn; Assn of J Librs, secy, 1948-58; Soc Amer Archivists; Linguistic Soc of Amer; Amer Numismatic Soc; Phi Beta Kappa. Contbr to Amer Jewish Yearbook, Jewish Book Annual. Hobby: ancient numismatics. Home: 240 Cabrini Blvd, New York, NY. Office: 165 E 56 St, New York, NY.

ALDEROTY, Zvi, Isr, municipal off; b. Tel Aviv, May 9, 1934; s. Moshe and Zipora; att: Ayanoth Agric Sch, 1949-53; Haifa U, 1968; m. Zehava, June 24, 1935; c: Ofer, Shay, Tal. Mayor, Migdal Ha'emek since 1959. Capt, Signal Corps, IDF, 1957-59. Recipient: Rozolio Prize, public admn, 1968. Home: Hativat Golani St, Migdal Ha'emek, Isr. Office: Ha'emek St, Migdal Ha'emek, Isr.

ALDOUBY, Zvi Jehudah, Isr, sculptor; b. Rupinka, Pol, Sep 15, 1904; s. Asher and Shprinza (Shechtver) Zupnik; in Isr since 1924; BA, Heb U, Jerusalem, 1934; tchr dipl, Heb Tchrs Sem, 1936; att schs of art, sculpture, Isr, It, 1934-40, 1946-48; m. Edith Irom, 1959; c: Yanir, Romam. Tchr, sculpture, hist of art, since 1947. Representations: Tel Aviv Mus; Ein Harod Mus; pvt collections, Isr, Eur, US, Austr. Co-found, mem, comm, art jury mem, Isr Artists Village, Ein Hod. Served Hagana. Mem: council, comm, Isr Artists, Sculptors Assn. Recipient: Haifa Munic Award, 1957; Dizengoff Award, Tel Aviv Munic, 1963; co-recipient, Intl Exhb, Monaco, 1964; Isr Army Award, Negev Fighters Monument project, 1966; acquisition award, Histadrut Exec Comm, 1967. Hobbies: collecting antiques, hist lit, Kabbala. Home: 38 Beeri St, Tel Aviv, Isr. Studio: Artists Village, Ein Hod, Isr.

ALEXANDER, Ernst, Isr, physicist; b. Berlin, Mar 19, 1902; s. Georg and Selma (Bader); DEng, Technische Hochschule, Berlin, 1928; m. Ernestine Dienstfertig, Aug 18, 1929; c: Shlomo, Dian. Prof, applied physics, head dept physics, Heb U, since 1933; asst, privat dozent, Freiburg U, 1929-33. Co-author: Chemical Analysis with X-rays, 1933; contbr to sci jours. Home: 14 Emek Refaim St, Jerusalem, Isr. Office: Heb U, Jerusalem, Isr.

ALEXANDER, Haim, Israel, musician, composer; b. Aug 9, 1915, Berlin, Ger; s. Emil and Elfriede (Schuftan); grad Pal Acad Music, Jerusalem, 1945; m. Ruth Rosenbaum, Jan 6, 1941; c: Gad, Ron, Dror. Acad tchr, Rubin Acad Music, Jerusalem, 1945. Mem: B'nai B'rith, David Yellin Lodge. Compositions for orch, choir, chamber music, publs on musical subjects. Recipient: Engel Prize, City of Tel Aviv, 1956; Pres

Prize, Zimryah, 1955. Home: 55 Tchernichovsky St, Jerusalem, Isr.

ALEXANDER, Martin, US, scientist, educator; b. Newark, NJ, Feb 4, 1930; s. Meyer and Sarah (Rubinstein); BS, Rutgers U, 1951; MS, U Wis, 1953, PhD, 1955; m. Renée Wulf, Aug 26, 1951; c: Miriam, Stanley, Prof, Cornell U, since 1966, mem fac since 1955; visiting prof, Heb U, 1961-62. Mem: Amer Acad Microbiol; Soil Sci Soc of Amer. Author: Introduction to Soil Microbiology, 1961; contbr numerous sci papers. Recipient: Soil Sci Award, Amer Soc Agron, 1966; Ind Research—100 Award, 1968. Home: 301 Winthrop Dr, Ithaca, NY. Office: Cornell U, Ithaca, NY.

ALEXANDER, Paul Julius, US, educator; b. Berlin, Ger, May 12, 1910; s. Carl and Anna (Mauthner); in US since 1935; DJ, U Hamburg, 1932; Licencié en droit, U Paris, 1934; PhD, hist, Harvard U, 1940; m. Eleanor Eyck, June 21, 1938; c: Ann, Lawrence, Michael. Prof, hist and comparative lit, U Cal, Berkeley, since 1968; lectr, prof, Hobart Coll, 1945-54; prof, chmn, hist dept, Brandeis U, 1954-58; prof, hist, U Mich, 1958-67. Mem: Amer Hist Assn; Medieval Acad. Author: The Patriarch Nicephorus of Constantinople, 1958; The Oracle of Baalbek, 1967; contbr to scholarly jours. Recipient, f: Guggenheim, 1951-52, 1965-66; Social Sci Research Fac, 1960-61; Fulbright Research, 1965-66. Home: 1521 Laloma, Berkeley, Cal. Office: Dept of Hist, U of Cal, Berkeley, Cal.

ALEXANDER, Shlomo, Isr, physicist; b. Freiburg, Ger, Sep 4, 1930; s. Ernest and Esther (Dienstfertig); in Isr since 1933; MS, Heb U, Jerusalem, 1956; PhD, Weizmann Inst of Sci, Rehovot, 1958; m. Esther Neuman, Nov, 1951; c: Michal, Nitza, Amir. Prof, physics, Heb U, since 1969; physicist, Weizmann Inst of Sci, 1954-69. Cpl, IDF, 1948-50. Contbr articles to profsl jours. Office: Heb U, Jerusalem, Isr.

ALEXANDRONI, Alexander, Isr, journalist; b. Warsaw, Pol, Sep 11, 1905; s. Shmuel and Malka (Malovanchik); in Isr since 1935; att U Warsaw; m. Sima Levy, Dec, 1945; c: Leora. Ed, Hadashot Hasport, sports daily, since 1954; sports journalist: Maariv, Heb daily, since 1948; Kol Isr Bc Co, since 1936; sports ed: Haboker, 1953-60; Jerusalem Bc, 1936-48. Haganah, 1936-48. Exec mem: Maccabi World Union; Maccabi Isr Hdqr; mem, Isr Journalists Assn; club, Rotary; fmr: mem: Ilanshil, Polio Cen Comm; cen comm, Soldier's Wfr Bd; exec comm, Isr Lawn Tennis Assn; club, Tel Aviv-Jaffa Rotary. Hobbies: tennis, collecting sports badges, flags. Home: 17 Ha'am Hazarfati, Ramat Gan, Isr. Office: 2 Tushiya St, Tel Aviv, Isr.

ALFANDARY, Isaac, Isr, physician; b. Shabac, Yugo, Dec 25, 1898; s. Mose and Esther (Adania); in Isr since 1945; MD, med sch, Strasbourg, Fr, 1926, specialist in nervous diseases, 1930; m. Gela Beograd. Chief, dept neur, Kupat Holim, Haifa, since 1946; phys, Neur Clinic, Belgrade, 1930-41; chief neur dept: J Hosp, Belgrade, 1941; Brit Mil Hosp, It, 1942-44. Vice-pres, Isr-Fr Med Soc, Haifa; off, Soc Dante Alighieri, Haifa; mem: of hon, Neur Soc of Fr; Soc Neur Psychol, Isr fmr, pres, Haifa br; Soc d'Oto-Neuro-Opthalmologie, Fr. Contbr sci articles to Fr, Heb periodicals. Recipient: Prix Dejeriue, Neur Soc of Fr, 1929; Prix Chauvin, Soc d'Oto-Neuro-Opthal, Fr. Home and office: 73 Hanassi Blvd, Haifa, Isr.

ALFASSI, Itzhak, Isr, author; b. Tel Aviv, Oct 13, 1929; s. Israel and Bela (Yacobovich); att Hebron Yeshiva, Jerusalem; Bar Ilan U, Ramat Gan; m. Adina Bretler; c: Zvi, Uri, Israel. Gen secy, B'nai B'rith in Isr, since 1954; secy: dept rel educ and culture, JA; to min of transp; mgr, off dep min of relief. Lt, Mil Rabbinate, IDF. Pres, Haroch lodge, B'nai B'rith; chmn, Young Adult sector, Mizrachi Org; mem: bd dir, soldiers comm; exec comm, Hapoel Hamizrachi; B'nai B'rith in Isr; B'rit Ivrit Olamit; natl leadership, Mizrachi Youth Org; names comm, Tel Aviv Munic. Author: Rabbi of Kozk, 1952; Rabbi Nachman of Braslev, 1953; Rishonim LeZion, 1956; Gur, 1957; HaSaba HaKadosh, 1958; Toldot HaHasidut, 1959; Tiferet Shebemalchut, 1961, 1967; Sefer Hadmorim, 1961; B'nai B'rith, 3 ed; HaChose MeLublin, 1969; HaHasidut, 1969; contbr numerous articles on various subjects; lectr, popular U, courses. Home: 9 Kazenelson St, Tel Aviv, Isr. Office: 10 Kaplan St, Tel Aviv, Isr.

ALHADEFF, Maurice, Republic of Congo, merchant; b. Rhodes Island, Sep 24, 1895; s. Abramo and Rachelle (Codron); in Congo since 1912; m. Ruth Ross (decd); c: Rachel Rosanes. Owner, M & J Alhadeff; trader and importer since 1918;

promotor, Afr art, exhibited at Orient Fair, 1962. Pres, Heb comty, Leopoldville, since 1954; first hon consul of Isr; club, Rotary, Leopoldville. Recipient: Chevalier de la Legion d'Honneur; Chevalier de l'Ordre de Leopold; Chevalier de l'Ordre du Lion, de l'Ordre du Leopard, de l'Ordre du Merite Centre Afrique. Home and office: PO Box 100, 3 ave du Kwango, Kinshasa, Congo.

ALHADEFF, Nissim I, Rhodesia, business exec; b. Rhodes Island, Sep 4, 1923; s. Saul and Perla (Levy); in Rhodesia since 1932; BCom, U Cape Town, 1947; m. Nelly Israel, Apr 11, 1954; c: Audrey, Evelyn. Co mgn dir, Crown Clothing Co Ltd, since 1950; mgn dir, Furncraft (Pvt) Ltd, 1948-50. Rhodesian, S Afr Forces, 1942-46. Mem: Rhodesian Zionist Youth; Sephardic Youth Soc, fmr chmn; Brit Empire Ex-Servicemen's League; Wingate Country Club; Rhodesian J Bd Deps, fmr vice-pres; Mashonaland regional comm, past vice-chmn; fmr vice-pres, Sephardic Heb Cong, Rhodesia; club, Wingate Country. Home: 16 Richmond Rd, Highlands, Salisbury, Rhodesia. Office: POB 854, Salisbury, Rhodesia.

ALHANATI, Daniel Josaphat, Greece, architect; b. Athens, July 17, 1922; s. Josaphat and Doudov (Azouvi); dipl, architect, Higher Sch for Architects, Polytechnium, Athens, 1945; m. Rosa Sciaky, Sep 12, 1954; c: Josaphat, Delia. Architectural engr since 1945; bldg constructor. Engr corps, Greek Army, 1949-51. Vice-pres, cen bd, J Comty of Greece; pres, J Schs in Athens; fmr, vice-pres, J Comty, Athens. Home: 10 Karpathov St, Athens, Greece. Office: 9 Aristidoy, Athens, Greece.

ALHANATIS, Daniel S, Greece, attorney; b. Athens, Sep 27, 1908; s. Samuel and Annette (Samuelides); att U Athens, 1924-28; m. Violette Behor Yessurun, Jan 21, 1943; c: Samuel, Moise. Pvt law practice since 1931. Off, Greek Army, Greek-Albanian War. Gen secy, Hellas-Isr League, since 1953; pres, Union Greek Zionists, since 1966; vice-pres, B'nai B'rith, since 1966; legal adv, Isr diplomatic delg in Athens, since 1953; legal adv, Greek J Comtys, 1935-42; vice-pres, Bd J Comtys of Greece, 1945-52; fmr, mem bd, J Comty, Athens. Home: 45 Blvd Alexandras, Athens, Greece. Office: 2 Nikis St, Athens, Greece.

ALIAV, Ruth, Isr, public relations officer; b. Kiev, Russ, Apr 27, 1916; d. Yitzhak and Rachel (Gross) Polisiuk; in Isr since 1929; LLB, U Vienna; PR, Columbia U, 1950. Dir, press, PR dept, ZIM Navigation Co, since 1949; JA repr, Hagana, Aliya B rescue, Balkan States, Turkey, Egypt, Eur, N and S Amers, 1938-49. Author: Never the Last Road, 1970. Chmn, PR Assn, Tel Aviv, S Br; exec mem: Intl PR Assn; Isr Advertisers' Assn; mem: B'nai B'rith, Shachar; Working Mothers' Org, Isr; found, chmn, Fed Profsl Working Women, Isr. Recipient: Decorations: Hagana; Komemiut; Aliya B; Aleh; Croix de la Lorraine, Fr Govt, 1954; Star of Hum Redemption, Liberian Pres, 1963; Afr Star, Ivory Coast. Home: 81 Bograshov St, Tel Aviv, Isr. Office: ZIM Co, 9 Ec had Ha'am St, Tel Aviv, Isr.

ALK, Isadore G, US, attorney; b. Green Bay, Wis, Aug 28, 1905; s. Lazarus and Sarah (Jacobs); JD, cum laude, U Wis, 1927; m. Marion Segal, June 9, 1935; c: Benita, Barbara. Pvt law practice: Wash DC, since 1947; Green Bay, Wis, 1927-42; atty, off, Gen Counsel, US Treasury Dept, 1942-44; chief counsel, Div of Fgn Funds Control, 1944-47; sr US Treasury repr Philippines and Japan, 1945; adv to US GHQ, SCAP, on financial and property controls, 1945. Mem: Amer, DC Bar Assns; Amer Soc for Intl Law; Intl Law Assn; Natl Geog Soc; ZOA; AJCong; B'nai B'rith; club, Woodmont Country. Contbr to profsl jours. Recipient: Medal of Freedom, 1946; Order of Crown, 1950, Order of White Elephant, both Thailand, 1955. Home: 2801 N Mexico Ave, NW, Washington, DC. Office: 4710 41 E St, NW, Washington, DC.

ALKAN, Walter J, Isr, physician; b. Berlin, Ger, May 12, 1911; s. Leopold and Adele (Wolfers); in Isr since 1935; att: U Freiburg; U Berlin; MD, Prague U, 1935; DTM and H, Sch of Hygiene and Tropical Med, London, 1938; m. Miriam Neugerg, 1935; c: Michael, David, Gideon. Dir, dept internal diseases, Asaf Harofe Govt Hosp, since 1949; mem med staff: Hadassah Hosp, 1930-39; Bikur Holim Hosp, Jerusalem, 1934-40. Lt col, Brit Army, dir mil hosps in It, Greece; maj, IDF. Contbr to med jours. Hobbies: numismatics, music. Home: 29 Ruppin St, Rehovot, Isr. Office: Asaf Harofe Govt Hospital, Zrifin, Isr.

ALLAN, Norman, US, merchant; b. Milw, Wis, May 31, 1921; s. Rev Louis and Sarah (Wilitzkin) Cohen; m. Esther Boyarsky,

June 16, 1935; c: Sally Alexander, Lawrence, Terrance (decd), Nancy Sturman. Diamond merchant since 1928; partner: Norman Allan & Co, since 1945; Norman Allan & Co, Naha, Okinawa, since 1949; pres: World Wide Jewelers, Detroit since 1956; E L Rice & Co, since 1958; partner, Allan's Jewelry Co, Baton Rouge, Mich, 1934-58; pres: Mercury Inves Co, 1954-62; Amer Supply Co, 1955-62. USN, 1945. Head, Norman and Esther Allan Found; vice-pres, JNF, Detroit, since 1960; chmn bd, Young Isr Council, Metrop Detroit, since 1964; vice-chmn, Detroit Isr Bond Comm, since 1952; pres, Adas Shalom Syn, 1963-65; life mem: JWV; Universal Yeshivah, Jerusalem; Amer Comm for Bar Ilan U, Isr, since 1957; mem: B'nai B'rith; Perfection Lodge 486, Masons; Moslem Temple, Shriners; Scottish Rite; VFW; clubs Town and Country. Hobby: yachting. Home: 18657 George Washington Dr, Southfield, Mich. Office: 17540 Wyoming Ave, Detroit, Mich.

ALLEN, Mel, US, sports broadcaster; b. Birmingham, Ala, Feb 14, 1913; s. Julius and Anna (Lieb) Israel; BA, U Ala, 1932, LLB, 1936. Sports commentator, radio and TV since 1937; for Fox Movietone News since 1946; broadcaster for radio and TV, Natl Collegiate Athletic Assn, since 1951; broadcaster, NBC since 1951; covered: All Star Games, 1939-43 and since 1946; World Series Games, 1938-43 and since 1947; Bowl Games: Rose, 1949, since 1952; Orange, 1950-51; Sugar, 1947; Natl Collegiate Athletic Assn football games, 1951-53; NY Giants, 1939-43; NY Yankees, 1939-43, and since 1946; instr, speech dept, debating coach, U Ala, 1936-37. Staff Sgt, US Army, 1943-46. Chmn, sports div: Gtr NY Fund; Boy Scouts of Amer; NY Cancer Fund; Natl Assn to Combat Blindness; Cerebral Palsy; UJA; Children to Pal; mem, Pres' Citizens Adv Comm on Fitness of Amer Youth; fmr pres, Sports Broadcasters Assn, 1950-51; gen chmn, Fight for Sight Campaign, 1952; mem: B'nai B'rith; Kappa Nu; clubs: Lambs; Friars. Co-author: It Takes Heart. Recipient: Order of the Rake, NY Advt Club, 1940; award, Sporting News, 1946-51; number one baseball broadcaster, Sporting News, 1946; Mel Allen Day, 1950; NY Times honor roll, 1947; award, Radio-TV Acad of Art and Scis, 1950-52; TV Award, Look Mag, 1950; citation, annual poll of TV-Radio eds, Radio Daily, annually since 1950; Fame Mag award, annually since 1951; gold medal, TV Guide; awards: radio-TV, Radio TV Mirror; Motion Picture Daily; top broadcaster, Radio-TV Daily; favorite broadcaster, TV-Radio Mirror; best broadcaster, Fame Mag, 1961; spec award, Look Mag, 1958; Sport Mag Award for special service to the sports field; voted salesman of year, Natl Assn Direct Selling Co, 1960. Home: Loop Rd, Bedford Village, NY. Office: Yankee Stadium, 161 St and River Ave, Bronx, NY.

ALLENTUCK, Marcia E, US, teacher; b. NYC, June 8, 1928; d. Isaac and Anna (Lipetz) Epstein; BA, summa cum laude, NYU, 1948; PhD, Columbia U, 1964; m. Jack Allentuck, Aug 5, 1959; c: Isaaca. Asso prof, Eng dept, CCNY, on fac since 1961; mem fac: Columbia U, 1955-57; Hunter Coll, 1957; visiting prof, Sarah Lawrence Coll, 1962-63. Mem: AAUP; Amer Assn U Women; MLA; Coll Eng Assn; Natl Council Tchrs Eng; Hist Sci Soc; Amer Soc for Aesthetics; Eng Grad Union; Phi Beta Kappa Alumnae; Renaissance Soc Coll Art Assn; Intl Fold Music Council; Intl Compara-tive Lit Assn; J Reconstructionist Found; Soc for Advance-ment Judaism; British Soc for Aesthetics; Anglo-J Hist Soc; Morningside Citizens Comm. Author: The Works of Henry Needler, 1961; Isaac Bashevis Singer, 1969; contbr to profsl jours. Recipient: Huntington libr f, 1968. Home: 5 W 86 St, New York, NY. Office: CCNY, New York, NY.

ALLIGER, Joseph K, US, business exec; b. Russ, Feb 22, 1896; s. Max and Fannie (Schmukler) Ailetcher; in US since 1898; m. Gladys Scheiner, Feb 21, 1921; c: Martin, Howard. Pres: Sterling Affiliates Inc, since 1958; Sterling Inves Corp, since 1929; chmn bd, Plaza Funding, since 1952. Pres, LI Zionist Region, 1956-57; vice-pres, Natl ZOA, 1956-58; chmn: UJA Gt Neck, 1950-51, 1956; Temple Isr Men's Club, 1952; Isr Bonds Drive, 1952-53, 1955; bd dirs: United HIAS Service; NCCJ; AJCong; J Info Bur; delg, WZC, 1956; club: ZOA Patrons. Home: 180 S Middle Neck Rd, Great Neck, NY. Office: 777 Northern Blvd, Great Neck, NY.

ALLMAN, David Bacharach, US, surgeon; b. Phila, Pa, July 11, 1891; s. Millard and Ray (Bacharach); MD, Jefferson Med Coll, Phila, 1914; hon: DSc, Temple U; LLD, Jefferson Med Coll; DHL, HUC; m. 2nd, Ann Lorenzen, July 19, 1965. Surg dir, Atlantic City Hosp, since 1942, sr cons surg chief, since 1950, mem bd govs; chief surg, vice-chmn, bd, Betty

Bacharach Home for Afflicted Children, since 1927, med dir, since 1927; cons surg, Atlantic City Hosp for TB, since 1920, mem bd mgrs and vice-pres; hon chief surg, Police and Fire Depts, Atlantic City, NJ; bd dirs, Guardian Savings and Loan Assn. USN, WW II. Vice-pres: 'US sect, Intl Coll Surgs; Cancer Soc; treas, Soc of Surgs, NJ; FACS; F: Intl Coll of Surgs; Acad of Med, NJ; AMA; dipl, Amer Bd Surg, founds group; mem: bd trustees, Jefferson Coll and Med Cen; bd mgrs, Temple Beth Isr; AAAS; Amer Trudeau Soc; ARC; Amer Hosp Assn; NY Acad Sci; NJ Hosp Assn; Atlantic City and NJ Civil Defense Councils; Atlantic Co Hist Soc; Elks; Masons; Shriners; Consistory; Grotto; life mem, Tall Cedars; Sojourners; Atlantic City chap, Reserve Offs of Naval Services; USCG Auxiliary; fmr: pres: State Bd Med Examiners, NJ; Jefferson Med Coll Alumni Assn; Atlantic Co Med Soc; NJ chap, Assn Mil Surgs; chmn, bd appeals, Selective Service, NJ; trustee, chmn bd, Med Soc of NJ; clubs: Tuna; Country; Racquet, all Atlantic City; Brigantine Yacht; Med of Phila. Hobbies: yachting, fishing. Home and office: 4105 Brigantine Blvd, Brigantine, NJ.

ALLON, Yigal, Isr, cabinet min, b. Kfar Tabor, Isr, Oct 10, 1918; s. Reuben and Haia (Schwartz) Paicovitch; att: Cadouri Agric Sch; Heb U, Jerusalem; Oxford U; m. Ruth Afisdorf, 1938; c: Nurit, Iftach. MK since 1954; dep PM since 1968, Min of Educ and Culture, since 1970, Min of Immigrant Absorption, 1968-70, mem: Cabinet Defence Comm, Econ Affairs Comm; Min of Lab, 1961-68; acting PM upon the death of Levi Eshkol, 1969. Active in Haganah, 1936-48; sgt, J Settlement Police, 1937-39; cdr, field units, Galilee dist, 1939, dir, instr, off sch; co-found, Palmach, 1941; cdr, spec underground activity, Brit Army, Syria, Leb, 1942; co-org, cdr, Haganah, Alia Bet, dep chief of command, 1943-45; chief of command, 1945-48; maj gen; cdr, major campaigns, Isr War of Independence, Upper Galilee Cen Front, S Front; mem Mil Adv Comm to PM during Six Day War. Author: Curtain of Sand; Arabs and Israelis Between War and Peace; The Palmach Story. Home: Kibbutz Genossar, Isr. Office: Min of Educ and Culture, Jerusalem, Isr.

ALLONY, Nehemia, Isr, orientalist; b. Warsaw, Pol, May 16, 1906; s. Naftali and Hanna (Borovski) Linde; in Isr since 1925; dipl Hebr Tchrs Coll, Jerusalem, 1931; att Friedrich Wilhelm U, Berlin, 1931-33; MA, Heb U, Jerusalem, 1937, PhD, 1944; m. Edith Trainin, Apr 29, 1956. Lectr, Heb Poetry and Lang in Middle Ages, Inst for Acad Studies, Heb U, Beersheva, 1950-63; dir, Inst Heb Manuscripts, Isr Min Educ, 1950-63; dir, Kindergarten Tchrs Sem, 1939-46; sci secy, Bibl Ency, 1944-47, both in Jerusalem; lectr, Semitic studies, Leeds U, Eng, 1947-49. Pres: Students Union, 1934-42; Hehalutz, Berlin, 1931-33; chmn, Hehalutz, Pol, 1924-26. Author: Poetry of Dunash ben Labrat, 1947; Scansion of Medieval Hebrew Poetry, 1950; Kitab 'Usul al-shi'r al-Ibrani, by R'an Se'ady Ga'on, Jerusalem, 1969; Kitab al Sabin Lafza, by Sh'ad Gaon, 1957; Studies in Medieval Hebrew Literature, 1957; contbr to scholarly publs; ed Niv haStudent, Jerusalem, 1934-37. Home: 41 King George Ave, Jerusalem, Isr.

ALLOUCHE, Felix Nissim, Isr, journalist; b. Sfax, Tunisia, Mar 17, 1901; s. Hayim and Yasmina; in Isr since 1956; att: Yeshiva, HS, Tunis; licencié ès lettres, Paris; m. Henriette Ankri, Apr 22, 1922; seven c. Ed, L'Information d'Israel, daily, Tel Aviv; spec corresp, Paris-Match; fmr: reporter, La Dépêche, daily, Tunisia; corresp in N Afr to Fr and Amer jours; found, dir: Le Réveil Juif; L'Echo Sioniste; La Gazette d'Israel; found, radio emission, Tunis Bc, Voix d'Israel, 1938-56. Arrested by Pétain govt, 1940, as J journalist and leader of Brith Trumpeldor; mem of résistance, Tunisia. Leader: zionist clubs; comty councils, KKL, all in Tunisia; delg, Revisionist Party, to ZCs; mem: Journalists Assn, Isr; Fgn Press Assn. Hobbies: literary critic; gardening. Home: 60 Balfour St, Bat Yam, Isr. Office: 52 Harakevet St, Tel Aviv, Isr.

ALLWEIL, Asher, Isr, engineer; b. Winniczki, Pol, Aug 20, 1909; s. Meir and Miriam (Milet); dipl engr, Poly Coll, Lwow, 1934; in Isr since 1935; m. Alisa Yehalom, Sep, 1938; c: Abraham, Mira. Dir, planning and engr dept, Min of Housing, since 1949; asso mem, academic staff, Technion, Haifa, since 1955; engr, Lwow, 1934-35; in practice, civil engr, Pal, 1935-41; exec engr, bridges and airfields, 1941-42; chief engr, Bldg and Techniques Research Inst, 1943-44. Mem: Natl Council for Research and Devl, since 1960, exec comm, Standards Inst, Isr, since 1961. Co-author: Habinyan miBeton Mezuyan, 1938, 1941; contbr to profsl publs; author, research reports on bldg methods and costs, published by Bldg Research Sta, Technion. Awards: A M Arnan Prize, Assn Engrs and Architects, 1968. Home: 3 Berliner St, Tel Aviv, Isr. Office: Min of Housing, Hakiryah, Tel Aviv, Isr

ALMAGOR, Dan, Isr, author; b. Ramat Gan, Isr, July 13, 1935; s. Zeev and Zehava (Katzenellenbogen) Elblinger; att Tel Aviv U, 1954-56; MA, Heb U, 1962; PhD, UCLA, 1968; m. Ella Appelrot, Feb 28, 1960; c: Orna, Elinoar. Author of plays, musical comedies, satires, songs, Heb adaptations: My Fair Lady, Fiddler on the Roof, Comedy of Errors; studies in medieval and modern Heb lit; Isr corresp: Gambit, London; Shakespeare Quarterly, NY; lectr, U Judaism, La, 1963-68. Served, IDF. Home: 4A Hatsofim St, Haifa, Isr.

ALMAGOR, Elisha, Isr, business exec; b. Vienna, Aus, June 7, 1914; s. Rudolf and Valery (Hajos); in Isr since 1935; att U Vienna, 1931-1933; BSS, LSE, 1935; m. Mollie Sonberg; c: Rafael, Simona Cohen. Dir gen, Tel Aviv Intl Trade Fair, since 1963; dep dir, dept educ, Haifa munic, 1951-56; dir, dept educ, Ashkelon dist, 1956-59; dir, ZOA House, 1959-63. Sgt, Brit Army, 1939-45; Capt, IDF, 1947-50. Home: 12 Atzmon St, Ramat Hasharon, Isr. Office: POB 21075, Tel Aviv, Isr.

ALMOG, David, Isr, investigator; b. Warsaw, Pol, June 2, 1915; s. Abraham and Milka (Palewsky) Sokolik; in Isr since 1924; ABTI, BTI, London, 1946; IAS, Inst of Applied Sci, Chgo, 1951; m. Tova Lipshitz, June 19, 1934; c: Adina Perlman, Zeeva Lipshitz. Dir, Argus Inves Service, since 1944; watchman, Netanya, 1930-31; mgr, David Tidhar and Co, 1934-40. Mem: Irgun Zvaei Leumi, 1935-39, detained several times by Brit Police; Acre, Mezra, Latrun Detention Camps; capt, security, IDF. Mem exec, B'nai B'rith, delg to convs in Isr, delg, Tri-annual World Conv, fmr: hon secy, B'nai B'rith, Isr, pres, Gideon Lodge; bd dirs, World Assn Detectives, ME gov, since 1963; hon mem, ADI, It; chmn, WSSA, Spain; gov for Asia, Assn for Brit Detectives; delg to intl congs: WSSA; WAD; IKD; ADI; mem, Haaguda Lemaan Hahayal; fmr chmn, various comms, Vaad Lemaan Hahayal. Author: Habalash Hamoderni, 1946; contbr to profsl mags. Recipient: Hon Brother Award, Gideon Lodge, B'nai B'rith, 1968. Home: 25 Pinsker St, Tel Aviv, Isr. Office: 16 Herzl St, Tel Aviv, Isr.

ALMOG, Joshua, Isr, diplomat; b. Jerusalem; s. Joseph and Julia (Albaranes); BA, Amer U, Beirut, 1945; att: Sorbonne U and Sch Political Sci, Paris, 1947. Repr, Min for Fgn Affairs, administered territories, since 1969; mem, educ missions for J Natl Instn to Fr, N Afr and Iran, 1946-50; political corresp for Hador daily, Teheran, 1950-51; pvt secy to Pres of Isr, I Ben-Zvi, 1955-58; toured US for UJA, 1958; first secy, consul, Isr legation in Greece, 1958-61; first secy, Isr Emb, Mali, 1961-62; dep dir, Afr Dept, Min for Fgn Affairs, 1963-64; counselor, Isr Embassy, Paris, 1964-68; mem, Isr delg to: UNCTAD, Geneva, 1965; UNESCO general assemblies, Paris, 1966, 1968; alternate Isr delg, Human Rights subcomm, Geneva, 1967; mem, Isr delg to Council of Eur, Strasbourg, 1968; visiting lectr, Sch of Political Sci, Paris, 1965-68. Brit Army, 1943-45; intelligence off, IDF. Recipient: silver medal, City of Paris, 1968. Home: POB 104, Jerusalem, Isr. Office: Min for Fgn Affairs, Jerusalem, Isr,

ALMOG, Michael, Isr, civic worker; b. Tel Aviv, Nov 27, 1923; s. Baruch and Malka (Kremin) Avrutsky; m. Niza Miller, Sep 10, 1946; c: Gonen, Dror, Nava. Chmn, technical comm, Isr Football Assn, since 1964; dir, dept munic affairs, Avoda Mapai party, since 1960; mgr, football sect, Hapoel, 1953-58. Sr staff off, Hagana, 1942-47; maj, IDF, 1948-51. Mem, central comm, Hapoel. Author: book of instructions for youth leaders; articles on sports. Home: Herzl St, Kfar Sava, Isr. Office: Avoda Party, 110 Hayarkon St, Tel Aviv, Isr.

ALMOGI, Joseph, Isr, cabinet minister; b. Poland, May 5, 1910; s. Zwi and Chana (Hoffman); in Isr since 1930; m. Schifra Weinblatt, 1934; c: Joram, Zwi. Min of Lab and Natl Ins, since June 1968; Min of Devl and Housing, 1962-65; Min without Portfolio, 1961-62; mem, Hagana Command, 1933-39; gen secy: Labor Council, Haifa, 1945-59; Mapai party, 1959-62. Brit Army, WW II. Home: 120 Arlosoroff St, Haifa, Isr. Office: Min of Lab, Jerusalem, Isr.

ALON, Azaria, Isr, journalist; b. Wollodars, Russ, Nov 15, 1918; s. Joseph and Sarah (Kipnis) Kozyrovsky; in Isr since 1925; Tchr Dipl, Seminar Hakibutzim; att U Tel Aviv, 1963-65; m. Ruth Diamant; c: Gilad, Avital, Yair. Mem, Kibbutz Beit Hashitta, since 1938; journalist, weekly column, Lamer-

hav daily since 1959; weekly prog, Nof Arzenu, Isr bc radii; Author: Pirhei har vagay; Al ezim v'al avanim; Al pnei Sinao. Aleph Bet shel Hayot; Aleph-Bet shel Ziporim; 77 Sihot al tera, A-B; Shvilim lamidlar; Israel, teva vanof; Natural History of the Land of the Bible. Mem: youth movement, Hamahanot Haolim, 1936-46; Kibbutz Hameuchad youth movement and cen, 1951-56; Nature Reserves Auth since 1963; cofound, Soc for Protection of Nature in Isr, 1953. Home: Kibbutz Beit Hashitta, Isr.

ALON, Gabriel, Isr, economist, journalist; b. Cologne, Ger, Mar 20, 1915; s. Richard and Clara (Elsberg) Eichelgrün; in Isr since 1933; att: HS, Cologne; Trade Sch, Technion, Haifa; m. Rena Karlsruher, Aug 4, 1941; c: Rachel Sagi, Tamar, Reuben, Naomi, Michael. Ed, Business Diary, since 1947; mem, Kibbutz Eylon, 1935-37; mgr, Hotel Emek, Haifa, 1937-42; income tax cons, 1942-47. Author: Palestine Income Tax Guide, 1945; World Commodity Trade Statistics, 1964-65. Hobby: econ theory, its hist. Home: 43 Oranim St, Kiryat Tivon, Isr. Office: 37 Hanamal S', Haifa, Isr.

ALON, Moni, Isr, educator; b. Vienna, Aus, Oct 4, 1914; s. Shlomo and Miriam (Rosenblum) Langermann; in Isr since 1934; att: LSE, London; Heb U, Jerusalem; m. Yael Loewisohn; c: Miriam Levy, Osnat, Shlomit. Tchr, Oranim, Kibbutz Tchrs Sem, since 1960; mem, Kibbutz Arzi Educ Bd, since 1960, secy, 1960-65; tchr, Mishmar Haemek HS, since 1945. Hagana, IDF since 1934. Mem: actions comm, Kibbutz Arzi; youth aliyah leader; secy, Hashomer Hatzair Youth movement, 1948-49; fmr youth aliyah repr to detention camps, Cyprus. Contbr articles on kibbutz educ. Spec interests: sociol, politics, lit, music. Home: Kibbutz Hazorea, Isr.

ALONI, Elchanan, Isr, engineer; b. Kreutzburg, Ger, Aug 23, 1922; s. Zwi and Jochebeth (Goschewsky); in Isr since 1938; BS, cum laude, Technion, Haifa, 1963; m. Michaela Stein, Mar 11, 1960; c: Irith, Ruth. Research engr, since 1963; owner, auto mech shop, 1945-53; tech designer, draftsman, Isr Elec Co, 1953-61. Automobile mech, Brit Army, 1941-44; cpl, IDF, 1947-49. Mem: Assn Engrs and Architects, Isr; Soc for Protection Nature, both Haifa. Hobbies: music, painting. Home: 2 Habroshim, Sabiniah, Kiryat Bialik, Isr. Office: Ministry of Defence, Kiryat Motzkin, Isr.

ALONI, Itzak, Isr, chess player, clerk; b. Bauhach, Pol, Apr 5, 1905; s. Eliyahu and Dina Schecter; in Isr since 1944; HS, Pol, 1922-24; m. Miriam Mussinger, 1935. Chess player, since 1915; chess instr, sch, clubs since 1949; participant, chess olympics, Holland, 1954; Moscow, 1956; Munich, 1958; Leipzig, 1960; Bulgaria, 1962; Tel Aviv, 1964; Cuba, 1966. Hagana, 1947-49. Chess champion: Isr, 1945,1962, 1966; Haifa, 1966; Jerusalem, 1946; Tel Aviv, 1969. Mem: Lasker Chess Club. Recipient: Isr Chess Org award. Home: 71 Derech Hashalom, Tel Aviv, Isr.

ALONI, Shulamit, Isr, legislator; b. Isr; b. David and Yehudit; tchrs cert, Tchrs Sem, Jerusalem; LLB, Heb U, Jerusalem; m. Reuben Aloni; c: Dror, Nimrod, Ehud. Chmn, Isr Consumer Council, since 1966; MK, 1965-70; columnist, Yediot Aharonot, Davar; ed, radio progs. Served, IDF. Author: Ezrah Umedinato, 1958, 4th ed, 1968; Zehuiot Hayeled Be' Israel, 1964; contbr to press. Home: 71A Derech Hasadot, Kfar Shmaryahu, Isr.

ALOUF, Haim, Isr, judge; b. Jerusalem, May 5, 1915; s. Mordekai and Ruhama (Simhon); law dipl, Law Sch, Jerusalem, 1945; att Heb U, Jerusalem; m. Suzette Amon, Sep 30, 1940; c: Daphne, Haggit, Ehud. Judge since 1954; police off, 1934-54. Home: 13 Yehuda Hamacabi St, Tel Aviv, Isr. Office: Law Courts, Tel Aviv, Isr.

ALOUF, Yehoshua, Isr, government official; b. Slonim, Russ, Mar 4, 1900; s. Isaac and Haya (Udaly) Wolpiansky; in Isr since 1912; grad, Govt Phys Educ Inst, Copenhagen, Den, 1924; m. Hynda Neumann, June 17, 1924; c: Ari. Ret since 1965; head sup, Phys Educ, Min Educ and Culture, 1957-65; instr, Maccabiah, Warsaw, 1916-20; chief org, Maccabiah games, 1932, 1935, 1950, 1953, 1957, tech adv, 1969; liaison off, JA and Brit Mandate authorities, Jerusalem, 1936-38; sup phys educ, Vaad Leumi schs, 1938-48; dir, phys educ dept, 1953-57. Mem: comm for phys educ terminology, Heb Lang Acad, since 1948; repr, Min of Educ, bd Isr Maritime League, 1952-65; delg: Paris Olympic games, 1924; tenth Sokol Festival, Prague, 1938; London Olympic games, 1948; Lingride, Stockholm, 1949; Helsinki Olympic games, 1952. Author: Munakei haHitamlut, 1940; Mish'hakei Tnua,

1941; Torat haHinukh haGufani, 1941; Hitamlut beSafsal uBeargaz, 1943; haMekhanika shel Guf haAdam, 1945; Sport, 1966; Torat Hatnuah, 1969; Da Shrirecha, 1969; pub, Bridge, mag in Heb, 1967-68. Recipient: Ot Hahagana,1958, Ot Hamishmar, 1963, Itur Lochamei Hamedinah, 1968. Home: 8 Renanim St, Ramat Gan, Isr.

ALPAN, Itzchak,Isr, engineer, educator; b. Yedinetz, Rum, Oct 25, 1919; BSc, Technion, Haifa, 1946, CE, 1947, MSc, 1956; PhD, London U, 1959; dipl, Imperial Coll, London, 1960; two c. Asso prof, civil engr, Technion, Haifa, since 1966, mem fac since 1946; structural engr, with cons engrs off, 1946-51; expert civil engr, soil mechs, UNESCO mission, with U Coll, Nairobi, Kenya, 1963-64; UNESCO expert, earthquake engr, Intl Inst Seismology and Earthquake Engr, Tokyo, Japan, 1965-66. F, Amer Soc Civil Engrs; mem: Assn Engrs and Architects in Isr; Instn Civil Engrs; Amer Geophysical Union. Contbr numerous sci papers and articles to profsl publs. Recipient: Fr Govt F in Paris, 1952-53. Office: Fac of Civic Engr, Technion, Haifa, Isr.

ALPER, Benedict Solomon, US, criminologist; b. Revere, Mass, June 28, 1905; s. Morris and Fredericka (Klatschken); AB, Harvard U, 1927; att Harvard Inst Criminal Law, 1932-33; m. Ethel Machanic, June 14, 1935; c: Fredrika. Lectr, criminology, Boston Coll; fmr lectr: Rutgers Law Sch; New Sch for Social Research; cons, UN Sect of Social Defense; research dir, Mass Child Council, 1935-39; NY State Leg Comm on Courts, 1941; field secy, Amer Parole Assn, 1942; spec asst to dir, Fed Bur of Prisons, 1942-43, 1946; with UN, 1946-51. Maj, US Army, 1943-46. Author: Criminal Youth and the Borstal System, 1941; Young People in the Courts of New York State, 1942; contbr to profsl jours. Home and office: Hatchville, Mass.

ALPER, Thelma G, US, psychologist, educator; b. Chelsea, Mass, July 24, 1908; d. David and Mollie (Herman) Gorfinkle; BA, Wellesley Coll, 1929; MA, Radcliffe Coll, 1941, PhD, 1943; m. Abraham Alper, Apr 1, 1932 (decd). Helen J Sanborn Prof Psych, Wellesley Coll since 1969, prof since 1954; cons, Judge Baker Guidance Cen, since 1959; lectr, Harvard U, 1946-48; asso prof, Clark U, 1948-52. Mem, exec comm, ACLU, Mass; pres, NE Psych Assn, 1970-71; mem bd, fmr pres, Mass Psych Assn; fmr mem, bd of trustees, Heb Tchrs Coll; f, Amer Psych Assn; mem: AAUP; Phi Beta Kappa; Sigma Xi; dipl, Amer Bd Examiners in Profsl Psych, since 1948. Co-ed, The Fighting Man, Infantry Jour, 1944; contbr to profsl jours. Home: 217 Kent St, Brookline, Mass. Office: Wellesley Coll, Wellesley, Mass.

ALPERIN, Goldie Green, US, attorney, law librl, association exec; b. Des Moines, Ia, Aug 16, 1905; d. Morris and Bessie (Miliwer) Green; LLB, Drake U Law Sch, Des Moines, 1927, JD, 1968; m. Moses Alperin, Dec 25, 1930 (decd); c: Herschel, Judith. Dir, Northwestern U Law Sch Libr, Chgo, since 1966; pvt practice, Des Moines, 1927-30; cert Sunday sch tchr, Chgo Bd J Educ, 1950-51; law libr, Chgo Bar Assn, 1951-63; dir, Defense Info Off, Chgo, 1963-65. Mem: Amer Assn Law Libr, fmr secy; Chgo Assn Law Libr, fmr mem exec bd, fmr ed; Amer Bar Assn; Natl Assn Women Lawyers, fmr region dir; Intl Assn Law Librs; Decalogue Soc Lawyers; Women's Bar Assn, Ill; hon mem, adv comm, Marquis Biographical Libr Soc; libr, Emanuel Cong. Ed, bull, Women's Bar Assn Ill, 1964-65; fmr asst ed, exec bd, Women Lawyers Jour. Recipient: named one of 20 repr US women lawyers, Women's Adjustment Bd, London, 1957. Home: 1238 Elmdale Ave, Chicago, Ill. Office: 357 E Chicago Ave, Chicago, Ill.

ALPERIN-WEINBERG, Menuha, Isr, author, journalist; b. Pinsk, Russ, 1898; d. Moshe and Zipora; att U Warsaw. Journalist, Yiddish newspapers; found, libr, Kiryat Motzkin; communal worker, Pinsk; lectr, Parents Club, Kiryat Motzkin. Author: first work published at age 14; Fun Hurban Efake; Robale; Palesier Yion; contbr to: Lamshzer Pinkas; Lamshzer Buch in Amerike; Buch Stalin; Hasidut; Yiddishe Zaitung. Mem: Yiddish Writers Assn. Home: Tel Mond, Isr.

ALPERN, Mathew, US, educator; b. Akron, O, Sep 22, 1920; s. Aaron and Goldie (Ray); att Akron U, 1937-38; OD, N Ill Coll Optometry, 1941; BME, U Fla, 1944; MSc, PhD, O State U; m. Rebecca Elsner, Aug 17, 1951; c: Bowen, Goldie, Barbara, Aaron. Prof: phys optics, Med Sch U Mich, since 1963; psych, U Mich, since 1963, on fac since 1955; asst prof, Pacific U, 1951-55. US Army, 1942-46. Mem: Amer

Comm Optics and Visual Phys; visual scis study sect, NIH; fmr Natl Acad of Scis repr, NRC and Natl Acad of Scis comm on vision; mem: Amer Phys Soc; Biophysics Soc; Optical Soc; asso res, vision and ophthal, Amer Psych Assn; Sigma Xi. Co-author: Sensory Processes; contbr to profsl and sci jours. Home: 3545 Woodland Rd, Ann Arbor, Mich. Office: U of Mich, Ann Arbor, Mich.

ALPERN, Zelthia R, US, organization exec, social worker; b. Buffalo, NY, Dec 27, 1911; d. Isadore and Esther (Fox) Ruben; BA, cum laude, Smith Coll, 1932; grad cert, U Buffalo, Sch of Social Work, 1943; m. Irwin Alpern, June 5, 1937; c: Michael, Lisbeth Ann. Exec dir, Planned Parenthood Center, Buffalo, since 1961; case worker: Monroe Co, Dept Public Wfr, Rochester, 1933-34; Children's Aid Soc, 1934-39; unit case sup, Erie Co Dept Social Wfr, 1939-43; psycht case worker, Buffalo State Hosp, 1961. Pres, Buffalo sect, Natl Council J Women, 1955-57, vice-pres, 1954-55; mem, Amherst League Women Voters; club, Social Worker's, Buffalo. Recipient: scholarship, Natl Council J Women, 1957. Home: 33 Bissell Dr, Eggertsville, NY. Office: 210 Franklin St, Buffalo, NY.

ALPERS, Bernard J, US, physician, educator; b. Salem, Mass, Mar 14, 1900; s. Samuel and Bessie (Swift); MD, Harvard Med Coll, 1923; ScD, med, U of Pa, 1930; m. Lillian Sher, Sept 11, 1927; c: Paul, David, Edward. Prof em, neur, Jefferson Med Coll, Phila since 1965, prof, head dept neur, 1938-65; neur, Jefferson Hosp, since 1938; cons, Pa Hosp and Wills Eye Hosp; neur and cons, Inst Pa Hosp; cons: VA; USN Hosp, Phila; dir: lab of neuropath, dept neurosurg, U of Pa, 1930-38; lab of neuropath, Inst of Pa Hosp, 1930-46. Fmr pres: Amer Neur Assn; Amer Bd Psycht and Neur; Amer Assn Neuropath; vice-pres, Cong Mikveh Isr; f: AMA; Amer Coll Phys; Amer Psycht Assn; mem: Assn for Research in Nervous and Mental Diseases; Coll of Phys, Phila; Phila Neur Soc; Pa and Phila Psycht Socs; Phila Co Med Soc; club, Harvard. Author: Clinical Neurology, 1946; Vertigo and Dizziness; contbr to med jours. Home: 500 Oak Rd, Merion, Pa. Office: 111 N 49 St, Philadelphia, Pa.

ALPERS, Lillian S, US, physician, educator; b. Toronto, Can, Aug 12, 1903; d. Charles and Ethel (Brody) Sher; in US since 1926; MD, U Toronto Med Sch, 1925; m. Bernard Alpers, Sep 11, 1927; c: Paul, David, Edward. Spec lectr: Women's Med Coll of Pa, since 1955, on fac since 1931; U of Pa, since 1955; asso in med, Women's Hosp of Phila, since 1930. Mem bd: Cong Mikveh Isr since 1959, pres Women's Group; Rebecca Gratz Club; Heb Sunday Sch Soc; natl bd, women's div, Amer Friends Heb U, since 1962; Pa Hosp Women's Auxillary; mem: Phila Co Med Soc; AMA; Amer Med Women's Assn; Hadassah; Ort; ZOA; AJCong; Delta Phi Epsilon. Recipient: woman of year award, women's div, Amer Friends Heb U, 1968; citation for comty service, Chapel of Four Chaplains, 1960, Hobbies: reading, theater, music. Home: 500 Oak Rd, Merion, Pa.

ALPERT, Carl, Isr, organization exec, journalist; b. Boston, May 12, 1913; s. Max and Flora (Effross); att Boston U, 1931-35; m. Nechamah Tennenbaum, 1940; c: Miryam, Joel, Ruth. Asst to pres, Technion, Haifa, since 1955, dir, exec vice-chmn, Bd of Govs, since 1964, dir, PR, 1952-1967; reporter, Jewish Advocate, Boston, 1932-35, asso ed, 1935-40; mgn ed, The New Palestine, 1940-46; dir, educ dept, ZOA, 1946-52; dir, vice-pres, Young Judea, 1936-40, pres, 1940-41. US Army, 1944-46. Natl pres, AACI, 1957-59. Author: Oracle, Jewish Reference Book, 1935; To the Land of Their Fathers, 1939; The Truth about the Jews, 1946; Palestine Between Two Wars, 1947; Guide to a New Life, 1956; asso ed, Universal Jewish Encyclopedia and World Scope Encyclopedia; intl syndicated weekly columnist and contbr to Anglo-J press in US, Can, S Afr. Hobbies: philately, J Americana. Home: 3 Kisch Ave, Haifa, Isr. Office: Technion, Haifa, Isr.

ALPERT, Herman S, US, psychiatrist; b. Potsdam, NY, Jan 17,1913; s. Israel and Sara (Lehrman); BA, U Rochester, 1934; MD, Eclectic Med Coll, Cincinnati, O, 1938; postgrad: Sch of Mil Neuropsycht, Eur Theater of Opr, US Army, Litchfield, Eng, 1944; NY Psycht Inst, 1946; NY Psychoanalytic Inst, 1948-51; m. Eileen Picker, Mar 31, 1946; c: Cheryl, Jeffrey. Pvt practice since 1947; asst clinical prof psycht, Mt Sinai Sch of Med, NY, CUNY, since 1967; visiting asso staff psycht, Hillside Hosp, Glen Oaks, NY, fmr adj att psycht; asst att psycht, Mt Sinai Hosp, since 1962, on staff since 1947; lectr, Inst Pastoral Psycht, 1948-52; qualified psycht, NY State Dept Mental Hygiene, since 1943; res psycht, Letchworth Village, Thiells, NY, 1939-42; chief, neuropsycht sect, Rhoads Gen Hosp, Utica, NY, 1945-46; sup psycht, Marcy St Hosp, Marcy, NY, 1946-47. Maj, US Army MC, 1942-46. Pres, NY State Hosps Med Alumni Assn, since 1968; mem bd dirs, Amer Soc Psychoanalytic Phys, since 1962; f: Amer Psycht Assn, since 1950; AMA; Amer Assn Mental Deficiency; Amer Bd Psycht and Neur, since 1946; mem: NY Soc Clinical Psycht; Assn Advancement Psychotherapy. Contbr to med jours. Special interest: collector of old violins. Home: 7 Briarfield Dr, Lake Success, NY. Office: 993 Park Ave, New York, NY.

ALPERT, Morton, US, scientist; b. NYC, June 10, 1924; s. Max and Julia (Milstein); BS, La State U, 1947; MS, O State U, 1948; PhD, U of Minn, 1952; m. Lois Salzman, Sep 5, 1948; c: Stephen, Sheri. Clinical researcher, Ames Co, Div of Miles Labs, Inc, Elkhart, Ind, since 1968; instr, anat, O State U, 1952, asst prof, 1952-59; asso prof, anat, Ind U Med Cen, 1959-68; educ author, Ind U Visual Aids Dept, 1959-68. US Army, 1942-46. Dem precinct committeeman, St Joseph City, since 1969; f: AAAS; Royal Microscopic Soc; mem: Amer Assn Anats; Histo-chem Soc; Soc for Experimental Biol and Med; Amer Soc for Cell Biol; Endocrine Soc; Assn for Advancement of Med Instrumentation; Instrument Soc of Amer; Alpha Epsilon Pi; Sigma Xi; fmr: co-chmn, adult educ comm, choir, Temple Beth El-Zedek, Ind; delg, Ind State Dem Conv, 1968; mem: J Comty Fund and Council, Columbus, O; Sinai Syn, S Bend, Ind, mem, adult educ comm; comm on leg, Gtr Ind Progressive Comm. Recipient: Hofheimer Prize, Amer Psycht Assn, 1961; Bronze Star Medal. Home: 53090 Haddington Dr, South Bend, Ind. Office: 1127 Myrtle St, Elkhart, Ind.

ALPERT, Seymour, US, physician, educational admnr; b. NYC, Apr 20, 1918; s. Louis and Ida (Freedman); AB, Columbia U, NY, 1939; MD, LI Coll of Med, Bklyn, 1943; m. Cecile Cohen, Sep 7, 1941. Vice pres, George Washington U, since 1969; prof, anesthesiology, George Washington U Med Sch, since 1961; asso chief, dept anesthesiology, George Washington U Hosp, since 1949; cons in anesthesiology: Walter Reed Army Hosp, since 1948; DC Gen Hosp, since 1948; VA Hosp, since 1956, all Wash, DC; chief med off in anesthesiology, Gallinger Munic Hosp, Wash, DC, 1946-47. Vice pres, Gtr Wash J Cmty Found, since 1967, mem bd dirs, since 1965; exec secy, Phi Delta Epsilon, fmr natl pres, ed, Phi Delta Epsilon News; mem: AMA; Amer Soc Anesthesiologists; Assn Amer Med Colls; Assn of U Anesthetists; DC Med Soc; Intl Anesthesia Research Soc; Jacobi Med Soc; MD-DC Soc of Anesthesiologists; Pan Amer Med Soc; Smith-Reed-Russell Med Soc; S Med Assn; Alpha Omega Alpha; bd mgrs, Adas Isr Cong; bd dirs, CJFWF; adv bd, Ind Devl Bank of Isr; bd dirs, Isr Investment Corp; natl bd govs, State of Isr Bonds; fmr: chmn: State of Isr Bonds Ambass' Ball; State of Isr Bonds, Gtr Wash; UJA of Gtr Wash. Contbr papers to profsl jours. Home: 2801 New Mexico Ave, NW, Washington, DC. Office: George Wash U, Washington, DC.

ALPERT, Uri, Isr, labor exec; b. Kovel, Pol, May 10, 1909; s. Meier and Zipora; in Isr since 1925; att Heb U, Jerusalem, 1928-29; m. Miriam Goldschmidt, May 15, 1942. Gen secy, Lab Council, Tel Aviv-Yaffa, since 1962. Brit Army, WW II; Haganah, 1942-46. Mem: Mapai party; Histadrut; bd mem: Shikun Ovdim; Mivtachim Otzar Hahayal; Philharmonic Orch; club, Brenner. Hobbies: pipes, gardening. Home: 15 Baron Hirsh St, Tel Aviv, Isr. Office: 5 Brenner St, Tel Aviv, Isr.

ALPERT, Warren, US, industrialist; b. Boston, Mass, Dec 2, 1920; s. Goodman and Tena (Harmon); BS, Boston U, 1942; MBA, Harvard Grad Sch Bus Admn, 1947. Pres, chmn, bd dirs: Warren Equities; Ritz Asso; 465 Park Corp; chmn, bd dirs: Natl Propane Co; Arren Studios, Barron Corp; Burns Realty; Liberty Enterprises; Pilgrim Enterprises; Plymouth Enterprises; Puritan Oil; Quaker Enterprises; Regal Petroleum; Drake Fuel; Drake Petroleum; Worcester County Oil; Cazeault Oil; Kenyon Oil; Northeast Corp; Oil Marketers; Windham Realty; Alwar Equities; Alwar Stations; Barry Stations; Higgenbotham Bros; McDuff Coal and Oil; Potter Fuel; Redwood Stations; Warren Petroleum; Warren Terminals; Westgate Stations. Signal Intelligence, US Army, 1943-45. Mem: bd trustees, Alcott Mgt Co; NY State small bus adv council, Small Bus Admn; exec comm, US for UN; dep asst admn, Agcy for Intl Devl, US State Dept; mem: bd dirs, Young Pres Org; exec council, Harvard Bus Sch Assn; clubs: Harvard, NYC, Boston, Providence; Sidney Hill, Newton, Mass;

Metacomet Country, RI; Commonwealth, Cal; Friars, NYC; Mid-Ocean Bath and Tennis. Home: Ritz Tower Hotel, Park Ave and 57 St, New York, NY. Office: 375 Park Ave, New York, NY.

ALROD, Dan, Isr, architect, town planner; b. Jerusalem, July 29, 1934; s. Zvi and Haya (Rotman) Axelrod; BArch, Technion, Haifa; m. Ilana Berinson, Feb 26, 1963; c: Dafna, Edan. Pvt practice since 1964; with Brumer Off, Denmark, 1962-63. Sgt, IDF, 1952-54. Mem: Assn Engrs and Architects in Isr; Architects Circle. Recipient: 6 architectural prizes. Hobby: sports. Home: 262 Rehov Hayarkon, Tel Aviv, Isr. Office: 1 Yoel St, Tel Aviv, Isr.

ALROD, Ilana Berinson, Isr, architect; b. Tel Aviv, Feb 2, 1936; d. Zvi and Hana (Wolf) Berinson; BArch, Technion, Haifa, 1957, dipl ing, 1961; m. Dan Alrod, Feb 26, 1963; c: Dafna, Edan. Pvt practice since 1963; architect, Novacap, Brasilia, 1967-68; chief designer, Arad, 1961-62. Off, engr corps, IDF, 1958-60. Mem: Isr Engrs and Architects Assn; Architects Circle. Hobby: sports. Home: 262 Hayarkon St, Tel Aviv, Isr. Office: 1 Yoel St, Tel Aviv, Isr.

ALROY, Efraim, Isr, administrator; b. Hamburg, Ger, Aug 13, 1915; s. Abraham and Perl (Felsenstein) Speigel; att HS, Hamburg; m. Esther Cohen, Aug 22, 1940; c: Geulah, Nili. Org jubilee celebrations, KH; judge, Histadrut, Haifa, 1949-61; mgr, Tahal, 1951-56; mission to Eur for World Zionist Org, 1959-61; mgr Haifa Sym Orch, 1961-68; mission to Ger, Magbit Cherum, 1968. Off, Hagana, 1933-48; capt, IDF, 1948-49. Home: 16 Leon Blum St, Haifa, Isr.

ALROY, Eli J, Isr, attorney; b. Radom, Pol, June 3, 1898; s. Itzhak and Cypa (Lewartowski) Kirschenbaum; in Isr since 1925; att: U Warsaw; Heb U, Jerusalem; Govt Law Sch, Jerusalem; m. Rachel Spielmann, 1948; c: Daona. Pvt practice since 1931. Served: Pol Army; Hagana; IDF, attached to transp unit, War of Independence. Mem, Govt legal comm, Leg on Road Transp; found, Safety First Soc of Isr, chmn, Tel Aviv br; co-found, vice pres, Aero Club of Isr; co-found, Prisoners Wfr Assn. Contbr to periodicals and daily press. Recipient: Paul Tissandier Diploma, for flying activities, 1957. Hobby: sports. Home: 31 Metudella St, Tel Aviv, Isr. Office: 38 Ahad Haam St, Tel Aviv, Isr.

ALSBERG, Paul Avraham, Isr, archivist; b. Wuppertal-Elberfeld, Ger, Mar 30, 1919; s. Alfred and Helen (Weinberg); in Isr since 1939; MA, Heb U, Jerusalem, 1943; PhD, 1958; m. Betti Keschner; c: Irith, Shimon. Dir, Isr State Archives, since 1957; chief asst, Cen Zionist Archives, 1949-57; lectr, grad libr sch, Heb U, Jerusalem since 1956. Mem: bd dir, Yad Veshem; exec council, Inst for Research on Zionism, Tel Aviv U; bd, Leo Baeck Inst, Jerusalem; council, Isr Hist Soc; vice-chmn, Isr Archives Assn; chmn, council B'nai B'rith Lodges, Jerusalem. Author: The Arab Question in Zionist Policy Before World War I; contbr to periodicals. Home: 8 Ben Labrat St, Jerusalem, Isr.

ALSCHULER, Leon S, US, attorney; b. Chicago, Ill, June 20, 1910; s. Leon and Myrtle (Barbe); BA, Antioch Coll, 1932; JD, Northwestern U, 1938; m. Evelyn Gardner, Jan 27, 1940; c: Robert, Susan. Partner, Schwartz & Alschuler, since 1952; atty: SEC, 1938-43; Loeb & Loeb, LA, 1946-51. Lt, USNR, 1943-46. Exec comm, AJComm, since 1947; bd trustee, Antioch Coll, 1962-65. Home: 303 N Swall Dr, Beverly Hills, Cal. Office: 9808 Wilshire Blvd, Beverly Hills, Cal.

ALSCHULER, Rose H, US, educator, author; b. Chgo, Ill, Dec 17, 1887; d. Charles and Mary (Greenebaum) Haas; att: Vassar Coll, 1905-06; U Chgo, 1904-05, 1906-07; m. Alfred Alschuler, Dec 17, 1907 (decd); c: Marion Despres, Frances Gudeman, Alfred, Richard, John. Cons: nursery educ since 1922; Winnetka Public Sch Nursery, Jr Kindergarten since 1941, org, staff dir, 1927-41; fmr cons org, staff dir: Franklin Pub Sch Nursery, 1926-31; Garden Apt Nursery Sch, Negro housing projects, 1927-33; Chgo Tchrs Coll Nursery Sch, 1931-40; 18 Works Progress Admn, Fed Emergency Relief Admn Nursery Schs, 1933-40; chmn Natl Comn Young Children, Wash, DC, 1941-43; cons, Fed Public Housing Auth, 1942-44. Secy, vice-pres, Natl Assn Nursery Educ, 1926-32; mem: bd dirs, Progressive Educ, 1928-40; exec bd, Fed J Charities, 1938-40; Council for Reconstruction Chgo Auditorium, 1961-67, N Shore chmn; chmn, N Shore Comm, Isr Bonds, 1952-58; mem: Amer Educ Research Assn. Author: Two to Six, 1933; The Child's Response to Life, 1937; Children's Center, 1942; Painting and Personality: A Study o

Young Children, 1947; contr to profsl jours. Recipient: citation: U Chgo, 1944; Roosevelt U, 1962; Govt of Isr Award, 1958; Eleanor Roosevelt Hum Award, 1966; N Shore St Isr Bonds Award; Technion, 1965. Home: 777 Sheridan Rd, Highland Park, Ill.

ALTAGAR, Zeev, Isr, journalist; b. Vilna, Pol, Sep 12, 1919; s. Zelig and Sonia (Moskovski) Kremer; in Isr since 1925; att Bar Ilan U, Ramat Gan; m. Tehila Krugman, Dec 27, 1949; c: Miron, Ra'anan, Niri, Sharon. Ed, Diplomat Mag, since 1963; cons, Liberian Emb, Isr, since 1959; chief reporter, Yediot Aharonot, 1949-56; fmr ed: Yediot Ramat Gan; Liberia Today; Maccabi World News; mil corresp, 1956; spokesman, Ramat Gan Munic, 1960-64; ed, West African News, 1961. Hon mem, Ghanian Party; mem, Isr Journalists Assn. Hobbies: music, collecting stamps. Home: 16 Sanhedrin St, Ramat Gan, Isr. Office: 7 Rama St, Kiryat Ono, Isr.

ALTBAUER, Moshe, Isr, educator; b. Przemysl, Pol, Nov 12, 1904; s. Baruch and Ita (Pechtalt); in Isr since 1935; att U Lwow; PhD, Cracow U, 1932; m. Ruth Junowiez, May 24, 1942; c: Dan, Yochanan. Asso prof, slavic ling, Heb U, Jerusalem, since 1969; dep ed, Heb Ency, since 1954; tchr, Wilno, 1927-35; staff, Tel Aviv Munic, 1936; found, dir, dep ed, cultural off, Hist Mus, Tel Aviv, 1966; research asso, Columbia U, 1966-67. Mem: Intl Slavists Comm; Intl Dialectologists Comm. Author: The Mutual Polish-Jewish Influences, Yiddish, 1933; Changes of Meaning, Heb, 1958; contr in several langs to periodicals. Recipient: award, Heb Lang Acad, 1958. Home: 90a Herzl Blvd, Jerusalem, Isr.

ALTER, Harry, US, editor, publisher, business exec; b. Youngstown, O, May 12, 1915; s. Czi and Dora (Bradlyn) att Youngstown U, 1940-41, 1946-47; m. May Lauar, Feb 14, 1945; c: Marsha. Ed, publisher, Youngstown Jewish Times, since 1946, sports ed, 1935-41; pres, Alter Asso, since 1948; asso ed, Buckeye Tavern News, 1946. US Army, 1941-46. Pres, J Comty Cen, 1960-62, bd mem, since 1948; bd mem, J Fed, 1957-67; Temple Anshe Emeth, 1950-61; mem: B'nai B'rith; JWV; Comty Chest; club, N Side Kiwanis. Home: 2339 Selma, Youngstown, O. Office: POB 777, Youngstown, O.

ALTER, Louis, US, composer; b. Haverhill, Mass, June 18, 1902; s. Simon and Mary (Rimmelman); att NE Conservatory of Music, 1919-21; m. Jeanne Gibbons, Feb 26, 1952; c: Allison, Adam. Mem, bd of review, ASCAP, since 1960; accompanist to Nora Bayes, 1924-27; songwriter for: Nora Bayes, Beatrice Lillie, Irene Bordoni, Helen Morgan, 1924-29; composer: motion picture musicals, Hollywood, 1929-31, 1935-45; Broadway musicals, 1931-34; soloist in own compositions, Hollywood Bowl Concerts, 1943-44; songs: Manhattan Serenade, 1928; My Kinda Love, 1929; 'm One of God's Children Who Hasn't Got Wings, 1930; Manhattan Moonlight, 1931; Manhattan Suite, 1931; Twilight o the Trail, 1935; You Turned the Tables on Me, 1936; Metropolitan Nocturne, 1936; Melody from the Sky, 1937; Rainbow on the River, 1938; Dolores, 1941; Nina Never Knew, 1953; orchestral suite, Jewels from Cartier Suite, 1956; New York, My New York, official state song, 1960; USAAF, 1942-43. Fmr vice-pres, Songwriters Protective Assn. Recipient: Bronze Medal, Venice Film Festival, 1936; Acad Motion Pictures Arts and Scis Award Nomination, 1936, 1941. Office: c/o ASCAP, 575 Madison Ave, New York, NY.

ALTERMAN, Israel, Isr, civil engr; b. Kishinev, Rum, Aug 22, 1920; s. Zvi and Dvora (Schwartz); in Isr since 1932; grad, Balfour Coll, Tel Aviv; att Inst Structural Engrs, London; DSc, MSc, Technion; m. Zippora Balaban, June 28, 1950; c: Ilan. Dir, Seker Tichun, since 1963; chief engr, partner, Engr Underground Structures Ltd, since 1969; head: dept structural design, Mekorot Water Co, 1950-58; Dan Region dept, Tahal Water Planning, 1953-58, dept, large pipe design, 1958-63. Maj, IDF Res, since 1948. Prin contrib: designed Jordan-Negev Pipeline, Eilat-Haifa Oil Pipeline. F, Royal Soc Health, London; vice-chmn, Shore Engr, Assn Engrs and Architects in Isr; Isr repr, Inst Structural Engrs, London; club, Lions, Savyon; fmr pres. Contr to profsl jours. Recipient: Kaplan Prize, Isr Govt; Arnan Prize, Assn Engrs and Architects in Isr. Home and office: 7 Brosh St, Savyon, Isr.

ALTERMAN, Zipora S, Isr, mathematician, geophysicist; b. Berlin, Ger, Aug 6, 1925; d. Leon and Regina (Wischnitzer) Balaban; in Isr since 1938; MS, Heb U, Jerusalem, 1949, PhD, 1953; m. Israel Alterman, June 6, 1950; c: Ilan. Prof head, dept, Environmental Sci, Tel Aviv U, dir, Inst Space and Planetary Sci, both since 1967; asso prof, Weizmann Inst

of Sci, since 1961, research sci, 1956-60; research sci, U Chgo, 1960-61; visiting prof: Heb U, 1961-65; Tel Aviv U, 1965-66; visiting mem, Courant Inst Math Sci, NYU, 1966-67. Capt, IDF, since 1948. Chmn, Isr Soc Geodesy and Geophys; hon secy, Isr Math Union, 1963-65; mem: Isr Natl Comm, Space Research; Amer Geophys Union; Amer Math Soc; Seismological Soc Amer; Isr Union for Data Processing. Contr of articles in sci jours and chapters in books. Home: 7 Brosh, Savyon, Isr. Office: Tel Aviv U, Ramat Aviv, Isr.

ALTMAN, Harry S, US, physician, educator; b. Narevke, Russ, Apr 3, 1899; s. David and Sophy (Topilofsky); in US since 1903; att NYU, 1915-17, MD, 1921; m. Gertrude Feurstein, June 12, 1927; c: Carole Henkoff, Kenneth. Pvt practice ped since 1924; asso clinical prof, ped, Columbia U, since 1950, mem fac since 1930; cons ped: Lincoln Hosp, NY, since 1957, dir ped, 1937-57; St Lukes Hosp, NY, since 1966; asso att ped, Babies Hosp, NY, since 1931; cons ped: Good Samaritan Hosp, Suffern, NY; St Barnabas Hosp, Bx, NY. Mem: Mayor's adv council on hosps and educ, NYC, 1956-58; Commn of Health's adv council during war on EMIC prog, 1948-58; chmn, NY State div, Amer Acad Ped, 1957-60; pres, Bx Ped Soc, 1938; mem, comm on med info, NY Acad Med, since 1948 and comm on admissions, since 1961; cons, Project Headstart, State of NY. Contr to ped jours. Home: 630 W 246 St, New York, NY. Office: Coll of Phys and Surg, Columbia U, New York, NY.

ALTMAN, Irving B, US, bank exec; b. Cleveland, O, Aug 18, 1901; s. Benjamin and Celia (Spieler); BA, NYU, 1922; m. Hazel Sammett, June 12, 1930; c: Donald, James. Exec vice-pres, dir, Freedom Natl Bank of NY, since 1964, field counselor, Mutual Security Agency, since 1949; ed, publisher, Dynamic America, 1935-41; radio, spec events commentator, 1935-41; candidate for Cong, 1940; vice-pres, cashier, Merchants Bank of NY, 1945-60; vice-pres, Amer Trust Co, 1960-63, all NYC. Mem: B'nai B'rith; Acad Political Sci, Columbia U; Amer Acad Political and Social Sci, U of Pa; Amer Mgmt Inst; Bank Auditors and Comptrollers' Conf; treas, dir, Parents' Assn, Syracuse U; club, Econ, NY. Contr to profsl jours. Home: 41 Peck Ave, Rye, NY. Office: 275 W 125 St, New York, NY.

ALTMAN, Max Menahem, Isr, physician; b. Potsdam, Ger, Jan 26, 1909; s. Herman and Martha (Lachman); in Isr since 1935; MD, U Berlin, 1934; m. Bera Adler, Jerusalem, 1937; c: Noemi Meshulam, David. Head, ear, nose, throat dept, Rambam Hosp, Haifa, since 1947; clinical lectr, Hadassah Med Sch, Jerusalem, since 1968; formerly: asst, ear, nose, throat dept, Hadassah Hosp; f, Lempert Inst of Otology, NY, 1955. Maj, RAMC, 1942-46; IDF, 1948-56. Bd mem, Otolaryngological Soc of Isr, chmn, Haifa br; chmn, Micha, for deaf children; mem: Isr chap, Intl Coll Surgs; Intl Rhinological Soc; Intl Audiological Soc. Contr to med jours. Spec interest: hist of Crusades. Home: 6 Melchett St, Haifa, Isr.

ALTMAN, Oscar L, US, economist; b. NYC, Jan 17, 1909; s. Benjamin and Rose (Sokoloff); BA, Cornell U, 1929; MA, 1930; PhD, U Chgo, 1936; m. Alberta Neblett, 1942; m. 2nd, Adeline Furness Roberts, 1952; c: Peter, Leslie, William. Traps, IMF, since 1966, dep dir, research dept, 1954-56, dir admn, 1946-54; head, banks trust, estates and research unit, Co Assessor's Off, Chgo, Ill, 1932-34; instr econ, Ohio State U, 1936-38; sr econ, SEC, 1938-40; prin econ, Natl Resources Planning Bd, 1940-42; off analysis and plans, Fr Supply Council, 1946. Lt col, USAAF, 1942-45. Mem: Amer Econ Assn; Amer Stat Assn; Phi Beta Kappa; Phi Kappa Phi; Tau Epsilon Phi; clubs: Army Navy Country; Cosmos. Author: Savings, Investment and National Income, 1941; contr to: Planning for America; The Dollar in Crises; profsl publs. Home: 2527 Queen Anne's Lane, NW, Washington, DC. Office: IMF, 19 and H Sts, NW, Washington, DC.

ALTMAN, Peter, US, engineer; b. Montreal, Can, Feb 24, 1902; s. Isador and Sarah (Bejenka); BA, U Detroit, 1925; first reg, Aeronautical Engr, State Mich, 1938; m. Jessie Ellenstein, July 21, 1929; c: William, Jerome, Susanne Zimmeirman, Marilyn Bronson. Engr cons since 1964; exec cons, Continental Motors Corp, since 1964, vice-pres, tech cons, 1948-64; prof, dir, aeronautics dept, U Detroit, 1925-40, chmn, research adv bd, 1960-67; dir, mfg reseach dept, Aviation Mfg Corp, 1940-43; engr cons, 1943-48; co-org, Helicopter Airways Services Inc, 1957, tech cons; bd dir, Lake Foundry Corp, Muskegon, Mich, 1966-70. RCAF Res, 1920-23. Prin contrib: participation in devl, design, mgf: Powell Racer, 1923-25; Stinson Biplane, 1925-26; other Stinson airplanes,

1927-40; Szekely Flying Dutchman, 1929-32; Derickson Trainer, 1928-30; Vervile Trainer, 1929-30; Detroit Aircraft, XP900, 1931; other airplanes, 1925-70; responsible devl new family of mil standard engines, precise power engine; generator sets. Dir: engr bd, U Detroit since 1969; Amer Tech Soc Detroit; Mich Aeronautics and Space Assn, since 1946; aviation comm, Gtr Detroit C of C; mem, Inst Aero Scis, fmr mem council; asso F, spec comm for fed, Amer Inst Aeronautics and Astronautics; mem, Natl Soc Automotive Engrs, fmr: chmn Detroit sect, natl air transp comm, natl aircraft activity, tech bd, spec adv to pres, 1935-69; fmr chmn prog, tech comms, Mich Aviation Week; fmr chmn, trends and devl, Engr Soc of Detroit; aviation hist comm, Mich State Dept of Aeronautics, resulted in publ Chronology of Aviation in Mich; Assn US Army; fmr bd trustees, Wayne Engr Research Inst; life mem, natl Phi Alpha; hon mem, Natl Mech Engr; mem, Pi Tau Sigma. Contbr tech papers; presentations; internal reports; lectrs; proposals to govt; articles to mags. Recipient, Trophies: Aero Digest; Dayton Daily News; Scientific Amer, all 1925, Intl Air Races. Hobby: aviation. Home: 626 New Center Bldg, Detroit, Mich. Office: 19884 Cranbrook Rd, Detroit, Mich.

ALTMANN, Alexander, US, educator; b. Kassa, Hung, Apr 16, 1906; s. Adolf and Malwine (Weisz); in US since 1959; MA, Manchester U; PhD, Berlin U, 1931; ordained rabbi, Rabb Sem, Berlin, 1931; hon DHL, HUC-JIR; m. Judith Franck, Dec 20, 1932; c: Fay Lunzer, Michael, Eve Yardeni. Phillip W Lown prof, J Phil, Brandeis U, since 1959, dir, Phillip W Lown Inst of Advanced Judaic Studies 1960-65; rabbi, J Comty, Berlin, 1932-38; lectr, Rabb Sem, Berlin, 1932-38; communal rabbi, Dist J Comtys Manchester, Eng, 1938-59; dir, Inst of J Studies, Manchester, 1935-59; F: Amer Acad Arts and Seis; Amer Acad J Research; mem, bd dirs, Leo Baeck Inst, NY. Author: Die Grundlagen der Weethik: Wesen, Wert, Person, 1931; Was ist Judische Theologie? 1933; Des Rabbi Moshe Ben Maimon More Newuchim imc Grundriss, 1935; Isaac Israeli, A Neoplatonic Philosopher of the Early Tenth Century, 1958; Studies in Religious Philosophy and Mysticism, 1968; ed; Journ of J Studies, London, Vols VI-IX; Between East and West, 1958; Scripta Judaica, Vols I-IV, 1961; Phillip W. Lown Inst Studies and Texts, Vols I-IV. Home: 126 Glen Ave, Newton Centre, Mass. Office: Brandeis, U, Waltham, Mass.

ALTSCHUL, Aaron Meyer, US, scientist; b. Chgo, Ill, Mar 13, 1914; s. Philip and Sophie (Fox); BS, U Chgo, 1934, PhD, 1937; hon DSc, Tulane U, New Orleans, 1968; m. Ruth Braude, Oct 24, 1937; c: Sandra Norman, Judy Bonderman. Spec asst, US Secy of Agric, for nutrition improvement, since 1969, spec asst for intl nutrition improvement, 1966-69, chief research chem, Seed Protein Pioneering Research Lab, 1958-66, both US Dept Agric, mem staff, since 1941; mem fac, dept chem, U Chgo, 1937-41. Prin contrib: Discovered Cytochrome (peroxidase); improved use of seed proteins for humans and animals; adv to: US agcys; govts; promoted increase in protein supplies to poor and underdeveloped countries. Mem: bd dirs, Temple Micha, Wash, DC; Phi Beta Kappa; Sigma Xi; Inst Food Technologists; Amer Chem Soc; Amer Soc Biol Chems; Amer Inst Nutrition; agric bd, NRC; fmr: pres, Communal Heb Sch, New Orleans; mem bd, New Orleans JWB. Author: 3 books; ed: Processed Plant Protein Foodstuffs, 1958; Proteins, Their Chemistry and Politics, 1965; symposium chmn, World Protein Resources, Amer Chem Soc, 1966; contbr articles and reviews to profsl publs. Recipient: Golden Peanut Award, Natl Peanut Council, 1964; Spencer Award, Amer Chem Soc, 1965; First Technion Award, Chgo sect, Amer Technion Soc, 1966; Underwood-Prescott Lecture, MIT, 1967. Home: 429 N St, SW, Washington, DC. Office: US Dept of Agric, Washington, DC.

ALTSZULER, Norman, US, educator; b. Suwalki, Pol, Nov 20, 1924; s. Meyer and Fay (Kalet); in US since 1937; BS, George Wash U, Wash, DC, 1950, MS, 1951, PhD, 1954; m. Rita Mintz, June 24, 1956; c: Henry, Paula. Prof, pharm, NYU Med Sch, since 1969, asso prof, 1964-69. US Army, 1943-46. Mem: Amer Physiological Soc; Endocrine Soc; Amer Soc Pharm and Experimental Therapeutics. Author: chap in Pharmacology in Medicine, 3rd ed; contbr numerous articles to sci publs. Recipient: USPHS Research Career Devl Award, 1959-69. Home: 18 Stuyvesant Oval, New York, NY. Office: 550 First Ave, New York, NY.

ALUMOT, Eugenia, Isr, chemist; b. Warszawa, Pol, June 18, 1919; d. Samuel and Cecilia (Golovthiner) Grajewski; in Isr

since 1949; MSc, Wroclaw U, Pol, 1947; PhD, Heb U, Jerusalem, 1956; m. Joseph Alumot, June 13, 1946; c: Zeev, David, Nina. Head, div animal nutrition, Volcani Inst Agric Research, since 1959, on staff since 1950; asst: U Wroclow, 1946-48; Centre National de Recherche Scientifique, Paris, 1948. Mem: Isr Chem Soc; Nutrition Soc, London. Contbr numerous papers to sci jours. Home: 4 Hamaapil St, Rehovot, Isr. Office: The Volcani Inst of Agric Research, Bet Dagan, Isr.

ALWEYL, Asher, Isr, engineer; b. Winniczki, Pol, Aug 20, 1909; s. Meir and Miryam (Millet) Allweil; in Isr since 1935; m. Alisa Yeahlom, Sep 15, 1938; c: Abraham, Mira Bal. Dir, engr div, Min of Housing, since 1960, chief engr, 1949-60; visiting lectr, postgrad sch, Technion, Haifa, since 1960; research engr, Bldg Research Sta, Technion, 1955-60. Mem: Natl Council for Research and Devl; exec comm, Standards Inst of Isr. Author: Engineering Economy in Building, 1967. Recipient: A M Arnan Prize, Assn Engrs and Architects in Isr. Home: 3 Berliner St, Tel Aviv, Isr. Office: Hakiryah, Tel Aviv, Isr.

AMAR, Moshe, Isr, attorney; b. Safed, Isr, May 21, 1922; s. David and Rivka (Anteby); att law sch, Jerusalem; m. Bracha Pomrock; c: Irith, Talya. Atty since 1948; councillor, Haifa Munic. Lt, IDF. Mem, political comm, Mapam; dep mem, Zionist Gen Council; chmn bd dirs, Govt and Munic Co for Slum Clearance in Haifa; mem exec comm, Sephardic Comty-Haifa. Home: 20 Pasteur St, Haifa, Isr. Office: 88 Ha'atz, maut St, Haifa, Isr.

AMDUR, Isadore, US, scientist, educator; b. Pittsburgh, Pa, Jan 24, 1910; s. Benjamin and Mollie (Silberblatt); BS, U, Pittsburgh, 1930, MS, 1930, PhD, 1932; m. Alice Steiner, June 16, 1935; c: Stephen, Nicholas. Prof, phys chem, MIT, since 1951, on fac since 1932; visiting prof, U Kyoto, Japan; visiting sci, US Japan Coop Sci Prof, both 1965-66. F: Amer Acad Arts and Sci; Amer Phys Soc; hon chmn, symposium on molecular beams at high, medium energy; mem: intl relations div, NRC; Amer Chem Soc; AAAS; Phi Lambda Upsilon Pi; Pi Lambda Phi; Sigma Xi, fmr pres, MIT chap; Phi Beta Kappa. Contbr to sci jours. Recipient: Guggenheim Memorial Found f, 1955-56. Hobbies: instrumentation, machine shop practice. Home: 47 Bay State Rd, Belmont, Mass. Office: MIT, Cambridge, Mass.

AMEN, Irving, US, artist; b. NYC, July 15, 1918; s. Benjamin and Bessie (Glusack); att: New Sch for Social Research; Acad de la Grande Chaumiere, Paris; Pratt Inst, Bklyn; Art Students League, NYC; m. Dora Beck, May, 21, 1941. Tchr: Pratt Inst, 1958; U Notre Dame, 1962. Numerous exhbs and oneman shows: US; Isr; Yugo; works included in: Metrop Mus Art; Mus Modern Art; Libr of Cong; Smithsonian Inst; Bibliotheque Nationale, Paris; Bibliotheque Royale, Brussels; Bezalel Natl Mus, Jerusalem; Victoria and Albert Mus, London; NY Public Libr; Phila Mus of Art; Albertine Mus, Vienna; Städtische Mus, Wilberfeld, Ger; perm works in: J Mus; Heckscher Found; Baltimore Mus of Art; Free Libr of Phila; De Cordoba Mus, Mass; Brooks Memorial Mus, Tenn; U of Me; Mills and Ore State Colls; in all Intl Graphic Exhbs, Yugo; subject of TV show, ADL, 1962. Mem: council, Soc Amer Graphic Artists; bd dirs, Artists Equity; Amer Color Print Soc; Audubon Artists; Wash Printmakers. Author: Irving Amen: Woodcuts, 1948-60. Hobbies: music, chess. Home: 120 E 90 St, New York, NY. Studio: 153 Waverly Pl, New York, NY.

AMI, Raoul Samuel, Isr, organization exec, author; b. Cairo, Egypt, Aug 10, 1906; s. Maurice and Fanny (Mieses) Krichewsky; in Isr since 1939; doctorate, political sci, Paris; dipl: oriental lang, journalist, Paris; m. Ida Amiel, Sep 24, 1939. Dir, JNF, Fr, since 1965; spec delg: KH, 1953-63; ORT, 1959-64. Mem: cen comm, Karen Kayemet-KH; B'nai B'rith, Jerusalem, Paris; Masons; first pres, Union des Juifs d'Egypte; club, Lions. Author: Les Juifs en Egypte; La Lybie et ses Juifs; Ce que j'ai vu et entendu en Espagne; Dans la Kéhilla dechirée de Grèce; 500 Pensees et Aphorismes; Les Juifs sous les Wisigoths d'Espagne; Quand David Retrouve Goliath; fmr political ed, Actualites. Recipient: Medaille d'Argent, Ville de Paris, 1969; Officier de l'Ordre d'Encouragement au Progrès, 1969. Home and office: France Sq, Jerusalem, Isr.

AMI, Yosef, Isr, business exec; b. Mukacevo, May 7, 1913; s. Eliezer and Pessel (Farbenblum) Salzberger; in Isr since 1939; att: U Prague; Heb U, Jerusalem; U Chgo; m. Lea Sud, Feb 4,

1939; c: Yehudit Susman, Batia, Esther. Vice-pres, Admn and Finance, Technion since 1965; mem, bd dirs, Isr Elec Co; econ: KH, 1946-47; PM's off, 1949-51; dep mgn dir, Ata Textiles Ltd, 1952-56; mgn dir, N area, Chemicals and Phosphates Ltd, 1956-64. Brit Army, 1942-46; Haganah; lt col, IDF. Author: Industrial Relations in Israel, 1955; co-author, Labor Relations in Israel, 1962; contbr articles on mgmt and econ. Home: 8 Netiv Ofakim, Ahuza, Haifa, Isr. Office: POB 4910, Haifa, Isr.

AMIAD, Ariel, Isr, government official; b. Rehovot, Aug 10, 1924; s. Joseph and Shara (Friman); BS, Cornell U, 1952, MPA, 1954; m. Rina Mirzakandoff, c: Tal, Orit, Esther. Dir gen, Min of Agric, since 1961, dep dir, settlement dept, JA, 1953-54; chmn: Water Devl Co, 1961-67; Huleh Valley Auth, 1961-65; pres, Agric Export Co, 1964. Col, IDF, signal corps, 1948-50; chief communications off, IDF, 1954-58. Prin contrib: took part in: org of Min of Agric, devl Isr export; devl agric in administered areas. Mem: Engr Assn, Tel Aviv. Spec interests: sci, nature. Home: 7 Zeitlin St, Tel Aviv, Isr. Office: Min of Agric, Hakiryah, Tel Aviv, Isr.

AMIAZ, Moshe, Isr, engineer; b. Kishinev, Russ, Sep 11, 1900; s. Nahum and Miriam (Grossman) Roitman; in Isr since 1925; att U Naples, 1920-22; CE, Sch of Civil Engr, U Gand, Belgium, 1924; m. Daniella Halperin, 1937; c: Meir (killed in action, Isr War of Independence, 1948). Cons engr, planning, bldg, munic engr, since 1966; chmn, Assn Jewish Students in Gand, 1923-25; city engr, Tel Aviv-Yaffa, 1952-66, acting city engr, 1950-52, dep city engr, 1939-50; civil defense adv, Tel Aviv, 1939-44. Mem: central comm, Assn Engrs and Architects, Isr; steering comm, Union Munic Engrs; Central Council for Beautiful Isr. Home and office: 6 Komemiyut St, Afeka, Tel Aviv, Isr.

AMIEL, Yaacov, Isr, organic chem; b. Bialystok, Pol, July 9, 1922; s. Avraham and Yokheved (Daichovsky); in Isr since 1936; PhD, Heb U, Jerusalem, 1956; m. Yehudith Zeitlin, March 17, 1953; c: Oran, Niva, Yokhai. Research asso, Weizmann Inst Sci, Rehovot, since 1959; research f, Yale U, Sterling chem lab, 1958-59; research dir, Tech Research Inst, Bangkok, Thailand, 1967-69. IDF, 1947-48. Mem, Isr Chem Assn. Contbr to sci publs. Home: 3A Bet Horon St, Tel Baruch, Tel Aviv, Isr. Office: Weizmann Inst of Sci, Rehovot, Isr.

AMIHUD, Itzhak, Isr, systems engr; b. Tel Aviv, Isr, Jan, 1937; s. Pinhas and Malca (Lerner); BSc, Technion, Haifa, 1958, MSc, 1963; m. Hana Haring, Apr 12, 1959; c: Zohar, Sara. Adv sys engr, IBM (Isr) Ltd, since 1967. Capt, IDF, 1959-63. Mem: Assn of Engrs and Architects, Isr; Info Processing Assn, Isr. Author: The Electronic Computer and Data Processing, 1968; Simulation-MPS Linear Programming, 1968. Recipient: outstanding service award, IBM, 1969; citation, Info Processing Assn, Isr, 1969. Home: 265 Modiin St, Ramat Gan, Isr. Office: 15 Lincoln St, Tel Aviv, Isr.

AMIQAM, Eliyahu, Isr, journalist; b. Wloclawek, Pol, Aug, 1915; s. Moshe and Itta (Rosenholz) Krzak; in Isr since 1935; att Heb U. Jerusalem; m. Ruth Schechter, Apr 1, 1947; c: Yair, Amnon. Parl corresp, Yedioth Aharonot, Heb daily, since 1965; mgn ed, El Am Pub Co, since 1964. Pilot, cdr, Irgun Zvai Leumi, co-found, Stern group, Irgun radio announcer; chief ed, Mivrak, paper of Lehi. Mem: Natl Fed Journalists in Isr. Contbr to Isr press. Home: 8 Megiddo St, Tel Aviv, Isr. Office: 5 Moses St, Tel Aviv, Isr.

AMIR, Menachem, Isr, criminologist; b. Tel Aviv, July 20, 1930; s. Zev and Esther (Peckash); BA, Heb U, 1953, MA, 1958; PhD, U of Pa, 1965; m. Delila Preversky, Mar 25, 1952; c: Orly, Gilly. Asso prof, criminology, U of Cal, Berkeley since 1969; head, research dept, Min of Social Wfr, Jerusalem, since 1968; research cons, Intl Studies in Juvenile Delinquency, HEW, 1965-68; lectr, Heb U, 1965-68; research cons, Pa Dept Correction, 1963-65; guest lectr, Carnegie Inst of Tech, 1964-65; asst prof, criminology and sociol, U Pittsburgh, 1963-65; lectr, U of Pa, 1963-65; sr researcher, Szold Inst, 1965-68; cons: Min of Educ; Min of Police, all in Isr. Off: Palmach, 1947-48; IDF, 1948-49. Mem: Isr Soc for the Prevention of Delinquency; Assn for Rehab of Prisoners; Amer Correctional Assn; Amer Soc of Criminology; Intl Soc Criminology. Author: Patterns in Forcible Rape, 1971; ed, Welfare, Isr Jour of Wfr, since 1968; contbr to sci jours. Hobbies: swimming, pipe collection, theater. Home: 5 Schachar, Jerusalem, Isr. Office: Sch of Criminology, Heb U, Jerusalem, Isr; U of Cal, Berkeley, Cal.

AMIR, Shimeon, Isr, diplomat; b. Lwow, Pol, Feb 15, 1921; s. Joseph and Chaja (Low) Enriech; in Isr since 1935; MA, Heb U, Jerusalem, 1950; PhD, Universidad Nacional Autonoma de Mexico, 1960; m. Shulamith Englander, Dec 11, 1947; c: Gilead, Dafna, Avital. Dir, div intl coop, Min for Fgn Affairs, since 1968; asst, Min for Fgn Aff, 1949-50; 1st secy, Isr legation, Buenos Aires, 1950-53, dir, personnel dept, 1953-56; counselor, Isr Emb, Mex, 1956-60; consul gen, Isr Emb, Port, 1960-62; dep dir, econ affairs, Min for Fgn Affairs, 1962-65; head, dir gen bur, 1965-67. Brit Army, 1941-46; IDF, 1948. Office: Min for Fgn Affairs, Jerusalem, Isr.

AMIR, Yehoshua, Isr, educator, translator; b. Duisburg, Ger, Dec 1, 1911; s. Manass and Martha (Neumark); in Isr since 1939; att Us: Bonn; Berlin; PhD, U Wuerzberg, 1937; ordained rabbi, Hochschule für die Wissenschaft des Judentums, Berlin, 1939; m. Margalith Lissauer, May 26, 1951; c: Joseph, Gideon, Rivka, Yehoyada. Sr lectr, J phil and classical studies, Tel Aviv U, since 1966; Heb techr, Ulpan Etzion, Jerusalem, 1949-66. IDF, 1948-49. Trans, books of: Buber; Rosenzweig; S Baron, into Heb; contbr: items to: Ency Biblica, Jerusalem; Germania Judaica II, Tübingen, Ger, 1968; articles on: ancient and modern J phil, Bibl studies, to scholarly jours. Home: 10 Smuts St, Jerusalem, Isr. Office: U of Tel Aviv, Ramat Aviv, Isr.

AMIR, Yehuda, Isr, psychologist; b. Vienna, Aus, May 2, 1926; s. Mordechay and Miryam (Retter) Koppe; in Isr since 1938; BA, Heb U, Jerusalem, 1953; MA, Yeshiva U, NY, 1954; PhD, NYU, 1959; m. Hempa Habas, Sep 30, 1955; c: Ehud, Michal, Yoav. Sr lectr, psych, Bar Ilan U, since 1960, coord, grad prog, social ind psych, since 1965; head, psych research dept, IDF, 1960-65, sr research off, 1959-60; gen secy, Isr Students Org in US, Can, JA, 1954-58. Lt, Palmach, 1948-50. Treas, Isr Psych Assn, exec comm, 1962-66; head, chap, Isr Scouts Youth Movement, 1944-45; mem, Intl Assn Applied Psych. Contbr to profsl jours. Home: 47 Hagen St, Ramat Hasharon, Isr. Office: Bar Ilan U, Ramat Gan, Isr.

AMIT, Jacob, Isr, editor; b. Kovno, Lith, Mar 25, 1904; s. Azriel and Miriam (Herskovitz) Gotlieb; in Isr since 1929; m. Breina Babilski, 1936; c: Eilon, Dina, Miriam. Ed, Al Hamishmar, Heb daily, since 1943; tchr: Kovno, 1927-29; Ben Shemen, Isr, 1932. Mem: gen council, exec, Histadrut; presidium, Gen Zionist Council; Ed's Bd of Isr Press. Home: Kibbutz Beit Zera, Emek Hayarden, Isr. Office: Al Hamishmar, Tel Aviv, Isr.

AMIT, Meir, Isr, business exec, Army off; b. Tiberias, Mar 17, 1921; s. Shimon and Haya (Levitin) Slutzky; MBA, Columbia U, 1961; m. Yona Kelman, June, 1942; c: Nitza, Anat, Eilat. Dir gen, Koor Ind, since 1969; brig gen, head, mil intelligence, chief, Isr secret service, 1961-68; joined Hagana, 1936; supernumerary policeman, 1941-48; participation in defense of Degania and liberation of Eilat; cdr battalion, 1948-49; brig cdr, 1950; chief oprs div, Gen Staff, 1951-53; off commanding, S Command, 1955-56; head, G br, Gen Staff, 1956-58; off commanding, Cen Area, 1958. Hobby: collecting dolls. Home: 55 Arlosoroff St, Ramat Gan, Isr. Office: 99 Ben Yehuda St, Tel Aviv, Isr.

AMITAY, Mordekhai, Isr, author; b. Beltzi, Bessarabia, June 8, 1914; s. Meyr and Henna; in Isr since 1935; att U Tel Aviv, 1967; m. Yocheved, 1938; c: Adam, Hagar. Mem, Kibbutz Sarid, since 1935. Author: Emek Emek, stories, 1945; haBakbuk haCachol, 1951; Ezlenu, poems for children; Mavvad haCsamim; Anshe Yachad; Ben Arbayim, novel, 1963; Sippure Stav, short stories, 1968; ed: Hashavua; Hedim; Mishmar L'iladim; trans from Yiddish: Manger; Gebirtio; Zimberg. Capt, Hagana, IDF, 1948-60. Mem: Acum; Union of Writers of Kibbutz Arzi. Recipient: Independence Award, Kishon Regional Council, 1964. Spec interests: drawing, hist of kibbutz movement. Home: Kibbutz Sarid, Isr.

AMITSUR, Shimshon A, Isr, mathematician, educator; b. Jerusalem, Aug 26, 1921; s. Jacob and Rashke (Zelkin); MSc, Heb U, Jerusalem, 1946, PhD, 1950; att Inst for Advanced Studies, Princeton, NJ, 1952-53; m. Sarah Frenkiel, Aug 5, 1947; c: Hannah, Michal, Elli. Prof math, Heb U, since 1960, on fac since 1947; visiting prof: U Notre Dame, Ind, 1958-59; U Chgo, 1965; sr fgn sci, US, 1965. Brit Army and J Brig, 1941-46; IDF, 1948-49. Mem: Amer Math Soc; Isr Math Union. Contbr research papers to Isr and fgn jours. Co-recipient: Isr prize for exact sci, 1953. Home: 43 Harav Harlap St, Jerusalem, Isr. Office: Heb U, Jerusalem, Isr.

AMMERMAN, Harvey H, US, physician; b. New Haven, Conn, Nov 5, 1917; s. William and Henrietta (Saltser); BS, George Wash U, 1939, MD, 1943; m. Lenell Goodman, Feb 28, 1943; c: Elaine, Bruce, Seth. Clinical prof, neur surg, George Wash U Sch Med; chief, neur surg, Sibley Memorial Hosp; cons: neur surg, Walter Reed Army Med Cen; VA Hosp; St Elizabeths Hosp, Freedmen's Hosp. Capt, US Army, 1945-47. First vice-pres, JCC, Gtr Wash; vice-pres, UJA, Wash; chmn: Bd J Educ, Gtr Wash; bd trustees, Sibley Memorial Hosp; f: Amer Coll Surgs; Intl Coll Surgs; dipl, Amer Bd Neur Surg; chmn, med legal comm, DC Med Soc; fmr pres, Wash chap sect, neur surg; exec comm, Amer Phys F, IMA; mem: Jacobi Med Soc, fmr pres; Amer Asso Neur Surgs; Phi Delta Epsilon, fmr pres. Co-author: Organizing for Dialogue in Medicine and Theology, 1969; articles on neur surg. Recipient: dist citation award, Jacobi Med Soc, 1967; man of year award, Temple Sinai, 1967. Home: 5511 Uppingham St, Chevy Chase, Md. Office: 730 24 St, Washington, DC.

AMMERMAN, Lenell Goodman, US, communal leader; b. Fond du Lac, Wis, Nov 5, 1918; d. Samuel and Ida (Swerdel); BA, U Wis, 1940; m. Harvey Ammerman, Feb 28, 1943; c: Elaine, Bruce, Seth. Lab econ, US Govt, 1941-53. Pres, Temple Sinai, Wash, DC, 1965-67; found, fmr admnr, Midweek Heb Sch; fmr chmn, hospitality cart service, Sibley Memorial Hosp, Wash, DC; mem, natl Isr comm, UAHC. Ed, Civic Assn Jour, Takoma Park, Md. Spec interests: art hist, touring art gals. Home: 5511 Uppingham St, Chevy Chase, Md.

AMPEL, Abraham, Isr, attorney; b. Zaleszczski, Pol, Dec 8, 1911; s. Leon and Elcie (Weintraub); in Isr since 1950; att U Czernowitz, 1929-34; m. Rachel Melzer, Nov 19, 1939. Asst adm gen, Min of Justice, since 1958; atty, 1935-48; legal adv, Ad Tor Gen, 1956-58. Pvt, IDF, 1951-56. Secy gen, Hayarden, Hazoar, Bucharest, 1946-48; mem: J Natl Acad Assn, until 1939; Isr Bar Assn. Hobbies: music, medicine. Home: 17 Balfour St, Jerusalem, Isr. Office: 4 Yedida St, Jerusalem, Isr.

AMRAM, Phillip Werner, US, attorney, author; b. Phila, Pa, Mar 14, 1900; s. David and Beulah (Brylawski); BA, U of Pa, 1920; BSA, Pa State Coll, 1922; LLB, U of Pa, 1927; m. Emilie Weyl, 1924; c: Mariana Fitzpatrick, David. Partner: law firm, Amram, Hahn and Sundlin, Wash, DC, since 1957; Wolf, Block, Shoor and Solis-Cohn, Phila, 1927-45; tchr, U of Pa Law Sch, 1929-42; asst gen, council, Bd of Econ Wfr, 1942-43, chief repr, S Pacific area, 1943; spec asst, US Atty Gen and spec counsel, Alien Property Custodian, 1943-45; US official observer: Eighth Hague Conf, 1956, Ninth Conf, 1960, mem Tenth Conf, 1964, Eleventh Conf, 1968. US Army, WW I. Chmn, HEW Council, Wash, DC, 1956-59; fmr trustee, J Pub Soc Amer; asso trustee, U of Pa Law Sch; mem: Amer, DC, Pa, Intl, Fed Bar Assns; Order of Coif; Phi Kappa Phi; Mil Order Fgn Wars. Author: Goodrich-Amram Procedural Rules Service, since 1938; Amram's Pennsylvania Common Pleas Practice, 6th ed, 1954; ed in chief, U of Pa Law Review, 1926-27; contbr to legal jours. Recipient: Chevalier Fr Legion of Honor. Home: 2601 31st St, NW, Washington, DC. Office: 700 Colorado Bldg, Washington, DC.

AMSEL, Abram, Can, psychologist, educator; b. Montreal, Can, Dec 4, 1922; s. Aaron and Anne (Levitt); BA, Queen's U, 1944; MA, McGill U, 1946; PhD, State U of Ia, 1948; m. Tess Steinbach, June 11, 1947; c: Steven, Andrew, Geoffrey. Prof, psych, U Toronto, since 1960; prof, Tulane U, New Orleans, 1948-60; sr postdoc f, NSF, U Coll, London, 1966-67. Pres: Tulane U chap, AAUP, 1958; f: AAAS; Amer Psych Assn; mem: Soc Experimental Psychols; Psychonomic Soc; Sigma Xi. Cons ed, Jour of Experimental Psych, since 1963; contbr to profsl jours. Home: 14 Clarendon Ave, Toronto, Can. Office: U of Toronto, Toronto, Can.

AMSTER, Shmuel Mordechai, Isr, lawyer; b. Mariampol, Galicia, Sep 8, 1909; in Isr since 1934; att: Carl IV U, Prague, 1930-33; Heb U, Jerusalem, 1934-35; LLB, Sch Law and Econ, Tel Aviv, 1939; m. Leah Litsky; c: Rina, Michal. Pvt practice since 1952; cdr, Betar Stanislavov, pres, students corp, Bar Kohba, 1936-48; natl secy, Revisionist Party, 1945-48; councilor, Petah Tikva Munic, 1951-55, mem, 1955-59. IDF, 1955. Mem: Cen Herut Movement; B'nai B'rith; Masons. Author: Pnei haMizrach, 1945; Toldot Shichrur Amim, 1948; Israel Shel Mata, 1959; fmr mem, ed bd, Novy Tchas, Nash Glos newspapers; contbr to newspapers. Home: 3 Montefiore St, Petah Tikva, Isr.

AMSTERDAM, Birdie, US, jurist; b. NYC, Mar 25, 1902; d. Joseph and Essie (Sperling); att CCNY; LLB, NYU, 1922. Judge: Supr Court, State of NY, since 1958, first woman jurist in this court; Munic Court, NY Co, 1940-54; City Court, City of NY, 1955-57, first woman jurist elected to both courts; pvt law practice, 1923-40. Hon chmn, exec comm, Women Lawyers Assn, NY State, since 1952; judicial mem: Assn Bar, NYC; NY, Bklyn, Bronx Co, NY State, and Queens Women's Bar Assns; Amer Judicature Assn; Assn Supr Court Justices, NY State; Natl Assn Women Lawyers; hon mem, Bklyn-Manhattan Trial Counsel Assn; mem: natl adv bd, Yeshiva U Women's Org; adv bd: Child Guidance League; NYU J Culture Found; dir, trustee, Comty Syn Cen; guest speaker, FJP, Gtr NY; hon bd mem: Infants' Wfr League Camps Inc; Sch Children's Wfr League; Assn for Help Retarded Children; hon mem: Guild, Home and Hosp, Daughters of Jacob; United HIAS Service; J Sanitarium and Hosp of Chronic Diseases; Iota Tau Tau. Recipient: gold key and scroll, NYU J Culture Found, 1947; scroll of honor, Amer Assn J Educ; citation, War Bond Drives, US Treasury, 1947; bronze plaque, outstanding woman of year, B'nai B'rith; scroll, woman of month, Amer Women's Assn; scroll, outstanding woman of year, Yeshiva U Women's Org; bronze plaque, outstanding woman of year, Masonic Order; scroll, woman of achievement, Sch Children's Welfare League; Justice Louis D Brandeis gold medal and scroll, J Forum, all in 1956; award of honor, NY State Women Lawyers Assn; trophy, Interfaith Movement Inc; scroll, City of Hope, all in 1957; scroll, NY Women's Bar Assn; achievement award, NYU Alumni Assn; citation plaque, J Home for Convalescents, all in 1958; bronze plaque and citation, Amer J Lit Found, 1960; medal, Rel Zionists Amer-Mizrachi-Hapoel Hamizrachi; scroll, Women's Dist 1, B'nai B'rith, both 1961; bronze plaque: Assn Trial Lawyers, NYC; Fed J Women Org; Assn Trial Lawyers, all 1962; Hunter Coll HS, 1967. Home: 170 Second Ave, New York, NY. Office: 60 Centre St, New York, NY.

AMZALAK, Moses Bensabat, Port, educator, author; b. Lisbon, Oct 4, 1892; s. Leao and Estela (Bensabat); att Lyceum and U Lisbon; hon D: Us: Paris; Toulouse; Lyon; Strasbourg; Bordeaux; m. Orovida Sequerra, 1925. Chancellor, Lisbon Tech U; dean, prof, Lisbon Sch Econ and Finance; prin, High Studies Inst, Lisbon; fmr: lectr, Heb U, Jerusalem; repr, delg to intl congs and convs. Mem, Port Acad. Recipient: Grand Officer: Polonia Restituta, Pol; St Olav, Nor; Orange and Nassau, Holland; Cdr, Légion d'Honneur, Fr; Grand Cross: Port Order of Public Instrn and Merito Industrial; Span Order of Alfonso El Sabio. Home: 58 rua Rodrigo da Fonseca, Lisbon, Port. Office: Lisbon Technical U, Lisbon, Port.

ANATI, Emmanuel, Isr, archaeologist, anthropologist; b. Florence, It, May 14, 1930; s. Ugo and Elsa Castelnuovo; in Isr since 1945; BA, Heb U, Jerusalem, 1954, MA, 1956; att Sorbonne, Paris, 1956-58; AM, Harvard U, 1959; Dr es lettres, Sorbonne, 1960; m. Ariela Fradkin, 1963; c: Daniel, Miriam. Dir, Centro di Studi Preistorici, It, since 1964; head, dept pre-hist, Tel Aviv U, since 1969; sr lectr, Heb U, since 1964; attaché, Natl Cen Sci Research, Paris, 1956-59. IDF, educ and culture br, 1948-49. Author: Camonica Valley, 1961; Palestine Before the Hebrews, 1963, Dutch ed, 1965; Origini della Civiltà-Camuna, 1968; Arte preistorica in Valtellina, 1968; Rock Art in Central Arabia, Vol I, II, 1968; Arte rupestre nelle regioni occidentali della penisola Iberica, 1968; ed in chief, dir, Bollettino del Centro Camuno di Studi Preistorici; Studi Camuni; Publicazioni del Centro Camuno di Studi Preistorici; Archivi de arte Preistorica; contbr to sci jours. Recipient: hon citizen, Capo Di Ponie, 1967; Cavaliere Della Repubblica, 1968. Spec interests: art, ancient books, artistic printing. Home: 5 Israel's St, Jerusalem, Isr. Office: Tel Aviv U, Ramat Aviv, Isr.

ANAU, Giullo, It, attorney, organization exec; b. Pisa, It, Sep 28, 1911; s. Angelo and Ada (Supino); law deg, U Rome, 1933. Secy, Unione Comunita Israelitiche Italiane, since 1956; atty, 1935-40; dir, Delasem, Rome, 1944-47; secy, Heb Comty of Rome, 1948-55. Office: Lungotevere Sanzio 9, Rome, It.

ANBAR, Michael, Isr, physical chemist; b. Danzig, Pol, June 20, 1927; s. Jehoshua and Chawa (Migdal); in Isr since 1933; MSc, Heb U, Jerusalem, 1950, PhD, 1953; m. Ada Komet, 1953; c: Ran, Ariel. Asso prof, Weizmann Inst of Sci, since 1961; dir, div chem, Isr Atomic Energy Research Lab, 1961-66; asst, chem, Heb U, 1949-50; visiting lectr, chem, U Chgo, 1953-55; dir, Radioisotope Training Cen, Rehovot, 1956-59;

sr research asso, Argonne Natl Lab, 1963-64; visiting prof chem, Stanford U, 1964-65; sr sci, Stanford Research Inst, Cal, 1968. IAF, 1943-50. Mem: Amer Chem Soc; Chem Soc of London; AAAS; Isr Chem Soc; Sigma Xi. Contbr to profsl jours. Recipient: Meir award, 1960; Zondek award, 1963. Home: 10 Neveh Weizmann, Rehovot, Isr. Office: Weizmann Inst of Sci, Rehovot, Isr.

ANGEL, Camillus, US, rabbi; b. Freisdorf, Lorraine, Fr, Dec 9, 1907; s. Nathan and Rachel (Meyerowitz); in US since 1908; BA, Harvard U, 1930; ordained rabbi, HUC, 1935, hon DD 1961; m. Shelma Greenberg, July 18, 1946; c: Naomi, Camille. Rabbi: Temple Beth David, Temple City, Cal, since 1961; Temple Sinai, Lake Charles, La, 1935-37; St George's Settlement Syn, London, Eng, 1937-39; Mt Sinai Cong, Texarkana, Tex, 1941-42; Beth Isr Cong, Hazleton, Pa, 1947-54; Temple Beth El, Pensacola, Fla, 1954-61. Chaplain, USAF, 1942-46. Mem: CCAR. Home: 722 E Camino Real Ave, Arcadia, Cal. Study: Temple Beth David, Temple City, Cal.

ANGEL, Rifka, US, artist; b. Lith, Sep 16, 1899; d. Raphael and Esther (Esterson) Angelevich; in US since 1913; att Art Students League, NYU; m. 2nd, Milton Douthat, June, 1929; c: Blossom. One-man shows: Knoedler Gal, Chgo, 1930, 1931; Increase Robinson Gal, Chgo, 1933; Carl Fischer Gal, NY, 1936; Findlay Gal, NY, 1937; Honolulu Acad Fine Arts, 1941; Roullier Gal, Chgo, 1944; ACA Gal, NYC, 1947; Van Diemen Lilenfield Gal, NYC, 1959; Roland de Aenlle Gal, NY, 1959; Park Ave Gal, 1963; Waddington Gal, Can, 1965; Jayson Gal, NY, 1966; exhb on invitation: Mus Modern Art; Whitney Mus Amer Art; Bklyn Mus; permanent collections: Rose Mus, Brandeis U; Chgo Art Inst; Honolulu Acad Fine Arts; Nelson Gal and Mary Atkins Mus of Fine Arts, Kansas City; librs; public schs and bldgs in Wash DC; pvt collections. Recipient: award, Chgo Art Inst, 1933; silver medal, Chgo Soc of Artists, 1933, prize, 1949. Home and studio: 79-81 Macdougal St, New York, NY.

ANGOFF, Allan, US, editor; b. Boston, Mass, July 30, 1910; s. Jacob and Anna (Pollack); BS, Boston U, 1932; MS, Columbia U, 1952; m. Florence Adelson, Mar 30, 1950; c: Jay, Naomi. Book review ed, Tomorrow Magazine, since 1957; dir, PR, Teaneck Public Libr, NJ, since 1965; found, ed, Teaneck Points of Reference, since 1965; feature writer, Boston, NY Newspapers, 1932-38; co-ed, contbr, The World Over, annual, 1938, 1939; ed staff, N Amer Rev, 1939-41; asso ed, Creative Age Press, 1945-46; mgn ed, Tomorrow Mag, 1946-51; W Eur repr, Tomorrow Creative Age, 1947-48; ed, Emerson books, 1951-52; asst dir, off of publs, NYU, 1951; ed in chief, NYU Press, 1955-57, ed on staff since 1953; reader's adv, reference dept, Montclair Free Public Libr, NJ, 1957-60; dir, Glen Rock Public Libr, NJ, 1965; asst reference libr, ed reference libr, NY Times, 1965-68; asst dir, Fair Lawn Public Libr, NJ, 1965-68; cons, Caxton Encyclopedia, London, NY, since 1968. Vice-pres, Bergen and Passaic Libr Assn, 1961-62; mem, bd trustees, Parapsychol Found; fmr cons, Ford Found; clubs: NYU fac; Natl Press, Wash, DC. Author: Hypnotism in USA, 1800-1900, in the series Abnormal Hypnotic Phenomena: A 19th Century Survey, 1968; ed, American Writing Today: Its Independence and Vigor. Home: 159 McCosh Rd, Upper Montclair, NJ. Office: Teaneck Public Libr, Teaneck, NJ.

ANGOFF, Charles, US, author, editor, educator; b. Minsk, Russ, Apr 22, 1902; s. Jacob and Anna (Pollack); in US since 1907; AB, Harvard U, 1923; m. Sara Freedman, 1943; c: Nancy Gollin. Prof: Eng, Fairleigh Dickinson U, since 1955; lit, NYU, 1957-66; lectr, fiction and Amer lit: Hunter Coll, 1949-54; New Hampshire U, 1949-61; Wagner Coll, 1961-69; mgn ed, The American Mercury, 1925-34, ed, 1934-35; ed, The American Spectator, 1935-36; mem, ed bd: The Nation, 1935; The North American Review, 1935-39; The Living Age, 1938-40; Scribner's Commentator, 1939; adv ed, Jewish Book Guild, 1949-56; exec ed, Mercury Publs, 1950-53; asso ed: JBCA, 1953-68; The Reconstructionist, 1954; ed, The Literary Review, since 1955; fac mem, B'nai B'rith Insts; novelist in res, Cal State Coll, LA, 1969. Pres, Poetry Soc of Amer, since 1969; mem: Natl Comm on Adult Educ; natl comm, JBCA; Authors League of Amer; club, PEN. Author: A Literary History of the American People, 2 vols, 1931; Palestrina, 1945; Fathers of Classical Music, 1946; The Book of Libel, 1947; Adventures in Heaven, 1947; When I Was A Boy in Boston, 1948; Journey to the Dawn, 1951; In the Morning Light, 1953; The Sun at Noon, 1954; Something about My Father and Other People, 1956; H L Mencken: A Portrait from Memory, 1956; Between Day and Dark, 1959; The Bitter Spring, 1961; Summer Storm, 1963; Memory

of Autumn, 1968; The Bell of Time, 1968; Memoranda for Tomorrow, 1968; Stories from the Literary Review, 1968; Winter Twilight, 1969; George Sterling: A Centenary Memoir, 1969; African Writing Today, 1969; plays: Something to Sing About, produc, Pasadena, 1941; Moment Musicale, produc, NY, 1943; chief ed, Fairleigh Dickinson U Press, since 1967; ed: Stradivari, 1938; The World Over, 2 vols, 1938, 1939, co-ed, 1939-40; co-ed, The American Mercury Reader, 1945; The World of George Jean Nathan, 1951; Stories from Many Lands, 1951. Recipient: Danoff Fiction Award, JBCA, 1954, 1969; spec award, maj contrib to J lit, FJP, NY, 1969. Home: 140 W 86 St, NYC.

ANGRIST, Alfred A, US, pathologist, educator; b. NYC, Mar 25, 1902; s. Isaac and Fannie (Levine); BS, CCNY, 1922; m. Sylvia Kasdan, June 9, 1932; c: Burton. Prof, chmn, dept path, Albert Einstein Coll of Med, since 1954; asso prof, clinical prof, NYU Med Coll, 1935-54; path, Queens Hosp Cen, 1935-54. Pres: Queens Co Med Soc, 1948; Queensboro Council for Social Wfr, 1951-53; NY Path Soc, 1954; mem, bd of dirs, exec comm, Health Ins Plan. Contbr to med jours. Hobby: photography. Home: 162-01 Powells Cove Blvd, Beechurst, NY. Office: Albert Einstein Coll of Med, New York, NY.

ANI, Yehuda, Isr, communal leader; b. Baghdad, Iraq, Mar 31, 1906; s. Ezra and Mazal; in Isr since 1935; m. Esther Aloof, 1939; four c. Dep mayor, Rehovot, since 1965; mem, Council, 1955-65; mem: Rel Council, Rehovot; chmn cen comm, Rehovot Munic; Rambam Comm of Sephardic Cmty; fmr: station master, Iraq RR, 1926-35; Naafi mgr, Pal Govt, 1940-47. Haganah, IDF, since 1935. Home: 62 Arlosoroff St, Rehovot, Isr.

ANIGSTEIN, Ludwik, US, parasitologist, educator; b. Warsaw, Pol, Feb 2, 1891; s. Isidore and Helen (Steinkalk); in US since 1939; PhD, U Heidelberg, 1913; MD, U Dorpat, Russ, 1915; MD, U Poznan, Pol, 1923; postdoc cert, London Sch Tropical Med and Hygiene, 1923; m. Luba Heller, Apr 16, 1916; c: Alice, Robert; m. 2nd, Dorothy Whitney, May 2, 1958. Prof, preventive med, public health, U Tex Med Br, Galveston, since 1946, on staff since 1940; cons, med div, Oak Ridge Inst for Nuclear Studies, US AEC, since 1950; lectr, communicable diseases, UNRRA Med Teaching Mission to Pol, since 1946; James W McLaughin f, to study tropical diseases, Peru, Brazil, 1955; surg, epidemiologist, Russ Red Cross, 1915-18; parasitologist, State Inst Hygiene, Warsaw, 1919-39; lectr: microbiol, State Sch of Hygiene, Warsaw, 1926-39; U Warsaw, 1929-39; mem, malaria commn, L of N, surveys, Eur, Asia, Afr, 1924-39; research, tropical med, Brit Malaya, 1929-31; malariologist, Thai Govt, 1931; health expert, Govt of Liberia, 1935-36; chmn, sect of tropical path, Third Intl Cong of Tropical Med, Amsterdam, 1938; research asso, lectr, U of Cal, 1940. Maj, Tex State Guard, 1943-46. F: Royal Soc Tropical Med and Hygiene; Amer Acad Microbiol; AAAS; Tex Acad Sci; NY Acad Scis: mem: Amer Soc Tropical Med and Hygiene; Amer Soc Experimental Path; Sigma Xi; Soc Experimental Biol and Med; The Sci Research Soc of Amer; Reticuloendothelial Soc; Phi Delta Epsilon; Mu Delta. Contbr to profsl publs. Home: 28 Manor Way, Galveston, Tex. Office: U of Tex Med Br, Galveston, Tex.

ANNENBERG, Walter Hubert, US, diplomat, editor, publisher; b. Milw, Wis, Mar 13, 1908; s. Moses and Sadie (Friedman); att U of Pa, 1931; hon: DJournalism, Temple U, 1951; DHumL, Pa Mil Coll, 1954; Albert Einstein Coll of Med, 1936; LLD: La Salle Coll, 1957; U of Pa, 1966; Dropsie Coll, 1968; m; c: Wallis; m. 2nd, Leonore Cohn, Sep 29, 1951. US Ambass to Gt Brit since 1969; fmr pres, Triangle Publs, Inc, which publishes: The Phila Inquirer, fmr ed and publisher; Seventeen Mag; TV Guide; Phila Daily News; Morning Telegraph, NY; Daily Racing Form; and operates stas: WFIL, AM, FM and TV, Phila; VNBF, FM, DM and TV, Binghamton, NY; WFBG, AM and TV, Altoona, Pa; WNHC, AM, FM and TV, New Haven, Conn; WLYH-TV, Lebanon, Pa; KFRE, KFRM, KFRE-TV, Fresno, Cal; bd dirs: Girard Trust Bank; Campbell Soup Co. Fmr cdr, USNR. Found, Annenberg Sch of Communications, U of Pa; donor: Walter A Annenberg Libr, Masters' House, both Peddie Sch, Highstown, NJ; pres: Phila Inquirer Charities, Inc; M L Annenberg Found, Inc; Annenberg Fund, Inc; mem, bd overseers, Albert Einstein Coll of Med, Yeshiva U; co-found, mem, bd trustees, Eisenhower Exch Fs, Inc; mem, bd corporators, Peddie Sch; mem: Sigma Delta Chi; Amer Soc Newspaper Eds; Amer Newspaper Publishers Assn; Newcomen Soc N

Amer; Fr Alliance, Phila; Cum Laude Soc, Peddie Sch; Friars Sr Soc, U of Pa; bd dirs, exec comm, Penn Cen Co; exec comm, Phila Council, Navy League; bd trustees, Phila area, United Fund; hon alumni, Heb U, Jerusalem; bd fed, JAs Gtr Phila; clubs: Lyford Cay, Nassau, Bahamas; Cent Country, White Plains, NY; Green Valley Country; Poor Richard; Midday; fac, U of Pa, all Pa; Hillcrest Country, Beverly Hills, Cal; Tamarisk Country, Palm Springs, Cal; Natl Press; Overseas Press. Recipient: Fr Legion of Honor; cdr: Order Merit of It Rep; Order of Lion, Finland; Order of Crown, It; Humanitarian award, Fed JAs. Home: Inwood, Wynnewood, Pa. Office: US Embassy, London, Eng.

ANNES, Paul G, US, attorney; b. Ekaterinoslav, Russ, July 28, 1900; s. Gersh and Minnie (Putterman) Anesh; in US since 1912; PhB, U Chgo, 1921, JD, cum laude, 1923; m. Ada Barac, Aug 29, 1930; c: George, Robert. Pvt practice since 1924. Natl vice-pres, AJCong, 1958-60 and since 1962, pres, Chgo Council, 1957-59, co-chmn, natl governing council, 1960-62; mem, natl exec comm, Natl Comty Relations Adv Council, since 1958; mem, bd dirs, Decalogue Soc Lawyers, pres, 1953-54; pres, Council Against Discrimination, 1950-52; bd dirs, Amer Friends Heb U; mem: Chgo Bar Assn; B'nai B'rith; club, City, Chgo, bd dirs, fmr pres; Covenant Ill, fmr bd dirs. Recipient: dist alumnus citation, U Chgo, 1952. Home: 3750 Lake Shore Dr, Chicago, Ill. Office: 134 N La Salle St, Chicago, Ill.

ANOFF, Isador Samuel, US, business exec; b. Cincinnati, O, Jan 8, 1892; s. Samuel and Pauline (Kohn); m. Florence Ginsberg, June 17, 1917; c: Seymour, Philip. Exec dir, Service Equipment Ind, since 1964; vice-pres, Franklin Products Corp, since 1957. Pres: Food Service Equipment Ind, 1933-47, chmn, exec comm since 1947; US Intl Trade Fair, Chgo, 1950; J Children's Bur, 1958-61, bd mem, since 1938; dir, Chgo Convention Bur, 1947-51, exec comm, since 1951, mem since 1940; vice-chmn, Bellefaire, Cleveland, since 1940, bd of trustees since 1931; dir, Off The Street Club, since 1949, exec vice-pres, since 1953; mem: B'nai B'rith; Masons; Zeta Beta Tau; club, Standard. Home: 1755 E 55 St, Chicago, Ill. Office: 1615 S Michigan Ave, Chicago, Ill.

ANOPOL, George, US, surgeon, educator; b. Siberia, Russ, Mar 24, 1893; s. Walter and Gitel (Gershenovich); in US since 1900; MD, U and Bellevue Hosp Med Coll, 1920; m. Annie Wagner, 1946. Prof, clinical orthopedic surg, Bellevue Med Cen, since 1948; prof, dir, orthopedic dept, NY Post Grad Hosp and Med Sch, 1938-48; on staff, 1922-48; dir: orthopedics, Wavecrest Convalescent Home, Bklyn Children's Aid, 1931-34; traumatic-orthopedic dept, Yonkers Gen Hosp, 1934-59. USN, 1941-45, ret as capt, MC, USNR, 1958. F: NY Acad Med; AAAS; Amer Coll Surgs; dipl, Intl Coll Surgs; mem: NY Co and State Med Soc; AMA; club, Interurban Orthopedic. Contbr to profsl jours. Recipient: Cong Selective Service Medal. Spec interests: gardening, mech. Home and office: 237 Valentine Lane, Yonkers, NY.

ANTIN, Arthur Paul, US, educator; b. NYC, June 27, 1926; s. Harry and Ruth (Klinger); BA, Goddard Coll, Vt, 1949; MA, Tchrs Coll, Columbia U, 1950, EdD, 1957; m. Jean Phillips, June 12, 1949; c: Joseph, William, Ruth. Supt schs, White Plains, NY, since 1969, asst prin, 1954-55, admn asst, 1955-65, asst supt, 1965-69; tchr, Richmond, Va, 1950-52. Cpl, US Army, 1944-46. Pres: NY Assn Sch Bus Officials; mem: State Commn Continuing Purchasing Comm; natl research comm on prog budgeting, Assn Sch Bus Officials; sch bd chmn, J Cmty Cen White Plains, trustee; mem: bd dirs, White Plains Libr; NEA; NY State Tchrs Assn; Amer Assn Sch Admnrs; club, Kiwanis White Plains, fmr pres. Hobbies: folksinging; boating. Home: 133 Longview Ave, White Plains, NY. Office: 5 Homeside Lane, White Plains, NY.

ANTOPOL, William A, US, pathologist, educator; b. NYC, Apr 6, 1903; s. Israel and Mata (Elman); BS, CCNY, 1923; MD, LI Coll Hosp, 1927; m. Bella Scholer, June 24, 1937; c: Michael, Stephen. Path, labs dir, Beth Isr Hosp, NYC, since 1949; dir research, Joseph and H Y Levy Found, since 1949; clinical prof path, NYU Coll of Med, since 1949; cons path: Bayonne Hosp and Dispensary since 1955, path, dir lab, 1930-35; Newark Beth Isr Hosp, NJ, since 1949, path and dir lab, 1935-49; chief cons, path, VA Hosp, Lyons, NJ, since 1947; prof path, Mt Sinai Med Sch, since 1966; adv bd, Lobund, U Notre Dame; f, path, Mt Sinai Hosp, NYC, 1928-30; path, dir lab, Hudson Co TB Hosp, 1932-36; visiting prof: U Montreal Inst for Experimental Med, 1966; U of Ky, 1967. Lt Col, US Army. F: NY Acad Med; Coll Amer Paths;

Amer Soc Clinical Path; mem: Assn Amer Paths and Bacts; Soc for Experimental Biol and Med; Amer Public Health Assn; Biochem Soc, Gt Brit; Amer Soc Cancer Research; Amer Assn Anatomists; Amer Soc Zool; Reticuloendothelial Soc; Sigma Xi. Ed bd, Jour of Mt Sinai Hosp; contbr to profsl jours. Recipient: commendation from Surg Gen, commendation ribbon, US Army; grant to investigate: cholinesterase, 1934; Shwartzman Phenomenon, 1936, both from AMA. Home: 350 First Ave, New York, NY. Office: 10 Perlman Pl, New York, NY.

APFEL, Harry, US, physician; b. Skalat, Aus, Dec 8, 1885; s. Morris and Peppi (Landesman); in US since 1898; MD, LI Coll Med, 1908; MS, U of Pa, 1927; m. Helene Gross, 1936; c: Florence Goodstein. Cons ped, Unity Hosp, Bklyn, since 1954, chief ped, 1927-54; lectr and instr, ped, NY Post Grad Med Sch and Hosp, 1918-20; med commn to Pol, JDC, 1920-21; dipl, Amer Bd Ped, 1936. Pres: East NY Med Soc, 1913-14; ped sect, Kings Co Med Soc and Acad of Med, Bklyn, 1936-37; mem: NY State Med Soc; AMA; Med Soc Kings Co. Contbr to med jours. Hobbies: music, lit. Home: Eaton's Harbor, Northport, NY.

APFELBERG, Benjamin, US, psychiatrist, educator; b. Vienna, Aus, Feb 28, 1897; s. Morris and Clara (Meissner); in US since 1898; MD, LI Med Coll, 1920; m. Gladys Kelley, 1939. Ret; asso dir, dept psycht, Bellevue Hosp, 1949-61, mem staff since 1930. Dipl in psycht; f: Amer Psychiatric Assn; NY Soc Clinical Psycht; mem, Sigma Xi. Contbr articles on forensic psycht. Home: 111-56 76 Dr, Forest Hills, NY.

APPEL, Gersion, US, rabbi, educator; b. Budapest, Hung, Jan 13, 1916; s. Juda and Celia (Perl); in US since 1924; BA, Yeshiva Coll, 1938; ordained rabbi, Rabbi Isaac Elchanan Theol Sem, 1940; DHL, Yeshiva U, 1945; PhD, Harvard U, 1962; m. Miriam Cohen, May 4, 1942; c: Dvora, Shlomo, Yakov, Ziporah, Rebecca, Esther. Prof, J phil, Stern Coll, Yeshiva U; visiting prof, Heb, NYU Grad Sch, Arts and Sci; rabbi: United J Orthodox Comty, Worcester, 1941-46; Cong Orach Chaim, NYC, 1946-48; Cong Bikur Cholim, Seattle, 1948-58; Kew Gardens Syn Adath Yeshurun, 1958-67. Vice-pres, RabCA, 1952. Author: Sefer haNeyar, 1960. Home: 2017 Ave M, Brooklyn, NY. Study: Stern Coll, Yeshiva U, New York, NY.

APPELBAUM, Emanuel, US, physician, educator; b. Pol, Apr 14, 1894; s. Harry and Rebecca (Gerstein); in US since 1906; AB, Columbia U, 1916, MD, 1918; m. Ruth Alpert, June 9, 1927; c: Arline Levinson, David. Prof, clinical med, NYU Med Sch, since 1956; att phys, U Hosp, since 1969; visiting phys, Bellevue Hosp, since 1938, asst visiting phys, 1926-38, path, 1921-28; asst visiting phys, Willard Park Hosp, 1943-55; chief, div acute infections cen nervous sys, NYC, Dept Health, 1941-43; cons phys: NY Infirmary, since 1946; Long Beach Memorial Hosp, since 1949; Meadowbrook Hosp, 1954-67; Knickerbocker Hosp, since 1957; Trafalgar Hosp, since 1959; Grand Cen Hosp, 1960-62; Beth Isr Hosp, Newark, NJ, since 1961; dir med em, Sydenham Hosp, since 1966, dir, 1948-66. Med Res Corps, US Army, 1918. Prin contrib: diagnosis and treatment of acute infections to the cen nervous system: chemotherapy and antibiotic therapy of acute infections. Co-chmn, higher educ div, UJA comm NYC, since 1958; chmn, Bellevue Hosp, UJA, 1945-55; f: NY Acad of Med; NY Acad of Sci; Amer Public Health Assn; Amer Coll Phys; mem: NY State Med Soc; AMA; AAAS; AHA; Brit Royal Soc of Med; Royal Soc of Health. Author: Acute Infections of the Central Nervous System, 1932; Prevention of Disease in Everyday Practice, 1955; Injuries of the Brain and Spinal Cord, 1960; Current Therapy, 1962; contbr to med jours. Recipient: Pulitzer Scholarship. Home: 40 E 83 St, New York, NY. Office: 910 Park Ave, New York, NY.

APPLBAUM, Joseph Stuart, US, rabbi; b. Bklyn, NY, June 11, 1944; s. Karl and Helen (Siegel); BA, Queens Coll, NY, 1965; ordained rabbi, Yeshiva Ch'san Sofer, 1965; m. Rhea Groob, Dec 26, 1964; c: Marc. Capt, J chaplain, SETAF, since 1967; asst rabbi, Ave M J Cen, Bklyn, since 1965, on leave; post J chaplain, Fort Ord, Cal, 1966-67. Dep natl chaplain, Res Off Assn, US; fmr pres, Mizrachi Hatzair, Queens chap; fmr chap repr, Young Isr Intercollegiates; mem: Mil Chaplains Assn, Vicenza chap; Assn US Army, Vicenza chap; Assn J Chaplains, NY chap; Royal Arcanum, NY chap; NY Bd Rabbis; Amer Bowling Cong, Vicenza chap; JWV, Queens chap; Amer Legion, Queens chap; club, Vicenza Audio. Hobbies: photography, stamps, coins, bowling. Home: 43A Villagio Della Pace, Vicenza, It. Office: Hqrs MSL SPT COMD, APO, NY 09221, Vicenza, It.

APPLBAUM, Karl, US, rabbi, attorney; b. Nasy Banya, Hung, Feb 10, 1910; s. Emanuel and Goldie (Eckstein); in US since 1922; BS, State Tchrs Coll, Cal, Pa, 1932; MS, CCNY, 1935; ordained rabbi, 1936; LLB, St Lawrence U, 1937; SD, 1939; MA, NYU, 1952; DHL, Yeshiva U, NYC, 1957; PhD, St Andrew's Ecumenical U Coll, London, Eng, 1956; DD, with hons, 1956; LLD, hc, Phoenix Acad, Bari, It, 1957; D Sociol, St Andrews, 1958; m. Helen Siegel, 1934; c: Elaine Feldman, Florence Laifer, Joseph. Rabbi, Ave M J Cen, Bklyn, since 1936; pvt practice, law, since 1939; prof, practical rabb, hist, various theol sems, 1950-56; lectr, phil, Queens Coll, NY, 1959-60. Lt col, Chaplains Corps, US Army, 1945-65. Pres: Queens Co JCC, since 1955; LI chap, Assn US Army, 1968-69; chmn, Queens Co Civic Improvement Council, since 1960; mem, local Sch Bd 25, Queens; active in: UJA; FJP; Young Isr, Kew Gardens Hills; bd govs: Natl Info Bur J Life; JKF Libr for Minorities; bd trustees: Independent Bukarester Sick Aid Assn; Sherishower Benevolent Assn; judge advocate, Queens Co chap, Reserve Off Assn, 1955-61; chaplain, various posts, JWV, since 1945; co-chaplain: Kings Co chap, 1946-48, Queens chap, 1962-63, dep natl chaplain, 1948-49, natl chaplain, 1965-66; mem: Hapoel Hamizrachi Amer; ZOA; Amer Public Wfr Assn; NY State Wfr Conf; Mil Chaplains Assn; Assn J Chaplains Armed Forces; RA; NY Bd Rabbis; Queens Co Bar Assn; NY State Bar Assn; B'nai B'rith; Amer Legion; Odd Fellows; KP; Royal Arcanum; clubs: Dem; Amer-Isr; Roslyn Country. Contbr to Bibl Ency, 1952. Recipient: received in pvt audiences by: Popes John XXIII, 1959; Pope Paul VI, 1968; Sarner Chaplaincy Award, 1962; Ky Col; meritorious service medal, 1970. Hobbies: chess, tennis, golf. Home: 136-80 71 Rd, Flushing, NY. Study: 1898 Bay Ave, Brooklyn, NY.

APPLBAUM, Martin Louis, US, rabbi; b. Bentlyville, Pa, Dec 1, 1926; s. Emanuel and Goldie (Eckstein); BA, Yeshiva Coll, 1948; ordained rabbi, Rabbi Isaac Elchanan Theol Sem, 1951; m. Sherry Steinberg, June 19, 1957; c: Yaakov, Nachum, Adena. Rabbi: Garden J Cen, since 1954; Brith Sholom Comty Cen, Phila, 1951-54. Mem: exec comm, LI Commn Rabbis, recording secy; NY Bd Rabbis; RabCA; Rabb Alumni, Yeshiva U. Author: Your Synagogue Journal, 1969. Home: 142-15 32 Ave, Flushing, NY. Study: 24-20 Parsons Blvd, Flushing, NY.

APPLE, Carl, US, ophthalmologist, educator; b. Libau, Latvia, May 5, 1895; s. David and Sarah (Kuf); in US since 1908; BS, U of Ill, 1921, MD, 1923; m. Minnie Kaplan, Feb 8, 1925; c: Darlene, Earl. Pvt practice since 1925; asso prof, U of Ill, since 1930; att ophthal, Edgewater Hosp. US Army, 1918-19. F: Amer Coll Surgs; Amer Acad Ophthal and Otology; AMA; mem, Ill and Chgo Med Soc; Chgo Ophthal Soc; Pan Amer Assn Ophthal; Intl Cong Ophthal; clubs: Covenant, Chgo; Twin Orchard Country. Contbr to med jours. Recipient: Cong Selective Service Medal, 1943. Home: 5801 N Sheridan Rd, Chgo, Ill. Office: 55 E Washington St, Chicago, Ill.

APPLE, Raymond, Eng, rabbi; b. Melbourne, Austr, Dec 27, 1935; s. Harry and Ada (Joachim); in Eng since 1958; BA, LLB, Melbourne U; dipl, J Coll, London; m. Marian Unterman, Dec 27, 1960; c: Simeon, Riva, Adina. Min Hampstead Syn, since 1965; dir, universities dept, Off Chief Rabbi, since 1968; headmaster, United J Educ Bd, Melbourne, 1953-58; rel dir, Assn for J Youth, London, 1959-63; min, Bayswater Syn, 1960-65. Chmn, J Marriage Educ Council; dep chmn, Solomon Wolfson J Sch; vice-pres, Union Anglo-J Preachers; council mem, B'nai B'rith. Author: Companion to the Machzor, 1964; The Hampstead Synagogue, 1892-1967, pub 1967. Home: 533 Finchley Rd, London, Eng. Study: The Hampstead Synagogue, Dennington Park Rd, London, Eng.

APPLEBAUM, Edmund, US, dentist, educator; b. NYC, Feb 1, 1899; s. Benjamin and Hanna (Harris); DDS, NY Coll Dent, 1922; m. Dorothy Frank; c: Joseph. Asso prof, dent histology, Sch Dent and Oral Surg, Columbia U, since 1950, with fac since 1928. Mem: Amer Dent Assn; Intl Assn for Dent Research; AAAS. Home: 40 W 77 St, New York, NY. Office: 630 W 168 St, New York, NY.

APPLEBAUM, Louis, Can, composer; b. Toronto, Can, Apr 3, 1918; s. Morris and Fanny (Frieberg); att: U Toronto; Royal Conservatory of Music, Toronto; m. Janet Hershoff, July 19, 1940; c: David. Dir, Composers, Authors, Publish-

ers Assn of Can, since 1957; music cons, St Lawrence Arts Cen, since 1968; dir music: Natl Film Bd, 1941-46; Stratford Festival, 1953-61; music cons; Natl Arts Cen, 1965-68. Composer: 3 Stratford Fanfares, 1966; The Stratford Scene, 1968; over 300 film scores, Hollywood, NY, Toronto; produc operas and operettas with Sir Tyrone Guthrie; composer, conductor: numerous radio and TV drama and variety shows; numerous festival drama series, Broadway, London, Stratford, Toronto. Found, Stratford Music Festival; dir: Can Music Cen; Can Music Council; chmn, Comm for Promotion of Can Music; trustee, Can League of Composers; fmr dir, Can Ballet Sch; mem: Le Cercle Universitaire, Ottawa; CAPAC, Toronto. Recipient: Acad Award Nomination, Motion Picture Acad, 1947; Centennial Medal, Can Govt, 1967. Hobbies: chess, sculpture. Home: 400 Walmer Rd, Toronto, Can. Office: 1263 Bay St, Toronto, Can.

APPLEBAUM, Morton M, US, rabbi; b. Toronto, Can, Aug 25, 1911; s. Joseph and Sarah (Leavit); in US since 1934; BA, U Toronto, 1934; BH, HUC, 1938, ordained rabbi, MHL, 1940, DD, 1965; m. Eleanor Wides, June 9, 1940; c: Lois, Bruce. Rabbi: Temple Isr, since 1953; Cong Shaarey Zedek, Lansing, Mich, 1940-43; Temple Beth El, Flint, Mich, 1943-53; Hillel counselor, Mich State Coll, 1940-43; chaplain: Pontiac State Hosp, 1944-46; Saginaw Vets Hosp, 1952-53. Mem bd: Akron Educ Comm; Child Guidance Comm; Mh Comm; Akron Dist Heart Assn; Legal Aid Soc; Citizens' Comm on Aging; Akron Jail Reform Comm; Comty PR and educ comm, Akron Police; fmr pres: Mich B'nai B'rith Council, 1946-47; Flint Lodge, B'nai B'rith, 1947-48; mem, exec bd: JCC; Comty Chest; YMCA; Urban League; Mental Hygiene; Family Counseling; Big Brothers, all Flint, Mich; mem: CCAR, mem exec bd since 1962; Commn on Church and State; Commn on Isr Projects; Beta Sigma Rho; club, Rotary. Author: What Everyone Should Know About Judaism, 1959; co-author, Sermonettes For Young People; contbr to periodicals. Home: 386 Delaware Ave, Akron, O. Study: 133 Merriman Rd, Akron, O.

APPLEBAUM, Samuel, US, violinist, educator; b. Passaic, NJ, Jan 15, 1904; s. Michael and Fannie (Levine); att Juilliard Sch of Music; m. Sada Rothman, Aug 19, 1927; c: Michael, Louis. Mem fac: Manhattan Sch of Music; Fairleigh Dickinson U. Author: Building Technic with Beautiful Music, 1954; Music for Two Violins, 1955; String Builder, 1960; University String Builder: String Clinic Recordings, Golden Crest Records, teaching films, U Wis; Amer ed, Strad Mag, London; co-author, With The Artists, 1956; composed arrangements for violin study. Fmr pres, NJ Music Educs Assn; vice-pres, Violin, Viola and Violoncello Tchrs Guild, NYC; 2nd vice-pres, NJ div, Natl Fed Music Clubs. Recipient: dist tchr of year award, Natl String Tchrs Assn, 1967. Home and studio: 23 N Terrace, Maplewood, NJ.

APPLEBAUM, Samuel Isaac, Eng, business exec; b. Zurardov, Pol, July 4, 1898; s. Chiam and Fanny (Goldfarb); in Eng since 1910; att Tech Sch, Liverpool; m. Tamara Solomon; c: Mindell, Ronald. Elec engr, United Fruit Co, US, 1923-27. Vice pres: chmn, JNF: Liverpool; Gt Brit; JPA; Liverpool Zionist Cen Council; mem, exec: ZF Council, Eng; WJC. Home: 7 Beauclair Dr, Liverpool, Eng. Office: 83 Islington St, Liverpool, Eng.

APPLEBAUM, Shimon, Isr, archaeologist, educator; b. Liverpool, Eng, Apr 21, 1911; s. Jacob and Clara (Goldberg); in Isr since 1939; BLitt, Oxford U, 1948, PhD, 1951; m. Shoshana Benchovski, 1956; c: Hava, Tzur, Mor. Prof, classical archaeol, Isr hist, Tel Aviv U, since 1969, on fac since 1960; sr lectr, Haifa U Coll, since 1960; research f, Heb U, Jerusalem, 1954-56. Sgt: Brit Forces, 1940-46; IDF. Prin contribs: excavations at: Beth Shean; Tiberias; Hadera; Timnah; Ein Bokek; studies in ancient Negev agric. Author: Jews and Greeks in Ancient Cyrene; Roman Britain in Agrarian History of England; contbr of numerous articles. Spec interests: criticism of social order. Home: 79a Rehov Hauniversita, Tel Aviv, Isr. Office: Tel Aviv U, Ramat Aviv, Isr.

APPLEBAUM, Shoshana, (pen name, **Yerushalmina Bat Zion**), Isr, author, teacher; b. Jerusalem, Apr 22, 1924; d. Abraham and Hava (Eisen) Bentchkovski; tchr dipl, Bet Hakerem Tchrs' Sem, 1948; dipl, Sch of J Scis, 1955; m. Shimeon Applebaum; c: Hava, Tzur, Mor. Author: Tiyul beHolot, 1956; Resisei Tal; Tlalim; Ne'arim Giborim, 1957. IDF, 1943-51. Volunteer mem, Magen David Adom. Hobbies: cooking, knitting. Home: 79a Hauniversita St, Tel Aviv, Isr.

APPLEBAUM, William, US, food distribution cons; b. Pruzana, Russ, Apr 24, 1906; s. Lipa and Esther (Volk); in US since 1920; BA, U Minn, 1931; research f, U Cincinnati, 1931-32; att U Minn, 1932-33; m. Celia Kiperstein, 1929 (decd); m. 2nd, Berenice Milgroom, Sep 18, 1960. Lectr em, food distribution, Harvard Grad Sch of Bus Admn, since 1968, lectr, 1960-68, visiting cons, 1954-60; dir: Hannoford Bros Co, Portland, Me, since 1960; Isr Pub Inst, Jerusalem, since 1966; Educ Pub Inst, NY, since 1967; Stop and Shop, Boston, since 1949, affiliated since 1938; chief, Market Research Dept, Kroger Co, Cincinnati, 1935-38, market research analyst, 1933-35; marketing cons since 1954. Dep chief, geog div, research and analysis br, Off Strategic Services, 1942-43, spec asst to br dir, 1943-44; exec off, br, 1944-45; capt, USMCR, 1943-45, maj, inactive Res, 1945-57. Chmn: public policy and rev bd, Amer Marketing Assn, 1958-59; spring conf, Amer Marketing Assn, 1946; comm on careers, geog, NRC and Assn Amer Geog, 1950-54; research adv comm, Super Market Inst, 1952-53; Natl Acad Sci and NRC, comm geog, 1960-61; pres, NE Chap, Amer Marketing Assn, 1946-47; delg, Fifth Gen Assembly, Pan Amer Inst Geog and Hist, 1950; mem: comm on comparative marketing, Amer Marketing Assn, since 1960; adv comm, Deciduous Fruit and Tree Nuts Research and Market, 1950; Agric Res Policy Comm, 1958-60; Natl Agric Research Adv Comm, 1961-64, all US Dept of Agric; exec comm, Prog in Food Marketing Mgmt, Mich State U, since 1960; sponsoring comm, Gottlieb Duttweiler Inst for Econ and Soc Studies, Ruschlikon, Zurich, since 1964; Food for Peace Mission, India, 1964; Food for Peace Mission, Yugo, 1965; cons, Research and Devl Bd, NSC, 1948-52; mem: Amer Marketing Assn; Amer Stat Assn; Assn Amer Geog; Amer Geog Soc; Regional Sci Assn; f, AAAS. Author: Store Location Strategy Cases; co-author: Cases in Food Distribution, 1964; Product Profitability Measurement and Merchandising Decision, 1965; Guide to Store Location Research With Emphasis on Super Markets, 1968; numerous monographs; mem, ed bd: Jour of Marketing, 1943-44; Jour of Retailing, since 1965; contbr to profsl jours. Recipient: citations, Super Market Inst, 1949, 1953; Hall of Fame in Distribution, Boston Conf on Dist, 1954; Amer Marketing Assn, National Award, 1950, Cincinnati Chap Award, 1956; citation of merit, Assn Amer Geog, 1959. Hobbies: cooking, gardening, photography, leather tooling. Home: 29 Tobey Rd, Belmont, Mass.

APPLEMAN, Hyman, US, rabbi; b. Russ, July 10, 1915; s. Dov and Esther (Kahn); in US since 1922; BA, Bklyn Coll, 1937; ordained rabbi, Yeshiva U, 1939; m. May Skurnick, Aug 6, 1944; c: Elaine, Jacob, Florence Asher. Rabbi, found, Sheepshead Bay J Cen, Bklyn, NY, since 1966; rabbi: Shore Park J Cen, Bklyn, since 1962; Young Isr of Pelham Pkwy, Bx, 1945-48; Zera Kodesh Cong, Norwalk, Conn, 1952-57; J Cen of Pelham Bay, Bx, 1957-62. Mem: Rabb Alumni, Yeshiva U; RabCA; fmr pres, Norwalk Mizrachi. Home: 3903 Nostrand Ave, Brooklyn, NY. Study: Sheepshead Bay J Cen, Nostrand Ave and Voohies Ave, Brooklyn, NY.

APTEKAR, Segulla Jacob, India, physician; b. Bombay, Oct 1, 1910; d. Jacob and Miriam (Jhirad); deg, St Xavier's Coll, Bombay, 1930; MB BS, Grant Med Coll, Bombay, 1935. Supt, Noor Hosp, Bombay, since 1968; hon obstet and gyn, Bombay Hosp, since 1951; hon cons obstet and gyn, W Railway Hosp, since 1960; supt, Cama and Albless Hosp, 1966-68, hon obstet and gyn, 1942-68; hon tchr, Grant Med Coll, Bombay U, 1942-68. FRCS; F, Royal Coll Obstet and Gyn; mem: reference comm, W India, Royal Coll Obstets and Gyns; mgn comm: Bombay Obstet and Gyn Soc; Assn Med Women in India; Bene Isr Stree Mandal; J Rel Union; B'nai B'rith Women's Auxiliary; Maharashtra State Women's Council; Maharashtra State Women Grad's Union; Bene Isr Conf Educ Fund; Bombay Red Cross; Bombay Presidency Radio Club; Indian Med Assn; Bombay Med Union; Grant Med Coll Soc; fmr: pres, Bombay Obstet and Gyn Soc; vice-pres, Bombay Women Grad's Union. Asso ed, Journal of Fed of Obstets and Gyns of India; contbr to med jours. Hobbies: classical music, reading, travel, natural hist. Home: Business Petal Chambers, French Bridge, Bombay, India. Office: Anik House, 5 Henry Rd, Bombay, India.

APTER, Nathaniel S, US, psychiatrist, educator; b. NYC, May 10, 1913; s. Louis and Sadie (Friedman); BA, Cornell U, 1933; MD, U Buffalo, 1938; m. Julia Tutelman, Dec 13, 1941; c: Marion, Eve. Pvt practice, psycht and psychan; professional lectr, psych, U Chgo, since 1955, on fac since 1946; att psycht, Michael Reese Hosp; cons: McLean Co Mh Clinic; Ill Dept Public Wfr; Manteno State Hosp, 1951; res neur, Kings Co

Hosp, Bklyn, 1940-42; house phys, asst psycht, Henry Phillips Psychiatric Clinic, Baltimore; asst psycht, Johns Hopkins U, both 1942-44; mem, neuro-psych cons div, US Surg Gen Off, 1946; att psycht, Cook Co Psychiatric Hosp, 1951; sr psycht Albert Merritt Billings Hosp, 1951-54. Capt, US Army, 1944-46. Pres, Ill Psychiatric Soc, 1958-59; vice-pres, Assn Psychiatric Facs, Chgo, 1952-53; f: Amer Psychiatric Assn; AAAS; dipl: Amer Bd Psych and Neur; Natl Bd Med Examiners; mem: bd of dirs, Ill Soc for Mh, 1953; Chgo Psychoanalytical Soc; Amer Psychosomatic Soc; AMA; mem, bd trustees, S Shore Temple, 1957-60. Contbr to med jours. Home: 7316 Paxton Ave, Chicago, Ill. Office: 111 N Wabash Ave, Chicago, Ill.

APTHEKER, Herbert, US, author, editor, educator; b, NYC, July 31, 1915; s. Benjamin and Rebecca (Komar); BS, Columbia U, 1936, AM, 1937, PhD, 1943; m. Fay Aptheker, 1942; c: Bettina. Instr, hist, Bryn Mawr Coll, since 1969; dir, Amer Inst for Marxist Studies, since 1964. Maj, US Army, 1942-46. Author: American Negro Slave Revolts, 1943; Essays on the History of the Negro People, 1945; The Negro People in America, 1946; To Be Free, 1948; A Documentary History of the Negro People in the United States, 1951; Laureates of Imperialism, 1954; History and Reality, 1955; Towards Negro Freedom, 1956; The Truth about Hungary, 1957; History of American People, Vol I, The Colonial Eng, 1959, Vol II, The American Revolution, 1960; The World of C Wright Mills, 1960; Dare We Be Free, 1961; ed: Political Affairs, 1955-63; Marxism and Democracy, 1965; Marxism and Alienatation, 1966; Mission to Hanoi, 1967; Marxism and Christianity, 1968; Autobiography of W E B DuBois, 1968; Nature of Democracy, 1968; asso ed, Masses and Mainstream, 1948-54. Mem: Author's League; Amer Hist Assn; Assn for Study Negro Life and Hist; Amer Acad Political Sci. Recipient: Guggenheim F in Hist, 1946-47. Home: 32 Ludlam Pl, Brooklyn, NY.

APTOWITZER, Willi Zeev, Isr, insurance exec; b. Vienna, Aus, Apr 3, 1918; s. Adolf and Rifka (Cirer); in Isr since 1938; ACII, Chartered Inst Ins, London, 1944; m. Marvit Stern, Sep 22, 1944. Chmn, bd dirs, Natl Ins Off Group since 1963, mgn dir since 1959; repr of Lloyds Underwriters, trustee in confidential investigation matters, since 1950; marine ins expert for several fgn ins co's; adv on ins: Fgn Min; Tel Aviv Mus; mgr, Hermon Ltd, Haifa, 1945-46; found partner, W W Aptowitzer and Co, 1946-49; co-mgr, dir: NIO, Ltd; Carmelia Ltd, both 1949-59: lectr in ins, courses sponsored by finance and tourist mins. Maj, IDF, 1947-68. Vice chancellor, Chaine de Rottisseurs, Haifa; mem: comm, Isr Cancer League, Haifa; Masons, fmr master; BBB, Haifa C of C; Isr Mgmt Cen; Isr-Amer Friendship League; Isr-Brit, Isr-Philippines, Isr-Ger C of C's; Micha, Variety Tent 51; Friends Tel Aviv Mus; Isr Ins Assn; clubs: Rotary, Mt Carmel, chmn, f comm; Isr Ins. Author: Insurance, A Political Weapon; contbr to daily press and mags. Hobbies: skiing; tennis; riding; music. Home: 16 Isaac Ave, Haifa, Isr. Office: 47 Ha'atzmauth St, Haifa, Isr.

ARAD, Abraham, Isr, organization exec; b. Pol, June 10, 1907; s. Mendel and Hana (Akselrod); att HS, Pol; m. Cila Teiber, 1945; c: Ofra, Menahem. Mem exec comm, trade union dept, Histadrut, mem exec, Mapai Party. Home: 46 Arlosoroff St, Holon, Isr. Office: 93 Arlosoroff St, Tel Aviv, Isr.

ARAD, Abraham, Isr, engineer; b. Haifa, Isr, Apr 29, 1926; s. Aharon and Bella Kipperman; dipl, engr, Technion, Haifa, 1950; m. Yona Hochman, Tel Aviv, Aug 21, 1951; c: Shy, Ron, Chen. Cons engr since 1965; planning and devl coord, Min of Devl, 1958-65; tech div, Vulcan Battery Works, Haifa, 1951-57; dir: Isr Mining Ind, 1960-65; Negev Phosphates Co, 1960-63; Dead Sea Bromine Co, 1955-60. Lt, IDF, 1948-50. Chmn, research comm, Assn Engrs and Architects in Isr, dir, bldg research inst; mem, Engrs Fed, Haifa, gen secy, 1957-58. Chief ed, Hamehandes, monthly publ, Isr Engrs Fed. Home and office: 14a Nitzaaim St, Haifa, Isr.

ARAD, Shimshon, Isr, diplomat; b. Dec 24, 1923; BA, New Sch for Social Research, NY; m. Bilhah Milson; three c. Ambass, The Hague, Holland, since 1968; prin aide, US div, Min for Fgn Affairs, 1952-56; first secy, Isr Emb, Wash, 1956-58; consul in NY, counselor, Perm Mission to UN, 1958-62; dir, US div, Jerusalem, 1962-64; ambass, Mexico, 1964-68. J Brig, Eur, WW II; off, IDF. Fmr ed, J Brig Heb daily newspaper. Office: Min for Fgn Affairs, Jerusalem, Isr.

ARANOFF, Sanford, US, physicist; b. Shenandoah, Pa, Nov 18, 1937; s. Abe and Rose (Gershman); BS, U Miami, 1958; att

Yeshiva U, NYC, 1954-58; PhD, NYU, 1965; m. Paula Halpern, 1966; c: Rena. Asst prof, physics, Rutgers U, Newark, since 1965, fac adv, student physics sect, since 1968; asso cons, Data Analysis Assos, since 1969; research asst, Union Carbide Corp, Parma, O, 1957; teaching asst, NYU, 1958-59; research asst, Courant Inst of Math Sci, NYU, 1961-65; mem, tech staff, Bell Telephone Labs, Whippany, NY, 1967; cons, Stanford Research Inst, 1968-69; lectr, various commercial and instl sems. Mem: Amer Phys Soc; Amer Assn Physics Tchrs; AAUP; Natl Physics Hon Soc. Contbr papers and publs to profsl and sci jours. Recipient: Natl Sci Found Coop Grad F, NYU, 1959-60; Courant Inst F, 1961-65; Regents Advanced Coll Teaching F, NYU, 1962-65; Research Council Summer F, Rutgers U, 1967. Home: 867 W 181 St, New York, NY. Office: Physics Dept, Rutgers U, 110 Warren St, Newark, NJ.

ARANOV, Saul Irwin, US, rabbi; b. Bklyn, NY, Feb 21, 1938; s. Louis and Sarah (Goodkin); BA, Yeshiva Coll, 1959; MHL, Bernard Revel Grad Sch, 1963; ordained rabbi, Isaac Elchanan Theol Sem, 1963. Rabbi, Cong B'nai Yitzhok, since 1965; coord, Beth Din, RabCA, Phila region, since 1968; rabbi, Cong Beth Shalom, Rego Park, NY, 1963-65. Chaplain, Assn for J Children, since 1967; vice-pres, RabCA, Phila region, since 1967; mem, Phila Bd Rabbis. Home: 3901 E Roosevelt Blvd, Philadelphia, Pa. Study: B St and E Roosevelt Blvd, Philadelphia, Pa.

ARANOW, Edward Ross, US, attorney; b. NYC, Apr 30, 1909; s. Harry and Sarah (Rosenfeld); BA, Columbia Coll, 1929; LLB, 1932; m. Rita Abrons, July 11, 1941; c: Vicki Klein, Judith, Robert. Sr partner, Aranow, Brodsky, Bohlinger, Einhorn & Dann, since 1947; pvt practice, 1939-42; asso: Colby, Brown & Pollack, 1932-34; Szold & Brandwen, 1934-39. Maj, Judge Advocate Gen's Corps, 1942-46. Pres, Columbia Law Sch Alumni Assn, 1965-67; mem, Columbia Law Sch bd visitors; bd trustee, Scarsdale Adult Sch; mem: Amer, Intl, NY State, NY Co, Fed, and NYC Bar Assns; Judge Advocates Assn; Phi Beta Kappa; club, Sunningdale Country. Co-author: Proxy Contests for Corporate Control, 1957, rev ed, 1968; contbr to profsl jours. Recipient: dist alumni service medal, Columbia Alumni Assn, 1962; Royal Order of Vasa, Sweden, 1968. Home: 47 Colby Lane, Scarsdale, NY. Office: 469 Fifth Ave, New York, NY.

ARAZI, Shlomo R, Isr, engineer; b. Zverinez, Pol, 1902; s. Zvi and Miriam (Reichert) Tenenbaum; in Isr since 1920; CE, Poly Inst, Freiburg ,Ger, 1928; m. Gisele Saphir, Mar 24, 1936; c: Ephraim, Dan. Tech adv: Min of Finance, since 1954; Min for Fgn Affairs, since 1967; Weizmann Inst of Sci; Hadassah Med Org; State Commn of Ceremonies; chmn commn on sports installations; chmn, Hakirya commn; asst architect, Public Works Dept, 1929-41; quantity surveyor, PWD, of Pal Govt, 1948-54; dir: Hakirya off, PM, 1948-54; Dept of State Property Div, Min of Finance, 1954-67. Served, Haganah. Mem: Hadassah Council of Isr; Council of World Fed YMHA; intl counselor, Lions Intl; exec comm, Assn Engrs and Architects in Isr, chmn, Jerusalem br; found off bearer, Grand Lodge, Masons, Isr; fmr mem, bd dirs, Pal Sports Assn; secy, Pal Football Assn; chmn, Maccabi Org, Jerusalem; found, secy, Pal Olympic Comm; mem, bd dirs, 1st and 2nd Maccabiah; clubs: Pal Automobile, vice-pres, Automobile and Touring of Isr, hon life pres. Contbr articles on sports motoring, building works to local press; sports commentator, Pal Bc, Isr Bc Service, 1936-50. Recipient: Commander of Orders of Oronje-Nassau, Netherlands; Star of Afr, Liberia. Home: 18 Marcus St, Jerusalem, Isr. Office: Min of Finance, Hakirya, Jerusalem. Isr.

ARAZI, Tuvia, Isr, diplomat; b. Lodz, Pol, Nov 16, 1912; s. Abraham and Miriam (Kusmirak) Tennenbaum; license-es lettres, Sorbonne U, Paris; dipl, Ecole de Langues Orientales, Paris; m. Gallia Georgette, Nov 18, 1947; c: Myriam, Michael, Dina. Head, div State econ planning, Min for Fgn Affairs, since 1969; defense and political dept, JA, 1940-45; fmr alternate Isr delg to UN; mem, Isr delg, Pal Concilliation Comm meeting, Lausanne, 1949; counselor: Isr Legation, Turkey, 1950-52; Isr Emb, Arg, 1952-56; Isr Ambass to Peru, Columbia, Ecuador, Bolivia, 1956-60; dir, Brit Commonwealth dept, Min for Fgn Affairs, 1960-62; Ambass to Cyprus, 1962-69. Served, Haganah. Hobbies: gardening; archaeol; oriental affairs. Office: Min for Fgn Affairs, Jerusalem, Isr.

ARBEL, Abir, Isr, engineer; b. Tel Aviv, Isr, Feb 7, 1937; s. Joseph and Leah (Eliel); BSc, with distinction, Technion, Haifa, 1960; MS, U Minn, 1963, PhD, 1968; m Nomi Hirsch-

mann, Feb 7, 1964; c: Ronen. Sr lectr, Technion, since 1968; research sci, Honeywell Corporate Research Cen, 1963-66; sr engr, Westinghouse Elec Corp, 1966-68. Cpl, IDF, 1954-57. Contbr to sci jours. Hobbies: swimming, sailing. Home: 25A Hatichon St, Haifa, Isr. Office: Technion, Haifa, Isr.

ARDAY, Eugene J, US, dermatologist; b. Czech, Apr 23, 1902; s. Simon and Karolyn (Gross); in US since 1921; AB, W Reserve U, 1924, MD, 1929; m. Margaret Goldstein, Oct 14, 1928 (div); c: Greta Klein, Judith Reich, David; m. 2nd, Florence Roth, Dec 5, 1955. Staff dermat and syphilologist, Patton State Hosp since 1967; visiting dermat, syphilologist, Cleveland City Hosp, 1932-46; demonstrator dermat, W Reserve U, 1934-37; syphilologist, USPHS Clinic, 1940-44; cons dermat, instr, Sch of Nursing, Lutheran Hosp, 1935-60. Mem: ZOA; B'nai B'rith; Amer Phys F Comm, IMA; World Med Assn; AMA; O State Med Assn; Phi Lambda Kappa. Home: 606 E Sunset Dr, Redlands, Cal. Office: Patton State Hospital, Patton, Cal.

ARDEN, Eugene, US, educational admnr; b. New York, NY, June 25, 1923; s. Harry and Gussie; BA, NYU, 1943; MA, Columbia U, 1947; PhD, O State U, 1953; m. Sandra Arden, Nov 7, 1948; c: Stacey, Jonathan. Dean, Grad Fac Arts and Scis, LIU, since 1964; prof, chmn, dept Eng, CW Post Coll, 1958-62, dean, 1962-64. Pvt to lt, US Army, 1943-46. Vice-pres, Cong Tiferet Isr; mem: natl comm, Academic Comm on Soviet Jewry; pres adv comm, Nassau/Suffolk Council, B'nai B'rith, fmr pres, Cen Nassau Lodge, mem: Academic Lodge; fmr mem, bd dirs, YM-YWHA. Contbr to various jours. Home: 92 Lancia Dr, E Norwich, NY. Office: LIU, Greenvale, NY.

ARDON, Michael, Isr, educator; b. Berlin, Ger, Dec 12, 1928; s. Mordecai and Miriam (Banet); in Isr since 1934; MSc, Heb U, Jerusalem, 1953, PhD, 1957; m. Ora Palti, Nov 11, 1952; c: Nili, Dalia. Asso prof, inorganic chem, Heb U, since 1959; research asso: Cornell U; U of Chgo, 1957-59; Stanford U, 1956-57; visiting chem, Brookhaven Naval Lab, 1957. Cpl, signal corps, Haganah, IDF, 1942-49. Head, coord comm, Org of Profs and Tchrs in Isr Us and Research Insts. Author: Oxygen, 1965. Home: 4 Alharizi St, Jerusalem, Isr. Office: Heb U, Jerusalem, Isr.

ARDON-EISENSTAEDT, Joseph D, Isr, engineer, technical advisor; b. Sopniewka, Pol, July 25, 1903; s. Menachem and Feyga (Troib); in Isr since 1932; att: Tech U, Darmstadt, Ger; U Toulouse; U Caen; U Paris, all in Fr, MS, 1926; m. Shoshana Eisenstaedt, July 25, 1927; c: Esther, Amiel, Menachem. Found, tech dir, Ran Ltd, since 1933, first electrical product factory in Isr; elec engr, electric power sta, Grajewo, Pol, 1927-28; produc mgr, PePeGe, Grudziadz, Pol, 1928-32. RAF, 1945. Mem: Assn Engrs and Architects in Isr; Electrochemical Soc, NY; AAAS; Assn for Advancement Sci in Isr; Natl Council for Prevention Accidents; Masons; clubs: Automobile and Touring of Isr. Contbr to profsl jours. Hobbies: painting, photography. Home: 40 Herzl St, Ramat Gan, Isr. Office: Tadiran, 3 Hashalom Blvd, Tel Aviv, Isr.

ARENDT, Hannah, US, author; b. Hanover, Ger, Oct 14, 1906; d. Paul and Martha (Cohn); PhD, U Heidelberg, Ger, 1929; in US since 1941; m. Heinrich Blücher, Jan, 1940. U prof, New Sch for Social Research, since 1967; research f, Notgemeinschaft der Deutschen Wissenschaft, 1931-33; gen secy, Fr br, Youth Aliyah, 1935-38; research dir, Conf on J Relations, NY, 1944-46; chief ed, Schocken Books, NY, 1946-48; exec secy, J Cultural Reconstruction, NY, 1949-52; Guggenheim F, 1952-53. Mem, bd dir: Conf on J Relations; J Cultural Reconstruction; Judah Magnes Found. Author: Der Leibesgriff bei Augustin, 1930; Sechs Essays, 1947; The Origins of Totalitarianism, 1951; Rahel Varnhagen—the life of a Jewess, 1957; The Human Condition, 1958; Between Past and Future, 1961; Eichmann in Jerusalem, 1963; Men in Dark Times, 1968; contbr to profsl mags. Home: 370 Riverside Dr, New York, NY.

ARENS, Mosheh, Isr, engineer; b. Kaunas, Lith, Dec 27, 1925; s. Theodore and Rose (Goldberg); in Isr since 1948; BS, MIT, 1947; MS, Cal Inst Tech, 1953; m. Muriel Eisenberg, July 12, 1949; c: Yigal, Raanan, Aliza, Ruth. Vice-pres, engr, Isr Aircraft Ind, since 1962; asso prof, dept aero engr, Technion, since 1957; farmer, Mvo'ot Betar, 1949-51; design engr, Knappen, Tippets, 1951-52; project engr, Curtiss Wright, 1953-57. Tech sgt, US Army Corps Engrs, 1944-46. Pres, Brith Trumpeldor, US, 1947-48; mem, AIAA. Contbr to profsl jours Home: 49 Hagerot St, Savyon, Isr. Office: Lod Airport, Isr.

ARENSON, Nathan, US, radiologist; b. NYC, Mar 27, 1912; s. Morris and Rose (Aaronson); BS, CCNY, 1933; MD, NY Med Coll, 1937; m. Alice Gilbert, Dec 24, 1936; c: Michael, Ronald. Radiologist: Sacred Heart Hosp, since 1948; Med Cen Clinic, since 1949; att cons radiologist, Escambia Gen Hosp, since 1948; cons radiologist: US Naval Air Sta Hosp, since 1949; Elgin Air Force Base Hosp, since 1954; att radiologist, Mac-Million Memorial Hosp, Brewton, Ala; radiologist, Va Hosp, Roanoak, Va, 1941-42; asso radiologist, Watts Hosp, Durham, NC, 1945-47; lectr, U of NC, 1945-47; asso radiologist, Touro Infirmary, New Orleans, La, 1947-48. US Army MC, 1942-45. F: Intl Acad Med; dipl: Natl Bd Med Examiners, 1939; Amer Bd Radiology, 1947; mem: Amer Coll Radiology; Escambia Co, Fla State Med Socs; AMA; Radiological Soc N Amer; NY Acad Sci; S Radiological Conf; Gulf Coast Clinical Soc; dir, Natl Rifle Assn; clubs: Kiwanis; Pensacola Riffle and Pistol; Azalea City Rifle, pres. Contbr to profsl jours. Recipient: Bronze Star, 1945. Home: 312 N Sunset Blvd, Gulf Breeze, Fla. Office: Med Cen Clinic and Sacred Heart Hosp, Pensacola, Fla.

ARENT, Albert Ezra, US, attorney, educator; b. Rochester, NY, Aug 25, 1911; s. Hyman and Sarah (Weller); BA, Cornell U, 1932; LLB, Cornell U Law Sch, 1935; m. Frances Feldman, Nov 23, 1939; c: Stephen, Margery. Partner, law firm, Arent, Fox, Kintner, Plotkin and Kahn, and predecessor firms since 1944; adj prof, taxation, Georgetown U Law Cen, since 1952; bd dirs: Macke Co; Kent Washington Inc; Linden Corp; Carl M Freeman Inc; Madison Natl Bank; research asst, NY State Law Revision Commn, 1934; atty, off chief counsel, US Bur Internal Revenue, 1935-39; spec asst, atty gen, US Dept of Justice, 1939-44, chief trial atty, Alien Property Litigation Unit, 1942-44; lectr fed taxation, Amer U, 1948-52. Chmn, Amer Bar Assn Comms on: procedure in fraud cases, 1949-51, pension and profit sharing trusts, 1951-52, court procedure, 1955-57, chmn, taxation sect; chmn, comm on equal opportunity, Natl J Comty Relations Council, since 1967, natl vice-chmn, 1967-70; pres, JCC, Gtr Wash, 1957-61; vice-pres, Amer Immigration and Citizenship Conf, 1965-66; mem: governing council, AJCong, since 1961, mem, Wash chap since 1944; bd dirs, overseas educ fund, League of Women Voters, since 1959; exec bd, UJA, Gtr Wash, since 1950; commn on social action, UAHC and CCAR, since 1962; bd mgrs, Wash Heb Cong, 1953-56, 1969-70; Telluride Assn; Bar Assn, Wash DC; Amer and Fed Bar Assns; John F Kennedy chap, B'nai B'rith; Amer Judicature Soc; Phi Kappa Phi; Phi Beta Kappa; clubs: Woodmont Country; Natl Lawyers, Wash; Cornell, Wash. Contbr articles on tax law. Recipient: Stephen S Wise Medallion Award, Natl Capital Chap, AJCong, 1965. Home: 3108 Rolling Rd, Chevy Chase, Md. Office: 1815 H St, NW, Washington, DC.

ARGAMAN, Yerachmiel, Isr, engineer; b. Haifa, Isr, Apr 21, 1937; s. Shalom and Bella (Wendlinger); BSc, Technion, Haifa, 1961, MSc, 1964; PhD, U of Cal, Berkeley, 1968; m. Chaya Stern, Aug 8, 1960; c: Ohad, Neta, Vered. Sr lectr, Technion, since 1968; research engr, Engr Sci Inc, 1968. Mem: Amer Soc Civil Engrs; Amer Water Works Assn; Amer Water Resources Assn; Water Pollution Control Fed; Chi Epsilon Frat. Contbr several papers to profsl jours. Home: 128 Hagalil St, Haifa, Isr.

ARGOV, Eliezer, Isr, organization exec, communal leader; b. Jerusalem, July 17, 1920; s. Jacob and Dina (Rashkowitz) Margovsky; att: Heb Tchrs Coll; Heb U; m. Aliza Valensky, Sep, 1947; c: Dina, Jacob. Overseas dir, JNF head off; mem exec, JNF head off, Jerusalem, with org since 1956; mem: natl employment service council, Min of Lab, since 1959; Civil Service Comm, for govt appointments, since 1956; PM Comm, for selection students abroad, since 1960; co-found, dir, Kol Zion Lagolah, overseas bc service, WZO, 1950-56; prin, HS, for clerks Histadrut, 1949-50; PR repr, Min of Defense, 1948-49. Info off, Haganah Hqr, 1945-48, judge in Haganah, War of Independence; Brit Army, WW II. Vice grand pres, Isr dist, B'nai B'rith, pres, Jerusalem lodge, head, Youth Org, Isr repr, World Intl Council, and B'nai B'rith Cabinet on Isr; mem: Conf J Org, ZC; chmn, Beit Ha'am Cultural Cen, Jerusalem; vice-chmn, Soldier's Wfr Comm; mem, world exec, B'rith Ivrith Olamith; missions to: US, Can, S Afr, Eng, Eur. Author: Begiyus Male, 1950; ed: Iton Hamagen, 1947-48; Israel and Diaspora, 1960; contbr articles and essays to Isr and fgn J press. Hobbies: sports, drama. Home: 14 Binyamin Mitudella St, Jerusalem, Isr. Office: POB 283, Jerusalem, Isr.

ARGOV, Michael, Isr, painter; b. Vienna, Aus, Sep 1, 1920; s. Zvi and Ethel (Isler) Singer; in Isr since 1933; att: Cadoory Agric Sch; art schs: Avni, Streichman and Steimatsky, Tel Aviv; Ecole Nationale des Beaux Arts, Paris; m. Michaela Dikovsky, Aug 29, 1955; c: Claude, Igal. One-man shows: Sherman Gal, Tel Aviv, 1947; Gal St Placide, 1951; Gal A Cazelles, 1953; Gal Suillerot, 1955, all Paris; Tel Aviv Mus, 1955; Mus Modern Art, 1955; Gal Suillerot, 1956; Gal Gerard Mourgue, Paris, 1958; Palais des Beaux Arts, Brussels, 1958; Helena Rubinstein Pavillion, Tel Aviv Mus, 1959; Munic Mus, Ger, 1960; Kunsthaus Lemperts, Cologne, Ger, 1960; Gal Isr, Tel Aviv, 1961, 1964; Hanegev Mus, Beersheva, 1965; Massada Gal, 1967; Gordon Gal, 1969, both Tel Aviv; group shows in: Fr; Isr; US; Eng; Belgium; Ger; Can; repr in collections: Fr Natl Mus; Munic Mus Modern Art, Paris; Mus of Wuppertal; Mus Tel Aviv; Mus Modern Art, Haifa; Mus Ein Harod; Mus Hanegev, Beer sheva; pvt collections in: Fr, US, Gt Brit; Belgium; S Amer; Isr; Ger; Can; tchr: Argov Art Studio, since 1962; Avni Art Inst, Tel Aviv, 1954-62; public lectr, modern art, art appreciation on radio, at educ insts. Recipient: first prize of Isr painting, Paris; Grand Prix, Uthon Friesz, Paris; Grand Prix de Deauville, Fr. Home: 1 Gordon St, Tel Aviv, Isr.

ARIAN, Asher, Isr, political sci, educator; b. Cleveland, O, Aug 4, 1938; s. Leo and Yetta (Begun); in Isr since 1966; BA, cum laude, W Reserve U, 1961; MA, Mich State U, PhD, 1965; div; c: Leor, Aviv. Asso prof, chmn, political sci dept, Tel Aviv U, since 1966; guest lectr, Communications Inst, Heb U, Jerusalem, 1967-70; asst prof, W Reserve U, 1965-66; visiting asso prof, U Minn, 1968. Mem: Amer Political Sci Assn; Isr Assn Fgn Policy Studies. Author: Ideological Change in Israel, 1968; co-author, Hopes and Fears of Israelis: Consensus in Israel, 1971; ed, Elections in Israel-1969, pub 1971; co-ed, Empathy and Ideology: Aspects of Administrative Innovation, 1966; contbr articles to profsl publs. Recipient: training f, Social Sci Research Council, 1964-65. Home: 87 Hauniversita St, Ramat Aviv, Isr. Office: Dept of Political Sci, Tel Aviv U, Ramat Aviv, Isr.

ARIAN, David, Isr, government official; b. Silesia, Ger, May 28, 1903; in Isr since 1933; DJur et rerPol, Breslau U; grad, Berlin Inst for Fgn Langs, 1928; att Us: Munich; Freiburg; Breslau; Berlin; m. Bat Sheva Mirvis, Sep 14, 1942. Local govt adv, Govt of Lesotho, on behalf of UN, since 1969; dep dir, Isr Min of Lab, since 1954; admnr, Imperial Ethiopian Cen Personnel Agcy, Addis Ababa, for UN, since 1962; dep personnel commn, PM's off, 1951-62, dir, planning dept, 1948-51; Assessor, Berlin Police Force and Prussian PM's off, 1928-33; mem staff, Gen Mortgage Bank of Pal Ltd, 1934-43; planning dept: JA, 1943-47; Isr Emergency Council, 1947-48. Home: Bet Hakerem, Jerusalem, Isr.

ARIAN, Philip, US, educator; b. Cleveland, O, Sep 6, 1928; s. Leo and Yetta (Begun); BA, Yeshiva, U 1950, MS, 1956; BD, JTSA, 1952, MRE, 1956; m. Judith Krieger, Mar 15, 1951; c: Adam, Alisa, Joel. Educ dir, Temple Isr since 1956; prin, Heb Acad, since 1963. Mem, exec: Natl Council J Educ; Educ Assembly; Natl Bd J Sch Cons. Author: four plays; co-author, The Story of the Prayerbook, 1968; contbr to J publs. Home: 223 Euclid Ave, Albany, NY. Office: New Scotland Ave, Albany, NY.

ARICHA, Joseph, Isr, author, editor; b. Oliavsk, Russ, 1907; s. Yehoshua and Miriam (Freilechman) Dolgin; in Isr since 1925; m. Rivka Shiffman-Ben Sira; c: Amos, Ofra. Author: Lechem veHazon, 1933; Kanfey Kesef, 1936; Ud Mazal, 1937; be-Sanverim, 1939; Maroth beKahol, 1941; Baaley Yetzrim, 1946; Psak Din, 1949; Yom veLaila, 1952; Zeadim B'esh, 1956; Senacherib Bihuda, 1958; Mul Cherev, 1962; Sofer Hamelech, 1967; Knafaim leCoulom, 1969; Pgisha B'yerushalim, 1969; ed, La-Koreh Hatzair, juvenile monthly since 1947; Selected Stories, 3 vols, 1966; contbr short stories to periodicals; books translated into Eng, Ger, Yiddish, Bulgarian and Arabic. Pres: PEN club, Isr since 1969; mem, cen comm, Heb Authors Assn, since 1949. Recipient: spec lit award, best short story of year, 1943; Holon Lit prize, 1954; Brenner prize, 1960; Miriam Talfir prize, 1969. Hobbies: painting, photography. Home: 10 Karni St, Ramat Aviv, Tel Aviv, Isr.

ARIELI, Mordechai, Isr, artist, educator; b. Suwalki, Pol, May 29, 1909; s. Jacob and Zelda (Murzinsky); in Isr since 1926; dipl, Bezalel Art Sch, Jerusalem; BA, Ecole des Arts Supérieure, Paris; m. Esther Norber, June 6, 1936; c: Gideon, Ohaliva. Tchr, Coll Tchr Sem for Painting, since 1955. Exhbs at: Bienvale Modern Mus, Sao Paulo, Brazil; NY; Chgo; Phila; Paris. Mem: Soc Isr Painters and Sculptors. Recipient: Dizengoff Award, Tel Aviv, 1961; several awards from Min of Culture. Home and studio: 8 Karni St, Ramat Aviv, Isr.

ARIELY, Amnon, Isr, advertising exec; b. Tel Aviv, Isr, June 6, 1922; s. Jacob and Rosa (Weingart); m. Rina Fein, Aug 15, 1943; c: Ron, Uri, Tamar. Pres, A Ariely Ltd Advt Agcy, since 1966; dir, partner, Tal Ariely, Ltd, 1950-65; lectr, Sch Advt in Isr. Capt, Brit Army, J Brig, 1942-46. Mem: SAWA; exec council, Isr Advt Assn; bd, Comm Isr Vet Tennis Assn. Hobbies: tennis, filming. Home: 15 Hateena St, Tel Aviv, Isr. Office: 7 Kaplan St, Tel Aviv, Isr.

ARIES, Robert S, Fr, business exec; b. Sofia, Bulgaria, July 21, 1919; s. Robert and Sophie (Presente); BA, Amer Coll, ofia, 1937; MEcon, U Minn; MS, Yale U; BChE, PhD, Bklyn Poly Inst, 1947; div; c: Elsie Hassid, Vivian, Lynn. Exec vice-pres, dir, Prochim SA, Monte Carlo, since 1958; pres, Société Française de Développement et Investissement; cons engr, Aries Assos, since 1945; adj prof, chem engr and econ, Bklyn Poly Inst, 1947-57. Holder, 100 intl patents. Mem, numerous profsl orgs in US and Can. Author: Chemical Engineering Cost Estimation, 1955; Rentabilité d'un Procédé Chimique, 1958; L'expertise scientifique des oeuvres d'art, 1965; i/c preparation, catalogue, works of Mané-Katz. Recipient: Army-Navy "E" for excellence, 1945; research medal, Pulp Chem Assos, 1956. Home: 1 rue Henri Dunant, Monte Carlo, Monaco. Office: 5 Avenue de L'Opéra, Paris, Fr.

ARKUSH, J Robert, US, attorney; b. NYC, Nov 25, 1906; s. Joseph and Janet (Hein); att Syracuse U, 1925-27; BA, UCLA, 1929; LLB, Stanford U Law Sch, 1932; m. Bertha Rosenberg, May 23, 1929; c: Lois Newiger, Roberta Schwartz. Pvt practice since 1932. Trustee, Wilshire Blvd Temple, since 1956; pres, Camp Hess Kramer, Inc, since 1960; fmr: pres: Natl Fed Temple Brotherhoods; S Cal Council; Beverly Fairfax J Comty Cen; Westside J Comty Cen; vice-pres, J Cens Assn; trustee: UAHC; HUC. Home: 390 S Hauser Blvd, Los Angeles, Cal. Office: 416 W 8 St, Los Angeles, Cal.

ARLOW, Jacob A, US, psychiatrist; b. NYC, Sep 3, 1912; s. Adolph and Ida (Feldman); BS, NYU, 1932, MD, 1936; m. Alice Diamond, Oct 31, 1936; c: Michael, Allan, Seth, Jonathan. Pvt practice, NYC, since 1942; clinical prof, psycht, SUNY, since 1962, mem fac since 1955; research asso psycht, Columbia U, since 1944; res neuropsycht, USPHS, 1938-39; asst psycht, Kings Co Hosp, 1941; asst, clinical neur, Montefiore Hosp, 1942-44; instr, neur, Coll Phys and Surgs, Columbia U, 1942-44; cons psycht, Pride of Judea Children's Home, 1940-45. Pres, Amer Psychoanalytic Assn, 1960-61; treas, Intl Psychoanalytic Assn, 1961-63; trustee, NY Psychoanalytic Inst; mem: AMA; Amer Psychiatric Assn; NY Psych Assn. Contbr to profsl jours. Home: 94 Wildwood Rd, Great Neck, NY. Office: 120 W 59 St, New York, NY.

ARMON, Haim Dov, Isr, author; b. Aug 8, 1896; in Isr since 1939; passed librarianship exams, Berlin. Co-found, dir, Rambam Circle, since 1955; fmr: clerk, J Comty, Berlin; asst to chief libr, J Libr, Berlin; social worker, Tel Aviv-Yaffa Munic. Aus Army, WW I. Author: Otzar Zuta; Masehet Derech Eretz Zuta; 20 monographs; adaptations and trans, legends on Rambam; pub selected chaps from Mishna Tora by the Rambam; contbr: to Yiddish press; to press in Isr and abroad. Home: 48 Bin Nun St, Tel Aviv, Isr.

ARNDT, Charles H, NZ, barrister; b. Wellington, NZ, Sep 23, 1905; s. Charles and Rae (Moeller); LLB, Vic U, Wellington, 1927, LLM, 1932; m. Rona Heinemann, Oct 21, 1953; c: Rosalie, Susan. Partner, C J O'Regan, Arndt & Peters, barristers, solicitors, since 1947; sr counsel of cases in NZ Supr Court and Court of Appeals, since 1947; partner, Ongley, O'Donovan and Arndt, barristers, solicitors, 1930-47. NZ Expeditionary Force, 1941-45. Hon solicitor, Wellington Heb Cong, since 1956; hon treas, NZ sect, Intl Commn of Jurists, since 1961; mem: Wellington Dist Law Soc; NZ Masonic Constitution; fmr master, B'nai B'rith; clubs: Racing of Wellington; Commercial Travellers of Wellington. Ed, supplement 10, MacDonalds Law of Workers' Compensation in New Zealand, 2nd ed. Hobbies: rugby, cricket, golf, bowls. Home: 41 Central Terr, Kelburn, Wellington, NZ. Office: 324 Lambton Quay, Wellington, NZ.

ARNHEIM, Rudolf, US, psychologist; b. Berlin, Ger, July 15, 1904; s. Georg and Betty (Gutherz); in US since 1940; PhD, U Berlin, 1928; m. Mary Frame, Apr 11, 1953; c: Margaret. Prof, psych of art, Carpenter Cen for the Visual Arts, Harvard U, since 1968; visiting prof, grad fac, New Sch for Social Research, 1933-68; mem, psych dept, Sarah Lawrence Coll, 1943-68. Pres, Amer Soc for Aesthetics, 1959-60, bd trustees, 1966-68; f, Guggenheim Found, 1941-42. Author: Art and Visual Perception, 1954; Film as Art, 1957; Picasso's Guernica, 1962; A Psychology of Art, 1966; asso ed, publs, Intl Film Inst, L of N, Rome, 1933-38; contbr to profsl jours. Home: 19 Garden St, Cambridge, Mass. Office: Carpenter Center for Visual Arts, Harvard U, Cambridge, Mass.

ARNON, Isaac, Isr, agricultural researcher, educator; b. Antwerp, Belgium, June 22, 1909; s. Salomon and Malka (Urbach) Aronovitch; in Isr since 1932; MSc, Fac of Agric, Gembloux; PhD, Heb U; m. Hilda Gunzig, 1929; c: Dan, Gideon. Dir: Research Center for Protected Crops, since 1968; Inst Field Crop Research, 1945-58; Agric Experiment Sta, Neve Yaar, 1945-58; Volcani Inst Agric Research, 1958-68. Lt, Cavalry, 1931-32. Prin contribs: modernization of crop produc in Isr. Chmn, panel experts org, agric research, FAO, Rome, mem, panel experts org, agric devl; corresp, Fr Acad Agric, Paris. Author: Organization and Administration of Agricultural Research, 1968; Crop Production in Dry Regions, 2 vols. Recipient: Isr prize for agric, State of Isr, 1971. Hobby: archaeol. Home: 12 Hazeitim St, Ramat Gan, Isr. Office: Volcani Inst of Agric Research, Bet Dagan, Isr.

ARNON, Jacob, Isr, economist; b. Amsterdam, Holland, Oct 3, 1913; s. Arjeh and Rosette (Asscher) van Amerongen; in Isr since 1948; DEcon, U Amsterdam, 1940; m. Louise Asscher, May 16, 1940; c: Arjeh, Josseef, Jehuda. Dir, Auth for Econ Planning, Min of Finance, dir Bur of Budget, 1952-56, fmr, dir gen; controller diamonds, Min of Trade and Industry, 1948-56. Fmr chmn: Dutch Zionist Youth Movement; Dutch Zionist Student Movement; Dutch Zionist Org; delg, WZC, Basle, 1946; hon mem, Diamond Control Commn, Holland. Contbr articles to journals. Home: 64 Herzl Ave, Jerusalem, Isr. Office: Min of Finance, Jerusalem, Isr.

ARNON, Joseph, Isr, educator; b. Lwow, Pol, Nov 15, 1911; s. Hertz and Laura (Hertzig) Halpern; in Isr since 1932; degs in psychol and educ: U Warsaw; Sem, Tel Aviv; postgrad studies, London, 1953-54; m. Carna Drenger, 1937; c: Asa, Avithal Milstein, Elisha. Lectr, psychol, secondary sch headmaster, Givathaviva, Hashomer Hatzair Study Cen, since 1949; mem Kibbutz Ein Hamifratz; insp, secondary schs, Kibbutz Arzi Movement, 1957-65; tchr, headmaster, Mossad Naaman, 1949-57. J Brig, Brit Army, 1941-45. Mem cen exec, Tchrs Org. Home: Kibbutz Ein Hamifratz, Isr.

ARNON, Michael, Isr, diplomat; b. Vienna, Aus, Apr 10, 1925; s. Israel and Melanie (Luft) Garfunkel; in Isr since 1938; dipl, intl affairs, U London; m. Hadara Strod, Feb 24, 1948; c: Ehud, Derit. Secy, Isr Cabinet, Jerusalem, since 1968; journalist, Jerusalem Post, 1945-48; press off, Min for Fgn Affairs, 1949-51; press attache, Isr Emb, London, 1951-54; dir, Isr Govt Press Off, 1955-56; counselor, Isr Emb, Wash, DC, 1956-61; dir, dept info, Min for Fgn Affairs, 1961-62; ambass to Ghana, 1962-65; consul gen, NY, 1965-68. IDF, 1948-49. Home: 32 Palmach St, Jerusalem, Isr. Office: Prime Minister's Office, Jerusalem, Isr.

ARNON, Ruth, Isr, biochemist; b. Tel Aviv, June 1, 1933; d. Alexander and Sarah (Perlman) Erez; MSc, Hebrew U, Jerusalem, 1954, PhD, 1960; m. Uriel Arnon, June 6, 1955; c: Michal, Yoram. Sr scientist, Weizmann Inst of Sci, Rehovot, since 1966; research asso, Rockefeller Inst, NY, 1960-63; visiting asso prof, U Wash, 1968-69. Lt, IDF Navy, 1955-56. Contbr pubs to tech profsl lit, jours, books. Mem: Isr Biochem Soc; NY Acad Sci. Home: 6 Frug St, Rehovot, Isr. Office: Weizmann Inst, Rehovot, Isr.

ARNSTEIN, Joseph M, US, business exec; b. Chgo, Ill, Jan 4, 1913; s. Julius and Sophie (Newman); PhB, U Chgo, 1933; m. Helen Gallagher, Jan 4, 1941; c: Joseph, Hugh, Mary, Judee. Sr vice-pres, Esquire Inc, since 1959, stat, 1935-51, circulation dir, 1951-55, vice-pres, circulation, 1955-59; stat, Walgreen Drug Co, 1934-35. Mem: Alumni Assn, U Chgo; Amer Stamp Dealers Assn; fmr, mem, bd dirs: United Givers Fund, Yonkers, NY; Henry S Richards Boys Club; Cen Registry, past chmn. Home: 37 Ridge St, Crestwood, Tuckahoe, NY. Office: 488 Madison Ave, New York, NY.

ARON, Milton, Can, rabbi; b. Trenton, NJ, Apr 19, 1917; s. Berl and Ida (Fishkin); desc of Gaon of Vilna; in Can since 1947; BA, U Chgo, 1937; ordained rabbi, Heb Theol Coll, 1940; DD, U Chgo Divinity Sch, 1941; m. Leona Kriloff,

Sep 7, 1941. Rabbi, Shaarey Zedek Syn, since 1947. Staff chaplain, lt col, USAF, 1940-45. Chmn, Council of Rabbis, Winnipeg, since 1956; natl pres, JNF, Can, since 1963; exec vice-pres, JNF of Amer, since 1966; natl chmn, JNF Found of Can, since 1958; exec dir, Hillel Found, 1945-47; mem: RA; Masons; B'nai B'rith; bd: Comty Chest; Boy Scouts; Family Bur; Alcohol Found; Handicapped Children; Art Found. Home: 352 Oxford St, Winnipeg, Can. Study: Wellington Crescent, Winnipeg, Can.

ARON, Raymond C F, Fr, educator, author, columnist; b. Paris, March 14, 1905; s. Gustave and Suzanne (Levy); agrégé de philosophie, Ecole Normale Supérieure, 1928; docteur es lettres, 1938; DHC: Harvard U, 1958; Basel U, 1960; Brussels U, 1962; Columbia U, 1966; Southhampton U, 1968; m. Suzanne Gauchon, 1933; c: Dominique Schnapper, Laurence. Dir, Ecole Pratique des Hautes Etudes, since 1968; prof, Sorbonne, 1955-68. Author: many books including: Introduction à la Philosophie de l'Histoire, 1938; L'Opium des Intellectuels, 1955; Paix et Guerre entre les Nations, 1962. Mem: Académie des Sciences Morales et Politiques; Amer Phil Soc; fgn hon mem, Amer Acad Arts and Sci. Recipient: Chevalier de la Légion d'Honneur. Home: 34 ave du Président Kennedy, Paris 16, Fr. Office: 6 rue de Tournon, Paris 6, Fr.

ARON, Roberto T, Isr, attorney; b. Arg, Nov 1, 1915; LLB, Santiago U, Chile; m. 2nd, Eva Coriat, Dec 14, 1948; c: Haim, Silvia, Daniel. Atty: initiator, promotor, Kiron project, Isr. Pres, Council World Gen Zionists, mem, World Zionist Action Comm; chmn: Aliyah Comm, Lib Party, fmr mem, Party exec; Isr Exec Comm; Isr Amer Med Cen, mem, bd dirs; Clal; Finance Bank, Isr; Otzar Maityashvut; fmr pres; ZF, Chile; Iamico; mem: presidium, Latin Amer Gen Zionist Confd. Contbr articles to jours. Home: 17 Nevo St, Ramat Gan, Isr. Office: 1 Melchet St, Tel Aviv, Isr.

ARON, Wellsley Pinhas, Isr, business exec; b. London, June 18, 1901; s. Maurice and Agnes (Gerechter); BA, Cambridge U, 1926; m. Rose Hoffman, Mar 21, 1927; c: Sharona Broza, Ylona Zedlitz. Dir, Hotel Devl, Isr, since 1967; cons, PR, Pan Am Airways, NY since 1950; tchr, Herzliya HS, Tel Aviv, 1926-27; asst political secy, WZO, 1927-30; mgn dir, Aron Advt Ltd, 1930-69. Maj, Royal Army Service Corps, 1939-45; Haganah, 1947-49; Isr mil mission, US, 1948-50. Chmn, Rotary Symposium, Problems of Peace, Jerusalem, 1970; found, Habonim, London; co-found, Bar Kochba Assn; fmr: head, Land and Lab, Pal, US; lectr, ZOA; vice-pres, J Ex-servicemen Assn, Eng; exec mem, Isr Maritime League; mem, athletic team repr Gt Brit, 1st Maccabiah games; capt, Pal Maccabee hockey team; clubs: Caesaria Golf and Country, fmr chmn; Rotary, Tel Aviv, fmr pres, fmr dist gov. Home: 18 Hazayit St, Tel Aviv, Isr. Office: 38 Ahad Ha'am St, Tel Aviv, Isr.

ARONFREED, Eva, US, educator, public relations cons; b. Phila, Pa, July 15, 1911; d. Joseph and Johanna (Scheindling); BFA, U of Pa, 1933, AM, 1947, PhD, 1958. Asso prof: Glassboro State Coll, on fac since 1962; social studies, Monmouth Coll, 1961-62. Women's Army Corps, 1942-45, maj, USAF, since 1957. Chmn, natl comm on case studies, Amer PR Assn, 1957-59; mem: Intl Union Local Auths; Amer Soc for Public Admn; Pi Gamma Mu; AAUP; Amer Assn U Women; Amer Political Sci Assn; PR Soc of Amer; Phila PR Assn; Amer Acad Political and Social Sci. Author: Public Relations As A Function of City Government, 1958; Public Relations As A Function of Local Government in The US, 1961; contbr to profsl jours. Recipient: cert appreciation, World Conf Local Govt, 1961. Spec interests: travel, theater, sports. Home: 403 S Cummings Ave, Glassboro, NJ. Office: Glassboro State Coll, Glassboro, NJ.

ARONIN, Jeffrey Ellis, US, architect; b. London, Eng, Aug 16, 1927; s. Joseph and Bertha (Danziger); in US since 1939; BArch, U Man, Can, 1949; MArch, McGill U, Montreal, Can, 1951. Pvt practice since 1949, own practice since 1957; lectr, architecture: Amer Inst Architects; U Meteorological Soc; U Cincinnati; U Miami; U Fla; U Va; Columbia U; U of Pa; Pa State U; U Man; Ga Inst of Tech; Ala Polytech Inst; Clemson Coll, SC; Travelers Research Inst; Pratt Inst, Kiwanis; B'nai B'rith; Us: Arizona State, Ball State; Case W Reserve; Howard; Ill; Kent State; Ky; Minn; Notre Dame; O; O State; Tulane; Va; Wash; Tuskegee Inst; moderator, radio series, Architecture for the Good Life and Architecture in the Space Age, sta WNYC, NY, and Voice of Amer; architect: Frank Grad & Sons, Newark, NJ, 1951-52; Shreve Lamb and Harmon, NYC, 1952-53; Voorhees, Walker

Foley & Smith and its successors, 1954-56; architect of syns; design of model residence on NBC Home Show, 1954; other projects include: Philippine Pavilion, NY World's Fair; Nigerian Emb; NY Public Libr, Edenwald br; US Gen PO, NY. F, Royal Inst British Architects; mem: Amer Inst Architects, vice-pres, 1969, fmr chmn, visitors comm, NY chap, publicity comm, 1967 conv, mem, comms on natural diaster and natl safety in bldgs, past chmn, speakers bur, NY chap; Mayor's Panel of Architects; Architectural League, NY, past chmn, fgn exhbs comm; NY Soc of Architects, mem, comms on admn bldg code, city planning and zoning, publs of state leg; Natl Inst of Architectural Educ, past chmn, activities comm; Royal Architectural Inst of Can; hon, Colegio Nacional de Arquitectos, Mexico; Sociedad de Arquitectos Mexicanos; Man Assn of Architects; Brit-Amer C of C; Danish-Amer Soc; Swed C of C in USA; Amer-Scandinavian Found; guest of hon, Sociedad Venezolana de Arquitectos, 1966. Author: Climate and Architecture, 1963; contbr to profsl and lay jours. Hobbies: chess, philately, swimming, golf, opera. Home: 389 Woodmere Blvd, Woodmere, LI, NY. Office: 101 Park Ave, New York, NY.

ARONOV, Aaron M, US, business exec; b. Montgomery, Ala, Dec 22, 1919; s. Jake and Nora (Varlow); att U Ala; m. Marjorie Schoenbaum, Sep 2, 1945; c: Jake, William, Teri. Pres: Aronov Realty Co; Aronov Tire, 1943-52; dir, Peoples Bank & Trust, Montgomery. Mem, bd dirs, Intl Council Shopping Cens; pres: Agudath Isr Syn, 1950-52; C of C, 1946; co-chmn, NCCJ, Ala; chmn: Water Works and Sanitary Sewer Bd, Montgomery, 1952; mem: Public Athletic Bd, Montgomery; Masons; Shriners; Elks; Montgomery Assn Home Builders; Montgomery Real Estate Bd; club, Sales Execs. Home: 2088 Myrtlewood Dr, Montgomery, Ala. Office: 532 S Court St, Montgomery, Ala.

ARONOVITCH, Michael, Can, physician; b. Montreal, Que, Can, Apr 15, 1910; s. Isaac and Minnie (Miller); BS, McGill U, 1931, MD, 1935; m. Katherine Silver, Dec 30, 1945; c: Jane, Stephen, Carole, Isaac. Pvt practice since 1946; med dir, Mt Sinai Sanitorium, since 1939; asst prof, med and clinical med, McGill U; phys: Grace Dart Hosp, 1940; Royal Vic Hosp, 1939; J Gen Hosp; cons, Dept of Vet Affairs, 1946, all Montreal. Maj, Royal Can Army MC, 1942-46. F: Royal Coll Phys, Can; Amer Coll Chest Phys; Amer Coll Phys; mem: Montreal Clinical Soc; Can Med Soc; Montreal Medico-Chirurgical Soc; contbr to med publs. Home: 1530 Dumfries Rd, Town of Mt Royal, Que, Can. Office: 4119 Sherbrooke W, Westmount, Que, Can.

ARONOWICZ, Dan, Isr, composer; b. Mlawa, Pol, Dec 25, 1909; s. Zvi and Chaja (Prusak); in Isr since 1947; att: Natl Sch of Music, Varsovie, 1929-31; Ecole Supérieure de Musique, Paris, 1936-40. Music critic, L'Information d'Israel. Composer, symphony, symphonic poems, Israeli suite, numerous overtures, quartets, songs. Mem: League of Isr Composers. Home: 25 Hauniversita St, Tel Aviv, Isr.

ARONOWICZ, Isaac, Isr, business exec; b. Lodz, Pol, Aug 27, 1923; s. Samuel and Yoheved (Laib); in Isr since 1934; master mariner, John Cass Sch Navigation, London, 1946; BSc, summa cum laude, Georgetown U Sch Fgn Service, Wash, DC, 1960; MBA, Columbia U Grad Sch Bus, 1961; m. Irene Bradfield, May 27, 1953; c: Ella, Ronit. Gen mgr, dir, Sefinot Ltd; dir, Mediterranean W Afr Lines Ltd, both since 1966; found, Sela, Kibbutz Meuchad Shipping Co; master, vessels, Zim Navigation Co Ltd, 1948-58. Home and office: 92 Gordon St, Tel Aviv, Isr.

ARONOWITZ, Alfred G, US, journalist; b. Bordentown, NJ, May 20, 1928; s. Morris and Lena (Goldman); BA, Rutgers U, 1950; m. Ann Wolkenheim, June 5, 1954; c: Myles, Brett, Joel. Music critic: New York Post, since 1969, feature writer, 1957-63, 1966-68; Life Mag, 1968; NY Times, 1966; ed, Lakewood Daily Times, NY, 1950-51; reporter, Newark Evening News, 1951-57; mgr, The Middle Class, rock'n roll band, 1963-65; contrib ed, Saturday Evening Post, 1957-63. Mem: Amer Newspaper Guild; Natl Soc Interior Designers; Phi Beta Kappa. Author: Ernest Hemingway, The Life and Death of A Man, 1961. Hobby: philately. Home: 1615 N Wood Ave, Roselle, NJ. Office: c/o William Morris Agency, 1350 Ave of Americas, New York, NY.

ARONOWITZ, Samuel E, US, attorney; b. Albany, NY, May 24, 1890; s. Max and Dora (Ettelson); BA, Dartmouth Coll, 1911; LLB, Albany Law Sch, 1914. Sr partner, O'Connell & Aronowitz, since 1924; dir: Natl Commercial Bank & Trust

Co, Albany, since 1939; Midland Abstract; trustee, City & Country Savings Bank. Mem, exec bd: Albany Med Cen Hosp; Mh Assn; JWF; JDC; JDA; Temple Beth Emeth, 1925-43; J Social Service, 1936-45; C of C, 1942-48; ARC, 1935-40; Interracial Council, 1927-39; pres, JCC, 1939-42, hon pres since 1943, all Albany; pres: Albany Co Bar Assn, 1937; Fed Bar Assn, 3rd Jud Dist, 1940; SUNY, Albany, Benevolent Assn, since 1949; chmn, banking law sect, NY State Bar Assn, 1962; mem, bd f, Brandeis U, since 1952; state cdr, Amer Legion, 1925; clubs: Albany-Colonie Country; Dartmouth, NYC. Home: DeWitt Clinton Hotel, Albany, NY. Office: 100 State St, Albany, NY.

ARONS, Arnold B, US, physicist, educator; b. Lincoln, Neb, Nov 23, 1916; s. Solomon and Esther (Rosen); ME, Stevens Inst Tech, 1937, MS, 1940; PhD, Harvard U, 1943; hon MA, Amherst Coll, 1953; m. Joan Rendall, Aug 17, 1942; c: Marion, Janet, Kenneth, Paul. Prof, U Wash, since 1968; trustee, Woods Hole Oceanographic Inst since 1963, asso, phys oceanography, since 1948, staff mem since 1943; asst, asso prof, Stevens Inst Tech, 1946-52; prof, Amherst Coll, 1952-68. Pres, Amer Assn Physics Tchrs, since 1967; f, AAAS; mem: Amer Phys Soc; Amer Geophys Union; Geochem Soc of Amer; Natl Sci Tchrs Assn; Tau Beta Pi; Sigma Xi; Commn on Coll Physics, 1962-68. Contbr to sci jours. Recipient, f: NSF, 1962-63; Guggenheim, 1957-58. Home: 10313 Lakeshore Blvd NE, Seattle, Wash. Office: Department of Physics, U of Wash, Seattle, Wash.

ARONS, Marvin Shield, US, physician; b. Derby, Conn, Feb 13, 1931; s. George and Pauline (Shield); BS, Yale U, 1951; DMD, Harvard U, 1955; MD, U of Md, Baltimore, 1957; m. Cyvia Russian, June 24, 1956; c: Mark, Jeffrey. Att plastic surg, Yale-New Haven Hosp, since 1965; asst clinical prof, plastic surg, Yale Med Sch, since 1965; clinical asso, Natl Cancer Inst, 1959-61; clinical asso, sr asst surg, NIH, USPHS; Bethesda, Md, both 1959-61; sr surg res, Georgetown U Hosp, 1961-62; res and chief res, plastic surg, U Tex Med Cen, 1962-65. Bd dir, New Haven JCC; secy, alumni off, Hopkins Grammar Sch, New Haven; mem, alumni schs comm, Yale; mem: Amer Cleft Palate Assn; Amer Coll Surg F, Oct 1970; Amer Fed Clinical Research; Amer Soc Maxillofacial Surg; Amer Soc Plastic and Reconstructive Surgs; Conn State Med Soc; NE Soc Plastic and Reconstructive Surg; New Haven Co Med Assn; New Haven Dent Assn; New Haven Med Assn; NY Regional Soc Plastic and Reconstructive Surg; Plastic Surg Research Council; Sigma Xi; Singleton Surg Soc; club, Yale, New Haven, mem, alumni schs comm. Contbr numerous papers to med jours. Recipient: awards, Amer Acad Dent Med, 1957; Amer Cancer Soc F, 1963-64, 1964-65. Home: 404 Wildwood Dr, Orange, Conn. Office: 2 Church St S, New Haven, Conn.

ARONSON, Boris Solomon, US, stage designer, artist; b. Kiev, Russ, Oct 15, 1900; s. Solomon and Dvora (Turfsky); father was chief rabbi, Kiev, later, Tel Aviv; in US since 1923; m. Lisa Jalowetz, June 5, 1945; c: Marc. Stage designer and artist since 1920; designed sets for numerous Broadway plays, including: The Crucible, 1953; My Three Angels, 1953; A View from the Bridge, 1955; The Diary of Anne Frank, 1955; Bus Stop, 1955; Orpheus Descending, 1956; J B, 1958; Coriolanus, 1959; Judith, 1962; Fiddler on the Roof, 1964; Cabaret, 1966; Mourning Becomes Electra, 1967; The Price, 1968; Zorba, 1968; represented in numerous exhibs; one-man shows of paintings in leading gals, NY, Cal, Eur; created art work: Temple Sinai, Wash, DC, 1961; Comty Cen Syn, Sands Point, LI. Mem: United Scenic Artists. Author: Marc Chagall, 1923; Modern Graphic Art, 1923. Recipient: Guggenheim F, 1950; award for stage designs, Amer Theatre Wing, 1950-51; Ford Found F, 1962; Tony Awards for: Rose Tattoo, 1952; Cabaret, 1967; Zorba, 1969. Home and office: 1 W 89 St, New York, NY.

ARONSON, David, US, rabbi; b. Ulla-Vitebsk, Russ, Aug 1, 1894; s. Yekuthiel and Yetta (Kudritzin); desc of Gaon of Vilna; in US since 1906; BA, NYU, 1916; MA, Columbia U, 1917; ordained rabbi, JTSA, 1919, DHL, 1946; DD, U Judaism, 1969; m. Bertha Friedman, May 1, 1927; c: Raphael, Hillel. Prof, rabbs, U Judaism, LA, since 1959, visiting prof, 1950; rabbi em, Beth El Syn, Minneapolis, Minn, since 1959, rabbi, 1924-59; rabbi: Camp Upton, US Army, LI, NY, 1917-19; Salt Lake City, Utah, 1920-21; Duluth, Minn, 1922-24; visiting lectr, JTSA, 1944-45. Mem: Minn Rabb Assn; League for Rel Lab; Amer Acad for J Research; J Natl Workers Alliance; Natl Commn on J Chaplaincy; Minn Citizens League; Metrop Inst of Art; delg, Amer J Conf,

1943-47: fmr: gov's Hum Rights Comm, Minn; study tours, J Comtys, Eur, Russ; repr to Far E, World Council of Syns; pres, RA; mem: bd dirs: Minn Fed for J Service; Round Table of Chr and J; ZOA; Amer Friends Heb U; Talmud Torah; J Family and Children's Service; bd trustees, JTSA; club, Standard. Author: The Jewish Way of Life, 1946; asso ed, American Jewish World, 1930-59; contbr to Eng-J press. Recipient: Solomon Schechter citation, JTSA, 1950; dist citizens award, Minn, 1959; dist communal service award, Minneapolis Fed for J Service, 1959. Home: 8555 Saturn St, Los Angeles, Cal. Office: 6525 Sunset Blvd, Los Angeles, Cal.

ARONSON, Joseph, US, interior architect; b. Buffalo, NY, Dec 22, 1898; s. Max and Jennie (Simon); BArch, Columbia Sch of Architecture, 1923; m. Henriette Mayer, Oct 24, 1930; c: Joseph. Cons, pvt practice, since 1922. US Army, 1918. Vice-pres, Victorian Soc in Amer; mem: Architects League, NY, Soc Architectural Hist; Intl Castles Inst, Amsterdam. Author: Book of Furniture and Decoration, 1936, rev eds, 1941, 1952; Ency of Furniture, 1938; New Ency of Furniture, 1967; contbr to profsl jours. Home: Townsend Hollow, Pine Hill, NY. Office: 118 E 37 St, New York, NY.

ARONSON, Samuel F, US, physician, educator; b. Seattle, Wash, July 15, 1910; s. Harry and Jenny (Shifrin); BS, U Wash, 1931; MD, Northwestern U, 1936; m. Elma Kahn, June 17, 1934; c: Judith Beck, Nina Cunningham. Pvt practice since 1937; asso clinical prof, U Wash Med Sch, since 1958, fac mem since 1952; electrocardiographer, cons, Kings Co Hosp, Seattle, 1947-61. Maj, US Army, 1940-47. Pres: Wash State Heart Assn, 1956-58; att staff, Kings Co Hosp, 1959-60; f: Amer Coll Angiology; Amer Coll Cardiology; Council on Clinical Cardiology; AHA; mem: Seattle Acad Internal Med; Wash State Soc Internal Med. Contbr to med jours. Home: 2815-69 Ave SE, Mercer Island, Wash. Office: 1316 Madison, Seattle, Wash.

ARONSON, Seymour, US, chemist; b. New Britain, Conn, Jan 23, 1929; s. Joseph and Ida (Isaacson); BA, Yeshiva U, NY, 1950; PhD, Bklyn Poly Inst, 1954; m. Judith Ralston; c: Debrah, Susan, Elaine. Asso prof, dept chem, Bklyn Coll, since 1968; research chem: Westinghouse Elec Corp, 1955-60; Brookhaven Natl Lab, 1960-68. F, Amer Inst Chems; mem: Amer Chem Soc; AAAS; fmr, chmn, educ comm, Heb Acad of Suffolk Co. Contbr publs to sci and tech jours. Home: 333 Laurel Rd, W Hempstead, NY.

ARONSTEIN, Georges, Belgium, attorney; b. Brussels, March 14, 1904; att Athenee de Saint-Gilles, Brussels; docteur en droit, licencie en sci politiques, U Libre, Brussels; m. Nina Semenova, Jan 7, 1932; c: Claude-Serge. Atty, Court of Appeals, since 1927; dir gen, ICA, London, Buenos Aires, Moscow, 1931-50. Maj, Belgian Army, 1940-45. Pres, Ligue Belge pour la Defense des Droits de l'Homme; bd dirs, Centrale d'Oeuvres Sociales Juives, and others. Recipient: OBE, and others. Home: 217 ave Brugmann, Brussels 18, Belgium.

ARROW, Kenneth J, US, economist; b. NYC, Aug 23, 1921; s. Harry and Lillian (Greenberg); BS, CCNY, 1940; MA, Columbia U, 1941, PhD, 1951; LLD, U Chgo, 1967; m. Selma Schweitzer, Aug 31, 1947. Prof, econ, Harvard U, since 1968; econ, Pres' Council Econ Advs, 1962; research asso, Cowles Commn for Research in Econ, 1947-49; prof, econ and stat, Stanford U, 1949-68. Capt, US Army Air Corps, 1942-46. F: Inst of Math Stat; Amer Stat Assn; Amer Acad Arts and Sci; mem: exec commn, Amer Econ Assn; Natl Acad Sci; Amer Phil Soc; fmr pres: Inst of Mgmt Sci; Econometric Soc. Author: Social Choice and Individual Values, 1951; co-author: Studies in the Mathematical Theory of Inventory and Production, 1958; Studies in Linear and Nonlinear Programming, 1959; A Time Series Analysis of Interindustry Demands, 1959. Recipient: John Bates Clark Medal, Amer Econ Assn, 1957; Army Commendation Ribbon. Office: Harvard U, Cambridge, Mass.

ARTOM, Eugenio, It, attorney, business exec, educator; b. Asti, It, Feb 17, 1896; s. Vittorio and Gemma (Pugliese); PhD, U Rome, 1919; m. Giuliana Traves, Apr 7, 1927. Atty, Supreme Court, It, since 1926; mgn dir, La Fondiaria Ins Co; vice-pres: La Presidente Ins Co; La Consorziale Ins Co, since 1945; prof modern hist, U Florence, since 1948; mem, Town Council of Florence, since 1948. Lt col, res, It Army, 1914-1918. Pres: Natl Assn Ins Enterprises, since 1953; Natl Inst for Blind, Florence; Inst for Profsl Instrn for Blind, 1947-63; Società Toscana per la storia del Risorgimento; mem: Natl Council for Lab and Econ; Società Leonardo de Vinci; natl council,

It Lib Party; fmr: vice-pres, Tuscan Comm for Natl Liberation; mem, Consulta Nazionale. Club, Rotary. Author: Lineamenti della Crisi Sociale, 1921; Lord Palmerston, 1945; Angelo Usiglie, 1949. Recipient: mil medal, War Cross, 1918. Home: 183 Via Masaccio, Florence, It. Offices: Via della Frezza 70, Rome, It; Piazza San Babila 1, Milan, It.

ARTZI, Itzhak, Isr, attorney; b. Siret, Bukovina, Rum, Nov 14, 1920; s. Gabriel and Fany (Katz) Herzig; in Isr since 1947; licence in lit, phil, Coll for J Students, Bucharest, 1945; dipl, atty, HS for Law and Econ, Tel Aviv, 1956; m. Margalit Liquornik, Sep 10, 1946; c: Shlomo, Naava. Chmn secretariat, Independent Lib Party, since 1968; mem mgmt, Sherut Hasidur Bc Co; fmr: mem exec, JA, head dept, Youth Aliyah; secy gen, Hanoar Hazioni, Rum; mem, illegal Zionist exec, Rum; mem, Vaad Ezra Ve'Hatzalah; spec delg for repatriation of children from death camps; mem, Hehalutz, missions to: Hung, Slovakia; W Ger; Fr; Yugo; org, illegal immigration, i/c immigrants of SS Knesset, 4000 persons; camp leader, Cyprus; mem: Kibbutz Bemaavak,1947-51; fgn service, 1952-54; service for internal revenues, Treasury, 1955-56. Served, IDF. Mem: adv bd, Yad VeShem; Theodore Herzl Lodge, B'nai B'rith; Irgun Hameuchad shel Iotzei Rum; mem exec, WJC; fmr vice-pres, Federation Internationale des Communautes d'Enfants. Author: The Way of Hanoar Hatzioni; mem, ed bd, Tmurot, monthly; dep ed, Zemanim; contbr to press. Hobbies: stamps, Rum affairs. Home: 31 Brandeis St, Tel Aviv, Isr. Office: 5 Beeri St, Tel Aviv, Isr.

ARTZI, Pinhas, Isr, assyriologist; b. Budapest, Hung, May 23, 1923; s. Joseph and Hajnal (Gluck) Landler; in Isr since 1950; ordained rabbi, Rabb Sem, Budapest, 1947; PhD, U Budapest, 1948; m. Fanny Bier, Apr 14, 1956; c: Ittay, Hillel, Jochanan. Asso prof: Bar Ilan U, Ramat Gan, since 1956, coorg, dept Heb and Semitic langs, mem, research council; Tel Aviv U, since 1961; chief rabbi Gyor dist, Hung, 1948-50. Lt, IDF, 1951-53. Mem: World Union J Studies; Groupe Francais Thureau Daufin, Paris. Co-author: Sumerian and Akkadian, Documents, 1965; ed, Assyriologic, Jour Near Eastern Studies; contbr to Bar Ilan U Yearbook series; articles to profsl jours. Recipient: Sinai Campaign medal; awards: J Bd Educ; J Bd Dep, Eng. Spec interests: hist, anthropology, drawing. Home: 1 Beit Hakerem, Jerusalem,Isr. Office: Bar Ilan U, Ramat Gan, Isr.

ARTZT, Walter W, US, business exec, author; b. Aus, Nov 11, 1904; in US since 1922; s. Kiva and Dora; att Wanamakers Inst, Phila; m. Betty Lesavoy, Aug 18, 1930; c: Paulette Howard, Karen. Chmn, Babygro of Scotland since 1964; pres, Babygro Inc, Allentown, Pa, 1938-64. Prin contrib: numerous inventions. Vice-pres, Amer Isr Cultural Found. Author: Ready Willing and Able, 1949; After the Holocaust, 1963; contbr, poetry in every ed, Undzer Aign Vinkel. Spec interests: Isr, poetry, Yiddish. Home: 116 E 68 St, New York, NY. Office: Empire State Bldg, New York, NY.

ARVEY, Jacob Meyer, US, lawyer; b. Chgo, Ill, Nov 3, 1895; s. Israel and Bertha (Eisenberg); LLD, John Marshall Law Sch, Chgo; hon DHL, Heb Theol Coll, Skokie, Ill, 1969; m. Edith Freeman, June 11, 1916; c: Erwin, Howard, Helen Bresky. Partner, law firm, Arvey, Hodes & Mantynband, since 1947; admitted to Ill bar, 1916; mem, law firm: Raber, Kostner, Herr & Arvey, 1920-29; McInerney, Epstein & Arvey, 1929-47; mem bd, Marina City Bank, Chgo; asst state atty, Cook Co, 1918-20; master in chancery, Circuit Court, Cook Co, 1930-34; alderman, 24 ward, Chgo, 1923-41; Dem natl committeeman, Ill, chmn, Cook Co, 1946-50. Lt col, US Army, 1941-45. Mem bd: Brandeis U; Natl Fed J Men's Clubs; Louis A Weiss Memorial Hosp, Chgo; Mt Sinai Hosp, Miami, Fla; J Home for Aged, Chgo and Miami; hon chmn, State of Isr Bonds Org, Chgo; fmr: mem: civic comm, De Paul U; citizens bd, Catholic Interracial Council; chmn, Catholic Youth Org campaign; various civic activities: U Chgo Research Found and Found for Emotionally Disturbed Children; Adlai E Stevenson Memorial Found; Amer Friends Heb U; Amer Friends Tel Aviv U; JDC; B'nai B'rith; UJA; JNF; JWB; J United Fund; Natl J Hosp, Denver, Colo; Amer ORT Fed; Amer Comm for Weizmann Inst of Sci; Amer Isr Public Affairs Comm; mem: Fed, Amer, Ill State, Chgo Bar Assns; Judge Advocates Assn; Decalogue Soc Lawyers; Navy League of US; Amer Vets Comm; JWV; Amer Legion; Masons; Elks; Loyal Order of Moose; Knights of Pythias; Asso Talmud Torahs, Chgo; Southwestern Silverlink Lodge 56; 100F; Isr Pub Inst; Ency Judaica Press, Inc; Aid Assn for Incurable Orthodox Js, Chgo; Res Off Assn; clubs: Variety,

Ill; Covenant, Ill; Standard; Bryn Mawr Country, Chgo; Westview Country, Miami Beach, Fla. Recipient: Bronze Star; US Legion of Merit; man of year: JNF, Chgo, 1957; Isr Bond Org, 1954, man of the century, 1964; award of merit, Decalogue Soc of Lawyers, 1950. Hobby: golf. Office: 1 N La Salle St, Chicago, Ill.

ARZI, Reuben, Isr, attorney; b. Mendzyrzec, Pol, May 11,1907; s. David and Sara (Finkelstein) Cedarbaum; in Isr since 1949; ML, Warsaw, 1931; att Inst for Judaica, Warsaw, 1929-32; m. Pesia Hoflat, July 9, 1933; c: Aviva, David. MK since 1965; political secy, Mapam, 1959-66, mem, cen comm, since 1950; gen secy, Hashomer Hazair, Pol, 1946-49. Mem: Zionist World Action Comm, since 1947; world bd, JNF, since 1956; bd, Yad Vashem, since 1964; Council ,Yad Vashem, since 1961; presidium, cen comm, Farbut Pol, 1936-39. Contbr to profsl jours. Hobby: chess. Home: 45B King George St, Jerusalem, Isr.

ARZT, Max, US, rabbi, educator; b. Stanislau, Pol, Mar 20, 1897; s. Hyman and Anna (Grossbach); in US since 1900; BS, CCNY, 1918; MA, Columbia U, 1921; ordained rabbi, MHL, JTSA, 1921, DHL, 1934, hon DD, 1950; m. Esther Podolsky, Mar 7, 1921; c: Miriam Teplitz, David, Raphael. Vice-chancellor, prof practical theol, JTSA, since 1951; asso, sem on rel, Columbia U, 1954; rabbi: Temple Beth El, Stamford, Conn, 1921-23; Temple Isr, Scranton, Pa, 1923-39. Pres: Council Social Agcys, Scranton, 1938-39; RA, 1939-40; vice-pres, Syn Council of Amer, 1939. Contbr: Talmudic studies in Jubilee vols of Profs Marx and Kaplan, JTSA, 1950, 1953; mem, comm, J Publ Soc, preparing new Eng trans Heb Scriptures, since 1955; contrib ed, Judaism. Home: 280 Riverside Dr, New York, NY. Study: 3080 Broadway, New York, NY.

ASBELL, Bernard, US, author; b. Bklyn, NY, May 8, 1923; s. Samuel and Minnie (Zevin); att U Conn, 1943-44; m. Mildred Sacarny, Jan 2 ,1944; c: Paul, Lawrence, Jonathan, Jordis. Reporter, Richmond (Va) Times Dispatch, 1945-46; mgn ed, Chicago Magazine, 1954-55; cons, educ and urban problems: Ford Found, 1963-69; Soc of Health, Educ and Wfr, 1965-66; US Off of Educ, 1966-68; Carnegie Corp, 1967; Intl Bus Machines Corp, 1966-68; tchr, non-fiction writing: Bread Loaf Writers Conf, Middlebury Coll,Vt, 1960, 1961; U Bridgeport, 1961-63; U Chgo. Sgt, US Army, 1943-45. Mem, Educ Writers Assn; fmr pres, Soc of Mag Writers. Author: When F.D.R. Died, 1961; The New Impoved American, 1965;contbr to: American Heritage; Harper's; Horizon; Lady's Home Journal; McCall's; NY Times Magazine; Redbook; Saturday Evening Post; Think; others. Recipient: Sch Bell Award, NEA, 1966; outstanding mag coverage of educ, Educ Writers Assn, 1966, 1968; best educ writing, Natl Council for Advancement Educ Writing, 1969. Home and office: 1359 Ridge Rd, North Haven, Conn.

ASCARELLI, Immanuel Manlio, Isr, educator; b. Ferrara, It, Nov 30, 1919; s. Giacomo and Wanda (Bernstein); in Isr since 1939; BSc, agric, Heb U, Jerusalem, 1950; PhD, 1956; postgrad studies: Natl Inst for Research in Dairying, Shirefield, Eng; Cornell U; MIT; m. Roma Wessel, May 19, 1946; c: Amihai, Michal. Sr lectr, animal nutrition, fac agric, Heb U, since 1963, on fac since 1951. Pvt, Brit Army, 1941-46; sgt, IDF, 1948. Mem: Nutrition Soc, London; Isr Biochem Soc; Assn for Nutrition and Food Tech, Isr; Poultry Sci Assn, US. Contbr papers on carotene and vitamin A metabolism and protein utilization. Recipient: Afr Star; It Star; Defence Medal; 6 Day War Medal. Home: 29 Vogel St, Rehovot, Isr. Office: Fac of Agric, Hebrew U, Rehovot, Isr.

ASCH, Sidney, US, jurist, legislator, educator: b. NYC, May 30, 1919; s. Bernard and Mildred (Roitman); BS, CCNY, 1940; LLB, Columbia U, 1943; PhD, New Sch for Social Research, 1956; m. Amy Cohen, Mar 18, 1951; c: Jane, Nancy. Judge, Civil Court, NYC, since 1961; prof law, NY Law Sch, since 1948; law asst, Judge B L Shientag, NYC, 1943; asso, law firm: Moses and Singer, 1944; Poletti, Diamond, Rabin, Freidin & McKay, 1946-48, both NYC; mem, NY State Assembly, 1952-61. Sgt, US Army, 1944-46. Mem: bd, Mt Eden Cen, since 1954; City Coll Alumni Assn; Concourse YMHA; Taft HS Cen. Author: Social Security in America, 1952, 1959; Police Authority and Rights of Individual, 1961; Civil Rights and Responsibilities Under the Constitution; co-author, Families and Children in Courts of NY, 1953; contbr to legal jours. Home: 940 Grand Concourse, Bx, NY. Office: 111 Centre S, New York, NY.

ASCHEIM, Charles N, US, advertising exec; b. Xenia, O, Apr 21, 1883; s. Jacob and Mollie (Flohr); m. Lyda Burton, Apr 7, 1908; c: Burton, Jay. Ret; vice-pres, Keelor & Stites, 1936-55; with: Lord & Thomas, 1904-13; JW Thompson Co, 1914-20; Burnet-Kuhn, 1921-35. Dir, Hatikvah Lodge, B'nai B'rith, Miami Beach; lecture forum comm, J Cen; pres, KK Bene Isr; mem: Temple Isr, Miami; publicity comm, J Wfr drs. Home: 639 Morton Towers N, Miami Beach, Fla.

ASCHER, Kurt Robert Simon, Isr, scientist; b. Nuremberg, Ger, Dec 24, 1923; s. Ludwig and Alice (Bodenheimer); in Isr since 1925; MSc, Heb U, Jerusalem, 1951; m. Anna Knobel-Lehrmann, Dec 12, 1948; c: Jacob, Jessica. Head, dept toxicology, Volcani Inst of Agric Research, since 1960; asst dept inorganic chem, Heb U, 1945-47; research f, Instituto Superiore di Sanita, It, 1957-60. Capt, research sci, IDF, 1948-57. Mem, cen comm, Centre International des Antiparasitaires, Rome, Zurich. Contbr numerous papers to sci research jours. Spec interests: hist of WW II; langs. Home: 10 Shmuel Hanagid St, Tel Aviv, Isr. Office: Bet Degan, Isr.

ASCHER, Mary Goldman, US, artist; b. Leeds, Eng, Dec 24, 1900; d. Jacob and Naomi (Goldsand) Goldman; in US since 1912; BBA, CCNY, 1923; MA, NYU, 1934; grad, guidance and admn, Columbia U, NYC, 1943; att: Art Students League; NY Sch Applied Design; Grand Cen Sch of Art; Hunter Evening Coll; Sch Chinese Brushwork; Famous Artists Fine Arts Sch; Provincetown Art Sch; m. David Ascher, Dec 24, 1926. Ar.ist, self-employed, lectr, since 1943; ed, Annual Newsletter, since 1962; tchr, Bd of Educ, NYC, 1925-39, 1st asst, chmn dept, 1939-46, dean of girls, dir of guidance; admn asst to prin, 1946-53. One-man travelling shows throughout US, with: Ltd Folio Ed of Lithographs; 12 Women of the Old Testament and Apocrypha; oils and mixed media; oils—hardedge; group shows in: Eng, Scotland, Fr, Mexico, Japan, Arg, Can, Isr, US; represented in collections: Natl Collection Fine Arts, Smithsonian Inst, Wash, DC; Norfolk, Va, Mus Fine Arts; US Natl Mus of Sport; Bat Yam Mus; Ein Harod Mus, both Isr; Interchurch Cen Libr, NYC; Fordham U Bx, NY; Rodeph Sholom Syn, NYC; many pvt. Mem: Natl Assn Women Artists; Amer Soc Contemporary Artists; NYC br, Natl League Amer Pen Women; Natl Soc Arts and Letters; Amer Assn U Women; Intl Platform Assn; life mem, Art Students League; f: Royal Soc of Arts, London; Metrop Mus Art; Mus Modern Art; Amer Fed Arts; Artists Equity; Natl Soc Arts and Letters; Natl Council on Arts; in J Life; in Govt. Author: Poetry-Painting, 1958. Recipient: Huntington Hartford Found F to complete 12 oil paintings on Women of the Old Testament and Apocrypha, 1961; medal of hon, Painters and Sculptors Soc, NJ, 1958; Marcia Brady Tucker Award, Natl Assn Women Artists, 1960; 1st prize modern watercolor and graphics, Profsl Artists Group, Natl League Amer Pen Women, 1962; McBurndy Corp Award, Oil, 18th NE Annual, 1967; career achievement award, arts, Baruch Alumni Soc, CCNY, 1968; 1st prize for poetry, NYC br, Natl League Amer Pen Women, 1968; Seligson Memorial Award, NAWA Natl Annual, oil and photography, 1969. Home and studio: 336 Central Park, New York, NY.

ASCHNER, Ernest, US, public relations, counsel; b. Berlin, Ger, Nov 9, 1912; s. Leopold and Hilda (Erlebacher); in US since 1946; PhD, U Berlin, 1934; m. Alice Kahn, Nov 3, 1939; c: Naomi, Judy. Pres, Aschner Asso, Inc, PR, since 1956; staff mem, The Palestine Post, Jerusalem, 1935-46, ch, Haifa bur, 1936-46; Reuters corresp, Agence Havas and Agence France Presse, 1936-46; freelance writer, 1946-49; i/c PR, econ dept, JA, Pal, NY, 1949-56; ed, Economic Horizons, monthly, 1949-56. Mem: PR Soc Amer; club, Overseas Press. Co-author: Journey to Israel. Home: 36 Barnum Rd, Larchmont, NY. Office: 10 E 44 St, New York, NY.

ASCHNER, Fritz Simon, Isr, mechanical engr; b. Breslau, Ger, Dec 23, 1903; s. Max and Eugenie (Oettinger); in Isr since 1936; att Realgymnasium, Breslau, 1920-21; hon DEngr, Tech Hochschule, Breslau, 1934; m. Margot Lewy; c: Ruth Berman, Reuben, Eshel. Asso prof, fac, mech engr dept, nuclear engr, Technion since 1966; design and planning engr, AEG, Berlin, 1927-36; mech devl and design engr, Isr Elec Corp. Mem, tech council, Assn Engrs and Architects, Isr; f, Inst Mech Engr, London; Elec Engrs, London. Author: Small and Medium Sized Steam Power Plants, 1935; contbr numerous papers to engr jours and intl congs. Hobbies: photography, stamps. Home: 26 Shoshanat Hacarmel St, Haifa, Isr. Office: Technion, POB 4910, Haifa, Isr.

ASCHNER, Paul William, US, surgeon, educator; b. NYC,

Apr 15, 1889; s. Herman and Mary (Wilhelm); BA, Columbia Coll, 1910; MD, Coll Phys and Surgs, Columbia U, 1912; m. Jeanne Blum, Apr 6, 1948. Cons urol, Brookdale Hosp, Bklyn, since 1955, chief urol, 1948-55; cons surg and urol, J Hosp, Bklyn, since 1949; urol, N Shore Hosp, Manhasset, NY, 1953-56; cons urol, LI J Hosp, New Hyde Park, NY, since 1954; instr, Columbia U, 1922-26; asst clinical prof, urol, LI Coll Med, 1935-48; att urol, Hosp for Jt Diseases, 1930-48; att surg and sr att urol, J Hosp, Bklyn, 1935-49. F: NY Acad of Med; Amer Coll of Surgs; dipl, Amer Bd Urol; mem: Nassau Co Med Soc; Nassau Acad Med; Bklyn Urol Soc; NY Urol Soc; Harvey Soc; NY Path Soc; Amer Urol Assn; Amer Gastroenterological Assn; Phi Beta Kappa; Alpha Omega Alpha; Phi Delta Epsilon; B'nai B'rith. Contbr to med jours. Home and office: 2 Stony Run Rd, Great Neck, NY.

ASHCANASE, Abe S, US, government official; b. Grand Forks, ND, June 24, 1919; s. Isaac and Rose (Fish); att Gonzaga U, Wash, 1936-37; E Wash Coll of Educ, 1938-40; BA, of Wash, U 1941; spec mgmt training, Harvard Grad Sch Bus, 1943; Sch of Mil Govt, Fr, 1945; Inst for Intl Devl, Johns Hopkins U, Sch Advanced Intl Studies, 1961. Dir training, US Agcy for Intl Devl mission to Saigon, Vietnam, 1967-68, asst dir, admn, New Delhi, India, 1962, chief, orientation activities, Wash, DC, 1963-66, exec off, Tunisia, 1966-67; engaged in merchandising, mgmt, 1931-41, 1947; info, ed specialist, US Forces, Aus, and Off High Commn for Aus, 1948-50; fgn service off, chief, mgmt and reports staff, US High Commn for Aus, Vienna, 1950-52; chief, reports staff, Tech Coop Admn, State Dept, 1953, fgn oprs admn, Iran desk, 1954; asst chief, comty devl div, US Oprs Mission to Iran, 1954; exec off, master jt fund oprs, Jt Fund for Tech and Econ Devl, Teheran, 1954-55; US Oprs Mission to Thailand, 1956; spec asst, housing, UN command, Off Econ Coord for Korea, 1957, SE area Coord, Pusan, 1958, cen area repr, Seoul, 1959, exec off, off contract relations, Intl Coop Admn, 1960-61. Maj, US Army, 1941-46. Life mem: Aleph Zadek Aleph; B'nai B'rith; mem: Sigma Alpha Mu: Masons, 32 deg; Shriner; asso mem, Brit Inst for Mgmt. Ed: Austria, A Graphic Survey, 1950-52; Study of Rehabilitation of Austria, 1945-47. Recipient: meritorious hon award, Agcy for Intl Devl; meritorious civilian service hon award, Dept of Army; Army Commendation Ribbon, Eur Theatre of Oprs Ribbon. Office: c/o R E Odom, 7200 Beechwood Rd, Alexandria, Va.

ASHE, David I, US, attorney; b. Bklyn, NY, Nov 13, 1910; s. Morris and Bessie (Newman); BSS, magna cum laude, CCNY, 1929; JD, Columbia U Law Sch, 1932; (div); c: Judi.h Handelman; Deborah Warheit; m. 2nd, Amelia Wexler, 1962; step-c: Richard Wexler, Susan Lahn. Mem, law firm, Ashe and Rifkin, since 1940; atty for intl and local lab unions; cons, ACLU, since 1942; counsel, United Parents Assns of NYC, since 1950; pres, 1948-50; instr, Trade Union Inst, Rand Sch of Social Sci, 1936-45. Mem: bd dirs, The New Leader, 1938-45; Rand Sch Soc Sci, 1940-44; Bd Higher Educ of NYC, since 1966; bd dirs, Research Found, CUNY and Research Found, City Coll, since 1966; gen counsel, The Workmen's Circle, since 1964; chmn: NY J Labor Comm, since 1966; mem, Natl admn comm; pres: Musicians Service Corp, since 1960; mem, Natl J Comty Relations Advisory Council, since 1965; natl panel of arbitrators, Amer Arbitration Assn, since 1950; Bar Assn, NYC; NY Co Lawyers Assn; Public Educ Assn; Citizens Union, NYC; bd dirs, NY Adult Educ Council, since 1966; natl comm, Workers Defense League, 1956-58; Phi Beta Kappa; Alumni Assns: CCNY, Columbia Law Sch. Author: Yellow Dog Contracts—Legal and Social Aspects, 1931; The Taft-Hartley Law-How it Affects Unions and Workers, 1947; The Labor—Management Reporting and Disclosure Act of 1959: An Analysis, 1959; adv ed, Parents Magazine, 1948-50; contbr to lab and educ publs. Home: 201 E 79 St, New York, NY. Office: 253 Broadway, New York, NY.

ASHE, Lillian H, US, educator, consultant; b. NYC, May 28, 1911; d. David and Anna (Wolkow) Hurwitz; BA, Barnard Coll, 1933; MA, Tchrs Coll, Columbia U, 1940, EdD, 1966; m. David Ashe, Jan 1933 (div); c: Judith Handelman, Deborah Warheit. Asso prof, sociol, Wis State U, La Crosse, since 1968; lectr, CCNY, Sch of Educ since 1961; cons, comty relations, since 1958; adv, United Parents Assn, NYC, since 1956, pres, 1952-56; educ liaison, Puerto Rican Social Services, since 1962; tchr, music, piano, 1933-48; area sup, US Bur of Census, 1960. Delg, NY State, White House Conf on Educ, 1955; mem, Bd of Educ, Commn on Integration, 1955-59; mem: League Women Voters; Citizens Housing and Planning Council; Adult Educ Assn. Co-author: Order of the Air, 1934; contbr, TV for children, Encyclopedia Yearbook, 1954;

profsl jours. Recipient: f, Fund for Adult Educ, Ford Found, 1960-61. Home: 402 N 8 St, La Crosse, Wis.

ASHEIM, Lester Eugene, US, librarian; b. Spokane, Wash, Jan 22, 1914; s. Sol and Bertha (Bergman); BA, U Wash, 1936, BLS, 1937, MA, 1941; PhD, U Chgo, 1949. Dir, Off for Libr Educ, Amer Libr Assn, since 1966; jr reference asst, U Wash Libr, 1937-41; libr, US Fed Penitentiary, McNeil Island, Wash, 1941-42; regional libr, US Fed Public Housing Auth, Seattle, 1946; asst prof, Grad Libr Sch, U Chgo, 1948-52, dean of students, 1951-52, dean and asso prof, 1952-61; dir, intl relations off, Amer Libr Assn, 1961-66. US Army, 1942-45. Mem: Spec Librs Assn. Author: The Humanities and the Library, 1957; Librarianship and the Developing Countries, 1966; ed: Forum on the Public Library Inquiry, 1950; The Core of Education for Librarianship, 1955; The Future of the Book, 1955; New Directions in Public Library Development, 1957. Recipient: dist alumnus award, U Wash Sch of Librarianship; Intellectual Freedom Award, Ill Libr Assn, both 1966; Scarecrow Press Award for Libr Lit, 1968. Hobbies: reading, film, popular culture. Home: 253 E Delaware St, Chgo, Ill. Office: 50 E Huron St, Chgo, Ill.

ASHENHEIM, Leslie Erle, Jamaica, solicitor; b. Kingston, Jamaica, Feb 5, 1899; s. Lewis and Estelle (de Cordova); MA, Wadham Coll, Oxford, Eng, 1921; m. Rita Brandon, 1925; c: Jill Andrews, Jack; m. 2nd, Helen Myers, 1944; c: Bryan. Solicitor and co dir; dir: Bank of Jamaica; Jamaica Public Service Co; Jamaica Telephone Co; Kingston Ice-Making Co; Coffee Ind Bd; chmn: Gleaner Co; Ins Co of Jamaica. Mem bd, mgmt, U Hosp of W Indies; f, Inst of Dirs, London; pres: Jamaica Employers Fed; Lawn Tennis Assn; vice-pres, Inc Law Soc of Jamaica, fmr pres; mem: United Grand Lodge of Eng; Friendly Lodge, Kingston, fmr Master. Hobbies: golf, bridge, tennis. Home: 12 Seaview Ave, Kingston 10, Jamaica. Office: 5 Port Royal, Kingston, Jamaica.

ASHENHEIM, Neville N, Jamaica, legislator; b. Kingston, Jamaica, Dec 18, 1900; BA, U Oxford, Eng. Mem, cabinet, Jamaican Govt; chmn, Ind Devl Corp, Jamaica Govt, 1952-57. Prin contrib: primarily responsible for restoration of Hunts Bay J Cemetery. Fmr: pres, United Cong of Israelites; pres, Children's Lunch Fund Council; chmn, Ger Ref Fund. Recipient: CBE; Knighthood, 1963. Home: Manor Court Apts, Penthouse 4, Kingston, Jamaica.

ASHER, Lila Oliver, US, artist; b. Phila, Pa, Nov 15, 1921; d. Benjamin and Mollie (Finkelstein) Oliver; cert, Phila Coll of Art, 1943; studied with Gonippo Raggi and Joseph Grossman; m. Sydney Asher Jr, May 5, 1946; c: Warren, Barbara. Asso prof, art dept, Howard U, since 1966, on fac since 1947; instr: DC Tchrs Coll, 1953-55; Montgomery Co adult prog, 1957-60. One man shows: Barnett-Aden Gal, 1951; Wm C Blood Gal, Phila, 1955; Arts Club, Wash, 1957; Collectors Gal, 1959; Garrett Park Public Libr, Garrett Park, Md, 1960; The Art Shop, Silver Spring, Md, 1961; Burr Gals, NYC, 1963; Gal 222, El Paso, Texas, 1965; exhibited at: Pa Acad of Fine Arts; Libr of Cong; Va Intermont Coll; U of Me; Natl Mus of Art; NY World Fair; B'nai B'rith, Wash; U of Va; represented: in perm collections: U of Va; Sweet Briar Coll; City of Wolfsburg, Ger; Corcoran Gal Art; Howard U Gal Art; Barnett-Aden Gal; in pvt collections; commissioned murals: Cong Rodeph Shalom, Pa, 1941; Bolling Field Officers Club, 1957; Wash Motel, 1958; Indian Springs Country Club, Glenmont, Md, 1959; commissioned portraits: Supr Court Justice Harold H Burton and Mrs Burton; Hon Cyrus S Ching; Hon Luther Evans; Joseph C Harsch; Congressman James Auchincloss. Chap recording secy, Artists Equity, since 1967; mem bd dirs, Montgomery Co Arts Cen; fmr pres, Soc of Wash Artists; recording secy, Soc of Wash Printmakers, since 1961. Recipient, prizes: Metrop Art Exhb, 1952; Corcoran Gal, 1955; Old Market Gal, 1961; Chevy Chase Art Exhb, 1961, 1962; and others. Home and studio: 4100 Thornapple St, Chevy Chase, Md.

ASHKANASY, Maurice, Austr, attorney; b. London, Eng, Oct 16, 1901; LLM, U Melbourne; m. Heather Epstein; c: Vivianne Davis, Aaron, Neal. Q.C. Lt col, Austr Army, 1940-45. Dep pres, Exec Council Austr Jewry; found, numerous J bodies, including Judean League of Vic; co-found, Mt Scopus Memorial Coll; trustee, Cultural Found; mem, council, WJC; COJO, dir, claims conf; fmr pres, Vic J Bd Deps. Recipient: Einstein Centenary Medal, 1956. Home: 36 Allenby Ave, E Malvern, Melbourne, Austr. Office: 205 William St, Melbourne, Austr.

ASHLEY, Charles D, US, attorney, business exec; b. Sun Prairie, Wis, Dec 11, 1899; s. David and Rose (Schutkin); AB, U Wis, 1921; LLB, Harvard Law Sch, 1924; m. Elenore Pinkhurst, Jan 23, 1940; c: Margot, David. Pvt practice since 1925; pres, treas, Terminal Storage Co; dir, Milw Pump and Tank Works; pres: Fidelity Bldg Corp; Mackie Bldg Co; Mitchell Bldg Co; Charles Realty Co. Vice-pres, Mt Sinai Hosp; dir, Amer Comm for Weizmann Inst; chmn, Milw Co Repub Party, 1951-53; mem, Electoral Coll, 1952-53; mem, bd trustees, Cong Sinai, fmr pres; Phi Beta Kappa; Delta Sigma Rho; Phi Sigma Delta; Milw Wis, and Amer Bar Assns; pres: Charles David Ashley Found; Charles Edgar Albright and Laura Uihlein Albright Found, fmr secy; fmr dir, Legal Aid Soc, Milw; clubs: U; Harvard, Milw. Homes: 2505 N Wahl Ave, Milwaukee, Wis; summer, Islandale, Oconomowic, Wis. Office: 611 N Broadway, Milwaukee, Wis.

ASIMOV, Isaac, US, author, educator; b. Russ, Jan 2, 1920; s. Judah and Anna (Berman); in US since 1923; BS, Columbia U, 1939, MA, 1941, PhD, 1948; m. Gertrude Blugerman, July 26, 1942; c: David, Robyn. Asso prof, bio-chem, Boston U Sch of Med, since 1955, on staff since 1949. US Army, 1945-46. Mem: Authors League of Amer; Amer Chem Soc. Author: numerous vols of sci fiction, non fiction; contbr to sci fiction mags. Home and office: 45 Greenough St, W Newton, Mass.

ASKIN, Arnold S, US, business exec; b. Utica, NY, Aug 21, 1901; s. Samuel and Leah (Rosenbloom); BA, Yale U, 1923; m. Fannie Halff, Mar 1, 1928; c: Edith Ehrlich, Audrey Rosenman. Vice-pres, The Askin Stores, Inc, 1926-60. US Army, 1942-45. Pres: NY Assn for New Amers, 1950-54; J Family Service, NY, 1954-58; vice-pres: Fed Employment Service, 1946-50; Hillside Hosp, pres, 1964-69; Family Service Assn of Amer, 1952-56; mem, Phi Beta Kappa; club, Yale, NY. Home: Cross River Rd, Katonah, NY. Office: Time and Life Bldg, New York, NY.

ASKOVITZ, Samuel I, US, physician; b. Phila, Pa, May 27, 1922; s. Charles and Esther (Goldberg); BA, U of Pa, 1941, MA, 1942, MD, Sch of Med, 1950; m. Fruma Kirzner, Oct 22, 1950; c: Avrohom, Rochel, Sarah, Hannah, Shoshannah, Miriam, Levi. Chief, tumor registry, Sch of Med, U of Pa, since 1955, f, therapeutic research, since 1952, lectr, med stat, sch of med, 1956-59, asso in ophthal, Grad Sch of Med, since 1952, Sch of Med, since 1960; instr, math, U of Pa, 1942-44; f, ophthal, Wills Eye Hosp, since 1954; mem, clinical staff, ophthal, Albert Einstein Med Cen, since 1954, hon cons, ophthal, since 1968, research f, 1952-60; med stat, 1955-59; cons, biostatistics: comm study of lung cancer, Phila Co Med Soc, since 1956; comm study of breast cancer, since 1958; partner, Statistical Consulting Services, since 1960. Sgt, USAAF, 1944-46. Vice-pres, Phila Mikvah Assn, since 1962, pres 1961-62; mem, bd dirs: Talmudical Yeshivah, Phila; Beth Jacob Schools of Phila; Wynnefield Heb Day Sch, Phila; mem, bd govs, Assn Orthodox J Sci; pres, Agudath Isr, Phila, 1963; f, AAAS; mem: AMA; Pa State, Phila Co Med Socs; Amer Public Health Assn; Assn for Research in Ophthal, AAUP; Sigma Xi. Contbr to profsl jours. Spec interests: study Bible, Talmud. Home: 5869 Overbrook Ave, Philadelphia, Pa. Office: 59 St, and Overbrook Ave, Philadelphia, Pa.

ASSAEL, Zvi, Isr, educational admnr; b. Uzhorod, Czech, 1919; in Isr since 1947; att Heb U, Jerusalem; m; four c. Dir, Dept for Torah Educ and Culture, for US and Can, JA, since 1969, dir, Eur Off, 1959-62; mem dept, since 1952; fmr engaged in teaching, and youth leadership. Served IDF. Fmr: mem, Bnei Akiva; active, Aliyah Bet, Czech; delg, ZC, Basle, 1946. Home: 71-49 169 St, Flushing, NY. Office: 515 Park Ave, New York, NY.

ASSAF, Michael, Isr, journalist, author; b. Lodz, Pol, May 3, 1896; s. Menahem and Hanna (Lzumiray); in Isr since 1920; att: Rel Coll, Lodz; Oriental Sem, Berlin; m. Miryam Lichtenstein, 1921, c: Ammron, Tamar Linder. Mem exec: Public Bd Culture and Art; Arab Pub House, Histadrut; mem, High Court, Lab Party; fmr: dir, Heb elem sch, Shalom Aleychem; mem 1st exec, Histadrut; mem exec, HaShomer Hatzair, Pol; secy, culture dept, Histadrut. Author: History of the Arabs in Palestine; Arab Rule in Palestine, Heb, 1935; The Arabs Under the Crusaders, 1942; The Arab Awakening and Flight, 1946-48; TH Lawrence—Life and Legend, 1967; 100 Years in Jewish History, 1840-1940, Arabic; chief ed: Al-Your, Arabic newspaper, 1948-60; Arab weekly of Histadrut, 1921-26; oriental ed, Davar daily; contbr: various pamphlets in several langs on the Arabic natl movement; numerous articles, trans, Heb, Arabic. Chmn, Isr Journalists Assn. Spec interests: langs, studied 11; hist. Home: 8 Peretz St, Tel Aviv, Isr.

ASSCHER, Clara Pinkhof, Isr, author; b. Amsterdam, Holland, Oct 25, 1896; d. Herman and Adeline (de Beer) Pinkoff; cert, Heb Tchrs Sem, Jerusalem, 1952; m. Avraham Asscher (decd); c: Eliezer, Menachem, Yitschak, Meir, Rosa Licht, Sophie Langer; m. 2nd, Asher Craczkes, 1958. Author: 12 children's books, 1918-28; 4 books for Youth, 1929-34; 4 novels, 1935-39; Sterrekinderen, 1946; De Koopbrief, 1953; Danseres zonder benen, 1966; Tirtsa, 1953, all in Dutch. Recipient: Aan Wal, Youth Lit Competition, 1932; award, W Ger Min of Educ, 1962. Home: 9 Tel Maneh, Haifa, Isr.

ASSEO, David, Turkey, rabbi; b. Istanbul, Aug 3, 1914; s. Isaac and Eugenie (Palombo); att rabb sem, Rhodes; ordained rabbi by Rabbi Raphael Saban; m. Elise Mesulam, 1944; two d. Chief rabbi, Turkey, since 1961; fmr, Heb tchr: Hasköy; Lycee Juif, Istanbul; secy, Rabb Council, then mem; chief rabb, Haydarpasa, Ortaköy, It-J comty of Istanbul; dir, Rabb Sem, 1955-62. Home: Sisli Büyükdere Cad, Ciftkurt apt 1, Istanbul, Turkey. Study: Yemenici Sokak 23, Beyoglu, Istanbul, Turkey.

ASSIA, Yehuda, Isr, banker; b. Baghdad, Iraq, 1917; s. Isaac and Hilwa (Malthalon); att bus ext dept, Columbia U; m. Jean Ainslie, Aug, 1950; c: David, Daliah, Daniela. Vice chmn, Fgn Trade Bank, Tel Aviv, since 1958; chmn, Fgn Trade Inves Co, Tel Aviv, since 1963; vice chmn, Eilat Pipeline Co Ltd, since 1959; chmn, Kiron Ltd, since 1962; mem bd dirs, Afr-Pal Inves Co Ltd, since 1963; mem bd, Amer Trust Co, since 1963; co-found, fmr mgn dir, Swis Isr Trade Bank, Geneva; fmr: export-import commn agt; owner, import-export firm, Baghdad and Japan; established Assia Ltd, Bangkok, Thailand; formed import-export firm, NYC. Vice chmn, Soc Bancaire et Financière, Paris since 1955; hon chmn, Iraq-Isr J Scholarship Fund, Isr, since 1953; hon pres, Sephardic Comty, Geneva; mem, intl hon bd, Ency Judaica, since 1963. Homes: Har Dafna St, Savyon, Isr; 3 rue Contamines, Geneva, Switz. Office: 15-17 Quai des Bergues, Geneva, Switz.

ASTOR, Alexander, NZ, rabbi; b. London, Eng, Aug 11, 1900; s. Theodore and Gertrude (Freedman) Ostroff; in NZ since 1926; att: Etz Chaim Theol Coll, 1912-20; J Coll, 1921-25, both London; BA, U of NZ, 1930; rabb dipl, Jerusalem, 1946; m. Rebecca Myers, Jan 19, 1926; c: Ruth Israelstram, Lorraine Shapiro. Chief min, Auckland Heb Cong, since 1931; sr chaplain, NZ Forces, since 1940; min, Dunedin Heb Cong, 1962-31. Found, pres, Auckland Judean Assn, since 1932; pres: Auckland Zionist Soc, since 1935; Friends Heb U, since 1939; United Comm for J Relief Abroad, since 1938; vice pres: Soc for Protection Women and Children, since 1932; Discharged Prisoners Aid Soc, since 1934; hon life mem, vice pres, mem bd govs, NZ League for Hard of Hearing, since 1933; fmr: official repr, JWB in NZ; att Anglo Amer Comm of Enquiry Pal; grand chaplain, Masonic Grand Lodge of NZ. Author: A History of Dunedin Jewry, 1931. Study: Synagogue Chambers, Greys Ave, Auckland, NZ.

ASTRACHAN, Max, US, statistician, educator, consultant; b. Rochester, NY, Mar 30, 1909; s. Israel and Lottie (Goldman); BA, U Rochester, 1929; MA, Brown U, 1930, PhD, 1935; m. Fannie Sherman, Dec 27, 1931; c: Gerald, David, Judith. Prof, quantitative methods, Sch of Bus, San Fernando Valley State Coll, Cal, since 1967; dir, Educ and Training Inst, Amer Soc Quality Control, 1965-67; math, logistics dept, Rand Corp, 1960-65; lectr, bus admn, Grad Sch Bus Admn, UCLA, 1961-65; prof, math, Antioch Coll, Yellow Springs, O, 1935-49; prof, stat, USAF Inst of Tech, Wright-Patterson Air Force Base, 1940-60, head, dept, acctnt and stat, 1955-60. Chmn, sch bd, Sinai Temple, LA, 1962; pres: Dayton Heb Inst, 1953-59; B'nai B'rith, Springfield, 1938; ZOA, O Valley Region, 1948-49; vice-pres, Beth Abraham Syn, Dayton, 1952; mem: Amer Stat Assn; natl bd dirs, Amer Soc Quality Control; Inst Math Sci; Oprs Research Soc Amer; Phi Beta Kappa; Sigma Xi. Co-author: Elementary Statistical Methods, 1950; contbr to prof mags. Home: 1737 Camden Ave, Los Angeles, Cal. Office: 18111 Nordhoff St, Northridge, Cal.

ATLAS, Samuel, US, educator; b. Kamai, Lith, Dec 5, 1899; s. Abraham and Beracha (Hurwitz); in US since 1942; att: Rabb Schs Slobodka and Poniewies, Lith, 1913-18; U Moscow,

1921; U Berlin, 1922-24; U Marburg, 1924; PhD, U Giessen, 1928; m. Celia Benjamin, 1934. Prof, phil, Talmud, HUC, Cincinnati, since 1942, JIR, NY, since 1951; lectr, phil and Talmud: Inst of Studies, Warsaw, 1929-34; Cambridge U, Eng, 1935-39; lectr, phil, Magdalen Coll, Oxford, 1936. Author: Epistemological Foundations of History, in Ger, 1928; To the Theory of Knowledge of Maimonides, in Heb, 1931; Philosophy of Maimonides and Its Systematic Place in History of Philosophy, 1936; Novellae of Abraham ben David, 1940; Rights of Private Property, 1944; Legal Fictions in Talmudic Law, in Heb, 1945; S Maimon's Treatment of the Problems of Antinomies, 1948; Maimon and Maimonides, 1952; Maimon's Doctrine of Infinite Reason, 1952; Solomon Maimon and Spinoza, 1952; From Critical to Speculative Idealism, The Philosophy of Solomon Maimon, 1964; Notes of Moses Ha-Kohen of Luxel on Maimonides' Code, 1969; articles on post-Kantian phil period, Ency of Philosophy, 1967; on legal status of Kings in Heb law, 1968. Home: 645 West End Ave, New York, NY. Office: 40 W 68 St, New York, NY.

ATLASZ, Robert, Isr, dental surg; b. Berlin, Ger, Sep 1, 1898; s. Arnold and Rosa (Pollak), in Isr since 1937; DMD, U Berlin, 1922; m. Charlotte Feder; c: Ruth Goldstein; Pvt practice, Tel Aviv, since 1937, Berlin, 1922-37. Lt, Aus-Hung Army, 1916-19. Hon vice-pres, Maccabi World Union; chmn, Maccabiah Games comm; mem, Isr Olympic comm; fmr sports dir, Maccabi, Ger; vet mem, Intl Amateur Athletic Fed; mem, B'nei B'rith Menora Lodge. Contbr lectures, articles on dent. Spec interests: music, navy. Home and office: 6 Pinsker St, Tel Aviv, Isr.

ATZIL, Aziz Menashe, Isr, advertising cons; b. Baghdad, Dec 15, 1919; s. Menashi and Lulu (Aslan); in Isr since 1928; att Amer U, Beirut, Lebanon, 1938-39; m. Camilla Peretz, Mar 25, 1942; c: Talila. Pres, Zurah Advt Ltd, since 1950; dir: Shefet Advt Ltd, since 1963; publ repr, Moaf Ltd, since 1951; org, dir annual courses in advt since 1953; lectr in advt; mgr: Menashi H Aslan Bankers, 1940-50; Near E Ind Supply Co, 1945-50. Chmn: Eliahu Hanavi B Syn; council, Isr Advt Assn, fmr pres; mem, Intl Advt Assn. Hobby: sports. Home: 42 Rembrandt St, Tel Aviv, Isr. Office: 3 Hashfela St, Tel Aviv, Isr.

ATZMON, Akiva, Isr, business exec, senior civil service off; b. Jerusalem, Feb 4, 1916; s. Baruch and Dvorah (Green) Wittenberg; att U de Firenze, It; DEng, Polytech di Torino, 1938; m. Henna Marcus, Feb 8, 1940; c: Dorit, Ordit, Daniela-Orit. Spec adv, Min of Trade and Ind, since 1957; gen dir, Mataeh Haumah Ltd, since 1966; dir, manpower dept, Min of Lab, 1954-55; dep dir gen, Min of Devl, 1955-57; mem bd dirs: Maskit Ltd, 1955-57; Negev Phosphates Ltd, 1955-58; Machtzavey Isr Ltd, 1955-58; Charsit Vehol Zach Ltd, 1955-57; Dead Sea Shore Devl Ltd, 1957-58. Haganah, 1932-46; Palmach, 1946-48; maj, IDF Engr Corps. Prin contribs: introduced in Isr intensive cultivation of Euroamerican popular trees for producing timber; invented and devl: methods on intl scale for following, and controlling, growth rate of trees; methods of irrigation and pest control; found, balneological cens on Dead Sea. Found: Gadna towns; Gadna Vegetable Producing Farms; Gadna Philharmonic Orch; Gadna units. Author: The Growing of Poplars for Windbreaks, 1967; The Poplars As Economical Trees, 1967. Home: 10 Palmach St, Hadera, Isr. Office: 4 Benjamin Blvd, Netanya, Isr.

ATZMON, Shmuel, Isr, actor, director; b. Bilgoray, Pol, June 29, 1929; s. Itzchak and Frida (Rapaport) Wircer; in Isr since 1948; att Drama Sch, Tel Aviv, 1948-51; m. Henia Roth, Aug 26, 1953; c: Anat, Itzchak. Actor, dir, Habimah Natl Theater, since 1968, actor, asst dir, 1953-68; found, mgr, actor, dir, Zavit Theater, 1959-68; actor, asst dir, Ohel Theater, 1951-53; directed: The Typist; Brecht on Brecht; The Foreposter; His Name Goes Before Him, Marko; acted in: No Exit; Glass Menagerie; Far Country; Altona; Creditors. Exec bd, vice-pres, Isr Cen, Intl Theater Inst, 1965-69, Isr repr, intl 7th Cong, NY; club, Variety, Isr. Recipient: Ford Foundation Travel Grant; Intl Theater Inst Award; Natl Council of Culture and Art Grant, 2nd prize, young dirs. Home: 6 Kikar Malkei Israel, Tel Aviv, Isr. Office: Habimah Theater, Tel Aviv, Isr.

AUERBACH, Carl Abraham, US, educator, attorney; b. Oct 2, 1915, NYC; s. Moritz and Rose (Auerbach); AB, LIU, 1935; LLB, Harvard Law Sch, 1938; m. Laura Kron, Sep 15, 1940; c: Linda, Eric. Prof, law, U Minn, since 1961; public mem, Admn Conf US since 1970, staff dir, comm internal org and procedure, 1961-62; atty: Ansell, Ansell and Marshall, 1938; US Lab Dept, 1938-40; asst gen counsel, OPA, 1940-43, gen counsel, 1946-47; asso gen counsel, US Off Econ Stabilization, 1946-47; prof, law, U Wis, 1947-61; cons, US Agcy Intl Devl, 1963-66; mem, US Commn Marine Scis, Engr, Resources, 1966-69. Lt, US Army 1943-46. Mem: US Natl Hwy Safety Adv Comm, since 1968; exec comm, div of behavioral scis, NRC, since 1967; Amer Law Inst; Amer Soc Intl Law; Law and Soc Assn; Citizens League of Minn. Co-author: The Legal Process, 1961; Federal Regulation of Transport, 1953. Recipient: Fulbright f: US, UK, 1953-54; f, Cen for Advanced Study in Behavioral Sci, 1958-59. Home: 3230 Kyle Ave N, Minneapolis, Minn. Office: Law Sch, U of Minn, Mineapolis, Minn.

AUERBACH, Charles, US, attorney, educator; b. Russ, July 15, 1898; s. Louis and Rachel (Armsham); in US since 1908; BA, W Reserve U, 1920, DJur, 1922; LLM, Cleveland-Marshall Law Sch, 1952; m. Celia Dworkin, June 30, 1927; c: David. Prof law, Cleveland Marshall Sch. Vice-chmn, candidates scanning comm, Cleveland Citizens League, 1952; chmn, juvenile court comm, Cleveland Bar Assn, 1966-68; mem: Amer Judicature Soc; UJA campaign comm; B'nai B'rith Hillel Found, 1953-56; admn comm, ZOA, 1947-50; J Consumptive Relief Soc, 1935-50; bd dirs, Bur J Educ; The Temple, 1948-49; bd trustees, J Family Service Assn, 1951-53; repr, Cleveland Wfr Fed, mem, study comm for HS and higher learning, 1962-63; mem, World Zionist Affairs Comm; lectr, Cen Amer, JA, 1945; J Comty Fed repr, Cleveland Tercentenary Commn, 1954; club, The Temple Men's, pres, 1952-53. Author: The Talmud-Gateway to Common Law, 1952; contbr articles to jours. Home: 18507 Newell Rd, Shaker Heights, O. Office: 531 Leader Bldg, Cleveland, O.

AUERBACH, Edgar, Isr, physician, researcher; b. Berlin, Ger, Aug 10, 1914; s. Herbert and Manya (Silbermann); in Isr since 1938; att Ger U, Prague; MD, St Joseph U, Beirut, Leb, 1946; m. Rena Mark, 1944; c: Judith. Asst prof, Hadassah-Heb U Med Sch, since 1958; dir, vision research lab, Hadassah Hosp, since 1957, research f, Cancer Research Lab, 1941-44, phys, eye, dept, 1947-52; research F: Harvard U, 1952-54, 1955-57; Ia State U, 1954-55. Maj, MC, IDF. Mem: Isr Phys and Pharm Soc; Isr Ophthal Soc; Isr Soc for Electroencephatography and Neurophys; Intl Soc for Clinical Electroretinography; Natl Acad Sci; NRC; Comm on Vision, Wash, DC; Assn for Research in Ophthal. Contbr to sci jours. Home: 27 Binyamin Mitudela St, Jerusalem, Isr. Office: POB 499, Jerusalem, Isr.

AUERBACH, Erich, England, photo journalist; b. Falkenau, Bohemia, Dec 12, 1911; s. Ignaz and Hermine (Zentner); in Eng since 1939; att, Phil fac, U Prague; m. Lucia Bodlaender, 1935; m. 2nd, Lizzy Tauber, 1946; c: Monica. Independent photo journalist since 1957; mem ed staff, Prager Tagblatt, 1931-38; official photographer, Czech govt in exile (London), 1941-45; sr staff photographer, Illustrated, London, 1945-57. Author: An Eye for Music, 1970. F, Royal Photographers' Soc, London. Hobby: music. Home and office: 29, Abercorn Pl, St John's Wood, London NW 8, Eng.

AUERBACH, Frank Helmut, Eng, artist; b. Berlin, Ger, Apr 29, 1931; s. Max and Charlotte (Borchardt); in Eng since 1939; deg, 1st class hons, silver medal, Royal Coll of Arts, London, 1955. One-man shows: Beaux Arts Gal, London, 1956-63; Marlborough Fine Art, London 1965-67; represented: Carnegie Intl Exhb, Pittsburgh, 1958-61; Dunn Intl, 1963; Gulbenkian Intl, 1965; Stuyvesant Collection, 1967, all London; public collections: Tate gal, Arts Council, both London; Contemporary Art Soc, Salvador Mus, Brazil; Natl Gal, Vic, Austr; Chrysler Mus, Provincetown, Mass; gals: Hull, Manchester, Nottingham, Oldham, and others. Office: c/o Marlborough Fine Art, 39 Old Bond St, London W 1, Eng.

AUERBACH, Isaac L, US, business exec, engineer; b. Phila, Pa, Oct 9, 1921; s. Philip and Rose (Levin); BS, Drexel Inst of Tech, Phila, 1943; MS, Harvard U, 1947; m. Nina Kaleska, Oct 9, 1921; c: Philip. Pres, Auerbach Corp for Info Sci's; chmn bd: Auerbach Info Inc; Bakkenist Auerbach NV, Amsterdam, Netherlands; Intl Programming Corp; lab asst, Midvale Co, 1937-41; devl engr, ITE Circuit Breaker Co, 1941-43; research engr, Eckert-Mauchly Computer Corp, 1947-49; mgr, spec producs div, Burroughs Research Cen, 1949-57. Served, USNR. Prin contribs: demonstrated 1st digital mercury delay line system for BINAC and UNIVAC computers, 1948; designed and devl static magnetic theory sys for ENIAC, 1952; devl radar target detection equipment

for SAGE air defense sys and for Atlas ICBM guidance computer, 1956. Found pres, Intl Fed for Info Processing, 1960-65, trustee, 1965-69; org, chmn, elec div, Allied J App, Phila, 1963-66; found, mem bd dirs, Phila chap, Amer Technion Soc, since 1948; f: Inst of Elec and Electronics Engrs; AAAS; bd dirs, J Publ Soc; bd trustees, Fed JA, Phila; exec comm, bd govs, Drexel U Alumni Assn; bd govs: Gtr Phila C of C Econ and Planning Council; adv bd, J student activities, Hillel Found; mem: bd advs, Cen for Strategic and Intl Studies, Wash, DC; natl council, Natl Planning Assn; citizens policy adv comm, Phila Bd of Educ, 1967-69; Research Soc of Amer; Young Pres' Org; Assn for Computing Machines; Amer Instrument Soc; Franklin Inst; Sigma Xi; Eta Kappa Nu; U Lodge, B'nai B'rith, Phila; Amer Soc for Cybernetics; club, Harvard U Alumni. Co-author: Handbook of Automation, Computation and Control, 1959; Computer Handbook, 1961; chmn, ed bd, Library of Computer and Information Sciences; contbr to tech jours. Recipient: Grand Medal, City of Paris, Fr, 1959; achievement award, Phila sect, Inst of Elec and Electronics Engrs, 1961; alumni citation; Drexel Inst of Tech, 1961; four service ribbons; humanitarian award, Fed JAs, Phila, 1966; Tower of David Award, State of Isr Bonds, 1969. Home: 700 Elkins Ave, Elkins Park, Pa. Office: 121 N Broad St, Philadelphia, Pa.

AUERBACH, Joseph, US, attorney; b. Franklin, NH, Dec 3, 1916; s. Jacob and Bessie (Reamer); BA, Harvard U, 1938; LLB, 1941; m. Judith Evans, Nov 10, 1941; c: Jonathan, Hope. Partner, Sullivan & Worcester, since 1952; dir: Tsai Mgmt Research Corp; Manhattan Fund; Hemisphere Fund; TMR Appreciation Fund; prin atty, SEC, Wash DC, 1941, 1948-50, Phila, 1942, 1946-47; adv, US chmn, Combined Steel Group, Allied High Commn for Ger, 1950-52. US Army, 1943-1946. Mem: Boston Legal Aid Soc; Assn of ICC Practitioners; Amer, Boston, Fed Bar Assns; clubs: Fort Hill; Sky; Harvard, NYC. Home: 23 Lime St, Boston, Mass. Office: 225 Franklin St, Boston, Mass.

AUERBACH, Leo, Isr, attorney; b. Tshernovitz, Russ, Aug 20, 1912; s. Baruch and Rosa (Gruenberg); in Isr since 1959; law deg, U Tshernovitz, Russ, 1934; PhD, political sci, Cluj, Rum, 1936; m. Esther Kotlear, May 10, 1944; c: Alisa, Heinrich. Official property collector, Min of Justice, since 1963; atty, Isr, since 1959, Rum, 1954-59; Atty gen, Cooperation Rum, 1949-54; fmr accts controller, Cen Control Bd, Va'ad Ha-poel, Histadrut. Mem: Isr Bar Assn. Home: 5 Bilu St, Petah Tikva, Isr. Office: Min of Justice, 39 Nachalat Benjamin St, Tel Aviv, Isr.

AUERBACH, Selig S, US, rabbi; b. Hamburg, Ger, Oct 20, 1907; s. Joseph and Rosa (Cahn); in US since 1940; ordained rabbi, Hildesheimer Rabb Sem, Berlin, 1933; PhD, Maxmilian U, Wurtzburg, Bavaria, 1933; m. Hilda Fromm, Dec 9, 1934; c: Hannah Issacs, Wilma Lebowitz, Nancy. Rabbi, Lake Placid Syn, Lake Placid, NY, since 1961; chaplain: Sunmount State Sch for Retarded, Tupper Lake, NY; NY State Hosp, Raybrook; Will Rogers Memorial Hosp, Saranac Lake, NY; asst rabbi, Wurzburg, prof rel, Tchrs Coll, 1930-34; regional rabbi, Recklinghausen, Westphalia, Ger, 1934-38; rabbi, Northamption, Eng, 1939-40; asst dir, Bd J Educ, Cincinnati, O, 1942; rabbi, Cong B'nai Issac, Aberdeen, SD, 1949-52; chaplain: Army Air Force Base, Rapid City, 1949-52; VA Hosp, Ft Meade, 1949-53; Hot Springs, 1949-52; asst chaplain, Ft Belvoir; rabbi, Beth El Cong, Torrington, Conn, 1958-61; J student adv, Paul Smith's Coll; NY lectr on Speaker's Bur, J Chautauqua Soc. Mem: RA, fmr mem, exec council, comm on J laws and standards, commn on coll youth; NY Bd Rabbis; treas, Natl Assn Mh Chaplains; ZOA; J Hist Soc; NY State Regional Advisory Bd, ADL; f, Lehman Inst on J Ethics; hon chaplain, Lake Placid Fire Brigade; clubs: Rotary, Saranac Lake; Lions, Lake Placid. Author: Rabbinical Assemblies of Rhine Communities During 13th Century; several responsa; contbr to J periodicals. Home: 30 Saranac Ave, Lake Placid, NY.

AUERBACH, Yoshua, Isr, business exec; b. Safad, Isr, June 15, 1923; s. Wolff and Hannah (Kahana); att: Fac de Filosofia, Sao Paulo; Escuelo de Ciencias Economica; Rio; Escuela Engenharia, Parana, all in Brazil; m. Paulina Gofman, July 18, 1948; c: Adir, Siona, Noar, Sagui. Gen dir: Tel Aviv Devl Co; Haifa Levant; Armol; fmr lectr, phil; fmr gen dir: Arca; Pasa; Armon; Magazines Modernos; fmr chmn, Haboker, Heb daily. Dir, Lib Party, Isr; fmr chmn: Zionist United Council; J Educ Org; Student org, Renascencia, all in Brazil; mem: World Zionist Action Comm; finance comm, JA. Ed: Menora; Porvir; Portuguese papers; collaborate, Heb Ency, Brazil and Portuguese issues; contbr articles on sociol, gen topics. Home: 6 Yeelim St, Ramat Gan, Isr.

AUFRICHTIG, Juan, Chile, merchant; b. Berlin, Ger, Sep 9, 1899; s. Max and Olga (Angres); m. Ilse Ehrenfried, Oct 27, 1931. Owner bus since 1939. Found, youth movement, Hakoah, Valparaiso, since 1941; dir, Comunidad Israelita, since 1942; pres, Centro Sionista, 1956-61; Chilean delg, WZC, Jerusalem, 1961; pres, Comunidad Israelita, Valparaiso, 1968-69; fmr: pres, B'nai B'rith lodge; active, Zionist orgs, Ger. Home: Cuarta Oriente 491, Casilla 480, Vina del Mar, Chile.

AUSTER, Lionel S, US, surgeon, oncologist; b. NYC, Aug 19, 1900; s. Max and Fanny (Sandler); AB, CCNY, 1919; MD, Cornell U, 1923; div; c: Natalie Levinson. Cons surg, asso in spec path, Bx Leb Hosp Cen, since 1964, on staff since 1932; surg, NYC Police Dept, since 1945; sci dir, Cancer Research Soc, Inc; visiting surg, NYC Cancer Inst, 1950-53. Lt, US Army, 1918; capt, USNR MC, 1941-46. F: Amer Coll Surgs; AMA; NY Acad Med; dipl, Amer Bd Surgs; mem: Phi Beta Kappa; AAAS; Amer Assn Cancer Research; NY Acad Sci; NY Cancer Soc; Soc, Med Jurisprudence; Intl Cancer Cong; NY Path Soc; Coll and Hosp Alumni Assn. Contbr to sci jours. Recipient: Pres Citation, USMC. Home and office: 2 E 88 St, New York, NY.

AUSUBEL, David Paul, US, psychiatrist, educator; b. Bklyn, NY, Oct 25, 1918; s. Herman and Lillian (Leff); AB, U of Pa, 1939; AM, Columbia U, 1940, PhD, 1950; MD, Brandeis U, 1943; m. Pearl Leibowitz, Nov 21, 1943; c: Frederick, Laura. Prof, prog head, educ psychol doctoral prog, CCNY, since 1968; prof, educ psychol, U of Ill, 1950-66; prof, psychol, educ, med educ, U Toronto, 1966-68; sr asst surg, USPHS, Wash, DC, 1945-47; chief med off, UNRRA, DP Assembly Cen, Ger, 1945-46; psycht res, USPHS Hosp, Ky, 1946-47; sr psycht, Buffalo State Hosp, 1947-48; lectr: psychol, LIU, 1948-49; psychol, psycht, Yeshiva U, 1948-50. Mem: Amer Psychol Assn; Soc Research in Child Devl; Mid West Psychol Assn; Natl Soc for Study Educ; Kappa Delta Pi; Sigma Xi. Author: Ego Development and Personality Disorders, 1952; Theory and the Problems of Adolescent Development, 1958; Drug Addiction: Physiological, Psychological and Sociological Aspects, 1958; The Psychology of Meaningful Verbal Learning, 1963; Educational Psychology: A Cognitive View, 1968; contbr to profsl publs. Recipient, Fulbright Research Grant, NZ, 1957-58. Home: 1902 G Huff Dr, Urbana, Ill. Office: U of Ill, Urbana, Ill.

AUSUBEL, Herman US, oral surgeon; b. Lezajsk, Aus-Pol, April 19, 1889; s. Israel and Frimet (Schiff); in US since 1905; DDS, NY Coll of Dent, NYU, 1911; Columbia U; m. Lillian Leff, Dec 25, 1915 (decd); m. 2nd Theresa Blechman, Apr 9, 1960; c: David, Hillel, Jean. Ret; tchr, lectr, clinician, oral surg, since 1920; chief oral surg, Bikur Cholim Hosp, Bklyn, NY, 1920-22; cons, oral surg, Long Beach Hosp, NY, 1924-30. Found: Ausubel revolving student loan fund; Ausubel prize, both Heb U. Fmr, pres: Bklyn Soc for Oral Diagnosis; League for Promotion Better Dent, org, 1917; Williamsburg and Kings Co Dent Soc; Amer League for Public Med; fmr vice-pres, Allied Dent Council; fmr chmn finance comm, Bklyn J Council; bd chmn, N Shore Zionist Dist, Fla, since 1957; pres, Weinberg discussion forum, Miami Beach, since 1958; Surfside citizens for lower taxes and better govt, 1958; mem, libr comm, Amer Friends Heb U; mem, natl admn comm, AJCong; Amer, state and local Dent Socs; Amer Assn for Advancement of Oral Diagnosis; ZOA; clubs: Sea Gate Comty, pres, 1933-36; Civic Affairs, pres, 1951-53. Asso ed, Odontologist, 1910-11; creator, phonograph, tape recording, Sleep Without Pills; contbr to profsl jours. Home: 9048 Froude Ave, Miami Beach, Fla.

AVENARY, Hanoch, Isr, musicologist; b. Danzig, Ger, May 25, 1908; s. Norbert and Anna (Begach] Lowenstein; in Isr since 1936; att: U Leipzig; U Munich; U Frankfurt; U Konigsberg; PhD, 1931; m. Thea Wrzeszinski, Jan 7, 1936; c: Tamar Givoli. Sr lectr, dept musicology, Tel Aviv U, since 1966; research f, musicology, Heb U, Jerusalem, since 1964. Maj, IAF, 1948-65. Prin contrib: research, hist of J and Near E music. Vice-pres, Isr Musicological Soc. Author: Hebrew Hymn Tunes—The Rise and Development of Musical Tradition, 1969; contbr to profsl jours and encys. Recipient: Zelig Altshul Research award, 1955-56. Hobbies: golf, gardening. Home: 136 Dizengoff St, Tel Aviv, Isr.

AVERBACH, Albert, US, attorney, author, lecturer; b. Bender, Bessarabia, Feb 22, 1902; s. Matus and Eva (Kirchen); in US since 1906; LLB, Union U, 1923. Mem, law firm, Gair and Averbach, since 1959, previously Gair, Finley, Averbach, Mahley and Hoffman, 1954-59; vice-pres, gen council: Rumsey Mfg Corp, 1941-47; Rumsey Products Inc, 1943-47; lectr: Law Sci Inst Symposiums, Austin, Tex, Chgo; Practicing Law Inst. Pres, Intl Acad Trial Lawyers, 1954-56; dir, chmn, leg comm, NY State Assn Plaintiffs Trial Lawyers; mem: Amer Judicature Soc; Amer, Fed, Onondaga Co, NY Bar Assns; Amer Soc Forensic Sci; Phi Sigma Delta; Chi Pi Phi, C of C; Comty Chest, AAAS; Law Sci Acad Amer; Intl Inst Arts Letters, Justinian Hon Law Soc; Masons, fmr master; hon f: Amer Coll Legal Med; Intl Acad Law and Sci; clubs: Demorcatic; Masonic Temple. Author: More About Traffic Jam in the Court, 1954; Medical Photography as a Boon to Trial Lawyers, 1954; Comparative Negligence-A Cure for our Congested Courts, 1955; The Problems of Traumatic Epilepsy as Viewed by the Trial Lawyer, 1955; The Modern Trial Lawyer, 1955; Tampering with our Jury System, 1956; Effective Courtroom Use of Medical Books, 1956; Finding an Expert for Your Case, 1957; Handling Accident Cases, vols 1—7, 1958-63; Handling Automobile Cases, 2 vols, 1960; asso ed, law jour, Natl Assn Claimants Compensation Attys since 1954; adv ed, negligence Compensation Service, since 1956; co-ed, Tort Medical Yearbook, 2 vols, 1961; The Verdicts Were Just. Hobby: golf. Home: RD 6, Auburn, NY. Offices: 30 State St, Seneca Falls, NY; 853 E Willow St, Syracuse, NY; Suite 1809, 50 Broadway, New York, NY.

AVIDA, Mordecai, Isr, government official; b. Plock, Pol, Oct 16, 1909; s. Yehuda and Sarah (Kalisher) Zlotnik; in Isr since 1930; BA, McGill U, Montreal, 1930; MA, Heb U, Jerusalem, 1935; m. Myriam Levkowitz, Aug 11, 1931; c: Ram, Uri. Dir gen, Ben Zvi Found since 1968; tchr, agric secondary sch, Pardess Hannah, 1935-36; asst controller, Heb progs, Pal BC Service, 1936-43, controller, 1943-48; dep dir, Brit Commonwealth dept, Min for Fgn Affairs, 1948-49; co-found and dir, Kol Zion Lagola radio, 1949-52; cultural attache, Isr legation, Buenos Aires, 1953-56; dir, S Amer desk, info div, Min for Fgn Affairs, 1956-58; min, counselor, Isr Emb, Buenos Aires, 1958-61; dir, cultural relations div, Min for Fgn Affairs, 1961-66; ambass to UNESCO, 1966-68. Pres, Casa Argentina—Tierra Santa; chmn, Heb U Alumni Assn. Recipient: Grand Off of Merit General San Martin, 1960. Home: 5 Palmach St, Jerusalem, Isr.

AVIDAN, David, Isr, essayist, playwright, painter, film maker; b. Tel Aviv, Feb 21, 1934; s. Dov and Pnina (Neikrug); att Heb U, 1952-54. Poet, painter, underground film-maker; head, experimental non-profit orgs; one of maj originators of avant-garde Isr poetry; first Heb poet to trans his own works into Eng; inventor, monoprojections, in painting; ed, TV, radio progs. Exhbs: Negative Stimuli, Massada-Dizengoff Art Gal, Tel Aviv, 1968; 10-Pro-Anti, 220 Gal, Tel Aviv, 1968; Mod Isr Art, 1969; Stop! Green, Gordon Art Gal, Artist's House, Jerusalem, 1969; Monoprojections, Isr Mus, Jerusalem, 1969; film: You Name It; record, David Avidan Reciting David Avidan; vol of poetry, Megaovertone, 1966; play, David Avidan Maggish Teatron Mufshat; poems in Heb: Brazim Afufei S'fatayim, 1954; Beayot Ishiyot, 1957; Sikkum Beinaim, 1960; Shirei Lahatz, 1962; Mashehu Bishvil Mishehu, 1964; Shirim Bilti-Efshariyim, Dorah Ishi Al Massa LSD, 1968; Anthology of Modern Hebrew Poetry, 1968. Mem: Assn Heb Writers, Isr. Recipient: grant, Isr Zangwill Fund, 1966; f, Eugene F Saxon Memorial Trust, 1967-68. Hobbies: sports, jazz, ballet. Home and office: 11 Shimshon St, Tel Aviv, Isr.

AVIDAR, Avraham, Isr, diplomat; b. Klodawa, Pol, Dec 5, 1918; s. Avigdor and Sara (Prost) Wroclawski; in Isr since 1947; att U London, 1941-42; BA, hons, Heb U, 1953; m. Malka Kastner; c: Giora, Raanan, Zafrira. Isr cousul gen, Chgo since 1966; secy, Hechalutz and Habonim movements, Danzig, 1937-39; org immigration to Pal from Nazi Danzig, 1938-39; secy, Hachshara, Tingrith, Brit; instr Aliyat Hanoar; repr, Hechalutz and Habonim in Scotland, all 1940-47; secy, Kibbutz Galed, prin, kibbutz sch, 1947-58; on diplomatic mission in Pol and USSR, 1958-61; at US desk, Min for Fgn Affairs, Jerusalem, 1961-62; on good will mission to US, 1962; dep spokesman, Min for Fgn Affairs, Jerusalem, 1962-63; consul of educ, NY, 1963-64, senior consul for political affairs, NY, 1964-66. Office: 936 N Michigan St, Chicago, Ill.

AVIDAR, Yemima Tshernovitz, Isr, writer; b. Wilna, Russ; d. Samuel and Bella (Feldman) Tshernowitz; att Us in Aus, Ger; m. Yosef Avidar; c: Rama, Dana. Author: Gan-Gani, The

Daughter; numerous books for children. Mem: Pioneer Women. Home: 5 Mevo Yoram St, Jerusalem, Isr.

AVIDAR, Yosef, Isr, diplomat; b. Keremenitz, Pol, May 7, 1906; s. Yoshua and Shprintza (Rochel); in Isr since 1925; m. Yemima Tschernovitz, Oct 1, 1932; c: Rama, Dana. Comptroller, Histadrut, since 1968; ambass, Russ, 1955-58; dir gen, Min of Lab, 1959-60; ambass, Argentina, 1961-65; dir, Govt Corp Auth, 1966-68. Haganah from 1925; mem, chief command, 1937-48; dir, mil ind, 1945-46; dep chief, gen staff, 1946-47; quartermaster gen, IDF, 1948-49; brig gen, cdr N command, 1949-52, cen command 1952-53; head, gen staff, 1954-55. Home: 5 Mevo Yoram St, Jerusalem, Isr. Office: 93 Arlosoroff St, Tel Aviv, Isr.

AVIDOM, Menahem, Isr, composer; b. Stanislawow, Pol, Jan 6, 1908; s. Isaac and Helen (Mahler) Kalkstein; in Isr since 1925; BA, Amer U, Beirut, 1928; att Natl Conservatory, Paris, 1928-31; m. Suzanne Soumi-Lyonais, Jan 31, 1935; c: Daniela Rabinovich, Miriam. Gen dir, ACUM Ltd, Isr Composers and Authors Assn, since 1956; fmr: gen secy, Isr Philharmonic Orch, 1946-52; art adv, Isr Gov, 1952-55. Composed: nine syms; three operas; three quartets; three concerti; vocal, instrumental and chamber music. Life f, Intl Assn for Arts and Letters, Zurich, since 1958; pres, Isr Composers League, since 1959; mem, Natl Arts Council, since 1962. Recipient: Press Prize, Intl Music Festival, 1934; two Engle Prizes for Music, Tel Aviv Munic, 1936, 1957; Isr Philharmonic Prize, 1952; Isr State Prize, 1961; ACUM Prize, 1964. Home: POB 11201, Tel Aviv, Isr. Office: 118-120 Rothschild Blvd, Tel Aviv, Isr.

AVIDOR, Arie, Isr, journalist; b. Roman, Rum, Sep 10, 1932; s. Eliezer and Etty (Katz) Hascalovici, in Isr since 1951; social sci deg, Heb U, Jerusalem, 1957; m. Liliane Weil, Jan 1, 1959; c: Anat, Lyat J. Ed, found, Aurora, since 1963; co-secy, Pecan Plantations Ltd, 1960-63. Sgt, IDF. Mem, Masons; fmr secy, Isr Hatzeriah; repr to Brazil, Bolivia, World. Confd Gen Zionists. Hobbies: photography; gardening; touring. Home: 24 Hacarmel, St, Ramat Hasharon, Isr. Office: 88 Hachashmonaim St, Tel Aviv, Isr.

AVIDOV, Zvi, Isr, educator; b. Znin, Ger, Nov 13, 1896; s. Moritz and Louise (Michel) Klein; in Isr since 1921; MSc, Heb U, Jerusalem, 1944, PhD, 1945; m. Elisheva Friedman, 1922; c: Noomi Lifshitz. Prof em, agric entomology, fac agric, Heb U, Rehovot, since 1965, prof, 1960-65, dean fac, 1958-62, on fac since 1951; asst entomologist, Agric Research Sta, 1923-30, entomologist, 1930-58. Author: Citrus Pests in Palestine, 1940; Pests of Vegetables in Palestine, 1941; Pests of Ornamental Plants in Israel, 1949; Plant Pests of Israel, Heb ed, 1961, rev Eng ed, 1969; contbr to profsl jours. Home: 3 Ussishkin St, Rehovot, Isr. Office: Fac of Agric, Hebrew U, Rehovot, Isr.

AVIGAD, Nachman, Isr, archaeologist, educator; b. Zawalow, Aus, Sep 25, 1905; s. Isak and Perl (Farb) Reiss; in Isr since 1925; MA, PhD, Heb U, Jerusalem; m. Shulamith Levin; c: Gad. Prof, head, dept archaeol, Heb U, 1954-68, mem fac since 1949. Prin contribs: archaeol excavations, studies in epigraphy. Mem: exec commn, Isr Exploration Soc, Archaeol Council, Isr; intl bd dirs, Isr Mus. Author: Ancient Monuments in the Kidron Valley, 1954; co-author, Genesis Apocryphon, 1956; contbr articles to profsl jours. Recipient: Bialik Prize, 1954. Home: 8 Ibn Shaprut St, Jerusalem, Isr. Office: Heb U, Jerusalem, Isr.

AVIGDOR, Isaac C, US, rabbi; b. Pol, Dec 2, 1920; s. Jacob and Rachel (Horowitz); in US since 1948; ordained rabbi, Rabb Coll, Stanislav, Pol, 1939; m. Esther Horowitz, June 14, 1949; c: David, Morton, Merrill, Jacob. Rabbi, United Syn of Gtr Hartford, since 1955; exec dir, Yeshiva Rabbi Solomon Kluger, 1948-52; prin, Yeshiva Acad, LI 1952-53; exec vice-pres, Hapoel Hamizrachi of Gtr NY, 1953-55. Mem: RabCA; Rel Zionists Amer; Yeshiva U. Author: Ten for Two, 1962; Six Reasons to Keep Kashruth. Home: 25 Overhill Rd, W Hartford, Conn. Study: 840 N Main St, W Hartford, Conn.

AVI-GUY, Zvi, Isr, legislator; b. Vienna, May 26, 1934; s. Zeev and Stella (Kronfeld) Icht; BA, LLB, Heb U, Jerusalem; m. Haviva Cruvi; c: Yoram, Gili, Amnon. Town clerk, Tel Aviv-Yaffa, since 1964; dir, mayor's off, spokesman, 1960-64; head, off, Min of Lab, 1956-59. Lt, IDF. Chmn, Assn for Promotion Tourism, Tel Aviv; mem: Gov bd, Haaretz Mus; publicity bd, Isr Philharmonic Orch. Co-Author: International

Relations; trans, Diplomacy by H Nicolson, into Heb, 1957. Hobbies: reading, tennis, swimming. Home: 36 Yehuda Hanasi St, Tel Aviv, Isr. Office: Munic of Tel Aviv Bldg, Kikar Malchei Isr, Tel Aviv, Isr.

AVIHAR (Eizenberg), Eliyahu Shmuel, Isr, journalist, sociologist; b. Pol, Jan 23, 1917; BA, HS for Social Sci; m. Esther Burstein; c: David, Giyora. Dir, intl project youth exch, Cen of Local Auth, Tel Aviv, since 1969; gen secy, Yessodot, Agric Educ Inst, 1951-57; lectr, Histadrut Clerks Sch; dir, Isr Tourist Off, Belgium, 1967-68. Mem, Public Council for Stat; fmr: vice pres, WW II Vet Org; mem, Yad Veshem Council. Ed, Plotzk, anthol; contbr to profsl jours. Home: 5 Hadaya St, Holon, Isr. Office: 3 Heftman St, Tel Aviv, Isr.

AVIMOR, Shimon, Isr, diplomat; b. Frankfurt, Ger, Aug 1, 1913; s. Hermann and Elsa; MA, cum laude, Heb U, Jerusalem, 1940; m. Rachel Janovsky, Feb 19, 1942; c: Yizraela, Yaakov. Dir, archives, Isr Min for Fgn Affairs, since 1968; first secy, Isr Emb, Dakar, Senegal, non-res consul, Gambia, 1962-65; Isr Ambass, Libreville, Gabon, 1965-68. Lt, IDF, 1948-49. Home: 14 Metudela St, Jerusalem, Isr. Office: Min for Fgn Affairs, Jerusalem, Isr.

AVINERI, Shlomo, Isr, educator; b. Bielsko, Silesia, Aug 20, 1933; s. Michael and Erna (Groner); in Isr since 1939; BA, MA, PhD, Heb U; m. Dvora Nadler, Oct 8, 1956; c: Maayan. Chmn, dept political sci, Heb U, since 1968, lectr, sr lectr since 1961; visiting lectr, Yale U, 1966-67. IDF, 1951-54. Mem: Intl Political Sci Assn. Author: The Social and Political Thought of Karl Marx, 1968; Karl Marx on Colonialism and Modernization, 1968. Recipient: Rubin Prize for Social Sci, 1968. Home: 50 Harlap, Jerusalem, Isr. Office: Dept of Political Sci, Heb U, Jerusalem, Isr.

AVINERY, Iddo, Isr, linguist; b. Tel Aviv, Isr, Feb 14, 1932; s. Itzhak and Judith (Nacht); BA, with distinction, Heb U, Jerusalem, 1952, MA, 1955; m. Marie Serfaty, Dec 16, 1965. Lectr, Semitic langs, Bar Ilan U, since 1965; fmr: tchr; writer, journalist; tchr, Heb, Arabic, Ma'ale Sch, Jerusalem. Contbr: articles to profsl publs; radio lectures. Recipient: Bialik Prize, Heb U, 1954; scholarship, Memorial Found for J Culture, 1970. Hobby: chess. Home: 43 Hamag St, Jerusalem, Isr. Office: Bar Ilan U, Ramat Gan, Isr.

AVINOAM, Reuben, Isr, poet, teacher, editor, civil servant; b. Chgo, Ill, Aug, 12 1905; s. Aharon and Miriam (Gorenstein) Grossman; in Isr since 1929; grad, NYU, 1928; m. Anna Shafir, 1925; c: Noam (killed in action, War of Independence), Edni. Tchr: Heb Acad Herzliah, NY, 1923-25; Tarbuth Tchrs Sem, NY, 1924-27; Herzlia Heb Coll, Tel Aviv, 1929-49; educ tour, US, 1945-46; lecture tours: Austr, 1951; US, 1955; repr, Isr Min of Educ and Culture, Shakespeare Conf, Stratford, Eng, 1951; sup, Eng lang instruction, Isr Min of Educ and Culture, 1950-52. Author: poetry: Shirim, 1930; Idyllyoth, 1934; Av uVito, 1934; Aley Dvai, 1948; Shirim uPoemoth, 1951; Etz Shatalti, 1958; Dmuyoth mini Kedem, poems, 1964; compiled Heb-Eng Dict, 1938; trans into Heb: Valley of the Moon, Jack London, 1930; Selected Tales, E A Poe, 1930; Dreamers of the Ghetto, Israel Zangwill; The Last Days of Shylock, Lewisohn; Fireflies, Tagore, 1942; Enoch Arden, Tennyson; King Lear, 1944; Antony and Cleopatra, Shakespeare, 1947; Samson Agonistes, Milton, 1950; Walden, Thoreau, 1962; compiled and trans into Heb: Mivhar Shirath America, Heb Anthol of Amer Verse, 1954; Mivhar Shirath Anglia, Heb Anthol of Eng Verse, 1957; co-ed: Shakespeare Tragedies, 1959 including trans: Romeo and Juliet; King Lear; Antony and Cleopatra; appd by PM Ben-Gurion as ed of lit and artistic works of the fallen soldiers of IDF since 1949; publ works, Gevilay Esh, Parchments of Fire, 3 vols, 1952-1958, 1961; ed, booklets for youth and poems relating to Feats of Valour in Isr wars. Mem: exec commn, Isr Writers Assn since 1954; secy, Isr PEN, 1942-46; delg, Intl PEN Congs, 1947, 1949, 1953. Recipient, Tchernichovsky Prize, Tel Aviv Munic, 1959. Home: 103 Rothschild Blvd, Tel Aviv, Isr.

AVISHALOM, Dov Issachar, Isr, educator; b. Kolo, Pol, June 25, 1910; s. Aron and Chana (Poznanski) Schultz; in Isr since 1935; BSc, Warsaw U, 1935; MSc, Heb U, Jerusalem, 1937; PhD, U Minn, 1963; m. Rachel Yudelevitz, Oct 16, 1945; c: Chana Hoffmann, Shoshana. Lectr, math, Heb U, since 1964; tchr, math, dir, real subjects, ORT Tech Coll, since 1951; tchr math: Bialik HS, 1937-38; Tchrs Sem, 1938-39; lectr, math: Bar Ilan U, 1957-61; St Thomas Coll, 1962-64; found, dir, HS, Netanya, 1939-40. Lt, Pol Army, Brit Army, IDF. Vice-pres, Jacob Frand Lodge, B'nai B'rith, Tel Aviv; mem: council, Academic Club, Histadrut; Assn for Symbolic Logic, US; Math Soc, Isr, US; fmr: charity dir, B'nai B'rith; secy, Kolo-Landsmanschaft; council mem, Tchrs Org. Author: four books on algebra, 1953; Calculus and Differential Equations, 1965. Recipient: cert of merit, Dict of Intl Biography, 1967. Spec interests: phil of math; symbolic logic; foundations of geometry; phil of Judaism. Home: 32 LaGuardia St, Tel Aviv, Isr. Office: Heb U, Jerusalem, Isr.

AVI-SHAUL, Mordechai, Isr, author, playwright; b. Solnok, Hung, May 17, 1898; s. Saul and Esther (Fisher) Mandel; in Isr since 1921; grad, Tchrs Training Coll, Budapest, 1917; att Heb U, Jerusalem, 1925-26; m. Lea Yedidia, May 18, 1919; c: Saul, Bruria, Naama. Author, playwright, trans, asso with Sifriat Poalim Pub Co, Tel Aviv, since 1948; contbr of: essays; poetry; lit criticism to Heb Newspapers, periodicals in Isr and abroad, since 1920; tchr, headmaster, schs and pedagogical insts: Hung and Yugo, 1917-21; Jerusalem, Ben Shemen, Tel Aviv, 1921-48. Author: 2 vols of poetry; 2 vols of plays, including Jew Suss; works of prose: Swiss Metamorphoses, 1963; King Karakash and other Profane Stories, 1965; The Graves Are Ready, 1968; essays on: Goethe; Heine; Thomas Mann; Brecht; Attila Jozsef; others; trans into Heb: works of: Jack London; Stefan Zweig; Lion Feuchtwanger; Julius Fucik; Jaroslav Hasek; Bertolt Brecht; Joseph Conrad; Thomas Mann; Goethe; Attila Joszef; Milkos Radnoti; Janos Arany. Mem: Heb Writers Assn; Société d'Auteurs, Compositeurs et Editeurs de Musique; League for the Rights of Man; Isr-USSR Friendship Org. Recipient: Tchernichovsky Prize for trans of classics, 1957; ACUM Prize for lit, 1966; Nordau Prize, 1967. Home: 8 Kiryat Sefer St, Tel Aviv, Isr. Office: POB 526, Tel Aviv, Isr.

AVISSAR, Pinhas, Isr, judge; b. Sudilkov, Russ, 1895; s. Ahron and Dvora (Bluvstein); in Isr since 1914; grad law, 1925; m. Pua Naidik; c: Hanna Giladi, Israel, (killed, War of Independence). Ret; Judge, Dist Court, Tel Aviv, 1948-65; pvt law practice, 1927-48. Turkish Army, 1916; Gdud Ivri, 1918. Home: 4 Feierberg St, Tel Aviv, Isr.

AVITAHL, Theodor, US, conductor; b. Bacau, Rum, Jan 13, 1933; s. Maier and Roza (Culer) Leibovici; in US since 1962; dipl of merit, State Conservatory of Music, Bucharest, 1955; m. Ursula Reyher, May 18, 1963; c: Nicole, Christian. Conductor, music dir, St Louis Philharmonic Orch, since 1963; perm conductor, Moldova State Philharmonic Orch, Rum, 1955-59; guest appearances, sym orchs: Belgium; Holland; Ger; Switz; Isr; US. Mem: Amer Sym Orch League; Amer Fed Musicians. Home: 9705 Hale Dr, St Louis, Mo. Office: Kiel Auditorium, St Louis, Mo.

AVITSUR, Shemuel, Isr, educator, organization exec; b. Baku, Russ, Jan 21, 1908; s. Itshak and Sheina (Zilberman) Gendler; in Isr since 1931; PhD, Heb U, Jerusalem, 1958; m. Pnina Lerner, July 27, 1934; c: Tsur, Nitsa. Dir: Ave-shalom Inst for Homeland Studies; Mus Adam ve Amalo, both since 1952; lectr, econ hist geog, Tel Aviv U, since 1969; asst secy, Histadrut Cultural Cen, Tel Aviv, 1932-36; instr, insp lab exch: local, Histadrut, Tel Aviv, 1937-40; natl, Histadrut Cen Control Comm, 1941-52. Mem: natl and local comns, Isr Geog Soc; Isr council, ICOM; council, Isr Exploration Soc; Natl Council for Parks and Natural Res; council, Isr Youth Hostel Assn; mgn bd, Mus Ha'aretz, Tel Aviv; fmr chmn, Isr Mus Assn. Author: The Yarkon, 1957; Water Power Installations in Eretz Israel, 1960; Survey of Water Power Installations in Eretz Israel, 1963, all in Heb; Water Power in Eretz Israel and Abroad, 1966; The Native Ard of Eretz Israel, 1965; both Heb with Eng summaries; The Origin of Industrialization in Eretz Israel, 1967; From Saddle to Wheel, 1968; contbr of numerous pamphlets, papers, and reviews. Recipient: Morris Katz Prize, Heb U, 1958; Pres Ben Zvi Prize, 1967. Home: 8 Bnei Moshe St, Tel Aviv, Isr. Office: 14 Beeri St, Tel Aviv, Isr.

AVI-YONAH, Michael, Isr, archeologist, educator; b. Lemberg, Aus, Sep 26, 1904; s. Solomon and Tamar (Weinbaum); in Isr since 1921; BA, U Coll, London, 1928, MA, 1941, PhD, 1958; m. Eva Boyko, Aug 2, 1955; c: Ruben. Prof, archeol and hist of art, Heb U, Jerusalem, since 1963; records off, dept antiquities, Pal Govt, 1931-38; research secy, dept antiquities, Isr Govt, 1948-53. Mem: exec comm, Isr Exploration Soc; archeol adv council, Min of Educ; Govt Names Comm; past chmn, Isr Numismatic Soc. Author: Mosaic Pavements in Palestine, 1932; Map of Roman Palestine, 1935, 1940; Abbreviations in Greek Inscriptions, 1942;

Oriental Elements in the Art of Palestine, 1944-48; Biyemei Roma uVizantion, 1946; Historia Geografit shel Eretz Israel, 1951; The Madaba Mosaic Map, 1954; Views of the Biblical World, Vol V; New Testament, 1962; Geschichte der Juden im Zeitalter des Talmuds, 1962; The Holy Land, 1966; Carta Atlas shel Tekufat ha-Bayit haSheni etc, 1967; Historia shel haOmanut haKlassit, 1969; co-author: Kadmonioth Arzenu, 1956; Our Living Bible, 1962; Macmillan Atlas of the Bible, 1968. Recipient: Bialik Prize, Tel Aviv Munic, 1956. Spec interest: 17th cent painting; 18th cent music. Home: 15 Bialik St, Jerusalem, Isr. Office: Heb U, Jerusalem, Isr.

AVIZEMER, Shimon, Isr, organization exec; b. Sanaa, Yemem, Apr 15, 1924; s. Shalom and Ora (Taibi) Shaer; in Isr since 1935; BA, Heb U, Jerusalem, 1954; m. Daliah Cubani, Tel Aviv, 1960; c: Ahiya, Haggai. Dir, Adult Educ Dept, Histadrut, since 1965; mem, Lab Party, co-found of its youth movement since 1950; Isr Consul: London, 1963-65; Bombay, India, 1962-63; dir, educ dept, chmn, scholarship comm, Histadrut, 1956-62; mgr, Magic Carpet Operation, flying Jews from Yemen to Isr, 1948-49. Maj, IDF, mil gov, Nablus, 1967. Mem: secretariat, United Lab Party; Zionist Action Comm; exec, WJC; chmn, Yemenite Immigrants Dept. Ed, Shluchot, newspaper; contbr articles on social, demographic, cultural subjects. Hobbies: writing poetry, keeping diary. Home: 31 Freedman St, Tel Aviv, Isr. Office: 93 Arlosoroff, Tel Aviv, Isr.

AVNER, Gershon, Isr, diplomat; b. Berlin, Ger, Nov 5, 1919; s. Arthur and Else (Deutsch) Hirsch; in Isr since 1933; att U Exeter, Eng, 1938-39; BA, U Oxford, 1942; MA, 1944; m. Yael Vogel, Mar 26, 1950; c: Michael, Ruth, Dan. Asst dir gen for Eur affairs, Isr Min for Fgn Affairs, since 1968; mem staff, political dept, JA, 1942-48; dir, W Eur dept, Min for Fgn Affairs, 1948-52; charge d'affaires, Budapest and Sofia, 1952-53; counselor, Isr emb, London, 1953-57; dir, US Dept, 1957-62; ambass: Norway, 1962-63; Canada, 1963-67. Pres, Oxford Union, 1941. Hobby: sports. Home: 1 Pinsker St, Jerusalem, Isr.

AVNER, Yehuda, Isr, diplomat; b. Manchester, Eng, Dec 30, 1928; s. George and Rivkah (Zelecovitz) Haffner; att Inst for Youth Leaders, Jerusalem; dipl, London Sch of Journalism; m. Miriam Cailingold, Feb 22, 1953; c: Daniel, Esther, Devorah, Yael. First secy, Emb of Isr, Wash, DC, since 1968; Isr consul, NY, 1967-68; fmr ed: political publs, Min for Fgn Affairs; State and Nation, JA; fmr, Isr corresp, Times of India. Served, IDF. Home: 1 Narkiss St, Jerusalem, Isr. Office: Isr Emb, Washington, DC.

AVNERY, Uri, Isr, legislator, author, editor; b. Beckum, Ger, Sep 10, 1923; s. Alfred and Hilda (Engelstein); in Isr since 1933; m. Rachel Gruenbaum, Oct 12, 1957. MK since 1965; chmn, Ha'olam Hazeh, New Force Party, since 1965; publisher, ed in chief, Ha'olam Hazeh weekly since 1950. Irgun Zvai Leumi, 1938-42, found, Bamaavak, mil youth org, 1946; cpl, Samson's Foxes Commando, 1948. Author: War or Peace in the Semitic Region, 1947; In the Fields of the Phillistines, 1949; The Other Side of the Coin, 1950; The Swastika, 1961; Israel without Zionists, The War of the Seventh Day, 1968. Home: 10 A Ruppin St, Tel Aviv, Isr. Offices: 12 Carlebach St, Tel Aviv, Isr; The Knesset, Jerusalem, Isr.

AVNI, Tzvi Jacob, Isr, composer; b. Saarbrücken, Ger, Sep 2, 1927; s. Samuel and Regina (Mandel) Steinke; in Isr since 1935; dipl, Music Acad, Tel Aviv, 1958; cert, Music Sem, Tanglewood, 1963; studies in electronic music; Columbia U, 1963-64; Toronto U, 1964; m. Pnina Grodnaith, Aug, 1949. Dir, cen music libr, Amers for Music Libr in Isr, since 1961; music adv, Bat Sheva, Bat Dor Ballet Groups; lectr, arranger, numerous Isr folk songs; dir, Lod Music Conservatory, 1958-61; music tchr: Music Tchrs Coll, 1966-68, other schs, 1954-58. Cpl, Isr Navy, 1951-53. Bd dirs: Amers for Music Libr in Isr; Isr League Composers, 1966-68. Compositions: Summer Strings, string quartet, 1961; Meditations on a Drama, 1966; Piano Sonata, 1961; Mizmorey Tehilim, psalms for choir, 1965; Wind Quintet, 1959; five Pantomimes, commissioned by Isr Composer's Fund, 1968; Jerusalem of the Heavens, choir and orch, 1968; The Destruction of the Temple, choir and orch, 1968; Akeda, chamber groups and narrator, 1969; Vocalise, electric music, 1969; recorded: Summer Strings; Meditations on a Drama; Vocalise; chief ed, Guittit, periodical, Isr Jeunesses Musicales, since 1966. Spec interests: handiwork, art exhbs, lecturing on music for youth. Home: 7 Zangwill St, Tel Aviv, Isr. Office: Mann Auditorium, Tel Aviv, Isr.

AVNI, Yaaqov, Isr, business exec; b. Pol, Oct 3, 1908; s. Menahem and Zipora (Biezynski); in Isr since 1935; att U's: Toulouse; Algier; m Naa Zeman, Oct 3, 1931; c: Dalith Shinaar. Gen mgr, Carmel Wine Co, since 1953, tech mgr, 1935-48. Maj, sci br, IDF, 1948-53. Mem: agric and bottling orgs. Author: Know Your Vineyard, 1942. Home: 8 Kfar Yona St, Tel Aviv, Isr. Office: Hayekev, Zikron Yaakov, Isr.

AVNIEL, Mordechai, Isr, attorney, artist; b. Parizi, Russ, July 18, 1900; s. Meir and Haya (Grobstein) Dickstein; in Isr since 1921; att Art Sch, Jekaterinburg, 1913-20; dipl, Govt Law Classes, Jerusalem, 1932; m. Nehama Drojan, 1923; c: Bezalel, Sara Avniel-Salomon. One-man shows in: Isr, US; Mex; Eur; works exhibited at: Biennale, Venice, 1958; Loeb Student Cen, NYC, 1962; Moss Gal; Waddington Gal, Can; represented in perm collections: Mus Modern Art, Haifa; Tel Aviv Mus; Bklyn Mus; Metrop Mus Art, NY; Mus Fine Arts, Boston; Mus Modern Art, NY; Phila Mus Art; Seattle Art Mus; Baltimore Mus; Carnegie Inst Fine Arts, Pittsburgh; Wadsworth Atheneum, Hartford, Conn; Fogg Mus, Cambridge, Mass; Smithsonian Inst, Wash, DC; Tropical Mus, Amsterdam, Holland; in pvt collections; represented Isr, Intl Art Sem, Fairleigh Dickinson U, NJ, 1962. Councilor, Haifa Munic Council, 1949-64; chmn: The Artist Colony, Safed; bd trustees, Haifa Munic Museums; pres, council, Painters and Sculptors Assn in Isr; mem: Cultural Art Council, Govt of Isr; cong court, WZO. Recipient: Herman Struck Prize of Art, Haifa, 1952; 10th Anniversary Prize of Water Colors, Ramat Gan Munic, 1958; Histadrut Prize, Jerusalem, 1961. Home: 18 Habroshim Blvd, Mt Carmel, Haifa. Studio: Artist Colony, Safed, Isr.

AVNIMELECH, Moshe Abraham, Isr, geologist, paleontologist, author; b. Warsaw, Pol, July 13, 1899; s. Abraham and Golda (Goldeewicht) Konigstein; in Isr since 1922; att: U Warsaw, 1919-20; Heb Tchrs Sem, Jerusalem, 1923-24; Free Polish U, 1927-29; U Gottinger, Ger 1932; PhD of Grenoble, Fr, 1935; m. Zipora Eisner, 1930; c: Yoram, Rina Michaely, Micha. Prof em, geology, paleontology, Heb U, since 1968, prof, 1963-68, chmn dept, 1964-65, on fac since 1929; dir, div paleontology, Isr Geological Survey, 1949-54; tchr, Heb Educ Org, Warsaw, 1926-28. Pol Army, 1919, Haganah, 1935-48; IDF, 1948. Mem, Isr Geological Soc; fmr: pres, Hashomer Hatzair Org, Pol; mem: Isr Workers Party (Mapai); Liberal Party. Author: several books, contbr to profsl jours. Home: 6 Ahad Ha'am St, Jerusalem, Isr. Office: Heb U, Jerusalem, Isr.

AVNIMELECH, Yoram, Isr, agronomist, educator; b. Jerusalem, Oct 3, 1933; s. Mosheh and Zipora (Eizner); PhD, agric, Heb U, Rehovot, 1964; m. Miriam Ben Ner, Nov 9, 1954; c: Nirit, Yaeer, Ram. Sr lectr, Technion, Haifa, since 1968, lectr, 1964-65, head fertilizers devl and soil fertilizing lab, since 1967; research asso, Amer Dental Assn, Natl Bur of Standards, 1965-67. Pvt IDF, 1950-52. Mem: Isr Soil Sci Soc; Amer Soil Sci Soc; Intl Soil Sci Soc. Contbr sci papers to jours. Home: 6 Hazalafim St, Haifa, Isr. Office: Technion, Haifa, Isr.

AVNON, Yaakov, Isr, diplomat; b. Vilno, Pol, Feb 26, 1919; s. Aharon and Esther (Zaczepinska) Kamieniecki; in Isr since 1937; att HS, Vilno; Technion, Haifa; m. Poriah Raffaeli, Sep 15, 1943; c: Daphna Nachmias, Ruth, Dan. Isr Ambass, Philippines, since 1968; first secy, Isr Legation, Stockholm, 1952-55; prin asst, div intl org, Min for Fgn Affairs, 1955-58; consul gen ,W States, US, 1958-61; ambass, Freetown, Sierra Leone, 1961-64; dir, PR div, Min for Fgn affairs, 1964-68; Isr repr, Gen Conf: UNESCO, New Delhi, 1956; ICAO, San Diego, Cal, 1959. Maj, J Brig, Brit Army, 1940-46; lt col, IDF, 1948-50. Hobbies: bridge, fishing, swimming. Home: 12/7 Ramat Danya, Jerusalem, Isr. Office: Emb of Isr, Manila, Philippines.

AVRECH, Avraham, US, rabbi; b. Yunov, Pol, June 4, 1919; s. Samuel and Miriam (Greenberg); in US since 1924; BA, Yeshiva Coll, 1940; ordained rabbi, Isaac Elchanan Theo Sem, 1943; MS, Yeshiva U, 1953; m. Minerva Keiler, Oct 31, 1943; c. Robert, Caron. Dir, alumni off, Yeshiva U, fmr dir, comty service dir; rabbi: J Comty House, Bklyn, since 1968; Cong B'nai Abraham, Auburn, Me, 1943-44; dir, S Tex area, Aberdeen Proving Grounds, Md, USO; chaplain, Perry Pt Vet Hosp, and Bainbridge Naval Base, Md, 1945-46; exec dir, Hapoel Hamizrachi Council, NY, 1946-48. Chaplain, Lt col, 353 Civil Affairs HQ "A", USAR; chaplain, US Army, 1950-55; special duty civilian chaplain for armed forces; Lab-

rador; Bermuda; Azores; Puerto Rico; Iceland: Nova Scotia. Chmn, Yeshiva U Athletic Assn; pres: Assn J Chaplains of Armed Forces, since 1968; Yeshiva Coll Alumni Assn, 1954-56; mem: bd educ Yeshiva of Flatbush, since 1965; Yeshiva U Athletic Assn since 1952; mem exec, RabCA since 1958. Recipient: 1st service award, Yeshiva Coll Alumni, 1959. Spec interest: J hist. Home: 1420 Ocean Pkway, Brooklyn, NY. Office: Yeshiva U, Amsterdam Ave and 186 St, New York, NY.

AVRECH, Dina, Isr, pianist; b. Tel Aviv, Oct 13, 1928; d. Shmuel and Luba (Polany); studied with: Rivka Shertok-Hoz, Bat-Sheva Goldstein, prof Leo Kestenberg, Isr; prof Seidelhofer, Vienna; maestro Michelangeli, It; MMus, Acad of Music, Vienna, 1960; m. Aaron Dolav, Oct 10, 1962. Concert pianist; numerous recitals, soloist with Isr and fgn symphonic orchs, in Isr and abroad. Home and studio: 9 Chen Blvd, Tel Aviv, Isr.

AVRIEL, Ehud, Isr, diplomat; b. Vienna, Aus, Oct 19, 1917; s. Israel and Helena (Segal); in Isr since 1939; m. Hanna Eliasberg, May 5, 1940; c: Dinah, Dorith, Ruth, Athalia. Chmn, WZC, since 1968; ambass to: Czech and Hung, 1948-50; Rum, 1950-51; dir gen, PM's off, 1951-52; dir gen, Treasury, 1952-53; MK, 1956-57; ambass, Ghana and Congo, Leopoldville, 1957-61; dep dir gen, Afr Affairs, Min for Fgn Affairs, 1961-65; ambass, It and Malta, 1965-68. Home: Neoth Mordechai, Upper Galilee, Isr.

AVRIEL, Mordechai, Isr, engineer; b. Budapest, Hung, Aug 8, 1933; s. Joseph and Lenke (Geber) Agoston; in Isr since 1949; BSc, MSc, Technion, Haifa; PhD, Stanford U, Cal, 1966; m. Hava Rosenthal, Sep 9, 1958; c: Dorith, Ron. Sr lectr: Technion, since 1968; Tel Aviv U, since 1969; cons: Isr Desalinization Comm, since 1968; Bechtel Corp, 1966-68; sr research engr, Mobile Oil Corp, 1966-68. Pvt, IDF, 1951-54. Exec secy, Isr Inst Chem Engrs; mem: Inst of Mgmt Scis; Oprs Research Soc of Amer; Amer Inst Chem Engr. Contbr to sci jours. Hobbies: classical music, sport. Home: 47 Horeb St, Haifa, Isr. Office: Technion, Haifa, Isr.

AVRON, Mordhay, Isr, scientist; b. Tel Aviv, Isr, Sep 29, 1931; s. Isaiah and Hava (Hanovsky) Abramski; BS, UCLA, 1953; PhD, 1955; m. Nira Mitrany, 1955; c: Boaz, Dana. Prof, biochem, Weizmann Inst of Sci, Rehovot, since 1966, on face since 1960. IDF, 1949-51. Contbr to sci jours. Home: 9 Neve Weizmann, Rehovot, Isr. Office: Weizmann Inst of Sci, Rehovot, Isr.

AVRUNIN, William, US, organizaion exec; b. Cleveland, O, Mar 4, 1911; s. Max and Anna Eisenstein; BS, O State U, 1933; att grad sch, W Reserve U, 1935-37; m. Frieda Farbman, Apr 6, 1941; c: Mark, Stephanie Waldman. Exec vice-pres, JWF, Detroit, since 1964, asso dir, 1948-64; regional dir, Council J Feds and Wfr Funds, 1945-47; exec dir, J Fed, Ft Wayne, Ind, 1943-45; case worker, sup, J Bd Guardians, NYC, 1937-43; asso ed, Friday Mag, Anglo-J monthly, 1934; lectr, Training Bur for J Communal Service, NYC, 1949; instr, U Mich, grad sch of social work, 1950, 1951, 1952. Bd mem, Mich Wfr League; mem: tech adv comm, Sch Communal Service, HUC-JIR; adv comm on overseas services, JDC; Sigma Delta Chi; Assn Cert Social Workers; fmr: pres: Natl Council of J Comty Service; Natl Comm for Big Brother Service. Author: Big Brother Manual, 1941; Study of Voluntary Fundraising in Israel, 1963; fmr chmn, ed bd, ed, profsl currents dept, Journal of Jewish Communal Service; contbr to profs jours. Recipient: award for outstanding conf paper, Natl Conf J Communal Service, 1958. Home: 10704 Ludlow St, Huntington Woods, Mich. Office: 163 Madison St, Detroit, Mich.

AXELBANK, Louis, US, mechanical engr; b. Novo Konstantin, Ukraine, Russ, Nov 3, 1894; s. Gdalia and Chaya (Mazur); in US since 1909; ME, Poly Inst, Bklyn, 1933; m. Rashelle Goldberg, Aug 19, 1950; c: Lucy Cifuentes, Martin. Ret; sr engr, NYC Dept of Public Works, 1938-66; engr, NYC Dept of Hosps, 1930-37; instr, Cooper Union, Sch of Architecture, NYC, 1947-1966. Mem: Natl Soc Profsl Engrs; Amer Soc Heating, Refrigerating and Air Conditioning Engrs; Amer Technion Soc. Author: Specification Standards Mechanical and Electrical, 1956; contbr to architectural and hosp jours. Hobbies: sculpturing, hiking, mt climbing. Home: 303 W 66 St, New York, NY.

AXELRAD, Albert Sidney, US, rabbi; b. Bklyn, Oct 22, 1938; s. Max and Rebecca (Brody); AB, Columbia College, 1960; BHL, MA, hons, HUC-JIR, NY, 1965; att Brandeis U; ordained rabbi; m. Berta Brooks, June 25, 1961; c: Marcy, Robin, David. J chaplain, Hillel dir, Brandeis U; Hillel dir, Wellesley Coll, both since 1965; asst to dir, B'nai B'rith Hillel Found, CCNY, 1963-65; lectr, HUC-JIR, 1964-65. Co-found: Gtr Boston br, J Peace F; mem natl exec comm; Havurat Shalom Comty Sem, Cambridge; mem, exec comm, Comm Rel Concern for Peace; cons, Clergy Cons Service on Problem Pregnancy; steering comm, Amer Movement Arab-Jewish Coop; mem: Natl Assn Hillel Dirs; SANE; CCAR; Cong Racial Equality; War Resisters League; F of Reconciliation. Contbr to New Frontiers For Jewish Life on the Campus, 1968; profsl jours. Home: 16 Peck Ave, Wayland, Mass. Office: 415 South St, Waltham, Mass.

AXELRAD, Jacob, US, attorney, author; b. Phila, Pa May 25, 1889; s. Abraham and Celia (Zion); LLB, NYU, 1912; LLM, 1913; m. Kate Gold, Nov 21, 1953; c: Muriel Klein. Pvt practice since 1913; asst prof, Eng, Associated Colls of NY, 1946-48; lectr, lit, sociol, Rand Sch Social Sci, 1948-49. Author: Anatole France: A Life Without Illusions, 1944; Patrick Henry: The Voice of Freedom, 1948; Philip Freneau: Champion of Democracy, 1969; Yankee Cavalier: Life and Times of Samuel Gridley; Endless Search, novel; Sparks from An Old Forge, 600 original aphorisms; Once Upon a Time: Legends of Liberty, portraits of famous Americans. Mem: ACLU; AAUP; NY, Mass, Fed Bar Assns. Homes: 55 W 11 St, New York; 15 Norwood Rd, W Hartford, Conn.

AXELROD, Abe E, US, biochemist, educator: b. Cleveland, O, June 10, 1921; s. Max and Rose (Leikin); AB, W Reserve U, 1933, MA, 1936; PhD, U Wis, 1939; m. Velma Hellerstein, Sep 12, 1939; c: Nancy, Philip. Asso dean, Sch of Med, U Pittsburgh, since 1965, prof, biochem, since 1954, asso prof, chem, 1945-51; research biochem, W Pa Hosp, 1942-51; asso prof, biochem, W Reserve U, 1951-54. Pres: Pittsburgh Soc Biol Research, 1958; mem: Inst of Nutrition, Soc of Immunologists; AAAS; Brit Biochem Soc; Soc Experimental Biol and Med. Contbr to tech and med jours. Home: 5821 Walnut St, Pittsburgh, Pa. Office: U of Pittsburgh, Pittsburgh, Pa.

AXELROD, Albert A, US, jurist; b. SF, Cal, July 2, 1901; s. Benjamin and Johannah (Rosenthal); JD, U of Cal, 1925;att Hastings Coll of Law, SF, 1922-25; m. Lucille Cohen, June 22, 1930; c: Joanne Gordon, Alan. Judge, SF Munic Court, since 1957, presiding judge, 1960; pvt law practive with Philip S Ehrlich, 1925-57. Vive-pres, found mem, Benjamin Swig Camp, Camp for Living Judaism; fmr pres, SF chap, Intl Footprint Assn; pres, Sinai Memorial Chapel; legal cons, Newhouse Found; mem: Masons, Elks, Shriners; B'nai Brith; bd trustees, Heb Free Loan Assn, fmr pres; Maimonides Health Cen; fmr: Mt Zion Hosp and Health Cen; fmr: pres, Cong Shearith Isr; N Cal region, UAHC, mem bd trustees; vice-chmn, SF Rep Co Cen Comm, mem Cal State Cen Comm; clubs: SF Sq; SF Trowel. Recipient: SF Chronicle Gold Medal for Service to SF, 1961; Legion of Honor Order of De Molay. Home: 135 Jordan Ave, San Francisco, Cal. Office: City Hall, San Francisco, Cal.

AXELROD, David, US, composer; b. LA, Cal, Apr 17, 1934; s. Morris and Pearl (Plaskoff); m. Saundra Kapelowitz, Mar 2, 1963; c: Michael, Scott, Dana, Brian. Exec produc, Capitol Records, Inc, since 1964; composer: Mass in F Minor,1967, used in motion picture, Easy Rider; Song of Innocence; Release of an Oath, 1968; Songs of Experience, 1969; Dead End Street; songs and arrangements for top recording artists including: Lou Rawls; Cannonball Adderley; David McCallum; and others. Natl trustee, Natl Acad Recording Arts and Sci, fmr mem, bd govs; patron: LA Co Mus of Arts; S Cal Chamber Music Soc; mem, Amer Fed Musicians. Recipient: nominations for several Grammy Awards. Hobby: mt climbing. Home: 5055 Amestoy Rd, Encino, Cal. Office: 1750 N Vine St, Hollywood, Cal.

AXELROD, Julius, US, pharmacologist; b. NYC, May 30, 1912; s. Isadore and Molly (Liechtling); BS, CCNY, 1933; MS, NYU, 1942; PhD, George Wash U, Wash, DC, 1955; hon DSc, U Chgo, 1966; m. Sally Taub, Aug 30, 1938; c: Paul, Alfred. Chief, pharm sect, Natl Inst Mh, since 1955; chem,Lab Ind Hygiene, 1933-46; research asso, Goldwater Memorial Hosp, NYU, 1946-49; chem, Natl Heart Inst, 1949-55; lectr: numerous symposiums and confs; med schs, US and Eur. Prin contribs: discovered about 15 enzymes in hormone metabolism; elucidated fate of noradrenaline and other hormones; biochemical actions in dineal gland; described actions of numerous drugs. F, Amer Coll Neuropsychopharmacology; mem: Amer Chem Soc; Amer Soc Pharm and Experimental Thera-

peutics; Amer Soc Biol Chems; Intl Brain Research Org; Sigma Xi; AAAS; panel, US Bd Civil Service Examiners; research adv comm, United Cerebral Palsy Assn; mem, ed adv bd: Life Sciences, since 1961; Currents in Modern Biology,since 1966; Journal of Neurobiology,since 1968; Pharmacological Research Communica,since 1968; Communications in Behavioral Biology, 1967; Rassegna di Neurologia Vegetativa, 1969; ed bd: Journal of Pharmacology and Experimental Therapy, since 1956; Circulation Research, since 1964; Journal of Medical Chemistry, 1961-66; contbr to profsl publs. Recipient: Natl Sci Found Travel Award, 1958; Intl Psychol Union Travel Award, 1961; Otto Loewi Memorial Lectr, NYU Med Sch, 1964; Dist Research Award, Assn for Research in Nervous and Mental Diseases,1965; Gairdner Found Award, 1967; Dist Achievement Award, George Wash U, 1968. Home: 10401 Grosvenor Pl, Rockville, Md. Office: Natl Inst Mh, Bethesda, Md.

AXELROD, Solomon Jacob, US, physician, educator; b.Gloversville, NY, Sep 25, 1912; s. Max and Ray (Semser). AB, magna cum laude, Dartmouth Coll, 1934; MD, Jefferson Med Coll, 1938; MPH, U of Mich, 1949; m. Pearl Guttman, June 30, 1935; c: Peter, Joan. Prof, public health econ, U of Mich, since 1957, chmn, dept med care org, since 1965, dir, bur public health econ,since 1960; med off, Health Dept,Tenn, 1941-43; off, USPHS, 1943-49; chief med off, migrant lab health prog, Dept of Agric, 1946-47. F, governing council, Amer Public Health Assn; mem, Phi Beta Kappa. Author: Public Assistan: Medical Care, 1960; co-author, Comprehensive Medical Services under Voluntary Health Insurance, 1958. Contbr to med jours. Home: 457 Barton N Dr, Ann Arbor, Mich. Office: Sch of Public Health, U of Mich, Ann Arbor, Mich.

AXER, Anatol, Isr, physician; b. Pshemishle, Pol, Mar 10,1914; s. Josef and Yohana (Traum); in Isr since 1941; deg phys,Jan Kazimierz Med Sch, Lwow, 1939; MD, St Joseph Med Sch, Beirut, 1942; m. Lea Luntz Fed, 1949; c: Ruth, Orit. Head, orthopedic dept, Assaf Harofe Govt Hosp, since 1951. Maj, MC, IDF. Mem: Société Internationale de Chirurgie Orthopédique et de Traumatologie; Isr Surg Soc; Brit Orthopedic Assn; f, Isr Orthopedic Assn. Contbr to profsl jours. Home: 10 Trumpeldor St, Tel Aviv, Isr. Office: Assaf Harofe Hosp, Zerefin, Isr.

AYALI, Meir, Isr, educational admnr; b. July 10, 1913; s. Juda and Esther (Kohn) Hirschler; in Isr since 1934; att: Rabb Coll, Frankfurt/M; U's: Frankfurt; Jerusalem; m. Naomi Gura, June, 1942; c: Efrat, Offer, Gilead. Prin, Yifat Regional HS, since 1943; found and ed, Igeret L'Chinuch, periodical on kibbutz educ, since 1952; fmr: agric worker; youth leader. Haganah, IDF, 1935-60. Mem various comms: Min of Educ; Kibbutz Movement; fmr: mem, JA mission, head, aliyah dept, to DP camps in Ger, Swed. Author: Chagim U'zemanim, 2 vols,1949;trans: Shakespearean Tragedy by George Brandes; poems by Nelly Sachs;contbr of articles on educ and J topics. Recipient: Independence Day Award, Kishon Regional Council, 1969. Spec interests: J studies; translation. Home: Yifat, Isr.

AYALON, David, Isr, educator, historian; b. Haifa, 1914; PhD, Heb U; att Amer U, Beirut. Prof, hist, Heb U, since 1952, dir, Inst Asian and Afr Studies, 1963-67, on fac since 1949; Arab affairs specialist, political dept, JA, 1938-48; mem, research dept, Min for Fgn Affairs, 1948-49; visiting prof: Princeton U; U of Cal, Berkeley, both 1967-68. Brit Army, 1941-44. Chmn, phys educ and sports comm, Heb U; mem, Isr Acad Sci. Author: Zion, 1937, 1939, 1946; Gunpowder and Firearms in the Mameluke Kingdom, 1956; co-author, Arabic-Heb Dict, 1947; contbr to profsl jours. Recipient: Rockefeller Found F, 1952, 1954-59. Home: 7 Magnes Sq, Jerusalem,Isr. Office: Heb U, Jerusalem, Isr.

AYALON, Zvi, Isr, government official;b. Russ, June 15,1911; s. Meir and Esther Leshtchiner; att: agric sch,Mikve Isr; Columbia U; m. Rachel Katznelson; c: Dalia, Boas. Head, licensing auth, Min of Transp, since 1967; spec repr, Min of Defence and spec attache, Isr Emb, London, 1959-64; with Isr Min, Bucharest, 1964-66. Instr with Haganah; later mem, high command; staff off, hqr, IDF, chief gen staff, 1947-48, cdr, cen sector, 1949-51; quartermaster-gen, 1951-53; commanding off, cen command, 1954-56. Home: 2 Daphne St, Tel Aviv, Isr.

AYGEN, Maurice Saban, Isr, physician; b. Tire, Turkey, Feb 1, 1925; s. Samuel and Judith (Galante); in Isr since 1962;

MD, Istanbul U, 1952; m. Simone Artini, 1962; c: Nitsa, Liora. Head, cardiopulmonary inst, Beilinson Hosp; sr lectr, Tel Aviv U, both since 1967. Lt, MC, IDF, 1952-53. Mem, Isr Heart Assn. Contbr articles to med jours. Home: Shikun Ovdei Beilinson, Petah Tikva, Isr. Office: Beilinson Hosp, Petah Tikva, Isr.

AZANIAH, Baruch, Isr, legislator, educator; b. Pinsk, Russ, Sep 18, 1905; s. Samuel and Zippora (Finkelstein) Eisenstadt; in Isr since 1933; att: Danzig Tech Inst, 1926-27; U Berlin; grad, Konigsberg U, 1931; m. Toni Simon, July 20, 1937. MK, 1951-69; chmn, Knesset Comm, 1955-59; mem, cen council, Mapai, since 1940, mem, presidium, parl group, Mapai and Lab Party, since 1951; court referee, Danzig, Berlin, 1931-33; tchr, leader youth groups, Ein Harod, Tel Yosef kibbutzim, 1934-35; tchr: Sem for Tchrs, Givat HaShlosha, 1945-51; Kfar Saba HS, 1948-50; dir, Berl Katznelson Memorial Sem, Kfar Saba, 1949-50; tchr, Tichon Hadash HS, Tel Aviv, 1950-1951. Mem, cen council, Ihud Hakevuzot ve ha-Kibbutzim, since 1951, mem secretariat, since 1959; fmr: mem, exec council, Histadrut; dir, youth dept, repr, Histadrut; Hakibbutz Hameuchad, Ger; mem: cen council, Hanoar Haoved; council, Hakibbutz Hameuchad; in Eur: chmn, Poalei Zion, Danzig; vice-chmn, Zionist Org, Danzig; secy JNF, Konigsberg; secy, Poalei Zion, Ger; delg to: 16th, 17th; 20th; 21st; 22nd ZCs. Home: Kibbutz Givat Hayim Ihud, Isr.

AZARIA, Hanania Mordehai, Greece, dental surg, educator; b. Verria, Greece, Aug 15, 1917; s. Mordehai and Rachel (Stroumsa); DDS, U Athens, 1940; m. Rachel Stroumsa, Aug 15, 1950. Prof, prosthetic dent, U Thessaloniki, since 1967. Pres, Stomatological Soc of N Greece, 1953-69; vice-pres, B'nai B'rith; mem: Greek-Isr League; Greek-Fr league. Contbr numerous papers on dent to Greek, It, Fr jours. Home: 139 Megalou Alexandron St, Thessaloniki, Greece. Office: 73 Ermou St, Thessaloniki, Greece.

AZIKRI, Nisim, Isr, actor; b. Varna, Bulgaria, Aug 7, 1939; s. Leon and Esther; in Isr since 1948; att Ohel Drama Sch; m. Fanny, Apr 15, 1964 (div). Actor: Habima Theater since 1960; Ohel Theater, 1956-57; Zera Theater, 1956-57; roles in Isr and fgn movies and theater. Armored corps entertainment, IDF, 1957-59. Home: 76 Hashmonayim St, Tel Aviv, Isr. Office: Habima Theater, Tel Aviv, Isr.

AZNEER, J Leonard, US, rabbi; b. Rum, May 26, 1921; s. Morris and Ida (Stein) Azneershansky; in US since 1922; BA, Yeshiva Coll, 1941; ordained rabbi, JTSA, 1945, MHL, 1949; PhD, U Pittsburgh, 1959; att Rabbi Isaac Elchanan Theol Sem, NY, 1938-41; m. Pearl Sacks, June 27, 1943; c: Jay, Reva, Ira. Rabbi: Anshe Emeth Temple, Youngstown,

O, since 1950; Temple Beth Isr, Warren, O; sr mem, grad fac, Youngstown State U, prof, phil and law, since 1951, asso prof, educ, head, dept Heb, 1952-62; rabbi: Temple Beth El, Allentown, Pa, 1944-45; J Comty Assn, Bay City, Mich, 1945-47; Knott Terr Syn, Schenectady, NY, 1947-50; visiting lectr, Albion Coll, 1946-47; lectr, Union Coll, 1948-49; conducted rel broadcasts, Search for Truth, radio stas WPTR, WBCA-FM, Schenectady, 1947-50. Pres, O region, RA, 1954-56, mem since 1945; mem: natl adv comm, JDC; natl bd, United Syn, fmr chmn, comm on small cmtys; Mahoning Valley Mh Assn; ZOA; B'nai B'rith. Author: Passover-A Programmed Text; Sukkot-A Programmed Text; Diabetic Acidosis-A Programmed Text; Resuscitation-A Programmed Text; Attitudes of Jewish Leaders to Question of Religion in Public Education; mem ed bd, Conservative Judaism, 1952-55; contbr to rel periodicals. Recipient: Harvey Goode award, JTSA, 1945. Home: 273 Norwood Ave, Youngstown, O. Study: 939 Elm St, Youngstown, O.

AZOULAI, Yaakov, Isr, jurist; b. Safad, Pal, Sep 1899; s. Izhak and Hana; LLB, Law Classes, Jerusalem, 1936; att Heb U, 1946; m; c: Itzhak, Abraham. Pres, Haifa Dist Court, since 1950, judge, since 1945; chief interpreter, dist courts, 1931-35; magistrate, 1935-45, chief magistrate with spec warrant Brit magistrate, Jerusalem, 1945-57. Chmn: Natl Comm for Release of Prisoners, since 1954; Comm for Released Prisoners Home; Prisoners Wfr Comm, Haifa, since 1949; Water Tribunal of Isr; Assn Sephardic Culture and Rel Instns, Mt Carmel, since 1956; Haifa br, Assn des Auditeurs et Anciens Auditeurs de l'Academie de Droit Intl de la Haye. since 1954; Haifa br, Isr Assn for UN, since 1957; mem exec comm, Natl Council for Blind; chmn: bd trustees, Rehab Cen for Blind, Migdalor, since 1951; Twin Cities Comm, Haifa-Marseille, since 1962; mem: Natl Juridical Council; B'nai B'rith; Assn for Support Scout Movement in Isr; lectr on judicial and gen subjects; fmr: chmn, Soldiers Wfr Comm; mem, council, JNF, KH, Haifa sect. Home: 20 Pinsky St, Mt Carmel, Haifa, Isr. Office: Dist Court, Haifa, Isr.

AZRAEL, Edward, US, attorney; b. Phila, Pa, June 30, 1907; s. Jacob and Rose (Bates); LLB, U Baltimore, 1929; m. Harriette Glasser, Nov 24, 1938; c: Jonathan, Richard. Pvt practice since 1930; mem, Azrael & Gann; vice-pres, Oak Ridge Devl Co Inc, since 1957; commn, Bd Munic and Zoning Appeals, Baltimore, 1942-63; instr, U Baltimore, 1942-44; pres, Family Mortgage and Loan Assn, since 1947. Mem: Dem State Cen Comm; Amer, Baltimore, Md State Bar Assns; B'rith Sholem; Amer Soc Planning Off; Chizuk Amuno Cong and Brotherhood; club, Bonnie View Country. Home: 7121 Park Heights Ave, Baltimore, Md. Office: 1154 Maryland National Bank Bldg, Baltimore, Md.

B

BAAR, Jacob, US, editor; b. NYC, July 25, 1904; s. Edward and Pauline (Finkelman); BS, NYU, 1926; MA, Columbia U, 1927; m. Ethel Paletz, Dec 23, 1945. Ed, Statistical Bull, Metrop Life Ins Co, 1940-66; ret. F, Amer Public Health Assn; mem: Amer Stat Assn; Population Assn of Amer; Amer Sociol Soc. Contbr to profsl jours. Home: 390 First Ave, New York, NY.

BABAD, Harry, US, chemist, educator; b. Vienna, Dec 3, 1936; s. Elias and Rebeca (Greenspan); in US since 1940; BS, Poly Inst, Bklyn, 1956; MS, PhD, U of Ill, Urbana, 1961; m. Joan Klein, Sep 24, 1965; c: Bruce, Nachael, Saul. Head, chem research sect, Ott Chem Co, since 1968; research asso, MIT, 1961-62; postdoc f, U of Chgo, 1962-63; asst prof, U of Denver, Colo, 1963-67. Prin contribs: research on ind products; patents. Mem: Sigma Xi; Phi Lambda Upsilon; AAUP; AAAS; Amer Inst of Chem; NY Acad of Sci. Contbr to profsl jours. Hobbies: sci fiction, gourmet cooking, fencing. Home: POB 13, Muskegon, Mich. Office: 500 Agard Rd, Muskegon, Mich.

BABAD, Joseph, US, educator; b. Lubaczow, Pol, June 17, 1908; s. Moses and Sarah (Rost); in US since 1940; PhD, U of Vienna, 1933; rabbi, Theol Sem, Vienna, 1934; ML, U of Pittsburgh, 1943; m. Pelke Rathaus, 1935 (decd); m. 2nd, Minnie Offman, 1959; c: Ada Morduchowitz, Rachel Bruckenstein. Dean of Students, Heb Theol Coll, Skokie, Ill, since 1952, prof, Bible, since 1945; rabbi: Aus, 1933-38; Tarentum, Pa, 1940-43; Wash, Pa, 1943-44; educ dir, Cleveland, O, 1944-45. Mem: natl adv comm, Histadruth Ivrith, Chgo, fmr pres; Hapoel Hamizrachi; RabCA. Author: History of Jews in Medieval Carinthia, 1944-45; Averroes, Contemporary of Maimonides, 1958; contbr to scholarly Ger, Eng, and Heb periodicals. Home: 7135 N Laramie, Skokie, Ill. Office: 7135 N Carpenter Rd, Skokie, Ill.

BABIN, Victor, US, pianist, composer, educator; b. Moscow, Russ; in US since 1944; grad, State Conservatory of Riga, Latvia, summa cum laude in piano and composition, 1927; postgrad, in piano under Artur Schnabel, in composition under Franz Shreker, Berlin Hochschule fur Musik, 1928-31; hon D, Fine Arts, U of NM, Albuquerque; m. Vitya Vronsky, 1933. Mem, two-piano team of Vronsky and Babin. Dir, Cleveland Inst of Music, since 1961; Aspen Sch of Music, 1951-54, mem fac since 1950; chmn: Tanglewood Inst; Piano Sem and Workshop, Berkshire Music Cen, 1965. US Army, WW II. Hon mem, Pi Kappa Lambda since 1965. Office: Cleveland Inst of Music, Cleveland, O.

BACH, Gabriel, Isr, attorney; b. Halberstadt, Ger, Mar 13, 1927; s. Victor and Erna (Benscher); in Isr since 1940; att Heb U, 1946-47; LLB, U Coll, London, 1950; barrister-at-law, Lincoln's Inn, London, 1950; m. Ruth Arazi, Oct 18, 1955; c: Orli, Yonathan, Michael. State Atty of Isr since 1969, dep state atty, 1956-69; fmr: asst state atty, Min of Justice, 1953-56; appd legal adv to Bur 6, conducting inves in Eichmann case, 1960, appeared as one of prosecutors in Eichmann trial. Capt, IDF, 1951-53. Mem, B'nai B'rith. Hobbies: play-reading, music. Home: 30 Radak St, Jerusalem, Isr. Office: Ministry of Justice, Jerusalem, Isr.

BACHI, Emilio, It, attorney; b. Turin, It, July 15, 1907; s. Donato and Alice (Todros); grad, law, U of Turin, 1928, grad, political, admn scis, 1929; m. Luisella Bachi, Dec 17, 1934; c: Marina Giordana, Simonetta, Daniela. Barrister, defender in High Court, since 1934; vice-pres, secy of council, Nebiolo Inc, since 1952; admn council, Soc Idroelettrica Piemonte, since 1957; Soc Reale Mutua Assicurazione, since 1958; repr of Province of Turin in admn of port of Genoa; fmr: journalist for Free It, La Voce Repubblicana; dir, radio news Turin, 1945; councillor, City of Turin, 1951, assessor for civil regulations and public works. Capt, US Army, 1944-45. Vice-pres, Popular U; counsel, It-Aus C of C; mem: council, Order of Barristers; admn council, Reale Riassicurazioni; fmr: pres, Turin sect; It Federalist Movement; mem council, Eur Commons. Recipient: Order of Merit of It Rep. Home: Via Massena 87, Turin, It. Office: Via Ponza 2, Turin, It.

BACHI, Roberto, Isr, civil servant, statistician, educator; b. Rome, It, Jan 16, 1909; s. Riccardo and Celia (Lampronti); in Isr since 1938; DJ, U of Rome, 1930; m. Vera Colombo, July 25, 1934; four c. Dir, Cen Bur Stat, Govt of Isr, since 1949; fmr: asst, econ dept, U of Rome, 1931; lectr, stat, U of Cagliari, 1932; U of Macerata, 1932-34; prof, stat: U of Sassari, 1934-36; U of Genoa, 1936-38; head, bur of stat, Hadassah Med Org, Pal, 1939-44; asst stat, dept of stat, Pal Govt, 1945-47; lectr, stat, Heb U, Jerusalem, 1945-47, prof, dean fac, social sci, 1953-54, pro-rector, 1959-60. F: Amer Stat Assn, Isr Natl Acad of Sci; mem: Intl Stat Inst; Intl Assn of Population Research. Author: International Migrations in Large European Towns; Statistical Methodology; The Demography of Italian Jews, 1600-37; Marriage and Fertility of Jewish Population in Palestine; Graphical Rational Patterns, 1968; contbr articles on methodology, gen demography, demography of J, med stat and sociostat. Home: 19 Hovevei Zion, Jerusalem, Isr.

BACHRACH, Alfred R, US, certified public acctnt; b. NYC, Jan 15, 1900; s. Irving and Henriette (Schmeidler); BS, Columbia U, 1921; m. Alice Rothschild, Dec 3, 1924; c: John, Robert, Ellin Gordon. Sr partner, Alfred Bachrach and Co, since 1934; pres, First Realty Capital Funds, since 1961; acctnt: Arnold Markel, 1921-24; own firm, 1924-28; exec dir: Trade Assn in Paper Ind, 1924-28; Robe and Allied Products Ind, 1932-34; cons, US Army Contract Renegotiation, 1940-42. USN, WW I. Hon pres, Cong Emanu-El, NY, since 1967, pres, 1956-67; bd dirs: FJP; Montefiore Hosp; asso: YM-YWHA's; Mosholu Comty Cen; mem: Amer Inst of Acctnts; NY State Soc of CPA's; Natl Assn of Cost Acctnts; NY Credit Men's Assn; Columbia Coll Council, since 1966; clubs: Metrop Country, White Plains, NY; Harmonie, NYC; Columbia U, NYC. Home: 33 E 70 St, New York, NY. Office: 770 Lexington Ave, New York, NY.

BACHRACH, Alice, US, communal worker; b. NYC; d. David and Dora (Stern) Rothschild; grad, NY Sch of Fine and Applied Arts, 1921; m. Alfred Bachrach, Dec 3, 1924; c: John, Robert, Ellin Gordon. Volunteer work since 1920. Was active in org women's div, JWB; chmn, 1942-45, hon chmn since 1955; Natl Adv Comm, Study on Recruitment and Retention of Volunteers; fmr: chmn: Amer Girl Mag; Girl Scouts; vice-pres: Natl USO, 1951-64; YWHA, NYC; Girl Scouts, 1953-57; fmr secy: ASAF; comm, Frank L Weil Inst, Advanced Studies of Rel and Hum; mem, bd govs, HUC-JIR; dir, mem, exec comm, NY Blood Cen; trustee, mem, exec comm, Parsons Sch Design; fmr: bd mem, FJP, NYC; fmr: mem: Conf on Volunteer Services to Psycht Patients; Women's Adv Council, Dept of Defense; Natl Civilian Adv Comm, WAC; Women's Adv Comm, info MSA; club, Women's City, NYC. Recipient: Frank L Weil Award, 1952. Home: 33 E 70 St, New York, NY.

BACHRACH, Paul B, US, psychologist; b. NYC, Aug 28, 1912; s. Samuel and Esther (Houshankoff); BBS, CCNY, 1933; MA, Columbia U, 1935, PhD, 1955; m. Edith Mednitzky, Jan, 1942; c: Jan, Eric. Asst prof, dept student services, CCNY, since 1958; asst chief, restitution br, Off of Mil Govt, 1947-49; research asso, Tchrs Coll, Columbia, 1956-57; lectr, Hunter Coll, 1956-57. Capt, IS, 1942-46. Mem: Amer Psych Assn; NY State Psych Assn. Co-author: Scientific Careers: Vocational Development Theory, 1957; contbr to psych jours. Recipient: Croix de Guerre, 1945. Home: 20 Tavano Rd, Ossining, New York, NY. Office: 137 M Street & Convent Ave, New York, NY.

BACHRACH, Uriel, Isr, educator; b. Heilbronn, Ger, Sep 9, 1926; s. Julius and Hanna (Würzburger); in Isr since 1933; MSc, Heb U, 1950, PhD, 1953; m. Esther Sacharin, Sep, 1954; c: Zelilah, Gilad. Asso prof, microbiol, Heb U, since 1965, fac mem since 1950; humanitarian trust f, U of Reading, Eng, 1953-55; visiting sci, NIH, Bethesda, 1960-62; research asso, Columbia U, 1967; visiting sci, NIH, 1968. Lt, IDF, 1948-49. Prin contribs: research on antibacterial substances, molecular biol of bacterial viruses. Mem: NY Acad Scis; Soc for Gen

Microbiol, Eng. Spec interest: archeol. Home: 4 Rav Chen St, Jerusalem, Isr. Office: Heb U-Hadassah Med School, Jerusalem, Isr.

BACK, Nathan, US, scientist, educator; b. Phila, Pa, Nov 30, 1925; s. Joseph and Freda (Goldhirsh); BS, Pa State U, 1948; MS, Phila Coll Pharm and Science, 1953, DSc, 1955; m. Toby Ticktin, June 17, 1951; c: Efrem, Aaron, Adina, Rachel, Sara. Prof, chmn, dept of biochemical pharm, U of Buffalo, since 1958; sr cancer research sci, Roswell Park Memorial Inst, since 1958; acting dir, Sch of Pharm, Heb U, Jerusalem; cons: Sidney Hillman Med Found, 1956-58; Ayerst Pharmaceutical Co, 1962-63; Ives-Cameron, 1960-62; State of Isr, 1948-50; research sci, Wyeth Inst for Med Research, 1950-51; instr, Phila Coll Pharm and Sci, 1954-55; visiting prof, Heb U; sci dir, Pharm Inst, NRC, Isr, 1969-70. Vice-pres, co-founder, Kadimah Day School, since 1960, pres, 1966-69; vice-pres, Intl Soc of Biochem Pharm; mem, bd, Temple Emanuel Syn, since 1959; f: AAAS; Royal Soc of Med; NY Acad of Sci; Intl Soc of Hematology; treas, Intl Cong of Pharm; mem: Amer Soc of Pharm and Therapeutics; Amer Soc of Experimental Biol and Med; Amer Assn for Cancer Research; Rho Chi; Sigma Xi; Amer Soc of Hematology; Intl Soc of Hematology; NYAcad of Sci; Reticulo-Endothelial Soc. Author: Laboratory Manual in Pharmacology, 1958; co-ed of books; contbr numerous articles to sci jours. Home: 172 Sterling Ave, Buffalo, NY. Office: U of Buffalo, NY.

BACK, Phillip Goldstein, US, advertising, public relations counselor; b. Little Rock, Ark, Oct 12, 1902; s. William and Sophia (Goldstein); grad Ky Mil Inst, 1920; Harvard Sch of Bus Admn, Sem on Advt/PR, 1958; m. Alice Lasker, Oct 12, 1925; c: Mimi Loeb, Marilyn Weinstein. Prop, Phillip G Back, Advt/PR, since 1945; fmr: dir advt, PR, Imperial Laundry-Cleaners, 1934-44; advt-sales promotion, Sears and Roebuck, 1931-34; mem, JD Back and Bros, dept store, 1920-31; all in Little Rock; part-time theatrical work; owner, Superior Attractions, bringing theatrical producs to Little Rock. Lt col, Ark Wing, Civil Air Patrol, USAF, dir info, active, search and rescue team. Pres: Cong B'nai Isr; Advt club; PR Soc of Amer, Ark Chap; Independent Order of B'nai B'rith, Little Rock lodge; J Wfr Agcy, Little Rock; bd mem, Amer Comm for Isr Affairs; Ark repr, ADL, B'nai B'rith; chmn: Bonds for Isr Comm; active worker, city, co, state political campaigns; mem: Masons, past dir; Shrine Band; PR dir, Scimitar Temple; fmr: dir, Salvation Army Ark Commn; secy, Ark Boy's Ind Schs; Commn, Ark Bd of Pardons and Paroles; off, mem bd: Heart Fund; March of Dimes; TB Christmas Seals; club, Westridge Country, pres. Recipient: various awards from communal, civic orgs. Home: One Fairfax Terrace, Little Rock, Ark. Office: 212 Louisana St, Little Rock, Ark.

BACKMAN, Jules, US, economist, educator; b. NYC, May 3, 1910; s. Nathan and Gertrude (Schall); BCS, NYU, 1931, MA, 1932; MBA, 1933; DCS, 1935; m. Grace Straim, Oct 18, 1935; c: Susan, John. Research prof, econ, NYU Sch of Commerce, since 1960, fac mem since 1938; mem, NYU Sen, 1962-65; vice-pres, Econ-Stat, Inc, 1933-35; research, Madden and Dorau, 1936-37; econ ed, Trusts and Estates Magazine, 1938-46, all NYC; asst dir, allotment inquiry, UJA, 1940-41; head econ cons, OPA, 1942-43; research, The Brookings Inst, 1943; ed writer, The NY Times, 1943-48; tech adv to ind mems, Pres Cost of Living Comm, 1944; econ adv to: steel ind in natl wage cases, 1944, 49, 52; Amer RRs in wage and rate cases, 1945-60; Temp State Commn to Study Rents and Rental Conditions, NY, 1953; mem: NY Milkshed Price Comm, 1948; Gov's Comm on Milk Marketing, 1961-65; visiting prof, U of Pittsburgh, 1957. Pres: Soc of Bus Advisory Professions, 1954-55; NYU Alumni Fed, 1954-56; chmn: bd, NYU Club, 1961-65; natl, Reform J Appeal, since 1966; co-chmn, bldg fund campaign, J Comty Cen, White Plains, NY; vice-chmn, mem bd govs, HUC-JIR, since 1962; hon f, Amer Stat Assn; dir: NYU J Culture Found, since 1949; Scarsdale Natl Bank and Trust Co, since 1959; mem, bd trustees, J Comty Cen, White Plains, NY, since 1951; mem: Amer Econ Assn; Beta Gamma Sigma; Phi Lambda Delta; Lambda Gamma Phi; Alpha Phi Sigma; clubs: Metrop Country; NYU. Author: Government Price Fixing, 1938; Surety Rate-Making, 1949; The Economics of Armament Inflation, 1951; Price Practices and Price Policies, 1953; Wage Determination, 1959; Economics of the Electrical Machinery Industry, 1962; Advertising and Competition, 1967; Economics of the Chemical Industry, 1969; co-author, War and Defense Economics, 1952; contbr to econ, ind publs. Recipient: NYU Meritorious Service Award, 1942; Madden Award, 1960; Man of the Year Award, Grad

Sch of Bus Admn, 1961. Home: 59 Crane Rd, Scarsdale, NY. Office: NYU, Washington Square, New York, NY.

BACOLAS, Sion Ezra, Greece, importer, commercial repr; b. Jannina, Greece, Aug 15, 1920; s. Ezra and Dina (Kalhamira); att U of Athens; m. Aimilia Kabili, Sep 4, 1945; c: Ezra, Hanna. Commercial repr, mgn dir, Introdictove des Montres; fmr merchant in fabrics. Mem, comm of clandestine org for rescue of J from Nazi persecution, 1942-44. Pres, spec comm for support, rehab of orphan girls, victims of Nazis, Jannina, 1945-47; mgn dir, org for support, rehab of J (OPAIE), Jannina, 1950-51; vice-pres, bd, J comty, Jannina, 1952-59; mem, gen assembly, J comty, Athens, 1966; secy gen, org for support and rehab of Greek J, since 1967, fmr vice-pres; mem: B'nai B'rith, Athens; C of C, Athens; Assn of Commercial Reprs. Home: Naxou 21, Athens, Greece. Office: Nikitara 10, Athens, Greece.

BACON, Yehuda, Isr, artist; b. Moravia, Czech, July 28, 1929; s. Israel and Ethel (Gross); in Isr since 1946; att Bezalel Acad, Jerusalem, 1946-52; Cen Sch of Arts, London, 1955-57, 1963-64, Ecole des Beaux Arts, Paris, 1957-58; div; c: Hannah. Head, lithography and etching dept, Bezalel Acad, Jerusalem, since 1959; one-man shows: Nora Gal, 1954-63; Artists House, 1961-69, both Jerusalem; Beersheba, 1963; Eilat, 1963; Johannesburg Whipman Gal; Cape Town New Art Gal, 1966, both S Afr; Ben Uri Art Gal, 1957; Cavendish Gal, 1964, both London; Antwerp, Belgium, 1964; Apeldoorn Mus, Holland, 1967; Charlottenburg Gal, Copenhagen, 1968; Stockholm, 1968; Vienna, 1968; intl and group shows: Young Artists Biennale, Paris, 1961; Biennale of Graphic Art, Tokyo, 1962; Royal Acad Summer Show, London, 1963; Intl Biennale of Graphic Art, Yugo, 1962, 68; itinerant Isr show, US, Scand, Australia, 1967; itinerant show of Isr Min of Educ and Culture, It, US, 1965, 68; First Biennale of Graphic Art, Pistoia, 1968; Second Pistoia Biennale, 1969; in mus and pvt collections: Isr Mus; Haifa Mus of Modern Art; Ein Harod Mus; Yad ve-Shem; Min of Educ and Culture, Isr; U Libr, Cape Town; Ben Uri Gal, London; Libr of Cong, Wash, DC; Pablo Casals, Marlene Dietrich, Nelson Rockefeller, others. Contbr illus for: Shin Shalom, 1964; Aharon Applefeld; Leo Baeck. Mem, Jerusalem Artists Assn. Recipient: Henrietta Szold scholarship, 1950; silver medal, hon mem, Acad Thomaso Campanelli, Rome. Hobbies: music, travel, chess. Home: 17 Yordei Hasira St, Jerusalem, Isr. Office: Bezalel Academy, Jerusalem, Isr.

BADER, Ira A, US, rabbi; b. NYC, Dec 6, 1942; s. Irving and Ruth (Appel); BA, Yeshiva Coll, NYC, 1964, ordained rabbi, 1967, MHL, 1967; MA, Fordham U, 1968. Chaplain, capt US Chaplain Corps since 1968; asst, psych lab, Yeshiva Coll, 1964-67; instr, Akiba acad, NY; 1964-67, chaplain, Fort Knox, Kty, 1968-69, Saigon, LongBinh and Mekong Delta Region, 1969-70. Mem: J Chaplains Assn; Assn of J Chaplains of Armed Forces; Psi Chi, Pi Delta Phi, Yeshiva U. Home: 700 W 178th St, New York, NY. Study: HQ, US Army Support Command, Saigon, Viet Nam.

BADER, Menahem, Isr, government official, business exec, author; b. Dukla, Aus-Hung, Sep 20, 1895; s. Josef and Hava (Langer); in Isr since 1920; grad, Bonn Law Sch, Ger; m. Dora Dodelson; c: Tamar. Mem, Kibbutz Misra, since 1920; fmr: dir gen, Min of Labor, 1948-49; MK, 1949-51; dir gen, Min of Devl, 1955-62. Co-found, Haganah. Mem exec comm: Mapam; Hakibbutz Haarzi; found, financial, commercial, ind div, JA; fmr: exec comm: Agric Cen; Histadrut; mem, Rescue Comm, JA, Istanbul, 1943-44. Author: Poalim Bamatzor, 1935; Haneshef, 1936; Aliya Bet, 1938; Michtav El Ima, 1940; Haim, 1941; Shlichujoth Azuwot, 1954; contbr of articles and poems. Home: Kibbutz Misra, Isr. Office: Central Office, Kibbutz Arzi, Tel Aviv, Isr.

BADT-STRAUSS, Bertha, US, journalist, author; b. Breslau, Ger, Dec 7, 1885; d. Benno and Martha (Guttmann) Badt; in US since 1939; PhD, Breslau U, 1908; studied in London, Breslau, Berlin, Munich; m. Bruno Strauss, May 8, 1913; s. Albrecht. Lectr, Breslau and Berlin, 1912–39. Author: Rahel und ihre Zeit, 1912; In Bne Berak und andere Erzaehlungen, 1920; Profiat Duran, 1920; Suesskind von Trimberg, 1920; Leon da Modena, Eldad und Medad, 1920; Moses Mendelssohn, Der Mensch und das Werk, 1929; Juedinnen, 1937; White Fire: The Life and Works of Jessie Sampter, 1956; ed, Hermann Cohen, Briefe, 1939. Home: 2 Dogwood Acres Drive, Chapel Hill, NC.

BAER, Gabriel, Isr, scholar; b. Berlin, Jan 13, 1919; s. Albert and Kaete (Freyer); in Isr since 1933; MA, Heb U, 1952, PhD, 1957; Amer U, Beirut, 1939–40; m. Eva Apt, June, 1946; c:Gideon, Tirzah. Asso prof, Heb U, since 1964; dir, Inst of Asian and Afr Studies, Heb U, since 1967. Maj, IDF, 1948–52. Author: A History of Land Ownership in Modern Egypt, 1962; Population and Society in the Arab East, 1964; Egyptian Guilds in Modern Times, 1964; Studies in the Social History of Modern Egypt, 1969; ed, Asian and Afr Studies annual; Hamizrah Hehadash quarterly. Hobbies: hiking, photography. Home: 17 Efrata St, Jerusalem, Isr.

BAER, Harold, US, jurist; b. NYC, Feb 11, 1905; s. Gustav and Ida (Blausten); BS, NYU, 1926, LLB, 1927; m. Edna Schofield Jacobus, Apr 17, 1928; c: Harold. Justice, Supr Court of State of NY, since 1968; law secy to Comptroller Joseph D McGoldrick, acting chief, law div, both 1942–45; partner, law firm, Baer and Gallın, 1945–54; lectr, munic govt and law, CCNY, Sch of Civic and Bus Admn, 1943–51; judge, City Court (Civil Court), NYC, 1954–58. Chmn: bd, Lexington Houses Nursing Sch (Wilhelm Weinberg Nursery Sch), 1956–61; munic affairs comm, Lib Party, 1945–54; pres: bd trustees, League Sch for Seriously Disturbed Children, since 1960; bd overseers, Acad of Judiciary; bd dirs, Play Schs Assn, since 1956; mem: Judiciary Relations Comm, Judicial Conf; adv comm, Civic Leg League; bd dir, Settlement Housing Fund Inc; United Neighborhood Houses; comm on soc services to Supr Court, Wfr and Health Council; adv council, NY State Jt Leg Comm on Mentally and Physically Handicapped; Citizen's Union; Grand St Boys Assn; NY Tchr Guild; Amer Bar Assn; NY Co Lawyers Assn; Amer Judicature Soc; Assn of Bar, NYC; KP, commn, 1948; club, Fairview Country. Home: 1049 Park Ave, New York, NY. Office: 60 Center St, New York, NY.

BAER, Jerry W, US business exec; b. Chicago, Ill, Nov 3, 1936; s. Jerome and Matilda (Levy); att Culver Mil Acad, Culver, Ind; BS, Ind U, 1958, MBA, U Chicago, 1963; m. Roggie Horwitz, Sep 5, 1961; c: Roggie, Julie. Pres, Dual-Wide Incorp since 1969; vice-pres, Pacific Amer Inds since 1969; sr financial analyst, Ford Motor Co, 1963-66; corp contr, Cole Nat Corp, 1966-69. 2nd lt, US Army, 1958-59. Home: 9100, Wilshire, Beverly Hills, Cal. Office: 156 N Willaman Dr, Beverly Hills, Cal.

BAER, Max Frank, US, organization exec; b. Frankfurt/Main, Ger, Nov 10, 1912; s. Bernard and Erna (Hoelzel); in US since 1921; att U of Ariz; LLB, Creighton U, Omaha, Neb, 1937; MA, Columbia U, 1942; EdD, George Wash U, 1947; m. Gertrude Smith, Feb 14, 1967; c: Richard Rosenbaum, Randye Low. Natl dir, B'nai B'rith Youth Org, since 1948; cons, US Employment Service and Social Security Admn; mem exec comm, World Org of J Youth; vice-pres, Council of Natl Org on Children and Youth; cons, evaluation comms, B'nai B'rith; mem: bd mgrs, Adas Isr Cong; exec comm, World Consultative Comm on J Youth; fmr: natl dir, B'nai B'rith Vocational Service; asst exec secy, AZA, B'nai B'rith; mem: Fed Adv Council, Bur of Employment Security; pres, Guidance and Personnel Assn, DC. Mem: Natl Assn of Social Workers, Wash, DC; Acad of Cert Social Workers; Amer Psych Assn; Amer Personnel and Guidance Assn; Natl Assn of J Communal Workers; Amer Assn of Group Psychotherapy; Natl Vocational Guidance Assn. Author: Occupational Information — Its Nature and Use, 1951; ed, Shofar, since 1948; found ed, Vocational Guidance Quarterly, 1951, contbr of numerous articles to jours, mags. Hobbies: reading, writing, lecturing, dancing. Home: 4201 Cathedral Ave NW, Washington, DC. Office: 1640 Rhode Island Ave NW, Washington, DC.

BAER, Rudolf L, US, physician, educator; b. Strasbourg, Alsace-Lorraine, Fr, July 22, 1910; s. Ludwig and Clara (Mainzer); in US since 1934; att U's: Frankfort, Heidelberg, Berlin, Vienna, Basel, 1928-34; MD; m. Louise Grumbach, Nov 6, 1941; c: John, Andrew. In pvt practice since 1940; prof, chmn, dermat dept, NYU Med Sch, since 1961, fac mem since 1946, dir, dermat, U Hosp and Skin and Cancer Unit, since 1961, att dermat and syphilologist, 1948-61, jr asst, 1939-41, asst att phys, 1941-46, asso, 1946-48; visiting phys, i/c of dermat and syphilology, Bellevue Hosp, since 1961, asso visiting phys, 1949-61; cons, dermat: VA Hosp, Manhattan, since 1961; Monmouth Memorial Hosp, NJ, since 1945; to Surg-Gen, US Army, since 1967; Natl Inst Allergy and Infectious Diseases, since 1967; FDA since 1968; active cons: Goldwater Memorial Hosp, since 1946; Elizabeth A Horton Memorial

Hosp, Middletown, NY; J Hosp for Aged, NYC; asst adj phys, Montefiore Hosp, NYC, 1937-39, adj phys, acting asso phys; visiting f, Cornell U Med Coll, 1942-46. F: Amer Acad of Allergy; AMA; Amer Acad of Dermat; Amer Coll of Allergists; NY Acad of Med; dipl, Amer Bd of Dermat, 1940, mem bd, since 1964; mem: NY Dermat Soc; Intl Comm of Dermat, since 1967; Comm on Cutaneous Diseases, Armed Forces Epid Bd, since 1967; AAAS; Amer Acad of Allergy; Amer Dermat Assn; NY Allergy Soc; NY Acad of Scis; NY Co and State Med Soc; Soc for Inves Dermat; corresp mem: Aus, Cuban, Danish, Fr, It, Swed Dermat Socs; hon mem: Brazilian, Brit, Finnish, Iranian, Israeli, Polish, Venezuelan Socs of Dermat and Syphilology. Author: Office Immunology, 1947; Atopic Dermatitis, 1955; Allergic Dermatoses due to Physical Agents, 1956; ed bd mem, Investigative Dermatology, 1950-62; Annals of Allergy, 1949-65; ed, Yearbook of Dermatology and Syphilology, 1955-65; asst ed, 1943-46, co-ed, 1947-55; contbr to med anthols; numerous articles to sci and med jours. Recipient: Dohi Memorial Medal, Japanese Dermat Soc, 1965. Home: 1185 Park Ave, New York, NY. Office: 550 First Ave, New York, NY.

BAER, Sidney Mordecai, US, business exec; b. Phila, Pa, June 17, 1910; s. Morris and Clara (Kennin); m. Belle Kimmelman, June 10, 1930; c: Bobbi Goldner, Alan, Nancy Teeter. Chmn, Baer Ins Agcy Inc, since 1930. Vice pres, Beth Zion-Beth Isr Syn; trustee, JTSA; mem: Children's Hosp of Phila; Allied J App; Dropsie Coll; United Fund; Amer Cancer Soc; Catholic Charities Appeal; Phila Orch; Emet Rabbi Herzog World Acad; Mary Bailey Inst for Heart Research. Home: 1901 Walnut, Philadelphia, Pa. Office: 1415 Locust, Philadelphia. Pa.

BAER, Yitzhak, Isr, educator, author; b. Halberstadt, Ger, 1888; s. Joseph and Rosa; in Isr since 1930; PhD, U of Freiburg, 1912; m. 1921. Prof, mediaeval J hist, Heb U, Jerusalem, since 1930; prof of gen mediaeval hist, 1932-45; tour of Spain to study Span-J hist, 1925-29; staff mem, Acad for Sci of Judaism, 1919-30; ed, Zion, hist quarterly review, since 1935. Author: Studies in the Jewish History of Aragon, 1913; Protocols of the Jewish Community of Duchy of Cleves, 1922; Jews in Christian Spain, 1929, 1936; The Religious-Social Trend of Sefer Hachasidim, 1938; History of the Jews in Christian Spain, Heb ed, 1945, Eng ed, 1961-66; Israel among the Nations, 1955. Home: 31 Alfasi St, Jerusalem, Isr. Office: Heb U, Jerusalem, Isr.

BAERNCOPF, Joseph B, US, certified public acctnt; b. NYC, Nov 18, 1889; s. Alexander and Sarah (Segar); grad, Pace Coll, 1915; m. Esther Efroymson, Dec 28, 1920; c: David, Robert. Ret; fmr: partner, George S Olive & Co, CPA's, 1932-65, sr acctnt, 1922-32; jr clerk, Hearts of Oak Benefit Soc, London, Eng, 1903-05; govt clerk, Bd of Agric, Eng, 1905-07; asst chief clerk, NY Telephone, Newark, NJ, 1907-09; computer, Worthington Machinery, Harrison, NJ, 1909-10; acctnt: Pa RR, 1910-15; Public Service, Newark, 1915-16; SH Wolfe, NY, 1916-17; asst secy, Amer Merchant Marines Ins, NY, 1917-22. US Army, 1918; USN, supervising auditor, 1942-45; US Army, spec repr, Off of Contract Settlement, 1945-47. Mem: Amer Inst CPA's; Ind Assn CPA's, past pres; Natl Assn Acctnts; Bus Hist Soc of Ind; Amer Accounting Assn; Amer Inst Mgmt; Athenaeum of Ind; B'nai B'rith; Masons; hon mem, Beta Alpha Psi, 1962; fmr: dir, vice-pres, United Cerebral Palsy of Cen Ind; mem, taxation comm, Ind C of C; fac asso, Ind U; chmn, troop comm, Boy Scouts of Amer; dir, J Comty Cen Assn; mem, auditing comm, trustee, dir, vice-pres, Ind Heb Cong; dir, vice-pres, JWF. Hobbies: fishing, painting, gardening. Home: 5312 N Illinois St, Indianapolis, Ind.

BAERWALD, Leo, US, rabbi; b. Saaz, Aus, Sep 20, 1883; s. Aron and Fanny (Lazarus); in US since 1940; PhD, U Erlangen, 1905; ordained rabbi, J Theol Sem, Breslau, 1911; m. Jenny Blumenthal, 1911 (decd); c: Ernest, Gabriele Vogel. Rabbi, Cong Beth Hillel, 1940-45; chief rabbi, Munich, Ger, 1918-40. Chaplain, Ger army, 1914-17. Mem: NY Bd of Rabbis; CCAR; Amer Fed of J for Cen Eur, exec comm. Author: Entwickelung der Lotzeschen Psychologie, 1905; co-author: 50 Jahre Hauptsynagoge München, 1937; contbr to periodicals. Home: 1372 Riverside Dr, New York, NY.

BAGNER, Alan Bernard, US, physician; b. Bklyn, Sep 29, 1911; s. Abraham and Esther (Hipsman); BS, NYU, 1932; MD, NY Med Coll and Flower Hosp, 1938; m. Harriet Wishy, July 8, 1947; c: Evan, Ronda. Phys, gen practice, since 1940.

Maj, US Army, 1941-46. Pres, Cong Beth Tikvah Knesset Israel; mem: AMA; NY State Med Soc; Kings Co Med Soc; KP lodge 439; fmr pres, Cong Beth Tikvah. Hobbies: photography, golf. Home and office: 1674 Remsen Ave, Brooklyn, NY.

BAHAT, Jacob, J, Isr, educator; b. Pol, June 2, 1910; s. Pinkas and Chaja (Kaminer) Bachstitz; in Isr since 1938; ordained rabbi, J Theol Sem, Vienna, 1938; att Us: Vienna, Jerusalem; m. Rachel, Apr 14, 1943; c: Nitza, Oded. Chmn, dept Heb lit and lang, Haifa U, since 1965; fmr: sr master, Heb, Tichon Hadash Sch, 1941-59; supt of HS's, Min of Educ, 1959-65. Educ off, IDF, 1948-49. Mem, U Tchrs Org; fmr mem, Supts of HSs. Author: Pirkei Gmara uFirkei Talmud, 1945; Kitsur Toldot Hasifrut Haklalit, 1945; Derech, 1959; Vedayek, 1960; Iyunei Mikra Bitsirat Agnon Vehaim Hazaz, 1962; contbr numerous research articles to lit mags. Home: 28 Einstein St, Haifa, Isr. Office: U Inst of Haifa, Mt Carmel, Haifa, Isr.

BAHCALL, John Norris, US, physicist; b. Shreveport, La, Dec 30, 1934; s. Malcolm and Mildred (Lazarus); PhD, Harvard U, 1961; m. Neta Assaf, Sep 21, 1966; c: Ron. Asso prof, theoretical physics, Cal Tech, since 1967. F: Sloan Found; Amer Physical Soc. Home: 2484 San Pasqual, Pasadena, Cal. Office: California Technology, Pasadena, Cal.

BAHIR, Arieh, Isr, organization exec; b. Odessa, Russ, May 1, 1906; s. Meir and Berta (Gnessin) Geller; in Isr since 1924; att Poly, Odessa, 1923-24; m. Esther Babushkina, Apr, 1928; c: Dan, Yigal. Mem: exec comm: Histadrut; Keren Hanegev, Midrashat Sdeh Boker; fmr: MK, 1st, 3rd and 6th Knesset; mem exec, Solel Boneh, 1956-59; secy, econ affairs, Kibbutz Afiqim, 1960-63; mgr, Kibbutzim Ind Org, 1963-66. Haganah, 1924-48. Mem: secretariat, Lab Org, since 1970; Public Council for New Immigrants, since 1969, Coop Council, since 1968; fmr: dir, Berl Katznelson Found, Bet Berl, 1945-65; first secy-gen, United Kibbutz and Kvutzot Org; secy, Rafi party, Knesset; mem, Lab Party Cen; org, lectrs, Mapai, 3rd Knesset. Home: Kibbutz Afiqim, Isr.

BAHLOUL, Yosef, Isr, attorney; b. Tiberias, Nov 18, 1923; s. Zion and Mazal (Benkiki); desc of Shmuel Benkiki, pres, Rabb Court, Tiberias; LLD, Jerusalem, 1950; m. Rebecca Abadi, Oct 19, 1952; c: Zion, Ariella, Nirit. Pres, Dist Contl, Nazareth, since 1969; frm: dep, asst, dist atty, Haifa and N dist; asst dist atty, Galilee, Tiberias; dist court judge, Haifa, 1968-69; lectr on criminal proced, Police Off Cen, 1958-69. Haganah, 1948-49; mem bd, Lions Club, Haifa, past pres; chmn, psycht comm; fmr: mem cen comm, Isr Bar Assn; repr, dist planning comm, Min of Justice; appd head, inves comm, to locate lost Yemenite children, 1949-52. Recipient: Jerusalem Signal; War of Liberation Signal; Sinai Campaign Signal. Home: 10 Lea St, Haifa, Isr. Office: District Court, Upper Nazareth, Isr.

BAHN, Benjamin Edward, US, dentist; b. Boston, July 22, 1893; s. Moses and Celia (Ebb); DMD, Harvard Dent Sch, 1913, postgrad, 1914, cert, dent public health, 1964; m. Mollie Abramson (decd); c: Arthur, Charles, Celia, Saul. Practising orthodentist, Boston and Plymouth; on staff, Forsyth Dent Infirmary, 1914-18. Dent examiner, Selective Service, WW II. Pres and org: Young Isr Movement of NE; (first) Roxbury Young Isr, 1922; Mizrachi Org of Roxbury, Dorchester, Mattapan and Milton, Mass; Union of Orthodox J Congs, NE Div, 1948-50; Young Isr of Gtr Boston, 1952-53; fmr: Roxbury Dent Soc, vice-pres; Regional Council of Young Isr, 1953; secy: Maimonides Inst; Daughters of Isr, Inc, Ritualarium, 1949-53; org, Children Sabbath Hour, 1934; f, Royal Soc of Health, London, since 1965; life mem, Mass Dent Soc; mem: NE Dent Soc; Gtr Boston Dent Soc; fmr asso mem, NE Soc of Orthodontists. Contbr to J and dent publs. Home: 369 Tappan St, Brookline, Mass. Office: 429 Blue Hill Ave, Roxbury, Mass.

BAILIN, Marvin Klein, US, attorney; b. Lennox, SD, July 21, 1924; s. Solomon and Huldah (Klein); PhB, U of Chgo, 1943; LLB, U of Pa, 1951; m. Janet Gellman, June 17, 1951; c: David, Devra, Steven. Partner, Christopherson, Bailin and Wilds, since 1951. Pvt, US Army, 1942-45. Commn, B'nai B'rith Commn on Comty and Vets Service; vice-chmn, plains states region, ADL; secy, Sioux Falls JWF Bd; trustee, Bellefaire Children's Residential Treatment Cen; mem bd: Family Service of Sioux Falls; United Comty Service of Sioux Falls; mem: Amer, State of SD Bar Assns; state corresp atty ACLU; B'nai B'rith of Sioux Falls; mem: Amer, State of SD Bar

Assns; Minnehaha Bar Assn; Amer Trial Lawyers Assn; state corresp atty, ACLU; B'nai B'rith, past pres: Sioux Lodge, SW Region Council; Masons; Consistory, Sioux Falls; pres: Sioux Falls Safety Council; Sioux Falls chap, and SD div, UN Assn; chmn: Cornbelt Bd, B'nai B'rith Youth Org; delgs assembly, United Comty Services of Sioux Falls; delg, B'nai B'rith Supr Lodge Convs; master, Trinity Lodge, No 200 AF and AM; mem bd, Sioux Council of Boy Scouts of Amer; pres, United Brotherhood Council of Sioux Falls. Recipient: dist service award, UN Assn of US, 1966; cert of service, outstanding contrib to minority races, NAACP, 1968; EAME theatre ribbon with three bronze stars. Home: 1410 Center, Sioux Falls, SD. Office: 509 Dakota Ave, Sioux Falls, SD.

BAILY, Nathan A, US, educator, author, consultant; b. NYC, July 19, 1920; s. Saul and Eleanor (Minz); BS, CUNY, 1940; MA, Columbia U, 1941, PhD, 1946; m. Judith Bernstein, June 20, 1946; c: Alan, Lawrence. Prof, bus admn, found dean, Sch of Bus Admn, Amer U, Wash, DC; econ, OPA; dir: Wash Mutual Inves Fund; Amer Wholesalers; Carl M Freeman Assos; Homer Hoyt Inst; tchr: Advanced Sch of Retail Mgmt, Natl Sales Exec; Amer Inst of Banking; hist, econ depts, CUNY; Fashion Inst of Tech. Dir: Friends US of Latin Amer; Pioneer Found; bd adv: Dist-Realty Title Ins Co; Fed Realty Inves Trust; Columbia Realty; trustee: Council on Opportunities in Selling; Middle Atlantic Assn, Coll of Bus Admn, secy, treas, pres; mem: Natl Educ Adv Comm, Amer Inst of Banking; Anti-Trust and Trade Regulation Comm, C of C; DC Small Bus Adv Council; Phi Beta Kappa; Amer U Honor Soc; Amer Econ Assn; AAUP; Amer Soc of Assn Execs. Contbr to jours. Recipient: Dist Salesman Award, Wash Sales Exec Club; f: E I duPont; Swift and Co; Danforth Found; Volker Fund. Home: 5516 Greystone St, Chevy Chase, Md. Office: Amer U, Massachusetts and Nebraska Aves, NW, Washington, DC.

BAIREY (BRONNER), Zev W, Mexico, business adv; b. Vienna, Aus, Mar 11, 1920; s. Jacob and Edith (Epstein) Bronner; in Mexico since 1957; BS, U of Cal, 1940; MA, U of the Americas, Mexico City, 1968; m. Elana Haydis, Sep 13, 1946; c: Daniel, Miryam, Ariela, Guita. Regional mgr, Investors Overseas Services, since 1961; instr, econ, U of the Americas, since 1966; sales mgr, Gumber, SA, 1958-62; Mex area dir, Bus Intl, 1966-68; numerous activities as bus adv in Isr, Eur, US. IDF, Cheil Mada, 1948-49. Past pres: Beth Isr Comty Cen, Mexico City; Alpha Omega Epsilon, Mex area chap; vice-pres, Cardozo Lodge, B'nai B'rith; mem: AAAS; Alpha Omega Epsilon. Ed, Tlatelolco Economic Monographs, Mex; contbr articles to jours. Hobbies: J hist, Heb ling, plant phys. Home: Montes Urales 610, Mexico City, Mex. Office: Apartado 10-756, Mexico City, Mex.

BAK, Benjamin, US, rabbi; b. Taragin, Lith, Feb 6, 1920; s. Herzel and Hene (Rabinowitz); in US since 1940; att Yeshiva U, 1940-43; ordained rabbi, Telshe Yeshivah, Lith, 1940; BS, 1952; MA, Johns Hopkins U, 1958; m. Muriel Alexander, June 13, 1943; c: Pinchos, Joseph, Herzel, Henie. Rabbi, Har Zion Tifereth Isr Cong, since 1944; dir, J Chaplaincy, State of Md, since 1962; coord, Beth Din, Rabb Council, 1961-63. Pres, Vaad Harabonim, 1956-60; RabCA, Md br, 1950-52; mem, Mh Chaplains. Home: 3407 Menlo Dr, Baltimore, Md. Study: 2706 Cheswolde Rd, Baltimore, Md.

BAKAN, David, US, psychologist, educator; b. NYC, Apr 23, 1921; s. Max and Rose (Rosenstrauch); AB, Bklyn Coll, 1942; MA, Indiana U, 1944; PhD, O State U, 1948; m. Mildred Blynn, Dec 24, 1942; c: Joseph, Jonathan, Daniel, Jacob, Deborah, Abigail. Prof, dept of psych, U Chgo, since 1961; U Montana, 1949-61; visiting lectr, clinical psych, Harvard, 1956-58. Author: Sigmund Freud and the Jewish Mystical Tradition; The Duality of Human Existence; On Method: Toward a Reconstruction of Psychological Investigation; Disease, Pain and Sacrifice: Toward a Psychology of Suffering. Home: 4809 Kenwood Ave, Chicago, Ill. Office: U of Chicago, Chicago, Ill.

BAKER, Abe B, US, neurologist, educator; b. Minneapolis, Mar 27, 1908; s. Solomon and Molly (Greenspan); BA, U Minn, 1928, BS, 1929, MB, 1930, MD, 1931, MS, 1932, PhD, 1934; m. Rose Witzman, May 7, 1933; c: Lowell, Elaine, Eleanor, Judith. Prof, head, dept neur, U Minn, since 1946; on fac since 1931. Mem: Amer Acad of Neur; Amer Neur Assn; Amer Assn of Neuropaths; Cen Neuropsycht Assn; Phi Beta Kappa; Alpha Omega Alpha; Sigma Xi. Author:

Outlines of Neuropathology; ed, Clinical Neurology, 1954, 4 vol, 1962. Home: 2900 Douglas Drive, Minneapolis, Minn. Office: U Hosp, Minneapolis, Minn.

BAKER, David, US, attorney, building exec; b. Columbia, SC, June 20, 1918; s. Frank and Clara (Kligman); BA, U of SC, 1940, LLB, 1946; m. Jo Ann Schreiber, June 25, 1950; c: Debra, Kenneth, John, Frank, Dale. Atty, since 1946; partner: Baker & Baker, since 1946; D & L Holding Co, construction firm, since 1950. Lt cdr, USN, 1941-46. Pres: Richland Kiwanis Club; Tree Of Life Temple; Columbia J Comty Cen; chmn: Comm of 100; Citizens Adv Comm; Cen City Steering Comm; secy, bd dirs, United Fund; bd dirs: Columbia C of C; adv, SC Natl Bank; secy: Natl Dem Party, SC, 1948; United Comty Services; mem: B'nai B'rith; ZOA; Richland Co, SC Bar Assns; State Fair Assn; Amer Legion. Home: 3540 Northshore Rd, Columbia, SC. Office: Midland Shopping Center, Columbia, SC.

BAKER, Saul Phillip, US, physician; b. Cleveland, O, Dec 7, 1924; s. Barnet and Florence (Kleinman); BSc, physics, Case Inst of Tech, 1945; biol, chem, psych, W Res U, 1947, both Cleveland, O; MSc, O State U, 1949, MD, 1953; PhD, Coll of Med, O State U, 1957, both Columbus ,O; div; c: Randall, Dean. Pvt practice, internal med, geriatrics, card, since 1962; asst visiting phys, dept of med, Baltimore City Hosp & Johns Hopkins Hosp, 1954-56; sr asst res, dept of med, U of Chgo Clinics, 1956-57; asst prof of med, Chgo Med Sch, 1957-62; asso prof of med, Cook Co Hosp Grad Sch of Med, 1958-62; head, dept of geriatrics, St Vincent Charity Hosp, 1964-67. USPHS, sr asst surg, res, 1954-56. Mem: adv comm, Golden Age Div, J Comty Cen; comm, Older People Wfr Fed; comm, Aging and Chronic Illness, Acad of Med, all Cleveland; sci council, Heart Assn, Northeastern O; profsl sect, Diabetes Assn, Gtr Cleveland; f: Amer Geriatrics Soc; Gerontological Soc; Amer Coll of Card; Council on Arteriosclerosis, AHA; AAAS; mem: Amer Phys Soc; Amer Fed for Clinical Research; NY Acad Sci; Soc for Experimental Biol and Med Sigma Xi; J Big Brother Assn; Golden Sq Masonic Lodge 32; Sigma Alpha Mu frat, pres, Cleveland Alumni Club; Phi Delta Epsilon med frat, grad club; Pi Delta Epsilon, natl hon journalism frat; Tau Kappa Alpha, natl hon forensic frat, holds, Case Hon Key; fmr, treas, El Al Lodge, B'nai B'rith. Lectr on speciality fields, on radio, TV; contbr numerous articles to profsl jours. Hobbies: bridge, golf. Home: 2300 Overlook Rd, Cleveland Heights, O. Office: 14077 Cedar Rd, Cleveland, S Euclid, O.

BAKST, Henry J, US, physician, educator; b. Providence, RI, May 19, 1906; s. Adolph and Sophie (Himowitz); PhB, Brown U, 1927; MD, Harvard Med Sch, 1931; m. Ruth Miller, June 23, 1933; c: David. Asso dean, Boston U Sch of Med, since 1965, prof, preventive med, chmn, dept, 1952-65; cons, Amer Bd of Preventive Med, since 1962; dir, outpatient dept and home med service, Mass Memorial Hosp, since 1949; asst visiting phys: Boston City Hosp, 1953; Mass Memorial Hosps, since 1948, chief, dept of ind rehab, since 1956; dir, div, health conservation, since 1960. Cdr, USN, res, 1940-46, ret. Chmn, Health Council, United Comty Services, Gtr Boston, 1953; secy-treas, Assn of Tchrs of Preventive Med, since 1960; f: Amer Coll Phys; Amer Public Health Assn; mem, bd dirs: Boston chap, AHA, 1953; J Family and Children Service, Boston, 1951; Mass Assn For Mh, 1954; mem: adv bd, Visiting Nurse Assn, Boston; AMA; Mass Med Soc; Cen Health Council, Mass; Sigma Xi; Public Health Training Council, USPHS, 1965-68. Contbr to med periodicals. Home: 285 Clinton Rd, Brookline, Mass. Office: Boston U School of Medicine, 80 E Concord St, Boston, Mass.

BAKWIN, Harry, US, physician; b. Utica, NY, Nov 19, 1894; s. Simon and Emma (Nadel); BS, Columbia Coll, 1915; MD, Columbia Coll Phys and Surgs, 1917; att U's: Vienna, Berlin, 1924-25; m. Ruth Morris, Feb 3, 1925; c: Edward, Patricia Selch, Barbara Rosenthal, Michael. Prof, clinical ped, NYU Sch of Med; men fac: Cornell U, 1919-24; Columbia U, Coll of Phys and Surgs, 1925-30; visiting phys, Bellevue Hosp, 1930-69. Lt, US Army, 1918-19. Mem: bd dirs, Amer Chess Found; Amer Ped Soc; NY Acad Med; AAAS; AMA; past pres, Amer Acad Ped. Author: Clinical Management of Behavior, Disorders in Children 3rd ed, 1966; Psychologic Care During Infancy & Childhood, 1942; contbr numerous articles to phys and behaviorial jours. Recipient: award in recognition of achievements, Coll of Phys and Surgs, Columbia U, 1967; 50 years service, Med Soc, State of NY,

1968. Hobbies: collecting paintings, chamber music, chess. Home and office: 132 E 71 St, New York, NY.

BALABAN, Miriam, Isr, communal leader; b. Phila, Pa, Dec 4, 1927; d. Zelig and Mathilda (Kallos); in Isr since 1949; BA, U of Pa; widow; c: Naomi. Pres, Isr Sci Services, since 1968; fmr: dir, natl sci pub house, Weizmann Sci Press, 1951-62; found, Isr Prog for Sci Trans, under contract with NSF and Jerusalem Acad Press. Mem: Conf of Biol Eds; Soc for Tech Writers and Publishers, Isr chap. Ed, Desalination, intl jour, since 1966; ed-in-chief, Research Council Publs and Weizmann Sci Press, 1951-62; dir, ed, Jerusalem Acad Press; ed, various sci jours. Hobbies: arts, crafts, nature. Home: 45 Herzog St, Jerusalem, Isr. Office: 19 Nili St, Jerusalem, Isr.

BALCOMBE, Frederick James, Eng, business exec; b. London, Dec 17, 1911; s. Sidney and Agnes (Harris); m. Clarice Cassel, Dec 22, 1936; (decd); m. 2nd, Rhoda Jaffe, June 29, 1956; c: Andrew Nicholas, Alison. Dir: A Cassel & Sons Ltd; Balcaston Construction; Castlemere Properties; cons, partner, Sidney Balcombe & Sons. Lt, RAF, 1939-45. Pres: Higher Blackley Comty Assn; Crescent Horticulture Soc; vice-pres: Blackley Amateur Football League; Disabled Drivers Assn; Manchester J Blind Soc; Manchester Hillel House; gov, King David Jews Sch; JP, Manchester City, Magistrates Bench; trustee, Higher Broughton Syn; treas, Heb U, Manchester House Appeal; hon mem, Commercial and Ind Club, Tel Aviv; found, mem, Variety Club of Isr; dep, Bd Deps of British Jews, 1960-65; councillor, Manchester City Council, 1958-67; mem: Ajex; Poale Zion; B'nai B'rith. Home: 58 Waterpark Rd, Salford, Eng. Office: 1/3 Teneriffe St, Salford, Eng.

BALDINGER, Milton I, US, attorney, educator; b. Olyphant, Pa, June 29, 1911; s. Philip and Anna (Zielger); BA, Pa State U, 1933; LLB, U of Pittsburgh, 1936; LLM, Georgetown U, 1939, SJD, 1941; m. Geraldine Cohen, Mar 29, 1944; c: Joan Cassin, Joseph. Vice-chmn, bd, gen counsel, First Fed Savings & Loan Assn, Wash, DC; fmr: atty, Fed Home Loan Bank Bd, 1937-38; asst counsel, Rural Electrification Admn, 1938-40; prof, law, Natl U, 1940-50; cons, Natl Hqrs, Selective Service Sys, 1942; lectr: Judge Advocates Gen Sch, 1942-44; Amer U Law Sch, 1950. Pres, Comm on Employment of Handicapped; chmn, Natl Capitol Area chap, Natl Found, March of Dimes; dir, Research Found of Wash Hosp Cen; dir and secy: Col Harland Sanders Found, Inc; Col Harland Sanders Charitable Org, Can; trustee, Baldinger Found; mem: DC Health and Wfr Council; Masons 33; Order of Coif; Tau Epsilon Rho; Zeta Beta Tau; Phi Kappa Phi; Delta Sigma Rho; Pi Delta Epsilon; Pi Gamma Mu; Amer Law Inst; Amer Bar Assn; bd dirs, DC Bar Assn; ZOA; fmr: pres, Adas Isr Heb Cong; pres, Argo lodge, B'nai B'rith; mem: exec, J Comty Council; bd trustees, UJA, both Gtr Wash; clubs: Natl Press; Capitol Hill; Woodmont Country. Author: Tax Chats, syndicated column; The General Welfare Clause, 1939; Constitutional Aspects of Selective Service System, 1941; Cases and Materials on Federal Income Taxation, 1947, and yearly supplement for several years; Estate Planning Notes, 1949-50; ed-in-chief, DC Bar Jour, 1959-66. Recipient: Selective Service Medal; cert of merit, Judge Advocates Gen Sch. Home: 4536 Linnean Ave, NW, Washington, DC. Office: 300 First Federal Savings Bldg, Washington, DC.

BALENSON, Michael A, US, denstist; b. Newark, NJ, Dec 21, 1936; s. Louis and Freida (Bressman); BS, U of Md, 1958, DDS, 1962; m. Cora Lefever; c: David, Brian, Jeffrey. Pvt practice since 1962. Lt, USNR, 1962-64. Asst treas, Alpha Omega Frat; mem: Amer Dent Assn; Md State Dent Assn; Young Men's Leadership Council, AJC; club, Mercantile, treas, 1969-70. Home: 3702 Clarinth Rd, Baltimore, Md. Office: 1668 E Belvedere Ave, Baltimore, Md.

BALFOUR, Gerald Arthur James Balfour, The 4th, Earl of, UK, landowner; b. Whittingehame, Haddington, Dec 23, 1925; s. 3rd Earl Robert and Jean (Cooke-Yarborough); great uncle, Arthur James Balfour, 1st Earl of Balfour; att HMS Conway, Wales, 1941-44; master mariner, Sir John Cass, London, 1953; m. Natasha Anton, Dec 14, 1956. Landowner; merchant navy, Ben Line, 1944-45; bldg ind, 1964-68. Home: The Tower, Whittingehame, Haddington, E Lothian, Scotland. Office: Whittingehame Estate, Haddington, E Lothian, Scotland.

BALINKY, Alexander, US, educator, economist; b. Odessa, Russ, Oct 24, 1919; s. Jacob and Esther (Swartz); in US since 1929; BA, U Cal, 1940; MA, PhD, Harvard U, 1947; m. Jean Lahn, Mar 29, 1951. Prof, econ, Rutgers U, since 1958; lectr, econ, since 1947. Econ, War Labor Bd, 1941-43, lab relations cons, 1943-45. Dir, Russ area prog, Rutgers U. Author: Albert Gallatin, Fiscal Theories and Policies, 1958; Planning and The Market in the USSR, 1967; Marx's Economics: Origin and Development, 1969; contbr to profsl jours. Home: 65 Hillcrest Rd, RD 1, Martinsville, NJ. Office: Dept of Econ, Rutgers University, New Brunswick, NJ.

BALL, Erna D, US, neuropsychiatrist, b. Berlin, July 11, 1849; d. Ernst and Bianca (Mendelsohn); in US since 1934; att: U Heidelberg; U Rostock; MD, U Berlin, 1918. Att psycht, Kew Gardens Gen Hosp, since 1954; att neur, Prof Cassirer Clinic, Berlin, 1920-26; asst neur, Vanderbilt Clinic, Columbia Med Cen, NY, 1934-40; psycht, J Fed Settlement, NY, 1936-42; att neuropsycht, NY Infirmary for Women, 1936-59; adj neuropsycht, Beth Isr Hosp, NY, 1938-50; phys i/c, Oceanside Gardens Sanatorium, Oceanside, LI, 1943-50; head, electroencephalographic dept, Assutah Hosp, Tel Aviv, 1950-54; asso visiting neuropsycht, Queens Hosp Cen, Jamaica, LI, 1954-64. Dipl, Amer Bd of Psycht and Neur; f, Amer Psycht Assn; mem: Acad of Neur; Assn for Advancement of Psychotherapy; Rudolf Virchow Soc; Amer Phys F for Isr Med Assn, Jerusalem Acad of Med; ZOA; Amer Comm of Ose; Soroptimist Intl Assn; Jamaica J Cen, Queens, NY; AMA; Queens Co Med Assn. Contbr in field of neur and psycht to sci publs. Home and office: 160-10 89 Ave, Jamaica, NY.

BALLENGER, A G, US, business exec; b. Chgo, May 9, 1893; s. Jules and Amanda (Foreman); BS, EM, Mich Coll of Mining and Tech, 1915; m. Doris Zeisler, June 28, 1924; c: Walter, William, Robert. Exec vice-pres, Morris Paper Mills and Morris Paper Mills Div, Fed Paper Bd Co, Inc, 1953-57, with co since 1916, presently ret; dir: Bank of Highland Park since 1961; Pure Filter, Ill, 1959-65. Capt, US Army, 1917-19. Co-chmn, Special Gifts, Highland Park Comty Chest, 1964; life trustee, Highland Park Hosp Found, pres, 1957-64; trustee: Ravinia Festival Assn; N Shore Cong Israel, Glencoe; past pres: J Fed Metrop Chgo, 1950-52; dir: Suburban Fine Arts Cen, Highland Park, Ill; Barren Found, Chgo; mem: City Council, Highland Park, 1965; Sch Bd 107, Elm Place Sch, 1930-39; Spec Comms for Sr Citizens, Wfr Council of Metrop Chgo; Amer Legion; VFW; Mil Order of Purple Heart; Sigma Rho; hon mem: Rotary Club, Highland Park; Zeta Beta Tau Found; clubs: Standard, Chgo, past pres; Northmoor Country, Highland Park, past pres; Chgo Fishing, Hayward, Wis, past pres. Recipient: Purple Heart for Meritorious Service, 1919. Home and office: 813 Moseley Rd, Highland Park, Ill.

BALLON, Sidney, US, rabbi; b. Pawtucket, RI, May 25, 1912; s. Israel and Sadie (Needle); BA, Brown U, 1932; ordained rabbi, HUC, 1938, hon DD, 1963; m. Jean Hymson, July 20, 1940; c: Jeffrey, Martha, Charles. Rabbi, Nassau Comty Temple, since 1951; regional rabbi, UAHC, 1938-39; rabbi, Tree of Life Syn, Columbia, SC, 1939-48; rabbi, Temple Adath Isr, Lexington, Ky, 1948-51. Chaplain, USAAF, 1942-45. Mem: CCAR; NY Bd of Rabbis; NY Assn of Reform Rabbis; ZOA; B'nai B'rith; club, Rotary Intl. Home: 356 Oakford St, W Hempstead, NY. Study: 240 Hempstead Ave, W Hempstead, NY.

BALSAM, Arthur, US, pianist; b. Warsaw, Pol, Feb 8, 1906; s. Maurice and Elly (Posnansky); in US since 1940; att: U Warsaw; Acad of Music, Berlin, 1928-31; m. Ruth Miller, U 1933. Recording artist for: Decca Records; Concert Hall Soc; London Records; Wash Records; Osieau Lyre; Musical Heritage; recorded all piano works of Mozart and Haydn; tchr: chamber music, U of Me; Boston U, since 1969; Kneisel Hall, summer sch for chamber misic, Blue Hill, Me, since 1953; Manhattan Sch of Music, since 1964; accompanist for: Francescatti, Milstein, Menuhin, Morini, until 1958; since 1958, only solo and chamber music concerts; asst artist for Budapest, Kroll, Vegh, Pascal Quartets; soloist with: NBC Sym, Philharmonic Orch of London, London Sym, Royal Philharmonic, Warsaw Philharmonic and Radio Orchs of BBC, London, Hilversum, Zurich, Warsaw. Mem, Albeneri Trio; club, Bohemians. Recipient: first prize, piano contest, Berlin, 1930; Mendelssohn-Bartholdy Award, 1931; Ford Found Grant, 1957. Home and office: 258 Riverside Dr, New York. NY.

BALSHAN, Amikam Joseph, Isr, chess champion; b. Kibbutz Ramat Hacovesh, May 3, 1948; s. Jacob and Ruth (Tverskey); att Bar Ilan U. Natl master in chess since 1969. IDF, 1966-69. Chess awards: 1st prize, Adult Championship, Petah Tikva, 1963; Ist place, Tel Aviv Youth Championship, 1963; Youth of Isr Championship, 1965; repr, Isr Chess Fed, Le Havre, Fr, won 1st prize; championship of IDF, 1967, 68, 69; 6th place, World Championship, Jerusalem, 1967; mem Isr team, World Students Olympics, 1968; 2nd place, Masters' Tournament, Natanya, 1969. Home: 160 Rothschild St, Petah Tikva, Isr.

BALTER, Dov, Uruguay, insurance broker; b. Montevideo, Uruguay, July 2, 1923; s. Jaime and Elena (Brisgal); att HS, IAVA, Montevideo; m. Serl Podhoretz, Mar 12, 1964; c: Arieh. Profsl ins broker. Gen secy, Scholem Aleichem Sch, Uruguay; mem: Hanoar Hatzioni; Hatjia; Fed Lib Sionista; past pres: Kehila Aszkenazi; Comité Central Israelita; past secy, Keren Hayesod, all Uruguay; mem, Partido Mapai, Uruguay. Hobbies: educ, reading, classical music. Home and office: Uruguay 1530/48, Montevideo, Uruguay.

BALTSAN, Hayim, Isr, journalist; b. Kishinev, Bessarabia, May 5, 1910; s. Ben Zion and Esther (Kremenstein); desc of Rabbi Maharal of Prague; in Isr since 1935; license en droit, Bucharest U, 1934; att Heb U, Jerusalem; admitted to Pal Bar, 1940; m. Ruth Garty, Apr 29, 1949; c: Reveetal, Aveekam, Astrith. Exec dir, chief ed, found, ITIM, natl Isr news agcy, since 1950; fmr chief, Jerusalem bur, chief news ed, Haboker, 1935-42; roving Eur corresp, Haaretz, 1942-48; both Heb dailies; dir: Turkey, Czech, HIAS of Amer, 1944-48. War Info Off, US Emb, Istanbul, 1942-43; War Info Bur, Brit Emb, Istanbul, 1943-45; active illegal immigration to Pal; with PR sect, IDF, 1948-49. Natl vice-chmn, Intl Press Inst; vice-chmn, League for Unequivocal Heb Orthography; mem: Isr Journalists Assn; Isr Bar Assn. Author: Colloquial Hebrew, in Eng, 1938; Six Years Activity of the Jerusalem Community, 1937; fmr, contbr of articles on Eur Jewry during WW II. Spec interest: reforming Heb orthography. Home: 23 Akkiva Aryeh St, Tel Aviv, Isr. Office: 10 Tiomkin St, Tel Aviv, Isr.

BALTZAN, David Mortimer, Can, physician; b. Leora, Bessarabia, May 10, 1897; s. Moses and Yetta (Bondar); in Can since 1903; MD, CM, McGill U, 1920; FRCP, 1931; FACP, 1932; hon LLD, 1969; m. Rose Cristall, 1927; c: Marcel, Don, Richard. Chief, staff, St Paul's Hosp, since 1951; prof, clinical med, U of Sask, since 1951, fmr chief, med dept; med cons: U Hosp; City Hosp; San Hosp; Can Natl RR; clinical cons, Baltzan Asso Med Clinic, since 1961; dir, Cancer Clinic, 1931-33. Royal Can Army, MC, WW II. Mem: Fed Royal Commn on Health Services; natl bd, dirs, CCJ, co-chmn, council; Can Author's Assn; Can repr, intl comm, Soc of Internal Med; fmr: pres: B'nai B'rith; Sask Med Assn; John Howard Soc; Acad of Med; trustee, Queen Elizabeth II Research Fund; vice-pres, W Can J Cong; dipl, Amer Bd of Internal Med. Author: Principles of Internal Medicine, 1944; contbr to med jours. Recipient: Hum Relations Award, CCJ, 1957; Coronation Medal, King George IV. Home: 219 Saskatchewan Crescent W, Saskatoon, Sask, Can. Office: 226 20 St E, Saskatoon, Sask, Can.

BAMBERGER, Bernard J, US, rabbi; b. Baltimore, Md, May 30, 1904; s. William and Gussie (Erlanger); BA, Johns Hopkins U, 1923; ordained rabbi, HUC, 1926, DD, 1929, hon DHL, 1950; m. Ethel Kraus, June, 1932; c: Henry, David. Rabbi em, Temple Shaaray Tefila, NY, since 1970, rabbi, 1944-70; Rabbi: Temple Isr, Lafayette, Ind, 1926-29; Temple Beth Emeth, Albany, NY, 1929-44. Pres: World Union for Progressive Judaism, since 1970, CCAR, 1959-60; Syn Council of Amer, 1950-51; vice-pres, J Book Council of Amer, 1951-52. Author: Proselytism in the Talmudic Period, 1939; Fallen Angels, 1952; The Bible - A Modern Jewish Approach, 1956; The Story of Judaism, 1957; ed, Reform Judaism, 1949; bd ed, New Jewish Translation of the Bible; contbr to periodicals. Home: 225 W 86 St, New York, NY. Study: 250 E 79 St. New York, NY.

BAMBERGER, Carl, US, orchestra conductor; b. Vienna, Feb 21, 1902; s. Gustav and Melanie (Prossnitz); in US since 1937; att U Vienna, 1920-24; m. Lotte Hammerschlag. Dir, orch and opera dept, Mannes Coll of Music, since 1938; conductor, Profsl Training Orch, New Sch, Phila, since 1968; opera conductor: Danzig, 1924-27; Darmstadt, 1927-31; music dir: Annual Spring Festival, Columbia, SC, 1943-50;

Little Sym, Montreal; guest conductor, philharmonic orchs, US; City Opera, NY; Buenos Aires; Paris; Eur; Philippines; Japan; China. Author: The Conductors Art, 1964; contbr to Americana Ency; concert hall records with Columbia, RCA Victor. Home: 171 W 79 St, New York, NY. Office: Mannes College of Music, New York, NY.

BAMBERGER, Fritz, US, college admnr, educator, author; b. Frankfurt-on-Main, Ger, Jan 7, 1902; s. Max and Amalie (Wolf); in US since 1939; PhD, U of Berlin, 1923; att Hochschule fuer die Wissenschaft des Judentums, 1925; m. Kate Schwabe, Mar 21, 1933 (decd); c: Michael, Gay; m. 2nd, Maria Nussbaum, Sep 29, 1963. Prof, intellectual hist, asst to pres, HUC-JIR, since 1962; research prof, Acad for J Research, 1926-33; prof, phil, Coll of J Studies, 1933-34; dir, Bd of Educ for J, 1935-38, all Berlin; pres, J Tchrs Coll of Prussia, 1934-38; prof, Coll of J Studies, Chgo, 1939-42; research, ed dir, Coronet Magazine, NYC, 1942-52; ed-in-chief, 1952-55; exec dir, Esquire and Coronet mags, 1955-61; cons to Esquire, 1962. Vice-pres, bd trustees, Leo Baeck Inst; past pres, Self-help; mem: Amer Acad of Political and Social Sci; Acad of Political Sci; bd govs, HUC, 1954-61; exec comm, Frank L Weil Inst of Advanced Studies in Rel and Hum; bd dirs, The Judeans; club, Overseas Press. Author: Entstehung des Wertproblems, 1924; Die Geistige Gestalt Moses Mendelssohns, 1929; Die Lehren des Judentums, 3 vols, 1928-30; Moses Mendelssohn's Gesammelte Schriften, 3 vols, 1929-32; Denkmal der Freundschaft, 1929; Das Buch Zunz, 1932; Das System des Maimonides, 1935; Herder's Blaetter der Vorzeit, 1936; Das Neunte Schuljahr, 1937; Zunz's Conception of History, 1941; Leo Baeck - The Man and the Idea, 1958; Books Are The Best Things, 1962. Home: 415 E 52 St, New York, NY. Office: 40 W 68 St, New York, NY.

BAMBERGER, Henry, US, rabbi; b. Albany, NY, June 1, 1935; s. Bernard and Ethel (Kraus); AB, Columbia, 1956; BHL, MA, ordained rabbi, HUC-JIR, 1956-61; m. Sheila Lister, June 21, 1959; c: Judith, Miriam. Rabbi, Vassar Temple, since 1966; student rabbi, Frederick Heb Cong, Frederick, Md, 1958-59; Monmouth Reform Temple, New Shrewsbury, NJ, 1959-61; rabbi, Temple Sinai, Sharon, Mass, 1961-66. Prog dir, UAHC, Camp-Inst for Living Judaism, 1959-60; treas, Dutchess Co chap, UNA; pres, Interfaith Council, Sharon, Mass, 1961-62; secy, Mass Bd of Rabbis, 1965-66; chmn, United Rabb Chaplaincy Comm, 1964-65; mem: CCAR; Assn of Reform Rabbis of NYC; Dutchess Co Min Assn; UAHC comm on camp education. Contbr to J jours. Recipient: Stephen S Wise memorial prize, HUC-JIR, 1958. Home: 16 Underhill Ave, Poughkeepsie, NY. Study: 140 Hooker Ave, Poughkeepsie, NY.

BAMBERGER, Itshak Dov, Isr, educator; b. Nurnberg, Ger, Feb 4, 1902; s. Itshak and Sara (Tachaver); in Isr since 1933; Rabb Sem, Berlin, 1921-23; att U of Berlin, London, Würz-(burg); 1924-32; PhD, Würzburg U, 1934; m. Esther Dym decd; c: Elhanan, Naomi Avesar; m. 2nd, Braha Sommer, 1968. Insp, Min of Educ and Culture; tchr, prin: schs, Ger and Isr, 1929-53. Isr Army, 1936-52. Mem, cen comm, Movement for Tora Judaism; treas, Isr Tchrs Union, 1946-51; mem, Hapoel Hamizrachi. Author: Der Prophet in der Englischen Literatur, 1933; Living English, Do and Say, 1957. Recipient: medals of Hagana, War of Independence, Sinai campaign. Hobby: music. Home: 5 Hakeshet, Jerusalem, Isr. Office: Ministry of Education and Culture, POB 202, Jerusalem, Isr.

BAMBERGER, Ruth Rachel, Isr, painter; b. Basel, Switz, Aug 10, 1905; d. Shlomo and Miryam (Löwenstein) Teplitz; married; c: Tamar Carmi. Fmr: painting tchr: Seeligsberg Hadassah Vocational Sch; Bezalel Art Sch; pvt lessons. One-man shows: Isr; Switz; NY; New Haven, Conn; St Louis, Mo; group shows: Isr; Switz; Brazil; US; Australia; Cité Intl des Arts, Paris. Home: 5 Ethiopia St, Jerusalem, Isr.

BAN, Béla (Adalbert), Isr, artist; b. Budapest, Hung, May 14, 1909; s. Geza and Rosa (Csillag) Blau; in Isr since 1963; att Coll of Ind Art; Fac of Graphic Arts; Coll of Fine Arts, Fac of Painting, all Budapest; m. Livia Adorjan; c: Eva Kallo, Marta. Painter and graphic artist; critic, Socialism Mag, Budapest 1938; tchr, Coll of Fine Arts, Budapest, 1950-55. Exhbs: Helsinki; Stockholm, both in 1942; Hung natl, 1945-1956; Galerie Creux, Paris, 1947, 1957; Surrealist World, 1947; Abstract World, 1947, all in Paris; Gal Antigona, Hebraica, all in 1958; Gal Van Riel, 1960, 1961; 1st Intl Modern Art, Arg, 1960; Galatea, 1962, all in Buenos Aires;

Group of Socialist Painters and Sculptors, 1934-44, Hung, 1964; one-man show: Tamas Gal, Budapest, 1944; Painters Assn Pavilion, Tel Aviv, 1965, Dugith Gal, 1968; Herzliya Mus, 1968-69, all in Isr; in pvt collections and mus. Compulsory lab service, 1942-43; compulsory lab service, Russ, 1944. Mem: Isr Assn of Fine Arts; fmr mem: New Assn of Practitioners of Fine Arts, 1931; Socialist Group of Artists, 1934-42; found, Europai Iskola, 1946-48; presidium and jury, Free Assn Hung Fine Art Practitioners, 1951-56, all in Budapest. Recipient: acknowledgement of excellence, Szinnyei Assn, 1938; 1st prize, fresco painting, Hung Social Democratic Party, 1942; Munkachy prize, 1951, 1953; all in Hung; 2nd prize, mosaic painting, Buenos, Aires, underground RR, 1958; Nordau prize, fine arts, Hitachdut Olei Hung, Tel Aviv, 1966. Home: HaRav Mordekhai Nurok, Ramat Elyahu, Isr.

BANAY, Yaakov Budnik, Isr, educator; b. Russ, Jan 1, 1896; s. Yitzhak and Golda (Shilman) Budnik; in Isr since 1921; att Pedg Coll, Russ, 1916-18; m. Eve Voznitsa, Mar, 1944; c: Yitzhak, Amitay, Nina Ben-Moshe. Educ counsellor, Cen Educ and Culture, Histadrut, since 1966; fmr: educ, dir, Isr Schs, 1924-50; dir, pedg dept, Educ Cen, Histadrut, 1950-65; chmn, cen pedg council, Cen Tchrs Org, 1956-66. Fmr chmn: Tarbut, cultural org; Zionist Org; Hechalutz, all Russ. Author: Real Pedagogy, 1938; Our Problems of Education, 1946; Avtolion's Letters, Experiment in Sex Education, 1947. Recipient: Zvi Eliov memorial award, Tchrs Org, 1966. Home: 75 Arlosoroff St, Holon, Isr.

BAND, Jordan Clifford, US, attorney; b. Cleveland, O, Aug 15, 1923; s. Samuel and Helen (Krause); BBA, W Reserve U, 1947, LLB, 1948; m. Alice Glickson, Apr 27, 1946; c: Terril, Stefanie, Claudia. Partner, Ulmer, Laronge, Glickman & Curtis, since 1948. Sgt, US Army, 1943-46. Natl chmn: Natl J Comty Relations Adv Council; natl exec bd, AJComm; vice-chmn: Public Wfr Comm, J Comty Fed of Cleveland; Atty Div, JWF Appeal of Cleveland; exec comm: Amer-Isr Public Affairs Comm; J Comty Fed of Cleveland; fmr: chmn: Natl Commn on Equal Opportunity, Natl J Comty Relations Adv Council; Gtr Cleveland Conf on Rel and Race; vice-pres, Fairmount Temple Young People's Cong; mem: Natl Steering Comm of Urban Coalition; conf, pres, major J orgs. Home: 18483 Parkland Dr, Shaker Heights, O. Office: 1100 Keith Bldg, Cleveland, O.

BANE, Henry, US, attorney; b. Sialiai, Lith, May 12, 1905; s. Benjamin and Sarah (Rause); in US since 1914; BA, Duke U, 1927; LLB, U of NC, 1930. Public guardian, Durham Co, since 1947; public admn, since 1945; US commn, Middle dist of NC, 1946-65; judge, Durham Co Civil Court, 1965-67. Past pres: B'nai B'rith lodge; Durham Co Bar Assn; ARC, Durham chap; Fed J Charities; Jr and NC Bar Assns; mem: Amer Bar Assn; Elks. Hobbies: golf, bowling. Home: 1815 Morehead Ave, Durham, NC. Office: 111 Corcoran St, Durham, NC.

BANESHIK, Percival Leon, S Afr, journalist, broadcaster, playwright; b. Johannesburg, Nov 6, 1915; s. Charles and Hettie (Wolfson). Arts ed, drama critic, Rand Daily Mail; sr announcer-produc, S Afr BC Corp, 1933-61, news ed, 1937-46; fmr, asst ed, S Afr Zionist Record; radio off, food and agric org, UN, 1947-48. Life mem, Johannesburg Repertory Players, mem, exec comm, 1943-53; master, Masons; clubs: PEN, Johannesburg; Transvaal Press; Transvaal Automobile. Author: plays: Elizabeth Wears a Wig; The Garden at the Threshold; Mr Midas; documentary films for UN; plays and pageants for S Afr Zionist Fed. Home: 1 Soldon Ct, 16 Olivia Rd, Berea, Johannesburg, S Afr. Office: Rand Daily Mail, POB 1138, Johannesburg, S Afr.

BANITT, Menahem, Isr, educator; b. Antwerp, Belgium, July 18, 1914; s. Samuel and Rebecca (Hirschkowitz) Berenblut; in Isr since 1949; lic es lettres, U Libre de Bruxelles, 1937; att: Rabb Sch, Paris, 1938-40; Ecole Pratique de Hautes Etudes, 1938-40; Isaac Elhanan Yeshiva, NYC, 1942-44; PhD, Columbia U, 1949; m. Irene Stern, Feb 6, 1945; c: Samuel, David, Ofer. Head, dept, Fr civilization, Tel Aviv U, since 1966; dean, students, since 1968; asso prof, Heb U, Jerusalem, since 1966, asst, 1954-57, instr, 1957-63, lectr, 1963-66; fmr: news writer, announcer, station OWI, NY, 1943-45; educ dir, J Cong, Newburgh, NY, 1946-49; tchr, JA Inst for Youth Leaders, Jerusalem, 1952-54; gen insp, Fr, Isr Min for Educ; Off Palmes Acad, 1967. Author: A Comparative Study of Judaeo-Italian Translations of the Bible, 1949; Fragments of

XIV Century Judaeo-French Biblical Glossary, 1960; Corpus Glossariorum Biblicorum Judaico-Gallicorum, 1969. Home: 36 Rabbi Yehuda Hanassi St, Tel Aviv, Isr. Office: Tel Aviv University, Ramat Aviv, Isr.

BANK, Harry, Isr, physician; b. S Afr, June 28, 1924; s. Abraham and Rebecca (Kahn); in Isr since 1948; MB, ChB, U of Cape Town, 1947; m. Myra Schweppe, July 4, 1948; c: Ilan, Ron. Head, dept med, Tel Hashomer Hosp, since 1966. Maj, MC, IDF, 1948-53. Hon pres, Soc of Internal Med; mem, Isr Endocrine Soc; fmr chmn, Isr Soc of Internal Med. Contbr to local and fgn jours. Home: 58 Kaf Tet b'November St, Tel Aviv, Isr.

BANOV, Leon, US, physician, educator; b. Suwalki, Pol, July 8, 1888; s. Alexander and Sonia (Danielewicz); in US since 1896; PhG, Med Coll of SC, 1907, MD, 1917, hon LLD, 1960; m. Minnie Monash, 1912; c: Leon, Morton, Roslyn Wyman (decd). Prof, preventive med, public health, Med Coll SC, since 1949, fac mem, since 1913; cons, State Bd Health and Charleston Bd Health, since 1961, on staff since 1918; spec cons, div chronic diseases, USPHS, 1950-53. Pres: Amer Public Health Assn, S Br, 1956; Charleston Co Med Soc, 1954; chmn: S Med Assn, 1930; Amer Public Health Assn, 1933; vice-pres, Amer Assn of Public Health Phys, 1954; exec secy, Charleston Co TB Assn, 1924-26; secy-treas, Intl Soc of Med Offs, 1937-39; dipl, Amer Bd Preventive Med and Public Health, 1949; mem: SC Public Health Assn; B'nai B'rith; Elks; Friendship Lodge, AFM, past master, 1916-17; delg, Intl Hygiene Cong, Dresden, Ger, 1930; club, Rotary. Weekly broadcaster, local radio and TV stas. Recipient: award, Dist Grand Lodge No. 5, B'nai B'rith, 1960; nominated for Lasker Award for dist service in Public Health, 1961; Service to Mankind Award, Charleston Club, 1961; award, S Br Amer Public Health Assn, for services as past pres, 1964. Home: 61 Campbell Dr, Byrnes Downs, Charleston, SC. Office: 334 Calhoun St, Charleston, SC.

BÄR, Walter J, Switz, banker; b. Basel, Mar 24, 1895; s. Julius and Marie (Ulrich); m. Marie-Blanche Halperine, Jan 15, 1924; c: Nicolas, Alfred, Roger, Ulrich. Partner, Julius Bär & Co, bankers, since 1922. Lt, Swiss Cavalry. Pres, Schweiz Isr Altersheim (Home for the Aged), Lengnau, since 1958; fmr treas, acting pres, Etania, Davos. Hobby: music. Home: 54 Bergstr, Zurich, Switz. Office: 36 Bahnhofstr, Zurich, Switz.

BARACH, Alvan Leroy, US, physician; b. Newcastle, Pa, Feb 22, 1895; s. Nathan and Jennie (Silman); CCNY, 1912-15; MD, Coll Phys and Surg, Columbia, 1919; m. Frederica Pisek, Apr 24, 1933; c: Jeffrey, John. Cons, med, em, Presbyterian Hosp, NY, since 1959, clinical prof, 1952-59, asst, med, 1922-31; asst, med, Coll Phys and Surg, 1922-25, instr, 1925-28, asso, med, 1928-35. Responsible investigation, OSRD, 1941-45. Devised oxygen chambers for treatment of pneumonia, cardiorespiratory diseases; introduced helium as new therapeutic gas in treatment of asthma and obstructive lesions in larynx and trachea. F: Amer Coll Chest Phys; AMA; NY Acad Med; mem: Nath Inventors Council, Dept of Commerce; Med Red Cross; Amer Soc Clinical Inves; Amer Phys Assn; Med Soc; Amer Acad of Allergy; Trudeau Soc; Alpha Omega Alpha; Omega Pi Alpha. Co-author: Pulmonary Emphysema, 1946, 1969; contbr to profsl jours. Recipient: bronze medal, AMA, 1936; scroll of hon, Intl Anesthesia Research Soc, 1936; Townsend Harris medal, CCNY, 1940; award of merit, Amer Assn Inhalational Therapists, 1960. Hobbies: reading, writing. Home: 72 E 91 St, New York, NY. Office: 929 Park Ave, New York, NY.

BARACK, Nathan A, US, rabbi; b. Belarodka, Russ, July 2, 1913; s. Philip and Etta (Cohen); in US since 1923; BA, Lewis Inst of Tech, 1934; ordained rabbi, Heb Theol Coll, 1936; DHL, JTSA, 1959; m. Lillian Astrachan, Feb, 1942; c: Sylvia Fishman, Judith, Sandra. Rabbi: Cong Beth El, since 1949; Sons of Abraham, 1937-38; Cong Beth El, Phoenix, 1939-44, 1946-49. Chaplain, US Army, 1944-46. Bd mem: MH Assn; J Wfr Council; Retarded Children Assn; mem: Hapoel Hamizrachi; B'nai B'rith; RA; J Chaplains; Sheboygan HS hum seminar staff. Author: The Tale of A Wonderful Ladder, 1943; Faith for Fallibles, 1952; Mount Moriah View, 1956; History of the Sabbath, 1965. Home: 2623 N 10 St, Sheboygan, Wis. Study: 1007 North Ave, Sheboygan, Wis.

BARAG, Dan Pinhas, Isr, archaeologist, educator; b. London, Eng, Sep 13, 1935; s. Gershon and Gerda (Gottheiner); desc of Barag; in Isr since 1935; BA, Heb U, Jerusalem, 1959, MA, hons, 1961; m. Hanna Altstaedter, Aug 21, 1958; c: Tamar.

Instr, dept archaeol, Heb U, Jerusalem, since 1969, asst, 1959-65. IDF, 1953-56. Co-author, Glass and Glassmaking in Ancient Mesopotamia, 1969; contbr to publs. Home: 22 Ben Maimon Blvd, Jerusalem, Isr. Office: Hebrew U, Jerusalem, Isr.

BARAK, Amitzur Zeev, Isr, engineer; b. Hadera, Isr, Mar 23, 1938; s. Abraham and Malka (Rot) Bruckner; BS, Technion, Haifa, 1960, MS, 1967; m. Leah Liberman, Aug 16, 1959; c: Hannah, Ester. Mgr, dept, distillation process, Isr Desalination Engr Ltd, since 1968, fmr, research engr; design engr, AVIRAM, 1961-62; research engr, Technion 1964-65. Off, IAF; maintenance engr, IDF, 1960-61. Prin contribs: invention and devl of vapor compression desalination process at low temp; devl and research, various desalination processes. Author: The VFVC (Zarchin) Process, 1967; The Flow in Ice Counterwashers, 1969. Home: 7 Um St, Tel Aviv, Isr. Office: POB 18041, Tel Aviv, Isr.

BARAK, Baruch, Isr, economist; b. Schweidnitz, Ger, May 5, 1928; s. Haim and Rachel (Feibelson) Brock; in Isr since 1937; BA, Heb U, Jerusalem, 1954; m. Hava Katz, Aug, 1951; c: Irith, Naomi. Econ consul to US, dir, Inves and Export Auth, NY, since 1967; dep dir, Inves Auth, Tel Aviv, 1961-64, dir for Eur, Zurich, 1964-66; dep dir gen, Min of Defence, 1966-67. Sgt maj, IDF, 1948-49. Prin contrib: planning, org and implementation of govt inves auth in Isr and abroad. Secy gen, Young B'nai B'rith, 1947-50; mem, Isr Mgmt Cen, Tel Aviv. Author: The German Penetration into the Middle East, 1954. Hobby: swimming. Home: Maoz Aviv, Binyan Rav Komot, Tel Aviv, Isr. Office: Investment Authorities, Shalom Bldg, Tel Aviv, Isr.

BAR-AM, Benjamin Bernhard, Isr, composer; b. Wiesbaden, Ger, July 20, 1923; s. Isidor and Rosa (Hermer) Behrmann, in Isr since 1936; att U London; studied music: with Paul Ben-Haim, 1945-49; Ecole Normale, Paris, 1950-51. Music critic: Jerusalem Post, since 1959; Mitteilungs Blatt, Ger weekly, since 1964; tchr, music theory, music hist: Ron Conservatory; Ramat Gan Conservatory; org: Isr Music Weeks; Isr Composer's Workshop; fmr org, 1st Intl Conf of J Liturgical Music, convened by Cantor's Assembly of Amer. Pvt, civil defense forces. Compositions: My Heart is Steadfast; Piccola Suite for Recorder and Harpsicord; liturgical works; various songs. Secy gen, League of Composers in Isr; hon secy: Soc Promotion Capella; Isr Pro Musica Antiqua; men: bd, Isr Assn Music Critics; ACUM; Isr chap, Intl Heinrich Schütz Soc; Milo Artist Club. Contbr of music articles to Isr music jours. Recipient: 1st prize for song, Zichru Oti, Histadrut, 1948; hon mention, spec prize for My Heart is Steadfast, Isr Chamber Choir Contest, 1965. Home: 9 Ben Shafrut, St, Tel Aviv, Isr. Office: 73 Nordau Blvd, Tel Aviv, Isr.

BARAM, Sioma, Isr, artist, art critic; b. Bessarabia, Aug 2, 1919; s. Berco and Rebecca (Katsowitch) Bubermann; att: Avni Studio, Tel Aviv, 1938-41; Louvre; Ecole des Beaux-Arts, Paris, 1950-51; m. Bella Brizel. One-man shows: gals: Isr, Fr, Switz, Eng, Spain, Japan, Algeria; Tel Aviv Mus; group exhbs: Fr, London, NY, Tokyo, Spain, biennials: Fr, Japan; exhb, numerous salons, Fr; art tchr, Rishon L'Zion, 1945-50. Brit Army, 1942-45; IDF, 1947-48. Prin contrib, org, Isr sect, Les Arts en Fr et dans le Monde, Paris. Mem, Soc Salon des Independants, Paris. Author: Arts, Bilan de L'Art Actuel; Documents, Sioma Baram, 1967; contbr to jours. Recipient: Isr Artists Award, Isr Consulate, Paris, 1960. Hobbies: fishing, tree planting. Home and studio: 41 rue de Seine, Paris, Fr.

BARANKIN, Edward W, US, mathematician, educator; b. Phila, Pa, Dec 18, 1920; s. Myer and Esther (Grossman); BA, Princeton U, 1941; MA, U Cal, 1942, PhD, 1946; m. Claire Chertcoff, 1941; c: Joseph, Barry. Prof, math, U Cal, Berkeley, since 1959, asso prof, 1952-59, dept stat, since 1954, fac mem, since 1947; physicist, Manhattan Project, Berkeley, Cal and Oak Ridge, Tenn, 1942-45; asst, Prof Hermann Weyl, Princeton, 1946-47; cons: USAF, Natl Bur Standards, and Off of Naval Research, since 1950; Rand Corp, 1951-52; Arthur D Little and Bell Telephone Labs, 1956; John Simon Guggenheim F, 1956-57; visiting prof, Inst Henri Poincaré, U Paris, 1956-57; cons to Mexican Govt, Mexico City, 1962; Fulbright research prof, Kyoto U, Japan, 1962-63; Fulbright-Hays visiting prof, Inst Maths, Natl U Mexico and Natl Inst Math Stats, Mexico City, 1964. F, Inst Math

Stat; chmn and org, Spec Comm for Devl of Communication with Negro Colls and Us, since 1964; mem: Econometric Soc; Inst Mgmt Sci; Amer Math Soc; Phi Beta Kappa; Sigma Xi; Japan Soc for Phil of Sci. Contbr of papers on pure and applied maths, probability, stats and theory of behaviour. Home: 20 Highland Blvd, Berkeley, Cal. Office: U of Cal, Berkeley, Cal.

BARANSON, Stanly, US, government official; b. NYC, Apr 14, 1917; s. William and Mary (Friedman); AA, George Washington U, 1945; m. Bertha Paul, Sep 18, 1938; c: Marc, Francis. Prog off and controller, Regional US AID for Afr, State Dept, since 1964; loan off for Cen Amer, AID, 1961-64; messenger, Dept of Agric, 1935-37; clerk, War Dept and Dept of Commerce, 1937-38; sr acctnt and ind analyst, Navy Dept, 1938-47; successively, commodity analyst, prog off and controller: Greece, Fr, Haiti, Taiwan, Iran, Francophone Afr and Wash, with AID and predecessor agcys, 1950-62; chief acctnt and asst to dir of immigration, JDC, Paris, 1947-50; acting dir, FOA Mission to Haiti, 1954; prog oprs off, Far East, for Peace Corps, Wash, 1961-62. Campaign worker, UJA; mem, Soc for Intl Devl. Hobbies: electronics, gardening. Home: 1501 Overlook Dr, Silver Spring, Md. Office: Agcy for Intl Devl Dept of State, Washington, DC.

BARANY, George, US, educator; b. Budapest, Hung, Apr 12, 1922; s. Ernest and Ernestine (Duschnitz) Fried; in US since 1956; MA, U of Colo, 1958, PhD, 1960; m. Susan Ziner, Oct 30, 1949. Prof, hist, U Denver, since 1969, asso prof, 1960-69. Mem: Amer Hist Assn; Amer Assn for Advancement of Slavic Studies; Mich Acad of Sci, Arts and Letters; Rocky Mt Social Sci Assn; Phi Alpha Theta; Delta Phi Alpha. Author: Stephen Széchenyi and the Awakening of Hungarian Nationalism, 1791-1841, 1968; contbr to profsl jours. Home: 2180 S Clayton, Denver, Colo. Office: University of Denver, Denvr, Colo.

BARASH, ZEEV, Isr, communal leader; b. Russ, 1913; s. Isac and Gitel (Rosenfeld); in Isr since 1933; BA, Gratz Coll, Phila, Pa; m. Leah Shpiro, 1939; c: Yoram, Haim. Chmn, bd dir, PPC Isr since 1970; asst gen secy, Histadrut since 1970, trade union exec, 1950-60, gen secy, public service union, 1960-66; Amer repr, exec bd, 1966-69. Mem, cen comm, Lab Party; bd dir, Zim; fmr: secy workers council Dead Sea; secy Hapoel; mem: Haifa lab council; trade union exec; gen council intl trasp workers fed exec bd, ITF; dep mem, jt maritime commn, ILO; fmr mem, Kibbutz Hulda. Home: 16 Ben Zion Israeli St, Givatayim, Isr. Office: 93 Arlosoroff St, Tel Aviv, Isr.

BAR-AVI, Israel, (Dore Wertenstein), Isr, author, editor; b. Mar 28, 1915, Ramnic Sarat, Rum; s. Julius and Sofia (Mayersohn) Wertenstein; in Isr since 1951; law deg, U Bucharest, 1937; m. Rahel Ismailer, Feb 3, 1946. Mgr, lit circle, Menorah, since 1958, ed: Menorah jour, 1959-65, Caietul pentru literatura si isotoriografie, since 1965; secy to hist, Moses Schwarzfeld and his J weekly, Egalitatea, Bucharest, 1934-40; admr, ed, Palestina, KH illus rev, 1938-39; contbr to Ency, J Bucharest Comty, 1942-43. Zuthor: Viata si opera lui Moses Schwarzfeld, Vol I, 1944; Vol II, 1953, Vol III, 1968-69; Cronicarii, 1945; Insemnari Istorice si Literare 1959; Dmuiot, 1960; Camene si Fapte, 1965; Din alte vremuri, 1965; Esseuri, 1965; Fil de antologie; contbr on Run-J hist to publs. Pres, gen secy, Kadimah, 1937; gen secy, Young J Union, Rum, 1945-48. Home: POB 763, Jerusalem, Isr.

BARBAN, Stanly, US, biochemist; b. NYC, Mar 16, 1921; s. Isidore and Pauline (Wagner); BS, CCNY, 1943; MS, U of Mich, 1950; PhD, Wash U, St Louis, 1952; m. Barbara Rosenberg, June 18, 1950; c: Beth, Lisa. Research biochemist, NIH, since 1954; bact, Syracuse Dept Public Health, 1950; instr, Upstate Med Coll, SUNY, Syracuse, 1952-53. Sgt, USAAF, 1943-46. Prin contribs: research in biochemistry of tumor viruses; mechanisms of drug resistance; biochemistry of tissue cell cultures; microbiol phys. Mem: Amer Soc Biol Chems; Amer Soc Microbiol; Sigma Xi; Phi Sigma; fmr, trustee, Temple Shalom. Contbr to sci jours. Recipient: USPHS F, 1953. Home: 6603 Phyle Rd, Bethesda, Md. Office: NIH, Bethesda, Md.

BARBASH, Jack, US, economist, educator; b. NYC, Aug 1, 1910; s. Louis and Rose (Titel); BS, NYU, 1932, MA, 1937; m. Kate Hubelbank, Mar, 1934; c: Louis, Fred, Mark. Prof, econ, lab educ, U Wis, since 1957; staff dir, sub-comm on lab and lab mgmt, US Sen, 1949-53; econ, legal dept, CIO,

1953-55; research, educ dir, ind union dept, AFL-CIO, 1955-57. Mem: Amer Econ Assn; Ind Relations Research Assn; League for Ind Democracy. Author: Labor Unions in Action, 1948; Unions and Telephones, 1952; Practice of Unionism, 1956; Labor's Grass Roots, 1961; American Unions Structure, Government and Politics, 1968. Spec interest: music. Home: 1836 Keyes Ave, Madison, Wis. Office: U Wis, Madison, Wis.

BARBEN, David J, US, dentist; b. NYC, Oct 7, 1919; s. Harry and Bessie; DDS, W Reserve U, 1920; m. Pvt practice since 1920. Prin contrib: developed remedy for Pyorrhea. USCG, 1917-20. Trustee, ZOA; mem: Amer Dent Assn; Alpha Omega; Masons. Contbr to dent jours. Home: 13995 Superior Rd, E Cleveland, Ohio. Office: 557 Leader Bldg, Cleveland, Ohio.

BARBER Stephen Shlomoh, Can, business exec; b. Rousinov, Czech, May 25, 1911; s. Hugo and Pauline (Steiner); in Can since 1954; LLD, U of Brno, 1934; m. Erika Tauber, Aug 7, 1957; c: Thomas, Bernard, Anna. Exec dir: Can-Isr C of C and Ind, since 1961; Can Soc for Weizmann Inst of Sci, since 1966; atty, Czech, 1934-38; head, relief, rehab dept, WJC, London, 1945-47; mgn dir: Lyon Mfg and Trading Co, London, 1948-54; Barcan, Montreal, 1954-61. Sgt, Czech Army, 1939-45. Pres, Reconstructionist Syn, Montreal; vice-pres, Amitiés Culturelles Can Francais-Isr; chmn, Comm on Archives and Research, Can J Cong; secy-gen, Assn Czech J in Fr, 1938-40; treas, World Union J Students, 1945-48; chmn, Assn J from Czech for Material Claims Against Ger, 1952-54; mem: B'nai B'rith; Soc for Hist of Czech J. Contbr articles on legal, political, econ, hist subjects to profsl jours. Home: 4600 Westmore Ave, Montreal, Can. Office: 1280 St Mark St, Montreal, Can.

BARCAY, Shmuel, Isr, banker; b. Obodovka, Russ, 1900; s. Itzhak and Feiga (Lifshitz) Berkovitch; in Isr since 1912; m. Rina Nick, Sep 10, 1923; c: Reuven, Idith, Orith. Mgr, Isr Amer Ind Devl Bank Ltd, since 1959; asst to gen mgr, Workers Bank Ltd, since 1950; dir, Bank Hapoalim (Workers' Bank), since 1966; delg Isr Min Fgn Affairs, mission to Ghana to advise on coop banking, 1958. J battalion, WWI; found mem, Haganah, 1922-48, Tel Aviv command, 1929-40, area cdr, 1940-44; lt col, IDF, 1948. Chmn, Natl Fed Haganah Vets, since 1966; mem, Histadrut; past master, Bezalel Free Mason Lodge. Home: 7 Hamishmar Haezrahi, Afeka, Tel Aviv, Isr. Office: 50 Rothschild Blvd, Tel Aviv, Isr.

BARCAYI, Simha Bunim, Isr, business exec; b. Lodz, Pol, July 26, 1898; s. Zvi and Haya (Hendlish); in Isr since 1919; grad, Intl Corresp Sch, London, 1932; Bus Admn Inst, Tel Aviv; m. Genia Bryczkowska, Nov 26, 1922; c: Ruth Shechter, Esther Shany. Ret, fmr dir, collecting dept, Isr Elec Corp, Ltd; fmr mem: Kibbutz Hulda, 1919-21; Kibbutz Gan Shmuel, 1921-23; guard, Mt Scopus, Jerusalem, 1923-25. Haganah; Isr Civil Defense Service. Co-found, Heb Scouts, Lodz, first repr to Gen Assembly; lectr, youth counsellor, Zionist orgs; fmr mem: B'nai B'rith; Masons; disciplinary comm, Pal Football Assn. Author: History, Development and Influences in Free Masonry, 1968; contbr to profsl jours and periodicals. Recipient: Haganah Decoration, 1958; Misrad Habitachon Decoration, 1968; Master Degree of Masonic Order, 1953-54. Hobbies: philately, J hist research. Home: 7 Natan Hehakham St, Tel Aviv, Isr.

BARDACKE, Gregory Joseph, US, organization exec; b. Harbin, China, June 22, 1912; s. Joseph and Anna (Goldfein); in US since 1923; BA, Syracuse U, NY, 1935; m. Beatrice Schoenberg, Jan 12, 1935; c: Judith, Ann, Jean. Exec dir, Amer Trade Union Council for Histadrut, since 1953. Mem: bd govs, League for Ind Democracy; bd dirs, Workers Defense League; ADA, NY. Home: 1073 Jackson St, Baldwin, NY. Office: 33 E 67 St, New York, NY.

BAR-DAVID, Israel, Isr, engineer; b. Simleul-Silvaniei, Rum, Apr 4, 1930; s. Zwi and Gizella (Marmorstein) David; in Isr since 1944; MS, Technion, Haifa, 1959; DSc, MIT, Cambridge, Mass, 1965; m. Dahlia Davidovic, May 20, 1954; c: Ayal, Gil, Shirli. Head, communications dept, sci dept, Min of Defence, Isr, since 1968; sr lectr, Technion, since 1965, on fac since 1958. Lt, IDF, Air Force, 1954-58. Secy, treas, Isr sect, Inst Elec and Electronic Engs, NY. Contbr, numerous papers in field of communication theory. Hobbies: music, camping, swimming. Home: 73 Hanassi St, Haifa, Isr. Office: Scientific Department, Ministry of Defence, Hakirya, Tel Aviv, Isr.

BAR-DAVID, Molly Lyons, Isr, author, journalist; b. Rosthern, Can, July 30, 1910; d. Harry and Ethel (Zaslowsky); in Isr since 1936; m. Yaacov Bar-David, Sep 5, 1939; c: Varda Mor, Geila Dickman, Ziona, Sharon. Columnist: Jerusalem Post; Orah Magazine, Montreal; Hadassah Magazine; Winnipeg Free Press; co-found, Bar-David Lit Agcy, repr authors, since 1947; fmr: lectr tours for: Hadassah; Can WIZO; culinary lectr tours, Eur; on lit assignment, Eur. Author: That's the Way It Is with Us, 1949; In Jerusalem's Corridor, 1950; Women in Israel, 1951; My Promised Land, 1953; What's Cooking in Israel's Melting Pot, 1963; Israeli Cookery, 1964; Jewish Cooking for Pleasure, 1965; Best of Jewish Cookery, 1969; pamphlets; film, fashion show scripts; radio skits; educ progs for orgs. Spec interests: folklore, cooking, sculpture, gardening. Home: Savyon, Isr. Office: POB 1104, Tel Aviv, Isr.

BARDIN, Shlomo H, US, educator, camp dir; b. Zhitomir, Russ, Dec 3, 1898; s. Hayim and Menia (Weissburd); in US since 1939; MA, Columbia U, 1930, PhD, 1932; m. Ruth Jonas, Oct 25, 1931 (div); c: David, Hillel. Exec dir, Brandeis Camp Inst, Brandeis Youth Found, both since 1941; dir, Camp Alonim, since 1953; found-dir: Haifa Tech HS, 1933-39; Haifa Nautical Sch, 1938-39, both Pal. Mem: Natl Council of J Educ; Phi Delta Kappa. Author: Pioneer Youth in Palestine, 1932; Jews and the Sea, 1940. Spec. interest: horses. Home: 1101 Pepper Tree Lane, Brandeis, Cal. Office: The Brandeis Inst, Brandeis, Cal.

BAREKET, Ytzhak, Isr, actor, director, educator; b. Bacau, Moldova, Rum, Dec 10, 1923; s. Abraham-Moshe and Sarah Bat Shamai (Ioseph) Brukmayer; in Isr since 1946; att Acad of Arts, Bucharest, 1942-45; m. Yael Zimmerman, Feb 2, 1956; c: Haghit, Sigal. Actor, munic theatre, Haifa, since 1966; dir, tchr, drama, Herzlia Coll, Tel Aviv, since 1960; fmr: actor, prin, mgr, Habimah Theatre and studio for adults and youth, 1951-65; prin of arts, dir, Massad, US, 1968; bc and movie actor: They Were Ten; Never on Saturday; master of ceremonies; dir: numerous performances with non-profsl actors: Anna Frank; Harpagon (The Miser); Peter and the Wolf; parts in plays: The Merchant of Venice; The Deputy; Royal Hunt of the Sun; Fortnight at Kinneret; US tours. IDF, 1948-51. Mem, exec council: Equity of Actors, Isr; Natl Union of Actors, Musicians and Dancers. Recipient: Ot Hakomamiut; Itur Lohamei Hamedinah; Ot Hahaganah. Spec interests: poetry, lit, philately, coins, medals, photography, sports. Home: 79A Hauniversita Rd, Tel Aviv, Isr.

BAR-ELAN, Chaim, Isr, business exec; b. Slonim, Pol, Dec 31, 1913; s. Moshe and Basia (Kamienomostki) Swietycki; grad Mikveh-Isr, 1933; dipl, Agric U, Vageninger, 1936; m. Ophira Schuffeld, Aug 15, 1950; c: Michal. Head, dept, agric ind, JA, since 1957; chmn, gen mgr, Alei-Tabak Ltd, since 1953; fmr: gen mgr, Rural Ind, mem bd dirs, Carmel Wines; mgr, Mikveh-Isr, Nurseries, 1933-36; chief trainer, horticulture, Fruit Growers Org, 1936-42; co-found, co-mgr, Isr Agric Extension Cen, 1956; gen mgr, Davar, cen workers daily, 1962-63. Prin contribs, intro of new varieties of fruits and tobacco to Isr. Volunteer, Brit Army, 1942-46; Haganah; IDF, 1948-49. Mem bd: Isr Bd of Wine-Grape Growers and Producers; Isr Bd of Tobacco Growers and Producers; Wine Growers, Rishon le Zion and Zichron Yaakov; bd dirs, Zerubavel-Bank, 1968; vice-mayor, Munic of Ramat Hasharon, 1966-68. Author: Experiments in Medical Herb Growing, 1964; Modern Wine Cellar for Adulam Region, 1965; Topics for Building Modern Wine Cellars, 1966; contbr of numerous articles on horticulture. Recipient: medals: War of Independence; 6-Day War; Haganah Aleh, Isr Govt, 1969. Hobbies: flowers, painting, philately. Home: 1 Ani Maamin St, Ramat Hasharon, Isr. Office: 5 Achuzat Bait, Tel Aviv, Isr.

BARENBOIM, Daniel, Isr, pianist, conductor; b. Buenos Aires, Arg, Nov 15, 1942; s. Enrique and Aida (Schuster); studied piano only with his father, composition with Nadia Boulanger; grad Santa Cecilia Acad, Rome, 1956; m. Jaqueline du Pré, June, 1967. First public concert at age 7; toured: US since 1957; Eur, Russ; Australia; Far E; soloist and conductor: Isr Philharmonic Orch; London Sym Orch; London Philharmonic Orch; Royal Philharmonic Orch, London; Berlin Philharmonic; performed several times cycle of all Beethoven and Mozart's sonatas; recorded for EMI, all Beethoven's sonatas, the five concerti, Choral Fantasy with Klemperer; two Brahms concerti with Barbirolli; Bartok's concerti with Boulez, all of Mozart's concerti conducted from the piano and all Mozart's syms conducting the Eng Chamber Orch. Recipient: Beethoven Medal, 1958; Paderewski Medal, 1963; laureate of two int competitions, Viotti and Casella. Office: c/o Hurok, 730 Fifth Ave, New York, NY.

BARENBOIM, Enrique, Isr, pianist, educator; b. Buenos Aires, Arg, Mar 17, 1912; att fac phil, Buenos Aires; m. Aida Schuster; c: Daniel. Fmr: lectr, Music Acad, Vienna; prof, postgrad pianists and profsls from Eur, US, S Afr, U's and coll's; four hands concerts with son Daniel. Author: Contribution to a Modern School of Piano; Misconceptions in Music; Permanent Values in Jewish Music; Introduction to Israeli Music. Homes: 27A Upper Montagu St, London, Eng; 19 Fichman St, Ramat Aviv, Isr.

BAREQUET, David, Isr, business exec; b. Tel Aviv, Sep 8, 1930; s. Issahar and Sara (Steinfeld) Bornstein; BS, elec engr, Technion, Haifa, 1955; BS, mech engr, Technion; BS, ARCST, metallurgy, Royal Coll of Sci and Tech, Glasgow, 1958; m. Ora Dan, Aug 30, 1955; c: Gill. Dir, David Barequet and Asso, since 1969; fmr: diesel supt, Isr RR, 1955-57; produc mgr, Isr Steel Works, 1959-62; repr to US, Govt of Isr Inves Auth, 1962-65; coord, ind div, Rassco Ltd, 1965-68. Lt, IS, IDF, 1948-50. Mem: Isr Mgmt Cen; Assn Engrs and Architects in Isr. Home: 8 Levitan St, Tel Aviv, Isr. Office: POB 22018, Tel Aviv, Isr.

BARGAL, Haim, Isr, artist; b. Koritz, Pol, May 30, 1922; s. Berl-Dov and Rosa (Hess) Bergal; in Isr since 1946; BA, Bezalel Art Sch, 1952; att Grand Schaumier Art Sch, Paris, 1962; m. Tirza Borkenfeld, 1947; c: Urith. Artist since 1946; art tchr, 1959-67. One-man shows: gals, mus, Isr; collective shows: Paris, London, Zurich, NY, 1962-69. Partisans, Russ, 1942-43; Haganah, 1946-48. Mem: cultural comm, Kibbutz Shaar Hagolan; Painters and Sculptors Ass, Isr. Contbr various publs to art albums and periodicals. Recipient: Partizanskaja Medall-Oteczestw, Wojna I-step; Za Botewyje Zaslugi; Debora Davidson grant, Isr, 1957; Independent Prize, Jordan Valley Regional, Isr, 1961. Home: Kibbutz Shaar Hagolan, Post Emek Hayarden, Isr.

BARGEBUHR, Frederick P, US, orientalist, educator; b. Hamburg, Ger, May 24, 1904; s. Arnold and Ida (Friedmann); in US since 1948; att U Bonn, 1930; U Frankfurt, 1931; U Paris, 1931; PhD, U Munich, 1933. Prof, Judaism, U of Ia, since 1951; architect, Naharia, Pardess Hanna, Jerusalem, Isr, 1934-47; instr: Putney Sch, 1948-49; Thomas Jefferson Sch, 1950-51; guest prof: U Berlin, 1959-61, 1964-65, Heidelberg, Bonn. Ling, British Army, Pal, WWII. Mem: Amer Oriental Soc; AAUP; Soc Bibl Lit; Research Club, U of Ia. Author: The Alhambra Palace of the Eleventh Century, 1956, Span, 1963; Die Bedeutung des Weltalls für Gott nach Ibn Gabirols Philosophischem Gedichte, 1954; Samuel han-Naghidh's White Whale, 1960; The Alhambra, A Cycle of Studies on the Eleventh Century in Moorish Spain, 1968; trans: Poems by Ibn Gabirol, 1936, Heb into Ger; Poems by Karl Wolfskehl, 1942, Ger into Heb. Recipient: research grants, Amer Phil Soc; scholarships, Bollingen Found; Fulbright grants. Office: School of Religion, U of Ia, Iowa City, Ia.

BAR-HAIM, Shaul Morris, Isr, diplomat; b. Bagdad, Iraq, Feb 13, 1924; s. Haim and Shulamith (Aharon) Aynatchi; LLB, Higher Sch of Law and Econ, Tel Aviv, 1956; m. Zioni Madmoni, June 7, 1945; c: Dalia Mcshay, Reuben. Isr ambass to Nicosia since 1969; fmr: dir: bur spec projects, 1965-66; ME dept, 1966-69, both Isr Fgn Min; min plen, Teheran, 1968-69; counsellor, Emb of Isr, Wash, DC; adv to Isr delg, UN; dir, Arabic Bc of Isr, 1949-60. Mem, Histadrut; fmr mem, Org of J from Iraq. Spec interests: radio commentary; teaching Arabic lang and lit. Home: 24A Motza Elite, Jerusalem, Isr. Office: Embassy of Israel, Nicosia, Cyprus.

BAR-HAVA, Nuri, Isr, executive; b. Tel Aviv, Aug 19, 1930; BA, Heb U, Jerusalem, 1957; deg, bus admn, 1960; m. Sima Sklar; c: Itai, Dan. Dir, finance, PM off, since 1966; chmn, Automation Comm, acct gen; secy, reg council, Beit Shaan, 1950-52; asst, Bur of Budgets, Heb U, 1954-57; Min of Finance, 1960-66. Pvt, Palmach, 1948-49. Mem, Lab Union, Heb U, 1956-58. Recipient, one-year UN scholarship, 1964-65. Home: 23 Ishai St, Jerusalem, Isr. Office: Ministry of Finance, Jerusalem, Isr.

BAR-HILLEL, Yehoshua, Isr, educator; b. Vienna, Sep 8, 1915; s. Israel and Sara (Dominitz) Westreich; in Isr since 1933; MA, Heb U, Jerusalem, 1938, PhD, 1949; m. Shulamith Aschkenazy, Aug 29, 1937; c: Maya, Miriam. Prof, logic, phil of sci, Heb U, since 1961; fmr: asst prof, asso prof, Heb

U; HS tchr, Jerusalem; research asso, MIT, US. J Brigade; lt, IDF. Pres, Isr Soc for Logic and Phil of Sci; past pres: Isr Soc Info Processing; Intl Union Hist and Phil of Sci; mem: Assn for Symbolic Logic; Amer Ling Soc; Isr Acad Sci and Hum; Phil of Sci Assn. Author: Foundations of Set Theory, 1958; Language and Information, 1964. Home: 30 Abarbanel St, Jerusalem, Isr. Office: Hebrew University, Jerusalem, Isr.

BAR-ILAN, Moshe, Isr, economist; b. Fuerth, Bavaria, Ger, July 31, 1909; s. Yehuda and Helene (Kahn) Birnbaum; in Isr since 1933; att HS of Econ, Berlin, 1929-32; m. Zippora Weinberg, July 16, 1943; c: Yael Gazit, Noemi. Dir, Urban Renewal Auth, since 1965. Lt, col, quartermaster gen, IDF, 1948-50. Home: 37 Hamatzbiim St, Zahala, Isr. Office: G 13 Hakirya, Tel Aviv, Isr.

BAR-ILAN, Tuvia, Isr, administrator; b. Berlin, Ger, Dec 28, 1912; s. Meir and Bella (Rabinowitz); desc of Naziv of Wolozin, famous head of yeshiva; in Isr since 1923; BChem, Bklyn Poly Inst, 1935; PhD, Heb U, Jerusalem, 1940; m. Florence Ribakove, Oct 15, 1937; c: Nafthali, Naama, Micha, Meir. Dir, Div Ext Studies, Bar-Ilan U, Ramat Gan, since 1965, dir, 1958-64; tchr, Mizrachi Tchrs Sem, Jerusalem, 1931; organic and biochem, Weizmann Inst Sci, 1936-43; found, dir, plastics cos, 1949-58. War Dept analyst and commanding off, Tech Experimental Sect, RE, Brit Army, 1943-46; cdr, Sci Corps, IDF, Jerusalem, 1948-49. Secy, Chems Org, Rehovot br; dir, Plastics Research Inst; chmn, Assn Plastics Extruders; mem, B'nai B'rith, past pres, lodge, Holon; fmr mem, Bd Higher Studies. Contbr articles to profsl jours. Recipient: Henrietta Szold Award for contbr in field of educ, 1962. Home: 3 Azar St, Holon, Isr. Office: Bar-Ilan University, Ramat Gan, Isr.

BARKAI, Yehuda, Isr, economist; b. Virbalis, Lith, June 11, 1925; s. Naftali and Tova (Pitluk); in Isr since 1935; BA, Sch Law and Econ, Tel Aviv, 1953; MA, New Sch, NY, 1958; m. Chaya Mishkov, Feb 15, 1946; c: Hadas, Dafna, Dan. Dir, Haargaz Ltd, since 1969; fmr: bus mgr, Habimah Natl Theatre, 1953-56; vice-pres, Ind and Commercial Bank, 1960-63; dir personnel, Kupat Holim, Health Serv, 1963-69. Lt, IDF, 1940-50. Intl commn, Isr Boy and Girl Scouts Fed; mem bd, Isr Assn Personnel Mgmt. Author: Basic Principles in Economics, 1962; Dictionary in Economics, 1969. Home: 6 Herzog St, Givatayim, Isr. Office: 94 Giborei Israel St, Tel Aviv, Isr.

BARKATT, Reuven, Isr, legislator; b. Taurage, Lith, June 15, 1905; s. Avraham and Dina; in Isr since 1926; att Us: Jerusalem; Strasbourg; Paris. m. Miriam Engel, Feb 12, 1933; c: Ariela Andresen, Aharon. Speaker, Knesset, since 1969; fmr mem, exec bur, head, intl Arab and cultural depts, Histadrut; ambass to Nor, 1960-61; gen secy, Mapai, 1962-66. Mem: Bur Socialist Intl; Assn Socialist Conf; exec, Intl Confd of Free Trade Unions; initiator, Afro-Asian Inst for Lab and Coop Studies. Contbr to lab press. Home: 56 Arlozorov St, Holon, Isr. Office: The Knesset, Jerusalem, Isr.

BARKAY, Richard M, Isr, economist, government official; b. Warsaw, Pol, Jan 2, 1918; s. Simon and Golda (Berlin); Royal U, Colonial Sci Inst, Milan, It; PhD, U Turin, 1953; m. Lilo Joseph, Sep 6, 1945; c: Yoel. Sr econ, Tahal Cons Ltd, Tel Aviv, since 1969; dist off and magistrate, Pal Govt, 1948-57; i/c econ research, Treas and State Controllers Off, Govt Isr; UN econ adv to Afr govts, 1958-61; head econ div, CBS, PM's off, Jerusalem, 1962-65; cons, Harvard U Adv Service, 1965-68; lectr, Tel Aviv U. Capt, Brit and J Brig Group, 1941-46. Participant: first Afr conf of Intl Army Assn for Research in Income, Wealth, econ commn for Afr, Addis Ababa, Ethiopia; UN Econ Commn for Eur conf, Geneva; DAS conf, Sorrento; mem: Intl Econ Assn; Ghana Research Council, 1956-60; Isr Stat Adv Council. Author: Central Banking in Underdeveloped Countries, 1953; The Public Sector in Israel, 1956; contbr: Stability and Progress in the World Economy, 1958; Economic Development of Africa, 1963; The Public Sector in Liberia, 1964-67; National Accounts of Liberia, 1964-67. Recipient: Grand Commander Star of Afr. Home: 5 Shalom Aleichem St, Talbieh, Jerusalem, Isr. Office: Tahal Consulting Ltd, 54 Ibn Gvirol, Tel Aviv, Isr.

BARKIN, Solomon, US, economist; b. NYC, Dec 2, 1907; s. Julius and Lillie (Kroll); BSS, CCNY, 1928; MA, Columbia U, 1929; att Columbia U, 1932-33; m. Elaine Rappaport, 1940; c: David, Roger, Amy. Prof, econ, U Mass, since 1968;

asst dir, research, NY State Commn on Old Age Security, 1929-33; asst dir, Lab Adv Bd, Natl Recovery Admn, 1933-36; chief, lab sect, div of ind econ, Dept of Lab, 1935-37; econ and tech adv to trade unions; dir of research, Textile Workers Union of Amer, 1937-63; adj prof, ind relations, Columbia U, 1959-62; head, soc affairs, div of OECD, 1963-67. F: Gerontological Soc; Wertheim F in Ind Relations, Harvard U; mem: Econ Assn; Ind Relations Research Assn; Natl Planning Assn. Author: The Older Workers in Industry, 1933; Toward Fairer Labor Standards, 1948; Textile Workers Job Primer, 1953; The Decline of the Labor Movement and What Can be Done About It, 1961; contbr to profsl publs. Home: Ling Hill Rd, Leverett, Mass. Office: U of Mass, Amherst, Mass.

BARLAS, Chaim, Isr, editor; b. Brest-Litovsk, Pol, Dec 18, 1898; in Isr since 1925; m. Zipora Lachower; c: Batia Cohen. Dir, Ency J Diaspora; fmr dir, Pal Off, Warsaw, 1919-25; secy, immigration dept, JA, later, dir; repr: JA, Geneva, 1939-40; JDC and WJCong, Turk, 1941-45; dir gen, immig dept, 1948-49; mem, rescue comm: JA; Va'ad Leumi. Contbr of numerous articles on immigration, Isr and fgn press. Home: 8 Saadia Gaon St, Jerusalem, Isr.

BAR-LEV, Adir, Isr, educator; b. Tel Aviv, Mar 5, 1929; s. Zalman and Tova (Leibman); BS, Technion, Haifa, 1952, MS, 1956, DSc, 1961; m. Esther Wahrmann, Sep 26, 1954; c: Ron, Nachum, Ayala. Asso prof, elec engr, Technion, since 1969, on fac since 1962; asst prof, Carnegie Inst of Tech, 1964-66. Signal corp, IDF, 1948-49. Prin contribs, devl microelectronic field, Isr. Mem, Microelec Comm, Min of Commerce and Ind; fmr secy, Technion Tchrs Assn. Contbr text books and sci papers to profsl publs. Home: 132 Hagalil St, Haifa, Isr. Office: Technion, Haifa, Isr.

BAR-LEV, Haim, Isr, Army off; b. Vienna, Nov 16, 1924; in Isr since 1939; att Columbia U, 1961-63; m. Tamar Maharshak c: Zohar, Omer. Rav Aluf, Chief of Staff, since 1968; cdr: Negev Campaign, War of Independence, 1948; Sinai Campaign, 1956, commanding off, armored corps, 1957-61; lt gen, 1964-66; second-in-command, 6-Day War. Office: IDF, Isr.

BARMOR, Benjamin, Isr, painter; b. Warsaw, Pol, July 20, 1934; s. Jacob and Rivka (Fridman) Bartmeser; in Isr since 1949; att Bezalel Art Acad, Jerusalem, 1954-56; Beaux Arts Acad, Paris, 1959-61; m. Tamar Rindzunsky, Dec 8, 1958; c: Ofer, Sharon. Mem, Isr Painters and Sculptors Assn. Home: 23 Rembrandt St, Tel Aviv. Isr.

BARNARD, Harry, US, biographer, researcher; b. Pueblo, Colo, Sep 5, 1906; s. David and Paula (Halpern) Kletzky; PhB, U of Chgo, 1928; att U of Denver, 1924-25; m. Ruth Eisenstat, Oct 23, 1943; c: Harry, Judith Papier, Karen, Ronald. Dir, research agcy, since 1969; fmr: mem, ed staff, various newspapers, Chgo, Detroit; PR cons for Henry Horner, Gov of Ill dir: research, City of Chgo Law Dept, 1935-41; press relations, U of Chgo, 1943; ed writer, Chicago Times, 1943; syndicated ed page column. Chicago Daily News, 1958-60; writer-in residence, Roosevelt U, Chgo, 1968. Author: Eagle, Forgotten, The Life of John Peter Altgeld, 1938; Rutherford B Hayes and His America, 1954; Independent Man, The Life of Senator' James Couzens, 1958; The Forging of an American Jew, The Biography of Julian W Mack, 1969; contbr to mags, encys. Home: 801 Lavergne St, Willmette, Ill. Office: 29 S La Salle St, Chicago, Ill.

BARNATAN, Yehuda, Isr, industrialist; b. Debica, Apr 25, 1903; s. Natan and Debora (Mahler) Gruenspan; in Isr since 1934; m. Claire Engelberg, Oct 1, 1937; c: Michael, Gabriel. Mgn dir: Natl Brewery Ltd, Nathanya, since 1954; Paca, Bat Yam, since 1946; dir: Oxygen Mfr, since 1934; Assis Alcohol Ind, since 1948; Amgo, aluminium tube ind, since 1950; Stewo, steel wool factory, since 1950; found or co-found of all above inds; mem, bd dirs: Isr Ind Bank; Ind Devl Bank. Mem presidium, Mfrs Assn Isr, since 1954, past chmn, exec comm. Home: 33 Ruppin St, Tel Aviv, Isr. Office: 118 Allenby Rd, Tel Aviv, Isr.

BARNEIS, Henry E, US, rabbi; b. NYC, Oct 2, 1908; s. Reuben and Ida (Leibowitz); BS, NYU, 1935, MA, 1937; MHL, ordained rabbi, HUC-JIR, 1951; m. Ruth Saravis, Aug 30, 1930; c: Zachary, Reuven. Rabbi: N Hills Syn, Cong B'nai Avraham, since 1969; Temple Beth El, Laurelton, NY, 1950-54; Cong Beth Isr, Greenville, SC, 1954-62; Temple Beth El

Itaca, NY, 1962-69; chaplain, Willard State Hosp, Willard State Sch, Willard, NY. Vice-pres, NC Assn of Rabbis, 1960-62; pres, Greenville dist ZOA, 1959-62; secy, NY Bd of Rabbis, 1951-53; mem: RA; alumni assn, HUC-JIR; Cincinnati Bd Rabbis. Home: 1410 Springfield Pike, Cincinnati, O. Study: 715 Fleming Rd, Cincinnati. O.

BARNES, Leo, US, economist; b. Denver, Colo, Nov 12, 1910; s. Benjamin Lazaroff and Bertha (Wittenberg); BBS, cum laude, CCNY, 1931; MA, Brown U, 1933; PhD, New Sch for Social Research, 1948; m. Regina Rosiny, May 27, 1932; c: Peter, Valerie. Prof, finance, chmn, dept of finance and inves, Hofstra U, since 1965; ed, analyst, Research Inst of Amer, 1942-46; chief econ, Prentice-Hall Inc, 1946-62; lectr: Rutgers U Sch of Bus Admn, 1947; New Sch for Social Research, 1948-63; visiting prof, econ, CCNY, 1963-65. Mem: Amer Econ Assn; Amer Finance Assn; Natl Assn of Bus Econ; Phi Beta Kappa. Author: Handbook of Production Controls, 1943; An Experiment that Failed, 1948; Handbook for Business Forecasting, 1950; Your Investments, 15 eds, 1954-68; Your Buying Guide to Mutual Funds and Investment Companies, 5 eds, 1956-60; Encyclopedia of Stock Market Techniques, 1965; contbr to: Bus-Finance Handbook, 1953; New Horizons in Bus. Home: 473 West End Ave, New York, NY. Office: Hofstra U, Hempstead, LI, NY.

BARNESS, Amnon, US, business exec; b. Tel Aviv, Isr, Oct 16, 1924; s. Nahum and I. (Muhimann); in US since 1947; att Heb U, Jerusalem, 1942; BA, Amer U, Cairo, 1947; MA, Syracuse U, 1950; m. Lillian Sarkin, June 20, 1947; c: Rena, Dalia, Daniel, Jordan. Pres, Intl Mercantile Corp, since 1960; chmn, bd, Daylin, since 1960; pres, Barness, Candiotty & Finkle Found; mem, bd, A&E Plastik Pak; vice-pres, ISECO Securities, 1950-57; dir, devl, Fed Mart Corp, San Diego, 1957-60. Pres: bd of dirs, W region, Amer Friends of Heb U; Fund for Job Corp Grads, 1966; chmn: LA Comm, Isr Bonds, 1968; bd, trustees, Isr Publ Soc; vice-pres, Brandeis Inst; dir: Sinai Temple, LA, 1967-68; US Capitol Hist Soc. Recipient: Knight Comm of Equestrian Order, Church of Holy Sepulchre, Jerusalem. Home: 628 N Arden Drive, Beverly Hills, Cal. Office: 9606 Santa Monica Blvd, Beverly Hills, Cal.

BARNESS, Lewis Abraham, US, physician; b. Atlantic City, NJ, July 31, 1921; s. Joseph and Mary (Silverstein); BA, Harvard Coll, 1941, MD, 1944; m. Elaine Berger, June 14, 1953; c: Carol, Laura, Joseph. Prof, ped, U of Pa, since 1962, asso prof, 1956-62; chief, ped, Hosp of U Pa, since 1958; Capt, US Army, 1944-46. Mem: Soc for Ped Research; Ped Soc; recorder, Amer Ped Soc, since 1966. Author: Manual of Pediatric Physical Diagnosis, 1957, 61, 66; ed, Computer Assisted Diagnosis in Ped, 1968. Hobby: music. Home: 130 Harvest Circle, Bala Cynwyd, Pa. Office: Hosp of U of Pa, 36 & Spruce Sts, Philadelphia, Pa.

BARNET, Samuel, US, jurist; b. NYC, Nov 27, 1890; s. David and Rebecca (Kugel); LLB, Boston U, 1912; m. Mollie Byer Barnet, Dec 28, 1915 (decd). Spec justice, Dist Court, Mass, since 1930; sr mem, law firm, Barnet & Barnet, since 1919; dir, Merchants Natl Bank of New Bedford, since 1958. First chmn, State of Israel Bonds, 1950-53; pres: Council of Social Agcys, 1948; New Bedford Ind Found, 1956; Tifereth Israel Cong, 1946-48; mem: New Bedford Sch Bd; State Comn for Fair Employment Practice; Amer Friends of Hebrew U; Masons; pres, Friends of Touro Syn; Kiwanis, pres, 1st gov, 1930-33. Home: 91 Rotch St. New Bedford, Mass.

BARNETT, Bernard Harry, US attorney; b. Helena, Ark, July 13, 1916; s. Harry and Rebecca (Grossman); DJur, Vanderbilt U, 1940; m. Marian Spiesberger, Apr 9, 1949; c: Charles. Pvt practice; spec partner, Woodward, Dawson, Hobson and Fulton, 1946-48; partner: Bullitt, Dawson and Tarrant, 1948-52; Greenebaum, Barnett, Doll and Matthews, 1952-70. Lt, USNR. Mem, Natl Exec Comm and Natl Campaign Cabinet from 1959; natl chmn, UJA, since 1967; gen chm, Isr Emergency Fund, Louisville, 1967; chmn: Louisville UJA, 1968-69; Advance Gifts, United Jewish Campaign, 1959-67; pres and and dir, Jerusalem Found; vice-pres and dir, Haifa U; mem: B'nai B'rith; bd overseers, U Louisville; bd counselors, Catherine Spalding Coll, Louisville since 1959; bd dir, Louisville Fund, since 1952; exec bd, Old Kentucky Home Council, Boy Scouts of Amer; mem: Ky Rep Finance Comm, 1956-60; Louisville and Jefferson Co Rep Exec Comm, 1954-65; Ky Rep State Cen Comm and Rep Finance Comm, chmn, 1955-60; adv group to Jt Comm Internal Revenue Taxation

of Cong, 1953-55; Comm on Ways and Means, House of Reprs, 1956-58; Amer, Ky State and Louisville Bar Assns. Recipient: Pres Unit Citation. Home: 800 S 4 St, Louisville, Ky. Office: 510 W Broadway, Louisville, Ky.

BARNETT, Harold Joseph, US, educator; b. Paterson, NJ, May 10, 1917; s. Abraham and Lena (Schiff); BS, U of Ark, 1939; MS, U of Cal, Berkeley, 1940; MA, PhD, Harvard U, 1946-48; m. Mildred Denn, Aug 4, 1940; c: Peter, Alexander, Katherine. Prof, econ, Wash U, St Louis, Mo, since 1963, dept chmn, 1963-66; asst econ, US Treas Dept, 1940-42; asst chief, Ger and Aus econ affairs, US State Dept, 1945-46; tech adv, US Dept Interior, 1948-52; head, Wash, DC, econ staff, Rand Corp, 1952-55; dir, econ growth studies, Resources for the Future, Inc, Wash, DC, 1955-59; prof, econ, chmn dept, Wayne State U, 1959-63; holds cons or adv positions with numerous firms, comms, govt offices. Maj, US Army, 1942-46. Mem: Amer Econ Assn; United World Federalists. Co-author: Scarcity and Growth, 1963; contbr of numerous articles, monographs, reviews to profsl jours. 51 Crestwood Dr, Clayton, Mo. Office: Washington U, St Louis, Mo.

BARNETT, Henry L, US, physician, educator; b. Detroit, Mich, June 25, 1914; s. Lewis and Florence (Marx); BS, Wash U Sch of Med, 1938, MD, 1938; m. Shirley Blanchard, Oct 19, 1940; c: Judith, Martin. Prof, chmn, ped, Albert Einstein Coll of Med, since 1955; instr, Wash U Sch of Med, 1940-43; asst prof, Cornell U, Med Coll, 1946-50, asso prof, 1950-55; mem, infant metabolism team to Netherlands and Swed, WHO, 1950. Capt, US Army, 1943-46. Mem: (hon) British Ped Assn; AAAS; Amer Acad Peds; Soc for Ped Research; Soc for Experimental Biol and Med; Harvey Soc; Amer Ped Soc; Amer Soc for Clinical Inves; Amer Physiological Soc. Co-author: textbook, Pediatrics, 1962; ed, Pediatrics, 14th ed, 1968; contbr numerous articles to med jours. Recipient: E Mead Johnson award for research in peds, 1949. Hobbies: viola, carpentry, farming. Home: 118 W 79 St, New York, NY. Office: Albert Einstein Coll of Med, New York, NY.

BARNETT, JOEL, Eng, government official; b. Manchester, Eng, Oct 14, 1923; s. Louis and Ettie (Cosofsky); AACCA, Brit Coll Acctnt, 1952; m. Lilian Goldstone, Sep 11, 1949; c: Erica. MP for Heywood & Royton since 1964; sr partner, JC Allen & Co, since 1953. Sgt, Brit Army, 1944-47. Home: 10 Park Lane, Whitefield, Eng. Office: 50 Princess, Manchester, Eng.

BARNETT, Louis, US, attorney; b. Bklyn, NY, Aug 4, 1904; s. Jacob and Lena (Weissman); att CCNY, 1922; LLB, NYU, 1925; m. Stella Leibowitz, Nov 11, 1934; c: Barbara Steinfeld, Brenda Solomon. Pvt practice since 1927. Govt appeals agt, Selected Service. Home: 949 Allen Lane, Woodmere, NY. Office: 175 Fulton Ave, Hempstead, NY.

BARNETT, Theodore, US, surgeon; b. Bklyn, Nov 1, 1913; s. Joseph and Esther (Friedland); BS, CCNY, 1932; MD, NYU, 1937; m. Sylvia Frisch, Oct 8, 1940; c: Philip, Janet, Lewis. Surg, J Hosp, Bklyn, since 1945; att surg, Adelphi Hosp, since 1947; chmn, Cen Med Group, Bklyn, since 1960, chmn, dept surg, since 1960. Maj, US Army, 1941-45. Chmn, J Hosp, Bklyn div, FJP, NY; co-chmn, UJA; FACS; dipl, Amer Bd Surg; mem: Bklyn Surg Soc; Phi Betta Kappa. Contbr to surg jours. Recipient: Glover C Arnold Surg Award, NYU Coll of Med, 1936. Home: 1105 E 19 St, Brooklyn, NY. Office: 345 Schermerhorn St, Brooklyn, NY.

BARNIR, Dov, Isr, journalist; b. Brussels, Belgium, Dec 3, 1911; s. Jacob and Hadassah (Rosengarten) Silberschatz; in Isr since 1932; att U of Brussels; m. Shirley Schenker; c: Avner, Hanna, Irith. Columnist, Al Hamishmar, Heb daily, since 1961; lectr, Afro-Asian Inst, since 1961; org secy: Hashomer Hatzair, Pal, 1946-48; Mapam, Isr, 1948-49; mem, first Knesset, 1949-51; gen secy, World Union of Mapam, 1956-61. Mem, natl council, Histadrut. Author: Trade Union Problems, 1941; Currents in Modern Art, 1954. Home: 4 Bloch St, Tel Aviv, Isr. Office: Al Hamishmar, Hamasger St, Tel Aviv, Isr.

BAR-NIV, Aharon, Isr, government official, accountant; b. Kishinev, Rum, Nov 30, 1918; s. Moshe and Gitel (Shkolnik) Branover; in Isr since 1939; grad, Inst of Public Admn, Isr, 1955; m. Genia Rechnitz, Oct 25, 1940; c: Yair, Ram. Chief controller, defence system, since 1965. Maj, IDF, 1948-66. Hobbies: music, sport. Home: 85 Sokolov St, Tel Aviv, Isr. Office: Ministry of Defence, Jerusalem, Isr.

BAR-NIV, Zvi, Isr, state atty of Isr; b. Lida, Pol, May 29, 1916; s. Mordecai and Sonya (Paveh) Nibulski; in Isr since 1936; att Heb U, 1936-39; LLD, Jerusalem Law Sch, 1941; m. Rina Plavner; c: Miryam, Irith. State atty of Isr; fmr, pvt practice, 1943-48; legal adv, Min of Lab, 1948-62; responsible for initiation, planning and formulation of lab and natl ins laws; spec adv, Intl Lab Org, 1958-60, Isr Govt repr, governing body, ILO, 1960-62, delg, annual confs, since 1949; chmn, application of convs comm, Intl Lab Conf, 1954; lectr, lab leg and social policy, Sch for Social Wfr, Jerusalem, 1941-58. Haganah; i/c contact with political prisoners; comptroller of manpower, War of Independence, 1948-49, Mem: Histadrut Lab Council, Jerusalem, 1941-46; Isr Bar Assn; Prisoners Wfr Comm; fmr, Histadrut Court of Hon. Author: National Insurance, 1953; contbr on lab leg to profsl publs. Home: Shahin House, Katamon, Jerusalem, Isr. Office: Ministry of Justice, Jerusalem, Isr.

BARON, Benjamin, Rhodesia, attorney; b. Bulawayo, Oct 16, 1904; s. Max and Dora (Lieberman); att Rhodes U, 1923; law cert, U of S Afr; m. Rachel Joffe, Sep 25, 1932; c: Marshall, Merle Guttman, Saone Crocker, Beverley Caplan. Atty, pvt practice, since 1926; fmr: MP, S Rhodesia, Bulawayo Dist. S Rhodesian Forces, 1939-45. Mem: exec, Bulawayo Dist Publicity Assn, since 1953; comm, Rhodesia U Assn, since 1950; exec, Rhodesian J Bd of Deps; chmn, Old Miltonians Assn; fmr: vice-chmn: Cen Afr J Bd of Deps; Bulawayo Heb Cong; chmn: Chovevei Zion Soc; J Guild; Young Isr Soc; clubs: Parkview Sports; Weizmann Country. Home: 19 Oxford Rd, Bulawayo, Rhodesia. Office: Kerne Bldg, Bulawayo, Rhodesia.

BARON, Harry, US, educator; b. New York, NY, Dec 31, 1908; s. Meyer and Rose (Shapiro); BS, Bates Coll, Maine, 1931; MS, NYU, 1935; DPM, NY Coll of Podiatry, 1947; PhD, Rutgers U, NJ, 1954; m. Laura Baelen, June, 1938; c: Cora, Eric. Dean and prof basic sci, Bklyn Coll, NY, since 1968, fac mem since 1960; prof, chem, Bklyn Coll of Pharm, 1960-68; fac mem, NY Med Coll, 1941-60; prof and chmn, basic scis, Lewi Coll of Podiatry, 1945-60. Mem: Amer Assn Clin Chem; Harvey Soc; Amer Chem Soc; NY Acad Sci; AAAS; Sigma Xi. Contbr of numerous articles to med jours. Home: 268 E 7th St, New York, NY. Office: 53 E 124th St, New York, NY.

BARON, Henry Arthur, Can, physician; b. London, June 25, 1904; s. Abraham and Minna (Fleischman); in Can since 1904; MD, McGill U, 1928; m. Brenda Joseph, Feb 8, 1946; c: Murray, Lois, Carole. Sr obstet, gyn, J Gen Hosp, Montreal, since 1948, staff mem since 1934; cons gyn: J Hosp of Hope; Maimonides Hosp and Old People's Home; Mt Sinai Hosp, all since 1942. Capt, RCA Res MC. Head, med div: YM-YWHA campaign, 1950; Fed campaign, 1951; pres: Montreal Soc Obstets and Gyns, 1956; Montreal Clinical Soc, 1948; f: Amer Coll Surgs, 1954; Amer Coll Obstets and Gyns, 1959. Contbr to med jours. Hobby: golf. Home: 4840 Côte St Luc Rd, Montreal, Can. Office: 6000 Côte des Neiges, Montreal, Can.

BARON, Rachel H, Rhodesia, communal leader; b. Johannesburg, S Afr, Sep 24, 1910; d. Harris (stepfather) and Judith Freedman; related to David Wolfson, Zionist leader; BA, Witwatersrand U, 1931; m. Benjamin Baron, Sep 25, 1932; c: Marshall, Merle Guttman, Saone Crocker, Beverley Caplan. Pres, Intl Relations and Peace Conf; fmr: found mem, chmn, Bulawayo Women's Zionist Soc; pres: Natl Council of Women of Rhodesia; Women's ZC of Cen Afr; Rhodesian Delg: World WIZO Confs; ACW Conf, Wash, DC; org, Rhodesia U fund dr. Home: Beth Rachel, 19 Oxford Rd, Hillside, Bulawayo, Rhodesia. Office: POB 1497, Bulawayo, Rhodesia.

BARON, Salo W, US, historian, educator, author; b. Tarnow, Aus, May 26, 1895; s. Elias and Minna (Wittmayer); in US since 1926; PhD, U Vienna, 1917, DRerPol, 1922, DJur, 1933; ordained rabbi, J Theol Sem, Vienna, 1920; hon degs: DHL, HUC, Cincinnati, 1944; LLD, Dropsie Coll, 1962; DLitt, Rutgers U, 1963; DLitt, Columbia U; m. Jeanette Meisel, June 12, 1934; c: Shoshana Tancer, Tobey Gitelle. Prof em, J hist, lit and instns, Columbia U, since 1963; dir em, Cen of Isr and J Studies, since 1968, dir since 1950; visiting prof, JTSA, since 1954; fmr: visiting lectr, prof, hist, acting libr, all JIR, NYC ,1926-30; visiting prof, hist, Heb U, Jerusalem, 1958. Hon pres, Conf for J Social Studies, past pres; pres, J Cultural Reconstruction, Inc, since 1947; mem, intl comm for sci and cultural hist of mankind, UNESCO, since 1952; fmr: pres, Amer Acad of J Research; Amer J Hist

Soc; chmn, cultural adv comm, Conf of J Claims Against Ger; chmn, academic council, Heb U; mem, citizens fed comm on educ, US Dept Educ; trustee, JIR. Author: A Social and Religious History of the Jews, 2nd ed, 1952-58, some vols trans into Heb and Fr; Bibliography of Jewish Social Studies, 1938-39, 41; The Jewish Community: Its History and Structure to the American Revolution, 3 vols, 1942; Modern Nationalism and Religion, 1947; ed: Essays on Maimonides, 1941; J Social Studies, quarterly, since 1939; ed-in-chief, A Documentary History of American Jews, since 1954. Homes: 29 Claremont Ave, New York, NY; Yifat Shalom, Canaan, Conn. Office Columbia U, New York, NY.

BARON, Samuel, US, musician; b. Bklyn, NY, Apr 27, 1925; s. Jacob and Bella (Deutsch); att: Bklyn Coll, 1940-45; Music Sch of Henry St Settlement, 1941-42, BS, Juilliard Sch of Music, 1948, all NY; m. Carol Kitzes, Dec 21, 1963; c: Pamela, David. Flutist, Bach Aria Group, since 1965; prof, flute and chamber music, SUNY, Stony Brook, since 1966; found, flutist, NY Woodwind Quintet, 1949-69; first flute, Minneapolis Sym, 1952-53; flutist, NY Chamber Soloists, 1958-65; has given first performances of numerous contemporary works of music; performer-in-residence, Summer Evenings of Music, U of Wis, 1954-68; prof, flute, Yale Sch of Music, 1965-67; recording artist: flute solo music, works of: Telemann, Bach, Mozart, Hovhanes, Riegger, Kupferman, Martino, Wigglesworth, Perle, Mamlok; chamber music, works of: Hindemith, Danzi, Rossini, Poulenc, Taffanel, Milhaud, Ibert, Carter, Schuller, Dahl, Etler, Barber; transcription of the art of the fugue by JS Bach, for chamber music performance, recorded, 1958-61; selected by State Dept for cultural prog: Latin Amer, 1956, 69; Orient, 1962. Composer: Bach Arias with Flute Obbligato; Chamber Music for Woodwinds. Home: 317 W 89 St, New York, NY.

BARON, Sydney Stuart, US, business exec; b. NYC, May 30, 1920; s. Hyman and Anna (Orlin); BS, St Johns U, 1942; m. Sylvia Schreibman, Oct 21, 1939; c: Barbara Balsam, Richard, Eric, Daniel. Chmn, bd, Sydney S Baron PR Corp, since 1955; PR cons: Aluminum Co of Amer; Amer Can Co; Associated Hosp Service, NY; Columbia U; Tishman Realty & Construction C; dir: United Aircraft Products Corp; Daitch-Shopwell Markets; Nan-Flower Corp; commn, NYC Dept Marine and Aviation, 1950-51; commn, promotion dir, NYC Dept Commerce, 1951-52; dir, PR, NY Dem Comm, 1952-55. Chmn, bd, Beth Jacob Schs and Tchrs Coll, since 1959; mem, bd trustees: Ord Wingate Inst, Isr since 1959; Maimonides Hosp, Bklyn, NY, since 1959; dir: Natl Org for Mentally Ill Children, since 1956; Interfaith Movement, 1950-54; natl civil rights commn, ADL, since 1959; co-chmn, Natl Sports for Isr Comm, since 1958; dir, PR, JNF, 1959; chmn, Kings Co chap, Amer Isr C of C, 1959; mem: PR Soc of Amer; Amer Mgmt Assn; pres council, Amer Inst Mgmt; clubs: Friars; Fenway Golf; Natl Dem; Loan Star Boat. Author: One Whirl, 1942; Men Without Humor, 1944; The Bells Ring Loudly, 1945; contbr to periodicals. Recipient: dist service award: JWV; VFW; FJP; gov award, UJA; perpetual scholarship award, Beth Jacob Schs; brotherhood award, Interfaith Movement; civil merit award, NYC. Hobbies: painting, writing poetry, archaeol, numismatics. Home: Scarsdale, NY. Office: 515 Madison Ave, New York, NY.

BAR-ON, Izhak, Isr, government official; b. Czech; s. Baruch and Bella (Berkovic) Braun; in Isr since 1940; att U Jerusalem, 1946-48; Staff Coll, Paris, 1951-52; m. Miryam, Dec, 1948; c: Naith, Zvi. Dir, intl coop and fgn liaison, Min of Defence, since 1968. Col, Haganah, IDF, 1962. Home: 16 Joav St, Zahala, Isr. Office: Ministry of Defence, Hakirya, Tel Aviv, Isr.

BAR-ON, Mordechai, Isr, retired army off; b. Tel Aviv, Dec 26, 1928; s. Abraham and Judith; BA, Heb U, Jerusalem; MIA, Columbia U; m. Ezella Zaizon; two c. Mem, IDF, War of Independence, served, southern front, infantry platoon cdr, then co cdr; appd opr off of brigade HQ; received rank of maj, age 21; org, dir, courses for officers: hist of political theory; mil leadership and educ problems; org, cdr, ROTC, Heb U; appd head, hist br, GHQ, IDF; personal asst to Moshe Dayan; since 1957, engaged in writing study on mil and political background of Sinai Campaign; nominated chief, educ, IDF. Prin contrib, devl system of leadership training for cdrs. Mem exec, WZO, JA, head youth, Hecalutz dept. Home: 7 Masaryk St, Jerusalem, Isr. Office: Jewish Agency, Jerusalem, Isr.

BAR-ON, Raphael Raymond, Isr, statistician; b. London, Eng,

Dec 4, 1927; s. Edward and Lillian (Silman); in Isr since 1951; BA, hons, Trinity Coll, Cambridge, Eng, 1947; MA, 1951; m. Jocheved Lurie, May 25, 1952; c: Sonia Shlomit, David. Chief, planning and devl, Directorate of Isr Cen Bur of Stat, since 1956; external lectr, Kaplan Sch, Heb U, Jerusalem, since 1958; fmr: head, research div, Isr Inst of Produc, 1952-54; stat, Shell-Mex and BP, 1954-55; asst prin, Gen Register Off. Council mem: Info Processing Assn of Isr; Assn for J Demography and Stat; vice-pres, Inter-U J Fed, UK, 1948-50; exec, Hitachdut Olei Britania, 1952-54; council, Histadrut of Social Sci Grads, 1961-64; fmr chmn, Cambridge U J Soc; f, Royal Stat Soc; asso mem, Oprs Research Soc of Amer; mem: Amer Stat Assn; Oprs Research Soc of Isr. Author: Seasonality in Israel, 1963; Seasonality and Trends in Israel Tourism, 1968; surveys on J U students; articles on measurement of rel observance among J; population census; record linkage; stat methods. Recipient: Open Exhibition, Trinity Coll, 1943. Spec interests: J stat, tourism. Home: 88A Herzl Blvd, Jerusalem, Isr. Office: Cen Bur of Stat, Jerusalem, Isr.

BAROUCH, Raphael, Isr, business exec; b. Tel Aviv, Dec 6, 1922; s. Shmuel and Rachel; MA, Heb U, Jerusalem, 1954; m. Avigail Marash, Oct 8, 1957; c: Shmuel, Yosef, Rachel. Gen mgr, Shalom Stores Ltd, Tel Aviv, since 1965; fmr: dep controller, fgn exch, Min of Finance, 1952-60; mgr, Mayer Investment, 1960-65. Vice-chmn, Isr Inst for Packaging and Design. Home: 46 Har Daphna, Savyon, Isr. Office: 9 Ahad Ha'am, Tel Aviv, Isr.

BAROWAY, Israel, US, educator; b. Baltimore, Aug 21, 1899; s. Solomon and Florence (Balser); BA, Johns Hopkins U, 1921, PhD, 1930; m. Frieda Berman, June 7, 1931; c: Malcolm, Helen. Ret; fmr prof, Eng, Queens Coll, Flushing, NY, 1954-65, on staff since 1937; instr: Johns Hopkins U, 1927-28; NYU, 1930-37. US Army, 1918. Mem: AAUP; MLA; Renaissance Soc; Phi Beta Kappa; club, Tudor-Stuart. Co-ed: Prose Masters, 1939; A Preface to Our Day, 1940; contbr to profsl jours. Recipient, grant, Fund for Advancement of Educ, 1952. Home: 42-66 Phlox Pl, Flushing, NY.

BARPAL, Joseph, Isr, business exec; b. Odessa, Russ, 1897; Itzhak and Haya (Rabinovitz); in Isr since 1925. Ret, fmr: vice-chmn, directorate, Zim Shoham, 1955-66; chmn, Yona Co; mem council, Nahshon. Fmr: delg, WZC s; secy, Hedera Workers Council; mem, Tnuva. Home: 116 Yefe Nof, Haifa, Isr.

BARR, Emil N, US, attorney; b. Vienna, Aus, Sep 9, 1891; s. Jacob and Fannie (Sonenschein); in US since 1893; BS, Columbia, 1913, LLB, Columbia U Law Sch, 1915, hon DHumL, HUC, 1965; m. Amelia Wasch, June 19, 1919. Mem, law firm, Barr, Bennett & Fullen, NYC since 1926; admitted to bar, 1916; assoc with Johnson & Galston, 1915-1920; pvt practice, 1921-26; justice, Supr Court, NY, 1931; Rep candidate, Borough of Bklyn, 1940. US Army, WW I, 2nd lt, US Army Res, 1926-1935. Hon lifetime chmn, UAHC since 1963, trustee, 1948, chmn, bd trustees, 1959-63; hon pres, J Hosp, Bklyn, 1948-54, hon chmn, bd since 1954; hon pres, U Temple, Bklyn, pres, 1941-49; bd of govs, HUC-JIR, fmr vice-pres, FJP; vic-pres, Bklyn JCC; trustee: Bklyn Inst Arts and Scis; United Hosp Fund, NY, Boys Welcome Hall; bd advs, NCCJ, Bklyn region; mem: Mason; Soc of Old Brooklynites; gov comm, Bklyn Mus; Bklyn Childrens Mus; clubs: Natl Rep; Bankers; Unity; Columbia U, all in NYC. Recipient: dist service, Men's League Bklyn, 1952; Amer Legion, King Co, 1952; Man-of-Year, Metrop Conf, Natl Fed of Temple Brotherhoods, 1963; Gold Medal, Downtown Bklyn Assn, 1964; Statesman Award, Syn Council of Amer, 1965. Home: 225 E 57 St, New York, NY. Office: 1 Battery Park Pl, New York, NY.

BARR, Simon, Isr, actor; b. Rum, Oct 26, 1927; s. Abraham and Ronia; in Isr since 1950; BA, U of Bucharest, 1946; m. Shoshana Landes, Mar 26, 1961; c: Daphne. Actor at Cameri Theatre. Pvt, IDF. Home: 1 Itamar Ben Avi, Tel Aviv, Isr. Office: Cameri Theatre, 101 Dizengoff St, Tel Aviv, Isr.

BAR-RAV-HAY, David, Isr, attorney, legislator; b. Njeshin, Russ, 1894; s. Jakob and Lea (Billig) Borovoj; in Isr since 1924; att Tech Coll, Brunswick, Ger, 1911-14; Inst for Intl Law, Odessa, Russ, 1919-20; law dipl, Govt Law Classes, Jerusalem, 1932; m. Shulamith Hess, 1919; c: Meir. In pvt practice since 1932; mem, cen comm, Mapai; secy, Hapoel Hatzair, 1924-25; Keren Kayemeth le Israel, 1925-26; MK,

Mapai, 1949-65. Mem: cen comm, Lawyers Assn of Isr; Law Council; dep chmn, J Comty of Haifa, 1931-49; mem: Va'ad Leumi, 1932-48; club, Trade and Maritime of Haifa. Contbr of articles to periodicals, Isr press; Almanac, 40 years of Hapoel Hatzair; pamphlet, Knesset. Spec interests: political sci, electoral laws, philately. Home: 26 Netiv Ofakim, Haifa, Isr. Office: 32 Herzl St, Haifa, Isr.

BAR-RAV-HAY, Meir Moura, Isr, attorney; b. Odessa, Russ, Aug 15, 1920; s. David and Shulamith (Heth) Borovoy; in Isr since 1924; att Jerusalem Law Classes, 1941-47; m. Yehudith Botkovsky, May 27, 1948; c: Dina, Noga, Rachael. Atty since 1948; partner, Bar-Rav-Hay, Erdstein & Bar-Rav-Hay law off, since 1950; legal adv to Technion, spec in local govt law. Haganah, 1936; sgt, British Army, Royal Engrs, 1941-46; major, Judge Advocates Br, IDF, 1948-50. Mem: exec bd, Isr War Veterans League; city council, Haifa, 1957-65; legal comm, World Veterans Fed; council mem, Isr World Veterans Fed, 1957-63; Isr Bar Assn. Hobby: philately. Home: 26 Netiv Ofakim St, Haifa, Isr. Office: 32 Herzl St, Haifa, Isr.

BAR-RAV-HAY, Shulamith, Isr, pediatrician; b. Hotin, Russ, Jan 1, 1895; d. Meir and Dina (Tovbin) Heth; in Isr since 1924; att: U of Montpellier, Fr, 1913-14; U of Kiev, Russ, 1914-18; m. David Bar-Rav-Hay, Oct 17, 1919; c: Meir. Pvt practice since 1927, ret, 1967. Chmn, WIZO, Haifa, mem exec comm. Home: 26 Netiv Ofakim St, Haifa, Isr.

BARROMI, Joel, Isr, diplomat; b. Rome, 1920; in Isr since 1939; MA, Heb U, Jerusalem; DJur, U Rome Law Sch; married; four c. Ambass, alternate repr, Permanent Mission of Isr to UN, ambass of Isr to Rep of Haiti, since 1963; appd dep dir, W Eur, Div of Fgn Min; dir, Latin Amer Div; fmr: tchr, JA Inst for Youth Leaders; research dept, W Eur, Latin Amer divs, Min for Fgn Affairs; first secy, later counsellor, Isr Emb, Buenos Aires; charge d'affaires ad interim: Montevideo, Uruguay; Havana; mem, several Isr delgs to Gen Assembly, UN; observer: UN subcomm for the Protection of Minorities and for the Elimination of Discrimination, UNESCO; UN Comm on Hum Rights, alternate repr of Isr; head, Isr delg to the inauguration of Pres of Panama; visited: Costa Rica; Nicaragua; Honduras; Guatemala, as ambass on a spec mission; observer to Inter-Amer Cultural Council, OAS, Wash, DC; ambass extraordinary and political adv, accompanied Zalman Shazar, Pres of Isr, on State visit to: Uruguay, Chile, Brazil. Office: 15 E 70 St, New York, NY.

BARRON, Jennie Loitman, US, jurist; b. Boston, Oct 12, 1891; d. Morris and Fannie (Castleman) Loitman; BA, Boston U, 1911, LLB, 1913, LLM, 1914, hon LLD, 1959; hon DSc, Lowell Tech Inst, 1964; m. Samuel Barron Jr, June 23, 1918; c: Erma Wernick, Joy Rachlin, Deborah Blazer (decd). Judge, Superior Court of Mass (life), since 1959, 1st woman jurist to be appd to this court; judge, Munic Court, Boston, 1st and only full-time woman judge in Mass appd for life, 1937; trial lawyer, 1914-37; admitted to bar: Mass, 1914; US Dist Court, 1915; Supr Court, 1921; 1st woman in Mass to present evidence to Grand Jury; served as Master in Superior Court; asst atty gen, Mass, 1934-35, 1st woman in Mass to prosecute criminal cases; off repr, USIA, people-to-people trip: India, Thailand, Hong Kong, Japan, 1962; by invitation of presiding judge, has sat as guest on Bench of Courts of London, Hong Kong, India, Russ, Isr, Brazil, Japan, Fr, Nigeria, numerous Afr and Scandinavian countries; off US delg, UN, first cong, crime and treatment of offenders, Geneva, Switz, 1955; lectr: for UJA, Hadassah, throughout US, on juvenile delinquency and crime. Pres: Coll Equal Suffrage League, 1910; Mass Assn of Women Lawyers, 1918; hon and 1st, women's auxiliary, Beth Israel Hosp; women's div, AJCong of Gtr NE; vice-pres, Boston J Comty Council; trustee, Temple Isr, Boston, Mass; del: Amer J Confs; Natl Crime Conf, 1934; Mid-Cent White House Confs on Child Wfr, 1950; from Natl League of Women Voters to Natl Conf on Uniform Laws for Marriage and Divorce; mem: natl bd, Hadassah; bd dirs, natl women's comm, Brandeis U; J Family and Children's Service; J Health Survey Comm; AJComm, Boston; NE Hosp; Washingtonian Hosp; hon life, bd trustees: Beth Isr Hosp; Assn J Philanthropies of Gtr Boston; bd dirs, Hillel Found, Boston U; natl comm, Cerebral Palsy Assn; NE Adv Comm to natl bd, NCCJ; Mass adv comm, Savings Bond Div; Natl J Tercentenary Comm; natl exec bd, People to People Civic Comm; Mass Post-war Law Inst; Boston, Mass and Amer Bar Assns; hon: Interracial F of Amer; Iota Tau Tau; Delta Kappa Gamma;

speaker on civil rights: TV and radio and before numerous groups in London, Hong Kong, India, Russ, Isr, Brazil, Japan, Senegal, Ghana, Nigeria, Kenya. Recipient: Alumni Medal, for dist public service, Boston U, 1951; Woman of the Week Award, Boston Traveler, 1952; Woman of the Year, Bus and Profsl Women's Club, Boston, 1954; Mother of the Year, State of Mass, 1959; Amer Natl Mother of the Year, 1959; Woman of Achievement, NE Soroptomist Award, 1959; citations: law libr shelf named in her honor in Stephen S Wise Cong House, NY, from NE women's div, AJCong, 1951; Mass Assn of Women Lawyers, on completion of 20 years on the bench, 1958; Mass Assn of Women Lawyers, on being first woman justice, Superior Court, 1959; Assn J Philanthropies, Mass Delta Kappa Gamma, AJCong, 1959; State Veterans Assn, 1963; Amer J Lit Found; Kiwanis Clubs; Boston C of C, as one of the ten outstanding women of Boston for work as champion of minority groups, civil rights, and work with juvenile delinquents; selected as Orator of the Day for Boston's Independence Day Celebration, by Mayor John F Collins, 1960. Home: 30 Clinton Rd, Brookline, Mass. Office: Superior Court of Mass, Boston, Mass.

BARRON, Milton L, US, sociologist, educator; b. Derby, Conn, Feb 25, 1918; s. Harry and Anne (Tevlin); MA, Yale U, 1942, PhD, 1945; m. Matilda Cogan, June 1, 1947; c: Benjamin. Prof, sociol, anthropology dept, CCNY, since 1960; fmr dept chmn; asst prof: Syracuse U, 1944-48; Cornell U, 1948-54; Fulbright visiting prof, Bar-Ilan U, Isr, 1962-63; visiting prof, Fresno State Coll, 1969-70. Mem: AAUP; Amer Sociol Assn. Author: People Who Intermarry, 1946; The Juvenile in Delinquent Society, 1954; The Aging American, 1960; ed: American Minorities, 1957; Contemporary Sociology, 1964; Minorities in a Changing World, 1967. Home: 51 Appleton Pl, Dobbs Ferry, NY. Office: College o City of New York, New York, NY.

BARRON, Moses, US, physician, educator; b. Russ, Nov 8, 1883; s. Jacob and Pauline (Jacobs); in US since 1889; BS, U of Minn, 1910, MD, 1911; m. Leah Fligelman, 1919; c: Louis, David, Jesse, Antoinette Stein. Prof em, med, Minn U, since 1952, on staff since 1913. Lt maj, US Army, MC Res, 1918-19. Mem, bd, J Fed, Minn; hon pres, Minn br, Amer Friends of Heb U; mem: AMA; Amer Coll Phys; Henn Co Med Soc, past pres; Cen Soc of Clinical Research; Minn Path Soc, past pres; Amer Assn Path and Bact; Minn Acad of Med; Minn Soc of Internal Med, past pres; Amer Diabetes Assn, hon; Amer Bd of Internal Med; Amer Assn for Cancer Research; AAAS; Alpha Omega Alpha; Sigma Xi, hon; hon f, Heb U of Jerusalem; club, Standard. Author: numerous publs on med and path; article which started Banting on discovery of insulin. Home: 2715 E Lake of Isles Blvd, Minneapolis, Minn. Office: 1127 Med Arts Bldg, Minneapolis, Minn.

BAR-SHAVIT, Shlomo, Isr, actor; b. Jerusalem, Dec 7, 1928; s. Aharon and Shulamit (Eliash) Friedman; att Mishmar Haemek, 1934-46; Habimah Actors Studio, 1946-48; m. Dita Navon; c: Ben, Michal. Profsl actor since 1948; radio monitor; play reader; author of children's radio and screen plays. IDF, 1948-49. Home: 4 Warburg, Tel Aviv, Isr. Office: Kikar Habimah, Tel Aviv, Isr.

BARTAL, Albert David, Isr, neurosurgeon; b. Sofia, Bulg, Jan 30, 1922; s. David and Rivka (Varon) Behmoaram; in Isr since 1949; att Fr Coll, Sofia; BS, Amer Coll, Sofia; MD, U of Sofia, 1948; m. Sara Krill, Jan 26, 1930; c: David, Relly. Head, dept, neur surg, Ichilov Hosp, Tel Aviv, since 1964; fmr: prosector, anat, med sch, Inst of Anat; lectr, phil, 1946-48; dir, Intl Student Camp, 1948; nominated aspirant asst, U Med Clinic, prof K Tchilov, 1948-49; fgn studies: Neur Inst, U of Freiburg, Ger, 1958; Natl Hosp for Neur Diseases, London, 1959; Yale U, New Haven, Conn, 1960-61. Mem: Natl Comm of Org of Kupat Holim Phys; Isr Surg Soc; Isr Neurosurg Soc; found, chmn, Tennis Club Beilinson. Contbr of sci publs in Bulg, Heb, Eng, in local and fgn med jours; sci trans from Russ to Eng. Home and office: 45 Chen Blvd, Tel Aviv, Isr.

BARTH, Alan, US, journalist; b. NYC, Oct 21, 1906; s. Jacob and Flora (Lauchheimer); PhB, Yale Coll, 1929; att Harvard U, 1948-49; m. Adrienne Mayer, July 1, 1939; c: Flora, Andrew. Ed writer, Wash DC Post and Times Herald, since 1943; ed writer, Beaumont Jour, 1937; Wash, DC, corresp, McClure Newspaper Syndicate, 1938-41; ed asst to US Secy of Treas, 1941; ed of reports, USOWI, 1941-43; visiting prof, U of Cal, Berkeley, 1958-59. Mem: natl comm, ACLU;

Sigma Delta Chi; clubs: Natl Press; Overseas Writers. Author: The Loyalty of Free Men, 1951; Government by Investigation, 1955; The Price of Liberty, 1961; contbr to Years of the Modern, 1950. Recipient: Amer Newspaper Guild award, 1948; Nieman F, Harvard U, 1948-49; Sigma Delta Chi award, 1949; Hillman Found award, 1951; OW Holmes award, CLU, Wash; Lasker award, CLU, NY. Home: 3520 Rodman St, NW, Washington, DC. Office: Wash Post & Times Herald, Washington, DC.

BARTH, George Zeev, Isr, journalist; b. Budapest, Hung, Sep 30, 1919; s. Alexander and Rudolfine (Wagner); in Isr since 1951; att Gymnasium, Nové Mesto; Commercial Acad, Piestany; m. Aviva Porges, Feb 20, 1949; c: Alexander. Co-ed, Yediot Chadashot, newspaper, since 1963; gen secy, Zionist Rev Org, CSR, 1945-49, Aus, 1949-51; ed, Yediot Hayom, newspaper, 1952-63; ed, Medinah Ivrit, Prague, 1949; staff, Neue Welt, Vienna, 1951. Mem: Isr Journalists Assn; B'nai B'rith, Bialik Lodge. Trans, numerous books from Heb to Ger. Spec interest: ME affairs. Home: 17 Moria St, Ramat Gan, Isr. Office: 66 Harakevet St, Tel Aviv, Isr.

BARTH, Helene, Isr, teacher; b. Halberstadt, Ger, July 7, 1891; d. Josef and Rosa (Dessau) Baer; in Isr since 1924; tchr cert, Tchr Sem, Halberstadt, 1911; att Acad, Frankfurt, 1911; U of Berlin, 1920-22; MA, oriental studies, Heb U, 1943; m. Leo Barth (decd). Ret since 1959; tchr, J schs, Ger, 1911-22; headmistress, Tchr Sem for Girls, 1924-30; sup, Schs Binyamina, 1931-50; dir, spec educ, Min of Culture, Jerusalem. Org sup, Mifal, for unschooled children; mem: Youth Play Grounds; Isr Assn Painters and Sculptors, Hist Soc, Isr; Isr Soc for Bibl Research; Archeol Soc; Heb U Grad Soc. Contbr of articles to pedg jours. Home: Narkiss St, House Harris, Jerusalem, Isr.

BARTOV, Hanoch, Isr, author, journalist; b. Petah Tikva, Isr, Aug 13, 1926; s. Simkha and Miriam; att Heb U, Jerusalem, 1946-51; m. Yehudith Shimmer, Feb 10, 1946; c: Gillat, Omer. Columnist, writer, Lamerhav, since 1956; fmr: diamond polisher, 1941-42; welder, 1942-43; researcher, Isr Inst for Applied Research, 1949-51; tchr, HS, 1951-56; counsellor, cultural off, Isr Emb, London, 1956-68. J Brig, 1943-46; IDF, 1948-49. Author: haCheshbon veHanefesh, 1953; Shesh Kenafayim laEchad, 1954, adapted for stage, produced, Habima, 1958, 1964, trans into Span, Eng, Fr; haShuk haKatan, 1957; Chatunat haKesef, radio play, 1958; 4 Israelim veChol America, 1961; Lev Chachamim, 1962; Sa haBayta, Yonathan, 1962, play produced by Zutta Theatre; Pits'ey Bagrut, 1965; Israelim baChatsar St James, 1969; trans, various books into Heb; contbr numerous articles to jours. Mem: bd dirs, Isr Bc; exec bd, Isr Writers Assn; Isr Journalists Assn; PEN. Recipient: Ussishkin Prize, Shesh Kenafayim laEchad; Shlonsky Prize, for Pits'ey Bagrut. Home: 91 University St, Ramat Aviv, Tel Aviv, Isr.

BARTUR, Moshe, Isr, diplomat; b. Pol, Oct 27, 1919; s. Shlomo and Hinda (Fishler); in Isr since 1938; m. Ursula Ruhemann, 1941; c: Dorith, Michal, Gad. Ambass to Japan and Korea since 1966; dep dir, econ dept, Min Fgn Affairs, 1949-52, dir, 1952-59, dep dir gen, 1959-61; ambass and head, Isr delg, UN Eur Off, Geneva, 1961-66; missions to Eur, US; munic counsellor, Jerusalem, 1965-66; mem, Isr Govt trade delgs to Eur, since 1950. Contbr of articles to jours. Office: Israel Emb, Tokyo, Japan.

BARTURA, Avraham Eliezer, Isr, educator, author, editor; b. Jerusalem, Sep 12, 1907; s. Jehuda and Miryam (Minzberg) Bergmann; BA, J Tchrs Sem, Würzburg, 1930; Nuremberg U; Yeshiva Zion, Jerusalem; Yeshiva Adath Israel, Nuremberg; econ coll, Nuremberg; m. Fanny Bernay (decd), Nov 7, 1932; c: Jacob. Sch insp, Min of Educ, since 1966; ed, Hazofe daily, 1944-48; bc, info off, Isr Bc, 1949-54; dir, Neve Hadassah Youth Colony, 1954-56; repr, educ and culture dept, JA, Ger, 1956-60; min of educ and culture, Jerusalem, 1960-61; dir, schs, Jerusalem, 1961-64; repr, Youth Aliya, JA, S Amer, 1964-66. Author, ed, trans of numerous books. Home: 7 Kiryat Moshe St, Jerusalem, Isr. Office: Min of Educ and Culture, Jerusalem, Isr.

BARUCH, Jordan J, US, engineer, educator; b. NYC, Aug 21, 1923; s. Solomon and Minnie (Kessner); MS, MIT, 1948, ScD, 1950; m. Rhoda Wasserman, June 3, 1944; c: Roberta, Marjory, Lawrence. Vice-pres, dir, Bolt Berane and Newman Inc, since 1955; pres, EDUCOM, since 1968; vice-pres, research devl, MIT, 1955-68, asst prof, 1950-55, lectr, 1955-68.

US Army, 1942-46. Prin contbr: inventions in instrumentation field. F: Acoustical Soc Amer, 1958; NY Acad Sci, 1960; Amer Acad Arts and Sci, 1963; Inst Elec and Electronic Engrs, 1966; mem: Eta Kappa Nu; Amer Phys Soc; AAAS. Home: 130 Dudley Rd, Newton Centre, Mass. Office: 100 Charles River Plaza, Boston, Mass.

BARUK, Henri Marc, Fr, physician, educator; b. St Avé, Fr, Aug 15, 1897; s. Jacques and Marie (Brechon); m. Suzanne Soriano. Prof, Faculté de Méd, Paris, since 1946; dir, research, École Pratique des Hautes Études, U of Paris, on staff since 1926; chief phys: Maison Nationale de Charenton, since 1931; psycht hosps, Fr, 1930. Fr Army, WWI, WW II. Pres: Société de Neur de Paris; Soc Méd-Psych; Soc des Amis de l'Université Héb de Jérusalem; Soc de la Méd Héb de Paris, 1946; Soc d'Hist de la Méd de Jérusalem, 1950; comm Fr-Isr, fac of med, 1951; vice-pres, OSE, Fr; f: Amer Intl Acad of Med, 1952, hon life mem; Royal Soc of Med, London, 1960; mem, several med assns including: Acad Natl de Méd, Paris; Intl Brain Research Org; It Acad of Med; Isr Med Assn. Author: numerous books and papers on psych, psycht, J civilization, Tzedek sci. Recipient: Officier de la Légion d'Honneur, 1939; Croix de Guerre, WWI; Commandeur de la Santé Publique, 1949. Home: 5 Quai de la République, 94 Val de Marne, près Paris, Fr.

BARWELL, Beatrice Jeannette, Eng, teacher; b. London, May 9, 1914; d. Mark and Leah (Dancyger); cert, Tchrs Training Coll, London, 1934. Head, Eng dept, HS, since 1962; sr tchr, Syn rel classes, since 1936. Hon life pres, Natl Union of Heb Tchrs, Gt Brit & Ir, found, pres, 1945-65; hon treas, ZF, Gt Brit & Ir, fmr, asst hon secy, hon secy; vice-pres, JPA comm, Wembley, fmr chmn; chmn: educ, youth comm, Bd Deps of British J; JNF commn, Wembley; vice-chmn, educ dept, JNF, Gt Brit; exec mem, Kosher Sch-Meals Service, London. Ed, Hamoreh, 1945-65; jt ed, 70 Years of Zionism; contbr to: J Chronicle; J Observer and ME Review; Zionist Year Book; Gates of Zion. Spec interest: educ, Zionism, lit, drama, music. Home: 22 Beechcroft Gardens, Wembley, Eng. Office: Mt Pleasant School, London E5, Eng.

BAR-YOSEF, Yehoshua, Isr, author, journalist; b. Safed, Isr, 1912; s. Yosef and Haya (Katz) Zehnwirth; m. Zipora Grunfeld, 1931 (decd); c: Yosef, Bilha Rubinstein, Itzhak; m. 2nd, Aviva Manheim, 1968. Columnist, weekly column in Yediot Aharonot, daily newspaper, since 1961; ed, co-found, Ha-Sifrut ha-Tzeira, lit weekly, 1939; mem, ed staff, Davar, daily, 1943-49; columnist, Maariv, daily, 1951-54. Mil corresp, IDF, 1948. Author: Kol ha-Yezarim, 1937; Av ha-Banot, 1941; Be-Simtaot Yerushalayim, play, 1942; Pgisha ba-Aviv, 1946; Ha-Ozar ha-Gadol, play, 1947; Sipurim, 1947; Me-Gufa shel Em, 1948; Ir Ksuma, trilogy, 1949-51; Haomdim al ha-Saf, 1953; Anshei Beit Rimon, 1956; Succat Shalom, 1958; collections of stories; plays. Recipient: Ussishkin Prize, 1951; Ramat Gan Prize, 1959; Safed Prize, 1961. Home: Artists Quarter, Safed, Isr.

BAR-YUDA, Moshe, Isr, journalist; b. Bratislava, Czech, Apr 19, 1934; s. Abraham and Blanka (Levber) Kastner; att Yeshivat Hebron, Jerusalem; ordained rabbi, Yeshivat Merkaz Harav, Jerusalem, 1954; m. Sarah Hacohen, Jan 29, 1964; c: Avraham, Aluma. Mem, ed staff, mgr, Panim El Panim, since 1966; fmr: repr, JA, Ethiopia, 1958-59; with sr service, Min of Defense, 1962-66. Capt, IDF, 1954-57. Author: Sefer Tiktin, 1961; contbr to periodicals. Hobby: classical music. Home: 90 Yehuda Halevi St, Tel Aviv, Isr. Office: 107 Lewinsky St, Tel Aviv, Isr.

BAR-ZACKAI, Nathan, Isr, jurist; b. Jerusalem, Aug 11, 1895; s. Joseph and Shaindl (Notkin) Bardaki; desc of Rav Shmuel Salant, Chief Rabbi, Pal; att law fac, U Istanbul; DJur, Paris, 1925; m. Rachel Gerter, July 15, 1930; c: Ari, Samuel. Pres, Tel Aviv-Yaffo Dist Court, since 1948; fmr: instr, law, Istanbul U, 1918-19; in pvt practice, Pal, 1926-27; prosecutor, Tel Aviv-Yaffo dist, 1928-34; asst, atty gen, Pal Govt, 1935-36; magistrate, Pal, 1936-39; lectr, criminal law, law courses, 1941-47; dist judge, all Jerusalem. Pres: court of hon, B'nai B'rith, Isr, since 1960; Org Rehab Prisoners and Offenders, since 1954; Gesher, since 1959; found, past pres, Isr-Fr Assn; found mem, Habonim Hahofshim. Author: La Conception Générale de la Responsabilité Civile en Droit Français et en Droit Turc, comparés, 1925. Recipient: Officier de la Légion d'Honneur, Pres of Fr, for Fr-Isr cultural activities, 1953. Hobby: horseback riding. Home: 86 Gordon St, Tel Aviv, Isr. Office: 14 Eilat St, Tel Aviv, Isr.

BAR-ZEEV, Jacob, Isr, judge; b. Cracow, Pol, May 28, 1913; s. Simon and Binah (Leibel) Wolf; in Isr since 1935; att Heb Coll; Jagellonian U, both Cracow; Heb U, Jerusalem; atty dipl, Govt Law Classes, Jerusalem, 1945; m. Lily Bendas, Dec 3, 1929; c: Irith, Simon, Avital. Chief judge, Magistrates Court, since 1954; fmr: chief Eng-Heb interpreter, Supr Court, 1945-47; asst legal adv, atty, Political Detainees Assn, Le Assirenu, 1947-48; dist atty's off, Haifa, 1949-52; judge, Magistrates Court, Tiberias, 1952-54. Capt, Pal Police Force, 1936-44; Haganah, 1947-48; IDF, 1949-65. Mem: Natl Council for Culture and Educ; Intl Commn of Jurists; Rotary Club, past pres, Tiberias br. Author: The Law Finder and Annotator, 1947; contbr of lectures and publs. Hobbies: bee-keeping, photography, sports. Recipient: decorations from Haganah for War of Independence, Sinai Campaign, Defence of Jerusalem. Home: David Remez St, Tiberias, Isr. Office: Law Courts, Tiberias, Isr.

BARZILAI, David, Isr, physician; b. Haifa, Isr, 1924; att Med Sch, Geneva, Switz, 1946-48; Heb U Med Sch, 1949-52. Dir, dept med "C" and endocrine unit, Rambam Med Cen, Haifa; sr lectr: hum biol, Isr Inst of Tech, Haifa; internal med, Heb U Med Sch; fmr: chief resident, internal med, dir, endocrine clinic, Rambam Govt Hosp; acting chief, internal med, Govt Hosp, Tiberias, since 1960; acting chief, internal med, Rambam Med Cen; travelling f to endocrine cens in Eur, US. British Army, 1942-46. Affiliated mem, Royal Soc of Med, 1964; mem: Isr Soc of Med; Isr Endocrine Soc; Isr Soc of Diabetes; Isr Soc of Fertility and Sterility. Contbr of numerous articles to profsl publs. Recipient: research f, Worcester Found for Experimental Biol, US, 1961-62; research grants: WHO; Children's Bur, USPHS; Isr Cancer Soc; Isr Research and Devl Grant. Home: 74 Hannasi St, Haifa, Isr. Office: Rambam Medical Center, Haifa, Isr.

BARZILAI, Joseph, Isr, hospital admnr; b. Czech, Aug 1, 1919; s. Herman and Etel (Ibel) Eisner; att: Masaryk U, med fac, 1937-39; Pazmany Peter U, Budapest, 1941-44; deg, hosp admn, Theol Sem of Gt Brit, Leeds U, 1960; m. Raja Dulitzky, Feb 7, 1950; c: Menashe, Zwi. Hosp admnr, Rambam Govt Hosp, Haifa, since 1956, fmr hosp admn clerk. Mem, Hosp Admnrs Org. Home: 22 Pasteur St, Haifa, Isr. Office: Bat Galim St, Haifa, Isr.

BARZILAY, Eliezer, Isr, journalist, writer; b. Transylvania, Russ, July 21, 1906; s. Jakob and Josefina (Singer) Kugel; in Isr since 1938; m; c: Amnon. Night ed, daily newspaper in Hung. Author: Dacoka Messzesegboi, poems, 1926; Meg Mindig, short stories, 1936; Csillas Ata'bor Folott, 1962; Reri Versek, Poesies 1968; Szakadek, novel, 1969. Mem, Hitachdut Olei Hungaria, Tel Aviv; secy, Nordau Prize Comm. Home: 3 Hazeitim St, Ramat Gan, Isr. Office: 52 Harakevet St, Tel Aviv, Isr.

BARZILAY, Michael, Isr, executive; b. Klausenburg, Transylvania, Rum, 1916; dipl, PR, Tel Aviv; BCS. Exec vice-chmn, Isr Affairs, Jt Pal Appeal, Gt Brit and Ir; fmr: consular repr, Isr Govt, Ger, 1948-49; secretariat, Mercas Hechalutz, Paris, 1949-52; Hanoar Hatzioni, Eur, 1952; missions on behalf of KH and JA to: Eur; Eng; N Amer; S Amer; S Afr, 1948-69; overseas dir, projects and PR of KH, Jerusalem, 1952-68. Hon treas, World Confd of Gen Zionists, 1950-52; found, chmn, PR Assn of Isr, 1956-62; Isr repr, council, Intl PR Assn, 1960-69; bd dirs, Govt Tourist Corp, 1954-66; council mem, World Maccabi Union, 1947-68. Home: 22 Aharon David St, Tel Aviv, Isr. Office: Jt Pal Appeal, Rex House, 4/12 Regent St, London SW1, Eng.

BARZILI, Seev, Isr, consulting engr; b. Vienna, Oct 23, 1922; s. Ovadia and Rivka (Bloch); in Isr since 1934; att Technion, Haifa, 1941-44; m. Lea Polski, Aug 27, 1946; c: Edna, Mia. Cons engr since 1962; sr devl engr, Isr Mining Ind, 1955-61. IDF, 1948-49. Prin contribs and projs: Port of Ashdod; Negev Phosphates, Oron; Isr Inst of Tech, Haifa; Australian Wool Ind, Ashdod; Chem and Food Inds; Entertainment Cen, Holon; Munics, Tel Aviv, Holon; Weizmann Inst, Rehovot; Timna Copper Mines; Lod Airport; Ein Bokek, Dead Sea; Tel Aviv U; preliminary inves and engr studies; preparation: gen diagrams, flowsheets, layouts, master plans, designs, specifications, analyses and recommendations. Adv comm, Registrar of Engrs and Architects, Min of Lab; fmr, cen comm, Assn Engrs and Architects, Isr. Home: 37 Yosef Tzwi St, Ramat Gan, Isr. Office: 90 Dizengoff St, Tel Aviv, Isr.

BAR-ZOHAR, Michael J, Isr, author; b. Sofia, Bulgaria, Jan 30, 1938; s. Jacques and Ines (Anavi); in Isr since 1948; BA,

Heb U, 1959; MA, Inst d'Études Politiques, U Paris, 1961; PhD, Found Natl de Sci Politiques, 1963; m. Galila Schlossberg, Oct 8, 1958; c: Gil. Press corresp, Lamerhav newspaper, 1961-64; press attaché, spokesman, Min of Defense, 1967. Sgt, IAF, 1956-58. Author: Suez Top-Secret, 1964; The Hunt for German Scientists, 1965; Ben-Gurion, The Armed Prophet, 1966; The Avengers, 1968; The Longest Month, 1968. Recipient: Sokolov Award for Jour, Tel Aviv Munic, 1965; Fr Acad Award, 1965. Hobby: scuba diving. Home and studio: 109 Rothschild Blvd, Tel Aviv, Isr.

BASER, Robert, Isr, painter; b. Athens, Greece, Apr 15, 1910; s. Benjamin and Rosalie; in Isr since 1934; att: Tsamiston Sch of Art; Acad of Fine Arts, Athens; m. Rivka Wizel; c: Hector. Prof, painting, WIZO Sch; fmr, publicity designer, Greca, Athens until 1934. Pvt J Brig. Recipient: 1st prize, painting, Athens, 1930; Dizengoff prize, 1948; Prize of the Sea, 1949; several Fr awards. 1949. Home: 18 Hachnaim, Givatayim, Isr. Office: WIZO School, Nahlat Yitzhak, Isr.

BASH, Marvin I, US, rabbi; b. Bklyn, NY, Dec 24, 1934; s. Saul and Celia (Kumim); BA, Yeshiva U, 1955; MA, Columbia U, 1959; ordained rabbi, JTSA, 1960; m. Deborah Blumenthal; c: Robert, Gila. Rabbi, Arlington Fairfax J Cong, since 1965; N Shore J Cen, E Setauket, NY, 1961-65. Treas, Wash Bd of Rabbis; mem, RA. Hobbies: sports, traveling. Home: 315 S Garfield, Arlington, Va. Study: 2920 Arlington Blvd, Arlington, Va.

BASKIN, Bernard, Can, rabbi; b. New Brunswick, NJ, Mar 9, 1920; s. Samuel and May (Guss); brother, Leonard Baskin, well-known Amer artist; BA, Bklyn Coll, 1943; MHL, JIR, 1947; hon LLD, McMaster U, 1969; m. Marjorie Shatz, May 9, 1949; c: Judith, David, Susan. Rabbi: Temple Anshe Shalom, Hamilton, Ont, since 1949; fmr: Temple Emanuel, Denver, Colo, 1945-57; Liberal Syn, Baton Rouge, La, 1947-49. Hillel counselor, McMaster U; chmn, Hamilton J PR Comm; mem, CCAR. Recipient: B'nai B'rith Humanitarian Award, 1954; Can Centennial Medal, 1967. Home: 50 Sanders Blvd, Hamilton, Ont, Can. Study: Cline Crescent and King St W, Hamilton, Ont, Can.

BASKIN, Samuel Jay, US, attorney; b. Russ, Sep 29, 1911; s. Jacob and Jennie (Laskin); in US since 1917; BS, Crane Coll, 1929; LLB, De Paul Law Sch, 1932; m. Hadassah Feuerstein, June 9, 1935; c: Sheldon, Judith Offer. Sr partner, law firm, Baskin and Server, since 1940. Vice-pres, Adult Educ Council of Gtr Chgo, since 1959; off, Hum Relations Comm, Highland Pk; vice-pres, Chgo Fed of Reform Judaism, since 1959; fmr: participant, World Peace Through Law Conf, Thailand, 1969; vice-pres, Chgo Bd J Educ; pres, S Shore Temple; chmn: Clarence Darrow Centennial, 1958; Hundredth Anniversary, J Family and Comty Service of Chgo, 1958; vice-chmn, J Tercentenary of Chgo, 1958; mem: natl bd, UAHC; Pi Gamma Mu; Nu Beta Epsilon; clubs, S ShoreMen's, past pres; Covenant, past pres. Co-author, chap on Chgo J lawyers, History of Chicago Jews, 1961; contbr to legal jours. Recipient: awards for J family and comty service: S Shore Temple, 1948; City of Hope, 1960; CJA, 1960; Isr Bonds, 1962. Home: 368 Moraine Rd, Highland Pk, Ill. Office: 188 W Randolph St, Chicago, Ill.

BASMAN-BEN-HAIM, Rivka, Isr, poet, educator; b. Vilkomir, Lith, Feb 20, 1925; d. Yechezkiel and Zipora (Haiman); in Isr since 1947; att: Tchrs Sem, Tel Aviv, 1951-54; Columbia U, 1961; m. Ben Haim, Aug 30, 1945. Govt employee, Min for Fgn Affairs, since 1962; fmr: tchr: Kibbutz Hama'pil, 1947-62; Isr Emb, Moscow, 1962-65. Haganah, 1947-48. Co-found, Young Isr, group of poets, writers; mem: Assn of J Writers, Isr br; Igud Yotzei Vilno. Author: collections of poems: Doves on the Well, 1959; Bleter Fun Wegn, 1968; publ poems in: Goldenekeit; Svive, NY; Almanac of Yiddish Writers. Hobbies: art, mus, lit, phil. Home: Shalom Aleichem St, Herzliya B, Isr.

BASOK, Chaim, Isr, advocate; b. Vilna, Russ, June 16, 1923; s. Yeheskel and Gita (Deul); desc of Rashi; LLD, Sch of Law and Econ, Tel Aviv, 1954; att Heb U, Jerusalem, 1956-58; m. Nachama Ben-Dov, July 19, 1953; c: Tova, Yeheskel, Deuel, Ishay, Shlomit. Dep Mayor, Tel Aviv Munic, since 1969; magistrate, Tel Aviv Munic Court, since 1959; in pvt practice since 1962; mem, Kibbutz Yavneh, 1947-52; legal adv, Min for Rel Aff, Chief Rabbinate, Isr, 1956-59; 1st pres, Mil Court, E Jerusalem, W Bank, 1967. Maj, IDF, 1951-56. Mem: legal adv, cen comm, Natl Rel Party; Natl Ins

Court; Govt Council on Petrol; co-found, mem, cen comms: United Synagogue, Isr; Council for Shabbat Observance; Lawyers Assn; pres. B'nai B'rith lodge. Contbr articles to jours. Hobbies: music, football. Home: 1 Amsterdam St, Tel Aviv, Isr. Office: 15 Mikve Israel St, Tel Aviv, Isr.

BASS, Hyman B, US, organization exec, author; b. Vilno, Pol, Nov 27, 1904; c: Rubin and Ida (Gilden); in US since 1922; att J Tchrs Sem, Vilno, and NYC; m. Rebecca Rosenblum, July 10, 1935 (decd); m. 2nd, Sulamitis Kreplak, Aug 22, 1952; c: Vivian. Exec dir, Cong for J Culture, since 1953, educ dir, 1948-53; lectr, J Tchrs Sem, NYC, since 1948, mem, bd dirs, since 1950; mem: ed adv bd, J Book Annual, since 1954; ed bd, J Audio-Visual Aid Materials Review, since 1950; bd dirs, Zukunft Lit Monthly, since 1953, co-ed since 1965; admn comm, CYCO Pub House, since 1953; council, Natl Found for J Culture, since 1960; trustee, Memorial Found for J Culture, since 1960; fmr: lectr: Arbeiter Ring, tchrs courses, 1935-48; overseas staff, JDC, 1945-48; profsl staff, United Services for New Amers, 1948; Inst for J Affairs, 1957-58. Treas, vice-pres, pres, JBCA; natl vice-pres, Arbeiter Ring; mem, planning comm, World Conf on J Educ, Jerusalem. Author: Der Ursprung Fun Pesach, 1926; Arbets Buch Far Yiddisher Geshichte, 1931; Yidn Amol, 1933; Yidn Amol Un Haint, 1937; Shprach Un Dertsiung, 1950; Program fun Yiddisher Geshichte, 1952; Undser Dor Muz Antsheidn, essays, 1950; co-author: Undzer Vort, 1932; Mein Shprach Buch, 2 vols, 1938, 42; Dos Yiddishe Vort, 1947; ed: Dertsiungs Entsiklopedie, 3 vols, 1957-59; Bleter Far Yiddisher Dertsiung, 1949-62; contbr to learned jours. Recipient: Shaban Lit Award, Cong for J Culture, 1950. Home: 164 E 78 St, New York NY. Office: 25 E 78 St, New York, NY.

BASS, Lipa, Isr, engineer; b. Teharan, Iran, July 1, 1928; s. Naftali and Batya (Lishinsky); in Isr since 1933; MS, Technion, Haifa; m. Noemi Oigman; c: Orna, Ronen. Dir, Jt Inst for Vocational Training, Min of Lab, ORT, since 1967; engr, IAF, 1957-59; mgr, engr, TIUS Co. Gen secy, Engr Org, 1960-62. Home: 2 Fichman St, Tel Aviv, Isr. Office: 39 David Hamelech, Tel Aviv, Isr.

BASS, Saul, US, designer; b. NYC, May 8, 1920; s. Aaron and Pauline (Feldman); att: Art Students League, 1936-39; Bklyn Coll, 1944-45; m. Elaine Makature, Sep 30, 1961; c: Robert, Andrea, Jennifer. Designer filmmaker; pres, Saul Bass & Assos Inc; free-lance designer, NYC, 1936-46; designer epilogue for motion picture Around the World in 80 Days, 1956; designs for: Man with the Golden Arm, 1955; Anatomy of A Murder, 1960; Exodus, 1961; others; repr perm collections, Mus of Modern Art; numerous one-man shows and group exhbs in US, Eur. Mem, exec bd, Intl Design Conf, Aspen, Colo, since 1955; hon mem, fac, Royal Designers for Ind; Royal Soc Arts, Eng, 1965; mem: Amer Inst Graphic Arts; Natl Soc Art Dirs; Alliance Graphique Internationale. Contbr numerous articles to profsl publs. Recipient: award for high artistic value in all work, Mus de Arte Moderna, Rio de Janeiro, 1959; citation for distinction to profession, Phila Mus Art, 1960; many medals and awards from various profsl orgs. Home: 337 South Las Palmas, Los Angeles, Cal. Office: 7039 Sunset Blvd, Los Angeles, Cal.

BATDORI, Shulamit, Isr, playwright, stage dir, lecturer; b. Warsaw, Pol, Dec 7, 1905; d. Yosef and Helena (Heinsdorf) Gutgeld; in Isr since 1925; grad: Max Reinhardt Sch of Dir, Vienna, 1934; Laban Cen Dancing Sch, Essen, Ger, 1933; att British Council course, directing, London, 1954; scholarship, Lee Strasberg's Actor's Studio, NYC, 1960; m. Reuven Zvi; c: Orna. Mem, Kibbutz Mishmar Haemek, since 1925; author, dir, plays for kibbutz movement theatre groups, profsl theatre; lectr, drama dept, Tel Aviv U. Author: plays: The Trial, 1939, produced in: Warsaw, Berlin, Buenos Aires; Ships Without Anchor 1942; Budapest, Cape Town; The Tractor, 1942; Huts and Moon, 1952; Sea and Home, 1953; Such Wells as Those, 1959; wrote, dir, open air performances: Till Eulenspiegel, 1955; Jephtha's Daughter, 1956; adapted, dir: Howard Fast's, My Glorious Brothers, 1952; Three Who Dreamt, musical festival; Dalia dance festival; Haifa festival, 1958,68, 10th, 20th anniversaries State of Isr; dir: From End to End, 1961, Tel Aviv; Music and Drama Festival, Isr, 1962; The Battle Diary of Givati, mil show, 15th anniversary, State of Isr, 1963. Mem: Govt Culture Council; Isr Authors Assn; Histadrut Stage Dirs Assn. Recipient: Ot Hahagana; Itur Lohmei Hamedina. Home: Mishmar Haemek, Isr. Office: Tel Aviv U, Isr.

BATKIN, Stanley Irving, US, business exec; b. NYC, Oct 18, 1914; s. Hyman and Bertha (Tenzer); att Wash Sq Coll, NYU, 1932-35; m. Selma Loinger, Nov 16, 1937; c: Alan, Gloria Schneider. Pres, Universal Folding Box Co Inc, Hoboken, NJ, since 1963; on staff since 1931. Recognized as expert in packaging field; holder of several patents for packaging improvements. Chmn, found, Beth El Comty Cen, 1948-58; chmn: Westchester-Hudson Valley Region, United Syn of Amer, 1958-62; New Rochelle Dist, Albert Einstein Coll of Med, 1959; New Rochelle dist, FJP, 1956-58; UJA, 1958-60; New Rochelle Dist, Devl Corp for Isr, since 1958; Westchester sect, Natl Patrons Soc, since 1966; Westchester sect, Isr Bond Org, since 1966; bldg comm, Beth El Syn, Westchester, since 1966; hon pres, Beth El Syn Cen, since 1965; pres, Beth El Syn, New Rochelle, 1959-65; secy, Metrop Concil, United Syn of Amer, 1958-62; mem, bd govs, J Mus, NY, 1963-66; mem, bd overseers, JTSA, since 1964; mem, bd trustees: Keren Yaldenu, 1958-63; Maimonides Hosp, Bklyn, 1959-62; Beth El Syn Cen, New Rochelle, since 1948; ZOA, New Rochelle div, since 1948; Solomon Schechter Sch of Westchester, since 1966; mem exec: cabinet, Natl Patrons Soc, since 1965; Amer mgmt Assn; Packaging Inst of NY; Graphic Arts Tech Found. Recipient: guest of honor, dinners tendered by: Beth El Syn Cen, 1956; Isr Bond Campaigns, 1957; FJP, 1960; ZOA, 1961; UJA, 1964; JTSA, 1968; Ist prize, Intl Photographic Contest, London Chronicle. Hobbies: book and stamp collecting, Judaica, photography. Home: 47 Taymil Rd, New Rochelle, NY. Office: Universal Folding Box Co, Inc, 13 and Madison Sts, New York, NY.

BATNITZKY, Jonathan, S Afr, journalist; b. Mariampol, Lith, Dec 15, 1899; s. Solomon and Rachel (Freiman); in S Afr since 1928; m. Haya Abramovitz, Jan 15, 1931; s. Solomon. Ed: South Africa Rosh Hashana Year Book, since 1949; Musaf Ivri, Heb supplement of Zionist Record, since 1966; ed: S Afr J Newspaper, 1933-36 and 1939-48; J Mail, 1937-38; Dapim, Heb monthy, 1950-54, corresp, Davar, Isr lab daily, 1950-62. Mem, Poalei Zion; fmr: gen secy, Histadrut Ivrit, both Johannesburg; secy, J Natl Council of Lith; gen secy, Hechalutz, Lith. Author, Israel Between East and West, in Yiddish, Eng, 1950; contbr to Amer-J jours. Home: 18 San Remo Ct, Bellevue, Johannesburg, S Afr. Office: POB 4263, Johannesburg, S Afr.

BATSHAW, Anne Tarshis, Can, physician; b. Ogdensburg, NY; d. Lewis and Szippa (Mechanic) Tarshis; BA, McGill U, 1921, MD, CM, 1924; m. Harry Batshaw, Jan 17, 1928; c: Zipporah, Lewis. Phys, J Gen Hosp, since 1938. Fmr: pres: Can Jr Hadassah; and mem, natl exec, Shaar Hashomayim chap, Hadassah. Home and office: 4336 Montrose Ave, Westmount, Can.

BATSHAW, Harry, Can, jurist; b. Dubrovna, Russ, Oct 14, 1902; s. Thomas and Golda (Gilman); in Can since 1905; BCL, McGill U, 1924; att U of Grenoble, Sorbonne; m. Anne Tarshis, Jan 17, 1928; c: Zipporah, Lewis. Judge, Can Superior Court, since 1950; pvt law practice for 25 years. Pilot off, RCAF Res, 1942-46. Pres, Can Friends, Alliance Isr Universelle; co-pres, Amitiés Culturelles Can Fr-Israel; co-chmn, Council of Chrs and Js; mem: Can Inst Intl Affairs; admn comm, UN Assn; pres, Young Judea, Can, 1931-34; hon vice-pres, ZOC, 1952; mem, World ZIonist Court of Honor, 1951; delg WZC, 1946, 1951; mem, Can delg, UN Conf Hum Rights, Teheran, 1968; fmr: trustee, Shaar Hashomayim Syn; secy, Baron de Hirsch Inst, Montreal; clubs: Montefiore; Lord Reading Yacht. Contbr articles on Zionist and legal subjects. Recipient: Medal of Merit, Govt of Fr. Home: 4336 Montrose Ave, Westmount, Can. Office: 85 St James St E, Montreal, Can.

BATSHAW, Manuel Gilman, Can, organization exec; b. Montreal, Can, Apr 17, 1915; s. Thomas and Goldie (Gelman); BA, McGill U, 1937; dipl, Montreal Sch Social Work, 1938; m. Rachel Levitt Dec 13, 1940; c: Mark. Exec dir, Allied J Comty Services, since 1967; J Comty Cen of Essex Co, NJ, 1940-57; dir, natl service, Natl JWB, 1964-67. Capt, MC, Can Army, 1941-44. Exec comm, Natl Conf J Communal Workers; past pres: Montreal Br, Can Social Workers; Natl Assn J Cen Workers. Home: 4300 Maisonneuve W, Westmount, Quebec, Can. Office: 493 Sherbrooke St W, Montreal Quebec, Can.

BATZ, Meir Rabinowitz, Isr, engineer; b. Moscow, Nov 7, 1917; s. Itzak and Ahuvah (Rabinowitz); desc of Shalom Aleichem (Rabinowitz); in Isr since 1929; civil engr dipl,

Technion, Haifa, 1940; m. Sara Agassi, 1944; c: Nitzan, Ahuvah, Ruth, Yigal. Dir, chief engr, s dist, div of planning, Dept of Interior, since 1964; fmr: chief instr, s dist, IDF, 1935; dir, chief engr, JA, 1945. British Defense Forces, WWII; lt, engr corps, IDF, since 1955. Prin contribs: regional planning, Negev; preliminary planning, alternative to Suez Canal. Chmn: Org of Architects and Engrs, s dist, Isr Lab Party, Beersheba, Negev; mem exec, IDF; vice-mayor, Beersheba 1955-59; dir, Intl Sem Planning, 1962-63; coord, dept of planning and bldg, Isr Fgn Off, dept of intl coop, 1962-64; vice-chmn, B'nai B'rith, gov bd, Beersheba; hon zanjero, Salt River Project, Arizona, 1965. Recipient: Rural Planning Award, 1965; Planning Intl Waterways Award, US Intl Coop Admn, 1965. Hobby: painting. Home: 127 Palmach St, Beersheba, Isr. Office: Min of the Interior, Beer sheba, Isr.

BAUER, Heinz, US, physician; b. Vienna, Aus, Nov 28, 1914; s. Alfred and Ida (Boscovitz); in US since 1946; att U of Vienna Sch of Med, 1933-38; MD, Emory U Sch of Med, Atlanta, Ga, 1951; m. Elizabeth Heller, Feb 4, 1939; c: John, Judith. Research asso, path, Walter Reed Army Inst Research, Wash, DC, since 1961; asso prof, path, Emory U Sch of Med, 1958-61. Pres, Atlanta dist, ZOA, 1960-61; mem: Atlanta Bd of J Educ; Atlanta Soc Path, pres, 1959-60; Coll Amer Path; NY Acad Sci; Alpha Omega Alpha Med Honor Soc. Contbr to profsl jours. Home: 8601 Manchester Rd, Silver Spring, Md. Office: Georgetown U Sch of Med, Washington, DC.

BAUER, Simon H, US scientist, educator; b. Kovno, Lith, Oct 12, 1911; s. Benzion and Golda (Betten); in US since 1921; BS, U of Chgo, 1931; PhD, 1935; m. Miriam Rosoff, June 25, 1938; c: Frederick, Linda, Ross. Prof, chem, Cornell U, since 1950; on fac since 1939; f, Cal Inst of Tech, 1935-37; instr, Pa State Coll, 1937-39; sr postgrad f, NSF, 1962. F: AAAS; Phi Beta Kappa; Sigma Xi; Amer Phys Soc; Amer Inst Chems; mem: Amer Chem Soc; Fed Amer Scis; Faraday Soc; NY Acad Scis. Contbr to profsl jours. Home: 312 Comstock Rd, Ithaca, NY. Office: Cornell University, Ithaca, NY.

BAUER, Yehuda, Isr, historian; b. Prague, Czech, Apr 6, 1926; s. Viktor and Gusta (Fried); in Isr since 1939; MA, hons, Cardiff Coll, U of Wales, 1950; PhD, Heb U, Jerusalem, 1960; m. Shula White, Dec 21, 1955; c: Danit, Anat. Lectr, dir, dept of holocaust studies; sci dir, oral hist, Inst of Contemporary J, since 1965; fmr, lectr, seminar Kibbutzim. Lt, IDF. Author: Diplomatia Umachteret, 1963; The Will to Live, 1970; ed bd, Moreshet; contbr of numerous articles on Zionist hist and holocaust. Home: Kibbutz Shoval, Negev, Isr. Office: Hebrew University, Jerusalem, Isr.

BAUM, Karl, Eng, journalist, public relations exec; b. Brno, Czech, Oct 6, 1907; s. Rudolf and Charlotte (Rischawy); in Eng since 1938; grad, State Acad Econ, Brno; m. Margot Gladtke, July 11, 1945. PR cons for industry and commerce since 1965; London corresp, Isr, Swiss, W Ger papers, since 1949; chief corresp, J Telegraphic Agcy, Czech, 1927-33; ed: Jüdische Volksstimme, Brno, 1925-27; Der Jüdische Sozialist, 1929-32; Der Neue Weg, 1933-34; chief ed, Moravia, Prager Tagblatt, Ostrauer Handelszeitung und Morgenblatt, Prager Abendblatt, 1933-38; chief, monitoring service, diplomatic corresp, exiled govts in London, Exch Telegraphic Co, 1940-47; found, head, WJC Eur Tracing Service for missing persons, 1945-48; ed, World J Affairs News and Feature Service, 1948-60; dir, WJC Info Dept for Eur, 1947-60. Chmn: Council J's from Czech in Gt Brit, since 1968; Haboneh, 1965-66; pres, Herder Young Adult Assn of B'nai B'rith, Brno, 1933-38; mem: Poale Zion; Inst PR; Fgn Press Assn; Natl Union of Journalists; Intl Fed Journalists. Hobbies: music, philately, Judaica Bohemia. Home and office: 30 Bracknell Gardens, London, Eng.

BAUM, Shepherd Z, US, rabbi, attorney; b. Memphis, Tenn, Sep 20, 1903; s. Solomon and Barbara (Schwebel) Zwetschkenbaum; att U of Chgo, 1921-23; ordained Rabbi, Rabbi Isaac Elchanan Theol Coll, 1924; att Syracuse U, 1926-27; LLB, Albany Law Sch, 1930; m. Esther Nussbaum, Aug 9, 1925; c: Judith Levenstein, Nahum, Amy Howard, Marla Mark. Chief sup, kosher law enforcement, NY State since 1934, org of first dept in US; rabbi: Temple Ashkenazi, Cambridge, Mass, 1924-27; New Beth Israel, Syracuse, NY, 1926-27; Sons of Abraham, Albany, NY, 1927-34. Capt, US Chaplain Corps, 1943-45. Pres: Bridge Inc since 1960; NY J Conf; Albany J Comm Center, 1932-35; natl dir, org, exec,

AJCong, 1946-47; dir, Albany Comty Chest, 1932-35; chmn, B'nai Zion-UJA; admn comm, Amer Red Mogen David; mem: Masons; Rabb Alumni, Yeshiva U. Hobbies: helping mentally ill and underprivileged people, sports. Home: 2050 Anthony Ave, Bronx, NY. Office: 93 Worth St, New York, NY.

BAUM, Werner A, US, meteorologist, educator; b. Giessen, Ger, Apr 10, 1923; s. Theodor and Beatrice (Klee); in US since 1934; BS, U of Chgo, 1943, MS, 1944, PhD, 1948; cert in Russ, U of Colo, 1946; m. Shirley Bowman, Jan 20, 1945; c: Janice, Sandra. Pres of U, prof physics, U of Rhode Island; research asst, instr, U of Chgo, 1946-47; research asso, asst prof, U of Md, 1947-49; prof, head dept, dir research, dean, grad sch, dean facs, Fla State U, 1949-63; vice-pres, academic affairs, prof meteorology, dean facs, U of Miami, 1963-65; vice-pres, sci affairs, prof meteorology, NYU, 1965-67; dep admnr, environmental sci services admn, US Dept Commerce, 1967-68. Ensign, weather and intelligence service, USN, 1944-46. Dir, Fund Overseas Research Grant and Educ; chmn, commn educ and manpower, Amer Meteorological Soc; Cert Cons Meteorologist; mem, adv bd, meteorological and geoastrophysical abstracts, Amer Meteorological Soc; Phi Beta Kappa; Phi Kappa Phi; Sigma Xi; Delta Sigma Pi; Chi Epsilon Pi; f: Amer Geophys Union; AAAS; Amer Meteorological Soc; fmr: trustee, corp secy, U Corp for Atmospheric Research; mem: comm, academic sci and eng, comm environmental quality, Fed Council Sci and Tech; comm marine research, Natl Council Marine Resources and Engr Devl; adv panel, atmospheric scis prog, NSF; asso dir, Fla Space Era Educ Study; comm sponsored research, Amer Council Educ; councilor, Oak Ridge Inst Nuclear Scis; councilor, AAAS; mem comm, climatology, adv, US Weather Bur; Natl Acad of Scis; chmn, adv comm, educ and training, US Weather Bur; mem, bd, Russ trans projects, Amer Geophys Union; trustee, Inter-U Communications Council; pres, Fla State U chap, AAUP; club, Cosmos, Wash. Contbr to profsl publs. Recipient: Hon Medal of Fla Acad of Sci, 1964; Carnegie Corp Admn F, 1964; spec citation, Amer Meteorological Soc, 1962. Home: 1909 Old Fort Dr, Tallahassee, Fla. Office: Fla State U, Tallahassee, Fla.

BAUMAN, Lionel R, US, attorney, real estate inves; b. NYC, Jan 25, 1911; s. Oscar and Mary (Lager); BA, U of Pa, 1932; LLB, Columbia Law Sch, 1935; m. Sylvia Dlugasch, Jan 23, 1936; c: Jeffrey, Patricia. In pvt practice since 1936. Pres, Amer Friends of Heb U, 1963-66, acting pres, 1962-63, dir, 1958-63, vice-pres, 1962-63; dir: Pal Purchasing Commn, 1947-49; Isr Communications Corp, 1949-51; mem: Rockrimmon Country and Harmonie Clubs. Home: 4 E 60 St, New York, NY. Office: 2 W 45 St, New York, NY.

BAUMAN, Zygmunt, Isr, educator; b. Poznan, Pol, Nov 19, 1925; s. Moshe and Sophie (Cohn); in Isr since 1968; BA, Acad of Political Sci, Warsaw, 1950; MA, U Warsaw, 1954, PhD, 1956, dozent, 1960; m. Janina Lewinson, Aug 18, 1948; c: Anna, Irith, Lilith. Prof, sociol, Tel Aviv U, since 1968; fmr: lectr, U Warsaw, head, chair of gen sociol. Mem, gov bd, Pol Sociol Assn, 1960-68. Author: Class, Movement, Elite, 1960; Outline of Sociology, 1962; Images of the Human World, 1964; Culture and Society, 1966; chief ed, Studia Socjologiczne, 1968; trans of various works; contbr to intl profsl jours. Home: 56 Neve Sharett St, Tel Aviv, Isr. Office: Tel Aviv University, Ramat Aviv, Isr.

BAUMANN, Leonard, Isr, engineer; b. Leipzig, Ger, May 16, 1911; s. Chaskel and Jenny (Cohn); deg, engr, Technikum, Oldenburg; att Bauhus, Dessau, 1930-32; m. Perla Slomowitz, Oct 13, 1942; c: Fella Carmi, Yael. Sr engr, Solel Boneh, Jerusalem, since 1952; public works dept, Haifa, 1936-39; chief engr, British War Dept, 1939-48; JA, Jerusalem, 1949-52. IDF, 1948-49. Connected with building of Hamashbir Bldg; Convention Hall; Jerusalem Theatre; Cen Bus Station, all in Jerusalem. Office: 20 Hoveve Zion St, Jerusalem, Isr.

BAUMGARD, Herbert M, US, rabbi; b. Norfolk, Va, Aug 3, 1920; s. Samuel and Sarah (Segal); BS, U of Va, 1942; MHL, ordained rabbi, HUC, 1950, DHL, 1962; att Columbia U, 1950-55; m. Selma Geller, June 20, 1948; c: Jonathan, Shira, Daniel. Rabbi: Beth Am Syn, since 1956; Temple B'nai Isr, Elmont, NY, 1950-56; dir, S Fla council, UAHC, 1956-59. Bd dirs: Gtr Miami J Fed; Gtr Miami J Comty Cen; Comty Relations Council; Econ Opportunity bd, Dade Co Comty Relations Council; pres: Gtr Miami Rabb Assn, 1964-65;

Interfaith Agcy for Social Justice of S Fla Inc, 1967-68. Author: What Is Liberal Judaism? 1954; Judaism and Prayer, 1962. Home: 6251 SW 62 Pl, S Miami, Fla. Study: 5950 N Kendall Dr, S Miami, Fla.

BAUMGARTEN-TRAMER, Franziska, Switz, psychologist, educator, author; b. Lodz, Pol; d. Raphael and Leonore (Lubliner) Baumgarten; PhD, U of Zurich, 1924; m. Moritz Tramer, May 17, 1924. Hon prof, U of Berne, since 1953. Author: Berufswünsche und Lieblingsfächer begabter Berliner Gemeindeschulkinder, 1921; Bibliographie zur psychologischen Berufsberatung, Berufseignungsforschung und Berufskunde, 1922; Arbeitswissenschaft und Psychotechnik in Russland, 1924; Beiträge zur Berufskunde des Versicherungswesens, 1925; Die Lüge bei Kindern und Jugendlichen, 1926; Die Berufseignungsprüfungen, 1928; Die Charakterprüfung der Berufsanwärter, 1929; Wunderkinder, 1930; Die Soziale Seite der Psychotechnik, 1931; Die Testmethode, 1933; Die Charaktereigenschaften, 1933; Die Dankbarkeit bei Kindern und Jugendlichen, 1936; Die Jugendliche und das Berufsleben, 1937; Beratung in Lebenskonflikten, 1943; Die Psychologie in kaufmännischen Berufe, 1943; Demokratie und Charakter, 1944; Psychologie der Menschenbehandlung im Betriebe, 2nd ed, 1946; Psychologie du voyageur de commerce, 1947; Zur Psychologie des Maschinenarbeiters, 1947; Die deutschen Psychologen und die Zeitereignisse, 1949; Das Heldentum der Akademikerinnen im Kriege, 1950; Zu Spät, 1952; Kinderzeichnungen in vergleichend psychologischer Beleuchtung, 1952; Der Lehrling und die Lehre, 1952; Testmaterial zur Prüfung von Berufseignung, 1952; Der Charakter und Charakterbildung, 1953; Die Regulierungskräfte im Seelenleben, 1955; Zur Berufswahl Schweizer Aerzte, 1959; Seelische Not und Vorurteil, 1961; Zur Geschichte der angewandten Psychologie in der Schweiz, 1961; books trans into numerous langs; ed: Intl Jour of Profsl Ethics, since 1953; Progrès de la Psychotech au cours des années de guerre, 1939-45, publ, 1950; La Psychotech dans le Monde Moderne, 1952. Inventor, 4 psychotech machines. Hon secy gen, mem exec, Intl Vereinigung für angewandte Psychologie; hon mem, Intl Vereinigung für Berufsberatung; Greek Jour for Psych. Home: Thunstr 33, Bern, Switz.

BAUMGOLD, Benjamin Zev, US, organization exec; b. Lodz, Pol, July 12, 1908; s. Victor and Frimet (Kirshenberg); in US since 1941; att Sorbonne; U of Paris, political sci, commerce, 1930-38; m. Deborah Berlinska, 1931; c: John, Janet. Dir, natl lab council, UJA, since 1952; natl asst secy, LZOA-Poalei Zion, 1942-48; gen secy, Lab Zionist Comm, Relief and Rehab, 1948-52. Natl vice-pres, LZOA; chmn, Lab Zionist Publs Comm; mem: exec, AZC; bd, Cong J Culture; tribunal, World Zionist Org, Jerusalem; fmr: gen secy, Lab Zionist Org, Fr; delg, ZC; mem: exec, Féd des Sociétés Juives, Fr; Zionist Actions Comm; natl exec, Farband Lab Zionist Order. Author: brochures on situation of refugees in Eur and Isr, 1949,50,51; contbr to J publs and Isr press. Home: 1112 Albemarle Rd, Brooklyn, NY. Office: 1290 Ave of the Americas, New York, NY.

BAUMOL, William J, US, educator; b. NYC, Feb 26, 1922; s. Solomon and Lillian (Itzkowitz); BSS, CCNY, 1942; PhD, LSE, 1949; m. Hilda Missel, Dec 29, 1941; c: Ellen, Daniel. Prof, Princeton U, since 1949; sr econ, Mathematica, since 1960; fmr: asst econ, Dept of Agric, 1942-43, 1946; asst lectr, LSE, 1947-49. US Army, 1943-46. Vice-pres, AAUP; mem: council, Econometric Soc; Inst of Mgmt Sci; fmr: pres, cen NJ chap, Amer Stat Assn; vice-pres, Amer Econ Assn. Author: Economic Dynamics, 1951; Welfare Economics and Theory of the State, 1952; Business Behaviour, Value and Growth, 1959; Economic Theory and Operation Analysis, 1960; The Stock Market and Economic Efficiency, 1965; coauthor: Economic Processes and Policies, 1954; Performing Arts: The Economic Dilemma, 1966; contbr to profsl jours. Hobby: painting. Home: 214 Western Way, Princeton, NJ. Office: Princeton U, Princeton, NJ.

BAVLY, Sarah, Isr, nutritionist; b. Amsterdam, Holland, Oct 18, 1900; d. Nathan and Lea (Meyersohn) Bawly; in Isr since 1926; DrChem, Amsterdam U, 1925; MS, Columbia U, 1929; PhD, 1947; m. Jehuda Bavly (Bromberg) 1930 (decd); c: Mirjam, Nathan. Dean, Coll of Nutrition and Home Econ, 1953-66; dir, nutrition dept, Hadassah, 1929-50; dir, nutrition dept, Min of Educ and Culture, 1950-61. Author: Poverty and Malnutrition Amongst the Jews of Jerusalem, 1943; Family Food Consumption in Palestine, 1946; Level of Nutrition in

Israel, 1951; Food Consumption and Nutrition of Urban Population in Israel, 1957; Food Consumption and Nutrition of Rural Population in Israel, 1960; Food Habits and their Changes in Israel, 1964; Nutritional Patterns Among Seven Rural Communities in Israel, 1966; Levels of Nutrition in Israel, 1966; Evaluation of Nutrition Education Programmes in Israel, 1969. Recipient: Szold Prize, Munic of Tel Aviv, 1951. Home: 24 Tudela St, Jerusalem, Isr.

BAWLY, Dan Abraham, Isr, certified public acctnt; b. Jerusalem, Aug 29, 1929; s. Lazare and Fannie (Smith); att: Heb U, Jerusalem, 1949-52; m. Ilona Zipstein; c: Yael, Gideon, Carmel, David. Exec partner, Bawly Millner and Co, since 1961; fmr, econ journalist, Jerusalem Post, 1955-57. Capt, IDF, 1948-50. Co-author: The Sandstorm, 1968; contbr articles on Arab affairs, econ problems. Home: 123 Haeshel St, Herzliya, Isr. Office: 5 Ahuzat Bait St, Tel Aviv, Isr.

BAWLY, Eliezer (Lazare), Isr, certified public acctnt; b. Amsterdam, Holland, Mar 24, 1895; s. Nathan and Lea (Meyersohn); in Isr since 1919; att Commercial Sch, Amsterdam; m. Fannie Smith, Oct 18, 1928; c: Dan, Abigail. Partner, certified public acctnt (Isr) firm, Bawly, Millner & Co, since 1933; secy, finance dept, Zionist Commn, Jerusalem, 1919-23; deputy treas, Zionist Exec, 1923-25, treas, 1925-27; head, settlement dept, JA, 1927-33; Acctnt-Gen to Govt of Israel, 1948-49; mem, financial delg to Eng, 1949-50; head, dept of claims against Pal Mandatory Govt. F, Assn of Certified and Corporate Acctnts, London; pres, Assn of Public Acctnts, 1941-46, 1948-49, 1950-52; chmn, Govt Comm for Public Acctnts Diplomas. Contbr to profsl jours. Home: Herzliya Pituah, Isr. Office: 5 Ahuzat Bait, Tel Aviv, Isr.

BAXT, Roland, US, organization exec; b. NYC, Jan 7, 1911; s. Jacob and Dora (Goodman); BS, Bklyn Coll, 1933; MS, Columbia U, 1935; m. Ruth Trutt, June 12, 1937; c: Sherwood, Paul, Robert. Exec dir, Fed Employment and Guidance Service, since 1941; NY State cert psych; dir, Adult Guidance Service, 1934-39; sr counselor: NY State Employment Service, 1939-40; Natl Ref Service, 1940-41; exec secy, J Occupational Council, 1951-61. Mem: bd, Cen Bur J Aged; comm, cardiovascular diseases in ind, NY Heart Assn; Pres, Comm Employment Phys Handicapped; comm, Boy Scouts Amer; Gerontological Soc; Natl Rehab Assn; KP; Ave N J Comty Cen; NY Personnel and Guidance Assn; fmr, pres, Natl Conf J Communal Service. Contbr articles on employment and vocational guidance. Home: 505 Ave O, Brooklyn, NY. Office: 215 Park Ave S, New York, NY.

BAY, Max Wolfe, US, certified public acctnt; b. Whitemouth, Man, Can, May 27, 1910; s. Leon and Esphira (Kaplan); att U of Man, 1925-26; Wayne U, 1928-35; m. Ada Kramer, Oct 10, 1935; c: Barbara Plummer, Susan. Partner: JK Lasser & Co, since 1965; Bay & Bay, 1942-65; instr, U of S Cal, 1948-54; lectr: Cal Soc CPA's; Amer Inst CPA's. Pres: J Cens Assn, LA, 1952-54; Beverly-Fairfax JCC, 1948-50; vice-pres, Natl JWB; treas, J Fed Council Gtr LA. Home: 3235, Earlmar Dr, Los Angeles, Cal. Office: 6380 Wilshire Blvd, Los Angeles, Cal.

BAYES, Harold, Eng, business exec; b. London, Feb 4, 1910; s. Chaim and Jane (Charing) Benkwich; m. Vivien Moss, Dec 12, 1937; c: Jeffrey, Alan, Rosalind Cohen. Chmn, mgn dir, A S Moss, Ltd, spec suppliers, trimmings for theatrical period costumes, since 1954. Vice-chmn, W London Zionist Soc, past chmn; mem, bd deps, council, United Syn; repr, Hammersmith Syn; fmr, chmn, Haleumim and Herzlia Young Zionist Socs; freeman, City of London; liveryman, Co, Carmen of London; mem, Freemasonry, Isr lodge; Mt Zion lodge, past master. Home: 3 Eversfield Rd, Kew Gardens, Surrey, Eng. Office: 9 Rathbone Pl, London W1, Eng.

BAYES, Jeffrey Joseph, Eng, attorney; b. London, Eng, Apr 21, 1939; s. Harold and Vivien (Moss); LLB, hons, London U; m. Joy Brecher, Sep 1, 1963; c: Gillian. Solicitor, partner, Clifford Watts, Compton and Co, since 1966. Exec council, Zionist Fed of Gt Brit; hon secy, Hampstead Garden Suburb Zionist Soc; Zionist Fed Day Schs and PR Comms; Fed of Zionist Youth, 1964-66; mem: Freeman of City of London; Freeman, Worshipful Co of Carmen. Hobbies: philately, criminology, cricket. Home: 9 Deansway, Hampstead Garden Suburb, London, Eng.

BAYLIN, George J, US, physician, educator; b. Baltimore, May 15, 1911; s. Morris and Pauline (Shulman); BA, Johns Hopkins U, 1931; MD, Duke U, 1937; m. Sarah Hartman,

July 10, 1938; c: Stephen, Jonathan, Eric. Prof, radiology, Duke Med Sch, since 1950, on staff since 1941; asst path, Guys Hosp, London, 1939; chief X-ray cons, VA Hosp, 1953. Dipl: Natl Bd of Med Examiners; Amer Coll Radiology; AMA; Amer Roentgen Ray Soc; NC Med Soc; Radiology Soc of N Amer; f: Amer Coll Radiology; Sigma Xi; AOA; NC X-ray Soc; dir, Duke Med Town Hall. Contbr to med jours. Recipient: medal, NC Med Soc, for best sci publ in med, NC State, 1948. Hobbies: music, ceramics. Home: 2535 Wrightwood Ave, Durham, NC. Office: Duke Hospital, Durham, NC.

BAZAK, Jacob, Isr, educator; b. Jerusalem, 1925; grad, Mizrachi Tchrs Training Coll, 1942; att Heb U, Jerusalem; grad, Govt Law Classes, Jerusalem, licensed atty, 1950; DJur, Heb U, 1961; m; four c. Sr lectr, Bar Ilan U, since 1968; legal mem, Psycht Dist Comm, since 1955; judge, Magistrate Court, Jerusalem, since 1954; fmr: tchr, elem schs, Jerusalem; practicing atty; tchr, Heb U. Author: Image of a Judge in Jewish Law, 1961; Criminal Responsibility and Mental Illness, 1963; Principles of Taxation in Jewish Law, 1964; ESP in Jewish Sources; ed, Jewish Law and the Jewish State, 1969; contbr of articles to legal publs. Home: 7 Gan Rehavia, Jerusalem, Isr.

BAZELON, David Lionel, US, jurist; b. Superior, Wis, Sep 3, 1909; s. Israel and Lena (Krasnovksy); att U of Ill, 1928-29; BSL, Northwestern U, 1931; hon LLD, Colby Coll, 1966; m. Miriam Kellner, 1936; c: James, Richard. Chief judge, US Court of Appeals, DC Circuit, since 1962, judge, 1949-62; prof, psycht, George Washington U, since 1966; sr mem, law firm, Gottlieb and Schwartz, 1940-46; asst atty-gen, US, 1946-49. Pres, Amer Orthopsycht Assn, 1968-69; mem: PHS, Natl Adv MH Council, 1967-71; DC, Chgo, Fed and Amer Bar Assns; bd trustees, Salk Inst, since 1962; club, Cosmos. Recipient: Isaac Ray Award, Amer Psycht Assn, 1960. Home: 3020 University Terrace, NW, Washington, DC. Office: US Courthouse, Washington, DC.

BAZELON, David T, US, attorney, educator, writer; b. Shreveport, La, Mar 2, 1923; s. Jacob and Florence (Groner); att U of Ill, 1940-41; U of Va, 1941-42; U of Chgo, 1942; BS, Columbia U, 1949; LLB, Yale U, 1953; div: s. Coleman. Prof, policy sci, SUNY since 1969: asso attorney: Hays, Podell, Algase, Crum and Feuer; Paul, Weiss, Rifkind, Wharton and Garrison; instr, Bard Coll, 1949-50; visiting f, Inst of Policy Studies, 1963-65; visiting prof, Rutgers Law Sch, 1965-67; Guggenheim f, 1967-68; writer-reporter for TV series; cons: Aspen Inst of Humanistic Studies; Rel and Lab Council of Amer; Amer Inst of Planners; Natl Humanities Fac. Mem: PEN; Authors Guild; League for Ind Democracy; Assn of Existential Psych and Psycht. Author: The Paper Economy, 1963; Power in America, 1967; contbr of articles and essays to revs, mags and anthols. Home: 849 Delaware Ave, Buffalo, NY. Office: 4224 Ridge Lea Rd, Room 30, Buffalo, NY.

BAZELON, Irwin Allen, US, composer; b. Evanston, Ill, June 4, 1922; s. Roy and Jeanette (Green); BA, De Paul U, Chgo, 1944, MA, 1945; Mills Coll, Oakland, Cal, 1945-47; m. Cecile Gray. Composer: Overture to Shakespeare's The Taming of the Shrew, performed by Natl Gal Orch, 1964; Concert Overture, at Carnegie Hall, 1965; Excursion for Orchestra, by Kan City Philharmonic Orch, 1966; Dramatic Movement for Orchestra, by Seattle Sym Orch, 1966; Short Symphony no 2, Testament to a Big City, Natl Sym Orch, Wash, DC, 1962; by Detroit Sym Orch, conducted by the composer, 1967; Symphony Concertante, clarinet, trumpet & marimba, Detroit Sym Orch, 1970; Symphony 6 Day War, to Isr, Kan City Philharmonic, 1970; numerous symphonies for piano and strings; chamber music, including: Brass Quintet; Duo for Viola and Piano; Early American Suite; String Quartet; music for films, including Jules Dassin's Survival, 1967; music for NBC-TV, including Budd Schulberg's classic novel, What Makes Sammy Run?; sonatas, pieces for piano, clarinet cello. Recipient: Natl & Fed Music Clubs prize, 1947-48; f, Edward MacDowell Assn. Home: 142 E 71 St, New York, NY.

BEANSTOCK, Sam, US, physician; b. London, Eng, Dec 4, 1907; s. Morris and Bluma (Piasetzky); in US since 1921; BS, NYU, 1929; MD, U of Md, 1933; m. Winifred Glennon, Sep 25, 1937. Chief, mental hygiene clinic, VA, San Antonio, Tex, since 1969; phys, VA Hosp: St Cloud, Minn, 1937; Danville, Ill, 1938-40; Chillicothe, O, 1940-42; dir, profsl services, VA Hosp: Roseburg, Oregon, 1952-55; Lebanon, Pa, 1955-57; hosp dir, VA Hosp, Chillicothe, O, 1958-69. Capt, MC, US Army, 1942-45. Dipl, Amer Bd Psycht and Neur; life f: Amer Psycht Assn; Disabled Amer Vets; service f, AMA; cert mental hosp admnr; mem, Ret Offs Assn. Home: 900 Burr Rd, San Antonio, Tex. Office: 307 Dwyer Ave, San Antonio, Tex.

BEAR, Jacob, Isr, engineer; b. Haifa, Feb 2, 1929; s. Isac and Ester (Sternberg); BS, summa cum laude, Technion, 1953, dipl ing, 1957; PhD, U of Cal, Berkeley, 1960; m. Siona Seton, June 14, 1951; c: Eitan, Alon, Iris. Asso prof, Technion, since 1960; head, hydraulics lab, fac civil engr, mem grad comm (option, hydraulic engr), all Technion; cons, hydrology: Water Planning for Isr Ltd, since 1960; Hydrological Serv, Min of Agric, since 1966; visiting prof, Cen for Research in Ground Water, Heb U, Jerusalem, since 1967; fmr: visiting prof, MIT, Mass; visiting lectr, Hydrology Inst, Princeton U; guest lectures and workshops: U of Cal, Berkeley; New Mexico Inst of Tech; USDA, Boise, Idaho. Prin contribs: research in: ground water movement by means of horizontal viscous flow analogy; artificial replenishment, sea water intrusion into coastal aquifers, regional ground water balances; seepage from rivers into layered soils, on transition zone between fresh and salt waters in coastal aquifers and a tensorial description of hydrodynamic dispersion in porous media; drainage of Jordan-Negev conduit; determination of hydraulic conductivity by means of infiltration rings; infiltration of flood water into sand dunes; solving ground water exploitation problems by means of an elec analog. Chmn: hydrology sect, Isr Assn Geodesy and Geophys; Intl Assn Hydraulic Research; mem: Natl Comm Hydrological Decade; Weizmann Inst for Publ Sci and Tech; Engrs and Architects Assn, Isr; adv comm, artificial recharge, Isr Min of Agric; fmr participant in numerous intl confs: Cal, Isr, Ill; mem, panel, Oceanography and Limnology, Isr Research and Devl Council. Mem, ed bd, Israel Jour Earth Scis; contbr of numerous articles to profsl jours. Home: 55 Disraeli St, Haifa, Isr. Office: Technion, Haifa, Isr.

BEBER, Meyer, US, physician, educator; b. Minsk, Russ, Dec 27, 1899; s. Israel and Rose (Greenglass); BS, U of Neb, 1920, PhD, 1925, MD, 1933; m. Lillian Rubenstein, Nov 25, 1926; c: Charles, Bernard. Admnr, Douglas Co Hosp, since 1963, med dir, since 1956; asso prof, internal med, Creighton U Sch of Med, since 1958; prof, internal med, U of Neb Coll of Med, since 1956, asso prof, biochem, since 1955; med staff: Bishop Clarkson Memorial Hosp; Immanuel Hosp. US Army, WWII. F: Amer Coll Phys; Amer Geriatrics Soc; Gerontological Soc; mem: Sigma Xi; Phi Beta Kappa; Alpha Omega Alpha; Zeta Beta Tau; AMA; AAAS; ACHA; Temple Isr. Home: 535 S 35 Ave, Omaha, Neb. Office: 4102 Woolworth Ave, Omaha, Neb.

BEBER, Sam, US, attorney, civic worker; b. Minsk, Russ, Sep 27, 1901; s. Israel and Rose (Greenglass); in US since 1908; LLB, magna cum laude, Creighton Law Sch, Omaha, Neb, 1923; m. Helen Riekes, Aug 2, 1925; c: Harley, Jane Abramson, Joan Katleman. Pres, Bank of Park Forest, Ill, since 1953; vice-pres: Oakbrook Shopping Cen; Oakbrook Utility Co; Old Orchard Shopping Cen; mem bd dirs: Bank of Overbrook; partner, law firm, Beber, Klutznick & Beber, Omaha, 1923-53; gen counsel, Omaha Housing Auth, 1940-50. Found, Aleph Zadik Aleph, B'nai B'rith, 1924, mem, natl exec comm, B'nai B'rith, 1926-41; UJA; pres, Beth El Syn, Omaha, 1929-31; J Philanthropies, 1930; Fed for J Service, 1943-45; mem: bd govs, Comty Chest, 1944-50; bd dirs, Comty Wfr Council, 1946-50, pres, 1947-49; exec comm, Omaha Round Table, NCCJ, 1940-49; bd dirs, Omaha Found, 1945-49; Nelb Adv Defense Comm, 1941-46; Selective Service Sys, WWII; vice-chmn, comm on housing, power and transp; chmn, Speakers' Bur, Omaha Plan; mem: Neb, Amer Bar Assns, Natl Assn of Housing Officials; clubs: Highland, Omaha; Standard; Ravisloe, Chgo. Home: 91 Monee Rd, Park Forest, Ill. Office: 30 Plaza, Park Forest, Ill.

BECK, Abe J, US, army off; b. Dallas, Texas, May 24, 1914; s. Jacob and Mollie (Pollack); LLB, Dallas Sch of Law, S Methodist U, 1939; m. Anne Michlin, Oct 21, 1945; c: Stephanie, Melanie, Darcy, John. Cdr, Warner Robins Air Material Area, since 1968; maj gen, USAF, since 1940; insp gen, SAC, 1963-64; dep chief of staff, material, 1964-66, weapons sys evaluation group, 1966-68. Vice-pres, Middle Ga Boy Scouts of Amer; dir: Macon C of C; United Givers Fund, Macon, Ga; mem, Bar Assn, Texas. Recipient: Legion of

Merit; DFC; AM; MC, British. Hobbies: fishing, hunting, flying. Home: 400 Officers Circle, Robins AFB, Ga. Office: Warner Air Material Area, Robins AFB, Ga.

BECK, Anatole, US, educator; b. NYC, Mar 19, 1930; s. Morris and Minnie (Rosenblum); BA, Bklyn Coll, 1951; MA, Yale U, 1951, PhD, 1956; m. Evelyn Torton, Apr 10, 1954; c: Nina, Micah. Prof, math, U of Wis, since 1966. Co-author: Excursions Into Mathematics, 1969. Home: 4221 Wanetah Trail, Madison, Wis. Office: U of Wisconsin, Madison, Wis.

BECK, Enrique, Switz, author; b. Cologne, Ger, Feb 12, 1904; s. Karl and Hedwig (Meyer). Author of poetry, prose, dramatic works; writer for theatre, radio, periodicals; trans of collected works of Federico Garcia Lorca into German, 9 ed between 1948 and 1969. Recipient, decoration: Ritterkreuz des Befreiungsordens der Spanischen Republik. Home: Klingentalgraben 31, Basle, Switz.

BECK, Samuel J, US, psychologist, author; b. Tecuciu, Rum, July 19, 1896, s. Abraham and Beatrice (Ciora); in US since 1903; BA, cum laude, Harvard U, 1926; MA, Columbia U, 1927, PhD, 1932; m. Anne Goldman, Sep 14, 1926; c: James, Ruth. Prof lectr: dept psycht, U Chgo, since 1948; cons, psych, Michael Reese Hosp, since 1950, head psych lab, 1936-50, fmr: sr res psychol, Boston Psychopathic Hosp, 1929-32; research asso, psycht, Harvard Med Sch, 1932-1933, 1935-1936; f, psycht, Rockefeller Found, 1933-35; prof lectr, dept psych Northwestern U, 1942-60. Pres, clinical div, Amer Psych Assn; Vice-pres, Intl Rorschach Test and Projective Techniques Soc; fmr: pres, Amer Orthopsycht Assn; vice-pres, Intl Soc MH. Author: Introduction to Rorschach Method, 1937; Personality Structure in Schizophrenia, 1938; Rorschach's Test; Vol I, Basic Processes, 1944, 49; Vol II, Variety of Personality Pictures, 1945; Vol III, Advances in Interpretation, 1952; The Six Schizophrenias, 1954; The Rorschach Experiment, 1960; Psychological Processes in the Schizophrenic Adaptations, 1965; co-author, Reflexed to Intelligence, 1959; asso ed, Amer Jour Orthopsycht; prin co-contbr, First Rochester Intl Conf, Origins of Schizophrenia, U Rochester, 1967. Recipient: first annual dist contribution award, clinical div, Amer Psych Assn, 1961; first annual award, Soc Projective Tech, 1965. Home: 5236 Greenwood Ave, Chicago, Ill. Office: U of Chicago, Chicago, Ill.

BECKER, Aharon, Isr, public servant; b. Russ, 1906; in Isr since 1924; m. Cyla Seltzer, 1930; c: Aviva Doron, Tamar Shin'ar, Itzchak. MK, chmn Peretz Naftali Fund; mem: Histadrut exec council; secretariat, Isr Lab Party (Mapai); council dirs, Bank Isr; dep mem, governing body, ILOs; fmr: mem: Kibbutz Ma'avar, 1925; bldg worker, 1926-28; secy, Ramat Gan Lab Council, 1929-32; secy, Union Textile Workers, 1933-34; mgn dir, ind dept, Coop Wholesale Soc, 1934-47; head, supply mission, Min of Defense, 1948-49; head, trade union dept, mem exec bur, Histadrut, 1949-61; secy-gen, Histadrut, 1961-69. Contbr numerous articles, booklets, to Isr and Brit press. Home: 66 Keren Kayemet Blvd, Tel Aviv, Isr. Office: Knesset, Jerusalem, Isr.

BECKER, James Herman, US, investment banker; b. Chgo, Dec 11, 1894; s. Abraham and Kate (Friedman); AB, Cornell U, 1917; m. Hortense Koller, June 4, 1928; c: Jane, Kate. Chmn, A. G. Becker & Co, since 1961, pres since 1947, dir since 1921; dir: Midas-Intl, since 1965; H Elkan, since 1968; Cyclops Steel Corp, 1937; City Stores Co, 1951; Parents, Inst, 1951; Enterprise Paint Mfg, 1958. Vice-chmn and dir, JDC, since 1926; hon trustee, Sinai Temple, Chgo; mem: Cornell U Council; Orch Assn. Home: 55 Oakvale, Highland Park, Ill. Office: 1 First Natl Plaza, Chicago, Ill.

BECKER, Lavy Mordecai, Can, business exec; b. Montreal, Can, Jan 22, 1905; s. Barnet and Jennie (Temchin); BA, McGill U, 1926; MHL, JTSA, 1930; MA, Columbia U, 1935; m. Augusta Shapiro, June 22, 1927; c: Hillel, Miriam. Pres: Marvel Ind, Ltd, Montreal; Lavy M. Becker Cons; vice-pres, Rubenstein Bros, Montreal; fmr: with JDC, Ger, NY, 1945-47; rabbi, Sunnyside, NY; social worker: Detroit, New Haven; Montreal; New Haven; New Eng regional sup, JWB. Pres, J Tchrs Sem, Montreal; life trustee, Allied J Comty Services; hon rabbi, pres, Fed of Reconstructionist, Reconstructionist Syns, US, Can and Curacao; governing council, WJC; bd dirs, J Telegraphic Agcy, NY; natl chmn, J Bicentenary Comm; clubs: Elmridge Country; U; fmr, chmn exec, Can J Cong. Home: 4831 Ponsard Ave, Montreal, Can, Office: 9393 Blvd St Laurent, Montreal, Can.

BECKER, Myer, US, business exec; b. Bialystok, Russ, June 2, 1898; s. Bernard and Freida (Smolian); in US since 1907; att Tulane U, 1914-15; U of Ala, 1916-17; BS, Columbia U, 1919; m. Sylvia Cohen, Jan 5, 1936; c: Jay, Brenda. Pres: Becker Apparel Corp, since 1945; Becker Trading Corp, since 1947. Cpl, US Army. Pres: B'nai B'rith Lodge, 1936-45; Va Assn Lodges, 1944; Beth Isr Cong, 1964-65; chmn bd, 1950, pres men's club, 1951; cdr, JWV post, 1941; chmn, UJA, Roanoke, 1943-44; natl adv council, student aid fund, Grad Sch of Bus, Columbia U, 1955-57; chef de gare, Amer Legion, 1946; mem: Phi Sigma Delta; Beta Gamma Sigma; Masons. Home: 2735 Richelieu Ave, Roanoke, Va. Office: 127 W Campbell Ave, Roanoke, Va.

BECKER, Ruth Henrietta, US, educator, registered nurse; b. Berlin, Mar 6, 1922; d Hans and Kate (Salzmann), in US since 1940; RN, Mt Sinai Hosp, 1945; BS, Columbia U, 1950, MA, 1952; m. Samuel Becker, June 14, 1953; c: Judith, Harold, Anne. Night sup, Mt Sinai Hosp Sch of Nursing, NYC, 1945-46; instr, 1946-52; med instr, U of Ia Coll of Nursing, 1952-54, research asso, 1956-62. Bd dir, treas, sup, Day Care Cen; mem bd, Johnson Co Dem Women's Club, since 1963, pres, 1967-68; various offs, Natl Assn for Retarded Children, Johnson since 1960; Hist Soc of Ia; Auxilliary of Goodwill Ind of SE Ia; Agudas Achim Syn; UN Assn; U Club. Recipient: award, Ia Assn Retarded Children, 1963. Home: 521 W Park Rd, Iowa City, Ia.

BECKER, Samuel L, US, educator; b. Quincy, Ill, Jan 5, 1923; s. Nathan and Rose (Dicker); MA, U of Ia, 1949, PhD, 1953; postdoc f, Columbia U, 1958-59; m. Ruth Salzmann, June 14, 1953; c: Judith, Harold, Anne. Chmn, dept of speech and dramatic art, U of Ia, since 1968; prof, communication research and bc, since 1950; dir, radio, U of Wyo, 1949-50; instr, radio, TV tech, State U of Ia, 1950-56, prof, dir, div of TV, radio, film, 1956. Bd dirs, Goodwill Inds of SE Ia; mem: Speech Assn of Amer; Natl Assn of Educ Bcs; Assn for Profsl Bc Educ; Natl Soc for Study of Communications; Amer Educ Theatre Assn; Natl Assn for Retarded Children; AAUP; Ia State Comm on Educ TV; Delta Sigma Rho; Pi Delta Epsilon. Author: Television: Techniques for Planning and Performance, 1958; A Bibliographical Guide to Research in Speech and Dramatic Art, 1963; ed, Speech Monographs; contbr to scholarly jours. Home: 521 W Park Rd, Iowa City, Ia. Office: U of Ia, Iowa City, Ia.

BECKER, Stephen David, US, author; b. Mt Vernon, NY, Mar 31, 1927; s. David and Lilian (Kevitz); AB, Harvard Coll, 1947; att Yenching U, Peking, China, 1947-48; m. Mary Freebrug, Dec 24, 1947; c: Keir, Julia, David. Author: The Season of the Stranger, 1951; Shanghai Incident, 1955; Juice, 1959; A Covenant with Death, 1964; The Outcasts, 1967; When the War is Over, 1969; non-fiction: Comic Art in America, 1959; Marshall Field III, 1964; trans from Fr, including, The Last of the Just, 1960; contbr to periodicals. Mem fac, Brandeis U, 1951-52; prof, U of Alaska, 1967; lectr at various Us. Pvt, USMC, 1945, Hobbies: sailing, navigation. Home: Todd Rd, Katonah, NY.

BECKER, Yakov, Isr, party official; b. Chelem, Pol, Mar 3, 1904; s. Israel and Rachel (Diamont); m. Faga Baum, 1937; m. 2nd, Froma Yakotivsky, 1954; c: Tova Levi, Moshe, Menahem. Mem, cen comm, Mapam; ed, Mapam Yiddish newspaper, since 1949. Pvt, Pol Army, 1925-27. Mem: Org of J Writers; fmr, munic council, Chelem, Pol; secy, Tailors Union. Home: 18 Kaplanski St, Tel Aviv, Isr. Office: 20 Yehuda Halevi St, Tel Aviv, Isr.

BECKER, Yechiel, Isr, virologist; b. Tel Aviv, June 29, 1931; s. Elimelech and Esther; MSc, with distinction, Heb U, Jerusalem, 1957, PhD, 1960; m. Miriam Rechavi; c: Rakefet, Oren. Asso prof, virology, Hadassah Med Sch, Jerusalem, since 1968; IDF. Author: Viruses as Molecules, 1969. Home: Shmaryahu Levin St, Jerusalem, Isr, Office: Hadassah Med Sch, Jerusalem, Isr.

BECKERMAN, Bernard, US, educator; b. NYC, Sep 24, 1921; s. Morris and Elizabeth (Sheftel); BSS, CCNY, 1942; MFA, Yale U, 1943; PhD, Columbia U, 1956; m. Gloria Brim, Aug 21, 1940; c: Jonathan, Michael. Prof, dramatic arts, chmn, theatre arts div, Columbia U, since 1965; chmn, drama, Hofstra U, 1955-65; visiting Fulbright pof, Tel Aviv U, 1960-61. Sgt, US Army 1943-45. Bd dirs, Amer Educ Theatre Assn. Author: Shakespeare at the Globe, 1962; Dynamics of Drama, 1970. Recipient: Bronze Star; 7th annual award, Amer Shakespeare Festival & Acad. Home: 27 W 67 St, New York, NY. Office: Columbia U, New York, NY.

BECKHARD, Julius, US, business exec, communal worker; b. Stuttgart, Ger, May 30, 1896; s. Gustave and Mathilde (Dreifuss); in US since 1923; m. Erna Sinn, Sep 3, 1922 (decd); m. 2nd, Vera Krueger, Aug, 20, 1948; c: Hanna Aron, Herbert, Eva Hommel. Head, found, The Bekhard Line, since 1924. Ger Army, 1914-18. Pres, LI Lodge, B'nai B'rith, 1954-55, vice-pres, metrop council, 1947-49, dist repr, natl services comm for armed forces and vets since 1947; bd founds, LI J Hosp, 1950; bd trustees, Natl J Hosp, Denver, Colo, 1958-60; bd govs, Jt Defense Appeal, 1958-62; vice-pres, adv bd, ADL, NY, adv bd, Eur Affairs Comm; creator, Henry Monsky Memorial Athletic Field, VA Hosp; natl commn, B'nai B'rith Vocational Guidance service, since 1962; chmn: comty, permanent exec bd, FJP, 1954-61; spec gifts, UJA, 1959-50; Henry Monsky Found, 1961; mem: Metrop Syn, NYC; club, Inwood Police Boys, pres, 1951-54, chmn, bd, since 1954. Hobbies: music, opera, photography. Home: 80 Park Ave, New York, NY. Office: 230 Fifth Ave, New York, NY.

BECKMAN, Theodore N, US, educator, author, consulting econ; b. Dzigovka, Russ, Sep 3, 1895; s. Nahum and Pearl (Treistman); in US since 1914; BS, O State U, 1920, MA, 1922, PhD, 1924; m. Esther Baker, 1920 (decd); c: Gloria Volk, Marilyn Myers, Joanne Cooper; m. 2nd, Sarah Langue, 1962; c: Yona Lowenthal, Edwin Langue, Marilyn Bress. Prof em, marketing, O State U, since 1966, fac mem since 1920; visiting prof, U of Colo, 1939-40; instr, Columbus chap, Natl Inst of Credit Men, 1921-25; dir, wholesale application prog, Allied Food Comm, Louisville, Ky, 1929; i/c of first wholesale census of distribution, Census Bur, 1929-32; cons: Census of Amer Bus, 1933-35; Dept of Commerce, 1934-36; Natl Defense Adv Comm, 1940; Dept of Lab, 1941, 54, 62; Off of Civilian Supply, War Produc Bd, 1942; Atty Gen's off, State of O, 1955; spec cons to eds of G and C Merriam Co (Webster's Dicts) on marketing terminology, 1956; cons econ for firms and trade assns on tax matters and anti-trust cases. F, Intl Inst of Arts and Letters; vice-pres: Amer Stat Assn, 1940; Amer Marketing Assn, 1939; bd dirs, devl fund, O State U; Presidents Club, OSU; hon chmn, Distribution Research and Educ Found; bd trustees: Natl Assn of Wholesalers, hon; Columbus Sym Orch; United J Fund and Council; mem: Amer J JDC; O State Alumni Assn; Hall of Fame in Distribution; Amer Ind Bankers Assn; Amer Legion; B'nai B'rith; Temple Isr; adv bd, Hillel Found; Newcomen Soc; Beta Gamma Sigma; Tau Delta Phi; Mu Beta Chi; hon mem, Sales Execs Club, Columbus, O; clubs: Cosmos, Wash, DC; Winding Hollow Country, Columbus, O; O State U Fac. Author: Credits and Collections: Management and Theory, 1924, 8th ed, 1969; Wholesaling, 1926; co-author: Marketing, 8th ed, 1967; asso ed, Jour of Marketing, 1935-38; contbr to bus and profsl mags, encys; US Govt printing off vols and monographs. Recipient: Paul D Converse award, Amer Marketing Assn, 1959; Cen O chap award, 1960; Marketing Educ of the Year, Sales and Marketing Exec Intl, 1962; O State U Alumni award for distinguished teaching, 1962. Home: 2158 N Parkway, Columbus, O. Office: Hagerty Hall, Ohio State U, Columbus, O.

BECKMANN, Albert Jules, US, physician; b. NYC, Mar 2, 1917; s. Charles and Rose Tepper (Clair); BA, Cornell U, 1938; MS, Sch of Public Health, U of NC, 1941; MD, Bowman Gray Sch of Med, Wake Forest Coll, 1945; m. Blanche Cooper, 1957; c: Robin, Randi. Asso prof, public health practice, Sch of Public Health and Admn Med, Columbia U, since 1968, fac mem since 1951; chief, ped, Franklin Gen Hosp, since 1963, pres, med staff, 1967; lectr, Pulitzer Sch of Journalism, Columbia U, since 1964; asst ped, Babies Hosp, Columbia U, since 1952; att phys, Meadowbrook Hosp, Nassau Co, since 1956; research asso, Sch of Public Health, Columbia U, 1949-51; asst chief, med service, Brooke Gen Hosp, Ft Sam Houston, Tex, 1946-47; chief, ped, Ft Clayton Gen Hosp, US Army, Caribbean, Panama Canal Zone, 1947-48; att ped, St John's Guild Floating Hosp, since 1952. Capt, US Army MC, 1946-48. F: Amer Public Health Assn; AAAS; Royal Soc of Health; mem: AMA. Contbr to med jours. Home and office: 111 Hempstead Ave, Malverne, Long Island, NY.

BEDERMAN, Nathan B, US, buisiness exec; b. Chgo, July 19,

1900; s. Michael and Clara (Berwin); att YMCA Coll, 1917-19; m. Virginia Stiefel, Jan 16, 1922; c: Alfred, James, Jeanne Aronson. Fmr pres, Arcole Midwest Corp. Cdr, US Navy, 1943-45. Vice-chmn, bd, Coll of J Studies, Chgo; dir, Lyric Opera, Chgo; fmr dir, J Comty Cens. Home: 22 Lakewood Pl, Highland Pk, Ill. Office: 580 Roger Willams Ave, Highland Pk, Ill.

BEEM, Hartog, Netherlands, teacher; b. Harderwijk, Dec 13, 1892; s. Abraham and Eva (de Vries); dipl, Ger lang and lit, U of Leiden, 1928; m. R Kannewasser, Aug 24, 1920. Tchr: HS, Leeuwarden, since 1929; Den Helder, Dordrecht secondary schools, 1917-29. Mem: ZF of Netherlands; exec comm, cen bd educ, Israelitisch Kerkgenootschap. Author: Tenach (trans), 1951; De Verdwenen Mediene, 1951, Yiddish in Holland, 1954; Jerosche, 1959; Het Jiddisj en zijn resten in Nederland, 1961; Woordenboekje van het nederlandse Yiddisch, 1967; contbr to periodicals. Home: 424 Diependaalse Laan, Hilversum, Netherlands.

BEER, A Robert, US, realtor; b. NYC, Apr 8, 1918; s. Alfred and Fannye (Heller); BS, Wharton Sch Finance and Commerce, U of Pa, 1939; att S Methodist U, 1952-53; Harvard Bus Sch, 1954; Ind U; U of Chgo; m. Geraldine Danzer, June 6, 1941; c: Alfred, David, Jonathan. Pres, Robert Beer and Co, Realtors; secy-treas, Real Estate Inst, Commercial Coll; vice-pres, treas, Miller-Beer, since 1952; treas, EM Kahn, 1947-52; lectr, S Methodist U. US Navy, 1943-46. Dir, Dallas Jr C of C; found mem, pres, SW Retail Controllers Assn; mem, large cities budgeting conf, CJFWF; treas, vice-chmn, dir, AJComm, Dallas chap; budget chmn, dir, J Wfr Fed, Dallas; speakers bur, NCCJ; steering comm, SW Intergroup Relations Council; exec comm, Neighbors for Fair Housing; Texas delg, World Cong, Brussels, 1949; pres, Dallas J Comty Cen, 1953-54; vice-pres, Temple Emmanuel Brotherhood, 1957; past dir, Dallas Bd Realtors; mem, Columbia Club. Hobby: photography. Home: 6542 Northwood Rd, Dallas, Tex. Office: 3131 Stemmons Freeway, Dallas, Tex.

BEERI, Eliezer, Isr, orientalist; b. Mannheim, Ger, Apr 29, 1914; s. Theodor and Anna (Strauss) Bauer; in Isr since 1937; att U Berlin; m. Lisel Reiss, July, 1937; c: Chanoch, Ruth, Gilead. Fmr dir: Arab workers' br, Isr Min of Lab, 1948-49; Arab dept, Mapam, 1952-55; Givat Haviva, Adult Educ Cen, Hashomer Hatzair, 1959-61. Haganah, IDF. Secy, Kibbutz Hazorea, 1956-61. Author: Hakatzuna ve-ha-schilton ba-'olam ha-'aravi, Army Officers in Arab Politics and Society. Home: Kibbutz Hazorea, Isr.

BEERI, Tuvia, Isr, painter; b. Topolcany, Czech, Aug 29, 1929; s. Moritz and Etel (Rosenbaum) Braun; in Isr since 1948; tchr, Oranim, Tivon, 1959. One-man shows: Katz Gal, 1961; Dugit Gal, 1965; Gal Contemporaine, Geneva, 1966; Gal Isr Arts, NY, 1967; Kunstkreis Leinfelden, Ger, 1968; Stuttgart U, 1969; La Nouvelle Gravure, Paris, 1969; Bineth Gal, Tel Aviv, 1969; group exhbs; NY, SF, Paris, Tel Aviv, Jerusalem, Sao Paolo, Haifa, Montreal, Firenze, Art tchr: Bezalel, Jerusalem, 1964-66; Avni Art Sch, Tel Aviv, 1964. Home and studio: 18 Hirshenberg, Tel Aviv, Isr.

BEERMAN, Herman, US, physician, educator; b. Johnstown, Pa, Oct 13, 1901; s. Morris and Fanny (Toby); BA, U of Pa, 1923, MD, 1927, DS, 1935; m. Emma Segal, May 13, 1924. Prof: dermat, U of Pa Sch of Med, since 1956, fac mem since 1929; Grad Sch of Med, U of Pa since 1947, chmn, 1949-67, fac mem since 1940; cons, Grad Hosp, U of Pa, since 1967, on staff since 1953; asso, Pepper Lab, since 1950; asst chief, dermat clinic, House U of Pa, 1938-65; asst dir, Inst for Study of Venereal Diseases, U of Pa, 1953-54; head, dept, dermat, Pa Hosp, 1947-67; hon cons, Phila Gen Hosp, 1953-68; dermat Skin and Cancer Hosp, 1947-54; cons, Coatesville VA Hosp, since 1967, on staff since 1953; cons: to lab, Children's Hosp, since 1949; Phila Psycht Hosp, 1950-57; USPHS, since 1937. Dipl, Amer Bd Dermat and Syphilology, 1935; Abbott f, chemotherapeutic research, 1932-46; f: Phila Coll Phys; Amer Coll Phys; AAAS; pres: Soc for Inves Dermat, 1947-48; Amer Soc Dermat, 1965-66; Amer Acad Dermat, 1965-66; Amer Dermat Assn, 1967-68; Assn of Profs of Dermat, 1967-68; Phila Dermat Soc, 1940-41, 1958-59; trustee: Dermat Found, 1963-68; Inst for Dermat Communication and Educ, since 1962; chmn, Comm on Infectious Diseases, 1968; mem: Phila Co Med Soc; Comm on Public Health and Med Studies; Comm on Medico-Legal Affairs;

Med Soc State of Pa; Amer Soc U Profs; Phys Soc of Phila; Amer Med Writers Assn; NY Acad of Sci; Amer Venereal Disease Assn; Tissue Culture Assn; Solomon Solis-Cohen Med Lit Soc; John Morgan Soc; Intl Soc of Tropical Dermat; (ed bd, Amer Jour of Med Sci, 1937-66; bd ed, Excerpta Medica); Phila Art Alliance; Phila Mus of Art; Sigma Xi; Phi Lambda Kappa; Med Club of Phila; hon men: Academia Espanola de Dermat y Sifilografia, Madrid; Dermat Assn of Pol; Deutsche Dermat Gesellschaft; Finnish Dermat Soc; Greek Dermat and Venereological Union; Intl Coll Experimental Dermat, U of Palermo; Iranian Soc Dermat and Venereology; Isr Dermat Soc; Laboratorio de Inves Leprologicas, Rosario, Arg; Pacific Dermat Assn; Societati Dermat Danicae; Sociedad Venezolana de Dermat, Venereologia y Leprologia, Caracas; corresp mem: Arg Dermat Assn; Swed Dermat Soc; fgn corresp mem, Soc de Dermat et de Syphiligraphia; hon life mem, Med Soc for Study of Venereal Diseases, London; hon mem, British Assn of Dermat. Mem, bd eds, Excerpta Medica, since 1950; ed bd, Amer Jour Med Sci, 1937-66; contbr to profsl jours. Recipient: Annual Herman Beerman Lecture, Soc for Inves Dermat, Inc, since 1960. Home: 2422 Pine St, Philadelphia, Pa. Office: 255 S 17 St, Philadelphia, Pa.

BEGIN, Menachem, Isr, statesman; b. Breast-Litovsk, Aug 31, 1913; s. Ze'ev-Dov and Chasia (Kossovsky); in Isr since 1942; MJ, U Warsaw, 1935; m. Aliza Arnold, 1939; c: Benyamin, Chasia, Leah. MK since 1949; mem, Govt Natl Unity, 1967-70; head, Betar Movement, 1939; arrested by Soviet Secret Police, 1940; deported, 1941, concentration camp Piechora-Lag; sentenced eight yrs for Zionist activities; released after Stalin-Sikorski agreement; joined Pol Army; cdr, Irgun Zvai Leumi, 1943 until Independence 1948; chmn, Herut (Freedom) party. Author: The Revolt; White Nights; Underground papers, 4 vols; contbr to Isr and fgn press. Office: Knesset, Jerusalem, Isr.

BEHAM, Yohanan, Isr, government official; b. Ger, Aug 9, 1918; s. Zeev and Franziska (Gimkiewcz) Boehm; in Isr since 1936; tchrs cert, Heb Tchrs Coll, Jerusalem, 1940; MA, Columbia U, NY, 1949; m. Bertha Bochner, 1959. Exec vice-chmn, Isr Mus, Jerusalem; fmr: tchr, Haifa HS, 1940-45; secy gen, Isr Min Fianance, 1949-52; econ edv staff, Govt of Isr, 1953-55; dir, Isr Govt Tourist Corp, 1955-61. Home: 5 Shalom Aleichem St, Jerusalem, Isr. Office: Israel Museum, Jerusalem, Isr.

BEHAR, Yakir, Isr, insurance agt, communal worker; b. Adrianople, Turkey, Apr 4, 1890; s. Joseph and Donna (Bahmoiram); in Isr since 1931; grad Us: Zurich; Venice; m. Bianca Cesana, Dec 14, 1919; c: Joseph. Independent ins agt, repr fgn co's, since 1952; fmr: prof, econ, law, Constantinople, 1913-1919; 1st J prof, Turkish Women's U; delg by Turkish Min of Educ to study at Swiss, Ger commercial colls; participated in loan negotiations, Turkish Govt, 1918-19; banker, It; mgr, Tel Aviv br, Banco di Roma; lectr, marine transp, Sch of Law and Econ; lectr, marine transp ins, Tel Aviv U; repr, Pal Mfrs Assn, commercial negotiations with Rum. Co-found, life pres, Tel Aviv-Yaffo Union of Sephardic Syns; life mem, Isr B'nai B'rith Lodge; mem exec, Natl Sephardic Council of Isr; mem: Va'ad Leumi; Emergency Fund Comm; Assn for UN, mission on behalf of Heb U to Egypt, Syria, Lebanon, 1942; mgr, Pardess Coop Soc; sr active mem, Tel Aviv Rotary Club; fmr: co-found, pres: Tel Aviv-Yaffo Sephardic Union; Tel Aviv-Yaffo Rel Council; mem, council for prep, Provisional J Govt in Diaspora; delg to consecration of Pal Dist XIV Lodges, B'nai B'rith, 1924; delg to conv, Atlantic City, co-found, Cen Eur Lodges, Prague; recd by Pope Benedictus XIV, 1919; mem loan comm, Tel Aviv-Yaffo Munic; clubs: Commercial and Ind; Rotary; life mem, Dante Alighiere Soc. Author: textbooks on law, econ, in Fr, Turkish, Heb; contbr of articles in Eng, Ladino. Home: 7 Bezalel Yaffe St, Tel Aviv, Isr.

BEHR, Werner Meyer, Eng, financial adv; b. Weissenfels, Ger, Dec 31, 1902; s. Max and Helene (Moses); att Gymnasium, Königstat, Ger; m. Sarah Luft; c: Marc. Owner, bus, financial adv; financial dir, N Israel, Berlin, 1923-39. Vice-chmn: Assn of J in Gt Brit, London; Council of Ger J; mem bd, Leo Baeck Charitable Trust; dir, Inst of Contemporary Hist & Wiener Libr; treas, Allocations Comm of Cen Brit Fund; chmn, Thank You Brit Fund; fmr, mem bd of dep, Brit J, Eng. Home: 2 Telegraph Hill, London NW3, Eng. Office: 6 Broad St Pl, London EC2, Eng.

BEHRMAN, Samuel Nathaniel, US, playwright; b. Worcester, Mass, June 9, 1893; s. Joseph and Zelda (Feingold); BA, Harvard Coll, 1916; MA, Columbia U, 1918; m. Elza Heifetz, 1936; c: Arthur. Playwright since 1927; asst ed, NY Times Book Review, 1918; contbr to: Smart Set; New Republic; Seven Arts; New Yorker; Masses. Author, plays: The Second Man, 1927, produced NYC, with Alfred Lunt and Lynn Fontanne, and London with Noel Coward; Serena Blandish, 1928; Meteor, 1929; Brief Moment, 1932; Biography, 1933; Love Story, 1934; Rain from Heaven, 1935; End of Summer, 1936; Amphitryon, adapted from Fr, 1937; Wine of Choice, 1938; No Time for Comedy, 1939; The Talley Method, 1941; The Pirate, 1942; Jacobowsky and the Colonel (with Franz Werfel), 1944; Dunnigan's Daughter, 1945; Jane, 1946; I Know My Love, 1949; Duveen, biography, 1952; Fanny (with Joshua Logan), 1954; The Cold Wind and the Warm, 1958; Lord Pengo, 1962; But For Whom Charlie, 1964; The Suspended Drawing Room, 1965; books: The Worcester Account, 1954; Portrait of Max, 1960; The Burning Glass, novel, 1968; numerous Hollywood films. Co-found, Playwrights Co, with Robert E Sherwood, Elmer Rice, Sidney Howard, Maxwell Anderson, John Wharton, 1938; mem, Natl Inst Arts and Letters. Office: 1185 Park Ave, New York, NY.

BEIER, Samuel K, US, attorney; b. NYC, Sep 22, 1901; s. David and Yetta (Hyman); BA, CCNY; LLB, NYU Law School; m. Min Price, June 19, 1932; c: David, Judith. Pvt practice since 1922; Spec Dep Atty Gen; candidate, US House of Reprs, 12th Dist, NY; commn, Condemnation and Appraisal, NY. Dir: W Side Instl Syn; Solomon Kluger Yeshiva; Beth Jacob Sch; Ohav Sholom; Ozor Hatorah; Shomrei Hadath; mem: NY Co Lawyers Assn, city court, criminal court, profsl comms; Theta Sigma Lambda; Amer, NY Co, and NY State Bar Assns; Masons; City Coll and NYU Alumni Assns; club, Fed Rep, fmr pres, bd dirs. Home: 334 W 86 St, New York, NY. Office: 250 Broadway, New York, NY.

BEIERFIELD, Sam J, US, manufacturers repr; b. Baltimore, July 16, 1902; s. Abraham and Mollie (Honigsberg); att: Baltimore City Coll, 1920; U of Md, 1924; m. Helen Fine, June 20, 1929; c: Abby. Mfrs repr, in commercial and ind lighting, since 1957; owner, High Rock Ginger Ale Co, 1929-57. Fmr chmn: Louisville Conf of J Org; United J Campaign; vice-pres: YMHA; Council for J Wfr Fed, SW region; mem: JWB; Amer Fund for Isr Instns; United Isr Appeal; B'nai B'rith; KP; Elks; Shriners; club, Standard Country. Home: 151 N Craig St, Pittsburgh, Pa.

BEIN ALEXANDER, Isr, historian, archivist, author; b. Steinach, Ger, Jan 21, 1903; s. Moritz and Lina (Bruckheim); in Isr since 1933; PhD, Berlin U, 1926; m. Betty Bildstein, 1928; c: Yohanan, Nehemia. State archivist, State of Isr, since 1956; dir, cen Zionist Archives, Jerusalem, since 1955; archivist, Deutsches Reichsarchiv, Potsdam, 1927-33; lectr, archives courses, Heb U, Jerusalem. Chmn, Isr Archives Assn; mem, exec commn, Inst for Zionist Research, Tel Aviv; Intl Council of Archives; mem bd, Isr Hist Soc; mem council, Yad ve Shem. Author: (in Ger) Die Staatsidee Alexander Hamilton in ihrer Enstehung und Entwicklung, 1927; Friedrich Hammacher, 1932; Der Zionismus und Sein Werk, 1939; (in Heb) Theodor Herzl, Biography, 2 vols, 1934, 39, rev ed, 1 vol, 1961 (Ger ed, 1934; Eng, 1940; 6th rev, illustrated ed, 1957; paperback ed, 1962); Arye Leib Motzkin, 1939; The Return to the Soil, A History of Jewish Settlement in Israel (Heb eds, 1943, 45, 51; Eng ed, 1952; also in Dutch, Hung, Rum, Yiddish); Herzl and Dreyfus, 1949; Israel's Charter of Freedom, 1949 (eds: Eng, Hung, It, Span, reprints, 1966); Nehemia de Lieme, 1950; With Herzl and in His Footsteps, 1954; Modern Antisemitism and its Place in the History of the Jewish Question (Heb, Eng, Ger), 1958; The Future of Our Past (Heb), 1963; The Jewish Parasite — Notes on the Semantics of the Jewish Problem (Eng, Ger, Heb), 1964-66; Franz Oppenheimer (Heb, Ger), 1965; ed, in Heb, The Motzkin Book, 1939; My Life and Work: The Autobiography and Diary of Arthur Ruppin, 2 vols, 1944, 47, new ed, 3 vols, 1968; Herzl's Complete Works, 1954; contbr to: Brockhaus Ency; Germania Judaica; Heb Ency; Ency Judaica; anthols; profsl mags; daily press. Home: 3 Benjamin Metudela St, Jerusalem, Isr. Office: POB 92, Jerusalem, Isr.

BEIN, Shlomo Siegfried, Isr, business executive; b. Steinach Saale Bavaria, Ger, Apr 11, 1897; s. Moritz and Lina (Bruckheim); in Isr since 1933; att Tech U, Berlin, 1923-26; m. Elizabeth Figner, (decd); m. 2nd, Elizabeth Bakker; c: Hilde

Nativ, Rachel Lux. Ret since 1968; mgn dir, S Bein and Co, Ltd, Haifa, 1934-68; mgr; Bayer Spiegelglasfabriken AG Bavaria, Ger, 1920-23; Bechmann Kupter AG, Berlin, 1924-30; Reinspiegel AH, Bonn, Ger, 1930-33; munic judge, Haifa, 1958-64; mem, Income Tax Consulting Comm, 1958-68. Lt. Ger Army, 1916-18; Haganah, 1936-48; vice-pres, BBB, Haifa; hon treas, Mt Carmel Comm, Haifa: mem exec cen, Independent Lib Party; Home: 57 Sea Rd, Mt Carmel, Haifa, Isr. Office: 11 Bank St, Hakfa, Ksr.

BEIN, William, US organization exec; b. Monor, Hung, Sep 21, 1898; s. Elias and Rosalie (Rosenstein); m. Ann Rudo, 1961; c: Ilona Urbach. Dir, spec progs, Conf on J Material Claims against Ger, since 1954; exec positions with JDC for over 30 years. Found, hon secy, Natl Parkinson Found; mem, bd trustees, Margaret Sanger Research Bur, NY. Recipient: Officer of Polonia Restituta, 1947; Officer of Ouissam Alaouite, 1953. Home: 50 E 72 St, New York, NY. Office: 3 E 54 St, New York, NY.

BEINART, Ben Zion, S Afr, advocate, educator; b. Melmesbury, S Afr, Oct 21, 1914; s. Israel and Gitel (Apter); BA, U of Cape Town, 1934, LLB, 1936; att LSE, U of London, 1937-39; barrister-at-law, Grey's Inn, London, 1940; m. Gladys Levy, June 22, 1945; c: Ann, William, Helen. WP Schreiner prof, Roman law, U of Cape Town, since 1950, asst prin, student affairs since 1969, dean, law fac, 1954-56, 1964-66; pvt practice, Grahamstown, 1945-49; prof, law, head dept, Rhodes U Coll, 1945-49; visiting prof: U Edinburgh, 1961, 1965; U Birmingham, 1968-69. Lt, S Afr Defense Force, 1940-44. Mem: comm, Civil Rights League, since 1950, past chmn; comm, Cape Town Soc, Friends of Heb U, since 1961; fmr mem, council, U of Cape Town; Royal Commonwealth Soc, London; Friends of It Assn; Wine Tasters' Guild; clubs: Owl, Cape Town; Albany, Grahamstown; fmr: chmn, S Afr Inst for Intl Affairs; mem exec, S Afr Inst Race Relations, W Cape regional chmn. Co-author: Stipulation and Theory of Contract, 1957; co-ed: DG van der Keessel: Dictata ad Institutiones, 1962; trans from Latin into Eng, Johannes Voet, Title 19.2, pub 1941; jt ed, Butterworths S Afr Law Review, 1954-57; gen ed, Acta Juridica, Cape Town, since 1958; mem, ed bd, Tydskif vir Hedendaagse Romeins-Hollandse Reg, since 1958; contbr articles to law jours and reviews. Home: Tusculanum, Upper Bowwood Rd, Claremont, Cape, S Afr. Office: U of Cape Town, Rondebosch, Cape, S Afr.

BEINART, Haim, Isr, historian, b. Pskow, Russ, Nov 14, 1917; s. Yoseph and Sheina (Zarchin) Leib; in Isr since 1937; att Gymnasium Ivri, Riga, Latvia; MA, Heb U, Jerusalem, 1947, PhD, 1956; m. Ruth Edelstein, Nov 7, 1951; c: Yael, Yosef, Haguith, Shlomo. Assoc prof, J medieval hist, Heb U, since 1966; acad adv, Inst for Higher Educ, Beersheva, since 1965; fmr: sci secy, Heb Bibl Ency, 1944-60; instr, lectr, sr lectr, Heb U, 1952-1966; hon secy, 5th World Cong of J Studies. IDF, War of Independence, Sinai Campaign. Prin contribs: research on J of Spain, Port; the Inquisition; the Sephardic dispersion. Author: Anusim beDin haInquisizia, 1965; contbr articles to reviews, jours. Recipient: A Ruppin award, 1966. Home: 11 Ibn Ezra St, Jerusalem, Isr. Office: Hebrew University, Jerusalem, Isr.

BEIRAN, David, Isr, physician; b. Tarnopol, Pol, June 8, 1920; s. Moses and Jetti (Herzog) Biberstein; in Isr since 1934; MD, U of Geneva, 1953; spec, Kaplan Hosp, Rehovoth; m. Talia Mehrer, Oct 13, 1953; c: Anat. Dir, Kaplan Hosp, since 1968, med cons, 1961-63; med adv, Govt of Malawi, 1964-67. Secy, Med Assn, Rehovoth; mem, Isr Med Assn. Contbr to profsl jours. Spec interests: J hist, lit. Home: 5 Gordon St, Rehovoth, Isr. Office: Kaplan Hosp, Rehovoth, Isr.

BEISER, Sam M, US, educator; b. NYC, June 6, 1923; s. Leon and Anna (Hisler); BS, CCNY, 1942; PhD, Columbia U, 1951; m. Evelyn Pachtman, Dec 27, 1947; c: Peter, Stephen, Michele, Andrea. Prof, microbiol, Columbia U, since 1965, on staff since 1953, Guggenheim f, 1962-63. Exec comm, Columbia U chap, AAUP, since 1960; mem: comm on cert, comm on immunology, Amer Acad Microbiol, since 1961; study sect, USPHS, 1964-68; AAAS; Amer Assn Immunologists; Genetics Soc; Soc of Amer Microbiols; Soc for Gen Microbiol; Harvey Soc; Sigma Xi. Asso ed, Immunology, since 1968; contbr to profsl jours. Recipient: f in med scis, NRC, 1951-53; Fulbright Research Award, 1962. Home: 92 Pleasant St, Dumont, NJ. Office: Columbia U, 630 W 168 St, New York, NY.

BEITELY, Leah, Isr, organization exec; b. Kishiniev, Russ, Sep 22, 1903; s. Yochanan and Batia (Kitzis) Svider; in Isr since 1920; att Fr Brevet Superieur, Fr Educ Dept, Cairo, Egypt; proficiency cert, Cambridge U, Eng; m. Israel Unterman; c: Nava Frankfurt, Tehila Kaly. Mem exec, WIZO, repr to Isr and fgn convs; mem, found comm, YWHA, Jerusalem. Hobbies: music, reading, travel. Home: 15 Modigliani St, Tel Aviv, Isr. Office: WIZO, King David Blvd, Tel Aviv, Isr.

BEJARANO, Simon, Isr, industrialist; b. Plovidv, Bulgaria, Sept 28, 1910; s. Michael, Julia (Romano); in Isr since 1936; grad, Bus Coll, Switz, 1928; m. Litty Lichtenstein, 1938; c: Ilana Reviv, Daniel. Mgn dir, Assis Ltd, since 1939; Mem; second, third Knesset, on behalf Gen Zionist Party; adv bd, Bank of Isr, 1954-69; presidium and exec, Isr Mfrs Assn, since 1941; bd dirs, Bank Leumi Le Israel. Club, Casesaria Golf. Home: 12 Alonim, Tel Benjamin, Ramat Gan, Isr. Office: POB 175, Tel Aviv, Isr.

BEKER, Simon, Venezuela, physician, educator; b. Maracaibo, Venezuela, Feb 6, 1929; s. Saul and Mina (Gorenstein); BM, Liceo Andres Bello, Caracas, 1947; m. Marisa Kohn, July 24, 1956; c: Toni, Ilana, Bernardo. Prof, gastroenterology, since 1966. Pres, Venezuelan Friends, Heb U, Jerusalem; fmr: vice-pres, gen secy, B'nai B'rith. Author: Portal Hypertension Syndrome, 1968; Insuficiencia Hepatica Fulminante, 1969; contbr numerous articles to profsl publs. Recipient: summa cum laudae, Cen U of Venezuela; premio gen, Venezuelan Soc of Gastroenterology. Home: Lomas San Rafael, La Florida, Caracas, Venezuela. Office: Sabana Grande, Caracas, Venezuela.

BEKERMAN, Adam, Isr, painter; b. Warsaw, Pol, Apr 4, 1915; s. Aharon and Leah (Kalenberg); desc of Rabbi Albek, Warsaw; in Isr since 1958; deg, High Art Sch, Warsaw; m. Lucina Kaufman, 1950; c: Carina. Painter, graphic artist; org, executed intl folklore and art pavilions, Posen, Pol, 1953-57; one-man and group shows: Isr, Pol; represented in pvt collections; executed: graphic presentation of book about soldiers who fell in Isr wars; monument, Bialystock, in memory of J ghetto rebellion, Pol. Leader, Assn Painters and Sculptors, Rishon Lezion; mem, Assn Painters and Sculptors, Isr; fmr mem, Assn Painters and Sculptors, Pol. Home: 4 Asher Levin St, Rishon Lezion, Isr.

BEKRITSKY, Morris, US, rabbi; b. NYC, Jan 18, 1915; ordained rabbi, Rabb Sem of Amer; BSS, CCNY; MA, NYU; m. Dorothy Horowitz; c: Bruce, Joy. Rabbi, Orthodox J Comty, Portland, Me, since 1948; lectr, nursing class, Me Med Cen; fmr, rabbi, Heb Acad, Utica, NY. Vice-pres: Va'ad Harabonim, Mass; New Eng region, Mizrachi, pres, Portland chap, Mizrachi; mem: exec comm, RabCA; Gov Reed's Comm on Children and Youth; Bur Social Wfr Adv Comm; Maine State Sub-Comm on Adoption; Beth Din Harabonim, Mass; repr, Conf on Racial Discrimination, Princeton U; White House repr, Conf on Children and Youth; regular TV prog, WCSH-TV, Portland; weekly radio prog, WCSH; chaplain, local hosps and nursing home; found, Portland Heb Day Sch; inspired founding of Shaarey Tphiloh Syn. Home: 76 Noyes St, Portland, Me.

BELAICHE, Marcel, Algeria, communal leader; b. Algiers, July 3, 1903; Docteur en Droit, U of Paris; m. Rolande Boukabza, 1929; two c. Hon pres, Consistoire Isr, Algeria; fmr: vice-pres: Algerian Assembly; Assn Natl des Conseils Généraux, Fr; mem, Conseil Supérieur Gouvernemental. Recipient: Médaille Militaire; Croix de Guerre. Home: rue Monseigneur Leynaud, El-Biar, Algiers. Office: 3 rue Littré, Algiers.

BELFER, Arthur B, US, business exec; b. Vodzislow, Pol, May 30, 1907; s. Benjamin and Linda (Plapla); in US since 1939; hon LHD, Yeshiva U, NY; hon LLD, U of Wyo; m. Diane Firkser, Feb 7, 1965; c: Selma Ruben, Anita Saltz, Robert. Chmn bd, Belco Petroleum Corp, since 1962, found, past pres; gen partner, 630 Third Ave Assn, since 1957; pres, Fundamental Bldg, since 1951; pres, Belfer, 1941-59; found, mgn partner, Belfer Natural Gas, 1954-59. Pres, Belfer Found; trustee, Yeshiva U; sponsor, Belfer Grad Sch of Sci, Yeshiva U; vice-pres, Sutton Place Syn; mem: bd overseers, Albert Einstein Coll, Yeshiva U; exec bd, AJComm; clubs: Town, NY; Elmwood Country, White Plains, NY. Office: 630 Third Ave, New York, NY.

BELFER, Robert Alexander, US, business exec; b. Chorzow, Pol, Mar 27, 1935; s. Arthur and Rachelle (Anisfeld); in US since 1942; BA, Columbia Coll, 1955; LLB, Harvard Law Sch, 1958; m. Renée Kones, Dec 3, 1960; c: Rachelle, Laurence. Pres, Belco Petroleum Corp, since 1965, vice-pres, 1958-64, exec vice-pres, 1964-65; partner, Belfer Natural Gas, 1958-59. Secy, Belfer Found; sponsor, Belfer Grad Sch of Sci, Yeshiva U; patron, Brandeis U; dir, Columbia Coll Fund; mem: Sigma Alpha Mu; W Park Racquet Club; fmr: trustee, FJP; mem, adv bd, Odyssey House; dir, Independent Petroleum Assn, Amer; trustee, Sutton Pl Syn. Office: 630 Third Ave, New York, NY.

BELFORD, Jacob, US, attorney; b. NYC, Aug 18, 1898; s. Harris and Annie (Schoenkopf); LLM, NYU, 1935; m. Blanca Leyva, 1958; c: Richard, Ronald. Atty, Belford & Belford. Pres, New Haven JCC; vice-pres, New Haven Men's ORT; natl bd dirs, Amer ORT Fed; mem: Amer, Conn Co Bar Assns; Masons; KP; B'nai B'rith; Probus Club. Home: 10 Burnt Swamp Rd, Woodridge, Conn. Office: 770 Chapel St, New Haven, Conn.

BELFORD, Richard Lyon, US, attorney; b. New Haven, Conn, May 6, 1927; s. Jacob and Johanna (Rosenthal); BS, Rutgers U, 1949; DJur, NYU Law Sch, 1952; m. Joyce Blixton, June 24, 1950; c: Bruce, Keith, Glenn, Karen. Atty since 1952; counsel, Conn Housing Inves Fund Inc, since 1968; exec dir, New Haven Commn of Equal Opportunities, 1965-67. USN, 1945-46. Pres, New Haven Hum Relations Council; vice-pres, New Haven Civil Liberties Council; mem: bd dirs: New Haven JCC; Clifford Beers Guidance Clinic; bd trustees, Cong Mishran Isr; steering comm, New Haven chap, AJCong; ADA; Amer, Conn, New Haven Co Bar Assns; Natl Assn Intergroup Relations Off; fmr, alderman, New Haven Bd Alderman. Home: 120 Alston Ave, New Haven, Conn. Office: 865 Chapel St, New Haven, Conn.

BELINE, George, US, artist; b. Minsk, Russ, July 23, 1887; s. Boris and Shima; in US since 1907; att Ecole des Beaux Arts, Fr; m. Miriam Himmelstein, Dec 24, 1916; c: Martin, Gloria Smith. Artist-painter and sculptor; fmr, tchr, NYC HSs. Exhibited in US and Fr; represented in perm collection, Natl Acad Design. Mem: bd dirs, Amer Artists Profsl League; bd govs, treas, Allied Artists Amer; B'nai B'rith; clubs: Salmagundi; Jewish. Recipient: prize, Salmagundi Club, 1966. Home and studio: 370 Central Park W, New York, NY.

BELKIN, Samuel, US, university pres; b. Swislicz, Pol, Dec 12, 1911; s. Solomon and Mina (Sattir); in US since 1929; ordained rabbi, Radun Theol Sem, 1929; att Harvard U, 1934; hon f, Brown U, 1935, PhD, 1935, hon DD, 1959; hon LHD, Dropsie Coll, 1964; m. Selma Ehrlich, Nov 10, 1935; c: Linda Schuchalter, Salo; m. 2nd, Abby Polesie, Jan 3, 1963. Pres, Yeshiva U, since 1943; dean, Rabbi Isaac Elchanan Theol Sem, since 1940, instr, Talmud, 1936-40; lectr, Talmud, New Haven Rabb Sem, Cleveland, O, 1929-30; instr, Greek, Yeshiva Coll, 1935-40; secy fac, Bernard Revel Grad Sch, 1937; exec comm, Yeshiva Coll, 1939; prof, Hellenistic lit, Yeshiva Coll, 1940-43. Bd dirs: Council of Higher Educ Instns in NYC; Youth Aid, Inc; adv comm, United Negro Coll Fund Inc; natl adv bd, United World Federalists; bd trustees, World Acad, Jerusalem; bd dirs, Soc of Friends of Touro Syn Natl Hist Shrine; bd f, Amer Acad J Research; adv bd, Amer Friends Heb U, Isr; adv council, Heb Culture Service Comm for Amer HS and Coll; publ comm, J Publ Soc, Amer; commn on chaplaincy, Natl JWB; intl comm, Remembrance Award; Amer Acad Political and Social Sci; Natl Council, Civic Responsibility; NY Acad Public Educ; Gtr NY Council for Fgn Students Inc; Natl Educ Assn, US; Acad Rel and MH; Amer Assn J Educ; Amer J Hist Soc; J Book Council of Amer; Jewish Acad Arts and Sci (hon mem); World Union Jewish Studies, Isr; Union Orthodox Rabbis of US and Can; RabCA, life mem; Rel Zionists of Amer; fmr mem, Mayor's Adv Comm on Sch Bd Nominations, NY; co-chmn, NY Citizens Comm on Housing; exec comm, Amer J Tercentenary; mem, Phi Beta Kappa. Author: Philo and Oral Law, 1940; Essays in Traditional Jewish Thought, 1956; In His Image, 1961; The Alexandrian Halakhah in Apologetic Literature; The Midrash Tadshe and Its Hellenistic Sources; The Onomastic Midrash in Philo; The Munchen Edition of the Tractate Nedarim; The Midrash Hanaelam of the Zohar and Its Source in Alexandrian Midrashic Literature; The Philonic Exposition of the Law in Light of Ancient Rabbinic Midrashim; Questions and Answers in Genesis and Exodus-The Oldest Recorded Palestinian Midrash; Philo and a Palestinian Midrashic Tradition; What Makes a Good Jew; Parent as Teacher and Teacher as Parent; Man and His Creator; The Philosophy of Purpose; The Four Dimensions of Higher Education; asso ed: Rabbinics; Universal Jewish Encyclopedia; contbr to: Journal of Biblical Literature; J Quarterly Review; Hapardes, Talpioth, Horeb, and Sura. Recipient: bronze medal for service to higher educ, NYC, 1963; gold medal for leadership in its founding and devl, Albert Einstein Coll of Med, Yeshiva U, 1965. Home: 101 Central Park W, New York. NY. Office: Amsterdam Ave & 186 St, New York, NY.

BELL, Daniel, US, editor, educator, author; b. NYC, May 10, 1919; s. Benjamin and Anna (Kaplan); BS, CCNY, 1938; grad study, Columbia U, 1939-40, PhD, 1959; div; c: Jordy; m. 2nd, Pearl Kazin; c: David. Prof, sociol, Harvard U; asso prof, Columbia U, 1959-62, prof, 1962-68; research cons, J Labor Comm, since 1947; staff writer, New Leader, 1940, mgn ed, 1941-44; mgn ed, Common Sense mag, 1944-45; instr, social scis, U of Chgo, 1945-48; lab ed, Fortune Mag, 1948-58; f, Cen for Advanced Studies in Behavioral Scis, 1959. Author: History of Marxian Socialism in Amer, 1952; The New Amer Right, 1955; Work and Its Discontents, 1956; The End of Ideology, 1960; The Radical Right, 1962; The Reforming of General Education, 1966; Toward the Year 2000, 1968; contbr to mags. Mem: Amer Comm for Cultural Freedom; Amer Sociol Soc; bd dirs, ACLU; J Lab Comm. Home: 65 Francis Ave, Cambridge, Mass. Office: Wm James Hall, Harvard U, Mass.

BELL, Leonard David, US, business exec; b. Lewiston, Me, Jan 19, 1927; BA, Bowdoin Coll, 1947; m. Phyllis Amsel; c: Nancy, Wendy, Jeffrey. Pres, Bell Mfg Co. Dir, Beth Jacob Syn; natl comm, Amer-Isr Public Affairs Comm; trustee: United Isr Appeal; and big gifts chmn, Lewiston-Auburn J Fed, past pres, campaign chmn; mem: adv bd, Franconia Coll; Philco-Ford Found, Navajo Indians; Fgn Policy Bus Execs Group; Amer Businessmen Abroad Comm; Natl J Wfr Bd Comm on open membership; admn comm, JDC; exec comm, ORT; natl exec, UJA; CJP, Boston, past chmn, metrop div; bd dirs: JDC; Amer Friends Heb U; Amer Friends Tel Aviv U; fmr: pres, Bowdoin Coll Alumni Club, Androscoggin Co; dir, financial secy, Lewiston-Auburn JCC; Androscoggin Co chmn, March of Dimes; div chmn, United Fund; natl chmn, UJA Young Leadership Cabinet; mem: Bowdoin Coll Alumni Council and Capital Fund Drive, Androscoggin Co. Recipient: Herbert H Lehman Young Leadership Award, 1967. Home: 10 Bowser Rd, Lexington, Mass. Office: 777 Main St, Lewiston, Me.

BELL, Renah, US, communal leader; b. Northadams, Mass, July 10, 1937; d. Moses and Magda (Schonfeld) Mescheloff; att: Stern Coll for Women, 1954-55; U of Ill, 1955-56; m. Alexander Bell, Sep 8, 1957; c: Meir, Esther. Pres: Yeshiva Toras Chaim, South Shore, PTA; Sharon chap, Hapoel Hamizrachi Women, 1959-64; Young Isr, Lawrence Cedarhurst Sisterhood, 1965-66; vice-pres, Massada chap, Mizrachi Women; mem, bd, Hi Li PTA, Young Isr, Lawrence-Cedarhurst. Hobbies: music, art, sci, anything connected with Isr. Home: 574 Grant Place, Cedarhurst, NY.

BELLAK, Leopold, US, psychiatrist, educator; b. Vienna, June 22, 1916; s. Siegfried and Marianne (Weiler); in US since 1938; att U of Vienna Med Sch, 1935-38; MA: Boston U, 1939; Harvard U, 1942; MD, NY Med Coll, 1944; dipl, NY Psychan Inst, 1950; m. Sonya Sorel, Dec 1952; c: Karola, Katrina. Pvt practice, psycht, NYC, since 1946; visiting prof, NYU, since 1965; cons: Westpoint Mil Acad, since 1965; Westchester MH Assn, since 1968; Rand Corp, since 1969; clinical prof, psycht, NY Med Coll, 1950-58, mem fac since 1946; lectr, New Sch, 1947-55; chief cons, psycht: Altro Health & Rehab Service, 1947-57; J Bd of Guardians, 1947-48; visiting prof, psych, CCNY, 1951-54, lectr, 1948-51; adj prof, psych, NYU, 1959-60; dir, psycht, City Hosp, Elmhurst, NYC, 1958-64. US Army MC, WWII. F: Amer Psycht Assn; mem: Amer and NY Psychan Assns; NY Acad Sci; Rorschach Soc, pres, 1957-58; Westchester Psychan Soc, pres, 1962-63. Author: Dementia Praecox, 1947; Manic Depressive Psychosis, 1950; TAT and CAT in Clinical Use, 1954; Schizophrenia, 1958; Contemporary European Psychiatry, 1961; Handbook of Community Psychiatry, 1963; The Broad Scope of Psychoanalysis, 1967; The Schizophrenic Syndrome, 1969; contbr numerous articles to profsl publs. Recipient: f: Austin; Rantouil, both Harvard U; annual

merit award, NY Soc Clinical Psych, 1964. Office: 22 Rockwood Dr, Larchmont, NY.

BELLAN, Ruben C, Can, educator; b. Winnipeg, Can, Oct 2, 1918; s. Harry and Lily (Kolovson); BA, U Manitoba, 1938; MA, U Toronto, 1941; PhD, Columbia U, 1958; m. Ruth Lercher, June 1, 1947; c: Paul, Lorne, Susan. Prof, econ, U Manitoba; mem, bd police commns, Winnipeg. RCAF, 1941-46. Author: Principles of Economics and the Canadian Economy, 1960; Fundamentals of Economics, 1962. Home: 628 Niagara St, Winnipeg, Can. Office: University of Manitoba, Fort Garry, Manitoba, Can.

BELLER, Aharon Y, Isr, neurosurgeon, educator; b. Grodisko, Pol, July 10, 1912; s. Uziel and Golda; in Isr since 1939; MD, U Vienna, 1938; m. Assia Ahronowicz, 1943; c: Ruth, Uziel. Prof, head, dept neurosurg, Hadassah-Heb U Med Sch, Jerusalem, since 1948; in pvt med practice, Jerusalem, since 1949. Contbr to profsl jours. Home: 12 Marcus St, Jerusalem, Isr. Office: Hadassah-Hebrew U Med Sch, Jerusalem, Isr.

BELLER, Harry E, US, physician; b. NYC, Sep 16, 1905; s. Max and Anna (Mezeritzky); MD, LI Coll of Med, 1928; postgrad studies: Kennedy VA Hosp, 1947-48; U Coll of Ga, Augusta, 1948-49; m. Beatrice Hyman, July 1, 1934; m. 2nd, Maysie Yates, Aug 26, 1948; c: Alexander, Linda. Asso prof, orthopedic surg, U of Miami Med Sch, Fla, since 1954; orthopedic surg: Jackson Memorial Hosp; Mercy Hosp; Variety Children's Hosp; Mt Sinai Hosp, all Miami, since 1949; mem staff, Cedars of Lebanon Hosp, Miami; asst orthopedic surg: Beth El Hosp, Bklyn, 1930-42; Kings Co Hosp, 1930-40; Bklyn J Hosp, 1930-42, both NY; res and instr, orthopedic surg, U of Ga, 1948-49. Maj, US Army, 1942-46. F, Amer and Intl Coll Surgs; dipl, Amer Bd Orthopedic Surgs; mem: Fla State Med Assn; Dade Co Med Assn; AAAS; Ga Acad Sci; Amer Acad Orthopedic Surgs; Fla Orthopedic Soc. Home: 1440 Alegriano, Coral Gables, Fla.

BELLER, Louis K, US, business exec; b. Bklyn, NY, Mar 22, 1900; s. Michael and Eva (Kritzman); m. Esty Feldman, Nov 14, 1927; s. Arthur. Pres, Public Service Tire Corp, since 1927. Fmr: bd dirs: Temple Beth El, Rockaway; Metrop Geriatric J Hosp; UJA; found, J Comty Cen, Saranac Lake; trustee, Automotive Union 797; mem: Unity Club, Bklyn; Masons 32. Home: 224 Beach 136 St, Belle Harbor, NY. Office: 1244 Bedford Ave, Brooklyn, NY.

BELLET, Samuel, US, physician, educator; b. Russ, Aug 21, 1902; s. Eli and Pauline (Tartakov); in US since 1909; BS, U of Pa, 1921; MD, Jefferson Med Coll, 1925; m. Jean Rosenthal, Jan 19, 1947; c: Joan. Pvt practice since 1934; prof, clinical card, Grad School Med, U of Pa, since 1954, dir, div cardiovascular diseases, 1948-63; dir, div card, Phila Gen Hosp, since 1951. Mem: Pres Commn on Heart Disease, Cancer and Stroke, 1964-65; AMA; Amer, Phila Colls Phys; AHA; Amer Coll Chest Phys; Amer Phys Soc; Amer Coll Card; Heart Assn of SE Pa; NY Acad Scis; AAUP; Sigma X. Contbr of numerous papers to med jours. Home and office: 2021 Spruce St, Philadelphia, Pa.

BELLITY, Meyer, Isr, advocate; b. Tunis, Sep 18, 1913; s. Moise and Emilie; in Isr since 1967; BLL, Fac de Droit, Aix-en-Provence, Fr; m. Marie Gabison; c: Michel, Juliette Gabison. Legal adv, Land's Govt, Gaza, since 1967; dir, Land Registration, Gaza and Sinai, since 1968; fmr: pres, ZF; mem munic council; mem, Conseil de l'ordre des Avocats, all Tunis; found; mem, ORT, Tunis. Resistance movements, Combat, fmr Liberte, and Lautreck, Tunisia, Fr. Mem, ZC, Isr delg; mem, comm of Zionist Activity; fmr: Tunisian delg to ZCs; secy, Socialist Students Org, Aix-en-Provence; fmr numerous Zionist activities, relations with WZC. Contbr: confs on Zionist topics; numerous articles to Tunisian press. Home: 11 Balfour St, Bat Yam, Isr.

BELLOW, Saul, US, novelist, educator; b. Lachine, Que, Can, June 10, 1915; s. Abraham and Liza (Gordon); in US since 1924; BS, Northwestern U, 1937; m. 3rd, Susan Glassman, 1961; c: Gregory, Adam, Daniel. Author: Dangling Man, 1944; The Victim, 1947; The Adventures of Augie March, 1953; Seize The Day, 1956; Henderson the Rain King, 1959; Herzog, 1964; Mosby's Memoirs & Other Stories, 1968; Mr Sammler's Planet, 1970; contbr to mags; Asst prof, Eng: gen educ div, NYU, 1950-52; creative arts dept, Princeton U, 1952-53; asso prof, Eng, U of Minn; asst prof, Eng, Bard

Coll, 1953-54; prof, comm on social thought, U of Chgo, 1962. Mem, Natl Inst Arts and Letters. Recipient: Guggenheim F, 1948-49; Natl Inst of Arts and Letters Award, 1952; Natl Book Award for Fiction, 1953, for Herzog, 1965. Home: 1126 E 59 St, Chicago Ill.

BELOVIN, Robert S, US, attorney; b. Bklyn, NY, Mar 10, 1944; s. Martin and Henrietta (Spindler); BA, LIU, 1965; JD, Bklyn Law Sch, 1968; m. Margaret Myers, Dec 25, 1966. Pvt practice since 1969; tchr of emotionally disturbed, since 1968. Mem: intl law frat, Phi Delta Phi; KP. Hobbies: tennis, skiing, reading. Home and office: 430 Ocean Parkway, Brooklyn, NY.

BELSITZMAN, Ilya, Isr, architect; b. Tiflis, Russ, June 5, 1917; s. Frederic and Clara (Gurevitch); in Isr since 1934; att Werner Siemens Gymnasium, Berlin; Ascola Gymnasium, Warsaw; Montefiori Tech HS, Tel Aviv; m. Naomi Feigenbaum, Mar 27, 1951; c: Amos, Anat. Architect, partner, Leitersdorf and Belsitzman; fmr: architect: with J Neufeld 1934-41; with Z Rechter, 1943-46; clerk of works with A Gut, bldg contractor, 1941-42. Capt, engr corps, IDF, 1948-49. Prin contribs: works executed: maternity and children's ward, Tel Hashomer Hosp, Tel Aviv; children's ward, outpatient clinic, lecture hall, Sharon Hosp; educ fac, Tel Aviv U; HS, trade schs, Petach Tikvah; theatres and cinemas: Petach Tikvah; Hadera; Tel Aviv; Rehovot; Samuel Hotel, Tel Aviv; maternity hosp, Govt of Gabon. Mem: Assn Engrs and Architects, Isr; Intl Hosp Assn, London. Hobby: photography. Home: 10 Dizengoff St, Tel Aviv, Isr. Office: 27 Remez St, Tel Aviv, Isr.

BELSKY, Robert A, US, business exec; b. NYC, Aug 9, 1914; s. Jacob and Brina (Parets); att Columbia U; m. Estelle Schultz, June 14, 1936; c: Barbara Vanefsky, Ilyne Herling. Pres, Banff Ltd, since 1954; chmn, bd, Sweater Bee, Banff, since 1967. Home: 25 Sutton Place S, New York, NY. Office: 1410 Broadway, New York, NY.

BELZ, Philip, US, business exec; b. Pol, Jan 15, 1904; s. Moses and Mary (Houserman); in US since 1910; m. Sarah Thomas, Nov 1, 1925; c: Jack, Paul, Leslie. Pres: Union Realty Co, since 1943; Belz Inves Co; dir, mem, exec comm, First Natl Bank of Memphis, since 1960. Chmn: Memphis Isr Bond Comm, since 1955; Cotton States for Isr Bonds, since 1955; mem: ZOA; Mizrachi; J Comty Cen; B'nai B'rith; natl bd, JWB, since 1962, past pres; natl cabinet, UJA; bd govs, B'nai B'rith Old Folks Home, since 1946; hon mem, Soc Hon Alumni, Heb U, Jerusalem; fmr: pres: Baron Hirsch Syn; Southeastern Conf Union Orthodox Syns; chmn, vice-pres, JWF; chmn, UJA; clubs: Furniture; Ridgeway Country; Lumberman's; Men's of Baron Hirsch Cong; 100 of Memphis; Executives, Memphis. Named: Man of the Decade, State of Isr Bonds Org, 1958; Man of the Year, Isr Bonds, 1969. Home: 4 Belleair Dr, Memphis, Tenn. Office: 1175 Morehead St, Memphis, Tenn.

BEN, Max, US, pharmacologist; b. Utica, NY, Oct 12, 1926; s. David and Sarah (Slakter); AB, Syracuse U, 1951; MA, Princeton U, 1953, PhD, 1954; m. Dorene Smith, June 15, 1952; c: Lisa, Edward, Ellen, Jennifer. Secy-treas, vice-pres, Research Health Scis Assos, Inc, since 1970; research asso: surg research, Harrison Dept, Sch of Med, U of Penn, 1954-56; endocrinology, neuropharm, Merck Inst of Therapeutic Research, 1956-58; sect head, endocrine research, Squibb Inst of Med Research, 1958; sr sci, Warner Lambert Research Inst, 1958-62; sr pharm, sci dir, pharm, Hazleton Labs, Inc, 1962-65; UN tech expert, pharm, adv to NCR on devl, PM Office, Isr, 1965-68; dir, spec projects, Bionetic Research Labs, 1969; secy, Natl Biol Congs, Amer Inst Biol Sci, 1969-70, assisted in org, pharm inst, Beilinson Hosp, Petah Tikvah, Isr. USN, MC, 1945-46. Bd dir, Temple Olam Tikvah; mem: Amer Phys Soc; AAAS; Amer Soc for Pharm and Experimental Therapeutics; NY Acad Scis; Sigma Xi; Amer Inst Biol Scis. Contbr of numerous articles and publs in med jours. Hobbies: amateur radio, golf, chess, bridge. Home: 9212 Talisman Drive, Vienna, Va.

BEN-ADERET, Noah, Isr, physician; b. Izmir, Turkey, Mar 18, 1925; s. Joseph and Rebecca; in Isr since 1952; MD, Istanbul U, 1948; m. Matilda Taranto, Jan 6, 1952; c: Igal, Orna, Nitza. Dir, dept obstet and gyn, Negev Cen Hosp, since 1960; chief res, dept obstet and gyn, Kaplan Hosp, 1953-60. Turkish Army, 1949; IDF, 1962. Mem: IMA; Soc of Fertility and Sterility; Lions Club. Contbr to profsl publs. Hobbies: cars,

philately. Home: 17/1 Shlomo Hamelech St, Beersheva, Isr. Office: Negev Central Hospital, Beersheva, Isr.

BEN-ADI, Herbert, Isr, author, journalist; b. Barcs, Yugo, July 22, 1904; s. Abraham and Ida (Stern); in Isr since 1948; m. Ora Labock; s. Yigal. Negev and Gaza corresp, Jerusalem Post, since 1949; contbr of articles to Isr, Amer mags. British Army; Amer Army of Occupation, Ger, 1944-46; IDF. Secy, Rotary Intl, Beersheva. Author: Israel's War for Peace, 1968. Hobbies: philately, archaeol. Home and office: 49 Smilanski St, Beersheva, Isr.

BENADY, Samuel, Gibraltar, attorney; b. Gibraltar, May 21, 1905; s. Mesod and Hannah (Serruya); MA, Jesus Coll, U of Cambridge, Eng, 1928; barrister-at-law, Inner Temple, London, 1926; m. Sadye Cohen, Sep 6, 1933 (decd); c: Pamela; m.2nd, Preciada Amselem, 1968. In pvt practice; QC since 1955; leader, Gibraltar Bar, since 1960. Squadron leader, RAF, 1940-45. Pres, Gibraltar J Comty, since 1956; city councillor, 1939. Hobby: travel. Home: 124 Main St, Gibraltar. Office: 3 Governor's Parade, Gibraltar.

BEN-AHARON, Itzhak, Isr, legislator, farmer; b. Zvinace, Aus, July 17, 1906; s. Aharon and Hanna (Perl) Eisenberg; in Isr since 1928; att Coll of Political and Econ Sci, Berlin, 1926-27; m. Miriam Avishai, 1932; c: Yariv, Yeshayahu. Sec, Isr, Gen Fed of Labor, since 1970; MK, Ahdut Haavoda, 1949-1970; mem: fgn affairs and defense comm; Min of Communications and Transp, 1959-62; Kibbutz Givat Hayim; exec comm, Histadrut; secretariat, Hakibbutz Hameuchad; fmr: mem, Haifa Lab Council; secy, cen off, Mapai; co-found, mem exec comm, Mapam; Hashomer Hatzair. Capt, J Brig, Brit Army, 1940; prisoner of war, Greece and Ger. Author: Letters to My Son, 1941; Listen Gentile, 1948; On the Eve of Change, 1968; ed, Baderekh, Bucarest, 1925-26; contbr to local press. Home: Kibbutz Givat Hayim, Isr. Office: Labour Party Hqr, Isr.

BENAIM, Moses E, Gibraltar, business exec; b. Gibraltar, Aug 6, 1919; s. David and Esther (Bibas); grandson of Raphael Haim Moses Benaim, chief rabbi of Gibraltar; four c; m.2nd, Esther Garson, Oct 16, 1967; one c. Mgn dir: D Benaim & Co Ltd, since 1952; Carmel Properties, since 1958; Overseas Motors, since 1961; Intl Hotels, since 1969; hon consul for State of Isr at Gibraltar since 1968. Pres, Etz Hayim Syn; trustee, Heb Poor Fund; mem: mgn bd, Heb Comty; clubs: J Social and Cultural; Casino Calpe; Calpe Rowing; hon secy, Gibraltar Music Soc. Hobbies: music, motoring. Home: 1E Baker's Passage, Gibraltar. Office: 3 City Mill La, Gibraltar.

BENAMI, Amnon, engineer; b. Haifa, Nov 27, 1927; s. Alexander and Aliza (Tzeplevich); BSc, Technion, 1952; MSc, Wash State Coll, Pullman, 1954; DSc, Technion, 1966; m. Tzvia Talil, Aug 16, 1955; c: Romi, Ran. Sr lectr, Technion, since 1968; research asst, Wash State Coll, 1952-54; visiting lectr, 1960-62, 1966-67. Sgt, IDF, 1948-49. Mem, Amer, Isr Socs of Agric Engrs. Contbr to profsl publs. Home: 32 Edmond Peleg St, Haifa, Isr. Office: Technion, Haifa, Isr.

BEN-AMI, Issachar, Isr, archivist; b. Casablanca, Morocco, Dec 14, 1933; s. Aaron and Esther (Levy); in Isr since 1954; BA, Heb U, Jerusalem, 1963; PhD, U of Göttingen, 1967; m. Paulina Rosenthal, Oct 3, 1960; c: Gad, Aviel. Dir, Isr Folklore Archives, Heb U, since 1968; research f, J folklore, Heb U, since 1968. IS corps, IDF, 1955-58. Treas, Jerusalem Soc for Social Rehab; mem: Amer Anthropological Assn; Isr Folklore Soc. Author: The Traditional Jewish Marriage in Morocco; ed, The Folklore, both forthcoming. Home: 9 Simon Bolivar, Jerusalem, Isr. Office: Hebrew University, Jerusalem, Isr.

BEN-AMI, Oved, Isr, communal leader; b. Petah Tikva, Isr, 1905; s. Meir and Shoshana (Zalelichin) Dankner; m. Yaffa Lerner, 1928; three daughters. Working on Undivided Land of Isr Movement; co-found, Heb daily, Maariv; chmn, bd dirs, Modiin Pub House Ltd, pub of Maariv; chmn, Kupat Am Bank, since 1966; fmr: found: Boy Scouts movement; Maccabi Org in Isr; mayor, City of Nethanya; Isr Diamond Cutting Ind, first pres, until 1950; corresp, Doar Hayom, first Jerusalem daily, mem ed staff, chmn bd dirs; co-builder, colony of Herzlia, with 25 settlers of B'nei Benyamin Org; secy gen, chmn, B'nei Benyamin; initiated settlements of Kfar Aharon, Even Yehuda; elected to 2nd Asefat Hanivcharim; mem, Vaad Leumi of Yishuv; participated in: establishment of JA; Aliyah

Bet, absorbing newcomers to Isr in City of Nethanya; rebuilding city of Ashdod, responsible for its planning and ind devl. Chmn, KBA Townbuilders Group Ltd; mem, bd govs: Heb U, Jerusalem; Weizmann Inst of Sci, Rehovoth; Tel Aviv U; Israel Mus; Wingate Inst of Physical Training, Nethanya; delg to 17th Zionist Cong; pres, Council for Beautification of Isr; participant, Undivided Land of Isr Movement. Office: Municipal Bldg, Nethanya, Isr.

BEN-AMITTAI, Israel, Isr, university exec; b. Petah Tikva, Isr, Nov 22, 1922; s. Yaakov and Naomi (Krochmalnik) Hendin; BA, Heb U, Jerusalem; m. Yeudit Moser, 1949; c: Ehud, Dan, Boaz. Dir gen, U of the Negev, Beersheva, since 1968. Col, chief cdr, artillery, IDF, 1948-67. Home: 52 Negba St, Beersheba, Isr. Office: University of the Negev, Beersheva, Isr.

BEN-AMITTAI, Levi, Isr, poet, teacher; b. Lahovitz, Russ, May 16, 1901; s. Mordechai and Nehama (Deretchinsky) Brevda; in Isr since 1920; att Heb U, Jerusalem, 1951-52; m. Lea Danziger; c: Yuval, Michal Eliaz, Hamutal Asaf. Tchr, Ulpan, Deganya B, since 1939. Haganah; IDF, 1967. Org, Kibbutz Writers' Circle. Author: Hashvicim Pnima, 1934; Leilot Bamatzor, 1936; Bakvutza, 1938; Sadot Sheba'emek, 1950; Oholiva, 1959; Midbar Matana, 1962; Osfei Kaitz, 1966; ed: Hasofer Bakvutza, 1956; Dganiot, 1958; Al Admatam, 1959. Recipient: Emek Hayarden award, 1958; Joseph Aharonovitz award, 1962; distinguished citizen award, from late Pres Ben Zvi, 1962; Ussishkin award, 1968. Home: Kibbutz Deganya B, Isr.

BEN-AMITTAY, Jacob, Isr, attorney; b. Luck, Ukraine, Russ, Sep 4, 1900; s. David and Esperanza (Gorenstein) Golub; in Isr since 1920; MJur, U of Kiev, 1920; LLD, Law Sch, Jerusalem, 1927; DRerPol, U of Berlin, 1960; m. Regina Chomska, Feb 17, 1952; c: Dalia Ben-Anath, Erella Rubinstein. Pres, U Econ and Social Studies, Tel Aviv, since 1968; in pvt practice since 1931; dir, numerous inves and econ co's; fmr, journalist. Lt, Aus Army, 1917; Irgun Zvai Leumi, 1947. Co-chmn, Ben-Amittay Scholarship Fund, Isr; chmn, intl relations comm, Lions Intl, Tel Aviv; mem: adv comm, WJC; B'nai B'rith; fmr: pres, Revisionist Party, Tel Aviv; mem exec, Isr Inst Intl Problems. Author: Political Science, 2 vols, 1935; The History of Political Ideas, 1967; fmr co-ed, International Problems; transl books, among others, of Bertrand Russel; contbr articles to jours. Hobbies: painting, photography, touring, sport. Home: 7 Modigliani St, Tel Aviv, Isr. Office: 2 Pinsker St, Tel Aviv, Isr.

BEN-AREE, Joshua H, Isr, legal adv; b. Turobin, Pol, Feb 11, 1914; s. Moshe and Zeldi (Mandelker) Silberklang; in Isr since 1935; att Yeshiva: Torat Hayim, Radom, Pol; Tomchei-Tmimim-Lubavich, Warsaw; dipl, jur, Tel Aviv U, 1956; m. Ayalah Tiomkin, May 1, 1945; c: Laveek, Yechiam. Legal adv, Min Police, since 1959; asst cdr, Min Police, since 1964; fmr: different posts in criminal inves; cdr, div forces, IDF; chief police prosecutor, Tel Aviv dist; found, lectr, High Offs Police Sch. Mem: Criminological Inst; Masons, Hakochov chap; B'nai B'rith, Dizengoff chap. Contbr to police jours. Recipient: Defense Medal, 1939-45; Oth Hamishmar; Independence Medal; Sinai Campaign Medal, 1956; 6-Day War Medal, 1967. Hobbies: chess, books. Home: 229 Dizengoff St, Tel Aviv, Isr. Office: 27 Hillel St, Jerusalem, Isr.

BEN-ARI, Mordechai, Isr, business exec; b. Transylvania, Rum, Sep 10, 1920; s. Itzhak and Elizabeth (Morton); in Isr since 1940; MA, Heb U, Jerusalem; m. Bilha Zukerman; c: Nitza, Yehuda. Pres, El Al Isr Airlines, since 1967, with firm since 1950. Haganah, War of Independence. Dir, Aliyah Bet, Aus, E Eur. Author: 20 Years of El Al, 1968; Role of an International Airline in the Service of a Small Community, 1969. Home: 7 Shneur St, Ramat Gan, Isr. Office: Lod Airport, Isr.

BEN ARI, Uri, Isr, business exec; b. Berlin, Feb 1, 1925; s. Max and Elisabeth (Markus) Banner; in Isr since 1939; m. Milca Hoff, Apr 11, 1965; c: Nurit Kaschtan, Gjora, Nimrod, Avner. Gen mgr, E Levin Epstein Ltd, publishers, since 1964; fmr: gen mgr, Elec Motors, 1958-64. Col, Haganah; Palmach; IDF, 1945-57. Home: 40 Harechesh St, Afeka, Isr. Office: 27 Rothschild St, Bat Yam, Isr.

BENARY, Jacob, Isr, executive; b. Burgas, Bulgaria, June 2, 1926; s. Joseph and Clara (Confino) Benrey; att Sch of Law and Econ, Tel Aviv; m. Edna Cohen, 1953. Dir, El Al Isr Airlines, br Arg, Uruguay, Chile, Peru, Bolivia; fmr journalist;

atty; head, freight devl sect, El Al Airlines. Home: 4025 Las Herras, Buenos Aires, Arg. Office: 464 Maipu St, Buenos Aires, Arg.

BEN-ARZI, Efraim, Isr, business exec; b. Slonim, Pol, July 19, 1910; s. Shamai and Rachel (Salucki) Kobrinsky; in Isr since 1924; EE, Grenoble U, Fr, 1935; m. Devora Gad, Sep 22, 1959. Pres, Madera Corp; chmn, Arad Chem Ind; mem bd, Sonol Isr; spec asst to PM, all since 1968; fmr: pres, chmn, El Al Isr Airlines, 1956-67; mgn dir, Mekorot Water. Lt col, Brit Army, WW II; maj gen, IDF. Exec comm, World ORT Union, since 1951; club, Caesaria Golf and Country, chmn since 1960. Recipient: mention in dispatches for gallantry, WW II. Home: 7 Chatam Soffer St, Tel Aviv, Isr. Office: Hadar Dafnah Bldg, 39 Sderot Shaul Hamelech, Tel Aviv, Isr.

BEN-ASHER, Chaim, Isr, labor org, b. Russ, June 6, 1904; s. Asher and Margalit Finkel; in Isr since 1924; att U of Odessa, 1920-22; Heb U, 1925-26; m. Hanna Mingelgrin, Dec, 1934; c. Shimshon, Iftah, Yael. Mem, Kibbutz Nezer Sereni, since 1950; mem secretariat, Kibbutz Hameuchad and Ihud Hakibbutzim, 1927-1954; MK, mem, Fgn Affairs and Security Comm, 1949-56; dir, Bet Berl Lab Coll. Capt, IDF, 1942-49. Author: Yesterday's World of Tomorrow, 1959. Home: 601/18, Eilat, Isr. Office: Kibbutz Nezer Sereni, Isr.

BENBASSAT, Alberto, Spain, business exec; b. Burgas, Bulgaria, Apr 9, 1911; s. Haim and Dorothea (Garti); in Spain since 1939; att Commercial Coll, Bulgaria; m. Regina Bassat Zara, Sep 16, 1948; c: Dorita, Elisita. Owner, chem import-export bus, Barcelona, since 1939; fmr: exec, Marco Garti, Sofia, Bulgaria, 1931-36; owner, Alberto Benbassat, Sofia, 1936-39. Pres, council Comunidad Isr de Barcelona, since 1965, pres, comunidad, 1959-65, mem comm, devl of new statutes, 1957-59, 1968-69; mem: C of C; Span trade and ind assns. Hobbies: music, skiing. Home: 333 Calle Balmes, Barcelona, Spain. Office: 30 Via Layetana, Barcelona, Spain.

BENCH, Nachman, US, business exec; b. Haifa, Feb 22, 1935; s. Benjamine and Esther Benchovsky; att Technion, Haifa, 1952-59; PhD, NYU, 1964; m. Adrienne; c: Adam. Pres, Spec Studies Inc; specialist in mgmt sci; cons, Off of Mayor, NY, 1967-68. Home: 240 Central Park S, New York, NY. Office: 55 W 44 St, New York, NY.

BEN-CHORIN, Jehuda, Isr, industrial adv; b. Breslau, Ger, May 30, 1915; s. Martin and Ella (Zarek) Brieger; in Isr since 1936; m. Sylvia Rautenberg, Oct 2, 1939; c: Ruth Lifschitz, Bilha Herzog, Amos. Ind adv, ind dept, Hakibbutz Ha'artzi, since 1968; mgr, Kibbutz Inds Assn, since 1968; gen mgr, Plastopil, Kibbutz Hazorea, 1964-68. Lt col, IDF; active in Palmach; Haganah. Mem, mission to Fr, Prague, 1948; Hakibbutz Ha'artzi, secretariat, exec comm. Home: Kibbutz Hazorea, Isr. Office: Hakibbutz Ha'artzi, 15 Leonardo da Vinci St, Tel Aviv, Isr.

BEN-CHORIN, Shalom, Isr, author, journalist; b. Munich, Ger, July 20, 1913; s. Richard and Marie (Schluesselblum) Rosenthal; in Isr since 1935; att U Munich, 1931-34; m. Avital Fackenheim, Aug 25, 1943; c: Tovia, Ariela. Jerusalem corresp, Yedioth Chadashot, since 1939; fmr war corresp, Mishmar Ha'am. Author: Die Antwort des Jona; Hamishim Shnot Zionut, 1946; David Frankfurtronkem, 1948; Juden und Christen, 1960; Im juedisch-christlichen Gespraech, 1962; Der unbekannte Gott, 1963; Jenseits von Orthodoxie und Liberalismus, 1964; Das Judentum im Ringen der Gegenwart, 1965; Aus Tiefen rufe ich, 1966; Zwiesprache mit Martin Buber, 1966; Wuenschet Jerusalem Friede, 1967, Juedische Existenz heute, 1967; Das bruederliche Gespraech, 1967; Bruder Jesus, 1967. Mem: B'nai B'rith, past vice pres, David Yellin Lodge; World Union for Progressive Judaism; Har-El Cong; fmr vice-pres, Isr Journalists Assn. Recipient: Leo Baeck prize, 1959; Bundesverdienst Kreuz, Ger Fed Rep, 1969. Home: 3 Ariel St, Jerusalem, Isr.

BEN-DAVID, Abba, Isr, linguist; b. Warsaw, Pol, Dec 3, 1911; s. David and Hannah (Rubinstein) Firestein; in Isr since 1934; MA, Heb U, 1939; att Conservatoire, Jerusalem, 1937-39. Ling adv, Jerusalem BC Service, since 1963; fmr: surveyor, cartographer (air photography), Photogrammetric Inst, Jerusalem, 1949-52; ed, Yad ve-Shem, Jerusalem, 1956-63. Cpl, British Army, 1942-46. Author: Biblical Hebrew and Mishnaic Hebrew, 1967. Recipient: Bialik prize, 1968. Spec interest: music. Home: 3 Shammai St, Jerusalem, Isr. Office: Kol Israel BC Sta, Jerusalem, Isr.

BEN-DAVID, Arieh, Can, business exec; b. Czernowitz, Aus, Jan 13, 1914; s. David and Sophie (Rosenbaum) Schuller; att Technion, Haifa; 1st m. c: Daniel, Ilan; m. 2nd, Eleonora Ekstein, Nov 15, 1948; c: Ariella, step c: Kalman Held. Gen mgr, Shopsy's Foods Ltd, since 1958; pres, Isr Philatelic Agcy of Can; owner, Tal Man, factory, Tel Aviv; m, Incode, Eritrea, 1955-56; co-owner, Chocolat Tobler, Vienna, 1956-58; Haganah. Pres: World Philatelic Cong of Isr, Holy Land & Judaica Soc; Can Assn for Isr Philately; Maccabi Tel Aviv, Soccer; hon vice-pres, Soc Isr Philatelists; mem: Royal Philatelic Soc of Can; Ar-Ge Isr in Ger. Contbr to philatelic jours. Recipient: postal hist research award, Amer Philatelic Soc; Berzion Bell award of postal hist research, IPPSA; Wolf award. Home: 7 Old Park Rd, Toronto, Ontario, Can. Office: 2 Huxley Rd, Weston, Ontario, Can.

BEN-DAVID, Avraham, Isr, communal leader; b. Czech, June 25, 1911; s. David and Sarah (Klugman) Mermelstein; in Isr since 1934; att U Bratislava; Heb U, Jerusalem; m. Bracha Zuk; c: Avshalom, Avihu. Head, ind dept, Hakibbutz Ha'arzi, Hashomer Hatzair, since 1966, mem, exec comm, secretariat; introduced first ind enterprises into kibbutz econ; delg of Hashomer Hatzair: Czech; Hung; delg in London, i/c econ activities of kibbutzim in Gt Brit; fmr: exec, Kfar Masaryk, 1934-42; mgn dir, Askar paint factory, 1942-47, 1955-63. Haganah, 1934-38. Active in Aliyah Bet; dir, Kibbutz Ind Assn; fmr, mem: hqr, Hashomer Hatzair, Czech; Hechalutz, Czech; Moatzat Poalei Haifa; delg to WZC, Geneva. Home: Kibbutz Kfar Masaryk, Isr. Office: 15 Leonardo da Vinci St, Tel Aviv, Isr.

BEN-DAVID, Itzhack, Isr, sociologist; b. Jerusalem, Dec 11, 1937; s. Eliahou and Margalit (Bitton); BA, Heb U, Jerusalem, 1966, MA, 1968; m. Devora Parnes, Apr 7, 1965; c: Hagit. Mem, Kibbutz Gevim, since 1967; lectr sociol, Bet Berl, Fac Agric, Rehovoth, 1966-69; secy, Kibbutz Gevim, 1967-68. IDF, 1955-58. Prin contribs, research in sociol of Kibbutzim. Mem: social comm, Ihud Hakvutzot veha Kibbutzim; ideolog circle, Lab Party; fmr mem ed bd, ba Ma'ale. Contbr to Kibbutz publs: Niv Hakvutzah; Heidim. Recipient: Even Zahav award, 1966. Home: Kibbutz Gevim, Shaar-Hanegev, Isr.

BEN-DAVID, Joseph, Isr, sociologist, educator; b. Györ, Hung, 1920; in Isr since 1941; dipl. social admn, LSE, 1949; MA, Heb U, Jerusalem, 1955; PhD, 1959; m. Miriam; c: Aaron, Gila, Uriel. Prof, Heb U, Jerusalem, since 1959; cons, Isr Natl Council for Research and Devl, since 1962; chmn, comm on Interdept Studies in Social Scis, since 1963; cons mem, OECD, Paris; f, Cen for Advanced Study, Stanford, U, Cal, 1957-58; visiting prof: U of Cal, Berkeley, 1964-65; U of Chgo, 1968, 1969. Fmr: secy, research comm, Intl Sociol Assn; AAAS; Amer Sociol Assn; Isr Sociol Assn; Isr Demographic Soc; Isr Hist Soc. Author: Society and Science, 1970; co-author, Introduction to Sociology, 1964; ed, Agricultural Planning & Village Community in Israel, 1964; mem, ed bds: Admn Sci Quarterly; Amer Jour Sociol; Minerva; fmr, mem, ed bd, Sociol of Educ. Office: Hebrew University, Jerusalem, Isr.

BEN-DAVID, Yehuda, Isr, government official; b. Youngstown, O, May 11, 1918; s. Zalman and Zipora (Brisker); in Isr since 1920; att: Montefiori Coll, Tel Aviv; Heb U, Jerusalem; Cdr and Staff Coll, Paris; m. Simone Werzberg, Dec 15, 1948; c: Rafael, Ram, Nurit. Dir, Merkaz HaHadracha, info off, since 1967; fmr, dir, Afr, Investment and Devl Co, Ltd; ambass: Fed of Mali; Rep of Senegal. Spec night squads; Haganah, cdr, field units, Tel Aviv dist; cdr, youth batallions, Tel Aviv, Jerusalem dists; second in command, Haganah, Ger, Aus, 1947-48; acting cdr, Fr, N Afr; lt col, IS, IDF; dep mil attache, Paris, 1957-60. Author: A Grain of Corn, 1967. Home: 14 Bat Yftah, Zahala, Isr. Office: Prime Minister's Office, Jerusalem, Isr.

BENDEL, Menahem, Isr, law officer; b. Isr, Aug 7, 1910; s. Yacob and Michal (David); m. Rachel Stern, Jan 16, 1940; c: Ron, Yacob. Head, inves br, N dist, Police Hqr, since 1928, asst cdr. Mem, Freemasons, Tel Aviv. Spec interests: hist books, fishing, hunting. Home: 10 Megiddo St, Haifa, Isr. Office: Police Headquarters, Nazareth, Isr.

BENDELSTEIN, Rubin H, US, rabbi; NYC, Sep 9, 1919; s. Abraham and Sarah (Pomerantz); BS, CCNY, 1938, MS, 1939; ordained rabbi, Rabb Sem of Amer, 1941; PhD candidate, TC, Columbia U; m. Florence Blachorsky, 1948; c: Alvin, Harold, Shulamith, Elena, Israel, Lavey, Sarah. Rabbi, Up-

town Syn, Bayonne, since 1941; chaplain: B'nai B'rith; KP; Rabb Sem of Amer, fac mem since 1945; Naval Base, Bayonne; Boy Scouts of Amer; Bayonne Mil Ocean Terminal; Caven Point Army Res Cen, Jersey City, NJ. Vice-pres, Bayonne Interfaith Housing Corp; chmn, Clergy Comm of United Fund; bd educ, United Heb Schs; co-chmn, rabb wfr, syn standards, marriage, family commn, RabCA, since 1954; hon pres, Bayonne chap, Mizrachi Org of Amer, since 1941; dir: Comty Chest, 1945-51; project dir, Bayonne Head Start; bd dirs: ARC; adv council, Boy Scouts of Amer; admn bd, Union of Orthodox Rabbis. Recipient: distinguished service award, B'nai B'rith, 1948. Home: 119 W 44 St, Bayonne, NJ. Study: 49 St and Ave C, Bayonne, NJ.

BENDER, Howard Marvin, US, business exec; b. Paterson, NJ, Oct 11, 1930; s. Jack and Dorothy (Blake); att Md U, 1948-50; m. Sondra Dosik, July 15, 1951; c: Barbara, Julie, Eileen, David. Exec vice-pres, Blake Construction Co Inc, since 1958, with co since 1950. Dir: Wash and Lee Savings & Loan Assn; Gtr Wash JCC; trustee: Radnor PTA; Isr Bonds; mem, Tau Epsilon Phi. Hobbies: golf, tennis, bowling. Home: 7400 Radnor Rd, Bethesda, Md. Office: 1120 Connecticut Ave, Washington, DC.

BENDER, Karpol, Isr, rabbi; b. Slonim, Pol, Feb 11, 1930; s. Philip and Mary (Bielous); in Isr since 1969; att U Cape Town, S Afr, 1948-49; BA, Yeshiva U, NY, 1953, ordained rabbi, 1957; m. Rena Zambrowsky, Jan 24, 1960; c: Amiel, Merryl. Dir, Off Diaspora Affairs, Bar Ilan U, since 1969; rabbi, Beth Isr Cong, Kingston, Can, 1959-69; dir, B'nai B'rith Hillel Found, Queens U, Kingston, Can, 1964-69; Heb chaplain, Fed Penitentiaries, 1959-69; rabbi, Seaview J Cen, Bklyn, NY, 1957-59. Vice-pres, Rabb Council, Can, 1966-69; mem exec, RabCA, 1966-68; fmr natl pres, Mizrachi Youth of Amer; fmr mem: ZOC Natl Council; Can Correctional Chaplains Assn; Can Inst Intl Affairs; B'nai B'rith; Natl Rel Wfr Comm, Jt Comty Relations Comm, Can J Cong. Home: 26 Hamaagal, Rimon, Isr. Office: Bar Ilan U, Ramat Gan, Isr.

BENDER, Morris B, US, physician, educator; b. Uman, Russ, June 8, 1905; s. Boris and Anna (Nemirowsky); in US since 1914; BS, U of Pa, 1927, MD, 1931; m. Sara Spirtes, June 28, 1936; c: Barbara, Adam, Barnaby, Victor. Prof, chmn, dept neur, Mt Sinai Sch of Med, since 1966, Henry P and Georgette Goldschmidt prof, neur, since 1968; prof, clin neur, NYU Coll of Med, 1951-66, on staff since 1938; clin prof, neur, Coll Phys and Surg, Columbia U, 1953; dir, neur service, Mt Sinai Hosp, since 1951, staff mem, since 1933; visiting neur psycht, Bellevue Hosp, asso att neur, 1946-49, dir neur service, 1951-61; cons neur, N Shore Hosp, Manhasset, NY, since 1953; sr cons neur, VA, 1946-61; asst alienist, Bellevue Psycht Hosp, NY, 1935-36; didactic psychan, 1935-36; Kings Co Mental Hygiene Clinic, Bklyn, 1936; research neuro-phys, Yale U, 1936-37; f: Abrahamson, in neuropsycht, NY, New Haven, 1935-37; hon research: Yale U, 1936-37; Josiah Macy Jr Found, NY, 1938-43; Dazian Found, NY, 1947-49; Cerebral Palsy Council, 1948-51; NRC, VA, 1948; Multiple Sclerosis Soc Comm, 1953; spec cons, USPH, 1962-64; S Cross of Brazil, 1967. Mem: Amer Neur Assn; Amer Phys Assn; Amer Psycht Assn; Amer Coll Phys; Assn for Research in Nervous and Mental Diseases; Soc for Biol Psycht; Amer Fed Clinical Research; NY Neur Soc; Harvey Soc; Soc Experimental Biol & Med; NY Co Med Soc; Sigma Xi; AAUP. Author of monographs and numerous sci articles and abstracts. Home: 400 E Shore Rd, Great Neck, Long Island, NY. Office: 1212 Fifth Ave, New York, NY.

BENDER, Morris C, S Afr, physician, farmer; b. Lith, Feb 14, 1902; s. Abraham and Zipporah (Joselowitz); in S Afr since 1910; MB, ChB, U of Witwatersrand, 1928; m. Leah Golub, Feb 21, 1933; c: Bernard, Audrey. Gen practitioner, Johannesburg, since 1929; farmer, Transvaal province, since 1943; mgn dir, Bender Holdings (Pty) Ltd, since 1953. Co-found, Cotlands Babies Sanctuary for Unwanted and Abandoned Babies, 1937, hon life vice-pres, 1953; hon phys, S Rand Hosp, Johannesburg, since inception until 1961; mem, bd trustees, exec off, Southeastern Heb Cong, Johannesburg, 1940. Home: Petunia St, Roseltenville, Johannesburg, S Afr.

BENDER, Myron L, US, educator; b. St Louis, Mo, May 20, 1924; s. Averam and Fannie (Leventhal); BS, Purdue U, 1944, PhD, 1948; m. Muriel Schulman, June 8, 1952; c: Alec, Bruce, Steven. Prof, chem, Northwestern U, since 1960; fac mem, Ill Inst Tech, 1951-60. F, Amer Inst Chem; mem: Natl Acad Sci; Amer Chem Soc; Sigma Xi; Phi Lambda Upsilon;

Chem Soc, London; Amer Inst Biol Chem; AAUP; AAAS. Contbr papers to profsl jours. Home: 2514 Sheridan Rd, Evanston, Ill. Office: Northwestern University, Evanston, Ill.

BENDHEIM, Charles H, US, business exec; b. Bklyn, NY, Nov 12, 1917; s. Siegfried and Nannette (Felsenstein); BS, Lafayette Coll, 1939; m. Els Salomon, June 21, 1942; c: Judith, Jack, Debra, Aviva, Philip, Edna, Karen. Pres, Phillipp Bros Chemicals Inc, since 1960. Mem, bd trustees: Yeshiva U; Cong Bachurei Chemed, Long Beach, LI, hon pres, 1950; treas, mem, bd trustees, Cong Shearith Israel, NY; vice-pres, Manhattan Day Sch; mem, intl bd of govs, Shaare Zedek Hosp, Jerusalem, Isr. Home: 101 Central Park W, New York, NY. Office: 10 Columbus Circle, New York, NY.

BENDIX, Reinhard, US, sociologist; b. Berlin, Feb 25, 1916; s. Ludwig and Else (Henschel); in US since 1938; MA, U of Chgo, 1943, PhD, 1947; m. Jane Walstrum, 1940; c: Karen, Erik, John. Prof, sociol, U Cal, since 1955, chmn, dept sociol, 1958-61; instr, U Chgo, 1943-46; asst prof, U Colo, 1946-47. Pres, Amer Sociol Assn, 1969-70; vice-pres, Intl Sociol Assn, 1966-70; mem, Amer Sociol Soc. Author: Work and Authority in Industry, 1956; Max Weber, An Intellectual Portrait, 1960; Nation-Building and Citizenship, 1964; co-author: Class, Status and Power, 1953; Social Mobility in Industrial Society, 1959; ed, State and Society; contbr to sociol jours. Recipient: Fullbright grant, 1953-54; MacIver award, Amer Sociol Soc, 1958; Carnegie Found f, 1961-62. Hobbies: music, gardening. Home: 3 Orchard Lane, Berkeley, Cal. Office: University of Cal, Berkeley, Cal.

BENDOR, Zvi, Isr, educational exec, educator; b. Bessarabia, Rum, Dec 24, 1916; s. Leib and Bluma (Tabatchnik) Dorfman; in Isr since 1936; tchr cert, State Tchrs Training Coll of Kibbutz Educ, 1950; MA, Heb U, Jerusalem, 1967; m. Naomi Bernstein, 1936; c: Noa Katz, Hadassah Shofti, Anat. Fmr: mem, bd dirs, State Tchrs Training Coll, lectr, Bibl lit, 1965-69; tchr, regional HS, Harei Ephraim, 1951-62; prin, educ work, Hashomer Hatzair, Isr, Eur. Haganah, 1949-50. Prin contrib: Bibl research. Mem: exec council, Kibbutz Hashomer Hatzair; council, Mapam Party; dept educ, Hakibbutz Haartzi; fmr secy, Kibbutz Dalia. Co-author: Sources of Kingdom in Ancient Israel; contbr of bibl articles; Kibbutz society; educ; Kibbutz Arzi periodicals. Home: Kibbutz Daliah, Isr. Office: Oranim, Kiriat Tivon, Isr.

BEN-DOV, David, Isr, diplomat; b. Haifa, Dec 31, 1923; s. Nachman and Ziporah (Braslavi); att Natl Defence Coll, Jerusalem; MA, Heb U, Jerusalem, 1951; m. Sarah Brown, May 21, 1947; c: Ofer, Daphna. Consul gen of Isr, SF, US; fmr news ed, Isr BC Service, 1951-53; tchr, dept sociol, Heb U, 1964-68. J Brigade, Brit Army; IDF. Home: 16 Hamagid St, Isr. Office: 105 Montgomery St, San Francisco, Cal.

BENEDIKT, Binyamin Zeew, Isr, educator, rabbi; b. Vienna, May 10, 1913; s. Samuel and Rosalia (Donath); in Isr since 1939; ordained rabbi, Yeshiva, Pressburg, 1936; MA, Heb U, Jerusalem, 1943, PhD, 1946; m. Jona Kopshtik, 1943. Rabbi of Ahuza, Haifa, since 1957; sr lectr, Talmud, Tel Aviv U; fmr rabbi: Dist of Vienna, 1933-39; Amsterdam, 1953-55; The Hague, 1955-57. Capt, IDF, 1940. Contbr of articles, medieval rabb lit, Maimonides, to scholarly publs. Home: 11 Gibeon St, Haifa, Isr.

BEN-EFRAIM, Isac, Isr, engineer; b. Piatra Neamtz, Rum, Dec 25, 1914; s. Froim and Penina (Segaler); in Isr since 1935; BS, MS, Inst of Tech, 1966; m. Nehama Sternziss, May, 1959; c: Yigal, Orit, Avishai. Cons engr; gen secy, Engrs Union, 1963-68. Parachute mission, Hagana, Rum, 1944; org illegal immigration from Rum for JA and Hechalutz, 1945-48; cdr, Briche, Rum, 1946. Home: 6 Levitan St, Tel Aviv, Isr. Office: 71 Weizmann, Tel Aviv, Isr.

BEN-ELIAHU, Bezalel, Can, organization exec; b. Montreal, Can, Jan 12, 1937; s. Harry and Eva (Lagunow) Yarosky; att Sir George Williams U, Montreal; m. Cherna Rosenberg, Jan 5, 1964; c: Leaht, Mayrav. Exec dir: ZOC; Can J Cong, maritime region, since 1969; fmr, mem, Moshav Ram-On, Isr. IDF, 1961-63. Spec interests: sheep farming, Bible study. Home: 1431 Lemarchant St, Halifax, Can. Office: 6239 Quinpool Rd, Halifax, Can.

BENENSON, William, US, physician, educator; b. Dniepropetrovsk, Russ, Sep 15, 1904; s. Jacob and Sonia (Mekler); in US since 1906; BA, Cornell U, 1925, MD, 1929; m. Esther

Siev, 1957; c: Michael, Sharon, Amy, Blanche. Cons phys, Queens Gen Hosp, since 1953; att phys, Flushing Hosp, since 1946; staff phys, Booth Memorial Hosp, 1955-66; phys emeritus, LI J Hosp, since 1960, staff path, 1953; asst phys, path, St John's Hosp, LI, 1931-46; asst prof, clinical med, NY Med Coll, since 1946. Lt col, US Army, WW II. Dipl, Amer Bd Internal Med; f, Amer Coll Phys; mem: AMA; NY State Med Soc; NY Card soc. Contbr to med jours. Home: 36-21 Parsons Blvd, Flushing, NY. Office: 36-17 Parsons Blvd, Flushing, NY.

BENESCH, Alfred A, US, attorney; b. Cleveland, O, July 3, 1879; s. Isidore and Bertha (Federman); AB, Harvard Coll, 1900, AM, 1901; LLB, Harvard Law Sch; hon LLD, Cleveland State U; hon LHD, HUC; hon LLD, W Reserve U; m. Helen Newman, Nov 29, 1906 (decd). Ret; fmr: partner, law firm, Benesch, Friedlander, Mendelson & Coplan. Fmr mem: Cleveland City Council; Public Safety Council; Cleveland Bd of Educ; mem: Cleveland JWF; Cleveland United Appeal; Mt Sinai Hosp; B'nai B'rith. Home: 2515 Kempen Rd, Cleveland, Ohio.

BENETAR, David L, US, attorney; b. NYC, Nov 19, 1906; s. Morris and Estella (Benetar); att NYU, 1923-25; LLB, Bklyn Law Sch of St Lawrence U, 1928; m. Beatrice Dalsimer, June 26, 1934; c: Carol Feinberg, Richard. Partner, law firm, Nordlinger, Riegelman, Benetar & Charney, since 1933; prin mediation off, Natl War Lab Bd, 1942-43; public panel mem, natl and 2nd regional War Lab Bd, 1943-45; guest lectr, lab law, Columbia, Rutgers, Fordham, NYU, Hofstra Coll, Practising Law Inst. Chmn, exec comm, J Bd Guardians, since 1960; bd trustees: FJP, NY, 1956-60; chmn: mem, lab mgmt adv panel, State Mediation Bd, appd by Gov Rockefeller; comm on lab and social security leg, Assn of the Bar, City of NY, 1950-53, vice-chmn, grievance comm, 1961-64, exec comm, 1957-60; chmn, lab mgmt relations comm, 1958-60; exec comm, NY C of C, 1966-68; chmn, comm on lab law, NY State Bar Assn, 1959-63; mem: NYC, State and Amer Bar Assns; bd dirs, Econ Devl Council of NYC, Inc; Cornell Club. Contbr to law jours. Home: 35 Sutton Pl, New York, NY. Office: 420 Lexington Ave, New York, NY.

BEN-EZER, Dov, Isr, engineer; b. Kovno, Lith, Sep 28, 1921; s. Ezra and Liza (Rudner) Pupkin; in Isr since 1933; dipl engr, mech engr, Technion, Haifa, 1945; m. Jafa Suchovolsky, Feb. 24, 1947; c: Liora, Idit. Cons engr since 1966; fmr: mech engr, 1946-54; mgr, engr dept, Electra Co, 1954-57; found, co-owner, tech dir: Alboa; Aveeram, 1958-66. Lt, IAF, 1948-49. Prin contribs: work in air-conditioning; refrigeration; vertical transp. Mem: Assn of Engrs and Architects, Isr; Ashrae, Amer Soc of Heating, Refrigeration and Air-Conditioning Engrs; Intl Inst of Refrigeration Engrs; Free Masons. Hobbies: photography, bridge. Home: 26 Daphna St, Tel Aviv, Isr. Office: 13 Levi Itzhak St, Tel Aviv, Isr.

BENFEY, Alice E, Australia, communal worker; b. Berlin, d. Martin and Gertrud (Seckelson) Fiatow, in Australia since 1939; DRerPol, U of Frankfurt/Main; widow; c: Marlis Cohen. Mem, ad personam: world WIZO exec; Australian ZF; fmr pres, Australian WIZO Fed. Spec interests: art, econ. Home: 8 Hansen St, Kew 3101, Melbourne, Australia.

BEN-GURION, Amos, Isr, business exec; b. London, Aug 23, 1920; s. David and Paula (Munvez); in Isr since 1922; grad, Kadoorie Agric Sch; m. Mary Callow, Feb 23, 1946; c: Galia Rafi, Alon, Ruth. Gen mgr, ATA Textile Co Ltd, since 1966; fmr dep chief, Isr Police, 1949-63. Maj, Brit Army, WWII; battalion cdr, IDF, 1948. Home: 53 Chorev St, Haifa, Isr. Office: POB 83, Kiryat Ata, Isr.

BEN-GURION, David, Isr, statesman; b. Plonsk, Pol, Oct 16, 1886; s. Avigdor and Sheindel (Friedman) Green; in Isr since 1906; received traditional rel educ; pvt tutoring in gen studies and langs; att Istanbul U, 1914; hon: DHL, JTSA, 1952; PhD, Heb U, 1957; LLD, Brandeis U, 1960; LLD, Rangoon U, 1961; DArch, Technion, 1962; m. Paula Munweis, 1917 (decd); c: Amos, Geula, Renana. Ret, Kibbutz Sde Boker; first PM and Min of Defense, Govt of Isr, 1948-53; proclaimed Independence of Isr, 1948; resigned 1953, settled at Kibbutz Sde Boker in the Negev, rejoined Govt as PM and Min of Defense, 1955-63. Fmr: co-found, Poalei Zion, Pol, 1903, mem, J Self-Defense, Pol, 1905; chmn, Poalei Zion conv, 1906; agric lab: Petah Tikva and Rishon-le-Zion, 1906-07;

Segera, 1907-09; co-found and chmn, Poalei Zion Constituent Conf, 1907; co-ed, Ha-Ahdut, monthly, 1910; mem, comm, Jewish Home Guard, 1915; exiled from Pal by Turkish admn, 1915; lived in US; co-found, Hechalutz, US, 1916; co-found, J Legion, served in its ranks, returned to Pal; co-found: Ahdut ha-Avoda, 1918; Histadrut (Gen Fed of J Lab in Isr), 1920, secy gen, 1921-35; Mapai (Isr Lab Party), 1930; delg: London Zionist Conf, 1920; Histadrut missions to Moscow, 1924, to US, 1927; Intl Lab Conf, Berlin, 1930; all WZCs since the 11th, 1913; mem, JA Exec, since 1933, chmn, 1935-48; delg to testify on behalf of the Yishuv (J population of Pal) before: British Inquiry Commn, 1938, 1946; Anglo-Amer Inquiry Commn, 1947; UN Inquiry Commn, 1947; following the UN Partition Resolution (Nov 29, 1947), elected chmn, Natl Admn i/c of security and defense; MK since 1949; state visits to: Eng, Greece, 1950; US, 1951; Fr, 1959; US, Eng, 1960; Fr, Belgium, Holland, 1960; Can, US, Eng, Fr, 1961; Burma, 1961; Scandinavian countries, 1962. Author: (maj publs) in Heb: Self-Government of Villayets, 1910; The Land of Israel, 1918; Ourselves and Our Neighbors, 1920; The Labor Movement and Revisionism, 1933; From Class to Nation, 1933; Mishmarot (essays on Labor Zionism), 1935; In the Struggle, 5 vols, 1949; Israel at War, 1951; Vision and Implementation, 5 vols, 1951; The Sinai Campaign, 1959; trans into Heb, Sombart's Studies on Socialism in the XIXth Century; co-author: Yizkor, in memoriam Hashomer heroes; in Eng: Rebirth and Destiny of Israel, 1954; in Span: Amanecer de un Estado, 1954; En la Patria Libre, 1954; in Ger: David und Goliath in unserer Zeit, 1961; contbr, numerous essays and articles. Recipient: Bublick Prize, Heb U, Jerusalem, 1949; Bialik Lit Prize for Judaica, 1952; Henrietta Szold award, Hadassah Women's Zionist Org of Amer, 1958. Home: Sde-Boker, Negev, Isr.

BEN-HAIM, Efraim, Isr, local leg; b. The Hague, Holland, Feb 23, 1916; s. Haim and Hanna (Wolfgang) Friedman; in Isr since 1939; licencié en sci agric, U Gand, Holland, 1938; m. Bertha Taustein, Mar 17, 1939; c: Ehud, Helal, Miryam, Ruth, Tirtsa. Dep head, regional council, Hof Hacarmel, since 1966; fmr: secy, Kibbutz Beit Oren, 1950; dir, HOM, HS, 1951-56; JA repr, i/c illegal immigration and self defense, N Afr; head, Afr dept, JA, 1949-50; Isr Ambass: Cen Afr Rep; Rep of Tchad. Instr, Palmach; IDF. Council chmn, mem head comm, Land of Isr Movement; fmr: council mem: Hakibbutz Hameuchad; Ahdut Ha'avoda; Mapam; secy, Zionist Youth Fed, Belgium. Author: History and Situation of Jewish Agriculture in Palestine, 1939; co-author, Chances for Aliyah and the Demographic Problem, 1969; contbr of articles on immigration, integration and social problems of Isr. Recipient: cdr, Order of Merit, Cen Afr, 1963; dist citizen, nominated by fmr Pres Ben Zvi, 1962. Home: Kibbutz Beit Oren, Isr. Office: Regional Council, Hof Hacarmel, Isr.

BEN-HAIM, Paul Shaul, Isr, composer; b. Munich, Ger, July 5, 1897; s. Heinrich and Anna (Schulmann) Frankenburger; in Isr since 1933; att Munich Acad of Music, 1915-16, 1919-20; m. Helena Acham, Aug 20, 1934; s. Yoram. Composer; pedg adv, Rubin Acad of Music, since 1961; two sym: Yzkor, sym poem for violin and orch; Concerto for strings; Concerto for piano and orch; Pastorale with Variations, for clarinet, harp and strings; String Quartet; Sonatina for piano; The Sweet Psalmist of Isr, for orch; Violin Concerto; Concerto for piano; Fri Evening Service; Three Psalms for SF; chamber music; songs; compositions for piano; arrangements of authentic Yemenite folk songs. Hon chmn, Isr Composers League. Recipient: Engel Award of Music, 1945, 1953; Isr Music Award, 1957. Home: 11 Aharonovitz St, Tel Aviv, Isr.

BEN-HAIM, Shmuel Mula, Isr, artist; b. Lida, Pol, July 30, 1916; s. Chaim and Fruma (Judelewicz) Kosciansky; in Isr since 1947; att: Gymnasium Tarbut, Lida; Avni Sch of Fine Arts, Tel Aviv, 1953-55; Acad de la Grande Chaumiere, Paris, 1955-56; m. Rivka Basman, Aug 30, 1945. Artist; exhb: Musee de Beaux Arts de la Ville de Paris, exhb of kibbutz artists; Ten Years of Israel's Painting, Tel Aviv Mus; Tenth Anniversary Exposition, Jerusalem; Mus of Mod Art, Paris; Chemerinsky Art Gal, Tel Aviv; fmr: cultural attaché, Isr Emb, Moscow, 1962-65. Pol army, 1938-45; mem of underground that helped Jews escape to Pal; off, Haganah, 1945-48. Past pres, Assn of Painters and Sculptors, Isr; past secy, Kibbutz Arzi Artists; past treas, tchr, Kibbutz Hamapil; mem bd, plastic arts, Isr Art Council; council mem, Isr Assn of Painters and Sculptors; mem, Isr Artists Assn. Recipient: Haganah Sign; Sinai War, Aleh. Hobby: music. Home: Herzlia B, Isr.

BEN-HAYIM, Zeev, Isr, educator; b. Mosciska, Pol, Dec 28, 1907; s. Hayim and Bluma (Nussbaum); in Isr since 1931; att JTS, Breslau, 1927-30, 1932-33; U of Breslau, 1928-30, 1932-33; Heb U, Jerusalem, 1931; m. Zippora Seiden, 1934; c: Gozal, Shelomit. Prof, Heb lang, Heb U, Jerusalem, since 1955; vice-pres, Acad of Heb Lang, since 1960; fmr, sci secy, Vaad Halashon Haivrith. Mem, Isr Acad of Sci and Hum, since 1966. Author: Studies in Traditions of the Hebrew Language, 1954; The Literary and Oral Traditions of the Hebrew and Aramaic Amongst the Samaritans, vols I, II, 1957; vol III, pt I, 1961, pt II, 1967; ed: Leshonenu, 1956-65; The Historical Dictionary of the Hebrew Language, in preparation, since 1961; contbr to profsl jours. Home: 117 Herzl Blvd, Jerusalem, Isr. Offices: Hebrew University; Academy of the Hebrew Language, Jerusalem, Isr.

BEN-HORIN, Eliashiv, Isr, diplomat; b. Sosnowic, Pol, Sep 4, 1921; s. Shmuel and Hella (Lisie); dipl law, Heb U; LLB, U of London; m. Nehama Kurzweil, Mar 23, 1948. Asst dir gen, Min Fgn Affairs, since 1968; adv, perm delg to UN, 1951; first secy, Isr Emb, Wash, DC, 1952-54; Legation, Ankara, 1954-55; dep dir, Asian-Afr div, Min for Fgn Affairs, 1955-57, dir, 1957-60; ambass to Burma, Nepal, Ceylon, all from 1960-63; Venezuela, Jamaica, Trinidad, all from 1963-67; dir, Latin Amer div, Min Fgn Affairs, 1967-68. British Army, WW II; IDF, Isr War of Independence. Home: 5 Palmach St, Jerusalem, Isr. Office: Min for Fgn Affairs, Jerusalem, Isr.

BEN-HORIN, M ir, US, educator, author; b. Königsberg, Prussia, Dec 31, 1918; s. Joseph and Dwoira (Polishuk) Schiffmann; BJP, Tchrs Inst, JTSA, 1941; MA, Columbia U, 1948, PhD, 1952; m. Alice Neugebauer, Sep 15, 1946; c: Judith, Joseph, Gideon. Prof, educ, chmn, sch of educ, Dropsie Coll, Phila, since 1957; mgn ed, J Social Studies, NYC, since 1957; inves, Dept of the Army, 1946-48; field dir, W Eur, J Cultural Reconstruction, Inc, 1949-50; mem, fac, acting registrar, Heb Tchrs Coll, Brookline, Mass, 1951-57; cons: Amer Assn for J Educ, since 1968; J Rel Educ, Reconstructionist Rabb Coll, since 1968. US Army, 1943-46; lt col, US Army Res. Vice-pres, Natl Council for J Educ, 1963; mem: Kappa Delta Pi; Phi Delta Kappa; Conf on J Soc Studies; AAUP; Mil Govt Assn; Rel Educ Assn of US and Can; Res Offs Assn of US. Author: Max Nordau, Philosopher of Human Solidarity, 1957; Through Jewish Eyes: Essays in Reconstructionist Judaism, 1969; co-ed, Studies and Essays (in honor of Abraham A Neuman), 1962; Judaism and the Jewish School, 1966; The Jew Faces the Modern World, 1969; mem, ed bd: The Reconstructionist; Judaism; J Educ; Jour of J Communal Service; contbr to scholarly and lit jours. Recipient: Joseph Bragin Memorial Prize, Tchrs Inst, JTSA. Home: 634 W Upsal St, Philadelphia, Pa. Office: Dropsie College, Philadelphia, Pa.

BEN-HUR, Nahum, Isr, plastic surg; b. Tel Aviv, Nov 24, 1928; s. Elkana and Sima (Abramobsky); MD, Heb U-Hadassah Med Sch, 1957; m. Miriam Peyser, June 15, 1951; c: Ehud, Tamir. Sr lectr, Heb U-Hadassah Med Sch, since 1967, perm chief phys, 1968; fmr: chief of surg, Malawi, Afr, 1963; plastic and maxillofacial surg, Hadassah U Hosp, 1964; f, NIH, NYU Med Cen, Inst of Reconstructive Plastic surg, 1965; cens on plastic surg, invited by Min of Health, Cyprus, 1968. Isr repr, Educ Found of Amer Soc Plastic and Reconstructive Surg; participant at numerous sems, symposiums, convs; pres, Isr Assn Plastic and Reconstructive Surg; mem: IMA; Isr Surg Soc; Isr Assn Plastic Surg; Transplantation Soc; British Assn Plastic Surg; Intl Soc for Burn Injuries; Amer Soc Plastic and Reconstructive Surg; Intl Coll Surgs; AAAS. Contbr of numerous articles to profsl publs. Recipient: Dr J Singer prize, Hadassah Med Sch, 1955; Pochovski Prize, IMA, 1965; prize of Educ Found, Amer Soc Plastic and Reconstructive Surg, 1968. Home: 15 Bait Vegan St, Jerusalem, Isr. Office: Hadassah-Hebrew University Hospital, Jerusalem, Isr.

BENJAMIN, David A, US, jurist; b. NYC, July 2, 1899; s. Joseph and Annie (Grossman); LLB, Fordham U Law Sch, 1919; m. Celia Weinstein, Nov 30, 1924; c: Ruth. Justice, Supr Court, State of NY, since 1955, assigned to Appellate Term, 1959; asst counsel, reapportionment comm, NY State Leg, 1936; spec asst, att gen i/c, Election Frauds, Bur, NY, 1945; judge, City Court, Kings Co, 1946-54; govt appeal agt, Local Draft Bd No 205, until 1946; assigned by Appellate Div to Condemnation, Tax Certiorari and Incompetency Proceedings, 1961; designated by Gov Rockefeller as asso justice, Appellate Div, 2nd dept, 1965. Mem bd trustees and vice-pres,

UJA, since 1958, fmr Bklyn chmn, city wide gen chmn; vice-pres, life trustee, mem exec comm, chmn, speakers bur, mem, communal planning and nominating comms, FJP; mem: bd dirs, Inst Applied Biol; bd trustees, Sara Delano Roosevelt House, Hunter Coll; bd dirs, ADL regional off; vice-pres, Youth United for Better Citizens of Tomorrow, Inc; Bklyn chmn: Albert Einstein Med Sch, Yeshiva U; Brandeis U Campaign Comm; hon dir, Bklyn J Hosp; hon trustee, YM-YWHA, NY; mem, bd trustees, Bklyn J Cen; f: Universal Brotherhood, JTSA; Brandeis U; hon citizen, Boys Town, Father Flanagan Boys Home; mem: St Vincent's Home for Boys Hundred Club; Unity Club, fmr pres and dir; bd, Amer ORT; Amer Legion; fmr: pres, Albert Einstein lodge, B'nai B'rith; chancellor, cdr, Criterion lodge, KP; chmn, Bklyn Comty Appeal; ARC; Bklyn chmn, Fed J Charities; chmn, law comm, Rep Party, Kings Co. Home: 20 Plaza St, Brooklyn, NY.

BENJAMIN, Julliet N, US, communal worker. Mem, natl bd, Hadassah; repr Hadassah on Amer Council of Volunteer Agcys for Foreign Service; secy and mem, bd dirs, JNF; fmr tchr, NYC HS's. Fmr: natl vice-pres, Hadassah; natl chmn, vocational educ comm, ed, Hadassah Newsletter; delg to WZCs; participant, Jubilee Mission to Isr, 1962. Home: 115 Central Park W, New York, NY. Office: 65 E 52 St, New York, NY.

BENJAMINI, Brachah, Isr, painter; b. Brody, Pol, Aug 6, 1901; d. Meir and Rosa (Freudmann) Andermann; in Isr since 1921; att Art Sch, Tel Aviv; cert tchr, Sem of Art Tchrs; m. Izchak Benjamini, 1925; c: Maya Kadishay, Yair. Art tchr, public schs. Haganah, 1930-48. Mem: Assn Painters and Sculptors, Isr; Histadrut Hamorim; fmr mem: Magen David Adom; Ilan (Isr Polio Found). Spec interest: lecturing on art. Home: Azar St, Ramat HaSharon, Isr.

BEN-JEHUDA, Jacob, Isr, business exec; b. Lodz, Pol, Oct 7, 1917; s. Jehuda and Szajndla-Stefania (Lubliner); in Isr since 1940; BSc, econ, Tel Aviv U, 1957; m. Bertha Mandelbaum, Mar, 1944; c: Chaim, Osnat. Mgn dir, Timna Copper Mines, since 1964; fmr head dept, Min of Defense, 1951-64. Palmach; Haganah, 1938-41. Org, mem, Kvutzat Usha, illegal immigration org: Persia; Turkey; Yugo; active in illegal immigration: Pol; Rum; Greece. Home: 1 Batei Berman, Eilat, Isr. Office: Timna Copper Mines, Eilat, Isr.

BEN-JOSEF, David, Isr, journalist; b. Slonim, Russ, 1909; s. Joseph and Zivya (Pasovski); in Isr since 1933; att Yeshiva, Russ; m. Bracha Bornstein, 1932; c: Chaim, Miriam. Mgr, social dept, Bank Lemelacha, since 1962; ed: Yozma; Miskhar Vekalkala; secy, Merchants Assn in Isr, 1953-62. Cdr, Haganah, Jerusalem 1946-49. Mem, cen comm, Mapai, candidate to 4th and 5th Knesset; asso mem, J of Pol; pres, Shedletz immigrants to Isr assn; mem, clerks cen comm, Histadrut; fmr, pres: Biala Yeshiva; Syn Bnei Brak. Author: official book on the Ministry of Defense, 1951; Hed Ha'Hagana, 1960; contbr articles in Heb and Yiddish to daily press. Hobby: social activities. Home: 11 Feierberg, Tel Aviv, Isr. Office: 9 Carlebach St, Tel Aviv, Isr.

BENKOVITZ, Miriam Jeanette, US, educator; b. Chattanooga, Tenn, Nov 16, 1911; d. Jake and Josephine (Bloomstein); BA, Vanderbilt U, 1932; MA, Peabody Coll, 1942; MA, Yale U, 1947, PhD, 1951. Prof, dept Eng, Skidmore Coll, Saratoga Springs, since 1946; partner, Saratoga Travel Bur, since 1958. Mem: MLA; Assn of U Women; Bibliographical Soc of Amer. Author: Bibliography of Ronald Firbank, 1963; Ronald Firbank, a Biography, 1969; ed, Edwy and Elgiva, by Madame d'Arblay, 1957; contbr to profsl jours. Hobby: collecting modern Eng first eds, letters. Home: 17 Ten Springs Dr, Saratoga Springs, NY. Office: Skidmore College, Saratoga Springs, NY.

BEN-MENAHEM, Ari, Isr, educator; b. Berlin, Nov, 1928; in Isr since 1934; MS, Heb U, Jerusalem, 1953; att Upsala U; PhD, Cal Inst of Tech. Prof, geophysics, applied math, Weizmann Inst of Sci, Rehovot, since 1965. Mem, NY Acad of Sci; Sigma Xi, AGU, SSA. Contbr of numerous articles on geophysics, applied math. Home: Yad Chaim Weizmann, Rehovot, Isr. Office: Weizmann Inst of Sci, Rehovot, Isr.

BEN-MENAHEM, Naphtali, Isr, librarian, author; b. Poieni sub Munte, Havasmezö, Hung, Jan 13, 1911; s. Menahem and Helen (Schwartz) Fried; in Isr since 1935; att U of Frankfurt/M, 1929-33; m. Bilha Tishby, Sep 20, 1938; c: Elhanan,

Amitai. Dir, Inst for Heb Bibliography, since 1960; mem, mgmt, Rabbi Kook Inst, since 1956, ed, 1951-59; dir, immigration dept, JA, 1948-51. Author: Sefer haTaamin shel Rabbi Abraham ibn Ezra, 1941; Megilat Starim, 1944; Gvilei Sefarim, 1947; Zmirot shel Shabat, 1949; Rabbi Moshe Haim Luzzato, 1951; Shirei Itzhak ibn Ezra, 1950; Me-Ginzei Israel be-Vatican, 1954; Misifrut Israel be-Ungaria, 1958; Hahmei Lita, 1959; Bshaarei Sefer, 1967; contbr of articles to profsl publs. Home: 8 Keren Kayemeth St, Jerusalem, Isr. Office: The Natl and U Libr, Jerusalem, Isr.

BEN-NAEH, David, Eng, communal leader; b. Jerusalem, Sep 14, 1936; s. Yehuda and Miriam; lt, Off Sch, 1956; m. Helen Nagari, Sep 1, 1964; c: Yaron, Shiy. Eur Shaliach, Hamishmeret Hatzeira, Mizrachi Hapoel Hamizrachi, Eng and Ir, since 1967; secy, Rel Cen of Educ, Isr, 1958-67; gen secy, Parents Assn, Elem Schs in Isr, 1965-67; guide, Isr tours, 1960-67. Zahal, 1955-58. Hon off: Natl Hamishmeret Hatzeira; Natl Mishmeret in Isr, 1960-67; mem, Educ Comm, Jerusalem Munic, 1966-67. Author: Guide To Elementary School Graduates, 1965. Hobbies: swimming, football. Home: 42 Vincent Ct, Bell Lane, London, Eng. Office: 345 Gray's Inn Rd, London, Eng.

BEN-NATAN, Asher, Isr, diplomat; b. Vienna, Feb 15, 1921, s. Nahoum and Bertha (Wiznitzer); att Inst des Hautes Etudes Intl, Geneva, 1951-53; m. Erika Frucht, 1940; c: Amnon, Miriam. Ambass, plen of Isr to Fr, since 1970; ambass to Ger, 1965-70 with: Hamosad La'alia, 1944-47; Fgn Office, 1948-53; dir gen, Chevrat Yam Suf, 1956-59; repr, Min of Defense to W Eur, 1956-59; dir gen, Min of Defense, 1959-65. Office: Embassy of Israel, Paris France.

BENNETT, Alfred Lester, US, attorney; b. Wash, DC, June 29, 1903; s. Louis and Flora (Yarlick); LLB, LLM, Georgetown U, 1924; m. Lillian Silverman, Dec 21, 1933; c: Jane Wilner. Sr partner, Bennett, Rosenfeld, & Schwartzbach, since 1960; dir, Amer Metrop Inves Co, 1958-69. Trustee, Gtr Wash J Comty Found; hon, bd dirs, J Comty Cen, Wash, DC; bd dirs, ADL; pres, B'nai B'rith lodge, 1940-41; mem: Amer, DC Bar Assns. Hobbies: golf, travel, civic affairs. Home: 4000 Massachusetts Ave, Washington, DC. Office: 420 Woodward Bldg, Washington DC.

BENNETT, Elsie Margaret, US, music arranger, teacher, studio mgr; b. Detroit, Mar 30, 1919; d. Sy and Ida (Carp) Blum; tchrs and performers cert, Ganapal Sch of Music, Detroit, 1941; BMus, Wayne U, 1945; MMus, Columbia U, 1946; m. Morton Bennett, June 20, 1937; c: Ronald, Kenneth. Music studio mgr and tchr, music arranger, since 1946; music tchr: Robotti Accordion Acad; Parkway Music Sch, both 1945-46. Pub works: Easy Solos for Accordion, 1946; Bass Solo Primer, 1948; Hebrew and Jewish Songs and Dances, for accordion, 1950, for piano, 1953; Hanon for Accordion; Accordion Music in the Home; Capriccio, It duet; Bei Mir Bist Du Schoen; Yossel, Yossel; Vos Du Vilst; Mein Shtatele Belz; Les Preludes; Viva la Compagne; Waltz of the Flowers; Ukrainian Dances; Waltz from Coppelia; Prayer of Thanksgiving; Ode to Joy; Dus Tolessel; Der Neier Yid, all 1953; William Tell Overture; Sleeping Beauty Waltz; Eisches Chail; Folk Melodies for Accordion; Five Finger Melodies, all 1954; Shene vi de Levonne, 1956; My Hero; In My Merry Oldsmobile; Smiles; Bass Chord Pattern Book; Put on Your Old Grey Bonnet, all 1957; March of Marionettes, 1958; Sway Southern Music; Mambo Jambo Southern; Besame Mucho Southern, all 1963; Granada Southern, 1965; Italian Folk Songs, 1965. Secy, Amer Accordionists Assn, past vice-pres, 2nd vice-pres; chmn, Composers Commissioning Comm; mem: Accordion Tchrs Guild; Bklyn Music Tchrs Guild, past secy. Recipient, awards: in recognition of contrib and faithful service to governing bd, Amer Accordionists Assn, 1948-60, in recognition of artistic accomplishments and contrib to music, 1962. Hobby: theater. Home and office: 694 Empire Blvd, Brooklyn NY.

BENNETT, Louis L, US, attorney, social worker; b. NYC, Jan 15, 1909; s. Maurice and Sarah (Brown) LLB, St John's U, 1931, BS, 1939; MS, NY Sch Social Work, Colimbia U, 1941; m. Estelle Goldman, June 8, 1929; c: Peter, Richard. Dep Regional commn, Social and Rehabilitation Service, HEW, NYC, since 1967; regional repr, Off of Aging, 1962-65; regional repr, Bur Family Service, prin wfr admn regional repr, 1965-67; dir, evening sessions, St John's U, 1927-41; pvt law practice, NYC, 1932-41 asst regional dir, US Off Comty War Service, NY, 1941-45, on detail to serve as exec dir, Vets Service Cen, NYC, 1944-45; cons to admnr, regional housing expiditer, Natl Housing Agcy, Washington, NYC, 1945-47; asst exec dir, AJComm, NYC, 1947-49; exec dir, NY Assn Assn for New Amers, 1949-52; asst exec vice-chmn, Natl UJA, 1952-56; exec dir, J Child Care Assn, NY, 1956-60; asst exec dir, Comty Council Gtr NY, 1960-62; cons, War Manpower Commn, 1942-45; lectr, NY Sch Social Work, 1942-45; adv bd, NY State Health Preparedness Commn, 1943; hon dep commn, NY State Civil Defense Commn, 1950; cons, US Off Educ, 1952-53. Chmn, family and child wfr comm, comty Council Gtr NY, 1956-60, bd mem, 1959-60; mem, bd dirs, Child Wfr League of Amer, 1960-62; mem bd, Assn Children's Instns, NY State, 1956-60; mem: jt bd comm, Council Social Work Educ-Natl Assn Social Workers, 1960-67; comm psychiatric service for children, Dept Hosps, 1962-65; Commn, since 1956; examining panel, NY State Civil Service Commn, since 1968; functional planning comm, FJP, NY, 1957-60; bd advs, spec comm divorce and marriage law, Natl Conf Commns on Uniform State Law; Natl Assn Social Workers, natl treas, bd, 1959-61; Amer Bar Assn; Amer Public Wfr Assn; Amer Soc Public Admnrs; Natl Conf J Communal Service; Amer Acad Political and Social Sc; NY Sch Social Work Alumni Assn, pres, 1945-48; Acad Certified Social Workers, Council Social Work Educ; Gerontological Soc; Amer Arbitration Assn; Natl Conf Social Work; Natl Conf Lawyers and Social Workers; asso mem, Natl Council Juvenile Cort Judges. Home: 2001 Ave P, Brooklyn, NY. Office: 42 Broadway, New York, NY.

BENNETT, Marshall, US, industrial realtor, developer; b. Chgo, Ill, Sep 19, 1921; BA, U Chgo, 1942; att: Wharton Sch, U of Pa, 1945; U Chgo Grad Sch Bus, 1946; m. Arlene Gettlemen, June 19, 1948; c: Barbara, Alice, Carole. Ind realtor, devl: Bennett & Kahnweiler, since 1949; Hart & Whetson, 1946-47; Milten, Bennett & Kahnweiler, 1947-49; pres, dir, Isbell Construction Co, Phoenix, Ariz, and Reno, Nev; dir: Consolidated Fundings Corp; Marmon Group; Mutual Franchise Corp; Main State Bank; Crane Carton Co; fmr dir: Rockwell Chocolate Co; Miller & Hart Meat Packing Co. USN, 1942-46, lt, USNR, 1942-54. Pres, St Alexius Hosp, Chgo; fmr pres, Chgo chap, Soc Ind Realtors; dir: Intl Soc Ind Realtors; Juvenile Protective Assn; Cong Solel Found; fmr dir, J Childrens Bur, Chgo; trustee: Ravina Festival Assn; Urban Land Inst; hon mem: Omega Tau Rho; Lambda Alpha; fmr commn, Highland Park Plan Commn. Home: 1405 Waverly Rd, Highland Park, Ill. Office: 120 S Riverside Plaza, Chicago, Ill.

BENNO, Benjamin G, US, artist; b. London, June 2, 1901; s. Abraham and Evelyn (Lemlern) Greenstein; in US since 1912; studied at: Modern Sch of Art, NYC under Robert Henri and George Bellows, 1912-16; NY Sch of Architecture and Beaux Arts under Solon Borglum, 1914-1917. Tchr, drawing and painting, Bklyn Childrens Muds since 1962, 1941-42, pvt classes, 1948-55, visiting prof, art, Montana St U, summer session, 1964; John Simon Guggenheim Memorial, 1932-33. Exhbs: gals: US, London; Paris; Oslo; Prague since 1913; one-man shows: gals: New, NYC, 1923; Galerie Pierre, Paris under Pablo Picasso, 1934; Castelucho-Diana Gals, Paris, 1935; Galeries Guggenheim Jeune, London, 1938; Arts Club, Chgo, 1939; SF Mus of Art, 1939; retrospective, Lotte Jacobi Gal, NYC, 1954; pastel retrospective, Collector's Gal, NYC, 1959; Amer Gal, 1961-62; black and white retrospective, Montana State U, 1964; retrospective, Galerie des Deux Mondes, TWA, NYC, 1967; repr in perm collections: Fogg Mus of Art, Cambridge. Mass; Bklyn Mus of Art, NYC; Baltimore Mus of Art; SF Mus of Art; pvt collections: Cal; Mex; S Amer; Eur. Home and studio: 434 Lafayette St, NYC.

BENNY, Jack, US, comedian; b. Waukegan, Ill, Feb 14, 1894; s. Meyer and Emma (Sachs) Kubelsky; m. Mary Livingstone, Feb 14, 1927; c: adopted, Joan. Film star since 1929; radio comedian since 1932; TV entertainer since 1949; debut as violinist, 1912; vaudeville actor, 1915; entertainer, overseas Armed Forces, 1943-45. Starred in motion pictures: To Be or Not To Be; George Washington Slept Here; Charley's Aunt; The Horn Blows at Midnight. Recipient: spec award for best male entertainer, Natl Acad of TV Arts and Sciences, 1957. Office: 9908 Santa Monica Blvd, Beverly Hills, Cal.

BENOR, Daniel, Isr, government official; b. Tel Aviv, Nov 14, 1927; s. Reuven and Miriam; BS, Heb U, Jerusalem; MS, Cornell U, NY; m. Tova, 1948; c: Orit, Edit. Dir, ext service, Min Agric, since 1968; fmr: dir, Eshbol Farm, 1954-61. Off,

IDF. Author: Degree of Specialization of Extension Agents in Israel. Home: 20 Haim Cohen St, Petah Tikva, Isr. Office: Min of Agric, Tel Aviv, Isr.

BENOR, Juda Leib, Isr, educational admn; b. Cairo, July 5, 1897; s. Isaac and Deborah (Shulman) Bloom; in Isr since 1914; BS, London U, 1932; m. Ethel Chodes, Jan 27, 1937; c: Daniel, David. Ret; fmr: civilian employee: Australian Red Cross, Cairo, 1914-15; gen staff intelligence, Egyptian Expeditionary Force, Brit, 1915-16; clerk: Public Security Dept, Min of Interior, Cairo, 1916-19; Occupied Enemy Territory Admn, Pal, 1919-1920; employee, educ dept, Govt of Pal, 1920-28; dist insp of J schs, dept of educ, Govt of Pal, 1928-48; insp of schs, dir, Arab educ, Min of Educ and Culture, Isr, 1948-52; asst dir gen, Min of Educ and Culture, 1952-62; lectr, Coll of J Studies, Los Angeles, 1962-63; cons, educ, World Bank, Wash, DC, 1963-64; sr cons, educ, UNESCO, Paris, 1964-65; secy, acting dean, Pal Bd of Higher Studies; sec gen, Isr Natl Commn for UNESCO; mem bd educ, Isr. Cpl. Haganah, 1942-47. Fmr: secy, chief commn, J Scouts, Pal; secy, Maccabi Athletic Club, Cairo; co-found, mem, exec comm, Isr Movement of Progressive Judaism; mem, Natl Commn, UNESCO, Isr. Contbr numerous articles on educ, Heb lang, Arab educ in Isr, progressive Judaism. Home: 4 Saadya Gaon St, Rehavia, Jerusalem, Isr.

BEN-PORAT, Yossef, Isr, government official; b. Lodz, Pol, 1906; s. Aharon and Shindel (Fortunski) Miedzyrecki; in Isr since 1925; m. Rachel Spiro, 1926; c: Giora, Varda. Dir, Min of Police, since 1968; fmr: sr cdr, Haganah, 1938-48; sr officer, Isr Police, 1948-58; asst insp gen, 1958-68. Home: 51 David Hamelech St, Tel Aviv, Isr. Office: Min of Police, Jerusalem, Isr.

BEN-REUVEN, Abraham, Isr, physicist; b. Tel Aviv, Sep 23, 1934; s. Josef and Ada (Assa); MSc, with distinction, Technion, 1961; PhD, Heb U, Jerusalem, 1963; m. Sara, Sept 11, 1958; c: Ehud, Gilli. Sr research asso since 1969; physicist, Natl Bur of Standards, Wash DC, 1963-65; research asso, Weizmann Inst of Sci, Rehovot, 1966-69. Lt, IDF, 1952-55. Prin contrib, research in molecular physics pertaining to gas and liquid dynamics. Mem: Isr Phys Soc; Soc for the Protection of Nature, Isr. Contbr to profsl jours. Hobby, philately. Home: 9 Gordon St, Rehovot, Isr. Office: Weizmann Inst of Sci, Rehovot, Isr.

BENRUBI, Haim, Greece, business exec; b. Salonica, Greece, July 14, 1896; s. Samuel and Ricoula (Hassid); diploma d'etudes commerciales, Mission Laique Française, Salonica, 1915; m. Alice Matarasso; c: Samuel, Nelly Abravanel. Exec: H Benrubi and Bros SA; Hellamyl SARL. Pres, JDC, Greece; councillor, Cen Bd J Comtys in Greece. Home: 5 Victoria Sq, Athens, Greece. Office: 155 I Drossopoulou St, Athens, Greece.

BEN-RUBI, Itzhak Bitti (Shimon Shimon), Isr, author; b. Serres, Greece, Mar 25, 1903; s. Bitti and Lutcha (De Botton); in Isr since 1945; att Lycée Français, Salonica; dipl, Cours Grandes Maitres du Dessin, Paris; Acad de Arte Dramatico, Cuba; m. Dora Camhy, Mar 25, 1928; c: Liliane Abastado Solomon, Moshe, Isaac. Author and journalist since 1950; contbr to Kol Israel Radio; chief ed, El Tiempo, 1950-67; gen secy, Austro Hellenique, S Amer, 1922-38; corresp, Voz Sefaradi, Mex, tobacco merchant, Greece, 1939-41. Greece Army, 1940-41. Author: El Secreto del Mudo; La Negrita de Rio; El Amor que Mata; Fuego, Sangre y Amor; Almas Juras; numerous poems trans into Fr, Greek, Heb; numerous radio sketches for Kol Isr; Aqui Os Habla Shimon Shimon; Locos con Seriedad, play; Metorafim Beritzinut; Maarhonim; Mes Douze Metiers en Israel. Fmr: gen secy Anti TB League, Greece; dir, UJA, Greece; mem: ACUM; Masons, Lumiere and Veritas lodges; spec envoy from KH to Latin Amer; pres, Isr-Greek Friendship League. Recipient: Caballero de la Ordre del Merito Civil; Officier de l'Ordre de Georges I de Grece. Spec interests: graphology; painting. Home: 170 Arlosoroff St, Tel Aviv, Isr. Office: 110 Hayarkon St, Tel Aviv, Isr.

BEN-SHAHAR, Haim, Isr, educator; b. Tel Aviv, June 26, 1935; s. Benyamin and Hinda (Feldman); BA, MA, Heb U, 1959; MBA, PhD, NYU, 1967; m. Yael Buks, June 10, 1956; c: Omri, Gili, Dan. Prof, econ, Tel Aviv U since 1967, dean, fac of social sci since 1968; lectr, bus admn, Heb U, 1961-67. Author, Interest Rates and the Cost of Capital in Israel, 1965; co-author, Efficient Economy, 1969; ed: Econ Quarter-

ly; Cost Accounting and Bus Econs. Home: 2 Levitak, Tel
Aviv, Isr. Office: Tel Aviv U, Tel Aviv, Isr.

BEN-SHAUL, Dvora Miranda, Isr, scientist; b. Houston, Tex,
May 10, 1929; d. Elwin and Ruth Valenchero; in Isr since
1958; BS, Oklahoma U, 1946; MS, Cal Inst of Tech, 1950;
MA, Winston Coll, Neb, 1953; m. Joseph Ben-Shaul, Oct 10,
1961; c: Rachel Lynn Miller (decd). Biol, Jerusalem Bibl Zoo
since 1965; nature ed, Jerusalem Post since 1967; biol: Heb
U, 1958-65; U Fla, 1958-59; animal husbandry sup, Marshall
Plan, 1953-58. Pvt, Machal, 1947-48. Prin contribs: research
on content of milk of wild animals; devl of hand-rearing
techniques for zoo animals. Bd dirs, Jerusalem Bibl Zool Soc;
asst secy, League to Prevent Rel Coersion in Isr; mem:
SPCA, Jerusalem; Isr Kennel Club. Author: The Use of Milk
Substitutes in Rearing Pigs, 1954; A Handbook for Pig
Breeding in the Tropics 1955; Night in the Wadi, 1969.
Spec interests: wildlife preservation, antique Bedouin
jewelry, Ger Shepherd dogs. Home: Hasan 015, New Beit
Narina-Nebe Jacob, Jerusalem, Isr. Office: Jerusalem Zoo-
logical Garden, Ltd, Jerusalem, Isr.

BENSHEM, Ruben, Isr, rabbi, educator; b. Pol, Feb 28, 1900;
s. Joseph and Rosa (Safrin-Lippa) Feldschuh; att U Vienna;
DTh, Theol Sem, Vienna; PhD, fac phil, U Vienna; m.
Ruth Halberstadt; c: Nekamiah, Joa. Dir, secondary sch,
Tel Aviv; prof, psych, U of Social Sci, Tel Aviv; fmr: chief
rabbi of Pol J. Mem cen comm, Independent Lib Org; pres:
Educ Comm, B'nai B'rith; mem, cen comm, Isr Coops; co-
found, Hashomer Hatzair, 1913; fmr: found, Student Org,
Masada; delg, Zionist Cong, 1929-37. Author: Palestine
Nights; Red Souls; Yiddish Social Lexicon; The Tent;
Silent Graves; Between the Ghetto Walls; Poland Burns;
The Third Incarnation; publ works in psych. Home: Givat
Shmuel, Isr.

BEN-SHEMESH, Shimeon, Isr, organization exec; b. Tel Aviv,
1915; s. Schmuel and Liza (Kaplunik) Spektorow; dipl,
Council of Legal Studies, Jerusalem, 1954; m. Chaya Wagman,
1946; c: Nurit, Schmuel. Dir gen, Keren Kayemeth LeIsrael
JNF since 1961; past dir, JNF Land Devl Auth; fmr, secy-
gen, land and soil devl dept, 1954-59. Home: Kfar Schmaryahu, Isr. Office: Keren Kayemeth LeIsrael, Jerusalem, Isr.

BEN-SIMHON, Shaul, Isr, trade union exec; b. Fez, Morocco,
Dec 29, 1929; s. Haim and Solika (Samoun); in Isr since
1948; m. Jacqueline Elmoslino, Feb 19, 1963; c: Galit, Eyal.
Mem, Histadrut Exec Bur, div ind safety and hygiene
vocational training since 1966; secy, Ashdod lab council,
1965-66; secy, Mapai Party, Ashdod, 1961; adv on lab and
coop, Govt of Senegal, 1963-65; active organ of Moroccan
immigrants. Home: 9 Rogozine St, Ashdod, Isr. Office:
Histadrut, 93 Arlosoroff St, Tel Aviv, Isr.

BENSIMON, Doris, Fr, sociologist; b. Vienna, Jan 9, 1924;
d. Victor and Merguerite (Bincer) Donath; in Fr since 1940;
licence, Us: Lyon, Lille, 1945-48; diplôme d'études supérieures,
U Aix-en-Provence, 1961; Dr d'état, Sorbonne, Paris, 1969;
m. I/c: research, Natl Cen Sci Research, Paris since 1963;
chargé de cours, U Cen of Oriental Langs since 1969; prof
modern letters, Natl Min of Educ, Paris, 1959-62. Research
on N Afr Jewry in Morocco, Isr, Fr. Author: Evolution du
Judaïsme Marocain sous le Protéctorat Français, 1968;
L'Intégration des Immigrants Nord-Africains en Israël, 1970;
contbr to profsl publs; Ency Judaica. Home: 28 rue St Fargeau,
Paris 20, Fr. Office: Centre d'Etudes Sociologiques, 82 rue
Cardinet, Paris 17, Fr.

BEN-SIRA, Rivka, Isr, artist; b. Vilna, Pol; d. Isaac and Touba;
grad Bezalel Art Sch, Jerusalem; m. Aharon; c: Ruth Asmon,
Isaac. One-man exhbs: Holon; Tel Aviv; Ashdod Yaakov;
several annual Isr exhbs. Mem, Assn of Painters and Sculptors,
Isr. Home and studio: 5 Cordova St, Tel Aviv, Isr.

BEN-SIRA, Yaakov, Isr, engineer, town planner; b. Kaniev,
Russ, Feb. 3, 1899; s. Pinchas and Ginni (Chudnowsky)
Shiffman; in Isr since 1913; att: Lida Yeshiva, Russ, 1903-13;
Herzlia Coll, Tel Aviv, 1913-18; BS, hons, London U, Eng;
m. Chaya Hurwitz, 1923; c. Moshe, Yitzhak. Cons in pvt
practice since 1951; agric worker, Petah Tikva and Galilee
until 1919; manual worker, rd construction, Galilee and Mt
Carmel, 1919-21; engr: Shell Oil Co, London, 1925; Solel
Boneh, Jerusalem, 1926-27; town planner, Jerusalem Munic,
1927-29; city engr and town planner, Tel Aviv Munic, 1929-
51; adv, Slum Clearance Auth. Volunteer, Pal Settlement

Police. Planner: Tel Aviv Slaughter House; Musrara Bridge;
Bilu and Bialik Schs; Levinsky Tchrs Sem; seashore promen-
ade; New Immigrants and Ex-Servicemen's Housing Scheme,
Tel Aviv; Maariv Printing House; Beit Sharon Off Bldg;
Cen Market Compound and Cold Storage; Ramleh Town
Planning Scheme; Artists' Village Ein Hod Devl Scheme;
Fmr pres, Isr Engrs and Architects Assn; fmr chmn, Bldg
and Technique Research Inst, Tel Aviv; secy, Maccabi Org,
1919; mem: bd dirs, Technion; Inst Civil Engrs; Inst Munic
Engrs; Royal Soc of Health; asso mem, Town Planning
Inst, Gt Brit. Contbr to local press. Home and Office: 133
Rothschild Blvd, Tel Aviv Isr.

BENTATA, Gabriel, Venezuela, lawyer; b. Tangier, Morocco,
Feb 17, 1934; s. Jacobo and Biddy (Sabah); in Venezuela
since 1942; LLD, summa cum laude, U Central, Caracas,
1958; ML, Harvard U, Cambridge, Mass, 1959; m. Judith
Rieber, Nov 16, 1963; c: Sergio, Jose, Bernardo. Lawyer,
asso partner, Estudio Bentata since 1959. Mem: B'nai B'rith,
Simon Bolivar lodge; Rotary, chap Chacao. Hobbies: tennis,
reading, classical music. Home: Quinta Remauso, 10 Trans-
versal Altamira, Caracas, Venezuela. Office: Citibank Bldg,
3 Piso, Caracas, Venezuela.

BENTES, Abrahao, Brazil, lawyer; b. Belém, Brazil, Mar 10,
1920; s. Isaac and Emilia; LLD, Sch of Law, Rio de Janeiro,
1945; m. Lola Nahon; c: Ricardo, Eliana. Pvt practice since
1945; newspaperman, public off, 1936-42. Pres bd, Asso Isr
Brasileira; mem comm, lectr, Hum Rights Comm: past
pres, Assn Comty Funds Isr; vice-pres, B'nai B'rith, Brazil
and Latin Amer; mem bd, B'nai B'rith, Belo Horizonto,
fmr chmn; fmr, PR, J aff, to govt offs. Contbr articles to
jours. Special interest, J hist research. Home: 876 rua Rio
Negro, Belo Horizonte, Minas Gerais, Brazil. Office: 424-5/
908, rua Carijos, Belo Horizonte, Minas Gerais, Brazil.

BENTON, Edward M, US, attorney; b. Bklyn, NY, Sep 18, 1906;
s. John and Celene (Richter) Bernstein; BA, cum laude,
Harvard Coll, 1928; JD, Harvard Law Sch, 1931; m. Esther
Koppelman, Apr 15, 1934; c: Alice, Jeremy. Pvt practice
since 1939; mem, law firm, Finkelstein, Benton & Soll;
vice-pres, dir, NY Majestic Corp, 1948-59. Vice-pres, Bklyn
dist ZOA, 1944-47; bd dirs, United HIAS Service since 1954;
bd dir, vice-pres, HIAS Immigrant Bank, 1952-64; HIAS,
1952-54; exec comm, gen counsel, Comm for Yiddish in HSs;
mem, AJComm. Home: 115 Central Park W, New York,
NY. Office: 515 Madison Ave, New York, NY.

BENTOR, Yaakov, K, Isr, geologist, b. Koenigsberg, Ger, Feb
13, 1910; s. Hugo and Jenny (Lazar) Winter; in Isr since 1933;
att U's: Koenigsberg; Berlin; Jerusalem; Zurich; Grenoble;
Paris; PhD, Heb U, 1945; DSc, Sorbonne, 1952; m. c: Amnon,
Yael, Elkana, Dir, Geological Survey of Isr, Min of Devl,
Jerusalem, 1955-67; prof, mineralogy-petrology, Heb U,
1957-63. Prin contrib, discovered copper, phosphate deposits
in Negev. Mem: Mineralogical Soc of Amer, Soc of Econ
Geologist, NY Acad of Sci, Geological Soc of Isr; council,
Intl Clay Assn. Author: La Chaine des Puys, 1955; Stratigraphy
of Israel, 1960; publ 6 vols, Geographical Map of Israel since
1951; mem ed bd, Geographical Map of World. Recipient,
Isr Prize 1955. Hobby, chess. Home: 6 B'nai B'rith St, Jerusalem, Isr. Office: Dept of Geology, Heb U, Jerusalem, Isr.

BEN-TOV, Arie, Isr, attorney; b. Bendzin, Pol, Aug 8, 1923;
s. Izchak and Frida (Makowski) Hassenberg; in Isr since 1947;
DJur, Law Fac, Jerusalem, 1956; m. Aviva Oldak, Apr 10,
1951; c: Ronit, Achituv, Hannah. Atty since 1957. Mem,
exec comm, Independent Lib Party; hon secy, Isr Fgn Policy
Assn; chmn, Bendzin Immigrants Assn in Isr; mem exec,
Pol J in Isr; mem, Chaine de Rotisseurs. Contbr to Heb,
Pol, Ger publs. Home: 83 Hazorea, Kfar Schmaryahu, Isr.
Office: 8 Frisch St, Tel Aviv, Isr.

BENTOV, Mordechai, Isr, legislator, journalist; b. Warsaw, Pol,
Mar 28, 1900; s. Yosef and Helena (Heinsdorf) Gutgeld; in
Isr since 1920; att Warsaw U; Inst of Tech, Warsaw, 1918-20;
Govt Law classes, Jeruaslem, 1925; m. Zippora Redlich, 1926;
c:Ora, Elisheva. MK, Mapam, signer of Isr Declaration of
Independence; Min of Lab and Reconstruction, Isr Provisional
Govt, 1948-49; Min of Devl, 1955-61; Min of Housing since
1965; Lab party since 1949. Mem: world exec, Hashomer
Hatzair; exec, Histadrut; Zionist Actions Comm; delg: Zi-
onist Congs; Round Table Conf, London, 1938; WJC, US,
1944; mem: political comm JA delg to UN, Lake Success,
1947. Author: The Case for a Bi-national Palestine, 1946; Is-

rael's Economy at Cross-Roads, 1965. Home: Kibbutz Mishmar Haemek, Isr. Office: Min of Housing, Jerusalem, Isr.

BENTSUR, Shmuel, Isr, diplomat; b. Cluj, Rum, 1906; s. Moshe and Zippora (Neuman) Peterfly; in Isr since 1934; att U Cluj; m. Sara Weinstein, 1930; c: Eytan. Insp gen, Isr Fgn Service, since 1967; dir, natl bur, JNF, Transylvania, 1927-34; gen secy, Zionist Org, Transylvania, 1930-34; laborer, Pal, 1934-45; official, Solel Boneh, 1945-57; on mission for Mapaite Hung, 1947-48 consul, Isr Legation, Budapest, Hung, 1948-50, chargé d'affaires, 1950-51; dep dir, E dept, Min for Fgn Affairs, Jerusalem, 1952, dir, 1953-56; Isr min to Aus, 1956-58; dep gen, Min for Fgn Affairs, 1958-62; ambass to Switz, 1962-67. Served, Haganah, 1934-48. Home: Givat Shahin, Jerusalem, Isr.

BENTWICH, Joseph Solomon, Isr, educator; b. London, Eng, Feb 3, 1902; s. Herbert and Susannah (Solomon); in Isr since 1925; MA, Trinity Coll, Cambridge U, 1923; Inst of Educ, London, 1924-25; m. Sarah Yofe, Sep 11, 1924; c: Shoshana Keini, Rahel Shavit, Michael, Zvi. Lectr, Oranim Tchrs Coll, since 1966; tchr: Gymnasia Herzlia, Tel Aviv, and Reali Sch, Haifa, 1925-28; insp, dept of educ, Pal Govt, 1928-43, asst dir, 1943-48; prin, Reali Sch, 1948-55; lectr, Sch of Educ, Heb U, Jerusalem, 1955-58; staff insp, Isr Min of Educ and Culture, 1960-65; tchr, secondary sch, Kfar Blum, 1965-67. Author: English Composition and Grammar, 1932; Elementary Mathematics, 1934; Scientific Method, 1954; Education in the State of Israel, 1960; Anthology of World Religions, 1964; Judaism, 1968; ed: Principles of Judaism, 1950; Petahim, jour of J thought, since 1967. Recipient: Isr prize, Min of Educ, 1962. Home: 6 Rashba, Jerusalem, Isr.

BENTWICH, Michael, Isr, educator; b. Jerusalem, Dec 22, 1930; s. Joseph and Sarah (Yoffe); BA, hons, Cambridge U, 1953; MS, Technion, 1956; PhD, U Mich, 1959; m. Ruth Pfau, Dec 14, 1960; c: Talia, Gur. Asso prof, Technion, since 1967, fmr: sr lectr, lectr, 1960-67; fmr: visiting asso prof, SUNY, 1967-69. IDF. Prin contribs: mechanics; fluid mechanics; math research. Fmr chmn, Technion Fac Org. Hobbies: folk dancing, guitar, squash, swimming. Home: 7 Nizanim St, Haifa, Isr. Office: Technion, Haifa, Isr.

BEN-TZUR, Avraham, Isr, journalist; b. Dortmund, Ger, Aug 1, 1924; s. Karl and Martha (Eichengruen) Steinweg; in Isr since 1939; m; c: Raanan, Gilad, Asa. Free-lance researcher, writer on ME Affairs; corresp, Al Hamishmar newspaer, 1960-61; ed, Al Mirssad, Arab weekly, 1963-65; mem, dept Arab affairs, Mapam, 1946-65. Haganah; IDF since 1950. Found mem, Kibbutz Lehavot Habashan, Upper Galilee. Author: Arab Socialism, Heb ed, 1965; rev Span ed, 1969; The Syrian Ba'ath Party and Israel, 1968; contbr of articles to Isr jours. Home: Kibbutz Lehavot Habashan, Isr.

BEN-URI, Joseph, Isr, educator; b. Drohobycz, Pol, Aug 16, 1908; s. Simon and Ruth (Rapaport); in Isr since 1934; Dipl, Engr, Tech U, Darmstadt, 1930, DEng, 1931; m. Pola Drexler, July 8, 1943; c: Raphael. Prof, EE, Technion since 1962, fac mem since 1952; cons engr since 1934; tchr, Imperial Coll, London, 1932-34; found, mgr, chief engr, Butagas Sholl Camps, 1936-46; controller, elec ind, Govt of Isr, 1948-50; mgr, Technion Research Found, 1953-55; visiting prof, Carnegie Inst Tech, 1958-60; mgr, chief engr, Koor Ltd, 1950-58. Contbr of numerous papers to profsl jours. Hobbies: photography, music, archaeol. Home: 1 Hazfira, Haifa, Isr. Office: Technion, Haifa, Isr.

BEN URI, Meir, Isr, architect; b. Riga, Russ, Mar 21, 1908; s. Moritz and Rosalie (Kron) Wasbutzky; in Isr since 1934; dipl eng architecture, Tech HS, Charlottenburg, 1934; m. Judith Bernstein, Jan, 1942; c: Nomie, Yael, Yair, Ofra, Tamar. Dir, Studio of Syn Arts since 1954; adv architect and artist; head, dept, phys planning, Isr Min of Ind and Trade, 1949-50; architect, town planner, Haifa; adv architect, Min of Rel Affairs, 1951-54; exhbs: Haifa; NY; Montreal; Ramat Gan. Prin contribs, research in Bible Syns; composer of rel songs, paintings and etchings; contbr to Heb, Eng periodicals. Recipient, first prize in numerous competitions. Home: 15 Bar Ilan St, Kfar Shmuel, Haifa, Isr.

BENUSIGLIO, Peppo (Joseph), Greece, business exec; b. Salonica, Greece, 1898. Found and dir, Helleni Optical Co; dir, Bank of Salonica, 1920-48. Mem, cen bd, World ORT Union; pres: ORT, Greece; loan fund JDC; Friends Alliance Isr Universelle; fmr: admnr: Communal Council, Salonica; Cen

Council, J Comtys, Greece; mem, admn council OPAIE Found, admn of Heirless Property and Rehab of Greek J. Home: Xenokratos 23, Athens, Greece, Office: 16 El Venizelou St, Athens, Greece.

BENVENISTE, David, Greece, business exec; b. Thessaloniki, Greece, Mar 1, 1921; s. Jacques and Henriette (Amar); m. Elisa Saltiel, June 12, 1949; c: Jacques, Erietta. Mgr, Furnishing Material Firm since 1958; acctnt, Steamship Agcy, 1939-41; dir, J comty, 1945-47; chief acctnt, Nissim Bros, 1951-58. Pvt, Greek Army, 1947-51. Pres, J Comty, Thessaloniki; mem, B'nai B'rith. Hobby, philately. Home: 15 Kalapotaki St, Thessaloniki, Greece. Office: 13 St Mina, Thessaloniki, Greece.

BENVENISTE, Irving Ely, US, physician, surgeon; b. Rhodes, It, Oct 7, 1903; s. Eliezer and Luna (Berro); in US since 1914; PhC, BS, U Wash, 1928; MD, Rush Med Coll, 1932; m. Jeanette Naon, Jan 14, 1957. Pvt practice since 1933; instr, urol, gyn, Sch of Nursing, San Joaquin Co Hosp, 1935-36. Pres: Sephardic Heb Cen, 1967-70; Cal chap, Alliance Israelite Universelle, 1959-61; chmn, Sephardic div, UJWF, 1951-69; bd dirs: J Fed Council, LA, 1959-65; S Cal Technion Soc, 1964-68; cabinet mem, Bonds of Isr, 1967-68. Hobbies: gardening, swimming. Home: 10654 Le Conte Ave, W Los Angeles, Cal. Office: 3753 E 1 St, Los Angeles, Cal.

BENVENISTI, David, Isr, educator; b. Salonica, Greece, Feb 25, 1897; s. Samuel and Luna; in Isr since 1913; tchr cert, Tchrs Coll, Jerusalem, 1918; MA, Heb U, Jerusalem, 1934; m. Lea Friedman; c: Meron, Raphael. Prin, elem sch; instr, Tchrs Coll. J Battalion of Brit Army, 1917; Haganah. Found, Rambler's Assn; mem exec, Isr Youth Hostels; Council of Tchrs for Keren Kayemet; mem comm, naming streets in Jerusalem; elected Honorable Citizen, Jerusalem. Author: geog books, Isr maps; Isr, Syrian and Leb guide books; publs on teaching of geog. Home: 11 Balfour St, Jerusalem, Isr.

BENVENISTI, Meron Shmuel, Isr, government official; b. Jerusalem Apr 21, 1934; s. David and Lea (Friedman); BA, BS, econ, Heb U, Jerusalem; m. Shoshana Lahav; c: Eyal. I/c E Jerusalem affairs since 1967; fmr dir, econ dept, Min of Tourism. Sgt, IDF, 1951-53. Fmr chmn, Heb U Students Assn; mem, Kibbutz Haniqra. Author: Crusader Castles in Israel, 1965; The Crusaders in the Holy Land, 1969. Home: 14 Coresh St, Jerusalem, Isr. Office: 23 Jaffa St, Jerusalem, Isr.

BEN-YAACOB, Abraham, Isr, author; b. Baghdad, Iraq, Sep 30, 1914; s. Yaacob and Khatoon; in Isr since 1925; att Tel Aviv Sch of Law and Econ; BA, Heb U, Jerusalem, 1964; m. Nava Nuriel, Oct 27, 1952; c: Ziva, Ora, Yair. Prin, Sch, Jerusalem since 1953; research writer, The History of the Eastern Jews. Author: Kehilot Yehudei Kurdistan, 1961; Yehudei Bavel Misof Yemei Hageonim Vead Yomeinu, 1965 and several other books; contbr: Ency Judaica; Heb Ency; Ency Lehalutsei Hayishuv Haivri Ubonav. Hon secy, court for induction problems, Jerusalem. Recipient: Itzhak Ben Zvi Award, 1961, 1965. Home: 3 Ben Dor St, Kiryat Moshe, Jerusalem, Isr.

BEN-YAACOV, Johanan, Isr, artist; b. Berlin, July 18, 1913; s. Caspar and Rosa (Levin) Jacubowicz; in Isr since 1933; att Bezalel Art Sch, 1940; m. Esther-Nelly Benilouche, Feb 14, 1951; c: Noam, Siv, Galia. Painter, sculptor for 35 years; works purchased by: Kew Gardens Conservative Cong Mus, NYC; Joel Starrels, Chgo; Dizengoff Mus, Tel Aviv; Mus for Music, Haifa; Army-Navy Mus, Haifa; Beth Wilfrid Isr Mus; Yad-Lebanim, Petah Tikva; J Kimchi, Savyon, Isr; settlement police, Isr, 1936-48. Mem: Isr Painters and Sculptors Assn; Painters and Sculptors of Hashomer Hatzair. Recipient: Dizengoff Award for art, 1951; Ruach Hazabar, 1955. Spec interests: music, archeol, psych. Home: Hazorea, Isr.

BEN-YAACOV, Yissakhar, Isr, diplomat; b. Hamburg, Ger, Dec 7, 1922; s. Salo and Paula (Felsen) Jacobson; in Isr since 1933; att U Munich, 1950-53; m. Priva Frischling, Mar 21, 1950; c: Naomi Tsofiya, Shlomo. Consul gen of Isr, Phila, Pa since 1966; pres, Consular Assn of Phila since 1968; chancellor, Consulate of Isr, Munich, 1948-53; asst dir, consular div, min for Fgn Affairs, 1953-56; dir, consular Dept, Isr Mission, Cologne, 1956-59; dep dir, dept for Intl Coop, Jerusalem, 1959-64. Educ off, Haganah, 1944-48. Secy and treas, Noar-oved, Working Youth Movement, 1941-44. Home: 6 Haarazim St, Jerusalem, Isr. Office: 225 15 St, Philadelphia, Pa.

BEN-YOHANAN, Asher, Isr, composer; b. Kavalla, Greece, May 22, 1929; s. Yohanan and Flora (Abravaya) Misrahi; in Isr since 1935; att NYU; teaching F, U Mich, MMus, 1970; studied composition with Paul Ben-Haim; won scholarship to study with Aaron Copeland; work with It composer Luigi Nono; att Intl Music Inst, Darmstadt; m. Shoshana Zwibel; c: Gilla. Instr: music theory, Acad of Music, Tel Aviv since 1962; and music dir, Thelma Yellin Music and Art HS, Tel Aviv. Compositions: Aria, for soprano and orch, 1952; Ode to Jerusalem, 1954; music for play, Uncle Tom's Cabin, 1956; Independence Day Parade, 1956; Festive Overture, 1957; Two Movements for Orchestra, 1959; Prelude and Toccata, for piano solo, 1960; String Quartet, 1962-64; Music for Orch, 1964, commnd by Isr Festival; Quartetto Concertato; choral pieces; most works recorded by Kol Isr bc sta; some pub by Isr Music Inst, Tel Aviv. Mem bd: League of Composers in Isr; ACUM; Milo, artists club. Home: 14 Louis Marshall St, Tel Aviv, Isr.

BENZEEV, Israel, Isr, educator, author; b. Jerusalem, Aug 20, 1899; s. Menachem and Sara Wolfenson; att: Tchrs Sem, Jerusalem, 1912-16; Arabic Training Coll, Alquds, 1919-21; Egyptian U, 1922-26; Frankfurt/M U, Friedrich Wilhelm U, Berlin, 1927-33; m. Shoshana Dinewitz, 1922; c: Ofra, Ruth, Talma. Ret; supt, Arabic HS, Min of Educ; prof, Semitic langs, Egyptian U, Dar El Ulum Coll, Cairo, Egypt, 1929-38; Arabic lit, Bar Ilan U, Ramat Gan, 1958-62. Author: Heb: The Jews in Arabia, 1929, 1942; Praying Problems in Present Jewish Life, 1929; Conversion to Judaism, 1961; Christian Missionary Activity in Israel, 1964; Who is Who in Jerusalem, 1965; Arabic: The Jews in Arabia before Mohammed, 1927; History of Semitic Languages, 1929; Maimonides: his Life and Essays, 1936; 5 vols, Arabic for Primary and Secondary Schools, 1942-57; Ger, Ka'ab al Ahbar und seine Stellung im Hadith und in der Islamischen Legendenliteratur, 1933; fmr, found, chmn: J Heb Club, Cairo; People Assn, Isr; World Union, Gerey Tzedek, propagation of Judaism. Contbr numerous articles on J problems. Home: 12 Ibn Ezra St, Jerusalem, Isr.

BEN-ZE'EV, Moshe, Isr, attorney; b. Russ, Dec 8, 1911; s. Wolf and Sara (Gelfand) Bodankin; in Isr since 1935; LLD, U Vilna, 1935; m. Zipora Kopel, Feb 7, 1939; c: Dan, Shaul, David, Sara. Pvt practice since 1968; fmr: dist court judge, 1958-63; atty gen of Isr, 1963-68. Maj, legal br, IDF, 1948-49. Fmr: chmn, Friends of Haifa Theatre; mem: cen comm, Isr Bar Assn; Law Council. Contbr to periodicals and press. Hobbies: chess, swimming. Home: 2 Mevo Yoram St, Jerusalem, Isr. Office: 2 Hasoreg St, Jerusalem, Isr.

BENZER, Seymour, US, biologist, educator; b. NYC, Oct 15, 1921; s. Mayer and Eva (Naidorf); BA, Bklyn Coll, 1942; MS, Purdue U, 1942, PhD, 1947; m. Dorothy Viosky, Jan 10, 1942; c: Barbara, Martha. Prof, biol, Cal Inst of Tech since 1967, visiting asso, 1965-67, research f, biophysics, 1949-51; inves, off of Sci Research and Devl, 1942-45; biophysicist, Oak Ridge Lab, 1948-49; Fulbright research scholar, Inst Pasteur, Paris, 1951-52; sr post-doctoral f, NSF, Cambridge U, 1957-58; Stuart prof, biol, Purdue U, 1961-67, f, 1942-45, instr physics, 1945-47, asst prof, 1947-52, asso prof, biophysics, 1952-58, prof, 1958. Mem: Natl Acad Sci; Amer Acad Arts and Sci; Amer Phil Soc; f, AAAS. Contbr to profsl jours. Home: 195 S Wilson, Pasadena, Cal. Office: Cal Inst of Tech, Pasadena, Cal.

BEN-ZION, US, artist; b. Ukraine, Russ, July 15, 1897; s. Hirsh and Sara (Gochban) Weinman; in US since 1920; att Yeshiva, Pol; m. Lillian Dubin, 1945. One-man exhbs: Artists Gal, 1936; Marion Willard Gal, 1937; Buchholtz Gal, 1946; Bertha Shaefer Gal, 1947-50; Curt Valentin, 1951, all NYC; one-man mus shows: Baltimore, Md; Portland, Ore; Taft Mus, Cincinnati; SF Mus; Smithsonian Inst, Wash, DC; Ia U; Bezalel Mus, Jerusalem; exhb of Bibl paintings, J Mus, NYC, 1948, 1951; repr at: Metrop Mus of Art, NYC; Whitney Mus; Mus of Modern Art, NYC; Chgo Art Inst; State Dept Art Abroad; Duncan Phillips Memorial, Wash, DC; Newark Mus, NJ; NY 42 St Public Libr; Tel Aviv Mus; Bezalel Mus; 25 year retrospective show, J Mus, NYC, 1959. Portfolios publ: etchings on Bibl themes, 1951-52; Prophets, 1953; Job, Song of Songs, Ruth, 1954; Drawings to Wisdom of the Fathers, 1960; Life of a Prophet, 1964; Gilgamesh and Enkidu, 1966; Self Portraits, 1968. Home and studio: 329 W 20th St, New York, NY.

BEN ZVI, Joseph, Isr, chemical engr; b. Berlin, Jan 6, 1927; s. Gregoir and Deborah (Wilensky) Farber; in Isr since 1936; dipl, Chem E, U of Lausanne, 1949, cert bact, 1950; Swiss Fed dipl of Public Analyst. Dir, chief chem, Cen Lab since 1959; dir, HSF Ltd Tel Aviv since 1969; consul of Malta; asst lectr, Technion, Haifa, 1956-58; research chem: IDF 1955-56; Isr AEC, 1953-55. Subaltern, Coast Guards, 1944-45, 2nd lt, since 1954. Prin contribs: discovery of new analytical methods for determining adulteration of food; trouble-shooting in ind; setting up new plants in chem, food ind. Mem, natl bd, Assn of Chem engrs; Jr C of C, Tel Aviv-Ramat Gan; fmr pres: Jr C of C, Tel Aviv; senate, past natl pres, Jr C of C, Isr. Recipient: Ot Hamishmar; Ot Lochamey Hamedina; Intl Relations Award, Jr Chamber Intl, 1963. Hobbies: fencing, tourism, chess. Home and office: 21 Pinsker St, Tel Aviv, Isr.

BEN-ZVI, Rachel Yanait, Isr, educator; b. Malin, Russ, 1886; d. Mayer and Shoshana (Moros) Lishansky; in Isr since 1908; att Jena U, Ger, 1904-05; agron engr, Nancy U, Fr, 1914; m. Itzhak Ben-Zvi (pres of Isr 1952-63) (decd); c: Amram, Eli (killed in action, War of Independence, 1948). First Lady of Isr, 1952-63; co-found: Poalei Zion Russia, 1906; Ahdut Ha'avoda, Pal, 1918; tchr, Heb HS, Jerusalem, 1908-10; research worker, Agric Experimental Sta, Atlit, 1915-16; mem cen comm, Pal Batallion, 1918-19; active mem, Haganah; found, Forestry Nursery, 1920; prin: Girls Farm, 1928; Havat ha-Limud (agric training farm for girls), 1933; Kfar Ha-noar (youth village), Ein Kerem, 1948; i/c of repatriation of J girls from Syria, Leb, to Pal farms, 1943. Mem: Hashomer; 1st, 2nd, 3rd Electoral Assemblies; delg: 7th, 9th, 11th, 15th, 19th, 25th, 35th, 52nd WZC; Socialist Trade Union Confs; Women's Workers Intl Cong, Paris, 1926. Author: Anu Olim, 1959; Coming Home; co-ed, Beyn Ha-Zmanim; Al ha-Saf; Ahdut; contbr to local press. Home: 10 Ibn Gevirol St, Jerusalem, Isr.

BER, Alter Maier, Eng, merchant; b. Baligrod, Pol, June 8, 1901; s. David and Taube (Berger); in Eng since 1940; m. Sarah Gross, Dec 18, 1932; c: Lea Josse, Ruth Rosenfelder. Dir, Ber & Lehrer, Ltd.Vice pres, chmn, UK JPA, Diamond JPA Comm; mem: Bd Deps, Fin Comm; Friends Heb U Council; dir, London Diamond Club. Home: 3 Frognal Lane, London NW3, Eng. Office: 88/90 Hatton Garden, London EC1, Eng.

BER, Artur, Isr, physician; b. Plock, Pol, Mar 25, 1908; s. Yeheskel and Dorota (Weinreich); in Isr since 1957; att U Warsaw, Pol, 1924-26, BS, 1931, MVD, 1935, MD, 1937; m. Irena Makowska, Dec 31, 1932; c: Kristine, Andre. Dir, endocrinological dept, Rogoff and Welcome Med Research Inst and Beilinson Hosp, Petah Tikva since 1957; prof of experimental endocrinology, Tel Aviv U since 1962; asst: dept bact, fac vetr med, dept of histology and embryology, fac med, Warsaw U, 1928-39; dir, biol dept, Boryszew Pharm Factory, Pol, 1932-36; asst to gyn depts, hosps, Warsaw, 1937-41; hosp dir, Plonsk, Pol, 1941-42; supernumerary prof, dir of dept of gen and experimental path, fac vetr med, U of Curie Sklodowska, 1945; dir, dept serum produc, State Inst of Hygiene, Pol, 1945; extraordinary prof endocrinology, fac med, U Lodz, Pol, 1945-47, full prof, 1945-47; dir, endocrinological dept, U and Med Acad, Lodz, Pol, 1945-57. Mem cen secretariat, Med Org, Histadrut since 1958; pres: Public Health Council, Histadrut; Cen Drug Comm, Kupat Holim; judge, supr court, Histadrut; mem Med Comm for Advancement Sci, Histadrut; found mem: Isr Endocrine Soc; Eur Soc for Comparative Endocrinology; affiliate, Royal Soc of Med, London; membre titulaire Soc de Therapeutique et de Pharmacodynamie, Paris; mem: Intl Fertility Assn; AAAS; Isr Fertility Assn; Isr Med Soc; Isr Union of WW II Vets; fmr pres: Pol Endocrinological Soc; Comm for Serobacteriological and Organopreparations of the III Pol Pharmacopea; Comm for Popular Sci Lectrs, U Lodz; lectrs, U of Lodz; ed, Pol Endocrinology; judge, Pol Med Assn; disciplinary off, Med Acad, Lodz. Recipient: Award of Vetr Cong in Pol, 1935; hon mem Czech Endocrinological Soc, 1949; Prize of Pol Endocrinological Soc, 1957; hon mem, Pol Endocrinological Soc, 1960. Hobby, sculpture. Home: 25 Dubnow St, Tel Aviv, Isr.

BERAN, Bruno, US, artist; b. Aus, 1888; at age 10, toured as violin virtuoso; att acads of fine arts: Vienna, Munich, Paris; studied under Claude Monet. Before WW I, exhibited at Salon, Paris; between WWs, portraitist, Fr, Ger, Spain, Czech; Eur exhbs; fled the Nazi regime to Spain, Fr, Can, US; portraitist: ambass at Wash, DC and other personalities, including: Van Kleffens of Holland; mesdames: Bonnet, Fr; Fartuhiani, It; Le Gallais, Luxembourg; Erkin, Turkey; Elath,

Isr; Lady Franks, Eng; Secy USAF, Robert Seamans; Justice William A Douglas; portraits for Supr Court and Art Gal, Yale U. Recipient: numerous awards, first prizes, medals, Art Acads. Home and studio: 600 Asylum St, Hartford, Conn.

BERC, Harold T, US, attorney; b. Chgo, Ill, Dec 8, 1914; s. Abraham and Sarah (Glassberg); att Northwestern U; LLB, De Paul U, Chgo; m. Mary Amtam, June 21, 1938. Pvt practice Chgo since 1937; fmr: mem, ed dept, Universal Intl News Service. Lt, USN, 1942-53. Fmr pres, Natl Blood Research Found; vice pres: US Assn, Ill; Decalogue Soc of Lawyers; natl cdr, AMVETS, 1959-60; US delg, World Vets Fed; charter mem, World Peace Through Law Cen; mem: Chgo Press Vets Assn; Amer, Ill, Chgo, 7th Fed Circuit Bar Assns; Chgo Commn on Hum Relations; Chgo Natural Hist Mus; Amer Arbitration Assn; Lex Legio, De Paul U; Lincoln Park Lodge, B'nai B'rith; Temple Sholom Brotherhood; clubs: City Club, pres; Chgo Press, charter mem. Contbr to legal jours. Recipient: Bronze Star; past natl cdrs dist service award, AMVETS, 1958. Home: 2842 Sheridan Rd, Chicago, Ill. Office: 33 N La Salle St, Chicago, Ill.

BERCOVICI, Isac, Isr, publicist; b. Braila, Rum, Apr 3, 1896; s. Leon and Sophie (Zins); in Isr since 1950; m. Florica Gruenspan, Nov 1934; c: Meron. Publicist; tchr, Aliath Hanoar, 1946-49. Mem, fmr vice-pres, B'nai B'rith Lodge; mem, Soc des Etudes Juives, Paris, 1927. Contbr to: Ency Judaica; Adam; Renasterea Noastra; Hasmoneea; Mantuirea; Viata Noastra; ed, Zion, 1918-20. Spec interests: hist of J people; phil, sociol of Judaism. Home: 3 Shalom Aleichem St, Bat Yam, Isr.

BEREK, Samuel I, US, business exec; b. Freemont, Neb, Feb 14, 1907; s. Jacob and Ida (Perlman); att Creighton U, 1925; BA, Midland Coll, 1929; MA, U Neb, 1931; m. Janet Braetz, June 23, 1940; c: Jonathan, Joyce. Mgr, Jake Berek Iron and Metal Co since 1930. Pres: Freemont Lodge, B'nai B'rith, 1945-48; Freemont Syn, 1951-52; chmn: Americanism comm, Optomist Club since 1951; state UN Day Comm since 1948; dist patriotism and civic affairs, Optimist Intl, 1953; local NCCJ since 1955; Freemont Flag Comm since 1954; state Natl Brotherhood Week; bd rev, Boy Scouts of Amer since 1957; Freemont Centennial Comm, 1967; mem: Gov's Comm on Hum Rights, 1955; educ comm, Sr C of C; AJCong; Dodge Co Hist Soc; Beth El Syn, Omaha; natl council, Boy Scouts of Amer; Mid-Amer council, Boy Scouts of Amer; merit badge counsellor, Boy Scouts of Amer since 1940. Recipient: gold cup award, Jr C of C, 1945; gold cert award, Freedoms Found, 1951; merit cert, Natl Found for Infantile Paralysis, 1956; Good Neighbor Award, 1956; service award, VFW, 1957; achievement award, Urban League, 1958; service award, Amer Legion, 1959; silver beaver award, Boy Scouts of Amer, 1959; merit award for outstanding service, State of Isr, 1950; Good Neighbor Award, Ak-Sar-Ben, 1956; service to mankind award, Freemont Sertoma Club, 1st recipient, 1964; Shofer award, natl council, J Scouts, 1968; hon citizen, N Bend, Neb, 1956; citations: Dept of Justice, Bur of Naturalization, 1945; NCCJ, 1958. Spec interest: writing songs. Home: 1620 N Nye Ave, Freemont, Neb.

BERELSON, Bernard, US, foundation exec, author, educator; b. Spokane, Wash, June 2, 1912; s. Max and Bessie (Shapiro); BA, Whitman Coll, 1934; BA, U Wash, 1936, MA, 1937; PhD, U Chgo, 1941; m. Elizabeth Durand, Apr 1, 1941, div; c: David; m. 2nd, Rosalind Kean, Sep 30, 1948, div; m. 3rd, Ruth Rappaport, Aug 6, 1953; step-c: Alice Palter; c: Lois, William, Jenny. Pres, Population Council since 1968, vice pres, 1963-68, dir, 1962-63; spec analyst, Fgn Broadcast IS, FCC, 1941-44; prof, libr sci, social sci, U Chgo, 1946, dean, Grad Libr Sch, 1947; sr staff off, Ford Found, dir, behavioral scis div, 1951-57; prof, U Chgo, 1957-60; dir, Bur Applied Social Research, Columbia U, 1960-61. Mem, Amer Sociol Soc; fmr pres, Amer Public Opinion Research Author: The Library's Public, 1949; Content Analysis, 1952; Graduate Education in the United States, 1960; co-author: What Reading Does to People, 1940; The People's Choice, 1944; Voting, 1954; Human Behavior, 1964; ed, Education for Librarianship, 1949; co-ed: Reader in Communication and Public Opinion, 1950; Family Planning and Population Programs, 1966. Home: 7 Ardsley Terr, Irvington, NY. Office: 230 Park Ave, New York, NY.

BERENBERG, David Paul, US educator, author; b. Bklyn, NY, Mar 17, 1890; s. Bernhardt and Lena (Theodor); BA, CCNY, 1912; m. Rose Zwickel, June 30, 1913; c: Naomi Leavitt,

Miriam Pincus. Headmaster, Franklin Sch, NY, 1932-51; lectr: lit, since 1951; lit, social scis, Rand Sch of Social Sci, 1915-36; found, ed, American Socialist Quarterly, 1932-35. Mem, Workmen's Circle. Author: The Letters of Glaucon and Sarai (poems), 1924; The Kid (poem), 1931; Socialist Fundamentals, 1932; America at the Crossroads, 1934; Chants (Poems), 1935. Home: 758 Dogwood Ave, Franklin Square, NY.

BERENBERG, William, US, physician, educator; b. Haverhill, Mass, Oct 29, 1915; s. Louis and Eva (Shapiro); BA, Harvard Coll, 1936; MD, Boston U, 1940; m. Blanche Berger, June 17, 1939; c: Jeffrey, Richard, Barbara. Clinical prof, ped, Harvard Med Sch; chief children's and infants med div, Children's Hosp since 1953. Pres, Amer Acad for Cerebral Palsy; dir: Boston Milk Comm since 1954; Soc for Prevention of Cruelty to Children, since 1957; Temple Emeth, since 1945; chmn: Amer Acad of Ped for Mass, since 1955; natl clinical adv comm, United Cerebral Palsy, since 1954; mem: Amer Acad of Ped; Amer Acad of Neur; Soc for Ped Research; Amer Ped Soc; Trudeau Soc; B'nai B'rith. Contbr to profsl jours. Recipient, Jacobi Award, AMA, 1950. Home: 50 Beresford Rd, Chestnut Hill, Mass. Office: 300 Longwood Ave, Boston Mass.

BERENBLUM, Isaac, Isr, scientist; b. Byalistock, Pol, Aug 26, 1903; s. Shraga and Michele (Slabotsky); in Isr since 1950; MD, Leeds U, Eng, 1920, MS, 1930; m. Doris Bernstein, Sep 30, 1928; c: Tirza Cohen, Ann Szoke. Prof, head dept, experimental biol, Weizmann Inst, Isr since 1950; Riley-Smith Research F, Leeds U, 1927-36; Beit Memorial Research F, Oxford U, 1936-40; lectr, dept path, Oxford U, 1940-49. Prin contribs, teaching and research in path and cancer. Chmn, Isr Cancer Assn; council mem, Intl Union Against Cancer; hon mem, Amer Assn Cancer Research; mem: World Acad Arts and Sci; Isr Acad Sci and Hum; hon life mem, NY Acad Sci. Author: Man Against Cancer, 1952; Cancer Research Today, 1967. Recipient: Weizmann Prize for Biol Sci, 1959; Rothschild Prize in Biol, 1966. Hobby, chess. Home: 33 Ruppin St, Rehovot, Isr. Office: Dept of Experimental Biology, Weizmann Inst, Rehovot, Isr.

BERENDSOHN, Walter Arthur, Swed, educator, researcher, author; b. Hamburg, Ger, Sep 10, 1884; s. Bernhard and Florette (Sonn); in Swed since 1943; PhD, U Kiel, 1911; m. Dorothea Eggert, June 27, 1918; c: Anne Romme, Karin Braun. Researcher, Swed Acad, since 1943; asst ed, Erasmus since 1952; fmr: asst, Ger Sem, Hamburg, 1914-20; pvt dozent, U Hamburg, 1920-26, prof, 1926-33; archive worker, Swed, 1943. Author: Der Impressionismus Hofmannsthals als Zeiterscheinung, 1920; Grundformen Volkstümlicher Erzählerkunst in den Kinder-und Hausmärchen der Brüder Grimm, 1922; Selma Lagerlöf, 1927; Knut Hamsun, 1929; Zur Vorgeschichte des Beowulf, 1935; Der lebendige Heine im germanischen Norden, 1935; Die Humanistische Front, Einführung in die deutsche Emigranten, vol 1, 1947, vol II, unpub; Registers to August Strindberg's Works and Letters since 1943; Strindberg-Problems (Swed), 1946; Strindberg's Last Four Years (Swed), 1948; Martin Andersen Nexö (Dan), 1949; Fancy and Reality in HC Andersen's Fairy Tales (Dan), 1955; Die Idee der Humanität in Vergangenheit und Gegenwart, 1961; Das Volk der Bibel im Land der Vaeter; Der Junge Staat Israel, 1962; Thomas Mann, Künstler und Kämpfer in bewegter Zeit, 1965; Humane Tendenzen im Atomzeitalter, 1965; August Strindberg und die Frauen, 1967; Briefe on Strindberg, 1968; Nelly Sachs Mysterienspiel vom Leiden Israels, 1969; Die Künstlerische Entwicklung Heines im Buch der Lieder, 1969; Gründung einer Forschungstelle für die Deutsche Literatur an Flüchtlingen aus dem Dritten Reich und Organisation der internationalen Zusammenarbeit, 1966-69. Home: Stramaljvagen 8, Bromma, Stockholm, Swed.

BERENGARTEN, Sidney, US, social worker, educator; b. Bklyn, NY, May 28, 1911; s. Adolph and Therese (Finkelstein); BA, NYU, 1932; MA, Clark U, 1933; MS, NY Sch of Social Work, Columbia U, 1943; m. Miriam Lindenbaum, 1932. Prof, social work, Columbia U Sch of Social work, since 1946, acting dean, 1967-69, asso dean, 1966-67, asst dean 1963-66; cons in soc work, neuropsycht, cons div, Off of Surg Gen, US Dept Army since 1948; lectr, nursing educ, Tchrs Coll, 1947-55; Amer specialist, Bur Cultural and Educ Affairs, US State Dept, 1965-66; cons, Fulbright Comm, Colombia, S Amer, 1965-66; research asst, US Dept Interior, 1934; field worker, asst case sup, NYC Dept of Wfr, 1934-41; case worker, sup, NY Comty Service Soc, 1942-43. Lt, Med Admn

Corps, US Army, 1943-46. Mem: adv comm, Children's Bur, Bur Public Assistance, HEW, 1953-59; cons, U Toronto Sch of Social Work, 1962-64; Natl Assn Social Workers; AAUP; Council on Social Work Educ. Author, Admissions Prediction and Student Performance in Social Work Education, Work Education, 1964; co-author: Social Work as Human Relations, 1949; Interviewing and Personality Assessment: Selection of Social Work Students, 1968; contbr to profsl jours. Home: 2200 85 St, Brooklyn, NY. Office: 2 E 91 St, New York, NY.

BERENSON, Ida, US, communal leader; b. Wolkowitz, Grodne, Russ; d. Samuel and Fanny (Starinsky) Kramer; m. Alexander Berenson, July 27, 1911 (decd). Ret; bd dirs, J Chronic Disease Hosp, Bklyn; mem: Yeshiva U Scholarship Fund; Chap 77, OES. Home: 226 W Broadway, Long Beach, NY.

BERENSON, Richard Arthur, US, business exec; b. Boston, Mass, May 12, 1908; s. Mashie and Fannie (Ricen); BA, Harvard Coll, 1928, MBA, 1930; m. Judith Woodbury, June 6, 1957; c: Marshall, Richard. Pres, Berenson Liquor Mart since 1935; treas: Revere Airways since 1946; Hotel Lenox since 1949; Revere Drive-In Theatre since 1947; Avon, since 1948. Pres: Intl Trade Cen, 1965-67, chmn of bd, 1967-68; Rotary, Boston, 1965-66; Northgate Shopping City since 1963; S Hooper-Richardson Co since 1963; Advt Club, 1956-57; dir: ARC since 1953; World Trade Cen, NE since 1957; vice-pres: Boston C of C, 1968-69, 1954-57; secy, Boston Arts Festival, 1957-60; trustee, CJA since 1953. Recipient, Chevalier de Merite Commercial Fr. Home: 26 Beech Road, Brookline, Mass. Office: 70 Summer St, Boston, Mass.

BERENSTEIN, Alexandre, Switz, judge, educator; b. Paris, Jan 19, 1909; s. Moise and Bluma (Monosson); licencié-en-droit, 1929, licencié-en-sociol, 1930, D-en-droit, 1936, U Geneva. Prof, lab law and ins, U Geneva since 1951, on fac since 1938; atty, Geneva Bar sine 1939; judge, Cour de Cassation, Geneva since 1966; dep judge, Fed Court for Social Ins since 1968. Pres: Intl Assn for Social Progress since 1967; Assn Suisse de Politique Sociale since 1961; secy gen, Intl Soc for Lab Law and Social Leg since 1958; mem, cen comm, Swiss Socialist Party. Author, Les Organisations Ouvrières, 1936; contbr of articles and pamphlets to profsl publs. Home: 29 bis de Miremont, Geneva, Switz. Office: 4 Place du Molard, Geneva, Switz.

BERENT, David, US, rabbi; b. NYC, Feb 28, 1907; s. Louis and Esther (Botchko); ordained rabbi, Etz Chayim Sem, Montreux, Switz, 1933; att: Dropsie Coll, Phila; Tchrs Coll, Columbia U; hon, DHum, Nasson Coll, Springvale, Me, 1957; m. Gertrude Weiner, Aug 5, 1934; c: Jonathan. Rabbi, Beth Jacob Cong, Lewiston, Me since 1940; adj prof, dept theol, St Joseph's Coll, Me; mem, phil dept, U of Me; rabbi, Cong Beth Judah, Wildwood, NJ, 1937-40. Chaplain, VA Hosp, Togus, Me since 1941; fmr: chaplain, Me State Guard; auxiliary chaplain: USN Air Sta, Brunswick, Me; USAF, Topsham, Me; civilian chaplain, Mil Police Battalion. J Chautauqua lectr, NE U's and Colls; pres, Rabb Assn of Me since 1959; delg, Mid-Cent White Conf on Youth; grand chaplain, Masons, Me; mem: State Bd Educ comm character bldg and Bible accreditation; State Bd Mediators-lab and mgmt; Amer Acad Political and Social Sci; govs comm, Veteran's and Child Health and Wfr since 1950; ZOA, vice pres, NE region; Mizrachi; Cmty Cen; B'nai B'rith; AJ Comm; asso mem, Amer Assn Marriage Counsellors; Mil Chaplains Assn; Mental Hosp Chaplains Assn; Young Isr; Masons; Shriners; Odd Fellows; KP. Contbr to: Eng-J Press; Universal J Ency. Recipient: Citation, outstanding citizen of Lewiston, by Elks, 1949; Boy Scouts Beaver Award, 1942; George Washington Medal and Prize, Freedom Fund, 1958,61; B'nai B'rith, Me, humanitarian award, 1961. Home: 12 Bardwell St, Lewiston, Me. Study: Beth Jacob Congregation, Lewiston, Me.

BERES, David, US, psychiatrist; b. Odessa, Russ, Apr 1, 1903; s. Nathan and Mary (Best); in US since 1905; BS, CCNY, 1923; MD, LI Med Sch, 1928; m. Dinah Schleifer, Dec 18, 1926; c: Paul, Robert. Pres, NY Psychan Soc since 1969; psycht, J Child Care Assn, NY, 1942-61. Pres: Amer Psychan Assn, 1963-64; NY Psychan Inst, 1964-66; vice-pres, Intl Psychan Assn, 1963-64. Contbr, articles to sci jours. Home and office: 151 Central Park W, New York, NY.

BERESIN, Victor Eugene, US, educator; b. Phila, Pa, May 29, 1916; s. Morris and Rebecca (Roitman); DDS, Temple U

Dent Sch, 1938; m. Marcella Suskind, Nov 24, 1948; c: Eugene, Alice. Asso clin prof, prosthetic dent, Temple U Dent Sch since 1965; att in prosthodontics, Albert Einstein Med Cen, Phila since 1953; asso, prosthetic dept, Grad Sch of Med, U of Pa, 1956-63. Maj, US Army, 1941-46. Dipl, Amer Bd of Prosthodontics; mem: Amer Dent Assn; Amer Equilibration Soc; Amer Prosthodontic Soc; Intl Assn for Dent Research; Amer Acad for Cleft Palate Rehabilitation; Phily Acad of Stomatology; club: Clinic, Phila, Phila Dent Studa. Contbr to profsl jours. Recipient, Bronze Star. Home: 436 Conshohocken St Rd, Bala-Cynwyd, Pa. Office: 275 S 19 St, Philadelphia, Pa.

BEREZIN, Adolpho, Brazil, banker; b. Sao Paulo, Brazil, Dec 8, 1926; s. Saia and Sarah; att tech sch of aviation, Sao Paulo; DDS, U Sao Paulo; m. Clara, July 1, 1951; c: Jairo, Rosely. Pres, Bank Renascenca SA since 1964; Brazil Air Force, 1943-46. Pres, Soc Isr de Beneficencia Ezra; vice-pres, Comm of Social Assis; mem: Rotary; Hebraica, both Sao Paulo. Recipient, Aviation Cross. Home: 370 Higienopolis Ave, Sao Paulo, Brazil. Office: 178 rua D José de Barros, Sao Paulo, Brazil.

BEREZIN, Martin A, US psychiatrist; b. Wrentham, Mass, Sep 14, 1912; s. Samuel and Fanny (Fliegelman); BS, Coll of Lib Arts, 1934; MD, Boston U, 1937; m. Evelyn Polan, Jan 14, 1942; c: Jane, Robert, Charles. Psychan, pvt practice since 1946; clinical asso psycht, Harvard Med Sch, asst clinical prof, psycht, Tufts Med Sch, 1951-63; psycht, Beth Isr Hosp, Boston since 1946; instr, Boston Psychan Soc and Inst since 1958; res, Medfield State Hosp, Harding, Mass, 1939-41; staff, Mass Gen Hosp, 1945-52; cons, VA, 1945-51; Murphy Army Hosp, 1948-50; dipl, Amer Bd Psycht and Neur, 1943. Col, US Army MC, 1941-46. Mem: Boston Psychan Soc and Inst; Amer Psychan Assn; Intl Psychan Assn; Amer Psycht Assn; Mass Med Soc; Gerontological Soc; pres, Boston Soc for Gerontologic Psycht, N NE Dist Branch Amer Psycht Assn, 1968-69. Contbr to med jours; ed-in-chief, Jour of Geriatric Psycht. Recipient: two combat Battle Stars, 1943; Pres Citation, 1943. Hobby, music. Home and office: 90 Forest Ave, W Newton, Mass.

BERG, Aaron W, US attorney; b. NYC, July 4, 1903; s. Jay and Rose (Weisberger); BA, Columbia Coll, 1924; LLB, Columbia U Sch of Law, 1927; m. Virginia Housman, Jan 16, 1935; c: Virginia Kahn, Carol Solomon. In pvt law practice, spec in surrogates court since 1927; asso: Wise and Seligsberg, 1927-29; Feiner and Skutch, 1929-37. NJ State Guard, 1941; USCG Res, 1942-52. Pres, Alcoholism Council, Monmouth Co since 1968; hon vice pres, Camp Emanuel, fmr dir, treas; hon dir, J Vacation Assn, fmr, treas; mem: comms, Fed Support J Philanthropic Socs, NYC; AJComm; Amer Council Judaism; Assn Bar, NYC; Zeta Beta Tau; Beth Miriam Temple, NJ; pres, Friends Long Br Librs; dir, Monmouth Co Mh Assn; trustee, Long Br Adult Sch; clubs: Columbia U; Ocean Beach; fmr dir: Boys Athletic League, NYC; Camp Ramapo, J Bd Guardians; secy, Fed Settlement; pres, Jr Fed; pres, Columbia Coll Alumni Assn, delg, Columbia U Alumni Trustee Nominating Conv; mem: Columbia Coll Alumni for Eisenhower; leg comm, United Neighborhood Houses; Monmouth Co, NJ, Rep Finance Comm; pres, Class 1924, Columbia Coll. Recipient: alumni medal, Columbia U, 1949; bicentennial medal, 1954, Dean's Award, 1945, Class 1924 award, 1954. Hobbies: rare book and print collecting, horticulture. Home: Hollywood Ave, Long Branch, NJ.

BERG, Abram Sulzberger, US, industrialist; b. Phila, Sep 7, 1902; s. Abram and Laura (Pollack); BA, U of Pa, 1924; m. Elsie Friedman, Nov 3, 1924; c: Alan, Lorna Hoopes. Bd chmn: Neatsfoot Oil Refineries Corp; Norco Products. Pres: Atlantic region, JWB, bd dir natl JWB; JWB Armed Services; Vet Comm USO, Phila, bd mem; mem, exec comty, natl council, USO; bd dirs: Fed of J Agcys since 1943; HIAS, vice-pres, 1940-45; natl exec comm, AJComm since 1946, admn comm since 1962; Jt Defense Appeal since 1948; bd dir, Cong Mikveh Isr; found chmn, hon chmn, Pa, Del, Md, AJComm; hon bd mem, J Family Service, Phila. Home: The Benson East, Jenkintown, Pa. Office: E Ontario and Bath Sts, Philadelphia, Pa.

BERG, Benjamin Nathan, US, surgeon, educator, research investigator; b. NYC, Dec 8, 1897; s. John and Rose (Lehr); BA, CCNY, 1916; MD, Columbia Coll of Phys and Surgtt 1920; m. Ethel Lichtenstein, Dec 28, 1924; c: Robert. As, surg, Hosp for Jt Diseases and Harlem Hosp since 1938;

cons surg, Hosp for Jt Diseases since 1961, Harlem Hosp since 1963; cons, histopath and teratology, Geigy Chemical Corp since 1964; research asso, Public Health Research Inst, 1963-64; asso path, Columbia Coll of Phys and Surgs since 1930; surg, internship, Mt Sinai Hosp, 1921-23; Blumenthal F, surg, 1927-30, instr, surg, 1927-30, Columbia Coll Phys and Surg; asst surg: Mt Sinai Hosp, 1923-27; Presbyterian Hosp, 1927-28; visiting surg, Vanderbilt Clinic, 1928-30; adj att surg: Sydenham Hosp, 1927-35; Beth Isr Hosp, 1929-35; Hosp for Jt Diseases, 1931-35; asso att surg: Harlem Hosp, 1930-38; Hosp for Jt Diseases, 1935-38. F: Amer Coll Surgs; NY Acad Med; AAAS; Amer Bd Surg, found; mem: bd dirs, Queensboro TB and Health Assn; Queens Div, Amer Cancer Soc; Teratology Soc; Harvey Soc; Soc Experimental Biol and Med; Soc Experimental Path; AMA; NY Co Med Soc; Gerontological Soc; Alpha Omega Alpha. Contbr of articles in fields of clinical and experimental surg and experimental path, with spec reference to diseases of stomach, liver, biliary tract, and pancreas; gerontological research on nutrition and longevity; publs on reproduction, fetal development and congenital malformations, as well as endocrine factors in fertility. Home and office: 40 E 88 St, New York, NY.

BERG, Harold F, US, surgeon; b. Bklyn, May 22, 1918; s. David and Rose (Graff); BA, U Louisville, 1939, MD, 1942; m. Pearl Greenberg, Sep 6, 1953; c: Amy, Dena, Karen, Lauren. Pvt practice since 1951; asst prof, surg, U Louisville, Sch of Med since 1961, on staff since 1949; cons, Oak Ridge Inst of Nuclear Studies, med div, since 1951; residency, Louisville Gen Hosp, 1950-51; research f, Damon Runyon Fund, 1951-57; att surg, VA Hosp, Louisville, Ky, 1951-60; chief surg, J Hosp, Louisville, 1958-61. Maj, US Army MC, 1943-46. Chmn: Louisville Adult J Educ Comm since 1968; Isr Bonds, Louisville, 1961-62; mem: Amer Coll Surgs; AMA; Cen Surg Assn; Ky State and Jefferson Co Med Assns; Ky Surg Soc; Louisville Surg Soc Cert, Amer Bd of Surg, 1951. Contbr to profsl jours. Hobbies: mosaics, ceramics. Home: 608 Jarvis Lane, Louisville, Ky. Office: 200 Med Towers Bldg, Louisville, Ky.

BERG, Louis, US, psychiatrist, author; b. London, June 19, 1901; s. Samuel and Ida (Steinberg); in US since 1904; AB, Coumbia U, 1920; MD, Jefferson Med Coll, 1923; grad study, U Vienna, 1926. Med dir, Henry Meinhard Memorial Health Cen since 1931; dist med sup, Dept of Health, NYC, since 1929; asso, neuropsycht, Beth David Hosp since 1936; asst phys, Manhattan State Hosp Insane, 1924-25; phys, NY Dept of Correction, Wfr I, 1928-35; instr, educ, NYU, 1929-34. Author: Prison Doctor, 1931; The Human Personality, 1932; Prison Nurse, 1934; Devil's Circus, 1934; Revelations of a Prison Doctor, 1934; Twilight Comes Early, 1939; Intolerance is a Symptom of Insanity, 1940; contbr to: Watkins Syndicate, 1935-37; periodicals on Mh. F, AMA; mem: Royal Soc Health; Amer Psycht Assn; NY Co and State Med Soc's; Masons. Home: Rocky Glen, Haviland Rd and Hunting Ridge, Stamford, Conn. Office: 17 E 70 St, New York, NY.

BERG, Raymond David, Eng, student; b. Glasgow, Scotland, Apr 29, 1945; s. Nathan and Gladys (Barnes); att Carmel Coll, Wallingford, 1957-62; Monkwearmouth Coll, Sunderland, 1962-65; HND Bus Studies, Bournemouth Coll, 1965-66; BS, Hull U, 1969. Pres, Hull U J and Isr Soc since 1967. Home: 14 Granville Court, Jesmond, Newcastle, Eng.

BERG, Roger, Fr, communal worker, editor; b. Nancy, Fr, Dec 22, 1910; s. Camille and Mathilde (Gompel); docteur en droit, U Nancy, 1934; m. Andrée Bloch, June 12, 1947. Ed-in-chief, Journal des Communautés since 1950; counsellor-at-law, Nancy, 1930-43; i/c practical studies, Fac de Nancy, 1931-32; gen secy: Consistoire Central des Isr de Fr, 1951-65; Conseil Repr des Juifs de Fr, 1952-65. Fr Army, WW II, prisoner of war, Ger, 1940-45. Author: Le Socialisme entre l'Economie Nationale et le Cosmopolitisme, 1935; La Persécution Raciale, 1946; La Voie Droite, 1960; Guide Religieux de la France, 1966; Guide Juif de France, 1967. Recipient, Concours Général de Legislation, l'Académie de Legislation, Toulouse. Home: 74 Bvd Richard Lenoir, Paris 11, Fr. Office: 17 rue St Georges, Paris 9, Fr.

BERG, Roland H, US, bacteriologist, author, editor; b. NYC, Feb 20, 1908; s. Davis and Millie (Hobsbawn); BS, Fordham U, NYC, 1927; att NYC Sch of Journalism, 1928-30. Sci and med ed, Look Magazine since 1954; bact, clinical and research worker at: J Hosp, Bklyn, NY, 1928-30; Manhattan Eye, Ear and Throat Hosp, NYC, 1930-44; dir, sci info, Natl Found for Infantile Paralysis, 1944-54; cons to: USPHS; Amer

Cancer Soc, 1944-52. Mem, bd dirs, Council Advancement Sci Writing; mem: Amer Public Health Assn; Authors Guild; Radio Writers Guild; Natl Assn Sci Writers; NY Acad of Scis. Author: Challenge of Polio, 1945; Polio and its Problems, 1949; contbr to natl mags; wrote and produced a series of radio and TV plays concerned with sci and med. Recipient, Ben Franklin Mag Award, 1956. Home: 240 Central Park S, New York, NY. Office: 488 Madison Ave, New York, NY.

BERG, Sydney Solomon, US, dentist; b. Boston, Mass, Jan 26, 1931; s. Louis and Jenny (Kursakisak); att Boston U, 1948-52; BJE, Heb Tchrs Coll, 1952; DMP, Tufts U Dent Sch, 1956; m. Mathilde Lipshitz, Oct 20, 1956; c: Daniel, Alan, Ethan. Pvt practice since 1968. Lt, USN, 1956-68. Chmn, bd educ, Temple Sinai, Marblehead, Mass, financial secy, 1961-62, chmn, sch comm, 1962-69; B'nai B'rith. Hobbies: sailing, collecting, stained glass. Home: 27 Sevinor Rd, Marblehead, Mass. Office: 66 Lewis St, Lynn, Mass.

BERGER, Abraham, US, librarian; b. Grzymalow, Galicia, May 30, 1903; s. Jacob and Gittel (Drimer); desc of David Solomon Eybeschuetz, Talmudic and Hasidic scholar; in US since 1921; BS, Columbia U, 1935, MS, Fac Libr Service, 1938; m. Pauline Kaplan, Oct 30, 1936. Fmr chief, J div, NY Public Libr, 1956-67, first asst, 1938-55. Pres, J Librs Assn, 1959-62; mem: Amer Acad J Research; Conf on J Social Studies; Amer J Hist Soc; YIVO Inst for J Research; Amer Libr Assn; Amer Friends Heb U. Contbr of articles to periodicals and encys. Spec interest, mythology. Home: 301 W 108 St, New York, NY.

BERGER, Elmer, US, rabbi, organization exec, author; b. Cleveland, O, May 27, 1908; s. Samuel and Selma (Turk); BA, U Cincinnati, 1930; ordained rabbi, HUC, 1932; m. Ruth Rosenthal. Exec vice-pres, Amer Council for Judaism since 1955, natl exec dir, 1943-55; dir, Amer Friends of ME; rabbi: Temple Beth Jacob, Pontiac, Mich, 1932-36; Temple Beth El, Flint, Mich, 1936-42. Mem, Phi Beta Kappa. Author: The Jewish Dilemma, 1945; A Partisan History of Judaism, 1951; Who Knows Better, Must Say So, 1955; Judaism or Jewish Nationalism, 1957; contbr, Ency Britannica Yearbook; Rel in Life; Chr Cent. Home: 912 Fifth Ave, New York, NY. Study: 201 E 57 St, New York, NY.

BERGER, Graenum, US, social work exec; b. Gloversville, NY, Apr 21, 1908; s. Harry and Bessy (Cohen); AB, U of Mo, 1930; MS, Grad Sch J Social Work, 1932; m. Emma Feinstein, Oct 16, 1928; c: Ramon, Baruch. Dir, Wiener Educ Cen, NY, since 1969; cons, J Comty Cen, Camps, J educ, FJP of NY, since 1949; exec dir, J Comty Cen, Staten I, 1932-38; headworker, Bx House, 1938-49; instr: NY Sch, Social Work, 1939-49; Yeshivah U, 1945-47; CCNY, 1945-47; Wurzweiler Sch, Social Work, 1965-66. Pres: Pelham J Cen, 1953-55; Natl Assn, J Cen Workers, 1946-48; Research Inst-Study of Group Work, 1958-65; bd dirs: Jerusalem YM and YWHA; NY Anti-Poverty Bd, 1964-66; LZOA, 1962-64; Natl JWB, 1962; mem: Natl Assn, Social Work; Acad Cert Social Workers. Author, Jewish Community Center, 1966; ed, Proceedings, Intl Cong J Communal Service, 1967; contbr to educ and J publs. Recipient, medals: Frank Weil, 1962; Naomi Lehman, 1968. Home: 340 Corlies Ave, Pelham, NY. Office: 130 E 59 St, New York, NY.

BERGER, Harold Joseph, US, attorney; b. Pottstown, Pa, Nov 10, 1921; s. Bernath and Goldie (Weiss); BA, Pa State U, 1942; LLB, U of Pa, 1958; m. Laurette Schwartz, July 1, 1947; c: Carol, Betsy, Lee, Mitchell. Atty, pvt practice since 1966; partner, Berger Bros since 1948. Past pres, Cong B'nai Jacob; dir, C of C; YMCA; chmn, Phoenixville Hum Relations Council; Kiwanis Club; United Fund, UJA; B'nai B'rith; mem: Chester Co; Pa; Amer Bar Assns. Home: N Russell Road, Phoenixville, Pa. Office: 235 Bridge St, Phoenixville, Pa.

BERGER, Heinrich Z, Isr, educator, orthodontist; b. Neisse, Ger, Feb 15, 1902; s. Eugene and Hannah; in Isr since 1933; DMD, U Berlin, 1927; m. Margarita Gottlieb, 1946; two c. Head, sec orthodontics, fac continuing med educ, Tel Aviv U since 1964; in pvt practice since 1933. Vice-pres, Eur Orthodontic Soc, 1959-62; found, pres, Isr Orthodontic Soc; mem: Isr Dent Assn; Intl Assn for Dent Research; Alpha Omega. Contbr to natl and intl profsl jours. Home and office: 69 Rothschild Blvd, Tel Aviv, Isr.

BERGER, Jean, US, composer; b. Hamm, Ger, Sep 27, 1909; in US since 1941; att U Vienna, 1928; PhD, U Heidelberg,

1932; studied with Louis Aubert, Fr, 1933-39; hon DMus, Pacific Lutheran U, Tacoma, Wash, 1969; m. Rita Holzer, 1944; c: Jonathan. Prof,Temple Buell Coll, Denver, Colo since 1967; composer; asso prof: Middlebury Coll, 1948-59; U of Ill, 1959-61; prof, U of Colo, 1961-68. Specializes in composition for chorus for churches, syns, schs, Us; civic choruses; published numerous works, most frequently performed include: Brazilian Psalms; Psalms of Penitence; Magnificat; Psalm 57; Skelton Poems; receives commissions from churches and syns; conducts own compositions throughout US. US Army, 1942-43. Mem, ASCAP. Hobby, skiing. Home and office: POB 429, Boulder, Colo.

BERGER, Ludwig, Isr, economist, author; b. Pol; in Isr since 1940; att Cracow U; Strasbourg U; PhD, econ. Econ adv; JA. Author: Problems of Foreign Trade, 1938; Industry in the State of Israel, 1958; Everything on Israel Economy, 1959; Studies in Israel Development Thought, 1961; Economic Liberalism in Israel, 1962; The Human Factor in Israel Economy, 1965; Sociological Problems of Absorption, 1966; A Foreign Study of Israel's Economy, 1968; Immigration Prospects: Short-Range and Long, 1969; Soviet Communism versus Judaism, 1969; ed: The Isr Yearbook; Econ Rev. Fmr chmn, Commn for the Reform of the Pol Ind Structure, 1936-38. Home: 5 Dizengoff St, Tel Aviv, Isr.

BERGER, M Marvin, US, attorney, business exec; b. NYC, July 24, 1908; s. Samuel and Rebecca (Neyer); BS, NYC, 1928, LLB, 1929; admitted NY Bar, 1930; m. Lillian Richel, Oct 10, 1937; c: Howard, Joel. Asso publisher, NY Law Jour; pres, dir, ABC Ind, Inc; vice-chmn bd dirs, vice pres, secy, NY Law Publ since 1963; secy, NY Post, 1945-63, gen counsel, chmn bd ed, NY State Bar Jour, dir, 1953-63; admitted Supr Court, 1961. Mem, natl council, United Syn of Amer since 1963; exec comm, Natl Civil Rights Comm, legal comm, PR Comm, Catholic-J Relations Comm, Bklyn, NY Diocese, ADL; mem, Syn Council of Amer, 1946-58, secy, 1954-58; mem, bd NCCJ, natl comm, Manhattan region; repr, Wartime Emergency Commn, United Syn, 1942-45; pres, life mem exec bd, Cong B'nai Jacob, Bklyn, 1948-49; pres, Hillcrest J Cen, Jamaica, NY, 1958-60, secy, 1953-55, vice-pres, 1955-58, mem bd trustees since 1954; mem: exec comm, ZOA; B'nai B'rith; NYU Almni Assn; bd: Civic Cen Syn, NY; mem: Amer, NY State, NYC, Queens Co; Fed Bar Assns; NY Co Lawyers' Assn; Inst of Judicial Admn; Amer Judicature Soc; NY Law Inst; clubs: Natl Press; Scribes; City of NY; Silurians. Author, articles on public and libel law. Home: 84-65 Avon St, Jamaica, NY. Office: New York Law Jour Building, 258 Broadway, New York, NY.

BERGER, Michael Jona, Isr, attorney, economist; b. Berlin, Nov 13, 1925; s. Alfred and Rivka (Kaufmann); father, cofound with Salman Shazar, Poalei-Zion, Ger, 1925; in Isr since 1933; MA, U Aberdeen, 1950; MJ, Heb U, Jerusalem, 1964; m. Salome Behr, Jan 7, 1954. Dir, control, State Controller's Off since 1962; sect head, Min of Fin, 1953-62. RAF, 1944-46; first lt, GHQ, IDF, 1950-53. Chmn, Jerusalem br, Union Grads Social Scis and Hum; hon treas, Friends Den in Isr; fmr dir of pubs, Student Council, U of Aberdeen. Recipient, Rubin Prize, Social Sciences. Hobbies: hist, cookery. Home: 40 Ramban St, Jerusalem, Isr. Office: 66 Rashi St, Jerusalem, Isr.

BERGER, Milton, US, attorney; b. Phila, Pa, Jan 2, 1904; s. Samuel and Fanny (Goldberg); BA, U of Pa, 1926, LLB, 1929; c: Alan, Hedy, Jane, Robert. Pvt practice since 1929; pres: Pa Papyrus Corp since 1950; Paper Research and Mach Inc; chmn bd, Natl Tube and Reel; secy-treas, Yarn Carrier. Pres, dist grand lodge No 3, B'nai B'rith, 1956-57; chmn, Natl Vocational Service Comm; Natl Found J Men's Clubs, 1943-44; budget comm, United Syn of Amer; vice-pres, World Council of Syns, 1957-61; delg, Supr Lodge Convs, B'nai B'rith, 1948-68; mem: natl council, Boy Scouts of Amer; exec comm, Phila Council, J Comm on Scouting; bd overseers, JTSA; hon bd dirs, Cong Adat Jeshurun, Elkins Park, Pa. Co-author, Roads to Jewish Survival; ed, The Torah, 1941-68. Recipient, Silver Bearer Award, Boy Scouts of Amer. Office: 1904 Gizard Trust Bldg, Philadelphia, Pa.

BERGER, Morroe, US, sociologist, educator; b. NYC, June 25, 1917; s. Morris and Frieda (Trotiner); BSS, CCNY, 1940; MA, Columbia U, 1947, PhD, 1950; m. Paula Wainer, Mar 7, 1943; c: Edward, Kenneth, Laurence. Prof, sociol, Princeton U since 1952, chmn, council on intl regional progs since 1968, dir, prog in Near E Studies, 1962-68, fac mem since 1952.

US Army, 1941-45. Pres, ME Studies Assn, 1967; mem: Amer Sociol Soc; Princeton J Cen. Author: Equality by Statute, 1952, rev, 1967; Racial Equality and the Law, 1954; Bureaucracy and Society in Modern Egypt, 1957; The Arab World Today, 1962; ed, trans, Madame de Stael, on Politics, Literature and National Character, 1964; contbr to: Intl Ency of the Social Sciences; Cambridge Hist of Islam. Home: 72 Clover Lane, Princeton, NJ. Office: Princeton U, Princeton, NJ.

BERGER, Murray Jacob, US, rabbi; b. Bklyn, NY, Oct 18, 1937; s. Joe and May (Kaplan); att W Reserve U, 1955-57; AB, U Cincinnati, 1959; BHL, MA, ordained rabbi, HUC, 1963; m. Roberta Schwartz, June 9, 1963; c: Karyn, Allan. Rabbi: Temple Ety Ahayem, Montgomery, Ala, since 1969; Temple B'nai Isr, 1965-69. Chaplain, US Army, 1963-65. Pres: NCCJ, Parkersburg; secy, B'nai B'rith; pres, Parkersburg Comty Service Council, 1967-68; mem: Assn J Chaplains Armed Forces; Natl Council, JDC; Masons; club, Lions. Home: 2450 Price St, Montgomery, Ala. Study: 725 Augusta St, Montgomery, Ala.

BERGER, Nathan, US, business exec; b. Frystzak, Pol, May 16, 1912; s. Leo and Hendel (Stein); in US since 1929; m. Dorothy Forman; c: Bruce, Miles. Pres, Berger & Berger Real Estate Corp since 1939, vice-pres, treas, 1933-38; pres, Mayflower Assos since 1962. Past pres: Concourse Cen, Isr; bd dirs: Riverdale J Cen; Riverdale Heb Day Sch; past bd dirs: Salanter Yeshiva; AJCong; past vice-pres, Salanter Yeshiva; vice-pres, Natl Hay Fever Relief Assn. Spec interest, cantorial music. Home: 630 W 246 St, New York, NY. Office: 2327 Grand Concourse, New York, NY.

BERGER, Ramon Francis, US, organization exec; b. Albany, NY, Aug 23, 1929; s. Graenum and Emma (Feinstein); BS, NYU, 1951, MA, 1955; m. Anita Fink, May 6, 1951; c: Elizabeth, Gideon. Exec dir, J Sponsored Camps Inc, since 1966; tchr, jr HS, NYC, 1955-57; asst exec dir, Surprise Lake Camp, NYC, 1957-64; camp dir, UAHC, 1964-65. Mem: exec comm, Metrop Assn J Cen Workers, fmr secy; Natl Assn J Cen Workers. Home: 237 E 20 St, New York, NY. Office: 31 Union Sq, New York, NY.

BERGER BARZILAY, Itzhak, Isr, educator; b. Crakow, Pol, Nov 29, 1904; s. Moshe and Rosa (Rabinovitz) Zlaznik; in Isr since 1920; Gymnasium, Bilitz, Ger; m. Esther Feldman; s. Yaakov. Sr research f, Bar Ilan U since 1969; invited to Moscow by Exec Comm of Communist Intl, 1931; sent to prison by Russ IS for 22 yrs. Author: Hayehudim Hasovietim Vegoralam, 1959; Zohar Bahatzot, 1961; Hatragedya Shel Hamahapecha Harusit, 1968; contbr to Heb press. Home: 29 Reading St, Tel Aviv, Isr. Office: Bar Ilan U, Ramat Gan, Isr.

BERGMAN, Bernard Aaron, US, editor; b. Chillicothe, O, July 8, 1894; s. Eleazer and Carrie (Weiler); BA, O State U, 1916; m. Frances Dellar, Mar 17, 1933 (decd). Ed: book div, Bulletin, Phila, since 1967, on staff since 1961; features ed, Pageant, since 1946; mgn ed, New Yorker, 1931-33; features, exec, Phila Record, 1935-42; dir, PR, Publicker Ind Inc, 1947-53; ed: Phila Daily News, 1956-58; J Exponent, 1958-60. Sgt maj, US Army, WWI, lt col, USAAF, WWII. Mem: Phi Beta Kappa; Zeta Beta Tau; Sigma Delta Chi; Phila PR Assn; Club, Franklin Inn. Co-author, The Smiling Corpse, 1935. Home: 1810 Rittenhouse Sq, Philadelphia, Pa. Office: 30th and Market Sts, Philadelphia, Pa.

BERGMAN, Harry, US, surgeon, educator, b. NYC, Oct 25, 1912; s. Sam and Polly (Freedman); att U Buffalo Arts Coll; MD, U Buffalo, 1934; m. Tillie Simon (decd); m. 2nd, Mollie Holzman, Apr 2, 1958; c: Ann Matasar, Judith Driban, Wendy Palley. Att urol: Bx Leb Hosp Cen; City Hosp since 1959; asso clinical prof, NY Med Coll; fmr: intern, Lebanon Hosp; res urol, Morrisania Hosp; clinical asst urol, Mt Sinai Hosp. Prin contribs: designed serial sect cancer biopsy instrument, 1947; new hemostatic catheter, 1958; found, Bergman's Sign for cancer of the ureter. Dipl: Amer Bd Urol; FACS; f: Amer Urol Assn; NY Acad Med; NY sect, Amer Urol Assn; mem, exec council, treas, past pres, Bx chap, Amer Coll Surg; AMA; Amer Phys Comm IMA; gen alumni bd, U Buffalo, past pres, Metrop Med Alumni; nominating comm, Bx Co Med Soc; ZOA (life); Masons; Magicians Guild Amer; Phi Lambda Kappa; Phys Sq Club Amer; Alpha Omega Alpha; fmr alternate delg, NY State Med Soc. Contbr to med jours; ed, The Ureter, 1967. Recipient, Pres citation for Selective Service. Hobbies: magic, movies, singing. Home: 24 Monterey Dr, Mt Vernon, NY. Offices: 1749 Grand Concourse, Bronx, NY; 27 Ludlow St, Yonkers, NY.

BERGMAN, Leo A, US, rabbi; b. Cleveland, O, Nov 23, 1913; s. Max and Mollie (Lefkowitz); BA, W Reserve U, 1934; ordained rabbi, MHL, HUC, 1940; DD, HUC-JIR, 1965; m. Adelaide Hubbard, Apr 1, 1942; c: Lee, William. Rabbi, Touro Syn since 1947; res lectr, J Chautauqua Soc, Loyola U, New Orleans since 1969; rabbi, Temple Beth El, Rockford, 1942-47. Past pres, RabC, New Orleans; chmn, church comm, Comty Chest; found: Interrace-Interfaith Comm; J Comty Lyceum Forum; New Orleans Clergyman's club, 1953; past pres, CCAR; mem: New Orleans J Comty Chest; Alumni Assn, HUC-JIR; Phi Beta Kappa; Amer Inter-Profsl Inst; club, Lakewood Country. Author: Master of our Fate, 1950; An American Story, 1952. Home: 2114 Jefferson Ave, New Orleans, La. Study: 4238 St Charles Ave, New Orleans, La.

BERGMAN, Moe, US, educator; b. Bklyn, NY, Mar 28, 1916; s. Max and Bessie (Stanzler); BA, U of Ill, 1937; MA, Columbia U, 1939, DEduc, 1949; m. Hannah Goodelman, Dec 18, 1938; c: Jay. Prof, dir communication sci prog, Inst of Health Sci, Hunter Coll, NY since 1969; prof and dir, Speech and Hearing Cen, 1953-66; visiting prof, Tel Aviv U Med Sch, 1968-69; prof, exec off, PhD prog, speech, grad div, CCNY, 1965-68; mem fac, first intl course, audiology, Swed, 1950. Lt, US Army, 1943-46. Prin contribs, research in audiology; planner and organizer of fgn audiology centers. Co-found: NY State Speech and Hearing Assn; and first chmn, Audiology Study Group, NY; mem: Amer Speech and Hearing Assn; AAAS; Amer Inst of Physics; Acoustical Soc Amer; hon mem: IMA; Laryngological Soc, 1968; hon pres, Isr Speech and Hearing Assn, 1964, 1968. Author: The Audiology Clinic, 1950; co-author, Auditory Rehabilitation for Hearing Impaired Blind Persons, 1965; contbr chaps in: Surgery in WW II, Otolaryngology and Ophthalmology, 1957; Rehabilitation of Deaf-Blind Persons, 1959; contbr numerous articles to profsl jours. Hobbies: music, sport. Home: 27 Gladstone Rd, New Rochelle, NY. Office: 695 Park Ave, New York, NY.

BERGMAN, Rebecca, Isr, nurse; b. Tisdale, Can, July 13, 1919; d. Harry and Ethel (Zaslow) Lyons; in Isr since 1936; BSc, NYU, 1951, MA, 1952; EdD, Columbia U, 1963; RN, Hadassah Sch of Nurisng, 1942; m. Shimon Bergman, Aug 10 1953. Head, dept of nursing, Tel Aviv U since 1968; cons, Kupat Holim since 1968; dir of nursing: Ger, 1946-48; Malben, 1952-61; head, nursing unit, dept social med, Heb U, 1963-67. Capt, Isr Army, 1948-49. Chmn, nursing comm, Natl Health Council; services comm, Isr Cancer Soc; exec, Isr Nurses Assn, 1964-67; curriculum comm, nursing div, Isr Min of ealth 1963-67. Contbr of numerous articles to nursing jours. Hobbies: theatre, music. Home: 55 Lochamai Galipoli, Tel Aviv, Isr. Office: Tel Aviv U, Tel Aviv, Isr.

BERGMAN, Sidney M, US, hospital cons; b. Roxbury, Mass, Nov 20, 1896; s. Joseph and Bertha (Tauber); att Harvard Coll, Med Sch; m. Esther Gabe, Jan 8, 1924; c: Charles. Em exec dir, life cons, Montefiore Hosp, Pittsburgh, since 1961; hosp cons since 1940; lectr, U Pittsburgh Sch of Public Health since 1946; hon research asso, sect of man, Carnegie Mus, Pitt, devl collection of ancient glass; fmr: acting dir, Beth Isr Hosp, Boston; exec dir, Sinai Hosp, Baltimore. Served, US Army. Prin contribs: inventor: first chest resporator, 1932; rubber wainscoting for hosps, 1929; Bergman-Bassinet, 1941; Bergman-Thorpe Eye Bed, 1957; Bergman post-operative bedside unit, 1961. F: Amer Coll Hosp Admnrs; Amer Public Health Assn; treas and trustee, Hosp Council, W Pa since 1955; mem exec comm, hosp liaison off, Soc Advancement Mgmt; life mem, Amer Hosp Assn, fmr regional chmn, natl gadget round table; mem: Intl Hosp Fed; Royal Soc Health; Mass Hosp Assn; AAAS; Amer Inst Archaeol; Amer Soc Natural Hist; Carnegie Inst; fmr: pres, SW Hosp Conf, Pa; vice-pres, Hosp Assn, Pa; chmn: comm, hosp facilities and vice-chmn, health div, Health and Wfr Assn, Allegheny Co; comm, Formulate Plans for Baltimore Council; treas, trustee, Md dist, Columbia Hosp Assn; mem exec comm, Pa Public Health Assn; secy, treas, Baltimore Hosp Conf; mem, NE Hosp Assembly; clubs: Harvard, Boston and W Pa; Harvard-Yale-Princeton. Recipient, Isabel P Kennedy Award, for dist service in the field of health and wfr, Allegheny co, 1961. Hobbies: travel, archaeol, photography. Home and office: 825 Morewood Ave, Pittsburgh, Pa.

BERGMAN, Simon, Isr, social worker; b. Brezany, Pol, Dec 26, 1913; s. Samuel and Rosalie (Seideman); in Isr since 1950; MS, Columbia U, 1963; m. Rebecca Lyons, Aug 20, 1953. Dep dir, Dept for Care of Aged, Malben since 1955; on staff since 1950; lectr, U Sch of Social Work, since 1965; dir, relief oprs, Amer Jt, Japan, 1951; dir, JDC Med Dept, Amer Jt, China, 1948-49. Pres, Isr Gerontological Soc; chmn, Social Policy Comm, Isr Assn Social Workers; vice-chmn, Council Social Services; past chmn: Far E Comm for JA for Isr; Zionist Org, Shanghai; natl exec, Isr Assn Social Workers; mem: Eur Social Research Comm; Intl Assn Gerontology; Natl Assn Social Workers; Gerontological Soc. Hobbies: Philately, art. Home: 55 Lohamey Galipoli, Tel Aviv, Isr. Office: 12 Kaplan, Tel Aviv, Isr.

BERGMANN, Arthur Aharon, Isr, banker; b. Berlin; s. Jehuda and Hedwig (Rosenzweig); in Isr since 1936; DJur, Friedrich Wilhelm U, Berlin, 1929; div mgn dir, Maritime Bank of Isr Ltd since 1962; dir of revenue, Govt of Isr, 1948-53. Author, Developing Countries and International Fiscal Law, 1969. Office: 94 Allenby St, Tel Aviv, Isr.

BERGMANN, Ernst David, Isr, educator, scientist; b. Karlsruhe, Ger, Oct 18, 1903; s. Yehuda and Hedwig (Rosenzweig); in Isr since 1934; PhD, U Berlin, 1925; DSc, Technion, U Montpellier; m. Anna Itin. Prof, organic chem, Heb U since 1953; sci dir, Weizmann Inst of Sci, 1933-51; dir, sci dept, Min of Defense, 1948-61; chmn, Isr AEC, 1952-66. Pres, Isr Standards Inst; chmn: sci sect, Isr Acad Sci and Hum; Natl Comms for Space Research and for Artificial Rain. Author: Textbook of Organic Chemistry; Acetylene. Recipient: Rothschild Prize; Israel Prize, 1968. Home: 8 Keren Kayemeth St, Jerusalem, Isr. Office: Dept of Organic Chem, Heb U, Jerusalem, Isr.

BERGMANN, Felix E, Isr, scientist; b. Frankfurt /O, Ger, Aug 17, 1908; s. Jehuda and Hedwig (Rosenzweig); in Isr since 1934; PhD, U Berlin, 1933, MD, 1933; m. Sarah Sulski, Oct 20, 1938; c: David, Hanna. Prof pharm and head dept, Heb U Med Sch, Jerusalem since 1956, asso prof, 1950-56; sr research asst, Weizmann Inst of Sci, 1934-47; research asso, Harvard Med Sch, 1949; visiting prof neur, Columbia U, 1958-59. IDF, 1948-49. Mem: Isr Acad Sci and Hum; Chem Soc, London; NY Acad of Sci; Isr Med Biochem, Chem, Phys, Neuro-phys Org; Société Chimique de France. Contbr papers on chem, biochem, phys and pharm to sci jours. Hobby, archaeol. Home: 3 Disraeli St, Jerusalem, Isr. Office: Heb U Med Sch, Jerusalem, Isr.

BERGMANN, Peter Gabriel, US, educator; b. Berlin, Ger, Mar 24, 1915; s. Max and Emmy (Grunwald); in US since 1936; att: Tech U, Dresden; U Freiburg; DRerNat, U Prague, 1936; m. Margot Eisenhardt, May 23, 1936; c: Ernest, John. Prof physics, Syracuse U, since 1947; research asst to Prof Albert Einstein, Inst for Advanced Study, Princeton, 1936-41; asst prof: Black Mt Coll, 1941-42; Lehigh U, 1942-44; chmn, dept physics, Yeshiva U, 1963-64. Prin contribs, research in theoretical physics. Trustee, New Lincoln Sch; mem: Intl Comm on Relativity and Gravitation; Amer Physics Soc; Amer Math Soc; AAAS; Fed of Amer Scis, fmr natl chmn; Ger, Eur Physics socs; NY Acad Sci. Author: Introduction to the Theory of Relativity, 1942; Basic Theories of Physics, 1949, 1951; The Riddle of Gravitation, 1968; contbr to sci publs, encys. Office: Syracuse U, Syracuse, NY.

BERGSON, Abram, US, economist, educator; b. Baltimore, Md, Apr 21, 1914; s. Isaac and Sophie (Rabinowits); BA, Johns Hopkins U, 1933; MA, Harvard U, 1935, PhD, 1940; m. Rita Macht, Nov 5, 1939; c: Judith, Emily, Lucy. Prof, econ, Harvard U since 1956; asst prof, U Tex, 1940-42; chief, econ div, subdiv Russ; mem, US delg, Moscow reparations conf, 1945; prof, Columbia U, 1946-56. Off of Strategic Services, 1944-46. F: Econometric Soc; Amer Acad Arts and Sci; mem: Amer Phil Soc; Amer Econ Assn; Phi Beta Kappa. Author: Structure of Soviet Wages, 1944; Economics of Soviet Planning, 1964; Essays in Normative Economics, 1966; contbr to econ jours. Home: 113 Walker St, Cambridge, Mass. Office: Harvard U, Cambridge, Mass.

BERGSON, Gershon, Isr, educational admnr; b. Serptz, Pol, Aug 21, 1913; s. Issachar and Lea (Zeligman); in Isr since 1947; att: Tchrs Sem, Vilno; Music Sch, Rovno; Heb U, Jerusalem; m. Malka Geifman, 1945; c: Sara, Avichai. Natl insp, Min of Educ since 1960, sch insp, Ashkelon, 1954, insp, S area, Beersheva, 1957; mem, pedg secretariat for primary educ; chmn, comm for sch Bc, i/c progs since 1962; tchr, Tarbut Schs, Pol, 1935-39; dir, econ dept, factory, Fergana-Uzbekistan; pedg dir, J Sch, Rovno; tchr, Ural; active, Zionist Org, Pol and Ger, ed, Voice of Zionism, 1946-47; found, educ dir, Alonei-Itzchak, Youth Aliyah Village, 1947-54. Served, Red Army. Chmn, comm for youth wing, Isr Mus; fmr, mem exec, Hanoar Hazioni. Author: Kaf ba-Tamuz, Haiav shel Herzl, in Yiddish, 1946; Ha-Minahel ba-Beth Sifro, 1963; Shlosha Dorot beSifrut ha-Yeladim ha-Ivrit, 1965; Beit Hasefer le-Yom Limudim Aroch, 1968; contbr numerous articles to profsl publs. Home: 5 Benjamin St, Jerusalem, Isr. Office: 34 Shivtei Israel St, Jerusalem, Isr.

BERINSON, Zvi, Isr, judge; b. Safad, Isr, 1907; s. Haim and Haya; dipl, Scots Coll, Safad, 1931; BA, hons, Jesus Coll, Cambridge, 1936; m. Hana Wolf, 1929; c: Ilana Alrod, Haim. Justice, Supr Court, since 1953; lectr, lab law and social ins, Heb U, Jerusalem, since 1952; tchr, Scots Coll, 1929-31; mem, Gray's Inn, London, 1936, advocate, 1936; legal adv, Gen Fed Lab, Histadrut, 1936-49; dir gen, Min Lab, 1949-53; head, Isr delg, ILO, Geneva, 1949-53, 1958-59. Chmn, Isr Opera Council; chmn, Isr Soc Criminology; mem, Soc for Rehab Offenders, Isr; vice-pres, Intl Prisoners Aid Assn. Home: 18 Marcus St, Jerusalem, Isr. Office: Supr Court, Jerusalem, Isr.

BERK, Harold, US, denstist, educator; b. Minneapolis, Minn, July 27, 1917; s. Wolf and Jenny (Sachs); att Loras Coll, 1935-37; DDS, Northwestern U, 1941; m. Helen Levin, Aug 2, 1942; c: Kenneth, Frederick, Donald. Asst prof, oral ped, Tufts U Sch of Dent Med since 1946; dent clinic, Forsyth Dental Infirmary, 1944-46; cons: Beth Isr Hosp, Boston, 1950-70; Childrens Hosp, Wash, DC, 1955-70. Lt cdr, USPHS, 1955-57. F: Amer Coll of Dent; Intl Coll of Dent; Amer Acad of Pedodontics; Amer Acad of Dent for Handicapped; mem: Amer Dent Assn; Mass Dent Soc; Gtr Boston Dent Soc; Amer Soc of Dent for Children; trustee, Combined J Philanthropies; hon life dir, Gtr Boston Brandeis Club, fmr treas, secy, vice-pres; found, bd, dirs, J Music Forum; Helen and Harold Berk Sch Fund, Boston U Grad Sch of Dent; Helen and Harold Berk Panographic X-ray Fund, Tufts U Sch of Dent Med; fmr chmn, Temple Ohabei Shalom, music comm. Contbr of numerous articles to profsl jours. Recipient, 'Diplome D'Honneur' for film, Vital Pulpotomy Technics, Paris, Fr. Home: 369 Dudley Rd, Newton Centre, Mass. Office: 1249 Beacon, Brookline, Mass.

BERKAL, Tobias, Ger, organization exec, attorney; b. Lodz, Pol, Jan 8, 1908; s. Abraham and Mary (Levitt); in Ger since 1950; LLD, U Warsaw, 1931; m. Gali Dubrowsky, May 27, 1946; c: Andrew. Gen secy, Fed J comties, Bavaria since 1953; court asst, 1931-34; asst atty, 1936-38; atty, 1939, all in Pol; Pol underground movement, Warsaw, 1943-45. Chmn: KH Magbith Cherum, Munich since 1938; Zionists Revisionists, Lodz, 1945-47, natl, 1948-50; mem: bd dirs, KH Magbith Cherum, Ger since 1967; Eur exec, Revisionists, Paris; World Union of Zionists Revisionists. Home: Schleissheimerstr 198, Munich Ger. Office: Giselastr 12, Munich, Ger.

BERKE, George, US, business exec; b. Smargon, Lith, Nov 23, 1900; s. Abraham and Rose (Simon); in US since 1917; m. Lena Bornstein, 1926; d. Betty Kravitz, Pres, Dixie Saving Stores, Inc, Chattanooga, Ten; on staff since 1932. Pres, SE Food Coop Assn, 1954-57; vice-pres, SE Grocers Coop Assn, 1952-55; mem bd, Natl-Retailer Owned Grocers, Chgo, 1949-55; pres, JWF, 1947-48, bd mem since 1947; vice-pres: J Comty Cen, 1955-57, one of found, 1944; chmn: ZOA, 1944; B'nai B'rith, 1946, bd mem, 1945-50; Emergency ZC, Chattanooga, 1942-49; vice-chmn, Zion Found; treas: B'nai Zion Cong, 1967-68; JWB, SE div since 1952; trustee, NCCJ since 1967; mem: allocation comm, United Fund, since 1960; natl affairs comm, Coop Food Distributors of Amer. Author, Study of Chattanooga Public Schools, 1957. Recipient: citation: as outstanding J citizen of the Year, J Comty Cen, 1950; by Chattanooga C of C for advancing the cause of educ, 1957, Service to Mankind Award, 1967. Home: 1209 Talley Rd, Chattanooga, Tenn.

BERKLEY, Elliot S, US, educational admnr; b. Kan City, Mo, Oct 12, 1924; s. Walter and Erni (Stulz) Berkowitz; cum laude, Harvard Coll, 1947; MA, Princeton U, 1949, PhD, 1952; m. Marcia Stevens Russell, June 28, 1958; c: Emily Dicksen, Eliot. Exec dir, Intl Relations Council, 1955-60, since 1965; asst to dir, Gtr Kan City Adult Educ Assn, 1954; admissions counselor, U Kan City, 1954; lectr, hist and govt, 1952-

59; instr, Kan City Art Inst and Sch of Design, 1956-59, dean of admn, 1959-60, vice-pres for devl, 1960-61, dean, coll, 1961-65; dir: Kan City assembly on US and Afr, 1959; Kan City assembly on US and E Eur, 1968; cons and asst to the dir, Minn Orientation Cen, U Minn, 1967. US Army, 1943-46. Chmn: Kan City Chap, AJComm, 1965-67, hon chmn since 1967; Fac Devl Grants Comm, Kan City Regional Council for Higher Educ, 1963-65; Mayor's UN Day Comm, Kan City, 1968; 2nd vice-pres, Intl Trade Club of Gtr Kan City, 1956; secy, Tension Envelope Found; mem, bd dirs: Kan City Br, NCCJ, 1952-62; Country Club Homes Assn, 1960-62; ACLU, W Mo; People-to-People Council, Gtr Kan City, 1961-64; J Vocational Service, Kan City; Urban League, Kan City, 1956-59; (hon) Rockhurst Coll; mem, bd councillors, Menorah Med Cen, 1956-57; mem: Mid-continent Adv Bd, Speaker Services for the UN; scholarship comm, Eddie Jacobson Found; citizens adv comm, Metrop Jr Coll, Kan City; Natl Comm of Comty World Affairs Orgs; Intl Studies Assn; Acad Political Sci; Amer Political Sci Assn; Amer Soc for Intl Law; Mid-W Political Sci Assn; Amer Acad Political and Soc Sci; Amer Hist Assn; Mo Political Sci Assn; Mo Assn Social Wfr; Jackson Co Hist Soc; Friends of Art; Kan City Mus Assn; Assn of Princeton Grad Alumni; mem, bd trustees, Conservatory of Music of Kan City, 1958-59; clubs: Princeton, Kan City; Harvard, Kan City. Home: 1014 W 63 St, Kansas City, Mo. Office: 210 Westport Rd, Kansas City, Mo.

BERKMAN, Aaron, US, artist, educator; b. Hartford, Conn, May 23, 1900; s. Harry and Sarah (Hartzmark); att Hartford Art Sch, 1919-21; Mus Art Sch, Boston, 1921-24; studied in Eur, 1924-26; m. Victoria Artese, Apr 13, 1933; c: Peter. Dir, em, YM-YWHA Art Center, since 1967, with cen since 1936; columnist, Art News, since 1955; numerous one-man shows. Mem: Artists Equity; Audubon Artists. Author: Art and Space, 1949; Functional Line in Painting, 1956. Recipient: f: Yaddo, 1957; Huntington Hartford Found 1958. Home: 230 E 88 St, New York, NY. Studio: 1305 Madison Ave, New York, NY.

BERKMAN, Jack I, US, artist; b. Wash, DC, Apr 10, 1908; s. Aaron and Fannie (Breeskin); deg, Corcoran Sch of Art, 1936; m. Eleanor Mensh, Dec 1932; c: Consuelo. Free-lance since 1959; dir, planning, Natl Capital Housing Auth, 1954-59; planner: US War Dept, 1929-37; Public Housing Admn, 1940-53. US Army, WWII. Pres: Thalian Assn, 1961-62; Wilmington Art Assn, 1960-62; vice-pres, Soc of Wash Artists, 1940-42; treas, Potomac br, Natl Housing and Redevl Officials, 1956-58; mem: Temple Emanuel, Greensboro, NC; Amer Inst Architects; NC Art Soc. Contbr to profsl jours; art lectr. Recipient: numerous first prizes for paintings. Home and studio: 518 Jefferson St, Greensboro, NC.

BERKOVITS, Eliezer, US, rabbi, author; b. Oradea, Rum, Sep 8, 1908; s. Bernard and Bella (Kosch); in US since 1950; att Frankfurt U, Ger, 1927-28; ordained rabbi, Hildesheimer Rabb Sem, Berlin, Ger, 1934; MA, PhD, U Berlin, 1933; m. Sali Bickel, Jan 6, 1933; c: Avraham, Shimshon, Bernard. Prof, chmn, dept J phil, Heb Theol Coll, Skokie, Ill since 1958; rabbi: Berlin, 1936-39; Leeds, Eng, 1940-46; Boston, Mass, 1950-58. Member, RabCA. Author: Hume und der Deismus, 1934; Was Ist der Talmud, 1938; Towards Historic Judaism, 1943; Between Yesterday and Tomorrow, 1945; God, Man and History, 1954; Judaism, Fossil or Ferment, 1956; A Jewish Critique of the Philosophy of Martin Buber, 1962; Prayer, 1962; Tnai Binisuin Ubeget, 1966; Man and God, Studies in Biblical Theories, 1966. Home: 8829 Monticellor Ave, Skokie, Ill. Office: Heb Theol Coll, 7135 Carpenter Rd, Skokie, Ill.

BERKOWITZ, Abram, US, attorney, business exec; b. Bklyn, NY, Apr 15, 1892; s. Morris and Bessie (Douglas); LLB, Boston U, 1916; m. Minna Kroll, Dec 7, 1917 (decd); c: Leonard, Dorothy Harvey White; m. 2nd, Jean Sholkin Golden, Jan 31, 1963. Partner, law firm, Ropes & Gray, Boston since 1930, with firm since 1916; dir: Emile Bernat & Sons Co; Fabreeka Products; Morse Shoe; Zayre. Trustee: Beth Isr Hosp Assn, Boston since 1944, pres, 1957-59, hon trustee since 1968; vice pres, Combined J Philanthropies, 1959; Boston Sym Orch, 1962; hon trustee, Temple Ohabei Shalom, Brookline, Mass; dir, Boston chap, Amer Soc for the Technion; fmr dir, Boy's Club of Boston; mem: Amer Bar Assn, Boston; Judicatures Soc; bd govs, HUC. Home: 80 Park St, Brookline, Mass. Office: 225 Franklin St, Boston, Mass.

BERKOWITZ, Bernard Markus, Isr, ship captain; b. Bremer-haven, Ger, Sep 29, 1921; s. Julius and Rosa (Isaack); in Isr since 1936; second mate dipl, Nautical Coll, Leith, Scotland, 1946; 1st off, Nautical Coll London, 1948, master mariner, 1950; m. Ruth Rosenberg; c: Ron, Daphne. Master, passenger vessel, M V Dan since 1968; has served as capt on all Isr passenger vessels of Zim Lines; fmr, capt, T.S.S. Shalom. Brit Navy, 1939-42. Mem, RGS, London; Ship Masters Assn, Haifa. Recipient, service ribbons: Afr Theatre; ETO. Hobbies: photography, recording music. Home: 1A Yair Katz St, Haifa, Isr. Office: 7-9 Haatzmaut Rd, Haifa, Isr.

BERKOWITZ, David S, US, educator; b. Pittsburgh, Pa, Aug 20, 1913; s. Abraham and Nellie (Sandler); AB, magna cum laude, Harvard U, 1938, AM, 1940, PhD, 1946; m. Jessie Cohen, Sep 8, 1940; c: Carl, Naomi. Prof, hist, Brandeis U, since 1949, asso prof, 1948-49, asst to pres, 1948-52, dir, U planning, 1948-52; cons to armed forces repr, Harvard U, 1942-44; visiting prof, Harvard U, 1957-58; liaison off, Comm on Need for State U, NY, 1946-48; exec off, Assn Coll and U, State of NY, 1946-48. Chmn: NE Renaissance Conf, 1965; Soc for Hist of Discovery; Oxford Bibliographical Soc; prog and personnel comm, Waltham Family Service Assn, since 1952, pres, 1959-61; sub-comm on budgets, Comm to Integrate Family Service Agcys, W Metrop Boston, 1961-62; personnel comm, Family Counselling Service; mem: Amer Hist Assn; AAUP; Phi Beta Kappa. Author: From Ptolemy to the Moon, 1965; Bibliotheca Bibliographica Incunabula, 1967; In Remembrance of Creation, 1968; Inequality of Opportunity in Higher Education, 1948; Bibliotheca Bibliographica Britannica, 1963; contr to profsl publs. Recipient: Washburn Prize, Hist; Rogers Travelling F. Home: 93 Beaumont Ave, Newtonville, Mass. Office: Brandeis U, Waltham, Mass.

BERKOWITZ, Edward, US, business exec; b. NYC, Dec 12, 1928; s. Irving and Ethel (Nirenstein); BA, Queens Coll, 1949; m. Rochelle Farber, June 21, 1953; c: Meryl, Ira,Gary. Pres: Island Container Corp, since 1969. Pvt, US Army, 1951-52. Vice-pres, Cong Shaaray Tefila; trustee, Hillel Sch. Hobbies: tennis, photography. Home: 170 Wildacre Ave, Lawrence, NY. Office: 900 Shepherd Ave, Brooklyn, NY.

BERKOWITZ, H Philip, US, rabbi; b. Boston, Mass, Aug 22, 1938; s. Louis and Ethel (Goldman); BJE, MHL, Heb Tchrs Coll, 1961; AB, EdM, Boston U, 1962; ordained rabbi,BHL, MAHL, HUC-JIR, 1966; m. Nancy Segel, Feb 15, 1965; c: Jeffrey, Judith. Rabbi, Temple Beth Jacob, since 1966; fac mem, Coll J Studies, Metrop Detroit, Fed of Reform Syns; chaplain, Pontiac State Hosp. Mem: Amer Coll, Jerusalem; Comty Relations Comm of JCC, Detroit, church state subcomm; Citizens Comm on Youth, Pontiac; CCAR; Police Trial Bd, Pontiac. Contr to sociol jours. Home: 59 S Genesee, Pontiac, Mich. Study: 79 Elizabeth Lake Rd, Pontiac, Mich.

BERKOWITZ, Louis, US, psychologist, social worker; b.NYC, Feb 15,1921; s. Aaron and Irene (London); AB, Columbia Coll, 1940; MSW, U of Pa, 1946; att JTSA, 1940-41; Columbia U Psych Grad Dept, 1940; U of Pittsburgh Grad Sch, 1941-42; NYU Grad Psych, 1955-56; NY Sch of Soc Research Clinic, 1956; Natl Psych Assn, 1956-62; m. Anita Solomon, 1942; c: Robert, David, Paul, Lester, Alan, Richard. Exec dir, Educ Alliance since 1960, asso asst dir, 1951-60; field instr, Yeshiva U, Wurzweiler Sch, since 1964; lectr, City U, Grad Sch Educ; psychan, in pvt practice, since 1958; prog dir: Cleveland E End Neighborhood House, 1946-49; Phila-Newark Neighborhood Houses, 1944-46; exec dir, Five Towns Comty House, Lawrence, LI, 1949-51; project dir: prog to keep potential drop-outs in sch, HEW support since 1964; Resocialization of ex-mental patients, 1963-66; family-centered socialization of ex-mental patients, since 1967; established first apt house for elderly under sect 202, US 1959 Housing Act, Educ Alliance; dir, Educ Alliance Prog, utilizing soc work and behavioural sci to make soc inst relevant to today's needs. Chmn: comm, Mobilization for Youth; comm of group measurement; Natl Assn Social Workers; vice-chmn and secy: Cleveland Assn of Group Workers; Cleveland Assn of Settlements, both from 1947-49; co-chmn, Lower E Side Neighborhood Assn, 1962-64; mem: various comms, Natl Assn J Cen Workers; NY Soc of Clinical Psychs; Natl Assn Social Workers; Natl Psych Assn of Psychan. Co-author, various papers to profsl jours. Spec interests: tennis, classical music. Home 341 Willets Rd, Roslyn Heights, NY. Office:Educational Alliance, 197 E Broadway, New York, NY.

BERKOWITZ, Samuel H, US rabbi; b. Brockton, Mass, Nov 26, 1915; s. David and Rose (Levert); BJE, Heb Tchrs Coll,

Boston, 1938; BA, Boston U, 1941; Rabbi, MHL, J Theol Sem, 1944, DHL, 1953; MA, Catholic U, 1949; m. Evelyn Birnbaum, Oct 5, 1941; c: Myer, Judith. Dir, B'nai B'rith Hillel Found, Phila since 1954; rabbi, Arlington J Cen, Va, 1943-45; dir, Hosp Service, Dept, JWB, Wash, DC, 1945-46. Mem: RA; Soc of Bibl Lit and Exegesis; Phi Beta Kappa. Home: 6243 N Camac St, Philadelphia, Pa. Office: 202 S 36 St, Philadelphia, Pa.

BERKOWITZ, William, US, rabbi; b. Phila, Pa, June 28,1924; s. Albert and Pauline; tchr deg, Gratz Coll, Phila, 1942; BS, educ, Temple U, 1948; ordained rabbi, MHL, JTSA, NYC, 1952; m. Florence Elster, Dec 22, 1946; c: Perry, Adena, Leah. Rabbi, Cong B'nai Jeshurun, NYC since 1951; found, dir, Inst of Adult J Studies; found, prin, Conservative Day Sch, Manhattan; radio bc, WEVD. Yeoman, USN, 1943-46. Vice pres: NY Bd Rabbis; B'nai Zion; mem: bd, govs, Isr Bonds; presidium, Histadruth Ivrith. Author: I Believe, 1963: Ten Vital Jewish Issues, 1964; Heritage and Hope, 1966; Let Us Reason Together, 1970. Home: 175 Riverside Dr, New York, NY. Study: 270 W 89 St, New York, NY.

BERLATSKY, Emanuel, US, executive social worker; b. Geneva, Switz, June 16, 1907; s. Joseph and Kate (Leaderman); in US since 1909; BA, U Minn, 1928; cert, Grad Sch for J Soc Work, 1929; m. Marjorie Roberts, Dec 30, 1930; c: Joel, Deborah Golden. Dir, field services, Natl JWB since 1961, Metrop Comtys since 1968, dir, bur of personnel and training, 1948-61; educ dir, J Comty Cen, Detroit, 1929-34; asst dir, Council Educ Alliance, Cleveland, 1934-38; exec dir, JWF, Winnipeg, Can, 1938-40; dir, prog, J Cen, Youngstown, O, 1940-41; field secy, mid-w sect, JWB, 1941-45; dir, prog, J Cen Div, JWB,1945-49. Pres, Natl Assn J Cen Workers, 1950-52; chmn: Natl Commn of Soc Work Careers; ed comm, Social Wfr Forum, 1959; mem: Amer Assn Soc Workers; Natl Conf J Soc Wfr; charter mem, Natl Assn Soc Workers. Contbr to profsl jours. Spec interest, European hist. Home: 115-25 Metropolitan Ave, Kew Gardens, NY. Office: 15 E 26 St, New York, NY.

BERLIN Chaim, Isr, physician; b. Minsk, Russ, Aug 28, 1890, s.Nehemia and Malka (Golodetz); in Isr since 1925; att U Zurich, Switz, 1911-14; MD, Em, U of Berlin, 1921; m. Fanny Badad (decd); c: Dan, Ariel. Head, dept dermat, Hadassah Hosp, Tel Aviv since 1934; visiting prof, Heb U, Jerusalem, 1957. Vice-pres Dermat Assn of Isr since 1930; corresp mem, Dermat Soc of Mexico. Contbr of numerous articles to profsl jours. Home and office: 15 Frug St, Tel Aviv, Isr.

BERLIN, Charles, US, librarian; b. Boston, Mass, Mar 17,1936; s.Joseph and Etta (Fox); AB, Harvard, 1958; MHL, Heb Tchrs Coll, 1959; PhD, Harvard, 1963; MS, Simmons Coll Sch of Libr Sci, 1964; m. Judith Armet, Mar 21, 1965; c: Anne. Lee M Friedman bibliographer, Judaica, Harvard Coll Libr, since 1962, head, Heb div, since 1962, lectr, 1962-65; instr, hist, Heb Tchrs Coll, 1958-62. Mem: Assn J Librs, fmr pres; subscription books comm, Amer Libr Assn; AAUP; trustee, Heb Tchrs Coll. Home: 15 Alden, Newton, Mass. Office: Harvard Coll Library, Cambridge, Mass.

BERLIN, David D, US, surgeon,educator; b. Odessa Russ, June 27, 1901; s. Mendel and Leah (Zeitlen); in US since 1904; MD, Tufts U, 1923. Em clinical prof, surg, Tufts U Sch of Med since 1966, on staff since 1930; hon surg, Boston City Hosp since 1966, cons, surg, 1945-66; cons, surg, Beth Isr Hosp since 1966; instr, surg, Harvard Med Sch, 1941-45; sr surg, res, USPHS, 1942-47. Pres, Gtr Boston Med Soc 1941; Alumni Assn, Boston City Hosp Contbr to profsl jours Home and office: 400 Commonwealth Ave, Boston, Mass.

BERLIN, Irving, US, lyricist, composer; b. Tumen, Russ, May 11, 1888; s. Moses and Leah (Lipkin) Baline; in US since 1893; m. Dorothy Goetz, Feb 1913 (decd); m. 2nd, Ellen McKay, Jan 4, 1926; c: Mary Barrett, Linda Emmet, Elizabeth Fisher. Pres Irving Berlin Music Corp since 1919; partner Ted Snyder Music, 1909-18. Sgt, US Army, WWI. Pop songs: Alexander's Ragtime Band; Oh How I Hate to Get Up in the Morning; When I Lost You; What'll I Do?; All Alone; Remember; Reaching for the Moon; When I Leave the World Behind; Always; Because I Love You; Blue Skies; Russian Lullaby; At Peace with the World; Any Bonds Today; White Christmas; Easter Parade; God Bless America; There's No Business Like Show Business; musical shows: This is the Army; The Coconuts, 1925; Ziegfeld Follies, 1927; Face the Music,1932; As Thousands Cheer, 1933; Top Hat (movie), 1935; On the

Avenue (movie), 1936; Follow the Fleet (movie), 1936; Alexander's Ragtime Band (movie), 1938; Second Fiddle (movie), 1939; Louisiana Purchase, 1940; Annie Get Your Gun; Miss Liberty; Call Me Madame; White Christmas (movie), 1954. Mem: Masons; Elks; clubs: Lambs; Friars; City Athletic. Recipient: Medal of Merit; Gold Medal from US Cong for 'God Bless America'. Office: 1290 Ave of Americas, New York, NY.

BERLIN, Moses Mendell, US, hospital admnr; b. Bklyn, NY, Oct 12, 1937; s. Lester and Mollie (Burgatz); att Yeshiva Etz Hayim, 1942-50; BA, cum laude, Yeshiva U, 1958; grad research asst, MIT, 1958-60; m. Roslyn Shelkowitz, June 22, 1959; c: David, Daniel, Joshua, Jonathan, Rachel. Asst vice pres, dir, Beaumont Hosp since 1968; fmr dir, med systems, Sylvania Electronics. Prin contribs: devl: and dir diagnostic progs for US Govt Intelligence Radar Computer Systems; systems analysis and design for hosp, bus, lab automation; and executed master plan for numerous bed med cen. Dir, Union of Orthodox J Congs in Amer; vice pres, Akiva Heb Day Sch, Mich; mem: J Cmty Council, Metrop Detroit; Assn for Computing Machinery; fmr: pres: Young Isr Syn, Brookline, Mass: NE reg, UJA; mem, J Council, Boston. Author, Computers in Medicine, 1962; contrib of articles to tech, med jours. Recipient, F, Outstanding Young Men in Amer, 1969. Hobbies: music, drama. Home: 14710 Rosemary St, Oak Park, Mich. Office: 3601 W 13 Mile Rd, Oak Park, Mich.

BERLIN, Nathaniel Isaac, US, physician; b. NYC, July 4, 1920; s. Louis and Gertrude (Sugarman); BS, W Reserve U, Cleveland, O, 1942; MD, LI Coll of Med, Bklyn, NY, 1945; PhD, U of Cal, Berkeley, 1949; m. Barbara Ruben, 1953; c: Deborah, Marc. Sci dir, Gen Labs and Clinics, Natl Cancer Inst since 1969; head, Metabolism Service, Gen Med Branch, NIH since 1956, Natl Cancer Inst since 1956, chief, 1959-61; clinical dir since 1961; res path, 1946-47; post-doctorate research f, Natl Cancer Inst, 1948-50, research f, 1949-50, research asso, 1950-51, instr, 1951, lectr and research asso, 1951-52; lectr and asso research med physicist, physics dept, U of Cal, 1952-53; research f, Natl Heart Inst, Natl Inst of Med Research, London, 1953-54; cons: USN Hosp, Bethesda, Md, 1955-65; Armed Forces Spec Weapons Project, 1957-59. US Army, 1942-45; naval med off, Armed Forces Spec Weapons Project, Dept of Defense, 1954-56. Contbr to research on erythroporesis in man and experimental animals; changes in gross body composition in neoplastic diseases of man. F: AAAS; NY Acad Sci; Intl Soc Hematology; mem: Amer Fed Clinical Research; Soc Experimental Biol and Med; W Soc Clinical Research; Amer Phys Soc; Biochemical Soc, Eng; Radiation Research Soc; Amer Soc Hematology, mem comm, 1967, exec comm since 1968; Amer Soc Clinical Inves; Alpha Omega Alpha; Sigma Xi; Zeta Beta Tau; Phi Delta Epsilon. Asso ed, adv bd, Cancer Research since 1968; ed, adv bd, Handbook; med adv comm, ARC; contbr to med jours. Recipient: Alumni Medallion, for dist service to Amer Med, SUNY Downstate Med Cen, 1966; Superior Service Award, HEW, 1966; Alumni Lectr, SUNY Downstate Med Cen, 1968. Home: 6600 Braeburn Pkwy, Bethesda, Md. Office: Natl Cancer Inst, NIH, Bethesda, Md.

BERLIN, Norman, US, business exec; b. Norfolk, Va, Apr 1, 1907; s. Alex and Anna (Blachman); AB, Cornell U, 1927, LLB, 1929; m. Harriet Garfunkel, Aug. 25, 1933; c: Linda Frierman. Pres, Berlin-Miles Inc since 1962; atty, Berlin-Hellman, 1935-48. Past pres, United J Fed, exec comm; exec bd, J Cmty Cen; past chmn, United J Fund; pres, B'nai B'rith, Norfolk, 1956; UJA, natl cabinet, 1955-57, UJA 1967 Isr Mission; natl bd govs, Isr Bonds, 1952-54; mem, Phi Epsilon Pi. Home: Hague Tower, Norfolk, Va. Office: 4545 Robin Hood Rd, Norfolk, Va.

BERLINER, Ernst, US, chemist, educator; b. Kattowitz, Ger, Feb 18, 1915; s. Joseph and Lucie (Ehrenhaus-Selinger); in US since 1940; att: U Breslau; U Freiburg; MA, Harvard U, 1941, PhD, 1943; m. Frances Bondhus, 1947; c: Susan. Prof, organic chem, Bryn Mawr Coll, since 1953, fac mem, since 1944; Guggenheim f, 1961-62. Mem: Amer Chem Soc; AAAS; British Chem Soc; Sigma Xi. Ed bd mem, Jour of Organic Chem, 1963-68; contbr of papers on physical-organic aspects of aromatic chem, kinetics of aromatic substitution; hyperconjugation. Recipient, Mfg Chems Assn Coll Chem, Tchr Award, 1963. Home: 219 N Roberts Rd, Bryn Mawr, Pa. Office: Bryn Mawr College, Bryn Mawr, Pa.

BERLINER, Joseph Scholom, US, educator; b. NYC, Sep 4, 1921; s. Michael and Yetta (Eisenberg); BA, Harvard U, 1947, PhD, 1953; m. Ann Korenbaum, Nov 7, 1943; c: Paul, Carl, Nancy. Prof, econ, Brandeis U since 1963; econ, Corp Econ and Ind Research, 1954-56; prof, econ, Syracuse U, 1956-63. Fmr: pres, Amer Assn Advancement Slavic Studies; exec secy, Assn Study of Soviet-type Econs. Author: Factory and Manager in the USSR, 1957; Soviet Economic Aid, 1958. Home: 3 Compton Circle, Lexington, Mass. Office: Brandeis U, Waltham, Mass.

BERLINER, Kurt, US, cardiologist, educator; b. Berlin-Charlottenburg, Ger, Aug. 9, 1899; s. Wilhelm and Regina (Klopstock); att U Heidelberg, 1918-19; U Goettingen, 1920; MD, U Berlin, 1922; in US since 1923; m. Ethel Beaver, May 15, 1955. Heart specialist, in pvt practice; asso prof, med, NY Med Coll since 1947; cons card, Sydenham Hosp, NY; asso att phys, Flower-Fifth Ave Hosp; asso, visiting phys, Metrop Hosp; intern, 4th U Hosp, Moabit Berlin, 1922-23; asst phys, Kings Park State Hosp, 1924-25; sr clinical asst phys and research asst, Mt Sinai Hosp, 1929-42; asso card, Broad St Hosp, 1931-34. Dipl, Amer Bd Internal Med; FACP, 1945. Contbr to med jours. Hobbies: art, hist, photography, music. Home: 1150 Park Ave, New York, NY. Office: 1235 Park Ave, New York, NY.

BERLINER, Selma M L, US, attorney; b. NYC; d. Theodore and Augusta (Munter) Lobsenz; BA, Hunter Coll, 1920; JD, NYU Law Sch, 1923; m. Ephraim Berliner, Oct 25, 1931; c: David. Partner, law firm, Schlesinger and Berliner, NYC since 1947; public mem, NY State Unemployment Ins Adv Council, 1944-58; first woman candidate, NY Supr Court Rep ticket, 1955. Pres: educ council, Hadassah, 1947-48, mem, prog comm, 1942-50; Assn Alumni, Hunter Coll, 1951–53; chmn, Ways and Means Comm, Women's Natl Rep Club since 1967; mem: comm on munic affairs, Assn Bar, NYC, 1958-61; Rep Co Comm since 1923; bd dirs, sisterhood, Span and Port Syn since 1932; clubs: Bus and Profsl Women's, pres, 1923-30; W Side Rep, pres, 1954-60. Author: Hearings Under NY State Workmen's Compensation Law, publ report of Comm on Admn of Justice, NY, 1934; Selection of Judges, publ report of NY State Constitutional Conv, 1938. Home: 365 West End Ave, New York, NY. Office: 30 Broad St, New York, NY.

BERLINGER, Elieser, Holland, rabbi; b. Illingen, Ger, Jan 27, 1904; s. Moses and Jettchen (Unna); in Holland since 1954; ordained rabbi, Hildesheimer Sem Rabbis, Berlin, 1928; m. Ruth Stern, May, 1928; c: Salomo, Jetta Chanow, Sara Fuchs. Chief rabbi, dist of Utrecht since 1956; rabbi: Schoenlanke, Posen, 1929–32; Malmoe, Swed, 1932–46; chief rabbi, Helsinki, Fin, 1946–52. Mem, B'nai B'rith. Recipient, Danska Frihetsmedaljen (Danish Medal of Liberty). Home: Edisonstraat 71, Amsterdam, Holland. Study: Springweg 164, Utrecht, Holland.

BERLINSKI, Herman, US, director of music; b. Leipzig, Ger, Aug 18, 1910; s. Boris and Deborah (Wygodzky); in US since 1941; soloist dipl, Landes Conservatorium, Leipzig, 1932; D Sacred Music, JTSA, NY, 1960; m. Sina Goldfein; c: David. Dir music, Wash Heb Cong, since 1963; organist, Temple Emanu-El, NY, 1954-60. Fr Army, 1939-41. Composer: works for orch: David and Goliath, 1946; Symphonic Visions, 1949; Concerto da Camera, 1951; For the Peace of Mind, 1952; Kiddush Ha-Shem, 1958; Avodat Shabbat, 1957-61; chamber music: Sonata for Flute and Piano; Petite Suite for Flute and Piano, 1942; Suite for Cello and Piano, 1948; Sonata for Violin and Piano, 1949; Quintet for String Quartet and Martenot, 1949; Quadrille, 1952; String Quartet, 1953; for piano: Allegretto Con Variazioni, 1937; Sonata Brevis, 1944; Petite Suite, 1950; Rhythm Ostinato, 1950; Variations on a Theme by Mozart, 1956; for organ: From the World of My Father, 1938; Sinfonia No 1, 1954; Prelude: And Behold, The Bush Burneth, 1956; Sinfonia No 2, 1958; In Memoriam, 1958; Elegy for Organ, in memory of Albert Einstein, 1958; Sinfonia No 3; liturgical works: Lecho Dodi, 1953; Who Is Like Unto Thee, 1954; It Is A Tree Of Life, 1955; anthems; cantatas; performer organ recitals; lectr on J music. Fmr, pres, J Music Forum, NY. Recipient, Croix du Combattant Volontaire. Home: 4000 Tunlaw St, Washington, DC. Office: Massachusetts Ave at Macomb St, NW, Washington, DC.

BERMAN, Aaron Z, S Afr, business exec, legislator; b. Laizevo, Lith, Feb 28, 1893; s. Sundel and Mina (Leftin); in S Afr since 1913; m. Jane Prisman, Aug 23, 1921; c: Harold, Cecile Engers, Mina Sennett. Dir, cos since 1922; public acctnt, 1922-40; senator, Rep of S Afr; councillor, City of Cape Town since 1932; mem, Cape Provincial Council (leader of the opposition), 1946–60. Maj, Union Defense Forces, WWII. Author, Municipal Enterprise, 1940. Recipient: Mention in Despatches, Coronation Medal. Home: 69 Upper Orange St, Cape Town, S Afr. Office: Atlantic House, Corporation St, Cape Town, S Afr.

BERMAN, Adolph A, Isr, psychologist; b. Warsaw, Pol, Oct 17, 1906; s. Isidor and Gustava (Berniker); in Isr since 1950; PhD, U Warsaw, 1931; m. Batia Temkin; c: Emanuel. Mem, cen comm, Isr Communist Party; MK, Isr Knesset, 1951-55; dir, J Psychotech Inst, Pol, 1933-39; gen secy, secret Pol council for help to Js; repr of fighting ghetto to Pol Underground, all 1939-45; MP, Pol, 1944-47. Chmn, Union of Anti-Nazi Fighters in Isr; mem, exec, Intl Fed of Resistance Movements; fmr: chmn, cen comm, J of Pol; mem, presidium, J Natl Comm in Pol. Author: Problems in Social Psychology, 1932; Social Psychology and Education, 1937; mem, ed bd, Frei Isr. Recipient: Grundwall Cross, high decoration of Pol govt, 1948; Liberation and Fighting Medal, Warsaw; Halohem baNazim Medal; Itur Lohamei Hamedina, both Isr. Home: 11 Bar Kochba St, Tel Aviv, Isr.

BERMAN, Alfred, US, attorney; b. NYC, Mar 28, 1908; s. Eli and Elizabeth (Izbitzky); PhD, Brown U, 1929; LLB, St Lawrence U, 1936, JDS, 1937; m. Nanette Dembitz, Feb 11, 1939; c: Jonathan, Joanne. Partner, law firms: Guggenheimer and Untermyer, NYC, since 1944; legal staff, SEC, 1938-42; Gen Counsel's Staff, War Produc Bd, 1942–44. Mem: Amer, NYC Bar Assns. Home: 55 East End Ave, New York, NY. Office: 80 Pine St, New York, NY.

BERMAN, Elaine Ruth, Isr, scientist; b. Chgo, Apr 2, 1923; d. Samuel and Minnie (Sachs) Seigel; in Isr since 1957; BS, U Chgo, 1943; MS, 1951; PhD, Northwestern U, 1955; m. Morton Berman, June 27, 1950; c: Susanna, Stephen, Samuel, David. Chief, Biochem Research Lab, dept, Ophthal, Heb U, Hadassah Med Sch since 1960; asso prof, biochem since 1969. Mem: Sigma Xi; Amer Assn for Research in Ophthal; Biochem Soc, Eng; Isr Biochem. Soc. Author, books and articles on biochem, ocular path. Recipient, Dr Erna Staner Award in Med Research, 1965. Home: 6 Berechyau St, Beth Hakerem, Jerusalem, Isr. Office: Hadassah U Hosp, Jerusalem, Isr.

BERMAN, Elihu H, US, attorney; b. Hartford, Conn, July 20, 1922; s. Saul and Emma (Kaplan); BA, Harvard Coll, 1944, LLB, 1948; m. Muriel Goldman, Jan 18, 1945; c: Rachel, Jonathan. Partner, Ritter & Berman since 1962. Lt, jg, USN, 1943-46. Pres: JNF Council, Hartford; Conn region, ZOA, 1966-68; Loomis Alumni Assn, 1964-65; hon vice-chmn, JNF; vice-chmn, Conn regional bd, ADL; secy, Harvard Club of N Conn; natl exec comm, ZOA; bd dirs: Amer ORT Fed; Hartford chap, ARC; past, Hartford J Comty Cen; comty relations comm, Hartford J Comm; mem: Farband Lab Zionist Org; KP; B'nai B'rith; NAACP, life; Rotary; Hartford Co, Conn and Amer Bar Assns; AJComm. Ed, Conn Bar Jour, 1954-56. Hobbies: tennis, golf, bowling. Home: 12 Fernwood Rd, W Hartford, Conn. Office: 266 Pearl, Hartford, Conn.

BERMAN, Etta, US, teacher, communal worker; b. Portland, Me, July 19, 1895; d. Aaron and Annie (Solmer); att, W State Normal Coll, Gorham, Me, 1918; Bay Path Inst, Springfield, Mass, 1922; BS, Boston U, 1933, MS, 1935. Ret; tchr, Cen High Sch, Manchester, NH, 1925-69. Vice-pres, NH, NE region, Hadassah, donor chmn, 1950, 1952, pres, Manchester chap, 1948-50, vice-pres, Brandeis chap, corresp secy, 1959; treas, Manchester League Women Voters, 1952-54; secy, J Comty Cen, Manchester, 1946, mem, bldg comm, 1945-54, mem bd dir, 1943-45; chmn women's div, UJA, 1949, 1951; pres auxiliary, B'nai B'rith, 1934-36, secy, 1933; Hillel chmn for NHU, 1946-50; secy, NH State Council, 1951-52; pres, YWHA, 1943-45; secy, Manchester Zionist Org, 1946; mem: Adath Yeshurun Cong; Adath Yeshurun Sisterhood, pres, 1946-48, secy, 1943-45; Temple Isr Sisterhood; Manchester Inst of Arts and Sci and Tchrs Guild; NH State Educ Assn; Tchrs NEA; NCCJ; NH Assn for the Blind; asso mem, YWCA; life mem: ZOA; Home for Aged, Portland, Me; clubs: pres, Coll Women's, 1946-48; Manchester Coll Women's. Home: 362 Hanover St, Manchester, NH.

BERMAN, Harry Louis, US, physician; b. Peoria, Ill, May 7, 1908; s. Max and Golda (Fogelman); BS, Bradley U, Ill, 1928; MD, Northwestern U Med Sch, 1932; m. Ellen Stein, June 24, 1934; c: Howard. Head, div radiotherapy and nuclear med,

Sinai Hosp, Baltimore since 1960; asst prof radiology, Johns Hopkins U Sch of Med; clinical asst prof, George Wash U Sch of Med, Wash, DC; in dermat practice, Pretoria, Ill, 1935-39; res, radiology: Walter Reed Gen Hosp, Wash, 1947-48; Presbyterian Hosp, NYC, 1948-50. Lt, US Army MC, 1939, ret with rank of col, 1960, prin assignments include: med instr, Mt and winter Warfare Sch, Colo, 1946-47; prof mil sci and tactics, Coll of Phys and Surgs, Columbia U, NY, 1948-50; radiologist: US Army Hosp, Ft Monmouth, NJ; 343 Gen Hosp, Japan; Atomic Bomb Casualty Comm, Hiroshima and Nagasaki, 1950-52. Pres, Baltimore Unit, Amer Cancer Soc; f: Amer Coll Radiology; Amer Geriatrics Soc; mem: Amer Med Writers Assn; Amer Phys F Inc, IMA; AMA; Baltimore City Med Soc; Radiological Soc N Amer; Amer Roentgen Ray Soc; Amer Radium Soc; Soc Nuclear Med; Md Radiological Soc; Amer Soc Therapeutic Radiologists; AAAS; Assn Amer Med Colls; Assn Mil Surgs US; Assn Advancement Med Instrumentation; Pan-Amer Med Assn; Inter-Amer Coll Radiology; Masons; Ret Off's Assn. Mem, ed bd, Military Medicine; contbr to profsl jours. Recipient: Legion of Merit; Commendation Ribbon with Cluster; Eur Theatre Medal with two battle stars, WW II; Korean Theatre Medal with three battle stars, Korean Conflict. Home: 2754 Deerfield Rd, Ellicott City, Md. Office: Sinai Hospital, Baltimore, Md.

BERMAN, Jacob K, US, surgeon, educator; b. Evansville, Ind, Oct 24, 1896; s. Isaac and Theresa (Kohn); BA, Ind U, 1919; MD, Jefferson Med Coll, 1921; m. Henrietta Kahn, Mar 29, 1923; c: Edward, Alice Roth, Theresa Bricker. Pvt practice since 1924; prof em, Ind Sch of Med and Dent, since 1967, on fac since 1923; chmn, research educ, Marion Co Gen Hosp, 1945-63; chief of staff, St Vincent's Hosp, 1946-48; past dir, surg educ, research, Indianapolis Gen Hosp; chmn, profsl standards, Methodist Hosp, since 1959; Sunnyside Sanitarium, 1961; dir, Charles J Wolf Found for Med Research, 1946-59; chief surg cons, VA Hosp, Fort Benjamin Harrison, 1958; consulting surg, VA Hosp for Chest Diseases, Indianapolis, 1953. Chmn, comm for Chair of Heb lang and lit, Ind U, 1962; trustee, Indianapolis Heb Cong; mem: Ind State Med Assn; Marion Co Med Assn; Amer Coll Surgs; Amer Bd Surg; Cen Surgical Assn; W Surg Assn, pres, 1962-63; Pan-Pacific Surg Assn; Intl Soc of Surg; Coll of Chest Phys; NY Acad of Scis; World Med Assn; Amer Cancer Soc. Author: Nursing in Emergencies, 1929; Synopsis of the Principles of Surgery, 1940; Principles and Practice of Surgery, 1950; A Syllabus of Surgical Principles, 4th ed, 1968; ed, Ind U Med Cen quarterly bull, 1939; contbr numerous articles to med jours. Home: 3939 Cooper Lane, Indianapolis, Ind. Office: 712 E 65 St, Indianapolis, Ind.

BERMAN, Julian Louis, US, physician; b. Minneapolis, Minn, July 8, 1937; s. Myron and Stepha (Shapiro); BA, U Minn, 1956, BS, 1959, MD, 1960; m. Gail Marcus, Mar 25, 1959; c: Reid, Lauren. Asso prof ped, Chgo Med Sch since 1969; dir, sect genet, Cook Co Hosp since 1968, att phys, 1967; co-dir, Phenylketonuria Clinic, U of Ill, Chgo since 1968; f in ped: Children's Memorial Hosp, Chgo, 1963-66; Queen Charlotte's Maternity Hosp, London, 1964-65; Laboratoire de Physiologie Comparée, Paris, 1965; dept ped, Karolinska Hosp, Stockholm, 1965-66, spec f, NIH and Children's Memorial Hosp, Chgo, 1965-66, chief res, 1962-63; asso ped, Northwestern U Med Sch and Children's Memorial Hosp, 1966-67. Mem: Midwest Soc Ped Research; Amer Fed Clinical Research; Amer Acad Ped; Sigma Xi; profsl adv bd, Research Found, Mentally Retarded Children. Contbr numerous papers to profsl publs. Home: 342 Skokie Ct, Wilmette, Ill. Office: 700 S Wood St, Chicago, Ill.

BERMAN, Karl G, Swed, business exec; b. Malmö, Swed, Apr 25, 1910; s. Jacob and Anna-Maria (Estherson); c: Bo-Rolf, Layla. Advt mgr; trade union mags since 1956; Albetet Malmo, 1932-45; sales mgr, Hermes Pub House, Stockholm, 1945-54. Mem: exec bd, WJC, Swed sect since 1948; hon mem, ZF of Swed since 1954; B'nai B'rith; Poalei Zion; found, NR-3 Club. Recipient: Armgirdel, Danish Underground, 1945; King Christian X Medal of Liberty, 1945; Knight of the Dannebrog, 1960. Home: Kvorngotan 14, Stockholm, Swed. Office: Barnhusgatan 10, Stockholm, Swed.

BERMAN, Louis, US, astronomer; b. London, Eng, Mar 21, 1903; s. George and Jennie (Esakowitz); in US since 1905; BA, U Minn, 1925, MA, 1927; PhD, U of Cal, 1929; m. Esther Goldberg, June 13, 1934; c: Susan. Lectr, astronomy, U of SF since 1968; instr, astronomy: Carleton Coll, Northfield, Minn, 1929-31; and math, Coll of San Mateo, Cal, 1931-35; City Coll, SF, 1935-68. Asst secy-treas, Astronomical Soc Pacific since 1968; mem: AAAS; Amer Astronomical Soc. Contbr to astronomical jours. Home: 1020 Laguna Ave, Burlingame, Cal. Office: U of San Francisco, San Francisco, Cal.

BERMAN, Mandell Leslie, US, business exec; b. Detroit, Mich, Nov 18, 1917; s. Julius and Esther (Moss); BA, magna cum laude, Harvard Coll, 1940; MBA, Harvard Bus Sch, 1942; m. Madeleine Brodie, Apr 18, 1950; c: Ann, Jonathan. Exec vice-pres, Bert L Smokler & Co since 1946; pres, Dreyfus Devl Co. Lt, USNR, 1942-46. Chmn bd: Amer Assn for J Educ; Comm for Planning for J Educ, CJFWF; vice-pres: Builders Assn, Metrop Detroit; JWF, Detroit; Cong Shaarey Zedek; bd dirs, Council J Feds and Wfr Funds Inc; mem, Detroit Regional Area Planning Commn, 1963-67. Home: 18065 Hamilton Rd, Detroit, Mich. Office: 200 Northland Tower W, Southfield, Mich.

BERMAN, Morris, US, engineer, inventor; s. Elias and Ethel (Kaplan); att: CCNY, Polytechnic Inst of Bklyn; Cooper Union; LLB, NY Law Sch. Inventor of Stressometer; designer, proposed world's 1st structure to the stratosphere; principle for long-range transmission TV towers. Chmn, Conf on Civil Service Leg; provisional chmn, 1st White House restoration comm; chmn: Natl Comm on Justice and Morality in Govt; Ccmm on Engr Progress; appealed to US Supr Court to declare voting in churches unconstitutional, 1966; mem: NY Soc Engrs; AJCong; club, Citizens Union. Mailing address: Box 115, New York, NY.

BERMAN, Morton M, Isr, rabbi, organization exec; b. Baltimore, Md, Aug 23, 1899; s. Morris and Rose (Frommer); BA, Yale U, 1921; ordained rabbi, MHL, JIR, 1926, DD, 1946; grad studies: Columbia U, 1929-30; U Grenoble, Fr, 1926; Heb U, Jerusalem, 1926-27; Hochschule fur die Wissenschaft des Judentums, Berlin, 1927; m. Grace Hofheimer, Oct 21, 1925 (decd); c: John; m. 2nd, Elaine Seigel Levy, June 27, 1950; c: Susanna, Stephen, David. Dir dept Eng speaking countries, KH head off, Jerusalem, 1957-67; hon dir since 1967; student rabbi, Danbury, Conn, 1923-26; rabbi, Temple Emanuel, Davenport, Ia, 1927-29; asst rabbi, Free Syn, NYC, 1929-37; dir field activities, JIR, 1929-37; rabbi, Temple Isaiah Isr, Chgo, 1937-57, rabbi em since 1957. Asst div chaplain, 6th Marine Div; chaplain, USNR. Mem: CCAR; bd, Amer Music Libr, Isr; Phi Beta Kappa; Phi Alpha; B'nai B'rith; fmr: natl vice pres, AJCong, pres, Chgo div, chmn admn comm; mem natl exec and admn comm, ZOA; dep, World Zionist Actions Comm, chmn, ZC; pres, Chgo Council, JNF; pres, Rabb Assn; asso gen chmn, CJA; mem: bd, Natl Housing Conf; exec, WJC; Gov's Comm, Youth and Communal Serv, Ill. Author: Index to Mielziner's Introduction to the Talmud, 1926; Jew's View at the Crucifixion, 1929; Role of the Rabbi, 1941; ed: Negro Community to the West, 1940; Our First Century, 1952; mem ed adv bd, Collier's Ency, 1951; AJCong Bulletins, 1933-34; asst ed, Ency Judaica since 1966; contributing ed, Opinion; contbr to periodicals. Recipient, Pres Unit Citation, Okinawa Campaign. Home: 6 Berachyahu St, Jerusalem, Isr. Office: POB 583, Jerusalem, Isr.

BERMAN, Moshe Eliahu, Isr, engineer; b. Jerusalem, Aug 7, 1907; s. Eliahu and Sara (Elstein); BS, hons, U Liverpool, Eng, 1930, MA, 1932; m. Cecile Sachs; c: Michal Cutler, Leora Shabek, Oded. Dir, engr serv, Min of Posts since 1938; tech asst, engr-in-chief, Pal Post, 1934-48; post grad apprentice, GEC, Eng, 1930-34. Contbr to erection of State radio; telephone; radio telegraph; domestic, intl commun; bc stations; initiated first Heb teleprinter, 1946. Chmn: Inst of EE, Isr br; Assn Architects and Engrs, Isr. Home: 128 Ben Yehuda St, Tel Aviv, Isr. Office: Ministry of Communications, Jerusalem, Isr.

BERMAN, Muriel Mallin, US, patron, collector; b. Pittsburgh, Pa, June 21, 1924; att: U of Pittsburgh; Carnegie Tech U; Cedar Crest Coll; Muhlenberg Coll; D, optometry, Pa State Coll; m. Philip Berman; c: Nancy, Nina, Steven. Vice-pres, fine arts chmn, Women's Club; prog chmn, Fgn Policy Assn, Lehigh Co; natl bd, Hadassah; chmn, prog comm, Lehigh Valley Educ TV, produc, Coll Speak-In series; art appreciation dir, lectr, Allentown Art Mus; treas, Annual Sym Ball; mem: League of Women Voters; YWCA; Dieruff HS Art Adv Comm; Phila Chamber Sym; Wellesley Club, NY. Found, donor, Carnegie-Berman Coll Art Slide Libr Exch;

trustee: Lehigh Co Comty Coll, also secy, bd dirs; Kutztown State Coll, vice-chmn bd trustees, 1965; NGO delg to UNICEF: Thailand, 1964; Ethiopia, 1966; att sem: Bangkok, 1964; Aspen Inst of Humanistic Studies: Aspen, Col, 1965; Tokyo, 1966; mem: Art Collectors Club of Amer; Amer Fed Art; Friends of Whitney Mus; Mus Modern Art; Mus Primitive Art; J Mus; Metrop Opera Guild; Lincoln Cen, all NY; Archives of Amer Art, Detroit; Allentown Art Mus; Hist Soc, Lehigh Co, Pa; Reading Art Mus. Loan exhbs from own collection, to Us, Colls, public bldgs, schs; writes catalogues, researcher and curator, Berman collection. Recipient: Woman of Valor citation, Bonds for Isr. Home: 20 Hundred Nottingham Rd, Allentown, Pa.

BERMAN, Philip I, US, business exec; b. Pennsburg, Pa, 1915; att Ursinus Coll; hon: LDH, Lehigh U, 1969; LLD, Ursinus Coll; m. Muriel Berman; c: Nancy, Nina, Steven. Pres and chmn, Hess's; chmn bd and exec comm, Commonwealth Inds, Inc; mem bd: First Natl Bank & Trust Co, Allentown; Capitol Products of Harrisburg; pres, Philip and Muriel Berman Found; elected underwriting mem, Lloyd's, London. USMC, WW II. Found bd mem: Allentown Housing Devl Corp; Lehigh Valley Adequate Housing Corp; chmn, Allentown Redevl Auth; bd mem: Allentown Sym Assn; Pa Bahia Partners of Alliance; mem exec bd, UAHC; natl bd mem, AJComm, fgn affairs comm; repr of Pa, Intl Exec Service Corps; fmr: found chmn, Citizens for Lehigh Co Progress; natl repr of Pa, Small Bus Admn; pres, Keneseth Isr Cong; US State Dept, UN delg to 43rd ECOSOC Meetings, Geneva, 1967; judicial inquiry and rev bd, State Pa, 1969-70; mem: Mayor's Citizen's Adv Comm; YMCA-YWCA Council; Amer Adv Council WJC; Reform J App, chmn, Pa; Natl Bd J Educ, Parents Educ Comm; Friends Whitney Mus; Amer Fed Arts; Allentown Art Mus; Lehigh Art Alliance; B'nai B'rith; J WV; Natl Comm for Judaism and Creative Arts; Amer-Isr Cultural Soc; Amer-Isr Public Affairs; Amer J League for Isr; AJCong; Amer Friends of Technion, Haifa; clubs: Lehigh Valley Motor; Berkleigh Country; Lehigh Valley; Pres; Cent. Recipient: Beta Gamma Sigma, hon bus frat, Lehigh U Delta Chap; f, Aspen Inst of Humanistic Studies; First Annual AJComm, Pa, Del, Md Region Award, dist work in area of hum rights; Allentown C of C, Dist Service Award; Outstanding Alumni Award, Upper Perkiomen Sch, 1968; 1968 Outstanding Civic Leaders of Amer Award. Hobbies: art collector, world traveler. Home: 20 Hundred Nottingham Rd, Allentown, Pa.

BERMAN, Philip Marvin, US, attorney; b. NYC, May 9, 1934; s. Jacob and Estelle (Wedeen); att NYU, 1956-57; LLB, JD, Bklyn Law Sch, 1960; m. Irene Labourdette, Mar 28, 1967, div. Pvt practice since 1960; admitted to practice, US Supr Court, 1967; arbitrator, Amer Arbitration Assn; govt asso appeals agt, US Draft Bd, Bklyn, NY; study comm, Monorail for NYC Comm, NY State Assembly, 1969; survey team, housing, employment and educ needs for GI's, NYC, 1969. US Army, 1954-57. Dir, Flushing Bland Comty Cen; mem: NY Civil Liberties Union; Amer Bar Assn; NY Co Lawyers Assn; NY Trial Lawyers Assn; Bklyn Law Rev Alumni Assn. Contbr of articles to legal jours. Recipient, Korean Service Medal. Hobbies: sailing, scuba diving, skiing. Home: 145 East 15 St, New York, NY. Office: 250 Broadway, New York, NY.

BERMAN, Reuben, US, physician, educator; b. Minneapolis, Minn, Feb 8, 1908; s. Alexander and Sarah (Cohen); BA, summa cum laude, U Minn, 1929, MB, 1932, MD, 1933; m. Isabel Rosenstein, July 26, 1931; c: David, Elizabeth Appelbaum, Samuel, Ruth, Theodore, Jean. Asso clinical prof, Med, U Minn, 1957; clinical prof since 1962, fac mem since 1955; pvt practice, internal med since 1937; cons, card, Minneapolis Vet Hosp since 1946; chief, Mt Sinai Hosp, 1951-52. Lt col, US Army, 1941-45. Pres, Minn Heart Assn since 1965; f: Amer Coll Phys; Amer Coll Card; mem: AMA; Amer Diabetic Assn. Contbr on cardiovascular diseases to med jours. Home: 5620 Edgewater Blvd, Minneapolis, Minn. Office: 1047 Medical Arts Bldg, Minneapolis, Minn.

BERMAN, William Barry, US, merchant; b. Minneapolis, Minn, Mar 25, 1905; s. Alexander and Sarah (Cohen); BS, U Minn, 1925; m. Zetta Goldberg, Apr 20, 1928; c: Jessie, John (decd), Harriet Glaser, Daniel. Owner, Pacific Fur and Wool Co since 1926. Pres: David Lubin Lodge, B'nai B'rith, 1934; Cong B'nai Isr, 1943-46; United JWF, 1948; JCC, 1948-52; vice-pres, Sacramento ZOA since 1962; bd dirs, J Fed since 1961. Home: 901 Fremont Way, Sacramento, Cal. Office: 1830 C St, Sacramento, Cal.

BERMAN, Yaakov, Isr, rabbi, educational admnr; b. Salant, Lith, Jan 2, 1878; s. Yehezkiel and Sprintza; in Isr since 1959; ordained rabbi, Telez Yeshiva, Lith; att Us Petersburg, Odessa; m. Leah Feitelovit; c: Itzhak, Shoshana Ein Gad. Pres: Theol Inst, Rehovot; Inst for Advanced Studies, Tchrs of Judaism; chief rabbi, Berditchev, 1910-21; prin, Netzah Isr Sch, 1922; chief insp, Natl Rel Schs; 1904-44. Mem: exec comm, Zionist Org; Intl Cen, Hamizrachi, Isr; fmr: delg, ZCs; asst dir, educ dept, JA, Va'ad Leumi. Author: Torat Hamedina BeIsrael, 1946; Halaha La'am, 3 vols, 1959; ed, with explanations for schs, Pirkei Shulcan Aruch; contbr, educ and rel to press. Recipient: Yekir Yerushalaim, 1968; Isr Award, 1969. Home: 16 Haraz St, Rehovot, Isr.

BERN, David S, US, attorney; b. Suwalki, Pol, Dec 30, 1908; s.Eliyahu and Miriam (Kuritzki); in US since 1942; LLM, Political Sci, U Stefan Batory, Vilno, Pol, 1931; DJ, De Paul U, Chgo, 1946; m. Ruth Gutkowski, June 28, 1934; c: Miriam Schencker. Atty, pvt practice since 1947; advocate, Pol, 1931-39; prin, Logan Sq Heb Sch, Chgo, 1945-59. Natl vice-pres, ZOA since 1963; mem, Hon Court World Zionist Org since 1964; pres: Chgo ZOA, 1963-65; First Chgo Isr InvesC orp, 1961-63; mem, Chgo and Ill Bar Assns. Home: 6101 N Sheridan, E Chicago, Ill. Office: 1 N La Salle St, Chicago, Ill.

BERNARDS, Solomon S, US, rabbi; b. Chgo, May 14, 1914; s. Abraham and Margaret (Josephman); att: Heb Theol Coll, 1927-38; Crane Jr Coll, 1931-33; BSA, Lewis Inst, Chgo, 1938; LLB, John Marshall Law School, 1937; admitted Ill Bar, 1937; rabbi, MHL, JTSA, 1942, DHL, 1949; m. Ruth Segal, Dec 26, 1948; c: Joel, Reena. Dir, dept interrel cooperation, ADL since 1961; rabbi: Kesher Zion Syn, Reading, Pa, 1942-44; Overbrook Park Cong, Phila, 1949-50; Cong Agudas Achim, Schenectady, NY, 1950-61. Chaplain, US Navy, 1944-46. Pres, Capitol Dist Bd Rabbis, 1957-59; mem: RA; ZOA; B'nai B'rith; Amer Acad Rel; SSSR; SBL; Rel Research Assn; AVCRW. Author: Who Is A Jew, A Reader; Jews in American Life, A Bibliographic Listing; The Living Heritage of Passover; The Living Heritage of the High Holy Days; The Living Heritage of the Sabbath; ed bd, The Reconstructionist Magazine; ed, Christian Friends Bulletin; contbr to J and Chr jours. Home: 528 B 136 St, Belle Harbor, NY. Study: 315 Lexington Ave, New York, NY.

BERNAYS, Doris F, US, public relations counsel; b. NYC, July 18, 1892; d. Samuel and Harriet (Rosenthal) Fleischman; BA, Barnard Coll, 1913; m. Edward Bernays, Sep 16, 1922; c: Doris Held, Anne Kaplan. Partner, PR firm, Edward Bernays since 1919; reporter, asst women's page ed, asst Sunday ed, NY Tribune, 1914-17. Vice-pres, Edward Bernays Found; clubs: Women Pays; NY Newspaper Women's; The College; Women's City, Boston. Author: A Wife is Many Women, 1955; ed, An Outline of Careers for Women, 1928; contbr to PR manuals; mags, texts, gen jours. Home: 7 Lowell St, Cambridge, Mass.

BERNAYS, Edward L, US, public relations counsel; b. Vienna, Nov 22, 1891; s. Ely and Anna (Freud); desc of Isaac Bernays, chief rabbi, Hamburg, 18-19 cent; nephew of Sigmund Freud; in US since 1892; BS, Cornell U, 1912; hon, DHum, Boston U, 1966; m. Doris Fleischman, Sep 16, 1922; c: Doris Held, Anne Kaplan. PR counsel, in partnership with wife, to ind and bus corps, trade assns, bc cos, newspapers, mags, founds, educ insts, govt since 1919; adj prof, Boston U, since 1968; free-lance writer for NYC newspapers, 1913-15; partner, Metrop Musical Bur, 1915-18; staff mem, US comm public info, US Govt, 1918-19; with reemployment of ex-servicemen campaign, War Dept, 1919; lectr, PR, NYU, 1923, adj prof, 1949-50; visiting prof, PR, U Hawaii, 1950. Pres, Edward L Bernays Found, Inc since 1946; chmn, natl comm for Adequate Overseas US Info Prog since 1953; mem of bd: NY State chap, Arthritis and Rheumatism Found; Hosp for Jt Diseases; Columbia Assns; Natl Cystic Fibrosis Research Found; Columbia U Sem Assn on Public Communication; sch of gen studies, Columbia U; sch of bus admn, Suffolk U; Natl Recreation Assn; Ditchley Found; adv comm. Letters Abroad; Natl Multiple Sclerosis Soc; clubs: Overseas Press; Cornell; Columbia Men's Fac. Author: Crystallizing Public Opinion, 1923 (with new preface, 1961)); Your Future in Public Relations, 1961; Biography of an Idea (memoirs), 1966; co-author: Broadway Anthology, 1917; Propaganda, 1928; Speak up for Democracy, 1940; Take your Place at the Peace Table, 1945; Public Relations, A Growing Profession, 1945; Public Relations, 1952; ed and contbr: Outline of Careers, 1927; Engineering of Consent, 1955. Recipient: Rank of

Officer of Public Instruction (Fr), 1926; King Christian X Medal (Dan), 1946; Cert of Commendation, U of Fla Sch of Journalism, 1954; Bronze Medallion and Awards, S Methodist U, 1954 Award of Appreciation, VFW, US, 1955; Bronze Medallion of Honor, NYC, of 1961. Home: 7 Lowell St, Cambridge, Mass.

BERNAYS, Paul Issak, Switz, mathematician; b. London, Oct 17, 1888; att: U of Berlin; U Göttingen; PhD, Göttingen, 1912. Lectr, in Phila, 1965; ret; privat-dozent, U Zurich, 1913-17; asst to prof Hilbert, Inst of Math, Gottingen, 1917-33; privat-dozent, U Gottingen, 1919, title prof, 1922; lectr, Eidgenosische Technische Hochschule, Zurich, 1934, extraordinary prof math since 1945, prof em since 1959; lectr, Princeton Inst, NJ, 1935-36; Phila, Pa, 1956, 61, 65. Consulting ed, Jour Symb Logic; bd dirs, Dialectica, intl phil review; mem: Norsk Videnskaps Akademi, Oslo; Acad Intl Sci, Brussels. Co-author: Grundlagen der Mathematik, vol I, 1934, 1968; vol II, 1939; Axiomatic Set Theory (monograph), 1959; contbr, series of papers, Jour of Symb Logic. Home: 11 Bodmerstr, Zurich, Switz.

BERNBAUM, Maurice Marshall, US, foreign service off; b. Chicago, Feb 15, 1910; s. Louis and Ann (Warsaw); SB, Harvard U, 1931; m. Elizabeth Hahn, Feb 5, 1942; c: Edwin, Marcia. Fgn service off, career min since 1961; US min to Arg, 1959-60; US ambass to: Ecuador, 1960-65; Venezuela, 1965-69. Mem: Amer Fgn Service Assn; club, Harvard, Wash. Home: 2401 Calvert St, NW, Wahsington, DC. Office: State Department, Washington, DC.

BERNE, Gustave Morton, US, attorney, communal worker; b. NYC, Mar 4, 1903; s. Nathan and Rose (Birnbaum) Bernknopf; AB, Columbia Coll, 1922; LLB, 1924; m. Janet Gibbs, Mar 7, 1934 (decd); c: Susan, Robert; m. 2nd, Selma Stetzer, May 8, 1966. Vice pres, AJComm, 1952-1971; pres, LI J Med Cen; dir, United Service New Amer since 1948; past chmn: NY Assn New Amer, 1952-71; coordinating comm, Jt Defense Appeal, 1948-52; treas, Natl Comty Relations Adv Council, 1952; found, dir, UJA, NY; pres, J Comty Services, LI, 1949-51; trustee, FJP, 1948-52; J Child Care Assn, 1952-58; clubs: Columbia, N Shore Country. Home: Beach Lane, Great Neck, NY. Office: 20-02 Seagirt Ave, Far Rockaway, NY.

BERNHARD, Ton, Isr, artist; b. Bucharest, Rum, Oct 21, 1915; s. Marcel and Rachael (Feurenstein); in Isr since 1964; att Acad Des Belles Arts, Bucharest, 1935-40; m. Edith Meisl, Sep 12, 1963. Exhbs: Bucharest, Isr, Paris, Johannesburg, NY, Frankfurt, Miami, LA, Montreal, Montevideo, Buenos Aires; painted: portrait of Chaim Weizmann owned by Knesset, Jerusalem; Union of Rels, owned by Dr R M W Kempner. Mem, masonic order Hashahar. Recipient, Plastic Arts Prize, Bucharest, 1948. Home: 7 Gordon St, Tel Aviv, Isr.

BERNHARDT, Maurice, US, attorney, jurist; b. NYC, June 28, 1899; s. Max and Celia (Berg); att CCNY, 1920; LLB, Columbia Law Sch, 1923; m. Ruth Schonziet, June 7, 1925; c: Helen Carr, Marcia Model, Joyce Siegel. Justice, State Supr Court, Family; fmr mem, law firm, Bernhardt, Sahn, and Epstein, NYC. Hon pres, Bklyn Coll Hillel Found; pres, Pride of Judea; bd mem, Bklyn JCC; treaz, Bklyn Women's Hosp; E NY and Brownsville, YUHA; Neighborhood Cen, E Flatbush; chmn: UJA, 1951; Bonds for Isr, 1952; asso chmn, FJP; chmn, Music Under Stars, Bklyn, 1950; mem: ZOA; B'nai B'rith; Amer Legion; JWV; club, 1934. Home: 890 E 23 St, Brooklyn, NY. Office: Supr Court Bldg, Brooklyn, NY.

BERNHEIM, Elinor K, US, volunteer wfr worker; b. NYC June 26, 1907; d. Alexander and Irma (Hernsheim) Kriden; BA, Vassar U, 1928; att NY Sch of Social Work, Columbia U, 1946-48; m. Leonard Bernheim, 1928. Volunteer social wfr worker since 1931. Vice pres: Natl JWB 1966; Comty Council, Gtr NY, 1968; Columbia U Sch of Social Work 1968; chmn, Social Work Recruiting Comm of Gtr NY since 1955, Natl Social Wfr Assembly since 1959; hon chmn, FJP since 1958, vice-pres, 1955-58, chmn bd, 1954-58; asso chmn, YM-YWHA's, Gtr NY; mem, adv bd, NY School of Social Work, Columbia U, since 1959; bd trustees, Natl JWB, Women's org div since 1954; mem, bd: Comty Council of Gtr NY since 1959. Mem: NYC Cultural Found; Lavenburg Found; Young Concert Artists; Women's City of NY; club, Cosmopolitan. Recipient: Columbia Bi-Centennial Medal, 1955; NY State gen award, 1959; Frank L Weil award, 1960;

gen award, Research Inst for J Group Work Agcys; Naomi Lehman Memorial Found award. Home: 930 Park Ave, New York, NY.

BERNHEIM, Hubert, Fr, industrialist; b. Mulhouse, Fr, May 8, 1899; s. Lucien and Cécile; m. Simone Israel, Feb 21, 1926; c: Gerard, Evelyne Blamont, Jean Francois. Pres and dir gen, Usines Ethel Malteries since 1959; pres, Bourse de Commerce, Strasbourg since 1952; vice-pres, Chambre Syndicale de la Malterie Francaise, 1960; mem: Chambre de Commerce, Strasbourg; Fr delg, Euromalt, EEC, Brussels; adv, Fr Fgn Comm dept. Pres, Fonds Social Juif Unifié, Bas-Rhin, Fr, 1952-66; mem, B'nai B'rith; clubs: Rotary Intl; Eur Circle, Strasbourg; Golf. Recipient, Officier de la Légion d'Honneur, 1953. Hobbies: ancient ceramics, painting. Home: 10 Quai Mullenheim, Strasbourg, Bas-Rhin, Fr. Office: Usines Ethel Malteries, Strasbourg, Bas Rhin, Fr.

BERNHEIMER, Franz Karl, Isr, artist, educator; b. Munich, May 16, 1911; s. Max and Karolina (Roos); in Isr since 1961; att: U Munich; Art Acad, Munich; U Zurich; studied sculpture with Herman Haller, Zurich; MA, art hist, MFA, Yale U, 1944; m. Aliza Hering, Feb 1, 1946; c: Anatol, Susanna. Artist and pvt tchr, since 1962; asst prof: Sweet Briar Coll, Va, 1946-58; Bklyn Coll, NYC, 1946. One-man exhbs: Art Alliance, Phila, 1943; Argent Gal, NY, 1950; Richmond Mus Fine Arts, Va, 1958; Katz Gal, Tel Aviv, 1962; Rina Gal, Jerusalem, 1963, 1967; group exhbs: US; Switz; It; Brazil; Isr; Eng; Isr Drawings, 1964; Graphic Biennale, Florence, 1968; Fall Exhb, Tel Aviv Mus, 1968; works in perm collection: Bklyn Mus; Isr Mus, Jerusalem; Mus of Modern Art, Haifa; Stoaliche Graphische Sammling, Munich; Graphische Kabinett, Zurich; Bibliothéque Royale, Brussels; Vic and Albert Mus, London; The Albertine Collection, Vienna; Mus Petach Tikvah; Ein Harod Mus; repr in pvt collections: Zurich; Winterthur; Cologne; Rome; Singapore; Phillip Cambridge; Va; Jerusalem; Tel Aviv; Haifa. Mem: Coll Art Assn Amer; Artists and Sculptors Assn Amer. Home and studio: 57B Alonim St, Tivon, Isr.

BERNICK, Sheldon Marvin, US, dentist; b. St Paul, Minn, July 10, 1940; s. Milton and Bernice (Brudnick); BS, U Minn, 1962, DDS, 1964; m. Judith Himmelstein, Aug 27, 1967. Pvt practice since 1968; tchr, Sch of Dent Med, U of Pa since 1968 att dent, Childrens Hosp, Phila since 1968, chief dent res, 1966-68; cons pedodent, USN Hosp, Phila. Lt cdr, USNR since 1960. Treas, Pa unit, Amer Soc of Dent for Children; ed, Chester Delower Dent Soc; tchr, Adath Isr Sch; mem: Amer Soc of Clinical Hypnosis; Acad of Dent for Handicapped; Amer Acad Pedodontics; Alpha Omega; Phi Epsilon Pi. Contbr of articles to dent jours. Hobbies: flying, sailing, photography. Home: 1401 W Chester Pike E4, Havertown, Pa. Office: 1230 Burmont Rd, Drexel Hill, Pa.

BERNS, Charles A, US, business exec; b. NYC, Aug 8, 1901; s. Abraham and Sophie (Basin) Bernfeld; BCS, NYU, 1922; LLB, NY Law Sch, 1926; m. Molly Rogat, 1932; c: Anthony, Abby Solmon, Susan Wolf. Chmn bd, co-found, Twenty-one Brands Inc since 1933. Vice-pres, Bx-Leb Hosp; dir, Distilled Spirits Inst; exec comm, NY Importers & Distillers; fund raising comm: FJP; JDC; B'nai B'rith; ARC; found, Jack Kriendler Memorial Found, 1948; mem: Masons; Shriners; Elks; NYU Gallatin Assn; clubs: NYU; Southampton Country; Madison Sq Garden. Recipient: Maddon award, NYU, helped create Sch of Hotel-Restaurant Mgmt, 1961. Home: 24 Central Park S, New York, NY. Office: 23 W 52 St, New York, NY.

BERNSOHN, Maurice Moshe, Isr, economist; b. Strasbourg, Fr, Mar 23, 1921; s. Samuel and Caroline (Salomon); in Isr since 1947; dipl, math, U Toulouse, Fr, 1941; dipl, finance and econ, Mgmt Inst, Tel Aviv, 1963; m. Miriam Steiner; c: Samuel, Ariella, Yael, Gil. Dir, co's since 1963; secy and treas, Kwoutzat Neve Ilan, 1949-55; dir, State of Isr Bonds, Fr and Belgium, 1957-59; gen mgr, Isr Official Inds, 1960-63. Fr underground, 1942-44; secret Fr Army, 1944-45. Mem Munic Council of Holon; exec pres, Union of Fr and Algerian Immigrants in Isr; natl leader, J Boy Scouts in Fr, 1946-47, Secy gen, Isr-Fr C of C, 1960-67. Author: David Ben Gurion, 1957; contbr of numerous articles to Le Monde, Paris, 1960-69. Home: 1 Brazzaville St, Holon, Isr.

BERNSTEIN, Abraham, US, physician; b. San Francisco, Oct 25, 1902; s. Joseph and Betty (Terkeltaub); BA, U of Cal, 1923, MD, Med Sch, 1927; postgrad study: Chgo Lying-

in Hosp and Dispensary, 1930; Bellevue Hosp, NY, 1931; Hosp for Women, Harvard Med Sch, 1931; hon DHumL, U Judaism, JTSA, 1966; m. Margaret Starcevic, June 18, 1944; c: Marcia, Richard. Pvt practice, obstet and gyn; mem sr courtesy staff, Mt Zion Hosp since 1946, res surg, gyn, 1927-29, adj, obstet, 1930-38; visiting gyn, Polyclinic Hosp since 1954; adv dir, Liberty Natl Bank since 1968; asst obstet and gyn, U of Cal Hosp and Clinic, 1930-51, instr, clinical obstet and gyn, Med Sch and Hosp, 1930-51; chief, obstet and gyn, Franklin Hosp, 1938-40; mem, active courtesy staff, Peninsula Hosp, Burlingame, Cal, 1955. Col, US Army, 1941-46. Dipl, Amer Bd Obstet and Gyn; found, f Amer Acad Obstet and Gyn; f: US chap, Intl Coll Surgs; Amer Geriatric Soc; Amer Acad Psychosomatic Med; Natl Gastro-Enterological Soc (asso); pres: United Syn of Amer, NW region since 1955; JNF, N Cal council since 1962; Friends of N Cal, Albert Einstein Med Coll since 1957; SF Heb Free Loan Assn since 1968; Grand Pres, Dist Grand Lodge 4, B'nai B'rith; mem natl bd dirs: United Syn of Amer; Fed of ORT, mem, SF bd; J Educ Soc, past vice-pres; mem bd dirs: JWF, SF; Cal Safety Council; mem: SF Co Med Soc; Cal State Med Soc; AMA; Assn Mil Surgs; asso, San Mateo Co Med Soc; J Comty Relations Council; SF Mus of Art; SF Acad Music; Masons; SF Bur J Educ; Cong Beth Sholom; SF Health Service Sys; chmn, Big Day, Bonds for Isr 1952; clubs: Commonwealth; Saints and Sinners; Intl. Contbr articles to med jours. Recipient: Army Commendation Ribbon for Meritorious Service with citation, 1945; cert of merit, United Syn of Amer, 1955; Akiba Award, B'nai B'rith, 1937, 1953; cert of recognition, JWF, SF, 1951; Big Day, Bonds for Isr Award, 1952; award for meritorious service, Saints and Sinners, 1952; Louis Marshall medal, JTSA, 1965. Home: 3767 Washington St, San Francisco, Cal. Office: 2266 Geary Blvd, San Francisco, Cal.

BERNSTEIN, Arthur, US, physician educator; b. NYC, Nov 15, 1909; s. Isaac and Lena (Sandman); BA, U of Pa, 1930, MS, 1931, MD, 1935; m. Grace Hoffman, June 26, 1935; c: Lory Greenbaum, Lawrence, Mark, Penny. Att in med, Newark Beth Isr Hosp since 1951, asso, cardiac clinic since 1937, asso, electrocardiography since 1937, research asso, card dept of labs since 1940; att card: Harrison Martland Med Cen since 1969, asst in med since 1952; Clara Maass Memorial Hosp; Babies Hosp unit, United Hosp, Newark; dir and att phys: Heart inst, Presbyterian Hosp unit, United Hosp, Newark; cons, card: Fitkin Memorial Hosp; Essex Mt Sanitarium; UOTS Children's Cardiac Home; Pleasant Valley Way Home for Aged; E Orange Gen Hosp; NY Rehab Comm; chief, cardiac clinic, Babies and Coit Memorial Hosp, 1948; asst surg, USPHS, Res 1943-46; asst instr, bact, Sch of Med, U of Pa, 1935-36; instr, card, Grad Sch Med, U of Pa, 1956-59, asso card since 1959; asso clin, prof med, NY Coll Med and Dent. F: Amer Coll Phys; Amer Coll Chest Phys, pres, NJ chap, 1959-60; Amer Coll Card, gov for NJ, 1958-62; Amer Coll Angiology; Amer Med Writers Assn; NY Acad Scis; dipl: Amer Bd Internal Med; subspeciality bd, Cardiovascular Diseases; pres: Essex Co, Heart Assn, 1952-53, mem bd trustees and exec comm since 1949; NY Heart Assn, 1965-67; mem: Essex Co and NJ State Med Socs; AMA; NJ Acad Med; SNJ State Heart Assn, bd trustees; Assn Mil Surgs; AAAS; NY Acad Sci; Alpha Omega Alpha; mem, bd trustees: J Comty Council; J Educ Assn; NJ mh Assn; Pleasant Valley Way Home Aged; J Comty Cen; Cong Adas Isr; Masons; clubs: Crestmont Country, U of Pa Alumni, N NJ. Contbr numerous articles to med jours. Recipient, Selective Service Medal, 1946. Hobbies: photography, collecting old silver, books, music recordings. Home: 100 Great Hills Rd, Short Hills, NJ. Office: 2130 Millburn Ave, Maplewood, NJ.

BERNSTEIN, Bernard, US. attorney; b. NYC, Nov 30, 1908; s. Henry and Annie (Goldstein); BA, Columbia U, 1928, Kent Scholar, Columbia Law Sch, 1927-30, LLB, 1930; m. Bernice Lotwin, 1938; c: Elinor Balka, Kate, Anne. Pvt Law practice since 1946; admitted to NY Bar, 1931; US Supr Court Bar, 1936; DC Bar, 1947; asso with Mitchell, Taylor, Capron and Marsh, 1930-33; atty, Treasury Dept, 1933-42, asst gen counsel, 1938-42; participated in all litigation relating to govt monetary policies, and in intl finance arrangements of Treasury Dept, and active in admn of fgn funds control; mem, drafting comm of experts, plans Inter-Amer Bank, 1939-40; US adv, Inter-Amer Conf on sys of econ and financial control, 1942. Lt-col, US Army, 1942, col, 1944; financial adv to Gen Eisenhower for Civil Affairs and Mil Govt, Eur and Mediterranean Theaters, 1942-45; financial adv, N Afr Econ Bd and Allied Forces, 1942-43; currency and exch adv, Allied Mil Govt and Allied

Control Comm, It and Sicily, 1943-44; jt dir, financial br, 6-5, SHAEF, 1944-45; dir, finance div and div on inves of cartels and external assets, US Group Control Comm for Ger, 1944-45. Legal adv, AJConf, 1946-48; chmn, working comm, J orgs for treaties with enemy countries, 1946-47; cons on behalf of Coord Bd of J Orgs to ECOSOC; chmn, Comm on Fgn and Intl Law, NY Co Lawyers Assn; mem: Temple Emanuel, NYC; B'nai B'rith; AJComm; NYC, 1964-69 NY State, and Amer Bar Assns; Amer Soc Intl Law; Mil Govt Assn, 1964-69; Tau Delta Phi; J Restitution Successor Org, 1946-48; club, Lawyers. Ed, Columbia Law Review, 1928-30. Recipient: Legion of Merit, Eur-Afr Theater ribbon; Legion of Honor; Croix de Guerre. Home: 34 Elm Ridge Rd, Great Neck, LI, NY. Office: 745 Fifth Ave, New York, NY.

BERNSTEIN, Bernice Lotwin, US, attorney, government official; b. Menomonie, Wis, Nov 26, 1908; d. Charles and Fannie (Fein) Lotwin; PhB U Wis, 1929, LLD, 1932; m. Bernard Bernstein, Aug 4, 1938; c: Elinor Balka, Kate, Anne. Dir, HEW, Region II since 1966; asst gen counsel, Social Security Bd, 1936-38; FSA, 1938-42; War Manpower Commn, 1942-45; asst solicitor, Dept of Lab, 1945-47; regional atty, HEW, 1947-65. Natl bd, Natl Council of Jewish Women, 1950-61, natl exec comm, 1955-61, natl treas, 1955-59; mem: Fed, Wis Bar Assns. Home: 34 Elm Ridge Rd, Great Neck, NY. Office: 26 Federal Plaza, New York, NY.

BERNSTEIN, Bertrand L, S Afr, barrister, business exec; b. Johannesburg, Aug 13, 1907; s. George and Ida (Abelheim); BA, LLB, hon LLD, U Witwatersrand; m. Barbara Leon, June 18, 1937. Dep chmn, Anglo-Transvaal Consolidated Inves Co Ltd, past legal adv, asst mgn dir, mgn dir; fmr: chmn, dir, gold mining and ind co's; practicing barrister, Johannesburg Bar. Served, S Afr Army. Mem: Witwatersrand Council of Educ, 1961 educ panel; trustee, Jan Smuts Memorial Fund; fmr: chmn: Council of Witwatersrand; S Afr Inst Med Research; vice-pres, Chamber of Mines; clubs: Rand; Johannesburg Country; Inanda; Flyfishers, Eng. Author: The Tide Turned at Alamein; Tomorrow is Another Day, hit novel of S Afr, 1652-1952. Hobbies: breeding pedigree cattle; fly fishing; ornithology. Home: 2 The Paddock, Sandown, Johannesburg, S Afr. Office: POB 7727, Johannesburg, S Afr.

BERNSTEIN, Charles Bernard, US, lawyer; b. Chgo, Ill, June 24, 1941; s. Norman and Adele (Shore); BA, U Chgo, 1962; JD, De Paul U Law Sch, 1965; m. Roberta Lesner, Aug 7, 1968. Mem firm, Max & Herman Chill since 1967; basketball pres dir, U Chgo, since 1967; mem firm, Axelrod, Goodman & Steiner, 1966-67. Mem, bd dirs: Cong Bicker Cholem, S Chgo; Richard E Gutstadt Lodge, B'nai B'rith, pres, 1969-70; Chgo Region B'nai B'rith Youth Org, 1967-70; mem: Amer J Hist Soc; Chgo, Ill State Bar Assns; J Fed, Metrop Chgo; Nu Beta Epsilon. Sports ed, Chicago Maroon, 1960-62; mem, bd eds, De Paul Law Review, 1964-65; ed: Ill State Bar Assn Sect on Public Utilities newsletter, 1964-65; Ill State Bar Assn Sect on Drainage and Levee Law newsletter, 1965-66; contbr to profsl publs. Recipient: Amer Jurisprudence award for excellence in legal phil, 1963. Spec interests: sports writing; collecting biographical material on famous Jews; studying genealogies of his J families; Amer J hist. Home: 5457 S Hyde Park Blvd, Chicago, Ill. Office: 100 W Monroe St, Chicago, Ill.

BERNSTEIN, Dagfinn, Nor, engineer; b. Oslo, Jan 22, 1928; s. Mendel and Elise; dipl Ing ETH; m. Judith Bodd, 1955; c: Knut, Ralph, Björn. Chief engr, Nor Bc NRK TV, Oslo. Past pres: Youth Soc, 1952-54, 1958-59; Scandinavian J Youth Assn, 1967-69. Home: Avlös, Bärum, Nor.

BERNSTEIN, David, US, physician, surgeon, educator; b. Minsk, Russ, Oct 20, 1910; s. George and Anna (Rosoff); in US since 1912; BS, NYU, 1930, MD, Coll of Med, 1935, teaching f, grad sch, 1930-31; m. Dorothy Ashery Skupsky, 1937; c: Helen Berman, Herbert. Chief, otolaryngology and otorhinolaryngologic plastic surg sci, Maimonides Med Cen since 1969; att otolaryngologist, otorhinoplastic surg, Maimonides, Coney Island Hosps, 1939-69; asso att otolaryngologist, otorhinoplastic surg, U Hosp, NYC since 1947; Bellevue Hosp since 1947, on staff since 1935; clinical prof, otolaryngology, and clinical plastic surg, NYU Meo Cen since 1955; att, otolaryngolosist, Bklyn Heb Home and Hosp since 1955. Maj, US Army MC, 1944-46. F: NY Acad Med; Amer Acad Facial Plastic and Reconstructive Surg; Amer Otorhinologic Soc Plastic Surg; Amer Acad Ophthal and Otolaryngology; Intl Coll Surg; dipl, Amer Bd Otolaryngology; chmn, sci prog,

Amer Soc Facial Plastic Surg, 1953; mem: bd trustees, Maimonides, Coney Island Hosps, 1959; Amer Med Soc, Vienna; moderator, Sem Cong, Plastic Microsurg, U Vienna 1969; bd govs, NYU Med Sch Alumni Assn; Amer Legion; Disabled Amer Vets and Ret Offs Assn; Masons, 32 deg; (320); Temple Emanuel, Bklyn; First Intl Cong Plastic Surgery, Stockholm, Swed; club, NYU, found mem. Contbr to med jours. Recipient, Amer Legion Medal, 1941, Home and office: 1342-51 St, Brooklyn, NY.

BERNSTEIN, David, US, newspaper ed, publisher; b. Hollis, NY, Mar 6, 1915; s. Herman and Sophie (Friedman); grad, Intl Sch, Geneva, 1932; m. Adele Teitelbaum, Aug 27, 1937; c: Adam. Ed, chmn bd, Binghamton Sun-Bull, since 1960; engaged in newspaper work, NYC, 1934-36; staff mem, AJComm, 1936-40; cons, Eur affairs, 1946-48; asst pres, Council for Democracy, NY, 1940-41; sr defense info writer, OWI, Wash, DC, 1942; org, dir, at invitation of Pres Manuel L Quezon, Off of Spec Services, Philippine Govt-in-Exile, Wash, DC, 1942-43; adv, Philippine Pres Sergio Osmena, Manila and Wash, DC, 1945-46; engaged in surveys of Eur conditions; jour purposes and US Govt, 1946-50; asst, admnr, US Fed Security Agcy, Wash DC, 1949-52; exec dir: Natl Citizens Comm for UN Day, Wash, DC, 1949; Amer J Tercentenary Comm, NYC, 1952-55; found, ed, pub, Middletown, NY Daily Record, 1956-60. US Army, 1943-45, ret with rank of 1st lt. Mem: bd dirs, ORT Fed since 1951; NY State Bd of Social Wfr since 1966; f, Dickinson Coll, SUNY, Binghamton; clubs: Natl Press, Wash; Overseas Press, NYC. Author, The Philippine Story, 1947; contbr to press and mags. Home: 5 Vincent St, Binghamton, NY. Office: 60 Henry St, Binghamton, NY.

BERNSTEIN, Dorothy Lewis, US, mathematician, educator; b. Chgo, Apr 11, 1914; d. Jacob and Tillie (Lewis); MA, U Wis, 1935; PhD, Brown U, Providence, RI, 1939. Prof, math, Goucher Coll, Baltimore since 1959, chmn, math dept, 1961-70; prof, U Rochester, mem fac, 1943-59. Mem: AAUP; Phi Beta Kappa; commn mem, Undergrad Progs, math; comm mem, MAA, on publs. Author, Existence Theorems in Partial Differential Equations; contbr to mags and profsl jours. Recipient: grants, scholarships, fs, all in math. Spec interest, computers in math educ. Home: 6857 Queens Ferry Rd, Baltimore, Md. Office: Goucher Coll, Baltimore, Md.

BERNSTEIN, Gerald, US, artist, teacher; b. Indianapolis, Ind, Aug 25, 1917; s. Nathan and Hilda (Sher); BA, NYU, 1948, MA, Inst of Fine Arts, 1950; att: Art Students League; John Herron Art Inst, Ind; m. Gladys Renfield. Owner, Island Art Cen, NY since 1958; curator of arts, Staten Island Inst Arts and Scis, 1950-56; instr, Staten I Comty Coll, until 1969; paintings exhibited in natl and local mus exhbs. Sgt, US Army, 1941-45. Pres, art sect, Staten I Inst Arts and Scis. Home and studio: 1639 Richmond Rd, Staten Island, NY.

BERNSTEIN, Harry, US, educator, author; b. NYC, Oct 13, 1909; s. Louis and Rose (Katz); BA, CCNY, 1933; MA, Columbia U, 1934, PhD, 1945; m. Florence Borenstein, June 2, 1936; c: Stefanie, Walter. Prof hist, Bklyn Coll, since 1958, mem fac since 1954; visiting prof: Columbia U, 1959-60; NYU, since 1960; U of Cal, Berkeley, 1962. Author: Origins of Inter-American Interest, 1945; Modern and Contemporary Latin America, 1952; Making an Inter-American Mind, 1961; Matias Romero: Modern Mexican, 1962, 1970; Brazil since 1800, pub 1963, 1970; contbr to encys and hist jours. F: NY Acad Scis; Ford Found, since 1953; Social Sci Research Council, 1943-44; mem, Amer Hist Assn. Recipient: Beveridge Prize, Amer Hist Assn, 1945; Columbia U Bicentennial Medal, 1954. Home: 191 Lexington Ave, Freeport, NY. Office: Bklyn Coll, Bklyn, NY.

BERNSTEIN, Henry C, US, attorney, organization exec; b. NYC, Mar 15, 1903; s. Joseph and Rose (Bellinker); LLB, St John's Coll, 1928; m. Martha Duff, Dec 2, 1928; c: Alan. Exec dir and exec vice-pres, UJA of Gtr NY since 1940; mem, natl UJA exec comm and campaign cabinet since 1949. Home: 115 Central Park W, New York, NY. Office: 220 W 58 St, New York, NY.

BERNSTEIN, Henry O, US, rabbi; b. Fürth, Ger, June 11, 1907; s. Jakob and Victoria (Obstfeld); in US since 1940; ordained rabbi: Yeshiva, Hung, 1929; Sem of Berlin, 1938; PhD, Sem Köln U, 1935; m. Estelle Siker, July 28, 1953; c: Joel, Jonathan. Rabbi: with life tenure, Cong Rodfe Zedek, Moodus, Conn, since 1955; J Comty Cen of Lower Middlesex Co,

Conn; mem, state adv bd, Family and Sex Educ, State of Conn; educ dir, Beth El, New London, Conn since 1949; dist rabbi, Cong Soest, Ger, 1935-39; rabbi: Union de Refugiados, Havana, 1939-40; Tikvah Chadosho, Baltimore, 1940-43; Asso de los Judeos, Lima, Peru, 1946-47. Fmr: pres: New London dist ZOA, Mins Assn of Lower Middlesex; vice-pres, Mins League of New London; mem, exec comm, Educ Assembly; mem, Rotary. Author: Die Entwicklung der Theologischen Ideen in der Frühzeit des Christentums, 1935. Home: 23 Colebrook St, Hartford, Conn.

BERNSTEIN, Herman W, US, attorney; b. NYC, Nov 12, 1900; s. Solomon and Rachel (Rasofsky); att CCNY; BS, NYU, 1921; LLB, Columbia U Law Sch, 1924; m. Annette Kaskel, Dec 17, 1931; c: George, Rachelle Schaffzin. Pvt practice, NYC since 1925. Hon vice-chmn, Night of Stars, United Isr Appeal, past gen counsel; co-found: UJA Gtr NY, vice-chmn, lawyers div; mem bd dirs, Amer J League for Isr; hon pres, 7th Zionist dist, ZOA, past pres; hon secy, J Info Bur; mem: Assn of Bar, NYC; NY Co Lawyers Assn; Amer Bar Assn, mem, numerous comms, including: round table; forum; courts; code; procedure; Brith Rishonim; bd dirs, JNF, and chmn, council of Mid-Manhattan, 1939-41; natl adv council, JDC; exec comm, bus and profsl group, AJCong; bd dirs, United Pal Appeal; Comm on Natl Unity for Pal; fmr: pres, League of J Youth of Amer; mem: org comm, Israel Friedlander classes, JTSA; natl comm, Pal exhb, NY World's Fair, 1938. Contbr to periodicals and jours. Home: 85 East End Ave, New York, NY.

BERNSTEIN, Irving, organization exec; b. NYC, Aug, 1921; s. Jacob and Ethel (Potasewitch); BA, CCNY, 1942; MA, Columbia U, 1946; m. Judith Munitz, Jan 2, 1952; c. Robert, Joseph. Exec vice-chmn, UJA since 1969, field repr, 1948-49, dir, W Coast region, 1950-61, asst vice-chmn, 1962-69; tchr, NYC, Public Sch Sys, 1946; with Dept of Wfr, 1947. US Army, 1942-45. Club, Lambs. Home: 1 Stoneleigh Rd, Scarsdale, NY. Office: 1290 Ave of the Americas, New York, NY.

BERNSTEIN, Leonard, US, conductor, composer, pianist, lecturer; b. Lawrence, Mass, Aug 25, 1918; s. Samuel and Jennie (Resnick); BA, Harvard U, 1939; grad, Curtis Inst of Music, 1941; studied: conducting with Fritz Reiner, Serge Koussevitzky; orchestration with Randall Thompson; piano with Helen Coates, Heinrich Gebhart, Isabella Vengerova; m. Felicia Montealegre Cohn, Sep 9, 1951; c: Jamie, Alexander, Nina. Music dir, NY Philharmonic, 1958-69; asst conductor, 1943-44; dir, Young People's Concerts since 1957; lectr, music series on TV programs, Omnibus, 1955-62; guest conductor, major orchs in US and abroad since 1944; head, orch and conducting dept, Berkshire Music Cen, 1951-55, mem, fac, 1946-51; asst to Koussevitzky, 1942; music dir, NYC Orch, 1945-48; prof, music, and dir, creative arts festival, Brandeis U, 1951-56. US repr, Prague Intl Festival, 1946; dir, Festival of the Americas, Hollywood, 1955. Conducted: opening concert, Mann Auditorium, Tel Aviv, 1957; transcontinental tour of Isr Philharmonic Orch in US, as guest conductor, 1951, with Koussevitzky. Maj compositions: Clarinet Sonata, 1942; Symphony No 1, Jeremiah, 1944; Fancy Free, ballet, 1944; On The Town, score for musical, 1944; Facsimile, ballet, 1946; Symphony No 2, The Age of Anxiety, 1949; Trouble in Tahiti, opera, 1952; Wonderful Town, musical, 1953; Serenade for violin and orchestra, commissioned by the Koussevitzky Music Found, 1953; West Side Story, score for musical, 1957; symphony No 3, Kaddish, 1963 (dedicated to the memory of Pres J F Kennedy) commissioned by Boston Sym Orch, premiered by Isr Philharmonic Orch; Chichester Psalms, for mixed choir and string orchestra (or organ), 1965. Author: The Joy of Music, 1959; Leonard Bernstein's Young People's Concerts for Reading and Listening, 1962; The Infinite Variety of Music, 1966. Recipient: Music Critics, NY Award for Jeremiah, 1944; Drama Critics Award, for Wonderful Town, 1953. Office: 205 W 57 St, New York, NY.

BERNSTEIN, Leopold, US, attorney; b. N Topeka, Kan, July 23, 1889; s. Louis and Rosa (Bitterman); BA, Christian Brothers, Memphis, Tenn, 1908; LLB, U Tenn, 1910; m. Lillian Klein, Dec 14, 1927; c: Rosalyn Hewey, Richard, Garland. Pvt practice since 1910; admitted, Cal State Bar, 1920; Dist Court, Cal, 1920; Supr Court, Wash, DC, 1954; US Army, WW I. Vice-pres, LA lodge, B'nai B'rith; mem: Masons; Phi Kappa Phi; LA Bar, S Cal; Rodef Shalom Cong. Home: 404 Sweetzer Ave, Los Angeles, Cal. Office: 756 S Broadway, Los Angeles, Cal.

BERNSTEIN, Louis, US, attorney; b. Portland, Me, Nov 26, 1900; s. Abraham and Sarah (Caplan); att Bowdoin Coll, Brunswick, Me, 1918-22; m. Selma Seligman, Jan 18, 1904. Atty since 1930; recorder, Portland Munic Court, 1948-52, judge, 1952-56. Maj, USAAC, 1942-45. Found, pres, J Comty Cen, 1938-42; trustee, Me Med Cen, 1958-69; overseer, Bowdoin Coll, 1958-69; mem, Amer, Me, Co Bar Assns. Home: 160 Caleb, Portland, Me. Office: 443 Congress, Portland, Me.

BERNSTEIN, Louis, US, rabbi; b. NYC, Apr 2, 1927; s. Samuel and Anna (Richman); BA, Yeshiva U, 1947, ordained rabbi, 1950; m. Pearl Moshel, Mar 13, 1955; c: Sara, David, Sima. Instr, Erna Michael Coll, Yeshiva U since 1968; rabbi: Young Isr of Windsor Park, 1955-68; Glenwood J Cen, Bklyn, 1950-52; instr, Yeshiva U HS, NY, 1954-68. Chaplain, US Army, 1952-54. Pres, Alumni Assn, Yeshiva Coll, 1960-62; chmn: Yeshivath Hadarom since 1961; chaplaincy comm, Rabb Alumni, Yeshiva U, 1961-62; secy, treas, vice-pres, RabCA since 1960; secy, Hapoel Mizrachi, Amer 1955; ed, Rabb Council Record since 1954; mem: J Chaplain Assn; Vaad Harabbonim, Queens. Hobby, tennis. Home: 64-52 Bell Blvd, Bayside, NY. Study: 67-45 215 St, Bayside, NY.

BERNSTEIN, Mark Richard, US, attorney; b. York, Pa, July 4, 1930; s. Phillip and Evelyn (Greenfield); AB, U of Pa 1952; LLB, Yale U, 1957; m. Elouise Kaufman, Mar 23, 1955; c: Phillip, Cary, Adam, Andrew, Jonathan, Evan. Partner: Grier, Parker, Pie, Thompson, Bernstein, Gage & Preston since 1968; Havnes, Graham, Bornstein & Baucom, 1960-68. Lt, US Army, 1952-54. Dir: Temple Beth El; Charlotte Sym Orch Assn; Charlotte Area Fund; pres: B'nai B'rith, Charlotte, 1959-61; Charlotte Civilian Club, 1966-67; chmn: B'nai B'rith Inst on Judaism, 1963; Temple Beth El, 1964-66; Charlotte Isr Bond Dr, 1966-68; mem: Phi Epsilon Pi; Phi Alpha Delta; club: Charlotte Athletic; Olde Providence Racket & Tennis. Home: 6619 Burlwood Rd, Charlotte, NC. Office: 1014 Law Building, Charlotte, NC.

BERNSTEIN, Marshall M, US, attorney; b. NYC, Apr 21, 1901; s. Saul and Sarah (Menline); AB, Columbia U, 1921, LLB, 1923; m. Beatrice Weilburg, Dec 28, 1926; c: Gerald, Carole, Brooks. Partner: Sirota, Bernstein & Steyer; Saul and Marshall M Bernstein, 1926-57; gen counsel, secy dir, Natl Container Corp, 1940-56; partner, Bernstein & Steyer, 1958-61. Mem bd of trustees, Cong Emanu-El, NYC; vice-pres, Cardozo Lodge, B'nai B'rith, 1950; NY exec comm, ADL, B'nai B'rith; club, Men's of Emanu-El, pres, 1937-41. Home: 91 Central Park W, New York, NY. Office 60 E 42 St, New York, NY.

BERNSTEIN, Martin, US, musicologist, educator; b. NYC, Dec 14, 1904; s. Joseph and Ida (Colodny); BS, NYU, 1925; BMus, 1927; m. Juliet Danziger, Nov 7, 1930 (dec); c: Ellen, James; m. 2nd, Virginia Lubkin, Aug 28, 1949; c. Roger, John. Prof, music, NYC, since 1947, head, music dept, since 1955, fac mem since 1926; mem: NY Philharmonic Orch, 1926-28; conductor, Amer Bach Soc, 1949-50. Intelligence off, US Army, 1943-46. Mem: AAUP; Amer Musicological Soc; Coll Music Soc; Soc for Publ of Amer Music. Author: Score Reading, 1932, 1951; co-author, An Introduction to Music, 1937, 51, 65. Recipient, Great Tchr Award, NYU, 1968. Home: 1 Blackstone Pl, New York, NY. Office: NYU, New York, NY.

BERNSTEIN, Marver Hillel, US, educator; b. Mankato, Minn, Feb 7, 1919; s. Meyer and Esther (Alpert); BA, MA, U of Wis; att, U Minn; PhD, Princeton U, 1948; m. Sheva Rosenthal, Sep 19, 1943. Prof politics and public affairs, Princeton U since 1958; guest scholar Brookings Inst since 1969; dean, Woodrow Wilson Sch, Princeton U, 1964-69, asso dir, 1961-64, chmn, dept politics, 1961-64. Chmn, B'nai B'rith, Natl Hillel Commn; mem: bd, Natl Civil Service League; Amer Soc for Public Admn; Natl Acad of Public Admn since 1968; AAUP; Amer Political Sci Assn; fmr: mem: adv council: comm for econ devl; comm for improvement of mgmt; Rockefeller Public Service Award Selection Comm; visiting comm, Kennedy Sch of Govt, Harvard U. Club, Princeton of NY. Author: Regulating Business by Independent Commission, 1955; The Politics of Israel, 1957; The Job of the Federal Executive, 1958; American Democracy, various eds since 1951. Home: 37 McCosh Cir, Princeton, NJ. Office: Princeton U, Princeton, NJ.

BERNSTEIN, Melvin Hillel, US, educator; b. NYC, Apr 21, 1914; s. Harry and Esther (Goodman); BA, CCNY, 1936;

MA, NYU, 1941, PhD, 1951; m. Mae Bellows, Sep 4, 1937, c: Harriet. Prof, Eng, Alfred U since 1949; instr, CCNY, 1939-43, 1946-49. USAF, 1943-46. Pres, Amer Studies Assn, NY State, 1958-59; counsellor, B'nai B'rith Hillel since 1949; mem, Natl Council Tchrs of Eng; ACLU; MLA. Contbr, short story, essays, anthols. Home: Alfred Station, NY. Office: Alfred U, Alfred, NY.

BERNSTEIN, Merton Clay, US, attorney, educator; b. NYC, Mar 26, 1923; s. Benjamin and Ruth (Kleeblatt); AB, Oberlin Coll, 1943; LLB, Columbia Law School, 1948; m. Joan Brodshang, Dec 17, 1955; c: Johanna, Inga, Matthew, Rachel. Prof, law, O State U since 1965; cons, Lab Dept, HEW; Off of Secy, Treasury Dept, 1962; counsel, subcomm on lab, US Sen, 1952; leg asst, Sen Morse, 1952-56; spec counsel, comm on lab and public wfr, US Sen, 1957-58; asso prof, law, U Neb, 1958-59; Walter E Meyer research f, Yale U, 1959-62; lectr, Law Sch, 1961-65; visiting prof, law, Columbia U, 1967-68. US Army, 1943-45. Mem: Ind Relations Research Assn; lab sect, Amer Bar Assn; Natl Acad of Arbitrators. Author: The Future of Private Pensions, 1964; Private Dispute Settlement: Cases and Materials on Arbitration, 1968; contbr to profsl jours. Home: Dublin, O. Office: Coll of Law, O State U, Columbus, O.

BERNSTEIN, Morris (pen name Morey), US, composer, author, poet; b. Capuline, Colo, Feb 29, 1916; s. Isaac and Minnie (Auerbach); m. Evelyn, Jan 10, 1940; c: Barry, Allan, Linda, Richard, Neil. Owner, Finer Arts Records and M Bernstein Music Pub Co since 1960; pres, MG Ent since 1963. Author and composer of numerous songs, including: Ziporah — The Lonely Butterfly, 1967; The Pony Mites, 1969; Julie d'Anne. Home and office: 60 S Glencoe St, Denver, Colo.

BERNSTEIN, Nahum Amber, US, attorney; b. NYC, Sep 5, 1907; s. Charles and Jennie (Steinberg); BSS, CCNY, 1929; LLB, Columbia Law Sch, 1931; m. Maxine Corman, Apr 20, 1941, div; c: Judith, Joan, Seth; m. 2nd, Shirley Evans, Jan 1, 1967; c: Richard, Anne, David. Mem, law firm, Bernstein, Seawell and Kaplan since 1932. Found, off: Amers for Haganah, 1947-48; Materials for Isr, 1947-54; Isr Speaks, publ, 1950-54; began first Amer law off in Isr, 1950; spec cons: Secy of Army, US, 1951-52; dir, Sekely-Hoffman Co, Tel Aviv; pres: Israeli Industries, Tel Aviv; Sol Bloom Family Found; Jerusalem Found; mem, Lawyers Club. Home: Amelia Earhart Lane, Rye, NY. Office: 18 Ahad Haam St, Jerusalem, Isr.

BERNSTEIN, Paul, US, educator; b. Phila, Jan 19, 1927; s. Abraham and Jennie (Geek); BS, Temple U, 1949, MEd, 1950; PhD, U of Pa, 1955; m. Irma Shuster, Apr 10, 1949; c: Jay, Lisabeth. Dean, Coll of Gen Studies and Grad Sch, Rochester Inst Tech since 1966; fmr: chmn, div social sci, Plattsburgh State U Coll, NY, 1964-66; chmn, social sci dept, Lock Haven State Coll, 1960-64; prof, Eur hist, 1955-64; hist tchr, Phila, 1949-55. US Army, 1944-47. Vice-chmn, Clinton Co Planning Comm since 1960; cons, Bucks and Lycoming Co schs; mem: Amer Hist Assn; charter, Soc for Fr Hist Studies; Société d'Histoire Moderne; Phi Alpha Theta; Elks. Author: History of Civilization: to 1640, 1960; History of Civilization since 1500, 1962; mgn ed, Lock Haven Bulletin since 1958; contbr to hist jours. Recipient, research grant in Ger hist, Amer Phil Soc, Phila, 1960. Hobby, philately. Home: 5 Candlewood Circle, Pittsford, NY. Office: Rochester Institute of Technology, Rochester, NY.

BERNSTEIN, Peretz, Isr, legislator, economist; b. Meiningen, Ger, June 12, 1890; s. Samuel and Minna; in Isr since 1936; m. Jenny Michaelson, 1912 (decd); c: David, Rachel, Judith, Moshe; m. 2nd, Adolphine Vigeveno, Aug, 1962. MK since 1949, repr Lib Party; ed, Haboker, daily, 1937-46; mem: ed bd, Pal Tribune, 1944-47; exec, JA, also head trade and ind dept, 1946-48; delg, spec comm to UN, 1947; Isr Provisional Govt Council, 1948-49; Isr Min of Comm and Ind, 1948-49. Pres, Lib Party since 1961; delg, ZCs; fmr: pres: Gen Zionist Party; Zionist Org, Holland; hon ed, Dutch Zionist weekly. Author: Der Antisemitismus als Gruppenerscheinung, 1925, Eng trans, 1951; Der Zionistische Gedanke auf Irrwegen, 1931; Joodse Problematik, 1936. Home: 25 Ben Maimon Blvd, Jerusalem, Isr.

BERNSTEIN, Philip, US, social worker; b. Cleveland, O, June 6, 1911; s. Jacob and Anna (Golufchin); BA, U Mich, 1932; MS, W Reserve U, Cleveland, 1934, hon DDL, 1966; m. Florence Michaelson, June 12, 1938; c: Joel, Paul, Judith.

Exec vice-pres, CJFWF since 1967, exec dir,1955-67, asso dir, dir field service, 1947-55; instr, comty org, 'V Reserve U; fmr: asst, dir, Cleveland J Comty Fed; exec secy, Cleveland JCC, 1935-43. Chmn, social issues and policies comm, mem bd dirs, Natl Assembly for Social Policy and Devl, Inc; mem, Council for Social Planning and Prog Devl; J co-chmn, steering comm, Natl Interfaith Consultation on Social Wfr; bd overseers, Sch of Advanced Social Studies, and adv comm, Inst of Contemporary J Affairs, both Brandeis U;N Amer mem, planning comm, 1971 Intl Conf of J Communal Service; exec comm, comm on comty action, spec comm on training, all Citizens Crusade Against Poverty; staff comm, Interrel Comm Against Poverty; adv comm, Comty Org Curriculum Devl Prog; Council on Social Work Educ; fmr: chmn execs conf, Natl Social Wfr Assembly; pres Natl Conf of J Communal Service; chmn, social service div: FJP, NY; UJA of Gtr NY; mem: ad hoc comm on public wfr, HEW; Empire Housing Found, NY; natl adv comm, AFL-CIO Comty Services Comm; bd and vice-pres, Natl PR Council for Health and Wfr Services; bd and exec comm, Natl Conf on Social Wfr. Contbr to encys, J and gen publs. Home: 320 Central Park W, New York, NY. Office: 315 Park Ave S, New York, NY.

BERNSTEIN, Philip Sidney, US, rabbi; b. Rochester, NY, June 29, 1901; s. Abraham and Sarah (Steinberg); BA, Syracuse U, 1921, hon DST, 1954; att Columbia U, 1922-25; Cambridge U, Eng, 1925; MHL, JIR, 1926; hon DD, Heb U, Jerusalem, 1946; hon DHum, Miami U; m. Sophy Rubin, Nov 6, 1925; c: Jeremy, Stephen, Alice Cannon. Rabbi, Temple B'rith Kodesh, Rochester, NY since 1926; adv, J affairs, US Army Cdrs, Europe, 1946-47. Pres, CCAR, 1950-52, hon chmn; Amer-Isr Public Affairs Comm, chmn, 1954-68; Natl Rabb ORT Comm; fmr pres: Rochester City Club; Rochester City Planning and Housing Council; mem, Monroe Co Hum Relations Comm. Author: What the Jews Believe, 1951; contbr of articles to mags and J publs. Recipient: Man of the Year, Rotary Club, 1958; Civic Medal, Rochester Mus, 1962; Annual Lit Award, Friends of Rochester Public Libr, 1967. Home: 140 Windemere Rd, Rochester, NY. Study: 2131 Elmwood Ave, Rochester, NY.

BERNSTEIN, Robert M, US, attorney; b. Phila, Oct 1, 1894; s. Ben Zion and Anna (Milekof); LLB, U of Pa Law Sch, 1914; m. Edith Levinson, 1919; c: Marshall, Deborah Silver, Samuel. Sr partner, Bernstein & Bernstein, Harrison & Kessler since 1916, specializing in personal injury litigation; delivered series of lectures under auspices of Practising Law Inst and Phila Bar Assn, dealing with handling of personal injury cases; conducted sem for sr law students, U of Pa; mem, sem sponsored by Legal and Med Inst of Amer; F, Heb U, Jerusalem, 1964, lectr. Chmn, Capital Needs Comm for Law Sch, U of Pa; vice-chmn: comm, civil procedure, Phila Bar Assn; Amer Bar Assn; Med-Legal Inst, Phila; devl fund, U of Pa Law Sch; hon dir, Cong Adath Jeshurun; dir, Amer J League for Isr; treas, Phila br, Amer Friends Heb U; f: Amer Coll Trial Lawyers; Intl Coll Trial Lawyers; fmr mem, bd mgrs, U of Pa Law Sch, 1959. Recipient: award, McKean Law Club, U of Pa, 1957; Tribute Dinner, State of Isr, 1962; Hall of Fame Award, S Phila HS, 1964; Alumni Award of Merit, 1964. Home: Cedarbrook Hill Apts, Wyncote, Pa. Office: 1000 Pennsylvania Lumbermens Bldg, Philadelphia, Pa.

BERNSTEIN, Saul, US, organization exec; b. Eng, Feb 10, 1909; s. Jacob and Ada (Bernstein); in US since 1922; m. Estelle Snapp. Admnr, Union of Orthodox J Congs of Amer since 1947; ed, J Life since 1947. Home: 117-01 Park Lane S, Kew Gardens, NY. Office: 84 Fifth Ave, New York, NY.

BERNSTEIN, Seymour, US, physicist, educator; b. Chgo, Feb 20, 1909; s. I S and Etta (Scher); BS, U of Ill, 1930; MS, U Chgo, 1937, PhD, 1939; m. Adelaide Rubin, 1938; c: Ruth Hyman, Irene. Prof, physics, U of Ill, Chgo Circle since 1964; engr, Bur of Engr, City of Chgo, 1930-35; instr, Austin Coll, 1939-42; research asso, Metallurgical Lab, U Chgo, 1942-44; chief research physicist, Oak Ridge Natl Lab, 1944-68; lectr, U Tenn, 1948-60; visiting prof: Isr Inst of Tech, 1955-56; U Miami, 1961-62; US delg, Intl Conf, Peaceful Uses of Atomic Energy, Geneva, 1955; visiting sci, Argonne Natl Lab, summers, 1965, 1967, 1968. F, Amer Phys Soc; mem: Sigma Xi, Tau Beta Pi. Home: 423 Homestead Rd, LaGrange Park, Ill. Office: U of Illinois, POB 4348, Chicago, Ill.

BERNSTEIN, Sidney R, US, editor, business exec; b. Chgo, Jan 29, 1907; s. Charles and Jennie (Greenblatt); att U of Ill, 1924-25; MBA, U Chgo, 1956; m. Adele Bass, Oct 5, 1930; c:

Jannet Wingis, Henry. Pres, Advt Publs Inc since 1964, on staff since 1938; ed dir, Advt Age since 1958, on staff since 1932; ed, Advt Requirements since 1958; visiting lectr, advt, Coll of Communication Arts, Mich State U since 1958; mem, adv comm, Coll of Commerce, Roosevelt U since 1959; asso ed, mgn ed, Hosp Mgmt, Chgo, 1925-31; lectr, advt, U Chgo, 1945-46. Dir, Amer Marketing Assn, 1946-47, vice-pres for marketing mgmt since 1958; mem: Alpha Delta Sigma; Sigma Delta Chi; Beta Gamma Sigma; clubs: Natl Press; Chgo Press; Arts, Chgo. Contbr of articles on marketing research, merchandising and advt. Recipient: Advt Man of the Year award, Chgo Fed Advt Club, 1961; Communications Man of the Year, Chgo Jr Assn of Commerce, 1961; elected to distribution hall of fame, Boston Conf on Distribution, 1961. Home: 534 Stratford Pl, Chicago, Ill. Office: 740 Rush St, Chicago, Ill.

BERNSTEIN, Sylvia, US, artist; b. Bklyn, NY; d. Charles and Anna (Finkelman) Schwartz; att Natl Acad of Design, 1941-46; m. Michael Bernstein, Mar, 1933; c: Davida, Holly, Deborah. One-man shows: Ruth White Gal, 1959, 1960; Silvermine Guild of Artists, Conn, 1960; exhbs: Whitney Mus Amer Art; NY; Butler Inst Amer Art; Portland Mus, Me; Hudson River Mus, NY; Columbia Mus Art, SC; Brick Store Mus, Me; City Cen, NY; Pa Acad Fine Arts; J & M Ringling Mus, Sarasota, Fla; Bklyn Mus; Soc Four Arts, Fla; Norfolk Mus Arts and Scis, Va; Parrish Mus, Southampton; Wadsworth Atheneum, Hartford, Conn; Amer Acad Arts and Letters; Nordess Gal; travelling shows of Amer Watercolor Soc; group shows, Allied and Audubon Artists; Ball State Tchrs Coll, Muncie, Ind; Springfield Mus, Mo; centennial "Hundred Years of Watercolor Painting in Amer", Metrop Mus; collections of: Adlai Stevenson Memorial Inst, Chgo; Whitney Mus Amer Art; Norfolk Mus Arts and Scis, Va; Hudson River Mus, NY; Parrish Mus; Columbia Mus, SC; Stanford U, Cal; Warner Libr, Tarrytown, NY; NYU pvt collections. Mem: Amer Watercolor Soc; Natl Assn Women Artists; Painters and Sculptors, NJ; Phila Watercolor Club; Soc Amer Painters and Sculptors; Knickerbocker Artists; Allied Artists; Audubon Artists; ZOA. Recipient: award, Natl Women Artists, 1954, 1957; N E annual Grumbacher Award, 1958; gold medal, Natl Arts Club, 1957; Nancy A Fuller Award, 1958; Grumbacher Award, Chautauqua Inst, NY, 1958; N E annual Laura M Gross Memorial Award, 1959; award, Parrish Mus, 1960; award, Soc Four Arts, Fla, 1960; Channing Hare Award, Palm Beach, Fla; Dawson Memorial Medal, Phila Watercolor Club. Home and Studio: 8 Circle Rd, Scarsdale, NY.

BERNSTEIN, Theodore Menline, US, journalist, educator; b. NYC, Nov 17, 1904; s. Saul and Sarah (Menline); BA, Columbia Coll, 1924; B Litt, Columbia U, 1925; m. Beatrice Alexander, Sep 2, 1930; c: Eric. Ed dir, Book Div, NY Times since 1969; asst mgn ed since 1952; staff mem since 1925; instr, asso prof, Sch of Journalism, Columbia U, 1925-50. Author: Watch Your Language, 1958; More Language that Needs Watching, 1962; The Careful Writer, 1965; co-author: Headings and Deadlines, 1933; Consultant on Usage, The Random House Dictionary; American Heritage Dictionary. Mem, Sigma Delta Chi. Recipient, dist service award, Journalism Alumni Assn, Columbia U, 1957. Home: 2 Fifth Ave, New York, NY. Office: 229 W 43 St, New York, NY.

BERNSTEIN, Victor Heine, US, journalist; b. NYC, Oct 7, 1904; s. Chanon and Eva (Finn); BA, Columbia U, 1924; BLitt, Sch of Journalism, 1925; m. Selma Krumgold, Oct 25, 1925. Free-lance writer since 1963; fmr: reporter, fgn corresp: NY Times; J TA; dir, PR, JA, NYC, 1949-51; mgn ed, The Nation, 1952-63. Author, Final Judgement: The Story of Nuremberg, 1947; co-author, The Inside Story of the Legion, 1948; contbr to periodicals. Home and office: 120 Chestnut Land Rd, New Milford, Conn.

BERNSTEIN, William Carl, US, surgeon, educator; b. Stillwater, Minn, Apr 12, 1904; s. Isaac and Jennie (Simon); BS, U Minn, 1925, MB, 1927, MD, 1928; m. Mildred Goldberg, Sep 25, 1933; c: William, Paula Hanauer, Jenelle Marcus. Clinical prof, U Minn since 1959, dir, proctology div since 1958; chief, div proctology: US Vet Hosp, 1946; Ancker Hosp, 1946. Maj, US Army MC, atomic bomb project, Oak Ridge, Tenn, 1943-46. Mem: St Paul and Minn Surg Socs; Amer Coll Surgs; Amer Proctological Soc; Phi Delta Epsilon. Contbr to med jours. Home: 740 River Dr, St Paul, Minn. Office: University Hospital, Minneapolis, Minn.

BERNSTEIN, Zvi, Isr, party exec; b. Lith, 1914; s. Chaim and Yocheved; in Isr since 1935; m. 1936; c: Elitsur. Leader, Hapoel Hamizrachi, Natl Rel Party of Isr since 1935; mem: Isr exec, WJC; council, Munic, Tel Aviv; ed bd, Hatzofe, daily newspaper; org agric training cen, Lith, 1931-35. Author: Pamphlets on rel subjects; admn, ed, Dos Yiddische Wort, weekly newspaper, Lith, 1932-35; pres, Pal Off, Kovno, 1932-35; ed, Netiva, 1940-43. Home: 51 Shadeh Hagesher St, Tel Aviv, Isr. Office: 166 Ibn Gvirol St, Tel Aviv, Isr.

BERNSTEIN-COHEN, Miriam, Isr, actress, author; b. Kishenev, Russ, Dec 14, 1895; d. Jacob and Debora (Bernstein) Cohen; in Isr since 1907; MD, Kharkov U, 1918; att Dramatic Sch, Kharkov; Philharmonia, Moscow, 1919-20; studied with Max Reinhardt and Leopold Jessner, Berlin, 1923-25; m. Michael Gor, 1922; c: David, Aviva. Mem, Chamber Theatre since 1952; co-found and actress: Teatron Ivri, 1921; Teatron Eretz Yisrael (Tai), 1923; Comedia Eretz Yisraelit, 1936; toured as one-woman-show, Eur and S Afr, 1927-34, 1938; JNF mission to Balkan countries, 1936-39. Mem, exec comm, Artists Assn of Isr; cultural affairs comm, Histadrut; Revisionist Delg, first Electoral Assembly, 1925; mem, Authors Assn of Isr since 1937. Author: Mephisto, 1937; Be-Eretz Ophir, 1938; Tav'era, 1947; Hava u-Bnoteha, 1953; Isha be-Drakhim, 1954; Olam Ha-Ashlayot, 1961; Dmamot (poetry), 1961; Mahu Teatron for Tevel u-Mloa Ency, 1962; Bein Yom l'Yom, 1967; trans: Poltava by Pushkin, 1946; Sefer Jacob Bernstein-Cohen, 1945; Journal of War by Henri Barbusse, 1949; ed, found, Teatron ve-Omanut, bi-weekly, 1924; contbr of poems, stories and articles to local press and periodicals. Home: 5 Bilu St, Tel Aviv, Isr.

BERNTON, Harry Saul, US, physician, educator; b. Ir, Jan 15, 1884; s. Philip and Rose (Davidson); in US since 1894; BA, Harvard U, 1904, MD, 1908; m. Rhea van Baalan Lowenberg, March 1, 1916; c: Ruth (decd), William, Horace. Pvt practice, allergy, since 1922; clinical specialist in allergy, Bur Agric Chem and Dept of Agric, Wash, DC, since 1936; clinical prof, med, Howard U, since 1948; asst, dir, Bender Lab, Albany, NY, 1909-14; path, RI Bd of Health, 1914-18; instr path, Harvard U, 1915-17; chief bur, preventable diseases, dir biol lab, Health Dept, DC, 1918-19; prof, med jurisprudence, George Wash U, 1919-24; hay fever expert, USPHS, 1922-25; allergist, VA, 1925-33; fac mem, lectr, hygiene, Georgetown U, 1919-21; asso prof, 1921-35, prof, 1935-51, Kober Memorial Lectr, 1956. F: FACP; Amer Coll of Allergy; Amer Acad of Allergy; mem: AMA; Amer Assn of Bacts and Paths; Med Soc of DC; Biol Soc of Wash, DC; S Med Soc; Amer Assn for Study of Allergy, pres, 1927-28; Royal Soc of Med; clubs: Cosmos; Harvard; Clinical; Intl Med; Pan-Amer Med. Contbr to med publs. Recipient, Fisk Prize, RI Med Soc, 1919. Home: 4000 Cathedral Ave, NW, Washington, DC.

BERRY, Louis, US, business exec; b. Liverpool, Eng, Oct 10, 1902; s. Harry and Gertrude (Ross); in US since 1922; m. Betty Eisenman, Sep 1, 1924; c: Harold, Selma Snider. Pres: Intl Hotels, Inc; Midwest Properties; dir, Public Bank of Detroit; pres, Raleigh Hotel, Wash, DC. Mem, natl bds: Weizmann Inst of Sci; UJA; mem, natl cabinet; Hillel Found; JDC; United Ser for New Amer; Amer ORT Fed; JTSA; chmn, natl planning comm: Bonds for Isr; treas, Cong Shaarey Zedek, mem, bd of trustees; mem, bd, J Social Ser Bur; J Wfr Fed; Sinai Hosp; all Detroit; clubs: Knollwood Country; Standard-City; Covenant. Home: 3086 Outer Dr, Detroit, Mich. Office: 3500 David Scott Bldg, Detroit, Mich.

BERSON, Solomon A, US, physician; b. NYC, Apr 22, 1918; s. Jacob and Cecelia (Leiberman); BS, CCNY, 1938; MSc, NYU, 1939, MD, 1945; m. Miriam Gittelson, Dec 24, 1942; c: Wendy, Debby. Prof, chmn, dir, dept of med, Mt Sinai Sch of Med, since 1968; sr investigator, VA, Bx, NY, since 1963, chief, radioisotope service, 1954-68; lectr, phys, Hunter Coll, 1942-45; cons, J Chronic Disease Hosp, Bklyn, 1953-56; bd of sci counselors, NIH, NIAMD, since 1966; natl adv council, 1961-64. Mem: Asso Amer Phys; Amer Soc Clinical Inves; Amer Physiological Soc; Harvey Soc of NY; Endocrine Soc; Soc for Experimental Biol and Med; Alpha Omega Alpha; Phi Beta Kappa; f: NY Acad Med; NY Acad Sci; AMA; AAAS. Contbr to profsl jours. Recipient: awards: 1s Eli Lilly, Amer Diabetes Assn; 1st William S Middleton Med Research; Banting Memorial Lectr and Banting Medal, Amer Diabetes Asso, 1965; Harvey Soc Lectr, 1966; Van Slyke, Amer Asso Clinical Chem 1968; NYU Med Alumni Achievement, 1969.

Home: 159 Yale St, Roslyn, LI, NY. Office: Mt Sinai Hospital, 11 E 100 St, New York, NY.

BERTINI, Aron, (pen name, **K A Bertini**) Isr, writer, teacher; b. Russia; June 14, 1903; s. David and Ella (Grinberg); Licence es Lettres, Sorbonne, Paris, 1927; m. Berta; c: Gary. Bd mem: Heb writers Assn, Tel Aviv, Isr PEN Cen. Author: T'mol Dehe, 1940; Milayil and Bokez, 1951; Mar'otal Haefer, 1954; Sh'evik Kahol, 1961: Bakbuk al pney Hamayim, 1969. Recipient: poetry award, ACUM, Isr, 1959; Jacob Fihman Award, Bessarbian Jewry World Org, Tel Aviv, 1966. Home: 19 Veidat Kattowitz, Tel Aviv, Isr.

BERTINI, Gary, Isr, conductor, composer; b. Bessarabia, May 1, 1927; s. Aron and Berthe (Licht); dipl, Inst of Musicology, Sorbonne, Fr, 1954; dipl, conducting, Paris Natl Conservatoire, 1954; studied composition under: M Seter, Tel Aviv; A Honegger, Paris; m. Rosette Berengole, 1955; c: Orith, Michal. Found, conductor, Rinat choir since 1955; tours: Intl Choir Festival, Paris, 1956; Festival of Sacred Music, It, 1960; US, 1962; fmr: found, musical dir, Israel Chamber Ensemble; guest conductor: Isr Philharmonic Orch; Kol Isr Orch; NY Philharmonic Orch; BBC Sym Orch; Eng Chamber Orch; London Sym; conductor: It; Fr; Switz; mem fac, Isr Acad of Music, Tel Aviv; found, Jeunesses Musicales youth concerts. Served, IDF. Compositions: symphonic music, music for numerous theatrical plays, radio, films. Mem: Natl Council for Culture and Arts; council, Isr Bc Auth. Home: 5 Basel St, Tel Aviv, Isr.

BERZON, Bernard L, US, rabbi; b. Plissa, Pol, Feb. 9, 1913; s. Abraham and Sarah (Sorkin); in US since 1925; ordained rabbi, Yeshiva U, 1935; m. Sylvia Goldentyer, Nov 5, 1935; c: Judith Greenwald, Chananya, Michael, Adina, Azarya. Rabbi: Cong Ahavath Isr since 1939; Bangor J Comty, Me, 1935-39. First vice-pres, RabCA, vice-pres, 1945-49; pres, Rabb Alumni, Yeshiva U, 1966-68; exec mem: NY Bd Rabbis, 1948-50, and since 1968; Hapoel Hamizrachi, 1942-51; vice-pres, Flatbush Council Rabbis since 1968; chaplain, Coney Island Hosp. Author: Non-Economic Elements in the Strike, 1940; Meshumadim, 1943; Good Beginnings, 1962; ed, Manual of Sermons, 1943. Home: 1152 E 26 St, Brooklyn, NY. Study: 2818 Ave K, Brooklyn, NY.

BESSIN, Hyman, Can, business exec; b. Ottawa, Can, Mar 7, 1910; s. Moses and Rachel (Wolinsky); m. Marion Friedman, May 31, 1942; c: Leya, Moshe, Berl, Hershel. Pres: Acklands Ltd, Winnipeg since 1959; McLennan, McFreely and Prior, Vancouver; Mindy's; Daly Inves; Ft Garry Ct; Shane Distributors; Winston Hall; B and V Mgmt Services; dir, Mizrachi Bank of Isr. Natl pres, Can Friends of Bar Ilan U since 1961, U trustee; mem, Natl Mizrachi Org of Can since 1935, natl chmn; dep mem, World Zionist Exec; fmr: pres, Ottawa JCC; mem: Munic Council; hydro-elec comm, both Winchester. Home: 438 Daly Ave, Ottawa, Can. Office: 1300 Michael St, Ottawa, Can.

BEST, David, Isr, architect, town planner; b. Liverpool, Eng, Mar 5, 1928; s. Percy and Rebecca (Silver); in Isr since 1951; dipl, reg architect, Manchester U, Eng, 1951; att MIT, 1967-68; m. Rina Bamral, Oct 20, 1952; c: Zohar, Ehud, Erez. Sr partner, David Best and Adam Eyac Architects and Town Planners since 1958; head, res bldg div, Isr Min of Housing, 1954-58. Brit Merchant Navy, 1945-46; res, engr corps, IDF since 1954. Planner of: Town of Arad; Dimona Civic Cen; Sharett HS, Upper Nazareth; Kibbutz Gonen; Soldier's Hostel, Beersheba; Urban Renewal, Askelon. F: Inst of Research of Architects Assn, Isr; Settlement Research Cen, Rehovot; natl comm: Isr Assn of Environmental Planning; Isr Architects. Author: Israel's Search for an Urban Environment; Shaping Tomorrow's Landscape, 1964. Hobbies: painting, art hist. Home: 15 Zfrania St, Ramat Chen, Isr. Office: 34 Sirkin St, Tel Aviv, Isr.

BETTELHEIM, Bruno, US, psychologist, educator; b. Vienna, Aug 28, 1903; s. Anton and Paula (Seidler); in US since 1939; PhD, U Vienna, 1938; m. Trude Weinfeld, May 14, 1941; c: Ruth, Naomi, Eric. Prof, educ psych, U Chgo since 1952, on fac since 1944; research asso, Progressive Educ Assn, U Chgo, 1939-41; asso prof, psych, Rockford Coll, Ill, 1942-44. F: Amer Psych Assn; Amer Orthopsycht Assn; mem: AAUP; Amer Sociol Assn; Chgo Psychan Soc; Amer Phil Assn. Author: Love is Not Enough, — The Treatment of Emotionally Disturbed Children, 1950; Symbolic Wounds — Puberty Rites and the Envious Male, 1954; Truants from Life — The Rehabilitation of Emotionally Disturbed Children, 1955; The Informed Heart, 1960; Dialogues with Mothers, 1962; The Empty Fortress, 1967; co-author, Dynamics of Prejudice, 1950. Home: 5725 Kenwood Ave, Chicago, Ill. Office: U of Chgo, Chicago, Ill.

BEUBE, Frank E, US, periodontist, educator; b. Kingston, Can, July 1, 1904; s. Jacob and Fanny (Florence); in US since 1930; LDS, DDS, U Toronto, 1930; m. Edith Schweitzer, Oct 5, 1930; c: Eric, Stephen. Head, periodontology div, Sch of Dent and Oral Surg, Columbia U, since 1948, prof since 1953, fac mem since 1930; head, periodontology dept, Presbyterian Hosp since 1941. Pres, Amer Acad Periodontology, 1965; dir, Amer Bd Periodontology; chmn: Comm on Insp and Educ Cens, 1968; pathodontia sect, 1st dist, Dent Soc, 1951; f: AAAS; Amer Coll Dent; NY Acad Dent; mem: Amer Dent Assn; Intl Assn Dent Research; Amer Acad Periodontology; Sigma Xi; Omicron Kappa Upsilon; Amer Acad Oral Path. Author: Periodontology: Diagnosis and Treatment, 1953; Gingivectomy, 1957; contbr to profsl jours. Home: 10 London Terr, New Rochelle, NY. Office: 730 Fifth Ave, New York, NY.

BEYER, Millard C, US, physician; b. Cleveland, O, Mar 26, 1905; s. Harry and Gertrude (Grossman); att: O State U, 1922-23; Adelbert Coll, 1923-26; BA, W Reserve U, 1926; MD, St Louis U, 1930; m. Gertrude Birnbaum, 1931; c: Barbara Black, Nancy Opler. Pvt practice since 1934; on staff, City Hosp, Akron, since 1934; med dir, Civil Defense, 1946. US Army, 1942-46. Pres, Summit Co Med Soc, 1953; vice-pres, Temple Isr, 1950-52; chmn: Summit Co Red Cross, 1954-58; PR Comm, 1946-49; mem, bd: Stan Hywet Found, 1957-59; Heart Assn, 1948-50; Crippled Childrens Soc 1959; United Fund, 1952-58; JWB, 1948-50; J Cen, 1947-49; mem, health commn, chmn, Ambulance Commn, City of Akron, both since 1967; clubs: City; Rosemont Country. Contbr to med jours. Recipient, awards: Sigma Delta Chi, 1956; United Fund, 1957. Home: 230 W Fairlawn Blvd, Akron, O. Office: Second National Bldg, Akron, O.

BEZEM, Naftali, Isr, artist; b. Essen, Ger, Nov 27, 1924; s. Itzhak and Sprinza (Zucker); in Isr since 1939; att Bezalel Sch of Arts and Crafts, 1943-46; m. Channa Liebermann, 1949; c: Itzhak, Shlomo. Exhbs: Biennale, Venice, 1954, 1960; Jerusalem, 1959; Tel Aviv, 1962; Haifa; Sao Paulo, Brazil, 1963; murals: Isr Pavilion, World Fair, Brussels, 1958; tchr, Bezalel Sch of Art, 1946-47. Publ: albums of lithography: Flowers in the Sun, 1959; Laments, 1962; Immigrants, 1964; Immigrant in Desert, 1966. Recipient, Dizengoff Award, Tel Aviv Munic, 1957. Home: 44 Louis Marshall St, Tel Aviv, Isr. Studio: Jaffa, Isr.

BIAL, Morrison David, US, rabbi, author; b. NYC, Aug 29, 1917; s. Jacob and Carrie (Dash); BA, Bklyn Coll, 1941; ordained rabbi, MHL, JIR, 1945; m. Dorothy Berman, Nov 6, 1954; c: Daniel, Anne. Rabbi: Temple Sinai, since 1953; Temple Emanuel-El, Lynbrook, NY, 1944-46; Beth Sholom People's Temple, Bklyn, 1946-50; Free Syn, Mt Vernon, NY, 1950-52. Author: Israel Reborn, 1949; The Passover Story, 1950; The Hanukkah Story, 1951; Hanukkah of the Maccabees, 1954; Passover Into Freedom, 1956; Offering of Prayer, 1962; Liberal Judaism at Home, 1967; co-author: The Rabbis' Bible, Vol I, 1967, Vol II, 1969. Chmn, Summit Clergy, 1955-58. Home: 44 Madison Ave, Summit, NJ. Study: Temple Sinai, Summit, NJ.

BIALER, Yehuda Leib, Isr, curator; b. Warsaw, Pol, Mar 5, 1896; s. Chanoch and Perla (Yekeles); in Isr since 1949; m. Yehudith Sirkis, Mar 1950; c: Neomi Boguslawski, Naftali. Chf curator, Wolfson Mus, Hechal Shlomo, Jerusalem, since 1958; mem, exec comm, Yad Vashem since 1956; dir, Rel Council Dept, Min for Rel Affairs, 1949-65. Mem, Bezal'el Mus Directorate. Author: Oisgetrifte Licht, 1949; Ir Lublin, 1952; Ashdot Yamim, 1957; Min haGnazim, 2 vols (bibliography), 1967, 1969; contbr to encys, mags. Home: 14 Radak St, Jerusalem, Isr. Office: Hechal Shlomo, 58 King George St, Jerusalem, Isr.

BIALKIN, Kenneth J, US, attorney; b. NYC, Sep 9, 1929; s. Samuel and Lillian (Kastner); att: Bucknell U, Lewisburg, Pa, 1947-48. LSE, Eng, 1952; BA, U Mich, 1950; LLB, Harvard Law Sch, 1953; m. Ann Eskind, Aug 19, 1956; c: Lisa. Partner, Willkie Farr & Gallagher, since 1961; lectr, 1965-69; adj asst prof, law, NYU, Law Sch since 1969; dir: Nelson Fund, Inc; Samson Fund; Paragon Natl; Computer Communications Network; U of Haifa Found, secy-treas. Chmn:

comm on securities exch, NY Co Lawyers Assn; sub-comm inves co's and inves advs, comm securities, Amer Bar Assn; vice chmn, natl civil rights comm, ADL; mem: law comm, domestic affairs comm, AJComm, NY; various bar assns; club: Harvard. Contbr to legal and financial jours; frequent speaker, legal forums. Home: 211 Central Park W, New York, NY. Office: 1 Chase Manhattan Plaza, New York, NY.

BIBERFELD, Philipp L, US, rabbi, author; b. Hamburg, Ger, Mar 17, 1901; s. Joshua and Lea (Cassuto); in US since 1939; att Yeshiva Galanta, Czech, 1919-21; JDS, U Hamburg, 1925; rabbi, Beth Hamedrash, Berlin, 1933; Yeshiva, Frankfurt/M, 1933; m. Malwine Caro, Aug 21, 1929; c: Helen Rauch, Dora Goldman, Joshua. Rabbi, Cong Agudas Yeshorim, NY, since 1939; lectr, Talmudical fac, Toralehranstalt, Yeshiva, Frankfurt/M, 1935-38. Author: Dina Dmalchuta Dina, 1925; Einführung in die Jüdische Geschichte, 1936; Der Jüdische Staat, 1937; Das Noachidsche Urrecht, 1938; Judaism and International Law (Israel of Tomorrow, ed, Rabbi Jung), 1946-49; Universal Jewish History, Vol 1, Ancient Jewish History, 1948; The Patriarchal Age, Vol 2, 1962. Home: 621 W 172 St, New York, NY. Study: 4046 Broadway, New York, NY.

BIBERFELD, Pinchas Paul, Isr, rabbi; b. Berlin; s. Chaim and Fanny (Deutchlander); att Rabb Sem; Hebron Yeshiva; Hildesheimer Rabb Sem, Berlin; Heichal Hatalmud, Tel Aviv; m. Malka Tversky; c: Chaim. Sup, Chinuch Azmai Schs; fmr: Youth guide, Yalde Teheran, Mikveh, Isr; dean, Yeshivat Beit Yosef, Tel Aviv; rabbi, syn Chassid Statopol, Tel Aviv. Mem: B'nai B'rith, Haroeh Lodge, Tel Aviv; Tel Aviv Rabbinate. Author: Menoucha Nechona; Yad Shaul; contbr to Men of Spirit by Dr Leo Young, NY; ed, Haneemon, organ of Yeshiva grads; contbr educ and lit essays to press and periodicals. Home: 14 Bilu St, Tel Aviv, Isr. Office: 28 David Yellin St, Jerusalem, Isr.

BIBERFIELD, Henry, Can, scientist; b. Berlin, Ger, Jan 6, 1912; s. Edward and Fanny (Deutschlander), in Can since 1942; MS, U Berlin; advanced deg Heb letters, Beth Hamidrash, Berlin; m. Erna Tauber, 1947; c: Miriam, Fanny, Julienne, Chaim. Chem, Wachtel AG, Leipzig, Ger, 1934-37; chief chem, Fisher, Ltd, London, Eng, 1938; dir, research, A Hollander and Son, Montreal, 1942-66. Pres: Ezra Youth Org, Leipzig, 1933-37; Assn of J Acad, Berlin, 1937; chmn: and co-found, Beth Jacob Sch for Girls, Montreal, 1951-55; publ comm, J Comty Council, Montreal; mem: presidium, Agudath Isr, Montreal; Corp of Profsl Chems; Que; Assn of Textile Chems of Amer and Can; exec, Assn of Orthodox J Sci of Amer; actions comm, Agudath Isr World Org. Lectr: Beth Jacob Tchrs Sem, 1964-65; on Bibl, J, and hist topics to various orgs. Author: The World of Prayer, 1954; David, King of Israel, 1959; The Kuzari, 1947, 3rd ed, 1957; ed (hon), Voice of the Vaad; contbr of articles to: J Life Mag; Can J Chronicle, etc; tech subjects to prof jours. Home and office: 660 McEachran St, Montreal, Que.

BIBERMAN, Ami, Isr, editor; b. Tel Aviv, Aug 7, 1930; s. Shmuel and Jehudith; BA, Tel Aviv U, 1968; m. Irith Shuldenrein, July 15, 1954; c: Osnath, Joram, Tamar. Head, div sci publs, Volcani Inst of Agric Research; mem, Kibbutz Hariel, 1949-55; chf asst, div, field crops, Fac of Agric, 1955-59. Samal, Palmach, 1948-49. Mem, Isr Periodicals Eds. Home: 11, Ben Zion Blvd, Rehovot, Isr. Office: POB 6, Beit Dagan, Isr.

BIBERMAN, Edward, US, artist; b. Phila, Oct 23, 1904; s. Joseph and Eva (Goldich); BS, U of Pa, 1924; att Pa Acad of Fine Arts, 1924-26; m. Sonya Dahl, 1938; d. Sonya Bray. Exhb first works, Autumn Salon, Paris, 1927; lectr, UCLA Extension, LA, 1950; works in Mus Phila; Houston; Orlando, Fla; Youngstown O; LA, Cal; Portland, Ore; Stanford U; in libraries; Tupperware; numerous one-man and group shows: 3 murals commns from US Sect of Fine Arts; Mem, Natl Soc Mural Painters. Authors: The Best Untold, 1954; Time and Circumstance, 1968; host, TV series, Dialogues in Art LA, 1968. Home and studio: 3332 Deronda Dr, Hollywood, Cal.

BIBI, Mordechai, Isr, government official; b. Baghdad, Iraq, July 1, 1922; s. Shlomo and Lily (Kookoo); in Isr since 1945; BLL, Tel Aviv U, 1955; m. Ruth Grajevsky, Sep 9, 1956; c: Amir, Michael, Uri. MK since 1959; Defense Min off, 1958. Lt, IDF, active mem, underground Zionist Movement, Iraq since 1942; i/c Aliya Beth, JA, 1945; continued project, 1949,

until J in Iraq were permitted to legally leave country. Hobbies: philately, carpentry, ceramics. Home: 38 Rokach St, Ramat Gan, Isr. Office: Knesset, Jerusalem, Isr.

BIBRING, Grete L, US, psychiatrist, educator; b. Vienna, Aus, Jan 11, 1899; d. Moritz and Victoria (Stengel) Lehner; in US since 1941; MD, U Vienna, 1924; hon DHumL, Brandeis U, 1968; m. Edward Bibring, Dec 1921 (decd); c: George, Thomas. Research cons, psychoanalytic psych, Radcliff Coll, Mass; cons, psycht service, Faulkner Hosp, Jamaica Plain, Mass; ed adv, Children's Hosp Ency of Child Care; clinical prof, psycht em, Fac of Med, Harvard; psycht-in-chief, em, Beth Isr Hosp, Boston; all since 1965; asst dir, Vienna Psychan Clinics, 1926-30; training analyst: Vienna Psychan Inst, 1933-38; British Psychan Inst, 1938-41; Boston Psychan Inst, 1941, chmn educ comm, 1952-54; spec lectr, psychan psych, Simmons Sch of Social Work, Boston, 1942; psycht cons, Children's Bur, Wash, DC, 1949-54. F, Amer Acad Arts and Sci's; vice-pres, Intl Psychan Assn since 1959, hon secy, 1950-52; mem: NY Acad Sci; Alpha Omega Alpha; Boston Psychan Soc and Inst, past pres; Intl Psychan Group Advancement Psycht; AAAS; fmr: pres, councilor, Amer Psychan Assn; asso mem, Vienna Psychan Soc, 1924, active mem, 1926. Mem, ed bd, Jour of Geriatric Psycht since 1965; contbr to profsl jours. Home: 47 Garden St, Cambridge, Mass. Office: 330 Brookline Ave, Boston, Mass.

BICK, Abraham Joshua, Isr, rabbi, author; b. Minsk, Russ, Apr 24, 1914; s. Schoel and Pearl (Perlow); in Isr since 1969; att Cen Universal Yeshiva, Jerusalem, 1932-35, ordained rabbi; m. Bella Unger, 1938; c: Irving. Rabbi, Adu Tur, Jerusalem. Author: books in Heb, Yiddish, Eng, lit criticism, theol, novels; contbr to Hatzofeh; Sinai; Lamerhav; Al Hamishmar; Hadoar; Jewish Day (Heb and Amer-J Press). Fmr: pres, Union of Ukrainian J in US and Can; mem: RabCA; Yiddish PEN club, US. Home: 45 Hebron Rd, Jerusalem, Isr.

BICK, Alexander N, US, surgeon; b. Yalta, Russ, Aug 9, 1901; s. Nahum and Sophie (Schlamowitch); in US since 1939; MD, Padua U, 1927; m. June 28, 1931; c: Isabella, Maria. Pvt practice since 1941; cons, Bellevue Hosp; asst, surg clinic: Turin U, 1928-31; Milan U, 1931-35; asso prof, surg path, Milan Surg Clinic, 1935-39; chief surg: Hosp of Sondrio, 1936-37; Hosp of Portoferraio, 1937-39; asst instr, clinical asst, dept coloproctology, NY Polyclinic Med Sch and Hosp, 1961-62. Pres, ZOA, 1956-57; mem: AMA; Med Soc, State NY; Med Soc, Co Albany; NY Soc Colon and Rectal Surgs; AGP; NY P Med Soc. Contbr to med jours in It. Hobbies: art collecting, music. Home and office: 1024 Madison Ave, Albany, NY.

BICK, Charles, US, accountant, communal worker; b. Ukraine, Russ, Sep 12, 1912; s. Chaim and Miriam (Horowitz); in US since 1925; att Yeshiva Rabbi Isaac Elchanan until 1932; BBA, CCNY, 1937; m. Sylvia Brill, 1939; c: Hillel, Joseph, Ezra. CPA, with Zemlock, Levy and Bick since 1940. Pres, Hapoel Hamizrachi of Amer, 1950-52; chmn: Amer-Zionist Youth Found since 1963; Rel Orgs for Aliyah, 1955-65; treas, AZC, 1953-63; bd govs: Rel Zionists of Amer, 1957, vice-pres, 1960-61; Amer Financial and Devl Corp for Isr; hon vice-pres, JNF; bd dirs, UJA; bd ed, J Horizon; mem, Zionist Actions Comm; delg: 22nd ZC, Geneva, 24th, 27th ZC, Jerusalem. Contbr to Eng-Heb press. Home: 67-42 Burns St, Forest Hills, NY. Office: 160 Broadway, New York, NY.

BICK, Edgar M, US, orthopedic surg; b. NYC, Apr 3, 1902; s. David and Bertha (Davidson); MA, Columbia U, 1923, MD, Med Sch, 1927; m. Estelle Cohen, Jan 30, 1930; c: Dale Carlson, Anne Ehrenkranz. Em clinical prof, orthopedic surg, Mt Sinai Med Sch since 1962; cons orthopedic surg: Mt Sinai Hosp since 1962; St Clare's Hosp since 1962; Blythedale Hosp since 1962; Brookhaven Hosp; orthopedic lectr: New Delhi; Hadassah Med Cen, Jerusalem, 1967. Lt col, US Army, 1941-46. F: NY Acad Med; Amer Acad Orthopedic Surgs; Amer Coll Surgs; hon mem, Assn Bone Surgs; Mexican Orthopedic Assn; mem: Amer Orthopedic Assn; Orthopedic Research Assn; Intl Soc Orthopedic Surg; Amer Rheum Assn; Latin Amer Orthopedic Assn; World Med Assn; Hist Sci Soc; Intl Soc Orthopedic Surg; adv comm, NY State Dept of Health, 1962; Temple Emanuel; VFW; Assn US Army; clubs: Columbia U; Harmonie. Author: Source Book of Orthopedics, 2nd ed, 1948, reprint 1968, No 30, Med Hist Classics, NYAM; Traumatic Lesions in the Aged, 1960; asso ed, Clinical Orthopedics; contbr, papers mainly on tumors of extremities, histologic devl of the human spine, trauma in the aged, hist of med. Recipient, Gold Medal, Amer Acad Orthopedic Surgs, 1950. Home: 975 Park Ave, New York, NY. Office: 30 E 60 St, New York, NY.

BICKEL, Alexander M, US, attorney, educator; b. Bucharest, Rum, Dec 17, 1924; s. Shlomo and Yetta (Schaefer); BS, CCNY, 1947; LLB, Harvard U, 1949; hon MA, Yale U,1960; m. Josephine Napolino, Oct 17, 1959; c: Francesco, Claudia. Chancellor Kent prof, law, legal hist, Yale U since 1966, fac mem since 1956; Holmes lectr, Harvard Law Sch, 1969; law off, State Dept, Frankfurt, Ger, 1950-51; mem, US Delg, EDC Conf, Paris, 1951-52; law clerk to Justice Frankfurter, 1952-53; spec asst, dir, policy planning staff, State Dept, 1953-54; research asso, Harvard Law Sch, 1954-56; US Army, 1943-45. Mem: Amer Bar Assn. Author: Unpublished Opinions of Mr. Justice Brandeis, 1957; Least Dangerous Branch, 1962; Politics and Warren Court, 1965; New Age of Political Reform, 1969; contbr ed, The New Republic since 1957; contbr to profsl jours. Home: 261 St Ronan St, New Haven, Conn. Office: Yale Law School, New Haven, Conn.

BICKEL, Shlomo, US, author, journalist; b. Uscieczko, Galicia, June 8, 1896; s. Isaac and Beile (Gefner); in US since 1939; DJ, U Czernowitz, Rum, 1922; m. Yetta Schaefer, Mar 6, 1923; c: Alexander. Staff, The Day J Jour since 1940; ed, Freiheit, Czernowitz, 1920-22; pvt law practice, Bucharest, 1923-39; co-ed: Unser Weg, 1926-27; Die Woch, 1934-35; Shoibn, 1936-38. Aust Army, WWI. Pres, Yiddish PEN Cen, 1956-59; chmn, comm of research, YIVO; presidium of bd dirs since 1945, vice chmn, exec comm, YIVO world council, 1935-39; mem: Farband; Yiddish Writers Union; IL Peretz World Council; admn comm, Cong for J Culture. Author: In Sich un Arumsich, 1936; A Shtot Mit Yidn, 1943; Detain un Sachhaklen, 1943; Di Yiddishe Essay, 1946; Yidn Davenen, 1948; Esseyen fun Yiddishen Troier, 1948; Drei Brider Zenen Mir Gewen, 1957; Schreiber fun Mein Dor, vol I, 1958, II, 1965, III, 1969; Rumenie, 1962; Family Ortchik, 1967; Heb trans, Mosad Bialik, 1967; Recipient: Libman Hersch Lit prize, 1964; Bimko prize; Ganapolski Lit award, Paris; H Leivick award, 1968. Home: 890 West End Ave, New York, NY. Office: 183 E Broadway, New York, NY.

BICKERMAN, Elias J, US, historian, educator; b. Russ, July 1, 1897; s. Joseph and Sarah (Margulies); in US since 1942; MA, St Petersburg U, 1918; PhD, Berlin U, 1926. Visiting prof, JTSA, since 1968, fmr research f; privat-dozent, U of Berlin; prof: École Pratique des Hautes Études, Sorbonne; École Libre, NY; U Judaism, LA; Guggenheim F; prof, ancient hist, Columbia U, 1952-67. Russ Army, 1916-18. Office: 3080 Broadway, New York, NY.

BIDNEY, David, US, anthropologist, educator; b. Ukraine, Russ, Sep 25, 1908; s. Samuel and Minnie (Guisman); in US since 1930; MA, U Toronto, 1929; PhD, Yale U, 1932; m. Evelyn Breslin, 1940; c: Martin, Rena. Prof, anthropology and educ, Ind U since 1950, instr, Yeshiva U, 1936-38; Sterling Research F, Yale Grad Sch, 1939-40, fac mem to 1942; research asso, Wenner-Green Found, Anthropological Research, NYC, 1942-50; Guggenheim F, 1950; Ford Found F, 1964. Mem: F, Amer Anthropological Assn, Royal Anthropological Inst; mem: Amer Phil Assn, Amer Folklore Soc. Author: Psychology and Ethics of Spinoza, 1940, 1962; Theoretical Anthropology, 1953, 1967; ed, Concept of Freedom, a symposium, 1963; contbr to phil and anthropological jours; symposia, ency. Spec interests: hist and theory of anthropology, mythology, folk rel, music, theatre. Home: 321 S Jordan Ave, Bloomington, Ind. Office: Indiana Universiry, Bloomington, Ind.

BIEBER, Samuel, US, scientist, educator; b. NYC, Feb 5,1926; s. Hyman and Pauline (Sussman); BA, NYU, 1944, MS, 1948, PhD, 1952; m. Rosalyn Hewitt, Dec 18, 1949; c: Susan, Scott. Campus dean, Fairleigh Dickinson U, Teaneck, NJ since 1969; dean, Richard L Conolly Coll, LIU, 1966-69, prof of biol, 1962-69; asso dean of grad fac, 1962-66; teaching f, NYU, 1948-51; research f, Wellcome Found, 1951-52; sr research biol, Burroughs, Wellcome and Co, 1952-62; asst chief, Radiological Service, CD, City of New Rochelle, 1954-57. Co-inventor and holder of patents relating to cancer chemotherapy. F, NY Acad Scis; mem: Amer Soc Zools; Soc Experimental Biol and Med; Soc Study Growth and Devl; AAAS; Amer Chem Soc; Amer Assn Cancer Research; Sigma Xi; Phi Sigma; Masons. Contbr to profsl jours. Hobbies: photography, piano, model railroading. Home: 1303 River Rd, Teaneck, NJ. Office: Fairleigh Dickinson U, Teaneck, NJ.

BIEDERMAN, Harry, US, dental surg; b. Boston, Mass, Nov 12, 1912; s. Morris and Emma (Dobrow); att Tufts Coll, 1932-34; DMD, Tufts Dent Coll, 1938; m. Anne Gale; c: Gerald, Robert. Pvt practice since 1938. Capt, USAC, 1943-46. Mem: Amer Dent Assn; club, Century. Hobbies: sports, reading. Home: 22 W Boulevard Rd, Newton Centre, Mass. Office: 153 Brighton Ave, Allston Mass.

BIEDERMAN, William, US, attorney; b. New York, July 15, 1914; s. Morris and Ethel (Abrahamowitz); att LIU, 1931-36; LLB, NYU Law Sch, 1937; m. Edna Platt, Nov 26, 1939; c: Jason, Robert. Pvt practice since 1937; lectr: Practising Law Inst, NYU Sch of Commerce. Chmn, Billmore-Merrick Syn Council since 1968; vice-pres, Brotherhood Council, Merrick since 1969; pres, Merrick J Cen, 1965-67; mem: Amer Bar Assn; Nassau Bar Assn; NY Co Bar Assn. Hobbies: tennis, golf. Home: 236 Merrick, Merrick, NY. Office: 280 Broadway, New York, NY.

BIEGEL, Herman Charles, US, attorney; b. New York, Aug 8, 1909; s. David and Tillie (Nusim); BS, cum laude, CCNY, 1930; LLB, Yale Law Sch, 1933; m. Shirley Gubert, June 24, 1930; c: Richard, Judy Sher. Sr partner, law firm Lee, Toomey &Kent since 1950; off chief counsel, Bur of Internal Revenue, 1934-37; partner, Alvord & Alvord, 1942-50; legal adv, Council of Profit Sharing Inds; mem, Pension Research Council, Wharton Sch of Finance, U of Pa; lectr, Tax and Law Insts. Lt cdr, USNR, 1944-46. Mem: NY Bar Assn; DC Bar Assn; Amer Bar Assn; Phi Beta Kappa. Co-author, Pensions and Profit Sharing; contbr, articles to legal jours. Home: 2838 Chesterfield Place, Washington, DC. Office: 1200 18 St N W, Washington, DC.

BIELE, Harry D, US, organization exec; b. Binghamton, NY, Apr 29 1908; s. Max and Ida (Ginsburg); BA, Johns Hopkins U, 1929; att Columbia U, 1936-39; Exec off, UJA since 1961, dir, trade and industry div, 1952-60; exec dir, Natl Comm for Resettlement of Fgn Phys, 1940-44; secy: Amer Comm for Displaced Med Scis, 1940-44; Latin Amer Comm, JDC and Agro-Jt, 1944-45; liaison off, JDC, Lisbon, 1945; dep dir, JDC oprs, Ger, 1945-47. Bd dirs: Amer Friends Heb U; bd trustees, Haifa U Found; club, Johns Hopkins. Home: 353 W 56 St, New York, NY. Office 1290 Ave of Americas, New York, NY.

BIELEY, Louis S, US, journalist; b. Bogopol, Russ, July 12, 1890; S. Solomon and Bessie (Sokolovsky); in US since 1906; att Columbia U; NYU; m. Fannie Orans, Jan 7, 1917; c: Sally. Research worker, underwriter, Union Cen Life Ins Co; bus mgr, J Daily News, 1925-28; circulation mgr, writer, J Morning Jour, 1928-53; weekly column, Doh, Dort und Yiberall, J Amer; contbr articles on Soviet Russ. Chmn: admn comm, Fed of Ukrainian J, 1940-49; pres: fmr, Rabbi Stephen Wise downtown br, Free Syn; Bogopoler Landsmanschaft; fmr chmn, admn comm, Fed of Ukrainian J; delg to Pres of US appealing to intercede on behalf of victims of anti-Jew pogroms; mem: ZOA; profsl div, AJCong; club, Bogopoler Verein. Home: 574 West End Ave, New York, NY. Office: 225 Broadway, New York, NY.

BIELSKI, Martin, Isr, editor; b. Breslau, Ger, July 5, 1921; s. Bruno and Eufemia (Rosenthal); in Isr since 1953; m. Elisabeth Glueckstadt, Mar 3, 1946; c: Reuben, Dan. Asst ed, Yedioth Chadashot daily, Tel Aviv since 1959; ed: Juedische Rundschau vom Illimani, 1945-47; Die Zeit, 1948-53; Hechs, 1948-53; all in Bolivia. Served IDF. Found, Assn for Relations Between Ger-Isr; mentor, B'nai B'rith, Bialik lodge; pres, Isr Info Assn; mem, Isr Journalists Assn; fmr: pres: Theodor Herzl Soc, Bolivia; Haim Nachman Bialik Lodge; vice-pres, Maccabi, Bolivia. Home: 174 Haaluf David, Ramat Gan, Isr. Office: 66 Harakevet Rd, Tel Aviv, Isr.

BIEN, Shlomo, Isr, chemist; b. Nagykanizsa, Hung, Apr 14, 1920; s. Gabor and Gizella (Kaufmann); in Isr since 1946; PhD, Pazmany Peter Tudoma'ny Egyetem, Budapest, 1944; m. Hana Weiss, May 14, 1944; c: Naava, Daniella. Sr lectr, Technion, Haifa since 1955; research chem: Potash Co, 1947-48; Shemen, 1950-55; research asso, Brandeis U, 1961-63. Mem: ACS; London Chem Soc; Isr Chem Soc. Contbr numerous articles to sci jours. Home: 67 Pinsker St, Haifa, Isr. Office: Technion, Haifa, Isr.

BIENENSTOK, Erwin, Eng, journalist, broadcaster; b. Wadowice, Pol, Dec 26, 1908; s. Max and Franciska (Schreiber); in Eng since 1940; LLM, Jagiellon U, Cracow, Pol, 1930;

m. Ruchla Ekchajser, Apr 11, 1948. Head, Heb sect, BBC External Service since 1959; first J corresp: Vienna, 1938; Prague, 1958; ed: J Chronicle News Service, 1947-59; Nouvelles Juives Mondiales; sr corresp, Reuters News Agcy, 1969. Pol Corps in Fr and Brit Armies, 1939-47. Fmr: mem exec comm, Histadrut, Poalei Zion, Pol; dir, J U Students Coop Soc. Author, Benataim Shevi, 1940-41. Recipient: Croix de Guerre with star; Polish Cross of Valor; Brit War Medals. Hobbies: reading, house plants. Home: 106 The Avenue, London NW6, Eng. Office: BBC Heb Service, Bush House, London WC2, Eng.

BIENSTOCK, Herbert, US, economist; b. NYC, Dec 25, 1922; s. Nathan and Anna (Flaum); BBA, CCNY, 1945; att NYU, 1945-47; m. June Klein, June 8, 1947; c: Ruth, Joshua. Regional dir, US Bur of Lab Stat since 1962, with Bur from 1945; adj prof, grad sch of educ, Hunter Coll since 1961; visiting lectr: Yeshiva U since 1967; Cornell U since 1968; instr, LIU, 1945-47. US Army, 1944. Pres, Heb Acad of N Queens; publicity chmn, NY chap, Amer Stat Assn; exec council, NY Stat Assn, 1960-61; bd mem, Bayside Hills J Cen, 1956-59. Author: Job World of 1960's, 1960; American Working Woman, 1961; Career Opportunities in Social Sciences, 1962. Recipient, Outstanding Performance Award, Bur of Lab Stat, 1958. Home: 53-12 Oceania St, Bayside, NY. Office: Dept of Labor, Bur of Lab Stat, 341 Ninth Ave, New York, NY.

BIENSTOCK, Victor Morris, US, journalist; b. Hartford, Conn, May 21, 1908; s. Samuel and Sophie (Bisko); BS, NYU, 1929; m. Rebecca Kosiner, Nov 28, 1936; c: Susan Burke, Marion Burnham. Vice-pres, ed, JTA since 1969, mem staff since 1935; ed, NY Herald Tribune News Service, 1931-33; fgn ed, Overseas News Agcy, also fmr, chief corresp; fmr, ed: London Morning Post; New York World; war corresp, US Army, 1943-45. Mem, Natl Press Club, Wash, DC. Recipient, ETO-ME Ribbon. Home: 47 Barlow Lane, Rye, NY. Office: 660 First Ave, New York, NY.

BIERINGER, Walter H, US, business exec; b. Boston, Nov 17, 1899; s. Leo and Sara (Wolfenstein); BA, Harvard U, 1921; m. Gertrude Kessel, Aug 5, 1922; d. Doris Hiatt. Exec vice-pres, Plymouth Rubber Co since 1922. Chmn, Gov's commn on Ref, Mass since 1948; pres, United Service for New Amer, 1944; natl chmn, UJA, 1953; vice-pres: Assn J Philanthropies; United HIAS Service; mem: bd of trustees since 1934; hon vice-pres, Urban League, 1953; bd of dirs: JDC; ORT; bd trustees, Howard U, 1953; club, Belmont Country. Home: 26 Wolcott Rd, Ext, Chestnut Hill, Mass. Office: Plymouth Rubber Co, Canton, Mass.

BIERMAN, Bernard, US, attorney, composer, author, business exec; b. NYC, Aug 26, 1908; s. Samuel and Dorothy (Adelman); pre-law deg, NYU, 1930; LLB, Bklyn Law Sch, 1932; m. Alice Epstein, July 6, 1933. Pres, Max Epstein Co, Inc since 1960; pvt practice, atty, 1932-42. Author-composer: Midnight Masquerade; My Cousin Louella; Vanity; What More Can I Ask For; The Love of Two Cabbages (children's album); Unless It can Happen With You; This is the Inside Story; Forgiving You; The Hills of Colorado; and others. Cpl, USAF, 1942-45. Vice pres, Assn Master Painters and Decorators, NY; mem: B'nai B'rith; ASCAP. Home: 50 Lenox Rd, Brooklyn, NY. Office: 1325 Utica Ave, Brooklyn, NY.

BIERMAN, Jacquin D, US, attorney, accountant; b. NYC, Jan 19, 1915; s. Alfred and Libbie (Silverstein); BS, summa cum laude, NYU, 1934; LLB, Yale Law Sch, 1937; m. Lema Spanier, Aug 20, 1939; c: Louise Oshatz, Alfred, Michael; m. 2nd, Gloria Freiman, Sep 19, 1967. Mgn partner, JK Lasser and Co since 1947; partner, Chase and Bierman since 1949; adj prof, taxation, div of gen educ, NYU since 1955, Law Sch since 1955, chmn tax study group, mem, adv and planning comm, lectr, inst on fed taxation since 1946; lectr, inst on fed taxation, U Miami since 1947; atty: Newman and Bisco, 1938-40; chief counsel's off, leg and regulation's div, penal div, Bur of Internal Revenue, 1940-45; asst head, Rev div, 1945-46. Mem: Amer Bar Assn; Beta Gamma Sigma; Order of Coif; clubs: Lotos, City Athletic. Author: Tax Shelter in Business, 1955; ed, JK Lasser's Excess Profits Taxes. Home: 31 Wildwood Dr, Kings Point, NY. Office: 666 Fifth Ave, New York, NY.

BIERMAN, Norman, US, attorney, civic worker; b. St Louis, Mo, July 1, 1907; s. Samuel and Hattie (Grossman); BA,

Wash U, 1929, LLB, 1929; m. Margaret Loeb, April 12, 1938; c: Mary Harris, James. Partner law firm, Anderson, Gilbert, Wolfort, Allen & Bierman since 1936; asso, 1929-36. Maj, USAAF, 1942-46. Pres, J Med Social Service Bur, 1947-51; Mo Assn Social Wfr, St Louis div, 1948; Mo Fed Merit System, 1938-43; vice-pres, J child Wfr Assn, 1950; J Orthodox Old Folks Home, 1954-55; vice-pres, Health and Wfr Council, St Louis, 1964; chmn budget comm, health and hosp div, Comty Chest, Gtr St Louis, 1950-52; vice-chmn: St Louis Child Wfr Adv Comm, 1952-55; Health and Hosp Div Planning Comm, Health and Wfr Council, Metrop St Louis since 1959; treas: J Fed, 1950; Citizens Comm for Civil Service, 1946-49; secy Counsel, J Hosp, 1954-59 and since 1967; mem: bd dirs: Vocational Counselling Service since 1957, life mem since 1961; J Hosp since 1951; J Child Wfr Assn, 1946-56; Sommers Children's Bur, since 1946; J Orthodox Old Folks Home, 1949-56; J Aid Assn, 1936-38; J Family Agcy, 1940-41; mem: bd govs, Comty Chest, 1953-57; Mo Council, Natl Civil Service League since 1940; St Louis Mo, State, Amer Bar Assns; Amer Judicature Soc; Judge Advocates Assn; Amer Soc Intl Law; Pi Lambda Phi. Contbr to profsl jours. Home: 7117 Cornell Ave, St Louis, Mo. Office: 705 Olive St, St Louis, Mo.

BIERMAN, William, US, physician, educator; b. NYC, Dec 10, 1893; s. Henry and Katharine (Durst); BA, Columbia U, 1915, MD 1917; m. Mae Friedlander, May 28, 1938. Prof Em, U of Cal, SF, since 1968, mem fac, since 1959; cons, physical therapy: AMA, since 1917; Dept of Hosps, 1936-44; att phys therapist, Beth Isr Hosp, 1930-35; asst clinical prof, therapeutics, NYU, 1936-44; att, phys med, Mt Sinai Hosp, NYC, 1937-59; asst clinical prof, phys med and rehab, Columbia U, 1945-59. Pres, NY Soc Phys Med and Rehab; mem: NY Acad Med; Harvey Soc; fmr pres: Amer Cong Phys Therapy; Soc Phys Therapy Physicians. Recipient: Chevalier, Fr Legion of Honor, 1937; Gold Key, Amer Cong Phys Therapy, 1941; medal, NY Soc for Phys Med and Rehab, 1955; Columbia U 200th Anniversary medal, 1967. Home: 750 Gonzalez Dr, San Francisco, Cal. Office: U of California, San Francisco, Cal.

BIEZUNSKI, Naomi, Isr, scientist; b. Plock, Pol; d. Hillel and Rachel; in Isr since 1938; MSc, Heb U, Jerusalem, 1955, MD, 1958. Research f, lectr, dept urol, Heb U Med Sch; research asso, Weizmann Inst of Sci, 1966-67; research f: Harvard Med Sch, 1965-66; Yale U Med Sch, 1963-65; intern, asst, dep ped, Hadassah Hosp, Jerusalem, 1958-63. Mem: IMA; Isr Biochem Assn. Contbr to profsl publs. Hobby, photography. Home: 40 Hapalmach St, Jerusalem, Isr. Office: Heb University-Hadassah Med Sch, Jerusalem, Isr.

BIHALJI-MERIN, Oto, Yugo, editor, author; b. Belgrade, Jan 3, 1904; s. David and Klara; att Sch of Plastic Arts; m. Elisabeth; c: Mirjana. Fmr: ed, lit mags. Interned, Ger war prisoners camps, 1941-45. Author: Juris u Vasionu (Eng ed, Conquest of the Skies); Spain between Death and Birth; Modern Ger Art, Do vidjenja u Oktobru (Au revoir in October); Misli i boje (Thoughts and Colours); Susreti sa mojim vremenom (Encounters with our Time); Modern Ger Art, Eng ed; theatre plays: Invisible Door; Mala zemlja izmedju svetova (A Small Country among Worlds); books on art: Yugoslav Sculpture in the Twentieth Cent; Byzantine Frescoes and Icons in Yugo; Art of the Primitives in Yugo; Das naive Bild der Welt (Eng ed, Modern Primitives, Masters of Naive Painting); co-author: Bogomil Art; Bogosav Zivkovic — The World of a Primitive Sculptor; Prodori moderne umetnosti (Abenteuer der modernen Kunst); monographs on artists; contbr: prefaces of catalogues; essays in mags; books appeared in Eur and USA. Home: Nemanjina 3, Belgrade, Yugo.

BIKEL, Theodore, US, folksinger, actor; b. Aus, 1924, lived in a kibbutz in Isr; in US since 1954; grad, Royal Acad Dramatic Art, London. Appeared on stage: The Lark; The Rope Dancers; The Sound of Music; Brecht on Brecht; Fiddler on the Roof; in movies: I Want to Live; The Angry Hills; The Defiant Ones; My Fair Lady; The Russians are Coming; My Side of the Mountain; Darker than Amber; starred in maj TV progs; recording artist for Elektra and Reprise Records. Found, mem, Cameri Theatre, Tel Aviv; fmr natl vice-pres, AJCong, chmn gov council; co-chmn, commn on J Affairs; delg. Plenary World J Cong, 1966; PM Conf, Jerusalem, 1969. Office: 25 Bank St, New York, NY.

BIKERMAN, Jacob Joseph, US, physical chem; b. Odessa, Russ, Oct 26, 1898; s. Joseph and Sarah (Morgulis) Bickerman; in

US since 1945; att U of St Petersburg, Russ, 1916-21; m. Valentina Leivand, Aug 31, 1933; c: Michael, Dina Schoonmaker. Research asso: Horizons, Inc, since 1964; MIT, 1956-64; held several acad and ind positions in Russ, Ger, Gt Brit and US. Mem: Amer Chem Soc; Brit Soc Rheology; Soc of Rheology. Co-author: Kapillarchemie, 1930, 1932; Surface Chemistry for Industrial Research, 1948; Foams, 1953; Surface Chemistry, 1958; The Science of Adhesive Joints, 1961, 2nd ed, 1968; contributions to Thermodynamics of Surfaces, 1961 and numerous papers. Home: 15810 Van Aken Blvd, Shaker Heights, O. Office: Horizons, Inc, Cleveland, O

BILDERSEE, Adele, US, educator; b. NYC, Sep 4, 1883; d. Barnett and Flora (Misch); BA, Hunter Coll, 1903; MA, Columbia U, 1912, PhD, 1932; DHL, Bklyn Coll, 1955. Ret; prof, Eng, Bklyn Coll, 1938-54, on fac since 1930; asso prof, Hunter Coll, 1926-30; acting dean, Bklyn br, Hunter Coll, 1926-30. Mem, bd of trustees: Bklyn Assn for Mh; Bklyn JCC; Bklyn J Hosp; JDC. Author: Jewish Post-Biblical History through Great Personalities, 1918; The Bible Story in the Bible Words, 1924-27; Imaginative Writing, A Course in College Composition, 1927; A Study of State Scholarship Students at Hunter Coll, 1932; The Hidden Books, Selections from the Apocrypha for the General Reader, 1956. Hobbies: music, theater, nature study. Home: 135 Eastern Pkwy, Brooklyn, NY.

BILDERSEE, Barnett, US, public relations exec; b. NYC, Apr 6, 1911; s. Isaac and Selena (Ullman); BL, Columbia U, 1932; m. Ada Kogan, June 30, 1934; c: Adele Feldman. Pres, Bildersee PR since 1963; reporter, NY Evening World, 1928-31, Providence Jour, 1933-34; London corresp, NY Post, Philadelphia Public Ledger Syndicate, 1932-33; cable ed, AP, NYC, 1934-40; fgn news ed, day city ed, PM and NY Star, 1940-49; vice-pres, Allied PR Associates, Inc, 1953-54; exec vice pres, 1954-56; dir, vice-pres, chmn, plans bd, Tex McCary, NYC, 1957-58; exec vice-pres, 1958-61; pres, Martial, 1961-63. Sr field repr, OWI, 1943. Mem: PR Soc of Amer; Soc Silurians; US Power Squadrons; Sigma Delta Chi; club, Advertising, NYC. Hobbies: photography, boating. Home: 205 West End Ave, New York, NY. Office: 18 E 41 St, New York, NY.

BILOVSKY, Maxwell M, US, business exec; b. Phila, Pa, Apr 5, 1901; s. Joseph and Frances (Folkman); att Drexel Inst, 1916; m. Betty Keller, June 7, 1935; c: Frances Turkish. Pres: Ind Elec Corp since 1942; Secnarf Realty; Magno Tronic; Crown Starter; mem, NY Stock Exch since 1937. Mem: Pa Soc; Monmouth Hist Soc; Mason-Shriner; clubs: Jumping Brook Country; Natl Rep; Buttonwood, NY Stock Exch; Downtown. Hobbies: collector of objets d'art, silverware, antiques, furniture. Home: 2 Spier Ave, Allenhurst, NJ. Office: 295 Halsy St, Newark, NJ.

BINDEMAN, J E, US, attorney; b. Baltimore, Md, Mar 24, 1913; s. Isaac and Sarah (Drobis); LLM, Georgetown U, 1939; m. Julia Paul, Mar 22, 1942; c: David, Stuart. In pvt practice since 1937. Chmn, Public Wfr Adv Council, DC; mem, bd dirs: AJComm; Wash Heb Cong, pres, 1958-60 Home: 3020 Brandywine St, NW, Washington, DC. Office. 606 Landmark Bldg, 1343 H St, NW, Washington, DC.

BIN-NUN, Yehiel, Isr, teacher, b. Rohatyn, Galicia, Apr 10, 1911; s. Yoel and Esther (Srohlicht) Fisher; in Isr since 1939; ordained rabbi, High Coll of Judaistics, Berlin, 1937; att U Berlin, 1929-32; PhD, U Heidelberg, 1936; m. Shochana Furst, 1943; c: Yoel, Elhanan, Zipora, Esther. Headmaster, Rel Govt Sem for Tchrs and Kindergarten Tchrs, Haifa, since 1950; lectr, Talmud, High Coll of Judaistics, Berlin, 1937-38; tchr, Reali HS, Haifa, 1939-50; headmaster, tchr, Rel Secondary Sch for Girls, Haifa, 1950-62. Haganah, 1949-48. Prin contrib: research work in Bible; Heb and Yiddish philol. Mem: Acad for Heb Lang, 1949-68; Bc Council in Isr, 1966-68; various comms, Min of Educ, Autho r: Das Yiddishe, 1938; contbr to profsl publs. Home: 10a Smolenskin St, Hiafa, Isr. Office: 101 Naweh Shaanan Rd, Haifa, Isr.

BINYAMINI, Israel, Isr, public servant; b. Rivnitza, Russ, 1911; in Isr since 1925; dipl engr, Fr, 1935; m. 2 c. With Solel Boneh since 1928; vice mayor, Ramat Gan since 1967; mem, Ramat Gan Munic Council since 1950. Found, mem secretariat, Isr Engrs and Architects Assn; chmn, City Planning Council, Ramat Gan Munic. Office: Ramat Gan Municipality, Isr.

BINZER, Herman S, US, attorney; b. Indianapolis, Ind, Jan 7, 1904; s. Michael and Elizabeth (Goldman); AA, U Toledo, 1924, BA, 1926, LLB, 1931; m. Bertha Desenberg, June 30, 1941; c: Renee, Herbert. In pvt law practice since 1930. Lt-col, US Army, 1942-46, off res, 1927-55, ret off, 1964. Mem: Amer, O State and Toledo Bar Assns. Hobbies: golf, baseball, football. Home: 2030 Richmond Rd, Toledo, O. Office: 1111 Edison Bldg, Toledo, O.

BINZER, Mildred Meyers, US, attorney; b. Peoria, Ill, Nov 30, 1909; d. Mandel and Gertrude (Stein) Meyers; att U Mich, 1926-29; JD, U Toledo, 1946; m. Royal Binzer, July 23, 1929. Mem, Zona Intl; past pres, and mem bd, Toledo Women's Traffic Council; Amer Acad Matrimonial Lawyers; mem, C of C; bd mem, Council J Women; Bus and Profsl Women's Club; World Peace Through Law Fed; State Fed, Bus and Profsl Women's Club; mem, bd League of Women Voters; Amer Assn U Women; Toledo-Lucas Co Safety Council; Amer Soc Intl Law; Commercial Law League; chmn, traffic safety, City of Toledo; fmr pres and mem, exec comm, out of state scholarship comm, U of Mich; mem: Lucas Co, Toledo; O State, Amer, and Intl Bar Assn; Natl Assn Women Lawyers; Federacion Internacional des Abogados; Kappa Betta Pi; Order Eastern Star; Natl Aeronautical Assn; Ohioana Soc; PAL auxiliary; Toledo Civic Playgoers Assn; clubs: Toledo Artists, Toledo Women's, Zona, past pres. Contbr to law jours. Home: 3105 Darlington Rd, Toledo, O. Office: 426 Spitzer Bldg, Toledo, O.

BINZER, Royal B, US, attorney; b. Indianapolis, Ind, Dec 19, 1899; s. Michael and Elizabeth (Goldman); BA, U Toledo, 1919; LLB, St John's U, 1920; m. Mildred Meyers, July 23, 1929. Pvt law practice since 1920; spec counsel to Atty Gen of O, 1932-68; admitted to: US Dist Court; US Court of Appeals; Supr Court; ICC. Mem: Amer, O State, Toledo Bar Assns; Lucas County Bar Assn, pres, 1939; past cdr, Amer Legion; past pres, Natl Sojourners; monarch O-Ton-Ta-La Grotto; Old Newsboys' Assn; C of C Masons; Eagles; Res Offs Assn; Commercial Law League of Amer; club, Rep. Home: 3105 Darlington Rd, Toledo, O. Office: 426 Spitzer Bldg, Toledo, O.

BIRK, Meir, Isr, physics engr; b. Rietava, Lith, Oct 7, 1924; s. Eliahu and Masha (Lipowitz); in Isr since 1926; att Yeshivat Ha Yishuv Hehadash, Tel Aviv, 1938-42; engr dipl, Technion, Haifa, 1949; PhD, Weizmann Inst, Rehovot, 1962; m. Yehudith Gershtanski, Feb 11, 1948; c: Itshak, Ohad-Shmuel. Asso prof, Weizmann Inst since 1965, research asso, sr sci, 1954-65; research asst, Princeton U, 1955-56; elec research engr, Lawrence Radiation Lab, U Cal, 1962-63. Capt, IDF, 1948-54. Prin contribs, devl of elec instruments for nuclear physics research. Publ papers in field of nuclear physics and nuclear instruments. Home: Yad Weizmann, Meonot Wolfson A, Rehovot, Isr. Office: Weizmann Inst of Sci, Rehovot, Isr.

BIRK, Yehudith, Isr, scientist; b. Grajevo, Pol, Sep 30, 1926; d. Itzhak and Frida (Browitz) Gershtanski; in Isr since 1935; MSc, Heb U, Jerusalem, 1950; PhD, Heb U, Rehovot, 1954; m. Meir Birk, Feb 11, 1948; c: Itshak, Ohad-Shmuel. Asso prof, Heb, U, Rehovot since 1966; instr, sr lectr, Heb U, 1956-66; post-doctorate f, Rutgers U, NJ, 1955-56; research biochem, U of Cal, Berkeley, 1962-63. Lt, IDF, 1948-49. Prin contribs, studies of the chem and nutritional significance of plant proteins and accompanying antimetabolites. Hon secy, Isr Biochem Soc, 1964-66. Contbr of articles in the field of research in bio-chem, nutritional jours. Home: Yad Weizmann, Meonot Wolfson A, Rehovot, Isr. Office: Heb U, Fac of Agric, Rehovot, Isr.

BIRNBAUM, Herbert, US, rabbi; b. Nürnberg, Ger, Oct 17, 1926; s. Bernhard and Frieda (Oppenheim); in US since 1940; BS, Johns Hopkins U, 1950; MA, George Washington U, 1954; EdD, U Md, 1963; Rabbi, Ner Isr Rabb Coll, Baltimore, 1952; m. Eva Altmann, Aug 12, 1951; c: Bernhard, Meyer, Eli. Dir, supervision and tchr placement, Bd of J Educ since 1967; prin: Petach Tikvah Heb Sch, 1953-57; Isaac Davidson Heb Sch, 1957-62; asst dir, Elem Heb Schs, Bd of J Educ, 1962-67. Pres, RabCA, Md Region, vice-pres, secy, 1965-67; mem, Heb Tchrs Assn. Contbr to rel publs. Home: 3414 Devonshire Dr, Baltimore, Md. Office: 5800 Park Hgts Ave, Baltimore, Md.

BIRNBAUM, Hermann, US, chemist; b. Gera, Thuringia, Ger, Apr 30, 1905; s. Juda and Rosa (Weisenthal); in US since 1935; PhD, U Leipzig, 1932; m. Minnie Wise, Jan 30, 1944;

c: Mark. Vice-pres, research and quality control, Carnegie Inst of Tech since 1961; research chemist since 1937, research asst, 1935-36; instr, Duquesne U, 1936-37. Prin contrib, inventor of process for continuous manufacture of concentrated monoglycerides. Contbr of articles to tech jours. Home: 5701 Munhall Rd, Pittsburgh, Pa. Office: 1300 Island Ave, McKees Rocks, Pa.

BIRNBAUM, Irwin, US, attorney; b. Rochester, NY, Jan 9, 1930; s. Harold and Reva (Levin); BA, Syracuse U, 1950, LLB, Coll of Law, 1952; m. Leta Kuppermann, Dec 23, 1951; c: Memdi, Daniel. Partner, law firm, Birnbaum & Harris since 1969; admitted to practice NY, 1953; asst dist atty, Onondaga Co, 1959-61; partner: Goldberg & Birnbaum, 1962; Rizzo, Aloi, Grasso & Urcinoli,1962-68; arbitrator, Amer Arbitration Assn, 1965-70; asso, Julien, Glaser & Blitz, 1968-69; cons, Onondaga Legal Services Corp, 1966-68. Mem: Amer Bar Assn; Onondaga Co Bar Assn, bd, dirs, 1966-67, chmn, family court comm, 1965, co-chmn, court house comm, 1967; Natl Dist Atty Assn; Amer Trial Lawyers Assn; NY State Bar Assn; Upstate Trial Lawyers Assn, bd, dirs, 1967-70; NY State Assn of Trial Lawyers; Syracuse Law Coll Assn; bd, dirs: Legal Aid Soc, 1970; Priority One Gtr Syracuse Inc, 1970; Syracuse U Alumni Interfraternity Council. Ed, Upstate Trial Lawyers Newsletter. Recipient: Alumnus Award, Syracuse U Interfraternity Council, 1966. Home: Old Farm Rd, Fayetteville, NY. Office: 925 University Bldg, Syracuse, NY.

BIRNBAUM, Milton, US, educator; b. Przemysl, Pol, June 6, 1919; s. Hyman and Theresa (Kleinhaus); in US since 1928; BA, CCNY, 1942; MA, NYU, 1948, PhD, 1956; m. Ruth Kushner, June 23, 1946; c: Ellen. Prof, chmn Eng dept, Amer Intl Coll, since 1962, on fac since 1948. US Army, 1942-45. Mem: AAUP; MLA; Natl Council of Tchrs of Eng; Coll Eng Assn; Kadimoh Cong; Phi Beta Kappa. Contbr of articles and revs to profsl jours. Hobby, music. Home: 132 Groveland St, Springfield, Mass. Office: Amer Intl Coll, Springfield, Mass.

BIRNBAUM, Philip, US, author; b. Zarnowiec, Kielce, Pol, Apr 15, 1904; s. Abraham and Roza; BA, Howard Coll; PhD, Dropsie Coll. Major works: The Arabic Commentary of Yefet ben Ali the Karaite on Book of Hosea, 1942; Maimonides' Mishneh Torah, 1944; HaSiddur HaShalem, 1949; Mahzor haShalem, 1951; The Passover Haggadah, 1953; A Treasury of Judaism, 1957; A Book of Jewish Concepts, 1964; Fluent Hebrew, 1966; High Holyday Prayer Book, 1963. Heb Eng ed, Maimonides' Mishneh Torah, 1967; contbr to Heb and scholarly jours. Dir: Asso Heb Sch; Sch Advanced J Studies; mem: ZOA; Histadruth Ivrith, Natl Council J Educ; The J Cen Syn, NYC; Farband Lab, Isr; Natl Assn Profs of Heb; Amer Acad J Research Home: 41 W 86 St, New York, NY. Office: 79 Delancey St, New York, NY.

BIRNBAUM, Z William, US, educator; b. Lwow, Pol, Oct 18, 1903; s. Ignacy (Isaac) and Lina (Nebenzahl); in US since 1937; LLM, U Lwow, 1925, PhD, 1929, postdoc research, U Goettingen, Ger, 1929-31, actuarial dipl, 1931; m. Hilda Merzbach, Dec 20, 1940; c: Ann, Richard. Prof, math, U of Wash, since 1939; dir, lab of stat research, since 1948; actuary, Phoenix Life Ins Co, 1931-37, in Vienna and Lwow; visiting prof: Stanford, 1951-52; U Paris, 1960-61; U Rome, 1964. Pres, Inst of Math Stat, 1963-64; f: Pol Inst of Actuaries, 1933; Amer Stat Assn; mem: Amer Math Soc; AAUP; J Family and Child Service; B'nai B'rith. Contbr to research publs and profsl jours; ed, Annals of Math Stat, since 1967. Home: 14620 SE 55, Hilltop Community, Bellevue, Wash. Office: U Washington, Seattle, Wash.

BIRNKRANT, Norman Howard, US, attorney; b. NYC, Aug 22, 1908; s. Maurice and Tilly (Schelberg); LLB, JD, Detroit Coll of Law, Mich, 1924-30; postgrad studies, U's: Mich; Detroit, 1928-32; grad, Sem J Studies, Temple Beth-el Coll, 1948; m. Phyllis Zelens, May 30, 1956; c: Terry Miller, Madge Grossman. Partner, law firm, Birnkrant, Birnkrant & Birnkrant; Aus Consul Gen for State of Mich, since 1953. Pres: Young People's Club, Temple Beth-El; JCI, Detroit and Windsor chap; US Jr C of C, 1939; Detroit chap, Federal Bar Assn; sr vice pres, Econ Cub, Detroit; mem: intl and comparative law sect, Amer Bar Assn; B'nai B'rith; spec intl adv, World Trade Club, US C of C. Author: Diploma for Diplomacy; Juvenile Welfare, 1939; Relief and Remedies of International Litigation, 1964. Spec interest, research in intl law. Home:

1525 Balmoral Dr, Detroit, Mich. Office: 1300 First National Bldg, Detroit, Mich.

BIRON, Jakob Markus, Eng, organization exec; b. Dukla, Pol, Nov 9, 1908; s. Brucha Fink; in Eng since 1939; att Höhere Handels Schule, Zwickau, Ger, 1923-26; m. Debora Freier, Oct 1931; c: Ruth Rogoff, Salman. Regional dir, JPA; regional org, JNF; gen secy, ZC, Leeds, all since 1944. Orig, F Groups, JNF, Leeds 1949, now many groups in Eng and abroad. Hon treas, gov, Selig Brodetzky J Primary Sch; chmn, Isr Settlers' Relatives Assn; exec mem J Repres Council; mem Council: Talmud Torah; United Heb Cong; Bd of Shechita, all Leeds; mem, bd govs, Habonim; financial secy, Blue & White Bazaar; mem mgmt comm, Moortown Syn; fmr: hon secy, marriage sect, Chassidishe Syn, mem, bd deps; mem: B'nai B'rith, 1055 Leeds. Hobby, communal and charitable activities. Home: 32 Broomhill Dr, Leeds, Eng. Office: Chapletown Rd, Leeds, Eng.

BIRSHTEIN, Yssel, Isr, author; b. Lublin, Pol, Sep 24, 1920; s. Noah and Malka (Jurberg); in Isr since 1950; m. Margaret Waisberg, June 14, 1941; c: Hannah Burstein, Nurit. Author: Under the Skies, Yiddish poems, 1949; Oif Shmule Trotuarn, 1958; A Mantle Fun A Printz, short stories, 1969; Tzipiyah (Heb), 1966. Fmr, secy, JNL Kadimah, Melbourne. Austr Army, 1941-45. Recipient: Award, Yiddish World Cong, Paris, 1960; Stolar Prize, Arg, 1959. Home: 49 Remez St, Kiriat Tivon, Isr. Office Heirut, Kiriat Tivon, Isr.

BISER, Erwin, US, operations research analyst; b. Felshtin, Ukraine, Russ, July 17, 1909; s. Samuel and Bertha (Sapir), desc of Baal Shem Tov; in US since 1921; BA, U of Pa, 1930, MA, 1931, PhD, 1938; c: Samuel, Loren, Sarah, Pamela. Chief, Oprs research analyst, Avionics Labs, US Electr Command, FT Monmouth; lectr, math, Monmouth Coll; prof, math: U of Kan City, 1946-47; Rutgers U, 1947-51. Mem: Oprs Research Soc Amer; Amer Math Assn; Masons; B'nai B'rith; Phil Assn; Phil Beta Kappa; Assn Symbolic Logic. Author: A General Schema for Natural Systems, 1938; Partition of Information Spaces, 1961; Cybernetic and Information Correlators, 1965; Time and the Physical World, 1952; Cybernetics and System Analysis, 1968; contbr to sci, phil and stat jours. Hobbies: piano, adult educ. Home: 103 Shark River Ave, Belmar, NJ.

BISGYER, Maurice, US, social worker, administrator; b. Bklyn, Aug 28, 1897; s. Joseph and Sarah (Flaumenhaft); BA, NYU, 1918, MA, 1919, Butler f, 1918-19; D HumL, hon, 1959; m. Hoda Rosenberg, July 7, 1925; c: Jay, Doris. Vice-pres, Natl Conf on Citizenship; exec vice-pres, B'nai B'rith, 1956-65, hon vice-pres since 1965, secy, 1937-65; secygen, Coordinating Bd of J Orgs, cons to UN since 1949; appointed by State Dept to US Commn, UNESCO, 1958; instr, NYU, 1918-19; pres, Natl Assn J Cen Workers, 1931-32. Mem: Natl Adv Comm of Educ; Atty Gen Comm, Juvenile Delinquency, 1946-47; Natl Conf J Social Wfr; Council, Amer J Hist Soc; Phi Beta Kappa. Author: Challenge and Encounter, 1967; co-author, Henry Monsky, The Man and his Work, 1947; ed bd, The American Zionist (ZOA). Home: 5500 Prospect St, Chevy Chase, Md. Office: 1640 Rhode Island Ave, NW, Washington, DC.

BISNO, Julius, US, organization exec; b. Memphis, Tenn, Apr 20, 1911; s. Jacob and Evelyn (Segal); PhB, Creighton U, Nebr, 1933; att: U Chgo; Amer U, 1933-34; George Washington U, 1938-39; m. Rose Cohen, Apr 16, 1935; c: Jay. Exec secy, J Comty Found, LA since 1955; Asso exes dir, J Fed Council of Citr LA since 1959 mem: bd dirs: Natl B'nai B'rith Youth Commn since 1962; J Hist Soc Amer since 1954; Natl Manuscript Soc since 1954; natl council JDC since 1950; natl council, J Comm on Scouting since 1945; CFJWF since 1950; bd regents, Brandeis U, Hyatt Inst since 1967; secy, S Cal Hist Soc; mem: J Hist Soc, Eng; B'nai B'rith; fmr: exec dir, United JWF, LA; natl dir, AZA, B'nai B'rith; natl exec dir, B'nai B'rith Youth Org; asst exec secy, LA JCC. Ed: The Shofar, 1933-45; AZA Program Guide, 1933-45; AZA Leader, 1940-45; mem natl ed bd, The Jewish Digest. Recipient: Sam Beber Award, AZA, 1953. Spec interest: collection of original autographs and manuscripts, specializing in Judaica. Home: 1616 San Ysidro Dr, Beverly Hills, Cal. Office: 509 N Vermont Ave, Los Angeles, Cal.

BISSELICHES, Moses, Isr, mechanical engr; b. Brody, Pol, Dec 29, 1878; s. Samuel and Rebecca (Klötzel); in Isr since 1949; att Rabb Sem, Budapest; ME, Tech HS, Budapest, 1902; m.

Franziska Greiner, Oct 26, 1919 (decd); c: Daniel, David. Fmr: mech engr, factory owner, Budapest; participated in rebuilding Danube Bridges after WWII. Hon pres, Herzl's Sons, Tel Aviv; sr off, Maccabi Zionist Students, Budapest, Isr; fmr pres, Zionist Org, Hung. Contbr articles on Zionism. Home: 41 Taiber St, Givatayim, Isr.

BISTRITZKY, (Agmon), Nathan, Isr, author, playwright; b. Zwenigorodka, Russ, Aug, 1896; s. Shmuel and Bella (Pelah); m. Haya Goodman, 1917; c: Samuel, Jacob. Author: Yomim ve Leiloth, 1924; Shabbeti Zvi, 1936; Yerushalaim ve Romi, 1941; Kismei Yabeshet, 1947; Leil Yerushalaim, 1950; Ecce Homo, 1954; Or Ganus, 1954; Theodore Herzl, 1955; Mahlafoth Avschalom; Herostrath, 1956; Don Quixote, 1956; The Vision of Man, 1957; trans into Heb: Don Quixote by Miguel Cervantes, poetry of Pablo Neruda. Recipient: title of academician, Royal Acad Fine Letters, Spain, for 1st complete trans, Don Quixote into Heb, 1958. Home: 9 Mevo Yoram, Jerusalem, Isr.

BITAN, Moshe, Isr, government official; b. Olomouc, Czech, Oct 17, 1918; s. Adolf and Helene (Deutch) Baumgarten; in Isr since 1939; att LSE, 1946-47; Harvard Sch of Bus, 1959; m. Leah Magnus, Aug 29, 1947; c: Elisha, Giora. Asst dir-gen, Min for Fgn Affairs since 1966; mgn dir, Koor, 1955-60; ambass of Isr to: Ghana, 1960-62; Swed, 1962-64. Home: 17 Washington St, Jerusalem, Isr. Office: Min for Fgn Affairs, Jerusalem, Isr.

BITKER, Bruno Voltaire, US, attorney; b. Milw, Wis, Feb 5, 1898; s. Jacob and Sara (Rubin); LLB, Cornell U, 1921; m. Marjorie Marks Mayer, 1957; adopted c: Robert. Pvt practice since 1921; mem, Sewerage Commn, Milw, 1931-53; spec counsel: Gov of Wis, 1937; State Banking Commn, 1938; chmn, Citizens Adv Comm, Greendale, 1938; cons, off of Produc Mgmt, Wash, 1941; Wis State counsel and dist dir, OPA, 1942-44; chmn, State Public Utility Arbitration Bd, 1947; mem and off: Gov's Commn on Hum Rights, 1947-56; Milw Commn on Hum Rights, 1948-55; chmn: Milw Commn on Living Cost and Food Conservation, 1947; Econ Study Commn, Milw, 1948; spec prosecuting atty, gambling inves, Milw, 1948; mem, Mayor's Commn, Hum Rights, 1948-57; US delg, Intl Conf Local Govts, Geneva, 1949; fed court trustee, Milw Rapid Transit Line, 1950-52; chmn: Munic Commn Mass Transp, 1954; Wis Bar Assn comm, World Peace Through Law, 1965-71; Wis adv comm, US Commn on Civil Rights since 1960; Gov's Comm, UN since 1959; mem, Pres's Commn, Hum Rights Year, 1968-69; US repr, UN Intl Conf, Hum Rights, Teheran, 1968; adv, US Dept of State, Bur Intl Org Affairs since 1968; mem, US Natl Commn UNESCO, 1965-71. Lt, US Army, WWI. Trustee, Milw Art Cen since 1957; charter mem, World Peace Through Law Cen, Geneva; mem: Bar Assns: Amer; Milw; Wis; Fed Bar Assn, past pres; Masons; clubs: University; Cornell Alumni, Wis. Contbr, articles to legal jours; reports and surveys on civic and gov admn. Recipient: City of Milw Citation for dist public service, 1944; Milw Amity Award, 1950; Hum Rights Commn Award, 1954; Milw Jr Achievement Award for Civic Affairs, 1959. Home: 2330 E Back Bay, Milwaukee, Wis. Office: 208 E Wisconsin Ave, Milwaukee, Wis.

BITNER, Harry, US, educator, law librarian; b. Kan City, Mo, July 22, 1916; s. Barney and Helen (Samberg); LLB, U of Kan City, Mo, 1939, BA, 1941; BS, U of Ill, 1942; m. Anne Goldstein, Sep 15, 1940; c: Lorraine. Prof law, law libr, Cornell U Law Sch, since 1965; asso law libr, Columbia Law Sch, 1946-54; libr, Dept of Justice, 1954-57; law libr, Yale Law Sch, 1957-65. Tech sgt, Signal Corps, US Army, 1943-46. Mem: Amer Assn Law Librs; council, Natl Libr Assns; fmr: secy, bd dirs, vice-pres, dir, New Haven JCC; secy, bd dirs, treas, dir, New Haven Bur J Educ; treas, dir, 2nd vice-pres, mem bd dirs, New Haven J Family Service. Co-author, Effective Legal Research, 3rd ed, 1969. Home: 406 Winthrop Dr, Ithaca, NY. Office: Myron Taylor Hall, Ithaca, NY.

BITTERMAN, Seymour Samuel, US, business exec; b. Newark, NJ, Oct 16, 1914; s. Isidore and Bertha (Goldman); att U of Ia, 1933-34; m. Roselyn Lichtenberg; c: Michael, Alan, Carol Paulnock. Corporate sr vice-pres, Curtiss Wright, Group Exec since 1968; dir, plant engr, 1958-67; corp vice-pres, 1967-68. Pres: Tifereth Isr Syn; Passaic Heb Med Aid Soc; mem: Amer Inst Plant Engr; Masonic. Home: 286 Aycrigg Ave, Passaic, NJ. Office: 1 Main St, Woodridge, NJ.

BITTKER, Boris Irving, US, jurist, educator; b. Rochester,

NY, Nov 28, 1916; s. Albert and Minnie (Rubens); BA, Cornell U, 1938; LLB, Yale Law Sch, 1941; m. Anne Stern, July 27, 1949; c: Susan, Daniel. Southmayd prof, law, Yale Law Sch since 1951, asst, asso prof, 1946-51; law clerk, Justice Jerome N Frank, US Court of Appeals, 2nd Circuit, 1941-42; atty, Lend-Lease Admn, 1942-43; Alien Property Custodian, 1945-46; visiting prof: Stanford Law Sch, 1951, 1955; NYU Law Sch, 1961, U Colo, 1966; Fulbright lectr: U of Pavia, U of Siena, both 1955. US Army, 1943-45. Mem: Amer Law Inst; Amer Conn Bar Assns. Author: Federal Income, Estate and Gift Taxation, 3rd ed, 1964; Federal Income Taxation of Corporations and Shareholders, 1959, 3rd ed, co-authored, 1966; co-author, US Taxation of Foreign Income and Foreign Persons, 1968; contbr to legal jours. Home: 445 St Ronan St, New Haven, Conn. Office: Yale Law Sch, New Haven, Conn.

BJELINSKI, Bruno, Yugo, educator, composer; b. Trieste, It, Nov 1, 1909; s. Pavao and Maria (Wakler); LLB, 1934; att Acad of Music, 1936; m. Ljerka Plestić; c: Dean, Alan. Prof, Music Acad, Zagreb, Yugo; atty until WW II. Composer: concertos for: piano and orch; 2 concertos for violincello and orch; flute and strings; oboe and strings; clarinet and strings; serenade for trumpet and pieces and strings; concerto for chorus and strings; violin and orch; bassoon and orch; cycles for voice and orch: Ciciban; The Nameless One; Without Return; piano solo, violin; two string quartets; sym; opera for children; 5 syms: ballets: Peter Pan; Pinoccio. Recipient: prize for music for children, piano solo, 1948; Balokovic Prize, for violin concert, 1954. Home: Susciceo trg 12, Zagreb, Yugo. Office: Music Academy, Gunduliceva 6, Zagreb, Yugo.

BLACK, Isadore Erwin, US, business exec; b. Griffin, Ga, Jan 18, 1908; s. Adolph and Mary (Gerinsky); BS, U of NC, 1928; m. Rita Olasov, Feb 2, 1937; c: Sharon Goldstein, Stephen. Pres: Texel Inds since 1945; Ind Textile Mills since 1951; mem: WPB, 1942-45; ind bd, OPA, 1942-45. Mem: Masons; Shriner; Tau Epsilon Phi; club, Columbian Country. Hobbies: golf, reading, travel. Home: 6235 Bandera, Dallas, Tex. Office: 1102 Kilpatrick, Cleburne, Tex.

BLACK, Leonard J, US, business exec; b. Bethlehem, Pa, Apr 26, 1919; s. Morris and Reba (Perlman); BS, Econ, U of Pa, 1941; m. Betty Glosser, June 21, 1942; c: Susan Eiseman, Jodie. Pres: gen mgr, Glosser Bros since 1969, mgr, 1954-60, vice-pres, gen mgr, 1960-69; Globe Wholesale since 1969, vice-pres, 1960-69; partner, Morris Black & Sons since 1948; secy, McKnight Devl since 1962. Lt cdr, USNR, 1941-46. Exec comm, Gtr Johnstown Comm; secy, Johnstown C of C; Cambria Co War Memorial Arena, pres, 1959; Johnstown Hockey Co; gen chmn, UJA campaign, Johnstown since 1968; trustee, Johnstown Savings Bank; mem: ARC; B'nai B'rith; Kiwanis; Pi Lambda Phi; fmr bd mem, Goodwill Inds Comm Chest. Hobbies: golf, athletics. Home: 2207 Spear St, Johnstown, Pa. Office: Franklin St, Johnstown, Pa.

BLACK, Max, US, educator, author; b. Baku, Russ, Feb 24, 1909; s. Lionel and Sophia (Divinska); in US since 1940; BA, Queens Coll, U Cambridge, 1930; att U Göttingen, 1930-31; PhD, U London, 1939, DLitt, 1955; hon DLitt, Colgate U, 1966; m. Michal Landsberg, Aug 21, 1933; c: Naomi Rosenbloom, Jonathan. Prof, phil, Cornell U since 1946; dir, Soc of Hum, Ithaca, NY since 1965; lectr, U London, 1936-40; prof, phil, U of Ill, 1940-46. Author: The Nature of Mathematics, 1933; Critical Thinking, 1946; Language and Philosophy, 1949; Problems of Analysis, 1954; Models and Metaphors, 1962; A Companion to Wittgenstein's Tractatus, 1965; The Labyrinth of Language, 1968; ed: Philosophical Review since 1950; Contemporary Philosophy Series of Cornell U Press; Jour Symbolic Logic, 1946-51. F: Amer Acad Arts and Scis; Inst Intl de Phil; Guggenheim Found, 1950-51; pres, Amer Phil Assn, E div, 1958. Hobbies: chess, music, hiking. Home: 408 Highland Rd, Ithaca, NY. Office: 308 Wait Ave, Ithaca, NY.

BLAINE, Allan, US, rabbi; b. NYC, Mar 4, 1931; s. Arthur and Frances (Perlmutter); BA, U Coll, NYU, 1952; dipl, Herzliah Heb Tchrs Inst, NYC, 1952; MHL, JTSA, 1957; m. Suzanne Iteld, Jan 28, 1962; c: Deena, Ari. Rabbi, Temple Beth-El, Rockaway Park, NY, since 1969; rabb tutor, Inst Rel and Social Studies; rabbi: Temple Beth Isr, Somerville, NJ, 1959-60; asso rabbi, E Midwood J Cen, 1960-69. Chaplain, US Army, 1957-59, spiritual adv, Munich J Comty. Secy: Bklyn Bd Rabbis; bd educ, Solomon Schechter HS; found, Habima Haktanah, semiprofsl experimental Heb theater, NYC; mem:

Econ, Cordoba, 1937, DEcon, 1942; m. Berta Menis, Oct 30, 1938; c: Hanna Kretchmer, Aharon, Yehudit. Sr tchr, stat, Tel Aviv U since 1960; gen mgr, Agrobank, 1954-59; head, research, Isr Inst Produc, 1959-68. Pres: Latin Amer Immigrant Assn in Isr; Hebraica; mem: Assn Française pour la Cybernetique Econ et Tech. Author: Popular Savings in Honduras, 1969. Home: 1 Shilo St, Tel Aviv, Isr. Office: Tel Aviv U, Tel Aviv, Isr.

BLEIBERG, Nina, US, physician, educator; b. Pol, Dec 14, 1911; d. Bernard and Regina (Weissberg); in US since 1940; MD, U Vienna Med Sch, 1938; MPH, Columbia U Sch Public Health, 1952; m. James Rudel, 1944. Chief, infant and pre-school div, Dept of Health, NY, since 1952; asso prof, preventive med and public health, NY Med Coll, since 1959; ped, NY Hosp, 1945-47. F, Amer Public Health Assn; Amer Acad Peds; dipl: Amer Bd Peds; mem, AMA; contbr to profsl jours. Hobby, painting. Home: 89-20 55 Ave, Elmhurst, NY. Office: Dept of Health, 125 Worth St, New York, NY.

BLEICH, Manning Harold, US, rabbi, civic worker; b. Yonkers, NY, Mar 6, 1911; s. Maurice and Pauline (Mittler); BS, NYU, 1932; ordained rabbi; NYC, 1934; m. Beatrice Kartzovnik, Oct 8, 1935; c: Judah, Aaron. Chaplain, Harlem Valley State Hosp, Wingdale, NY since 1968; rabbi: Cong Schomre Hadath, Poughkeepsie, NY since 1961; rabbi: Tarrytown Heb Cong, 1934-37; Ohev Sholom Syn, Lewistown, Pa, 1937-58; admnr, Yonkers Heb Acad, NY, 1958-61. Mem bd dirs: Poughkeepsie Cmty Heb Sch; JWF; J Cmty Cen; Poughkeepsie Commn on Hum Relations; Sr Citizens Housing Commn; Dutchess Co Boy Scout Council; Dutchess Co Ministerial Assn; mem: natl council, United Isr Appeal since 1938; natl comm, JDC since 1939; exec bd, Amer Cancer Soc since 1949; vice-pres and secy, Rabb Alliance of Amer since 1959; fmr: pres: NYU Menorah Soc; Intercollegiate Menorah Assn; natl council, J Youth Org; collegiate br, Union of Orthodox J Congs; Cen Pa Council B'nai B'rith; Mifflin Co Libr Assn; chmn, Interfaith Council, NYU; prin, J Cen Williamsbridge; vice-pres, E Pa Zionist region; exec dir, UJA of Lewistown; vice chmn, Mifflin Co Round Table of NCCY; vice chmn, mem exec bd, Juniata Valley Council, Boy Scouts of Amer; chmn: Amer Zionist Council, Cen Pa; 1945 Appeal, Mifflin Co chap, ARC; co-chmn, United Hosp Fund; secy, Conf of Orthodox Rabbis of Pa; mem: exec comm, Union of Orthodox J Congs of Amer; fac, Adult Coll of J Studies, Yonkers; bd dirs, Juniata Valley Found for Blind; Pa Libr Assn; Pa Seaboard Region, JNF; Mifflin Co Comty Fund; club, Kiwanis, Lewistown, mem bd dirs. Recipient: Silver Beaver Award, Boy Scouts of Amer, 1950; citation, ARC, 1940. Home: 55 B Carroll St, Poughkeepsie, NY. Study: Station A, Wingdale, NY.

BLEIER, Richard, M, US, business exec; b. NYC, Dec 29, 1913; s. William and Irma (Stiefel); BS, Cornell U, 1935; m. Jeanette Guinzborg, Sep 5, 1938; c: Richard, Steven, Ralph. Chmn bd, I. B. Kleinert Rubber Co since 1967, pres, 1962-67, with firm since 1945; pres, New Castle Water since 1949, past supt; service mgr, Amer Machine and Foundry, 1935-41. Maj, US Army, WW II. Chmn, Westchester div, AJ Comm since 1962; mem: bd govs, AJ Comm since 1965; bd dirs, Fed Employment and Guidance Service since 1966, vice-pres since 1966; fmr: chmn, notions div, speaker's bur FJP; pres: Temple Beth-El; Natl Notion Assn; clubs: Town, New Castle, NY, fmr pres; Sheldrake Yacht. Home: 715 King St, Chappaqua, NY. Office: 350 Fifth Ave, New York, NY.

BLEY, Paul, US musician; b. Montreal, Can, Nov 10, 1932; s. Joseph and Betty (Cohen); in US since 1959; att Juillard Sch of Music, 1950-54; McGill U, 1954-58; div; c: Augustine. Pres, chmn, Synthesizers Inc since 1970: formed trio, 1958, toured, Eur, Far E and US; concerts: Town Hall, NYC, 1969; Philharmonic Hall, Lincoln Cen, NY, 1969; recorded numerous LP albums as pianist; numerous musical compositions. Mem: NARAS; AFM. Home: 639 1/2 Hudson St, New York, NY. Office: 22 King St, New York, NY.

BLITZER, Leon, US, educator, physicist; b. NYC, Dec 13, 1915; s. Jacob and Rebecca (Tropp); MS, U Ariz, 1939; PhD, Cal Inst Tech, 1943; m. Pauline Meyer, June 21, 1942; c: Charles, Miriam. Prof, physics, U Ariz since 1950; cons, TRW Systems, LA, since 1955; instr, physics, Cal Inst of Tech, 1943-46; physicist, Off of Sci Research and Devl,

Cal Inst, 1941-46; cons USN Ordnance Test Sta, 1946-55. Mem: Amer Phys Soc; Amer Assn Physics Tchrs; Phi Beta Kappa; Sigma Xi; AAAS; Cong Anshei Isr. Co-author: Exterior Ballistics of Rockets, 1954; contbr to sci jours; asso ed, Amer Jour of Physics, 1957-60. Hobbies: piano, numismatics. Home: 2902 Calle Glorietta, Tucson, Ariz. Office: U of Ariz, Tucson, Ariz.

BLOCH, Alexander, US, violinist, teacher, conductor, composer; b. Selma, Ala, July 11, 1881; s. Edward and Elizabeth (Long); att Columbia U, 1897-98; studied violin with Sevcik, Vienna, 1910-12; Leopold Auer, St Petersburg, Russ, 1912-14; m. Blanche Bloch, Nov 1, 1914; c: Alan, Janet. Concertmaster, soloist, Tiflis Sym Orch, Caucasus, 1913; NY debut, 1915; concertized in E and S in Sonata recitals for violin and piano, first to play the entire Beethoven Cycle in US; asst to Prof Leopold Auer, US, 1917-27; head, violin dept: Wash Coll Music, Wash, DC; Rollins Coll Conservatory, Winter Pk, Fla; conductor: Alliance Sym Orch, NYC, 1927-30; Chatham Choral Soc, 1929-34; Cen Fla Sym Orch, Winter Pk, Fla, 1937-43; guest conductor: Natl Sym Orch, Wash, DC; NBC Sym Orch, NYC; org: Summer Sch Music, Springhill Farm, Hillsdale, NY, Alexander Bloch String Quartet, 1936-41; conductor, Fla W Coast Sym Orch, Sarasota, Fla, 1949-61. Mem: Natl Assn Amer Composers, Conductors; Beethoven Soc; Bohemians; Phi Beta. Composed: Roeliff's Dream, children's operetta, 1932; The Lone Tree, Christmas opera, 1934; orch transcription of the Vitali Chaconne; numerous songs; author: three technical works for violin; contbr to musical mags. Homes: 126 Garden Lane, Sarasota, Fla; Springhill Farm, Hillsdale, New York.

BLOCH, Arnold, Austr, solicitor; b. Portsmouth, Eng, Aug 8, 1928; MA St Johns Coll, Cambridge, 1948, LLB, 1949; LLB, Melbourne U, 1950. In pvt practice. Chmn, Vic J Bd Deps since 1962; pres, Mt Scopus Memorial Coll. Home: 37 Howitt Rd, Caulfield, Victoria, Austr. Office: 167 Queens St, Melbourne, Austr.

BLOCH, Blanche, US, pianist, lecturer, author; b. NYC, Dec 20, 1890; d. Godfrey and Jeannette (Fried); m. Alexander Bloch, Nov 1, 1914; c: Alan, Janet. Concert pianist, touring with Alexander Bloch, spec in violin and piano sonata recitals, 1913-36; dir music dept, Roeliff Jansen HS, Hillsdale, NY, 1932-34; Out of Door Sch, Sarasota, Fla, 1934-37; lectr under the auspices of the Central Fla Symphony Orch, Winter Pk, 1936-43; mem fac, Rollins Coll Conservatory, Winter Pk, 1937-40; lectr on programs of Alexander Bloch, conductor Fla W Coast Sym Soc, Sarasota 1950-61. Mem: Hillsdale, Co Comty, Columbia Co, NY; Friends Berkshire Music Cen, Tanglewood, NJ; Author: The Bach Festival Murders, 1942; The Strange Case of Mr Crawford, 1948; contbr of articles on music, teaching, and horticulture. Hobby: gardening. Homes: 126 Garden Lane, Sarasota, Fla; Springhill Farm, Hillsdale, New York.

BLOCH, Charles B, US, cantor; b. NYC, Aug 15, 1916; s. Barnett and Rose (Silberman); dipl, Bklyn Conservatory of Music; LLB, St John's U, Bklyn; att JTSA Cantors Summer Inst; studied with: Rev Simon Raisen; Mario Rubini-Reichlin; Fausto Cleva; Joseph Garnett; m. Evelyn Rubin, June 25, 1939; c: Robert, Heni Abramowitz, Joel. Cantor, Temple Ansche Chesed, NYC since 1967; practicing atty; cantor: Temple Emanu-el, Boro Pk, 1944-49; Temple B'nai Sholom, Rockville Cen, 1949-55; J Cen of Kew Gardens Hills, 1959-67; appeared in concerts: US; Can; S Amer; Isr; soloist: Carnegie Hall; Concert of First Intl Conf of Liturgical Music, Isr; Bar Ilan U, Isr, 1967; concerts: Town Hall; Bklyn Acad of Music, NYC; weekly TV prog, Morning Chapel; appeared extensively on radio; recording artist. Hon chmn, Metrop Region, Cantors Assembly; mem: exec bd, Natl J Music Council; Cantors Assembly of Amer, past mem exec council; J Cantors Mins Assn of US and Can; J Liturgical Music Soc; fmr, repr of Cantors Assembly, Syn Standards Comm, United Syn of Amer. Composer, cantorial and choral settings to V'Shomru and Mogen Ovos, 1959; contributing author, Guide to Congregational Standards of United Synagogue of America; co-ed, Bibliography of Jewish Vocal Music; contbr composer to Zamru Lo, anthol, 1955, 1960. Hobby, collecting old violins. Home: 845 West End Ave, New York, NY. Office: 100 St and West End Ave, New York, NY.

BLOCH, Charles J, US, attorney; b. Baton Rouge, La, Oct 10, 1893; s. Michel and Lena (Blum); AB, U of Ga, 1913; hon, DJ, Suffolk U, 1959; m. Marie Lena Klein, Nov 8, 1917;

c: Eleanor Small, Marian Hecht. Mem, firm: Bloch, Hall, Hawkins and Owens since 1968; Hall & Grice 1914-20; Hall, Grice & Bloch, 1920-33; Hall & Bloch, 1933-53; div counsel: Ga S & Fla RR Co, 1945; S R R Co (Ga) since 1957. US Offs Training Camp, Fort McPherson, Ga, 1917. Chmn, Amer Bar Assn comm on individual rights and mem, comm, jurisprudence and law reform since 1961; treas, students' loan commn, Ga Bar Assn since 1939; secy-treas, 1939-44, pres, 1944-45; chmn, rules comm, Supr Court of Ga since 1947; chmn, Judicial Council, Ga, 1947-57; f: Amer Coll of Trial Lawyers; Amer Bar, Found, mem: Natl Assn RR Trial Counsels; Macon Bar Assn; Elks; Phi Kappa Phi; Phil Delta Phi; clubs: Idle Hour Country, Commerce, Atlanta. Author, States' Rights—The Law of the Land, 1958; contbr to legal jours. Home: 2703 Hill Crest Ave, Macon, Ga. Office: 710 Walnut St, Bldg, Macon, Ga.

BLOCH, David P, US, educator, researcher; b. Chgo, Ill, Feb 10, 1926; s. Peter and Clare (Perskie); BS Northwestern U, 1948; PhD, U Wis, 1952; m. Jacqueline de Goumois, Oct 31, 1952; c: Peter, Deirdre, Elizabeth. Prof, botany, U Tex, since 1961; research asso, Columbia U Coll Phys and Surg, 1952-56; asst prof, zool, U of Cal, 1956-61; research in cell biol; Guggenheim f, U Geneva, 1964-65. USAAF, 1944-45. Mem: AAAS; Amer and Intl Soc of Cell Biols; Soc of Gen Phys. Contbr to profsl journals. Recipient: research f: Amer Cancer Soc, 1953-55; Damon Runyon Found, 1956. Home: 3709 Gilbert St, Austin, Tex. Office: U of Tex, Austin, Tex.

BLOCH, Eric, US, scientist; b. Munich, Ger, Apr 4, 1928; s. Alexander and Hilda (Loeb); in US since 1939; BS, CCNY, 1948; MA, U Tex, 1950, PhD, 1953; m. Pnina Grunberg, July 30, 1961; c: Talia. Asso prof, biochem in obstet, gyn, Albert Einstein Coll of Med since 1965, asst prof, 1958-65; staff biochem, Worcester Found for Experimental Biol, 1952-57; research asso, asst, Children's Cancer Research Found, Harvard Med Sch, 1957-58. Mem: Amer Soc Biol Chems; Soc Gyn Inves; Amer Chem Soc; Endocrine Soc; NY Acad Sci; AAS; Sigma Xi; Phi Lambda Upsilon. Contbr to biochem and endocrinology jours. Recipient, Research Career Devl Award, 1960. Home: 3215 Arlington Ave, New York, NY. Office: Albert Einstein Coll of Med, Bronx, NY.

BLOCH, Ernst, Ger, philosopher, educator; b. Ludwigshafen/Rhein, July 8, 1885; s. Maximilian and Berta (Freitel); att U's: Munich; Wurzburg; PhD, 1908; m. Karola Piotrkowska, Nov 12, 1934; c: Jan. Prof, U Tübingen since 1961; free-lance phil writer until 1949; prof, U Leipzig, 1949-61. Author: Geist der Utopie, 1918; Thomas Münzer als Theologe der Revolution, 1922; Spuren, 1930; Erbschaft dieser Zeit, 1933; Freiheit und Ordnung, 1946; Subjekt-objekt Erlauterungen zu Hegel, 1951; Avicenna und die Aristotelische Linke, 1952; Christian Thomasius ein deutscher Gelehrter ohne Misere, 1953; Das Prinzip Hoffnung, 1959; Philosophische Grundfragen, 1960; Naturrecht und menschliche Würde, 1961; Verfremdungen, 1962; Tübinger Einleitung in die Philosophie, Vols I and II, 1963; Literarische Aufsätze, 1965; Widerstrand und Friede, 1968; Uber Karl Marx, 1968; Atheismus im Christentum, 1968, Philosophische Aufsätze, 1969. Home: 35 Im Schwanzer, Tübingen, Ger.

BLOCH, Felix, US, physicist, educator; b. Zurich, Switz, Oct 23, 1905; s. Gustav and Agnes (Mayer); in US since 1934; att Swiss Fed Inst of Tech, 1924-27; PhD, U Leipzig, Ger, 1927; f: Lorentz Found, Holland, 1930; Oersted Found, Den, 1931; Rockefeller Found, It, 1933; m. Lore Misch, Mar 14, 1940; c: George, Daniel, Frank, Ruth. Prof physics, Stanford U, since 1936; acting asso prof, 1934-36; lectr, U Leipzig, 1932; research for US govt at Stanford U, Harvard U, Los Alamos, 1942-45; dir: Eur Nuclear Research Cen, Geneva, 1954-55. Prin contribs, theoretical and experimental research in atomic and nuclear physics. Pres, Amer Phys Soc, 1965-66; mem: Royal Society of Edinburgh; Royal Dutch Acad Sci; Natl Acad Sci; Amer Acad of Arts and Scis. Contbr to Amer and Eur sci publs. Recipient, Nobel Prize in Physics, 1952. Home: 1551 Emerson St, Palo Alto, Cal. Office: Stanford U, Palo Alto, Cal.

BLOCH, Fritz E, Ger, rabbi; b. Munich, Mar 21, 1903; s. Julius and Eugenie (Hochstädter); att J Theol Sem, Breslau, 1923-26; PhD, U Breslau, 1926; ordained rabbi: Sem, Berlin; Yeshiva Telsche, Lith; Yeshiva Mir, Pol; m. Anna Grosswirth, 1931; c: Abraham, Jakob, Meny, Miriam Dubnikow. Rabbi, Wuerttemberg since 1953; tchr, Heb sch, Telsche, 1926-29; rabbi: J comty, Aschaffenburg, 1932-38; Achdut

Cong, Bat Yam, Isr, 1940-48; govt official, Jerusalem, 1950-53. Study: Hospitalstr 36, Stuttgart, Ger.

BLOCH, Georges, Fr, manufacturer, communal worker; b. Mulhouse, Fr, June 22, 1898; s. Benoit and Regine (Levy); m. Simone Weil, Sep 27, 1922; c: Jacques, Pierre. Diamond cutter since 1948. First vice-pres: J Comty, Strasbourg, since 1950; KH since 1950; mem, exec comm, United J Social Fund; Président-Fondateur de la Fondation Elie Cohen Bourses pour étudiants. Recipient: Croix de Guerre, 1928; Médaille des Evadés, 1928; Chevalier de la Légion d'Honneur, 1954. Home: 7 rue de Franqueville, Paris 16, Fr.

BLOCH, Henry Simon, US, economist; b. Rheinbischofsheim, Kehl, Ger, Apr 6, 1915; s. Edward and Claire (Bloch); in US since 1937; LLD, Econ, Nancy U, Fr; post-doctorate f, Acad Intl Law, The Hague, 1937; D, hon causa, econ, politics, social sci, Brussels, 1969; c: Miriam. Jr vice-pres, G M Warburg, Pincus and Co, since 1970; dir, E M Warburg and Co, Inc since 1967; pres, Zinder Intl, 1962-66; adj prof, public law, Columbia U since 1962, lectr, law, 1955-62; appd by secy-gen, UN dep commn, tech assistance, 1962, sect chief, Dept Security Council Affairs, 1946-49, acting dir, later dir, Fiscal Div, 1949-55, dir, Fiscal and Financial Br, Bur of Econ Affairs, 1955-62, dir, Bur of Tech Assistance Oprs, 1959-62, adv, UN Consultative Comm, Asian Devl, Bangkok, Thailand, 1965; instr and research sup, US Army civil affairs training sch, U Chgo, 1942-45; prin econ, Treasury Dept, 1945-46, n m, Treasury delg, negotiate tax treaties in W Eur, 1946; cons, Fgn Econ Admn, 1945; missions to: Isr, Somalia, Haiti, Bolivia, Colombia, Mexico, Chile, Thailand, Pakistan, India, Ghana, Ethiopia, 1950-62; mem, Bunche Mission, Congo, 1960. Mem adv bd, Intl Inst Fiscal Documentation, Amsterdam since 1954; Acad Political Sci; Amer Soc Intl Law; mem, Intl Inst Public Finance; Amer Econ Assn; Amer Friends Heb U; hon mem, Royal Econ Soc, Belgium; clubs: Columbia U; Men's Fac, Columbia U; Cosmos, Wash, DC. Author, La Théorie des Besoins de Carl Memnger, 1937; co-author; Taxation and the Social Structure, 1944; Economics of Military Occupation, 1944; The Progress of Underdeveloped Countries, 1952; Tax Policy and the Gold Problem, 1961; The Global Partnership, International Agencies and Economic Development, 1968; Financial Strategy for Developing Nations, Afterthoughts to the Amsterdam Panel, 1969; contbr to Ency Britannica and profsl jours. Office: 60 Broad St, New York, NY.

BLOCH, Herbert R, Jr, US, business exec; b. Cincinnati, O, Oct 29, 1916; s. Herbert and Jean (Kaufman); BA, Yale U, 1939; m. Jane Meinrath (decd); c: Peter; m. 2nd, Jean Rosenthal, Jan 1, 1969. Exec vice-pres, Shillito's, staff mem since 1939; pres, Shillito Store Found; dir: Wolf Machine Co; Cincinnati Credit Bur; OPA, Wash, DC, 1941-42. Lt, USAF, 1942-45. Vice-chmn, bd govs, HUC-JIR; treas; J Fed, Cincinnati; chmn, JWF campaign, 1969, fmr treas; mem bd, CJFWF; vice-chmn, bd, Bellefaire, Cleveland; mem: Cincinnatus Assn; BBB; Isaac M Wise Temple; Comty Chest and Council, Cincinnati; ARC, Hamilton Co chap, fmr treas; J Vocational Service, fmr pres; Financial Exec Inst; Cincinnati Org Study Comm; Emergency Public Transit Comm, Cincinnati; clubs: Losantiville Country; Bankers of Cincinnati; Queens City. Home: 1617 E McMillan St, Cincinnati, Ohio. Office: Seventh & Race St, Cincinnati, Ohio.

BLOCH, Herman S, US, research chemist; b. Chgo, June 15, 1912; s. Aaron and Esther (Broder); BS, U Chgo, 1933, PhD, 1936; m. Elaine Kahn, July 4, 1940; c: Aaron, Janet, Merry. Asso dir, research, Universal Oil Produc Co since 1963, with con since 1936. Mem, Bd Educ, Skokie Sch Dist, 1958-64; chmn: Skokie Human Rel Comm, since 1965; Educ Activities Comm, Mfg Chem Assn, 1969-71; Comm Phys Sci, Ill Bd Higher Educ, 1969-70; pres, Phi Beta Kappa Assn, Chgo, 1968-69; f: Amer Inst of Chem; NY Acad Sci; Ill Acad of Sci; AAAS; Soc Chem Ind; mem: Amer Chem Soc; commn, Cook Co Housing Auth, 1969-71. Contbr of papers on catalysis, petroleum refining, petrochem, Home: 9700 N Kedvale Ave, Skokie, Ill. Office: 30 Algonquin Rd, Desplaines, Ill.

BLOCH, Menachem, Isr, business exec, publisher; b. Mukacevo, Czech, Apr 28, 1926; s. Simcha and Yael (Axelrad); in Isr since 1949; tchrs dipl, Tchrs Inst, Yeshiva U, NY, 1943; B A, Yeshiva U, 1947; MA, Columbia U, 1949; m. Syma, July 12, 1957; c: Yehuda, Varda, Hedva. Dir, Yachdav Pub Firm since 1960; registrar: Bar Ilan U, 1955-59; Mishlav,

Histadrut Sch, 1952-55. Sgt maj, IDF, 1951. Exec secy, Book Pub Assn of Isr. Author, Highway to English, 2 vols, 1958, 1969; ed. HaSefer BeIsrael, Heb bull. Home: 9 Kalai St, Givatayim, Isr. Office: 29 Carlebach St, Tel Aviv, Isr.

BLOCH, Moshe R, Isr, scientist; b. Usti, Czech, Aug 2, 1902; in Isr since 1936; att U Leipzig; PhD, U Bern, 1926; m; c: David, Andrew. Chmn, sci staff, Negev Inst, Arid Zone Research, Beersheba; fmr head, research and devl, Dead Sea Works, Ltd. Prin contribs, research on potash; bromine; geochem of exaporites; solar energy. Recipient: Heirmann Prize, Munic of Tel Aviv, 1965; Isr Prize, 1965. Spec interest, hist. Home: 11 Simchoni St, Beersheba, Isr. Office: POB 1025, Beersheba, Isr.

BLOCH, René M, Fr, navy off; b. Frankfurt/M, Ger, Feb 18, 1923; s. David and Irma (Benjamin); att Ecole Polytechnique, Paris, 1946; licencie es sci, U Paris, 1946; MA, Harvard U, 1947; att: Ecole Natl Super du Genie Maritime, Paris, 1949; Cen de Perfectionnement dans l'Admn des Affaires, Paris, 1950; Advanced Mgmt Prog, Harvard U, 1968. Rear adm, Fr Navy, dir, Atlantic Missile Range; For Free Forces, N Afr, It, Fr, 1942-45; asst dir, overhaul and repair, Fr Naval Air Sta, Toulon, 1950-52; tech dir, Fr Naval Aviation, Paris, 1952-61; asst dir aeronautics, Fr Min of Defense, 1961-65, div Intl Affairs, 1965-66. Mem bd: ORT, Paris; Alliance Israelite Universelle, Paris; f, Royal Aeronautical Soc, London; asso f, Amer Inst Aeronautics and Astronautics; mem: Amer Inst Elec and Electronics Engrs; AFITAE, Paris; past vice pres, B'nai B'rith, Paris. Recipient: Officier de la Legion d'Honneur; Combattant Volontaire de la Resistance; Medaille de la France Libre; Medaille de l'Aeronautique; Medaille de Monte Casino; Grand Cross Order of Merit, Fed Rep of Ger; Cdr Royal Oder of Orange, Nassau of Netherlands. Hobbies: skiing, water sports, music. Home: 66 rue Bénonville, Paris, 16e, Fr. Office: 14 rue Saint-Dominique, Paris 7e, Fr.

BLOCH, Robert G, US, physician, educator; b. Nuremberg, Ger, Mar 3, 1894; s. Sally and Gutta (Rosenberg); MD, U Munich, 1922; in US since 1923; m. Lotte Donnerstag, Dec 28, 1925; c: Francis, Peter. Chief, div pulmonary diseases, Montefiore Hosp, Bx, NY, 1951-62, cons; ret clinical prof med, Coll of Phys and Surgs, Columbia U; asst, U of Munich Clinics, 1922-23; instr: surg, U of Ill, 1926-27; med, U Chgo, 1927-28; asst prof, 1928-30, asso prof, 1930-42, prof, 1942-51, chief, div pulmonary diseases, 1927-51; dir, Edward Sanatorium, Naperville, Ill, 1928-30. Ger Army, 1914-18. F, Amer Coll Phys; mem: AMA; NY Acad Med; NY Acad Sci; Assn for Thoracic Surg; Soc for Clinical Inves; Amer Trudeau Soc; Soc for Experimental Biol and Med; Sigma Xi. Contbr to profsl jours in the field of pulmonary diseases. Home: 5 E 73 St, New York, NY, and Yorktown Heights, NY. Office: Montefiore Hosp, Bronx, NY.

BLOCH, Robert W, US, public relations cons; b. NYC, Mar 21, 1928; s. Maurice and Madeline (Neuberger); BS, NYU, 1949; m. Deborah Garfunkel, June 23, 1955; c: Andrea. Pres, Robert W Bloch PR since 1946; reporter; radio-TV writer-produc since 1945. Mem: admn comm, HUC-JIR since 1966; bd trustees, Amer J Soc for Service since 1958; public info comm, Cong Emanu-El since 1958; PR Soc Amer; Intl Radio TV Soc; overseas affiliate, Inst of PR, London; club, Harmonie. Recipient, Letter of Commendation, Marine Corps, 1953. Home: 179 E 70 St, New York, NY. Office: 1 E 57 St, New York, NY.

BLOCH, Uzi, Isr, labor exec; b. Jerusalem, May 13, 1930; s. Shmuel and Rivka; MJ, Heb U, 1952; dipl, Grad Inst Intl Studies, Geneva; m. Niza Yekeles; c: Shirli, Yaron. Dir, div acad affairs, Histadrut since 1962; chmn, Histadrut Fund for Encouragement of Research since 1966; gen secy, World Union of J Students, 1957-58. Lt, IDF, 1947-49. Mem: exec comm, Histadrut; cen body, Lab Party; chmn, Isr Union of Students, 1952-53; bur mem, Intl Union Socialist Youth, 1955-56; mem: Isr Law Chamber; Research Assn Lab Studies. Author: Cases in Income Tax, 1964; Intrioducton to Jurisprudence, 1968. Hobby, gardening. Home: 28 Hapoel, Herzlia, Isr. Office: 93 Arlozoroff, Tel Aviv, Isr.

BLOCH-FRANKENTHAL, Leah, Isr, educator; b. Jerusalem, Nov 16, 1903; d. Isaac and Sarah (Salasnik) Frankenthal; desc of Moshe Frankenthal, Talmudist; MS, Heb U, Jerusalem, 1937, PhD, 1939; m. Bruno Bloch, Apr 13, 1945. Asso prof, biochem, Heb U Hadassah Med Sch since 1967,

on fac since 1950; asst, Heb U, 1930-40. Mem: Isr Biochem Soc; Isr Chem Soc; Isr Assn U Women. Contbr of articles to sci jours. Home: 3 Molcho St, Jerusalem, Isr. Office: Heb Hadassah Med School, Jerusalem, Isr.

BLOCHMAN, Lawrence G, US, journalist, novelist, translator; b. San Diego, Cal, Feb 17, 1900; s. Lucien and Haidee (Goldtree); BA, U of Cal, 1921; m. Marguerite Mailard, 1926. Free-lance writer since 1929; journalist: San Diego Evening Tribune; Japan Advertiser, Tokyo; Far Eastern Review, Shanghai; S China Morning Post, Hong Kong; The Englishman, Calcutta; Chicago Tribune, Paris and Nice; Paris Times; San Diego Sun; NY Herald Tribune, Guatemala, 1921-29; OWI, overseas br, 1941-46; chief, radio prog bur, VOA, NY, London, Paris, Luxembourg, 1943-45; Fgn Service Selection Bds, State Dept, USIA, 1962, 1964, 1967. Author: Midnight Sailing, 1938; Blowdown, 1939; Wives to Burn, 1940; See You at the Morgue, 1941; Diagnosis: Homicide, 1949; Rather Cool for Mayhem, 1950; Recipe for Homicide, 1951; Doctor Squibb: The Life and Times of a Rugged Idealist, 1958; Clues for Dr Coffee, 1965; Understanding Your Body, 1968; co-author: Alone No Longer, 1963; The Power of Life or Death, 1965; Second Choice, 1966; Wake Up Your Body, 1969; trans, from Fr: The Unknown Warriors, by Benouville, 1949; Caroline Cherie, by C St Laurent, 1951; In Search of Man, by A Missenard, 1957; Heroes of God, by Daniel-Rops, 1959; Three Beds in Manhattan, by Georges Simenon, 1964; numerous stories and novelettes for Amer mags; cinema; radio, TV progs. Clubs: Overseas Press, Amer; Mystery Writers Amer; PEN. Home: 370 Riverside Dr, New York, NY.

BLOCK, Adolph, US, sculptor; b. NYC, Jan 29, 1906; s. Henry and Dora (Wolpin); att Beaux-Arts Inst of Design, 1921-27; Fontainebleau Sch of Fine Arts, Fr, 1927; m. Tilda Frishman, June 29, 1930. Asst to A Sterling Calder, Herman A McNeil; instr, sculpture, Natl Acad of Design, since 1959; exhbs: numerous works in various public insts; designed: Spencer and Brady Medals, Amer Chem Soc; Long Lines medal, Amer Telegraph and Telephone Co; Karl Taylor Compton medal, Amer Inst of Physics; William Allen medal, Amer Soc Hum Genet; 63rd Issue, Soc Medalists, 1961; bronze busts of Spinoza and Simon Barer; eight figure panels for Natl Shrine of Immaculate Conception, Wash, DC, 1959; Georgetown U, Medal of Honor, 1964; Washington Irving Medal for NYU Hall of Fame series, 1968; Dr F.J. Kallmann memorial plaque, Columbia Presbyterian Med Cen, NY, 1967. Pres, Natl Sculpture Soc, 1963-65; mem, bd dirs, Fine Arts Fed, NY, 1955-62; Allied Artists Amer, pres, 1964-65; mem: Architectural League, NY; Hudson Valley Art Assn; elected academician, 1967, Natl Acad Design; f, Natl Sculpture Soc. Ed, Natl Sculpture Review since 1958. Recipient: Lindsay Morris prize for medals, 1956, 1958, 1963, 1969; Theresa Richard memorial award, religious sculpture, 1964, Allied Artists Amer; Hudson Valley Art Assn, 1961; Herbert Adams memorial medal and citation for outstanding service to Amer sculpture, 1961; gold plate award, Amer Acad Achievement, Cal, 1961; award, for portrait bust, Natl Arts Club, 1969; Nathan Hale coin medal, Natl Commemorative Soc, 1969. Home: 319 W 18 St, New York, NY. Studio: 400 W 23 St, New York, NY.

BLOCK, Cy, US, insurance exec; b. Bklyn, NY, Apr 5, 1919; s. Abraham and Jennie; m. Harriet Spektor, Apr 8, 1943; c: Bette Simonson, Margy, Nancy. Life insurance salesman since 1948; profsl baseball player, 1938-51, Chgo Cubs, 1942-48; coach, US Sports for Isr, baseball, 1965-69. USCG, 1942-45. Mem: B'nai B'rith; pres: Okla Little League, 1949-54; Lake Success Little League, 1956-57; comm, League for Girls, 1959-69. Hobby, sports. Home: 4 Old Field Lane, Lake Success, NY. Office: 60 E 42 St, New York, NY.

BLOCK, Eugene B, US, organization exec, editor, author; b. Oakland, Cal, Jun 12, 1890; s. Joseph and Juliette (Haas); m. Ruth Weinschank, Mar 27, 1915; c: George, Edwin, Charles. Ed, publisher, J Comty Bull, 1946-69; city ed, asst mgn ed, SF Call-Bulletin, 1920-39; exec dir, J Comty Relations Council, SF, 1939-65. Author: The Wizard of Berkeley, 1958; Great Train Robberies in the West, 1959; Great Stagecoach Robbers of the West, 1962; May God Have Mercy, The Case Against Capital Punishment, 1962; The Vindicators, 1964; Fifteen Clues, 1965; Famous Detectives, 1966; Fabric of Guilt, 1968. Secy, Bur of J Educ since 1960; treas, SF Council on Alcoholism, 1959-68; mem: bd, Cong Emanu-El, 1960-66; Council Civic Unity; Cong Chr and J; Booker T

Wash Comty Cen; SF Br, NAACP; bd, Parole Commns. Home: 2533 Turk St, San Francisco, Cal.

BLOCK, Joseph L, US, business exec; b. Chgo, Ill, Oct 6, 1902; s. Leopold and Cora (Bloom); att Cornell U, 1920-22; hon LLD; St Joseph's Coll, Collegeville, Ind, 1957; Bradley U, Peoria, Ill, 1959; Roosevelt U, Chgo, 1965; Ill Inst of Tech, Chgo, 1968; Northwestern U, 1968; hon DEng, Rose Poly Inst, Terre Haute, Ind, 1961; m. Lucille Eichengreen, Jan 19, 1924; c: Joseph (decd), Susan Rubnitz. Ret; chmn, exec comm, Inland Steel Co, since 1967, with co since 1922; steel div, War Produc Bd, Wash, DC, 1941-44. Pres: J Fed Chgo, 1947-50; Chgo Assn of Commerce and Ind, 1957-59; Chgo Comty Fund, 1961-63; chmn, adv comm, Cook Co Dept of Public Aid; chmn, bus adv council, YMCA, Metrop Chgo; dir: First Natl Bank of Chgo; Commonwealth Edison Co; Chgo Bd of Trade; trustee: Mus of Sci and Ind; Ill Inst of Tech; Comm for Econ Devl; mem: Pres adv comm, lab mgmt policy, 1961-66; Ill State Bd of Higher Educ; sr council, Chgo Assn of Commerce and Ind; adv council, Northwestern U Grad Sch of Bus; govs, Ill, adv commn, lab mgt policy for public employees, 1966-67; clubs: Chgo; Commercial; Executives; Standard; Tavern; Mid-America; Lake Shore Country, Glencoe, Ill. Home: 1325 Astor St, Chicago, Ill. Office: 30 W Monroe St, Chicago, Ill.

BLOCK, Lester H, US, attorney; b. Buffalo, NY, Sep 14, 1906; s. Barnett and Dora (Herring); BA, U of Va, 1928; LLB, U of Ga, 1931; grad studies, Yale U, 1931-32; m. Anna Maisel, Nov 11, 1933; c: Bruce, Brian. Pvt practice since 1933; NYC, 1931-33; sr mem, Block, Colucci, Callanan & Crangle. Pres: Temple Beth Zion Men's Club, 1953; Rose Coplon Home, 1966-68; Alpha Epsilon Pi, 1932-33; Montefiore Club, 1958, secy, 1953; bd mem, United J Fed of Buffalo, treas, 1968; mem, Masons. Home: 78 Hallam Rd, Buffalo, NY. Office: Genesee Bldg, Buffalo, NY.

BLOCK, Marvin Avram, US, physician; b. Buffalo, NY, Jan 11 1903; s. Robert and Sarah (Sernoffsky); BS, MD, SUNY, 1919-25; m. Lillian Kevitt, Nov 29, 1933. Asst prof, clinical med, Sch of Med, SUNY, Buffalo since 1935; affiliated with Buffalo Gen Hosp; cons: HEW; Natl Inst MH; Intl Inst on Alcohol and Alcoholism, Geneva, Switz; Natl, Cong Parents and Tchrs; NY State Dept Health of Motor Vehicle Drivers; Amer Psycht Assn; Buffalo Police Dept; Malvern Inst, Pa. Chmn: sub-comm, alcohol and drugs, Pres Comm on Traffic Problems; comm on alcoholism, Erie Co Med Soc; vice-pres, Amer Med Soc Alcoholism; mem: comm on alcohol and drug dependence, council on Mh, AMA; bd dirs: Natl Council Alcoholism, past vice-pres; Buffalo Area Council Alcoholism, past pres; Buffalo Council World Affairs; Jellinek Memorial Fund; adv bd: Erie Co Mh Assn; adv comm on narcotics, NY State Dept Health; gov's adv council on alcohol, NY State Dept Mental Hygiene; AMA repr, Comm on Alcoholism, Amer Hosp Assn; mem: Buffalo Acad Med; Acad Psychosomatic Med; AAAS; Amer Acad Political and Social Sci; NY Acad Sci; Amer Public Health Assn; NY State Public Health Assn; Assn Amer Med Colls; NY State Soc Med Research; US comm, World Med Assn; natl council, JDC; Mayor's Comm on Hum Relations, Buffalo; NY State Assn Profsls; Amer Geriatrics Soc; W NY Geriatrics Soc; N Amer Assn Alcoholism Progs; Erie Co Soc Prevention of Cruelty to Animals; Amer J Phys Comm; Salvation Army Assn; AJComm; Alumni Assn, U Buffalo; Amer Red Mogen David; ZOA; Amer Educ Found; ARC; Temple Zion, Buffalo; Maimonides Med Soc; Automobile Club, Buffalo; Buffalo Fine Arts Acad; Buffalo Philharmonic Orch Soc; Buffalo Chamber Music Soc; fmr: found, pres, NY State Council Comms Alcoholism; mem, bd dirs: Meyer Memorial Hosp; U Buffalo Rehab Cen; Rosa Coplon J Home and Infirmary; Buffalo and Erie Co Comty Chest; J Fed Social Service; Erie Co Comty Wfr Council; clubs: Montefiore; Westwood Country; Automobile. Author: Alcoholism — Its Facets and Phases, 1965; Alcohol and Alcoholism — Drinking and Dependence, in print; mem, ed bd: Group Medicine; Encyclopedia of Problems of Alcohol; contbr numerous med publs. Recipient: M & R Award, natl, 1953; outstanding citizen, Buffalo Evening News, 1955; Lane Bryant Citation, 1958; Malvern Inst Citation of Merit, 1962; Wisdom Award of Honor, Wisdom Soc and Wisdom Mag, 1966. Hobbies: tennis, sculpture, writing. Home and office: 371 Linwood Ave, Buffalo, NY.

BLOCK, Melvin A, US, business exec; b. NYC, May 28, 1908; s. Alexander and Tilly (Goetz); BS, U of Pa, 1931; m. Anita

Rowe, May 8, 1934; c: James, Susan. Pres, Block Drug Co, Inc since 1945; mem, bd dirs, Reed and Carnrick. Capt, US Army, WW II. Mem: bd dirs, Assn YM-YWHA's, Gtr NY since 1957, past pres; Phi Sigma Delta; fund raising comm, UJA; drug div, NY Fed Charities; fmr: trustee, Mt Sinai Hosp; mem, exec comm, natl council ADL, mem, E regional bd; chmn, Gtr NY Jt Defense Appeal; club, Hollywood Golf. Home: 778 Park Ave, New York, NY. Office: 257 Cornelison Ave, Jersey City, NJ.

BLOCK, Robert J, US, business exec; b. Seattle, Wash, Oct 20, 1922; s. Max and Esther (Parker); att Stanford U, 1940-42; U of Wash, 1942-43; m. Dorothy Wolens, Aug 11, 1946 (decd); c: Jonathan, Adam, Daniel, Kenan, Susanna Genss, Mary. Pres: Columbia Cascade Corp since 1958; Block Shoe Stores, 1946-53, 1954-58; cons, area redevl admn, Dept of Commerce since 1962; fmr: reg repr, Walston and Co, 1953-54; USAAF, 1942-45. Pres: Block Found; Allied Arts Found; Allied Arts of Seattle, mem exec comm since 1958; mem bd trustees: J Publ Soc of Amer since 1956; World Affairs Council of Seattle since 1948, mem exec comm since 1956; Neighborhood House, Seattle since 1962; Cent 21 Corp since 1960; mem: Natl Defense Exec Res, Off of Emergency Preparedness; Natl Budget and Consultation Comm; natl exec bd, AJ Comm since 1958, chmn, Seattle chap since 1962; natl council, USO since 1958; exec comm, Kings Co chap, Natl Found since 1956; exec bd, Armed Services YMCA, Seattle since 1954; marketing conf comm, Wash Trade Fair, chmn, bus tours sub-comm, both 1958; bd dirs, Seattle Area Ind Council since 1958, chmn, ind promotion div since 1959; Civic Cen Adv Comm since 1955; comm studying fgn water-borne commerce, Wash Ports since 1957; fmr mem: Seattle Park Bd Commnrs; finance comm, Independence Day Celebration, Post No 1, Amer Legion; clubs: Wash Athletic; Harbor, both Seattle; Spokane; Arctic. Author, Journey to Russia, 1961. Recipient, Citation, for outstanding contrib to 20th Air Force, 1945. Home: 1617 E Boston Terr, Seattle, Wash. Office: 500 Union St, Seattle, Wash.

BLONDHEIM, Solomon Hillel, Isr, physician; b. Baltimore, Md, Mar 25, 1918; in Isr since 1951; BS, CCNY, 1938; MD, Cornell U Med Sch, NYC, 1942; m. Syril Appleton, Mar 25, 1950; c: David, Debra, Menahem, Daniel. Chief asst phys, dept internal med, Hadassah Hosp, Jerusalem since 1960, chief, metabolic unit and lab since 1960; asso prof, internal med, Hadassah Med Sch; research asso, Rockefeller Hosp, Inst for Med Research, 1949-51. Capt, US Army MC, 1943-46. Mem: Phi Beta Kappa, CCNY; Alpha Omega Alpha, Cornell Med Sch. Home: 9 Balfour St, Jerusalem, Isr. Office: Hadassah Hosp, Jerusalem, Isr.

BLOOM, David, US, physician; b. Warsaw, Pol, Oct 21, 1892; s. Mordecai and Salomea (Otterman)Pfeferblum; in US since 1920; MD, U Bern, Switz, 1919; m. Lida Delajour, 1923. Cons dermat, Sydenham Hosp since 1965, dir, dermat, 1949-65, mem staff since 1940; cons, dermat, Del Valley Hosp, Walton, NY since 1951; att dermat, NYU med clinic, 1926-36; visiting dermat, Bellevue Hosp, 1954-61; att dermat, U Hosp, 1954-61; prof, clinical dermat, NYU, 1957-61. Fmr, chmn: Bx Dermat Soc; Manhattan Dermat Soc; chmn, delg, NY State Med Soc, dermat sect; f: NY Acad Med; Amer Acad-Dermat; mem: Soc for Inves of Dermat; Amer Soc Hum Genet; AAAS; frm: mem, secy, dermat sect, NY Acad Med. Contbr, chap on Genodermatoses, Medical Clinics of North America, 1959; contbr numerous articles mainly in field of genet dermat. Home: 235 E 22 St, New York, NY. Office: 135 E 50 St, New York, NY.

BLOOM, Harold, US, educator; b. NYC, July 7, 1930; s. Willam and Paula (Lev); BA, Cornell, 1951; PhD, Yale, 1954; att, Cambridge U, Eng, 1954-55; m. Jeanne Gould, May 11, 1958; c: Daniel, David. Prof, Eng, Yale, since 1965. Author: Shelley's Mythmaking, 1959, 1969; The Visionary Company, 1961, 1962, 1971; Blake's Apocalypse 1963, 1970; Yeats, 1970; The Ringers in the Tower, 1971; Wallace Stevens, 1971. Home: 179 Linden St, New Haven, Conn. Office: 2976 Ezra Stiles Coll, Yale U, New Haven, Conn.

BLOOM, Herman Irving (pen-name, Harmon Bellamy), US, business exec, author; b. Springfield, Mass, Oct 14, 1908;s. Meyer and Anne (Hurwitz); att Northwestern U, 1925-29; m. Julia Prosansky, Mar 1, 1942 (decd); c: Miriam, Muriel; m. 2nd, Nellie Korsakov, Jan 13, 1957. Treas, dir, Bloom's Photo Supply Inc, since 1948; treas, Good Block Realty Corp, since 1955; dir, Ins Finance Co, Dince 1963; trustee,

Rona-Mel Realty Trust, since 1954. Author: The Seventh Commandment, 1942; The Transgressor, 1933; Bedmates, 1934; Skin Deep, 1934; Bodies Are Different, 1935; Struggle, 1935; Sacrifice, 1936; Leap Year Madness, 1937; Sweet and Lovely, 1938; A Fine Romance, 1938; Let's Read, anthology, 1939; Tune in on Love, 1940; Frenchy, 1949; Night of Passion, 1949; Pick-Up, 1949; Midnight Sinners, 1949; Flesh and Females, 1950; Lover Boy, 1950; Hard Boiled, 1950; A Body To Own, 1952; Lovers Bewitched, 1952; Girl Hungry, 1952; ed, Authors Publ, Inc, 1932-34; newspaperman, Newark Evening News, 1952-61; contbr to mags. Mem: JWV; B'nai B'rith; J Comty Cen; Temple Beth El; bd dir, Cong Kodimoh; Springfield C of C; Springfield Advt Club; Mystery Writers of Amer; Natl Assn of Credit Men; Kodimoh, Beth El Brotherhoods; capt, Putnam Phalanx, Hartford; club, Crestview Country. Recipient, Victory Medal. Hobbies: philately, photography. Home: 85 Pinewood Dr, Longmeadow, Mass.

BLOOM, Israel C, US, attorney; b. Burgettstown, Pa, Sep 2, 1897; s. Charles and Tilly (Caplan); BA, U Pittsburgh, 1920; LLB, 1922; m. Ida Lample, Dec 15, 1935; c: Sigmund, Carole, Charles. Partner, law firm, Bloom, Bloom, Rosenberg and Bloom. Served, WW 1. Fmr pres: B'nai B'rith; Beth Isr Syn; Wash Co Bar Assn, 1951; Pittsburgh Law Alumni, 1962-63; chmn, co-chmn, UJA; chmn, Isr Bond Dr; delg, Pa Constitutional Rev Conv, co-chmn, Admn and Finance Comm; mem: Pa State, Amer Bar Assns; Assn ICC Practitioners; ZOA; Amer Legion; Elks; Islam Grotto; Masons; Tall Cedars of Leb; Consistory; Shrine; Phi Lambda Phi; clubs: Nemacolin Country; Playhouse; Concordia; Rolling Hills Country; Rotary. Home: 145 Wilmont Ave, Washington, Pa. Office: 200 Washington Trust Bldg, Washington, Pa.

BLOOM, Paul Irving, US, rabbi; b. Hattiesburg, Miss, Nov 30, 1931; s. Herman and Florence (Kaplan); BA, U Cincinnati, 1952; BHL, MHL, HUC, 1956; MA, U Cincinnati; m. Patricia Frankel, Aug 30, 1955; c: Jonathan, Judith. Rabbi, Spring Hill Ave Temple since 1960; asst rabbi, Temple Sinai, New Orleans, 1958-60. Chaplain, USAF, 1956-58. Vice-pres, SE Assn of CCAR; bd mem: Eye Bank; Interfaith Comm for Hum Concern; Mh Cen; Cerebral Palsy Found; Mobile JWF; B'nai B'rith; pres, Mobile Min Assn, 1964-65; mem: Amer Acad Political and Social Scis; Acad Rel and Mh; Assn of J Chaplains; club, Rotary. Home: 209 Childree Dr, Mobile, Ala. Study: 1769 Spring Hill Ave, Mobile, Ala.

BLOOM, Pauline, US, writer, teacher; b. Poltava, Russ; d. Max and Meta (Landau); att Hunter Coll; NYU; Bklyn Coll. Tchr writing, Bklyn Coll; leader, writers' workshops to various resort areas; fmr, lectr: Columbia U; Rutgers U; Town Hall; conducts corresp course in fiction writing; lectr, writers confs throughout US. Author: Toby, Law Stenographer, 1959; Study of Vanity Fair, 1967; contbr to major natl mags. Treas, Natl League Amer PEN Women, Inc, past state pres; mem bd, Mystery Writers of Amer, past secy; fmr, mem council, Authors' Guild. Home and office: 60 Plaza St, Brooklyn, NY.

BLOOM, Samuel Michael, US, physician, educator; b. Portland, Me, Dec 27, 1908; s. Max and Bessie (Baum); BS, cum laude, NYU, 1932; MD, 1935; postgrad studies, Columbia U, 1939-40, 1951-52, 1955-57; m. Zita Greene, June 17, 1945; c: Lloyd, Betty. Asso clinical prof, Mt Sinai Sch of Med since 1966; asso att otolaryngologist, Mt Sinai Hosp since 1960, chief, rhinoplasty clinic since 1962; asso att phys, City Hosp Cen, Elmhurst, NY since 1965; mem fac rhinoplasty, Page and William Black Postgrad Med Sch since 1967; pvt practice, NY since 1947; clinical asst, asst att otolaryngologist, Mt Sinai Hosp, 1939-40, 1946-60; asst otolaryngologist: Chesapeake and O Hosp, Clifton Forge, Va, 1940-41; Bellevue Hosp, 1947-48; mem: postgrad fac, rhinoplasty, Columbia U, 1952-66; fac, rhinoplasty sems, Amer Acad Facial Plastic and Reconstructive Surg, Cook Co Grad Sch, Chgo and Cedars of Lebanon Hosp, 1968. Capt, maj, US Army MC, 1941-46. Dipl, Amer Bd Otolaryngology; f: Amer Acad Ophthal and Otolaryngology; Amer Coll Surgs; Amer Laryngological, Rhinological and Otological Soc; NY Acad of Med; treas, Amer Acad Facial, Plastic and Reconstructive Surg; mem: AMA, NY Co, State Med Socs; Alpha Omega Alpha; Amer Phys F; IMA; Amer Phys Comm; B'nai B'rith; JWV; Park Ave Syn; ZOA; fmr natl cdr, Amer Defenders Bataan and Corregidor. Contbr to med jours. Home: 150 E 77 St, New York, NY. Office: 123 E 83 St, New York, NY.

BLOOM, Simon, US, publisher, editor; b. New Haven, Conn,

Sep 7, 1902; s. Israel and Ida (Schiff); LLD, Denver U Law Sch, 1922; m. Jeanette Rubin (decd); c: Martin, Elaine. Found, ed, publisher, J Ledger, Newark, NJ since 1946; found, publisher: Westchester J Post, NY since 1959; LI J Journal, since 1957; practicing atty, Denver, Colo, 1922-28. US Army, 1940. Mem: natl exec comm, 1969-70, life mem, ZOA, past pres, Weequahic-Clinton Hill dist, NJ, past vice-pres, NJ region, all ZOA; mem: JWV; NAACP; AJCong; Colo Bar. Home: 109 Parker Ave, Maplewood, NJ. Office: 79 Orchard St, Newark, NJ.

BLOOM, Stanley Simon, Eng, business exec; b. London, Jan 18, 1924; s. Solomon and Hannah (Solomons); BSc, econ, LSE, 1948; m. Salomé Charlupski, Sep 4, 1949. Chmn, mgn dir, City of London Launderette (Holdings) Ltd, since 1967; dir, W London Launderettes since 1952. War service, coal-miner, volunteer, 1944-47. Chmn: U Lib Club, 1943-44; Fed Zionist Youth, 1948-49; council mem, ZF, Gt Brit, 1948-49; org secy, JNF, Gt Brit, 1948-54; vice-chmn, Launderette Trade Assn, 1956-59; mem: Inst of Dirs; Royal Automobile Club. Home: 33 Bryanston Sq, London W1, Eng. Office: 4 Sebert Rd, London E7, Eng.

BLOOMBERG, Allan Ellia, US, physician, educator; b. Pittsburgh, Pa, Oct 7, 1908; s. S. S. and Sadie (Klebansky); BS, cum laude, Harvard U, 1929, MD, 1933; m. Sue Herts, Nov 23, 1933; c: Jon, Paul, Seth. Asso prof, thoracic surg, Albert Einstein Coll of Med since 1958; att thoracic surg: Bx Munic Hosp Cen since 1954; Montefiore Hosp since 1942; Grand Cen Hosp since 1957; Hosp for Jt Diseases and Med Cen, asso, 1960; Trafalgar Hosp, asso, 1960; French Hosp; cons, thoracic surg, Manhattan and Bx State Hosps; asso att thoracic surg, Beth Isr Hosp 1946. US Army, 1943-45. Dipl: Amer Bd of Surg; Bd of Thoracic Surg; f: Amer Coll Surgs; Amer Coll of Phys; NY Acad of Med; mem: Amer Assn for Thoracic Surg; Amer Trudeau Soc; Intl Cardiovascular Soc; NY Soc for Cardiovascular Surg; NY Soc for Thoracic Surg; Phi Delta Epsilon. Contbr to med jours. Recipient, Pres Unit citations. Home: 199 Palisade Ave, Dobbs Ferry, NY. Office: 1095 Park Ave, New York, NY.

BLOOMFIELD, Bernard Manfred, Can, business exec; b. Montreal, Oct 16, 1904; s. Harry and Sadie (Davis); att McGill U, 1927; PhD, HC, Heb U, Jerusalem, 1966; LLD, HC, St Francis Xavier U, Antigonish, NS; m. Nery Loewy, June 8, 1943; c: Harry, Evelyn. Pres: Can Mfrs Sales Co; Isr Continental Oil; dir, various co's. Pres: Eldee Found; Lady Davis Med Research Inst, J Gen Hosp, Montreal; vice-pres: dir, Amer Comm for Lab Isr; E Can region, and natl treas, J Immigrant Aid Services; natl pres, Can Histadrut Campaign; natl treas: Can Friends Heb U; Can-Isr Maritime League; gov: Institut de Cardiologie de Montreal; J Gen Hosp; life gov: J Peretz Sch; J Peoples Sch, both Montreal; Bialik Heb Sch, Toronto; chmn: JNF; Can Centennial Forest; found, past natl treas, Can-Isr C of C in Isr; a found, Can Forest, Isr; hon dir, Baron de Hirsch Inst and Child Wfr Bur; mem: exec, UIA; Montreal Bd Trade, intl bd govs, Heb U, Jerusalem; Que Provincial Council of St John Ambulance, mem adv bd; bd govs, St Francis Xavier U, NS; adv comm on fund raising and chmn, intl adv comm, Coady Inst; hon adv council, Shaar Hashomayim Syn, 1968; delg, PM's Econ Conf, Isr, 1968; mem, Phi Lambda Phi; clubs: Montefiore; United Service. Author, Israel Diary, 1950. Recipient: Histadrut Humanitarian Award, 1965; Cdr Brother of the Order, by Gov Gen, Can, 1965; Guest of Hon, Bernard M Bloomfield Negev Dinner, JNF, Can, 1968; Order Knight of Grace, Most Venerable Order of Hosp of St John, Jerusalem. Home: 3180 St Sulpice Rd, Montreal, Can. Office: 1010 Beaver Hall Hill, Montreal, Can.

BLOOMFIELD, Gerard M, US, attorney, civic worker; b. NYC, Dec 4, 1905; s. Max and Johanna (Tannenbaum); LLB, NYU Law Sch, 1927; m. Kathryn Federman, 1937; c: Marshall, Edward, Matthew. Practising atty since 1928; admitted to practice before: Supr Court, US; US Emergency Court of Appeals; Dept of Justice, bd of immigration appeals; Dist Court, US for S and E Dists, NY. Chmn: property, Salvation Army; Bx Campaign, Natl Found Infantile Paralysis, 1945-46; lawyers comm, Fed for Support of J Philanthropies, Bx, 1946; spec gifts comm, Bx Co, Girl Scouts Council, Greater NY, 1959; finance comm, Boy Scouts, Bx, 1961; lawyers div, ARC, 1958; Bx chap, NCCJ, 1946-47, Bx div, natl bd of dir; bd of trustees, Rotary Found; secy, Misericordia Hosp Assn; mem, bd dirs: Heb Home for Aged; Multiple Sclerosis; Bx Bd of Trade since 1936; UJA since 1949;

mem, bd mgrs, Bx YMCA; mem: exec comm, Gtr NY Fund since 1943; exec comm, Jt Defense Appeal since 1945; Bx Cancer Comm; J Bd Guardians; Amer UN Overseas Appeal for Children; Council Sch Dists; State Commn Against Discrimination; exec comm, JDC; natl comm, Citizens Comm, Re-org Exec Br of Govt; Bx Co Bar Assn; NY Co Lawyers Assn; Bar Assn, State of NY; Fed Bar Assn; NY, NJ, Conn Bar Assns; Amer Judicature Soc; Amer Acad Political Sci; club, Rotary, Bx, pres, 1955-56. Hobbies, boating and yachting. Home: 4680 Fieldston Rd, Riverdale, NY. Office: 349 E 149 St, New York, NY.

BLOOMFIELD, Louis M, Can, attorney; b. Westmount, Quebec, Aug 8, 1906; s. Harry and Sadie (Davis); BA, McGill U, 1927; LLM, cum laude, U Montreal, 1930; LLD, St Francis Xavier U, 1964. QC; specialist in intl law; dir, Isr Continental Oil Co Ltd; guest lectr: Ford Found, McGill U; Tel Aviv U; Inst of Air and Space Law. Maj, Royal Can Army. Hon counsel, WJC, London; judge, WZC tribunal; vice-chmn, bd, Credit Suisse (Can); vice-pres, Reddy Memorial Hosp; pres, Can br, Intl Law Assn, London; charter patron, Intl Bar Assn; mem: Can Bar Assn; Bar, Province of Quebec; vice-pres, World Wildlife Fund, Can. Author: The British Honduras-Guatemala Dispute, 1953; Egypt, Israel and the Gulf of Aquaba in International Law, 1957; Grundung und Afbay Kanadischer Aktiengesellschaften, 1960; La Convention de Varsovie dans une optique canadienne, 1961; co-author, Boundary Waters Problems of Canada and the United States, 1958. Home: 3 Westmount Sq, Westmount, Quebec, Can. Office: 930 Royal Bank Bldg, Place Ville Marie, Montreal, Can.

BLOOMFIELD, Morton Wilfred, US, educator; b. Montreal, Can, May 19, 1913; s. Samuel and Hannah (Brown); in US since 1936; BA, McGill U, Montreal, 1934, MA, 1935; att U London, 1935-36; PhD, U Wis, 1938; m. Caroline Lichtenberg, Mar 16, 1952; c: Micah, Hanna, Samuel. Prof, Eng, Harvard U since 1961; asst prof, Eng, U Akron, O, 1939-46; prof, O State U, 1946-61. Sgt, US Army, 1942-46. Mem: adv comm, Intl Assn U Profs Eng; fmr, exec council, MLA. Author: Piers Plowman as a Fourteenth Century Apocalypse, 1962; The Seven Deadly Sins, 1952; co-author, A Linguistic History of English, 1963. Recipient: Guggenheim F, 1949-50, 1964-65; Haskins Medal, Medieval Acad Amer, 1965. Home: 13 Kirkland Pl, Cambridge, Mass. Office: Harvard U, Cambridge, Mass.

BLOUSTEIN, Edward J, US, educator; b. NYC, Jan 20, 1925; s. Samuel and Celia (Einwohner); BA, NYU, 1948; PhB, Oxford U, Eng, 1950; PhD, Cornell U, 1954, LLD, 1959; m. 2 c. Pres, Bennington Coll since 1965; lectr, phil of law and social phil, Bklyn Coll, 1950-51; political analyst State Dept, 1951-52; instr, logic and phil, Cornell U, 1954-55; law clerk, Judge Stanley Fuld, NY State Court of Appeals, 1959-61; prof law, NYU Law Sch, 1961-65. Mem, Phi Beta Kappa. Co-author: Dimensions of Academic Freedom, 1969; fmr ed-in-chief, Cornell Law Quarterly; contbr to reports, jours. Recipient: Fulbright scholar to Oxford U. Home and office: Bennington Coll, Bennington, Vt.

BLUESTEIN, Richard N, US, hospital exec; b. Indianapolis, Ind, Dec 30, 1914; s. Si and Hannah (Nathan); BA, U Cincinnati, 1936, LLB, 1938; m. Eleanor Getzug, Apr 2 1939; c: Barbara, Louis. Exec vice-pres, Natl J Hosp, Denver since 1962; dir, NE Regional Off, ADL, 1939-43, natl coord, 1943-44; dir, comty relations comm, Cincinnati JCC, 1944-49; asst to pres, JUC-JIR, 1949-58; asst to pres, Brandeis U, Waltham, Mass, 1958-62. First pres, Natl Fed Temple Youth, 1939-41; pres and found, Cincinnati F House, 1945-48; treas, Cincinnati Mayor's Friendly Relations Comm, 1945-48. Home: 19 Random Rd, Englewood, Colo. Office: 3800 E Colfax Ave, Denver, Colo.

BLUESTONE, E Michael, US physician, hospital cons; b. NYC, Dec 26, 1891; s. Joseph and Sarah (Bluestone); BS, Columbia U, 1913, MD, 1916; m. Bertha Rodetsky, July 7, 1922. Cons, Montefiore Hosp, NYC since 1951, dir, 1928-51; prof, public admn, NYU; asst prof, hosp admn, Columbia U since 1945; pvt practice one year; asst dir, Mt Sinai Hosp, 1920-26; dir, Hadassah Med Org, Pal, 1926-28; chmn, Straus Health Cen, Jerusalem, 1926-28; expert examiner, Munic Civil Service Commn, NY, 1934, 1936, 1937,1941, 1951; cons, Off Vocational Rehab, Fed Security Agcy, Wash, DC, 1944-50. Lt, US Army MC, 1917-19. Prin contrib, originator of Home care prog. Pres: Gtr NY Hosp Assn, 1935-37; Amer Assn Hosp

Consultants, 1951-53; chmn, med reference bd, Hadassah and Heb U, 1939-50; cert: Amer Bd Preventive Med and Public Health; Royal Soc Health, Eng; f: AAAS; Amer Public Health Assn; charter f, Amer Coll Hosp Admnrs; mem: state adv council, Jt Hosp Survey and Planning Comm, NY; exec comm, IMA; Amer Acad Dent Med (hon) ;Alpha Omega (hon); expert panel on med care, WHO, 1955-67. Mem, ed bd, The Modern Hospital, Chgo, since 1929; adv ed bd Jour Gerontology since 1945; ed council, Hospitals, jour of Amer Hosp Assn, 1941-43; contributing ed, Hospital Management; tech adv, Commn Chronic Illness; delg: Intl Hosp Cong, Vienna, 1931; Paris, 1937; prin speaker: Brussels, 1951; London, 1953; Lucerne, 1955; Lisbon, 1957; Edinburgh, 1959; Venice, 1961; Dr E M Bluestone f in hosp admn, Hadassah, 1950; Bluestone Inst for Med Research, NY, 1968. Contbr numerous papers on med care, public health and hosp admn. Recipient: Dist Service Award, Amer Hosp Assn, 1961. Hobbies: travel, books, poetry. Home and office: 773 Pelham Rd, New Rochelle, NY.

BLUHM, Solomon, US, educator; b. Bklyn, Feb 9, 1894; s. Max and Rosalie (Geisenberg); BA, CCNY, 1914; MA, Columbia U, 1915; att W Reserve U, 1928-30; PhD, NYU, 1950; m. Emma Honor, Aug 26, 1917; c: Sylvia Kline. Ret, prof, dept educ, Hunter Coll, NYC, 1930-59; ret, lectr, NYU, 1938-39; educ, Dropsie Coll, 1956-57. US Army, WW I. Mem: AAUP; Soc Experimental Study Educ; AAAS; NY Acad Public Educ; NCCJ; Phi Delta Kappa; Phi Beta Kappa. Author: Genesis of NYC's Board of Education, 1845-1855, 1951; A Temporal Footnote to a Century of Educational Distinction, 1941; Studies of Superintendents of Schs in NYC; first ed, The J Cen, 1922-24; lit ed, The J Review and Observer, 1925-27; asso ed, The Reflex, 1928-30; contbr of articles on Comenius, Pestalozzi, Herbart and Froebel in Ency of Education, 1970. Home: Park W Village, 792 Columbus Ave, New York, NY.

BLUM, Albert H, US, jurist; b. Baltimore, Md, June 25,1900; s. Philip and Annie (Goldstein); BA, Johns Hopkins U, 1920; LLB, U of Md, 1923; m. Eva Brown, Oct, 1964; c: Sunny. Asso judge, Munic Court, Baltimore since 1961; pvt practice, Baltimore, 1923-61; asst, State's Atty, 1930-34; co-org, co-dir, Domestic Relations Court, 1930-34; police magistrate, Baltimore City, 1940-42; lectr, 3rd Annual Law Enforcement Inst, U of Mo, 1960. Students Army Training Corps, WW I; lt cdr, USN, 1942-45; liaison officer with Brit Navy in It. Pres, J Family and Children's Service, 1950-52; vice-pres, Bar Assn of Baltimore, 1952; chmn, adv bd, Vet Pardons, State of Md, 1946-47; vice-chmn, Md State Accident Fund, 1947-52; dir, NCCJ, 1959-62; mem, bd: Dept of Public Wfr; Levindale Heb Home and Infirmary, both 1946-49; Assn J Charities, 1950-52; mem: Masons; Scottish Rite; Phi Sigma Delta; trustee, Md Acad of Scis. Recipient: Commendation Ribbon, USN, 1945; Order of the Crown of It, 1946. Spec interests: athletics, photography, lecturing on travels. Home: 3401 Greenway, Baltimore, Md. Office: Munic Court, Baltimore, Md.

BLUM, Baruch, Isr, neuro-physiologist; b. Zichron-Yaacov, Isr, Aug 25, 1926; s. Nahaman and Frida (Powsner); BA,U Minn, 1948, MS, Grad Sch, 1951; att U of Cal, SF, 1951-52; PhD, Georgetown U, Wash, DC, 1955; m. Ruth Joseph; c: Rachel, Barak, Alisa, Yael. Sr phys, dept phys and pharm, Tel Aviv U Med Sch, Beilinson Hosp since 1968; i/c neurophys and pharm unit, dept, exp biol, Weizmann Inst of Sci, 1955; med research f, Montreal Neur Inst, McGill U, Can, 1960-61; visiting asso prof, pharm, McGill U Sch of Med, 1961-62; visiting sci, Natl Inst of Neur Diseases and Blindness, NIH, Bethesda, Md, 1962; appt sr sci, Weizmann Inst of Sci, 1965; visiting sci, dept neur surg, U Wash Med Sch, Seattle, 1965-66; research asso, Mt Zion Neur Inst, Mt Zion Hosp, SF, Cal, 1966-67; visiting asso prof, dept pharm, U Minn Sch of Med, 1967-68. IDF, 1948-49. Prin contribs, inventions: new micrometric device; new head holder; a stereotaxic instrument with ancephalic reference points; a multiple microelectrode manipulator. Mem: Isr Soc Phys and Pharm; Isr Soc EEG; participant: 2nd Intl Pharm Meeting, Prague, 1963; Amer Pharm Soc, Syracuse, 1966; Fed Amer Socs Exp Biol and Med; Amer League Against Epilepsy; Isr Soc Advancement Sci; Amer Phys Soc, Wash, DC, 1967; Amer EEG Soc, Denver, Colo; W Pharm Soc, Cal; Symp on neur in anesthesiology, Seattle, Wash, 1966; 2nd Intl Symp on Stereoencephalotomy, Copenhagen, 1965; 6th Intl Cong of Electroencephalography and Clinical Neurophys, Vienna, 1965. Contbr: chaps in: Microelectrode Studies, 1966; Sports, Science and Medicine, 1969; numerous spec lectures at various instns. Recipient: grants and research contracts as prin investigator: Amer Acad Arts and Scis, 1962; Ford Found, 1968-69; LE Louis Found for Psychobiological Research, 1969; Dist Scholarship Award, U of Cal Grad Sch, 1950; Intl Brain Research Org Travelling F to US, 1968. Hobby, hiking. Home: 46 Hamazbiim St, Zahala, Isr. Office: Tel Aviv U Sch of Med, Ramat Aviv, Isr.

BLUM, Gerald Henry, US, business exec; b. San Francisco, Dec 3, 1926; s. Abe and Mildred (Loewenthal) BA, Stanford U. 1950; m. Sidney Kellas, Oct 25, 1969; c: Shelly, Todd. Vice pres, gen mgr, Emporium, SF since 1955. Cpl, USAF, 1945-48. Chmn, CARE, Fresno Co; dir: BBB, Fresno; Fresno Conv Bur: Fresno State Coll Press Club; Downtown Assn, Fresno, pres, 1957-58, 1961-62; fmr pres, Stanford Alumni Assn, 1951-52; trustee, United Crusade, Fresno; Valley Employers Council; Jr Achievement, Fresno Co; trustee, Valley Childrens Hosp; Fresno Philharmonic Sym Assn; Fresno Arts Cen; mem: Mayors Biracial Comm; clubs: University; San Joaquin Country; Sequoin Country; Rotary; Fresno; Boys, pres. Recipient, Man of Year, Fresno Jr C of C, 1959. Hobbies: golf, fishing, astronomy. Home: 1310 W Dovewood, Fresno, Cal. Office: Fulton Mall, Fresno, Cal.

BLUM, Gerald Saul, US, educator; b. Newark, NJ, Mar 8, 1922; s. Benjamin and Augusta (Cohen); BA, Rutgers U, 1941; MA, Clark U, Mass, 1942; PhD, Stanford U, Cal, 1948; m. Myrtle Wolf, Mar 3, 1946; c: Jeffrey, Nancy. Prof, chmn, dept psych, U of Cal, Santa Barbara since 1968; prof, psych, U Mich, 1948-68. Sgt, USAF, 1942-46. Dipl, experimental psych, Amer Bd Examiners in Profsl Hypnosis; mem: Sigma Xi; Phi Beta Kappa; AAAS; Amer Psych Assn. Author: The Blacky Pictures, 1950; Psychoanalytic Theories of Personality, 1953; A Model of the Mind, 1961. Home: 1227 Viscaino Rd, Santa Barbara, Cal. Office: U of Cal, Santa Barbara, Cal.

BLUM, Jerome, US, educator; b. Baltimore, Apr 27, 1913; s. Moses and Fannie (Herzfeld); BA, Johns Hopkins U, 1933, PhD, 1947. Prof, hist, Princeton U since 1961, dept chmn, 1961-67, master, grad coll since 1958, fac mem since 1947; Lawrence Lectr, Conn Coll, 1968. US Army, 1942-46; capt, res, 1945-51. Pres, NJ State Home for Girls, 1965-69; chmn, NJ State Ad Hoc Comm on Services Children, 1966-68; mem, bd mgrs, NJ State Home for Girls since 1964; trustee, mem ed bd, Princeton U Press since 1967; mem, bd dirs: Morrow Assn Correction since 1968; mem: Amer Hist Soc; Econ Hist Assn; AAUP; exec comm: Agric Hist Soc since 1967; Council on Research in Econ Hist since 1968; clubs: Nassau, Princeton, Cosmos, Wash, DC. Author: Noble Landowners and Agriculture in Austria, 1948; Lord and Peasant in Russia, 1961; co-author, The European World, 1966; mem, bd ed, Jour Modern Hist, 1956-58; mem, ed bd, Jour Econ Hist, 1963-68; contbr to learned jours. Recipient: Guggenheim F, 1950-51; Shreve F, 1951; James Madison Preceptor, Princeton U, 1952-55; sr f, Council of Hum, Princeton, 1959-60; H B Adams Prize, Amer Hist Assn, 1962. Home: Graduate College, Princeton, NJ. Office: Princeton U, Princeton, NJ.

BLUM, Leon L, US, physician; b. Telschi, Lith, May 4, 1908; s. Karl and Eta (Rabinowicz); in US since 1934; att U Heidelberg, 1928; MD, U Berlin, 1933; m. Ernestine Berman, 1936; c: Leonore, Carolyn. Path and dir, labs: Asso Phys and Surgs Clinic since 1936; Union Hosp since 1937, both at Terre Haute, Ind; found, sr partner, Terre Haute Med Lab since 1947; visiting path: Clay Co Hosp, Brazil, Ind since 1950; Putnam Co Hosp, Greencastle, Ind since 1951; Freeman-Greene Co Hosp, Linton, Ind since 1956; Vermillion Co Hosp, Clinton, Ind since 1956; dir: Ind State U-Union Hosp Sch of Med Tech; adj prof, life scis, Ind State U since 1967; found and dir, Terre Haute Sch of Certified Lab Assts; cons, Vigo Plant, Chas Pfizer and Co, 1958-69; res path, Mt Sinai Hosp, Chgo, 1934-36; acting and asst dir, South Bend Med Labs, 1936; att path, St Anthony Hosp, Terre Haute, 1944-54. Dipl, Amer Bd of Path, 1939; f, Amer Soc Clinical Paths; found f: Coll Amer Paths; Intl Acad Path; pres, Ind Assn Paths; mem: AMA; Amer Assn Blood Banks; Ind State Med Assn; Amer Cancer Soc; Aesculapian Soc Wabash Valley; Terre Haute Acad Med; Vigo Co Med Soc; IMA; Jerusalem Acad Med; B'nai B'rith. Contbr to med and sci jours. Recipient, Annual Achievement Award (path), 1961. Hobbies: chess, bridge, golf, photography. Home: 3200 Ohio Blvd, Terre Haute, Ind. Office: 1505 N 7 St, POBox 1468, Terre Haute, Ind.

BLUM, Richard J, US, business exec; b. Pittsburgh, Pa, Feb 7,

1901; s. Max and Bertha (Kaufmann); att U of Pa, 1921; m. Carolyn Barbara Winkler, Apr 2, 1924 (decd); m. 2nd, Ernestine Ackerman Bandler, May 2, 1951; c: Kenneth, Robert. Bus cons, NYC since 1957; secy, treas, controller, Gimbels, Pittsburgh, 1921-37; with Macy's Dept Store, St Louis, Mo, spec asst to pres, until 1948; mem, bd dirs, Gimbel Bros, NYC and vice-pres, Saks, and exec head, Saks 34th until 1957. Clubs: Cent Country, Purchase, NY; Advt, NY; Stourport Yacht, Eng. Home: 12 Burgess Rd, Scarsdale, NY. Office: 400 Madison Ave, New York, NY.

BLUM, Uri, Isr, author; b. Vienna, June 30, 1904; s. Arie and Iente; in Isr since 1929; m. Batyah Wagenberg, Jan 1, 1929; c: Naama, Barselai. Tchr, Tchrs Coll since 1943; ed, Oarim since 1941. Author: Limud veyezira; Dereh haHora'a; Madrihim. Home: 14 Nordau Blvd, Tel Aviv, Isr. Office: POB 303, Tel Aviv, Isr.

BLUMBERG, David M, US, insurance agt; b. Forrest City, Ark, July 6, 1911; s. Louis and Rose (Davis); BA, Wash U, St Louis, 1936, LLB, 1936; m. Miriam Reich, Nov 28, 1937; c: James. Gen agt Mass Mutual Life Ins Co since 1955, with co since 1953; instr, Life Underwriter Training Council, 1951-55. Lt, USN, 1942-45. Pres: Knoxville Assn of Life Underwriters, 1953; Tenn Assn of Life Underwriters, 1956; Natl Assn of Life Underwriters, 1962; pres: Council of Comty Services, 1959-60; s section, JWB, 1957-59; Temple Beth El, 1939-40; chmn, Knoxville, gen campaign, United Fund, 1961; mem, bd trustees: Knoxville Public Libr, 1955-58; U of Tenn, Sch of Rel, since 1958; secy, Knox Co chap, ARC, 1955; mem: Juvenile Court Adv Comm, 1960-61; delg, White House Conf on Youth and Children, 1959-60; mem: Million Dollar Round Table, 1956-57; Scottish Rite, 33 degree Mason; clubs: Tenn Leaders of Life Underwriters, first pres, 1954; Kiwanis; Knoxville Sales and Marketing Execs. Recipient: C of C, Man of Year, Knoxville, 1961; civic and comty service award, Rel Heritage Found Amer, 1963; Man of the Year, Tenn Assn Life Underwriters, 1964. Home: 1222 Lakeland Dr, Knoxville, Tenn. Office: 304 Fidelity Bank Bldg, Knoxville, Tenn.

BLUMBERG, Gerald, US attorney; b. NYC, July 25, 1911; s. Saul and Amelia (Abramowitz); BA, cum laude, Cornell U, 1931; JD, cum laude, Harvard Law Sch, 1934; m. Rhoda Shapiro, Jan 7, 1945; c: Lawrence, Rena, Alice, Leda. Pvt practice since 1937; staff mem, NY State Mortgage Comm, 1934-37. Mem: NY State Bar Assn; Amer Intl Bar Assn; NY Co Lawyers Assn; Harvard Legal Aid Bur; Phi Beta Kappa; Phi Kappa Phi. Home: Baptist Church Rd, Yorktown Heights, NY. Office: One Rockefeller Plaza, New York, NY.

BLUMBERG, Harry, US, educator, author; b. NYC, Aug 27, 1903; s. Philip and Hannah (Sabsevitz); dipl, Tchrs Inst, JTSA, 1920, att grad div, 1920-24; BS, NYU, 1924; MA, Columbia U, 1925; PhD, Harvard U, 1929; m. Ann Kamber, Oct 25, 1931; c: Judith, Paul. Prof em, adj prof, Hunter Coll, since 1969, on fac since 1956; prin: W Side Heb Sch, Phila, 1929-32; Cong Nahlath Zion Heb Sch, Bklyn, 1933-36; instr, Flatbush Yeshiva, NY, 1936-39; tchr, Heb, James Monroe HS, Bx, NY, 1939-56; instr, Heb, div, CCNY, 1948; JTSA, 1948-52; asst examiner, Heb, Bd Educ, NYC, 1951; chmn, Coll Entrance Examining Bd for Heb, 1959-62; visiting prof, Heb lit and phil, Tel Aviv U, 1969-70. Pres: Achiever Soc B'nai Zion, 1957-58; Amer Assn Tchrs Heb, 1967-69; mem: exec comm, Natl Assn Profs Heb, 1959-62, pres, 1967-69; bd govs,Hunter Coll Chap, AAUP, 1960-62; Amer Oriental Soc; Mediaeval Acad Amer; Amer Fed Modern Lang Tchrs; MLA; Tchrs Guild; Soc Intl Pour l'Etude de la Phil Medievale; ZOA; Histadruth Ivrith; Amer Friends Heb U, Jerusalem; club, Humanities (Hunter Coll), pres, 1960-61. Author: Modern Hebrew Grammar and Composition, 1955; co-author: Mi-Sifruth Ha-Dorot, 1942; Ivrith Hayyah, 2 vols, 1946, 1952; ed, Sefer Ha-Hush ve-ha-Muhash le Abu'l Walid ibn Rushd, 1954; J Heb Studies since 1969; co-ed, Averrois Cordubensis Compendia Librorum Aristotelis Qui Parva Naturalia Vocantur, 1949, Eng trans with introduction and notes, 1961; contbr to learned Heb and Eng periodicals. Office: Tel Aviv U, Ramat Aviv, Isr.

BLUMBERG, Julia Baum, US educator, communal worker; b. Hazleton, Pa; c: Benjamin and Ida (Lurie) Baum; PhB, summa cum laude, Muhlenberg Coll; post-grad: NYU, Columbia U; m. Leo Blumberg, Aug 9, 1938. Pres: B'nai B'rith Women, Bethlehem; B'nai B'rith Women, Dist No 3; mem, fac, Sr HS, Bethlehem; dir, placement of graduates, bus dept; mem, natl exec bd, 1953-57; Gtr Beth Emeth Sisterhood, pres, 1952-53;

Natl Fed Temple Sisterhoods; natl exec bd,1953-57; Gtr Wilmington Fed Women's Org: pres, 1963-65, dir, 1965-69 and 1969-73; mayor's comm for UN, 1963-65 and 1969; mem, UN Assn, 1963-68; UNICEF comm, 1966-68; bd dirs: Hillel Found Bldg Fund Corp of Pa; Hadassah; Natl Council of J Women; charter mem: Brandeis U; Kutz Home for the Aged; mem, Phi Sigma Iota; Del Nature Educ Cen Inc; Recreation, Promotion and Service; Mh Assn; Del Correctional Inst; club, Wilmington New Cent, intl relations comm, 1958-68, 1968-70, chmn, admissions comm, 1968-70. Author: Aims and Objectives; Philosophy of Secondary Education. Home: 4 E 14 St, Wilmington, Del.

BLUMBERG, Leo, US, engineer, educator; b. Wilmington, Del, July 22, 1894; s. Morris and Gertrude (Block); BS, U of Del, 1927; ME, Purdue U, 1929; att Temple U, 1935-37; DSc, Pa Mil Coll, 1955; m. Julia Baum, Aug 9, 1938. Prof, elec and mech engr, chmn, engr div, Pa Mil Coll since 1946; cadet engr, Gen Elec Co, 1916-18; gen engr, Aetna, 1918-19; instr, math,YMCA, 1921-24; asso prof, dept engr, U of Del, 1919-47; gen cons engr, Hercules Powder, 1941-57; engaged in cons work since 1941. US Army,WWI; conducted defense training course, WWII. Found, Del Soc for Profsl Engrs and Land Surveyors; chmn: Del Licensing Bd for Mech and Elec Engr; Del State Bd of Boiler Rules; mem: natl council, State Bds of Engr Examiners; Amer Soc Mech Engrs; Amer Inst Elec Engrs; Amer Soc for Engr Educ; Pi Mu Chi; AAUP; Men of Sci; Phi Kappa Phi; Tau Beta Pi; Temple Beth Emeth, exec council, bldg comms, 1955; Amer Legion; clubs: Engrs; Triangle. Home: 4 E 14 St, Wilmington, Del.

BLUMBERG, Nathan, US, physician, educator; b. Phila, Pa, May 25, 1887; s. Harris and Rebecca (Krause); MD, Jefferson Med Coll, 1907; postgrad studies: NYU; Harvard Med Sch; m. Rectavia Duitch, Jan 4, 1914; c: Jack, Theodore. Prof, clinical med and geriatrics, Hahnemann Med Coll; chief, med service, and med dir, Home for J Agen; med dir: E State Penitentiary; B'rith Sholom; cons in med: Einstein Med Center; sr att phys, 1937-52; Phila Gen Hosp; att phys, chest diseases, 1923-53; cert internist, Bd of Internal Med, 1937. Lt, WWI. Natl pres, B'rith Sholom, 1930; trustee: Home for J Aged; York House; mem, bd of dirs, Phila Co Med Soc; house of delgs, Pa State Med Soc; f: Amer Coll Phys; Amer Coll Chest Phys; Amer Coll Cards; Amer Coll Geriatrics; AMA; Mem: Gerontological Soc; AHA; AAAS; Rodeph Sholom Cong; ZOA; B'nai B'rith; Masons. Contbr to med publs. Home and office: 1901 Walnut St, Philadelphia, Pa.

BLUMBERG, Phillip Irvin, US, attorney, educator; b. Baltimore, Md, Sep 6, 1919; s. Hyman and Bessie (Simons); AB, magna cum laude, Harvard U, 1939, LLB, magna cum laude, 1942; m. Janet Mitchell, Nov 17, 1945; c: William, Peter, Bruce, Elizabeth. Prof, Boston U Sch of Law since 1968; chmn, finance comm, Fed Devl Co since 1968; dir: Verde Exploration Ltd; Mitchell-Rand Mfg; partner, Szold, Brandwen, Meyers and Blumberg, 1949-66; pres, United Ventures, 1962-67. USAAC, WWII. Mem, bd trustees: Natl Assn Real Estate Inves Funds; Edward A Filene Good Will Fund; treas, Harvard Law Review, 1941-42; mem: Dem Comm, Essex Co, 1956-57; Assn Bar, NYC; Amer Bar Assn; NY Co Lawyers Assn; Phi Beta Kappa; Delta Upsilon; clubs: Harvard of NY; Wall St of NY. Home: 35 Foxcroft Rd, Winchester, Mass. Office: 765 Commonwealth Ave, Boston, Mass.

BLUME, Alvin Leonard, US, insurance exec; b. NYC, Mar 10, 1893; s. Samuel and Mary (Beckerman); att CCNY, 1 10; LLB, NYU Law Sch, 1914; m. Dorothea Sieburth, Oct 30, 1928; c: Ellen, Mary. Vice-pres, Paige, Obrion & Russell. Dir, J Bd Guardians' Camp Ramapo since 1930; chmn, fund raising campaigns, UJA, Fed J Charities, HUC; mem, bd govs, HUC since 1951; dir, J Big Brother Assn, NYC, 1917-45. Home: 1095 Park Ave, New York, NY. Office: 110 William St, New York, NY.

BLUMENFELD, Harold, US, journalist; b. NYC, July 12, 1908; s. Jacob and Jennie (Schaerin); att NYU, 1923-27; m. Gerry Krasner, Feb 21, 1932; c: Judith Dolgins, Daniel Dolgins. Dir, spec projects, Acme Newspictures, since 1968, exec newspicture ed since 1952; ed, mgr, 1924-52. Prin contrib, pioneered use of 35 mm cameras in news photography. Mem: Natl Press Photographers Assn; Soc of Silurians; Photo Admnrs Inc; Sigma Delta Chi; Kappa Alpha Mu; Alpha Mu Sigma; Circle of Confusion. Co-ed, numerous non-fiction books. Recipient: Ed of Year Award, 1959; Joseph Spragut

Award, 1969, both from Natl Press Photographers Assn. Hobbies: photography, teaching. Home: 320 Central Park W, New York, NY. Office: 220 E 42 St, New York, NY.

BLUMENFELD, Irwin, US, public relations exec; b. Seattle, Wash, Jan 16, 1909; s. Charles and Hanna (Freudenberger); BA, U of Wash, 1930; m. Freda Raban, Nov 27, 1942; c: Charles. Dir public info, U of Wash, since 1953; ed and publisher, Granite Falls Forum, Sumas News, 1933-42. Pvt to capt, US Army, 1942-46, lt col, res, since 1960. Pres: Snohomish Co Printers Assn, 1935; Sumas C of C, 1940; mem: Sigma Delta Chi, pres, Seattle chap, 1948, 1958; Sigma Alpha Mu; club, Sumas Lions, pres, 1941. Home: 2553 25 Ave, N Seattle, Wash. Office: U of Wash, Seattle, Wash.

BLUMENFELD, Meyer, US, rabbi; b. Kielce, Pol, Dec 16, 1905; s. Solomon and Frida (Kredowitz); in US since 1927; ordained rabbi, Mesivta, Warsaw, 1923; m. Esther Schiff, Sep 1927; c: Solomon, Aaron, David. Rabbi, Cong Talmud Torah since 1930. Pres, Fed Pol J of Amer, past vice-pres; mem: Agudas Harabonim, US, Can; RabCA. Author: Pri Shlomo, 1926; Minchas Meyer, 1948; Torath Chaim, 1951; Simchath Olam, 1954; Or Chodosh, 1957; Mishnath Israel, 1960; Or Torah, 1962; N'sivoth N'viym, 1963; Sha'ar Hamelech, 1967; Ohr Olom, 1968; contbr to rabb jours. Home and study: 29 Pomona Ave, Newark, NJ.

BLUMENFELD, Samuel M, US, educator, author; b. Letichev, Russ, Sep 13, 1901; s. Max and Fanny (Waxman); in US since 1919; BS, CCNY, 1925; MA, Columbia U, 1926; rabbi, MHL, JIR, 1930, DHL, 1943; hon DD, HUC, 1957; m. Rose Mazel, Jan 8, 1930; c: Tamar, Rena, Naomi. Prof, Heb lit and culture, Hofstra U; fac mem, New Sch for Social Research, since 1958; registrar, dean, pres, Coll of J Studies, Chgo, 1930-53; dir, ext dept, supt, Bd J Educ, Chgo, 1930-53; dir, dept educ and culture, JA for Isr, 1954-67. Author: Master of Troyes, 1946; Maimonides the Educator, 1952; Hevra vehinuch B'Yahadut America, 1966. Recipient: Talmud prize, JIR, 1930; citation, J Book Council, Chgo, 1943; named, Ky Col, 1957. Home: 1330 E 17 St, Brooklyn, NY. Office: 515 Park Ave, New York, NY.

BLUMENKRANZ, Bernhard, Fr, author, educator; b. Vienna, June 12, 1913; s. David and Ettel (Blaser); PhD, U Basle, 1945; dipl, Ecole Pratique des Hautes Etudes, Sorbonne, 1955; docteur-es-lettres, Paris, 1958; m. Noëmi Onimus, June 12, 1947; three c. Maitre de Recherches, Centre National de la Recherche Scientifique, Paris. Author: Die Judenpredigt Augustins, 1946; Altercatio contra Synagogam, 1954; Gisleberti Crispini Disputatio Iudei et Christiani, 1956; Juifs et Chrétiens dans le Monde Occidental, 1960; Bibliographie des Juifs en France, 1961; Les Auteurs Chrétiens Latins du Moyen Age sur les Juifs et le Judaisme, 1963; Juden und Judentum in der mittelalterlichen Kunst, 1965; ed: Archives Juives; contbr to: Revue des Etudes Juives; Revue du Moyen-Age Latin; Jour J Studies; Année Sociol. Pres, Fr Dept J Archives. Home: 12 rue Emile Faguet, Paris 14e, Fr. Office: Ecole des Hautes Etudes, Division des Aires Culturelles, 20 rue de La Baume, Paris 8e, Fr.

BLUMENTHAL, Aaron H, US, rabbi; b. Montreal, Can, Feb 7, 1908; s. Abraham and Bessie (Jacobowitz); in US since 1928; BA, McGill U, 1928; ordained rabbi, JTSA, 1932, hon DD, 1960; m. Jane Spitzer, Feb 7, 1937; c: David, Judah, Eve, Joshua. Rabbi: Cong Emanu-el, Mt Vernon, NY since 1946; Beth Isr Cen, St Albans, LI, 1932-36; J Cen, Bayshore, LI, 1936-37; Temple Beth-El, Houston, 1937-46. Chaplain, capt, US Army, 1943-46. Pres, RA, 1956-58; chmn: Comm, J Chaplaincy, 1959-62; Mt Vernon Comty Tensions Seminar, 1962-66; delg, WZC, Geneva, 1939; mem: RA; JWB. Contbr to rabb and educ jours. Home: 5 Willow Pl, Mt Vernon, NY. Study: 261 E Lincoln Ave, Mt Vernon, NY.

BLUMENTHAL, Hans Elchanan, Isr, rabbi; b. Fulda, Ger, May 16, 1915; s. Jacob and Clara (Hecht); att Yeshivoth of Telsh, Slobodka, Kelmi, all in Lith; att London U, 1938-40; BA, MA, PhD, Melbourne U; m. Ingeborg Last, Sep 19, 1943; four c. Rabbi and educ emissary, J Comty, Munich; rabbi: Elwood Heb Cong, Austr, 1942-45; J Comty, Claremont, Cape Town, S Afr, 1947-53; lectr, Tchrs Sem, Beth Hakerem, Jerusalem; lectr, on pedg and Bible, for Min of Educ, Jerusalem and Eva de Rothschild HS. Mem: B'nai B'rith, Jerusalem. Contbr monographs and articles on educ. Home: 6 Hatibonim St, Jerusalem, Isr.

BLUMENTHAL, Henry, US, educator, author; b. Graudenz, Ger, Oct 21, 1911; s. Edwin and Regina (Cronheim); in US since 1938; BA, U Berlin, 1933; MA, U of Cal, 1943, PhD, 1949. Dean, Rutgers U, prof hist, on fac since 1959. US Army, 1943-46. Mem: Org Amer Hists; AAUP; Amer Hist Assn. Author: A Reappraisal of Franco-American Relations, 1830-1871, 1959; France and the United States: Their Diplomatic Relations, 1789-1914; contbr of articles and book reviews to profsl jours. Spec interest, music. Home 505 Elizabeth Ave, Newark, NJ. Office: Rutgers U, Newark, NJ.

BLUMENTHAL, Herman T, US, physician; b. NYC, Apr 8, 1913; s. Samuel and Jennie (Applebaum); BS, Rutgers U, 1934; MS, U of Pa, 1936; PhD, Wash U, St Louis, Mo, 1938, MD, 1942; m. Eleonore Gottlieb, Aug 18, 1940; c: Daniel, Frederick. Research prof, gerontology, dept psych, Wash U; dir, clinical research prog on aging, VA Hosp, Jefferson Barricks, Mo, 1962-65; dir, labs: J Hosp, Louisville, Ky, 1946-47; J Hosp, St Louis, Mo, 1950-57; asst, asso prof, path, St Louis U, 1947-50; dir, Inst Experimental Path, 1957-62. Commanding off, Med Lab, US Army, 1943-46. Treas: Intl Assn Gerontology since 1961; Gerontological Soc since 1961; mem: Amer Soc Paths and Bacts; Amer Soc Cancer Research; AHA; NY Acad Sci; Amer Soc Experimental Path; Sigma Xi; fmr: mem, Charter Comm, Kirkwood, Mo; chmn, Mo div, Soc Experimental Biol and Med, mem natl council. Co-author, Pancreatitis, a Clinico-Pathological Correlation, 1959; ed, Medical and Clinical Aspects of Aging, 1962; contbr numerous articlesto sci jours. Recipient, Alexander Berg Prize in Microbiol, Wash U, 1940. Home: 1940 Geyer Rd, Frontenac, Mo. Office: 216 S Kingshighway, St Louis, Mo.

BLUMENTHAL, Leonard Mascot, US, mathematician; b. Athens, Ga, Feb 27, 1902; s. George and Henriette (Hirschfield); BS, Ga Inst Tech, 1923; MS, U Chgo, 1924; PhD, Johns Hopkins U, 1927; natl research f, Inst for Advanced Study, Princeton, 1933-34; intl research f, U Vienna, 1934-35; m. Eleanor Begger, June 23, 1926. Prof, U of Mo since 1942, fac mem since 1936; research asst, Inst for Advanced Study, 1935-36; cons, Inst Numerical Analysis, Natl Bur Standards, 1951-52; Fulbright lectr: U Leiden, Netherlands, 1954-55; U of Madrid, 1962-63; U of Buenos Aires, 1967. Mem: Real Academia de Ciencias, Spain; bd govs, Math Assn Amer; mem: AAUP; Amer Math Soc; Circolo Matematico di Palermo; Sigma Xi; Pi Mu Epsilon. Author: Distance Geometrics, 1938; Theory and Applications of Distance Geometry, 1953; A Modern View of Geometry, 1961; asso ed, Amer Math Monthly, 1942-51; contbr, math jours. Home: 205 Ridgely Rd, Columbus, Mo. Office: U of Mo, Columbus, Mo.

BLUMENTHAL, Pinchas E, Isr, educator; b. Berlin, May 10, 1912; s. Elchanan and Paula (Gotthelft); in Isr since 1935; LLD, U Cologne; tchrs dipl, U London; att Heb U, Jerusalem; widower; c: Rachel Hildesheimer, Naomi Seevi, Elchanan, Shlomit. Dir, dept sec schs tchr training and service training, Min of Educ since 1967; fmr: tchr; sch insp, lectr; dir, Isr Educ TV. Haganah; IDF. Author: Ein Su Agadah, Herzl biog; Ishim Upoalam; anthols of Eng, Amer lit; textbooks on hist and Eng; articles on Shakespeare. Home: 27 Balfour St, Jerusalem, Isr.

BLUMENTHAL, Warren B, US, chemist; b. New Orleans, La, Nov 9, 1912; s. Julian and Xariffa (Barnett); BA, Cornell U, 1933; m. Helen Sayetta, Mar 26, 1939; c: Julian. Chief chem, research, Titanium Alloy Mfg Div, Natl Lead Co since 1948 research chem, Ansbacher-Siegle, 1934-45. Prin contribs: preparations and applications of titanium and zirconium compounds, delineation of the chem of zirconuim. Chem, Amer Inst Chem, Niagara chap, 1955, natl councillor, 1956; Phi Delta Mu; vice-pres, Temple Beth El, Niagara Falls, NY, 1958; mem: Heb Cultural Circle, Manhattan, bd trustees, 1940; AJComm; Amer Chem Soc, natl councillor, 1966-68; Amer Inst Chem. Author: The Chemical Behavior of Zirconium, 1958; Branch of Almond: The Life and Times of Jeremiah, 1961; contbr of articles to chem jours; Ency of Sci and Tech, and Ency of Chem Tech. Spec interests: study and teaching Bible; boating. Home: 747 Ohio Ave, N Tonawanda, NY. Office: Natl Lead Co, Niagara Falls, NY.

BLUMGART, Herrman L, US, physician, educator; b. Newark, NJ, July 19, 1895; s. David and Sophie (Hiller); BS, Harvard U, 1917; MD, Harvard Med Sch, 1921; hon SD, Harvard U, 1962; m. Margaret Stein, July 1931; c: Ann. Dir, dept, med research, Beth Isr Hosp, Boston since 1928, phys-in-chief,

1946-62, phys-in-chief em, 1962; prof med, Harvard Med Sch, 1946-62, prof em, 1962, on fac since 1924; visiting phys, Beth Isr Hosp, 1928-46; cons, internal med and tropical diseases, NE area, Va, 1950-56; cons med, NE Hosp for Women and Children, 1952; visiting prof, med, King George Med Coll, Lucknow, India, 1958. Col, US Army MC, 1943-46. F, Amer Coll Phys; past mem: bd dirs, AHA, hon f, since 1963; adv bd, Psychosomatic Med; chmn, sect on internal med, AMA, 1953; mem: found group, Amer Bd Internal Med and Amer Bd Cardiovascular Diseases; Amer Assn Phys; Amer Soc Clinical Inves; Amer Acad Arts and Scis; clubs: Harvard, Boston; Interurban Clinical. Ed bd, NE jour of Med since 1950; ed-in-chief, Circulation, jour of AHA; fmr asso ed, Amer Jour of Med; contbr of articles on heart disease. Recipient, Legion of Merit with Oak Leaf Cluster. Home: 138 Irving St, Cambridge, Mass. Office: 330 Brookline Ave, Boston, Mass.

BLUMSTEIN, Molly G, US, civic worker; b. Phila, Pa, June 29, 1904; d. Charles and Esther (Lieberman) Goldman; BA, U of Pa, 1925; MA, 1932; m. George Blumstein, Dec 22, 1935; c: Charles. Hon mem, bd dirs, J Family Service; secy, bd dirs, J Y's and Cens; chmn, council, women's auxiliary, Albert Einstein Med Cen, 1958-60; mem: Natl Council of J Women; Amer, E Pa, Phila Psych Assns; Rorschach Inst; Hadassah; ORT; Brandeis Women; women's div, Amer Friends Heb U; J Publ Soc. Home: 5219 Wayne Ave, Philadelphia, Pa.

BOAS, George, US, educator, author; b. Providence, RI, Aug 28, 1891; s. Herman and Sarah (Eisenberg); BA, Brown U, 1913, MA, 1913, MA, Harvard U, 1915; PhD, U of Cal, 1917; LLD: Wash and Lee U, 1949; U of NM, 1951; LHD: Wash Coll, 1958; Johns Hopkins U, 1966; m. Simone Brangier, June 22, 1922. Prof em, hist of phil, Johns Hopkins U since 1957, prof since 1933; instr, forensics, 1915; visiting prof phil, Harvard, 1949, both U of Cal. Lt, US Army, 1917-19; lt cdr, 1943-44, cdr, 1944-45, USNR. Author: French Philosophies of the Romantic Period, 1925; Never Go Back, 1928; The Major Traditions of European Philosophy, 1928; Our New Ways of Thinking, 1930; A Critical Analysis of the Philosophy of Emile Meyerson, 1930; The Happy Beast, 1933; Philosophy and Poetry 1933; A Primer for Critics, 1937; Essays on Primitivism and Related Ideas in the Middle Ages, 1948; Wingless Pegasus, 1950; Dominant Themes in Modern Philosophy, 1957; The Inquiring Mind, 1958; Some Presuppositions of Aristotle, 1959; The Limits of Reason, 1960; Rationalism in Greek Philosophy, 1961; The Heaven of Invention, 1962; The Challenge of Science, 1965; The Cult of Childhood, 1966; co-author: Primitivism and Related Ideas in Antiquity, 1935; trans: Claude Monet, by Georges Clemenceau, 1930; Emerson, The Enraptured Yankee, by Regis Michaud, 1930; The Hieroglyphics of Horapollo, 1950; The Mind's Road to God, by St Bonaventure, 1953; ed: Courbet and the Naturalistic Movement, 1938; The Greek Tradition, 1939; Romanticism in America, 1940. Mem: Amer Phil Assn; Amer Phil Soc; S Soc Phil and Psych; Amer Soc Aesthetics; Associé d'Académie Royale de Belgique. Home: Ruxton, Md.

BOAS, Harold, Austr, architect, town planner; b. Adelaide, Australia, Sep 27, 1883; s. Abraham and Elizabeth (Solomon); att Prince Alfred Coll, 1896-99; m. Sadie Cohen, Mar 29, 1911; c: Pegg, Marjorie. Town planning adv: City of Fremantle; Munic of Geraldton; Merridin and other local auth, all W Austr, sr partner, Oldham, Boas, Ednie-Brown & Partners, architects, Perth; JP since 1931; councillor, City of Perth, 1914-43. J repr, YMCA in Australian Army, 1916-20. Pres: W Austr div, Save the Children Fund; Assn for UN, 1949-51; vice-pres, Royal Austr Inst Architects, 1947 f, 1946; Austr Amer Assn, 1953-54; co-found, life mem, Temple David Cong, Perth; chmn, Metrop Town Planning Commn, 1928-30; vice-chmn, Austr Inst, Intl Affairs, 1952-54; f, Planning Inst, Austr; club, Perth. Author: The Australian YMCA with the Jewish Soldier of the Australian Imperial Forces 1916-20; Australian Jewry-Book of Honor. Recipient, KBE, 1969. Home: 1A Cliff St, Perth, W Austr. Office: 64 Kings Park Rd, Perth, W Austr.

BOASSON, Charles, Isr, attorney, scholar; b. Amsterdam, Holland, Jan 25, 1912; s. Joseph and Margaretha (Boasson); in Isr since 1939; LLM: Amsterdam U, 1935; London U, Eng, 1938; m. Corry MacGillavry Sep 30, 1936; c: Margalith, Jedida Khayat, Joseph, Hanan, Jadon. Acad work, Truman Cen for Advancement of Peace since 1968; sr partner, law firm, Boasson and Argov since 1959; fmr, law practice, Jerusalem; asso prof, Intl Legal Org, Sydney U,

1967-68. Haganah, IDF. Pres, Jerusalem Rotary Club, 1951-58; Jerusalem Chamber Music Soc, 1961-62; legal adv: Isr Soc for Mh; Isr SPCA; Irgun Olei Holland; mem: World Acad Arts and Scis; Isr Bar assn. Author: Sociological Aspects of Law and International Adjustment, 1950; Approaches to Studies of International Relations, 1963; contbr of major chaps to books, articles in profsl jours. Recipient, Knighthood Order of Oranje Nassau, conferred by Queen of Netherlands, 1956. Home: 49 Hechalutz St, Jerusalem, Isr. Office: 10 Ben Yehuda St, Jerusalem, Isr.

BOBER, Sam H, US, farmer, agricultural merchant; b. Borzova, Ukraine, Nov 14, 1891; s. Benjamin and Hannah (Sonnenschein); att Baron de Hirsch Agric Sch, Woodbine, NJ, 1911; Mich State Coll, 1912-13; SD State Coll, 1916; Harvard U, summer, 1937; homesteading in Butte County, SD, 1915; hon DSc, SD State U, 1966; m Rose Stolar, 1916; c: Louis, Jack, Mira Lee; m. 2nd, Raychell Silverman, Oct 1968. Fmr operator, 15,000 acre ranch, Newell, SD; chmn: US Experiment Farm Adv Comm since 1948; dist adv comm, Farm Credit; Natl Adv Comm, Natl Farm Loan Assns, 1949-54; sci asst, US Experiment Sta, 1915-24; org: first co-op telephone co, SD, 1916; first Farm Bur group, W SD, 1917; mem: State Coll Seed Certification Comm since 1935; Natl Field Crops Comm, 1948; Fed Farm Credit Bd, 1955, reappd, 1956. Chmn: Butte Co, ARC, 1941-45; W SD, UJA, 1948-49; mem: Masons, past master; Shriners; Newcomer Soc N Amer; natl council, Natl Planning Assn; Angus Cattle Breeders Assn; Amer Farm Bur Fed. Author, booklet on Farm Credit Progress, 1958; collaborator for the Farm Credit Act passed by Congress, 1953; subject of an article in Reader's Digest, 1949, The Remarkable Story of Sam Bober. Recipient: over 300 first prizes at state and intl shows; honoured by SD State Coll for contributions to agric, 1950. Home: 3473 E Seneca, Tuscon, Ariz.

BOBROFF, Harold, US, attorney; b. NYC, Apr 29, 1920; s. Max and Mary (Platt); BBA, CCNY, 1947; LLB, NY Law Sch, 1951; m. Marion Hemendinger, Nov 25, 1945; c: Caren Spital, Fredric. Partner, Bobroff, Olonoff & Scharf since 1952; chief dep co atty, Nassau Co, 1962-64; chief counsel, NY State Constitutional Conv, 1967; leg counsel, NY State Leg, 1968-69. Capt, US Army, 1942-45. Dir, Comm Coll; state committeeman, assembly dist chmn, Dem Party; vice-pres, Temple Sinai, LI; mem: Masons; B'nai B'rith; NY Co and Nassau Co Bar Assns. Recipient: Pres Unit Citation. Home: 795 Hampton Rd, Woodmere, NY. Office: 122 E 42 St New York, NY.

BOCHNER, Salomon, US, mathematician, educator; b. Podgorze, Pol, Aug 20, 1899; s. Joseph and Rude (Haber); in US since 1933; PhD, U Berlin, 1921; m. Naomi Weinberg, 1937; c: Deborah. Edgar Odell Lovell Prof, math, Rice U since 1968; Henry Burchard Fine Prag of Math, prof em, Princeton U since 1968, fac mem since 1933; mem, Inst for Advanced Study, 1945-48; f, Math Educ Bd: Copenhagen, Oxford, Cambridge, 1924-26; lectr, U Munich, 1927-33; visiting lectr, Harvard U, 1947; visiting prof, U of Cal, Berkeley, 1954; cons: Los Alamos Project, Princeton, 1951; NSF, 1952. Mem: Amer Math Soc; Natl Acad Sci. Author: Fouriersche Integrale, 1932, eng trans, 1959; Harmonic Analysis and Theory of Probability, 1955; The Role of Mathematics in Rise of Science, 1966; Eclosion and Synthesis, Perspectives on the History of Knowledge, 1968; Selections of Mathematical Papers of Salomon Bochner; co-author: Several Complex Variables, 1948; Fourier Transforms, 1950; Curvature and Betti Numbers, 1953; ed, Dictionary of the History of Ideas; contbr to sci jours and texts. Home: 184 Springdale Rd, Princeton, NJ. Office: Princeton University, Princeton, NJ.

BODENHEIMER, Hannah Henriette, Isr, teacher, author; b. Cologne, Ger; d. Max and Rosa (Dalberg); in Isr since 1933; att Lyceum, Cologne; U of Bonn; certs: Prussian Min of Agric, 1931; Preuss Provinzschulkollegium, 1932. Tchr; established and managed sch, Wolfratshausen b Munich, found des Juedischen Frauenbundes, Min of Educ, Bayern, 1926-32. Arranged father's Zionist archives which have been publ in Heb, Eng and Ger; author and contbr of numerous studies to Ha'olam; works include: Max Bodenheimer, Lebensbeschreibung, 1951; Bereschith Hatnu'ah, 1965; The Statutes of the Keren Kayemeth, 1964-65; Im Anfang der zionistischen Bewegung; eine Dokumentation auf der Grundlage des Briefwechsels zwischen Theodor Herzl und Max Bodenheimer, 1965. Home: 8 Sa'adya Ga'on St, Jerusalem, Isr.

BODKIN, Sally Grosz, US, sculptor; b. Aus-Hung, Nov 11, 1900; d. Lawrence and Hani Grosz; in US since 1906; att: Arts Students League; Natl Acad; m. Irving Bodkin, 1918; c: Robert. Instr, sculpture, Adult Educ, Great Neck, NY, 1950-56; exhbs, pvt collections. Mem: Sculpture Cen, NY, found; Natl Assn Women Artists; Artists Equity. Recipient, Sculpture Prize, Natl Assn Women Artists, 1948. Home and studio: 10 Apple Tree Lane, Great Neck, NY.

BODNER, Sol Rubin, Isr, scientist; b. NYC, Mar 7, 1929; s. Irving and Nettie (Finkelstein); in Isr since 1964; BCE, Poly Inst, Bklyn, NY, 1950; MSc, NYU, 1953; PhD, Poly Inst, Bklyn, 1955; m. Nechama Vardi, Nov 1, 1952; c: Neal, Alan, Oran, Bettina. Head, dept of materials engr, Technion, Haifa since 1968; prof since 1964; asst prof, Brown U, 1959-64; asst prof, Brown U, 1956-59. Prin contrib, initiated and org dept materials engr, Technion. F, Guggenheim Found, 1962; mem, Sigma Xi. Pub numerous sci papers on materials and structures. Home: 62 Derech Hayam, Haifa, Isr. Office: Technion, Haifa, Isr.

BOEHM, Werner W, US, educator; b. Ger, June 19, 1913; s. Karl and Bertha (Oppenheimer); in US since 1937; LLB, Dijon U, Fr, 1936, Des Lettres, 1937; MSW, Tulane U, 1941; m. Bernice Roseburg, June 5, 1942; c: Andrew. Dean and prof, Rutgers U Grad Sch of Social Work, New Brunswick, NJ since 1963; prof, social work, U Minn, 1958-63; fac mem since 1951; asst prof, U of Wis, 1946-51; dir, coord, soc work curriculum study, Council on Social Work Educ, NYC, 1955-58; cons: UN Tech Assistance Sect, 1952; Isr Min of Social Wfr, 1952; Heb U, 1959; vice-chmn, 2nd commn, Intl Conf of Social Work, Rome, It, 1961; rapporteur, Intl Conf of Schs of Social Work, Rome, 1961; Natl bd: Natl Assn of Social Workers, 1966-69; NJ Wfr Council, 1963-66; Natl bd: Council on Social Work Educ; chmn, comm on Educ Services since 1964; 1st vice-pres, Natl Conf on Social Wfr, 1969-70; AAAS; Soc for Psych Study of Social Issues; visiting lectr, Inst de Service Social et de Recherches Sociales, Montrouge, Fr, 1968; State Dept Spec in Social Work, Brazil, 1967. Author: Objectives of the Social Work Curriculum of the Future, 1959; The Social Case-Work Method in Social Work Education, 1959; contbr to numerous books and profsl jours. Recipient, Cassidy Memorial Research Award, U Toronto, 1959. Home: 35 N Eighth Ave, Highland Park, NJ. Office: Rutgers U Graduate School of Social Work, 536 George St, New Brunswick, NJ.

BOGEN, Stanley Maurice, US, stockbroker; b. NYC, May 11, 1937; s. Max and Marcy; BEcon, U of Pa, 1958; MBA, NYU, 1959; m. Joy Supine, Oct 23, 1960; c: Lauren, Edmund. Vice-pres, First Devonshire Corp. Served, USAF. Gov, Heb U; dir: Amer-Isr Cultural Found; Sponsors for Educ Opportunity. Home: 655 Park Ave, New York, NY. Office: 67 Broad St, New York, NY.

BOGIN, Maxwell, US, physician; b. Bklyn, NY, Dec 26, 1901; s. Harry and Mary (Handelman); BS, Yale U, 1923; MD, Sch of Med, 1926; m. Edith Hoffman; c: Deborah Cohen, Abby Kenigsberg. Cons, ped, Bridgeport Hosp since 1966, chief of service, ped dept, 1949-66; asst res, ped, 1928-29, res, 1929-30. Pres, Children's Med Group since 1964; chmn, med adv bd, Crippled Children's Clinic; Conn State chmn, Amer Acad Ped, 1955-57. Contbr to med jours. Hobby, photography. Home: 333 Cornell Rd, Fairfield, Conn. Office: 340 Capitol Ave, Bridgeport, Conn.

BOGNER, Sidney M, US, rabbi; b. NYC, Sep 9, 1909; s. Abraham and Minnie (Spiegel); BSS, CCNY, 1934; rabbi, MHL, JIR, 1938; m. Florence Lifshitz, 1937; c: Susan, Minna, Marcia, William. Rabbi, Cong B'nai Isr of Kearny and N Arlington, NJ; fmr rabbi, Bellrose J Cen, LI, NY. Pres: Essex Co Bd of Rabbis, 1961-63; Suffolk Co Assn of Rabbis, 1945-47; B'nai B'rith lodge, 1941-42; Bay Shore dist, ZOA, 1947-48; secy, Rabb Assembly of LI, 1948-51; vice-pres, Rabb Assembly of NNJ; civilian chaplain, Govs I, 1942-45; chaplain: maj, NJ Wing Civil Air Patrol; Sq Club, NJ. Mem: Child Wfr League; Masons; KP. Author: Jewish Attitude Toward Palestine in the 18th Century, 1938. Home: 16 Grand Pl, Kearny, NJ. Study: Cong B'nai Isr of Kearny and N Arlington, Kearny, NJ.

BOGORAD, Lawrence, US, biologist; b. Tashkent, Russ, Aug 29, 1921; s. Bernard and Florence (Bernard); in US since 1922; BS, U Chgo, 1942, PhD, 1949; hon MA, Harvard U, 1967; m. Rosalyn Sagen, June 29, 1943; c: Leonard,

Marsha. Prof, biol, Harvard U since 1967; visiting inves, Rockefeller Inst, 1951-53; prof, U Chgo, 1961-67, mem fac, 1953-61; f: NCR-Merck, 1951-53; Fullbright, 1960; NSF, 1961. Lt, US Army, 1943-46. Mem: Amer Soc Plant Phys, pres, 1968-69; Amer Acad Arts and Scis; Amer Soc Cell Biol; Amer Soc Biol Chem; Botanical Annual Rev of Plant Phys, 1963-67; contbr of articles to biol and biophys jours. Recipient: Research Career Award, NIH, 1963; Quantrell Award, U of Chgo, 1959. Home: 2 White Pine Lane, Lexington, Mass. Office: Biol Labs, Harvard U, 16 Divinity Ave, Cambridge, Mass.

BOGORAD, Samuel Nathaniel, US, educator; b. New Bedford, Mass, Apr 7, 1917; s. Sidney and Rebecca (Eisenstadt); AB, summa cum laude, Brown U, 1939, MA, 1941; PhD, 1949; hon MA, Harvard U, 1946; m. Ruth Pollack, Sep 10, 1944. Frederick Corse Prof Eng Lang and Lit, U of Vt, since 1968, chmn Eng dept since 1961, on fac since 1957; asst in Eng, Brown U, 1939-41; instr Eng, U F, Northwestern U, 1942-45; visiting asst prof, Brown U, 1948-49; visiting prof Eng: Coll of William and Mary, 1951; U Colo, 1958. Pres, NE region, united chaps, Phi Beta Kappa, mem comm on qualifications; natl dir, Coll Eng Assn, fmr pres, NE chap; mem: Commn on Insts of Higher Educ, NE Assn Colls and Secondary Schs; MLA; Natl Council Tchrs Eng; AAUP. Co-author: The College Miscellany, 1952; Atlantic Essays, 1958; contbr to scholarly jours. Home: 1425 Hinesburg Rd, S Burlington, Vt. Office: Dept of Eng, U of Vt, Burlington, Vt.

BOGRAD, Harriet Mary, US, attorney; b. Paterson, NJ, Apr 6, 1943; d. Samuel and Pauline (Klemes); BA, Bryn Mawr Coll, 1963; LLB, Yale Law Sch, 1966. Project dir, Childrens Circle Planning Corp since 1970; project dir, Dixwell Legal Rights Assn Inc, 1965-66; instr, Albert Einstein Coll of Med since 1967; atty, Montefiore Hosp, 1966-70. Found, dir, S Teaching Prog Inc, 1963-65; atty, Comm for Comty Controlled Daycare. Contbr of articles to profsl jours. Home: 785 West End Ave, New York, NY. Office: 530 E 169 St, Bronx, NY.

BOHM, Jack Nelson, US, lawyer; b. Sharon, Pa, July 5, 1924; s. Joseph and Aranka; att Us: Pa; Ga; Kan City; DJur, Wash U, St Louis, Mo, 1948; m. Elizabeth Viscofsky, Sep 27, 1947; c: Robert, Richard, Lorie. Mem, law firm, Glass, Bohm, Hirschman & Rostov since 1963; atty-at-law since 1948. Lt col, US Army, 1942-46, res since 1948. Mem: intl bd govs, B'nai B'rith; bd: J Fed and Council, Kan City; Cong Beth Shalom, Kan City, past pres, Men's Club; Amer Bar Assn; Mo Bar Assn; Kan City Bar Assn, chmn, lawyer referral comm; Lawyers Assn of Kan City; Masons, Rockhill chap; Res Offs Assn; Plains States Regional Bd, ADL; Meadowbrook Country Club, Kan City; Phi Alpha Delta; Phi Eta Sigma; fmr: pres: Dist Grand Lodge 2, B'nai B'rith, Kan City Lodge 184; mem: natl commn, B'nai B'rith Youth Org; Mayor's Commn on Personnel Practices, Kan City; bd, Leo N Levy Memorial Hosp, Ark; club, Meadowbrook Country. Recipient, Eur Theatre, with 3 battle stars. Home: 610 W 67 Terrace, Kansas City, Mo. Office: 1006 Grand St, Kansas City, Mo.

BOHNEN, Eli Aaron, US, rabbi; b. Toronto, Can, Sep 16, 1909; s. Max and Nellie (Brill); in US since 1931; BA, U Toronto, 1931; MHL, rabbi, JTSA, 1935, DHL, 1953, DD, 1967; LHD, U of RI, 1967; m. Eleanor Rosenthal, July 2, 1939; c: Judith, Michael. Rabbi, Temple Emanu-el since 1948; asst rabbi, Cong Adath Jeshurun, Phila, 1935-39; rabbi, Temple Emanu-El, Buffalo, 1939-48. Chaplain, US Army, 1943-46. Pres, RA, 1966-68; mem, Masons. Home: 500 Elm Grove Ave, Providence, RI. Study: 99 Taft Ave, Providence, RI.

BOHROD, Aaron, US, artist; b. Chgo, Nov 21, 1907; s. George and Fanny (Feingold); att Crane Coll, Chgo, 1926; Chgo Art Inst, 1927-28; NY Art Students League, 1929-31; m. Ruth Bush, 1929; c: Mark, Georgi, Neil. Artist in res: U of Wis since 1948; U of S Ill, 1942-43; artist, war corresp, Life Magazine, 1943-45. Represented in perm collections at: Metrop Mus Art; Whitney Mus Art; Bklyn Mus; Detroit Art Inst; Art Inst, Chgo; Boston Mus Fine Arts; Pa Acad Art; Corcoran Mus, Wash, DC; Butler Art Inst, Youngstown, O; Cranbrook Acad, Mich; Walker Art Cen, Minneapolis and others. Painted: cover designs for Time Magazine; series on Amer rels, Look Magazine. Author: A Pottery Sketch Book, 1959; A Decade of Still Life, 1966. Recipient: Guggenheim F in Creative Painting, 1936-38; prizes: Cal

Water Color Soc, 1940; Pa Acad Fine Arts, 1940; Carnegie Intl Mus, 1941; Metrop Mus Art, 1943; Chgo Art Inst, eight prizes, 1941-47; Corcoran Mus, 1943; Natl Acad of Design, 1961, 1965; Gov's Award for Art, Wis, 1969. Home: 4811 Tonyawatha Trail, Madison, Wis. Studio: U of Wisconsin, Madison, Wis.

BOIM, Leon, Isr, educator; b. Vladimir-Volynsk, Pol, Apr 2, 1910; s. Mordchai and Rachel (Alperson); in Isr since 1957; MJur, U Warsaw, 1936; PhD, Heb U, Jerusalem, 1961; m. Bronislava Martenfeld, Feb 4, 1936; c: Marek. Sr lectr, pub law and pol sci, Tel Aviv U since 1958; i/c research, State Compt Off, 1957-58; chief ed, Studies in State Contr; pvt law practice, 1945-49; prof: pol sci, Sch of Admn and Econ, Pol, 1949-51; Constitutional law, Fac Law, Vroclav, Pol, 1957-58. Mem: Inst Leg Research and Comp Law; Inst of Intl Relations, Isr; Soc Pol Sci; Friends of UN; Soc Criminology. Author: The Government of USSR, 1955; The Ombudsman, 1965; The Party-State Control in the Soviet Union; contbr of numerous articles to legal publs. Recipient, award, Pol Min of HS, 1956. Hobby, photography. Home: 5 Brodi St, Ramat Aviv, Isr.

BOKSER, Ben Zion, US, rabbi, author; b. Lubomi, Pol, July 4, 1907; s. Morris and Gittel (Katz) in US since 1920; BA, CCNY, rabbi, JTSA, 1931; MA, Columbia U, PhD, 1935; m. Kallia Halpern, July 21, 1940; c: Miriam, Baruch. Rabbi: Forest Hills J Cen since 1935; Cong Kehillat Isr, Bx, NY, 1931-32; Cong, Vancouver, 1932-33; ed, NBC radio prog, Eternal Light since 1950; visiting prof, homiletics, JTSA, 1952; lectr since 1953; mem, Conf on Sci, Phil and Rel. Author: Pharisaic Judaism in Transition, 1935; The Legacy of Maimonides, 1950; The Wisdom of the Talmud, 1951; From the World of the Cabbalah, 1954; Judaism and the Modern Man, 1957; The Weekday, Sabbath and Festival Prayer Book, 1957; The Gift of Life, 1958; The High Holy Day Prayer Book, 1959; Profile of the Faith, 1963; Judaism and the Christian Predicament, 1966. Home: 110-40 70 Ave, Forest Hills, NY. Study: 106-06 Queens Blvd, Forest Hills, NY.

BOKSER, Kallia H, US, radio commentator; b. Denver, Colo, Oct 16, 1915; d. Ephraim and Frima (Hammer) Halpern; BA, Hunter Coll, 1935; grad study, NYU, 1940-41; m. Ben-Zion Bokser, July 21, 1940; c: Miriam, Baruch. Commentator, radio sta WEVD since 1958. Chmn bd, Queens div, UJA since 1956, mem cabinet, women's div, Gtr NY since 1954; mem bd, Natl Women's League since 1954, chmn, natl prog, 1956-57; HDA, NYC, asst to dir, Off of Problem Housing; housing spec and urban planner, Comty Council, Gtr NY, 1964-69; mem: exec comm, Natl J Music Council; Mizrachi Women's Org; Hadassah; AJCong. Hobby, collecting J ceremonial objects. Home: 110-40 70 Ave, Forest Hills, NY. Office: WEVD, 117 W 46 St, New York, NY.

BOLOTOWSKY, Ilya, US, artist, educator; b. Petrograd, Russ, July 1, 1907; s. Julius and Anastasia (Shapiro); in US since 1923; att: St Joseph, Constantinople, Turkey, 1920-23; Natl Acad of Design, NYC, 1924-30; U of Wyo, 1949-51; m. Meta Cohen, Sep 17, 1947; c: Andrew. Prof, art: State Coll, New Paltz, NY since 1957; Southampton Coll, LIU, NY since 1965, chmn art dept; head, art dept, Black Mt Coll, Black Mt, NC, 1946-48; asso prof, art, U of Wyo, 1948-57; visiting prof, art: Bklyn Coll, 1954-56; Hunter Coll, 1963-64; U of Wis, 1968; adj prof, U of NM, Albuquerque, 1969. USAAF, WW II. Represented in: Mus of Modern Art; Whitney Mus of Amer Art; Phila Mus; Solomon R Guggenheim Mus; Yale U Gal; Munson-Williams-Proctor Inst; Lyman-Allyn Mus, New London, Conn; Brandeis U; RI Sch of Design; NYU; Duncan Phillips Gal; Rock Springs HS, Wyo; Coll of Agric, U of Wyo; Dr Frederick Olsen's Found; Chase-Manhattan Bank; Continental Grain Co; Union Carbide Co; Mus of Modern Art, Ceret, Fr; Gotheborg Mus, Swed; Calcutta Mus of Art, India; Albright-Knox Gal, Buffalo, NY; U of NM, Albuquerque, NM; NC Mus of Art, Raleigh, NC; Jerusalem Mus, Isr; pvt collections: Richard B Baker; Amory H Bradford; Lionel Baumann; Miller Co; Dennis Paddock; Henry R Hope; Mrs Edward Root, George H Warren; Onya La Tour; Mrs J B Neumann; Jan Mitchell; Leo Castelli; George L K Morris; Mrs Grace Brandt; Mrs Grete Schultz; Jose de Rivera; murals: Williamsburg Housing Project, 1936; NY World's Fair Hall of Med Sci, 1939; Hosp for Chronic Diseases,Wfr I, NYC, 1940; Theodore Roosevelt HS, 1940; G D Thompson, Pittsburgh, Pa, 1946; Rugoff Theatres, Cinema I-Cinema II, NYC, 1962. One-man shows: New Art Circle, 1946, 52; Pinacotheca, 1947, 1950; Grace Borgenic Gahtl:

1954, 1956, 1958, 1959, 1961, 1963, 1966, 1968. Compiled Russian-English Dictionary of Painting and Sculpture, 1963. Charter mem, co-found: Amer Abstract Artists since 1936, fmr pres; Fed Modern Painters and Sculptors since 1939; mem, Gallatin Assn, NYU; asso mem, Sharon Art Assn, Sharon, Conn. Recipient: first prize, Natl Acad of Design, 1924, 25; Hallgarten prize, 1929, 30; first prize, ed and trans work on Military Dictionary, 1942; scholarship, Tiffany Found, 1929, 30; Yaddo, 1934; Guggenheim f, 1941; grants for experimental filmwork: U of Wyo Coll of Grad Studies, 1953, 56; SUNY Research Found, 1959, 1960; Sharon Annual Art Festival Award, 1959; first prize, experimental film, Metanoia, Midwestern Film Festival, Chgo, 1963. Home: John St, Sag Harbor, Long Island, NY. Office: Southampton Coll of LIU, Southampton, Long Island, NY.

BONDI, Aron A, Isr, scientist, educator; b. Vienna, Feb 16, 1906; s. Hugo and Martha (Gumpertz); in Isr since 1934; PhD, U of Vienna, 1929; m. Eva Merkin, 1937; c: Elchanan, Margalith. Prof, animal nutrition and biochem, fac agric, Heb U, Rehovot, since 1956; head of lab, Agric Research Sta, Rehovot, 1934-59. Contbr to sci jours. Recipient, Laureate, Rothschild Award for Agric, 1967. Office: Fac of Agric, Heb U, Rehovot, Isr.

BONDY, Curt W, Ger, psychologist, educator, author; b. Hamburg, Ger, Apr 3, 1894; s. Salomon and Marie (Lauer); PhD, U Hamburg, 1921. Prof em, psych, social pedg, U of Hamburg since 1959, prof, 1950-59; research asso, Inst of Educ, U of Gottingen, 1923-25, prof, dept phil, 1930-33; guest lectr, sch for social work, adult educ, 1923-33; ref work in Ger, Holland, Eng, Belgium, US, 1933-40; instr, psych, Coll of William and Mary, Richmond, Va, 1940-42, asst prof, 1943-44, asso prof, head, psych dept, 1944-47, prof, 1948-50. Mem: Amer Psych Assn; Deutsche Gesellschaft für Psychologie. Author: Die Proletarische Jugendbewegung in Deutschland, 1922; Pädagogische Problemen im Jugendstrafvollzug, 1925; Pädagogische und psychologische zum Lüneburger Fürsorgeerziehungsprozess, 1931; Einführung in die Psychologie, 1967, 3rd ed, 1969; contbr of essays on psych, pedg problems to jours. Home: 18A, Oberstrasse XI, Hamburg, Ger.

BONEH, Eliezer, Isr, executive; b. Zloczow, Pol, Feb 9, 1912; s. Moses and Yetti (Hoffman); in Isr since 1932; BA, Tel Aviv U, 1954, MA, 1958; PhD, U of Lyon, Fr, 1963; m. Batia Prisand, May 1, 1934; c: Arnon, Nitza. Dir: Taxation Dept, Haifa Munic since 1957, Sanitation Dept, 1952-57. Served, Haganah. Chmn: Haifa Acad Assn of Social Scis; Isr Olei Zloczow Organ. Author: Political Economy, 1960; Principles of Money, 1962; ed, Haifa Munic Employees Jour. Recipient, Ot Haganah, Aleh. Hobbies: chess, swimming, table tennis. Home: 14 Keller St, Haifa, Isr. Office: Municipality of Haifa, Isr.

BONI, Albert, US, publisher; b. NYC, Oct 21, 1892; s. Charles and Bertha (Saslavsky); att: Cornell U, 1909-1910; Harvard U, 1910-12; m. Nell vanLeeuwen. Pres, Readex Microprint Corp since 1950; vice-pres, Boni & Liveright, 1917-20; pres, A & C Boni, 1923-35; first publ, paperbacks, 1928; originator and founder, Modern Library. F, Mus of Arts and Scis, Rochester, NY; Natl Microfilm Assn; mem: Soc of Motion Picture & TV Engrs; Natl Microfilm Assn; Amer Libr Assn; Royal Photographic Soc of Gt Brit; Soc of Photographic Scis and Engrs; Amer Inst of Physics. Author: Modern Book of French Verse, 1920; Photographic Literature, 1962. Recipient, Pioneer Medal, Natl Microfilm Assn, 1952. Home: 59 W 12 St, New York, NY. Office: 5 Union Sq, New York, NY.

BOOKATZ, Samuel, US, artist, sculptor; b. Phila, Pa, Oct 3, 1910; s. Barnet and Anna (Cohn); att: John Huntington Polytech Inst, Cleveland, O; Cleveland Mus Inst of Art; Mus Sch Fine Arts, Boston, Mass; Harvard U Med Sch; Grande Chaumiere, Collorossi, both Paris; Amer Acad in Rome; studied with: Alexander Jacovleff, Oskar Kokoschka, Ivan Mestrovic; m. Helen Meyer, Oct 14, 1964. Dir: Samuel Bookatz Georgetown studio, since 1943; Shenandoah Studio-Wildcat Mt-Blue Ridge Mt; chms. Cdr, USN, USNR, 1943-65. One-man shows: Amer Acad, Rome, 1938, 1940; Paris, 1939; Inst of Art, Cleveland; Corcoran Gal of Art, 1948; Smithsonian Inst, Natl Mus, 1950; I F A Gal; Artist Mart, 1945-62, all Wash, DC; Monede Gal, NY, 1963, 1964; exhbs: mus, gals, Us, Art Insts, throughout US; in perm collections: Corcoran Gal of Art; Phillips Gal; US Bur Med and Surg; The White House; Barnet Aden Gal; Smithsonian Inst; Armed Forces Med Mus; Court of Appeals, all Wash, DC; US Naval Hosp: Bethesda, Md; Portsmouth, Va; Print

Club; and in numerous other gals and mus's in pvt collections throughout US and abroad. During WW II, by his sketches aided plastic surg on facial injured soldiers; spoke out for black Amers' civil rights; contbd painting Hallelujah to dr for rebldg Alabama Baptist Church; designed poster, Hail O Israel, raising funds for med supply to Isr Six Day War. Recipient: scholarships: Cleveland Inst of Art, 1931-35; Boston Mus Sch of Art, 1935-37; William Paige Award, Boston Mus, for study abroad, 1937-39; Prix de Rome, 1937-39; Inst Allende, San Miguel, Mexico, 1954; Ford Grand in Hum's, Ford Found, 1962; numerous prizes from mus' throughout the world. Home and studio: 2700 Que St NW, Washington, DC.

BOOKBINDER, Jack, Isr, artist, educator; b. Odessa, Russ, Jan 15, 1911; s. Israel and Rebecca (Braun); in Isr since 1922; BFA, U of Pa, 1934; MFA, Temple U, 1946; m. Bella Braverman, Sep 16, 1936; c: Michael, Carl. Art dir, Phila phblic schs, since 1959, spec asst to art dir, 1945-59; lectr: esthetics, hist of art, Barnes Found, Merion, Pa, 1937-44; art educ, U of Pa, 1946-59; hist of art, PA Acad Fine Arts, 1949-61; art educ, Pa State U, 1950; cons, educ div, Phila Mus of Art, 1944-45; asso dean, Long Beach I Found Arts and Sci, 1951. Repr in perm collections: Pa Acad Fine Arts; Phila Mus of Art; Libr of Cong; Natl Gal of Art, Wash, DC; Yale U Art Gal; New Britain, Conn, Inst; Tyler Collection, Temple U; Kutztown Stae Coll, Pa; Woodmere Art Gal; Converse Coll, SC; Mus Fine Arts, Abilene, Tex; Reading, Pa, Mus and Art Gal; one-man shows: PA Acad Fine Arts, 1952; Phila Art Alliance, 1954; Woodmere Art Gal, 1955; Nessler Gal, NYC, 1961. F, Tyler Sch Fine Arts, Temple U; mem: Amer Watercolor Soc; Natl Art Educ Asn; E Arts Assn; Artists Equity Assn; Phila Art Alliance; Woodmere Art Gal; Pa Acad Fine Arts F; Phila Art Tchrs Assn; Audobon Artists; clubs: Phila Watercolor; Phila Print. Author: Industrial Arts in Education; Invitation to the Arts; History of Sculpture; The Gifted Child: His Education in the Philadelphia Public Schools; TV progs: Fifteen Steps in the World of Art; Artists USA; Art and the Artist; Profiles in Art; contbr to Compton's Ency; profsl jours. Recipient: f: in psych, PA Sch Social Work, 1935-36; for study and documentation in Mex, UN Council, Phila, 1948; scholarship for art study abroad, Barnes Found, 1938-39; 1st prize: Tyler Sch Fine Arts Alumni, 1947; Phila Art Tchrs Assn; Assn, 1950; Fifth Annual Exhb, Temple U Alumni, 1951; Pa Acad Fine Arts F Exhb; 1952; purchase prize: Lambert Fund, Pa Acad Fine Arts, 1947, 1953; Yale U Mus, 1949; Tyler Sch Fine Arts Alumni, 1950; Libr of Cong, 1951; silver medal, DaVinci Alliance, 1949; Clarence Wolf memorial prize, 1952; third prize: Print Club, Rochester, 1948; Cheltenham Art Cen Annual, 1949; John Pennell Memorial Medal, Phila Watercolor Club, 1957; Mong Q Lee Memorial Award, Amer Watercolor Soc, 1961; Jos Dixon Crucible Co Award for Graphics, 1962; gen alumni award, Temple U, 1964; annual DaVinci Art Alliance Award, 1964; Wm Church Osborn Memorial Award, Amer Watercolor Soc. 1948. Office: 323 S Smedley St, Philadelphia, Pa. Office: Bd of Educ, Phildadelphia, Pa.

BOOKBINDER, Hyman H, US, economist, foundation exec; b. NYC, Mar 9, 1916; s. Louis and Rose (Palger); BSS, CCNY, 1937; postgrad studies: New Sch for Social Research, 1940-42; NYU, 1947-49; m. Bertha Losev, Dec 25, 1938; c: Ellen, Amy. Wash repr, AJComm since 1967; econ, asst dir of research, Amalgamated Clothing Workers Amer, NYC, 1940-43, 1945-50; spec asst, dir, Manpower Off, Natl Security Resources Bd, Wash, DC, 1950-51; dep asst admnr, Natl Production Auth, Commerce Dept, Wash, DC, 1951-53; chief, cong research, CIO, Wash, DC, 1953-55, leg repr, AFL-CIO, 1955-61; spec asst, Secy of Commerce, Luther H Hodges, 1961-62; dir, Eleanor Roosevelt Memorial Found, 1962-63; asst dir, OEC, 1964-67; spec asst to Vice-Pres Hubert Humphrey, 1965-67. USN, 1943-45. Trustee, Amer Immigration and Citizenship Conf; secy, Civil Lib Clearing house; Wash chmn, ad hoc, Comty Genocide and Hum Rights Treaties; vice-chmn, Council of Wash, DC; UNA repr; trustee: Jt Action in Comty Services; Interrel Comm Against Poverty; B'nai B'rith; Workmen's Circle; Natl Urban League; Natl Assn Inter-group Relations Officials. Author, To Promote the General Welfare, 1950. Office: American Jewish Committee, 818 18 St, Washington, DC.

BOOKSPAN, Martin, US, music critic and commentator; b. Boston, Mass, July 30, 1926; s. Simon and Martha (Schwartz); BS, Harvard U, 1947; m. Janet Sobel, 1954; c: Rachel Raissa, David, Deborah. Coord, Concert and Symphonic Activities, ASCAP, since 1968; critic-at-large for WNAC-TV Channel 7

in Boston, since 1969; contbr ed, Stereo Review Magazine, since 1957; columnist and reviewer, The New York Times, 1961-1964; dir, music dir, prog dir, prog cons, WQXR, NY, 1956-68; coord, radio, TV, recordings, Boston Sym Orch, 1954-56; exec dir, NE Opera Theatre, 1952-54. Mem: adv comm, Natl Acad Recordings Arts and Sci, 1962-66; blue ribbon panel, Natl Acad TV Arts and Sci, 1967-68; adv bd, Music for Westchester Inc 1962-67; adv bd, Westchester Conservatory of Music since 1965; men's comm, NY Assn for Blind since 1961; cons: Rockefeller Found, 1963-67; American Fed of TV and Radio Artists since 1948. Contbr to prof jours. Author: 101 Masterpieces of Music and Their Composers, 1968. Home: 65 Parkview Dr, Eastchester, NY. Office: 575 Madison Ave, NYC.

BOOKSTEIN, Isadore, US, jurist; b. Albany, NY, Feb 12, 1891; s. Hyman and Lillie (Gallup); LLB, Albany Law Sch, 1912; m. Edith Friedman, Nov 23, 1913; c: Stanley, Selma Dubb, Edward. Ret; justice, NY Supr Court, 1946-68; counsel to law firm, Kohn, Bookstein and Karp, since 1968; fmr: asst dist atty, 1920-21, co-judge, 1921-22, both Albany; lectr, Albany Law Sch, 1923-46, trustee since 1954; asst counsel, Jt Leg Reapportionment Comm, 1943-45. Fmr: chmn, UJA; pres: Temple Beth Emeth Brotherhood; Gideon Lodge, B'nai B'rith; chmn, Albany Co Rep Comm; mem: Masons; KP; Elks; Zeta Beta Tau; Tau Epsilon Rho. Contbr to law jours. Recipient: B'nai Birith Award, 1947; Man of the Year, JWV, 1957. Home: 19 Stonehenge Lane, Albany, NY. Office: 100 State St, Albany, NY.

BOORSTIN, Daniel J, US, historian, educator, author; b. Atlanta, Ga, Oct 1, 1914; s. Samuel and Dora (Olsan); BA, summa cum laude, Harvard Coll, 1934; Rhodes Scholar, Oxford U, 1934-37; BA, first class hons, 1936, BCL, first class hons, 1937; studied, Inner Temple, Eng, barrister-at-law, 1937; JSD, Yale U, 1940, Sterling F, 1937-38; admitted Mass Bar, 1942; m. Ruth Frankel, Apr 9, 1941; c: Paul, Jonathan, David. Preston and Sterling Morton Dist Service Prof, hist, U Chgo since 1968, mem fac since 1944, Walgreen lectr, 1952; instr: hist and lit, Harvard Coll; hist, Radcliffe Coll, both, 1938-42; legal hist, Harvard Law Sch, 1939-42; asso prof, hist, Swarthmore Coll, 1942-44; sr atty, Off Lend-Lease Admn, Gen Counsel, Wash, DC, 1942; Amer hist ed, Ency Britannica, 1951-55; cons, Social Sci Research Cen, U Puerto Rico, 1955; Fulbright visiting lectr: U Rome, 1950-51; Kyoto U, Japan, 1957; first incumbent of chair of Amer hist, Sorbonne, Paris, 1961-62. Author: The Mysterious Science of the Law, 1941, paperback reprint, 1958; The Delaware Cases, 1792-1830, 3 vols, 1943; The Lost World of Thomas Jefferson, 1948, paperback reprint, 1960; The Genius of American Politics, 1953; The Americans: The Colonial Experience, 1958; America and the Image of Europe, 1960; The Image or What Happened to the American Dream, 1962; The Americans: The National Experience, 1965; An American Primer, 1966, paperback, 1968; The Landmark History of the American People, 1968; ed, Chicago History of American Civilization, 30 vols; contbr of articles and book reviews to lit, hist and legal publs. Mem: Colonial Soc, Mass; Amer Hist Assn; Mass Valley Hist Assn; S Hist Assn; Mass Bar Assn; Inner Temple, London; Int House, Japan; Phi Beta Kappa; appointed by Pres Johnson to Amer Revolution Bi-Centennial Commn, 1966; clubs: Elizabethan of Yale; Quadrangle; Cosmos; Wash, DC; Reform, London. Recipient: Bancroft Prize, Columbia U, 1959; awards: Friends of Lit, 1959; Soc of Midland Authors, 1959; Parkman Prize, 1966. Home: 5609 Woodlawn Ave, Chicago, Ill. Office: University of Chicago, Chicago, Ill.

BORDON, Abraham S, US, jurist, business exec; b. Piater, Russ, Oct 7, 1891; s. Samuel and Libby (Passeulis); in US since 1898; LLB, Cornell, U, 1914; LLD, hon, U of Hartford, 1965; m. Mindel Harris, Aug 14, 1917; c: Anne Meyer, Nancy Mellman. Judge, Superior Court, Conn, since 1950; justice, Supr Court, Conn, 1960; dir, Hartford Fed Savings Loan Ass, 1934; vice-pres, Atwater Mfg Co, 1931. Pres: J Fed, 1948-50, and 1962-64, dir since 1940; J Comty Council, 1938; dir, Hartford J Comty Cen since 1940; vice-chmn, United Service Org, 1940-41; mem: Corporator Inst for Living; Adult Probation Commn, 1956; Bd of Parole, 1961; Zeta Beta Tau; club, Tumble Brook. Recipient: awards: Man of the Year; Zeta Beta Tau, 1949; B'nai B'rith, 1953. Home 887 Farmington Ave, W Hartford, Conn. Office: Superior Court, Hartford, Conn.

BOREK, Felix, US, scientist; b. Crakow, Pol, May 5, 1926; s.

Joel and Stephanie (Kronengold) Rubinstein; in US since 1947; att Jagiellonian U, Crakow, 1946-47; BS, cum laude, Hobart Coll, Geneva, NY, 1950; MA, Harvard U, 1952; PhD, Rutgers U, 1955; m. Carmia Ganz, 1957. Asst prof, dept, microbiol and immunology, Albert Einstein Coll of Med, Bx, NY since 1967; asso biochem, Armed Forces Inst of Path, Wash, DC, 1958-63; visiting sci, Weizmann Inst of Sci, Isr, 1963-65, sr sci, 1965-67. Prin contribs: research work in immunology and immunochem; teaching med and grad students in immulogy and microbiol. Mem: Amer Assn of Immunologists; British Soc for Immunology; Isr Biochem Soc; Amer Chem Soc; AAAS; Sigma Xi. Author: Delayed-Type Hypersensitivity to Synthetic Antigens in Current Topics of Microbiology and Immunology, vol 43, 1968; ed, Immunogenicity, 1970; contbr of numerous articles to sci jours. Hobbies: music, photography, archaeol. Home: 400 Central Park W, New York, NY. Office: Dept of Microbiol and Immunology, Albert Einstein Coll of Med, Bronx, NY.

BORETZ, Benjamin Aaron, US, composer, editor, critic; b. NYC, Oct 3, 1934; s. Abraham and Leah (Yollis) Coll, 1954; MFA, Brandeis U, 1957; MFA, Princeton U, 1960, PhD, 1969; m. Naomi Messinger, Sep 1, 1954; s. Avron. Asst prof, music, Columbia U since 1969; ed, Perspectives of New Music since 1962, founding co-ed; music critic, The Nation since 1962; mem fac, music depts: U of Cal, 1957-59; Princeton U, 1959-68; Brandeis U, 1962-63; NYU, 1964-69. Composer: Chamber Concerto, 1954; Piano Variations, 1955; Wind Quintet, 1956; Violoin Concerto, 1957; Donne Songs, 1959-60; String Quartet, 1958-59; Ensemble Variations, 1962-64; Group Variations, I, 1966-68, II, 1968-69. Found chmn, Amer Soc U Composers, fmr, exec secy; mem: Amer Composers Alliance, fmr mem, nominating comm; Amer Musicological Soc; dir, Group Computer Synthesis, NYU; mem panel, Cong Intl Musicological Soc, Aus. Ed, Perspectives on Schoenberg and Stravinsky, 1968; contbr to musicological jours. Recipient: Fromm Found Award, for Violin Concerto, 1956; Award Musical Studies, Ingram-Merrill Found, 1966. Home: 225 W 86 St, New York, NY. Office: Columbia U, New York, NY.

BORG, Sidney F, US, engineer, educator; b. NYC, Oct 3, 1916; s. Herman and Pauline (Leibman); BS, Cooper Union, 1937; MCE, Poly Inst, Bklyn, 1940; DEngr, Johns Hopkins U, Baltimore, 1950; hon MEngr, Stevens Inst of Tech, 1958; licensed profsl engr, NY, NJ states; m. Audrey Elliott, Apr 4, 1944; c: Nicholas, Andrew, Jill, Kenneth. Head, civil engr dept, Stevens Inst of Tech since 1952; cons to ind firms and State of NJ in field of applied mech; with War Dept, 1940-41; engr, Turner Construction Co, 1942-43; asst prof, CE, U of Md, 1943-44; asso prof, Naval Postgrard Sch, Annapolis, Md, 1945-51; research engr, Grumman Aircraft, Bethpage, LI, 1951-52; Fulbright visiting prof, applied mech, Dan Tech U, Copenhagen, 1965-66; visiting prof: Technische Hochschule, Stuttgart, Ger, 1966; Pol Acad of Sci, 1968; Mem: Amer Soc for Engr Educ; Sigma Pi; Tau Beta Pi; f: AAAS; Amer Soc Civil Engr. Author: An Introduction to Matrix Tensor Methods in Theoretical and Applied Mechanics, 1956; Fundamentals of Engineering Elasticity, 1962; Matrix Tensor Methods in Continuum Mechanics, 1963; co-author: Advanced Structural Analysis, 1959; chaps in: Ency Americana; Handbook of Applied Mechanics; ed, textbook series, The Van Nostrand U Series in Civil Engineering and Applied Mechanics; contbr to profsl jours. Recipient: NSF Research Grant, 1956-57, 1958-60; Dist Alumnus Award, Poly Inst of Bklyn, 1957. Home: 2 Ninth St, Hoboken, NJ. Office: Stevens Inst of Tech, Hoboken, NJ.

BORGENICHT, Grace, US, art dealer; b. NYC, Jan 25, 1915; d. Samuel and Jeanette (Salny) Lubell; MA, Columbia U, 1937; studied painting, Paris, 1935; m. Jack Borgenicht, 1938 (div); c: Jan, Berta, Lois; m. 2nd, Norman Sachs, 1956 (div); m. 3rd, Warren Brandt, 1960. Found and pres, Grace Borgenicht Gall, NYC; sponsored exhb to foster contemporary art. Contbr to art publs. Recipient, first prize, Natl Assn of Women Artists, 1949. Hobbies: music, gardening. Home: 138 E 95 St, New York, NY. Office: Grace Borgenicht Gallery, 1018 Madison Ave, New York, NY.

BORGHI, Lamberto, It, educator, author; b. Leghorn, It, Jan 9, 1907; s. Augusto and Eva (Sonino); PhD, U of Pisa, 1929; DSS, New Sch for Social Research, NYC, 1948; marriage annulled; c: Carlo, Liana Coope. Prof educ, dir, Inst di Pedagogia, U Florence since 1955; fmr: visiting f, Yale U; prof educ: Us: Palermo; Torino; visiting prof, New Sch for

Social Research, NYC; mem, Eur Comm of Educators appd by Gov of Puerto Rico, survey educ and sch conditions in Commonwealth. Mem: intl council, Educ F; War Resisters Intl, London; Wider F of Soc of Friends. Author: Humanism and Religious Conception in Erasmus, 1935; Education and Authority in Modern Italy, 1951; John Dewey and Contemporary Educational Thought in USA, 1951; Essays on Psychology of Education, 1951; The Project Method, 1953; Foundations of Activity Education, 1952; John Dewey's Educational Ideal, 1955; Education and Schools in Italy Today, 1958; The Educational Thought in Italy During the Risorgimento, 1958; Education and Social Action, 1962; School and Community, 1963; School and Milieu, 1964; co-author, Education in United States, 1949; ed: School and City; Non-Violent Action. Home: Via Baciocchi 30, Leghorn, It. Office: U of Florence, It.

BORICHANSKY, Yehochua, Isr, educator; b. Bobrouisk, Russ, Mar 29, 1897; s. Samuel and Malka (Baksht); in Isr since 1948, att Inst d'Electrotech et de Mecanique Appliquee, Nancy, Fr, 1926-27; m. Miriam Kelman; c: Joseph, Natanya Kovo. Part time lectr, Technion, Haifa since 1965; with Henri Potez Aeroplanes, 1930-48; insp, profsl schs, exec comm, Histadrut, 1954-66. Mem: Oleh l'aoleh, Histadrut; Oleh Russia Org. Author: Problems of Physics; Springs; Theory of Vibrations. Home: 12 Rav Tsair, Tel Aviv, Isr.

BORNE, Mortimer, US, artist; b. Rypin, Pol, Dec 31, 1902; s. Harry and Lena (Warshaw); in US since 1916; att: Natl Acad of Design; NYC; Art Students League, NYC; Beaux-Arts Inst of Design, NYC; m. Rachel Sylvia Zipes, 1929. Profsl artist, sculptor, etcher, painter, since 1926; art lectr New Sch for Soc Research, since 1945; author, plan for interchange of artists, US State Dept, 1939; participant, U of Air Progs, US State Dept, 1947; Works exhb at: Chgo Art Inst; Bklyn Mus; Metrop Mus Art; Carnegie Inst; Mus Modern Art; one-man shows: Jerusalem, Isr, 1935; Intl Coll, Springfield, Mass, 1940; Cedar Rapids, Ia Art Assn, 1940; Corcoran Gal of Art, Wash, 1941; Mus Fine Arts, Montreal, Can, 1942; Grand Cen Art Gals, NY, 1943; Smithsonian Inst, Wash, 1944; Currier Gal, Manchester, 1945; Connoisseur Gal, NY, 1959; Rotary Intl Conv, Toronto, Can, 1964; Tel Aviv, 1965; works represented in perm collections: Libr of Cong US Natl Mus; NY Pub Libr; Riverdale J Comty Cen; Metrop Mus of Art (more than 100 etchings, black and white, and in color); famous pvt art collectors. Dir, Tappan Zee Art Cen, Nyack, NY, since 1960; mem, Amer Etchers' Soc. Contbr of articles on art to art jours. Recipient, Noyes Prize for best print in US, Soc of Amer Etchers. Club, Rotary, Nyack, chmn, intl service comm, since 1960. Home and studio: 107 S Broadway, Nyack, NY.

BORNSTEIN, Esther, Isr, tourist guide; b. Milan, It, July 23, 1936; d. Moshe and Sima (Arditi); in Isr since 1953; cert nurse, IDF Sch, 1955; cert guide, Tourist Guide Sch, Tel Aviv, 1968; m. Eliezer Bornstein, Jan 1, 1969; c: Ilan, Nurit. Tourist guide; ambulance driver, Magen David Adom, 1960-68. Nurse, IDF, 1954-55; aided paratroopers during liberation of E Jerusalem, 1967, called Angel of Mandelbaum Gate, White Angel. Mem, WIZO. Recipient, citations: Chief of Staff, IDF, 1955; Pres of Isr, 1967. Home: 23 Hameyasdim St, Jerusalem, Isr.

BORNSTEIN, Hyman, US, metallurgical engr; b. Chgo, Ill, Sep 3, 1891; s. Morris and Anna (Segal); BS, Armour Inst of Tech, 1911; LLB, John Marshall Law Sch, 1915; m. Carolyn Landauer, Jan 15, 1936; c: Ann. Cons metallurgist, since 1953; engr chem, City of Chgo, 1912-17; mgr materials, engr dept, Deere & Co, Moline, Ill, 1920-51, chief tech cons, 1951-53; metallurgical adv to Isr, Tech Assistance Admn, UN, 1952-53. Capt, US Army, 1917-19. Pres, Amer Foundrymen's Soc, 1937-38; Temple Emanuel, Davenport, Ia, 1932-34, 1958-60; mem: Amer Chem Soc; Amer Soc Metals; Amer Inst Mining and Metallurgical Engrs; Amer Soc for Testing Materials; clubs: Rock I Arsenal Golf; Outing. Hobby, gardening. Home: 2105 19 Ave, Rock Island, Ill.

BORNSTEIN, Leo Arthur, Isr, plastic surg; b. Jersey City, NJ, Dec 1, 1911; s. Charles and Freda (Posner); in Isr since 1948; BS, U of Ala, 1932; MD, U Edinburgh, Scotland, 1937; m. Victoria Zamore, Aug 19, 1949; c: Elhanan, Ilan, Oded. Chief, plastic surg; Tel Hashomer Hosp; Tel Aviv U Med Sch, both since 1950. Capt: US Army MC, 1943-46; IDF, 1948-51. Chmn, Comm of Educ, Intl Confd Plastic Surgs; pres: Isr Plastic Surgs Org, 1956-61; Rotary, Savyon, 1961-63; mem:

Amer, Brit and Isr Assns Plastic Surgs. Home: 43 Bnayahu St, Zahala, Tel Aviv, Isr. Office: 34 Tchernichovsky St, Tel Aviv, Isr.

BORNSTEIN, Siegbert, US, pathologist, educator; b. Berlin, June 7, 1903; s. Hugo and Henriette (Weinberg); in US since 1936; MD, U Berlin, 1926; m. Charlotte Brauns, Sep 28, 1937. Cons path, Chilton Memorial Hosp, since 1967, path, 1961-67; path, J Hosp, Berlin, 1936; asst bact, Beth Isr Hosp, NYC, 1937-42; asst path, Bklyn J Hosp, 1943; instr, clinical path, Hunter Coll, 1943; asst prof, path, Jefferson Med Coll, 1958-66; chief, lab service, VA Hosps: Oteen, NC, 1946-50; Montrose, NY, 1950-57; Phila, 1957-61. Maj, US Army, 1943-46. Dipl, Amer Bd Paths, 1944; found f, Amer Coll Path; f: Amer Coll Phys; Amer Assn Clinical Path; mem: Soc for Experimental Biol and Med; Pompton Lakes J Cen, NJ. Contbr to profsl jours. Home: 184 Hamburg Turnpike, Pompton Plains, NJ.

BOROS, David, S, US, rabbi; b. Czepa, Czech, Apr 11, 1914; s. Ignac and Netti (Berczi); in US since 1960; att Masaryk U, Brno, Czech, 1939; BA, Sir George Williams Coll, Montreal, Can, 1953; ordained rabbi, J Coll, London, 1949; rabb dipl, Merkaz Hatorah, Montreal, 1954; PhD studies, Dropsie Coll, Phila, 1964; m. Adele Schreiber, June 23, 1957. Rabbi, prin: B'nai Jacob Syn Cen since 1967; Adath Isr Cong, Oswego, NY, 1960-64; rel adv, B'nai B'rith Hillel State U, Oswego, NY, 1960-64; rabbi, prin, Adath Isr Cong, Millville, NJ, 1964-67. Chaplain: B'nai B'rith Valley Forge Chap; Borough Council, Phoenixville, Pa; mem: RabCA; Assn Alumni, Sir George Williams U; Dropsie Coll Student Org; Oswego Hist Soc. Hobby, chess. Home: 1101 S Gay St, Phoenixville, Pa. Study: Starr and Manavon, Phoenixville, Pa.

BOROW, Aaron, US, rabbi; b. Phila, Pa, Nov 6 1933; s. Abraham and Minnie (Janin); BA, Yeshiva Coll, NY, 1955; BRE, Yeshiva U, NY, 1955; ordained rabbi, Isaac Elchanan Theol Sem, MY, 1959; m. Pearl Karalitzky, Dec 12, 1955; c: Rebecca, Ephraim, Jacob, Israel. Rabbi, Cong Nusah Hari-B'nai Zion. dir, St Louis Sunday Torah Sch, both since 1964; Heb tchr: Clearview J Cen, 1956-57; Lincoln Park J Cen, 1957-59; rabbi, Cong Agudath Isr. 1959-64. Vice-pres: Rabb Council, St Louis; J Comty Relations Council, St Louis; mem: RabCA; Rel Zionists of Amer. Home: 1137 N McKnight St, University City, Mo. Study: 8630 Olive Blvd, University City, Mo.

BOROWITZ, Eugene Bernard, US, rabbi; b. NYC, Feb 20, 1924; s. Benjamin and Molly (Shafranik); BHL, MHL, DHL, HUC, 1948; EdD, Columbia U Tchrs Coll, 1958; m. Estelle Covel, Sep 7, 1947; c: Lisa, Drucy, Nan. Prof, educ, J rel thought, HUC-JIR since 1962; visiting lectr, JTSA, since 1967; rabbi, Comty Syn, Port Wash, 1957-62; natl dir, educ, UAHC, 1957-62; adj prof, Temple U, 1962-65; visiting prof: Columbia U Tchrs Coll, 1966; Princeton U, 1965-68. Chaplain, USN, 1951-53. Vice-pres, Rel Educ Assn; adv comm, Judaism, Quarterly Jour of J Thought. Author: A Layman's Introduction to Religious Existentialism, 1965; A New Jewish Theology in the Making, 1968; Choosing A Sex Ethic, 1969; What Can A Jew Say About Faith Today, 1969. Home: 19 Reid Ave, Port Washington, NY. Study: 40 W 68, New York, NY.

BORSKY, Arthur, US, musician, composer; b. Phila, Pa, Nov 29, 1918; s. Israel and Anna (Stark); BMus, U of Md, 1967; MMus, Wash Musical Inst, 1969; m. Leah Gripon, Sep 13, 1964. Instr, piano & theory, Wash Musical Inst since 1968; lectr: Wash Comm Sch since 1969; Temple Isr, Md, 1956. Mem: ZOA, Brandeis, Wash DC br; Heritage Lodge, B'nai B'rith; publicity chmn, Havruta Heb Speaking Club, DC; Natl Assn Music Tchrs; Natl Conf Music Educs; Amer Fed Musicians. Composer of numerous musical works, Contbr of articles to musical jours. Recipient: Natl Cent Music Tchrs Natl Assn, 1968; Ford Found F Grant, contemporary music project, 1969. Home and Office: 8109 Tahona Dr 303, Silver Spring, Md.

BORSOOK, Louis, Can, manufacturer; b. London, Apr 12, 1903; s. Simon and Sarah (Goldberg); in Can since 1907; BA, U of Toronto, 1926; m. Dorothy Lipschitz, Sep 17, 1926; c: Elsa, Beryl. Owner, chmn bd, Dorothea Knitting Mills Ltd, since 1967; pres, Parkhust Realty. Hon vice-pres, YM, YWHA, Home: 500 Avenue Rd, Toronto, Can. Office: 20 Research Rd, Toronto, Can.

BORVICK, Irwin Stanley, US, rabbi; b. Brockton, Mass, June 8, 1934;; s. Abraham and Taube (Gold); BA, Yeshiva Coll

1957; MHL, Bernard Revel Grad School, NYC, 1960; ordained rabbi, Yeshiva U, 1960; m. Judith Cohen, Feb 5, 1959; c: Aviva, Sari, Gordon. Rabbi: Lido Beach J Cen since 1969; Young Isr, Syracuse, 1967-69; Cong Degel Isr, Lancaster, Pa, 1962-67. Chaplain, capt, US Army, 1960-62. Mem, exec bd, RabCA; vice-pres, Rabb Alumni Yeshiva U, 1965-67; mem: NY Bd of Rabbis; Rabb Council of Long Beach. Contbr to rel jours. Recipient: chaplain award, Yeshiva U, 1962; cert of achievement, US Army. Home: 841 E Walnut St, Long Beach NY. Study; 1 Fairway Rd, Lido Beach, NY.

BORWICZ, Michel Maximilien, Fr, author; b. Cracow, Pol, Oct 11, 1911; s. Adolf and Anna (Rosenwald) Boruchowicz; in Fr since 1947; BA, U of Cracow, 1937; docteur ès lettres, Sorbonne, 1953. Author: numerous books in Pol, 1937-47; A l'Echelle Inhumaine, 1950; Ecrits des Condamnés à Mort, 1954; L'Insurrection du Ghetto de Varsovie, 1966; Terreur en Europe, 1968; Vies Interdites, 1969; Arische Papieren ayrens, 3 vols, 1955; Dort Wo Seis Meivein Andersh, 1955; Zwanzig Jahr Später, 1964, all in Yiddish; contbr to numerous Fr, Pol and Yiddish jours. During Ger occupation WWII: in extermination camp, Janowski; chief of clandestine net; cdr, socialist maquis, Miechow region, mem J Combat Org: contbr to clandestine jour; wrote poems sent by underground to the free world, reprinted in NY as Piesni Ghetta (Poems of the Ghetto), trans into several langs. Fmr: dir. hist commn, Cracow, co-dir, hist cen J commn, Pol; expert, High Court, judging war criminals; dir, Centre d'Etudes, l'Histoire des Juifs en Pol et Paris. Home: 67 Vaugirard Blvd, Paris 15e, Fr.

BOSAK, Meir, Isr, author, educator; b. Cracow, Pol, May 21, 1912; s. Yehuda and Esther (Fugelhot); in Isr since 1949; att U Warsaw, 1931-35; MPh, Inst Hohmat Isr, Warsaw, 1931-35; MPed, U Cracow, 1937; m. Sara Panzer, 1946. Tchr, HS, Rehovot; in several concentration camps, WWII. Author: Benoga Hasne, 1933; Kohvei Simcha'ot, 1953; Ve'ata Eini Ra' atcha, 1958; Berikud Keneged Halevana, 1960; Ahar Esrim Shana, 1963; Besha'ar Tahanat Hadmama, 1969; Ke'alim Baruach, 1966; contbr, J hist in Pol. Mem, Heb Writer's Assn. Recipient, MH Shapira Award, 1966. Home: 37 Shimon Tarsi, Tel Aviv, Isr. Office: Menuha Venahala St, Rehovot, Isr.

BOSMI, Nahum, Isr, police off; b. Baghdad, Iraq, Dec 27, 1921; s. Menashe and Yaffa (Bek); desc of Herb Curer, Baghdad, 1858-1920; Nahum Ishak Bek, Baghdad, 1859-1917; in Isr since 1922; architecture deg, Brit Inst, Jerusalem, 1940; m. Alegra Levy, Mar 14, 1955; c: Noga, Ofra, Talia. Police off, chief supt, head spec br, s dist spokesman, Isr Police Force since 1967; fmr; head, Arab rural sect, info serv, Haganah, 1941-48; intell off, IDF, 1948-49; participated in capture of terrorist groups. Fmr: scout leader; mem, Menora Club. Spec interests: Jerusalem hist, Bible, stamps. Home: Shikun Vatikei Hagana, 17 Sokolov St, Jerusalem, Isr. Office: Police District Headquarters, Maalee Gat Shimon, Jerusalem, Isr.

BOSS, Jochanan, Isr, physician; b. Cottbus, Ger, Dec 10, 1926; s. Walter and Esther (Baer); in Isr since 1934; MD, U of Zurich, Switz, 1954; m. Esther Heymann, 1952; c: Daphne, Gabriel, Amarel. Sr lectr, Heb U Hadassah Med Sch, Jerusalem since 1964; Beilinson Hosp, Petah Tikvah, Isr, 1956-61; Harvard Med Sch, Boston, Mass, 1961-62; U of Pitt, Pa, 1962-64. Lt IDF MC. Mem: Intl Acad Path; NY Acad Sci; Intl Assn Nephrology. Contbr of numerous papers in med field. Home: 36 Hapalmach St, Jerusalem, Isr. Office: Heb U Hadassah Med Sch, Jerusalem, Isr.

BOTEIN, Bernard, US, attorney; b. NYC, May 6, 1900; s. Herman and Sarah (Leonson); att CCNY, 1917-19; LLB, Bklyn Law Sch, 1924; hon: LLD, NY Law Sch, 1960; NYU, 1964; JTSA, 1965; Yeshiva U, 1965; Bklyn Law Sch, 1966; m. Marian Berman, Oct 13, 1940; c: Stephen, Michael. Sr partner, Botein, Hays, Sklar & Herzberg, since 1969; presiding justice, Appellate Div, 1st dept, NY Supr Court, 1958-69, appd justice, Supr Court, 1941, elected 1942, appd assoc justice, Appellate Div, 1953; asst dist atty, NY Co, 1929-36; headed city-wide accident fraud inves, 1936-37; headed state ins fund inves, 1938-39; chief counsel to Frederick Crane, Moreland comm inves state printing. Prin contribs: innovations in court procedures including: Manhattan and Bail and Summons projects; mh info service; impartial med testimony project; 24-hour arraignment court, court reorg which became effective in 1962. Pres, Assn Bar, NYC, since 1970; chmn: bd eds, NY Law Jour; bd trustees, NYC-Rand Inst; Mayor's Comm on Racial and Rel Prejudice; adv council, NY State Jt Leg Comm

on Crime; fmr chmn, Departmental Comm on Jud Admn, 1st dept; asso chmn, NYC Criminal Justice Coord Council; dir: NY Legal Aid Soc; Amer Arbitration Assn; Brotherhood-in-Action; Cen for NYC Affairs; Natl Legal Aid and Defender Assn; Council on Law-Related Studies; trustee: Practicing Law Inst; Vera Inst of Justice; Law Cen Found, NYU; William Nelson Cromwell Fund; f, Amer Coll Trial Lawyers; mem: Amer, NY State Bar Assns; NY Co Lawyers Assn; Amer Judicature Soc; Cent Assn; fmr mem, Jud Conf, NY State. Author: The Slum and Crime, 1936; Trial Judge, 1952; The Prosecutor, 1956; co-author, The Trial of the Future, 1963; contbr to law revs and ins periodicals. Recipient: Medal, Assn Bar, NYC, 1963, 1970; Chief Justice Stone Award, 1965; award for dist service to NYC, New Sch for Social Research, 1965; Judge Joseph Proskauer award, 1965; medal of merit, NY Co Grand Jurors Assn, 1968; gold medal, NY State Bar Assn, 1970; William Schieffelin award, Citizens Union. Home: 1010 Fifth Ave, New York, NY. Office: 200 Park Ave, New York, NY.

BOTKIN, Benjamin A, US, Folklore scholar, editor; b. Boston, Mass, Feb 7, 1901; s. Albert and Anna (Dachinick); BA, magna cum laude, Harvard Coll, 1920; MA, Columbia U, 1921; PhD, U Neb, 1931, DLitt, 1956; m. Gertrud Fritz, Aug 30, 1925; c: Dorothy Rosenthal, Daniel. Free lance, writer since 1945; ed in chief, Rediscovering Amer series, Folklore and Society Series, Johnson Reprint Corp, since 1967; mem, subcomm on folk music, off Cultural Presentation, US State Dept, since 1967; instr, asst prof, asso prof, Eng, U Okla, 1921-40; asst instr, U Neb, 1930-31; asst prof: Mont, 1932; NM Normal U, 1933; cons, natl resources comm, Comm on Population Problems, US Govt, 1936; folklore ed, Fed Writers Project, 1938-39; chief ed, writers' unit, Libr of Cong Project, 1939-41; asst i/c, chief, Archives of Amer Folk Song, Libr of Cong,1942-45; lectr, folklore: Columbia U, 1948; NY State Hist Assn Sems on Amer culture, 1950. Author: The American Play-Party Song, 1937, 1963; ed: Folk-Say, 1929, 1930, 1931, 1932; The Southwest Scene, 1931; A Treasury of American Folklore, 1944; Albums 7-10, Folk Music of the United States, from Records in the Archives of American Folk Song, 1945; Lay My Burden Down; A Folk History of Slavery, 1945; A Treasury of New England Folklore, 1947, rev ed, 1965; A Treasury of Southern Folklore, 1949; A Treasury of Western Folklore, 1951; Sidewalks of America, 1954; A Treasury of Mississippi River Folklore, 1955; New York City Folklore, 1956; A Treasury of American Anecdotes, 1957; A Civil War Treasury of Tales, Legends and Folklore, 1960; co-ed: A Treasury of Railroad Folklore, 1953; The Illustrated Book of American Folklore, 1958; contrib ed: NY Folklore Quarterly, since 1946; Southwest Rev, 1929-37; poetry ed, My Oklahoma, 1927-28; ed, publisher, Space, 1943-35; asso ed, Recall, since 1960; guest ed, Recall II, 1961; ed cons: The Life Treasury of American Folklore, 1961; The Badmen, Columbia Records Legacy Collection, 1963; cons, games, Random House Dict on the English Language, 1966; contbr to: Funk & Wagnall's Standard Dict of Folklore, Mythology and Legend, 1949-50; Colliers Ency, 1950; World Book Ency, 1960; various symposia, anthols, quarterlies, newspapers, record albums. Pres: Amer Folklore Soc, 1944-45, f since 1962; Okla Folklore Soc, 4928-40; Okla Writers, 1927-28; hon vice-pres, NY Folklore Soc, since 1949; chmn, bd dirs, Workshop for Cultural Democracy, 1956-58; bd dirs, Natl Folk Festival Assn, since 1967, natl adv council, since 1934; mem, found comm, J Heritage Found, since 1958; co-found 1st chmn, Jt Comm on Folk Arts, Works Progress Admn, 1938-39; delg, 3rd natl conf, US Natl Comm for UNESCO, NYC, 1952; mem: Intl Folk, Music Council; Manuscript Soc; Phi Beta Kappa. Recipient: f, grants: fac research, U Okla, 1932; Julius Rosenwald Found 1937-38; Libr of Cong, 1941-42; Guggenheim Found, 1951-52; Louis M Rabinowitz Found, 1966; medal, Civil War Roundtable, NY, 1963; sr f, Natl Endowment for Hums, 1968. Home and office: 45 Lexington Dr, Croton-on-Hudson NY.

BOTKIN, Henry A, US, artist, b. Boston, Apr 5, 1896; s. Albert and Anna (Dachinik); att Mass Sch of Art, Boston, 1914-17; Art Students League, NY, 1918-22; m. Rhoada Lehman, 1930; c: Toinette Laurant, Glenn. Painter, asso, Fine Arts Assns Gal, NYC; adv, numerous leading art collectors; represented by Frank Rehn Gal, NYC; held numerous one-man shows in: Billiet Gal, Paris; Phillips Gal, Wash, DC; Denver Mus; Arts Club, Chgo; U of Okla; U of Neb; Walker Gal; Stendahl Gal, LA; Corvoisier, SF; Assn Amer Artists; Marie Harriman Gal; represented in perm collections in numerous muss: Metrop Mus of Art; Phillips Memorial Gal, Wash, DC;

Mus Modern Art, NYC; Wadsworth Athenium, Hartford, Conn; Mus of Fine Arts, Boston; Akron Art Inst, O; Colby Coll Art Mus, Me; Norfolk Mus of Art, Va; Holyoke Coll, Mass; Whitney Msu Amer Art, NY; Bklyn Mus, NY; Newark Mus, Riverside Mus, NYC; Dallas Mus Fine Arts, Walker Art Cen, Minn; Norton Gal, Fla; Smith Coll Mus Art, Mass; State Mus Art, Munich; Rochester Memorial Art Gal, NY; U of Okla; Wash Co Mus of Fine Arts, Md; Chrysler Mus of Provincetown, Mass; Mus of Tel Aviv, Isr; The Butler Art Inst, O; U of Neb; Ain Harod Mus, Isr; Abbott Labs; Bat Yam Mus of Arts, Isr; Denver Art Mus, Colo; NYU Art Collection; U of Mich; Brandeis U; Rose Art Mus, Waltham, Mass; Syracuse U, NY; U of Mich; Libr of Cong, Wash, DC; Mobile Art Gal, Ala; La Jolla Mus of Art, San Diego, Cal; represented in touring exhbs: US, Eng, Japan, Ger, Fr, Can, Yugo, S Amer, Isr, S Afr, It. Pres: Fed Modern Painters and Sculptors since 1958; and found, Gal 256, Provincetown, Mass; Amer Abstract Artists, 1954-55; NY Artists Equity Assn, 1951-52; f, Intl Assn Plastic Arts; f, Intl Inst Arts and Letters. Lectr and participant, speaker on radio and TV, including Voice of Amer; conductor of forums in many cities with leading art personalities; org of many gal and mus exhbs in US and abroad; tchr, writer and critic of art. Recipient, Natl Inst Arts and Letters, 1967. Home and Studio: 56 W 11 St, New York, NY.

BOTNER, Benjamin, US, insurance exec; b. Hartford, Conn, Aug 3, 1900; s. Samuel and Fannie (Sandler); LLB, NYU Law Sch, 1929; chartered life underwriter, U of Pa, 1945; m. Frieda Rosenberg, Sep 29, 1928; c. Mrs. Peter Davies. Mgr, life ins agcy since 1969, asst sales mgr, Metropolitan Life Ins, 1931-65; volunteer worker, Vera Inst of Justice, 1967. Secy, NY Law Sch Alumni Assn; pres, Sidney Liptzen Found, 1950-51; vice-pres, Order of Lions, 1945-46; mem: B'nai B'rith. Contbr of articles to ins jours. Home: 1199 Park Ave, New York, NY. Office: 1180 Avenue of the Americas, New York, NY.

BOTTLEMAN, Raymond Raphael, US, engineer; b. NYC, May 30, 1913; s. Max and Celia (Gruzman); BS, Syracuse U, 1939; m. Ida Bader, Mar 15, 1950; c. Charles. Vice-pres, engr, Tupperware Co since 1960; chief engr, Great Amer Plastics, 1951-56; asst supt, Leviton Mfg Co, 1956-60; tchr, plastics, Rhode I Jr Coll. Mem: Soc Plastic Engrs, fmr pres: Soc Plastics Ind; Masons. Hobbies: photography, golf. Home: 86 Vassar Ave, Providence, RI. Office: POB 751, Woonsocket, RI.

BOTZER, Avraham, Isr, naval officer; b. Lukov, Pol, July 25, 1929; s. Josef and Frida (Levin) Botchan; in Isr since 1937; att: Heb U, 1966-67; Navy Command and Staff Course; m. Tamar Cahany; c. Galia, Orna. Cdr in chief, Isr Navy since 1968; mem, Sea br, Palmach at age 17; IDF Navy since War of Independence; captured Egyptian ship, Ibrahim-el-Awal, during Sinai Campaign; commanded force which was first to arrive at Sharm-el-Sheikh in Six Day War; fmr chief Navl Oprs.

BOUDIN, Leonard B, US, attorney; b. NYC. July 20, 1912; s. Joseph and Clara (Hessner); BSS, CCNY, 1933; LLB, St John's U, 1935; m. Jean Roisman, Feb 20, 1937; c. Michael, Kathy. Partner, law firm, Rabinowitz, Boudin, and Standard since 1947; atty, Mortgage Comm, State of NY, 1935-36; admitted to: NY Bar; US Court of Appeals 2nd, 5th, DC Circuits; US Dist Court, S Dist, NY, DC; Supr Court; Treas Dept; Customs Court, NY; Bd of Immigration Appeals and Immigration and Naturalization Service. Mem, bd trustees, Downtown Comty Sch since 1944, chmn 1944-47; Amer Arbitration Assn; Natl Panel of Arbitrators; Natl Lawyers Guild; Amer Fgn Law Assn; British Inst of Intl and Comparative Law; London Inst of World Affairs; Amer Soc of Intl Law; mem: ed bd; Lawyers' Guild Rev since 1944; St John's Law Rev 1934-35; Intl Juridical Assn Bull, 1934-37. Contbr to law jours. Home: 12 1/2 St Lukes Pl, New York, NY. Office: 30 E 42 St, New York, NY.

BOUKSTEIN, Maurice M, US, attorney; b. Cohoes, NY, Oct 24, 1905; s. Elias and Ida (Fish); att NYU, 1929-32; LLB, St Lawrence U Law Sch, 1935; LLM, 1936; m. Anna Horstein, Aug 20, 1931; c: Sara, Dina. Prin partner law firm, Guzik and Boukstein, since 1951; legal adv, JA for Isr, since 1946; gen counsel, Counsulate Gen of Isr, NY, since 1948. Delg, Claims Conf in the negotiations with Fed Rep of Ger on reparations, The Hague, 1952; counsel, Conf on J Material Claims Against Ger, since 1953; gen counsel, mem exec comm, Memorial

Found for J Culture; mem: exec comm, World Found of J Culture. Admn Comm, ZOA, 1940-45, exec comm, 1941-45; chmn, Platform Comm ZOA for Amer J Conf, 1943; AZEC, 1942-45; bd dirs, Amer Econ Comn for Pal, since 1934; bd dirs, J Restitution Successor Org, since 1947, chmn, exec comm, 1962; bd dirs: United Pal Appeal, 1941-45; KH, 1943-45; JNF, 1941-45; gov and mem exec council, Weizmann Inst of Sci, Rehovot, Isr, since 1949; bd dirs and exec comm, Amer-Isr Cultural Found; delg, 23rd WZC, Jerusalem, 1951; secy, Amer Econ Comm for Pal, 1933-37; secy, Pal Econ Corp, 1940-41; cons, Bd Econ Warfare of US, Wash DC, 1942; mem: Amer Bar Assn; NY County Lawyers Assn; Amer Acad Political Sci; clubs: Putnam Country, NYU. Home: 1040 Park Ave, New York, NY. Office: 37 Wall St, New York, NY.

BOURLA, Henri, Isr, business exec; b. Salonica, Greece, 1891; s. David and Palomba (Hasson); in Isr since 1935; m. Carmen Saporta 1921; 2c. Mgn dir, Isr Discount Bank Ltd; dir: Discount Bank Investment; Devl and Mortgage Bank; Industrial Devl Bank of Isr; Property and Bldg Corp; vice-pres, Tel Aviv Stock Exch; mem, various govt comms for stock exch and monetary problems; adv comm, Bank of Isr for banking affairs; fmr, pvt banker: Paris, 1911-1914. Greece, 1914-35. Contbr to Isr press. Home: 42 Balfour St, Tel Aviv, Isr. Office: 27/29 Yehuda Halevy St, Tel Aviv, Isr.

BOURLA, Oded, Isr, artist, educator; b. Jerusalem, June 23, 1915; s. Yehuda and Miriam (Goldberg); att Agric Coll, Mikve Isr, 1930-33; New Bezalel Sch, Jerusalem, 1935-38; m. Talia Hillman, Nov 16, 1946; c: Leeron, Tamir. Art tchr since 1960; tchr, Heb Schs, 1950-54; fabric designer, Lowenstein, 1955-58. Pvt, IDF, 1948-50. Exhbs of paintings: NY; Wash; Boston; New Bedford; Madrid; Alicante, Spain. Mem, ACUM Author: Michtavim Leliora, 1960; Shirim Mikol Hazvaim, 1964; Alef Bet Shel Susim, 1964; Kmo Sipurim, 1968; a record, Songs from the Bible, folkways, 1953; trans, La Vie Quotidienne à Rome à L'Apogée de l'Empire by Jérôme Carcopino, 1967; contbr short stories, articles. Home: 8 Hoffien St, Ramat Aviv, Isr.

BOXER, Harold H, US, attorney; b. Chgo, Ill, Apr 24, 1907; s. Joseph and Dorothy (Lindner); BS, St John's U, 1928; PhD, Midwestern U, 1932; m. Enid Aussenberg, Mar 9, 1946. Law secy, Supr Court Justice, Queens Co since 1969; referee, Small Claims Court, Civil Court, NYC since 1956; spec asst atty gen, Election Frauds, NYC, 1932. Pres: Trylon Dem Assn since 1968; Forest Hills Hapoel Hamizrachi since 1959; Queens Inst J Studies,1951-52; First Bklyn Hung Aid Soc, 1950; chmn: Jt Youth Commn, Union Orthodox J Congs of Amer since 1952; RabCA since 1952; Natl Conf of Syn Youth Monthly since 1952; vice-chmn, Coord Comm, Fed J Philanthropies, Queens; UJA Forest Hills Div, since 1950; delg, Syn Council of Amer since 1954; mem: Natl Council, JWB since 1956; Admissions Comm, Queens Co Bar Assn since 1952; Award Comm, Edison Found, 1954-58; HIAS; Ind Order B'rith Abraham; KP; Masons; Club, Lawyers of Queens. Recipient: FJP Award, 1960; Kether Shem Tov Award, Union Orthodox J Congs of Amer, 1964; Home: 104-21 68 Dr, Forest Hills, NY. Office: 39 Broadway, New York, NY.

BOXER, Murry, US, physician, attorney, educator; b. NYC, June 14, 1901; s. Joseph and Dorothy (Lindner); LLB, St Lawrence U, 1922; JSD, Bklyn Law Sch, 1924; BS, NYU, 1926; MD, Coll Phys and Surgs, 1932; PhD, Midwestern U; m. Edna Rothman, Dec 9, 1926; c: Joyce Rothman, Barbara Tindel. Judge, Spec Sessions Cour, Rockland Co, NY since 1962; pres, Midwestern U. Pres, Heb Sch of Williamsburg, 1924-26; found, Yeshiva of Crown Hgts, Bklyn; dir, Kiwanis Intl; dep grand master, Odd Fellows; pres, Amer Phys Assn; life mem, Elks; mem: Amer, Fed, Bklyn Bar Assns; HIAS; ZOA; J Bd of Educ; J Tchrs Assn; Masons; KP; Sigma Tau Mu, chancellor, 1926-28; Frat Socs of Chile; clubs, Natl Dem. Ed, Jour of Healing Arts. Home: 85 Washington Ave, Spring Valley, NY. Office: 225 Broadway, New York, NY.

BOYKO, Hugo, Isr, ecologist, b. Vienna, Aus, Oct 6, 1892; in Isr since 1935; att Akademisches Gymnasium, Off Sch and U, Vienna, Aus; PhD, U of Vienna, 1930; m. Elisabeth Spitzer, May 25, 1920; c: Hava, Avi-Yona, Maya, Herbert. Coordinator, pres, World U Cen, utilization, of saline and waste water, since 1968; ecological cons: Isr; India UNESCO; US, from 1961; pvt sci, desert ecology, ME countries, 1936-44; ecologist, Pal Govt, 1944; head, perm team, biol, ME, Colonial

Off, 1947; ecological adv: Min of Agric, PM Off, 1948. Off, Aus Army, 1911-1919. Prin contribs; principles and new methods in plant ecology for productivizing deserts. Pres, World Acad of Art and Sci since 1965; hon cons, UNESCO since 1952; f: World Acad of Arts and Scis since 1960; AAAS since 1956; mem: Intl Ecological Commn, ICUN since 1960; correp mem: Swed Phytogeog Soc since 1951; Acad of Arts and Scis, Puerto Rico since 1962; fmr: dean, Council, World Acad Art and Sci; hon secy gen, WAAS; chmn: Intl Commn on Applied Ecology, IUBS; Intl Comm on Ecological Climatology, ISB; vice-pres, Intl Soc of Bio-Meteorology; mem: Sevenmem Intl Adv Commn, UNESCO, Arid Zone Research; hon, Intl Soc for Tropical Ecology. Author and contbr of numerous articles on natural laws in ecological climatology; hydrology; plantsociology; global salt circulattion to sci jours. Recipient: John Fleming Medal, 1959; Medal of Honor in gold, Order of Merit for Research and Invention, Fr, 1966; William F Petersen Award, sci accomplishments in field of salt water irrigation, U Intl Biometerological Cong, Montreux, 1969. Home: 1 Rupin St, Rehovot, Isr.

BRACHMAN, Abraham J, US, rabbi; b. Jacobstadt, Latvia, June 7, 1900; s. Marcus and Chaye (Vershok); in US since 1905; att, Marietta Coll, 1917-19; BA, U Pittsburgh, 1925; ordained rabbi, JIR, 1946; hon DD, Marietta Coll, 1955; m. Sarah Ruby, Nov 14, 1935; c: Merom, Areve Alexander. Rabbi, Heb Inst, Fort Worth, since 1946. US Army, 1918. Pres, chmn, bd, Cong Ahavath Sholom, 1937-45; secy and pres, Kallah of Tex Rabbis, 1953-57; chmn, publs comm, HUC-JIR Alumni Assn, 1953-56; vice-chmn, Natl Rabb Council since 1953; mem: bd of trustees, JIR, 1943-48; bd of dirs, Heb Theol Coll, Chgo since 1943; bd of govs, HUC-JIR, 1949-58; AJCong, 1938; B'nai B'rith Lodge, 1923; ZOA, 1936-41; Ed, and publisher, J Theol Southwest, since 1959; contbr annual research papers to Kallah, 1948-59; rel periodicals. Home and study: 2308 Warner Rd, Fort Worth, Tex.

BRACHMAN, Leon H, US, business exec; b. Marietta O, July 21, 1920; s. Elias and Ella (Beren); BS, cum laude, Harvard Coll, 1942, tching f, elec, Harvard U, 1942-44; m. Fay Rosenthal, Aug 10, 1941; c: Deborah, Ellen, Marshall, Wendy. Pres: Petrochemicals Co, Inc, 1968; Marco-Chemical, 1960, secy-treas, 1946-60; radar engr, Consolidated Vultee Aircraft, 1944-46. Pres, Fort Worth ZOA, 1948-50; vice-pres SW region, 1949-53; Amer Oil Chems Soc; mem: natl campaign cabinet, UJA; natl bd, JDC; bd, Fort Worth J Fed, pres, 1957-59; bd, All Sts Hosp. Hobbies: flying, camping, music. Home: 3720 Autumn Dr, Fort Worth, Tex. Office: 2001 N Grove, Fort Worth, Tex.

BRACHMAN, Malcolm K, US, business exec; b. Fort Worth, Tex, Dec 9, 1926; s. Solomon and Etta (Katzenstein)); BA, Yale U, 1945; MA, Harvard U, 1947, PhD, 1949; m. Minda Delugach, Sep 4, 1951; c: Lynn, Lisa, Malcolm. Pres: Pioneer Amer Co since 1961; Northwest Oil since 1956; vice-pres, dir, The Producers Supply and Tool since 1954; asst prof, physics, S Methodist U, 1949-50; asso physicist, Argonne Natl Labs, 1950-53; mem research staff, Tex Instruments, 1953-54. Pvt, US Army, USAC, 1944-46; capt, US Army Res, 1949-55; Dir: St Marks Sch of Tex; UN chap, Tex Life Conv; Home for J Aged; Comty Chest; chmn bd, Jarvis Christian Coll; mem, bd devl, S Methodist U since 1962; f: Amer Phys Soc; Grad Research Cen; mem: Phi Beta Kappa; Sigma Xi, Harvard Found Council; Harvard Alumni Assn; Masons; Amer Assn Petroleum Geol; Soc Exploration Geophysicists; NY Soc Security Analysts; Inst Radio Engrs. Contbr to to profsl jours. Home: 10036 Hollow Way Rd, Dallas, Tex. Office: 2730 Republic National Bank Building, Dallas, Tex.

BRACHMAN, Solomon, US, business exec; b. Jacobstadt, Latvia, Dec 15, 1896; s. Marcus and Chaye (Vershok); in US since 1905; BA, Marietta Coll, 1918; LLD, Tex Chr U, 1968; m. Etta Katzenstein, Oct 31, 1921; c: Malcolm, Marilyn Hoffman. Pres, The Producers Supply and Tool Co since 1935; chmn, bd, Pioneer Amer Inst since 1946; vice-pres, treas, NW Oil. Pres: J Fed, 1944-50; Beth El Cong, 1952-53; dir, CJFWF, 1945; trustee, Tex Chr U since 1950; mem, bd: Harris Methodist Hosp since 1952; UAHC since 1953; mem, Phi Beta Kappa. Home: 4312 Bellaire Dr S, Apt 102, Fort Worth, Tex. Office: Trans-Amer Life Bldg, Fort Worth, Tex.

BRACHYAHU, Elhanan, Isr, engineer; b. Rogovo, Lith, June 1, 1890; s. Aharon and Sarah (Frame); desc of Rabbi Abba Jakov Boruchow; in Isr since 1914; BS, MIT, 1922; m. Rivkah

Muller, 1927; c: Dinah Mayraz, Ofra Kastner. Ret; fmr, chief engr, head, tech dept, JNF, Jerusalem, 1926-58. Prin contrib: water supply and drainage of JNF lands, including Huleh swamps and lake. Contbr to profsl jours. Home: 81 Hanassi Blvd, Haifa, Isr.

BRADLOW, Frank R, S Afr, business exec, author; b. Johannesburg, June 19, 1913; BCom, U Witwatersrand, 1935; m. Edna Rom, Nov 14, 1945; c: Diana Anthony, Hugh. Regional dir, Bradlows Stores Ltd since 1946, secy 1935-39. War service, 1939-43. Natl vice-pres, S Afr J Bd Deps, past treas, Cape comm; chmn, Friends, S Afr Libr since 1962; govt appd trustee: S Afr Libr; William Fehr Art Collection; asso, Chartered Inst Secys; Chmn, Cape Town PEN club since 1961; fmr chmn, Cape div, S Afr Furniture Retailers Assn; vice chmn, Rosecourt J Youth Cen; clubs: Civil Service; Cape Town Rotary; Clovelly Country. Co-author: Thomas Bowler of The Cape of Good Hope; Here Comes the Alabama: The Career of the Confederate Raider; Baron Von Ludwig and the Ludwigsburg Garden, 1965; Thomas Bowler, His Life and Work, 1968. Recipient, Cape Tercentenary Found Award, 1968. Home: Sha-anan, Shetland Rd, Rondebosch, S Afr. Office: 69 Plein St, Cape Town, S Afr.

BRAGINSKI, Yehuda, Isr, educator; b. Konotop, Czeznigov, Russ, Sep 17, 1897; s. Yitshak and Chilna (Woolman); in Isr since 1929; att U Kijew, 1916-22; m. Batya Kipriss; c: Yitshak, Nimrod. Tchr, Heb, children and adult immigrants; with Kibbutz Archives. Red Army, 1920; IDF; active Aliyah Bet. Mem: Zionist World Actions Comm; Histadrut HaZionit Haolamit since 1915; ZF "Tzor Vakolov" Hitachdut Poalei Zion; JA past head, absorp dept; Kvutzat "Et Leganot" delg, ZCs; fmr mem: Cen Hechalutz; gen mgmt, UJA; repr, HaHistadrut veha Hanabah HaZionit to Hahechalutz, all Pol. Author, Am hoter el hof (People Striving to the Shore). 1965. Home: Kibbutz Givat HaShlosha, Isr.

BRAHAM, Jackson, Isr, physician; b. Leeds, Eng, Aug 14, 1914; s. Israel and Annie (Masson); in Isr since 1949; MD, Leeds med sch, 1939; m. Tamara Reindorf, 1945; c: Philip, Dan. Head, neur dept, Tel Hashomer govt hosp, Tel Aviv since 1969. Mem: Neuropsycht Soc; EEG Soc; fmr mem, MRCP, Leeds. Contbr of articles on neurological subject to med lit. Home 21 Maaleh Hatsofim, Ramat Gan, Isr. Office: 18 Bialik St, Tel Aviv, Isr.

BRAHAM, Randolph L, US, educator, author; b. Rum., Dec 20, 1922,; MS, CCNY, 1949; PhD, New Sch, NYC, 1952; m. Elizabeth Sommer. Asso prof. CCNY, since 1959; tchr: Fairleigh Dickinson U, Hunter Coll, Hofstra U, 1956-59. Mem: Amer Political Sci Assn. Author: Education in Communist Rumania, 1958; Jews in the Communist World, 1961; Eichmann and the Destruction of Hungarian Jewry, 1961; Eichmann es a magyar zsidosag pusztulasa, 1963; The Hungarian Jewish Catastrophe, 1962; The Destruction of Hungarian Jewry, 1963; Education in Rumanian People's Republic, 1964; Soviet Politics and Government, 1965; Hungarian-Jewish Studies 1966; Israel: A Modern Education System, 1966; Documents on Major European Governments, 1966; The Synagogues of Hungary, 1968; Hungarian-Jewish Studies, 1969; The Eichmann Case, 1969; Education in the Hungarian People's Republic, 1969; contbr to political and J jours. Home: 114-07 Union Turnpike, Forest Hills, NY. Office: CCNY, New York, NY.

BRAININ, David Neumark, US, attorney; b. NYC, Apr 19, 1925; s. Joseph and Salomea (Neumark); BA, Columbia Coll, 1948; JD, NYU Sch of Law, 1958; m. Sharon Sema, June 21, 1962; c: Jo, Laurie, David, Peter, Julia. Partner, law firm: Rubin, Wachtel, Baum & Levin since 1963; Brainin & Longo, 1959-60; asso Wachtel & Michaelson, 1960-62; lectr, Practicing Law Inst; mem, appellate div, Supr Court, NY State. USN, 1943-46. Mem: Amer Bar Assn; NY State Bar Assn, exec secy, Corp Law Comm, 1959-60; NY Bar Assn; Phi Beta Kappa. Contbr of articles to legal jours. Home: 70 Hamilton Ave, New York, NY. Office: 598 Madison Ave, New York, NY.

BRAJKOVIC, Vladimir, Isr, scientist; b. Slav, Pozega, Yugo, July 20, 1897; s. Ziga and Dragica (Scheyer) Breyer; in Isr since 1950; MPharm, U of Zagreb, 1919; Engr Chem, Tech HS, Zagreb, 1923; m. 2nd, Blazica Scheyer, Jan 13, 1949; d. Liora Harel. Chief pharmacist-chem, Ikapharm Ltd, 1950-67; tech dir, chem factory: Jogofarmacija, 1923-28; Kastel, 1928-42; Pliva, 1945-49, all of Zagreb, Yugo; commercial dir, Beograd, 1949-50. Yugo partisans, 1943-45. Mem, Masons; fmr: hon mem, Pharmaceutical Soc of Yugo; pres, Yugo Chem Soc; mem: Commn for Yugo Pharmacopaeia; sci bd, Min of Public Health, Yugo; bd, Yugo Ind Chamber. Contbr of articles to fgn profsl jours; fmr ed, Farmaceutski Vjesnik, Zagreb. Home: 14 Hashmonaim St, Ramat Gan, Isr.

BRAMSON, David Jay, US, merchant; b. Chgo, Nov 1, 1937; s. Leo and Ann (Travis); att U of Colo, 1955-58; m. Suzan Sloan, Feb 7, 1963; c: Nancy, Jeffrey, Max. Pres, Bramson Inc and Subsidiaries since 1962; partner, Gold-De Brow-Bramson Farms since 1964. Mem, Standard Club; Fmr, chmn, women's apparel div, CJA, Chgo; Club, Standard. Recipient, Isr PM Medal, women's apparel div, Chgo Bonds Isr. Hobbies: fishing, handball, farming. Home: 3750 N Lake Shore Dr, Chicago, Ill. Office: 160 N Michigan St, Chicago, Ill.

BRAND, Hyman, US, manufacturer, communal worker; b. Pol, Aug 2, 1892; s. Kalman and Pessel (Nagelbusch); in US since 1909; m. Clara Stern, Mar 31, 1917; c: Arthur, Frances Levitch. Mgn partner, Brand & Puritz since 1928. Pres: Heb Acad of Gtr Kan City since 1966; Kan City Mfrs Assn; Kan City Mfrs Assn, both since 1940; mem: JA for Isr, since 1963; B'nai B'rith; AJComm; ZOA; Masons; bd, Rockhurst Coll since 1954; fmr: pres: J Fed and Council; Beth Shalom Syn, parnas since 1951; vice-pres, Comty Chest; regional chmn, UJA; natl vice-pres, United Syn of Amer; chmn, vice-pres, natl bd overseers, Midwest region, JTSA; mem bd: United Funds; Kan City Art Inst; Starlight Theater; C of C; Urban League; United J Social Service; Home for J Aged; J Comty Cen; mem, bd councillors, Menorah Hosp; clubs: Oakwood Country, Men's of Beth Shalom Syn. Recipient: citation, Catholic Comty Service, 1952; citation of merit, Kan City chap, Hadassah, 1954; Louis Marshall award; award, NCCJ, 1958; Isadore Bierfeld award, Kan City J Comty Cen. Home: 633 W Dartmouth Rd, Kansas City, Mo. Office: 313 W 8 St, Kansas City, Mo.

BRAND, Irving Rubin, US, attorney; b. Minneapolis, Minn, Dec 23, 1918; s. Harry and Ruth (Rubin); BSL, U of Minn, 1941, LLB, 1943; m. Ruth Miller, 1953; c: Judith, Johanna, Jonathan, Jethra, Joshua. Partner, law firm, Maslon, Kaplan, Edelman, Borman, Brand and NcNulty, since 1967; Judge; Dist Court, Hennepin Co, Minn, 1955-66; prof lectr, Sch of Dent, U of Minn since 1947, adj prof, Law Sch since 1953; law clerk, US Circuit Court judge, 1943-44; with Dept of Justice, Wash, DC, 1944-45; judge, Munic Court, Minneapolis, 1951-55. Chmn: Comm on Jury Instrn guides, Minn Dist Judges Assn since 1959; Hennepin Co Jr Bar Assn, 1950-51; pres, Minn Chap, Amer Friends Heb U, 1957; dir, Hillel Found, U of Minn since 1951; mem, bd trustees, Mt Sinai Hosp, Minneapolis since 1952; mem, bd, Minneapolis Fed for J Service, 1952-55; mem: Hennepin Co, Minn, Amer Bar Assns; Amer Judicature Soc; Amer Law Inst. Contbr to med jours. Home: 4300 Forest Rd, St Louis Park, Minn. Office: 1200 Builders Exch Bldg, Minneapolis, Minn.

BRAND, Oscar, US, writer, composer, performer; b. Winnipeg, Can, Feb 7, 1920; s. I Z and Beatrice (Shulman); in US since 1945; BA, Bklyn Coll, 1942; div; c: Jeannie, Eric, Anthony. Pres: Harlequin Productions, Inc; Gypsy Hill Music, both since 1959. Composer: original producs: In White America; How to Steal an Election; The Education of Hyman Kaplan; A Joyful Noise; The Golden Chariot of the Sun; The Bridge of Hope; Broadway musical, The Male Animal; writer, composer, performer: numerous LP albums; three off-Broadway shows; two Broadway shows; numerous motion pictures; numerous books, articles; reviewer, Saturday Review; pub works include: Singing Holidays; Western Guitar; Bawdy Songs; Ballad Mongers: Folksongs for Fun; Courting's a Pleasure. US Army, 1942-45. Adv: YMCA, music div, Coord, Folk Music - NYC; Pres' Comm, Nutrition; Educ TV; fmr: mem, pub comm, UAHC; moderator, The Dissenters. Recipient: awards: Golden Lion: Venice; Edinburgh; SF; Golden Reel: Emmy; Peabody; O State; Scholastic; Thomas Alva Edison; Valley Forge; Freedom Found; Festival Citations; public service citations, Hadassah; NYC (La Guardia to Lindsay). Hobby, sailboating. Home: 4 Perry St, New York, NY.

BRAND, Philip, US, rabbi; b. NYC, Apr 10, 1914; s. Max and Molly (Fleischer); BA, Yeshiva U, 1933; MS, CCNY, 1935; rabbi, Rabbi Isaac Elchanan Theol Sem, 1939; m. Mollie Rosen, Mar 28, 1943. Rabbi; Cong B'nai Jacob, Avnel, NJ since 1959; Ohave Sholom, Gardner, Mass, 1940-43; Queens

J Cen, Queens Village, NY, 1943-52; Temple Beth-El, Cranford, NJ, 1952-57. Pres, Cranford Clergy Council, 1954-55; vice-pres, United Clergy, Woodbridge Area, NJ; mem: Hum Rights Comm, Woodbridge; RabCA; NY Bd Rabbis; Alumni Assn, Yeshiva Coll, Rabb Alumni. Author: Causes of WWI as treated in Secondary Schools Textbooks of Eng, Ger, Neutral Powers and US, 1935; Contbr monthly column, Cranford Citizen and Chronicle since 1952. Hobby, philately. Home: 380 Lord St, Avenel, NJ. Study: Cong B'nai Jacob, Avenel, NJ.

BRANDLER, Mark, US, jurist; b. Antwerp, Belgium, Nov 9, 1909; s. Samuel and Sarah (Gutwirth); in US since 1915; att CCNY; LLB, Bklyn Law Sch, St Lawrence U, 1932; m. Estelle Weinberg; d. Diane. Judge, Superior Court, LA Co, Cal since 1957; pvt practice, 1932-37; asst dist atty, LA Co, 1937-53; judge, Munic Court, LA, 1953-57. US Army, 1942-45. Mem: regional adv bd, ADL; LA JCC; B'nai B'rith; Elks; Eagles; LA, NY, Cal Bar Assns. Home: 1000 Lexington Rd, Beverly Hills, Cal. Office: Dept 107-Superior Court, Hall of Justice, Los Angeles, Cal.

BRANDT, Henry George, Eng, rabbi; b. Munich, Ger, Sep 25, 1927; s. Friedrich and Margot (Frey); in Eng since 1951; BS, hon, Queen's U, 1955; rabbi, Leo Baeck Coll, 1960; m. Sheila Phillips, Aug 21, 1955; c: Lynda, Michael, Naomi, Jonathan. Rabbi, Sinai Syn, Leeds, Eng since 1960; sr min, Assn Reform Syns since 1967. Lt, Isr Navy, 1948-51. Chmn, Assembly of Mins, Reform Syns of Gt Brit; hon vice-pres, JNF, Leeds Commn; Leeds J Inst; mem, B'nai B'rith. Contbr to rel jours. Recipient, Isr War of Independence Medal, 1948. Home and study: 59 The Drive, Leeds, Eng.

BRANDT, Peter H, US, attorney; b. NYC, Feb 6, 1896; s. Jacob and Rose (Korn); BS, Case W Reserve, 1919, MEd, 1922; LLB, Fordham Law Sch, 1927, LLD, 1969; m. Elsie Finestone, June 27, 1926; c: Hubert, Carol Ferranti. Partner, law firm, Peter H & Hubert J Brandt since 1928. US Army, 1918. Emergency chmn, UJA Bx Co; pres: Riverdale J Cen; Nathan Straus J Cen; ZOA dist 64; fmr: chmn: Sch Bd 22, NYC; Selective Service Bd 18; secy, NYC Comm on Tax Exemption; mem: Masons; Bx Bar Assn; Amer Legion; JWV; Amer Soc of Appraisers. Contbr articles to profsl jours. Hobbies: Americana, Judaica. Home: 3701 Henry Hudson Pkwy, Riverdale, NY. Office: 350 Fifth Avenue, New York, NY.

BRANDWEIN, Bernard Jay, US, educator; b. Chgo, Ill, Apr 19, 1927; s. William and Eleanor (Adelman); MS, Purdue U, 1951, PhD, 1955; m. Despina Sbarounis, Feb 23, 1951; c: Robert, David, Karen. Prof, chem, SD State U, mem, grad fac, since 1960; grad research asst, Purdue U, 1952-55. Cons, SD Ind Devl Expansion Agcy; mem: Amer Chem Soc; Inst Food Techs; NY Acad Sci; SD Acad Sci; AAAS; Phi Lambda Upsilon; Sigma Xi; Intl Brotherhood Magicians. Author, Elementary Organic Chemistry Laboratory Manual, 1967; contbr research papers to food sci jours. Home: 414 State Ave, Brookings, SD. Office: Dept of Chem, South Dakota State U, Brookings, SD.

BRASCH, Rudolph, Austr, rabbi, author; b. Berlin, Nov 6, 1912; s. Gustav and Hedwig (Mathias); in Austr since 1949; att U Berlin, 1931-35; PhD, Wuerzburg U, 1936; ordained rabbi, Hochschule für die Wissenschaft des Judentums, Berlin, 1938; hon DD, HUC, Cincinnati, 1959; m. Liselotte, Feb 16, 1952. Found, N Shore Temple Emanuel, Sydney, 1957; chief min, dir Heb educ, Temple Emanuel since 1949; fmr: rabbi: N London Syn, 1938-48; and co-found, Southgate and Enfield Progressive Syn, both London, 1944-48; Dublin Progressive Syn, 1946-47; Springs and Dist J Reform Cong, S Afr, 1948-49; dir, PR, S Afr Bureau for Progr Judaism, 1948-49. Chaplain, civil defense, London Blitz, 1939-45. Life vice pres, Austr and NZ Union Progressive Judaism since 1960; mem: Friends Heb U; PR comm, NSW Bd Deps; governing body, World Union for Progressive Judaism since 1948; fmr: pres J Libr Assn NSW; vice pres, Moses Montefiore Home, Sydney; vice chmn: Soc Study of Rel, London; guest lectr, Heb, St Andrews Coll, Sydney U, 1952-53. Author: The Midrash Shir ha-Shirim Zuta, 1936; The Jewish Question Mark, 1945; A Little Book of Comfort for Jewish People in Times of Sorrow, 1946; The Irish and the Jews, 1947; The Star of David, 1952, 1956, 1965; The Eternal Flame, 1958; Sir John Monash, 1959; How Did It Begin? 1965, 1967, 1968, 1969; Mexico - A Country of Contrasts, 1966, 1967; Dreimal Schwarzer Kater, 1968; In the Beginning 1968;

The Jewish Heritage, 1969; The Unknown Sanctuary, 1969; ed: The Progressive, S Afr, 1948-49; The Temple Emanuel Haggadah, Sydney, 1953; contbr to mags; broadcaster and telecaster. Recipient, OBE, 1967. Home: 14 Derby St, Vaucluse Sydney, Austr. Study: 7 Ocean St, Woollahra, Sydney, Austr.

BRASLAVSKY, Yosef, Isr, lecturer, teacher; b. Romny, Russ, Feb 15, 1896; s. David and Sara (Naimark); in Isr since 1905; att: Herzlia Coll, Tel Aviv; U of Berlin; m. Miriam Grünspan, Feb 21, 1941; c: Sara, David. Tchr: Levinsky Sem, Tel Aviv since 1940; adult courses, Kibbutzim, 1920-22; lectr, Palestinology since 1923; lectr, guide, Histadrut inst since 1923; fmr: lectr, research worker, tour, Eng; lectr, Pioneer Movement Cen, Pol; conducted sem's, Palestinology; lectr, grad class, Yeshiva U, NY, on behalf of JA dept of educ in Diaspora. Off, interpreter, Turkish Army, 1918-20. Mem: Govt Comm, Names for Settlements since 1951; adv comm, Isr Exploration Soc since 1932; Isr Soc for Bibl Research since 1950; council, Dept of Antiquities, Govt of Isr since 1962. Author: Do You Know the Country, 6 vols, 1940-64; Galilee and the Northern Valleys, 1956; The Land of the Negev, 1956; Around the Dead Sea, 1956; To Eilat and the Red Sea, 1956; Between Tabor and Hermon, 1960; The Human Panorama in Galilee since Prehistory, 1968; The Wars and the Defense of the Jews in Palestine After the Rebellion of Bar Kochba, 1942; Studies of Our Country — Its Past and Relics, 1954; From the Gaza Strip to the Red Sea, 1956; contbr to: local press; mags; profsl publs; Ency Judaica. Recipient: Hankin Prize, JNF, Jerusalem, 1947; Bialik Prize, Tel Aviv Munic, 1960; Ben Zvi Prize, 1965. Home: 19 Keren Kayemeth Blvd, Tel Aviv, Isr.

BRAUDE, Baruch, Isr, chartered acctnt; b. Jerusalem, Oct 6, 1914; s. Isaiah and Ella (Strauss); att St Joseph's Coll, London; BSc, U Coll, London U, 1935; m. Faigel Wolsky, 1941; c: Delia, Alon. Sr partner, Braude & Co, CAs, since 1939. F, inst of CAs. Home: 110 Haeshel St, Herzliya on Sea, Isr. Office: Haatzmaut Bank Bldg, Montefiore St, Tel Aviv, Isr.

BRAUDE, Jacob, Eng, business exec; b. Fürth, Ger, Dec 14, 1902; s. Israel and Regina (Rosenstein); DLaw, U Leipzig, summa cum laude, 1930; m. Ruby Braude, 1930; c: Bernard, Andrew. Codir, Tobias Braude & Co Ltd. Exec vice-pres, Mizrachi Fed of Gt Brit; pres, Hendon Adath Isr Cong; chm, Friends of Midrashia, Isr; vice-pres; WJC, Brit sect; mem, Bd Deps. Ed bd, chmn, J Review; contbr of numerous articles to J publs. Special interests: J educ and demography. Home: 14 Gloucester Gardens, London NW11, Eng. Office: 27 Creechurch Lane, London EC3, Eng.

BRAUDE, Jacob M, US, jurist, editor; b. Chgo, Ill, Dec 13, 1896; s. Emil and Anna (Kaplan); BA, cum laude, U Mich, 1918; att Northwestern U Law Sch, 1919; JD, U Chgo, 1920; m. Adele Covy Englander, Feb 22, 1946; c: Ann Englander, Jan Berkson. Judge, Circuit Court, Cook Co, Ill, since 1956; mem, Ill Hwy Safety Commn, 1934; chmn, Natl Conf State Liquor Admnrs. 1934; Cen State Gasoline Tax Conf, 1933; asst atty gen, Ill, under Govt Otto Kerner; judge, Munic Court, Chgo, 1934-56; presided over Boy's Court, dealing with youth 17-21 years old. US Army, World War I. Mem: adv bd, div for youth and comty service, Dept Public Wfr, 1945, comm, child wfr leg; delg at large, Wfr Council, Metrop Chgo; mem, bd dirs, Juvenile Protective Assn; vice-pres, Ill Soc for Mental Hygiene; f, fmr pres, Ill Acad Criminology; chmn, Chgo Common Alcoholism; pres, Portal House; fm pres; ZOA; JNF; Young men's J Council, Life dir, natl vice, chmn, Comm for Advancement of Judaism; mem, bd trustees-Chgo Sinai Cong; mem, adv bd: J Children's Bur; World Youth mag; mem bd, Natl Assn for Gifted Children; chmn, bd, Bishop Bernard J Shell Youth Award, since 1952; chmn, Chgo br, AJComm; mem: Chgo, Ill, Amer Bar Assns; Amer Judicature Soc; Amer legion; Masons; Decalogue Soc of Lawyers; Phi Beta Phi; Forty and Eight. Author: I Like Bad Boys, 1939; Speaker's Encyclopedia of Stories, Quotations and Anecdotes, 1957; Braude's Handbook of Humor for all Occasions, 1958; New Treasury of Stories for Every Speaking and Writing Occasion, 1959; Speaker's Encyclopedia of Humor, 1961; Lifetime Speaker's Encyclopedia, 1962; Speaker's Desk Book of Quips, Quotes and Anecdotes, 1963; Braude's Treasury of Wit and Humor, 1964; Complete Speakers and Toastmasters Library, 8 vols, 1965; The Complete Speaker's Index to Selected Stories for Every Occasion 1966; Braude's Handbook of Stories for Toastmasters and Speakers, 1967; Braude's Source Book for Speakers and Writers, 1968; contbr to mags. Home: 1000 Lake Shore Plaza, Chicago Ill. Office: Chgo Civic Cen, Chicago, Ill.

BRAUDE, William G, US, rabbi; b. Telsiai, Lith, Apr 25, 1907; s. Isaac and Rachel (Halperin); in US since 1920; BA, U Cincinnati, 1929; ordained rabbi, HUC, 1931; MA, Brown U, 1934, PhD, 1937; hon: DD, Brown U, 1955; DHL, HUC-JIR, 1959; LHD, U of RI, 1960; m. Pearl Finkelstein, June 19, 1938; c: Joel, Benjamin, Daniel. Rabbi: Cong Sons of Isr and David (Temple Beth El) since 1932; Rockford, Ill, 1931-32; fmr lectr, Bibl lit and his of rels, Brown U. Mem; bd govs, HUC-JIR, 1950-56; exec bd, CCAR, 1945; fmr pres, World Affairs Council, RI; delg, 3rd World Cong J Studies, Jerusalem, 1961; mem: commn on J educ, UAHC and CCAR, 1943-58; Amer Acad for J Research; Phi Beta Kappa; Athenaeum, Providence. Author: Jewish Proselyting, 1940; Liberal Judaism in a Reactionary World (monograph), 1942; Relevance of Midrash (monograph), 1955; trans: Midrash on Psalms, 1959, 1960; Pesikta Rabbati, 1968; initiated and conducted radio prog, Ask the Rabbi; initiated TV prog, The Book We Live By; contbr ed, Judaism; mem, ed bd, CCAR Jour since 1952. Home: 93 Arlington Ave, Providence, RI. Study: 70 Orchard Ave, Providence, RI.

BRAUER, Alfred T, US, mathematician, educator; b. Berlin, Ger, Apr 9, 1894; s. Max and Caroline (Jacob); in US since 1939; att U of Heidelberg, 1913; U of Berlin, 1913-14; PhD, 1928; m. Hildegard Wolf, Sep 4, 1934; c: Ellen Kaplan, Carolyn Hudson. Kenan prof math, U of NC since 1959, on fac since 1942; asst, U of Berlin, 1926-35, privat-dozent 1932-35; asst, Inst for Advanced Study, Princeton, NJ, 1939-42; lectr, NYU, 1940-42. Mem: Sigma Xi; Amer Math Soc; Math Assn of Amer; NC Acad Sci; Elisha Mitchell Sci Soc. Recipient, Sci Research Award, Oak Ridge Inst of Nuclear Studies for significant contrib to sci in S, 1948. Home: 410 Patterson Pl, Chapel Hill, NC. Office: U of NC, Chapel Hill, NC.

BRAUER, Efrem, US, locations analyst, real estate devl; b. NYC, June 10, 1922; s. Solomon and Ida (Karpman); BA, NYU, 1943, att Grad Sch of Arts and Scis, 1946-48; m. Rhoda Tauber, 1945; c: Janet, Nancy, Andrew. Real estate devl, Goldman Builders, Inc, Union, NJ, since 1967; instr, stat, Newark Div, Rutgers U, 1951-59; dir, mem, JWV, 1947-54; locations analyst, Food Fair Stores, 1954-67. US Army, 1943-46. Vice-pres, Ridgefield Park Blood Assn; chmn, bd trustees, Temple Emanuel Ridgefield Park, 1958-60, pres, 1960-62; co-chmn, Mayor's Comm on Brotherhood, 1961-62; cdr, JWV, Palisades Park, NJ, 1950-51; mem: Bd Commns, Ridgefield Park; Ridgefield Park Planning Bd, 1964-68; Citizens Comm on Planning for Ridgefield Park, NJ, 1961-62. Recipient, Asiatic Pacific Campaign Medal, 1945. Home: 17 Barnes Drive W, Ridgefield Park, NJ. Office: 1880 Morris Ave, Union, NJ.

BRAUN, J Werner, US, scientist; b. Berlin, Nov 16, 1914; s., Simon and Edith (Brach); in US since 1936; PhD, U Göttingen, Ger, 1936; m. Barbara Melnikow, June 7, 1942; c: Renee Augins, Stephanie Blythe, Robin. Prof, microbiol, Rutgers U since 1955; cons, govt and ind orgs; research asso, U of Cal, 1936-48; chief, genet br, Army Biol Labs, 1948-55; visiting prof, Heb U, Jerusalem, 1962-63. Prin contribs in: genet; microbiol; immunology. Mem: Amer Soc Microbiol, past pres; Genet Soc Amer; NY, NJ, Acads Sci; past pres, Theobald Smith Soc. Author, Bacterial Genetics, 1953, 2nd ed, 1965; ed: Bacterial Endotoxins, 1964; Nucleic Acids in Immunology, 1968; Immunological Tolerance, 1969; contbr numerous articles to sci jours. Home: 72 Mason Dr, Princeton, NJ. Office: Rutgers U, New Brunswick, NJ.

BRAUN, Karl, Isr, physician, educator; b. Czech, May 24, 1912; s. Shmuel and Rosa (Lustig); in Isr since 1938; MD, Gratz U, Aus, 1935; m; c: Ilana, Abraham. Asso prof, med, Heb U-Hadassah Med Sch, Jerusalem since 1955, on fac since 1951, chief, cardiovascular research lab, Hadassah Hosp, Jerusalem since 1949; asso phys, 1938-47; staff mem: U Hosp, Gratz, Aus, 1935-38; Michael Reese Hosp, Chgo, Ill; Bellevue Hosp, Mt Sinai Hosp, both NY, 1947-49. Chmn: Isr Cardiac Soc since 1951; Isr br, Intl Card Soc. Author: Research on Heart Diseases; mem ed bd, Amer Heart Jour; fgn cons ed, Amer Jour of Card; contbr to med jours. Home: 10 Alharizi St, Jerusalem, Isr. Office: Heb U-Hadassah Med Sch, Jerusalem, Isr.

BRAUN, Sidney D, US, educator; b. NYC, May 10, 1912; s, Max and Helen (Brown); dipl, Sorbonne U, 1932; MA, NYU, 1935, PhD, 1945; att: U of Mex; Columbia U; m. Miriam Kadish, June 8, 1941. Prof, Fr, Yeshiva U since 1952; chm div langs and lit, 1952-54, 1958-59, mem fac since 1936; chargé de cours, U Francaise de NY, since 1955; prof Fr, Lehman Coll, CUNY, since 1968, chmn, dept, Romance langs, since 1969; visiting asso prof, Romance langs, LIU, 1945-49 visiting prof, U of Wash, Seattle, 1963-64; Fulbright research scholar, Paris, 1964-65; prof, Fr, Wayne State U, 1965-68. Mem: MLA; Amer Assn Tchrs Fr; Amer Assn Tchrs Span; Société des Prof Francais en Amérique; AAUP. Author: The Courtisane in the French Theatre from Hugo to Becque, 1947; Zola's Esthetic Approach and the Courtesan, 1947; Peguy and Bernard Lazare — A Common Mystique, 1950; Dictionary of French Literature, 1958; Correspondance André Gide, André Suarès, 1963; Source and Psychology of Sartre's Le Mur, 1965; André Suarès's Unpublished Early Notebooks, 1967; co-ed, coll ed, Anatole France's Le Crime de Sylvestre Bonnard, 1958. Recipient: Grande Médaille D'Argent de la Ville de Paris; Chevalier dans l'Ordre des Palmes Académiques. Home: 90 LaSalle St, New York, NY. Office: Lehman Coll, Bedford Park Blvd W, New York, NY.

BRAUN, Siegfried, Isr, publicist; b. Brauenberg, Ger, Nov 3, 1885; s. Daniel and Johanna (Hess); in Isr since 1939; att: U of Munster; U of Bonn; PhD, U Cologne, 1923; m. Elisabeth Mond, May 15, 1918; c: Gerhard, Walter. Hist and publicist since 1941; tchr, 1906-39; ed, Jud Schulzeitung, 1934-38; journalist, 1906-69; guide; lectr; research on the hist of the Yishuv. Mem bd: Synagogengemeide Köln; Jüdische Lehrerverband, Ger; mem, B'nai B'rith Lodge, Tel Aviv. Author: Jahrbuch der Synagogengemeide Köln, 1934; Lesebuch fur jud Schulen, 1938. Home: Kibbutz Maayan Zvi, Isr.

BRAUN, Simon, Isr, scientist; b. Vienna, Aug 19, 1933; s. Aaron and Esther (Austerlitz); in Isr since 1945; BS, Technion, Haifa, 1958, MS, 1951, DSc, 1967; m. Miriam Aftergood, Oct 20, 1965; c: Dalit, Orit. Sr lectr, Technion since 1968. Contbr to various sci publs. Home: 18 Raanan St, Haifa, Isr. Office: Technion, Haifa, Isr.

BRAUN, Stevan, (pen name, Kvazimodo Braun István), Yugo, jurist, author; b. Yugo, Aug 20, 1908; s. Henrik and Kata (Gotlib); att Fac of Law, 1927-31; deg, 1932; m. Erzebet Petrik, Sep 26, 1946; c: Andris. Supr judge, Supr Court, Vojvodina, fmr judge, Dist Court; law practice, 1937-41. Author: plays: Case Magdich, in Hung, 1953; Neobicna generalna proba, 1957; novels: Testamentum, 1954; Chinese Room, in Hung, 1960; comedy, Please a Kindly Face, in Hung, 1961. Recipient: lit award, 1953, 1957; Order of Work; October Prize, Town Subotica, 1968. Home: Trg Oktobarske Revolucije 10, Subotica, Yugo. Office: Supr Court of Vojvodina, 3 Sutjeska St, Novi Sad, Yugo.

BRAUN, Yehezkel, Isr, composer; b. Breslau, Ger, Jan 18, 1922; s. Abraham and Judith Schopf; in Isr since 1924; cert tchr, Tchrs Coll, Tel Aviv, 1949; BA, Music Acad, Tel Aviv, 1953; m. Shulamith Glasman, 1948; c: Raphael, Goorie, Rotem. Lectr: Isr Acad of Music; Music Tchrs Coll, Tel Aviv since 1954; music tchr, State Tchrs Coll, 1952-61. Prin compositions: Concerto for Flute and Orchestra, 1957; Psalm for Strings, 1959; A Symphony of Dances, 1963; Solo Sonata for Flute, 1957; Three Sketches for Harp, 1962; The Jordan Valley Music for Ballet, 1961; Piano Sonata, 1957; Pedals on Vacation, for harp, 1965; Piano Pieces for Young Musicians, 1968; contbr of various collections of songs and choral compositions. Hobbies: classical studies, bird watching. Home: 13 Karni St, Tel Aviv, Isr.

BRAUNER, Artur, Ger, film produc; b. Lodz, Pol, Jan 8, 1918; s. Moshe and Brana (Brandes); m. Teresa Albert, Nov 1946; c: Henry, Fela. Film produc since 1946; films include: The Rats; Soldier Schwejk; Morituri; 20 Juli; Sunset; documentary films. Recipient: 1st prize for The Rats and Sunset, from Berlin Film Festival; prize for 20 Juli, from Ger Fed, Govt; prize for Soldier Schwejk, from SF Golden Globe. Home: Konigsallee 18, Berlin-Grunewald, Ger. Office: CCC Films, Berlin-Spandau, Ger.

BRAUNSCHVIG, Jules A, Morocco, industrialist; b. Ste Marie-aux-Mines, Fr, June 21, 1908; s. Georges and Laure (Simon); dipl, political sci, U of Paris, 1929; eng lic, Sorbonne Paris; m. Gladys Toledano, 1947; c: Daniel, Myriam, David. Pres, Etablissement Braunschvig, Casablanca. Vice pres, Alliance Israélite Universelle, 1946; hon pres, Assn Maimonide, 1951; vice-pres, J Material Claims against Ger; co-chmn, Consultative Council of J Orgs. Home: 97 Hassan Seghir Blvd, Casablanca, Morocco. Office: Alliance Israélite Universelle, 45 Rue La Bruyère, Paris 9e, Fr.

BRAUNSTEIN, Baruch, US, business exec, rabbi; b. New Castle Pa, Mar 3, 1906; s. Peter and Esther (Pazer); BS, O State U,

1926; ordained rabbi, MHL, JIR, 1930; PhD, Columbia U, 1936; m. Gladys Belmont, June 19, 1928. Mgr, Fields Co since 1951; rabbi: Beth Shalom Cong, NY, 1927-29; Cong Keneseth Isr, Allentown, Pa, 1943-49; Cong Beth Isr, Atlantic City, NJ, 1950-51; mem teaching staff, U of Cal Ext Div, 1952; counselor, J students, Columbia U, 1928-34; spec lectr, Amer U, Beirut, Leb, 1933; guest preacher, spec lectr: Amer Us and Near East Sch of Theol, Beirut; U City of Madrid; served as cons and narrator, radio progs. F, Natl Council on Rel in Higher Educ since 1927; mem: CCAR; Amer Acad Political and Social Sci; Amer Hist Assn; Forum Soc; Delta Sigma Rho; fmr: dir, World Affairs Forum of the Air, Phila, 1936-37; active, overseas relief campaigns, 1938-43; mem, exec staff, Emergency Peace Campaign, Amer Friends Service Comm, 1936-37. Author, The Chuetas of Majorca, 1936; contbr: Universal Jewish Ency; periodicals. Home: 3005 Garber St, Berkeley, Cal. Office: 2800 Telegraph Ave, Berkeley, Cal.

BRAUNTHAL, Julius, Eng, author; b. Vienna, Aus, Aug 27, 1889; s. Maier and Clara (Gelles); m. Ernestine Gernreich; c: Friedrich, Otto. Author: Need Germany Survive? 1943; In Search of the Millenium, 1945; The Paradox of Nationalism, 1946; The Tragedy of Austria, 1948; L'Antitesi Ideologica fra Socialismo e Comunismo, 1956; The Significance of Israeli Socialism and the Arab-Israeli Dispute, 1958; Il Socialismo in Asia, 1959; Otto Bauer, Ein Lebensbild, 1961; Victor Adler and Friedrich Adler, 1965; History of the International 1864-14, 1914-43, 1943-64, 1961-70; ed, Yearbook of the Intl Socialist Lab Movement, 1956. Lt Aus-Hung Army, 1914-18; lt col, Army, Aus Rep, 1918-20. Med, bd dirs, Intl Inst of Social Hist, Amsterdam; gen secy, Socialist Intl, 1949-56; mem: Friends Heb U, Jerusalem; Soc For Study of Lab Hist; Fabian Soc. Recipient, Gt Silver Medal for Bravery. Hobby, music. Home: 20 The Grove, Teddington, Middlesex, Eng.

BRAUNWALD, Eugene, US, educator; b. Vienna, Aus, Aug 15; 1929; s. William and Clare (Wallach), in US since 1939; BA, NYU, 1949, MD, 1952; m. Nina Starr, May 25, 1952; c: Karen, Allison, Adrienne. Prof, chmn, dept med, U of Cal, San Diego, since 1968; chief, card br, clinical dir: Natl Heart Inst, 1966-68; dir, Public Health Service, 1955-64. Prin contribs, cardiovascular research. Pres, Amer Fed for Clinical Research; vice-pres, AHA; fmr vice-pres, Amer Coll Card. Author: Mechanism of Contraction of Heart, 1968; Principles of Internal Medicine, 1969. Recipient: Fleming award, Dept HEW, 1964; Abel award, Pharm Soc, 1965. Home: 9702 La Jolla Farms Rd, La Jolla, Cal. Office: 255 W Dickinson St, San Diego, Cal.

BRAV, Stanley R, US, rabbi; b. Phila, Pa, Nov 22, 1908; s. Herman and Hattie (Mitchell); BA, U Cincinnati, 1931, MA, 1935; BH, HUC, 1930, ordained rabbi, 1934, hon DD, 1959; PhD, Webster U, 1939; m. Ruth Englander, 1932; c: Harriet Baum, Susanne Waltzer, Judith Sher, Henry. Rabbi, Temple Sholom, Cincinnati, O, since 1954, found, 1954; asst rabbi, Temple Emanu-El, Dallas, Tex, 1934-37; rabbi: Temple Anshe Chesed, Vicksburg, Miss, 1937-48; Rockdale Ave Temple, Cincinnati, 1948-54. Pres: Alumni Assn, HUC-JIR, 1959-60, mem, bd govs, 1958-61; Miss Social Hygiene Assn, 1947-48; O Valley Region CCAR, 1966-68; Social Health Soc, 1965-67; chmn, Miss conf, B'nai B'rith, 1940; found, exec secy, JWF, Vicksburg, 1937-48; treas: Fayette-Haywood Workcamps, since 1967; Metrop Area Rel Coalition of Cincinnati, since 1968; mem: first bd, S Regional Council, B'nai B'rith, 1945-48; JCC; Comty Relations Comm; J Family Service; natl exec bd, J Peace F; clubs: Pearlcasters; Torch of Cincinnati; Cosmic, pres, 1953-55. Author: Jewish Family Solidarity, 1940; Wife of Thy Youth, 1946; Since Eve, 1959; Telling Tales Out of School, 1955; ed, Marriage and the Jewish Tradition, 1951; contbr to profsl publs. Home: 399 W Galbraith Rd, Cincinnati, O. Study: 3100 Longmeadow Lane, Cincinnati, O.

BRAVER, Bernhard, Aus, editor, journalist; b. Chodrow, Pol; s. Itzhak and Zipora (Farb); att HS, Stanislau, Pol; m. Antonia. Chief ed, Die Stimme; fmr, Creditanstalt, Vienna. First chmn of revived J Comty, Vienna, after WWII, found, Vienna J Comty future activity; found, chief ed, Der Neue Weg, first jour in Vienna after 1945; found, gen secy, Zionist Org, Vienna, after WWII, and its jour, Die Stimme; pres, Aus Ort; vice-pres, Keren Kayemeth; chmn bd, Kreditgen, Vienna. Contbr to: Dr Bloch's Wochenschrift; Jüdischer

Arbeiter; various evening jours, Vienna. Home: Grosse Neugasse 32, Vienna, Aus.

BRAVERMAN, Jay, US, educational dir; b. NYC, Aug 5, 1937; s. Samuel and Ida (Cohen); BA, MA, ordained rabbi, all Yeshiva U; m. Sandra Drozen, June 21, 1959; c: Deborah, Jeffrey, Rochelle. Educ dir, United Talmud Torahs since 1970; fmr: dean, Detroit Coll of J Studies, Mich; prin, United Heb Schs, Detroit. Chmn, comm on test preparation, Natl Bible Contest; mem: bd dirs, Talmud El Am; Natl Council for J Educ; RabCA. Recipient: Regents Coll Teaching F, 1959-61; F, Memorial Found for J Culture, 1963-65; f, Natl Found for J Culture, 1961-62, 1964-65. Home: 13321 Northfield, Oak Park, Mich. Office: 4850 St Kevin Ave, Montreal, Can.

BRAVERMAN, Libbie Levin, US, educational cons; b. Boston, Dec 20, 1900; d. M A and Pauline (Drucker) Levin; BS, W Reserve U, Cleveland, 1935; grad work: Harvard U; U Pittsburgh; widowed. J educ cons since 1952; Educ dir: Euclid Ave Temple, 1946-52; Temple Sinai, Stamford, Conn, 1966-67. Med bd govs, Coll J Studies; mem: bd, Bur J Educ; hon bd, Hadassah; fmr: vice-pres, Natl Council for J Educ; pres: O-Mich-Ind Rel Tchrs Assn; Cen States Region, Hadassah; head councellor: Camp Tabor; Camp Carmelia. Co-author: Activities in the Religious School; Children of the Emek, 1931; Religious Pageants, 1941; Children's Services 1948; Children of Freedom, 1953; Six Day Warriors, 1969; Teach Me to Pray, Books 1 and 2; chap in Purim Anthology, 1949. Home: 2378 Euclid Hgts Blvd, Cleveland, O.

BRAVERMAN, Samuel, Isr, chemist; b. Falticeni, Rum, May 23, 1934; s. Zvi and Rivka (Smilovici); in Isr since 1952; BSc, cum laude, Bar Ilan U, Isr, 1960; PhD, U Alberta, Can, 1963. Chmn, dept chem, Bar Ilan U since 1968; sr lectr since 1968. Cpl, IDF, 1953-58. Mem, council, Isr Chem Soc. Contbr: numerous sci papers to chem jours. Home: 6 Aaronson St, Bnei Brak, Isr. Office: Bar Ilan U, Ramat Gan, Isr.

BRAWER, Abraham J, Isr, geographer, author; b. Stryj, Galicia, Mar 30, 1884; s. Michael and Lea (Zeimer); in Isr since 1911; att Theol Sch, Vienna, 1909; PhD, U Vienna, 1909; m. Sarah Mayersohn, (decd); c: Moshe, Judith, Hulda Liberanome. Chief geog, Heb Ency, Jerusalem since 1950; tchr: HS, Tarnapol, Galicia, 1910-11; Tchrs Sem, Jerusalem, 1911-14; sch dir, rabbi, Constantinople, Turkey, 1914-18. Volunteer, police service, Pal. Author: Galizien Wie Es an Oesterreich Kam, 1910; Haaretz, textbook, geog of Pal, 5 eds, 1927-54; Avak Drakhim, voyages in Leb, Syria, Iraq, Persia, 2 vols, 1931, 35; School Atlas, 1938; contbr to: Hashiloah (Heb); Joseph II and the Jews of Galicia, vol 23, 1910; A New Source of History of Frank and His Adherents, vols 23, 38, 1919, 1922; Zichronot Av- Rabbi Michael Braver — uVno A.V. Braver; Galitzya Viyehudeah; constant contbr to Haaretz daily since 1920; to sci publs. Mem, geog names comm, Pal, 1921-48, Isr Govt since 1950; co-found, first secy, J Soc for Exploration of Pal. Recipient, Medal of Honor, Yakir Yerushalaim, Jerusalem Munic, 1966. Spec interest, Heb rel lit. Home: 24 Reines St, Tel Aviv, Isr.

BRAWER, Moshe, Isr, geographer; b. Vienna, Nov 3, 1919; s. Abraham and Sara (Mayersohn); desc of Rabbi Meir Mayersohn, Talmudic auth; in Isr since 1920; att Heb U, Jerusalem; BS, MS, PhD, U London, 1945-52; m. Rina Arison, Dec 16, 1951; c: Gilli, Orit, Solli. Vice-dean, fac hum, Tel Aviv U since 1967, head dept, geog since 1966; fgn ed, Hatzofe, 1952-67; geog ed, Ency Hebraica. F, Royal Geog Soc, London; natl comm mem, Isr Geog Soc. Author: Israeli High School Atlas, 1952; Atlas of the Middle East, 1963; Hebrew Historical Atlas, 1965; contbr of numerous maps and articles on geog and political subjects. Home: 23 Hameaa Veahad St, Ramat Chen, Isr. Office: Dept of Geog, Tel Aviv U, Ramat Aviv, Isr.

BRAYER, Menachem M, US, psychologist, educator; b. Strusov, Pol, Mar 9, 1922; s. Joseph and Mollie (Morgenstern) in US since 1948; ordained rabbi, Yeshiva of Kishineff, 1940; BA, U of Iassy, 1945; MHL, Yeshiva U, 1949, DHL, 1950, PhD, 1958; m. Mimi Friedman, 1952; c. Yigal, Nehama, Dov. Prof, Bibl lit and educ, Ferkauf Grad Sch, Yeshiva U, since 1966, fac mem since 1948, cons psychol, Yeshiva Coll since 1958; asst prof, Bibl lit, Stern Coll, since 1955; dir, cultural dept, Hapoel Hamizrahi, Bucharest, 1944-47; cons psychol, J Educ Comm, since 1958. F, Soc for Psychoanalytic Study and Research; mem: Amer, NY State Psych Assns;

Amer Acad for J Studies; Soc of Bibl Lit and Exegesis; Heb PEN Club; Histadruth Ivrith. Contbr to Heb, Eng, Yiddish, and Rumanian Publs. Recipient: awards: Sr Prof, Yeshiva Coll, 1962; Sr Prof, Tchrs Inst, Yeshiva U, 1967. Hobbies: poetry, music, travel. Home: 812 W 181 St, New York, NY. Office: Amsterdam Ave and 187 St, New York, NY.

BRAZ, Isaac, Isr, political leader; b. Tel Aviv, Aug 8, 1926; s. Joseph and Dvora; LLB, LLM, U of London; m. Rina Segal; c: Shifra, Rivka, Aron, Josepha. Chmn: Lib Party, Petah Tikva since 1965; Council of Maccabi since 1954. Maj, Pres Mil Court. Chmn, popular sport comm, Maccabi, Isr; pres, supr court, Basketball Assn; mem: cen comm, Lib Party; supr court, Isr Sport Orgs; dist comm, Bar Assn, Tel Aviv. Home and office: 12 Ahad Haam, Petah Tikva, Isr.

BRECHER, Michael, Can, educator; b. Montreal, Mar 14, 1925; s. Nathan and Gisella (Hopmeyer); BA, with honors, McGill U, 1946; MA, Yale U, 1948; PhD, 1953; m. Eva, Danon, Dec 7, 1950; c: Leora, Diana, Seegla. Prof, political sci, McGill U since 1963, on fac since 1952; asst dir, Asian Div, Min for Fgn Affairs, Jerusalem, 1950-51. Mem: Can Inst Intl Affairs; Can Political Sci Assn; Assn Asian Studies; Asian Soc. Author: The Struggle for Kashmir, 1953; Nehru: A Political Biography, 1959, abridged ed, 1961; The New States of Asia, 1963; Succession in India, 1966; India and World Politics, 1968; Political Leadership in India, 1969. Recipient, Watamull Award, for book, Nehru, Amer Hist Assn. Home: 4925 Ponsard Ave, Montreal, Can. Office: McGill U, Montreal, Can.

BREGER, Marcus, US, rabbi; b. Bucovina, Aus, May 18, 1905.; s. Jacob and Liebe (Druckmann); in US since 1939; PhD, U Breslau, Ger, 1930; ordained rabbi, J Theol Sem, Breslau, 1931; m. Bertha Rittenberg, July 10, 1933; c: Liba Feuerstein. Rabbi, Cong Anshei Isr, Tucson, Ariz, since 1939; prof, Talmud and hist, Collegio Rabbinico, Rhodes, It, 1932-38. Chaplain, maj, US Army, 1943-46. Pres, Ariz Rabb Council, since 1959; mem: ZOA; Rabb Assn of Amer; JWV; B'nai B'rith; Mil Chaplains Assn; Assn of J Chaplains; club, Rotary. Author: Beitraege zur Handelsgeschichte der Juden in Polen im 17 Jahrhundert, 1932; contbr: Ency Judaica; Ger periodicals. Recipient, Army, commendation ribbon, Okinawa, 1946. Home: 5829 E Burns St, Tucson, Ariz. Study: 5550 E Fifth St, Tucson, Ariz.

BREGMAN, Benjamin B, US, business exec; b. Boston, Mass May 13, 1909; s. Harry and Esther (Brodsky); AB, magna cum laude, Tufts Coll, 1931; m. Irene Faller, July 24, 1934; c: Harry, Cydne, Sheila Morgo. Pres, treas, Tru-Stitch Moccasin Corp, div of Wolverine World Wide; gen mgr: Macht Shoe Corp, 1934-37; Consolidated Footwear Corp, 1937-40. Served, Natl Guard. Pres: Temple Beth El, 1944-52; Winter Series Cultural Org, 1950-51; chmn, fund drive, UJA, 1942-61; mem, natl cabinet, 1950-62; dir: Franklin Co TB and Heart Assn, pres, 1952-53; N NY Trust Co; vice-pres, Alice Hyde Memorial Hosp. dir, C of C, 1946-52; Amer Heart Soc; Comty Chest; Red Cross; chmn bd, Malone Cen Sch Dist; chmn: Regional Dr, N NY State, NCCJ; N NY dr for Eisenhower Libr; Soc for Prevention of Cruelty to Animals, all Malone; mem: Phi Beta Kappa; Elks; Masons; clubs: Malone Discussion; Rotary; Malone Country. Home: 75 Elm St, Malone, NY. Office: 123 Catherine St, Malone, NY.

BREIDENBACH, Lester, US, surgeon, educator; b. NYC, Dec 21, 1897; s. Gustav and Sophie (Guckenheimer); BS, NYU, 1921, MD, 1922; m. Carla Rhonheimer, Dec 24, 1925; c: Lester, Rhona Landorf. Dir, surg, Grand Cen Hosp, 1942-63; att surg: Misericordia Hosp, since 1933; Doctors Hosp, since 1950; asso prof, clinical surg, NYU Bellevue Med Cen since 1939; dir, Emergency Services, U Hosp; cons surg, Bellevue Hosp. USN, WWI. Mem: Amer Coll Surgs; Amer Bd Surg; NY Soc Cardiovascular Surg; Amer Assn Surg of Trauma; AMA; local, state and natl med socs; NY Surg Soc; NY Acad Med; Alpha Omega Alpha. Contbr to med jours. Home: 25 Sutton Pl S, New York, NY. Office: 169 E 69 St, New York, NY.

BREINDEL, Joseph H, US, physician; b. Zablotow, Pol; s. Leizer and Rachel; in US since 1938; MD, U Rome, 1938; m. Sonia Weissenberg, 1953; c: Monique, Eric. Pvt practice since 1944; att phys, NY Infirmary; asso att phys, Columbus Hosp. F: Intl Coll Surgs; Amer Soc Abdominal Surgs; Amer Coll Obstet and Gyn; dipl, Amer Bd Obstet and Gyn; mem: AMA; NY State, NY Co Med Socs; NY Acad Sci: Intl

Fertility Assn. Contbr to med jours. Home: 45 Gramercy Park, New York, NY. Office: 54 Gramercy Park, New York, NY.

BREINER, Richard H, US, attorney; b. Milw, Wis, Feb 28, 1935; s. James and Fannie (Appel); AB, LLB, U of Mo Law Sch; att Wash U, St Louis, Mo; m. Dorothy Landau, Oct 30, 1960; c: Daniel, Deborah. Dep city atty, Tiberon, Cal since 1965; dep public defender, Marin Co, Cal since 1965. Lt, US Army, 1957-59. Pres, dir, Cong Rodef Shalom; dir, ACLU, Marin Co chap; mem: Dem Cen Comm, Marin Co; Phi Beta Kappa; Zeta Beta Tau. Contbr of articles to law reviews. Home: 31 St Francis St, San Rafael, Cal., Office: 1534 Fifth St, San Rafael, Cal.

BREITEL, Charles David, US, jurist; b. NYC, Dec 12, 1908; s. Herman and Regina (Zuckerberg); AB, U Mich, 1929; LLB, Columbia U Sch of Law, 1932; LLD, hon, LIU, 1953; m. Jeanne Hollander, Apr 9, 1927; c: Eleanor Zabel, Vivian. Asso judge, Court of Appeals since 1966; adj prof, law, Columbia U Sch of Law since 1963, mem bd of visitors; deputy dist atty, Thomas E Dewey spec Rackets Inves, NY Co, 1938-41; asso with Thomas E Dewey, in pvt practice, 1942; counsel to Gov Dewey, 1943-50; NY State Post War Public Works Planning Commn; Jt Leg Comm on Munic Revenues and Reduction of Taxes; appd justice of State Supr Court, 1950, reappd, 1951, elected, 1951, designated asso justice, Appellate Div, First Dept, 1952, redesignated, 1957, 1962-66, re-elected, 1965; Leary lectr, U of Utah Law Sch, 1966; Earl F Nelson Memorial lectr, U of Mo Law Sch, 1960. Mem: adv comm, Amer Law Inst; Fed Commn, Intl Rules of Judicial Procedure, 1958-66; pres commn, Law Enforcement and Admn of Justice; Amer Law Inst; Council of Amer Law Inst; Inst of Judicial Admn; Assn Bar, NYC; NY Co Lawyers Assn; NY State Bar Assn; Columbia U Law Sch Alumni Assn, past pres. Home: 146 Central Park W, New York, NY. Office: Court of Appeals, 74 Trinity Pl, New York, NY.

BREITSTEIN, Zvi, Isr, editor; b. Lodz, Pol, May 9, 1916; s. Josef and Sara (Pajecka); in Isr since 1935; m. Esther Vilenska, 1943; c: Sara, Josef. Ed, Kol Haam, daily newspaper, cen organ of Communist Party of Isr since 1947. Brit Army, 1942-46; Home: 6 Dik St, Kiryat Shalom, Tel Aviv, Isr. Office: Kol Haam, Eilat St, Tel Aviv, Isr.

BRENER, Leo, US, rabbi; b. New Orleans, La, May 11, 1909; s. Elias and Fannie (Lew); PhB, U Chgo, 1928, MA, 1930; rabbi, Heb Theol Coll, Chgo, Ill, 1934; m. Nannette Freeman, June 30, 1940; c: Nathan, Meyer, Etta. Rabbi, Cong Agudath Achim, Shreveport, La, since 1934. Pres, Shreveport dist, ZOA, 1942, secy, 1936-40; B'nai B'rith, 1937. Mem, bd dirs: Shreveport J Fed; NCCJ; mem, RabCA. Home: 718 College, Shreveport, La. Study: 1707 Line Ave, Shreveport, La.

BRENER, Mark I, US, rabbi; b. Pol, Oct 5, 1927; s. Abraham and Anne (Cukier); in US since 1946; BA, Yeshiva U, 1951, MA, 1960; ordained rabbi, Rabbi Isaac Elchanan Theol Sem; 1954; m. Lenore Krojansky, June 14, 1953; c: Ester, Zipporah. Rabbi: Cong Etz Jacob since 1962; Chaplain, Good Samaritan Hosp, LA; Heb Comty Cen, Fla, NY, 1954-59; Seaview J Cen, Bklyn, 1959-62. Vice-pres, Bd Rabbis of S Cal; corresp secy, Rabb Council of Cal; past treas, NY Bd Rabbis; exec bd: Cal Bd Rabbis; Yeshiva U Rabb Alumni; RabCA; orthodox relief comm, City of Hope; mem: Assn Orthodox J Sci; Amer J Hist Soc. Recipient, grant for research: in hist of Jews in Lima, Peru, Lucius N Littauer Found, 1961; B'nai B'rith Hillel Found, 1965. Home: 7934 W Fourth St, Los Angeles, Cal. Study: 7659 Beverly Blvd, Los Angeles, Cal.

BRENER, Pynchas N D, Venezuela, rabbi; b. Pol, July 27, 1931; s. Abraham and Chana (Cukier); in Venezuela since 1967; tchrs dipl, Yeshiva U, 1951, BA, 1952, ordained rabbi, 1955; MA, Columbia U, 1955; m. Henny Bernstein, Nov 21, 1956; c: Daniel, Michael, Jonathan. Chief rabbi, Union Israelita de Caracas since 1967; rabbi, Holliswood J Cen, 1955-67; instr math, NY Comty Coll, 1962-67; visited J comtys in S Amer as repr of Union of Orthodox J Congs and RabCA, 1962. Mem: intl affairs comm, NY Bd Rabbis, 1962-63; exec comm, Rabb Alumni, Yeshiva U since 1960; RabCA; LI Comm of Rabbis; pres, Rabb Council, Venezuela; chaplain, J Scouts, Venezuela. Home: El Dorado Ave, Los Proceres, San Bernadino, Caracas, Venezuela. Study: Union Israelita de Caracas, Avenida Marques del Toro, Caracas, Venezuela.

BRENER, Roy, US, psychologist; b. New Orleans, La, May 1, 1913; s. Elias and Fannie (Lew); PhB, U Chgo, 1933, MS, 1935, PhD, 1939; m. Golda Altschul, Aug 8, 1937; c: Elliot, David. Chief, psych, VA Hosp, since 1946; lectr, Loyola U, since 1964; psychol, fed exec devl prog, U Coll, U Chgo, 1948-63; neur, psycht, Northwestern U Med Sch, since 1954. US Army, 1943-46. Dipl, Amer Bd Examiners in Profsl Psych; f: Amer Psych Assn; mem: Ill Mh Planning Bd since 1967; Midwestern Psych Assn; Ill Psych Assn. Contbr to profsl jours. Home: 812 N Grove Ave, Oak Park, Ill. Office: VA Hospital, Hines, Ill.

BRENNER, Daniel L, US, attorney; b. Kan City, Mo, Sep 9, 1904; s. Adolphe and Tillie (Brenner); BA, U of Mo, 1925; JD, U of Mich Law Sch, 1927. Sr mem, Brenner, Lockwood and O'Neal and predecessor firms since 1959; asso, Borders and Borders, 1939; partner, Roach and Brenner, 1939-48; circuit judge, Kan City, 1943-44; partner: Roach, Brenner and Wimmell, 1948-51; Brenner, Van Valkenburgh and Wimmell, 1951-59. Pres: J Fed and Council of Gtr Kan City, 1956-59; B'nai B'rith Dist Grand Lodge, 1950-51; vice-pres, Supr Lodge of B'nai B'rith, since 1956, mem, bd govs, since 1956; dir, Rockhurst Coll since 1958; natl commnr, Hillel Founds, since 1953; charter trustee, U of Mo Hillel Found; mem: bd trustees, B'nai B'rith Found, since 1962; bd dirs: Comty Chest and United Funds, Inc, since 1956; Leo N Levi Memorial Hosp, Hot Springs, Ark, since 1951; Bellefaire, Cleveland, O, since 1952; NCCJ, since 1951; Beth Shalom Cong, since 1951; Amer, Mo State and Kan City Bar Assns; Amer Judicature Soc; Legion of Honor, Order of DeMolay, since 1945; clubs: Oakwood Country; Native Sons of Kan City. Recipient, award and citation for outstanding work in hum relations, NCCJ, 1956. Contbr to legal jours. Home: 311 E 70 St, Kansas City, Mo. Office: 800 Lathrop Bldg, Kansas City, Mo.

BRENNER, Jacob, Isr, attorney; b. Aus, Apr 25, 1903; s. Samuel and Fanny (Isserls); desc of 16th cent Rema Rabbi Moshe Isserls; in Isr since 1944; PhD, law, U Vienna, 1929; m. Elizabeth Rubenstein, Aug 3, 1944; c: Irith. Consul of Aus in Tel Aviv since 1944, in pvt law practice with wife since 1949; atty, notary since 1949; atty, Vienna, 1936-38. British Army, 1943-44; IDF, 1949-52. Head, Zionist Ref Comm, Brussels, Belgium, 1938-40; mem: B'nai B'rith, Theodor Herzl Lodge, Tel Aviv. Home: 14 De Haas St, Tel Aviv, Isr. Office: 6 Levontin St, Tel Aviv, Isr.

BRENNER, Mortimer, US, attorney; b. Bklyn, NY, July 5, 1889; s. Jacob and Louise (Blumenau); BA, Columbia U, 1910, LLB, 1912; m. Sylvia Freehof, June 17, 1915; c: Louise, Janet, Naomi. Mem, law firm, Rohrlick, Solomon and Hoffner. Dir, Bklyn JCC; co-chmn, jt adv comm, Syn Council of Amer and Natl Comty Relations Council; fmr pres: Council for Social Planning; United J Aid Socs of Bklyn; Cong Beth Elohin, mem, bd of trustees; fmr chmn: Kings Co Council, State Commn for Hum Rights; grievance comm, Bklyn Bar Assn; comm on uniform state laws, NY Co Lawyers Assn; mem: NY State Bar Assn; Bar Assn, NYC. Home: 160 Parkside Ave, Brooklyn, NY. Office: 30 Broad St, New York, NY.

BRENNER, Reeve Robert, US, rabbi; b. NYC, May 20, 1936; s. Abraham and Eva (Schwartz); desc, Ludwig Zamenhof, creator of Esperanto; BA, CCNY, 1957; ordained rabbi, BHL, MHL, HUC-JIR, NY, 1958-64; m. Joyce Rosman, June 18, 1959; c: Neeva, Nurete. Rabbi: Princeton J Cen since 1968; Beth Hillel, Queens, NY, 1962-64; Beth Am Temple, 1966-68; chaplain, Torrance State Hosp, 1967-68; instr, St Vincent Coll and Sem, La Trobe, Pa, first J scholar to become mem of staff of this Catholic instn, 1967-68. Chaplain, US Army, 1964-66. Co-found, pres, Found Advanced Psychotherapy, NY; chmn, Leadership Conf Civil Rights, NY; pres, Princeton Clergy Consultation Comm; mem, CCAR; fmr chmn: Hum Rights Commn; Independent Citizens Comm. Author: An Unveiling, short story; Reflections on a Heart, poem; Holocaust and Hiroshima; American Jews and Germany; A Riddle, poem; Expo 67, a review; The Golden Rule Controversy; Rabbi on Campus; Jewish Social Worker and Religious Divorce; Reform Responsa; American Jewry and the Rise of Nazism. Recipient: Binder Memorial Prize, HUC, 1964; YIVO Inst for J Research Award, 1968. Home: 21 Forester Dr, Princeton, NJ. Study: 435 Nassau St, Princeton, NJ.

BRENNER, Uri Nissan, Isr, farmer; b. Jerusalem, July 25, 1914; s. Josef and Chaia (Braude); att Sem of Social Scis, Ef'A,

Hakibbutz Hameuchad, 1954-56; m. Nessia Golubov, 1936; c: Michal Sella, Jochai, Tirtza Soria, Aielet. Mem, co-found, Kibbutz Maoz Haim since 1937; fmr secy; co-found: Kvutzat Hachugim, Raanana; Potash works, Sdom; youth group leader, secy, youth movement Hamacanot Ha'olim; mem secretariat, Hakibbutz Hameuchad; mem council, Hak-Ham. Dispatch rider, Haganah; unit cdr, Pal Scheme, 1942; co-cdr, regiment cdr, second-in-cd, brigade cdr, all Ha'olim; Palmach; lt col, IDF. Home: Kibbutz Maoz Haim, Isr.

BRESLAU, David, Isr, educator; b. Jacksonville, Fla, Jan 7, 1914; s. Louis and Bessie (Cohen); in Isr since 1949; att: Gratz Coll, Phila, Pa; Temple U, Phila; NYU. Asso dir, Hillel Found, Heb U, Jerusalem since 1960; tchr, prin, Beth El Sch, Camden, NJ, 1931-40; exec dir, prin, Habonim Inst, 1940-47; exec dir, Lab Zionist Youth Commn, 1948-49; asst educ dir, Berl Katzenelson Inst, Kfar Saba, 1949-53; JA Shaliach to Habonim, Amer, 1953-56; dir, youth, young adults workshop Isr, 1953-56; Ichud Olami Shaliach to LZOA, 1956-58, mem, secretariat; chmn, Lab Zionist Commn on Youth and Aliya; dir, Eng dept, Mapai, 1959-60. Served, USAF. Found mem: AACI, past natl pres; Chug Mevakshei Derech, vice-pres; mem secretariat, World Lab Zionist Movement; alternate delg, WZCs; dep mem, actions comm, WZO; chmn, Jerusalem council, W Immigrants Assn. Ed: Adventure in Pioneering, 1957; Arise and Build, Story of Amer Habonim, 1961; ed secy, Hagesher, 1960; mem, ed bd, Israel Seen From Within; Isr ed bd, Reconstructionist. Spec interests, all activities asso with absorption of newcomers to Isr. Recipient, Henrietta Szold Award. Home: 4 Yehoash St, Jerusalem, Isr. Office: 4 Balfour St, Jerusalem, Isr.

BRESLAU, Franklin Charles, US, rabbi; b. Chgo, May 5, 1944; s. Frederick and Gisella (Goldschmidt); BHL, Heb Theol Coll, Skokie, 1965; BSE, Ill Inst of Tech, 1965; MEE, NYU, 1970. Chaplain, capt, US Army since 1967; asso elec engr, IBM Corp, 1965; chaplain, Vietnam, 1967-70; 1st airborne J chaplain in US Army hist. Mem: 101st Airborne Div Assn; Inst of Elec Engrs; JWV. Recipient: Bronze Star, Army Recommendation Medal, Vietnam Campaign Medal, Vietnam Service Medal. Home: 200 W 86 St, New York, NY.

BRESLOW, Israel, US, labor exec; b. Dashev, Ukraine, 1906; in US since 1934; m; one c. Mgr, NY Dressmakers Union Local 22, ILGWU since 1958, vice-pres since 1962; chmn, Local 22, 1944-50, bus agt, 1948-58. Pres, Workmen's Circle; chmn, Workmen's Circle div, UJA, NYC, 1958; vice-chmn, J Lab Comm; mem: J Socialist Ferband; Forward Assn. Contbr on lab problems to Yiddish press. Home: 330 W 28 St, New York, NY.

BRESS, David G, US, attorney; b. NYC, June 7, 1908; s. Abraham and Elizabeth (Geto); BS, U of Va, 1928; LLB, Harvard U, 1931; m. Flora Lyon, Sep 20, 1941; c: Pamela, David. Partner, Ginsburg, Feldman & Bress; US atty for DC, 1965-69; pvt practice, 1931-65; fac mem, Wash Coll Law, Amer U, 1932-50; prof, Georgetown Law Sch, 1950-62; instr, Practising Law Inst. Cdr, USNR, 1941-45. Past pres, Wash Heb Cong, 1963-66; bd dirs: natl Capitol area council; Criminal Law Inst, Georgetown U; f: Amer Coll Trial Lawyers; mem: exec comm, Wash chap, AJComm; Amer Bar Assn; Bar Assn DC. Home: 3126 Ellicott St NW, Washington, DC. Office: US Court House, Washington, DC.

BRETTSCHNEIDER, Bertram Donald, US, educator; b. Bklyn, NY, May 7, 1924; s. Joseph and Fannie (Cohn); BA, Tulane U, 1947, MA, 1948; MA, Columbia U, 1951; PhD, NYU, 1956; m. Rita Fischman, June 25, 1950; c: Jane, Joseph. Prof, phil, Hofstra U since 1963, f, phil, New Coll, since 1967, fac mem since 1959; asst, psych, Tulane U, 1947-48; instr, phil, U of Conn, 1949-50. Sgt, US Army, 1943-46. Mem: Amer Phil Assn; Soc for Phenomenology and Existential Phil; Amer Soc Aesthetics. Author: Philosophy of Samuel Alexander: Idealism in Space, Time and Deity, 1964; The Goliath Head, 1971. Recipient, outstanding tchr award, Hofstra U, 1968. Home: 6 Lendale Place, Huntington, NY. Office: Hofstra U, Hempstead, NY.

BREUER, Mordechai Marcus, Isr, principal; b. Frankfort, Ger, Apr 8, 1918; s. Isaac and Jenny (Eisenmann); in Isr since 1936; att London U (ext), Jerusalem, 1943; BA, MA, PhD, Heb U, Jerusalem, 1957-67; m. Fanny Levy, Aug 1943; c: Dina, Shlomo, Miriam, Zippora, Chava, Tamar, Yizchak.

Prin: Horeb Schs, Jerusalem since 1961; Kfar Eliyahu, 1950-57; Even Ha'ezer, 1958-60; lectr, Heb U, 1961-68. Mem: Isr BC Auth; Isr Inst for Sacred Music; Hist Soc of Isr; Soc of Composers; several tchrs and prins socs. Co-ed, Ha'ma'ayan, Orthodox J quarterly; contbr of articles on J hist and educ phil to periodicals. Spec interests: J hist, educ, music. Home: 54 Ben Maimon Ave, Jerusalem, Isr. Office: Horeb Schools, King George Ave, Jerusalem, Isr.

BREUER, Shamshon, Isr, actuary, government official; b. Frankfurt, Ger, Apr 22, 1891; s. Salomon and Sophie (Hirsch); in Isr since 1933; att: Yeshivah of Frankfurt, 1909-12; U of Heidelberg, Strassburg, Frankfurt, 1912-15; ScD, U of Frankfurt, 1915; U of Gottingen, 1919; m. Else Fraenkel, 1920 (decd); m. 2nd, Agatha Jeidel, 1928 (decd); m. 3rd, Lisa Aron Wechsler; c: Mardohkai, Zeev, Zippora Henschke, Hanna Bachrach, Haya Sternfeld, Shlomo, Aron. Ret; chief actuary, Natl Ins Inst, 1954-66; prof, math, Karlsruhe Tech U, 1925-33; prof, actuarial sci, Frankfurt U, 1928-33; chief actuary, Migdal Ins Co, Ltd, Jerusalem, 1934-48; supt of ins, Isr Min of Finance, 1949-54. Mem: Inst of Actuaries, London; Isr Assn Actuaries. Author: Methods of Capitalization According to the National Insurance Law, 1953; The Civil Wrongs Ordinance, 1944; trans, Drei Abhandlungen über die Auflösung der Gleichungen, 1928; contbr to profsl jours. Home: 3 Alharizi Rd, Jerusalem, Isr.

BREVIS, Anna Bear, US educator; b. Rechitza, Russ, Dec 24, 1899; d. Moses and Bessie Bear; in US since 1906; att: Buffalo Tchrs Training Sch; U of Buffalo; Columbia U; m. Harry Brevis, 1932. Prin, public sch, Buffalo, 1929-58. Prin contrib: devl new method of teaching reading; devl Judaism-in-the-Home movement, for educ prog of Natl Women's League, United Syn of Amer. Mem: Elem Prin Assn, Buffalo, NY; NY State Tchrs Assn, Natl Educ Assn; Hadassah. Contbr to Reconstructionist Mag; educ mags. Home: 11740 Wilshire Blvd, Los Angeles, Cal .

BREVIS, Harry J, US, rabbi; b. Kochanovo, Russ, Mar 9, 1898; s. Isaac and Hode (Wahl); in US since 1911; BA, U of Mich, 1923; LLB, Detroit Coll of Law, 1919; MA, Columbia, 1932; admitted Mich Bar, 1923; ordained rabbi, MHL, JIR, 1929; hon DD, HUC-JIR, 1959; m. Anna Bear, 1932. Instr, U of Buffalo; rabbi, Temple Beth El, Batavia, 1942-62; chaplain: VA Hosp, Buffalo, 1952-62; Attica Prison, 1945-62; lectr, Cal Sch, HUC, 1963-66. Past pres, Buffalo ZOA; bd govs, J Fed; bd trustees: Bur of J Educ; Devl Heb Braille Code, 1933. Author: Heb Braille Chrestomathy, 1935; Anthology of Hebrew Literature, 1966; Story of Hebrew Braille in Amer J Archives, 1969; contbr to J and gen mags. Home: 11740 Wilshire Blvd, Los Angeles, Cal.

BREZNIAK, Hyam, Austr, writer, journalist, editor; b. Miedzyrzec, Pol, June 20, 1914; s. Jehudah and Sarah; in Austr since 1939; EE, Technion, Vilna, 1930; m. Paula Taft, 1952; c: Daniel, Michael. Ed, The Bridge, quarterly, since 1964; fmr: vice-pres, Council to combat Fascism and Antisemitism. Author: The Song of the Warsaw Ghetto, 1965; Pinchas Goldhar, 1968; Six Sydney Jewish Artists, 1970; contbr, articles to local J press. Mem, NSW J Bd of Deps. Home: Sunnyside Cr, Castlecrag, Sydney, Austr. Office: 104 Bathurst St, Sydney, NSW, Austr.

BRIANSKY, Rita, Can, artist; b. Pol, July 25, 1925; d. Pincus and Eva (Goldstock); in Can since 1929; att: Montreal Mus of Fine Arts; Ecole des Beaux Arts, Montreal; Art Students League of NY; m. Joseph Prezament, Apr 29, 1949; c: Anna, Wendy. One-man shows: Montreal Mus of Fine Arts, 1957, 1962; Upstairs Gal, Toronto, 1959; Elca London Studio, Montreal, 1963, 1965; Gal Pascal, Toronto, 1964, 1966, 1969; Alice Peek Gal, Ont, 1964; Artlenders, Montreal, 1964; Glenhyrst Arts Council, Ont, 1965; West End Art Gal, Montreal, 1967; Gal 1640, Montreal, 1969; exhbs: Intl Biennial Exhb of Prints, Tokyo; Intl Women's Exhb, Vichy, Fr; repr in perm collections: Mendel Art Gal, Saskatoon, Sask; Art Gal of Hamilton, Ont; London Art Mus, Ont; Burnaby Art Soc; St Joseph Tchrs Coll, Montreal; Thomas More Inst, Montreal; McMaster U, Hamilton; Sarnia Public Libr, Ont; Vancouver Art Gal; New Brunswick Mus; CNR Exec Train; Reader's Digest, Montreal; Alberta Coll of Art; exhb in group shows in every maj cen in Can since 1945. Mem: Can Soc Graphic Arts; Can Painters-Etchers and Engravers; Royal Astronomical Soc of Can. Recipient: 3rd prize, etching, First Natl Print Show, Burnaby, BC, 1961, 1963; hon mention, Intl Womens Exhb, Fr,

1961; grant, Can Council, 1962, 1967; Purchase Award, St Joseph Tchrs Coll, Montreal, 1963. Home and studio: 4832 Wilson Ave, Montreal, Can.

BRICHTO, Herbert Chanan, US, rabbi; b. Jerusalem, Jan 22, 1925; s. Shlomo and Rivka (Frankel); in US since 1931; BSS, CCNY, 1948; ordained rabbi, MHL, HUC, 1950; PhD, U of Pa, 1962; m. Mira Pollak, Nov 2, 1946; c: Johanna, Kathryn, Herschel. Prof, Bible, HUC since 1966, on fac since 1962; rabbi, Temple Sinai, 1953-55. Chaplain, US Army, 1951-53. Mem: CCAR; Soc Bibl Lit; Amer Oriental Soc. Home: 1018 Avondale, Cincinnati, O. Study: 3101 Clifton Ave, Cincinnati, O.

BRICK, Daniel, Swed, editor; b. Stockholm, Mar 23, 1903; BA; m. Anna Riwkin, 1929. Ed, Judisk Kronika, monthly since 1932; found, dir, Judiska Kulturinstitutet since 1957; fmr: ed: The Menora; The Exodus; Via Suecia, both for inmates of concentration camps. Fmr: secy chmn, J Youth Club; Zionist Soc of Stockholm; pres, Scandinavian J Youth Assn; secy gen, Swed ZF; dir, Pal Off, Stockholm; first Isr repr in Scandinavia and Iceland; dir Isr Passport Off, Stockholm. Author: Varför anklagar man judarna? 1939, 1944; co-author: Palestina, 1948; Israel i gar, i dag, i morgon, 1955, eng ed, Israel Yesterday, Today, and Tomorrow, 1958; ed, Mot anti-semitismen (Swed authors opinions on anti-semitism) 1943; trans into Swed: Auto-Emancipation by Leon Pinsker, 1937; novels and short stories from Yiddish and other langs; pub, Zionismen, by Prof Hugo Valentin, 1933. Office: Valhallavhägen 104, Stockholm, Swed.

BRICKMAN, Jay R, US, rabbi; b. NYC, Oct 19, 1924; s. David and Dorothy (Ricklin); BA, U of Mich, 1943; MHL, JIR, NYC, 1947; MA, U of Wis, 1960; m. Rita Warschauer, June 15, 1951; c: Clifford, Harriet, Andrew. Fac, Marquette U since 1967; rabbi: Cong Sinai since 1955; Temple Isr Staten Island, NY, 1948-55. Chaplain, US Army, 1950-52. Home: 8041 N Linksway, Milwaukee, Wis. Study: 8223 N Port Wash Rd, Milwaukee, Wis.

BRICKMAN, William W, US, educator, editor; b. NYC, June 30, 1913; s. David and Sarah (Shaber); BA, CCNY, 1935; PhD, NYU, 1938; m. Sylvia Schnitzer, 1958. Prof, educ hist and comparative educ, U of Pa, since 1962; summer sessions: U of Cal, 1953-54; U of Ill, 1958; U of Toledo, 1959; Teachers Coll, Columbia U, 1964; U of Pittsburgh, 1965; U of Wyoming, 1968; ed, School and Society, since 1953; tutor, Ger, CCNY, 1937; instr, Ger, U of Pa, 1945; asst mgn ed, Modern Lang Jour, 1942-46; ed, Educ Abstracts, 1942-44; asso prof, chmn, dept of hist of educ, NYU, 1952-57; prof, educ, 1957-62; visiting prof, educ, Yeshiva U, 1953-57, 1964; Loyola Coll, 1962; educ hist and comparative educ, U of Hamburg, 1957. US Army, 1943-46. Mem: bd of educ, Rabbi Jacob Joseph Sch, 1952; Natl Fulbright Selection Comm, 1952-53; Amer Hist Soc; Natl Soc for Study of Educ; AAAS; Hist of Sci Soc; AAUP; Natl Soc Coll Tchrs of Educ; Amer Acad Political and Social Scis; Renaissance Soc of Amer; Hist Assn, Eng; Young Isr; Union of Orthodox J Congs of Amer; Torah Umesorah; Phi Delta Kappa; trustee, Payne Educ Sociology Found, 1953-59; adv, Torah Umesorah, since 1949. Author: Educational Systems in the US, 1964; co-author: John Dewey: Master Educator, 1959; The Changing Soviet School, 1960; The Countdown on Segregated Education, 1960; Religion, Government and Education, 1961; A Century of Higher Education, 1962; Automation, Education, and Human Values, 1966; A History of International and Comparative Education: Nineteenth Century Documents, 1968; contbr: year-books of Ency Britannica; Ency of Educ Research; Dict of Amer Hist; scholarly, profsl J jours. Recipient, Battle Star, 1945. Home: 2227 N 52 St, Philadelphia, Pa. Office: U of Pa, Philadelphia, Pa.

BRICKNER, Balfour, US, rabbi; b. Cleveland, O, Nov 18, 1926; s. Barnett and Rebecca (Aaronson); BA, U Cincinnati, 1948; ordained rabbi, MHL, HUC, 1952; m. Barbara Michaels, June 20, 1954; c: Elsa, Barnett, Adam. Dir, Commn for Interfaith Activities for Reform Judaism; asso dir, Commn on Social Action of Reform Judaism, both UAHC, both since 1961; rabbi, Temple Sinai, Wash, DC, 1952-61; J Chautaqua Soc lectr, Amer U, Wash, DC, 1955-61. Natl co-chmn, Natl Rel Cabinet, State of Isr Bonds; chmn, Interrel Affairs Comm, Syn Council of Amer; appd by Pres of US to Natl Citizens Comm on Comty Relations Service; host, weekly radio prog, Adventures in Judaism; mem: bd, Upper Park Ave Comty Assn; exec comm, Natl Comm of Clergy and

Laymen Concerned About Vietnam; Negotiation Now; fmr: initiated and led teaching mission to W Ger to teach Judaism to 7,500 non-Jewish Ger HS students; lectr mission on behalf UJA: Fr, Ger, Eng, It, N Afr; mem staff, Natl Fed of J Temple Youth Camp Leadership Inst, with wife, led youth tour to Isr; dir, B'rith Hillel Found, Cincinnati, O. Contributing author: Christians and Jews: The Tragic Past and the Hopeful Future; (pamphlet) As Driven Sands, 1957; contbr of numerous articles to jours and mags. Recipient, Merrill Found Grant to study race relations in the South, 1961-62. Home: 2 Sackett Circle, Larchmont, NY. Office: 838 Fifth Ave, New York, NY.

BRILL, Harold M, US, surgeon; b. Peoria, Ill, Sep 26, 1905; s. Charles and Rochel (Levin); BS, Northwestern U, 1930, BM, BS, 1932, MD, 1932. Pvt practice since 1932; asso prof, obstet and gyn, Chgo Med. Sch; cons, obstet and gyn, Chgo Health Dept. Cdr, MC, USNR, 1942-46. F: AMA; Amer Coll Surgs; Intl Coll Surgs; Amer Coll Obstet and Gyn; dipl, Amer Bd Obstet and Gyn; mem: Chgo Gyn Soc; Cen Assn Obstet and Gyn; Phi Delta Epsilon; Sigma Xi. Contbr to med jours. Home: 2933 Sheridan Rd, Chicago, Ill. Office: 55 E Wash St; 6201 N Cal Ave, Chicago, Ill.

BRILL, Hyman Carl, US, educator; b. NYC, Apr 14, 1912; s Charles and Fannie (Stein); BJP, JTSA, 1934; BSS, CCNY, 1936, MSciEd, 1939; m. Helen Stern, Dec 25 1938; c: Rebecca Snyder, Hinda Fuchs. Tchr, elem sch, NYC Bd of Educ since 1963; asst prin, Rabbi Jacob Joseph Sch, since 1944; Heb sch tchr, 1940-44. First pres, org, Forest Park J Cen, hon pres; fund raiser: Isr Bonds; Yeshiva U; mem, Cen Queens Council of Orthodox Congs. Recipient, outstanding service plaque, Isr Bonds, 1966; cert, Yeshiva U, 1962, 1969. Home: 83-75 Woodhaven Blvd, Woodhaven, NY. Office: 84 Shaffer, New York, NY.

BRILL, Isidor C, US, cardiologist, educator; Vladimiretz, Russ, Oct 1, 1888; s. Abraham and Deborah (Cherniac); in US since 1903; BA, Columbia U, 1912, MD, 1914; m. Ruth Lowengart, 1923 (decd); c: Madeline Nelson, Eleanor Stern; m. 2nd, Isobel Skoborg, 1956. Cons phys, U of Ore Med Sch; staff phys: St Vincent's Hosp since 1917; Holladay Park Hosp since 1940; Good Samaritan Hosp; prof med em, U of Ore Med Sch; instr: Stanford U, 1914-15; U of Cal, 1915-16; research, Harvard U, 1923; Research Inst, Cedars of Lebanon Hosp, LA, 1949. Pres , J Educ Assn, 1942-52; mem, bd govs, Amer Coll of Card, 1957-60; Alpha Omega Alpha; Sigma Xi; clubs: Pacific Interurban Clinical; Tualatin Country. Co-author: The Auricular Arrhythmias, 1952; contbr to med jours. Home: 1975 SW Montgomery Dr, Portland, Ore. Office: 2220 SW First Ave, Portland, Ore.

BRILLIANT, Moshe D, Isr, journalist; b. W Hoboken, NJ, Apr 26, 1915; s. Max and Ida (Propp); in Isr since 1933; m. Sylvia Abrams, June 25, 1939; c: Joshua, Hedva. Corresp, The Times, London since 1949; res corresp, NY Times since 1949; mem ed staff, Jerusalem Post, 1934-53. Contbr, Harpers Mag; American Mercury. Home: 21 Chen Blvd, Tel Aviv, Isr.

BRILLIANT, Nathan, US, educational exec; b. Kalish, Pol, Sep 4, 1894; s. Jacob and Hannah (Moskowitz); in US since 1902; BS, CCNY, 1918; MA Tchrs Coll, Columbia U, 1930. Ret; dir, Cleveland Bur of J Educ, 1946-60; prin, B'nai Shearith Juda, NY, 1925-26; educ dir, Euclid Ave Temple, Cleveland, O, 1927-46. Pres: O, Mich, Independent Rel Sch Tchrs Assn; Natl Council for J Educ, 1956-57; mem, ed bd, J Educ Mag, 1938-45; mem, exec bd: Zionist Dist; Natl Council for: J Educ; J Comty Council; JWF Comm; social agcy comm, J Comty Fed; Inst of J Studies; Rel Educ Assn, regional; Adult Educ Council; all of Cleveland; mem: B'nai B'rith; ZOA; Histadruth Ivrith. Co-author: Let's Celebrate Purim; Maimonides; Religious Pageants for Jewish Schools, 1941; Children's Services, 1948; Supplement to Activities in the Religious Schools, 1950; Activities in the Religious School, 1951. Home: 5 Island Ave, Miami Beach, Fla

BRILLING, Bernhard, Ger, historian; b. Tremessen, Posen, June 3, 1906; s. Samuel and Pauline (Scheftelowitz); rabb dipl, Jüdische Theol Sem, Breslau, 1933; PhD, Münster, 1958; m. Eva Redlich, 1939. Found, dir, dept, hist of Ger J, U of Münster since 1958; archivist, J comty, Breslau, 1928-39. Author, Geschichte der Juden in Breslau (1454-1702), 1960; co-author: Westfalia Judaica I, 1967; Juden in Münster (1933-45), 1960; contbr to Ency Judaica; Germania Judaica II on hist of J in Ger; Heb printing; J Archives; Rabbi Jonathan Eibenschutz; connections with Eretz Isr before the Zionism, in HUA, Studies in J Bibliography and Folklore. Home: Hollenbeckerstrasse 23, Münster 44, Ger.

BRIN, Alexander, US, educator, editor; b. Zaslav, Russ, June 15, 1893; s. Joseph and Zlata (Applebaum) Gottland; in US since 1907; m. Bertha Kastor, June 12, 1927; c: Barbara, Frederica. Ret; dean, Mass State Bd of Educ, 1949-62; ed, publisher, The J Advocate since 1917. Fmr: chmn, Natl Bd of Review on GI Accreditation of Schs and Colls; Bay State repr, Citizens Fed Comm, US Off of Educ; repr Mass at Pan-Amer Educ Cong, Havana, Cuba, 1941; sponsor, Pan-Amer Book Fair; resolution chmn, prog comm, Mass-Wash Bi-centennial Commn, 1932; vie-pres, Gtr Council, Boy Scouts of Amer, 1941; Mass repr, White House Conf on Educ since 1930; mem, Boston panel of arbitrators, NY Stock Exch; vice pres, Mass Crime Comm since 1952; life trustee, Beth Isr Hosp, Boston; Cathedral of Pines; life dir, Combined J Philanthropies of Gtr Boston; Incorporator, Childrens' Med Cen, Boston; mem: Pres's Council, Brandeis U; Bay State Coll Bd and State Vocational Bd; training comm, Boy Scout Inst of Leadership; club, New Cent. Recipient: Dist Service Medal, Mass-Wash, Bi-Centennial Commn, 1932; Dist Service Award, Mass Tchrs Assn, 1963. Home: 60 Babcock St, Brookline, Mass. Office: 251 Causway St, Boston, Mass.

BRIN, Herbert Henry, US, editor; b. Chgo, Feb 17, 1915; s. Sol and Fannie (Goroway); att: DePaul U and Law Sch, 1933-37; Crane Jr Coll, 1933; U of Chgo, 1939-40; c: Stanley, David, Jeremy. Ed-publisher, owner, Heritage Pub Co (publisher of four J newspapers, annual J Comty Directory) since 1954; reporter, City News Bur, Chgo, 1942-47; feature writer-reporter, LA Times, 1947-54; accredited to: Summit Conf, Paris, 1960; Eichmann Trial, Jerusalem, 1961; lectr and reader of poetry at various Call Colls and to W Coast Temple groups. US Army, 1943-46. Found and dir, Westside Poetry Cen, LA; found: Pacific SW brs, Union of Orthodox J Congs of Amer, 1957; Jr Blind, 1953-69; mem: exec comm, armed services comm, JWB, since 1959; bd, Hillel Heb Acad, 1959-60; Beth Jacob Cong, Beverly Hills, since 1957; mem: AJComm; Farband; AJCong; ZOA; JWV. Author: Wild Flowers, 1965; Justice, 1967. Recipient: Award of Merit, JWV, 1955, 1956; Three-Bell Award, Cal Assn for MH, 1958; Torch of Hope, City of Hope, 1959. Home: 18450 Clifftop Way, Malibu, Cal. Office: 2130 S Vermont Ave, Los Angeles Cal.

BRIN, Myron, US, educator; b. NYC, July 1, 1923; s. Philip and Frances (Kraut); BS, Cornell U, 1947; M, Nutrition Sci, 1948; PhD, Harvard U, 1951; m. Phyllis Blecher, June 4, 1944; c: Kenneth, Steven, Mitchell. Asst dir, clinical nutrition, Hoffman-La Roche Inc, Nutley, NJ, since 1969; research asso, Harvard Med Sch, 1953-56; chief biol, Food and Drug Labs, 1956-58; asso prof, biochem, SUNY Med Sch, 1958-68; prof, nutrition, U of Cal, Davis, 1968-69. Lt, USAF, 1943-45. Pres, J F of Davis, Cal; mem: Amer Soc Biol Chem; Amer Inst Nutrition; Amer Soc Clinical Nutrition; Soc for Experimental Biol and Med; Royal Med Soc, London; AAAS; NY Acad Sci; Amer Chem Soc; Amer Inst Chem; Sigma Xi; Phi Kappa Phi. Contbr numerous publs to sci jours. Recipient, A Cressy Morrison Award, NY Acad Sci, 1962. Home: 30 Wellington Rd, Livingston, NJ.

BRINBERG, Charles H, US, physician; b. Aus, May 1, 1900; s. Morris and Caroline (Horowitz); in US since 1905; BA, Columbia U, 1920; MD, Syracuse U, 1924; m. Lillian Levin, June 26, 1926; c: Michael Burnhill, Marian Mintzer. Chief, dept female sex endocrinology, Bklyn J Hosp since 1932, gyn dept, 1928-49, mem staff since 1924; res obstet, Fordham Hosp, NY, 1926; instr, Kings Co Med Soc, 1934-52. US Army, 1918. F, Amer Coll Obstet and Gyn; dipl, Intl Bd Surg; mem: AMA; Kings Co Med Soc; Amer Soc Study Fertility; Endocrine Soc; Harvey Soc; NY Acad Sci; Intl Fertility Soc; Intl Obstet and Gyn Soc; Coll of Surgs. Author, Female Sex Endocrinology, 1949; contbr numerous articles to med and sci jours. Hobbies: photography, fishing. Home and office: 191 Ocean Ave, Brooklyn, NY.

BRISEL, Bella, Fr, artist; b. Jerusalem, July 23, 1929; d. Aaron and Haya (Mintsberg); in Fr since 1950; att Ecole des Beaux-Arts, Paris; m. Sioma Baram. One-man shows: gals: Paris, London, Tokyo, Osaka, NY, Yaffo, Balearic Islands, Spain; Tel Aviv Mus; salons: Tokyo, Spain, Eng, Algeria, Morocco,

Japan, US. Pub works: stone reliefs, Yehuda Halevi's Shirei Kodesh, 1955; Bella Brisel, Documents, 1961; Bella Brisel, Twentieth Century Masters, 1962. IDF, 1947-48. Recipient: UFAI, Intl Exhb, Gen Isr Painters, Paris, 1953; Isr Consulate, 1955. Home & studio: 41 Rue de Seine, Paris, Fr.

BROCHES, Aron, US, attorney; b. Amsterdam, Netherlands, Mar 22, 1914; s. Abraham and Chaja (Person); in US since 1939; LLM, Amsterdam U Sch of Law, 1936, JD, 1939; LLB, Fordham U, 1942; m. Catherina Pothast, May 2, 1939; c: Ida Calabro, Paul. Gen counsel, Intl Bank for Reconstruction and Devl since 1959, staff mem since 1946; secy gen, Intl Cen for Settlement of Inves Disputes since 1967; legal positions with Netherlands Govt, 1942-46. Exec council, Amer Soc of Intl Law, Wash, DC: trustee, Intl Legal Cen, NY; mem: Netherlands Soc for Intl Law; World Peace Through Law; clubs: Cosmos, Wash, DC; Societeit De Witte, Hague, Netherlands. Contbr to legal jours. Hobbies: music, theatre. Home: 2600 Tilden Pl, Washington, DC. Office: 1818 H St, Washington, DC.

BROCK, Samuel, US, neuropsychiatrist, educator; b. NYC, Oct 8, 1893; s. Charles and Julia (Barcus); MD, NYU, 1916; m. Marie Westhoff, June 30, 1919. Prof, neur, NYU, Coll of Med, 1940-61; att neuropsycht, Bellevue Hosp, 1940; cons, neur, Beth Isr Hosp, all of NYC. Mem: NY Acad of Med; Amer Neur Assn; AMA; Amer Psycht Assn; Assn for Research in Nervous and Mental Diseases; NY Neur Soc; NY Soc of Clinical Psycht; Amer Acad of Neur. Author: Injuries of the Brain and Spinal Cord, 4th ed, 1960; The Basis of Clinical Neurology, 4th ed, 1963; contbr to sci jours. Home: 315 E 68 St, New York, NY. Office: 115 E 61 St, New York, NY.

BRODETSKY, Manya, Eng, communal worker; b. Bialystok, Pol, June 23, 1890; d. Paul and Michal (Slabodsky) Barenblum; in Eng since 1914; att Bristol U, psych, 1914-15; m. Selig Brodetsky, Jan 13, 1919, decd; c: Paul, Adèle Kitrick. Life pres, Ladies' Zionist Assn, Leeds; hon life pres, Women's ZC, Leeds; hon pres, Selig Brodetsky Zionist Soc, Harrow & Kenton; hon vice-pres: WIZO; W London Zionist Soc; Friends of Isr Philharmonic Orch; Union Maccabi Assn; vice-pres: British Council, Shaare Zedek Hosp, Jerusalem; British Maccabiah Org Comm; found-mem, WIZO House, London; council mem, Women's Voluntary Service, Leeds, taught Russ, Fr, WW I, WW II. Spec interest, Isr Philharmonic Orch. Home: 55 The Moors, Kidlington, Eng.

BRODIE, Bernard Beryl, US, pharmacologist; b. Liverpool, Eng, Aug 7, 1909; s. Samuel and Esther (Ginsburg); in US since 1931; BS, McGill U, 1931; PhD, NYU, 1935; hon DS: U of Paris, 1963; Phila Coll of Pharm Sci, 1965; U of Barcelona, 1967; hon DM, Karolinska Inst, 1968; hon DS, NY Med Coll, 1970; m. Anne Smith, Aug 31, 1950. Chief, chem pharm lab, George Washington U Med Sch, since 1949, prof lectr; prof lectr, Georgetown U Med Sch; cons, grad council, George Washington U; asso prof, biochem, asst prof, pharm, instr, dept med, NYU Med Sch, 1941-50. Pres: Amer Coll of Neuropsychopharm, 1965; mem: Amer Soc Biol Chem; Amer Soc Pharm Experimental Therapy; Harvey Soc; Sigma Xi; NY Acad Scis; Soc for Experimental Biol & Med; Amer Assn of Clinical Chem; Amer Chem Soc; AHA; AAAS; Royal Soc of Med, London; Pavlovian Soc of Amer; Intl Soc of Biochem & Pharm; Intl Pharm Soc. Author: Metabolic Factors Controlling Duration of Drug Action, 1963; Drug Enzyme Interactions, 1964; found, Life Scis; ed bd: Advances in Pharmacology Intl Jour of Neuropharm; Circulation; Eur Jour of Pharm; adv bd: Pharm Research Communications; Ency of Pharm & Therapeutics; contbr of numerous articles to jours. Recipient: Oscar B Hunter Memorial Award, Amer Therapy Soc, 1970; Golden Plate Award, Amer Acad Achievement, 1970. Home: 4977 Battery Lane, Bethesda, Md. Office: 9000 Rockville Pike, Bethesda, Md.

BRODKIN, Henry A, US, surgeon; b. Russia, Feb 15, 1901; s. Isaac and Anna (Kantrowitz); in US since 1905; MD, Jefferson Med Coll, 1924; m. Eva Topkins, Sep 6, 1925; c: Hyla Garlen, Richard, Roger. Att thoracic surg, Newark Beth Isr Hosp, since 1952; on cons staff, E Orange Gen, Irvington Gen Hosps, Newark Eye and Ear Infirmary; chief med dir, NJ Dept of Lab and Ind, 1946-59; med, admn cons, NJ Rehab Comm, 1946-59; State Surg, NJ Dept of Defense, 1947-61. Col, US Army MC, 1940-45. US delg, 11th Intl Cong Mil Med and Pharm, 1947, Basle, Switz; mem: Amer Coll Surgs; Intl Coll Surgs; Amer Coll Chest Phys; Belgian Soc Surgs; NY Thoracic

Surg Soc; NJ Soc of Surgs. Contbr of numerous articles to profsl jours. Recipient: Silver Medal, U of Liege, Belgium, 1945. Home: 377 S Harrison Rd, Irvington, NJ. Office: 40 Union Ave, Irvington, NJ.

BRODKIN, Martin Freeman, US, attorney; b. Chicago, Ill, July 7, 1916; s. Louis and Celia (Freeman); AB, Northwestern U, 1940; LLB, Chgo-Kent Law Sch, 1944, JD, 1969; m. Zerna Kogan, June 15, 1958; c: Dory, Brandon. Atty and asst, corp council, city of Chgo, since 1956; pvt practice; dir: Power Tools, Inc; King Mfg; asst state atty, City of Chgo, 1945-56. Mem: bd dirs, Hollywood Park B'nai B'rith; munic court comm and criminal law comm, Chgo Bar Assn; Amer Judicature Soc. Home: 6256 N Avers Ave, Chicago, Ill. Office: 134 N LaSalle St, Chicago, Ill.

BRODSKY, Harry, US, artist; b. Newark, NJ, July 20, 1908; s. Samuel and Dora (Bakelenik); att: Pa Mus Sch of Ind Art, 1928-31; U of Pa, 1931; m. Ida Mockrin, 1936; c: David, Dorothy. In pvt bus of design; fmr: art dir: Mid City Press; TV Guide; instr, adv art, vocational HSs, Phila, 1938-44, 1949-50; exhbs: Acad of Fine Arts, 1934, 1948-50; Cong Libr, 1943-46; Carnegie Inst Natl Show, 1945-46; Natl Acad, 1946-48; Bklyn Mus, 1947-48, 1950-51; Whitney Mus, 1934; Art Alliance, Phila; Cincinnati Mus; with State Dept show exhb in Paris, Rome, Milan; USIA, overseas, 1963-64; prints now exhb throughout S Amer by State Dept; perm collections: Bklyn Mus; Springfield Mus; Bezalel Mus, Isr; one-man shows: Print club, Phila, 1948; Westcott and Thomson Gals, Phila, 1951; Donovan Gals, 1953; Art Alliance, 1953; Women's City Club, 1962. Pres, Artists Guild of Del Valley, 1965; club, Print. Recipient, Purchase award, Bklyn Mus, 1947. Home: 6633 N 8 St, Philadelphia, Pa. Office: 27 and Ranstead St, Philadelphia, Pa.

BRODSKY, Irving, US, social worker exec; b. Bklyn, NY, June 7, 1915; s. Abraham and Lena (Levine); AB, Bklyn Coll, 1937; grad, Columbia U Sch of Social Work, 1940; post grad study, Columbia U, 1940-42; m. Jeanne Blum, Mar 12, 1944; c: Ellen, Robert. Exec vice-pres, Asso YM-YWHA's of Gtr NY since 1957; adj prof, Hunter Coll Sch of Social Work since 1958; fmr: exec dir: J Assn for neighborhood Cens, 1946-57; E NY YM-YWHA, 1944-45; lectr: social work, NYU Sch of Educ, 1949-52; social wfr admn, Adelphi U, 1952-55; cons to comty studies conducted for Greenleigh Assos and NJWB. Cpl, mil psycht social worker, US Army, 1945-46. Chmn, prog comm, Research Cen of Natl JWB and Brandeis U; mem: exec comm and bd dirs, Natl JWB; adv council, Hunter Coll Sch of Social Work; Natl Assn of Social Workers; Natl Assn of J Cen Workers; Acad of Cert Social Workers; fmr, chmn, public recreation, Comty Council, Gtr NY. Co-author: Adventure in Mental Health, 1946; Manual for Board Members, Natl JWB, 1957; contbr numerous articles to profsl and J jours in US and abroad. Hobbies: gardening, boating. Home: 30 Lake Rd, Rye, NY. Office: 33 W 60 St, New York, NY.

BRODSKY, Nathan, US, economist; b. Phila, Pa, Sep 22, 1916; s. Alfred and Pauline (Sennett); BS, Temple U, 1937; att U of Pa, 1938-40; PhD, Amer U, 1958; m. Margaret McStay, Dec 27, 1946; c: James, David, Barbara. Dir, educ progs and mgmt training, Dept of Defense since 1966, staff mem since 1967; U lectr since 1948. Col, US Army, 1940-46. Pres, local PTAs and civic assns; mem: Amer Econ Assn; Amer Acad of Political Sci; Inst of Mgmt Sci. Contbr of articles to econ and educ jours. Recipient: civilian Meritorious Service Medal, Dept of Defense, 1970; Bronze Star. Home: 2840 Lorcom Lane, Arlington, Va. Office: Pentagon, Washington, DC.

BRODSKY, Ralph Howard, US, oral surg; b. NYC, Feb 25, 1900; s. George and Rose (Horwitz); DMD, Harvard U, 1922; m. Ruth Anshen, 1923; c: Judith. Pvt practice of dent and oral surg, NYC since 1922; prof em, dent, Mt Sinai Sch of Med; oral surg, Mt Sinai Hosp since 1922; cons oral surg, Dept of Hosps, NYC since 1946; vice-pres, Vitron Research Corp since 1950; oral surg, dir, Hecksher Found Dent Clinics, 1924-31; dir, dept oral surg, Sea View Hosp, 1934-46; lectr, NYU Grad Med Sch, 1947-50. Prin contribs: extensive research in dent caries and oral TB; introduced Grenz Ray to dent, the cold curing plastic, several instruments. Dipl, NY Bd Oral Surg; f, NY Acad Sci; mem: Amer Dent Assn; Pan Amer Odontological Assn, found, past pres; NY Acad Sci; Intl Assn for Dent Research; Amer Assn Dent Eds; hon mem, S Amer dent assns. Fmr book ed, papers; pub, The Atlas of

Oral and Facial Lesions. Home and office: 14 E 81 St, New York, NY.

BRODY, Abraham A, Swed, educator; b. Banovce, Czech, Sep 27, 1901; s. Heinrich and Sara (Handler); in Swed since 1925; PhD, Royal U, Uppsala, Swed, 1936; ordained rabbi, Lehranstalt für die Wissenschaft des Judentums, Berlin, 1938; m. Eva Gurewitsch Goorin, Feb 28, 1923; c: Sam, Simon, Isser. Tchr, Mosaiska Comty, Swed since 1928; asso prof, Stockholm U, since 1936. Pres, Gen Zionist, Swed since 1951; vice-pres, Zionist Fed, Swed, since 1951; found pres, Heb Club, Stockholm; pres, Brit Ivrit Olamit, Stockholm, since 1925; mem, Die Giessener Mischna. Author: Memories of Aaron Isaac, 1932; Der Mishna Traktat Tamid, 1936; Development and Shifting of Motives in the Israelite-Jewish Conceptions of Clean and Unclean, 1948; The History of the Jews, 1950; Swedish Jewish Pioneers and Ancestors, 1956. Home: 55 Sveavägen, Stockholm, Swed. Office: Mosaiska Förmamlingen, 3 Wahrendorffsgatan, Stockholm, Swed.

BRODY, Henry, US, physician; b. NYC, May 14, 1905; s. Moses and Nady (Brick); BS, CCNY, 1926; MD, U of Rochester, Sch of Med and Dent, 1932; m. Margaret Breuer, Aug 24, 1934; c: Alice, Daniel. Dir of labs, Albert Einstein Med Cen, N div, since 1950; asso prof, path: Med Sch, Temple U; Grad Sch of Med, U of Pa; f, tutor, instr, biol dept, CCNY, 1925-39; f, phys dept, Sch of Med and Dent, U of Rochester, 1928-29; asso, path, Beth Isr Hosp, NY, 1937-50; instr, path, Med Coll, NYU, 1939-47. Maj, MC, US Army, 1942-46. Pres: Phila Path Soc; clinical path sect, Co Med Soc, Phila, 1956-57; mem: Coll of Amer Path; Amer Assn of Path and Bact; Amer Soc of Clinical Path; Intl Acad of Path; NY Acad of Scis; Phila Coll of Phys; AAAS; Alpha Omega Alpha; Sigma Xi. Contbr to med jours. Home: 721 Meetinghouse Rd, Elkins Pk, Pa. Office: Albert Einstein Med Cen, Philadelphia, Pa.

BRODY, Martin, US, business exec; b. Newark, NJ, Aug 8, 1921; s. Leo and Renee (Kransdorf); BA, Mich State U, 1943; m. Florence Gropper, Nov 22, 1946; c: Marc, Renee. Chmn, pres, Restaurant Assos Inc since 1963; dir: Caldor since 1961; Bishop Inds since 1964; Dollar Savings Bank since 1969; pres, AM Cap Corp, 1961-63. Capt, US Army, 1943-46. Vice-pres, Temple Bnai Abraham; chmn, young mens div, Essex Co, UJA; mem, Young Pres Org, NJ. Home: 30 Kean Rd, Short Hills, NJ. Office: 1540 Broadway, New York, NY.

BRODY, Selma R, US, geriatric cons; b. NYC, June 1, 1926; d. Herman and Rose (Appelbaum) Rich; BA, Hunter Coll, 1946; m. Elroy Brody, Sep 18, 1949; c: Madeleine, Robert. Partner, Selroy Music Co; pres, Miller-Brody Prod; author, composer, for TV and children's recordings; writer-publisher of several hundred songs for children, dir, artists and repertoire, Peter Pan Records, 1961-68; chmn, bd dirs, Senior Citizens Center of Mt Vernon, Inc, 1954-62, profsl dir, 1958-61; sup, Sr Citizens Activities of Westchester Co Recreation Commn, 1955-58. Cons to Gov of NY on problems of aging, 1958; designer, Sr City, a model for aged, NY State Fair, 1958; mem: Natl Recreation Assn; NY State Recreational Assn. Author: American Encyclopedia of Learning Through Music, 1958-60; Senior City at the New York State Fair (pamphlet). Home: 290 Collins Ave, Mt Vernon, NY. Office: 342 Madison Ave, NYC.

BRODY, Sidney F, US, business exec; b. Des Moines, Ia, Nov 15, 1915; s. Abraham and Lena (Freedman); BS, Harvard Coll, 1937; m. Frances Lasker, Aug 14, 1942; c: Christopher, Susan. Pres, Brody Inves Co, since 1953; mem, bd dirs: Amer Elec since 1961; Westland Capital since 1962; Security Pacific Natl Bank; Gen TV. Lt col, USAF, 1941-45. Mem, bd dirs, pres, LA County Mus of Art; UCLA Art Council, chmn finance comm; bd trustees, Thacher Sch; past mem, bd trustees, Leo Baeck Temple. Recipient, Croix de Guerre. Hobbies: sports, art. Home 360 S Mapleton Dr, Los Angeles, Cal. Office: 9477 Brighton Way, Beverly Hills, Cal.

BRODY, William, US, administrator; b. Bklyn, NY, Dec 24, 1908; s. Max and Bertha (Neustadt); BS, NYU, 1930, MA, 1939, MPA, 1943; m. Sylvia Stanler, June 28, 1936; c: Barbara Richmon, Ronald. Dep dir, Natl Multiple Sclerosis Soc, since 1965; dir, personnel: US Natl War Lab Bd, 1944-46; NYC Dept of Health, 1945-51; personnel adv, US Econ Stabilization Agcy, 1951-53; asst to exec dir, Natl J Hosp, Denver, 1953-57;

dir, admn, Phila Dept of Public Health, 1957-65. Pres, NY Munic Personnel Soc, 1948-50; mem: Public Personnel Assn; Amer Soc Public Admn; Amer Public Health Assn. Author, Personnel Administration in Public Health Nursing, 1951; contbr to profsl jours. Home: 30-60 Crescent St, Astoria, NY. Office: 257 Park Ave S, New York, NY.

BROIDA, Herbert P, US, physicist; b. Aurora, Colo, Dec 25, 1920; s. Theodore and Lucy (Shatz); BA, U of Colo, 1944; MA, Harvard, 1945, PhD, 1949; m. Ina Burnes, Aug 8, 1948; c: John, Allison. Prof, U of Cal since 1962; chief, free radicals sect and coord free radicals prog, Natl Bur Standards, 1956-62, on staff since 1949. Prin contribs in fields of molecular spectroscopy, upper atmosphere physics, laser physics, chem kinetics, energy exch. F: AAAS; Amer Phys Soc; Optical Soc Amer; chmn, Intl Comm on Free Radicals Symposia, 1968; mem: Amer Assn Physics Tchrs; Amer Chem Soc; Combustion Inst; exec comm, W Spectroscopy Assn; Fed Amer Sci; Phi Beta Kappa; Sigma Xi; club, Cosmos. Recipient: Fleming Award, 1956; Dept of Commerce Gold Medal, 1960. Home: 4071 Naranjo Dr, Santa Barbara, Cal. Office: Physics Dept, U of Cal, Santa Barbara, Cal.

BROIDO, Lucy K, US, communal leader, educator; b. Pittsburgh, Pa, Mar 21, 1900; d. Theodore and Florence (Schwarz) Kaufmann; BA, cum laude, Vassar Coll, 1921; MA, U of Pittsburgh, 1925; m. Louis Broido, Aug 1, 1923; c: Theodore, Joseph. Mem bd: Natl Council of J Women; med council, Downstate Med Cen, SUNY; JDC; Assn for New Amers; treas, Intl Council J Women; hon pres, Natl Council J Women; vice-pres, J Educ Comm, 1946-53; instr, Eng dept, U of Pittsburgh, 1923-25; Hunter Coll, NYC, 1927-30. Home: 20 Sutton Pl S, New York, NY.

BROMBERG, Abram Izchak, Isr, rabbi, author; b. Ostrov Mazowiezk, Pol, Apr 14, 1898; s. Natan and Rosa (Shidlowska); in Isr since 1940; att Yeshiva, Warsaw, Pol; Tchrs Sem, Warsaw, 1919-23; U Warsaw, 1923-26; m. Liba Gurewitcz, 1926; c: Jacob, Feiga; wife and children perished under Nazi regime. Hamizrachi Intl Cen since 1950, cen for rel educ; fmr: rabbi, Grudzondz, 1930-39; research worker in Talmudic lit; insp of educ, rel schs, Isr, 1948-68; chaplain, Pol Army, 1940-45. Author: Hamusar Hayehudi, 1939; Homat Yerushalayim, 1943; Rashi Veyerushalayim, 1945; Mekorot Lefiskei Harambam, 1947; series of monographs, Migdolei Hatora Vehahasidut, 1947-69; contbr of numerous articles to learned publs. Mem, Heb Writers Assn. Recipient, hon award, Jerusalem Munic, 1969. Home: 5 Keren Hayesod St, Jerusalem, Isr.

BROMBERG, Eleazer, US, mathematician, administrator, educator; b. Toronto, Can, Oct 7, 1913; s. Aaron and Miriam (Hadler); BS, CCNY, 1933; MA, Columbia U, 1935; att U of Toronto, 1935-37; PhD, NYU, 1950; m. Edith Weiss, Mar 28, 1948; c: Dan, Michael, Jeremy. Prof, applied math, NYU, since 1953; instr, physics: Worcester Poly Inst, 1941-42; NYU, 1942-43; research math: Columbia U, 1943-44; NYU, 1944-45; math, Reeves Instrument Corp, NYC, 1945-50, 1952; head, mechanics br, Off Naval Research, 1950-53; physicist, Los Alamos Sci Lab, 1956-57; asst dir, Courant Inst of Math Scis, 1957-66. Mem: Amer Math Soc; Math Assn of Amer; Soc for Ind and Applied Math. Contbr of papers on elasticity, computing techniques. Home: 30 Young Ave, Pelham, NY. Office: 251 Mercer St, New York, NY.

BROMBERG, Henri Louie, Jr, US, attorney; b. Dallas, Tex, Jan 15, 1911; s. Henri and Felice (Fechenbach); BA, U of Tex, 1932; JD, Northwestern U Law Sch, Chgo, 1935; m. Janice Mayer, Apr 12, 1936; c: Henri. Partner, Johnson, Bromberg, Leeds & Riggs since 1958; dir: North Park Natl Bank, Dallas since 1965; Peoples Amer Bank, Atlanta since 1968; Dallas Market Cen Co since 1955; many pvt corps; Carrington, Gowan, Johnson, Bromberg & Leeds, 1946-58. USAF, 1942-46, lt col, 1946. Dir: AJComm, Dallas chap since 1951, chmn, 1951; Dallas Grand Opera Assn, and secy since 1946; Dallas Co Comty Action Comm since 1965; Temple Emanu-El since 1950, pres, 1959-61; found, mem first and all subsequent bds dirs since 1967, secy since 1968; fmr: pres and dir, W Dallas Social Cen; JWF, Dallas; vice-pres, dir, Tex Psycht Found; dir: Dallas Co Assn Blind; Council Social Agcies, Dallas; natl vice-chmn, Jt Defense Appeal Natl Council; mem natl bd dirs, Council J Feds and Wfr Funds; mem natl bd, NCCJ, co-chmn, Dallas chap; mem: S Methodist U Law Sch Bd of Visitors; bd govs, HUC-JIR; gov comm, 1960 White House Conf, Children and Youth; delg, White House Conf Intl

Coop, 1965; mem: Amer Judicature Soc; Archaeol Inst Amer; Dallas Art Assn; C of C, Dallas; Amer, Dallas, Tex, Bar Assns; clubs: Columbia, Dallas, dir, 1946-59, pres, 1949; Dallas; City; Commonwealth, all Dallas; Confrerie Des Chealiers Du Tastevin since 1967. Recipient, Army Commendation Medal. Home: 4842 Brookview Dr, Dallas, Tex. Office: 211 N Ervay, Dallas, Tex.

BROMBERG, Manuel, US, artist; b. Centerville, Ia, Mar 6, 1917; s. David and Tonata (Sobul); dipl, Cleveland Sch of Art, 1937; cert, Colo Springs Fine Arts Cen, 1940; m. Jane Dow, Dec 23, 1941; c: Susan, Christine. Portrait painter; visiting prof, NY State Coll, New Paltz since 1957; instr, Colo Springs Fine Arts Cen, 1938-40; head, art dept, Salem Coll, 1947-49; asso prof, design, NY State Coll, 1949-54; dist research f, SUNY, 1967; commissioned to make drawing of NATO Fgn Mins meeting Paris, 1955. War artist, Eur Theater of Oprs, US Army, 1942-45. Pres, SE Coll of Art Conf, 1951-52; chmn, Woodstock Artists Assn; f: Guggenheim Found; Fuller Research, 1950; Woodstock Found, 1959; mem, Woodstock Artists Conf. Paintings reproduced in mags and jours; exhbs: US, Can, Eng, Fr, Australia; murals: POs of: Tahlequah, Okla; Greybull, Wyo; Geneva, Ill; Keesler Field, Miss; Coll Union Bldg, NC State Coll. Recipient, US Army Legion of Merit, 1945. Home and studio: Woodstock, NY.

BROMBERG, May V, US, civic worker; b. Bklyn, May 22, 1912; d. Baruch and Clara (Richman) Vladeck; BA, U of Pa, 1937; m. Norbert Bromberg, July 31, 1930; c: Charney, David, Sarina. Trustee, bd of Coop Educ Services of Westchester, since 1966; hon chmn, women's div, J Lab Comm, 1952; pres, PTA, 1955-57; mem, exec bd, 1953-67; secy, exec bd, Bursey Sch, 1953; treas, League of Women Voters, 1953; Bd Educ of the Tarrytowns, 1957-66; mem, bd dirs: comm on Mh, Westchester Assn, 1953; Heb and Sunday Sch, 1952-55; samplemakers employment service, ILGWU, 1937; research and adult educ, ORT, 1939-41; mem: co comm, Lib Party, 1950-57; exec and admn comm, women's div, J Lab Comm since 1947; Workmen's Circle; Urban League; Phelps Memorial Hosp; asst to: B C Vladeck, councilman, Manhattan, 1938; George Backer, councilman, Manhattan, 1938-39. Home: Gunpowder Lane, Tarrytown, NY.

BRONFENBRENNER, Martin, US, economist, educator; b. Pittsburgh, Pa, Dec 2, 1914; s. Jacques and Martha (Ornstein); BA, Wash U, 1934; PhD, U of Chgo, 1939; cert in Japanese, USN, U of Colo, 1944; m. Teruko Okuaki, Nov 13, 1951; c: Kenneth, June. Prof, chmn econ, Carnegie-Mellon U, since 1962; econ, Treas Dept, 1940-42; econ, Fed Res Sys, 1945-47; prof, econ: U of Wis, 1947-57; Mich State U, 1957-58; tax econ, Supr Cdr for Allied Powers in Japan, 1949-50; cons econ, UN Econ Commn for Asia and Far E, Bangkok, 1952; prof, econ, U of Minn, 1958-62; f, Cen for Advanced Studies in Behaviorial Scis, Stanford, 1966-67. Mem: Amer Econ Assn; Econometric Soc; Amer Stat Assn; AAUP; ACLU; Phi Beta Kappa. Contbr of articles on econ theory, Far E area. Home: 6612 Forward Ave, Pittsburgh, Pa. Office: Grad Sch of Ind Admn, Carnegie-Mellon U, Pittsburgh, Pa.

BRONFMAN, Allan, Can, industrialist, communal leader; b. Brandon, Manitoba, Can, Dec 21, 1895; s. Ekiel and Minnie (Elman); BA, U Man, 1915, LLB, 1919; hon, PhD, Heb U, Jerusalem, 1957; hon LLD, U Man, 1967; m. Lucy Bilsky, June 28, 1922; c: Edward, Mona Sheckman (decd), Peter. Vice-pres and dir: Distillers Corp-Seagrams Ltd, Montreal; Distillers, Montreal; Calvert Distillers, Amhertsburg, Ontario; Seco Investments, Montreal; dir, Joseph E Seagram & Sons, Waterloo, Ont; pvt law practice, Man, 1919-24. Hon pres, J Gen Hosp, Montreal since 1955, pres, 1933-55, mem, exec comm and chmn, jt conf comm; natl pres, Can Friends Heb U, Jerusalem since 1944; mem, bd govs, Heb U since 1950, dep chmn, 1955; mem, natl council and natl exec, ZOC; natl chmn: Herzl 50th Year Commencement; for Can, Isr 10th Anniversary Celebrations, 1958-59; mem, natl exec, United J Relief Agcs; hon vice-pres and mem Dominion Council, Can J Cong; mem: natl council, Boy Scouts; bd dirs: Assn Paraplegics; Concerts Sym; Montreal Festivals; Montreal Opera Guild; Asso Brother Off, Order of St John of Jerusalem; pres: campaign, CJA, Montreal, 1941; J Orphanage and Children's Aid, W Can, 1921-24; mem: Masons; B'nai B'rith; Pi Lambda Phi; Winnipeg Budget Bd, 1922; exec comm, Fed J Comty Services, Montreal, 1925, vice-chmn, 1927, mem, bd of trustees, 1925, chmn, 1928-31; mem, bd trustees: YM-YWHA, 1958; Ency Judaica Research Found; hon chmn, Que Soc

Crippled Children, 1935-60; clubs: Montefiore, Elm Ridge and Country, Montreal; socs: IOBB; Lodge of Covenant, AF & AM; Pi Lambda Phi; frat, Alumni (McGill). Recipient: Grand Cross del Merito of Order of Malta, 1949; Chevalier, Legion of Honor, Fr Govt, 1948; Humanitarian Award, Can B'nai B'rith, 1958; Isr Bond Man of the Year, 1964. Home: 9 Belvedere Rd, Westmount, Que, Can. Office: 1430 Peel St, Montreal, Can.

BRONFMAN, Charles R, Can, industrialist; b. Montreal, Can, June 27, 1931; s. Samuel and Saidye (Rosner); att McGill U; m. Barbara Baerwald, May 7, 1962. Pres, House of Seagram Ltd; chmn, dir, Supersol, Isr; vice-pres, dir, Seagrams; pres, Cemp Investments; dir: Gramercy Holdings, Toronto; Bank of Montreal; Can Pacific Airlines. Vice-pres, Allied J Comty Services of Montreal; life gov, J Gen Hosp, Montreal; gov: Montreal YM-YWHA; Jr C of C of Dist, Montreal; mem: Young Pres' Org, fmr NE vice pres; Montreal Bd of Trade; Gen Council of Ind; Natl Adv Council on Fitness and Amateur Sport; Shaar Hashomayim Syn; Temple Emanuel, both Westmount; clubs: Elm Ridge Golf and Country; Greystone Curling, Montreal; Hollywood Golf, Deal, NJ. Home: 4300 de Maisonneuve Blvd W, Westmount, Montreal, Can.

BRONFMAN, Gerald, Can, business exec; b. Yorktown, Sask, Dec 22, 1911; s. Harry and Ann (Gallaman); BCom, McGill U, 1935; m. Marjorie Schechter, Feb 9, 1941; c: Joan, Corinne, Judith, Jeffrey. Pres: Kensington Ind, Inc since 1943; Gerbo, Roslyn Devls; fmr: dir: Dominion Dairies; Stressteel. Squadron leader, RCAF, WWII. Hon vice-pres, Can Red Cross Soc, Que div; dir, Montreal Sym Orch; councillor, Montreal Mus of Fine Arts; life gov: Verdun Protestant Hosp; J Gen Hosp; J Hosp of Hope; Montreal Childrens Hosp; Camp B'nai B'rith; mem: bd trustees, YMHA; Sen, Stratford Shakespeare Festival Fund of Can; natl council, JDC; bd dirs, Mt Sinai Sanatorium, Montreal; Pi Lambda Phi; Mu Sigma; McGill Grad Assn; clubs: Montefiore; Elmridge Country; Greystone Curling. Recipient, Off US Legion of Merit. Homes: 475 Roslyn Ave, Westmount, Montreal, Can; Quebec and Ste-Adèle du Nord, Quebec, Can. Office: 1245 Sherbrooke St W, Montreal, Can.

BRONFMAN, Samuel, Can, industrialist, communal leader; b. Brandon Can, Mar 4, 1891; s. Ekiel and Minnie (Elman); hon LLD; U Montreal, 1948; U Waterloo, Ont, 1961; m. Saidye Rosner, June 29, 1922; c: Edgar, Charles, Minda, Phyllis. Pres: Distillers Corp-Seagram Ltd, since 1934; Distiller Corp Ltd, Org 1924; Thomas Adams Distillers Ltd, Vancouver BC, Four Roses Distillers Ltd; Glove Bedding Co, Ltd, Winnipeg, Can; Seagram Overseas Corp Ltd; dir: Calvert of Can Ltd; Joseph E Seagram &s Sons, Ltd. Chmn, bd govs, Can J Cong, pres, 1938-62; pres: United J Relief Agcys; Can Isr Corp; Can Isr Devl Lt; hon pres; ZOC; Fed J Comty Service Montreal, fmr pres; CJA, Montreal, a found; hon chmn, jt campaign, CJA-United Isr Appeal, Montreal; vice-pres: WJC, chmn, N Amer sect: Conf on J Material Claims Against Ger; World Fed YMHA and J Comty Cens; Natl Found for J Culture; hon vice-pres: J Publ Soc of Amer; Quebec council, Order of St John of Jerusalem, asso cdr brother; mem, bd govs: McGill U; Can Council, Intl C of C mem: Can Council, 1957-61; natl council, Boys Scouts of Can; adv council Sch of Commerce, McGill U; adv bd, Rehabilitataion Inst Montreal; exec comm, JDC; dir, Can Mh Assn; asso mem, central council, Can Red Cross Soc; Mt Royal Lodge, B'nai B'rith; Masons; clubs: Montefiore; Elm Ridge Golf and Country; Can, Montreal, Quebec; Cent Country. Recipient: Stephen S Wise Award, AJCong, 1965; Companion Order of Can, 1967. Homes: 15 Belvedere Rd, Montreal, Can; 723 S Broadway, Tarrytown, NY. Office: 1430 Peel St, Montreal, Can.

BRONSTEIN, Aaron J, US, attorney; b. Baltimore, Md, May 6, 1905; s. Max and Rosa (Lebow); BA, Harvard Coll, 1925, LLB, 1928; m. Gertrude Nagels, July 5, 1930 (decd); c: Judith Rubin; m. 2nd, Jeanette Lyons, Apr 19, 1944. Sr partner, Brown, Rudnick, Freed & Gesmer. Pres: J Comty Fed, Gtr Lyons, Mass Inc, 1962-67; J Comty Council, Metrop Boston, 1959-61; NE div, AJCong, 1955-59; NE Zionist region, 1947-49; Brookline-Brighton-Newton Zionist dist, 1947-49; Kehillath Isr Brotherhood, 1939-41; vice-pres, JNF, NE, 1950-52; natl vice-pres, Natl Fed of J Men's Clubs, 1941-43; natl council, JDC since 1949; natl exec comm, ZOA, 1950-52; clubs: New Cent; Harvard Varsity. Home: 28 Atlantic Ave, Swampscott, Mass. Office: 85 Devonshire St, Boston, Mass.

BRONSTEIN, Arthur J, US, educator, author; b. Baltimore, Mar 15, 1914; s. Gershon and Bessie (Kirschenbaum); BA, CCNY, 1934; MA, Columbia U, 1936; PhD, NYU, 1939; m. Elsa Meltzer, 1941; c: Nancy, Abbot. Prof, speech and linguistics, Lehman Coll; exec off, doctoral prog, speech, CUNY; mem, ed adv comm, The American College Dictionary since 1947; educ cons, pronunciation, Collier's Encyclopedia since 1962; cons, pronunciation, Random House Dictionary of the English Language since 1962; mem fac staff: CCNY, 1935-36, 1937-38; O State U, 1936-37; U Hawaii, 1963; prog dir, asso dir, childrens camps, Me, 1952-54, 1956-57; prof, speech, Queens Coll, CUNY, 1938-67; Fulbright prof, Eng lings, Tel Aviv U, 1967-68; chmn, voice phonetics, lings group, Speech Assn Amer, 1962-63. Capt, Adj Gen Div, USAAF, 1955-58. Author: The Standard of American Pronunciation in the Nineteenth Century, 1949; The Pronunciation of American English, 1960; co-author, Your Speech and Voice, 1967; ed, lings and phonetics sect, Biographical Dictionary of Speech Education since 1962; contbr to profsl jours and mags. Mem: AAUP; MLA; Speech Assn Amer; Amer Speech and Hearing Assn; Speech Assn E States; Ling Circle, NY; fmr, mem, gen comm, ACLU. Home: 36 Brokaw Lane, Great Neck, NY. Office: CUNY, Grad Cen, New York, NY.

BRONSTEIN, Daniel A, US, attorney; b. Baltimore, Md, Dec 12, 1942; s. Lewis and Elaine (Mandel); BA, Johns Hopkins U, 1963; LLB, U of Md Law Sch, 1966; att U of Mich Law Sch, 1970-71. Pvt practice, 1966-70; legal adv, Baltimore Comm Relations Commn, 1965-67; research asso, U of Md Law Sch, 1968-69. Secy, Baltimore Small Business Devl Cen, 1967-68; mem: Amer Bar Assn; Md State Bar Assn. Author, Chesapeake Bay in Legal Perspective, 1970; 2 works in Vol 25, Md Law Rev; asst ed, Md Law Rev, 1965-66. Recipient, Amer Jurisprudence Prize, Lab Law, 1966. Hobbies: golf, chess, camping. Home: U of Mich Law Sch, Ann Arbor, Mich.

BRONSTEIN, Daniel J, US, educator; b. NYC, Dec 11, 1908; s. Anatole and Liza (Wegman); BS, CCNY, 1928; AM, Harvard, 1930, PhD, 1933; m. Betty Grossman, Sep 29, 1940; c: Gene Hayden. Prof phil, CUNY since 1953, on fac since 1931, Fmr pres, AAUP chap; mem: Amer Phil Assn; Mind Assn; Phi Beta Kappa. Co-author: Approaches to the Philosophy of Religion, 1954; Basic Problems of Philosophy, 3rd ed, 1964; contbr to books and scholarly jours. Home: 536 Ogden Ave, W Englewood, NJ. Office: 133 St and Convent Ave, New York, NY.

BRONSTEIN, I Pat, US, pediatric endocrinologist, educator; b. Chgo, Aug 10, 1901; s. Henry and Leah (Lehr); BS, U Chgo, 1923, MD, 1925; m. Sofia Lome, Aug 8, 1927; c: Alice, Susan. Prof em, U of Ill Med Sch since 1953; chief, ped endocrine clinic, U of Ill Hosps, since 1940, on staff since 1930; sr att ped, Michael Reese Hosp; cons, ped endocrinologist, Cook Co Hosp; on staff since 1940; pvt practice since 1927; dir, ped med educ, Ill Masonic Med Cen. Pres, Chgo Ped Soc, 1962-63; licentiate, Bd of Ped; mem: AMA; Ill and Chgo Med Socs; Acad of Ped; Sigma Xi; Phi Delta Epsilon. Contbr numerous papers on ped endocrinology. Home: 260 E Chestnut, Chicago, Ill. Office: 30 N Michigan Ave, Chicago, Ill.

BRONSTEIN, Siegbert, US, pathologist, educator; b. Berlin, Ger, June 7, 1903; s. Hugo and Henriette (Weinberg); in US since 1936; MD, U Berlin, 1926; m. Charlotte Brauns, Sep 28, 1937. Cons path, Chilton Memorial Hosp since 1967, path, 1961-67; res, Munic Hosp, Berlin, 1927-33; path, J Hosp, Berlin, 1936; asst bact, Beth Isr Hosp, NYC, 1937-42; asst path, Bklyn J Hosp, 1943; instr, clinical path, Hunter Coll, 1943; asst prof, path, Jefferson Med Coll; chief lab service, VA Hosps: Oteen, NC, 1946-50; Montrose, NY, 1950-57; Phila, 1957-61. Capt, maj, US Army, 1943-46. Dipl, Amer Bd of Paths, 1944; found f, Amer Coll Paths, 1947; f: Amer Coll of Phys; Amer Assn of Clinical Paths; AAAS; AMA; mem, em, Soc for Experimental Biol and Med; mem: Pompton Lakes J Cen, NJ. Contbr to profsl jours. Home: 184 Hamburg Turnpike, Pompton Plains, NJ.

BRONSTON, Jack E, US, attorney, legislator; b. Plainfield, NJ, Jan 10, 1922; s. Harry and Yetta (Cohen); AB, magna cum laude, Harvard U, 1942, LLB, 1948; LLM, taxation, NYU, 1952; m. Adele Schwartz, June 17, 1948; c: David, Deena, Rhoda. State senator, NY since 1958; dir, secy, Basic Properties, Inc since 1961, vice-pres, 1963; secy: Diefendorf Comm on Sch Financing, 1960-63; Dem Co Comm, 1960-61. Lt, USMC, 1942-46. Natl dir, NCCJ since 1967; mem: NYC Bar Assn; Acad for Rel and Mh; Phi Beta Kappa; Hillcrest J Cen; B'nai B'rith, past vice-pres, Jamaica chap; fmr: vice-pres, Cen Queens Allied Civic Council; chmn: spec gifts comm, UJA; UJA Hillcrest J Cen; mem, bd trustees, Pal Endowment Fund. Author, monographs on educ financing. Recipient, Man of the Year in Jamaica, Jt Defense Appeal, 1961. Home: 184-37 Hovenden Rd, Jamaica, NY. Office: 51 E 42 St, New York, NY.

BRONZ, George, US, attorney, government official; b. NYC, July 7, 1910; s. Louis and Sarah (Paley); BS, CCNY, 1929; LLB, Columbia U, 1932; m. Pearl Holly, Apr 15, 1938; c: Stephen, Elizabeth. Pvt practice since 1954; research asst, Columbia Law Sch, 1930-33; atty: Natl Recovery Admn, 1933-35; Dept of Agric, Resettlement Admn, 1935-37; chief legal adv, Dept of Interior, Bituminous Coal Consumers Counsel, 1939-43; spec asst to gen counsel, Treasury Dept, 1943-54; Anglo-Amer Financial and Trade Conf, 1945; mem, US delgs: UN Conf on Trade and Employment, Havana, 1947-48; preparatory comm, London, 1946, Geneva, 1947; spec mission to Thailand, 1946; Gen Agreement on Tariffs and Trade, Geneva, Annecy, Torquay, 1948-52; chmn, comm on Spec Exch Agreements, London, 1950; lectr, Harvard Law Sch, 1954. Mem: Amer Bar Assn; Fed Bar Assn; Natl Lawyers Club; DC Bar Assn; Phi Beta Kappa. Ed, Columbia Law Review, 1930-32; contbr to law jours. Home: 3315 Rowland Pl, NW, Washington, DC. Office: 888-17 St, NW, Washington, DC.

BROOK, Benjamin H, US, social worker; b. NYC, Jan 31, 1913; s. Hyman and Doris (Birnbaum); MA, NYU, 1936; MSW, Columbia U, 1947; m. Elizabeth Berg, Dec 25, 1938; c: Robert, Mark. Exec vice-pres, Tucson JCC, since 1949; country dir, It, JDC, 1945-47; field dir, ARC Field Services, 1943-45; lectr in public admn, U Ariz, 1966-69; asst prof, social work, Cal State Coll, 1968. Pres: Ariz Conf Social Wfr; referee, Pima Co, Juvenile Court; bd mem, Tucson Commn on Hum Relations; Exec Assn United Comty Campaign, 1967-69, liaison repr, 1965-67; social action chmn, Natl Assn Social Workers, Tucson, 1965-67; mem, Amer Acad of Political Sci. Recipient: Award, Pope Pius XII, 1945; Award of Hon, JCC, 1964. Home: 4325 E 13 St, Tucson, Ariz. Office: 102 N Plumer, Tucson, Ariz.

BROOK, Jerachmiel, Isr, power engr; b. Tolchin, Russ, Dec 25, 1903; s. Shmuel and Esther (Altshuler); in Isr since 1924; deg, power engr, Polytech Inst, Moscow, 1924; m. Hava Zeitlin; c: Dahlia Dagan. Ret since 1967; shift engr, Pal Elec Corp 1925-34, mgr Jordan Hydro power plant, 1938-43; mgr and chief engr, tech div, Isr Elec Corp, N Isr, 1943-67. Prin contribs, building and exploitation of all power plants in north. Mem: cen comm, Mech Engrs of Isr, Haifa. Contbr to profsl jours. Home: 4 Hanadiv Ave, Haifa, Isr. Office: POB 10, Haifa Isr.

BROOKES, Murray, Eng, university reader; b. Salford, Eng, Jan 26, 1926; s. Jack and Julia (Reikan); MA, BM, BCh, Bradsenose Coll, Oxford, 1949; DM, Guy's Hosp Med Sch, London, 1962; m. Esther Levine, Mar 24, 1957; c: Alison, Sally, Jacelyn, Max. Reader, anat, U London since 1966; research f, 1954-55; lectr, 1955-61, at U of Liverpool; sr lectr, Guy's Hosp, 1962-66. Capt, RAMC, 1952-54. Princ contrib: inves into blood supply of the skeleton; original discoverer of the physicochem control of osteogenesis. Vice-chmn, Southgate Yavneh Kindergarten and Nursery; mem: Anat Soc; British Orthopedic Assn; Bone and Tooth Soc. Author: Blood Supply of Bone, 1970; contbr, chap in Modern Trends in Orthopaedics, IV, 1964 and to sci jours. Home: 68 Lakenheath, Southgate, London N14, Eng.

BROOKES, Reuben Solomon, Eng, rabbi, educator; b. Buenos Aires, Arg, July 8, 1914; s. Abraham and Bela (Posner); att Talmudical Coll: Manchester, Liverpool; dipl theol, U Birmingham; m. Blanche Ackerman, Oct 19, 1941; c: Eta Stirzaker. Min, dir, educ since 1950; asst min: Telzer and Kovno Cong, Manchester, 1937-39; Southport Heb Cong, 1939-50. Pres, Young Isr Soc; vice-pres, U Birmingham Soc; chmn, Birmingham ZC; mem, Cen Council of J Educ; Royal Soc of Lit; chaplain, Birmingham U; fmr pres, B'nai B'rith; f: Royal Soc of Arts; Royal Asiatic Soc; Phil Soc of Eng. Author, Dictionary of Judaism, 1959; co-author, A Guide to Jewish Knowledge, 1956. Spec interests: orientalism, writing, lecturing. Home: B2 Calthorpe Mansions, Fiveways, Bir-

mingham 15, Eng. Study: Heb Cong, Singers Hill, Birmingham 1, Eng.

BROOKS, Sidney H, US, rabbi; b. Buffalo, NY, Apr 3, 1920; s. Sidney and Irma (Bing); BA, U Cincinnati, 1942; BHL, HUC, 1942, MHL, ordained rabbi, 1946; m. Jane Heyman, June 29, 1944; c: Miriam, Joel. Rabbi, Temple Isr sine 1952; asst rabbi, Temple Beth Ahabah, 1944-45; Temple Sholom, Springfield, O, 1946-52; instr, comparaitive rel, U Omaha, 1954-59. Chmn, comm on resolutions, CCAR, 1967-70, chmn, comm on youth since 1962, exec bd mem, 1962-64; exec bd: Govs Comm on Youth, 1960; natl comm of alumni overseers, HUC-JIR, 1962-64; bd trustee, UAHC, 1968-72; mem: Acad Rel and Health; Chgo Bd Rabbis; B'nai B'rith; Masons; Scottish Rite; club, Rotary. Recipient, George Wash medal, Freedom Found, 1957, 1961. Home: 8668 Cedar, Omaha, Neb. Study: 7023 Cass St, Omaha, Neb.

BROSH, Pinchas, Isr, engineer; b. Tel Aviv, Feb 4, 1925; s. Itschak and Esther (Boruchovitz); dipl engr, Tech Hochschule, Munich, 1949; m. Varda Zilberman, 1949; c: Zohar, Miriam. Structural designer and adv since 1962; town engr, Ashkelon, 1952-53; designer, Jordan Valley Project, 1953-56. Projects: Weiss Auditorium, Heb U, Jerusalem; ORT Training Cen; El Al Bldg; Cameri Theatre; Habima Theatre; Migdalot Hotel, all Tel Aviv; Church of Annunciation, Nazareth; Argaman Factory Complex, Javne; Inst Farina, Bethlehem; shopping cen, Beersheva. Mem: Assn Engrs and Architects, Isr; Tel Aviv Country Club. Recipient, Terrae Sanctae Custodia, 1969. Home and office: 5 Zlocisti St, Tel Aviv, Isr.

BROSH, Zvi, Isr, diplomat; b. Berlin, July 6, 1922; s. Paul and Edith (Friedlaender) Boroschek; in Burma since 1968; m. Audrey Goldston, Oct 26, 1948; c: Edward, Liora. Ambass of Isr, Burma and Maldive Rep since 1968; Min of Isr to Ceylon since 1968; asst controller, news, Pal BC Service, 1946-48; dir, fgn lang broadcasts, Kol Isr, 1948-50; mem, Isr Govt Study Mission on TV, US, Can, UK, Fr, 1952-53; mil commentator, Kol Isr, 1955-60; political commentator, 1963-66; press couns, Isr Mission, Cologne, Ger, 1960-63; dep dir, Info Dept, Min for Fgn Affairs, Jerusalem, 1963-64, acting dir, Intl Coop Dept, 1965-66; Isr delg, UNESCO Cong of Educ Mins, Tehran, 1965; charge d'affairs of Isr, Ceylon, 1966-68. Royal Navy, 1942-46; Hagana, 1946-48; maj, lt col, IDF, 1950-60. Chmn, Fgn Min Staff Comm, Jerusalem; mem: Bd Mgmt, Settlement Study Cen, Rehovot; club, Rotary, of Colombo. Hobby, yachting. Home: 57 Prome Rd, Rangoon, Burma. Office: 49 Prome Rd, Rangoon, Burma.

BROSHI, Magen I, Isr, archaeologist; b. Jerusalem, Isr, Aug 27, 1929; s. Azriel and Esther (Wollach); BA, Heb U, Jerusalem, 1953, MA, 1958; m. Ofra Ezrahi, Sep 26, 1954; c: Michal, Oded, Yoav. Curator, Shrine of the Book, Isr Mus, Jerusalem since 1965; IDF. Prin contribs, numerous archaeol excavs. Author, From the Beginning, 1968; contbr numerous articles to jours. Home: 18 Sd Hameiri, Jerusalem, Isr. Office: Israel Mus, Jerusalem, Isr.

BROTHERS, Joyce D, US, psychologist; b. NYC; d. Morris and Estelle (Rapoport) Baer; BS, Cornell U, 1947, MA, 1950, PhD 1953; hon DHL, Franklin Pierce Coll, 1969; m. Milton Brothers, July 4, 1949; c: Lisa. Pvt practice since 1950; columnist: Good Housekeeping Magazine since 1964; Bel McClure Syndicate since 1964; NBC radio network, 1966-70; research f, UNESCO, 1949-50; instr, Hunter Coll, 1949-52; asst, psych, Columbia U, 1948-52. Mem: Fed of J Womens Org; Sigma Xi. Author: Ten Days to a Successful Memory; Woman. Home and Office: 350 E 86 St, New York, NY.

BROTMAN, Robert H, US, dentist; b. Newark, NJ, Mar 16, 1896; s. Benjamin and Rosa (Kassan); DDS, Baltimore Coll Dent Sch, 1922; m. Sadie, Sep 6, 1914; c: Norton, Rosa Fink, Valeer Sass. Pvt practice since 1922. Mem: Amer Dent Assn; Baltimore City Dent Soc; Alpha Omega; Baltimore Alumni; Masons; Odd Fellows; exec bd. Beth Jacob Cong; club, Ritchie Civic, fmr pres. Author: Let's Look at Your Teeth, 1933; The Family Book of the Mouth, 1967; contbr of articles to jours. Home and office: 5901 Glen Ave, Baltimore, Md.

BROTT, Alexander, Can, musician, educator; b. Montreal, Can, Mar 14, 1915; s. Sam and Annie (Fixman); att Julliard Sch of Music, NYC; licentiate of music, McGill U; hon DMus, Chgo Conservatory Coll; laureate, Acad de Musique de Quebec; m. Lotte Goetzel, 1943; c: Boris, Dennis. Prof, head, instrumental dept, McGill Conservatory of Music, since 1949; found, conductor, musical dir, McGill Chamber Orch since 1939; conductor, musical dir: Montreal Pops Orch since 1958; and found, Concert Under the Stars since 1958; fmr: concertmaster, asst conductor: Montreal Sym Orch; Les Concerts Symphoniques de Montreal; guest conductor: with maj orchs in Eur since 1948; spec Can Day bc, BBC, London; maj orchs in Can; Orch of Amer, NYC; Montreal Festivals; London Philharmonic Sym Orch; Can repr, Prague Festival, 1946; invited to conduct in Russ, cultural exch prog, 1962; maj compositions: Concordia; Royal Tribute (for coronation of Queen Elizabeth II); From Sea to Sea; Delightful Delusions; War and Peace; Violin Concerto; Spheres in Orbit; Arabesque for Cello and Orchestra; Lullaby and Procession of the Toys; Three Astral Visions; works were performed under direction of: Thomas Beechman; Otto Kemperer; Leopold Stokowski; Pierre Monteux; Ernest MacMillan; Vladimir Golschmann. Recipient: Elizabeth Sprague Coolidge Prize, for chamber music composition, 1937, 1938; Loeb Memorial Prize, for chamber music performance, 1937, 1938; Lord Strathcona Prize, 1939; Pan Amer Conductors 1st Prize, 1958; Olympic Medal, 1948, award, 1952; Sir Arnold Bax Gold Medal, 1961; Dr Harry J Stern award, 1969. Home: 5459 Earnscliffe Ave, Montreal, Can. Office: McGill U, Montreal, Can.

BROWDY, Alvin, US, attorney; b. Kan City, Mo, Sep 19, 1917; s. Harry and Rosa (Levin); BS, U of Ill, 1937; LLB, Georgetown U, 1949; m. Leatrice Lowen, Mar 15, 1942; c: Roger, Wendy, Craig. Patent atty since 1949; lt, USNR, 1943-46. Vice-chmn, Bd J Educ of Gtr Wash; secy, Capitol of Gtr Wash; bd dirs: Montgomery Co JCC; Men's Club, Montgomery Co; mem: B'nai B'rith; J Hist Soc; Friends of Kennedy Cen; Dist and Amer Bar Assns; Amer Patent Law Assn; Phi Epsilon Pi. Home: 3313 Brooklawn Terr, Chevy Chase, Md. Office: 1233 Munsey Bldg, Washington, DC.

BROWN, Arthur J, US, business exec; b. Chgo, Apr 14, 1911; s. Boris and Kate (Bakalor); m. Frieda Gordon; c: Margot, Gordon. Pres, ABC Freight Forwarding Corp since 1941. Life-time hon chmn, bd dirs, Bayside J Cen; active in rehab of handicapped and former inmates of penal insts; adv, commn, econ devl; Queens Co, NY. Home: 1 W 81 St, New York, NY.

BROWN, Fred, US, psychologist; b. Pressburg, Aus, May 18, 1905; s. Max and Ethel (Wolkowitz); in US since 1907; MA, Ohio State U, 1930, PhD, 1933; m. Minerva Lehman, Apr 10, 1937; c: Janet, Daniel. Prof psycht, Mt Sinai Sch of Med, CUNY, since 1967; chief psychol: Mt Sinai Hosp, since 1946; Minneapolis Public Schs, 1936-43; cons: psych, VA; Yeshiva Mh Project; mem, ed bd, Psychosomatic Med; pvt practice, psychodiagnostics, since 1946; asst prof, psych, Pa State Coll, 1935-36; adj prof, psych, NYU, 1948-60; chief psychol, Alfred Wilson Children's Cen, 1934-35. Lt to maj, USAAF, 1943-46. F: Amer Psych Assn; div of abnormal and clinical psych, Amer Psychosomatic Soc; E Psych Assn. Co-author: Sex Questions and Answers, 1950; co-ed: Training for Clinical Psychology, 1959; contbr to profsl jours. Recipient, Whittlesey House sci award, 1959. Home: 1200 Fifth Ave, New York, NY. Office: Mt Sinai Hosp, 100 St and Fifth Ave, New York, NY.

BROWN, Herbert Charles, US, chemist, educator; b. London, May 22, 1912; s. Charles and Pearl (Stein); in US since 1914; BS, U of Chgo, 1936, PhD, 1938, DSc, 1968; c: Charles. Richard B Wetherill prof of chem, Purdue U, since 1959, fac mem since 1947; chem cons: Ethyl Corp since 1943; Esso Research and Engineering since 1960; f, Eli Lilly post-doctorate research, U of Chgo, 1938-39; instr, chem, 1939-43; co-dir, war research projects for US Army, Natl Defense Research Comm, and Manhattan Project, all U of Chgo, 1940-43; asst prof, chem, Wayne U, 1943-46, asso prof, 1946-47; visiting prof: UCLA, 1951; O State U, 1952; visiting lectr: Natl U of Mexico, 1954; U of Berkeley, Cal, 1957; U of Colo, 1958; SUNY, Stonybrook, LI, NY, 1966; U of Cal, Santa Barbara, 1967; Heb U, Jerusalem, 1969. Mem: AAAS; Amer Chem Soc; Ind Acad of Scis; Natl Acad of Scis; Amer Acad of Arts and Scis; Chem Soc, London; bd govs, Heb U, Jerusalem; Phi Lambda Upsilon; Sigma Xi. Contbr to profsl jours. Recipient: letter of commendation, War Dept, 1948; research award, Sigma Xi Chap, Purdue U, 1950; Nichols Medallist, 1959; Award for Creative Research in Organic Chem, 1960; SOCMA Medallist, 1960; H.N. McCoy Award, 1966; Linus Pauling Medallist, 1968; lec-

tureship awards: Harrison Howe, 1953; Friend E Clark, 1953; Freud-McCormack, 1954; Centenary Lecturer, Eng, 1955; Julius Stieglitz, 1958; Max Tischler, 1958; A.D. Little, 1968; Baker, 1969. Home: 1840 Garden St, W Lafayette, Ind. Office: Purdue U, Lafayette, Ind.

BROWN, Himan, US, motion picture produc and dir; b. NYC, July 21, 1910; s. Samuel and Dora (Arkis); BA, Bklyn Coll; LLB, St Lawrence U; m. Mildred Geller, Apr 9, 1933; c: Barry, Hilda. Pres: Produc Cen Inc, NYC; Galahad Produc, NYC; produced, dir: Chanukah Festival for 18 yrs on behalf of State of Isr Bonds; motion pictures dealing with J life and problems; prop, largest motion picture stages and facilities in NYC; dir, creator of radio dramatic series. Vice-pres, FJP of NY; trustee: UJA of Gtr NY; AJCong; United HIAS Services; JDC; Isr Bonds. Hobbies: collecting art, fund raising, speechmaking. Home: 285 Central Park W, New York, NY. Office: 221 W 26 St, New York, NY.

BROWN, Isabelle G, US, communal worker; b. Mobile, Ala, Aug 18, 1910; d. Benjamin and Sarah (Levenberg) Gup; BS, Flora Stone Mather Coll, 1931; m. Ronald Brown, Feb 24, 1933; c: Bennett, Barry. Vice-pres, Natl Council J Women since 1959, past pres, Cleveland sect; mem: Cleveland exec comm, AJComm; Cleveland Wfr Fed; fmr: pres, treas, Intl Council J Women; first chmn, Women's Org, J Comty Fed, mem, Cleveland exec bd. Hobby, travel. Home: 13435 N Park Blvd, Cleveland, O.

BROWN, Leon, US, architect; b. Blackville, SC, Sep 25, 1907; s. Isador and Sadie (Cohen); BArch, Ga Tech, 1929; MArch, U of Pa, 1933; m. Marguerite Kahn, Aug 30, 1944; c: Warren. Architect, Brown and Wright, since 1949; prof, architecture, Howard U, Wash, DC, since 1947; architect, Brown, Wright and Mano, 1967. Capt, Engrs Corps, US Army, 1942-46. Pres: Forest Hills City Assn, 1966-68; Wash DC Metrop Chap, Amer Inst of Architects, 1956, corp mem since 1940; regional bd of architects, DC, 1967-69; Natl and Amer Panels of Arbitrators, Wash Bldg Cong; Zeta Beta Tau; Pi Tau Pi; Wash Heb Cong; mem: bd, NE Settlement House, since 1952; Metro-Wash-DC Planning and Housing Assn, since 1953; mem, exec comm, AJComm, Wash DC chap, since 1953; natl bd dirs, NCCJ, 1967; 1st comm chmn, Wash DC chap, NCCJ, 1968; chmn, bd of appeals and rev of licensing and inspections, DC Govt, 1956-60; admissions comm, Natl Amer Inst of Architects, 1959; Coll of F, AIA, 1969; mem, Wash DC Urban Coalition, 1968; clubs: Cosmos; Woodmont Country. Co-author, R Brognard Okie, Architect of Philadelphia, 1954; contbr to tech jours. Recipient: award for houses designed in the Wash area, Amer Inst of Architects; Evening Star award for Britten House; award for Robert Black House, Potomac Valley Chap, Amer Inst of Architects; award for Sheridan Terrace Housing Project. Home: 4158 Linnean Avenue, NW Washington, DC. Office: 1640 Wisconsin Avenue, NW Washington, DC.

BROWN, Louis M, US, lawyer; b. Los Angeles, Sep 5, 1909; s. Emil and Anna; AB, cum laude, U of S Cal, 1930; LLB, Harvard, 1933; m. Hermione Kopp, May 30, 1937; c: Lawrence, Marshall, Harold. Partner, Irell and Manella, LA since 1947; admitted to Cal bar, 1933; US Supr Court, 1944; adj prof of law, U of S Cal since 1960; lectr, law: Southwestern U; U of Cal, LA; U of S Cal; mem, planning comm, Tax Inst since 1948; pvt practice, 1933-35. F, Amer Bar Found; mem: Amer, Beverly Hills, LA Co, SF bar Assns; State Bar Cal; Amer Judicature Soc; Amer Bus Law Assn; Town Hall, LA; Order of the Coif; Mason; B'nai B'rith; fmr pres, Friends of Beverly Hills Public Libr; found, admnr, Emil Brown Fund Preventive Law Prize Awards since 1963; club, Harvard, S Cal. Author: Preventive Law, 1950; How to Negotiate a Successful Contract, 1955; ed, Major Tax Problems, 3 vols, 1948-51; contbr to legal jours. Hobbies: music, photography. Home: 606 N Palm Dr, Beverly Hills, Cal. Office: Gateway E Bldg, Century City, Los Angeles, Cal.

BROWN, Lucy, US, musician, teacher; b. Yonkers, NY, Nov 19, 1913; d. Louis and Paula (Cohn); att, Ecole Normale de Musique, Paris; m. Jesse Wallach, Dec 13, 1945. Pianist since 1927; tchr: Metrop Music Sch, 1944-45; Turtle Bay Music Sch, 1950-51; Ind Hill Music Workshop, 1960; recitalist, soloist; Carnegie Hall Pops Concerts, and Radio City Music Hall; musical dir, composer: John Butler Chamber Ballet, Festival of Two Worlds, Spoleto, It; accompanist and musical asst: Ballet Theatre, Ballet Intl, NYC Ballet; accompanist and vocal coach: NYC Cen Opera; mem, orchs: New

World, Little Orch Soc, Metrop Opera; music ed of documentary films for: Pan-Am, Amer Friends Service Comm, Come Back Africa; pianist and asst to conductor, Bdwy shows: Let's Make an Opera, 1950; Sandhog, 1954; performer of TV background music: Hallmark Hall of Fame, Bell Telephone Hour; radio and recordings. Bd govs, Amer Guild of Musical Artists; mem: NY Singing Tchrs Assn; fmr: sponsor, Metrop Music Sch. Recipient: cert of honor, Min of Fine Arts, Fr, 1931; official pianist, Dmitri Mitropoulous Intl Competition,FJP. Home and studio: 514 West End Ave, New York,NY.

BROWN, Matthew, US, attorney; b. NYC, Mar 26, 1905; s. Jack Goddard and Pauline (Roth)); BS, 1925; LLB, Harvard Law Sch, 1928; m. Edna Goodrich, June 8, 1932; c: Patricia. Mem, law firm, Brown, Rudnick, Freed & Gesmer; mem, bd dirs: Norfolk Co Trust Co; Winde-McCormick Lumber since 1953. Vice-pres: Combined J Philanthropies; Temple Israel, mem, bd trustees, since 1946; pres, JCC, Metrop Boston, 1954-55; mem: natl exec, AJComm since 1951; bd of Selectmen, Brookline since 1956; Fed and Supr Court Bars; Boston, Mass and Amer Bar Assns; Pi Lambda Phi; clubs: Boston, Mass Rep; Belmont Country,vice-pres, 1951. Home: 419 Clinton Rd, Brookline, Mass. Office: 85 Devonshire St, Boston, Mass.

BROWN, Melvin Frommel, US, attorney, business exec; b. Carlinville, Ill, June 4, 1935; s. Ben and Selma (Frommel); AB, Wash U, Mo, 1957, JD, Law School, 1961; m. Jacqueline Hirsch, Sep 2, 1962; c: Benjamin, Mark. Corp secy, asso legal counsel, ITT Aetna Corp, St Louis, Mo since 1965; atty-at-law, 1961-62; asst to Gen Counsel, Union Elec, 1962-65. Capt, US Army, 1967-68. Pres, St Louis chap, AJ-Comm; mem: exec comm, J Comty Relations Council, St Louis; Dem Commn on Party Reform, Mo; hon col, Gov's Staff, Mo, 1964, 1968; fmr, chmn, young lawyers sect, Bar Assn, Metrop St Louis. Contbr to legal publs. Home: 7449 Oxford Dr, St Louis, Mo. Office: 212 S Central Ave, St Louis, Mo.

BROWN, Minerva L, US, communal worker; b. Harrisburg, Pa, Feb 20, 1916; d. Louis and Sara (Sachs) Lehrman; BA, Pa State U, 1938; MSW, NY sch of Social Work, Columbia U, 1945; m. Fred Brown, Apr 10, 1938; c: Janet, Daniel. PR off, Mt Sinai Hosp, Dept of Psycht, since 1967; registrar, postgrad sch of med, Mt Sinai Sch of Med. Mem: Natl bd, Natl Council of J Women, 1953-65; Natl Assn of Social Workers; Natl Citizens Comm on Careers in Social Work; Council on Social Work Educ; natl exec comm, White House Conf on Children, 1960; vice-pres, Women's Club, 1960-61. Contbr of Articles on Mh workshops. Home: 1200 Fifth Ave, New York, NY. Office: Mt Sinai School of Medicine, New York, NY.

BROWN, Nathan, US, educator; b. Hung, Nov 24, 1912; s. Armin and Fannie (Mittelman); in US since 1913; BSS, CCNY, 1934, MS, 1935; PhD, NYU, 1954; m. Mari Shapin, June 20, 1937; c: Walter, Susan. Exec dep supt, NYC Public Schs, since 1966; prin, HS for Fashion Inds, 1950-60; asst supt of schs, Bd of Educ, 1961-65; asso dir, Cen for Urban Educ, 1965-66. Prin conribs: helped build Yahud Comprehensive HS, Isr; devl res training prog for drop-outs at Camp Madison Felicia. Vice-pres, J Tchrs Comty Chest; exec bd: Genesis Heb Cen; mem: Amer Orthopsycht Assn; Amer Personnel and Guidance Assn. Co-author, The High School Counselor Today, 1966; contbr to jours on guidance. Recipient, Man of Year in Educ, Assn of Chairmen, 1967. Home: 501 E 79 St, New York, NY. Office: 110 Livingston St, Brooklyn, NY.

BROWN, Rafael Meir, Isr, (profsl name, Rafi Brown), antiquities restorer; b. Haifa, Isr, Sep 23, 1936; s. Jonah and Rachel (Solomon); desc of Yoel Moshe Solomon; att Heb U, Jerusalem; m. Sarah Daniel, 1960; c: Gil, Ofer. Head, Restoration Lab for Antiquities. Sgt, IDF, 1954-56. Mem: IIC; ICOM. Spec interest, archaeol. Home: 51 Tchernichovsky St, Jerusalem, Isr. Office: Israel Mus, Jerusalem, Isr.

BROWN, Ronald, US, management cons; b. Chgo, Oct 4, 1900; s. Charles and Florence (Cohn); att Dartmouth Coll, 1918-19; m. Isabelle Gup, Feb 24, 1933; c: Bennett, Barry. Fmr vice-pres, dir, Fremco Mfg Co, 1928-60. Prin conribs: devl of successful techniques for devl of first echelon sups in marketing field. Vice-chmn, adv bd, Cuyahoga Co Juvenile Court; trustee, Cleveland Hgts-U Hgts Public Libr; fmr: pres, Cleveland Hgts Bd of Educ; vice-pres, J Comty Cen; trustee, J Comty Fed, Author, From Selling to Managing, 1968. Home: 13435 N Park Blvd, Cleveland Hgts, O.

BROWN, Sidney A, US, business exec; b. Malden, Mass, Aug 9, 1907; s. Abraham and Anna (Needle); BS, MIT, 1928; m. Sydney Rabinovitz, June 17, 1932; c: Jay, Caroline. Profsl engr vice-pres, Rogers Corp since 1945; mem: Masons; Soc Advancement Mgmt, past pres, Hartford chap; Tech Assn Pulp and Paper Inds; past pres, Temple Beth Shalom. Home: 15 Coburn Rd, Manchester, Conn. Office: Rogers Corporation, Rogers, Conn.

BROWNSTEIN, Bernard, US, business exec; b. NYC, Sep 27, 1910; s. Julius and Molly (Gross); att: CCNY; NYU; LLB, Bklyn Law Sch, 1932; m. Harriet Wolfberg, June 5, 1949; c: Lynn, June. Pres: Berlang Co Inc, since 1945; Berlang Steel Corp, 1946-70; Browning Export Corp, 1946-69; Dale Metals Corp, 1952-70. Bd trustee, Park E Syn, Cong Zichron Ephraim, pres, Men's Club; bd, Midtown Lodge, B'nai B'rith; cabinet, Manhattan div, State of Isr Bonds; co comm, Dem Party, since 1959; bd dirs: ADL appeal; Yorkville Dist, ZOA; vice-pres, Ocean Pkwy dist, 1946-49, co-chmn, political comm, 1948-49, speakers comm, 1948-49; Gtr Flatbush Civic League; Ocean Pkwy J Cen, 1935-49; mem: NY Bd of ADL; Assn of Steel Distributors; Wall St Syn; Millinery Cen Syn; YMHA; clubs: Pine Ridge Country; Knickerbocker Dem; HH Psych, Pres, 1938-39. Contbr to trade jours. Home: 1040 Park Ave, New York, NY. Office: 274 Madison Ave, New York, NY.

BRUCH, Hilde, US, psychiatrist, psychoanalyst; b. Ger; d. Hirsch and Adele (Rath); in US since 1934; ped training, Leipzig U; psycht training, Johns Hopkins U, 1941-43; psychan training, Wash Baltimore Inst, 1941-45. Prof psycht, Baylor Coll, since 1964; ped, Babies Hosp, NYC, 1934-53; asso psychan, Psychoanalytic Clinic for Training and Research, Columbia U, 1947-64, asso clinical prof, Coll Phys and Surgs, 1953-58, clinical prof, 1958-64; att psycht, NY State Psychiatric Inst, 1954-64, dir, children's service, 1953-55, psychotherapeutic sup, 1955-64; pvt practice psychan and chil psycht, NYC until 1964. Prin contribs: psychosomatic studies of obesity and anorexia nervosa; family interaction in schizophrenia. Dipl: Amer Bd Ped; Amer Bd Child Psycht; f: Amer Psychiatric Assn; Amer Orthopsychiatric Assn; Amer Acad Child Psycht; mem: Amer, intl psychoanalytic assns. Author: Don't Be Afraid of Your Child, 1952; The Importance of Overweight, 1957; Studies in Schizophrenia, 1959; contbr to profsl jours. Home: 1600 Holcombe Blvd, Houston, Tex. Office: Baylor Coll of Med, Houston, Tex.

BRUCKMAN, Arthur S, US, attorney; b. NYC, Jan 6, 1907; s. David and Helen (Newman); BS, CCNY, 1927; LLB, Fordham U, 1930; m. Tamar Chertok, June 3, 1934; c: George, Robert. In pvt practice since 1931; mem, law firm, Bruckman and Bruckman. Mem: natl bd, Natl Fed J Men's Clubs since 1945, past natl pres, past pres, NY Metrop region; natl bd dirs, United Syn of Amer since 1945, pres, NY Bd Educ since 1956, past vice-pres, NY Metrop region; NY Bd of Rev and Conciliation; bd overseers, JTSA since 1949; adv comm, J Cen Lectr Bur since 1949; Natl Comty Relations Adv Council, mem, comm, discrimination in housing and immigration since 1953; Natl Acad J Studies since 1954; bd dirs, J Educ Comm, NY; NYC, Bx, State Bar Assns; fmr: secy, treas, Syn Council, Amer; vice-pres, NY Metrop region; mem bd dirs, natl council, Natl JWB; pres, Temple Emanuel, Parkchester, NY. Asso ed, Torch Mag since 1956. Home: 20 Metropolitan Oval, New York, NY. Office: 250 Broadway New York, NY.

BRUNN, David S, Isr, banker; b. Miloslaw, Pol, Nov 7, 1895; s. Abraham and Bertha (Flatau); in Isr since 1933; m. Margarete Goldberg, Feb 26, 1923; c: Miriam Clyman, Hanna Levy. Dir, Ellern's Inves Corp Ltd and other financial corps. Served, Ger Army, 1914-18. Chmn, Assn of Blind; mem: council, Isr Philharmonic Orch; Tel Aviv comm, KH; Isr Amer Soc. Recipient: Iron Cross, 1918. Home: 36 Givati St, Ramat Chen, Isr.

BRUNO, Michael, Isr, educator; b. Hamburg, Ger, July 30, 1932; s. Hans and Lottie (Samson); in Isr since 1933; BA, MA, King's Coll, Cambridge, Eng; PhD, Stanford U, Cal, 1962; m. Ofra Hirshenberger, Oct 7, 1958; c: Yael, Ido. Asso prof, Heb U since 1967, chmn dept econ since 1968; govt cons on econ policy; fmr: jt dir, research dept, Bank of Isr, 1964-67; visiting prof, MIT, 1965-67; sr lectr, Heb U, 1965-67. IDF, 1950-52. Prin contribs, research on econ devl and growth. F, council mem, Econometric Soc; mem:

council, Intl Assn for Research in Income and Wealth; fmr: various govt comms; Kibbutz Hatzerim. Author, Interdependence, Resource Use and Structural Change in Israel, 1962; contbr to econ jours. Hobbies: music, hiking. Home: 15 Hovevi Zion St, Jerusalem, Isr. Office: Hebrew University, Jerusalem, Isr.

BRUNSCHVIG, Georges, Switz, attorney; b. Bern, Feb 21, 1908; s. Henri and Selma (Guggenheim); DJur, U of Bern; m. Odette Wyler, Oct 24, 1935; c: Pierrette Braunschweig, Monique Bloch. In pvt law practice. Pres, Schweizerischer Israelitischer Gemeindebund, since 1946, active since 1933; pres, J Comty of Bern, 1940-48. Author: Vernichtung einer Fälschung (Kollektivehrverletzung); Publikation über den Prozess der Protokolle der Weisen von Zion. Home: 53 Friedheimweg, Bern, Switz. Office: 51 Marktgasse, Bern, Switz.

BRUNSCHVIG, Jean Sally S, Switz, attorney; b. Geneva, May 17, 1914; s. Arnand and Suzanne (Meyer); licencié en droit, U of Geneva, 1936; dipl, comparative legal studies, U of Cambridge, Eng, 1939; m. Yvonne Sipos; c: Jacqueline, Michèle. Atty at law, Brunschvig & Badel since 1941. Pres, W Switz United Jew Appeal; Consul Gen of Monaco since 1968; fmr: co-pres, Geneva chap, World Brotherhood; pres, J Comty, Geneva; mem, bd dirs, Fed of Swiss J Comtys. Home: 27 Quai du Mont Blanc, Geneva, Switz. Office: 78 rue du Rhone, Geneva, Switz.

BRZEZINSKA, Eva Neuman, Isr, artist; b. Lodz, Pol, Dec 11, 1911; d. Isaac and Sarah (Przedborska); in Isr since 1949; m. 1948. Exhbs: Warsaw, Lodz, Krakow, all Pol; Munich, Ger; Tel Aviv Mus; Bat Yam, Isr; pvt gals in Isr. Mem: WIZO; Women Social Workers. Home: 9 Anilewicz, Bat Yam, Isr.

BUCHBAND, Martin, US, physician; b. Przemysl, Pol, Aug 5, 1895; s. Adolf and Ella (Salzberg); in US since 1938; MD, U of Vienna, 1924; m. Lily Steinfeld, Dec 25, 1924; c: George. Pvt practice, specialty, ear, nose and throat; teaching staff, Med Sch, U of Vienna, 1924-36; dir, ear, nose, throat dept, Rothschild Hosp, Vienna, 1936-38; instr, ear, nose and throat, Coll Physicians and Surgs, Columbia U, 1939-49. F: AMA; NY Co Med Soc; Intl Coll of Surgs. Contbr to profsl publs. Recipient: Knight of the Greek Elotarian Order, Commander Cdr of the Corona Romanie. Home: 241 Central Park W, New York, NY. Office: 30 Central Park S, New York, NY.

BUCHTHAL, Fitz, Den, physician, educator; b. Witten-Ruhr, Ger, Aug 19, 1907; s. Sally and Hedwig (Weyl); in Den since 1945; att U's of Freiburg; Stanford; MD, Berlin, 1931; DHC, Münster, 1960; m. Margaret Lennox, Aug 19, 1957. Dir, Inst of Neurophys, U of Copenhagen since 1946. Contbr to sci papers in muscle and nerve phys. Recipient, Ridder of Dannebrog. Home: Copenhagen-Gentofte, Den. Office: Inst of Neurophys, U of Copenhagen, Copenhagen, Den.

BUCKWALD, Harold, Can, attorney; b. Winnipeg, Manitoba, Can, Feb 22, 1928; s. Frank and Bessie (Portigal); BA, U of Manitoba, 1948, LLB, 1952, LLM, 1957; m. Darlene Besbeck, June 5, 1960; c: Jeffrey, Richard. Sr partner, Buchwald, Henteleff & Zitzerman since 1966; jr partner, Matlin, Kushner & Buchwald, 1954-61; lectr, corporate law, Man Law Sch, 1958-62; sr partner, Matlin, Buchwald & Co, 1961-66; spec counsel, Govt of Province of Manitoba, Consumer Protection, 1965-69. Pres, Winnipeg chap, Can Friends Heb U; vice-pres, YMHA Comty Cen, Winnipeg; alternate mem, Intl Bd Govs, Heb U; bencher, Law Sch of Man; natl vice-chmn, taxation sect, Can Bar Assn, 1968-70, 1st vice-pres, past 2nd vice-pres, secy, treas, chmn, leg comm; appd by PM, Consumer Council of Can, 1968-70; dir, Winnipeg Football Club, 1965-70; mem: Sigma Alpha Mu; Sigma Xi; Glendale Country Club; fmr: hon solicitor Winnipeg Sym Orch; chmn: B'nai B'rith Summer Camp, cen Can region; adv bd, B'nai B'rith Hillel Found, U of Manitoba; panelist: annual confs, Can Tax Found; annual meetings, Can Bar Assn; lectr, continuing legal educ, Man Bar Assn. Author, Administration and the Carter Report, 1967; weekly column in: Toronto Globe; Mail Daily Newspaper, 1966-68; contbr to legal publs. Recipient, QC, Province of Manitoba, 1966. Home: 800 Campbell St, Winnipeg, Manitoba, Can. Office: 259 Portage Ave, Winnipeg, Manitoba, Can.

BUCHWEITZ, Menachem, Isr, judge; b. Cracow, Pol, Oct 29,

1910; s. Jacob and Perla (Matzner); in Isr since 1943; att U Cracow, 1933; Grad Sch Political Sci, Cracow, 1934; DJ, 1936; m. Zisa Cohen, 1944; c: Margalit. Judge since 1958; dep dist atty, 1952-58; chief asst, secy of govt, 1950-52; gen secy, Min of War Relief, 1948-50; lectr of commercial, political law, Acad for Public Admn, Tel Aviv. Mem exec comm, chmn cultural div, B'nai B'rith; pres, Rambam Lodge, Free Masons; mem exec bd, Hazohar, Pol, 1932-39. Author: Mandate of the League of Nations Over Palestine (in Pol), 1938; Local Government in Isr, 1965; ed, Trybuna Narodowa, Zionist weekly, Cracow, 1933-39. Home: 3 Haifa Rd, Tel Aviv, Isr.

BUDICK, Isidore, US, rabbi, educator; b. Komanestie, Aus-Hung, 1914; s. Benjamin and Clara (Whitman); in US since 1920; BSS, CCNY, 1932, MS, 1935; MHL, ordained rabbi, JIR, 1940; PhD, Dropsie Coll, 1949; att Fordham U; NYU; m. Miriam Halperin, Dec 24, 1950. Lectr, modern hist, Bklyn Coll since 1961; rabbi, Milville, NJ, 1940-42; asso prof, org, dir, Hillel Found, Okla U, 1943-45; dir, Hillel Found, U of NC, 1945; instr: Graetz Coll, Phila, 1946-53; Akiba Heb Acad, 1951-53; rabbi, Phila, 1949-53; dir, J Culture Found; instr, NYU, 1953-54; lectr: Herzl Inst, NYC; political sci, ext dept, NYU; NY HS tchrs on Western Man's Heritage; civilian chaplain, WW II. Vice-pres, Natl Info Bur for Life Inc; bd dirs: Amer Assn Heb Profs; B'nai B'rith; AAUP; RA; Phi Beta Kappa. Torch and Scrolls; mem, Amer Hist Assn. Author, The Dynamics of Western Man's Isms, 1965. Home: 1820 Cortelyou Rd, Brooklyn, NY.

BUDIN, Alexander H, US, rabbi; b. Pol, Aug 10, 1905; s. Louis and Sarah (Dvoretzky); in US since 1921; rabbi, Isaac Eichanan Theol Sem, 1929; BBS, CCNY, 1930; DHL, Yeshiva U, 1942; m. Celia Lazarus, 1937; c: Annette, Joel. Rabbi, Cong Ohab Zedek, Rockaway Park, NY since 1935. Mem: RabCA; NY Bd of Rabbis; Mizrachi Org; B'nai B'rith; ZOA. Author, Exegesis of Immanuel of Rome, 1942. Home: 223 Beach 135 St, Belle Harbor, NY. Study: 13401 Rockaway Beach Blvd, Rockaway Park, NY.

BUDNITZ, Edward, US, cardiologist; b. New Britain, Conn, May 8, 1907; s. Alexander and Naomi (Bassewitz); BS, magna cum laude, Yale U, 1928; MD, Harvard, 1932; m. Rebecca Gass, Dec 13, 1936; c: Harriet, Susan, Sandra, Albee. Chief card, Worcester City Hosp, since 1967, on staff since 1937; asst in med, Harvard Med Sch, 1935-46. US Army, 1942-45. Dir, Worcester Fed Savings and Loan Assn since 1957; FACP; f, Worcester Dist Med Soc; dipl, Amer Bd Internal Med; trustee, Temple Emanuel; YMCA; mem: B'nai B'rith; ZOA; JWV; Masons. Contbr to profsl jours. Home: 285 Salisbury St, Worcester, Mass. Office: 37 Fruit St, Worcester, Mass.

BULAWKO, Henry, Fr, journalist; b. Lyda, Lith, Nov 25, 1918; s. Zalman and Golda (Szpilkowsky); att Rabb Sch, Paris. Ed, Amitiés France-Israel, since 1951. Pres: Hashomer Hatzair since 1945; Amicale des Anciens Déportés Juifs de France since 1968; Cercle Bernard Lazare since 1954. Author: Les Jeux de la Mort et de L'Espoir, 1955; Crimes sans Châtiments, 1962; Le Défi Sioniste; children's stories. Recipient, Médaille de la Déportation. Home: 11 rue Le Regrattier, Paris 4e, Fr. Office: 17 rue de la Victoire, Paris 9e, Fr.

BULZ, Emmanuel, Luxembourg, rabbi; b. Vienna, Mar 6, 1917; s. Moses and Bertha (Fingerhut); att Sorbonne, 1937-38; ordained rabbi, Rabb Sch of Fr, Paris, 1942; licencié en droit, licencié es lettres, U of Lyon, 1946; Docteur en Droit, U of Neuchâtel, Switz, 1954; m. Hélène Engelard, June 18, 1944; c: Noemi, Elisabeth, Michel. Chief rabbi, Luxembourg, since 1959; rabbi: Lyon, Fr, 1946-48; La Chaux de Fonds, Switz, 1949-59. Mem, B'nai B'rith. Author, Le Divorce en Droit Rabbinique dans ses Rapports avec le Droit Laïque Moderne, 1954. Recipient, Croix de la Résistance. Home: 59 route d'Arlon, Luxembourg.

BULZ, Hélène, Luxembourg, communal worker; b. Sieniawa, Pol, July 4, 1923; dipl, commercial HS, 1944; m. Emmanuel Bulz, June 18, 1944; c: Noemi, Elisabeth, Michel. Pres, WIZO, Luxembourg since 1961. Home: 59 route d'Arlon, Luxembourg.

BURACK, Abraham S, US, publisher, editor; b. NYC, Jan 31, 1908; s. Jacob and Elizabeth (Effross); m. Sylvia Kamerman, Nov 28, 1940; c: Janet, Susan, Ellen. Ed and publisher: The Writer, mag; plays, drama mag for young people; publisher, textbooks since 1933; asso, Sch of Publs, Simmons Coll since 1949; instr, jour div, Sch of PR, Boston U, 1950-57; in mail advt bus, 1925-33; lectr, schs and colls on writing and publishing. Ed: 100 Plays for Children, 1949; Four-Star Radio Play for Teenagers, 1959; Writing Detective and Mystery Fiction, 1967; The Writers Handbook, 1969; Four-Star Plays for Boys, 1969. Past pres, B'nai B'rith lodge. Home: 72 Penniman Rd, Brookline, Mass. Office: 8 Arlington St, Boston, Mass.

BURAS, Nathan, Isr, engineer; b. Burlad, Rum, Aug 23, 1921; s. Baruch and Ethel (Weiser); in Isr since 1938; cert, Mikveh-Isr, 1941; BS, highest hons, U Cal, Berkeley, 1949; MS, Technion, Haifa, 1957; PhD, UCLA, 1962; m. Netty Stivel, Apr 13, 1951; c: Nir. Asso prof, Technion since 1966; fmr dean, fac agric engr, Technion, 1966-68; sr lectr, 1962-66; asst research engr, UCLA. Served, Royal Engrs, Brit Army, 1942-46; capt, engr corps, IDF, 1950-51. Prin contrib, devl of sys analysis in water resources engr. Secy, Water Resources Systs Working Group, Intl Assn of Sci Hydrology; pres, Isr Students Assn, U of Cal, 1947-49; vice-pres, Hillel, U of Cal, 1948-49; mem: Amer Soc of Civil Engrs; Isr Soc for Geodesy and Geophys. Author: Advances in Hydroscience, vol III, 1966; Scientific Allocation of Water Resources. Recipient, campaign medals: Afr; It; Sinai Ribbon; Laureat du Congres, 6th Intl Cong of Agric Engrs, 1964. Home: 5 Einstein St, Haifa, Isr. Office: Technion, Haifa, Isr.

BURG, Yosef, Isr, cabinet min; b. Dresden, Ger, Jan 31, 1909; s. Abraham and Ziwia (Stockhamer); in Isr since 1939; PhD, U Leipzig, 1933; tchrs dipl, Ped Inst, Leipzig, 1934; ordained rabbi, Hildescheimer Rabb Sem, Berlin, 1939; m. Rivka Slonim, 1943; c: Zvia, Ada, Abraham. Min of Interior; Min of Social Wfr, Govt of Isr 1959-70; Min: of Health, 1951-52; of Posts, 1952-58; vice-chmn, first Knesset, 1949-51; tchr, Herzlia HS, Tel Aviv, 1941-46. Fmr mem: Zionist Actions Comm; exec, Mizrachi Youth Aliyah, Ger; exec comm, Pal Off, Berlin. Contbr of essays and articles. Home: 6A Ben Maimon St, Jerusalem, Isr. Office: Ministry of Social Welfare, Jerusalem, Isr.

BURGAUER, Werner, Switz, business exec; b. St Gallen, May 28, 1917; s. Willi and Gretel (Uhlman); textile engr deg, Textile Sch, Wattwil, 1936; textile chem deg, Manchester Poly, Eng, 1939; m. Janine Dreyfuss, Aug 8, 1946; c: Liliane, Pierre, Edith. Dir, Dirk Burgauer and Co AG, textile mfrs since 1955; tech mgr, Britannia Mill, Blackburn, Eng, 1939. Served, Swiss Army. Mem, bd dirs, admn examination bd, J Comty, past pres; pres, Verein zur Erhaltung des Jüdischen Friedhofs Hohenems since 1960; mem: Masons; speaker and BC corp mem, Kaufmännische Directorium, St Gallen. Hobbies: golf, skiing, numismatics, filming. Home: Peter and Paulstr 33, St Gallen, Switz. Office: St Gallen, Switz.

BURKE, Allan, Eng, organization exec, editor; b. Manchester, Eng, Dec 7, 1914; s. Joseph and Betsy; att Manchester U; FCCS, Corp of Secys, London; m. Molly Aizec; c: Maureen Freedman. Gen secy, Anglo-Isr C of C since 1953; ed, Anglo-Israel Trade Jour since 1957; fmr, produc dir, family bus. Lt cdr, Royal Navy, 1936-46; volunteer, Isr War of Independence, 1948; cdr, chief naval oprs, Isr nav; only volunteer from abroad in command of a man-of-war in a fgn navy; only non-Isr appd to command of Israeli maj war vessel. Recipient: stars: Atlantic; Afr; It; Fr; Ger; 1939; War Service Medal; Isr decorations: Medal of Independence; Freedom Fighters Medal. Spec interest, Isr. Home: 194 Turnpike Link, Park Hill Village, E Croydon, Surrey, Eng. Office: Kern House, 36 Kingsway, London WC2, Eng.

BURKE, Henry G, US, attorney, accountant; b. Baltimore, Oct 29, 1902; s. Max and Rose (Cohen); BCS, Baltimore Coll of Commerce, 1923; LLB, U of Md, 1927; PhD, Johns Hopkins U, 1933; m. Alberta Hirshheimer, Dec 26, 1930. Partner: acctnt firm, Burke, Landsberg & Gerber since 1923; law firm, Burke, Gerber & Wilen since 1951. Mem: Md Assn CPAs, past pres; Amer Inst Acctnts; Baltimore Bar Assn; bd dirs, Asso J Charities; Johns Hopkins Club; fmr: chmn, Asso J Charities and Wfr Fund Campaign; mem: bd dirs, Amer Assn Attys and CPAs; bd mgrs, YMCA schs; bd dirs, JWF, Baltimore; pres: HIAS, Baltimore; J Family and Children's Bur; club, Johns Hopkins. Contbr to profsl jours. Home: 116 W University Pkwy, Baltimore, Md. Office: 326 St Paul Pl, Baltimore, Md.

BURMAN, Daniel, US, physician; b. NYC, May 7, 1910; s. Isidor and Gussie (Levine); AB, George Wash U, 1933, MA,

1934; MD, Howard U, 1938; m. Beatrice Lookstein, May 24, 1942; c: Matthew, Danby, Dorothy. Pvt practice since 1941; att ophthal: Fordham Hosp, NYC, since 1951; Heb Hosp for Chronic Illness since 1951; visiting prof, scis, Amer Coll, Jerusalem; asst otolaryngologist, Harlem Hosp, NYC, 1950; cons, Dept of Wfr, NYC, 1951; att ophthal, Home and Hosp of Daughters of Jacob, 1951; adj ophthal, Mt Sinai Hosp, 1951; asso ophthal: Royal Hosp, 1948; Manhattan Eye, Ear and Throat Hosp, 1957; Misericordia Hosp, 1958; Bx Eye and Ear Hosp, 1958; Pelham Bay Gen Hosp, 1960. US Marine Res, 1934-38; US Army, 1942-44; USCG, 1949. Dipl: Amer Bd Ophthal; Amer Bd Otolaryngology; f: Amer Coll of Surgs; Intl Coll of Surgs; Acad Amer Ophthal and Otolaryngology; NY Soc for Clinical Ophthal; Assn for Research in Ophthal; Amer Acad Dent Med; Amer Acad Plastic Surg of Head and Neck; Kappa Pi Med Scholarship Soc; pres, life mem, ZOA; mgr, Genesis Zionist Inves Assos; pres, Histadrut Summer Camps in Isr; mem: AMA; Bx Co, Westchester Co Med Assns; NY State Howard U Med Alumni Assn; Jerusalem Acad of Med; IMA; Elks; Masons; f: chmn, ADL; mem, Genesis Heb Cen, vice-pres, PTA; clubs: Kiwanis; Physicians Sq. Spec interests: social and communal affairs, world-wide travel, public speaking on med problems and Isr affairs, active in interracial and interfaith groups: Afr, Isr; S Amer. Home: 1860 Grand Concourse, New York, NY. Office: 1938 Grand Concourse, New York, NY.

BURMAN, Herman J, US, physician, educator; b. Russ, July 14, 1898; s. Isidor and Gussie (Levine); in US since 1906; BSM, Fordham U, 1919; MD, Tufts Med Sch, 1923; m. Anne Feinstein, July 27, 1948; c: Don, Alice Post. Dir, otolaryngology, bronchoscopy, esophagology, Harlem Hosp since 1929; clinical prof, otolaryngology, NY Med Coll since 1944; cons, otolaryngology, Harlem div, Columbia U; dir, otologic microsurg, Bx Eye and Ear Hosp; asso visiting otolaryngologist, Flower and Fifth Ave Hosps since 1948; cons, Metrop and Bird S Coler Hosps since 1948. Served WWI. Pres, Bx Otolaryngology Soc, 1947; f: Amer Coll of Surgs; Amer Acad Ophth and Otolaryngology; dipl, Amer Bd of Otolaryngology. Author, Textbook of Diseases of Nose and Throat, 1935; contbr to Jackson and Jackson's Diseases of Nose and Throat; articles on otolaryngology. Home: 891 Park Ave, New York, NY. Office: 1235 Grand Concourse, New York, NY.

BURMAN, Louis Robert, US, dentist, teacher; b. NYC, Aug 23, 1906; s. Isidor and Gussie (Levine); PhG, Fordham U, 1924; BS, NYU, 1934; AM, George Washington U, 1935; DDS, NYU, 1940; m. Frances Cohen; c: David, Lester. Asso prof, periodontia and oral med, fmr asst prof, anat, NYU Coll Dent, fac mem since 1940; postgrad instr, 1st Dist Dent Soc since 1941; past visiting periodontist, Morrisania City Hosp, Grand Cen Hosp. Pres, Parents Assn, NYU Coll Dent; past pres, Amer Acad Oral Med; Bx Co Dent Soc, past intl pres, Alpha Omega Frat; dipl: Amer Bd Periodontology; Amer Bd Oral Med; f: Amer Coll Dent; Amer Acad Oral Med; NY Acad Dent; AAAS; Soc of Gerontology; mem: Sigma Xi, Sci Research Soc Amer; Amer Dent Assn. Fmr bus mgr, Jour of Dent Med; co-author three textbooks, contbr of numerous articles to med and dent jours, visiting lectr. Home: 165 West End Ave, New York, NY. Office: 200 Central Park S, New York, NY.

BURMAN, Samuel Seidel, US, attorney; b. Pinsk, Russ, Oct 12, 1902; s. Isidor and Gussie (Levine); in US since 1905; LLB, NY Law Sch, 1923; m. Lee Goldstein, Feb 7, 1931; c: Jane. Pvt law practice; law secy to Justice Julius Miller, 1st jud dept, Supr Court, NY, 1943-50; asst US atty, s dist, NY, 1951-53; admitted to practice in: US Court of Appeals; S and E Dist Courts, all in 1925; US Supr Court, 1929; Treas Dept, 1940; US Customs Court; Subversive Activities Control Bd; PO Dept; bd of immigration appeals and immigration and naturalization service, US Dept of Justice; VA; Tax Courts of US; FCC; US Court of Mil Appeals; War Claims Commn; ICC, all in 1953; appd commn, referee in divers proc, NYC. USCG Res, 1945-46, lt, NY Guard, 1946-47. Exec secy: Amsterdam Dem Club, Fifth Assembly Dist Co Comm, both 1949-54; mem: NYC Bar Assn; arbitration and conciliation, and law reform comms, NY Co Lawyers Assn; Fed Bar Assn; Bx Co Bar Assn; Fifth Div, Off s Assn; NY Guard; W Side Instl Syn; Elks; ZOA; Grand St Boys Assn; club, W Side Lions Intl, dep dist gov zone chmn, pres. Contbr to Legal Aspects of Installment Selling, 1936. Home: 100 W 57 St, New York, NY. Office: 200 W 57 St, New York, NY.

BURNS, Arthur F, US, economist, educator; b. Stanislau, Aus, Apr 27, 1904; s. Nathan and Sarah (Juran); BA, Columbia U, 1925, MA, 1925, PhD, 1934; D honoris causa: Lehigh U, 1952; Rutgers U, 1955; Brown U, 1956; Dartmouth Coll, 1956; Oberlin Coll, 1956; Wesleyan U, 1958; Swarthmore Coll, 1958; U of Pa, 1958; LIU, 1960; U Chgo, 1960; U Rochester, 1963; m. Helen Bernstein, Jan 25, 1930; c: David Joseph. Chmn, Fed Res Bd since 1969; counsellor to Pres Nixon, 1969; John Bates Clark prof, Columbia U since 1959; pres, mem res staff, Natl Bur Econ Research, fmr, dir research; mem, Pres Adv Comm on Lab Mgmt Policy since 1961; prof, Rutgers U, 1927-44; chief stat, RR Emergency Bd, 1941; cons: Treas Dept; Natl Security Council; Dept of Defense; State Dept; Lab Dept; Fed Res Bd; chmn: Pres Council of Econ Advs, 1953-56; Adv Bd on Econ Growth and Stability, 1953-56; Cabinet Comm on Small Bus, 1956; mem adv council on social security financing, 1957-58; Millar lectr, Fordham U; Murary lectr, State U of Ia; Fairless lectr, Carnegie Inst of Tech; mem: Temporary State Commn on Econ Expansion, 1959-60; Gov's Comm on Minimum Wage, NY, 1964. Pres, Acad Political Sci; corresp, Inst de Sci Econ Appliquee; Trustee, Twentieth Cent Fund; Tax Found Inc; Mutual Life Ins Co of NY; past pres, Amer Econ Assn, f; dir: Nationwide Securities; Dividend Shares, f: Amer Stat Assn; Econometric Assn; Amer Acad Arts and Scis; mem: Amer Phil Soc; Council on Fgn Relations; Pilgrims Soc; clubs: Cosmos, Wash, DC; Cent Assn, NYC; Men's Fac, Columbia U. Author: Production Trends in the United States since 1870, 1934; Economic Research and the Keynesian Thinking of Our Times, 1946; Frontiers of Economic Knowledge, 1954; Prosperity without Inflation, 1959; The Management of Prosperity, 1966; contbr to profsl publs Home: 2 Tudor City Pl, New York, NY. Office: 261 Madison Ave, New York, NY.

BURROWS, Abe, US, playwright, director; b. NYC, Dec 18, 1910; s. Louis and Julia (Salzberg); att CCNY, 1928-29; NYU, 1929-31; m. Carin Smith, Oct 2, 1950; c: James, Laurie. Co-author and dir, Broadway plays: Can-Can, 1953; Three Wishes for Jamie, 1953; Say, Darling, 1958; How to Succeed in Business Without Really Trying, 1962; co-author: Guys and Dolls, 1950; Silk Stockings, 1954; dir: Two on the Aisle, 1951; Reclining Figure, 1954; Happy Hunting, 1956; Golden Fleecing, 1959; author of screen play, Solid Gold Cadillac, 1955; author and dir: First Impressions, 1959; Cactus Flower, 1965. Author, Abe Burrows Song Book, 1955; numerous radio and TV appearances. Mem: Dramatists Guild; Writers Guild of Amer; Amer Fed of TV & Radio Artists; Dirs Guild of Amer; Soc of Stage Dirs & Choreographers; ASCAP. Recipient: NY Drama Critics Circle Award, 1950, 1962; Antoinette Perry Award, 1950, 1962; Pulitzer Prize for Draama, 1962. Home and office: c/o Wm Morris Agency, 1350 Sixth Ave, New York, NY.

BURROWS, Selig S, US, industrialist; b. NYC, June 1, 1913; s. Louis and Julia (Salzberg); att Fordham U, law sch, qualifying cert; NYU Law Sch; m. Gladys Spatt, Sep 18, 1938; c: Kenneth, Jonathan, Patricia. Pres, dir, NY Globe Laundry, Inc since 1950; exec vice-pres, dir: Cen Coat, Apron and Linen Service, NYC; Amer Coat and Apron Laundry, Schnectady, NY; pres, dir: Cen Coat Linen and Apron Service, Baltimore; Noxall and US Linen Supply, Paterson, NJ; partner: Cen Laundries, Jersey City, NJ; Spatt Textile and Trading, Jersey City, NJ; pres, Real Estate Industrials, NYC. Dir, United Cerebral Palsy Research Found; mem, bd trustees: LI J Hosp since 1958; N Shore Hosp since 1958; Bklyn Heb Home and Hosp for Aged since 1955; chmn, Jt Defense Appeal, LI; vice-pres, FJC, LI since 1950; mem, exec comm, UJA, LI, since 1950; charter mem, bd dirs, NY Worlds Fair; dir, exec adv council, United Cerebral Palsy Found; found, Einstein Med Coll, NY; mem: council, Whitney Mus Amer Art; clubs: Lotos, NY; Dutch Treat, NY; Fresh Meadow Country; Palm Beach Country, Fla; Art Collectors Amer. Recipient, presidential appointment, US Treas Dept, assay comm, 1963. Home: 96 Merrivale Rd, Great Neck, NY. Office: 514 W 49 St, New York, NY.

BURSON, Josephine, US, communal worker; b. Memphis, Tenn, Dec 23, 1915; d. Charles and Clara (Blecker) Wainman; att Memphis State U; m. Leo Burson, Sep 3, 1939; c: Mrs H Kirke Lewis, Charles. Mem, natl bd, Hadassah since 1956, natl vice-pres, 1962-64, past pres, s region, Memphis chap, fmr mem, natl service comm; participated in Hadassah leadership tour of Isr, 1959; mem, natl org comm, natl Zionist Affairs Comm; delg to 25th, 26th and 27th WZC, Jerusa-lem, dep mem, actions comm; pres, J Comty Relations Council, Memphis, 1963-67, co-org, 1958; chmn, UJA, Women's Div, 1950; bd trustees, United Isr Appeal; appd mem, Govs Cabinet, State of Tenn, 1967; commr, Employment Security since 1967; chmn, Govs Commn Migratory Lab; mem, Govs Commn, Status of Women; vice-pres, Interstate Conf, Employment Security Admnrs. Home: 2228 Henry Ave, Memphis, Tenn. Office: 536 Cordell Hull Bldg, Nashville, Tenn.

BURSTEIN, Ada Landman, Peru; communal leader; b. Lima, Peru, Apr 26, 1926; d. Luis and Dora (Rosenfeld) Landman; m. Manuel Burstein, Dec 19, 1948; c: David, Felipe, Benjamin, Janet. Pres, Fed WIZO Peru since 1963. Secy, local J Help, 1961-65; mem: Magbit, 1967; Comite Damas Leon Pinelo, 1962-65. Home: 240 Ugarte y Moscoso, Magdalena, Lima, Peru. Office: POB 2280, Lima, Peru.

BURSTEIN, Charles L, US, physician, educator; b. Paris, Fr, Apr 22, 1906; c: Jacob and Pearl (Gersik); in US since 1916; BS, NYU, 1928; MD, U of Paris, 1934; m. Loretta Lipschitz, Sep 14, 1930; c: Joan. Chief, dept anesthesiology, Hosp for Spec Surg, NY, since 1947, mem staff since 1937; asso clinical prof, anesthesiology: Cornell Med Sch since 1955; NYU Post-Grad Med Sch, 1950-55; att cons in anesthesia, VA Hosp, Bx, NY, since 1947; f in anesthesia, NYU Med Sch, 1936-37, instr, 1937-50; asst visiting anesthetist, Bellevue Hosp, 1937-50, mem staff since 1935. Maj, US Army MC, 1942-46. Mem: Amer Soc of Anesthesiologists; AMA; chmn, comm or clinical anesthesia study commns, since 1962; NY Co Med Soc; Soc for Experimental Biol and Med; Sigma Xi; hon mem, sect on anesthesiology, Kings Co Med Soc. Author, Fundamental Considerations in Anesthesia, 1949, 1955; contbr numerous articles to med jours. Recipient, Bronze Star for Meritorious Service, 1945. Home: 47 Clinton St, Mt Vernon, NY. Office: 535 E 70 St, New York, NY.

BURSTEIN, Harvey, US, consultant, attorney; b. St Louis, Mo, Jan 3, 1923; s. Morris and Rachel (Johannes); LLB, Creighton U and Law Sch, 1948; m. Ina Bebchick, 1947. Pres, Harvey Consultants Corp since 1963; vice-pres, The Norman Co since 1962; spec agent, FBI, 1948-53; chief, inves and security, Dept of State, 1953-54; atty and security cons, self-employed, 1954-61; security off, MIT, 1956-61; asst to pres, Norman Jaspan Assos, 1961-62; admitted to practice: Neb, Mass, NY and Fed Courts; guest lectr: MIT, 1959-60; Ind U, since 1960; Mich State U, 1963. US Army, 1943-46. Chmn: civil rights and liberties comm, Boston Chap, AJComm, 1957-58; speakers bur, AJComm, 1958-61; admn vice-chmn, AJComm, 1959-61; exec comm, Westchester Chap, AJComm, 1963-64; coll liaison comm, Larchmont Temple, 1962-64; ext comm, Pi Lambda Phi, 1958-62; MIT Frat Advs Group, 1959-60; pres, Pi Lambda Phi, 1962-63; chief of staff, dept of Mass, JWV, 1956-57; mem: exec comm, Temple Ohabei Shalom Brotherhood, 1955-56; speakers bur, Boston Bar Assn, 1959-61; comm on profsl criteria, Amer Soc for Ind Security, 1959-61; Amer Bar Assn; Amer Inst of Mgmt; Intl Assn of Chiefs of Police; Soc of Fmr FBI Agents; Masons; Scottish Rite; Amer Arbitration Assn; Boston Bar Assn; NY Co Lawyers Assn; Soc of Profsl Mgmt Cons. Rel ed, Larchmont Temple News, since 1965; contbr to bus, law enforcement and legal jours. Home: 21 N Chatsworth Ave, Larchmont, NY. Office: 99 W Hawthorne Ave, Valley Stream, NY.

BURSTEIN, Herbert, US, attorney; b. Phila, Pa, Dec 15, 1914; s. Joseph and Millie (Rotwein); BA, cum laude, LIU, 1935; JD, St Lawrence U, 1939, JDS, magna cum laude, 1942; att NYU; m. Beatrice Sobel, June 18, 1938; c: Karen, Ellen, Patricia, Jessica, John, Judd. Partner, law firm, Zelby & Burstein since 1942; instr, LIU; lectr: Practicing Law Inst; NYU; Southwestern U; CUNY; counsel, US House of Reprs. Mem: Amer Bar Assn; Amer Judicature Assn; NYC Bar Assn. Author, Women in War; ed, trade jours; contbr of articles to legal jours. Home: 62 Causeway, Lawrence, LI, NY. Office: 30 Church St, New York, NY.

BURSTEIN, Julius, US, physician, educator; b. New Haven, Conn, Sep 10, 1900; s. Simon and Pauline (Berman); AB, Columbia U, 1921; MD, W Reserve U, 1924; m. Blnache Korones, June 21, 1927; c: Harriet Jackson, Irma Ascher, Susan. Asso card, U Memorial Hosp since 1935; asso clinical prof, med, NY Med Sch since 1949; card: Riverside Hosp, 1935-50; St Elizabeth Hosp, dir, cardiovascular service, Morrisania City Hosp, 1952. Mem: AMA; AHA; J Acad Arts and Scis; Masons; f, Amer Coll Card. Author, Illustrative Electro-cardiography, 1935, 1940, 1948; contbr to med jours. Hobby, photography. Home: 90 Seacord Rd, New Rochelle, NY. Office: 233 E 69 St, New York, NY.

BURSTEIN, Michael Lawrence, Isr, actor, singer; b. NYC, July 1, 1945; s. Paul and Lillian (Lux); in Isr since 1962; att HS of Music and Art, NYC, 1960-62; m. Edith Pupisky, July 20, 1968; c: Peter. Appearances: Yiddish theatre for 17 years; Isr film, Two Kunilemls; Isr musical, The Megilla of Itzik Manger. Recipient: Kinor David, Yediot Aharonot, 1966; Isr Song Festival, 1st Prize, Kol Isr, 1967. Hobbies: photography, law, tennis. Home and studio: 18 Hildesheimer St, Tel Aviv, Isr.

BURSTEIN, Moshe, Isr, bookkeeper; b. Pol, 1907; in Isr since 1926; m. Sara, 1933; c: Dvora, Sima, Naomi. Bookkeeper, Natl Ins since 1954; fmr: agric worker; mem, Kibbutz Givat Hashlosha; Haganah, 1928-48. Chmn village, Kfar Sirkin, 1939-69; dep chmn, regional council Mifalot Afek; active, econ instns, Kfar Sirkin; fmr: affiliated with: Poalei Zion; Hechalutz; Lab Org, all Pol. Home: Kfar Sirkin, Isr. Office: National Insurance Office, Petah Tikva, Isr.

BURSTEIN, Samuel M (Shmuel Barav), US, rabbi; b. NYC, Apr 4, 1921; s. Abraham and Stella (Cohn); BA, Columbia U, 1941, MA, 1945; BHL, JTSA, NYC, 1941; MHL, ordained rabbi, 1945; m. Pearl Shmidman, July 1, 1951; c: Ilana, Alissa. Rabbi: Beth Emeth Syn, Larchmont, NY since 1968; Cong Tifereth Isr, Lincoln, Neb, 1945-46; Agudath Achim, Pittston, Pa, 1946-47; mem, Kibbutz Ein Hanatziv and Kfar Darom of Kibbutz Hadati, Isr, 1948-51; rabbi, Agudath Isr Cong, Ottawa, Can, 1951-59; Agudas Isr Cong, Hazelton, Pa, 1959-68. Chaplain, lt, US Army, 1947-48; pilot instr, author of tech manuals, IAF, 1948-51. Found, Ottawa Hillel Councillorship, 1957; charter mem, Parl Lodge, B'nai B'rith, 1958; chaplain and instr, meteorology and navigation, Civic Air Patrol; chaplain, Post 287, JWV since 1959; mem: Mh Assn; JCC; ZOA; Comty Chest; YMCA Bldg Campaign; UJA; J Comty Cen; Boy Scouts; State of Isr Bonds; exec council, RA, 1959-62; Rel Zionists of Amer; Assn of J Chaplains; NY Bd of Rabbis; Airplane Owners and Pilots Assn; Amer Assn for UN; Phila Bd Rabbis; ACLU; NAACP; Mahala Min Assn; NRA; SANE; Rel Educ Assn; on speakers burs of: ZOA and ZOC; Comty Chest; J Federated Dr; Cavalcades of Judaism; club, Kiwanis Intl. Author: Rabbi with Wings, 1965; ed: A Teenager's Introduction to Judaism, 1957; contbr of articles to periodicals. Recipient: Ger Occupation Medal, US Army, 1948; Isr Liberation Medal, 1951. Hobbies: flying, photography. Home: 21 Birch Lane, Larchmont, NY. Study: 111 Boston Post Rd, Larchmont, NY.

BURTON, John Harvey, Eng, solicitor; b. Berkhamsted, Eng, May 5, 1946; s. Stanley and Sadie (Davis); grad, Coll of Law, London. Solicitor since 1969. Chmn, Cen Young Zionist Soc, fmr, vice-chmn, fund raising off; bus mgr, Young Zionist Mag, Fed Zionist Youth, mem, secretariat. Hobbies: golf, drawing, painting, deltiology, music, travel, J and gen Zionist activities. Home: 16 Cloister Gardens, Edgware, Middlesex, Eng. Office: 160 Piccadilly, London, Eng.

BUSCHKE, Franz J, US, physician, educator; b. Berlin, Aug 24, 1902; s. Abraham and Erna (Frankel); in US since 1934; att Med Sch, U of Freiburg; MD, U of Berlin Med Sch, 1927; m. Ruth Minkowski, Jan 2, 1930; c: Herman, Esther Federman, James, Frances. Prof, radiology, U of Cal, Sch of Med since 1957; asso prof, Tumor Inst of Swed Hosp, Seattle, Wash, 1939-56. Co-author: Krebs und Verebung, 1935; Cancer: Its Diagnosis and Treatment, 1938; Supervoltage Roentgentherapy, 1950; ed, Progress in Radiation Therapy, 1958, 1962, 1965. Home: 2465 Union St, San Francisco, Cal. Office: U of Cal, Med Center, San Francisco, Cal.

BUSH, Gerald Stanley, US, business exec; b. Bklyn, NY, May 21, 1935; s. Murry and Reva (Fishbein); BSEE, The Citadel, 1957; MEE, U of Cal, 1960; MBA, U of Buffalo, 1965; m. Tamara Bluth, June 10, 1962; c: Elan, Orlie, Aviva, Ronna. Exec vice-pres, Info Techs Inc since 1969; controller, AMF, 1963-67; Garan Inc, 1967-68; vice-pres, Gen Sci, 1968-69. Capt, USAF, 1957-61. Home: 17 Chipping Lane, Norwalk, Conn. Office: 83 East Ave, Norwalk, Conn.

BUTTENWIESER, Benjamin J, US, banker; b. NYC, Oct 22, 1900; s. Joseph and Caroline (Weil); BA, Columbia, 1919; m. Helen Lehman, Oct 3, 1929; c: Lawrence, Carol (decd), Peter, Paul. Lt partner, Kuhn, Loeb & Co, since 1952, with firm since 1918; dir: Revlon; Chock Full o'Nuts; Tishman

Realty & Construction; Title Guarantee; US Asst High Commn for Ger, 1949-51; natl bank code commn, Natl Recovery Act, 1933. USN, 1942-45; cdr, USNR. Bd trustees: FJP; Lenox Hill Hosp; mem: Columbia U; Fisk U; NY Philharmonic; Parkinson's Disease Found; clubs: Midday; Cent Country. Home: 450 E 52 St, New York, NY. Office: 40 Wall St, New York, NY.

BUTTENWIESER, Lawrence B, US, attorney; b. NYC, Jan 11, 1932; s. Benjamin and Helen (Lehman); BA, U of Chgo, 1952, MA, 1953; LLB, Yale Law Sch, 1956; m. Ann Lubin, July 13, 1956; c: William, Carol, Jill, Peter. Partner, law firm since 1966. Chmn, bd, Asso YM-YWHA, Gtr NY Inc; treas, City Cen of Music and Drama; vice-pres, Citizens Housing and Planning Council, NY; dir: Interfaith City Wide Coordinating Comm Against Poverty; FJP, NY; Montefiore Hosp and Med Cen; United Neighborhood Houses of NY Inc; Dalton Sch. Home: 1080 Fifth Ave, New York, NY. Office: 575 Madison Ave, New York, NY.

BUXBAUM, Henry, US, obstetrician, gynecologist, educator; b. Chgo, Ill, Feb 19, 1894; s. Herman and Dora (Spiegel); MD, Loyola U, Chgo, 1917; m. Ruth Polakoff, Apr 18, 1920; c: Howard, Eileen Schwartz. Pvt practice since 1919; asso prof em, Northwestern U, Chgo, on fac since 1950; sr att obstet and gyn, Michael Reese Hosp; found, Chgo Maternity Cen; cons: Louis Weiss Hosp; Jackson Park Hosp; sup phys, Chgo Bd of Health. Dipl, Amer Bd of Obstet and Gyn, 1932; pres, Chgo Gyn Soc, 1953-54; f: Amer Coll of Surg; Cen Assn of Obstet and Gyn; mem: AMA; Amer Coll of Obstet and Gyn. Contbr to med jours. Hobby, travel. Home: 1642 E 56 St, Chicago Ill. Office: 8 S Michigan Ave, Chicago, Ill.

BYCHOWSKI, Gustav, US, psychiatrist, educator; b. Warsaw, Pol, Aug 21, 1895; s. Zygmunt and Gizela (Horwitz); in US since 1941; MD, U of Zurich, 1919; MD, U of Warsaw, 1923; postgrad study, Zurich and Vienna; MD, State Bd, NYC, 1943; m. Maria Aurbach, 1906; c: Krystyna Earles, Monica Holmes. In pvt practice psycht since 1923; prof, diagram preceptor, Dept of Psycht, Mt Sinai Hosp; asst clinical prof, psycht, NYU since 1950; asso clinical prof, psycht, SUNY since 1956; training analyst; asso visiting neuropsycht, Bellevue Hosp since 1950; dir, psycht, Inst for Crippled and Disabled, NYC, 1945-50; asst psycht, J Hosp, Warsaw, 1924-26; phys-in-chief, Sch System for retarded and psychopath children, 1928-32; legal psycht, Court of Appeal, Warsaw, 1928-39; asso prof, psycht, U of Warsaw, 1934-39. F, Amer Psycht Assn; mem: NY Soc for Clinical Psycht; Amer Psychan Assn; Amer Acad of Sci; pres, Schilder Assn since 1953. Author: Metaphysics and Schizophrenia, 1923; Textbook of Psychoanalysis, 1928; Slowacki and His Psyche, 1930; Dictators and Disciples, 1949; Psychotherapy of Psychoses, 1952; Evil in Man: The Anatomy of Hate and Violence, 1968; ed, Specialised Techniques in Psychotherapy 1952; contbr to profsl jours. Home and office: 1148 Fifth Ave, New York, NY.

BYLAN, Hyman J, US, business exec; b. Milw, Wis, Apr 18, 1898; s. Rubin and Minnie (Winkelman); BA, U of Wis, 1922; m. Esther Schwartz, June 18, 1926; c: Nancy Bratman. Pres, B & B Beer Distributing Co; dir: Mich Beer & Wine Wholesalers Assn, 1934-35; Natl Beer Wholesalers Assn, 1953-54; US Army WW I. Pres, J Comty Fund, 1946-48; chapter chmn, ARC, 1951-53, mem, bd dirs, 1945-54; cochmn, NCCJ, 1942-45; campaign chmn, UJA, 1947; Mich delg, Amer J Conf, 1947; dir, Metrop Planning Commn, 1945-48; pres, Temple Emanuel, 1941-43, 1951-53; mem: bd dirs, Comty Chest; exec comm, natl bd, UAHC, since 1956, pres, Great Lakes region, 1955-60; bd dirs: Amer Cancer Soc; Grand Rapids Art Mus; Aquinas Coll; mem-at-large, natl bd of delg, AJComm, since 1945; Amer Legion, cdr post, 1946; Phi Sigma Delta; Scabbard and Blade; Elks; Masons; clubs: Rotary; Army and Navy; Standard, Chgo; Peninsular; Green Ridge Country. Home: 900 Santa Barbara Dr, Grand Rapids, Mich. Office: 201 Matilda St, NE, Grand Rapids, Mich.

BYRON, Al, US, lyricist; b. NYC, Sep 16, 1932; s. Moe and Beatrice (Kalenscher) Schwartz; BA, Bklyn Coll, 1954. Lyricist: hit song of 1960, Happy-Go-Lucky Me; hit song of 1962, Roses are Red; songs recorded by: Elvis Presley; Della Reese; Bobby Vinton; John Gary; author, play, The Idiot Savants; fmr, tchr, Bd Educ. Mem, ASCAP. Recipient, Gold Record Award, for Roses are Red, 1962. Hobby, art collecting. Home and office: 330 W 45 St, New York, NY.

C

CABASSO, Victor Jack, US, biologist; b. Egypt, June 21, 1915; s. Jacques and Fortunée (Bouskela); in US since 1946; att Heb U, Jerusalem, 1935-38; Sorbonne, Paris, 1939-40; DSc, U of Algiers, 1941; m. Anna Cooper, June 26, 1948; c: Jacqueline, Phillip. Dir, microbiol research, Cutter Labs since 1967; research, Pasteur Inst: in Paris, 1939; in Tunis, 1940-43; spec inves, public health, Offro, Tunis, 1943-44; head, lab sect, UNRRA, ME mission, 1944-45, Greece mission, 1945-46; head, virus immunological research dept, Lederie Labs, 1958-67; F, NY Acad of Sci. mem: examination and licensing comm, public health virologists, Amer Acad of Micro-biol since 1960; NY Soc of Tropical Med; Amer Soc for Microbiol; Amer Public Health Assn; AAAS; Temple Beth El, Spring Valley, NY; asso mem, Pasteur Inst, Tunis; contbr numerous profsl jours. Home: 490 Tharp Dr, Moraga, Cal. Office: Cutter Labs, Berkeley, Cal.

CAFTORI, David, Isr, painter; b. Jaffa, Isr, July 13, 1923; s. Ben Zion and Lea (Perera) Button; att: Avni Arts Sch, Tel Aviv, 1954-57; Arts Tchrs Sch, Tel Aviv; 1958-59; Louvre Arts Sch, Paris, 1961-63; m. Mali Gerasi; c: Netiva, Nir. Art tchr, Avni Arts Sch, since 1959; exhbs: Katz Gal, Tel Aviv, 1958; Tel Aviv Mus, 1958, 1959, 1960, 1961; NY, 1960; Paris, 1962-68; Compiegne, 1962; Monte Carlo, 1962; Goteberg, Sweden; repr in pvt collections: Eur, Isr, Palmach, Haganah; IDF, 1942-46. Mem Isr and Fr Assn of Painters. Recipient: 1939-45 stars, Afr, It, 8th Army. Home: 24 Hakeshet St, Tel Aviv, Isr.

CAHANA, Jean, Fr, physician; b. Vaslui, Rum, Mar 20, 1908; s. Isac and Perla (Weinberg); in Fr since 1928; MD, Fac Med, Paris U, 1935; MD, Institut de Stomatologie, Paris, 1936; m. Toni Goldenberg, Aug 28, 1934; c: Micheline, Jean. Pvt practice, stomatology and dent, since 1935. Fr Army, 1944-55. Hon pres, med comm, UJA, Fr; pres, B'nai B'rith Lodge, Fr; past pres: Union des Médecins, Dentistes et Pharmaciens, Amis d'Israel; Amitiées Odonto-Stomatologiques Franco-Israeliennes; Friends of Isr Dent Schs. mem: exec, ZF; exec comm, JNF, WJC. Ed, Union (UMDPAI), J Med Rev, since 1968. Recipient, Croix de Guerre, 1945. Home and office: 34 rue Bassano, Paris 8, Fr.

CAHEN, Julius F, Isr, engineer, educator; b. Hertogenbosch, Holland, Feb 10, 1899; s. Ferdinand 'and Libetha (Hartog); in Isr since 1947; MSc, Tech U, Delft, Holland, 1922; m. Frederika de Jong, 1930; c: Gideon, Ruth Manassen, Hanan Vleeschhouwer (adopted), Abel, Yudith; Pres, mgmt cons, Ind Service Corp, Haifa, since 1950; asso prof of ind mgmt engr, Technion, Haifa, since 1952; adv, Min of Finance, Econ Devl Bd, Singapore since 1960; engr, cons off of ind org, Amsterdam, 1922-26; stone quarry man, Kibbutz Migdal Zedek, Pal, 1926-27; engr, Minerva Motorcar Mfg Co, Antwerp, Belgium, 1927-28; engr, controller, Philips Glow-lamp Works, Eindhoven, Holland, 1928-38; chief engr, controller, Netherlands Railways, Utrecht, Holland, 1938-45; adv, Netherlands Treasury, head, org ser, Netherlands Govt, 1945-47; vice-pres, Pal Corp Inves Co and Union Bank of Isr, both 1947-50. Netherlands Army. Princ contribs: design and introduction of budgeting and costing sys, inventory control, org theory to industry and govts. Fmr, pres Netherlands Zion Students Org, 1920-21; mem, bd, Netherlands Zion Org, 1930-36; head, tech, educ dept, Netherlands Hachshara, 1930-40. Mem, Netherlands Royal Inst of Engrs. Home: 27 Yefe Nof St, Haifa, Isr. Office: POB 1717, Haifa, Isr.

CAHMAN, Werner U, US, sociologist; b. Munich, Ger, Sep 30, 1902; s. Sigwart and Hedwig (Schuelein); in US since 1940; BA, U Munich, 1925; PhD, 1927; postgrad studies, U Chgo, 1940-42; m. Gisella Levi, 1943; Prof sociol, Rutgers U; mem fac, New Sch for Social Research since 1963; chmn, Amer Comm for Dachau, since 1962; research asso, Inst for Welt-wirtschaft, U Kiel, 1929; exec secy, Cen Verein of Ger J, Munich, 1929-34; lectr, Fisk U, Nashville, Tenn, 1943-45; research asso, Natl JWB, 1946; media evaluation analyst, Voice of Amer, 1951-53; secy, Conf on J Studies, 1954-56;

visiting prof: Vanderbilt U; Atlanta U; Bklyn Coll; lectr, Yeshiva U, 1958-62. Mem: Amer Sociol Assn; E Sociol Soc; Population Soc of Amer; Amer Political Sci Assn; U Chgo Alumni Assn; J Info Bur, bd mem, since 1954; Inst for Medi-terranean Affairs, bd mem, since 1954; child guidance comm, and black J comm, FJP of NY since 1960; Park Ave Syn. Author: Der Oekonomische Pessimismus und das Ricardosche System, 1929; Die Duetsche Seifen-und Parfumerie-Industrie, 1931; Intermarriage and Jewish Life, 1963; Ferdinand Toemics on Pure and Applied Empirical Sociology, 1969; Jews and Gentiles, 1969; co-author: How Cities Grew, 1959-61; Sociology and History, 1964; contbr to books; Report on Palestine Refugees, 1958; Von Juden in Muenchen, 1959; Judentum in Geschichte und Gegenwart, 1964; profsl and J publs; asso ed, Reconstructionist, since 1956. Recipient: grand: Diamond Jubilee Fund, 1941; Julius Rosenwald Fund, 1943; Wenner Gren Found for Anthropological Research, 1948; award, Conf on J Material Claims Against Ger, 1955. Hobbies: swimming; mountain climbing. Home: 67-71 Yellowstone Blvd, Forest Hills, NY. Office: Rutgers U, Newark, NJ.

CAHN, Frances T, US, organization exec; b. SF, Cal, Feb 16, 1907; d. Meyer and Irma (Tricst); BA, Mills Coll, Cal, 1928, MA, U of Cal, 1930. Cons: Off, Comm of Wfr, HEW, 1963-64. Children's Bur, 1964-65, UNICEF since 1962, pres Comm on Juvenile Delinquency, 1961-62; mem: research staff, Bur Public Adm, U of Cal, 1930-37; asst prof, U Utah, 1937-38; tech adv, Bur Public Assistance, Social Security Bd, 1938-40; sr staff mem, Natl Resources Planning Bd, 1940-41; cons, comty resources, OPA, 1941-42, sr econ, eligibility for autmobile rationing, 1942-43, Off, Dep Admnr Rationing, prin econ, 1943-46; mem, div admn mgmt, Bur of Budget, 1946; sr mem, staff, Brookings Instn, 1947-48; Comm on Financing Higher Educ, 1949-51; exec assn, Fund for Advancement Educ, 1951-53; cons, bd Regents, SUNY, 1954-55, exec dir, Natl Council J Women, 1955-59; dir prog planning, White House Conf on Children and Youth, 1959-60; cons; HEW, Off of Spec Asst, Juvenile Delinquency, Off of Secy, 1961-62; Off Commn Wfr Dept, 1963-64; Child-ren's Bur, 1964-65; Pres' Juvenile Delinquency and Pres' Study Group on a Natl Service Corps, 1962-63; provisional course cons, Jr League of City of NY, 1965-66; full time cons, UNICEF and Div Social Devl, UN, 1967-69. Mem: Pres Comm on Employment of Physically Handicapped, 1956-59; bd dirs, Amer Immigration Conf, 1956-59; exec comm, wo-men's orgs, div, Natl JWB, 1956-59; Natl Comm on Literacy, 1957-59; house delgs, Council on Social Work Educ, 1959-60; mem: Amer Econ Assn; Natl Conf Social Wfr; AAUP, Natl Conf J Communal Service; Phi Beta Kappa. Author: Incidence of Juvenile Delinquency in Berkeley, 1930-32, pub 1934; Federal Employees in War and Peace, 1949; co-author, Welfare Activities of Federal, State and Local Governments in California, 1850-1934, pub 1936; contbr to fed govt and wfr periodicals. Home: 111 E 56 St, New York, NY.

CAHN, Joseph, US, surgeon; b. Hamburg, Ger, Nov 9, 1897; s. Davis and Nanny (Munk); in US since 1940; att Berlin U, 1918-19; MD, Hamburg U, 1923; m. Ann Horowitz, Oct 24, 1941. Clinical surg asst, Mt Vernon Hosp. Ger Army, 1916-19. F, Westchester Acad of Med; mem: NY State, Westchester Co, Mt Vernon Med Socs; B'nai B'rith. Recip-ient: Iron Cross; Hanseaten Cross. Hobby, photography. Home: 245 Langdon Ave, Mt Vernon, NY. Office: 245 E 4 St, Mt Vernon, NY.

CAHN, Judah, US, rabbi, educator; b. NYC, Dec 19, 1912; s. Samuel and Sadye (Rosenzweig); BS, NYU, 1933; MHL, ordained rabbi, HUC-JIR, 1939; MA, Columbia U, 1940; DD, Springfield Coll, 1953; m. Evelyn Baum, Oct 10, 1936; c: Steven, Victor. Rabbi, Metrop Syn of NY since 1959; fac mem, New Sch for Social Research since 1966; rabbi: Sinai Temple, Springfield, 1936-42; Temple Isr, Lawrence, NY, 1946-59; instr, govt, U of Mass, 1936-42; Hillel dir, Smith

Coll, and U of Mass, 1936-42; natl admnr, Hillel Found, 1942-46; visiting prof, Springfield Coll, 1953; instr, sch of educ, HUC-JIR, 1959-66. Natl vice-pres, NAACP, 1953-65; chmn: NY State Higher Educ Assistance Corp, dir, 1958; comm on public educ, NY Bd of Rabbis, 1968; comm on ME affairs, ADL, 1967; spec cons, NY State Educ Dept, 1964-68; mem: NY Bd of Rabbis; B'nai B'rith; CCAR. Home: 211 Central Park W, New York, NY. Study: 10 Park Ave, New York, NY.

CAHN, Ralf Bernard, Isr, dental surg; b. Cologne, Ger, May 22, 1924; s. Hugo and Paula (Markus); in Isr since 1934; DDS, U Geneva Switz, 1952; m. Erika Glunfeldt, May 13, 1965; d. Daphna. Head, Cleft Palate, Rambam Hosp, Haifa, since 1965. Maj Isr Navy. Prin contrib, found, head, only cleft palate treatment cen in ME. Mem: Isr Dent Assn; Yeorit Dent Health Cen, Haifa; Alpha Omega; Eur Orthodontic Soc. Hobby, golf. Home: 6 Ein Gedi St, Haifa, Isr. Office: Rambam Hosp, 4 Sha'ar Lebanon St, Haifa, Isr.

CAHN, Sammy, US, lyricist; b. NY, June 18, 1913; s. Abraham and Alice (Reiss); div; c: Steven, Laurie. Lyricist: Please Be Kind; I'll Walk Alone; Poor Little Rhode Island (official state song); It's Been a Long, Long Time; Love and Marriage; All the Way; Come Fly with Me; High Hopes, Pres Kennedy's campaign song; Call Me Irresponsible; My Kind of Town; Three Coins in a Fountain; It's a Woman's World; The Tender Trap; The Best of Everything; The Long Hot Summer; night club scores: Connie's Hot Chocolates Of 1936; New Grand Terrace Revue; Cotton Club Parade, 1939; Broadway stage scores include: High Button Shoes; Walking Happy; Skyscraper; scores for 22 motion pictures and many title and theme songs; fmr, violinist, vaudeville orch; co-org, with Saul Chaplin, dance band. Mem, ASCAP. Recipient: Emmy Award, for Love and Marriage, 1955; Acad Award for: Three Coins in the Fountain, 1954; All the Way, 1957; High Hopes, 1959; Call Me Irresponsible, 1963. Home: 704 N Canon Dr, Beverly Hills, Cal. Office: c/o Edward Traubner, 1901 Ave of the Stars, Los Angeles, Cal.

CAHNMANN, Hans J, US, chemist; b. Munich, Ger, Jan 27, 1906; s. Sigwart and Hedwig (Schulein); in US since 1941; licensed pharm, U Munich, 1930, PhD, chem, 1932; licensed food chem, 1933; m. Ruth Heilbronner, Sep 8, 1945; c: Catherine, Vivian, Stephen. Research chem, NIH, USPHS, since 1950; dir, research labs Crinex, Paris, 1936-39; research asst: Fr Public Health Service, 1939-40; U Aix-Marseille, 1940-41; dir, research devl, Biochem Products Corp, 1941-42; research asso, Mt Sinai Hosp, 1942-44; sr chem: Givauden-Delawanna, 1944-47; William R Warner, 1947-49. Mem: J Social Wfr Agcy; Amer Chem Soc; Fed Amer Sci. Contbr to profsl jours. Home: 5430 Beech Ave, Bethesda, MD. Office: NIH, Bethesda, Md.

CAINE, Leon J, US, merchant; b. Chgo, Ill, Nov 4, 1895; s. Jacob and Bessie (Gershkovitz); m. Hannah Etshokin, May 22, 1917; c: Lola Jaffee, Selma Marcus, Violet, Eugene, John. Steel merchant, Caine Steel Co since 1922. Mem, bd dirs, Michael Reese Hosp, since 1947; clubs: Standard, Bryn Mawr. Home: 505 N Lake Shore Dr, Chicago, Ill. Office: 730 N La Salle St, Chicago, Ill.

CAINE, Marco, Isr, urological surg; b. London, May 23, 1923; s. Theodore and Bella (Fedderman); in Isr since 1959; MB, MS, St Bartholomew's Hosp Med Sch, U London; FRCS; FACS; m. Deborah Binstock, Nov 25, 1945; c: Geoffrey, Stuart, Edward. Head, dept of urol, Hadassah U Hosp, Jerusalem, since 1959; asso prof urol, Heb U Med Sch, since 1965; sr surg registrar: St Paul's Hosp, 1950-51; N Middlesex Hosp, 1953-59; hon lectr, Inst of Urol, U London, 1956-59, all London. Pres, Isr Urol Soc; mem: bd and exec comm, Hechal Shlomo, Rel Cen, Jerusalem; several urol and surg assns. Co-author, The Ureter, 1967; ed, Urologia Internationalis; contbr, numerous sci publs in Isr, intl med jours. Hobbies: music, art, handicrafts. Home and office: 2 Hovevei Zion St, Jerusalem, Isr.

CAIS, Michael, Isr, chemist; b. Vaslui, Rum, Oct 10, 1924; s. Zvi and Rachel (Cohin); in Isr since 1941; BSc, Leeds U, 1950; DSc, Technion, Haifa, 1955; postdoc, Wayne U, Detroit; m. Judith Amidi, Dec 19, 1945; c: Daphne, Ruth. Prof, chem, Technion since 1958; research chem, Ethy Corp, Detroit, 1957-58; visiting prof, Cal Inst of Tech, 1965-66. Prin contribs: research in organo-metallic chem. Pres, Isr Chem Soc; chmn, Intl Conf on Coord Chem, 1967-68; mem:

Isr Natl Council for Research and Devl, Amer; Chem Soc, London. Author, Progress in Coordination Chemistry, 1968; ed bd: Inorganica Chimica Acta; Isr Jour of Chem; contbr to sci jours. Office: Technion, Haifa, Isr. Home: 21 Smolenskin St, Haifa, Isr.

CALAHORRA, Yizhak, Isr, architect, sculptor; b. I of Crete, Jan 1, 1910; s. Leon and Rachel (Constantin); desc Salomon Calahorra, king's phys, Cracow, 1600; in Isr since 1944; grad, Ecole des Beaux Arts, Paris; m. Miriam de Cazes, June 17, 1944; c: Arieh, Rachel, Elon. Prof, Inst Plastic Arts, Bat Yam, since 1960; Isr corres, Architectoniki, art rev, Athens, since 1959; mem, Isr Tech Assistance Mission, Govt of Mali, 1964-68; adv, visual arts, Town Planning Comm, Athens, 1938. Lt: Greek Army, 1940-41; IDF, 1948-49. Fmr gen secy, Greek Sculptors Inst; mem: comm, J Youth Assn, 1935-38; Isr Engrs and Architects Assn; cen comm, Isr Painters and Sculptors Assn; Greek Sculptors Assn; Soc Salon d'Automne, Paris; B'nai B'rith; Masons. Recipient: 1st, 2nd, 3rd prize, competition for liberation monument, Volos, Greece; 3rd prize, Hadassah Civic Cen competition, Jerusalem, 1955. Home and studio: 2 Anilewitz St, Bat Yam, Isr.

CALARASHO, Andrei, Isr, theater dir; b. Botosani, Rum, May 30, 1922; s. Zalman and Etty (Cheis) Gropper; in Isr since 1965; Dipl Dir, Inst Film and Drama, Bucharest, 1948; m. Olga Miskowic, Sep 8, 1946. Film, radio, theater, TV dir since 1948; dir, army theater, Bucharest, 1948-52; prof, Acad Film and Drama, 1950-60; dir of films, Bucharest, 1952-65 Mem: Acad Film and Theater Drama, Rum; Isr TV, Gen Fed of Lab in Isr. Author: films: Eagle 101, 1956; Hello, I Got Wrong Number, 1958; several features, numerous documentary films; appearances at film festivals in Japan, Venice. Home: 62 Rothschild Blvd, Petach Tikva, Isr. Office: TV House, Romema, Jerusalem, Isr.

CALLEN, Herbert B, US, scientist, educator; b. Phila, Pa, July 1, 1919; s. Abraham and Mildred (Goldfarb); BS, Temple U, 1941, MA, 1942; PhD, MIT, 1947; m. Sara Smith, Jan 21, 1945; c: Jill, Jed. Prof, physics, U Pa since 1948; cons, Univac div, Sperry Rand Corp since 1952; physicist: Kellex, Manhattan Project, 1944-45; Princeton U, 1945; research asso, MIT, 1947-48. Div councillor, F, Amer Phys Soc, 1966-70 mem, exec comm, div solid state physics, 1965-70; mem: and chmn, adv panel for physics, NSF, 1967-70; Amer Assn Physics Tchrs; AAUP; Sigma Xi; fmr: mem: and chmn adv comm, Natl Magnet Lab; magnetic sub-comm, Amer Inst Elec Engrs. Author, Thermodynamics, 1960; contbr to tech jours. Recipient, Naval Ordnance Devl Award, 1945. Home: 2136 St James Pl, Phildadelphia, Pa. Office: U of Pa, Philadelphia, Pa.

CALLMAN, Rudolf, US, attorney, author; b. Cologne, Ger, Sep 29, 1892; s. Max and Clara (Meyer); in US since 1936; LLD, U Freiburg, Ger, 1919; LLB, Harvard Law Sch, 1939; m. Maria Hess, Apr 20, 1919; c, Ellen. Pvt practice, specializing in unfair competition, trademark, copyrights and antitrust laws since 1943; fmr: pvt practice, Cologne, Ger, 1922-36; hon prof, U of Cologne, 1954. Pres, later chmn bd, Amer Fed J from Cen Eur Inc; vice-pres, mem, exec comm, Conf on J Material Claims Against Ger, since 1955; mem: exec, Leo Baeck Inst; Amer, NYC Bar Assns; Amer Assn Intl Law; NY Patent Law Assn; US Trade Mark Assn. Author: Unfair Competition and Trade Marks, 1929, 1932; The German Cartel Law, 1933; Unfair Competition and Trade Marks, 1st ed, 3 vols, 2nd ed, 5 vols, 1950, 3rd ed, 5 vols under title Unfair Competitions, Trade Marks and Monopolies, 1967; contbr to legal and econ periodicals. Home: 117-14 Union Turnpike, Kew Gardens, LI, NY. Office: 10 E 40th St, New York, NY.

CALVIN, Joseph K, US, physician; b. Chgo, Ill, Nov 24, 1895; s. Julius and Stella (Kaiser); BS, U Chgo, 1916; MD, 1918; m. Pauline Harris, June 9, 1926; c: Robert, Caryl Rubin. Sr att phys, Michael Reese Hosp since 1953; asst prof peds, U of Ill, 1926-38; intern, Cook Co Hosp, 1918, res, 1919-20, att phys, 1926-38. Pres: Chgo Ped Soc, 1935; ped sect, Ill Med Soc, 1933; mem: Ill, Chgo Med Socs; AMA; Amer Acad of Peds; Chgo Inst of Med; Phi Betta Kappa; Alpha Omega Alpha; Phi Delta Epsilon; KAM Temple. Contbr to textbooks, med jours. Home: 4800 Chicago Beach Dr, Chicago, Ill. Office: 1954 E 73 St, Chicago, Ill.

CANAAN, Gershon, US, architect; b. Berlin, Ger, Jan 19, 1917; s. Ernst and Hedwig (Davidson) Kortner; BA, Technion,

Haifa, 1938; MA, U Texas, 1952, BA, city planning, 1954; m. Doris Smith, May 23, 1954; c, Robert. Prin, architecture and planning, Dallas, since 1958; spec architectural adv US Public Housing Admn, since 1962; consul, Fed Rep Ger, since 1963; apprentice: Erick Mendelsohn, Isr, 1937; Frank Lloyd Wright, US, 1947; instr, architectural design, U Tex, 1950-51. Off, J Brigade, Brit Army, 1942-45; off, Hagana; capt, IDF, 1948-50. Prin contrib, memorial designs throughout US for 6 million J killed during Nazi Regime. First child of Henrietta Szold Youth Aliyah to Isr, 1934, Kibbutz Ein-Harod. Initiator, annual celebration, Ger Day in Tex, 1963; chmn, Tex-Ger Day Council, 1963-67; found, pres, Dallas Goethe Cen, 1964-67; Ambass of Goodwill, appd by Gov John Connally, Tex, 1965. mem: Amer Inst Architects; Soc Am Mil Engrs; Dallas Consular Corps; C of C; Soc of Architects, Tex. Author: Rebuilding the Land of Israel, 1954. Recipient: Afr, It, Pal, 1942-45 medal; Victory Medal; Campaign Stars; Volunteer and War of Independence medals, Isr; Presidential Citation, 1965; Superior Service Award for Public Housing; hon citizen of Tex and Dallas; Key to City. Home: 4700 St Johns Dr, Dallas, Texas. Office: 610 Simons Bldg, Dallas, Texas.

CANE, Melville, US, attorney; b. Plattsburgh, NY, Apr 15, 1879; s. Henry and Sophia (Goodman); AB, Columbia U, 1900, LLB, 1903; widower. Atty, Ernst, Cane, Berner & Gitlin, since 1905. Author, numerous vols of poetry and prose, pub 1926-68; contbr to legal and scholarly publs. Recipient, Medal for Excellence in Law and Lit, Columbia U, 1948. Home: 400 E 57 St, New York, NY. Office: 5 W 45 St, New York, NY.

CANTAROW, Abraham, US, biochemist, educator; b. Hartford, Conn, Jan 27, 1901; s. Joseph and Helen (Karp); att Tufts Coll, 1917-20; MD, Jefferson Med Coll, 1924; m. Elizabeth Stern, 1932; c, Ellen. Prof em, Jefferson Med Coll since 1966, prof, head biochem dept, 1945-66; fac mem since 1927; cons, bur of med and surg, USN Hosp, Phila, since 1948; biochem, Jefferson Hosp, 1932-45; asst phys, 1940-45. Mem: Amer Phys Soc; Assn for Cancer Research, pres, 1969; Endocrine Soc; Amer Pharm Soc; Soc Experimental Biol and Med; NY Acad Sci; Phila Coll Phys. Author: Calcium Metabolism, 1935; Lead Poisoning, 1945; Textbook of Biochemistry, 3rd ed, 1962; Clinical Biochemistry, 6th ed, 1962; contbr to sci jours. Home: 2939 Van Ness St NW, Washington, DC. Office: Natl Cancer Inst, Bethesda, Md.

CANTER, Albert M, US, artist; b. Norma, NJ, June 1, 1892; s. Louis and Edith (Levin); grad, Phila Mus Sch of Ind Art, 1914; att: Pa Acad Fine Arts, 1914-16; Acad Colarossi, Paris, 1924, 1929-32; Acad de la Grande Chaumière, Paris, 1929-32; Newark Tchrs Coll, 1942-44; Rutgers U, 1944; m. Florence Smith, June 21, 1925; c: Edith Traurig, Dorothy Kreitzberg, Howard. I/c, fine and ind arts dept, W Paterson Public Schs, W Paterson, NJ since 1955; partner, Canter & Bayha, Phila and NY, 1920-24; owner, Canteur Art Gals, 1927-29; studies in Paris and NY, 1929-40; art tchr, Orange HS, NJ, 1943-46; paintings exhbs at: Paris Salon; Acad Fine Arts, Vienna; Pa Acad Fine Arts; Phila Water Color Soc; Munic Art Gal; Montclair Mus; repr, Graphic Sketch Club; pvt collections. Co-found, Boys Sym Orch, Phila, 1911; now The Sym Club; F, Pa Acad Fine Arts; mem: Amer Acad Political and Social Sci; J Cen, W Orange; Masons. Recipient: vote of artists, most popular painting, Munic Gal, NYC, 1936; hon mention, Montclair Acad, NJ State exhb, 1936. Home and studio: 10 Dawson Ave, W Orange, NJ.

CANTER, Hyman, E, US, obstetrician, gynecologist; b. Lith, Mar 27, 1902; s. Solomon and Sara (Boyarski); Kanterowicz; in US since 1912 BS, W Va U, 1921; MD, Temple U, 1924; MS, U of Pa, 1929; m. Evelyn Weil Marks, Nov, 1958; c: Patricia, John. Sr obstet and gyn, Montefiore Hosp, Pittsburgh since 1934. Chmn: phys div, United J Fund, 1952-57; collections, Isr Bonds, 1953-58; rel ritual group, Beth Shalom, 1961-63; ZOA; f: found: Amer Coll of Obstets and Gyns; Amer Soc of Abdominal Surgs; Pittsburgh Obstet and Gyn Soc. Dipl: Amer Bd of Obstet and Gyn; Intl Coll: Surg; Obstetrics and Gynecology; mem, exec bd, Amer Phys f for IMA. Contbr to med jours. Home: 5700 Bunkerhill St, Pittsburgh, Pa. Office: 3600 Forbes Ave, Pittsburgh, Pa.

CANTOR, Alfred J, US, physician; b. Syracuse, NY, Mar 14, 1913; s. Abraham and Fanny (Sirlin); BA, Syracuse U, 1933, MD, Coll of Med, 1936; m. Eleanor Weschler, June 9, 1938; c: Pamela, Albert. Pvt practice, since 1936; dir research, Unitrol Inst for Research in Geriatrics; cons surg, proctology,

Jersey City Med Cen, 1957. Prin contribs: invented surg and diagnostic instruments; devised new oprs in proctology. Found and found pres, Intl Acad Proctology, 1947, intl secy-gen, since 1948; found and pres, Acad of Psychosomatic Med, 1954, presently, pres Em; found and dir, research in proctology, Intestinal Research Inst, since 1955; f, Amer Med Writers Assn, since 1953; mem: Natl Proctological Assn; Natl Gastroenterological Assn; Phi Beta Kappa; Phi Kappa Phi; Alpha Omega Alpha. Author: Ambulatory Proctology, 1946, 2nd ed, 1952; Cancer Can Be Cured, 1946; Painless Rectal Surgery, 1951; Handbook on Psychosomatic Medicine, 1951; Psychosomatic Aspects of Surgery, 1956; Immortality, 1958; How to Lose Weight the Doctor's Way, 1959; Unitrol, The Healing Magic of the Mind, 1965; Ridding Yourself of Psychosomatic Health Wreckers, 1965; Dr Cantor's Longevity Diet, 1967; ed-in-chief, Jour of Proctology, since 1950; contbr to med jours. Hobbies: magic, mind reading. Home: 96 Wildwood Rd, King's Point, Gt Neck, NY. Office: 147-41 Sandford Ave, Flushing, NY.

CANTOR, Arthur, US, producer, publicist; b. Boston, Mass, March 12, 1920; s. Samuel and Lillian (Landsman); m. Deborah Rosmarin, Nov 18, 1951; c: David, Jacqueline, Michael. Theatrical produc since 1959; pres: Advance Public Relations Inc since 1958; Entertainment Advt since 1951; producer: Broadway plays: The Tenth Man, 1959; All The Way Home, 1960; Gideon, 1961; A Thousand Clowns, 1962; Passion of Josef D, 1964; Trigon, 1965; World of Gunter Grass, 1966; The Concept, 1968; films: The Golden Age of Second Avenue, 1968; Tango, 1969; press rep, Playwrights, 1947-50. Lt, USAAF, 1942-46. Clubs: Harvard; Players. Home: 1 W 72 St, New York, NY. Office: 234 W 44 St, New York, NY.

CANTOR, Irving David, US, business exec; b. Bklyn, NY, Sep 28, 1912; s. Samuel and Jenny; att Bklyn Coll; m. Irma Mayer, June 4, 1947; c, Sharon. Pres, Cantor Bros Glass Corp since 1949. Sgt, USAF. Pres: United Glaziers of NY; Suffolk Co Shrine Club; Awixa Pond Art Cen; treas, Sunrise lodge, B'nai B'rith; chmn: UJA; Bay Shore Music for LI; dir: Bay Shore C of C; Auto Glass Dealers Assn; mem: Bay Shore J Cen; Bay Shore C of C; Masonic Lodge 1043; B'nai B'rith 2056; Royal Arch Penataguit chap; Kismet Shrine Temple; Bay Shore Elks; Grand Street Boys Assn; Bay Shore Lions Club; E Sportsmen's Club Inc; fmr: trustee, J Cen of Bay Shore. Recipient: leadership award: B'nai B'rith, 1957, 60; Awixa Pond Art Cen, 1964; State of Isr Bonds, 1963; Jt Defense Appeal, 1960; UJA, 1963. Spec interests: pr; performing arts. Home: 39 Bay Way, Bay Shore, NY. Office: 57 Park Ave, Bay Shore, NY.

CANTOR, Irwin, US, jurist; b. Chgo, Ill, June 20, 1924; s. Abraham and Sylvia (Katzman); BS, Bradley U, 1947; LLB, U of Ill, 1949, JD, 1949; m. Alena Kleiner, Dec 19, 1948; c: Michael, Garry, Kim. Judge, Superior Court of Maricopa Co, since 1963; staff mem, leg council, Ariz State Leg, 1955; chmn, Ariz Commn on Uniform Laws, 1959-63. Pres, Temple Sholom, 1957, 1958, 1960, bd trustees, 1955-64; vice-pres, B'nai B'rith, 1957; chmn, ADL, 1959-62; bd dirs Temple Beth Isr. Home: 1808 Palmcroft Way, NW, Phoenix, Ariz. Office: Maricopa Co Court House, Phoenix, Ariz.

CANTOR, James, US, insurance broker; b. Lawrence, Mass, Oct 28, 1906; s. Jacob and Bessie (Boches); BA, Brown U, 1939; m. Sara Kaplan, Jan 3, 1937; c: Judith, Ethan. Partner Cantor & Co since 1930; treas, Cantor Ins Agcy since 1942. Pres: Ins Brokers Assn of Mass; Assn Ins Agts, 1953-55; UJA, 1948-55; Heb Comty Cen, 1948-50; Temple Beth El, 1948-50; Pouzzner Lodge, B'nai B'rith, 1937-39; Brown U Club since 1958; Kiwanis, 1950; exec comm: ADL; AJComm; trustee, Lowell Instn for Savings; mem, Masons; Shriners; KP; MDRT. Home: 26 W View Rd, Lowell, Mass. Office: 174 Central St, Lowell, Mass.

CANTOR, Samuel C, US, attorney; b. Phila, Pa, Mar 11, 1919; s. Joseph and Miriam (Ginzberg); BSS, CCNY, 1940; JD, Columbia U, 1943; m. Dorothy Van Brink, Apr 9, 1943; c: Judith, Barabara. Vice-pres, gen counsel, Mutual Life Ins Co, NY since 1967, 2nd vice-pres, gen solicitor, 1964-66; NY State vice-pres, Amer Life Convention, since 1965; mem, Supt of Ins, special comm, holding co's, 1967-68; pres, Ins Fed of NY 1967-68; 1st deputy supt, ins, NY State, 1959-64; acting supt of ins, NY State, 1963-64; counsel, NY State Sen, 1949-59; asst dist atty, NY Co, 1943-48; counsel, NY State Sen, 1949-59; partner: Newcomb, Woolsey & Cantor, Esqs, 1952-55;

Newcomb & Cantor, Esqs, 1955-59. F, Amer Bar Found; lectr, Coll Ins, NYC; mem: Masons: B'nai B'rith; KP; NY State Dist Attys Assn; Amer, NY State Bar Assns; Bar Assn, NYC; Amer Judicature Soc; Club: Fairview Country. Home: Audubon Lane, Greenwich, Conn. Office: 1740 Broadway, New York, NY.

CANTOR, Shulamith L, Isr, educational admnr, nurse; b. Beirut, Leb, Mar 5, 1894; d. Aharon and Camila (Aboulafia) Yedid-Halevy; in Isr since 1918; tchrs cert, Amer Cert for Girls, 1914; RN, Amer U Sch of Nursing, 1918; both Beirut; att Columbia U, NY; m. Louis Cantor, June, 1920 (decd); c: Daniel, David, Judith Kerner. Ret since 1959; dir: nursing educ and service, Hadassah Med Org, 1934-48; nursing div, Isr Min of Health, 1948-57, chmn, Hadassah Luncheon Fund; Isr repr, Intl Council of Nurses; mem: bd dirs, WIZO, Jerusalem since 1962; fmr: exec comm, Heb Women's Org. Contbr on nursing to local and fgn press. Hobby, gardening. Home: 13 Palmach Rd, Jerusalem, Isr.

CANTOR, William, US, insurance exec; b. Haverhill, Mass, Dec 27, 1897; s. Jacob and Bessie (Boches); BA, Harvard U, 1920; hon D of Oratory, State Coll, 1950. Partner, Cantor & Co, since 1921; gen agent, The Fidelity Mutual Life Ins; chmn of bd, Cantor Inst Agcy. Pres, Mass State Chamber of Commerce, 1961-70; found; now hon life pres, Harvard-Radcliffe Hillel Found; Boston U Hillel House; dir, Camp Allen for the Blind; fmr pres, Cen NE Council, B'nai B'rith, past chmn, metrop Boston council, B'nai B'rith; mem, bd of dirs, NE regional bd ADL of B'nai B'rith; Combined J Appeal; J Vocational Service; adv comm, Boston State Tchrs Coll; found and pres, Kiwanis Founds of NE; pres: Lowell Kiwanis, Boston Kiwanis, gov, NE dist; fmr dir: Brandeis U Assn; TB & Health Assn; C of C Lowell; treas, Cambridge Cen for Adult Educ; hon life trustee and bd mem, Cathedral of the Pines, NH; established and endowed Jacob & Bessie Cantor scholarship with Harvard Club, Lowell; clubs: Brandeis U; Shriner; Harvard, Boston and Lowell. Home: 7 Francis Ave, Cambridge, Mass. Office: 126 State St, Boston, Mass.

CAPELL, Preston, US, business exec; b. Butte, Mont, Dec 1, 1901; s. Carl and Johanna (Rindsberger); BS, Northwestern U, 1924; m. Olive Owen, Oct 25, 1945 (decd). Pres, Preston Capell Co Inc since 1948; mayor of Nampa, 1951-57. Lt comdr, USN Res, WWII. Mem: bd dirs, fmr pres, Nampa C of C; Idaho comm, AJComm; chmn: Gov's Comm on Public Assistance; charities allocation comm, United Fund; fmr: Gov's appointee to Pres Comm on Aging; state chmn, Natl Found; Elks; B'nai B'rith, Boise, Idaho; club: Rotary. Home and office: 132 Davis Ave, Nampa, Idaho.

CAPELOUTO, Reuben, US, entomologist; b. Atlanta, Ga, Nov 7, 1920; s. Gabriel and Seignoru (Galanti); desc of Abram Galanti, leader in Turkish revolt of Sultan Hamid; BSA, U of Fla, 1947, MSA, 1949; m. Rachel Franco, May 28, 1953; c: Grant, Raymond, Carl, Sue. Pres, Capelouto Termite & Pest Control Inc since 1964; fac mem, Fla A & M. Pres, B'nai B'rith, Tallahassee; mem: Fla Pest Control Commn, 1963-66; Fla A & M; Scottish Rite Bodies; Shrine, Morocco. Home: 1114 Lothian Dr, Tallahassee, Fla. Office: 1933 Thomasville Rd, Tallahassee, Fla.

CAPLAN, Albert Joseph, US, university admnr; b. Phila, Pa, Feb 2, 1908; s. Joseph and Frances (Belber); BS, educ, Temple U, 1929, law deg, 1931; m. Sylvia Bayuk, Mar 13, 1932; c: Judith Gould, Jerome, Stephen. Dean, Charles Morris Price Sch of Advt and Journalism since 1966; partner: Bayuk Bros, Phila-Baltimore Stock Exch, 1944-51; Albert J Caplan and Co, 1951-60; pres, Charles A Taggert and Co, mem, NY Stock Exch, 1960-65. Specialist, USN, 1944-46. Dir: Cong Adath Jeshurun; Temple Beth Zion, Isr. Home: 135 19 St, Philadelphia, Pa. Office: 1319 Locust, Philadelphia, Pa.

CAPLAN, Fred Harry, US, justice; b. Clarksburg, W Va, Dec 3, 1914; s. Henry and Hannah (Seigelman); AB, W Va U, 1939; LLB, U Richmond, 1941; m. Miriam Kessler, Nov 12, 1941; c, Betty. Judge, W Va Supr Court of Appeals, since 1962; mem, W Va House Delgs, 1949, 1951; asst atty gen, State of W Va, 1953-61, chmn, Public Service Commn, State of W Va, 1961-62. Tech sgt, US Army, 1941-46. Vice-pres: U Richmond Law Sch Assn; B'nai B'rith, Charleston; treas, W Va Jud Assn; mem: W Va State Bar; W Va, Amer, Harrison Co Bar Assns; VFW; Moose Club; B'nai B'rith; fmr: pres: Exch Club, Clarksburg; Zionist Org, Clarksburg. Home:

4218 Noyes Ave, Charleston, W Va. Office: State Capitol, Charleston, W Va.

CAPLAN, Harry, US, educator; b. Hoag's Corner, NY, Jan 7, 1896; s. Jacob and Sarah (Tolchin); BA, Cornell U, 1916, MA, 1917, PhD, 1921. Prof em, Dept of Classics, Cornell U, since 1967, Goodwin Smith prof, 1941-67, on fac since 1919; visiting prof: U Wis, 1925; U Mich, 1932; Northwestern U, 1938; Stanford U, 1942, 1948, 1969; U Chgo, 1945; Columbia U, 1946; U Pittsburgh, 1967, 1968; U Wash, 1968; Brandeis U, 1968, 1969; U Minn, 1969. US Army, 1918-19. Pres, Amer Philol Assn, 1955; f: John Simon Guggenheim Memorial Found, 1928-29, 1956; Mediaeval Acad, Amer Cen for Advanced Studies, Wesleyan U, 1962-63; mem: AAUP; Ling Soc of Amer; MLA; Natl Assn Tchrs of Speech; Classical Assn, Eng and Wales; Renaissance Soc of Amer; Phi Beta Kappa, Delta Sigma Rho; Phi Delta Kappa; Phi Delta Phi; Phi Eta Sigma. Author and ed: A Late Mediaeval Tractate on Preaching, 1925; Gianfrancesco Pico della Mirandola on the Imagination, 1930; Mediaeval Artes Praedicandi, 1934; A Supplementary Hand List, 1936; Rhetorica ad Herennium, 1934; co-author: Pulpit Eloquence—English, 1955; Pulpit Eloquence—German, 1956; jt ed, Cornell Studies in Classical Philology, since 1930; asst ed, Quarterly Jour of Speech, 1923; contbr to profsl jours. Home: E Greenbush, NY. Office: 121 Goldwin Smith Hall, Ithaca, NY.

CAPLAN, Herman, US, business exec; b. Pittsburgh, Pa, Sept 10, 1896; s. Guttman and Rebecca (Blumberg); AB, cum laude, Harvard U, 1919; m. Jean Singer, May 30, 1922; c: Geraldyn Siegel, George. Pres, Grant Steel Corp since 1945. Ensign, USNR, 1917-19. Mem: Phi Beta Kappa; clubs: Concordia; Westmoreland Country. Home: 1447 Inverness St, Pittsburgh, Pa. Office: 1200 Keenan Bldg, Pittsburgh, Pa.

CAPLAN, Leslie, US, psychiatrist; b. Steubenville, O, Mar 8, 1908; s. Isaac and Ethel (Schochet); BA, O State U, 1933, MD, 1936; grad studies: U Mich, 1938-40; U Minn, 1946-49; m. Arline Steiner, Oct 12, 1947; c: Carol, Laura. Pvt practice since 1948; staff hosps: Mt Sinai; St Mary's; Fairview; Methodist; Glenwood Hills; asso clinical prof, U Minn; cons, Minn State Reformatory. Flight surg, USAAF, 1941-46. Contbr to mil books and med jours. Recipient: Seven Battle Stars, Legion of Merit, Purple Heart. Home: 5301 Newton Ave S, Minneapolis, Minn. Office: 1946 Med Arts Bldg, Minneapolis, Minn.

CAPLAN, Louis, US, attorney; b. Sep 15, 1886; s. David and Rachel; LLB, U Pittsburgh, 1912, hon LLD, 1966. Pvt practice since 1912; mem: firm, Sachs & Caplan, 1919-45; bd dirs: May, Stern & Co, Pittsburgh, since 1945; Commercial Bank & Trust since 1962; Ruben Furniture Co, McKeesport, Pa, since 1923. Lt, US Army, 1919-45. Hon pres, J M Gusky Heb Orphanage and Home, W Pa, since 1939 mem, bd dirs: AJComm since 1962; natl pres, 1961-62; Action Housing, Pittsburgh, since 1957; bd govs, HUC-JIR, 1949-69, hon mem for life since 1969; trustee: Pittsburgh United J Fed, pres, 1956-58; Leon Falk Family Trust; Lehman-Epstine Trust; dir, Pittsburgh Assn for Improvement of the Poor since 1947; pres, Louis J and Mary E Horowitz Found; mem: Amer, Pa, Allegheny Co Bar Assns; Third Circuit Jud Conf; Amer Law Inst. Recipient: award, NCCJ, 1953; Louis Caplan lectures in J Law established in his honor: U Pittsburgh Law Sch, 1942; HUC-JIR, 1966; annual Louis Caplan Hum Relations Award, Pittsburgh chap, AJComm. Home: Royal York Apts, 395 Bigelow Blvd, Pittsburgh, Pa. Office: Grant Bldg, Pittsburgh, Pa.

CAPLAN, Ruben, US, attorney; b. Baltimore, Md, Jan 19, 1908; s. William and Frieda (Applestein); JD, U of Md, 1927; BCS, Baltimore Coll of Commerce, 1932; m. Bessie Greenberg, Jan 27, 1935; c: Irvin, Jay. Att since 1929. Dir, Greenspring Valley Syn; city councilman, Baltimore City Council; past master, B'rith Sholom; fmr: chmn, bd, Shranei Tfizah Syn; dir: Histadrut; Zionist Org. Recipient: Pres Award, Union Orthodox Congs Assn, 1965. Home: 6306 Pimlico Rd, Baltimore, Md. Office: 218 E Lexington St, Baltimore, Md.

CAPLAN, Samuel, US, editor; b. Russ, Mar 10, 1895; s. David and Anne; in US since 1905; att U Pittsburgh, 1914-16; Columbia U Sch of Journalism, 1916-17; m. Hannah Levin, Sep 4, 1921; c: Joseph, Leonard. Ret; ed, Congress Weekly, NYC, from its founding, 1940-66; mgn ed, J World, Cleveland, 1920-22; ed; J Leader, Boston, 1923-25; New Pal, NY, 1934-40. US Army, 1917-19. Mem: ZOA; AJCong; Sons of Isr,

Woodmere. Author: The Great Jewish Books, 1953. Home: 237 Club Dr, Woodmere, NY.

CARAS, Roger Andrew, US, author; b. Methuen, Mass, May 24, 1928; s. Joseph and Bessie (Kasanoff); att Northeastern U, Boston: W Reserve U, Cleveland; AB, U of S Cal, 1954; m. Jill Langdon Barclay, May 9, 1954; c: Pamela, Barclay. Author, columnist, lectr, broadcaster, conservationist, naturalist since 1968; exec asst to vice-pres, Columbia Pictures Corp, 1954-1965; vice-pres; Polaris Products, NY; Hawk Films Ltd, London, both 1965-1968. Staff sgt, US Army, 1946-48, 1950-51. Author: Antarctica: Land of Frozen Time, 1962; Dangerous to Man, 1964: Wings of Gold, 1965; The Throwbacks, 1965; The Custer Wolf, 1966; Last Chance on Earth, 1966; North American Mammals, 1967; Sarang, 1968; Monarch of Deadman Bay, 1969; Panther! 1970; Source of the Thunder, 1970; nationally-syndicated column, Our Only World, Register and Tribune Syndicate; CBS radio show, Pets and Wildlife; lecture series under mgmt of Intl-Famous Agcy, Inc, NYC. Bd dirs: Fund for Animals; Humane Soc, US; f, Royal Soc of Arts, London; mem: Authors Guild; Authors League; Outdoor Writers Assn of Amer; Mensa. Hobbies: natural hist, exploration, photography. Home: 46 Fenmarsh Rd, E Hampton, NY. Office: 84-01 Main St. Kew Gardens, NY.

CARDIN, Benjamin Louis, US lawyer,; b. Baltimore, Md, May 10, 1943; s. Meyer and Dora (Green); BA, U Pittsburgh, 1964; JD, U of Md, 1967; m. Myrna Edelman, Nov 11, 1964; c: Michael, Deborah. Mem, House Delgs, State Leg, Md since 1967; pvt practice since 1967; mem, Govs Comm, Minimum Housing Standards. Mem: bd, Safety First Club, Md; JFK Dem Club; comm, JNF; ABA, Md Bar Assn; Jr Bar Assn; St Johns Lodge, Masons; clubs: Golden Eagle Sq and Compass Yedz Grotto. Home: 2509 Shelleydale Dr, Baltimore, Md. Office: 211 St Paul Pl, Baltimore, Md

CARDIN, Meyer M, US, jurist; b. Baltimore, Md, July 14, 1907; s. Harris and Anna (Cherry); LLD, U of Md, 1929; m. Dora Green, Dec 23, 1936; c: Howard, Benjamin. Judge, Supr Bench, Baltimore City, since 1961; mem, law firm, Cardin & Cardin, 1929-61; mem, Md House Delgs, 1935-39; chief police magistrate, traffic courts, 1957-58, both Baltimore. Pres, Benjamin Green Found; chmn, wfr comm, Yedz Grotto, since 1960, mem bd since 1941; fmr monarch; mem: comms on evidence and uniform laws for Fed Courts; Scottish Rite; Scottish Rite KCCH; bd, B'nai B'rith; fmr chmn: Isr Bond Dr High Holiday Campaign; Workmen's Compensation Commn, Md; Gov's Study on Workmen's Compensation; liaison comms: Employment Security Bd; Supr Bench Family Court for Bar Assn, Baltimore; bd mem, Tfiloth Cong, fmr pres, Brotherhood; finance comm, Beacon chap, Order E Star, fmr patron; fmr master, St Johns Lodge; clubs: Golden Eagle Sq and Compass, fmr pres; Mercantile. Recipient: Man of year: B'nai B'rith, 1963; Golden Eagle Sq and Compass, 1964; forest planted in Isr in hon Cardin family. Home: 6210 Park Heights Ave, Baltimore, Md. Office: Supr Court, Baltimore, Md.

CARELLI, Gabor P, US, opera singer; b. Budapest, Hung, Mar 20, 1915; s. Bela and Lenke (Deutsch) Krausz; in US since 1939; att Music Acad Franz Liszt, Budapest, 1934; DJ, U of Peter Pazmany, 1937. Soloist, tenor with Metrop Opera, since 1950; soloist: NBC Sym Orch under Toscanini; Dallas, Minneapolis Sym Orch under Dorati; appeared with: New Orleans Opera; Phila Opera; State Opera, Budapest; Opera House, Frankfurt; Isr Philharmonic Orch under Ferenc Fricsay, 1954, 1956; prof voice, Manhattan Sch of Music since 1964. Bd dir, Amer Guild of Musical Artists. Home: 41 W 86 St, New York, NY. Office: Metrop Opera Assn, New York, NY.

CARES, Reuben M, US, physician, laboratory dir; b. NYC, Aug 24, 1903; s. Ely and Dora (Moseyev); BS, CCNY, 1925; MD, LI Coll of Med, 1928; cert specialist in path, Amer Bd Path, 1941 and forensic med, 1960; m. Sylvia Marrow, Dec 25, 1933; c: Herbert, Arnold. Dir, labs, Kings Park State Hosp since 1949; Lakeside Hosp since 1952; asst clinical prof, NY Med Coll since 1956; cons path since 1953; dir labs, Harlem Valley St Hosp, 1946-48. Lt col, US Army, WWII. Pres, NY State Assn Public Health Labs, 1965-66; f, NY Acad of Med; depl, Natl Bd Med Examiners; Amer Bd Path; f, mem: AMA; Amer Assn Paths and Bact; Amer Soc Clinical Paths; Intl Assn Paths and Bact; Amer Soc Clinical Paths; Intl Assn Med Mus; Audio-Engr Soc; Suffolk Acad Med, secy bd, charter trustee; Assn Research in Nervous and Mental Dis-

eases; B'nai B'rith; fmr chmn ADL chap; Ed, Bull & Book of Suffolk Co Med Soc, 1953; contbr to med jours on path and lab subject and to audio-engr jours; Minkler's Path of Nervous System. Hobbies: audio elec, photography. Home: Cottage 2, Kings Park, NY. Office: Kings Park State Hosp, Kings Park, NY.

CARIN, Uri, Isr, attorney; b. Galicia, Pol, June 5, 1914; s. David and Adela (Kranzman) Stockhamer; in Isr since 1939; tchrs cert, Tchrs Sem, Lwow, Pol, 1936; MJur, Heb U, Jerusalem, 1954; m. Judith Bleiberg, Dec 26, 1946; c: Elinoar, Shulamith. Dep dir, econ dept, JA, since 1963, on missions abroad on behalf JA: Paris; Marseilles; London; Scandinavia. Irgun Zvai Leumi, 1946-48; J Brig, Brit Army; illegal immigration, Aliyah Bet. Mem, Freemasons Grand Lodge of Isr; fmr: dep dist cdr, Betar, Pol off, area command, Betar, Lwow; mem exec, Union of Zionist Revisionists. Established, ed, Chad Ness, monthly of Betar, Pol, 1937-38; corresp, Hamashkif, daily, 1946. Hobbies: hist, collection of silver miniatures. Home: 13 Hakeshet St, Jerusalem, Isr.

CARLEBACH, Felix, Eng, rabbi; b. Lubeck, Ger, Apr 15, 1911; s. Simson and Rosa (Graupe); ordained rabbi, U and Sem, Cologne, Ger; MA, U Manchester; m. Babette Kohn; c: Judith Klener, Sulamith Leon; Naomi. Rabbi and min, S Manchester Syn. Chaplain: to 2 J lord mayors, Manchester; J Blind Soc; pres, B'nai B'rith Lodge. Home: 5 Longton Ave, Manchester, Eng.

CARLIN, David R, US, lawyer; b. NYC, Dec 23, 1933; s. Mordecai and Mildred (Pepper); BA, Syracuse U, 1955; LLB, Bklyn Law Sch, 1958; DNF, Cambridge U, 1961; LLM, NYU, 1970; m. Judith; c: Montgomery, Alexander. Pvt practice since 1958. Lts since 1958-59. Mem: J Big Brother; Masons. Home: 320 Riverside Dr, New York, NY. Office: 401 Brodway, New York, NY.

CARLIN, Gabriel S, US, business exec, author; b. NYC, Mar 19, 1921; s. Samuel and Lena (Franco); BS, NYU, 1951; MBA, 1954; m. Rosalind Goldberg, Apr 17, 1943; c: Donald, Beverly. Sr vice pres, dir, Savin Business Machines Corp since 1964; dir, Automated Information Systems since 1969; Army-Navy purchasing coord, US Dept Defense, 1947-50; gen sales mgr, Old Town, 1950-60; gen mgr, Xerox, 1960-64. Lt, US Army, 1942-46. Mem, Natl Mgmt Assn. Author: The Power of Enthusiastic Selling, 1962; How to Motivate People and Persuade People, 1964. Hobbies: tennis, golf, travel. Home: 1807 Long Ridge Rd, Stamford, Conn. Office: 161 Sixth Ave, New York, NY.

CARLIN, Jack Raymond, US, business exec; b. NYC, Dec 28, 1924; s. Louis and Gussie (Rubin); BS, CCNY, 1945; m. Rhoda Klenetsky, June 25, 1947; c: Ira, David, Joseph, Daniel. Pres, research products div, Miles Labs, Inc, since 1966; dir, Miles-Yeda, since 1967; fmr: man dir, Miles Chems Isr; pres: Nuclear Ind; co-found: and pres, Atomic Assos; NE Nuclear; Atomic Personnel; Sharp Labs; Atomic Devl and Machine. Home: 1539 Springbrook Dr, Elkhart, Ind. Office: 1127 Myrtle St, Elkhart, Ind.

CARMEL, Shaul, Isr, author: b. Stefanesti-Botosani, Rum, July 6, 1937; s. Marcu and Mindla (Sapira) Croitoru; in Isr since 1965; m. Isabella Schonfeld, Aug 20, 1957; d. Francisca. Author: Journal de Front, 1967; Florile Nisipului, 1968; Drumuri Rascruci; Canalia. contbr of articles to Revista Mea weekly, Caef Pentru monthly; Mem, Menorah Home: 22/15 Arba Haartzot Rd, Holon, Isr. Office: 8 Haarbaa St. Tel Aviv, Isr.

CARMEL, Yosef, Isr, University admnr, army off; b. Odessa, Russ, Aug 1, 1924; s. Moshe and Zehava (Barakh) Kremer: desc of Haim Nahman Bialik; in Isr since 1925; studied law, econ; m. Sheila Selzer, Apr 17, 1950; c, Shai. Dir, PR Dept, Tel Aviv U since 1964; appd exec vice chmn, bd gov, Tel Aviv U, 1968; Military Aide de Camps to late pres of Isr, Yitzhak Ben Zvi, 1952-63; various missions to Far E; Burma, 1959; Afr, 1961; accompanied pres Ben Zvi to Liberia, 1963. Col, IDF since 1948. Author: With the Scattered in the East, Heb ed, 1960, later trans: Eng, Yiddish; A Trip to the Dispersed Brethren; Yitzhak Ben Zvi, 1967. Hobby: collector of bells. Home: 44 Hashoftim St, Tel Aviv, Isr. Office: Tel Aviv U, Ramat Aviv, Isr.

CARMELY, Harold W, US, organization exec; b. Wolkowysk, Pol, Jan 29, 1899; s. Jacob and Esther (Freeman) Weinstein;

in US since 1922; att, Yeshiva Lida, Pol; grad, Ger tchrs courses, Pol, 1917; m. Esther Tamarin, 1923; d. Naomi Jacobson. Admnr vice-pres, ZOA 1958-59, chmn, admn bd since 1960; hon vice-chmn and vice-pres, JNF since 1962; bd dirs, Bklyn JCC, since 1956; Bklyn Cabinet, UJA, since 1956; mem: presidium, Histadrut Ivrit, since 1960; gov council, WJC since 1960; actions comm, World Zionist Org; delg to Zionist Cong, 1961, 1964, 1968; vice-chmn, ZC, since 1963. Prin, Heb Schs, Pal, 1918-22; dir, KH, NYC, 1923-28; supt, Daughters of Isr Home and Hosp, NYC, 1928-32. Recipient, grove of 10,000 trees planted in Isr in his name by Zionist Org, 1960. Home: 93 Armour St, Long Beach, NY.

CARMI, Ady, Isr, advocate, journalist; b. Rum, Mar 4, 1933; s. Joseph and Clara (Abramovici); in Isr since 1950; MJ, Heb U, Jerusalem; m. Licu Markovitz; c: David, Michael. Contbr to: Viata Noastra, daily; Facla, weekly; Diplomatic Observer, monthly; L'Information d'Israel, daily; and Isr radio progs. Gen secy, Rum Olei in Isr. Home: 14 Schmuel Hanaghid St, Jerusalem, Isr. Office: 12 Shamai St, Jerusalem, Isr.

CARNOVSKY, Leon, US, educator; b. St Louis, Mo, Nov 28, 1903; s. Isaac and Jennie (Stillman); AB, with distinction, U of Mo, 1927; PhD, U Chgo, 1932; m. Marian Satterthwaite, Aug 25, 1939 (decd); m. 2nd, Ruth French, June 7, 1967. Prof, Grad Libr Sch, U of Chgo, since 1944, mem fac, since 1932; asst to libr, Wash U, 1928-29. Mem: Amer Libr Assn; Assn Amer Libr Schs; club, Quadrangle. Author: Library Service in a Suburban Area, 1936; A Metropolitan Library in Action, 1940; ed: Library Quarterly, 1943-61; The Medium-Sized Public Library, 1963; The Public Library in the Urban Setting, 1968; Library Networks: Promise and Performance, 1969. Recipient, Melvil Dewey Medal, 1962. Home: 5805 Dorchester Ave, Chicago, Ill. Office: U Chicago, Chicago, Ill.

CARO, Ernest F, Eng, business exec; b. Berlin, Ger, Apr 30, 1894; s. Israel and Rosa (Jaroczynski); m. Ella Littman, Oct 26, 1924; c: Gunter, Ingeborg. Mgn dir, Loretta Cigars Ltd since 1945; shirt mfr, Ger, 1922-38. Vice-chmn, Geulah Zionist Soc since 1949; vice-pres, JPA comm since 1952; mem, Bar Kochba J Sport Club since 1908, sport warden, Berlin, 1919-27. Home: 8 James Close, Woodlands, London NW11, Eng.

CARP, Bernard, US, social work exec. b. NYC, Nov 24, 1908; s. Morris and Minnie (Greenberg); BS, Tchrs Coll, Columbia U, 1930, MA, 1935, PhD, 1944; m. Helen Goldstein, Dec 23, 1932; c: David, Joel. Exec dir, JCC, Providence, RI since 1957; chmn, govs bd of registration of social workers, RI, 1966-69; mem: fac, Bklyn Ethical Culture Sch, 1930-35; Bklyn Coll, 1937; dir Troy JCC, 1937-39; Staten I JCC, 1939-41; staff, Natl JWB, 1941-57; music cons, natl USO, 1943; mem: ext staff, NY State Sch for Lab and Ind Relations, Cornell U, 1953-57; chmn, inst of liturgical music, Temple EmanuEl, NYC, 1948; recreation and group work execs, RI Council of Comty Service, 1959-60. Found, Natl J Music Council, 1944, pres, 1944-46; chmn, UN Fund Execs, 1962-64; mem: exec comm, Soc for Advancement of J Liturgical Music, 1944-46; ZOA, J Reconstructionist Found, Progressive Educ Assn; Amer Assn Group Workers; adult educ dept, NEA; Natl Assn Tchrs Speech; Kappa Delta Pi; Sinfonia Sigma Alpha Nu. Author: Personal Factors and a Speech Judgement, 1944; Jewish Themes for Discussion, 1944; Jewish Center Songster, 1950; Jewish Comty. Center Annual Meeting, 1954; Your Annual Meeting, 1955. Home: 16 Roberta Ave, Pawtucket, RI. Office: 170 Sessions St, Providence, RI.

CARP, Louis, US, surgeon; b. NYC, Mar 29, 1893; s. Isidor and Rose (Strassman); att CCNY, 1909-11; MD, Columbia U Coll of Phys and Surgs, 1915. Fac, Sch of Public Health and Admn Med, Columbia U; cons surg, Goldwater Memorial Hosp since 1956, visiting surg, 1939-54; Nyack Hosp since 1957; US Marine Hosp, Ellis I, NY since 1934; surg-in-chief, Good Samaritan Dispensary, 1919-24; att surg, Presbyterian Hosp, 1919-28; instr in surg, Columbia U, Coll Phys and Surgs, 1919-28; att surg and chief, surg clinic, Hosp for Jt Diseases, 1925-31; Hosp for Jt Diseases, 1928-39. Capt, MC, US Army, 1918-19, maj, med reserve corps, 1920-43, maj, MC, 1942; cons in surg and orthopedics, Armed Forces Induction Stations, 1942-47. Pres: Metrop Med Soc, 1924-26; secy, 1921-23; clinical soc, Hosp for Jt Diseases, 1930-31; f: Amer Coll Surg, mem, NY credentials comm; Acad Med in Surg; AMA, Amer Geriatric Soc; Gerontological Soc; dipl, Amer Bd of Surg; bd dirs: City Cen of Music and Drama, Inc; Men's

command adv council, Vets Music service; mem: bd visitors, Rockland State Hosp, since 1936, pres since 1952; mem: comm on admission, NY Acad Med, 1943-45, secy, 1944; secy, surg section, 1943, chmn, 1943-44; med bd, Riverside Hosp, 1926-46; comm on mem, NY Co Med Soc, 1939-60; adv council, Dept of Hosps, NY, 1936-44; NY Surg Soc; NY Soc for Thoracic Surg. ea Contribs to surgical jours; articles on music and natural hist to periodicals. Hobby, music. Home and office: 1016 Fifth Ave, New York, New York.

CARPI, Daniel, Isr, educator; b. Milan, It, Aug 3, 1926; s. Leone and Louisa (Modena); in Isr since 1945; BA, MA, PhD, Heb U, Jerusalem; postgrad studies, U Rome; m. Jehudith Treitel, May 5, 1950. Sr lectr, J hist, Tel Aviv U, dir, Inst for Zionist Research, in memory of Chaim Weizmann. Capt, IDF. Contbr of numerous articles to profsl publs. Home: 3 Pasternak St, Tel Aviv, Isr. Office: Tel Aviv U, Ramat Aviv, Isr.

CARROLL, Arthur, US, certified public acctnt; b. Phila, Pa, Apr 25, 1920; s. Samuel and Fannie (Creppa); BS, Temple U, 1947; m. Lorna Mandell, Dec 30, 1945; c: Phyllis, Sheryl, Larry, Ronald. CPA, sr partner, Arthur Carroll & Co since 1965; partner: C Henry Pols & Co, 1956-61; Winderman, Caplan & Carroll, 1961-65. Pvt, US Army. Pres, Cong Beth El Suburban; exec comm, JCRC, Main Line Br; bd educ comm on ethics, United Syn Amer; pres, Temple Bnai Aaron Men's Club, 1956-58; mem: B'nai B'rith; Amer Inst CPA's; Pa Inst CPA's. Home: 1725 Sue Ellen Dr, Havertown, Pa. Office: 2 Penn Center Plaza, Phildaelphia, Pa.

CARSON, Saul, US, journalist, author, lecturer; b. Russ, June 29, 1895; s. Meyer and Rose (Schliefer); in US since 1908; att U Mich, 1920-21, 1922-23; U Rochester, 1921-22; m. Bettina Dayna, 1937; c: Alfred, Herbert, Paul. UN corresp, Fairchild News Service and Fairchild Broadcast News, since 1968; columnist, UN Newsletter, since 1954; radio, TV script ed, documentarist since 1945; writer, produc, dir, "This is the UN, It's Actual Voices," 1950, 1955; Voices Toward Peace, documentary hist of the UN, 1960; reporter, feature writer, newspapers, Phila, 1923-34; mgn ed, The Thinker, Popular Biography, The American Short Story, 1929-31; PR dir, Bklyn Fed J Charities, Natl Assn of J Soc Work, 1934-38; ed, wfr publs, State of NY, Dept of Soc Wfr, 1938-40; writer, PM, 1940, contbr ed, Time Mag, 1943-44; on radio staff, Variety, 1944-47; columnist, New Republic, 1947-52; exec ed, Billboard Mag, 1950-52; radio, TV ed, The Compass, 1952, UN corresp, JTA, 1953-68. Author: Of Human Freedom, 1940; Return to the Roots, 1959; contbr to: The Thinker, Popular Biography; The Nation; The New Republic; Holiday. Mem: UN Corresps Assn; Amer Newspaper Guild. Home: 370 Riverside Dr, New York, NY. Office: Press Sect, UN, New York.

CARTER, Everett, US, educator; b. NYC, Apr 28, 1919; s. Ben and Myra (Rosenberg); BA, U of Cal, LA, 1939, MA, 1943, PhD, 1947; m. Cecile Doudna, June 29, 1940; c: Dale Timothy. Prof, Eng, U of Cal, Davis, since 1966; Fulbright lectr: U Copenhagen, 1954-55, 1961-62; U Strasbourg, 1966-67; visiting lectr, Harvard U, 1957-58; vice chancellor, 1959-63, spec asst to pres, 1963-64, U dean of research, 1964-66, all U of Cal, Davis. Mem: PMLA; ASCAP. Author: Howells and the Age of Realism, 1954; Harold Frederic's The Damnation of Theron Ware, 1960. Recipient: Commonwealth Medal for Non-Fiction, Commonwealth Club, Cal, 1955; Guggenheim F, 1961. Home: 734 Hawthorne St, Davis, Cal. Office: U of Cal, Davis, Cal.

CARTER, Victor M, US, business exec; b. Rostov, Russ, Aug 21, 1910; s. Mark and Fanya; in US since 1921; m. Andrea Zucker, July 15, 1923; c: Fawn Silverton. Chmn, bd, Isr Devl Corp; dir: Beneficial Standard Life Ins; United Cal Bank; Isr Cen Trade and Inves Co; Isr Corp; pres, bd chmn, Republic Corp, 1959-65; fmr pres: Gaffers & Sattler;, Pioneer Mfg Co. Regional chmn, US, World Econ Conf, Jerusalem; pres: J Fed Council, Gtr LA; United Way; Japan-Amer Soc, S Cal; Japanese Philharmonic Orch, LA; Victor M and Andrea Carter Found; vice-pres, dir, Greek Theatre Assn; dir: Cedars-Sinai Med Cen; City of Hope; LA C of C; LA World Affairs Council; Plastic Surg Found, Cal; Urban League; Vally Presbyterian Hosp; Young Musician's Found; Gtr LA Urban Coalition; LA Hillel Council; United Isr Appeal; mem, bd govs: Tel Aviv U; Heb U; Wfr Found, LA; mem, admnrs br, Acad Motion Pictures Arts and Sci; fmr: pres: City of Hope and Natl Med Cen; J Comm for Personal Service; LA Fire Commn; Braille Inst; chmn,

State of Isr Bonds, 1962-65; gen chmn; United Crusade, 1967; United J W JWF Campaign, 1961. Recipient: hon f, Heb U, Jerusalem; Shield of David award, State of Isr; Order Sacred Treasure, Emperor of Japan. Home: 10375 Wilshire Blvd, Los Angeles, Cal. Office: 7250 Franklin Ave, Los Angeles, Cal.

CASPI, Eliahu Shraga, Isr, physician; b. Ostrolenka, Pol, Dec 20, 1928; s. David and Sarah (Makovsky); in Isr since 1934; MD, magna cum laude, U Brussels, 1958; m. Zehava Stern, Sep 8, 1954; c: Arza, Jacob; Yael. Asst chief, obstet and gyn, Assaf Harofe Hosp since 1960; asst, Kaplan Hosp, 1958-60. Maj, MC, IDF. Mem: Assn Obstets and Gyns, Isr; Assn Sterility and Infertility, Isr. Author: Injury of Velamentous Vessels, 1962; Carcinoma of the Fallopian Tube, 1964. Home and Office: 22 Weizmann St, Tel Aviv, Isr.

CASPI, Elkana, Isr, business exec; b. Kibart, Lith, Apr 24, 1924; s. Yehuda and Shoshana (Greengrass); in Isr since 1925; Grad: Mgmt Sch, Technion, 1963; Harvard Bus Sch, 1969; m. Levana Matarasso, June 7, 1946; c: Elan, Oren. Mgn dir, Tadiran Isr Elect Indus Ltd, since 1959; mem, official govt, Isr mission to US, 1950-53, 1957-59. Maj, IDF, 1941-59. Home: 7 Emanuel Blvd, Tel Aviv, Isr. Office: 3 Derech-Hashalom St, Tel Aviv, Isr.

CASS, Millard, US, government official, attorney; b. Norfolk, Va, Nov 8, 1916; s. Sigismund and Ridia (Schreier); BS, U of Va, 1938, LLB, 1940. m. Ruth Marx, 1943; c: Sandra Burt, Ronald, Pamela. Dep Undersecy, US Dept of Lab, since 1955, on staff since 1946. Pvt practice, Portsmouth, Va, 1940-41; atty; SEC, 1941; NLRB, 1941-46, legal asst to Gen Counsel, 1945-46; chmn, mem, various depts lab and interagcy comms; mem, US Govt delgs, Intl Lab Confs, 1946-48, official observer, 1955; co-chmn, Natl Lab-Mgmt Manpower Policy Comm, since 1963. Pres, Montgomery Council of PTA's, 1962-64; mem, bd mgrs, Md Cong of Parents and Tchrs, 1962-64; mem, bd dirs: Montgomery Co Scholarship Fund, 1962-64; Intl Syn, John F Kennedy Airport, NY; pres, Wash Heb Cong since 1970; pres, Sligo Jr High Sch, PTA, 1959-61; mem: bd of eds, Va Law Review, 1938-40; Montgomery Co Curriculum Study Comm, 1960-61; Va State, Amer Bar Assns; Phi Beta Kappa; Omicron Delta Kappa; Order of the Coif; Raven Soc. Contbr to legal, labor, mgmt, govt publs. Recipient, awards: Arthur S Flemming, 1955; Dist Service, Dept of Lab, 1960; Rockefeller Public Service, 1966; Hornbook, Montgomery Co Assn; 1968. Hobbies: woodwork, writing. Home: 2103 Plyers Mill Rd, Silver Spring, Md. Office: Dept of Lab, Washington, DC.

CASS, Samuel, Can, rabbi; b. Toronto, Can, May 1, 1908; s. Aaron and Toba (Zeldin); BA, CCNY, 1929; ordained rabbi, JTSA, 1933, DHL, 1948; MSW, McGill, U, 1970; m. Annabel Goldfine, Dec 7, 1943; c, Ely. Rabbi: Beth Israel Cong, Vancouver, BC, 1933-41; Herzl Conservative Cong, Seattle, Wash, 1941-42; dir, B'nai B'rith Hillel Found, McGill U, 1946-67. Sr chaplain, maj, Can Army, 1942-46; hon chaplain, Dominion Command, Royal Can Legion since 1947; chaplain: Brig F Kirsch Br, No 97, Royal Can since 1947. Chaplain Assn JWU of Can, since 1968; Montreal metrop dist, Can Boy Scouts, 1951-67; natl chmn, youth, chalutziut comm, United ZC, Can, 1950-52; mem, youth,educ comm, Can Friends of Heb U, 1950-68; pres, Gt Montreal Bd of J Mins, 1951-53; chmn, rel wfr comm, Can J Cong 1951-53; mem: natl exec, ZOC, 1950-55; Natl Assn Hillel Dirs; RA since 1933; pres, Vancouver Lodge, B'nai B'rith, 1935-36. Home: 1520 McGregor Ave, Montreal, Can.

CASSEL, Curtis Emanuel, Rhodesia, rabbi; b. Opole, Ger, Nov 9, 1912; s. Emil and Paula (Levy); in Rhodesia, since 1957; ordained Rabbi, Hochschule fur die Wissenschaft des Judentums, Berlin, 1939; att Berlin, Breslau Us; m. Cecilia Witkowski, Aug 26, 1936; c: Charles, David. Rabbi, Bulawayo Progressive Cong, since 1957; 2nd min, W London Syn, since 1948; rabbi: Glasgow Progressive Syn, 1945-48; Frankfurt, 1936-39. S Sgt, Royal Pioneer Corps, 1940-45. Fmr pres, hon mem: 1st Lodge of Eng, Bn'ai B'rith; Soc for J Study; chmn, Afr Wfr Soc; vice chmn, Council for Adult Educ; exec mem: Cen Afr J Bd Deps; J Old Aged Home; hon secy, J Hist Soc of Eng; mem of council: Anglo J Assn; Citizens' Advice Bur; Council for Social Service; mem: bd trustee, Hum Trust; Rotary. Study: 104 Rhodes St, Bulawayo, S. Rhodesia. Home: 44 Weir Ave, Bulawayo, S. Rhodesia.

CASSIN, René Samuel, Fr, statesman, author; b. Bayonneè Oct 5, 1887; s. Henri and Gabrielle (Dreyfus); licencié ès,

lettres, 1908, DJur, Faculté de Droit, Paris, 1914; D, HC: Oxford U, 1945; Mainz, 1962; Heb U, Jerusalem, 1968; m. Simone Yzombard. Mem: Conseil Constitutionnel, since 1960; Institut de Fr, Academie des Scis Morales et Politiques, since 1947; barrister-at-law, Paris, 1909; lectr, Faculté de Droit, Aix, 1916; prof: Lille, 1920; Paris, 1929; Min of Justice and Educ, Fr War Govt, 1940-43; mem, consultative assembly, pres, judicial comm, Algiers, 1944; hon vice pres, Conseil d'Etat de France, 1949-60; Fr repr: hon, League of Nations, 1924-38; UN, 1946-51; UNESCO, 1945-62; War Crimes Commn, 1943-45; mem and pres, UN Commn on Hum Rights, since 1946, prin ed, Universal Declaration of Hum Rights adopted by UN Assembly, 1948; judge, past pres, Eur Court of Hum Rights, 1959. Pres: bd trustees, École Nationale d'Admn, since 1945; Alliance Israélite Universelle, since 1943; Consultative Council of J Org, since 1946; hon pres, Union Française des Anciens Combattants, since 1945; mem: Acad of Bologna; La Law Inst; fmr, pres: Intl Inst Admnr Scis; Soc of Comparative Leg. Author: L'Exception d'Inexécution dans les Contrats; Les Droits de l'Etat dans les Successions en Suisse, 1914; Le Domicile dans le Conflit des Lois, 1930; La Déclaration Universelle et la Mise en Oeuvre des Droits de l'Homme, 1951; Livre Jubilaire du Conseil d'Etat, 1952. Recipient: Nobel Peace Prize, 1968; Croix de Guerre, 1915; Médaille Militaire, 1918; Compagnon de la Libération, 1941; Officier de la Résistance, 1945; Grande Croix de la Légion d'Honneur, 1958. Home: 36 quai de Béthune, Paris, Fr. Office: Conseil Constitutionnel, Palais Royal, Paris, Fr.

CASSIRER, Eric, US, merchant; b. Breslau, Ger, Mar 26, 1917; s. Martın and Lisbeth (Lasker); m. Ilse Weinberg; c: Frank, Martin, Susanna. Pres: Automobile Exch, since 1948; Northwest Nash Inc, 1945-48. Pres, J Council, Ventura, 1953; chmn, UJA, five times; mem, ZOA. Author: Used Cars a Goldmine, 1956. Home: 1149 Church St, Ventura, Cal.

CASTEL, Calev, Isr, physician; b. Cuneo, It, June 18, 1914; s. Gustavo and Aurelia (Colombo) Castelbolognesi; in Isr since 1939; MD, U Padova, Milan; dipl, Acad Arts, Padova; m. Liana Polacco, 1939; c: Gad, Ora, Yael. Repr, JA missions to: N Afr, 1944-45, 1947-48; Cyprus, 1946. IDF: War of Independence, 1948; Sinai Campaign 1956. Mem: Med Org, Isr; Ped Org, Isr; Painters Assn, Isr. Author: Hakodosh, 1947; contbr to Isr and It jours; participant in painting exhbs. Home: Kibbutz Netzer Sereni, Isr.

CASTLEMAN, Benjamin, US, pathologist, educator; b. Everett, Mass, May 17, 1906; s. Samuel and Rose (Michaelson); BA, Harvard Coll, 1927; MD, Yale U Med Sch, 1931; hon MD, U of Goteburg, Swed, 1966; m. Anna Segal, Dec 22, 1935; c: Ruth Griffin, Jean Chase. Chief, dept path, Mass Gen Hosp, Boston, since 1953; path, Emerson Hosp, Concord, Mass, since 1941; cons path: Mass Ear and Eye Infirmary, since 1937; Boston Vets Hosp, since 1952; Memorial Hosp, Worcester, since 1952; prof path, Harvard Med Sch, since 1961; fmr: cons path, Cushing Vets Hosp, Framingham, Mass; instr, Tufts Med Sch. Dipl, Natl Bd Med Examiners; F, Amer Acad Arts and Scis; mem: Amer Assn Paths and Bacts; Intl Acad Path, past pres; Amer Soc Clinical Paths; NE Cancer Soc; Mass Med Soc; fmr: pres, NE Path Soc; secy, Boston Med Libr; chmn, NE regional comm, Coll of Amer Paths; club, Harvard, Boston. Ed, Case Records of Mass Gen Hosp, since 1943; mem ed bd, NE Jour of Med, since 1946; contbr to med jours. Home: 335 Marsh St, Belmont, Mass. Office: Mass General Hosp, Boston, Mass.

CATANE, Moshe, Isr, librarian, author, educator; b. Mulhouse, Fr, July 11, 1920; s. Alexandre and Marguerite (Meyer) Klein; in Isr since 1949; deg, archivist, paleographer, Ecole Nationale des Chartes, Paris, 1949; D, U Strasbourg, 1967; m. Shulamit Feist, Dec 21, 1941; c: Raphael, Esther Horowitz, Dina Klein, Myriam, Berouria, Siona, Bath-Sheva, Yoel, Ahinoam, Hananel, Tsouriel. Sr Libr, chief cataloguer, J Natl U Libr since 1956; sr lectr, Fr lit and civilization, Bar Ilan U since 1969; chief bibliographer, Heb Ency since 1966; lectr, Grad Libr Sch, Heb U, Jerusalem since 1960; pub column, Lettre de Jérusalem, Tribune Juive, Strasbourg since 1954; libr, Bibliothèque Nationale, Paris, 1946-49; tchr, interim dir, Alliance HS, Jerusalem, 1949-56. Author: Toledot ha-Yehudim (1900-50), 1956; Les Juifs dans le Monde, 1962. Mem: comm, Movement for Torah Judaism, ed, movement's periodical, Mahalekhim; fmr: chmn, Traditional J Youth, Fr; mem, Kiriat Sefer Ed Bd. Recipient, Palmes Académiques, Fr Govt, 1959. Spec interests: J liturgy, writing on J subjects.

Home: POB 864, Jerusalem, Isr. Office: J Natl and U Libr, Jerusalem, Isr.

CATARIVAS, David, Isr, diplomat; b. Istanbul, Turkey, Aug 10, 1921; s. Samuel and Claire (Jerusalmi); in Isr since 1950; Law (license) humanities, Sorbonne, 1942; Maimonides Coll, Paris, 1939; m. Hannah-Irene Schwabach, Dec 14, 1948; c: Tamar, Samuel; dep dir, div info, Min for Fgn Affairs since 1968; dir, Fr Bc, Isr Bc Sys, 1952-56; secy gen, ZF, Paris, 1956-58; counsellor, Isr Emb, Paris, 1958-63. Author: Israel, 1957; Les Juifs, 1963; Histoire de Jerusalem, 1965; corresp, Fr press; secy gen, World Union of J Students, 1947-49. Home: 5 Degania St, Jerusalem, Isr. Office: Min for Fgn Affairs, Jerusalem, Isr.

CATRAN, Joseph, Isr, attorney; b. Damascus, Syria, Jan 5, 1915; in Isr since 1934; educ, HS of Law and Econs, Tel Aviv; m. Rachel Bousaglo; 3 c. Mayor, Acre Munic; fmr, Town Clerk. Pres, Isr-Fr Assn; fmr, pres, Rotary, Acre. Contbr to press and lectr on munic topics. Recipient, UN F to Switz and Fr to study munic admn. Office: Acre Munic Bldg, Acre, Isr.

CATS, Chaim Itzhak, Isr, business exec; b. Antwerp, Belgium, Oct 27, 1910; s. Abraham and Rosa (Ginzberg); desc of Gaon of Vilna; in Isr since 1934; licencié ès sciences, Inst Supérieur de Commerce, Belgium, 1932; DEcon, U Strasbourg, Fr, 1934; m. Chana Mouschine, Apr 11, 1937; c: Rachel Friedman, Mordechai Friedman, Ora. Dep chmn, bd dirs, since 1968, mem mgmt bd, since 1956; Isr Elec Corp; guest lectr, Technion, Haifa, 1954-67. Prin contribs: planning of rate structure of electricity supply in Isr; planning Isr elec sys. Mem: Govt Sea-Water Conversion Commn; power and water comm, Isr AEC; Govt Control Commn on Restricted Bus Practices; bd, Isr Assn of Grads in Social Scis; fmr mem: AEC; Jt US-Isr Sea-Water Desalting and Power Team. Author, A Study of Price Indices in Palestine, 1939; contbr articles on econ and power econ to profsl jours. Home: 18 Freud St, Haifa, Isr. Office: Isr Elec Corp, Haifa, Isr.

CATSMAN, David P, US, attorney; b. Flint, Mich, Dec 12, 1910; s. Philip and Anna (Gittleman); BA, U Mich, 1933; m. Elinor Roth, June 25, 1941; c: Ellen Frieden, Julie. Pvt practice since 1937. Lt, USNR, 1943-45. Vice-pres: Gtr Miami J Fed; Sinai Hosp, Gtr Miami Inc; chmn: Peace Through Law Comm, Florida Bar Assn, Real Property Probate and Trust Law Sect, 1957-58, 1st chmn, Marketable Recording Title Act and Uniform Title Standards Comms; dir: J Family and Childrens Services, Gtr Miami; Temple Isr; clubs: Bayshore Exch, fmr pres: Westview Country, vice pres. Contbr to legal jours. Home: 250 E San Marine Dr, Miami Beach, Fla. Office: SE Second Ave, Miami, Fla.

CATZMAN, Frederick M, Can, attorney; b. Toronto, Jan 1, 1907; s. Oscar and Pauline (Shapiro); BA, U of Toronto, 1926; Barrister-at-Law, Osgoode Hall Law Sch, 1929; m. Irene Meyers, June 28, 1934; s. Marvin. Mem law firm, Catzman and Wahl, since 1939. Pres: B'nai B'rith lodge; Zionist Council; vice-pres, Beth Tzedec Cong, since 1952; chmn; jt pr comm, Can J Cong and B'nai B'rith, since 1950; bd govs, Goel Tzedec Cong, fmr: vice chmn, commercial law sect, Can Bar Assn; dir: Heb Free Loan Assn; Heb Free Sch; clubs: Lawyers; Primrose; Northwood Golf and Country. Author: The Bulk Sales Act of Ontario, 1950; The Personal Property Security Act, 1967. Recipient, Queen's Counsel, 1950. Home: 5 Forest Ridge Dr, Toronto, Can. Office: 133 Richmond St W, Toronto, Can.

CEDARBAUM, Bernard, US, attorney; b. New Haven, Conn, Sep 1, 1928; s. William and Elsie (Schuster); AB, Yale Coll, 1950; LLB, Harvard Law Sch, 1953; LLM, Yale Law Sch, 1966; m. Miriam Goldman, Aug 25, 1957; c: Daniel, Jonathan. Partner, law firm, Carter, Ledyard & Milburn, since 1965, mem fir, since 1959; atty, Dept of Justice, 1956-59. Cpl, US Army, 1953-55. Mem: Assn Bar, NYC: NY State Bar Assn; club, Town, Scarsdale, NY. Home: 125 Brewster Rd, Scarsdale, NY. Office: 2 Wall St, New York, NY.

CEDARBAUM, Israel, Isr, educator; b. Warsaw, Pol, Feb 4, 1910; s. Elias and Felicia (Spiro); MS, U Warsaw, 1930; dipl, EE, Inst of Tech, Warsaw, 1934; candidate, tech sci, Inst of Energy, Moscow, 1946; PhD, Imperial Coll, U London, 1956; m. Deborah Rosenzweig, June 13, 1937; c: Elana Elikedem, Yoram. Dean, Fac Elec Engr, Technion, since 1965, Carl Fechheimer Prof of Elec Engr since 1964, on fac

since 1963; leader, computer research group, sci dept, Isr Min of Defense, 1950-63; visting asso prof, Columbia U, 1960-61; visiting prof, U of Cal, Berkeley, 1961-62. Chmn: Isr sect, URSI; Isr sect, IRE, 1953; f, IEEE; mem: Assn Engrs and Architects, Isr; Assn Applied Geometry, Isr; NY Acad Sci; club, Tensor, Gt Brit. Author, numerous sci publs. Home: 8 Morad Hazamir, Mt Carmel, Haifa, Isr. Office: Technion, Haifa, Isr.

CEGLA, Wolf, Isr, business exec; b. June 24, 1919; DJ, studied intl law, Ger; Acad Intl Law, The Hague; m. Elga Cegla. Dir: J Cegla and Co Ltd; Olive Oil Factory. Mem exec, chmn, Overseas Mem Div, Mfrs Assn; past counselor, Rotary Intl for Isr, Iran, Turkey; past gov Rotary Dist, Isr; chmn: Cen Fodder Assn of Pal, 1942; ALIN, Isr Soc for Crippled Children; Mossad Abrahams. Author: Palestine's Wartime Fodder Control Scheme, 1945. Home: 24 Soutine St, Tel Aviv, Isr. Office: 25 Rothschild Blvd, Tel Aviv, Isr.

CELNIK, Max, US, librarian; b. Berlin, Ger, June 15, 1933; s. Leib and Gitla (Schnall); in US since 1939; BA, Bklyn Coll, 1955; BHL, JTSA, Coll J Studies, 1957; MLS, Rutgers U, 1956; m. Faith Caplan, Mar 25, 1958; c: Eliezer, Gershom. Mgn ed, libr cons, PCMI Libr Info Sys, Natl Cash Register Co, since 1969; asst prof, libr admn, Yeshiva U, since 1967, fac mem since 1957; libr cons: Crowell Collier MacMillan since 1966; FJP since 1965; chief libr, Cong Shearith Isr since 1956; research libr, NY Public Libr, 1956-57; libr cons: United Syn of Amer, 1959-60; Yeshiva U HS since 1961; org, yeshiva elementary, hs, syn and comty cen librs. Prin contrib: Celnik Libr Classification Sys of Judaica. Natl secy, Assn J Librs since 1967; vice-pres, Yeshiva U chap, AAUP, 1961-63; mem: Amer Coll and Research Librs Assn; Amer Libr Assn; FJP, NYC. Author: The Synagogue Library: organization and Administration, 1960; A Bibliography on Judaism and Jewish-Christian Relations, 1965; ed: Physician's Book Compendium, 1969; Jews in American Life, 1967-68, 1968-69; contbr to profsl and scholarly jours. Recipient: dist service award, 1965. Home: 2186 Cruger Ave, Bronx, NY. Office: 355 Lexington Ave, New York, NY.

CENTNER, Otto, Yugo, jurist; b. Brcko, Bosnia. Yugo, July 29, 1905; s. Samuel and Aurelia (Goldman); dipl, Fac of Law, Zagreb; m. Marta Druker. Judge, Supr Court of People's Rep of Croatia, pres, Criminal Council since 1954. Joined the partisans in 1943. Exec bd, Assn of Lawyers, sect for criminal law, People's Rep of Croatia since 1958; vice-pres, J Comty, Zagreb since 1959; pres, Old Age Home, Fed of J Comtys since 1962; fmr secy, J Academic Soc, Judea, and Fed J Youth Socs, Yugo; fmr ed, Hanoar, J youth periodical. Home: 239 Proleterskih Brigada, Zagreb, Yugo.

CEYTLIN, Uri, Isr, engineer; b. Warsaw, Pol, May 25, 1915; s. Akiba and Nechama (Rabkiewicz); in Isr since 1933; dipl, mech and teaching, Heb Tech Inst, Haifa, 1939; m. Ernestine Hellreich, May 1940; c: Ruth Beck, Jona. Dist engr, Haifa Public Works Dept, Min of Lab, since 1964; design engr, power sta dept, Pal Elec Corp Ltd, 1946-48; erection engr, Isr Shipyards, Haifa, 1962-64. Lt, Brit Army, ME Forces, 1939-46; lt col, IDF, 1948-61. Mem: Engrs Union; Royal Engrs Army Assn; asso mem, Amer Soc of Mech Engrs. Recipient: Desert-Star; It Star; 1939-48 Star; Defence Medal; Victory Medal, both by Brit Army; all IDF campaign ribbons. Hobby, racing car construction. Home: 101 Hatishbi St, Haifa, Isr. Office: 3, Carmel Ave, Haifa, Isr.

CHABCHAY, Marie Fr, museum curator; b. St Petersbourg, Russ, 1890; d. Lazar and Rachel Averbach (Biske); in Fr since 1927; dipl ès lettres, U St Petersbourg, Sch of Beaux Arts, 1915; m. Alexander Chabchay (decd), 1909. Curator of Musée d'Art Juif, Paris, since 1948; artist painter; libr for sci research, Russ Natl Libr, 1917-22; co-found, with late husband, First J Art Mus, Russ, 1914, (appropriated by Soviet govt); lectures on Hist and Hist of Art, Petrograd; several one-man shows; exhbs in Salons, group exhbs, Paris. Mem Assn des Artistes Juifs de Fr. Home: 18, rue Lally Tolendal, Paris 19, Fr. Office: 42, rue des Saules, Paris 18, Fr.

CHADABE, Solon Myle, US, attorney; b. Lith, June 2, 1903; s. Benjamin and Rebecca (Goldschmidt); in US since 1909; BSS, CCNY, 1924; LLB, Columbia U, 1927; m. Sylvia Cohen, June 6, 1931; c: Joel, Susan. Pvt practice since 1928. Mem: Bd Trial Lawyers Assn, NYC since 1958. Fmr pres: Benj N Cordozo Lodge, B'nai B'rith; Mens Club, Cong Emanu-El, NYC; Metrop Conf on Natl Fed Temple Brotherhoods;

chmn, Child Wfr and Activities Project; natl life mem comm, J Chautauqua Soc; bd, Stanley Safian Found; mem comm, Cong Emanu-El Mens Club; JGS; mem, Manhattan dist, Grand Lodge No 1, B'nai B'rith; dir: Youth Activities; regent, Schuyler Council Royal Arcanun, DD Grand Regent; master, Independent Lodge Masons, counsel, Merchant Marine Vet Found Export-Import div, Off of Price Stabilization; mem: bd, Natl Fed Temple Brotherhoods; natl vice-pres; NY Co Lawyers Assn; camp comm, Camp for Living Judaism; consistory, Mason, Shriner, Mecca Temple; clubs: Columbia; Good Fellowship, NYC, bd, fmr pres. Author: The Lodge of Tomorrow; Organizational Planning. Recipient: Outstanding B'nai B'rith Service Award; citations: US Treas Citation 1946, Pres Citation and Cong Medal for Service as Govt Appeal Agt, Selective Service Sys, 1941-1947. Home: 1025 Fifth Ave, New York, NY. Office: 342 Madison Ave, New York, NY.

CHAIKIN, Joseph, US, actor, director; b. Bklyn, NY, Sep 16, 1935; s. Abraham and Leah (Tikochinsky); att Drake U, Des Moines, Ia. Dir, Open Theater, since 1963; prof, New Sch; actor in Eur and US in leading roies of plays by Brecht, Beckett, Ionesco, Pirandello, others; dir: in Eur and US, including: The Serpent; America Hurrah; Sweeney Agonistes; Terminal Ward; Royal Shakespeare Co; lectr: Harvard; Columbia U; Yale U; Colgate U. Councellor, Resist-Support in Action. Contbr to drama reviews. Recipient: (4 times) Obie Award; Vernon Rice Award, 1969. Spec interest, sign lang for the deaf. Home: 15 E 12 St, New York, NY. Office: 402 E 10 St, New York, NY.

CHAIN, Sir Ernst Boris, Eng, educator, biochemist; b. Berlin, Ger, June 19, 1906; s. Michael and Margarete (Eisner); in Eng since 1933; MA (Oxon); DPhil (Berlin); PhD (Cambridge); DPhil (Oxon); D HC: U Liège, 1946; U Bordeaux, 1947; U Turin, 1954; U Paris, 1959; Albert Einstein Coll of Med, 1961; U La Plata, Arg; Montevideo, Uruguay; Brazil, 1962; Chgo, 1965; Yeshiva U, NY; Phila Coll of Pharm; m. Anne Beloff, 1948; three c. Prof, biochem, U London, Imperial Coll, since 1961; research, Sir William Dunn Sch of Path, Oxford, since 1935. Research: chem dept, Inst of Path, Charité Hosp, Berlin, 1930-33; Sch of Biochem, Cambridge, 1933-35; U demonstrator, lectr, chem path, U Oxford, 1936-48; sci dir, Intl Research Cen for Chem Microbiol, Istituto Superiore di Sanità, Rome, 1948-64. Prin contrib, initiated, jointly with Prof H W Florey, work on penicillin that led to the discovery of its curative properties. Hon f: Royal Coll of Phys; Inst of Biol; Weizmann Inst of Sci, Isr; Natl Inst Scis, India; Società Chimica Italiana; Microbiol Soc, Isr; Finnish Biochem Soc; Fitzwilliam Coll, Cambridge; FRS, 1949; FRSA, 1963. hon life mem, NY Acad Sci; hon mem, NY Acad Med; mem, Société Philomatique, Paris; mem corresp, Natl Acad of Med, Paris; Contbr to sci jours. Recipient: Nobel prize for Phys and Med, 1945; Harmsworth Memorial Fund, 1946; Berzelius medal in silver, Swed Med Soc, 1946; Pasteur medal, Institut Pasteur, Paris, 1946; Pasteur medal, Société de Chimie Biologique, 1946; Paul Ehrlich Centenary prize, 1954; Gold medal for Therapeutics, Worshipful Soc Apothecaries, London; Marotta medal; Carl Neuberg medal; Commandeur de la Légion d'Honneur; Grande Ufficiale al merito della Repubblica Italiana. Hobby, music. Office: Dept of Biochem, Imperial Coll of Sci, Imperial Institute Rd, London SW7, Eng.

CHAIT, Aaron, US, communal leader, author, editor; b. Stolpze, Pol, May 13, 1908; s. Abraham and Ziva (Inselbuch); in US since 1938; MJur, U Stefan Batory, Pol, 1936; m. Celia Rockove, Dec 1944; c: Herschel, Abraham. Dir pr, Bialy stoker Cen & Home for Aged since 1948, ed, Bialystoker Stimma; rabbi, Poale Agudath Isr, Bklyn, since 1960; weekly feature writer, columnist, Day-J Journal since 1939; part-time lectr, UJA; instr, Poale Agudath Isr, E Flatbush; fmr radio performer, Sta WEVD. Author: Sharfsin, J wit quiz book; Reizele dem Shochets; Two Worlds; Israel; Wizard Wheel, quiz game; Judaica, quiz game. PR dir, yeshivas and communal orgs; mem: RA; United Heb Comty, NYC. Spec interests: writing; public speaking; radio progs; artistic layouts. Home: 1662 Carroll St, Brooklyn, NY. Office: 228 E Broadway, New York, NY.

CHAIT, William, US, librarian; b. NYC, Dec 5, 1915; s. Max and Mollie (Miller); BA, Bklyn Coll, 1934; BLS, Pratt Inst, 1935; MS, Columbia U, 1938; m. Beatrice Faigelman, June 13, 1937; c: Edward. Dir, Dayton and Montgomery Co Public Libr, since 1956; asst br libr, Bklyn Public Libr, 1935-45;

chief, in-service training, personnel control, Milw Public Libr, 1946-48; dir, Kalamazoo Public Libr, 1948-56; visiting lectr: W Mich U; U of Ill; Kent State U; Fulbright prof, libr sci, U Teheran, Iran, 1969-70. Service command libr, US Army, 1945-46. Pres: Dayton City Beautiful Council, 1968-69; O Libr Assn; Public Libr Assn Amer; bd dir: Dayton Mus of Natural Hist, since 1958; NCCJ; Amer Libr Assn, since 1968; treas, Montgomery Co Hist Soc, since 1968; first vice-president, area council services, Comty Wfr Council, 1959-61; fmr pres: Cong B'nai Isr, 1953-55; Council of Social Agcys, Kalamazoo, 1954-55; Mich Libr Assn, 1955-56; mem: B'nai B'rith; Temple Isr; Beta Phi Mu; clubs: Kiwanis; Torch, pres; Dayton Discussion, pres, 1966-67. Hobbies sailing, gardening. Home: 2931 Ensley Ave, Dayton, Ohio Office 215 E 3 St, Dayton, Ohio.

CHAJES, Julius T, US, musician; b. Lwow, Pol, Dec 21, 1910; s. Josef and Valerie (Roth); in US since 1937; att: U of Vienna, 1929; Music Conservatory, Vienna; m. Annette Schoen, Mar 30, 1964; s. Jeffrey. Music dir, J Comty Cen since 1940; tchr, Wayne State U; head, piano dept, Beit Leviim, Tel Aviv, Isr, 1934-36. Co-chmn, Detroit Round Table for Catholics, J, Prot; mem: B'nai B'rith; Detroit Bohemians; Mich Tchrs Assn; Detroit Musicians' League. Composer of numerous compositions. Hobbies: chess, bridge. Home: 18014 Warrington, Detroit, Mich. Offices: 18100 Meyers, Detroit, Mich.

CHALEF, Rita, US, psychiatrist; b. NYC, July 7, 1925; d. Samuel and Beatrice (Berman) Mendelson; BA, NYU, 1945; MD, Women's Med Coll of Pa, 1950; m. Morton Chalef, 1950; c: Emily, Michael, Steven. Staff psycht, LI J Hosp, since 1959; adj att psycht, Hillside Hosp, Glen Oaks, NY, since 1959; cons, psycht, Deepdale Gen Hosp, since 1966; f, child psycht, Mt Sinai Hosp, 1955-56; res in psycht: St Elizabeths Hosp, Wash, DC, 1951-52; Perry Point VA Hosp, Md, 1952-53; Bklyn, NY, VA Hosp, 1953; cons: Pride of Judea Childrens Home, 1953-55; J Comty Services of LI, 1955-60; Merrick Sch Dist, Merrick, NY, 1957-62; psycht, Mh Clinic, Paterson, NJ, 1954-55; prof, Adelphi Coll, 1958-59. Pres, Women Phys, Nassau Co since 1960; program chmn, Merrick's Citizens Comm for Better Schs since 1960; chmn, comty aspects comm, Nassau Psycht Soc since 1961; mem: AMA; NY State Med and Nassau Med Socs; Amer Psycht Soc; LI J Hosp Staff Soc. Contbr to med and psycht jours. Home and office: 212 Robby Lane, Manhasset Hills, NY.

CHALFIN, Morris, US, business exec; b. NYC, Apr 18, 1918; s. Harry and Pauline (Kaminker); att St John U; m. Miriam Poltarack, Dec 27, 1941 (decd); c: Arlene Lite, Mitchell, Amy. Bus exec since 1942. Cpl, US Army, 1942-43. Mem: Gt Neck Syn; W Side J Cen; Garment Cen Cong; Beth Jacob Schs; Beth El J Cen of Flatbush; Childrens Day Nurseries, Jer; UJA; Masons. Home: 18 Locust Dr, Great Neck, NY. Office: 318 W 39 St, New York, NY.

CHALK, Roy O, US, business exec; b. London, Eng, June 7, 1907; s. Bennett and Sophie (Stem); in US since 1910; admitted, NY Bar, 1932; m. Claire, Dec. 24, 1931; c, Barbara. Pres, chmn bd, Transp Corp of Amer since 1945; pres, chmn bd: DC Transit Sys, Wash, DC; Trans Caribbean Airways; pres, chmn, Radio San Juan; Tele San Juan, Puerto Rico; ed, publisher: Wash, DC Examiner; El Diario La Prensa newspaper, NY; dir Wash DC Bd of Trade, 1957. Civilian cons, training divs, USN; USAF; cons, IAF, 1945-49; Found. Albert Einstein Coll of Med; Amer Korean Found, vice-chmn; Lincoln Cen, NYC; JTSA, mem exec comm; Independent Mil Air Transp Assn, US; mem, pres council: Georgetown U; Catholic U of Puerto Rico; bd trustees: Finch Coll; Eleanor Roosevelt Cancer Found; mem bd Coll of Virgin I; NCCJ; natl chmn, AJComm; chmn, finance comm, US Comm for UN. Recipient: award of merit, Bur of Aeronautics, USN, 1945; hon citizen, Govt of Korea, 1957; Natl Medal of Honor, Govt of Korea; achievement award, Advt Club, Wash, DC, 1958. Home. 1010 Fifth Avenue, New York, NY. Office: 714 Fifth Avenue, New York, NY.

CHALL, Jeanne S, US, educator; b. Pol, Jan 1, 1921; d. Hyman and Eva (Kreinik) Sternlicht; BBA, CCNY, 1941; PhD, 1952; m. Leo Chall, June 8, 1946; div. Prof educ, Harvard Grad Sch of Educ since 1965; asst Inst of Psych Research, Tchrs Coll, Columbia U, 1943-45; research asst to research asso and instr, bur of educ research, O State U, 1945-49; summer session fac: State Tchrs Coll, New Palz, NY, 1954-56; Teachers Coll, Columbia U, 1958, 1960; visiting asso prof Grad Sch of Educ, Harvard U, 1963; lectr to prof of educ,

CCNY, 1959-65. Chmn pre-conf insts 1958-61; bd dir: Intl Reading Assn 1961-64; Sociol Abstracts, Inc, 1962-64; pres, Natl Conf on Research in Eng, 1963; Natl adv comm, Dyslexia and related reading disorders, 1968-69, adv council, Title III, Commonwealth of Mass; chmn prog comm, Natl Assn for Remedial Tchrs 1955; f: Amer Psych Assn; AAAS; AAUP; Pi Lambda Theta; Beta Gamma Sigma; mem: NY Acad Sci; Amer Educ Research Asso; Natl Soc for Study of Educ, Author: Readability: An appraisal of Research and Application 1958; Learning to Read: The Great Debate, 1967; co-author, Dale-Chall Formula for Predicting Readability, 1948; Roswell-Chall Diagnostic Reading Test, 1956; contbr to profsl jours. Spec interest: psych and teaching of reading, research in communications and learning. Home: 1558 Massachusetts Ave, Cambridge, Mass. Office: 202 Larsen Hall Harvard U, Cambridge, Mass.

CHAMIEL, Haim Itzchak, Isr, educator, author, poet; b. Ostrolenka, Pol, Jan 18, 1917; s. Efraim and Bella (Ziman); in Isr since 1939; PhD, Heb U, Jerusalem, 1952; m. Hava Hertz; c: Efraim, Nira Daniel. Dir, dept for Torah educ and culture in the diaspora, WZO since 1953; lectr, educ, Bar Ilan U since 1968; tchr, youth leader Kfar Hanoar Hadati, 1939-44; ed, rel sect, Youth and Hechalutz Dept, WZO, 1956-59. Pvt, IDF, 1948-49. Prin contribs, org and devl of J educ in diaspora at all levels; series of pedg vols, "Mayanot". Exec mem, World Heb Union; bd dir, Hashomer Hadati, Author: Benofei Hayom, lyrics and poems, 1966; Poems of Samuel Ibn Sasson with commentary, 1962; 4 vols of poetry: MeOfek El Ofek, 1952; Avivim, 1958; Moked Venir, 1960; Nerot Bamoledet, 1966; Essays on Jewish Education. Recipient: Klausner Prize, Tel Aviv, 1950, Rudolph Kaplan and Rabbi Ashlag Prizes, Heb U, 1954. Spec interest: poetry, Bible research. Home: 7a Narkis St, Jerusalem, Isr. Office: JA, Jerusalem, Isr.

CHAMLIN, Max, US, physician; b. Loev, Russ, Dec 21, 1908; s. Jacob and Mary (Siegel); in US since 1910; BA, Columbia Coll, 1930; MD, NYU and Bellevue Med Coll, 1934; m. Jeanette Arzt, June 28, 1934; c: Matthew, Richard. Att ophth, Montefiore Hosp; cons ophth: NY Eye and Ear Infirmary; Bx VA Hosp; researcher in field of neurophth; prof and chmn dept, ophth, Albert Einstein Coll of Med, Yeshiva U, 1956-69. Contbr to med jours. Home: Oxford Rd, New Rochelle, NY. Office: 8 E 77 St, New York, NY.

CHAMPAGNE, Marian G, US, attorney, author; b. Schenectady, NY, Dec 17, 1915; d. Joseph and Rae (Greenberg) Grosberg; BA, Smith Coll, 1936; LLB, Albany Law Sch, Union U, 1955; JD, 1967; m. Herbert Champagne, Aug 18, 1940; c: Emily, Margot. Pvt practice since 1955; adv staff, LaSalle Inst, Chgo. Mem: NY Bar Assn; Authors' Guild; Writers' Alliance; Parents Without Partners; Alumnae Assn, Smith Coll; Alumni Assn, Albany Law Sch; Natl Council J Women; Temple Beth Emeth. Author: The Cauliflower Heart, 1944; Quimby and Son, 1962; Facing Life Alone, 1964, paperback, 1969; contbr of short stories to gen jours. Hobbies: collecting china, design needlework. Office: 199 S Allen St, Albany, NY.

CHANIN, Abe S, US, sports writer, publisher; b. NYC, Sep 19, 1921; s. Isadore and Anna (Jaffe); BS, U Ariz, 1947; m. Mildred Perelman, Aug 4, 1946; c: Beth. Publisher, ed: The Arizona Post, 1956-1966; Collegiate Baseball since 1957; sports ed, Arizona Daily Star since 1945. US Army, 1943-45. Pres: Natl Collegiate Baseball Writers Assn, 1961; Arizona Daily Star sportsmen's fund, since 1947; vice pres: J Comty Cen, 1958-60; mem, bd dirs, JCC, 1956-60; Cong Anshei Isr, 1957-58; dir, PR, CJA since 1956; Amer Assn Coll Baseball Coaches since 1956. Recipient, Awards: natl baseball writing, Amer Assn, Coll Baseball Coaches, 1950, 1951, 1954, 1955; Arizona Newspapers Assn, 1959-61; Silver baseball, Amer Assn Coll Baseball Coaches, 1962; Rockney Club of Amer service 1963. Home: 5625 E Ninth St, Tucscon, Ariz. Office: Box 12666, Tucson, Ariz.

CHANOFSKY, David Harry, US, rabbi; b. NYC, Feb 3, 1932; s. Alter and Becky (Malinowitz); BA, Yeshiva Coll, 1953; ordained rabbi, Rabbi Isaac Elchanan Theol Sem, 1956; m. Leah Emil, May 24, 1953; c: Dona, Jordan. Rabbi: Monsey J Cen since 1966; Cong of Bennington, Vt, 1956-58; Degel Isr Syn, Watertown, NY, 1958-61; Temple Isr, Riverhead, NY, 1961-66; student Rabbi, Jackson Hgts J Cen; Young Isr of Parkchester; Heb tchr; youth worker: Young Isr of Manhattan; Camp Deal for Boys; W End Country Club. Mem:

RabCA; NY Bd of Rabbis; Yeshiva U Rabb Alumni; Rotary; Suffolk Co Cmty Council; Heb Acad of Suffolk Co; found, mem bd dirs, educ bd, past pres, all E LI J Assns; bd of rel advs to LIU; volunteer dir, Hillel activities, Southampton Coll; civilian chaplain, Suffolk Co Air Base, Westhampton; trustee, LI Commn of Rabbis; fmr mem, bd dirs: Jefferson Co Mh Assn; Sr Citizens; Comm of Alcoholism; co-found, first sch for retarded children in Vt. Home: 20 Carlton Rd, Monsey, NY. Office: 101 Route 306, Monsey, NY.

CHANOVER, Hyman, US, rabbi, educator, author; b. Makow, Pol, Apr 19, 1920; s. Abraham and Anna (Certner); in US since 1921; tchrs diploma, Tchrs Inst, Yeshiva U, 1939; BA, summa cum laude, Yeshiva Coll, 1941; ordained rabbi, MHL, JTSA, 1945; MEd, Temple U, Phila, 1947; m. Alice Fischer, 1944; c: Leonard, David. Cons educ, NY FJP since 1969; dir: dept comty planning, Amer Assn for J Educ since 1966, dept comty service, 1964-66, dept personnel services, 1955-64; mem at-large, Natl Bd of License since 1964, comm for standards for tchr training since 1957, exec secy, 1955-57, 1959-64; rabbi: Cong Ahavath Isr, Oaklane, Phila, 1947-52; Temple Isr, Albany, NY, 1952-54. Prin contribs: devl: Tchrs Day Observance in US, natl pension plan for J and educ personnel, natl prins' cert prog for J schs. Research asso, AJComm, 1941-42; chmn, found, sch comm, United Syn, 1952-62; exec comm, Natl Council for J Educ since 1968, 1956-59, 1962-65; United Syn Commn on J Educ, 1952-61; comm tchrs educ, UAHC, 1966-68; at-large, natl council, Boy Scouts of Amer, 1941-47; Assn for Childhood Educ; Natl Conf J Communal Workers; RA. Author: Happy Hanukah Everybody, 1954; Planning for Threes to Eights in the Hebrew School, 1954; Blessed Event, 1956; My Book of Prayers, 2 vols, 1959; A Book of Prayer for Junior Congregations, 1959; A Curriculum Guide for the Kindergarten, 1960; Intensifying the Primary Program, 1962; A Haggadah for the School, 1964; Teaching the Haggadah, 1964; Jewish Education in Houston, 1968; Communal Allocations for Jewish Education (1936-66), 1968; Community Grants to Jewish Schools, 1969; ed, Our Teacher, 1958-63; ed, supervised, 22 comty studies of J educ since 1965 asso ed, The Synagogue School, 1954-61. Home: 5 Sylvester Pl, Lynbrook, NY. Office: Amer Assn for J Educ, 101 Fifth Ave, New York, NY.

CHAPIRO Marc, Switz, educator; b. St Petersburg, Russ, 1895; s. Dr Bernard and Isabella (Poliakoff); Licencie en Droit, U Geneva, 1917, PhD, 1941. Privatdozent, U Geneva, since 1958; mem staff, ILO, (BIT), Geneva, 1935-48; mem, ling services, WHO, (OMS), Geneva, 1948-57. Author: L'Illusion Comizue, 1940; La Révolution Originelle, 1958; Le Judaisme incompris, 1961; trans, Frères Karamazov, by Dostoievsky, 1946; other Russ novels. Mem: Société Romande de Philosophie; comm, Assn des anciens fonctionnaires intl; comm, B'nai B'rith Lodge, Henri Dunant. Home: 15 rue Marignac, Geneva, Switz.

CHAPLIN, George, US, newspaper ed; b. Columbia, SC, Apr 28, 1914; s. Morris and Netty (Brown); BS, Clemson Coll, SC, 1935; Nieman f, Harvard U, 1940-41; m. Esta Solomon, Jan 26, 1937; c: Stephen, Jerry. Ed, Honolulu Advertiser, Hawaii since 1959; city ed, Greenville, SC, Piedmont, 1936-41; mgn ed: Camden, NJ Courier Post, 1946-48; San Diego Jour, 1948-49; New Orleans Item, 1949-50, ed, 1950-58. US Army, 1942-46, off i/c Stars and Stripes, Mid-pacific Ed, 1944-45. Mem bd of dirs: Pacific and Asian Affairs Council; Honolulu Sym Soc; Hawaii JWB; mem, Temple Emanuel; club, Pacific Honolulu. Recipient, Star of Solidarity, It Govt, 1952. Home: 4437 Kolohala St, Honolulu, Hawaii. Office: Honolulu Advertiser, Honolulu, Hawaii.

CHAPMAN, Arieh Cyril, Isr, government official; b. Bristol, Eng, Apr 6, 1925; s. Lawrence and Claire Levy (Reed); in Isr since 1954; m. Hannah Freund, June 6, 1956; c: Joab, Daphne. Dep dir, tourist sect, Bur for Promotion of Aliyah Projects since 1968; fmr: dir, JPA, Manchester; secy, Zionist Cen Council, 1965-68; Eng absorption dept, JA, 1962-65; dir, Aliyah Dept, NE, 1960-62. Natl treas, Hitachdut Olei Britannia, past secy; secy gen, Achdut 1965-68. Home: 3 Schlesinger St, Tel Aviv, Isr. Office: 70 Ibn Gvirol St, Tel Aviv, Isr.

CHAPMAN, Bernard M, US, surgeon, author; b. Chgo, Ill, Jan 4, 1914; s. Mendel and Kate (Chapman); MD, U of Ill, 1937; m. Rose Glukman, Oct 15, 1939; c. Fern Pelton, Marcia. Pvt practice since 1947; att surg, Edgewater Hosp; asso surg, Chgo Med Sch; tumor cons, VA, 1947-53; path, Chgo Eye and Ear Hosp, 1953. Capt, US Army, MC, 1943-46.

Author: Massive Gastric Hemorrhage Associated With Aberrant Pancreas in Stomach, 1947; Dyserminoma of the Ovary, 1947; Subarachnoid Hemorrhage Secondary to a Tumor of the Hypophysis, 1948; Unusual Complications of Amebiasis, 1947; Modern Aids to Cancer Diagnosis for The General Practitioner, 1950; Cancer Diagnosis in a Small Community Hosp, 1950; Rectosigmoidal Polyps, 1951; Cytological Diagnosis of Rectal and Colon Conditions, 1959. F, Int Coll Surgs; dipl, Amer Bd Path, 1946; Amer Bd Abdominal Surg, 1960; mem: AMA, Chgo and Ill State Path Socs; Intl Soc Paths; AAAS; B'nai B'rith. Home: 6645 N Kimball Ave, Lincolnwood, Ill. Office: 5707 N Ashland Ave, Chicago, Ill.

CHAPMAN, Morris B, US, rabbi; b. NYC, Jan 27, 1909; s. Oscar and Esther (Amerling); BA, CCNY, 1929; BJP, JTSA, 1928, ordained rabbi, MHL, 1933, DHL, 1953, DD, hon, 1965; MA, Columbia U, 1938. Rabbi, Cong B'nai Isr, since 1947; Cong Beth Jacob Lewiston, 1933-35; Cliffside Park NJ Cong, 1937-39; Cong Emanu-El, Port Richmond, Staten I, 1939-41; J Cen, Merrick, 1941-42. Chaplain, US Army, 1942-47. Pres, SE region RA; dir: SE region, United Syn Amer, 1958-61, youth activities, 1953-58; exec bd, ARC; mem: Assn J Chaplains; Mil Chaplains Assn; Assn Fla Rabbis; JWV; ZOA; B'nai B'rith; Fla Conf Social Wfr. Home: 6020 Fifth Ave N, St Petersburg, Fla. Study: 301 59 St N, St Petersburg, Fla.

CHARASH, Uri, Isr, electronics engr; b. Tel Aviv, Isr, Dec 12, 1937; s. Menachem and Raya; BSc, Technion, Haifa, 1962. Head, research and devl group, Defense Min since 1966. Sgt, IAF, 1956-58. Recipient: Isr Defense Prize, 1968. Hobbies: photography, music, sailing. Home: 48 Shoshanat HaCarmel St, Haifa, Isr.

CHARGIN, Louis, US, physician; b. Minsk, Russ, May 1, 1880; s. Marcus and Mary (Turetzky); in US since 1891; MD, U of Med, 1902. Cons: dermat and syphilologist: Mt Sinai Hosp; Lebanon Hosp; Kingston Ave Hosp, Bklyn; venereal diseases, Dept of Health, NYC. Mem, Amer Dermat Assn; NY Soc for Inves Dermat; Acad of Med; AMA; Contbr, numerous papers to profsl jours. Home and office: 1 W 85 St, New York, NY.

CHARIFAI, Zaharira, Isr, actress, author; b. Tel Aviv, Isr, Dec 12, 1929; d. Chaim and Chana (Levintov); att Tel Aviv Drama Sch, 1951-53; m. Shlomo Schwartz (pen-name S Shva'), Oct 23, 1956; c. Aya. Main roles: Grousha, Brecht's Caucasian Chalk Circle, 1963 Venice Bienale; Mute Catherine, Mother Courage; Antigone, Sophocles' Antigone; Inez, Sartre's No Exit; Agafia Tichonovna, Gogol's Marriage. Palmach, IDF, 1946-50. Co-author, Nodedei Lail, 1965. Recipient, Klausner Award, 1964. Home and office: 14 Zekharya St, Tel Aviv, Isr.

CHARLOP, Zevulun, US, rabbi; b. Bx, NY, Dec 14, 1929; s. Jechiel and Ida (Schocher); BA, Yeshiva Coll, 1951; ordained rabbi, Yeshiva U, 1954; MA, Columbia U, 1959; m. Judith Rosner, Dec 27, 1954; c: Pesha, Rochelle, Anna, Shoshana, Zev, Alexander. Rabbi, Young Isr of Mosholu Pkwy, since 1954; instr Talmud, James Striar Sch, Yeshiva U; visiting lectr, Amer hist, Yeshiva U. Pres, Council Young Isr Rabbis; chaplain, Free Sons of Isr; dir, Amer Cancer Soc, NY comm; mem, RabCA. Fmr ed, Chavrusa, publ of Yeshiva U. Home: 3037 Bainbridge Ave, Bronx, NY. Study: 100 E 208th St, Bronx, NY.

CHARLTON, Israel Joseph, Eng, business exec; b. Sunderland, Eng, Mar 26, 1922; s. Morris and Rosie (Morris); att Bede Glammer Sch, Sunderland, m. Elaine Graham, Feb 7, 1950; c: Doreen, Jonathan, Marion. Chmn, mgn dir, M Charlton Ltd since 1964; secy, dir, M Charlton, 1946-67.Pres, Sunderland Chamber of Trade, 1956-58; chmn, N Region Fed of J Youth, 1949-51; treas, Sunderland Talmud Torah, 1961-63; secy: Sunderland Beth Hamedrash, 1963-66, Sunderland Bd of Shechita; Home: 6 Victoria Rd, Sunderland, Eng. Office: 6-9 Towans Rd, Sunderland, Eng.

CHARMATZ, Konrad, Brazil, publisher, editor; b. Ostrowiec, Pol, Dec 21, 1910; s. Majer and Esther (Waksman); att HS, Pol; m. Sara, Mar 12, 1950; c: Esther, Marlene. Owner, chief ed, O Novo Momento, newspaper, Sao Paulo, since 1964; ed newspapers: Notre Parole, Paris, 1945-46; Imprensa Israelita, Rio de Janeiro, 1947-1964. Mem: Organização Sionista Unificada; Federacão Israelita; Cong of J Culture.

Home: 1538 rua Bela Cintra, ap 21, Sao Paulo, Brazil. Office: 449 rua Julio Conceiçao, Sao Paulo, Brazil.

CHARNEY, Hanna K, US, educator; b. Vienna, Jan 8, 1931; d. Leopold and Frida (Wolf) Kurz; in US since 1948; AB, Hunter Coll, 1951; MA, Smith Coll, 1952; PhD, Columbia U, 1956; m. Maurice Charney, June 20, 1954; c: Leopold. Chmn, Fr Dept, Hunter Coll since 1967, prof, since 1969. Mem: MLA; AAUP; Amer Assn Tchrs, Fr: Société de Professeurs Français en Amerique; Phi Beta Kappa. Author: Le Scepticisme de Valéry, 1969; contbr to educl jours. Recipient: Shirley Farr F, Amer Assn U Women, 1960-61; Fulbright research grant to Fr, 1960-61; Home: 168 W 86 St, New York, NY. Office: Hunter Coll, 695 Park Ave, New York, NY.

CHARNEY, Maurice M, US, educator; b. Bklyn, NY, Jan 18, 1929; s. A Benjamin and Sadie (Stang); AB, magna cum laude, Harvard Coll, 1949; MA, Princeton U, 1951; PhD, 1952; m. Hanna Kurz, June 20, 1954. Prof Eng Rutgers U since 1967; instr, Hunter Coll, 1953-54; exch prof, Fulbright prog, U Bordeaux and Nancy, 1960-61. US Army, 1954-56. Mem: Malone Soc; MLA; Shakespeare Assn of Amer. Author: Shakespeare's Roman Plays, 1961; ed of Timon of Athens, 1965, and Julius Caesar, 1969; Style in Hamlet, 1969; Now to Read Shakespeare, 1970; contbr to lit jours. Home: 168 W 86 St, New York, NY. Office: Rutgers U, New Brunswick NJ.

CHARNY, Carmi (T Carmi), Isr, poet, translator; b. NYC, Dec 31, 1925; s. Bernard and Anna (Aichenbaum); in Isr since 1947; dipl, Tchrs' Inst, Yeshiva U, NYC, 1944; BA Columbia Grad Sch, 1946, Heb U, Jerusalem, 1951; m. Tamara Rikman; c: Gad (by previous m.), Daniel. Ed, children's sect, Am Oved Publ, since 1963; mem, repertoire comm, Habima, 1958-60; co-ed, children's sect, Sifriat Poalim, 1958-62. Capt, IAF, 1947-49. Author: Mum Vehalom, 1951; Ein Prahim Shehorim, 1953; Hayam Ha'Aharon, 1958; Nehash Hanehoshet, 1961, (Eng, Heb, Fr, Ger eds); Haunicorn Mistakel Bamar'a, 1967; Tvi'a, 1967; co-ed, The Modern Hebrew Poem Itself, 1965; trans: A Midsummer Night's Dream; Farquhar's Beaux' Stratagem; Sophocles' Antigone; Chritopher Fry's The First Born; Albee's Zoo Story; Behan's The Hostage; Osborne's Look Back in Anger; Brecht's Herr Puntila und sein Knecht Matt; Mechel de Ghelderode's Pantagleize; Master's Spoon River Anthology. Mem: Heb Writers Assn; ACUM. Recipient, Shlonsky Prize for Poetry, 1958. Home and office: 10 Aminadav St, Jerusalem, Isr.

CHARRY, Elias, US, rabbi; b. Bklyn, NY, Feb 4, 1906; s. Marim and Dora (Romm); BSS, CCNY, 1926; ordained rabbi, MHL, JTSA, 1930; m. Ruth Epstein Revsen, Dec 31, 1930; c: Marim, Adina, Dana. Rabbi: Germantown J Cen, since 1942; fmr: Indianapolis, Ind; Youngstown, O. Pres; Phila bd Rabbis; vice-pres, Phila ZOA, since 1944; O Valley Zionist Region, 1942; Gov Commn on Educ, Ind, 1938; chmn: United Syn Commn on J Educ, 1951-53; div, comty services, 1960-63; secy, RA, 1944; found, Akiba Heb Acad, 1947, chmn, educ comm, since 1949; bd dirs, Gratz Coll, since 1944; bd overseers, JTSA, 1948-51. Co-author: The Eternal People. Home: 6626 McCallum St, Philadelphia, Pa. Study: 400 W Ellet St, Philadelphia, Pa.

CHASE, Louis A, US, attorney; b. Pol, Mar 26, 1904; s. Morris and Fanny (Hillman); in US since 1905; LLB, Depaul U; m. Rose Steinpress, May 23, 1931; c: Michael, Judith Franzblau. Atty in Ill and Cal since 1926. Pres: Beaconsfield Club, 1933; Temple Emanuel of Beverly Hills, 1952-56; Pacific SW Council, UAHC, 1954-59; vice-pres, J Comty Found since 1966; vice-chmn, UAHC, 1959-63; treas, J Fed Council LA, 1957-59; bd dirs, J Fed Council; bd govs, Cedars-Sinai Med Cen; bd trustees, City of Hope; mem: AJComm; B'nai B'rith; club, Hillcrest Country. Home: 710 N Trenton Dr, Beverly Hills, Cal. Office: 9201 Wilshire Blvd, Beverly Hills, Cal.

CHASEN, Mignon C, US, psychiatrist; b. Moscow, Russ, Jan 5, 1911; d. Daniel and Anna-Chaya (Kissin) Charney; in US since 1938; MD; Royal U, Palermo, It, 1936; m. William Chasen, Apr 10, 1942; c: Barbara, Laura. Asst psycht: McLean Hosp, Waverly, Mass; Harvard Med Sch; Mass Gen Hosp, Boston; clinical instr, psycht, Tufts Med Sch; cons, Brockton VA Hosp, 1962-66; cons, Boston State Hosp; sr res, psycht, Boston VA Hosp, 1954-55; phys i/c child health sta, NYC Dept of Health, 1944-46. Dist councillor, Amer Psycht Assn since 1961, NE dist, 1965; dipl, Amer Bd Psycht and Neur; f, Amer Psycht Assn; mem: AMA; Mass Med Soc; Amer Group Psychotherapy Assn; Soc of Research in Psycht. Contbr to profsl jours. Spec interest: lit, art, swimming. Home and office: 111 Cedar St, Newton Center, Mass.

CHASEN, William H, US, physician; b. Augusta, Ger, May 3, 1907; s. Samuel and Leah (Alderstein); in US since 1913; MD, U Lausanne, 1937; m. Mignon Charney, Apr 10, 1942; c: Barbara, Laura. Chief, arthritis clinic, VA hosp, since 1947; chmn Research, Educ comm, 1966-69, clinical instr, med, Boston U Sch of Med, 1960; moderator, "Ask the Doctor" radio series, Station WBZ, Boston, 1958-61. Col, US Army Res MC, 1953-67. Chmn, Mh comm, Mass Acad of Gen Practice since 1958, pres, 1955-56; f, NY Acad Sci since 1966; mem: Govs Adv Council on Health and Task Force on Aging; med and sci comm, NE Arthritis and Rheumatism Found since 1954; MH comm, Mass Med Soc, 1961; natl surg, JWV, 1954-55; Amer Geriatrics Soc; Amer Rheumatism Assn; AMA; NE Rheumatism Soc; AAAS; Assn Mil Surgs; trustee, Mass Mh Cen, 1969; clubs: Rotary, Newton-Brighton, Brookline. Contbr to profsl jours. Recipient, Army Commendation Medal, US Army. Home: 111 Cedar St, Newton Center, Mass. Office: 17 Court St, Boston, Mass.

CHASIN, Simon T, US, dental surg; b. Phila, Pa, Nov 18, 1904; s. Charles and Anna (Radbill); DDS, Temple U, 1934: postgrad studies: Temple U; Amer Cancer Soc; m. Esther Chasan, Jan 28, 1928; d. Dianne Wenstrom. Pvt practice since 1934; Mfr, jewelry, David Hillerson, 1918-22; window decorator, Lit Bros, 1923-24; dir, spec projects, Frank & Seder, 1929-31; art student: Allen Lane Art Cen; Cheltenham Art Cen; Arlington Cultural Cen; Phila Mus of Art; one-man painting exhbs: Glenside Free Libr; W Phila Fed Saving & Loan Assn; participated in numerous group art exhbs. Pres, W Oak Lane Art League; chmn: educ comm, NW br, Phila div, Amer Cancer Soc, fmr sect leader, Crusade Campaign; dent comm, Friends of 50th Ward Comm Ambulance Assn: vol leader, hobby classes: Shallcross Sch; Stanton Childrens Sch; mem: Amer Dent Assn; Phila Co Dent Assn; clubs: W Oak Lane Lions; Limekiln Golf. Recipient: cert of merit for Dist Service in Public Wfr Activities; numerous certs and letters of appreciation from Wfr Assns. Home and office: 1847 E Washington Lane, Philadelphia, Pa.

CHASET, Nathan, US, urologist, surgeon; b. Providence, RI, May 7, 1911; s. Benjamin and Eva (Goldstein); PhB, Brown U, 1932; MA, Boston U, 1935, MD, 1936; m. Rosalind Kimball, May 15, 1941; c: Richard, Paul, Ellen. Chief, urol dept: Miriam Hosp, since 1946; Lying-In Hosp, since 1955; cons: RI Hosp; Roger Williams Hosp, VA Regional Off; VA Hosp, Davis Park. Maj, US Army MC, 1942-46. Pres, Providence Med Assn, 1969; dipl, Amer Bd Urol; f: Amer Coll Surgs; mem: RI Med Soc; AMA; Amer Urol Assn; Pan Amer Med Assn. Contbr to profsl jours. Recipient: official commendation, Govt of Iran, 1946. Home: 52 Emeline St, Providence, RI. Office: 105 Keene St, Providence, RI.

CHASINS, Abram, US, pianist, composer, author, radio music dir; b. NYC, Aug 17, 1903; s. Saul and Elizabeth (Hochstein); att, Columbia U, 1919-21; studied music at Juilliard Found, 1919-26; Curtis Inst of Music, 1926-29; m. Constance Keene, Apr 22, 1949. Ret, 1965; music dir, WQXR, radio stats of the NY Times, 1943-65; commentator, Sym Hall Series and others since 1943; debut in 1928, soloist with Phila Sym Orch in own First Piano Concerto; appeared in recitals and as soloist with leading orchs throughout US and Eur, 1927-47; radio artist, CBS and NBC, initiated Master Class of the Air, 1932-39; mem, Curtis Inst Fac, 1926-35; Berkshire Music Cen, Tanglewood, 1940-41; was first contemporary Amer composer to have works performed by Toscanini, 1931; his research findings are incorporated in sci and musical text books. Chmn, music juries judging performance and compositions for awards offered by: Leventritt Found; Naumburg Award; Natl Fed: NY Philharmonic Projects. Publ numerous works including: Three Chinese Pieces; Parade; Period Suite for Orchestra; two concertos. Author: Speaking of Pianists, 1957, 9th edition, 1962; The Van Cliburn Legend, 1958; The Appreciation of Music, 1966, contbr, NY Times Mag Ed Book Rev; natl mags. Mem: ASCAP; club: Bohemians; Manhattan Chess. Spec interests: research, chess, bridge. Office: 200 E 78 St, New York, NY.

CHASNOFF, Jack M, US, lawyer; b. St Louis, Mo, July 23, 1921; s. Jacob and Julia (Linenthal); att, U Chgo, 1938-41;

LLB, Wash U, St Louis, 1948; m. Alice Wides, Oct 11, 1942; c: Judith, Joseph, John. Pvt practice since 1947; partner, Tucker & Chasnoff, since 1950; secy, dir: Natl Chair & Furniture Co since 1960; Western Mfrs Bldg Co, since 1958; fmr: asso, Lowenhaupt, Waite, Chasnoff & Stolar, 1948-50; sec, Gen Aviation Supply Co, 1955-61. Lt, USNR, 1942-45. Mem: Amer, St Louis, Mo Bar Assns, Order of Coif. Recipient, DFC, Air Medal with gold star, lt, USNR, 1942-45. Home: 1 Paxton Lane, St Louis, Mo.

CHASNOFF, Jacob, US, lawyer; b. Mitchell, SD, June 21, 1883; s. Moses and Mary (Agrant); AB, U of Mo, 1903, MA, 1904; LLB, cum laude, Harvard Law School, 1909; m. Ally Linenthal, Apr 1, 1910, (decd); c. Jane Olmer, Josephine Webber, Jack, Jules. m. 2nd, Evelyn Cohn, Dec 31, 1954. Pvt practice since 1909; mem, firm Lowenhaupt, Mattingly, Chasnoff, Freeman & Holland since 1955; fmr: asso, Donald & Taylor, 1909-15; mem: Taylor & Chasnoff, 1915-18; Taylor, Chasnoff, Willson & Cunningham, 1941-43; Lowenhaupt, Waite, Chasnoff & Stolar, 1943-55; prof Law, St. Louis U, 1915-17; admitted to US Supr Court Bar, 1917; Sr Counsellor, Supr Court of Mo, since 1955; fmr pres, Voness Realty Co. Mem: Amer, Mo and St. Louis Bar Assns, Amer Judicature Soc; Harvard Law Sch Assn; life mem, B'nai B'rith; fmr: trustee, Cong Temple Isr; master, St. Louis Lodge 20, Masons; found, Menorah Soc, Harvard; mem, bd of ed, Harvard Law Review, 1907-08; clubs: Westwood Country, St. Louis Harvard. Home: 1129 Surrey Hills Dr, Richmond Heights, Mo. Office: 408 Olive St, St Louis, Mo.

CHASNOFF, Julius, US, physician, educator; b. NYC, July 25, 1902; s. Isaac and Pearl (Feinberg); BS, CCNY, 1922; MD, Cornell U, 1926; m. Nora Feder, July 18, 1933 (decd); 2nd m. Julia Warsh, Dec 30, 1968; c: Amy Finkston, Paul. Pvt internal med practice since 1930; asso clinical prof, med, NY Med Coll; cons in med, Metrop Hosp since 1968, staff since 1937; asso clinical prof, att phys, Flower & Fifth Ave Hosps since 1966; att phys, Beth Isr Hosp since 1961; instr, biol CCNY, 1923-40; phys to local draft bd, 1940-42; Beth Isr Hosp f; res, path, Stadt Krankenhaus am Urban, Berlin, 1929-30; med, Wenckebach Klinik, Vienna, 1930. Chief, med service, US Army Hosps, 1942-46; col, USAR, 1946-62. Depl, Amer Bd Internal Med; f: Amer Coll Phys; NY Acad Med; NY Diabetic Assn; mem: AMA; NY Acad of Sci; Assn Mil Surgs; US; Amer J Phys Comm; Phi Beta Kappa; Alpha Omega Alpha; Omega Pi Alpha; Phi Delta Epsilon. Contbr to med jours. Recipient: Army Commendation Ribbon. Home and office: 315 E 70 St, New York, NY.

CHASSLER, Seymour M, US, editor; b. Bklyn, NY, Nov 8, 1919; s. David and Henrietta (Becker); BA, NYU, 1941; MA, Columbia U, 1942: m. Natalie Goldfarb, Apr 2, 1943; c: Joseph, Philip, Deborah. Ed-in-chief, Redbook Mag since 1960; vice-pres, McCall Publ Co: asso ed, picture ed, Collier's Mag, 1950-55; ed-in-chief, Pageant Mag, 1955-60: ed, dir, This Week Mag, 1955-60. Mem, Amer Soc of Mag Eds. Home: 51 Villa Rd, Larchmont, NY. Office: 230 Park Ave, New York, NY.

CHAVEL, Charles B, US, rabbi; b. Ciechanow, Pol, July 14, 1906; s. Isaac and Feiga (Zaushnitz); in US since 1920; ordained rabbi, Heb Theol Coll, 1928; PhB, U of Chgo, 1928; MA, U Louisville, 1932, LLB, 1935; DHL, J U of Amer, Chgo, 1959; m. Florence Krasna, June 20, 1933; c: Cyrella Langer, Isaac. Rabbi: Cong Shaare Zedek since 1946; Cong Anshei Sfard, Louisville, 1924-45; fmr dir, syn activities, Union Orthodox J Congs of Amer. Mem: RabCA; Mizrachi Org; NY Bd Rabbis. Author: The Book of Divine Commandments of Maimonides, 1940; Sefer Ha-Chinuch, 1952; Perushei Haramban al Hatorah, 1959; Rambam, His Life and Teachings, 1960; Kitvei Harambam, 2 vols, 1936; The Commandments, 2 vols, 1967; Peirush Rabbenu Bachya al Hatorah, 3 vols, 1968; Kad Hakemach and all other smaller works, by Rabbenu Bachya, 1969; Chidushei Haramban to Tractate Abodah Zarah, 1969; ed, Hadorom, RabCA, since 1957; contbr to scholarly jours. Recipient, Harav Kook, City Tel Aviv, 1955. Home: 333 Beach 28 St, Edgemere, NY. Study: 3617 Edgemere Ave, Edgemere, NY.

CHAYEN, Joseph, Eng, biologist, researcher; b. Southend-on-Sea, Essex, Eng, Dec 25, 1924; s. Samuel and Rebecca; BSc, Imperial Coll, U London, 1948; att U Cambridge; PhD, U London, 1951; DSc, 1961; m. Sonja Beruh, 1953; c: Ann, Susan. Head, Cellular Biol Div, Kennedy Inst of Rheumatology, since 1966; Lillian May Coleman Research F, Royal Col of Surg, Eng, 1955-66. Prin contribs: chem and functional basis of disease; early diagnosis of cancer; causes of arthritis; cellular biophys and biochem micro-techniques. Co-author: Biophysical Technique, 1968; A Guide to Practical Histochemistry, 1969. Contbr numerous articles, chaps to jours and books. Home: 207 Western Rd, Leigh-on-Sea, Essex, Eng. Office: Kennedy Inst of Rheumatology, Bute Gdns, London, Eng.

CHAYEN, Mark, Isr, anaesthetist; b. Essex, Eng, Mar 3, 1916; s. Samuel and Rebecca (Yampolsky); in Isr since 1951; MB, BS, U Coll and Hosp, London, 1940; m. Lea Fuchs, c: David, Benjamin, Michal. Head, dept of anaesthesia and resuscitation, Tel Aviv Munic Hosp, since 1957; clinical asso prof, anaesthesia and resuscitation, Tel Aviv U since 1966. Capt, Brit Army; maj, IDF. F, Royal Soc of Med; mem: Isr Anaesthetist's Assn; IMA. Contbr, articles to Heb, Amer, Eng jours. Recipient: Mil Cross. Hobbies: sailing, camping. Home: 4 Hasulam St, Ramat Gan, Isr. Office: Tel Aviv Munic Hosp, Isr.

CHAYEN, Moses Jeremiah, Isr, educator; b. London, Eng, Nov 15, 1917; s. Samuel and Rebecca (Pomeranz); in Isr since 1947; BA, U London, 1939, PhD, 1969; m. Elvira Feldman, Dec, 1945; d. Naomi. Lectr: Heb U since 1965; Bar Ilan U since 1956; capt, Brit Army, 1940-46; capt, cdr Jerusalem Area, IDF, 1948-49. Mem: Ling Soc Amer; Intl Phonetics Assn. Author: Cours de Francais I, 1951; Cours de Francais II, 1952. Recipient: Fulbright Scholarship, MIT, 1963-64. Home: 4 Abarbanel St, Jerusalem, Isr. Office: Dept of Eng, Heb U, Jerusalem, Isr.

CHAYEN, Ralph, Isr, chemist; b. Southend-on-Sea, Eng, June 13, 1928; s. Samuel and Rebecca (Yampolsky); in Isr since 1964; BSc, ARCS, ARIC, Imperial Coll, London, 1952; PhD, DIC, 1955; FRIC, 1960; m. Edna Greenburgh, Dec 21, 1961; c: Samuel, Nurit. Head, endocrine lab, Ichilov Hosp since 1966; asso prof, chem, Bar Ilan U since 1968; lectr, U Coll, London, 1955-64; sr research biochem, Ichilov Hosp, 1964-66; visiting asso prof, Tel Aviv U, 1966-68. RAF, 1947-49. Mem: Biochem Soc; Royal Inst of Chem. Co-author, Modern Methods of Chemical Analysis. 1965; contbr to sci jours. Home: 4A Rehov Tor Hazahav, Herzlia, Isr. Office: Ichilov Hosp, Tel Aviv, Isr.

CHAYES, Abram, US, attorney, educator; b. Chgo, Ill, Jul 18, 1922; s. Edward and Kitty (Torch); AB, Harvard Coll, 1943, LLB, 1949; m. Antonia Handler, Dec 24, 1947; c: Eva Abigail, Lincoln, Sarah, Angelica. Prof, law, Harvard U since 1965; asst prof on fac since 1955; legal aid to Gov of Conn, 1949-50; asst gen counsel, US Pres Materials Policy Comm, 1950-51; law clerk, US Supr Court, 1951-52; asso atty, Covington and Burling, 1952-55; legal adv, Dept of State, 1961-64. US Army, 1943-46. Pres, Harvard Law Rev, 1949; mem Phi Beta Kappa; Amer Acad Arts and Scis. Co-author, International Legal Process, 1968; contbr to legal jours and books. Home: 3 Hubbard Park, Cambridge, Mass. Office: Harvard Law Sch, Cambridge, Mass.

CHAZANOF, William, US, educator; b. NYC, Aug 23, 1915; s. Morris and Sarah (Gold); BS, Albany Coll, NYU, 1938; MA, Columbia U, 1941; PhD, Syracuse U, 1955; m. Helen Wohl, June 22, 1941; c: Esther, Shifra, Jansen, Allen. Prof host, SUNY since 1959, fac mem since 1948. USAF, 1942-45. Chmn, Taxpayer's Party, 1957-59; pres; Temple Beth El, 1964-66, fmr chmn rel educ comm, vice-pres, 1955-58; Coll Instr Council; Amer Coll Assn for U Profs, Fredonia chap, 1955; dir, Fac Assn, SUNY, 1959-62; mem: Village Planning Bd since 1958; AAUP; Amer, Mass Valley Hist Assns; Natl Council for Social Studies. Contbr to profsl jours. Recipient: Five bronze stars, WWII. Home: 41 Cottage St, Fredonia, NY. Office: SUNY, Fredonia, NY.

CHAZEN, Bernard, US, attorney; b. NYC, Sep 14, 1923; s. Nathan and Esther (Sandberg); LLB, Columbia U, 1948; LLM, Rutgers U, 1951; m. Bernice Bassewitz, Feb 21, 1954; c: David, Jonathan, Sarah. Attorney, partner, Baker, Garber, Chazen and Duffy since 1954. Cdr, USNR, 1964-67. Pres: Bd of Educ, City of Englewood, 1965-69, bd mem since 1964; chmn: NJ State Bar Assn, Citizens' Conf or NJ Courts, 1970; leg action comm, NJ State Bar Assn, fmr chmn, intl and comparative law comm; trustee, NJ YMHA-YWHA Camps; mem: Amer, Hudson Co Bar Assns; Temple Emanu-El; Amer Soc of Intl Law; Natl Assn of Claimants Compensation Atts; Maritime Law Assn of the US. Home: 331 Starling Rd, Englewood, NJ. Office: 1 Newark St, Hoboken, NJ.

CHAZIN, Maurice, US, educator; b. LI City, NY, Apr 12, 1905; s. Aron and Lena (Rothberg); BS, NYU, 1926, MA, 1926; PhD, Johns Hopkins U, 1929; m. Mary Berry, Dec 22, 1931; c: Joel, Judith. Prof romance langs, Queens Coll, since 1952, chmn dept, 1938-52; Johnston Scholar, Johns Hopkins U, 1926-29, 1931-32; lectr, Columbia U, 1932-37; instr, CCNY, 1934-38. Mem: Phi Beta Kappa; AAUP; MLA; Comparative Lit Assn of Amer; mem: exec comm, Amer Assn of Tchrs of Fr; comm on higher educ, UJA; educ comm, Jamaica and Hillcrest J Cen's; fmr, chmn, comparative lit sect, MLA. Contbr to profsl jours. Home: 177-41 Edgerton Rd, Jamaica, NY. Office: Queens Coll, Flushing, NY.

CHEIN, Isidor, US, psychologist, educator; b. NYC, Mar 5, 1912; s. Max and Rebecca (Zatal); BS, CCNY, 1932; MA, Columbia U, 1933; PhD, 1939; m. Norma Cohen, 1937; c: Orin, David, Judith, Deborah. Prof, psych, NYU, since 1952; cons, tech research advisory comm, Natl JWB; J Bd of Guardians; J Educ Comm; Natl Comty Relations Adv Comm; CJFWF; Rel Educ Assn, NYC Youth Bd, NY State Commn for Youth; instr, CCNY, 1937-44, lectr, 1944-49; research asso, Mayor's Comm on Unity, NYC, 1945-46; comm on comty inter-relations, AJ Cong, 1946-47, asso dir 1947-50, dir, 1950-52. Pres, Soc, for Psych Study of Social Issues, Amer Psych Assn, 1962-63, div of Phil Psych, 1968-69; NY State Psych Assn, 1964-65; f: Amer Psych and Sociol Assns; mem, Council, Society for Sci Study of Rel, 1962-65. Contbr profsl and sci jours. Home: 66-15 Thornton Pl, Rego Park, NY. Office: NYU, Washington Sq, NYC.

CHELOUCHE, Aviezer, Isr, advocate, government official; b. Tel Aviv, Isr, July 28, 1923; dipl advocate, Law Sch, Jerusalem, 1947; postgrad and political sci studies, Paris; m. Rachel Garfinkel; two c. Asst dir gen, Min for Fgn Affairs, since 1968, with Min, since 1948; second secy: Isr Legation, Bucharest, 1948-50; Isr Embs: Brussels, 1950-51; Paris, 1951-53; prin asst, E Eur Div, 1953-55; first secy, Isr Emb, Moscow, 1955-58; asst dir, Econ Div, 1958-59; dir, 1959-60; dir, W Eur Div, 1960-61; Min of Isr, Yugo, 1961-63; ambass, Nigeria, 1963-65; dir, Econ Div, 1965-68. Home: 13 Hovevei Zion St, Jerusalem, Isr. Office: Min for Fgn Affairs, Jerusalem, Isr.

CHEN, Louise, Isr, scientist; b. Galatz, Rum, Mar 11, 1938; d. Zissu and Golda (Galperin) Boiato; in Isr since 1950; MSc, Tel Aviv U, 1962; PhD, Weizmann Inst of Sci, Rehovot, 1966; m. David Chen, Dec 7, 1965; c. Orly. Visiting research F, Oxford U, since 1968; f, sr common room, Wolfson Coll, since 1969; fmr, research F, Weizmann Inst. Sgt, MC, IDF, 1951-53. Prin contribs: research on mechanism of leukemia induction in mice; a new method of immunizing mice against cancer cells, using hybrid cells. Contbr numerous articles to Isr and intl sci jours. Hobby, music. Home: 20 Moskowitz St, Rehovot, Isr.

CHEN, Nira, Isr, music tchr; b. Ein Harod, Isr, Mar 8, 1924; d. Eliezer and Sara (Chen) Ben-Ezra; att: Music Acad, Jerusalem; Tchrs Coll, Tel Aviv; m. Avraham Lifschitz; c. Irith Stekelmacher. Music tchr, since 1949; recorded folksongs; pub several books and records; choir conductor, Kibbutz Cultural Comm, coord musical events and concerts in kibbutz. Mem: ACUM; Music Tchrs Union. Home and office: Ein Harod, Isr.

CHERKASKY, Martin, US, hospital admnr; b. Phila, Pa, Oct 6, 1911; s. Samuel and Sarah (Kosharsky); MD, Temple U Med Sch, 1936; att Gratz Heb Training Coll, 1928-32; m. Sarah Griffin, 1941; c: Karl, Marny, Michael. Dir, Montefiore Hosp, NY since 1951, on staff since 1937; clinical asso prof, NYU, since 1956; cons, Commn of Hosp, Dept of Hosp, NYC; NY State Hosp, Rev and Planning Council since 1961; tech adv, Comm on Chronic Illness, 1953; Health Ins Plan of Gtr NY; mem, adv comm on devl and expansion of psycht services in gen hosp, NY State Dept of Mh; in pvt practice, 1939-40; dipl, Amer Bd of Preventive Med and Public Health; f, NY Acad of Med; mem: adv bd, AJDC; Amer Public Health Assn; Amer Hosp Assn; AHA; ed bd, Jour of Chronic Diseases; The Commonwealth and Intl Libr of Sci, Tech and Engr. Contbr to profsl jours. Home: 150 E 210 St, Bronx, New York. Office: Montefiore Hosp, 210 St and Bainbridge Ave, Bronx, New York, NY.

CHERNIAK, Abraham, Isr, artist, engineer; b. Korma, Russ, Sep 13, 1904; s. Asher and China (Katznelson); in Isr since 1926; ME, Mendeleff Tech Inst, Moscow, 1925; dipl architect,

Tech Inst, Haifa, 1929; m. Ziporah Fania Neufeld; c: Dorita Shapiro, Ada Koren, Joseph Tzafnat, Asher Tzafnat. Ret; dir, tech dept, Min of Housing, 1950-68; exec engr, Heb U, Mt Scopus, Jerusalem, 1946-49. Mem, Assn of Engrs and Architects in Isr. Author, Jerusalem Ink Drawings, Nofei Yerushalaim, 1968. Hobbies: poetry, painting, drawing. Home: 16 Eben Shapruth St, Jerusalem, Isr.

CHERNIAK Joseph, Isr, author; b. Khotimsk, Russ, Aug 10, 1895; s. Chaim and Riva (Chornaya); in Isr since 1965; att: Natl Educ Inst; pedg deg, Liebknecht Pedg Inst, Moscow, 1920; wife and children perished under Nazi regime, Russ. Political prisoner, Russ, 1949-55. Tchr, Yiddish, Khotimsk, 1918; pedg, ethnograph, Moscow, 1920; dir, insp, Crimea, 1930. Author: pedg works in Russ; folklore works, in Yiddish; contbr to: Yiddishe Shriften; Yikuf; Yivo; critics on Yiddish lit. Mem: Russ Writers Union; Yiddish Lit Union; Cong J Sci, Jerusalem. Home: Malben, 15 Shapiro St, Netanya, Isr.

CHERNICK, Sidney S, US, biochemist; b. Winnipeg, Can, Mar 6, 1921; s. Harry Albert and Rose (Segal); BA, UCLA, 1943, MA, 1945, PhD, 1948; m. Sada Dolhinow; c: Kathy, Paul, Lawrence. Sr sci, USPHS, Natl Inst of Arthritis and Metabolic Diseases, NIH, since 1953; fmr: phys, U of Cal Med Sch, 1948-51; prof, phys, pharm, N Dakota St Coll, 1951-53. Mem: Amer Soc of Biol Chems; Soc for Experimental Biol and Med; Sigma Xi. Contbr on diabetes, intermediary metabolism in nutritional and hormonal states. Home: 6703 Melville Pl, Chevy Chase, Md. Office: Natl Inst of Arthritis and Metabolic Diseases, NIH, of Bethesda, Md.

CHERNIN, Eli, US, educator, scientist; b. NYC, Sep 12, 1924; s. Jeremiah and Sonia (Vassilevitzky); BS, CCNY, 1944; MA, U Mich, 1948; ScD, Johns Hopkins U, 1951; m. Judith Gamoran, June 17, 1956; c: Joshua, Lisa, Michael. Asso prof, tropical public health, Harvard Sch of Public Health, since 1962, mem fac, since 1951; mem, tropical med and parasitology study sect, USPHS, since 1966. US Army, 1944-46. Mem: NY Acad Sci; AAAS; Amer Soc Parasitologists; Amer Soc Tropical Med and Hygiene; Royal Soc Tropical Med and Hygiene; Sigma Xi. Mem, ed bd, Jour of Parasitology, since 1968; contbr numerous articles to profsl jours. Recipient, Bailey K Ashford Award in tropical med, Amer Soc Tropical Med and Hygiene, 1962. Home: 109 Highland Ave, Newtonville, Mass. Office: Harvard Sch of Public Health, Boston, Mass.

CHERNISS, Harold F, US, classical scholar, educator; b. St Joseph, Mo, Mar 11, 1904; s. David and Theresa (Hart); BA, U of Cal, 1925, PhD, 1929; att: U Chgo, 1926; U Gottingen, 1927; U Berlin, 1928; Hon DHL: U Chgo, 1950; HUC-JIR, 1959; m. Ruth Meyer, Jan 1, 1929. Prof, Inst for Advanced Study, Princeton, NJ, since 1948; instr, classics, Cornell U, 1930-33; asso prof Greek, Johns Hopkins U, 1936-46; prof Greek, U of Cal, 1946-48. pvt to capt, US Army, 1942-46. Mem: Amer Phil Soc, Brit Acad; Royal Acad Arts and Scis (Goteborg); AAAS; Classical Assn, Gt Brit; Acad Arts and Scis, Cordoba, Amer Philol Assn; Phi Beta Kappa; Delta Sigma Rho. Author: The Platonism of Gregory of Nyssa, 1930; Aristotle's Criticism of Presocratic Phil, 1935; Aristotle's Criticism of Plato and the Acad, 1944; The Riddle of the Early Acad, 1945; Plutarch's De Facie Quae in Orbe Lunae Apparet, 1957. Contbr to Scholarly publs. Home: 98 Battle Rd, Princeton, NJ. Office: Inst for Advanced Study, Princeton, NJ.

CHERNOBLE, Samuel F, US, printer, business exec; b. Odessa, Russ, Jan 17, 1905; s. David and Leah (Tonkonogy); in US since 1914; att Bklyn Coll, 1957-59; m. Ethel Shapiro, Aug 23, 1928; c: Jonathan, Elizabeth, Daniel. Pres, Graphic Arts Management Corp; cons, on graphic arts. Prin contrib, to the devl of dry offset process. Trustee: Brotherhood Syn; Franklin F, Royal Soc of Arts; mem, natl panel, Amer Abitration Soc; past chmn, Printing Ind of Metrop NY; co committeeman, Rep Party. Contbr: trade jours. Home: 40 W 10 St, New York, NY. Office: 200 Varick St, New York, NY.

CHERNOFF, Amoz Immanuel, US, researcher; b. Malden, Mass, Mar 17, 1923; s. Isaiah and Celia (Margolin) Chernichovsky; BS, Sheffield Sci Sch, Yale U, 1943; MD, Sch of Med, 1947; m. Renate Fisher, Jan 25, 1953; c: David, Susan, Judith. PIR Memorial Research Cen, U of Tenn, since 1964; prof research, since 1958; prof med, U Tenn Coll of Med, Memphis since 1965; asst, resident med, Barnes Hosp, St Louis, 1948-49;

asso phys, 1951-56; research f, Michael Reese Hosp, Chgo, hematology, dept of hematologic research, 1949-51, asst dir, research lab, 1950-51; f med, Amer Coll Phys, Wash U Sch Med, 1951-52; spec research f, USPHS, Sch of Med, 1952-53, instr med, 1952-54, asst prof med, 1954-56; mem, USPHS cancer chemotherapy study sect, Bethesda, Md, 1958-63; cons, St Louis City Hosp, hematology, 1953-56; asso prof med, Duke, U Sch of Med, 1956-58; VA Hosp, Durham, NC, chief, hematology sect, 1956-58; adv bd, Blood, Jour of Hematology, 1961-65; bd educ, Heska Amuna Syn, Knoxville, Tenn since 1962; f, Amer Coll Phys; f, IMA; mem: Amer Fed Clinical Research; Soc for Experimental Biol and Med; Cent Soc for Clinical Research; Amer Soc for Clinical Inves; NY Acad of Sci; Intl Soc of Hematology; S Soc of Clinical Research; Amer Soc of Hum Genet; Sigma Xi; Alpha Omega Alpha; contbr to med and sci jours. Recipient, Research Career Award, USPHS, 1962. Home: 8017 Bennington Dr, Knoxville, Tenn. Office: U of Tenn, Alcoa Hwy, Knoxville, Tenn.

CHERNOFF, Hyman M, US, physician; b. Springfield, Mass, Jun 3, 1918; s. Isaiah and Celia (Margolin); BS, Yale U, 1939; MD, NYU, 1943; m. Shulamith Scharfstein, Aug 29, 1948; c: Deborah, Naomi, David, Jonathan, Daniel, Joshua. Asso prof, clinical med, Yale Sch of Med since 1969; fmr, asst clinical prof med; att card, Grace-New Haven Hosp since 1951; att physician since 1948; dir, dept of electrocardiography, Memorial Unit, Yale New Haven Hosp since 1967; research F, USPHS, 1947-48; pvt practice, internal med 1948-67. Capt, US, Army MC, 1945-47. Mem: AMA, Sigma XI; Phi Delta Epsilon. Contbr to profsl jours. Home: 2151 Chapel St, New Haven, Conn. Office: Yale New Haven Hos, New Haven, Conn.

CHERNOFF, Lewis M, US, business exec; b. New Brit, Conn, Apr 4, 1912; s. Menas and Sonia (Wintz); att NYU, 1931-33, m. Helen Sondik, June 4, 1939; c: Pamela Berger, Linda Willner; Treas: Hodgson Houses Inc, Amer Mobile Homes and Americans' Homes of North Carolina, Inc. Owner, Chernoff-Lockwood Ins Agcy, 1933-47; treas: High Produc Machine, 1942-49; Sondik divs, 1947-64; Bd trustee and found Beth El Temple, of W Hartford, pres, 1957-58; B'nai Isr Syn, 1947-51; Emanuel Syn, 1951-53; vice-pres, Natl Ramah Commn, United Syn of Amer, 1960-62; mem, bd educ, City of New Brit, 1940-46; bd dirs, Jayark Corp; mem: Cliffside Country Club. Home: 59 Norwood Rd, W Hartford, Conn. Office: 2944 Main St, Hartford, Conn.

CHERNOFSKY, Morris I, US, attorney, accountant, educator; b. Bklyn, NY, Dec 2, 1922; s. Max and Bertha (Cohen); BA, Yeshiva U, 1943; MBA, NYU, 1945; CPA: NY, 1950; Conn, 1956; JD, NY Law Sch, 1958, LLM, 1963, JSD, 1964; m. Ruth Gershbaum, May 30, 1946; c: Philip, Neil, Bennett. Asst prof, accountancy, Baruch Coll, CUNY since 1965; fac mem since 1947; pvt practice since 1965; att, 1959-65; CPA, 1950-65; admitted: NY Bar 1959; Bar of Tax Court 1960; US Supr Court 1964. Mem: Amer Inst of CPA's; NY State Soc of CPA's; Amer Bar Assn; NY Co Lawyers' Assn; Amer Assn of Atty-CPAs; AAUP; Beta Alpha Psi. Author: Administering Cash and Funds, 1953. Home: POB 242, Flushing, NY. Office: 17 Lexington Ave, New York, NY.

CHEROFF, Irving S, US, educator, organization exec; b. Bklyn, NY, Aug 11, 1914; s. Max and Bertha (Matz); BS, Bklyn, Coll 1935; MA, Tchrs Coll, Columbia U, 1936; MA, social work, admn, O State U, 1949; hon: LLD, Burton Coll, Sem, Colo, 1958; DLitt, Wm Carter Bible Coll, Goldsboro, NC, 1959; grad work: NYU, Hunter Coll, Boston U; m. Isabelle Rosenbollm, 1940; c. Richard. Prof, sociol, social work, Fayetteville State Coll since 1965; area dir, United Service Org, J WB, NC since 1952; caseworker, dir athletics, NYC Dept of Wfr; tchr, NYC Bd Educ; fmr playground dir, NYC Dept of Parks; field instr, Sch of Social Admn, O State U, 1946-50; dir, Schonthal Cen and Camp, Columbus, O, 1946-50; J Comty Cen, Worcester, Mass, 1950-51; US Army, 1943-46, i/c phys, educ reconditioning, US Hosp, Camp Edwards. Treas, Council of Social Service Agcys, Cumberland Co since 1953; instr, NCCJ; mem, bd dirs: NC Assn J Men since 1959; ADL; state exec comm, B'nai B'rith; steering comm, PR chmn, bi-centennial, Fayetteville Cumberland Co, since 1954; Ft Bragg-Fayetteville Mil Affairs Comm, 3rd Army Advisory Comm, since 1953; Acad Cert Soc Workers; Natl Assns; Social Workers; J Cen Workers; masons ed, bd, J Cen Worker, 1950-52. Contbr articles to Anglo-J Publs. Recipient: Commendation medal, Victory Medal, 1946; Freedom Found award, 1951; Tercentenary Medal, 1954; cert, Vet Admn,

1956; Man of the Year, B'nai B'rith, Fayetteville, NC, 1960. Hobbies: sailing, coaching soccer, baseball, basketball. Home: 422 McPhee Dr, Fayetteville, NC. Office: POB 897, Fayetteville, NC.

CHERRICK, Bernard, Isr, rabbi, org exec; b. Dublin, Ire, Nov 16, 1914; s. Hertz and Emma (Brodie); in Isr since 1947; BA, U Manchester, 1936; MA, 1937; research f, 1937-38; postgrad research, London Sch of Econ, 1938-40; ordained rabbi, Liverpool Yeshiva. Vice Pres, Heb U, Jerusalem, since 1968, i/c Dept Info and Public Affairs since 1947; fmr exec vice-pres, rabbi, New Syn, London, 1938-40; lectr, div, Heb U: Australia; NZ; Can; Gt Brit; S Afr; Latin Amer, USA. Served chaplain, Brit Army. Dir: JNF, 1942-47; United Pal Appeal 1942-47; both Gt Brit. Office: Hebrew U, Jerusalem, Isr.

CHERTKOV, Morris, US, attorney, administrator; b. Russ, Jan 5, 1909; s. Harry and Rebecca (Kallick); in US since 1921; PhB, U Chgo, 1931; JD, 1933; m. Ruth Cohen, Dec 2, 1953; c. Boren. Pvt practice in trade regulation and admin law since 1968; prof, Coll of Econ and Bus, U Wash, 1935-42; sr and supervisory atty: OPA, 1942-43, 1946-47; CAB, 1947-61, exec dir, 1961-63; chmn, exec dir, Alaska Public Service Commn, 1965; cons common carrier regulatory field, 1966-67. US Army, 1943-45. Home: 9030 Sligo Creek Pkwy, Silver Spring, Md. Office: 1730 Rhode Island Ave NW, Washington, DC.

CHERTOFF, Mordecai Samuel, US, executive, rabbi, editor; b. NYC, Sep 7, 1922; s. Paul and Esther (Barish); BS, CCNY, 1943; ordained rabbi, MHL, JTSA, 1964, DHL, 1968; m. Lily Sefton, Feb 20, 1951; c: Daniel, Jocelyn. Exec dir, Amer Histadrut Cultural Exch Inst, NYC, since 1969; cons, Ktav Pub House, NY; ed, Shocken Books, NYC, 1946; fgn news ed, Pal Post, Jerusalem, 1947-49; ed, Frontline, IDF mag, 1948-49; UN corresp, Hador, 1949-50; pr staff, Isr Consulate Gen, NYC, 1950; instr, Heb civilization and lang, U Tex, 1952-53; rabbi: Temple Beth El, Portland Me, 1954-55; Temple Beth El, Harrisburg, Pa, 1955-58; instr, Heb lit, Bible, Baltimore Heb Coll, 1958-61; rabbi, B'nai Isr, Pittsburgh, 1961-66; dir, Amer-Isr Secondary Sch Prog, 1965-69. Served, Haganah, IDF, 1947-50. Pres, ZOA, Austin, Tex, 1951-52; mem: Acad Political Sci; Amer Acad for J Research; RA; NY Bd Rabbis. Editor, The New Left and the Jews, 1971; trans, Yedidi Haya'ar by Donia Rosen; contbr: Ency of Zionism and Isr; J periodicals. Home: 390 Riverside Dr, New York, NY. Office: 33 E 67 St, New York, NY.

CHESLOCK, Louis, US, musician, composer, teacher; b. London, Sep 9, 1899; s. Jacob and Rebecca (Neumark); in US since 1901; tchrs cert: violin, 1917, harmony, 1919, artist dipl, composition, 1921, Peabody Conservatory Coll of Music, Baltimore; D MusA, honoris causa, 1964, Peabody Inst; m. Elise Hanline, May 31, 1926; c. Barry. Tchr: Peabody Conservatory of Music, violin since 1916, composition harmony, counterpoint, orchestration, form since 1922, chmn, theory dept since 1950; first violinist, asst concertmaster, Baltimore Sym Orch, 1916-37; compositions performed: N and S Amer; Eur; Isr; Philippines; orchestral works performed: Singapore, Bombay, 1967. Composer: opera, sym, concertos, sonatas, ballet, string quartets, oratorios; works for: voice, violin, cello, piano, Fr horn; works: Violin Vibrato, 1931; The Jewel Merchants, opera, 1940; The Congo, choral work with orch, 1942; Cinderella, ballet, 1946; Graded List Violin Music, 1948. Mem: Amer Musicological Soc; Amer String Tchrs Assn, pres, Md chap; AAUP. Author, H L Menken on Music, 1961. Recipient: Peabody Alumni award, 1921; hon mention, Chgo Theater symphonic contest, 1923; Chgo Daily News awards for compositions, piano, violin, violoncello, orch, 1923-24; hon mention, NY Women's sym orch contest, 1938; Natl Composer's Clinic Contest award, choral composition, 1942; elected, Baltimore City Coll Hall of Fame, dist achievement, music, 1960. Home: 2318 Sulgrave Ave, Mt Washington, Baltimore, Md. Office: Peabody Conservatory of Music, Mt Vernon, Pl, Baltimore, Md.

CHESNIN, Leon, US, agronomist, soil chem, educator; b. NYC, Mar 28, 1919; s. Samuel and Anna (Melcher); BS, U of Ky, 1940; PhD, Rutgers U, 1948; m. Esther Katz, Sep 28, 1940; c: Sidney, Harold, Nancy, Gary. Asso prof, U Neb since 1947; Cons, Fertilizing Cos on Micronutrients and farm prod problems; soil surveyor, Soil Conservation Service, 1941-42; insp, powder and explosives, War Dept, 1942; sup, chemurgic research dept, Joseph I Seagram & Sons, 1942-44;

research asst, soils, NJ Agric Experiment Sta, 1944-47. Pres, B'nai B'rith lodge, 1952; educ dir, Tifereth Isr Syn since 1959; mem: Natl Micronutrient Comm, Amer Council on Fertilizer Application; Syn Youth Comm; prog comm, ed bd, Natl Fertilizer Solutions Assn; charter mem: Natl Agric Youth Inst; Agric Careers; mem: Amer Soc Agronomy; Soil Sci Soc Amer; Intl Soil Sci Soc; Gamma Sigma Delta; Sigma Xi. Contbr to profsl jours. Spec interests: farm mgmt, youth work. Hobbies: chess, photography. Home: 2645 C St, Lincoln, Neb. Office: U of Neb, Lincoln, Neb.

CHESNIN, Samuel, US, business exec; b. May 1, 1889; s. Sidney and Ethel (Bennenson); in US since 1905; m. Anna Melcher, Mar 13, 1914; c: Leon, Sidney (decd). Ret; pres, Chesnin and Leis Inc, 1933-52. Col, Blue Star Brigade, Air Warden Service. Chmn, landsmanschaften div, Histadrut, 1943-48; chmn, pres, Lincoln, Neb, chap, JWF, 1951-59, bd mem, 1956-62; trustee, bd dirs, Tifereth Isr Syn, 1953-62, fmr vice-pres; life mem, Lincoln C of C; mem, B'nai B'rith, Van Courtlandt Lodge, life hon pres. Home: 3520 S 37 St, Lincoln, Neb.

CHEYETTE, Irving, US, educator; b. NYC, Aug 1, 1904; s. Samuel and Fanny (Levy); BS, Tchrs Coll, Columbia U, 1929, MA, 1930, EdD, 1936; m. Ruth Netter, 1925; c: Herbert, Fredric. Composer of music; dir, music educ, SUNY, Buffalo since 1955; instr, music, Horace Mann, Lincoln Schs, NY, 1928-35; public schs, Mt Vernon, NY, 1930-38; dir, music, State Tchrs Coll, Ind, Pa, 1938-48, Syracuse U, 1948-54; Fulbright Prof, Tokyo U of Arts, Japan, 1954-55; conductor, adjudicator, music festivals, US, Can Japan, 1932-62. Pres, music sect, Pa State Educ Assn, 1939-40; chmn, coll sect, NY State Sch Music Assn, 1960-62; music coord, J Cen, Mt Vernon, NY, 1934-38; Buffalo, NY, 1959-60; mem: ethics comm, NEA, 1939-40; exec bd, Music Educ Natl Conf, 1946-50; AAUP; NY State Educ Assn; Erie Co Music Educ Assn; NEA; NY State Sch Music Assn; Music Educ Natl Assn; Conf; Phi Delta Kappa; Phi Mu Alpha; Kappa Delta Pi; clubs: B'nai B'rith. Author of musical textbooks. Contbr to musical publs. Home: 95 North Dr, Eggertsville, NY. Office: SUNY, Buffalo, NY.

CHIEL, Arthur A, US, rabbi; b. Taylor, Pa, Dec 16, 1920; s. Solomon and Frieda (Binik); BA, Yeshiva U, 1943; ordained rabbi, JIR, 1946; DHL, JTSA, 1960; m. Kineret Dirnfield, Oct 21, 1944; c: Deborah, Daniel, Naomi, David. Rabbi, Cong B'nai Jacob, Woodbridge since 1962; research f, AJCong, 1946-47; asst prof, Judaic Studies, U Man, 1950-52; rabbi: Rosh Pina Cong, Winnipeg, Can, 1952-57; Genesis Heb Cen, Tuckahoe, NY, 1957-62. Mem: Amer J Hist Soc; Man Hist Soc. Author: Jewish Experiences in Early Manitoba, 1955; The Jews in Manitoba, 1961. Home: Northrop Rd, Woodbridge, Conn. Study: Cong B'nai Jacob, Rimmon Rd, Woodbridge, Conn.

CHIEL, Samuel, US, rabbi, b. Taylor, Pa, June 6, 1927; s. Solomon and Frieda (Binik); BSS, CCNY, 1949; MHL, ordained rabbi, JTSA, 1952; m. Jeanette Eisenberg, 1949; c: Hillel, David, Jonathan. Rabbi: Temple Emanuel, Newton Cen, Mass, since 1968; Malverne J Cen, 1956-68; Temple Beth El, Quincy, Mass, 1954-56. Chaplain, US Army, 1952-54. Fmr pres, United Syn Comm, J Educ; mem: exec council, RA; Comm on J chaplaincy, Natl JWB. Fmr prog ed, Eternal Light TV series, JTSA; contbr to, Best J Sermons. Recipient: Outstanding Young Man of Quincy Award, Quincy Jr C of C, 1956. Home: 510 Ward St, Newton Center, Mass. Study: 385 Ward St, Newton Center, Mass.

CHILL, Channing D, US, attorney; b. Newburgh, NY, Aug 14, 1936; s. Abraham and Libby (Kaplan); BA, Yeshiva U, 1957; LLB, Yale Law Sch, 1960; m. Vivian Jacobs, Feb 16, 1963; c: Michael, Adam. Partner, law firm, Quint, Marx & Chill since 1966; chief counsel, minority leader; NY State Assembly since 1968, counsel, standing comm on housing, 1966-67; repr, State of NY, 63rd annual conf, Natl Tax Assn, 1970. Dir, chmn, comm on law and leg, Union of Orthodox J Congs of Amer; NY regional chmn, Yale Law Sch Fund. Contbr of articles to jours. Home: 42 West End Ave, Brooklyn, NY. Office: 66 Court, Brooklyn, NY.

CHINICH, Bessie, US, attorney; b. Newark, NJ; d. Barnet and Nettie (Chinich) Chinich; grad, Plaut Memorial Heb Sch, Sch, 1923; LLB, Rutgers U Law Sch, 1930; admitted to NJ Bar, 1931; m. Harry Federbush, May 28, 1933; c: Paul, Roberta. Contracting off, Defense Supply Agcy, Defense

Dept, since 1965; contract specialist with NY Procurement Dist, US Army, since 1953; concert pianist, played Town Hall, NYC; in gen law practice, 1931-44, 1948-51; conferee, salary stabilization unit, Treasury Dept, 1944-46; investigator, Civilian Produc Admn NYC, 1946-47; claims examiner, War Assets Admn, 1947-48; investigator, Natl Produc's Admn, Dept of Commerce, Newark, NJ, 1951-53. Mem: Essex Co, NJ State, Amer Bar Assns; Rutgers U Alumni Assn; Intl Platform Assn; Natl Council Juvenile Court Judges; Amer Judicature Soc; fmr: mem: speaker's bur on Referenda for Rev NJ State Constitution; Temple B'nai Abraham; active in: YMHA; Girl and Boy Scouts; orphanages, homes for aged; off in various political orgs; counsel, Newark Comm for Neighborhood Conservation and Rehab. Home: 580 S 11 St, Newark, NJ. Office: 240 Route 22, Springfield, NJ.

CHINITZ, Benjamin, US, economist, educator; b. NYC, Aug 28, 1924; s. Abraham and Mollie (Resnick); AB, Yeshiva U, 1946, DHumL, 1969; AM, Brown U, Providence, RI, 1951; PhD, Harvard U, 1954; m. Ethel Kleinman, Oct 15, 1950; c: Adam, Michael. Prof econ, chmn dept, Brown U, since 1966; prof, chmn dept econ, U Pittsburgh, asst dir, Cen for Regional Econ Studies; dep asst secy, US Dept of Commerce, 1965-66; mem, Pres Johnson's Task Force on Transp Policy, 1964; US repr, meeting, Sr Econ Advs, Econ Commn for Eur, Geneva; Fulbright visiting scholar, U Glasgow, Scotland; cons: UN; Pres Council of Econ Advs; RAND Corp; other public and pvt agcys; official guest of State of Isr. Sgt, USAF, 1946-49. NE, repr, Jt Council on Econ Educ; pres, Regional Sci Assn; org, Research Conf on Urban Econ; chmn, Adult Educ, Bur J Educ, Providence, mem bd: JNF, RI; Gen J Comm, RI. Author: Freight and the Metropolis, 1960; City and Suburb, 1965; co-author, Region in Transit. Home: 42 Intervale Rd, Providence, RI. Office: Brown U, Providence, RI.

CHINITZ, Jacob, US, rabbi; b. Starobin, Russ, Jan 30, 1921; s. Abraham and Mollie (Resnick); in US since 1924; BA; ordained rabbi, Yeshiva U, 1945; m. Ruth Jacobs, 1947; c: David, Penina. Rabbi: Temple Beth Ami, Phila, Pa since 1959; Cong B'nai Isr, Pontiac, Mich, 1949-52; Cong Ahavas Achim, Detroit, Mich, 1952-58; fac, Amer Coll, Jerusalem, sem 1969. Chmn, Radio-TV Comm, Bd Rabbis; vice-chmn, RA; produc of TV program, "Ask the Rabbi"; mem: bd dir, J Comty Relations Council, 1962; Rabb Alumni, Yeshiva U; Phila Bd of Rabbis; RA; B'nai B'rith; UJA mission to Isr, 1964; UJA Rabb Cabinet. Ed: Voice Still Speaks, sermons of Rabbi Morris Robi; rabbi's page, J Exponent, 1968-69; contbr: Natl J jours, including, Amer Rabbi, Reconstructionist, J Spectator, Recipient: Talmud prize, Yeshiva Coll, 1944; Bonds for Isr Certificate Year of Negev Award, 1963. Home: 9115 Dale Rd, Philadelphia, Pa. Study: 9201 Bustleton Ave, Philadelphia, Pa.

CHINOY, Ely, US, sociologist; b. Newark, NJ, Sep 5, 1921; s. Solomon and Bella (Traskanoff); BA, Rutgers U, 1942; PhD, Columbia U, 1953; m. Helen Krich, June 6, 1948; c: Michael, Claire. Prof, chmn, dept sociol and anthropology, Smith Coll since 1961; instr, personnel relations, Newark Coll of Engr, 1942-44; sociol, NYU, 1945-46; lectr, sociol, U Toronto, 1947-51; visiting prof, U Leicester, Eng, 1963-64. Mem: AAUP; Amer Sociol Assn; E Sociol Soc; Phi Beta Kappa; ACLU. Author: Sociological Perspective, 1954, 2nd ed, 1968; Automobile Workers and the American Dream, 1955; Society: An Introduction to Sociology, 1961, 2nd ed, 1967; cons ed, Atherton Press, NYC since 1964; publs, asso ed, Amer Sociol Review, 1961-64; contbr to profsl jours. Recipient: F, Social Sci Research Council, 1946-47. Home: 230 Crescent St, Northampton, Mass. Office: Smith Coll, Northampton, Mass.

CHITAYAT, Abrahm Akram, Isr, lawyer; b. Baghdad, Iraq, July, 1914; s. Aboudy and Loulou (Eliahou); in Isr since 1951; LLB, Tel Aviv U; m. Regina Saleh Hougui, Aug 12, 1953; c: Obadia, Aharon, Tamar, Yoram. Pvt practice since 1965; mem, City Council, Ramat Gan, since 1959. Secy: Mapai, 1953-54; Histadrut, 1955-60; fmr secy, Iraq J Org. Hobbies: politics, stamps. Home: 27 Yarden St, Ramat Gan, Isr. Office: 56 Herzl St, Ramat Gan, Isr.

CHOD, Leon, S Afr, physician; b. Buenos Aires, Arg, Aug 21, 1894; s. Jacob and Elizabeth (Dubin) Chodorsky; vetr surg, Imperial Vetr Coll, Warsaw, 1916; MB, Med Fac, U Odessa; att St George Hosp Med Sch, London, 1925; m. Rosalia Slotar, June 28, 1915; c: Mrs, Eugene Muskat. Ret since 1949; pvt practice, Pretoria, 1926-49; London, Eng, 1925-26. LRCP; MRCS; mem, Med Assn, S Afr. Home: 26 White House, 263 Schoeman St, Pretoria, S Afr.

CHOMSKY, Noam, US, educator; b. Phila, Pa, Dec 7, 1928; s. William and Elsie (Simonofsky); BA, MA, U of Pa, Phila, 1951; PhD, ling, 1955; hon LHD, U of Chgo, 1967; hon DL, U London, 1967; m. Aviva; c: Diane, Harry. Ferrari P Ward prof, modern langs and lings, MIT, since 1966, asst prof, 1955-58, asso prof, 1958-61, prof, 1961-66; research F, Harvard U, since 1962; asst instr, U of Pa, 1950-51. Mem: Amer Acad of Arts and Scis; numerous profsl socs; steering comm, Resist. Author, books and articles on lings, phil, intellectual hist, contemporary issues. Office: Room 20C-132, MIT, 77 Mass Ave, Cambridge, Mass.

CHOMSKY, Samuel W, US, rabbi; b. Russ, Jan 28, 1909; s. Jacob and Nancy (Vinograd); in US since 1913; BA, U Cincinnati, 1931; ordained rabbi, HUC, Cincinnati, 1934; att Heb U, Jerusalem, 1934-37; DD, HUC-JIR, 1959; m. Ida Knigoff, June 29, 1934; c. Nina. Chaplain, VA, LA, since 1946; regional dir, commn J chaplaincy, JWB, 1945-55; rabbi, Cong Beth Sholom, Topeka, Kan, 1937-41. Chaplain, US Army, 1942-46; sr J chaplain, SW Pacific; mem, theater staff, Gen MacArthur; col, Army Res, 1958. Pres: S Cal chap, Mil Chaplains Assn, 1958-59; S Cal Assn Lib Rabbis, 1954-55; mem: CCAR; JWV, state chaplain; Amer Legion, dept chaplain; Res Off Assn, state Chaplain. Home: 456 N Bowling Green Way, Los Angeles, Cal. Study: VA Center, Los Angeles, Cal.

CHOMSKY, William, US, educator; b. Russ, Jan 15, 1896; s. Meyer and Esther (Korman); in US since 1913; BA, Johns Hopkins U, 1921; MA, U of Pa, 1925; PhD, Dropsie Coll, 1926; DHL, Gratz Coll, 1969; m. Elsie Simonofsky, Aug 19, 1927; c: Noam, David. Prof em, Gratz Coll, since 1969; chmn, fac, 1949-69, prof since 1954, on fac since 1924; prof, Heb and J Educ, Dropsie Coll, 1955. Mem: Amer Acad for J Research; Natl Council for J Educ; LZOA; Histadrut Ivrith; Mikveh Isr Cong; World Union J Studies, Conf on J Studies. Author: How to Teach Hebrew, 1947; David Kimhi's Hebrew Grammar, 1952; Hebrew: The Eternal Language, 1957; Teaching and Learning, 1959; Ha-Lashon ha-Ivrit b'Darkhei Hitpathuthah, 1967; Darkhei Hora'ah u'Lemidah, 1968; contbr to profsl jours. Home: 6417 N Fairhill St. Philadelphia, Pa.

CHOREV, Amos, Isr, Military off; b. Jerusalem, Feb, 1924; s. Eliahu and Tova (Sochazewer); MS, MIT, 1952, ME, 1954; m. Shoshana, 1946; c: Yechiam, Nira. Maj-Gen, Chief of Logistics, IDF, since 1968; chief: Oprs, S Front, 1949-50; Ordnance Corps, 1955-56; Dep Chief Sci, Defense Min, 1966. Mem, Sigma Xi. Home: 8 Hagefen St, Ramat Hasharon, Isr.

CHOURAQUI, Andre Nathan, Isr, jurist; b. Ain Temouchent, Algeria, Aug 11, 1917; s. Isaac and Lila (Meyer); in Isr since 1958; LLD, Paris U; Dipl, Superior Studies Public Law and Political Econ Islamic Law, Algiers U; m. Annette Levy, 1958; c: Emmanuel, Elisheva, Yael, David, Mikhal. Dep Mayor, Jerusalem, since 1965; perm delg, Alliance Israelite Universelle since 1953; advocate, judge, Algiers Dist Court of Appeal. Fr Resistance, 1942-45. Pres: Isr Sect, World F Rel Brith Am; Fr Sect, Brith Ivrit Olamit, 1955-60; hon, Assn Immigrants from N Afr; pres of honor, Assn Immigrants from Algeria; vice-pres, Comm Non-Govt Org of UNICEF-UNAC, 1950-56; hon secy, Comm for Interfaith and Understanding; dir, Sinai Series Press, U of Fr; counselor, PM of Isr, Ben Gurion, problems ingathering exiles, 1959-63. Author: La condition Juridique de l'Israelite Marocain, 1950; Introduction aux Devoirs des Coeurs, 1950; Les Juifs d'Afrique du Nord, 1952; Le Cantique des Cantiques, 1952; Les Psaumes, 1956; L'Etat d'Israel, 1956; Histoire du Judaisme, 1957; Cantique pour Nathanael, poems 1960; Theodore Herzl, 1960; La Pensée Juive, 1965; Les Juifs, 1966; Introduction aux Livres Sapientiaux de la Bible, 1966; Lettre à un ami arabe, 1966. Recipient: Prize: City of Paris for Civil Law; Audiffret 1952; Louis Marin 1956; Knight, Legion of Honor. Home: Ein Rogel St, Jerusalem, Isr. Office: Jaffa Rd, Jerusalem, Isr.

CHUDOFF, Earl, US, jurist; b. Phila, Pa, Nov 16, 1907; s. Morris and Jennye (Rubin); BS, U of Pa, 1929; LLB, U Pittsburgh Law Sch, 1932; m. Bess Cohen, Dec 24, 1936; c: Stephen, Diane. Judge, Court of Common Pleas, No 1, Phila Co since 1958; bldg and loan examiner, Pa State Dept Banking, 1936-39; mem: Pa State Leg, 1941-48; 81st, 82nd, 83rd, 84th, 85th US Cong, chmn: public works, resources; subcomm, on Govt oprs. USCG Res. Pres, Phila chap Fed Bar Assn; natl vice-pres for 3rd circuit; mem: AJCong, B'nai B'rith, Brith Sholom; Masons; Phila ZOA; Lehigh Consistory, AASR; Geo B McCracken Memorial Chap, USCG League;

Amer Judicature Soc; Tau Epsilon Rho; Beta Gamma Sigma; F Commn; clubs: Golden Slipper Sq, treas; 21 Jewel Sq, pres. Recipient: Alpha Lodge, B'nai B'rith annual achievement award, 1954; Max Slepin Award, JWV, 1956, humanitarian award: Histadrut, 1957; ZOA, 1958, B'nai B'rith, 1957, 1958. Home: 2401 Pennsylvania Ave, Philadelphia, Pa. Office: 242 City Hall, Philadelphia, Pa.

CHURGEL, Moshe, Isr, actor; b. Lodz, Pol, Jan 1, 1901; s. David and Beila (Sauitzki); in Isr since 1925; m. Fruma Reider, Pol; c: Dory, Bilha Yagil. Actor, Chamber Theatre since 1953; fmr, actor Matatee Theatre. Performed in Pygmalion; The Price. Served, Pol Army; Haganah. Recipient: Milo award: performance in The Price, The Rainmaker, The Good Soul of Techman. Home: 13 Ein Harod St, Tel Aviv, Isr.

CHURGIN, Gershon Abraham, US, educator; b. Pohost, Russ, Dec 3, 1903; s. Reuben and Divsha (Hochstein); in US since 1932; BS, Columbia U, 1929, MA, 1931; PhD, Johns Hopkins U, 1939; m. Ida Feinstein, 1939; c: Anita, Jonah. Prof, J Phil, Heb lit, Yeshiva U, NYC since 1950, instr, 1939-50; prin, W Talmud Torah, Baltimore, Md, 1930-39; club, Heb PEN. Author: Currents in Modern Philosophy, 1959; Horizons of Thought; Studies in Jewish and General Philosophy, 1968; contbr to: Sefer Hashanah, Vol VII, 1944; Bitzaron, 1944; Hatekufah, Vol XXXIV-XXXV, 1949; Talpioth, 1953; SURA, Israel-Amer Annual, 1953-54, 1956; Zeramin, 1959; Heb periodicals; co-ed, Bitzaron. Spec interest, lit criticism. Home: 92 Pinehurst Ave, New York, NY. Office: Yeshiva U, Amsterdam Ave and 186 St, New York, NY.

CIDOR, Hanan A, Isr, economist; b. Berlin, Ger, Nov 12, 1905; s. Hendrik and Ellen (Philippi) Citroen; in Isr since 1952; dipl, Grad Inst Intl Studies, Geneva, 1947; m. Ruth Vallentin, Oct 2, 1925; c: Tamar Shoshan, Raphaël, Eliana Tadmor. Econ adv: U Notre Dame, Ind; fgn cos with econ interests in Isr since 1967; dir: div for migration, UN Intl Ref Org, 1947-52; div for Intl Orgs, Isr Min Fgn Affairs, 1953-57; Isr Ambass to Netherlands, 1957-63; dir, Isr Export Inst, 1963-65. Mem, Bd dirs: Independent Lib Party; Tourist Ind Devl Corp since 1965. Author: Les Migrations Internationales, 1948; Overseas Migrations, Past and Future, 1951. Home: 16 Hameyasdim, St, Jerusalem, Isr.

CIECHANOVER, Joseph, Isr, attorney; b. Haifa, Isr, Oct 1, 1933; s. Isaac and Bluma (Lubanshevsky); cert, Heb U Sch of Bus, 1963; MJur, Heb U, 1956; LLM, U of Cal Law Sch, Berkeley, 1967; m. Atara Pchor, May 15, 1962; c: Tamar, Dafna. Legal adv, Min of Defense since 1968; found, Coop Ins Corp since 1966; fmr: legal adv, personnel mgr, Min of Agric; drafted most of agric laws of Isr up to 1968. Vice-pres, Tel Aviv Bar Assn. Home: 112/1 Neve Rassco, Ramat Hasharon, Isr. Office: Min of Defense, Isr.

CITRIN, Walter J, Hong Kong and Japan, business exec; b. Kiev, Russ, June 2, 1912; s. Joseph and Helen (Golenpolsky); att U of BC, 1932; BS, U Hong Kong, 1936; m. Judith Zirinsky, Aug 9, 1938; c: Jacob, David, Daniel. Dir: United Paper Co Ltd; United Agcys, both Hong Kong; mgn dir; Intl Textiles, Asso Agcys, both Japan. Interned by Japanese, 1942-45. Hon immigration off, Hong Kong; hon repr: immigration dept, JA; JDC; fmr: pres: J Comty, Japan; UJA, Japan; chmn: bd, Shanghai J Sch; Far East Pal Off; Shanghai ORT; clubs: Shanghai J, pres. Home: 24 Hachiyama-cho, Shibuya-ku, Tokyo, Japan. Offices: 410/411 Kokubu Bldg, Nihombashitori, Chu-ku, Tokyo, Japan; 425 Alexandra House, Hong Kong.

CITROEN, Paul, Netherlands, artist; b. Berlin, Ger, Dec 15, 1896; s. Hendrik and Ellen (Philippi); studied art, Berlin, 1914-15; Bauhaus, Weimar, 1922-24; m. Celine Bendien, Dec 18, 1929; c. Paulien Bruggeman. Artist-painter of portraits, landscapes; prof, Acad of the Hague, 1935-61; Author: Palet, 1931; Material, 1933; Richard, 1940; Tekeningen en Aantekenningen, 1941; Jacob Bendien, 1890-1933, pub, 1940; Licht in Groene Schaduw, 1941; De Tekenaar Henk Hartog, 1915-1942, publ, 1947; Schetsboek voor Vrienden, 1947; Kunsttestament, 1952; Een Tekenies, 1954; Introvertissimento, 1956; Notities van een schilder, 1966; Wir Maler heurte and die Kunsttradition, 1969. Mem, Paulchri Studio, the Hague. Home: 100 Oostdorperweg, Wasenaar, Netherlands.

CITRON, Samuel J, US, educator; theater dir, playwright; b. Ciechanow, Pol, Jan 24, 1908; s. Irving and Sarah (Kwiat); in US since 1920; att: Tchrs Inst, JTSA, 1923-31, Dramatic Workshop, New Sch for Social Research, 1939-40; LLB, St John's U Sch of Law, 1931; BS, NYU, 1951; MA, 1954; PhD,

1963; m. Deborah Shpall, 1934; c. Aaron, Sharon. Admitted to NY Bar, 1932. Dir, sch dramatics dept, J Educ Comm, NYC since 1944; found, dir, J Theater for Children, NY since 1945; dir, dramatics dept, Bur J Educ, 1934-40; educ dir Temple Gates of Prayer, Flushing, NY, 1941-44; dir, Brandeis Camp Inst of E, Winterdale, Pa, 1951. Found, dir, first Heb lang radio progs in US, WEVD, 1949-50; exec secy, Golden Pen Playwriting Contest; mem: Natl Council for J Educ; Amer Educ Assn; Children's Theater Conf; Writers Guild of Amer; ZOA; NEA; Phi Delta Kappa. Author: Ost Jude, 1937; New Marranos, 1940; Still They Come, 1941; Little People, 1944; Cave of the King, 1946; Rich Man, Poor Man, 1949; Peretz Trio, 1951; To Wake the King, 1954; Headline Parade Series, since 1946; Dramatics the Year Around, 1956; Dramatics for Creative Teaching, 1961; History of Hebrew and Yiddish Drama, sect in A History of Modern Drama, 1947; The Golden Slippers, 1967; Israel-Dream and Fulfillment 1968; TV scripts. Recipient: award, Best J TV prog, 1958; award for years of creative service in J drama and J audio-visual educ, 1964, both from Natl Council for J Audio-visual Materials. Home: 29-59 167 St, Flushing, NY. Office: 426 W 58 St, New York, NY.

CITRON, William Michael, US, attorney, legislator; b. New Haven, Conn, Aug 29, 1896; s. Benjamin and Deborah (Newmark); BA, Wesleyan U, 1918; LLB, Harvard U Law Sch, 1921; m. Helen Brodow, Sep 25, 1942; c: Nannette, Lynda. State adv, Selective Service; repr, Conn State Leg, minority leader, 1927, 1931; corp counsel, City of Middletown, 1928-34; mem: Commn for Old Age Pensions, State of Conn, 1929-34; US House of Reprs, 1934-38, mem, Judiciary Comm. Lt, US Army, 1918-19, maj, 1942-44. Chmn, Ethics Comm for Lawyers, Middlesex Co; pres: Middlesex Co Bar Assn, 1950-52; Bar Libr, 1960-64; B'nai B'rith, 1924; chmn, UJA 1956; mem: council, Conn State Bar Assn, 1961-65; Disabled Amer Vets, cdr, Dept of Conn, 1948-49; Adath Isr Syn; Masons; Odd Fellows; Elks; ZOA; AJComm. Home: 124 High St, Middletown, Conn.

CLARK, H Sol, US, attorney; b. Savannah, Ga, Dec 29. 1906; s. Sam and Ella (Raskin); BA, Cornell U, 1928, LLB, 1930; m. Matilda Shapiro, May 14, 1933; c: Fred, Janet (decd), Atty since 1930; partner, Brannen, Clark & Hester; asst city atty, 1944-47. Found, pres, Savannah Legal Aid Off, 1946-49; pres: Savannah Bar Assn, 1952; J Educ Alliance, 1936; chmn: Co Bd Public Wfr; bd, Salvation Army; March of Dimes; gen chmn, SE Ga, UJA campaign, 1947; trustee, Telfair Art Acad, 1959-62; compiler, Ga Masonic Code; f: Amer Bar Found; Intl Acad Trial Lawyers, dean 1969; Amer Coll Probate Counsel; bd dirs: Ga Heart Assn; fmr: Amer Judicature Soc, 1960-64; Natl Legal Aid and Defender Assn, 1949-59; Ga Ind Loan Adv Bd, 1955-59; mem, Masons, 33 deg. Recipient: Savannah's J man of year award, 1958; Reginald Heber Smith Award, 1961; Emory U designated H Sol Clark F, 1968. Home: 109 E 44 St, Savannah, Ga. Office: 204 Georgia State Bank Bldg, Savannah, Ga.

CLARK, Harry Edmund, Can, business exec; b. Montreal, May 26, 1911; s. Samuel and Polly (Fink); dipl, commercial educ, McGill U, Montreal Bd Trade, 1936; att Sir George Williams U, 1945-55. Pres, Overseas Chemicals Co Ltd, since 1945; past pres, St. Lawrence Toastmasters club; Masons; YMHA, gov. Clubs: Montefiore; Lachute Golf; YMCA, Bus and Profsl Men's; Wentworth Golf. Home: 6010 Cote St Luc Rd, Montreal, Can. Office: 2485 St Patrick St, Montreal, Can.

CLAYMAN, Abe Donald, US, business exec; b. Des Moines, Ia, Jan 6, 1912; s. Mendel and Rae (Renewich); m. Betty Hyman, June 1945 (decd); c: Linda Silverstein, Ronald; m. 2nd, Sophie Rutman, July 11, 1959; c. Howard Rutman, Gail Resnick, Vivian Givant. Dir: United Fed Savings and Loan since 1952; secy, Oak Creek Park Co Inc since 1964; treas, VIP Motor Homes, since 1969; trustee, Betty Clayman Trust since 1949; pres, Louis Corp. Chmn, Ia State, Isr Bonds since 1959, chmn, Des Moines drive, 1958; exec bd, comm, Tall Corn area council, Boy Scouts since 1959; pres: Des Moines lodge, B'nai B'rith, 1957, E Ia council, 1959, dist chmn, Isr comm, 1962, UN Comm, 1963, bd mem, Found of US; J Social Service, 1959-63; J Comm Cen, 1965; JWF, Des Moines, 1959-67; chmn, bd, Beth El Jacob Syn, 1950-53; treas, Tifereth Isr Syn, 1949-53; chmn, All in One Wfr Fed drive, 1960, co-chmn, 1959; mem: Masons; hospitality comm, Des Moines C of C; Mayors Youth Comm, 1963-64; Judicial Dist Nominating Comm, 1963-69. Recipient: Man of Year award, B'nai B'rith, 1965, found award, 1964. Home: 1800 Grand, W Des Moines, Ia.

CLAYTON, Aubrey Maurice, Eng, business exec; b. Manchester, Eng, Feb 9, 1917; s. Joseph and Esther (Kauffman); att Gen Grammar Sch for Boys, 1928-34; m. Cecelia Lewis; c: Esther, David, Bernard. Exporter. Chmn: King David Sch, Manchester since 1964; Mather Coll of Educ since 1968; hon treas: Manchester J. Day Cen and Club since 1963; Manchester House Heb U Manchester since 1960; Friends of Histadrut, Manchester since 1958; hon secy, Friends of Isr Philharmonic Orch, Manchester since 1954; trustee: Nathan Laski Memorial Trust since 1960; Kind David Schs Scholarship Endowment Fund since 1960; Alderman Abraham Moss Memorial Trust since 1964; magistrate, City of Manchester since 1966; educ comm mem, City of Manchester since 1961; mem council: Manchester and Salford J since 1958; Prestwich Heb Cong, 1948-66; hon corresp, Gov King David Schs since 1950; bd mem, Bd Dep Brit J, 1964-67. Home: 59 Hilton Lane, Prestwich, Manchester, Eng. Office: 37 Peter St, Manchester, Eng.

CLEEMAN, Paul, US, business exec; b. Antwerp, Belgium, Jan 26, 1934; s. Eli and Miriam (Rubenstein); in US since 1943; BA, Yeshiva Coll, NY, 1955; dipl., construction estimating, Mech Inst, NY, 1958; m. S Trina Dyckman, June 6, 1961; c: Jewel, Raymond, Michael, Edmond. First vice-pres, Walter Scott and Co, Inc since 1963; vice-pres, Universal Improvements since 1966. Vice pres, Riverdale Heb Day Sch, NY; bldg chmn, mem, bd trustees, Salanter-Akiva Riverdale Acad; mem: bd trustees, Yeshiva Beth Abraham, Jerusalem; Communal Taxpayers Assn; numerous trade, profsl, J orgs; fmr: pres, Young Adults Cong Oheb Zedek, NYC; mem bd trustees: Yeshiva Rabbi Moses Soloveichik; Cong Oheb Zedek. Recipient: Man of the Year, Yeshiva U, 1969; Sarei Alofim, Yeshiva Rabbi Moses Soloveichik, 1969. Hobbies: fencing; skiing. Home: 415 Hawthorne Ave, Yonkers, NY. Office: 225 W 57 St, New York, NY.

CLURMAN, Harold, US, stage dir, theater critic; b. NYC, Sep 18, 1901; s. Samuel and Bertha (Saphir); att: Columbia U, 1919; U Paris, 1923; hon DL; Bard Coll, 1957; Carnegie Inst of Tech, 1962; hon D, Boston U, 1969; m. Stella Adler, 1943; d, Ellen.Visiting prof, Hunter Coll; critic: The Nation since 1952, New Republic, 1948-52; actor, stage mgr, Theater Guild, 1924-31; found Group Theater, 1931, dir, 1931-42; dir: Awake 1935; Golden boy, 1937; Rocket to the Moon, 1938; Gentle and Sing, People, 1938; Deadline at Dawn, 1945; A Member of the Wedding, 1950; The Autumn Garden, 1951; Desire Under the Elms, 1951; The Time of the Cuckoo, 1952; Mademoiselle Colombe, 1954; A Touch of the Poet, 1958; A Shot in the Dark, 1961-62; Incident at Vichy, 1964; Long Day's Journey Into Night, 1965; The Iceman Cometh, 1968, Tokyo, 1968; Uncle Vanya, LA; co-produc, All My Sons, 1947. Author: The Fervent Years, 1945; Lies Like Truth, 1958; The Naked Image, 1966. Recipient, Chevalier, Legion d'Honneur, Fr, 1956; award, George Jean Nathan, 1958; Song prize, Knox Coll, 1968. Home: 205 W 57 St, New York, NY.

CLURMAN, Richard M, US journalist; b. NYC, Mar 10, 1924; s.Will and Emma (Hertzberg); PhB, U Chgo, 1946; m. Shirley Potash, Apr 13, 1957; c: Richard, Michael, Susan, Carol. Chief of corresps, Time and Life Publ, since 1961; press ed, Time, 1949-55; asst ed, Commentary, 1946-49; ed dir, Newsday, 1955-58. US Army, 1942-46. Chmn bd, NYC Cen of Music and Drama. Home: 11 Fifth Ave, New York, NY. Office: Time and Life Bldg, Rockefeller Center, New York, NY.

COBURN, Seymour K, US, engineer; b. Chgo, Dec 21, 1917; s. Henry and Kate Brownstein; BS, U Chgo, 1940; MS, Ill Inst of Tech, 1951; m. Elsa Freed, Dec 6, 1948; c: Karen, Kenneth, Monica, Valerie, Marshall. Asso research cons, since 1959; auth on atmospheric corrosion of metals; cons to NYC, Chgo, Air Pollution Atmospheric Monitoring Test; responsible for bldg first skyscraper in weathering steel, Chgo Civic Cen, 1967; participated in last open air atomic bomb test, Yucca Flats, Nevada, 1955; corrosion engr, US Steel Corp, since 1959; chem engr, Assn of Amer RR, 1951-59; chem, Lever Bros, 1944-51. Mem: B'nai B'rith; Dor Hadassah Cong; Amer Chem Soc; Natl Assn Corrosion Engrs; Amer Soc for Testing Materials; Amer Soc for Metals; Sigma Xi; Phi Lambda Epsilon. Contbr to sci and engr jours. Home: 5733 Northumberland Rd, Pittsburgh, Pa. Office: 125 Jamison La, Monroeville, Pa.

CODEL, Martin, US, TV-radio cons; b. Duluth, Minn, May 18, 1902; s. Morris and Sarah (Fagie); AB, U Mich, 1924; m. Ella April, July 1, 1927; c: Sue Seligson, Martha, Nancy (decd),

Richard. TV-radio cons since 1959; staff mem: AP, NY, 1925-26, S Amer, 1964-65; US Daily, Wash, 1926; columnist, N Amer Newspaper Alliance, 1927; org, mgr, Radio News Bur, 1927-35; found, ed, Broadcasting Mag, 1931-44; found, publisher, TV Digest 1945-59; surveyed: TV potential of Afr for RCA, 1960; TV-radio, W Hemisphere, Time Inc, 1960-62, Asia, 1963, S Amer, 1964-65. Adv, council on TV-radio, Wis State Hist Soc; mem: adv comm, O State Inst for Educ by TV and Radio; exec comm, AJComm; Phi Sigma Delta; Sigma Delta Chi; clubs: Natl Press; Overseas Writers. Author: Radio and Its Future, 1930. Home: 2734 34 Pl NW, Washington DC. Office: 505 Grange Bldg, Washington, DC.

COFNAS, Jerachmiel, Eng, Rabbi; b. Olkienik, Pol, Dec 27, 1912; S. Kalmen and Basia (Etel); desc Rabbi of Moldechney, Pol; att Radum and Grodno Yeshivoth, Pol; m. Bertha Sternberg, c: L Cofnas, Yulia Warshawsky, Sylvia. Rabbi, New Syn. Spec interests: gen communal wfr work, adult educ. Home: 107 Edgbaston Rd, Birmingham, Eng. Study: 11 Park Rd, Moseley, Birmingham, Eng.

COGAN, David Joseph, US, business exec,; b. Kishiniv, Rum, Feb 7, 1923; s. Morris and Helen; in US since 1925; BBA, St Johns U, NY, 1945; att CCNY, 1939-40; m. Ferne Milder, Feb 11, 1945; c: Sharon, Carol. Theater owner; Broadway, motion picture produc; fmr partner, Cogan, Bell and Co; produc: A Raisin in the Sun; In the Counting House; Odd Couple; Midnight Sun. Cpl, US Army, 1942. Mem: bd dirs: Heb Sch for Music and Dance; Family Inst; bd govs, League of NY Theaters; club, Lone Star Boat. Recipient, NY Drama Critics Award, 1958. Hobbies and spec interests: music, theater, movies. Home: 350 Fifth Ave, New York, NY.

COGAN, Leo Judah, US, rabbi, business exec; b. Bklyn, NY, Apr 1, 1918; s. Harris and Dinah (Ratush); BA, Bklyn Coll, 1943; MS, Columbia U, 1946; ordained rabbi, Yeshiva Beth Joseph, Bialystock, Pol, 1939; m. Ruth Kiel, June 24, 1945; c: Rebecca, Jesse, Harris. Pres, Arrow Knitting Mills; rabbi: Cong Tifereth Isr, W Flatbush, 1940-43; Mapleton Park Heb Inst, 1943-48; Cong Tifereth Isr, Mapleton Park, 1948-56. Pres, Hapoel Hamizrachi of Amer; bd dirs: Heb Inst of LI: Cong Ohab Zedek; Belle Harbor J Cen; mem: Soc Bibl Lit and Exegesis; Amer Acad for J Research; Amer J Hist Soc; RabCA; NY Bd Rabbis; ZOA; Mizrachi Org. Home: 192 Beach 124 St, Belle Harbor, NY Office; 350 Fifth Ave, New York, NY.

COGAN, Nathan, Isr, actor; b. Baku, Russ, May 14, 1914; s. Josef and Gusta (Wasserman); att Dramatic Sch & Conservatorium, Bucharest, 1934-35; in Isr since 1935; m. Vardana Horowitz, Aug 21, 1952; c: Hamutal, Ayelet. Mem: Chamber Theatre since 1946; Sadan Theatre, 1936-38; Matate Theatre, 1938-39; Teatron Ivri, 1939; Pal Opera, 1940-41; Do-Re-Mi Theatre, 1941; J. Brigade, Brit Army, 1942-46. Mem, Actors Union. Home: 28 Frug St, Tel Aviv, Isr. Office: Chamber Theatre, Tel Aviv, Isr.

COGAN, Robert David, US, composer; b. Detroit, Mich, Feb 2, 1930; s. Leon and Merrium (Gottschalk); BMus, MMus, U Mich, 1947-52; MFA, Princeton U, 1956; att Staatliche Hochschule für Musik, Hamburg, Ger, 1958-60. m. Pozzi Escot July 1, 1959. Chmn, theoretical studies, mem fac composition, NE Conservatory, since 1963. Musical works include: Fantasia for Orchestra, 1951; Composition for String Trio, 1959; Sounds and Variants, 1961; Spaces and Cries, 1964; whirl...ds I, 1968; whirl...ds II, 1969; musical works performed by: Cleveland Orch; Hamburg Radio Orch; RIAS Orch, Berlin; Berkshire Music Cen Orch; N Ger Radio; W Ger Eadio; Rothschild Found; Fromm Music Found; conductors: Gunther Schuller; Jacques t-Louis Monod; New Event Ensemble; Jan de Gaetani; U's: Ill; Mich; Colo; Oregon; Eastman Sch of Music; Composers Forum of NY; NE Conservatory. Mem: Phi Beta Kappa; US sect, Intl Soc for Contemporary Music. Contbr to: music jours; Ency Americana. Recipient, Guggenheim F, 1968. Home: 24 Avon Hill St, Cambridge, Mass. Office: 290 Huntington Ave, Boston, Mass.

COGEN, Charles, US, teacher; b. NY, Oct 31, 1903; s. Joseph and Bessie (Wishnick) Cohen; AB, Cornell U, 1924; LLB, Fordham U, 1927; MA, Columbia U, 1931; m. Tess Schnittkramer, Feb 9, 1930; c: Joel, Edward. Cons: Amer Fed of Tchrs, since 1968; past pres; Design for Learning, Inc, since 1969; pres: Econ Tchrs Assn NYC; AssnTchrs of Social Studies, NYC; United Fed Tchrs, 1952-64; chmn, dept social studies,

Bay Ridge HS, 1952-64; Natl secy, J Lab Comm; hon vice-chmn; Amer Trade Union Council, Natl Council for Lab Isr; vice-pres, League for Ind Dem; delg, US natl comm for UNESCO; vice-pres, Council of AFL-CIO Union of Sci, Profsl and Cultural Employees; mem; exec bd, Workers Defense League; Amer Econ Assn; fmr: pres, Amer Fed of Tchrs; vice-pres, ind dept, AFL-CIO. Author: Review Materials in Economics, 1935; Economics in Our Democracy, 1950. Hobbies: theater, music, chess. Home: 185 Park Row, New York, NY.

COHEN, Abraham H, US, public relations counselor; b. Preluk, Russ, April 15, 1900; s. Issac and Chernia (Haft); in US since 1905; m. Dora Hackman, 1925 (decd); c: Elihu, Matanah. Counsel, in PR, NYC since 1934; in actuarial dept, Mutual Life Ins Co, 1917-19; mgr, Navy Knitting Mills and Camel Sportwear, 1921-24; exec dir, LI Pal Found Fund, 1924-27; org dir, J Educ Assn, NY, 1927-32; exec dir AJCong, 1932-34; an org, Forest Hills J Cen; org: bd dir, Amer Assn for J Educe since 1937; and first pres, ZOA, Forest Hills Dist, 1937-42; Centennial Celebration, Temple Emanuel, NYC; Heb Home for Aged, Riverdale, NY, secy, World J Conf, Geneva, Switz, 1932; natl chmn, JNF on behalf of ZOA, 1941-43; bd dirs, JNF and UPA 1940-48; chmn, admn comm, JBCA, exec bd since 1940; natl treas, 1948-54, pres, NY Metrop J Book Council, 1944-50, hon pres since 1950; bd dirs, JWB, NYC; trustee Tchrs Sem and Peoples U; Herzlia Tchrs Inst; Amer Mus J Culture; Rabb Sem of Amer: mem, Intercoll Menorah Soc; Amer PR Assn found; ZOA; Forest Hills J Cen; B'rith Rishonim of US; Amer Geriatrics Assn; pres J Club 1937-42, 1945-47, 1949-51, 1958-69. Contbr articles to De Haas Ency of Jewish Knowledge. Spec interests: J Educ, Isr, Zionism, geriatrics. Home: 7131 Manse St, Forest Hills, NY. Office: 250 W 57 St, New York, NY.

COHEN, Aharon, Isr, lecturer, author, orientalist; b. Bessarabia, Russ, June 3, 1910; s. Yosef and Rachel (Kliger) Kegan; in Isr since 1929; m. Rivka Ghivelder, June, 1931; c: Tirtza, Yosef. Mem, Kibbutz Sha'ar Ha'amakim. Author: Israel Veha'olam Ha'aravi, 1964, Eng ed, 1969; Hamizrach Ha'aravi, 1955, 2nd ed, 1957, 3rd ed, 1960; Ha'olam Ha'aravi Shel Yameinu, 1958; 2nd ed, 1960; Tmurot Mediniyot Ba'olam Ha'aravi, 1959; 2nd ed, 1965; contbr to Ency of Social Sci. Secy, Magdiel Workers Council; fmr: delg: Histadrut Confs; 19th ZC; mem: exec comm, Arab dept, Histadrut; exec comm, Kibbutz Arzi; co-found, mem cen comm, Mapam; secy, League for J-Arab Friendship and Coop. Home: Kibbutz Sha'ar Ha'amakim, Isr.

COHEN, A David, S Afr, attorney; b. Outdshoorn, S Afr, June 13, 1913; s. Simon and Jeannie (Manaschewitz); m. Joyce Josephson, Nov 2, 1952. Atty, Supr Court, S Afr, since 1935. State chmn, Lions Intl; fmr pres, Heb Order of David. Home: 3 Ajax Rd, Dalview, Brakpan, S Afr. Office: 101/115 Sheffreel House, Prince George Ave, Brakpan, S Afr.

COHEN, Alan Norman, US, business exec; b. Clifton, NJ, Dec 19, 1930; s. Samuel and Ida (Phillips); BA, Columbia Coll, 1951; JD, Columbia Law Sch, 1954; m. Joan Fields, Nov 25, 1953; c: Laurie, Gordon. Sr vice-pres, dir, Kinney Natl Services Inc since 1970; partner, law firm, Paul Weiss, Goldberg, Rifkind, Wharton & Garrison, 1957-70; US Army, 1955-57. Chmn, personal income tax comm, NY State Bar Assn, 1969-70; vice-pres, treas, Temple Shomrei Emunah; trustee, Temple Beth Tikva, Wayne, NJ; mem, Bd of Adjustment, Montclair. Hobbies: tennis, politics. Home: 77 Myrtle Ave, Montclair, NJ. Office: 10 Rockefeller Plaza, New York, NY.

COHEN, Alan Seymour, US, educator; b. Boston, Mass, Apr 9, 1926; s. George and Jennie (Laskin); AB, magna cum laude, Harvard U, 1947; MD, magna cum laude, Boston U Sch of Med, 1952; m. Joan Elizabeth Prince, Sep 12, 1954; c: Evan, Andrew, Robert. Prof, med, Boston U Sch of Med, since 1968, head, arthritis and connective tissue disease sect, U Hosp, since 1960; cons, rheumatology: Commonwealth of Mass, since 1964; Arthritis Found, since 1965; spec cons, USPHS, since 1966; teaching and research F in med, Harvard Med Sch, 1953-55; registrar in med, St Andrew's U Med Sch, Scotland, 1955-56; research and clinical F in med, Mass Gen Hosp, 1956-58; instr, med, Harvard Med Sch, 1958-60; Wellcome Research Travelling F, Isr, 1960; surg, USPHS, 1953-55. Prin contribs: patient care; rheumatology; anyloid disease. F, Arthritis and Rheumatism Found, 1956-59; mem: exec comm, Amer Rheumatism Assn, chmn, publ,

criteria comms; bd dirs, governing comm, med admn comm, Arthritis Found; Amer Soc for Clinical Inves; Amer Fed for Clinical Research; Electron Microscopy Soc of Amer; Amer Soc Experimental Path; Amer Soc for Cell Biol; Phi Beta Kappa; Alpha Omega Alpha; NY Acad Sci; Soc for Experimental Biol and Med; Mass Med Soc; past pres, NE Rheumatism Soc. Club, Harvard, Boston. Author, Laboratory Diagnostic Procedures in the Rheumatic Diseases, 1967; co-ed, Amyloidosis, 1968; contbr numerous articles to med publs. Recipient: Maimonides Award, Gtr Boston Med Soc, 1952; One of 4 Outstanding Men in Mass, Mass Jr C of C, 1961. Hobby, tennis. Home: 54 Winston Rd, Newton Cen, Mass. Office: 750 Harrison Ave, Boston, Mass.

COHEN, Albert, Switz, author; b. Corfu, Greece, Aug 16, 1895; s. Marc and Louise (Ferro); in Switz since 1947; m. Bella Berkowich, Feb 21, 1955. Author: Parole Juives, poems, 1920; Solal, novel, Fr, Ger, Eng, 1930, Ezechiel, play, produced at Comédie Française, 1933; Mangeclous, novel, Fr, Eng, 1938; Le Livre de ma Mère, Fr, Swed, Span, Port, 1954; Belle du Seigneur, novel, awarded Grand Prix du Roman, Académie Française, 1968. Legal adv, intergovernmental comm on refs, London; dir, protection div, IRO, Geneva. Recipient: Commandeur de l'Ordre de Léopold II; Chevalier de la Légion d'Honneur. Home: 7 Avenue Krieg, Geneva, Switz.

COHEN, Alex, US, government official; b. Arnheim, Holland, May 28, 1897; s. Michael and Margaret (Jacobson); in US since 1916; m. Rita Guerra, Apr 9, 1947; c: Margaret, Rita, Alex. Ret; 1st secy, Emb, political, lab off, San Jose, Costa Rica, 1961-63, with State Dept since 1942; with mil intelligence, War Dept, 1922-29, 1932-42. USN, 1917-19; US Army, 1919-22. Mem: Masons, life; Scottish Rite; club, Collectors, NY. Recipient: Medal of Freedom, War Dept, 1947; superior service award, State Dept, 1958. Hobbies: Mozart, philately, orchids. Home: 1233 NW 36 Dr, Gainesville, Fla.

COHEN, Alfredo David, Guat, business exec; b. Guat City, Guat, May 16, 1925; s. Alberto and Raquel (Cohen); att: Eng-Amer Bus Sch, Guat; Soulé Bus Sch, New Orleans; m. Emmy Moryde, Mar 25, 1962; c: Felix, Miriam, Daniel. Life Ins broker and exec, since 1966; acctnt, Pan-Amer Life, off mgr, 1944-56; gen broker, US Life Ins Co, 1959-66. Prin contribs: training, devl of brokers; lecturing, monitoring of employees. Pres: Magen David, fmr, mem, bd dirs; Dynamo Club-Pan-Amer Life Ins; treas, cen council J comty, 1967-69. Author, Florilegio (selected pieces of lit), 1960. Mem: Aeroclub, Guat; Million Dollar Round Table. Recipient: Air Race Championship, Club de Magos, Guat, 1954; Honor Roll Man of Year, Ins Salesman, 1965. Hobbies: airplane piloting, carpentry, organ playing. Home: 19-29 9 Ave, Guatemala City, Guat. Office: 6-20 1a C, Guatemala City, Guat.

COHEN, Archibald C, US, physician; b. Clark's Harbour, Can, Feb 13, 1909; s. Abraham and Rachel (Smofsky); in US since 1924; BA, Harvard U, 1928, MD, 1933; m. Shulamith Rabb, Aug 30, 1942. Chief, med service VA Hosp since 1962, staff since 1947; staff phys: VA Hosps, Oteen, NC; Indianapolis and Aspinwall, Pa, 1950-54; res: TB Hosps; Montefiore Sanatorium, Bedford Hills, NY, 1934-35, 1938-39; White Haven Sanatorium 1937-38. Maj, US Army, 1944-46; col, US Army Res, 1946-48. Pres: Butler Co TB Soc, 1957-60; Pa Trudeau Soc, 1956-57; Pa chap, Amer Coll Chest Phys, 1960-61; dir, Butler Co Philatelic Soc, 1950-62; mem: AMA; Natl TB Assn; Amer Thoracic Soc; ZOA; Rel Zionists Amer; Amer Topical Assn. Author, The Drug Treatment of Tuberculosis, 1966; contbr: sect on Tuberculosis, Encyclopedia of Medicine, Surg and Specialities; numerous pulmonary diseases to med jours. Hobby, philately. Home: 8 King David Court, Butler, Pa. Office: VA Hosp, Butler, Pa.

COHEN, Armond E, US, rabbi, author; b. Canton, O, June 5, 1909; s. Samuel and Rebecca (Lipkowitz); BA, NYU, 1930; ordained rabbi, JTSA, 1934; MHL, 1937, DD, 1966; hon f, Heb U Jerusalem, 1969; LLD, Cleveland Marshall Law Sch, 1969; m. Anne Lederman, June 28, 1934; c: Rebecca Long, Deborah (decd), Samuel. Rabbi, Park Syn since 1934; visiting prof, JTSA since 1965; lectr, Amer Found of Rel and Psycht since 1953. Pres: JNF, 1938-40; Zionist dist, 1940-42; hon, natl vice-pres, ZOA; dir: Amer Cancer Soc; JWF; trustee: Cleveland Mh Assn; Consumers League, O; bd govs, Amer Found Rel and Psycht; mem, Unemployment Compensation Comm, O since 1938. Author: Outline in Medieval Hebrew

Literature, 1937; Selected Reading in Zionism, 1938; All God's Children, 1945; ed bd, Jour of Rel and Health. Home: 3273 Euclid Hts Blvd, Cleveland Heights, O. Study: 3325 Euclid Hts Blvd, Cleveland Heights, O.

COHEN, Arthur A, US, business exec, author; b. NYC, June 25, 1928; s. Isidore and Bess (Junger); BA, U Chgo, 1946, MA, 1949; att JTSA, 1951-53; m. Elaine Firstenberg, Oct 6, 1956; c, Tamar. Cons ed, E P Dutton and Co and Viking Press since 1968; co-found, mgn dir, Noonday Press, 1951-55; found, pres, Meridan Books, 1955-60; vice-pres, World Publ, 1960-61; dir, rel dept, Holt, Rinehart and Winston, 1961-63; ed-in-chief, vice-pres, gen book div, 1964-68. Author: Martin Buber, 1958; The Natural and The Supernatural Jew, 1962; The Carpenter Years, 1966; The Myth of the Judeo-Christian Tradition, 1970; Error: Arguments and Doctrines, 1970; Faith: Theological Essays of Milton Steinberg, 1960; ed, Judaism since 1969; bd adv, Congress Bi-Weekly; contbr to: Religion and the Free Society, 1958; American Catholics; A Protestant-Jewish View, 1959; Religion and Contemporary Society, 1963; contbr to J and gen periodicals. Adv council mem, Inst for Advanced Judaic Studies, Brandeis U. Spec interest, collecting primitive art. Home: 160 E 70 St, New York, NY.

COHEN, Ben, US, business exec; b. Baltimore, Md, Jan 27, 1900; s. Isaac and Marsha (Pondfield); att Franklin Sch of Acctnt, Baltimore; m. Zelda Greenberg, Jan 29, 1928; c: Rosalee Davidson, Charlotte Weinberg. Pres, House Engr Co, Baltimore, asso real estate bldg and devls since 1939; vice-pres, Charg-it, Fla, since 1960; secy-treas, Md Jockey Club, Pimlico Race Track since 1952. Pres, Herman and Ben Cohen Charity Found since 1949; life mem, bd dirs, Oheb Shalom Cong since 1950; mem: comms, Assn J Charities; club, Suburban Country. Hobby, thoroughbred breeding and racing stables. Home: 6701 Park Hgts Ave, Baltimore, Md. Office: 1229 Mt Royal Ave, Baltimore, Md.

COHEN, Benjamin, Isr, judge; b. Strasbourg, Fr, July 17, 1913; s. Moshe and Rachel (Nessel); in Isr since 1920; Licencie en Droit, U Lyon, 1934; m. Tamar Frank, Sep 20, 1934; c: Yael, Naomi Barzilai, Alon. Judge, Dist Court of Tel Aviv since 1950; advocate, pvt practice, 1938-50. Chief legal off, Isr Army, 1948-49. Contbr to law jours. Home: 4 Yehuda Halevi St, Tel Aviv, Isr. Office: Dist Court of Tel Aviv, Tel Aviv, Isr.

COHEN, Benjamin V, US, attorney, government official; b. Muncie, Ind, Sep 23, 1894; s. Moses and Sarah (Ringold); PhB, U Chgo, 1914, JD, 1915; JDS, Harvard U, 1916; hon LLD, Dropsie Coll, 1952. Secy, US Circuit Judge Mack, 1916-17; atty, US Shipping Bd, 1917-18; counsel, Amer Zionist Peace Conf, 1919-21; pvt law practice, NYC, 1922-23; asso gen counsel, Public Works Admn, Wash DC, 1933-34; natl gen counsel, Power Policy Commn, 1934-41; spec asst, US Atty-Gen, 1934-41; adv, US Emb, London, Eng, 1942-43; gen counsel, Off War Mobilization, 1943-45; counselor, US State Dept, 1945-47; legal adv, Intl Monetary Conf, 1944; delg, Dumbarton Oaks Conf, 1944; US delg: Berlin Conf, 1945; Council of Fgn Mins: London, 1945; Moscow, 1945, 1947, Paris, 1946, NYC, 1946; Peace Conf, Paris, 1946; sr adv, US Delg to UN, 1946; alternate repr: US to UN, 1948-52; UN Disarmament Comm, 1952; US repr, Intl Court of Justice, The Hague, 1950. Mem, Phi Beta Kappa. Author: United Nations, Constitutional Developments, Growth and Possibilities (the Holmes Lectures), 1961. Recipient: The Niles Memorial Lecture, Heb U, Jerusalem, 1965. Home: 1727 Massachusetts Ave, Washington, DC.

COHEN, Benno, Isr, attorney, legislator; b. Ger, Sep 30, 1894; s. Abraham and Bertha (Foerder); LLB, U Breslau, 1922; m. Susi Tugendhat, 1933; c, Yehudit. MK, repr, Lib Party since 1961; lectr on public admn, Sch of Law and Econ, Tel Aviv; dir org of immigrants from Ger, 1939-47; pres, Disciplinary Court of Isr, 1951-59; co-found, political parties: Aliya Hadash; Progressive Party; Lib Party; official, Off of PM, 1949-59. Chmn: org of immigrants from Cen Eur; Zionist Org, Berlin, Ger. Home: 4 Hakerem St, Tel Aviv, Isr.

COHEN, Bernard, US, educator; b. NYC, Nov 21, 1927; s. Mendel and Elka (Stuchinski): AB, SF State Coll, 1951; att, U of S Cal, 1954; MA, W Mich U, 1965; m. Phyllis Fleck, July 3, 1955; c: Jeffrey, Martin. Trades training counsellor, since 1968; fmr: speech therapist: Muskegon Area Sch Dist, 1963-68; E St Louis, Ill, Sch Dist, 1958-63; mem, Pilot

Project, Sask Dept of Public Health, 1961; prog comm mem, Mich Speech and Hearing Assn, 1966-67; fmr: film theater mgr, Ill Council for Exceptional Children, adv comm, Exceptional Children Week; film chmn, Speech Correctionists, E St Louis Public Schs. Pvt, US Army, 1946-47. Pres: Abraham Rosen Lodge 818; Chokia chap CEC; pres elect, W Shore Council for Exceptional Children; mem: Emanuel Epstein B'nai B'rith Lodge; NEA; Wise, Kenosha Educ Assns; Amer, Wis Personnel and Guidance Assns; Intl, Wis Assns for Pupil Personnel Workers; Wis Assn for Children with Behavioral Disorders; fmr: bd dirs, United Cerebral Palsy Assn, Gtr St Clair and Madison Co; treas, Gtr St Louis Speech and Hearing Assn. Hobbies: records, books. Home: 8524 18 Ave, Kenosha, Wis. Office: 611 56 St, Kenosha, Wis.

COHEN, Bernard Eli, Isr, pediatrician; b. Cape Town, S Afr, Dec 26, 1919; s. Max and Sarah (Penn); in Isr since 1952; MB, ChB, U Cape Town, 1941, Public Health Cert, 1946; DCH, MRCP, Liverpool, Edinburgh; m. Blanche Schneider; c: Shai, Shelli. Dir: dept ped and assessment cen for retarded, Phenylketonuria Unit, Tel Hashomer Govt Hosp since 1952; fmr: mem adv comm for retarded, Isr Min of Health; visiting prof ped, Albert Einstein Coll Meds, NY; WHO cons, PKU Collaborative Project; prin inves of mental retardation in Isr, grants from Wfr Admn, Children's Bur, Wash, DC. Capt, S Afr Army MC; IDF Res Med Corps, 1954-68. Mem exec, ped br, IMA; Jerusalem Acad of Med; fmr: co-chmn, Intl Symposium PKU and Allied Metabolic Disorders; council of admn, Intl League of Soc for Handicapped, Brussels; councillor, bd, Intl Assn of Sci Study of Mental Deficiency. Contbr to sci publs. Recipient, Dr, Joseph Meir Award, Histadrut Sick Fund, 1962. Hobbies: music, golf. Home: 15 Hagederoth St, Savyon, Isr. Office: Tel Hashomer Hosp, Tel Hashomer, Isr.

COHEN, D Walter, US, dentist, educator; b. Phila, Pa, Dec 15, 1926; s. Abram and Goldie (Schlein); DDS, U of Pa, 1950; m. Betty Axelrod, Dec 19, 1948; c: Jane, Amy, Joanne. Pvt practice periodontics since 1951; prof, chmn dept, periodontics, U of Pa Sch of Dent Med since 1962, dean for academic affairs, 1969; visiting prof, periodontics, Boston U Sch of Grad Dent since 1965; guest lectr, Temple U Sch of Dent since 1954; visiting prof, U of Ill Coll of Med, 1962; cons: periodontics, Ft Dix Army Base since 1960; VA since 1961; chief, periodontics, Phila Gen Hosp since 1960; staff, Einstein Med Cen since 1953; natl cons, periodontics, USAF, 1965-69. USN, 1945-46. Dir, Amer Bd Periodontology since 1966; pres: Amer Soc Periodontists, 1966-67; Phila Soc Periodontology, 1959-60; Phila secy, Intl Assn for Dent Research, 1959-60; f: Amer Coll Dents; Amer Acad Oral Path; mem: Sigma Xi; Omicron Kappa Upsilon; Alpha Omega; Varsity, U of Pa. Co-author: Periodontia, 1957; Introduction to Periodontia, 1959, 1969; Periodontal Therapy, 1968. Home: 124 Colwyn Lane, Cynwyd, Pa. Office: 4001 Spruce St, Philadelphia, Pa.

COHEN, Daniel C, US, lawyer; b. Phila, Pa, Aug 11, 1927; s. Hyman and Clara (Rosenfeld); LLB, Harvard Law Sch, Cambridge, Mass, 1951; BHL, Gratz Coll, Phila, 1956; m. Louise Dine, Oct 7, 1956; c: Jonathan, Eve, Judith, Benjamin. Partner, Wolf, Block, Schorr and Solis-Cohen, since 1951; USNR, 1945-46; Lt, US Army Jagcorps, 1952-54. Pres: Cong Mikveh Isr; HIAS and council migration service, 1963-66; vice-pres, Gratz Coll; trustee, Fed of J Agcys; mem: Amer Judicature Soc; Amer, Pa, Phila and Fed Bar Assns. Home: 7610 Mountain Ave, Elkins Park, Pa. Office: 12th floor, Packard Bldg, Philadelphia, Pa.

COHEN, David, Isr, author; b. Russ, 1894; s. Avraham and Roshka; in Isr since 1924; m. Luba Goldberg; c: Mula, Oorie, Rachel Peled. Ret; fmr: tchr; journalist. Author: legends: Asher Shamati Vesaparti; Agadot Kinneret; Rinat Haneurim; Lamed Vav Agadot; Shearim Nivtechim; books trans into Yiddish, Span; travels throughout Isr to tell his legends: Agadot Mitnagot put to music by Yoahim Stuchewsky; contbr to press in Isr and abroad. Found, Working Youth Org in Isr, educ; Working and Learning Youth of Histadrut. Home: 17 Modigliani St, Tel Aviv, Isr. Office: 93 Arlosoroff St, Tel Aviv, Isr.

COHEN, David, Isr, investment banker; b. Tel Aviv, Isr, Oct 21, 1929; s. Haim and Sarah (Selimansky); BA, Ill Coll, 1951 MIA, Columbia U, 1952; PhD, LSE, London, 1960; m. Judith Kanner, June 15, 1957; c: Rona, Shelly. Co repr i/c, First Hanover Corp, Tel Aviv br, since 1969; dir, Dorit Inves since

1964; lectr, Heb U, 1953-54, 1957-58; econ dept, JA, London, 1958-60, dir cos bur, 1961-64. Pvt, IDF, 1952. Mem: Cen Comm Lib Party; Financial Soc Isr; Ind and Commercial Club of Tel Aviv. Contbr of econ articles to profsl jours. Recipient: Sinai Campaign and 6-Day War insignias. Home: 16 Chissin St, Tel Aviv, Isr. Office: 70 Ibn Gvirol St, Tel Aviv, Isr.

COHEN, David Z, Isr, business exec; b. Tel Aviv, Isr, Feb 27, 1927; s. Abraham and Glika (Goldfinger); BS, Columbia U, 1954; MS, Princeton U, 1956; m. Zivia Bergner; c: Eyal, Tamar. Gen mgr, IBM Isr, since 1967; chief computer engr, Min of Defence, 1959-64; project mgr, RCA, Camden, NJ, 1956-59. Maj, IDF, 1947-50. Prin contribs: patents in computer circuits and sys designs. Dir, Amer-Isr C of C. Home: 17 Lidsky St, Tel Aviv, Isr. Office: 15 Lincoln St, Tel Aviv, Isr.

COHEN, Douglas Harry, Austr, surgeon; b. Sydney, Austr, Feb 10, 1920; s. Leslie and Susan (Solomon); MB, BS, U Sydney, 1942; MS, 1950; f, Royal Australasian Coll of Med, 1950; m. Lysabeth Cohen, Feb 15, 1943; c: Susan, Richard. Sr ped surg, Royal Alexandra Hosp for Children, since 1965. Capt, Austr Army, 1944-46. Author, Malignant Disease in Childhood. Mem. Court of Examiners, treas, State Comm, Royal Australasian Coll of Surgs; mem: Austr Ped Assn; Brit and Pacific Assn of Ped Surgs; clubs: U, Sydney; Royal Sydney Yacht Squadron. Contbr numerous articles to profsl jours. Hobbies: sailing, painting. Home: 40 Shirley Rd, Wowstonecraft, NSW, Austr. Office: Royal Alexandra Hospital for Children, Camperdown, NSW, Austr.

COHEN, E Richard, US, physicist; b. Phila, Pa, Dec 14, 1922; s. Harry and Rose (Brodsky); AB, hons, U of Pa, 1943; MS, hons,Cal Inst of Tech, 1946; PhD, physics, magna cum laude, 1949; m. Gilda Rosenblatt, Oct 18, 1953; c, Shelly. Asso dir sci cen, N A Rockwell since 1962; sr asso, Engr and Applied Sci. Cal Inst of Tech since 1964, with Inst since 1944; instr physics: U of Pa, 1943-44; Atomics Intl, 1949-62. Prin contribs: co-holder patent on small nuclear heat source. Mem: comm, fundamental phys constants, NRC; adv bd, Off Critical Tables; Intl Union Pure and Applied Physics, commn on atomic masses, 1960-69, secy, 1969-72; ed adv bd, Nuclear Sci and Engr Jour, Amer Nuclear Soc; adv comm, reactor physics, AEC, 1954-69; delg: Intl Conf on Peaceful Uses of Atomic Energy, Geneva, 1955, 1958; Congresso Internationale sulle Constanti Fondamentali della Fisica, Torino, 1956; mem: Assn for Computing Machinery; AAAS; Sci Research Soc of Amer; Pi Mu Epsilon; Sigma Xi; f: Amer Nuclear Soc; Amer Phys Soc. Author: Methods of Least Squares, Ency Britannica, 1955; co-author: Physical Units, Ency Britannica, 1956; Fundamental Constants of Physics, 1957; mem, ed adv bd, Jour of Stat Physics, 1968; contbr to profsl books and jours. Recipient: Ernest Orlando Lawrence Memorial Award, 1968. Home: 17735 Corinthian Dr, Encino, Cal. Office: 1049 Camino Dos Rios, Thousand Oaks, Cal.

COHEN, Edward, US, foundation adv; b. NYC, Jan 21, 1930; s. Joseph and Marilyn (Cohen); BSS, CCNY, 1951; att Columbia U, 1951-52; m. Elizabeth Birtwell, Dec 31, 1952; c: John, Ann, Susan, Alicia, Pamela. Dir, Two Years Colls, NJ Dept Higher Educ; sup, group work, YM-YWHA, Bklyn, NY, 1955; press off, Amer Emb, Belgrade, Yugo, 1957-61; asst cultural affairs off, educ affairs, US Govt, Caracas, Venezuela, 1962-63; vice-pres, Intl Devl Found, 1963-68. Sgt, US Army, 1952-54. Ed, US Cultural Rev, Pregled, Belgrade, 1957-61. Recipient: meritorious service award, USIS, 1961; commendation ribbon. Hobbies: hiking, boating. Home: 43 Eglantine Ave, Pennington, NJ. Office: 225 W State St, Trenton, NJ.

COHEN, Edward I, US, attorney, business cons; b. NYC, Apr 30, 1943; s. Alfred and Irma (Doris); BA, Cornell U, 1964; MBA, 1967, JD, 1968; m. Sylvia Golbin, June 11, 1967. Pvt practice since 1968; cons, Metal Purchasing Co since 1965; asst, atty gen, NY State, 1966: mem, intl dept, Der Danske Provinsbank, Copenhagen, Den, 1967. Mem: Assn for Intl Exch of Students in Econ and Commerce, org, Cornell, 1966-67; Amer Fgn Law Assn; Amer Bar Assn; NY State Bar Assn; Inst on Taxation of Fgn Income; Practicing Law Inst; Alumni Class Council of 1965; fmr: co-found, Cornell Soc Intl Law; chmn: inv price fixing comm, Cornell U; Friends of Silver Fox, 1965-68; mem, Phi Alpha Delta. Author: Scarsdale High School Handbook, 1961. Home: 100 Split Tree Rd, Scarsdale, NY. Office: 175 W 13 St, New York, NY.

COHEN, Edward M, US, foreign service off; b. Bklyn, NY, Oc 25, 1931; s. Benjamin and Irene (Greenblatt); BA, Bklyn Coll, 1953; att: NYU, 1955; U of Cal, 1962-63; m. Elly Kempler, Nov 22, 1952; c: Diana, Wendy, Ned. Chief, econ and commercial sect, US Consulate Gen, Dacca, E Pakistan, since 1967; press off, State Dept, Wash, DC, 1956-58; Amer vice-consul, Niagara Falls, Ont, 1959; consul, Hamilton, Bermuda, 1959-62; econ off, US Emb, Athens, Greece, 1963-67. Home: c/o Kempler, 8635 21 Ave, Brooklyn, NY. Office: Amer Consulate Gen, Dacca, E Pakistan.

COHEN, Edward Milton, US, business exec; b. Uniontown, Pa, Sep 5, 1909; s. Max and Lillian (Shirk); BS, U Pittsburgh, 1931; m. Emily Weinberg, May 28, 1933; c: Miles, Lois Sodokoff. Pres, secy treas, Cohen Furniture Co; treas, Brunton Knitting Mills, 1958-60. Chmn bd, Natl Retail Furniture Assn, 1962; dir, Uniontown Comty Chest since 1948; Uniontown Credit Bur; Uniontown Hosp, 1952-60; Pa Retailers Assn, 1957-61; pres, Temple Isr, 1938-49; Uniontown C of C, 1956-57; clubs: Pittsburgh Furniture; Uniontown Exch; Westmoreland Country. Home: 5407 Beacon St, Pittsburgh, Pa. Office: 19 Beeson Blvd. Uniontown Pa.

COHEN, Emil L, US, attorney; b. Buffalo, NY, Mar 8, 1911; s. Samuel and Rose (Laufer). LLB, cum laude, U Buffalo, 1933; m. Bernice Kaiser, June 28, 1935; c: Susan, Nancy, Bruce. Pvt practice since 1934; asso mem, Philip Halpern, 1935-43; spec tax foreclosure atty, Corp Counsel, City of Buffalo, 1936; mem, research staff, majority leader, NY State Constitution Conv, 1938; asst atty gen, State of NY, 1943-52; confidential law asst, Supr Court Justices, 8th jud dist, Buffalo, 1952-53; secy, NY State Supr Court Justice R Foster Piper, 1953-55; lectr: bus law, U Buffalo Sch of Bus Admn, 1948; appellate advocacy, Sch of law, 1952-54; counsel, Erie Co Reo Comm, 1956-62; NY State Estate Tax Atty, 1959-62; justice, Supr Court, State of NY, 1962; NY State Comm for Hum Rights, 1966-68. Fmr: pres and dir: Temple Emanu-El; Montefiore Lodge, B'nai B'rith; Pres and chmn bd, Bay Beach Comty Cen Assn; mem: Amer, NY State, Erie Co, Bar Assns; Temple Beth Zion; Masons; club, Lawyers. Hobbies: gardening, swimming, bridge, golf. Home: 81 Chatham Ave, Buffalo, NY. Office: 1236 Prudential Bldg, Buffalo, NY.

COHEN, Esther S, US, educator, artist; b. NYC, Dec 29, 1913; d. Solomon and Maryita (Beshunsky); BS, NYU, 1941, MA, 1949; profsl deg, Alfred U, 1952. Asso prof E Conn State Coll since 1967; asst prof, art, Willimantic State Coll since 1949; dir: Lenox Hill Pottery, 1936-44; Pottery Workshop, 1947-49; instr: Herzlia Tchrs Sem, 1944-52; Fieldston Sch, 1946-47; NYU, 1947-49. Exhb ceramics: NY World's Fair, 1939; Barbizon Plaxa Gal; Cooper Union Mus. Bd govs, Inst for Study of Art Educ, NYU; mem: Natl Educ Assn; Artist-Craftsmen Soc; Heb League; Natl Soc for Educ in Art; E Art Assn; Natl Art Educ Assn. Contbr to educ jours. Home: 466 Prospect St, Willimantic, Conn. Office: E Conn State Coll, Willimantic, Conn.

COHEN, Ethel Silberman, US, communal leader; b. NYC, Feb 14, 1895; d. Joseph and Esther (Greenberg) Silberman; att J Tchrs Inst, JTSA; BA, MA, summa cum laude, NYU; m. Frank Cohen, Jan 31, 1921, c, Amos. Chmn: Mailamm, Amer-Isr Music Assn, J Music Council, JWB; mem: Natl Council of J Women; AJ Cong; Reconstructionist Found; fmr: mem bd, Hadassah; chmn, mem bd, overseas comm, Natl Council of J Women; chmn educ comm, Intl Council of J Women; pres, Esco Fund Comm Inc. Author, Yiddish Folk Songs, 1929. Home: 88 Central Park W, New York, NY.

COHEN, Eugene J, US, rabbi; b. NYC, Aug 22, 1918; s. Philip and Rose (Cohen); ordained rabbi, Yeshiva U, 1942; PhD, Boston U, 1954; m. Ada Twersky, Jan 12, 1944; c: Burton, Bethsheva, Leeber. Chaplain: Intl Syn since 1966; Bklyn VA Hosp since 1969; rabbi, Cong Derech Emunah, 1948-66. Chaplain, capt, US Army, 1945-47: active with Bricha underground movement during mil service. Secy, Rel Z of Amer; fmr pres, J Chaplains of US; mem: RabCA; NY Bd of Rabbs; Rabb Alumni, Yeshiva U. Home: 258 Riverside Dr, New York, NY. Study: Kennedy Airport, Jamaica, NY.

COHEN, Frederick Baum, US, attorney; b. Bremerton, Wash, Feb 3, 1913; s. Jacob and Mildred (Baumwohl); LLB, U Wash, 1935; m. Marguerite Quitslund, May 11, 1941, (decd); c: Marilyn, Priscilla, Margo; m. 2nd, Katherine Wolfe Watson, Dec 14, 1962; stepd, Diane. Pvt practice since 1935; prosecut _ ing atty, Kitsap Co, Wash, 1941-47. Chmn, Kitsap Co Fed J Fund, 1946-48; dem state committeeman, mem, Kitsap Co Dem Cen Comm, 1936-52; past pres, Kitsap Co Bar Assn; natl council, JDC since 1948; exec dir, Bremerton Power Squadron; mem: B'nai B'rith; Masons; Elks; C of C; Kitsap Co, Wash State, Amer Bar Assns; clubs: Wash Assn Young Men's Bus; Port Orchard Yacht; Bremerton Shrine. Home: 1412 17 St, Bremerton, Wash. Office: 309 Frst Federal Bldg, Bremerton, Wash.

COHEN, Gabriel Murrel, US, publisher; b. Louisville, Ky, Aug 31, 1908; s. Isaac and Jennie (Rosenbaum); BA, U of NC, 1930; m. Helen Aronovitz Sep 22, 1938; c: Lawrence, Theodore, Miriam, Debbie, Ben Zion, Jennie, Hermine, Rena. Publisher, Post and Opinion since 1931. Home: 6140 Kingsley Dr, Indianapolis, Ind. Office: 611 N Park, Indianapolis, Ind.

COHEN, George W, US, attorney; b. Redondo Beach, Cal, June 10, 1895; s. Isaac and Emma (Stencel); BA, U of Cal, 1917, JD, 1921; att, Harvard Law Sch, 1919-20; m. Carolyn Furth, Mar 12, 1923; c: Donald, Richard. Partner, Law firm, Kaplan, Livingston, Goodwin, Berkowitz and Selvin, 1963-67; atty, Jesse H Steinart, SF, Cal, 1921-22; partner: Loeb, Walker and Loeb, 1924-28; Loeb and Loeb, 1938-44; pvt practice, 1944-52; partner, Cohen and Roth, 1952-57; pvt practice, 1957-63. Perm pres, Class of 1917, U of Cal; fmr: pres, LA Comty Relations Comm; vice-pres, Harvard Law Sch Assn of S Cal; dir, Wfr Fed of LA; trustee, LA Co Bar Assn; mem: LA JCC; bd trustees, Leo Baeck Temple; bd govs: Beverley Hills Bar Assn; State Bar of Cal. Home: 322 S Arden Blvd, Los Angeles, Cal. Office: 300 S Beverley Dr, Beverley Hills, Cal.

COHEN, Gerson David, US, educator; b. NYC, Aug 26, 1924; s. Meyer and Nellie (Goldin); BA, hons, CCNY, 1944; BHL, JTSA, 1943, MHL, ordained rabbi, 1948; PhD, Columbia U, 1958; m. Naomi Wiener, May 26, 1948; c: Judith, Jeremy. Prof, hist, Columbia U, since 1967, dir, cen Isr and J studies, since 1968, Gustave Gottheil lectr, Semitic Langs, 1950-60; asst prof, J lit and instns, JTSA, 1953-63. Secy, Amer Acad for J Research; bd dirs, Leo Baeck Inst, Conf on J Social Studies; publ comm, J Publ Soc; mem: Amer Oriental Soc; Medieval Acad, Amer. Author: Great Ages and Ideas of the Jewish People, 1956; Proceedings of the American Academy of Jewish Research, 1959; Messianic Postures of Ashkenazim and Sephardim, 1967; Sefer haCabbalah, 1967. Home: 416 W 255 St, Bronx, NY. Office: 608 Kent, Columbia U, New York, NY.

COHEN, Harry, US, surgeon; b. Aus, Oct 1, 1885; s. Samuel and Betty (Holzer); in US since 1885; MD, Cornell U, 1907; postgrad studies, Columbia U; hon degs: DS, Avatar intl U, Eng; Universidad Latino Americano, Cuba; DL; Accademia di Studio Superiore Phoenix, Accademia studiorum Minerva, Bari, It; DCL, St Andrews U Coll, London; LLD, Intl Acad, London; Western U; PhD, Acad Androfofica, San Marino; Wash, Intl Acad Rome, It; Coll of Applied Psych, Fla; D Psych, Natl U of Therapeutics, India; m. Flora Levy, 1921; c: Robert, Michael. Pvt practice, NYC, cons surg, Columbia Hosp; att surg, Manhattan Gen Hosp; med insp, NY Dept of Health, 1912-13; on staff, Sydenham Hosp, 1913-16; att surg, People's Hosp, 1914-35; chief surg clinic, Beth Isr Hosp, 1919-34; asso surg Wickersham Hosp. Prin contrib, inventor of the Clamp Tourniquet and surg instruments. F: NY Acad Med, life; Amer Coll Surgs; Intl Coll Surgs; Intl Acad Proctology; Amer Geriatric Soc; AMA; dipl, Intl BD Surg, fmr pres: E Med Soc; NY Phys Med Soc; Beth Isr Hosp, Alumni Assn; Natl Council Bus and Profsl Men: J Forum Assn, NY Fed of Philanthropic Soc; Amer J Phys Comm; Yeshiva U Med Sch; IMA; mem, Cardinal's Comm of the Laity; Found of Catholics for Human Brotherhood; mem: NY State, Co Med Socs; Cornell U Alumni Assn; Amer Med Writers Assn; Amer Assn for UN; hon mem, numerous societies all over the world; chancellor; Philathea Coll, London, Ont, Can; Chatham Hill Coll, W Va; St Andrews Coll, London; provost, Amer Intl Acad NY; club, US Power Squadron, Navigators, NY. Author: Simon Bolivar and the Conquest and Liberation of South America; India and the Taj Mahal; Religion of Benjamin Franklin; asso ed: J Cyclopedia, 1943; American Jews, their Lives and Achievements, 1947, 1959; intl med chmn, Who's Who in World Jewry, 1955; 1964; ed-in-chief, Amer J Lit Found, 1954-59; co-ed, J in the World of Sci, 1957. Recipient: Grand Prix Humanitaire de Belique; hon cross, Union Philanthropique des Oeuvres Françaises;

apostolic benediction, His Holiness Pope Pius XII, Pope John XXIII; Knights of the Order, St John of Jerusalem; Order of Malta; Order Nunez Vasco de Balboa, Panama; Crown of Stuart, Scotland, Order Crown of It; Cross de Lorraine, Fr; Chevalier Renaissance Française; Order White Lion, Czech; hon academician Acad di Santa Brigida, Swed. Home: 320 Central Park W, New York, NY. Office: 45 Gramercy Park, New York, NY.

COHEN, Harry, US, attorney; b. NYC, Mar 4, 1904; s. Benjamin and Celia (Pedes); LLB, NYU, 1924; m. Rose Blankfein, Feb 12, 1940; c: Bernice, Cecille. Pvt practice since 1927; unit head, atty, rent control, OPA, Bx co, 1943-48; govt appeal agt, Selective Service, 1941-46. Pres; ZOA, 1951-53; B'nai B'rith, Rehoboth Lodge, 1943; chmn: Council of Nursing Sch Comms, Dept of Hosps, 1954-55; natl shekel campaign, 1951; lay adv bd, Morrisania City Hosp since 1957; mem: coord comm, Assn Bar, NYC, 1965-68; AZC, 1965-68. Ed, The Advocate since 1953; contbr to J publs. Home: 135 W 168 St, Bronx, NY. Office: 260 E 161 St, Bronx, NY.

COHEN, Harry A, Isr, rabbi; b. NYC; s. Herman and Dora (Gordon); in Isr since 1958; BS, CCNY, 1915; PhD, Columbia U, 1918; ordained rabbi, JTSA, 1919; MHL, 1929; m. Batya Katz, Aug 10, 1922. Rabbi em, Savyon since 1965, rabbi, 1960-64; lectr, Bar Ilan U; rabbi, Jacksonville J Cen, Fla, 1926-30; head, dept fgn langs and social studies, Norwich Free Acad, Norwich Conn, 1930-46; exec dir, Temple on Heights, Cleveland, O, 1947-50; rabbi, Sons of Jacob Syn, Waterloo, Ia, 1953-58. Mem: RA; NE Classical Assn; B'nai B'rith; AJCong; ZOA. Author: Influence of Jewish Commentators on the English Bible, 1922; Commentary of Rabbi David Kimhi on Hosea, 1929; Minimum Vocabulary in Social Studies, 1935; Key Terms in Social Studies, 1937; A Basic Jewish Encyclopedia, 1965. Home: 8 Magal St, Savyon, Isr.

COHEN, Herbert L, US, attorney; b. Bridgeport, Conn, Apr 18, 1905; s. Samuel and Esther (Schine); BA, Yale U, 1925; LLB Yale Law Sch, 1928; m. Ruth Steinkraus Dec 26, 1962; c: Carol Becker, Mary Weisman, Partner, Cohen and Wolf, since 1955. Trustee, counsel, U Bridgeport; repr, Coun Cen Assembly; chmn NE reg, CJFWF; dir, US Assn for UN; mem: Amer Bar Assn; World Peace Through Law; fmr: pres: Bridgeport: J Comty Council; Service Bur; United Fed J Campaign. Home: Darbrook Rd, Westport, Conn. Office: 955 Main St, Bridgeport, Conn.

COHEN, Herman, US, endocrinologist; b. NYC, Mar 1, 1915; s. Morris and Tillie (Rosenberg); BS, NYU, 1938, MS, 1942, PhD, 1951; m. Bernice Luber, Mar 21, 1942; c: Robert, Lawrence. Vice-pres, research, Princeton Labs since 1952; research asso, E R Squibb and Sons, New Brunswick, NJ, 1946-52. F: NY Acad Sci; AAAS; mem: Amer Chem Soc; Endocrine Soc; Amer Phys Soc; NY Acad Sci; Soc for Experimental Biol and Med; Sigma Xi. Contbr to profsl jours. Home: 549 Jefferson Rd, Princeton, NJ. Office: Princeton Laboratories, Box 534, Princeton, NJ.

COHEN, Herman, US, educator; b. Superior, Neb, Dec 29, 1924; s. Morris and Dora (Schwartz); MA, State U Ia, 1948, PhD, 1954; m. Marlee Hollander, Aug 24, 1947; c: Matthew, David, Robert, Anthony. Prof speech, U Mass since 1967; prof, U Ore, 1965-67, on fac since 1949. US Army, 1943-46. Mem: AAUP; ACLU; Speech Assn of Amer; W Speech Assn. Co-author, Fundamentals of Speech, 1963; ed, Quarterly Jour of Speech; cons ed, Western Speech since 1960, ed, 1964-67; contbr to profsl jours. Home: 2 Eaton Ct, Echo Hill, Amherst, Mass. Office: U of Mass, Amherst, Mass.

COHEN, Herman Howard, US, accountant, attorney; b. NYC, Jan 5, 1903; s. Samuel and Anna (Kowalski); BCS, NYU, 1923, MCS, 1924, BS, 1927, JD, 1930; m. Goldie Blum, Dec 21, 1929; c, Susan Axelrod. Sr partner, Cohen & Field, since 1924; cons ed, Research Inst of Amer; staff acctnt, Samuel Heller, 1920-22; sr acctnt, Frendel & Brown, 1922-24. Vice-pres, Harlyn Found; treas, Colony of Hope; mem, presidium, Natl Comm for Futherance of J Educ; chmn, mem, Emet Rabbi Herzog World Acad; div chmn: UJA; Isr Bonds; mayor's comm, NY Shakespeare Festival; dir: NY State Soc CPA's; W Side Instn Syn; Manhattan Day Sch; Riverside Sch; Amato Opera Theatre; Vascular Research Found; mem: Amer Inst CPA's; NY State Soc CPA's; Niagara Soc; clubs: Grant St Boys; Acctnts. Author: Legal Tax Savings Methods, 1936; Guide to Tax Economy, 1937; contbr to profsl jours. Hobby, music. Home: 12 W 72 St, New York, NY. Office: 565 Fifth Ave, New York, NY.

COHEN, Horace R, Can, business exec; b. Montreal, Feb 12, 1895; s. Lyon and Rachel (Friedman); dipl of commerce, BA, McGill U; m. Jennie Heilleg, June 20, 1922; c: Lazarus (decd), Judith Gainsbury, David. Pres, The Freedman Co Ltd, since 1948. Admnr of fine clothing, War Time Prices and Trade Bd, WW II. Capt, Can Overseas Mil Forces. Hon pres: Shaar Hashomayim Syn, since 1947; United Talmud Torahs, since 1951; Can Legion Post, since 1950; hon vice-pres, ZOC, since 1955; hon vice chmn, CJA, since 1954; trustee, YM-YWHA, Montreal, since, 1950, past vice-pres; dir: NCCJ, Can, since 1958; J Gen Hosp, since 1934; Boys Farm Training Sch, since 1938, hon vice pres, since 1965; mem bd overseas, JTSA, since 1952; JP, since 1951; f, Royal Commonwealth Soc; mem bd govs: Verdun Protestant Hosp; Notre Dame Hosp; Childrens Memorial Hosp; Montreal Gen Hosp; J Gen Hosp; fmr: pres, chmn, centennial comm, Baron de Hirsch Inst; pres, Mt Royal Lodge, Dist Grand Lodge 1, both B'nai B'rith; mem, bd govs, Supr Lodge, B'nai B'rith; treas, Camp B'nai B'rith; master, Masons; Grand Jr Deacon, Grand Lodge of Que; clubs: United Services; Montefiore. Recipient: OBE, 1946; citation, JTSA, 1950; Solomon Schechter Medal for ethical leadership, 1959; Citation, B'nai B'rith, 1950, 1961. Home: 4332 Westmount Ave, Westmount, Quebec, Can. Office: 5300 Molson St, Montreal, Can.

COHEN, Howard Allen, US, attorney, teacher; b. Newark, NJ, Feb 10, 1941; s. Frank and Lillian (Klappholz); AB, Rutgers U, 1963, PhD, 1965; m. Barbara Underwood, June 24, 1964. Dep asst, secy, wfr leg, HEW since 1969; adj prof, leg, Georgetown Law Cen, Wash DC since 1968; teaching f, Boston Coll Law Sch, 1965-66; instr, Dickinson Sch of Law, Carlisle, Pa, 1966-67; leg counsel, Donald Runsfeld, US Cong, 1968-69. Mem: Fed Bar Assn; Amer Political Sci Assn; Amer Public Wfr Assn; Ripon Soc; fmr pres, Student Govt, Rutgers U. Recipient, Cong F, Amer Political Sci Assn, 1967. Hobbies: photography, oenology. Home: 811 N Carolina Ave, SE, Washington, DC. Office: HEW, Washington, DC.

COHEN, Howard Elmer, US, actor, b. Nashville, Tenn, Jan 2, 1926; s. Alex and Julia (Minsky); BS, Columbia U, 1950; att CCNY; m. Joan-Ellen Drosin, Dec 12, 1954; c, Lyle. Actor since 1946. USN, 1944-46. Pres: Martin Strauss Soc; Temple Shaarei Tfilah, NYC; mem, bd dirs: Project 58, Inc, theater workshop; Clinic for Emotionally Disturbed Children; NY League, Natl Fed Temple Youth; San Fernando Valley chap, Assn for UN; Valley Fair Housing Council; Cal Jr Sym Assn; LA Co Mus Art; ACLU; mem: Acad Motion Picture Arts and Sci; Acad TV Arts and Sci; Actors Equity Assn; Amer Fed TV and Radio Artists; Screen Actors Guild; life mem, Actors Fund of Amer; fmr mem: Equity Libr Theater W; w coast adv bd, Actors Equity Assn; club, Lambs. Home: 12745 Milbank St, Studio City, Cal.

COHEN, I Bernard, US, educator, author; b. Far Rockaway, NY, Mar 1, 1914; s. Isador and Blanche (Bernstein); grad, Valley Forge Mil Acad, 1933; BS, Harvard U, 1937; PhD, 1947; LLD, Poly Inst, Bklyn, 1964; m. Frances David, June 23, 1944; c, Frances. Prof, instr, asso prog, hist of sci gen educ, physics, phys sci, Harvard U, on fac since 1942; Visiting overseas f, Churchill Coll, 1968. Author: Benjamin Franklin's Experiments, 1941; Roemer and the First Determination of the Velocity of Light, 1944; Phys Lab Manual, 1944; Science Servant of Man, 1950; General Education in Science, 1950; Benjamin Franklin, His Contribution to the American Tradition, 1953; Franklin and Newton, 1956; Isaac Newton's Papers and Letters on Natural Philosophy, 1958; Birth of a New Physics, 1960; A Treasury of Scientific Prose, 1963; ed, Isis, 1953-59, mgn ed, 1947-52; contbr: articles, book revs to jours: Pres: Intl Union, Hist and Phil of Sci, 1969-72; Hist of Sci Soc, 1960-62; chmn, US Natl Comm, Hist and Phil of Sci, 1961; f, AAAS; mem: Amer Acad Arts and Sci; Amer Assn Hist of Med; Amer Hist Assn; Intl Acad Hist of Sci; Amer Antiquarian Soc; Sigma Xi; Phi Beta Kappa. Home: 22 Gray Gardens E, Cambridge, Mass. Office: Harvard U, Cambridge, Mass.

COHEN, Idov, Isr, legislator, journalist; b. Milhaleni, Rum, Nov 17, 1909; s. Aharon and Hannah (Butnar); in Isr since 1939; m. Lea Rechbach, 1934; c: Naomi, Eliezer, Elhanan. Fmr: MK; councilman, Tel Aviv Munic; dir, Gen Organic Fertilizers Corp Ltd; ed: Shtiri, Illustratiunea Evreasca;

Renashterea; Hasmonea; Adam, all in Rum; ed: Haoved Hatzioni; Karnenu, Pal; co-found, Hatechiya, Rum lang newspaper. Pres, United Rum Jews in Isr; found and pres, comm for reunification of families, Rum-Isr; co-found, Rum Immigrants Assn, Pal; dir: JNF, Rum; info dept, JNF Jerusalem; mem exec council, Histadrut, chmn, appeals bd; mem exec, World Parl Assn, London; fmr: dep mem, Provincial Govt Council, Isr; co-found, mem natl and political comms, Progressive Party. Author, Oif'n Eigenem Weg, 1949; trans into Heb: books by Huxley, Stefan Zweig, A Schnitzler, Saroyan; contbr to mags. Home: 40 Basle St, Tel Aviv, Isr.

COHEN, Irma, US, psychologist; b. Frankton, Ind, May 14, 1901; d. Adolph and Flora (Isaac) Loeb; MA, O State U, 1926, PhD, 1927; m. Samuel Cohen, Apr 1, 1942; c: Alan, Richard, Sandra Dee. Clinical psych, Mt Sinai Hosp and Cleveland Guidance Cen, 1927-30. Pres, vice-pres, recording secy, Cleveland Council for Mh, 1950-55; pres: E Side Comm Maternal Health Assn; Women's Auxiliary, Cleveland Dent Soc, 1950; mem, delg assembly, J Comty Fed, 1950-69; mem: adv comm, AJComm, vice-pres, 1953; bd trustees, Council on Hum Relations, 1945-69; Amer Assn U Women; Natl Council J Women; Alpha Omega Auxiliary, pres, 1954-55; Alpha Epsilon Phi, natl pres, 1948-55, natl treas, 1929-46. Author: The Intelligence of Jews as Compared with Non-Jews, 1927; Verbalization in the Solution of Problems of the Multiple Choice Type, 1927. Home: 3307 Chadbourne Rd, Shaker Heights, O.

COHEN, Irun Robert, Isr, physician; b. Chgo, Ill, Sep 1, 1937; s. Samuel and Sara (Wineberg); in Isr since 1968; BA, Northwestern U, 1959, MD, med sch, 1963; m. Yael Yarom, June 23, 1959; c: Michal, Tamar. Visiting sci, Weizmann Inst of Sci, Rehovot, since 1968; asst res, f, dept ped, Johns Hopkins Hosp, Baltimore, 1966-68; postdoc f, Arthritis Found; surg, Natl Communicable Disease Cen, USPHS, Atlanta, Ga, 1964-66; intern, Hadassah U Hosp, Jerusalem, 1963-64. Lt dx dcr, USPHS, 1964-66. Prin contribs: research in immunology and ped. Mem. AOA Med Hon Soc. Contbr to profsl jours. Home: 36 Eisenberg St, Rehovot, Isr. Office: Weizmann Inst of Sci, Rehovot, Isr.

COHEN, Irwin Herbert, US, attorney, certified public acctnt; b. NYC, Dec 12, 1927; s. Hyman and Annie (Gilik); BBA, CCNY, 1949; LLB, Bklyn Law Sch, 1953; m. Selma Unger, Nov 19, 1950; c: Barbara, Joel. In pvt practice. Pvt, mil police, US Army, 1946-48. Chmn, bd govs, Scott Tower Housing Co Inc Coop, fmr vice-chmn and mem; mem: Amer Bar Assn; NY State Soc of CPA's. Recipient: Victory Medal; Army of Occupation Medal, Japan. Home: 3400 J, Paul Ave, New York, NY.

COHEN, Isadore, US, botanist, educator; b. Haverhill, Mass, May 31, 1911; s. Hyman and Lena (Shapiro); MS, Tufts Coll, 1933; PhD, U of Pa, 1936; m. Florence Steinberg, Nov 24, 1949. Prof, dept head, biol, Amer Intl Coll since 1951, mem fac since 1946. US Army, 1941-45. Mem: Amer Botanical Soc; Sigma Xi. Contbr of papers on cytology and nuclear stains. Home: 93 Osceola Lane, Longmeadow, Mass. Office: Amer Intl Coll, Springfield, Mass.

COHEN, Isadore Roy, US, business exec; b. Bethel, NY, Jan 10, 1922; s. Morris and Bessie (Sheftel); BS, Cornell U, 1948, MS, 1949; m. Joan Goodman, Nov 26, 1959; c: David, Shari, Bonni. Vice-pres, S B Penick & Co, div of CPL Intl Inc since 1967, pres, Legear Labs Inc, a subsidiary since 1968, mem, bd dirs since 1968, mgr, antibiotics feed div, 1963-67; microbiol research sci, 1949-53; advt mgr, animal nutrition div, 1953-54, asst mgr, 1954-58; mgr, 1958-63, all at Commercial Solvents Corp. Home: Gracemere, Tarrytown, NY. Office: 100 Church St, New York, NY.

COHEN, Israel, Isr, journalist, editor, author; b. Ulszakowcze, Aus-Hung, May 2, 1905; s. Itzhak and Gitel (Perlmutter); in Isr since 1925; grad, Tchrs Sem, Vienna, 1924; m. Zvia Gordon; c: Nurit, Hagit. Ed, Hapoel Hatzair, since 1948, co-ed, 1934-48; ed, Niv ha-Kvutza. Author: Evaluations and Reflections, 1938; monograph on IE Zalkinson, 1942; Face to Face, 1949; Gateways, 1954; Parallel Proverbs, 1954; Bridges, 1955; Biblical Portraits, 1958; Dictionary of Parallel Proverbs, 1961; Collected Works, 4 vols, 1962; Monograph on Matatya Shoham, 1965; Mirrors, 1968; co-ed, Lessons in Political Economy, 1940; trans into Heb: Psychoanalytisches Volksbuch, by Paul Federn-Meng, 1932; A Young

Man's Diary, by F Lasalle, 1946; A Proclamation for Socialism and Revolution, by Gustav Landauer, 1951; Socialist Thought by GDH Cole, 1956; contbr, essays, articles to local press and lit periodicals. Mem: exec comm, Heb Author's Assn; PEN Club; head, Inst for trans of Heb Lit; natl comm, Mapai Party. Home: 54 Harav Reines St, Tel Aviv, Isr. Office: 110 Hayarkon St, Tel Aviv, Isr.

COHEN, Itzhak, Isr, judge; b. Brody, Pol, Nov 15, 1913; in Isr since 1935; ML, U Lvov, Pol, 1935; m. Adina; c: Ruth Zonenfeld, Neomi Tzisick, Hava. Judge, Dist Court, Haifa, since 1953; judge, Magistrate's Court, Haifa, since 1950; lectr, Haifa U since 1950; advocate, pvt practice, 1940-50. Office: District Court, Haifa, Isr.

COHEN, J Stanley, US, physician, educator; b. Lancaster, Pa, Jan 12, 1903; s. Abraham and Dina (Sorkin); BS, Franklin & Marshall Coll, 1923; MD, U Cincinnati Med Sch, 1927; m. Helen Hirsh Manheimer, Aug 4, 1937; c: Robert, Suzanne, Jeffrey. Em att obstet and gyn, Albert Einstein Med Cen, Phila; sr att dept obstet and gyn: Rolling Hill Hosp, Elkins Park, Pa; Oxford Hosp, Phila; em asst prof, obstet, gyn, Temple U, asst prof 1940-47; pres: Equitable Builders Inc; Eden Rock Devel Corp; Stanley Inves; Safeway. Pres, Lancastor Lodge, B'nai B'rith, 1934-35; E dist of Pa, 1935-36, gen comm, 3rd dist, 1936-39; bd Salvation Army, 1937; J Comty Relations Council, 1940-45. F Amer Coll Surgs; Intl Coll Surgs; Amer Coll Obstet and Gyn; dipl, Amer Bd Obstet and Gyn; mem: Amer, Pa, and Phila Co Med Socs; Amer Fertility Soc; Pan Amer Cancer Cytology Soc; Obstet and Endocrine Socs; Rodeph Shalom Temple; club, Philmont Country. Contbr to med jours. Home: 503 Spring Ave, Elkins Park, Pa. Offices: Tabor Med Bldg, York and Tabor Rds, Philadelphia, Pa; Balston and Medford Ave, Parkwood, Philadelphia, Pa.

COHEN, Jerome B, US, educator; b. NYC, Jan 18, 1915; s. Charles and Estelle (Bauland); BSS, cum laude, CCNY, 1934; MA, Columbia U, 1935; PhD, 1947; m. Mina Salmon, June 18, 1941; c, Carla. Prof, econ and finance, Bernard M Baruch Sch of Bus and Public Admn, CUNY since 1947, dean since 1969; prof, econ and finance, Baruch Coll, CUNY, 1968; cons, anti-trust, 1960-68; pres, Metrop Econ Assn, 1954-55; participant, Merrill Cen for Econ, 1959, 1961; mem: Amer Econ Assn; Amer Finance Assn; Natl Tax Assn; AAUP; Council on Fgn Relations; Natl Assn Bus Econ; Royal Econ Soc; Phi Beta Kappa, 1st vice-pres, 1969; Beta Gamma Sigma. Author: Japan's Economy in War and Reconstruction, 1949; Economic Problems of Free Japan, 1952; Japan's Postwar Economy, 1958; Personal Finance: Principles and Case Problems, 1964; co-author: The Financial Manager, 1966; Investment Analysis and Portfolio Management, 1967; contbr to profsl jours. Recipient: Rockefeller Found Grant, 1956; Social Sci Research Council Grant, 1963, 1964; Townsend Harris Medal, 1967. Home: 135 E 74 St, New York, NY. Office: 17 Lexington Ave, New York, NY.

COHEN, John Solomon, Eng, business exec; b. Feb 23, 1901; s. Joseph and Esther (Rose); m. Golda Brenner, Feb 28, 1928; c: Josephine, Johnson, Richard, Elizabeth. Chmn, Investment Surveys Ltd; fmr: pres, admn council, co-pres, dir comm, Rodwell Group; pres: Monarch Securities; City & Southwark Properties; Survey House. Mem: bd govs, exec admn and finance comm, Heb U, Jerusalem; exec, cons, United Syn; Friends Heb U; Friends London J Hosp; treas, Evelina de Rothschild Sch; patron: UN Assn; Eur Movement. Hobbies: walking, conversation, sailing. Home: 5 Carlton Gardens, London SW1, Eng.

COHEN, Joseph, US, attorney; b. Kan City, Mo, Mar 23, 1902; s. Barnett and Hulda (Marcus); LLB U of Kan City Sch of Law, 1925; m. Margaret Pollack, Aug 21, 1927; c: Barton, Hildred Hoffman, Miles. Pvt practice since 1925; chmn, Rosedale State Bank since 1949; chmn bd, Metcalf State Bank, Overland Park, Kan since 1962. Pres: J Council, Gtr Kan City 1948-54; Comty Chest, Kan City, 1949; United Comty Fund, Wyandotte, Co Kan, 1953-55; Dist Grand Lodge 2, B'nai B'rith, 1933-34; Wyandotte Co Bar Assn, 1968. Contbr to legal publs. Home: 3030 W 67 Terr, Mission Hills, Kan. Office: 711 Huron Bldg, Kansas City, Kan.

COHEN, Joseph Horace, US, chemical engr, industrialist; b. Kovna, Lith, Nov 14, 1890; s. Morris and Ida (Chaitt); in US since 1895; BS, MIT, 1913; m. Rose Stone, 1916; c: Joseph, Ira, Nancy Silberstein. Ret; gen mgr, Atlantic

Gelatin Co, div Gen Foods, 1946-55, on staff since 1919; chem, Amer Glue, 1914-19. Pres: Gen Research Soc of Amer, since 1919; Temple Isr; hon life; bd trustees, Beth Isr Hosp, hon life; Heb Union Sch Educ and Sacred Music, NY; UAHC, 1947-55; bd mgrs, CJP; mem: Amer Chem Soc; AAAS; Soc Motion Picture Engrs; Optical Soc of Amer; Masons; Shriners; clubs: New Cent, pres, 1937-38; Belmont Country, Boston; Standard, Chgo; Chemist. Home: 180 Beacon St, Boston, Mass.

COHEN, Joseph Louis, US, attorney, government official; b. Omaha, Neb, Apr 6, 1908; s. Louis and Clara (Glassman); LLB, Creighton Law Sch, Omaha, 1932, JD, 1968; m. Alta Elkin, Mar 15, 1938; c: Lawrence, Ellen, Dennis, Michael. Regional personnel off, US Gen Services Admn, Region 8, since 1950; pvt law practice, 1932-41; fmr: field examiner, sr investigator, hearing off, mem, loyalty rev bd, all Civil Service Commn; employee relations off and personnel off, War Assets Admn. Vice-chmn, vocational service commn, Supr Lodge, B'nai B'rith, since 1962, fmr: pres, dist lodge; mem, bd dirs, supr lodge; pres, Denver lodge, dist dep; mem, bd govs, dist grand lodge; mem natl armed services comm; delg, supr lodge convs, Isr, Wash, DC, appd mem Supr Lodge personnel policy comm, 1965; mem: natl bd, JWB, since 1950; bd dirs, hon chmn, Rocky Mt USO-JWB since 1950; bd dirs, Denver USO-JWB, since 1958, past chmn; bd trustees, Beth Joseph Cong, since 1956; regional adv bd, ADL, since 1950; bd dirs, J Comty Cen, since 1950; Metrop Council for Comty Service; Colo-Wyoming Fed Personnel Council; Denver Fed Cen Health Bd; Neb Bar Assn; trustee, Natl J Hosp, Denver; Denver Tennis Club; fmr: div chmn, Allied J Council; chmn: Fed Personnel Council; public div, Comty Chest; United Fund; Fed Bus Men's Assn, all Denver. Recipient: 1st Fed Bus Men's Assn annual award to fed employee who contributed most to civic, comty affairs, 1955; Natl Civil Service League merit citation, outstanding career in public service. Home: 5530 E Second Ave, Denver, Colo. Office: Bldg 41, Denver Federal Center, Denver, Colo.

COHEN, Julius, US, educator; b. NYC, Oct 27, 1910; s. Saul and Mollie (Sidler); MA, W Va U, 1932, LLB, 1937; LLM, Harvard Law Sch, 1938; att Columbia Law Sch, 1936; m. Lillian Tyson, 1945. Prof, law, Rutgers Sch of Law since 1957; U Neb Sch of Law 1946-47; legal and admn aide to gov W Va, 1940-42; chmn, W Va State Election Comm, 1941-1943; legal div, War Manpower Commn, 1942-44; Alien Property Custodian, 1944-45; visiting prof, U Ind Law Sch, 1950, 1953, 1954; Yale Law Sch, 1958-59. Guggenheim F, 1963-64. Author: Materials and Problems on Legislation 1949; co-author, The Community and the Law, 1958; co-ed, The Law School of Tomorrow, 1968; contbr to profsl jours. Home: 16 Clover Lane, Princeton, NJ. Office: Rutgers Sch of Law, Newark, NJ.

COHEN, Lawrence B, US, educator; b. Pottstown, Pa, Feb 12, 1916; s. Robert and Cecelia (Laber); MA, U of Pa, 1937; PhD, Columbia U, 1950; m. Naomi Epstein, Nov 24, 1938; c: Edward, Jonathan, Frederick. Prof, dept chmn, IE, Columbia U; visiting prof, Technion, Isr, 1967-68; cons, arbitrator. Mem: Amer Econ Assn; Ind Relations Research Assn. Author: Work Staggering for Traffic Relief. Home: 322 Central Park W, New York, NY. Office: Columbia U, New York, NY.

COHEN, Leo, Isr, banker; b. Ger, Aug 3, 1894; s. Abraham and Rosa; in Isr since 1921; att: U Berlin; U of Munich. Dir, Gen Mortgage Bank Ltd; mem bd dirs: Isr Mortgage Bank; Ichud Ins Agcy; Blumenton Found; Neoth Aviv. Mem, bd govs, Heb U, Jerusalem; UJA; Keren Kayemeth; KH; Isr Sym Orch. Home: Herzlia B, Isr.

COHEN, Lester B, US, merchant; b. Uniontown, Pa, Apr 10, 1907; s. Max and Lillian (Shirk); BA, U of W Va, 1926; BS, U Pittsburgh, 1930; m. Ethel Levy, 1931; c: Maxine, Stanton. Pres, Cohen Furniture Co, Brownsville, Pa, since 1950; interior decorator since 1956. Pres: B'nai B'rith, 1943-47; Tri-State Zionist Region, 1947-50, hon pres since 1950; Temple Isr, since 1962; Comty Cen, 1962; chmn, ADL, since 1947; bd dirs: Salvation Army, since 1942; United J Fed, since 1940; Comty Cen, since 1945; C of C, since 1950; mem: exec comm, Comty Chest, since 1950; natl exec comm, ZOA, since 1948; Phi Epsilon Pi; natl regional vice-pres, Natl Soc Interior Designers; clubs: Uniontown Exch, pres, 1944-47; Merchants, pres, 1949-51; Fayette Co Sportsman's, pres, 1942-49; U Pittsburgh Three-Letterman; U Pittsburgh Cap and Gown. Recipient: named letterman of dist, U Pittsburgh, 1969; made hon life mem, local Salvation Army bd, 1969. Hobby, sports car racing. Home: 125 Belmont Circle, Uniontown, Pa. Office: Cohen Furniture Co, Beeson Blvd, Uniontown, Pa.

COHEN, Lewis, US, physician; b. Columbus, O, Mar 23, 1918; s. Harry and Florence (Lebeson); BA, O State U, 1938, MD, 1942; postgrad course, orthopedic surg, Ia City, 1946-47, cerebral palsey, 1947; m. Betty Bosniak, 1949; c, Judith. Dir, dept phys med, rehab, Detroit Hosps: Grace; Sinai; Receiving; Memorial; cons, Mich Multiple Sclerosis Cen, 1950-52. Capt, US Army MC, 1943-46. Dipl, Amer Bd Phys Med and Rehab; Baruch F: Mayo Clinic; Columbia Presbyterian Med Cen; NYU; Bellevue Inst of Phys Med and Rehab; f, Amer Coll Phys; secy, Beth Aaron Syn, 1953; found mem, Amer Assn Electromyography and Electrodiagnosis; mem, Amer Acad Phys Med and Rehab. Co Contbr to med jours. Home: 26602 Dundee, Huntington Woods, Mich. Office: 20905 Greenfield Rd, Detroit, Mich.

COHEN, Lou, US, merchant; b. Florence, SC, Apr 25, 1895; s. Mendel and Rebecca (Rubinstein). Owner, M Cohen & Son, since 1933; pres, Winmar Orchard since 1934; vice-pres, Berkely Upholstering since 1937. Pres, City Hosp, bd trustees. Spec interest, art. Home: 133 N Queen St, Martinsburg, W Va. Office: 131 N Queen St, Martinsburg, W Va.

COHEN, Louis Arthur, US, research chem; b. Boston, Mass, July 12, 1926; s. Jacob and Jenny (Goldenberg); BS, Northeastern U, Boston, 1949; PhD, MIT, 1952; m. Susan Altman, Oct 9, 1955; c, Peter. Research chem, NIH, since 1954; chief, div biochem mechanisms since 1965; dir, Found for advanced Educ in Sci since 1967, chmn, chem dept since 1962; visiting prof, chem, Howard U, Wash, DC, since 1956; instr, Yale U, 1952-54. Mem: Amer Chem Soc. Contbr to profsl jours. Hobbies: music, horticulture. Home: 9814 Inglemere Dr, Bethesda, Md. Office: NIH, Bethesda, Md.

COHEN, Manuel Frederick, US, attorney; b. Bklyn, Oct 9, 1912; s. Edward and Lena (Kartzman); BSS, Bklyn Coll, 1933; LLB, Bklyn Law Sch, 1936, hon LLD, 1962; hon LLD, Babson Inst of Bus Admn, 1968; DHL, HUC, Cincinnati, 1969; m. Pauline Grossman, Apr 20, 1940; c: Susan Borman, Jonathan. Sr partner, law firm, Wilmer, Cutler & Pickering since 1969; profsl lectr, law, George Washington U Law Sch since 1968; staff mem, SEC, 1942-61, mem Commn, 1961-64, chmn, 1964-69; dir, Intl Chem and Nuclear Corp; secy: Intl Research and Devl, SA; Stires, Winston & Co. Mem: Amer Fed Bar Assns; Amer Law Inst; Amer Soc of Intl Law; Amer Acad Political and Social Sci; Amer Judicature Soc; Acad of Political Sci; Société Royale D'Economie Politique de Belgique; adv bd, Bur of Natl Affairs; Natl bd advs, Practising Law Inst; hon, Order of the Coif; clubs: Cosmos, Wash, DC; Intl; Woodmont Country. Cons ed, Finance Mag. Recipient awards: Rockefeller Public Service Award, Princeton U, 1956; Career Service Award, Natl Civil Service League, 1961; Dist Alumnus Medal, Bklyn Coll, 1962; Dist Service Award, SEC, 1965; Brotherhood Award, NCCJ, 1965. Home: 6403 Marjory Lane, Bethesda, Md. Office: 900 17 St, NW, Washington, DC.

COHEN, Maurice, Austr, attorney, business exec; b. Tel Aviv, June 30, 1915; s. Leon and Miriam (Alsaig); in Austr since 1927; LLB, Melbourne U, 1937; LLM, 1939; m. Thelma Libow, June 14, 1941; c: Barbara, Jocelyn. Lt, Austr Army, 1940-44. Mem exec, Friends Heb U since 1939, fmr gov, Heb U; fmr pres, Austr Friends Heb U; pres: Hillel Found, Vic; Melbourne HS Old Boys Assn; J Patriotic Auxiliary; chmn: sch council, Melbourne HS; JNF, Vic; vice-chmn, State ZC, Vic; ZF, Austr and NZ; Vic Zionist Org; hon solicitor: Magen David Adom; Yeshiva; Mizrachi; hon asst secy, Kadimah; mem: exec, KH; Youth Aliyah Appeal; clubs: Cranbourne Country; Grads Union; Royal Automobile; Vic. Home: 56 Kooyong Rd, Caulfied, Austr. Office: 473 Bourke St, Melbourne, Austr.

COHEN, Maurice Seymour, Can, rabbi; b. Winthrop, Mass, Nov 13, 1919; BA, Harvard U, 1941; MA, 1942; BJE, Heb Tchr's Coll, Boston, Mass, 1939; ordained rabbi, MHL, JTSA, 1945. Rabbi: Shaare Zion Cong, Montreal, Can since 1946; Rodeph Sholom Cong, Bridgeport, Conn, 1944-45. Chmn, J Chaplaincy Bd, Montreal; mem: natl exec comm, Can J Cong; Fed J Comty Services; e region: ZOC; Can J Cong. Home: 5015 Circle Rd, Montreal, Can.

COHEN, Max, US, attorney; b. Rochester, NY, Jan 14, 1907; s. Philip and Minnie (Ruben); LLB, Albany Law Sch, 1928; m. Marcella Davis, June 24, 1930, (decd); c: Carol, Arthur, m. 2nd, Sara Shuman, Aug 28, 1955. Pvt practice since 1929; gen counsel, Amer Carnivals Assn since 1933; mem, Cohen & Gould, 1936-52; sr mem, Cohen, Gould, Farbo & Gleiner, 1953-59; dep corp counsel, City of Rochester, 1938-43; admitted NY Bar 1929; Fed, US Supr Courts, 1934. Pres, Cong Beth Sholom, 1961-64; exec comm, 13th ward Rep; secy, 14th ward Rep, comm, 1933-62, chmn, 1962-64; mem: Amer, NY State, Monroe Co Bar Assns; Decalogue Soc of Lawyers; Amer Jud Soc; Justinian Hon Law Soc; Moose, gov, 1935-38, state pres, 1937-38, secy-treas, 1950-56; Elks; Eagles, Masons; KP, dist dep grand chancellor, 1938. Home: 47 Culver Rd, Rochester, NY. Office: 39 State St, Rochester, NY.

COHEN, Maynard Manuel, US, physician, educator; b. Regina, Can, May 17, 1920; s. Aleck and Dora (Pinsk); AB, U Mich, 1941; MD, Wayne State U, 1944; PhD, U Minn, 1953; m. Doris Rosenshine; c: Deborah, Elena. Prof, head div neur, prof pharm, U of Ill Coll of Med since 1963; chmn, dept neur, Presbyterian St Lukes Hosp, Chgo; dir, Cen Cerebrovascular Research, Rush Presbyterian St Lukes Hosp Med Cen since 1969 cons; NIH since 1959; neuropath, Oslo Comty House, established neuropath lab Oslo, Nor, 1951-52; research asso, U Oslo Clinics, 1951-52; Cen for Cerebrovascular Research, dir, 1962-63, mem fac, 1950-63; prof, neur, U Minn, 1959-63. US Army 1946-47; path, 42 Gen Hosp, Korea, 1946-47. Chmn, sect on neurochem, Amer Acad Neur since 1961, past vice-pres, secy; profsl adv bd, Epilepsy Found since 1964; fmr: secy, Minn Soc Neur Psycht; med adv bd, Hennepin Co Multiple Sclerosis Soc; pres, Assn U Prof Neur; mem: Amer Assn Neuropath; Biochem Soc, Eng; Assn Research Nervous and Mental Diseases; Intl Brain Research Org; Intl Soc Neurochem; Amer Soc Neurochem; Nor Neur Assn; Sigma Psi; Alpha Omega Alpha. Ed, Monographs in Basic Neurology; co-ed, Morphologic and Biochemical Correlates of Neural Activity, 1963; asso ed: World Neur since 1962; Jour of Neur Scis; contbr to: Clinical Neur, 1955; med jours. Recipient, dist service award, Wayne State U Sch of Med, 1964. Spec interests: viola, prints. Home: 1000 Chestnut Ave, Wilmette, Ill. Office: Rush Presbyterian St Lukes Hosp, Chicago, Ill.

COHEN, Menachem, Isr, engineer, architect; b. Riga, Latvia, May 27, 1931; s. Jacob and Regina (Jadlowker); in Isr since 1938; BSc, Technion, Haifa, 1955; m. Ada Horman, Oct 17, 1940; c: Jacob, Alma. Pvt practice since 1958; part-time sr lectr, Technion. Sgt, IDF, 1948-50. Mem, Assn Engs and Architects in Isr. Recipient: 1st prize for planning: Tel Aviv City Hall, 1957; Comprehensive Sch, Tiberias, 1969; Commercial Center, Arad. Home: 115 Jabotinsky St, Tel Aviv, Isr. Office: 16 Nahum St, Tel Aviv, Isr.

COHEN, Morris, US, metallurgist, educator; b. Chelsea, Mass, Nov 27, 1911; s. Julius and Alice (Ovson); BS, MIT, 1933, DSc, 1936; m. Ruth Krentzman, Jan 24, 1937; c: Barbara, Joel. Ford Prof, materials sci and engr, MIT, since 1962, prof, phys metallurgy, 1946-62, asso dir, Manhattan Project, 1943-46, on fac since 1936; investigator, off for Sci Research and Devl, 1942-43. F: Amer Acad Arts and Sci; Amer Inst of Mining, Metallurgical and Petroleum Engrs; NY Acad Sci; mem: AAAS; British Inst of Metals; Japan Iron and Steel Inst; Natl Acad Sci; British Iron and Steel Inst; hon mem, Indian Inst of Metals; Amer Phys Soc; Sigma Xi; Amer Soc for Engr Educ; hon mem, Amer Soc for Metals, past vice pres, fmr, chmn Boston chap, trustee. Author: Heat Treatment of High Speed Steel, 1946; Titanium in Steel, 1949; contbr to profsl jours on: phase transformations, metallography, heat treatment; solid state diffusion; thermodynamics; mech behavior of metals; tool steels; age hardening. Recipient: H M Howe Medal, Amer Soc for Metals, 1945, 1949; Sauveur Memorial Lecture and Award, 1947; Campbell Memorial Lecture, 1948, both Amer Soc for Metals; Inst of Metals Award, Amer Inst of Mining and Metallurgical Engrs, 1950; Kamani Medalist, Indian Inst of Metals, 1952; Mathewson Gold Medal, Amer Inst of Mining and Metallurgical Engrs, 1953; Inst of Metals Lecture, 1957; Burgess Memorial Lecture, 1958, Sauveur Memorial Lecture, Phila chap, Woodside Lecture, Detroit chap, Amer Soc for Metals; Clamer Medal, Franklin Inst, 1959; Coleman Lecture, 1960; Hondremont Memorial Lecture, Intl Inst of Welding, 1961; Howe Memorial Lecture, 1962; Hatfield Memorial Lecture, 1962; Gold Medal, Amer Soc for Metals, 1968. Home:

491 Puritan Rd, Swampscott, Mass. Office: MIT, Cambridge, Mass.

COHEN, Morris H, US, educator; b. Cincinnati, O, Apr 28, 1917; s. Isadore and Esther (Appelbaum); BA, U Chgo, 1939; att Harvard U, 1940-41; PhD, U Chgo, 1950; m. Margrit Koeckemann, 1962. Chmn, dept govt and intl relations, Clark U, since 1969, prof since 1966, on fac since 1947; Fulbright lectr, Amer govt and politics, U Amsterdam, Holland, 1955-56; Ford Found F, 1951-52; B'nai B'rith Hillel counselor, Worcester Coll, 1953-55. US Army, 1942-45. Pres: Clark chap, AAUP, 1944-45; Clark chap, Phi Beta Kappa, 1958-59; Worcester Plan E Assn, 1960; mem: bd dirs, J Family Service since 1957; Amer Political Sci Assn; B'nai B'rith; tech cons, Worcester J Fed on study of Worcester J population, 1957-58. Spec interest: J hist; natural hist. Home: 16 Tatnick Gardens, Worcester, Mass. Office: Clark U, Worcester, Mass.

COHEN, Morris L, US, educator, librarian; b. NYC, Nov 2, 1927; s. Emanuel and Anna (Frank); BA, U Chgo, 1948; JD, Columbia U Law Sch 1951; MLS, Platt Grad Libr Sch, 1959; m. Gloria Weitzner, Feb 1, 1923; c: Havi. Daniel. Biddle law libr and prof law, U of Pa Law Sch, since 1963; lectr, librarianship; Drexel Inst of Tech; Columbia U Grad Libr Sch: cons on libr building and planning to several U's. Pres, Amer Assn Law Librs; mem: exec bd, Phila chap, ACLU; Amer Bar Assn; Bibliographical Soc of Amer; Amer Libr Assn; Amer Soc for Info Sci; fmr: pres, U of Pa chap, AAUP; chmn, law and political sci sect, Amer Libr Assn; mem bd dirs, lower Merion Syn. Author: Legal Biography Briefed, 1965; Legal Research in a Nutshell, 1968. Recipient: grant, Natl Endowment for Hums, 1968, 1969; Contemporary Achievement Award, Pratt Inst, 1969. Home: 2285 N 51 St, Philadelphia, Pa. Office: U of Pa Law School, Philadelphia, Pa.

COHEN, Myer, US, international public official; b. Wash, DC, Nov 9, 1907; s. Myer and Helen (Wolf); BA, Swarthmore Coll, 1929; att: Cambridge U; Yale Law Sch; PhD, Yale Grad Sch; m. Elizabeth Elson, Aug 21, 1933; c: Arthur, Judith Kretzmann. Asst admnr, dir, bur of oprs and prog, UN Devl Prog since 1968, dir bur oprs, 1959-68; instr, Sch of Social Studies, 1935-40; asst regional dir, Farm Sec Admn, 1940-44; chief, DP oprs, UNRRA, 1944-47; asst dir gen, IRO, 1947-52; tech asst bd rep, UN, 1952-56; dir, prog div, UNTAA, 1956-58. Mem: Phi Beta Kappa. club; Yale. Author: Selected Supreme Court Decisions, 1937. Home: 2 Peter Cooper Rd, New York, NY. Office: United Nations, New York, NY.

COHEN, Nahum Donald, Isr, rabbi, educator; b. Scranton, Pa, Aug 31, 1932; s. Abe and Corinne (Gonfine); in Isr since 1968; BS, NYU, 1954; BHL, ordained rabbi, JTSA; m. Friedel Morton, June 10, 1958; c: Sara, Judy, Reuven. Educ dir, Yemin Orde Youth Village since 1968; dir, NY Metrop Region, United Syn of Amer, 1964-68; asst dir, 1960-64. Maj, chaplain, US Army, 1958-69. Mem: bd, Assn J Chaplains; Rabb Assn; Res Offs Assn. Author: Programming With a Purpose, 1965; A Guide to Men's Club Programming, 1967; Manual for Synagogue Leaders, 1967. Hobby, lectr on philatelic Judaica. Home and office: Yemin Orde Youth Village, Hof Hacarmel, Isr.

COHEN, Nathan E, US, educator; b. Sep 29, 1909; s. David and Ada (Cottler); AB, Harvard U, 1931, MA, 1932, PhD, 1934, Sheldon F, 1934-35; m. Sylvia Golden, 1934; c: David, Edward, Susan. Vice pres, W Reserve U, 1963-64; dean, Sch of Applied Soc Sci, 1958-64; prof, social work, UCLA, 1964-68, dean, Sch Social Wfr, 1968-69, prof, social work and chair, doctoral prog, 1968-69; dir, LA Riot Study of 1967; exec dir, YMHA, Boston, 1935-37; J Comty Wfr Fund and Council, Springfield, Mass, 1937-39; dir, leadership training and research, JWB, 1939-41, prog and J Cen Divs, 1941-45; prof, social work, NY Sch of Social Work, Columbia U, 1945-54, asso dean, 1955-58. Pres, Natl Conf on Social Wfr, 1963-64; Natl Assn Soc Workers, 1955-57; vice-pres, Amer Assn Group Workers, 1946-50; chmn, Natl Council Soc Work Educ, 1949-52; adv bd, O Dept of Public Wfr; spec cons to dir Natl Inst Mh, since 1963; mem, AAUP; Natl Assn Social Workers. Author: An Overall Look, Columbia U Bicentennial Series, 1955; Social Work in the American Tradition, 1958; Social Work and Social Problems, NASW, 1964; ed, The Citizen Volunteer, 1960. Recipient: Bicentennial medal, Columbia U, 1955; spec award, Natl Assn of J Cen Workers, 1956. Hobbies: sports, carpentry. Home: 13288 Chalon Rd, Los Angeles, Cal. Office: Sch of Social Wfr, UCLA, Los Angeles, Cal.

COHEN, Nina F, Can, communal leader; b. Glace Bay, NS, Mar 17, 1907; d. Max and Rose (Hausner) Fried; att Mt Allison Ladies Coll, 1923-24; hon LLD, Mt Allison U, 1936; m. Harry Cohen, Mar 28, 1928; c, J Stuart. Pres: Cape Breton March of Dimes; Cape Breton Council Cancer Soc; hon pres: Can Hadassah; WIZO; Bus and Profsl Women; vice-pres, NS Polio Soc; chmn; Cape Breton Red Cross Armed Services Comm; Cape Breton Miners Found and Mus; natl tourism chmn, Federated ZOC; natl chmn, migration and immigration, Natl Council of Women, Can; found: and hon pres, Miners Folk Soc; Miners Mus, Glace Bay, NS; "Men of the Deeps", miner's chorus; hon gov, Heb U; mem, WZO. Recipient: Red Cross Medal of Merit; Nina Cohen Village Award, Isr; NS Woman of the Cent, 1867-1967; Can Centennial Standard; two Can Centennial Medals; CBS Lloyd MacInnis Hum Award, 1968; Medal of Service; Order of Can; Heb U, Jerusalem. Hobbies: gardening, travel, photography. Home: 35 Howe St, Sydney, NS, Can.

COHEN, Noah Judah, US, educator, linguist, communal worker; b. Bklyn, NY, Sep 13, 1917; s. Alex and Gussie (Pitlevnik); BA, NYU, 1938; MA, Catholic U, Wash, DC, 1953; PhD, 1959; m. Dena Langer, 1948; c: Sharon, Abram, Michael. Cons, ling, US govt; instr J subjects, Beth Shalom Cong, Talmud Torah since 1959; bd educ, Heb Acad of Wash since 1960; chmn, bd educ, Wash Highlands J Cen, 1946-55, bd dirs, 1948-52. US Army, 1941-46, lt col, US Army Intelligence Res. Pres, Council Orthodox Syns, Gtr Wash since 1964; chmn, exec comm, Seaboard Region, Union Orthodox Congs of Amer since 1966; bd dir, Beth Shalom Cong and Talmud Torah since 1960; exec comm, JCC Gtr Wash; Wash Bd J Educ, Policy Planning comm, Natl Asso Profs Heb, since 1965; Amer Oriental Soc; J Hist Soc; Delta Phi Alpha; Educ Council, Wash, DC; youth activities chmn, Council of Orthodox J Congs for Wash, DC. Author: The Jay Treaty of 1794—A Study of American Violations of Earlier Commitments to France in 1778, pub, 1949; The Concept of Tsa'ar Ba'ale Hayyim—Its Bases, Development and Legislation in Hebrew Literature, 1953, rev, 1959; contbr to scholarly jours and encys. Recipient: Chinese decoration, 1945; Natl Meritorious Achievement Award, Natl Conf Syn Youth, 1964; Comty Service Award, Union Orthodox J Cong Amer, 1966; Meritorious Service Award, appd hon mem fac, US Army Intelligence Sch, 1966. Home: 7605-14th St, Washington, DC.

COHEN, Oscar, US, organization exec; b. Dundas, Can, June 1, 1908; s. Harry and Ida (Ziskind); in US since 1946; BA, U Toronto, 1929; att Columbia U, 1929-30; m. Marjorie Merlin, Feb 8, 1947; c: Myra, Deborah, Judith. Natl prog dir, ADL, since 1954; ed, J Standard, 1932-34; dir, Can J Cong, 1935-41, both Toronto; dir: JCC, Detroit, 1946-49; comty services dir, ADL, 1949-54. Lt col, Can Army, 1941-46. Mem: Amer Sociol Assn; Soc for Study of Social Problems; Inter-Amer Soc Psych; Soc for Psych Study of Social Issues; B'nai B'rith; Amer Vets Comm; Natl Assn Intergroup Relations Off; Urban League; NAACP; bd, Rel Research Assn. Contbr to social sci and gen jours. Recipient, MBE. Home: 27 W 86 St, New York, NY. Office: 315 Lexington Ave, New York, NY.

COHEN, Paul Pincus, US, attorney; b. Ellicottville, NY, Mar 26, 1896; s. Isaac and Sarah (Kallet); BA, magna cum laude, Harvard U, 1916; LLB, cum laude, 1918; m. Frances Proskauer, Feb 21, 1943; c, Virginia. Mem, law firm, Cohen Swados Wright Hanifin and Bradford since 1954; chmn, bd, N Tonawanda Enterprises Inc; mem, adv bd, Marine Midland Trust, W NY Niagara area off since 1945; pres, Old Fort Niagara Assn since 1946; dir: Niagara Share Corp since 1950; secy to Judge Julian W Mack, 1918; asso, Hawkins Delafield & Longfellow, 1918-19; lectr govt, U Buffalo, 1921-22; in banking, Amer Inst Banking, 1922-24; mem, firms, Franchot, Runals, Cohen, Taylor & Mallam, 1927-50; Cohen, Fleischmann, Augspurger, Henderson & Campbell, 1951-53. Vice-pres and bd trustees, Temple Beth Zion, Buffalo, NY, 1953; mem: council ADL since 1951; bd govs, United J Fed, 1953; chmn, Buffalo chap, AJComm, 1953-54, natl exec comm since 1954; vice-chmn, United J Fund Appeal, Niagara Falls, 1941-43; mem: Council, Buffalo State U Coll, 1966; bd trustees, Niagara U, 1968; Amer, NY State, Erie Co and Niagara Co Bar Assns; Phi Beta Kappa; clubs: Westwood Country, Harvard, Buffalo. Ed, Harvard Law Rev, 1916-18, contbr of articles on govt and finance, The Lincoln Libr, 1924. Recipient, Silver Medal of Honor, Fr, 1958. Home: 150 New Amsterdam Ave, Buffalo, NY. Offices: 256 Third St, Niagara Falls, NY; 70 Niagara St, Buffalo, NY.

COHEN, Philip P, US, biochemist, educator; b. Derry, NH, Sep 26, 1908; s. David and Ada (Cottler); BS, Tufts Coll, Mass, 1930; PhD, U Wis, 1937, MD, 1938; m. Rubye Tepper, 1935; c: Philip, David, Julie, Milton. H C Bradley Prof of Phys Chem, U Wis Med Sch since 1968, fac mem since 1941; NRC F; U Sheffield, Eng, 1938-39; dept Phys Chem, Yale U, 1939-40; cons, biochem, State Dept, U Mex, 1958. Mem: Pres' Public Health Service Hosp Comm, 1965; chmn; Comm on Growth, NRC, 1954-56; Wis Sect, Amer Chem Soc, 1951; mem: exec comm, div med sci, NRC, 1954-56; research adv council, Amer Cancer Soc, 1956-58; bd sci counsellors, Natl Cancer Inst, 1957-59; Phys Chem Study Sect, NIH, 1958-62; Natl Advisory Cancer Council, NIH, 1963-67; adv comm, Biol and Med, US AEC, 1963; chmn, 1969; adv comm on Med Research, PAHO, 1967; Sci Soc; Amer Soc Biol Chems; AAAS; Biochem Soc of Eng; Sigma Xi, pres, Wis Chap, 1968; Harvey Soc, hon; Sociedad Arg de Investigacion Bioquimica, hon. Contbr to research jours and sci books of works on biochem research. Recipient, Commonwealth Fund Award, 1958. Home: 1117 Oak Way, Madison, Wis. Office: U of Wis Med Sch, Madison, Wis.

COHEN, Ralph, Isr, business exec; b. Bridgeport, Conn, Jan 27, 1919; s. Morris and Dora (Karpilow); in Isr since 1950; att: Mikveh Isr Agric Sch; Yale U; m. Florence Golden, 1951; c: Mark, Doron, Yoav. Vice-pres, Isr off, Ampal-Amer-Isr Corp, Isr Devl Corp since 1950; mem, bd dirs: Sefen Fibre Bd; Tarit, Lake Galilee Canneries; Lapidoth, Isr Oil Prospectors; Naphta, Isr Petroleum Corp; Yahkin Mataiim; Isr Securities; Magal-Isr Gas Enterprises; secy, Isr Amer Ind Devl Bank. Natl dir, div communal workers, LZOA, 1947-48; natl dir, Natl Assembly for Lab Isr, 1948-50. Home: Shikun Olei America, Herzlia Pituach, Isr. Office: Ampal, 50 Rothschild Blvd, Tel Aviv, Isr.

COHEN, Reba B, US, communal worker; b. Baltimore, Md, Mar 6, 1901; d. Isadore and Caroline (Jacobson) Blustein; att Syracuse U, 1919-22; m. Charles Cohen, June 12, 1922; c: Ruth Wasserman, Carol Marks. Supt, Women Builders Morris Harvey Coll since 1963; chmn, State Bd Rehab for Blind since 1962; mem: State Bd for Handicapped since 1961; State bd Rehab for Blind, since 1962; Co Bd Camp Gallahad for Crippled Children. Natl ritualist, Alpha Epsilon Phi since 1957; Supt, Temple Isr Rel Sch, 1928-68; fmr pres: Natl Council J Women; Temple Isr Sisterhood; State Fed of Temple Sisterhoods, state parl, 1950-56; secy, natl found, Alpha Epsilon Phi, 1958-60. Home: 1576 Virginia St, Charleston, W Va.

COHEN, Reuven, Isr, farmer; b. Odessa, Russ, Mar 14, 1900; s. Alexander and Tova; in Isr since 1924; dipl agronom, High Inst for Agric, Kharkov, 1923; m. 1923; c: Aza, Eitan, Nir. Secy, Kibbutz Ein Harod since 1961, mem since 1924; mem secretariat, secy comm for settlement, Hakibbutz Hameuchad; cen comm, Lab Party of Isr. Served, Haganah. Mem, numerous bd JNF; cen bd Org of Agric Workers. Author: Foundations of the Kibbutz. The Kibbutz Settlement—Principles and Processes. Home: Ein Harod, Meuchad, Isr.

COHEN, Richard Loeb, US, dentist; b. Cleveland, O, Dec 30, 1932; s. Samuel and Irma (Loeb); att Bowling Green State U, O; DDS, O State U, 1957; m. Judith Rosenblum, June 15, 1958; c: David, Rachel, Jonathan, Jennifer. In pvt practice since 1967; sr cons, prosthodontist, Mt Sinai Hosp, Cleveland. Capt, US Army, 1957-62. Exec secy, Amer Pin Implant Soc; trustee, Suburban Temple; f, Intl Coll of Dent; mem: Mt Sinai Hosp Cleft Palate Team; Alpha Omega, treas, study group; Acad of Gen Dent; Amer Prosthodontic Soc; Amer Dent Soc; Cleveland Dent Soc; Boy Scouts of Amer, chmn, troop comm; Amer Cleft Palate Assn. Hobbies: skiing, tennis, sailing, music. Home: 22699 Douglas Rd, Shaker Heights, O. Office: Severance Med Arts Bldg, Cleveland Heights, O.

COHEN, Richard S, US, publicist; b. NYC, July 21, 1923; s. Louis and Leah (Diamond); BA, CCNY, 1943; m. Jeanne Carpe, May 9, 1948; c: Joelle, Leslie, Nina. Asso exec dir, PR dir, since 1958; AJCong; reporter, NY Times, NY Herald Tribune, 1942-43; publicity writer, JDC, 1945-49, pr dir, Eur hqrs, 1949-53; ed, Research Inst Amer, 1954-55; ed, commentator, J TV Chronicle, 1965-66; commentator, WBAI-FM, 1966; WEVD, 1968-69. USAAF, 1943-45. Pres, Amer J PR Soc; secy, Baldwin J Cen, 1960; club, Overseas Press. Author, Sunday in the Sixties, 1962; co-author: School Segregation Northern Style, 1961; School in Crisis, 1969; contbr to mags. Home: 1514 Coolidge Ave, Baldwin, NY. Office: 15 E 84 St, New York, NY.

COHEN, Robert Abraham, US, psychiatrist; b. Chgo, Ill, Nov 13, 1909; s. Ezra and Catherine (Kurzon); BS, U Chgo, 1930, PhD, 1935, MD, 1935; m. Mabel Blake, Mar 21, 1933; c: Donald, Margery. Dir, clinical invest, Natl Inst of Mh, since 1952; bd dir, Chestnut Lodge Inc, Rockville, since 1951, clinical dir, 1946-52. Cdr, USNR, 1941-46. Pres: Wash Psychan Soc, 1951-53, chmn, 1962-63; Wash Psycht Soc, 1958-59; chmn, bd dir, Found Fund for Research in Psycht, 1960-63; dir, Wash Psychan Inst, 1959-62; mem: Amer Psycht Assn; Amer Psychopath Assn. Contbr to profsl jours. Home: 4514 Dorset Ave, Chevy Chase, Md. Office: Natl Inst of Mh, Bethesda, Md.

COHEN, Robert Sonne, US, educator, scientist; b. NYC, Feb 18, 1923; s. Mordechai and Mabel (Reinschreiber); BA, Wesleyan U, 1943; MS, Yale U, 1943, PhD, 1948; m. Robin Hirschhorn, June 18, 1944; c: Michael, Daniel. Prof, chmn dept physics, Boston U, since 1958; visiting prof, hist and phil of sci, Amer U, summers, since 1958; visiting prof: phil of sci, MIT, 1958-61; hist of ideas, Brandeis U, 1959-60; visiting f, phil of sci, Pol Acad of Sci, 1962; asst prof, physics and phil, Wesleyan U, 1951-57; Ford F, phil of sci, Cambridge U, Eng, 1955-56; instr, physics and phil, Yale U, 1944-45, 1949-51, mem research staff, Div War Research, Columbia U and Jt Communications Bd, Us Jt Chiefs of Staff, 1944-46. Chmn: Boston Coll for Phil of Sci; Amer Inst for Marxist Studies; trustee, Wesleyan U; mem: bd dirs, Inst for Unity of Sci; natl council, Emergency Civil Liberties Comm; exec comm, Boston Area Fac Group on Public Issues; Phi Beta Kappa; Sigma Xi; Amer Assn Physics Tchrs; Amer Phys Soc; Amer Phil Assn; Phil of Sci Assn; Hist of Sci Soc; AAUP; NAACP. Co-author: Modern Philosophies and Education, 1955; The Validation of Scientific Theories, 1956; The Philosophy of Rudolf Carnap, 1963; Marxism and Democracy, 1965; Ernst Mach—Physicist and Philosopher, 1969; contbr to sci and phil jours. Home: 44 Adams Ave, Watertown, Mass. Office: Boston U, Boston, Mass.

COHEN, S Ralph, US, publicist; b. Elizabeth, NJ, July 9, 1917; s. Aaron and Lillie (Brody); BA, Union Coll, Schenectady, NY, 1937; m. Enid Nemy, Aug 31, 1951. Asst to pres, Scandinavian Airlines Sys, Inc, NY, since 1963; newspaper reporter, Schenectady and Albany, NY, 1934-37; press relations, Hudson River Navigation, NY, 1937; leg corresp, NJ State House, 1937-43; dir, AJCong, NJ div, 1937-38; Trenton Housing Auth, with LJ Lanning, 1942-43, both NJ; Natl Aeronautics Assn of US, 1943-46; publicity dir, G R Wilson for US Sen, 1942; ed, Natl Aeronautics Mag, Wash, DC, 1943-46; dir, pr, Intl Air Transp Assn, 1946-63; war corresp, UK, Fr, Ger, 1945; studied Brit civil aviation on invitation of Brit Govt, 1945. US Army, 1941. Mem: bd, Thanks to Scandinavia Found; pr adv comm, Boy Scouts World Bur, Geneva; council, Montreal Mus of Fine Arts; Aviation Writers Assn; Can PR Soc; Inst PR, UK; Can Inst Intl Affairs; hon mem, It Press Relations Assn; secy, Intl Airlines PR Confs, 1947, 1949, 1954, 1958, 1960, 1962; clubs: Natl Press, Wash; Overseas Press; Wings; Lotus, all NYC. Author: IATA: The First Three Decades, 1969; contbr to US fgn publs. Office: 555 Fifth Ave, New York, NY.

COHEN, Samuel I, US, communal leader; b. Asbury Park, NJ, Apr 17, 1933; ordained rabbi, Mesivta Rabbi Chaim Berlin Rabb Acad, 1956; BA, Bklyn Coll, 1955; MRE, Yeshiva U, 1959, EdD, 1967; m. Mira Hager, Sep, 1960; two c. Dir, mem dept, B'nai B'rith Dist No 1 since 1966, regional dir, 1961-66; lectr, Manhattan Comty Coll since 1968; exec dir, LI Zionist youth Comm, 1957-61; adj asst prof, sociol, LIU, 1967; lectr, Queensborough Comty Coll, 1968. Mem: Young Isr Syn, Wavecrest and Bayswater; Rabb Alliance of Amer; Amer Sociol Assn; Adult Educ Assn; Natl Conf J Communal Service. Contbr to educ and J publs. Home: 2904 Bayswater Ave, Far Rockaway, NY. Office: 315 Lexington Ave, New York, NY.

COHEN, Samuel Isaac, Eng, physician; b. Cardiff, Wales, Nov 22, 1925; s. Gershon and Ada (Samuel); BSc, MD, U Wales, Cardiff, 1948; FRCP; m. Vivienne Wolfson, May 24, 1955; c: Michael, Elizabeth. Cons psycht; London Hosp since 1963; London J Hosp since 1969; lectr, med, U of Wales, 1952-56; psycht, the Maudsley Hosp, London, 1956-62. Chmn, Doctors and Dentists Comm, JPA, London. Contbr to med jours. Home: 8 Linnell Dr, London, Eng. Office: London Hosp, London, Eng.

COHEN, Samuel Selig, US, dentist; b. Providence, RI, Aug 22,

1899; s. Abraham and Anna (Greenberg); DDS, O State U, 1927; m. Irma Loeb, 1924; c: Alan, Richard, Sandra Dee. Pvt practice, dent, since 1927; dir, prosthetic dent dept, Mt. Sinai Hosp, Cleveland, O since 1946, mem staff since 1928; dent cons, Bellefaire Home for Disturbed Children, J Children's Bur since 1953; prosthodontist, Edward Reiter Cleft Palate Clinic since 1945; lectr clinician, dent prosthetics and mouth rehab, US, Can since 1932; Intl Dent Cong, Rome, 1957; Pan-Amer Dent Assn, Mex, 1958; Heb U, Jerusalem; Isr Dent Soc, Tel Aviv; Dent Sch, Bangkok, 1960. Sr chmn, dental div, JWF Dr, 1949-55; chmn, non-alumni div, Western U Fund Dr, since 1959; capt, dent div, O State U devl fund dr, since 1950; f: Amer Coll Dents, Intl Coll of Dents, Gtr NY Acad Prosthodontics; dipl, Amer Bd Prosthodontics, pres, Amer Prosthodontic Soc, 1955-56; Cleveland Dent Soc, 1950-51; Cleveland Chap, Alpha Omega, 1937; mem: Chgo Dent Soc; Amer Dent Assn: Dent for Children; Amer Equilibration Soc; Pierre Fauchard Acad; Amer Acad Plastic Research; Royal Soc Health; Omicron Kappa Upsilon; Masons; B'nai B'rith; Home: 3307 Chadbourne Rd, Shaker Heights. O. Office: Severance Med Arts Bldg, Cleveland Heights, O.

COHEN, Saul, US. attorney; b. LA, Cal, June 19, 1927; s. Jack and Sarah (Ostrofsky); AB, UCLA, 1950; JD, Stanford U, 1953; m. Anne-Lise Engel, Dec 6, 1954; c: Adam, Mikala, Elizabeth. Partner, Selvin and Cohen since 1963; fmr lectr, Loyala U Law Sch. Cpl, US Army, 1945-46. Mem: Amer, Cal, LA Co, Beverly Hills Bar Assns; Amer Judicature Soc; Copyright Soc of US; LA Copyright Soc; fmr: pres, Friends UCLA Libr; bd trustees: Comty TV of S Cal; Inner City Cultural Cen; clubs: Sierra; Zamarano. Co-author, An Author's Guide to Scholarly Publishing and the Law, 1954; contbr to legal jours. Hobbies: book collecting, primitive art, sculpture. Home and Office: 544 San Antonio St, Santa Fe, NM.

COHEN, Saul Bernard, US, educator; b. Malden, Mass, July 28, 1925; s. Barnet and Anna (Kaplan); AB, Harvard U, 1948, AM Harvard U, 1949, PhD, 1955; m. Miriam Friederman, June 11, 1950; c: Deborah, Louise. Dir, prof, sch geog, Clark U, since 1965, dean, Grad Sch, since 1967; adv: social sci div, NSF; bur for educ personnel devl, US Off of Educ; prof, Boston U, 1952-64. Cpl, US Army, 1943-46. Councillor, Assn Amer Geogs, past exec secy; chmn: comm on geog, Natl Acad Scis, NRC; Consortium of Profsl Assns for Study of Spec Tchr Improvement Progs; coord, co-chmn, US-Isr Geog Research Symposium, Jerusalem, 1969; mem: Amer Geog Soc; AAAS; fmr, chmn: Commn on Coll Geog; Comm on Geog and Afro-Amer; club, Cosmos. Author: Geography and Politics in a World Divided, 1964, 65; American Geography-Problems and Prospects, 1968; contbr numerous articles and monographs. Recipient, Service Award, Assn Amer Geogs, 1969. Home: 50 Solon St, Newton, Mass. Office: Main St, Worcester, Mass.

COHEN Saul G, US, chemist, educator; b. Boston, Mass, May 10, 1916; s. Barnet and Ida (Levine); MA, Harvard U, 1938, PhD, 1940; m. Doris Brewer, Nov 26, 1941; c: Jonathan, Elisabeth. Chmn, dept chem, Brandeis U since 1959, on fac since 1950; cons, Polaroid Corp since 1950, chief chem, 1950-55; instr, Harvard U, 1941-42; Mem: Phi Beta Kappa; Sigma Xi; Amer Acad Arts and Scis; Amer Chem Soc; Chem Soc, London; AAAS; Technion Soc; ZOA; sr Fulbright scholar, UK, 1958-59. Contbr to profsl jours on organic and phys organic chem. Home: 39 Moon Hill Rd, Lexington, Mass. Office: Brandeis U, Waltham, Mass.

COHEN, Seymour Jay, US, rabbi; b. NYC, Jan 30, 1922; s. Philip and Rose (Cohen); BSS, cum laude, CCNY, 1942; MA, Columbia U, 1949; PhD, U Pittsburgh, 1953; ordained rabbi, JTSA, 1946, MHL, 1949; m. Naomi Greenberg, 1946; c: Grace, Marc, Leeber. Rabbi; Anshe Emeth since 1961; Patchogue J Cen, 1947-51; B'nai Isr Cong, Pittsburgh, 1951-61; f, Lehman Inst of Talmudic Ethics since 1958. Chmn: Amer J Conf on Soviet J since 1965; campaign, United J Fed, Pittsburgh, 1957, hon chmn, 1958; co-chmn, Young Judea, 1949-52; pres, Chgo Bd of Rabbis since 1968; vice-pres, Syn Council of Amer, 1965-67; secy, RA, 1962-64; mem: natl exec bd, ZOA, natl rabb cabinet, JTSA since 1953; Amer Zionist Youth Commn, 1948-50; Phi Beta Kappa. Author: Monetary Problems of the Middle East, 1939-52; Judaism and the World of Business and Labor, 1961; Negro-Jewish Dialogue, 1963; Religious Freedom and the Constitution, 1963; A Time to Speak, 1968; trans, Paths of the Righteous,

1969; contbr to jours. Recipient, ZOA F, Heb U, 1946. Home: 3800 Lake Shore Dr, Chicago, Ill. Study: 3760 N Pine Grove, Chicago, Ill.

COHEN, Seymour Stanley, US, biochemist, educator; b. Bklyn, NY, Apr 30, 1917; s. Herman and Lena (Tanz); BS, CCNY, 1936; PhD, Columbia U, 1941; m. Elaine Pear, July 12, 1940; c: Michael, Sara. Prof, biochem, U of Pa, Sch of Med, since 1954; Hartzell Prof, chmn, dept therapeutic research, since 1963, on staff since 1943; Charles Hayden prof, Amer Cancer Soc, 1957; Jesup lectr, Columbia U, 1967; F: Abbot Labs, 1940; NRC, Rockefeller Inst, 1941-42; Guggenheim, Pasteur Inst, 1947-48; Lalor, 1951, 1952; Amer Acad Arts and Sci. Pres, Soc of Gen Phys, 1967-68. Mem: Amer Chem Soc; Amer Soc Biol Chem; Amer Soc of Bacts, AAAS; Corp of Marine Biol Lab; Sigma Xi; Natl Acad Sci, 1967. Author: Virus Enzymes, 1968; asso ed, Virology, 1955-60; ed Bact Revs since 1969; bd, Jour of Biol Chem since 1960; Contbr to sci publs. Recipient: Eli Lilly Medal, bact, 1951; Mead Johnson Award, ped, 1952; Newcombe Cleveland award, AAAS, 1955; Borden Award, Amer Assn of Med Colls, 1967. Home: 43 Rockglen Rd, Philadelphia, Pa. Office: U of Pa, School of Med, Philadelphia, Pa.

COHEN, Shalom, Isr, journalist; b. Baghdad, Iraq, Feb 12, 1926; s. Eliahu and Flora (Cohen); att Vic Coll, Egypt; m. Ora Heller, May 11, 1955; c: Ron, Ariel. Mgn ed, Haolam Hazeh, mag, since 1968, on staff, since 1950; MK; secy gen, Haolam Hazeh, New Force Party. Cpl, IDF, 1948-50. Home: 37 Yavetz St, Kiriat Matalon, Petah Tikva, Isr. Office: 12 Carlebach St, Tel Aviv, Isr.

COHEN, Shear-Yashuv J, Isr, rabbi, educator; b. Jerusalem, Nov 27, 1927; s. David and Sarah (Etkin); ordained rabbi, Rabbi Kook Yeshiva, 1947; MJ, Heb U Law Fac, Jerusalem, 1954; m. Naomi Goldstein, Jan 20, 1953; c: Eliraz. Dep mayor, Jerusalem, heading educ, culture, youth depts; dir, Harry Fischel Inst For Research in J Law, found Sem for, Rabbis and Rabb Judges, Jerusalem since 1955; vice chmn, Emet World Acad for J Studies since 1962. Chaplain, IDF 1949-53; chief chaplain, IAF, 1953-54; maj, IDF, Isr War of Liberation, prisoner of War, siege of Jerusalem (Old City). Mem: Jerusalem City Council since 1956; mem exec since 1960; cen bodies Natl Rel Party; Isr comm, UNESCO since 1958, mem exec since 1960; B'nai B'rith; B'nai Zion; Chug Mishpatanim Datiim; Irgun Havrei haHaganah. Ed, rev ed, Yesod ve-Shoresh ha-Avoda, 1960; ed bd, Halacha Pesuka-Restated Code of Jewish Law, 1st vol, 1962; contbr articles to periodicals. Recipient: Ot Yerushalaim; Semel Haneche; Ot Aleh. Home: 21 Balfour St, Jerusalem, Isr. Office: Harry Fischel Inst, Jerusalem, Isr.

COHEN, Sheldon J, Can, business exec; b. London, Ont, May 23, 1905; s. Isaac and Anna (Steinberg); BA, Queens U, Kingston, Ont, 1927; m. Fagel Gordon; c: Norda, Dana. Pres, I Cohen, & Co, Ltd; vice-pres, Morco Products, since, 1953. Hon pres, Beth Isr Cong, Kingston, since 1965, past pres; pres, JCC, since 1947; mem: bd govs, Kingston Gen Hosp; Can Inst Intl Affairs; Kiwanis Club; fmr: pres: Comty Chest; Cancer Soc, both Kingston; chmn, adv comm, Hillel Found, Queens U; exec mem: E Can council, B'nai B'rith; Red Cross Soc; mem, bd dirs, Children's Aid Soc. Home: 117 King St W, Kingston, Ont. Office: POB 290, Kingston, Ont, Can.

COHEN, Sheldon Stanley, US, attorney government official; b. Wash, DC, June 28, 1927; s. Herman and Pearl (Jaffe); AB, hons, George Wash U, 1950, JD, hons, 1952; m. Faye Fram, Feb 21, 1951; c: Melinda, Laura, Jonathan, Sharon. Commn, Internal Revenue Service since 1956, leg atty, 1952-56, chief counsel, 1964-65; partner Arnold, Fortas & Porter, 1960-64. USN, 1945-46. Pres, Inter-Amer Cen of Tax Admnrs, 1967-68; dir; J Comty Cen; J Social Service Agcy; Natl Found for J Culture; bd mgrs, Adas Isr Cong; bd dirs: Natl JWB; United Syn of Amer; mem: George Wash U Council for Sch of Govt and Bus Admn; Order of Coif; Masons; DC Inst of CPA's, hon; Amer and Fed Bar Assns; Phi Delta Phi; Phi Sigma Delta. Recipient: Arthur S Flemming Award, Jr C of C, Wash, DC. Home: 5518 Trent, Chevy Chase, Md. Office: Suite 400, 1730 M St, NW Washington, DC.

COHEN, Shimon, Isr, musician; b. Tel Aviv, Oct 14, 1937; s. Dov and Chavatselet Ben Zeev; att Acad of Music; Composer, arranger, conductor, pianist. Home: 25 Pinsker St, Rishon-le-Zion, Isr.

COHEN, Simon, US, librarian; b. Baltimore, Md, Feb 26, 1894; s. Benjamin and Rebecca (Sinsheimer); AB, U Cincinnati, 1914; DD, HUC, 1924; att: Brown U, 1917-19; m. Dagmar Abramson, May 10, 1944; c, Marthamae Schlow. Reference, serial libr, cataloger, Klau Libr, HUC-JIR since 1952; libr; Cong Mishkan Isr, Selma, 1922-25; Temple Beth-El and Temple Emanuel, NYC, 1925-28; dir research, Universal J Ency, NYC, 1928-44; HUC Sch for Tchrs, 1929-31. Mem, Soc Bibl Lit. Author: Essence of Judaism, 1932; Seven-branched Light, 1944; Shaaray Tefilia, 1945; contbr of numerous articles to standard reference works and profsl jours. Home: 2200 Victory Pkwy, Cincinnati, O. Office: 3101 Clifton, Cincinnati, O.

COHEN, Sol W, US, attorney; b. NYC, Oct 22, 1902; s. David and Antoinette (Tannenbaum); att CCNY; LLB, NY Law Sch, 1925; m. Mollie Spitzer, Dec 19, 1931; c: Alan Cober, Diane Teplitzky. Pvt practice since 1927. Pres, off, various civic and legal orgs; Criminal Bar Assn, NYC; NY Co Lawyers Assn. Home: 210 E 15 St, New York, NY. Office: 134 Centre St, New York, NY.

COHEN, Stuart A, US, business exec; b. Chgo, Ill, Mar 20, 1936; s. Jack and Bernice (Steadman); BS, metallurgical engr, Purdue U, 1957; MBA, U of Chgo, 1965; m. Ruth Marcus, Feb 8, 1959; c: Cathy, Edward, Howard, Laurie, Brian, Barbara. Vice-pres, mfr since 1966. Pvt, US Army, 1958. Mem: Sigma Alpha Nu; Sigma Eta. Hobby, golf. Home: 80 Ferndale, Deerfield, Ill. Office: 4528 Division, Chicago, Ill.

COHEN, Sylvan M, US, attorney; b. Phila, Pa, July 28, 1914; BA, U Pa, 1935, LLB, Law Sch, 1938; m. Alma; s: Steven Mark, Sr partner, Cohen, Shapiro, Berger, Polisher and Cohen, since 1939; sr enforcement atty, OPA, 1941-42; pres and trustee, Pa Real Estate Inves Trust; mem, bd dirs: Ind Valley Bank and Trust Co; Sci Resources; Fla Palm-Aire; Belmont Ind. Lt, combat intelligence off, USAAC, 1941-46. Pres, mem, bd trustees, Fed J Agcys of Gtr Phila; first pres, Meadowlands Country Club; vice-pres: mem bd govs, Natl Assn of Real Estate Inves Funds; mem bd trustees, Albert Einstein Med Cen; Beth Jacob Schs of Phila; Amer Friends of Heb U, Phila chap; co-chmn, Bi-Partisan Com for Merit Selection of Judges; asso chmn, bd govs, Phila comm, State of Isr Bonds; chmn: Pension comm for Phila Gas Works; comty participation unit, Council on Youth Opportunity; State Leg comm of NAREIF; fmr chmn: Admn Judge Liaison comm, chmn, Civil Jud Procedure comm, mem, supr Court Adv comm, of Phila Bar Assn, mem, bd govs, 1965-67; bd dirs: Technion Soc; JDC; Variety Club Camp for Handicapped Children; Beth Sholom Cong; U Pa Varsity and Football Clubs; Bd of Ethics, City of Phila; natl panel of arbitrators, Amer Arbitration Assn; mem: Phila, Pa, Amer, Fed Bar Assns; Socio-Legal Club; Phila Lawyers Club; exec comm, chmn's comm, bd trustees, United Fund; bd dirs, Natl Found, March of Dimes; bd trustees, United Isr Appeal, Inc, Ed staff, Collier on Bankruptcy; fmr, note ed: Amer Bar Assn Bill of Rights Rev; and leg ed, U Pa Law Rev. Home: 1000 Serpentine Lane, Wyncote, Pa. Office: 12 S 12 St, Philadelphia, Pa.

COHEN, Theodore, Japan, business exec, communal leader; b. NYC, May 31, 1918; s. Isidor and Fanny (Chernuchin) Cohan; in Japan since 1946; BSS, CCNY, 1938; AM, Columbia U, NY, 1939; att: U Mich; Cornell U; m. Mitsu Watanabe, Nov 3, 1949; c: Frederick, Dorothy, Maury. Vice-pres, M I Greisman and Son Ltd, Can since 1953; mgn dir, Marshall Scott since 1954; chief, Japanese lab sect, US Fgn Econ Admn, 1944-45; chief, lab div, GHO Supr Cdr for Allied Powers, Tokyo, 1946-47; econ adv to Gen MacArthur, 1947-50; mem, hist dept, fac, CCNY, 1938-40; delg, UN Econ Commn for Asia and Far E; 1949; with Off of Strategic Services, Wash, DC, 1941-44. Co-found, Japanese Comm for Cultural Freedom; vice pres, J Comty of Japan, since 1962, fmr acting pres; co-found, exec bd, Tokyo J Comty; chmn, Isr Emergency Fund Dr, Japan, 1967; mem: Phi Beta Kappa; Columbia U Alumni Assn; Japan; fmr: repr of J Comty, Tokyo USO Comm. Author of considerable Japanese lab leg including present Lab Relations Adjustment Law: contbr to encys, periodicals. Recipient, Commendation for Meritorius Civilian Service, US Govt, 1950. Hobbies: swimming, music, J hist. Home: 3-6-4 Moto Azabu, Tokyo, Japan. Office: Sanshin Bldg, Yurakucho Chiydoa-ku, Japan.

COHEN, Vera L, Austr, communal leader; b. Brisbane, Sep 25,

1902; d. Aaron and Selina (Jacobs) Emanuel; att Auckland Tech Coll, NZ; m. Bernard Cohen, June 15, 1927; c: Laurelle Renof, Neville. Natl pres, Natl Council J Women, Austr, 1955-67, past pres, local charities comm, active in council's intl relations; co-vice-pres, Intl Council J Women, Jerusalem, 1969; pvt secy, Commnr Crown Lands, Lands Dept, Auckland, 1920-27; mem exec: Natl Council Women; NSW J Bd Deps; women's div, Bi-Centenary Celebration Landing Capt Cook; mem: Fed JNF; Sydney Opera House; life gov: Food for Babies Fund; Sir Moses Montefiore Home; Benevolent Soc; delg, State ZC, Australia and NZ. Recipient, Queen's Coronation Medal, 1953. Home: 29 Dans Ave, Coogee, NSW, Austr.

COHEN, Victor W, US, research physicist; b. NYC, 1911; s. Morris and Mary (Ryshpan); BS, CCNY, 1931; PhD, Columbia, 1935; m. Grace Jonas, 1940; c: Richard, Dorothy, Ruth. Staff: Brookhaven Natl Lab since 1947; USN Dept, 1940-44; Natl Bur of Standards, 1944-47; research asso, U of Ia, 1934-37; instr, CCNY, 1939-40. F, Amer Phys Soc; mem: Epsilon Chi; Sigma Xi. Contbr to sci jours. Recipient, citation, Navy Dept. Home: Patchogue, NY. Office: Brookhaven Natl Lab, Upton, NY.

COHEN, Wallace M, US, attorney; b. Norton, Va, July 11, 1908; s. Jacob and Annie (Hyman); BS, Harvard Coll, 1929; att Harvard Law Sch, 1929-31; LLB, Cornell Law Sch, 1932; m. Sylvia Stone, 1932; c: Anne Winkelman, Edward, David. Partner, Landis, Cohen and Singman since 1951; pvt practice, Boston, Mass, 1932-38; atty, NLRB, 1938-39; counsel to admnr, Wage and Hour Div, Lab Dept, 1939-40; atty, Council Natl Defense, 1940-41; gen counsel, Shipbuilding Stabilization Comm, 1940-41; regional admnr, OPA, 1942-43; dir, liberated areas, Lend Lease Admn, 1943; asst dir, Fgn Econ Admn, 1943-44. Mem: natl bd, AJComm; Montgomery Co Housing Auth; f, vice-chmn, Brandeis U; clubs: Lonesome Pine; Woodmont Country; Fed City; Intl; Natl Press; Natl Lawyers. Contbr to profsl jours. Home: 444 Massachusetts Ave, NW, Washington, DC. Office: 1910 Sunderland Pl, NW, Washington, DC.

COHEN, Wilbur Joseph, US, educator; b. Milwaukee, Wis, June 10, 1913; s. Aaron and Bessie (Rubenstein); PhD, U Wis, 1934; LHD, Adelphi Coll, 1962; LLD, U Wis, 1966; LHD, Yeshiva U, 1967; m. Eloise Bittel, Apr 8, 1938; c: Christopher, Bruce, Stuart. Dean, prof, U Mich Sch of Ed since 1969; Secy, HEW, 1968-69, asst secy, 1961-65, under secy, 1965-68; prof, public wfr admn, U of Mich, 1956-61; staff researcher, Roosevelt Cabinet Comm on Econ Security, 1934; tech adv, Social Security Admn, 1935-54; dir, research stat div, 1954-56; pres, Kennedy Task Force on Health and Social Security, 1960; chmn: Pres' Comm on Population and Family Planning, 1968; Pres' Air Quality Adv Bd, 1968. Pres, Natl Conf on Social Wfr, 1970; mem: Mich Bd Health; Amer Econ Assn; Amer Public Wfr Assn; Ind Relations Research Assn; Amer Public Health Assn; Natl Assn Social Workers. Author, Retirement Policies Under Social Security, 1957; co-author: Readings in Social Security, 1948; Social Security: Programs, Problems and Policies, 1960; Income and Welfare, 1962. Recipient: dist service award, HEW, 1956; annual award, Natl Conf Social Wfr, 1957; outstanding service award, Group Health Assn, 1956; Florina Lasker Award, Natl Conf Social Wfr, 1961; Terry Award, Amer Public Wfr Assn, 1961; Blanche Ittleson Award, Social Work Recruiting Comm, NY, 1962; awards: Natl Assn for Mentally Retarded Children, 1965; Assn of Phys Med, 1965; Bronfman Public Health Prize, 1967; Rockefeller Public Service, 1967; Murray-Green, 1968. Home: 620 Oxford, Ann Arbor, Mich. Office: Sch of Educ, U of Mich, Ann Arbor, Mich.

COHEN, William, US, public relations counsel; b. Vergennes, Vt, Sep 3, 1912; s. Abraham and Zelda (Fishman); PhD, U of Vt, 1934; MPA, NYU, 1956; m. Jessie Turberg, July 4, 1942; c, Nina. PR counsel, NYC; liaison off, Off of Econ Devl, City of Newark, NJ; dir: Amer Technion Soc, 1948-53; Alexander's Dept Stores, 1953-54; pr expert and city mgr, Amer Devl Corp, 1953-54; pr dir, Amer Friends Heb U, 1955-59. USAF, 1942-46. Mem: Newspaper Guild, NY; Amer J PR Soc. Ed, found, Wing Tips, AAF, 1942-46; ed, sci and tech jours, 1948-53. Hobby, archeol. Home: 310 First Ave, New York, NY. Office: 18 E 50 St, New York, NY.

COHEN, William, US, rabbi; b. NYC, Dec 17, 1919; s. Samuel and Dora (Marcus); BA, Yeshiva U, 1941; ordained rabbi,

Rabbi Isaac Elhanan Theol Sem, 1943; m. Miriam Irom, Apr 11, 1943; c: Devra, David, David Israel. Rabbi, Beth David Syn, W Hartford Conn, since 1946; counselor, B'nai B'rith Hillel Found, Trinity Coll, since 1951; rabbi: Cong Beth David, Lynbrook, LI, 1943-44; Cong Adath Isr, Middletown, Conn, 1944-46. Pres, Rabb Council, Conn; bd dirs: Hartford J Fed; Hartford J Cmty Cen; Yeshiva, Hartford; Conn Project Equality Inc; mem: natl exec, RabCA; Yeshiva U Rabb Alumni, past vice pres; fmr, pres, Mizrachi Org, Hartford. Ed, Sermon Manual of RabCA, 1967. Recipient: Dist Alumnus Award, Yeshiva U, 1965; B'nai B'rith Citation, 1961. Home: 134 Penn Dr, Hartford, Conn. Office: 20 Dover Rd, W Hartford, Conn.

COHEN, William, US, educator; b. Scranton, Pa, June 1, 1933; s. Maurice and Nellie (Rubin); BA, U of Cal, 1953, LLB, 1956; m. Betty Stein, Sep 13, 1952; c: Barbara, David, Rebecca. Prof, law, UCLA since 1962, visiting asso prof, 1959-60, asso prof, 1960-62; visiting prof, Stanford Law Sch, since 1968; law clerk, Asso Justice Wm O Douglas, US Supr Court, 1956-57; asst prof, U Minn, 1957-58, asso prof, 1958-60. Home: 16878 Severo Pl, Encino, Cal. Office: Law Sch, UCLA, Los Angeles, Cal.

COHEN, Yaacov, Isr, civil servant; b. Jerusalem, Jan 3, 1929; s. Gershon and Eliza (Cohen); att: Yeshivot; Porat Yosef; Aluma, both Jerusalem; Bar Ilan U, Ashkelon br, 1967-69; m. Yael Levy, Aug 10, 1955; c: Yuri, Tamar, Ely. Dist off, Ashkelon, Min of Interior, since 1969, with min since 1954; fmr: with Hadassah Guggenheim Org, Jerusalem; head, local council, Ofakim, 1960-62. Haganah: lt, IAF, 1950-54. Chmn, Ashkelon dist, Natl Council for Prevention of Accidents; vice-pres, B'nai B'rith, Ashkelon; mem, local philanthropic orgs. Hobbies: botany, folk dancing, lit. Home: 52 Hashikma St, Ashkelon, Isr.

COHEN, Yaakov Y, Isr, author, educator; b. Bklyn, NY, Mar 21, 1919; s. Isidor and Helen (Grossman); in Isr since 1961; BA, Bklyn Coll, 1940; ordained rabbi, BHL, MHL, JTSA, 1943; att, Heb U, 1947-48; PhD, Columbia U, 1958; m. Rhoda Levine, Dec 23, 1945; c: Michal, Jeremy, Adeena. Dir, B'nai B'rith Hillel Found in Isr; fmr: educ dir, rabbi, Soc for Advancement of Judaism, NYC; instr, phil of rel, JTSA, NYC. Dir, J Reconstructionist Found, NY; educ dir, Park Syn, NY. Author: Jewish Education in Democratic Society, 1955; The Case for Religious Naturalism, 1958; chaps in Mordechai M Kaplan: An Education; Intermarriage and Jewish Life; Varieties of Jewish Belief; Illustrated History of the Jews; A History of Jewish Education in the US; Judaism and the Jewish School; Chinuch le-Emunah ve le Masoret; book on Yaakov Meir; Roads to Jewish Survival; co-author, The Reconstructionist; Petachim. Office: 4 Balfour St, Jerusalem, Isr.

COHEN, Yahya, Singapore, surgeon, educator; b. Singapore, Apr 1, 1920; att, King Edward VII Coll of Med, Singapore, deg with distinction: Med Jurisprudence, Surg, Obstet, Gyn, 1947; postgrad training, UK, 1951-54; m. Janina Horowitz. Sr surg, Gen Hosp, Singapore, since 1960; external examiner, Anat, U Singapore; examiner, Surg, Ped Surg, Singapore Nursing Bd, sr lectr, U Malaya, Singapore; visiting prof, Tel Aviv U, 1965. Fmr pres, Singapore Med Assn; pres, Singapore Surg Soc; fmr: mem, council, U of Singapore; chmn, Nurses State Examination Comm; scribe, Acad of Med Council; f, Royal Soc of Med; mem: Singapore Med Council; Malayan Med Council; British Assn of Plastic Surgs; master, Acad of Med. Office: General Hosp, Singapore 3.

COHEN, Yardena, Isr, dancer; choreographer, dance therapist; b. Isr; d. Pinhas and Miriam (Raphaelkes); att Dance Acad, Vienna; m. Ernest Grunwald, 1934; c: Daniel, Edith. Head, dance studio, Isr; cons on dance therapy to psychs; fmr dance tchr, Dresden, Ger. Prin contrib: Revived ancient styles of dance and instruments. Author: be Toff ube Madid. Home: 10 Jerusalem st, Haifa, Isr. Studio: 10 Golomb St, Haifa, Isr.

COHEN, Yehezkel, Isr, educator; b. Montreal, Can, Nov 4, 1925; s. Abraham and Ida (Stock); in Isr since 1949; MA, Heb U, Jerusalem, 1953; EdD, Columbia U, 1964; m. Fayge Kravitz, Sep 5, 1946; c: Gila, Raanan, Gidon. Dean students, Heb U, Jerusalem, since 1966; exec secy, World Heb Union, 1956-60; overseas students adv, Heb U, 1964-66. RCAF, 1943-46. Vice-chmn, Adult Educ Assn Isr. Home: 35 Tchernichovsky St, Jerusalem, Isr. Office: Heb U, Jerusalem, Isr.

COHEN, Yehuda, Isr, musician; b. Prague, Czech, Mar 14, 1910; s. Avigdor and Emilia (Fischel); in Isr since 1936; studied music and engr in Prague; m. Shoshanna Slomovic, May 19, 1938; c, Hanna Liron. Ed, musical progs, Isr Bç Sta; lectr on music for subscribers of Isr Philharmonic Orch; fmr: invited by It Govt for Research work; lectr, Fac of Beyreuth Festival Master Classes. Music critic, Yedioth Chadashoth, daily newspaper; music corresp abroad. Recipient, medal by It Govt for cultural activity in diffusing It lang and music. Home: 9 Zamenhof St, Tel Aviv, Isr. Office: Hakiryah, Tel Aviv, Isr.

COHEN, Yehuda, Isr, judge; b. Safed, Isr, Jan 23, 1914; s. Menachem and Lea (Landman); BA, math, Amer U, Beirut, Leb, 1934; grad, Govt Law Sch, Jerusalem, 1940; m. Shulamit Proter, Jan 30, 1945; c: Raphael, Varda, Ehud. Judge, Dist Court, Jerusalem since 1954; clerk, Halvaah Vehisachon Bank, 1935-41; pvt law practice, 1947-49; judge, Magistrate's Court, Jerusalem, 1949-54. Lt, Brit Army, 1942-46; maj, IDF, 1947-49. Vice-pres, B'nai B'rith, Isr; chmn: Comm Soldiers Wfr Org; Ot Hamutzar Council both in Jerusalem; mem: financial council, Ezrath Nashim Hosp; comty council, YMCA; Beth Hillel Comm, all Jerusalem. Hobby, stamps. Home: 8 Shmuel Hanagid St, Jerusalem, Isr. Office: Courts Bldg, Russian Compound, Jerusalem, Isr.

COHEN, Yona, Isr, journalist, editor; b. Jerusalem, Isr, Aug 1, 1920; s. Gershon and Aliza; m. Victoria Cohen, 1946; c: Eytan, Gad, Emuna, Nily. Parl corresp, Hatzofe newspaper since 1948; ed, Dapei-Aliyah monthly. Author: Eynaim (stories for children) 1961; Yosele, 1962; Milhemet Hamagen V'Hayshua, 1968; Hahan Gershon M'Nahalat Shimon, 1968; Ben-Ezrah Limdinah, 1962. Chmn, Parl Corresp Assn of Isr; mem: cen comm, gen council, Natl Rel Party; exec, Isr Soc Eds of Periodicals. Home: 3 Yael St, Jerusalem Isr. Office: Hatzofe Newspaper, 3 Strauss St, Jerusalem, Isr.

COHEN, Yves Yvan, Fr, educator; b. Tunis, Tunisia, Oct 6, 1927; s. Henri and Mathilde (Nataf); in Fr since 1946; licénciè ès sci, pharm, U Paris, 1950, DSc, 1955; m. Nicole Monnot, July 28, 1951; c: Henri, Anne, Jean. Prof, fac pharm, U Paris, since 1962; attaché de recherches, CNRS, Paris, 1951-55; prof, Sch of Med and Pharm, Rouen, 1955-62. Lt, Service de Santé. Mem, several sci socs. Co-author, Médicaments Organiques de Synthèse, vol 1, 1969; contbr numerous publs in biol, radiopharm, radioactivity. Office: 4 Ave de l'Observatoire, Paris Fr.

COHEN-HARTOG, Eva, Netherlands' communal worker; b. Oss, Nov 11, 1889; m. Salomon Cohen (decd); c: Hans, Marjanna. Recipient: Order of the Oranje-Nassau. Home: 11 Van Beuningenstr, Rotterdam, Netherlands.

COHN, Adele, US, librarian; b. Shreveport, La, Aug, 25, 1907; d. Jacob and Jeanette (Kline); BA, Converse Coll, Spartanburg, SC, 1929; natl tchrs cert, Natl Bd, UAHC. Head circultion dept, Birmingham Public Libr, since 1948, asst: W End Br, 1930-34; reference dept, 1934-38, head, Cen Pk br, 1938-48. Rel sch tchr, Temple Emanu-El since 1929; mem, choir, libr comm, Temple Sisterhood, since 1951; mem bd, since 1952; mem, SE Libr Assn; Birmingham Libr Club, past pres; fmr chmn leg comm, Amer Libr Assn. Recipient: for 40 yrs of continuous service, Temple Emanu-El, 1969. Home: 1313 Woodland Ave, SW, Birmingham, Ala. Office: 2020 7th Ave, N, Birmingham, Ala.

COHN, Albert Marcus, US, educator; b. Providence, RI, Nov 10, 1912; s. Henry and Emma (Pincus); BE, RI Coll of Educ, 1940; MA, W Res U, 1947. Asso prof, Eng, RI Sch of Design, since 1964. asst prof, 1956-64; instr, drama, Emerson Coll, 1947-49, asst prof, 1949-55. USAAF, 1942-45. Mem: AAUP; Amer Educ Theater Assn. Contbr to profsl jours. Recipient: Asiatic Pacific Theater Campaign Ribbon Philippine Liberation Ribbon; Amer Theater Campaign Ribbon. Home: 64 Carr St, Providence, RI. Office: RI Sch of Design, Providence, RI.

COHN, Arthur, US, musician; b. Phila, Pa, Nov 6, 1910; s. Bernard and Pauline (Weissblatt); att: Combs Conservatory of Music; Juilliard Grad Sch of Music, NY; studied with: William F Happich; Sascha Jacobinoff; m. 2nd Lois Hoffman, June 1959; c: Alan, Deborah Persoff, Leslie. Dir, serious music, MCA, NY, since 1966; music dir, conductor, Sym Club, Phila, Pa, since 1942; conductor, Haddonfield Sym Orch, NJ, since 1958; numerous guest performances and own music performed throughout the world; curator, dir, Fleischer Music Collection, Free Libr of Phila, 1934-52, head, libr's music dept, 1946-52; exec dir, Settlement Music Sch, Phila, Pa, 1952-56; head, fgn and sym depts, Mills Music, NY 1956-66. Composer: Declamation and Toccata; Hebraic Study, both for bassoon and piano; Quotations in Percussion; author: The Collector's 20th Century Music in the Western Hemisphere, 1961; Twentieth Century Music in Western Europe, 1965; Musical Quizzical, 1969; critic: Rochester Times, NY; Trade Union; Modern Music Tempos; Amer Record Guide. Treas, Amer Music Cen; head, admissions comm, MacDowell Colony; mem, ASCAP. Recipient, prizes: for Chamber Music, Amer Soc Ancient Instruments, Phila, 1940; for Orchestral Music, Natl Sym Orch, Wash, DC, 1942. Hobby, sport. Home: 200 W 86 St, New York, NY. Office: Park Ave, New York, NY.

COHN, Clarence, US, biochemist; b. Phila, Pa, Dec 7, 1910; s. Harris and Hetty (Cramer); BS, U of Pa, 1932; att MIT, 1932-33; MD, Jefferson Med Coll, 1938; m. Pauline Schwartz, Dec 14, 1946; c: Terry, Marilyn, Nina. Dir, div nutritional sci, med res inst, Michael Reese Hosp and Med Cen since 1965; staff mem since 1941, dir, dept biochem, 1946-65; asso prof, clinical path, Chgo Med Sch since 1956. US Army MC, 1942-46. Mem: AAAS; Endocrine Soc; Amer Phys Soc; Amer Diabetes Assn; Amer Assn Clinical Chem; Soc Experimental Biol and Med; Amer Fed Clinical Research. Contbr to textbooks and profsl jours. Home: 1174 Ash St, Winnetka, Ill. Office: Michael Reese Hospital, Chicago, Ill.

COHN, David V, US, biochemist; b. NYC, Nov 8, 1926; s. Ralph and Claire (Schenkman); BS, CCNY, 1948; PhD, Duke U, 1952; postdoc F, W Reserve U, 1952-53; m. Evelyn Turner, Apr 3, 1947; c: Robert, Emily. Prin sci, radioisotope research service, VA Hosp, Kan City, Mo, since 1953. USNR, 1945-46. Mem: AAAS; Amer Soc Biol Chems; Amer Chem Soc. Contbr to profsl jours. Home: 10041 Fontana, Overland Park, Kansas. Office: 4801 Linwood Blvd, Kansas City, Mo.

COHN, Donald M, US, business exec; b. Rochester, NY, Dec 9, 1915; s. Harry and Dorothy (Meyer); BA, U Mich, 1937, JD, 1940; m. Elizabeth Lipton, Mar 28, 1942; c: Frederick, Louise, Rhea. Mgmt cons, exec off: Chemtrox Corp; Qualtron Inds; both since 1969; vice-pres, asst gen mgr, Superba Cravats, 1954-69. US Army, 1941-45. Mem: exec bd, AJComm; exec comm, U Rochester Assn; bd trustees, J Home and Infirmary; Mich State Bar; C of C; club, Rotary. Recipient: spec commendation, Counterintelligence Corps, WWII. Home: 163 Warrington Dr, Rochester, NY. Office: 620 Meigs St, Rochester, NY.

COHN, Edward E, US, organization, exec; b. Milw, Wis, Sep 5, 1919; s. Hyman and Beckie (Adashek); BS, U Wis; m. Marion David, Dec 4, 1947; c: Steven, by previous m; Carol. Exec secy, Dist Grand Lodge 6, B'nai B'rith, Chgo, since 1965, on staff since 1939. Capt, US Army, 1942-46. Mem, bd trustees, Cong Beth Sholom, Park Forest, 1951-56, chmn, bldg comm 1951-55; mem, natl adv bd, B'nai B'rith Youth Services; found, Park Forest B'nai B'rith; co-chmn, J App, S Cook Co, 1955-56; treas, Bd J Educ, Park Forest, 1951; mem: Amer Legion; VFW; Mil order of WWs; club, Res Offs Assn, Covenant, Ill. Recipient: Pres Unit Citation. Hobby: philately. Home: 6833 N Kedzie Ave, Chicago, Ill. Office: 228 S Wabash Ave, Chicago, Ill.

COHN, Eli, Isr, scientist; b. Danzig, Aug 2, 1932; s. Siegfried and Paula (Mendel); in Isr since 1950; MSc, agric, Heb U, Jerusalem and Rehovot, 1960. PhD, Heb U, Rehovot, 1965; m. Ruth Offer, Oct 25, 1960; c: Ayala, Shmuel, Adi. Head, div of nematology, Volcani Inst of Agric Research, since 1967. Cpl, IDF. Mem: Eur Soc of Nematologists; Soc of Nematologists; Isr Phytopath Soc. Co-author, Plant Parasitic Nematodes in Israel and Their Control, 1963; mem, ed bd Isr Journal of Agric Research; contbr of numerous papers to sci jours. Home: 29 Meyzan St, Tel Aviv, Isr. Office: Volcani Inst of Agric Research, Bet Degan, Isr.

COHN, Haim H, Isr, jurist; b. Lübeck, Ger, Mar 11, 1911; s. Zeev and Mirjam (Carlebach); grandson of Solomon Carlebach, Rabbi of Lübeck; nephew of Josef Carlebach, Rabbi of Hamburg, in Isr since 1930; att: U Munich, 1929-30; Heb U and Rabb Coll, Merkaz Harav, 1930-32; Referendar, U Frankfort, 1933; m. Else Benjamin, 1933, div; c: Eliahu, Jehudit Bar Chen; m. 2nd, Michal Smoira, 1966. Judge Supr

Court since 1960, admitted to bar, Pal, 1937; secy, legal council, Emergency Commn, JA for Pal, 1947-48; state atty, Min of Justice, 1948-49, dir gen, 1949-50; Min of Justice, 1952; atty gen, State of Isr, 1950-60. Head delg, UN Commn: Intl Criminal Jurisdiction, 1951; Enforcement of Maintenance Obligations, 1956; Intl Commercial Arbitration, 1958; chmn, Isr-Den Friendship League, since 1961; mem, exec council, Heb U, Jerusalem, since 1955; vice-chmn: Council of Higher Educ, Isr, since 1958; chmn, Isr sect, Intl Commn of Jurists; mem: UN Commn on Hum Rights, 1957-59, 1965-67; Perm Court of Arbitration, The Hague; Assn Bar, NYC; Amer Fgn Law Assn; Intl Law Assn. Author: The Foreign Laws of Marriage and Divorce, 1937; Glaube und Glaubensfreiheit, 1967; The Trial and Death of Jesus, Heb, 1968; contbr of articles to Isr, fgn jours. Home: 36 Tchernichovsky St, Jerusalem, Isr. Office: Supr Court, Jerusalem, Isr.

COHN, Henry Jacob, Eng, educator; b. Hendon, Eng, Feb 5, 1936; s. Ernst and Marianne (Rosenbaum); MA, PhD, U Coll, Oxford, 1954-60; att Us: Cologne; Heidelberg; m. Ruth Harris, Aug 7, 1960; d. Carolyn. Lectr, Hist, U Warwick, since 1967; asst, U Glasgow, 1960-61; asst lectr, lectr, U Leicester. Fmr, hon secy, Friends Heb U, Jerusalem, Leicester Br; f. mem, Royal, J, Hist Socs. Author: The Government of the Rhine Palatinate in the Fifteenth Century, 1965; Government in Reformation Europe, 1970; contbr articles to profsl jours, Ency Britannica. Hobby, Eur Architecture before 1800. Home: 50 Canr on Close, Coventry, Warwicks, Eng. Office: U of Warwick, sch of Hist, Coventry, Eng.

COHN, Herluf, Den, advocate; b. Copenhagen, Den; s. Georg and Elfriede (Bamberger); Gymnasium Copenhagen; m. Nira Jacobson, Aug 21, 1960; c: Jonna, Eva, Irene, Charlotte. Advocate since 1958; entitled to conduct cases for the Supr Court of Den. Contbr articles to jours. Home and office: 57, Fredericiagade, Copenhagen, Den.

COHN, Hilde D, US, educator; b. Goerlitz, Ger, Feb 8, 1909; d. Ludwig and Meta (Klinkowstein); in US since 1937; att U Berlin; U Munich; U Heidelberg, 1928-33; PhD, U Heidelberg, 1933. Prof, modern lang dept, Swarthmore Coll since 1967, asst prof, 1948-54, asso prof, 1954-67; instr, Bryn Mawr Coll, 1938-48. Mem: MLA; Amer Assn Tchrs of Ger; AAUP; ACLU. Contbr to profsl jours. Home: 302 N Chester Rd, Swarthmore, Pa. Office: Swarthmore College, Swarthmore, Pa.

COHN, Hillel, US, rabbi; b. Berlin, Ger, Sep 4, 1938; s. Franklin and Miriam (Finkelstein); in US since 1939; AB, UCLA, 1959; BHL, HUC, LA, 1959, ordained rabbi, 1963; m. Rita Jarson, 1960; c: Elana, Marc. Rabbi, Cong Emanu-El, since 1963; chaplain, Marion Correctional Inst, O State Prison, 1960-63; visiting lectr, U Redlands, 1968-69. Pres: San Bernardino Area Mh Assn, 1965-67; Family Service Agcy, San Bernardino, since 1968; chmn: Solo Parents Project Comm, Arrowhead Soc Planning Council, 1963-65; budget panel, Arrowhead United Fund/United Comty Services, since 1967; Support of Churches Comm, San Bernardino Kiwanis Club, since 1966; mem, bd dirs: Inland chap, ARC, 1964-67; Planned Parenthood Assn, San Bernardino, 1966-68; Inland Area Urban League, 1966-68; Inland Adolescent Clinic, San Bernardino, since 1966; San Bernardino United J Wfr Fund, since 1963; S Cal B'nai B'rith Youth Adv Council, 1966-68; mem: pub affairs comm, Cal Assn for Mh, 1967-68; J Reconstructionist Found; J Peace f; Health Educ Adv Comm, San Bernardino City Unified Sch Dist; adv bd, Dopers Anonymous Rehab through Educ prog, since 1968; CCAR; Pacific Assn of Reform Rabbis; S Cal Assn Lib Rabbis; Bd Rabbis, S Cal; Natl Assn Temple Educ. Author: The Movements of Jewish Life, 1966; S'lichos Service, 1963, rev ed, 1965; Haggadah for Children, 1964, rev ed, 1966; Handbook for Parents, 1965, rev ed, 1967. Recipient: award: Emanuel Gamoran, Natl Assn of Temple Educs, 1965; Dist Service, Outstanding Man-of-the-Year, San Bernardino Jr C of C, 1966. Home: 25902 18 St, San Bernardino, Cal. Study: 3512 North E St, San Bernardino, Cal.

COHN, Howard, US, editor; b. NYC, Nov 1, 1922; s. Morris and Vivian (Siegel); BA, Amer U, Wash, DC, 1947; m. Regina Cohn, Apr 2, 1949; c: Steven, Robert. Exec ed, Med World News Mag, since 1968; asso ed, Collier's, 1951-56; exec ed, Pageant Mag, 1959-63; mgn ed, True Mag, 1963-68. US Army, 1943-46. Mem, Soc of Mag Writers. Home: 35 Shirley Lane, White Plains, NY. Office: 299 Park Ave, New York, NY.

COHN, Irwin I, US, attorney; b. Detroit, Mich, Sep 22, 1896; s. Samuel and Maly (Fellman); LLB, U Mich, 1917; hon deg, Bar Ilan U, Isr; m. Sadie Levin, Jan 14, 1923; c: Avern, Rita Kogan. Atty, Honigman, Miller, Schwartz & Cohn since 1961; pvt practice until 1961; Secy, Sinai Hosp of Deroit; pres: Detroit Urban League; Hillel Found, U Mich; vice-pres, United Heb Schs in Detroit; sup, Wayne Co Bd Sups; adv bd, United Found of Detroit; chmn, Isr Emergency Fund; bd dirs, JWF of Detroit; comm mem, Mich State Bar Assn Legal Aid: mem: City Plan Commn of Detroit; Metrop Detroit Regional Planning Commn; Detroit Bar Assn; State Bar of Mich; Pres Club, U Mich. Home: 700 Whitmore, Detroit, Mich. Office: 2290 First Natl Bldg, Detroit, Mich.

COHN, Isidore, US, surgeon, educator; b. W Baton Rouge Parish, La, Apr 9, 1885; s. Henry and Sophie (Farrnbacher); BS, La State U, 1903; MD, Tulane Sch of Med, 1907; m. Elsie Waldhorn, Apr 5, 1910; c: Babette Golden, Elsie Rosenthal, Isidore. Prof em, clinical surg, La State U, since 1952, prof: grad sch, 1937-44, clinical surg, undergrad sch, 1944-52; cons: Touro Infirmary since 1946; Charity Hosp of La since 1950; asst demonstrator, Tulane U Sch of Med, 1908-09, prof: clinical surg, undergrad sch, 1919-37, dir, dept surg, grad sch, 1932-37. Pres: Alumni Soc, La State U, 1943-44; La Surg Soc, 1949-50; vice-pres, S Surg Soc, 1932; mem: Amer Coll Surgs; Amer Assn: Surg of Trauma; Study of Endocrinology; AMA; Intl Soc Surg; S Surg Assn; Soc Experimental Biol, Med; NY Acad Scis; SE Surg Assn; La Surg Assn; La State Med Soc; New Orleans Surg Assn; Orleans Parish Med Soc; Peru Acad of Surg (hon); Alpha Omega Alpha; Phi Kappa Phi; Phi Delta Epsilon; ODK frat, La State U; clubs: Round Table; Intl House of New Orleans. Contbr to med jours. Home: 5535 Clairborne Ave, New Orleans, La.

COHN, James M, US, composer, musicologist; b. Newark, NJ, Feb 12, 1928; s. Morris and Cecile (Neuhaus); att Eastman Sch of Music, NY; Cornell U, Ithaca, NY; BS, Juilliard Sch of Music, NY, 1949, MS, 1950, both in composition. Musicologist, ASCAP, since 1955, with ASCAP since 1950. Composer: The Fall of the City, one-act opera, 1955; Sym No 3, 1959; Variations on The Wayfaring Stranger, for orch, 1962; Variations on John Henry, for sym or concert band; Reflections, for chorus; Statues in the Park, choral song-cycle on poems by Felicia Lamport, 1969; syms; string quartets; piano sonatas; various shorter works, for orch, band, chorus, solo instruments and instrumental chamber ensembles. Recording secy, Music & Performing Arts Lodge, B'nai B'rith; mem: Amer Fed of Musicians, local 802; Amer Music Cen, NYC. Recipient: Two prizes, Natl Fed of Music Clubs, for violin sonatina and piano variations, 1944; Queen Elizabeth of Belgium prize, for Sym No 2, 1953; U of O award, for The Fall of the City, 1955; It Assn for Dissemination and Educ in Music award, for Sym No 4, 1960. Hobbies: photography, painting, sculpture, drama, ballet, books walking, good conversation. Office: c/o ASCAP, 575 Madison Ave, New York, NY.

COHN, Josef, US, organization exec; b. Berlin, Ger, Sep 6, 1904; s. Louis and Emma (Petzall); PhD, U Heidelberg, 1929. Eur repr, Wiezmann Inst of Sci since 1955; secy to Weizmann, 1933-48. Author: England and Palestine, in German, 1931. Mem: ZOA, List Soc, Eur. Home: 240 Central Park S, New York, NY. Eur address: Huegels 6, Zurich 8002, Switz.

COHN, Jules, US, educator, management con; b. New Brunswick, NJ, June 18, 1930; s. Edward and Mae (Rose); BA, Rutgers U, 1951, MA, 1954, PhD, 1958. Cons, McKinsey and Co Inc, NYC since 1968; sr Research Sci, NYU since 1968, mem fac since 1965; cons, NYC Housing and Redevl Bd since 1962; lectr, Rutgers U since 1962; US Fulbright lectr in Finland, 1960-61; instr: Bard Coll, 1954-58; Bklyn Coll, 1958-61; official repr, NYU to Inter-U Consortium for Political Research, Ann Arbor, Mich, 1966-67; cons, Comprehensive Plan, Comty Renewal Prog, City Planning Dept, NYC; Housing Task Force, NY Urban Coalition, 1965-68; Social Studies Curriculum Devl Project, Grad, Sch of Educ, Harvard, 1964-65; dep to exec coord of prog and policy devl, Off of Mayor, NYC, 1962-64; dir, div of Research, Planning and Training, Neighborhood Conservation Bur, Housing and Redevl Bd, NYC, 1962-64. Mem: Pres's Ad Hoc Adv Panel on Urban Problems, NYU, 1965-68; Amer Political Sci Assn; Amer Studies Assn; Phi Alpha Theta; NY Hist Soc; Urban Hist Group, U of Wis; Urban Studies Group, U Leeds, Eng; Natl Assn of Housing and

Redevl Officials; Amer Soc for Public Admn; Pi Sigma Alpha; Intl Political Sci Assn; clubs: Harvard, NYC; 4th NAD, Reform Dem, NYC, pres, 1961. Author: The Muqaddima of Ibn Khaldun, 1958; Politics as Process, 1959; Politics in the City, 1968; contbr, The Govt of NYC: Roles and Resources, a report commissioned by Comty Renewal Prog, NYC; Municipal Politics, a case study, Amer Educ Publs, Columbus, O, 1967; Man, Culture, and Society, ed by Charles Lawrence, Carl Nordstrom and Jules Cohn; ed, adv cons, Bollinger Series, Bollinger Found, NY. Home: 3P 4 Wash Sq Village, New York, NY. Office: 245 Park Ave, New York, NY.

COHN, Marcus, US, attorney; b. Omaha, Neb, Sep 20, 1913; s. Sam and Rose (Forman); AB, U Chgo, 1935, JD, cum laude, 1939; LLM, Harvard Law Sch, 1940; m. Harryette Nightingale, Aug 20, 1939; c: Lawrence, Barbara. Partner, Cohn & Marks since 1945; chief, field off, legal dept, FCC, 1941-44; Pres, Wash, DC chap, AJComm since 1962, natl exec comm since 1962; treas and exec comm, Fed Communications Bar Assn since 1960; mem: Exec comm, Wash JCC; Phi Beta Kappa; Sigma Alpha Mu; clubs: Natl Press; Fed City; Intl. Home: 4031 Oliver St, Chevy Chase, Md.

COHN, Max Arthur, US, artist; b. London, Eng, Feb 3, 1904; s. Morris and Jeanette (Rorkes); in US, since 1906; att Art Students League, 1921-25; Colarossi Acad, Paris, 1927; m. Sarah Waldstein, Feb, 3, 1934; c, Jane. Owner, Graphic Art Studios, 1948-62; numerous one-man shows; represented in Albany; Phila; Metrop Mus Art; William Rockhill Nelson Gal; Howard U; Dallas and US, Embs. Treas, Del Valley Artists Assn; life mem, Art Students League; mem, Serigraph Soc. Author, Silk Screen Techniques, 1958; co-author, Silk Screen Stenciling as a Fine Art, 1942. Home and Studio; 311 W 24 St, New York, NY.

COHN, Michal Smoira, Isr, musicologist; b. Tel Aviv, Feb 13, 1926; d. Moshe and Esther (Hurwitz); Dipl, Isr Acad Music, 1947; PhD, Upssala U, Swed, 1958; m. Haim Cohn; c: Tamar, Gad. Dir music, Isr Bc since 1968; lectr, Tel Aviv U since 1967; ed, Bat-Kol, music bimonthly 1953-64; pedg admn, Isr Acad Music, 1961-66; music critic, Ha-aretz, 1963-66. Chmn, Sharet Fund for Young Artists; bd dirs, Isr Musicological Soc; mem, music sect, Isr Council for Art and Sculpture. Author: Folksong in Israel, 1964; Music, An Historical Introduction, 1966; contbr to profsl jours. Home: 36 Tchernichovsky St, Jerusalem, Isr. Office: Isr BC, Jerusalem, Isr.

COHN, Morris M, US, public health engr; b. Schenectady, NY, Nov 21, 1898; s. Jacob and Rebecca (Cohn); BS, Union U, 1921, MS, 1931, hon, DSc, 1954; dipl environmental engr; m. Rose Gold, 1923 (decd); c: Grace Cohen, Jay. Natl Defense Exec Res Em; cons engr since 1946; cons: AEC, Knolls Atomic Power Lab; NY State Leg; USPHS; Gen Elec Research Lab; ed research dir, Water Works Engr, 1954-63; Reuben H Donnelly Corp, 1955-63; Waste Engr since 1936; sanitary chem, City of Schenectady, 1921-24, sanitary engr, 1924-25, dir, environmental sanitation, 1946-51, city mgr, 1952-54; lectr, Albany Med Coll, 1950-54; adj prof, CE, CCNY, 1954-56; Brackett lectr, Union U, 1954-55; lectr: U of Ill; Ga Inst Tech; cons: NY State Health Dept; Amer Public Works Assn; NY State Pure Water Assn. US Army, WWI. Chmn: Northeast Interstate Water Pollution Control Comm, 1950-51; Mohawk Valley Sanitation Council, 1945; NY State Commn since 1950; secy, Mohawk River Adv Commn, AEC, since 1955; f, Amer Public Health Assn; pres, Amer Soc CEs, Mohawk-Hudson sect, 1944; Schenectady Co chap, NY State Soc Profsl Engrs, 1936; NY State Sewage Works Assn, 1935; vice-pres, dir, Fed Sewage and Ind Wastes Assn, 1940, chmn, wastes practice comm since 1944; life mem: Amer Public Health Assn; Amer Public Works Assn; Amer Soc CEs, mem: Natl Soc Profsl Engrs; NY State, NJ Water Pollution Control Assns; Natl Defense Exec Res; Intl Assn City Mgrs; Md-Del Water and Sewage Assn; Inter-Amer Assn Sanitary Engrs; Conf Munic Engrs; Amer Soc Public Admn; NY State Public Health Assn; Park Ave Syn, NYC; Nott Terrace Syn, Schenectady; Amer Legion; Sigma Xi; Schenectady Boy Scout Council. Author: Sewers for Growing America, 1967; contbr to profsl jours. Recipient: Kenneth Allen, Arthur S Bedell, Charles Alvin Emerson awards, all Water Pollution Control Fed; Samuel A Greeley award, Amer Public Works Assn, 1951. Home: 1100 Madison Ave, New York, NY. Office: 466 Lexington Ave, New York, NY.

COHN, Nate, US, business exec; b. Cedar Rapids, Ia, June 1, 1907; s. Esac and Eva (Berg); att Coe Coll, Cedar Rapids, 1925; U of Ia, 1926; m. Beatrice Levitzky, Sep 3, 1939; c: David, Marilyn. Vice-pres: Dearborn Brass Co; Eagle Inves Co; secy, E Cohn & Sons, Inc; pres, Cedar Rapids Pump and Supply Co, all Cedar Rapids, Ia. Mem: bd, St Luke's Hosp; bd trustees, Coe Coll; Ia Home for Aged, Des Moines; Plumbing Brass Inst, Chgo; bd dirs, C of C, Cedar Rapids; Elks. Home: 2222 First Ave NE, Cedar Rapids, Ia. Offices: Dearborn Brass Co, Cedar Rapids, Ia; Plumbing Brass Inst, Chgo, Ill.

COHN, Nathan, US, attorney; b. Charleston, SC, Jan 20, 1918; s. Samuel and Rosa (Baron); LLB, SF Law Sch, 1947; m. Carolyn; c, Norman. Pvt practice. Lt, USAF Res. Co-author, Criminal Law Seminar, 1-3. Office: 1255 Post, San Francisco, Cal.

COHN, Norman, Eng, author, educator; b. London, Eng, Jan 12, 1915; s. August and Daisy (Reimer); MA, Christ Church Sch, Oxford, 1939; DLitt, Glasgow; m. Vera Broido, Sep 3, 1941; c, Nik. Professorial F, U of Sussex since 1963; found, dir, Cen for Research in Collective Psychopath, since 1963; prof, U Durham, 1960-63; F, Cen for Advanced Study in Behavioral Scis, Stanford, 1966. Capt, Brit Army, 1939-46. Author: The Pursuit of the Millennium, 1957, rev ed 1970; Warrant for Genocide, 1970; trans: Gold Khan and Other Siberian Legends; contbr to profsl jours. Mem, Athenaeum. Recipient, Wolf-Anisfield Prize for Race Relations, 1968 Hobbies: walking, travel. Home: 61 New End, London NW3, Eng. Office: 3 Henrietta St, London WC2, Eng.

COHN, Roy M, US, attorney; b. NYC, Feb 20, 1927; s. Albert and Dora (Marcus); BA, Columbia U, 1946, LLB, 1947. Partner, Saxe, Bacon and Bolan since 1959; dir, Baltimore Paint and Chem Co; asst, US Atty, NYC, 1948-50, confidential asst, 1950-52; spec asst, Atty Gen McGranery, 1952; chief counsel, US Sen permanent inves sub comm, 1953-54; mem, US prosecution vs William Remington, 1950; vs Julius and Ethel Rosenberg, 1951. Pres, Amer J League Against Communism; regent, St Francis Coll; mem: Assn Bar, NYC; Amer, NY State Bar Assns; NY Co Lawyers Assn; B'nai B'rith; Cen Syn. Recipient, annual award, lawyers div, FJP, 1952. Home: 1165 Park Ave, New York, NY. Office: 20 Exchange Pl, New York, NY.

COHN, Sigmund A, US, educator, jurist; b. Breslau, Ger, June 6, 1898; s. Georg and Sofie (Hamburger); in US since 1939; JUD, magna cum laude, U Breslau, 1919; JD, summa cum laude, U Genoa, It, 1934; m. Susanne Lewy, 1925; c: Eva Galambos, Marianne Freeman. Prof Em, Law, U of Ga Law Sch since 1964, fac mem since 1939; mem, Min of Justice, 1923-30; judge, Circuit Court of Appeals, 1930-33, both at Berlin; asst prof, U Genoa Sch of Econ, 1934-38; counselor, Justice Dept, W Ger, ret, 1951, adv comm, Ga Corp Code, 1966-68. Mem: Amer Soc Intl Law; AAUP; Phi Kappa Phi; Phi Delta Phi; Tau Epsilon Phi. Author: Cases on Torts and Traffic Law, 1923-33; co-author: Commentary on German Laws for the Protection of the Republic, 1930; Commentary on German Laws for the Use of Arms, 1931. Spec interest, comparative and intl law. Home: 320 South View Dr, Athens, Ga. Office: U of Ga, Sch of Law, Athens, Ga.

COHN, Victor Edward, US journalist, science reporter; b. Minneapolis, Minn, Aug 4, 1919; s. Louis and Lillian (Bessler); BA, magna cum laude, U Minn, 1941; m. Marcella Rigler, 1941; c: Jeffrey, Deborah, Phyllis. Sci ed, Wash Post since 1968; fmr: sci reporter, Minneapolis Tribune, 1947-67, reporter, copy-reader, 1946; ed, Minn Daily, U of Minn, 1940-41; desk man, Minneapolis Star, 1941-42; visiting lectr, U of Minn Sch of Journalism, 1956-67. Lt, USN, 1942-45. Pres, Natl Assn Sci Writers, 1961-62; f, AAAS; mem: comm on public understanding of sci, AAAS, 1959-67; Council for Advancement of Sci Writing, since 1960; Amer Newspaper Guild; Phi Beta Kappa. Author: 1999: Our Hopeful Future, 1956; contbr of syndicated newspaper articles and to mags. Recipient: George Westinghouse Award for Dist Sci Writing, AAAS, 1951, 1959; Sigma Delta Chi Dist Service Award, 1952, 1956, 1959; citation, Minn State Med Assn, 1955; Albert Lasker Med Journalism Award, 1958; Natl Headliner Award, 1959, 1962; Dist Citizen Award, Phi Beta Kappa Assn, Minn, 1966; Harrington Trophy, Minn Pub Health Assn, 1966. Home: 4701 Willard Ave, Chevy Chase, Md. Office: 1515 L St, NW, Washington, DC.

COHN, Werner, Can, sociologist; b. Berlin, Ger, Mar 24, 1926; s. James and Else (Rosenbaum); in Can since 1960; BSS, CCNY, 1951; MA, New Sch for Social Research, 1954, PhD, 1956; m. Rita Pressner, Dec 23, 1951; c: Judith, Jonathan, James, Naomi, Rachel. Asso prof sociol, U of BC since 1964, asst prof, 1960-64; mem fac, Northland Coll, 1956-60; f, Conf on J Material Claims Against Ger, 1954-55; research f, Can Council, 1969. USN, 1944-46. Chmn, UJA, Ashland, Wis 1959-60; f, Amer Sociol Assn; mem: Pacific Sociol Assn; Soc for Sci Study of Rel; Amer corresp, Gypsy Love Soc. Contbr to profsl jours. Home: 4726 W Fourth Ave, Vancouver, Can. Office: U of BC, Vancouver, Can.

COHN-HAFT, Louis, US, educator; b. NYC, Nov 13, 1919; s. Harry and Goldie (Haft) Cohn; BA, Columbia Coll, 1941; MA, Columbia U, 1949, PhD, 1955; m. Athena Capraro, Apr 23, 1942; c: Hera, Anthony, Mario. Prof, hist, Smith Coll since 1963; instr, hist, Columbia U, 1950-53. Dir, NDEA Inst for HS tchrs of Hist, 1967-69; mem: Hampshire Co chap, Civil Liberties Union, Mass; chmn, 1958-60; Amer Hist Assn; Amer Philo Assn; Hist of Sci Soc; Archaeol Inst of Amer; AAUP. Author: The Public Physicians of Ancient Greece, 1956; Source Readings in Ancient History, 1965; contbr to hist jours. Home: 54 Kensington Ave, Northampton, Mass. Office: Smith Coll, Northampton, Mass.

COHON, Beryl David, US, rabbi; b. Lith, Feb 12, 1898; s. Solomon and Rachel (Kushner); in US since 1905; BA, U Ill, 1921; ordained rabbi, HUC, 1925, hon DD, 1950; m. Sally Kivelson, June 30, 1929; s. Albert. Found, rabbi, Temple Sinai since 1939; visiting lectr, Tufts Coll since 1947; rabbi: Pensacola, Fla, 1925-27; Cumberland, Md, 1927-29; Temple Isr, Boston, 1929-39. Exec bd, CCAR since 1953. Author: Introduction to Judaism, 1929; The Prophets, 1939; Judaism, in Theory and Practice, 1948; From Generation to Generation, 1952; Out of the Heart, 1957; Jacob's Well; Some Sources and Parallels to the Sermon on the Mount, 1956; Gods Angry Men, 1961; My King and My God, 1963; Vision and Faith, 1967; Men at the Crossroads, Between Synagogues and Church, Jerusalem and Rome, 1969; contbr to J publs. Home: 134 Sewall Ave, Brookline, Mass. Study: 50 Sewall Ave Brookline, Mass.

COLBERT, Ralph A, US, attorney; b. Cleveland, O, Nov 29, 1907; s. Joseph and Helen (Steiner); BA, W Reserve U, 1928, LLB, 1930; m. Hazel Haas, 1934; c: Richard, Jean. Partner, Squire, Sanders, Dempsey and Cleveland, since 1967, and partner, predecessor firm, since 1946, asso since 1930; admitted to O Bar, 1930. Col, USAAF, air intelligence, staff of Gen Arnold, Wash, DC, 1942-44; US Strategic Bombing Survey, 1944-46. Pres, Cleveland chap, AJComm, 1947-50, natl exec bd; 1949-60; chmn, Comty Relations comm, 1950-56; bd trustees: J Comty Fed, 1951-56; Montefiore Home, 1948-61; The Temple, 1947-49; Council on World Affairs, since 1950; Cleveland Playhouse, since 1963, all in Cleveland; mem: Amer, O State, Cleveland Bar Assns; Phi Beta Kappa; Order of Coif; Delta Sigma Rho; Pi Epsilon Delta; Zeta Beta Tau; Tau Epsilon Phi; club, Oakwood. Recipient: Bronze Star, Legion of Merit, both 1945. Home: 2980 Fontenay Rd, Shaker Heights, O. Office: 1800 Union Commerce Bldg, Cleveland, O.

COLBI, Paul Saul, Isr, government official; b. Trieste, It, Jan 30, 1908; s. Arnoldo and Teresa (Levi); in Isr since 1939; PhD, Law fac, Rome U, 1926; m. Leah Spiegler, 1944; c: Michal, Tamar. Head, div of Chr Affairs, Min of Rel Affairs since 1948; fmr: atty, It; farmer, Isr. Haganah, 1941. Fmr mem: It Zionist Org; Keren Kayemeth, It; bd, J Comty, Trieste. Author: A Short History of Christianity in the Holy Land, 1965; Christianity in the Holy Land, Past and Present, 1969; Commander of St Gregory the Great, 1964. Home: 3 Bialik St, Jerusalem, Isr. Office: 23 Shlomo Hamelech St, Jerusalem, Isr.

COLE, Sidney I, US, engineer, business exec; b. Chgo, Ill, Aug 15, 1907; s. Benjamin and Henrietta (Swarzman); BS, Armour Inst of Tech, 1928, ME, 1933; m. Sally Brilliant, Aug 9, 1931. Pres, Ind Erectors Inc, since 1951, with firm since 1928. Natl treas, UAHC, fmr pres, Union Inst; fmr chmn, jt apprenticeship comm, trust fund, Chgo Structural Iron Workers; bd dirs, Chgo Bd J Educ; mem: Amer Soc ME, life; W Soc Engrs; Natl and Ill Socs profsl Engrs; Amer Ordnance Assn; Amer Arbitration Assn; Temple Beth Isr; Masons; Technion; B'nai B'rith; Tau Epsilon Phi; clubs: Covenant; Builders; Exec. Home: 6833 N Kedzie Ave, Chicago, Ill. Office: 1316 W Cermak Rd, Chicago, Ill.

COLE, Sylvan, US, business exec; b. LA, Cal, Sep 2, 1889; s. Nathan and Fannie (Prager) Cohn; m. Dorothy Stein, Mar 5, 1917; c: Sylvan, Charles, Richard (decd). Ret, 1961; chmn bd Natl Shirt Shops of Del and subsidiary Cos (now merged into McCrory Corp) since 1960, serving in adv capacity, co-found, Co first named Dollar Shirt Shops, 1911, pres, 1935-42. Mem: admn and exec comms, AJComm since 1951, found chmn, Palm Beach chap; Soc of Four Arts; Palm Beach Art Inst; club, Breakers Cubana. Hobbies: photography, travel. Home: 250 Bradley Pl, Palm Beach, Fla.

COLEMAN, Aaron Barnet, US, attorney; b. NYC Nov 11, 1896; s. Barnet and Mollie (Kohlman); BA, Columbia Coll, 1917; LLB, 1921; m. Martha Levy, Apr 17, 1924; c, Paul. Atty since 1921; lectr, CCNY, 1928-65; fmr prof, Bklyn Law Sch; asso, Wollman & Wollman, Esqs, 1923-36, partner, 1936-43; asst corp counsel, NYC, and presiding off, OPA, 1943-48. US Army, 1918. Mem: B'nai B'rith; NY Co Lawyers Assn; AAUP; Phi Beta Kappa. Hobby, piano. Home: RR I, Box 279, New Canaan, Conn. Office: 74 Trinity Pl, New York, NY.

COLEMAN, Clarence L Jr, US, business exec ; b. Chgo, Ill, Aug 31, 1903; s. Clarence and Bella (Freund); AB, Princeton U, 1924; m. Lillian Suffrin, Feb 21, 1927; c: Thomas, Nancy White, Patricia. Vice-pres, secy, Coleman Floor Co; dir, exec comm, Old Rep Life Ins Co. Chmn, bd, Amer Council for Judaism, since 1966; past pres, life bd mem, Lakeside Cong for Reform Judaism; clubs: Standard; Sky-Line; Lake Shore Country. Home: 850 Lamson Dr, Winnetka, Ill. Office: 3100 Tollview Dr, Rolling Meadows, Ill.

COLEMAN, Jules V, US, psychiatrist, educator; b. Bklyn, NY, Nov 2, 1907; BA, Cornell U, 1928; MD, U Vienna Med Sch, 1934; m. Victoria Schwanfeldt, Jan 9 1932; c: Ann Mandelbaum, Jeremy. Chief, Mh sect, dept of epidemiology and public health, Yale U/Sch of Med, since 1962, clinical prof, since 1952; psycht, Pleasantville Cottage Sch, 1937-40; dir, E Harlem Unit Bur of Child Guidance, NYC, 1940-42; cons, Foster Home Bur and Bklyn Children's Aid Soc, 1940-42; head, mental hygiene div, U Colo Med Cen, and prof psycht U Colo Med Sch, 1946-50; asso dir, Bur Mental Hygiene, Conn State Dept Health, 1950-52; fac mem: Inst on Mh in Public Health, Berkeley, Calif, 1947; Gulfport Miss, 1948; Salt Lake City, Utah, 1950, Amsterdam, 1953; cons: comty services comm natl Mh Adv Bd, USPHS, 1947-48; VA Mental Hygiene Clinic, Denver, 1946-50; Natl J Hosp, 1946-50; Winter Gen Hosp, Topeka, 1947-50; Fitzsimons Gen Hosp, Denver, 1947-50; Colo State Dept Health, 1948-50; mental hygiene clinic, dept health, Yale U, 1950-52; chief, psycht clinic, Grace New Haven Comty Hosp, 1952-62. Psycht, Lawson Gen Hosp, US Army, 1942-43; psycht, 38th Infantry Div, US Army, maj, 1943-45. Pres, Amer Assn of Psycht Clinics for Children, 1949-51; vice-pres, Conn Assn for Mh, 1962-63; bd trustees, Commn on Alcoholism, State of Conn, chmn 1959-61; f: Amer Psycht Assn; Amer Orthopsycht Assn; AAAS; dipl, Amer Bd of Psycht and Neuro; mem: psycht training review comm, Natl Inst of Mh, 1965-69, chmn, 1968-69; Group for Advancement of Psycht; Amer Acad Child Psycht; Amer Psychan Assn; W NE Psychan Soc; chmn, Conn State Bd of Mh, since 1969. Contbr to profsl jours. Home: 14 Briar Lane, New Haven, Conn. Office: 135 Whitney Ave, New Haven, Conn.

COLEMAN, Philip, N, US, industrialist, philanthropist; b. Savannah, Ga, Mar 22, 1882; s. Charles and Eugenia (Nathans); m. Ray Kauffman, June 28, 1911. Pres: Amer Cross Arm Co, Fla, Ga Pa, Ore; Amer Celcure Wood Preserving Corp, since 1950; Coleman Evans Wood Preserving Corp, since 1954; Continental Cross Arm; Chgo, since 1950. Pres: Ahavath Chesed Temple, 1959-60; Jacksonville chap, Sons of Amer Revolution, 1960-61; JCC; PN and Ray K Coleman Found; State chmn, AJComm, 1956-60; vice-chmn, UAHC, 1954-68; adv bd, Jacksonville U; dept ind and commerce, US C of C, bd dirs, YMCA; dept mfrs, NAM. Home: 2309 River Rd, Jacksonville, Fla. Office: POB 1255, Jacksonville, Fla.

COLEMAN, Shalom, Austr, rabbi; b. Liverpool, Eng, Dec 5, 1918; s. Samuel and Fruma (Margolin); in Austr since 1961; Heb tchrs dipl, J Coll, London, 1939; Min Dipl, 1954, ordained rabbi, 1955; BA, hons, U Liverpool, 1940; BLitt, 1941; MA, U S Afr, 1956; PhD, U Orange Free State, S Afr, 1960; m. Anna Daviat, Mar 29, 1941; c: Romaine, Martin. Chief rabbi, Perth Heb Cong since 1966; head, Perth Bet Din; lectr, Bibl studies, U W Austr Adult Educ Dept; Justice-of-the-Peace for W Austr; part-time Heb chaplain to W Command, US Communications Sta, Exmouth; lectr, post-Bibl Heb, U Sydney; hon dir, David J Benjamin Inst of J Studies; radio, TV broadcaster; lectr to comty service, church orgs; chief min, S and head dists, Heb Cong Dayan Sydney Beth Din. Chaplain to S Afr Army Cen Command; RAF, WWII. Mem bd deps, exec, ZC; fmr vice pres, NSW Bd of J Educ. Author: Bloemfontein Jewry Hashomer Jubilee, vol, 1953; Mosaic Trends in Midrash and Talmud, 1956; Habakkuk in Rabbinic Doctrine, 1964; Malachi in Midrashic Analysis; Speakers Notes for the Lecture Service of NSW of Deps; ed, vols I, II, proceedings of David J Benjamin Inst; contbr of Blook critiques, numerous articles in local overseas jours. Recipient: Sir Robert Waley (Int) Memorial Scholarship, 1964; Cert of Merit of Memorable Order of Tin Hats (MOTHS). Spec interest: advancement of inter-faith relationships; archaeol of Bible. Home: 71 Graham Rd, Mt Lawley, West Austr. Study: Brisbane Street Synagogue, Perth, West Austr.

COLEMAN-COHEN, Reginald Herbert, Eng, business exec; b. Hastings, Eng, Sep 23, 1902; s. Hyam and Esther (Szapira); deg, Coll of Estate Mgmt, 1926; m. Joan Maurice, July 12, 1938. Exec dir, Alliance Bldg Soc, since 1923, secy 1929-66; pres, Corp of Ins Agts, since 1969, fmr secy. Pres: JPA; Intl Friendship League; chmn, Technion MDA; dep chmn, Spastics Soc; trustee, Lib Syn, all Brighton & Hove; chmn, Nursing Assn, Brighton Dist; mem: Brighton Rotary; Intl Union Bldg Socs; f: Chartered Auctioneers & Estate Agts Inst; Corp of Secs; Bldg Soc's Inst; Corp of Ins Agts; clubs: Inst of Dirs; Eng-Speaking Union. Recipient: Arva medal, JNF; award, Intl Insurance, U Austin, Tex, 1964. Home: 40 New Church Rd, Hove, Sussex, Eng. Office: Alliance Building Soc, Hove Park, Hove, Eng.

COLIN, Ralph F, US, attorney, business exec; b. NYC, Nov 18, 1900; s. William and Elizabeth (Benjamin); BA, CCNY, 1919; LLB, Columbia U Law Sch, 1921; m. Georgia Talmey, June 2, 1931; c: Ralph Jr, Pamela. Mem, law firm, Rosenman, Colin, Kaye, Petschek, Freund & Emil; dir, gen counsel: CBS Inc, since 1927; Columbia Artists Mgmt, since 1930; Parke-Bernet Galleries, 1959-64; Carnegie Coating, since 1961; dir: Alfred A Knopf, 1936-66; Calvert Petroleum, 1957-61; Rotary Elec Steel, 1944-58; admn vice-pres, Art Dealers Assn of Amer Inc, since 1962. Dir: Shelter Rock Found since 1943; Rockmeadow Found since 1952; Amer Arbitration Assn, 1932-56; William S Paley Found, 1936-69; JDC, 1943-49, exec comm, 1943-46, admnr comm, 1942-46; dir, bd of trustees and vice-pres; The Philharmonic Sym Soc of NY, 1942-56; bd of trustees and hon secy, Baron de Hirsch Fund, 1934-56; trustee, vice-pres, Mus Modern Art, NYC, vice-pres of intl council, since 1956; Amer Fed Arts, 1946-56; visiting comm for dept of fine arts and Fogg M, Harvard U; adv comm, The Arts Cen Prog, Columbia U; bd of trustees, NY FUP; exec comm, 1951-52; chmn, radio Bc div, Natl War Fund, 1943, 1944. Vice-pres, Assn of the Bar of NYC, 1958-59; mem: NY Co Lawyers Assn, NY State, Amer, and Fed Communications Bar Assns; Radio Pioneers. Contbr to legal jours. Home: 941 Park Ave, New York, NY. Office: 575 Madison Ave, New York, NY.

COLLENS, William S, US, physician, educator; b. NYC, June, 5, 1897; s. Jacob and Rebecca (Skolnick); BS, CCNY, 1917; MD, Cornell U Med Coll, 1921; m. Clara Lerner, May 15, 1930; c: Joanna Berger, Richard. Clinical asst prof, SUNY, Downstate Med Cen, since 1953; cons phys, Maimonides Hosp, NYC, chief diabetic clinic, chief peripheral vascular disease clinic; cons, metabolic diseases, Rockaway Beach Hosp; att phys, J Sanitarium, Hosp for Chronic Diseases. Med off, draft bd, WW II. Licentiate, Amer Bd Internal Med; chmn: phys comm, Maimonides Hosp; f: Amer Coll Phys; NY Acad of Med; NY Acad of Sci; AAAS; mem: AHA; Soc for Experimental Biol, Med; Amer Soc for Study Arteriosclerosis; Amer Diabetes Assn; Intl Soc of Angiology; Endocrine Soc; Kings Co Med Soc; AMA; Bklyn Soc for Internal Med; clubs, Unity; The Bohemians. Author, Manual for the Jewish Diabetic, 1931; co-author: Peripheral Vascular Diseases, 1939, 1953; Modern Treatment of Diabetes Mellitus, 1946; Helpful Hints to the Diabetic, 1949; contbr to med and sci jours. Hobbies: painting, photography. Home and office: 123 Eighth Ave, Brooklyn, NY.

COLLINS, David Eng, school-master; b. Ilford, Eng, Mar 19, 1946; s. Jack and Grace (Balcombe) Jacobs; tchr's dipl,

Brentwood Coll of Educ, Brentwood, 1967. Asst master, since 1967; tchr, Heb and Rel, Ilford Dist Syn, Essex, since 1963. Vice-chmn, Fed Zionist Youth, fmr, fund-raising; fmr, chmn, Ilford Young Zionist Soc. Home: Quebec, 3, Toronto Rd, Ilford, Essex, Eng. Office: Forest Gate HS, Forest St, Forest Gate, London, Eng.

COLLOMS, Albert L, Eng, attorney; b. Denver, Colo; s. Morris and Sarah (Smirnow); in Eng since 1961; BSc, Yale, 1925; LLB, Yale, 1927; MSc, Columbia U, 1940; m. Branda Stenning, Aug 8, 1961; c: Michael, Martin. Atty since 1927; sr atty, US Housing Auth, 1938-40; prin atty, OPA, 1941-46. Educ chmn, Croton J Cen, 1940-50; co-chmn, Westchester Amer Lab Party, 1946-55; Hon secy, Mapam, Gt Brit; council mem, ZF; exec council mem, Amers for Progressive Isr, 1944-45; mem: Natl Lawyers Guild, NYC; Haldane Soc, London; Yale Club, London. Author: Eleemosynary Institutions and Public Utilties; Workmens' Compensation Law; Strangers Return, a play, NYC, 1937. Home and office: 123 Glouncester Ave, London, NWI, Eng.

COLMAN, Henry Irving, US, obstetrician, gynecologist; b. Boston, Mass, Nov 7, 1906; s. Morris and Goldie (Savitz); MD, Tufts Med Sch, 1931. Att obstet, gyn, LI J Hosp, New Hyde Park, LI since 1955; clinical asst prof, SUNY, Downstate Med Cen, Bklyn, NY since 1960. Capt, US Army MC, 1942-43. Dipl, Amer Bd Obstets and Gyn; f: Amer Call Obstets and Gyn; Queens Gyn Soc; Amer Coll of Surgs; Intl Coll of Surgs. Contbr to med jours. Home: 20 Canterbury Rd, Great Neck, NY. Office: 69-60 108 St, Forest Hills, LI, NY.

COLOMBO, Yoseph, It, educator; b. Leghorn, It, Nov 21, 1897; s. Samuele and Clelia (Luzzati); PhD, U of Pisa, 1920; m. Berta Bonfiglioli (decd); c: Anna Stern, Sara Viterbo, Samuel, Clelia. Prin, sch since 1946; lectr: on J phil, Instituto Superiore Mayer, Milan; on J lang and lit, U of Milan; prof phil, hist, Licei Statali, 1922-35; prin: Liceo Scientifico, Ferrara, 1935-38; Scuola Ebraica, Milan, 1938-45. It Army, 1917-19. Mem: bd, ORT, It fmr Eur exec, B'nai B'rith. Author: Jewish Conceptions and Modern Theories, 1926; The Foundations of Maimonides' Moral, 1932; Pages of Jewish Morals, trans of Pirkey Aboth, 1932; The Philosophical Thoughts of Elia Benamozegh, 1950; School Organization in the State of Israel; Tradition of Culture in the History of Italian Jewry, 1966; A Bergson's Concept in Hebraic Texts, 1965; The Polemic Luzzatto-Benawoseph about the Kabbala, 1965; ed, Rassegna mensile d'Israel; contbr to: Ency It; other encys; articles on pedg to It periodicals. Recipient: Cavaliere Ordine della Repubblica Italiana; Medaglia d'oro, Scuola e cultura. Home: Pl Aquileia 6, Milan, It.

COLORNI, Vittore, It, educator; b. Mantua, It, July 19, 1912; s. Emanuele and Emma (Levi); desc of Abraam Colorni, engr, author, 1544-99; law deg, U Bologna, 1933; m. Alda Morpurgo, Apr 4, 1943; c: Emanuele, Angelo. Prof, It hist jurisprudence, fac law, U Ferrara, since 1956, past chargé de cours. Pres, Accademia Virgiliana of Sci's, Letters and Arts, Mantua; mem: communal bd for bldg regulations, Mantua, since 1957; Acad Sci's, Ferrara; Lombard Inst of Sci's and Letters, Milan; Acad Sci's, Alessandria, It. Author: Legge ebraica e leggi locali, 1945; L'eguaglianza come limite della legge nel diritto intermedio e moderno, 1946; Per la Storia della pubblicita immobiliare e mobiliare, 1954; Gli Ebrei nel Sistema del diritto comune fino alla prima emancipazione, 1956; Il territorio mantovano nel Sacro Romano Impero, vol I, 800-1274, pub 1959; L'uso del greco nella liturgia del guidaismo ellenistico e la Novella 146 di Giustimano, 1964; Le tre leggi perdute di Roncaglia ritrovate in un ms parigino (Bibl Naz Lat 4677) 1966. Home: 17 Corso Umberto I, Mantua, It.

COLTON, Joel, US, historian, educator; b. NYC, Aug 23, 1918; s. Philip and Theresa (Cotler); BA, CCNY, 1937, MS, 1938; MA, Columbia U, 1940, PhD, 1950; m. Shirley Baron, May 8, 1942; c: Valerie, Kenneth. Prof, chmn, dept hist, Duke U, mem fac since 1947; lectr, hist, Columbia U, 1946-47; visiting prof, U Wis, 1961. Mil Intelligence Off, US Army, 1942-46. Pres, Duke U chap, Phi Beta Kappa, 1955-56; mem: Amer Hist Assn; Soc for Fr Hist Studies. Author: Compulsory Labor Arbitration in France, 1936-39, 1952; Léon Blum: Humanist in Politics, 1966; The Twentieth Century, in Time-Life Great Ages of Man series, 1968; co-author, A History of the Modern World, 1956, 1965; bd eds, Jour of Modern His. Recipient: Guggenheim f, 1957; Rockefeller, f, 1962; Mayflower non-

fiction award, 1967. Home: 1616 Pinecrest Rd, Durham, NC. Office: Duke U, Durham, NC.

COLTON, Lawrence Michael, US, rabbi; b. Detroit, Mich, Oct 2, 1940; s. Harry and Josephine (Cohen); BA, Wayne State U, 1962, Tchrs Cert, 1962; ordained rabbi, BHL, MAHL, HUC, 1967; m. Roberta Fishman, June 30, 1963; c: Howard. Asst rabbi, Touro Syn, New Orleans, since 1969; rabbi, Temple Beth Boruch, Richmond, Ind, 1963; Temple Beth El, Fairmont, W Va, 1964-68; Temple Sinai, New Bedford 1967-69. Bd dirs: JWF; New Bedford Convalescence Home; Big Bros; Model Cities Educ Task Force; mem, Exch Club. Home: 844 Wilshire Blvd, Metairie, La. Study: 1501 Gen Pershing St, New Orleans, La.

COMAY, Michael, Isr, diplomat; b. Capetown, S Afr, Oct 17, 1908; s. Alexander and Clara (Ochberg); in Isr since 1946; BA, U Capetown, 1928, LLB, 1931; m. Joan F Solomon, Dec 22, 1935; c: Yael Stern, Yochanan. Ambass to Gt Brit; perm repr of Isr to UN, 1960-67; chmn, Isr delg to UN, 1960-67; asst dir gen, Fgn Min, 1951-53, 1957-59; first ambass of Isr to Can, 1953-57; dir, Brit Commonwealth Div, Fgn Min, 1948-51; spec repr in Pal of S Afr ZF in political dept of JA, Jerusalem and at UN, with spec missions to Australia, NZ, S Afr and Can, 1946-48; repr of Isr at intl confs: Civil Aviation, Montreal, 1956; Atomic Energy, Vienna, 1957; Law of the Sea, Geneva, 1958; Trade and Devl, New Delhi, 1968; Hum Rights, Teheran, 1968. Maj, S Afr Forces, 1940-45. Office: Min of Fgn Affairs, Jerusalem, Isr.

CONE, Ceaser, US, business exec; b. NYC, Jan 30, 1908; s. Ceaser and Jeanette (Siegel); BA, U of NC, 1928; MBA, Harvard U, 1930; m. Martha Abercrombie, Nov 19, 1938; c: Ceaser, Martha, Laurence. Chmn, Cone Mills Corp since 1966, treas, 1946-56, pres, 1956-66. Dir: Amer Textile Mfrs Inst, 1956-59, 1961-64; Natl Assn of Mfrs 1966-68; pres: Greensboro C of C, 1955; Greensboro United Fund, 1966; secy, Greensboro High Point Airport Auth, 1942-67; mem: B'nai B'rith; Elks; Rotary. Home: 506 Cornwallis Dr, Greensboro, NC. Office: Cone Mills Corp, Greensboro, NC.

CONE, Edward T, US, musician, educator; b. Greensboro, NC, May 4, 1917; s. Julius and Laura (Weill); BA, Princeton U, 1939, MFA, 1942. Prof, Princeton U since 1960, fac mem since 1947; Woodrow Wilson f, Princeton U, 1945-47. US Army, 1942-45. Composer, unpubl orch, choral, chamber compositions; adv ed, Perspective of New Music since 1968, co-ed, 1965-68; author, Musical Form and Musical Performance, 1968; contbr to musical jours. Treas, Amer sect, Intl Soc for Contemp Music, 1950-52; club, Nassau of Princeton. Home: 1 Queenston Pl, Princeton, NJ. Office: Dept of Music, Princeton U, Princeton, NJ.

CONN, Jacob Harry, US, psychiatrist, educator; b. Baltimore, Md, Jan 20, 1904; s. Nathan and Mollie (Lurie); BA, Johns Hopkins U, 1925; MD, U of Md Med Sch, 1929; m. Beatrice Blum, 1935; c: Rosalind, Margaret. Asst prof, Johns Hopkins U, since 1942, fac mem since 1931; pvt out-patient service, since 1948; diagnostic clinic, psycht-psychosomatic service, since 1941; psycht-in-charge, Silver Cross Home for Epileptics, Reistertown, Md, 1939-53; cons: USPHS, US Dist Court, since 1937; adj att, neuro-psycht, Sinai Hosp, Baltimore, since 1940, lectr, Sch for Nurses, 1934-37; mem, staff of Seton Psycht Inst, Baltimore since 1945, chmn, visiting staff, 1961-62; pvt practice since 1933; intern, Boston Psychopathic Hosp, 1930-31. Psycht, Army Induction Bd, 1942-47; cons: Selective Service, since 1942; neuro-psycht, VA, 1946-50. Pres: Md Assn Pvt Practising Psychts, 1950-51; Soc for Clinical, Experimental Hypnosis, 1959-61; Amer Psycht Assn, 1940; Amer Acad Child Psych, 1953; Soc for Clinical and Experimental Hypnosis, 1954; dipl: Amer Bd Neur and Psycht, 1935; Child Psycht, 1959; Med Hypnosis; mem: AMA; Phi Lamda Kappa. Ed, bd, jours: Tice Sys of Med, since 1942; Nervous Child, since 1948; Clinical and Experimental Psychopath, since 1951; Archives of Criminal Psychodynamics, 1954; Clinical and Experimental Hypnosis, since 1955; contbr to sci, consumer jours. Recipient: award of merit, 1960; Bernard B Raginsky bronze plaque, 1961; awards: Schneck, 1964; President's award of Appreciation, 1966; Adolf Meyer Centenary Lecture, 1966; best paper on Clinical Hypnosis, 1968. Home: 7900 Stevenson Rd, Pikesville, Md. Office: 812 Med Arts Bldg, Baltimore, Md.

CONSTANTINIS, Raphaël, Greece, journalist, editor, government official; b. Zante, Greece, July 17, 1892; s. David and

Mazaltov (Mordo); grad, U Athens, 1913; m. Donna Rousso, Jan 28, 1931; s. David. Dir: Evraiki Estia, fortnightly paper 1947-63; The Voice of Israel, monthly mag, 1934-39; intl accounts, Greek Min of Posts, Telegraph and Telephone, 1914-50. Fmr: pres: JNF, Greece; JNF, Athens; JCC, Athens; Union of Zionists of Greece; secy-gen, Greece-Isr Friendship League; club, Bene Zion. Home: 28 Alicarnassou St, Athens, Greece.

CONWELL, Esther M, US, physicist, educator; b. NYC, May 23, 1922; d. Charles and Ida (Korn); BA, Bklyn Coll, 1942; MS, U Rochester, 1945; PhD, U Chgo, 1948; m. Abraham Rothberg, 1945. With Gen Telephone and Elect Labs since 1952; visiting prof, Ecole Normale Supérieure, Paris, 1962-63; instr, physics, Bklyn Coll, 1946-54. F: Amer Physical Soc; AAAS; mem: Phi Beta Kappa; Sigma Xi; Pi Mu Epsilon. Author: High Field Transport in Semiconductors, 1967; contbr to profsl jours. Recipient: annual award, Soc of Women Engrs, 1959. Office: Gen Telephone and Elect Lab Bayside, NY.

COOK, Michael L, US, attorney; b. Rochester, NH, Mar 5, 1944; s. Israel and Molly (Landes); AB, Columbia U, 1965; JD, NYU, 1968. Atty, asso, law firm, Weil, Gotshal & Manges since 1970; tchr, law, Lehman Coll, CUNY since 1968; atty assoc, law firm, Richard E Bauman, 1969-70. Mem: Amer, NY State, NY Co Bar Assns; AAUP, Lehman chap; NY ACLU. Recipient, Amer Jurisprudence Prize, Lawyers Coop Publ Co, 1968. Home: 166 W 22 St, New York, NY. Office: 727 Fifth Ave, New York, NY.

COOK, Samuel, US, rabbi; b. Phila, Pa, June 8, 1907; s. Morris and Elsie (Sophi); BA, Haverford Coll, Pa, 1927; att: Thomas Wister Brown Grad Sch, Haverford, 1927-28; ordained rabbi, HUC, 1934; hon DD, 1959; m. Ray Clara Marcus, Jun 12, 1938; c: Michael, Joel. Exec dir, UAHC, dept coll educ, since 1967, dir: Natl Fed of Temple Youth; vicepres, Natl Young Judea, 1931-32; asst rabbi, Cong Keneseth Isr, Phila, 1937-40; rabbi, Temple Beth Isr, Altoona, Pa, 1940-46; dir, B'nai B'rith Hillel Found, U of Ala, 1934-36, fac mem, 1935-36. Chaplain, US Army, 1943-46. Exec bd mem, CCAR; mem, Phi Beta Kappa. Home: 141-02 68 Dr, Flushing, NY. Office: UAHC, 838 Fifth Ave, New York, NY.

COOK, Thomas, US, business exec; b. Nov 8, 1887; s. Isaac and Chaia (Kraus) Kooks; in US since 1909; att ORT Vocational Training Sch, Russ, 1899-1903; m. Esther Noll, June 17, 1910; c: Harry, Henrietta Sklar. Pres, Ann Arbor Foundry Co since 1948, charter org, with firm since 1920. Natl bd dirs, Amer ORT Fed; delg, World Conf, Montreal, 1968; exec bd, Ann Arbor UJA; bd dirs, Mich B'nai B'rith ADL; founder: Workmen's Circle, Detroit; I L Peretz Schule, Detroit; active, Yivo, research; publ comm; Cong J Culture; J Hist Soc; mem: City of Hope; AJComm; Amer Foundryman's Soc; Gray and Ductile Iron Foundry Soc; Natl Foundry Soc; Masons; Elks; Ann Arbor J Comty Cen; J Publs Soc. Hobbies: chess, music. Home: 300 Linda Vista, Ann Arbor, Mich. Office: 1327 Jones Dr, Ann Arbor, Mich.

COONS, Isidor, US, communal work exec; b. Wilkes-Barre, Pa, June 14, 1889; s. Joseph and Ella (Constine); PhB, Lafayette Coll, 1910; m. Ruth Greenwald, Dec 27, 1921; s. George. Independent fund-raiser since 1955; ed, Wilkes-Barre Evening News, 1910-17; city chmn, Dem Party, 1912; Lt, US Army, 1917-19. Dir: fund raising campaigns until 1925; natl fund raising, JDC, 1925-38; found, exec vice chmn natl campaign, UJA, 1939-49; exec vice-chmn, combined campaign, UAHC and HUC, 1949-55; mem: fmr, mem bd, JWB; Amer Hist Soc; B'nai B'rith; Amer Legion. Home: 774 Addison St, Woodmere, NY.

COOPER, Bernard Labe, US, businessman; b. Hampton, Va, Sep 27, 1922; s. Morris and Rose (Harris); att, U Va; m. Pearl Strauss, Nov 23, 1947; c: Sharman, Wayne, Marla. Owner, Cooper's Dept Store since 1969. Tech sgt, USAAC, 1943-46. Pres, B'nai Isr Cong, Hampton, Va; mem: Monitor Lodge 197, Masons; Newport News Consistory 32 deg, Scottish Rite, Va; Khedive Temple, Shrine Club; BPO Elks, Lodge 366; Amer Legion; fmr: treas, pres, Phoebus Civic Assn; dir, Hampton Retail Merchants Assn. Home: 104 Eggleston Ave, Hampton, Va. Office: 14-16 E Mellen St, Hampton, Va.

COOPER, Joseph D, US, educator, industrial cons; b. Boston, Mass, May 25, 1917; s. Samuel and Hinde (Bryner); AB,

George Wash U, 1944; MA, Amer U, 1947, PhD, 1951; m. Ruth Zeidner, Feb 11, 1942; c: Lenore, Byron. Prof, govt, Howard U since 1964; mgmt cons since 1960; exec dir, Salary Stabilization Bd, 1951-53. Author: Handbook for Sales Meetings, 1959; How To Communicate Policies and Procedures, 1960; The Art of Decision Making, 1961; How To Get More Done in Less Time, 1962; Woman's Guide to Part-Time Jobs, 1963; contbr, articles on med econ, photography. Hobbies: photography. Home and office: 2810 Blaine Dr, Chevy Chase, MD.

COOPERMAN, Hasye, US, author, lecturer; b. NYC, Feb 2, 1909; d. Ephraim and Miriam (Scholar); BA, Hunter Coll, 1927; MA, Columbia U, 1928, PhD, 1931; m. NB Minkoff, Apr 1931 (decd); c: Amram, Eli. Poet and author since 1925; lectr: lit and esthetics, in Yiddish and Eng, since 1928; Amer, comparative, Yiddish lit, New Sch for Social Research,since 1951, head dept, 1961-67. Author: Yagd, Yiddish, 1929; poems, The Chase, 1932; The Aesthetics of Stephane Mallarme, 1933; Men Walk the Earth, 1953; NB Minkoff Memorial Volume, Yiddish, 1959; article on Yiddish lit in The American Jew, a Reappraisal, 1964; contbr: articles, J Heritage Reader, 1965; poetry: Beliot Poetry Jour; Voices, Intl Midstream and other periodicals, Mem: Poetry Soc of Amer; James Joyce Soc of Amer. Recipient: Natl Award for Poetry, The Mists are Rising Now, Amer Lit Assn, 1957. Home: 334 W85 St, New York, NY. Office: 66 W 12 St, New York, NY.

COOPERSMITH, Harry, US, educator; b. Russ, Dec 5, 1902; in US since 1911; BS, MA, Columbia U; att Julliard Sch of Music; m. Ethel Kane; c: Penina. Music dir, J Educ Comm, NY since 1940; asso prof, Herzlia J Tchrs Sem; music dir: Chgo Bd J Educ, 1926-32; Anshe Emeth Syn, Chgo, 1932-40. Pub works: The Songs We Sing; The New Jewish Songster. Home: 17 Manor House Dr, Dobbs Ferry, NY. Office: 426 W 58 St, New York, NY.

COOPERSTEIN, Louis, US, educator; b. Boston, Mass, Apr 4, 1912; s. Harry and Esther (Posner); AB, Harvard Coll, 1933; att Harvard Grad Sch Arts and Sci, 1933-36, AM, 1934; m. Ida Geller, July 30, 1939; c: Ruth. Chmn, modern langs dept, Northeastern U since 1965, prof modern langs since 1962, on fac since 1938. OWI, psych warfare, 1958-59. Chmn, adult J educ comm, Temple Emanuel, Newton; dir, natl council, Northeastern U; fac adv, Alpha Epsilon Pi; pres, Northeastern U Fac Club, 1957-58; mem: MLA; NE MLA; Amer Assn Tchrs Ger; Phi Beta Kappa. Hobbies: art, music. Home: 44 Whitney Rd, Newtonville, Mass. Office: Northeastern U, Boston, Mass.

COPE, Mitchel, US, business exec; b. Portland, Me, Jan 29, 1917; s. Joseph and Pya (Rozen); m. Thelma West, Jan 13, 1952; c: Ronna, David, Debra. Pres, The Minat Corp since 1948. Lt, USAC, 1945-46. Chmn, Me Commn on Intergovt Relations; corporator, Me Savings Bank; trustee, Me Regional Memorial Hosp; dir: Temple Beth El; J Home for Aged; pres, Marine Home Builders Assn; natl repr: Natl Assn, Home Builders; Natl Comm for Support of Public Schs; mem: Portland Bd Realtors; Portland J Comty Cen; Shaarey Tphiloph Syn; B'nai B'rith; KP. Hobby, skiing. Home: 66 Pya, Portland, Me. Office: 34 Proble, Portland, Me.

COPELAND, Charles Michael, Isr, executive; b. Manchester, Eng, Nov 25, 1938; S. Benjamin and Lily (Goldstone); in Isr since 1963; BSc, LSE, 1961; dipl personnel mgmt, 1962; m. Judith Brodie, Mar 14, 1968; c: Sharon. Co-found, dir, World Union J Students Inst, Arad, since 1967. Fmr chmn, Inter-U J Fed of Gt Brit, Ir; mem, Inst of Personnel Mgmt. Home and office: World Union of J Students Inst, Arad, Isr.

COPELMAN, Louis, Isr, physician; b. Bucharest, Rum, Apr 28, 1911; s. Samuel and Debora; MD, Fac of Med, 1935, MD, summa cum laude, Fac of Phil, 1936, both in Bucharest; Chercheur, College de France, 1936; m. Liliane Fromant, Oct 8, 1939. Psycht, neuro-endocrinologist since 1935; mem, Intl Bd of Eds, Excerpta Medica, Psych since 1966; prof, Coll for J Students, Bucharest, 1940-44; head, research dept, Fac of Med, 1944-48; prof, Inst for Social Researches, Bucharest, 1946-50. F, J Claims Conf, NY; mem: Cultural Inst of the Choral-Temple, Bucharest; NY Acad of Scis; Eur Acad for Allergology; AAAS; Amer Soc for the Psychopath of Expression; Conseil Intl de la Société de Psychopathologie de l'Expression, Paris; hon, Société de Psychologie de l'Université de Panama; fmr pres, 1st sect, Congress International d'Historie de la Medecine, Sienna, It, 1968. Author: The Psycho-galvanic Reflex and Its Applications, 1936; The Rorschach-Psychodiagnostic, 1937; co-author: Music and Medicine, 1958; Psychology and Gerontology, 1962; Painters, Witnesses of Their Soul, 1968; Art et Psychiatrie, 1969; bd eds: Soc for Cycle Researches; Société Française de Phlebologie; ed, University Cours for Psychology and Endocrinology, Bucharest, Fac of Med, 1946; contbr of numerous psychopath articles to sci jours. Recipient: 3 prizes, Acad de Medicine de Paris, Laureat de l'Histadrut, 1964; f, Centre National de la Recherche Scientifique, Isr-Fr, 1968. Home: 154 Dizengoff St, Tel Aviv, Isr.

COPLAN, Robert Charles, US, attorney; b. Cleveland, O, Apr 12, 1918; s. Morris and Camille (Benesch); BA, O St U, 1939, LLB, law sch, 1942; m. Shirley Solomon, May 7, 1943; c: Marianne, Elizabeth. Mgn partner, Benesch, Friedlander, Mendelson and Coplan since 1945; vice pres, dir, gen counsel, Pa Life Ins; fmr law clerk, Fed Dist Court, O. Lt, USN. Pres, Cleveland Scholarships Progs; trustee, chmn, O Law Opportunity Fund; man trustee: Natl Council, O St U Law Sch; Roy and Eva Markus Found; mem: Amer Judicature Soc; Amer, O, Cleveland Bar Assns; budget comm, Campaign Cabinet, J Cmty Fed; fmr: trustee, Bellefaire; cocapt: Cleveland Cmty Fund; Cleveland chap, Amer Cancer Soc. Home: 2951 Drummond Rd, Shaker Heights, O. Office: 1100 Citizens Bldg, Cleveland, O.

CORAN, Diana Bernstein, US, organization exec; b. NYC, July 28, 1926; d. Rubin and Mollie (Huchlerin); BA, Hunter Coll, 1943; MA, Columbia U, 1944; Rel Sch Cert, Sch of Educ, HUC-JIR, 1952. Dir, women's org div, Natl JWB, since 1957; fmr: research writer, AJComm; profsl, i/c contemporary J affairs, Natl Council of J Women; exec, dept mem, admn services, Natl Fed of Temple Sisterhoods. Mem: Amer Hist Soc; Amer J PR Soc; speakers bur, UJA. Contbr of: filmstrips; scripts; pamphlets; articles; book reviews. Hobbies: painting, music. Home: 735 Pelham Pkwy N, New York, NY. Office: 145 E 32 St, New York, NY.

CORCOS, David, Isr, business exec, historian; b. Mogador, Morocco; s. Jacob and Hannah (Abulfaia); in Isr since 1959; BCom, BBA, Lycee Lyautey, Inst Commercial, Casablanca; BA, Inst des Hautes Etudes, Rabat; m. Georgette Afriat, 1948; c: Sidney, Jack. Dir, Isr Independent Trust and Inves Co, since 1963; dept ed, hist, Ency Judaica. Mem council, Sephardic J Comty, Jerusalem. Contbr to: hist and J publs; Ency Judaica. Home: 38 Hatayassim Rd, Jerusalem, Isr. Office: 35 Remez St, Tel Aviv, Isr.

COREN, David David, Isr, educator; b. Jerusalem, Isr, June 4, 1917; s. Asher and Malka (Eliashar) Anshel; att tchr sem, Jerusalem, 1952-53; m. Chana Panet, Mar 10, 1940; c. Yechiel, Shani, Tamar, Ruth. Chmn, regional council, Sulam Tzor; fmr: mukhtar secy, Beth Ha'Arava; secy, Gesher HaZiv; sch prin, Gesher HaZiv. Head, admn, IAF; brig gen, Nahal. Mem: Merkaz Mapai; Merkaz Rafi; Merkaz Avoda, Ihud. Home: Kibbutz Gesher HaZiv, Mobile Post, Galilee, Isr.

CORNBLEET, Theodore, US, dermatologist, educator; b. St Louis, Mo, Mar 10, 1899; s. Morris and Sarah (Mett); BA, Mo U, 1919; MS, St Louis U, 1921, MD, 1923; PhD, U of Ill, 1937; m. Dea Tietelbaum, Jan 6, 1935; c: Suzanne, David. Chief, dermat, Cook Co Hosp since 1959, on staff since 1933; cons, Mt Sinai Hosp since 1950, on staff since 1930; prof, U of Ill since 1945, fac mem since 1928. US Army, 1918. Pres: Amer Soc Inves Dermat, 1953-55; Chgo Dermat Soc, 1951; bd dirs, Amer Acad Dermat, 1951; mem: AAAS; AMA; Amer Inst Med; Alpha Omega Alpha; Sigma Xi. Author: Dental Art and Science, 1938; Medical Uses of Soap, 1945; ed, Dermat Digest; ed bd: Clinical Med; Jour of Clinical Pharm; Med Digest; contbr to med jours. Recipient: Bronze medal, Ind State Med Soc, 1955; cert of merit, AMA, 1958; silver medal, Amer Acad Dermat, 1968. Home: 3300 Lake Shore Dr, Chicago, Ill. Office: 30 N Michigan Ave, Chicago, Ill.

CORNFELD, Gaalyahu, Isr, editor, publisher; b. Rosh Pina, Isr, May 1902; s. Leon and Sarah (Korsonsky); m. Lillian Kert, 1924; c: Givon. Dir, chief ed, Hamikra Baolam Ltd, since 1957; ed, independent pub; ed, journalist, 1942-47; acting dir, Twersky Pub House, Tel Aviv, 1945-48; pvt bus, 1950-52. Author and co-ed: Adam to Daniel, 1960; Epic of the Maccabees, 1962; Daniel to Paul, 1962; Pictorial Bibl Ency, 1964. Mem: Pal Exploration Fund, London; Amer Sch Oriental

Research, Jerusalem; fmr dir, Heb Book Pubs Assn. Spec interests: Bible, archaeol, graphic arts. Home and office: 145 Hayarkon St, Tel Aviv, Isr.

CORNFELD, Lillian, Isr, nutritionist; b. Montreal, Can, June 1, 1902; in Isr since 1922; att: McGill U, Montreal, Columbia U, NY; m. Gaalyahu Cornfeld, 1924; c: Givon. Nutritional adv, Malben JDC, since 1950; tchr, Evelina de Rothschild Sch, Jerusalem, 1922; found, first children's playgrounds, Jerusalem. Adv on nutrition: ARC and US Army in Pal, WW II; UNNRA; mem, food adv comm, Isr Army, 1958-59. Author: How to Cook in Wartime, 1942; Ani Mevashelet, 1947; Hamitbach Hameshubach, 1960; Hamitbach Hatov, Maarav .ve Misrach, 1968; Diet Book, 1969, all in Heb; Israeli Cooking, 1962; ed, food prog, Jerusalem Radio and columns in Haaretz and Jerusalem Post. Home: 145 Hayarkon St, Tel Aviv, Isr.

CORRE, Alan David, US, educator; b. London, Eng, May 2, 1931; s. Jacob and Edith (Taylor). in US since 1955; BA, hons, U London, 1951; MA, U Manchester, 1953; PhD, U Pa, 1962; m. Nita Levy, Dec 18, 1957; c: Jacob Giselle, Raquel, Isaac. Chmn, dept Heb Studies, U Wis, since 1968, prof since 1963; min, Cong Mikveh Isr, Phila, 1955-63. Comm mem, Coll Entrance Exam Bd, Heb Examiners Comm; mem: Ling Soc Amer; Amer Assn Sefardic Studies. Author: Anatomy of a Decipherment, 1967; Phonemic Problems in the Masora, 1968. Recipient: 1st prize, research in hum, Wis Acad, 1967; NEA f for Younger Scholars, 1967-68; spec interests: Sephardic studies, Judeo-Arabic studies. Home: 3309 N 45 St, Milwaukee, Wis. Office: U of Wis, Milwaukee, Wis.

CORWIN, Norman, US, author, director, producer; b. Boston Mass, May 3, 1910; s. Samuel and Rose (Ober); m. Katherine Locke; c: Anthony, Diane. Regents lectr: UCBS; UCLA; U of S Cal; in res, U of NC; writer: for film co's including: MGM; 20th Cent Fox; RKO, all since 1948; for legitimate theater, since 1957; writer, dir, produc, CBS, 1938-48. Author: Thirteen by Corwin, 1938; They Fly Through the Air, 1938; More by Corwin, 1942; Untitled and Other Plays, 1944; On a Note of Triumph, 1945; The Plot to Overthrow Christmas, 1951; Dog in the Sky, 1952. The Rivalry, 1957; The World of Carl Sandburg, 1962; Overkill and Megalove, 1963; Yes Speak Out Yes, 1968, commissioned by UN; Prayer for the 70's, 1969; screenplays: The Blue Veil, 1951; Scandal at Scourie, 1953; Lust for Life, 1956; The Story of Ruth, 1960; dir, The Chinese Wall, 1962. Chmn, documentary awards comm, Acad of Motion Pictures, since 1963; mem: Authors League Amer; Screen Writers Guild; Dramatists Guild; affiliated, Brandeis Inst. Recipient: Peabody Medal, 1942, 1945; Bok Medal, Advt Council of Amer, 1943; grant, Amer Acad Arts and Sci's, 1943; freedom award, NCCJ, 1944; World Flight Award, Freedom House, 1946. Hobbies: mineralogy, Bibl lit. Home: 14145 Greenleaf St, Sherman Oaks, Cal. Office: 10401 Wellworth Ave, Los Angeles, Cal.

COWAN, Henry Jacob, Austr, educttor; b. Glogow, Ger-Pol, Aug 21, 1919; s. Arthur and Erna (Salisch); in Austr since 1953; BSc, U Manchester, Eng, 1939, MSc, 1940; PhD, U Sheffield, Eng, 1952, DEng, 1963; m. Renate Proskauer, 1952; c: Judith, Esther. Prof, head dept architectural sci, U Sydney, since 1953; lectr, U Sheffield, 1943-53; visiting prof, Cornell U, NY, 1962; dean architecture, U Sydney, 1966-67. Royal Engrs, 1940-45. Pres: Technion Soc, Bldg Sci Forum, both Austr; fmr pres, sect architecture and engr, Australian and NZ Assn for Advancement of Sci; chmn, Austr Group, Intl Assn for Bridge and Structural Engr; f: Inst Engrs, Austr; Amer Soc Civil Engrs; mem, Instn Structural Engrs, London. Author: Theory of Prestressed Concrete Design, 1956; Design of Reinforced Concrete, 1963, 1968; Reinforced and Prestressed Concrete in Torsion, 1965, Span ed, 1967; An Historical Outline of Architectural Science, 1966; Design of Prestressed Concrete, 1966; Models in Architecture, 1968; ed: Archttectural Sci Rev since 1958; Vestes, mag of Fed of Austr U Staff Assns since 1965; contbr numerous articles to profsl jours. Recipient, R W Chapman Medal, Inst of Engrs, Austr 1956. Hobby, collecting books. Home: 93 Kings Rd, Vancluse, Austr. Office: U of Sydney, Austr.

COWAN, Jack, Can, business exec; b. London, Eng, Feb 27, 1900; s. Harris and Annie (Gollom); in Can since 1906; m. Anna Soltz, July 19, 1921; s. Bernard. Dir, 30 cos, mainly real estate. Natl pres, United J People's Order, Can; past pres, Toronto Lodge, B'nai B'rith. Mem ed bd, Can J Outlook. Home: 242 Hillhurst Blvd, Toronto, Can. Office: 825 Eglinton Ave, Toronto, Can.

COWAN, Marcy Hamilton, US, attorney; b. Bklyn, NY, July 22, 1904; s. Meyer and Matilda (Abrams); AB, Columbia Coll, 1924; JD, Fordham Law Sch, 1927; MSS, New Sch for Social Research, NY, 1938; m. Jennie Taleisnik, Aug 9, 1930 (decd); c: Edward, Neil, Richard. Atty in pvt practice; tchr, prin, elementary sch since 1952. Vice-pres, Assn Tchrs Social Studies; secy, pres, Econs Tchrs Assn; pres, Ditmas Chap, Amer Assn Retired Persons; mem: Schoolmer's Lodge, B'nai B'rith; ACLU, Bklyn chap. Hobbies: reading, theater. Home: 1259 E 26 St, Brooklyn, NY. Office: 245 W 57 St, New York, NY.

COWAN, Martin B, US, attorney; b. NYC, June 6, 1935; s. Joseph and Yetta (Wilkowitz); AB, Columbia Coll, NY, 1957; LLB, Columbia Law Sch, 1959; m. Dorrit Blech, Dec 20, 1959; c: Alison, Jillian, David. Partner, law firm, Wien, Lane & Malkin since 1968; asso, Casey, Lane & Mittendorf, 1960-62; trial atty, Tax Div, Justice Dept, 1926-66; asso, Reanis & McGrath, 1966-69; lectr, Practicing Law Inst, NYC. Vice-pres, Westchester Day Sch, Mamaroneck, NY; secy, Cong Young Isr of Westchester; mem: tax sect, comm on personal income taxation, NY State Bar Assn, subcom on charitable contrib; tax comm, Bar Assn, NYC; tax sect, comm on real estate problems, Amer Bar Assn. Contbr to legal jours; fmr, mem, ed bd, Columbia Law Rev. Home: 2 Cameron Pl, New Rochelle, NY. Office: 60 E 42 St, New York, NY.

COWEN, Anna W, US, clinical psychol; b. Aus, June 24, 1905; d. Max and Mary (Schapira) in US since 1908; AB, Pembroke Coll, 1927; MA, Brown U, 1931; Cal Licensed Psychol; diplomate in clinical psych, Amer Bd Examiners in Profsl Psych; m. Morris Cowen, Aug 7, 1928; c: Hope Solomons, Donald. Pvt practice; vocational counselor, J Vocational Service; clinical psych, Cranston Child Guidance Clinic and sch psych for Cranston's 23 public schs, since 1958; fmr: guidance tchr, E Providence Sch Dept; Psychometrist, vets guidance cen, Brown U, 1945-56; psychol, RI Psych Services; clinical psych, RI Mental Hygiene Services; visiting lectr: RI Coll; Catholic Tchrs Coll, 1961-62.Vice pres, Nathan Bishop PTA; mem: hon life, RI Cong Parents and Tchrs; LA Co Psych Assn; LA Soc of Clinical Psychols; Natl Assn Rehab; RI Psych Assn; Cranston Tchrs Assn; RI Educ Assn; Amer Psych Assn; Phi Beta Kappa; Sigma Xi; fmr: prog chmn: Hadassah; Natl Council J Women; Henry Barnard Mothers Club; secy, sisterhood, Temple Emanu-El. Home: POB 27758, Los Angeles, Cal. Office: 1900 Dracena Dr, Los Angeles, Cal.

COWEN, Eugene Sherman, US, government official; b. NYC, Feb 5, 1925; s. Jacob and Shirley (Sherman); BA, magna cum laude, Syracuse U, 1949; MA, 1952; m. Phyllis Wallach, Jan 29, 1948; c: James, Stephanie. Spec asst to US Pres since 1969; reporter, Syracuse-Herald Jour, 1948-52; mem, Newhouse Newspaper Wash Bur, 1952-53; staff mem, Congresswoman Bolton, O, 1953-56; staff, HEW, 1956-58; press cons, Senator Hugh Scott, Pa, 1958, admn asst, 1967-69. Off, UAAC, WWII. Hon chmn, Govt Div, UJA; mem, Temple Emmanuel, Kensington, Md; Phi Beta Kappa; fmr: dir: Pa Rep Primary Campaign for Raymond P Shafer; campaign for dist atty, Arlen Specter; Senator Scott's campaign. Home: 920 Loxford Terr, Silver Spring, Md. Office: The White House, Washington, DC.

COWEN, Jack P, US, ophthalmologist, educator; b. Chgo, Ill, Feb 22, 1906; s. Isadore and Doris (Posner); BS, cum laude, U Chgo, 1927; MD, Rush Med Coll, 1931; postdoc study, ophthal, U Vienna, 1934. Att ophthal, Michael Reese Hosp, Chgo, since 1935; cons ophthal: USN Hosp, Great Lakes, Ill; Weiss Memorial Hosp, Chgo; fgn asst, Elschnig Clinic, U Prague, Czech, 1935; off asso, Dr Harry S Gradle; asso, Ill Eye and Ear Infirmary; clinical asst prof, ophthal, U of Ill, 1947-57. Cdr, USNR, 1942-46. F: Chgo, Amer, Ill Med Socs; Amer Coll of Surgs, Chgo Ophthal Soc; Pan-Amer Cong of Ophthal; Amer Acad Ophthal; Amer Bd Ophthal; Inst Med of Chgo; Assn for Research in Ophthal; Alpha Omega Alpha; Ill, Natl and Tropical Audubon Socs; Chgo Acad of Sci; Chgo Art Mus; mem: Tau Delta Phi; Phi Delta Epsilon; clubs: City, Cliff Dwellers, Lit. Contbr to: Amer Ency; med jours; guest lectr. Hobbies: ornithology, painting, archaeol. Home: 1448 N Astor St, Chicago, Ill. Office: Ill. N Wabash Ave, Chicago, Ill.

COWEN, Maurice L, US, attorney, business exec; b. Chgo, Ill, Feb 18, 1912; s. Wolf and Fannie (Mueller); LLB, Chgo Kent Coll, 1936; m. Rosalie Small, May 18, 1942; c: Bruce, Jon-Paul, Peter, William. Pvt practice since 1936; pres: Gelatin Corp of Amer; Cowen Pharm; W Pharm Assn; vice-pres, Corel Distributors; chmn bd: Atlas Pharm; Cleary-Lloyd Oil; half-owner, Standard Realty & Mgmt; bd dirs: Excelsior Pharm; Dental Pharm Corp Amer. Life mem, Chgo Hist Soc; mem: Amer, Ill, Chgo Bar Assns; Amer Jud Soc; Amer Acad Political and Social Sci; Natl Assn Chain Drug Stores; Chgo Council Fgn Relations; Art Inst, Chgo; clubs: Standard, Merchants and Mfrs; City of Chgo. Contbr to legal jours. Home: 205 Westmoreland Dr, Wilmette, Ill. Office: 33 N LaSalle St, Chicago, Ill.

COWEN, Zelman, Aust, educator, attorney; b. Melbourne; Vic, Oct 7, 1919; s. Bernard and Sara (Granat); BA, U Melbourne, 1939, LLB, 1940, LLM, 1941; Rhodes Scholar for Vic, 1941; Supr Court Prizeman, 1941; BCL, Ma, Oxford U, 1947; Vinerian Scholar, 1947; f, Oriel Coll, Oxford, 1947-50; DCL, Oxford U, 1968; hon LLD, Hong Kong U, 1967; CMG, 1968; m. Anna Wittner, June 7, 1945; c: Simon, Nicholas, Katherine, Benjamin. Barrister, Gray's Inn and Vic; prof em, U Melbourne; mem Devl Corp, NSW; vice chancellor, U of NE, since 1967; fmr: prof public law, dean fac law, U Melbourne; visiting prof: U Chgo; Harvard Law Sch; Fletcher Sch of Law and Diplomacy; U Utah; George A Miller visiting prof, U of Ill; dist visiting prof, Wash U, St Louis; cons, constitutional problems, Brit Control Comm for Ger, US Mil Govt. Lt, Aust, Naval Volunteer Res. Fgn hon mem: Amer Acad Arts and Sci; mem: Social Sci Research Council of Austr; Sydney Opera House Trust. Author, Federal Jurisdiction in Australia, 1959; Australia and the United States: Some Legal Comparisons, 1954; American Australian Private International Law, 1957; Federal Jurisdiction in Australia, 1959; The British Commonwealth of Nations in a Changing World, 1965; Isaac Isaacs, 1967; co-author: Cowen and Carter Essays in the Law of Evidence, 1956; Cowen and Mendes da Costa Matrimonial Jurisdiction in Australia, 1950; ed, Intl Law Quarterly, 1950; co-ed, Conflict of Laws, 6th ed; contbr to Eng, Can, Amer, Austr legal publs. Office: U of New England, Austr.

CRACOVANER, Arthur J, US, physician, educator; b. NYC, July 2, 1901; s. Henry and Anne (Segal); BA, Columbia U, 1922; MD, Coll Phys and Surg, 1925; postgrad study, U Vienna, 1928; m. Liska Brauner, Nov 23, 1932; c: Linda. Practicing phys, adv surg, dept broncho-esphagology and laryngeal surg, NY Eye and Ear Infirmary, since 1952; cons otolaryngology, Lenox Hill Hosp; clinical prof, otolaryngology, Post Grad Med Sch, NYU-Bellevue Med Cen, since 1952; bronchoscopist, Bellevue Hosp, 1938-56; cons otolaryngologist, USPHS, SI; cons in orl, City Hosp Cen, Elmhurst, NY. Lt col, USAAF, WW II. Dipl, Amer Bd Otolaryngology; f: Amer Coll Surgs; Amer Coll Chest Phys; Amer Acad Ophthal and Otolaryngology; Amer Laryngological, Rhinological and Otological Soc Inc; Amer Laryngological Assn; Amer Soc for Head and Neck Surg; Intl Broncho-Esophagological Soc; Amer Geriatrics Soc; mem: Amer Broncho-Esophagological Assn; Amer Assn for Thoracic Surg; NY Acad Med; AMA; NY Med Soc; NY Soc for Thoracic Surg; World Med Assn; Pan-Amer Assn Orl and Broncho-Esophagology. Author: monograph, Nose and Throat Surgery, 1942; contbr to med jours. Hobby: painting. Home: 1100 Park Ave, New York, NY. Office: 103 E 78 St, New York, NY.

CRAMER, Joseph, B, US, psychiatrist, educator; b. Rochester, NY, Aug 24, 1914; s. Benjamin and Ida (Robfogel); BA, U Rochester, 1936; MD, NY Med Coll, 1941; m. Hope Woronock, Mar 23, 1946; c: Marcia, Carol. Dir, child psycht, prof, Albert Einstein Coll Med since 1955; instr, NYU, 1946; cons: Sheltering Arms Children's Service, 1948; NY Training Sch, 1949-51; Rochester Guidance Cen, 1951; instr, child psycht, U Pittsburgh, 1951-55. US Army 1942-46. Mem: Amer Psycht Assn; Amer Psychan Assn; Amer Orthopsycht Assn; AAUP; Assn Amer Colls; AAAS; NY Council on Child Psycht; Chgo Psychan Soc. Author: The Management of Social Adjustment and Behavior Problems in Adolescence, 1958; The Common Neuroses of Childhood, 1959; Sublimation and Sexual Gratification in the Latency Period of Girls, 1949; contbr to profsl jours. Home: 200 E 71 St, New York, NY. Office: Morris Park Ave and Eastchester Rd, New York, NY.

CRAVITZ, Leo, US, microbiologist; b. Chelsea, Mass, Nov 26, 1918; s. William and Sadie (Aronow); BS, Boston U, 1941; D, Public Health, MIT, 1944; m. Marcia Saperstein, May 10, 1944; c: Elaine, Barbara, Anne. Med microbiol, Rochester Gen Hosp; since 1946; cons: Strasenburg Labs, Castle Co; Park Ave Hosp, Rochester; Myers Comty Hosp, Sodus, NY; lectr, Forsythe Dental Clinic, Boston, 1943-44. Lt, USN, 1944-46. Bd dirs: Day Care Cen for Handicapped Children; MacEllven Nowrock Memorial Found; pres, Rochester Regional Soc for Lab Med, 1953-54; mem: Amer Soc Microbiol; Amer Public Health Assn; AAAS; NY State Assn Public Health Labs; Sigma Xi; clubs: MIT, Rochester Philatelic Assn. Contbr to profsl jours. Recipient: Cert of merit, Rochester Eye Bank & Research Soc, Inc, 1960. Home: 31 Rockhill Rd, Rochester, NY. Office: 1425 Portland Ave, Rochester, NY.

CREMIN, Lawrence A, US, educator; b. NYC, Oct 31, 1925; s. Arthur and Theresa (Borowick); BS, CCNY, 1946; MA, Columbia U, 1947, PhD, 1949; m. Charlotte Raup, 1956; c: David, Joanne, Frederick. A P Barnard Prof of Educ, Tchrs Coll, Columbia U, since 1961; fac mem since 1949. USAAF, 1944-45. Pres, Natl Acad of Educ, since 1969; pres, Natl Soc of Coll Tchrs of Educ, 1961-62; pres, Hist of Educ Soc, 1960-61. Author: The American Common School, 1951; A History of Education in American Culture, 1953; A History of Teachers College, Columbia University, 1954; Public Schools In Our Democracy, 1956; The Republic and The School, 1957; The Transformation Of The School, 1961; The Genius of American Education, 1965; gen ed, Classics in Education. Recipient: Guggenheim f, 1957-58; Bancroft Prize in Amer Hist, Columbia U, 1962. Home: 35 E 85 St, New York, NY. Office: Tchrs Coll, Columbia U, New York, NY.

CRESKOFF, Jacob J, US, structural engr; b. Belz, Russ, Mar 30, 1900; s. Louis and Toba (Lerner); in US since 1905; BS, CE, U of Pa, 1922; m. Mildred Blumenthal, Mar 16, 1935; c: Stephen, Ruth. Pres: Vacuum Concrete Corp of Amer since 1960; Thermo Fluid since 1952; cons, construction div, Dept of Defense since 1952; guest prof, engr seismology, Grad Sch of Engr, Villanova U since 1962; vice-pres: Vaccum Concrete, 1938-42, 1948-52; McCloskey and, 1942-46. Pvt, US Army, 1918; cdr, USN, WWII. Mem: Amer Concrete Inst; Main Line Reform Temple. Author: Dynamics of Earthquake Resistant Structures, 1934; contbr to tech mags. Recipient: Dist engr, U of Pa, 1955. Home: 200 N Wynnewood Ave, Wynnewood, Pa. Office: 6111 Lancaster Ave, Philadelphia, Pa.

CREZELLITZER, Franz, Isr, composer; b. Berlin-Charlottenburg, Nov 1, 1905; s. Fritz and Martha (Shoenfliess); related to: Gertrud Kolmar, poet; Walter Benjamin, philosopher; in Isr since 1934; att Stern Conservatory, Berlin; m. Sima Antman. Free-lance composer. Major works: The Pied Piper of Hamelin, ballet, 1944-46; 2 Sonatas for Violin and Piano, 1948; Piano Quintet, 1949; Piano Concert, 1950; 2 symphonic phantasies for orch; phantasy for violin and orch, 1960; for violoncello, 1962; 2 String quartets, 1953,63; concerto for 2 pianos, 1966; concerto for viola, 1967; preludes for piano, 1947-67-68; 2 suites for string orch, 1952-68; trio for piano, violin, cello, 1968. Hobbies: painting, constructing mechanical toys. Home: 12 Hagilboa St, Tel Aviv, Isr.

CRIEP, Leo H, US, physician, educator; b. Jassy, May 26, 1896; s. Herman and Gertrude (Zuckerman); in US since 1914; BS, U Pittsburgh, 1918; MD, 1920; m. Merla Rosenfield, Dec 15, 1942; c: Susan, Leo Jr. Asso prof, U Pittsburgh Med Sch since 1936; fgn asst in med: U Paris, 1925; U Coll Hosp, 1925-26; sr att phys: Montefiore Hosp, 1929; Presbyterian Hosp, 1938; cons, US VA, 1932. Pres, Amer Acad Allergy, 1939; mem: AMA; Soc Amer Immunologists; AHA; Soc Biol Research; Phi Delta Epsilon. Author: Essentials of Allergy, 1945; Allergy and Clinical Immunology, 1962, 1969; Dermatologic Allergy, 1967; contbr to med jours. Home: 1212 Malvern St, Pittsburgh, Pa. Office: Bigelow Blvd and Tunnel Pl, Pittsburgh, Pa.

CRIST, Judith, US, educator, critic; b. NYC, May 22, 1922; d. Solomon and Helen (Schoenberg) Klein; AB, Hunter Coll, 1941; MS, Columbia U, 1945; m. William Crist, July 3, 1947; c: Steven. Adj prof, journalism, Grad Sch, Columbia U, since 1959; reporter, feature writer, asso critic, 1945-60, film critic, ed for arts, 1960-63, asso drama critic, 1963-66, all NY Herald Tribune; f, State Coll, Wash, 1942-43. Instr, USAAF,

1943-44. Mem: natl bd, Women's Med Coll; Amer Newspaper Guild; Phi Sigma Mu; Sigma Tau Delta. Author, The Private Eye, the Cowboy and the Very Naked Girl, 1968; film critic: TV Guide, since 1966; NY Mag, since 1968; and theater critic, NBC-TV Today Show, since 1963. Recipient: George Polk Award, LIU, 1951; awards: Educ Writers Assn; Amer Newspaper Guild; NY Newspaper Guild; NY Newspaper Women's Club, 1955, 1959, 1963, 1965, 1967. Home: 180 Riverside Dr, New York, NY. Office: 230 W 41 St, New York, NY.

CRIVAN, Harry Edward, Scotland, metallurgist; b. Edinburgh, Nov 9, 1907; s. Solomon and Bertha (Bay); BSc, 1st class hon, U Glasgow, 1929. Vice-prin, Tech Coll, Coatbridge since 1959, on staff since 1948; foundry metallurgist, Colvilles Ltd, 1939-48; metallurgical cons, UNESCO; educ mem, Iron & Steel Ind, training bd. Mem: exec, Scottish Assn for award of natl certs and dipls; council, Educ Inst of Scotland; Scottish tchrs salaries comm; pres: Glasgow J Inst; mem bd govs, Glasgow Habonim; vice-pres, Glasgow Zionist Org; chmn, Scottish-Isr Friendship League; f: Inst Metallurgists; Royal Inst of Chem; found mem, sole Scottish repr, comm, British Iron and Steel Research Assn, setup in WW II; mem: Scottish Council, Bridge for Brit and Isr. Author: Casting in Steel, 1955; contbr articles to profsl jours. Hobby: communal work. Home: 146, Camphill Ave, Glasgow, Scotland. Office: Tech Coll, Coatbridge, Lanarkshire, Scotland.

CROHN, Burrill B, US, physician, author; b. NYC, June 13, 1884; s. Theodore and Leah (Baum); BA, CCNY, 1902; MD, Columbia U, 1907; m. Rose Blumenthal, June 30, 1948; c: Ruth Dickler, Edward. Pvt practice, internal med; cons in gastroenterology, Columbia U, since 1946, on staff since 1920; cons gastroenterologist, Mt Sinai Hosp, since 1946, chief of clinic, out-patient dept, on staff since 1911; Prof em of Med, Mt Sinai Sch of Med; cons phys: St Joseph's Hosp, Far Rockaway, LI; Beth Isr Hosp, Newark, NJ. Mem: Amer Gastroenterologic Assn, pres, 1933-34; Soc for Experimental Bio and Med; Amer Proctological Assn; Intl Gastroenterological Assn; Amer Coll of Phys; Amer Bd of Internal Med; Arg Gastroenterological Soc; Arg Proctological Soc; Harvey Soc; Pan-Amer Gastroenterological Assn (hon); Sigma Xi; FJP. Author: Affections of the Stomach, 1927; Understand Your Ulcer, 1943, 3rd ed; Regional Ileitis, 1947, 2nd ed, 1958; contbr to profsl jours. Recipient: Townsend-Harris Medal, CCNY, 1948; Julius Friedenthal Medal, Amer Gastroenterological Assn, 1953; Jacobi Medal, Mt Sinai Hosp, 1962. Spec interest: farming, hist, Civil War Round Table. Home: 18 E 84 St, New York, NY. Office: 1000 Park Ave, New York, NY.

CROHN, Lawrence, US, communal worker; b. NYC, Feb 22, 1892; s. Theodore and Leah (Baum); m. Jennie Brodie, 1920; c: David, Leah, Harris. Pres, JCC, of Metrop Detroit, 1958-60; fmr: pres, Zionist Org of Detroit; pres, found, ZC of Detroit. Contbr ed, Reconstructionist. Home: 19186 Whitcomb, Detroit, Mich.

CROHN, Nathan N, US, surgeon, educator; b. Chgo, Ill, June 12, 1900; s. Morris and Lena (Schwied) Crohn; BS, U Chgo, 1921, MD, Rush Med Coll, 1923; att, U Vienna, 1927; m. Lera Amlingmeyer, Oct 6, 1934; c: Natalie. Pvt practice since 1927; chmn, att surg, dept of surg, and Michael Reese Hosp, 1946-62, on staff, since 1924; clinical prof, surg, Chgo Med Sch since 1954; asst prof, Northwestern U, 1952-54, on staff since 1928; sr att surg, Mt Sinai Hosp since 1952; research f, Nelson Morris Inst for Med Research, 1926; asso surg, Rush Med Coll, 1932-41, asso surg, Cook Co Hosp, 1932-34, all Chgo. Lt, Med Res Corps, 1934, recommissioned, 1939; surg, USPHS, Res, 1944-49. F: Amer Coll of Surgs; Intl Coll of Surg; dipl, Amer Bd Surg; mem: AMA; Ill, Chgo Med Socs; Phi Delta Epsilon. Contbr to med jours. Home: 844 Junior Terr, Chicago, Ill. Office: 104 S Mich Ave, Chicago, Ill.

CROLL, David Arnold, Can, legislator, barrister; b. Moscow, Russ, Mar 12, 1900; BA, LLB, U Toronto. Mem, Can Sen, since 1955, first J Cabinet mem and Senator in Can; QC; mayor, Windsor, Ont, 1930-34, 1938-40; Min of Lab, Public Wfr and Munic Affairs for Province of Ont, 1934-37; mem, Can House of Commons, 1945-55. Office: Toronto-Dominion Cen, Toronto, Ont, Can.

CROSS, Ephraim, US, educator, linguist; b. Boston, Mar 6, 1893; s. Abraham and Rose (Vandenberg); BA, CCNY, 1913; MA, 1914; PhD, Columbia U, 1930; JD, NYU Sch of

Law, 1929; m. Mary Hochlerner, 1940. Prof, dept romance langs, CCNY, asst prof, 1936-58, mem fac since 1931; tchr NYC high schs, 1914-17, 1922-31. F, Amer Geog Soc; delg, 8th Intl Cong of Ling, Oslo, Nor, 1957; 10th Intl Cong of Ling, Bucharest, Rum, 1967; mem: NY State Bar Assn since 1933; Alumni Assn, CCNY; Ling Soc of Amer; Amer Oriental Soc; exec comm mem, Ling Circle of NY; Tchrs Union; Natl Lawyers Guild; NY State Fed Modern Lang Tchrs; ACLU; Amer Soc Intl Law; Amer Philo Assn; Amer Name Soc; Algemeen Nederlandsch Verbond; Société de linguistique de Paris; Société des Études Latines; People's Lobby; Alliance Francaise de NY; NAACP. Author: Your Name, 1926; Syncope and Kindred Phenomena, 1930; Language Study and the Armed Forces, 1944; The Case Against Professor William E Knickerbocker, 1949; contbr to ling jours. Home: 215 W 98 St, New York, NY. Office: CCNY, Convent Ave, New York, NY.

CROWN, Alan David, Austr, educator; b. Leeds, Eng, Sep 28, 1932; s. Abraham and Sarah (Addlestone); in Austr since 1959; BA, 1954, U Leeds, Eng, MA, with distinction, 1957; att Birmingham U, post-grad, art, educ, 1954-55; PhD, U Sydney, 1967; m. Sadie Rose, Oct 2, 1958; c: Ann, Aviva. Sr lectr in Semitic Studies, U Sydney since 1968, on fac since 1962. Sgt, Royal Army Educ Corps, 1955-57. Pres, NSW Friends of Heb U; dir, Hillel Found, NSW; asst ed, The Bridge; co-found, convenor, Austr Academics for Peace in ME; adv, J orgs; exec. NSW State Zionist Council; libr comm, Gt Syn; fmr: educ comm, J Bd of educ; bd govs, King David Sch; mem, B'nai B'rith, Sir John Monash lodge. Contbr, TV, series of lectures on Bibl themes and modern Isr; articles to profsl and popular jours. Home: 2/63 Victoria Rd, Bellevue Hill, Austr. Office: Dept of Semitic Studies, U of Sydney, Austr.

CROWN, Henry, US, business exec; b. Chgo, June 13, 1896; s. Arie and Ida (Gordon); m. Rebecca Kranz, Aug 12, 1920 (decd); c: Robert, Lester, John; m. 2nd, Gladys Kay, Mar 1946. Chmn bd, Henry Crown and Co; chmn finance comm, mem exec comm, dir, Chgo, RI and Pacific RR; mem exec comm, dir: Hilton Intl; Waldorf Astoria Corp; vice-pres, dir, 208 S La Salle St Bldg; clerk, Chgo Fire Brick, 1910-12; traffic mgr, Union Drop Forge, 1912-16; partner, S R Crown, 1916-19; pres, chmn bd, Materials Service, 1921-41; chmn, exec comm, dir, Gen Dynamics, 1959-66. Dir, Chgo Boy Club; trustee: Syracuse U; De Paul U; U Chgo Cancer Research Found; asso and f, Brandeis U; f, St Joseph's Coll, Ind; mem: Chgo Civil Defense Corps; natl council, Boy Scouts of Amer; Mill Order WWs; Loyola U Citizens Bd; U Ill Citizens Comm; Northwestern U Assns; Medinah Shrine, Masons, 33 deg; club: La Qunita Country, dir; Mid-Day; Standard; Execs; Tavern. Home: 900 Edgemere Ct, Evanston, Ill. Office: 300 W Washington St, Chicago, Ill.

CUBA, Joseph, US, attorney, accountant; b. Atlanta, Ga, Sep 21, 1909; s. Joseph and Etta (Kaufman); BCS, Ga Sch of Tech, 1930; LLB, Atlanta Law Sch, 1933; m. Ida Miller, 1938; c: Philip, Larry, Sarah. CPA since 1930; partner, Max M Cuba and Co, CPA's since 1940; Cuba, Cuba and McNatt, attys, since 1960. Maj, USAAF, 1942-45. Pres: Atlanta Bur of J Educ, 1962; Gate City Lodge, B'nai B'rith, 1963; Cong Ahavath Achim, 1955-58; vice-pres: J Home for Aged since 1966; Heb Acad of Atlanta, 1956-57; chmn: New Bldg, Planning and Construction Comm since 1965; Pacesetters Div, Atlanta J Wfr Div, 1967-68; construction comm, Camp Barney Medintz, 1961; secy, Standard Town and Country Club since 1966; mem: Amer Inst CPA's; Amer Bar Assn; ZOA; Atlanta J Comty Cen; Masons; club, Progressive, pres, 1939-41. Home: 1867 W Wesley Rd, NW, Atlanta, Ga. Office: 45 Eighth St, NE, Atlanta, Ga.

CUBA, Max M, US, attorney, certified public acctnt; b. New York, NY, Dec 10, 1905; s. Joseph and Etta (Kaufman); BS, Ga Inst of Tech, Atlanta, Ga, 1923; LLB, Woodrow Wilson Coll of Law, Atlanta, Ga, 1932. Sr partner: Max M Cuba & Co, CPA's; Cuba, Cuba, & McNatt, tax atty's. Vice-pres, Amer Assn for J Educ; chmn, Simon Wolfe Endowment Fund; mem bd: Atlanta-Fulton Co Jt Planning Bd, past chmn; NCCJ; Atlanta J Comty Council; J Social Services Fed; Heb Acad; Atlanta JWF; Atlanta J Wfr Fund; J Children Services, fmr pres; trustee, Ahavath Achim Syn, fmr pres, co-chmn, bldg comm; mem, natl bd: United HIAS Service; natl council, JDC; Large City Budgeting Conf; mem: Amer, Ga, Atlanta Bar Assns; State Bar, Ga; Amer Inst CPA's; Ga Soc CPA's; Heb Benevolent Cong; Masonic

Lodge, past worshipful master; Scottish Rite Freemasonry; B'nai B'rith; AJComm; Ga Tech Alumni Assn; Ga State Coll Alumni Assn; BBB; Atlanta C of C; Amer Soc Planning Officials; Natl Assn Cos; fmr mem: Atlanta City Council; Ga Gov's staff; clubs: Progressive, fmr pres; Standard. Recipient: man-of-year, JWV, 1960; dist service award, B'nai B'rith, 1961; brotherhood medallion, NCCJ, 1966; natl award, JTSA, 1966. Home: 1270 Peachtreet St, NW, Atlanta, Ga. Office: 45 Eight St, NE, Atlanta, Ga.

CUKOR, George, US, motion picture dir; b. NYC, July 7, 1899; s. Victor and Helen (Fross). Motion picture dir, Selznick Intl since 1937; asst stage mgr, NYC, 1921; stage dir, mgr, Lyceum Theatre, Rochester, NY, 1921-28; stage dir, Empire Theatre, NYC, 1926-29; co-dir, Paramount Pictures, 1929; dir, MGM, 1933-34; PKO, 1934-36. Dir: plays: The Constant Wife; The Cardboard Lover; The Great Gatsby; motion pictures, dialogue dir: All Quiet On the Western Front; River of Romance; co-dir: Grumpy; The Virtuous Sin; The Royal Family; dir: The Tarnished Lady; Girls About Town; One Hour With You; Dinner At Eight, 1933; Little Women, 1934; David Copperfield, 1935; Romeo and Juliet, 1936; Holiday, 1937; Zaza, 1938; Two-Faced Woman; The Women, 1939; Susan and God, 1939; Philadelphia Story; The Twins; The Keeper of the Flame, 1942; Gaslight, 1943; Winged Victory, 1943; Double Life, 1947; Edward My Son, 1948; Adam's Rib, 1949; A Life of Her Own, 1950; Born Yesterday, 1950; The Model and the Marriage Broker; The Marrying Kind; Pat and Mike; Fame and Fortune; It Should Happen to You, 1954; A Star is Born, 1954; Bhowani Junction, 1955; Les Girls, 1957; Wild is the Wind, 1957; Heller in Pink Tights, 1958; Let's Make Love, 1959; Chapman Report, 1962; My Fair Lady, 1964; Justine, 1969. Home: 9166 Cordell Dr, Los Angeles, Cal.

CUMMINGS, Nathan, US, business exec; b. St Johns, NB, Can, Oct 14, 1896; s. David and Esther (Saxe); in US since 1939; hon: D Hum, Philathea Coll, 1953; LLD, Fla S Coll, 1954; m. Ruth Kellert, 1919 (decd); c: Herbert, Alan, Beatrice Mayer; m. 2nd Joanne Toor, Aug 9, 1959. Found, hon chmn, chmn, exec comm, Consolidated Foods Corp since 1947; chmn, Asso Prod since 1947; dir, Maurice L Rothchild and Co since 1957; acquired C D Kenny, Baltimore, 1941; with McCormick's, Can, 1932-38. Patron-benefactor, Metrop Mus of Art, NY; patron and governing mem, Minneapolis Fine Arts Soc; governing life mem, Chgo Art Inst; mem: NY State C of C; rel comm, City of Chgo; clubs: Montefiore, Montreal; Econ, NY; Canadian, NY; Standard, Chgo; Marco Polo, NY. Recipient: Chevalier of the Legion of Honor, Fr, 1957; Cavalier of the Order of Merit, It, 1957; Comendador of the Order of Merit, Peru, 1957; dedicated the Ruth Cummings Research Pavilion, Michael Reese Hosp, Chgo, 1958. Hobby, collecting paintings of Fr impressionist artists and Peruvian pre-Columbian objects. Home: Waldorf Towers, 100 E 50 St, New York, NY. Offices: 135 S La Salle St, Chicago, Ill; 375 Park Avenue, New York, NY.

CUPERMAN, Sami, Isr, physicist; b. Piatra-Neamtz, Rum, Oct 5, 1928; s. Abraham and Tzipora (Zinger); in Isr since 1956; MSc, C I Parhon U, 1955; PhD, Heb U, Jerusalem, 1960; m. Iaffa-Sheny Marcus, July 16, 1949; c: Ioram, Ionatan. Sr lectr, Tel Aviv U, since 1965; researcher in: nuclear physics, Weizmann Inst, 1957-60; thermonuclear plasmas, Euratom, Paris, 1960-62; thermonuclear research: ORNL, US, 1962-64; Isr AEC, 1964-66. IDF, 1960. Prin contribs in: nuclear physics; thermonuclear physics; astrophys plasmas; stellar dynamics. Mem, Amer, Isr Physics Socs. Contbr of numerous publs to profsl jours. Home: 75 Zahal St, Kiriat Ono, Isr. Office: Tel Aviv U, Ramat Aviv, Isr.

CURIEL, Isaac, Uruguay, business exec; b. Izmir, Turkey, Aug 1, 1921; s. Moises and Esther (Segura); desc of Rabbi David Algranati; in Uruguay since 1938; att Alliance Is-raelite Universelle, Izmir; m. Clara Margounato; c: Raul, Jorge, Hugo. Bus exec. Pres, Cen J Comm, Uruguay; B'nai B'rith, Oriental Lodge since 1963, dir, gt dist XX Lodge since 1969; delg: Importer Chambre, ALALC; Free Commerce Latin Amer Assn; fmr: pres, Central J Comm of Uruguay, vice-pres counselor; vice-pres, B'nai B'rith, Oriental Lodge, guardian, treas, mentor; counselor: Sepharody J Comty of Uruguay, treas; Bd trustees, IAVA; secy, B'nai B'rith Regional Council, Plata Zone; Youth Assn; La Bonne Volonte, Izmir. Home: Blvd España 2386/301, Montevideo, Uruguay. Office: Juncal 1414/11, Montevideo, Uruguay.

CUSHMAN, Edward H, US, attorney, author; b. Phila, Pa, Jan 22, 1897; s. Arthur and Katie (Levy); LLB, Temple U, 1920; m. Martha Gerson, Jan 1, 1930; c: Robert, Kenneth, Carol. Pvt practice since 1920; gen counsel, Natl Assn Surety Bond Prods, Natl exec comm, UAHC, 1950-63; pres: Pa council, UAHC, 1951-55; Cong Temple Judea, 1953-55; natl exec comm, AJComm, 1950-59, chmn, Phila chap, 1949-51; master, William B Hackenburg lodge, Masons; mem: Phila, Pa, and Amer Bar Assns. US Army WW I. Author: Law of Mechanics Liens in Pa, 1925; Bonds on Public Improvements, 1932, rev annually, contbr to law jours. Home: 707 Chelton Ave, Philadelphia, Pa. Office: 123 S Broad St, Philadelphia, Pa.

CUSHMAN, Jerome, US, educator; b. Chgo, Ill, June 1, 1914; s. Maxwell and Lottie (Rositzky); AB, Eng, Park Coll, Mo, 1940; BS, libr sci, La State U, 1941; m. 2nd, Marion Gurkewitz, Aug 24, 1969; c, from 1st m.: Keith, Deborah, Sarah, Evan. Sr lectr, Children's lit, Sch of Libr Service and Dept of Eng, UCLA, since 1965; chief libr, public libr, Salina, Kan, 1945-61; chief libr, New Orleans Public Libr, 1961-65. US Army, 1941-43. Pres: Kan Libr Assn; Mt Plains Libr Assn; mem: Amer Libr Assn, past mem exec bd; ACLU; AAUP; fmr: local repr, JWB; comty chest bd, Salina, Kan Comty Chest; NAACP, Salina, Kan. Author: Marvellas Hobby, 1962; Tom B and the Joyful Sound, 1970; coord ed (periodically), children's sect, LA Times; reviewer: adult poetry, Lib Journ; juvenile books, LA Times; children's storyteller; tchr, courses, ext dept, UCLA; contbr to profsl publs. Recipient, Brotherhood Award, Frontiers Club, 1965. Hobbies: book collecting, art, music. Home: 7447 Sausalito St, Canoga Pk, Cal. Office: UCLA, Los Angeles, Cal.

CUTLER, Lawrence Mark, US, physician; b. Old Town, Me, Oct 22, 1906; s. Edwin and Rachel (Rawinski); BA, U of Me, 1928; MD, Tufts Med Sch, 1932; m. Catherine Epstein; c: Eliot, Joshua, Joel. Pvt practice since 1946; cons staff, E Me Gen Hosp since 1968, chief, med service, 1950-68, staff since 1936; house off, Boston City Hosp, 1933-35. US Army, 1941-46. Chmn, bd trustees, U of Me; exec council, Amer J Hist Soc; state delg, White House Conf on Educ, 1955; council mem, Arthritis and Metabolic Disease Adv Council, NIH, 1951-55; chmn, Gov's Adv Comm on Educ, 1957-58; bd dirs, E Me Guidance Cen, 1960-64; mem: State Comm on Coord Higher Educ; Amer, Me and Penobscot Co Med Assns; Amer Soc Intl Med. Home: 33 Grove, Bangor, Me. Office: 31 Grove, Bangor, Me.

CUTLER, Max, US, surgeon; b. Jitomir, Russ, May 9, 1899; s. Sam and Esther (Tchudnowsky); in US since 1907; BS, U of Ga, 1918; MD, John's Hopkins U, 1922; post-grad studies: Curie Inst, Paris; Radiumhemmet, Stockholm; m. Bertie B, Apr 12, 1946; c: Nina, Nancy, Susie. Pvt practice, specializing in cancer; cons in cancer, VA, 1931-46; asso surg, Northwestern U Med Sch, Chgo, 1935-45; dir, tumor clinic, Michael Reese Hosp, Chgo, 1931-37; found, Chgo Tumor Inst, 1938; mem, Natl Adv Cancer Council, 1939-42; first pres, Amer Assn for Study of Meoplastic Diseases, 1933-34. Mem: AMA; Amer Radium Soc; Amer Assn for Cancer Research; Intl Coll Surgs; NY Acad Med; Chgo Med Soc; fgn radiological socs; Phi Epsilon Pi; Phi Delta Epsilon; Phi Beta Kappa; Alpha Omega Alpha. Co-author: Tumors of the Breast, 1931; Cancer its Diagnosis and Treatment, 1938; Tumors of the Breast (rev), 1962. Home: 38550 Florence St, Beaumont, Cal. Office: 436 N Roxbury Dr, Beverly Hills, Cal.

CUTTER, William R, US, rabbi, educator; b. St Louis, Mo, Feb 9, 1937; s. Jack and Gladys (Frank); AB, Yale U, 1959; BHL, MHL, ordained rabbi, HUC; att: Heb U, Jerusalem; UCLA. Asst dean, HUC, Cal Sch, since 1969, asst prof, Heb lang and lit, since 1969. Secy, Hoover Urban Renewal Adv Comm; mem: bd J Youth Council, J Fed, LA; exec bd, Pacific Assn Reform Rabbis; Yale Alumni Schs Comm; ACLU; CCAR; Pacific Assn Amer Rabbis; Hobbies and special interest: reading; modern Heb lit; Amer novl; sailing. Home: 2888 Nichols Canyon, Los Angeles, Cal. Office: 8745 Appian Way, Los Angeles, Cal.

CYNOWICZ, Hersh Z, India, merchant, communal leader; b. Yedwabne, Pol, 1907; s. Yoseph and Szyrka-Reisla (Krasnoborski); in India since 1941; MJur, U Stefan Batory, Wilno. Mgn dir, J Chamber of Trade; fmr: repr of Prof Weizmann in negotiations with Indian Govt; in pvt law practice, Pol. Pres, Cen J Bd of India; hon pres, Bombay Zionist Assn; chmn, United Isr Appeal; found, chmn, Pal off, India; repr: for JA; for J faith, all Rels Conf, India; delg: ZCs, WJC Assemblies; WJC to UNESCO Conf; mem: Zionist Actions Comm; world exec, WJC; fmr: mem: Rabb Council; cofound, Shul-Kult; Chevra Madait Ivrit; Hist-Ethnographic Soc; Cen Comm of J Trade, all Pol. Recipient, inscription in JNF Golden Book by J Comty of Afghanistan. Home: Amarchand Mansion, 16A Mayo Rd, Bombay, India.

CYNOWICZ, Moshe Leib, Isr, author, civil servant; b. Yadwabne, Pol, 1905; s. Yosel and Szyrka (Krasnoborski); in Isr since 1935; att: Yeshivot; Lomza; Mir; U Frankfurt/M; disciple of: Chaim Ozer Grodzenski, last Vilno Gaon; Rabbi Dr Chaim Heller, Berlin. Educator; lectr, writer, author monographs on J comtys and talmudic personalities of E Eur; Contbr to ency and jours. Found, Tzeirei Mizrachi. Home: 48A Ben Yehuda St, Tel Aviv, Isr.

CZAPSKI, Gidon, Isr, chemist; b. Berlin, Mar 28, 1932; s. Walter and Grete (Milgrom); in Isr since 1934; MSc, Heb U, Jerusalem, 1955, PhD, 1959; m. Eilat Ytran. Asso prof phys chem, dir linear accelerator lab, Heb U, since 1964, fac mem, since 1954; asso prof chem div, Tel Aviv U since 1964; fmr: chem tchr, HS; research asso, Brookhaven Natl Lab, NY; lectr, Boris Kidrich Inst Vinca Beograd, Yugo; visiting asso sci, Argonne Natl Lab, US; guest of Democritus Nuclear Research Cen, Athens. Prin contribs: research in reactions of H atoms in solutions; radiation chem of aqueous solutions with the use of flow methods and pulse radiolysis; flash photolysis of aqueous systems; kinetics of fast reaction using a flow system. Author: in Heb: Course of Lectures in Thermodynamics, 1965; Course of Lectures in Chemical Kinetics, 1967; contbr of numerous articles to profsl jours. Home: 44 Tchernihovsky St, Jerusalem Isr. Office: Heb U, Jerusalem, Isr.

CZERNIAK, Pinchas, Isr, physician; b. Horodec, Pol, Sep 14, 1909; s. Arie and Szyfra (Jarmuk); in Isr since 1950; MD, Fac of Med, Montpellier, Fr, 1936; Grad Sch of Hygiene, Montpellier, 1936; m. Genia Feldstein, 1940; c: Irith, Zila, Abraham, Judith. Head, Dept Radiotherapy and Isotopes, Tel Aviv U Med Sch, Tel Hashomer Hosp, since 1965 and Baruk's Inst for Radioclinical Research, Tel Hashomer, 1967; head, dist hosp, Antopol, Pol, 1945-47; dir, VD U Clinic, Wroclaw, Pol, 1948-50; asst, Hadassah Radium Inst, Jerusalem, 1950-54. Principal contribs in the field of atomic med and radiotherapy. Mem: Isr Roentgenology Assn; Soc of Nuclear Med; Société d'hygienistes Atomiques. Author of 3 books Nuclear Medicine; contbr of numerous articles to profsl jours. Recipient: Prix Dubreuilh, 1936; Prix Dr Meyer, 1957. Home: 3 Shulamit St, Tel Aviv, Isr. Office: Tel Hashomer Govt Hosp, Isr.

CZERSKI, Alexander, Isr, mining engineer, author; b. Kattovice, Pol, Dec 6, 1920; s. Marek and Elfriede (Luftig); in Isr since 1957; Mining Eng, Gleiwitz Politech, 1952; m. Isabella Topiel, Apr 3, 1925 (decd); c: Eva, Ilana. Helped numerous immigrant families settle in Isr. Authors: Colors in the Fog, 1963; Flame, Ashes and Smoke, 1964; Believing and Doubt; film scenarios. Red Army, 1941-43. Recipient: Pol Gold Cross, devl Pol mining ind; Order of Courage, Red Army; Isr Prize, Short Stories, 1960. Home and office: 8 Gordon St, Tel Aviv, Isr.

D

DACHOWITZ, Pincus, US, rabbi; b. Vilna, Pol, Jul 21, 1920; s. Hirsh and Leah (Schechter); in US since 1923; att CCNY, 1937-38; BA, Yeshiva Coll, 1941; att W Reserve U Law Sch, 1943-45; ordained rabbi, Rabbi Elchanan Theol Sem, 1942; m. Seyma Sacksner, Mar 4, 1952; c: Cynthia, Moses, Emily. Rabbi: Cong B'nai Isr, Midwood, Bklyn, since 1945; Oheb Zedek Cong, Cleveland O, 1943-45. Mem: RabCA; Union of Orthodox Rabbis of US and Can; ZOA; Rel Zionists of Amer; B'nai B'rith. Contbr to rabb publs. Home: 4301 Ave, J, Brooklyn, NY. Study: 4815 Ave I, Brooklyn, NY.

DACK, Simon, US, cardiologist, educator; b. NYC, Apr 19, 1908; s. Isadore and Rebecca (Beitch); MD, NY Med Coll, 1932; m. Jacqueline Rosett, Jan 23, 1949; c: Leonard, Jerilyn. Asso clinical prof, med: Mt Sinai Sch of Med, since 1966, fac mem since 1948; NY Med Coll; Flower Fifth Ave Hosp, both since 1958; lectr, card, Columbia U, since 1936. Maj, US Army MC, 1942-46. F: Amer Coll Card, gov, metrop NY, 1966-68; Amer Coll Phys; Amer Coll Chest Phys; NY Acad Med; mem: Alpha Omega Alpha; Amer Fed for Clinical Research; AHA; NY Heart Assn; NY Cen Syn. Ed-in-chief, Amer Jour Card, since 1958; author: Medical Complications of Pregnancy, 1960; Coronary Heart Disease, 1963; contbr to encys and profsl jours. Home: 85 East End Ave, New York, NY. Office: 1111 Park Ave, New York, NY.

DAGAN, Avigdor, Isr, diplomat; b. Czech, June 30, 1912; s. Moshe and Frieda (Ehrenstein) Fischl; in Isr since 1949; DRerPol, U Prague, 1938; m. Stella Berger, Apr 10, 1938; c: Daniel, Gabriel. Dir, E Eur dept, Min of Fgn Affairs, Jerusalem, since 1968; fmr: J parl secy, Czech parl, 1936-39; first secy, legation, Tokyo, 1955-58; emb counsellor, Rangoon, 1959-60; ambass to Pol, 1961-64; min to Yugo, 1965-67. Author: Czech books; ed, Zionist Weekly, Zidovske Spravy, Czech, 1935-39. Hobby: painting. Home: 4 Rabbi Benjamin St, Jerusalem, Isr. Office: Min for Fgn Affairs, Jerusalem, Isr.

DAGAN, Gedeon, Isr, scientist; b. Galatz, Rum, Dec 24, 1932; s. David and Janet (Schachter); in Isr since 1962; dipl, Inst of Civil Engr, 1956; BSc, U of Bucharest, 1956; DSc, Technion, 1964; m. Ora Sneh, 1962; c: Sigal, Noga. Sr lectr, Technion since 1965, fac mem since 1963; fmr: research sci: Inst of Hydro Research, Rum, 1956-59; Hydronautics Inc, US, 1967-68. Contbr to profsl jours. Home: 45 Einstein St, Haifa, Isr. Office: Technion, Haifa, Isr.

DAGONI, Shaul, Isr, physician; b. Bochnia, Pol, Jan 28, 1907; s. Moshe and Regina (Jassen) Landfisch; in Isr since 1942; MD, U of Cracow, 1931; m. Elis Weinberg, 1948; c: Ilana, Eyran. Dist med off, Workers Sick Fund, Haifa, since 1951. Served, Pol and Brit armies; maj IDF, MC, all 1939-50. Mem, IMA; pres, Judaica Philatelic Hist Soc, Isr br. Author: Judaica Guide, 1965; contbr to philatelic jours. Recipient: DSC, Pol. Home: 58 Sderot Hanassi, Haifa, Isr. Office: Kupat Cholim, Haifa, Isr.

DAGUT, Merton, Isr, teacher; b. Manchester, Eng, Jan 16, 1921; s. Harry and May (Simon); in Isr since 1951; MA, Oxford U; m. Hinda Bloom, July 31, 1947; c: Rahel, Ronit, Ilan. Sr tchr, Eng dept, Haifa Coll, since 1965; fmr: lectr in Heb, Leeds U, 1949-51; tchr, Eng, Reali Sch, Haifa, 1953-65. Spec interests: semantics. Home: 28 Margalit, St, Haifa, Isr.

DAINOW, Joseph, US, attorney, educator; b. Montreal, Can, July 5, 1906; s. Aaron and Pearl (Sourkes); in US since 1935; BA, McGill U, 1926; BCL, 1929; Docteur en Droit, U of Dijon, Fr, 1931; SJD, Northwestern U, 1938, hon LLD, U of Ghent, 1964; m. Frieda Fineman, Aug 23, 1933; c: Jariel, Keren. Prof, law, La State U, since 1947, on fac since 1938; dir, Inst of Civil Law Studies, La State U, since 1967; lectr, McGill U, 1931-32; research assn, Northwestern U, 1933-35; prof, Loyola U, 1935-38. Lt col, Judge Advocate Gen dept, US Army, 1942-46; mem, legal staff, Amer prosecution, Nuremberg, 1945. Mem: bd dirs, Amer Assn for Comparative Study of Law; council, La State Law Inst; AAUP; Amer and La Bar Assns; Amer Soc of Intl Law; Amer Fgn Law Assn;

Lib Syn; Order of the Coif; Gamma Eta Gamma. Ed bd, Amer Jour of Comparative Law; ed: Civil Code of La, 1947, 1961; Civil Property Cases and Materials, 1956, 2nd ed, 1968; Security Devices Cases and Materials, 1956, 2nd ed, 1969. Author: Essays on the Civil Law of Obligations, 1969; contbr to legal jours. Recipient: Guggenheim f, 1954; Fulbright lectr: Fr, 1954; Belgium, 1962-63. Home: 1956 Glendale Ave, Baton Rouge, La. Office: La State U Law Sch, Baton Rouge, La.

DALITH, Fritz, Isr, radiologist; b. Frankfurt/Main, Ger, Apr 27, 1910; s. Isidor and Fanny (Lorsch) Saalberg; in Isr since 1937; m. Else Dahl, Apr 4, 1937; c: Michael. Head, dept of diagnostic radiology, Tel Hashomer Hosp, since 1948; asso prof, chmn, dept of diagnostic radiology, Tel Aviv U, since 1968. Haganah; lt-col, IDF MC, 1948-66. Mem: intl socs of radiology, card, and nephrology. Author: Roentgenographic Positions, 1967. Office: Tel Hashomer Hosp, Ramat Gan, Isr.

DALSHEIMER, Helen Miller, US, communal leader; b. Baltimore, Md, Apr 16, 1900; d. Solomon and Minnie (Kaufman) Miller; att Goucher Coll; m. Hugo Dalsheimer, Oct 31, 1921; c: Roger, George. Pres, World Fed of YM-YWHA's; mem bds: UAHC; JWB, vice-pres; NCCJ; vice-pres, Hosp for Women of Md; pres, Baltimore Heb Cong. Home: Leisure Hill, Baltimore, Md.

DALSIMER, Samuel, US, business exec; b. NYC, Nov 13, 1908; s. Nathan and Carolyn (Baum); att Cornell U, 1926-29; m. Shirley Wasch, Jan 17, 1935; c: James, Andrew. Vic-chmn, bd, Grey Advt Inc, since 1964, with firm since 1955; vice-pres: Husband & Thomas, 1934-40; Cecil & Presbrey, 1940-50, exec vice-pres, 1950-55. OWI, 1944-45. Chmn, natl prog comm, exec comm, natl commn, ADL, since 1959; club: Collector's. Hobby: philately. Home: 20 Sutton Pl S, New York, NY. Office: 430 Park Ave, New York, NY.

DAMARI, Shoshana, Isr, folk singer; b. Yemen; d. Zekharia and Ayalah; m. Shlomo Bosmi; c: Nava. Intl star performer, stage, screen, radio, TV; stage debut with Li-La-Lo Theater, Tel Aviv, 1946; toured DP camps, Cyprus, 1948; appearances for Isr Troops; concert tours and recitals: US, coast-to coast, 1951-54, 1960-63; Scandinavia, 1958; Eur, 1956-58; S Afr and Rhodesia, 1956, 1961; films: Hill 24 Does Not Answer, Hatikva; records: Columbia, Vanguard, Warwick. Home: 16 Klonimus St, Tel Aviv, Isr. Office: c/o Gideon Ben-Ami Prods, 425 Central Park W, New York, NY.

DANE, Maxwell, US, advertising exec; b. Cincinnati, O, June 7, 1906; s. Abraham and Sophie (Sall); m. Belle Sloan, Apr 4, 1933; c: Henry. Chmn, exec comm, Doyle Dane Bernbach, Inc, found and dir since 1949; exec, Dorland Intl, 1937-39; advt promotion mgr: Look Mag, 1939-41; WMCA, 1941-44; pres, Maxwell Dane, 1944-49. Vice-chmn, ACLU, NY, 1959-67; co-chmn, advt and publ div, UJA, since 1945; trustee: Havorford Coll; FJP, co-chmn, advt and pub div, 1950-69; vice-chmn mgmt comm, Amer Assn of Advt Agcys, since 1959; mem: Cen Syn; Bnai B'rith; AJCong; AJComm; ADL, chmn, natl program comm, 1969; publ comm, Commentary Mag; clubs: Old Oaks Country; City Athletic; Harmonie. Home: 650 Park Ave, New York, NY. Office: 20 W 43 St, New York, NY.

DANENBERG, Leigh, US, newspaper publisher; b. NYC, Sep 23, 1893; s. Ury and Bertha (Filer); BA, NYU, 1913; att Columbia Sch of Journalism, 1914; m. Nina Purdy, 1921; m. 2nd, Elise Nicholas, 1928 (div); c: Shirley Manasevit, Dale, Leigh, Elsa, Darryl. Pres, Bridgeport Herald Corp, since 1929; fmr: publisher, ed, Bridgeport Sunday Herald, since 1929; reporter: NYC, Wash, DC, SF, 1914-17; corresp, Ger, 1921-23; ed, Norwalk Sentinel, 1923-29. Sgt, US Army MC, 1917-18. Clubs: Natl Press; Natl Dem; Overseas Press. Home: Westport, Conn. Office: 299 Lafayette St, Bridgeport, Conn.

DANGEL, Edward M, US, attorney, publisher; b. Boston, Mass, July 9, 1891; s. Julius and Rachel (Goldstein); LLB, Boston U,

Law Sch, 1912; m. Sadie Linsky, 1914; c: Edward. Pvt practice since 1913; owner, Wilson Hill Publishers, since 1949; owner and ed: The Legalite, since 1949; Police and Firemen's Jour, since 1949; prof, law, Boston U, 1941-59. Fmr pres:Boston U Law Sch Assn; Mass Law Soc; Amer Soc Intl Law; Mass Trial Lawyers Assn; mem: Amer Law Inst; Masons. Author: The Real Estate Broker, 1928; Civil and Criminal Conspiracy, 1929; Lawyers Manual, 1932; Motor Vehicles, 1937; Contempt, 1939; Labor Unions 1941; Criminal Law, 1951; Mass Business Corp, 1953, Home: 18 Dean Rd, Brookline, Mass. Office: 101 Tremont St, Boston, Mass.

DANIEL, Leon, US, journalist; b. Jassy, Rum, Mar 30, 1901; s. Nathaniel and Marie (Edelstein); in US since 1935; att Tech U, Berlin, Ger; m. Edith Fried, Mar 25, 1954 (decd); Pres, Pix Inc,since 1935; fmr: staff, NY Times photo service, 1926-28; Cen Eur mgr, Pacific and Atlantic Photos; AP pohto dept; both 1928-35. Club: Overseas Press. Contbr to profsl jours. Home: 200 E 78 St, New York, NY. Office: 236 E 46 St, New York, NY.

DANIELI, Haim, Isr, business exec; b. Pol, Apr 12, 1911; s. David and Lea (Danhirsch); in Isr since 1935; att, Poly, 1931-33; m. Bilha Feld, 1935; c: Yael, Shlomo. Mgr, Diamond Mfr Assn, since 1950. Chmn: Kfar Silver; Molly Goodman Academic HS; fmr mem: Munic Council, Tel Aviv, 1950-59; exec comm, Gen Zionist Party, Isr, until 1960. Home: 75 Einstein St, Tel Aviv, Isr. Office: 3 Jabotinsky St, Ramat Gan, Isr.

DANIELS, Alfred Harvey, US, business exec; b. Pittsburgh, Pa, Mar 14, 1912; s. Harry and Irene (Finn); BS, magna cum laude, Harvard, 1933, MBA, hons, 1938; m. Ada Schoenberg; c: James, Molly; m. 2nd, Stella Goldstein, July 1, 1959. Dept store exec since 1968; dir, exec comm, Natl Retail Merchants Assn,1952-65; dir, Asso Merchandising Corp, 1959-69; pres, chmn of bd, Burdine's, Miami, 1958-65; bd dirs, Fed Dept Stores, 1969; group pres, Fed Dept Stores, 1969. Vice-chmn, J Fed, Bklyn, 1952-53; bd dirs, asst treas, J Family Service of NY, 1951-56; bd dirs, J Family Service of Miami, 1963-64; bd trustees: U of Miami, 1964-68; United Fund of Miami, 1961-68; off, CJA, 1960-67; mem: AJComm; clubs: Lotos; Harvard; Miami. Contbr to merchandising jours. Hobbies: contemporary art, tennis, golf. Home: 2 Owenoke Park, Westport, Conn. Office:Fed Dept Stores, 222 W 7 St, Cincinnati, O.

DANISHEFSKY, Isidore, US, biochemist; b. Pol, Apr 3, 1923; s. Jacob and Anna (Gorelik); in US since 1924; BA, Yeshiva U, 1944; ordained rabbi, Rabbi Isaac Elchanan Theol Sem, 1945; MS, NYU, 1947, PhD, 1952; m. Madeleine Weinstein, Sep 5, 1951; c: Kenneth, Avis, Prof, NY Med Coll, since 1964, pres, fac sen, fac mem since 1958; research asso: Poly Inst of Bklyn, 1951-52; Columbia U Med Sch, 1952-58. Bd dirs, Yeshiva Soloveitchik, since 1968, pres, bd of educ, 1965-68; mem: Amer Assn for Cancer Research; Amer Soc Biol Chem; AAAS; Amer Chem Soc; Sigma Xi; Phi Lambda Upsilon. Contbr to books, encys and sci jours. Recipient: travel award, NSF, 1958; lectr, Gordon Conf, 1958; Bernard Revel Memorial award, Yeshiva U, 1962; award, Amer Coll of Angiology 1964. Home: 3850 Hudson Manor Terr, New York, NY. Office: Fifth Ave at 106 St, New York, NY.

DANNETT, Sylvia G L, US, author; b. NYC, Dec 25, 1909; d. Abraham and Hannah (Weinberg) Liebowitz; BA, NJ Coll for Women, 1930; m. Emanuel Dannett, June 29, 1933; c: Kenneth, Wendy. Author: Mr Bilge of the Aquarium, 1942; Tell the Truth Mickey, 1942; Defy the Tempest, 1944; Down Memory Lane, 1954; Noble Women of the North, 1959; She Rode With the Generals, 1960; A Treasury Of Civil War Humor, 1963; Profiles of Negro Womenhood, 1619-1965, 2 vols; And the Show Goes On-in the Confederacy; Lincoln and the Fine Arts; Traitor or Patriot-Rebecca Wright; The Door to the Tower; Confederate Surgeon. Mem: bd trustees, Temple Isr Cen; Authors League of Amer; Overseas Press Club of Amer; The Woman Pays Club; Amer J Hist Soc; Hadassah; NY,Westchester Hist Socs; NAACP; Manhattan Women's div, Brandeis U; ARC; fmr: secy, alumnae class, Douglass Coll; chmn, ritual comm, Beth Shalom Syn; mem ladies comm, Civil War Centennial. Home: 9 Reimer St, Scarsdale, NY.

DANON, David, Isr, scientist, educator; b. Pazrdjik, Bulgaria, Oct 17, 1921; s. Moshe and Regina (Bassan); in Isr since 1925; grad, med sch, Geneva, 1952; m. Arlette Behar-Meir, Dec 14, 1959; c: Daphna, Ilan Noga. Head, sec of biol

ultrastructure, Weizmann Inst, since 1964, asso prof since 1962, staff mem since 1955; fmr: asst, biophysics, Geneva U, 1952-55; sabbatical, Columbia Med Cen, NY, 1962. Served, Irgun, 1942-48; med off, IAF. Contbr to profsl jours. Recipient: Partick E Gorman prof, 1966. Hobbies: painting, guitar. Home: 16 Henkin St, Rehovot Isr. Office: Weizmann Inst, POB 26, Rehovot, Isr.

DANON, Oskar, Yugo, composer, conductor; b. Sarajevo, Yugo, Feb 7, 1913; s. Solomon and Ana (Baruh); dipl, Acad of Music, Prague, 1936; PhD, U of Prague, 1938; m. Vjera Bonacić, May 1945; c: Maja. Conductor, Belgrade Philharmonic Orch, dir and conductor, Belgrade Opera, since 1944; choir and orch conductor, Prague, 1935-39; philharmonic orch and choir conductor, Sarajevo and Belgrade, 1939-41; concerts: Eur,US, Asia. Mem, Natl Liberation Army, 1941-44. Composer: choir and sym orch, solo songs. Recipient: war medals; Order of Work. Home: 1 November 29 St, Belgrade, Yugo. Office: Opera Belgrade, Belgrade, Yugo.

DANSKER, Raphael M, US, investment exec; b. Bkln, NY, Sep 25, 1917; s. William and Lena (Riskin); BS, Franklin and Marshall Coll, 1937; DDS, U of Pa, 1941; m. Shirley Koven, Nov 18, 1945; c: Leslie, Steven, Bruce. Pres, Inves Funding Corp of NY, with firm since 1950; dir: The Citadel Life Ins Co of NY; P Ballantine & Sons; Surety Bank and Trust Co, Security Title and Guaranty Co. Capt, US Army, 1942-45. Trustee, dir,J Memorial Hosp; mem: Temp.e Rodeph Sholem; Natl Dem Club; Amer Legion; Grand St Boys Assn; Masons; 32nd deg; Shriners; clubs: Hampshire Country; Rockefeller Center Luncheon. Recipient: medals, five battle stars, US Army. Home: 70 E 77 St, New York, NY. Office: 630 Fifth Ave, New York, NY.

DANTON, Charles, US, attorney; b. Petoskey, Mich, Feb 22, 1902; s. Alex and Celia (Glazer); AB, U of Mich, 1921, JD, 1926; m. Mildred Nicklas, Mar 28, 1943; c: Daniel, Dana Ashendorf. Pres, Charles Danton Investment Councellors, since 1960; fmr: staff, Sonnenschein, Berkson, Lautmann, Levinson & Morse, Chicago, 1926-31; mem: Becker & Danton, 1931-45; Danton & Lazar, 1947-59. Ensign, US Navy, WWI, capt, mil govt, US Army, WW II. Mem: Miami Beach, Dade Co, Fla, Ill, and Amer Bar Assns; Masons, 32nd degree; Shriners; Elks; Intl Platform Assn; clubs: Intl Press; El Centro; Lawyers, U of Mich. Contbr to bus and profsl jours. Home: 3333 NE 34 St, Fort Lauderdale, Fla. Office: 2810 E Oakland Park Blvd, Fort Lauderdale, Fla.

DANZIG, Hyman, US, rabbi; b. NYC, May 29, 1917; s. Eli and Ida; BA, Bklyn Coll, 1940; m. Belle Moses, July 1, 1947; c: Rita, Florence. Rabbi; Temple B'nai Isr, since 1950; Cong B'nai Isr, Greensburg, Pa, 1946-48; Cong Beth Shalom, Columbia, SC, 1948-50. Pres, Bd of Rabbis of Essex Co, NJ, 1967-69; secy: Nutley Clergy Fellowship; RabCA, NJ chap, 1956; mem, bd trustees, JCC, Essex Co, 1969-1970; mem: Rotary. Home: 48 Freeman Pl, Nutley, NJ. Study: 192 Centre St, Nutley, NJ.

DA-OZ, Ram, Isr, composer; b. Berlin, Ger, Oct 17, 1929; s. Haim and Miriam (Freudenberg) Daus; in Isr since 1934; grad: Agric Sch, Givat Hashlosha, 1948; Acad of Music, Tel Aviv, 1953; m. Sari Grosz, Nov 1, 1950. Composer since 1955; piano tuner since 1954. IDF, lost eyesight, Isr War of Independence, 1948. Composer: Changing Phantoms, for chamber orch, 1967; Of Grief and Consolation, for orch, 1960; Suite in Old Style, for strings, 1958; Trio for Strings, 1961; Concertfor Violin and Strings, 1961; Suite for Cembalo, Oboe, Flute and Cello, 1962; Capricio for Piano, 1962; Nine Dance Movements for Piano, 1963; Trio for Strings, 1963; Trio for Piano, Violin and Cello, 1964, 1965; Three String Quarters; Two Sonatas for Piano; Two Song Cycles; Prologue, Variations and Epilogue for Piano, 1968. Mem: Isr League of Composers; ACUM. Home: 41 Neve Shaanan St, Haifa, Isr.

DAROFF, Joseph Alfred, US, business exec; b. Phila, Pa, Dec 18, 1899; s. Harry and Ethel (Stavitsky); att, U of Phila; m. Sylvia Gaber, June 7, 1922; c: Lynn Lane. Pres, H Daroff & Sons, Inc; vice-pres and mem, bd dirs, Botnay Inds; bd dirs: Sanitized Sales Co of Amer; Clothing Mfrs of Amer. Exec comm, Phila Clothing Mfrs Assn, 1967; bd dirs, City Trusts, City of Phila; vice-pres, Amer Assn for J Educ; bd overseers, JTSA; bd dirs, Amer Friends Heb U; vice-chmn, Pa ADL, regional adv bd; mem bd: and vice-pres, Lucien Moss Rehab Hosp; Phila Fellowship Commn; treas: Cens; JWB, Middle Atlantic sect, since 1942; vice-pres, Beth Jacob Schs; fmr:

pres, chmn, bd trustees, Cong Adath Jeshurun; pres, bus and profsl group, AJCong; vice-pres, Gtr Phila chap, AJCong; hon vice-pres, YMHA; chmn, Phila F Commn Membership Enrollment; mem, Unity lodge, Masonic Temple; clubs: Locust; Philmont Country; Golden Slipper Sq; Saints & Sinners, Ed Wynn Tent, Delaware Valley. Inaugurated, Joseph A Daroff Older Adult Campus at YMHA. Recipient: awards: Bus and Profsl Group, AJCong, 1957; Comty Service, JTSA, 1961; JNF, 1961; man-of-the-year, Phila Men's Apparel Assn, 1964; Stephen Wise, AJCong, 1964; Natl Brotherhood, NCCJ, 1964; Natl J Hosp, 1964; Syn Council of Amer, 1968; citations: Gratz Coll; Middle Atlantic sect, JWB, Home: 220 W Rittenhouse Sq, Philadelphia, Pa. Office: 2300 Walnut St, Philadelphia, Pa.

DAROFF, Michael, US, business exec; b. Phila, Pa, Dec 11, 1903; s. Harry and Ethel (Stavitsky); hon deg, Phila Coll of Textiles; m. Esther Fruchbom, May 22, 1924; c: Norman, Deborah. Chmn bd, pres, Botany Industries, Inc, since 1955; chmn bd, H Daroff & Sons, since 1946. Mem: bd dirs, Brand Names Found; bd trustees: Phila Coll of Textiles and Sci; Yeshiva U; Perkiomen Sch; mem: bd, Albert Einstein Med Cen; adv bd of lay trustees, Villanova U; fmr: dir: Clothing Mfr Assn of Amer; Phila C of C; chmn bd, Amero Inst of Men's and Boys' Wear; clubs: Philmont Country, dir; Locust-Midcity. Recipient: man-of-the-year; Phila Men's Apparel Assn, 1946; Textile Vets of Amer, 1967; torch of hope, City of Hope, Natl Med Cen, Cal, 1968; Albert J Ettelson Humanitarian award; Brotherhood award, NCCJ; Lighthouse award. Home: 700 Westview St, Philadelphia, Pa. Office: 2300 Walnut St, Philadelphia, Pa.

DASCAL, Adolfo, Brazil, business exec; b. Suceava, Rum, Jan 13, 1912; s. Sloima and Gitel (David); in Brazil since 1930; att Cernauti HS, Rum; m. Sarah Schwartz, Jan 18, 1940; c: Claudio, Marcelo. Exec, Aronzon & Dascal, since 1936. Pres, KH, Brazil; vice-pres: Federacão Israelita, Sao Paulo; Chevra Kadisha; mem of council, past dir, Associacão Braci-leira A Hebraica, Sao Paulo. Fmr: mem, Youth Movement Beitar, Rum; found mem, Beitar, Brazil; dir, Escola Israelita Luiz Fleitlich. Recipient: medal from Ze'ev Jabotinsky. Home: 1175 Rua José Maria Lisboa, Sao Paulo 5, Brazil. Office: 27 Rua Silva Jardim, Sao Paulo, Brazil.

DAUBE, David, UK, educator, author; b. Freiburg, Ger, Feb 8, 1909; s. Jakob and Selma (Ascher); DJ, with distinction, Göttingen U, Ger, 1932; PhD, Cambridge, U, 1935; DCL, Oxford U, 1955; hon degs: Edinburgh U, 1958; Sorbonne, 1962; Leicester U, 1963; m. 1936; c: Jonathan, Benjamin, Michael. Regius prof of civil law, U of Oxford, f, All Souls Coll, since 1955; f, Caius Coll and lectr in law, Cambridge U, 1938-51; prof, U Aberdeen, 1951-55; spec lectr in talmudic law, London Sch of Oriental Studies, 1948-49; Roman law, Heb U, Jerusalem, 1949; Frankfurt U; Heidelberg U; Erlangen U; Paris U; Jordan Bequest lectr, London U, 1952; Gifford lectr, U Edinburgh, 1962-63; sr f, Yale U, 1962; Ford prof, U Cal, Berkeley, 1964; visiting prof Konstanz U, Ger 1967; f, Brit Acad since 1937; Korresp Mitglied Akad. Wiss. Göttin-gen, 1964, Bayer Akad Wiss, Munich, 1966; mem: academic bd, Inst of J Studies, London, since 1953. Author: The Aramaic Gospels, 1945; Studies in Biblical Law, 1947; The New Testament and Rabbinic Judaism, 1956; Forms of Roman Legislation, 1956; The Exodus Pattern in the Bible, 1963; The Sudden in the Scriptures, 1964; Collaboration with Tyranny in Rabbinic Law, 1969; contbr to scholarly jours. Office: All Souls College, Oxford, Eng.

DAUS, Milton T, US, attorney; b. Sharon, Pa, Jan 10, 1904; s. Max and Jessie (Marx); BS, U of Pa, 1925; LLB, John Marshall Law Sch, 1929; m. Jeanne Rosenfeld, Nov 30, 1931; c: Thomas, Alan, Margaret. Partner, Daus, Schwenger & Kottler, since 1933. War Dept, 1941-44. Treas, Cleveland chap, ARC, 1933-40; exec comm, 1933-57; chap chmn, AJ Comm; Cleveland J Vocational Service; bd trustees: Suburban Temple; U of Pa, 1967-75; Oakwood Club, 1964-70; treas, Panel of Amers; exec bd, Council Gardens of Cleveland; mem: United Appeal of Cleveland; Cleveland Bar Assn; clubs: U of Pa Alumni; Commerce; Mid-Day. Home: 13800 Shaker Blvd, Shaker Hgts, O. Office: 1290 Union Commerce Bldg, Cleveland, O.

DAUTCH, Charles, US, attorney; b. Buffao, NY Aug 10, 1896; s. Louis and Esther (Amdur); LLB, U of Buffalo, 1917; m. Charlotte Wallach, Oct 16, 1923; c: Phyllis Heilbrun, Nancy Urdan. Partner, law firm, Aaron, Dautch, Sternberg & Lawson; gen counsel, Buffalo Real Estate Bd. Pres, United J

Fund, 1946-48; chmn, Fed Campaign, 1940; dir, Temple Beth El; mem, bd govs, J Fed for Social Service, 1922-51, all of Buffalo. Mem: Amer, NY State Bar Assns; Erie Co Bar Assn; Masons; Fed Ins Counsel; Temple Beth Zion; Temple Beth El; club: Lawyers. Author: Little Biographies of Big People, 1925; Facts Worth Knowing, 1928; Lawyers Indemnity Insurance, 1941. Hobbies: walking, travel. Home: 745 La-fayette Ave, Buffalo, NY. Office: 500 Walbridge Bldg, Buf-falo, NY.

DAVID, Amnon, Isr, physician; b. Tel Aviv, Isr, Sep 22, 1930; s. Zwi and Esther (Kasowsky); BA, cert of phys chem, U Montpellier, 1949; MD, Faf Med, Paris, 1956; dipl, in repro-ductive biol, Hosp of U Penn, 1968; m. Lily Jortner, Jan 15, 1959; c: Guy, Yuval. Tchr, anat, Tel Aviv U Med Sch, since 1968; sr clinical asst, obstet and gyn, Tel Hashomer Hosp, since 1964; fmr: res in anesthesiology, Hadassah Hosp. Lt, MC, IDF, 1957-59. Prin contrib, invention of Urigator, appa-ratus for automatic flushing of urinary bladder, 1969. Mem: Isr Soc of Obstet and Gyn; Isr Fertility Assn; Isr Soc of Bio-Med Engr; Intl Fertility Soc; Soc for Study of Fertility, London; Intl Soc of Research in Biol of Reproduction. Contbr to profsl publs. Hobbies: photography, music. Home: 43 Yahalom St, Ramat Gan, Isr. Office: Tel Hashomer Govt Hosp, Ramat Gan, Isr.

DAVID, Benjamin, US, manager, producer, composer; b. NYC, Oct 15, 1899; s. Abraham and Anna (Smolensky). LLB, LLM, NYU, 1920-22; m. Bozena Foune, Mar 1, 1923; c: Lionel. Composer; fmr: pvt law practice, 1922-26; org, BD Nice Music Publishers, 1926-30; mgr: Eddy Duchin, Leo Reisman, Emil Coleman, Al Goodman; Max Meth; producer: for screen and Broadway stage; composer: for Ziegfeld Follies, Greenwich Village Follies, Shubert Passing Shows; songs: Wond'ring; Where the Volga Flows; Just A Bit of Heaven In Your Smile. Office: ASCAP, 575 Madison Ave, New York, NY.

DAVID, Filip Friderik, Yugo, author; b. Kragujevac, Yugo, July 4, 1940; s. Friderik and Roza (Judić); deg, Fac of Philol, 1964; Acad of Dramaturgy, 1966; both Belgrade; m. Vera Gajić, Apr 3, 1968. Dramatist: TV Belgrade, since 1967; Con-temporary Theatre, Belgrade, 1965-67. Author: Bunar u Tamnof Sumi, 1964; Zarisi o Stvarnom i Nestvarnom, 1969. Mem, Assn of Yugo Writers. Recipient: prizes: casopis Ucadost, 1964; casopis Telegram, 1965. Home: 16 Visegrad-ska, Belgrade, Yugo. Office: TV Belgrade, 10 Takovska, Belgrade, Yugo.

DAVID, Meir S, Isr, physician; b. Baghdad, Iraq, Feb 25, 1912; s. Shaoul and Naima (Reuben); in Isr since 1950; MD, Amer U, Beirut, 1937; DTM, London Sch of Tropical Med and Hygiene, 1938; m. Zelma Grunberg, Feb 18, 1947; c: Sami, Dalia. Chief phys, Kupat Holim Maccabi, since 1961. Fmr: dep mayor, Ramat Gan, 1961-64; munic counselor, 1955-64. Chmn: Isr Cancer Assn; IMA, exec mem; Natl Council for Preventing Road Accidents. Hobby: gardening. Home: Men-des St, Ramat Gan, Isr. Office: 4 Arlosoroff St, Ramat Gan, Isr.

DAVID, Suhar, Eng, businessman, communal leader; b. Rum, May 15, 1902; s. Israel and Yvette (Braunstein); in Eng since 1920; BSc, 1925; m. (decd); c: Ghita Cohen. Ret bus exec, fmr sr dir, Gestetner, Ltd. Chmn, Ravenswood Found; treas, Soc for J Studies; gov, Inst of J Studies; f, Royal Soc Arts. Recipient: OBE, Brit Govt; Off, Order Leopold II, Belg. Home: 43 Hallam Court, 77 Hallam St, London W 1, Eng.

DAVID, Yonah, educator, poet; b. Jassy, Rum, Sep 8, 1919; s. Mordehai and Hene-Reiza (Matus); in Isr since 1949; MA, U Bucharest, 1946; PhD, Heb U, Jeursalem, 1965; m. Dalya Sason, Dec 27, 1962; c: Isrsel, Vered. Asst prof, Heb lit, Tel Aviv U, since 1966; fmr mem, Kibbutz Ein Zietim. IDF, 1949-69. Mem: Intl Org J Sci; World Union of J Studies; fmr: Zionist Histadrut Comm; Aliya Beit; haBonim Youth movement; all Rum. Author: Bamikchol, 1956; Shirim Al lo Ahava, 1961; ed, contbr: anthologies, Ency Judaica, period-icals. Home: 1 Shahar St, Jerusalem, Isr. Office: Tel Aviv U, Ramat Aviv, Isr.

DAVIDOFF, Leo Max, US, surgeon; educator; b. Talsen, Lat-via, Jan 16, 1898; s. Israel and Liebe (Lemkus); in US since 1905; MD, Harvard Med Sch, 1922; hon DHL, Yeshiva U, 1953; m. Ida Fisher, Oct 3, 1926; c: Helen Wallach, Leonore Lockwood, Frank Fisher, Mary Houts. Prof em, Albert Ein-stein Coll of Med, Yeshiva U, since 1968, fmr prof, chmn, dept neur surg, asso dean since 1961; surg to Byrd-MacMillan

Arctic Expedition, 1925; dir, surg, J Hosp of Bklyn, 1937-45; chief, neuro-surg, Montefiore Hosp, NYC, 1945-49; prof, Coll of Phys and Surgs, Columbia U, 1945-49; clinical prof, neuro-surg, NYU Med Coll, 1949-53; neuro-surg, Mt Sinai Hosp, NYC, 1951-53; dir, neuro-surg, Beth Isr Hosp, NY, 1949-53. F, Amer Coll of Surgs; dipl, Amer Bd Neur Surg, past vice-chmn; mem: Hadassah med adv bd; bd dirs, Amer Friends Heb U; med adv bd, Yeshiva U, Soc Neur Surgs, past pres; AMA; Amer Neur Assn; Harvey Cushing Soc, past pres; missions, Unitarian service comm, 1946, 1948. Author: Brain Tumors, 1928; Normal Encephalogram, 1940; Abnormal Pneumoence-phalogram, 1950; contbr to profsl jours. Recipient: hon medal, U of Prague, 1946; Order of White Lion, Czech, 1946. Hobbies: sculpture, gardening. Home: 73 Marshall Ridge Rd, New Canaan, Conn. Office: Albert Einstein Coll of Med, New York, NY.

DAVIDOFF, Philip, US, attorney, public education admnr; b. Phila, Pa, Feb 28, 1910; s. Samuel and Lea (Goldstein); BS, Temple U, 1932, JD, 1936, MS, 1948; m. Ruth Kahnowitz, Dec 25, 1958; c: Susan. Dir, for grievances and disputes, sch dist of Phila, since 1964; prin, Jr HS and elementary schs, 1946-65, tchr, 1930-42. US Maritime Service, USNR, 1942-45. Pres, Temple Sinai; chmn, scholarship comm for Phila, press Jt bd, ILGWU; mem: Sch Admnrs Alliance; NEA; Pa Educ Assn; AJCong; B'nai B'rith; Phila Orch Assn; fmr chmn, bd trustees, House of Correction, Phila. Contbr to profsl jours. Recipient: Hoyer Lafferty award, Phila Normal Sch, 1930; Phila Bd of Educ scholarship, Phila sch dist, 1930. Home: 906 Plainfield St, Philadelphia, Pa. Office: 219 N Broad St, Philadelphia, Pa.

DAVIDON, William Cooper, US, scientist, educator; b. Ft Lauderdale, Fla, Mar 18, 1927; s. Jack and Ruth (Simon); BS, MS, PhD, U of Chgo, 1945-54; m. Ann Morrissett, Dec 6, 1963; c: Alan, Ruth, Sarah. Prof, physics, Haverford Coll, since 1961; dir of research, Nuclear Chgo, 1948-54; research sci: U of Chgo, 1954-56; Argonne Natl Lab, 1956-61. USN, 1945-46. Educ chmn, Soc for Social Responsibility in Sci; steering comm, Resist; natl bd, Sane; fmr vice-pres, Fed of Amer Scis; mem, Sigma Xi. Author: Without Arms Control, 1959; Nth Country Problem, 1970; contbr to sci jours. Home: 7 College Lane, Haverford, Pa. Office: Haverford Coll, Haverford, Pa.

DAVIDOVIĆ, Solomon, Yugo, surgeon, educator; b. Belgrade, Yugo, May 26, 1891; s. David and Alligretti (Farchy); MD, U of Vienna, 1919; m. Ella Koen, May 28, 1928; d. Greta Terzić. Ret; prof, surg, U of Belgrade, 1949-62; asst prof, Surg Clinic, 1919-41. Mem: em, Intl Assn Surgs; Fr Assn Surgs; Serbian Assn Surgs, Yugo. Contbr to Yugo and fgn profsl jours. Home: Vojvode Milenka 20a, Belgrade, Yugo.

DAVIDOVITCH, David, Isr, museum dir; b. Pabianice, Pol, July 29, 1905; s. Joseph and Rachel (Wonchocker); in Isr since 1933; dipl ing, U of Strasbourg, 1928; m. Noemi Hirschberg, 1938; c: Yoram. Dir, Mus of Ethography and Folklore, Tel Aviv, since 1961; fmr: engr, tech dept, Munic of Tel Aviv. Haganah, 1938-48. Mem, Assn of Engrs and Architects in Isr. Author: Synagogues in Poland and Their Destruction, 1960; Synagogues in Poland, 1961; Wall Paintings of Synagogues in Poland, 1968; The Ketuba, Jewish Marriage Contracts Through the Ages, 1968; Wandmalereien in Alten Synagogen, 1968. Home: 192 Arlosoroff St, Tel Aviv, Isr. Office: Mus of Ethnography, Tel Aviv, Isr.

DAVIDSON, Albert Milton, US, business exec; b. Milw, Wis, Nov 23, 1911; s. Mandel and Sophia (Dunn); att Ind U, 1930-34; BS, 1958. Pres, Aldason Corp, since 1952. Asst field commnr, Boy Scouts of Amer, 1945-47; pres, Temple Isr, 1953-54; dir, Ind U Alumni Assn, 1953-54; past vice-pres, B'nai B'rith; bd dirs, YMCA; mem, ZOA; clubs: Lions; Elcona Country; Covenant; Miami Beach Yacht Power Squadron. Recipient: award, YMCA. Home: 2760 N Bay Rd, Miami Beach, Fla. Office: 730 W Franklin St, Elkhart, Ind.

DAVIDSON, Charles Joseph, US, rabbi; b. Boston, Mass, May 28, 1932; s. Max and Rose (Garber); BA, U of Denver, 1952; BHL, MHL, HUC, 1958; att Heb U, Jerusaelm, 1955-56; m. Sandra Ullian, Dec 22, 1957; c: Joshua, Jonathan, Sara. Dir, spec services, UJA, since 1968; asst rabbi, Cong Emanuel, NYC, 1960-62; rabbi: Village Temple, 1962-65; Cong B'nai Isr, Bayport, Conn, 1966-68. Lt, USN, 1958-60. Pres Judaic Studies Found; natl bd, AJComm. Home: 2140 Burr St, Fairfield, Conn. Study: 1290 Ave of the Americas, New York, NY.

DAVIDSON, Gustav, US, author, publisher; b. Warsaw, Pol, Dec 25, 1895; s. Max and Frieda (Barasch); in US since 1897; MA, Columbia U, 1920; hon DLitt, U Libre, Pakistan; m. Mollie Strauss, Mar 22, 1942. Found, dir, Fine Editions Press, since 1940; vice-pres, Davidson Printing Corp, since 1940; secy em Poetry Soc of Amer; fmr staff mem, NY Daily Mirror, Phila Inquirer, Wash Star. Mem, Walt Whitman Birthplace Assn; Brit Poetry Assn. Author: Melmoth the Wanderer, 1915; Songs of Adoration, 1919; Half Century of Sonnets, 1926; Lilith, 1928; First Editions in American Juvenilia, 1939; Bird of Time, 1940; The Most Tragic Story in Mathematics, 1940; Mortal Hunger, 1943; Thirst of the Antelope, 1945; The Great Adventure, 1945; Moment of Visitation, 1950; Ambushed by Angels, 1965; illus, A Dictionary of Angels, 1967; contbr of poetry and critical articles to mags. Found, ed: The Madrigal, 1917-18; Rhythmus, 1922-23; found, publ, Poetry Chap Book, 1942-53. Recipient: medal, Poetry Soc of Amer, 1947; Lyric Found award, 1950; poet-in-residence, Poets House, New Harmony, 1962; gold medal, Govt of Philippines; Knighthood of Order of St Nicholas Thaumaturgus; $3500 di Castagnola award. Home: 200 E 36 St, New York, NY.

DAVIDSON, Henry A, US, psychiatrist; b. Newark, NJ, May 27, 1905; s. Louis and May (Tannenbaum); BA, Columbia U, 1925; MD, Jefferson Med Coll, 1928; MS, U of Pa, 1931; m. Adelaide Heyman, Oct 20, 1936; c: Laurence, Ellen. Supt, Essex Co Overbrook Hosp, since 1957, staff mem since 1954; chief, prog dev, psycht service, VA, 1950-54; chief, psycht, VA Office for NJ, 1947-50. Maj, US Army, MC, 1942-47. F, Amer Psycht Assn; pres: NJ Psycht Assn, 1949-50; NJ Medi-colegal Assn, 1956-57; vice-pres, NJ Wfr Council, 1949-51; parliamentarian, Amer Psycht Assn, since 1950. Ed, Jour of Med Soc, NJ, 1939-51. Author: A Short Story of Chess, 1949; Forensic Psychiatry, 1952; Handbook of Parliamentary Procedure, 1954; Guide to Medical Writing, 1956. Contbr to med and popupar mags. Home: POB 500, Cedar Grove, NJ. Office: Essex Co Overbrook Hosp, Cedar Grove, NJ.

DAVIDSON, Irving, US, attorney, educator, humorist; b. Novidvor, Vilna Guberne, Pol, Jan 15, 1904; s. Edward and Lillian (Amstibovski) Shilupsky; in US since 1906; BSS, CCNY, 1924; LLB, Fordham Law Sch, 1928; LLD; m. Adele Pearlman, July 2, 1939; c: Judith Liebermann, Janet Davidson. Atty, educ, humorist, since 1931; prin, rel sch, Park Ave Syn, NY; lectr, contemporary J wit and humor, J Cen Lecture Bur of JWB, NYC. Pres, NY Natural Hygiene Soc; 2nd vice-pres, Amer Natural Hygiene Soc; dir: activities: Oheb Shalom Cong, Newark, NJ; Temple Ansche Chesed, NYC; life mem, ZOA. Hobbies: humor, health, pedg. Home and office: 1810 Ave N, New York, NY.

DAVIDSON, Irwin D, US, jurist; b. NYC, Jan 2, 1927; s. Lafayette and Tillie (Bechstein); BS, NYU, 1927; LLB, 1928; m. Berenice Feltenstein, June 4, 1936; c: James, Mark; m. 2nd, Marion Doniger, May 31, 1965. Judge, Supr Court of NY State, since 1957; pvt practice, 1929-35; counsel, NY State Leg Bill Drafting Commn, 1935-37; mem, NY State Leg, 1937-48; judge, Court of Spec Sessions, 1949-54; mem, US House of Rep, 1955-56. Trustee: FJP: Rodeph Sholem Temple; Amer Hosp, Denver; NY Philanthropic League for Crippled Children; chmn, speakers bur, UJA, 1954; Manhattan Fed for Support of J Philanthropies, 1951-54; bd mem, Visitors for Wash Square Coll of Arts and Sci; mem: NY State and NYC Bar Assns; NY Co Lawyers Assn; Metrop Trial Lawyers Assn; Army-Navy Union; Tau Delta Phi. Author: The Jury is Still Out, 1959. Hobbies: painting, travel. Home: 785 Fifth Ave, New York, NY. Office: 100 Centre St, New York, NY.

DAVIDSON, Joseph Terence, Isr, physician; b. Dublin, Ir, May 3, 1928; s. Aaron and Bunie (Cohen); in Isr since 1959; LRCP, Glasgow U; FRCS, London; m. Debora Gillon; c: Claire Birkham, Philip, Elyad. Chief phys, anesthesiologist, sr lectr, Hadassah U Hosp, since 1959. RAF, 1952-54. Pres, Isr Soc of Anesthesiologists. Recipient: research f, NIH. Home: 6 Berekhyau St, Jerusalem, Isr. Office: Hadassah U Hosp, Jerusalem, Isr.

DAVIDSON, Morris, US, artist, educator, author; b. Rochester, NY, Dec 16, 1898; s. Harris and Sophie (Ellis); studied: Art Inst of Chgo; Paris; m. Anne Schlessinger, Aug 24, 1927; c: Eric, Lucy. Dir, Morris Davidson Sch of Modern Painting, Provincetown, since 1935; fmr instr: Minneapolis Sch of Art; Roerich Mus Sch; fmr head, dept of painting, Schenectady Mus; cons, art educ, Schenectady Public Sch System, 1943-60. One-man shows: San Diego Mus; Baltimore Mus of Art;

Pa Acad Fine Arts; Kleeman Gal; perm collections: Sarah Lawrence Coll; NYU; Bezalel Mus, Jerusalem. Fmr pres, Fed of Modern Painters and Sculptors; mem, bd trustees, Provincetown Art Assn, 1961-63. Author: Understanding Modern Art, 1931; Painting for Pleasure, 1938; An Approach to Modern Painting, 1948; Painting with Purpose, 1964. Home: 7 Orchard Terr, Piermont, Rockland Co, NY. Studio: Miller Hill Rd, Provincetown, Mass.

DAVIDSON, Robert M, US, business exec, atty; b. NYC, Feb 1, 1904; s. Maurice and Blanche (Reinheimer); BA, magna cum laude, Harvard Coll, 1925, LLB, Law Sch, 1928; m. Luise Scheiner, Sep 29, 1931; c: Bruce, Marcia. Pres, Sanib Corp since 1962; asst counsel: Magistrates Courts Inves, 1930; Invest of Affairs of NYC, 1931; mem, law firm: Davidson and Mann, 1936-48; Maurice P and Robert M Davidson, 1948-52; spec counsel, law firm, Greenbaum, Wolff & Ernst, 1953-54; with Amer Overseas Finance, 1956-58. Pres, Woodrow Wilson lodge, B'nai B'rith, 1953-55; mem: exec comm and comm on leg, Citizens Union, NYC; Amer Bar Assn; NY Co Lawyers Assn; club: Harvard, LI. Home: 117-01 Park Lane S, Kew Gardens, NY.

DAVIDSON, Sidney, US, accountant, educator; b. Chgo, Ill, May 29, 1919; s. Mendel and Eva (Slosberg); MBA, U of Mich, 1941, PhD, 1950; m. Freda Sendler, June 23, 1946; c: Jonathan, Victoria. Arthur Young prof, acctnt, grad sch of bus, U of Chgo, dir, inst profsl acctnt, both since 1962, fac mem since 1958, acting dean since 1969; prof, Johns Hopkins U, 1949-58. Lt, USNR, 1942-46. Pres, Amer Acctnt Assn, 1968-69; mem: Amer Inst CPA's; Ill Soc CPA's; Amer Econ Assn; Oprs Research Soc Amer; club: Quadrangle. Author: Studies in Accounting Theory, 1962; Hand-Book of Modern Accounting, 1970; contbr to profsl jours. Home: 5719 S Kenwood, Chicago, Ill. Office: U of Chgo, Chicago, Ill.

DAVIDSON, Sol M, US, business exec, author; b. Newark, NJ, Dec 13, 1924; s. Isidor and Helen (Black); BA, La State U, 1946; MA, NYU, 1954, PhD, 1959; m. Hermia Goldfinger, June 19, 1949; c: Cliff, Ron, Brian. Vice-pres, dir, oprs, Dial Finance Co, since 1967, with co since 1959; asst educ dir, Beneficial Finance since 1959, with co since 1948. USN, 1945-47. Vice-pres, Ia Bd of Intl Educ; mem: comty relations comm, JWF; adv bd, B'nai B'rith; ACLU; fmr: chmn: Hum Rights Comm; Adult Educ Adv Council, Public Schs; Broadlawns Hosp Adv Comm, all in Des Moines. Author: The Cultivation of Imperfection, 1965; The Power of Friction, 1967; contbr to mags. Recipient: award, Des Moines, Public Schs, 1963. Spec interest: student of comic strips, book in progress. Home: 5200 Shriver Ave, Des Moines, Ia. Office: 207 9 St, Des Moines, Ia.

DAVIES, Arthur Michael, Isr, physician; b. Wallasey, Eng, Feb 11, 1924; s. Samuel and Dora (Frost); in Irr since 1950; MB, BCh, MD, U Manchester; MRCS; LRCP, U of London, Eng; m. Betty Benjamin, July 15, 1946; David, Jonathan. Head, dept prev ecology, Heb U Med Sch, since 1964; fmr: research f in preventive med, Harvard Med Sch, 1956-57; coord, USPHS, Rep of Liberia, 1960-61; chief epidemiologist, Isr Min of Health, 1958-60, visiting sci, USPHS; mem, expert comms, study groups, WHO. Capt, RAMC, 1947-49. F: Amer Public Health Assn; Royal Soc of Med; Royal Soc of Tropical Diseases and Hygiene; mem: exec, Intl Epidemiological Assn; sci council on epidemology, Intl Soc of Card. Ed bd: Medical Care; contbr to profsl jours; co-ed: Health Services in Developing States, 1968. Home: 12 Ussishkin St, Jerusalem, Isr. Office: POB 1172, Jerusalem, Isr.

DAVIES, J Clarence, US, business exec; b. NYC, Mar 6, 1912; s. J Clarence and Rosalie (Loewi); AB, Dartmouth Coll, 1934; m. Helen Wolfe, June 10, 1934; c: J Clarence III, Alan. Pres and dir: J Clarence Davies Realty Co, Inc; Fordham-Concourse Corp, 1934-58, and since 1962; mem, bd trustees, Excelsior Empire Savings Bank, since 1964. Lt, USAF, 1942-45; maj gen, USAF Res, since 1966. Chmn, Housing and Redevl Bd, NYC, 1960-62; pres, United Neighborhood Houses; NY Diabetes Assn; bd trustees: Cong Shaarey Tefila; Horace Mann Sch for Boys; Home for Aged and Infirm Heb of NY; mem: Amer Soc Real Estate Counselors; Amer Inst and NY State Soc Real Estate Appraisers; NY Real Estate Bd; Natl and State of NY Real Estate Assns; Commerce and Ind Assn of NY; NY State C of C; Theta Chi; fmr: bd dirs: NY State Comm on Discrimination in Housing; chmn: Air Reserve Policy Bd, Air Defense Command; steering comm, NYC Youth Bd; pres: Citizens Housing & Planning Council, NYC, chmn bd dirs; Manhattan chap, Reserve Offs Assn; vice-

pres: YM-YWHA, trustee; NY chap, AJComm, mem, exec comm; bd trustees, Montefiore Hosp, vice-chmn, exec comm; mem: US Lawn Tennis Assn, fmr pres; natl enrollment comm, Dartmouth Coll; clubs: Dartmouth Coll; Harmonie; Racquet. Home: 215 E 68 St, New York, NY. Office: 331 Madison Ave, New York, NY.

DAVIS, Bernard David, US, physician, educator; b. Franklin, Mass, Jan 7, 1916; s. Harry and Tillie (Shain); AB, Harvard U, 1936, MD, 1940; m. Elizabeth Menzel, June 19, 1956; c: Franklin, Jonathan, Katherine. Adele Lehman prof, bact phys, Harvard Med Sch, dept head, 1958-68; intern, f, Johns Hopkins Hosp, 1940-42; commissioned off, USPHS, 1942-54; prof, pharm, NYU Med Sch, 1954-57; head, dept of bact and immunology, Harvard Med Sch, 1957-68. Mem, med adv bd, Heb U-Hadassah Med Sch; mem: Amer Soc Biol Chem; Amer Soc Microbiol; Amer Soc Cell Biol; Amer Acad of Arts and Sci; Natl Acad Sci. Contbr to sci jours. Recipient: Waksman medal, Soc of Amer, Bacts, NJ br, 1954. Home: 23 Clairemont Rd, Belmont, Mass. Office: Harvard Med Sch, Boston, Mass.

DAVIS, Bernard David, Eng, accountant; b. London, Eng, Sep 27, 1929; s. Harry and Rose (Bloch). Chartered acctnt since 1951. RAF, 1951-53. Chmn: Eur bd, World Union for Progressive Judaism; vice-chmn, Reform Syns of Gt Brit; jt treas, Leo Baeck Coll; fmr: chmn, SW Essex Reform Syn, 1956-59, pres, 1959-65. Home and office: 100 Ashmill St, London, NW1, Eng.

DAVIS, Bernard G, US, publisher, editor; b. Pittsburgh, Pa, Dec 11, 1906; s. Charles and Sarah (Harris); att: U of Pa; Columbia U; BS, U of Pittsburgh, 1927; m. Sylvia Friedman, Nov 20, 1930; c: Joel, Carol Teten. Pres: Davis Publications Inc, since 1957; Sci and Mechs Publ, since 1959; fmr: pres, dir, WB Ziff, 1946-57, with firm since 1927. Chmn and dir, PR comm, J Fed, Chgo, 1945-52; treas: ZO, Chgo, 1940-42; Magazine Publ Assn, since 1959; dir, J Fed, Chgo, 1943-52; mem: natl panel of arbitrators, Amer Arbitration Assn, since 1956; Amer Council on Educ for Journalism; Pi Beta; Sigma Delta Chi; clubs: Ocean Beach. Home: 15 Chateau Chaumont, 2180 Ibis Isle Rd W, Palm Beach, Fla. Office: 229 Park Ave S, New York, NY.

DAVIS, Daniel L, US, rabbi; b. Baltimore, Md, Aug 22, 1903; s. Isaac and Fannie (Levin); BA, Johns Hopkins U, 1923; ordained rabbi, HUC, 1926; hon DD, HUC-JIR, 1961; m. Sonia Kochman, June 23, 1926; c: Baruch. Dir, NY Fed of Reform Syns, since 1947; rabbi: Cong Beth-El, Hammond, Ind, 1926-27; Cong Shaarai Shomayim, Lancaster, Pa, 1927-47; club: Johns Hopkins. Author: Understanding Judaism, 1958. Home: 320 Riverside Dr, New York, NY. Office: 838 Fifth Ave, New York, NY.

DAVIS, Eli, Isr, physician; b. Birzai, Lith, June 1, 1908; s. Haim and Rose (Bergel); in Isr since 1946; BSc, U of Manchester, 1919, MSc, 1920; MB, BCh, 1933, MD, 1935; m. Elise Rosenbloom, Jan, 1939; c: Naomi, Chaim. Head, med outpatient dept C, Hadassah Hosp, since 1951; mem staff since 1947; asso prof of med, Heb U-Hadassah Med Sch, since 1965; fmr: head, dept of med, St Andrews Hosp, Bow, London, 1942-46. Dep dir, Hadassah Med Org, 1946-48, dir, 1946-51; bd of mgmt, Heb U-Hadassah Med Sch, 1948-51; comm: Eur Microcirculation Soc; Isr Rheumatic Fever Soc; secy, Isr Microcirculation Soc; chmn, org comm, ZF, Eng, 1940; mem: Royal Coll of Phys, London; Isr Health Council, 1949-51. Author: Rheumatic Fever-Clinical, Ecological and Familial Aspects, 1969; co-author: Clinical Capillary Microscopy, 1966; contbr to sci jours. Recipient: $10,000 award, Hadassah Research Fund, 1951. Hobbies: walking, J folk art. Home: 9 Shlomo Molcho St, Jerusalem, Isr. Office: Hadassah Rothchild U Hosp, Jerusalem, Isr.

DAVIS, Elliott, US, geologist, business exec; b. Kansas City, Mo, Jan 9, 1915; s. Herman and Miriam (Kahan); BS, U of Okla, 1937; m. Hannah Foreman, 1937; c: Barry, Lee, Mark, Timothy. Pres, Alliance Bus Inves Co, since 1959; secy: Davis Inds, since 1959; Interstate Royalties of Okla, since 1949; mgr, New Era Royalties, since 1954; 1st geologist, Shamrock Oil and Gas, Amarillo, Tex, 1936-37. Maj, US Army, 1942-45. Mem, natl bd, Regional Assn of Small Bus Invest, since 1959; pres: Downtown Tulsa Unlimited, 1965-67; Temple Isr, 1966-68; B'nai B'rith, Okla, 1954; B'nai B'rith, Tulsa, 1953; J Comty Council, 1955-57; exec comm, SW region, ADL; mem: Amer Assn of Petroleum Geologists; Tulsa Geological Soc; Phi Beta Kappa; Sigma Gamma Epsilon.

Recipient: Bronze Star. Home: 4444 S Zunis St, Tulsa, Okla. Office: 510 McFarlin Bldg, Tulsa, Okla.

DAVIS, Esther Michelson, US, artist, art cons, editor; b. Brunswick, Ga, Aug 10, 1893; d. Morris and Zella (Hirsehfield) Michelson; tchrs dipl, Parsons Art Sch, NYC, 1914; att: New Sch for Social Research, NY: Columbia Grad Sch; studied with Norman Raeben, Chaim Gross; m. Harold Davis, Apr 30, 1919 (decd); c: Richard, James, Betty Cummins. Dir, Comty Gal, NYC; fmr: art dir, advt mgr: Lane Bryant, NYC, 1917-19; Bamberger's, NJ, 1919-20; free-lance artist, cons, ed, 1922-69. One-man shows, painting and sculpture: New Gal; Bodley Gal; Roko Gal; perm collections: Colby; Syracuse Mus; Drew U. Mem: Amer Acad Political and Social Sci; Advt Club, NY; participant, benefit art shows, Hashomer Hatzair; exhb mem: Artists Equity; Amer Fed of Art and Allied Artists; past pres, United Order of True Sisters. Ed: The Echo, 1925-45; Art Books, 1965-69; contbr to mags, press. Recipient: 1st prize, 4 group shows, New Sch for Social Research. Home and studio: 10 Park Ave, New York, NY.

DAVIS, (Ben David), Gerald, Isr, physicist; b. London, Eng, Aug 30, 1928; s. David and Mary (Levene); in Isr since 1954; BSc, hons, Imperial Coll, London, 1950; ARCS, 1950, PhD, 1953; m. Irene Dombrowsky, 1953; c: Michael. Head, nuclear physics div, Isr Atomic Energy Commn, since 1961, on staff since 1958; psso prof, physics dept, Bar-Ilan U, since 1963; lectr in physics, Technion, 1954-58, head nuclear engr lab, 1958. Pres, Isr Phys Soc, 1969-70. Contbr to sci jours. Home: 25 Dubnov St, Tel Aviv, Isr. Office: Soreq Nuclear Research Cen, Yavneh, Isr.

DAVIS, Jacob, US, business exec; b. Pittsburgh, Pa, Oct 4, 1897; s. Barnett and Annie (Jacobs); BA, Harvard Coll, 1919; m. Florence Bachrach, June 21, 1924 (decd); c: Richard (decd), Caroline (decd), Suzanne Lubell; m. 2nd, Mildred Claster, Dec 30, 1952. Pres, Barnett Davis Inc, diamond importers. Pres: United J Fund, 1952-54; Council on J Educ, 1953-59; Coll of J Studies, 1953-62, hon pres since 1962; bd govs, Amer Assn of J Educ; bd of overseers, JTSA; clubs: Concordia; Westmoreland Country; Century; Harvard. Home: 128 N Craig St, Pittsburgh, Pa. Office: Clark Bldg, Pittsburg, Pa.

DAVIS, Maurice, US, rabbi; b. Warwick, RI, Dec 15, 1920; s. Jacob and Sadie (Marks); AB, U of Cincinnati, 1945; BHL, MHL, HUC, 1949; LHD, honoris causa, Marian Coll, 1969; m. Marion Cronbach, Dec 10, 1944; c: Jay, Michael. Rabbi: J Comty Cen, White Plains, since 1967; Indianapolis Heb Cong, 1956-67; Euclid Ave Temple, 1949-51; Temple Adath Isr, 1951-56; chaplain, USPHS Hosp for Drug Addicts, Lexington, Ky, 1951-56. Found, pres, Ind Commn on Hum Relations, 1961-64; bd dirs: Westchester MH Assn; natl: AJCong; HUC Alumni; natl chmn, CCAR commn on family, 1962-67; dean, natl leadership training inst, Natl Fed Temple Youth, 1951-64; hon chmn, NAACP, 1965-66; govs commn: Youth, Aging and Aged, Migratory Labor, 1961-67. Contbr to rel jours. Home: 56 Winslow Rd, White Plains, NY. Study: 252 Soundview Ave, White Plains, NY.

DAVIS, Moshe, Isr, historian, educator; b. Bklyn, NY, June 12, 1916; s. William and Ida (Schenker); in Isr since 1959; BS, Tchrs Coll, Columbia, 1936; BJP, Tchrs Inst, JTSA, 1937, MHL, 1942; ordained rabbi, 1942; PhD, Heb U, Jerusalem, 1945; m. Lottie Keiser, June 11, 1939; c: Zev, Tamar Benzur. Head, Inst of Contemporary Jewry, Heb U, since 1959, asso prof, since 1963, Stephen S Wise chair, Amer J hist and Insts, since 1965; research prof, Amer J hist, JTSA, since 1964; dir, Amer J Rel Archives, since 1967; co-dir, Amer J Hist Cen, since 1953; fmr: provost, JTSA, 1950-59, staff mem since 1942; visiting prof, Heb U, Jerusalem, 1959-63; prog ed: Eternal Light, NBC radio, 1942-52; Frontiers of Faith, NBC-TV, 1951-53. Vice-pres: Amer J Hist Soc; mem: publ comm, J Public Soc; exec mem: Isr Hist Soc; Assn for J Demography and Stats; found: Histadrut Hanoar Haivri, 1936; Leaders Training f, 1946; mem: Amer Acad of J Research; Amer Hist Assn; NEA; Natl Council for J Educ. Author: Jewish Religious Life and Institutions in America, 1949; The Shaping of American Judaism, 1951; The Emergence of Conservative Judaism, 1963; co-author: The Birthday of the World, 1959; ed: Mordecai M Kaplan Jubilee Volumes, 1951; Israel: Its Role in Civilization, 1956; co-ed: The Writing of American Jewish History, 1957; The Illustrated History of the Jews, 1964; The Regional History Services of the American Jewish History Center, vol I, 1963; cons ed and contbr, Ency Judaica, 1968; contbr, Ency Britannica. Recipient:

Lena Sokolow f, 1937-38; Louis LaMed award, 1951; Guggenheim f, 1956, 1959. Hobbies: piano, dramatics, art. Home: 14 Balfour St, Jerusalem, Isr. Office: Inst of Contemporary Jewry, Heb U, Jerusalem, Isr.

DAVIS, Moshe, Eng, educator; b. Eng, June 19, 1926; s. Israel and Rebecca (Hurwitz); m. Lola Goldfinger, Jan 30, 1949; c: Esther, Naomi. Dir, educ, JNF, Gt Brit and Ir, since 1960, PR off, ZF, Gt Brit and Ir, since 1968. Sgt-maj, Brit Army, 1945-48; chaplain, 1954-60. Author: Journeys of the Children of Israel, 1966. Hobby: sculpture. Home: 5 Regents Court, Stonegrove, Edgware, Middlesex, Eng. Office: Rex House, Regent St, London, Eng.

DAVIS, Norman, US, business exec; b. NYC, July 13, 1918; s. Louis and Sayde (Kaplan), U of Va, 1939; m. Leslie, Friedman, July 22, 1944; c: Warren, Bruce, Gary. Res vice-pres, Walston & Co Inc; registered repr, Merrill Lynch, Pierce, Fenner & Smith, 1945-56. Maj, USAAC, 1941-44. Pres: Natl J Hosp; Allied J Council; chmn, Rocky Mnt Inves Bankers Assn, 1962. Recipient: DFC, 1942; Air Medal, 1942; Pres Citation, 1942. Home: 222 Cherry St, Denver, Colo. Office: Denver US Natl Bank Cen, Denver, Colo.

DAVIS, Sam, US, manufacturer; b. Providence, RI, Feb 28, 1894; s. George and Fanny (Munter); m. Beatrice Sass, Apr 28, 1930; c: Malcolm, George, Theodore. Pres: Universal Found; Diana Found; Diana Corset and Brassiere Co; Belmar Brassiere and Girdle Co; dir, Blauner's Inc. Vice-pres: ZOA; Temple Beth El, Cedarhurst, hon; co-chmn, Bonds for Isr, S Shore Five Towns; natl council, JDC; adv council, UJA; bd dirs: W Side Inst Syn, NYC; Garment Cen Syn, NYC; FJP; J Fed of Cedarhurst; Brotherhood-in-Action. Home: 6 Auerbach Lane, Laurence, LI, NY. Office: 358 Fifth Ave, New York, NY.

DAYAN, David, Isr, author, editor; b. Tel Aviv, Isr, Mar 29, 1935; s. Jacob and Malka (Bistry); att Heb U, Jerusalem, 1962-66; m. Haua Gauze, Sep 9, 1958; c: Esther, Jacob, Rina. Sr ed, radio progs, since 1965; asst-ed, IDF weekly, since 1968; fmr: asst-ed, Gadna weekly, 1956-60; corresp, Haaretz daily, 1960-62; ed, Gali-Zahal, IDF, 1956-68. Sgt, IDF youth brigade. Author: Strike First, 1968; From Hermon to Suez, 1967; Security Without Peace, 1968; A Guerra dos Seis Dias, 1967. Home: 6 Urim St, Holon, Isr. Office: 1 Ein Dor St, Tel Aviv, Isr.

DAYAN, Moshe, Isr, government official; b. Kibbutz Degania, Isr, May 20, 1915; s. Shmuel and Devora; att sr off sch, Eng, 1951; BSc, School of Law and Econ, Tel Aviv U, LLB, 1959; m. Ruth Schwartz, 1935; c: Yael Sion, Ehud, Assaf. Min of Defense, since 1967; MK, Min of Agric, 1959-64; MK, Rafi party, 1965, Lab party since 1968. Haganah, 1928-48; dep cdr, Wingate's Raiders, 1937; co-found, Palmach, 1941; instr, J parachutist units in Eur, 1942-45; 1t col, cdr of oprns, IDF, 1948; repr, IDF, Rhodes peace talks, 1949; chief, gen staff, IDF, Sinai Campaign, 1958. Author: Diary of the Sinai Campaign, 1966. Home: 11 Yoab St, Zahala, Tel Aviv, Isr. Office: Min of Defense, Tel Aviv, Isr.

DAYAN, Ruth, Isr, home industries exec; b. Merhavia, Isr, Mar 6, 1917; att handicraft courses, London, 1950-53; m. Moshe Dayan, 1935; c: Yael Sion, Ehud, Assaf. Mgn dir, Maskit Ltd, since 1954. Fmr: head, crafts dept, Isr min of Lab; fmr mem: Kibbutz Shimron; Moshav Nahalal. Prin contrib, promoted home ind in frontier settlements during mass immigration, 1949. Home: 11 Yoab St, Zahala, Tel Aviv, Isr. Office: 32 Ben Yehuda St, Tel Aviv, Isr.

DEAN, Abner, US, artist, author; b. NYC, Mar 18, 1910; s. Louis and Deana (Grozcky) Epstein; BA, Dartmouth Coll, 1931; att Natl Acad of Design, NYC. Artist and sculptor. Author: It's a Long Way to Heaven, 1945; What Am I Doing Here? 1947; And on the Eighth Day...., 1949; Come As You Are, 1952; Cave Drawings for the Future, 1954; Wake Me When It's Over, 1955; Not Far From the Jungle, 1956; Abner Dean's Naked People, 1963; contbr to public and ind periodicals. Spec interests: building systems, mass produced housing. Mem: Soc of Illus. Home: 166 E 61 St, New York, NY.

DECTER, Aaron, US, rabbi, communal leader; b. Odessa, Russ, Aug 26, 1913; s. Jacob and Pauline (Fischel); in US since 1920; BA, Yeshiva U, 1933; MHL, ordained rabbi, JTSA, 1937; candidate, PhD, Dropsie Coll; grad studies: Harvard U; Boston U; Heb U; Sorbonne; m. Penina Goldman; c: Avi, Gabriel; adopted c: Jeffrey, Michael, Sylvia Ledis. Rabbi, Garment Cen Syn, NYC, since 1967; natl coord, Amer Histadrut Devl Found, since 1967; fmr: rabbi: Adath Shalom Syn, Phil, 1960-67; Comty Syn, Atlantic City, NJ, 1951-54; Temple Beth Isr, Phila, 1940-44. Sr chaplain, US Army, Eur, 1943-46; active in war-time Haganah activities, 1943-46. Delg, WZC, 1939; official observer: Anglo-Amer Commn, 1946; UN Spec Comm on Pal, Jerusalem, 1947; spec asst to natl exec dir, coord of activities, Penn-Seaboard Region, JNF; natl secy, Amer Comm for Writers' Cen in Isr, 1956-69; mem: exec, Histadrut Ivrit, Heb Culture Found; RA; NY Bd of Rabbis; Phila Bd of Rabbis; B'nai B'rith, Fashion Capitol lodge; fmr: natl admn council, ZOA; natl exec, League for Rel Lab in Isr; natl council, JDC; natl org comm, Emergency Conf to Save J People of Eur; mem: J Hist Society; NAACP; J Execs League; NCCJ; Natl Assoc for J Educ; Rabb F of the Reconstructionist; club: Linwood Country. Ed, J Record of Can, 1935-36; ed and ed dir, Israel Speaks, 1950-56; contbr to periodicals. Recipient: citations: Protestant Mag; NCCJ; man-of-the-year, Isr Histadrut campaign. Hobbies: tennis, chess. Home: 2500 Johnson St, Riverdale, NY. Study: 205 W 40 St, New York, NY.

DEECH, Ruth Lynn, Can, educator; b. London, Eng, Apr 29, 1943; d. Josef and Dora (Fraenkel); MA, St Anne's Coll, Oxford, 1965; MA, Brandeis U; called to Bar, Inner Temple, 1967; m. John Deech, July 23, 1967. Asst prof, fac of law, U of Windsor, Ontario; fmr, staff, Royal Law Commn, London. Past pres, Oxford J Soc. Contbr to Can Bar Rev. Home: 1933 Riverside Dr W, Windsor, Ontario, Can.

DEGANI, Meir H, US, physicist, educator; b. Warsaw, Pol, Jan 4, 1909; s. Dov and Haya (Goldman); in US since 1928; BS, MIT, 1932, MS, 1941, ScD, 1942; m. Edith Schumacher, Dec 23, 1948; c: Vivian, Lynne. Prof, physics, chmn, sci dept, SUNY Maritime Coll, since 1946, acting dean, 1966-67; asst prof, geophys, Pa State U, 1942-43; chief instr, meteorology, Amer Export Airlines, 1943-44. Aerographer, USN, 1944. Mem: Amer Phys Soc; AAUP; Amer Geophys Union; Amer Technion Soc; LZOA; Heb Circle of Manhattan; Amer Friends of Heb U. Author: Astronomy Made Simple, 1955; contbr to profsl jours. Recipient: medal, NY State. Office: SUNY Maritime Coll, Ft Schuyler, NY.

de GROOT, Ralph, Eng, underwriter; b. London, Eng, Sep 30, 1920; s. Moses and Rose (Rosetski); BCom, LSE, 1941; m. Lily Sherr, 1968; five c. Mem, pres div, Mfrs Life Ins Co of Can, since 1955; gen secy, Zionist Cen Council, Manchester, 1949-55, pres. British Army, 1941-46. Dir, JPA; mem: Achdut; Moses Caster lodge, B'nai B'rith. Hobby: archaeol. Home: 16 New Hall Rd, Salford, Eng. Office: St Andrews House, Portland St, Manchester, Eng.

DEHAN, Meyer, Isr, executive; b. Tiberias, Isr, Apr 18, 1910; s. Michael and Channa; att Amer U, Beirut; m. Simcha Cohen, June 30, 1931; c: Dalia Goren, Shibolette Keuhller, Ruth Brookman. Dir, Kupat Holim Maccabi, Jerusalem, since 1963. Fmr: secy, Sudan Govt, 1927-31; chief clerk, Pal Govt dist courts, 1931-35; mgr, Petco-Bleico, 1936-46. Mem exec, Isr-Amer Friendship Soc; Isr UN orgs; clubs: Lions, bd dir; KP, chancellor, cdr. Author: Planning is Free Enterprise. Spec interests: music, touring, langs, ME hist. Home: 14-16 Ussishkin St, Jerusalem, Isr. Office: 5 King George St, Jerusalem, Isr.

DeJONG, Louis, Netherlands, historian; b. Amsterdam, Apr 24, 1914; s. Godfried and Batsy (Aleng); PhD, U Amsterdam, 1953; m. Elizabeth Cost Budde, June 9, 1939; c: Joost, Matthys, Roelof, Annemarie. Dir, Netherlands State Inst for War Documentation, since 1945; prof, contemporary hist, Netherlands Sch of Econ, Rotterdam; fgn ed, Groene Amsterdammer, weekly, 1938-40; contributing ed, broadcaster, Netherlands Govt Bc, Radio Oranje, London, 1940-45. Mem: Royal Netherlands Acad Sci; fgn policy council, Dutch Lab Party. Author: Je Maintiendrai, 4 vols, 1941-45; De Duitse Vijfde Colonne in de Tweede Wereldoorlog, 5 vols, 1953; De Bezetting, 5 vols; Het Koninkrijk der Nederlanden in de tweede Wereldoorlog, first 2 vols, 1969; mem; ed bd, Delta, Dutch quarterly; mem bd, Het Parool, daily. Recipient: Off of Order of Orange-Nassau. Home: Lijnbaansgracht 294, Amsterdam, Netherlands. Office: Herengracht 474, Amsterdam, Netherlands.

DEKEL, Efraim, Isr, government official; b. Lityn, Russ, Nov 15, 1903; s. Moshe and Sheindel (Geitelman) Krasner; in Isr since 1921; m. Shoshana Alyagon, Dec 5, 1931; c:

Ram, Nurit Az, Ruth Kritchman. Ret. Dir gen, Jaffa Port 1952-66; fmr: served Pal Police, 1922-32; commr, Tel Aviv Fire Brig, 1937-53; chief, Isr Fire Brig, 1943-53; dir, Navy sect, Min of Defense, 1950-52, with org since 1949. Cdr info service, Haganah 1925-47; JA repr on Gen Wingate's staff, 1938; cdr, Bricha, 1946-48. Author: haKabaut, 1945; haKabaut haMaasit, 1952; Alilot Shai, 1953; Shai-The Exploits of Haganah Intelligence in Palestine, 1959; beNetivei haBricha, 2 vols, 1959; haKabaut Bimei Shalom VeSh'at Herum, 1960; Sridei-Cherev, 2 vols, 1963. Home: 20 Amsterdam Ave, Tel Aviv, Isr.

DELMAN, J David, US, attorney; b. NYC, May 22, 1899; s. Moses and Sarah (Samler); BA, CCNY, 1919; DJ, NYU, 1923; m. Ida Garber, 1927; c: Joseph, Blossom. Pvt practice since 1924. US Army, 1918-19. Hon pres, Natl Council of Young Isr; dir: JWB; J Comty House, Bensonhurst, NY; co-found, UJA, NY, 1946; del, Amer J Conf, 1943; mem: admn comm, JDC; exec comm, AJCong; mem: NY Co Lawyers Assn; club: Sioux lodge, KP, chancellor cdr. Lawyers; Comty, pres. Contbr to mags. Home: 135 Ave P, Brooklyn, NY. Office: 130 W 42 St, New York, NY.

DELVALLE, Frank, Netherlands, Antilles; communal leader; b. Curacao, Sep 7, 1910; s. Elias and Sarah (Penso); m. Rebecca Robles, Mar 22, 1953; c: Sheila, Susan. Dir, Salinja Trading Co, 1967-68; comptroller, Marchena, Moren and Co, 1947-68. Pres: Cong Mikve Isr Emanuel, since 1967; B'nai B'rith, Curacao, 1968; Curacao Lions Club, 1952, 1955. Hobby: painting. Home: Mahaaiweg 26, Willemstad, Curacao, Netherlands Antilles. Office: Heerenstraat 23, Willemstad, Curacao, Netherlands Antilles.

DEMBITZ, Lewis N, US, economist; b. Wash, DC, Sep 1, 1910; s. A Lincoln and Sara (West); BA, George Wash U, 1930; MBA, Harvard U, 1932; m. Florence de Haas, May 10, 1937; c: Susan Katz, Abigail Meyer; m. 2nd, Grace Ralston; step c: Marian, Henry Halley. Dir, research, Carter H Golembe Assos Inc, since 1968; fmr: asso adv, div of research and stat, Federal Res Bd, 1956-65, staff mem since 1934; sr asso, Robert R Nathan Assos, Inc, 1966-68. Prin econ analyst, US Bd of Econ Warfare, London, 1943-45; US prin adv on Ger debts, Intergovt Study on Ger, London, 1950-51. Mem: Amer Finance Assn; Amer Econ Assn; Amer Stat Assn; ZOA. Contbr to profsl jours. Home: 3414 Garfield St NW, Washington, DC. Office: 1225 Connecticut Ave, Washington, DC.

DEMBO, Morris, US, government official; b. Bklyn, NY, June 20, 1918; s. Abraham and Yetta (Herschkowitz); BBS, CCNY, 1939; att Columbia U, 1939-42; U Pa, 1954-55; m. Doris Roth, Dec 23, 1946; c: Jonathan, Micah, Rose, Joshua. Research cons, Amer Emb, New Delhi, since 1968; vice-consul, Bombay, 1948-49; 2nd secy, Emb: Pretoria, 1949-53; Karachi, 1955-58; research analyst, State Dept, 1958-63; Isr secy: Emb Nairobi, 1963-65; New Delhi, 1966-68. Mem: Alumni Assn of CCNY; Amer Fgn Service Assn. Home: 4638 Spruce St, Philadelphia, Pa.

DEMUTH, Richard Holzman, US, international offical; b. NYC, Sep 11, 1910; s. Leopold and Dora (Holzman); AB, Princeton U, 1931; LLB, Harvard Law Sch, 1934; m. Eunice Burdick, June 14, 1947; c: Nancy Chase. Sr off, World Bank, Intl Bank for Reconstruction & Devl, since 1946, now dir, devl service dept; atty, Simpson, Thatcher & Bartlett, 1935-39; spec asst, Off of Solicitor Gen, 1939-42. Lt Col, US Army, 1942-46. Mem: adv comm, Woodrow Wilson Sch, Princeton U, 1957-66; budget comm, Health and Wfr Council, Wash DC, 1960-64; chmn, govt div, UJA, 1941-42; bd trustees, Hudson Guild, NYC, 1936-39. Mem: NY Bar Assn; Phi Beta Kappa; clubs: Metrop; Princeton, Wash DC and NY. Recipient: Legion of Merit, WW II. Home: 5404 Bradley Blvd, Bethesda, Md. Office: 1818 H Street, NW, Wash, DC.

DENHOF, Miki G, US, designer, editor; b. Trieste, It, Jan 1, 1912; d. Bernard and Olga (Krieger) Bardach; in US since 1938; att Gymnasium; pvt art sch, both Vienna; Reiman Art Sch, Berlin; m. Hans Denhof, Aug 1938. Asso ed, House and Garden Mag, since 1970; promotion art dir, The Condé- Nast Publ Inc, 1945-55; art ed, Glamour Mag, 1955-60, art dir, 1960-70. Works repr: Art Dirs Shows; Graphic Arts File Mus of Modern Art. Mem: Mus of Modern Art; Metrop Mus of Art; Opera Guild; ZOA; Guild Hall, E Hampton, NY. Home: 227 Central Park W, New York, NY. Office: 420 Lexington Ave, New York, NY.

DENNERY, Phyllis S, US, civic worker; b. NYC, Mar 25, 1919; d. Henry and Freida (Seydel) Sugarman; m. Moise Dennery, June 7, 1941; c: Harry, Richard. Mem, natl bd, Natl Council J Women, since 1959; natl conv chmn, 1959; natl delg comm, AJComm, since 1957; delg comm, JDC since 1955; pres, bd trustees, educ TV sta WYES TV, since 1967; mem: bd trustees: New Orleans Public Libr; Natl Citizens Comm for Public Bc, 1967-68; exec comm, Adult Educ Assn of La; bd dirs: Cultural Attraction Fund; JWF, 1958-62; New Orleans Urban League. Home: 2303 Broadway, New Orleans, La.

DE-PHILIPPE, Edis, Isr, singer; b. NYC; Found, dir, Isr Natl Opera since 1947; leading roles, Isr and abroad; produced and appeared in over 35 operas. Home: 88 Aluf David St, Ramat Hen, Isr. Office: Israel Natl Opera, 1 Allenby St, Tel Aviv, Isr.

DERE'I, Hananya, Isr, rabbi; b. Marakesh, Morocco, 1930; in Isr since 1950; ordained rabbi, High Yeshiva, Morocco, 1949; m. Ruth Amzaleg; c: Yoav, Rachel, Yehiel, Geula, Nissim. Rabbi to moshavim, appointed by Chief Rabbinate of Isr; fmrly active in immigration of Moroccan Jews to Isr. Prin contbr: Aids deserted J women to get rel divorce; found and converted ex-Jews in fmr Arab territory. Contbr to rel jours. Spec interests: Falashite, Karaite and Shomronite Jews. Home: 159 Sderot Yerushalaim, Yaffo, Isr.

DERESIEWICZ, Herbert, US, scientist, educator; b. Brno, Czech, Nov, 5, 1925; s. William and Lottie (Rappaport); in US since 1939; BME, CCNY, 1946; MS, Columbia U Sch of Engr, 1948, PhD, 1952; m. Evelyn Atlman, Mar 12, 1955; c: Ellen, Robert, William. Prof, mech engr, Columbia U, since 1962, mem fac since 1951, U f, 1949-50; mem, sr staff, applied physics lab, Johns Hopkins U, 1950-51; Fulbright Sr Research Scholar, It, 1960-61; Fulbright lectr, Weizmann Inst, Isr, 1966-67. Sgt, US Army, 1946-47. Mem: AAAS; Amer Soc Mech Engr; Seismological Soc Amer; NY Acad Scis; Sigma Xi; Tau Beta Pi. Home: 366 Broad St, Englewood, NJ. Office: Columbia U, New York, NY.

DERMAN, Herbert, US, pathologist; b. Bklyn, NY, May 22, 1921; s. Isidor and Lillian (Schwartzberg); BS, La State U, 1941, MD, 1943; m. Mary Coughlin, Apr 12, 1944; c: Letty, Ellen, Jane. Dir, City of Kingston Lab, since 1950; lectr, path, Albany Med Coll, since 1961; att path: Benedictine Hosp; Kingston Hosp; cons path, Vet Memorial Hosp, Margaretville Hosp; att path, Liberty Maimonides Hosp, 1958-64. US Amry WW II Chmn, Coll Amer Path; bd trustees: Kingston Savings Bank; Hudson Valley Philharmonic Soc, 1960-62; vice-chmn, Citizens Survey Comm, Ulster Co, since 1964; pres: Assn of Clinical Scis, 1961; NY State Soc Path; dipl: Amer Bd Path; Amer Soc Clinical Path; NY Acad Med; mem: NY Path Soc; NY State Soc Path; AMA; J Comty Cen, bd dir, 1952-62; B'nai B'rith. Contbr to med books, profsl jours. Home: RR 3, Kingston, NY. Office: City of Kingston Lab, Kingston, NY.

DERSHOWITZ, Alan Morton, US, attorney, educator, author; b. Bklyn, NY, Aug 1, 1938; s. Harry and Claire (Ringel); BA, magna cum laude, Bklyn Coll, 1959; LLB, magna cum laude, Yale Law Sch, 1962; m. Sue Barlach; c: Elon, Jamin. Prof,law, Harvard U, since 1967, mem fac since 1964; atty-at-law since 1962; law clerk to Justice Goldberg, US Supr Court, 1963-64. Treas, Boston Hillel; mem: Phi Beta Kappa; Order of Coif. Author, Psychoanalysis, Psychiatry and Law, 1967; ed-in-chief, Yale Law Jour, 1961-62; contbr to legal jours. Home: 21 Robinson St, Cambridge, Mass. Office: Harvard Law Sch, Cambridge, Mass.

DERSHOWITZ, Milton, A, US, rabbi; b. Bklyn, NY, Oct 31, 1910; s. Louis and Ida (Maultasch); BSS, CCNY, 1933; MS, 1934; ordained rabbi, Rabb Sem of Amer, 1936; m. Anne Deresiewicz, 1939; c: Alexander, Martin, Zachary. Chaplain, Middletown State Hosp, since 1954; tchr, Mesifta HS, Bklyn, 1933-37; rabbi: Ohev Zedek, Albany, 1937; Cong Adath Jeshurun, Newport News, Va, 1940-42; Cong Sons of Abraham, LaCrosse, Wis, 1942-44. Chaplain: Fort Eustis, Langley Field, Va, 1940-42; Camp McCoy, Wis, 1942-44. Mem, mid-E region, Assn of Mental Hosp Chaplains, 1962-63. Contbr to rel and Mh jours. Home: 188 W Main St, Middletown, NY. Study: Middletown State Hosp, Middletown, NY.

DESER, Stanley, US, physicist, educator; b. Rovno, Pol, Mar 19, 1931; s. Norman and Miriam (Melamed); BS, summa cum laude, Bklyn Coll, 1949; MA, Harvard, 1949, PhD, 1953; m. Elsbeth Klein; c: Toni, Clara, Abigail. Prof, physics, Brandeis U, since 1965, fac mem since 1958; mem: Inst Advanced Study, Princeton U, 1953-55; Inst Theoretical Physics, Copenhagen, 1955-57; lectr, Harvard, 1958. Mem: Amer Phys Soc; ed bd, Jour Math Phys, 1961-64. Recipient: fs: Parker, 1953; Jewett, 1954; NSF postdoc; Fulbright; Guggenheim. Home: 45 Whitney St, Newton, Mass. Office: Brandeis U, Waltham, Mass.

DESHE, Eliezer, Isr, business exec; b. Brno, Czech, Nov 30, 1922; s. Meshulam and Ada (Nadel) Dische; in Isr since 1939; att U London; Tel Aviv Law Sch; m. Yaffa Yakubovitz, Dec 25, 1945; c: Daniela Benary, Ari. Ins broker since 1958; fmr: dep commn of prisons, Min of Police, 1954-58. Maj, mil police, IDF, 1948-54. Chmn, Isr Assn of Ins Brokers; gov, Rotary dist 199, Isr; mem: Ins Council to Min of Finance; Assn for After-Care of Prisoners; B'nai B'rith. Hobby: music. Home: 12 Zfania St, Ramat Gan, Isr. Office: 41 Lilienblum St, Tel Aviv, Isr.

DESHE, Michael, Isr, teacher, author; b. Russ, May 27, 1915; s. Shachna and Malka (Nachamtzik) Eisenstadt; in Isr since 1925; tchrs cert, Tchrs Coll, Jerusalem, 1939; BA, Heb U, 1954; MA, Wayne State U, 1961; m. Yael Zimbal, Apr, 1944; c: Orit, Arnon. Tchr, HS and Seminary, since 1950; sup, elem schs. Lt, IDF, 1947-49. Author: Shaharit, 1941; Urim beLev Yam, 1946; Ad ha Yareach haZe, 1951; Orit Mesaperet, 1954; Da et haNegev, 1955; Sipurim veLikcham, critique, 1952; haNer vehaShemesh, children's stories, 1955; Mi Madlik et haBarak, 1958; laDuchiphat de Ichpat, both children's poems; Ulat Yamin haAdama, poems, 1958; Ron miShomron, children's stories, 1962; Yafe miKol Shir, poems, 1964; Alexander Ish haMidbar, 1969; Chinuch Lekraih Tova, 1969; contbr to jours, daily press. Mem: Authors Org; Histadrut. Recipient: Davar award, 1952. Hobby: gardening. Home: Shdema, Emek Sorek, Isr. Office: HS Seminary, Gedera, Isr.

DESHEN, Shlomo Avraham, Isr, social anthropologist; b. Frankfurt, Ger, June 13, 1935; s. Ludwig and Charlotte (Cohn) Idstein; in Isr since 1949; BA, Heb U, 1961; PhD, Manchester U, Eng, 1968; m. Hilda Goldberg, 1962; c: Eliezer, Elisha, Hillel. Lectr, social anthropology, Tel Aviv U, since 1968; rural sociol, Land Settlement Dept, 1961-64; asst, dept sociol, Heb U, 1960-61; research f, Manchester U, 1964-68. Sgt, IDF, 1954-56. Mem, Movement for Torah Judaism; hon mem, Assn of Immigrants from Djerba and S Tunisia. Author: Immigrant Voters in Israel, 1970; contbr to scholarly jours. Home: 73 Bait Ve'Gan St, Jerusalem, Isr. Office: Tel Aviv U, Ramat Aviv, Isr.

DESSAU, Gabor, It, geologist, geophysicist; b. Perugia, It, June 27, 1907; s. Bernardo and Emma (Goitein); (uncle Hermann Dessau, archeologist and epigraphist); att: U of Pisa; Technische Hochschule, Berlin; DEngr, mining, U of Rome, 1929. Chargé de cours, mineral deposits, U of Pisa, since 1957; fmr: i/c mineral investigations, It Bur of Mines, Sicily; asst, Politecnico,Turin; chief, geological and geophysical br, Gen Mining Inspectorate, It, E Afr, Addis Ababa; state geologist, mining engr, mining dept, Jaipur, India; geophysicist i/c, Geological Survey of India, Calcultta; chief geologist, It Geological Survey, Rome; chargé de cours, mineral deposits, U of Naples; UNESCO tech asst expert, Technion, Haifa; research f, dept geology, Harvard U; f, Inst of Sci, It; mem: It, Swiss, Fr, Geological Socs; It, Swiss, Brit Mineralogical Socs; Eur Assn of Exploration Geophysicists; Soc of Econ Geologists; Soc of Exploration Geophysicists; Amer Inst of Mining, Metal and Petroleum Engrs; Amer Geophysical Union; Can Inst of Mining and Metallurgy; Mining, Geological and Metallurgical Inst of India; fmr vice-pres, Eur Soc of Econ Geologists. Contbr sci papers to It and fgn profsl jours. Recipient: scholarship, Marco Besso Found, Rome, 1930; Premio Molon, It Geological Soc, Rome, 1935; title Libera Docenza, U of Rome, 1937; silver medal, Mining, Geological and Metalurgical Inst, India, 1948. Office: U of Pisa, Via S Maria 53, Pisa, It.

DESSER, Abraham A, US, government exec; b. Lask, Pol, May 31, 1902; s. David and Rose (Jacobs); m. Hanna Fried, Aug 20, 1941; c: Joan. Commnr, Fed Meditation and Conciliation Service, since 1952; intl rep, ILGWU, AFL, 1935-42; sup, collective bargaining research, Natl Ind Conf Bd, 1942-48; asst econ commnr, Econ Coop Admn, Paris, 1949-50; attaché, US Emb, Burma, 1951-52. Mem: Ind Relations Research Assn; Workmen's Circle; Dipl and Consular Offs Ret Inc. Contbr to profsl jours. Home: c/o NYU Fac Club, New

York, NY. Office: Fed Mediation and Conciliation Service, 26 Federal Plaza, New York, NY.

DESSLER, Nachum Wolf, US, rabbi, educational dir; b. Kelem, Lith, Feb 27, 1921; s. Elyohu and Bluma (Ziv); in US since 1940; att Telshe Yeshiva Coll, Telsche, Lith, 1934-40, Cleveland, O, 1943; m. Miriam Finger, June 5, 1945; six c. Rabbi, educ dir, Heb Acad of Cleveland, since 1943. Natl vice-pres: Torah Umesorah; Natl Yeshiva prins comm. Home: 2634 Bishop Rd, Wickliffe, O. Study: 1860 S Taylor Rd, Cleveland Hgts, O.

DETTELBACH, Arthur H, US, attorney,; b. Cleveland, O, Jan, 1904; s. Henry and Hattie (Hyman); AB,W Reserve U, 1924, LLB, 1926; m. Isobel Keller, June 1, 1929; c: John, Kenneth, Betsy. Pvt practice since 1926; pres, Electronics, Inc. Mem, bd of dirs, J Comty Center, since 1959; bd mem, AJComm, since 1952, chmn: Cleveland chap, 1957; UJA since 1948; Cleveland J Wfr, 1958; United World Federalists, 1958-61; Suburban Temple, 1954-61; mem: Cleveland Council of World Affairs; Zeta Beta Tau; B'nai B'rith; Tau Epsilon Rho; Delta Sigma Rho; Masons; clubs: Oakwood; City; Commerce. Home 2540 N Moreland Blvd, Shaker Hgts, O. Office: Leader Bldg, Cleveland, O.

DEUTCH, Sydney S, US, ophthalmologist; b. Liverpool, Eng, Mar 8 1906; s. Harris and Shana (Albert); in US since 1921; BS, Tufts U, 1931, MD, 1934; m. Marcella Seta, May 28, 1946; c: Jacqueline, Joann. Pvt practice since 1937; instr: Tufts U Med Sch; Boston U Med Sch; sr eye surg, Boston City Hosp; visiting eye surg: Union-St Annes Hosp; U Hosp, Boston; cons to Surg Gen, US Dept of Defense. Capt, US Army, 1943-46. Pres, Fall River Med Soc; vice-regent, Intl Coll Surgs; mem: Amer Coll Surgs; Amer Acad Ophthal; NE Ophthal Soc. Home and office: 321 N Main St, Fall River, Mass.

DEUTSCH, Alfred Leonard, US, business exec; b. NYC, Apr 13, 1914; s. Adolph and Nina (Warady); AB, U of Mich, 1934; JD, Detroit Coll of Law, 1937; m. Berice Rosenberg, Sep 17, 1946; c: Robert, Dennis, Morris. Pres, Amer Savings Assn; chmn, Citizens Mortgage Corp; pres, Mich Savings & Loan League, 1963; vice-chmn, Fed Home Loan Bank, Indianapolis, 1964-68. Lt, US Army, 1942-46. Treas, United J Charities; bd dirs: JWF; Sinai Hosp; past chmn, Allied J Campaign of Detroit; past pres: Cong B'nai Moshe; Children's Orthogenic Sch; mem, Phi Epsilon Pi; clubs: Standard-City; Savoyard; Franklin Hills Country. Hobbies: golf, music, art. Home: 1200 Ardmoor, Birmingham, Mich. Office: 600 Woodward, Detroit, Mich.

DEUTSCH, Babette, US, novelist, poet; b. NYC, 1895; d. Michael and Melanie (Fisher); BA, Barnard Coll, 1917; Hon DLitt, Columbia, 1946; m. Avraham Yarmolinsky; c: Adam, Michael. Lectr, poetry, Sch of Gen Studies, Columbia U, since 1944. Author: Banners, 1919; Honey Out of the Rock, 1925; A Brittle Heaven, 1926; In Such a Night, 1927; Potable Gold, 1929; Fire for the Night, 1930; Epistle to Prometheus, 1931; Mask of Silenus, 1933; This Modern Poetry, 1935; One Part Love, 1939; Heroes of the Kalevala, 1940; It's a Secret, 1941; Walt Whitman, Builder for America, 1941; The Welcome, 1942; Rogue's Legacy, 1942; Take Them, Stranger, 1944; The Reader's Shakespeare, 1946; Poetry in Our Time, 1952, 1956, 2nd ed, 1963; Animal, Vegetable, Mineral, 1954; Poetry Handbook, 1957, 3rd ed, 1969; Coming of Age: New and Selected Poems, 1959; Collected Poems 1919-1962, 1963; Poems of Samuel Taylor Coleridge, 1967; The Collected Poems of Babette Deutsch, 1969; trans, The Book of Hours, by Rilke; co-trans: Pushkin's Eugene Onegin; Two Centuries of Russian Verse, 1966. Mem: PEN; Natl Inst of Arts and Letters. Home: 300 W 108 St, New York, NY.

DEUTSCH, Samuel, US, educational dir, editor, publisher; b. NYC, Dec 30, 1912; s. Jochanan and Blanche (Zuckerbrod); BA, Yeshiva Coll, 1934; cert, NYU, 1935; att Training Bur for J Communal Service, 1939-41; m. Helen Sobel, June 13, 1943; c: Eli, Reena. Ed and publisher: J Current Events; educ dir: Oakland J Cen, Bayside NY; Heb Inst, Englewood, NJ, 1941-49; Temple Beth El Zedeck, Indianapolis, 1949-56; Oxford Circle J Comty Cen, Phila, 1956-59; Cong B'nai Isr, Woonsocket, RI, 1959. Exec comm, Educ Assembly of United Syn of Amer; corresp secy, Natl Council for J Educ. Author: Pupil's Guide to the Bible, 1955; The Jewish Calender, 1956; The Jewish Home, 1956; The Jewish Holidays, 1957. Home: POB 418, Oakland Garden Sta, Flushing, NY. Office: Oakland J Cent, Bayside, NY.

DeWOSKIN, Irvin S, US, business exec; b. St. Louis, Mo, Oct 27, 1909; s. Leon and Fannie (Prensky); BS, Wash U, St Louis; m. 1937, div, 1955; m. 2nd, Eleanor Ritchie, 1960; c: Steven, Kenneth, Nancy, Robert. Pres: Beltx Corp; Allergenic Products; Orthoband. Mem, adv council, St Louis Commn Planned Industrial Expansion; mem: Mo State Tech Service; Orthodontic Found; C of C; Shaare Emeth; J Fed; Masons, 32nd deg; Shriners; Omicron Delta Gamma; Beta Gamma Sigma; Alpha Epsilon Pi; 51 Club. Home: 4466 W Pine Blvd, St Louis, Mo. Office: 1000 Washington Ave, St Louis, Mo.

DGANY, Amos, Isr, farmer, legislator; b. Tel Aviv, Isr, May 23, 1926; s. Shmuel and Batya (Yeruchimovits); att Heb U, 1961-62; m. Judith Svarts, July 8, 1951; c: Tirza, Dalia. MK since 1958; mem secretariat: Moshavim Movement; Lab Party; fmr: mem secretariat, Rafi Party; org, youth group, Mapai; youth counsellor, Hanoar Haoved; leader, instr, new immigrants, Negev. Haganah; segen, IDF, 1948-49. Home: Kfar Vitkin, Isr.

DIAMOND, Aaron M, US, attorney; b. NYC, Apr 9, 1918; s. Isaac and Minnie (Rainess); LLB, St Lawrence U; m. Gertrude Stone, Jan 9, 1944; c: Mitchell, Stuart. Partner, law firm, Diamond & Golomb since 1953. Dir, ACLU, Nassau chap; mem: FJP; B'nai B'rith, mid-town lodge; tax comm, NYC Lawyers Assn; tax comm, Amer Bar Assn; fmr: pres: LI Consumer Coop Soc; Young Israel Chap; ADA; dist pres, ZOA. Home: 819 Hampton Rd, Woodmere, NY. Office: 99 Park Ave, New York, NY.

DIAMOND, David Leo, US, composer; b. Rochester, NY, July 9, 1915; s: Osias and Anna (Schildhaus); att: Eastman Sch of Music; Cleveland Inst of Music; Dalcroze Sch of Music; studied with Nadia Boulanger, Paris. Prof, chmn, dept composition, Manhattan Sch of Music, since 1965. Composed: eight syms, introduced by leading conductors; three violin concertos; piano concerto; cello concerto; eleven string quartets; composed and conducted score, Margaret Webster's production of The Tempest, Broadway, 1944-45. Composed score: Romeo and Juliet; The Rose Tattoo. Recordings: Columbia; Capitol; CRI. Mem, Natl Inst of Arts and Letters. Works commissioned by: Louisville Orch; Rockefeller Found; Fromm Found; Park Ave Syn. Recipient: three Guggenheim fs; Prix de Rome cash award; Juilliard Publ award; Paderewski prize; Rheta Sosland award; citation, Music Critics Circle of NY; grant, Natl Acad of Arts and Letters; Fulbright prof at U Rome, Harvard U; ASCAP-Stravinsky award, 1965. Contbr to music jours. Hobbies: painting; swimming; lang studies. Home: 249 Edgerton St, Rochester, NY.

DIAMOND, Freda, US, designer, home furnishings cons; b. NYC; d. Jack and Ida (Levine); grad, Woman's Art Sch; Cooper Union; studied architecture, decorative design in Fr; It; Belgium; Swed; Den; m. Alfred Baruch. Designer and home furnishings cons for dept stores and mfrs; on govt sponsored mission to It for rehab of craftsman; adv on handicraft and small ind to Min of Intl Trade and ind, Japanese Govt, 1957 and 1968. Mem: Natl Home Fashions League; Ind Design Inst; Amer Inst of Decorators; Fashion Group. Author: The Story of Glass, 1953; contbr to Your Future in the Fashion World. Home and office: 140 E 37 St, New York, NY.

DIAMOND, Malcolm L, US, educator; b. Bklyn, NY, Nov 6, 1924; s. Walter and Jeanette (Luria); BE, Yale U, 1945; PhD, Columbia U, 1956; m. Barbara Reingold, 1953; c: Michael, Jonathan. Prof, rel, Princeton U, since 1968; fac mem since 1953; fac, Sarah Lawrence Coll, NY, 1950-51; adj asst prof, NYU, 1951-53. USN, 1943-46. Author: Martin Buber: Jewish Existentialist, 1960. Recipient: E. Harris Harbison Teaching award, 1970. Home: 393 Walnut Lane, Princeton, NJ. Office: Princeton U, Princeton, NJ.

DIAMOND, Norman H, US, rabbi; b. Buffalo, NY, Nov 1, 1905; s. Morris and Nelly (White); BA, U of Cincinnati, 1932; ordained rabbi, HUC-JIR, 1935, BHL, 1931, hon DD, 1960; m. Cora Cohen, Dec 15, 1946; c: Nikki, Judith. Rabbi: Temple Beth El, since 1961; Temple Isr, New Castle, Pa, 1935-42; USO-JWB, 1942-44; Temple B'nai Jehoshua, Chgo, 1945-50; Temple Anshe Sholom, Chgo Hgts, 1950-52; Temple Sholom, Springfield, O, 1953-61. Bd mem: Citizens Scholarship Found; Halifax Min Assn; Child Day Care Cent; United Fund; Planned Parenthood, Urban Renewal Comm; Child Guidance Clinic; Family Service Agcy; JWF; regional

ADL; CCAR; J Fed. Home: 1035 Belaire Dr, Daytona Beach, Fla. Study: 507 Fifth Ave, Daytona Beach, Fla.

DICKENSTEIN, Abraham, US, banker, industrialist; b. Wishniewa, Pol, June 15, 1902; s. Benjamin and Frieda (Rabinowitz); m. Frida Yoshpe, Jan 23, 1923; c: Leah, Ruth. Pres, AMPAL-Amer Isr Corp; Isr Devl Corp; mgn dir, Bank Hapoalim; chmn, bd, Isr Amer Ind Devl Bank; pioneer laborer in Pal, 1921-24; found, mgr: Audit Union of Credit Coops, Pal, 1925-29; Audit Union of Consumer's Coops, 1925-29; Transp Coops, 1927-39, both in Pal; asst dir, Worker's Bank, Ltd, 1924-38. Delg, WZCs, 1939, 1951. Contbr to periodicals. Home: 375 West End Ave, New York, NY. Office: AMPAL, 17 E 71 St, New York, NY.

DICKENSTEIN, Israel, Isr, industrialist; b. Chernigov, Russ, July 10, 1910; s. Hanan and Hana (Cherwin); in Isr since 1923; m. Judit Israeli, Aug 11, 1935; c: Talia Wolfson, Roni. Gen mgr, Albar Ltd, since 1956; chmn, Netivei Neft, since 1967; fmr: gen mgr, Metco Ltd. Maj, Haganah, 1928-51. Prin contrib: pioneered aluminum rolling in Isr. Mem bd: Nafta Oil Co; Lapidot Oil Co; Isr Petroleum Inst; mem, past pres, Rotary, Givatayim. Home: 18 Hameitar St, Ramat Gan, Isr. Office: POB 20, Kfar Saba, Isr.

DICKER, Herman, US, rabbi; b. Jasina, Hung, Jan 30, 1914; s. Osias and Sara (Spindel); in US since 1938; ordained rabbi, U Zurich, 1937; PhD, Libr Sch, Pratt Inst, Bklyn, 1968, MLS; m. Eileen Last, July 29, 1945; c: Anna, Eli. Head, circulation and reference libr, JTSA since 1968. Chaplain, US Army, 1943-67, lt col, 1960, ret, 1967. Mem: Rel and Cultural comm, JDC; comm, arts and lit in J life, Commn on syn relations, FJP; Speakers Bur, UJA; Assn J Chaplains; Assn J Librs; Intl Libr Sci Honor Soc; Beta Phi Mu. Auhor: History of Jews in Ulm, Germany in the Middle Ages, 1938; Wanderers and Settlers in the Far East, A Century of Jewish Life in China and Japan, 1962. Home: 52-12 Parsons Blvd, Flushing, NY. Office: 3080 Broadway, New York, NY.

DICKSTEIN, Benjamin, US, pediatrician; b. Phila, Pa, Oct 28, 1915; s. Harry and Anna (Levitz); BA, U of Pa, 1936, MD, 1940; m. Joan Borteck, Dec 24, 1939; c: Howard, Kenneth, Mary Ann. Chief ped: Jeanes Hosp; John F Kennedy Memorial Hosp; ped: Florence Crittendon Home; Children's Aid Soc of Phila; sr att ped, Einstein Med Cen; asso visiting phys, Children's Hosp of Phila; asst prof, U of Pa Med Sch and Grad Sch, since 1947; med dir, Assn for J Children of Phila since 1961. Lt col, USAAF, 1942-45. Dipl, Amer Bd Ped; f: Amer Acad Ped; AMA; Coll Phys of Phila; bd trustees, FJP of Phila; bd dirs, Amer Friends of Heb U; mem: Phila Ped Soc; Phila Hematology Soc. Home: 8325 Fairview Rd, Elkins Park, Pa. Office: 6810 Castor Ave, Philadelphia, Pa.

DIENAR, Baruch, Isr, film producer and dir; b. Ger, Apr 2, 1920; in Isr since 1934; att: Tchrs Sem, Jerusalem; Heb U; Columbia U; m. Janky Ginsberg. Films: Tent City; They Were Ten; Land of a Thousand Faces; The Sand Curtain; The Seventh Day; Speaking of Israel; Bon Voyage. Recipient: Venice Film Festival award, Grand Prix, Cannes, 1961; Prix CIDALC, Mannheim, 1961; 1st prize, Intl Festival of Folklore, Monaco, 1965; gold medal, Intl Film Festival, US, 1969. Home: 44 Kedoshey Hashoa St, Herzlia-Pituach, Isr.

DIESENDRUCK, Leo, US, physicist; b. Vienna, Aus, July 1, 1920; s. Zevi and Lilli (Kohn); BA, U of Cincinnati, 1941; PhD, Johns Hopkins U, 1943, postgrad studies, 1946-49; m. Judith Abarbanel, June 20, 1942; c: Tamar, Miriam, Jonathan, Naomi. Prof, Physics, Queens Coll, CUNY, since 1962; U of RI, 1949-59; prin sci, Gen Dynamics Corp, 1959-62. Natl pres, LZOA, since 1968; fmr, chmn, comty action comm; mem: Amer Phys Soc; Amer Acoustical Soc; AAUP; Amer Assn Physics Tchrs; Sigma Xi; Phi Beta Kappa; Amer Profs for Peace in ME; fmr, mem exec comm, Assn Amers and Cans for Aliyah. Contbr to physics jours. Home: 16 Drury Lane, Great Neck, NY. Office: Queens Coll, CUNY, Flushing, NY.

DIETZ, David H, US, editor, author, journalist; b. Cleveland, O, Oct 6, 1897; s. Henry and Hannah (Levy); BA, W Reserve U, 1919, hon DLitt, 1948; LLC, Bowling Green State U, 1954; m. Doro hy Cohen, Sep 26, 1918; c: Doris Turner, Patricia Morris, David. Sci ed, Scripps-Howard Newspapers, since 1921; mem, ed staff, The Cleveland Press, since 1915; lectr, gen sci, W Reserve U, since 1926. US Army, WW I; cons to Surg Gen of the Army, 1944-47; Charter mem and first pres, The Suburban Temple, 1947-52; Natl Assn of Sci Writers, 1934; f, Sigma Delta Chi, since 1966; AAAS; O Acad of Sci; Royal

Astronomical Soc; guest f, Pierson Coll; Yale U, 1942; mem, Amer Astronomical Assn; Soc Astronomique de France; Sigma Xi; Zeta Beta Tau; clubs: City; Oakwood; Rowfant; Natl Press, Wash, DC. Author: The Story of Science, 1931; Medical Magic, 1937; Atomic Energy in the Coming Era, 1945; Atomic Science, Bombs and Power, 1954; All About Satellites and Space Ships, 1958; All About Great Medical Discoveries, 1960; All About the Universe, 1965; Stars and the Universe, 1968. Recipient: Pulitzer prize, 1937; Zeta Beta Tau New Orleans trophy, 1938; Goodrich award, 1940; War Dept cert, 1945; Dist Sci Writers award, Westinghouse, 1946; Lasker Med Journalism award, 1954; Ohioana medal, 1958; James T Grady gold medal, 1961. Spec interest: violin. Home: 2891 Winthrop Rd, Shaker Heights, O. Office: The Cleveland Press, Cleveland, O.

DINERMAN, Helen S, US, business exec; b. NYC, Dec 25, 1920; d. Maurice and Lillian (Blau) Schneider; BA, Hunter Coll, 1940; MA, Columbia U, 1948; m. James Dinerman, May 20, 1945; c: Robert, Alice. Chmn, exec comm, Intl Research Assos. Vice-pres, World Assn for Public Opinion Research; mem: Phi Beta Kappa. Contbr to profs l jours. Home: 179 E 70 St, New York, NY. Office: 1270 Ave of the Americas, New York, NY.

DINES, Michael, Eng, author, editor; b. Manchester, Eng, Feb 2, 1916; s. Gabriel and Miriam (Siverstone) Dinerstein; att Talmudical Coll, Manchester, 1928-32; m. Rosemarie Freedman; c: Steven, Gail, Ruth, Jonathan, Ed. Jewish Life, since 1964. Cpl, RAF, 1941-46. Author: Operation-Deadline; Operation-To Kill A Man; Operation-Kill or Be Killed; one-act plays; short stories, TV, radio scripts. Mem: Screen Writers Guild; Crime Writers Assn. Recipient: Afr Star; Long Service medal. Home: 37 Ringley Rd, Whitefield, Eng. Office: 4 Wells St, Manchester, Eng.

DININ, Samuel, US, educator; b. Zarawitz, Russia, Oct 10, 1902; s. Julius and Esther (Krafchick); in US since 1909; BA, CCNY, 1922; MA, Columbia U, 1923, PhD, 1933; hon DHL, JTSA, 1953; m. Bessie Bernstein, 1934; c: Miriam, Michael. Vice-pres and chmn of the facs, U of Judaism since 1963, dean, 1957-63; fac mem, since 1947; resgistrar, asso prof, educ and hist, Tchrs Inst, JTSA, 1921-45; exec-dir, Bur of J Educ, J Comty Council, LA, 1945-57. Pres: Assn of J Communal Execs of LA, 1952-54; Natl Council for J Educ, 1937-39; NY Zionist Soc, 1940-43; vice-pres, S Cal Chap, Amer J Hist Soc, secy, W states region, Amer Assn for J Educ, 1947-52, mem, bd govs, 1954-68. Author: Judaism in a Changing Civilization, 1933; Zionist Education in the US, 1945; contbr to The Reconstructionist; chaps in books: M M Kaplan-An Evaluation; The Tercentenary and After; The Educating Among Jewish Teachers; The Curriculum of the Hebrew Teachers Colleges. Recipient: awards: JTSA, 1945, 1966. Home: 712 N Kings Rd, Los Angeles, Cal. Office: 6525 Sunset Blvd, Los Angeles, Cal.

DINITZ, Simcha, Isr, diplomat; b. Tel Aviv, Isr, June 23, 1929; s. Joseph and Bruria Beder; att U Cincinnati, BSc, cum laude, Georgetown U, Wash, DC, 1954, MSc, intl law, 1956; m. Vivian Kingsburg, Sep 19, 1954; c: Doreet, Tamar, Michael. Min of Info, Isr Emb, Wash, DC, since 1968; dir, off of dir gen, fgn off, 1961-63, mem, Isr delg to UN Gen Assembly, 1963-65; dir, cabinet, political secy to fgn min, 1963-66; min, Isr Emb, Rome, 1966-68. Pvt, IDF, 1948-50. Contbr to legal jours. Recipient, Dr Cotinho award in Geopolitics, Georgetown U, 1954. Home: 40 Nayot St, Jerusalem, Isr. Office: 1621 22 St, Washington, DC.

DINNES, Jacob M, US, attorney; b. NYC, Apr 10, 1908; s. Abraham and Rachel (Zucker); att CCNY, 1923-26; LLB, cum laude, Bklyn Law Sch, St Lawrence U, 1929; m. Marjorie Wolgel, Feb 20, 1935; c: Carol. Pvt practice since 1946; law secy, Justice of Supr Court, NY State, since 1963. Chmn of bd, LI Zionist Found, Inc, since 1966; pres, LI Zionist Region, 1953-55, fmr exec mem, ZOA; mem: Philonomic Council; Masons. Contbr to law jours. Home: 117-01 Park Lane South, Kew Gardens, NY. Office: 292 Madison Ave, New York, NY.

DINSTEIN, Zvi, Isr, government official; b. Tel Aviv, 1926; att Heb U, Geneva U; m. Aya Rupin; three c. MK; dep min of finance, since 1969; controller, fgn exch; fmr Eur Missions for immigration, arms, supply purchase, 1948-53; asst dir, Devl Auth; head, fgn aid bur, Min of Finance; dir, Inves Auth; dep Min of Defense, 1965-67. Home: 44 Bloch St, Tel Aviv, Isr. Office: Min of Finance, Rupin Rd, Jeusalem, Isr.

DINUR, Ben Zion, (Ben Levi), Isr, historian, educator; b. Khorol, Russ, Jan 2, 1884; s. Shneor and Naomi (Eskinbein) Dinaburg; in Isr since 1921; ordained rabbi, J Theol Sem, Dinaburg, 1912; MA, U of Berlin, 1917; att U's: Bern; Petrograd; m. Bella Feingold, 1910 (decd); c: Yeshayahu. Prof em, modern J hist, Heb U, since 1947, fmr chmn, Inst of J Studies, dean, Fac Hum, fac mem since 1936; fmr: chmn, lit council, Bialik Inst; tchr, Russ, 1902-21; prin, instr, Beth Hakerem, Tchrs Sem, Jerusalem, 1921-46; MK, 1949-55; Min of Educ and Culture, 1951-55. Pres, intl council, World Union of J Studies; mem, Isr Acad of Sci and Hum; cen comm, Heb Tchrs Assn; cen comm, Heb Authors Assn; fmr: pres, Isr Hist Soc; court of appeal, Histadrut; delg, WZC. Author: Eretz Israel in the Year 5623, 1924; Israel in Exile, 7 vols, 2nd ed, 1959-68; haRambam, 1935; The Hibbat Zion Movement, 2 vols, 1939; Pioneers of Eretz Israel, 1947; beMifnei haDoroth, 1955; Arakhim uDerakhim, 1957; baOlam she-Shaka, 1958; Zakhor, 1958; Bnei Milchama uMahapecha, 1961; Bnei Dori, 1964; Herzl, 1968; chmn ed bd: The Yishuv Book; The Haganah Book; co-ed: Zionist Quarterly; Shivat Zion, annual; contbr to hist and pedagogical jours. Home: Histadrut Quarter, Kiriat Moshe, Jerusalem, Isr. Office: Heb U, Jerusalem, Isr.

DIRECTOR, Herman, US, business exec; b. Bremen, Ger, May 15, 1915; s. Simon and Bertha (Yeserski); in US since 1934; m. Lillian Rosenzweig, Mar 22, 1945; c: Steven, Dennis, Toby. Pres: ABC Furniture Stores, Savannah, since 1957; Merchants Finance Corp since 1956; Town and Country Furniture since 1957; Buck Furniture since 1959. Staff intelligence off, USAAF, 1942-46. Pres: Retail Furniture Assn, 1959-61; Savannah J Council, 1960-61; Bd of Educ, 1968-69; chmn: Bonds for Isr, 1960-61; UJA and Fed, 1958-59; bd mem: ARC, 1960-62; United Comty Services since 1961; Home: 4710 Fairfax Dr, Savannah, Ga. Office: 125 W Broad St, Savannah, Ga.

DISHON, Judith, Isr, educator; b. Berlin, Ger, Mar 5, 1937; d. Moses and Susanne (Drimmer) Harz; in Isr since 1938; tchrs cert, Gordon Tchrs Training Coll, 1957; BA, MA, with distinction, Heb U, 1959-63; PhD, hons, Columbia U, 1967; m. Menachem Dishon, Oct 21, 1958. Lectr, Bar Ilan U, since 1967. Mem: Amer Sch for Oriental Research; Isr Soc for Bible Research. Contbr to jours. Spec interests: ancient ME langs and cultures; J lit in Spain during the middle ages; Bible research. Home: 13 Modigliani St, Tel Aviv, Isr. Office: Bar Ilan U, Ramat Gan, Isr.

DLUZNOWSKY (Dunow), Moshe, US, author; b. Tomashov-Mazow, Pol, Feb 22, 1906; s. Henoch and Esther (Pius); in US since 1942; m. Berta Klebanow, 1946; c: Esther, Henry. Author: dramas produced in several countries, novels, and short stories trans into several langs: The Wheel of Fortune, 1949; The Well on the Road, 1953; Autumn in the Vineyard, 1956; The Potter's Daughters, 1952; A House on West End Ave, 1955; The Forgotten Man, 1955; Men and Masks, 1957; A Tree in the Field, 1958; The Wanderer of Morocco, 1958; Marionettes, 1961; The Chariot (children's stories), 1958; The Lonesome Ship, 1957; Der Falsher Mishpot, 1953-54; The Spice Merchant of Safi, 1956; The Banquet, 1959; Der Kuntzenmacher, 1959; Windmills, 1963; The Lonesome Ship, 1964; The Eleventh Inheritor, 1964; Under the Shadow of the Atlas Mountains, 1965; Doors and Windows, 1966; Men in a Cage, 1968; A Guest from a Distant Way, 1969; contbr to Yiddish, Anglo-J and Heb periodicals. Mem: IL Peretz Writers Union; Yiddish Pen Club; The Dramatist Guild; Cong for J Culture; J Natl Workers Alliance; Workmen's Circle. Recipient: Zvi Kessel Lit prize, 1949. Home: 225 W 86 St, New York, NY.

DOBIN, Rubin R, US, rabbi; b. Bklyn, NY, Oct 12, 1915; s. Harry and Luba (Lupowitz); att: U of Tex; U of Newark; Rutgers U, 1934-38; ordained rabbi, NY Theol Coll, 1938; cert, Talmudic Acad, Yeshiva U; m. Dorothy Welsch, Jan 25, 1937; c: David, Daniel, Robert, Judith Brilligi, Harriet. Dir, spec projs, JNF of Amer, since 1968; chmn, J Comty Council, since 1959; rabbi: NJ and Tex, 1936-41; pres: Childhood Nursery Products, Inc, 1944-50; Two Guys from Massapequa, 1950-64, Rubin R Dobin, Asso, since 1964. Chaplain, US Army, 1941-44. Vice-pres: Gustav Hartman YMHA, Far Rockaway; NJ RabCA, 1938-41; chmn, J Comty Council, Far Rockaway; LI Peace Corps Service Council; J Culture Council, NY J Educ Comm; Intl Secretariat for Voluntary Service; Spec Comm for Poverty Program Planning; natl UN-Rotary Intl Jerusalem Book Proj; fmr Far Rockaway Friday Night Forum Series; vice-chmn, Mayor Lindsay's NYC Comm of Exec Volunteers; mem, bd: LI Arts Cen; Cong Shaarey Tefila, Far Rockaway; mem: NY metrop sect, JWB; cabinet, Syn Commn, NY FJP; Intl Syn, J F Kennedy Airport, NY; fmr instr, Coll of J Studies; club: Rotary. Author: Gems of Jewish Wisdom, 1966; Moscow Chief Rabbi Reports, 1968; Our Jewish Heritage, 1968. Recipient: commendation, US Army, 1944; cert of merit, Mayor Lindsay, NYC, 1966; commendation, Yeshiva U, 1967. Spec interests: reading, world travel, J hist, Isr memorabilia. Home: 124 Broadway, Lawrence, LI, NY. Office: 42 E 69 St, New York, NY.

DOBKIN, Alexander, US, artist, illustrator, teacher; b. Genoa, It, May 1, 1908; s. Dmitri and Katherine (Kanter); in US since 1922; BS, CCNY, 1931; MA, Columbia U, 1934; att Art Students League, NY; m. Mabel Mount, Aug 25, 1951; c: Katherine. Dir, Art Sch of Educ Alliance, since 1954; fmr lectr, instr: Cent of Progress, Chgo, 1935; Poppenhusen Inst, Coll Point, 1935-39; New Art Sch, NY, 1937-41; Whitman Sch of Interior Decoration, 1947-49; CCNY, adult educ div, 1948-50. One-man shows: ACA Gal, NY; Forum Gal; exhbs: Bklyn Mus; Art Inst, Chgo; Carnegie Inst; Corcoran Gal, Wash, DC; Mus of Modern Art, NYC; Marie Harriman Gal; Pa Acad; perm collections: Butler Art Inst; Newark Mus; Tel Aviv Mus; Mus of Modern Art; Phoenix Fine Arts Assn; Phila Mus Art; Libr of Cong, Wsah, DC; Joseph H Hirschhorn collection, Smithsonian Inst. Author: Principles of Figure Drawing, 1949, 3rd ed, 1961; Travel Sketchbook, 1966. Recipient: St Gaudens medal, 1934; Roosevelt Memorial award, 1947; purchase awards: Childe Hassam, Amer Acad Arts and Letters, 1956; J and E R Pennel Collection, Libr of Cong, 1949, 1955. Home: 737 Greenwich St, New York, NY. Office: 197 E Broadway, New York, NY.

DODEK, Miriam S, US, author, radio and TV performer; b. Detroit, Mich, May 29, 1909; d. David and Bessie (Cohn) Selker; BA, U Mich, 1928; MA, W Reserve U, 1929; JD, Northwestern U Sch of Law, 1934; m. Samuel Dodek, 1936; c: Mariamne Brauzer, Samayla Deutch. Writer, performer, radio progs, "World of the Poet", and "The Golden Gods", since 1950; fmr: tchr, Eng lit, Cleveland, 1930-31; writer, dir, Kappa Beta Pi, Hadassah, Temple Anshe Emet, Chgo, 1931-53; atty, resettlement admn, gen counsel's off, US Govt, 1935-36. Author: River of Wonders, 1952, 2nd ed, 1967; contbr to mags. Pres, Amer Friends of Heb U, 1954-60; chmn, women's div, UJA, 1953, speakers' bur, 1947-52; first vice-pres and dir of educ, Hadassah, 1933-35; vice-pres, Found of Rheumatic and Arthritic Diseases, 1952-54, all Wash, DC; co-found: Argo, B'nai B'rith Women's Auxiliary, 1939; chmn, women's div, State of Isr Bonds, 1952; trustee, Wash Coll of J Studies, 1952; mem bd: Brandeis U Alumni Assn; chmn, philanthropy comm, UJA, 1947; both Wash DC; mem: Chi Delta Phi; Kappa Beta Pi; Portia Honorary Lit and Public Speaking Soc; League of Amer Penwomen; Assn of U Women. Hobbies: travel, archaeol. Home: 2930 Woodland Dr, Washington, DC.

DODEK, Samuel M, US, physician, educator; b. Chgo, Ill, June 14, 1902; s. Mayer and Lena (Ettinger); BA, George Washington U, 1923; MD, Jefferson Med Coll, 1927; MA, W Reserve U, 1931; m. Miriam Selker, 1936; c: Mariamne Brauzer, Samayla Deutch. Clinical prof, obstet and gyn, Sch of Med, George Wash U, since 1950, on fac since 1932; att obstet and gyn, George Wash U Hosp, since 1936; admn chmn, depts obstet and gyn, Wash Hosp cen, 1958-64; fmr: demonstrator, obstet and gyn, Sch of Med, W Reserve U, 1930-32; att gyn, Gallinger-Munic Hosp, 1932-56; att obstet, Garfield Memorial Hosp, 1936-67. Chmn, obstet bd, Wash, DC, 1964-69; dipl, Amer Bd of Obstet and Gyn; Intl Bd of Surg; chmn, Med Adv Comm on Planned Parenthood, Wash, DC, 1963-67; f: Amer Coll of Surg; Intl Coll of Surg; AMA; Wash Gyn Soc; Amer Coll Obstet and Gyn; Amer Bd Obstet and Gyn; dir, Amer J Phys comm, since 1949; mem: AAAS; Research Soc of Amer; AAUP; Intl Med Club; Amer Friends of Heb U; Wash Heb Cong; NY Lying-in Alumni Assn; Phi Sigma Delta; Phi Delta Epsilon; Sigma Xi; clubs: Bass Rocks Beach; Woodmount Country; Natl Press. Author: Shakespeare's Knowledge of Medicine, 1932; contbr to med jours. Recipient: hon mention, Intl Cong Obstet and Gyn, 1950; award, DC Med Soc Sci Assembly, 1961; Gold Headed Cane award, Wash Hosp Cen, 1969. Home: 2930 Woodland Dr, NW, Washington, DC. Office: 1730 Eye St, Washington, DC.

DOFT, Benjamin J, US, business exec; b. Aus, Feb 21, 1902; s. Beryl and Sarah (Ginsburg); in US since 1921; BA, Wash Sq Coll, NYU, 1934; m. Anne Schein, 1926; c: Emily, Martin,

Lucy, Bernard. Vice-pres, Burlington div, Princeton Mills, 1934-59. Pres, LI Zionist region, 1948-52; mem: bd of dirs, UJA; exec bd, AZC; bd of trustees, Herzliah Heb Tchrs Inst; exec, Isr commn, natl B'nai B'rith; bd, Culture Found, NYU; visiting bd, Wash Sq Coll, NYU; asso treas: ZOA; United Isr Appeal, 1948-60. Home: 379 Broadway, Lawrence, LI, NY.

DOFT, Max, US, business exec; b. Szczerzec, Pol, Jan 10, 1890; s. Beryl and Sarah (Ginsberg); in US since 1906; Talmudic educ, Lemberg, Pol; m. Madeline Rosengarten, Nov 25, 1917; c: Elliot, Frank (decd). Ret; pres, found, Princeton Knitting Mills, 1913-60; found, Textile Mill, Isr, 1929. Found: Aus-Hung ZOA; LI Sym Orch; UJA Isr Bonds; Intl Relief Drives; AJCong; LI J Hosp; Amer Friends of Heb U, Jerusalem; Amer-Isr C of Cs; Boy's Town, Jerusalem; chmn, exec comm, Brandeis Sch, Lawrence, LI, NY; natl chmn, Stephen Wise Memorial Fund Comm; mem: bd, Amer-Isr Culture Found; bd, Cong Sons of Isr, Woodmere, NY; Amer Bd of Arbitration; bd govs, alternate, Heb U, Jerusalem; fmr natl treas, AJCong. Hobbies: golf, music, painting. Home: 512 Jorgen, Lawrence, LI, NY.

DOLAV, Aaron, Isr, journalist; b. Tel Aviv, Isr, Jan 1, 1928; att, Columbia U, 1950-51; m. Dina Avrech, Oct 10, 1962. Sr corresp, Ma'ariv, Heb daily, since 1953; staff mem since 1952; fmr: staff mem: Bamachane; Haolam Hazeh. Introduced in Ma'ariv the elaborate spec assignment feature. Interviewed Russian PM Bulganin in Russ, 1956. Sgt, IDF, 1948-50. Contbr to jours, periodicals. Recipient: Jabotinsky award. Home: 3 Chen Blvd, Tel Aviv, Isr. Office: Ma'ariv, 3 Carlebach St, Tel Aviv, Isr.

DOLGIN, Simon Arthur, US, rabbi; b. Chgo, Ill, Mar 26, 1915; s. Isadore and Dina (Horowitz); BS, Lewis Inst Tech, 1939; ordained rabbi, Heb Theol Coll, 1939, DHL, 1959; ThD, U of S Cal, 1954; m. Shirley Gorodeisky, Aug 14, 1943; c: Saralee, Gaola (decd), Sharon, Marcia, Michael, Jess. Rabbi, Beth Jacob Cong, since 1939. Vice-pres, RabCA, 1966-68; Bur J Educ of LA, 1949-55, 1968; dir, J Comty Council, LA, 1949-55; natl council, Hapoel Hamizrachi of Amer, 1943-55; vice-chmn, Natl Council of Rel Zionists of Amer. Ed: Rabb Council Sermon Manual, 1954; contbr to theol jours. Home: 474 S Wetherly Dr, Beverly Hills, Cal. Study: Beth Jacob Cong, Beverly Hills, Cal.

DOLIN, Albert H, attorney; b. Chgo, Ill, Nov 28, 1912; s. Harry and Esther (Klitzky); BS, Northwestern U, 1936; LLB, Loyola U, 1943; m. Rivy Hoffing, June 14, 1936; c: Barry. Exec vice-pres, secy, Goldblatt Bros Inc, since 1968, with firm since 1951; dir, Prospect Plaza State Bank, Mt Prospect, Ill; gen counsel, Heart Research Found. Dir, Civic Fed; chmn, bd of trustees, N Suburban Syn Beth-El; trustee: Cancer Research Found, U Chgo, secy-dir since 1957; Coll of J Studies; dir, midwest region, Technion; mem, bd of govs, State of Isr Bonds, since 1961. Recipient: State of Isr Bonds award, 1961. Hobbies: photography, music. Home: 68 Lakeview Terr, Highland Park, Ill. Office: 333 S State St, Chicago, Ill.

DOLLINGER, Isidore, US, jurist, attorney, legislator; b. NYC, Nov 13, 1903; s. Emanuel and Jennie (Weidler); BCS, NYU, 1925, LLB, 1928; m. Rose Zahn, Sep 1, 1929; c: Edmund. Justice, Supr Court, State of NY since 1969; fmr: mem: NY State Assembly, 1937-44; NY State Sen, 1945-48; US House of Reprs, 1949-59; dist atty, Bx Co, 1960-69. Mem, Bx Co Bar Assn. Home: 1020 Grand Concourse, Bronx, NY. Office: 851 Grand Concourse, Bronx, NY.

DOMAN, Leon H, US, attorney; b. Phila, Pa, Aug 26, 1899; s. Bernard and Sarah (Frankel); BA, CCNY, 1920; MBA, 1922; JD, NYU, 1928; m. Edith Morse, Jan 24, 1942; c: Ruth, David. Gen counsel, Amer Fgn Ins Assn, 1942-64, with assn since 1929. US Army, WW I. Mem: Amer, NY State, NY Co Bar Assns; Ins Soc; Intl Law Assn; Fgn Law Assn; Assn of Bar of NYC; Amer Soc of Intl Law; Acad of Political Sci; Econ Round Table; Masons, 32 deg; Scottish Rite; club: Lawyers. Conthr to profsl jours. Home: 110-50 71 Rd, Forest Hills, NY.

DOMKE, Martin, US, attorney, author; b. Berlin, Ger, Sep 11, 1892; s. Leopold and Meta (Lebram); in US since 1941; att, U Berlin Law Sch, 1911-14; DJ, U Greifswald, 1915; m. Eva Dienst; c: George. Vice-pres, Amer Arbitration Assn, 1943-68; mem: Berlin Bar, 1923-33; cons, fgn and intl law, Paris, 1933-40; adj prof, law, NYU Sch of Law, 1950. Trustee,

Consular Law Soc, 1959; dir, Fgn Law Assn, 1953; mem: Assn of Bar of NYC; Amer Soc of Intl Law; Intl Law Assn. Author: Trading with the Enemy in World War II, 1943; The Control of Alien Property, 1947; American-German Private Law Relations, 1956; Commercial Arbitration, 1965; The Law and Practice of Commercial Arbitration, 1968; ed-in-chief: The Arbitration Jour, 1946; contbr to jours. Home: 370 E 76 St, New York, NY.

DON, Yehuda, Isr, economist; b. Budapest, Hung, June 21, 1930; s. Jacob and Antonia (Filut); in Isr since 1947; BA, Heb U, 1953, MSc, 1957; PhD, LSE, 1961; m. Malka Raff, Apr 4, 1954; c: Shlomith, Jeremy, Jacob. Sr lectr, econ, Bar Ilan U, since 1965, head of dept, 1966-69, on staff since 1961; visiting prof, SF State Coll, since 1969; econ, Min of Trade, 1957-58. Served on border settlement, 1948-54. Bd dirs, Isr Coop Coll; mem: sci comm, Intl Research Cen for Rural and Coop Comtys; Isr Natl Council of Lab Force; econ comm, Natl Rel Party, 1966-69. Ed: Public and Coop Econ in Isr, 1968; contbr to profsl jours. Hobby: gardening. Home: 3 Arnon St, Kiryat Ono, Isr. Office: Bar Ilan, U, Ramat Gan, Isr.

DONAGI, Alexander Emanuel, Isr, scientist; b. Grajewo, Pol, Apr 5, 1929; s. Arieh and Tova (Katz) Waks; in Isr since 1931; BSc, Technion, 1954, dipl engr, 1955; MPH, U Pittsburgh, 1960; DSc, ind health, U Cincinnati, 1962; m. Rachel Sher, June 2, 1955; c: Ran, Alon. Head, unit of environmental nuisances prevention, Min of Health, since 1968, with org since 1957; adj sr lectr, Technion, since 1964. Lt, IAF, 1948-50. Chmn, honor and award comm, Intl Radiation Protection Assn; mem: Isr Radiation Protection Assn; Air Pollution Control Assn; Assn for Promotion of Sanitation in Isr. Contbr to profsl jours. Recipient, Public Health Practice award, U Pittsburgh, 1960. Home: 15 Kdoshei-Kahir St, Holon, Isr. Office: 27 Prof Shor St, Tel Aviv, Isr.

DONALDA, Pauline, Can, singer, teacher; b. Montreal, Can, Mar 5, 1882; d. Michael and Fanny (Goldberg) Lightstone; att Royal Vic Coll; studied voice with Prof Clara Lichtenstein; Duvernoy, Paris; hon DMus, McGill U, 1954; m. Mischa-Leon Haurowitz, 1926 (decd). Prof of singing; opera debut, McGill U Conservatorium, 1904; appeared: La Monnaie, Brussels, 1905-06; Hammerstein's Manhattan Opera House, NYC, 1906-07; L'Opera Comique, Paris, 1907; Covent Garden, London, 1905-14, 1919. Pres, Opera Guild Inc, Montreal; life mem, Can Red Cross. Recipient: Officier de l'instruction publique, Paris, 1927; Order of Canada, 1967; Centennial medal, 1967. Home: 3410 Atwater Ave, Montreal, Can.

DONBROW, Max, Isr, educator; b. London, Eng, Jan 9, 1920; s. Ralph and Polly (Eckstein); in Isr since 1965; BPharm, BSc, PhD, U London; m. Milly Freed, Nov 7, 1944; c: Pauline, Pamela. Visiting prof, head, dept pharm, Heb U, Jerusalem, since 1965; research asst, May Baker Ltd, Eng, 1941-44; asst, sr prin lectr, Sch of Pharm, Chelsea Coll, London, 1946-64. F: Royal Inst of Chem; Chem Soc; Pharm Soc; mem: Isr Pharm Assn; Spectrophotometric Group, Eng; Polarographic Soc, Eng; fmr: secy, Friends of Heb U; chmn, Pharm Group, Eng. Author: Instrumental Methods in Analytical Chemistry, vol I, 1966, Vol II, 1967. Contbr to profsl jours. Hobbies: photography, theatre, walking. Home: 3 Ibn Gvirol St, Jerusalem, Isr.

DONIGER, Lester Laurence, US, publisher; b. Raczki, Pol, Oct 15, 1909; s. Moses and Celia (Jalkut); in US since 1920; BA, NYU, 1931; att Columbia U; m. Rita Roth, Sep 29, 1937; c: Jerome, Anthony, Wendy. Pres: Book Club Guild, Rel Book Club Inc, 1957-68; Channel Press Inc, Doniger and Raughley Inc, 1954-65; ed, The Pulpit Digest, 1937-45. Pres: Bd of Educ, Great Neck, 1962-64; Sex Info and Educ Council of US, 1967-68; Phi Beta Kappa Alumni, LI, 1958-60; asso, New Coll, Hofstra Coll, 1960; f, Intl Inst of Arts and Letters, 1961-62; asso trustee, N Shore Hosp, Manhasset, NY, since 1965; clubs: Overseas Press, Advt. Home: 26 Wildwood Dr, Great Neck, NY.

DONIN, Hayim Halevy, US, rabbi; b. NYC, June 3, 1928; s. Max and Eva (Smolensky) Dolnansky; BA, Yeshiva U, ordained rabbi; MA, Columbia U, PhD, Wayne State U, 1966; m. Tzivia Hanover, June 24, 1951; c: Cheryl, David, Rena, Miriam. Rabbi: Cong B'nai David, since 1953; Cong Kesher Isr, 1951-53. Chmn, Bd License for Heb Tchrs, Metrop Detroit, 1967-69; co-chmn: Comty Relations Comm, JCC; Parent-Youth Guidance Commn; adv, syn and sch sect,

Allied J Campaign; exec comm, RabCA; adv cabinet, B'nai B'rith, ADL; bd dirs: Midrasha Coll J Studies; Mich Soc Mental Health; JNF; Syn Council for Isr Bonds, mem, Gov Ethical and Moral Panel; found, rabb chmn, Detroit Friends of Yeshiva U. Author: Beyond Thyself, 1965; contbr to J press. Home: 17639 George Washington Dr, Southfield, Mich, Study: 24350 Southfield Rd, Southfield, Mich.

DOPPELT, Frederic A, US, rabbi; b. Sanok, Austria-Hung, Dec 14, 1906; s. Hyman and Sara (Amster); in US since 1920; BA, U Cincinnati, 1930; ordained rabbi, HUC, 1931, hon DHL 1956; hon DD, Wilberforce U, 1947; m. Lucille Greenebaum, June 21, 1936; c: Carolyn. Rabbi, Cong Achduth Vesholom, since 1940; lectr, hist, phil of rel, Ind U Cen since 1947; rabbi: Saginaw, Mich, 1931-34; Elmira, NY, 1934-40. Exec council, Amer J Hist Soc; bd overseers, HUC-JIR; responsa comm, CCAR, since 1936; natl vice-chmn, ARC campaign, 1962; mem: NY State Housing Commn, 1937-40; ZOA; B'nai B'rith; AJComm; HUC Alumni Assn; clubs: Quest; Fortnightly; Ft Wayne Country; Rotary. Author: The Contribution of Hassidism to Prayer, 1931; Dialogue with God, 1942; co-author, A Guide for Reform Jews, 1957. Home: 2500 Randall Rd, Fort Wayne, Ind. Study: 5200 Old Mill Rd, Fort Wayne, Ind.

DORENBAUM, Jennie Shaine, US, business exec, communal worker; b. Bristol, RI, Sep 24, 1895; d. William and Annie (Landay) Shaine; LLB, Boston U, 1916; m. Philip Dorenbaum, Nov 5, 1934; c: Frances. Pres, Springfield Photo Mount Co, Holyoke, Mass, since 1951. Mem bd, and 1st pres, women's div, Gen J Comm; Miriam Hosp; Hadassah; fmr: pres: Council of J Women; 1st dist, B'nai B'rith Women, mem, women's supr council. Home: 65 Intervale Rd, Providence, RI. Office: 475 Canal St, Holyoke, Mass.

DORFF, Sol Ervin, US, civil engr; b. Pol, Dec 2, 1908; s. Henry and Anna (Gordon); in US since 1921; BS, U of Wis, 1929, BCE, 1937; m. Anne Nelson, Aug 21, 1938; c: Elliot, Elaine. Pres, Dorff and Co, Contractors and Engrs, since 1945; fmr engr: Froemming Bros; Mason and Hanger; City of Milw. Pres: J Family and Children's Service; Wis Conf of Conservative Syns; commnr, Bd of Harbor Commnrs, past pres; trustee: J Home for Aged; Bd of J Educ, past vice-pres; mem: B'nai B'rith; Wis Soc of Profsl Engrs; bd dirs: Milw JWF; Isr Bond Comm; Beth El Ner Tamid Syn, past pres. Recipient: plaque, Isr Bonds, 1968. Home and office: 3400 N 56 St, Milwaukee, Wis.

DORFMAN, Albert, US, physician, educator; b. Chgo, Ill, July 6, 1916; s. Aron and Anna (Schwartzman); SB, U of Chgo, 1936, PhD, 1939, MD, 1944; m. Ethel Steinman, Sep 1, 1940; c: Abby, Julie. Prof, bio-chem, U of Chgo, since 1961, chmn, dept of ped, since 1962, prof, 1957-61; dir, LaRabida-U of Chgo Inst, 1952-69; chief, bio-chem, Army Med Sch, Wash, 1946-48. Mem: Amer Acad of Arts and Scis, 1966; Amer Chem Soc; Amer Soc Biology Chems; Soc Experimental Biol and Med; AHA; Amer Rheumatism Soc; Soc Ped Research; Amer Ped Soc; Amer Council on Rheumatic Fever. Contbr to sci jours. Recipient: E Mead Johnson award, 1957. Home: 2231 E 67 St, Chicago, Ill. Office: 920 E 59 St, Chicago, Ill.

DORFMAN, Ben David, US, economist; b. Portland, Ore, Feb 16, 1902; s. David and Tillie (Korman); AB, Reed Coll, 1924; MA, U of Cal, 1927, PhD, 1932; m. Hilda Rotenberg, 1934; c: David, Harriet Aurora Reisman. Econ cons, since 1965; fmr: chmn, instr, U of Hawaii, 1924-25; dir, fgn trade lab, U of Cal, 1925-27; asst prof, U of ND, 1930-31; econ adv, L of N Comm of Enquiry of Far E, 1931-32; mem, Philippine Survey comm, US Govt, 1935-36; chmn, US Tariff Comm, 1961-65, with org since 1934. Liaison off, bd of econ warfare, 1941-42; cons, war produc bd, 1942-43. Adv, US rep, ECOSOC, UN, 1947; i/c of US Tariff Delg to GATT, Fr, 1949, Eng, 1950-51, Tokyo, 1959. Mem: Amer Econ Assn; Phi Beta Kappa; Beta Gamma Sigma; Omicron Delta Gamma; Pan Xenia; club: Cosmos, Wash, DC. Contbr to periodicals. Recipient: Wm Harrison Mills f, U of Cal, 1930-32. Home: 4719 30 St, NW, Washington, DC.

DORFMAN, Joseph, US, educator, author; b. Ramanovska, Russ, Mar 27, 1904; s. Mendel and Etta (Reznick); in US since 1905; BA, Reed Coll, 1924; MA, Columbia U, 1925, PhD, 1935; m. Sarah Sorrin, 1932; c: Susan, Mark. Prof, econ, Columbia U, since 1948, fac mem since 1931; econ, Natl Ind Conf Bd, NYC, 1927-28; f, New Sch for Social Research, NYC, 1929-31. Pres: Econ Hist Assn; Assn for

Evolutionary Econ, 1968; mem: Amer Econ Assn; Econ Hist Assn; Royal Econ Soc; Amer Hist Assn. Author: Thorstein Veblen and His America, 1934; Economic Mind in American Civilization, 5 vols, 1946-59; co-author: Early American Policy, 1960; ed: Relations of the State to Industrial Action; Economics and Jurisprudence, both by Henry Carter Adams, 1954; Types of Economic Theory, by WC Mitchell, vol 1, 1967; mem, ed bd, Political Sci Quarterly; Hist of Political Economy; contbr to profsl publs. Recipient: Seligman prize, Columbia U, 1937; Guggenheim f, 1953-54; Ford Fac Research f, 1959-60. Home: 39 Claremont Ave, New York, NY. Office: Columbia U, New York, NY.

DORFMAN, Ralph I, US, biochemist, educator; b. Chgo, Ill, June 30, 1911; s. Aron and Anna (Schwartzman); BS, U of Ill, 1932; PhD, U of Chgo, 1934; m. 2nd, Margaret Cameron, 1965; c: (by 1st m) Gerald, Ronald. Sr vice pres, Syntex Research, since 1964, dir, Inst of Hormone Biol, since 1964; visiting prof pharm, Stanford U Sch of Med, since 1967; fmr: research asst, U of Chgo; instr, pharm, La State U; asst prof: Yale U; W Reserve U; dir labs, Worcester Found for Experimental Biol; research prof, biochem, Boston U; prof chem, Clark U. F: AAAS; Amer Acad of Arts and Sci; hon f, Chilean Med Soc; mem: Sigma Xi; Phi Lambda Epsilon; Amer Chem Soc; Soc for Experimental Biol and Med; Amer Soc for Cancer Research; Amer Soc of Biol Chems; Amer Stat Soc; Endocrine Soc; AMA; publ comm, Soc for Study of Reproduction; Mexican Endocrine Soc; Pan Amer Med Assn; Dan Soc for Endocrinology. Author: Metabolism of Steroid Hormones, 1953, revised ed, 1965; Androgens, 1956; The Human Adrenal Gland, 1961; ed, Methods in Hormone Research, vols I-V, 1962; asso ed, Can Jour of Biochem; contbr numerous papers on biochem, endocrinology, productive fertility. Recipient, Dist Service award, Med Alumni Assn, U Chgo, 1967. Home: 10465 Berkshire Dr, Los Altos Hills, Cal. Office: Syntex Research, Stanford Ind Park, Palo Alto, Cal.

DORFMAN, Robert, US, economist; b. NYC, Oct 27, 1916; s. Samuel and Mina (Gordon); BA, Columbia, 1936, MA, 1937; PhD, U of Cal, Berkeley, 1948; m. Nancy Schelling, Nov 6, 1949; c: Peter, Ann. Prof, econ, Harvard U, since 1935; fmr: asso prof econ, U of Cal, 1950-55. Oprs analyst; USAAF, 1943-46; USAF, 1948-50. Author: Application of Linear Programming to the Theory of the Firm, 1951; The Economic Status of the Aged, 1947; The Price System, 1964; Prices and Markets, 1967; co-author: Linear Programming and Economic Analysis, 1958; Design of Water Resource Systems, 1962; ed, Measuring Benefits of Government Investments, 1965. Home: 81 Kilburn Rd, Belmont, Mass. Office: Harvard U, 325 Littauer Cen, Cambridge, Mass.

DORFMAN, Saville, S Afr, engineer, town planner; b. Johannesburg, S Afr, May 16, 1910; s. Aaron and Rebecca (Bloom); BSc, U of Witwatersrand, 1931, dipl, town planning, 1945; dipl, traffic engr, Yale U, 1939; m. Sheba Cramer, Aug 17, 1938; c: Malcolm. Chief Traffic Off, City of Johannesburg, since 1954, traffic engr and dep engr, 1943-54; fmr: civil engr asst: Rand Water Bd, 1932-33; City Council of Johannesburg, 1933-38, traffic engr, 1940-43. Pres, Inst Traffic Offs, 1953-54 and since 1961, mem exec; mem: Road Safety Council; Inst Town Planners, S Afr; Inst Traffic Engrs, US; asso mem: Inst CEs, Gt Brit; Inst Munic Engrs, Gt Brit; internal mgmt comm, Syt Syn, United Heb Cong, Johannesburg; Old Edwardian Soc. Contbr to profsl jours. Hobbies: bowling, gardening. Home: 302 Bretton Woods, Killarney, Johannesburg, S Afr. Office: Traffic Dept, Bree and Harrison Sts, Johannesburg, S Afr.

DORI, Yaakov, Isr, educator, army off; b. Haifa, Isr, Oct 8, 1899; s. Zvi and Miriam Dostrovsky; dipl ing, U of Ghent, 1925; m. Badana Pintoff, 1929; c: Jerahmiel, Zvi, Eytana. Pres, Technion, Haifa, 1951-65; staff engr, tech dept, Pal Zionist Exec, 1926-31; head, research and devl dept, Govt of Isr, 1950-51. Served J Legion, 1918; off, Haganah, 1921-22, cdr, Haifa dis, 1931-39; org, training courses, Wingate's Night Squads, 1938; chief of staff: Haganah, 1938-47; IDF, 1948-50. Contbr to press. Home: 103 Hatishbe St, Haifa, Isr.

DORIAN, Frederick, US, musicologist, educator; b. Vienna, Aus, July 1, 1902; s. Alois and Therese (Neumann) Deutsch; in US since 1936; PhD, U Vienna, 1925; att State Acad of Music, Vienna; Arnold Schoenberg Sem of Composition, Vienna; m. Sadie Pearlman, Aug 9, 1940. Prof, music, Carnegie -Mellon U, since 1936. Author: The Fugue in the Instrumental and Vocal Works of Beethoven, 1927; The History of Music in

Performance, 1942; The Musical Workshop, 1947; Commitment to Culture, 1964. Mem: Amer Musicological Soc; Intl Musicological Soc; Intl Soc for Contemporary Music. Home: 4921 Forbes Ave, Pittsburgh, Pa. Office: Carnegie-Mellon U, Pittsburgh, Pa.

DORMAN, Gladys M, US, attorney; b. Bklyn, NY, July 18, 1911; d. Benjamin and Blanche (Rosenthal); BA, Cornell U, 1931; MA, Columbia U, 1933; LLB, cum laude, Bklyn Law Sch, 1936; m. Benjamin Raphael, Feb 12, 1939; c: Stephen, Alan. Pvt practice since 1936; partner, Raphael & Dorman, since 1950; asso ed, Bklyn Barrister, since 1954; NY State Bar Bulletin, 1957-58. Chmn, surrogate sect, Bklyn Bar Assn, since 1959; trustee, Bklyn Bar Assn, since 1966; mem, NYC, Bd of Higher Edn, since 1949; chmn, Bklyn Coll admn comm, since 1956, chmn, law comm, since 1960, exec comm, since 1956; pres, Bklyn Women's Bar Assn, 1944-46; hon pres, since 1946; mem: NY Bar Assn; Alpha Epsilon Phi; FJP; Philomonic Council; club: Lawyers, dir since 1946. Home: 8801 Shore Rd, Brooklyn, NY. Office: 26 Court St, Brooklyn, NY.

DORON, Aharon, Isr, architect; b. Vienna, Aus, May 15, 1917; s. Josef and Esther (Zwiling) Groskopf; att Ecole Natl Supérieure D'Architecture; MA, architect, town planner, Inst Supérieure D'Arts Décoratifs, Brussels; m. Sara Sandler, Nov 4, 1941; c: Dafna Shneur. Pvt practice, architect and town planner, since 1941; fmr, asso: Henry Van de Velde; Jean Jules Eggericy, Brussels. Home: 52 King David St, Tel Aviv, Isr. Office: 15 Soutine St, Tel Aviv, Isr.

DORON, Aharon, Isr, administrator, army off; b. Ludwigshafen, Ger, Feb 17, 1922; s. Siegfried and Franzi (Neuburger); m. Hanna Harari, May 25, 1948; c: Ehud, Nurit. Vice-pres, Tel Aviv U, since 1965. Served Haganah, 1939-48; supernumerary police, 1941-46; cdr: army training base, IDF, 1948-50; Nahal, 1950-52; infantry battalion, 1952-54; brig gen, head of personnel, IDF, 1959-63. Home: 33 Hazayit St, Ramat Hasharon, Isr. Office: Tel Aviv U, Ramat Aviv, Isr.

DORON, Alexander, Isr, bank exec; b. Rum, Feb 6, 1906; s. Herrmann and Fridda Moscovitz; in Isr since 1910; att: Herzliah Gymnasia, Tel Aviv; Highgate Sch, London; m. Shoshana Harlap, 1932; c: Daniel, Naomi. Secy, Bank Leumi leIsrael, since 1938; co-mgr, Otzar Hityashvut Hayehudim Ltd; co-secy, J Colonial Trust; fmr: personal secy to gen mgr, Anglo-Pal Bank, Tel Aviv. Served Haganah; capt, Brit Army, 1940-45; liaison off to fgn press, IDF. Chmn, Isr Assn of Inc Secys; f, Corp of Secys, London; mem bd, Advt Assn of Isr. Home: 4 Hatamar St, Tel Aviv, Isr. Office: Bank Leumi leIsrael, head office, Tel Aviv, Isr.

DORON, Asher (Dascalu), Isr, engineer; b. Mastacan, Rum, Sep 25, 1910; s. Elias and Eva (Rubin) Eisicovici; in Isr since 1957; dipl, CE, Poly Sch, Bucharest, 1936; m. Aura Iuster, Nov 11, 1945; c: Alexander. Cons engr since 1958; town planner, master plan team of Tel Aviv, since 1964; fmr: asso prof, Inst for Bridges and Roads, Bucharest, 1948-49; planning dir, Min of Bldg, Rum, 1950-53. Mem: cen comm, United Workers Party, Mapam; Assn of Engrs and Architects in Isr; ZF, fmr mem, exec comm; MP, Rum, 1946-48; secy, Interparliamentary group; found leader, Zionist Socialist Party, Mishmar, 1945-48; mem presidium, J Cmty's Fed, 1947-49, all in Rum. Home: 50 Brodetski St, Tel Aviv, Isr. Office: 19 Har Nevo St, Tel Aviv, Isr.

DORON, Eliezer, Isr, diplomat; b. Kishinev, Russ, July 19, 1910; s. Asher and Haia (Fridman) Spector; in Isr since 1931; att: Heb Coll, Magen David, Kishinev; Coll for Judaic Studies, Berlin 1934-35; U of Frankfurt, 1935-36; New Sch for Social Research, NY, 1952-54; m. Yehudith Yedidia, Sep 2, 1943; c: Yael, Esther. Ambass of Isr, to Arg, since 1969; fmr: secy, off workers union, Histadrut, Jerusalem, 1936-38; dir, youth dept, Pal Found Fund 1938-48; press and info off, Isr Min for Fgn Affairs, 1948-49; Isr consul: Zurich, 1949-52; NYC, 1952-54; dir, cultural relations div, Min for Fgn Affairs, 1954-58; ambass to Chile, 1958-63; dir: Latin Amer div, Min for Fgn Affairs, 1963-64, E Eur div, 1964-67; ambass to Rum, 1967-69. Author: Characteristics of Palestine Youth, 1947; Quiz Book on Judaism, Zionism, and Palestine, 1947; The Negev-What Are We Fighting For?, 1949; Arachim, 1950; In the Israeli Diplomatic Service, 1956. Home: Shlomo Molcho St, Jerusalem, Isr. Offices: Emb of Isr, Buenos Aires, Arg; Min for Fgn Affairs, Jerusalem, Isr.

DORON, Gabriel, Isr, diplomat; b. Rehovot, Isr, Feb 9, 1914; s.

Herman and Fridda (Strass) Moscovitz; att Herzliya Coll, Tel Aviv; m. Fay Orgel, 1937; c: Avital. Min of Isr to Cuba, since 1968; consul to Australia, 1949-51; chief of personnel, Min of Fgn Affairs, 1951-53; consul to India, 1953-56; consul gen to S Afr, Rhodesia, Nyasaland, 1956-59; dir gen, Commercial Bc Isr, 1960-64; dir, Off of Pres, Isr, 1964-65; min to Brazil, 1965-68. Brit Army, WW II; maj, IDF, 1948-49. Hobbies: sculpture, philately, photography, golf. Home: Avenida 25, No 15814, Cubanacan, La Habana, Cuba. Office: Min for Fgn Affairs, Jerusalem, Isr.

DORON, Haim Rafael, Isr, public health official; b. Buenos Aires, Arg, Mar 26, 1928; s. Moshe and Hanah (Orlean) Derechinsky; in Isr since 1953; MD, Fac de Ciencias Medicas, U Buenos Aires, 1952; dipl, public health, Sch of Tropical Med and Hygiene, U London, 1961; m. Noemi Gutman, Oct 18, 1952; c: Amos, Hanah, Ishaiaau. Head, med dept, Kupat Holim, since 1968; fmr, regional med off, Negev, Kupat Holim. Served IDF. Mem: Secretariat, Isr Lab Party; Isr Health Council; Cen Natl Radio and TV Council; IMA; Org of Public Health Drs. Home: 38 Gershon St, Beersheva, Isr. Office: Kupat Holim, 101 Arlozoroff, Tel Aviv, Isr.

DORON, Jacob, Isr, attorney, diplomat; b. Leningrad, Russ, Oct 24, 1914; s. Issac and Esther (Paenson); in Isr since 1933; dipl, Govt Law Sch, 1942; m. Judith Laskov, May 9, 1936; c: Ellamy, David, Daniel, Tamar. Asst to Isr repr, UN, since 1971; fmr: pvt law practice, 1943-59; consul gen to S Afr, Rhodesia, 1959-63; dep, acting legal adv, Min for Fgn Affairs, Jerusalem, 1963-67; ambass to Venezuela, 1967-71. Maj, IDF, 1948-49. Fmr mem, Haifa Bar Assn; club: Rotary. Contbr to jours. Hobby: tennis. Home: Mt Carmel, Haifa, Isr. Office: Min of Fgn Affairs, Jerusalem, Isr.

DORON, Shalom, P, Isr managing dir; b. Vienna, Aus, May 11, 1917; s. Leon and Sophie (Ingber) Dikman; in Isr since 1936; LLB, Heb U; grad, Govt Law Sch; m. Carmela Gluecksohn, Aug 19, 1952; c: Gal-Aryeh, Adiel. Mgn dir, Isr Land Developing Co, Ltd; mem, bd dirs, several inves and devl corps; budget comm, Isr Bc Services. Off, J Battalion, Brit Army, WW II; capt, IDF. Bd of govs, World B'nai B'rith; chmn, Isr bd, B'nai B'rith Women of Amer Children's Home in Isr; Hon treas, Isr Soc for Political Sci. Contbr to jours. Hobbies: philately, journalism. Home: 1 Sa'adiagaon St, Rehavia, Jerusalem, Isr.

DORON, Shaul, Isr, engineer; b. Braila, Rum, July 6, 1907; s. Herman and Fridda (Strass) Moscovitz; in Isr since 1910; BSc, E London Coll, London U, 1927; m. Elizabeth Kirschner, Aug 28, 1931; c: Zvi, Hadara. Dep, dir gen, Tahal, Water Planning for Isr, Ltd, since 1956, with org since 1955; asst mgr, chief engr: Pal Mortgage and Credit Bank Ltd, 1931-48; Pal Water Co, 1933-49; chief engr, irrigation dept, JA, 1949-51; engr adv: Min of Transp, 1951-53; Min of Devl, 1953-54. Served Haganah, 1932-48; maj, IDF, 1948-49. F, Amer Soc of CEs; mem: Assn of Engrs and Architects in Isr; Inst of Civil Engrs, London. Home: 32 Magal St, Savyon, Isr. Office: Tahal, 54 Ibn Gvirol St, Tel Aviv, Isr.

DOROT, Moshe Shemuel, Isr, hotelier; b. Vienna, Aus, Apr 18, 1915; s. Anton and Frida (Winkler) Deutsch; in Isr since 1938; deg Handelsakademie, Vienna, 1929-33; grad Hotel Direktoren Schule, Vienna, 1937-38; m. Edith Engelbert, Apr 17, 1940; c: Daniel, Raphael. Mgn dir, Ashkelon Hotels Co, Dagon Hotel, since 1954; mgr, Windsor Hotel, Haifa, Jerusalem Hotel, Jaffa, 1940-47; head, purchasing dept, Malben. Prins contrib: Founder and first commanding off, Shekem, Isr army post exchange service. Capt, British Army, 1942-46, lt col, IDF 1948-50. Mem: bd dir, Isr Hotel Assn; Tadmor Isr Hotel Sch; Rotary, past pres; Freemasons. Office: Dagon Hotel, Ashkelon, Isr.

DOROTH-DUESTERWALD, Avraham W, Isr, economist, author; b. Berlin, Ger, Aug 6, 1900; s. Leopold and Adele (Spanier) Düsterwald; in Isr since 1934; att Us of Freiburg, Berlin and Heidelberg; m. Ella Striemer. Lectr in pub fin, fac of soc sci, Heb U, Jerusalem, since 1948; fmr: econ editor: Leipziger Tagblatt, 1924-25; Vossische Zeitung, Berlin, 1925-34; secy, training sec, Ger Imm Assn, 1935-37; ed, Meshek Leumi, 1936-41; sr research econ: JA, 1940-48; Min of Fin, 1948-50; dir, research dept, Govt Invest Center, 1950-52; sci econ adv, State Comptroller, 1952-59; fmr mem: Isr Curr Planning comm, Min of Fin; exam bd for chartered pub acctnts, Min of Justice; guest lectr: U Berlin, 1959; U Freiburg, 1968. Mem: exec council, Isr Political Sci Assn; fmr: Isr exec council, Intl Fiscal Assn; Pub Comm for Budget Standards. Author: Foreign Investment in Palestine, 1937; The Social Economic Background of Professional Life in Palestine, 1946; The National Wealth, 2nd ed. 1950; Problems of Public Financing in Developing Countries, 1958; 10 Years Development of Israel's National Wealth, 1958; Principles of Public Finance and Financial Policy, 10th ed, 1966; Principles of Monetary Policy, 1959; Deficit Spending, 1960; Financial Problems of Public Housing, 1962; Economic Aspects of Prohibited Dwellings, 1968. Contbr: Ency Heb; Isr Econ Annual; Philo Lexicon, profsl jours in Isr and abroad. Home: 81 Keren Kayemeth Blvd, Tel Aviv, Isr.

DORSEN, Norman, US, educator; b. NYC, Sep 4, 1930; s. Arthur and Tanya (Stone); BA, Columbia U, 1950; LLB, Harvard Law Sch, 1953; att LSE, London, 1955-56; m. Harriette Koffler, Nov 25, 1965; c: Jennifer, Caroline. Prof, law, dir, Arthur Garfield Hays Civil Liberties prog, NYU Law Sch, since 1961; fmr: law clerk to Justice John Harlan, US Supr Court, 1957-58; lawyer, NYC, 1958-60. Lt, judge advocate gen's corp, US Army, 1953-55. Comm chmn, Amer Bar Assn; bd dirs: Bill of Rights Found; ACLU, gen counsel; Phi Beta Kappa; fmr, bd govs, AJCong; mem: Amer Law Inst. Author: Frontiers of Civil Liberties, 1968; co-author: Political and Civil Rights in the US, 2 vols, 1967; contbr to jours. Recipient: cert of merit, Point Park Coll, 1967. Home: 298 W 11 St, New York, NY. Office: 40 Washington Sq, New York, NY.

DOSTROVSKY, Arieh, Isr, dermatologist, educator; b. Caro, Russ, Feb 25, 1887; s. Moshe and Yoheved (Schreiber); in Isr since 1919; MD, U Basle, 1915; m. Sonya Polyskin, 1908; c: Yoheved Dostrovsky-Kupernik, Israel, Ruth Sagher. Cons, dermat, Heb U-Hadassah Med Hosp and Sch; prof em, dermat and venereology, Heb U-Hadassah Med Sch, Jerusalem, since 1956, head, dept of skin and venereal diseases, 1920-56; dean, 1948-53, fac mem since 1938; fmr, med dir, Hosp for Hansen's Disease, Jerusalem. Pres, Isr Dermat Soc, 1927-1968; mem, expert adv panel, venereal infections and treponematosis, WHO. Co-ed, Intl Dermatologica, Basle; contbr to Isr and fgn med jours. Home: 19 Alharizi St, Rehavia, Jerusalem, Isr. Office: Heb U-Hadassah Med Sch, POB 499, Jerusalem, Isr.

DOTAN, Aron, Isr, educator; b. Stuttgart, Ger, Jan 12, 1928; s. Nissan and Klara (Spindel) Deutscher; in Isr since 1933; MA, PhD, Heb U, 1947-52; m. Ruth Ventura, Nov 19, 1952; c: Zevi, Haya, Tamar. Sr lectr, head, Heb lang dept, Tel Aviv U, since 1964, vice-dean, fac of hum, 1966-67; sr lectr, Heb lang, Bar Ilan U, since 1964; research secy, Acad Heb Lang, Heb U, Jerusalem, 1951-64; visiting prof, Sorbonne, 1967-68. Adv mem, Acad Heb Lang, Jerusalem. Author: Dikduke hate'-amim of Aharon Ben Asher, 1967; contbr to profsl jours. Home: 89 Hauniversita St, Tel Aviv, Isr. Office: Heb Lang Dept, Tel Aviv U, Ramat Aviv, Isr.

DOTHAN, Joseph, Isr, management cons; b. Hung, Feb 13, 1914; s. Shmuel and Feige (Fuchs) Deutsch; in Isr since 1939; att Budapest U; m. Ahuva Dichter; c: Shmuel, Miriam Chosen. Adv, i/c, org and methods, Tel Aviv-Jaffa Munic, since 1957; instr, mgmt, to Afr groups studying in Isr; fmr: produc and org mgr, Pal Textile Printing, 1939-48; adv, org and methods: Min of Transp and Communications, 1949-51; Civil Service Commn, 1951-54; Histadrut Kupat Cholim, 1954-57. Haganah; off, IDF, 1948-49. Co-found, Isr Inst Productivity; f: Isr Assn Mgmt Cons; Isr Assn Social and Econ Scis; Inst Work Study Practitioners, Brit; asso, Brit Inst Mgmt; mem: Isr Mgmt Cen; Inst Off Mgmt; Assn Tchrs of Mgmt, both Brit; sr mem, Amer Inst Ind Engrs. Contbr to profsl jours in Isr and abroad. Recipient: medal, civil service comm, Govt of Isr. Home: 202 Modein St, Givatayim, Isr. Office: POB 2299, Tel Aviv, Isr.

DOTHAN, Moshe, Isr archaeologist; b. Cracow, Pol, Sep 13, 1919; s. Salomon and Helen (Gutfreund) Hammer; in Isr since 1938; MA, Heb U, 1951, PhD, 1960; m. Trude Krakauer, Apr 11, 1950; c: Daniel, Uriel. Dir, excavations and survey, Dept of Antiquities, since 1954, with dept since 1950. Served Brit Army; IDF. Contbr to profsl jours. Home: 25 Kaf Tet Benovember St, Jerusalem, Isr. Office: POB 586, Jerusalem, Isr.

DOUBEN, Jouey Buchenwald-Behrmann, UK, executive, actor, consultant; b. Windawa, Latvia, June 25, 1925; s. Abraham and Sarah (Behrmann); in Eng since 1934. Dir, hist info and political intelligence, Research Inst of The Holocaust, London, since 1945; found, Comm for Inves of Nazi Crimes in Baltic States, since 1945. Fmr inmate: extermination camps: Bu-

chenwald, Stuthoff-Danzig, Kaiserwald, Dondangen (only survivor); adv to prosecution, first rebuttal witness, Buchenwald Trials, Dachau, Munich, 1947. Served US Army and US Mil Govt in Ger, 1945. Actor: part with Frank Sinatra, "Naked Runner". Mem: British Actors Equity Assn; Union of Victims of Fascism and Nazism; fmr: press off, Assn of Nazi Camp Survivors, Gt Brit; exec mem, Union Victims of Fascism in Ger. Contbr to intl publs. Home: 34 Elm Tree Rd, London NW8, Eng. Office: 8 Harley St, London, W1, Eng.

DOUER, Yair, Isr, civil servant; b. Damascus, Syria, Mar 11, 1917; s. Eliyahu and Sarah (Sakal); in Isr since 1924; BA, Heb U, 1964; m. Lydie Chich, Aug 2, 1950; c: Gad, Tal, Ayala. Dir, Nahal div, Min of Defense, since 1960; fmr: mem, Kibbutz Alumot, 1935-42; Kibbutz Ramat Yohnan, 1942-56; emissary, JA, Tunisia, 1948-50; dir, youth immigration dept: Tunisia, 1952-53; Morocco, 1954-55. Cdr, immigration camp, Fr, 1948; Haganah; lt, IDF, 1948-49. Mem bd: Ind Nahal Found; Public Tender Commn for Civil Service. Recipient: Ot Mishmar; Notroot. Home: 12 Sde Boker St, Givatayim, Isr. Office: Hakiryah, Tel Aviv, Isr.

DOVRAT, Aharon, Isr, business exec; b. Buenos Aires, Arg, Sept 30, 1931; s. Shlomo and Rosa (Dzeghitman); in Isr since 1958; att: Heb Tchrs Coll, Buenos Aires, 1942-49; U Buenos Aires, 1949-53; m. Dalia Tsur, Jan 5, 1952; c: Anat, Shlomo. Mgn dir, CLAL Isr Inves Co Ltd, since 1956; fmr: dep dir, Inves Cen, 1959-62; dir, div of ind, Min of Commerce and Ind, 1962-65. Home: 11 Mavoh Yoram St, Jerusalem, Isr. Office: 32 Ben Yehuda St, Tel Aviv, Isr.

DOWEK, Ephraim, Isr, diplomat; b. Cairo, Egypt, Nov 9, 1930; s. Solomon and Adrienne (Coen); deg, Farouk U, Cairo; att Tel Aviv U; m. Sarah Tobie, Feb 18, 1951; c: Ada, Shmuel. Ambass to Dahomey, since 1965; treas, Kibbutz Yogev 1951-53; mayor, Beit Shean, 1955-63; ambass to Chad, 1963-65; mem exec, Mapai, 1955-63; MK, 1965. Fmr: mem: Natl Educ Bd; exec, local councils; Vaad Hapoel, Histadrut; club: Rotary. Hobby, philately. Office: Min for Fgn Affairs, Jerusalem, Isr.

DRABKIN, Murray, US, attorney; b. NYC, Aug 3, 1928; s. Max and Minnie (Masin); AB, Hamilton Coll, 1950; LLB, Harvard Law Sch, 1953. Pvt practice, NYC and Wash DC, since 1968; dir, Conn Revenue Task Force, since 1969; cons, Stanford Research Inst, since 1969; counsel, comm on the judiciary, US House of Reprs, 1957-65; chief counsel, Spec Congressional subcomm on State Taxation, 1961-65; spec cons, tax policy, to Mayor Lindsay, NYC, 1965-66, spec asst, 1966-68. Lt cdr, USNR, 1953-57. Prin contribs: architect of 1966 overhaul of NYC tax sys. Mem: tax comm, C of C, NY, since 1968; Natl Bankruptcy Conf since 1968; Assn of Bar of NYC; Phi Beta Kappa; Delta Sigma Rho; fmr: mem: adv council, Tax Inst of Amer; NYC Adv Comm on tax admn; delg, Gov Rockefeller, Annual Conf of Natl Tax Assn; club: Harvard, NYC. Author: State Taxation of Interstate Commerce, 1965; contbr to legal jours. Hobby: sailing. Home: 56 Washington Ave, New York, NY. Office: 277 Park Ave, New York, NY.

DRACHE, Samuel J, Can, attorney; b. Winnipeg, Can, Dec 11, 1906; s. Mordechai and Etta (Olberg); BA, U Man, 1926, LLB, 1929; m. Marjorie Tadman, Apr 27, 1933; c: Arthur. Ret, 1963; pvt law practice, 1930-63; appd: Kings Counsel, 1951; Q.C. Fmr: found: Zionist Cultural Inst, 1949; Zionist Research Found, 1959; chmn, Zionist Educ Trust, 1962; hon life pres, ZOC; co-org, local chap, UJA; W vice-pres, HIAS; delg: first post-war world conf, WZO, London, 1945; delg, WZCong, Jerusalem, 1956, 1960; dir: Patriotic Salvage Org, 1940-45; Winnipeg Little Theatre, 1950-55; Winnipeg Sym Orch; Comty Chest, 1954-60; mem: adv bd, Min of Ind and Commerce, 1958-60; clubs: Glendale Country; Montefiore; Wig and Pen, London. Home: 128 Montrose St, Manitoba, Can. Office: 209 Notre Dame Ave, Winnipeg, Can.

DRACHLER, Norman, US, educator; b. Pol, May 20 1912; s. Israel and Rose (Saperstein); in US since 1923; MA, Wayne State U, 1939; PhD, U Mich, 1951; m. Evelyn Taxey, Apr 1, 1937; c: David, Judith Handel, Ruth. Supt, Detroit Public Schs, since 1967, staff mem of sch system since 1937; rel educ dir, Temple Beth El, 1951-66; cons, US Off Educ, 1966-69. Bd dirs: JCC; Boy Scouts, Detroit area; pres, Natl Assn Temple Educs, 1954-56; mem, LZOA. Spec interests: collector of Judaica, Amer educ hist. Home: 18971 Littlefield, Detroit, Mich. Office: 5057 Woodward, Detroit, Mich.

DRACHLISS, Eliezer, Isr, banker; b. Ukraine, Russ, Aug 22, 1904; s. Moshe and Freida (Serebrenick); in Isr since 1926; att HS; Sem Courses of Econ and Control, all in Russ; m. Gosia Kilisky, 1932; c: Shlomit Atter. Mgn dir, Isr-Brit Bank Inves Co Ltd, since 1964; mem, bd dirs: Mobilia Pistons Ltd; Natl Co for Devl and Inves; Universal Protein Establishment, Unimark, Isr; other co's; fmr: road laborer; ed, She'-arim, Tel Aviv Munic Workers mag; head, control body, all ind and commercial establishments of Histadrut, 1952-57. Served Haganah. Mem: Histadrut Haovdim; Ind and Commercial Club; Isr Mgmt Cen; natl council, Histadrut, delg to confs; natl council, Tel Aviv dist council, Mapai delg to confs; fmr: delg, Conf of Employee Org; mem bd, Pal Aviation Enterprises; financial secy, world WIZO; gen secy, cen comm, KH, Beersheba. Contbr to: local press; econ publs. Hobbies: chess, philately. Home: 19 Weizman St, Tel Aviv, Isr. Office: 31 Lilienblum St, Tel Aviv, Isr.

DRACHMAN, Julian M, US, educator, author; b. NYC, Feb 17, 1894; s. Bernard and Sarah (Weil); BS, CCNY, 1915; MA, Columbia U, 1916, PhD, 1930; m. Emily Deitchman, May 1, 1927 (decd); c: Richard, Jonas, Daniel. Ret; lectr: New Sch of Social Research, 1961-64; tchr, Eng, Morris HS, 1936; chmn, dept, Eng, New Utrecht HS, 1936-62; lectr: humanities, Grad Sch of Educ, CUNY, summer sessions: 1959, 1960, 1963, 1964. Sgt, US Army MC, 1918-19. Author: Studies in the Literature of Natural Science, 1930; Spelling for Secondary Schools, 1941; Making Friends with Words, 1956; Just For Now, poetry, 1969; contbr to periodicals and mags. Bd govs, J Tchrs Comty Chest; fmr pres: J Tchrs Assn; Assn of Chmn of Eng; Menorah Alumni; mem: Cong Zichron Ephraim; Manhattan Beach J Cen; Citizens Union; World Federalists; Natl Council of Eng Grad Union; ZOA; LZOA; fmr: head counsellor: Surprise Lake Camp, Camp Tabor. Recipient: Best Short Play, J Drama Guild, 1955. Hobby: art. Home: 225 E 57 St, New York, NY.

DRACHSLER, Leo M, US, attorney; b. Czech, Sep 6, 1899; s. Jacob and Charlotte (Neugeboren); in US since 1903; BA, CCNY, 1920; LLB, Columbia Law Sch, 1924; att: grad fac, political sci, Columbia U, 1935-42; New Sch for Social Research, 1935-42; m. Helene Tannenbaum, Nov 26, 1936; c: Peter, David. Pvt practice, intl law, since 1925; adj prof, NY Law Sch, since 1965; fmr: asso counsel, judiciary comm, US House of Reprs, 1933; spec counsel, NYC Charter Rev Commn, 1938; acting regional atty, sr hearing off, Natl War Lab Bd, 1943-45; atty, anti-trust div, US Dept of Justice, 1945-46; mem, prosecution staff, Intl Mil Tribunal, Nuremberg, Ger, 1946-47; spec adv, US DP Commn, Munich, Ger, 1948-49; judge, US Mil Govt Courts for Ger, 1949-50. Mem: leg comm, Citizens Union, NYC; Citizens Housing Council, NYC; Amer Bar Assn; Amer Fgn Law Assn; Consular Law Soc; NY, NJ, Conn, Fed Bar Assns; Amer Soc Intl Law; Dem Party, NY, Co; Amer Arbitration Assn; NY chap, AJComm. Co-author: Anti-Trust Delimma-Why Congress Should Revise the Anti-Trust Laws, 1969; contbr to legal jours. Home: 55 Park Terrace E, New York, NY.

DRAGER, Marvin, US, public relations exec; b. NYC, May 10, 1920; s. Harry and Fanny (Katzman); BS, St John's U, 1940; MA, Columbia U, 1942; m. Lenore Schwam, 1943; c: Sharon, Laura, Iris. PR cons since 1947; fmr: reporter, NY Post, 1942-43; photo ed, AP, 1943-46; asst PR dir, Columbia Records, 1946-47. Hobbies: photography, golf. Home: 40 W 86 St, New York, NY. Office: 420 Madison Ave, New York, NY.

DRAPKIN, Israel Senderey, Isr, criminologist; b. Rosario, Arg, July 17, 1906; s. Isaac and Louise (Senderey); in Isr since 1959; BA, MD, U Santiago, Chile, 1923-29; postgrad studies: U Paris, 1935; U London, 1945-46; m. Rebecca Gidekel, Sep 9, 1936; c: Luisa Zeldis, Allan. Prof criminology, dir, Inst Criminology, law fac, Heb U, since 1959; fmr: chief, psychosomatic outpatient clinic, Natl Health Service, Chile, 1947-59; lectr, Criminal Police Sch, Chile, 1942-59; prof, criminology, law fac, U Chile, 1950-59; found and dir: Chilean Inst of Criminology, 1936-59; Inst of Criminology, Heb U, 1959. Vice-pres, Intl Soc Criminology, Paris; hon pres: Dist Grand lodge, B'nai B'rith, Chile; Panama City; mem, Free Masons, Chile; fmr: mem bd dirs, Intl Soc of Criminology, Paris; grand pres, Dist Grand lodge; B'nai B'rith, Latin Amer. Author: Manual de Criminologia, 1944; Prensa de Criminalidad, 1958; contbr to intl profsl jours. Recipient: scholar and f, British Council, 1945-46; Oscar Freire decoration, State of Sao Paulo, Brazil, 1968; Spec interest: archaeol, enthnography of pre-Columbian Amer; photography; music.

Home: 48 Harlap St, Jerusalem Isr. Office: Heb U, Jerusalem, Isr.

DRAZIN, Nathan, US, rabbi; b. NYC, Mar 17, 1906; s. Aaron and Malka (Leboff); ordained rabbi, Yeshiva U, 1933; BS, Columbia U, 1932, MA, 1933; PhD, Johns Hopkins U, 1937; m. Celia Hoenig, Dec 26, 1933; c: Israel, Joseph, Sura Ungar. Rabbi, Shaarei Tfiloh Cong, 1933-64; pres, Talmudical Acad Baltimore, 1958-68. Pres, Mizrachi, seaboard region, since 1947; praesidium, Council Orthodox Rabbis since 1954; dir, JWF, 1958-61; mem, Bur Kosher Meat and Food Control, since 1949. Author: History of Jewish Education, 515 BCE-220 CE, 1940; Marriage Made in Heaven, 1958; contbr to mags. Spec interest: marriage counselling. Home: 3622-B Fords Lane, Baltimore, Md.

DREHER, Carl, US, author, engineer; b. Vienna, Aus, Feb 16, 1896; s. Julius and Cecilia (Friedmann); in US since 1899; BS, CCNY, 1917; m. Rose Genodman, Apr 13, 1925. Author and writer since 1937; fmr: engr, RCA, 1917-29; dir of recording, RKO Studios Inc, 1929-37. Major US Army, 1942-45. F, Inst Radio Engrs; Inst Elec and Electronics Engrs. Author: The Coming Showdown, 1942; Automation, 1957; staff writer, The Nation, since 1957; contbr to mags. Home: RD 5, Brewster, NY.

DREILING, David A, US, surgeon, educator; b. Bklyn, NY, June 5, 1918; s. Louis and Rose (Lusty); BA, Cornell U, 1938; MD, NYU, 1942; m. Muriel Oppenheimer, June 25, 1942; c: David jr. Prof, surg, Mt Sinai Sch of Med, since 1967, dir, experimental surg, 1962-67; chief of surg: Elmhurst Hosp, since 1964; Greenpoint Hosp, 1926-1964; asso prof, clinical surg, Albert Einstein Sch of Med, 1956-64. Mem: AMA; Acad of Med; Acad of Sci; Amer Coll Surgs; Intl Coll Surgs; Amer Soc Clinical Research; NY Surgs Soc; Amer Phys Soc. Author: Mallatie del Pancreas, 1960; Pancreatic Inflammatory Disease, 1964; co-ed, Amer jour Gastroenterology; contbr to profsl jours and books. Home: 171 W 57 St, New York, NY. Office: 19 E 98 St, New York, NY.

DREWS, Robert S, US, psychiatrist; b. Bklyn, NY, Dec 25, 1900; s. Jacob and Ida (Singer); MD, Wayne U, 1925, MD, 1926; MS, U Mich, 1935, D Public Health, 1938; postgrad studies: Wayne Co Gen Hosp; Johns Hopkins; Columbia U; Temple U; Neuropsycht Inst, U Mich; m. Josephine Sandorf, June 21, 1925; c: Sonya Raimi. Pvt practice, psycht, since 1946, gen practice, 1926-46; fmr: mem staff, Children's Hosp and Women's Hosp, 1927-36; instr, neuropath, Wayne U, 1926-31. F: Amer Geriatrics Soc; Assn Phys and Surgs; co-found: Amer Acad Psychosomatic Med; Amer Ontoanalytic Soc; Amer Soc for Social Psycht, past pres; mem: Amer Soc for Research in Clinical Hypnosis; AAAS; Inst for Gen Semantics, med sect; Amer Sociol Assn; Acad of Psychotherapy; Intl Cong Psycht; Intl Cong of Criminology; Founders Soc; Detroit Inst of Arts; Detroit Phil Soc; Detroit Sci Mus; Detroit Roundtable Catholics, Jews, Protestants; Masons; Shriners; Phi Epsilon Delta; pres: Amer Soc Group Psychotherapy and Psychodrama, Detroit chap, Intl Soc for Gen Semantics; dir, Mich Inst Group Psychotherapy and Psychodrama; co-found, first pres, Amer Acad Group Psychotherapy and Psychodrama; asso, Moreno Inst, NYC; clubs: Factfinders; Monad; Specialists; Bohemian. Contbr ed: jour of Existential Psycht; Jour of Group Psychotherapy. Recipient: asso f, Mich State Med Soc, 1938, f, 1939; 1st prize for essays, Amer Phys Lit Guild, 1937, 1938. Home and office: 12500 Broadstreet Blvd, Detroit, Mich.

DREYER, Edward Leo, US, business exec; b. NYC, Mar 11, 1918; s. Samuel and Anette (Spilberg); BS, U of Va, 1939; m. Rose Morey, June 11, 1944; c: John, Nancy. Pres, Adamas Carbide Corp, since 1945; mem, bd dirs: Newark Brush Co; Morey Machy, LI; purchasing agt, Jacques Kreisler Corp, 1939-41. Lt, USN, 1941-45. Mem: Employment Assn of Northern NJ, past pres; bd, Union Council, Boy Scouts of Amer; exec comm, NJ ADL, past chmn; chief exec forum, Young Pres Org, past vice-pres; mem: Amer Soc Tool Mfr Engrs; Soc Carbide Engrs; AJComm; B'nai B'rith. Home: 15 Troy Dr, Short Hills, NJ. Office: Adamas Carbide, Kenilworth, NJ.

DREYFUSS, Fritz, Isr, physician, educator; b. Fuerth, Ger, May 23, 1910; s. Albert and Alice (Oppenheimer); in Isr since 1934; MD, U Basel, 1934; m. Adinah Lachovitsky, Aug, 1942; c: David, Gideon, Arnon. Chief, dept of med "B", Ichilov Hosp, Tel Aviv, since 1963; asso prof med, Heb U-Hadassah Med Sch, since 1955; prof, med, Tel Aviv U Med

Sch, since 1965; fmr: chief phys, Hadassah Hosp, Jerusalem, 1946-63; dean fac, continuing med educ, Tel Aviv U, 1962-68. Contbr to profsl jours. Home: 50 Be'eri St, Tel Aviv, Isr. Office: Ichilov Munic Hosp, 6 Weizman St, Tel Aviv, Isr.

DREYFUSS, Henry, US, industrial designer; b. NYC, Mar 2, 1904; s. Louis and Elise (Gorge); hon degs: Occidental Coll, 1953; Pratt Inst,1963; Otis Art Inst,1968; m. Doris Marks, July 26, 1930, c: John, Gail Wilson, Ann. Corporate cons, since 1969, clients include: Hallmark Cards, Amer Tel & Tel Amer Airlines, Polaroid; fmr, owner, ind design firm, 1929-69. Vice-pres, Hollywood Bowl Assn; bd, dirs, Educ Facilities Lab; bd trustees, Ford Found; mem fac: Cal Inst of Tech; UCLA; council chmn, Performing Arts Ind Designers Soc of Amer; Benjamin Franklin f, Royal Soc of Arts: visiting comm, Harvard U Grad Sch of Design; past pres, Amer Soc of Ind Designers; mem: bd overseers, Harvard Coll; Amer Soc of MEs. Architectural League of NY; found, Natl Council of Arts. Author: Designing for People, 1955-67; The Measure of Man, 1960-67; entbr to natl mags and profsl jours. Recipient: gold medal award, Architectural League of NY, 1951; Order of Orange-Nassau, Queen Juliana, 1952; award, Soc of Ind Designers, 1960; award, Phila Mus Coll of Art, 1962; design in steel award, Amer Iron and Steel Inst, 1965; Ambass award for achievement, Eng, 1965; spec interest: preparing intl symbol dict. Home: South Pasadena, Calif. Office: 4 W 58 St, New York, NY; 500 Columbia St, Pasadena, Cal.

DRILLMAN, Solomon E, US, rabbi; b. Beuthen, Ger, Aug 2, 1921; s. Isaac and Mindel (Wolf-Shifman); in US since 1946; ordained rabbi, Yeshiva U, 1949, MRE, 1958; m. Chaya Tversky, June 21, 1950; c: Yaakov, Yehiel, Yehoshua. Rabbi, Glenwood, J Cen, since 1952; instr, Bklyn br, Yeshiva U, since 1949. Pres, Vaad Harabonim of Flatbush, since 1966; exec comm: JNF, Bklyn; educ comm: Yeshiva Rambam; Yeshiva of E Pkwy; planning comm, Isr Bond dr, Bklyn; mem: RabCA; Union Orthodox Rabbis of Amer. Home: 956 E 54 St, Brooklyn, NY. Study: 888 E 56 St, Brooklyn, NY.

DROOKER, Joshua Charles, US, physician, educator; b. Boston, Mass, Dec 8, 1907; s. Noah and Freida (Chait); BS, Tufts Coll, 1929, MD, 1933; m. Emile Levy, July 3, 1947; c: David, Nancy. Prof and chmn, tept of otolaryngology, Tufts U Med Sch, since 1958, on fac since 1946; instr, otolaryngology, Harvard U Med Sch, since 1938. Lt col, US Army MC, 1942-47. Mem; Amer Acad of Ophthal and Otolaryngology; Amer Otological, Rhinological and Laryngologic Soc. Contbr to med publs. Home: 20 Edgehill Rd, Brookline, Mass. Office: 285 Commonwealth Ave, Boston, Mass.

DROPKIN, David, US, educator; b. Vitebsk, Russ, Sep 13, 1908; s. Abraham and Minna (Pearlstein); in US since 1923; ME, Cornell U, 1933; MME, 1935, PhD, 1938; McMullen Research Scholar, 1936-38; m. Sophie Kutzko, Sep 15, 1940; c: Marilyn, Lloyd. Prof, mech engr, Cornell U, since 1957, on fac since 1943; McMullen Research Scholar, 1936-38; Westinghouse research asso, 1938-41; visiting engr, Brookhaven Natl Lab, 1949-50; sr sci, Avco Corp, 1957. Mem: AAUP; Cornell Soc Engrs; Amer Soc for Engr Educ; Amer Soc Mes; Amer Soc Heating, Refrigerating and Air Conditioning Engrs; Sigma Xi; Pi Tau Sigma; Tau Beta Pi; Atmos; Temple Beth El; AAAS; NY Acad of Scis; Phi Kappa Phi; clubs: Statler; Cornell, Ithaca; Cornell, NY. Contbr to profsl jours. Home: 210 Eastwood Ave, Ithaca, NY. Office: Cornell U, Ithaca, NY.

DROPKIN, John, J, US, physicist, educator; b. Bobruisk, Russ, Feb 22, 1910; s. Samuel and Celia (Levine); in US since 1912; BA, Columbia U, 1930; MS, Bklyn Poly Inst, 1947, PhD, 1948; m. Zelda Stern, 1933 (decd); c: Frances, Vivian; m. 2nd, Ruth Warshavsky Zeitlin, 1957; stepc: Devorah, Jonathan. Prof, physics, Bklyn Poly Inst, since 1955, head of dept, 1957-65, Thomas Potts Prof of Physics, since 1957, fac mem since 1948; fmr math tchr, NYC HS, 1936-48. F: Amer Phys Soc; Amer Physics Tchrs; Phi Beta Kappa; Sigma Xi. Contbr to profsl jours. Home: 473 E 18 St, Brooklyn, NY. Office: 333 Jay St, Brooklyn, NY.

DROR, Benjamin, Isr, business exec; b. Stanislawow, Pol, June 6, 1900; s. Jacob and Hinda; m. Judith; c: Rifka. Mgr, milk div, Tnuva Ltd. Fmr: mgr, Solel Boneh Ltd; bd dirs, Hamashbir Coop Ltd. Mem: high court, Histadrut; Intl Assn of Milk, Food and Environmental Sanitarians. Home: Kibbutz Bet Alfa, Isr. Office: Merkaz Tnuva Ltd, Tel Aviv, Isr.

DROR, Igal, Isr, business exec; b. Beer-Yaacov, Isr, June 29, 1922; s. Nachum and Sara (Prober) Ziviluk; att Herzliya Gymnasia, Tel Aviv; m. Edith Amzalek; c: Orit, Nachum. Head of oprs, Port of Ashdod, since 1965; fmr insp, Yachin, 1949-57; Citrus Market Bd of Isr, 1957-65. Lt col, IDF. Chmn, munic, Ganei Yehuda; club: Rotary, Savyon, fmr pres. Home: 8 Hashikma St, Ganei Yehuda, Isr. Office: Port of Ashdod, Isr.

DROR, Yehezkel, Isr, educator; b. Vienna, Aus, Aug 12, 1928; s. Isidor and Stephania (Altman) Friemann; in Isr since 1938; BA, MJur, Heb U, 1953; LLM, SJD, Harvard U, 1955; m. Rachel Elboim, Feb, 1953; c: Asrael, Otniel, Itiel. Prof, head, public admn div, Heb U, since 1964; govt cons on policy making, planning, admn, since 1964; f, Cen for Advanced Study in Behavioral Scis, 1962-63; sr staff mem, Rand Corp, 1968-70. Staff off: Haganah, IDF, since 1944. Chmn: acad council, Mgmt Coll; public admn, Isr Mgmt Cen; vice-chmn, Isr Cen for Policy Studies; mem, Intl Future Research Comm. Author: Public Policymaking Re-examined, 1968; Ventures in Policy Sciences, 1970; co-author: Israel: High Pressure Planning, 1966. Recipient: f, UN, Eur, 1958; Rosolio award, Public Admn Conf, 1965. Home: 48 Shimoni St, Jerusalem, Isr. Office: Heb U, Jerusalem, Isr.

DRORI, Zephania, Isr, rabbi; b. Isr, Mar 13, 1937; s. Itzhak and Rachel (Ratz) Munin; att: Yeshivat B'nei Akiva, Kfar Haroeh, 1950-53; Yeshivat Kerem B'Yaune, Yavneh, 1953-56; ordained rabbi, Yeshivat Merkaz Harav Kook, Jerusalem, 1963; m. Chaya Samson, Oct 24, 1963; c: Emuna, Eliyahu, Leah. Chief Rabbi, Kiryat Shmona, since 1968; fmr: lectr, Judaic studies, JA, 1956-67; head, Yavneh grad prog, JA, 1963-66; head, Yeshivat Yerushalaiym leZerim, 1966-68; co-found, Yeshivat Kerem Bi'Yavne. Mil Rabbinate, 1959. Fmr mem: Natl Council of B'nei Akiva; natl exec, Mishmeret Hatzeira. Author: laAmelim laTora, 1963; lectr, Kol Isr Radio, weekly bc, Popular Halacha, since 1968. Spec interest: phil of Rabbi Kook. Home: 10/8 Yehuda Halevy St, Kiryat Shmona, Isr. Study: Rel Council, Kiryat Shmona, Isr.

DRORY, Mordechai, Isr, diplomat; b. Jerusalem, Isr, Feb 16, 1931; s. Meir and Jaffa; att, U Paris; BA, Heb U, 1962; m. Shoshana Goltz, 1951; c: Joseph, Alon, Consul gen, Marseille, Fr, since 1968; fmr: mem, Isr emb, Paris, 1956-58; official, Min of Defense, 1959-60; dir, dept finance, Min for Fgn Affairs, 1964-67; chief, div of personnel, 1967-68. IDF, 1948-50. Office: Min for Fgn Affairs, Jerusalem, Isr.

DROSSIN, Julius, US, educator, cellist; b. Phila, Pa, May 17, 1918; s. Alexander and Rachel (Rosenberg); BMus, U of Pa, 1938; MA, W Reserve U, 1951, PhD, 1956; m. Esther Weinstock, May 17, 1941 (decd); m. 2nd, Barbara Wolpaw, Feb 4, 1967; c: Beverly Siegel, Alexander, Phyllis, Laurie, Penny, Ellen. Chmn, prof, music dept, Cleveland State U, since 1956; fmr: cellist, Cleveland Sym Orch, 1948-57; instr, Villa Maria Coll, Erie, Pa, 1951-58. Sgt, US Army, 1943-45. Mem, bd trustees, vice-pres, Koch Sch Music; delg, Cleveland JWF; bd dirs, Cleveland Philharmonic Orch; adv comm, Cleveland Bd Educ; mem: Amer Musicological Soc; shmn, Cleveland Composers Guild. Author: The Perceptive Listen 1970. Composer: 4 syms; Kaddish for Chorus and Orch; 8 String Quartets; 5 Sonatas; chamber music. Recipient: Pres citation, 3 battle stars. Home: 3141 Somerset Dr, Shaker Hgts, O. Office: Cleveland State U, 24th and Euclid Ave, Cleveland, O.

DRUCKER, Daniel Charles, US, engineer, educator; b. NYC, June 3, 1918; s. Moses and Henrietta (Weinstein); BS, Columbia U, 1937, CE, 1938, PhD, 1940; m. Ann Bodin, 1939; c: David, Miriam Baker. Dean, coll of engr, U of Ill, since 1968; instr, mech engr, Cornell U, 1940-43; supr, mech solids, Armour Research Found, 1943-45; asst prof, mech, Ill Inst Tech, 1946-47; chmn, phys sci council, Brown U, 1961-63, prof, engr, since 1950, mem fac since 1947. USAAF, 1945-46. Mem, exec comm, applied mech div, Amer Soc MEs; chmn: Intl Cong Experimental Mechs; US delg, Intl Union of Theoretical and Applied Mechs, 1966-68; mem: Gen Assembly Engrs J Council, 1966-68; Soc for Experimental Stress Analysis, fmr pres; Inst Aerospace Sci; ASCE; Amer Soc Engr Educ; Natl Acad Engrs; Soc of Rhenology; NRC; Tau Beta Phi; Sigma Xi; Amer Acad Arts and Scis; Amer Technion Soc, southern NE chap, 1953-54; mem bd, J Comty Cen, Providence, 1957-59. Author: Introduction to Mechanics of Deformable Solids, 1967; tech ed, Jour of Applied Mechs, 1956-68; mem, ed bd, Quarterly of Applied Math, since 1957; contbr to tech and sci jours. Recipient: Guggenheim f, 1960-61; von Karman medal ASCE, 1966; Marburg lectr,

ASTM, 1966; Laame medal ASEE, 1967; Murray lectr, SESA, 1967; Fulbright travel grant, 1968; NATO Sr Sci f, 1968. Office: Dean, coll of engr, U of Ill, Urbana, Ill.

DUBIN, Bernard, US, organization exec; b. Phila, Pa, Mar 21, 1915; s. Samuel and Mollie (Gumberg); BS, Temple U, 1936; MSW, U of Pa, 1938; m. Sarah Kurtzman, July 21, 1940; c: Don, Stephen. Exec dir, J Fed Camden Co, since 1947; fmr: asst to dir, J Family Service, Phila, 1938-42; dir: Personal Aid Bur, 1942-43; natl services, United Service for New Amer, 1943-47. Chmn, exec inst, intermediate cities, Council of J Fed and Wfr Funds, 1962-63; chmn, Assn of United Fund Execs, Camden Co, 1963-65; mem: Camden Co Citizens Adv comm, Survey of Detention and Correctional Facilities; Natl Assn of Social Workers. Contbr to profsl jours. Home: 875 Edge Park Dr, Haddonfield, NJ. Office: 2395 W Marlton Pike, Cherry Hill, NJ.

DUBIN, Harry E, US, biochemist, pharmaceutical exec; b. Russ, Mar 4, 1891; s. Abraham and Fanny (Gold); in US since 1895; BS, CCNY, 1912; PhD, U of Pa, 1916, f, research med; m. Estelle Schacht, June 14, 1917; c: Warren, Alan, Elinor. Cons, Walker Labs, Mt Vernon, NY, 1953-62; fmr: chief chem, Grain Chem Co, NYC, 1918-20; dir, biochem dept, HA Metz Lab, 1923-32, with firm since 1920; pres, HE Dubin Labs, 1933-46; tech dir, US Vitamin Corp, 1936-46; pres, HED Pharmaceuticals, 1951-53. Prin contrib: isolated active principles of cod liver oil in concentrate containing fat-soluble anti-rachitic and anti-ophthalmic vitamins. Mem: Amer Chem Soc; Soc for Experimental Biol and Med; Amer Soc of Biol Chems; NY Acad of Scis; Biochem Soc of Eng. Home: 43 Calton Rd, New Rochelle, NY.

DUBINER, Betty V, Isr, communal worker; b. London, Can, June 3, 1912; d. Alexander and Batsheva (Siskind) Zimmerman; in Isr since 1950; att, London Tech and Commercial Schs, Can; m; c: Donna Wolberger, Daniel, Deborah. Chmn, Sports Club for Handicapped Children; dir, vice-chmn, fund raising, Isr Found for Handicapped, ILAN; mem, exec, Natl Comm for Soldiers Wfr. Home: 33 Nevo, Ramat Gan, Isr.

DUBINSKY, Harold W, US, real estate exec; b. Springfield, Ill, Apr 8, 1908; s. Jack and Ethel (Greenberg); BA, U Wis, 1929; m. Myra Friedman, June 24, 1936. Partner, Jack Dubinsky and Sons, since 1936. Pres, St Louis, J Comty Relations Council, since 1969; vice chmn, exec bd, UAHC, since 1967; hon life pres, Natl Fed of Temple Brotherhoods, since 1964; natl pres, J Chautauqua Soc, 1951-55; clubs: Westwood Country; Mo Athletic. Hobby: photography. Home: 10 Country Estates, Frontenac, Mo. Office: 701 Chestnut St, St Louis, Mo.

DUBSKY, Moshe Zdenek, Isr, organization exec; b. Prague, Czech, Aug 29, 1919; s. Ludvik and Kamilla (Weisbach); in Isr since 1968; m. Sylvia Tcherny, May 10, 1947; c: Peter, David. Dep dir, head off, British ZF, since 1968; fmr: PR off, ZF, UK; mgr, Zionist Year Book; secy, Gen Zionist Admn Off, ZF, UK, 1947-68. Czech Army, 1942-46. Found: Anglo-Isr Friendship League, UK; British Immigrants Parents Assn. Hobbies: photography, music. Home: 6/6 Tor Hazahav St, Herzliya, Isr. Office: 76 Ibn Gvirol St, Tel Aviv, Isr.

DUER-ADLER, Shoshana, Isr, actress; b. Damascus, Syria; d. Eliahu and Sarah; in Isr since 1925; att, Habima Dramatic Sch; w; c: Rina Carmeli, Ilan Adler. Actress, stage, TV, radio; mem, Habima Theatre. Home: 5 Meggido St, Tel Aviv, Isr. Office: Habimah Theatre, Tel Aviv, Isr.

DUFF, Abraham Beer (Dov), Isr educator; b. Jassy, Rum, Feb 1, 1899; in Isr since 1938; élève titulaire, Ecole Pratique des Hautes Etudes, Paris, 1922-23; Lic ès L, U Montpelliere, 1929; PhD, U Jassy, 1932; PhD, honoris causa, U Montpellier, 1956. Prof em, Fr civilization, Heb U, since 1968; fac mem since 1938; mem, archaeol expedition, excavations at Jerusalem, Tel-el-Djesari, 1923-24. Hon pres, Asso Intl des Etudes Françaises, Paris, since 1955, pres, 1952-54. Co-ed, Etudes Gobiniennes, Strasbourg since 1966. Recipient: U Jassy scholarship, 1933; Officier de la Légion d'Honneur. Home 1 Washington St, Jerusalem, Isr.

DUFFIELD, Walter, Australia, organization exec; b. London, Eng, Apr 2, 1921; s. William and Deborah (Piasetsky); in Australia since 1945; BA, U of Hong Kong 1942; m. Ruth Simha Gubbay, Feb 12, 1951; c: Deborah, Judith. Gen secy: State ZC of Vic, since 1947; State ZC, NSW, 1946-47; ZF of Austr and NZ, 1950-54, 1958-62, 1966-70. Brit Army, 1941-45, POW, Japan, 1942-45. Delg, Vic J Bd of Deputies,

since 1948, mem, prog sect, YMHA, Sydney; past pres, S Caulfield Heb Cong, Melbourne; clubs: Vic J Ex-servicemen's; Royal Automobile. Home: 37 Balaclava Rd, E St Kilda, Melbourne, Austr. Office: 584 St Kilda Rd, Melbourne, Austr.

DUKER, Abraham G, US, editor, historian, educator; b. Rypin, Pol, Sep 27, 1907; s. Asher and Feiga (Gorodensky); in US since 1923; BA, CCNY, 1930; PhD, Columbia U, 1956; m. Lillian Sandrow, 1940; c: Nahum, Sara, Dvora. Dir of librs, prof of hist and social instns, Yeshiva U, since 1963; fmr: research librr, Grad Sch for J Social Work, 1934-38; instr, hist: Sem Sch for J Social Studies, 1941-43, 1946-48; Heb Union Sch of Educ and Sacred Music, 1946-56; New Sch For Social Research, 1950-55; Columbia U, 1953-56; pres, prof, Coll of J Studies, Chgo, 1956-62; visiting prof, Columbia U, 1966-67. Mem: bd dirs, YIVO, since 1948; Amer Acad J Research; Isr Hist Soc; J Acad Arts and Scis; Amer Hist Soc; ZOA; LZOA; B'nai B'rith; fmr: exec comm: Natl Council for J Educ; Natl Conf J Communal Service. Author: Eged Agadoth, 1930; Evreiskaia Starina, 1932; The Situation of the Jews in Poland, 1936; Jewish Survival in the World Today, 1939-41; Emerging Cultural Patterns in American Jewish Life, 1950, 1962; Jewish Community Relations, 1952; Workshop in Jewish Community Affairs, 1952; The Great Polish Emigration and the Jews, 1956; The Impact of Zionism on American Jewish Life, 1958; An Evaluation of Achievement in American Jewish Local History Writing, 1960; The Mystery of the Jews in Mickiewicz, 1962; ed: J Social Studies, since 1958; Contemporary Record (now Commentary), 1938-41; contbr to jours. Jome: 90 Laurel Hill Terrace, New York, NY. Office: Yeshiva U, New York, NY.

DULKIN, Sol I, US, biochemist; b. Chgo, Ill, Dec 17, 1915; s. Nathan and Fannie (Fine); BS, Lewis Inst, 1940; MS, U of Ill Coll of Med, 1947; PhD, Northwestern U Med Sch, 1951; m. Emma Sechooler, June 6, 1936; c: Julia, Ellen. Owner, dir, Chem-Tech Labs, since 1952; QM Food & Container Inst, 1947-51. Chmn, S Cal sect, Amer Assn of Clinical Chems, 1962-63; dipl, Amer Bd of Clinical Chem, 1955; mem: Amer Chem Soc; Amer Inst Chems; Inst Food Techs; Amer Assn Clinical Chems; Sigma Xi; B'nai B'rith; AAAS; Amer Assn Bioanalysts; Assn Vitamin Chems. Contbr to profsl jours. Home: 13139 Valleyheart Dr, Sherman Oaks, Cal. Office: 236 S Robertson Blvd, Beverly Hills, Cal.

DULZIN, Leib (Leon), Isr, organization and business exec; b. Minsk, Russ, Mar 31, 1913; s. Moshe and Miryam (Dreizer); in Mex 1928-56; in Isr since 1956; m. Annette Gutman Harrow, Jan 31, 1962; c: Debora, Alon. Treas, mem exec, JA, head, co and inves bur; mem: world directorate, KH; bd dirs, Rassco, Rural and Suburban Settlement Co Ltd; Yakhin Hakal; Ozar Hataassiya; gov: Bank Leumi leIsrael; Pal Land Devl Co. Vice-pres, World Confd of Gen Zionists; mem: cen, political comms, Lib Party; exec, Gahal; fmr, pres, Zionist Org of Mex, 1938-42; mem, exec, Confd of Gen Zionists Latin Amer, 1951-56; jt pres, KH, Independence Bonds Dr in Mex; delg: chmn, world conf, WJC, 1944, chmn, political comm: 23rd, 24th, WZCs. Author: The Economic Role of the Middle Class; The Middle Classes and Their Role in the Productive Absorption of Immigrants; What Can Bring About the Middle Class Immigration; The Economic Absorption of New Immigrants in Israel Yearbook, 1958-61; contbr to periodicals. Home: 11 Mapu St, Tel Aviv, Isr. Office: JA, 17 Kaplan St, Tel Aviv, Isr.

DUNNER, Joseph, US, educator, author: b. Fuerth, Ger, May 10, 1908; s. Samuel and Ella (Laske); in US since 1935; MA, U of Frankfurt, Ger, 1931; PhD, U Basel, 1934; m. Ada Bier, Dec 24, 1935. Sr prof, political sci, Yeshiva U, since 1964; lectr, sch of overseas admn, Harvard U, 1943-44; chief, intelligence sect, OWI, London, 1944-46; dir, Inst Intl Affairs, Grinnell Coll, 1946-58, prof, 1946-63. F: U of Frankfurt; Brookings Inst; life f, Intl Inst Arts and Letters; natl exec comm, ZOA; exec comm, Midwestern Assn Political Sci; natl council, Amer Friends of Hebrew U. Author: Die Gewerkschaften im Arbeitskampf, 1935; If I Forget Thee, 1937; Major Aspects of International Politics, 1948; The Republic of Israel, Its History and Its Promise, 1950; Democratic Bulwark in the Middle East, 1953; Baruch Spinoza and Western Democracy, 1955; Dictionary of Political Science, 1943; A Handbook of World History, 1967. Home: 156-08 Riverside Dr W, New York, NY. Office: Yeshiva U, Amsterdam Ave and 186 St, New York, NY.

DUNSKY, Israel, Isr, business exec; b. Lith, July 20, 1908; s. Judah and Miriam (Butkovsky); in Isr since 1959; BA, U of

S Afr, 1936; m. Irene Hack, 1936. Mayor, Kfar Shmaryahu; bd dir, Isr Cycle Mfr Ltd, since 1959; mgn dir, Belfast Dress Mfr, Jeryl's (Pty), both in S Afr, 1949-59. Chmn, S Afr ZF Comm, Isr, since 1960; fmr pres: Student Zionist Assn; Zionist Youth Council; KH; United Isr Appeal; Zionist Fed; Germiston United Heb Cong; all in S Afr; repr S Afr at WZC; fmr mem, WZCs. Home: 56 HaOranim St, Kfar Shma·yahu, Isr. Office: Mayor of Kfar Shmaryahu, Isr.

DUNSKY, Shimshon, Can, author, teacher; b. Yasinovka, Russ, Aug 18, 1899; s. Avraham and Chaya (Liverant); in Can since 1922; m. Esther Stilman, Dec 7, 1923; c: Menahem, Zipporah Rabinovitch. Vice-prin, tchr, mem bd dirs, J People's Schs, since 1923. Author: Imunei Dikduk, 2 parts, 6th ed; Midrash Rabbah Echah, (Lamentations); Yiddish trans and explanatory notes, 1956; Midrash Rabbah-Esther and Ruth, Yiddish trans and explanatory notes, 1962; Midrash Rabbah-Koheleth (Ecclesiastes), Yiddish trans and explanatory notes, 1967; contbr to Yiddish educ jours. Mem: J Writers Assn, Montreal; Farband Lab Zionist Order; Keren Hatarbut of Can; Yiddish Pen Club; J Public Libr, Montreal. Recipient: H M Caiserman Lit award, Can J Cong, Can J Cong. Home: 6567 De Vimy, Montreal, Can. Office: 5170 Van Horne Ave, Montreal, Can.

DURBACH, Saul, S Afr, civil engineer; b. Boshof, S Afr, Feb 6, 1917; s. Abraham and Annette (Shapiro); in Lesotho, Afr, since 1967; BCE, U Witwatersrand, 1938; m. Mona Friedberg, Jan 11, 1944; c: Janet, Ronald, Elaine. Chief conservation off, Dept Agric, since 1967; fmr irrigation engr: S Afr Govt, 1945-49; Rhodesian Govt, 1950-56; chief conservation engr, Govts of Rhodesia and Zambia, 1956-67. Capt, S Afr Engr Corps, 1940-45. Mem: S Afr Inst Engrs; Rhodesian Inst Engrs. Recipient: Afr Star; British Defense Medal. Hobby: tennis. Home: 38 Maseru W, Maseru, Lesotho, Afr. Office: Dept of Soil Conservation, Maseru, Lesotho, Afr.

DURWOOD, Maureen W, US, communal worker; b. Providence, RI, June 14, 1931; d. William and Julianna (Schmelz) Wolkoff; att Pembroke Coll, 1949-52; m. Richard Durwood, June 2, 1950; c: Keith, Jan, Dana. Asso chmn, gen solicitation, J Fed, since 1962, spec gifts chmn, 1968-69; bd mem, Natl Council J Women, chmn, PR; corresp secy, Kan City chap, women's comm of Brandeis U, since 1961; bd mem, AJComm, since 1962, vice-chmn, Kan City chap, 1969, 1970; bd mem, sisterhood, Temple B'nai Yehudah; mem: Natl Council J Women; League Women Voters; Menorah Hosp Auxiliary. Hobby: antiques. Home: 6100 Mission Dr, Shawnee Mission, Kan.

DUSHKIN, Alexander M, Isr, author, educator; b. Suwalki, Pol, Aug 21, 1890; s. William and Rachel (Strevlian); in Isr since 1949; BA, CCNY, 1911; MA, Columbia U, 1913; PhD, 1917; cert, JTSA, 1916; m. Julia Aaronson, July 4, 1921; c: Kinereth Gensler, Avima Lombard. Spec prof, J Educ in Diaspora, Inst for Contemporary Jewry, Heb U, since 1962, prof em, since 1959; fmr: prin, W side Heb HS, NYC, 1913; tchr, Heb Tchrs Sem, Jerusalem, 1920; insp, J Schs, Govt of Pal, 1920-21; dir bd J Educ, Chgo, 1922-34; lectr, educ and Judaica, U Chgo, 1922-34; found, instr, Coll of J Studies, 1922-34; asso dir, NY Bd J Educ, 1922-35; prin, Heb Secondary Sch, Beth Hakerem, Jerusalem, 1934-39; dir, Michael Friedsdam Endowment, J Educ Comm NY, 1939-49. Mem: Natl Council J Educ; ZOA; NEA. Author: Jewish Education in the US, 1958; Jewish Education in the Diaspora, Problems of Teachers and Teaching, Heb, 1968; ed: Ency Hinuchit, vol III; Studies in Education, Scripta Hierosolymitana, 1963; contbr to mags. Home: 56 Ben Maimon St, Jerusalem. Isr. Office: Hebrew U, Jerusalem, Isr.

DWORETSKY, Joseph H, US, educator, accountant; b. Bklyn, NY, May 9, 1912; s. Harry and Sophie (Leckowitzki); att CCNY, 1933; BS, LIU, 1946; MBA, NYU, 1952; m. Jennie Finkelstein, June 16, 1935, c: Ethel, Samuel, Miriam, Abigail. Acting dean, Sch Bus Admn, Bklyn Cen, LIU, since 1969, prof, acctnt, since 1958, fac mem since 1946; partner, Dworetsky Bros & Co, CPA's since 1946; bd dirs, E Bklyn Savings and Loan Assn, since 1958; instr, acctnt, Bklyn Coll, 1944-46; chmn, bd dirs, United Ind Bank, 1955-67. Asso vice-pres, Natl Council of Young Isr; bd dirs, Ridgewood C of C; mem: NY State Soc of CPA's; Amer Acctnt Assn; AAUP; Natl Assn of Cost Acctnts; Amer Econ Assn; NEA; Amer Acad of Political Sci; Bus Hist Soc; Econ Hist Assn; J Publ Soc; Amer J Hist Soc; Young Isr of Rugby; Yeshivah Torah V'Das; club, Madison Dem. Home: 810 E 51 St, Brooklyn, NY. Office: LIU, Brooklyn, NY.

DWORETZKY, Murray, US, physician, educator; b. NYC, Aug 18, 1917; s. Samuel and Frieda (Newhoff); BA, U of Pa, 1938; MD, LI Coll Med, 1942; MS, U of Minn, 1950; m. Barbara Ratner, June 11, 1943; c: Thomas, Joan. Pvt practice, internal med, allergy; clinical prof, Cornell U Med Coll since 1966; att phys and phys-in-charge, allergy clinic, NY Hosp, since 1966. Capt, US Army MC, 1943-46. Pres: Amer Acad Allergy, since 1968; NY Allergy Soc, 1962-63; f: Amer Coll Allergists; Amer Coll Phys; NY Acad Med; dipl, Amer Bd Internal Med and Allergy; mem: AMA; AAAS; Amer Assn Immunologists; Amer Fed Clinical Research; Soc Experimental Biol and Med; Sigma Xi. Contbr to med jours. Home: 21 E 87 St, New York, NY. Office: 115 E 61 St, New York, NY.

DWORSKY, Florence G, US, communal worker; b. Cheteen, Russ, July 27, 1897; d. Eli and Adele (Zipperman) Goldenberg; in US since 1898; m. Philip Dworsky, 1921; Hon pres, S Cal chap, Amer Friends of Heb U, dsince 1950, secy since 1963, pres, 1941-50, charter mem since 1931; charter mem and pres, Hadassah, Minneapolis, Minn, 1929-33; pres, Isr Women's Org for J Educ, LA, 1950-51; bd govs, Bonds for Isr; Council of J Women; Helping Hand; Hadassah; ARC; Comty Chest; UJF; Vista Del Mar Orphanage; Lit Guild; Temple Isr Sisterhood; org, Youth Aliyah in S Cal, 1938. Home: 865 Comstock Ave, Los Angeles, Cal.

DYEN, Isidore, US, educator; b. Phila, Pa, Aug 16, 1913; s. Jacob and Dena (Bryzell); BA, U of Pa, 1933, MA, 1934, PhD, 1939; m. Edith Brenner, June 11, 1939; c: Doris, Mark. Prof, Malayo-Polynesian and compartaive lings, Yale U, since 1958, mem fac since 1942; ling, sci inves of Micronesia, Pacific Sci Bd, NRC, 1947, 1949. Mem: Ling Soc Amer; Amer Oriental Soc, vice-pres 1965-66; Amer Anthropological Assn; Conn Acad Arts and Scis; Temple Miskkan Isr. Author: Spoken Malay, 1945; The Proto-Malayo-Polynesian Laryngeals, 1953; A Sketch of Trukese Grammar, 1965; A Lexicostatistical Classification of the Austronesian Languages, 1965. Recipient: Guggenheim f, 1949, 1964. Home: 1955 Paradise Ave, Hamden, Conn. Office: Hall of Grad Studies, Yale U, New Haven, Conn.

DYKIERMAN, Nathan Rubin, Eng, secretary; b. Dresden, Ger, Sep 12, 1924; s. Mayer and Brandla (Hejnochowicz); in Eng since 1939; m. Margot Hirsch, Aug 3, 1947; c: Rochelle. Secy, Bachad Fellowship, London, since 1966. Pvt, British Army, 1944-47. Exec mem: Hapoel Hamisrachi Fed, Gt Brit, Ir; United Syn Dist Council; warden, Kingsbury Dist Syn; treas, Wembley lodge, B'nai B'rith; mem: council, British Assn, Pal-Isr Philatelists; J Ex-Service Men, Women, Wembley Br. Home: 91 Dorchester Way, Kenton, Middx, Eng. Office: 276 Willesden Lane, London NW2, Eng.

E

EAGLE, Harry, US, physician, medical researcher; b. NYC, July 13, 1905; s. Louis and Sadie (Kushnov); BA, Johns Hopkins U, 1923, MD, Med Sch, 1927; hon MS, Yale U, 1948; hon DSc, Wayne State U, 1965; m. Hope Whaley, Aug 21, 1928; c: Kay Kyle. Prof, cell biol, Albert Einstein Coll of Med, NYC, since 1961; intern, Johns Hopkins Hosp, 1927-28, asst in med, 1929-30; instr, 1930-32; asso, bact, U of Pa Med Sch, 1933-35; lectr, Johns Hopkins Sch of Med, 1936-37; dir, venereal diseases research lab, Johns Hopkins Hosp, 1936-46; lab of experimental therapeutics, Johns Hopkins Sch of Hygiene, Public Health, 1946-47; sci dir, Natl Cancer Inst, Bethesda, Md, 1947-49; adj clinical prof, George Wash U Med Sch, Wash, DC, 1948-60; chief, lab cell biol, Natl Inst of Allergy and Infectious Disease, NIH, Bethesda, 1949-61. Comm off, USPHS, since 1936. Dipl: Amer Bd of Path; Amer Bd Preventive Med; fmr pres, Soc for Clinical Invest; trustee, Found for Microbiol, Rutgers U; mem: Soc Amer Bacts; Amer Soc Immunologists; Amer Soc Biol Chems; Amer Assn of Phys; Amer Acad Arts and Sci. Contbr to sci jours. Recipient: Ely Lilly award; Alvarenga prize; Pres Cert of Merit; Gold Medal award, Phi Lambda Kappa; Albert Einstein Commemorative award. Office: Albert Einstein Coll of Med, New York, NY.

EAGLE, Herbert David, US, business exec; b. Boston, Mass, Jan 2, 1918; s. Leon and Sadie (Lewis); att, St Johns U, NY, 1935-37; BA, UCLA, 1939; m. Mildred Tepper, May 25, 1940; c: Lynne. Vice-pres, marketing, Transamerica Corp, since 1969; guest lectr: UCLA; U of S Cal; U Ariz; sr vice-pres, marketing, Occidental Life of Cal, 1968-69, mem firm since 1948. Capt, USAAF, 1941-46. Dir: Sales and Marketing Execs Assn, LA, fmr pres; mem, exec comm, Sales and Marketing Execs Intl; mem: UCLA Alumni Assn; Amer Marketing Assn; B'nai B'rith; fmr: panel moderator, discussion leader, Health Ins Assn, Amer Group Forums Corp; chmn, Citizens Comm for Rapid Transit in LA Co; gen chmn, Jr Achievement, S Cal Fund Campaign; mem, regional adv bd, Pacific Coast ADL. Hobbies: golf, reading. Home: 1301 Nimrod Pl, Los Angeles, Cal. Office: 1150 S Olive St, Los Angeles, Cal.

EASTON, Harold, US, attorney; b. Los Angeles, Apr 11, 1913; s. Jacob and Sadie (Cohen); AB, UCLA, 1934; JD, U of Cal, Berkeley, 1937; m. Celine Silver, Nov 6, 1937; c: Lisa. Pvt practice since 1937; chief counsel, food enforcement div, OPA, Wash, DC, 1941-46. Regional pres, Pacific SW United Syns of Amer, 1952-54, 1960-67; pres, Sinai Temple, 1967-69; mem: bd overseers, U Judaism, since 1950; bd dirs, Camp Ramah in Cal, since 1955; Amer, Cal Bar Assns; Phi Beta Kappa; Pi Sigma Alpha; Pi Kappa Delta; Pi Gamma Mu; Mason, 32 deg; Shriner; Order of Coif. Contbr to profsl jours. Home: 1100 Sutton Way, Beverly Hills, Cal. Office: 4201 Wilshire Blvd, Los Angeles, Cal.

EATON, Herman Joseph, US, insurance broker; b. NYC, Mar 7, 1912; s. Louis and Rose (Smoller) Epstein; att NYU, 1929-30; Rutgers U, 1935-36; dipl, Chartered Life Underwriter, Amer Coll Life Underwriters, 1956; m. Ida Polishook, Oct 11, 1936; c: Lewis, Sara. Agt, Berkshire Life Ins Co, since 1946; mgr, W Union Telegraph Co, 1934-36, 1937-41, commercial repr, 1936-37; agt, Prudential Ins 1941-43; pres, Herman J Eaton, Inc 1947-66. Pres: B nai B rith, 1942-44; J Comty Cen, 1948-49; JCC, 1952-56; Heb Sch, 1952-56; chmn: JWF, 1953, 1965; Ulster Co Heart Fund, 1964-65; Daughters of Sarah Home, 1958-66; mem: bd dirs, Talmud Torah, 1956-58; ZOA, Masons; Shrine; Cong Agudas Achim; C of C; budget comm, Comty Chest, 1958-59; Million Dollar Round Table, 1963-65; Temple Beth Shalom. Ed, Kingston J Commentator, 1939-40. Home: 1865 79 St, Causeway, Miami Beach, Fla. Office: 100 Biscayne Blvd, Miami, Fla.

EBAN, Abba S, Isr, diplomat, government official; b. Capetown, S Afr, Feb 2, 1915; s. Abraham and Alida (Sacks); MA, Queens Coll, Cambridge U, 1938; hon: DHL, LLD; m. Susan Ambache, Mar 18, 1945; c: Eli, Gila. In Isr since 1940. Min for Fgn Affairs since 1966; Brown research f in Arabic, Heb, and Persian, Pembroke Coll, Cambridge U, 1938; lectr, Arabic and Oriental studies, 1938-40; liaison off, Allied Hdqrs

and J population, Jerusaelm, 1942-44; chief instr, ME Cen of Arabic Studies, Jerusalem, 1943-44; mem, political dept, JA for Pal, 1946; liaison off, UN Spec Commn on Pal, Lake Success, NY, 1947; participated in final talks with Pal Mandatory Govt, London; appointed by Provisional Govt of Isr as repr to UN, 1948; perm repr Isr to UN, with Min rank, 1949-59; Isr Ambass to US, 1950-59; pres, Weizmann Inst of Sci, Rehovot, 1958-66; Min without Portfolio, 1959-60; Min of Educ and Culture, 1960-63; Dep PM, 1963-66. F: World Acad Arts and Sci; Amer Acad Arts and Sci. Author: preface to new edition of Leo Pinsker's Auto-Emancipation, 1939; The Modern Literary Movement in Egypt, 1944; Maze of Justice, 1949; Voice of Isreal, 1957; Tide of Nationlism, 1959; My People, 1968; contbr articles and lectures on political and educ topics. Office: Min for Fgn Affairs, Jerusalem, Isr.

EBENSTEIN, William, US, educator; b. Aus, May 11, 1910; s. Samuel and Gittel (Godapper); in US since 1936; LLD, U Vienna, 1934; PhD, U Wis, 1938; m. Ruth Jaburek, 1938; c: Philip, Robert, Andrew, Alan. Prof, political sci, U Cal, Santa Barbara, since 1962; mem fac: U of Wis, 1938-46; Princeton U, 1946-62. Author: Today's Isms, 6th ed, 1970; Great Political Thinkers, 4th ed, 1969. Home: 2685 Glendessary Lane, Santa Barbara, Cal. Office: U of Cal, Santa Barbara, Cal.

EBENZOHAR, Simcha, Isr, labor organization official; b. Russ, 1905; s. Yitshak and Miriam; in Isr since 1925; m. Edis de Philipe; three c. Secy, exec comm, Histadrut, since 1925; admn dir, mem: exec bd, council, Isr Natl Opera, since 1947. Found head, illegal Bc stats in Pal and abroad; head of communications, org, Haganah illegal immigrant ships. Found, chmn, Prisoner's Wfr Soc, on behalf of Va'ad HaLeumi. Home: 88 Aluf David, Ramat Chen, Isr. Office: 93 Arlosoroff St, Tel Aviv, Isr.

EBIN, Robert Felix, US, attorney; b. Boston, Sep 26, 1940; s. Leo and Ruth (Shapiro); AB, Brown U, Providence, RI, 1962; LLB, cum laude, Columbia U Law Sch, 1965; att NYU Sch of Bus Admn; m. Lois Rosenberg, Aug 15, 1965; c: Lauren. Asso atty, law firm, London, Buttenwieser & Chalif, since 1968; secy, Blasius Ind, Inc, NYC, since 1968; and dir, Revere Smelting & Refining Corp, Newark, NJ, since 1970; student asst, US Atty Off, S Dist NY, 1964; asso atty, Wickes, Riddell, Bloomer, Jacob & McGuire, 1965-68. Mem: Assn Bar, NYC; NY State Bar Assn; fmr: spec council, Citizens for Clean Air, Inc, NYC. Founding ed, Jour of Law and Social Problems, NYC; contbr to legal jours. Recipient, Harlan Fiske Stone Scholar, Columbia U Law Sch, 1965. Hobbies: photography, philately, sailing, skiing. Home: 550 W 252 St, New York, NY. Office: 575 Madison Ave, New York, NY.

ECKER, Arthur D, US, neurologist, neurosurgeon, educator; b. NYC, Jan 29, 1913; s. Murray and Olga (Edelstein); BA, Dartmouth Coll, 1931; MD, Johns Hopkins U, 1934; MS, U Minn, 1938; PhD, 1938; m. Marcia Schlesinger, Sep 15, 1935; c: Sandra Kaplan, Jonathan. Pvt practice since 1939; sr att neurosurg, Syracuse Memorial Hosp, since 1948; chief neurosurg, Comty Gen Hosp, Syracuse, since 1963; fmr clinical prof, State U Coll of Med; chief neurosurg, Syracuse U Coll 1939-55. US Army, 1942-46. Mem: Amer Coll Surg; AMA; of Med, Assn for Research in Nervous and Mental Diseases; Syracuse Acad of Med, fmr pres; Harvey Cushing Soc; NY Acad of Med; Amer Acad of Neur. Author; The Normal Cerebral Angiogram, 1951; co-author: Arteriographic Localization of Intracranial Masses, 1955; contbr to profsl jours. Hobbies: badminton, archaeol, old maps. Home: 603 Crawford Ave, Syracuse, NY. Office: 407 University Ave, Syracuse, NY.

ECKERLING, Benjamin, Isr, physician; b. Soroki, Pol, June 8, 1915; s. Zvi and Rivka (Rum); in Isr since 1945; MD, U It, 1939; m. Shoshana Simon, Jerusalem, 1955; c: Dorit, Zvi. Head, dept obstet and gyn, Beilinson Hosp, Petah Tikva, since 1968; prof gyn, Tel Aviv U, since 1969. Mem, Intl Coll

Surgs, FISCS chap, Isr. Contbr to profsl jours. Hobby: gardening. Home: 5 Hagyvah St, Savyon, Isr. Office: Beilinson Hosp, Petah Tikva, Isr.

ECKSTEIN, Otto, US, educator; b. Ulm, Ger, Aug 1, 1927; s. Hugo and Hedwig; AB, Princeton U, 1951, LLD, 1966; AM, Harvard U, 1952, PhD, 1955; m. Harriett Mirkin; c: Warren, Felicia, June. Prof, econ, Harvard U, since 1963; pres, Data Resources, since 1969; tech dir, Jt Econ Comm, US Cong, 1959-60; mem, Pres Council Econ Advs, 1964-66. US Army, 1946-47. Mem, Amer Acad Arts and Scis. Author: Water Resource Development: The Economics of Project Evaluation, 1958; Public Finance, 1967. Recipient: Guggenheim F, 1960. Home: 24 Barberry Rd, Lexington, Mass. Office: Harvard U, Cambridge, Mass.

ECKSTEIN, Shlomo, Isr, economist; b. Wiesbaden, Ger, Nov 1, 1929; s. Mordechai and Gusti (Raber); in Isr since 1960; lic econ, Natl U Mexico, 1956; PhD Harvard U, 1959; m. Lea Zollman, Mar 3, 1957; c: Eitan, Sara, Rivka. Sr lectr, chmn, dept econ, Bar Ilan U, since 1961; bd dirs: Isr Founds Trustees; Isr Chemicals, Ltd, subsidiary cos of Inorganic Div; i/c Bachad Hachshara, NJ, 1953-54, cons to Govt Mex on agrarian reform policies on behalf OAS, 1966-68; coord on sub-comm on agric econ, Natl Council for Research and Devl, Isr, 1964-65; lectr tours on agric cooperation, devl in Latin Amer on behalf govt of Isr, 1964-66; cons, invited as intl expert by FAO to World Land Reform Conf, convened by FAC and UN, Rome, 1966. Head, B'nai Akiva Org, Mex; mem: Amer Econ Assn; Soc Mex de Geografia y Estadistica. Author: Collective Farming in Mexico, Span, 1966; The Macroeconomic Framework of the Mexican Agrarian Problem, 1968; Inter-village Cooperation in Agricultural Services in Israel, Heb, 1969. Spec interest: classical and popular music. Home: Faculty Housing, Bar Ilan U, Ramat Gan, Isr. Office: Bar Ilan U, Ramat Gan, Isr.

EDEL, Abraham, US, educator; b. Pittsburgh, Pa, Dec 6, 1908; s. Simon and Fannie (Malamud); BA, McGill U, Montreal, 1927, MA, 1928; BA, Oxford, Eng, 1930; PhD, Columbia U, 1934; m. May Mandelbaum, Jan 30, 1934 (decd); c: Matthew, Deborah. Prof, phil, CUNY, on fac since 1931; professorial lectr, SUNY, Downstate Med Cen, 1958-69; visiting lectr: Barnard Coll, 1931-32; U of Cal, 1947-48; Columbia U, 1949, 1950, 1961; Swarthmore Coll, 1954; Sarah Lawrence Coll, 1956; New Sch for Soc Research, 1956-57, 1959; U of Pa, 1965-66; W Reserve U, 1966. Mem: Amer Phil Assn; Metaphys Soc of Amer; Amer Soc for Political and Legal Phil. Author: Aristotle's Theory of the Infinite, 1934; The Theory and Practice of Philosophy, 1946; Ethical Judgment, 1955; Science and the Structure of Ethics, 1961; Method in Ethical Theory, 1963; Aristotle, 1967; co-author: Anthropology and Ethics, 1959, 1968; contr to profsl jours. Recipient: Butler Silver Medal, Columbia U, 1959; f: Moyse Travelling, McGill U, 1928; Columbia U, 1930-31; Guggenheim, 1944-45; grants: Rockefeller Found, 1952-53; NSF, 1959-60. Home: 171-07 84 Rd, Jamaica, NY. Office: CUNY, New York, NY.

EDEL, Yitzhak, Isr, composer; b. Warsaw, Pol, Jan 1, 1896; s. Samuel and Esther (Helemer); in Isr since 1929; att conservatories: Warsaw, Kiev, Moscow; m. Fanny Billig, Tel Aviv, Dec 17, 1930. Tchr, Tel Aviv Conservatory since 1965; fmr: conductor, lectr: Janush Korczak Inst, Taubet Schs; conductor, Hashomer Hatzair choir; lectr, choir conductor, Lewinsky Tchrs Sem; tchr: Acad of Music, Tel Aviv; Sem Hakibbutzim. Compositions for orch: Capriccio; Andante and Hora; Rikud Israeli; Sinfonietta Rusticana, oratorium; Lamitnadvim Ba'am; Mourning Cantata; Laben, cantata in seven movements; The Golden Feather, children's suite for voice and orch; 12 string quartets; Quartet for oboe, clarinet, bassoon, piano; Piano and Violin Pieces; Songs with Piano or Orch Accompaniment; Sonatina for Oboe and Piano; String quartet and Soprano; Trio for piano, violin, cello; Triplyque for piano; The Base of Music; The Song of Israel. Fmr, secy, Composer's Union; found, J Music Assn, Warsaw. Music critic: Doar Hayom, lit mag. Recipient: Engel Prize, 1955; Tenth Anniversary Radio Prize; Dipl di Merito, It, 1952; first prize for song, Shir Haroeh, Heb U, and NY Assn for Music in Isr; Milano Prize, 1968. Home and studio: 52 Balfour St, Tel Aviv, Isr.

EDELMAN, Arthur Jay, US, business exec; b. NYC, July 19, 1925; s. Samuel and Beatrice (Helfgot); BA, Sarah Lawrence Coll, NY, 1950; m. Theodora Joffe, May 28, 1950; c: Sam, Sally, Antonia, David, Mary, John. Pres, Heming Joffe Ltd. Yeoman, USNR, 1943-46. Recipient: Natl Shoe Retailers

Award, 1963; Coty Award, Amer Fashion Critics, 1963; Neiman Marcus Award, 1965. Home: Alligator Farm, Spring Valley Rd, Ridgefield, Conn. Office: 387 Park Ave S, New York, NY.

EDELMAN, Daniel J, US, business exec; b. NYC, July 3, 1920; s. Selig and Selma (Pfeiffer); m. Ruth Rozumoff, Sep 3, 1953; c: Richard, John, Renee. Pres, Daniel J Edelman, Inc, since 1952; news writer, CBS, 1946-47; dir, pr, Toni Co, 1948-52. US Army, 1942-46. Mem: bd dirs, ADL, since 1959; publicity. Gov Comm on Employment Physically Handicapped, 1952; comm, Columbia Coll Fund; bd dirs, Ill Assn for Crippled; PR Society of Amer, chmn, counselors sect, prog chmn, 1968 conv; Phi Beta Kappa; Zeta Beta Tau; club, Standard. Recipient: Outstanding Achievement Award, Amer PR Assn, 1954, 1957; award, Publicity Club of Chgo, 1961; place of honors list for dist alumni, Grad Sch of Journalism, Columbia U, 1963; 4 battle stars; Commendation Medal, both WW II. Home: 1315 N Astor St, Chicago, Ill. Office: 221 N LaSalle St, Chicago, Ill.

EDELMAN, Isidore S, US, physician, educator; b. NYC, July 23, 1920; s. Abraham and Fanny (Thaler); BA, Ind U, 1941, MD, 1944; m. Florence Jaffe, Aug 30, 1942; c: Arthur, Joseph, Susan, Ann. Samuel Neider Research Prof of Med, U of Cal Sch of Med, since 1967, on staff since 1952; asso dir, Cardiovascular Research Inst, since 1960; fac research lectr, U of Cal, SF, 1967-68; res phys, neoplastic diseases div, Montefiore Hosp, NYC, 1947-48; research f: Dazian Found at Montefiore Hosp, 1948-49; US AEC, 1949-50; AHA 1950-52; both at Peter Bent Brigham Hosp and Harvard Med Sch, Boston; established inves, AHA, 1952-59; chief, U of Cal Med Research, SF Hosp, 1956-58; sr research f, chem, USPHS, Cal Inst of Tech, 1958-59; visiting sci, Weizmann Inst of Sci, Rehovot, Isr, 1965-66. Capt, US Army MC, 1944-46. Mem: Amer Phys Soc; Biophys Soc; Amer Soc for Clinical Inves; W Assn of Phys; W Soc for Clinical Research; AAAS; Assn of Amer Phys; fmr: chmn W div, Amer Fed for Clinical Research; mem research comm, Cal Heart Assn. Ed bd: Jour of Clinical Inves, 1959; Amer Jour of Phys, 1961; Jour of Applied Phys, 1961; contbr papers to sci, profsl jours. Recipient: Moses Prize, Montefiore Alumni Assn, 1953; Eli Lilly Award, Endocrine Soc, 1969. Home: 40 Linares Ave, San Francisco, Cal. Office: U of Cal, San Francisco, Cal.

EDELMAN, John W, US, labor exec; b. Forest Hill, NJ, June 27, 1893; s. John and Rachelle (Krimont); m. Kate Van Eaton, 1921; c: Alison Carter, Arnold, Anne Stephansky. Pres em, Natl Council of Sen Citizens, since 1969, pres, 1963-69, pres, Natl Consumers League, 1948-68; Wash repr, Textile Workers' Union of Amer, CIO, 1943-63; music, drama critic, Springfield, Mass, Repub 1915-18; reporter, NYC newspapers, 1921-22; publicity dir, BW Huebsch Pub Co, 1922-24; labor ed, Tribune, Reading, Pa, 1924; campaign mgr for Robert M Follette, Pa, 1924; telegraph ed, Camden Post Telegram, 1925-26; publicity, research dir, Amer Fed Hosiery Workers, 1926-39; secy, Natl Lab Housing Conf, 1933-36; delg, ILO, Geneva Conf, 1936; asst dir, info, US Housing Auth, 1939-40; cons, Natl Defense Adv Council, 1940-42; CIO liaison off, OPA, 1942-45; pres, Old Dominion Housing Corp, Va, 1946-48. Mem, natl comms: CIO leg; Amer Labor Educ Service Policy; Comm for Nation's Health; Natl Consumers' League; Natl Housing Conf; OPA, Lab Policy; Comm on Children in Wartime; US Children's Bur; charter mem; Amer Newspaper Guild; ADA. Home: 813 S Veitch St, Arlington, Va.

EDELMAN, Lily P, US, educational admnr, editor; b. San Francisco, Sep 2, 1915; d. Morris and Rachel (Margolis) Podvidz; BA, Hunter Coll, 1936; MA, Columbia U, 1938, profsl dipl in adult educ, Tchrs Coll, 1954; m. Nathan Edelman, May 30, 1936; c: Jean Louise (decd). Dir, dept adult educ, B'nai B'rith, since 1961, ed asso, 1967-61; ed, J Heritage, since 1961; educ dir, E and W Assn, 1941-51; free-lance writer, State Dept, 1952-53; exec secy, Natl Acad Adult J Studies, United Syn, 1954-57. Mem: Phi Beta Kappa; Lillie Straus chap, B'nai B'rith Women; Adult Educ Assn, USA; bd: Md Assn of Adult Educ; Natl Council J Audio-Visual Aids. Author: Japan in Story and Pictures, 1953; Hawaii, USA, 1954; The Sukkah and the Big Wind, 1956; Israel: New People in an Old Land, 1958, rev ed, 1969; mem ed bd, J Digest; contbr to jours. Home: 560 Riverside Dr, New York, NY.

EDELMAN, Murray Jacob, US, educator; b. Nanticoke, Pa, Nov 5, 1919; s. Kalman and Sadie (Wiesenberg); BA, Bucknell U, Pa, 1941; MA, U Chgo, 1942; PhD, U of Ill, 1948; m.

Bacia Stepner, Jan 15, 1952; c: Lauren, Judith, Sarah. Prof, political sci: U of Wis, since 1966; U of Ill, 1948-66. Staff sgt, US Army, 1942-45. Mem, Amer Political Sci Assn. Author: The Licensing of Radio Services in the United States, 1950; Channels of Employment, 1952; National Economic Planning by Collective Bargaining, 1954; The Symbolic Use of Politics, 1964; The Politics of Wage-Price Decisions, 1965; contbr to profsl jours. Recipient: Fulbright grants, 1952, 1956; Guggenheim F, 1962-63. Home: 1824 Vilas Ave, Madison, Wis. Office: U of Wis, Madison, Wis.

EDELMAN, Paul S, US, attorney; b. Bklyn, NY, Jan 2, 1926; s. Joseph and Rose (Kaminsky); AB, Harvard U, 1947, LLB, 1950; m. Rosemary Jacobs, June 15, 1951; c: Peter, Jeffrey. Partner, Kreindler and Kreindler, since 1953. US Army, 1944-46. Chmn: admiralty sect, Amer Trial Lawyers Assn; maritime comm, Fed Bar Council; cons, Natl Council on Maritime Resources; mem, exec comm, NY chap, AJComm, since 1963; dir, Camp Moonbeam Assn; mem: Maritime Lawyers Assn; Co Lawyers Assn; fmr: mem comm, NY chap, Natl Assn Claimants Counsel of Amer; chmn, young attys div, UJA. Author: Maritime Injury and Death, 1960; contbr to profsl jours. Recipient: 5 Eur Theatre Opr Ribbons, WW II. Home: 57 Buena Vista Dr, Hastings, NY. Office: 99 Park Ave, New York, NY.

EDELMAN, Samuel D, US, physician, educator; b. Meriden, Conn, Oct 4, 1891; s. Charles and Sarah (LeVine); MD, O State U, 1914; m. Jessie Cecile, July 6, 1922; c: Jeanne Israel. Pvt practice, ped since 1914; asso prof, clinical ped, O State U since 1945; chief ped, St Ann's Hosp, since 1943; White Cross Hosp, 1930-35; Grant Hosp, 1935-37; sr att ped: Children's Hosp; U Hosp, all Columbus, O. Lt, US Army, MC, 1917-19. Pres: Cen O Ped Soc, 1958; B'nai B'rith, 1926-27; Temple Brotherhood. 1940-42; Hillel Found, O State U, 1946-48, all Columbus; mem: bd, J Cem; Masons; Amer Legion; JWV; ZBT; Phi Chi; club, Winding Hollow Country. Contbr to med jours. Home: 1620 E Broad St, Columbus, O. Office: 327 E State St, Columbus, O.

EDELMANN, Abraham, US, scientist, educator; b. NYC, Sep 5, 1915; s. Samuel and Ida (Levy); BA, Johns Hopkins U, 1936; MSc, NYU, 1939; PhD, O State U, 1947; m. Rita Duker, June 14, 1942; c: Beth, Samuel. Lectr, Grad Sch of Public Health, U of Pittsburgh, since 1961; sr lectr, Carnegie-Mellon U, since 1961; vice-pres, Nuclear Sci and Engr Corp, since 1960, cons since 1966, mgr, dept biol and med, 1955-60; research asso, O State Med Sch, 1940-46, instr, 1946-47; sci, Brookhaven Natl Lab, 1947-55; dir, div radiation biol, Allegheny Gen Hosp, 1964-66, asst and asso att radiation biol, 1964-66. F: NY Acad Sci; O Acad Sci; Amer Nuclear Soc; Sigma Xi; mem: Radiation Research Soc, past secy; Soc for Experimental Biol and Med; Endocrinology Soc; Aeromed Assn; Amer Phys Soc; AAAS. Ed, Radioactivity for Pharmaceutical and Allied Lab, 1960; contbr numerous articles to sci jours. Home and office: 1634 Beechwood Blvd, Pittsburgh, Pa.

EDELMANN, Rafael, Den, librarian, educator; b. Reshitza, Latvia, Jan 7, 1902; s. Chajim and Miriam (Metter); PhD, U Bonn, 1928; PhD, HC, U Copenhagen, 1966; att: U Berlin; Rabbiner Sem, Berlin; m. Elisabeth Levi, May 24, 1932; two c. Head, J dept, Bibliotheca Simonseniana, Royal Libr, Copenhagen, since 1938, asst, 1933-38; lectr, U Copenhagen, since 1948; asst, U Bonn, 1927-33; adv, Dan delg to UNESCO Gen Assembly, Paris, 1946. Chmn, Assn of Librs of Judaica and Hebraica in Eur, since 1955; mem: council, World Union of J Studies, since 1961; bd delgs, J Comty, Copenhagen, 1946-49. Author: Heimat, Alter und Bestimmung der synagogalen Poesie, 1932; Zur Frühgeschichte des Mahzor, 1934; Maimonides on Medicine, 1952; On the Arabic Versions of the Pentateuch, 1953; Jödisk Mystik, 1954; Jödisk litteratur gennem 2000 ar, pub, 1961; Jüdisches Geistesleben am Rhein von den Anfängen bis 1945, pub, 1963; Das "Buch der Frommen" als Ausdruck des volkstümlichen Geisteslebens der deutschen Juden im Mittelalter, 1966; Jiddisch Krestomati, 1966; Soferim—Massoretes; "Massoretes"—Nakdenim, 1969; Jdedommen, 1968; Hebraica From Denmark, 1969; ed: Corpus Codicum Hebraicorum Medii Aevi, 1954; Subject Concordance to the Babylonian Talmud, by L Goldschmidt, 1959; Old Hebrew Manuscripts in Facsimile, 1969; Grace After Meals and Other Benedictions, with introduction, 1969; contbr to periodicals. Recipient, Order of Dannebrog, 1953. Home: 65 Rosenörns Alle, Copenhagen, Den. Office: Royal Libr, Copenhagen, Den.

EDELSBURG, Yitzhak, Isr, business exec; b. Pol, Nov 11, 1924; s. Schmuel and Paulina (Farber); in Isr since 1935; MA, U London, 1950; m. Rina Amity, 1947; c: Jacob, Ariel. Gen dir: L Edelsburg and Sons Ltd; Cen Export and Ind Devl Co. Off, IAF. Mem, bd dir: Isr natl comm, ICC; Tel-Aviv Jaffa C of C; life senator, JCI; found, pres Isr ICI (intl repr), dist gov, Lions, Isr 356. Home: 2 Hevra Hadasha St, Tel Aviv, Isr. Office: 57 Herzl St, Tel Aviv, Isr.

EDELSON, David, US, administrator; b. NYC, Jan 28, 1919; s. Max and Freida (Epstein); BA, NYU, 1948; MA, Columbia U, 1950; MHA, Northwestern U, 1958; m. Miriam Osnovitz, Apr 3, 1943; c: Richard, Jeffrey. Supt, Dixon State Sch, Div, Mental Retardation Services, Dept Mh, State of Ill, since 1962; asst supt, admn, E Moline State Hosp, 1958-62; dir, social service, Evansville State Hosp, Evansville, Ind, 1956-57; lectr, behavioral disabilities, U Wis. Adj, USAAC, 1942-45. Mem: bd, Lee Co Mh Assn; bd, Dixon C of C; Amer Assn on Mental. Deficiency; Council for Exceptional Children; B'nai B'rith; fmr: Ill govs adv council on Retardation; Ind govs ad council on Geriatrics. Recipient: Leadership award, Ill Assn for Mentally Retarded, 1968. Home and office: 2600 Brinton Ave, Dixon, Ill.

EDELSTEIN, David (Duda), Isr, sculptor; b. Seidlce, Pol; s. Mordecai and Rivka; in Isr since 1932; att: H Hertz Inst; Inst of Arts, both Tel Aviv; Art Sem: Paris; Florence; m. Maj. Works: busts prominent persons: David Ben Gurion; Abba Eban; Pres Kennedy; Pres Johnson; figures: Bibl; Yemenite; realistic and styled; medallions: Chaim Weizmann; Itzchak Ben-Zvi; A H Silver; Pres Truman; woodcarvings; sculptural reliefs; ornamentation of public bldgs. Mem: Isr Inst of Painters and Sculptors, Tel Aviv. Home: 13 Arba Aratzot St, Tel Aviv, Isr. Studio: 12 Maharal St, Tel Aviv, Isr.

EDELSTEIN, David Simeon, US, educator, historian; b. NYC, Jan 19, 1913; s. William and Clara (Brener); BA, CCNY, 1932; MA, Columbia U, 1933, PhD, 1949; grad studies: CUNY; Hunter Coll; Tchrs Coll, Columbia U; NYU Sch of Educ; Fordham U; Oxford U; Bd of Educ, NYC; m. Frances Fisher, June 4, 1939; c: Helen Freedman, Henry, Daniel. Asso prof, educ, W Conn State Coll, since 1967; adj asso prof, hist, Fordham U, Bx, NY, since 1967; tchr: HS, 1934-38; social studies, NY Sch of Printing, 1938-42; social studies, and acting dept chmn, Alfred E Smith Vocational HS, 1942-45; chmn, Eng and social studies, Manhattan Vocational and Techn HS, 1945-51; chmn, Eng and Social studies, Grace Dodge Vocational HS, 1951-58; jr prin, Public Sch 13, Bx, 1958; asst examiner, Bd Examiners, NYC Bd of Educ, 1948-67; field sup, federally funded after sch study cen, 1966-67. Vice-pres, Solomon Schechter Day Sch, White Plains, NY; chmn; bd dirs, Wakefield Fusion Club, 1931-32; sch bd, Genesis Heb Temple, Tuckahoe, NY; mem: sch bd, Temple Emanuel, Parkchester; Natl Urban League; NAACP; Harlem Neighborhoods Assn; Amer Assn of Sch Admns, Amer Hist Assn; AAUP; NY State Assn of Elem Sch Prin; NYC Elem Sch Prin Assn; Natl Council Local Admnrs Vocational Educ; Phi Alpha Theta; Phi Delta Kappa; Social Studies Council; active in: Boy Scouts of Amer; Hutchison River Council; ARC. Author: Joel Munsell: Printer and Antiquarian, 1950; contbr articles on educ and graphic arts to profsl jours. Recipient: cert of merit, Dict of Intl Biography, 1967. Spec interest: travel, gardening, tennis. Home: 84 Avondale Rd, Yonkers, NY. Office: 181 White St, Danbury, Conn.

EDELSTEIN, Mortimer S, US, attorney; b. Paterson, NJ, Mar 1, 1904; s. Abram and Ida (Lapat); BS, U Pa, 1926; LLB, hons, Cornell U, 1931; m. Rosabelle Winer, May, 1941; c: Jana. Partner, law firm, Young, Kaplan and Edelstein, since 1950; dir and off, several bus corps; lectr: Practicing Law Inst, since 1949; Duke U Law Sch; asst gen counsel, asst exec dir, Port of NY Auth, 1940-44; partner, law firm, Paul, Weiss, Wharton and Garrison, 1944-49. Vice-pres, dir, counsel, Boys Town, Jerusalem, Inc; mem: Phi Beta Kappa; Order of Coif; clubs: Cornell of NY; Harmonie, NY. Author: The Bride Laughed Once, 1943; ed, Cornell Law Quarterly, 1930-31; contbr to profsl jours. Homes: 245 E 72 St, New York, NY; 7 Highwood Rd, Westport, Conn. Office: 277 Park Ave, New York, NY.

EDELSTEIN, Sydney M, US, business exec, chemist; b. Chattanooga, Tenn, Jan 22, 1912; s. Samuel and Frances (Leventhal); BS, MIT, 1932; hon DSc, Lowell Inst, 1956; m. Mildred Citron, Nov 29, 1931; c: Ruth. Pres, tech dir, Dexter Chem Corp, since 1944; researcher, textiles and chems, Dixie

Mercerizing, 1932-35; research asso, Amer Assn of Textile Chems and Colorists, 1935-37. Holder, cellulose and textile patents. Natl chmn, UJA; chmn, Bonds for Isr; mem, bd dirs, J Comty Cen, both Englewood, NJ; f: Amer Inst of Chems; Textile Inst, Gt Brit; secy, div hist of chem, Amer Chem Soc; mem: Amer Assn Textile Technologists; Hist of Sci Soc; Bibliographical Soc; Amer Soc of Autograph Collectors. Contbr numerous articles on textile chem. Hobby: golf. Home: 338 Hillcrest Rd, Englewood, NJ. Office: 845 Edgewater Rd, New York, NY.

EDELSTEIN, Yehoshua Abraham, Isr, organization exec; b. Vienna, Aus, July 20, 1919; s. David and Lea (Donner); BSc, Leeds U, Eng, 1942; m. Shoshanna Kahn, Mar 31, 1955; c: Leora, Uriel, Efrat. Repr: youth and hechalutz dept, JA, US, since 1968; in Gt Brit, 1955-68; treas, farm mgr, Kibbutz Kfar Hanassi, 1949-55; dir, Habonim Foundry, 1959-68. Mem: Habonim World Secretariat; Council of Kibbutz Inds; regional council, Upper Galilee. Office: 515 Park Ave, New York, NY.

EDEN, Bracha, Isr, musician; b. Jerusalem, Isr, July 15, 1928; s. Haim and Yehudit (Kramerovsky) Orr; grad hons, Acad of Music, Jerusalem, 1952; m. Gamliel Eden, 1946; c: Yoram. Prof, Rubin Acad of Music, since 1958; dir, Targ Music Cen, Jerusalem, since 1969; numerous recordings for Decca Records; nominated for Grand Prix du Disques; first recording of piano version of Stravinsky's Rite of Spring; over 10 years of concerting: Eur; US; Can; Pol; S Afr; benefit concerts for J and Isr orgs. Recipient: Silver Medal, Vercellini Intl Competition, It, 1956. Home: 15 Shamai St, Jerusalem, Isr. Office: POB 410, Jerusalem, Isr.

EDER, Howard A, US, physician, educator; b. Milw, Wis, Sept 23, 1917; s. Samuel and Rebecca (Abram); BA, U Wis, 1938; MD, Harvard Med Sch, Boston, Mass, 1942; MPH, Harvard Sch Public Health, 1945; m. Barbara Staus, July 15, 1954; c: Rebecca, Susan, Michael. Prof, med, Albert Einstein Coll of Med, since 1957; cons: USPHS, since 1961; Brookhaven Natl Lab, since 1956; asst phys, Rockefeller Inst, 1946-50; asst prof med, Cornell U Med Coll, 1950-53; inves, Natl Heart Inst, 1953-55; asso prof med, SUNY Coll of Med, 1955-57. USPHS, 1943-55. Chmn, sect on med, NY Acad of Med, 1961-62; mem: NY State Bd of Med Examiners; Council on Atherosclerosis; AHA; Amer Soc for Clinical Inves; Amer Soc for Biol Chems; Royal Soc of Med; Biochem Soc, London; Amer Phys Soc; Assn Amer Phys; Phi Beta Kappa; Alpha Omega Alpha. Ed bd, Jour of Lipid Research, since 1960; Gen Clinical Research Centers Comm, since 1961; contbr to med jours of articles on renal disease and the metabolism of fats in relationship to arteriosclerosis. Home: 4683 Waldo Ave, New York, NY. Office: Albert Einstein Coll of Med, Eastchester Rd & Morris Park Ave, New York, NY.

EDERY, Habib, Isr, pharmacologist; b. Rosario, Arg, Dec 25, 1923; s. Simon and Rahel; in Isr since 1954; DVM, La Plata, Arg, 1947; postgrad studies: Paris, Natl Inst for Med Research, London, 1960-62; m. Clara, Mar 20, 1951; c: Daniel, Rahel. Asso prof, pharm, Tel Aviv U Med Sch; chmn, Isr Phys and Pharm Socs; both since 1969; head, dept of pharm, Isr Inst Biol Research, since 1954; visiting lectr, sci meetings: Florence, It; Sao Paulo, Brazil. Contbr numerous research papers. Hobbies: archaeol, painting, music. Home: 19 Wiezmann St, Rishon Le Zion, Isr. Office: PO Box 19, Ness Ziona, Isr.

EDERY, Mordecai, Arg, rabbi; b. Tangier, Morocco, Apr 19, 1928; s. Jalifa and Esther (Levinia); in Arg since 1956; ordained rabbi, Rabb Sem, Torah Vehaim, Tangier; m. Aida Burman; c: Ruth, David, Ariel. Rabbi, Sephardic Comty Chalom, Buenos Aires, since 1962; vice-rector, Seminario Rabinico Latinoamericano, since 1962; co-dir, Instituto Academico Hamid Rasha Haivrit, since 1962. Author of Span version Sidur; Machzor, Ashkenaz; Machzor, Sephardic. Spec interest, Bibl research. Home: 2510/8-B, Virrey Olaguer, Buenos Aires, Arg.

EDREI, Meir, Isr, communal leader; b. Tiberias, Isr, Sep 29, 1918; s. Machlouf and Hana (Hayon); corresp student, Bennett Coll; m. Esther Blanca; c: Michael, Joseph, Jacob. Mayor Tiberias, since 1965; fmr: i/c post, telegraph, Isr Govt, 1935-53; dist mgr, Amidar 1953-65. Haganah, 1934-48. Treas: Merkaz Marpeh Vetayarout; Igud Arim, Fire Brig; fmr prin, Maccabi sport club. Contbr to jours, Isr press. Home: Shchunat Ovdim, Yalag St, Tiberias, Isr. Office: Tiberias Munic, Tiberias, Isr.

EDWARDS, Jesse Efrem, US, pathologist; b. Hyde Park, Mass, July 14, 1911; s. Max and Nellie (Gordon); BS, Tufts Coll, Bedford, Mass, 1932; MD, Tufts Med School, Boston, 1935; m. Marjorie Brooks, Nov 12, 1952; c: Ellen, Brook. Chief path, Miller Hosp, St Paul, Minn, since 1960; prof, path, U Minn, since 1960; cons, Mayo Clinic, Minn, 1946-60; prof, path, Mayo Found, 1946-60. Lt col, US Army, MC, 1942-46. Bd mem, Family Service, St Paul, Minn; mem: AMA; Amer Ped; Natl Amer Socs in Path and in Card; fmr pres: AHA; Minn Heart Assn; Internal Acad Path. Author and co-author: numerous books on heart disease; contbr to sci jours. Recipient: Modern Med Award, Modern Med, 1964; Gold Heart Award, AHA, 1970. Home: 1565 Edgecombe Rd, St Paul, Minn. Office: 125 W College Ave, St Paul, Minn.

EDWARDS, Leo, US, songwriter, composer, showman; b. Posen, Pol-Ger, Feb 21, 1886; s. Maurice and Johanna (Simon); in US since 1891; m. Olga Weiner, June 6, 1921 (decd); m. 2nd, Gertrude Zimmerman, Oct 15, 1946. Asso with brother, Gus Edwards; proteges include: Eddie Cantor, George Jessel, Groucho Marx, Phil Silvers, Ray Bolger; composer of songs: Isle d'Amour; Sweetheart Let's Grow Old Together; That's What the Rose Said to Me; Fanny Brice Songs in numerous Ziegfeld Follies; operetta, Blue Paradise; Shubert's Wintergarden Produc; The Midnight Rounders, The Merry Whirl, Jesse Lasky's Trained Nurses; Tomorrow's America, Army, Navy and Air Force songs, endorsed by late Pres Roosevelt; entertained and furnished entertainment for Armed Forces, WWs I and II. Charter mem, ASCAP; hon life mem, Beth Abraham for Incurables; club, Lambs. Home: 27 W 72 St, New York, NY. Office: ASCAP, 575 Madison Ave, New York, NY.

EFRATI, Pinhas, Isr, physician, educator; b. Czech, Apr 9, 1907; s. Moshe and Hanna (Shimonovitcz); in Isr since 1933; MD, Ger U, Prague, 1931; m. Avivah Hoffmann, 1942; c: Anat, El'ad, Amiram. Head, dept med, dir lab, blood morphology and cytology, Kaplan Hosp, since 1953; lect, hematology, Bar Ilan U, since 1959; asso prof, Hadassah Hosp, since 1965; dir and head, dept med, Schweizer Memorial Hosp, 1939-49; head, dept med, Govt Hosp, B'nai Brak, 1949-53. Off, Haganah, 1933-48. Sci bd, IMA; mem: NY Acad Sci; Swiss Soc of Hematology; corresp mem, It Soc of Hematology. Contbr to med jours. Home and office: Kaplan Hosp, Rehovot, Isr.

EFRON, Benjamin, US, education dir; b. Bobroisk, Russ, Mar 10, 1908; s. Israel and Sarah (Simonofsky); in US since 1913; BSS, CCNY, 1929; MA, Columbia U, 1937; m. Lillian Westerman, June 20, 1935; c: Richard, Sheila. Dir of educ, Cong Emanu-El Jeshurun, since 1968; cons, KTAV Publ, since 1963; dir educ: Temple Beth-El, Providence RI, 1955-59; Temple Sinai, Roslyn, NY, 1959-65; dir, Coll J Studies, LA, 1965-68. Prin contribs: devl curriculum prog for J Rel Sch from Grades K to 12, and various textbooks. Vice-pres, Natl Assn Temple Educs; chmn, Sch Council, Bur J Educ, 1957-59; mem: Amer J Hist Soc; AJCong. Author: Story Without End, 1949; Pathways Through The Prayerbook, 1961; Message of the Torah, 1963; ed: Currents and Trends in Contemporary Jewish Thought, 1965; Fundamentals of Judaism; co-author, Your Bar Mitzvah, 1963; contbr to J jours. Recipient: award for Curriculum Design, Natl Assn Temple Educs, 1960; award for Rel Sch Textbooks, 1963. Hobbies: children's theater, Yiddish lang. Home and office: 2419 E Kenwood Blvd, Milwaukee, Wis.

EFRONI, Yehuda, Isr, actor; b. Tel Aviv, Isr, Jan 18, 1931; s. Avraham and Mina (Chodosh) Efroniass; att London Acad Music and Dramatic Art, 1953-56; m. Uli Schocken, Aug 25, 1953; c: Leor, Yoseffa. Mem, Habimah, Isr Natl Theatre, since 1951; actor, Chamber Theatre; played with Chisbatron Theatre; toured Isr in one-man performance; toured Eur with wife; parts in Isr films; parts in plays: The Merchant of Venice; Caesar and Cleopatra; Dybbuk: toured US; Can; Eng; participated in Intl Drama Festival: Comedy of Errors; The Parisienne; The Little Murders; Othello; The Marriage. Palmach mil entertainment group, 1948-51. Home: 9 Frishman St, Tel Aviv, Isr. Office: Habimah Theatre, Tarsat Blvd, Tel Aviv, Isr.

EFROS, Israel I, Isr, poet, educator; b. Ostrog-Volyn, Russ, May 28, 1891; s. David and Gitel (Krusman); in Isr since 1955; att NYU, 1913, BA, Columbia U, 1914, MA, PhD, 1915; hon DHL, JTSA, 1937; m. Mildred Blaustein, Dec 20, 1925; c: Gitel. First rector, Tel Aviv U, 1955-59, hon pres since 1959; found, Baltimore Heb Coll and Tchrs Training Sch, 1918, dean, 1918-28; prof Heb U, Buffalo, 1929-41; visiting prof, JTSA, 1937-39; prof: Heb, Hunter Coll, 1941-55; J phil, Heb lit, Dropsie Coll, 1941-55. Author: The Problem of Space in Jewish Medieval Philosophy, 1917; The Bloody Jest, 1922; Philosophical Terms in Moreh Nevuhim, 1924; Millon Angli-Ivri, 1929; Shirim, 1932; Vigvammim Shotkim, 1933; Maimonides' Treatise on Logic, 1938; Zahav, 1942; Anahnu daDor, 1945; Heimlose Yidn, 1947; Goral uPitom, 1954; haFilosofia haYehudit haAtika, 1959; Bein Hofim Nistarim, 1962; 2 vols on ancient and modern J phil, 1965; 4 vols Heb verse, 1966; trans: Shakespeare's Hamlet, 1942; Timon of Athens, 1953; Coriolanus, 1959; Bialik's poetry, 1948. Recipient, awards: Lamed Poetry, 1942, 1954; Tchernichovsky, 1961; JBCA, 1965; Bialik, 1966. Home: 11 Mapu, St, Tel Aviv, Isr.

EFROYMSON, Clarence W, US, educator; b. Indianapolis, Ind, Nov 1, 1897; s. Gustave and Mamie (Wallenstein); BA, Harvard U, 1919; PhD, U Vienna, 1932; BHL, HUC, 1959; m. Elizabeth MacClintock, July 8, 1935. Prof em, econ, Bulter U, on fac since 1918. US Army, 1918. Established: chair for Bible studies in memory Dr Yehezkiel Kaufmann, Heb U, Jerusalem, 1963; Bar Ephraim Fund, JTSA, for publ contemporary works on J phil and theol, 1963. Mem: bd, UAHC, 1951-59; intl hon bd, Ency Judaica, since 1963; Phi Beta Kappa; AAUP; Royal Econ Assn; Amer Econ Assn; hon mem, bd govs, Heb U, Jerusalem; club, Indianapolis Lit. Home: P O Box 292, RR2, Carmel, Ind.

EGER, Akiva, Isr, educator; b. Königsberg, Ger, Apr 15, 1913; s. Izhak and Anita (Frenkel); in Isr since 1935; att U's: Freiburg, 1931; Frankfurt, 1931-32; Königsberg, 1932-33; Paris, 1933-35; LSE, 1953-55; m. 2nd, Lea Raesener; c: Miriam Kedar, Anat, Daniel.Prin: Afro-Asian Inst for Coop and Lab Studies, Tel Aviv, since 1961; prin, sem, 1958-60; emissary, Youth and Hechalutz Educ, JA, Fr, Egypt, Swed, US, Can, N Afr, UK, Ir, 1939-55. Mem: Intl dept, Histadrut; coop council, Min of Lab; Soc for Intl Devl; Histadrut; fmr: mem: exec, Ihud haKibbutzim, Isr; council, Ihud haKvutzot vehakibbutzim; council, HaKibbutz HaMeuchad. Author: The Role of Cooperation and Labor in the Development of Young States, 1965. Hobbies: gardening, books, philately. Home: Kibbutz Netzer-Sereni, Isr. Office: 7-9 Nehardea St, Tel Aviv, Isr.

EGER, Joseph, US, musician; b. Hartford, Conn, July 9, 1925; s. Abraham and Clara (Ellovich); grad: Curtis Inst of Music; Tanglewood. Conducted series of sym concerts: Carnegie and Philharmonic Halls, NY; Sinfonia, London; Haifa Sym, Isr; solo Fr horn, NY and LA Philharmonic orchs; concert artist, world tours; found, music dir, Eger Players and Camera Concerti Chamber Orch, 1956-61; found, conductor, Westside Sym and NY Orch Soc since 1961; asso conc, to Leopold Stokowski and Amer Sym, 1965-68; conducted sym orchs: Pittsburgh, LENA, Midland, Victoria, Long Beach, Vienna Radio, NY; mem, fac: Peabody Conservatory; Aspen. S/Sgt, USAAF. Contbr to Assn Consolidated and Intl Publishers, music jours; recordings: RCA Victor, Westminster, Charisma. Found: Joseph Eger's Crossover; Eger Youth Concerts and Harlem Project. Home: 40 W 67 St, New York, NY.

EHRENFELD, Ernest Nachum, Isr, physician; b. Prague, Czech, Dec 25, 1912; s. Salomon and Cecile (Levy); in Isr since 1940; MD, Ger U, Prague, 1935; cert specialist in internal med, 1939; m. Gerda Bibo, Mar 15, 1942; c: Michael, Ruth, Uri. Asso prof med, Heb U, Hadassah Med Sch, since 1965; chief phys, dept internal med, Hadassah U Hosp, since 1949; head, endocrinology clinic, since 1955; Magnes f, Cornell U Med Sch, NY, 1952-53. Maj, RAMC, 1942-46; Asso f, Amer Coll Card. Contbr to sci jours. Home: 34 Ramban Rd, Jerusalem, Isr. Office: Hadassah U Hosp, Jerusalem, Isr.

EHRENPREIS, Irvin, US, educator; b. NYC, June 9, 1920; s. Louis and Edith (Lipman); BA, CCNY, 1938; MA, Tchrs Coll, Columbia U, 1939; PhD, 1944; D hon causa, U of Besancon, Fr, 1965; m. Anne Henry, Aug 19, 1961. Commonwealth Prof Eng, U of Va, Chalottesville, since 1968; fac mem since 1965; prof, Eng, Ind U, Bloomington, Ind, 1961-65; fac mem since 1945; sr f, Natl Endowment for the Humanities, 1968; visiting research f, Merton Coll, Oxford, 1968. Mem: MLA; Bibliographical Soc, London, Eng; Intl Assn U Prof Eng. Author: The Personality of Jonathan Swift, 1958; Swift, vol 1, 1962, vol 2, 1967; contbr to lit jours. Recipient: Fulbright award, 1949-50; Guggenheim, 1955-56, 1961-62; f, Amer Council of Learned Soc, 1958-59. Office: U of Va, Charlottesville, Va.

EHRENREICH, Bernard, US, business exec; b. NYC, Dec 8, 1896; s. Moritz and Sarah (Kelner); att CCNY, 1914-18; m. Emma Park, June 24, 1923; pres, Beryl Mills Inc, since 1927. Trustee: B'nai B'rith Found of US, since 1960; Lawrence White Found, since 1959; Natl, J Hosp, Denver, Colo, since 1959; mem bd govs, Jt Defense Appeal, since 1957; vice-chmn, Camp B'nai B'rith, since 1967; mem, exec comm, ADL, since 1960, natl civil rights comm, since 1952, E region bd, since 1943, chmn, metrop council B'nai B'rith for ADL, i/c NYC, Westchester, and LI, 1943-47; org and pres, Defenders Lodge, B'nai B'rith, 1939-60; mem, Natl Youth Adv Bd; delg to world conv, B'nai B'rith, Isr, 1959; chmn, metrop council, UJA, for B'nai B'rith, i/c NYC, Westchester, and LI; mem, NY cabinet, UJA, 1947-52; mem, Masons: NY Grand Lodge Comm on Masonic Educ; org, charter mem, Felicity Lodge, 1928; pres, 8th dist, grand master, 1939-40; chmn, war services; chmn bd, B'nai B'rith publ, Metrop Star, 1957-59; club Cent, chmn, 1954-56 and since 1959. Home: 55 Park Ave, New York, NY.

EHRENREICH, Emma, US, artist; b. NYC, Sep 19, 1906; d. William and Rose (Koch) Park; att: CCNY, LIU; Hunter Coll Grad Sch; Natl Acad Design; Art Sch, Bklyn Mus; Art Students League; m. Bernard Ehrenreich, June 24, 1927. Exhbs in mus: Bklyn, intl watercolor, 1953, 1955, 1957, 1959, 1961; Whitney; Natl Acad; Provincetown Soc of Arts, Audubon Soc; Natl Watercolor Soc, Cleveland; Corcoran; Pa Art; Dayton; Columbus; Riverside; repr in natl exhb of J Tercentenary 1955; invited from Butler Mus annual 1958 exhb by the Pittsburgh Plan for Art, for 1 year; Bklyn Mus, biennial graphic exhb, 1958, to traveling print show, by Amer Fed of Arts; traveling exhbs: Contemporary Arts, Inc; Bklyn Soc of Artists; Natl Assn of Women Artists; Natl Assn of Painters in Cassein, Studio Guild; Amer Fed Arts; Japan, 1960; group traveling show, S Amer, 1961; one-man shows: gal: Contemporary Arts, Inc, 1953, 1955, 1959, 1962, 1964, 1966; Silvermine Guild for Artists, Conn, 1958; Art Guild, Utica, NY, 1963; Vendome, Phila, 1966; repr at: Brandeis U; Governors' Hosp, NY; Freedom House, NY; Denver Mus of Arts; pvt collections: Bruce Gimbel; Myrtle Frank; Richard Herson; M Northrop-Fisher. Mem: Natl Assn Women Artists; Natl Assn Painters in Cassein; Bklyn Soc of Artists; Artists Equity; NY Soc Women Artists, treas: Provincetown Art Soc; Contemporary Arts, Inc; Hadassah; B'nai B'rith; ORT. Recipient: Berth Barstow prize, Natl Assn of Women Artists, 1950; Grumbacher, 1st prize in cassein, Bklyn Soc of Artists, 1951, 2nd prize in oils, 1953, watercolor 2nd prize, 1963; anonymous purchase award to a mus for woodcuts, Natl Assn of Women Artists, 1954, creative watercolor prize, 1955; Watercolor Medal of Honor, 1962, Lillian Cotton Award, 1963, Marion Haldenstein Prize, 1969; watercolor chosen, Inst of Design Show, Designing a Room around a Painting, Silvermine Guild, Conn, 1956; anonymous prize in oils, 2nd award, Bklyn Soc of Artists, 1957, 1st prize for watercolor, 1958; oil painting, Victor Wyler Found, 1961; medal of honor, Audubon Artists Inc, 1962; Hydenryk Prize, 1964, Watercolor, 1968, Natl Soc of Painters in Cassein; prize 1965, Print etching, 1965, Riverside Mus, ASCA; Oil, 1966, acylic, 1968, Natl Acad, Natl Assn of Women Artists; Oil, 1968, Natl Acad, Audubon. Home: 55 Park Ave, New York, NY. Studio: 817 Broadway, New York, NY.

EHRENREICH, Joseph Willard, US, educator; b. NY, Dec 21, 1920; s. Isaac and Bertha (Lazaroe); BBA, CCNY, MBA, U of S Cal; PhD, NYU; m. Isabel Resler, Mar 7, 1948; c: Edward, Mark, Ava, Beth. Prof, bus econ, dir Research Inst for Bus Econ, U of S Cal, since 1964; dir, planning and research, Prudential Ins Co, 1948-64. Lt cdr, USNR, 1943-46. Pres, Pasadena J Temple and Cen; mem, Beta Gamma Sigma; fmr: chmn: econ sect, Town Hall of Cal; S Cal Research Council. Author: Text for Employee Benefit, 1969; contbr to social sci jours. Recipient: Founder's Day Award, NYU, 1963; Dean's Award, U of S Cal, 1965. Home: 737 Berkshire Ave, Pasadena, Cal. Office: U of S Cal, Los Angeles, Cal.

EHRENTREU, Jona Ernest, Eng, rabbi; b. Munich, Ger, May 12, 1896; s. Chanoch and Ida (Feuchtwanger); PhD, U's: Munich, Berlin, Königsberg, 1924; m. Jenny Heckscher; c: Henry, Shimon, Israel, Esther Jacobovitz, Ruth Levi, Hannah Bamberger. Rabbi: Kehal Adath Yeshurun, since 1947; Etz Chaim Syn, Berlin, 1920; Pressburg Yeshivah, Beth Din, 1923-26; Beth Din, Munich and Dist, 1926-39, resistance activity against Nazi attacks; UK ref on SS Duncia, camps in Hay and Tatura, Austr, 1940-42; Beth David Cong, Mizrachi Adath, 1942-46. Cpl, Ger Army, 1916-18. Found: Beth Jacob movement, lectr, tchr training course, Pol, 1925;

Ezra youth movement, Berlin, 1920. Contbr to rel jours. Recipient: Iron Cross. Home: 23 Grosvenor Gardens, London, Eng.

EHRENWALD, Jan, US, psychoanalyst; b. Bratislava, Czech, March 13, 1900; s. Eduard and Melanie (Spielmann); in US since 1946; MD, U Prague, 1925; m. Anny Stein, Dec 13, 1933; c: Barbara Krohn. Cons psycht and practising psychan: NYC, since 1947; Roosevelt Hosp, since 1952; asso psycht, neuropsycht dept, U Vienna, 1928-31; practising psycht, Bratislava, 1931-39; asst med off, Springfield Mental Hosp, London, 1942; acting med off, Royal W Counties Inst, Eng, 1943-45; mem, med mission to Czech, 1945-46; instr chapl, Coll of Med, SUNY, 1948-52. Capt, Home Guard, Eng, 1942-44. F: Royal Soc of Med, 1942; Amer Psycht Assn; NY Acad of Med; Assn for Advancement of Psychotherapy; trustee, Amer Soc for Phys Research; mem: Amer Acad for Rel and MH; B'nai B'rith. Author: Uber den Sogenannten Judischen Geist, 1938; Telepathy and Medical Psychology, 1947; New Dimensions of Deep Analysis, 1953; From Medicine Man to Freud, 1957; Neurosis in the Family, A Study of Psychiatric Epidemiology, 1962; Psychotherapy: Myth and Method, 1966; contbr to prof jours. Home and office: 11 E 68 St, New York, NY.

EHRLICH, Abel, Isr, composer; b. Cranz, Ger, Sep 3, 1915; s. Arthur and Else (Eichelbaum); in Isr since 1939; dipl, tchr composition, Music Acad, Jerusalem, Isr, 1944; att summer courses, new music, Darmstadt, Ger, 1959, 1961, 1963, 1967; m. Leah Klauber, April 1, 1947; c: Jehudith, Daniel. Composer since 1931; tchr composition, Acad of Music, Tel Aviv U since 1964; tchr: Erez Isr Music Acad, Jerusalem, 1940-53; Tchrs Coll, Oranim, 1953-68. Cpl, IDF, 1964. Prin compositions: Bashrav for Violin Solo; Work for Orch; Passing Shapes for String Quintet; Radiations Book A and B; Shaharit, piano; Damaged Moon; Trio for Violin, Cello and Piano; The Dream of the Double Cry; Time Sculptures, for string orch; music for Antigone; From Ahab's Diary; 5th String Quartet; Habayit Haze; Music for Flute and Piano; Quartet for Four Percussion Players; Book of Creation; Andante for Violin and Piano; Bashrav; Testimony; The Letter of Hiskia; Don't Be As Your Father; 4th String Quartet. Recipient: two commns by Isr Composer's Fund; 10 years, Rinat Choir Prize; Libervon Prize, 1968, 1969. Home: 13 Tagore St, Ramat Aviv, Isr. Office: Acad of Music, Tel Aviv U, Ramat Aviv, Isr.

EHRLICH, Abraham J, US, rabbi; b. Jerusalem, Isr, Aug 10, 1923; s. Nachum and Esther (Cohen); BA, Wooster Coll, ordained rabbi, MST, Hebron Yeshivah, Jerusalem; m. Pearl Ulman, Dec 28, 1947; c: Michael, Michelle. Rabbi: Temple Beth Isr, since 1959; Wooster O Temple, 1949-54; Temple Beth Isr, Bristol, Conn, 1954-59; pres, Shiurim Publ Co. Pres, Nassau-Suffolk Region, RA, 1966-68; comm mem, J Law and Standards, RA. Author: Shiurim, texts for rel schs. Home: 63 Essex Ct, Port Washington, NY. Study: Ash Pl, Port Washington, NY.

EHRLICH, Charles, Fr, merchant; b. Haguenau, Fr, June 26, 1905; s. Jacques and Melanie (Klein); m. Louise Levi; c: Nicole, Martine, Nadine. Asso with Jacques Ehrlich & Son, Houblons, since 1927. Pres: J comty, Strasbourg; Assistance Sociale Juive, Strasbourg; Eur Union of Commerce; Natl Union of Commerce, both Houblons; mem: Consistoire Israelite du Bas-Rhin; B'nai B'rith; club, Rotary. Office: 142 Grand'Rue, Haguenau, Fr.

EHRLICH, Hyman, US, attorney; b. Stanislau, Aus, Aug 29, 1905; Elias and Gussie (Stark); in US since 1915; LLB, St Johns U Law Sch, Bklyn, NY, 1928; m. Tess Greenberg, July 2, 1932; c: Sheldon and Robert. Pvt practice since 1929. Home: 65-14 110 St, Forest Hills, NY. Office: 217 Broadway, New York, NY.

EHRLICH, Jerrold I, US, attorney; b. Bklyn, NY, Jan 21, 1934; s. Harvey and Belle (Crames); AB, Oberlin Coll, 1955; LLB, Yale, 1958; m. Elaine Bergman, Dec 26, 1954; c: Mark, Bruce, Alan, Philip. Asso atty, Harry H Lipsig, since 1967; vice-pres, Research Devl Techniques Intl, Inc, since 1970; asso atty, Burke & Groh, 1959-66; asst dist atty, Queens Co, NY, 1967. Treas, Couples Club, Stephen E Wise Free Syn; Amer Trial Lawyers Assn; NJ State Bar Assn; NY State Bar Assn; Fed Bar Council; NY State Dist Attys Assn; NY City Lawyers Assn; Queens City Bar Assn; fmr dir: Queens Council on the Arts; Jamaica Sym Orch; United Cerebral Palsy of Queens. Recipient: C LaRue Munson award, Yale U,

1957. Spec interests: comty political activity. Home: Valley View Dr, Montville, NJ. Office: 100 Church St, New York, NY.

EHRMAN, Arnost Zvi, Isr, author, editor; b. Kralovsky Chlumec, Czech, Apr 22, 1914; s. Samuel and Bertha (Lauer); in Isr since 1962; att Yeshivot, Hung; LLD, dipl, political sci, U Berne, Switz, 1946; ordained rabbi, J Coll, London, 1949; m. Esther Unger, Apr 12, 1961; c: Eric, Miriam, Etta. Ed in chief, El-Am Talmud, Tel Aviv, since 1964; rabbi: Nairobi, Kenya, 1953-59; Bristol, Eng, 1959-62; research f, Talmudic Law, Heb U, Jerusalem, 1963-64. Prin contrib: promoting study and research, Talmud, J law. Fmr: mayor's chaplain, Nairobi; hon chaplain, Brit Legion; visiting chaplain, HM Prisons, Bristol, Eng; mem: Isr Bar Assn; B'nai B'rith. Contbr numerous articles on Talmudic, legal subjects. Recipient: f, J's Coll, London. Hobby: debating. Home: Faculty Housing, Bar Ilan U, Ramat Gan, Isr. Office: 25 Stand St, Tel Aviv, Isr.

EHRMAN, H Bruce, US, rabbi; b. Boston, Mass, June 1, 1918; s. Herbert and Sara (Rosenfeld); AB, Harvard U, 1939; BHL, HUC, 1944, MHL, ordained rabbi, 1948; m. Nancy Lehman, Aug 25, 1946; c: Ann, David, Johanna. Rabbi, Cong Isr, Brockton, Mass, since 1948; J chaplain, VA Hosp, Brockton, since 1954; acting rabbi, Cong Gemiluth Chassodim, Alexandria, La, 1945-47. Trustee, Brockton Public Libr; mem: fmr mem exec bd, CCAR; Rotary Club; fmr: pres, Eastern NE Conf Lib Rabbis; vice-pres, secy: Rabb Assn, Gtr Boston, Mass Bd Rabbis; pres, vice pres, treas, Birch Island, Me, Improvement Assn; dir, ARC. Home: 47 South St, Brockton, Mass. Study: 184 W Elm St, Brockton, Mass.

EHRMAN, Sender, US, business exec; b. Pruchnicku, Pol, Feb 22, 1897; s. Meyer and Chana (Ehrman) Schumer; in US since 1941; m. Mathilda Weinberg; c: Gershon, Maurice, Jacob, Hilda Frommer, Rachel Goldwasser. Pres: Sender Ehrman Co Inc; S Ehrman & Sons; mgn dir: Rebna Realty Co; Ehrman Assos. Trustee, Tchebiner Yeshiva Kochav Miyaakov; vice-pres, United Lubavitcher Yeshivoth; off, Colel Hibath Jerusalem; club, Diamond Dealers, NY. Home: 725 W 184 St, New York, NY. Office: 71 W 47 St, New York, NY.

EHRMANN, Eliezer Leo, US, educational admn, author; b. Tarnow, Aus, July 22, 1903; s. Moses and Toni (Friedler); in US since 1938; Prussian State Tchrs Dipl, Berlin, 1928; PhD, U Berlin, 1929; att, Hochschule fuer die Wissenschaft des Judentums, Berlin; m. Marli Heimann, 1936; c: Frank. Supt, Bd J Educ, Chgo, since 1944; cons, research asso, educ dept, Reichsvertretung der Juden in Deutschland, Berlin, 1936-38. Vice-pres, Histadrut Ivrit, Chgo, 1962; mem, exec comm: Natl Council on J Audio-Visual Materials, since 1952; Natl Council for J Educ, since 1957. Author: Der englische Kampf gegen die fremden Bankiers im dreizehnten Jahrundert, 1929; Sukkot and Simhat Tora, 1937; Purim, 1937; Chanukka, 1937; Pesach, 1938; Das Fest der Mazzot in Erzaehlungen und Schilderungen, 1938; Rosch haSchana und Yom Kippur, 1938; Arbeits-plaene fuer die Festtage, 1936-38; Mafteakh leHora'at Toldot Yisrael, 1940; The Conflict with Hellenism, 1944; Jewish Life under Roman Rule, 1946; Visual Aids in Jewish Education, 1951; contbr to profsl jours. Home: 706 N Kenilworth Ave, Oak Park, Ill. Office: 72 E 11 St, Chicago, Ill.

EHRMANN, Herbert B, US, attorney; b. Louisville, Ky, Dec 15, 1891; s. Hilmar and Ernestine (Heissman); BA, Harvard U, 1912, LLB, 1914; m. Sara Rosenfeld, May 12, 1917; c: Bruce, Robert. Partner, law firm, Goulston and Storrs, Boston, Mass, since 1921; dir, US Trust Co; with Boston Legal Aid Soc, 1915-17; partner, Ehrmann and Bloom, 1916-17; asso, Hale and Dorr, 1919-21; counsel, with William G Thompson, for Sacco and Vanzetti, 1926-27; chmn, Women's Clothing Wash Bd of Mass, 1915-19; mem, War Lab Policies Bd, 1918-19; dir, ind relations div, US Shipping Bd, 1919; mem: Mass Jud Council, 1934-37; Mass Civil Service Comm, 1939-43; referee, panel chmn, Natl War Lab Bd, 1942; arbitrator, Amer Arbitration Assn, 1945. Pres: AJComm, 1959-62; hon pres, since 1962; Hale House Assn; Gtr Boston Fed Neighborhood Houses, 1934-37; chmn, Boston J Tercentenary Comm, 1954; secy-treas, Civic Educ Found; trustee: Mass Training Schs, 1933-37; Soc Law Libr; Assn J Philanthropies; mem: admn comm, J Comty Council, 1954; Council of Boston Bar Assn; bd mgrs, Old South Assn; Amer, Mass, Norfolk, and Boston Bar Assns; C of C; Delta Sigma Rho; club, Harvard, Boston. Author: The Criminal Courts of Cleveland, Ohio, 1921; The Untried Case, 1933, The Case That Will Not Die, 1969; Under This Roof, play, produc on Broadway, NY,

1942; contbr to prof jours. Home: 14 Irving St, Brookline, Mass. Office: 131 State St, Boston, Mass.

EIBER, Harold B, US, physician, educator; b. NYC Mar 29, 1915; s. Solomon and Frieda (Katzman); BA, NYU, 1936; att Royal Coll Phys and Surgs, Edinburgh, 1936-39; MD, U Lausanne, Switz, 1940; m. Audrey Collier, June 27 1948; c: Marcy, Shelley, Selwyn; m. 2nd, Helen Eiber, Sep 15 1967. Asso prof med, NY Med Coll, since 1953; dir, Gilman Lab, since 1953; att phys: Flower and Fifth Ave Hosp; Beth Isr Hosp; Metrop Hosp; Bird S Coler Hosp. Maj, US Army. Prin contrib: Preparation of radioactive heparin, 1959; F: Amer Coll Angiology; NY Acad of Med; Intl Coll Angiology; AAAS; mem: Soc Experimental Biol and Med; AHA; AMA; trustee, Lorge Sch, NYC. Contbr to med, biochem, other sci jours. Recipient: research grants: AEC; NIH-USPHS; AHA; Croix de Guerre; Legion of Honor. Hobby: philately. Home and office: 48 E 75 St, New York, NY.

EICHELBAUM, Stanley, US, journalist; b. NYC, Oct, 5, 1926; s. Sam and Rebecca (Rosen); BA, CCNY, 1947; MA, Columbia U, 1948; cert d'études, Sorbonne, Paris, 1949. Film, theater critic, San Francisco Examiner, since 1960, mem staff since 1958; instr, dramatic art, U of Cal Ext, SF since 1968; reporter, researcher, New Yorker Mag, 1949-58; contbr drama revs to various publs, including: Hollywood Reporter; Playbill. Mem: prog comm, SF Art Inst; Cal Hist Soc. Hobby: painting. Home: 333 Green St, San Francisco, Cal. Office: 110 Fifth St, San Francisco, Cal.

EICHHORN, Antonija Geiger, Yugo, pianist, educator; b. Rzeszow, Jan 2, 1893; d. Henrik and Ernestine (Neuman); dipl, Acad of Music, Vienna, 1909, teaching dipl, 1912; m. Marcel Eichhorn, Apr 21, 1918; c: Edgai. Prof, Acad of Music, Zagreb, since 1945, and 1920-40; piano debut, Zagreb, 1902; Budapest, 1904; Prague, 1907; Vienna, 1908; Berlin, 1911; London, 1912; soloist with sym orchs: Zagreb; Belgrade; Rijeka, all Yugo. Interned, camp, in It, 1941-45; club, U Profs. Recipient: 1st prize, Acad of Music, Vienna, 1909; 1st prize, piano, Aus State prize, 1912; several prizes in Yugo, including Nazor prize for life work, 1966. Home: Saveska cesta 8, Zagreb, Yugo.

EICHHORN, David Max, US, rabbi; b. Columbia, Pa, Jan 6, 1906; s. Joseph and Anna (Zivi); BA, Cincinnati U, 1928; ordained rabbi, HUC, 1931, DD, 1938; hon DHL, JIR, 1956; m. Zelda Socol June 23, 1935; c: Jonathan, Michael, Jeremiah, Judith. Chaplain for J Scis, Cape Kennedy Space Cen, Apr to Sept each year; dir, field oprs, comm on J chaplaincy, Natl JWB, NY, 1945-68; rabbi: Sinai Temple, Springfield, Mass, 1932-34; Mt Sinai Cong, Texarkana, Ark, 1935-38; dir, Fla Hillel Founds, Tallahassee, Fla, 1939-42. Chaplain, US Army, 1942-45, lt col, US Army Res. Fmr pres; Alumni Assn, HUC; Assn J Chaplains Armed Forces; mem: Masons; Amer Vet Comm; CCAR. Author: A History of Christian Attempts to Convert the Jews of the US and Canada, 1938; Cain, Son of the Serpent, 1957; Musings of the Old Professor, 1936; Conversion to Judaism: A History and Analysis, 1965. Homes: 85-14 66 Ave, Rego Park, Long Island, NY; Cape Kennedy Space Cen, Fla.

EICHHORN, Gunther Louis, US, chemist; b. Frankfurt; Slash Main, Ger, Feb 8, 1927; s. Fritz and Else (Weiss); in US since 1938; BA, U Louisville, 1947; MS, U of Ill, 1948, PhD, 1950; m. Lottie Neuhaus, 1964; c: David, Sharon. Chief, sect on molecular biol, Gerontology Research Cen, Natl Inst Child Health and Human Devl, NIH, City Hosps, Baltimore, Md, since 1958; teaching asst, U of Ill, 1947-49; asst, asso prof, inorganic chem, La St U, 1954-57; commissioned off, USPHS, NIH, 1954-57; asso prof, Georgetown U, 1957-58. F: AAAS; Amer Chem Soc; B'nai B'rith; Phi Lambda Upsilon; NY Acad Sci; Sigma Xi; Phi Kappa Phi. Auhtor: Coordination Compounds in Natural Products, 1953; The Role of Metal Ions in Enzymatic Reactions, 1959; contbr to profsl jours. Recipient: postdoc f, O State U, 1951-52; grants: Research Corp, 1950-54; NIH, 1957-58. Home: 6703 97 Ave, Seabrook, Md. Office: NIH, Baltimore City Hosps, Baltimore, Md.

EICHLER, Joseph L, US, builder, developer; b. NYC, June 25, 1900; s. David and Hannah (Strauss); BCS, NYU, 1922; m. Lillian Moncharsh, Oct 5, 1924; c: Richard, Edward. Pres: J L Eichler Assoc Inc, since 1967; Eichler Homes, Inc, 1947. Mem: Gov Brown's Comm on Metrop Area Problems; Golden Gate Auth Commn; bd trustees, SF Mus Modern Art; Bay Conservation & Devl Commn; clubs: Lake Merced Golf; Commonwealth, SF. Recipient: Man of Year, City of

Hope, 1959; Citizen of Merit, Sun Reporter, 1958; numerous other awards. Home: 1860 Willow Road, Palo Alto, Cal. Office: 343 Second St, Los Altos, Cal.

EIDELBERG, Ludwig, US, physician, educator; b. Zlocow, Pol, Dec 27, 1898; s. Ithamar and Helena (Selzer); in US since 1940; MD, U Vienna, 1925; m. Marthe Elkann, Sep 6, 1939; c: Philippe. Clinical prof psycht, NY Psychoanalytic Inst. Pres, Psychoanalytic Assn, NY, 1959-60. Author: Studies in Psychoanalysis, 1952; An Outline of a Comparative Theory of the Neuroses, 1954; Take off your Mask, 1960; Dark Urge, 1961; ed in chief, Ency of Psychan; contbr sci papaers. Home and office: 25 E 86 St, New York, NY.

EIDELSBERG, Joseph, US, physician, educator; b. NYC, Apr 19, 1896; s. Isadore and Rose (Grossman); MD, NYU, 1918; m. Bessie Strauss, Dec 26, 1920; c: Robert. Asso prof, clinical med, Columbia U, NYC, 1928-47, NYU, since 1947; att phys, U Hosp and Bellevue Hosp, NYC; lectr, endocrinology, NYU Post Grad Med Sch. US Army MC, WWI. Mem: AMA; Assn for Study of Internal Secretions; Alpha Omega Alpha. Contbr to med jours. Home: 50 E 78 St, New York, NY. Office: 895 Park Ave, New York, NY.

EIDINGER-FUCHS, Sidonie, Isr, painter; b. Czernowitz, Rum, Apr 26, 1929; d. Moses and Fany (Herzig) Fuchs; in Isr since 1960; BA, Timisoara Coll, 1947, MA, State Acad Fine Arts, Cluj, Rum, 1955; m. Manfred Eidinger, Feb 19, 1952; c: Maya. Painter and free graphician since 1955; tchr, free graphics, Wizo Sch, since 1964; asst prof, graphic dept of Acad, 1954-59; dir, graphic dept Inst of Fine Arts, Bat Yam, Isr, 1961-68; participant, group show, Warsaw; one-man shows: Bucharest; Budapest; Stockholm; exhbs, Isr Assn Painters and Sculptors. Mem, Isr Assn Painters and Sculptors. Spec interest: hist of art. Home: 33 Shapira St, Petah Tikva, Isr.

EIGEN, Herman Arnold, US, organization exec; b. NYC, Mar, 26, 1910; s. Maxwell and Augusta; MSW, Columbia U, 1939; m. Sadie Salutsky, Sep 15, 1940; c: Maxene Rocker, Joel. Exec dir: J Comty Cen of Cleveland, since 1954, Buffalo, 1947-54; head social worker, U Settlement House, Cleveland, 1934-42; tchr: W Reserve U, 1940-42; U Buffalo, 1950-54. Capt, US Army, 1942-47. Fmr pres, Midwest region, Natl Fed Settlement Workers; fmr vice-pres, Natl Assn J Cen Workers; mem: Natl Assn Social Workers. Contbr to profsl jours. Home: 3790 Washington Blvd, University Heights, O. Office: 3505 Mayfield Rd, Cleveland Heights, O.

EIGEN, Maurice, US, organization exec; b. Bklyn, NY, May 18, 1912; s. Max and Gussie (Katz); BS, LIU, 1932; MA, Columbia U, 1934; att NY Sch of Social Work, 1936-39; m. Edna Cooper June 12, 1938; c: Deborah. Dir: Heb U-Technion Joint Maintenance Appeal, since 1956; Brit zone in Ger, Amer JDC, 1945-47; fund raising, United HIAS Service, 1954-56; asst dir, HIAS, 1947-54; asso sup in Gt Brit, ARC, 1942-45. Mem: intl comm on social work, Natl Conf J Communal Service; Assn Fund Raising Dirs; fmr: mem: planning comm, UNRRA; DP's study comm, finance comm, Amer Council of Voluntary Agcys for Fgn Service. Contbr to profsl jours. Home: 849 E 17 St, Brooklyn, NY. Office: 11 E 69 St, New York, NY.

EIGER, Norman N, US, jurist; b. Chgo, Ill, Aug 6, 1903; s. Isaac and Rachel (Brender); LLB, De Paul U, 1924; m. Leona Wolan, Dec 31, 1935; c: Lawrence, Rodney. Judge, Circuit Court, Cook Co, since 1964; mem, exec staff, Capital Stock Tax Assessor, Ill State Tax Commn, 1932-36; asst to Corp Counsel, City of Chgo, 1936-47; chmn, Ill State Bd of Rev, Lab Dept, 1948-52. US Coast Guard Res, WWII. Arbitrator, mem panel, Amer Assn Arbitrators; vice-pres: Adult Educ Council of Metrop Chap; Ill Judges Assn; hon life trustee, Temple Isaiah Isr; co-chmn, Conciliation Comm, Chgo fed, UAHC; secy, Patriotic Found Chgo; mem: Chgo Bar Assn, exec, civil practice comm; natl conf state trial judges, Amer Bar Assn; Decalogue Soc of Lawyers; Sponsors of Wash, Morris, Solomon Monument; Navy Club of Chgo; adv bd, Ill Police Res; awards comm, B'nai B'rith Org; hon mem, adv bd, New World; fmr: vice-pres: and mem bd trustees, Coll of J Studies; and mem bd dirs, Bd J Educ; Chgo B'nai B'rith Council, pres, Jackson B'nai B'rith Lodge; chmn, lawyers div, CJA; fmr grand chancellor, Nu Beta Epsilon. Home: 5485 Hyde Park Blvd, Chicago, Ill. Office: Munic Court, Chicago, Ill.

EILON, Samuel, Eng, educator; b. Oct 13, 1923; s. Abraham and Rachel; att Technion, Haifa, Isr; PhD Imperial Coll,

London, 1955, DSc engr, 1963; m. Hannah Samuel, 1946; four c. Prof, Ind Mgmt, head, Mgmt Engr Sect, Imperial Coll of Sci and Tech, U of London, since 1963, mem fac since 1952; fmr: asso prof, Technion, Haifa, 1957-59; prof research f, Case-W Reserve U, Cleveland, 1967-68. Off, IDF, 1948-52. Mem and past mem, comms of Produc Engr, Dept of Educ and Sci; mem council, Operational Research Soc. Author: Element of Production Planning and Control, 1962; Inventory Control Abstracts, 1968; co-author: Industrial Engineering Tables, 1962; Exercises in Industrial Management, 1966; Industrial Scheduling Abstracts, 1967; ed, Management Studies Series; contbr numerous sci papers. Recipient: Joseph Whitworth Prizes for two papers, both 1960. Hobbies: theater, tennis, walking. Home: 1 Meadway Close, London NW 11, Eng. Office: Imperial Coll, Exhibition Rd, London SW 7, Eng.

EINFELD, S Charles, US, motion picture exec; b. NYC, Oct 25, 1901; s. Richard and Celia (Baruch); att Columbia U, 1920; m. May Band, June 15, 1927; c: Richard, Lise Connell, Linda Sigel. Vice-pres: Twentieth Century Fox Film Corp, since 1948; Warner Bros Pictures, 1929-46; pres, Enterprise Producs, 1946-48. Mem: Assn of Motion Pictures Advertisers; Acad of Motion Picture Arts and Scis. Home: Casa Delta, Ascona, Switz. Office: 342 Madison Ave, New York, NY.

EINFELD, John I, Austr, att; b. Sydney, Austr, Dec 21, 1915; s. Marcus and Doris (Garbel); Solicitor and Atty, Supr Court, NSW, 1939; Commn for affidavits; m. Maadi Sussman, Oct 18, 1945; c: Louise, Stephen, Denise. Sr partner, John I Einfeld & Co, since 1962; vice-pres, Moriah Coll, since 1967; articled law clerk, 1934-39; partner, law firm, Rishworth, Dodd & Einfeld, 1946-61. Capt, Austr Imperial Force, 1940-46. Pres, J Ex-Servicemen and Women Assn, 1950-58; dir wfr, Co-op Bldg Soc Group, since 1959; patron, Fed J Ex-Servicemen and Women, Austr, fmr pres; chmn, King David Sch, since 1967; mem: comm on mgmt, exec council, Austr Jewry, since 1960; exec, J Bd Deps, since 1949; fmr: mem council, J War Memorial; mem bd mgmt, NSW div, YMHA. Recipient: mention in dispatches, 1947; Queen's Coronation Medal, 1953. Home: 13 Black St, Vaucluse, NSW, Austr. Office: Natl Bank Bldg, 251 George St, Sydney, Austr.

EINFELD, Sydney David, Austr, legislater, communal leader; b. Sydney, Austr, June 17, 1909; s. Marcus and Doris (Garbel); m. Rose Appelboom, June 2, 1934; c: Marcus, Robyn. MP, NSW, since 1965, dep leader, Opposition, since 1968; JP. Pres: Fed Austr J Wfr Soc, since 1951; Fed YM-YWHA in Austr, since 1950; Austr Comm for ORT, since 1956; vice-pres, NSW J Bd Deps, since 1952; World Fed YM-YWHA and Cmty Cens, since 1949; exec mem, WJC, since 1951; chmn: Austr Council for Overseas Aid, since 1966; bd dirs, 17 coop bldg socs, since 1953; mem bd mgmt, Gt Syn, since 1953; fmr: pres, exec council, Austr Jewry; dep chmn, Austr Natl Comm:World Ref Year; Freedom from Hunger Campaign; dir, Conf on J Material Claims Against Ger, Inc; vice-pres: Austr Comm for Intl Ref Campaign; Austr Natl Comm for Ref; world vice-pres, Intl Council Voluntary Agcys; led 3-man delg to Viet Nam on survey for requirements for civilian aid to S Viet Nam. Home: 162 Military Rd, Dover Heights, Austr. Office: Parl House, Macquarie St, Sydney, Austr.

EINHORN, Herbert A, US, attorney; b. NYC, Feb 5, 1913; s. William and Sadie (Reich); BA, cum laude, Ohio U, 1933; LLB, Columbia U Law Sch, 1935; m. Roslyn Appel, Feb 11, 1940; c: Eric, Diane. Partner, Aranow, Brodsky, Bohlinger, Einhorn and Dann, since 1946; asso, Livingston and Livingston, 1935-38; sr counsel, NY State Ins Fund, 1938-40, spec counsel, inves, 1940-41; asst atty gen, NY State, 1943-45. Pres, Brotherhood, 1952; dir, asst treas, Camp Loyaltown, since 1962; mem: Columbia Law Sch Alumni Assn; O U Trustees Acad; B'nai B'rith; NYC and NY Co and Amer Bar Assns; clubs: Friars, NYC; Hampshire Country; NYU. Co-author: Proxy Contests for Corporate Control, 1957, rev, 1968; contbr to legal jours. Recipient: B'nai B'rith Award, 1951. Home: 12 Glen Eagles Dr, Larchmont, NY. Office: 122 E 42 St, New York, NY.

EINHORN, Jerzy, Swed, educator; b. Czestochowa, Pol, July 26, 1925; s. Pinkus and Sarah (Blibaum); in Swed since 1946; BM, Uppsala U, 1949; MD, Kardinska Inst, Stockholm, 1954; m. Nina Rajmic, Oct 1, 1954; c: Lena, Stefan. Prof, radiotherapy, dir, Radiumhemmet since 1968; phys, 1954-61, dep dir head, isotope dept, 1962-67; prof radiotherapy, Kardinska Inst, since 1959. Lt, Swed Army; mem, exec comm WJC, Swed sect; holds offices and mem in various profsl orgs. Contbr numerous articles to sci publs. Home: 13 Gen-

vagen St, Danderyd, Swed. Office: Radiumhemmet, Karolinskasjukhuset, Stockholm 60, Swed.

EINHORN, Joseph H, US, attorney; b. NYC, May 1, 1906; s. Samuel and Ida (Jassem); BA, Union Coll, Schenectady, NY, 1928; LLB, Albany Law Sch, 1931, JD, 1968; m. Rose Weinberg, Jan 2, 1933. Pvt practice since 1931; referee to examine the accounts of incompetents, Albany Co, 1946-58. Fmr pres: and mem, bd trustees, Temple Beth Emeth Brotherhood; Albany JCC; Gideon lodge, B'nai B'rith, mem, gen comm Dist 1, pres, Up-State NY Council; natl treas, Kappa Nu; chmn: Assn Red Cross chaps, Capital Dist, since 1959; natl resolutions comm, 1969, ARC, fmr: bd sups, Albany Co, vice-chmn, fund chmn; Albany chap, AJComm since 1962; NY State Jt Defense Appeal; fmr, relations comm, JCC, men's div, JWF campaign; fmr: mem, bd: Council of Comty Services; J Home for Aged; Natl Judge Advocate, Chem Warfare Service; Hudson Valley Council, Girls Scouts of Amer; mem: Amer, NY State and Albany Co Bar Assns; Albany Inst of Hist and Art; Amer Legion; Amer Vets of WW II, JWV; Disabled Amer Vets; Elks; Tau Epsilon Rho; Tau Kappa Alpha; clubs: Kiwanis, fmr pres; Torch. Fmr ed: Albany J Comty Year Book, 1945-52; Albany Bar Assn Handbook, 1948. Home: 152 Rosemont St, Albany, NY. Office: 90 State St, Albany, NY.

EINHORN, Nathan H, US, physician, b. Bakau, Rum, Apr 9, 1901; s. Morris and Fannie (Rosenblatt); in US since 1902; BA, U Colo, 1923; MD, 1926; MSc, med, U of Pa, 1934; DSc, 1936; m. Rose Levitt, July 29, 1934; c: Philip. Clinical prof em, ped, Hahnemann Med Coll, since 1966, prof, 1956-66; pvt med practice since 1946; civilian cons, ped, Valley Forge Army Hosp, since 1948; mem exec comm, Phila Gen Hosp, since 1950, dir med educ, since 1965, visiting phys, 1946-1966, pres med staff, 1959-61; sr endocrinologist; Einstein Med Cdn, 1955-66, J Hosp, 1939-59. Lt to col, US Army, 1941-46. Mem bd govs, Beth David Reform Cong, since 1957, past pres; Amer Acad Ped; FACS; mem: Pa, Phila Co Med Socs; AMA; Phila Ped Soc; Phi Delta Epsilon, fmr grand consul; Sigma Xi; Phi Sigma Delta; Masons. Contbr numerous articles to profsl jours. Recipient: Billings Gold Medal Award, AMA, 1937; Leg of Merit, 1946. Home: 6374 Drexel Rd, Philadelphia, Pa. Office: Civic Centre Blvd, at 34 St, Philadelphia, Pa.

EISEMAN, Myron J, US, business exec; b. NYC, Feb 28, 1919; s. Aaron and Estelle (Alexander); BBA, NYU, 1937; m. Marjorie Koenig, Dec 8, 1953 (decd); c: Patricia, Nancy; m. 2nd, Adrienne Kaster, Jan, 1966; c: Richard, Robin. Vice-pres, United Merchants and Mfgs, Inc, since 1958; dir, United Merchants and Mfgs, London, Eng, since 1959; chmn, bd, United Intl Corp, since 1954, on staff since 1945; dir: Pan Ameritex de Panama, since 1948; Springlass Ltd, Eng, since 1960; Brit Silk Dyers, since 1961; chief exec off, fgn div, Cohn Hall Marx, 1937-45. US Army, 1942-45. Mem: AJComm; FJP; Pan Amer Soc; Ecuadorian Assn; C of C, Latin Amer; club, Beach Point Country. Recipient: Medal of Verdun, 1944. Hobbies: woodworking; audio. Home: Sunny Ridge Rd, Harrison, NY. Office: 1407 Broadway, New York, NY.

EISEMANN, Meier S, US, educator; b. Frankfurt, Ger; in US since 1953; ordained rabbi, Eitz Chaim and Liverpool Yeshiva, 1948. Prin: Torah Acad since 1955; fmr prin, Progressive Heb Day Sch, Toledo, O; visiting lectr: U Minn Sch Libr Sci; St Johns U; Concordia Coll; Coll of St Catherine; midwest coord, Torah Umesorah. Vice-pres: Natl Assn Yeshiva Prin; fmr vice-pres, Phyllis Wheatley Comty C; chmn, Mayor's Adv Comm to N Side Planning Commn; past dir, United Fund of Hennepin Co; natl bd dirs, Heb Day Sch PTA's; mem Educ Assn; adv local radio sta on rel progs. Contbr to scholarly jours. Office: 4000 Golden Valley Rd, Minneapolis, Minn.

EISENBACH, Shalom Leyb, US, rabbi; b. Jerusalem, Pal, Apr 4, 1919; s. Abraham and Rachel (Eisebach); in US since 1929; BA CCNY, 1942; ordained rabbi, Messifta Tiphereth Jerusalem, 1944; att: Dropsie Coll, 1945-50; Yeshiva U, 1948; MA, U Conn, 1960; m. Anita Smith, Feb 18, 1945; c: Kenneth, Gil, Ava, Eileen. Prin, Wilmington Gratz Heb HS, Wilmington, Del, since 1967; educ dir, Beth Shalom, Wilmington, since, 1967; tchr, Heb, Mesifta Tifereth Jerusalem, NY; Beth Midarash L'Amorot, NY; Span-Port Syn, NY, 1943-45; rabbi, tchr, Beth Hillel Cong, Millville, NJ, 1945-50; dir, B'nai B'rith Hillel Found, U of Conn, Storrs, 1950-60; chaplain, Mansfield Training Sch and Hosp, 1950-60; registrar, lectr, Bible and Heb, Coll J Studies, Chgo, Ill, 1960-64. Vice-pres, Histadruth Ivrit, Chgo; mem: bd dirs, ADL, Conn; exec bd,

NCCJ, 1953-54; educ assembly: B'nai B'rith; J Hist Soc; Natl Council J Educ; Rel Educ Assn; Rel Counsellors Org, U Conn. Home: 1202 Wilson Rd, Mayfield, Wilmington, Del. Study: Coll of J Studies, 72 E 11 St, Chicago, Ill.

EISENBERG, Azriel, US, educator, author; b. Russ-Pol, Aug 29, 1903; s. Elazar and Mindel (Shpetric); in US since 1914; att Tchrs Inst, JTSA, 1922; BS, NYU, 1926; PhD, Columbia U, 1935; hon DHL, JTSA, 1959; m. Rose Leibow Aug, 19, 1928; c: Sora Landes, Judah. Dir em, J Educ Comm of NY; dir info, Bur J Educ: NY, 1968, dir: Cincinnati, 1935-40; Cleveland, 1940-45; dir, Phila Council J Educ, 1946-49; acting dean, Graetz Coll, Phila, 1946-49; dir, World Council of J Educ, 1966-68; served J educ in Iran, JDC, 1969; fmr pres: Natl Council for J Educ; J Tchrs Assn, NY; NE O Rel Educ Assn; chmn, United Syn Comm on J Educ; co-chmn, Natl Zionist Educ Comm; org, intl conf on J educ, Eur, under auspices JDC, 1956. Author: Children and Radio Programs, 1936; Into the Promised Land (guide), 1936; Jewish Literature since the Bible, 2 vols, 1943, 1946; Hundreds of Pictures, 1951; Tzedakah and Federation, 1952; Dear Parents, 1953; The Great Discovery, 1956; The Story of the Jewish Calendar, 1958; Voices From the Past, 1958, Fr ed, 1962, Heb ed, 1962; My Jewish Holidays, 1958; The Dead Sea Scrolls, in Heb, 1958; Readings in the Teaching of Hebrew, 1961; Kolot Mini Kedem; Olamot Shenelinu Veniglu; Jewish Historical Treasures; Jerusalem United, A Manual for Schools; The Secret Weapon, Stories on Prayer; co-auther: Teacher's Guide, 1940; Teaching Jewish History, 1954, Fr ed, 1961; Story of the Prayer Book; Sabra Children; ed: The Bar Mitzvah, 1952; The Confirmation Reader, 1954; Yerushalayim, 1955; Modern Jewish Life in Literature, 1956; Accent on Hebrew, 1960; Eyewitness to Jewish History; Tzedakah and Community; contbr to J mags. Home: 68-52 Juno St, Forest Hills, NY. Office: 426 W 58 St, New York, NY.

EISENBERG, David, US, sports commentator; b. NYC, Oct 31, 1907; s. Miron and Rose (Bromberg); BS, NYU, 1933; m. Barbara DePoris, Dec 27, 1932; c: Vidabeth Bensen, Phoebe Kerness. Sports commentator, radio sta WOR, NYC, 1957-67; sports writer: NY Jour Amer, 1929-66; NY World Jour Tribune, 1966-67. Pres: Metrop Basketball Writers Assn, 1950-51; Metrop Golf Writers Assn, 1966-67, hon pres since 1967; mem, B'nai B'rith. Co-author: Swing the Clubhead, 1952. Hobbies: theatre, history, opera, concerts, golf. Home: 2823 Avenue M, Brooklyn, NY.

EISENBERG, Dov, Isr, engineer; b. Haifa, Isr, July 22, 1929; s. Mordechai and Frida (Lubeshovsky); BSc, Technion, Haifa, 1956; engr deg, 1958; MSc, 1960; m. Esther Perach, Haifa, Isr, 1957; c: Yoad, Gili. PWD dist engr, Judea, Samaria, since 1967, asst dist engr, S dist, 1965-67; lab tech, Bldg Research Lab Tech, 1945-56; designing engr, Solel Boneh, Haifa, 1956-57; research engr, Bldg Research Lab, Technion, 1957-60; project mgr, Solel-Boneh, Ethiopia, 1960-65. Served IDF, 1950-52. Mem: comm, Engrs Org of Histadrut; Assn Engrs and Architects, Isr; Lions Club, Negev br. Home: 22A Izhak Sade St, Beersheva, Isr. Office: 2, Lincoln St, Tel Aviv, Isr.

EISENBERG, Henryk, Isr, scientist; b. Berlin, Ger, Mar 7, 1921; s. Simha and Inna (Gurieva); in Isr since 1939; MSc, Heb U, Jerusalem, 1949, PhD, 1952; m. Hanna Shechter, Sep 19, 1943; c: Shai, Dan. Prof, Weizmann Inst Sci, since 1968, on fac since 1962; visit f: Yale U, 1951-52; Mellon Inst, Pittsburgh, 1958-60; NIH, Bethesda, 1965-66. Sgt, Royal Engrs, WW 11, 1941-46; sci corps, IDF, 1948-49. Prin contribs: research in phys chem of polymers and electrolytes; nucleic acids and enzyme sys; aspects of water structure; thermodynamics. Mem: Faraday Soc; Isr Biochem Soc; Amer Chem Soc; Chem Soc, London. Contbr to sci jours. Hobbies: hiking, tennis. Home: 8 Neveh Weizmann, Rehovot, Isr. Office: Weizmann Inst of Sci, Rehovot, Isr.

EISENBERG, Izhak, Isr, journalist; b. Pinsk, Russ, Dec 30, 1913; s. David and Hodel (Ratkewitz); in Isr since 1934; att: U Warsaw, 1934; Heb U, Jerusalem, 1934-35; m. Tova Ruda, Oct 17, 1939; c: Abraham, David. Found, mem, ed bd: Haboker, daily, Tel Aviv, since 1935; Gesher; corresp, Yiddish newspapers: Die Presse, Arg; Die Yiddishe Zeitung, Brazil; Barkai, S Afr; Letzte Neis, Tel Aviv; lectr, cultural and political topics; missions for KH: Brazil, 1954; Belgium, 1962. Mem: exec, WJC, since 1959; exec comm: Isr Lib Party; Isr Org for UN; Isr natl council: KH; Friends of the Heb U; council, exec, Lib Party, sect in Histadrut; world exec, B'rith Ivrit Olamit; Histadrut court of honor; vice-

chmn, cen comm, Maccabi, Isr. Co-ed, Maasaf Isr, 1958. Home: 21 Margolin St, Tel Aviv, Isr. Office: Haboker, 32 Harakevet St, Tel Aviv, Isr.

EISENBERG, Jacob, US, business exec; b. Frankfurt, Ger, Dec 16, 1898; s. Chaim and Gittel (Zitronenbaum) Hirsch; in US since 1938; m. Esther Kestenbaum, May 5, 1924; c: Leon, Margot Schnall. Vice-pres, secy, treas, Desco Shoe Corp, since 1941; exec, M and J Eisenberg Factors, 1938-42; part owner, Tissage Epontis, Fr, 1931-1939. Pres, Yeshiva Dov Revel, Forest Hills, NY; co-found, Yeshiva HS of Queens; mem: natl council, JDC; Mizrachi; Amer Schs of Oriental Research. Spec interests: J educ; Bibl archael. Home: 63-39 Yellowstone Blvd, Forest Hills, NY. Office: 16 E 34 St, New York, NY.

EISENBERG, Judah Moshe, US, physicist, educator; b. Cincinnati, O, Dec 17, 1938; s. Azriel and Rose (Leibow); AB, Columbia Coll, 1958; PhD, MIT, 1962; m. Marion Capriles, Aug 27, 1961; c: Deborah, Noami, Daniel. Dept of physics, U of Va, since 1970, chmn, dept physics, U of Va, since 1970, prof, since 1968, on fac since 1962. Sesquicentennial Asso, 1969; Sir Thomas Lyle research f, U Melbourne, 1965. Mem: gov bd, Temple Beth Isr; Amer Phys Soc; Va Acad Sci. Co-author: Nuclear Excitation Mecha-nisms, 1969; Nuclear Medals, 1970; contbr on nuclear structural physics, to tech jours. Home: 2514 Hillwood Pl, Charlottesville, Va. Office: Dept of Physics, U of Va, Charlottesville, Va.

EISENBERG, Leon, US, psychiatrist; b. Phila, Pa, Aug 8, 1922; s. Morris and Elizabeth (Sabreen); BA, U of Pa, 1944, MD, Med Sch, 1946; AM, hon, Harvard U, 1967; m. Ruth Bleier, June 10, 1948; co Mark, Kathy; m. 2nd, Carola Blitzman Guttmacher; c: Larry, Alan. Prof, psycht, Harvard Med Sch, since 1967; psycht in chief, Mass Gen Hosp, since 1967; prof, child psycht, Johns Hopkins U, 1961-67, fac mem since 1952; psycht i/c, children's psycht service, Johns Hopkins Hosp, 1961-67; instr, phys, U of Pa, 1947-48. Capt, US Army MC, 1948-50. Pres: MD Psycht Assn, 1958-59; Johns Hopkins Chap, AAUP, 1960-61; Psychiatric Research Soc, 1969-70; mem: AAAS; Amer Acad Peds; Aer Acad Child Psych; Phi Beta Kappa; Sigma Xi; Amer Acad Arts and Scis; Mass Med Soc. Ed, Amer Jour Orthopsycht; ed bd: Jour Child Psych-Psycht; Jour Psycht Research; Child Devl. Home: One Sparks Pl, Cambridge, Mass. Office: Mass Gen Hosp, Boston, Mass.

EISENBERG, Maurice, US, concert cellist, teacher, author; b. Koenigsberg, Ger, Feb 24, 1900; s. Samuel and Fannie (Berlin); att Peabody Conservatory of Music, Baltimore, Md; studied with: Prof Alexanian, Eeole Normale de Musique, Paris; Prof Julius Klengel, Leipzig, Ger; Prof Hugo Becker, Berlin; Pablo Casals, Barcelona, Paris; m. Paula Halpert, June 6, 1921; c: Pablo, Marta Friedler. Prof, violoncello, Juilliard Sch, NYC, since 1964; found, artistic dir, Intl Cello Cent, London since 1952; prof, Pablo Casal Class, Ecole Normale de Musique, Paris, 1929-39; prof, Intl Master Classes, Cascais, Port; visiting prof, U of S Cal, 1942, 1943; visiting prof, Longy Sch of Music, Cambridge, Mass since 1951; concert lectr, Assn of Amer Coll. Soloist with: Boston Sym; Phila Orch; LA Sym; and with leading orchs in Gt Brit and Eur. Mem: The Bohemians; NYC; The Violoncello Soc, NYC, vice-pres, Author: Cello Playing of Today, 1957; contbr to music periodicals. Recipient: Peabody Dist Service Award, 1965; NJ Sym 1966 Art Award; Violoncello Soc of NY Award, 1969. Home: 119 Cypress St, Millburn, NJ. Office: Juilliard Sch of Music, Lincoln Center Pl, New York, NY.

EISENBERG, Meyer, US, attorney; b. Bklyn, NY, Dec 15, 1931; s. Samuel and Bella (Fishman); BA, Bklyn Coll, 1953; LLB, Columbia U, 1958; m. Carolyn Schoen, Dec 26, 1954; c: Julie, Ellen. Asso gen counsel, SEC, since 1969, on staff since 1962; exec asst, chmn Manuel F Cohen, SEC, 1968-69; legal asst, Commn EN Gadsby, 1961; counsel, Inves Co Study, since 1962; law clerk, Chief Justice William M McAllister, Supr Court, Ore, 1958-59; counsel: Off Gen Counsel, 1959-61; Spec Study of Securities Markets, 1962. US Army, 1954-56. Chmn, ADL, Natl Capital Area, 1968-69; vice-pres, Natl Capital Assn, B'nai B'rith; mem: Amer Bar Assn; Delta Sigma Rho; exec comm, JCC, Gtr Wash, 1968-69; Md State Comm on State Aid to Non-Public and Parochial Schs, 1969. Contbr to law revs. Home: 1810 Metzerott Rd, Adelphi, Md. Office: SEC, Washington, DC.

EISENBERG, Moses J, US, dentist, researcher; b. NYC, July 22, 1895; s. Franz and Eva (Evans); DMD, Harvard U, 1917;

m. Violet Hirshon, June 29, 1929; c: Frederick, Judith. Pvt practice and research since 1917; chief dent service, J Memorial Hosp, Boston, Mass, since 1939; asst, dept of dent research, Harvard U, 1917, dent research f, 1933-40; acting chief, dept of dent orthopedics, Forsythe Inst, 1923-25. F: Royal Microscopical Soc, London; AAAS; mem: Temple Isr; Mishkan Tefila, past off, trustee, both Boston. Contbr to dent jours; composed: consecration hymn, The Fear of the Lord is the Beginning of Knowledge, for soloist organ and choir, 1958; musical scores: for a Hanukka play, 1959; two Purim plays; 1960, 1961; fmr asso ed, American Dental Surgeon. Recipient: medal, Harriet Newell Soc for Dent Research, Harvard, 1917; Freedoms Found Award, 1951. Home: 171 Wallis Rd, Chestnut Hill, Mass. Office: 444 Warren St, Roxbury, Mass.

EISENBUD, Jule, US, physician, educator; b. NYC, Nov 20, 1908; s. Abraham and Sarah (Abramson); BA, Columbus Coll, 1929. MD, Coll Phys and Surgs, 1934; m. Molly Lewis, Dec 31, 1937; c: Joanna, John, Eric. Pvt practice, psycht, since 1938; asso clinical prof, psycht, U Colo Sch of Med, since 1950; asso, psycht, Columbia Med Sch, 1938-50. Mem: Amer Psycht Assn; Amer Soc-Psychical Research; Amer Psychoanalytic Assn. Contbr to profsl jours. Home and office: 4634 E Sixth Ave, Denver, Colo.

EISENDRATH, Joseph Louis, US, business exec; b. Chgo, Ill, June 12, 1908; s. Joseph and Laura (Sloman); PhB, U Chgo, 1929; m. Gladys Rothafel, Apr 9, 1936; c: John, Peter. Pres, chmn bd, Banthrico Inds Inc, since 1955. Dir, Highland Park-Highwood Comty Chest; treas, Evanston N Shore Area Council, Boy Scouts of Amer, mem, natl council; fmr vice-pres; mem: Zeta Beta Tau; fmr: pres, Chgo Civil War Round Table; Amer Air Mail Soc; clubs: Chgo Press, Northmoor CC. Ed in chief, Amer Air Mail Catalogue, since 1970; ed, Air Post Jour, both of Amer Air Mail Soc, 1955-63. Recipient: award: Walter J Conrath, Amer Air Mail Soc, 1963; Richard E Bohn, Aerophilatelists, 1969. Hobby: philately, Lincolniana. Home: 4615 W Roosevelt Rd, Chicago, Ill. Office: 17 N Desplaines St, Chicago, Ill.

EISENMAN, Zvi, Isr, author; b. Warsaw, Pol, Sep 20, 1920; s. Moshe and Elca (Viherlock); in Isr since 1949; att Folkshul Sch, Warsaw; m. Ehudith Federman, Mar 7, 1916. Author: The Train, in Yiddish, trans into Heb, 1956; Mazoles, 1968; Mazalath, 1969; fmr asst ed, Volksblatt. Mem, Young Isr Group of Yiddish Writers. Home: Kibbutz Alonim, Isr.

EISENPREIS, Alfred, US, business exec; b. Vienna, Aus, June 16, 1924; s. Zygmunt and Claire (Silbermann); in US since 1939; att: Bucknell U, 1940-42; New Sch for Social Research, NY, 1955-60; AB, St Thomas Coll, Scranton, Pa, 1943; m. Elizabeth Long, June 18, 1956; c: Steven. Vice pres, Allied Stores Corp, since 1963, dir research, 1958-63, asst group mgr, 1957-58, asst mgn dir, Pomeroy's Inc, 1954-57, fmr dir, Jamaica devl corp. Trustee: Wilkes Coll, PA; UAHC; Reece Sch, NYC; Natl Retail Found; dir, mem exec: Amer, Retail Feds; Natl Retail Merchants Assn; cons: Exec Off, US Pres, Off for Emergency Preparedness; Bus Defense Services Admn, Commerce Dept; chmn, Natl Mgmt Council for Distributive Educ; dir, 82-83rd St Corp; exec comm, Natl Marketing Adv Comm, Commerce Dept; dir, Men's Club, Cong Emanu-El, NY; alternate mem, steering comm, Natl Urban Coalition, Wash, DC; natl comm, bus policy, NPA; chmn, sub-comms on educ and research, Comm on Consumer Interests, US C of C; mem: NY Acad Sci; Amer Marketing Assn; Amer Stat Assn; Amer Sociol Assn; Natl Assn Bus Econ; AJ Comm, NY; Dept Urban Transp Research, Hwy Research Bd; comm, second regional plan, NY Regional Plan Assn; Ritual Comm, Cong Emanu-El; marketing planning council, Amer Mgmt Assn; Census Adv Comm, US Dept Commerce; Natl Adv Council, Urban Amer; Newcomen Soc in N Amer; research and operating comm, Natl Assn of BBB's; hon mem, Retail Research Soc; fmr: vice pres, pres, Brotherhood, Cong B'nai B'rith; chmn bd, Retail Research Inst; chmn adv comm, Natl Planning Assn; trustee: Fed Stat Users Conf; NY Metrop Region Stat Cen; clubs: Forecasters, NY; Advt. Author, contbr Marketing Through Retailers, 1966; Handel und Wissenschaft; Store Location Research; contbr to profsl jours. Recipient, Silver Plaque Award, Natl Retail Merchants, Assn, 1967. Hobbies: painting, collector of rare books. Home: 40 E 83 St, New York, NY. Office: 401 Fifth Ave, New York, NY.

EISENSCHER, Jacob, Isr, artist, engraver; b. Bukovina, Rum; in Isr since 1935; grad, Vienna Acad of Art. Tchr, Bezalel Sch of Arts, Jerusalem. Prin works, colored woodcuts, exhb

at: Paris, 1935; Sao Paulo Biennale, 1953; O'Hana Gal, London, 1954; Venice Biennale, 1957; Intl Exhb of Art and and Lab, Geneva, 1957; Isr Artists Exhb in: Nor; Swed; Finland; Aus; Turkey; Austr; NZ, 1958; group exhbs: Chile; Venezuela, 1961; one-man show: Tel-Aviv; Haifa. Recipient: Haifa Prize, Haifa Munic, 1958. Home and studio: 12 Smolenskin St, Tel Aviv, Isr; summer home: Artists Colony, Safad, Isr.

EISENSHTAT, Sidney, US, architect; b. New Haven, Conn, June 6, 1914; s. Morris and Ella (Sobole); BArch, U of Cal, 1935; m. Alice Brenner, Dec 19, 1937; c: Abby Tessa, Carole Oken. Owner, architect, Sidney Eisenshtat, AIA, Architect and Assos, since 1950; partner, Eisenshtat and Lipman, 1946-50; architect: Temple Emanuel, 1955; Hillel Heb Acad, 1963; Union Bank, 1960; Citizens Bank Bldg, 1950, all Beverly Hills, Cal; Sinai Temple, 1960; Westside JCC, 1954; Kaiser Found Admn Cen, 1961; Home of Peace Bldg, 1960, all LA, Cal; Temple Isr, Hollywood, Cal, 1955; Sven Lokrantz Sch for Handicapped Children, Reseda, Cal, 1961; Temple Mt Sinai, El Paso, Tex, 1962. Chmn bd: W Coast Talmudical Sem, since 1958; Torah U, 1961-62; architects, engrs div, UJA, 1958-60; Key Men, vice-pres, 1959-60; pres, Beth Jacob Cong, 1958-60; dir: U of Judaism, 1954-61; Union Orthodox Congs of Amer, 1960-63; J Cen Assn, 1954-55; Guardians of J Homes for Aged, 1954-61; Hillel Heb Acad, 1957-61; architectural cons, UAHC, since 1960; mem: Amer Inst Architects; Architects Guild. Recipient: Honor Award, Amer Inst Architects, 1960; awards for designs of Home of Peace Bldg; Sven Lokrantz Sch for Handicapped Children. Home: 2736 Motor Ave, Los Angeles, Cal. Office: 144 S Beverly Dr, Beverly Hills, Cal.

EISENSON, Jon, US, educator; b. NYC, Dec 17, 1907; s. Abraham and Sarah; BSS, CCNY, 1928; MA, Columbia U, NY, 1930, PhD, 1935; m. Freda Francke; c: Elinore, Arthur. Prof, speech and hearing scis, dir, Inst for Childhood Aphasia, Stanford U Sch of Med, since 1962; Eng tchr, Bd Educ, NYC Schs, 1928-35; tuotr to asst prof, Bklyn Coll, 1935-42; prof, Queens Coll, 1946-62. Lt to Maj, 1942-46; set up, supervised, Lang Rehab Prog for Surg Gen's Off, WW II. Mem: subcomm, Hum Communication and Its Disorders, Natl Inst Neur Diseases and Blindness; research comm, Speech Path and Audiology, VA; original mem, Research Group on Devl Dyslexia and World Illiteracy, World Fed of Neur; cons, Vet's Admn; f, Amer Pshych Assn; dipl, Clinical Psych, Amer Bd Examiners in Profsl Psych; mem, Phi Beta Kappa, Gamma chap; fmr: pres, Amer Speech and Hearing Assn; Amer Speech and Hearing Found; chmn, Educ Adv Comm, United Cerebral Palsy; mem, Med and Sci Comm. Author: Confirmation and Information in Rewards and Punishments, 1935; The Psychology of Speech, 1938; Examining for Aphasia, 1946; Basic Speech, 1950; Improvement of Voice and Diction, 1957; co-author: The Psychology of the Physically Handicapped, 1940; The Defective in Speech, 1942; Speech Disorders, 1956; Speech Correction for the Schools, 1957; Psychology of Communication, 1963; Basic Speech, 1950; ed, contbr, Stuttering: A Symposium, 1958; contbr to profsl books and periodicals. Recipient, Hons, Amer Speech and Hearing Assn, 1967. Home: 853 Mayfield St, Stanford, Cal. Office: Sch of Med, Stanford U, 300 Pasteur Dr, Palo Alto, Cal.

EISENSTADT, Heinz B, US, physician; b. Berlin, Ger, Dec 15, 1905; s. Ludwig and Elise (Schmulewitz); in US since 1937; MD, Freidrich Wilhelm U, 1929; m. Ruth Haase, Dec 16, 1934; c: Rita. Phys, specialist, internal med, since 1930; co-owner, Med Clinic, Port Arthur, Tex, since 1946. F: Amer Coll of Phys; Amer Coll of Chest Phys; Amer Coll of Card; Amer Coll of Gastroenterology. Pres, Temple Rodef Shalom, 1940; trustee, Coll of Gastroenterology; mem: Soc of Nuclear Med; Tex Acad Internal Med. Author: numerous sci papers; contbr to book on Electrocardiography. Hobbies: photography, music, antique collecting. Home: 210 Fourth Ave, Port Arthur, Tex. Office: 2301 Procter St, Port Arthur, Tex.

EISENSTADT, Shmuel N, Isr, educator; b. Warsaw, Pol, Sep 10, 1923; s. Michael and Rosa (Boruchin); in Isr since 1935; MA, Heb U, Jerusalem, 1944, PhD, 1947; postgrad, LSE, 1947-48; m. Shulamit Yaroshevski, 1948; c: Michael, Irith, Alexander. Prof, sociol, Heb U, since 1959, fac mem since 1948, chmn dept, 1951-68, dean fac of social sci, 1966-68; visiting prof: U Oslo, 1958; U Chgo, 1960; MIT, 1962-63; chmn, Council on Comty Devl, Isr, 1962-66; visiting prof, Harvard U, 1966, 1968-69. Mem: Isr Acad of Sci and Hum;

Amer Acad Arts and Sci; Comms on Research, Training and Teaching; Intl Sociol Assn; Amer Sociol Assn; F, Royal Anthropological Inst. Author: The Absorption of Immigrants, 1954; From Generation to Generation, 1956; Essays on Sociological Aspects of Economical and Political Development, 1961; The Political Systems of Empires, 1963; Essays on Comparative Institutions, 1965; Modernisation, Protest and Change, 1966; Israeli Society, 1968; The Prot stant Ethic and Modernisation, 1968; Political Sociology of Modernisation (in Japanese), 1968; ed: Political Sociology, 1955; Comparative Perspectives on Social Change, 1968; Charisma and Institution Building, Selections from Max Weber, 1968; adv bd, Intl Ency, Social Sci; contbr to profsl jours. Home: 30 Radak St, Jerusalem, Isr. Office: Hebrew U, Jerusalem, Isr.

EISENSTARK, Abraham, US, educator; b. Warsaw, Pol, Sep 5, 1919; s. Isadore and Sarah (Becker); in US since 1921; BA, U of Ill, 1941, MA, 1942, PhD, 1948; m. Roma Gould, Jan 27, 1948; c: Romalyn, David, Douglas. Prof, microbiol, Kan State U, since 1959. US Army, 1942-46. Contbr to profsl jours. Recipient: Guggenheim F, 1948; sr post doct F, NSF, 1967. Home: 2082 College Hgts Rd, Manhattan, Kan. Office: Kan State U, Manhattan, Kan.

EISENSTEIN, Alfred, US, business exec, composer, author; b. Brody, Pol, Nov 14, 1899; s. Marcus and Louise (Sokol); in US since 1939; deg, civil eng: Tech U, Vienna, 1928; Tech U, Berlin, 1929; m. Mercedes Malespin, Feb 21, 1952. Pres: Construction Corp, since 1960; A Eisenstein, since 1960; pres, treas, Pops Music, since 1965; among works executed: new youth bldg, Rego Park J Cen; Solomon Schechter Sch; Firehouses, Libr, for NYC. Composer: Adagio Lamentoso, 1964; Impromptu, 1967; and other Orch Works; pieces for violin and cello; works recorded by Wiener Rundfunk Orch. Mem: NY State Soc Profsl Engrs; ASCAP; fmr: master, Free Masons, Isr; mem, Soc Mil Engrs. Recipient: Spec Award, ASCAP, annually since 1965; Bronze Plaque, C of C, 1968. Home and office: 94-30 59 Ave Elmhurst, NY.

EISENSTEIN, Ira, US, rabbi, editor; b. NYC, Nov 26, 1906; s. Isaac and Sadie (Luxenberg); BA, Columbia Coll, 1927; ordained rabbi, JTSA, 1931; PhD, Columbia U, 1941; hon DD, JTSA, 1958; m. Judith Kaplan, June 10, 1934; c: Miriam, Ann. Pres: Reconstructionist Rabb Coll, since 1968; J Reconstructionist Found, since 1959; ed, The Reconstructionist, since 1959, on staff since 1935; rabbi, Soc for the Advancement of Judaism, NYVC, 1931-54; Anshe Emet Syn, Chgo, Ill, 1954-59; visiting prof, homiletics, JTSA, 1951; lectr, U Chgo; Northwestern U; U Pittsburgh; U of Colo; La State U. Pres: RA, 1952-54; vice-pres, Chgo RA, 1959. Author: Creative Judaism, 1936, rev 1953; What We Mean by Religion, 1938; Ethics of Tolerance, 1941; Judaism under Freedom, 1956; ed, Varieties of Jewish Belief, 1968; co-ed: New Haggadah; Sabbath Prayer Book; High Holiday Prayer Book; Mordecai M Kaplan: An Evaluation; contbr to publs. Hobbies: music, photography. Home: 845 West End Ave, New York, NY. Study: 15 W 86 St, New York, NY.

EISENSTEIN, Judith K, US, musicologist; b. NYC, Sept 10, 1909; d. Mordecai and Lena (Rubin) Kaplan; BS, Tchrs Coll, Columbia U, 1928, MA, 1932; PhD, HUC, JIR, 1966; m. Ira Eisenstein, June 10, 1934; c: Miriam, Ann. Instr, Sch for Sacred Music, HUC-JIR; Tchrs Inst, JTSA, 1929-54; Coll J Studies, Chgo, 1958-59. Mem: Amer Musicological Soc; J Liturgical Music Soc; Natl J Music Council; Soc for Ethnomusicology; Natl Folk Song Soc; Sigma Alpha Iota. Author: Gateway to Jewish Song, 1939; Music for Jewish Groups, 1940; Festival Songs, 1943; co-author, cantatas: What is Torah? 1942; Our Bialik, 1945; Seven Golden Buttons, 1947; Reborn, 1952; Thy Children Shall Return, 1954; contbr to mags. Hobbies: painting, ceramics. Home: 845 West End Ave, New York, NY.

EISINGER, Chester E, US, educator; b. Chgo, Ill, May 11, 1915; s. Harry and Clara (Brownstein); BA, UCLA, 1937; MA, U Mich, 1938, PhD, 1945; m. Marjorie Kendall, July 31, 1937; c: Peter, Steven, Joel. Prof, Eng, chmn, Comm of Amer Studies, Purdue U, since 1959, fac mem since 1945. Pres, Amer Studies Assn, Ohio-Ind Chap, 1959-60; mem: MLA; ACLU; AAUP. Author: Fiction of the Forties, 1963; Introduction to Mailer, The Naked and the Dead, 1968; contbr studies on Amer lit to lit jours. Recipient: Fulbright grant to teach Amer Lit: U Innsbruck, Aus, 1960-61; Cairo U, Egypt, 1951-52; grant, Purdue Research Found, 1956-65. Home: 1729 Sheridan Rd, W Lafayette, Ind. Office: Purdue U, W Lafayette, Ind.

EISNER, Bruno, US, pianist, educator; b. Vienna Aus, Dec 6, 1884; s. Adolf and Rosa (Silberstein); in US since 1936; att: Vienna Acad of Music, 1936; m. Olga Mauksch, May 7, 1922. Tchr: Hochschule fuer Musik, Berlin, 1930-33; piano master class, YMHA, NY, 1937-42; Westchester Conservatory, 1945; NY Coll of Music, 1947-48; Music Acad, Phila, 1948-50; visiting prof: Sch Music, Ind, U, 1951-54; State U, Colo, 1956-57. Concert pianist, played throughout Eur, including Salzburg Festival, Isr, and US. Aus Army, WW I. Arranger: of Carl Maria von Weber's piano works; arias by Handel, for violin and piano. Club, The Bohemians. Home: Ansonia Hotel, Broadway at 73 St, New York, NY.

EISNER, Henry W, US, advertising exec; b. Nordhausen, Ger, July 3, 1920; s. Walter and Elsa (Stern); in US since 1940; att: U Zurich, 1938-39; London Poly, 1939; Johns Hopkins U, 1941-48; m. Harriet Sauber, July 11, 1943; c: Nancy, Steven. Pres, SA Levyne Co since 1965, vice-pres, 1960-65. Sgt, USAAC, 1943-46. Chmn, Amer Assn Advt Agcys; cabinet mem, Assoc J Charities; mem: bd: J Family and Children Bur; Chamber Music Soc, Baltimore; clubs: Suburban; Cen, all in Baltimore. Home: 5806 Greenspring Ave, Baltimore, Md. Office: 343 St Paul, Baltimore, Md.

EISNER, Herman, US, rabbi; b. Kusnica, Czech, July 14, 1918; s. Salamon and Ruchamah (Friedman); in US since 1947; att: Yeshiva Horomah, Dune Szerdohel, Czech, 1939; ordained rabbi, Tifereth Jerusalem Rabb Sem, NYC, 1949; BS, MS, Yeshiva U, 1959; m. Malvina Gerlich, Aug 11, 1946; c: Moshe. Rabbi, Cong Ezrath Isr, Ellenville, NY, since 1949; chaplain, Catskill Reformatory, State of NY. Chmn, bd educ, Heb Day Sch, Sullivan, Ulster Cos; mem: RabCa, RA; Amer Chaplains Assn; B'nai B'rith; UJA; JDC. Recipient: Citizen of Year, Ellenville, NY, 1966; testimonial dinner, Isr Bonds, 1968. Home: 36 Center, Ellenville, NY.

EISNER, Max John, US, investment banker; b. Pittsfield, Mass, June 15, 1918; s. Michael and Rose (Lake); att, Williston Acad, Easthampton, Mass, 1934-37; BA, Union Coll, Schenectady, NY, 1941; m. Doris Sands, July 13, 1942; c: Ellen, Michael, Richard, Patti, Julie, Kathy. Exec vice-pres, Hartzmarck & Co, Inc; vice-pres, Jury Verdict Research Co, both since 1962; pres, Sands Mfg, 1946-62; dir: Globe Amer; Inarco. Capt, US Army, 1942-45. Pres, The Temple, Cleveland, O; fmr: vice-pres, Montefiore Home; dir, NCCJ; clubs: Oakwood; Cleveland Bond; Kappa Nu. Home: 2932 Broxton Rd, Shaker Hts, O. Office: 1000 E Ohio Bldg, Cleveland, O.

EISNER, Otto Zvi, Eng, educator; b. Czech, Jan 12, 1911; s. Yehudah and Ida (Rosenbaum); in Eng since 1939; BA, hons, U, London, 1949; PhD, law, Prague U; m. Ingeborg Mann, Sep 7, 1946; c: John, Deborah. Sr lectr, U Bradford, since 1964; lectr, Coll of Commerce, Liverpool, 1957-64; asst ed, structure reports, Intl Union of Crystallography, 1955-57; asst lectr, U Coll Cardiff, 1947-55. NCO, Czech Army, 1935-45. Author: Gedichte, 1938; co-trans from Nezval's poetry; contbr to periodicals, jours and other publs. Spec interests: langs, trans of poetry; frequent visits to Isr. Home: 19 Bodmin Ave, Shipley, Yorks, Eng. Office: U of Bradford, Eng.

EITINGER, Leo S, Nor, psychiatrist; b. Lomnice, Dec 12, 1912; :.Shlomo and Helene (Kurtz); in Nor since 1939; MD, Masaryk U, Czech, 1937; DMS, Oslo U, 1958; m. Lisl Kohn, July 1, 1946. Head, psycht dept, Oslo U Hosp; prof psycht, U of Oslo, both since 1966; chief psycht cons, Nor Armed Forces, since 1952; sub-dir, Rönvik Hosp, Bodo, Nor, 1946-48. Nor MC, 1950. Chmn, postgrad educ comm, Nor Psycht Assn, since 1960, fmr pres, assn, fmr mem, social comm bd; mem: research team on concentration camp survivors, Oslo U; Oslo J Comty Bd; Nor Med Assn; Nor Med Acad; Nor Polio Assn; IMA; corresp f, Amer Psycht Assn. Author: The Influence of Military Life on Young Norwegian Men's Mental Health, 1954; Psychiatric Investigations Among Refugees in Norway, 1958; Theories on Neuroses, 1962; Concentration Camp Survivors in Norway and Israel, 1964; co-author: Nervous Diseases and Mental Health, 1955; Norwegian Concentration Camp Survivors, 1968; Textbook on Neuroses, 1969; contbr numerous papers to Nor and fgn publs. Recipient: King of Nor Gold Medal, 1954. Home: Övre Ullern Terrasse 67, Oslo, Nor. Office: Psykiatrisk Klinik, Vinderen, Oslo, Nor.

EITINGON, Nadia Reichert, Isr, pianist; b. Kiev, Russ, 1906; s. Alter and Fania (Goldberg) Ingon; in Isr since 1927; att Natl Conservatory, Kiev; studied with: Prof Teichmiller;

Arthur Shnabel; m. June 5, 1928. Appeared with: Isr Philharmonic in Isr; Aus; Fr; Eng; Pol; Leb; Crypus. Mem: Milo Club; judges panel, Amer-Isr Found which gives scholarships to young artists. Hobby: story and joke telling. Home: 22 Dizengoff St, Tel Aviv, Isr.

EISENDRATH, Maurice N, US, rabbi, religious leader; b. Chgo, Ill, July 10, 1902; s. Nathan and Clara (Oesterreicher); BA, U of Cincinnati, 1925; ordained rabbi, HUC, 1926, hon DD, 1945; m. Rosa Brown, Nov 24, 1926 (decd); m. 2nd, Rita Hands Greene, 1964. Pres, UAHC, since 1943; life tenure since 1952; rabbi: Virginia St Temple, Charleston, W Va, 1926-29; Holy Blossom Temple, Toronto, Can, 1929-43. Vice-pres, World Union for Progressive Judaism; natl chmn, PR, United J Comty of Can; co-found, Can Conf Chr and J, Inc; dir: Natl JWB; J Chatauqua Soc; asso chmn, Amer J Tercentenary Comm; chmn, inter-rel comm, and mem, exec comm, Natl Comty Relations Adv Council; mem: bd govs, HUC-JIR; exec bd, CCAR; Syn Council of Amer; theologians' comm, Amer Assn for Intl Off of Educ; natl council, JDC; clubs: Harmonie; Standard, Chgo. Author: The Never Failing Stream, 1939; Home: 465 Park Ave, New York, NY. Study: 838 Fifth Ave, New York, NY.

EJGENBERG, Bernardo Mario, Uruguay, communal leader; b. Montevideo, Uruguay, Nov 19, 1943; s. Mendel and Ana (Mekler); BM, IAVA, Montevideo, 1962; fac of med, 1963. Prof, piano, since 1964. Secy gen, Zionist Org, Uruguay, since 1968, several activities since 1961; coord, PR, S Amer U ZF; mem: WJC; World Union J Students; Youth ZF; Assn Med Students; leader, Kadimah U Union. Hobbies: music; sports; J studies. Home: Ciudadela, 1174/602, Montevideo, Uruguay.

EKSZTAJN, Yeshayahu S, Isr, business exec; b. Warsaw, Pol, Aug 28, 1923; s. Isaac and Haya (Folbaum); in Isr since 1940; BSc, Technion, Haifa, 1944; dipl Ing, 1949; m. Hanna Gesundheit, 1950; c: Haggit, Avigdor. Dir, Ya'al Assos Ltd, mgmt cons, Tel Aviv, since 1953: fmr, lectr, produc mgmt, Heb U, Jerusalem, 1958-66. Off, IAF, 1948-51. F, Inst of Work Study Practitioners; mem: Inst of MEs, both in London; mem: council, Isr Assn of Mgmt Cons; chmn: comm: educ comm, Isr Inst of Productivity; chmn: comm on training in mfg mgmt, Isr Mgmt Cen; fmr: mem: bd dirs, Technion; mgn comm, Technion Alumni Assn. Contbr to profsl mags. Home: 50 Weizmann St, Tel Aviv, Isr. Office: POB 6128, Tel Aviv, Isr.

ELAN, Yaffa, Isr, business exec; b. Bialystock, Russ, Sep 15, 1914; d. Isser and Cila (Kagen) Greenfeld; in Isr since 1921; BSc, U of Caen, Fr; m. Ephraim Elan, June 1942; c: Vardit. Dir: milling, weaving, dyeing, cotton wool factories, Isser Greenfeld and Sons since 1936. Prin contrib: research work in entomology, vegetables, especially on parthenogenesis of coccidae. Mem bd govs, B'nai B'rith, Isr; gen secy, cen bd, B'nai B'rith; secy, Isr-Aus Friendship League; fmr pres, B'nai B'rith, Hashachar Lodge; delg, world conv, B'nai B'rith, 1969. Home: 15 Mazeh St, Tel Aviv, Isr. Office: 7 Bar Yochay St, Tel Aviv, Isr.

ELATH, Eliahu, Isr, diplomat, public servant; b. Snosk, Russ, July 31, 1903; s. Menahem and Rivka (Ripp) Epstein; in Isr since 1925; att: Kiev U, 1922; Heb U, Jerusalem, 1928; BA, Amer U, Beirut, 1931; hon PhD: Dropsie Coll, Phila, 1949; Brandeis U 1962; Wayne State U, Detroit, 1964; PhD, 1969; m. Zehava Zalel, Aug 4, 1931. Pres, Heb U, Jerusalem, 1962-68; agric worker, Rehovot, Beer Yaakov, 1925-28; bldg worker, Transjordan, 1929-30; corresp, Reuters, Heb newspapers, Syria, Lebanon, 1931-34; head, ME div, political dept, JA, Jerusalem, 1934-45; dir political dept, Wash DC, 1945-48; first ambass of Isr to US, 1948-50; mem Isr delg to UN, 1948-50; ambass of Isr to Eng, 1950-59; chmn, bd govs, Afro-Asian Inst for Lab Studies, Isr, 1959-62. Pres: Isr Oriental Soc, since 1960; Magen David Adom; Isr Asian Friendship League; vice-pres, ICA. Author: haBedouim, Hayeihem uMinhageihem, 1933; Ukhlesei Ever haYarden, 1934; Israel and Her Neighbors, 1957; Haj Amin el-Husseini, The Man and His Rise to Power; contbr to sociol and political jours. Home: 17 Bialik St, Beth Hakerem, Jerusalem, Isr.

ELAZAR, Daniel Judah, US, educator; b. Minneapolis, Minn, Aug 25, 1934; s. Albert and Nettie (Barzon); att: Midrasha, Coll of J Studies; Wayne State U, Detroit, Mich, 1950-54; MA, U Chgo, PhD, 1959; m. Harriet Fienberg, Jan 22, 1961; c: Naomi, Jonathan. Prof, political sci, Temple U, since 1964, dir, Cen for Study of Federalism, since 1967; head libr,

United Heb Schs, Detroit, 1951-59; asst prof, govt and public affairs, U of Ill, 1959-63; visiting asst prof, political sci, U Minn, 1963-64; visiting prof, Amer studies and political sci, Heb U, 1968-69. Prin contribs: pioneers and leader, Amer Federalism, cons, Adv Commn on Intergovernmental Relations; devl, field of J political studies: Adv comm, J Communal Affairs, dept Amer J Comm; coll comm, Phila Fed JAs, vice-chmn, educ comm, Solomon Schechter Day Sch, Phila; cons: Atty Gen, Minn; Educ Commn of States; chmn, State Political Cultures Comm; lectr, US Civil Service Commn; fmr: pres, B'nai B'rith Hillel Found, U Chgo; chmn, Allocations Comm J Fed, Champaign, Urbana, Ill Regional Exec Comm, ADL, planning comm, J Comty Cen, Minneapolis; mem: Beth El Cong, Minneapolis; Har Zion Temple, Phila; Amer Political Sci Assn; Amer Soc for Public Admn; AAUP; AAAS; Org of Amer Hists; W Hist Assn; Pa Political Sci, Public Admn Assn; Minn Acad Sci; Hist Socs: Minn, Colo, Ills Mont, Amer J; Phi Beta Kappa. Author: The American Partnership, 1962; American Federalism, 1966, 1968; Cities of the Prairie, 1969; ed: The American System: A New View of Government in the United States, 1966; The Politics of American Federalism, 1968; co-ed: Cooperation and Conflict: A Reader in American Federalism; co-author, 1st comprehensive classification sys for Judaica librs; contbr: books, monographs, articles to profsl jours. Recipient: Leonard D White Award, for best dissertation in field of public admn, Amer Political Sci Assn, 1960; numerous Fs and grants. Home: 2334 N 50 St, Philadelphia, Pa. Office: Cen for Study of Federalism, Temple U, Philadelphia, Pa.

ELDAD, Israel, Isr, author, ed, educ; b. Pol, Nov 11, 1910; s. Fruma and Scheib; in Isr since 1940; att rabb sem, Vienna; PhD, U Vienna; m. Batia Washitz; c: Na'ama Marbach, Arie. Lectr, humanities, Technion, Haifa; ed: Hazit, Zot ha'Aretz, chronicles. Author: Ma'aser Rishon, 1951; Hegionot haMikra, 1953; trans into Heb: Nietzsche; Will Durant; Sidney Honig; David Kaufman; co found, Movement for Integrated Isr, 1967; fmr mem, Lohamei Herut Isr. Home: 30 Abarbanel St, Jerusalem, Isr.

ELDER, Emil Marshall, US, business exec; b. Cleveland, O, Nov 14, 1897; s. Jennie (Krauss); m. Edna Lebowitz, May 8, 1921; c: Robert, Richard, Howard. Chmn bd, Great Lake Sash & Door Co, since 1969, vice-pres, 1935-69. Vice-pres: Mt Sinai Hosp, fmr treas; United Cemetery; fmr: pres: Fairmont Temple; J Family Service Assn; Heb Free Loan; vice-pres: J Comty Fed; J Vocational Service; club, Oakwood Country. Home: 3270 Warrensville Center Rd, Shaker Heights, O. Office: 1968 66 St, Cleveland, O.

ELEFANT, Moshe Y, US, rabbi; b. South Fork, Pa, Nov 5, 1914; s. Gershom and Hensha (Klein); AB, ordained rabbi, Yeshiva U, 1938; m. Aliza Blaustein, Aug 24, 1948; c: Esther, Peshe, Rivka, Hensha, Yosef, Shaya. Tchr, handicapped who are homebound, Bd Educ, NYC, since 1962; rabbi, congs, 1938-44, 1948-60; dean, Yeshiva of Hartford, Conn, 1944-48. Mem, United Fed Tchrs, NYC; fmr: mem: bd educ, Yeshiva Ohel Yakov, Bklyn, NY; RabCA; NEA; chmn, bd educ, Yeshiva Adath B'nai Isr, Cleveland, O. Contbr to jours. Home: 1851 50 St, Brooklyn, NY.

ELFENBEIN, Elsie, US, organization exec; b. NYC, Aug 21, 1899; m. Hiram Elfenbein, Sep 2, 1919; c: Laurence. Pres, Natl Council J Women, Jersey City, 1933-34; natl chmn, social leg and publ comms, 1938-44; natl vice-chmn, PR comm, 1945; exec dir, 1946-55; natl vice-pres, Women's Intl League for Peace and Freedom, 1944-46; chmn: dist leg, Birth Control League of Amer; civic and pub wfr, ninth dist, NJ State Fed of Women's Clubs; Hudson Co Women's Div, NRA; asso natl secy, Workers Defense League, 1942-43; secy-treas, Intl Council J Women, 1949-51; exec-dir, Post War World Council, 1943-46; mem: steering comm, Natl Peace Conf; exec comm, Natl Perm Fair Employment Practices Comm; exec comm, Citizens Comm on DPs. Home: Huguenot, NY.

ELFENBEIN, Julien, US, communications consultant, editor; b. Chgo, Ill, Aug 12, 1897; s. Isaac and Elizabeth (Berez); att: U Tex Law Sch, 1917-19; Art Students League, 1920-21; m. Lucy Reed, 1924; c: John, Julien. Corporate communications cons; reporter, Scripps-Howard newspapers, 1919-20; artist, NY Times, 1920; pres, Julien Elfenbeing, Inc, advt agcy, 1922-26; dir sales promotion, Ir and Scottish Linen Guild, 1926-30; adj asso prof, bus, journalism, NYU, 1965-68; chief ed, Housewares Review, 1931-60; chmn, ed, comm, Haire Pub Co, 1955-60; Publisher Profit Parade, 1954. Mem:

found, advt post, Amer Legion; Intl Panel Arbitrators, Amer Arbitration Assn; Assn for Educ in Journalism; Sigma Delta Chi; Delta Sigma Rho; Sigma Upsilon; Kappa Tau Alpha; US Consumer Goods Mission to Fr, 1963; fmr pres: Housewares, NY; Greenhaven Rye Assn. Clubs: Fac, NYU; Greenhaven Yacht, Commodore; U Club of Mamaroneck; Deadline. Author: Business Journalism, 1945, 3rd ed, 1959, 4th ed, 1969; Businesspaper Publishing Practice, 1952, 2nd ed, 1969; Business Letters and Communications, 1967; Handbook of Business Form Letters, 1969; contbr to Ency Britannica. Recipient: seven times winner of Jesse Neal and Ind Market awards for outstanding journalism; illuminated scroll, FJP; Medal C of C, Bordeaux; Cdr, L'Ordre du Bontemps Graves-Modoc. Office: 1028 The Parkway, Mamaroneck, NY.

ELFIN, Mel, US, journalist; b. Bklyn, NY, July 18, 1929; s. Joseph and Bess (Margolis); AB, Syracuse U, NY, 1951; AM, Harvard U, 1952; att: New Sch for Social Research, NY, 1954-58; m. Margery Lesser, June 21, 1953; c: David, Dana. Chief, Wash bur, Newsweek Mag, since 1965, mem staff since 1961; asst city ed, LI Press, 1956-58, mem staff since 1954. Capt, USAF, 1952-53, Res, 1953-69. Mem: Phi Beta Kappa. Co-author, Bricks and Mortarboards; contbr to mags. Recipient: George Polk Memorial Award, for reporting, 1957; NY Newspaper Guild Page One Award, 1957. Home: 2804 29 St, NW, Washington, DC. Office: 1750 Pennsylvania Ave, Washington, DC.

ELFMON, Samuel L, US, physician; b. Russ, Mar 27, 1911; s. Louis and Sara (Levine); in US since 1919; BS, U Richmond, Va, 1932; MD, Med Coll of Va, 1935; m. Lillian Shain, Nov 28, 1938; c: Linda, Shila. Phys: pvt practice since 1935; Highsmith Hosp, since 1937; instr, Duke U Sch Med, since 1949; cons: VA Hosp, Fayetteville, NC, since 1947; US Army Hosp, Fort Bragg, NC, since 1953. US Army MC, 1942-45. Pres: Cumberland Med Soc, 1940, 1954; Better Health Found, 1960; chmn bd, Beth Isr Cong, 1948, 1952; mem bd dirs: S Natl Bank, since 1960; Mid-S Ins Co, since 1960; YMCA, since 1961; NC State Bd of Mh, since 1963; mem: Kiwanis, pres, 1959; NC Soc of Internal Med; Amer Coll Phys; AMA; Masons. Contbr to profsl jours. Hobby: golf. Home: 117 Stedman St, Fayetteville, NC. Office: 225 Green St, Fayetteville, NC.

EL-HANANI, Aba, Isr, architect; b. Warasw, Pol, Jan 26, 1918; s. Ezriel and Tova (Schnitzer); engr dipl, architecture, Technion, Haifa, 1940; m. Hanna Rezinkov, Mar 5, 1943; c: Edith, Ehud. Pvt practice since 1946; maj works: Worker's Club, Social Cen, Eilat; sch bldgs: Jerusalem, Tel Aviv, Rishon le Zion; pres palace, Jerusalem; various bldgs: Ashkelon, Tel Aviv, Jerusalem. Haganah, 1936-48, IDF, 1948-49. Mem cen comm, Assn of Engrs and Architects in Isr. Ed, Tvai, quarterly for architecture, town planning; contbr to local and fgn profsl jours and press. Recipient: numerous prizes for architectural competitions. Hobbies: painting, archaeol. Home: 17 Maale Hashahar St, Ramat Gan, Isr. Office: 27 Shlomo Hamelech St, Tel Aviv, Isr.

ELHANANY, Abraham Haim, Isr, journalist, author; b. Larissa, Greece, Aug 2, 1909; s. Haim and Sara (Sasson) Alhanaty; in Isr since 1912; att, Heb U, 1945-46; m. Hana Mendelsohn; c: Rephael, Oded. Newspaper corresp, Davar Daily, Jerusalem, since 1933; fmr newspaper corresp, Doar Hakon. Author: Ish veSsiho; Sihat Sofrim. Recipient: Agron Prize, Munic of Jerusalem. Home: 6/4 Kiryat Moshe, Jerusalem, Isr. Office: 16 Hillel St, Jerusalem, Isr.

ELIA, Albert Moussa, Isr, lawyer; b. Beirut, Leb, Nov 7, 1920; s. Moussa and Lisa (Yerouchalmy); in Isr since 1964; dipl, atty, fac law, Beirut, 1942; PhD, U de Lyon, Fr, 1956; m. Hassiba Moussally, Sep 19, 1954; c: Elsa, Myriam, Daniella, Moussa, Fouad. Pvt practice since 1967; adv to public auth on Arab Criminal Law, 1969; appd by Mil Courts for defense of Arab terrorists, 1968-69; pvt practice, Leb, 1944-64. Past mem: B'nai B'rith; Beirut, J Comm of Personal Status, J Cen Communal Council; leader, Young Orthodox J Org, all in Beirut. Author: Book on Rules of Israeli Civil Procedure, 1969; Contribution jurisprudentielle à la Legislation spéciale des Loyers au Liban, 1957. Spec interest, rel youth educ. Home: 6/12 Tor Zahav St, Herzliya, Isr. Office: 94 Yehuda Halevy St, Tel Aviv, Isr.

ELIACHAR, Eliahou, Isr, business exec, communal worker; b. Jerusalem, Oct 10, 1899; s. Itzhak and Rosa (Navon); att: Fr U, Leb; Cairo Law Sch; Jerusalem Law Sch; m. Hava Bialik; c: Isaac. Ed, publisher, Hed haMizrah, since 1942;

co-found, mgn dir: Pal Milling and Trading Co; Pal Airways; Buildco; Jerusalem Devl; fmr: official receiver; Trade and Ind Dept, Govt of Pal; dep mayor, Jerusalem, 1951-54; MK. Turkish Army, 1915-1918. Co-found, vice-pres, World Sephardi Fed; pres, Sephardi Comty, Jerusalem; mem, B'nai B'rith; fmr; pres, Jerusalem Comty Council; mem: Electoral Assembly; Vaad Leumi; Yishuv Security Comm. Author: A Jew of Palestine Before the Royal Commission, 1936; First Industrial Census of Palestine; contbr to local and fgn press. Hobby: chess. Home: 42 Jabotinsky St, Jerusalem, Isr. Office: POB 582, Haifa, Isr; POB 617, Jerusalem, Isr.

ELIACHAR, Victor, Isr, diplomat; b. Jerusalem, Isr, Apr 18, 1913; s. Moreno and Rachel (Navon); att: Amer U; St Joseph U, both Beirut; Sorbonne, Paris; m. Elda Barukh, Nov 16, 1956. Ambass of Isr, Bogota, Colombia, since 1969; traffic mgr, Pal Airways, 1937-40; mgn dir, Pal Tarvel and Trading Co Ltd, 1946-48; first Isr consul at Istanbul, Turkey, 1949-52; consul, Marseilles, Fr, 1952-56; dep dir, W Eur div, Min for Fgn Affairs, Jerusalem, 1956-59; counsellor, Isr Emb, Brussels, 1959-61; Isr Ambass to Senegal, 1962-64; Isr Min to Bulgaria, 1967. Haganah, 1935-47; Brit Army, 1941-46; IDF, 1947-49. Mem, B'nai B'rith. Recipient: Afr Star; It Star; War Medal; IDF Ot Haatzmaut; Ot Hahitnadvut. Office: Apartado Aereo 14494, Bogota, 1, Colombia; Min for Fgn Affairs, Jerusalem, Isr.

ELIAKIM, Marcel, Isr, physician; b. Plovdiv, Bulgaria, June 2, 1921; s. Albert and Rosalie (Nahmias); in Isr since 1949; att med fac, Sofia; MD, Heb U Hadassah Med Sch, 1952; research f, U of Pa, 1961; m. Caroline Susman, Dec 7, 1947; c: Abraham, Alon. Prof med, Heb U-Hadassah Med Sch, since 1963; dir, Inst of Post-Grad Med Training, Heb U, 1962-66. Lt, sci corps, IDF, 1952-54. Chmn, research comm, Asian-Pacific Soc Card, since 1968; mem numerous local and intl med orgs. Asso ed, Isr Jour of Med Scis, since 1968; contbr numerous articles to jours in Isr and abroad. Recipient: Ben-Ari Award, 1950; Federgreen-Zwilling Award, 1964, 1965. Home: 34 Keren Hayesod St, Jerusalem, Isr. Office: Hadassah U Hosp, Jerusalem, Isr.

ELIAS, (M) Hans, US, researcher, educator; b. Darmstadt, Ger, June 28, 1907; s. Michael and Anna (Oppenheimer); in US since 1939; PhD, U Giessen, 1931; m. Anneliese Buchtal, Oct 11, 1936; c: Peter, Thomas. Prof, anat, Chgo Med Sch, since 1949; chief, lab for histology and cinematography, Consiglio Nazionale delle Ricerche, It, 1936-38; prof, histology, Middlesex Vetr Sch, 1939-45; sci film production sup, USPHS, Communicable Disease Cen, Atlanta, Ga, 1945-49. Pres, Intl Soc for Stereology, 1961-67, hon pres since 1967; f, AAAS; mem: Amer Soc Zoologists; Amer Assn Anats; Società Italiana di Anatomia; Anatomische Gesellschaft. Author: Plate Structure of Liver, 1948; Human Microanatomy, 1960; Vital Character of Human Cancer, 1962; Morphology of the Liver, 1969; Basic Human Anatomy, 1970; contbr numerous articles to profsl jours. Recipient: three awards for sci exhbs, AMA. Spec interest: sci illus. Home: 2670 Birchwood Lane, Deerfield, Ill. Office: 2020 W Ogden Ave, Chicago, Ill.

ELIAS, Herbert, US, physician, educator; b. Vienna, Aus, Apr 30, 1885; s. Salomon and Helene (Kauders); in US since 1939; MD, U Vienna, 1909; m. Ada Hirsch, Feb 23, 1936; c: Hanna, Kurt. Ret since 1965; pvt dozent, Vienna, 1919; prof med, U Vienna, 1929-38; chief, med dept: Kaufmännisches Spital, 1936, Rothschild Hosp, 1936-38, both Vienna; clinical prof med, NY Med Coll, 1954-65, mem fac since 1939; visiting, cons phys, Metrop Hosp, 1939-59; att phys, Flower and Fifth Ave Hosp, 1952-65; dir, clinic, Bird S Coler Hosp, 1952-65, all NYC. Aus Army, WW I. F, Amer Coll Card; hon pres, Amer Fed J from Aus, since 1950, fmr pres; mem: NY Acad Scis; AMA; Co, State, NY Med Socs; NY Diabetic Soc; Amer Soc Eur Chems; Amer Assn Hist of Med; NY Med Circle; Amer Phys F for IMA; B'nai B'rith; AJCong; fmr: pres: Rudolf Virchow Med Soc, NY; KH; J Phys Assn, both Vienna; mem, adv comm for Aus, WJC, NYC. Author: books, contbr numerous articles to Ger, Amer med jours and archives. Home: 35 W 81 St, New York, NY.

ELIAS, Irving, US, business exec, communal leader; b. Janina, Greece, Dec 22, 1899; s. Elihu and Stamo (Sebathay); in US since 1910; m. Ann Negrin, June 24, 1922; c. Leonard, David, Estelle. Pres, Irving Elias Assos; chmn bd, Allstate Paper Box Co, Inc, both since 1967; limited partner, Russell and Saxe Stock Brokerage House, since 1939; hon chmn bd, Asso Fashion Ind's, since 1966; pres, E D Leonard; dir, Standard

Safe Deposit; pres: Artistic Paper Box, to 1967, Set-Up Paper Box Mfrs Assn, 1935-46; dir, Public Natl Bank, 1935-42. Vice-pres: Span and Port Syn, trustee Sephardic Home for Aged, Trustee co-found, Sephardic Studies Prog, Yeshiva U; chmn, Manhattan div, Isr Bonds; fund raising chmn, David and Tamar de Sola Pool Village; Isr trustee, treas, Emanuel Lodge 654, Mason; mem: KP; Grand St Boys Club; Shield of David Home for Retarded Children; fmr pres, Men's Club, Span and Port Syn. Home: 11 Riverside Dr, New York, NY. Office: 50 Broad St, New York, NY.

ELIAS, Paul, Isr, physician; b. Rum, May 16, 1924; s. Felician and Cecilia (Goldring); in Isr since 1963; MD, U Bucharest; m. Alisa Raviv, Feb 3, 1964; c: Anca, Dana. Med dir, Rehovot Maternity Hosp, since 1968. Mem: Rotary, Isr; Isr Bridge Fed. Contbr to med jours. Home: 37-39 Benjamin St, Rehovot, Isr. Office: Rehovot Maternity Hosp, Rehovot, Isr.

ELIASBERG, Wladimir G, US, psychiatrist, author; b. Wiesbaden, Ger, Dec 10, 1887; s. Samuel and Rachel (Eliasberg); in US since 1938; un U Berlin, 1906-10; MD, U Heidelberg, 1911; PhD, U M atth, 1924; m. Esther Talbot; c: Eva Hareli, Hanna Avriel, siciriam Rosenzweig, Susanne. Pvt practice, psycht and neur, Mince 1919; ship's dr, Far East, 1913; phys Hosp for Brain Diseases, Munich, 1919-23; att phys, supt, Hosp for Nervous and Mental Diseases, Munich-Thalkirchen, 1928-30; lectr, forensic psycht, Munich Bar Assn, 1932; visiting prof, Academie des Sciences Politiques, Prague, 1937; psycht, out-patient dept, Mt Sinai Hosp, NY, 1941-44; lectr, psych, Rutgers U, 1946; psycht cons, Bulova Watch Co, 1946; med dir, Bklyn Citizens Comty Treatment and Guidance Clinics, 1953. Capt, Mc, Ger Army, 1914-18. F: NY Acad Med; AMA, life; Amer Psycht Assn; dipl, Amer Bd Psycht and Neur; fmr pres: Amer Soc Psycht Phys; Assn for Psycht Treatment of Offenders; vice-pres, Amer Mh Found, since 1958; mem: NY Soc for Clinical Psycht; Amer Psych Assn; Amer Sociol Assn; Soc of Criminology; Amer League to Abolish Capital Punishment; Acad Political and Social Scis; NY Soc of Amer Jurisprudence; E Psycht Assn; E Sociol Assn; NY State Assn of Psycht; Assn for Hist of Med; E Psycht Research Assn; Rudolph Virchow Med Soc; hon mem: Allgemeine Aerztl Gesellschaft fuer Psychotherapie, Vienna; Prague Inst for Psychotechs; Vienna Assn of Spec in Advt, Propaganda and PR; found, gen secy, Ger Congs for Psychotherapy, 1926; delg, 7th Intl Cong for Psychotech, Moscow, 1931; chmn, div for ind path, 8th Intl Cong, Prague, 1934. Author: Outlines of a General Pathology of Work, 1924; The Problem Child, 1931; From Reason to Rationalization, 1932; Psychology and the Administration of Law and Justice, 1933; Sciences of Propaganda and Advertising on the Basis of Sociology, Economics and Psychology, 1936; Women and Propaganda, 1936; Physicians and Propaganda, 1936; Psychiatry and Propaganda, 1945; Forensic Psychology, 1946; Corruption and Bribery, 1951; Art, Immoral and Immortal, 1954; Speaking and Thinking, 1954; Towards a Philosophy of Propaganda, 1957; Psychotherapy and Society, 1959; Social Psychiatry, 1959; Parkinsonism, 1962; Wills in Stroke and Aphasia, 1963; Lie Detector, 1967; Violence, 1969; co-author, Studies on Pathology of Work and Motivation Theory, 1930; contbr to med, sci jours; ed, Allgemeine Aerztl Zeitschrift fuer Psychotherapie, 1928-31; ed bd, Archives of Criminal Psychopathology, 1950; asso ed, Jour of Group Psychotherapy, 1954. Recipient: Iron Cross, 1st and 2nd classes, WW 1. Home and office: 151 Central Park W, New York, NY.

ELIASOPH, Paula R, US, artist, teacher, author; b. NYC, Oct 26, 1895; d. Joseph and Ann (Machlis) Rubin; att: Pratt Inst Fine Arts, 1914-18; Columbia U, 1923-25; Art Students League, NYC, 1930-32; m. Joseph Eliasoph, Jan 4, 1920 (decd); c: Herbert, Eugene, Janet. Art sup, instr for children, Yeshiva of Cen Queens Elem Sch and Jr HS, Jamaica. since 1949; pvt studio since 1938; art instr, Forest Hills J Cen Adult Sch of Study, since 1951; Adult Recreations Cen Public HS 131, Jamaica, 1949-51 evening sessions; lectr: Queens Coll; in service credit lectures to tchrs, Bd Educ, NYC since 1949; research: U Minn Psych Dept, summer 1967; U of Mo Dept Hist in Art, 1969; chmn: adv mus comm, Borough of Queens, since 1947; Jamaica Armory Exhb of Golden Jubilee, 1948; Mayor's Plan Comm for Exhbs and Festivals, since 1949; mem, Comm for Study of Art in Educ, NYU, 1949. Repr in perm exhbs of: Metrop Mus Art; Bklyn Mus Art; NY Public Libr; Libr of Cong; pvt collections: exhs in mus and gal throughout US and Can; one-man shows: Leonard Clayton Gal, 1930, 1933; Bklyn Mus of Art, 1930; Guild Hall, E Hampton, LI, 1932; Montros Gal, 1936; Belle and Fletcher Gal, Boston, Mass, 1937; Argent Gal, NY, 1938;

Town Hall Club, 1939; Wildenstein Gal, Fed Modern Painters and Sculptors, 1940-48; Queensborough Public Libr, 1946; Lindenauer and Simon, 1944; Dominion Gal, Montreal, 1949; Van Wyck Cong Church, 1953; Forest Hills J Cen, 1951-54; Kew Gardens Art Cent, 1952-53; Queens Botanical Gardens Art Festival, since 1949; Exhb of Art, US, 1958; Riverside Mus, NY, 1955-62; Lever House Gal, NY, 1963, NY Women's Council Hashomer Hatzair, NYC; Fed Modern Painters and Sculptors, Union Carbide Bldg Gal, 1964, 1966, 1967, 1968; Natl Acad, Amer Watercolor Soc, 1964-69; Amer Watercolor Soc, Metrop Mus of Art, 1967. Chmn, Jamaica Armory Art Found, 1948; vice-chmn, Recreation Council for Juvenile Aid, Queens, 1947-49; treas, incorporating trustee, Fed Modern Painters and Sculptors, 1941-49; secy, Natl Assn Amer Pen Women, 1952-54; mem: Amer Watercolor Soc, NYC; Art Students League, NYC; Art League of LI; Tchrs Comm J Educ; comm on art educ, Mus of Modern Art; Hadassah; natl Women's Comm, Brandeis U. Author: Etchings and Dry Points of Childe Hassam, 1933; Space-Time as the Artist Sees It, 1935; Modern Art Movements, 1936; Understanding Abstract Art, 1937; Manual on Art Teaching to Adults, Art Psychology of the Child and Art Curriculum for Teaching Children in Elementary Parochial School; contbr to art mags and other jours. Recipient: 1st and 2nd prizes for etchings, YWCA, 1943; bronze medal for painting, Art League of LI, 1950; bronze medal, Borough of Queens for chmn activity in Queens Jubilee Armory Art Exhb, 1949. Home and studio: 148-25 89 Ave, Jamaica, NY.

ELIASOV, Eli, Rhodesia, business exec, accountant; b. Venterstad, S Afr, Dec 5, 1913; s. Simon and Rosie (Mindel); Inc Secy; Inst of Estate Agts and Valuers, Rhodesia; Asso Inst of Shipping and Forwarding Agts; m. Peggy Rubinstein, Jan 30, 1941; c: John, Jocelyn. Secy, dir, Fed Bd of Executors and Trust Co, Ltd, since 1954; self employed, 1945-54. Lt, Royal Rhodesian Regiment, 1939-45. Treas, J Bd of Deps since 1949, vice-pres since 1963, pres, 1958-62; secy: Bulawayo Chevra Kadisha, since 1949; Rhodesian Clothing Council, since 1949; fmr pres, Cen Afr J Bd of Deps; mem: Soc Inc Secretaries; clubs: Parkview; Weizmann Sports, fmr chmn. Hobby: bowling. Home: 71 Duncan Rd, Subarko, Bulawayo, Rhodesia. Office: Box 1017 Bulawayo, Rhodesia.

ELIAV, Arie L, Isr, government official; b. Moscow, Nov 21, 1921; in Isr since 1924; grad, cum laude, Heb U, Jerusalem; att Reading, U; Cambridge U, Eng: m. Tanya Zvi; c: Zvi, Ofra, Eyal. Secy gen, Lab party, since 1969; asst to Levy Eshkol: settlement dept, JA, Min of Agric, Min of Finance, 1949-53; instr, immigrants village, Moshav Nevatim, 1954; first dir, Lachish regional project, 1955-57; first secy, Isr Emb, Moscow, 1958-60; first dir: Arad regional project, 1960-62; Chazvin project, Jran, 1962-63; mission on behalf of Beit Hillel, US, 1964; head, Mapai Org Dept, 1965; MK, 1965; dep Min, Commerce and Ind, 1966-67; dep Min of Immigration and Absorption, 1969; Lt Col, IDF, 1947-49; Brit Army; worked for illegal immigration to Pal; Sinai Campaign, i/c rescue evacuation of J from Port Said. Author: Between Hammer and Sickle (under name of Ben-Ami), 1965; The Voyage of the Ulua, 1967; New Targets for Israel, 1968; contbr to local, fgn publs. Home: 3 Karl Netter St, Tel Aviv, Isr. Office: Labor Party, Hayarkon St, Tel Aviv, Isr.

ELIAV, Binyamin, Isr, journalist, editor, government official; b. Riga, Latvia, Apr 26, 1909; s. Elias and Fanny Lubotzky; in Isr since 1925; att U's: Berlin, Vienna, Paris; m. Berta Finkelman; c: Yael, Miriam. Asso ed, Ency Judaica, since 1967; political adv, Min for Fgn Affairs 1953-62; Isr En,b, Buenos Aires, Arg, 1954-55; political ed, Fgn Min, 1962-66; dir info services, PM off, 1966-67; mem, vice-chmn, Isr Bc Auth, 1967-68; ed bd, haYarden daily, 1935-36; ed, haYarden, weekly, 1936-38; bd, HaMashkif, 1940-44; chmn, Tenuat Haam, 1944-48; Asefat haNish'arim, 1946-48; Yediot Ahronot, 1948; haDor, 1949-52; ed 1952-53; consul gen in NYC, 1960-61. Home: 10 Brodi St, Jerusalem, Isr.

ELIEL, Ernest Ludwig, US, chemist; b. Cologne, Ger, Dec 28, 1921; s. Oskar and Louise (Tietz); att U Edinburgh; DSc, U Havana, 1946; PHD, U Ill, 1948; m. Eva Schwartz, Dec 23, 1949; c: Ruth, Carol. Prof, chem, U Notre Dame, since 1960. Mem: Sigma Xi, AAAS, Phi Kappa Phi, Phi Lambda Upsilon, Amer Chem Soc, Chem Soc of London. Home: 17305 Parker Ave, South Bend, Ind. Office: U of Notre Dame, Notre Dame, Ind.

ELIEZER, Isaac, Isr, chemist; b. Sofia, Bulgaria, Jan 19, 1934; s. Nissim and Mathilda (Diba); in Isr since 1943; MSc, Heb

U, Jerusalem, 1956, PhD, 1960; m. Naomi Stein, June 30, 1960; c: Eran, David. Asso prof, chem, Tel Aviv U, since 1967; sci, Isr AEC, 1960-63; sr sci, Sorek Nuclear Research Cen, 1963-65; research asso, U of S Cal, 1965-67. Mem, Isr Chem Soc. Contbr numerous publs to sci jours. Hobbies: books, music. Home: 3 Gordon St, Rehovot, Isr. Office: Tel Aviv U, Ramat Aviv, Isr.

ELIEZER, Victor, Greece, merchant; b. Arta, Greece, 1915; s. Victor and Hanna (Soussi); att commercial HS, Corfu, Greece; m. Rebecca Yohana; c: Hanna, Victor. Merchant, Eliezer Bros, Athens; fmr: Gross Commercial Ltd; Agric Bank of Greece. Vice-pres, org for assistance and rehab of J (OPAIE); mem bd, Hevra Kadisha, Athens; past secy gen: Gen Comm for Assistance for all J, Greece; ORT; past mem, gen assembly J Comty, Athens; past mem bd, J Comty, Athens; mem, B'nai B'rith, Filon, Athens. Home: Mithimnis 58, Athens, Greece. Office: Athinaidos 4a, Athens, Greece.

ELISCU, Frank, US, sculptor; b. NYC, July 13, 1912; s. Charles and Florence (Kane); att: Beaux Arts Inst of Design, Pratt Inst, 1930-33; m. Mildred Norman, 1942; c: Norma Banas. One-man exhb, Mexico, 1955; repr in collections: Brookgreen Gardens, SC; Aeronautical Hall of Fame; other works: Stevens Inst; Cornell Med Sch; Olin Hall, NY; Heisman Memorial Trophy; statue, Naiad, at 100 Church St, NY; Atoms for Peace figure, Ventura, Cal; The Torah, Temple Mt Sinai, Bergtulo; The Astronauts, Headley Mus, Lex, Ky. Pres, Natl Sculpture Soc, 1967-70, vice-pres, 1955-58. Author: Sculpture, Three Techniques—Wax, Clay, Slate, 1960; Direct Wax Sculpture. Designed the Collaborative Medal of Honor for the Architectural League, NY. Recipient: Edith S Moore prize, sculpture, 1948; Bennet prize, Natl Sculpture Soc; silver medal, Architectural League, 1958. Home: 440 Rockhouse Rd, Easton, Conn.

ELKAN, Wolf, US, surgeon; b. Mannheim, Ger, July 9, 1913; s. Benno and Hedwig (Einstein); in US since 1939; att: U Frankfurt, 1930-33; U Heidelberg, 1933-34; MD, ChD, U Rome, 1938; licentiate: Royal Coll of Surgs and Phys, Edinburgh, 1939; Royal Fac of Phys and Surg, Glasgow, 1939; m. Beverly Macey, Sep 29, 1946; c: Anthony, Mathew. Asst clinical prof surg, NY Med Coll; asst att surg, Flower and Fifth Ave Hosp; asso att Surg, Metrop Hosp; all NY; asso surg, cardiovascular service, Harlem Hosp since 1956; 1st asst to Prof Rudolph Nissen, 1945-52; clinical asst surg, Mt Sinai Hosp, 1945-55; asst surg, Montefiore Hosp, 1935-56. Dipl: Amer Bd Surg; Intl Bd Surg; Amer Bd of Abdominal Surg; f, Intl Coll of Surgs; pres, Rudolph Virchow Med Soc since 1962, fmr secy; mem, AMA; Mt Sinai and Montefiore Hosp Alumni Assns. Contbr to profsl publs; report on heart wound oprs, Life Mag, 1956. Hobbies: sailing, skiing; watercolors; sculpture. Home: 131 Riverside Dr, New York, NY. Office: 57 W 57 St, New York, NY.

ELKAVETZ, Israel, Isr, youth leader; b. Dedemotichon, Greece, Aug 10, 1937; s. Yaaqov and Esther; in Isr since 1941; att Oranim, Kibbutz Tchrs Sem; m. Irit, Aug 5, 1963; c: Eyal. Natl, exec secy, Heb Scout Youth Movement, 1965-67; secy, Kibbutz Tel Katzir, 1967-68. Pvt, IDF, 1954-57. Fmr, mem exec,Jordan Valley Regional Council. Recipient: service badge, Isr Scout Youth Movement. Spec interest: youth educ. Home: Kibbutz Tel Katzir, Jordan Valley, Isr.

ELKIN, Benjamin, US, educator, author; b. Baltimore, Md, Aug 10, 1911; s. Samuel and Leah (Sachs); BS, Lewis Inst, Chgo, 1932; MA, Northeastern U, 1947, PhD, 1950. Prin, Rogers Sch, since 1948; with personnel off, VA and Social Security Bd, 1936-39; tchr: Eng, Harrison HS, 1939-41; Eng, econ, Von Steuben HS, 1941-48. Author: Loudest Noise in the World, 1954; Gillespie and the Guards, 1956; Six Foolish Fishermén, 1957; True Book of Schools, 1958; Big Jump and Other Stories, 1958; True Book of Money, 1960; King's Wish and Other Stories, 1960; Man Who Walked Around the World, 1961; Lucky and the Giant, 1964; Al and the Magic Lamp, 1963; Why the Sun Was Late, 1966; Such is the Way of the World, 1967; Wisest Man in the World, 1968; Magic Ring, 1969, all books for children. Staff sgt, US Army, 1942-65. Mem, B'nai B'rith; fmr, Ill state chmn, Natl Assn Gifted Children. Recipient: Citation of Merit, Natl Assn Gifted Children, 1966. Home: 1205 Sherwin Ave, Chicago, Ill. Office: 7345 N Washtenaw Ave, Chicago, Ill.

ELKIN, Milton, US, physician, educator; b. Boston, Mass, Feb 24, 1916; s. Philip and Rose (Dexter); BA, Harvard U, 1937, MD, 1941; m. Gloria King, Nov 12, 1943; c: Philip,

Karen, Laura. Prof, chmn, dept radiology, Albert Einstein Coll of Med, since 1954; dir radiology, Bx Munic Hosp, since 1954; Cambridge. City Hosp, 1925-35; asso radiologist, Cedars of Leb Hosp, 1953-54. Maj, USAAF, 1942-46. F, Amer Coll of Radiology; mem: Amer Roentgen Ray Soc; Radiological Soc of N Amer; NY Roentgen Soc; Assn U Radiologist. Contbr to med jours and books. Home: 13 Kingston Rd, ?carsdale, NY. Office: 1300 Morris Park Ave, Bronx, NY.

ELKINS, Dov Peretz, US, rabbi; b. Phila, Pa, Dec 7, 1937; s. Edward and Bertha (Byer); BA, Temple U, 1959; ordained rabbi, MHL, JTSA, 1946; m. Elaine Rash, June 12, 1960; c: Hillel, Jonathan, Shira. Rabbi, Har Zion Temple, since 1966. Capt, chaplain, US Army, 1964-66. Author: So Young To Be A Rabbi, 1969; co-author: Worlds Lost and Found, 1964; Treasures From The Dust, 1970. Recipient: award, best juvenile book, JBCA, 1964, 1964. Home: 455 Matsonford Rd, Radnor, Pa Study: 639 County Line Rd, Radnor, Pa.

EL KODSI, Baroukh, US, physician; b. Cairo, Egypt, Aug 24, 1923; s. Moussa and Zohra (Aslan-Cohen) Yerushalmi-Levy; in US since 1957; MD, Cairo U Sch of Med, Cairo, 1945; cert: Amer Bd Internal Med, 1964; Subspecialty Bd, Gastroenterology, 1969; m. Marie Menasha, Mar 26, 1960; c: Sylvia, Robert, Karen, Dir, Gastroenterology, Maimonides Med Cen, Bklyn, NY since 1968, att phys since 1969; att phys, Coney Island Hosp, since 1967, asso att phys, 1965-69, asso dir med services, 1965-67; asst prof med: SUNY, Downstate Med Cen, Bklyn, NY, since 1969, on fac since 1965; att phys, Kings Co Hosp, since 1965; asst dir, med, Framingham Union Hosp, Boston, Mass, 1964-65; asst phys: Boston City Hosp, 1962-65; Framingham Union Hosp, 1964-65; instr med, Boston U Sch of Med, 1962-65; pvt practice; att phys, J Hosp, Cairo Egypt,1950-57. Sr mem, Amer Fed for Clinical Research; mem: Amer Coll of Phys; AMA; Mass Med Soc; NY State Med Soc; Bklyn Gastroenterological Soc. Contbr to profsl publs. Hobbies: tennis, music. Home: 35 Seacoast Terr, Brooklyn, NY. Office: 4802 Tenth Ave, Brooklyn, NY.

ELKOSHI, Gedalyahu, Isr, author, educator; b. Ostrow-Mazowieck, Pol, 1910; s. Zeev and Zipporah (Bachrach) Elkes; in Isr since 1932; att: U Warsaw; Warsaw Inst J Sci, both 1930-32; MA, Heb U, Jerusalem, 1936, PhD, 1944; m. Ruth Bravmann, Aug 16, 1937; c: Ehud, Zeev. Prof, Heb lit, Tel Aviv U, since 1967, sr lectr, 1956-67; libr, Natl and U Libr, 1934-44; tchr, lit, Rehavia HS, both Jerusalem, 1944-55; asst ed, Ency Hebraica, Jerusalem, 1946-66. Author: Biblical Anthology, 1953; Thesaurus Proverbiorum Latinorum, 1959; Letters from P Smolenskin to Y L Gordon, 1959; Nahlath Zevi, 1966; Hebrew Press of Vilna in the 19th Century, 1967; ed in chief, Ency Massada, Tel Aviv, 1958; trans into Heb: Greek Religion, 1951; Greek Culture, 1956, both by T Zielinski; ed: Selected Works of S D Luzzatto, 1948; Selected Works of N H Wessly, 1951; Selected Works of Bar-Tobiah, 2 vols, 1964; contbr essays on modern Heb lit. Home: 15 Alfasi St, Jerusalem, Isr. Office: Tel Aviv U, Ramat Aviv, Isr.

ELL, Leon J, US, attorney, communal worker, b. Pol, May 17, 1896; s. Peltiel and Zepora (Jacobi); in US since 1910; LLB, Northwestern U Law Sch, 1920; m. Alice Katz, May 24, 1931; c: Sandra Dalkin. Inves cons since 1943; columnist, Miami Times, Miami, Fla; atty, Chgo, Ill, 1920-43. Mem, Fla Rep Natl Conv Delg. US Army, WW I. Mem: exec comm, JNF, since 1961, fmr mem bd dirs; Gtr Miami J Fed, since 1950; United Fund and Mh Inst, since 1960; pres council, JNF of Gtr Miami, since 1960; mem: White House Conf on Ref, since 1956; US Ref Comm, since 1960; Fla delg, Rep Natl Conv, 1956, 1968; hon life mem, Temple Beth Sholom, fmr pres; fmr: mem bd dirs, UAHC; trustee, HUC; repr US Govt at Geneva on Intergovt Comm on Eur Migration; Fla St Rep Chmn for Minorities. Author: Events that Shaped History; contbr to local press. Home: 16 Island Ave, Belle Isle, Miami Beach, Fla. Office: 1451 N Bayshore Dr, Miami, Fla.

ELLENBERG, Edward, Isr, journalist; b. Vienna, Aus, Feb 28, 1925; s. Simon and Bertha (Tannenbaum); in Isr since 1962; LLB Fac Law, Bucharest, 1949; PhD, political, social sci, Etudes Universitaires Internationales, Luxembourg, Zurich, 1964; m. Gisele Melixon, May 11, 1944; c: Egon, Erwin. Ed in chief, publisher, gen mgr: Mednews Agcy; Business News Service; Mediterranean Observer Group; Business Observer; Diplomatic Observer; Tourism and Travel Observer, since 1963; asst ed, FACLA; corresp Eur jours; fmr: press off: Swed Finnish Legations, Bucharest. Vice-press: Natl J Party,

Rum, 1945-47; Hasmonaea, 1945-47; pres, Natl Zionist Students Org, Rum, 1945-47; mem: Intl Fed Journalists; Natl Fed Journalists, Isr; Fgn Press Assn, Isr. Author: Slaves of the Twentieth Century, 1946; Israel (Let Us Know Our Homeland), 1965; Behind the Scenes of the Six Day War, 1967. Hobbies: philately, painting. Home: 5 Ein Yahav St, Holon, Isr. Office: POB 7025, Tel Aviv, Isr.

ELLENBERG, Egon, Isr, journalist; b. Bucharest, Rum, Oct 12, 1947; s. Edward and Gisele (Melixon); in Isr since 1962; att U Econ and Social Studies, Tel Aviv; m. Jocheved Scheiner, Jan 19, 1969. Mgn ed: The Diplomatic Observer; The Business Observer, since 1966; Isr corresp, Intl Reports News Agcy, NY, since 1967. Sgt, engr corps, IDF. Hobbies: lit; cinema; philately. Home: 50 Mivtza Sinai St, Ramat Yosef, Isr. Office: POB 7025, Tel Aviv, Isr.

ELLENBERG, Max, US, physician; b. NYC, Jan 29, 1911; s. Phillip and Sarah (Yablon); BS, cum laude, CCNY, 1931; MD, NYU Coll of Med, 1935; m. Mary Lemon, Dec 1, 1942; c: Richard, Robert, William. Asso clinical prof med, Mt Sinai Sch of Med; att phys, Mt Sinai Hosp, since 1950, on staff since 1935; instr med, Coll Phys and Surgs, NYC, since 1948. Lt col, US Army MC, 1942-46. Pres, dir, NY Diabetes Assn; f, NY Acad of Sci; FACP; mem: AMA; Amer Bd Internal Med; Alpha Omega Alpha; Phi Beta Kappa. Sr ed, Clinical Diabetes Mellities. Contbr numerous articles to profsl jours. Home: 799 Park Ave, New York, NY. Office: 936 Fifth Ave, New York, NY.

ELLENBOGEN, Henry, US, jurist; b.Vienna, Aus, Apr 3, 1900; s. Samson and Rose (Franzos); BA, Duquesne U, Pittsburgh, Pa, 1922, LLB, 1924; JD, Duquesne U; m. Rae Savage, Dec 18, 1927; c: Naomi, Judith. Pres Judge, Court Common Pleas, Allegheny Co, Pa, since 1963, on court since 1938; mem, US House of Repr, 1932-38; served on Price Control Bd; mem, Natl War Lab Bd, WW II. Prin contrib: while in Cong sponsored: low cost housing bill; first contributory old-age pension resolution; wrote and secured passage, Unemployment Compensation Bill for DC. Chmn: fund raising dinners for Pittsburgh Council, JNF; fund raising campaign, United Negro Coll Fund, Pittsburgh; campaign, Amer Friends Heb U, for Pittsburgh and Tri-State area; fmr natl vice-pres, ZOA; mem: life, bd dirs, YM-YWHA, Pittsburgh. US Delg to UN Comm on Narcotics, Geneva, Switz, 1959, NYC, 1961; club, Westmoreland Country. Contbr articles to mags. Office: City-Co Bldg, Pittsburgh, Pa.

ELLENBOGEN, Maximilian, US, educator; b. Vienna, Aus, July 2, 1924; s. Isidor znd Rosa (Wagschal); desc of Rabbi Elimelech of Lizansk, co-found of Hassidism; in US since 1950; MA, Columbia U, 1953, PhD, 1957; m. Alexandra Kosseff; c: Dina, Sharon. Prof, Heb, Queens Coll, NY, on fac since 1960; lectr: Hunter Coll, NYC, 1956-59; Columbia U, 1959-60. Served, WW II. Mem: Soc Bibl Lit and Exegesis; Amer Oriental Soc; AAUP; Natl Assn Profs of Heb. Author: Foreign Words in the Old Testament, Their Origin and Etymology, 1962; Sound and Meaning, Essay Concerning the Origin of Human Speech, 1963; Dum Spiro Spero, 1964; The Common Prehistoric Origin of Certain Non-Synonymous Semitic Roots, 1967; Associative Fields Radiating From The Concepts "Throat Neck", 1968; Root Enlargement in Semitic Speech, 1969. Home: 910 Smith St, Uniondale, NY. Office: Queens Coll, Flushing, NY.

ELLENBOGEN, Otto, Isr, artist; b. Vienna, Aus, Sep 19, 1922; s. Ignatz and Rosa (Wagschal); in Isr since 1938; att Sch for Applied Arts, Vienna; m. Rachel Leibovitz, Mar, 1951; c: Amir, Amos. Perm contbr to Natl Exhb of Isr Artists, Tel Aviv, Helena Rubenstein Pavilion; one-man shows in Isr since 1950; repr in pvt collections in Isr and abroad; invited by Herzl Inst, NY for exbs in US; fmr mem, sci team of Hazor Archaeol Excavations. Mem: cen comm, natl exec, Isr Painters and Sculptors Assn; Intl Assn of Plastic Arts; Isr br repr and delg to gen assembly of all intl artists assns, 1969, Holland. Home: 40 Shlomzion Hamalka, Tel Aviv, Isr.

ELLENBOGEN, Saul, US, organization exec; b. Hoosick Falls, NY, Apr 27, 1901; s. Nathan and Anna (Cantor); m. Hilda Goldberg, Mar 9, 1924; c: Raphael, Shirley Schwartz. Exec dir:Temple Beth Shalom, since 1968; Young Isr of Flatbush, 1929-35; Ocean Pkwy J Cen, 1935-43, 1956-61; YM-YWHA of Williamsburg, 1943-56; Yeshiva Ohel Moshe, 1962; Valley Stream J Cen, 1962-64; Bayside J Cen, 1965-67. Pres, Blvd J Cen, since 1959; mem: life ZOA; Natl Assn Syn Admnrs; Natl Assn Temple Secys; charter, intl Conf Social

Wfr; UJA of Gtr NY. Ed, feature writer, The Synagogue Center. Recipient: citation, Natl Assn J Cen Workers. Home and NY office: 1407 Linden Blvd, Brooklyn, NY.

ELLERN, Hermann, Isr, banker; b. Karlsruhe, Ger, Oct 4, 1892; s. Ignaz and Claire (Feuchtwanger); in Isr since 1933; grad Coll of Commerce, Ger; m. Bessie Loewenthal (decd); c: Usiel ,Menahem, Miriam, Joshua; m. 2nd Eva Nussbaum. Found, chmn: Ellern's Bank Ltd; Ellern's Inves; Elgar Inves; Ellis AG Zurich; bd chmn, Moller Textile; dir, Gen Mortgage Bank; Ind Devl Bank of Isr; co-owner, Ignaz Ellern, bankers, Ger, 1919-33. Fmr pres, B'nai B'rith lodge, Ramat Gan; club, Rotary. Home: 4 Haparsa St, Ramat Gan, Isr. Office: Shalom Tower, Tel Aviv, Isr.

ELLIMORE, Gershon, Isr, journalist; b. Lith, Aug 11, 1900; s. Eliyahu and Sima (Lipov) Valkovski; m. Marysha Lipski, Dec 29, 1960; c: Aliz, Micael, Levita Tadmor. Ret since 1966; fmr: secy, Lith Consulate Gen; acting Consul Gen; journalist, newspapers: in Lith: Yiddishe Shtime; Lietuvos Aidas; Lietuvos Zinios; in Isr: Ha'aretz; Lamerchav; Davar; Omer. Mem, MILO. Author: Mul Eitanei haResha; co-author, Yahaduth Lita. Spec interests: lit; chess. Home: 118 A, Derech Hanitzahon, Tel Aviv, Isr.

ELLIOT, Simon (Eliakimowicz), Mexico, attorney, industrialist, writer; b. Wilno, Pol, 1912; LLB, NYU, 1945, DJ, 1968; m; two c. Exec vice-pres, Fibras Vitricas Mexicanas, SA; fmr head and co-owner: Kenaf Mexicano; Amer Textil; Industrias Sorel. Active, Dem Party, NY, org, New Amer political groups for leading dems; repr fiber ind at intl convs; chmn, textile commn, intl Kenaf conf. Contbr, weekly column to Sztime, Mexico; numerous articles on textile to US, Eur, Span jours. Mem: OSE and ORT org, repr Mexico at its World Confs; vice-pres, Pre bar Assn, NYU Law Sch; fmr: pres, academic frat Jordania, Wilno, found by Jabotinsky. Home: Monserrat 23, Puerte de Vigas, Edo de Mexico, Mexico. Office: Mesones 129 5 To. Piso, Mexico 1, Mexico.

ELLIS, Michael, US, theatrical produc; b. Phila, Pa, Oct 25, 1917; s. Alexander and Mollie (Fein) Abrahamson; grad, Wyo Sem, 1935; BA, Dartmouth Coll, 1939; att Us: Grenoble, 1937; Sorbonne, 1937-38, both Fr; m. Neva Patterson, Mar 22, 1953 (div); m. 2nd, Mary Walker, May 10, 1958; c: Sandra, Gordon, Thomas. Actor, stage mgr, with James Russo, Broadway Shows, 1948-53; owner, operator, Bucks Co Playhouse, 1954-64, State Theatre of Pa, 1959. Produc: Come Blow Your Horn, 1961; The Advocate, 1963, both with William Hammerstein; The Beauty Part, 1962; Absence of a Cello, with Jeff Britton, 1964; The Paisley Convertible, 1967; The Girl in the Freudian Slip, 1967. Mem, adv bd, Hopkins Cen, Dartmouth Coll. Home: Box 80, RD 2, New Hope, Pa.

ELLIS, Morris S, US, chemist; b. Golta, Cherson, Russ, Jan 3, 1882; s. Yosef and Malka (Abidor) Yelisavetsky; BS, Cooper Union, NYC, 1917; m. Edith Greenspan, May 4, 1907 (decd); c: Ruth Taub, Miriam Geller, Tamar Weiss, Joseph. Ret; fmr: research and analytical chem, Ellis Labs; research chem: Marietta Refining Co; Lederle Labs. Prin contribs: devl methods for the mfg of dyes; devl of the organic chem ind in US. Mem: Natl Exec bd, B'nai Zion, fraternal ZOA; Temple B'nai Zion, Bloomfield, NY; hon pres, JNF, Newark, NJ, hon vice-pres, NJ Region. Ed, contbr, Bull, Temple B'nai Zion. Recipient: F, Amer Inst Chems, 1923; Golden Legion, Cooper Union, 1965; Natl Bulletin Award, United Syn Amer, 1967. Home: 2307 Aetna, Woodland Hills, Cal.

ELLISON, Arnold Daniel, US, executive dir; b. Charleston,SC, Mar 4, 1917; s. Charles and Frances (Reisman); AB, U of NC, 1937, MA, 1940; m. Anne Witten, Sep 11, 1943; c: Paula Woolf, Elaine. Exec dir, Dist Grand Lodge B'nai B'rith since 1963; bus mgr, Fla League of Munic, 1945-46; mgr, Globe Shoe Stores Inc, 1946-58; dist membership dir, B'nai B'rith, 1958-63. Sgt, US Army, 1940-45. Mem: Pi Sigma Alpha. Home: 1738 N Holly Lane NE, Atlanta, Ga. Office: 805 Peachtree St NE, Atlanta, Ga.

ELLISON, Cyril Lee, US, advertising exec; b. NYC, Dec 11, 1916; s. John and Rose; m. Anne Nottonson, June 4, 1941. Vice-pres: Franklin and Joseph Advt Agcy, since 1969; advt dir: American Artist Mag; Art Director's Annual; Art School Directory, 1939-62. Served WW II, 1942-46. Chmn, bd trustees, pres, Westbury Heb Cong, 1955; cdr, Advt Mens post, Amer Legion, 1954-60. Contbr to profsl jours. Recipient: Gray-Russo Advt Man of Year, 1957; award, Amer Legion. Home: 444 E 82 St, New York, NY. Office: 641 Lexington Ave, New York, NY.

ELLMAN, Shimon, Isr, engineer, business exec; b. Minsk, Russ, Dec 10, 1905; s. Hellman and Malca (Eisenberg); grad Polytech Inst, Leningrad, 1925; dipl, agric, chem engr, U Nancy, Fr,1932; m. Aviva Ismojik, Aug 28, 1930; c: Yael Moritz, Dan. Mgn dir: AMPA, Ltd; AMPA Inves; mgr, partner: Amcor; Amron Elecs; Pleese Mech Works; Amzur (Rock Wool); Redmond Amcor (Motors), all since 1953; fmr: instr, Agric Research Sta, Rehovot; agron, settlement dept, JA for Pal; mgn dir, Gen Trade and Engr Ltd; mgr, Isr Inves and Finance; Gen Tyre and Rubber; Isr Commercial Consortium; Mehadrin; mem: purchasing mission, Min of Defence, in Can and US; adv econ council, Govt of Isr. Pres, Export Inst of Isr, since 1961; mem: presidium, Mfrs Assn, Isr; fmr: pres, Isr Importers and Wholesalers Assn; vice-pres, Isr C of C. Contbr articles to agric jours. Recipient: Gold medal, Agric Inst, Nancy, Fr, 1932. Spec interest: agric research. Home: 6 Rembrandt St, Tel Aviv, Isr. Office: 16 Petah Tikva Rd, Tel Aviv, Israel.

ELLMANN, Richard, US, educator, author; b. Highland Park, Mich, Mar 15, 1918; s. James and Jeanette (Barsook); BA, Yale U, 1939, MA, 1941, PhD, 1947; B Litt, Trinity Coll, Dublin, Ir, 1947; m. Mary Donahue, Aug 12, 1949; c:Stephen, Maud, Lucy. Goldsmiths' Prof, Eng lit, Oxford U, since 1970; prof, Eng, Yale U, 1968-70; Franklin Bliss Snyder Prof, Eng, Northwestern U, 1963-68, fac mem, since 1951; instr, Harvard U, 1942-43, 47-48, Briggs-Copeland asst prof, Eng, 1948-51; f, Sch of Letters, Ind U, 1956, 1960, sr f, since 1966; visiting prof, U Chgo, 1959, 1969. USN, 1943-45. Cons, Ford Found, 1959; chmn, Eng Inst, 1961-62; f, Amer Acad Arts and Scis, since 1969; mem: exec council, MLA 1960-64; Phi Beta Kappa; Chi Delta Theta. Author: Yeats: The Man and the Masks, 1948; The Identity of Years, 1954; James Joyce, 1959; Eminent Domain, 1967; ed bd, MLA, since 1968. Recipient: Rockefeller F, 1946; grant, Amer Phil Soc, 1953; Kenyon Rev F, 1954; Longview Found Award, 1955; Guggenheim F, 1950, 1958; Natl Book Award 1960. Home: New College, Oxford U, Eng.

ELLMANN, William Marshall, US, lawyer; b. Highland Park, Mich, Mar 23, 1921; s. James and Jeannette (Barsook); att: Occidental Coll, 1939-40; U Mich, 1940-46; LLB, Wayne State U, 1951; m. Sheila Frenkel, Nov 1, 1953; c: Douglas, Carol, Robert. Partner, Ellmann & Ellmann; spec asst atty gen, Detroit, Mich, since 1964; chmn, spec comm atty gen, to study use of state troops in emergencies. US Army, 1942-46. Mem: Detroit Bar assns, past vice-chmn, PR comm; commn, Mich State Bar, past pres; Amer Arbitration Assn; Sigma Nu Phi; delg, House of Delgs, Amer Bar Assn; bd dirs, Hillel Day Sch; ADL, Detroit; JNF; Shalom Post, JWV; fmr, mem exec comm, Inst for Continuing Legal Educ. Contbr to legal jours. Home: 28000 Weymouth St, Farmington, Mich. Office: 1800 Penobscot Bldg, Detroit, Mich.

ELLNER, Charles, US, attorney; b. NYC, Aug 12, 1901; s. Saul and Clara (Osias); BA, cum laude, Columbia U, 1922, JD, Law Sch, 1925; m. Adelaide Taub, 1930 (decd); c: Peter, Caryl Rubenfeld; m. 2nd, Minna Goldberg, June 10, 1952. Pvt practice, Jamaica, NY, since 1925; govt appeal agt, Selective Service, 1944-47; asso agt, Registrant's Adv Bd, 1941-42, asso mem, 1942-46; spec dep atty gen, NY State Elections and Fraud Bur, 1944; counsel, Jamaica Natl Bank, NY, 1930-35; spec counsel: NY State Dent Soc, 1949; First Jud Dist Dent Soc, 1948; Tenth Jud Dist Dent Soc, 1955-56. F: Intl Inst Arts and Letters, 1961; Intl Acad Law and Sci; arbitrator, Amer Arbitration Assn, since 1941; mem: NY State Trial Lawyers Assn; Amer, NY State ,Queens Co, Bar Assns; NY Co Lawyers Assn; Acad Political Sci; Jamaica C of C; Briarwood J Cen; Queens Council, Boy Scouts; Columbia Coll, Columbia Law Sch, Queens Co Columbia Law Sch Alumni Assns; Phi Beta Kappa; fmr: mem: B'nai B'rith; Jamaica Estates Assn; Co committeeman, election dist capt, Dem Party, Queens Co, NY; delg, NY State Dem Jud Conv; co-found, pres, Public Sch 131 Comty Cen; Jamaica chmn, Phi Beta Kappa Defense Drive; Jamaica estates chmn, Boy Scouts Fund Drives; co-org, Boy Scouts Cub Pack 130; clubs: Jefferson Dem; Jamaica Lawyers; Queens Lawyers of FJP; fmr: Econ; Lions; City; Commercial of Queens Village. Contbr to profsl jours. Recipient: Hubbard Math Medal, 1919; Pulitzer, Regents and Law Sch Scholarships; Selective Service Medal, 1947. Hobbies: sculpture, painting, photography, fishing. Home: 140-10 84 Dr, Jamaica, NY Oflce: 161-19 Jamaica Ave, Jamaica, NY.

ELMAN, Irving, US, writer, producer; b. Paterson, NJ; s. Joseph and Anne (Nirenberg); BS, CCNY; att: NYU; Columbia U;

m. Mildred McDaniel, Sep 28, 1946; c: Jeffrey, Corey. Vice-pres, prog devl, Arena Producs, for TV: supervisory produc, High Chaparral; produc: Slattery's People; Ben Casey; The Eleventh Hour; writing credits: TV: High Chaparral; Ben Casey; Slattery's People; Eleventh Hour; Hallmark Hall of Fame; Studio One; US Steel Hour; Kraft Theatre; Alcoa-Goodyear; Armstrong Circle Theatre; Pulitzer Prize Playhouse; Celanese Theatre; Alfred Hitchcock Presents; Climax; Line-Up; Danger; Zane Grey Theatre; Janet Dean; June Allyson Show; Bourbon Street Beat; Matinée Theatre; My Three Sons; Cain's Hundred; The Rifleman; Mama; The Invisible Man; Appointment With Adventure; His Honor, Homer Bell; Tales of Tomorrow; Man Against Crime; Follow The Sun; Claudia; True Story; The Mask; The Investigator; Crime Photographer; The Legionaire; Suspense; A Date With Judy; Way of the World; plays: on Broadway: Uncle Willie; The Brass Ring; The First Million; off Broadway: Three Kisses; Strangers and Lovers; feature pictures: Backlash; Strange Journey; The Crimson Key; Roses are Red; Challenge; Thirteen Lead Soldiers; Accomplice; Jewels of Brandenburg. Cpl, US Army, 1942-43. Mem: Writers Guild of Amer; ASCAP; Natl Acad TV Arts and Scis; Natl Acad Recording Arts and Scis. Recipient: Emmy nominations: outstanding dramatic series, Slattery's People; outstanding dramatic prog: Rally Round Your Own Flag, Mister; Golden Globe Nomination, outstanding dramatic prog, The Eleventh Hour; Alexander Graham Bell Award, outstanding dramatic contrib, A Woods Full of Question Marks, Ben Casey. Home: 430 Puerto del Mar, Pacific Palisades, Cal.

ELMAN, Philip, US, lawyer; b. Paterson, NJ, Mar 14, 1918; s. Jacob and Anne (Nirenberg); AB, CCNY, 1936; LLB, Harvard U, 1939; m. Ella Shalit Dec 21, 1947; c: Joseph, Peter, Anthony. Commn, FTC, since 1961; law clerk to Judge Calvert Magruder, US Court of Appeals, Boston, Mass, 1939-40; atty, FCC, 1940-41; law clerk to Justice Felix Frankfurter, US Supr Court, 1941-43; with: Off Fgn Econ Coord, Dept of State, 1943-44; Solicitor Gen's Off, Justice Dept, 1944-45; legal adv, Off of Mil Govt, Berlin, Ger, 1945-46; asst to Solicitor Gen, Justice Dept, 1946-61; argued numerous cases before US Supr Court. Mem: DC, Amer, Fed Bar Assns; Amer Law Inst; Harvard Law Sch Assn; Phi Beta Kappa, CCNY. Ed, Of Law and Men, papers and addresses of Felix Frankfurter, 1965. Recipient: Rockefeller Public Service Award, 1967. Home: 6719 Brigadoon Dr, Bethesda, Md. Office: FTC, Washington, DC.

ELOIT, Jacques (Eljasiewicz), Fr, roentgenologist; b. Le Puy, Fr, Apr 14, 1943; s. Herzla and Liba (Schubert); BSc, U, Nancy, Fr, 1961, DM, 1969. Roentgenologist, Nancy Hosp, since 1967, on staff since 1964; res: Maison Neuve Hosp, 1969-70; Inst of Card, 1970, both Montreal, Can. Vice-pres, Nancy sect, Union des Médecins, Dentistes, Pharmaciens, Amis d'Israel, mem: natl council, Fr; Fr-Can Assn. Hobbies: photography, skiing. Home: 13, rue Jeanne d'Arc, Nancy, Fr. Office: Hôpital Central, Nancy, Fr.

ELON, Menachem, Isr, educator; b. Düsseldorf, Ger, Nov 1, 1923; s. Shimeon and Sarah (Brand) Fetter; in Isr since 1935; ordained rabbi, Yeshivat Hebron, 1944; dipl, Tel Aviv Sch of Law and Econ, 1948; MA, Heb U, 1954, DJur, fac law, 1961; m. Ruth Buxbaum, Mar 9, 1949; c: Arie, Joseph, Benjamin, Avital, Mordechai. Prof, J law, Heb U, dir, Inst for Research in J Law, since 1963; secy to Finance Comm, Knesset, 1950-51, atty, 1951-54; sr prin asst to atty gen, 1954-62; adv on J law, Isr Min of Justice, 1958-66; guest lectr, Oxford U, 1967. Lt, Mil Advocate Unit, IDF, 1948-49. Adv bd, Inst of J Studies; lectr in Talmud, study group, Knesset; Disciplinary off, Heb U, 1965-66; mem: B'nai B'rith; comm appd by Min of Justice: on replacement of charters of the Mejelle; to prepare a bill on principles of Law and Contracts. Author: Freedom of Debtor's Person in Jeewish Law, 1964; Religious Legislation in the Laws of the State of Israel and Within the Jurisdiction of The Civil and Rabbinical Courts, 1968; ed, Indices to the Responsa of Jewish Law, 1965; div ed, Div of J Law, Ency Judaica, 1967; contbr articles to jours. Recipient: Moritz and Charlotte Varburg Memorial Fund for J Studies, 1961. Home: 12 Ibn Shaprut St, Jerusalem, Isr. Office: Hebrew U, Jerusalem, Isr.

ELOUL, Kosso, US, sculptor; b. Russ, Jan 22, 1920; s. Leib and Hanna (Shapira) Skorohod; att Chgo Art Inst; m. Rita Letendre. One-man exhb: Tel Aviv Mus; Jerusalem Artists Assn Pavillion; Gal Rina, Jerusalem; Gal Topazia Alliata, Rome; Gal Camille Hebert, Montreal; David Stuart Gals, LA; Gal of Isr Art, NY; J Mus, NY; Jerrold Morris, Toronto; Gordon Gal, Tel Aviv; group shows: Jerusalem; Haifa; Tel Aviv; Isr 10th Anniversary; Tel Aviv Mus; Venice; Antwerp; Aus; Yugo; Paris; Spoleto; Milan; Ein Harod Mus; Berlin; Vienna; Art Isr, toured US and Can; Montreal; Pittsburgh Intl; London; Paris; Detroit; Cal; LA; graphics: Tokyo; LA; Wash, DC; selected commissions: Heb U, Jerusalem; Tel Aviv 50th Anniversary Exposition; Yad Vashem; El Al Airlines Bldg; Fed Steel Corp, Long Beach, Cal; Brandeis U. Fmr artist-in-res, Cal State Coll. Mem, Academia Tiberina, It. Home: 55 W 74 St, New York, NY.

ELOVIC, Albert, It, business exec; b. Sobrance, Czech, Sep 13, 1917; s. Jakob and Mina (Grünstein); in It since 1967; law deg, Charles U, Prague, 1939; m. Ada Benco, Dec 12, 1947. Gen mgr, vice pres, Hotel Corp of Amer, since 1958; vice chief of staff, Czech Army in Russ, 1942-45; diplomatic envoy, Czech govt, to UNRRA, Rum, 1945-48; pres, Soimarin Export-Import, 1948-58. Col, Czech Army, 1942-45; was three times condemned to death, by Ger, Russ, Hung; last condemnation commuted to forced lab, Russ; set free, joined Czech Army in Russ, 1942; as delg to UNRRA, helped J getting illegally to Isr. Recipient: numerous high Russ and Czech decorations. Home: 78 Aleardi St, Mestre Venezia, It. Office: Hotel Sonesta, 12 Galvani St, Milan, It.

ELOVITZ, Mark Harvey, US, rabbi; b. Pittsburgh, Pa, May 20, 1938; s. Meyer and Lillian (Werner); BA, NYU, 1960; att Heb U, Jerusalem, 1962-63; MHL, ordained rabbi, JTSA, 1964; m. Helen Altheim, Oct 13, 1963; c: Rachel, Michal. Rabbi, Cong Beth El, Fairfield, since 1969; asst rabbi, Temple Beth El, Cedarhurst, Conn, 1967-69. Chaplain, capt, USAF, 1964-67. Mem: RA; Conn Valley RA; Acad Rel and Mh; Assn J Chaplains; Phi Beta Kappa, NYU. Contbr to J mil, rel jours. Recipient: Commendation medal, USAF, 1967. Hobby: tennis. Home: 128 Drake Lane, Fairfield, Conn. Study: 1200 Fairfield Wds Rd, Fairfield, Conn.

ELROM, Gideon, Isr, business exec; b. Jerusalem, July 20, 1922; s. Matityahu and Pnina (Kleinert) Gordon; grad: JA Inst, Jerusalem, 1948; att staff coll, USAF, Ala, 1952; MBA, Columbia U, NYC, 1963; m. Erella Ziv, Dec 1, 1963; c: Shironne, Sahar, Heelat. Pres, Teshet Ltd, since 1968; vice-pres El Al Isr Airlines, since 1968, with El Al since 1964. Col, IAF, 1953-64. Home: 3 Haofek St, Savyon, Isr. Office: 32 Ben Yehuda St, Tel Aviv. Isr.

ELSON, Alex, US, attorney; b. Kiev, Russ, Apr 17, 1905; s. Jacob and Rebecca (Brodsky); in US since 1906; PhB, U Chgo, 1925, JD, 1928; m. Miriam Almond, July 6, 1933; c: Jacova, Karen. Pvt practice, since 1945; lectr, Northwestern U Law Sch, since 1960; mem, panel of arbitrators, Fed Mediation and Conciliation Service, since 1945; charter mem, Natl Acad of Arbitrators, since 1947; trial atty, Legal Aid Bur and United Charities, Chgo, 1929-34; lectr: Northwestern U Law Sch, 1931-39; U of Chgo, 1933-50; Yale U Law Sch, 1946; asso with Tolman, Chandler and Dickinson, law firm, 1934-38; regional atty, wage and hour div, US Dept Lab, 1938-41; asst gen counsel and regional atty, Chgo OPA, 1941-45; public mem, War Lab Bd, 1945; chmn, Chgo City Rent Comm, 1947-48; referee, RR Adjustment Bd, 1951. Pres, J Family Comty Service, 1951-54; chmn: devl of law comm, 1949-52; candidates' comm, since 1958, both Chgo Bar Assn; Ill Bd Mh Comms, since 1961; vice-chmn: Ill Comm on Children, 1953-58; Ill Div, ACLU, 1959; mem: Amer Law Inst; bd mgrs, Chgo Bar Assn, 1945-46; adv comm, Wfr Council of Metrop Chgo, Chgo Housing Auth, 1956; bd trustees, Hull House; cons, Ford Found. Author: Civil Practice Forms, 1934; co-author: Civil Practice Forms, Ill-Fed, 1952, rev, 1965. Home: 5642 S Dorchester Ave, Chicago, Ill. Office: 11 S LaSalle St, Chicago, Ill.

ELSON, David, Isr, biochemist; b. Kane, Pa, Aug 7, 1919; s. Charles and Sheba (Shatzkin); in Isr since 1955; BA, U of Pa, Phila, 1941; att NYU, 1946-47; PhD, Columbia U, NY, 1951; m. Pnina Spitnik, July 26, 1956; c: Ari. Research sci, biochem, Weizmann Inst, Rehovot, since 1955; research sci, Columbia U, 1951-55. US Army, 1942-45. Mem: Eur Molecular Biol Org; Isr Biochem Soc; Isr Chem Soc; Amer Soc of Biol Chems. Contbr to profsl jours. Home: Neveh Weizmann, Rehovot, Isr. Office: Weizmann Inst, Rehovot, Isr.

ELSON, Harry, US, business exec, communal, civic worker; b. Albany, NY, Aug 2, 1909; s. Myer and Sadie (Lincoln); att St Johns U Sch of Law; m. Esther Cohn, Oct 14, 1929; c: Edward. Owner, Atlantic News Agcy Inc, since 1953, pres since 1957; exec vice pres, treas, Amer Service Co, since

1961; pres, Airport News Corp, since 1960; exec vice-pres, Amer Publs Overseas, since 1960; partner, Elson Book Stores; gen mgr, Norfolk News Agcy, 1936-53. Found, first chmn and trustee natl bd, AJComm; PR Bur, Norfold Cmty Council; co-chmn, Cmty Chest, commercial div; dir, past treas, Oheb Sholom Temple, all Norfolk; trustee, JPSA; mem: bd: NCCJ; J Children's Service; Council for Periodical Distributors Assn; natl exec, AJComm; C of C; Va Camellia Soc; B'nai B'rith; Atlantic Coast Independent Distributors Assn; Natl Tercentenary Comm; Amer J Hist Soc; Soc Friends Touro Syn; fmr: pres: Vaad Hakashruth; JCC; vice-pres, J Comty Cen; co-chmn, UJA; delg, Natl Comty Relations Adv Council; clubs: Standard; Commerce, both Atlanta; Hague; Downtown of Norfolk; Elks; Airport Exec. Home: 3649 Peachtree Rd, Atlanta, Ga. Offices: 3875 Green Industrial Way, Chamblee, Ga; 878 Memorial Dr SE, Atlanta, Ga; 21 rue de Berri, Paris, Fr.

ELTON, Geoffrey Rudolph, Eng, educator, historian; b. Tübingen, Ger, Aug 17, 1921; s. Victor and Eva (Sommer) Ehrenberg; in Eng since 1939; BA, U London, PhD, 1943; DLitt, Cambridge U, Eng; m. Sheila Lambert, Aug 20, 1952. Prof, Eng Constitutional Hist, Cambridge, since 1967, on fac since 1949. Author: The Tudor Revolution in Government, 1953; England under the Tudors, 1955; Star Chamber Stories, 1958; The Tudor Constitution, 1960; Reformation Europe, 1963; The Practice of History, 1967; The Body of the Whole Realm, 1969; Sources of History: England 1200-1640, pub 1969; ed: New Cambridge Modern History, Vol 2, 1958; Renaissance and Reformation, 1963; contbr to profsl jours. F: Royal Hist Soc; Brit Acad. Hobbies: squash rackets, joinery, gardening. Home: 30 Millington Rd, Cambridge, Eng. Office: Clare Coll, Cambridge, Eng.

EMIOT, Israel, US, writer; b. Pol, Jan 15, 1909. Coord, cultural events in Yiddish, J Cen of Rochester. Author: 4 books of poetry; contbr poems and short stories to mags, to press, to Yiddish Daily, all Pol, 6 books of poetry and short stories, US; contbr to J Forward, Yiddish newspapers, mags. Recipient: Prize, best book of poetry, JBCA, 1962; Kessel Prize, Mex; prize, World Cong J Culture, for book of poetry. Home: 173 Comkey Ave, Rochester, NY. Office: 380 Andrews St, Rochester, NY.

EMSHEIMER, Arthur, Switz, attorney; b. Pforzheim, Ger, Mar 8, 1900; s. Oskar and Alice (Weil); att U's: Heidelberg; Munich; Berlin, 1918-22; D Jur; div; c: Herbert, Hanna Lewis. Dir, Schweizenische Zentialstelle fin Tlischtlingsholfe, Zurich, since 1967; fmr ed, info service bull, legal council; fmr, judge, Ger. Mem: Kartell Convent. Home: Apt House Seefeldquai 1, Zurich, Switz. Office: Kinkelstr 2, Zurich, Switz.

ENDE, Asher Harry, US, attorney, government admnr; b. NYC, Nov 8, 1914; s. Isidor and Julia (Korner); BA, Bklyn Coll, 1934; LLB, Bklyn Law Sch, 1937; MPA, NYU, 1940; m. Jeanne Greenberg, July 2, 1939; c: Kenneth, Neil. Dep chief, common carrier bur, FCC, chief off, satellite communications, hearing examiner, 1961-64; chief, rates and revenue requirement, Common Carrier Bur, 1950-61; chmn, US delg to confs of Intl Telecommunications Union, since 1951. Lt, USAF, 1943-46. Prin contrib: helped draft Communications Satellite Art; mem delg: which drafted intl agreements for satellite communications; numerous interagcy comms on all facets of communications policy; participated in drafting basic policies in communications field by FCC. Asst secy, UJA, Wash, DC; mem: bd trustees, JCC, Wash, DC; J Comty Cen, Wash, DC; fmr: bd trustees: UJA; Cong Beth El, Montgomery Co, Md. Recipient: awards for exceptional performance duties, FCC. Home: 5845 Marbury Rd, Bethesda, Md. Office: 1919 M St, Washington, DC.

ENGEL, George L, US, physician, educator; b. NYC, Dec 10, 1913; s. Adolph and Esther (Libman); BA, Dartmouth Coll, 1934; MD, Johns Hopkins U, 1938; m. Evelyn Lipman, Oct 30, 1938; c: Peter, Betty. Prof, psycht, U Rochester Sch of Med, since 1957, fac mem since 1946; lectr, SUNY, since 1959; asst prof, med and psycht, U Cincinnati, 1945-46, fac mem since 1942; asst att psycht, Cincinnati Gen Hosp, 1943-44, on staff, 1942-44; cons: neuropsycht, Off US Surg Gen, 1948-49; Natl Adv Mh Council, USPHS, both 1949-53. Pres, Amer Psychosomatic Soc, 1952-53, 1953-54, and since 1969; mem: f comm, Found Fund for Research in Psycht, 1956-61; Amer Soc for Clinical Inves; Amer Psychan Assn; AAAS; Amer Soc for Electroencephalography; Amer Psycht Assn; AAUP; Rochester Acad of Med; Monroe Co Med Soc; NY

Acad of Scis; W NY Psychoanalytic Soc; asso mem, Chgo Psychoanalytic Soc, since 1956. Author: Fainting, 1950, 2nd ed, 1962; Psychological Development in Health and Disease, 1962; ed bd: Jour of Psychiatric Research, since 1959; Perspectives in Biol and Med, since 1957; Psychosomatic Med, since 1954. Contbr to med jours. Recipient: Research f, Dazian Found, 1941; Alexander Award, Inst for Psychan, 1962. Home: 91 San Gabriel Dr, Rochester, NY. Office: 260 Crittendon Blvd, Rochester, NY.

ENGEL, Gerald, US, organization exec, rabbi; b. NYC, Aug 10, 1919; s. Marcus and Lena (Jabloner); BA, Yeshiva Coll, 1940; ordained rabbi, Rabbi Isaac Elchanan Sem, 1944; MA, U of Me, 1947; EdD, Tchrs Coll, Columbia U, 1954; m. Marilyn Kopelowitz, July 7, 1952; c: Liba, Mayer, Moshe, Yehudah. Dir, B'nai B'rith Hillel Found, Purdue U, since 1955; asso dir, Boston Area, 1944-45; state dir, Me, 1945-47; dir, U of Fla, 1947-49. Delg, State of Ind, White House Conf on Children and Youth, 1960; fmr pres, Ind Bd Rabbis, 1959-60. Author: study of Amer perm res in Isr in 1967; of Amers who returned from Isr, 1968; contbr to psych and J jours. Hobbies: camping, photography. Home: 448 Littleton St, W Lafayette, Ind. Office: 912 W State St, W Lafayette, Ind.

ENGEL, Irving M, US, lawyer, communal leader; b. Birmingham, Ala, Oct 19, 1891; s. Michael and Sophie (Kronenberg); LLB, cum laude, Yale Law Sch, 1913; hon: D Litt, Dropsie Coll for Heb Cognate Learning, 1958; DHum L, HUC-JIR, 1958; m. Katherine Asher, Jan 14, 1926 (decd); c: Susan Levy. Mem, Konta, Kirchwey and Engel, NYC, 1926-43, successor firm, Engel, Judge and Miller, NYC, since 1944; pvt practice in Birmingham, Ala, until 1913; lectr, real estate and taxation for: Practising Law Inst; Amer Bar Assn; NYU; dir: Hudson and Manhattan RR Co, 1936-46; Lawyers Title, Corp, NY, 1946-48; mem: title ins adv comm, Title Guarantee; bd of govs, 1948-51, arbitration bd, leg comm, Real Estate Bd of NY; candidate for Cong, Dem and Lib Parties, NYC, 1950. Pres: AJComm, 1954-59, hon pres, since 1959; and found, Ala Jr C of C, 1920; fmr pres, Educ Found for J Girls; mem, Truman's Spec Mission, inauguration Pres Remon of Panama, 1952; chmn: exec comm, AJComm, 1949-54; bd, Educ Found for J Girls; J Defense Appeal Campaign, NYC, 1952 policy bd, Citizens Comm on DPs, 1947-50; NY Comm for Dem Voters, 1960-61; adv council, since 1962; policy and planning comm, NY Citizens for Kennedy and Johnson, 1960; co-chmn: governing bd, Consultative Council of J Orgs accredited to UNESCO, 1954-59; NYC Comm on Amer J Tercentenary, 1955; vice-chmn, mem policy comm, Amer Comm for Isr Tenth Anniversary Celebration, 1958; mem, bd dirs: Natl Comm Against Discrimination in Housing; Citizens Comm on DP; Natl Comm on Segregation in Nation's Capital; President's Comm on Govt Contract Compliance, 1951-53; mem: Council on Fgn Relations; fgn policy subcomm, Natl Adv Coun il, Dem Natl Comm; State Comm on Public Security, 1956-58; delg, Ger-Amer Conf on E-W Tensions, Bad Godesburg, Ger, 1959, Wash, DC, 1961, Berlin, Ger, 1962; alternate delg, from NY Co, Dem Natl Conv, 1952, 1956; headed missions for AJComm to: Paris, Tunisia, Algeria and Morocco, 1954; Paris, Rome, Isr, Tunisia and Morocco, 1957; Arg, Brazil, Chile and Peru, 1958; clubs: Harmonie; Yale; U. Author: Justice Black After Seven Years, 1944; Income Tax and Real Estate, 1945; ed, Yale Law Sch Jour. Recipient: Grand Officer of Order of Micham Iftikhar (Tunisian Legion of Honor), 1954; Chevalier of French Legion of Honor, 1957. Home: 24 Central Park S, New York, NY. Office: 52 Vanderbilt Ave, New York, NY.

ENGEL, Joseph Henry, US, operations analyst; b. NYC, May 15, 1922; s. Arthur and Jennie (Gotthilf); BMath, CCNY, 1942; att Yale U, 1946; MA, U Wis, 1947; DMath, 1949; m. Beverly Rosenblum May 2, 1943; c: Wendy, Stern, Eric, David. Dir, Planning and Research Services, since 1968; mem: bd trustees: Cybernetics Research, since 1969; Inst for Creative Studies, since 1969; bd dirs, Columbia Computer Corp, since 1968; dir, operation evaluation group, Cen for Naval Analyses, 1962-65, asst chief sci, 1965-67; spec tech asst to vice-pres, COMSAT, 1967-68. Lt, US Army Air Corps, 1942-46. Prin contribs: devl: important math models of various aspects of mil, mineralogical, other ind operations; computer-based financial forecasting sys. F, AAAS; trustee, Wash Operations Research Council; cons, operations research, Fulbright Hays Adv Screening Comm in Math; US repr, NATO adv panel on operational research; mem: council, Oprs Research Soc of Amer, past pres; Sigma Xi; Pi Mu Epsilon; fmr: pres, Woodburn Elem

Sch PTA; secy, mem, bd dirs: Holmes Run Acres Recreation Assn; Mil Operations Research Soc; club, Cosmos. Author: The Mathematics of Combat, 1970; contbr to Jour of Oprs Research Soc of Amer. Recipient: Tremaine Gift, 1940; hon mention, Belden Math Competition, 1941, both CCNY; decorations: DFC; Air Medal; AP Theatre Ribbon; Amer Theatre Ribbon; WW II Victory Medal. Hobbies: chess, swimming, reading, travel, politics. Home: 7200 Selkirk Dr, Bethesda, Md. Office: 950 L'Enfant Plaza S, SW, Washington, DC.

ENGEL, Karel Nathaniel, Eng, geologist; b. Prague, Czech, May 23, 1921; s. Frederick and Nelly (Thieberger); desc of Rabbi Akiva Eger; in Eng since 1939; BSc, Leeds U, 1944; m. Ruth Cohen, Dec 30, 1946; c: Uri, Shulamith, Daniela, Tamar, Shimon. Dir, Elmat Ltd, chartered engr, since 1965, mgr, 1947-65; tech dir, Mason and Barry Ltd, 1960-64. J Brig, WW II. Prin contribs: invention of various devices for off-shore drilling, underwater construction; originator of intl nomenclature for large diameter rotary core drilling equipment. F, Geological Soc; mem, Instn of Mining and Metallurgy. Author: Rotary Core Drilling Equipment, 1965. Home: 67 Roehampton Lane, London, SW 15, Eng. Office: 32 Maida Vale, London, W9, Eng.

ENGEL, Lehman, US, composer, conductor; b. Jackson, Miss, Sept 14, 1910; s. Ellis and Juliette (Lehman); att: Cincinnati Conservatory of Music, 1926-27; Cincinnati Coll of Music, 1927-29; grad, Juilliard Sch, 1934; hon DMus, Boguslawski Coll of Music, Chgo, 1944. Conductor, theater: Lil Abner; Shangri-La; Fanny; Wonderful Town; Gilbert and Sullivan Operettas; A Month of Sundays; Bless You All; The Liar; Alive and Kicking; Macbeth; Bonanza Bound; Call Me Mister; Shadow Play; The Little Dog Laughed; Johnny Johnson; Destry Rides Again; Goldilocks; Jamaica; The Consul; musical dir, State Fair Musicals, Dallas, Tex, 1949-52; Broadway Plays; Call Me Madame; Student Prince; The Wizard of Oz; Carousel; A Tree Grows in Brooklyn; Miss Liberty; The Merry Widow; Song of Norway; I Married an Angel; Where's Charlie? Annie Get Your Gun; Desert Song; Roberta; Brigadoon; Maytime; High Button Shoes; Showboat; Chocolate Soldier; Pal Joey; Bitter Sweet; Bloomer Girl; Rose Marie; Up in Central Park; concert conductor: The Soldier, Carnegie Hall, 1956; Bklyn Acad of Music; Libr of Cong, Wash, DC; William and Mary Coll; Wells Coll; State Tchrs Coll of Va; Bklyn Inst; Mus Natural Hist; Sarah Lawrence Coll; Fordham U; NY World's Fair; guest conductor: Sym Orch, Jackson, Miss, 1951; NY Philharmonic, Lewisohn Stadium, 1951; Dallas Sym, 1951; Town Hall, NY, 1958; Boston Sym Orch, 1969; Turkish State Opera, 1969; composed and conducted music for films; composer, dance music for: Martha Graham; Doris Humphrey, Charles Weidman; Radio City Music Hall Ballet; Gluck Sandor; Felicia Sorell composed and conducted music for TV shows; many recordings on Victor, Columbia, Decca labels; lecturer, Cincinnati Coll Conservatory of Music; mem, fac, Salzburg Sem in Amer Studies, Salzburg, Aus, 1968. Pres: Arrow Music Press, Inc, since 1938; Concert Artists Guild, Inc, since 1957; mem: adv bd, Sch of Performing Arts; bd dirs, Everyman Asso; composers commn, League of Composers; adv bd, Music Sch, Henry St Settlement; Bc Music, Inc; Sigma Alpha Mu. Author: The American Musical Theater-A Consideration, 1968; contbr to mags and profsl jours. Recipient: Antoinette Perry Award, 1950, 1953; gold medal, City of Jackson, Miss, 1958; decoration from the Repub of Aus, 1968; Scroll from the Consular Law Soc for Outstanding Achievement in the Theater, 1968. Home: 350 E 54 St, New York, NY.

ENGELBERG, Louis, US, rabbi; b. NYC, June 28, 1910; s. Philip; BA, MA, Yeshiva U; m. Hannah Katz, Dec 9, 1943; c: Abraham, Etta Einstadter, Jacqueline, Abigail, Philip. Rabbi: Taylor Rd Syn, since 1939; Elmira, NY, 1937-39. Capt, US Army, 1943-46. Pres, Yeshiva Coll Alumni Assn; vice-pres, RabCA; exec bd, Rel Zionists Amer; mem: B'nai B'rith; UA Interrel Council. Home: 3485 Blanche Rd, Cleveland Heights, O. Study: 1970 S Taylor Rd, Cleveland Heights, O.

ENGELBERG, Peter Jose, Guat, industrialist; b. Rzeszow, Pol, Apr 3, 1920; s. Chaim and Berta (Karp); in Guat since 1947; att Lwow Coll, Pol, 1939-41; m. Regina Stelcner, Mar 14, 1948; c: Betty Terun, Fryda, Jaime. Co-prop: Engelberg, Benchoam and Cia, since 1959; Rene Lemus and Cia, since 1966; Engelberg and Monzon Cia, 1948-56; prop, Tinorieria Iris, 1956-59; found and co-prop: Fabrica de tejidos Iris;

Fabrica de enguatados Relepen. Pres, Centro Hebreo de Guatemala, directive, 1960-62, mem triumvirate, 1962-64; vice-pres, Consejo Central de la Comunidad Judia de Guatemala; delg, Economic Conf Jerusalem, 1968; mem: Camara de Industria; Club Deportive Israelita. Home: Av Las Americas 17-71, Guatemala City, Guat. Office: 50 Calle 17-39, Guatemala City, Guat.

ENGELMAN, Nestor Ariel, Uruguay, communal leader; b. Salto, Uruguay, Mar 5, 1938; s. Martin and Berta (Loschkin); LLD, DSS, dipl, Fac of Law, Montevideo, 1969; m. Perla Gerstenfeld, Oct 22, 1966; c: Shulamit. Exec secy, J Cen Comm, J Hist prof, J Inst, both since 1967; gen secy, J Students Org, 1958-63; pres, J Youth Council, 1964-67; dir, La Voz Semanal, weekly, 1967-69; found, Zionist Students S Amer Fed (FUSSA); lectr, communal orgs; att: Sem for fgn students' leaders, Isr, 1962; World J Youth Planning Conf, NY, 1965; participant confs of J Youth: Arg, 1960; Uruguay, 1961; Brazil, 1965. Exec mem, Uruguayan Zionist Org; plenum mem, Tnuat Aliah; fmr: pres, J Youth Cen; co-pres, Latin Amer J Youth Council; presidium mem, UJA, Youth div. Contbr articles to J press; mem: J Grads Assn, Chaim Weizmann; Bar Assn. Home: Br España 2921, Montevideo, Uruguay.

ENGELSOHN, Harold Shmuel, US, educator; b. Bklyn, NY, Sep, 13, 1938; s. William and Ethel (Simckes); BA, Bklyn Coll, 1959; att Yale U, 1959-60; MA, NYU, 1968; m. Esther Dick, Mar 9, 1964; c: Rochayl, Naeema, Moshe. Coord Math, Kingsborough Comty Coll, since 1968, dep chmn, math, 1966-68; lectr, math, Bklyn Coll, since 1964. Pres, Canarsie J Cen; vice pres, Assn Orthodox J Tchrs, NYC; mem: Sigma Xi; Amer Math Assn; Math Assn of Amer; NY State Tchrs Math; Natl Council Tchrs Math; Pi Mu Epsilon, Bklyn Coll, past pres. Co-author: set of math textbooks; contbr to book revs in math, Judaica. Recipient: Woodrow Wilson F Award, 1959. Home: 680 E 79 St, Brooklyn, NY. Office: Kingsborough Comty Coll, 1200 Oriental Blvd, Brooklyn, NY.

ENGLANDER, Benjamin H, US, rabbi; b. Pal, Sep 20, 1908; s. David and Esther (Stampfer); desc of Joshua Stampfer, found of Petah Tikva Colony in Pal; in US since 1911; BS, Lewis Inst of Tech, Chgo, 1929; ordained rabbi, JTSA, 1934, MHL, 1947; DD, 1967; m. Deborah Weitz, June 23, 1935; c: Daniel, Shulamit. Rabbi: Temple B'nai Isr, Irvington, NJ, since 1947; Cong Shaare Shomayim, Phila, 1934-37; Cong B'nai Jacob, Bklyn, NY, 1937-47. Pres: Rabb Assembly of NJ, 1958-60; Glenwood Dist, ZOA, 1944; vice-pres: Bklyn Bd Rabbis, 1946; Syn Council of Essex Co, 1949-53; Bklyn Min Assn, 1946-48; mem, exec bd, NJ Br, United Syn of Amer, since 1955; an org, J Council, Irvington; mem: NY Bd Rabbis; Hapoel Hamizrachi; Hum Relations Council, Irvington; RA. Home: 93 Park Pl, Irvington, NJ. Study: 706 Nye Ave, Irvington, NJ.

ENGLANDER, Roger, US, TV producer-dir; b. Cleveland, O, Nov 23, 1926; s. Will and Frieda (Osteryoung); PhB, U Chgo, 1948; att: Chgo Musical Coll, 1944-48; Goodman Theatre of the Arts Inst, 1947-48. Independent TV produc and dir since 1961; produc, NBC-TV, 1948-50; dir, ABC-TV, 1950-51; produc-dir, CBS-TV, 1951-61; visiting prof: Parsons Coll, Ia; NYU; U of SC, Columbia, SC. Produc-dir for TV: NY Philharmonic Young People's Concerts, with Leonard Bernstein; Vladimir Horowitz at Carnegie Hall; S Hurok Presents; Show of the Month, NBC-TV; NBC Opera Theatre; Omnibus; Twentieth Century; Odyssey; Candid Camera; Let's Take a Trip; Bell Telephone Hour; Startime; Lincoln Center Presents; Festival of the Performing Arts; Concert of the Week; Look Up and Live; Lamp Unto My Feet; live theatrical producs: Salute to the American Musical Theatre, for Pres Johnson, White House, Wash, DC; all-star benefits: Music Theatre, Lincoln Cen Found for Intl Child Health, NY Assn for Brain-Injured Children; stage dir, NYC Opera Co; produc, NY Philharmonic Promenade Concerts. Pres, Amer Dance Theatre, Inc; St Lukes Place Assn; trustee; Dance Notation Bur; Mannes Coll of Music; Profsl Children's Sch; cons, NY State Council on the Arts; mem: bd, Intl Music Cen, Paris; Natl Endowment for the Arts, Wash, DC; gov, Natl Acad TV Arts and Scis. Contbr to profsl publs; lectr at numerous Us. Recipient: Emmy Awards, TV Acad of Arts and Scis, 1961, 1962, 1965; Bc Perceptor Award, 1967; Produc's Awards, O State U, 1960, 1961. Home: 15 St Lukes Place, New York, NY. Office: 524 W 57 St, New York, NY.

ENGLMAN, Binyamin Robert, Isr, physicist; b. Budapest, Hung, Dec 7, 1930; s. Max and Elisabeth (Weltner); in Isr since 1963; BSc, ARCS, Imperial Coll, London, 1954; PhD, Queen Mary Coll, London, 1957. Head, theoretical solid state group, Sorek Research Labs, Isr AEC, since 1963; fmr: research f, MIT, 1962-63; lectr, Technion, Haifa, 1958-61; asso visiting prof, Tel Aviv U, 1967-68. Fmr mem comm, Org of Orthodox J Scis. Contbr sci papers to profsl mags. Hobbies: Bible; lithurgy; sports. Home: 21 Beri St, Rehovot, Isr. Office: Sorek Research Lab, Isr.

ENOCH, Paul, Isr, linguist; b. Darmstadt, Ger, July 18, 1913; s. Moshe and Sarah (Bronner); in Isr since 1949; att med sch, U Frankfort, Ger, 1931; cert tchr, J Sem for Tchrs and Rabbis, Paris, 1937; BS, fac sci, Technion, Haifa, 1960; dipl, Fr Lang and Lit, Sorbonne, Fr, 1961; dipl, tech of lang labs, U Besançon, Fr, 1965; PhD, 1965; m. Hannah Isay, Nov 15, 1933; c: Constance Barak, Pierre, Anne. Sr lectr, i/c lab of applied, dept of gen studies, Technion, since 1967, guest lectr, lectr, Fr, 1955-57; tchr: Talmud Torah Sch, Paris, 1937-38; Heb, J Comty, Brussels, 1938-40, 1945-48; Judaism, HS of Forest, Brussels, 1948-49; Fr, chem, Hugim HS, Haifa, 1950-55. Capt, Free Fr Army, 1940-45. Prin contribs: devl of audiovisual Heb lang teaching; research in acoustics and applied phonetics, 1967; research in lexicology for elaboration of basic word lists of colloquial Isr Heb, 1968. Corresp etranger, Assn Nat des Combattants Volontaires de la Résistance Française; comm mem, Friendship Assn, Isr-Belgium; mem: Intl Soc of Phonetic Scis; Assn Fr de Linguistique Appliquee; Assn Intl de Linguistique Appliquee; Assn Intl Pour l'Enseignement des Langues Vivantes par les Méthodes Modernes; Deutsche Gesellschaft für Sprechkunde und Sprecherziehung EV; corresp de: Le Français dans le Monde; Tendances; fmr: corresp mem, Credif. Author: Méthode audio-visuelle d'Hébreu, ler degré; Livre de l'élève; Livre du maître, 1967, supplement, 1967; Livret écriture lecture, 1967; contbr articles to profsl jours. Recipient: Citoyen d'Honneur, Belgium, 1947; Gratitude Award, Fr Govt, 1948; Officier d'Académie, 1953; Chevalier de la Légion d'Honneur, 1965; Itur Lochamay Hamedinah, Min of Defense, Isr, 1968. Home: 7 Rehov Kadima, Mt Carmel, Haifa, Isr. Office: Technion, Haifa, Isr.

ENZER, Hyman A, US, educator; b. Elizabeth, NJ, July 29, 1916; s. Isak and Regina (Rosenberg); BA, Union Coll, 1938; MA, NYU, 1955, PhD, 1963; m. Sandra Solotaroff, 1952; c: Lisa, Ethan. Asso prof, chmn, dept sociol, Hofstra U, since 1950; reporter, Elizabeth Daily Jour, 1941-50; cons, Roslyn, NY Sch Bd, 1958-59. USAAC, 1943-46. Mem: AAUP; Amer Sociol Assn; fmr: chmn, state publicity, NJ Assn for Retarded Children; mem, NY Jt Leg Comm on Mental Deficiency. Recipient, DFC. Home: Hempstead, NY. Office: Hofstra U, Hempstead, NY.

EPHRAIM, Jerome W, US, business exec; b. Chgo, Ill, Dec 14, 1901; s. Falk and Rose (Himes); BCS, NYU, 1923; m. Muriel Abrahams, Dec 18, 1930; c: Pamela, Rosemary. Pres: Ephraim and Co, since 1928; Ephraim Freightways, since 1952, both Denver, Colo. Dir, Colo Motor Carriers Assn, 1954-56; mem, adv bd, Colo Planning Div, 1964-65. Author: Take Care of Yourself, 1936; Guide to Health, 1940; Guide to Beauty, 1940; contbr to mags. Home: 740 Pearl St, Denver, Colo. Office: 1385 Umatilla St, Denver, Colo.

EPHRATI, David, Isr, diplomat; b. Vienna, Aus, Oct 5, 1927; s. Ephraim and Malcia (Sucher) Seiden; in Isr since 1945; att: Heb U, Jerusalem; Tel Aviv U; m. Betty Garfunkel, June 20, 1950; c: Yaira, Romit. Consul gen, Montreal, Can, since 1971; ambass extraordinary and plen, Libreville, Gabon, since 1968-71; counsellor, chargé d'affaires, Emb of Isr, Addis Ababa, 1967-68; sr asst to dir, W Eur Dept, Min for Fgn Affairs, Jerusalem, 1964-66, with Min of Defense, Tel Aviv, 1949-63. Lt, IDF, 1948-50. Fmr mem, Aliyat Hanoar, Kibbutz Merchavia. Hobbies: music, philately. Home: 6 Jabotinsky St, Jerusalem, Isr. Office: Isr Consul, Montreal, Can.

EPHROS, Gershon, US, cantor, teacher, composer; b. Serotzk, Pol, Jan 15, 1890; s. Abraham and Feiga (Kizelstein); in US since 1911; studied with: Prof AZ Idelsohn, Jerusalem, Pal, 1909-11; Prof Herman Spielter, NYC, 1919-22; Joseph Achron, 1929-33, NYC; m. Rose Hurwitz, May 31, 1912; c: Helen, Abraham. Cantor em, Temple Beth Mordecai, Perth Amboy, NJ, since 1957, cantor, 1927-57; instr, Heb Schs, Bur J Educ, NYC, 1911-13; cantor: Cong Beth El, Norfolk, Va, 1918; Temple Beth Elohim, Bx, NY, 1919-27; fmr instr, Sch of Sacred Music, HUC, NYC. Ed and author: Cantorial Anthology, syn music, 1929, 6th vol, 1966; composer: Children's Suite, 1944; Three Jewish Folk Songs, 1946; Biblical Suite, 1951; New Birth of Freedom, 1953; Ihyu le Rotzon, 1956; hymns for revised US Army and Navy Hymnal; Second String Quartet, Aeolian, 1962; Suite Hebraique for Symphony Orchestra, 1966; le om haShabbat, 1966; Lel Shabbat, 1966; Hallel veZimrah, to memory, Rabbi Abba Hillel Silver, 1967; piano variations: Introduction, Andante Fugue for string quartet; Havdalah; piano sonata, Hinay Ma Tov for chorus and piano; commissioned by Temple of the Hgts, Cleveland, to write Selichot Service. Pres, J Music Forum; mem: bd, J Music Council, JWB; ASCAP; Amer Musicological Soc; Amer Assn for Composers and Conductors; Cantors Assembly; Cantors Assn of Amer. Recipient: title, Hazan Mechubad b'Yisrael, HUC, 1953; f, Cantors Inst, JTSA, 1954. Home: 98-15 Horace Harding Expressway, Rego Park, NY.

EPPLER, Elizabeth Esther, Eng, archivist; b. Budapest, Hung, Feb 21, 1921; d. Alexander and Rosalia (Weisz) in Eng since 1947; Licencie ès Lettres, U Paris, 1939; PhD, U Budapest, 1942. Sr research off, Inst J Affairs, since 1960; archivist, WJC since 1954; libr, Hung Natl Mus, 1942-48; cultural org, Mizrachi Women's Org, 1948-50; research asst, Publ Firm, 1950-54. Natl council, WJC, Brit sect; mem, Intl Fed U Women. Contbr to books and publs. Hobbies: music, photography. Home: 8 Strathray Gardens, London, NW3, Eng. Office: 13-16 Jacob's Well Mews, George St, London, W1, Eng.

EPPSTEIN, Uri, Isr, musicologist; b. Saarbrücken, Ger, Feb 3, 1925; s. Irvin and Herta (Kahn); in Isr since 1935; MA, Heb U, Jerusalem; att: Rubin Acad of Music, Jerusalem; Tokyo U Fgn Studies; research scholarship, Tokyo U Arts; m. Kikue Iguchi, Jan 2, 1965; s. Isaac. Music critic, haAretz, Heb daily, since 1963; secy, J Music Research Cen, Heb U, Jerusalem, since 1966; prog writer, Isr Bc Service, 1946-69; ed staff mem, music critic, Zmanim daily, 1953-55. Pvt, IDF, 1948-49. Mem, control comm, Isr Musicological Soc; Japan-Isr Friendship Soc. Author: Japanese Music Through the Eyes of Meiji Era Musicians, 1961; Japanese Music through Meiji Eyes, 1967; asst ed, Herzl's Collected Works, 1958. Home: 79 Herzog St, Jerusalem, Isr. Office: Hebrew U, Jerusalem, Isr.

EPPSTEIN, Victor, US, educator; b. Peoria, Ill, Jan 22, 1901; s. Henry and Molly (Livingston); BA, U of Cal, 1926; att, Columbia U, 1926-28; ordained rabbi, MHL-JIR, 1929, hon DD, 1954; m. Solveig Abrahamson Dahl, 1947; c: John. Prof, Heb lang and civilization, U Okla, since 1956; rabbi, United Heb Cong, Havana, Cuba, 1929-31; Temple Emanuel, Kingston, NY, 1931-32; Madison Ave Temple, Scranton, Pa, 1932-36; dir, B'nai B'rith Hillel Found: Pa State Coll, 1944-45; CCNY, 1945-52; U Ind, 1952-56; U Okla, 1956-58; asst regional dir, US off Defense Wfr Services, 1941-42; dir, summer rabb inst, JIR, 1947-48. Mem: CCAR. Home: 1012 Brookside Dr, Norman, Okla.

EPSTEIN, Arthur W, US, physician, educator; b. NYC, May 15, 1923; s. Jacob and Anne (Bass); AB, Columbia U, 1944, MD, Coll Phys and Surg, 1947; m. Leona Cruce, Mar 2, 1955; c: David, Nona Kathryn, Emily Vera, James. Prof, psycht and neur, Tulane U, since 1964, fac mem, since 1952. Lt cdr, USNR, MC, 1956-58. F: Amer Psycht Assn; Amer Acad Psychan; AAAS; Amer Acad Neur. Author: An Anatomist's Dream of Love; contbr to med jours. Home: 1664 Robert St, New Orleans, La. Office: 1430 Tulane Ave, New Orleans, La.

EPSTEIN, Benjamin, US, statistical cons; b. Boston, Mass, Mar 5, 1918; s. Harry and Fanny (Rabinowitz); BS, MIT, 1937, MS, 1938; PhD, U of Ill, 1941; m. Molly Hoffman, Sep 8, 1940; c: David, Carl, Sibyl. Cons in stat, since 1960; f, math, U of Ill, 1938-39, asst ,1939-41, instr, 1941-42; math and stat, Frankford Arsenal, 1942-44; staff stat, Westinghouse Elec Corp, 1944-45; mem staff, Coal Research Lab and lectr, dept math, Carnegie Inst Tech, 1945-48; prof, math, Wayne State U, Detroit, Mich, 1955-60, on fac since 1948; visiting positions: asso prof, math, U of Cal, Berkeley, 1950; asso prof, stat, Stanford U, 1951, prof, 1955-56, 1957-60; prof, dept ind Eng and oprs Research, U of Cal, Berkeley, 1965-66. Prin contribs: engaged in probability and stats, particularly in connection with problems arising in sci and engr; has made theoretical and applied contribs to bioassay, tests of increased severity, extreme values, order stats, particle size distributions, quality control, sampling inspection, stat theories of fracture and fatigue, ling, life testing, math models for reliability and maintainability, Poisson and more general stochastic processes. F: AAAS; Inst of Math Scis; Amer Stat Assn;

Amer Soc for Quality Control; mem: Intl Assn for Stats in the Physical Scis; Oprs Research Soc of Isr; Amer Math Soc; Math Assn of Amer; Soc for Ind and Applied Maths; Oprs Research Soc of Amer; AAUP; Sigma Xi. Asso ed, technometrics; rev, for math and applied mechs revs; contbr to profsl jours. Home and office: 768 Garland Dr, Palo Alto, Cal.

EPSTEIN, Bernard Mordecai, US, attorney; b. Hammond, Ind, June 10, 1902; s. Hyman and Sarah (Goodman); JD, Northwestern U, 1922; att U Chgo, 1919-27; m. Melba Browarsky, Sep 27, 1936; c: Nona. Pvt practice; partner, Stone, Epstein, Lynch & Corby. Pres, J Info Soc Amer; bd mgrs,YMCA, Hyde Park Dept; mem: exec comm, Amer J Hist Soc; fmr: pres: Hyde Park; Council of Churches and Syns; Conf Brotherhood Temple; club, Standard, Chgo. Contbr to legal jours. Spec interest, J hist evaluation. Home: 5000 E End Ave, Chicago, Ill. Office: 111 W Monroe St, Chicago, Ill.

EPSTEIN, David Mayer, US, musician; b. New York, NY, Oct 3, 1930; s. Joshua and Elizabeth (Mayer); AB, Antioch Coll, 1951; M Mus, NE Conservatory, Boston, 1954; MFA, Brandeis U, 1954; PhD, Princeton U, 1956; m. Anne Merrick, June 21, 1953; c: Eve, Beth. Asso prof, music, MIT, since 1965; dir, Acoustic Research Contemporary Recording Project, since 1969; music critic, Musical America, 1956-57; asst prof, music, Antioch Coll, 1957-62; music dir, Educ Bc Corp, 1962-64; guest conductor: Cleveland Orch; Berlin Radio Sym Orch; Czech Radio Orch; NY City Cen; NJ Sym; found, first conductor, Youth Sym Orch, NY, 1963-66. Composer: Four Songs for Soprano, French Horn, String Orchestra, 1964; String Trio, 1969; music for: orch, chamber ensembles, theater, film, TV. Mem: bd, Amer Soc U Composers; adv bd, NE Lyric Theatre; musical adv bd, Eur Lang Inst; bd: Young Audiences, Boston; Adirondack Arts Found; mem: Amer Fed Musicians; Amer Sym Orch League; Amer Music Cen; ASCAP; Intl Webern Soc. Recipient: Louisville orch Award, 1955; Fromm Found Award, 1955; BC Music Award, 1956; US Junior C of C Man of the Year, 1964; Arthur Shepherd Award, 1965; Rockefeller found commn, 1969. Hobbies: reading, travel, sailing. Home: 54 Turning Mill Rd, Lexington, Mass. Office: MIT, Cambridge, Mass.

EPSTEIN, David S, US, journalist; b. Taurogen, Lith, Aug 2, 1908; s. Haym and Ethel (Neuwidel); in US since 1924; att: Yeshiva U, 1925-28; Mizrachi Tchrs Inst, Jerusaelm, 1928-29; City Coll, St Louis, 1933-37; m. Helena Silverman, Feb 2, 1943; c: Rena Solomon, Hayim, Daniel. Mgn dir, Hadoar, Heb weekly, since 1955; mgn ed, Jewish Record, St Louis, 1935-39; ed, Our Path, 1939-41; chief copy writer, Joseph Jacobs Advt Agcy, 1940-42, 1946-48; ed, Isr Digest, 1952-53. Mem admn comm, United Zionist Revisionists of Amer, fmr exec dir; secy, US Cen Shekel and Election Bd, since 1950; mem: exec comm, AZC, since 1952; bd dir, JNF, since 1950; admn comm, Histadrut Ivrith of Amer, since 1956; Yiddish Writers Union; delg, ZC, Jerusalem; dep mem, Gen Council, WZO, since 1965; world exec comm, Heruth Zionists Revisionists World Union. Author: Fifty Years of Reconstructive Work, Yiddish, Eng; A History of the Orthodox Jewish Community in St Louis, 1938. Home: 895 West End Ave, New York, NY. Office: 150 Fifth Ave, New York, NY.

EPSTEIN, David Weiss, US, pediatric dentist; b. Indianapolis, Ind, Oct 16, 1914; s. Maurice and Ruby (Weiss); AB, U Wis, 1962; DDS, Ind U Sch of Dent, 1968; MSD, Ind U-Purdue U Sch of Dent, 1970; m. Cheryl Shmalo, Aug 9, 1969. Asst prof, ped dent Ind U-Purdue U Sch of Dent, since 1970, on fac since 1969. Mem: Amer Dent Assn; Amer Soc Dent for Children; Alpha Omega Dent Frat. Hobbies: bridge, handball, tennis. Home: Fenn-Woode Apts, Newington, Conn. Office: 4 Holcomb St, Hartford, Conn.

EPSTEIN, Edward Jay, US, author; b. NYC, Dec 6, 1935; s. Louis and Betty; MA, Cornell U, 1965; att, Harvard U. Teaching f, Harvard U. Author: Inquest: The Warren Commission and the Establishment of Truth, 1964; Counter Plot, 1969; contbr to: New Yorker, Esquire; NY Times; Commentary; Book World. Home: 295 Harvard St, Cambridge, Mass.

EPSTEIN, Elias Louis, US, educator; b. Estonia, Sep 5, 1907; s. Betzalel and Hannah (Czyz); in US since 1926; BA, U Cincinnati, 1931, MA, 1932; PhD, U Chgo.1941; m. Roselyn Touff, Apr 29, 1937; c: Charlotte Biegelsen. Prof, Heb lang and lit, HUC since 1943, chmn, grad dept since 1963, ed, Heb Union Coll Annual, 1957-68; mem: CCAR; Amer Oriental Soc; Soc Bib Lit. Home: 5300 Hamilton Ave, Cincinnati, O. Office: 3101 Clifton Ave, Cincinnati, O.

EPSTEIN, Ervin, US, physician, educator; b. Vallejo, Cal, May 17, 1909; s. Nathan and Lilly (Levin); AB, U of Cal, 1931, MD, 1935; m. Selma Zinman, July 16, 1936; c: Ervin, Kenneth. Asso clinical prof, dermat, U of Cal Med Sch, since 1962; asso, clinical prof, med, Stanford U Med Sch, since 1957, asst, 1950-57; chief, dermat, Alameda Co Hosp, since 1955; cons, dermat, USAF VA, since 1946. Capt, US Army MC, 1942-45. Pres, Pacific Dermat Assn, 1957-58; pres, secy: SF Dermat Soc, 1940-42, 1946-47; sect, Cal Med Assn, 1947-49, 1956-57. Author: Skin Surgery, 1956, 2nd ed, 1962; Regional Dermatologic Diagnosis, 1960; Radiodermatitis, 1962, contbr numerous papers on dermat. Home: 5 Sotelo Ave, Piedmont, Cal. Office: 477-29 St, Oakland, Cal.

EPSTEIN, Frederick Hermon, US, physician; b. Frankfurt/M, Ger, July 24, 1916; s. Ernst and Klara (Redelsheimer); in US since 1956; att: U of Zurich, Switz, 1934-36, BA, MA, Cambridge, 1940, MB, B Chir, MD, 1943; MRCS, LRCP, U London Hosp Med Sch; div; c: Andrew, Anthony. Prof, epidemiology, U Mich Sch of Public Health, since 1963, mem fac since 1956; res phys, hosps Gt Brit, 1943-48; with NYU Coll of Med, 1948-56. Prin contrib, research in cardiovascular disease. Chmn, council on epidemiology; mem, bd dirs, AHA; dir, cardiovascular research cen, U Mich; affiliated with numerous natl and intl med orgs; fmr: cons, WHO; mem: comm on epidemiology, Natl Acad Scis; med research council, bd trustees, Mich Heart Assn. Author: chaps in med books, contbr to med and sci jours. Recipient: Research Career Award, Natl Heart Inst, 1962. Home: 400 Maynard St, Ann Arbor, Mich. Office: U of Mich Sch of Public Health, Ann Arbor, Mich.

EPSTEIN, Jacob, Isr, sculptor; b. Pol, Feb 14, 1921; s. Nahman and Sarah (Gorenbuh); in Isr since 1959; art sculptor with distinction, Art Acad, Lvov, 1941; m. Tova Orgun, July 25, 1948; c: Bella, Rachel. Headmaster, sculpture sect, Art Inst, Bat Yam, since 1960; co-found, head, Inst Plastic Art, Bat Yam, since 1960. Monuments: Russ Entrance Gate to Triumph Mt; Heroes Graves, Lvov; Entrance Gate to Munic Garden, Lvov; portraits in munic mus: Shevtzenko; Gogol; Krilov; Pol; repr: at mus: Ha'aretz, Tel Aviv; Kibbutz Hakuk; Beit Yatziv; Beersheva; pvt collections: Tel Aviv; Ein Harod; Ramat Gan; Beersheva; Wash DC; NY; Cleveland; Paris; rel work, Syn, Ramat Yosef. Recipient: art award: Bat Yam Munic; Ist award: Monument for Lvov's heroes; monument for fallen soldiers of Six-Day War. Home: 33 Mivtza Sinai, Bat Yam, Isr.

EPSTEIN, Joseph, US, physician; b. New Haven, Conn, Aug 23, 1899; s. Abram and Simme (Sulkess); PhB, Yale U, 1920, MD, Sch of Med, 1923; m. Lillian Shapiro, Apr 10, 1930; c: Simon, Fred, Abram. Pvt practice, neur and psycht, since 1923; asst clin prof, psycht, NYU-Bellevue since 1962; cons psycht, Kings Park State Hosp since 1960; med off specialist, neur and psycht, VA, 1926-31; att neur, NY Neur Inst, 1930-50. F: life, Amer Psycht Assn; AAAS; dipl, Amer Bd Neur and Psycht. Mem: B'nai B'rith; ZOA; Masons. Contbr to med publs. Home: 340 E 64 St, New York, NY.

EPSTEIN, Julius A, US, business exec; b. NYC, Apr 26, 1923; s. Isidor and Ida (Lelchuk); att: CCNY, 1943-46; George Wash U, Wash, DC, 1941-43; m. Rose Lansman, June 30, 1947; c: Ellen, Lawrence. Chmn, bd, Fala-Mailman Marketing Services, since 1969; found, vice-pres, Direct Mail in NY Inc, since 1968; produc mgr, O E McIntyre, 1950-52; mgmt cons, Fairbanks Assoc, 1952-54; pres, Mailman Inc, 1954-69; vice-pres, Mid Westchester YM and YWHA, Scarsdale, since 1965; chmn, FJP, New Rochelle; mem, leg comm, Direct Mail Advt Assn; bd, Iona Coll Inst of Arts, since 1967; bd, Postmaster Gen Mailers Tech Adv Comm, since 1966; fmr pres: Mail Advt Service Assn Intl; NY chap; Tom Paine lodge, B'nai B'rith, New Rochelle; Direct Mail Marketing Lodge, B'nai B'rith, NY; fmr: mem: bd, Asso 3rd Class Mail Users; New Rochelle Mayors Govt Oprs Comm. Recipient: Charles S Raizen Award, FJP, New Rochelle, 1969. Home: 154 Daisy Farms Dr, New Rochelle, NY. Offices: 641 Ave of Americas, New York, NY; 185 Price Parkway, Farmingdale, NY.

EPSTEIN, Lee, US, attorney, educator; b. Union, City, NJ, Apr 25, 1909; s. Simon and Lena (Langer); BS, NYU, 1930; LLB, Harvard Law Sch, 1935; SJM, NYU Law Sch, 1947; m. Beatrice Greenberg, June 28, 1940; c: David, Phoebe. Atty, lab arbitrator, since 1935; prof, econ, CCNY, 1958-65; lectr, Pratt Inst, since 1953. Judge advocate gen, US Army, 1943. Mem: Natl Acad of Arbitrators; City Bar Assn; club, Har-

vard. Contbr to legal periodicals. Recipient: US Army Commendation ribbon. Home: 150 E 89 St, New York, NY. Office: 660 Madison Ave, New York, NY.

EPSTEIN, Leo, Brazil, business exec; b. Kenzingen, Ger, May 27, 1915; s. Michael and Karolina (Dreyfuss); in Brazil since 1936; Acctnt, Commercial Sch, Emmendingen, 1934; m. Graça Levy, May 27, 1942; c: Alfredo, Eli, Piedade. Co-owner, Mining Co; co-owner, exec, construction, real estate bus, since 1943; financial cons, geological surveys, Geoexploracões Ltd; acctnt, Guenzburger Co, 1931-36; sales mgr, A Steffen, 1936-37; ind sales mgr, 1937-43. Pres, council, Asso Rel Isr do Rio de Janeiro; dir council, Fed Soc Isr do Rio de Janeiro; council mem: Keren Kaiemet Leisr; Gen Zionist Org; exec comm, KH; pres, B'nai B'rith. Home: Pr Flamengo 224, Rio de Janeiro, Brazil. Office: Av Rio Branco 156 s/1009, Rio de Janeiro, Brazil.

EPSTEIN, Leon D, educator; b. Milw, Wis, May 29, 1919; s. Harry and Anne (Lekachman); BA, U Wis, 1940, MA, 1941; PhD, U Chgo, 1948; m. Shirley Galewitz, 1947. Prof, political sci, U of Wis, since 1969, dean, Coll Letters and Sci, 1965-69, fac mem since 1948; jr and asst econ, US Govt, 1941-42; asst prof, political sci, U Ore, 1947-48. Capt, US Army, WW II. Mem: Amer Political Sci Assn; AAUP; Phi Beta Kappa. Author: Britain-Uneasy Ally, 1954; Politics in Wisconsin, 1958; British Politics in Suez Crisis, 1964; Political Parties in Western Democracies, 1967; contbr to political sci jours. Hobby: tennis. Home: 2806 Ridge Rd, Madison, Wis. Office: U of Wis, Madison, Wis.

EPSTEIN, Louis R, US, business exec; b. Sharon, Pa, Jan 28, 1926; s. Samuel and Bess (Rosenblum); BA, U Rochester, 1950; m. Marlene Lurie, Aug 13, 1950; c: Richard, Susan, Georgia. Dir, merchandising, Golden Dawn Foods, since 1958. US Army, 1943-46. Chmn: Shenango Valley Isr Bond Dr; Shenango Valley United Fund, treas, 1969; Shenango Valley J Fed, 1961-62; pres: W Pa Conf of Temple Brotherhoods, 1959-60; Shenango Valley Comty Concert Assn, 1969; vice-pres, Youngstown Sym Bd; fmr financial secy, Temple Beth Isr, Sharon, Pa; mem: bd govs, Tri-State Isr Bonds; natl bd, Natl Fed Temple Brotherhoods; club, Kiwanis. Home: 1754 McDowell St, Sharon, Pa. Office: 385 Shenango Ave, Sharon, Pa.

EPSTEIN, Manuel, US, attorney; b. Bklyn, NY, Mar 15, 1937; s. Simon and Cora (Kotick); BA, Bklyn Coll, NY, 1956; LLB, JD, Bklyn Law Sch, 1959; m. Sara Berlin, Apr 7, 1969. Pvt practice since 1960; atty: NY State, 1961-67; Corporate Growth, 1968-69. Capt, US Army, 1959-60. Res since 1961. Dir: Amers for J Action; Interfaith; chmn, legal comm, United Peoples; mem: Res Offs Assn, NY; Mil Assn, NY; clubs: Wall St; Syn Luncheon, co-chmn, 1968-69. Hobby: writing. Home: 85 E 43 St, Brooklyn, NY. Office: 574 E 93 St, Brooklyn, NY.

EPSTEIN, Morris, US, editor, author, scholar; b. Newark, NJ, July 7, 1921; s. Isaac and Gittel (Minzter); BA, Yeshiva Coll, 1942; Tchrs Dipl, Tchrs' Inst, Rabbi Isaac Elchanan Theol Sem, 1942; MA, Columbia U, 1944; PhD, NYU, 1957; m. Shifra Herschfus, May 29, 1949; c: Guita, Sherry. Ed, World Over Mag, since 1949, on staff since 1947; prof and chmn, Dept of Eng, Yeshiva U Stern Coll for Women, since 1966; fac mem since 1955; PR dir, lit ed publs, J Educ Comm, NY, 1958-66; author, World Over Playhouse, NBC, 1948-50; commentator, WXRT, Chgo, 1948-50; mgn ed, J Educ Mag, Natl Council for J Educ, 1954-58. Author: books for children: My Holiday Story Book, 1952; Tell Me About God and Prayer, 1953; All About Jewish Holidays and Customs, 1958; A Pictorial Treasury of Jewish Holidays and Customs, 1959; A Book of Torah Readings, 1960; A Picture Parade of Jewish History, 1963; Tales of Sendebar, the Hebrew Version of the Seven Sages, 1967; asso ed, The Samuel K Mirsky Memorial Volume, 1970; drama reviewer, Show Business; ed adv bds, J Digest, In Jewish Bookland. Pres: Yeshiva Coll Alumni Assn, 1956-58; Amer J PR Soc, 1963-65; mem: exec comm, Natl Council for J Educ, 1957-60; lit comm, NCCJ; juvenile book comm, J Publ Soc; steering comm, Eng Grad Assn, NYU; exec bd, JBCA; Radio Writers Guild; Eng Grad Union, Columbia U; AAUP; MLA; Medieval Acad of Amer; Coll Eng Assn; Intl Assn U Profs Eng; club, Medieval, NY. Recipient: grants to lectr at World Congs J Studies, 1961, 1965, Amer Council Learned Socs; Founds' Day award, NYU, 1958; Horeb Award, 1962, Bernard Revel Award, 1964, both Yeshiva U. Home: 207 W 86 St, New York, NY.

Offices: 426 W 58 St, New York, NY; 253 Lexington Ave, New York, NY.

EPSTEIN, Moshe Yehiel Halevi, Isr, rabbi; b. Ozerov, Pol, 1890; s. Avraham; desc of rabbi Jacob Joseph, the Hose of Lublin; ordained rabbi, Admor, Ozerov; Rabbi in Isr since 1953; a head, Agudat Isr. Author: Esh Dat, 11 vols; Be'er Moshe, 3 vols; Bamidbar; Dvarim. Recipient: Isr Award, 1958.

EPSTEIN, Norman N, US, dermatologist, educator; b. SF, Cal, June 14, 1896; s. Nathan and Lillian (Levin); MD, U of Cal, 1923; m. Gertrude Hirsch, Jan 19, 1934; c: William, John, Eugene. Pvt practice since 1926; Clinical prof em, dermat, U of Cal Med Sch at SF, on fac since 1950; sr, hon staffs of several hosps in SF. US Army, WW I. Fmr: pres, Pacific Dermat Assn; vice-pres, sect on dermat, AMA; pres, SF Dermat Assn; pres, sect on dermat, Cal Med Assn; mem: AMA; Cal Med Assn; Soc for Inves Dermat; Amer Acad of Dermat; Amer Dermat Assn. Contbr to med publs. Home: 101 Alma St, Palo Alto, Cal. Office: 450 Sutter St, San Francisco, Cal.

EPSTEIN, Pauline, US, attorney; b. Bklyn, NY, Aug 17, 1907; d. Samuel and Ida (Rosenfeld); LLB, Southwestern U, 1933; m. Edward Crabtree (div); c: Samuel. Atty since 1933; acctnt since 1946. Chmn, bd dirs, Exceptional Children's Opportunity Sch, since 1950; treas, LA-Beverly Hills chaps, Natl Lawyers Guild; life mem: J Natl Home for Asthmatic Children; Mahnia Silverberg chap, City of Hope; NAACP; f, Amer Assn on Mental Deficiency; mem: Intl Fed Women Lawyers; Intl Conf on Social work; Women's Intl League for Peace and Freedom; Women for Leg Action; Cal Assn for Health and Wfr; AJCong; Israela; B'nai B'rith; Hollywood Bowl Assn; S Cal Chamber Music Soc; Wilderness Soc; fmr: vice pres, S Cal Women Lawyers; chmn, legal aid comm, Natl Assn Women Lawyers; clubs: Mothers of City Terr Folk Shule, fmr pres: Lawyers of LA; Globetrotters of Ceylon. Home: 2131 N Cahuenga Blvd, Hollywood, Cal. Office: 3028 Wabash Ave, Los Angeles, Cal.

EPSTEIN, Raymond, US, business exec; b. Chgo, Ill, Jan 12, 1918; s. Abraham and Janet (Rabinowitz); att: MIT, 1934-36; BS, U of Ill, 1936-38; m. Betty Jadwin, Apr 7, 1940; c: Gail, David, Norman, Harriet. Chmn bd, A Epstein and Sons Inc, since 1961, vice-pres, 1947-59, pres, 1959-61. Pres, JWF, Metrop Chgo; chmn bd, J United Fund; life dir, Mt Sinai Med Research Found, mem, bd trustees, Chgo Med Sch; mem: steering comm, large city budgeting, Council J Fed and Wfr Funds, Inc; Chgo comm, Fund for the Rep; Loyola U Citizens Bd; housing comm, Mayor's Comm for Sr Citizens; Amer Soc of Civil Engrs; Soc Amer Reg Architects; Amer Concrete Inst; W Soc of Engr; Natl Soc Profsl Engrs; Ill Soc of Profsl Engrs; Structural Engrs Assn of Ill; Construction Specifications Inst; Fr Engrs in US, Inc; fmr pres,Young Men's J Council; fmr mem, bd dirs, chmn budget comm, vice-pres, JWF, Metrop Chgo; fmr chmn,. Group Reviewing Comm and Budget Comm, Comty Fund, Chgo; fmr, bd dirs: Chgo Bldg Cong; U of Ill Found; fmr natl council, JDC; fmr bd mem, CJFWF; fmr bd mem, secy, J Fed, Metrop Chgo; fmr treas, bd mem,Wfr Council, Metrop Chgo; clubs: Standard; Illini; MIT, Chgo; Pi Lambda Phi. Hobbies: Rare books, wines, coins. Home: 4950 S Chicago Beach Dr, Chicago, Ill. Office: 2011 W Pershing Rd, Chicago, Ill.

EPSTEIN, Samuel, US, business exec; b. Bobroisk, Russia, Mar 15, 1900; s. Louis and Fanny (Yerenberg); in US since 1905; m. Mollie Caplan, Jan 23, 1927; c: Norman, Myra Schaftel. Pres, L Epstein and Sons, since 1946. Pres, Beth Tfiloh Cong, Baltimore since 1958; mem, bd: Sinai Hosp; Amer Assn for J Educ; commn: Parks Bd, Baltimore since 1962; Sch Bd, 1959-62; mem: JNF; UJA; Asso J Charities; ZOA; B'nai B'rith; Masons. Home: 11 Slade Ave, Baltimore, Md. Office: 3818 Eastern Ave, Baltimore, Md.

EPSTEIN, Samuel, US, author, editor; b. Boston, Mass, Nov 22, 1909; s. Joseph and Sarah (Gershofsky); BL , Rutgers U, 1932; m. Beryl Williams, Apr 26, 1938. Asst dir, NJ State Writers Project, 1935-41; sci ed, NJ Agric Experiment Sta, 1942-45; fed cons, dept microbiol, Rutgers U, 1946-50. Tech writer, US Army Signal Corps, 1944-46. Author (under pseudonym Charles Strong): Stranger at the Inlet, 1946; How to Develop, Print and Enlarge Pictures, 1947; The Secret of Baldhead Mountain, 1946; The Riddle of the Hidden Pesos, 1948 (pseudonym Bruce Campbell); The Secret of Skeleton Island, 1949; The Riddle of the Stone Elephant, 1949; The Black Thumb Mystery, 1950; The Secret of Hangman's Inn, 1951;

The Mystery of the Iron Box, 1952; The Clue of the Phantom Car, 1953; The Mystery of the Galloping Horse, 1954; The Mystery of the Green Flame, 1955; The Mystery of the Grinning Tiger, 1956; The Mystery of the Vanishing Magician, 1957; The Mystery of the Shattered Glass, 1958; The Mystery of the Invisible Enemy, 1959; The Mystery of Gallows Cliff, 1960; The Clue of the Silver Scorpion, 1961; The Mystery of the Plumed Serpent, 1962; pseudonym Adam Allen, in collaboration with wife: Tin Lizzie, 1937; Printer's Devil, 1939; Dynamo Farm, 1942; Water to Burn, 1943; Dollar a Share, 1943; New Broome Experiment, 1944; pseudonym Douglas Coe in collaboration with wife: Pioneer of Radio, 1943; Road to Alaska, 1943; The Burma Road, 1946; Seashells, 1963; The International Red Cross, 1963; Spring Holidays, 1964; Medicine from Microbes, 1965; The Game of Baseball, 1965; Stories of Champions, 1965; Young Paul Revere's Boston, 1966; The Sacramento, 1968; European Folk Festivals, 1968; Harriet Tubman, 1968; Take This Hammer, 1969; Who Says You Can't, 1969; The First Book of the World Health Organization, 1964; The First Book of Switzerland, 1964; The First Book of News, 1965; The Picture Book of Franklin Delano Roosevelt, 1969; co-author: Miracles from Microbes, 1946; Houdini: Magician Extraordinary, 1950; The Real Book about Inventions, 1951; The Real Book about Benjamin Franklin, 1952; The Real Book about Alaska, 1952; The Real Book about Pirates, 1952; The Real Book about Spies, 1953; The Real Book about Submarines, 1954; William Crawford Gorgas, 1953; The First Book about Electricity 1953; The Real Book about the Sea, 1954; The First Book of Hawaii, 1954; The First Book of Words, 1954; The First Book of Glass, 1955; The First Book of Mexico, 1955; The First Book of Printing, 1955; The Rocket Pioneers, 1955; Francis Marion, 1956; Prehistoric Animals, 1956; The Andrews Raid, 1956; All about the Desert, 1957; The First Book of Codes and Ciphers, 1956; The First Book of Italy, 1958; The First Book of Maps and Globes, 1959; Jackknife for a Penny, 1959; All about Prehistoric Cavemen, 1959; The First Book of Measurement, 1960; The First Book of Washington, DC, 1961; The First Book of the Ocean, 1961; The First Book of Teaching Machines, 1961; Meet North Africa, 1957; Meet South Africa, 1958; George Washington Carver, 1961; David Fairchild, Plant Explorer, 1961. Mem: Author's League of Amer. Home: Southold, NY. Office: c/o McIntosh and Otis, 18 E 41 St, New York, NY.

EPSTEIN, Samuel, US, physician; b. NYC, Nov 14, 1912; s. Hyman and Minnie (Aboff); BS, NYU, 1931; MD, U and Bellevue Med Coll, NYC, 1934; m. Blanche Mendlowitz, Aug 25, 1940; c: Judy, Robert. Pvt practice since 1937; att phys, Maimonides Hosp, 1964, chief card OPD, since 1967, on med staff since 1937; clinical asst, prof med, SUNY, Downstate Med Cen, since 1961, clinical instr, 1959-61; visiting phys and med dir, Coney I Hosp, since 1958, mem staff since 1937; on staff, Harbour Hosp, 1937-50. Cert, Amer Bd Internal Med and sub-specialty Bd Cardiovascular Diseases; f: Amer Geriatrics Soc; Amer Coll Phys; Amer Coll Card; Amer Coll Chest Phys; mem: AMA; Kings Co Med Soc; AHA; NY Heart Assn; NY Card Aassn; NY Acad Scis; Bklyn Soc Internal Med; AAAS: Amer Fed for Clinical Research; Ocean Med Soc, pres, 1959. Contbr, to med jours. Hobbies: photography; J hist. Home: 3101 Bedford Ave, Brooklyn, NY. Office: 700 Ocean Ave, Brooklyn, NY.

EPSTEIN, Samuel P, US, business exec; b. NYC, May 25, 1896; s. Louis and Celia; m. Jane Norman, Nov, 1919; c: Lewis, Esta. Dir, Ponce Hotel, Puerto Rico, since 1959; exec, vice-pres, Bulova Watch Co, 1919-58; pres, Clinical Facilities, 1959-62. USN, 1917-18. Mem, bd trustees, Leb Hosp; vice-chmn, jewelry divs: UJA; FJP of NY; club, Town, NY. Home: 333 Sunset Ave, Palm Beach Fla.

EPSTEIN, Samuel S, US, chemist, business exec; b. Russ, July 14, 1906; s. Samuel and Krana (Turcott); BS, RI State U, 1929; MS, Ia State Coll Grad Sch, 1932, PhD,1934; m. Evelyn Boehm, Feb 22, 1935; c: Raymond. Vice-pres: Kirsch Beverages Inc, since 1944, chem since 1939; No-Cal, 1955; chief bio, Schwartz Lab, 1934-37; dir, research, Germ Proof Paint, 1937-38; cons chem, bact, Foster D Snell Food Research Lab, 1938-42. Prin contrib: originator No-Cal, dietetic carbonated beverages, 1950. Mem: Amer Public Health Assn; Amer Inst Food Tech; AAAS; Soc Amer Bact; Royal Soc Health, Brit; Soc Soft Drink Tech; Amer Chem Soc; Sigma Xi; Phi Kappa Phi; Masons; B'nai B'rith; Temple Petach Tikvah; J Hosp for Chronic Diseases. Contbr to sci jours. Recipient: Chesterman Award for contribs to soft drink ind, 1951. Hobby: chess. Home: 97-28 57 Ave,Corona,NY. Office:921 Flushing Ave,Brooklyn,NY.

EPSTEIN, Samuel W, US, business exec; b. Sheffield, Pa, Nov 24, 1893; s. William and Lena (Bender); BS, U of Pa, 1917; m. Bessie Rosenblum, June 20, 1922. Exec, Golden Dawn Foods, since 1922; pres, Harry M Pollock Co, Kittanning, Pa since 1953; head chem, rubber div, chem sect, US Bur of Standards, 1917-20. Chmn: sales to banks, unions, spec funds, Tri-State Isr Bonds Comm, past mem, regional planning bd; mem, regional bd, ADL, since 1959; fmr: pres, Pa Regional Council Reformed Syns; chmn, mem exec bd, J Fed Campaign; pres, mem bd dirs, Beth Isr Temple, Sharon, Pa; mem, natl bd, UAHC; club, Sharon Country. Home: 558 Boyd Dr, Sharon, Pa. Office: 385 Shenango St, Sharon, Pa.

EPSTEIN, Seymour, US, writer, teacher; b. NYC, Dec 2, 1917; s. Joseph and Jenny (Pomerantz); att CCNY; NYU; m. Miriam Kligman, May 5, 1956; c: Alan, Paul. Asso prof, Eng dept, U Denver, since 1969. M/Sgt, USAF, 1941-45. Author: Short Story 1, 1958; The Pillar of Salt, 1960; The Successor, 1961; Best Short Stories of 1962, pub 1963; Leah, 1964; A Penny for Charity, 1965; Caught in that Music, 1967. Recipient: Edward Lewis Wallant Memorial Book Award, 1964; Guggenheim F, 1965. Home: 2035 S Monroe St, Denver, Colo. Office: U of Denver, Denver, Colo.

EPSTEIN, William, Can, barrister, UN official; b. Calgary, Can, July 10, 1912; s. Harry and Bella (Geffen); BA, U Alberta, 1933; LLB, 1935; postgrad study, LSE, 1937-38; m. Edna Hyman, Sep 22, 1946; c: Mark. Dir, disarmament affairs div, UN Secretariat, since 1967, chief, armaments control and enforcement measures sect, since 1951; secy, Disarmament Commn, since 1952; tech cons, repr, Secy Gen for Demilitarization of Latin Amer, 1965-69; chmn, Secy Gen's group cons expert on chem and biol weapons, 1969; secy, political and security comm, UN Gen Assembly, 1962, asst secy, 1946-59; personal repr Secy Gen, conf on discontinuance of nuclear weapons tests, Geneva, 1959; dep personal repr, Secy Gen, conf of 10 Nation Comm on Disarmament, Geneva, since 1962; in pvt law practice, Can, 1935-42; travelling scholarship in Eur, 1938; secy, Can Claims Commn, London, 1944-46; sr political affairs off, UN Pal Commn with Bernadotte and Bunche missions, 1948; chief, ME and Afr affairs sect, UN Dept of Political Security Council Affairs, 1951, acting chief, 1949-51. Can Army, 1942-46. Mem: Alberta Law Soc; Can Bar Assn; Amer Soc Intl Law. Contrb to legal, political publs. Home: 400 E 58 St, New York, NY. Office: UN, New York, NY.

EPSTINE, Harry M, US, business exec; b. Chillicothe, O, Apr 2, 1899; s. Benjamin and Bella (Adolph); att, U Mich, 1922; m. Jane Metzger, Apr 6, 1936; c: Beatrice Morrison, Marianna Specter. Pres: May Stern and Co, since 1948, mem co since 1931; Epley Land, since 1948; Porter-Gratiot Realty, since 1938; mem bd, B G Foods, since 1955; asst gen mgr, Summerfield and Hecht, Detroit, 1919-30. US Army, 1917-18. Hon pres, United Vocational and Employment Service, since 1942; mem, bd trustees: W Pa Blue Cross, since 1957; WinchesterThurston Sch, since 1958; St Vincent's Coll, since 1959; Maurice Falk Med Found, since 1963; Montefiore Hosp, 1942-63; mem: bd dirs, United J Fund, 1936-62; admn comm, AJComm, since 1956; FJP; YM-YMHA, 1942-50; clubs: Furniture; Standard, both Chgo; One Hundred; Westmoreland; Concordia, all Pittsburgh. Home: 803 Devonshire St, Pittsburgh, Pa. Office: 914 Penn Ave, Pittsburgh, Pa.

ERDELYI, Arthur, Eng, educator, researcher; b. Budapest, Hung, Oct 2, 1908; s. Ignác and Friderike (Roth); in Eng since 1964; D Rer Nat, Prague U, 1938; DSc, Edinburgh U, Scotland, 1940; m. Eva Neuberg, Nov 4, 1942. Prof, Edinburgh U, 1939-1949 and since 1964; prof math, Cal Inst of Tech, 1949-64; visiting prof, applied math, Heb U, 1956-57. Sci cons, Brit Admiralty, WW II. Chmn on revision fundamental math tables, NCR; mem: Assn U Tchrs; London Math Soc; Edinburgh Math Soc; ZOA; academic council, Friends Heb U; fmr: vice pres, Edinburgh Zionist Assn; chmn, Bur J Educ, Pasadena, Cal; mem council, Amer Math Soc; f, Royal Soc, Edinburgh; fgn mem, Acad of Sci, Torino; invited lectr, Intl Cong of Maths. Author: Asymptotic Expansions, 1956; Operational Calculus, 1962; ed and coauthor: Higher Transcendental Functions, 3 vols, 1953-55; Tables of Integral Transforms, 2 vols, 1954; mem ed bd: Journal of Soc of Ind and Applied Math; other math jours; contrb to profsl jours. Hobbies: music, walking. Home: 26 Gilmour Rd, Edinburgh, Scotland. Office: U of Edinburgh, Scotland.

ERDREICH, Marius, Isr, physician; b. Bucharest, Rum, May 31, 1929; s. Bernard and Sarah (Getzel); in Isr since 1950; MD, Heb U Med Sch, Jerusalem, 1956; m; c: Anat, David; m. 2nd, Amalia Zimerman, Apr 20, 1966; c: Adi. Med dir, dept dir, Govt Hosp, Acre, Isr, since 1962; mem, Appeal Comm, Natl Assurance; phys, Talbieh Hosp, 1956-57. Med off, IDF. Prin contribs: org clinical, teaching approach in psycht; improvement in cmty org mental hosps. Mem: Lyons Int; Isr Med Org; Neuro-Psycht Assn; Med Dirs of Hosps. Author: Prolytic Activity of Plasma in Different Pathological Conditions. Home: 24 Leon Blum St, Haifa, Isr. Office: Govt Hosp, Haganah St, Acre, Isr.

ERELL, Avraham, Isr, organization exec; b. Lodz, Pol, Aug 28, 1912; s. Chaim and Yita (Landau) Engel; in Isr, since 1925; att, Mikve Israel, Agric Sch; m. Dina Yoskovitz, Dec 26, 1957. Dir, Magen David Adom, Tel Aviv, since 1955. Maj, Brit Army, 1940-46; Rav Seren, IDF, 1948-53. Hobby: music, lit. Home: 8 Pinkas St, Tel Aviv, Isr. Office: 13 Mazeh St, Tel Aviv, Isr.

EREM, Moshe, Isr, legislator; b. Ladi, Russ, July 8, 1896; s. Shaul and Bluma (Besin) Kazarnovsky; in Isr since 1924; att Psychoneur Inst, Petrograd, 1916-18; Law Sch, U Moscow, 1918; m. Rivka Regensberg, 1917; c: Shimon, Mina. MK since 1949, chmn, Lab Comm, Knesset; mem: exec, Histadrut, since 1939; cen secretariat, Histadrut, since 1961; head, dept vocational training, Amal, since 1961; tchr, Russ, 1918-22; mem: Lab Council, Tel Aviv, 1924-35; Munic, Tel Aviv, 1926; dir: dept mil mobilization, vets, Histadrut, 1939-45; dept, relations between minorities and J, 1948-49. Mem: Poalei Zion; Zionist Actions Comm, 1939-55; exec, WJC, head, cultural dept, Isr Sect; delg: Working Pal Cong, Berlin, 1931; WZC; on mission to US, 1935-37. Author: Front Kegen Front, 1921; Di Blutike Geshenishen in Eretz Israel, 1929; leBaayat haSheela haAravit, 1935; HaZionut haZeira haBein Leumit, 1947; trans from Russ: haMilhama vehaSocialism; haMada vehaDat, both by Lenin; contbr to Isr press. Home: 7 Shimshon St, Tel Aviv, Isr. Office: The Knesset, Jerusalem, Isr.

EREN, Yehuda, Isr, writer, lecturer; b. Pol, 1906; s. Shalom and Yocheved; in Isr since 1933; att Art Conservatory, Vienna; m. Hana Greenwald; c: Ziva Ben Porat. Art adv, dir, Drama Dept, Cultural Cen, Va'ad Hapoel, since 1947; fmr: recitation performances: Eur; Latin Amer; actor, Wilner Truppe. Off, IDF, 1948-49. Author: Omanut haKri'a, 1960; Verteidigung der Alltäglichen Worte, 1937. Home: 187 Dizengoff St, Tel Aviv, Isr.

EREZ, Yehuda, Isr, editor; b. Novomirgorod, Russ, May 1, 1900; s. Fishel and Rivka Rejnitchenko; in Isr since 1923; c: Gad, Rivka. Ed, co-ed, Pub Cos: Nayot, Am Oved; mem: Kibbutz Giv'at Haim, since 1939; Kibbutz Tel Yosef, 1924-39; fmr ed, meHayeinu newspaper. Prin contribs: promoter publishing works of: Berl Katzenelson, Itzhak Ben Zvi, Eliyahu Golomb, Levi Eshkol, David Ben Gurion, and others. Ed: Sefer Z"S beRusia, 1963; Sefer ha'Aliya haShlishit, 1964; Zion Vatzedek, 1971; Igrot Berl Katznelson, 1970; Igrot Ben Gurion, 1971; contbr to newspapers and mags. Delg: 17th, 18th ZCs; Histadrut missions to Eur, 1928-29; 1933-34; 1937-38; mem: secretariat, Hakibbutz Hameuhad; Histadrut Council; Goud Ha'avoda Joseph Trumpeldor. Home: Kibbutz Giv'at Haim, Isr. Office: 64 Mazeh St, Tel Aviv, Isr.

ERHARD, Moshe Walter, Isr, insurance exec; b. Berlin, Ger, Jan 18, 1899; DEcon, U Freiburg; m. Margalit Solomon; three c. Chmn: Migdal-Binyan Ins Co; Maoz Ins Co, Life Assurance Assn. Mem bd: Sela Ins; Afr Isr Inves. Fmr: chmn, JNF, Ger; mem: Anglo-Isr C of C; Govt Ins Council; Isr-Swiss Friendship Assn; Migdal-Binyan, Eng. Home: 52 Hakeshet St, Ramat Gan, Isr. Office: POB 1888, Tel Aviv, Isr.

ERLANGER, Gustav, US, physician; b. Ichenhausen, Ger, Apr 21, 1886; s. Aaron and Dilly (Bayersdorf); MD, U Berlin, 1910; in US since 1935; m. Martha Wertheimer, Sept 25, 1947; c: Herbert. Ophthal, pvt practice; eye dept, U Munich, asst and dir, children's dept, eyes, U Hosp, Munich 1911-12; asso, privy councillor, Dr Paul Silex, St Maria Vic Hosp, Berlin, 1912-20; with: clinic, Manhattan Eye, Ear, Nose and Throat Hosp, 1936-37; Manhattan Gen Hosp, 1937-38, both NYC. Found, pres, Soc of Research on Iontophoresis, Inc, 1947; f: AAAP; AAAS; mem: Amer Assn Fmr Eur Chems; AMA; NY Co Med Soc; NY Acad Scis; Soc for Research on Iontophoresis; Natl Council Bus and Profsl Men; R Virchow

Med Soc. Contbr to med jours. Home and office: 20 W 77 St, New York, NY.

ERLANGER, Philippe, Fr, author, public servant; b. Paris, July 11, 1903; s. Camille and Irène (Hillel-Manoach); desc of Count Abraham Camondo; licencié en droit, diplomé des sciences politiques, licencié es lettres, Sorbonne, Paris. Ministre Plénipotentiaire, oprs pertaining to the arts, Min for Fgn Affairs, since 1946; found, Intl Film Festival, Cannes, Fr; mem, cen comm, Alliance Israélite Universelle, since 1932. Author: Henri III; Le Régent; Charles VII; Louis XIII; Buckingham; Monsieur, Frère de Louis XIV; Diane de Poitiers; L'Etrange Mort de Henri IV; Le Massacre de la Saint Barthélemy; Louis XIV; Cinq Mars ou la Passion et la Fatalité; Richelieu; Clemenceau. Recipient, among others: Officier de la Légion d'Honneur; CBE; Commandeur des Arts et Lettres. Home: 45 Croisette, Cannes, Fr.

ERON, Leonard D, US, educator; b. Newark, NJ, Apr 22, 1920; s. Joseph and Sarah (Hilfman); BS, CCNY, 1941; MA, Columbia U, 1946; PhD, U Wis, 1948; m. Madeline Marcus, May 21, 1950; c: Joan, Don, Barbara. Prof, psych, U of Ill, since 1969; asst prof psych, Yale U, 1948-55; lectr, Smith Coll Sch for Social Work, 1950-62; Fulbright lectr, Free U of Amsterdam, Holland, 1967-68; dir research, Rip Van Winkle Found, 1955-62; prof, psych, U of Ia, 1962-69. Lt, US Army, 1942-45. F: Amer, NY State, Mid Western, Ia, Psych Assns; mem: Phi Beta Kappa, Sigma Xis; dipl, Amer Bd of Examiners in Psych; fmr pres, Hudson Area Cmty Chest; pres, Ia Psych Assn. Co-author: An Experimental Approach to Projective Techniques; Relation of Theory to Practice in Psychotherapy; Classification of the Behaviour Disorders; contbr to psych jours. Office: U of Ill, Chicago Circle, Chicago, Ill.

ERON, Madeline M, US, psychologist; b. New Brunswick, NJ, Sep 8, 1920; d. Israel and Rae (Becker) Marcus; BA, NYU, 1941; MA, Columbia U, 1942; m. Leonard Eron, May 21, 1950; c: Don, Joan, Barbara. Dir, psych services, U of Ia Comprehensive Evaluation and Rehab Cen, since 1968; psych cons, Cedar Rapids, Ia, public schs, 1963-67; sr clinical psychol: Inst for Crippled and Disabled, NYC, 1944-50; Rip Van Winkle Clinic and Found, Hudson, NY, 1957-61; Berkshire Farm for Boys, Canaan, Conn, 1961-62. Mem: Amer, NY State, E, Midwestern, and Ia Psych Assns; Psych Assn of Northeastern NY; Council for Exceptional Children; League Women Voters; Sisterhood, Agudas Achim Cong; Psi Chi, Hadassah; past mem bd dirs, Hudson, NY chap, U Clubs; past pres, parent-tchr group, Union Free Sch, Claverack, NY. Contbr to profsl jours. Office: c/o Prof Leonard Eron, U of Ill, Chicago Circle, Chicago, Ill.

ERSNER, Jack S, US, physician; b. Phila, Oct 12, 1906; s. Samuel and Sara (Siegel); att Haverford Coll; BS, Temple U, 1927, MD, 1930; m. Anne Cohen, Mar 29, 1934; c: Roberta. Endocrinologist, gyn in pvt practice since 1931; chief em, endocrinology, Albert Einstein Med Cen, since 1969, asso chief, 1955-69; mem staff, Mt Sinai Hosp, 1938-49. Mem: AMA; Phila Co, Pa Med Assns; Endocrine Soc; pres, natl Phi Lambda Kappa, since 1949; mem bd govs, since 1939; ed, frat's quarterly and med directory; clubs: Phys Sq, mem bd govs since 1950, past pres, ed jour, Natl Medico-Masonicus, since 1955; Phila Alumni. Author: Treatment of Obesity, 1950; Treatment of the Underweight, 1943; Use of Benzedrine Sulfate in the Armed Forces, 1943; Hexestrol, A Synthetic Hormone, 1944; Treatment of Endocrine Disturbances in the Male, 1947; Endocrine vs Cellular Rejuvenation Implantation, 1960; Treatment of Cryptorchidism, 1961; Oral Contraceptives, 1962; ed, Medical Jour of Albert Einstein Med Cen, 1955-58. Home: 411 Meadowbrook Lane, Erdenheim, Pa. Office: Cen Med Bldg, Philadelphia, Pa.

ESENOFF, Carl M, US, accountant; b. Chgo, Ill, July 22, 1907; s. Elliot and Annie (Slavick); att San Diego State Coll; BS, U of Cal, 1929; m. Bernice Muskat, May 24, 1936; c: Ronda. Partner, Peat, Marwick, Mitchell and Co, cert public acctnts, since 1961; Everts and Esenhoff, cert public acctnts, 1938-61. Pres, Comty Found, United J Fund, since 1967; San Diego chap, CPA's, 1943; Fed JAs, 1950-55; secy, B'nai B'rith, 1935-37; treas, J Wfr Soc, 1947-48; Heb Home for Aged, 1944-54; chmn, United J Fund Drive, 1953; mem bd, United Comty Services, 1960-69; Temple Beth Isr, since 1966; Citizens Interracial Comm, since 1964; Cal Soc CPA's 1944-45; comm on auditing procedure, Amer Inst CPA's, 1950-53; Family Service Assn, 1947-50; mem bd trustees, Cal Western U, 1954-65; mem, Cal State Bd Acctncy, 1945-53; comm on

acctnt procedure, 1957-59; J Wfr Soc, 1947-48; Comty Wfr Council, 1948; adv bd, State Coll, since 1950; State Coll Alumni, 1934-37; Comty Chest, 1939-42; co council, Boy Scouts of Amer, 1943-52; C of C, San Diego, Cal, 1964-68; Beta Alpha Psi; Masons, Shrine; club, Rotary. Contbr to profsl mags. Home: 1150 Anchorage Lane, San Diego, Cal. Office: 1850 Fifth Ave, San Diego, Cal.

ESHEL, Jacob, Isr, business exec; b. Berlin, Ger, Mar 10, 1929; s. Kalman and Sarah (Richter); BSc, Tel Aviv U, 1959; grad studies, mgmt sem; m. Miriam Rot, May 26, 1953; c: Judith, Zvia. Dep mgr, Discount Bank Investment Corp Ltd, since 1969; fmr: mem bd dirs: Amer-Isr Paper Mills; Elron Electronic Ind; Elbit Computers; Monsel Electronic Instruments; Mimex; United Tours; Tambour Paints: Suliatan; vice pres, PEC Isr Econ, 1968; asst vice-pres, 1964-68; asst mgr, United Sran Plastics, 1955-60. Maj, IDF. Mem, Isr Mgmt Cen. Home: 3 Zahal St, Givatayim, Isr. Office: 16 Beit Hashoeva St, Tel Aviv, Isr.

ESHEL, Nimrod, Isr, government official; b. Ein Harod, Isr, July 27, 1925; s. Yehosua and Shlomith (Golomb); Nautical Educ degs; m. Bracha, 1952; c: Gidon, Tamar. Dir, shipping and ports div, Min of Transp, since 1968; fmr: 2nd mate on ship; master; head, emergency org of sea transp. Palmach, Haganah, underground immigration ships, taken prisoner for underground activity. Office: Min of Transp, Dept of Shipping and Ports, Haifa, Isr.

ESHKOL, Dov, Isr, hotel mgr; b. Karlsruhe, Ger, June 19, 1914; s. Haim and Bina (Silberfaden) Weintraub; in Isr since 1939; m. Yehudit Zarankin, May 5, 1942; c: Noah, Uri, Johai. Mgr, guest house, Kibbutz Ayelet Hashahar, since 1960. Lt col, IDF, 1959. Bd dirs: Histour; Pri Hagalil; Isr Hotel Assn. Recipient: man of year, 1967, Sk'al Club; Work Price, Histadrut, 1969. Home and office: Kibbutz Ayelet Hashahar, Upper Galilee, Isr.

ESHKOL, Yosef, Isr, journalist; b. Isr, Jan 18, 1929; s. Reuben and Hayah Limonik; m. Zipora Hadad; c: Giora, Uri, Zvi. Ed: Bamahaneh, since 1967; Bemahaneh Gadna, 1957-59; vocal progs, Isr Army Radio, 1959-62; Skira Mqusit, monthly, 1962-67. Sgt IDF, 1947-49. Author: Six Day's War, official report, pub by Min of Defense, 1967. Home: 63 Einstein St, Tel Aviv, Isr. Office: 1 Ein Dor St, Tel Aviv, Isr.

ESON, Morris E, US, educator; b. Montreal, Can, Apr 18, 1921; s. Max and Rose (Grusby) Isenberg; in US since 1937; BS, Ill Inst Tech, 1942; AM, U Chgo, 1944, PhD, 1951; ordained rabbi, Heb Theol Coll, 1945; m. Joy Platt, Mar 21, 1943; c: Charles, Elizabeth, Marc, Judd. Prof, chmn, psych dept, SUNY, since 1951; research asst, U Chgo, 1943-45; lectr, 1949-51; prin, Agudath Achim, Chgo Heb Sch, 1947-51. Chaplain, US Army, 1945-47. Pres, Psych Assn Northeastern NY, 1959-60; vice-pres, bd, Temple Isr, since 1961; mem, bd, J Social Service, 1953-61; f: Amer Psych Assn; AAAS; mem: Natl Soc Study of Educ. Author: Educational Psychology, 1963; contbr to profsl jours. Recipient: Fulbright Research Scholar, Heb U, 1957-58; visiting scholar, Isr Inst of Applied Social Research, 1967. Home: 817 Lancaster St, Albany, NY. Office: SUNY, 135 Western Ave, Albany, NY.

ESSRIG, Harry, US, rabbi; b. Safed, Pal, Aug 16, 1912; s. Isaac and Hannah (Trovitz); in US since 1920; BS, Tchrs Coll, Columbia U, 1932; cert, tchrs inst, JTSA, 1934; MHL, ordained rabbi, HUC, 1940; PhD, U Mich, 1957; hon DD, HUC, 1965; m. Rose Baskin, Aug 14, 1946; c.: Miriam, Ronald. Rabbi, U Syn, LA, Cal, since 1964; Hillel dir: U Chgo, 1940-42; Harvard U, MIT, both 1946-47; visiting instr, educ HUC, 1948-50; dir, Gt Lakes Council, UAHC, 1955-59; intern, psychotherapy and counseling, Merril-Palmer Inst, 1962-64; rabbi, Temple Emanuel, Grand Rapids, Mich, 1947-64. Asst staff chaplain, USMC, WW II. Mem: Amer Psychol Assn; Amer Assn Marriage Counselors. Co-author: Medinat Yisrael: Israel Today; contbr to: One America, 1962; Anglo-J jours. Home: 1943 Westridge Terrace Rd, Los Angeles, Cal. Study: 11960 Sunset Blvd, Los Angeles, Cal.

ESTERMANN, Immanuel, Isr, educator; b. Berlin, Ger, Mar 31, 1900; s. Arie and Rachel (Brenner); in Isr since 1964; DSc, U Hamburg, 1921; m. Roza Chwolles, 1923; c: Hannah Bergman, Eva. Prof, physics, Technion, Haifa, since 1964; lectr, U Hamburg, 1922-23; prof, physics, Carnegie-Mellon U, 1933-50; sci dir, USN Dept, 1950-64. Prin contrib: research in atomic and solid state physics. Mem bd: Tree of Life Cong, Phila, Pa, 1935-50; Heb Inst of Pittsburgh, 1940-50; club,

Cosmos, Wash, DC. Author: Methods of Experimental Physics, 1939; Research in Molecular Beams, 1959. Recipient: Silver Medal, Paris, 1962; Dist Civilian Service Award, Navy Dept, 1964. Home: 18 Hursha St, Haifa, Isr. Office: Dept of Physics, Technion, Haifa, Isr.

ESTERSON, Sidney Israel, US, educator; b. Baltimore, Md, Aug 28, 1902; s. Joseph and Rebecca (Fantuch); BA, Johns Hopkins U, 1924; PhD, 1931; Tchr Cert, Baltimore Heb Coll, 1923, BHL, 1924; m. Rose Abrahamowitz, July 26, 1931; c: Lonna Kahn, Judith Chernak, Marilyn, Joseph. Dir: Beth Jacob Sch and Cen, since 1948; Dept Info and Research, Baltimore, Bd of J Educ, since 1948; prin: Ezra Heb Sch, 1924-25; Isaac Davidson Heb Sch, 1925-46; dir, United Heb Schs, Dallas, 1946-48. Secy, Baltimore Prins Assn; pres: Baltimore Young Judaea, 1925-29; Heb Tchrs Assn; vice-pres, Natl Young Judaea; exec comm, Natl Council for J Educ; mem: ZOA; AJCong; Natl Conf J Communal Service. Contbr to J publs. Recipient: Harry Greenstein Award, Baltimore Heb Coll, 1968. Home: 6605 Park Heights Ave, Baltimore, Md. Office: 5713 Park Heights Ave, Baltimore, Md.

ESTRIN, Herman A, US, educator; b. N Plainfield, NJ, June 2, 1915; s. Morris and Ida (Bender); AB, cum laude, Drew U, 1937; AM, Tchrs Coll, Columbia U, 1942; prof dipl, dir of guidance, 1950, EdD, 1954; postdoc studies; m. Pearl Simon, June 26, 1949; c: Robert, Karen. Asso chmn, grad, undergrad divs, Newark Coll Engr, since 1950, prof, Eng, since 1958, on fac since 1946; instr, social studies, Grant Sch, S Plainfield, NJ, 1938-42; visiting prof, summer sessions, grad div, Cal Western U. US Army, 1942-46, capt, hon res corps, since 1946. Pres, NJ Assn Tchrs Eng, 1966-70; AAUP; Gtr NY Regional Coll Eng Assn, 1958-59; chmn, Amer Lit Landmarks Comm, NCTE; exec secy, NJ Engrs Council for Student Guidance, since 1953, exec comm, ed bd; second vice-pres, Natl Council Coll Publs, Adv, since 1961; mem: Amer Soc for Eng Educ; Natl Council for Tchrs of Eng; NJ Assn Tchrs Eng; Speech Assn of Amer; MLA; Conf on Coll Composition and Communication; NJ Collegiate Press Assn; NJ Personnel and Guidance Assn; Comm on Composition, Natl Council Tchrs of Eng; Sigma Tau Delta; Alpha Phi Omega; Phi Delta Kappa; Kappa Delta Phi; Omicron Delta Kappa; Pi Delta Epsilon; Tau De Delta Phil. Author: The New Scientist, 1962; Higher Education in Engineering and Science, 1963; Technical and Professional Writing, 1963; College and University Teaching, 1963; Freedom and Censorship of the College Press, 1966; The American Student and His College, 1967; The College Freshman, 1970; contbr to scholarly jours. Recipient, awards: Alumni Achievement in Arts, Drew U, 1957; medal, merit, Pi Delta Epsilon, 1957; meritorious plaque, NJ Collegiate Press Assn, 1958; nominee for George Westinghouse, Newark Coll of Engr, 1958; Vector Plaque Newark Coll Engr, 1961; citation, Newark Coll Engr, and Class of 1964, 1961; cert of award, NJ Collegiate Press Assn, 1961; Gold Key, Columbia Scholastic Press Assn, 1962; Cert of Commendation for Advancement of Coll Instruction, Tau Beta Pi, 1967. Hobbies: music, gardening. Home: 315 Henry St, Scotch Plains, NJ. Office: Newark Coll of Engr, Newark, NJ.

ESTRIN, Thelma, US, research engr; b. NYC, Feb 21, 1924; d. Isadore and Mary'(Ginsburg) Austern; att CCNY; PhD, U Wis, EE, 1951; m. Gerald Estrin, Dec 21, 1941; c: Margo, Judith, Deborah. Research engr, Brain Research Inst, UCLA, since 1960; engr, Weizmann Inst, 1954-56. Mem: bd, Amer Prof Peace in ME, LA chap; IEEE; Biomed Engr Soc; Electroencephalographic Soc; AAAS; Sigma Xi; AJCong. Recipient, F: Fulbright, US Govt, 1963; Ellen Sahn, Amer Assn U Women, 1951. Home: 500 Warner Ave, Los Angeles, Cal. Office: Anat Dept, UCLA, Los Angeles, Cal.

ETKIN, William N, biologist, educator; b. NYC, Dec 10, 1906; s. Israel and Dora (Rothenberg); BS, CCNY, 1928; MA, Cornell U, 1930; PhD, U Chgo, 1934; m. Ann Fliederbaum, 1932; c: Judith Levy, Asher. Prof em, anat, Albert Einstein Coll of Med, since 1955; prof em, biol, Yeshiva Coll, CCNY. Mem: ZOA; B'nai B'rith, pres, Educs Lodge, 1942. Author: College Biology, 1950; Social Behaviour of Vertebrates, 1964; contbr to med and zool jours. Spec interests: phil of sci, rel. Home: 630 Shore Rd, Long Beach, NY. Office: Albert Einstein Coll of Med, New York, NY.

ETRA, Max J, US, attorney; b. Galicia, Aus, Apr 24, 1903; s. Aaron and Sarah (Goldman); in US since 1907; BS, CCNY, 1924; LLB, Fordham U, 1928; LLD, Yeshiva U, 1958. Pvt law practice since 1929. Chmn bd trustees, Yeshiva U;

hon pres, Union Orthodox J Congs of Amer; pres: Yeshiva Syn Council of Amer; hon, Cong Kehilath Jeshurun; found, mem bd overseers, Albert Einstein Coll of Med; chmn, Amer J Tercentenary; vice-pres, Beth Isr Hosp; mem: bd trustees, Ramaz Sch; natl council, Boy Scouts of Amer; Assn Bar, NYC; NY Co Lawyers Assn; life, Mizrachi-Hapoel Ha-Mizrachi; Amer J Hist Soc; AJ Cong; CCNY: Alumni; Friars; Grand St Boys Assn; Elks. Home: 21 E 87 St, New York, NY. Office: 745 Fifth Ave, New York, NY.

ETTELSON, Harry W, US, rabbi; b. Lith, Oct 2, 1883; s. Samuel and Mollie (Harris); in US since 1884; BHL, HUC, 1900, ordained rabbi, 1904; BA, hons, U Cincinnati, 1904; PhD, Yale U, 1916; hon LLD, Southwestern U, Tenn, 1941; DD, HUC-JIR, 1954; m. Nell Schwab, Nov 20, 1924; c: William. Rabbi em, Temple Isr, Memphis, Tenn, since 1954, rabbi, 1925-54; rabbi: Achduth Vashalom, Ft Wayne, Ind, 1909-10; Beth Isr, Hartford, Conn, 1910-1919; Rodeph Shalom, Phila, Pa, 1919-25. Mem: exec, CCAR, hon life mem since 1954; chmn, comm on info on Judaism, UAHC since 1945; population bd, JPSA, since 1923; fmr: chmn, Juvenile Commn; found, United J Charities, both Hartford; pres: Bd J Mins, Phila; HUC Alumni Assn; Profsl and Church Social Workers Assn, Memphis; clubs: Cross-Cut, Memphis, found, pres; Yale, Ridgeway Country, Rotary of Memphis, Phi Beta Kappa, Memphis. Author: Integrity of I Maccabees, 1925; Ecclesiastes Quatrains, 1904; Leopold Stein, Centenary Paper, 1906; Love's Avowals, poems, 1927. Recipient: Newberger Cup, outstanding J citizen of year, Temple Isr Jrs, 1937; spec medallion, outstanding work in interfaith f, NCCJ, 1954. Home: 1023 A School Lane House, Philadelphia, Pa.

ETTENHEIM, Sarah C, US, civic worker; b. Richmond, Va, Mar 23, 1911; d. Jacob and Naomi (Silverman) Cohn; BA, physics, U Richmond, 1930; MS, political sci, U Wis, 1963; m. George Etterheim, Oct 10, 1933; c: George, Elizabeth Brandzel. Instr, Inst Govt Affairs, U Wis, Milw, since 1963; pres, Settlement Cook Book Co, since 1951. Pres, Milw Plan Comm, 1963-66; secy, United Comty Services, since 1967; mem bd: natl, regional, NCCJ, since 1948; Urban Day School, since 1967; Planned Parenthood Assn, since 1952; Milw J Council, since 1953; J Comty Cen, since 1959, 1946-48; YMCA, since 1958; Child Care Cens, 1946-56; Wis Mh Assn, 1954-58; Fed J Women's Orgs, 1950-52; J Vocational Service, 1953-56; Milw Found, 1960-68. Recipient: interfaith award, B'nai B'rith, 1955; spec service award, J Vocational Service, 1956; civic award, NCCJ, 1960; Skirting Politics award, presented by Milw Sentinel for civic service, 1964; Women's service award, for public service, 1965; Theta Sigma Phi civic Munic Award 1967. Hobby: handicraft. Home: 1260 N Prsopect Ave, Milwaukee, Wis.

ETTLINGER, Charlotte, Swed, civic worker; b. Kaunas, Lith, June 10, 1923; d. Isser and Ella (Lurie) Braude; in Swed since 1942; att U's: Uppsala; Stockholm, both Swed; m. Joseph Ettlinger, Dec 17, 1944; c: Kaj Manfred, Mirjam. Pres, WIZO, Swed, since 1957; cultural chmn and vice pres, 1953-57, mem, world exec, WIZO; mem bd, Natl Council Women in Swed; delg: cong, Intl Council of Women, Athens, 1951; WZC, Jerusalem, 1961; mem: exec, ZF, Swed; J Info Comm, Swed. Home: 7 Östermalmsgatan, Stockholm, Swed.

ETTLINGER, Hyman J, US, educator; b. St Louis, Mo, Sep 1, 1889; s. Abraham and Pearl (Shucart); BA, Wash U, St Louis, Mo, 1910; MA, Harvard U, 1911; PhD, 1920; m. Rosebud Segal, Sep 1, 1918; c: Martin. Prof, math, U Tex, since 1920, fac mem since 1913. US Signal Corps, 1917-19. Pres: Beth Isr Cong, 1943-44; J Council, 1946-52; B'nai B'rith lodge, 1938-39, all Austin, Tex; vice-pres, Southwest JCC, 1946-52; delg, White House Conf on Educ, 1955; mem: AAAS; Math Soc of Amer; Amer Math Soc; Tex Acad Sci; NRC; Phil Soc of Tex; Grass Roots Educ League of Tex; NCCJ; Phi Beta Kappa; Sigma Xi. Author: textbooks on maths; co-author, The Calculus, 1942; contbr articles on math to jours in US; Eng; Japan; Pol. Recipient: Byrd Found Award for stimulating youthful talent in sci, 1955. Hobbies: sports, travel. Home: 3110 Harris Park Ave, Austin, Tex. Office: PO Box 7512 U Station, Austin, Tex.

ETTLINGER, Joseph, Swed, businees exec; b. Stockholm, July 6, 1923; s. Jacob and Jeannette (Philip); engr, U Stockholm; m. Charlotte Braude, Dec 17, 1944; c: Mirjam, Kaj Manfred. Mgn dir, Mettal & Bergprodukter, Stockholm, since 1953; research chem under Profs Euler and Adler, 1944-46. Chmn: Hellel J Day Sch; Cong Adas Yisroel; mem: bd deps, Misrachi. Home: 7 Ostermalmsgatan, Stockholm, Sweden. Office: Mettal & Bergprodukter, Stockholm, Swed.

ETZION-HOLZBERG, Jitzchak Raphael, Isr, educator, author; b. Kovno, Russ, Apr 4, 1885; s. Feiba and Relke (Soloveitchik); in Isr since 1933; BA, Charkov U, Russ, 1912; m. Feige Yoffe, Aug, 1908; c: Joseph, Benjamin, Yecheskel. Ret; chief insp of rel schs, 1935-54; fmr: lectr, math, Charkov U; MP, Lith; asst prof, Tech HS, Charkov; dir: tchrs training coll; girls grammer sch, both Yavneh, 1921-33. Author: A Collection of Commentaries to the Torah, 1939; Axiomatics and Principles of Non-Euclidean Geometry, 1941; The Teaching of Arithmetics in the Junior Schools, 1946; Epistles to Parents on the Religious Education of their Children, 1956; The Foundations of Various Systems in the Teaching of Reading, 1957; The Great Universe in Which We Live, 1965; The Existence of God as the Principle of Judaism, 1961; The Study of the Problems of Religion, 1969; The Theory of Evolution From the Standpoint of Modern Exact Science, 1968; The Unity of the Creator as the Principle of Judaism and as the Fundament of Jewish Moral. Recipient: Knighthood of Gedimin Order, Lith, 1930; Prize for Educ, Tel Aviv Munic, 1967. Home: 30 Zfania St, Jerusalem, Isr.

ETZIONI, Amitai, US, educator; b. Cologne, Ger, Jan 4, 1929; s. Willi and Gertrude (Hanauer) Falk; in US since 1957; BA, Heb U, 1954, MA, 1956; PhD, U Cal, Berkeley, 1958; m. Minerva Morales, Sep 14, 1965; c: Eitan, Oren, Michael. Prof, sociol, Columbia U, since 1959, chmn, dept since 1969. Served, IDF. Author: Befrotz Haportzim Heb, 1952; A Comparative Analysis of Complex Organizations, 1961; The Hard Way to Peace: A New Strategy, 1962; The Active Society, 1968; Political Unification, 1965; contbr to profsl jours, periodicals. Mem, Amer Sociol Assn. Recipient: Guggenheim F, 1968-69. Home: 420 W 118 St, New York, NY. Office: Columbia U, New York, NY.

ETZIONI, Moshe, Isr, jurist; b. Jabno, Aus, Aug 28, 1908; s. Yaakov and Sheindel (Grossbard) Klapholz; in Isr since 1936; MJ, U Cracow, 1932, DJ, 1935; att, Jerusalem Law Classes; m. Yehudit Span, June 17, 1943; c: Yaakov, Amos. Pres, Dist Court, Haifa, since 1969; fmr relieving pres; in pvt law practice, 1942-45; atty, legal adv, War Produc and Heavy Ind Dept, 1945-48; magistrate, Tel Aviv, 1948; chief magistrate, Haifa, 1948; judge, dist court, 1949-59; temp Judge, Supr Court, Haifa, 1966. Mem: Isr bd, Intl Commn of Jurists; Rothschild Comty Cen, Haifa; ORT; fmr, chmn, govt and public comms of inquiry: Tivon Comm; Shatta Prison Comm; Wadi Salib Comm. Ed, Nasza Walka, Pol, 1923-36; contbr to Pol press. Spec interests: archaeol; hiking. Home: 4 Leonardo Da Vinci St, Haifa, Isr. Office: Dist Court, Haifa, Isr.

ETZIONY, Mordecai, Can, physician; b. Wioclawek, Pol, Feb 6, 1905; s. Samuel and Brayna (Lubianecki); in Can since 1922; BA, McGill U, 1928, MA, 1931, MD, 1938; m. Bella Forman, Nov 7, 1931. Mem, staff: J General Hosp, since 1941; J Hosp of Hope, since 1942; Herzl Dispensary, 1940-48; asst prin, J People's Schs, 1929-30; tchr, 1922-30; lectr, psych and first-aid, Yiddisher Folks U, 1942. Hon med off, Consulate Gen of Isr; curator, libr-mus, Shaar Hashomayim Syn, Montreal, since 1967; dir, Unzer Camp and Kindervelt, Farband Labor Zionist Org, 1932, 1934, 1936; chmn, med div, Histadrut campaign, 1950-54; mem: Can Med Assn; Montreal Medico-Chirurgical Soc; perm archivist, Montreal Clinical Soc; Amer Assn Hist Med; Friends Heb U; Amer Phys F Comm, IMA; YIVO; LZOA, Poale Zion; J Writers Assn, Montreal; med div, UJA; corresp mem, Isr Soc Hist of Med and Sci; f, Amer Geriatric Soc. Contbr to J Daily Eagle since 1930; med jours. Home and office: 4765 Edouard Montpetit Blvd, Montreal, Can.

EULAU, Milton B, US, attorney; b. NYC, Feb 26, 1912; s. Julius and Hortense (Bachenheimer); BA, Cornell U, 1933; JD, NYU, 1936; m. Harriet Katz, Nov, 1945. Partner, Liebman, Eulau, Robinson & Perlman, since 1937; with NY Co Dist Atty's off, 1935-36. Vice-pres: and mem, bd trustees, Family Location Service, past pres; and chmn, exec comm and mem bd, Asso YM-YWHAs, Gtr NY, since 1945, pres since 1967; mem, bd trustees, FJP, since 1946; fmr: pres, bd trustees, Madison House, NYC; vice-pres, mem, bd trustees: J Assn of Neighborhood Cens; J Family Service. Home: 875 Park Ave, New York, NY. Office: 32 E 57 St, New York, NY.

EVANS, Clifford, US, television news exec; b. NYC; s. Joseph and Rebecca (Calvert); att CCNY; m. Ruth Wolf. Dir,

Wash News Bureau, RKO Gen Bc, since 1966; spec reporter, assoc produc, Today program, NBC TV, 1952-60; vice-pres, Sports Network, 1960-62; produc, moderator, Ladies of the Press, TV and radio, 1962-67. Mem, White House Corresp Assn; club, Natl Press, Wash, DC. Recipient: awards: UN, journalism, UN Assn, 1945; Page One, Newspaper Guild, NY, 1947; Golden Eagle, Film Documentation, NEA, 1965; Human Relations Award, B'nai B'rith, 1966; Lasker, Variety. Home: 4201 Cathedral Ave, NW, Washington, DC. Office: 5100 Wisconsin Ave, NW, Washington, DC.

EVANS, Emanuel J, US, business exec, city official; b. Plainfield, NJ, May 2, 1907; s. Isaac and Sarah (Newmark); BA, U of NC, 1928; m. Sara Nachamson, June 19, 1928; c: Robert, Eli. Pres, Evans United Dept Stores, since 1930; mayor, City of Durham, since 1951; dir, Wachovia Bank, Durham, since 1948; Colorcraft Corp, since 1969; WRDV-TV, Durham, since 1968. Pres: Merchants Assn, 1950; Comty Chest, 1946; hon life, Beth El Syn, since 1951; NC Munic League, 1958; vice-pres: Durham C of C, 1969; Watts Hosp, 1969; chmn: NC Bonds for Isr, 1969; United Fund, Durham,1964; state chmn, UJA, 1944; bd, U of NC Alumni Assn, 1968-70; chmn, U of NC Alumni Giving Council, 1958-60; mem, Council, US Conf of Mayors, 1956-62; club, Kiwanis, vice-pres, 1945. Recipient: young man of year award, Jr C of C, for services to the comty, 1942; Durham civic hon award, 1964; nominated hon citizen of Jerusalem, Isr, 1953. Home: 1401 Fairview, Durham, NC. Office: 118½ E Main St, Durham, NC.

EVANS, Raymond Bernard, US, songwriter; b. Salamanca, NY, Feb 4, 1915; s. Philip and Frances (Lipsitz), 1936; BS, U of Pa, 1936; m. Wyn Ritchie, Apr 19, 1947. Songwriter, Livingston & Evans, since 1940. Maj songs: Buttons & Bows; Mona Lisa; Que Sera Sera; To Each His Own; Golden Earrings; Silver Bells; Tammy; Bonanza; Dear Heart; music for: numerous Hollywood movies; Broadway shows: Oh Captain; Let It Ride. Mem: Beta Sigma Rho; ASCAP; Acad Motion Picture Arts and Scis; Natl Acad Recording Arts and Scis; Composers and Lyricists Guild. Recipient: Acad Awards, for: Buttons & Bows, 1948; Mona Lisa, 1950; Que Sera Sera, 1956. Hobbies: sport, lit, politics, travel. Home and office: 1255 Angelo Dr, Beverly Hills, Cal.

EVANS, Sara N, US, business exec, communal worker; b. Baltimore, Md; d. Eli and Jennie (Bloom) Nachamson; att: Goucher Coll, Baltimore; Duke U, Durham, NC; m. Emanuel Evans, June 19, 1928; c: Robert, Eli. Secy-treas: Evans United Dept Stores Co, since 1935; Evans Inves, since 1953; Jefferson Inves, since 1948; mem, bd dirs, Cape Fear Feed Products, since 1960. Pres: Seaboard Region, Hadassah, 1942-44; hon Durham Chap, Hadassah, 1952, hon life mem; Durham Fed J Charities, 1958-61; natl vice-pres, Hadassah,1954-57; chmn, NC Women's Div, UJA, 1958; mem, bd dirs: natl, United Isr Appeal, 1960; natl Hadassah, 1942-51; United Fund since 1960; women's div, Durham Comty Fund, 1952; mem: NC State Bd, Amer Assn for UN, 1961-63; Durham Assn for UN; NCCJ; League Women Voters; United Fund, Durham; NC Sym Orch; bldg comm, Beth El Synagogue, 1958; clubs: Women's, Durham; Bus and Profsl Women's. Recipient: Leadership Award, UJA, 1958; award, State of Isr Bonds, 1962; spec award, Tau Epsilon Phi. Home: 1401 Fairview, Forest Hills, Durham, NC. Office: 118½ E Main St, Durham, NC.

EVEN, Joseph K, Isr, business exec; b. Bialystok, Russ, May 3, 1916; s. Wolfe and Tauba(Warhaftig) Kamieniecki; BSc, Technion, Haifa, 1941; m. Tamar Varon, July 10, 1946; c: Hermona Soreq, Yael, Matityahu. Mgn dir, Hahofer, Isr Ltd since 1967; dir: Jerusalem Quarries; Hartuv Quarries; and asso firms, since 1962; dir: bldg div, Min of Defense, 1954-57; Lime and Stone, 1958-62; design and construction, Hartuv Quarry, 1962-67. J Brig, 1943-46; IDF, 1948-57. Mem bd govs, exec council, Technion; mem: Assn Engrs and Architects, Isr; Soc for Rock Mech; fmr: pres, Alumni Assn, Technion; chmn, Munic Emergency Comm, Rishon le Zion; mem: panel of judges, supr mil court; clubs: Rishon le Zion br, Rotary, fmr pres; Engrs, Tel Aviv, fmr pres; mem, ed bd, Jour of Assn of Engrs and Architects, Isr. Spec interests: hist, sci. Home: 16 Jerusalem St, Rishon le Zion, Isr. Office: 44 Petah Tikva Rd, Tel Aviv, Isr.

EVENOR, Hanna, Isr, judge; b. Warsaw, Pol, Jan 17, 1919; d. Nahum and Sabina (Goldmacher) Nir; in Isr since 1925; att law classes, Jerusalem, 1939-45; m. Eshel Evenor, 1945; c: Roni, Irith, Michal. Judge, Tel Aviv dist court, since 1964; advocate, 1945-49; dep dist atty, 1952-62; dist atty, 1962-64, all Tel Aviv; lectr, law fac, Tel Aviv U, since 1962. Mem: cen comm, Isr Bar Assn; comm, Women Lawyers Assn. Co-author: Civil Wrongs—The Law and Precedents, Part I, 1957; contbr articles to profsl jours. Home: 15 Bar Kochba St, Ramat Gan, Isr.

EVEN-SHOSHAN, Avraham, Isr, educator, author, linguist; b. Minsk, Russ, Dec 25, 1906; s. Chaim and Roshka Rosenstein; in Isr since 1925; grad, Heb Tchrs Sem, 1928; MA, Heb U, 1942; m. Zivia Kagan, July 15, 1931; c: Yuval, Daphna. Instr, Isr Min of Educ, 1952-53; prin, David Yellin Heb Tchrs Coll, 1954-67. Council mem, Isr Tchrs Assn, since 1928. Author: The New Illus Heb Dict, 1947-51; juvenile lit: A Hundred and One Wonders, 1930; The Book of Wonders, 1944; Let's Solve the Puzzle, 1940. Co-author: Stories of the Bible, 1934; Torah with Rashi for Schools, 1946; The Concordance of Bialik's Poetry, 1961; ed: Itonenu, children's weekly, 1932-1937. Home: 15 Arlosoroff St, Jerusalem, Isr.

EVEN-TOV, Ori, Isr, electric engr; b. Jerusalem, Sep 16, 1927; s. Meir and Hanna; BSc, Columbia U, 1956; MS, Drexel Inst of Tech, Phila, 1959; m. Mina Fuhrman, Apr 17, 1958; c: Tamar, Daniel. Mgr, Plant B, Isr Aircraft Ind; engr, Remington Rand Univac, 1956-58; chief devl engr, B & F Control Systems, 1958-60. Capt, IDF, 1947-52. Prin contrib: research and devl means of war. Mem, IEEE, Isr. Recipient: Isr Defense Award, 1966; Jerusalem Decoration. Home: 40 Hagderot St, Savyon, Isr. Office: Yahud, Isr.

EVER, Isaac Hirsh, US, rabbi; b. Warsaw, Pol, Feb 27, 1913; in US since 1925; s. Hyman and Celia (Plotzker); ordained rabbi, New Haven, Cleveland Orthodox Rabb Sem of Amer, 1935; hon DL, Burton Coll, Colo, 1955, PhD, 1956; m. Ethel Levenberg, Mar 8, 1936. Rabbi, Agudath Isr Heb Inst, since 1951; found and chancellor, Talmudic Theol Coll of Amer, since 1962; prin, Beth Jacob Sem of Amer, 1938-40; rabbi, Saratoga Heb Cen, Bklyn, NY, 1940-47; southeastern dir, Yeshiva U, Miami Beach, 1949-51. Mem, World Rel Mizrachi Movement. Author: The Biography of Rabbi Judah H Levenberg, 1939; Holiday Symbols, 1947; Two Worlds, 1956; Life Dream, 1961. Home: 525-78 St, Miami Beach, Fla. Study: 7801-7811 Carlyle Ave, Miami Beach, Fla.

EVER-HADANI, Aharon, Isr, poet, author, editor; b. Pinsk, Russ, Apr 25, 1899; s. Nissan and Shoshana (Shemrinski) Feldman; in Isr since 1913; grad, agric coll, Holland, 1926; m. Hemda Stern, 1923; c: Rachel, Arieh. Free-lance writer since 1930; chief ed, Chaklauth beIsrael,Min of Agric monthly, since 1955; agric worker, Pal, 1921-24; instr, agric settlements, 1924-30; mem ed staff, Boustani, weekly, 1932-40; ed, ha-Meshek haChaklai, monthly, 1940-44. Author: The Wooden Shack, 1930; The Enterprise in the Wilderness, 1931; The Volunteer Tapuchi, 1936-38; Shomrim, produced by Habimah Theatre; A People at War, 1947; The Sixty Years' History of Hadera, 1951; With Valor and Spirit, 1952; History of Benyamina, 1953; Fifty Years of Settlement in Lower Galilee, 1950-54; Shimon the Locust-Fighter; Kol Asher Neshama be Apo, 1963; book on PICA (1882-1957); Selected Works, 1967,68,all in Heb. Home: 21 Hissin St, Tel Aviv, Isr.

EVRON, Ephraim, Isr, civil servant; b. Haifa, Isr, June 12, 1921; s. Shlomo and Dvora (Goldsweig) Epstein; att Heb U, Jerusalem, 1939-41; govt law classes, Jerusalem, 1945-48; m. Rivka Passman, Sep 14, 1943; c: Tamar, Dan. Ambass to Can since 1969; political secy to Fgn Min Moshe Sharett, 1949-51; secy to PM David Ben-Gurion, 1951-53; second secy, Emb of Isr, Wash DC, 1953; chef de cabinet, Defence Min Pinhas Lavon, 1954-55; Histadrut repr to N Amer, bd dirs, Solel Boneh, both 1955-61; first counsellor, later min plen, Isr Emb, London, 1961-65; appd min, Emb of Isr, Wash DC, 1965-68; ambass, Swed, 1968-69. Brit ME Forces, 1941-46; IDF, 1948. Office: Min for Fgn Affairs, Jerusalem, Isr.

EVYATAR, Asriel Andre, Isr, mathematician; b. Antwerp, Belgium, June 14, 1926; s. Elias and Helene (Knoblauch) Gutwirth; in Isr since 1951; SC, 1951, Lic sci, 1948, U Libre, Brussels; m. Hena Kohn, Apr 10, 1949. Dean, fac math, Technion, Haifa,since 1969, fac mem since 1954; research asso, Northwestern U, 1958-59; U of Cal, 1959-60; asso prof, U Mass, 1963-64, sr lectr, 1964-65. Lt, IDF. Pres, Technion Tchrs Assn, 1964-66; found mem, Isr br, Amer Prof for Peace in ME; mem: Isr Math Union; Amer Math Soc. Contbr to sci jours. Home: 98 Shoshanat Hacarmel St, Haifa, Isr. Office: Technion, Haifa, Isr.

EWEN, David, US. author, musicologist; b. Lwow, Aus-Hung,

Nov 26, 1907; s. Isaac and Helen (Kramer); att CCNY, 1924-27; musical educ, pvt tutors and spec courses, Columbia U; m. Hannah Weinstein, Sep 11, 1936; c: Robert. Adj prof music, U Miami, since 1966; free-lance writer; music ed: Cue Mag, 1937-38; Universal J Ency, 1939-43; serious record music critic, stage, 1938-39; dir, Allen, Towne and Heath, publishers, 1946-49; US Army, 1944-45; authorized to write hist Amer paratroopers. Author: The Unfinished Symphony: Story of Franz Schubert, 1931; Hebrew Music, 1931; From Bach to Stravinsky, 1933; Composers of Today, 1934; The Man of the Baton, 1935; Twentieth Century Composers, 1936; Men and Women Who Make Music, 1939, last ed, 1949, trans into Heb; Pioneers in Music, 1940; Living Musicians, 1940; Music Comes to America, 1942, 1947; The Book of Modern Composers, 1942, 1951; Dictators of the Baton, 1943, 1948; The Story of George Gershwin, 1943, trans into Heb; Music for the Millions, 1944, 1954; Men of Popular Music, 1944, 1952; Tales from the Vienna Woods, 1944; Listen to the Mocking Words, 1945; Haydn: A Good Life, 1945; Songs of America, 1947; American Composers Today, 1948; The Story of Irving Berlin, 1950; The Story of Arturo Toscanini, 1952; The Complete Book of 20th Century Music, 1952; The Story of Jerome Kern, 1953; European Composers Today, 1954; Encyclopedia of the Opera, 1955; Panorama of American Popular Music, 1957; Richard Rogers, 1957; The Complete Book of the American Musical Theatre, 1958; Encyclopedia of Concert Music, 1959; The World of Jerome Kern, 1960; Leonard Bernstein, 1960; The Story of America's Musical Theatre, 1961; History of Popular Music, 1961; New Book of Modern Composers, 1961; Ewen's Lighter Classics of Music, 1961; The World of Great Composers, 1962; David Ewen Introduces Modern Music, 1962; The Book of European Light Opera, 1962; The Life and Death of Tin Pan Alley, 1964; The Complete Book of Classical Music, 1965; American Popular Songs: From the Revolutionary War to the Present, 1966; The World of Twentieth Century Music, 1967; co-author: Musical Vienna, 1939; Fun with Musical Games and Quizzes, 1952, trans into Heb; The Milton Cross Ency of Great Composers, 1953, trans into Heb; books have been trans into many langs; reprinted in Armed Services eds; contracted by VOA to write and co-produce numerous broadcasts on hist of Amer popular music, 1962; Kol Isr, Jerusalem, Jerusalem Conservatory, 1962. Home and office: 2451 Brickell Ave, Miami, Fla.

EWIG, Arthur B, US, attorney; b. Warsaw, Pol, Oct 1, 1903; s. William and Regina (Pasternak) Ewigkeit; in US since 1906; LLB, Fordham U, 1924; m. Mahnyna Seidlin, Feb 24, 1929; c: Joan, Barbara. Practising atty, Ewig and Beck since 1925; spec city judge, Kingston, NY, since 1958; fmr: atty, NY State Tax Commn for Ulster Co; Ulster Co Town Atty; Corp Counsel for City of Kingston. Pres: Ulster Co Bar Assn; J Comty Council; past pres: Temple Emanuel; B'nai B'rith; all Kingston; mem: bd trustees, Kingston Hosp; bd dirs, Ulster County Chest; Civil Service Commn, Ulster Co. Hobbies: photography, gardening. Home: 261 Pearl St, Kingston, NY. Office: 286 Clinton Ave, Kingston, NY.

EYLON, Abraham, Isr, government official; b. Vilkovishkes, Russ, Dec 21, 1894; s. Isaac and Theresa Idelson; in Isr since 1927; PhD, U Leningrad, 1921; m. Nadiezda Mordvinov, 1918; one c. Isr Govt printer, 1948-65; dir, Assn of Coop J Banks, Lith, 1923-26; found: Mischar veTaasiya Co Ltd; Levant Fairs, Tel Aviv; Pal Airways; org, Pal fgn trade exhbs. Fmr: chmn, Hahever, Zionist Students Assn, Russ; mem, cen comm, Zionist Org, Russ and Lith. Contbr to Isr and fgn press. Home: 214 Ben Yehuda St, Tel Aviv, Isr.

EYLON, Izhak, Isr, civil engr; b. Warsaw, Pol, Jan 11, 1899; s. Jeshajah and Blima (Ritter) Landstok; in Isr since 1930; dipl, CE, Poly U, Warsaw, 1927; m. Minna Zarecki, June 5, 1932; c: Alexander. Ret; asst munic engr, Givatayim, Isr, 1947-53; asst chief engr, Rassco, Tel Aviv, 1953-68. Sgt, Pol Army, 1918-1921. Pres, Org Warsaw J in Isr, since 1954; mem: exec, Fed Pol J in Isr, since 1964; Assn Engrs and Architects in Isr; Histadrut, engrs sect; B'nai B'rith; fmr: pres: Academicians Org; Hatechijah; mem, exec, Zionist Org, all in Pol; delg, ZCs; pres, J Students Org, Warsaw, Poly U; found, first pres, Halutz Baalei Melacha, Pol. Home: 185 Ben Yehuda St, Tel Aviv, Isr.

EYLON, Pinhas Jacob, Isr, communal leader; b. Opochno, Pol, Apr 6, 1909; s. Yechezcel and Chaya (Sppaizman) Zuker; in Isr since 1930; m. Miriam Landsberg, Feb 2, 1930; c: Hagai, Drora. Mayor, Holon, since 1953. Off, Haganah, 1930-52. Chmn, Union of Local Auth in Isr; delg, Intl Mayor

Congs, Rome, Isr, Wash, Warsaw, Belgrade, Stockholm, Vienna. Mem: Cen Comm, Lab Party; B'nai B'rith; hon mem, Rotary Club. Recipient: hon citizen, Suresnes, Fr. Home: 104 Bialik St, Holon, Isr. Office: Munic of Holon, Inc, Isr.

EYTAN, Eli, Isr, educator; b. Munich Ger, July 25, 1908; s. Jacob and Sara (Körber); in Isr since 1934; att U: Leipzig; Vienna, 1926-27; PhD, U Munich, 1932; m. Ruth Lewin, Dec 31, 1933; c: Edna Liban. Sci secy, Heb Lang Acad, co ed, Leshonenu la'Am, since 1945; sr lectr, Tel Aviv U, since 1957; tchr, secondary schs,Tel Aviv, Haifa, 1934-42; journalist, Haboker, 1936-39. Fmr mem, Soc for Advancement of Sci. Contbr to ling jours. Home: 50 Yair St, Ramat Gan, Isr. Office: 6 Kaplan St, Tel Aviv, Isr.

EYTAN, Rachel, Isr, author; b. Tel Aviv, May 4, 1932; d. Yaakov and Sarah (Zewig) Litai; att Tchrs Sem: Levinsky; Ha-Kibbutzim; m. Dan Eytan, 1952 (div); c: Omry, Hamutal; m. 2nd Jerry Fishman, Oct 2, 1967. Author: ba Rakia ha Hamishi, 1962; contbr short stories to newspapers; lectr, Heb lit; fmr tchr. Recipient: Brenner prize, 1966. Homes: 14 Him St, Tel Aviv, Isr; 227 Central Park W, New York,NY.

EYTAN, Reuven, Isr, organization exec; b. Munich, Ger, Sep 22, 1909; s. Jacob and Sara (Koerber); in Isr since 1934; PhD, Us: Leipzig; Munich; Vienna; m. Francisca; c: Daniel, Ayala. Dir, org, info depts, World Zionist Org; secy, Zionist Gen Council; fmr: secy: Zionist Org; Keren Kayemet leIsr, both Ger; org of Zionist activities: Isr, Asia, US, Eur. Contbr pamphlets and papers on Zionism and hist of art. Hobby, art. Home: 37 Jabotinsky St, Jerusalem, Isr.

EYTAN, Walter, Isr, diplomat; b. Munich, Ger, July 24, 1910; s. Maurice and Hedwig (Kahn); in Isr since 1946; att St Paul's Sch, London; BA, Queens Coll, Oxford, 1932, MA, 1934; m; c: David, Ruth, Jonathan; m. 2nd Beatrice Levison, Apr 2, 1958. Political adv to Fgn Min, since 1971; lectr, Ger, Queens Coll, Oxford, 1934-46; prin, Public Service Coll, Jerusalem, 1946-48; dir gen, Isr Min for Fgn Affairs, 1948-59; head Isr Delg: Armistice Negotiations with Egypt Rhodes, 1949; Lausanne Conf, 1949; Atoms for Peace Conf, Geneva, 1955; ambass to Fr 1960-71. Author: The First Ten Years: A Diplomatic History of Israel, 1958. Office: Min for Fgn Affairs, Jerusalem, Isr.

EZEKIEL, Mordecai JB, US, economist, UN, US official; b. Richmond, Va, May 10, 1899; s. Jacob and Rachel (Brill); BS, U of Md, 1918; MS, U Minn, 1923; PhD, Robert Brookings Grad Sch, Wash, DC, 1926; m. Lucille Rinsterwald, Dec 24, 1927; c: David, Jonathan, Margaret. Cons econ: Agcy for Intl Devl; U Ariz; FAO Indicative World Plan, all since 1967; spec asst to dir gen, Food and Agric Org, UN, 1961-62, agric econ to dir gen i/c econ dept, 1947-61; with US Census Off, 1920-22; jr, later sr econ, Dept Agric, 1922-30; asst chief econ, US Fed Farm Bd, 1930-33; econ adv to secy, Dept, Agric, 1933-46; econ, US Agcy for Intl Devl, 1962-67. Lt, US Army, 1918. F: Amer Stat Assn; Intl Conf Agric Econs; Econometric Soc; Amer Farm Econ Assn; Amer Econ Assn; fmr mem bd, Overseas Sch of Rome. Author: Methods of Correlation Analysis, 1929, 1940, 1959; $2500 a Year from Scarcity to Abundance, 1936; Jobs for All, 1939; Towards World Prosperity Through Economic Development, 1947; contbr to profsl jours. Hobbies: hiking, gardening, skiiing. Home: 5312 Allandale Rd, Washington, DC.

EZEKIEL, Nissim, India, educator, poet, playwright; b. Bombay, Dec 16, 1924; s. Moses and Diana (Jhirad); BA, hons, Wilson Coll, 1945; MA, U Bombay; m. Daisy Jacob, Nov 23, 1952;

three c. Head, Eng dept, Mithibai Coll of Arts, Bombay, since 1961. Secy, India br, PEN club. Author: A Time to Change and Other Poems, 1952; Sixty Poems, 1953; The Third, poems, 1958; The Unfinished Man, poems, 1960; The Exact Name, poems, 1966; ed: An Emerson Reader, 1966; A Martin Luther King Reader, 1969; Poetry India, quarterly; cons ed, Paperback Pub Prog, India Book House. Hobbies: performing and visual arts. Home: The Retreat, Bellasis Rd, Bombay, India. Office: Mithibai Coll of Arts, Vile Parle, W Bombay, India.

EZEKIEL, Walter N, US, industrial microbiol, plant path; b. Richmond, Va, Apr 26, 1901; s. Jacob and Rachel (Brill); BS, Md State Coll, 1920; MS, U of Md, 1921, PhD, 1924; att: US Dept Agric Grad Sch, 1922-24; U Minn, 1925-27; m. Sarah Ritzen; c: Herbert, David, Joseph, Raphael, Miriam Bernhardt. Microbiol, Bur Mines Research Cen, College Park, since 1964; asst plant path, Md Agric Experiment Sta, 1920-25; natl research f, biol scis, U Minn, 1925-27; plant path, Tex Agric Experiment Sta, 1928-44; mycologist i/c, fungus and moisture proofing prog, Navy Dept, 1944-54; technologist, microbiol, Bur of Mines, Interior Dept, 1955-64. Vice-chmn, gov div, UJA, since 1968, on exec comm since 1951; chmn, Brazos Co, Tex, UJA, 1940-44; vice-chmn, UJA, for Dept of Navy, 1946-54; chmn for Interior Dept, 1957-64; mem: div agric and colonization, Econ Research Comm, ORT, since 1941; Natl Council for Pal, under UPA, Wash Coll J Studies; Wash chap, Amer Technion Soc; f: AAAS, Tex Acad Sci; mem: Amer Phytopath Soc; Mycological Soc of Amer; Sigma Xi; Soc for Ind Microbiol; Wash Botanical Soc; Soc Tech Writers and Publishers; Amer Inst Biol Scis; Amer Soc for Microbiol; ZOA; Friends Heb U; mem, Va Bicentenary Commn, 1938; chmn, comm preparing exhbs for Tex Centennial Exposition, 1936. Contbr numerous papers to profsl publs. Recipient: postdoc f, NRC, 1925-27; meritorious civilian service award and citation, Bur of Ordnance, 1946. Home: 3105 34 St, NW, Washington, DC. Office: Research Cen, College Park. Md.

EZER, Alexander, Isr, government official; b. Priluki, Russ, May 10, 1894; s. Emanuel and Miriam (Silifka) Ezerov; in Isr since 1921; att Psychoneurol Inst, St Petersburg, 1913-15; fac law, U Tomsk, 1917; m. Rivka Wolkenstein; c: Manuella Gabriel. Govt adv for tourism since 1964; dir, Binyanei Ha'uma, Ltd, Jerusalem, since 1949; mgn dir, Heb Librs Distribution, since 1952; fmr: found, dir, Trade and Ind Pub and Exhb; Levant Fair, Pal Exhbs, Press and Publicity; org, Pal exhbs abroad; dir: J Ind Council; econ dept, JA; Conquest of the Desert Exhb; fmr mem: Cen Zionist Comm Siberia and Ural; J Natl Comm, Siberia; Siberian Parl, repr Siberian J, 1917-19. Found and ed: Trade and Industry, 1923-36; Palestine and the Middle East, 1926-36; Palestine Trade Catalogue, 1945-46. Home: 90 Herzl Blvd, Jerusalem, Isr.

EZRAHI, Yariv, Isr, composer, musician; b. Jerusalem, Isr, Dec 31, 1904; s. Modechay and Batya Krishepski; in Isr since 1904; att Commercial Sch, Tel Aviv; grad, Music Acad, Vienna; att Conservatory of Music,Vienna; m. Hana Diesenhaus; c: Ofra Magen, Yaron. Dir, Ron Conservatory, since 1938; prof music, violin; music critic: Hayom, Yediot Acharonot, Heb dailies. Served, Haganah. Composer: Songs with Piano; 2 Suites for Youth, String Orch; The Wild Shepherd, violin with piano accompaniment; Art and Popular Songs; Suites for Strings. Pres, Music Critics Assn; hon secy, Music Tchrs Assn; adv mem prog comm, ZOA House. Recipient: first prizes, London Intl Competitions. Hobbies: sports, isometrics. Home: 103 Ibn Gvirol St, Tel Aviv, Isr.

F

FABIAN, Alfred, Austr, minister; b. Breslau, Ger, Aug 27, 1910; s. Leo and Ella (Baron); in Austr since 1939; LLD, U Breslau, 1933; ordained rabbi, J Theol Sem, Breslau, 1939; m. Ilse Sternberg, Dec 1, 1940; c: Miriam, Diana, Carmel. Chief min, N Shore Syn, Sydney, since 1962; sr J chaplain, Commonwealth Mil Forces, since 1962, chaplain, N Command, since 1953; min, Adelaide Heb Con, 1940-47; chief min, Brisbane Heb Cong, 1947-62. Hon treas, Assn J Mins of Austr; vice pres: UN Assn; Marriage Guidance Council; Comty of Sydney Wfr Services; mem: Scouts Council, Queensland; club, Brisbane Rotary, 1953-62. Hobby, music. Home: 8 Kenilworth Rd, Lindfield, Austr. Study: 15 Treatts Rd, Lindfield, Austr.

FABRICANT, Solomon, US, economist, educator; b. Bklyn, NY, Aug 15, 1906; s. Sam and Sarah (Plotkin); BCS, NYU, 1926; BS, CCNY, 1929; MA, Columbia U, 1930, PhD, 1938; m. Bessie Blacksin, Feb, 1934; c: Ruth, Peter, Sarah. Prof, econ, NYU, since 1948; staff mem, Natl Bur of Econ Research, 1930-53 and since 1965, acting dir research, 1953-54, dir, 1954-65; council mem, Intl Assn for Research in Income and Wealth, since 1965; chmn, research adv bd, Comm for Econ Devl, 1960-62; cons, Bur of Budget, 1945-52 and 1962-65; Bur of Census, 1945-50 and since 1960; NY State Tax Commn, 1951-52; HEW 1966-69; Pres, Task Force on Sci Policy 1969. Mem: Amer Acad of Arts and Scis; Amer Econ Assn, vice-pres, 1960-61; Amer Phil Soc; Amer Stat Assn; Econometric Soc; Econ Hist Assn, trustee, 1952-56; Royal Econ Soc; Soc of Bus Adv Professions, vice-pres, 1961-65. Asso ed, Jour of Amer Stat Assn, 1950-51. Author: Capital Consumption and Adjustment, 1938; Output of Manufacturing Industries, 1940; Employment in Manufacturing, 1942; Trend of Government Activity, 1952; The Economic Consequence of Size of Nations, 1960; Primer on Productivity, 1969; Philanthropy in the American Economy, 1969; co-author: Economic Principles and Problems, 1936; Studies in Income and Wealth, 1937, 1946, 1949, 1950, 1958, 1969; War and Defense Economics, 1952. Contbr to sci jours. Home: 157 Brite Ave, Scarsdall, NY. Office: Nat Bur of Eco Research, 261 Madison Ave, New York, NY.

FACHER, Irwin Lee, US, attorney; b. Newark, NJ, Sep 13, 1939; s. Saul and Sylvia (Brody); AB, Dartmouth Coll 1961; JD, Harvard Law Sch, 1964; m. Marylou Portnoy, May 29, 1966; c: Scott. Atty, partner, Zucker, Lowenstein, Gurny and Zucker, since 1965; jud clerk, State of NJ, 1964-65. Chief counsel, Essex Co chap, ACLU; class agt, class comm man, Dartmouth Coll; mem: Essex Co, NJ, Amer Bar Assns; Phi Beta Kappa. Home: 24 Harding Dr, S Orange, NJ. Office: 744 Broad, Newark, NJ.

FACKENHEIM, Emil L, Can, rabbi; b. Halle, Ger, June 22, 1916; s. Julius and Meta (Schlesinger); in Can since 1940; ordained rabbi, HS for Sci of Judaism, Berlin, 1939; PhD, U Toronto, 1945; LLD, Laurentian U, 1969. Prof, phil, U Toronto, since 1961, mem fac since 1948; rabbi, Cong Anshe Shalom, Hamilton, Ont, 1943-48. Author: Paths to Jewish Belief, 1960; Metaphysics and Historicity, 1961; The Religious Dimension in Hegel's Thought, 1968; Quest for Past and Future: Essays in Jewish Theology, 1968; God's Presence in History, 1969; contbr to scholarly publs. Home: 563 Briar Hill Ave, Toronto, Can. Office: U Toronto, Toronto, Can.

FAERBER, Meir M, Isr, journalist; b. Moravska Ostrava, Czech, Apr 29, 1908; s. Rubin; in Isr since 1934; m. Sara Tutelman; c: Aron, Daniel. Co-ed, Yediot Hadashot; Isr corresp for: Das neue Israel, Israelitisches Wochenblatt, Zurich; Munchener Judische Nachrichten, Munich; Die Gemeinde, Vienna. Author: Auf der Flucht erschossen, 1933; Residenz Schuschan, 1944; Dr Emil Margulies, 1949; Das Parlament Israels, 1958; Marchen und Sagen aus Israel, 1959; contbr vols of poetry, books for children. Fmr found, chmn, Isr-Aus Assn, 1956-63; B'nai B'rith lodges: Theodore Herzl, 1962-63; Haboneh Hazioni 1967-68; fmr, co-found, mem, Revisionist Movement, J State Party, Czech. Home: 56 Yitzhak Sadeh St, Tel Aviv, Isr.

FAGIN, Emmanuel Lazarus, Isr, organization exec; b. Liverpool, Eng, June 23, 1900; s. Solomon and Rose (Isaacs); desc of: Tosefot Yomtov; Moses Mendelsohn; m. Lily Glass, Feb 20, 1929; c: Joyce Cohen, Hilary Greenberg. Hon life pres, Liverpool Zionist Cen Council; hon secy, mem Natl exec, Histadrut Olei Britannia, Haifa br; chmn, Va'ad Hanhalah, Moadon Ha'oleh, Haifa; fmr: mem exec comm, J Repr Council; pres, Liverpool Jr Zionist Assn; found, 1st pres, Jr Zionist Movement, Gt Brit and Ir; pres: Liverpool Shivath Zion; LCZ; chmn, trustees, Zion House, Liverpool, chmn, Isr Info Comm; found, vice pres, Merseyside Anglo-Isr Club; gen secy, Liverpool ZCC; reg dir, JNF, JPA; mem: select comm, Liverpool Old Heb Cong; Masons, Mt Carmel br; Royal Arch Masons, Mt Carmel 6, both Haifa. Army res, WW I; civil defense WW II. Author: Memoirs of N I Adler, 1948; Jubilee of Liverpool Zionism, 1950; contbr to jours. Hobbies: gardening, photography, handicrafts, painting. Home: 15 Kol Israel Haverim St, Ramat Shaul, Haifa, Isr.

FAGIN, N Bryllion, US, educator, author; b. Russ, June 15, 1892; s. Nissen and Matla (Neistadt); in US since 1900; AB, Tchrs Dipl, George Wash U, 1922, AM, 1923; PhD, Johns Hopkins U, 1931; m. Mary Berkowitz, June 4, 1916; m. 2nd, Clarissa Mogilevsky-Pearlman, Apr 29, 1965. Lectr, World Drama, New Coll, Sarasota, Fla, since 1966; asso prof em, Eng, drama, Johns Hopkins U, 1958-66, fac mem since 1946; clerk, US Govt, Wash, DC, 1916-21; instr, Eng, U of Md, 1923-24, asso prof, 1924-25; prof, U Baltimore, 1926-32; visiting prof: Amer Studies, Salzburg Sem, 1951, 1958; Eng, U Rochester, 1953-54; LeMoyne Coll, 1958-59. Pres: Edgar Allan Poe Soc, 1955-57; Tudor and Stuart Club, 1956-58; secy, Studies Soc, 1954-55; mem: found, Writers League of Wash; Amer Educ Theatre; Authors League of Amer; Coll Eng Assn; AAUP; MLA; Natl Council Tchrs Eng. Author: Short Story Writing; An Art or a Trade? 1923; The Phenomenon of Sherwood Anderson, 1927; William Bartram: Interpreter of the American Landscape, 1932; The Histrionic Mr Poe, 1949; co-ed, Eugene O'Neill and his Plays, 1961. Recipient: grant, Amer Phil Soc, 1948; John Hay Whitney Award, 1958. Home: 2707 Queen Anne Rd, Baltimore, Md. Office: Johns Hopkins U, Baltimore, Md.

FAHN, Abraham, Isr, educator; b. Vienna, Aus, Aug 8, 1916; s. Selig and Sarah (Rosenmann); in Isr since 1935; MSc, Heb U, 1942, PhD, 1948; m. Nehama Ekhajzer, Apr 13, 1948; c: Miriam, Naomi. Prof, chmn, botany dept, Heb U, since 1965, dean, fac sci, 1963-65; visiting sci, Jodrell Lab, Kew, UK, botany sch, Cambridge, 1952-53; research f, Harvard U, 1956; visiting sci, ETH, Zurich, 1962. Lt, IDF, 1948-49. Author: Plant Anatomy, Heb, 1962, Eng, 1967; co-author, Cultivated Plants of Israel, 1957; contbr papers to sci jours; adv bd, Phytomorphology. Home: 7 Gat St, Jerusalem, Isr. Office: Hebrew U, Jerusalem, Isr.

FAIGENBAUM, Harold M, US, chemist, educator; b. Watervliet, NY, Sep 4, 1902; s. Morris and Minnie (Smith); Chem E, Rensselaer Poly Inst, 1923, PhD, 1926; m. Edith Sanders, Dec 19, 1937; c: Mark. Prof em, Rensselaer Poly Inst, since 1967, prof, inorganic chem, 1940-67, head, dept, 1949-67, on fac since 1926; chief chem and cons, NY State Biol Survey, 1929-40. Chmn, jt commn on syn admn, UAHC and CCAR, since 1962; trustee, UAHC, since 1950, vice-chmn, since 1967; bd dirs, Rensselaer Co chap, ARC, since 1953; exec council, United Comty Service, Mohawk-Hudson area, since 1959; mem: Amer Chem Soc; Sigma Xi; Phi Lambda Upsilon; Phi Sigma Delta. Home: 1912 Burdett Ave, Troy, NY. Office: Rensselaer Poly Inst, Troy, NY.

FAIN, Samuel S, US, musicologist, conductor; b. Chgo, Ill, Dec 25, 1909; s. Morris and Ella (Magidson); BMusE, Northwestern U, 1940; MA, U of Ariz, 1951; DMus Arts, U of S Cal, 1956; m. Elizabeth Miller, Jan 14, 1955; c: Joan, Marilyn. Prof, music, U Ariz, since 1941; band, orch dir, Chgo Public Schs, 1930-40; instr, Amer Conservatory, 1936-40; visiting band dir, Mich State U, 1949; conductor, Tucson Sym Orch, 1945-49; visiting prof: U of S Cal, 1955,

1956; Mich State U, 1949, 1965. Hon life mem: Phi Mu Alpha; Kappa Kappa Psi; mem: Phi Delta Kappa; Music Educ Natl Conf. Contbr to profsl jours. Hobbies: hist, sports. Home: 4934 E 12 St, Tucson, Ariz. Office: U of Ariz, Tucson, Ariz.

FAINE, Solomon, Austr, microbiologist, educator; b. Wellington, NZ, Aug 17, 1926; s. John and Luba (Ketko); in Austr since 1959; PhD, Oxford U, Eng, 1955; MD, Otago U, NZ, 1959; m. Eva Rothschild, May 17, 1950; c: Miriam, Susan, Jonathan. Prof, chmn, dept microbiol, Monash U, since 1968; cons microbiol, Alfred Hosp, Melbourne; lectr, Otago U, 1950-58; asso prof, U Sydney, 1959-68; visiting sci, Isr Inst for biol research, Nes Ziona, Isr, 1963-64. Research in med microbiol and immunology. Pres, Austr Soc for Microbiol; mem: Amer Soc for Microbiol; AAAS; Soc Cen Microbiol. Contbr articles to sci jours. Recipient: Peter Bancroft Prize, U Sydney, 1965. Hobbies: music, photography. Home: 2 Murray St, Armadale, Melbourne, Austr. Office: Dept of Microbiol, Monash U, Alfred Hosp, Prahran, Melbourne, Austr.

FAITLOWICZ, Sarah Gliksman, Isr, artist; b. Lodz, Pol, Dec 17, 1915; d. Wolf and Liza (Bereskin) Meirowicz; in Isr since 1957; att Acad Arts, Warsaw, Pol; m. Jacob Faitlowicz. Represented in numerous exhbs in Pol; one-man shows: Warsaw, Krakow, Lodz; Artists Pavilion, Tel Aviv, 1958, 1964; Chagal House, Haifa, 1959; Hadany Gal, Rehovot, 1965; Kuastim Widerstand, Dresden, Ger, 1968; paintings done in Lodz Ghetto, now in Yad Vashem Mus. Mem, Isr Painters and Sculptors Assn. Recipient: Town Prize, Lodz; medal of distinction, Min Culture and Art, Pol, 1955. Home: 18 Motzkin St, Tel Aviv, Isr.

FAJANS, Kasimir, US, chemist, educator; b,. Warsaw, Pol, May 27, 1887; s. Herman and Wanda (Wolberg); att U Leipzig, 1904-07; PhD, U Heidelberg, 1909; postgrad studies: Zurich, 1909-10; U Manchester, 1910-11; m. Salomea Kaplan, 1910; c: Edgar, Stefan; in US since 1936. Prof em, chem, U Mich, since 1957, prof, 1936-57; asst and privatdozent, physical chem, Technische Hochschule, Karlsruhe, 1911-17; prof, U Munich, 1925-35, dir Inst for Physical Chem, 1932-35; sci collaborator, Glass Sci Research, Found, 1944-47; cons Owens-Ill Glass Co, Toledo, O, 1948-55; Baker Lectr, Cornell U, 1930; Foster lectr, Buffalo U, 1939; conducted grad seminar at: Shell Devl Co, Emeryville, Cal, 1953; Minnesota Mining and Mfg Co, St Paul, Minn, 1959. F, Amer Physical Soc. Mem, council: Deutsche Chemische Gesellschaft, 1921-22; Bunsengesellschaft, 1929-32; Amer Chem Soc, 1944; chmn, U Mich, sect, 1947; mem: AAAS; Faraday Soc; Amer Crystallographic Assn; Soc for Freedom in Sci; Sigma Xi; Acads of Sci at: Leningrad, 1925; Munich, 1927; Cracow, 1929; Polish Inst Arts and Scis in Amer, 1942. Hon mem: Chem Soc, Karlsruhe; Soc of Doctors of Madrid; Spanish Soc for Physics and Chem; Royal Inst of Gt Brit; Phi Lambda Upsilon; Societas Physico-Medica Erlangensis; Polish Chem Soc; Mexican Chem Soc; Soc, Nuclear Med. Author: Radioaktivität und Neuste Entwicklung der Lehre von den Chemischen Elementen, 1919; Radio-elements and Isotopes, Chem Forces and Optical Properties of Substance, 1931; Adsorptionsindikatoren für Fällungstitrationen, 1935; co-author: Physikalisch-Chemisches Praktikum, 1929; Refractometry in Physical Methods of Organic Chem, 1945; ed: Elektrochemie, in Handbuch der Experimentalphysik, vol XII/1, 1932; vol. XII/2, 1933; asso ed, Jour of Physical and Colloid Chem, 1948-49; co-ed, Zeitschrift für Kristallographie, 1924-39; mem, ed bd, Zeitschrift für Elektrochemie, 1932-33; contbr to jours on chem, physics and crystallography. Recipient: Victor Meyer Prize, Heidelberg, 1909; Medal, U Liege, 1948; honored by establishment of the Kasimir Fajans Award in Chem, U of Mich, 1956. Home: 1016 Lincoln Ave, Ann Arbor, Mich. Office: Dept of Chem, U of Mich, Ann Arbor, Mich.

FALK, Emanuel E, US, business exec; b. Newport News, Va, July 23, 1904; s. Maurice and Carolyn (Seesholtz); att U of Va, 1921-23; m. Jean Berman, July 23, 1941; c: David. Partner, Drucker and Falk, ins-real estate , since 1938; Natl pres, Inst of Real Estate Mgmt, since 1960. Pres: B'nai B'rith, 1940-42; JCC, 1946; Travelers Aid Soc, 1949; Comty Chest, 1953; Peninsula Wfr Council, 1954; Temple Sinai, 1955-56; treas, Rodef Sholem Cong, 1949-50; state chmn, UJA, 1948; vice-pres, Peninsula Assn of Commerce, 1950; secy, Peninsula Ind Comm since 1957. Home: 27 Garland Dr, Newport News, Va. Office: 131 26 St, Newport News, Va.

FALK, Gerald Y, Austr, business exec, lighting cons and engr;

b. Plymouth, Eng, July 8, 1918; s. Leib and Fanny; in Austr since 1922; FIES, Sydney Tech Coll. Governing dir, Planned Lighting Co Pty Ltd, since 1945; fmr with Austr Gen Elec Pty Ltd. Sgt, Austr Civilian Mil Forces, 1936-39, capt, Austr Imperial Forces, 1939-45. Pres: Illuminating Engr Soc, Austr; exec council, Austr Jewry, 1968-70; NSW J Bd Deps, 1967-69; NSW J War Memorial, 1953-56; Austr delg, WJC, Brussels, 1966; mem: Returned Service League, Austr; Good Neighbor Council, NSW; B'nai B'rith; Masons; Royal NSW Bowling Assn; clubs: Tattersalls; Dover Hgts Bowling; Progressive Sports, fmr vice-pres. Home: 31 Weonga Rd, Dover Heights, NSW, Austr. Office: 38 Market St, Sydney, Austr.

FALK, Isidore Sydney, US, public health official; b. Bklyn, NY, Sep 30, 1899; s. Samsin and Rose (Stolzberg); PhB, Yale U, 1920, PhD, grad sch, 1923; m. Ruth Hill; c: Sydney, Stephen. Exec dir, Comty Health Cen Plan, New Haven, since 1968; prof, bact, U of Chgo, 1929; dir, bur of research and stat, US Social Security Admn, 1940-54; prof em, public health, Yale Sch of Med, since 1968, prof, 1961-68; US Army, 1918. Prin contribs: participant in devl US Social Security prog, natl health progs, US, other countries. F: AAAS; Amer Ph Assn chmn, tech comm, Comm for Natl Health Ins; fmr active in various profsl assns; mem: many profsl assns. Author: The Costs of Medical Care, 1933; Security Against Sickness, 1936, other books recently pub; wrote numerous profsl articles and monographs. Home: 472 Whitney Ave, New Haven, Conn. Office: Room 209, 135 College St, New Haven, Conn.

FALK, Leon Jr, US business exec; b. Pittsburgh, Pa, Sep 23, 1901; s. Leon and Fanny (Edel); att Phillips Exeter Acad; BS, Yale U, 1924; hon LLD, U Pittsburgh, 1952; m. Katherine Sonneborn, June 24, 1926; c: Ellen, Sara, Sigo, David, Susannah; m. 2nd, Josephine Ross, Dec 23, 1948; m. 3rd, Loti Gerard, Jan 27, 1963. Pres, dir, Chatham Cen Inc; Webster Hall Hotel Corp; dir: exec comm, Natl Steel; Duquesne Light; Pa Ind Chem; fmr: i/c copper refining, later, of purchases, Federated Metals; chmn bd, Falk & Co, 1948-52, with firm since 1926; dir, fgn commodities div, vice pres, Commodity Credit, Wash, DC, 1943; chief, fats and oils bur, War Food Admn, 1943-44; Amer repr, chmn, sub-comm on fats and oils, Combined Food Bd, 1943-44. Trustee, vice chmn, U Pittsburgh; chmn bd, Maurice Falk Med Fund; trustee, exec comm, Presbyterian U Hosp, Pittsburgh; mem exec comm, Allegheny Conf on Comty Devl; vice pres, United Fund, Allegheny Co, Pa; mem: Phi Lambda Phi; clubs: Westmoreland Country, Pittsburgh; Concordia; Harvard-Yale-Princeton; Chems, NYC. Recipient: Order of Juan Pablo Duarte, Dominican Rep, 1941; Fr Legion of Honor, 1952. Home: Chatham Center, Pittsburgh, Pa. Office: Grant Bldg, Pittsburgh, Pa.

FALK, Randall M, US rabbi; b. Little Rock, Ark, July 9, 1921; s. Randall and Lucile (Kronberg); BA, U Cincinnati, 1944; MHL, ordained rabbi, HUC-JIR 1947, MA, Vanderbilt U, 1966; m. Edna Unger, Dec 21, 1952; c: Randall, Jonathan, Heidi. Rabbi, Temples: Ohabai Sholom, since 1960; Isr, Tulsa, 1945-46; Anshe Hesed, Erie, Pa, 1947-60. Vicechmn, S Regional Council, ADL; bd alumni overseers, HUC-JIR; mem commn, Interfaith Activities of UAHC; mem bds: Family and Children's Service; ARC; Sr Citizens Inc; Hum Relations Commn; Project Equality, Tenn chap, vice-chmn; Rel Heritage Found; UN Assn; hon life mem, Natl Fed Temple Youth, since 1959; mem: CCAR; B'nai B'rith; club, Rotary. Recipient: Comty brotherhood award, Erie, Pa, 1959. Home: 1209 Canterbury Dr, Nashville, Tenn. Study: 5015 Harding Rd, Nashville, Tenn.

FALK, Ze'ev Wilhelm, Isr, educator; b. Berlin, Ger, May 11, 1923; s. Meyer and Frieda (David); in Isr since 1939; advocate, govt law classes, Jerusalem, 1951; MA, PhD, Heb U, Jerusalem, 1958; m. Miriam Strauss, Oct 29, 1962; c: Haim, Orah. Sr lectr, Tel Aviv U, since 1964; f, Heb U, Jerusalem, since 1959; found, dir, Sem Heb Law, Fac of Law, Tel Aviv U; pvt law practice, 1952-55; legal adv, Min of Social Wfr, 1955-60; judge, advocates' chamber supr tribunal, 1962-66; visiting lectr: U London, Oxford, Glasgow, Murgia, Navarra, 1966; bd dir, govt legal service union, 1960-67; lefgal adv, Min of Interior, 1960-67. IDF, 1948-49. Co-dir, Keren Yeladenu; mem: Isr Advocates' Chambers; Movement Torah Judaism; IURA, Rivista Internazionale di Diritto Romano e Antico; Société F de Visscher pour l'Histoire des Droits de l'Antiquité. Author: Nisu'in veGerushin, 1961; Hebrew Law in Biblical Times, 1964; Jewish Matrimonial Law in Middle Ages, 1966; Halacha veMa'ase beMedinat Israel, 1967; ed bd, Matat; contbr to jours. Recipient, Isr Fighters' Decoration. Home: 10 Rav Berlin St, Jerusalem, Isr.

FALLIK, Alexander, Isr, physician; b. Galicia, Aus, Aug 26, 1917; s. Eliezer and Ita (Becher); in Isr since 1939; att, U Bologna; MD, U Rome, It, 1947; m. Rina Bernstein, Mar 22, 1949; c: Orit, Elazar. Dir, Govt Psycht Hosp, Nes Ziona, since 1954; org, Mh unit, Jehuda dist. Sgt, Pal Regiment, 1940-45; maj, IDF, 1948-49. Mem: Neuro-Psycht Soc, pres, Tel Aviv sect. Contbr articles to profsl jours. Home: 75 Yavne Rd, Rehovot, Isr. Office: POB 1, Nes Ziona, Isr.

FALSTEIN, Louis, US, author; b. Nemirov, Ukraine, May 1, 1909; s. Joseph and Bessie (Kammerman); in US since 1925; att NYU, 1945-47; m. Shirley Gesser, Apr 9, 1949; c: Jessica, Joshua. Author: novels: Face of a Hero, 1950; Slaughter Street, 1953; Sole Survivor, 1954; Spring of Desire, 1959; Laughter on a Weekday, 1965; The Man Who Loved Laughter, biography of Shalom Aleichem, 1968; ed: The Martyrdom of Jewish Physicians in Poland, 1963; Their Brothers' Keepers, 1957; contbr to B'nai B'rith Great Jewish Personalities. Staff sgt, USAF, 1943-45. Mem, Authors Guild. Recipient: Purple Heart, Air Medal, with 3 oak-leaf clusters; 9 battle stars. Home and office: 368 Eastern Pkwy, Brooklyn, NY.

FANTL, Henry, Can, economist; b. Ceske Budejovice, Czech, Feb 4, 1912; s. Josef and Elsa (Weiner); in Can since 1968; LLD, Masaryk U, Brno, Czech, 1935; m. Sima Kreitstein, May 5, 1943; c: Joseph, John. Research econ, Ont Dept of Lab, since 1968; head, econ sect, Inst for Tech and Econ Info, Prague, 1960-68. I/c youth activities, J Rel Comty, Prague, Czech, 1965-58. Home: 10 Hogarth St, Toronto, Can. Office: 8 York St, Toronto, Can.

FARAGO, Ladislas, US, author, journalist; b. Csurgo, Hung, Sep 21, 1906; s. Arthur and Irma (Lang); related to Theodor Herzl; in US since 1937; grad, Acad of Commerce and Consular Affairs, Budapest, 1926; m. Liesel Mroz, Mar 22, 1934; c: John. Journalist, Hung; with NY Times World -Wide Bur, Berlin, Ger; spec corresp, AP, Ethiopia; fgn ed, Sunday Chronicle, London, Eng, 1935; dir, research, Comm on Natl Morale, 1940-42; ed, Corps Diplomatique, 1946; sr ed, UN World, 1947-50; chief, desk X, Radio Free Eur, 1950-52. Mem, staff, US Off Naval Intelligence, 1942-46. Author: Abyssinia on the Eve, 1935; Abyssinian Stop Press, 1936; Palestine at the Crossroads, 1937; The Riddle of Arabia, 1937; German Psychological Warfare, 1940; Axis Grand Strategy, 1942; Behind Closed Doors, 1950; War of Wits, 1954; Burn After Reading, 1961; Strictly From Hungary, 1962; The Tenth Fleet, 1962; It's Your Money, 1964; Patton: Ordeal and Triumph, 1964; The Age of Scoundrels, 1965; The Broken Seal, 1967. Home: Carmen Hill No 1, New Milford, Conn. Office: 1225 Park Ave, New York, NY.

FARBER, Emmanuel, US, physician, educator; b. Toronto, Can, Oct 19, 1918; s. Morris and Mary (Madorsky); in US since 1946; MD, U Toronto, Can, 1942; PhD, U of Cal, Berkeley, 1949; m. Ruth Diamond, Apr 16, 1942; c: Naomi. Prof, chmn, Dept of Path, U Pittsburgh Sch of Med, since 1961; Amer Cancer Soc F, Cook Co Hosp, Chgo, 1949-50; instr, asst, asso prof, path, Tulane U Med Sch, 1950-59; prof, Amer Cancer Soc, 1959-61; visiting prof, Charity Hosp of New Orleans, La, 1959-61; chmn, Path "B" Sect, NIH, 1962-66; Surg gen's adv comm on smoking and health, 1962-64. Lt to capt, Royal Can Army MC, 1943-46. Cons, Div Chronic Diseases, HEW, since 1964; pres, Histochem Soc, 1966-67; mem: bd dirs, Amer Asso for Cancer Research, 1964-67; Comm on Path, Div Med Scis, Natl Acad Scis, NRC, 1965-66; Adv Panel 5 on Med Sci of US-Japan Coop Sci Prog, 1965; Natl Adv Council, USPHS 1966-70; Amer Soc Biol Chems; Amer Chem Soc; Amer Assn for Cancer Research; Amer Assn Experimental Path; Amer Assn Paths and Bacts; Biochem Soc; Intl Acad of Path; AAAS; NY Acad of Sci; Sigma Xi; Soc for Experimental Bio and Med. Contbr to med jours; chaps in research books. Recipient, Awards: 2nd annual Parke-Davis, 1958; 4th annual Bertha Goldblatt Teplitz memorial, 1961. Home: 5454 Beacon St, Pittsburgh, Pa. Office: 716A Scaife Hall, U of Pittsburgh Sch of Med, Pittsburgh, Pa.

FARBER, Emanuel Philip, US, physician; b. Kingston, NY, Feb 6, 1915; s. Isaac and Mary (Goldstein); AB, Cornell U, 1936; MD, LI Coll of Med, 1941; m. Thelma Krevitz, Jan 9, 1944; c: Richard, Arthur. Co-chmn, dept of obstet, gyn, Rolling Hill Hosp, Elkins Park, Pa; Staff mem: Frankford Hosp; Einstein Med Cen; St Joseph Hosp; Kensington Hosp;

Oxford Hosp; St Agnes Hosp. Found f, Amer Coll Obstets and Gyns; f: Amer Coll of Surgs; Intl Coll of Surgs; dipl, Amer Bd Obstets and Gyn; mem: AMA; Phila Obstet Soc; Phila Co, Pa Med Socs; Phi Lambda Kappa; Masons. Contbr to med jours. Home: 8314 Fairview Rd, Elkins Park, Pa. Office: 6823 Castor Ave, Philadelphia, Pa.

FARBER, Isadore E, US, psychologist; b. St Joseph, Mo, May 21, 1917; s. Jacob and Rose (Malkin); BA, MA, U of Mo, 1936-39; att: St Joseph Jr Coll; HUC, 1937-38; PhD, U of Ia, 1946; m. Billie Gulko, May 5, 1942; c: Ronna, Deborah. Prof, psych, U of Ill since 1964; asst prof, prof, U of Ia, 1947-64; research prof, U of Okla, med res educ, 1956-57; research cons, Air Force Personnel and Training Res Cen, San Antonio, Tex, 1949-56; training cons, VA, Ia City, 1957-64; visiting prof: psych, U Wis, 1955; Stanford U, 1960. USAAC, adj gen off, 1940-45. Exec council: Amer Prof for Peace in ME, Chgo region; AAUP, U of Ill, since 1969; Mid-W Psych Assn, council 1956-58, secy, treas, 1958-61, pres, 1961-62; mem: Natl Inst Mh, study sect for psychopharm, 1962-66, chmn, 1966-67; LZOA of Chgo; Phi Beta Kappa; Sigma Xi. Ed, Jour Experimental Research in Personality since 1964; cons ed, psych, Dodd, Mead and Co; contbr to numerous psych jours. Home: 7912 Church, Morton Grove, Ill. Office: Morgan and Harrison Sts, Box 4348, Chicago, Ill.

FARBER, Joseph, US, attorney; b. Bklyn, NY, Jan 31, 1944; s. David and Hannah (Beckhoff); BS, LIU, 1965; DJur, Bklyn Law Sch, 1968; m. Evelyn Caspari, Mar 23, 1967. Sr partner, Feder and Farber, since 1969; fmr, atty i/c matrimonial law, Queens Legal Services; tchr sci, NYC Bd Educ, 1968-70. Prin contrib, devl and instituting procedures and forms for matrimonial practice in poverty law. Fmr pres, youth group, Cong Ahavath Isr; vice-pres, LIU Law Soc; mem: Amer Bar Assn; Queens Co Bar Assn; Bklyn Law Sch Alumni Assn; LIU Alumni Fed; Alpha Phi Omega, pres, consul, Tau Delta Phi. Contbr to legal jours. Spec interest, legal assistance for poor. Home: 35 Penn St, Port Jefferson Sta, NY. Office: 2 Pennsylvania Plaza, New York, NY.

FARBER, Lionel, US, biochemist; b. Chgo, Ill, Sep 7, 1908; s. Morris and Mary (Madorsky); BA, U Toronto, 1930, MA, 1931, PhD, 1934; m. Freda Saiger, Dec 16, 1934; c: Lewis, William. Prof, biochem, Cal Coll Ped Med, since 1969; research biochemist, Seafood Research Lab, Hooper Found, U of Cal, 1946-69, on staff since 1937; prin contribs: fish preservation tech, detecting methods to determine shell fish spoilage. F, AAAS; mem: Amer Chem Soc; Amer Soc of Microbiol; Pacific Fisheries Technologists; Inst Food Technologists; Amer Fisheries Soc. Home: 75 Circle Ave, Mill Valley, Cal. Office: 1770 Eddy St, San Francisco, Cal.

FARBER, Sarah E, US, communal worker; b. Phila, Pa, Apr 1, 1904; d. Samuel and Bertha (Karr) Efter; tchrs cert, Phila Normal Sch, 1924; att Temple U, 1928-30; m. Albert Farber, May 28, 1931; c: Joel, Judith Blumenthal. Natl vice-pres, women's div, Amer Friends Heb U, since 1962; mem: natl exec bd, women's div, State of Isr Bonds, since 1951. Mem: bd dirs: women's council, Council of J Fed Agcys, Gtr Phila, since 1960; Elkins Park Free Libr, since 1959; Women's div of Dropsie Coll; non-govt delg, repr, World Union for Progressive Judaism, Hum Rights Commn of UN, 1952. Author: Confessions of a Volunteer Fund Raiser, in American Judaism, 1958. Recipient: Woman of Valor award, State of Isr Bonds. Home: 7933 Park Ave, Elkins Park, Pa.

FARBER, Saul Joseph, US, physician, educator; b. NYC, Feb 11, 1918; s. Isidore and Mary (Bunim); AB, NYU, 1938; MD, NYU Sch Med, 1942; m. Doris Balmuth, Mar 13, 1949; c: Joshua, Beth. Nathan Friedman Prof, med, chmn, dept med, NYU Sch Med, since 1966, on fac since 1948; dir, Bellevue and U Hosps, since 1966; on staff both hosp since 1959; established investigator, AHA, 1955-60; career sci, Health Research Council, NYC, 1960-65; cons, research and educ comm, VA Hosp. Lt, USN, MC, 1943-46. Mem bd, Amer Bd Internal Med, since 1968; dipl, since 1955; f: Amer Coll Phys; NY Acad Med; mem: Amer Soc for Clinical Inves; Assn Amer Phys; Amer Physiological Soc; Harvey Soc; Soc for Experimental Biol and Med; Amer Fed for Clinical Research; Sigma Xi; Alpha Omega Alpha; Assn Profs Med; NY Soc Nephrology; Soc Urban Phys; NY Heart Assn; Natl Inst Arthritis and Metabolic Diseases; natl adv research resources council, USPHS; basic sci adv comm, Natl Cystic Fibrosis Found; med adv comm, Irvington House; adv council, NY State Kidney Disease Inst; AHA; Health Research Council, NYC; Inter-Soc Commn for Heart Disease Resources; NY

Metrop Regional Med Prog for Heart Disease, Cancer, Stroke, Related Diseases; Hosp Corp Task Force, NYC; Comm on Research in Corp Hosps; adv council, med bds, Munic Hosps; clubs: Salt and Water, Interurban Clinical. Ed, Amer Jour of Med Scis, since 1970; contbr to numerous sci publs. Home: 25 Plaza St, Brooklyn, NY. Office: 550 First Avenue, New York, NY.

FARBERMAN, Harold, US, composer, conductor; b. NYC, Nov 2, 1930; s. Louis and Lena (Kramer); BS, Julliard Sch of Music, 1951; MMus, NE Conservatory of Music, Boston, Mass, 1955; m. Corinne Curry. c: Thea, Lewis. Music dir, Colo Springs Sym, since 1966; guest conductor, orchs: Miami Sym; BBC, London; New Philharmonic; Eng Chamber; Denver Sym; NY Philharmonic; Percussionist, Boston Sym, 1951-53. Compositions include: operas: Medea; The Loosers; syms for large orch; chamber pieces for mixed smaller ensembles; percussion music for small or large ensembles; recorded: first ed ever done by single conductor of Charles Ives 4 syms; and for: Capitol Recods; Columbia; RCA; Boston Records; Cambridge Records; Serenus Records; received commns from: Denver Sym Orch; Julliard Sch of Music; Lincoln Cen (opera); Council for the Arts. Mem, ASCAP. Home and office: 470 West End Ave, New York, NY.

FARBMAN, Aaron A, US, surgeon; b. Odessa, Russ, Apr 2, 1902; s. Samuel and Bertha (Rubin); in US since 1903; AB, Columbia Coll, 1923; MA, Columbia U, 1924, MD, Coll of Phys and Surgs, 1928; m. Marie Prager, July 23, 1944; c: Leslie, Robin. Pvt practice since 1930; att surg, Detroit Mem Hosp; asso, att surg, Sinai Hosp; mem, surg staff, Cottage Hosp, Grosse Pointe, Mich; med dir, Continental Motors war plant, 1940-47. Chmn, phys educ comm, YMCA, mem, mgt comm; natl exec comm, Amateur Chamber Music Players; chmn, finance comm, citizens' adv comm, Detroit Bd of Educ; f: Amer Coll Surgs; Intl Coll Surgs; Amer Geriatric Soc; mem: AMA; Mich State Med Soc; Wayne Co Med Soc; clubs: Econ, Detroit; Columbia; Mich. Contbr to surg lit and exhibits. Hobbies: violin, chamber music. Home: 809 Berkshire Rd, Grosse Pointe Park, Mich. Office: 14515 Kercheval Ave, Detroit, Mich.

FARBMAN, Leonard X, US, engineer, contractor; b. NYC July 28, 1910; s. Morris and Martha (Danashewitz); BS, Carnegie Inst of Tech, 1932;m. Ruth Rubin, Nov 4, 1933; c: David. Exec, M Farbman & Sons, since 1933. Chmn: Jt NYC and Lincoln Sq Comty Planning Action Comm; Jt Plumbing Ind Bd, Manhattan and Bx, 1961-64; Assn of Plumbing Contractors, NYC, 1961-64; acting chmn, Lower W Side Anti-Poverty Corp, 1966-1968; Boro Pres Comty Planning Bd, 1960-62; dir, Citizens Watch Dog Comm, Lincoln Sq, 1958-60; pres, Riverside Neighborhood Assembly, 1954-56; chmn, Lib Party 3rd Assembly Dist, 1948; mem: Mayor Wagner's Comm on Housing, 1956; co-committeeman, Dem Party. Home: 91 Central Park W, New York, NY. Office: 592 W 126 St, New York, NY.

FARBSTEIN, Leonard, US, attorney, legislator; b. NYC, Oct 12, 1902; s. Louis and Yetta (Schlanger); att CCNY, 1919; HUC, 1920; LLB, NYU, 1924; m. Blossom Langer, Sep 19, 1947; c: Louis. Mem, US House of Reprs, 1957-70; mem, NY State Leg, 1933-57; fmr mem, temporary Commn on the Courts, State Jud Conf and State Jud Council; USCG Res, WW II. Fmr chancellor, KP; mem: Amer Jud Soc; NY Co Lawyers Assn; NY State Bar Assn; Amer Bar Assn; Assn Bar, NYC; B'nai B'rith; AJCong; Lower E Side Dem Assn; E Side C of C; Bial stoker Syn. Home: 500A Grand St, New York, NY. Office: 276 Fifth Ave, New York, NY.

FARELL, David M, US, obstetrician, gynecologist, educator; b. Newport News, VA, Aug 23, 1905; s. Max and Jenny (Levinson); AB, Johns Hopkins U, 1924; MD, Jefferson Med Coll, 1928; att schs of grad studies: Rotunda Hosp, Dublin, Ir; Frauenklinik U, Berlin, Ger, both 1931; m. Elizabeth Polin, June 30, 1929; c: Davida. Dir, dept gyn, Jefferson Med Coll Hosp, since 1961, co-dir, pelvic malignancy clinic, since 1961; prof, obstets and gyn, Jefferson Med Coll, 1961-63, on fac since 1950; att gyn, Phila Gen Hosp. Bd dirs: Beth David Temple, Phila, 1951-52; Beth Tefila, Yeadon, Pa, 1954-55. F: Amer Coll Surgs; Amer Coll Obstets and Gyn; Phila Coll Phys; dipl, Amer Bd Obstets and Gyn; mem: Assn Profs Gyn and Obstets; Phi Alpha; Phi Sigma Delta; Phi Delta Epsilon. Contbr to profsl jours. Home: 812 Longacre Blvd, Yeadon, Pa. Office: 1912 Spruce St, Philadelphia, Pa.

FARKAS, Tibor, Isr, organization exec; b. Sucany, Czech, Nov 22, 1902; s. Josef and Johanna (Schlesinger); Jur Academie, Pecs, 1921; Mil Academi, M Weisskirchen, 1925; m. Berta Rosner, 1948. Gen secy, Hitachdut Olej Hungaria, since 1963; dir, Hotel Imperial Kassa, 1939-44; Kassa Bus, 1944-48; Malben, 1949-63. Maj, Czech Army, 1924-39. Pres, Svaz protifasistickych veznov, Kosice, 1945-48; mem: Munic of Kosice, 1946-48; B'nai B'rit. Recipient: decorations: division, 1928, 1938; partisan, 1946. Home: 168 Ibn Gvirol St, Tel Aviv, Isr. Office: 61 Hayarkon St, Tel Aviv, Isr.

FARNBOROUGH, Louis Henry, Ger, lawyer; b. Neustadt, Ger, Feb 26, 1905; s. Sigmund and Emma (Moos) Farnbacher; LLD, U Würzburg, Ger, 1927; m. Hilde Rothmann, Aug 24, 1938; c: Margaret Dolleman, Stuart. Lawyer, Court of Appeal, since 1952; clerk of court, British mil govt for Ger, 1945-46; sr legal off, Brit control comm for Ger, 1947-51. Staff sgt, Pioneer Corps, 1940-46. Pres: JNF, Ger; J Loan Fund, N Rhine Westphalia; mem bd: J Comty, Düsseldorf; Assn J Comtys, N Rhine Westphalia; mem, Brit Legion; fmr chmn, Brit Businessmen's club, Düsseldorf. Author: Kommentar zum Wiedergutmachungs Gesetz, 1951, 1967; contbr articles on pvt intl law. Recipient: Battle of Brit crosses; D-Day Medal. Hobbies: arts, sport. Home: 2 Drake St, Düsseldorf, Ger. Office: 100, Königsallee, Düsseldorf, Ger.

FARR, Myra, US, civic worker; b. Auburn, Me, Apr 25, 1915; d. Harry and Jeanette (Magid) Goodkowsky; m. Aaron Farr, Mar 27, 1938; c: Harvey. Natl vice chmn, ways and means comm, Natl Council J Women, since 1961, fmr natl vice pres, natl vice chmn, nominating comm since 1961, fmr: pres, S interstate region, pres, Miami sect, mem, natl bd, since 1959; hon trustee, Temple Sholom, Miami Beach, since 1959, fmr mem bd, rel sch; mem exec comm, Miami chap, AJComm since 1962, parliamentarian, Mt Sinai Hosp Women's Auxiliary since 1961; mem: United Fund, Dade Co, since 1962; Gtr Miami J Fed, since 1951; exec comm, Miami Women's div, NCCJ, since 1955; fmr: pres: Homemaker Service, Dade Co; Conf J Women's Orgs, Dade and Broward Cos; Sisterhood, Temple Beth Sholom; vice pres, mem adv bd, interfaith chmn, Fed J Women's Orgs; co-found, vice-pres, Brandeis U Women's Comm, Miami chap; dir: PTA, Biscayne Elem, Nautilus Jr High, Miami Beach HS; J Family Service, Gtr Miami; chmn, women's div, CJA; asso chmn, United Fund, Miami Beach; co-chmn, Sheltered Workshop, sponsored by Natl Council J Women and Gtr Miami J Fed; mem: exec, family and child care div, Wfr Planning Council, Dade Co; by laws comm, Dade Fed Women's Clubs. Recipient: Comty Headliner Award, Theta Sigma Phi, 1968; Gtr Miami Sect, NCJW Hannah G Solomon Award, 1965. Home: 934 79 Terr, Miami Beach, Fla.

FASMAN, Oscar Z, US, rabbi, educator; b. Chgo, Ill, Mar 23, 1908; s. Samuel and Beatrice (Horwitz); PhB, U Chgo, 1928; ordained rabbi, Heb Theol Coll, 1929; hon DD, Yeshiva U, 1955; m. Jeanette Rubin, July 10, 1932; c: Chaim, Avis Sugarman, Millicent Drebin, Reuven. Rabbi, found, Beth Torah Cong, Lincolnwood, since 1964; prof em, Heb Theol Coll, since 1964, pres, 1946-64; rabbi: Cong Bnai Emunah, Tulsa, 1930-40; Vaad Ha'Ir, Ottawa, 1940-46. Chaplain, Can Army, 1942-45. Mem: RabCA, Mizrachi. Author: An Epistle on Tolerance by a Rabbinic Zealot, 1939; The Sabbath, The Cornerstone of Judaism, 1941; The Attitude of the Hafetz Hayyim Toward Labor, 1946. Home: 5016 Jarlath, Skokie, Ill. Study: 4721 Touhy Ave, Lincolnwood, Ill.

FAST, Howard, US, author; b. NYC, Nov 11, 1914; s. Barney and Ida (Miller); att Natl Acad Design, 1932; m. Bette Cohen, June 6, 1937; c: Rachel, Jonathan. Author: Two Valleys, 1933; Strange Yesterday, 1934; The Children, 1935; Place in the City, 1939; Conceived in Liberty, 1939; The Last Frontier, 1941; The Unvanquished, 1942; Citizen Tom Paine, 1943; Freedom Road, 1944; The American, 1946; Clarkton, 1947; My Glorious Brothers, 1948; The Proud and the Free, 1950; Spartacus, 1951; The Passion of Sacco and Vanzetti, 1953; Silas Timberman, 1954; Moses, Prince of Egypt, 1958; The Winston Affair, 1959; The Golden River, 1960; April Morning, 1961; Power, 1962; Agrippa's Daughter, 1964; The Hill, 1964; Torquemada, 1966; The Hunter and the Trap, 1967; The Jews: Story of a People, 1968. Mem: J Peace F; F for Reconciliation. Recipient: Breadloaf Award, 1935; Schomburg Race Relations Award, 1944; Page One Award, Newspaper Guild of Amer, 1947; J Book Guild Award, 1949; Intl Peace Prize, Russ, 1953; Screenwriters Annual Award, 1960; annual book award, Secondary Educ Bd, 1962. Home and office: Box 85, Florida Hill Rd, Ridgefield, Conn.

FAUST, Jacob, US, chemist, researcher; b. Rohatyn, Pol, June 14, 1902; s. David and Debora (Loew); in US since 1931; att U Cracow, Pol, 1922-24; MS, chem ing, Deutsche Technische Hochschule, Prague, Czech, 1928; att: Bklyn Polytech Inst, 1932-34; Princeton U, 1941-42; m. Hedda Waldinger, Mar 15, 1931; c: Stanley, Eleanor. Sr research chem, Witco-Sonneborn Chem Corp, since 1935. Prin contribs: holder of patents in US and numerous fgn countries, on mfr of petroleum products, use of petroleum oils and additives. Contbr to profsl jours. Hobbies: Holy Scriptures, photography. Home: 293 Greylock Pkwy, Belleville, NJ.

FEDDER, A Herbert, US, rabbi; b. Dinewitz, Russ, June 4, 1900; s. Joseph and Anna (Kleinman); in US since 1901; PhD, Johns Hophins U, 1924; Rabbi, JTSA, 1929; cert in group counseling. Civic Center Clinic, Bklyn, 1959; cert marriage counselor, 1968; m. Harriet Solomon; div; c: Norman, Marianne; m. 2nd, Ethel Ritt, Oct 21, 1956; c: Robert. Chaplain, Bx Vet Hosp, since 1960; rabbi: Flint J Cen, 1929; Laurelton J Cen, 1931-46. US Army, 1944-46. Asso mem, Amer Assn Marriage Counselors; mem: RA; JWV; Tau Alpha Omega; Amer Soc Group Psychotherapy and Psychodrama, Soc Sci Study of Sex. Home: 71-39 165 St, Flushing, NY. Office: Bx Vet Hosp, Bx, NY.

FEDER, Aaron, US, physician, educator; b. NYC, May 1, 1915; s. Herman and Fannie (Trenner); att NYU, 1931-34; MD, U of Md Sch of Med, 1938; exch scholar, Harvard U Med Sch, 1937; m. Beatrice Wallance, Dec 25, 1941; c: Carol, Jane. Pvt practice since 1940; clinical prof med, Cornell U, 1959, mem fac since 1941; att phys, LI J Hosp; cons phys, Booth Memorial Hosp; visiting phys, Bellevue Hosp; att phys, NY Hosp, att staff, Hosp for Jt Diseases, 1940-51; card cons NYC Dept Health, 1946-51; cons phys, N Shore Hosp, Long Beach Memorial Hosp. Lt to maj US Army, 1942-46. Dipl, Amer Bd Internal Med; examiner: Amer Bd Internal Med; 1955-57; Natl Bd Med Examiners, f: NY Acad Sci; Amer Coll Physicians; NY Acad Med; Amer Coll Card; fmr bd of dirs: NY Card Soc; Amer Phys Comm; med bd, LI, J Hosp and Bellevue Hosp; mem, med adv bd, Heb U and Hadassah; exec comm, FJP, Queens; LI phys comm, UJA; chmn, Queens and Jackson Hgts phys comm, United Hias Service; mem: AMA; Amer Fed for Clinical Research; AAAS; AHA; Intl Soc Internal Med; Amer Soc for Tropical Med and Hygiene; Assn Amer Med Colls. Contributor to med publs. Recipient: Philippine liberation and bronze star. Hobby: painting. Home: 28 Meadow Woods Rd, Great Neck, NY. Office: 4042 75 St, Jackson Heights, NY.

FEDER, Saul E, US, attorney; b. Bklyn, NY, Oct 8, 1943; s. Joseph and Toby (Brooks); BS, NYU, 1965; DJur, Bklyn Law Sch, 1968; m. Marcia Weinblatt, Feb 25, 1968. Sr partner, Feder and Farber, NYC, since 1969; staff atty Queens Legal Services Corp, since 1969; spec invest, Atty Gen Off, Bur Election Frauds, 1966; acctnt partner, Dube and Feder, 1967-70. Vice-chmn, bd dirs, Young Isr, Briarwood, NY; sponsor, Isr Bond Campaign; fmr: comm chmn, Young Isr, Boro Park; leader, Boy Scouts Amer; mem: Amer Bar Assn; Queens Co Bar Assn; club, Briarwood Couples, vice-pres, exec comm. Author: You and Your Landlord, 1970; contbr numerous articles on poverty law. Recipient: Areopagus Honor Soc, NYU, 1965; Scholastic Achievement award, NEDT, 1959. Spec interests: State of Isr; law reform; comty, civic, philanthropic orgs. Home: 84-01 Main St, Briarwood, NY. Office: 2 Pennsylvania Plaza, New York, NY.

FEDERBUSH, Simon, US, rabbi, author; b. Narol, Aus, Feb 15, 1892; s. Hersch and Czarna (Hirsh); in US since 1940; att: U Cracow; U Lwow; PhD, U Vienna, 1923; ordained rabbi, Theol Sem, Vienna, 1923; m. Miriam Horowitz, 1928; c: Uriel, Emanuel. Rabbi, Salanter Syn, Bx, NY, since 1940; mem, Pol Parl, 1923-28; chief rabbi, Finland, 1930-40. Pres, Mizrachi Org, Galicia, Pl, 1924-30; co-found, Tora Va'Avoda movement; hon pres: Hapoel Hamizrachi of Amer, since 1942; Hadoar, weekly, NYC; chmn, Histadruth Ivrith of Amer; chmn, exec, B'rith Ivrith Olamit; mem: exec, WJC, since 1943; World Zionist Action Comm; World Council of Mizrachi; presidium, World Fed Pol Jews; Union Orthodox Rabbis of US and Can; pres: Religious Writers Soc; Publ Soc Moria. Author: Shlemut haYahudut, 1928; Lyunim, 1929; The Protocols of the Elders of Zion in the Light of Truth, 1933; Hikrey Talmud, 1936; haMusar ve haMishpat beIsrael, 1946; Mishpat haMelucha beIsrael, 1952; Benethivoth Hatalmud, 1954; Hikrei Yahadut, 1965; Helashon Haivrit beIsrael Veamim, 1967; ed: Mizracha, Gilionoth and Yiddishe Bletter, Lwow; Jewish Horizons,

NYC; Maimonides Vol, 1956; Jewish Concept of Labor, 1957; Rashi Vol, 1958; Hochmath Israel, 2 vols, 1958; World Jewry Today, 1959; Hazon Tora veZion, 1960; Tora-Umlucha, 1961; Hasiduth veZion, 1963. Recipient: award, Mizrachi Exec; LaMed Prize, 1953, 1957. Home: 2105 Ryder Ave, Bronx, NY.

FEDERMANN, Xaver Yekutiel, Isr, business exec; b. Chemnitz Ger, Nov 14, 1914; s. David and Zipora (Kupfermintz); att, Lehranstalt für Wissenschaft des Judentums, Berlin, 1936; m. Bella Reiner, Aug 30, 1939; c: Michael, Irith. Pres, Federmann Enterprises; found, Isr Miami Group, owners, Dan Hotel Chain in Isr; Isr-Amer Enterprises Corp Ltd; Isr partner, Isasbest; Carmel Mortgage and Invest Bank. Bd govs, Weizmann Inst of Sci; fmr active: zionist youth org, Habonim, Hechalutz, in Ger; youth aliya; club, Caesarea Golf and Country. Contbr articles on econ subjects. Home: 89 Sea Rd, Mt Carmel, Haifa, Isr. Office: 51 Haatzmaut Rd, Haifa, Isr.

FEFFER, Solomon, US, educator; b. Warsaw, Pol, Sep 28, 1907; s. Hyman and Pessa (Borenstein); in US since 1916; grad, Tchrs Inst, Yeshiva U, 1924; AB, CCNY, 1930; MA, Columbia U, 1931; m. Bessie Press, Sep 2, 1930; c: Amnon, Jonathan. Chmn Dept of Hebraic Studies, Rutgers U, since 1966; instr JTSA, 1944-66; chmn, dept of fgn langs, George Wash HS, 1954-68. Secy, Amer Assn of Tchrs of Heb, 1945-47; mem, Assn Fgn Lang. Contbr to educ and bibliographical jours. Hobbies: collecting ceremonial objects. Home: 350 Central Park W, New York, NY. Office: Rutgers U, Newark, NJ.

FEHER, George, US, physicist; b. Bratislava, Czech, May 29, 1924; s. Ferdinand and Sylvia; in US since 1946; BS, U of Cal, Berkeley, 1950, MS, 1951, PhD, physics, 1954; m. Elsa Rosenvasser, June 19, 1961; c: Laurie, Shoshana, Paola. Prof, physics, U of Cal, La Jolla, since 1960; research physicist, Bell Telephone Co, 1954-60; asso prof, Columbia U, 1959-60. Prin contribs in fields of: paramagnetic resonance; masers; nuclear polarization; primary processes in photosynthesis; inventor, ENDOR tech. Mem: bd govs, Technion, Haifa; Amer Phys Soc; Amer Biophys Soc; Sigma Xi. Contbr to sci jours. Recipient, Amer Phys Soc Award, 1960. Home: 2710 Bordeaux Ave, La Jolla, Cal.

FEHR, Uri, US, geophysicist; b. Jerusalem, July 18, 936; s. Hans and Miriam (Shaltiel); in US since 1962; MSc, Heb U, Jerusalem, 1962; PhD, UCLA, 1966; m. Gila Lachman, July 16, 1962; c: Yael, Rahm. Research asso, Lamont Geophys Labs, Columbia U, since 1967; sr cons geophysicist, since 1968; sys analyst, PM's Off, Jerusalem, 1960-62; research asst, U of Md, 1962-63; sr engr, UCLA, 1963-67. IAF, 1954-57. Mem: Amer Geophys Union; Amer Meteorology Soc; Marine Tech Soc; Acoustical Soc of Amer; Amer Inst Aeronautics and Astronautics; AAAS. Contbr to sci jours. Office: 41 Riverside Ave, Westport, Conn.

FEIBELMAN, Julian Beck, US, rabbi; b. Jackson, Miss, Mar 23, 1897; s. Abraham and Eva (Beck); BA, Millsaps Coll, 1918; hon LLD, 1946; ordained rabbi, HUC, 1926, hon DD, 1955; MA, U of Pa, 1929, PhD, 1939; m. Mary Fellman, Oct 20, 1938; c: Julian B. Rabbi em, Temple Sinai, New Orleans, since 1970, rabbi, 1936-1970; asst rabbi, Temple Knesseth Isr, Phila, Pa, 1926-36; lectr, Tulane U, 1950-53. Sgt, US Army, WW I, volunteer Red Cross Field Service. Adv, NCCJ, since 1945; mem: Interfaith Comm Mins to study race relations since 1958; prison interfaith bd mins for parolees; bd overseers, HUC; bd, social wfr planning commn, ADL; bd: Volunteers of Amer; Kingsley House; Metrop Area Comm; lay bd, DePaul Hosp; Boy Scouts of Amer; J Fed; J Children's Home; J Comty Cen; ed comm, J Publ Soc; Eng Speaking Union; Fgn Policy Assn; Mayor's Adv Comm; New Orleans Crime Commn, all New Orleans; Amer Assembly, Columbia U; Lakewood C of C; fmr: pres: La Soc for Mh; La Soc for Social Hygiene; HUC Alumni Assn; New Orleans Family Service Soc; chmn: Home Service Comm; interfaith comm, CCAR; appd by Gov Earl Long to State Interfaith Commn for Prison Rehabilitation; repr, First Intl Conf on Anti-semitism, Switz, 1947; clubs: Rotary, past pres; Round Table. Recipient: citation, Millsaps Coll; annual medal for dist service, St Mary's Dominican Coll; Weiss Award, NCCJ; Times-Picayune Loving Cup Award, 1967. Home: 530 Walnut St, New Orleans, La. Study: 6227 St Charles Ave, New Orleans, La.

FEIBLEMAN, James Kern, US, educator, author; b. New Orleans, La, July 13, 1904; s. Leopold and Nora (Kern); att

U of Va; studied privately in Eur; m. Dorothy Steinam, Dec, 1928 (div); m. 2nd, Shirley Grau, Aug 4, 1955; c: Peter, Ian, Nora, William, Katherine. Chmn, phil dept, Tulane U, since 1957; W R Irby Prof, phil, since 1969, fac mem since 1943; lectr, dept psycht, La State U Sch of Med, 1958-67; partner, Leopold Inves, since 1954; asst mgr, L Feibleman and Co, 1930-54. Pres: Peirce Soc, 1948-49, treas, 1946-47; New Orleans Acad of Sci, 1958-59; vice-pres, Phi Sigma Tau, 1956-57; mem: AAUP; Amer Math Soc; Amer Phil Assn; Amer Soc for Aesthetics; Assn Symbolic Logic; AAAS; Brit Soc for Phil of Sci; Jordan Soc; Metaphys Soc of Amer; Mind Assn; MLA; Phi Beta Kappa; Royal Inst Phil; S Cen MLA; S Soc for Phil and Psych. Author: numerous books, most recent being: The Dark Bifocals, 1953; The Institutions of Society, 1956; The Pious Scientist, 1958; Inside the Great Mirror, 1958; Religious Platonism, 1959; The Foundations of Empiricism, 1962; Bisocial Factors in Mental Illness, 1962; Mankind Behaving: Human Needs and Material Culture, 1963; The Two-Story World, 1966; Moral Strategy, 1967; contbr to profsl jours. Office: Tulane U, New Orleans, La.

FEIDEN, Murray T, US, jurist; b. Phila, Pa, Dec 7, 1904; s. Hyman and Mary (Thau); LLB, Bklyn Law Sch, 1926; m. Claire Axelrod, Apr 2, 1938; c: Rica, Robert. Justice, Supr Court, NY, since 1965; counsel to J Leg Comm, NY State Leg, 1936; secy to: Judge A H Geismar, 1936-38; Judge J H Livingston, 1939-42; libr, cons, opinion clerk, Kings Co Court, 1942-49; justice, City Court, NY, Kings Co, 1950-65. Pres, Infants Home, Bklyn, Inc; trustee, Bklyn J Cen; Temple Petah Tikva; mem cabinet, UJA, since 1955; chmn, FJP, Bklyn. Home: 225 Adams St, Brooklyn, NY. Office: Supr Court, Brooklyn, NY.

FEIFFER, Jules Ralph, US, cartoonist, writer; b. NYC, Jan 26, 1929; s. David and Rhoda; att: Art Students League, NYC, 1946-47; Pratt Inst, Bklyn, 1947-50; m. Judith Sheftel, Sep 17, 1961; c: Kate. Pub works: Sick Sick Sick, 1959; Passionella, 1960; The Explainers, 1969; Harry the Rat with Women, 1963; Boy Girl-Boy Girl, 1964; Hold Me!, 1965; Feiffer's Album, 1966; The Unexpurgated Memoirs of Bernard Mergendeiler, 1967; Feiffers Marriage Manual, 1968; Feiffer on Civil Rights, 1967; The Great Comic Book Heroes, 1967; Little Murders, 1968; The White House Murder Case, 1970; Pictures at a Prosecution, 1970; syndicated cartoons appear in numerous US and fgn newspapers. Pvt, US Army, 1951-53. Sponsor: Comm for Public Justice; Amnesty Intl, US; SANE; mem: Dramatists Guild; Authors Guild; Authors League; Screenwriters Guild; club, PEN. Recipient: awards: George Polk Memorial, 1961; Metrop Council, AJCong, 1962; Capital Pres Club, 1966; Obie, 1969; Outer Critics Circle, 1969, 1970. Office: Publishers-Hall Syndicate, 30 E 42 St, New York, NY.

FEIGA, Wilfred B, US, attorney; b. Worcester, Mass, Jan 25, 1895; s. Leon and Pauline (Beeder); AB, cum laude, Harvard Coll, 1915, LLB, 1918; m. Claire Goodman, 1963. Ret; asst clerk courts, Worcester Co, 1942-65; auditor Superior Court, 1934-42. Concert Master, Harvard U Orch; exhibited paintings in Worcester and Fitchburg Club. Pres: J Home for Aged, 1941-60; Free Public Libr, 1931-32, 1966; dist grand lodge, B'nai B'rith, 1936-37; vice-pres, Civic Music Assn; exec comm; Zionist Dist; Worcester Club; bd dirs, JWF. Home: 9 Woodmer Rd, Worcester, Mass.

FEIGENBAUM, Aryeh, Isr, educator, physician; b. Lwow, Aus, 1885; in Isr since 1913; MD, Vienna, 1911; PhD, HC, Heb U, Jerusalem; m. Rachel Meyouhas; 2 c. Prof em, ophthal, Heb U, Jerusalem, chmn, pre-fac med, Heb U, 1937-44; asst, Prof Hirschberg's Eye Clinic, Berlin, 1913; head, eye dept: J Health Bur, Jerusalem; Hadassah U Hosp, 1922-54. Prin contribs: research in jt field of ling and depth psychol; studies on glaucoma; papers on trachoma and conjunctivitis; relation between eye and nose; endocrinic, neur and vascular disturbances and the eye. Mem, Ophthal Soc of UK; hon mem: Ophthal Soc of N Greece; Hellenic Ophthal Soc, Athens; chmn: Isr Ophthal Soc, since 1955; Isr Soc for Hist of Med and Sci; fmr: chmn, Jerusalem Med Soc; co-found, Pal J Ophthal Soc. Author, ha'Ayin, 1927, first med textbook in modern Heb; found: haRefuah, 1920; Intl Folia (later Acta) Ophthalmologica Orientalia, 1932-40; Acta Medica Orientalia, 1942, new Isr Med Jour; ed, Report of Trachoma Conf, first med book in modern Heb, 1915; mem ed bd: Ophthalmologic, Basle; Excerpta Medica, Amsterdam; Ophthalmic Literature, London; contbr numerous papers to profsl jours. Recipient: Szold Prize for Med and Public Hygiene, 1964. Home: 3 Hahabashim St, Jerusalem, Isr.

FEIGIN, Dorothy L, US, artist; b. NYC, Mar 8, 1904; d. Julius and Kate (Ginsburg) Lubell; att: Art Students League of NY, 1923-26; courses, Tchr's Coll, Columbia U, 1923-30; m. Solomon Feigin, Mar 6, 1927; c: Simon. Ret; chmn, Fine and Ind Arts, NY, 1926-61. In perm collection: Libr of Cong, Wash, DC, lithograph and woodcut; Metrop Mus of Art, NYC, lithograph; exhbs in US and Eur. Vice-pres, NYC HS Art Tchrs' Assn, 1952-54; treas, Fed, Modern Painters and Sculptors, since 1959; dir, NY Soc of Women Artists, since 1959. Mem, Amer Graphic Artists. Recipient: awards for outstanding oil painting, Natl Assn Women Artists, 1947, 1950; water color award, Natl Assn Women Artists, 1951. Home: 99 E 4 St, New York, NY.

FEIGIN, Dov, Isr, sculptor; b. Lugansk, Russ, 1907; s. Zalman and Haia; in Isr since 1927; att Ecole Superieure des Arts Decoratifs à Paris, 1933-37; m. Eugenie; c: Dan, Gavriel. Exhbs: Pesel Bagan, Haifa, 1951, 1959; Beinnale, Venice, 1948, 1962; Antwerp, 1959; Sculpturing Symposium, Mitzpe Ramon, 1962; one-man show, Helena Rubinstein Mus, 1960; monuments: For the Fallen Soldiers of War of Independence, 1949; Wall Relief, Shalom Boat, 1963; Holy Ark, Midrashiat Noam Syn, Pardes Hanna, 1965; Sculptural Wall, Yad Kennedy, Jerusalem, 1966; Wall Relief, ORT Sch, Kfar Saba, 1967. Mem: Painters and Sculptors Assn; Ofakim Hadashim Assn. Recipient: Awards: Dizengoff, 1942, 1946; Haifa Munic 1953; Milo, 1968. Home and studio: 11A Nitzana St, Givatayim, Isr.

FEIGIN, Irwin H, US, neuropathologist, educator; b. NYC, May 13, 1915; s. George and Rose (Herman); BA, Columbia Coll, 1934; MD, NYU, 1938; m. Mollie Kanowitz, June 30, 1949; c: Joel, Diane. Prof, neuropath, NYU, since 1959, asso prof, 1956-59; asst prof, neuropath, Columbia U, 1952-56. US Army, 1942-46. Pres, Munic Concerts, Inc, since 1958; mem: Phi Beta Kappa; Alpha Omega Alpha; Assn Path and Bact; Histochem Soc. Contbr to sci jours. Home: 54-24 Browvale Lane, Douglaston, NY. Office: NYU Med Cen, 550 First Ave, New York, NY.

FEIGLIN, Jacob, Isr, engineer, business exec; b. Melbourne, Austr, June 25, 1928; s. Chaim and Matia (Kaplan); in Isr since 1960; dipl, Chem E, U Melbourne, 1952; AMI, Chem E, Royal Inst Chem E, London, 1956; m; Esther, Nov 28, 1950; c: Naomi, Yael, Moshe. Mgr, Austr Wool Ind Ltd, Ashdod, since 1962; fmr: research engr, Isr Mining Ind, Haifa; tech mgr, Universal, Austr. Prin contribs: research into possible utilization and diversification of Isr based minerals. Chmn, parents comm, Rehovot Rel HS; fmr secy, Brit Ivrit Olamit, Austr. Home: 29 Hanasi Harishon St, Rehovot, Isr. Office: Austr Wool Ind Ltd, Ind Zone, Ashdod, Isr.

FEIL, Harold, US, cardiologist, educator; b. Bay Shore, NY, June 26, 1889; s: George and Lillian (Stein) Cohen; MD, O Wesleyan U, 1911; BA, U Denver, 1914; m. Nellie Elgutter, July 29, 1915; c: George, Mary Hellerstein, Edward. Pvt practice since 1913; clinical prof em, med, W Reserve U, since 1955, on fac since 1921; visiting phys, Cleveland City Hosp, 1921-33; phys-in-chief, Mt Sinai Hosp, 1948-50; asso, phys, U Hosp, Cleveland, 1933-55. Mem: AMA; AAAS; Cen Soc for Clinical Research; AHA; The Temple; clubs: Rowfant; Oakwood. Contbr articles on investigative and clinical card to med publs. Home: 2343 Ardleigh Rd, Cleveland Heights, O. Office: 25 Prospect Ave, SW, Cleveland, Ohio.

FEILCHENFELD, Hans, Isr, chemist, educator; b. Berlin, Ger, Apr 6, 1919; s. Hugo and Edith (Heller); in Isr since 1938; MSc, PhD, Heb U, Jerusalem; m. Hannah Weiler, Oct 25, 1954; c: Noomi, David, Michal, Ephrat. Prof, applied chem, Heb U, Jerusalem, since 1967; head, research dept, IAF, 1949-50; dir, Timna Copper Mines; research dir, Isr Research Council, 1951-66. Maj, IAF, 1948-50. Fmr chmn, Isr Chem Soc, 1965-66; mem: Sigma Xi; Faraday Soc. Home: 3 Mapu St, Jerusalem, Isr. Office: Hebrew U, Jerusalem, Isr.

FEIN, A Edwin, US, marketing and management cons; b. NYC, Apr 9, 1898; s. Samuel and Anne (Fein); att: NYU, 1919-26; Columbia U, 1925-26. Bd chmn, Research Co Amer, since 1959, mgn dir since 1939; vice-pres, secy, United Ind, Corp since 1969; colonial mgr, William H Knox, 1919-22; pres, gen mgr, Sparklets, 1925-35; sales, tech cons, Walter Kidde, 1935-37; dir sales, Doughnut Corp Amer, 1937-39. US Army 1918-19. Vice-pres, distribution, Soc for Advancement in Mgmt; mem: Amer Mgmt Assn; Amer Marketing Assn; Amer Assn for Public Opinion Research; Natl Sales Execs; club, Sales Execs. Author: The Exchange Situation, 1920;

An Outline of Radium and Its Emanations, 1924; Basic Marketing Chart of United States, 1942-54; National Survey of Brewing Industry, 1941-68; How Consumers Spend Their Income, 1947; Research With a Practical Accent, 1953; This is My Life, 1956; Management Research, 1962. Home: 303 E 57 St, New York, NY. Office: 660 Madison Ave, New York, NY.

FEIN, Abraham, Isr, business exec; b. Kowno, Lith, Mar 7, 1931; s. Mordechai and Chana (Salanski); in Isr since 1947; MA, Heb U, Jerusalem, 1959; m. Miriam Harburger, Mar 9, 1961; c: Tamar, Mordechai. Mgn dir, Bank Lemelacha, since 1965; econ adv, Min of Commerce and Ind, 1961-65; Pvt, IDF 1948-52. Ed bd, Quarterly Banking Rev, since 1966. contbr econ articles to jours. Home: 23 Krauze St, Holon, Isr. Office: 9 Carlebach St, Tel Aviv, Isr.

FEIN, Arnold L, US, jurist; b. Boston, Mass, Apr 22, 1910; s. Jacob and Annie (Kanter); BS, NYU, 1931, JD, 1933; m. Margaret Roach. Justice, Supr Court, NY State, since 1968; pvt practice, 1934-56; spec counsel, US Sen Crime Inves Comm, 1951; div counsel, Off Price Stabilization, 1951; counsel to pres, NYC Council, 1952-53; judge, Civil Court, NYC, 1965-68. US Army, 1942-46; war crimes prosecutor, Manila and Tokyo. Fmr chmn, NY Comm for Dem Voters; fmr vice-chmn, NY State ADA; mem: Amer Vets Comm; Citizens Union; NAACP; ACLU; club, E Midtown Reform Dem. Recipient: Army Commendation Ribbon; Dist Unit Badge. Home: 601 E 20 St, New York, NY. Office: 60 Center St, New York, NY.

FEIN, Bernard, US, business exec; b. NYC, Jan 15, 1908; s. Samuel and Anna; LLB, St Lawrence U, 1929; m. Elaine Schneir, 1948; c: Kathy, Lawrence, Susan, Adam, David. Pres, chmn bd: United Ind Corp; Affiliated Hosp Produc, Can; pres: IB Kleinert Rubber, Affiliated Med Producs, Can; dir, AAI. Asso dir, men's council, J Comty Cen, White Plains, NY. Home: Garden Rd, Scarsdale, NY. Office: 660 Madison Ave, New York, NY.

FEIN, Irving A, US, business exec; b. Bklyn, NY, June 21, 1911; s. Harry and Fannie (Milstein); att: Colby Acad; U Baltimore; U Wis; LLB, Bklyn Law Sch, 1936; m. Florence Kohn, Dec 25, 1941; c: Michael, Patricia. Pres, J & M Producs Inc, since 1956; exec produc, Jack Benny Show, since 1958; publicist, Warner Bros, 1933-41, dir exploitation, 1944-46; asst publicity dir, Samuel Goldwyn Producs, 1941-42; dir: exploitation, Columbia Pictures, 1942-44, 1946-47; PR, Amusement Enterprises, 1947-51; public exploitation, CBS Radio, Hollywood, 1951-53, PR, 1953-55, vice-pres, 1955-56. Recipient: Emmy Award for Jack Benny Show, 1961. Home: 1100 N Alta Loma Rd, Los Angeles, Cal. Office: 9908 Santa Monica Blvd, Beverly Hills, Cal.

FEIN, Isaac M, US, educator, historian; b. Russ, Aug 16, 1899; s. Meir and Matia (Sirchis); in US since 1923; PhD, Dropsie Coll, 1934; m. Chaya Wertheim, Apr 18, 1920; c: Rashi, Leibel. Prof em, Baltimore Heb Coll, since 1964; prof, 1943-64; curator, J Hist Soc of Med, since 1960. Mem: Natl Council for J Educ; Amer J Hist Soc; Farband; ACLU; ADA. Contbr to scholarly publs. Recipient: intercultural educ, U of Cal, Natl Council for J Culture. Home: 7628 Carla Rd, Baltimore, Md. Office: 5800 Park Heights Ave, Baltimore, Md.

FEIN, Leah Gold, US, psychologist; b. Minsk, Russ, Dec 10, 1910; d. Jacob and Sara (Meltzer) Gold; DH, Forsythe Tufts, 1927; BS, Albertus Magnus Coll, 1939; MA Yale U Grad Sch, 1942, PhD, 1944; dipl, Gram Amer Bd in Profsl Psych, dipl, clinical psych, 1964; m. Alfred Fein, June 10, 1944; c: Ira. Pvt practice, clinical and cons psych and therapist, since 1948; staff mem, Bur Child Guidance, Bd of Educ, NYC, since 1968; research asso, Children's Intl Summer Villages, since 1953; vice-pres, Alfred G Fein Sales Corp; dir, testing services, Carleton Coll, Minn, 1944-46; research asso, Conn Inter-racial Commn, 1946-47; asst prof, U Bridgeport, 1946-47, lecturing prof, psych, 1952-58; cons, comty relations, Bridgeport J Council, 1946-47, 1952-56; clinical cons, Conn Comm on Alcohol, Stamford Clinic, 1952-60; research cons, Norwalk Hosp, Conn, 1960-64; clinical cons, psychotherapist, Norwalk Psycht Clinic, 1954-64; dir, Cerebral Palsy Assn, Waterbury, Conn, 1964-65; asso prof, psych and sociol, Quinnipiac Coll, Hamden, Conn, 1965-66; cons psych, instr med staff, NY Hosp, Cornell Med, 1966-67; dir, psych dept, Psycht Treatment Cen, NYC, 1967-68; research psychol to child psycht, Roosevelt Hosp, NYC, 1968-69. Mem: natl bd on comty relations, AJCong; Amer Psych Assn; Inter-Amer

Soc Psych; Fairfield Co Soc Clinical Psychols; Natl Council J Women; f: Amer Acad Psychotherapy; Soc for Projective Techniques; fmr: chmn, PR, Intl Council Psychols, vice-pres, chmn, profsl relations among psychols throughout world; educ cons, Hadassah, Seattle, Wash chap; vice-pres, Assn for Gifted Children. Author: The Three Dimensional Personality Test, 1960; contbr to profsl jours. Recipient, Marion Talbot F, Amer Assn U Women, 1943. Home: 1050 Park Ave, New York, NY. Office: Bldg Educ Bur Child Guidance, New York, NY.

FEIN, Leonard J, US, educator; b. Bklyn, NY, July 1, 1934; s. Isaac and Clara (Wertheim); BA, MA, U Chgo, 1951-58; PhD, Mich State U, 1962; m. Zelda Kleiman, June 19, 1955; c: Rachel, Naomi, Jessica. Asso dir, MIT-Harvard Jt Cen for Urban Studies, dir research, since 1968; asso prof, political sci, MIT, since 1967, fac mem since 1962. Mem: exec comm: AJCong; Amer-Isr Public Affairs Comm; ed council, Conf on J Social Studies; bd trustees, Amer Zionist Youth Found. Author: American Democracy, 1965; Israel: Politics and People, 1968. Home: 149 Buckminster Rd, Brookline, Mass. Office: 66 Church St, Cambridge, Mass.

FEIN, Norman N, US, physician; b. Milw, Wis, Aug 27, 1903; s. Sol and Lena (Suran); BS, U Wis, 1928; MD, 1930; m. Clare Grabin, Sep 2, 1931; c: Harlyn, Leslie. Pvt practice since 1954; chief, ear, nose, throat dept, VA Hosp, since 1950; chief, otolaryngology service: State Hosp of Ark; Mo Pacific Hosp; chief res, Johnston Emergency Hosp, 1932-34; in otology, Johns Hopkins Hosp, 1934-35, res, 1935-38; chief, ear, nose, throat dept, Trinity Hosp and Clinic, Little Rock, 1946-54; asso prof, otolaryngology, U Ark Med Sch, 1948-53. Mem: Pulaski Co Med Soc; Ark Med Soc; AMA; Amer Acad Ophthal and Otolaryngology; Johns Hopkins Hosp and Surg Assn; S Med Assn; B'nai B'rith; B'nai Isr Temple; club, Westridge Country. Home: 1001 Fawnwood Road, Little Rock, Ark. Office: 520 Waldon Bldg, Little Rock, Ark.

FEIN, Samuel L, US, attorney; b. Minsk, Russ, June 8, 1899; s. Abraham and Sarah (Schwartz); in US since 1906; LLB, NYU Law Sch, 1922; m. Mildred Sherman, Dec 31, 1922; c: Phyllis Perelman Serman. Sr mem, Fein, Cavanaugh, Kimball, since 1950; first asst city solicitor, 1934-35; comm, Bd Public Works, 1938-47; mem, Planning Bd, 1939-45, all Springfield, Mass; govt appeal agt, Selective Service, local bd 142, 1940-47, local bd 14, 1951-54, mem bd, since 1954; admitted to practice, Mass, US Dist and Supr Courts; Interstate Commerce Comm. Lt col, Mass Wing, Civil Air Patrol. Former gov, Amer Trial Lawyers Assn; pres: Cong Beth El, 1941-43, 1948-49, B'nai B'rith lodge, 1928; vice-pres, Hampden Co Bar Assn, 1950-52; chmn, ward 3 Rep City Commn, 1935-47; dir, Comty Council, since 1950; mem: Tau Epsilon Phi; Amer Mass Bar Assns; Soc of Amer Intl Coll; Mass Trial Lawyers Assn; Springfield J Civic Agcys; Amer Legion; JWV; Independent City of Homes Assn; ZOA; KP; Masons; Shriner; Elks; NAACP; Boy Scouts of Amer, Hampden Council; clubs: Probus; The Airways, Inc; Natl Travel; Brandeis U; Crestview Country, Springfield; NYU Alumni, W Mass, past pres; Westover Offs' Open Mess; Natl Fed J Men's. Ed, ATLA Law Jour. Recipient: Selective Service Medal, 1947. Home: 240 Longmeadow St, Longmeadow, Mass. Office: 1421 Main St, Springfield, Mass.

FEINBERG, Abraham, US, banker; NYC, Mar 7, 1908; s. Jacob and Eva (Wolin); LLB, Fordham U, 1929; LLM, NYU, 1936; hon LLD, Brandeis U, 1961; m. Lillian Farber, Sep 3, 1929; c: Eliazar, Judith. Chmn bd, Cen Bottling Co, Ltd, Isr; vice-chmn bd and chmn exec comm, Amer Bank & Trust Co, since 1963; pres, Devl Corp for Isr since 1951. Pres: Amer Comm, Weizmann Inst Sci, 1952; Amers for Haganah, 1947; chmn, bd trustees, Brandeis U, 1954-61; clubs: City Athletic; Harmonie; Old Oaks Country. Home: Elmsmere Rd, Mt Vernon, NY. Office: 562 Fifth Ave, New York, NY.

FEINBERG, Banice, US, physician; b. NYC, Jan 5, 1901; s. Morris and Ida (Goldberg); MD, Tufts U, 1922; hon, DMS, Brown U, 1969; m. Laura Sydney, Sep 10, 1933; c: Helen Schneider, Albert, Lloyd. Pvt practice, ped, since 1925; chief ped, RI Hosp, since 1955; cons, dept ped: Providence Lying-In Hosp; St Joseph's Hosp; Pawtucket Memorial Hosp; fmr, chief: Crawford Allan Memorial Hosp; Convalescent Hosp for Rheumatic Children, 1940-55. Lt cdr, USNR, WW II. Chmn, RI sect, Amer Acad Ped, 1956-59; pres, NE Ped Soc, 1961-62; fmr pres: Children's Heart Assn, RI; RI Heart Assns; mem: AMA; RI Med Soc; Providence Med Assn; Amer Acad Ped; bd dir, AHA, 1960-66. Contbr to med jours. Home:

245 Slater Ave, Providence, RI. Office: 225 Waterman St, Providence, RI.

FEINBERG, Charles E, US, business exec; b. London, Eng, Sep 27, 1899; s. Samuel and Jane (Stocker); in US since 1923; LHD, S Ill U, 1955; m. Lenore Brown, Jan 30, 1927; c: Bartley, Suzanne Ness, Judith Kuehne. Ret; vice-pres, Speedway Petroleum Corp, 1958-62; mgr, Regal Shoe, 1923-25; salesman, mgr, Silent Automatic, 1925-28; vice-pres, pres, Argo Oil, 1928-51, pres, 1951-58. Pres, Detroit Assn, Phi Beta Kappa; mem: libr council, U Notre Dame; bd, Friends U Detroit Libr, fmr pres; Mich Hist Commn; natl J comm, Boy Scouts of Amer, exec bd, Detroit area council; natl comm on J Americana, B'nai B'rith; J Hist Soc; Council, Friends Princeton Libr; bd dirs, Amer Friends Heb U; Bibliographical Soc, U Va; Bibliographical Soc of Amer; Huntington Libr; U Ky Librs; Syracuse Libr Assn; Manuscripts Soc; Free Libr Phila; Columbia U Libr; bd trustees, Detroit Hist Soc; bd dirs, Howard Home; clubs: Franklin Hills Country; Franklin; Mich; Grolier; Albert Gallatin Assos. Author: Notes on Whitman Collections and Collectors, 1955; A Whitman Collector Destroys a Whitman Myth, 1958. Recipient: cert of merit, USIA, 1954; Detroit Probus Club Brotherhood Award, 1959; dist citizen, Detroit Hist Soc, 1959; comty service pin, Boy Scouts of Amer, 1961. Hobby: collecting manuscripts, letters, books by or about Walt Whitman. Home: 872 W Boston Blvd, Detroit, Mich.

FEINBERG, Gerald G, US, chiropodist; b. Malden, Mass, Feb 14, 1909; s. Morris and Ida (Goldberg); att: RIU; Bryant Coll; RI Coll of Podiatry; DSP, NE Coll of Podiatry, 1933; m. Esther Ackerman, Aug 27, 1939; c: Daniel, Leslie. Pvt practice since 1933; mem, bd examiners in chiropody, RI, since 1941. Pres: RI Chiropodist Soc, 1947; ZOA, 1947; vice-pres, Judah Touro Lodge, 1946-48; secy, J Comty Fund, 1941-49; treas, Touro Syn, 1946-57; chmn, war service, B'nai B'rith, 1941-46, all in Newport, RI; mem: bd, Soc Friends Touro Syn; RI Heart Soc, 1950-55; UJA; Natl J Hosp, Denver, Colo, 1948-50; USO Council, 1942-46; Amer Radio Relay League, asst dir since 1966; KP; NAACP; ZOA; B'nai B'rith; Natl Assn Chiropodists; club, Newport Country Radio, pres, 1953, and since 1958. Contbr to profsl jours. Home and office: 344 Broadway, Newport, RI.

FEINBERG, Horace B, US, school admnr; b. NYC, Oct 12, 1902; s. Henry and Mildred (Valenstein); BSS, CCNY, 1922; LLB, Bklyn Law Sch, 1928; MA, NYU, 1943; JD, Bklyn Law Sch; m. Mae Korn, Dec 27, 1938; c: Mildred Grossberg, Michael. Prin, Public Sch 198, Bklyn, since 1953. Div chmn, UJA; adv bd, E Midwood J Cen, Bklyn; mem, bd educ, Cong Shaare Torah, Bklyn; bd trustees, Crown Hgts Yeshivah, Bklyn. Home: 1143 E 19 St, Brooklyn, NY. Office: 4105 Farragut Rd, Brooklyn, NY.

FEINBERG, Joseph M, US, attorney; b. New Haven, Conn, June 13, 1907; s. Hymen and Celia (Segal); LLB, Rutgers U, 1928; m. Mildred Greenberg, Nov 28, 1931; c: David. Pvt practice since 1929; partner, Feinberg, Feinberg and Tritsch; asst, NJ State counsel and acting chief counsel, Home Owners Loan Corp, 1933-35; counsel on tax matters, City of Rahway, 1939-43; munic court judge, 1948-51. Pres: Heb Cong, 1945-48; J Young People's League, Elizabeth; mem: exec council, Boy Scouts. JDC, ZOA; AJComm; Amer Union Co, NJ Bar Assns; Rutgers U Alumni Assn; clubs: Kiwanis Boys Key; Shackamaxon; Rahway. Home: 955 Minnisink Way, Westfield, NJ. Office: 1447 Campbell St, Rahway, NJ.

FEINBERG, Mortimer Robert, US, psychologist; b. NYC, Aug 26, 1922; s. Max and Frieda (Siegel); att CCNY, 1940-44; MA, Ind U, 1946; PhD, NYU, 1950; m. Gloria Granditer, June 22, 1948; c: Stuart, Todd. Prof, psych, Baruch Coll, CUNY, since 1950; prof: Bklyn Coll, 1950-51; chief psychol, Research Inst of Amer, 1955-60; Columbia Grad Sch, 1960-61; cons, ind psychol; USAF; USMC; Gen Elec Corp; Eastman Dillon; Chase-Manhattan. Cpl, US Army, 1943-44. F, AAAS; pres, BFS Psychol Assos, since 1960; mem: bd trustees, Temple Isr, N Westchester; AAUP; dipl, ind psych, progchmn, Amer Psych Assn. Author: Developing People in Industry, 1950; Psychology for Executives, 1965. Hobbies: photography, golf, gardening. Home: 34 Brook Lane, Peekskill, New York, NY. Office: 17 Lexington Ave, New York, NY.

FEINBERG, Nathan, Isr, attorney, educator; b. Kovno, Lith, June 6, 1895; s. Leon and Henia (Ratner); in Isr since 1924; DJ, U Zurich, 1918; dipl, Grad Inst of Intl Studies, Geneva, 1930; m. Yehudith Ostrovsky, 1925. Prof em, intl law and relations, Heb U, Jerusalem, since 1965, fac mem since 1945, dean, fac law, 1949-51; Isr mem, Perm Court of Arbitration, Hague, Netherlands, since 1962; secy, Comm of J Delgs, Paris, 1922-24; in pvt practice, Isr, 1925-27, 1934-45; journalist accredited to L of N, 1928-33; privat-dozent, Law Fac, U Geneva, 1931-33; lectr: Hague Acad of Intl Law, 1932, 1937, 1952. F, Intl Inst Arts and Letters; mem: Inst Intl Law; bd govs, Heb U, Jerusalem; Amer Soc Intl Law; Isr bd, Intl Law Assn; Isr sect, Intl Comm of Jurists; David Davies Memorial Inst Intl Studies, London; council, Yad Vashem; fmr: co-found, mem, J Pal L of N Soc; legal adv, Comm J Delgs, before L of N in the Bernheim Petition, 1933; hon magistrate, Tel Aviv war profiteering court, WWII; chmn, study group, Heb U, for preparation of report, Isr and UN, 1956. Author: La Question des Minorités à la Conférence de la Paix 1919-20 et l'action juive en faveur de la Protection Internationale de Minorités, 1929; La Juridiction de la Cour Permanente de Justice Internationale dans le Systeme des Mandats, 1930; La Pétition en Droit International, 1933; Some Problems of the Palestine Mandate, 1936; Charter of the United Nations and Statute of the International Court of Justice, Heb trans with introduction, 1946; L'Admission de Noveaux Membres à la Société des Nations et a l'Organisation des Nations Unies, 1952; The Jewish Struggle Against Hitler in the League of Nations; the Bernheim Petition, in Heb, 1957; The Legality of a State of War after the Cessation of Hostilities—under the Charter of the United Nations and the Covenant of the League of Nations, 1961; Palestine under the Mandate and the State of Israel—Problems in International Law, in Heb, 1963; The Jewish League of Nations Societies, A Chapter in the Struggle of the Jews for their Rights, in Heb, 1967; ed: Studies in Public International Law in the Memory of Sir Hersh Lauterpacht, 1961; co-ed, The J Year Book of Intl Law, 1949; contbr to fgn and local legal jours. Home: 6 Ben Labrat St, Jerusalem, Isr. Office: Heb U, Jerusalem, Isr.

FEINBERG, Samuel Maurice, US, physician, educator; b. Yurburg, Russ, Mar 28, 1895; s. George and Anna (Shulman); in US since 1907; BS, U Wis, 1917; MD, Rush Med Coll, 1919; m. Cecile Stern, Mar 19, 1922; c: Alan, Robert, Ruth, Helene. Dir, Allergy Research Lab, Evanston Hosp, since 1965; prof em, med, Northwestern U Med Sch, since 1965; prof, 1950-65, mem fac since 1921; att phys, Cook Co Hosp, 1926-28; chief area cons in allergy, VA, 1948-61. US Army, 1918. Prin contribs: in field of allergies; original discoveries: importance of moulds as cause of asthma and hay fever, 1933; the use of anti-histamines in allergic disease, 1945; the role and mechanism of infection and other measures in inhibiting allergic phenomena, since 1950; mechanism of induction of new allergy and relationship of immediate to delayed type. Mem: Amer Acad Allergy, fmr pres; Intl Assn Allergology; Subspecialty Bd Allergy; Chgo Soc Allergy; Amer Coll of Phys; Phi Beta Kappa; Sigma Xi; N Shore Cong Isr; hon mem, Eur and S Amer Allergy Assns; fmr mem, training grant comm, Natl Inst of Allergy and Infectious Disease, NIH. Author: Asthma, Hay Fever and Related Disorders, 1933; Allergy in General Practice, 1934; Allergy in Practice, 1944, 2nd ed, 1946; the Antihistamines, 1950; Allergy, Facts and Fancies, 1951; Living with Your Allergy, 1958; mem ed bd: Journal of Allergy; Clinica Europea; contbr to profsl jours. Recipient: Medaille d'argent de la ville de Paris, 1958. Hobbies: oil painting; traveling. Home: 750 Green Bay Rd, Winnetka, Ill. Office: 739 Clavey Rd, Highland Park, Ill.

FEINBERG, Solomon M, S Afr, physician; b. Johannesburg, May 26, 1918; s. Joe and Martha (Wolpe); MB, BCh, U Witwatersrand, 1941; m. Eillen Lucey, Mar 23, 1946 (decd); c: Lynette, Sharon; m. 2nd, Isabel Cave, June 2, 1965; c: Kathryn, Kevin. Med off of health, Ramsgate, since 1951; med off i/c blood transfusion, since 1965; lectr, Red Cross Soc, since 1946; asst railway med off, since 1948; asst dist surg, since 1948; fmr: house surg, Non-Eur Hosp, Johannesburg, 1941-42; sr med off, Grey's Hosp, Pietermaritzburg, 1943-46. Vice-chmn, Margate Players Dramatic Soc, since 1960; fmr: elected councillor, Borough of Margate, 1947; dep mayor, Margate, 1951-52, mayor, 1952-53; Margate Council repr: Publicity Assn of Margate and C of C; Margate repr, S Coast Public Bodies; hon mem, Port Shepstone Hosp Bd; chmn: S Afr Assn of Arts 1960; vice-chmn: S Afr Natl TB Assn; Football Assn; hon mem, Sch Adv Bd; first chmn, Lower S Coast Heb Cong; clubs: Rotary, past pres, ed mag; Margate Country. Hobbies: oil painting, philately, horticulture. Home: Marine Dr, Ramsgate, S Afr. Office: POB 200, Margate, S Afr.

FEINBLATT, Ebria, US, museum curator; b. Hadera, Isr, d. Isaac and Mary (Glaser); in US since 1919; BA, NYU, 1945; MA, U of Cal, 1947. Curator, prints and drawings, LA Co Mus of Art, since 1948, adv, graphic arts council; visiting lectr, U of S Cal, 1968. Bd dirs: Print Council of Amer, since 1959; Tamarind Lithography Workshop, since 1959; mem Amer Assn Art Hists. Contbr to art jours. Recipient: Fulbright f, 1950-52; Ford Found grant, 1962. Home: 136 S Sweetzer Ave, Los Angeles, Cal. Office: LA Co Mus of Art, Los Angeles, Cal.

FEINBLOOM, Abe, US, business exec; b. Binghamton, NY, Jan 13, 1901; s. Simon and Rachel; m. Helen, 1927; c: Harold. Chmn bd, Champion Products Inc; mem, bd dirs, Cen Trust Co. Fmr pres, Mfrs-Natl Assn Coll Stores; vice-pres: AJComm, Rochester; YM-YWHA; JWB; World Fed; Amer-Isr Public Affairs Comm; US Comm Sports in Isr; mem, bd dirs: Temple Brith Kodesh; Child Day Care Cen for Retarded Children; mem: B'nai B'rith; Masons; Elks; club, Rotary. Hobbies: boating, golf. Homes: 820 East Ave, Rochester, NY; 9101 E Bay Harbor Dr, Miami, Fla. Office: 15 College Ave, Rochester, NY.

FEINBLOOM, William, US, optometrist; b. NYC, Jan 10, 1904; s. Louis and Eva (Ewall); att Columbia U, Optometry Sch, 1923; BS, CCNY, 1927; MA, Columbia U, 1933; m. Evelyn Eron Diamond; c: Louise Herz, Stephanie Friedman, Ellen Gottfried, William, Richard. Cons: NY State Vocational Rehabilitation Service For the Blind, since 1953; NYC Optometric Soc Clinic, 1927-30; Bx Optometric Soc Clinic, 1928-31; NJ Optometric Soc Clinic, 1929-32; first dir, Public Health Bur, Amer Optometric Assn, 1940-42; asso in optometry, Columbia U, 1952-53. F: Amer Acad Optometry; NY Acad Sci; NY Acad Optometry. Intl Soc Contact Lens Specialists, since 1963. Mem: NY State Bd Optometry, 1955-65, pres, 1960-65; bd trustees, NY Optometric Cen; Amer Optometric Assn; Optical Soc of Amer; Amer Psych Assn; AAAS; Omega Epsilon Phi; Sigma Xi. Author: numerous articles on visual aids to partially blind, to optometric jours. Recipient: Herschel Gold Medal, 1963. Office: 138 E 36 St, New York, NY.

FEINGOLD, David Sidney, US, scientist, educator; b. Chelsea, Mass, Nov 15, 1922; s. Louis and Miriam (Young); BS, MIT, 1944; PhD, Heb U, Jerusalem, Isr, 1956; m. Batia Haber, Nov 15, 1949; c: Oded, Anat, Michele. Prof, microbiol, Dept Microbiol, Sch of Med, Fac of Arts and Scis, both U Pittsburgh, since 1966; asst research biochem, Dept Biochem, U of Cal, Berkeley, 1957-60; asst prof, biol, Dept Biol, U Pittsburgh, 1960-63, asso prof, 1963-66, chmn, PhD Prog. Prin contribs: research in biochem and microbiol; work on: structure and biosynthesis of naturally occurring saccharides in micro-organisms, plants, and animals; metabolism of carbohydrates in plants and micro-organisms; mechanism of action of enzymes; role of microbial endotoxin in viral interferon; educ in the field of biochem and microbiol; devl of lecture and lab courses; devl of grad prog leading to deg of PhD in Microbiol. USNR, 1944-46. F, Amer Inst of Chems; mem: Amer Chem Soc; Amer Soc Biol Chems; Amer Soc for Microbiol. Contbr, chaps to: Methods in Enzymology; Modern Methods in Plant Analysis; articles to: Acta Medica Orientalia; Amer Heart Jour; Archives of Biochem and Biophysics; Biochem and Biophys Research Communications; Biochem Jour; Biochem; Biochimica Biophysica Acta; British Jour of Experimental Path; Bull of the Research Council of Isr; Dermatologia; Fed Proc Jour of the Amer Chem Soc; Jour of Bact; Jour of Biol Chem; Immunochem; Nature; Proc of the Natl Acad of Sci, US; Proc of the NY Acad of Sci; Jour of Virology. Recipient: Isr Prize, State of Isr, 1957; Career Devl Award, USPHS, 1965. Home: 6420 Bartlett St, Pittsburgh, Pa. Office: Dept of Microbiol, U of Pittsburgh Sch of Med, Pittsburgh, Pa.

FEINGOLD, Jessica, US, organization exec; b. New Orleans, La, Dec 28, 1910; d. Meyer and Jessie (Schwabacker); BA, Vassar Coll, 1931; MA, Columbia U, 1933. Admn secy, JTSA, exec vice-pres, conf on sci, phil, rel; dir, inst for rel and social studies; exec secy, inst on ethics, all JTSA. Recipient, first medal, conf on sci, phil and rel, JTSA, 1956. Home: 327 Central Park W, New York, NY. Office: 3080 Broadway, New York, NY.

FEINGOLD, Norman, Eng, business exec; b. Manchester, Eng, Feb 3, 1925; s. Philip and Sarah (Levy); PMG cert, Coll Radio Tech; m. Zela Harris; c: David, Vivienne. Dir, Normans. Radio off, merchant marine, 1941-46. Found chmn, natl

chmn, Achdut, Gt Brit; provincial exec: ZF, Gt Brit and N Ir; Zionist Cen Council; exec vice-chmn, JPA, Manchester; exec, ZF, Gt Brit. Home: 10 Ravensclose, Prestwich, Lancashire, Eng. Office: 897 Rochdale Rd, Manchester, Eng.

FEINGOLD, Robert, US, attorney; b. NYC, Dec 19, 1904; s. Samuel and Anna (Friedman); LLB, Bklyn Law Sch, 1926; m. Bertha Feldman, Sep 20, 1929. Pvt practice since 1929. Prin contrib, prepared 2nd code under NRA. Pres: S Shore YM and YWHA; Freeport JCC; mem, Mayors Citizen Comm on Planning; fmr: chmn bd, Lemberger Home for Aged; bd, Reform J App. Home: 70 N Grove St, Freeport, NY. Office: 16 Court St, Brooklyn, NY.

FEINGOLD, S Norman, US, psychologist, organization exec; b. Worcester, Mass, Feb 2, 1914; s. William and Aida (Salit); AB, Ind U, 1937; AM, Clark U, 1940; EdD, Boston U, 1948; m. Marie Goodman, Mar 24, 1947; c: Elizabeth, Margaret, Deborah, Marilyn. Natl dir, B'nai B'rith Vocational Service, since 1958; ed, Counselor's Info Service, since 1960; dir, J Vocational Service, Boston, 1940-43, exec dir, 1946-58, exec dir, adjustment cen, Boston, 1957-58; spec lectr, instr, Boston U, 1953-58. Chief psych, US Army, 1943-46. Chmn, Commonwealth of Mass, Council on Employment of Aging, 1957-58; mem: Pres Comm on Employment of Physically Handicapped; Amer Personnel and Guidance Assn; Amer, E, Mass, and Md Psych Assns; Natl Vocational Guidance Assn, pres, 1968-69; AAAS; Gerontological Soc, Inc; Natl Rehab Assn; Phi Delta Kappa; clubs: Monday Luncheon, off, 1956; New Cent, off 1957-58; Torch. Author: The Vocational Expert in the Social Security Program, 1969; Scholarships, Fellowships and Loans, Vol I-Vol IV, 1949-62; How to Choose that Career—Civilian and Military, 1954; Words for Work, 1958; How to Get College Scholarships, 1958; coauthor: How to Get that Part-Time Job, 1958; Finding Part-Time Jobs, 1962; Occupations and Careers, 1969; College and Career Plans of Jewish High School Youth. Recipient: Meritorious service insignia, US Army; George Biven Found award, 1937; citations: Commonwealth of Mass, Div Blind; B'nai B'rith; Monday Luncheon Club; J Vocational Service. Hobby: photography. Home: 9707 Singleton Dr, Bethesda, Md. Office: 1640 RI Ave, NW, Washington, DC.

FEINGOLD, Victor, US, lawyer; b. Bklyn, NY, Feb 19, 1912; s. Isadore and Rebecca (Wolkowiski); AB, CCNY, 1933; JD, Fordham U Law Sch, NYC, 1936; LLM, NYU Law Sch, 1955, towards JSD, 1955-57; m. Elizabeth Postman, Aug 13, 1939; c: Jane Goldman, Lisa Cohen. Pvt practice since 1936; fmr gen counsel for lab unions; lectr, lab relations. Profsl adv, Parents Without Partners Inc; various comms, Amer Bar Assn; NY Co Lawyers Assn; mem, B'nai B'rith, Spirits Lodge, NY. Fmr mem, bd ed, Fordham Law Rev; contbr to legal jours. Recipient, Alumni Service Medal, CCNY, 1967. Hobbies: outdoor sports, travel, gardening. Home: 125 Oxford Rd, New Rochelle, NY. Office: 405 Lexington Ave, New York, NY.

FEINMARK, Louis, US, attorney; b. New Haven, Conn, Aug 13, 1896; s. Morris and Esther (Lefkowitz); BA, Yale U, 1916, LLB, 1918; m. Ida Shelnitz, June 29, 1924; c: Minna Land. Pvt practice since 1918. Pres: Slum Clearance Council, New Haven, 1940-41; Gtr New Haven Housing Council, 1946-51; Conn J Comty Relations Council; New Haven J Comty Cen, 1959-61; NE region, CJFWF, 1957-60; mem, Mayor's Charter Revision Commn, 1955; vice-chmn, Natl Comty Relations Adv Council, 1960-62; treas, 1961-62; chmn, Comm on Discrimination in Employment; dep chmn, Conn Commn on Hum Rights and Opportunities, vice-pres since 1950; mem, exec comm, AJCong, since 1957; hon mem, bd trustees, Cong Mishkan Isr; mem: Amer and Conn State Bar Assns. Home: 364 Central Ave, New Haven, Conn. Office: 152 Temple St, New Haven, Conn.

FEINSILVER, Alexander, US, rabbi; b. Tel Aviv, Isr, Jan 18, 1910; s. Morris and Rachel (Schulman); in US since 1915; BA, W Reserve U, 1931; BHL, HUC, 1933; ordained rabbi, 1937; DD, HUC-JIR, 1962; Cert Marriage Counsellor, 1967; m. Lillian Mermin, Sep 23, 1946; c: David, Ruth. Rabbi: Temple Covenant of Peace, Easton, Pa, since 1955; Temple Isr, Paducah, Ky, 1937-41; B'nai Isr, Sacramento, Cal, 1941-46. Mem, bd, Easton Family Service; United Fund, Easton; CCAR; Comm on Rel Work in US; B'nai B'rith; HUC Alumni Assn; club, Rotary. Author, In Search of Religious Maturity, 1960. Contbr to J periodicals. Hobby:

music. Home: 510 McCartney St, Easton, Pa. Study: Temple Covenant of Peace, Easton, Pa.

FEINSILVER, Lillian Mermin, US, writer; b. New Haven, Conn, Oct 15, 1917; d. Charles and Merchame (Rosen) Mermin; att U Chgo, 1941, 1942; New Sch for Social Research, 1945; m. Alexander Feinsilver, Sep 23, 1946; c: David, Ruth. Secy, Yale U, 1937-39; asst secy, Comm on Hygiene of Housing, Amer Public Health Sch, Yale Sch of Med, 1939-44; research asst, John Wiley & Sons Publ, 1944-46. Author: The Taste of Yiddish, 1970; studies on Eng usage, impact of Yiddish since 1943; birth control; food processing and labeling; contbr numerous articles, verse, features to profsl jours. Publicity chmn, Sisterhood, Temple Covenant of Peace; fmr, bd dirs: Easton Planned Parenthood Cen; Pa-Jersey Camps; mem: Hadassah; Deborah. Home: 510 McCartney St, Easton, Pa.

FEINSILVER, Oscar, US, physician; b. Worcester, Mass, Oct 23, 1908; s. Samuel and Ida (Alpert); MA, Clark U, 1931; MD, Tufts U, 1935; m. Goldie Gans, Sep 4, 1932; c: David, Samuel, Rachel. Sr visiting phys, St Vincent Hosp, since 1950; cons, chest diseases, Fairlawn Hosp; bronchoscopist, med cons, Rutland State Sanatorium, 1937-66; med dir, Rutland Training Cen, 1943-64. F: Amer Coll Phys; Amer Coll Chest Phys; life mem, ZOA; mem: AMA; Amer Acad Allergy; AHA; Amer Trudeau Soc; B'nai B'rith. Contbr to books and jours on pulmonary diseases. Hobby, photography. Home: 7 Colony Lane, Paxton, Mass. Office: 390 Main St, Worcester, Mass.

FEINSTEIN, Abraham Morris, US, attorney, b. Bklyn, NY, Aug 28, 1909; s. Israel and Bella (Menaker) Hyman; LLB, Bklyn Law Sch, 1930; m. Lillian Goldstein, Mar 12, 1960; c: Brian. Pvt practice since 1931; arbitrator, small claims part, Civil Court NYC, since 1954. Fmr: grand-chancellor, KP, NY; pres: YM-YWHA, E Flatbush-Rugby; Utica, Church Merchants Assn; mem: Bklyn Bar Assn; pres, Council Fraternal Orgs, State of Isr Bonds; hon mem, Rugby Post 1011, Amer Legion. Recipient, awards: FJP; State of Isr Bonds. Home: 2716 E 66 St, Brooklyn, NY. Office: 5024 Church Ave, Brooklyn, NY.

FEINSTEIN, Josephine, Isr, publicist; b. Galatz, Rum, Jan 1, 1896; d. Ferdinand and Sophia (Hascalovici) Feldman; in Isr since 1950; m. Itzhac Feinstein, Jan 26, 1928; c: Josepha Rauch, Mircea Juster, Harry Juster (decd). Chmn, WIZO Br Amidar, Bat Yam, since 1952; mem, cultural comm, Fr-Isr League; fmr: chmn WIZO, Bucharest; comm mem, Iubirea de Oameni Hosp, Bucharest. Author: Povesti De Pretutindeni; Basmele Lumii; Intreura si Omenie; ed, Struma; contbr to local, fgn newspapers; lectr, Voice of Isr radio progs. Home: 9 Sokolov St, Bat Yam, Isr.

FEINSTEIN, Louis, US, biochemist, government official; b. Phila, Pa, Apr 20, 1912; s. Jacob and Katie (Levin), BA, U of Pa, 1933, BS, 1934, MS, 1939; PhD, Georgetown U, 1946; m. Florence Waldman, Apr 14, 1935; c: Jay, Henry. Br chief, marketing research div, US Dept Agric, since 1967, with dept since 1939; research chem, Barrett Co, 1934-35; chem, U of Pa Sch of Med, 1935-39. Prin contrib, fields of animal composition, insecticides, vitamins. Mem: Amer Chem Soc; Amer Inst Chems; AAAS; Assn Official Agric Chems; Sigma Xi. Home: 1013 W Nolcrest Dr, Silver Spring, Md. Office: US Dept of Agric, Hyattsville, Md.

FEINSTEIN, Monte A, US, business exec; b. Providence, RI, Aug 3, 1898; s. Bernett and Bessie (Potter); BS, U of Pa, 1920; m. Ruth Moss, Nov 22, 1940; c: Marvin, Ronald. Pres: Marvin Properties Trust, since 1943; Amer Elec Cable Co, 1943-63, ret. USN, 1918, cdr, 1941-46. Mem: NE bd, ADL, since 1956; pres: Sinai Temple, 1949-51, 1953-55, 1966-67; UJA, Holyoke, Mass, 1953-55; clubs: Shriners; Masons, 32 deg; Rotary. Home: 120 Crestview Circle, Longmeadow, Mass.

FEINSTEIN, Robert N, US, researcher; b. Milw, Wis, Aug 10, 1915; s. Jacob and Jennie (Cohen); BS, U Wis, 1937, MS, 1938, PhD, 1940; m. Betty Greenbaum, May 15, 1941; c: Ann, Jean. Sr biochem, Argonne Natl Lab, since 1960, on staff since 1947; research asso: U Chgo, dept biochem; Michael Reese Hosp, 1940-41; May Inst for Med Research, Cinn, O, 1946-47. Maj, med admn corps, US Army, 1941-46. Mem: Soc Biol Chems; Amer Chem Soc; Amer Soc for Experimental Biol; Radiation Research Soc; AAAS. Contbr to sci jours. Recipient: Guggenheim F, Institut du Radium, Paris, 1959-60. Home: 4624 Highland Ave, Downers Grove, Ill. Office: Argonne Natl Lab, Argonne, Ill.

FEINSTEIN, Rosaline, US, communal worker; b. Altoona, Pa, July 18, 1901; BA, Goucher; MA, Eng Lit, U of Pa; LHD, HC, Gratz Coll, 1969; m. Myer Feinstein (decd); c: Peggy Freedman, Samuel. Vice-pres: Fed JAs, Gtr Phila; Amer Friends Heb U, Phila chap; Gratz Coll; Settlement Music Sch, Queen St br; mem: Fed JAs Women's Council Exec Comm; Hon Alumnae Assn Heb U; bd govs: Dropsie Coll, Phila; Heb U, Jerusalem; admn comm, Heb Union Coll's Bibl and Archaeol Sch, Jerusalem; natl bd, Women's Div, UJA; bd: J Employment and Vocational Service; Neighborhood Cen, J Yeshivas and Cen br. Pres, Myer and Rosaline Feinstein Found, through Isr Educ Fund, established Public Libr, Eilat; contbr establishment of IEF-HS, kibbutz Sde Boker, Isr; life mem, Hadassah; donated: Myer Feinstein floor, Alice Seligsberg Comprehensive HS, Hadassah, Jerusalem; day nursery for children of staff mems; donor, Gan Horim, Jerusalem. Recipient: Woman of Valor Award, State of Isr, 1962; Eleanor Roosevelt Humanitarian Award, 1968. Spec interest, J educ. Home: 220 W Rittenhouse Sq, Philadelphia, Pa.

FEINSOT, Aaron, US, business exec; b. Elizabeth, NJ, Nov 25, 1923; s. Philip and Ella (Berger); AB, Union Coll, Schenectady, NY, 1946; MA, NYU, 1951, PhD, 1965; m. Louise Finkelstein, May 8, 1957; c: Paul, John, Lauren. Pres, learning and info div, Cahners Pub Co, since 1968; dir, Brazilian Inst, NYU, 1961-68, dir, off spec service, 1956-68. US Mil Govt, Eur, 1943-46. Mem, Amer Sociol Assn. Home; 29 Washington Sq, New York, NY. Office: 205 E 42 St, New York, NY.

FEINSTONE, W Harry, US, research exec; b. Pol, Oct 1, 1913; s. Samuel and Sophia (Satz); in US since 1920; BS, U Ark, 1936; ScD, Johns Hopkins U, 1939; m. Goldye Wilder, July 3, 1938; c: Jeremy, Linda, Stephen. Vice-pres, sci admn, Plough Inc, since 1958; dir, biol chemotherapy, Amer Cyanamid Co, 1939-43; research, Nepera Chem, 1943-47; sci dir, CB Kendall, 1949-58; cons to pharmaceutical ind, 1947-58. Home: 3745 S Galloway Dr, Memphis, Tenn. Office: 3022 Jackson Ave, Memphis, Tenn.

FEIRING, Emanuel H, US, neurosurgeon, educator; b. NYC, Oct 29, 1913; s. Max and Jenny (Schneider); BS, CCNY, 1932; MD, NYU Coll of Med, 1936; m. Hilda Goldberg, Dec 24, 1942. Asso prof, surg, Albert Einstein Coll of Med, since 1954; att neurosurg, Bx Munic Hosp Cen; neurosurg, Montefiore Hosp. US Army, 1943-46. Mem: AMA; Harvey Cushing Soc; NY Neur Soc; NY Soc Neurosurg; Assn for Research Nervous and Mental Diseases; Amer Acad of Neur; Phi Beta Kappa. Co-author, Practical Neurology, 1955; contbr to profsl jours. Spec interest: art, music. Home: 393 West End Ave, New York, NY. Office: 40 E 89 St, New York, NY.

FEIS, Herbert, US, historian, author; b. NYC, June 7, 1893; s. Louis and Louisa (Waterman); BA, Harvard U, 1916, PhD, 1921; hon LHD: Princeton U, 1961; U Mich, 1965; U Cincinnati, 1966; m. Ruth Stanley-Brown, Mar 25, 1922; c: Mary. Mem, Inst for Advanced Study, Princeton, since 1948; adv on intl econ affairs, State Dept, 1931-44; spec cons, Secy of War, 1944-47. Lt JG, USN, WW I. Author: Europe: The World's Banker, 1931; The Road to Pearl Harbor, 1951; The China Tangle, 1953; Churchill-Roosevelt-Stalin-The War They Waged and the Peace They Sought, 1957; Between War and Peace: The Potsdam Conference, 1960; Japan Subdued: The Atomic Bomb and End of Pacific War, 1961; Foreign Aid and Foreign Policy, 1965; 1933: Characters and Cows, 1966; Japan Confessed, 1967. Home: York, Maine.

FEIT, Charles, US, attorney, educator; b. NYC, June 7, 1912; s. Abraham and Bessie (Singer); BA, CCNY, 1931; LLB, Columbia U, 1934; m. Hadassah Abelow, Dec 23, 1937; c: Joanne. Pvt practice since 1934; lectr, law, CCNY, since 1946; adj prof, law, Pace Coll, since 1953; chief counsel, regional rationing atty, OPA, 1942-47. Pres, Roosa Music Sch Assn; dir, Bklyn Hgts Comty Bldg Inc; trustee, Cong Mt Sinai; mem: NY Co Lawyers Assn; CCNY and Columbia Law School Alumni Assns; Phi Beta Kappa; Assn Bar, NYC. Author: The Enoch Arden: A Problem in Family Law, 1938; asst rev Vol V, Collier's on Bankruptcy. Home: 215 Adams St, Brooklyn, NY. Office: 41 E 42 St, New York, NY.

FEIT, Elliot Michael, US, attorney; b. NYC, Jan 30, 1942; s. Dudley and Hattie (Koenig); BBA, CCNY, 1963; JD, Bklyn Law Sch, 1966; LLM, NYU Law Sch, 1969; m. Anitra Johnson, Dec 11, 1966; c: Laurie. Atty, law firm, Johnson,

Zimbalist, Tannen and Katzman, since 1969; real estate salesman, Schlang Brothers and Co, 1963-65; tchr, bd educ, NYC, 1966-69. Chmn, seder comm, FJP; co-chmn, Comty Planning Bd 12, NYC; bd dirs: Young Isr of Flatbush; Midwood Comty Council; loan comm, bd dirs, Gemilath Chasodim of Flatbush; fmr: pres, treas, Intercollegiate Council of Young Isr-Young Adults; co-chmn, N Amer J Youth Council; mem: Bklyn Bar Assn; NY Co Lawyers Assn; Amer Judicature Soc; CCNY Alumni Assn; Baruch Coll Alumni Assn; NYU Law Sch Alumni Assn; Bklyn Law Sch Alumni Assn; 70th Precinct Youth Council; club, Flatbush Dem, bd dirs. Home: 1075 Ocean Pkwy, Brooklyn, NY. Office: 401 Broadway, New York, NY.

FEITELL, Arthur, US, proctologist; b. NYC, Sep 27, 1911; s. Abraham and Fannie (Wolk); BS, LIU, 1932; MD, Baylor U Coll of Med, 1936; m. Joyce Prichap, Sep 12, 1939; c: Alan, Francyne. Chief, proctology, Stuyvesant Polyclinic, since 1952, pres, 1955-57; asso surg proctology, Beth Isr Hosp, since 1967; asst clinical prof surg, Flower and Fifth Ave Hosp, since 1966; asso surg, Sydenham Hosp; asso visiting surg, Metrop Hosp; asst att surg, NY Med Coll, instr, proctological surg, 1958-66. Maj, US Army, MC, 1941-46. F: Intl Coll Surg; NY Soc Colon and Rectal Surgs; dipl: Amer Bd Colon and Rectal Surg; Pan Amer Med Asso; mem: Amer Proctological Soc; AMA; NY State Med Soc; NY Med Soc; E Side Clinical Med Soc, pres, 1956-57; Masons; Natl Assn Amer Composers and Conductors; Phi Delta Epsilon, LIU Alumni Assn; NY Grad; club: Temple Beth Emeth Mens. Contbr to med jours. Home and office: 60 Gramercy Park N, New York, NY.

FEITELSON, Dina, Isr, educator; b. Vienna, Aus, May 28, 1926; s. Joseph and Hedwig (Koralek) Schur; in Isr since 1934; MA, Heb U, Jerusalem, 1951; PhD, 1956; postdoc studies, Cambridge U, Eng, 1954-55; m. Jehuda Feitelson, July 24, 1950; c: Eran, Dror. Lectr, Heb U, since 1965, on staff since 1956; sch insp, Min of Educ, since 1962; tchr, David Yellin Sch, 1946-51; educ researcher, Szold Found, 1951-54; visiting scholar, U Chgo, 1964-65. IDF, 1948-49. Prin contrib, devl method, teaching initial reading adapted to the spec features of the Heb lang. Author: Causes of School Failure Among First Graders, 1953; I Too Can Read, 1960; Improving the Teaching of Hebrew in the Primary School, 1964; I Read Already, 1967; School and Home, 1968. Pres, Isr Reading Assn; mem: Isr Psych Assn; Isr Phil Soc. Recipient: Isr Award, 1953. Home: 4 Sa'adya Gaon St, Jerusalem, Isr. Office: Heb U, Jerusalem, Isr.

FEITELSON, Jehuda Leo, Isr, educator; b. Riga, Latvia, March 23, 1922; s. Isaac and Vera (Levias); in Isr since 1946; att Riga U; PhD, Heb U, Jerusalem, 1954; m. Dina Schur, July 24, 1950; c: Eran, Dror. Asso prof, Heb U, Jerusalem, since 1968, on fac since 1963; research asso, U Chgo, 1964-65. Sgt, IDF, 1947-49. Prin contrib, in fields of molecular spectroscopy and biophysics. Mem, Faraday Soc. Contbr to sci jours. Hobby, photography. Home: 4 Sa'adia Gaon St, Jerusalem, Isr. Office: Heb U, Jerusalem, Isr.

FELD, Benj, US, business exec; b. Houston, Tex, Sep 3, 1913; s. Sebastian and Miriam (Feld) Lomanitz; BS, Rice U, 1934; m. Evelyn Begnaud, Feb 9, 1936, div; c: Carol Jerry; m. 2nd, Effie Shoemaker, Apr 20, 1968. Res sales exec, St Regis Paper Co, with firm since 1934; dir, Perman Basin RR Co, Odessa, Tex; USNR, 1944-46. Vice-pres, dir, Pacific Found; mem, SW region exec comm, ADL; dir, JCC; mgmt comm, Metrop YMCA; club, Houston. Hobby, photography. Home: 4384 Varsity Lane, Houston, Tex. Office: PO Drawer 2160, Houston, Tex.

FELD, Hans Nathan, Eng, business exec; b. Berlin, Ger, July 15, 1902; s. Herrmann and Hermine (Reiner); in Eng since 1935; DJur, U's of Berlin, Freiburg, Wuerzburg, 1920-24; m. Kate Behr, May 24, 1928; c: Ernst. Dir, co, since 1937; ed: Film Kurier, 1926-32; Die Kritik, 1933-35; World Film News, 1935-36. Chmn: Hampstead Zion House; Theodore Herzl Soc; vice-chmn, Poale Zion, London; mem: Org Comm, ZF; Royal Inst, Intl Affairs, Chatham House; Soc of Authors; C of C. Contbr articles to jours. Hobbies: film, drama. Home: 26 Heath Dr, London NW3, Eng. Office: 10 East Cheap, London EC3, Eng.

FELD, Jacob, US, consulting engineer; b. Rzeszow, Aus, Mar 3, 1899; s. Israel and Gussie (Haarzopf); in US since 1906; BS, CCNY, 1918; CE, MA, U Cincinnati, 1921, PhD, 1922; m. Ethel Gold, Jan 26, 1928; c: Judith. Cons CE, since 1926;

spec cons, USAF since 1953; chief engr, Brader Construction Co, 1936-40; US del, intl tech conf, Eur, S Amer; engr designs: NY Coliseum; Guggenheim Mus; Yonkers Raceway; radio towers, Shanghai; radio telescope structures; Bellevue Hosp Cen; Lincoln Cen for Performing Arts, garage, plaza and bridge; Manhattan Water Pollution Control Project; constructions: Sixth Ave subway, NYC; Sampson Naval Training Sta, Geneva, NY; Stewart Air Field, Newburgh, NY. Bd dirs: Technion, Isr, since 1960; Cejwin Camp; mem: Amer Technion Soc, dir, 1945-60; Amer Conf J Relations, since 1950; f: Amer Soc CEs; Phi Beta Kappa Assos; AAAS; NY Acad Sci, chmn, engr div, 1959-61, pres, 1965-66; found, Westchester lodge, B'nai B'rith, 1940; mem: Amer Concrete Inst; Highway Research Bd; Natl Soc Profsl Engrs; Phi Beta Kappa; Sigma Xi; Tau Beta Pi; Xi Epsilon. Recipient: Collingwood award, 1924, Engr of the Year award, 1955, Amer Soc CEs; White award prize 1931, Engr of Year award, 1959, Bklyn Engrs Club; Clemmens Award, Boston Soc CEs, 1956; Steinman award prize, NY Acad Sci, 1959; spec award, Conn Soc CEs, 1963; Fr Order of Merit, off, 1963; Silver Medal, Rep of Fr, 1966; dist alumni award, U Cincinnati, 1969; Townsend Harris Medal, CCNY Alumni, 1960; dist engr alumni award, CCNY, 1969. Home: Yorktown Heights, New York. Office: 114 E 32 St, NYC.

FELD, Joseph M, US, mathematician, educator; b. Pol, Dec 12, 1907; s. Israel and Rose (Lerner); in US since 1907; AB, Columbia U, 1921, ChemE, 1923, PhD, 1931. Prof, math, Queens Coll, since 1941; instr, Columbia U, 1927-31; lectr, Bklyn Coll, 1931-41. US Infantry, 1943. Pres, Queens Coll chap, AAUP; mem: Amer Math Soc; Math Assn of Amer; Hist of Sci Soc; Council for Basic Educ; Phi Beta Kappa. Contbr to math jours. Home: 143-07 Sanford Ave, Flushing, NY. Office: Queens Coll, 65-30 Kissena Blvd, Flushing, NY.

FELD, Lipman G, US, business exec; b. Kan City, Mo, Jan 16, 1914; s. Emel and Celia (Goldman); BS, Harvard Coll, 1935; JD, U of Mo, 1938; m. Anne Brozman, Apr 30, 1942; c: Robert, Celia. Vice-pres: Cent Acceptance Corp, since 1946; Cencur since 1968; Protective Life Ins, 1957-60; bd dir, ins, finance, tax and employment service cos; atty, Butler Disman, 1938-41. Maj, US Army, 1941-46. Trustee, Cong B'nai Jehudah, 1961-68; treas, Young Audiences, 1961-64. Contbr to mags. Home: 1233 W 69 St, Kansas City, Mo.

FELDBERG, Irving, US, physician; b. NYC, July 21, 1904; s. Louis and Anna (Karp); BS, CCNY, 1926; MD, NYU, 1931; m. Edith Cohen, Oct 11, 1934; c: Stephen. Practicing ophthal, since 1953; ophthal: VA Hosp, Hines, Ill, 1941-45; VA Hosp, Bath, NY, 1945-53. Maj, US Army, 1944-46. F, Amer Acad Ophthal and Otolaryngology; dipl, Amer Bd Ophthal; FACS; mem, Elks; fmr: pres, med staff, St James Hosp, Hornell, NY; mem, planning commn, N Hornell, NY. Contbr to med jours. Home: 426 Cleveland Ave, N Hornell, NY. Office: 28 Elm St, Hornell, NY.

FELDENKRAIS, Moshe Pinchas, Isr, executive, author; b. Baranowicze, Pol, May 6, 1904; s. Aryeh and Sheindel (Pshater); in Isr since 1918; dipl Eng, ETP, Paris; PhD, Eng, Sorbonne, Paris; div. Dir, Feldenkrais Inst; mem, group 4, CNRS, Paris; sci off, Admiralty Sci and Tech Pools, UK. Dir, elec dept, IDF. Author: Body and Mature Behaviour; Der Aufrechte Gang; several communications to Acad des Sci, Paris; numerous books on Judo; recd several patents. Home: 27 Frug St, Tel Aviv, Isr. Office: 49 Nachmani St, Tel Aviv, Isr.

FELDER, Gedalia, Can, rabbi; b. Pol, May 7, 1921; s. Hersch and Esther (Schorr); in Can since 1937; ordained rabbi; m. Anna Teichner, 1942; c: Aaron, Joseph, Esther, Rachel, Yacov. Rabbi, Shomrei Shaboth Cong, since 1949; fmr, rabbi: Ahavas Isaac, Sarnia, Ont; Sons of Jacob, Belleville, Ont; Beth David, Brantford, Ont. Chmn, Vaad Hakashrut, Toronto, since 1960; mem: exec, RabCA, since 1963; exec and rabb body, Can J Cong; Natl Beth Din Tzedek, RabCA; fmr: vice pres, Rabb Council of Can; mem exec, pres, Ont div, RabCA. Author: Yesodei Yeshurun, 6 vols, 1954-62; Nachlat Tzvi, 1959; contbr to rabb publs. Home: 107 Viewmount Ave, Toronto, Can. Study: 585 Glengrove Ave, Toronto, Can.

FELDER, Raoul Lionel, US, attorney; b. NYC, May 13, 1934; s. Morris and Millie (Goldstein); BA, Wash Sq Coll, 1955; att, U Bern, Switz, 1955-56; JD, NYU Law Sch, 1959; m. Myrna Anenberg, May 26, 1963; c: Rachael. Pvt practice since 1964; asst US atty, Justice Dept, 1961-64. F, Amer

Acad Matrimonial Lawyers; mem: Assn Bar, NYC; Amer Bar Assn; NY State Bar Assn. Author: Handbook on Divorce, 1971. Home: 123 E 75 St, New York, NY. Office: 342 Madison Ave, New York, NY.

FELDMAN, A L, US, business exec; b. Hartwell, Ga, Mar 17, 1896; s. Morris and Minna (Shobelstock); m. Jennie Saul, Mar 28, 1920; c: Carlyn Fisher, Brena Frey. Chmn, bd, Puritan Chem Co, Atlanta, Ga, affiliated corps, found co, 1920. Chmn: Fulton Co Heart Fund; JWF; numerous local and natl wfr bds; mem: bd, Ga State Coll Found, adv council; adv comm, Atlanta-Fulton Co Vocational Educ Schs; trustee, Miles Coll, Birmingham, Ala; US Chamber Adv Panel on Manpower Training; trustee, St Josephs Hosp, Atlanta; mem, bd dirs, Health Careers Council, Ga; mem, Ga Nuclear Adv Commn; fmr: bd mem, Comty Chest; first educ comm chmn, Ga State C of C; found, Tchr Recognition Prog; chmn, Ga Tchr Scholarship Plan, produc, film on educ; mem: Jr C of C, life; Alpha Kappa Psi; club, Rotary. Recipient: citation, Comty Chest, 1931; Man-of-Year, B'nai B'rith, 1953; service award, Kappa Phi Kappa, 1957. Spec interest: better educ. Home: 3596 Castlegate Dr, NW, Atlanta, Ga. Office: 916-932 Ashby St, NW, Atlanta, Ga.

FELDMAN, Albert, US, rabbi; b. Baltimore, Md, June 6, 1928; s. Arthur and Anna (Polishook); ordained rabbi, Rabbi Chaim Berlin Rabb Acad, Bklyn, 1951; m. Estelle Silverman, May 24, 1953; c: Cheryl, Alisa. Rabbi, Beth Hamedrash-Westville Syn, since 1954; chaplain, VA Hosp. Pres: Vaad Horabonim, New Haven; Rabb Council, Conn, 1960-61; mem: Rabb mission to Isr, 1952; spec dep sheriff, Co of New Haven; exec bd: Bur of J Ed; J Comty Council; RabCA. Home: 122 Brooklawn Circle, New Haven, Conn. Study: 74 W Prospect St, New Haven, Conn.

FELDMAN, Edward, US, attorney; b. NYC, Feb 28, 1907; s. Leo and Rose; LLB, Southwestern U, La, 1932; m. Helen Gottfried, Oct 1, 1933; c: Lane, Karen Goldberg. Pvt practice since 1933; fmr: lectr and trial atty; judge pro-tem, Superior Court of LA; instr, law. Fmr pres: Guardians J Home for Aged; LA Trial Lawyers Assn; mem, natl bd arbitrators, Amer Arbitration Assn; fmr chancellor, cdr, KP; mem: Amer J Fed; legal staff, J comm for personal service, Gateways; LA, Beverly Hills, Cal Bar Assns; Med, Legal Assn; fmr mem, Wilshire Bar Assn, Wilshire C of C; Tau Delta Phi; Legion Lex; both S Cal; club, Westside Trojan, dir. Home: 342 S Bentley Ave, W Los Angeles, Calif. Office: 6505 Wilshire, Los Angeles, Cal.

FELDMAN, Emanuel, US, rabbi; b. Newburgh, NY, Aug 26, 1927; s. Joseph and Sarah (Felner); BS, Johns Hopkins U, 1950, MA, 1952; ordained rabbi, Ner Isr Rabb Coll, 1952; m. Estelle Samber, Nov 25, 1952; c: Han, Jonathan, Amram, Orah, Geulah. Rabbi, Cong Beth Jacob, since 1952; guest lectr, Bar-Ilan U, Tel Aviv, 1966-67. Vice-pres, RabCA. Author: The 28th of Iyar, 1968; asso ed, Jewish Horizon Magazine; ed-in-chief, Sermon Book of RabCA, 1962; book ed, Tradition Mag; contbr to J periodicals. Home: 1459 Biltmore Dr NE, Atlanta Ga. Study: 1855 La Vista Rd, NE, Atlanta, Ga.

FELDMAN, Estelle E, US, educator; b. NYC, Sept 30, 1895; d. Max and Minnie (Firestone); BS, Boston U, 1927; MA, Yale U, 1930, PhD, 1936. Ret; fac mem, New Haven Public Schs, 1913-48, dir, pupil service, 1948-62; tchr: Panama Canal Zone, 1919-21; New Britain State Tchrs Coll, 1943-45; New Haven State Tchrs Coll, 1946-48; Conn U, 1946; U of Vt, 1949; U of Me, 1963-66. Vice-chmn, Hum Relations Council of Gtr New Haven; secy, New Haven Hum Relations, since 1966; dir: J Bur Educ; Psych Service Inc; Farnam Neighborhood House; natl chmn, Natl Vocational Guidance Assn; trustee, hist, Conn Personnel and Guidance Assn; mem: J Family Service; Cong Mishkan Isr; Amer Personnel and Guidance Assn; Amer Sch Counselors Assn; Assn for Councelor Educ and Supervision; Natl Assn Ret Tchrs; club, Yale, New Haven. Author: An Introductory Course in Foreign Language, 1930; A History of the Connecticut Personnel and Guidance Association, 1967; contbr to educ jours. Home: 733 Elm St, New Haven, Conn.

FELDMAN, Eugene, US, attorney; b. NYC, May 24, 1927; s. Nathan and Rose (Kopf); BS, 1948; LLB, Harvard Law Sch, 1952; LLM, NYU Law Sch, 1965; m. Anne Gross, Aug 31, 1956; c: Simon, Nancy, Joshua. Pvt practice, since 1953; instr, Queens Coll, since 1965; asst dist atty, Queens Co, 1962-66. Pres, Carroll St Assn; treas, First St Nursery Sch;

fmr treas, Intl Nursery Sch; mem: Assn Bar, NYC; NY State Bar Assn; Asst Dist Attys Assn; Amer Natural Hist Soc; Harvard Law Sch Alumni Assn. Hobbies: tennis, politics, poetry. Home: 736 Carroll, New York, NY. Office: 217 Broadway, New York, NY.

FELDMAN, Freda, S Afr, communal worker; b. Johannesburg; d. Joseph and Leah (Ginsburg); att: J Govt Sch, Johannesburg; New Castle Convent, Natal; m. Richard Feldman, May 27, 1931 (decd); c: Josse, Mona. Natl chmn, Women's United Communal Fund; vice chmn, S Afr J Appeal; vice-pres, exec mem, Union J Women of S Afr; found, women's sect, S Afr ORT-OZE, past chmn, hon pres, vice chmn, ORT, S Afr; mem: exec: S Afr J Bd Deps; planning comm, United Communal Fund; and mem cen bd, World ORT Union; Intl Women's ORT, Geneva. Home: 15 Fourth Ave, Lower Houghton, Johannesburg, S Afr.

FELDMAN, Harry A, US, physician, educator; b. Newark, NJ, May 30, 1914; s. Joseph and Sara (Pivnick); AB, George Wash U, 1935, MD, 1939; m. Lillian Maltz, June 14, 1939; c: Ronald, Donna, Jeffrey, Robert. Prof, chmn dept preventive med, SUNY, Upstate Med Cen, Syracuse, since 1957; chmn test comm, preventive med, Natl Bd Med Examiners, since 1968; mem: expert panel, coccal diseases, WHO; fmr: sr f, virus diseases, NRC; dir research, Weiting-Johnson Hosp. US Army, MC, 1942-46. Pres: cen NY chap, Soc Experimental Biol and Med; cen NY chap, Arthritis and Rheumatism Found, since 1961; mem bd: Onondaga Health Assn, since 1961; Heart Assn, Onondada Co, since 1961; secy, treas, Amer Epidemiological soc, 1968; mem: adv council, Vetr Coll, Cornell U; bd counsellors, div biol standards, Natl Inst Health, 1963- 7; comm on taxoplasmosis, Intl Cong Microbiol; Amer Soc Immunologists; AHA; Amer Rheumatism Soc; Soc Amer Microbiols; f: Amer Public Health Assn; Amer Acad of Microbiol; Amer Ped Soc; dipl, Amer Bds Internal Med and Biol; fmr: secy-treas, Council of Academic Soc's, AAMC; pres, Assn Tchrs of Preventive Med. Contbr to med and sci jours. Home: 704 Crawford Ave, Syracuse, NY. Office: SUNY Upstate Med Cen, Syracuse, NY.

FELDMAN, Irving M, US, educator, poet; b. Bklyn, NY, Sep 22, 1928; s. William and Anna (Goldberg); BSS, CCNY, 1950; MA Columbia U, 1953. Prof: Eng, SUNY, Buffalo since 1964; Kenyon Coll, 1958-63; instr, Eng, U Puerto Rico, 1954-56; Lecteur Americain, U Lyons, 1957-58. Author: Works and Days and Other Poems, 1961; The Pripet Marshes and Other Poems, 1965; Music Papers and Other Poems, 1970; contbr to lit jours. Recipient: Kovner Memorial Award for Eng poetry, JBCA; 1962. Home: 349 Berryman Dr, Buffalo, NY. Office: Dept of Eng, SUNY, Buffalo, NY.

FELDMAN, Israel, Isr, attorney, municipal official; b. Tel Aviv, Isr, Oct 2, 1921; s. Rubin and Chana (Leitman); LLM, Sch Law and Econs, Tel Aviv, 1942; D Law, Dipl, D'etudes and Superieures en Econ-Politique, U de Lyon; m. Chaya Rivlin; c: Chana, Amir, Odeda, Hadas, Eilath. Mayor, Ramat Gan Munic, since 1969; fmr dep mayor, councillor, Munic Council; atty since 1950. Mem: Council Lib Party; Dist Court Bar Assn. Home: 16 Kish St, Ramat Gan, Isr. Office: Municipality, Ramat Gan, Isr.

FELDMAN, Jerome Stanley, US, business exec, consultant, engineer; b. St. Louis, Mo, Dec 13, 1926; s. Phillip and Ioa (Singer); BS, IE, BS, BA Wash U, St Louis; att St Louis U Law Sch; broker's licence, ins and real estate, State of Mo; m. Arlene Greenberg; c: Mark, Karen, Bruce, Lawrence, Michael, Cindy. Sup oprs, Bianco Mfg Co, subsidiary of Holiday Inn of Amer; power of atty for Legal and Mortgage Co Estate; pres, Frontier Home Mortgage Corp. Capt, USAAC, 1944-46. Councilman, City of Olivette, fmr mayor; pres: B'nai B'rith, Ebn Ezra Lodge; Gtr St Louis B'nai B'rith Council; B'nai B'rith, Mo State Assn; mem: Engrs Club of St Louis; VFW; Disabled Amer Vets; JWV; AF Assn; bd dirs: Jr Achievement, St Louis; Shaare Zedek Syn; fmr: mem: Youth Comm, Olivette; planning and zoning comm, St Louis Co. Recipient: Air Medal, Soldiers' Medal; Commendation Award; Purple Heart; Jr C of C Award, State of Tenn, 1952. Hobbies: sports; reading; politics. Home: 844 Woodmoor Dr, Olivette, Mo. Office: 2736 Victor St, St Louis, Mo.

FELDMAN, Joseph D, US, pathologist; b. Hartford, Conn, Dec 13, 1916; s. Max and Rebecca (Hurewitz); BS, Yale U, 1937; MD, LI Coll Med, 1941; m. Naomi Granott, Mar 4, 1949; c: Orna, Danah, Ruth. Mem, Scripps Clinic and Research Found, since 1961; f, USPHS, Yale U, 1948-50; lectr, Heb U-Hadassah Med Sch, 1950-54; asso prof, U Pittsburgh, 1954-56; prof, 1956-61. Maj, US Army, 1942-46. Exec bd, United J Fed, San Diego. Contbr articles to profsl jours. Office: 476 Prospect St, La Jolla, Cal.

FELDMAN, Joseph W, US, business exec; b. NYC, May 26, 1906; s. Nathan and Ray (Wallach); BS, NYU, 1928; m. Dorothy Appel, Aug 12, 1928; c: Wallace, James. Chmn, Feldman, Kahn and sutton, since 1958; advt dir, Warner Bros Theatres, 1929-41, pres, Pittsburgh J Publication and Educ Found, 1962; bd mem: Health and Wfr Assn, Allegheny Co, 1968-70; Gov's Comm on Rehabilitation Study, NW Pa, 1966-68; United Fed, Pittsburgh, 1958-62; J Comty Relations Council, 1950-62, chmn, 1953-58; United Fund, Allegheny Co, 1950-62; FJP, 1954-58; UJF, 1948-70; mem: B'nai B'rith; Pi Lambda Phi. Short story writer. Home: Villa Raphael, 2871 N Ocean Blvd, Boca Raton, Fla. Office: 717 Liberty Ave, Pittsburgh, Pa.

FELDMAN, Leon Aryeh, US, educator; b. Berlin, Ger, Oct 25, 1921; DHL, Yeshiva U, 1957; DTheol, Amsterdam U, 1965; PhD, Columbia U, 1967; m; 2 c. Prof, Hebraic studies, Rutgers U, since 1965, fmr chmn dept; cons: Natl Found J Culture, since 1968; J Educ Comm, NY, 1951-52; FJP, NY, 1954-62; Natl Council J Women, 1956-58; Herzliah Heb Tchrs Sem, 1960-62. Mem: Natl Assn Profs of Heb; AHA; Amer J Hist Soc; Amer Acad J Research; Soc of Bibl Lit; Amer Oriental Soc; Conf J Social Studies, past mem exec; Isr Hist Soc; Medieval Acad Amer; Natl Council J Educ, past mem exec; Rel Educ Assn; f: Amer Sociol Assn, 1960; Amer Council of Learned Socs, 1964; Memorial Found for J Culture, 1967; Rutgers Research Council Fac, 1968. Author: Studies in the Life and Times of Nissim ben Reuben Gerondi of Barcelona; Kuntresim-Josef Corcos on Ketuboth; Rabbenu Nissim's Commentary on Ketuboth; Rabbenu Nissim's Commentary on the Bible; Abraham ben Isaac Halevi; Commentary on Lamentation; Proverbs and the Song of Songs; Fragments of the Book of Esther; Letters and Lithurgical Poems Exchanged by Nissim Gerondi, Cresques ben Shesheth and Hasdai Crescas; Rabbenu Nissim's Homily on Leviticus 1:1; Twelve Homilies by Nissim Gerondi; Changing Aspects of the Sociology of the Jews in the United States; Resources for Jewish Living in American Society; Jewish Experiences in America. Recipient: Henryk Kauffman F, 1959. Office: Rutgers U, New Brunswick, NJ.

FELDMAN, Leon Henry, US, physician; b. Baltimore, Md, June 10, 1910; s. Harry and Rose (Cohen); PhG, U of Md, 1930, BS, 1932, MD, 1934; m. Ruth Johnston, Oct 17, 1937; c: Ronda, Barbara, Leon. Pvt practice since 1938; staff mem: Memorial Mission Hosp; Aston Park Hosp; NC cons phys, US Dept of Justice, since 1939; chief of staff, St Joseph's Hosp, 1952-54, exec bd, 1939-64. Mem: NC Boxing and Wrestling Commn, 1952-58; B'nai B'rith; vice-pres, adv bd, Salvation Army, 1952-58; natl councils; Joint ADL Appeal; UJA; JDC; pres NC chap, Amer Coll Chest Phys, 1952-54; f, Amer Coll Chest Phys; mem: AMA; AHA; S Med Soc; NC State Med Soc; World Boxing Assn; vice-pres, Natl Wrestling Assn, 1957. Home: 18 Beaver Brook Rd, Asheville, NC. Office: Flatiron Bldg, Asheville, NC.

FELDMAN, Lilian, US, painter; b. Bklyn, NY, July 8, 1916; d. Samuel and Minnie (Nathanson) Horowitz; att: Cooper U; Pratt Inst, both NY; m. Abe Feldman, June 25, 1939; c: Scott, Russel. Exhbs: Hofstra; Hecksher Mus; USA '58; Dem Art Show; Douglaston Art Assn; Natl Art Assn, NY; N Shore Comty Art Assn; Art Unlimited; Manhasset Art Assn; Sea Cliff Settlement House; Panoras Art Gals; Nassau Comty Coll; Molloy Coll; Adelphi U; House of Reprs, Wash, DC; LI Art Festival, Post Coll; Eton Gals, NY; Donnell Libr; RAA Gal; NY State Pavilion, Worlds Fair Grounds, NY; Baiter Gal, Huntington, NY; Salisbury Pk; LIU; Tanglewood Preserve; repr in: perm collections: Nassau Comty Coll; Profsl Artists Guild of LI; pvt collections. Secy, Profsl Artists Guild; fmr chmn, Temple Sinai Sisterhood. Home: 214-12 16 Ave, Bayside, NY.

FELDMAN, Louis, US, physician; b. Siberia, Russ, July 4, 1897; s. Jacob and Hinda (Speigel); in US since 1900; MD, cum laude, Tufts Med, Boston, 1919; m. Ina Rabinowicz, June 1, 1919 (decd); c: Ernest, Leonard. Chief, phys med, dir and coord, Med Rehab J Memorial Hosp; Cons: Soldier's Home; NE Sinai Hosp; Brookline Hosp; State Mental Hosps; Foxboro, Medfield, Taunton, Westboro, Paul Dever, Walter E Fernald and Boston State Hosp; fmr: pvt practice; dir, pvt Ind Clinic; asst, med, Tufts Med Sch; prof, phys med,

Middlesex U; mem, Med Adv Bd; secy, chmn, Sect Phys Med, Mass Med Soc; pres, NE Soc Phys Med; Specialty Bd Eligibility. Chief, Civilian Defense, approved med examiner (Fed), WW II. Found, charter mem, vice-pres, Tufts Med Hon Soc; Amer Phys F Comm; IMA; fmr: vice-pres, Brotherhood Temple B'nai Moshe; chmn, Med Group for United Comty Fund; mem: AMA; NE Soc Phys Med; Amer Cong Phys Med and Rehab; Mass Med Soc; Suffolk Co Med Soc; Assn Med Rehab Dirs and Coords; Rehab Council United Fund; Temple Lodge Masons; club, New Cent Club, J profsl chap. Recipient: 50 Year Gold Medal, Mass Med Soc, 1969; 25 Year Gold Medal, Amer Cong of Rehab Med, 1969. Hobbies: dramatics, painting. Office: 1516 Commonwealth Ave, Boston, Mass.

FELDMAN, Louis H, US, educator; b. Hartford, Conn, Oct 29, 1926; s. Sam and Sarah (Vine); MA, Trinity Col, 1947; PhD, Harvard U, 1951; m. Miriam Blum, Mar 8, 1966; c: Moshe, Sarah. Prof, classics, Yeshiva Coll, since 1966, fac mem since 1955. Ford found teaching f, Trinity Coll, 1951-52, instr, 1952-53; instr: Hobart Coll, 1953-55; Stern Coll, 1955-56; F, Guggenheim, 1963-64. Mem: Classical Assn Atlantic States; Amer Classical League; Amer Philol Assn; Phi Beta Kappa. Author: Scholarship on Philo and Josephus, 1937-62; Josephus, Jewish Antiquities, Books 18-20, Loeb Classical Library, Vol 9; asso ed, The Classical World, 1955-57, mgn ed, 1957-59; contbr to scholarly jours. Home: 915 West End Ave, New York NY. Office: Yeshiva Coll, Amsterdam Ave and 186 St, New York, NY.

FELDMAN, Mildred, US, communal worker; b. Milvale, Pa, Nov 11, 1911; d. Joel and Lena (Garfinkel) Cohen; m. Meyer Feldman, Dec 26, 1937; c: Stuart, Stephanie, Judith. Exec bd, B'nai B'rith, since 1960; chmn, adv bd, Hillel Founds, Pittsburgh, 1959-60, mem, Natl Hillel Commn. Home: 6363 Douglas St, Pittsburgh, Pa.

FELDMAN, Milton H, US, scientist; b. NYC, Mar 17, 1918; s. Harry and Bertha (Samuel); BA, NYU, 1939, PhD, 1944; m. Mildred Greenberg, Feb 3, 1946; c: Jonathan, Joan Judith, Jessica. Chief, chem, biol, oceanography, Pacific NW Water Lab; sci, Oak Ridge Natl Lab, 1946-49; adv sci, Bettis Atomic Lab, Pittsburgh, 1953-59; dep tech dir, Defense Atomic Support Agcy, Wash DC, 1959-60. Prin contribs: co-discoverer, shielded isotopes in fission, 1947; discoverer, new radiation effect, 1952. Contbr of published and classified works on radiation effects, radio chem, reactor techn. Home: 3625 NW Roosevelt Dr, Corvallis, Ore. Office: 200 SW 35 St, Corvallis, Ore.

FELDMAN, Myer, US, attorney; b. Phila, Pa, June 22, 1917; s. Israel and Bella (Kurland); BS, U of Pa, LLB, 1938; m. Silva Moskovitz, Oct 26, 1941; c: Jane, James. Sr partner, law firm, Ginsburg and Feldman, since 1965; exec asst to chmn, SEC, 1952-53; counsel to US Sen banking comm, 1954-57, spec counsel to SEC, 1957-58; leg asst to Senator Kennedy, 1958-60; dir, research and progs, Kennedy-Johnson campaign, 1960; counsel to US Pres, 1961-65, US Army, 1942-46. Gov, Weizmann Inst of Sci, hon chmn, UJA, since 1965; trustee: J Publ Soc; Eleanor Roosevelt Memorial Fund, since 1962; dir: Flame of Hope, Inc; The Flying Tiger Line; Royal Resources Corp; mem: bd overseers, Coll Virgin I, since 1962; Tau Epsilon Rho; Order of the Coif. Author: Standard Pennsylvania Practice, 4 vols, 1955-58; contbr to jours. Recipient: outstanding alumnus, Girard Coll, Phila, 1961; man of year: B'nai B'rith Women, Phila, 1962; Natl Council of Young Isr, 1963. Home: 2828 Ellicott St, NW, Washington, DC. Office: 1700 Pennsylvania Ave, NW, Washington, DC.

FELDMAN, Pinchus, Austr, rabbi, educational admnr; b. Bklyn, NY, Oct 17, 1944; s. Mendel and Rochelle (Simpson); in Austr since 1968; att, Lubavitch Rabb Colls: NY; Montreal; Kfar Chabad; m. Pnina Gutnick, Mar 13, 1967; c: Yosef, Fruma. Rabbi, Yeshiva Syn; prin, Yeshiva Coll, both since 1968. Home: 55 Anglesea St, Bondi, Austr. Study: 32-36 Flood St, Bondi, Austr.

FELDMAN, Stephen, D, US, business exec; b. Budapest, Hung, June 19, 1916; s. Eugene and Freida (Fenakel) von Feldman; in US since 1932; att: Stevens Inst Tech, 1935-37; NYU, 1937-39; BA, S Methodist U, 1967; m. Pearle Lindblad, Mar 15, 1953. Vice-pres, Intercontinental Mfg Co Inc since 1955, with co since 1951; chief produc engr, Luscombe Airplane, 1941-49; pres, The Joggler, 1951-55. Dir: Visual Aid Volunteers; YMCA lt gov, Tex dist, Civitan Intl, 1962; co-chmn, Tiferet Bachurim, Budapest, 1930-31; org, natl head, Shomer Hadati,

Hung, 1931-32; vice-pres, Heb Alliance, 1938-39; exec dir, Heb Fed, Carteret, NJ, 1939-41; chmn, Comty Chest, Garland, 1959-60; mem: Amer Astronautical Soc; Amer Ordnance Assn; Garland Ind Council; Garland Personnel Dirs Assn; C of C; Amer Soc Ind Security; Cong Tiferet Isr; Temple Immanuel; clubs: Civitan; E Hills Country; Rotary. Spec interests: psychol, phil. Home: 1700 Robin Lane, Garland, Tex. Office:PO Box 949, Garland, Tex.

FELDMAN, Walter S, US, artist, educator; b. Lynn, Mass, Mar 23, 1925; s. Hyman and Fannie (Gordon); MFA, Yale U, 1951; MA, Brown U, 1959; m. Barbara Rose, June 1950; c: Steven, Mark. Prof, art, Brown U, since 1953; instr, Yale U, 1951-53; numerous one-man shows in US, It, Mex; participated in exhbs throughout US and in Jerusalem. Represented in perm collections: Wichita; Youngstown; Jerusalem; Libr of Cong; Lehigh U; Troy; Mus Modern Art; NY; Metrop Mus Art, NY; Princeton U. US Army, 1943-46. Recipient: Alice Kimball English traveling f, 1950; print prize, Metrop Mus of Art, 1953; gold medal for foreigners, La Ia Mostra Dell'Autoritratto, Milan, 1957; Tonner prize, Amer Color Print Soc, 1958; Howard Found f, 1961-62. Home: 224 Bowen St, Providence, RI. Office: Brown U, Providence, RI.

FELDMAN, William, US, physicist; b. New London, Conn, Sep 15, 1917; s. Morris and Freda (Pelenberg); BS, Purdue U, 1939; PhD, U of Pa, 1942; m. Marilyn Gorin Apr 3, 1949; c: Nelson, Catherine, Robert. Prog mgr, research and engr, lunar orbiter prog, Eastman Kodak Co, since 1966, with firm since 1956; sr physicist, radiation lab, U of Cal, 1942-43; asst supt, Eastman Kodak Co, Oak Ridge, 1943-45; asst supt, eng devl, guided missiles sect, Naval Ordnance Div, 1951-56, research physicist, 1945-51; mem: Amer Inst Physics; Amer Phys Soc; AAAS; Armed Forces Communication and Elec Assn; NY Acad Sci; Rochester C of C; Rochester Engr Soc. Recipient: NASA Public Service award, 1967. Home: 88 Palmerston Rd, Rochester, NY. Office: Eastman Kodak Co, Rochester, NY.

FELDMANN, Harry S, Switz, psychiatrist, educator; b. Lancy, Switz, May 19, 1919; s. Joseph and Hannah (Wolfsohn); MD, U Geneva, 1950, laureate, fac med, 1951, dipl, specialist in neur, psycht, psychotherapy; m. Denise Gutmann, Sep 30, 1946; c: Serge, Anne, Carole. Asst prof, psychopath of children, U Geneva, since 1952; tchr, clinical psychol, Bon Sécours Hosp, since 1953; in pvt practice, neuropsycht, since 1954; prof, École d'Études Sociales, since 1958; phys, asst, med clinic, Hôpital Cantonal, Geneva, 1946-47, asst dept neur, 1947-49; asst neuro-psycht dept for children, Hôpitaux de Paris, 1949-50; first asst, head neur clinic, Hôpital Cantonal, 1950-52. Pres: youth commn; social comm, both J Cmty of Geneva; mem: Soc Med de Genève; Soc Suisse de Neur; Soc Suisse de Psycht; Soc Suisse de Pédo-psycht; Soc Med Suisse de Pshychotherapie; Assn de Psychol Scientifique de Langue Fr; Assn Intnl de Psycht Infantile et des Professions Affiliées; Brit Soc for Study of Addiction to Alcohol and Other Drugs; World Fed for Mh; Intl Council for Group Psychotherapy. Contbr numerous articles to profsl publs; numerous lectures at profsl, lay confs. Home: 23 Chemin du Salève, Petit-Lancy, Geneva, Switz. Office: 6 Cours de Rive, Geneva, Switz.

FELDMANN, Maurice, US, economist, public relations counsel; b. Vienna, Aus, July 24, 1914; s. Samuel and Gisela (von Fiderer); in US since 1939; D Rer Pol, U Vienna, 1932. Pvt practice since 1945; financial ed, Der Wiener Tag, 1933-38; staff mem: Tidningen, Stockholm, Swed, 1938-39; King Features Syndicate, 1940; Chr Sci Monitor, 1940-42. US Army, USAAC 1942-45. F, Inst of Dirs, London, Eng; since 1956; vice-pres, Intl Operatic Soc, Bad Ischl, Aus, since 1959; mem: B'nai B'rith; Air Force Assn; PR Soc of Amer; club, Temple Emanuel Men's. Author: Economic Barriers of Europe, 1942. Office: 745 Fifth Ave, New York, NY.

FELDNER, Chaim, Isr, agricultural researcher, plant breeder; b. Russ, Jan 2, 1903; s. Shlomo and Pearl (Zeuger); in Isr since 1923; m. Chayah Bedolski, May 15, 1929; c: Nira Gal, Shlomo, Shulamit. Agric researcher, plant breeding, Experimental Agric Stat, Beit Shean, since 1964; fmr: agric worker; Kibbutz Ganigar, 1928-32; Kibbutz Ramat Yohanan, 1932-40; plant breeder, Kibbutz Beit Alfa, 1940. Pvt, Haganah, 1924-48. Prin contribs: Devl new varieties of cauliflower, onion and garlic. Mem, union and garlic comms, Dept of Agric; fmr mem, profsl comm for seed growing, Hazera, seed growers and distributors. Contbr to Hasadeh, agric jour. Recipient award: First Prize for Cactus, 8th Intl Flower Show,

Haifa, 1959; Work, Histadrut, 1956; Hazerah, 1962; Kaplan, Isr Min of Lab, 1969. Home: Kibbutz Beit Alfa, Isr. Office: Experimental Farm, Beit Shean, Isr.

FELDS, Rachel A, communal worker; b. Oakland, Cal, Mar 18, 1907; d. Alexander and Deborah (Lobree) Hirshberg; att U of Cal .1924-25; m. Murray Felds, Oct 25, 1936; c: Alexandra Warshaw, James. Mem, Natl Council of J Women, since 1937, fmr: natl bd mem, pres, Oakland sect, vice pres, W regional conf, repr to Natl J Council exec bd, chmn PR, Nassau Co, bd mem, Long Beach sect; bd mem, Sisterhood, Temple Emanuel, Long Beach; publicity chmn, PTA, Long Beach; dir, USO-JWB activities, Oakland J Cmty Cen; PR chmn, Nassau Co coord comm, Cub Scouts; fmr: mem natl bd, natl vice pres, Natl Council of J Jrs, also, natl chmn, rel educ, natl mem comm; mem bd, League of Women Voters. Bd, This is Long Beach; circulation mgr and ed asst, Long Beach (NY) Progress; cert Braillist, Libr of Cong. Hobbies: Braille, gardening. Home: 466 W Fulton, Long Beach, NY.

FELDSTEIN, Benjamin, Isr, mechanical engr; b. Warsaw, Pol, Nov 30, 1904; s. Moshe and Esther (Jaffe); in Isr since 1934; dipl engr, Tchrs Coll of Warsaw; m. Eugenie Bukszpan, May 21, 1935; c: Moshe, Varda Zonder. Lectr, tech insts; cons engr; fmr head, tech educ, training dept, Isr Elec Corp. Mem: Engrs and Architects Assn in Isr, tech council, repr of assn in Acad Heb Lang, repr in Technion, Haifa, fmr: mem, cen comm, repr in engr council. Author: Introduction to Internal Combustion Engines, 1955; Steam Boilers Textbook, 1964; contbr articles to profsl jours. Home and office: 21 Shapiro St, Givatayim, Isr.

FELDSTEIN, Dalton George, US, business exec; b. Dubuque, Ia, Nov 12, 1904; s. Jacob and Ethel (Sterngartz); m. Joyce Mell, Oct 13, 1940; c: June, Sabra, Heidi. Pres: Dalton Motors Inc; Metrop Warehouse, LA; Dalton Leasing; Dalton Inves, Sacramento. Pres, Sisters of Mercy Hosp; fmr pres: Temple B'nai Isr; Amer Cancer Soc, Sacramento; Comty Chest, Sacramento; mem: Sacramento State Coll; Pres Council, Brandeis U; Natl Comty Chest and Councils; United Crusade; Mercy Hosp; Appeals Rev Bd; Gov Comm for Employment of Physically Handicapped; City of Hope; Elks; Shriners; clubs: Sutter; St Francis Yacht; Delta Yacht, fmr commodore; pres, council Brandeis U; City of Hope. Home: 1318-45 St, Sacramento, Cal. Office: 1520 K St, Sacramento, Cal.

FELHEIM, Marvin, US, educator, author; b. Cincinnati, O, Oct 9, 1914; s. Louis and Bessie (Goodman); AB, U Cincinnati, 1936, AM, 1937; PhD, Harvard U, 1948. Prof, Eng, U Mich, since 1962, mem fac since 1948; home visitor, Cincinnati Bd Educ, 1937-40; instr, U of Mo, 1945-47; Smith-Mundt lectr, Natl Taiwan U, 1954-55; spec lectr, US State Dept, Nagano Sem, Japan, 1955; Fulbright lectr: Pau Summer Inst, Fr, 1958; U Athens, Greece, 1962-63; visiting prof, U Hawaii, 1964; C B Cockfair Chair of Continuing Educ, U of Mo, Kan City, 1966-68; hon f, Shakespeare Inst, Stratford-upon-Avon, 1957-58. Capt, USAAC intelligence, 1942-45. Author: Modern Short Stories, 1952; The Theatre of Augustin Daly, 1956; comedy: Theories, Plays, Criticisms, 1962; contbr to lit jours; trans of plays by: Sartre, Camus, Pagnol. Mem: Phi Beta Kappa; Tau Kappa Alpha; Phi Kappi Phi; MLA; Coll Eng Assn; bd: Ann Arbor Art Assn; Dramatic Arts Cen; club: Research, U Mich. Recipient: sr class orator, U Cincinnati, 1936; class of 23 award for teaching, U Mich, 1954. Hobby: collecting modern art. Home: 1124 Hill St, Ann Arbor, Mich. Office: U of Mich, Ann Arbor, Mich.

FELLER, Noah, Isr, surgeon; b. Kovno, Lith, 1908; in Isr since 1933; MD, Govt U, Kovno, 1933; m; c: Shaul, Amirah, Edna. Med supr and head surg dept, Hasharon Hosp, Petah Tikva, since 1942; res, surg dept, Hadassah Hosp, Tel Aviv, 1933-35; first asst, surg dept, Kupat Holim, Tel Aviv, 1935-36; Beilinson Hosp, 1936-42. FICS; mem, IMA. Ed bd, Dapim Refuiim; contbr to med jours. Recipient: FICS Award, 14th Annual Conv, Intl Coll of Surgs, Atlantic City. Home: Alter Mihud St, Petah Tikva, Isr. Office: Hasharon Hosp, Petah Tikva, Isr.

FELLMAN, Abraham, Isr, certified public accnt; b. Jaffa, Pal, Mar 25, 1906; s. Haim and Haya (Lederberg); att London U, 1930-31; grad, Assn of Cert and Corporate Acctnts, Eng, 1931; Chartered Inst of Secys, Eng, 1930; m. Zipora Branitsky, Feb 20, 1934; c: Gila Meshulam, Haim, Noga. Owner, Abraham Fellman and Co, CPA, since 1934; sr clerk, Whinney Murray and Co, CAs, Haifa, 1931-33; secy, Pal Plantations Ltd, Lord Melchett's estate in Pal, 1933-34. F: Assn Cert and Corporate Acctnts; asso, Chartered Inst of Secys; Royal Econ Soc; asst grand master, Grand Lodge, Masons, Isr, asst secy gen, Supr Council 33 for Isr; grand prin, Grand chap of Royal Arch Masons, Isr; mem: Assn CPA's in Isr; club, Commercial and Ind, Tel Aviv. Author: Pioneers of Citrus Growers in Eretz-Isr, 1937; Palestine Income Tax Law and Practice, 1946; The Law of Income Tax, 1949-50; The Income Tax Law and Practice in Israel, 1950-52; The Law and Practice of Cooperative Societies, 1953; The Law and Practice of Income Tax in Israel, 1955; Principles and Practice of Company Law in Israel, 1960; The Law and Practice of Winding Up, 1969; contbr to profsl jours. Hobbies: photography, archaeol. Home: 12 Chen Blvd, Tel Aviv, Isr. Office: 48 Rothschild Blvd, POB 53, Tel Aviv, Isr.

FELLMAN, David, US, educator, author; b. Omaha, Neb, Sep 14, 1907; s. Jacob and Brandel (Gubermann); MA, U Neb, 1930; PhD, Yale U, 1934; LLD, U Neb, 1966; m. Sara Dinion, Aug 6, 1933; c: Laura, Michael. Prof, political sci, U Wis, since 1947; instr, asst, asso prof, U Neb, 1934-47. Author: The Censorship of Books, 1957; The Defendant's Rights, 1958; The Limits of Freedom, 1959; The Supreme Court and Education, 1960; The Constitutional Right of Association, 1963; Religion in American Public Law, 1966; The Defendant's Rights Under English Law, 1966; ed: Post-War Governments of Europe, 1946; Readings in American National Government, 1947, 1950; Midwest Jour of Political Sci, 1957-59; contbr to profsl jours. Natl pres, AAUP, 1946-66, pres, Wis chap, 1950-51, natl council, 1958-61, comm on acad freedom and tenure, since 1958, chmn 1959-64; pres, Midwest Conf Political Scis, 1955-56; exec bd, ACLU, since 1952; vice-pres, Amer Political Sci Assn, 1959-60; comm mem, commn on law and social action, AJCong since 1957; ed bd, Amer Political Sci Rev, 1947-49; mem: Govt's Commn on Hum Rights, 1959-65; Phi Beta Kappa; Sigma Alpha Mu, natl scholarship chmn, 1943-48. Recipient, awards: Centennial for dist service, Mich State U, 1955; sr fac research in govt research, Social Sci Research Council, 1959-60; Fulbright research, LSE, 1961-62; Sam Beber, B'nai B'rith, 1966. Home: 1911 Kendall Ave, Madison, Wis. Office: U of Wis, Madison, Wis.

FELSENHARDT, Alexandre, Fr, communal worker; b. Bordeaux, Oct 22, 1882; licencié ès sci math, U Bordeaux; m. Germaine Hecht, 1920; c: Renee. Banker, ret. Pres, local comm, Fonds Social Juif Unifié, since 1958; vice-pres, Assn des Déportés Résistants Patriotes de Bordeaux, since 1946; mem, Consistoire Central des Israélites de Fr. Home: 3 rue Ravez, Bordeaux, Fr.

FELSENTHAL, Edward George, US, business exec, attorney; b. Chgo, Ill, July 8, 1886; s. Eli and Nettie (Goldsmith); AB, U Chgo, 1908, JD, 1910; m. Mildred Hartman, Feb 5, 1913; c: George, Elizabeth Kornblith. Ret; partner, Felsenthal & Coleman, inves dealers, 1938-52; atty, pvt practice, 1910-20; vice-pres and treas, Hartman Corp; pres, Realty Mgmt Co, 1920-37. Federal Res Militia, 1918-20. Active in numerous comty orgs; mem, Ill Interracial Commn, 1948-52; club, Standard. Home: 1335 Astor St, Chicago, Ill. Office: 33 N LaSalle St, Chicago, Ill.

FELSHER, Isaac Myron, US, physician, educator; b. Retschen, Russ, Nov 17, 1896; s. Max and Libby (Maskalik); in US since 1907; BS, U Chgo, 1924, MD, 1928; postgrad cert, dermat, Northwestern U, 1939; m. Hannah Felsher, Nov 22, 1930 (decd); m. 2nd, Ezerial Schwartz, Feb 20, 1952. Practicing derm, Chgo, since 1933; asso prof em, Northwestern U Med Sch; sr att dermat, non-active, Michael Reese Hosp. Mem: Ill Med Assn; AMA; Chgo Med Soc; Chgo Dermat Soc, fmr pres; Amer Geriatrics Soc; Amer Acad Dermat; Assn Amer Med Colls; Soc for Investigative Dermat; Inst of Med, Chgo. Contbr to med jours. Hobby, photography. Home: 7921 Bloomingdale Ave, Elmwood Park, Ill. Office: 5720 W Fullerton Ave, Chicago, Ill.

FELSON, Benjamin, US, radiologist, educator; b. Newport, Ky, Oct 21, 1913; s. Solomon and Esther (Bissell); BS U Cincinnati, MD, 1935; m. Virginia Raphaelson, Mar 18, 1936; c: Stephen, Nancy, Marcus, Richard, Edward. Prof, dir, dept radiology, U Cincinnati, since 1950, fac mem since 1945; dir, dept radiology: Cincinnati Gen Hosp, since 1950; with dept since 1935; Drake Hosp; Children's Hosp; Holmes Hosp; Dunham Hosp; cons: Walter Reed Army Hosp; Armed Forces Inst of Path; Sur Gen, USAF; VA; Sr Gen, US Army;

USPHS; Dayton VA Hosp; chief cons, radiology, mem, dean's comm, Cincinnati VA Hosp; f, cancer therapy, Indianapolis City Hosp, 1940-41. Maj, US Army MC, 1942-45. Mem, natl bd dirs, Amer J Phys Comm, since 1955, chmn, Cincinnati chap, 1955-58; first vice-pres, Radiological Soc of N Amer, 1959; f: Amer Coll Radiology; Amer Coll Chest Phys; mem: Cincinnati Acad Med; O State Med Assn; O State and Gtr Cincinnati Radiological Socs; Assn U Radiologists; Amer Friends Heb U, mem, natl bd dirs, since 1955, chmn, Cincinnati chap, 1955-58; Alpha Omega Alpha; Pi Kappa Epsilon; hon mem: Tex, Phila, Detroit and Cuban Radiological Socs; Natl Acad of Med of Columbia; Can Assn Radiologists; Brazilian Coll Radiology. Author: Fundamentals of Chest Roentgenology, 1960; Principles of Chest Roentgenology-Programed Learning, 1965; Case of Day Book, 1966; ed: Diseases of the Chest, 1962; Manual Roentgenology Techniques in the Lab Animal, 1968; Seminars in Roentgenology; corresp ed, Annales de Radiologie; contbr numerous sci papers, chaps to med vols. Recipient: Mt Scopus citation, 1968. Hobby, sports. Home: 3994 Rose Hill Ave, Cincinnati, O. Office: Cincinnati Gen Hosp, Cincinnati, O.

FELSTEIN, Benjamin, US, economist; business exec; b. NYC, June 30, 1921; s. Gershon and Sarah (Altschuler); BA, Bklyn Coll, 1942; m. Mary Weintraub, May 30, 1947; c: Judith, Janet. Staff asst to vice-chmn of bd, Food Fair Stores Inc since 1966, on staff since 1947; sr bus econ, OPA, 1942-47. Pres, Oak Lane Civic Assn; police affairs comm, Crime Commn; chmn, Food Distributors Assn; bd adjuntos, Cong Mikveh Isr; bd dirs: Mercy Douglass Hosp; Comty Leadership Sem Active Alumni; mem: Natl Assn Bus Econs; Amer Econ Assn; Amer Stat Assn; Amer Marketing Assn; Amer Mgmt Assn; Bklyn Coll Alumni Assn; C of C, Phila; Alpha Phi Omega. Home: 816-69 Ave N, Philadelphia, Pa. Office: 3175 JF Kennedy Blvd, Philadelphia, Pa.

FENDLER, Harold A, US, attorney; b. St Louis, Mo, Feb 19, 1902; s. Henry and Grace (Altman); AB Stanford U, 1922; JD Stanford Law Sch, 1923; postgrad studies, Harvard Law Sch, 1923-24; m. Miriam Olden, Mar 8, 1933; c: Robert, Douglas. Sr partner, law firm, Fendler & Warner, since 1955; mem, law firm: Carpenter, Babson & Fendler, 1930-39; Fendler, Weber & Lerner, 1945-55; lectr, law of lit property, Stanford Law Sch, 1948-50; drafted, Cal Statutes on Lit Property, 1947-49. F, Intl Trial Lawyers Assn; mem: leg comm, Amer Bar Assn, 1950-60, copyright comm, 1945-62; conf delg, LA Bar Assn, 1944-50; Delta Sigma Rho; club, Brentwood Country LA; LA Lawyers, mem, exec bd 1940-44. Contbr to legal jours. Hobbies: golf, sailing, boys clubs. Home: 735 Bonhill Rd, Los Angeles, Cal. Office: 9465 Wilshire Blvd, Beverly Hills, Cal.

FENICHEL, Seymour, US, rabbi, attorney; b. NYC, May 5, 1924; s. Harry and Miriam (Feuer); ordained rabbi, Yeshiva U, 1948; BS, CCNY, 1946; MA, NYU, 1954; LLB, JD, Bklyn, Law Sch, 1959; m. Naomi Kerper, Nov 27, 1949; c: Moses, Deborah. Atty, law firm, A Alan Lane, since 1961; rabbi: Cong Te Fares Isr, Kan City, Mo, 1949-51; Cong Shaan Isr, Bklyn, 1952-69. Treas, Rabb Bd, Flatbush, Bklyn; fmr, mem, exec comm, RabCA; mem: KP, Harmony Lodge. Home: 5317 Beverly Rd, Brooklyn, NY. Office: 635 Madison Ave, New York, NY.

FENYVES, José (pen name Pepe Pinar), Uruguay, estimator; b. Berindie, Hung, Aug 30, 1910; s. Mayer and Cecilia (Feinkuchen); in Uruguay since 1928; att HS, Arad, Rum. Estimator of quotations, Barraca Suiza, since 1967, with firm since 1949; prin, Furniture Finishing Shop, 1931-45; spec finisher, Olympic Factory, LA, Cal, 1946-47. Pres, youth and minor div, Basketball Fed of Uruguay, off overseer, 1st div; dir gen, sports, mem bd, Hebraica-Macabi Assn of Uruguay, Montevideo, past secy gen; dir, Shalom, monthly; fmr: pres, Table Tennis Assn, Uruguay, also outstanding player, winner several prizes, 1932-44; pres, Macabi-Hacoah Assn, Montevideo; dir gen, sports; coach, Football team; head delg to Basketball Fed, Uruguay; org, through Hebraica Macabi, 1st Mini-Basketball Championship, Uruguay, 1968; head and coach, Hebraica Macabi Basketball Team, to 8th Macabiah, Isr, 1969; fmr: secy, J Hung Culture Assn, Uruguay, found and leader, Youth div; dir, actor, numerous theatre performances, Span, Yiddish, Hung; mem: J Comty; J Home for Old and Orphan; Lib Zionist Org; New Zionist Org; J Hung Assn; J Mutual Med Assn, all Montevideo; clubs: Wanderers Football; U of Uruguay; Barraca Suiza, all Montevideo; Hobbies: books on J topics; sport; philately. Home: 1027

Durazno St, Montevideo, Uruguay. Office: Barraca Suiza SA, 2180 Gral Flores Ave, Montevideo, Uruguay.

FERBER, Robert, US, economist, educator; b. NYC, Feb 13, 1922; s. Samuel and Dinah (Rosenthal); BS, CCNY, 1942; MA, U Chgo, 1945, PhD, 1951; postgrad studies, Columbia U; m. Marianne Abeles, Aug 18, 1946; c: Don, Ellen. Research prof, econ, dept econ, bur econ and bus research, U of Ill, since 1956, on fac since 1948, dir survey research lab; research asst, Cowles commn for research in econs, U Chgo, 1943-45; Edward Hillman, 1944-45; chief stat, Ind Surveys Co, 1943-45; econ, stat, I Devegh & Co, 1945-47. f, Amer Stat Assn; mem: Amer Econ Assn; Amer Marketing Assn; Econometric Soc; Inst of Meth Stat. Author: Statistical Techniques in Market Research, 1949; A Study of Aggregate Consumption Functions, 1953; The Railroad Shippers Forecasts, 1953; The Employers' Manpower Forecasts, 1958; co-author: Marketing Research-Selected Literature, 1952; Problems and Cases in Marketing Research, 1954; Research Methods in Economics and Business, 1962; ed, Jour of the Amer Stat Assn; ed, applications sect, Amer Marketing Assn; co-ed, Motivation and Market Behavior, 1958. Recipient: award for outstanding contrib to marketing, Amer Marketing Assn, 1950. Home: 606 S Western Ave, Champaign, Ill. Office: Box N, Sta A, U of Ill, Champaign, Ill.

FERBER, William L, US, urologist; b. Newark, NJ, June 4, 1903; s. Abraham and Nettie (Kornbluth); BS, NYU, 1923; MD, Cornell U, 1927; postgrad studies in urol, Baltimore, 1930-31; m. Diana Behrman, June 17, 1928; c: Andrew, Betty. Pvt practice since 1927; dir urol: City Hosp, Elmhurst, NY; Sydenham Hosp, NYC; att urol, Home and Hosp, Daughters of Isr; cons urol, J Bd Guardians; asst att urol, Mt Sinai Hosp. Maj, US Army MC, 1942-46. F, Amer Coll Surgs, 1941; dipl, Amer Bd Urol, 1939; hon police surg, NYC Police Dept; mem: AMA, NY State and Co Med Soc; NY sec, Amer Urol Assn; Amer Psychosomatic Soc; Alpha Omega Alpha; Phi Beta Kappa; club, Harmonie, NYC. Contbr to med publs. Home: 225 W 86 St, New York, NY. Office: 40 E 83 St, New York, NY.

FERENCZ, Benjamin B, US, attorney; b. Soncuta-Mare, Rum, Mar 11, 1920; s. Joseph and Sarah (Schwartz); in US since 1920; BSS, CCNY, 1940; LLB, Harvard Law Sch, 1943; m. Gertrude Fried, Mar 31, 1946; c: Carol, Robin, Donald, Nina. Mem, law firm, Taylor, Ferencz & Simon; counsel, Intl Council B'nai B'rith, 1958-61; spec counsel: Supr Lodge, B'nai B'rith, since 1951; Conf on J Material Claims against Ger since 1958, dir for Ger, 1953-56; counsel, Amer OSE, 1959-61; exec counsel, off, Chief of Counsel for War Crimes, Nuremberg, 1946-48; chief prosecutor for the US, war crimes trial against Nazi extermination squads, 1947; dir gen, Restitution Successor Org, 1948-56; dir of oprs, United Restitution Org, Ltd, 1954-56; spec legal adv at Hague reparations negotiations Ger-Israel, 1952. US Army, 1943-45. Mem: NY Bar Assn; Amer Soc of Intl Law. Contbr to intl legal jours. Home: 14 Bayberry Lane, New Rochelle, NY. Office: 60 E 42 St, New York, NY.

FERGUSON, Robert S, US, film exec; b. NYC, May 8, 1915; s. Samuel and Augusta (Horowits); BS, NYU, 1936; m. Helene Berlin, Aug 1, 1940; c: Carole, Sandra. Vice-pres, Columbia Pictures, since 1963; fmr: Warner Bros Pictures; Scripps Howard Newspapers. Pres: Temple Sinai, since 1961; Screen Publicists Guild, since 1948. Home: 761 W Broadway, Woodmere, NY. Office: 711 Fifth Ave, New York, NY.

FERMAN, Joseph W, US, publisher; b. Lida, Lith, June 8, 1906; s. Wolfe and Esther (Little); in US since 1914; BCS, NYU, 1927; m. Ruth Eisen, Jan 29, 1931; c: Edward. Publisher: The Magazine of Fantasy and Science Fiction, since 1954; Venture Science Fiction; publisher, pres and dir, Mercury Publs, since 1954; pres and dir: Jonathan Press, since 1954; Fantasy House, since 1954; treas and dir, Leasehold Assn, since 1958; dir, Chapin Jr Corp, since 1959; ed, Bestseller Mystery Mag, since 1959; vice-pres and gen mgr: Mercury Mystery Books, 1937; Ellery Queen's Mystery Mag, 1941; Bestseller Books, 1940; circulation mgr, The Amer Mercury, 1926-39, vice-pres and dir, 1940-50. Charter mem, Comm for World Hum Rights, 1968; mem Mag Publishers Assn; clubs: Hundred Million; Nassau Co Unity. Home: 20 Addison Pl, Rockville Centre, NY. Office: 347 E 53 St, New York, NY.

FERSTER, Bernard, Austr, business exec; b. Warsaw, Pol, Jan 21, 1909; s. Joseph and Felicia (Bram); BCom, Hochschule für Welthandel, Vienna, 1931; m. Rodia Wislicki, 1938;

c: Felicia, Alexandra, Renée. Mgn dir, Advance Plastics Ltd, since 1949; with Stepan SA, Warsaw, 1933-39; forest laborer, Ural, Russ, 1939-41; econ, sr acctnt, Samarkand, Russ, 1941-46; off mgr, Paris, 1947-49. Pres, State ZC of NSW, since 1966; vice-chmn, United Isr Appeal, since 1965; councillor, Exec Council of Australian Jewry, since 1968; mem, Sydney Lodge, B'nai B'rith; hon treas, ZF of Austr and NZ. Home: 72 A Dowmalbyn Rd, Bellevue Hill, Sydney, Austr. Office: 70-74 Wilson St, Newton, Sydney, Austr.

FERSTER, Samuel Stanley, Austr, business exec; b. Warsaw, Pol, Jan 9, 1911; s. Joseph and Felicia (Bram); in Austr since 1947; att Sch of Econ, Vienna; m. Frances Finkelstein, Mar 1938; c: Ronald, Anita Rychter. Co dir since 1948; dir: Advance Plastics, since 1950; Advance Ind, since 1969, Austr Inst of Mgmt, since 1964. Treas, Friends Heb U, Jerusalem; exec mem, United Isr Appeal; chmn dept, State ZC, all NSW; fmr council mem, J Bd of Deps; mem, lawn tennis assn. Home: 1 Thornton St, Darling Point, Sydney, Austr. Office: 70 Wilson St, Sydney, Austr.

FERTIG, Joseph, US, chemist; b. Berlin, Ger, Jan 6, 1931; s. Aaron and Sarah (Goldberg); in US since 1957; BSc, N Poly U, London, 1954, PhD, 1957; m. Lisa Schnerb, Oct 12, 1958; c: Naomi, Aaron, Shoshanna. Sr group leader, Merck Chem Div, since 1967; research sect leader, Natl Starch & Chem Corp, 1958-67. Prin contribs: chem of monomers and polymers, plastic additives, catalysts; holder of numerous patents. Pres, NJ chap, Assn Orthodox J Sci; secy Agudath Isr of Amer; bd govs, J Educ Cen; mem: Amer Chem Soc; AAAS. Contbr to sci jours. Home: 752 Murray St, Elizabeth, NJ. Office: Merck & Co Inc, Rahway, NJ.

FESHBACH, Herman, US, educator; b. NYC, June 2, 1917; s. David and Ida (Lapiner); BS, CCNY, 1937; PhD, MIT, 1942; m. Sylvia Harris, Jan 28, 1940; c: Carolyn, Theodore, Mark. Prof, physics, MIT since 1954, dir, Cen for Theoretical Physics, instr, 1941-45, asst prof, 1945-47, asso prof, 1947-54; Guggenheim F, 1954-55; Ford CERN f, 1962-63. Mem: NRC; Amer Phys Soc; Acoustical Soc; Natl Acad Sci; Amer Acad Arts and Sci. Co-author, Methods of Theoretical Physics, 1953; asst ed, Annals of Physics. Home: 5 Sedgwick Rd, Cambridge, Mass. Office: MIT, Cambridge, Mass.

FEUCHTWANGER, Meir Max, Isr, educator; b. Frankfurt/M, Ger, July 18, 1904; s. Jakob and Zerline (Hackenbroch); in Isr since 1936; MSc, U Frankfurt, 1929; m. Julie Bamberger; c: Rahel Kastro, Shimeon, Hannah, Israel, Itshak, Nehamah, Shelomoh, Shifra. Sr lectr, Tel Aviv U, since 1962; sch headmaster 1933-52. Home: 24 Pumbadita St, Tel Aviv, Isr. Office: U of Tel Aviv, Ramat Aviv, Isr.

FEUCHTWANGER, Moshe Michael, Isr, surgeon, educator; b. Munich, Ger, June 14, 1927; s. Heinrich and Henrietta (Feuchtwang); in Isr, since 1936; att Zurich Sch of Med, 1946-48; MD, Hadassah Med Sch, Jerusalem, 1952; m. Dina Levanon, Nov 22, 1949; c: Dalia, Naomi. Head, dept surg, Negev Cen Hosp, since 1968; sr lectr, Heb U, Jerusalem; fac mem, sch of med, Tel Aviv U; chief phys, Hadassah Hosp, Jerusalem, 1960-67; research f, U of S Cal, 1961-62. Lt, Isr MC, IDF, 1948-49. Secy gen, Isr Surg Soc; IMA; Société Internationale de Chirurgie; Isr Surg Soc. Contbr to profsl jours. Recipient, Medals: Defense; Jerusalem insignia; Independence; Sinai; Isr Warriors. Home: 67 Negba St, Beersheba, Isr. Office: POB 151, Beersheba, Isr.

FEUCHTWANGER, Walter, Ger, business exec, banker, judge; b. Munich, Ger, 1916; s. Sigbert and Riwkah (Gluskinos); m. 2nd, Chris Campbell, 1958; c: Ruth, Susan. Judge, Commercial Court at Landgericht Munchen I; partner, W Feuchtwanger Bank KG, Munich; pres, Feuchtwanger Corp of NY; dir: Feuchtwanger London Ltd; Kommerzial-bank AG, Zurich; City of Sao Paulo Improvement and Freehold Land Co Ltd; Leumi Financial, NY; several enterprises in Isr, It, Can; fmr mgr, Palestina Amt, Munich. Vice pres, Makkabi, Ger; treas, Youth Aliyah, Ger; mem: bd, UJA, Ger; Haganah, B'nai B'rith; Maccabi World Union. Home: 55 Sollner St, Munich, WGer. Office: 6 Maximilianstr, Munich, WGer.

FEUER, Henry, US, chemist, educator; b. Stanislvow, Aus-Hung, Apr 4, 1912; s. Jacob and Julie (Tindel); in US since 1941; PhD, U of Vienna, 1936; postdoc f, Sorbonne, 1939; m. Paula Berger, Jan 19, 1946. Prof, chem, Purdue U, since 1961, on fac since 1946. Mem: Amer Chem Soc; Brit Chem Soc; AAAS; Amer Rocket Soc; AAUP; Phi Lambda Upsilon. Contbr to profsl jours. Hobby, mountain climbing. Home:

726 Princess Dr, W Lafayette, Ind. Office: Purdue U, Lafayette, Ind.

FEUER, Herbert Jerome, US, attorney, business exec; b. NYC, Sep 6, 1923; s. Edward and Rose (Berger); BA; St Johns U, Bklyn, 1949; DJur, NY Law Sch, 1949; m. Helen Denny, June 3, 1951; c: Edward, Ruth. Pvt practice since 1950; asst counsel, ways and means comm, NY State Assembly, 1965; mem, NY State Assembly, 1966. USAAC, 1942-46. Dist leader, Dem party, 76th Assembly dist, Bx; mem: Masons, Felicity lodge 1100; B'nai B'rith, Redemption lodge 1358, fmr pres. Home: 17 Parkfield Rd, Scarsdale, NY. Office: 342 Madison Ave, New York, NY.

FEUER, Leon I, US, rabbi; b. Hazelton, Pa, May 23, 1903; s. Isaac and Rose (Gluckman); BA, U Cincinnati, 1924; BHL, ordained rabbi, HUC-JIR, 1927, DD, 1955; m. Hortense Morgenstern, Dec 8, 1928; c: Leon. Rabbi, Collingwood Ave Temple, since 1935; min, rel educ, The Temple, Cleveland, 1927-35. Pres, CCAR, 1936-65; vice-pres, ZOA, 1948-58; exec mem, JA, since 1966; hon mem, Phi Kappa Phi; mem: Phi Sigma Delta; Tau Kappa Phi. Author: The Jew and His Religion, 1932; Jewish Literature Since the Bible, 1935; Why a Jewish State? 1943; On Being a Jew, 1947. Hobby: painting. Home: 2608 Valley Brook Dr, Toledo, O. Study: 2335 Collingwood Ave, Toledo, O.

FEUER, Lewis S, Can, educator, author; b. NYC, Dec 7, 1912; s. Joseph and Fannie (Weidner); BS, CCNY, 1931; MA, Harvard U, 1932; PhD, 1935; m. Kathryn Beliveau, Oct 13, 1946; c: Robin. Prof, sociol, U Toronto, since 1966; instr, phil, CCNY, 1939-42; instr, lectr, asst, asso prof, phil: Vassar Coll, 1946-51; U Vt, 1951-57; Ford f for the Advancement of Educ, 1954-55; prof, phil, social sci, U of Cal, Berkeley, 1957-66. Author: Psychoanalysis and Ethics, 1955; Spinoza and the Rise of Liberalism, 1958; The Scientific Intellectual, 1963; The Conflict of Generations, 1961; ed, Marx and Engels, Basic Writings on Politics and Philosophy, 1959. Mem: AAUP, pres, Vt chap, 1955-56; Amer Phil Assn; Vt Hist Soc. Recipient: Bowdoin Medal, Harvard, U, 1935. Home: 29 Roxborough St E, Toronto, Can. Office: U of Toronto, Toronto, Can.

FEUER, Mortimer, US, attorney; b. NYC, Nov 25, 1909; s. William and Gussie (Goldenberg); BS, CCNY, 1928; LLB, Columbia U Law Sch, 1931; m. Louise Gottschall, July 29, 1937; c: Richard, Thomas. Partner, law firm, Hays, Feuer, Porter, and Spanier, and predecessors, since 1939; dir, Varifab Inc, since 1967; pres, dir, Dextra Baldwin McGonagle Found, since 1968; dir, Condec Corp, since 1955; fmr: asso, Hays Podell and Shulman, 1931-39; lectr, corporate law, Practicing Law Inst, 1954, 1958. Delg-at-large, Dem Natl Conv, 1960; alternate delg, State of NY Dem Conv, 1964; mem: NY State and NYC Bar Assns; NY Co Lawyers Assn; Grand St Boys Assn; Sha'aray Tefila Syn; clubs: Dem; Lawyers; Amsterdam Dem, vice-chmn bd govs. Author: Personal Liabilities of Corporate Officers and Directors, 1961; Handbook for Corporate Directors, 1965; ed, Columbia Law Rev, 1929-31; contbr to law jours. Home: 270 West End Ave, New York, NY. Office: 445 Park Ave, New York, NY.

FEUEREISEN, Charles, US, business exec; b. NYC, May 18, 1918; s. Henry and Regina (Fuchs); att CCNY, 1935-38; m. Helene Auerbach, May 3, 1953; c: Henry, Patricia. Partner, Service Brokerage Co, since 1965; salesman, Gen Mills Inc, 1938-48; sales mgr, Vanity Fair Paper Co, 1948-65. Sgt, US Army, 1942-45. Natl Cdr, JWV; pres, Food Ind lodge, B'nai B'rith, 1965-66; mem: Sales Execs, Grocery Mfrs. Recipient: Silver Star, Bronze Star, Purple Heart, Dist Unit Citation. Home: 430 Grant Ave, Oradell, NJ. Office: 1326 Lawrence St, Rahway, NJ.

FEUERSTEIN, Emil, Isr, author, journalist; b. Kiskoros, Hung, Apr 21, 1914; s. Phillip and Ella (Vogler); att: U of Breslav; Rabb Sem Breslau; U Basel; U Berlin; J Coll, London; m. Fella Kagan; c: Benjamin, Maya Halpern. Free-lance journalist since 1941; fmr: mem ed Staff; Hatzofe; Haboker; Yedioth Aharonot Heb Dailies; theatre critic; Gazith, Hatzofe. Head, Dramatic Critics Circle; mem: Intl Theatre Inst, Isr; Soc of Tech Writers and publishers, masons: Assn of Heb Journalists. Author: Encyclopedia of World Literature, 6 vols, 1945-50; Biography of Shakespeare, 1952; Jewish Nobel Prize Winners, 1954; Jewish Scientists 1956; Famous Jews, 1958; Historical Discoveries, 4 vols, 1959-62; Winners of the Nobel Prize in Literature, 1960; Jewish Writers, 1960; Jewish Soldiers, 1961; Jewish Discoverers and Inventors, 1962; Historical Inventions 4 vols; 1001 Historical Personalities; Jewish Women; Famous Jews in the Theatre; films; trans of novels and plays. Home: 18 Daphna St, Tel Aviv, Isr.

FEUERSTEIN, Moses I, US, business exec; b. Boston, Mass, Mar 10, 1916; BA, Yeshiva Coll, NY, 1936; MBA, Harvard U, 1938; m. Shirley Shapiro, 1943; c: Mordecai, Joanne, Henry, Esther. Pres, Malden Mills Sales Co, Inc, NYC, since 1940; vice-pres, Malden Knitting Mills, Malden, Mass, since 1938. Pres, Union Orthodox J Congs of Amer, since 1954; Yeshiva Coll Alumni Assn, 1942-43; vice-pres, Hapoel Hamizrachi of Amer, 1950-51; treas, Natl Council for Young Isr, 1952-53; mem: bd dirs, Torah Umesorah, since 1951; Natl Soc for Day Schs, since 1951; Harvard Bus Sch Alumni Assn. Home: 42 Beech Rd, Brookline, Mass. Offices: 303 Eastern Ave, Malden, Mass.

FEUERSTEIN, Sidney S, US, surgeon; b. Boston, Mass, Sep 13, 1920; s. Victor and Anna (Rubin); MD, Yale U, 1945; m. Charlotte Clein, Oct 1, 1945; c: Ronnie, Henry. Att surg, Mt Sinai Hosp, since 1958; clinical prof, otolaryngology, Mt Sinai Med Sch, since 1967; lectr, Albert Einstein Med Sch, 1968. Capt, USAF, 1945-48. Vice-pres, Fifth Ave Syn; Amer Coll Surgs; AMA; Amer Acad Otolaryngology; chmn, Amer med comm, Shaare Zedek Hosp, Jerusalem; mem, Amer Laryngological, Rhinological and Otological Soc. Contbr to med jours. Recipient, cert of merit, AMA, 1958. Home: 630 Park Ave, New York, NY. Office: 860 Fifth Ave, New York, NY.

FEUERSTEIN, Tobie, Fr, dental surg; b. Metz, Fr, Nov 7, 1925; s. Kalman and Dobe (Singer); PhB, 1943, DDS, U Strasbourg, 1947; m. Laure Herbst, Feb 27, 1947; c: Claude. Pvt practice since 1949; hon pres, Talmud Thora comm, pres 1957-67; vice-pres: J Cultural Assn; B'nai B'rith; all Grenoble; secy, Comité Magbit Aide à Israel, 1948-49. Home: 46 rue Thiers, Grenoble, Fr. Office: 8 rue Lieutenant Chanaron, Grenoble, Fr.

FIBERT, Berndt, Swed, merchant; b. Norrköping, Swed, Feb 20, 1915; s. Filip and Ester-Lea (Brick); m. Anna Jacobsohn, Sep 23, 1943; c: Ester, René, Dan. Mgr, Fibe-Textil AB, Kallered, since 1944; trade studies, Finland, Estonia, Holland, Fr, until 1940. Chmn: United Isr Appeal of Göteborg, since 1947; JNF, since 1944; mem, bd deps, J Comty of Göteborg, since 1962; fmr: secy, B'nai B'rith; chmn: Zionist Org of Göteborg; J Youth Org, Stockholm. Home: Sylvestergatan 4, Göteborg, Swed. Office: POB 44, Kallered, Swed.

FIDLER, Michael M, Eng, business exec; organization exec; b. Salford, Lancs, Eng, Feb 10, 1916; s. Louis and Goldie (Sherr); att Royal Tech Coll, 1932-33; m. Maidie Davis, Aug 27, 1939; c: Jan, Linda. Bus cons: mgn dir: H and H Fidler Ltd, since 1941; Michael Lewis, since 1942; San Remo Properties, 1951-66; Wibye Ltd, 1968. Pres, Bd Deps Brit J, since 1967; Fed J Youth Socs, Gt Brit, since 1951; Middleton, Prestwich and Whitefield Div Conservation Assn, since 1965; Holy Law Cong, Manchester, since 1967; Manchester Union of J Socs, since 1964; vice pres: Union of Young Isr Socs of Gt Brit, since 1950; Manchester J Wfr Service; Manchester J Bd Guardians; Brit Red Cross Soc, N Manchester, since 1957; Hillel Found, Gt Brit, since 1968; chmn: Divisional Educ Exec, div 19 of Lancashire Co Council, since 1967; trustees, Chaim Weizmann Youth Cen, Manchester, since 1967; dep chmn: Prestwich Finance and Policy Comm, since 1967; Manchester Vic Memorial J Hosp, since 1967; JP for Co of Lancaster, since 1958; lectr, Extra Mural Dept, Manchester U, since 1966; treas, Inst of J Studies, since 1956; gov: Stand Grammar Sch's, since 1955; St Peter's Roman Catholic Grammar Sch, since 1965, f: Royal Geog Soc; Royal Asiatic Soc; Royal Econ Soc; Inst of Ind and Commercial Acctnts; chmn, Prestwich Parks and Public Bldgs Comm, since 1956; pres: Prestwich Heys Amateur Football Club, since 1965; Prestwich and Dist Chrysanthemum Soc, since 1957; patron Prestwich Combined Football Assn, since 1964; mem: N Manchester Hosp Mgmt Comm, since 1962; exec comm, Council of Chr and J, Manchester br, since 1966; fmr: dir, Manchester C of C, chmn garment mfrs sect; pres, Council of Manchester and Salford J; councillor, Borough of Prestwich; Mayor of Prestwich; dep chmn: Prestwich Local Council Reorg Comm; Prestwich Cen Area Re-devl Comm; jt chmn, Natl Jt Clothing Council of Gt Brit; vice chmn, British Rainwear Mfrs Fed; chmn, Natl Assn of British Mfrs, Manchester br; lectr, Min of Info; vice chmn, Friends of Heb U, Manchester br; vice chmn, NW Regional Bd for Ind, Manchester and Dist; mem: clothing adv comm, British Bd for Trade; grand council, Confd of Brit Ind; clubs: Emb, London; Milverton Lodge, Manchester. Author: One Hundred Years of the Holy Law Congregation, 1964; La Puissance Economique de la Grand Bretagne, 1966. Spec interests: politics, travel, reading, fgn affairs, educ. Homes: San Remo, Sedgley Park Rd, Prestwich, Manchester, Eng; 51 Tavistock Ct, Tavistock Pl, London, Eng. Office: Woburn House, Upper Woburn Pl, London, Eng.

FIDLER, Milton Manning, US, attorney; b. NYC, Feb 22, 1919; s. Joseph and Pauline (Mitzner); att St Johns U; LLB, St Johns U Law Sch, Bklyn, 1947; m. Sylvia Glick, Sep 22, 1946; c: Ronna Elliot, Lewis. Pvt practice since 1947; arbitrator, NYC Civil Court, since 1960; Amer Arbitration Assn, since 1970; asso govt appeal agt, US Selective Service, since 1967. Lt, US Army, 1942-46; chief legal off, US Mil Govt, Hakodate, Japan, 1945-46; US Army Res, 1946-53. Dir: Asso Health Found; Fraternal Med-Specialist Panel; sponsor, Fund for Neuromuscular Diseases and Genetic Research; org, pres: Wfr Assn Utopia Lodge Inc, since 1948; also dir, Utopia Blood Bank, since 1957; Utopia Fed Credit Union, since 1969; mem, comm law, Grand Lodge, KP since 1960, past asst chief dep, mem, Utopia Lodge, Bklyn; mem: PTA; St John's Alumni Assn, Cong Shaari Isr, Bklyn, guest lectr; E Flatbush Civic Assn. Contbr, law rev articles, St Johns Law Rev. Recipient: life mem, KP; Philippine Liberation Medal, Combat Infantryman Badge. Home: 855 E 48 St, Brooklyn, NY. Office: 26 Court St, Brooklyn, NY.

FIEDELMAN, Joel B, US, attorney; b. Sheboygan, Wis, Oct 4, 1918; s. Sam and Esther (Berg); BA, U Wis, 1942, LLB, 1942; m. Norma Wasserman, June 7, 1947; c: Ira. Pvt practice since 1945; atty: Lab Dept; Justice Dept OPA, all 1942-45; acting munic judge, 1952-53. Pres, Cong Beth El, since 1962; JP, Sheboygan, since 1951; chmn: B'nai B'rith Inst for Judaism, Eagle River, Wis, 1967; Sheboygan J Wfr Council, 1967-68; Natl Found for Infantile Paralysis, Sheboygan Co, 1952-53; vice-pres, Child Care Cen since 1953; exec secy, J Wfr Council, 1948-51; bd dirs, Comty Fund, Sheboygan, 1954; mem: Bd of Zoning Appeals, since 1962; ZOA; Wis and Sheboygan Bar Assns. Home: 2718 N 26 St, Sheboygan, Wis. Office: 815 New York Ave, Sheboygan, Wis.

FIEDLER, Leslie Aaron, US, author, educator; b. Newark, NJ, Aug 3, 1917; s. Jacob and Lillian (Rosenstrauch); BA, NYU, 1938; MA, U of Wis, 1939, PhD, 1941; att Harvard U, 1946-47; m. Margaret Shipley, Oct 7, 1939; c: Kurt, Eric, Michael, Deborah, Jennie, Miriam. Prof, eng, SUNY, since 1963; visiting prof: U Rome, 1951-52; Bologna, 1952-53; Princeton, 1956-57; Athens, 1961-62; prof, eng, dir, hum, Mont State U, 1941; visiting prof, U of Sussex, 1967-68. Author: An End to Innocence. 1955; The Art of the Essay, 1957; The Images of the Jew in American Fiction, 1957; Love and Death in the American Novel, 1960; No! In Thunder, 1960; Pull Down Vanity, 1962; The Second Stone, 1963; The Continuing Debate, 1964; Waiting for the End, 1964; The Last Jew in America, 1966; The Return of the Vanishing American, 1968; Nude Croquet, 1969; Being Busted, 1970; contbr stories, essays, poems to: Encounter; Preuves; Partisan Rev; Kenyon Rev; asso ed, Ramparts; Eng adv, St Martin's Press. Japanese interpreter, USNR, 1941-45. Pres, Missoula J Comty, 1960-63; mem: MLA; Dante Soc; Phi Beta Kappa; club, PEN Club. Recipient: Rockefeller, Fulbright, Kenyon Rev and Princeton U Fs; award, excellence in creative writing, Inst of Arts and Letters, 1957. Home: 154 Morris Ave, Buffalo, NY.

FIELD, Irwin Saul, US, business exec; b. Detroit, Mich, May 3, 1935; s. Walter and Lea (Damsky); BS, UCLA, 1957, MBA, 1960; m. Joanna Sinaiko, Sep 8, 1957; c: Edward, Ronald. Asst to pres, Liberty Vegetable Oil Co, since 1961; pres, NM Paint Mfg, since 1957; dir: Mac-O-Lac Paints; Kolorfast Paint. Natl vice-chmn, UJA Young Leadership Cabinet; co-chmn, comm on leadership devl, J Fed Council, LA, mem bd; mem: United JWF Comm of LA; budget and allocations comm, J Fed Council; Council on J Feds and Wfr Funds, natl comm on leadership devl and coll youth; Natl Inst Oilseed Producs; W Coast Oilseed Devl Comm; fmr: chmn, comty service comm; mem, bd, LA Hillel Council. Recipient: Robert Greenberg Leadership Award, J Fed-Council of LA, 1962. Home: 115 S McCadden Pl, Los Angeles, Cal. Office: 15306 S Carmenita Rd, Santa Fe Springs, Cal.

FIELD, Maxwell, US, trade association exec; b. Boston, Mass, Feb 22, 1912; s. Samuel and Sarah (Gruber); BA, Dartmouth

Coll, 1933; MCS, Amos Tuck Sch of Admn and Finance, 1934; m. Ruth Leavitt, June 28, 1935; c: Jane Munick, Sally Patkin, Richard. Exec vice-pres: New Eng Footwear Assn; Amer Footwear Mfrs Assn; dir, Natl Shoe Fairs of Amer, since 1964. Fmr dir, NE chap, NCCJ; fmr pres, dir: NE chap, Quartermaster Assn; Boston chap, Amer Soc of Assn Execs; mem: Amer Econ Assn; Amer Stat Assn; Defense Orientation Assn; Temple Emanu-El, Marblehead; clubs: Dartmouth; Kentwood Country. Contbr of articles on footwear ind. Home: 370 Puritan Rd, Swampscott, Mass.

FIELD, Walter Lichtenfeld, US, business exec; b. Pol, Apr 3, 1902; s. Isaac and Sarah (Schoenbard) Lichtenfeld; in US since 1920; m. Lea Damsky, May 28, 1929; c: Harriet Siden, Irwin. Paint mfr exec, since 1931; pres, Mocahac Paints Inc since 1931. Bd dirs: JWF; Cong Shaarey Zedek; Amer Technion; ZOA; Hillel Day Sch; Wayne State U Press; Detroit J Hist Soc; mem: Detroit Public Libr; AJCong; B'nai B'rith; Amer Friends Heb U; AJComm. Author: More Truth Than Poetry, 1956; A People's Epic, 1963; Symphony of Threes, 1966. Spec interest, J Hist. Home: 19346 Berkeley, Detroit, Mich. Office: 5400 Nevada, Detroit, Mich.

FIERMAN, Louis B, US, psychiatrist; b. Cleveland, O, May 11, 1922; s. Benjamin and Rebecca (Ghidaleson); BS, W Reserve U, 1944, MD, 1946; m. Ella Yensen, Sep 25, 1947; c: Dan, Lauren. Asso prof, psycht, Yale U, since 1961, res, Yale dept of psycht, 1951-53; chief, psycht service, VA Hosp, W Haven, Conn, since 1960, staff, psycht, 1953-60. Capt, US Army MC, Army of Occupation, Japan, 1947-49. Pres, Conn dist br, Amer Psychiatric Assn, 1962-63; mem: AMA; Conn State Med Soc; New Haven Co Med Assn; Phi Delta Epsilon; Alpha Omega Alpha. Contbr to med jours. Home: Enoch Dr, Woodbridge, Conn. Office: 210 Prospect St, New Haven, Conn.

FIERST, Miriam, US, communal worker; b. Montreal, Can, Sep 8, 1891; d. Hirsh and Sarah (Fierst) Cohen; m. Harry Fierst, Sep 21, 1913; c: Herbert, Leba, Leonard. Fmr natl vice-pres, perm hon council mem, Hadassah, fmr chmn natl speakers bur and natl membership chmn; fmr fund-raising chmn, Hadassah Med Org; natl vice-pres, JNF; bd dirs: Amer Zionist Youth Commn; UJA; J Fed; delg: ZC, 1957; 25 WZC, Jerusalem, 1960. Home: 340 W 57 St, New York, NY.

FIGLER, Bernard, Can, attorney, author, Zionist leader; b. Bender, Russ, June 16, 1900; s. Israel and Paya (Goldman); in Can since 1909; MSW, McGill U; LLM, U de Montréal; m. Sadie Serchuk, July 3, 1928; c: Miriam Shadmon, Israel, Ghita Wolff. Admitted to Que Bar, 1925; Q.C; head, Judgement Dept, Provincial Court, Montreal; fmr: tchr, J People's Sch's; adult educ dir, Montreal YMHA; field org, prog dir, ed, Can Zionist; exec dir, Zionist Order Habonim, Can Young Judea; natl exec secy, JNF, Can. Author: Job Analysis in Group Work Agency, 1946; From Mandate to State, 1951; History of Zionist Ideal in Canada, 1961; Canadian Jewish Biographies: Lillian and Archie Freiman, 1962; Hananiah Meir Caiserman, 1962, Louis Fitch Q.C, 1969; Samuel William Jacobs KC, MP, Lyon Cohen, Rev Dr Herman Abromowitz; Abraham Ansel Levin; Poetry in Canada's Parliament. Hobby, music, Home: 5854 Decelles Pl, Montreal, Can.

FILBERBAUM, Milton B, US, cardiologist, educator; b. Bklyn, NY, Jan 29, 1904; s. Louis and Anna (Friedman); AB, Columbia U, 1923, MD, 1928; m. 2nd, Rose August, Jan 20, 1961; c, by previous m: Lewis. Clinical asst prof med, SUNY Downstate Med Cen, 1950-62; cons phys: Mather Memorial Hosp, Port Jefferson, NY; Suffolk Hosp, Riverhead, NY; Southside Hosp, Bay Shore, NY; Smithtown Gen Hosp, Smithtown, NY; att phys, Brookhaven Memorial Hosp, Patchogue, NY. Lt cdr, USNR, 1942-45. F: Amer Coll of Phys; Amer Coll of Chest Phys; clinical card, AHA; dipl, Amer Bd Internal Med, cert in cardiovascular disease; mem: AMA. Contbr to med jours. Home: 8 Oakland St, E Patchogue, NY. Office: 4 Schoenfeld Blvd, Patchogue, NY.

FILER, Leonidas (Leo Filer), Isr, actor, film dir; b. Buenos Aires, Arg, May, 1929; s. Julio and Clara (Schliapnik); in Isr. since 1950; att U Buenos Aires Sch of Engr, 1947-49; cert: Amer Theatre Wing, NY, 1956; RCA-TV, NY, 1969; m. Hadassa Avni, Aug 9, 1954; c: Avnit. Films: dir, The Miracle, 1968; asso exec produc, sup dir, The Boy Across the Street, 1966; co-dir, Girls to Eilat, 1964; dir, independent produc, numerous documentary, educ films; script writer: Eldorado; Simchon's Family; Girls to Eilat; TV: script writer: Puerta al

Suspenso; Telecine, both Mex TV; actor, Mex TV; asts dir, Puerta al Suspenso; theatre: dir, numerous stage producs, 1958-68; guest actor, dir: Habima Theatre, Tel Aviv; Ohel Theatre, Tel Aviv; dir of own play, LaEsfera Theatre, Mex; leading actor, Mexico City; actor, one man show touring Latin Amer, Span Morocco; perm mem, Habimah Theatre; radio: dir, progs, Voice of Isr, Curtain Rise series, adaptations of full length plays; writer, narrator of 230 Panoramas de Israel, Bc in Latin Amer; writer, leading actor, sci fiction series, Opr Inter X, Mexico; IDF, 1967. Mem: Intl Theatre Inst, Isr; SMPTE, NY. Recipient: Silver Lion of San Marco, Venice, 1966, Gold Plaque, Teheran Festival, 1966 for The Boy Across the Street; mentioned by Mex radio and TV as one of three best TV actors for performance in: The Caine Mutiny; The Diary of Anne Frank. Home: 21 Chissin St, Tel Aviv, Isr; 825 West End Ave, New York, NY.

FILLER, Louis, US, educator, author; b. Odessa, Russ, May 2, 1912; s. Pit and Sarah (Kutcher); in US since 1914; BA, Temple U, 1934; MA, Columbia U, 1941, PhD, 1943; m. Sheila Flaherty, Aug 19, 1964; c: Stuart, Victor, Judith; by previous m: Stephen, Abby, Helen. Prof, Amer civilization, Antioch Coll, since 1946; cons, Notable Amer Women, since 1960; research hist, Amer Council Learned Socs, 1942-44; hist, off, Quartermaster Gen, War Dept, 1944-46; book ed, Antioch Review, 1948-55; cons: New Century Cyclopedia of Names, 1954; Dictionary of American Biography, 2nd supplement, 1958; Fulbright lectr: U of Bristol, Eng, 1950-51; State U of Ia, dept Eng, 1960; CCNY, 1968-69; summer sessions: hist dept: U of Wyoming, 1947; CCNY, 1948; Roosevelt U, Chgo, 1955; W Reserve U, 1957; Colo Coll, 1958; LIU, 1961; Eng dept: Wash U, St Louis, 1950; Pa State U, 1952; U of Utah, depts Eng and hist, 1953; SF State Coll, social sci div, 1960; Sonoma State Coll, social sci div, 1962; f: U, Amer hist, Columbia, U, 1941-42; Amer Council Learned Soc and Social Sci Research Council, 1953-54; Mem: Amer, Miss Valley Hist Assns; Newberry Conf in Amer Studies, 1952-58; elector, Amer Studies Assn, 1952-53. Author: Crusaders for American Liberalism, 1939, 1961; Randolph Bourne, 1943, 1963; The Crusade Against Slavery, 1960; Dictionary of American Social Reform, 1963; The Unknown Edwin Markham, 1966; ed: The New Stars, by Manie Morgan, 1949; Chatterton, by Ernest Lacy, 1952; Mr. Dooley: Now and Forever, by F P Dunne, 1954; The World of Mr Dooley, 1962; Late Nineteenth Century American Liberalism; others; contbr to gen and profsl publs. Recipient, Ohioana Book Award, for non-fiction, 1961, for biography, 1967. Home: 1345 Meadow Lane, Yellow Springs, O. Office: Antioch Coll, Yellow Springs, O.

FILLER, Robert, US, educator; b. Bklyn, NY, Feb 2, 1923; s. Alfred and Ethel (Schwab); BS, CCNY, 1943; MS, U of Ia, 1947, PhD, 1949; m. Lael Rosenbloom (decd); m. 2nd, Miriam Holland, Sep 20, 1959; c: Susan, Rebecca, Debby, Daniel; step c: Michael. Prof, chmn dept chem, Ill Inst of Tech, since 1968, on fac since 1955; cons: fluorine chem, IIT Research Inst, 1963-64; U of Ill Coll of Med, 1959-60; research asso, Ben May Lab for Cancer Research, U Chgo, 1956-57; asst prof, O Wesleyan U, 1953-55; research chem, Wright Air Devl Cen, 1951-1953; postdoc research f, Purdue U, 1950-51, NIH spec postdoc f, U of Cambridge, Eng, 1962-63. Pfc, US Army, 1944-46. Mem: Sigma Xi; exec comm, div of flourine chem, Amer Chem Soc; fmr cdr, JWV, Gary Ind chap. Contbr numerous articles to profsl jours. Recipient: Amer Theatre Ribbon. Hobbies: reading; politics; sports; neighborhood activities. Home: 6935 S Chappel Ave, Chicago, Ill. Office: Ill Inst of Tech, Chicago, Ill.

FILMUS, Tully, US, painter; b. Ataki, Bessarabia, Aug 29, 1908; s. Michael and Eva (Gustoff); in US since 1913; BA, Pa Acad of Fine Arts, 1927; m. Gladys Nodiff, June 18, 1939; c: Michael, Stephen. Represented in perm collections including, Whitney Mus; Metrop Mus Art; MIT; Tel Aviv Mus, Isr; Biro Bidjan Mus, Russ; Syracuse U Mus; Yeshiva U; Orleans Gayl Inst, Haifa, Isr; Sholom Aleichem Inst, Tel Aviv, Isr; Holyoke Mus; one-man exhbs: ACA Gal, Rome, It, 1964; Harbor Gal, Cold Spring Harbor, NY, 1966; Cen Gal, New Haven, Conn, 1966; ACA Gal, NY, 1967; Kenmore Gal, Phila, Pa, 1968; numerous exhbs in US; Rome; instr: Amer Artists Sch, 1937-39; Cooper Union Sch of Art, 1938-50; letters and documents deposited in Syracuse U Manuscript coll. Mem: Artists Equity Assn; Audubon Artists; bd dirs, N Shore Comty Arts Cen. Recipient: Cresson Award, F Prize, both PA Acad Fine Arts; Salmagundi Prize, 1969. Home and studio: 17 Stuart St, Great Neck, NY. Summer home: Becket, Mass.

FINCI, Zak, Yugo, educator; b. Sarajevo, Yugo, 1921; s. Leon and Rosa (Altarac); att, Agric Fac, Belgrade, 1939-47; m. Loni Musafija, 1948; c: Leo, Rudi. U prof, since 1948; prof, Fac of Agric, Sarajevo U. Fought in People's Liberation War, Yugo, 1942-45. Author: Traktorizacija poljoprivrede Bosne i Hercegovine, 1953; Ekonomika inokosnih gazdinstava, 1960; Organizacija kombajniranja žita i siliranja krme, 1961; Univerzitetski udžebenici (3 books), 1964, 1966, 1969; Dugoročne razvojne tendencije poljoprivredne proizvodnje Jugoslavije, 1968; Ekonomika proizvodnje sjemenskog krompira, 1970; Usmjeravanje razvitka naučnog rada, stručne službe i školstva, 1970. Recipient: Order of Valour, Order of Merit for People, 2nd class, Order of Frat, Memorial Sutjeska 1943; Town Sarajevo Award. Home: 5 Sutjeska, Sarajevo, Yugo. Office: Poljoprivredni Fakultet, 18 Zagrebačka, Sarajevo, Yugo.

FINE, Allan, Can, singer, concert artist, tchr; b. Schaulen, Lith, Aug 13, 1926; s. Joseph and Miriam (Gesselsohn) Fingerhut; in Can since 1949; BSc, U Munich, 1949; att Music Conservatory, Montreal; LMus, McGill U, 1966; m. Judy Silverstein, June 23, 1951; c: Howard. Lectr, voice produc, McGill U, since 1967; cantor, Beth Isr, Hartford, Conn, since 1963; RCA recording artist, since 1968; performances with: Montreal Sym Orch; Hartford Sym; Opera Guild; on radio and TV; recitals and concerts; released album of Hebraic melodies in six langs. Mem: B'nai B'rith; Survivors of Nazi Oppression, Montreal br. Hobbies: sports, photography, travel. Home: 6670 Coolbrook Ave, Montreal, Can.

FINE, Alvin I, US, rabbi; b. Portland, Ore, Oct 25, 1916; s. Henry and Sophie (Weinstein); BA, Reed Coll, Portland, 1937; ordained rabbi, MHL, HUC; DHL, hon causa, Santa Clara U, 1964; m. Elizabeth Ackerman, May 1, 1949; c: Lloyd, Jonathan, Deborah. Rabbi, Cong Emanu-El, since 1948; prof, SF State Coll, since 1965; rabbi, Cong Beth Emeth, Wilmington, Del, 1942; mem fac, asst to pres, HUC, 1946-48; mem bd trustees, all HUC. Chaplain, US Army, 1943-46. Pres, Bd of Rabbis of N Cal; mem: SF Hum Rights Commn; bd trustees: Grad Theol Union, Berkeley; Reed Coll, Ore; natl adv councils: UJA, JDC; natl gov council, AJCong; bd dirs: JWF; Council for Civic Unity; World Affairs Council of N Cal; ARC; bd govs, J Educ Soc; exec comm, Bonds for Isr; org comm, Fed Fund; chaplaincy comm: CCAR; LZOA; fmr Cal State Comm on Public Educ; bd trustees, HUC; hon chmn, SF Histadrut; chmn bd, ACLU of N Cal. Recipient: JNF-JFK Award, 1964; Liberty Bell Award, SF Bar Assn; United World Federalists Adlai E Stevenson Award. Home: 3330 Jackson St, San Francisco, Cal. Office: Arguello and Lake Sts, San Francisco, Cal.

FINE, Arnold, US, journalist, educator; b. NYC, Jan 15, 1924; s. Morris and Beatrice; MA, LIU, 1949; m. Edith Rubin, Aug 27, 1950; c: Jay, Brian, Martin. Ed: Bklyn Daily; Herald Tribune; J Press; syndicated columnist, newspapers, educ jours; writer: cartoon series; Our Heritage, Stories of King Solomon; Stories of the Sages; Israel's Underground Fighters; pres, bd educ, Isaiah Day Schs; tchr, mentally retarded children, NYC; prof, LIU, 1950-54. USN, US Army. PR dir: Guide Dog Found for Blind; educational multi-media coord, Articulated Multi-Media Physics course for NY Inst of Tech; mem, Masons. Recipient, Awards: Ed and Publ, 1960; Bklyn Womans Bar Assn, 1961; Educ Council, Devl Computer Training Arithmathink Learning Machine and Concrete Values System of Arithmetic. Home: 134-40 230th St, Laurelton, NY. Office: 2427 Surf Ave, Brooklyn, NY.

FINE, Benjamin, US, educator, author, editor; b. NYC, Sep 1, 1905; s. Charles and Rebecca (Goldin); ES, U of RI, 1928; MS, Sch of Journalism, Columbia U, 1933, MA Tchrs, Coll, 1935, PhD, 1941; hon deg: DE, Bryant Coll, 1946; HDumL, Yeshiva U, 1949; DE, U of RI, 1950; LLD, Leb Valley Coll, 1951; DLitt, U Toledo, 1951; Des Lettres, Union Coll, 1952; DS, U Tampa, 1953; m. Lillian Chafetz, Oct 11, 1936; c: Ellen, Jill Mainelli, Carla Reiss, Janet. Dean, Coll of Journalism, U Palm Beach, Fla; educ ed: N Amer Newspaper Alliance since 1959; Bell McClure Syndicate since 1960; asst, Pulitzer Sch of Journalism, 1932; reporter, NY Post, 1933; asst pr, Tchrs Coll, Columbia U, 1933-36; educ reporter, educ ed, NY Times, 1937-58; dean, Grad, Sch of Educ, NYC-Ford Found Tchr Training, 1958-60; chmn, dept of journalism, Point Park Jr Coll, Pittsburgh, 1961-62; headmaster, Sands Point Acad and Country Day Sch for Gifted Children, 1962-70. Mem: Authors League of Amer; Silurians; NY Reporters Assn; NEA; Amer Assoc Sch Admnrs; Soc Amer Hist; NY Acad of Public Educ; Sigma Delta Chi; Phi Delta Kappa; Kappa Delta Pi;

Alpha Epsilon Pi; Mayor Wagner's Comm on Scholastic Achievement, Mayor's Comm on Evaluation of Juvenile Delinquency, natl pr comm, Girl Scouts of Amer; Masons, 32 deg; trustee: Lafayette F Found; Natl Bus and Profsl Council; dir: Natl Assoc for Gifted Children; Libr Club of Amer; Roosevelt Sch, Conn; exec bd, Amer Assoc for UN; past-pres, Educ Writers' Assoc; cons, NY State Citizens' Comm for Public Schs; clubs: Overseas Press. Author: A Giant of the Press, 1933; College Publicity in the United States, 1941; Educational Publicity, 1943; Democratic Education, 1945; Admission to American Colleges, 1946; Our Children are Cheated, 1947; Opportunities in Teaching, 1952; Fine's American College Counselor and Guide, 1955; 1,000,000,Delinquents, 1955; The School Administrator and the Press, 1956; The School Administrator and His Publications, 1957; How to be Accepted by the College of Your Choice, 1957; How to Get the Best Education for Your Child, 1958; Modern Family Guide to Education, 1962; Teaching Machines, 1962; Profiles of American Colleges, 1963; Stretching Their Minds, 1965; Underachievers, 1967; Your Child and School, 1968; New Ways to Study and Learn; Now It Can be Told, 1969; How I Got That Story; How to Get the Most Out of College, 1970; contrb to jours and mags; author of three weekly columns syndicated in several hundred newspapers; ed bd, Educ Forum; assoc ed, Gifted Child Quarterly. Recipient: Numerous awards in fields of educ, journalism, including Pulitzer Award for NY Times articles, 1944; Frederick Z Lewis Medal, Tchrs Wfr League of NY State, 1947; Natl Sch Bell Award, 1962; citation, Educ Writers Assn for "outstanding interpretation of education to the public," 1962; f, Creative Educ Found, 1969. Office: 660 Fern St, W Palm Beach, Fla.

FINE, Charles S, US, physician, educator; b. Toronto, Can, Dec 7, 1911; s. Louis and Esther (Freeman); in US since 1937; MD, U Toronto, 1937; m. Reva Baker, June 6, 1937; c: Susan, Jeffrey. Pvt practice since 1941; clinical asso prof, dept obstet and gyn, U Wash, since 1949; asst res, obstet, Baltimore City Hosp, 1938-39; f, gyn path, Johns Hopkins Hosp, 1939; chief res, obstet and gyn, Michael Reese Hosp, 1940-41. Maj, US Army, 1943-46. Pres: Seattle J Fed, 1967-68; Seattle Gynecological Soc, 1955; vice-pres, Fed J Fund, Seattle, 1959, 1961, secy, 1962; campaign chmn, Amer and Interntl Infertility Soc, 1965; dipl Amer Bd Obstet and Gyn; f: Amer Coll Obstet and Gyn; Amer Coll Surgs; mem: NW Pacific Obstet and Gyn Soc; Pacific Coast Infertility Soc. Contrb to med jours. Home: 445-140 NE Bellevue, Wash. Office: 340 Stimson Bldg, Seattle, Wash.

FINE, Isadore V, US, educator; b. Columbia, Mo, May 23, 1918; s. Solomon and Ida (Corenbaum); BS, RI Coll, 1942; MS, Columbia U, 1947, PhD, 1952; m. Selma Lightman, Oct 14, 1945; c: Stephen, Debra. Prof, business admn, U Wis, since 1947; business cons, lectr; instr, Bklyn Coll, 1947. Lt col, USAAF, 1942-46. Dir, Hillel Found, Madison, since 1960; financial secy, Temple Beth El, since 1966; budget comm, Madison Wfr Council, since 1961; mem: Amer Marketing Assn; Natl Assn of Purchasing Agts; Alpha Epsilon Pi; Phi Kappa Phi. Author: Industrial Purchasing 1955, 3rd ed, 1969; Ital ed, 1961, Japanese ed, 1962; contrb to profsl jours. Home: 826 S Midvale Blvd, Madison, Wis. Office: U of Wis, Madison, Wis.

FINE, Jacob, US, surgeon, educator; b. Brockton, Mass, Feb 10, 1900; s. Myer and Sarah (Weinstein); AB, Harvard Coll, 1920, MD, 1924; m. Anna Rosenblatt, June 22, 1922 (decd); c: David, Jonathan; m. 2nd, Ann Sokol, Apr 19, 1960. Dir, surg, Beth Isr Hosp, Boston, since 1948, mem, surg staff, since 1931; prof em, Harvard Med Sch, since 1966, fac mem, since 1932; responsible investigator, OSRD, 1941-45. ROTC, US Army WW I. Mem: adv bd, Heb U Hadassah Med Sch, 1950; adv and bd trustees, Heb Tchrs Coll; Amer, Intl, Boston Surg Socs; Soc Experimental Biol and Med; NRC; Natl Med Research Council; FACS; f, NY Acad of Sci; fmr: secy, Boston Comm on Med Emigrees; mem: bd, Tel Aviv Med Sch; bd govs, Weizmann Inst; Amer Acad Arts and Sci. Author: Care of Surgical Patients, 1950; Bacterial Factor in Shock, 1954; contrb to med and surg jours. Home: 8 Wolcott Rd Ext, Chestnut Hill, Mass. Office: Beth Isr Hosp, Boston, Mass.

FINE, Morris, US, editor; b. Warsaw, Pol, Mar 3, 1914; s. Hyman and Pearl (Taub); in US since 1921; BA, Drew U, 1936; MS, Columbia U Sch of Libr Service, 1954; postgrad studies, Columbia U and Sorbonne, 1946-49; m. Beatrice Weiss, Sep 15, 1940; c: Margery, Lawrence, Richard. Mem, exec

staff, AJComm, since 1937; ed, Amer Jewish Yearbook, since 1947. US Army, WW II. Mem: Natl Conf J Communal Service; Amer Libr Assn. Home: 231 Seaman Ave, Rockville Centre, NY. Office: 165 E 56 St, New York, NY.

FINE, Morris Eugene, US, metallurgy engr, educator; b. Jamestown, ND, Apr 12, 1918; s. Louis and Sophie (Berrington); B Metallurgical Engr, with distinction, U Minn, 1940; MS, 1942, PhD, 1943; m. Mildred Glazer, Aug 13, 1950; c: Susan, Amy. Walter P Murphy Prof, Material Sci, Northwestern U, since 1964, chmn, 1954-60, chmn, Materials Research Cen, 1960-64; instr, U Minn, 1942-43; sci, Manhattan Project, 1943-45; mem, tech staff, Bell Telephone Labs, 1945-54; visiting prof, material sci, Stanford U, 1967-68. Chmn: Chgo Chap, Amer Soc for Metals, 1963; local comm, Intl Conf on chem physics of non-metallic crystals, Northwestern U, 1961; pres, Northwestern U chap, Sigma Xi, 1961-62; mem: fmr, Materials Adv Bd, Natl Acads of Sci and Engr; exec comm, Inst of Metals Div, Amer Inst of Mining, Metallurgical and Petroleum Engrs, since 1960, chmn, 1967-68; dir, Metallurgical Soc of Amer, since 1967; Amer Ceramic Soc; AAAS; Sigma Alpha Sigma; f, Amer Phys Soc. Author: Phase Transfusion in Condensed Systems; contbr numerous sci and tech papers Recipient: Chicagoan of the Year in Sci, 1960. Home: 1101 Manor Dr, Wilmette, Ill. Office: Northwestern U, Evanston, Ill.

FINE, Phil D, US, attorney, banker; b. Brooklyn, Mass, Aug 20, 1925; s. Joseph and Ann (Rosenblum); LLB, Boston U, 1950; m. Norma Loew, Dec 28, 1952; c: Susan, Lauri, Debra. Sr partner, Fine & Ambrogne; chmn, bd dir, Commonwealth Natl Bank, Boston; 1st vice-pres, dir, Hull Coop Bank, Hull, Mass; dep admnr, Small Business Admn, 1961-62; cons, US Dept of Commerce, 1968; lectr: Amer Mgmt Assn; Practicing Law Inst; dir: Intl Ind Inc; Hi-G, Inc; Computer Environments Corp; Valle's Steak House. Dir: Boston Patriots; mem, bd trustees, Newton Free Libr, vice-chmn, Newton Housing Auth, 1960-1961; mem: Natl Planning Assn, Washington, DC; chmn: Speakers Bur, steering comm, J Tercentenary Comm; Asso Philanthropies; Kirstein Scholarship Fund; mem: Amer, Mass, Boston, Bar Assns; clubs: Bankers; NY; Fed City, Wash, DC; Natl Press, Wash; PineBrook Country, Boston. Home: 42 Annawan Road, Waban, Mass. Offices: 1 State St, Boston, Mass; 1700 Pennsylvania Ave, NW, Washington DC.

FINE, Reuben, US, psychoanalyst, chess master; b. NYC, Oct 11, 1914; s. Jacob and Bertha (Nedner); BS, CCNY, 1933; PhD, U of S Cal, 1948; m. May Medziber, Dec 25, 1953; c: Benjamin, Ellyn; m. 2nd, Charlotte Margoshes, Apr 20, 1963. Pvt practice since 1948; dir training, Metrop Inst for Psychoanalytic Studies; dir, Cen for Creative Living; psychol: VA, 1948-50; Post Grad Cen for Psychotherapy, 1950-51; prof, psych, CCNY, 1953-58; chess master, 1930-50; visiting prof: LIU, 1965-68; U Amsterdam, 1961; U Florence, 1968; Adelphi U, since 1969. Research cons, USN, 1944-45. Mem: Amer Psychol Assn; Soc for Projective Techs; Natl Psych Assn for Psychan; NY State Psych Assn; Theodor Reik Clinic. Author: The Psychology of the Asthmatic Child, 1948; Freud: A Critical Reevaluation, 1962; The Healing of the Mind, 1970; contbr to profsl jours. Recipient: Cert of Dist Service to Naval Ordnance. Home and office: 225 W 86 St, New York, NY.

FINE, Sidney, US, educator, author; b. Cleveland, O, Oct 11, 1920; s. Morris and Gussie (Redalia); BA, W Reserve U, 1942; MA, U Mich, 1944, PhD, 1948; m. Jean Shechter, Dec 5, 1942; c: Gail, Deborah. Prof, hist, U Mich, since 1959, on fac since 1948. USNR, 1942-46. Author: Laissez Faire and the General Welfare State, 1956; Recent America, 1962; The The Automobile Under The Blue Eagle, 1963; Sit-Down: The General Motors Strike of 1936-37, pub 1969; co-author, The American Past, 1961; contbr to hist jours. Bd, Beth Isr Comty Cen, 1955-58; mem: Amer Hist Assn; Lab Hist Group; AA UP; Mich Acad of Arts, Sci and Letters; Org of Amer Hists; Phi Beta Kappa; Phi Kappa Phi. Recipient: Guggenheim F; Dist Fac Achievement Award, 1969. Home: 825 Russet Rd, Ann Arbor, Mich. Office: U of Mich, Ann Arbor, Mich.

FINE, Sidney H, US, government official; b. Yonkers, NY, Dec 11, 1906; s. Max and Anne (Steinberg); att: Columbia U, 1929-30; Amer U, 1941-42; Georgetown U, 1957-58; BA, Amer U, 1963; m. Margery Wood, Aug 2, 1947; c: Barbara, David. Press attache, US Emb, Belgrade, Yugo, since 1966; newspaper reporter: Newark (NJ) Star Eagle, 1926-29; NY Inves News, 1929-32; NYC News Assn, 1933-41; ed, FCC, 1941-45; cultural affairs off, Amer Emb, Moscow, USSR,

1945-46; info off, Commerce Dept, 1946-48; press off, US delg to NATO, Paris, Fr 1948-54; dir, off of public info, USIA, 1954-57; public info dir, Amer Natl Exhb, Moscow, 1959; first secy, Amer Legation, Sofia, 1960-62; public affairs adv, Bur Afr Affairs, State Dept, 1962-66. Mem: Wash Heb Cong; Pi Sigma Alpha; club, Natl Press. Home: 6041 Rossmore Dr, Bethesda, Md. Office: Amer Emb Belgrade, Yugo.

FINEBERG, S Andhil, US, rabbi, organization exec; b. Pittsburgh, Pa, Nov 29, 1896; s. Nathan and Libby (Landau); BA, U Cincinnati, 1917; ordained rabbi, HUC-JIR, 1920, hon DD, 1958; PhD, Columbia U, 1932; m. Hilda Cohen, 1925. Comty relations cons: NCCJ since 1965; AJComm, 1939-64; rabbi: Temple Beth El, Niagara Falls, 1920-24; J Comty Cen, White Plains, 1926-29; Sinai Temple, Mt Vernon, 1931-37; natl chaplain, JWV, 1931-37. USMC, 1917-19. Pres, Assn J Comty Relations Workers, 1952-55; chmn, profsl standards comm, Natl Assn Intergroup Relations Officials, 1952-53; mem: NY Bd Rabbis; CCAR. Author: Biblical Myth and Legend, 1932; Overcoming Anti-Semitism, 1943; Punishment without Crime, 1949; The Rosenberg Case, 1953; Defrauding Minority Groups, 1957; The Fallacies of Communism, 1958; Deflating the Professional Bigot, 1960; contbr to: Commentary; Reader's Digest; gen mags. Recipient: Anisfeld-Wolf Lit Award, 1950. Home: 19 William St, Mt Vernon, NY. Office: 43 W 57 St, New York, NY.

FINEBERG, Shlomo Z, US, rabbi, psychologist; b. Memphis, Tenn, July 4, 1903; s. Morris and Jeanette (Manis); rabbi, Heb Theol Coll, 1930; Rabb ordination by Rabbi Moshe Epstein, A I Kook and PH Frank, all of Jerusalem; BS, Heb U, Jerusalem, 1932; MHL, Jewish U, Skokie, Ill, 1961, DHL, 1968; DHL, grad sch Heb Theol Coll; m. Naomi Wainger May 8, 1928; c: Janice Paul, Sondra Kraff, Leon. Rabbi, B'nai Isr, Austin, Chgo, since 1943; rel psych, U Chgo, since 1960; rabbi: Adath Isr Cong, Evansville, Ind, 1928-30; B'nai Isr Cong, Flint, Mich, 1932-43. Mem, bd trustees, B'nai B'rith, hon lt cdr, JWV, Chgo; mem: bd gov, State of Isr Bonds; pres, JNF, Flint, Mich, 1937-38; found, Flint Nachla, Isr, 1936-37; past off: Chgo Rabb Council; Chgo Bd Rabbis; Chgo Rabb Council; Loops Syn; club, Covenant. Recipient: State of Isr Bonds award, 1938; plaque, City Council of Chgo. Home: 6833 N Kedzie Ave, Chicago, Ill. Study: 2927 W Touhy, Chicago, Ill.

FINEGOLD, Wilfred J, US, physician; b. Pittsburgh, Pa, July 31, 1909; s. Jules and Celia (Gruber); BS, U Pittsburgh, 1931; MD, U London, Eng, 1936; m. Marcella Leyton, Nov 24, 1939; c: Alan, Nan. Asso clinical prof, U Pittsburgh Med Sch, on fac since 1960; chief, dept obstet, Montefiore Hosp, since 1958; sr staff, Eliz Steele Magee Hosp, since 1959; chief, div of infertility clinic, Pittsburgh Planned Parenthood Clinic, since 1945; treas, 3500 Fifth Ave Corp, 1952-62; secy, Intl Soc Study Fertility, 1956-60. F: Pittsburgh Obstet Soc; Amer Soc Study Infertility; dipl, Amer Coll Obstet and Gyn; mem: AMA; Allegheny Co Med Soc; Masons; Phi Epsilon Pi; clubs: Concordia; Westmoreland Country; U Pittsburgh. Author: Artificial Insemination, 1964. Home: 4940 Baynard St, Pittsburgh, Pa. Office: 3500 Fifth Ave, Pittsburgh, Pa.

FINEMAN, Irving, US, novelist, playwright; b. NYC, Apr 9, 1893; s. Joseph and Rebecca (Blanc); BS, MIT, 1917; BS, Harvard, 1917; m. Helene Hughes, 1935 (div); c: Joseph, Jonathan. Practicing engr until 1930; mem: fac of engr, U of Ill, 1925-28; fac lit, Bennington Coll, 1932-38; screen writer for MGM, Warner Bros, Columbia Pictures, 1932-46; ed cons Rand Corp, Cal, 1957. Lt, USN, 1917-22 and 1940. Mem, Sigma Alpha Mu, fmr natl pres. Author: This Pure Young Man, 1930; Lovers Must Learn, 1932; Hear, Ye Sons, 1933; Doctor Addams, 1939; Jacob: An Autobiographical Novel, 1941; Ruth, 1949; Akiba, play, 1949; Fig Tree Madonna, play, 1950; Woman of Valor; The Life of Henrietta Szold, 1961; contbr of poems, articles, stories in Harpers, Nation, Yale Rev, Partisan Rev, Saturday Rev. Recipient: Longmans prize, 1930; Stevens award Dramatists Alliance, 1951. Home: Maple Hill Rd, Shaftesbury, Vt.

FINERMAN, Uzi, Isr, communal leader; b. Ein Harod, Isr, Sep 9, 1924; s. Itzhak and Rachel (Friman); m. Hana Israel; c: Tamar, Eliyahu, Orit. Secy gen, Tnu'at Hamoshavim, Moshav Movement, since 1961; farmer, Kfar Yehezkel. Col, IDF. Home: Moshav Kfar Yehezkel, Isr. Office: 6 Reines St, Tel Aviv, Isr.

FINESTEIN, Israel, UK, barrister, author; b. Hull, Yorks, Eng, Apr 29, 1921; s. Jeremiah and Rosa (Bernstein); MA,

Trinity Coll, Cambridge; m. Marion Oster, Dec 17, 1946. Author: Short History of Anglo-Jewry, 1957; Sir George Jessel, 1958; ed: Sketches of Anglo-Jewish History by James Picciotto, 1956. Hon secy, Hillel Found, since 1954; chmn, J Coll Libr, since 1956; mem council, J Hist Soc, since 1956; mem: Bd Deps, since 1944, comms: exec, law and parl, Eretz Isr; fmr mem, fgn affairs comm; fmr: pres, Cambridge U J Soc; chmn, Inter-U J Fed; vice-chmn, standing conf, J Youth. Home: 4 Fairhazel Mansions, Fairhazel Gardens, London, NW6, Eng.

FINGER, Elliott, US, physician, business exec; b. Orangeburg, SC, Sep 26, 1909; s. Morris and Sarah (Pliskin); BS, Med Coll of Charleston, 1931; MD, Med Coll of SC, 1933; postgrad studies: Cook Co Sch of Med; Tulane Sch of Med; div; c: Joyce Barth (decd), Stephanie Rushton, Daryl Laricks, Ronald. Owner, Finger Clinic Hosp, SC, since 1937; pvt practice limited to surg and gyn; pres, Peedee Bldg Inds, since 1953; fmr, alderman, councilman, City of Marion, mayor pro-tempore, 1961. Maj, US Army, 1940-45. Pres, Medico, Inc; dipl, Intl Acad Proctology; mem: Amer Fracture Assn; Amer Soc Abdominal Surgs; S Med Assn; bd trustees, Temple Isr, Florence, SC, since 1949, past pres; AMA; SC Med Assn; Peedee Med Assn, past pres; Marion Co Med Soc. Home: 301 Harmon Park, Marion, SC. Office: 208 Harllee St, Marion, SC.

FINGER, Harold Ben, US, engineer, administrator; b. NYC, Feb 18, 1924; s. Beny and Anna (Perlmutter); BS, CCNY, 1944; MS, Case Inst of Tech, Cleveland, O, 1950; m. Arlene Karsch, June 11, 1949; c: Barbara, Elyse, Sandra. Asst secy, research and tech, Dept Housing and Urban Devl, since 1969; asso chief, compressor research br, NACA, Lewis Research Cen, Cleveland, O, 1954-57, mem staff, since 1944; mgr, space nuclear propulsion off, dir, space power and nuclear syss, 1960-67, dir, space nuclear sys div, 1965-67, both NASA-AEC; asso admn, org and mgmt, NASA, 1967-69. Trustee, Temple Sinai, Wash, DC. Recipient, awards: James H Wyld Propulsion, AIAA, 1968; co-recipient, Soc of Automotive Engrs Manley Memorial, 1957. Home: 6908 Millwood Rd, Bethesda, Md. Office: 451 7th SW, Washington, DC.

FINGER, Seymour Maxwell, US, diplomat; b. NYC, Apr 30, 1915; s. Samuel and Bella (Spiegel); BS, Ohio U, 1935; att U Cincinnati, 1942; Littaur Sch Public Affairs, Harvard U, 1953-54; m. Helen Kotcher, Apr 5, 1956; c: Mark. Consul Gen, US Mission to UN, since 1963; Ambass, sr adv to Perm US Repr to UN since 1967, sr adv, econ, social affairs, 1956-63; tchr, 1937-38; br mgr, asst to vice pres, Photo Reflex Studies, 1935-46; vice consul, Amer Emb, Stuttgart, Ger, 1946-49; 2nd secy, Amer Emb, Paris, 1949-51; 2nd secy, econ off, Amer Legation, Budapest, Hung, 1951-53; econ off, Amer Emb, Rome, It, 1954-55; 1st secy, chief, political sect, Amer Emb, Vientiane, Laos, 1955-56; US repr to trusteeship council, to spec comm on colonization. US Army, 1943-45. Mem: Phi Beta Kappa; Kappa Delta Pi; Cen Syn of Nassau Co; Council on Fgn Relations; clubs: Amer, Paris and Rome. Author: The Escape Clause in Public Policy, vol VI, 1955. Home: 476 Morris Ave, Rockville Centre, NY. Office: US Mission to UN, 779 UN Plaza, New York, NY.

FINK, Aaron H, US, business exec; b. Union City, NJ, Apr 1, 1916; s. Jacob and Tessie (Dubow); AB, Johns Hopkins U, 1938; m. Roslyn Lamb, Dec 6, 1942; c: Elliot, Ilene. Pres: Essex Paper Box Mfg Co, since 1948; NJ Boxcraft Bur; mem, bd trustees, NJ Paper Box Mfrs Assn; mem, adv bd, Amer Inst of Mgmt; US delg, Conf of Mfrs, Paris, Fr, 1954; mem, Spec Econ Mission, It, 1954. Mem: Amer Soc of Quality Control; Tech Assn of Paper and Pulp Inds; NAM; Amer Mfg Assn; Natl Soc for Bus Budgeting; Confrerie de la Chaine Rotisseurs; Amer Forestry Assn; Amer Geophys Union; Natl Geog Soc; Amer Material Handling Soc; clubs: Crestmont Country, mem, bd govs, 1955-61; Great Oak; Newark Athletic. Hobby, sailing. Home: 20 Crestwood Dr, Maplewood, NJ. Office: 281 Astor St, Newark, NJ.

FINK, Jenny, US, communal worker; b. Biebrich, Ger, Aug 28, 1886; d. Moritz and Marie (Dreyfuss) Sender; in US since 1941; m. David Fink, Apr 16, 1912; c: Miriam Hochstein, Phyllis Weissman, Theodore. Pres, NY chap, Mizrachi Women's Org, since 1956, mem, natl admn bd, since 1951; pres, J Child Care, Antwerp, Belgium, 1923-40; women's auxiliary, Jesodah Hatorah Sch, Antwerp, 1921-34; vice-pres, Council of J Women, Antwerp, 1928-40; mem, Ohab Zedek Sisterhood. Home: 300 Central Park W, New York, NY.

FINK, Mina Miriam, Austr, communal leader; b. Bialystock, Pol, Dec 5, 1913; d. Nathan and Frieda (Kaplan) Waks; in Austr since 1932; att HS, Bialystock, Pol; m. Leo Fink, Sep 20, 1932; c: Freda Freiberg, Nathan. Pres, Natl Council J Women, Austr, since 1967; dir, Austr J Wfr and Relief Soc; pres: ladies group, United J Overseas Relief Fund, 1945-47; Victorian Natl Council J Women, 1958-60; dir, UJORF, 1943-47. Home: 516 Toorak Rd, Toorak, Vic, Austr. Office: 466 Punt Rd, S Yarra, Melbourne, Austr.

FINK Morton Joel, US, business exec; b. Bklyn, NY, Nov 5, 1933; s. William and Estelle (Hahn); BA, NYU, 1955; m. Barbara Schop, June 24, 1956; c: Lisa, Dana. Pres, TV Presentations Inc, since 1958; vice pres, Sterling Communications, mem bd dir; asst mgr, network film prog dept, ABC TV, 1955-57. Pvt, US Army Signal Corps, 1957-58. Hobbies: gold, swimming, photography. Home: 224-77 76 Rd, Bayside, NY. Office: 375 Park Ave, New York, NY.

FINK, Paulette W, US, communal leader; b. Mulhouse, Fr, Oct 22, 1911; d. Jean and Blance (Salomon) Weill; in US since 1946; certs: Sorbonne, 1930; Coll de Fr, 1931; m. Yves Oppert (decd); c: Nadine Harris, Francelyne Lurie; m. 2nd, Israel Fink, Sep 14, 1954. Natl chmn, women's div, UJA, since 1960, mem, men's exec comm, since 1960; speaker for UJA and JDC, 1946-54; org Children's Home, Fr, 1944-46; Red Cross war nurse, 1939-41; mem, bd: Hadassah; Minneapolis Fed for J Services; State of Isr Bonds; Hillel Found; fmr Brandeis U; Temple Isr; clubs: Oak Ridge Country; Standard. Recipient, awards: Minneapolis Fed for J Services; State of Isr Bonds; UJA; Eleanore Roosevelt Humanity. Hobbies: music; gardening; fencing. Home: 3716 Washburn Ave S, Minneapolis, Minn.

FINK, Sol P, US, investment counsel; b. NYC, Mar 2, 1898; s. Henry and Pesha (Golomb); m. Betty LeKashman, Feb 1, 1922; c: Carol Richman, Nancy Baer. Ret, 1958; vice-pres, Major Press, Inc, 1920-30; asso, Hirsch and Co, mem NY Stock Exch, 1930-49, invest counsel, 1930-58; vice-pres, dir, Merritt-Chapmen & Scott, 1949-52; dir, Omnibus Corp, 1950-51. US Cavalry, 1912-15; capt, US Army, WW I, col, Signal corps, WW II; commandant, US Army Eur Signal Sch, 1952-55. Mem: Mil Order of WW, 40 and 8; Grand St Boys, Res Off's, Fgn Policy Assns; Acad, Political Sci; Soc Amer Wars; Amer Natl Theatre Acad; Masons; Shriner; B'nai B'rith; ACLU. Recipient: Legion of Merit, 1946; Commendation Medal, War Dept, 1946. Home: River Rd, Essex, Conn.

FINKEL, Herman Jacob, Isr, agricultural engr; b. Chgo, Ill, Mar 9, 1918; s. Morris and Henrietta (Israelson); in Isr since 1949; BS, U of Ill, 1940; MSc, Technion, 1960; PhD, Heb U, 1957; m. Jeannette Galler, June 20, 1941; c: Moshe, Aliza. Prof, agric engr, Technion, since 1959; head, dept of agric engr, 1959-1963; dairy farm insp, Health Dept, St Louis, Mo, 1941-42; CE, US Army Engrs, Gt Lakes dir, Chgo, 1942-43; agric engr, US Soil Conservation Service, Canastota, NY, 1943-46; structural engr: Consoer, Townsend and Assos, Chgo, 1946-47; Ford, Bacon and Davis, Chgo, 1947; Schmidt, Garden and Erikson, Chgo, 1947-49; chief engr, Soil Conservation Service, Isr Min of Agric, 1949-52; Missions Isr Govt, UNESCO in many countries; adviser, UN committees. Contbr to professional and govt publs. Home: 42 Einstein St, Haifa, Isr. Office: Technion, Haifa, Isr.

FINKEL, Irving, US, manufacturer; b. Vilna, Lith, Sep 3, 1894; s. Max and Gittel (Frankel); in US since 1913; BS, CE, Cooper Union, NY; widower; c: Sheila Walterbaum, Leonard. Pres, Ladies Intimate Wear Concern, since 1927; fmr civil engr. Pres, Bitzaron, Heb monthly; dir, UJA; chmn bd educ, Ezra Acad, Bklyn; mem: bd trustees, Temple Beth El, Manhattan; Manhattan Beach J Cen; natl exec, ZOA; B'nai B'rith; Bklyn region, ZOA; fmr: dir, JNF; pres, Manhattan Beach ZOA. Author: Verdant Melody, Heb poems, 1967; contbr: poems to press in US, Isr; essays to various jours. Recipient, UJA, ZOA awards. Spec interests: poetry; music; Heb culture. Home: 286 Coleridge St, Brooklyn, NY. Office: 38 E 30 St, New York, NY.

FINKEL, Shimon, Isr, actor, theatrical dir; b. Grodno, Russ, Dec 8, 1905; s. Zvi and Chaia (Shapiro); in Isr since 1924; att Max Reinhardt Dramatic Sch, Berlin; m. Monika (decd); c: Marta Avinoam. Mem: Habimah Theatre since 1927; Tai Theatre, 1922-27; dir, Habimah Theatre: On the Plains of the Negev; Ghosts; Day and Night; actor, maj roles: Süss, Jew Süss; Mannheim, Professor Mannheim; Shylock, Mer-

chant of Venice; Gessler, William Tell; Reubeni, Reubeni, Prince of Jews; Raskolnikoff, Crime and Punishment; Tuvia, Tuvia the Milkman; Hippolyte, Phaedra; Hamlet, Hamlet; Oswald, Ghosts; Oedipus Rex; Iago, Othello; The Father; Peer Gynt; Ceaser, Ceaser and Cleopatra; King Lear; Henry IV; Pirandello; Otto Frank, Diary of Anne Frank; Cornelius Melody, The Touch of the Poet; Pius II, The Deputy; Nathan, Nathan the Wise; Edgar, The Dance of Death. Author, On Stage & Backstage, 1968. Recipient, Prizes: JA, for Hamlet, 1946; Tel Aviv Munic, for King Lear, 1956; Menachem Gnessin, for Melody in Touch of the Poet; Isr for Achievements, 1969. Home: 28 Dov Hoz St, Tel Aviv, Isr. Office: Habimah Theatre, Tel Aviv, Isr.

FINKELSTEIN, Chaim, Isr, educator, organization exec, author; b. Brisk, Pol, May 5, 1911; s. Aharon and Rahel; in Isr since 1968; m. c: Daniel, Gita Monash, Rahel. Mem exec, head, dept for educ and culture in diaspora, JA since 1968; fmr: initiator, found, gen pedg dir, network of educ insts named after Shalom Aleichem, until 1968. Chmn, pedg council, J Educ Comm, Arg; active in Zionist Movement, Arg, secy gen, Achdut Ha'avoda Poalei Zion, Arg; delg, ZC's since 1946; mem, Zionist Gen Council, since 1951. Author: Vizie, Vort un Var; numerous articles, pamphlets, on educ, Zionist lit, gen J topics. Home: 17 Jabotinsky St, Jerusalem, Isr. Office: FOB 92, Jerusalem, Isr.

FINKELSTEIN, David, US, physicist, educator; b. Bklyn, NY, July 19, 1929; s. I idor and Ester (Rubenstein); BS, CCNY, 1949; PhD, MIT, 1953; Ford F, Cern, Geneva, 1958-59; m. Helene Cooper, 1949; c: Daniel, Beth, Eve. Prof, physics, Yeshiva U since 1964, on fac since 1960; asst prof, Stevens Inst, 1955-57, asso prof, 1957-60. Contbr papers on gen relativity, quantum mech, plasmas, high-energy particle accelerators. Home: 333 Liberty Rd, Teaneck, NJ. Office: Yeshiva U, New York, NY.

FINKELSTEIN, Isaac Nathan, Eng, business exec; b. Piotrkow, Tryb, Pol, Jan 20, 1914; s. Leib and Baila (Gold); in Eng since 1945; att J Gymnasium, Piotrkow, 1924-31; m. Gertrude Weinstein, Mar 16, 1947; c: Lionel, Anita. Mgn dir, Bautricht Ltd, since 1961; Conworth Inves, since 1963; Tempo Furniture. War prisoner, Piotrkow, Bugaj, Buchenwald, Coldida, Theresienstadt, 1939-45, org transp young children under UNRRA and J Ref Orgs to Eng. Chmn, JNF Stanmore, Middlesex; vice-pres, 45 Aid Soc; mem, Local Bldg Fund, Blue and White Comm; brochure chmn, Kingsbury JNF Comm, 1956-64; CBF; JPA. Spec interest: Isr and local charities. Home: 10 Bowls Close, Stanmore, Middlesex, Eng. Office: 3/4 Varley Parade, Edgware Road, London, NW9, Eng.

FINKELSTEIN, Jacob J, US, orientalist, educator; b. Bklyn, NY, Mar 22, 1922; s. Morris and Augusta (Liebhart); BA, Bklyn Coll, 1948; PhD, U of Pa, 1953; m. Dorothee Metlitsky, 1956. William M Laffan Prof, Assyriology, Babylonian lit, Yale U, since 1965, research asst, Assyriology, 1953-55; Guggenheim f, 1955; prof, U of Cal, Berkeley, 1964-65; chmn, dept of Near E Langs, 1961-65, on fac since 1956. USAAF, 1942-46. Mem: Amer Oriental Soc; Amer Sch of Oriental Research. Co-author: The Sultantepe Tablets I, 1957; asso ed, Jour of Amer Oriental Soc, 1961-64; contbr in fields of Mesopotamian texts, law and hist. Office: Hall of Grad Studies, Yale U, New Haven, Conn.

FINKELSTEIN, Jerry, US, public relations counsel; b. NYC, Jan 26, 1916; s. Albert and Ethel (Kaufman); LLB, NY Law Sch, 1936; m. Shirley Marks, Mar 18, 1942; c: Andrew, James. Found, publisher, Civil Service Leader, since 1939; pres chmn bd, Struthers Wells Corp; chmn bd: Struthers Sci and Intl; NY Law Publ, Sci and Govt Publs, dir, Commercial Bank N Amer, staff, spec prosecutor, Thomas E Dewey, 1935-36; reporter, civil service ed, NY Mirror, 1937-39; mem: State Bd of Regents, 1941; research dir, NY State Sen, 1938-41; chmn, planning commn, city planning dept, NYC, 1950-51. USCG, 1943-45. Trustee, NY Law Sch; bd overseers, JTSA; chmn, fine arts gift comm, Natl Cultural Cen; mem: AJComm; Soc Silurians; Newspaper Reporters Assn; clubs: Natl Dem; Overseas Press; Advt. Recipient: Decorated Knight, Order of Merit, It, 1958. Home: 812 Park Ave, New York, NY. Office: 630 Fifth Ave, New York, NY.

FINKELSTEIN, Lawrence S, US, educator; b. NYC, Mar 11, 1925; s. Frank and Sylvia (Lemkin); BA, Columbia U, 1944, MA, 1947; m. Marina Salvin, Aug 4, 1951; c: Susan. Secy, Cen for Intl Affairs, Harvard U, since 1969; acting dean,

Grad Sch of Arts and Sci, Brandeis U, Waltham, Mass 1967-69; Dep Asst Secy of Defense for intl security affairs, dir, 1965-66; Case-W Reserve U Study, 1966-67; vice-pres, Carnagie Endowment for Intl Peace, 1959-65, project dir, dir of studies, 1952-62; div asst, Div of Dependent Areas Affairs, State Dept, 1944-46; political affairs analyst, Trusteeship Div, UN Secretariat, 1946-47; research asst, lectr in govt, Columbia U, 1947-49; mem staff, Council on Fgn Relations, 1949-50. F, Social Sci Research Council; mem: Inst for Strategic Studies, London; Intl Studies Assn; Amer Political Sci Assn; Amer Soc Intl Law. Author: US Policy Toward SE Asia, 1951; Arms Inspection, 1962; co-author, Collective Security, 1965; bd eds, International Organization; contbr articles to publs. Home: 4 Upland Rd, Lexington, Mass. Office: Brandeis U, Waltham, Mass.

FINKELSTEIN, Louis, US, rabbi, educator, religious leader; b. Cincinnati, O, June 14, 1895; s. Simon and Hannah (Brager); AB, CCNY, 1915, PhD, Columbia U, 1918, rabbi, JTSA, 1919; hon deg: STD, Columbia U, 1944; DL, Boston U, 1950; DHL, Dropsie 1961; MIT, 1966; HUC, 1968; D Laws: Temple, 1963; Manhattan, 1965; Fordham, 1966; STD, NYU, 1967; m. Carmel Bentwich, Mar 5, 1922; c: Hadassah Davis, Ezra, Faith Katzenstein. Chancellor, JTSA, since 1951, on fac since 1931; pres: Inst for Rel and Social Studies; dir: Conf on Sci, Phil and Rel, since 1939; rabbi, Cong Kehilath Isr, NYC, 1919-31. Ambass to papl coronation, 1963; mem, exec council: RA, pres, 1928-30; United Syn of Amer; Syn Council of Amer; JDC; bd trustees, NCCJ; bd dir, Amer Friends Hebrew U, adv bd, Inst for Advancement of Cultural and Spiritual Values; appd by Pres Roosevelt to succeed Cyrus Adler, as repr of Judaism to advise the Pres on steps for world peace, 1940; f, and vice-pres, J Acad Arts and Sci; f: Amer Acad for J Research, fmr pres; Amer Acad Arts and Sci; hon vice-chmn, Amer Tercentenary Comm; alumnus mem, Phi Beta Kappa. Author: Jewish Self-Government in the Middle Ages, 1924; The Development of the Amidah, 1925; The Pharisees, Their Origin and Their Philosophy, 1925; Prolegamena to the Edition of the Sifre, 1932; The Mekilta and Its Texts, 1934; Maimonides and Tannaitic Midrashim, 1935; Akiba, Scholar, Saint, Martyr, 1936; Tradition in the Making, 1937; The Pharisees: The Sociological Background of Their Faith, 1938, 1963; Beliefs and Practices of Judaism, 1941; Pre-Maccabean Documents in the Passover Haggadah, 1943; co-author: Religions of Democracy, 1941; Faith for Today, 1941; ed: Kimchi's Commentary on Isaiah, 1926; The Sifre on Deuteronomy, 1935, 1936; Rab Saadia Gaon: Studies in his Honor, 1944; The Jews: Their History, Culture and Religion, 1949-60; Abot of Rabbi Nathan, 1950; co-ed, Science, Philosophy and Religion, symposia, 1942-62; vice-pres, mem, ed bd, Universal Jewish Encyclopedia; contbr to theol and phil jours. Recipient: Townsend Harris Medal, 1940; natl service award, Phi Epsilon Pi, 1952. Home: 340 Riverside Dr, NYC. Office: 3080 Broadway, NYC.

FINKELSTEIN, Michael, Isr, endocrinologist, educator; b. Sosnowiec, Pol, Dec 15, 1916; s. Eliezer and Bela (Zmigrod); in Isr since 1934; PhD, Heb U, Jerusalem, 1946; m. Nehama Gilmovsky, Mar 27, 1947; c: Elazar, Elona. Prof, endocrinology, Hadassah Med Sch, Jerusalem, since 1967, head, endocrinology dept, since 1962. Haganah, dep cdr, Mt Scopus, 1947-48. Prin contribs: clarification of biochem defects in congenital sexual anomalies in man; regulation of human reproduction. Mem, several med socs. Author: Research on Steroids, 1968; contbr numerous sci papers to profsl jours. Recipient: Henrietta Szold Prize, Tel Aviv Munic, 1961. Home: 36 Hapalmach St, Jerusalem, Isr. Office: Hebrew U, Hadassah Med Sch, Jerusalem, Isr.

FINKELSTEIN, Nisson Ascher, US, business exec; b. Milton, Mass, June 11, 1925; s. Benjamin and Tena (Kadetsky); AB, Harvard U, 1945; PhD, MIT, 1949; m. Rona Glassman, Sep 3, 1950; c: Jesse, Adam, Loren, Andrew. Pres, ILC Ind, since 1966; vice-pres, resources and devl, Glen Alden Corp since 1968; dir, resources and devl, Bausch and Lomb, 1950-59; vice-pres, resources and engr, Gen Dynamics, 1959-64; vice-pres, Intl Latex, 1964-66. Co-chmn, NCCJ, cen Del; adv council, mem, Gov of Del; chmn, Kent Co Theater Guild; fmr chmn, J Fed of Del campaign; mem: AAAS; Inst of Elec and Electronic Engrs; Amer Phys Soc; Amer Optical Soc; Amer Acoustical Soc; clubs: Cosmos, Wash, DC; Harvard, NYC. Contbr to sci jours and periodicals. Home: Fox Hall Dr, Dover, Del. Office: 350 Pear St, Dover, Del.

FINKELSTEIN, Reuben, US, physician; b. Kaunas, Lith, Sep

13, 1883; s. Simon and Hannah (Brager); in US since 1886; MD, LI Coll Hosp, 1906; m. Mayne Manischewitz, Oct 28, 1909 (decd); c: Leonard (decd), Dorothy Cohen, Bertrand, Natalie Bronster. Cons: med, Metrop J Geriatric Cen, since 1955; gastroenterologist: Kingsbrock J Med Cen, since 1936; Brookdale Hosp Cen, since 1949; post-grad work, Harvard U Med Sch, 1915; internal med, Charité Hosp, Berlin, 1922. F: life: Amer Coll of Phys; AMA; Natl Gastroenterological Assn; Amer Geriatrics Soc; mem: Kings Co Med Soc; Bklyn Acad of Med; E NY Med Soc, pres, 1922; Bedford Med Soc, pres, 1926; NY State Med Soc; Bklyn Soc of Internal Med; NY Gastroenterological Assn; IMA; Amer Bd of Internal Med; mem, OPA, Bklyn, 1942-45; hon chmn, Bklyn Phys comm, UJA, since 1945; trustee, Bklyn J Cen, a found, 1918; mem, ZOA, pres, Brownsville chap, 1904-08; Masons, Fortitude Lodge, No. 14; Cong Ohave Sholom; club, Phys, Sq, Bklyn. Contbr to med jours. Home and office: 41 Eastern Pkwy, Brooklyn, NY.

FINKELSTEIN, Sidney W, US, author, art critic; b. Bklyn, NY, July 4, 1909; s. Harold and Bessie (Liberchein); BA, CCNY, 1929; MA, Eng lit, Columbia U, 1932; MA, hist of art, NYU, 1955. Author: Art and Society, 1949, trans into Heb; Jazz: A People's Music, 1950; How Music Expresses Ideas, 1952; Charles White—American Artist, 1954; Realism and Art, 1954; Composer and Nation, 1960; Existentialism and Alienation in American Literature, 1965; Sense and Nonsense of McLuhan, 1968; contbr to: American Dialogue; Mainstream; Massachusetts Review; Problems of Philosophy, USSR. US Army, 1942-45. Home: 522 Stanford Rd, Brooklyn, NY.

FINKLE, Joseph M, US, advertising exec; b. Providence, RI, July 8, 1902; s. Morris and Etta (Epstein); BAcc, Bryant Coll, 1922; m. Esther Bass, Aug 1, 1937; c: Karen. Partner, Joseph Maxfield Co, since 1937. Pres, Comm on Minoity Housing, since 1966; mem: Providence Hum Relations Commn, since 1967; pres, dist grand lodge, B'nai B'rith, 1955-56; chmn, NE ADL, 1956-57; bd trustees: Miriam Hosp; Temple Beth El; J Bur of Educ; Gen J Comm; NCCJ. Home: 51 Savoy St, Providence, RI. Office: 144 Westminster St, Providence, RI.

FINKLER, Rita S, US, endocrinologist; b. Kherson, Russ, Nov 1, 1888; d. Wolf and Sara (Hoppner); in US since 1919; att Law Sch, U St Petersburg, Russ, 1909; MD, Women's Med Coll of Pa, 1915; m. Samuel Finkler, 1913 (decd); c: Sylvia Becker. Chief em, dept endocrinology, Newark Beth Isr Hosp, since 1950, with dept since 1934; pvt and hosp practice since 1919; lectr. Chmn, Isr Bonds, Essex Co Med Soc; co-chmn, UJA; mem: AMA; NJ State Med Soc; Acad of Med, N NJ; Endocrine Soc; Amer Soc for Study of Sterility; AJCong; Hadassah; Pioneer Women; f comm, Amer Phys, IMA. Contbr to med and sci publs. Home: 26 Troy Dr, Short Hills, NJ. Office: 116 Millburn Ave, Millburn, NJ.

FINN, David, US, public relations counselor; b. NYC, Aug 30, 1921; s. Jonathan and Bessie (Borgenicht); att CCNY; m. Laura Zeisler; c: Kathy, Dena, Peter, Amy. Chmn bd, Ruder and Finn Inc, since 1948. Lt, USAF. Chmn bd, The J Mus; treas, MacDowell Colony; adv bd, Council for Study of Mankind; trustee: JTSA; City of Hope; Amer Friends Heb U; grad adv bd, CCNY; adv comm, NYC Off of Cultural Affairs; Manpower Opportunities in Isr. Author: Public Relations and Management, 1960; The Corporate Oligarch, 1969. Hobbies: sculpture, painting. Home: 90 Wellington Ave, New Rochelle, NY. Office: 110 E 59 St, New York, NY.

FINN, Samuel L, US, attorney; b. NYC, June 3, 1890; s. Samuel and Ida (Schwartz); admitted to O bar, 1914; att U of Dayton, 1920-22, hon DHum, 1957; m. Lillian Evans, Sep 15, 1917; c: Chester, Celeste Klein. Sr partner, Eastbrook, Finn & McKee, since 1940, with firm since 1920; pres: Chester Inves Co; Ludlow Realty, vice-pres, dir: Mercer Foundry, Natl Foundry & Furnace; Victor Realty; secy, dir: Grays Realty; Burton Sanfort Inves. Adv bd for registrants, US Selective Service Sys, WW II. Pres: Educ and Musical Arts, Inc, since 1947; lay bd, U Dayton, bd trustees, since 1942; exec, Dayton Found, since 1947; dir: C of C; ARC, Art Inst since 1942, all Dayton; mem: Amer Council of Judaism; NCCJ, mem, bd trustees, Dayton chap; Dayton, O State and Amer Bar Assns; Temple Isr, Dayton; KP, Masons; YMCA; Newcomen Soc of US; Pres's Adv Council of Brandeis U; AJComm; clubs: Meadowbrook Country, past pres; Discussion, past pres; Bicycle, Queen City, Cincinnati; Stroop Trout, Towne, Dayton. Recipient: cert of appreciation, Pres F D Roosevelt.

Home: 1200 Amherst Pl, Dayton, O. Office: Hulman Bldg, Second and Ludlow Sts, Dayton, O.

FIORENTINO, Emmanuel Henri, Isr, journalist; b. Tunis, July 9, 1913; s. Yehouda and Clotilde (Nunez); in Isr since 1953; m. Gilda, June 12, 1942; c: Rina Meiraz, Yehouda. Journalist since 1938. Vice pres, Immigrants from N Afr Org, Isr; mem, Isr ZC; fmr secy, Tunisian ZF. Home: 10 Noah St, Ramat Aviv, Isr. Office: 57 Harakevet St, Tel Aviv, Isr.

FIRESTONE, Milton M, US, editor; b. NYC, June 8, 1927; s. Louis and Anna (Fleiderbaum); att Kan City Jr Coll, 1943-44; BEcon, U Kan, 1946; m. Bea Blumenthal, May 30, 1954; c: David, Michael, Judith. Ed, publisher, J Newspaper; comptroller, Columbia Glass Co, 1953-63. US Army, 1950-52. Treas, Amer J Press Assn, fmr vice-pres; org, found, bd dir: Heb Acad of Gtr Kan City; Beth Shalom Syn, Kan City; mem: B'nai B'rith; World Fed J Journalists, Jerusalem; Phi Beta Kappa; Pi Sigma Alpha; fmr, J Students Union, Kan City. Recipient: Comty Service Award, Heart of Amer B'nai B'rith Lodge, 1964; Man of Year, Heart of Amer chap, B'nai B'rith Women, 1965. Hobbies: geog, photography. Home: 711 E 80 St, Kansas City, Mo. Office: POB 8709, Kansas City, Mo.

FIRST, Joseph M, US, attorney, business exec; b. Phila, Pa, Apr 1, 1906; s. Louis and Sarah (Selig); BS, Wharton Sch, U of Pa, 1927; LLB, U of Pa, 1930, LLM, 1932; m. Helen Gross, Dec 27, 1931; c: Elsa, Abigail, Jonathan. Vicepres, secy, Triangle Publs, since 1940; bd mem, Cen Penn Natl Bank, Phila. First pres, hon pres, bd dir, Albert Einstein Med Cen; pres, J Publ Soc; trustee, Temple U; vice-pres, secy, Annenberg Sch of Communications; secy, treas, Annenberg Fund, Inc; vice-pres, secy: Annenberg Found; Phila Inquirer Charities; mem: Merion Civic Assn; FJP of Phila; Amer Friends Heb U and Technion, Phila chap; Brandeis Lawyers Soc; bd, Cen Penn Natl Bank of Phila; adv bd, State of Pa, Liberty Mutual Ins; Soc TV Pioneers; Scribes; Phila, Pa, Amer Bar Assns; Amer Newspaper Pubs Assn; natl panel of arbitrators, Amer Arbitration Assn; bd trustees, Dropsie Coll; life trustee, Har Zion Temple; legal asst, Amer Law Inst; Order of Coif; Gowen F; fmr: chemn publs comm, Pa Bar Assn; pres, Wharton Sch Alumni Soc. Case ed, U Pa Law Rev; ed em, Pa Bar Assn Quarterly. Recipient: U Pa Alumni Award of Merit, 1958; McKean Law Club, U Pa, Outstanding Almms Award, 1959; Pa Bar Assn Dist Service Award, 1961. Pa Bar Assn Spec Citation, 1968. Home: 230 Orchard Way, Merion Station, Pa. Office: 400 N Broad St, Philadelphia, Pa.

FIRSTENBERG, Harold S, US, business exec; b. Bx, NY, May 20, 1914; s. Louis and Anna (Siegel); att U of Ga, 1932-33; NYU, 1933-34; m. Lillian Cohen, Aug 16, 1939; c: Beverly, Barbara. Pres, Machinery and Equipment Co Inc, since 1938; found, Ind Machinery, Winston Salem, NC, 1935-37. Bd dirs, Peninsula J Comty Cen, pres, 1947-48; Temple Beth Jacob; pres, Peninsula and Redwood B'nai B'rith, 1945; mem, Cen Cal Conf, B'nai B'rith, pres, 1949; Peninsula Coord Comm, pres, 1946; ZOA; AJComm; Hillel Assoc; US, Cal and SF C of C. Hobbies: photography, sports. Spec interest, fraternal club work. Home: 90 Melrose Place, Redwood City, Cal. Office: PO Box 3132, San Francisco, Cal.

FISCH, Harold, Isr, educator; b. Birmingham, Eng, Mar 25, 1923; s. Solomon and Rebecca (Swift); in Isr, since 1957; BA, hons, Sheffield U, 1946; DLitt, Oxford U, 1948; m. Frances Roston, Aug 26, 1947; c: Malcolm, David, Brian, Shifra, Eliezer. Repr J cons in US, Bar Ilan U, since 1971, rector, 1968-71, prof, Eng, since 1964; on fac since 1957; visiting prof, U of Md, since 1971; lectr, Harvard, Brown, Ind U, since 1971; lectr, U of Leeds, 1947-57; visiting prof: Brown, RI U, 1965. Author: The Dual Image, 1959; Jerusalem and Albion, 1964; co-ed, Mans Mortalities, 1968; trans: Haggada, Eng, 1965; The Five Books of the Tora and the Haftarot, 1967. Fmr chmn, Intl U J Fed, Gt Brit, Ir; mem: natl exec, Isr Amer Soc; Land of Isr Movement. Hobby: Bible trans. Home: 18 Sokolow St, Petah Tikva, Isr. Office: Bar Ilan U, Ramat Gan, Isr.

FISCHEL, Edward E, US, physician; b. NYC, July 29, 1920; s. Joseph and Liza (Herman); BA, Columbia U, 1941, MD, Coll Phys and Surgs, 1944, ScD Med, 1948; m. Pauline Dunieff, Dec 26, 1943; c: Robert, Janet. Dir, dept med: Bx Leb Hosp Cen, since 1962; asso clinical prof, med, Albert Einstein Coll Med, since 1957; res, Presbyterian Hosp, 1945-47; asso in med, Columbia U, 1950-55; cons, USPHS;

f: NY Acad Med, fmr chmn, sect on microbiol; AAAS, council mem; dipl, Amer Bd Internal Med; FACP; fmr pres, sect of Arthritis Found, Amer Rheumatic Assn; mem: research comm, Amer Council on Rheumatic Fever and Cogenital Heart Disease; AMA; AHA; Amer Soc for Clinical Inves; Soc of Experimental Biol and Med; Amer Assn Immunologists; NY Rheumatism Assn, past pres; Harvey Soc. Contbr to med jours. Home: 337 Engle St, Tenafly, NY. Office: Bx Leb, Hosp Cen, 1276 Fulton Ave, Bronx. NY.

FISCHEL, Henry (Heinz) Albert, US, educator; b. Bonn, Ger, Nov 20, 1913; s. Adolf and Anna (Suessengut); in US since 1948; ordained rabbi, Hochschule fd Wissenschaft des Judentums, Berlin, 1939; PhD, U Edinburgh, 1944; m. Sylvia Morris, 1949. Prof, Near E Studies, Ind U, since 1964, fac mem, since 1961; educ and rabb positions, Can, 1943-48; fmr lectr, hist, ling, rel, U of Ala; dir, Hillel, rabbi, Temple Emanuel, Tuscalosa, Ala, 1948-56; dir, Pittsburgh Dist, Hillel, 1956-58; asst prof, Brandeis U, 1958-61. Pres: Soc Bibl Lit and Exegesis, Can Sect, 1947-48; Dominion Council, Can J Cong, 1944-47; natl prog chmn, Judaism, Amer Acad of Rel; MLA; natl bd, Coll Entrance Exams, since 1959; Amer Acad J Research; Amer Oriental Soc; B'nai B'rith; Isr Hist Soc; Natl Assn Profs, Heb; Conf J Soc Studies; World Union J Studies; Ling Soc of Amer; Assn Profs Judaica. Author: First Book of Maccabees, 1948; Diaspora 1963; Cynicism and the Ancient Near East, 1969; contbr articles on Bibl Hellenism, J hist and lit. Recipient: Herman Vogelstein Award, 1938; Nathanson Scholarship, 1942-43. Research Grants: Carnegie, Ford Found, 1963-65; Guggenheim F, 1969-70. Home: 1512 Clifton Ave, Bloomington, Ind. Office: Ind U, Bloomington, Ind.

FISCHEL, Otto, Eng, business exec; b. Mor Ostrava, Czech, Nov 25, 1914; s. Jacob and Frieda (Stark); in Eng since 1939; m. Katerina Strenitz, Apr 29, 1943; c: Lucy. Co dir since 1952. Vice chmn, Council of J from Czech in Gt Brit; fmr leader, Herzlia Youth Group, London. Home: 34 Clairemont Pk, London N7, Eng. Office: 18 Market Rd, London N3, Eng.

FISCHEL, Walter J, US, orientalist, educator, author; b. Frankfurt/M Ger, Nov 12, 1902; s. Hugo and Zerline (Kahn); D Rer Pol, U Frankfurt, 1924; PhD, U Giessen, 1925; m. Irene Markrich, June 13, 1954; c: Corinne. Prof, Semitic langs and lit, U of Cal, Berkeley, since 1945, chmn, dept of Near E langs, 1948-58, chmn ed bd, publs in Semitic philol since 1949; fac mem, Sch of Oriental Studies, Heb U, Jerusalem, 1926-45; sci expeditions to ME countries including: Turkey, Iraq, Kurdistan, Persia; delg, Intl Orientalists Congs. Pres, Pacific Coast Sect, Soc of Bibl Lit and Exegesis, 1949-1; 5 mem exec comm, w br, Amer Oriental Soc, 1951-53; f: Royal Asiatic Soc, Gt Brit; Amer Acad for J Research. Author: Bibliography of the Publications of Joseph Horowitz, 1930; The Origin of Banking in Medieval Islam, 1933; The History of the Marrano Community in Persia, 1936; Jews in Medieval Islam, 1937; 2nd, ed, 1968. The Karimi Merchants, 1937, 1960; A Journey to Kurdistan, Persia and Babylon, 1940; The Jews of Kurdistan, 1944; Khorasan in Medieval Hebrew and Islamic Literature, 1945; The Jews under the Qajar Dynasty, 1949; Jews and Judaism at the Court of the Moghul Emperors in India, 1950; Semitic and Oriental Studies, 1951; Ibn Khaldun's Activities in Egypt, 1951; The Bible in Persian Translation, 1952; Ibn Khaldun and Tamerlane, Their Historic Meeting in Damascus in 1401, publ 1952; Isfahan, 1953; Azerbaijan in Jewish History, 1953; Jews of Bukhara, 1953; The Newly Discovered Hebrew Scrolls, 1953; Ibn Khaldun and Josippon, 1954; Ibn Khalduniana (Bibliography), 1954; The Jews of India, Their Contribution to the Economic and Poitical Life (Jerusalem), 1960; Israel in Iran, 1960; Cochin in Jewish History, 1962; Early Zionism in India, 1963; Mulla Ibrahm Nathan, 1958; The Jewish Merchant-Colony in Madras /1960; A Jewish Merchant House in Bengal, 1964; William Popper—His Contribution to Islamic Scholarship, 1964; From Cochin to New York, 1965; The Immigration of "Arabian" Jews to India in the Eighteenth Century, 1965; The Rediscovery of the Jewish Community at Firuzkuh, 1965-66; The Indian Archives, 1967; Ibn Khaldun and Tamerlane, The Rotenburg Family in Dutch Cochin, 1967; The Jewish Merchant: 1765-1791, pub, 1967; The Exploration of the Jewish Antiquities in Cochin 1967; Ibn Khaldun in Egypt, 1967; The Haggadah of the Bene Israel of India, 1968; trans: Die Pharisaer by R Travers-Herford into Ger; Jesus von Nazareth by Jospeh Klausner, into Ger; contbr to: Ency Hebraica; Universal J Ency; profsl jours. Recipient: Guggenheim f for research on the hist of the J in Asia 1959-60; Fulbright award, both 1963-64. Home: 2954 Russell St, Berkeley, Cal. Office: U of Cal, Berkeley, Cal.

FISCHER, Eric, US, geographer, educator, author: b. Vienna, Aus, Jan 13, 1898; s. Max and Olga (Pollaczek); in US since 1941; PhD, U Vienna, 1921; m. Irene Kaminka, Dec 21, 1930; c: Gay, Michael. Ret: sr researcher, Army Map Service, 1951-65; lectr, George Wash U, since 1952; prof, Coppin State Coll, 1965-68; prof, Aus, 1925-28; instr, Bard Coll, 1943-44; researcher, Off of Strategic Services, US Dept of State, 1944-47; lectr, U of Va, 1947-50; prof, NYU, 1950-51. Aus Army, WW I. Author: A Question of Place, The Development of Geographic Thought, 1967, 1969; The Passing of the European Age, 1943, 1947; co-author: Karl Glave-Kolbielski, Ein Politischer Abendteureer, 1937; German and English Glossary of Geographic Terms, 1949; A Geography of Europe, 1957, 1962; Principles of Political Geography, 1958; contbr to profsl jours. Mem: Amer Geographical Soc; Assn of Amer Geographers; Amer Hist Assn; Amer J Hist Soc; Wiener geographische Gesellschaft. Home: 301 Philadelphia Ave., Takoma Park, Md.

FISCHER, Eva, Belgium, communal leader; b. Antwerpen, Belgium, Sep 2, 1895; d. Abraham and Toba (Weinberg) Goldstein; att Coll, Antwerpen; m. Maximilaan Fischer(decd), June 19, 1919; c: Thea Zucker, Bernard. Pres, WIZO, Belgium-Luxembourg, since 1946; mem, World WIZO Exec, since 1951, hon life mem since 1966; fmr: pres, Union des Femmes Juives; Oeuvre Nationale de l'Enfance. Mem, B'nai B'rith, 770 Mentor. Home: 32, Charlottelai, Antwerpen, Belgium.

FISCHER, Golda (Joslyn), US, pediatrician, educator; b. Pol, Mar 28, 1913; d. Joel and Esther(Srzelisker); in US since 1940; MD, Med Coll of State of SC, 1943; m. Maynard Joslyn, Apr 19, 1947. Pvt practice; ped, Alameda Co Hosps, since 1960; mem staff: Children's Hosp, since 1945; Children's Hosp, E Bay, since 1947; Berkeley Gen Hosp, since 1947, all SF Bay Area; prof, food tech, U of Cal, Berkeley; mem staff, Maternal and Child Wfr Clinic, 1946-48; res: Babies Hosp, Phila, 1944; Queens Gen Hosp, NY, 1945; chief res, Children's Hosp, SF, 1946-47. Life mem: Hadassah, fmr educ chmn, Berkeley chap; Pioneer Women; hon mem, Women's Med Assn of Isr; corresp mem, IMA; mem: bd, Amer Phys F, IMA, exec bd, life mem since 1966; fmr: active: ZOA; Women's Drs Assn in Isr; Young WIZO, Vienna, 1931-38, Cardiff, Wales, 1938-40. Contbr articles on Judaism and Isr to J periodicals, med jours. Home: 1317 Spruce St, Berkeley, Cal.

FISCHER, Irene K, US, geodesist; b. Vienna, Aus, July 27, 1907; d. Aharon and Clara (Loewi) Kaminka; in US since 1941; att Inst of Tech, 1927-29; MA, U Vienna, 1931; m. Eric Fischer, Dec 1930; c: Gay, Michael. Chief, geoid br, Army Map Service, since 1961; geodesist, since 1952. Mem: Amer Geophys Union; Intl Union for Geodesy and Geophys; contbr to profsl jours. Recipient: Medals: Army Meritorious Civilian Service; Research and Devl Achievement; Awards: Exceptional Civilian Service; Dist Civilian Service, Dept of Defense. Home: 301 Philadelphia Ave, Takoma Park, Md. Office: c/o Topographic Command, 6500 Brooks Lane, Washington, DC.

FISCHER, Leo G, Den, attorney; b. Copenhagen, Den, Sep 5, 1902; s. Josef and Paula (Eichel); law deg, U Copenhagen, 1926; m. Anna Lion, 1939. Pvt practice since 1931; mem, bd dirs, bus enterprises. Chmn bd, J Comty, Copenhagen, since 1964, mem bd, since 1956, mem, bd delgs, 1936-40, 1948-56, vice chmn, 1948-56; chmn bd, J Old People's Home; mem, Danish comm, ORT; pres, Den Lodge, B'nai B'rith; vice pres, Dist Grand Lodge of Eur; active, Danish and Scandinavian Youth Fed. Home: Worsaaesvej 24, Copenhagen, Den. Office: Gothersgade 109, Copenhagen, Den.

FISCHER, Louis, US, author; b. Phila, Pa, Feb 29, 1896; s. David and Shifra (Kantsopolsky); Grad, Sch Ped, Phila, 1916; m. Bertha Mark, Dec, 1922; c: George, Victor. On fac, Princeton U; fgn corresp, Amer, Eur jours, since 1921. Author: Oil Imperialism, 1926; The Soviets in World Affairs, 1930; Why Recognize Russia, 1933; Machines and Men in Russia, 1934; Soviet Journey, 1935; Why Spain Fights On, 1937; Stalin and Hitler, 1940; Men and Politics: An Autobiography, 1941; Dawn of Victory, 1942; A Week with Gandhi, 1942; Empire, 1943; The Great Challenge, 1946; Gandhi and Stalin, 1947; The Life of Mahatma Gandhi, 1950; The Life and Death of Stalin, 1952; This is Our World, 1956; Russia Revisited, 1957; The Story of Indonesia, 1959; Russia, America and the World, 1961; The Life of Lenin, 1956; Fifty Years of

Soviet Communism: An Appraisal, 1967; Soviet Russia's Road From Peace to War, Soviet Foreign Policy from Nov 7, 1917, to June 22, 1941, pub 1969; ed: Thirteen Who Fled, 1949; The Essential Gandhi, An Anthology, 1962. Recipient: Natl Book Award, 1965. Home: 42 S Stanworth Dr, Princeton, NJ. Office: Woodrow Wilson Sch, Princeton U, NJ.

FISCHER, Maurice, Isr, physician; b. Bielsko, Pol, Nov 23, 1921; s. Haim and Julia (Mandel); in Isr since 1952; MD, med sch, Basel, Switz, 1951; MPH, Heb U, med sch, Jerusalem, 1965; m. Sylvia Smaragd, Feb 23, 1943; c: Alexander, Rachel, Oded. Asst med dir, Assaf Harofe Hosp, Beer-Yaacov, Isr, since 1964. Lt, IDF, 1955-57. Chmn, Anti-Cancer League, Holon, Isr; mem: Comm for Cultural and Rel Activities; IMA; fmr mem, munic rel comm; club, Rotary, Holon. Contbr of med papers. Home: 42 Hankin St, Holon, Isr. Office: Assaf Harofe Hosp, Beer-Yaacov, Isr.

FISCHER, Norman, US, oral surg; b. Phila, Pa, June 25, 1936; s. Bernard and Hannah (Weiner); AB, UCLA, 1957; DDS, U of S Cal, 1961, cert oral surg, Sch of Dent-LA Gen Hosp, 1966; m. Adrienne Rotenberg, July 30, 1967; c: Stacey. Pvt practice since 1966; staff mem, Cedars Sinai Hosp, LA. Capt, US Army, 1961-63. Amer Bd Oral Surg; Alpha Omega; S Cal Acad Oral Path, both San Fernando Valley. Home: 133 N Swall Dr, Beverley Hills, Cal. Office: 22030 Sherman Way, Canoga Park, Cal.

FISCHER, Sharon P, Isr, physician; b. Bucharest, Rum, Mar 10, 1922; d. Sebastian and Rose (Tenenbaum); in Isr since 1958. Chief, hematology, Jaffa Govt Hosp, since 1953; f, Wash U, 1962-63; hematologist, asst prof, Temple U, 1969. Contbr numerous papers to Amer, Eur jours. Home: 18 Keren Kayemeth Blvd, Tel Aviv, Isr. Office: Govt Hosp, Jaffa, Isr.

FISCHLER, Ben Zion I, Isr, educator; b. Vienna, Aus, May 4, 1921; s. Joseph and Bertha (Rubin); in Isr since 1949; att Heb U, Jerusalem. Dir, Heb div, WZO, comm, Jerusalem exam, since 1964; cons, Heb, Can, 1958-61; lectr, Heb: Sir George William U, Montreal, 1961; New Sch for Social Research, NY, 1961-64; sup, Heb Schs, Can Assn for Heb Educ and Culture, 1958-61, dir, Ulpan Cen, Herzl Inst, NY, 1961-64; cons, Heb, audio-visual aids, dept educ, culture, JA, NY, 1961-64; tchr: Cyprus, 1947-49; Ulpan Motzkin, Haifa, 1951-58; head tchr, camps for immigrants, Isr, 1949-51; fmr dir, Tchrs Sem, Can. IDF. Adv mem: Brit Ivrit Olamit; World Assn for Heb Lang and Culture; Adult Educ, Isr; ad hoc comm, Heb U, fgn off. Contbr articles on lang lab, Ulpan teaching sys. Home: 9 Yotam St, Jerusalem, Isr. Office: 45 King George St, Jerusalem, Isr.

FISCHLER, Henryk, Isr, engineer; b. Bochnia, Pol, Apr 19, 1922; s. Avigdor and Rachel (Faber); in Isr since 1957; MSc, Tech U, Wroclaw, 1950; PhD, Heb U, 1964; m. Elza Oppenheim, Oct 21, 1950; c: Ram, Marta. Research f, Weizmann Inst of Sci, since 1969, research asso engr, 1957-64; design engr, head, design sect, Radio Plant M Kasprzak, Warsaw, 1950-57; visiting staff, Communications Biophysics Group, MIT, 1965-66. Cpl, Pol Army, 1943-45. Prin contribs: studies in electroneur on mech transfer function of middle ear in perception of hearing; devl instrumentation for bio-med research and clinical use: radio-telemetry of biol phenomena apparatus for measuring vibrations of ear parts, radio heart and baro-pacemakers, controlled heart pacing. Mem: Elec Inst and Elec Engrs; Intl Fed for Med and Biol Engr. Contbr to tech jours. Home: 6 Frug, Rehovot, Isr. Office: Dept of Elec, Weizmann Inst of Sci, Rehovot, Isr.

FISH, Sidney Meshulam, US, educator; b. Sanok, Pol, June 8, 1908; s. Yehuda and Zipora (Fish); in US since 1925; Jüdisches Paedagogium, Vienna, 1924-25; Boston Heb Tchrs Coll, 1927; BS, Boston U, 1932; PhD, Dropsie Coll, 1948; m. Rose Hershfield, June 25, 1934; c: Louise, Sylvia Wachtel, Jonathan. Asso prof, hist, Bible, Gratz Coll, since 1949; exec dir, Heb Sunday Sch Soc, Phila, since 1969, and 1961-67; tchr, prin: Newburyport, Mass, 1929-32; Lawrence Heb Sch, 1938-44; exec dir, United Heb Schs of Phila, 1967; prin contrib: found, Hashomer Hatzair movement, Boston. Pres, Histadruth Ivrith of Phila; natl vice-pres, Histadruth Ivrith; secy: Gratz Coll Fac; Dropsie Coll Alumni Assn; mem: Hist Soc Pa; Natl Council for J Educ; Assn JA Execs, Phila; Natl Council J Communal Service. Author: Reshith Binah, 1947; Barnard and Michael Gratz, Their Life and Times, 1949; Aaron Levy: Founder of Aaronsburg, 1951; The Weekly Torah Reader, 1960. Home: 28 Aberdale Rd, Bala Cynwyd, Pa. Office: Gratz Coll, 10 St and Tabor Rd, Philadelphia, Pa.

FISHBEIN, Irwin H, US, rabbi; b. Providence, RI, Aug 4, 1931; s. Ralph and Saide (Rich); BHL, MHL, Brown U, Providence, RI, 1952; ordained rabbi, HUC, 1956; m. Barbara Tcath, June 15, 1952; c: Jonathan, Linda, David, Robert. Rabbi: Temple Beth El, since 1964; Temple Isr, N Westchester, Croton-on-Huudson, NY, 1958-60; Temple Isr, Nyack, NY, 1960-61; asst rabbi, Cong Rodeph Shalom, Phila, Pa, 1961-64. Chaplain, USN, 1956-58. Pres, NJ Assn Reform Rabbis; vice-pres: Concerned Clergy of Elizabeth; NJComm Against Discrimination; chmn, Mayors Commn on Human Relations, Elizabeth, 1965-67; mem: CCAR; club, Rotary. Contbr to J periodicals. Recipient: Stephen S Wise Prize, HUC, 1954; Best Sermon of the Year Award, 1954. Hobbies: tennis, swimming, woodworking. Home: 128 E Dudley Ave, Westfield, NJ. Study: 1374 North Ave, Elizabeth, NJ.

FISHBEIN, J I, US, editor, publisher; b. Chgo, Ill, Oct 27, 1912; s. Frank and Anna (Meltzer); BA, Northwestern U; m. Lillian Desow; c: Wendy, Shelly. Ed-in-chief, The Se .el, since 1943; staff mem: Chgo Tribune, 1930-31; Chgo American, 1931-32; Fmr pres, Amer J Press Assn. Office: 216 W Jackson Blvd, Chicago, Ill.

FISHBEIN, Meyer H, US, archivist; b. NYC, May 6, 1916; s. Jacob and Celia (Brownstein); BSS, Amer U, 1950; MA, 1954; m. Evelyn Centner, March 30, 1947; c: Daniel, Diane. Dir, records appraisal div, Natl Archives since 1968, chief, bus econ br, 1958-61, records appraiser, 1962-68. Pres, Natl Archives Employees Credit Union, 1957-58; bd dirs, govt dir, UJA, 1956-61; f, Soc of Amer Archivists; mem: Amer Hist Soc; Org of Amer Hist. Author: Early Business Statistics of the Federal Government, 1958; ed adv, Business Hist Rev; contbr to profsl jours. Home: 3900 Littleton St, Silver Spring, Md. Office: Natl Archives, Washington, DC.

FISHBEIN, Morris, US, editor, author, physician; b. St Louis, Mo, July 22, 1889; s. Benjamin and Fanny (Clück); BS, U Chgo, 1910; MD, Rush Med Coll, 1912; hon: Pharm D, Rutgers U, 1942; LLD, Fla S Coll, 1957; m. Anna Mantel, July 7, 1914; c: Barbara Friedell, Morris (decd), Marjorie Marks, Justin. Cons med ed, Doubleday Co, since 1950; med ed, Encyclopedia Britannica, since 1948; mem, bd chief eds, Excerpta Medica; intl chief ed, Revista de la Confederacion Medica Panamericana, 1952-57; ed, World-Wide Abstracts of General Medicine, since 1958; contbr ed, Postgraduate Medicine, since 1950; prof em: U Chgo, since 1954, fac mem, 1916-54; U of Ill Coll Med, since 1924; house phys, Durand Hosp, McCormick Inst for Infectious Diseases, 1912-13; ed, Jour of AMA, 1924-50, on staff since 1913; ed: Bulletin of Soc of Med Hist, Chgo; Hygeia, 1924-50. F: Amer Public Health Assn; Amer Geriatrics Soc; Royal Soc Med, London; mem: gen adv comm, Natl Found, since 1937, comm on profsl educ and publs, vice-pres, mem adv comm, Intl Polyomyelitis Cong; bd mem: Natl J Hosp, Denver; La Rabida Sanitarium, Chgo; Hektoen Inst Med Research; bd govs, Chgo Heart Assn; pres: Amer Med Writers' Assn; Chgo Med Soc, 1961-62; AMA; Chgo Path Soc; Inst of Med; Soc Med Hist, Chgo; AAAS; Phi Delta Epsilon; Alpha Omega Alpha; Alpha Omega, hon; Sigma Delta Chi; clubs: Standard; Tavern; Chgo Lit; Quadrangle; Variety; Ravisloe Country; Lotos, NY; Rotary. Author: The Medical Follies, 1925; Mirrors of Medicine, 1925; The New Medical Follies, 1927; The Human Body and Its Care, 1929; An Hour of Health, 1929; Doctors and Specialists, 1930; Shattering Health Superstitions, 1930; Fads and Quackery in Healing, 1932; Frontiers of Medicine, 1933; Syphilis, 1937; Your Diet and Your Health, 1937; Do You Want to Become a Doctor?, 1939; The Natural Nutrition, 1942; History of the American Medical Association, 1947; Medical Writing: The Technic and the Art, 3rd ed, 1957; Popular Medical Encyclopedia, 1953; New Advances in Medicine, 1956; Handy Home Medical Adviser and Concise Medical Encyclopedia, 1957; co-author: Handbook of Therapy, 1925; First Aid Training, 1943; Health and First Aid, 1944; Crusading Obstetrician, 1949; ed: Your Weight and How to Control It, 1927; Common Ailments of Man, 1945; Doctors at War, 1945; Medical Uses of Soap, 1946; Tonics and Sedatives, 1949; Reducing: Your Weight and How to Control It, 1951; Children for the Childless, 1954; Successful Marriage, 1955; Modern Home Medical Adviser (revised), 1953, 54, 55, 56, 57, eds in Eng and Holland); Illustrated Medical and Health Encyclopedia, 1957; Modern Marriage and Family Living, 1957; Modern Family Health Guide, 2 vols, 1959; co-ed, Why Men Fail, 1928; contbr to mags. Recipient: Knight Cdr of the Crown, It, 1933; Order of Carlos Finley, Cuba, 1942; Cdr, Civil Order of Health, Spain, 1952; citation, for unselfish and effective service to

comty, nation and humanity, coll div, Alumni Assn U Chgo, 1943; cert of merit for outstanding efforts as chmn, comm on info, NRC, Pres Truman, 1948; Officer's Cross in Order of Orange-Nassau, Holland, 1954; med alumni dist service award, U Chgo, 1956; dist service award, Amer Med Writers' Assn, 1956; dist lectr award, Phi Beta Kappa, 1957; annual award, Midwest Pharmaceutical Advt Club, 1958; alumni medal, U Chgo, 1962; heart and torch award, AHA, 1962; off, Order of Phoenix, Greece, 1968; Jesse L Rosenberger Medal, U Chgo, 1968. Hobbies: travel, bridge, golf, music. Home and office: 5454 S Shore Dr, Chicago, Ill.

FISHBERG, Arthur M, US, physician, educator; b. NYC, June 17, 1898; s. Maurice and Bertha (Cantor); BA, Columbia U, 1919, MD, 1921; m. Irene Levin, June 16, 1933. Phys-in-chief, Beth Isr Hosp; cons phys, St Joseph's Hosp; clinical prof, med, NYU; cons Army Med Cen, Wash, 1947-54. Mem: AMA; AHA; Amer Soc for Clinical Inves; NY Acad of Med; hon: Buenos Aires Med Soc; Brazilian Card Soc. Author: Hypertension and Nephritis, 1930; Heart Failure, 1937; contbr to med jours. Home and office: 1136 Fifth Ave, New York, NY.

FISHBONE, Herbert, US, attorney; b. NYC, Aug 12, 1921; s. Samuel and Anna (Blumenkrantz); AB, Lafayette Coll, Easton, Pa, 1941; LLB, Cornell U, NY, 1949; m. Vivian Manperl, Oct 23, 1966; c: David, Deborah, Daniel. Pvt practice since 1950. Lt, USGC, 1942-46. Chmn: Ɨa-Del-Md region, AJComm; Lehigh Del Devl Council, Easton, Pa; mem, Northampton Co, Pa, Amer, Bar Assns; fmr: pres, bd trustees, Easton Hosp; exec comm, Pa J Comty Relations Council. Home: 423 Paxinosa Rd E, Easton, Pa. Office: Easton Natl Bank and Trust Co Bldg, Easton, Pa.

FISHEL, Stanley I, US, advertising exec; b. NYC, Jan 2, 1914; s. Max and Mollie (Schulman); BS, Columbia U, 1934. Exec vice-pres, treas, Fairfax, Inc; vice-pres, treas, Jasper, Lynch and Fishel, 1938-49. Lt, USCG, 1942-46. Natl pres, Zeta Beta Tau, 1956-60; mem, youth services, comm, JWB; fmr chmn, advt div, FJP; mem, exec comm, advt div, UJA; bd dirs: Henry Kaufmann Campgrounds. Home: Park Sheraton Hotel, New York, NY. Office: 270 Madison Ave, New York, NY.

FISHENFELD-DIAMANT, Janette, Brazil, author; b. Niteroi, Brazil, Sep 28, 1931; d. Aron and Luiza (Solomon) Diamant; PhD, U Rio de Janeiro; m. Laizer Fishenfeld, Jan 10, 1953; c: Suzette, Rejane. Author: Os Dispersos, 1968; The Miracle, story, 1968; tchr, HS, 1951-52; journalist, Qonde Vamos?, weekly mag, 1965-70; contbr poetry to, 4000 Years of Poetry, Collection Brazilian J Poetry, 1969. Vice-pres, WIZO, secy, J Sch, 1965-67. Spec interests: educ, psych, J hist. Home: Otavio Carneiro St, 130/1101, Niterói, Brazil.

FISHER, Bernard, US, surgeon, educator; b. Pittsburgh, Pa, Aug 23, 1918; s. Reuben and Anna (Miller); BS, U Pittsburgh, 1939, MD, 1943; m. Shirley Kruman, June 5, 1947; c: Beth, Joseph, Louisa. Prof, surg, dir, surg research lab, U Pittsburgh, since 1958; John and Mary Markle scholar in med sci, 1953-58. Chmn, Natl Surg Adj Breast Project; mem: Soc of U Surg; Cen Surg Assn; Soc of Vascular Surg; Amer Coll of Surg; Amer Cancer Soc; Amer Surg Assn; Bre st Task Force, Natl Cancer Inst; Soc Surg Alimentary Tract; Soc of Experimental Biol and Med; Amer Phys Soc. Ed bd, Transplantation jour; Cancer jour; numerous articles to med jours. Recipient: C of C man of year award in med, 1966. Home: 5636 Aylesboro Ave, Pittsburgh, Pa. Office: U of Pittsburgh, Pittsburgh, Pa.

FISHER, Esther, Isr, journalist; b. Lodz, Pol, Sep 19, 1926; d. Mordechai and Suhifra (Flancbaum) Abramowicz; in Isr since 1949; att HS, Ghetto Lodz; m. Gershon Fisher, Dec 12, 1951; c: Shifra. Reportages to Yediot Aharonot and its weekly, on deflections of the soul in man in gen, the young man in particular; stories on great deeds of small people. Recipient; Commendation for screenplay, Bd of Arts and Culture. Home: 21 Daniel St, B'nai Brak, Isr.

FISHER, Gerald Saul, US, business exec, attorney; b. Bx, NY, Mar 24, 1931; s. Abraham and Rose (Richards); AA, Worcester Jr Coll, Mass, 1950; BBA, Clark U, Mass, 1952; LLB, Boston U Law Sch, 1955; m. Sue Chidakel, Apr 7, 1957; c: Stevan, Jody, David. Pres, Copper Penny Family Coffee Shops, since 1969; counsel, corp finance div, SEC, 1955-58; asso dep, admn, 1964-67; admn vice-pres, 1967-69, both US Small Bus Admn; with admn since 1958. Mem: Amer Bar Assn;

Bars: Mass, DC, US Supr Court; fmr, bd dirs, Heb Home for Aged, Wash, DC. Contbr to legal publs. Recipient, several awards for dist service to US Govt. Hobbies: fishing, golf. Home: 4450 Callada Pl, Tarzana, Cal. Office: 13701 Riverside Dr, Sherman Oaks, Cal.

FISHER, Hans, US, educator; b. Breslau, Ger, Mar 4, 1928; s. George and Johanna (Gotteheiner); in US since 1941; BS, Rutgers U, NJ, 1950; MS, U Conn, 1952; PhD, U of Ill, 1954; m. Ruth Hirschberg, Aug 24, 1950; c: Deborah, David, Daniel. Chmn, prof, dept nutrition, Rutgers U, since 1967, on fac since 1954. Prin contribs: devl amino acid diets for animals; studies on protein quality; research in nutritional aspects of arteriosclerosis. Pres, Rutgers chap, AAUP; vice-pres, YMHA, Highland Pk; trustee, Highland Pk Temple and Cen; dir, J Fed; mem: Amer Inst of Nutrition; AAAS; Brit Nutrition Soc; NY Acad of Scis; Poultry Sci Assn; fmr vice-pres, Cong Ahavat Achim. Author, chap, New Methods in Nutritional Biochemistry, 1967; contbr numerous publs to sci jours. Recipient, Awards: Research, Poultry Sci Assn, 1957; Nutrition, Amer Feed Mfrs Assn, 1959. Hobby, music. Home: 216 N Third Ave, Highland Pk, NJ. Office: Rutgers U, New Brunswick, NJ.

FISHER, Isadore, US, dermatologist; b. Duluth, Minn, Aug 26, 1910; s. Marcus and Ida (Greenfield); BS, U Minn, 1932; MB, 1936, MS, 1948; m. Rhea Wolfson, Sep 24, 1961; c: Roberta, Carol, Stephen, Nancy Unterman. Pvt practice since 1948; chief dermat, Mt Sinai Hosp, since 1951; asso prof, med, U Minn, asst prof, 1953; chief dermat, VA Hosp; att dermat: St Barnabas Hosp; Mt Sinai Hosp; Deaconess Hosp; Asbury Methodist Hosp. Mem: AMA; Amer Acad of Dermat; Minn Dermat Soc; Minneapolis Acad Med; Minn State Med Assn; Minn Med Assn; Hennepin Co Med Soc; Soc for Inves Dermat; Noah Worcester Dermat Soc; Sigma Xi. Contbr to med jours. Home: 4633 Sunset Ridge, Minneapolis, Minn. Office: 1948 Med Arts Bldg, Minneapolis, Minn.

FISHER, Leonard Everett, US, painter, author, illustrator; b. NYC, June 24, 1924; s. Benjamin and Ray (Shapiro); att Bklyn Coll; BFA, Yale U, 1949, MFA, 1950; m. Margery Meskin, Dec 21, 1952; c: Julie, Susan, James. Fmr dean, Whitney Art Sch. Prin exhbs: Rockefeller Cen; Seligmann Gal, NY; Amer Fed Arts Natl Tours; Whitney Mus; Springfield Mus, Mass; Silvermine Guild of Artists, Conn; New Haven Paint and Clay Club; Rochester Inst of Tech; Soc of Illustrators, NY; NE Annual; Fairfield U Invitational; Pa State U Invitational; repr in collections: Libr of Cong, Wash, DC; Kerlan Collection, U Minn; Leonard Everett Fisher Archive, libr, U Ore; Fairfield U; U of S Miss; Elmira Coll; Housatonic Cmty Coll; Free Libr of Phila; illus works include projected 20 vol ed Colonial Americans for children. Pres, New Haven Paint and Clay Club; dir ex officio, Arts Council of Gtr New Haven; mem: bd dirs, Westport-Weston Arts Council; Amer Inst of Graphic Arts; Silvermine Guild of Artists; Authors Guild; Soc Conn Craftsmen. Recipient: Pulitzer Art award, Natl Acad of Design and Columbia U, 1950; Premio Grafico, Intl Book Fair, Bologna, It, 1968; Winchester f, Yale U, 1949; citations: textbook design, children's book illustrations, Amer Inst of Graphic Arts; Ten Best Illustrated Children's Books award, NY Times, 1964; Carl L Blenner Prize for Painting, 1969. Hobby: piano. Home and studio: 7 Twin Bridge Acres Rd, Westport, Conn.

FISHER, Max, US, attorney; b. Reading, Pa, July 20, 1896; s. Harry and Bertha (Hirschman); LLB, Dickinson Law Sch, 1919; m. Rose Mendelsohn, Dec 25, 1921; c: Sara, Richard. Pvt practice since 1920. US Army, WWI and II. Pres, JCC, 1933-37 and since 1950; Kesher Zion Syn, 1938-41, 1946-47; chmn, UJA, 1948; co-chmn, 1951; dir, mem, exec comm, Birks Co United Fund, since 1958; mem bd, J Home Northeastern Pa; pres, B'nai B'rith, 1935, all Reading. Home: 521 Carsonia Ave, Pennside, Reading, Pa. Office: 538 Court St, Reading, Pa.

FISHER, Max M, US, business exec; b. Pittsburgh, Pa, July 15, 1908; s. William and Molly (Brody); BS, O State U, 1930; hon PhD: Bar Ilan U, Isr; Albion Coll, Mich; m. Sylvia Krell (decd); m. 2nd, Marjorie Switow, July 1, 1953; c: Jane Sherman, Majorie, Julie, Philip, Mary. Bd dirs: Mich Con Gas Co; Mich Bell Telephone Co; Dayco; Mfrs Natl Bank, Detroit, Mich; Fruehauf Corp; Marathon Oil; chmn, bd: Fisher-New Cen; Safran Printing. Pres, UJA; vice-pres, CFJWF; chmn, exec comm: JWF, Detroit, past pres, bd govs; United Found; bd, AJComm; bd, New Detroit, Inc;

mem bd, Sinai Hosp; clubs: Franklin Hills Country, past pres; Standard; Econ, Detroit, mem bd; City; Hundred of Detroit; Great Lakes; Bloomfield Open Hunt; Palm Beach Country. Home: 27751 Fairway Hills Dr, Franklin, Mich. Office: 2210 Fisher Bldg, Detroit, Mich.

FISHER, Michael Ellis, US, educator; b. Fyzabad, Trinidad, W Indies, Sep 3, 1931; s. Harold and Jeanne (Halter); in US since 1966; BSc, first class, King's Coll, London, Eng, 1951, PhD, physics, 1956; m. Sorrel Castillejo de Claremont; c: Caricia, Daniel, Martin, Matthew. Prof, chem and math, Cornell U, since 1966, mem fac since 1958. Flying Off, RAF, 1951-53. Mem: Inst Physics; Phys Soc; Soc for Ind and Applied Math; Amer Phys Soc; Math Assn Amer. Author: Analogue Computing at Ultra-High Speed, 1962; The Nature of Critical Points, 1964; contbr to profsl publs. Office: Cornell U, Ithaca, NY.

FISHER, Myer, Eng, physician; b. Dublin, Eire, Apr 22, 1901; s. Simon and Fanny (Atlas); MB, BCh, BAO, Natl U, Eire; LM, U Coll, Dublin, 1926; m. Annie Silverstone; c: Ruth Banin, Cyril. Phys, i/c Phys, Med and Rehab, St Mary's Hosp Luton; Queen Victoria Memorial; asst phys, Lister Hosp, Hitchin; fmr: Highlands Hosp, London; Welwyn Hosp, Herts, MO, i/c div 225; lectr, ARP Services and Brit Red Cross. Exec mem, Bachad F; vice-pres, Hapoel Hamizrachi; found, Palmers Green and Southgate, Yavneh Nursery, Kindergarten; fmr: chmn: JNF; Mizrachi Org, both Dublin; Mizrachi Org, Manchester, London; mem exec, Magen David Adom, London; f, Royal Soc Med, London; mem: Brit Assn Phys Med; Amer Assn Phys Med and Rehab. Contbr numerous papers to profsl publs. Hobbies: reading, athletics, walking, rugby football, cricket, gardening. Home: 22 River Ave, London, N 13, Eng.

FISHER, Samuel, Eng, business exec; b. London, Eng, Jan 20, 1905; s. Bernard and Dora (Freedman); m. Millie Gluckstein, Oct 21, 1935; c: Marilyn Taylor. Vice-pres, exec, London Diamond Bourse, since 1949; Brit repr, Intl Diamond Confs. Sr vice-pres, Bd deps, Brit J; pres, J Assn for Physically Handicapped; sr trustee, United J Friendly Soc; chmn, London Lab Mayors Assn, since 1953; dep chmn, magistrate JP, W Cen Div; chmn, Betting and Licensing Magistrates Bench; mem, B'nai B'rith, First Lodge of Eng. Recipient: Knight Bachelor, Queen Elizabeth II, 1967. Hobbies: writing book reviews, reading biographies and hist. Home: 15 High Point Flats, London N6, Eng. Office: 32/33 Haton Garden, London EC1, Eng.

FISHMAN, Asher, Eng, attorney; b. London, Eng, May 6, 1919; s. Samuel and Fanny (Winegarten); LLB, hons, U Coll, 1940; m. Sylvia Krausz, Sep 14, 1948; c: Elkan, Cynthia. Pvt practice since 1945. Lt, Royal Army Ordnance Corps, 1941-45. Pres: London Bd for Shechita; Natl Council Shechita; chmn, London Bd J Rel Educ; bd govs, JFS Comprehensive Sch; mem: Bd Deps Brit J's; council: Beth Hamedrash Comm of United Syn; J's Coll; Kerem Schs; elder, United Syn. Home: 33 Linden Lea, Hampstead Garden Suburb, London, N2, Eng. Office: 26/28 City Rd, Finsbury Sq, London, EC1, Eng.

FISHMAN, Fred N, US, attorney; b. NYC, Aug 21, 1925; s. Arthur and Frederica (Greenspan); BS, summa cum laude, Harvard Coll, 1946, LLB, Magna cum laude, Law Sch, 1948; m. Claire Powsner, Sep 19, 1948; c: Robert, Nancy. Partner, law firm, Kaye, Scholar, Fierman, Hays and Handler, since 1962; law secy to Chief Judge Calvert Magruder, US Court of Appeals, First Circuit, 1948-49; law secy to Asso Justice Felix Frankfurter, US Supr Court, 1949-50; atty, law firm Dewey, Ballantine, Bushby, Palmer and Wood, NYC, 1950-57; asst vice-pres, Freeport Sulphur Co, 1959-61, joined co as atty, 1957. Trustee, past chmn exec comm, Public Educ Assn, NYC, vice-pres, since 1960, fmr chmn, comm on sch admn and leg; mem: exec comm NYC Bar Assn, past chmn, comm on admn law, fed, state leg, munic affairs, corporate law; NY State Bar Assn, comm on admn law; NY Co Lawyers Assn; Amer Bar Assn; Phi Beta Kappa; Harvard Club, NYC; fmr: mem comm, Harvard Law Sch-Isr Coop Research for Isr Legal Devl; club, Harvard, NYC. Ed, Harvard Law Rev; contbr to legal publs. Home: 17 E 89 St, New York, NY. Office: 425 Park Ave, New York, NY.

FISHMAN, Harold C, US, dermatologist; b. Yonkers, NY, Oct 1, 1913; s. Jacob and Fay (Rosenbloom); AB, U of Cal, 1934, MA, 1935, MD, 1940; postgrad studies, NY Postgrad Med Sch and Hosp, Skin and Cancer Unit, 1946-47; m.

Flora Lazard, Dec 3, 1939; c: Michael, William. Sr att dermat em; LA Co-U of S Cal Med Cen; att dermat Cedars of Leb Hosp; Culver City Hosp; Mt Sinai Hosp, LA; staff, Inst for Med Research; Cedars of Leb Hosp; lectr, postgrad dermat, U of S Cal Med Sch. US Army, 1941-46. Pres: Westwood Acad Med and Dent; Metrop Dermat Soc of LA, 1952; vice-pres: dermat sect, Cal Med Assn, 1955; Irving Thalberg Lodge, B'nai B'rith, since 1948; dipl: Amer Bd Dermat; Amer Acad Dermat; Pacific Coast Dermat Assn; Soc Inves Dermat; AMA; LA Co Med Assn; Inst Soc Trop Derm; Noah Worcester Derm Soc; Beverly Hills Acad Med, pres, 1961; S Cal B'nai B'rith Hillel Council; Phi Delta Epsilon; Psi Chi; Wilshire Blvd Temple Brotherhood, pres, 1961. Contbr to med jours. Home: 705 N Alpine Dr, Beverly Hills, Cal. Office: 10921 Wilshire Blvd, Los Angeles, Cal.

FISHMAN, Herman, US, certified public acctnt; b. Bx, NY, Feb 15, 1920; s. Abraham and Minnie (Abraham); BBA, CCNY, 1947; m. Vivian Kilimnik, Sept 30, 1944; c: Barry (decd), Eileen, Joanne. Pvt practice since 1954; CPA, business cons, Leonard Levine, CPA, 1943-54. Mem: Amer Inst of CPA's; NY State Soc of CPA's. Hobby: J folklore. Home: 2840 Sedgwick Ave, Bronx, NY. Office: 310 Madison Ave, New York, NY.

FISHMAN, Seymour, US, psychologist, organization exec; b. Newark, NJ, Feb 10, 1915; s. Samuel and Ethel (Raffman); MA, Clinical Psych, CCNY; m. Sylvia Shemel, Feb 14, 1937; c: Simon, Judith. Exec vice-pres, Amer Friends Heb U, since 1964; fmr: Pacific Ocean Area Dir, USO, Hawaii, org 1st Hawaiian J App, 1944, established 1st syn in Honolulu; city mgr, Minneapolis, Chgo for Isr Bonds; clinical psychol, Bellevue Hosp; f, psych dept, NYU. F, Amer Psych Assn. Recipient: Civilian citation, for contrib to morale of US Servicemen in Pacific, US War Dept, 1946. Office: 11 E 69 St, New York, NY.

FISHMAN, William H, US, biochemist, educator; b. Winnipeg, Can, Mar 2, 1914; s. Abraham and Goldie (Chmelnitsky); in US since 1940; BS, U Sask, 1935; PhD, U Toronto, 1939; postdoc study: U Edinburgh, Scotland, 1939-40; Cornell U Med Sch, 1940-41; m. Lillian Waterman, Aug 6, 1939; c: Joel, Nina, Daniel. Prof, path, oncology, Tufts U Sch of Med, since 1960, research prof, biochem, 1948-60; dir, cancer research, Tufts-NE Cen Hosp, since 1958; lectr, steroid training, Clark U, Worcester, Mass, since 1956; asst prof, biochem, Bowman-Gray Sch of Med, NC, 1943-45; research asso, U Chgo, 1945-48; NSF, travel award to Japan, 1959, guest speaker, Fifth Glucuronic Acid Research Cong, Tokyo, 1959. Mem: Amer Soc of Biol Chem; Biochem Soc (London); Amer Chem Soc; Amer Soc for Cell Bio; Sigma Xi; Soc for Experimental Biol and Med; NY Acad of Scis; Amer Assn for Cancer Research; Amer Fed Clinical Inves; The Histochem Soc; The Endocrine Soc; Laurentian Hormone Conf; Royal Med Soc, affiliate. Author: The Chemistry of Drug Metabolism, 1961; co-author, The Physiopathology of Cancer, 1953, 1959; Metabolic Conjugation and Metabolic Hydrolysis; chaps in med books; contbr to med publs. Home: 56 Mason Terr, Brookline, Mass. Office: Tufts-NE Cen Hosp, Boston, Mass.

FISHMAN, William Samuel, US, business exec; b. Clinton, Ind, Jan 26, 1916; s. Max and Fannie (Dumes); att, U of Ill, 1932-36; grad work, U Chgo, 1936-37; hon DBA, Bryant Coll, Providence, RI, 1968; hon LLD, Lincoln Memorial U, Harrogate, Tenn, 1969; m. Clara Silvian, 1936; c: Alan, Fred, David. Pres, ARA Services Inc, since 1964, sr vice-pres, 1959-63, exec vice-pres, 1963-64; dir, Fidelity Bank of Phila; pres, Authomatic Merchandising Co, 1956-59. Pres, bd, J Publ Soc Amer; exec comm, FedJA, Gtr Phila; natl bd, Big Brothers Amer; trustee, Bryant Coll; dir: Natl Automatic Merchandising Assn, since 1949, pres 1958-59; Phila Orch Assn; Phila Music Acad; Fidelity Bank of Phila; Amers for Competitive Enterprise Sys; Crime Commn Phila; Gtr Phila C of C; exec comm: Phila US Savings Bond Campaign; mem: Natl Restaurant Assn; Phi Beta Kappa; Phi Kappa Phi; Delta Sigma Rho; clubs: Locust; Philmont Country; Sunday Breakfast; Phila; Standard; Chgo; Harmonie, NYC. Recipient: F, Brandeis U; Service to Youth, Pop Warner Little Scholars, 1969; NAMA's John S. Mill Award, 1955. Hobbies: flying, photography, fishing. Home: 2124 Delancey, Philadelphia, Pa. Office: 2503 Lombard, Philadelphia, Pa.

FITELSON, H William, US, attorney; b. NYC, Jan 21, 1905; s. Isidore and Gertrude (Greenhouse); att Columbia U; LLB, NY Law Sch, 1927; m. Anita Morrow, Sep, 1930; c: David,

Margaret, Robin. Partner, law firm, Fitelson & Mayers, specializing in communications; mgn dir, Theatre Guild, TV and radio. Mem, bd dirs, numerous public service orgs. Author: Theatre Guild on the Air, 1947. Home: 46 Morton St, New York, NY. Office: 580 Fifth Ave, New York, NY.

FLAMM, Donald, US, business exec; b. Pittsburgh, Pa, Dec 11, 1899; s. Louis and Elizabeth (Jason); att NYU, 1917; m. Etelle Schiller, Dec 29, 1947. Owner, chmn bd, radio sta WMMM, Westport, Conn, since 1960; fmr: owner, mgn dir, WMCA, NY; pres, mgn dir, Inter-City Network; co-owner, WPAT, NJ. Spec liaison off, OWI, WW II, originated plan for ABSIE (Amer Radio Station in Eng), publicized anti-Nazi movements in US, Eng. Pres, Mt Neboh Cong, NY; chmn, NJ Civil War Centennial Commn, since 1960; bd dirs: Oscar Lewenstein Plays Ltd, London; Actor's Studio, NY; Heb Free Loan Soc, since 1948; NY exec comm, ADL; and found, J Theatrical Guild; mem: hon, Catholic Actor's Guild; PR comm, UAHC; Grand St Boys Assn; Cinema Lodge; B'nai B'rith; United Hunts Racing Assn; charter found, Eleanor Roosevelt Inst for Cancer Research; clubs: Lambs; Friars; Alpine Country; Circus Saints and Sinners; Rockefeller Luncheon. Home: Villa Nevele, Anderson Ave, Closter, NJ. Office: 25 Central Park W, New York, NY.

FLAPAN, Simha, Isr, editor; b. Tomaszow, Pol, Jan 27, 1911; s. Israel and Deborah (Bongart); m. Sarah Szeps, 1935; c: Amram, Yael Shachar, Naamah. Ed, found, New Outlook, since 1957; mem exec, Mapam, since 1949; dir, J-Arab Inst, Givat Haviva, since 1963; fmr: Natl secy, Arab dept, Mapam, 1949-52; dir, 1954-65; Eur repr, Mapam, 1965-68; natl council, Histadrut, 1949-64; natl exec mem Kibbutz Arzi, Ha-Shomer Hatzair; secy, Kibbutz Gan Shmuel. Author: La Guerre Israele-Arabe de 1967; contbr of essays, articles. Hobbies: music, chess. Home: Kibbutz Gan Shmuel, Isr. Office: 8 Karl Netter St, Tel Aviv, Isr.

FLAX, Arnold Jack, Isr, communal exec; b. Manchester, Eng, May 12, 1926; s. Solomon and Eva (Moscovitch); BSc, U Coll of N Wales, 1947; m. Esther Newman, Apr 20, 1952; c: Yehuda, Sara, Yair, Elisha. Dir, youth and hechalutz dept, JA, since 1968. Mem, Kibbutz Beth Haemek, Nahariya, since 1952. Office: 4/12 Lower Regent St, London, Eng.

FLEISCHAKER, Joseph, US, business exec; b. Louisville, Ky, Jan 9, 1910; s. Siegfried and Sophie (Lippold); BS, U Miami, 1932; m. Marie Sales, June 14, 1937; c: Carol Westerman, Susan Silber, Joan Evers. Dist sales mgr, Columbus Stove Co, since 1962; vice-pres, Will Sales, Louisville, 1937-63. Lt, supply corps, USNR, 1942-46. Pres, Brith Sholom Temple, 1953, 1954, 1955; mem, bd dirs: J Hosp; Louisville Heb Home for Aged; YMHA; co-chmn, Jr div, UJA, 1933-34; mem: Amer Legion; Urban League, AJComm; NCCJ; Phi Epsilon Pi; Rho Beta Omicron; fmr pres, Ky Appliance Dealers, 1954-57; Natl Appliance Radio-TV Dealers Assn, 1958-59; clubs: Kiwanis; Brith Sholom Men's, pres 1947-49; Standard Country, vice-pres, 1952-60. Home: 665 S Kinker Blvd, St Louis, Mo. Office: 401 S 4 St, Louisville, Ky.

FLEISCHER, Ezra (pen name, I Goleh), Isr, educator, author; b. Timisoara, Rum, Aug 7, 1928; s. Judah and Zilla (Wittman); in Isr since 1960; BA, Law Fac, U Bucarest, 1950; PhD, Heb U, Jerusalem, 1964; m. Anat Rappaport, Nov 1, 1955; c: Judah. Lectr, Medieval, Heb Lit, Heb U, Jerusalem, since 1964; ed secy, Tarbitz ,quarterly for J studies; adv mem, Acad, Heb Lang. Author: Meshalim, 1957; Masa Gog, 1959; be-Hehalek Laila, 1961; contbr to profsl jours. Recipient: Isr Award for Masa Gog, 1959. Home: 5 Radak St, Jerusalem, Isr. Office: Hebrew U, Jerusalem, Isr.

FLEISCHER, Michael, US, chemist; b. Bridgeport, Conn, Feb 27, 1908; s. Julius and Flora (Reinitz); BS, Yale U, 1930, PhD, 1933; m. Helen Isenberg, Aug 5, 1934; c: Walter, David. Geochem, US, Geol Survey, since 1939; asst chem, Geophys Lab, Carnegie Inst, 1936-39; lectr, George Wash U, 1957-63. Pres: Geochem Soc, 1964; Geol Soc, Wash, 1968, vice-pres, 1953; Intl Union Chem, 1953-56, commn on geochem, vice-pres, 1951-53; Mineralogical Soc Amer, 1952, vice pres, 1951; bd dirs, Amer Geol Inst, 1950-51; mem: Sigma Xi; Amer, Brit,

Fr, Swiss, It, profsl socs. Asso ed, Amer Mineralogist, 1941-53; asst ed, Chem Abstracts, since 1940; asst to ed, Dana's System Mineralogy, 1935; contbr to profsl jours. Home: 3104 Chestnut St, NW, Wash- ington DC. Office: US Geol Survey, Washington, DC.

FLEISCHER, Robert Louis, US, physicist; b. Columbus, O, July 8, 1930; s. Leo and Rosalie (Kahn); AB, Harvard U, 1952, AM, 1953, PhD, 1956; m. Barbara Simons, June 10, 1954; c: Cathy, Elizabeth. Physicist, Gen Phys Lab, Gen Elec Research and Devl Cen, Schenectady, NY, since 1960; asst prof, metallurgy, MIT, 1956-60; sr research f, phys, Cal Inst Tech, 1965-66; adj prof, phys and astronomy, Rensselaer Polytech Inst, 1967-68; visiting lectr, Dept of Geophysics, U of W Ont, 1968-69; cons, US Geological Survey. Pres, Zoller Sch PTA; mem, bd dirs, Citizens League, Schenectady; mem: Amer Astronomical Soc; Amer Phys Soc; Amer Geophysics Union; AAAS; Meteorological Soc; Sigma Xi; AAAS. Contbr to tech jours. Recipient: spec award for Dist Service, advancement nuclear sci, Amer Nuclear Soc, 1964. Home: 1356 Waverly Pl, Schenectady, NY. Office: General Elec Research Lab, Schenectady, NY.

FLEISCHMAN, Harry, US, organization exec, ed; b. NYC, Oct 3, 1914; s. Abraham and Rachel (Kohn); att, CCNY, 1931-33; m. Natalie Wiencek, June 18, 1937; c: Martha, Peter, Marid. Dir, natl lab service, AJComm, NYC, since 1953, race relations coord, since 1963; org, Amalgamated Clothing Workers, 1937-38; natl secy, Socialist Party, 1942-50 campaign mgr, Norman Thomas pres campaign, 1944-48. Natl vice-chmn, Workers Defense League, since 1962, chmn, natl bd, 1957-62; chmn exec comm, League for Industrial Democracy, since 1962; trustee, Levittown Public Libr, NY, since 1967; mem, exec bd, Assn J Communal Relations Workers, since 1968; chmn: AJComm Staff Org; lab educ sect, Adult Educ Assn, 1963-65; mem, exec bd: Post World Council,1942-67; Rel and Lab Council of Amer, 1953-65; Workers Educ Local 189, Amer Fed of Tchrs, 1955-64; Norman Thomas Fund, 1969; mem: Amer Newspaper Guild; Socialist Party; ADA; PTA; NAACP; Workmen's Circle; ACLU; Natl Assn of Intergroup Relations Officials. Author: Let's Be Human, 1960; Norman Thomas: A Biography, 1964, 1967; 1969; pamphlets: Labor's Fight for Equality; Anti-Semitism in USA; Negro Anti-Semitism and the White Backlash; The Civil Rights Story; co-author, pamphlets: We Open the Gates; Security, Civil Liberties and Unions; Labor Looks at Civil Liberties; columnist, Let's Be Human, monthly column, since 1953; ed, Socialist Call, 1942-50; lab ed, Voice of Amer, 1950-53. Hobby: photography. Home: 11 Wedgewood Lane, Wantagh, NY. Office: 165 E 56 St, New York, NY.

FLEISCHMANN, Peretz, Isr, physician; b. Kiev, Russ, Mar 3, 1900; s. Simon and Martha (Brill); in Isr since 1936; MD, U Königsberg, 1927; m. Charlotte Brill, 1928; c. Alisa Ben-Horin, Rena Gamish. Ret; med dir, Cen Emek Hosp, Afula, phys-in-chief, internal med dept, 1941-68; clinical asso prof internal med, Heb U, Hadassah Sch of Med, Jerusalem, 1966; research worker: 4th U Med Clinic, Berlin, both 1925-33; phys, Kupat Holim, Tel Aviv, 1936-41. Mem: IMA; Is Soc Internal Med; Isr Card Assn; Intl Soc Internal Med. Contbr articles on biochem, card, clinical med to Isr, fgn profsl jours. Home: 40 Wedgewood Ave, Haifa, Isr.

FLEISHER, David, US, educator; b. NYC, Feb 8, 1911; s. Ephraim and Sarah (Charmas); BS, NYU, 1930; MA, Harvard U, 1931, PhD, 1941; div, c: Michael; m. 2nd; c: Martin. Prof, Eng, Yeshiva U, since 1951; asst prof, asso prof, 1944-51; instr CCNY, 1939-44; visiting asst prof, NYU, 1948-49. Mem: Phi Beta Kappa; MLA; club, Harvard, NY. Author: William Godwin: A Study in Liberalism, 1951. Home: 790 Dearborn Teaneck, NJ. Office: Yeshiva U, Amsterdam Ave and 186 St, New York, NY.

FLEISHER, Elizabeth H, US, architect; b. Phila, Pa, Aug 28, 1892; s. Harry and Minnie (Rosenberg) Hirsh; BA, Wellesley, Coll, 1914; M, Arch, Smith Coll, 1929; m. Horace Fleisher, June 8, 1916; c: Harriet Berger, Susan, Peggy Suckle. Ed asst, ed-in-chief, Archives of Environmental Health 1960-67; part-ner, Roth & Fleisher, 1941-59. Bd dirs: F House and Farm, since 1956; Montgomery Co TB and Health Assn, 1961-65; corporater, Women's Med Coll of Pa, since 1942; Adv Board New School of Music 1969; mem: adv bd, New Sch of Music, since 1969; Amer Inst Architects; Mus Modern Art; Phila Art Mus; Phila Art Alliance; Woodmere Art Gal; YWHA; Phi Beta Kappa Associates. Hobby: painting and travel. Home: 4030 Apalogen Rd, Philadelphia, Pa.

FLEISHER, Leon, US, pianist; b. San Francisco, July 23, 1928; s. Isidor and Berta; studied with Artur Schnabel; m. Dorothy Druzinsky, Dec 30, 1951; m, c: Deborah, Richard, Leah; m. 2nd, Risselle Rosenthal, Apr 1, 1962; c: Paula, Julian. Concert pianist since 1943; made official orch debut with SF Orch under Pierre Monteux, 1943; prof piano, Peabody Con-servatory of Music, Baltimore, Md; mem summer fac, Music Acad of W; master classes in various U's; played with: all major orchs throughout N, S Amer, Eur, Scandinavia and at all maj festivals; appeared on Telephone Hour, NBS radio. Records: Epic, Columbia. Bd dirs: Cen Stage, Baltimore; Naumberg Found. Recipient, 1st Amer winner, Concours Musicale Reine Elisabeth de Belgique, 1952; served on juries of numerous competitions. Office: c/o Columbia Artists Mgt, Inc, 165 W 57 St, New York, NY.

FLEISS, Milton Lester, US, lawyer; b. Bklyn, NY, July 11, 1908; s. Henry and Mollie (Breuer); AB, Columbia Coll, 1928; DJur, Columbia Law Sch, 1930; m. Bernice Hecht, Apr 14, 1938; c: Susan Loewenstein, Judith Darin, David. Pvt practice since 1931. Comm chmn, Bklyn Bar Assn; trus-tee, Cong Beth Elohim, Bklyn; comm mem, NY State Bar Assn; fmr pres: ZOA, Bklyn chap; Avukah, Bklyn chap; Cassia Found Inc; mem: Masons; Cassia Lodge 445, master 1953. Hobbies: sailing, cycling. Home: 75 Henry St, Brooklyn, NY. Office: 188 Montague St, Brooklyn, NY.

FLETCHER, Neville Hyman, Eng, physician; b. Dublin, Ir, Nov 17, 1931; s. Samuel and Eva (Phillips); att, Wesley Coll, Dublin, 1945-59; MB, BC, U Dublin, 1955; m. Renita Kersh, Mar 8, 1959; c: Heather, Stephanie. Factory dr, Min of Lab, Salford and Manchester; med adv: Rootes Motors; Green-gate and Irwell Rubber Co, both in Manchester; Eaton En-velope, Worsley; Royal Ballet Co, London; ship's surg, Blue Funnel Line, 1957. Chmn, Friends Heb U, med br, Manches-ter; hon phys, Manchester; J Blind Soc. Hobbies: bridge, med lectures. Home: 2 Pearl Ave, Salford, Eng. Office: 23 Derby St, Salford, Eng.

FLEXER, Akiva, Isr, geologist; b. Tel Aviv, Isr, Dec 31, 1933; s. Haim and Rachel (Morgan); MSc, Heb U, Jerusalem, 1960, PhD, 1965; m. Zipora Yanay, Mar 18, 1954; c: Amit, Hagai. Lectr, Heb U, since 1965; partial lectr, Haifa, Beer-sheva U's; fmr, tchr. Educ br, IDF, 1967. Prin contrib, re-search in geology of Isr. Vice pres, Geologial Soc of Isr, fmr pres; mem: Société Géologique de Fr; Intl Paleontological Union. Author: Geology, 1961; Introduction to Geology, 1967; Geology, Principles and Processes, 1969; contbr to geological jours. Recipient, Best Lectr, Fac Agric, 1968. Hobbies: drawing, field trips. Home: 10 Aluf Simhoni St, Jerusalem, Isr. Office: Dept Geology, Heb U, Jerusalem, Isr.

FLEXNER, Louis B, US, anatomist, educator; b. Louisville, Ky, Jan 7, 1902; s. Washington and Ida (Barkhouse); BS, U Chgo, 1923; MD, Johns Hopkins Med Sch, 1927; m. Josefa Barba, 1937. Prof, anat, since 1951, chmn, dept anat, dir, U Inst Neur Scis, 1951-67, both U of P; research asso, Carnagie Inst, Wash, DC, since 1951, mem staff since 1941; mem staff, Johns Hopkins Med Sch, 1929-41. Secy-treas, Amer Assn Anats, since 1955; mem: Natl Acad Scis; Amer Soc Arts and Scis; Amer Phys Soc; Amer Soc Biol Chems. Contbr to profsl jours. Hobby: sailing. Home; 4631 Pine St, Philadelphia, Pa. Office: Sch of Med, U of Pa, Philadelphia, Pa.

FLEXSER, Leo A, US, chemist; b. NYC, June 20, 1910; s. Morris and Kate (Gordon); BA, Columbia U, 1931, MA, 1932, PhD, 1935; m. Bertha Simberloff, Dec 29, 1939; c: Arthur. Vice-pres, Hoffmann-La Roche, Inc, since 1963, with co since 1941; research chem, Montrose Chem, Newark, 1935-36, staff until 1938; research, devl chem, NY Quinine and Chem, 1938-41. Prin contrib: devl of vitamins and pharmaceutical chems Bd trustees, Jersey City State Coll, 1968-74; f, Amer Inst. Chem; mem: Amer Chem Soc; AAAS; Amer Inst Chem Engrs; Soc Chem Ind. Home: 3 The Fairway, Upper Montclair, NJ. Office: Roche Park, Nutley, NJ.

FLIEGEL, Hyman J, US, attorney; b. Amdur, Pol, Sep 16, 1898; s. Harry and Sarah (Weiner); in US since 1907; BS, CCNY, 1920; LLB, Columbia U, 1922; m. Mollie Schwartz, June 27, 1926; c: Sylvia Nachtigall. Trial counsel, Tenzer, Greenblatt, Fallon & Kaplan, NYC, since 1944; counsel, B'nai Zion, NYC, since 1939; prin, NYC Comty Cens and Vacation Playgrounds, 1920-27. USN, 1918; USNR, 1918-21. Natl pres, B'nai Zion, 1959-61; natl vice-pres, ZOA, 1959-60; pres: Cong Shaare Torah, 1951-55; delg, Amer J Conf,

1943-47; ZOA, Biltmore conf, 1942; admn council, AJCong, since 1949; admn comm, ORT, since 1947; exec bd, Bklyn Zionist Region since 1944, pres, 1962-66; Bklyn JCC, since 1954; KH, since 1946, comm, Zionist Archives and Libr, since 1946; bd overseers, JTSA, since 1957; delg, WZC, 1961; dep mem, Zionist Action Comm, since 1961. Author: The Life and Times of Max Pine, 1959; ed: B'nai Zion Voice, since 1951; Radiant Light, KP, 1923-26; contbr to periodicals. Recipient, Awards: Treasury Dept 1942, 1943; Civilian Defense, NYC, 1945. Home: 141 E 21 St, Brooklyn, NY. Office: 235 E 42 St, New York, NY.

FLIEMAN, Moshe, Isr, engineer, public official; b. Ukraine, Russ, July 20, 1905; in Isr since 1930; dipl, elec engr, Electro-Mech Inst, Moscow, 1928; m. Rivka Starkman; c: Rachel, Nurit, Daniel. Mayor, Haifa, since 1969, dep mayor, 1955-69, mem city council, 1950; with Elec Corp, 1932-59; fmr mem, Hechalutz. Home: 32a Vitkin St, Haifa, Isr. Office: Haifa Munic, Haifa, Isr.

FLIGELMAN, Julius, US, business exec; b. Minneapolis, Minn, Oct 22, 1895; s. John and Antoinette (Friedman); att U Minn; m. Molly Sapero, Nov 20, 1920; c: Joan Travis, Mona Brandler. Chmn: LA Period Furniture Co; Exec Life Inst Co of Beverly Hills; First Exec Corp of Beverly Hills. a found: Isr Fgn Trade Credits Corp, NY; Electrochemical Inc, Haifa. Chmn: United JWF campaign, 1948; LA Bonds Isr campaign, 1955; U of Judaism; pres, Isr Histadrut Campaign, W coast region; natl bd dir: Reconstructionist Found; Natl Comm Labor Isr; JDC; co-found, J Reconstructionist Soc of Cal; bd dir: Isr Pub Inst Jerusalem; World J Bible Soc Found; Amer Technion Soc; Heb U, Jerusalem; Temple Isr; bd overseers: JTSA; natl gov council, Amer Asso J Educ; bd gov, State Isr Bonds; natl comm, Amer Isr Public Affairs. Home: 800 Sarbonne Rd, Los Angeles, Cal. Office: 1838 E Santa Barbara Ave, Los Angeles, Cal.

FLOCH, Joseph, US, artist; b. Vienna, Aus, Nov 5, 1895; s. Samuel and Jenny (Mauksch); in US since 1941; MA, Acad Fine Arts, Vienna, 1919; m. Hermine Fränkl, May 12, 1934; c: Jenny, Marguerite. Paintings represented in perm collections: Mus Modern Art, Paris; Jeu de Paume, Paris; Mus of Lille; Mus of Grenoble; Mus City of Paris; Mus of Mulhouse, all Fr; Whitney Mus; Metrop Mus, both NYC; N H de Young Mus, SF; Toledo Mus of Art; William Rockhill Nelson Gal, Kan City; Springfield Mus Fine Arts; Montclair Art Mus; Mus of Vienna; Albertina Mus, Vienna; Mus of Tel Aviv; Mus of Jerusalem; one-man shows in Eur; US; prof, New Sch of Social Research, 1962. Mem: Salon d'-Automne, Paris; Fed of Modern Painters and Sculptors, NY; Natl Acad of Design. Recipient: gold medal, Intl Exhb, Paris, 1937; Lippincott prize, Pa Acad of Fine Arts; award, Amer Acad Arts and Letters, 1954; Breevort Eickemeier award, Columbia U, 1955; William Palmer memorial prize, 1960; Chevalier of Fr Order of Arts and Letters; Isidor Meml gold medal, Natl Acad, 1963; first prize, E States Exhb, Mus of Fine Arts, Springfield, Mass, 1966; Saltus Gold medal of merit, Natl Acad, 1967. Home: 61 W 74 St, New York, NY. Studio: 54 W 74 St, New York, NY.

FLOCKS, Rubin H, US, urologist, educator; b. NYC, May 7, 1906; s. Morris and Rose (Blackman); BA, Johns Hopkins U, 1926, MD, 1930. Prof, head dept urol, U of Ia, since 1949, prof, urol, 1946-49; urol in chief, U Hosps, Ia City. Mem: AMA, past chmn, urol sect; Amer Urol Assn; Amer Assn Genito-Urinary Surgs; Clinical Soc Genito-Urinary Surg; Phi Beta Kappa; Sigma Xi; Alpha Omega Alpha; bd trustees, Amer Bd Urol. Hobbies: tennis, golf. Home: 514 Grandview Court, Iowa City, Ia. Office: U Hosps, Iowa City, Ia.

FLOHR, Roman, Isr, business exec; b. Lwow, Pol, Aug 22, 1910; s. Sigmund and Lola (Polak); in Isr since 1935; att Poly Coll, 1929-32; m. Simone de Lathouwer, 1946; c: Uri, Dan. Gen secy, Koor Inds, since 1951; dir: Intl Tracing Service, Geneva, 1948; Isr Min of Defense Regional Off, Haifa, 1948; secy, Soltam Ltd. Capt, J Brig, 1940-46. Exec dir, United Isr Appeal, Vic, 1966-67; secy PR Soc, 1959-64. Home: 36 Zirelson St, Tel Aviv, Isr. Office: 99 Ben Yehuda St, Tel Aviv, Isr.

FLORMAN, Alfred L, US, physician, educator; b. Jersey City, NJ, Oct 11, 1912; s. Samuel and Daisy (Schluger); AB, Princeton U, 1934; MD, Johns Hopkins Med Sch, 1938; m. Ruth Ludeke, Apr 26, 1944; c: Deborah, Sue, Amy. Prof, ped, NYU Med Sch, since 1968; research f, bact, Har-

vard Med Sch, 1940-42; visiting inves, virology, Hosp of Rockefeller Inst, 1946-47; dir, ped, N Shore Hosp, Manhasset, 1953-68; asso att ped, Mt Sinai Hosp, NYC, 1955-68; asst clinical prof, ped, Columbia U, 1959-63. Capt, US Army, 1943-46. Chmn, med adv comm, N Nassau Natl Found, since 1961; mem: Phi Beta Kappa; Amer Ped Soc; Soc for Ped Research; Amer Acad of Ped; AMA; Amer Assn Immunologists; NY Acad of Med. Contbr to profsl jours. Home: 46 Barberry Lane, Roslyn Heights, NY. Office: 550 First Ave, New York, NY.

FLOWERS, Harold Marvin, Isr, chemist; b. Leeds, Eng, Feb 6, 1927; s. Ben and Sara (Wagenheim); in Isr since 1953; BSc, hons, U of Leeds, 1947, PhD, 1950; m. Sylvia Polli Uri, Sep 15, 1952; c: Zvia, Sarona. Sr sci, Weizmann Inst of Sci, since 1965; Fulbright scholar, 1961-63; visiting prof, U of Cal, Berkeley, 1967-68. Pvt, Isr Army, 1952-53. Headmaster, Study Cen, Habonim, Eng, 1951-52; org, tchr, Youth Training, Educ Prog, Habonim, Eng, 1950-51; mem, Amer Chem Soc. Hobbies: photography, mt climbing. Home: 38 Beeri, Rehovot, Isr. Office: Weizmann Inst of Sci, Rehovot, Isr.

FLUEGELMAN, David B, US, insurance agt; b. NYC, Feb 6, 1903; s. Henry and Tessie (Bleier); BS, CCNY, 1923; m. Evelyn Cardozo, June 25, 1939; c: Andrew, Betty Kahn. Gen agt em, Conn Mutual Life Ins Co since 1968; fac mem, Chartered Life Underwriters Inst, U Conn. Pres: Natl Assn Life Underwriters, 1952-53; NY State Assn Life Underwriters, 1947-48; NYC Life Underwriters Assn, 1946-47; fmr chmn, NY State Adv Bd, Life Ins Examination, mem since 1947; life mem, Million Dollar Round Table, since 1943; mem, bd, Estate and Trust Council; mem: Phi Epsilon Pi, Grand Councilor, 1942-46; clubs: City Athletic; Old Oaks. Home: 23 Hotel Dr, White Plains, NY. Office: 342 Madison Ave, New York, NY.

FLUM, Yael, Isr, psychologist; b. Aussig, Czech, Apr 8, 1916; d. Adolf and Ada (Kraus) Kompert; in Isr since 1938; m. Max Flum, Apr, 1943; c: Handh, Tirza. Lectr, Heb U, since 1965; vocational counselor, Histadrut, 1942-56; psych sup, Min of Educ, 1957-61. Prin contrib: initiated counselor educ at Heb U. Mem, natl comm, Psychological Assn. Contbr articles to profsl publs. Home: 8 Bustenai St, Jerusalem, Isr. Office: Heb U, Jerusalem, Isr.

FOA, Eliahu, Isr, chemist; b. Torino, It, Sep 4, 1915; s. Moise and Anita; in Isr since 1939; PhD, U Genoa, It, 1937; m. Hanna Usigli, Mar 1, 1948; c: Hanita, Ruth ,Neomi. Head, applied radiation research dept, Sorek Nuclear Research Cen, since 1965; research prof, chem dep, Bar Ilan U, since 1968; head: inorganic chem dept, Isr AEC, 1950-56, sci personnel dept, 1958-60; external relations dept, 1958-66. Lt, IDF, 1948-63. Prin contribs, devl process for extraction of uranium from low grade ores; ind and other uses of radioisotopes; uses of radiation from large radiation sources. Contbr to sci jours. Home: POB 1126, Rehovot, Isr. Office: Sorek Nuclear Research Cen, Isr.

FOGEL, Ephim Gregory, US, educator; b. Odessa, Russ, Nov 15, 1920; s. Harry and Elizabeth (Mitnik); in US since 1923; BA, CCNY, 1941; MA, NYU, 1947; PhD, O State U, 1958; m. Charlotte Finkelstein, May 17, 1941; c: Daniel, David, Rebecca. Prof, Eng, Cornell U, since 1966, chmn, Eng dept, 1966-70, dir ,grad studies in Eng, 1963-65, on fac since 1949. Sgt, US Army, 1942-46. Hon Adv, Jt Comm for Summer Sch, UK; Supervisory Comm, Cornell Concordance; chmn, selection comm, George Jean Nathan Drama Award, 1966, 1969; mem: Pres Commn on Educ and Student Role in U; AAUP; MLA, Renaissance Soc of Amer; Shakespeare Assn; Phi Beta Kappa, CCNY, Cornell, clubs, Statler. Author: Othello in Teaching Shakespeare, 1969; Introduction to reprint of J L Cardozo, The Contemporary Jew in Elizabethan Drama, 1971; co-author, Evidence for Authorship, 1966; contbr: Shakespeare Quarterly, Bulletin of the NY Public Libr, Jour of Higher Education; Studies in Honour of Margaret Schlauch, 1966; Bicentenary Wordsworth Studies in Honor of John Finch, 1971; poems in: A Treasury of Jewish Poetry, Cross Section, Atlantic Monthly, Poetry. Recipient: grant, Natl Endowment for Hums, 1967; f, O State U, 1947; Regents Scholar, NY State Bd Regents, 1937-41; Tremaine Scholar, CCNY, 1938-41; Leon Medal for Best Record in Eng, CCNY, 1941. Spec interests: Shakespeare, Sir Philip Sidney, Amer Poetry. Home: 812 Triphammer Rd, Ithaca, NY. Office: Dept of Eng, Cornell U, Ithaca, NY.

FOGEL, Herbert Allen, US, attorney; b. Phila, Pa, Apr 20, 1929; s. Frank and Ethel (Weinstein); AB, U of Pa, 1949,

LLB, 1952; m. Alexandra Wolf, June 16, 1957; c: Alexa, Marya. Partner, Obermayer, Rebmann, Maxwell & Hippel, since 1959. Vice-chmn: Sitting Judge, Comm, Phila Bar Assn; 125 Anniversary, Intl B'nai B'rith Hum award Dinner for Hugh Scott; Citizens Charter Comm of Phila; Comm for New Fed Court House, Phila Bar Assn; bd mgrs, Moore Coll of Art; bd govs: Lawyers Club; Moss Rehab Hosp; bd dirs: Phila chap, Young Audiences, Inc, solicitor; Eagleville Hosp and Rehab Cen; SF Hope; Phila chap, AJComm; natl exec comm, Amer J Hist Soc; bd trustees: Phila Orch Pension Fund Found; FJA; constitution revision comm, Pa Bar Assn; mem: Bench-Bar Comm, Phila Bar Assn. Home: 6540 Wissahickon Ave, Philadelphia, Pa. Office: 1418 Packard Bldg, Philadelphia, Pa.

FOGELMAN, Lazar, US, journalist; b. Neswish, Russ, May 27, 1891; s. Simha and Adele (Sacker); in US since 1921; JD, Imperial U, Warsaw, 1912; att Psychoneur Inst, Petrograd, 1913-15; LLD, Fordham Law Sch, 1927; m. Sarah Damesek, 1920 (decd); c: Edwin; m. 2nd Elsie Nimetz (decd). Ed, The Jewish Daily Forward, since 1962, ed, feature writer, 1961-62; dir, J Tchrs Sem, 1924-27; ed, Zukunft, Yiddish mag, 1939-41. Mem: World Memorial for J Martyrs; J Lab Comm; J Culture Cong; fmr: pres, J Writers Union; treas, Workmen's Circle. Author: Paul Axelrod, 1928; Booker T Washington, 1930; Workman's Circle, short hist, 1931. Home: 1884 Summit Ave, St Paul, Minn.

FOGELMAN, Morris J, US, surgeon, educator; b. Chgo, Ill, Feb 22, 1922; s. Joseph and Tillie (Schwartz); AB, U of Ill, 1942, MD, 1944, MS, 1948; m. Marilyn Marr, Jan 6, 1958; c: Evan, Joe, Margot. Clinical prof, surg, U of Tex, Southwestern Med Sch, since 1957, on fac since 1948; research f, dept, clinical sci, U of Ill, Coll of Med, 1947-48; asst phys, 1947-48; sr att surg, Parkland Memorial Hospital, Dallas; cons phys, surg: VA hosps, Dallas, McKinney, Tex; att surg: Baylor Hosp; St Paul's Hosp; Gaston Hosp; Parkland Memorial Hosp. Capt, US Army, MC, 1945-47. F, Amer Assn for Surg of Trauma; dipl, Amer Bd of Surg; mem: bd dirs, Dallas Sym Orch; Civic Opera Assn; mem: Dallas Citizens Traffic League; Dallas Council World Affairs; Amer Assn for the Hist of Med; Amer Coll Surgs; AAAS; AMA; Dallas Co Med Soc; Dallas Soc of General Surgs; Dallas S Clinical Soc; NY Acad of Sci; Tex Med Assn; Tex Traumatic Surg Soc; Sigma Xi. Home: 7608 Woodthrush, Dallas, Tex. Office: 712 N Washington, Dallas, Tex.

FOIGHEL, Isi, Den, educator; b. Chemnitz, Ger, Dec 21, 1927; in Den since 1933; DJ, U Copenhagen; m. Vera Hecksler, Mar 5, 1953; c: Hanne, Allan. Prof, law, U Copenhagen, since 1951; visiting scholar, Harvard U, 1969. Danish delg, OECD Legal Expert Group, since 1961; pres: Danish Ref Council; Danish ORT; legal adv, Danish delg at ICJ Northsea Continental Shelf Case; exec comm, UN Delg for Ref, 1968; found, secy, Danish-Isr Soc. Author: Naturalization of Foreign Property, 1957; Nationalization and Compensation, 1961; several books on intl and Danish law. Home: Jaegersborg Alle 136, Copenhagen, Den.

FOLDES, Eugene, US, physician, educator; b. Budapest, Hung, May 6, 1891; s. David and Rose (Lanzman); in US since 1925; MD, Royal Hung U, 1914; m. Henny Fechner, July 14, 1925. Pvt practice, internist, since 1926; clinical prof, em, NY Polyclinic Med Sch and Hosp, since 1959; asst prof, med, Royal Hung U, Budapest, 1922-24. F, Amer Coll Gastroenterology; dipl, Amer Bd of Internal Med, since 1936, mem: Intl Gastroenterology Soc; Intl Soc Internal Med; NY Card Soc; NY Acad of Scis; AMA; NY State Med Soc; NY Soc Internal Med; Royal Soc of Health, Eng. Author: A New Approach to Dietetic Therapy, 1933; contbr to med jours. Home: 7 E 85 St, New York, NY. Office: 898 Park Ave, New York, NY.

FOLDI, Andrew Harry, Switz, singer, music dir; b. Budapest, Hung, July 20, 1926; s. Alexis and Ann (Rothman); in Switz since 1961; MA, U Chgo, PhB, 1948; m. Leona Levy, Aug 10, 1947; c: David, Nancy. Opera and concert singer, performed: La Scala, Milan; Wiener Festwochen; Bayerische Staatsoper, Munich; Grand Théatre, Geneva; SF Opera; Chgo Lyric Opera; Luzerner Festwochen; Aldeburgh Festival; Orchs: Stravinsky Festival; Concertgebouw of Amsterdam; Chgo Sym; Pittsburgh Sym; Gulbenkian, Lissabon; Aus TV Network; BBC, London; Bayerische, Radio; Radio Beromünster, Zurich, etc. Prof, grad, musicology, 1949-52; prof of voice, 1950-57; dir, Opera Workshop, 1951-57, all DePaul U, Chgo; lectr, Hum, Fine Arts, dir, music prog, dept of Adult Educ, U Chgo, 1951-61; cantor, music dir: Temple

Isaiah Isr, Chgo, 1948-61; Eng speaking J Comty, Geneva, since 1966. Mem: Amer Musicological Soc; Natl Assn Tchrs of Singing. Author: An Introduction to Music, 1959; Music Criticisms, Chgo Times, 1947-48. Home: 11 Ch des Crêts de Champel, Geneva, Switz.

FOLKMAN, Jerome Daniel, US, rabbi; b. Cleveland, O, Sep 25, 1907; s. Ben and Rose (Tronstein); BA, U Cincinnati, 1928; BHL, HUC, 1928, ordained rabbi, 1931; grad sch, U Mich, 1934-36; hon DD, HUC, 1957; PhD, O State U, 1953; m. Bessie Schomer, Dec 14, 1930; c: Moses, David, Joy Moss. Rabbi Temple Isr, since 1947; adj prof, sociol, O State U since 1963; rabbi: Temple Beth Isr, Jackson, Mich, 1931-36; Temple Emanuel, Grand Rapids, Mich, 1937-47; mem, bd dirs, Mins Life and Casualty Union; bd govs, HUC 1952-56; lectr, Englander Memorial, 1957. F, Amer Sociol Assn; mem: bd trustees: Columbus Hosp Fed; Grant Hosp; bd dirs: Franklin Co, Heart Assn; Columbus adv Council, naval affairs since 1958; Alpha Kappa Delta; AAUP; club, Fac, O State U. Author: The Cup of Life, 1955; Design for Jewish Living, 1955; co-author, Marriage has Many Faces, 1969; contbr to scholarly jours and popular mags. Recipient: Gov award, State of O, 1968. Home: 2538 Maryland Ave, Columbus, Ohio. Study: 5419 E Broad St, Columbus, Ohio.

FOLMAN, Mordechai, Isr, chemist, educator; b. Lodz, Pol, Apr 14, 1923; s. Arie and Lea; in Isr since 1950; MSc, chem engr, Lodz Polytech, 1950; DSc, Technion, Haifa, 1955; PhD, Cambridge U, Eng, 1958; m. Wanda Rein, Aug 17, 1944; c: Dorit, Orna, Ariel. Prof, chmn, dept, Technion, Haifa, since 1964; lectr, sr lectr, 1955-64; visiting sci: Natl Bur Standards, Wash, 1966-67; Bristol U, 1967-68. Prin contrib, research in phys and surface chem. Mem: Faraday Soc, Eng; Isr Chem Soc. Contbr numerous articles to sci publs. Home: 42a Tel Maneh St, Haifa, Isr. Office: Technion, Haifa, Isr.

FONDILLER, William, US, engineer; b. Igarella, Russ, Dec 21, 1885; s. Herman and Rachel (Barish); in US since 1886; BS, CCNY, 1903; EE, Columbia U, 1909, MA, 1913; hon DSc, Isr Inst of Tech, 1949; m. Naomi Bernfeld, Aug 3, 1915; c: Robert, Danial, Gloria Atlas. Cons engr since 1951; lab engr, W Elec Co, 1909-24, head, phys lab, 1923; dir of elec apparatus devl, Bell Telephone Labs, 1925-43, asst vice-pres and treas, 1943-50; research asso, Columbia Sch of Engr, 1935-50; cons, Off Research and Devl, US Govt, 1942-45. Holder, patents for loading coils, transformers, cables. Hon pres, Amer Technion Soc, 1950; trustee, NY Inst of Tech, 1958; bd dirs, Amer Assn for UN, Wash, DC, 1957-59; f: Amer Inst of EE; AAAS; NY Acad of Sci; clubs: Cosmos, Wash, DC; Columbia U, NY. Contbr to tech jours. Recipient: Medals: Townsend Harris, CCNY, 1944; U, Col U, 1945; Egleston, Col Engr Alumni, 1967. Home and office: 262 Central Park W, New York, NY.

FORKOSCH, Morris David, US, educator, author, attorney; b. NY, Feb 26, 1908; s. Samuel and Yetta (Heimovitz); LLB, St Johns U, NY, 1930, LLM, 1932; BA, NYU, 1936, MA, 1938, JSD, 1948; PhD, Grad Fac, New Sch for Social Research, 1952, MSS, 1956; m. Selma Milner, Nov 26, 1934 (decd); c: Joel, Jonathan. Prof, law, chmn, dept public law, Bklyn Law Sch, since 1949; practicing atty since 1931; admitted: to NY bar 1931; to US Supr Court, 1939; prof, econ, Latin Amer Inst, 1946-49; prof, bus math, Hervey Jr Coll, 1946-49. Lt, US Army, 1944-46. Mem: natl bd dirs, Amer Soc for Legal Hist, NE States br, past pres; presidency, Internationales Institut für Kommunalwissenschaften; grievance panel, AAUP; Assn Bar, NYC; Amer Political Sci Assn; fmr, mem natl bd dirs and cen counsel, Anti-Nazi League for Hum Rights. Author: Antitrust and the Consumer, 1956; A Treatise on Administrative Law, 1956; Carmody-Forkosch New York Practice, 7th ed, 1963; A Treatise on Labor Law, 1953, 2nd ed, 1965; Constitutional Law, 1963, 2nd ed, 1969; ed: The Political Philosophy of Arnold Brecht, 1952; Essays on Legal History in Honor of Felix Frankfurter, 1966. Hobbies: scuba diving, skiiing. Home and office: 250 Joralemon St, Brooklyn, NY.

FORMAN, Max L, US, rabbi; b. Albany, NY, Mar 6, 1909; s. Isaac and Celia (Bernstein); BA, U of Pa, 1930; ordained rabbi, JTSA, 1934, MHL, 1949, DD, 1966; m. Diana Slavin, July 4, 1933; c: Gayl Shechter, Cyrelle, Barr, Donna. Rabbi: Hollis Hills J Cen, since 1955; Temple B'nai Aaron, Phila, 1944-45. Pres, RA, Queens div, 1960-62; mem: NY Bd Rabbis; ZOA; B'nai B'rith; Histadruth Ivrith. Author: Capsules of Wisdom, 1948; Ideas That Work, 1952; World's

Best Thought, 1969. Home: 80-51 Bell Blvd, Jamaica, NY. Study: 210-10 Union Turnpike, Flushing, NY.

FORMAN, Phillip, US, jurist; b. NYC, Nov 30, 1895; s. Morris and Tilly (Peters); LLB, Temple U, 1919; m. Pearl Karlberg, Apr 12, 1937. Judge, US Court of Appeals, Third Circuit, since 1959; US dist atty, 1928-32; judge, US Dist Court, 1932-58; chief judge, 1951-59. Pres, bd mgrs, NJ State Hosp, 1947-58; trustee, Rutgers U, 1947; mem, bd: AJComm; JDC; JWB; J Fed, Trenton. Home: 5 Belmont Circle, Trenton, NJ. Office: Fed Bldg, Trenton, NJ.

FORMIGGINI, Gina, It, author, journalist; b. Verona, It, Aug 23, 1902; d. Arnaldo and Giulia (Padovani) Voghera; att Brera acad, Milano; m. Arrigo Formiggini, Oct 4, 1922; c: Giorgio, Arnaldo, Arturo, Paola Parrella. Author: Einstein Nella Vita E Nell' Ebraismo, 1950; Franco Sogna, for children, 1952; haTikva, Il Canto Della Speranza, 1955, trans into Span, 1956; Vita in Vetrina, 1961; Attraverso la Republica Democratica Tedesca, 1967; Apocalisse Sull'Europa, 1969; various monographies, anthols, journalist since 1950; contbr numerous articles to various jours. Mem: Adei WIZO, past vice-pres; letters' comm, FIDAPA, Lyceum; fmr, mem of comm, Consiglio della donna; Soroptimist Intl Assn; Comunita Europea degli Scrittori. Recipient: Penna d'Oro, Accademia d'Arte di Bergamo, 1954; Presidence Prize, Presidenza Consiglio Ministri, 1956; Gold Medal, narrative prize, FIDAPA, 1964; Archeol prize, Acad Archeol It, 1966; gold medal, lit prize, Tarquinia-Cardarelli, 1969. Hobbies: theatre, archaeol. Home: 186 Via Cimarosa, Naples, It.

FORSHER, Bruno Jossel, US, spacecraft engr; b. Vienna, Aus, Nov 16, 1914; s. Moses and Cornelia (Berger); in US since 1938; att Technische Hochschule, Vienna, 1932-38. Mem: tech staff, Reliability Engr for Nuclear Power Action ,Spacecrafts and Aircraft since 1954; Gen Dymanics, Pomona; Aerospace Corp, USAF; Lockheed Missiles Space. Prin contrib: research on all orbital satellites, bio-satellite sci prog of NASA. Vice-pres, Soc Isr Philatelists; dir: Workshop Philatelic Exhbs of S Cal; Inst Environmental Sci, 1953-63; mem: Writers Guild of Amer Philatelic Soc; club, LA Philatelic. Author: The Interim Period Stamps of Israel, March to July, 1948; Supplement to the Tabs of Israel, 1963; The Reliability of Space Craft Systems, 1964; contbr to philatelic publs. Hobby: Isr interim period stamps. Home: 16446 Bircher St, Granada Hills, Cal. Office: 1800 N Highland Ave, Hollywood, Cal.

FORSTER, Arnold, US, attorney, author; b. NYC, June 25, 1912; s. Hyman and Dorothy (Turits) Fastenberg; LLB, St John's U, 1935; m. May Kasner, Sep 29, 1940; c: Stuart, Jane. Dir, civil rights,gen counsel, ADL, since 1940; police justice, Suffolk Co, 1953-56. Author: Anti-Semitism, 1947, 2nd ed, 1948; A Measure of Freedom, 1950; Report from Israel, 1969; co-author: Troublemakers, 1952; Cross-Currents, 1956; Some of My Best Friends, 1962; Danger on the Right, 1964; Report on the Ku Klux Klan, 1965; Report on the John Birch Society, 1966; The Radical Right, 1967. Mem: NY State Bar; US Supr Court Bar; B'nai B'rith. Hobby: painting. Home: 79 Wykagyl Terr, New Rochelle, NY. Office: 315 Lexington Ave, New York, NY.

FORTI, Emilio, It, physician, educator; b. Verona, It, May 25, 1901; s. Samuel and Bice (Lombroso); att U Bologna, Padova, Modena, 1912-18, MD; MD, Mass License, Boston, 1940; m. Egle Ancona, Sep 5, 1929. Docent, obstet, gyn, Modena U, since 1947 and 1931-38; asso obstet, gyn, clinic, U Perugla, 1931-38; surg, USPHS, 1945-46; asso surg clinic, U Roma, 1947-56. Mem: AMA; It Soc Surg; It Soc Obstet and Gyn; Roman Med Soc; IMA; pres, KH, It, 1954-62; vice-pres, Natl Blood Donors Assn, It, 1938; f, Intl Coll Surgs. Hobby: antique glasses, pottery. Contbr to med jours. Home and office: Via Lima 48, Rome, It.

FORTUNA, Luba, Isr, jurist; b. Lith, Oct 29, 1918; d. Jacob and Cecilia (Friedlander) Rosenthal; in Isr since 1939; dipl, atty, U Fac of Law, Lith; m. Immanuel Fortuna, July 1, 1937; c: Gilead, Cilla, Arnon, Nizzan. Judge. Haifa Courts, since 1954; Haifa Dep Dist Atty, 1948-52; fmr pvt law practice. Pres, Comm for Wayward Girls; org, leg aid burs in Isr; mem, Soroptimist Org. Author: Legal Aid Comparative Study. Home: 43 Panorama St, Haifa, Isr.

FOX, Alan Martin, Eng, civil servant; b. London, July 5, 1938; s. Sidney and Clarice (Solov); BSc, hons, PhD, Queen Mary Coll, London, 1956-63; m. Sheila Pollard, June 20, 1965;

c: Victoria. Prin, Min of Tech, since 1963. Mem, council, ZF, Gt Brit and N Ir, fmr vice-pres, ZF; fmr: chmn, Fed Zionist Youth; pres, Students Union, Queen Mary Coll. Home: 46 Wynchgate St, London, Eng. Office: Min of Tech, London, Eng.

FOX, Isaac Solomon, Eng, physician; b. Cracow, Pol, Nov 25, 1896; s. Jacob and Rosalie (Trenner); desc of Byalystokker Maggid; in Eng since 1902; MB, ChB, U Med Sch, Liverpool, 1921; m. Gladys Lightman, June 27, 1927; c: Joan Levinson, Victor, Mervyn. Pvt practice. Hon vice-pres, ZF of Gt Brit; pres, Syn Council ZF, Gt Brit; chmn: Friends ZF Educ Trust; Day-Sch Comm, ZF of Gt Brit; chmn bd govs; Rosh Pinah J Primary Sch; Mathilda-Marks-Kennedy Primary Sch; Hillel House Schs, both London; gov, Carmel Coll, Wellingford; f, Royal Soc Med, London; fmr: sheriff, City of Chester, 1931-32, mayor, 1932-33; life pres, Muswell Hill Heb Cong; exec, London Bd J Rel Educ; mem council, United Syns, London; mem, Bd Deps Brit J. Co-ed: Excerpta Medica, sect Neur and Psycht; Second Eur Cong of Neur Surg; fmr chmn ed bd: Gates of Zion; Zionist Year Book. Office: 9C Bedford Towers, Kings Rd, Brighton, Sussex, Eng.

FOX, John Jacob, US, business exec, civil engr; b. Tokay, Hung, Feb 22, 1896; s. Lester and Kate (Freiman); in US since 1901; deg, Civil Eng, Cornell U, Ithaca, NY, 1917; m. Rose Greenberg, Sep 21, 1924; c: Laurel Vlock, Marian Wexler. Pres, Fox Steel Corp, since 1950, chmn bd, Fox Steel, since 1950. Chmn, Isr Bond Comm, Gtr New Haven; fmr pres: New Haven JCC; Cong B'nai Jacob; Conn Zionist Region. Home: Ansonia Rd, Woodbridge, Conn. Office: 312 Boston Post Rd, Orange, Conn.

FOX, Louis J, US, merchant; b. Baltimore, Md, June 8, 1911; s. Robert and Sylvia (Miller); m. Dorothy Newman, Sep 11, 1933; c: Shirley, Ellinor (decd). Owner, Fox Chevrolet Sales Inc, Baltimore, Md, since 1933. Sgt, US Army, 1944-46. Pres: J Comty Cen, 1951-53; JWF, Baltimore, 1955-57, fmr vice-pres, natl chmn, large city budgeting conf, 1959-62; CJFWF, since 1966; Baltimore Heb Cong, since 1952; mem: natl cabinet, UJA; Pi Tau Pi; clubs: Suburban; Phoenix, all of Baltimore. Home: 7706 Seven Mile Lane, Pikesville, Md. Office: 2020 Hanover St, Baltimore, Md.

FOX, Marvin, US, educator, author; b. Chgo, Ill, Oct 17, 1922; s. Norman and Sophie (Hershenhorn); BA, Northwestern U, 1942, MA, 1946; ordained rabbi, Heb Theol Coll, Chgo, 1942; PhD, U Chgo, 1950; m. June Trachtenberg, Feb 20, 1944; c: Avrom, Daniel, Sheryl. Prof, phil, O State U, since 1948; visiting prof, Heb Theol Coll, 1955. US Army 1942-46. F, Amer Council Learned Socs, 1962-63; mem: Amer Phil Assn; Medieval Acad of Amer, AAUP. Author: Kant's Fundamental Principles of the Metaphysic of Morals, 1949; Diversity of Methods in Dewey's Ethical Theory, 1951; Kierkegaard and Rabbinic Judaism, 1953; Moral Facts and Moral Theory, 1954; The Trials of Socrates, 1956; Buber's Moral Philosophy, 1962; Theisitic Bases of Ethics, 1963; Religion and Human Nature in the Philosophy of David Hume, 1964; Prolegomenon to Cohens, The Teachings of Maimonides 1968; The Meaning of Theology Today, 1968; Maimonides and Aquinas on Natural Law, 1969; contbr ed, Judaism, since 1954; asso ed, J Parent, since 1956; mem, ed bd: Horizon, since 1956; Tradition, since 1958. Recipient: Elizabeth Clay Howald postdoc f, 1956-57. Home: 128 S Ardmore Rd, Columbus, O. Office: O State U, Columbus, O.

FOX, Raymond, Isr, physicist; b. NYC, July 17, 1932; s. Morris and Bertha (Rosenfeld); in Isr since 1961; BS, CCNY, 1950-53; MA, Harvard U, 1955, PhD, 1958; m. Barbara Smith, Sep 4, 1955. Asso prof, physics, since 1967; sr physicist, U of Cal, Livermore, 1958-61; NSF F, Weizmann Inst, 1961-62; sr lectr, Technion, 1962-67. Mem: Phi Beta Kappa; Sigma Xi. Contbr numerous articles to sci jours. Recipient: NSF F, US Govt, 1961. Hobby, singing. Home: 67a Einstein St, Haifa, Isr. Office: Technion, Haifa, Isr.

FOX, Samuel J, US, rabbi, educator; b. Cleveland, O, Feb 25, 1919; s. Joseph and Yetta (Mandel); att Talmudical Acad, 1936; BA, Yeshiva Coll, 1940; ordained rabbi, Rabbi Isaac Elchanan Theol Sem, 1941; MA, Butler U, 1944; PhD, Harvard U, 1959; m. Edith Muskin, Jan 25, 1942. Rabbi, Cong Chevra Tehilim, since 1960; prof, hist, phil, Sout - eastern Mass Tech Inst, N Dartmouth, Mass; prof, theol, Merrimack Coll; rabbi: United Heb Cong, Indianapolis, 1941-51, Cong Anshei Sfarad, Lynn, 1951-58. Pres: Orthodox Rabb Council of Gtr Boston; Mass Council Rabbis; exec vice-pres, NE region, Rel Zionists Amer, since 1959; chmn United Rabb Chaplaincy Commn of Mass; natl exec comm, RabCA; bd dir, Gen Theol Libr; mem, Blue Ribbon Commn, Gov Commn to study public aid to pvt educ instn in Mass; AAUP. Ed-in-chief, RabCA sermon manual; columnist: JTA; Horizon; host, moderator, TV prog; contbr to J publs. Home: 27 Harwood St, Lynn, Mass. Office: 611 Washington St, Boston, Mass.

FOX, Samuel L, US, physician, educator; b. Baltimore, Md, Dec 27, 1914; s. Jacob and Ida (Sahm); Pharm G, U Md, 1934, BS, 1936, MD, 1938; m. Drusilla Wolff, Dec 30, 1948; c: Samuel, Richard. Pvt practice, specialising in: eye, since 1960, eye, ear, nose and throat, 1940-60; assts prof, pharm, U Md Med Sch, since 1964, asst prof, phys, 1949-64; lectr phys, U Md Dent Sch, since 1963; dir, dept ophthal, S Baltimore Gen Hosp, since 1968; visiting lectr, U Md Sch of Pharm, since 1951; mem, med bd, US induction sta, Baltimore, 1940-46. Dipl: Amer Bd of Otolaryngology; Amer Bd of Ophthal; FACS; f: Intl Coll of Surgs; Assn Amer Med Colls; Amer Acad Ophthal and Otolaryngology; Amer Otorhinologic Soc for Plastic Surg; AAAS; Amer Soc of Ophthal and Otolaryngologic Allergy; Amer Assn for Hist of Med; Ind Med Assn; Amer Laryngological, Rhinological and Otological Soc; Amer Acad Plastic Surg Head and Neck; AMA; pres, mid-Atlantic council, UAHC, since 1964, chmn comm on census and redistricting, since 1967, bd trustees since 1964, exec comm since 1966, fmr, nominating, prog comms; hon life trustee, Temple Oheb Shalom, past pres; chmn med staff and exec comm, S Baltimore Gen Hosp; pres elect, Md Ind Med Assn; mem : Med and Chirurgical Fac of Md; Baltimore City Med Soc; S Med Assn; Rho Chi; Masons; Scottish Rite; Shriners; Civitans. Author: Comments on US Pharmacopoeia XI and the National Formulary VI, 1937; contbr numerous articles to med jours. Hobby: gardening. Home: 3518 Barton Oaks Rd, Pikesville, Md. Office: 1205 St Paul St, Baltimore, Md.

FOX, Sanford J, US, lawyer, educator; b. NYC, Sep 28, 1929; s. Herman and Martha (Cohen); AB, hons, U of Ill, 1950; LLB, Harvard U, 1953; m. Vivian Daitz, Apr 3, 1954; c: Gregory, Michael, Diana. Prof, law, Boston Coll Law Sch, since 1959; cons on juvenile court, Pres Johnson's Commn on Law Enforcement and Admn of Justice; teaching f, Harvard U, 1957-58; asst dir, project for effective justice, Columbia U, 1958-59. Legal off, USN, 1954-57. Chief draftsman, NH criminal code; co-reporter, Mass Revised criminal code; mem: World Mh Assn; Acad Social and Political Sci; Mass Crime Commn; Gov's Comm on Jails and Houses of Correction, 1961-62; Intl Soc of Criminology; NY State, DC Bar Assns. Author: Science and Justice, 1968; contbr to legal jours. Recipient: Natl Inst of Mh, F in psycht and delinquency, 1960-61; Ford Found f, 1961-62, 1963-64. Home: 15 Englewood Ave, Brookline, Mass. Office: Boston Coll Law Sch, Brighton, Mass.

FOX, Sidney A, US, ophthalmologist, educator; b. Russ, Jan 30, 1898; s. Louis and Rebecca (Albert); in US since 1904; BA, Brown U, 1919; MD, St Louis U, 1931; MSc, U of Pa, 1935; m. Dorothea Doctors, 1931. Pvt practice, NYC, since 1935; clinical prof, ophthal, NYU, Med Sch, since 1955; cons: Goldwater Mem Hosp: Vet Hosp, NY; Hosp for Jt Diseases. Lt col, US Army MC, since 1943. F: Amer Coll of Surgs; AMA; Amer Acad of Ophthal and Otolaryngology; NY Acad of Med; Amer Bd of Ophthal; mem: Alpha Omega Alpha. Author: Your Eyes, 1944; Ophthalmic Plastic Surg, 1952; Affections of the Lids, 1964; Surgery of Ptosis, 1968; contbr to sci publs. Recipient, Legion of Merit Award, 1946. Home and office: 11 E 90 St, New York, NY.

FRAENKEL, Aviezri Siegmund, Isr, mathematician; b. Munich, Ger, June 7, 1929; s. Joel and Esther (Pineas); in Isr since 1939; BSc, Technion, Haifa, 1953, MSc, 1957; PhD, UCLA 1961; m. Shaula Babad, June 7, 1956; c: Jedidja, Jigal, Amir, Jael, Abraham. Sr sci, Weizmann Inst of Sci, since 1962, elec engr, 1954-57; head, dept math, asso prof, Bar Ilan U, since 1966; res asst engr, UCLA, 1957-61; asst prof, math, U Ore, 1961-62. Lt, IDF. Prin contrib: found, dir, experimental full text electronic retrieval sys for responsa. Chmn, IPA Comm for HS Computer Educ; bd dirs, IPA Info Process Assn, Isr; mem: Amer Math Soc; Math Assn of Amer; Assn Computing Machinery; Inst Elec and Electronics Engrs; secy, Agudat Mitzvah Walev. Contbr sci papers. Recipient: Fulbright travel grant, US Govt, 1957. Home: Neveh Weizmann, Rehovot, Isr. Office: Weizmann Inst of Sci, Rehovot, Isr.

FRAENKEL, Gottfried S, US, educator; b. Munich, Ger, Apr 23, 1901; s. Emil and Flora (Weil); in US since 1948; PhD, U Munich, 1925; m. Rachel Sobol, Dec 15, 1928; c: Gideon, Dan. Prof, entomology, U of Ill, since 1948; asst, Heb U, Jerusalem, 1928-30; privatdozent, comparative phys, U of Frankfurt, 1931-33; lectr, phys, Imperial Coll Sci and Tech, U London, 1935-48; visiting prof: U Minn, 1947; Heb U, Jerusalem, 1968; U Paris, 1968; sci adv, Isr Inst of Biol Research, Ness Ziona. Mem, Natl Acad of Sci. Author: Decorative Title Pages of Music, 201 Examples from 1500 to 1800, pub 1968; co-author, The Orientation of Animals, 1940, 1961; contbr numerous publs to profsl jours. Home: 606 W Oregon, Urbana, Ill. Office: Dept of Entomology, U of Ill, Urbana, Ill.

FRAENKEL, Henry, Den, architect; b. Copenhagen, Den, May 23, 1900; s. Louis and Sophia (Blasberg); MAA, Royal Acad of Art, Copenhagen, 1928; m. Eva Lachmann, 1931. Pvt practice since 1928; works include: Titan machinery factory; Cloetta Chocolate Factory; Town Hall, Vreta Kloster; old age home of N J Fraenkels Found; pvt, ind, official bldgs in Den, Swed; exhb: Charlottenborg; Copenhagen; Trienale, Milan. Mem bd, Swed Ind Housing Soc, 1945-67. Found, ed, The Handbook of Building Industry, 1930-64; contbr to profsl jours. Home: Carl Plougsvej 7, Copenhagen, Den. Office: Frederiksberggade 27, Copenhagen, Den.

FRAENKEL, Josef, Eng, journalist, author; b. Ustrzyki-dolne, Pol, June 11, 1903; s. Moses and Taube (Weinberger); in Eng since 1939; att Vienna U, 1927-32; m. Dora Rosenfeld; c: Ruth. Dir, press dept, WJC, since 1945; secy, J Record Off since 1957; head JTA, Czech, 1937-39; contbr to J papers and publs in maj cities. Delg: WZCs, 1929-39, London, 1945; WJC, first session, 1936; hon secy: Aus br WJC, 1936-38; Council Continental Zionists, 1939-48; Assn J Journalists and Authors, Gt Brit, 1940-68; Jacob Ehrlich Soc, since 1953; found, World Union, J Journalists; coord, prep comm, World Conf J Journalists, Jerusalem, 1959-60; chmn: J State Party, Gt Brit, 1940-46; Nahum Sokolow Soc, 1939-47; co-found, Unity Group, 1940-47; head, Boycott Comm Against Ger, Vienna, 1936-38; exec comm mem: ZF, 1942-46; YIVO, 1948-60; world exec comm, Zionist Revisionists, 1946. Author: Theodor Herzl, des Schöepfers erstes Wollen, 1934; Herzl, 1936; Palästina Lacht, 1936; Siegmund Werner, ein Mitarbeiter Herzls, 1939; Theodor Herzl, 1946; Robert Stricker, 1950; History of the Shekel, 1952; Louis D Brandeis, 1959; Mathias Acher, 1959; Jewish Libraries of the World, 1959; Lucien Wolf and Theodor Herzl, 1960; Jewish Press of Gt Brit, 1823-1963, pub 1963; Dubnow, Herzl and Ahad Haam, 1963; Nahum Goldmann, 1967; Jewish Press of the World, 6th ed, 1967; Jews of Austria, 1967; co-author, Man and Legend, 1963. Home: Larkhall Rise, London, SW4, Eng. Office: 55 New Cavendish St, London W1, Eng.

FRAENKEL, Joseph A, Isr, engineer; b. Schweidnitz, Silesia, Sep 16, 1891; s. Moritz and Malwine (Friedlaender); att U Munich, 1910-14; Dipl, Engr, U Hanover, 1920; m. Lore Hirschfeld; c: George. Cons engr since 1965; bldg cons engr, Berlin, 1920-34; transp, traffic adv to bus coops, Haifa, Tel Aviv, 1939-48; chief engr, Isr Min Transp, 1948-65. Asso mem, Inst of Transp, Eng; mem: Engrs and Architects Assn in Isr; Inst of Traffic Engrs, US; club, Rotary. Contbr to profsl jours. Hobbies: drawing, painting, photography. Home and office: 29 Yehudah Hayamit St, Tel Aviv, Isr.

FRAENKEL, Malka, Isr, organization exec; b. Baarn, Holland, July 31, 1892; in Isr since 1929; att Amsterdam U; m. A H Fraenkel; four c. Pres, Keren Yaldenu, Jerusalem. Recipient, Outstanding Citizen of Jerusalem, 1961. Home: Bet Hama'alot, Jerusalem, Isr.

FRAENKEL, Stephen J, US, research engineer; b. Berlin, Ger, Nov 28, 1917; s. Max and Martha (Plessner); in US since 1938; BS, with distinction, U Neb, 1940, MS, 1941; PhD, Ill Inst of Tech, 1951; m. Josephine Rubnitz, June 28, 1941; c: Richard, Charles, Martha. Gen mgr, research and devl, container div, Container Corp of Amer, since 1964; engr: Pittsburgh Des Moines Steel, 1941-44; Link Belt, Chgo, 1944-46; mgr, dept of propulsion and structural research, Armour Research Found, Chgo, 1946-55; dir, research and devl, Stanray, 1955-63; dir, engr research, Continental Can, Chgo, 1962-64. Pres, Amer Rocket Soc, Chgo sec, 1957-58; mem, bd trustees: Beth Emet Syn, Evanston, 1955-56; Wilmette Village Caucus, 1958-60; chmn, Chgo sec, Fed Assn Pulp and Paper Ind, 1968-69; mem: Sigma Xi; Sigma Tau; Tau Beta Pi; Chi Epsilon; Amer Mgmt Assn; Amer Ordnance Assn;

Navy League; Soc for Experimental Stress Analysis; AJComm. Contbr to tech jours. Recipient: cert of achievement, Jt Task Force III, US Govt, 1951. Home: 1252 Spruce St, Winnetka, Ill.

FRAENKEL, Yehuda, Isr, attorney; b. Russocice, Pol, July 18, 1899; s. Mayer and Eva (Lipszyc); in Israel since 1920; att Ger Coll, Lodz 1914-17; U Warsaw, 1917-20; grad, Law sch, Jerusalem, 1925; m. Frymeta Dunkelblum, Jan 11, 1938. Pvt practice, since 1925; mem, law firm: Y Fraenkel and Co; Dunkelblum and Fraenkel, 1925-48, later Fraenkel and Pratt; legal adv: JA, Tel Aviv Munic, both 1927-40; magistrate, Tel Aviv, 1929-47; legal ed, Haaretz Heb daily, 1937-38; appellate div, disciplinary court. Vice pres, Intl Bar Assn, fmr, mem exec; mem, council, Friends Heb U; fmr chmn, Tel Aviv munic elections; mem, Isr Law Council. Contbr articles to Heb press. Home: 79 Keren Kayemet Blvd, Tel Aviv, Isr. Office: 15 Ahad Haam St, Tel Aviv, Isr.

FRAENKEL, Zeev, Isr, physicist; b. Munich, Ger, June 15, 1925; s. Alfred and Bertha (Enrentreu); in Isr since 1937; EE, Technion, 1948; MS, Columbia U, 1952, DSc, 1956; m. Sarah Pelchovitch, Feb 18, 1953; c: Michal, Avraham, Tamar. Asso prof, physics, Weizmann Inst of Sci since 1956. Lt, IDF, 1948-51. Contbr to sci jours. Home: 10 Eisenberg St, Rehovot, Isr. Office: Weizmann Inst of Sci, Rehovot, Isr.

FRAIBERG, Louis Benjamin, US, educator; b. Detroit, Mich, Sep 18, 1913; s. Meyer and Anna (Lazner); BA, Wayne State U, 1937, MA, 1939; MSW, U Mich, 1946, PhD, 1956; m. Selma Horwitz, Mar 11, 1945; c: Lisa. Prof, Eng, U Toledo, since 1963, chmn, dept, 1963-66; instr, Wayne State U 1953-57; lectr, U Mich 1957-58; asso prof, La State U, New Orleans, 1958-63. Mem: MLA; Natl Council Tchrs Eng; Intl Comparative Lit Assn; Amer Studies Assn; AAUP. Author: Psychoanalysis and American Literary Criticism, 1960. Home: 2888 Bayridge Dr, Ann Arbor, Mich.

FRAIBERG, Selma, US, educator; b. Detroit, Mich, Mar 8, 1918; d. Jack and Dorella (Newman) Horwitz; BA, Wayne State U, 1939, MSW, 1944; m. Louis Fraiberg, Mar 11, 1945; c: Lisa. Prof, child psychan, U Mich, lectr, 1945-50, asso prof, 1963; pvt practice, child analysis, since 1945; asso prof, social work, Tulane U, 1957-62; supervising child analyst, Baltimore Psychoanalytic Inst. Author: The Magic Years, 1958; contbr numerous articles on psychan child devl, lit criticism and parent educ. Recipient, Awards: Child Study Assn, 1959; dist alumni, Wayne State U, 1960. Home: 2888 Bayridge Dr, Ann Arbor, Mich. Office: Childrens Psycht Hosp, U of Mich, Ann Arbor, Mich.

FRAM, Leon, US, rabbi; b. Raseinas, Lith, Dec 12, 1895; AB, MA, U Cincinnati, O, ordained rabbi, HUC, 1920. Rabbi, found, Temple Isr, Detroit, Mich, since 1941; rabbi: Temple Beth El, Detroit, 1925-41, Temple Judea, Chgo, 1920-25. Prin contribs: devl Temple HS, Adult Educ movement, Reform Temples, US. Pres, Rabb Commn, Detroit; hon chmn, Mich council, AJCong; mem, CCAR; fmr: pres, Detroit Public Libr Commn; natl chmn: ZOA. Home: 5440 Cass St, Detroit, Mich. Study: 17400 Manderson St, Detroit, Mich.

FRANCIS, Norman Charles, US, physicist; b. Rochester, NY, Nov 27, 1922; s. Morris and Jennie (Levy); BA, U Rochester, 1948, PhD, 1952; m. Beverly Cohen, May 31, 1947; c: Cynthia, Karen, Martha. Mgr, ADA Theoretical Physics, Knolls Atomic Power Lab, since 1963; adj prof, Rochester Physics Inst, since 1963; research asso, Ind U, 1952-55. USN, 1944-46. Prin contrib, devl of nuclear model and reactor, physics methods. Pres: Northeast, NY Sect, Amer Nuclear Soc, 1966-67; Schenectady chap, U Rochester Alumni Club, 1965-66; sch, bd, Temple Gates of Heaven; Amer Phys Soc. Contbr to sci jours. Hobbies: swiming, traveling. Home: 2311 Plum St, Schenectady, NY. Office: Knolls Atomic Power Lab, River Rd, Schenectady, NY.

FRANCK, Isaac, US, organization exec; b. Zozov, Russ, Mar 15, 1909; in US since 1923; s. George and Minnie (Babin); BS, NYU, 1934; att: Harvard U, 1937-40; U Mich, 1940-43; Columbia U, 1947-49; PhD, U of Md, 1966; m. Pearl Crystal, Oct 21, 1934; c: Walter, Phyllis. Exec vice-pres, JCC, Gtr Wash, since 1949; prof, phil, sociol, Amer U, 1956; bus mgr, Shevillei haHinuch, educ monthly, 1928; libr, Herzliah Heb Acad, tchr, HS dept, 1928-29; tchr, Heb schs, 1929-34; dir, clubs, J Cen, Port Chester, NY, 1934-37; exec dir, J Comty Cen, Manchester, NH, 1937-39; educ dir, J Comty Cen, Detroit, Mich, 1939-41, exec dir, JCC, Detroit, 1941-46; spec

instr, political sci dept, Wayne State U, 1943-46; exec dir, Bklyn J Council 1946-47; exec secy, Amer Fund for Isr Instns, 1947-49; cons, State Dept, Intl Info Admn, 1951-54; study tours of W Ger and Isr, guests of the govts, 1957; lectr, conductor, sems at U's, prof societies and acads. Mem: Amer Phil Assn; Amer Political Sci Assn; Amer Sociol Assn; Assn for Public Opinion Research, Natl Conf J Communal Service; ZOA; NAACP; Urban League; Natl Assn of Intergroup Relations Officials; Assn J Comty Relations Workers; Natl Council for J Educ. Author: pamphlet, Jewish Religious Life in US, in Ger, 1951, in Eng, 1953; co-author: Amer Jewry: The Tercentenary and After, 1955; Community Organization, 1958; Trends and Issues in Jewish Social Welfare in the US, 1899-1958, pub 1966; contbr articles, book revs to mags and newspapers. Recipient, Stephen S Wise Medallion, AJCong, 1962. Home: 1415 Crestridge Dr, Silver Spring, Md. Office: 1330 Massachusetts Ave, Washington, DC.

FRANCO, Marcel, US, business exec; b. Milas, Turkey, Feb 3, 1897; s. Jaime and Estrella (Menasce); in US since 1945; att U Lausanne, Switz. Res repr in Mex, Amer Bank and Trust, Co of NY. Pres, Amer Friends, Alliance Israélite Universelle, since 1954; vice-pres, cen comm, Paris, Fr, since 1948; asso treas, United HIAS Service, since 1957; vice chmn, Consultative Council J Orgs, since 1953; pres: Grand Rabbinate, Turkey, 1935-38; J Cmty of Istanbul, 1934-38; B'nai B'rith lodge, Istanbul, 1934-38; clubs: Harmonie; Bankers, NY; Hacienda, Mex. Recipient: Fr Legion of Hon, 1955; Cdr Ouissam Alaouite, Morocco; Hon Consul Gen of Morocco in Mex. Home: Santa Anita No 310, Lomas Hipódromo, Mex. Offices: Avenida 5 de Mayo No 29, Mex; 61 Broadway, New York, NY.

FRANK, Bernard, US, attorney; b. Wilkes-Barre, Pa, June 11, 1913; s. Abraham and Fanny; PhB, Muhlenberg Coll, 1935; LLB, U of Pa, 1938; postgrad, NYU, 1940-42; m. Muriel Levy, 1938; c: Roberta, Allan. Pvt practice since 1939; dir: Allen Organ Co; Hess's Inc; asst US atty, E Dist of Pa, 1950-51; first asst city solicitor, Allentown, Pa, 1956-60. US Army, WW II. Chmn: Allentown Housing Bd of Rev, since 1960; Isr Bonds, Allentown, 1952-55; bd, Temple Beth-El, 1948-49; B'nai B'rith Natl Adult J Educ Commn, 1961-63; dep chmn, Fed Bar Assn Commn on Ombudsman; pres: lodge, B'nai B'rith, 1942-43; E Pa Council, 1947-48; Comty Action Comm of Lehigh Valley, Inc, 1966-68; 94th Infantry Div Assn, US Army, 1953-54, hon mem, 1954; found, Aleph Zadik Aleph Dist 3, 1934; mem, bd, J Day Sch; mem: Amer Bar Assn Comm on Ombudsman; Lehigh Co, Pa, Amer and Fed Bar Assns; participant, Arden House Conf on Ombudsman, 1967. Author: Proposals for Pennsylvania Ombudsman, 1967; The British Parliamentary Commissioner for Administration—the Ombudsman, 1968; The Ombudsman and Human Rights, 1969. Recipient: Awards: Sam Beber, B'nai B'rith, 1934. Allentown B'nai B'rith, 1962, AJCong, 1968. Home: 745 N 30 St, Allentown, Pa. Office: 517 Hamilton St, Allentown, Pa.

FRANK, Bertram A, US, business exec; b. Buffalo, NY, Dec 2, 1909; s. Myer and Dodye (Lyon); U Baltimore, 1927-29; m. Lillian Goldberg, June 5, 1947; c. David, Jane. Sr vice-pres, bd dirs, Sun Life Ins Co of Amer. US Army 1943-45. Chmn bd, Gen Agents and Mgrs Round Table, 1906; pres: Baltimore J Council, 1956-59; chmn, steering comm, since 1959; Baltimore bd dirs, chap, Chartered Life Underwriters, 1958-59; vice-chmn, ins div, Asso J Charities, bd electors, vice-pres, Baltimore Heb Cong, exec bd, JCC, since 1959; bd delg, AJComm; mem, Pi Tau Pi; club, Suburban, bd mem. Home: 2433 Everton Rd, Baltimore, Md. Office: 20 S Charles St, Baltimore, Md.

FRANK, Edith S, US, civic worker, free-lance writer; b. Madison, Wis, July 16, 1902; d. Isaac and Sarah (Goldberg) Sinaiko; BA, U Wis, 1924; att: Wheeler Sch of Music, Madison, Wis; Cosmopoloitan Sch of Music, Chgo, Ill; m. David Frank, June 24, 1924 (decd); c: Suzanne Freund. Mem bd govs, Metrop Housing and Planning Council, Chgo, since 1960; mem: Intl Platform Assn; Amer Sym Orch League; fmr: pres, Theta Sigma Phi; dir, Near N Comty Council, Chgo; pres: Women's Council for City Renewal; League of Women Voters, W Va and Toledo, O, also state dir for W Va and Ill; Friends Toledo Public Libr; NW dist O Fed of Music Clubs; vice-pres, Toledo Regional Planning Assn; mem: coord comm, public wfr, W Va State Planning Bd; bd, UN Assn, Toledo; bd trustees, Toledo Sym Orch; women's comm, Chgo Sym Orch; women's auxiliary, Amer Soc of Mech Engrs; bd dirs, council social work and leader, Charleston, W Va, Girl Scouts of Amer; chmn, women's div, Kanawha Co, United War and

Comty Fund Dr; 1st vice-pres, Chgo br, Amer Assn U Women; clubs: Chgo Womens, vice-chmn, fine arts; U; Arts, Chgo; Madison Press, fmr secy. Recipient, Awards: service, Munic Defense Council, Charleston, W Va, 1945; outstanding citizen, Toledo, O, Newspaper Guild, 1951. Hobbies: music, art. Home: 1515 Vilas Ave, Madison, Wis.

FRANK, Elaine Spiesberger; US, communal leader; b. Chgo, Ill, Mar 14, 1917; d. Sam and Irene (Hofheimer); BA, U Chgo, 1938; m. Zollie Frank, Jan 1, 1938; c: James, Charles, Nancy Kaplan, Laurie Lieberman. Hon life pres, Women's Auxiliary, JCC, Chgo, since 1958, pres, 1952-58; pres, JCC, since 1968; bd dirs, Wfr Council of Metrop Chgo; chmn: Spec Adv Comm on Day Camp for Handicapped Children, Spalding Sch; Cook Co Comm on Children and Youth; co-chmn, Manpower Commn, Natl JWB; bd trustees, Chgo Sym Orch; bd dirs, Girl Scouts of Chgo, 1963-66. Home: 361 Hawthorn Lane, Winnetka, Ill.

FRANK, Emily S, US, artist, teacher; b. NYC; d. Robert and Lena (Machson); att: NYU; Art Students League; hon deg, Ecole de Bella Arte, Rome, It, 1952; m. Matthew Shapiro, Sep 1924; c: John. Art techr, NYC Bd Educ, since 1950; pvt tchr since 1948; connected with White House Gal; one-man shows: NY; Miami; Dallas, Tex; LA, Cal; Eur; repr in pvt collections: works in oil and mixed media; portrait of JFK in White House; repr in perm collections: Evansville Mus, Ind; Dallas Mus, Tex; Mus in Isr; designer of creative clothes: Ash and Seitie, 1924-28; Pattollo, 1920-24; Lang and Kohn, Mem: Artists Equity; Amer Artists Group; Contemporary, 1930-36. Painters of Metrop Mus of Art, NYC. Recipient: 1st Prize for painting, Berlin Exhb, 1954; testimonial from House of Knights, Malta, Rome, 1949. Hobbies: music; phil. Home and studio: 43 Fifth Ave, New York, NY.

FRANK, Freidel, US, communal worker; b. NYC; d. George and Annie (Slonimsky) Itskowitz; att: CCNY, 1931-33; J Tchrs Sem, 1933-35; m. Murray Frank, Apr 7, 1935; c: Paul, Davis, Judith. Prin, Chaim Weizmann Sch, since 1955; substitute tchr, jr and sr HS's, since 1948; actress, Yiddish Art Theatre, 1928-32; asst buyer, Lansburgh's Dept Store, 1936-39; spec asst, Heb sect, Libr of Cong, 1950-52; instr: adult educ courses, Temple Sinai, 1958, 1962; Tifereth Isr Syn, 1959. Pres, Council of Pioneer Women, Gtr Wash, mem, larger natl bd, 1962-65, vice-pres J Lab Comm, 1948-49; mem: exec bd, JCC, Gtr Wash, 1950, 1963. Natl bd dirs, Natl Comm for Lab Isr, mem, speaker's bur, women's div, UJA, 1948; pres, Sisterhood Cong Beth Isr, 1947-49; club, Progressive Women's, affiliate of Workmen's Circle, found and pres, 1937-44. Home: 7810 16 St, NW, Washington, DC.

FRANK, Harry B, US, jurist; b. NYC, Mar 6, 1905; s. Samuel and Sarah (Levenson); LLB, NYU Sch of Law, 1926; m. Helen Leef, Feb 15, 1931; c: Ned, Norma Frankel. Justice, NY Supr Court, since 1965, acting justice, 1957-65; pvt practice, 1928-54; chief counsel, NY Dist Off Price Stabilization, 1952; justice, City Court of NY, New York Co, 1954-57. Chmn, Comm on Rules and Practice, City Court of NY, 1956-57; pres: Alumni Class of 1926, NYU Law Sch, 1956-63; NYU Law Alumni Assn, pres 1969-70; fmr pres: Council of Orgs of AJCong; Men's Group of the Godmother's League; vice-pres, Metrop Council, UJA; chmn: W Side Sym Orch; co-chmn: Comm on the UN, 1959-60; mem: Ins Comm, Assn Bar, NYC, 1958-61; Empire State Chap, Fed Bar Assn; City and Co Bar Assns; NY Co Lawyers Assn; bd dirs, NYU Law Alumni Assn, 1963-65; fmr adv council, NYU Law Alumni Assn; bd dirs, NY J Child Care Council; Freedom Lodge, B'nai B'rith; Grand St Boys; Arcana Lodge No 246; Masons; Young Men's Philanthropic League. Home: 300 E 74 St, New York, NY. Office: 111 Centre St, New York, NY.

FRANK, Isaiah, US, educator; b. NYC, Nov 7, 1917; s. Henry and Rose (Isserles); BBS, CCNY, 1936; BHL, Sem Colı J Studies, 1937; MA, econs, Columbia U, 1938, PhD, 1960; m. Ruth Hershfield, Mar 23, 1941; c: Robert, Kenneth, William. Clayton Prof Intl Econs, Johns Hopkins U, since 1963; cons: World Bank; State Dept; Treas Dept; Agcy for Intl Devl; Comm for Econ Devl; mem: Adv Comm, UN Conf on Trade and Devl; Adv Council, Inst for Latin Amer Integration; research asso, Columbia U Council for Research in Social Scis, 1936-39; instr, Amherst Coll, 1939-41; Carnegie F, Natl Bur of Econ Research, 1941-42; cons, War Produc Bd, 1942; sr econ, Off Strategic Services, 1942-1944; on leave from State Dept as dep dir for fgn areas of Pres' Materials Policy Commn, 1951-52; State Dept repr on Jt Ind Govt Iron and Steel Mission to Eur, 1947; cons, Off Spec Repr for Eur

Recovery Prog, Paris, 1948; econ adv, US Delg to 10th Inter-Amer Conf of Mins of Finance and Econ, Rio de Janeiro, 1954; head, US Delg to Confs on Dollar Liberalization of OEEC, Paris, 1955, 1956; econ adv, US Delg to Mins Meetings, OEEC, Paris, 1956, 1957, 1958; head, US Delg to cons on balance-of-payments restrictions, under auspices of Gen Agreement on Tariffs and Trade, Geneva, 1957, chmn, US Delg, meeting, Geneva, 1958; econ adv, Conf of US Ambass in W Eur, Paris, 1958; adv, Conf of US Sr Econ Offs in W Eur, W Berlin, 1958; mem, US Delg, meeting of US-Can Jt Cabinet Comm on Trade and Econ Affairs, Ottawa, 1959; spec mission, Mexico, five Cen Amer Reps to advise on integration of their econs, 1959; cons, Sen Interstate and Fgn Commerce Comm, 1960; mem, Council on Fgn Relations Study Group on Eur Common Market, 1960; chmn, US Delg, ind and resources, Econ Commn for Asia and Far E, Bangkok, 1961; US repr: 4th meeting of Devl Assistance Group, London, 1961, 5th meeting, Tokyo, 1961; London meeting on Devl Assistance to India, 1961; adv: US Delg to Intl Bank and Monetary Fund meetings, Vienna, 1961; US Delg, Min meetings, Org for Econ Coop and Devl, Paris, 1961; chmn, US Delg, meeting on Pakistan's Fgn Exch Situation, Paris, 1961; mem: Brookings Instn Adv Comm on Grants, Loans and Local Currencies, 1961; Pres' Task Force on Fgn Econ Assistance, 1961; adv: CED Comm on Commercial Policy of Atlantic Comty, 1962; meeting of econ policy comm, Org for Econ Coop and Devl, Paris 1963; chmn, US Delg to preparatory comm, UN Conf on Trade and Devl, 1963; dep asst secty, econ affairs, State Dept, 1962-63, dir, off of intl trade, off of intl finance and devl affairs, 1945-63; lectr, Amer Studies, Sulzburg Sems, 1969. 1st lt, US Army, 1944-45. Mem: Council on Fgn Relations; Amer Econ Assn; Phi Beta Kappa. Author: The European Common Market, 1961; co-author, The Growth and Fluctuation of the British Economy, 1953; contbr to profsl jours. Recipient, Rockefeller public service award, Princeton U. Home: 3102 Hawthorne St, NW, Washington, DC. Office: Sch of Advanced Intl Studies, Johns Hopkins U, 1740 Massachusetts Ave, NW, Washington, DC.

FRANK, Jack D, US, rabbi, educator; b. Frankfurt, Ger, July 9, 1926; s. Ludwig and Judith (Van Gelder); in US since 1940; ordained rabbi BHL, Heb Theol Coll, 1956; MA, U Chgo; cert, U Jerusalem; m. Rochelle Sachs, Nov, 27, 1954. c: Judith, Bathsheva, Aviva, Elana. Rabbi, Kehilath Jacob Beth Samuel, since 1961; dir, guidance, IDA Crown J Acad, since 1963; dir, testing, Asso Talmud Torahs, since 1965; rabbi, Anshe Sholom, 1956-57; prin, Hillel Torah Day Sch, Lakeshore, 1958-63. Mem: Torah Tchrs Assn; Chgo Rabb Council; Natl Conf Yeshiva Prins; Rel Zionists Amer. Home: 6715 N Avers Ave, Lincolnwood, Ill. Study: 2828 W Pratt, Chicago, Ill.

FRANK, Joseph N, Can, executive, communal leader; b. Manchester, Eng, Nov 11, 1906; s. Maurice and Eva (Alexander); in Can since 1910; m. Rachel Berlin, Jan, 1932; c: Eleanor, Barbara. Pres, J N Frank Asso Inc; dir: Real Estate Inves Corp; Can-Isr Devl; vice pres, Can-Isr Securities; asso clothing admnr, Wartime Prices and Trade Bd, 1940-45. Pres, ZOC; dir: World Maccabiah Union; Can J Cong; JNF, Can; Adath Isr Cong; gov: Weizmann Inst of Sci; Heb U, hon f; Bar Ilan U; Technion, all Isr; Amer-Isr Cultural Found; YW-YMHA; United Talmud Torahs, Montreal; life gov, J Gen Hosp; mem: Shaar Hashomayim Syn; actions comm, WZO; Masons; B'nai B'rith; St James Lit Soc; fmr: pres, Can Young Judea; chmn, UJA; co-treas, CJA; Montreal; clubs: Montefiore; De Sola. Home: 28 Sunset Ave, Montreal, Can. Office: 4141 Sherbrooke St W, Montreal, Can.

FRANK, Murray, US, journalist; b. NYC, May 10, 1908; s. Paul and Pauline (Waxman); att: J Tchrs Sem, NYC, 1929-33; BA, George Wash U, 1936; MA, Amer U, 1937; m. Frieda Itzkowitz, Apr 7, 1935; c: Paul, David, Judith. Admn asst, US Repr William L St Onge, since 1963; corresp for: The Day—Jewish Jour, since 1953; J Morning Jour, 1940-43, merged with The Day, 1953; Jewish Chronicle, Yiddishe Zeiting, Buenos Aires since 1945; Davar, Isr, 1945-50; Amer Zionist, 1944-47; Nat J Post, 1950-52; tchr, Wash, DC Schs, 1937-41; econ analyst, Commerce Dept 1941-52; US Fgn Econ Admn, 1942-45; lectr, J hist, Coll J Studies, Wash, DC, 1949-51; natl dir info, B'nai B'rith, 1945-47; adv, J Affairs, to US Repr Sol Bloom 1945-49; admn asst; US Repr Abraham J Multer, 1949-51; US Repr Victor I Anfuso, 1955-65; lectr, J Hist, post-bibl J lit, Temple Sinai adult educ courses, 1956-58. Pres, Farband LZOA, Wash Br, 1962-68; vice-pres, Wash Comm for Shaare Zedek Hosp in Jerusalem; vice-chmn, UJA, govt div; repr: Amer J Conf, 1945-46; Amer ZC,

1949-51; mem, bd dirs: JCC, 1941-44; J Social Service Agcy, 1944-46; Heb Acad of Wash, 1950-54; Amer J Tercentenary Comm, 1953-54; Chaim Weizmann Sch; Natl Comm for Lab Isr; mem, bd trustees; Wash UJA; mem: educ comm, JCC; Workmen's Circle; J L Peretz Yiddish Writers Union; YIVO; Amer Historical Assn; Amer Acad of Political Social Sci; Cong Press Gal; White House News Corresps; State Dept Corresps Assn. Author: Fisheries of Latin America, 1944; The War Refugee Board, 1945; This is B'nai B'rith, Book of Facts, 1947, 2nd ed, 1949; co-author, Industrialization of Latin America, 1946, ed, B'nai B'rith News, 1945-47; contbr to periodicals in US, Gt Brit, Isr; dir, announcer, Voice of Isr, weekly radio prog, WDON and WASH-FM, Wash, DC, 1958-61. Home: 7810 16 St, NW, Washington, DC. Office: c/o Congressman William L St Onge, House Off Bldg, Washington, DC.

FRANK, Reuven, US, journalist; b. Montreal, Can, Dec 7, 1920; s. Moses and Anna (Rivenovich) Reichenstein; in US since 1940; att U Coll, Toronto, 1937-40; BS, CCNY, 1942; MS, journalism, Columbia U, 1947; m. Bernice Kaplow, June 9, 1946; c: Peter, James. Pres, NBC News, since 1969, exec vice-pres, 1967-69, mem staff since 1950; reporter, Newark Evening News, 1947-49, night city ed, 1949-50; news ed, Camel News Caravan, 1951-54; produc, Huntley-Brinkley Report, 1956-62; exec produc, 1963-65. Writer-produc: Berlin-Window on Fear, 1953; The Road to Spandau, 1954; Outlook, series, 1956-59; Time Present, series, 1959-60; Chet Huntley Reporting, series, 1960-63; Israel-The Next Ten Years, 1958; The S-Bahn Stops at Freedom, 1958; The American Stranger, 1958; The Requiem for Mary Jo, 1959; The Big Ear, 1959; Our Man in the Mediterranean, 1959; Where is Abel, Your Brother?, 1960; Our Man in Hong Kong, 1961; The Land, 1961; The Many Faces of Spain, 1962; Our Man in Vienna, 1962; Clear and Present Danger, 1962; The Tunnel, 1962; A Country Called Europe, 1963; The Problem with Water is People, 1963. Mem: Writers Guild of Amer; Amer Newspaper Guild; Natl Acad TV Arts and Scis; Radio and TV Corresps Assn. Recipient, awards: TV news writing, Sigma Delta Chi, 1955; Robert E Sherwood, 1958, 1959; George Polk, LIU, 1961; dist service, Columbia Journalism Alumni, 1961; 1st person, Inst Educ by Radio-TV, O State U, 1963, Emmy, best news prog, 1958, 1959, 1960, 1961, 1962, 1964, best documentary prog, 1963, prog of year, 1963. Office: 30 Rockefeller Plaza, New York, NY.

FRANK, Rudolph, Switz, author, translator, lecturer; b. Mainz, Ger, Sep 16, 1886; s. Carl Theodor and Mathilde (Ebertsheim); in Switz since 1937; att U: Munich, Zurich, Heidelberg, all 1904-09; DJ, 1909; m. Anna Klein, July 3, 1939; c: Renate, Vincent, Rony. Lectr, modern lit, Radio Basel, since 1950; stage mgr, actor, Ger, Rum, Switz, It, Aus, 1909-51. Author: Moderne Lyriker, 1907; Lucinde und Vertraute Briefe von Schleiermacher, 1908; Goethe für Jungens, 1910; Geisselbrechts Puppenfaust, 1911; Ackersmann aus Boehmen, 1919; Das expressionistische Drama, 1920; Das Moderne Theatre, 1927; Der Schädel des Negerhäuptlings Makaua, 1931; Ahnen und Enkel, 1936; Mont Soleil, 1937; Kraft durch Feuer, 1939; Spielzeit meines Lebens, 1960; Das Doktorshaus in der Judengasse, 1961; trans of 50 vols, 1922-56; contbr to: Vossische Zeitung, Berliner Tageblatt, 1910-33; Basler National Zeitung, 1948-55; Basler Abendzeitung, since 1947. Mem: Christlich-jüdische Arbeitsgemeinschaft; PEN club. Home: Schützenmattstr 42, Basel, Switz.

FRANK, Samuel B, US, dermatologist, educator; b. Cleveland, O, Sep 7, 1909; s. Jacob and Yetta (Bergman); BA, W Reserve U, 1930, MD, 1933; grad f, Columbia U Coll Phys and Surgs, 1935-38; m. Eleanor Koosed, June 12, 1934; c: Joyce, Amy. Prof, clinical dermat, NYU Post-Grad Med Sch, since 1963; fac mem since 1937; att dermat: White Plains Hosp, since 1946; U Hosp; NYU Med Cen, both since 1937; cons: Blythedale Hosp, since 1948, Hawthorne-Cedar Knolls, since 1949, Pleasantville Cottage Sch, since 1956, Hillcrest Home, since 1957, Dobbs Ferry Hosp, since 1952. Col, US Army, 1941-45. Mem: Soc for Inves Dermat; Amer Acad Dermat, Westchester Acad Med; NY Acad Med; Dermat Soc of Gtr NY; AMA; NY State Med Soc; Westchester Dermat Soc; J Comty Cen; JWV; B'nai B'rith; club, Colectors. Contbr to med jours. Home: 3 Fairway Dr, Mamaroneck, NY. Office: 170 Maple Ave, White Plains, NY.

FRANK, Solomon, Can, rabbi; b. NYC; s. Abraham and Gerta (Epstein); LLB, U Buffalo, 1922, BS, 1923; MA, U Man, 1929, PhD, 1943; ordained rabbi; m. Elsie Brook, 1935; c: Karen. Min, Span and Port Syn, Montreal, since 1947. Fmr

vice-pres, Can J Cong; mem: B'nai B'rith; Masons; KP. Home: 5500 Campden Pl, Montreal, Can. Study: 5471 Lemieux Ave, Montreal, Can.

FRANK, Victor H, US, oral surg; b. Phila, Pa, Apr 26, 1900; s. Albert and Roseta (Lowenstein); DDS, U of Pa Dent Sch, 1921; m. Lee Weiss, Oct 8, 1923 (decd); c: Patricia, Carey, Victor. Staff Grad Hosp, U of Pa, since 1925, on staff since 1961; chmn, dept of dent, Albert Einstein Med Cen, S div, since 1939, chief dent services, Wolffe Hosp; courtesy staff, Chestnut Hill Hosp. Dent, Dent ARC Disaster Preparedness Comm; hon vice-pres, Big Brother assn; bd dirs, J Comty Relations Council; Phila Mouth Hygiene Assn; Comm of Seventy; hon mem, bd dirs, Neighborhood Cen; pres, N Phila Assn Dent, 1929-30, 1944-45; Phila Co Dent Soc, 1938-39; Pa Assn Dent Surgs, 1945-46; U of Pa Dent Alumni, 1946; Phila Soc Exodontists and Oral Surgs, 1951-52; Phila sect, Amer Coll Dent, 1951-52; Pa Dent Assn, 1958-59; E Dent Soc, 1944-45; f: Amer Coll Dents; Intl Coll Dents; dipl Amer bd Oral Surg; mem: Amer Dent Assn; Amer Soc Oral Surgs, Great Lakes Soc Oral Surgs; Acad Stomatology; Fed Dentaire Internationale; club, Philmont Country, pres, 1958-61. Contbr to profsl jours. Home and office: 1800 Pine St, Philadelphia, Pa.

FRANK, Werner Louis, US, business exec; b. Ger, June 4, 1929; s. Arthur and Bertha (Weingartner); in US since 1937; BS, Ill Inst of Tech, Chgo, 1951; MS, U of Ill, Urbana, 1955; m. Phoebe Mannel, Aug 21, 1955; c: Dori, Judith, Daniel. Sr vice-pres, business exec, Informatics, since 1962, co-found; sr staff, Thompson Ramo Wooldridge, 1955-62. US Army, 1952-54. Chmn, computer comm, Jerusalem Econ Conf; past chmn: Mid-W region, Intercollegiate ZOA; Assn Computing Machinery, San Fernando chap; mem: Assn Computing Machinery, Wash, DC: Soc for Mgmt Info Sys. Contbr numerical analysis and data processing subjects to jours. Home: 5701 Lenox Rd, Bethesda, Md. Office: 4720 Montgomery Lane, Bethesda, Md.

FRANK, Zollie S, US business exec, b. Dayton, O, Jan 1, 1907; s. Charles and Lena (Kessler); att O State U; m. Elaine Spiesberger, Jan 1, 1938; c: James, Charles, Nancy Kaplan, Laurie Lieberman. Pres, owner, Z Frank Inc, since 1939; Five Wheels and Laurie James Corp, since 1944; chmn bd: Wheels, since 1959; Four Wheels, since 1962. Vice-pres, N Shore Cong, Isr; life mem, Brandeis U; bd mem, trustee: Lyric Opera, Chgo; Michael Reese Hosp, Chgo; trustee, Steven David Epstein Found; mem: pres adv comm, Gen Motors; Citizens Bd, Loyola U; active in CJA, Chgo. Home: 361 Hawthorn Lane, Winnetka, Ill. Office: 6200 N Western Ave, Chicago, Ill.

FRANKEL, Arnold Judah, US, business exec; b. NYC, Mar 17, 1922; s. Solomon and Rose (Blitz); BChE, CCNY, 1942; MChE, Poly Inst, Bklyn, 1949; m. Miriam Drexler, Oct 29, 1944; c: Hinda, Janet, Alan. Chmn, Aceto Chem Co In , since 1962, co-found, 1947. Chmn, NE Queens Far Housing Comm, 1962-64; mem: Temple Beth Sholom, Amer Chem Soc; AAAS; Amer Inst of Chem; Sigma Xi, Fordham U chap; club, Chem, NY. Recipient: f, Amer Inst Chem, 1968. Home: 33 162 St, Flushing, NY. Office: 126-02 Northern Blvd, Flushing, NY.

FRANKEL, Charles, US, educator, author; b. NYC, Dec 13, 1917; s. Philip and Estelle (Cohen); AB, Columbia U, 1937, PhD, 1942; m. Helen Lehman, 1941; c: Susan, Carl. Prof, phil, Columbia U, since 1956, fac mem since 1939; Guggenheim, f, 1953-54; Fulbright Research profsl U Paris, 1953-54; Carnegie Corp f, 1959-60; US Asst Secy of State, Educ and Cultural Affairs, 1965-67. Chmn, comm on profl ethics, AAUP, 1956-59; mem: Phi Beta Kappa; Amer Phil Assn; Institut International de Philosophie Politique; Council on fgn relations; club, PEN; Cent Assn. Author: The Faith of Reason, 1948; The Bear and the Beaver, 1951; The Case for Modern Man, 1956; The Power of the Democratic Idea, 1960; The Democratic Prospect, 1962; The Love of Anxiety, 1965; The Neglected Aspect of Foreign Affairs, 1966; Education and the Barricades, 1968; ed-at-large, Saturday Rev, since 1968; ed: Introduction to Contemporary Civilization, 1941; Rousseau's Social Contract, 1947; The Uses of Philosophy, 1955; Issues in University Education, 1959; The Golden Age of American Philosophy, 1960. Recipient, Woodbridge Prize, 1947. Home: 317 Phillips Hill Rd, New York, NY. Office: Columbia U, New York, NY.

FRANKEL, Harry H, US, business exec, organization exec; b. Jacksonville, Fla, Aug 22, 1895; grad, Wharton Sch, U of

Pa; m. Lillian Gordon. Off, dir, Isr Inves Corp; dir, Ind Devl Bank of Isr; chmn bd, Judith Muller Ltd, Haifa. Served, WW I, II; vice-pres, Amer Comm for Weizmann Inst; supervising instr, ARC, Camp Clairborn, La, 1943-44. Natl bd govs, Isr Bond Org; org, first chmn, O Valley Zionist Region; bd gov, Weizmann Inst of Sci; found: Truman Peace Cen, Jerusalem; Amer J League for Isr; dir: Amer Friends Heb U; UJA, Gtr NY; fmr: UJA chmn for E region; NY St; numerous spec missions to Isr. Chmn ed bd, American Israel Review. Home: 5151 Collins Ave, Miami Beach, Fla.

FRANKEL, Jonathan, Isr, educator; b. London, Eng, July 15, 1935; s. Ernest and Ella (Goitein); in Isr since 1964; BA, MA, PhD, Cambridge U, Eng, 1954-61; m. Edith Rogovin, Nov 10, 1963; c: Leora. Lectr, Heb U, Jerusalem, since 1964; research f, Jesus Coll, Cambridge, 1960-63; sr f, Columbia U, 1961-62; visiting asst prof, Bklyn Coll, 1964-69. Ed, Vladimir Akimov Dilemmas of Russian Marxism, 1969; contbr to profsl jours. Home: 2 Neve Granot, Jerusalem, Isr. Office: Heb U, Jerusalem, Isr.

FRANKEL, Lois R, US, communal worker; b. NYC, Mar 21, 1929; d. Albert and Darcy (Grean) Rauch; att: Wellesley Coll, 1945-47; m. Harding Frankel, June 26, 1947; c: Richard, James, Douglas. Mem, bd: natl women's div, UJA; Houston Comty Council, United Fund; sisterhood, Cong Beth Isr; AJComm, women's comm for Brandeis U; Amer Med Cen at Denver, 1956-58; Council J Women, 1953-55; exec comm, JCC; chmn, women's div, United J Campaign, 1959-61, all Houston; club, Wellesley. Home: 3608 Rio Vista St, Houston, Tex.

FRANKEL, Max, US, journalist; b. Gera, Ger, Apr 3, 1930; s. Jacob and Mary (Katz); in US since 1940; AB, Columbia U, 1952, MA, political sci, 1953; m. Tobia Brown, June 19, 1956; c: David, Margot, Jonathan. Wash bur chief, NY Times, since 1968. Home: 5607 Montgomery St, Chevy Chase, Md. Office: 1920 L St NW, Washington DC.

FRANKEL, Rafael, Isr, agronomist; b. Beuthen, Ger, Jan 18, 1922; s. Shmuel and Martha (Blumenthal); in Isr since 1937; BS, U of Cal, Davis, 1956; PhD, Heb U, Jerusalem, 1961; m. Miriam Rubin, July 1954; c: Tal. Head: dept agronomy and garden coop, since 1958; div of genet and breeding, since 1961, both at Volcani Inst of Agric Research, Bet Dagan; dir, Agric Research Sta, Neve Yaar, 1956-58. Mem, several sci socs. Contbr numerous sci papers to profsl publs. Home: 18 Havradim St, Yahud, Isr. Office: Volcani Inst of Agric Research, Bet Dagan, Isr.

FRANKEL, Rudolf L, S Africa, business exec; b. Johannesburg, Nov 15, 1908; s. Jacob ad Mathilde (Buxbaum); BA, U Witwatersrand; m. Nora Lomey, May 20, 1935; c: Jillian Wolpert, Jonathan. Chmn, Tiger Oats & Natl Milling Co, Ltd, since 1944. Capt WW II. Chmn, S Afr Friends Heb U; mem, bd govs, Heb U. Hobby: golf. Home: Hathaway, Christopherson Rd, Ranelagh Estate, Johannesburg, S Afr. Office: Schlesinger Centre, 222 Smit Street, Braamfontein, Johannesburg, S Afr.

FRANKEL, Samuel Benjamin, US, naval off; b. Cincinnati, O, July 14, 1905; s. Jonas and Bertha (Sass); BS, US Naval Acad, 1929; m. Tellervo von Hellens, June 2, 1936; c: Susan. Ret, 1964; Rear Adm, USN, chief of staff, Defense Intelligence Agcy, 1961-69, naval off since 1929; navy attaché: Russ, 1941-44, China 1948-50. Recipient: Dist Service Medal, 1942. Home: 2220 20 St, NW, Washington, DC.

FRANKEL, William, Eng, editor, attorney; b. London, Eng, Feb 3, 1917; s. Isaac and Anna (Lecker); LLB, hons, London U, 1943; m. Gertrude Reed, Apr 16, 1939; c: Anne, John. Barrister, Middle Temple, S E Circuit, since 1944; dir: Vallentine Mitchell and Co Ltd, since 1957; J Gazette; ed, The J Chronicle, since 1958. Mem: Athenaeum, London; MCC. Home: I Linden Gardens, London W2, Eng. Office: 25 Furnival St, London EC4, Eng.

FRANKENSTEIN, Carl, Isr, educator; b. Berlin, Ger, Feb 16, 1905; s. Emil and Rosalie (Czempin); in Isr since 1935; PhD, Erlangen U, 1927; Berlin U, 1923-26; m. Rechumah Druckman, April 29, 1949. Prof em educ, Hebrew U, since 1969; prof, 1959-61; prin probation off, Pal, 1937-46; dir, Henrietta Szold Found for Child Wfr and Research, 1947-53. Author: Molitors Metaphysische Geschichtsphilosophie, 1928; Waywardness in Children, 1947; Die Ausserlichkeit des Lebensstils, Psychopathy, 1959; Persönlichkeitswandel, 1964;

The Roots of the Ego, 1966; Psychodynamics of Externalization, 1968; ed: Child Care in Israel, 1950; Between Past and Future, 1953; Studies in Education, 1963; found, jour, Megamot; contbr numerous articles to jours. Mem state and munic comm on wfr, educ, Mh, profsl training. Recipient: Isr State Prize for Educ, 1965. Home: 23 Shmaryahu Levin St, Jerusalem, Isr. Office: Heb U, Jerusalem, Isr.

FRANKENTHAL, Kate, US, psychiatrist; b. Kiel, Ger, Jan 30, 1889; d. Julius and Cecilia (Goldmann); att Us: Kiel, Heidelberg, Erlangen, Munich; MD, U of Freiberg, 1914; in US since 1936. Practicing psycht and psychan, since 1938; asst Charité Hosp, Berlin, Ger, 1919-24; city health off, Berlin, Ger, 1928-33, magistrat-medizinalrätin, ret, 1953; dir, emigration comm, Prague, 1936; psycht, State Farm for Women, Conn, 1937-38; inst, psycht, Columbia U, 1946-47; mem fac, William Allanson White Inst of Psycht, 1946-47. Phys, Aus Army, 1915-18. Mem: City Council, Berlin, 1920-32; Prussian State Parliament, 1929-32; dipl Amer Bd Psycht, 1947; f: AMA, Amer Psychiatric Assn; mem: Amer Psychoanalytic Assn, Amer Acad Political and Social Scis; World Fed of Mh; Fgn Policy Assn; Natl Council Family Relations. Author: Background for Tomorrow, 1953; contbr articles to med and political jours. Home and office: 41 Central Park W, New York, NY.

FRANKL, Viktor E, Aus, psychiatrist, author; b. Vienna, Aus, Mar 26, 1905; s. Gabriel and Elsa (Lion); m. Eleonore Schwindt, July 18, 1947; c: Gabriele. Head neur dept: City Policl nic, since 1946; J Hosp, 1940-42, both Vienna; prof neur, psych, U Vienna, 1955; visiting prof: Harvard U summer sch, 1961; S Methodist U summer session, 1966. Pres, Aus Med Soc for Psychotherapy, since 1950; found, leader, Youth Work Cen, 1928-38. Author: Aerztliche Seelsorge, 1946; Ein Psycholog erlebt das Konzentrationslager, 1946; ... trotzdem Ja zum Leben sagen, 1946; Die Psychotherapie in der Praxis, 1947; Die Existenzanalyse und die Probleme der Zeit, 1947; Zeit und Verantwortung, 1947; Der unbewusste Gott, 1948; Der unbedingte Mensch, 1949; Homo patiens, 1950; Logos und Existenz, 1951; Die Psychotherapie im Alltag, 1952; The Doctor and the Soul, 1955, 1965; Pathologie des Zeitgeistes, 1955; Theorie und Therapie der Neurosen, 1956; Das Menschenbild der Seelenheilkunde, 1959; From Death-Camp to Existentialism, 1959; Man's Search for Meaning, 1962; Psychotherapy and Existentialism, 1967; The Will to Meaning, 1969. Home: Mariannengasse 1, Vienna, Aus. Office: Marianengasse 10, Vienna, Aus.

FRANZBLAU, Abraham N, US, psychiatrist, educator, author; b. NYC, July 1, 1901, s. Manes and Esther (Blau); BS,CCNY, 1921; PhD, Columbia U, 1934; MD, U Cincinnati Coll of Med, 1937; hon LHD, HUC-JIR, 1958; m. Rose Nadler, Dec 21, 1923; c: Michael, Jane Isay. Pvt practice since 1949; preceptor in psycht, Mt Sinai Hosp, since 1962, asso att psycht, 1958-62; lectr, Mt Sinai Med sch, since 1965; dean em, HUC-JIR, since 1958, prof: J educ, 1931-37; past ral psycht, 1937-46, both Cincinnati, dean pastoral psycht, NY, 1946-58; dir, commn on research, UAHC, 1928-:0; psych, bur reference, research and stat, Bd Educ, N\C, 1921-23; prin, HUC Sch for Tchrs, NYC, 1923-31. Maj, Surg Gen Off, USPHS, 1943-46. Mem, bd overseers, NY State Rehabilitation Hosp, Haverstraw, 1962; f: Amer Psychiatric Assn; NY Acad Med; Amer Psychosomatic Assn; Amer Geriatric Assn; mem: AMA; NY Soc for Clinical Psycht, pres, 1970; NY Co Med Soc; Kappa Delta Pi; Alpha Omega Alpha. Author: Reform Judaism in the Large Cities, 1931; 25 Years of Training Rabbis, 1933; Religious Belief and Character, 1935; The Road to Sexual Maturity, 1954; Liebe und Reife, Ger, 1957; A Primer of Statistics for Non-Statisticians, 1958; A Sane and Happy Life, 1963; contbr to profsl jours. Home and office: 1 Gracie Terr, New York, NY.

FRANZBLAU, Rose N, US, psychologist; columnist, radio commentator; b. Vienna, Aus, Jan 1, 1905; d. Meyer and Rachel (Breitfeld) Nadler; in US since 1905; BA, Hunter Coll, 1925, MA, Columbia U, 1933, PhD, 1935; m. Abraham Franzblau, Dec 21, 1923; c: Michael, Jane. Daily columnist, human relations, New York Post, since 1947; radio commentator, Dr. Franzblau's World of Children, WCBS, since 1965; feature writer, You and Your Family, Family Circle, since 1967, dir: girls activities, Natl Youth Admn, 1943-44, overseas personnel training, UNRRA, 1944-46, Wash; outplacement, OPA, NY, 1946-47. Chmn: adv council, Home Term Courts; co-chmn, WAIF, NY, Intl Rescue Service;

chmn, Girlstown of It adv bd, dept psych, U Jerusalem; bd dirs: Lorge Sch, NYC; Oliver Wendell Holmes Found; hon life mem: NAACP, Hadassah. Author: Race Differences in Mental and Physical Traits, 1935; co-author: Final Report, Natl Youth Admn, 1944; Tensions Affecting International Understanding, 1950; A Sane and Happy Life, 1963; The Way It Is Under Twenty, 1964. Recipient: Woman of Year, Child Guidance League, 1959; Judy award, Albert Einstein Coll of Med, 1960; Joey award, Asthma Research Found, 1962. Home: 1 Gracie Terr, New York, NY.

FREED, Simon, US, biochemist. neurochemist; b. Lodz, Pol, Nov 11, 1899; s. Abraham and Rachel (Kohn); in US since 1905; SB, MIT, 1920; Sorbonne, Paris, 1920-21; PhD, U of Cal, Berkeley, 1927; m. Sybil Brainerd, 1943. Research prof, biochem, neur, NY Med Coll, since 1967; research asso, instr, U of Cal, 1928-30; f, John Simon Guggenheim Found, Leiden, Holland, 1930-31; asst prof, chem, U Chgo, 1937-43, 1945-46; SAM Lab, Columbia U, 1943-45; chief chem, Oak Ridge Natl Lab, 1946-49; sr sci, Brookhaven Natl Lab, 1949-65; prof, phys, Mt Sinai Med Cen, NY, 1966-67. Mem: Assn Med Colls; AAAS. Asso ed, Jour of Chem Physics, 1941-43; contbr to profsl jours. Office: NY Med Coll, Fifth Ave and 106 St, New York City, NY.

FREEDEN, Herbert H, Isr, journalist; b. Posen, Ger, Jan 22, 1909; s. Isidor and Elise (Havelland) Friedenthal; in Isr since 1950; att U's: Goettingen; Munich; Berlin; PhD, U Leipzig, 1933; m. Marianne Hochdorf; c: Michael. Publicity dir, Keren Kayemeth le'Israel, since 1950; dir PR: JNF of Gt Brit and Ir, and Jt Pal Appeal, 1941-50; fgn corresp. Mem: B'nai B'rith; club, PEN. Author: The Invisible Link, 1936; A Ship on Its Way, 1938; The Everlasting Nay, 1944; Grist to God's Mill, 1947; Jewish Theatre in Nazi Germany; contbr essays and short stories; co-found, ed, AJR Info, Eng, 1944-50. Home: 15 Ha'ari St, Jerusalem, Isr. Office: Keren Kayemeth Le-Israel, Jerusalem, Isr.

FREEDLANDER, Samuel O, US, surgeon; b. Wooster, O, July 30, 1893; s. David and Anna (Arnson); AB, Adelbert Coll, W Reserve U, 1915, MD, Sch of Med, 1918; m. Adeline Kaden, 1931 (decd); c: Mina Gibans, Jeanne Abrahams; m. 2nd, Edith Hays, 1960. Cons, surg: Mt Sinai Hosp, Cleveland, since 1959, dir, 1945-59; Forest City Hosp, since 1945, mem, bd dirs, 1958-62; cons in thoracic surg: St Luke's Hosp, 1950; Cleveland Metrop Hosp; asso clinical prof surg, W Reserve U Med Sch, 1940-59; chief of surg div, chief thoracic surg, Cleveland City Hosp, 1932-53; chief surg, Sunny Acres Sanitarium, 1932-59; dir, Katz Sanders Lab for Surg Research, 1945-59. F, dipl: Amer Coll Surgs; Amer Bd urg, found; mem: Amer Coll Chest Phys; Amer Bd Thoracic Surg, found mem; Cuyahoga Co Med Soc; AMA; Amer Assn Thoracic Surg; Cen Surg Assn. O State Med Assn; Trudeau Soc; Amer Public Health Assn; Group Health Assn; Phi Beta Kappa; Alpha Omega Alpha; Sigma Psi; bd dirs, Acad of Med, 1936-39; trustee, Cleveland Med, Libr 1949-52, life f, since 1951; pres, Cleveland Surg Soc, 1958: club, Cleveland City, 1961-62. Home: 13710 Shaker Blvd, Cleveland, O. Office: Community Health Found, 11717 Euclid Ave, Cleveland, O.

FREEDLESS, Nahum Leon, Isr, rabbi; b. Warsaw, Pol, 1898; in Isr since 1963; BA, U Cincinnati, 1925; ordained rabbi, HUC, 1927; m. Miriam. Ret; fmr: rabbi, Roanoke, Va; pvt bus, NYC. Prin contrib: instrumental through Brisker Landsmanschaffen to bring financial aid to Kibbutz Gal On, which had been destroyed by Egyptians in War of Independence. Fmr: spiritual guide, parents group, whose children had emigrated to Isr as mems Hashomer Hatzair; active: ZOA; Haganah. Recipient: official cert, Kibbutz Gal On. Home: 18 Michah. St, Tel Aviv, Isr.

FREEDMAN, Abraham L, US, jurist; b. Trenton, NJ, Nov 19, 1904; s. Louis and Annie (Goldman); LLB, Temple U Law Sch, 1926; hon LLD, Temple U, 1966; m. Jane Sunstein, Jan 23, 1939; c: Robert , Margery. US Circiut Judge, 3rd Circuit Court of Apeeals, since 1964; in pvt practice law, 1926-61; fmr partner, Wolf, Block, Schorr and Solis-Cohen; gen counsel, then cons, Phila Housing Auth, 1938-49; counsel, Phila Housing Assn, 1940-61; city solicitor, Phila, 1952-56; spec counsel: Housing for the Pa Post-War Planning Commn, 1944-46; Redevl Auth, Phila, 1946-47; Housing for the Pa State Planning Bd, 1949-51; City of Phila, Girard Coll case, 1956-58; prof. domestic relations and Pa practice, Temple U Law Sch, 1931-44; lectr, family law, U of Pa Law Sch, 1955; US judge E dist Pa, 1961-64. Co-chmn, Gtr Phila

Movement, 1960-61; hon pres, J Comty Relations Council, since 1944; vice-pres, incorporator, Phila F Commn, since 1945; pres, Fed JAS, Gtr Phila, 1956-59; mem, bd dirs, United Fund and Health and Wfr Council; chmn: Phila Council for Comty Advancement, since 1961; mem: Citizens Charter Comm; Phila Charter Commn; draftsman, Pa Urban Redevl Law, 1945. Author: Law of Marriage and Divorce in Pa, 2nd ed, 3 vols, 1957. Home: 1014 W Horter St, Philadelphia, Pa. Office: US Court House, Ninth and Market Sts, Phiadelphia, Pa.

FREEDMAN, Alfred M, US, psychiatrist; b. Albany, NY, Jan 7, 1917; s. Jacob and Pauline (Hoffman); AB, Cornell U, 1937; MD U Minn, 1942; m. Marcia Kohl, 1943; c: Paul, Daniel Prof psycht, dept chmn, NY Med Coll, since 1960; dir psychiatric services; Flower and Fifth Ave Hosp; Metrop Hosp; Bird S Coler Hosp, since 1960; child psycht, U Hosp, NYC, 1952-53; dir pediatric psycht, asso prof psycht, SUNY, Downstate Med Cen, 1955-60. Maj, US Army MC, 1942-46. Pres, NY Soc of Clinical Psycht, 1967-68; bd dirs: Amer Orthopsychiatric Assn; AMA; Amer Psychiatric Assn; Sigma Xi; Amer Public Health Assn; Collegium Internationale Neuro-Psychopharmacologicum; World Fed for Mh; fmr mem, bd dirs, Walden Sch. Co-ed, Comprehensive Textbook of Psychiatry; contbr to med jours. Home: 161 W 86 St, New York, NY. Office: NY Med Coll, Fifth Ave and 106 St, New York, NY.

FREEDMAN, Doris Chanin, US, government admnr; b. Bklyn, NY, Apr 25, 1928; d. Irwin and Sylvia (Schofler) Chanin; BS, Albright Coll, Reading, Pa, 1950; MSW, Columbia U, 1953; m. Alan Freedman, June 3, 1951; c: Karen, Nina, Susan. Dir, org, NYC Dept Cultural Affairs, since 1967; social worker, NY Guild J Blind, 1953; spec projects dir, Comty Council, Gtr NY, 1954-55; partner, Tanglewood Press, 1964. Mem: bd: Mosholu Montefiore Comty Cen; Scholarship Educ and Defense Fund for Racial Equality; exec bd, Columbia U Sch of Social Work Alumni Assn; Pi Gamma Mu; fmr: chmn, parents assn, Ethical Cultural Sch; prog chmn, Encampment for Citizenship; mem, exec bd, Ethical Fieldston Fund; club, Women City. Author, Can Government "Get With It" in the Arts, 1968. Recipient, awards: Alumni, Outstanding Sr, Albright Coll, 1950; Louise Waterman Wise, AJCong, 1968. Hobbies: tennis, Cloisonné jewelry, collector of contemporary Amer art. Home: 25 Central Park W, New York, NY. Office: 830 Fifth Ave, New York, NY.

FREEDMAN, Emanuel R, US, editor; b. York, Pa, Dec 2, 1910; s. Abe and Annie (Liverant); BA, Columbia U, 1931, BL, 1932; m. Eva Magyar, Apr 10, 1949; c: Eric, Alix. Asst mgn, ed, NY Times, since 1964, copy ed, fgn desk, 1934-42, news ed, London, 1945-48, fgn news ed, 1948-64; with OWI, Wash, DC, 1942-45. Mem: Council on Fgn Relations; Intl Press Inst; clubs: Overseas Press; Dutch Treat. Home: 1000 Park Ave, New York, NY. Office: 229 W 43 St, New York, NY.

FREEDMAN, Harold L, US, physician; b. Luzerne, Pa, Dec 21, 1913; s. Max and Bertha (Berkowitz); BA, U Mich, 1934, MD, 1941; postgrad, Walter Reed Hosp Sch of Tropical Med, 1943; m. Gladys Hornung, Aug 22, 1937; c: Richard. Pvt practice since 1947; dir, Coronado Med Clinic, since 1959; sr aviation med examiner, Fed Aeronautical Assn, base surg, AEC, Sandia Base, Albuquerque, 1946-47; prin med off, Zia Co, Los Alamos, 1947; med dir, NM Life Ins Co, 1954-57. State co-chmn, NCCJ, 1954-60; pres, JWB, NM, 1954-47, vice-pres, NM br, NAACP, 1958; med adv, Gov Traffic Safety Council, 1958; delg, World Brotherhood Bldg Dedication, 1956; Gen Assembly of Judaism, 1958; natl sponsors comm, Back to the Syn Movement, 1958-60; mem: ZOA; Civil Defense Council, State Police; AMA; Ind Med Assn; Amer Acad Gen Practice; B'nai B'rith; Shriners. Co-recipient: UN award for NM, 1959. Home: 4934 Burton Dr SE, Albuquerque, NM. Office: ·3500 Constitution NE, Albuquerque, NM.

FREEDMAN, Harry L, US, psychiatrist; b. Boston, Mass ,Dec 14, 1899; s. Max and Rebecca (Kofsky); MS, MIT, 1923; MD, Harvard, 1928; m. Iris Worden, June 6, 1933; c: Lenore Cohen, Geraldine. Chief, psychiatric service, Clinton Prison, Dannemora, NY, since 1950; psycht, dept correction, NY State prisons, since 1932. Lt col, US Army, 1941-47, Life f, Amer Psycht Assn; mem, Natl Assn Mh, Inc. Recipient: Army Legion of Merit; Army Commendation Medal. Contbr to profsl jours. Home: 152 Broad St, Plattsburgh, NY. Office: Clinton Prison, Dannemora, NY.

FREEDMAN, Jacob, US, geologist, educator; b: Manchester, NH, Mar 28, 1911; s. Morris and Sarah (Gorin); BS, U of NH, 1938; MA, Harvard U, 1940, PhD, 1948; m. Bertha Book, Jan 16, 1944; c: David, Marsha Ginsburg. Prof, geology, Franklin and Marshall Coll, Lancaster, Pa, since 1947, chmn, dept geology, 1955, 1957-59, 1961-63; exec secy NAGT-US Geological Survey Coop Summer Field Training Prog, since 1966; asst instr, geology, U of NH, 1937-38; geologist, Alaskan br, US Geological Survey, 1942-45; asst instr, Harvard U, 1946-47; research geologist, mil geological br, US Geological Survey, 1947; field geologist, fgn geology br, Tel Aviv, Isr, 1953-54, geologist, Pa Geological Survey, 1958-64; resources research br, US Geological Survey, geochem exploration for silver around Lancaster, Pa, 1966-68. Vice-pres, mem bd: J Comty Cen, 1948-56; Temple Beth El, 1949-52; JCC; adv, Hillel at Franklin and Marshall Coll; mem: AAUP, mem, exec comm, vice-pres, local chap, 1956-57; Assn Geology Tchrs, vice-pres Northeast sect, 1965, pres, 1966; Mineralogical Soc of Pa; Pa Acad of Sci; mem ed comm of proc, 1948-50; Geochem Soc; Geological Soc of Amer; Phila Geological Soc; Amer Geological Inst; Sigma Xi. Men's of Temple Beth El Club, past pres. Contbr to: bull, US Geological Survey; profsl jours; Source Book of Geology for Elem and Secondary Sch Tchrs. Hobbies: golf, swimming, skiing, camping. Home: 2414 Helena Rd, Lancaster, Pa. Office: Franklin and Marshall Coll, Lancaster, Pa.

FREEDMAN, John, US, radiologist; b. NYC, Oct 6, 1902; s. Samuel and Molly (Rappaport); MD, U of Mich, 1926; m. Geraldine Berger, May 20, 1928; c: Florence Wolf, Donald, Helen Weiser. Ret; fmr dir, X-ray dept, N Detroit Gen Hosp; instr, radiology, U of Ill, Chgo, 1931-32. Maj, US Army MC, 1942-46. Contbr to med journals. Home: Box 952, Palm, Springs, Cal.

FREEDMAN, Joseph Leopold, Eng, solicitor; b. London, Eng, Nov 3, 1903; s. Jacob and Hannah (Beirnstein); MA, LLB, Christ's Coll, Cambridge, 1924; m. Rosa Bosman, Mar 20, 1932; c: Harold, Michael. Cons, J L Freedman and Co, since 1969, partner 1928-68; JB, Middlesex Area, Gtr London; alderman, Borough of Barnet; mayor, Borough of Hendon, 1950-51. Chmn, NW Reform Syn; past asst grand registrar, United Grand Lodge of Eng; solicitor, Supr Court of Judicature, Eng, 1927. Home: 2 Woodward Ave, Hendon, London NW4, Eng. Office: 20 Station Rd, Edgware, Middlesex, Eng.

FREEDMAN, Lew, Austr, communal leader, author; b. Mezritch, Pol, Jan 31, 1911; s. Alexander and Rebecca (Bromberg); in Australia since 1948; BComm, Prin Coll Commerce, Warsaw, 1932; m. Cyla Shein, 1940. Gen secy, J Cultural Cen, Kadimah, Melbourne, since 1949; fmr: research F, YIVO, 1936-37; lectr, HS, both Pol, 1937-38; ed, J Post, weekly, Melbourne, 1948-49. Author, in Yiddish: Research on Some Aspects of Economic Structure of the Jews in Poland, 1937; Life of the Jews in Mezritcher Ghetto and their Annihilation, 1947; Madam Adler, play, 1967; ed, Third Australian Jewish Almanac, Yiddish, 1966; contbr to J mags. Recipient, Award for play, Madam Adler, World Cong for J Culture, NY, 1967. Hobbies: lit, arts, theatre. Home: 310 Alma St, Caulfield, Vic, Austr. Office: 9 Gordon St, Elsternwick, Vic, Austr.

FREEDMAN, Louis, US, biochemist, business exec; b. New Haven, Conn, Jan 28, 1894; s. Joseph and Paulina (Tatarsky); PhB, Yale U, 1915, MS, 1917; PhD, Columbia, U, 1922; m. Bertha Gallup, July 24, 1923; c: Joel, David, Paul. Research cons, US Vitamin and Pharm Corp, since 1965 vice-pres i/c research, 1947-65, with firm since 1936; research chem: Metz Labs, NY, 1919-27; Winthrop-Metz Research Lab, 1927-36. Prin contrib: co-discoverer and holder more than 100 patents in field of vitamins, organic chem, nutrition, pharm; with Dr Casimir Funk, made 1st synthetic adrenalin in US, 1919; invented: process for extraction vitamins direct from fish livers on commercial scale, 1938; process for solubilizing fat soluble vitamins, A, D, E, 1947; palatable sodium free salt; found: Louis and Bert Freedman Found Patent Award, Amer Inst Chems, 1966; Freedman F in biochem, Yale U; donor, Louis Freedman Postgrad Cen for Pharm Sci, Heb U. Vice-pres, mem bd govs, Amer Friends Heb U; chmn, exec comm, Lipotropic Research Found, since 1963; f, life mem: Amer Inst Chems; NY Acad Sci; mem: ind adv comm, Natl Vitamin Found; Amer Chem Soc; Soc for Experimental Biol and Med; Soc for Clinical Research; Sigma Xi; Yale Engr Assn; exec comm ZOA, Mt Vernon, NY; co-chmn, Gtr NY drug div, UJA. Contbr to: annual vitamin revs; Ency Americana, since 1965; numerous articles to sci and

profsl jours. Hobbies: photography, travel. Home: 139 E 63 St, New York, NY.

FREEDMAN, Marion Kaye, Can, communal leader, educator; b. New Brit, Conn, Apr 2, 1916; d. Issac and Sadelle (Shapiro); att Sergent Coll, Mass; BS, Arnold Coll, New Haven, Conn; MEd, U Conn; m. Jack Freedman; c: Richard, Linda Margolese. Mem: exec, Intl B'nai B'rith Women; bd dirs, J Immigration Aid Soc; natl council, Can J Cong; J General Hosp; Hillsdale Golf and Country Club; Shaare Zion Syn; commn: Isr Commn; Hillel Commn; found, Urban Camp for Underprivileged Children; mem: bd: Red Feather; Red Cross; natl women'a div, State of Isr Bonds; fmr: asst natl exec dir: ORT; Can Friends Bar Ilan U; pres, B'nai B'rith Dist; off, Talmud Torah; B'nai B'rith Youth Comty; prog chmn, Jt PR, Can J Cong, B'nai B'rith. Recipient awards: women of year, Lamentation Region Youth; outstanding comty service; Leadership; Can Govt for Women's Voluntary Service. Spec interests: educ, writing. Home: 3555 Cote des Neige, Montreal, Can.

FREEDMAN, Martin, US, rabbi; b. Newark, NJ, Nov 13, 1926; s. Solomon and Yetta (Tornheim); BA, NYU, 1949; BHL, HML, ordained rabbi, HUC-JIR, 1955; m. Frances Lipman, Dec 18, 1955; c: Francessca. Rabbi, Cong B'nai Jeshurun, Nathan Barnert Memorial Temple, since 1956; lectr, J culture Found, Columbia U; found rabbi, Temple Beth El, Elizabeth, NJ, 1951-55; instr, Bible and Judaism, HUC Sch of Educ, 1954-56. Adv bd, SANE; mem: NJ ACLU; Amer Indian Fund; NAACP; bd dirs, Paterson State Coll, chmn, commn on justice and peace, UAHC. Home: 345 E 42 St, Paterson, NJ. Office: 152 Derrom Ave, Paterson, NJ.

FREEDMAN, Morris, US, educator, author; b. NYC, Oct 6, 1920; s. Boris and Anna (Katz); BA, CCNY, 1941; MA, Columbia U, 1950, PhD, 1953; m. Charlotte Kopelman, 1945; c: Paul, Iris. Prof, Eng, head dept, U of Md, since 1966; prof, U of NM, 1962-65, fac mem, since 1955; instr, Eng, CCNY, 1945-54. USAAF, 1943-45. Author: Confessions of a Conformist, 1961; Chaos in our Colleges, 1963; Compact English Handbook, 1965; The Moral Impulse: Modern Drama from Ibsen to the Present, 1967; ed: Essays in the Modern Drama, 1964; Fact and Object, 1963; Contemporary Controversy, 1965; Controversy in Literature, 1968; asso ed, Commentary, 1953-55; contbr, numerous articles on drama, Milton, and Dryden, short stories to periodicals and mags. Office: U of Md, College Park, Md.

FREEDMAN, Rosa Annie, Eng, communal leader; b. London, Eng, Aug 13, 1908; d. Harold and Julia (Cohen) Bosman; dipl, Borrdige House; m. Joseph Freedman, Mar 20, 1932; c: Harold, Michael. Councillor, London Borough Barret; chmn, Health and Wfr Comm. Chmn, Barret Overseas Students Leadership Assn; pres, J Friendly Circles; life mem, Council League of J Women; natl pres, 1961-64; fmr: chmn, Childrens Comm, Middlesex Comty Council; secy, Conservative Assn of Middlesex Comty Council; mem, Intl Council J Women. Spec interests: working for refug, overseas students. Home: 2 Woodward Ave, Hendon, London, Eng.

FREEDMAN, Samuel, Can, jurist; b. Russ, Apr 16, 1908; s. Nathan and Ada (Foxman); in Can since 1911; BA, U Man, 1929; LLB, Man Law Sch, 1933; hon LLD; Assumption U, Windsor, 1960; U Windsor, 1960; Heb U, Jerusalem, 1964; ND State U, 1965; U Toronto, 1965; U Man, 1968; Brock U, 1968; McGill U, 1968; Queen's U, 1969; hon DCnL, St John's Coll, Winnipeg, Man, 1967; m: Claris Udow, 1934; c: Martin, Susan Silverman, Phyllis. Judge, Court of Appeal, Man, since 1960; Q.C; mem, law firms: Steinkopf, Lawrence and Freedman, 1933-45; Freedman and Golden, 1946-52, both Winnipeg; lectr Man Law Sch, 1941-59; judge, Court of Queen's Bench, Man, 1952-60. Chancellor, U of Man, 1959-68; pres: Man Bar Assn, 1952; YMHA, 1936-37; B'nai B'rith, 1943-44; vice-pres, Comty Chest, 1946; bencher, Law Soc Man, 1949-52; chmn: Can Inst Intl Affairs, 1947-48; Can Friends Heb U, 1953; govr, Heb U, Jerusalem, since 1955; mem: Can found: Can Bar Assn; club, Glendale Country. Hobbies: public speaking, golf. Home: 425 Cordova St, Winnipeg, Can. Office: Court House, Winnipeg, Can.

FREEDMAN, Samuel Z, US, surgeon; b. Pol, Apr 7, 1896; s. Harris and Jennie (Kopita); in US since 1899; MD, NYU, 1918; m. Martha Kaplan, June 27, 1926; c: Walter. Cons urol: Gouverneur Hosp; Polyclinic Hosp; Beth Isr Hosp. Dir, div standards of med care, Med Soc, State of NY; bd dirs, United Med Service since 1956. Contbr to med jours .

Home: 541 E 20 St, New York, NY. Office: 750 Third Ave, New York, NY.

FREEDMAN, Saul J, US, business exec; b. Phila, Pa, July 24, 1934; s. Daniel and Gertrude (Glazier); BS, U of Pa, 1956; m. Peggy Feinstein, June 24, 1956; c: Andrew, Paul, Myra. Pres, Pa Fed Savings and Loan Assn since 1965. USNR, 1956-58. Pres, Phila chap, Amer-Isr C of C; vice-pres, J Y's and Cens, Gtr Phila; treas: Rebecca Gratz Club; Mercy Douglass Hosp; Oak Lane Day Sch; Neighborhood Cen; secy, Phila Friends of Lubavitcher; chmn: Isr comm, J Comty Relations Council; Phila Volunteers for Isr; mem: exec comm: Natl UJA Young Leadership Cabinet; Natl Comm on Leadership Devl, CJFWF; Phila council, Boy Scouts of Amer; bd trustees, Fed of JA's; bd govs, Insured Savings and Loans of Gtr Phila; coord chmn, trade council, Allied J App. Recipient, Myer Feinstein Young Leadership Award, Fed of JA's of Phila, 1965. Home: 1230 Wrack Rd, Meadowbrook, Pa. Office: 1627 Walnut St, Philadelphia, Pa.

FREEDMAN, Walter, US, attorney; b. St Louis, Mo, Oct 30, 1914; s. Sam and Sophie (Gordon); BA, Wash U, St Louis, 1937, LLB, 1937; LLM, cum laude, Harvard U, 1938; m. Maxine Weil, June 23, 1940; c: Jay, Sandra. Partner, Freedman, Levy, Kroll & Simonds; cheif counsel, Off Export Control, Fgn Econ Admn, 1942-44, dir, export, control, 1944-45. Mem: Amer Bar Assn; Fed and DC Bar Assns; Amer Law Inst; Wash Heb Cong, bd of mgrs, 1952-55; club, Woodmont Country. Contbr to legal jours. Home: 3554 Appleton St, NW, Washington, DC. Office: 1730 K St, NW, Wahsington, DC.

FREEDMAN, Warren, US, attorney; b. Scranton, Pa, May 2, 1921; s. Samuel and Sarah (Spitz); AB, Rutgers U, 1943; att: Cornell U Sch of Law, 1942-43; Yale U, 1943-44; LLB, Columbia Law Sch, 1949; m. Esther Rosenbluth, May 3, 1944; c: Debby, Miriam, Douglas. Counsel, Bristol Myers Co, since 1963, house counsel, asst gen mgr, Clairol div, since 1953; pvt law practice since 1949; lectr: Practicing Law Inst Amer Mgmt Assn, Commerce and Ind Assn, NY, since 1957; New Sch for Social Research, NYC, 1957-66; mem, law fac, Rutgers U Law Sch, 1949-51; atty examiner, FTC 1950-53; partner, law firm, Margolis, Freedman and Shire, 1961; fac mem, NYU Sch of Continuing Educ, 1966. Dir: Guidance Cen, New Rochelle; Beth El Comty Cen, since 1954; natl commn, ADL, 1968-71; mem, NY regional bd, Westchester Co steering comm, chmn, Westchester Co, PEARL, mem, Metrop council comm; bd govs, Dist l, B'nai B'rith, 1968; mem, exec Metrop Council, B'nai B'rith, chmn Hillel comm, 1968; fmr chmn, Westchester Co Adult J Educ Comm, B'nai B'rith, 1967; dir, Empire Region BBYO bd dir, 1968; swp, Mt Vernon Lodge, B'nai B'rith, 1968; fmr pres, Tom Paine Lodge, 1964; found, chmn: Tom Paine Forums; chmn, New Rochelle div, UJA, 1968; active leader: FJP; ADL Appeal. Author: Richards on Insurance, 4 vols, 1952; Freedman on Allergy and Products Liability, 1961; two treatises: Society on Trial, 1965; Societal Behavior, 1965; law rev articles; ed, Monthly Products Liability Digest, 1958. Home: 81 Stratford Rd, New Rochelle, NY. Office: 630 Fifth Ave, New York, NY.

FREEHOF, Solomon B, US rabbi, author; b. London, Aug 8, 1892; s. Isaac and Golda (Blonstein); BA, U Cincinnati, 1914; ordained rabbi, DD, HUC, 1916; hon DHL, HUC-JIR, 1945; m. Lillian Simon, Oct 29, 1934. Rabbi em, Rodef Shalom Temple, since 1968; rabbi, 1934-68; rabbi: Kehillat Anshe Maariv Temple, Chgo, 1924-34; tchr, rabb, HUC, 1915-24. Chaplain Amer Expeditionary Forces, 1917-19. Author: Commentary on the Book of Psalms, 1938; Modern Jewish Preaching, 1941; The Small Sanctuary, 1942; Reform Jewish Practice, 1944; Preface to Scripture, 1950; The Book of Job, A Commentary, 1952; Reform, Recent, and Current Reform Responsa. Hon life pres, World Union for Progressive Judaism, pres, 1962-67; fmr pres, CCAR; exec bd mem: UAHC; rei activities comm, JWB. Home: 128 N Craig St, Pittsburgh, Pa. Study: 4905 Fifth Ave, Pittsburgh, Pa.

FREEMAN, Bernard, Austr, business exec; b. Sydney, Sep 1, 1896; s. Adolf and Malvina; m. Marjorie Bloom, Feb 16, 1926; c: Geoffrey, Pamela. Found: Metro-Goldwyn-Mayer, Austr, NZ, S Pacific, 1925, mgn dir, 1925-66, chmn dirs, 1967. Austr Army, WW II; inaugurated free films to Austr Troops, 1939-45. First mem chmn, N Motion Picture Distributors' Assn, Austr, 1939-41, 1963; life mem, RSS and AILA State Br, since 1945; life gov: Royal NSW Inst for Deaf and Blind Children; Vic Ear & Eye Hosp; Vic Sch for Deaf Children; chmn: Anzac House Trust, since 1947; Anzac House Appeal, 1945-47; Miss Austr Quest, 1948-49; UN Appeal for Children,

1953; World Ref Year, NSW Comm, 1960; US Intl House Appeal, since 1962; mem: Lord Mayor's Patriotic Fund, 1939-45; Films Adv Comm to Fed Govt, 1939-45; Admn Comm, British Cen, 1944-46; Sydney Opera House Trust Exec Comm; Exec Mgmt and Music, Drama Comm; bd mgmt, Intl House Sydney U; bd mgmt, Intl House NSW U; chmn, NSW Comm, Anzac Memorial & Forest , Isr; clubs: Austr-Amer Assn; Amer Soc; Amer Natl; Austr Flying Corps Assn; City and Coogee Bowling; Rotary, Sydney, past pres; Tattersalls; Journalists'. Recipient: CBE, 1956; Knight Bachelor, 1967. Home: 85 Yarranabbe Rd, Darling Point, Austr.

FREEMAN, David, Isr, insurance broker, author; b. Manchester, Eng, 1901; s. Marks and Jennie; in Isr since 1946. Secy, Pal Potash Ltd, 1946-48; dep controller fgn exch, N Dist, 1948-49; mem: Haifa Port Enquiry Comm, 1952; ports stevedoring rate-fixing comm, 1953. Pres, Moriah Cong, since 1955; chmn, Moadon Haoleh, since 1967; mem bd dirs, World Council of Syns; fmr: found, chmn; BBB; mem comm, Anglo-Isr C of C; mem: Bd Deps Brit J's, law and parl comm; exec council, ZF, Gt Brit; exec council, Manchester and Salford Js; hon secy: Friends Heb U; Heb Educ Bd; instr, Habonim, all Manchester; Isr delg, biennial conv, United Syn of Amer; lectr tour, J comtys, USA; N regional trades mgr, Trades Adv Council, Eng; clubs: Rotary, Haifa; Masons, past master. Author: The Day Will Come, 1936; Theodor Herzl, 1937; The Glory of Israel, 1939; A Little Spiel, 1939; Passover, The Jewish Spring Festival, 1940, BBC Broadcast; The Scholar, 1940; War Time Evacuation of Jewish Children, an enquiry, 1941; In Galilee, 1940; Prof Hermann Schapira, on the centenary of his birth, 1940; The Jubilant Voice, 1942; Dreyfus-A Study in Anti-Semitism, 1945; Abraham Lincoln, 1959; Jacobus H Kann, 1965; Justice L D Brandeis, 1967; fmr: Manchester corresp, J Chronicle; jt ed, Rama, B'nai B'rith monthly; contbr to local and fgn press. Home: 47 Disraeli St, Ahuza, Haifa, Isr. Office: 35 Hameginim St, Haifa, Isr.

FREEMAN, Frank S, US psychologist , educator; b. St Louis, Mo, Oct 11, 1898; s. Isaac and Anna (Levine); BS, Harvard U, 1920; EdD, 1926; m. Esther Worthington, June 19, 1928; Ret; prof psych, Cornell U, 1940-65, prof, educ, 1935-40; on fac since 1965; practice psych since 1925; educ, cons, Bur Aeronautics, USN, 1942; visiting prof: Denver U, 1948; U S Cal, 1949; Ore Coll of Educ, 1967; U Hawaii, 1963-64; cons in psych to educ socs. F, AAAS; fmr vice-pres, exec comm mem, NY State Psych Assn; exec comm mem, Natl Soc Coll, Tchrs Educ; chmn NY State Bd Examiners of Psychols, 1956-60, mem, 1960-62. Author: Development and Learning, 1942; Theory and Practice of Psychological Training, 1950, rev ed, 1955, 3rd ed, 1962; co-author: Psychology and Education, 1939; contbr to profsl jours. Home: 1414 N Lake Shore Dr, Sarasota, Fla.

FREEMAN, Harold S, Can, attorney, b. Manchester, Eng, Dec 8, 1902; s. Hyman and Matilda (Jacobson); BA, McGill U, 1923; LLB, U Montreal, 1926; m. Lillian Gold, Mar 26, 1946; c: Martin, Alan. Pvt practice since 1926; QC since 1961. Mem: Shaare Zion Syn; fmr: pres, Lord Reading Soc; chmn, publs comm, ZOC, mem exec; pres: B'nai B'rith lodge; Camp B'nai B'rith for Underprivileged Boys; chmn, J Comty Camps; natl vice pres, Zionist Order Habonim, pres, Mt Carmel Lodge; campaign vice-chmn, United J Camps; control chmn, campaign for J Gen Hosp; mem: jt PR comm, Can J Cong; exec, perm comm, CJA, delg, Can J Cong convs, 1947, 1949, 1951; club, Hillsdale Golf and Country Club. Home: 5034 Grosvenor Ave, Montreal , Can. Office: Gordon Brown Bldg, Montreal, Can.

FREEMAN, Lucy, US, author; b. NYC, Dec 13, 1916; d. Lawrence and Sylvia (Sobel) Greenbaum; BA, Bennington Coll, 1938; m. William Freeman Oct 7, 1946; div. Free-lance writer since 1952; reporter, NY Times 1941-52. Author: Fight Against Fears, 1951; Hope for the Troubled, 1953; Before I Kill More, 1955; Hospital in Action, 1956; Search for Love, 1957; So You Want to be Psychoanalyzed, 1958; Troubled Women, 1959; Story of Psychoanalysis, 1960; Children Who Kill, 1961; The Abortionist, 1962; Remember Me to Tom, 1963; The Available Woman, 1968; The Cry for Love, 1969; Farewell to Fear, 1969. Mem: ed bd, Natl Council on Crime and Delinquency; Natl Assn of Sci Writers; Amer Orthopsycht Assn; Soc of Mag Writers; Amer Mystery Writers Assn; club, PEN. Hobbies: theatre, movies, dancing, horse-racing, golf. Home and office: 120 Central Park S, New York, NY.

FREEMAN, Samuel D, US, organization exec; b. Brockton Mass, Jan 23, 1912; s. Morris and Tillie (Denenberg); **BS.**

Bklyn Coll, 1933; MS, CCNY, 1939; MSSW, NY Sch of Social Work, 1949; DEd, Columbia U, 1953; m. Ruth Oxenhorn, Aug 1, 1934; c: Jay, Elisa. Dir: adult prog services dept, JWB, since 1951; lecture bur since 1946; tchr, Puerto Rico, Naguabo, 1935-36, Caguas, 1936-37; field dir, United Service Org, Panama CZ, 1944; Natl Prog dir, Armed Services, JWB, 1946. Exec comm, Council Natl Orgs, 1952-53; pres, NY Adult Educ Council, 1964; bd dirs, NY Adult Educ Council, since 1958; mem: delg Assembly, Adult Educ Assn; Natl Assn, J Cen Workers. Author: Adult Education in Jewish Comminity Center, 1952; ed-in-chief, J Audio-Visual Rev. Home: 196 Rockaway Pkwy, Brooklyn, NY. Office: 145 W 32 St, New York, NY.

FREEMAN, Simon, Eng, physician; b. Edinburgh, Scot, Apr 29, 1904; s. Joseph and Reva (Lipetz); in Eng since 1931; LRCPS, Edinburgh, 1931; m. Mimi Daniels, Oct 24, 1936; c: Anthony, Peter. Pvt practice since 1931; med referee, Min Health and Social Security, since 1948; police surg, Manchester City Police, 1958-64; med vice-pres, Assn for Prevention of Addiction, 1964-66; Lt col, RAMC, 1939-54. Chmn, Manchester div, BMA, 1965-68; corresp surg, St John Ambulance Assn; f, Manchester Med Soc; mem: Manchester Health Exec Council; Brit Acad Forensic Sci. Contbr to med and profsl jours. Recipient, OBE, 1963. Spec interests, drug dependence problem, drunken driver problem. Home: 3 Thornhill Rd Heaton Mersey, Cheshire, Eng. Office: 1080 Stockport Rd, Manchester, Eng.

FREEMAN, Stan, US, composer, pianist; b. Waterbury, Conn, Apr 3, 1925; s. Nathan and Augusta; att Julius Hart Sch of Music, Hartford, Conn. Musical dir for Marlene Dietrich; composer, scores: I Had a Ball, 1967; Teahouse of the August Moon, 1970; piano soloist with: Cincinnati Sym Orch; Memphis Sym; NY Philharmonic Orch; recordings: Columbia; Project Three Records. Sgt, USAC, 1943-46. Hobbies: collecting: rare books; records of old show bus personalities. Home: 214 E 78 St, New York, NY.

FREEMAN, William, US, physician; b. Boston, Mass, July 27, 1901; s. Jacob and Anne (Metcalf); BChE, Northeastern U, 1924; att Boston U, 1924-25, MD, Sch of Med, 1929; m. Gertrude LeClair, 1935 (decd); m. 2nd, Pauline Murray, June 26, 1947; c: Anne Robbins, William LeClair, Susan, Frederick. Chief path, dir labs, Truesdale Hosp and Clinic, since 1946; asst prof path, Boston U Med Sch, since 1931; path, dir labs: Worcester State Hosp and Neuro-endocrine Research, 1931-46; Worcester Hahnemann Hosp, 1932-46; dir, Worcester Med Soc comty blood bank. Lt, ret, US Army, MC, Res. Pres, Fall River Med Soc; med dir, Fall River Civil Defense, since 1951; dir, Fall River Cerebral Palsy Rehab Cen, since 1958, fmr pres; mem: AMA; Amer Coll Phys; Coll Amer Path; Amer Soc Clinical Path; Intl Acad Path; Mass Med Soc; regional and State path soc's; dipl: Natl Bd Path, 1931; Amer Bd Path, 1937; fmr: pres: RI Soc Path; NE Assn Blood Bank Drs, 1956-58. Contbr to med jours. Hobby: floraculture. Home: 93 Garners Neck Rd, Swansea, Mass. Office: Truesdale Hosp, Fall River, Mass.

FREI, Ephraim Heinrich, Isr, physicist, educator; b. Vienna, Aus, Mar 2, 1912; s. Siegmund and Franzisca (Wiener); in Isr since 1938; PhD, U Vienna, 1936, att postgrad, 1936-38; sr scholar, Heb U, Jerusalem, 1938-42; m. Yael Rosenfeld, May 9, 1948; c: Leah, Michael. Prof elec, Weizmann Inst of Sci, since 1960, head dept since 1961; asst, physics, Heb U 1946-48; head dept elec, Min Defense, 1948-50; mem, engr, Inst for Advanced Study, Princeton U, 1950-52, head, dept elec, 1956, asso prof, 1957; Intl Stanford Research Inst, 1959-60. Civilian engr, Brit Army 1942-47; IDF, 1948-49. Mem: Amer Phys Soc; Isr Phys Soc; f, IEEE; chmn, Isr Soc Biomed Engrs. Contbr, sci publs on magnetism, solid-state physics, biomed engr. Home: 5 Ruppin St, Rehovot, Isr. Office: Weizmann Inst of Sci, Rehovot, Isr.

FREIBERG, Joseph A, US, orthopedic surg, educator; b. Cincinnati, O, Oct 3, 1898; s. Albert and Jeanette (Freiberg); BA, Harvard U, 1920; MA, U Cincinnati, 1922, MD, 1923; m. Louise Rothenberg, Oct 6, 1928 (decd); c: Richard, Elinor. Prof em, U Cincinnati, Coll of Med, since 1969, prof surg, dir, orthopedic div, 1964-69, on fac since 1928; pvt practice since 1940; dir, orthopedic service: Cincinnati Gen Hosp; Holmes Hosp; Cincinnati Children's Hosp; cons: VA Hosp, Cincinnati; Hamilton Co Drake Hosp; Dunham Hosp. Hon f, Brit Orthopedic Soc, 1967; dipl, Amer Bd Orthopedic Surg; f, Amer Coll of Surg; mem: Amer Orthopedic Assn, pres, 1962; Amer Acad Orthopedic Surg; Amer and O Med Assn; Orthopedic

Forum; Sigma Xi; Alpha Omega Alpha; clubs: Losantiville Country, U; Harvard; Cincinnati. Contbr to med jours. Home: 7154 Knoll Road, Amberley Village, Cincinnati, O. Office: 2939 Vernon Pl, Cincinnati, O.

FREIDBERG, Alan Elliot, US, organization exec; b. Phila, Pa, Dec 13, 1936; s. Joseph and Kay (Krasick); BA, Penn State U, 1957; att: Heb U, Jerusalem, 1957-58; HUC-JIR, NY, 1958-60. Admnr, Amer-Isr Cultural Found, since 1967; trainee, Van Raalte Co, 1960-61; merchandise coord, Ohrbach's, 1961-66; buyer, Abraham & Straus, 1966-67. Mem: exec comm, Amer Alumni Assn, Heb U; J Bd Guardians; Alpha Phi Omega; Beta Sigma Rho. Hobbies: music, reading, travel. Home: 70 W 95 St, New York, NY. Office: 4 E 54 St, New York, NY.

FREIDKES, Nahum, Isr, educator, editor, certified public acctnt; b. Bielsk-Podlaski, Pol, Mar 6, 1931; s. Kalman and Sheina (Kowinski); in Isr since 1950; m. Ribka Schreiber, Sep 9, 1958; c: Dina, Anat. CPA since 1959; lectr, Tel Aviv U, since 1958; ed, Jour of Inst of CPA's in Isr, since 1967; f lectr, Heb U, 1960-62. Vice-pres, Inst of CPA's in Isr; cen comm, Isr Independent Lib Party. Contbr on taxation, accountancy, mgmt to periodicals and press. Home: 11 Shomron St, Holon, Isr. Office: 21 Sharon St, Tel Aviv, Isr.

FREIFELD, Sidney A, Can, government official, journalist; b. Toronto, Can, Sep 2, 1910; s. Louis and Jessie (Schipper); BCom, U Toronto, 1932; att: LSE, 1932-34; Natl Defense Coll, Can, 1962-63; m. Crenia Sandler, Aug 25, 1939; c: Riva, Miriam. Chargé d'affaires, Can Emb, Uruguay, since 1969; corresp, US, Can press, Eur and NY, 1936-39; press off, AJComm, NYC, 1939-41; dir, press and info services, Can Consulate Gen, NYC, 1943-51, and Can delg to UN, NYC, 1947-52; chief press off, 1952-54, head, US desk, 1954-55, Dept External Affairs, Ottowa; first secy, Can Emb, Mexico City, 1955-58; counsellor, Can Emb, Dublin, 1958-61; chief spokesman, head, press div, Dept External Affairs, Ottawa, 1962-63; counsellor, Can Mission to UN, 1964-69. Address: Casilla Posta 852, Montevideo, Uruguay.

FREILICH, Ellis B, US, physician, educator; b. Chgo, Ill, Jan 17, 1891; s. Moses and Mindel (Wolf); MD, U of Ill, 1914; m. Mildred Kamerman, Sep 3, 1916; c: Joseph, Muriel Shacknov. Prof em, med, U of Ill, since 1956, on fac since 1943; att phys: Mt Sinai Hosp, past pres, med staff; Cook Co Hosp; chief, TB staff. Co-chmn, phys div, CJA; dir: J Fed of Metrop Chgo; Mt Sinai Med Research Found; FACP; dipl, Amer Bd of Internal Med; mem, Phi Delta Epsilon; club, Standard. Author: A Manual of Physical Diagnosis, 1941; contbr to med jours. Home: 320 S Plymouth Court, Chicago, Ill. Office: 55 E Washington St, Chicago, Ill.

FREILICH, Joseph K, US, physician; b. Chgo, Ill, Feb 10, 1918; s. Ellis and Mildred (Kamerman); BS, U Chgo, 1938, MD, 1941; m. Shirley Berlau, Dec 15, 1946; c: Robert, Charles, Jane. Pvt practice, internal med, since 1956; att phys, chief thoracic med sect, dir dept inhalation therapy and pulmonary phys lab, St Joseph Hosp; dir, Park View Home. US Army, 1942-45. Mem: AMA; Ill State and Chgo Med Socs; Amer Coll Phys; Phi Delta Epsilon; Phi Sigma Delta; Phi Beta Kappa. Author: Pericarditis Current Therapy, 1954; co-author, Textbook of Physical Diagnosis, 1947; contbr to med jours. Hobbies: golf, photography. Home: 2648 Lakeview, Chicago, Ill. Office: 55 E Washington St, Chicago, Ill.

FREILICH, Michael Leon, US, art gallery dir; b. Czestochowa, Pol, May 1, 1912; s. Sam and Sophie (Schwartzberg); in US since 1914; BA, CCNY, 1935; att: Columbia U, 1935-36; CCNY, 1937-38; Dir, owner, Roko Gal, since 1946; lectr: Bklyn Mus; Village Art Cen; Fairleigh Dickinson U, NJ; Brook Guild Artists, Westchester; Baranik Studio Work Shop, White Plains, NY; YM-YWHA, NY; frequent juror, art competitions: Hudson River Mus, Yonkers, NY; Bklyn Mus; McGraw Publs; Albert Einstein Med Inst; others; accredited appraiser of art collections; collector of contemporary Amer, Oriental art; group worker, arts and crafts, Madison House; lectr, Mus of Modern Art, 1938-39; corresp, lectr, VA, 1943-46. Prin contribs: discovery and devl contemporary Amer painters, sculptors, graphic artists. Exec chmn, art comm, Karen Horney Clinic; art adv, NY Clinic for Mh; art cons, Cen for Urban Studies, NY. Author: numerous introductions to art catalogues. Hobbies: psychol, tennis, ice skating, dance. Home and office: 407 E 77 St, New York, NY.

FREIMAN, Lawrence, Can, business exec, communal leader; b. Ottawa, Feb 4, 1909. Pres, gen mgr, A J Freiman Ltd. Hon chmn, Ottawa Isr Bond Comm; bd dirs, Red Cross; bd govs, Victorian Order of Nurses; regional adv comm, Can Wfr Chest. Home: 250 Sylvan Rd, Rockcliff Park, Ottawa, Can. Office: 69 Rideau St, Ottawa, Can.

FRENKEL, Eliezer, Isr, architect; b. Paris, Fr, Oct 29, 1929; s. Itzhak and Miriam (Anisfeld); in Isr since 1935; BArch, Pratt Inst, NY; m. Nora Rubenfeld; 1954, c: Tamar, Miriam. Architecht since 1959; architectural critic, Jerusalem Post, since 1966; designed and executed: urban renovations: Old City of Jaffa; Old City of Jerusalem. Mem: Architects and Engrs Assn, Isr, since 1962; Isr Assn for Environmental Design, since 1966. Recipient, Awards: Israel Rokach, Tel Aviv Munic 1966; Uzi Rosen, Isr Assn Engrs and Architects. Home and office: 15 Hildesheimer St, Tel Aviv, Isr.

FRENKEL, Lawrence, US, business exec; b. NYC, July 2, 1918; s. Louis and Margaret (Phillips); att: U of SC, 1941-42; Stanford U, 1942-44; Grad Sch of Social Research, NYC, 1946-49; m. Helga Nygaard, Sep 11, 1943; c: Margaret Goldstein, Louis. Partner: Frenkel Mailing Service, since 1953; Frenkel Assos, since 1953; publisher, Amer J Orgs Directory, since 1956; chief public health off, UNRRA, Aus, 1945-46. Mil IS, strategic bombing survey, US Army, 1941-45. Pres, Natl Assn PO and Gen Service Maintenance Employees, Amer Fed of Lab, local 58, 1952-53; dir, Beth Jacob Sch, Heb Tchrs Coll, since 1960; chmn, NY Metrop Council, since 1961; transp chmn, Manhattan Boro Pres Comty Planning Bd; mem: Chinese Amer Art Soc; China Inst; Mail Advt Service Assn; club, Gen Douglas McArthur Repub. Contbr to Hoover Libr, Stanford U. Office: 24 Rutgers St, New York, NY.

FREUD, Anna, Eng, psychoanalyst; b. Vienna; Aus, d. Sigmund and Martha (Bernays); att coll, Vienna; hon degs: LLD: Clark U, Worcester, Mass, 1950; U Sheffield, Eng, 1966; ScD: Jeeffrson Med Coll, Phila, 1964; U Chgo, 1966; Yale U, New Haven, 1968. Dir, Hampstead Child Therapy Course, Clinic. Author, The Writings of Anna Freud, 7 vols. Recipient, CBE, 1967. Home: 20 Maresfield Gardens, London NW3, Eng.

FREUD, Moshe, Isr, physician; b. Koenigsberg, Ger, Mar 10, 1924; s. Isaac and Paulina (Fortuna); in Isr since 1925; MA, Amer U, Beirut, Lebanon, 1946; MD, Med Sch, Geneva, Switz, 1951; m. Hassia Yarkoni, Sep 6 1949; c: Irith, Dan. Head, med dept, Cen Emek Hosp, Afula, since 1969; asst head, med dept A, Beilinson Hosp, since 1965; on staff, since 1951. Capt, IDF, res forces, since 1961. Mem: IMA; Isr Soc for Internal Med; Isr Gastroenterological Soc. Contbr numerous articles on internal med and gastroenterology to local and fgn jours. Hobbies: music, photography. Home and office: Cen Emek Hosp, Afula, Isr.

FREUD-MARLÉ, Lilly, Eng, professional entertainer; b.Vienna, Aus; d. Maurice and Marie (Freud) Freud; niece of Sigmund Freud; in Eng since 1939: att Tchrs Sem, Stern Conservatory, both Berlin; studied with: K K Hofschauspieler, Otto Sommerstorff; Oscar Sauer, Otto Brahm Theatre; m. Arnold Marlé, July 4, 1917; c: Omri, Aviva Harari. Intl entertainer and actress; recitals: world lit in poetry and prose, in Ger, Fr, Eng langs; with Rabindranath Tagore, his Ballad, in original Bengali; famous interpretor of Anderson's Fairy Tales; lectured at Us: Hamburg, Berlin, Copenhagen, Jerusalem. First artist to introduce E poets to W world, including: Li-tai-pe; R Tagore. Home: 404 Clive Court, Maida Vale, London W 9, Eng.

FREUDENHEIM, Milton B, US, journalist; b. New Rochelle, NY, March 4, 1927; s. Milton and Patricia (Kroh); AB, U Mich, 1948; m. Elizabeth Ege, Mar 7, 1951; c: Jo, Susan, John, Tom. Natl, fgn ed, Chgo Daily News, dir, fgn service, since 1966, columnist, UN corresp, 1956-66; reporter, Courier-Jour, Louisville, 1948-49; Akron Beacon Jour, 1949-53; Wash, DC, corresp, Knight newspapers Inc, 1953-56. Pres, UN Corresps Assn, 1966; mem, Temple Jeremiah. Home: 1202 Lake Ave, Wilmette, Ill. Office: 401 N Wabash, Chicago, Ill.

FREUDENTHAL, Alfred M, US, engineer, educator; b. Stryj, Pol, Feb 12, 1906; s. Simon and Gustafa (Mueller); in US since 1947; CE, Technische Hochschule, 1929; MS, Charles U, 1930; DSc, Technische Hochschule, 1930, all of Prague; m. Mary Silberstein, 1939; m. 2nd, Maria Roney, 1962; c: Pierre. Prof, civil and materials engr, George Wash U, Wash, DC, since 1969; design engr, Prague, Czech, 1930-34; engr, Warsaw, Pol, 1934-35; res engr, Port of Tel Aviv, Pal, 1935-45; engr

cons, Brit Army in Pal and Transjordan, 1941-44; cons engr, Tel Aviv, 1945-47; prof, civil engr: Technion, Haifa, 1937-47; Columbia U, 1949-68; fmr mem since 1948. Mem: Amer Soc CEs; Inst Aeronautic and Astronomical Soc Rheology; Intl Assn Bridge and Structural Engrs; Sigma Xi, Perm Intl Assn of Navigation Congs; Sigma Xi; Tau Beta Pi. Author: Verbundstuetzen für Hohe Lasten, 1933; Inelastic Behaviour of Engineering Materials and Structures, 1950; Introduction to Solid Mechanics, 1966; ed: Proceedings, Intl Conf on Fatigue in Flight Structures, Columbia U, 1956; Proceedings, Intl Conf on High Temperature Structures and Materials, Columbia U, 1964; Proceedings, Intl Conf on Structural Safety and Reliability, Smithsonian Inst, Wash DC, 1969. Recipient, Medals: Norman, Amer Soc CEs, 1948, 1957; Swed Royal Aeronautical Soc, 1957. Office: George Washington U, Wshington, DC.

FREUDENTHAL, Carmen K, US, communal worker; b. Sedalia, Mo, Feb 8, 1898; d. Arthur and Clemence (Joseph) Kahn; att Wash U, St Louis, 1916-18; BA, Smith Coll, Northhampton, Mass, 1920; grad work, St Louis Sch of Social Wfr, 1920; m. Louis Freudenthal, Mar 28, 1932; c: Elsa Altshool, Max. Pres, Dona Ana Co Planned Parenthood Assn, since 1962; secy NM Adv Comm, US Civil Rights Comm, since 1962; bd mem, Comty Action Agcy, OEO, Dona Ana Co, since 1965; publicity chmn, mem, bd dirs, Las Cruces Comty Concert Assn, 1946-66; mem: regional adv bd, ADL; bd dirs, Dona Ana Co Mh Assn, since 1961; pres Las Cruces br, Amer Assn of U Women, 1947-49; Women's Improvement Assn, Las Cruces, 1940-41; org, fmr pres, women's auxiliary, Comty Hosp. Recipient: human rights award, NM Br, Amer Assn for UN, 1964. Home: 539 W Las Cruces Ave, Las Cruces, NM.

FREUDENTHAL, Heinz, Swed, conductor, musician; b. Danzig, Pol, Apr 25, 1905; s. Max and Else (Lichtwitz); in Swed since 1928; att Staatskonservatorium der Musik, Würzburg; BA, U Würzburg, 1927; m. Elsbet Hippéli, Aug 22, 1927; c: Otto, Peter. Chief conductor, Town Orch, Kristiansand, Nor, since 1969; prin viola player; Landeskapelle, Meiningen, 1927-28; Gothenburg Orch Soc, 1928-36; conductor, artistic leader, Norrköping Radio Orch, 1936-53; chief conductor, Isr Bc Service, Jerusalem, 1954-61; dir, Town Music Sch, Karlstad, 1961-69. Home: Vallingdal, Rimforsa, Swed.

FREUND, Arthur J, US, attorney; b. St Louis, Mo, Apr 17, 1891; s. Fred and Fannie (Wurzel); BA, Wash U, St Louis, 1914, LLB, 1916; m. Margaret Drey, 1925; c: Edith Binder, Emily Ullman. Pvt practice since 1916; spec asst atty gen, Mo, 1920-24; mem:bd police commns,1925-29; bd election commns, 1932-33, both St Louis. Fmr pres: YM-YWCA, St Louis; United Service Orgs, St Louis; chmn, sect on criminal law, mem, comm on organized crime, Amer Bar Assn, 1951-52; fmr secy, JF, St Louis, mem exec comm; f, Amer Bar Found; mem: exec comm, JWB, since 1942; Amer Law Inst; Inst Jud Admn; Order of Coif; Amer Council for Judaism, 1943-50; bd, Wash U YM-YMCA, 1942-50; Inter-Amer Bar Assn; Mo Bar Assn; Bar Assn, St Louis; Seldon Soc; adv comm on rules of civil procedure, US Supr Court; co-found, Sect Individual Rights, Amer Bar Assn, fmr mem, council. Contbr: articles on fed statutes, including authorship of fed kidnapping act. Recipient: St Louis Award for dist public service, 1937; dist alumni award, Wash U, 1956; award of merit, United Service Org, 1961; civil liberties award, 1964. Home: 6235 Washington Blvd, St Louis, Mo. Office: 7 N Seventh Ave, St Louis, Mo.

FREUND, Hirsch E L, US, rabbi; b. Oct 15, 1898; s. Jacob and Bessie (Hollander); BA, U Cincinnati, 1921; att, U Chgo,1926, 1930; BHC, ordained rabbi, HUC, 1928, DD honoris causa, 1962; Harvard Chaplains Sch, 1942; m. Serita Scheineson, Aug 3, 1926; c: Myron. Chaplain: VA, since 1952; US Merchant Marine Acad, Kings Point; dir, internal J relations, ADL, 1946-48; exec dir, Syn Council of Amer, 1948-52; asso ed, Ind J Chronicle, 1930-33. Maj, US Army, 1942-46. Pres, B'nai B'rith Lodge, Anderson, Ind, 1931-32; mem, adv bd, ADL, Metrop NY, 1955-58; mem: chaplaincy commn, CCAR, 1952-56; exec bd, Mil Chaplains Assn, 1960-61; NY Co chaplain, JWV, 1955-58; mem: J Chaplains Assn; NY Reform Rabbis Assn; HUC Alumni Assn; Masons. Contbr to Anglo-J mags. Home: 2 Spruce St, Great Neck, NY. Office: Bklyn VA Hosp, Brooklyn, NY.

FREUND, Miriam, US, communal leader; b. NYC; d. Harry and Rebecca (Zindler) Kottler; BA, Hunter Coll, 1925; MA,

NYU, 1927, PhD, 1936; m. Milton Freund, July 3, 1927; c: Matthew, Harry. Ed, Hadassah Mag, since 1966; natl Isr Bond, chmn, Hadassah, since 1960; natl pres, Hadassah, 1956-60, mem, natl Youth Aliyah comm, 1953-56, mem, natl bd, 1940, mem natl exec comm, 1945, natl chmn, vocational educ comm, 1948-53; natl chmn, Amer Zionist Youth Activities, 1943-48; vice-pres, natl bd mem, Brandeis U, vice-pres, women's comm, 1949, 1950; found and charter mem, Brandeis Youth Found, 1948; delg, Amer J Conf, 1942; org, Intercollegiate ZF of Amer, 1945; mem, natl bds; JNF, exec comm, World Council of Syn, since 1966; KH; chmn, exec comm, Amer Zionist Council; mem praesidium, actions comm, WZO; fmr tchr, New Utrecht, Abraham Lincoln, Wash Irving HS; lectr. Author: Jewish Merchants in Colonial America, 1936; Jewels for a Crown—the Chagall Windows; contbr articles to publs. Recipient: citation, JWB. Home: 200 E 71 St, New York, NY. Office: 65 E 52 St, New York, NY.

FREUND, Paul A, US, jurist, educator; b. St. Louis, Mo, Feb 16, 1908; s. Charles and Hulda (Arenson); BA, Wash U, St Louis, 1928; LLB, Harvard U, 1931; DJS, 1932; hon LLD: Columbia U, 1954; U Louisville, Ky, 1956; Wash U, St Louis, 1956; U Chgo, 1961; hon MA Cambridge U, Eng, 1957; hon LHD, HUC, 1961. Carl M Loeb U Prof, Harvard U Law Sch, since 1958; prof law, since 1939; law clerk, Justice Brandeis, US Supr Court, 1932-33; atty Dept Treasury and Reconstruction Finance Corp, 1933-35; spec asst to US Atty Gen, 1935-39, 1942-46; visiting prof, Stanford U, 1950; visiting Pitt prof of Amer hists and instns, Cambridge U, Eng, 1957-58; vice-pres, Salzburg Sem in Amer Studies. Mem: Amer Law Inst; Amer Acad Arts and Scis; ACLU; Mass Hist Soc; Amer Phil Soc; AJComm; ZOA; clubs: St Botolph; Saturday. Author: On Understanding the Supreme Court, 1949; The Supreme Court of the United States, 1961; co-ed, Constitutional Law: Cases and Other Problems, 1955; On Law and Justice, 1968; ed in chief, History of the US Supreme Court; contbr to Ency Britannica, legal jours. Home: 995 Memorial Dr, Cambridge, Mass. Office: Harvard Law Sch, Cambridge, Mass.

FREUNDLICH, Leo, US, chemist; b. Schiffierstadt, Ger, Feb 4, 1899; s. Isidor and Lina (Wolf); in US since 1923; att U Heidelberg, 1919-20; PhD, U Würzburg, 1923; m. Illa Weiler, May 2, 1948. Cons chem chocolate and cocoa ind, since 1951; chem research and plant control, Auramine Corp of Amer, 1924-25; chem for research and devl and difficult analysis, Ekroth Labs, 1925-29; chief chem: Runkel Bros, 1929-31; Hotton Chocolate Co, 1931-51. Dist pres, ZOA, 1940-45; treas, 1946-60; chmn: Gtr Newark dist, JNF, since 1955; E Orange UJA, 1956-57; f, Amer Inst of Chem; mem: Amer Chem Soc; Amer Assn of Candy Techs; Cong Sharey Tefilot; ZOA. Contbr to tech jours, Hobby: philately. Home and office: 175 Prosepect St, E Orange, NJ.

FREYER, A B (Abraham) US, attorney; b. St Joseph, Mo, Aug 9, 1887; s. Bernard and Rosa (Fedder); grad, La Poly Inst, 1905; m. Etta Alltmont, Aug 20, 1913; c: A B, Sam, Carroll Zusak. Mem, law firm; Freyer and Freyer, since 1953; Wise, Randolph and Rendall, 1910-15; Wise, Randolph, Rendall and Freyer, 1915-48; sr mem, Freyer, Goode, Nelson and Freyer, 1948-53. Mem: Amer, La Bars; org, Shreveport Bar Assn, first pres; Lodge B'nai B'rith, fmr pres, Grand Lodge 7, fmr pres, dist counsel, Intl Supr Lodge, fmr vice pres, mem, exec comm; bd govs, B'nai B'rith Home, Memphis; counsel, natl bd trustees, B'nai B'rith Henry Monsky Found; natl bd trustees, Leo N Levi Memorial Hosp, Hot Springs, Ark, fmr vice-pres; Shreveport Masons, fmr master; Shreveport, Scottish Rite Bodies, fmr Venerable Master, fmr Wise Master, fmr Master of Kadush, 33 deg; El Karubah Temple Shrine; bd trustees, Shriners Hosp for Crippled Children, Shreveport; Shreveport Court 26, Royal Order of Jesters; AJComm, mem gen comm; fmr: mem: legal comm, Mid Continent Oil and Gas Assn; Natl Hillel Commn; ADL Commn; exec comm, Caddo War Chest Council; exec comm, United Comty Orgs, Shreveport and Caddo Parish; bd, Shreveport C of C; natl commn, United Seaman's Service; JDC; natl council, Jt Defense Appeal; pres, SW region, UAHC, found, first co-chmn, Shreveport chap, NCCJ. Recipient: testimonial, NCCJ, 1960; B'nai B'rith Found of US, established AB Freyer Youth F in recongnition of contribs to Amer Jewry, 1961. Home: 3515 Madison Park Blvd, Shreveport, La. Office: 611 Sklar Bldg, Shreveport, La.

FRIDMAN, Gideon, Isr, educator; b. Leningrad, Russ, Mar 1, 1917; s. Yehoshua and Miriam (Menin); in Isr since 1933;

BSc, Technion, Haifa, 1940; m. Shoshana Borkowsky, Aug 23, 1945; c: Tsoor, Miriam. Sr lectr, descriptive geometry, Technion, since 1959, coord, descriptive geometry courses, since 1962, on fac since 1949. Mem, chmn of council, Technion Fac Assn, 1960-61; mem, bd of govs, Technion, 1966-68. Mem: Isr Math Union; Haganah, Vet Assn. Home: 6 Ha'asif St, Haifa, Isr. Office: Technion, Haifa, Isr.

FRIED, Alexander, US, music and art critic; b. NYC, May 21, 1902; s. Henry and Sarah (Perlis); BA, Columbia Coll, 1923; MA, Columbia U, 1924; m. Edith Trumpler, Jan 29, 1949; c: Madelyn, Harriet. Music, art critic, SF Examiner, since 1934; mgn ed, Musical Digest, 1925-26; music art ed, SF Chronicle, 1926-34. Mem, SF-Oakland Newspaper Guild; club, Il Cenacolo. Contbr to profsl jours. Hobbies: langs, travel. Home: 22 Crown Terr, San Francisco, Cal. Office: San Francisco Examiner, 110 Fifth St, San Francisco, Cal.

FRIED, Amnon, Isr, surgeon; b. Vienna, Aus, Nov 24, 1912; s. Joseph and Chaja (Kuttner); in Isr since 1938; MD, U Vienna, 1937; m. Ruth Erlich, Mar, 1945; c: Miriam, Dinah. Chief, orthopedic dept, Beilinson Hosp, Petah Tikva, since 1955; cons, Beth Lowenstein Hosp for Rehab, sr lectr, Tel Aviv U Med Sch; demonstrator, anat, U Vienna, 1934-37; fmr res: Vienna Hosp; Beilinson Hosp, asst to: Dr E Spira, Prof Friberg, Stockholm; head, orthopedic dept, Hasharon Hosp, Petah Tikvah, 1948-55. Mem: Isr Surg Soc; Soc Orthopedic Surgs; Intl Coll Surgs; Société Internationale de Chirurgie Orthopedique et de Traumatologie. Contbr articles to profsl jours. Home: 13 Kiriat Sefer St, Tel Aviv, Isr. Office: 16 Cremieux St, Tel Aviv, Isr.

FRIED, Helen, US, communal worker, educator; b. Port Chester, NY, Mar 6, 1912; d. Joseph and Rose (Boehm) Feiner; BS, NYU, 1934, MA, 1938; m. Albert Fried, June 30, 1935; c: Arthur, Michael. Pres, Natl Women's League, United Syn of Amer, since 1962, vice-pres, 1958, hon pres, Bklyn br, since 1958; natl dir, Speakers Training for Natl Women's League; fmr pres: Marine Park Cen Sisterhood; Bklyn Cen Sisterhood; bd dirs: Council of Amer; World Council of Synagogues; JTSA—J Braille Inst; area chmn, UJA, 1949; NGO delg, UN; fac mem, CCNY; tchr, HSs, 1935-43. Mem: Women's div, Isr Bonds; NAACP; Amer Assn Jr Colls; Speech Assn of Amer; Intl Platform Assn; E States Speech Assn; Hadassah; club, Copake Country. Home 2071 E 35 St, Brooklyn, NY.

FRIED, Paul H, US, physician; b. Burgettstown, Pa, June 20, 1915; s. Aaron and Anna (Kepecs); BS, U Pittsburgh, 1935; MD, Jefferson Med Coll, 1939; m. Grace Greenfield, June 11, 1939; c: Carlie, Nancy, Alice. Sr att phys, obstet-gyn, since 1945; att obstet-gyn, Jefferson Med Coll Hosp, since 1939, instr since 1941. Capt, US Army, 1943-46. Found f, Amer Coll Obstets and Gyns, 1954; hon mem: Congresso Brasiliero; comm mem: PR; Phila Med Soc; mem, bd dirs, Cent Coty Res Assn; capt, Allied J App, 1953; mem: Pa Co Med Soc; AMA; Amer bd Obstet and Gyn; Amer Coll Surgs; Intl Fertility Assn; NY Acad Scis; Amer Common Maternal Inc; Jefferson Soc for Clinical Inves, Fed Amer Soc for Experimental Biol; Fertility Research Found; Phila Mus of Art; Pa Acad of Fine Arts; J Chautauqua Soc; Natl Tree Farmers Assn; F Commn; clubs: Pitt Alumni, Metrop Phila; Men's Rodeph Sholom Syn, first vice-pres, 1961-62. Contbr numerous articles to med jours. Recipient: McRae Award, Jefferson Soc for Clinical Inves 1952. Spec interest: tree farming. Home: Dorchester Apts, Rittenhouse, Sq, Philadelphia, Pa. Office: 275 S 192 St, Philadelphia, Pa.

FRIED, Theodore, US, artist; b. Budapest, Hung, May 19, 1902; s. Samuel and Margaret (Rosenstock); in US since 1942; att Royal Acad of Fine Arts, Budapest, Hung, 1920-24; m. Maria Engelharth, 1950; c: Christopher. One-man shows in Eur and US; repr in perm collections: Albertina, Vienna; Kunsthalle, Jena; Musée Natl d'Art Modern, Paris; Musée des Augustins, Toulouse; Walker Art Cen, Minn; Butle-Inst of Amer Art; Youngstown; Memorial Art Gall, Rochester; Oesterreichische Gal, Vienna, and in pvt collections. Fmr vice-pres, Fed Modern Painters and Sculptors. Hobby: violin. Home and studio: 463 West St, New York, NY.

FRIEDBERG, Maurice, US, educator; b. Rzeszow, Pol, Dec 3, 1929; s. Isaac and Ida (Jam); in US since 1948; BS, Bklyn Coll, 1951; AM, Columbia U, 1953; PhD, 1958; m. Barbara Bisguier, Mar 18, 1956; c: Rachel. Prof, Slavic langs and lit, Ind U, since 1966, dir, Russ, E Eur Inst, since 1967; Fulbright visiting prof, Russ lit, Heb U, Jerusalem, 1965-66;

asso prof i/c Russ div, Hunter Coll, 1955-65; asso, Russ Research Cen, Harvard U, 1953; visiting prof, Columbia U, NYU. Vice-pres, UJCmty, Bloomington, Ind. Author: Russian Classics in Soviet Jackets, 1962; The Party and the Poet in the USSR, 1963; A Bilingual Edition of Russian Short Stories, vol I, 1964, vol II, 1965; div ed, Ency Judaica; contbr to mags. Recipient: research and travel grants from: Ford Found; Amer Council of Learned Soc's; Oxford U; Inst for Study of Russ; Harvard U; Fulbright-Hays Award. Home: 4426 Sheffield Dr, Bloomington, Ind. Office: Indiana U, Bloomington, Ind.

FRIEDBERG, Simon, US, structural engr; b. Jaroslaw, Pol, Oct 6, 1932; s. Isaac and Ida (Jam); in US since 1948; BCE, CCNY, 1954; MCE, Columbia U, 1956; DJur, NYU, 1967; m. Myrna Schreiber, Jan 31, 1965; c: Deena, Miriam, Joshua. Project dir, structural engr, Urban Devl Corp, since 1969; CE, NYC Housing Auth, 1963-69, chief structural sect, 1969; lectr, adult educ, Bklyn Coll, 1958-63. US Army, 1957. Fmr chmn, social activities, corresp secy, Mark Twain House, Bklyn Coll, house plan asst, Hillel; mem: Amer Soc CE; Cong Mackrike Horav, Bklyn; various rel and philanthropic groups; Chi Epsilon frat. Recipient: dean's list of honor students, NYU Law Sch, 1967; Amer Jurisprudence Prize, Lawyers Coop Co, 1969. Spec interests: Talmud, problems J natl communal interests. Home: 688 E 7 St, Brooklyn, NY. Office: 1345 Ave of the Americas, New York, NY.

FRIEDE, J George, US, business exec; b. Warsaw, Pol, Sep 12, 1920; s. Maximillian and Stefania (Anker); in US since 1941; att Cambridge U, Eng, 1939-41; m. Felicia Pressner, Dec 28, 1952; c: Andrew, Stephanie, Margaret, Caroline. Partner, Seaward Commerce Co; pres, Seaward Co; treas, Combined Owners Inc. US Army WWII. Mem: US Co of C; Commerce and Ind Assn; US Power Squadrons; E Cruiser Assn; Equity Libr Theatre; World Trade Club of NY; pres, Premium Point Park Assn, 1959-60. Home: 210 W 90 St, New York, NY. Office: 19 W 44 St, New York, NY.

FRIEDE, Maximillian, US, business exec; jurist; b. Warsaw, Pol, Mar 7, 1887; s. Adolf and Teofila (Szyszko); in US since 1941; att State Coll, Warsaw, 1907; m. Stefania Anker, July 7, 1914; c: George. Sr partner, Seward Commerce Co, NYC since 1945; found, sr partner, Pomeranc, Kahan and Friede, Warsaw, 1912-39; dir: Warsaw Sugar Refineries Corp, 1932-39; Gnaszyn Textile, 1929-39; Electricitaet Chem, Zombkowice, 1930-39; Klucze Paper and Pulp Mills, 1927-39; Gnaszyn, Colored Paper, 1929-39; Universal Fiduciary, Warsaw, 1928-39; judge, Dist Court, Commercial Div, Warsaw, 1921-39; hon consul gen, Ecuador, in Pol, 1937-40; consul gen for Peru, Ecuador; Pol Govt in exile, London, 1940; chmn: Fed Assns of Commercial Agts and Reprs, 1926-39; C of Cs: Pol-Pal, 1930-39; law comm and mem, Court of Hon, c Ind, Warsaw, 1929-39; dir, Warsaw Stock Exch,1923-39; Pol-Brit C of C, 1937-39; Intl C of C, Paris, 1933-41; Intl League Commercial Agts Repr, Amsterdam, 1927-33; vice-chmn: Pol-Hung C of C 1934-39; Assn of Pol Exporters, 1937-39; head, first Pol Trade Delg to Eng, 1935; mem: exec comm, Warsaw C of C, 1928-39; exec, council, Pol Min of Finance, 1932-39; Pol delg, intl commercial treaty negotiations, 1928-38; sponsor, Trade and Vocational Schs, Warsaw, 1925-39. Chmn, Club of Pol J, NYC, since 1949; vice-chmn, Comm for Econ. Self Help in Pol; mem: AJComm; AJCong; US C of C, Wash, DC; Commerce and Ind Assn, NY. Recipient: Gold Cross of Merit, 1928; Order of Polonia Restituta, 1933: Home: 246 West End Ave, New York, NY. Office: 19 W 44 St, New York, NY.

FRIEDEL, Samuel N, US, legislator; b. Wash, DC, Apr 18, 1898; s. Philip and Rose (Franklin); m. Regina Johnson, Mar 8, 1939. Mem, US House of Repr, since 1953; house delg, Md State Leg, 1935-39; city councilman, Baltimore, 1939-47, 1951-53. Mem: Mt Wash Improvement Assn; Har Sinai Brotherhood; Petach Tikvah Syn; Elks. Home: 2201 South Rd, Baltimore, Md. Office: 2110 Rayburn Office Bldg, Washington, DC.

FRIEDENBERG, Daniel Meyer, US, business exec; b. Mt Vernon, NY, Feb 24, 1923; s. Samuel and Rose (Klein); BS, Wharton Sch Finance and Commerce, U of Pa, 1943; m. Maria Jay; c: Samuel, Danielle; m. 2nd, June Daniels; c: Jay, Bertand. Pres, John-Platt Realty Corp, since 1957; curator, coins, medals, J Mus of NY, since 1963; guest lectr: Yale U; Columbia U; Swarthmore Coll. US Army, 1943-44. Patron: JTSA; Isr Cultural Found; delg, Intl Real Estate Bd; mem: ACLU; Metrop Mus of Art; NY Botanical Garden, life; Amer Numis-

matic Soc; Amer Numismatic Assn. Author: Great Jewish Portraits in Metal, 1963; Jewish Medals from the Renaissance to the Fall of Napoleon, 1503-1815, pub 1969; contbr articles, short stories, poems, lit criticism to jours and books. Home: 79 Byram Shore Rd, Byram, Conn. Office: 13 Platt St, New York, NY.

FRIEDENBERG, S Charles, US, business exec; b. Baltimore, Md, Nov 3, 1902; s. Nathan and Sarah (Friedman); BCS, La Salle U, 1921; m. Mollie Abrams, June 12, 1924. Pres, gen mgr, Overbrook Egg Nog Corp, since 1947, with firm since 1933; secy and treas: Jersey Ice Cream, 1924-30; Jersey Ice Cream Products, 1930-33. Mem: Baltimore Assn of Commerce; Natl Fed Temple Brotherhoods; Oheb Shalom Cong; Masons; Shriners; B'nai B'rith; ZOA; Phi Sigma Delta; JIR; UAHC; fmr, mem, bd dirs, Beth Tfiloh Cong. Home: 11 Slade Ave, Pikesville, Md. Office: 2810 W Saratoga St, Baltimore, Md.

FRIEDENSON, Meyer, US, physician; b. Polotsk, Russ, May 15, 1905; s. Samuel and Fanny (Abramson); in US since 1906; BS, Yale U, 1924, MD, 1927; m. Faye Cohen, Aug 8, 1928 (decd); c: Harriet Burger, Jay; m. 2nd, Dorothy Nenner, Mar 29, 1958; step-c: Barbara Goodman. Pvt practice since 1929; clinical visiting instr, preventative and environmental med, Albert Einstein Coll of Med, 1958-66; asso phys, Montefiore Hosp, since 1930; lectr, med, Columbia Coll Phys and Surgs, 1940-64. Maj, US Army MC and chief, cardiovascular sect, in US, 1942-46. FACP; dipl, Amer Bd Internal Med; mem: AHA; NY Heart Assn; NY State Med Soc; NY Co Med Assn; AMA. Contbr to med jours. Home: 43 Rodman Oval, New Rochelle, NY. Office: 47 E 67 St, New York, NY.

FRIEDFELD, Louis, US, physician; b. NYC, Aug 27, 1906; s. Max and Anne (Welinsky); BS, NYU, 1927; MD, U and Bellevue Hosp, Med Coll, 1930; postgrad, Tulane U, 1943; m. Mildred Allenson, June 26, 1955; c: Pauline, Sanford. Att phys, Beth Isr Hosp, NY; phys, 1932-52; med dir, Home of Old Isr. Capt, US Army MC, 1942-44. Mem: NY Mayor's Adv Comm on Care of the Aged; citizen's comm on aging, Comty Council, Gtr NY; dipl, Amer Bd Internal Med; FACP; f: Amer Geriatric Soc; NY Acad of Med; Amer Coll of Angiology; mem: AMA; AHA; NY Acad Sci; Park Ave Syn; club, Fairview Country. Contbr to med jours. Hobby: photography. Home: 211 Central Park W, New York, NY. Office: 121 E 60 St, New York, NY.

FRIEDHABER, Zvi, Isr, folklorist; b. Worms, Ger, Oct 3, 1925; s. Zeev and Malka (Kilstock); in Isr since 1934; m. Bracha Ludmier, Apr 8, 1951; c: Malka, Amira, Amichai. Folklorist, found, head, Archive for J Dances, since 1950; secy, Haifa Dist Court, since 1952. Served IDF. Fmr delg: Fifth World Cong of J Studies; Yeda Am Conv; Conv for Rel Music. Author: HaMachol haYehudi, 1968; Mecholot ha'Am BeIsrael, 1969; contbr researches, articles, bibliographies to profsl publs. Home: 78 Harishonim St, Haifa, Isr. Office: Dist Court, Haifa, Isr.

FRIEDLAND, George, US, business exec; b. Lith, Sep 15, 1901; in US since 1905. Ret since 1959; vice-chmn, bd, Food Fair Stores, Inc, 1953-59, pres, 1941-53; dir, Food Fair Properties. Pres: George Friedland Found; hon pres: Temple Adath Isr of Main Line; Beth Jacob Schs of Phila; vice-pres: Allied J Appeal; treas, bd overseers, JTSA; trustee: Albert Einstein Med Cen; Greenstone Found; hon, Phoenix Art Mus; chmn, Devl Fund, Uptown Home for the Aged, Phila; dir: Food Stores Found; mem: Founds Harry S Truman Cen for Advancement of Peace, Heb U, bd dirs, Amer Friends Heb U; found, Albert Einstein Coll Med, Yeshiva U, NY; Phila Mus of Art; bd overseers, Fine Arts, Brandeis U; exec comm, J Comty Relations Council; exec bd, Phila Lyric Opera Co; Fed J Agcys, Phila; Pa Soc; Franklin Inst; Pa Acad Fine Arts; Newcomer Soc in N Amer; Pa Commn; Crime Prevention Assn of Pa; Pa Housing Assn; AJComm; clubs: Green Valley Country; Golden Slipper Sq; Locust-Mid-City. Recipient: Awards: dist service, Govt of Isr, 1952; achievement: Mary Bailey Heart Inst, 1955; B'nai B'rith Supr Lodge, Pres Gold Medallion Humanitarian Award, 1964. Home: Bluebeard's Castle Hotel, St Thomas, Virgin Islands.

FRIEDLANDER, Albert Hoschander, Eng, rabbi, educator; b. Berlin, Ger, May 10, 1927; s. Alex and Sali (Hoschander); in Eng since 1966; PhB, U Chgo, 1946; BHL, ordained rabbi, HUC, Cincinnati, 1952; PhD, Columbia U, 1966; m. Evelyn Phillipp, July 9, 1961; c: Ariel, Michal. Rabbi, Wembley Lib Syn, since 1966; lectr in hist, Leo Baeck Coll, London, since 1966, f, 1966; rabbi: United Heb Temple, Fort Smith, Ark, 1952-56; Temple B'nai B'rith, Wilkes-Barre, Pa, 1956-61; instr, phil, Wilkes Coll, Wilkes-Barre, 1957-61; rabbi, J Cen of the Hamptons, E Hampton, NY, 1961-66; counselor, rabbi, Columbia U, 1961-66. Chmn: Eur Conf Progressive Rabbis; Jt Chaplaincy Commn to Progressive Students; exec mem, Eur Bd, World Union for Progressive Judaism; chmn, Commn on Art and Lit, CCAR, 1963-65; bd dir, exec comm, Amer Bd, World Union for Progressive Judaism, 1963-66; civic offs: Mh, United Fund; mem: B'nai B'rith; Rabb Conf, Union Progressive and Liberal Syns; fmr mem: Amer J Hist Soc; Leo Baeck Inst. Author: Isaac M Wise; The World of My Books, 1954; Serial History of Reform Judaism, 1957; annotated trans, Leo Baeck's, This People Israel, 1963; ed, Never Trust a God Over Thirty, 1967; Out of the Whirlwind: Holocaust Literature, 1968; Teacher of Theresienstadt, the Theology of Leo Baeck, 1968; Contbr ed, Jews From Germany in the US, 1955; contbr to rel and gen jours. Recipient: B'nai Jeshurun Prize for PhD study in Judaism, Columbia U, 1968. Home and study: Preston Rd, Harrow, Middlesex, Eng.

FRIEDLANDER, Dov, Isr, demographer; b. Dusseldorf, Ger; s. Nahum and Ester (Grumberg); in Isr since 1936; PhD, LSE, 1962; m. Yonina Cahana, Nov 6, 1956; c: Hamutal, Rama. Sr lectr, Kaplan Sch, Heb U, since 1964; research f, Cen for Urban Studies, U Coll, London, 1962-64. Mem, Intl Union for Sci Study of Population. Contbr to profsl jours. Home: 21 Oren, Haifa, Isr. Office: Hebrew U, Jerusalem, Isr.

FRIEDLANDER, Emanuel, Isr, business exec; b. Breslau, Ger, Apr 11, 1926; s. Ernst and Alma (Markowicz); in Isr since 1940; m. Shoschana Katz, Feb 19, 1953; c: Eliad, Raanan. Gen mgr, Agric Coop Soc, since 1956; secy gen, Ihud Chaklai, since 1962. IDF, Sinai Campaign, Six Day War. Mem: exec: Lib Party, chmn, comm of econ problems; planning auth, Min of Agric; adv council for coop's, Min of Lab; council, Min of Absorption; budget comm, JA; exec, PASA; local council, Beit Yitzhak; secy, Miflagei Ichud Chalukai; exec, Teme Coop Marketing Soc. Home: Beth Yitzak, Isr. Office: Agric Coop, Beth Yitzhak, Isr.

FRIEDLANDER, Herbert N, US, researcher; b. Chgo Hts, Ill, Mar 12, 1922; s. Harry and Bertha (Tartak); BS, U Chgo, 1942, PhD, 1947; m. Sophie Thoness, Oct 10, 1943; c: Miriam, Carl, Ira. Dir, tech oprs, Chemstrand Research Cen, since 1967, mgr, basic polymer sci research 1962-65, dir, new products research and devl, 1965-67; research asst, chem dept, U Chgo, 1947-48; asst project chem, research devl dept, Standard Oil Ind, 1948-61; research asso, Amoco Chems, 1961-62; cons, Natl Council for Research and Devl, State of Isr, 1962. Holder, 15 US patents. Pres, Park Forest Bd J Educ, 1968, dir, 1953-59; dir: Comty Council, Wake Co; NE Engr Found; mem: Soc of Aerospace Material and Process Engrs; Fiber Soc; NCCJ; Amer Chem Soc; AAAS; Phi Beta Kappa; Sigma Xi. Contbr to sci jours. Hobbies: sailing, photography, ceramics, swimming. Home: 2409 Rock Ridge Court, Raliegh, NC. Office: Chemstrand Research Cen, PO Box 731 Durham, NC.

FRIEDLANDER, Lawrence U, US, business exec; b. Brieg, Ger, Apr 13, 1925; s. Siegmar and Lottie (Bach); in US since 1947; m. Marian Mendelson, Oct 3, 1953; c: David, Steven, Linda. Pres, Gt Amer Chem Corp, since 1967; dist mgr, Chemex Ind, 1962-67. Treas, Temple Isr; lt gov, Optimist, Fla Dist; chmn, N Fla Muscular Dystrophy Dr; vice-pres, Temple B'nai Isr, 1958-59; mem: Comm of 100; C of C; club: Capital Cen Optimist, 1967-68. Hobbies: golf, youth work. Home: 706 Lothian Dr, Tallahassee, Fla. Office: 623 Industrial Dr, Tallahassee, Fla.

FRIEDLANDER, Saul, Switz, educator; b. Prague, Czech, Oct 11, 1932; s. Hans and Elisabeth; MA, Sch of Political Sci; PhD, Sch of Intl Studies, Geneva; m. Meiry Hagith, Aug 20, 1959; c: Elhanan, David. Prof, contemporary hist, Grad Inst of Intl Studies, since 1963; chmn, dept of intl relations, prof, contemporary hist, Heb U, Jerusalem, until 1961. Author: Pius XIII and the Third Reich, 1966; Prelude to Downfall; Hitler and His United States, 1968; Kurt Gerstein, The Antiquity of Good, 1969; Réflexions sur l'avenir l'Israel, 1969. Home: 50 rue Moillebian, Geneva, Switz. Office: Grad Inst of Intl Studies, Geneva Switz.

FRIEDLANDER, Sidney Irwin, US, insurance exec; b. Utica, NY, Nov 24, 1928; s. Max and Dorothy (Franklin); att Utica Coll, Syracuse U, 1946-48; m. Naomi Wishman, Mar 30, 1958; c: Ellen, Karen. Owner, Max Friedlander Gen Ins

Agcy, since 1948. Seaman, USN, 1953-54. Gen chmn, J Comty Cen Bldg Dr; past pres: JCC and Cen, 1966-68; past regional vice-pres, JWB, 1967-68; past treas, Charles T Sitrin Home for Aged, 1956-57; past vice-chmn, UJA; past bd dirs, Utica Youth Bur. Hobbies: golf, tennis. Home: 2653 Edgewood, Utica, NY. Office: 325 Genesee St, Utica, NY.

FRIEDLANDER, Walter J, US, physician; b. Los Angeles, June 6, 1919; s. Jacob and Gussie (Gold); BA, UCLA, 1941, MD, 1945; m. Florence Eastburn, June 14, 1943; c: John, Jessie, Joseph. Prof, chmn neur dept, U Neb Coll of Med, since 1966; chief: electroencephalography lab, NIH, Bethesda, 1952-53; neur sect, VA Hosp, SF, 1953-56, Natl Vets Epilepsy Cen, Boston, 1956-61; prof, neur, Albany Med Coll, 1962-66. Mem: Amer Acad Neur; Amer Epilepsy Soc; AAAS; Amer Electroencephalography Soc; NY Acad Sci; Acad Aphasia. Contbr to med jours. Office: U of Neb College of Med, Omaha, Neb.

FRIEDLER, Egon, Uruguay, journalist; b. Vienna, Aus, Aug 13, 1932; s. Adolfo and Paula (Rosner); in Uruguay since 1939; att sem of activists, Hashomer Hatzair, Isr, 1955, cert, proficiency in Eng, Cambridge, 1961; m. Ethel Kanovich; c: Talma, Rasia. Exec dir, J-Uruguayan Inst of Hum Relations, repr since 1967; fmr: exec dir, Amer-J comm, Uruguay; music critic, El Pais, Marcha; political journalist. Treas, Chamber of Critics, Classical Records; found, Assn for Friendship, Uruguay-Isr, secy gen, 1961-66; cons mem, WJC, 1962-67; mem, Press Assn. Author: Cooperativism in Israel, 1963, 2nd ed, 1965; trans: from Heb, books by: David Ben Gurion, Lea Goldberg, Meir Talmi; poems by: Bialik, Tchernichovsky, Rachel; from Ger, poems by Nelly Sachs; from Eng, the Accusation of Gideon Hausner in Eichmann's Process; poems by Benjamin Britten; tales by Bernard Malamud; confs and press confs of Isr personalities; active writing on Soviet J problem. Hobbies: music, politics, lit. Home: S Antuna 2749/101, Montevideo, Uruguay. Office: Florida 1128, Montevideo, Uruguay.

FRIEDLICH, Herbert A, US, attorney; b. Rochester, NY, Dec 21, 1893; s. Abraham and Nettie (Bloch); AB, Harvard Coll, 1915, LLB, Law Sch, 1917; m. Margaret Becker, Mar 10, 1923; c: John, Mary Florsheim. Partner, Mayer, Friedlich, Spiess, Tierney, Brown & Platt, since 1932. US Army, 1917, 1942-45. Recipient: Carnegie Hero silver medal, 1922; Legion of Merit, 1945. Home: 2424 St Johns Ave, Highland Park, Ill. Office: 231 LaSalle St, Chicago, Ill.

FRIEDMAN, Abe, S Afr, merchant; b. Strand, Cape, S Afr, Feb 22, 1919; s. Benjamin and Anna (Cohen); m. Micky Raubman, Feb 12, 1939; c: Merle, Benjamin, Barry. Dir: Friedman and Cohen (Pty) Ltd, since 1936; Strand Timber and Hardware, since 1954; Strand Travel Bur; HH Laundry; munic councillor since 1958; dep mayor, Strand since 1961. S Afr Forces, 1941-45. Charter pres, Hottentots Holland B'nai B'rith, 1967-68; chmn: W Zionist Soc; C of C, Strand Somerset W, since 1951; clubs: Strand Gold; Rotary found, pres. Home: Tambuza, Debeers Rd, Strand, Cape, S Afr. Office: Main St, Strand Cape, S Afr.

FRIEDMAN, Albert B, US, educator; b. Kan City, Mo, Aug 16, 1920; s. Jay and Ida (Barron); BA, summa cum laude, U of Mo, 1941; MA, Harvard U, 1942, PhD, 1950; att: Oxford U, 1941; London U, 1951-52; Paris U, 1957-58. William Starke Rosenzug III Prof, Eng, Claremont Grad Sch, Cal, since 1969, prof, 1960-69, on fac since 1960; visiting prof, U of Cal, 1962; asst prof, Harvard U, 1955-60; Derby f, Harvard, 1942; Guggenheim f, 1957-58, 1965-66; Fulbright f, 1951-52, 1957-58; Brit Govt Scholar, 1950-51; dir, Eng Inst, Columbia U, 1964-67. Mem: Medieval Acad of Amer; Amer Folklore Soc; Cal Folklore Soc; vice-pres since 1965; chmn, comparative lit sect, MLA, 1960; secy, arthurian lit sect, 1969. Author: Folk Ballads, 1956; Literary Experience of Superior Students, 1957; The Ballad Revival, 1961; Creativity in Graduate Education, 1952; Ywain and Gawain, 1964; ed, W Folklore, since 1959. Recipient: Legion of Merit; Silver Star; Royal Order of George I; Order of the Phoenix; Kaiser-i-Hind, second class; Intl Folklore Soc prize, 1962. Hobby: old master drawings, seals, medals. Home: 900 Butte, Claremont, Cal. Office: McManus Hall, Claremont, Cal.

FRIEDMAN, Arnold P, US, physician; b. Portland, Ore, Aug 25, 1909; s. Carl and Lena (Levy); BA, U of S Cal, 1932, MA, 1934; MD, U of Ore Med Sch, 1939; m. Sara Fritz, 1939; c: Carol. Att phys, neur div, Montefiore Hosp since 1949, phys i/c, headache unit, 1947; res, neur, LA Hosp, 1940-42; asst phys, Boston Psychopathic Hosp, 1942-43; f, neur, Harvard Med Sch, 1943; research asso, Boston City Hosp, 1943-44; clinical prof, neur, Columbia U Coll Phys and Surgs, 1954; asso, att phys, Neur Inst, Presbyterian Hosp, 1949; cons, neur, VA, NY, 1949. Dipl, Amer Bd Psych and Neur; f: AMA, cons, new and non-official drugs since 1960, vice-chmn and mem, exec comm, sect on nervous and mental diseases, since 1962; NY Acad of Med, mem, Friends Rare Book Room; Amer Acad Neur, mem, bd of trustees, 1958; Amer Psych Assn; NY State and C Med Soc; Amer Neur Assn; NY Neur Soc; Amer Assn of Neuropaths; Soc of Biol Psych; Amer Psychosomatic Soc; Psi Chi; Assn for Research in Nervous and Mental Disease; Amer League Against Epilepsy; LA Co Med Soc of Neur and Psych; hon surg, Police Dept, NYC, since 1961; mem, US Pharmacopeia Scope Panel on Neuropsycht, 1960-65; chmn, panel on headache, Natl Inst Neur Diseases and Blindness, 1961-62; chmn-secy, Research Group M, Headache and Migraine, World Fed Neur; club, Harvard. Author: Modern Headache Therapy, 1951; co-author, Headache: Diagnosis and Treatment, 1959; contbr to med jours. Home and office: 71 E 77 St, New York, NY.

FRIEDMAN, Benjamin, US, ophthalmologist; b. Russ, Aug 30, 1900; s. Hyman and Bertha (Haytin); in US since 1905; MD, NYU, Bellevue Med Coll, 1924; m. Bassami Raskin, 1925; c: Ronnie Woog, Ellin Grossman. Prof em, NY Med Coll, fac mem since 1957; cons, opthal; Metrop Hosp; Bird S Coler Hosp. Served, WWI; cdr, USN MC, 1943-46. Fmr pres, NY Soc Clinical Opthal; f: NY Acad Med; Amer Coll Phys; sr mem, Amer Acad Ophthal and Otology. Contbr to med jours. Hobby, fishing. Home: 8 E 96 St, New York, NY. Office: 3 E 74 St, New York, NY.

FRIEDMAN, Bernard Robert, US, business exec; b. E Chgo, Ind, May 27, 1903; s. Julius and Mayme (Maremont); banking deg, U of Ill, 1925; m. Miriam Rothschild, Mar 4, 1927; c: Juell Kadet, Marilyn Parfenoff. Pres, Rogers Jewelers, since 1943; profsl musician; gen mgr, produc, theatrical performances, U of Ill, 1921-25. Dir: Natl B'nai B'rith; NW Ind JWF; Temple Isr, Gary, Ind; life mem, Elks; mem: Natl B'nai B'rith Commn of Youth Work; bd govs, coord, Dist 2, B'nai B'rith, past pres, mem, Supr Lodge bd govs; life mem, Musicians Union, Gary, Ind; volunteer worker, Mt Sinai Hosp, Miami Beach, Fla; fmr, pres: Ind State Assn and Gary, Ind, both B'nai B'rith. Home: 1423 Glenwood Ave, Griffith, Ind. Office: 201 E 154 St, Harvey, Ind.

FRIEDMAN, Bernard Samuel, US, research chem; b. Chgo, Ill. Apr 1, 1907; s. Nathan and Fanny (Baskin); AB, U of Ill, 1930, PhD, 1936; m. Estelle Freund, 1938; c: Alice, Joyce, Richard. Research asso, Sinclair Oil Corp since 1960, asso dir, chem research, 1948-60; group leader, Universal Oil Producs, 1936-44; dir, chem research, Phila Depot US Quartermaster, 1946-48. Fmr chmn: Chgo chap, Amer Inst Chems; Amer Chem Soc; fmr pres, Chgo Tech Socs Council; mem: Chgo Bd Educ; Zeta Beta Tau; Phi Beta Kappa; Sigma Xi. Author: Friedel Crafts and Related Reactions, 1964; contbr papers to sci jours; holder of numerous patents on new petroleum producs and processes. Home: 7321 S Shore Dr, Chicago, Ill. Office: 400 E Sibley Blvd, Harvey, Ill.

FRIEDMAN, Charles, US, stock broker; b. Passaic, NJ, Aug 29, 1902; s. Samuel and Sara (Mishkind); BS, U of Pa, att Wharton Sch of Finance, 1924; m. Helen Lamport, June 5, 1928; c: Sandra Blum, Carla Berry, John. Maj, USAC, WW II. Hon trustee, Temple Isr; found pres, hon mem, bd dirs, Isr Brotherhood; N Amer bd, World Union for Progressive Judaism, treas; hon chancellor, J Chautauqua Soc; dir, treas, United Fund of N Westchester; dir, vice-pres, Braille Inst of Amer; past pres, Pound Ridge Assn; hon mem, bd dirs, Natl Fed Temple Brotherhoods; exec bd, NY Fed Reformed Temples; bd dirs, UJA, Gtr NY, chmn, UJA, New Rochelle, 1936-40; found, Jr League, Lighthouse, 1927; mem, Pound Ridge Planning Bd. Recipient: Bronze Star, 1945. Home: Trinity Pass Rd, Pound Ridge, NY. Office: Darien, Conn.

FRIEDMAN, Charles, US, writer, director; b. Russ, Sep 20, 1902; s. Louis and Anna (Zeid); in US since 1910; m. Irene Battenfield, 1946. Dir, writer: Pins and Needles; My Darlin' Aida; dir: Carmen Jones, musical; Street Scene; produc, dir, TV Shows of: Eddie Cantor; Fred Allen; Abbott and Costello; writer-dir: Broadway, 1938-50; Hollywood: 20th Cent Fox, MGM, 1938-42; NBC-TV, CBS-TV, 1940-60. US Army, 1942. Mem: Dramatists Guild; ASCAP. Hobby, painting. Home and office: 372 Central Park W, New York, NY.

FRIEDMAN, Daniel M, US, government official; b. NYC, Feb 8, 1916; s. Henry and Julia (Freedman); AB, Columbia Coll, 1937; LLB, 1940; m. Leah Lipson, Jan 16, 1955. Dep solicitor gen, Justice Dept since 1968, with dept since 1951; mem, SEC, 1942-51. US Army, 1942-46. Mem, Fed Bar Assn. Contbr to legal jours. Home: 325 Constitution Ave, NE, Washington, DC. Office: Justice Dept, Washington, DC.

FRIEDMAN, Edward L, US, attorney; b. NYC, July 27, 1916; s. Edward and Louise (Kuttner); BSS, CCNY, 1937; LLB, Columbia U, 1940. Gen atty, NY Telephone Co since 1967, with Cox since 1954; law clerk, Chief Justice Stone, US Supr Court, 1943-45; with Root, Clark, Buckner & Ballantine, 1945-54. Counsel, secy, Citizens Comm to Keep NYC Clean Inc since 1955. Home: 4 Washington Sq Village, New York, NY. Office: 140 West St, New York, NY.

FRIEDMAN, Emma F, US, editor; b. Chgo, Ill, Feb 16, 1904; d. Max and Rose (Plofsky) Fleischman; att U of Ill, Champaign, Ill, 1922-24, 1925-26; m. Samuel Friedman, July 3, 1927; c: Howard, Sandra Czarlinsky. Ed, The SW J Chronicle, since 1933. Home: 2612 NW 14 St, Oklahoma City, Okla. Office: 822 Okla Mortgage Bldg, Oklahoma City, Okla.

FRIEDMAN, Harold, US, business exec; b. Bklyn, NY, Mar 14, 1911; s. Max and Tillie; att: St John's Coll, Bklyn, 1928-29; NYU, 1965-66; m. Sylvia Nirenberg; c: Lewis, Diane. Mgn partner, Abraham & Co, NY Stock Exch, Amer Stock Exch, since 1969; mgn partner, Sutro Bros, brokerage firm, 1928-62; pres, Edward A Viner & Co Inc, 1963-68. Pres, United HIAS Service; mem: NY Soc and Amer Inst of CPA's; KP. Home: 993 Park Ave, New York, NY. Office: 120 Broadway, New York, NY.

FRIEDMAN, Harold B, US, chemist; b. Montgomery, Ala, Oct 13, 1904; s. William and Etta (Lipson); BA, U Ala, 1923; PhD, U of Va, 1927; m. Maxine Cohen, Mar 1, 1953; c: Martin, Carol, Cathy. Chief, research and devl, Zep Mfg Corp, since 1945; instr, chem, U of M, 1927-28; research asst; Columbia U, 1928-29; asst, asso prof, Ga Inst of Tech, 1929-42. Research, devl tech div, US Army Chem Corps, 1942-45; US Army Res, 1928-58, ret, lt col. Amer Inst of Chems. Mem: educ comm, Atlanta C of C, fmr chmn; Phi Beta Kappa; Sigma Xi; Phi Kappa Phi; bd, the J Temple; Amer Chem Soc; Ga Acad of Sci, fmr pres; Chem Specialties Mfrs Assn. Contbr to sci, ird jours. Recipient: 30 year Res Ribbon; Army Commendation Ribbon. Hobbies: philately, photography. Home: 2690 Margaret Mitchell Dr, NW, Atlanta, Ga. Office: 1310 Seaboard Ind Blvd, NW, Atlanta, Ga.

FRIEDMAN, Harold E, US, attorney; b. Chgo, Ill, Apr 14, 1907; s. Emil and Margaret (Hirsch); att: Crane Coll, 1924-26; U of Ill, 1926-30; LLM, Marshall Coll of Law, 1931; m. Helen Meyer, Aug 13, 1933; c: Charles. Pvt practice since 1931; chief, legal staff, Chgo procurement and contract termination div, Signal Corps, US Army, 1944-46. Pres: Chgo Fed, UAHC; mem, natl bd; Chgo Assn Retarded Children, 1964-67; KAM Temple, 1963-65; mem, bd: J Vocational Service; Psychiatric Aid Soc; Retarded Children's Aid, Inc, 1956-64; Mt Mayriv Cemetery Assn, Chgo, 1958-64; chmn, folk org div, CJA, Chgo, 1958-64, mem admn comm, 1956-64; mem: Pi Lambda Phi; Ill State, Amer Bar Assns; Decalogue Soc of Lawyers; B'nai B'rith; Masons; Progressive Order of W. Recipient: meritorious service award, Psychiatric Aid Soc, Chgo, 1959; meritorious service citation, Signal Corps. Hobby: photography. Home: 5435 Hyde Park Blvd, Chicago, Ill. Office: 10 S LaSalle St, Chicago, Ill.

FRIEDMAN, Henry M, Austr; organization exec; b. Melbourne, Austr, Apr 8, 1915; s. Ephraim and Fanny (Rosen); m. Leila Harris, Dec 4, 1945; c: Eric, Graham. Secy, Melbourne Heb Cong since 1947; corresp, Beth Din, 1948. Life mem, Victorian Assn J Ex-Servicemen and Women. Home: 43 Rosemont Ave, Caulfield, Austr. Office: Syn Chamers, Toorak Rd, S Yarra, Austr.

FRIEDMAN, Howard Irwin, US, attorney; b. Chgo, Ill, Apr 21, 1928; s. Samuel and Emma (Fleischman); BA, U Okla, 1948; MA, U Chgo, 1949; LLB, Yale U, 1952; m. Wilma Mann, June 24, 1951; c: Lesey, Harry, Beth. Partner, Loeb and Loeb, since 1957; teaching F, Stanford U Law Sch, 1954-55; dep atty gen, Cal Justice Dept, 1955-57. Capt, USAF, 1952-54. Chmn, AJComm, LA chap; rel comm, J Fed Council, LA; bd-trustees, Temple Judea, Tarzana, Cal; fmr pres, Temple Kol Olam; mem: Amer Cal State, LA Co Bar Assns; Amer Judicature

Soc. Contbr, articles, NYU Law Rev. Home: 16237 Meadow Ridge Rd, Encino, Cal. Office: 1600 One Wilshire Bldg, Los Angles, Cal.

FRIEDMAN, Jacob (pen name, **J Namdizf**), Isr, author; b. Ukraine, Aug 15, 1910; s. Joseph and Margalit (Twersky); in Isr since 1948; m. Keniam Lammd, July 6, 1936; c: Chana. Author: Oisgestrekte Hent 1933; Adam, 1935; Pastecher in Israel, 1967. Mem, PEN Club. Recipient: Poetry Award, Cultur Cong, 1954; Sholem Aleichem, Frischman Award, 1960. Spec interest, phil. Home and studio: 3 Fihman St, Ramat Aviv, Tel Aviv, Isr.

FRIEDMAN, Joseph J, US, surgeon; b. Bklyn, NY, Nov 9, 1905; s. Jacob and Regina (Schoen); BA, Cornell U, 1926; att: Dartmouth Med Sch, 1926-28; MD, Johns Hopkins Med Sch, 1930; m. Frances Gluck, Oct 18, 1933; c: Alan, Jay. Specialist in: ophthal, since 1946; otolaryngology, 1934-42; att surg: Sanitarium and Hosp for Incurables, since 1947; J Chronic Diseases Hosp, since 1947; asst att surg, Bklyn Eye and Ear Hosp, since 1950. Maj, US Army MC, 1942-46. F: Amer Coll of Surgs, since 1951; AMA, since 1950; Acad of Ophthal and Otolaryngology, since 1946; Bklyn Opthal Soc, since 1946; dipl, Amer Bd Ophthal since 1950; mem, Phi Delta Epsilon. Home: 322 Glendale Rd, Scarsdale, NY. Office: 57 Midwood St, Brooklyn, NY.

FRIEDMAN, Lawrence Abraham, US, dentist; b. NYC, Apr 23, 1937; s. Samuel and Lillian (Wittes); BA, NYU, 1958; DDS, U of Pa, 1962; m. Loretta Falk, May 14, 1960; c: Jonathan, Andrew. Asst mem, Dent Sci Inst, since 1968; pvt practice, periodontics, since 1967. Capt, USAF, 1962-64. Bd dirs: Men's Club, Cong Beth Yeshurun; Downtown B'nai B'rith; mem: Tau Epsilon Phi; Alpha Omega. Home: 5227 Lymbar, Houston, Tex. Office: 902 Frostwood Dr, Houston, Tex.

FRIEDMAN, Leon, US, surgeon; b. Phila, Pa, July 26, 1915; s. Jacob and Sima (Sussman); BA, U of Pa, 1934, MD, 1938; m. Beatrice Weissman, July 14, 1940; c: Jerald, Jaye. Chmn, exec comm, Warren Hosp, Phillipsburg, NJ, since 1967, active att surg since 1959, staff mem, since 1945; mem, bd dirs, Consolidated Activities Inc since 1958; surg, Gen Hosp, Monroe Co, 1941-45; asso chief surg, acting chief thoracic surg, Easton Hosp, Easton, Pa, 1954-58. Life F: Amer Coll of Surgs; Intl Acad Proctology; f, Intl Coll Surgs; dipl, Amer Bd of Surg; pres, B'nai B'rith Judea Lodge, 1952-54; mem, bd dirs, B'nai Abraham Syn, since 1945; mem, bd activities, J Comty Cen, 1950-54, all Easton, Pa; life mem ZOA; asso mem, Med Soc, Warren Co, NJ; mem: Med Soc, Northampton Co, Pa; Herbert Horthorne Surg Soc, Grad Sch, U of Pa; Interns and Res Soc, Hosp of U of Pa; Alpha Omega Alpha; clubs: Carib Ocho Rios, Sea and Country, 1st vice-pres since 1960. Contbr to med jours. Recipient, Med Alumni Award, U of Pa, 1938. Homes: 632 Chestnut Terrace, Easton, Pa; Carib Ocho Rios, Jamaica, West Indies. Office: 1725 Northampton St, Easton, Pa.

FRIEDMAN, Leon, US, lawyer, author; b. NYC, June 2, 1933; s. Morris and Fannie (Shames); AB, Harvard Col, 1954; att Harvard Grad Sch, 1954-55; LLB, Harvard Law Sch, 1960; div. Gen counsel, Chelsea House Pubs, since 1968; atty, Kaye, Scholer, Fierman, Hayes & Handler, 1960-67. Sgt, US Army, 1955-57. Prin contribs, Supr Court arguments in civil rights and civil liberties cases. Author: Southern Justice, 1965; Civil Rights Reader, 1967; The Justices of the United States Supreme Court 1789-1969, Their Lives and Major Opinions, 1969; contbr to periodicals. Home: 22 W 56 St, New York, NY. Office: 70 W 40 St, New York, NY.

FRIEDMAN, Leopold, US, attorney, business exec; b. Ger, June 10, 1887; s. Abraham and Rosalie (Lederman); in US since 1892; LLB, NY Law Sch, 1908; m. Ruth Holzman, Oct 26, 1939; pvt practice since 1911; secy, vice-pres, counsel, Loew's Inc (MGM), 1919-54; vice-pres, pres, chmn, bd, Loew's Theatres, 1954-60. USN, 1917. Vice-pres, mem, bd trustees, Hosp for Jt Diseases; pres, mem, bd trustees, Cen Syn; clubs: Harmonie; Quaker Ridge Country. Home: 480 Park Ave, New York, NY. Office: 745 Fifth Ave, New York, NY.

FRIEDMAN, Lillian, US, business exec; b. St Louis, Mo, Oct 14, 1909; d. Jacob and Rose (Zalman); div; c. Toby. Vice-pres, Brentano's since 1960; book buyer, 1951-60; book buyer, Stix Baer & Fuller, St Louis, Mo, 1940-50. Co-author: Europe Looks at the Civil War, 1960. Home: 86 W 12 St, New York, NY. Office: 586 Fifth Ave, New York, NY.

FRIEDMAN, Louis Frank, US, attorney; b. Baltimore, Md, May 26, 1941; s. David and Miriam (Sugarman); BS, U of Md, 1962, DJur, 1965; LLM, Georgetown U, 1968; m. Phyllis Cole, Dec 25, 1968. Partner, Miles and Friedman, since 1968, asso since 1965. Panelist, estate planning sem, Comm for Continuing Legal Educ; mem: Md Bar Assn; Baltimore City Jr Bar Assn; young lawyers div, Asso J Charities; young men's leadership div, Asso J Charities. Recipient: Amer Jurisprudence Award in Equity, 1964; Amer Jurisprudence Award in Estate Planning, 1966; Order of the Coif, U of Md, 1965. Home: 6607 Sanzo Rd, Baltimore, Md. Office: 1805 First Natl Bank Bldg, Baltimore, Md.

FRIEDMAN, Martin, US, artist; b. Budapest, Hung, Apr 24, 1896; s. Bernard and Rose (Heller); in US since 1905; att: Natl Acad Design, 1913-14; Beaux Arts, NYC, 1925-26; m. Barbara Borrous, Sep 7, 1928; c: Arnold. One-man shows: Brownell-Lamberton Gals, NY, 1932; Artists' Gal, NY, 1942, 1944; Perls Gal, NY, 1945; Babcock Gal, NY, 1951, 1955, 1959, 1964; Phila Art Alliance, Phila, Pa, 1951; Cowie Gal, LA, Cal, 1952, 1961; Mansfield State Coll, 1966; exhbs: Whitney Mus, NY; Carnegie Inst, Pittsburgh; Worcester Mus; Toledo Mus, Neb U; U of Ill; Corcoran Art Gal, Wash, DC; Pa Acad of Fine Arts; Dallas; Richmond, Va; Art for Victory, and Water Color Shows, Metrop Mus, NY; Butler Art Inst, Youngstown, O; Natl Acad of Design, NY; World's Fair, 1935; Childe Hassam Fund at Acad Arts and Letters, NY; Provincetown Art Assn; E End Gal, Provincetown, Mass; Rudolph Gal, Woodstock, NY, and Fla; Woodstock Art Assn; represented in perm collections: Mansfield State Coll; Ogunquit Mus, Me; U Ariz; Rochester Mus; Brandeis U; Butler Art Assn; Mission San Juan Capistrano; Tel Aviv Mus; Lichtenstein Mus, Safad, both in Isr. Recipient: Gold Medal, Audubon Soc of Artists: for oil, 1952, for casein, 1954, John Newman Medal for oil, 1955; hon mentions and Gold Medal for water color, Bkln Mus, 1957; dir's prize, Soc for Painters in Casein, 1957. Home and studio: 530 W 113 St, New York, NY.

FRIEDMAN, Maurice, US, business exec; b. NYC, Aug 15, 1915; s. Louis and Dora (Bergstein); AB, NYC, 1936; MS, 1938; m. Gertrude Wiener, Feb 19, 1939. Vice-pres, dir Sci Components, since 1968; asso chem, Signal Corps Engr Lab, 1941-45; chief engr PR Mallory and Co, 1945-49; vice-pres, Microtone, 1949-53; Gen Instrument, 1953-65; gen mgr, semiconductor div, Sperry Rand, 1965-68. Holder numerous patents. Mem: Electrochem Soc; Amer Chem Soc; NY Acad Sci; Tau Alpha Omega. Contbr to profsl jours. Home: 182 Parsonage Hill Rd, Short Hills, NJ. Office: 350 Hurst St, Linden, NJ.

FRIEDMAN, Maurice S, US, educator, author; b. Tulsa, Okla, Dec 29, 1921; s. Samuel and Fannie (Smirin); BS, magna cum laude, Harvard U, 1943; MA, O State U, 1947; PhD, U Chgo, 1950; hon LLD, U of Vt, 1961; m. Eugenia Chifos, Jan 17, 1947. Prof: rel, Temple U, since 1967; phil, Manhattanville Coll, 1966-67; Pendle Hill Cen for Dialogue and Study, 1957, 1959, 1964, 1965, 1967; Sarah Lawrence Coll, NY, 1951-65; lectr: New Sch for Social Research, NY, since 1954; Wash, DC, Sch of Psycht, since 1957; guest lectr, William Alanson White Inst, NY, 1958-60; f, comm on hist and culture, Chgo U, 1947-49; instr, masterpieces of world lit, Wash U, St Louis, 1949-50; phil, O State U, 1950-51; visiting prof: rel phil, HUC, Cincinnati, 1956-57; phil of rel, Union Theol Sem, 1965-67; visiting lectr, Vassar Coll, 1967. Chmn, Amer Friends of Ichud, 1956-58; mem: ed comm, Comm on Higher Educ since 1956; Amer Phil Assn; Rel Educ Assn; Phi Beta Kappa; Amer Metaphys Soc; Frank L Weil Inst of Rel and Hum; AAUP; Frank Rosenzweig Soc; J Phil Soc. Author: Martin Buber: The Life of Dialogue, Brit publ, 1955, US, 1955, 1960; The Covenant of Peace, 1960; Problematic Rebel, 1963; The Worlds of Existentialism, 1964; Martin Buber, Vol 1—The Road to I and Thou, 1968; To Deny our Nothingness; Contemporary Images of Man, 1968; ed trans, works of Martin Buber; ed bds: Judaism, Rel Educ, and Rev of Existential Psychology and Psychiatry; contbr: articles on Martin Buber to Ency Britannica; articles on phil, Judaism to scholarly and lay jours. Recipient: first prize, L of N Assn, 1939; grant, Lucius N Littauer Found, 1960. Hobby: piano. Home: 73 Bronxville Rd, Bronxville, NY. Office: Temple U, Philadelphia, Pa.

FRIEDMAN, Milton, US, radiologist, educator; b. Newark, NJ, Sep 13, 1903; s. Samuel and Sarah (Goldberg); MD, George Wash U, 1926; m. Marian Mendelson, 1928 (div); c: Susan; m. 2nd, Elna Linborg, Dec 21, 1947. Prof, radiology, NYU

Coll of Med, since 1937, asso prof, clinical radiology, since 1950, on fac since 1937; dir, supervoltage radiation dept, Hosp for Jt Diseases, since 1945, att radiation therapist, since 1946, adj roentgenologist, 1932-46; att radiologist, Bellevue Hosp, since 1928, research f, 1932-34, asso, radiation therapy, 1937-52; cons, radiation: AEC, since 1954; Clara Maas Memorial Hosp, Newark, since 1953; USPHS, since 1950; Walter Reed Army Hosp, since 1948; Natl Bur of Standards, since 1948; Newark City Hosp, since 1948, mem staff since 1926; NJ State Health Dept Comm, investigating radium poisoning in watch-dial workers; chief cons, radiation, VA, since 1946; asso radiologist, Sydenham Hosp, 1931-38; instr, US Army Sch of Roentgenology, 1942; chief, radiation therapy, Walter Reed Gen Hosp, 1942-45; cons, Halloran VA Hosp, 1948-51. Lt col, US Army MC, 1942-45. Pres: Amer Radium Soc, 1966-67; Radiological Soc, NJ, 1938; NY Cancer Soc, 1959-60; Amer Radiotherapy Soc, 1960-61; vice-pres, NJ Assn Tumor Clinics, 1940; med dir, Lila Mottey Cancer Found; chmn, Comm for Devl Isotope Sources, AEC, since 1959, chmn prog comm, supervoltage sem at Oak Ridge, Tenn, 1956; f, Amer Coll of Radiology; AMA; dipl, Amer Bd of Radiology; mem: adv comm distribution of radium, Natl Cancer Inst; sub-comm on cancer, Gov's Comm for Public Health and Wfr, NJ, 1939; natl comm on radiation protection, Natl Bur Standards, 1947; exhibit comm, Amer Radium Soc, since 1949; civilian defense panel, State of NY, 1951; cancer adv comm, NYC Health Dept, 1959; cancer control comm, NJ Med Soc, 1937-39; bd govs, NY chap, George Wash U Alumni Assn, since 1952; mem: AAAS; Brit Inst Radiology; Amer Assn for Cancer Research; Inter-Amer Coll Radiology; Pan-Amer Med Assn; Soc Nuclear Med; NY Roentgen Ray Soc; Radiological Soc of N Amer; Amer Roentgen Ray Soc; NY Acad of Sci; Harlem Med Soc; NY Inst Oral Clinical Path; Acad of Med, Northern NJ; Sigma Xi; Phi Delta Epsilon; club, Intl of Radiotherapy. Contrib author: Gynecological Roentgenology, 1931; Tumors of the Skin, 1939; Principles and Practice of Plastic Surgery, 1950; Clinical Therapeutic Radiology, 1950; numerous monographs; co-author, ed, Roentgen, Rads and Riddles, US AEC publ, since 1959; ed, Amer Lectures on Radiation Therapy, 1950, 1953; contbr to sci publs. Recipient: cert of merit, NJ State Med Soc, 1937; cert hon mention: Intl Conv of Radiology, 1937; NJ State Med Soc, 1940; Radiological Soc N Amer, 1941; Legion of Merit, 1946; silver medal, Amer Roentgen Ray Soc, Wash, DC, 1951; third award, Med Soc of NJ, 1952. Hobbies: art, music, photography. Home: 20 E 68 St, New York, NY. Office: U Hosp, 566 First Ave, New York, NY.

FRIEDMAN, Milton, US, economist, educator; b. NYC, July 31, 1912; s. Jeno and Sara (Landau); BA, Rutgers U, 1932; MA, U Chgo, 1933; PhD, Columbia U, 1946; hon LLD: Rikkoyo U, Japan, 1963; Kalamazoo Coll, 1968; Rutgers U, 1968; Lehigh U, 1969; hon DHL Rockford Coll, 1969; m. Rose Director, June 25, 1938; c: Janet, David. Paul Snowden Russell Dist Service Prof Econ, U Chgo, since 1962, prof, econ, since 1948; on fac since 1946; mem, research staff, Natl Bur of Econ Research, since 1948; columnist, Newsweek Mag since 1966; visiting prof, econ, U of Wis, 1940-41; prin econ, div of tax research, Treasury Dept, 1941-43; asso dir, stat research group, Div War Research, Columbia U, 1943-45; visiting Fulbright lectr, Cambridge U, Eng, 1943-54; visiting Wesley Clair Mitchell Prof, Columbia U, 1964-65. F: Amer Stat Assn; Econometric Soc; Inst Math Stat; Cen for Advanced Study in Behavioral Scis; vice-pres, Mont Pelerin Soc; adv bd, Amer Enterprise Assn since 1956; mem: Amer Econ Assn, past pres, bd ed, 1951-53; Royal Econ Soc, club, Quadrangel; fmr mem bd dirs. Author: Essays in Positive Economics, 1953; A Theory of the Consumption Function, 1957; A Program for Monetary Stability, 1959; Price Theory, 1962; Capitalism and Freedom, 1962; Dollars and Deficits, 1968; The Optimum Quantity of Money and other Essays, 1969; co-author: Income from Independent Professional Practice, 1946; Sampling Inspection, 1948; A Monetary History of the United States, 1867-1960, pub ,1963; The Balance of Payments, 1967; ed, Studies in the Quantity Theory of Money, 1956; columnist, Newsweek Mag, since 1966. Recipient: John Bates Clark Medal, Amer Econ Assn, 1951. Home: 5825 Dorchester Ave, Chgo, Ill. Office: U of Chgo, Chicago, Ill.

FRIEDMAN, Milton H, US, attorney; b. Elmira ,NY, Nov 11, 1905; s. Louis and Celia (Bladen); AB, Cornell U, 1926; LLB, Yale U, 1928; m. Marjorie Block, Feb 4, 1938; c: Catherine, Margaret, Ann. Pvt practice since 1928. Mem: Erie Co, NY State Bar Assns; Amer Law Inst; Amer Judicature Soc; fmr pres: Temple Beth Zion; Bur J Educ 1950; clubs:

Montefiore; Westwood Country. Home: 325 Middlesex Rd, Buffalo, NY. Office: Prudential Bldg, Buffalo, NY.

FRIEDMAN, Milton R, US, attorney; b. Hartford, Conn, Jan 16, 1904; s. Max and Amalie (Pinkus); BA, Yale U, 1925, LLB, 1928; m. Dorothy Guiterman, Aug 3, 1934; c: Alan. Partner, Parker, Duryee, Sunino, Malone and Carter, since 1958; lectr: real estate law, NYU, since 1951; Practicing Law Inst, NY, since 1942; law secy, Judge Learned Hand and Thomas W Swan, 1928-29; asso, firm, Mitchell, Capron, Marsh, Angulo & Cooney, 1929-58. Fmr chmn, real property law commn, Assn Bar, NYC, mem, state leg, rent control commns; mem: Amer Law Inst, 1967; clubs, Yale, NY. Author: The Business and Commercial Rent Control Laws of NY, 1946; Contracts and Conveyances of Real Property, 1954, 2nd ed; Preparation of Leases, 10th ed, 1962; contbr to legal jours. Home: 115 W 73 St, New York, NY. Office: 1 E 44 St, New York, NY.

FRIEDMAN, Miriam R, US, communal worker; b. Cincinnati, O; d. Julius and Gertude (Hirshchorn) Rothschild; m. Bernard Friedman, Apr 3, 1927; c: Juell Kadet, Marilyn Parfenoff. Choreographer for churches, temples, schs, since 1921; profsl dancer, tchr, 1921-32. Natl repr, B'nai B'rith Women, since 1956, fmr: pres: dist 2, Gary chap; Ind St Assn; secy, dist 2, B'nai B'rith Youth Council; mem: Ind regional bd, ADL since 1957; found, B'nai B'rith Youth Canteen; org, Gary B'nai B'rith Girls; bd dirs: Temple Isr Sisterhood; Temple Beth El Sisterhood; Hadassah; JWB Gary, past chmn, gen gifts campaign; YMCA since 1953, fmr chmn, public affairs, vice-pres; Brandeis Women; Natl Council J Women; Psi Iota Xi; nurses aid, ARC; capt, Cancer Drive; org, Brownie and Girl Scout Troops, Miller Beach, Ind. Home: 1423 N Glenwood, Griffith, Ind.

FRIEDMAN, Morris S, US, surgeon; b. Russ, Sept, 15, 1914; s. David and Sonia (Friedman); in US since 1921; BS, U Chgo, 1936; MD, Rush Med Coll, 1938; m; div; c: Sheldon, Stephen, Susan; 2nd m. Mary Jane; c: Tim, Kurt, Pam. Pvt practice, specialization, orthoped surg since 1947. US Army, WW II. F: Amer Coll of Surgs; Acad of Orthoped Surgs; mem: AMA; Ind Soc of Orthoped Surgs; bd mem: UJA; United Heb Sch; Temple Beth El, all S Bend, Ind. Home: 1617 E Jefferson Blvd, South Bend, Ind. Office: 919 E Jefferson Blvd, South Bend, Ind.

FRIEDMAN, Murry N, US, physician, educator; b. Bklyn, NY, Apr 8, 1919; s. Harry and Bessie (Fried); BA, NYU, 1939, MD, 1943; m. Elinor Bloom; c: Amy, Betsy, Geri, Nancy. Clinical asso prof, surg, SUNY Downstate Med Cen, Bklyn, since 1955; att visiting surg, Kings Co Hosp; cons surg, Bklyn Vets Hosp; asso att surg, LI Coll Hosp. Capt, US Army MC, 1944-46. F: Amer Coll of Surgs; Bklyn Surgs Soc; dipl, Amer Bd of Surgs. Contbr to med jours. Home: 55 Deepdale Dr, Great Neck, NY. Office: 142 Joralemon St, Brooklyn, NY.

FRIEDMAN, Newton J, US, rabbi; b. Cleveland, O, Feb 13, 1909; s. Anton and Jennie (Rogen); AB, cum laude, W Reserve U, 1928; DHL, HUC, 1932, ordained rabbi, 1934, DD HC 1959; ThD, Burton Sem, 1955; att Harvard U, 1939; m. Rosalie Kanter, Mar 26, 1935; c: Gary, Jeffrey. Rabbi, Temple Emanuel, Beaumont, Tex, since 1957; dir, Hillel Found, U Tex, 1941-45; rabbi: Temple B'nai B'rith, Wilkes Barre, Pa ,1945-53; Temple Beth Isr, Macon, Ga, 1953-57; instr, Lamar Tech, 1963-66. Secy, SE region, UAHC, 1953-57; natl Americanism commn, ADL; mem: exec comm: Beaumont UJA; Temple Emanuel Brotherhood; bd dirs: pres, Beaumont chap, ARC Crippled Children's Soc, Beaumont; bd trustees, two terms, HUC Alumni Assn; speakers bur: J Defense Appeal; J Chautauqua Soc; natl sup comm on comty relations, AJComm; NCCJ; adult educ comm, Beaumont YMCA; prog comm, Beaumont Min Assn, pres; social justice comm, CCAR, pres, SW region; clubs: Beaumont Country; Zeta Beta Tau. Author: The Life of Joseph Nasi, 1934; The History of Macon, Georgia, Jewry, 1955. Home: 5895 Clinton, Beaumont, Tex. Study: 1120 Broadway, Beaumont, Tex.

FRIEDMAN, Newton S, US, attorney; b. Minneapolis, Minn, Dec 20, 1911; s. Samuel and Lillian (Waxman); BA, U Minn, 1931; LLB, Columbia U, 1934; att U Basel, Switz; m. Danna Michaels, Dec 12, 1950; c: Joy Dale, Karen. Pvt practice since 1953; chief, denazification div, Mil Govt for Württenberg, Ger, 1947-48; lab off, US Fgn Service, Stuttgart, Ger, 1948-53; atty, civil admn, Mil Govt, Ger. US Army, 1943-46. Chmn, Duluth br, Workmen's Circle; state chmn, since 1961, natl exec bd; state vice-chmn, J Lab Comm; natl committeeman, AJComm; dir, atty, Duluth Coop Soc; publicity dir, folk festival Intl Inst, 1955; mem, state bd of dirs, ACLU since 1958; mem, bd dirs, Duluth JF; natl delg, ORT; mem: NY, Minn, and Amer Bar Assns; clubs: Saturday Lunch, pres, 1955-56; Duluth JF, secy, 1954-55. Spec interests: civil liberties, politics. Home: 4114 Pitt St, Duluth Minn. Office: 417 Torrey Bldg, Duluth, Minn.

FRIEDMAN, Norman, US, educator; b. Boston, Mass, Apr 10, 1925; s. Samuel and Eva (Nathanson); att Bklyn Coll, 1943; MIT, 1943-44; BA, Harvard, 1948, MA, 1949, PhD, 1952; m. Zelda Nathanson, June 7, 1945; c: Michael, Janet. Prof, Eng, Queens Coll, since 1968, fac mem since 1963; instr, asso prof, U Conn, 1952-63. Mem: Natl Council Tchrs Eng; MLA; AAUP; Phi Beta Kappa. Author: EE Cummings: The Art of His poetry, 1960; EE Cummings: The Growth of a Writer, 1964; co-author: Poetry: An Introduction to Its Form and Art, 1961; Logic, Rhetoric and Style, 1963; contbr of fiction, poems, articles to profsl jours. Recipient: Bowdoin prize, 1948; grants-in-aid, Amer Council Learned Societies, 1959-60; Fulbright grant, U Nantes, Nice, 1966-67; NW Rev annual poetry prize, 1963, Borestone Mt poetry awards, 1964, 1967. Home: 33-54 164th St, Flushing, NY. Office: Dept of Eng, Queens Coll, Flushing, NY.

FRIEDMAN, Norman H, Can, business exec; b. Montreal, Can, June, 28, 1900; s. David and Miriam (Jacobs); BCom, McGill U, 1921; m. Rose Matts, Apr 3, 1940. Vice-pres, C S Allen and Co, Ltd; fmr gen mgr, pres. Donor, Kipling and Leacock collections to McGill U Libr. F, Royal Soc of Scouts, London, Eng; gov trustee, YM-YWHA; home commn, Montreal region, Boy Scouts of Can, joined Boy Scout movement, 1928; life mem: Natl Geog Soc; Amer Philatelic Soc; Montreal Amateur Athletic Assn; mem: Zeta Beta Tau; Masons; club, Montefiore. Recipient: Medal of merit, Boy Scouts Assn, 1942; Silver Acorn Award, presented by Gov Gen, Can, 1957; Silver Wolf Boy Scouts of Can Award, 1968. Office: 250 Clarke Ave, Westmount, Can.

FRIEDMAN, Orrie M, US, educator, researcher; b. Grenfell, Can, June 6, 1915; s. Jack and Gertrude (Shulman); in US since 1946; BS, U Man, Can, 1935; BS, McGill U, 1941, PhD, 1944; m. Laurel Leeder; c: Mark, Gertrude, Hugh. Pres, treas, Collaborative Research, Inc; vice-pres, United Chemist Co, Ltd; spec cons on cancer chemotherapy; NIH; USPHS, since 1962; jr research chem, NRC, Can, 1944-46; research f, chem dept, Harvard U, 1946-49; research asso, Harvard Med Sch, 1949-52; asso, surg research, Beth Isr Hosp, Boston, Mass, 1949-52; asst prof, Harvard Med Sch, 1952-53; prof, chem, Brandeis U, 1960-64, on fac since 1953. Prin contrib: research in chem of high explosives, alkaloids and organophosphorus compounds, studies in chemotherapy of cancer and mental illness. F: AAAS; Chem Soc, London, Eng; mem: Amer Chem Soc; Amer Assn for Cancer Research, Inc; Radiation Soc; Assn of Harvard Chems; Sigma Xi. Contbr to med and sci jours. Home: 49 Warren St, Brookline, Mass. Office: Collaborative Research, Inc, 1365 Main St, Waltham, Mass.

FRIEDMAN, Paul S, US, radiologist; b. NYC, Aug 5, 1914; s. Lewis and Dorothy (Kantrowitz); BA, Columbia Coll, 1933; MD, NYU Coll of Med 1937; m. Elise Kohn, May 20, 1948; c: Ellen, Peter, Steven. Pvt practice since 1945; cons, Valley Forge Army Hosp, since 1949; instr, grad sch of med, U of Pa, since 1950; all Phila; f, res, Jefferson Hosp, 1940-41; asso: J Hosp, 1945-49; Episcopal Hosp 1953-55; radiologist, Rush Hosp, 1948-61, pres med staff, 1958-60. Capt, US Army, 1941-45. Chmn: comm on leg, Phila Co Med Soc, also comm on med and rel, since 1952; local AJComm; f: Coll of Phys; Amer Coll of Chest Phys; Amer Coll of Legal Med; Coll of Radiology; mem: bd trustees, Phila State Hosp; speakers bur: AMA; Pa Med Soc; bd dirs, Pa Med Political Action Comm; Roentgen Ray Soc; Radiology Soc of N Amer; Laennec Soc; Pa Radiological Soc; Amer Trudeau Soc; Alpha Omega Alpha; Phi Beta Kappa; clubs: Locust-Mid-City; Rydal Course. Contbr to med jours. Hobbies: photography, golf. Home: 8107 Cedar Rd, Elkins Park, Pa. Offices: 1422 Chestnut St, Philadelphia, Pa; 7852 Montgomery Ave, Elkins Park, Pa.

FRIEDMAN, Philip, US, businessman; b. Ostrow, Pol, Aug 24, 1906; s. Hershel and Rachel (Burstein); att Heb sch, Pol; m. Jennie Rosenstein, Apr 16, 1932. Restaurant owner. Pres, group, B'nai Zion, exec mem. Recipient, award for various

contribs to Zionist movement. Home: 440 Neptune Ave, Brooklyn, NY.

FRIEDMAN, Samuel D, US, publisher; b. Peoria, Ill, May 14, 1902; s. David and Rebecca (Wind); att Bradley U, Peoria, Ill, 1920-22; m. Emma Fleischman, July 3, 1927; c: Howard, Sandra Czarlinsky. Publisher, bus mgr, Southwest J Chronicle, since 1933; advt mgr: rotogravure sect, Peoria Jour-Transcript, 1923; Ill State Jour, Springfield, Ill, 1924-25; spec eds mgr, advt dept, Chgo Daily News, 1926. US Army, 1918. Pres, Okla City Zionist dist, since 1958; mem, bd dirs: Okla City JCC, since 1958; Leo N Levi Memorial Natl Arthritis Hosp, Hot Springs, Ark, since 1966; secy, Emanuel Heb Cemetery Assn, since 1959; city team capt, United Fund of Okla City, since 1940; team capt, YMCA mem campaign, since 1930; treas, Okla Comm, Natl J Hosp at Denver; city chmn, Kiwanis Jr Police, 1936; state chmn: B'nai B'rith, 1936, United HIAS Service, 1938; mem: Masons; Shriners; Elks; club, Okla City Sales Execs. Home: 2612 NW 14 St, Oklahoma City, Okla. Office: 822 Okla Mortgage Bldg, Oklahoma City, Okla.

FRIEDMAN, Shama, US, rabbi, educator; b. Phila, Pa, Mar 8, 1937; s. Joseph and Dorothy (Deitch); BA, U of Pa, 1958; BHL, Gratz Coll, Phila, 1958; ordained rabbi, MHL, PhD, JTSA, 1966; m. Rachel Swergold, Aug 20, 1961; c: Sara, Adina, Jonathan. Asst prof, rabb, JTSA, since 1967, acting libr, since 1969. Contbr articles to Ency Judaica. Home: 3025 Netherland Ave, Bronx, NY. Office: 3080 Broadway, New York, NY.

FRIEDMAN, Shirley M, US, journalist; b. Providence, RI, June 16, 1923; d. Harry and Pearl (Reffkin); BS, Simmons Coll, 1945; MS, Grad Sch of Journalism, Columbia U, 1946; m. Bernard Roffman, June 28, 1952; c: Seth, Faith. Ed, home furnishings, Newark News, since 1946; instr, Rutgers U, 1946-52, 1961-62. Mem: Amer Inst of Interior Designers; Natl Home Fashions League; Natl Soc of Interior Designers; club, Simmons Coll of NJ. Contbr to: Better Homes and Gardens; Good Housekeeping; American Family. Recipient: Dorothy Dawe-Amer Furniture Mart, natl award for dist newspaper reporting in the home field, 1949. Home: 20 Oval Rd, Millburn, NJ. Office: 215 Market St, Newark, NJ.

FRIEDMAN, Sidney, US, banker, attorney; b. Bklyn, NY, Dec 1, 1907; s. Wolf and Sarah (Silver); LLB, Yale U, 1931, PhB, Brown U, 1928, MA, 1931; m. Blanche Nanner, 1930. Chmn bd, chief exec off, Natl Bank of N Amer, since 1964; dir: CIT Financial Corp, since 1966; Mitchell Field Devl Corp, since 1967. Asso trustee, N Shore Hosp, since 1966; mem: Bd of Ethics, Nassau Co, since 1968; Phi Beta Kappa Assos. Recipient: Metrop Award Yeshiva U, 1966; Tree of Life Award, Boys Town, Jerusalem, 1967; citizen of year award; Adelphi-Suffolk Coll, 1968; NCCJ, Suffolk, 1969. Home: 15 Wensley Dr, Great Neck, NY. Office: 44 Wall St, New York, NY.

FRIEDMAN, Sidney N, US, business exec; b. Detroit, Mich, Sep 26, 1918; s. Julius and Anna (Robin); AB, U Mich, 1940, MBA, 1950; m. Ada Goldman, Dec 6, 1942; c: Joel, Alan. Vice-pres, finance and corp secy, Samsonite Corp, since 1940; bd dir, Altrd SA de CV, Mexico City; asst secy: Samsonite of Can; Design W Inc, La. Lt, USNR, 1942-46. Dir: Traveler's Aid Soc; Colo Public Expenditures Council; Downtown Denver Improvement Assn; Adams Co Mh Assn; mem: Temple Emanuel; State of Colo, treas dept adv comm; fmr: vice-pres, Detroit lodge, B'nai B'rith; comm chmn: Allied J Campaign; United Fund; mem: Financial Exec Inst; Natl Assn Acctnts, both Rocky Mt. Hobbies: golf, reading. Home: 3175 S St Paul, Denver, Colo. Office: 11200 45 Ave, Denver, Colo.

FRIEDMAN, Sol B, US, rabbi; b. NYC, Apr 6, 1890; s. Joseph and Rose (Friedman); LLB, Cleveland Law Sch, 1914; MA, Columbia U, 1919; ordained rabbi, Yeshiva, U, 1919, PhD, 1961; m. Clare Goldstein, Sep 5, 1922; c: Lionel, Ezra. Rabbi, Young Isr, Wash Hgts, since 1949; exec secy, NY State Adv Bd for Kosher Law Enforcement; rabbi: Poale Zedek Cong, Pittsburgh, Pa, 1920-32; Wash Hgts Cong, NYC, 1932-40; rabb cons, Beth Isr Hosp, since 1943, chaplain since 1947. Vice-pres, Manhattan region, RabCA; found: Agudath Kehiloth, 1920; Women's League for Traditional Judaism, 1921; Rabb Bd, 1922; Sinai Club for J Youths, 1926; Agudath Isr br, 1926, all Pittsburgh; mem, exec, Agudath Isr of Amer since 1939, vice-pres since 1961, mem, political comm and repr at UN, Agudath Isr World Org, since 1946;

pres, Conf Orthodox Rabbis of Amer, 1933-35; mem: NY Bd Rabbis, 1933, exec, 1940; RabCA, 1936, exec, 1938; Union Orthodox Rabbis, US and Can, 1948, exec since 1960; Union Orthodox J Congs of Amer, 1923; Histadruth Talmide Yeshiva Ungarn; Tomche Torah since 1938. Author: Roman vs Jewish Law, 1919; An Historic Review of the Laws of Kashruth, 1961. Home: 286 Ft Washington Ave, New York, NY. Office: NY State Kosher Adv Bd, 93 Worth St, New, York, NY.

FRIEDMAN, Tuviah Samuel, Isr, journalist; b. Radom, Pol, Jan 23, 1922; s. Jakob and Haya (Lender); att Us: Vienna, Zurich; m. Anna Guttman, Sep 14, 1952; c: Ronit. Found, dir, chief, Documentation Inst in Isr, since 1957; chmn, Intl J Org Nazis Sufferers; dir, Documentation Inst, Vienna, Aus, 1946-52. Partisan fighter, Pol, 1944; 1t, Pol Army, 1945-46; mem, Haganah, Vienna, 1946. Prin contrib: Caught about 2,000 war criminals who were brought to trial. Author: The Hunter, 1961; We ShallNever Forget, 1964; documentary pamphlets on Nazi criminals he caught; contbr to newspapers, mags. Recipient, medals: Haganah; War of Independence; Sinai; War Against Nazis; Six Day War; Lohamei Hamedina. Address: POB 4950, Haifa, Isr.

FRIEDMAN, Wilbur Harvey, US, attorney; b. NYC, Feb 5, 1907; s. Isidor and Zara (Sloat); AB, Columbia Coll, 1927; LLB, Columbia Law, 1930; m. Frances Margolis, May 21, 1943; c: Joan, Roy. Sr partner, Proskauer, Rose, Goetz and Mendelsohn, since 1955, solicitor gen, since 1932; law secy, US Supr Court, 1930-31; atty, Justice Harlan F Stone Off, 1931-32; lectr tax law. Vice-pres, NY Co Lawyer's Assn, fmr chmn: comm on taxation, comm on group ins; exec comm, NY State Bar Assn, sect on taxation; mem: Amer Bar Assn; Bar Assn, NYC; Phi Beta Kappa; Tau Delta Phi; clubs: Lotos; Columbia U. Author: Estate Tax Handbook; NYU Institute on Federal Taxation, 1943, 1965. Home: 1016 Fifth Ave, NewYork, NY. Office: 300 Park Ave, New York NY.

FRIEDMAN, William W, US, dentist; b. Zborov, Czech, Feb 1, 1920; BS, YMCA Coll, Chgo, 1940; DDS, Loyola U Dent Sch, Chgo, 1944; m. Geraldine Rosenbaum, Sep 10, 1944; c: Rochelle, Sandra, Joan. Pvt practice since 1946; mid-w chmn, Found Advancement Implant Research, since 1968. Vice-pres, Exras Isr Cong; chmn: JNF dent div; Isr Bonds, dent div; fmr: pres, secy, Chgo Acad Dent Research, mem: Amer Dent Assn; Amer Soc Implant Dent; Chgo Acad Dent Research; Alpha Omega. Author: Parent Approach to Child Patient, 1955; Personal Approach in Hypnosis, 1958; Dental Consideration in Pregnancy, 1960; The Aging Patient, 1962; Psychological Approach to the Difficult Patient, 1963; ed, Memorial Book, since 1956. Recipient: Asiatic, Pacific, Phillipine Liberation; American, Victory medals. Hobbies: writing, sculpturing. Home: 7417 N Talman Ave, Chicago, Ill. Office: 7442 N Western Ave, Chicago, Ill.

FRIEDMANN, Abraham, Isr, business exec; b. Haifa, Isr, Nov 6, 1905; s. Aaron and Sara; grad, HS of Commerce, Tel Aviv; m. Dvora Kook, Jan 22, 1929; c: Edna Tocatly, Izhak. Mgn dir, Isr Cen Trade and Inves Co Ltd, since 1954; chmn: Nesher-Cement Ltd; Urdan Metallurgical Works Ltd; Samson Tire and Rubber Co; bd dir: Swiss-Isr Ltd; Kitan Dimona Ltd; Leyland Triumph Ltd; Clal-Isr Inves Co; Consolidated Near E Co of Isr; Isr Chem Fibres Ltd; Ind Devl Bank of Isr; KBA Townbuilders Group, Ltd; hon consul of Finland in Isr. Bd dir: Mfrs Assn in Isr; Isr Port Auth; Friends Tel Aviv U; Friends Technion, Haifa; Wingate Inst for Phys Educ. Home: 26 King David Blvd, Tel Aviv, Isr. Office: 39 Lilienblum St, Tel Aviv, Isr.

FRIEDRICH, Salomon, Fr, journalist, communal worker; b. Rymanow, Pol, Apr 14, 1921; m. Shoshana Szrajbhand, Mar 17, 1950; c: Samuel, Ilana, Maurice. Dir gen: Alliance Fr-Isr; Comité de Solidarité Française avec Isr; pres, union of E Eur J; dir, Anti-racist World Union; mem: world exec, Herouth Hatzohar; Comité d'Action Sioniste. Home: 9 rue Parrot, Paris 12e, Fr.

FRIEND, Chaim H, US, organization exec; b. Atlanta, Ga, Oct 14, 1919; s. David and Celia (Elfenbein); MA, CCNY, 1941; att Cleveland Yeshiva, 1937-39; ordained rabbi, Yeshiva Rabbi Isr Meyer Hacohen, Bklyn, NY, 1942; div; c: Gil, Julie. Exec vice-chmn, Reform J App, UAHC-HUC-JIR, since 1965; dir, UJA, 1950-60; exec, Emerald Ptg, 1960-65. Member: ZOA. Home: 444 E 82 St, New York, NY. Office: 838 Fifth Ave, New York, NY.

FRIEND, Paltiel, US, rabbi; b. NYC, Dec 15, 1916; s. David and Celia (Elfenbein); BS, Bklyn Coll, 1942; MA, Yeshiva U,

1967; ordained rabbi, Rabb Sem of Amer, 1945; m. Goldie Blumenreich, Nov 20, 1944; c: Dvora. Dean, Yeshiva Gedola, Montreal, since 1968; instr, Yeshiva Rabbi David Leibowitz, 1957-65; rabbi, Young Isr of Bushwick, 1958-67. F, Ner David Rabb Grad Inst; licensed, NY Bd of Milah; mem: Union Orthodox Rabbis, US, Can; Alumni Org of Rabb Sem of Amer; Metrop Bd Rabbis; Young Isr Council of Rabbis. Contbr to rabb jours, asso ed, Haor, 1938-39. Home: 95 Clymer St, Brooklyn, NY. Study: 62-35 Hillsdale Rd, Montreal, Can.

FRIENDLY, Edwin S, US, newspaper exec; b. Elmira, NY, June 15, 1884; s. Myer and Sarah (Meyerfeld); m. Henrietta Steinmeir, Dec 26, 1914; c: Helen Foster, Edwin. Vice-pres, Westchester Co Publishers Inc, 1954-64; clerk, NY Times, 1909, financial advt mgr, 1911, asst bus mgr, 1913-22; bus mgr: NY Herald, later Herald-Tribune, 1922-24; The Sun, 1922-41, gen mgr, 1941-44; vice-pres, dir, 1944-50; vice-pres, NY World Telegram and Sun, 1950-54. Chmn, comm on advt agts, Amer Newspaper Publishers Assn, 1926-31; comm i/c bur of advt, 1932-41; US Victory Waste Paper Campaign, 1943-45; hon dir for life, BBB, NYC; dir: Advt Council; Brand Names Found; NY Conv and Visitors Bur; mem: natl advt council, Boston Conf on Distribution, 1968; bd govs, Hundred-Year Assn, NYC; club, Advt. Recipient: Dist Service Citation, Amer Newspaper Publishers Assn, 1946; citations: War Dept, Navy Dept, Va, ARC, War Production Bd, 1946. Hobbies: golf, riding, swimming. Home: Hotel Surrey, 20 E 76 St, New York, NY.

FRIENDLY, Henry J, US, jurist; b. Elmira, NY, July 3, 1903; s. Myer and Leah (Hallo); BA, Harvard Coll, 1923; LLB, Harvard U Law Sch, 1927; m. Sophie Stern, Sep 4, 1930; c: David, Joan Goodman, Ellen Simon. Judge, US Circuit Court, since 1959; law clerk to Justice Brandeis, US Supr Court, 1927-28; asso, Root, Clark, Buckner & Ballantine, 1928-36, partner, 1937-45; vice-pres, gen counsel, Pan Amer World Airways, Inc, 1946-59; partner, law firm, Cleary, Gottlieb, Friendly & Hamilton, 1946-59; Oliver Wendell Holmes Lectr, Harvard Law Sch, 1962. Trustee-at-large, FJP; fmr pres, Harvard Alumni Assn; mem: Council of Amer Law Inst; clubs: Harmonie; Harvard; Cent. Home: 1088 Park Ave, New York, NY. Office: US Court House, NewYork, NY.

FRIESNER, Simon, Eng, dental surg; b. Stanislavov, Pol, Jan 7, 1911; s. Leon and Berta (Gerner); in Eng since 1946; deg, dent surg U Strasbourg, Fr, 1937; m. Helena Roch; c: Irena Brauner. Dent surg, since 1937. Lt, dent corps, Pol Army. Chmn: Pol-J Ex-Servicemen's Assn; Beer Yaacov Children's Village Assn; vice chmn, Jabotinsky Inst, London; mem: exec, WJC, British sect; British Dent Assn; Friends Assn for Soldier's Wfr in Isr. Recipient: Monte Cassino Cross; Silver Cross of Merit; War Star; It Star; War Medal. Hobbies: photography, philately. Home: 100 Shoot-Up-Hill, London NW 2, Eng.

FRISCH, Leonard H, US, editor, publisher; b. Suvalki, Pol, Apr 20, 1890; s. Joseph and Sarah (Herman); in US since 1901; BA, U Minn, 1912; att U Montpellier, Fr, 1919; m. Bessie Miliman, Jan 15, 1928; c: Charles, Daniel. Ed, publisher, Amer J World, since 1912; supt, Minneapolis off, Galveston Immigration Bur, 1913-14. US Army, 1918-19. Vice-pres, Amer J Pres Assn, since 1952; pres: Talmud Torah, Minneapolis; ZOA; Minneapolis Fed for J Service, 1932-57; mem: Minn Newspaper Assn; Minneapolis C of C; B'nai Brith; AJCong; AJComm; Masons, Adath Jeshurun and Beth El Syns; club, Standard. Hobbies: hiking, fishing. Home: 4820 Hwy 7, Minneapolis, Minn. Office: 822 Upper Midwest Bldg, Minneapolis, Minn.

FRISHMAN, Daniel, US, scientist, inventor; b. Bklyn, NY, Oct 19, 1919; s. Michael and Anne (Shafter); BA, Bklyn Coll, 1940; MSc, Catholic U, Wash, DC, 1947, PhD, Georgetown U, 1950; m. Ruth Bolker, Feb 1, 1942; c: Michael, Steven, Laura, Robert. Tech adv, Reid Meredith, since 1965; project mgr, Harris Research Labs, 1951-55; dir, research and devl, Malden Mills, 1955-62; pres, dir research, Fibersearch Corp, 1962-65. Prin contrib: patented inventions relating to textile chem, textile prod, furs, hair pieces. Mem: Andover Sch Comm; NE bd, ADL; confchmn, Merrimack Valley Dialogues Inc; bd govs, Temple Emanuel, educ chmn, plastics comm, Jerusalem Econ Conf; fmr: chmn, bd trustees, trustee, Andover Public Libr; chmn, Andover Educ Conf; mem: Amer Chem Soc; AAAS; Fiber Soc; Amer Assn Textile Chem and Colorists; contbr numerous tech articles and patents. Recipient: Meritorious Service, Defense Dept, 1945; Andover Educ Assn, 1964. Home: 14 Castle Hgts Rd, Andover, Mass. Office: 300 Canal St, Lawrence, Mass.

FRISHMAN, Yitzhak, Isr, physicist; b. Zamosc, Pol, Sep 13, 1938; s. Nathan and Zippora (Weintraub); in Isr since 1949; BSc, Heb U, Jerusalem, 1962, MSc, 1964; PhD, with distinction, Weizmann Inst, Isr, 1966; m. Yehudit Goldberg, Mar 22, 1966. Sr physicist, Weizmann Inst since 1969; fmr: research asso, Stanford Linear Acceleration, 1966-68; mem, Inst for Advanced Study, Princeton, NJ, 1968-69. Sgt, IDF, 1956-59. Prin contrib: research in high energy physics and elem particles. Contbr to research reports. Office: Weizmann Inst of Sci, Rehovot, Isr.

FROCHT, Max M, US, educator, scientist, consulting engineer; b. Russ-Pol, June 3, 1894; s. Meyer and Eva (Egerwald); in US since 1912; BS, U Mich, 1922, PhD, 1931; MS, U Pittsburgh, 1926; hon LLD, Ill Inst of Tech, 1968; m. Dora Lipkin, Oct 16, 1918. Prof em, Ill Inst of Tech, since 1964, research prof, mech, dir, experimental stress analysis, 1946-64; fac, dept of mechs, Carnegie Inst of Tech, 1922-46; visiting lectr: Technion, Haifa; U Leningrad; U Moscow; Soc of ME, Warsaw; Jap Soc of ME, Tokyo, 1967. Princ contribs: presentation to Technion at Haifa, Isr photoelasticity collection of thousands of negatives and slides. F: AAAS; Amer Soc of Mech Engr; mem: Soc Experimental Stress Analysis, hon; AAUP; Amer Soc engr educ; Sigma Xi; Pi Tau Sigma; Tau Beta Pi; org, Intl Symposium on Photoelasticity, 1961, ed of proceedings. Author: Photoelasticity, Vol I, 1941, Vol II, 1948, trans, Russ, Span, Chinese; Strength of Materials, 1951; contrib numerous sci papers to jours. Recipient: Wm Murray Lectureship, Soc for Experimental Stress Analysis, 1959; Natl annual MM Frocht Award for highest achievement in educ of experimental mechs, SESA, 1968; publ, Selected Scientific Papers, from jt research with his colleagues, 1968. Home: Parker Dorado, 3180 S Ocean Dr, Hollandale, Fla.

FROESCHEL, George, US, novelist, playwright; b. Vienna, Aus, Mar 9, 1891; s. Salomon and Malvine (Engelsmann); in US since 1936; LLD, U Vienna, 1917; m. Elsa Schulke, Nov 6, 1922. Writer, MGM Studios, since 1939; ed, Ulstein Publs, Berlin, 1924-33. Cavalry off, Aus Army, 1911-18. Author: ten novels, three collections of short stories; screenplays: Waterloo Bridge; The Mortal Storm; Mrs Miniver; Random Harvest; Command Decision; Scaramouche; Story of Three Loves; Betrayed; Me and the Colonel. Club, Jewish. Recipient: Acad Award for screenplay, Mrs Miniver. Home: 1146 San Ysidro Dr, Beverly Hills, Calif.

FROESCHELS, Emil, US, physician; b. Vienna, Aus, Aug 24, 1884; s. Sigmund and Johanna (Tintner); MD, U Vienna, 1907; m. Gertrude Toepfer, Jan 7, 1915; pvt practice, specializing in speech and voice therapy, since 1912; hon prof, Pace Coll, since 1968; prof, ear, nose, throat dept, head, clinic for logopedics, U Vienna, 1924-38; research prof, Wash U, St Louis, 1939-40; dir, speech and voice clinic: Mt Sinai Hosp, NYC, 1940-49; Beth David Hosp, NYC, 1950-55. Fmr pres, Aus Soc for Phonetics; found, hon life pres, Intl Assn Logopedics and Phoniatrics; pres, NY Soc Speech and Voice Therapy, since 1947; f, Assn for Advancement of Psychotherapy; hon mem: Arg Soc Logopedics and Phonetics; Aus Otolo and Laryngo Soc; Pirquet Soc Clinical Med; life mem, AMA. Author: numerous books and articles. Recipient: Aus Cross of Hon. Home: 687 Lexington Ave, New York, NY. Office: 133 E 58 St, New York, NY.

FROHMAN, Dov Zisman, Isr, attorney, social worker; b. Bendzin, Pol, Nov 8, 1929; s. Arie and Ester (Traiman); in Isr since 1945; att Mikveh Isr Agric Sch, 1945-47; deg, profsl social worker, Sch of Social Work, Isr, 1952; MJur, Heb U, Jerusalem, 1962; m. Jona Klayner, June 21, 1955; c: Jehuda, Ester, Amnon. Dir, Youth Protection Auth, Min Social Wfr, since 1969; town dir, social services devl town, Beth Shemesh, 1965; dir, Haifa and N dist, Min Social Wfr, 1965; dir, Jerusalem and S dist, 1965-69. Social service br, IDF, 1952-56. Author: Law, Government and Services, 1963; Supervision, Tutorship, Consultation, 1967; What is Supervision in Social Services?, 1967. Home: 19 Herzog St, Jerusalem, Isr. Office: 18 Haemek St, Jerusalem, Isr.

FROMBERG, Gerald, US, artist, educator; b. Bklyn, NY, July 19, 1925; s. Charles and Anna (Feldman); BA, Bklyn Coll, 1946; att: Bklyn Mus Art Sch, 1949; New Sch for Social Research; MA, U of NM, 1951; m. Laverne Ray, Sep 13, 1952; c: Paul, Robert, Steven. Asso prof art, Bradley U, Peoria, Ill, since 1963; artist: Metro Assos Services, 1946-47; partner, Fromberg and Charles, 1947-49; Marwel Advt, 1949; Advt Aides, 1951; acting instr, U of Wash, 1952-53; instr, Dillard U, 1953-55. One-man shows: NM State Mus, 1951; U of NM,

1951; Henry Gal, Seattle, 1954; Contemporary Artists Gal, Peoria, 1956, 1960; Barone Gal, NY, 1957; N Ill U, 1959; Lincoln Coll, Ill, 1959; Bradley U, 1961, 1962; Lakeview Cen, Peoria, 1966; Bradley U, 1967; two-man shows: Contemporary Gal, Dallas, Tex, 1968; Fulton Gal, NY, 1969; group shows: Contemporary Arts Gal, NY, 1951, 1952; Northwest Annual, Seattle, 1953; Momentum Midcontinental, Chgo, 1954; New Cen Orleans Art Assn, 1954, 1955, 1956; 1955, 1961; Ill Valley Artists Annual, Peoria, 1955, 62; Audubon Artists Annual, NY, 1956, 1957, 1962; Butler Inst of Art, 1957; Denver Annual W Artists, 1958, 1962; Heart of Ill Fair, 1958, 62; Ill State Fair, 1961; Quincy Soc of Fine Arts Annual, 1961; Natl Exhb of Small Paintings, 1962; New Horizons in Sculpture, 1966; Ill Sculptors, 1968, 1970. Mem, Peoria Art Cen; fmr mem: Artists, Equity, bd dirs, Seattle chap; Coll Art Assn. Recipient: 1st prize, oil, Pacific NW Arts and Crafts Fair, Bellevue, Wash, 1952, 53, 54; medal of honor, oil, Audubon Artists, 1957; hon mention: Cen Ill Artists Annual, 1956, 57, 59; Ill Valley Annual, 1956, 3rd prize, 1961, 1st prize, 1963; 2nd prize: Peoria Art Cen Mem's Show, 1957, 1959, 1st prize, 1962, 1963; Heart of Ill Fair, 1958, 1959, 1st prize, 1962, 1963; 2nd prize, watercolor, Ill State Fair, 1961; 2nd prize, Natl Exhb of Small Painting, 1962; 1st prize, Peoria Art Guild Area Show, 1965. Hobby: golf. Home: 2024 S Mahark La, Peoria, Ill. Office: Bradley U, Peoria, Ill.

FROMCENKO, Abe Gerson, Isr, business exec; b. Porhov, Russ, Aug 4, 1916; s. Eliahu and Sophie (Kopilov); in Isr since 1934; BSc, Technion, 1938; m. Ruth Taube, Feb 28, 1946; c: Tamara Pelosoff, Livia. Pres, gen mgr, Elite Isr Chocolate & Sweets Mfg Co Ltd, since 1961; chmn of bd, The Nazareth Candy Co, since 1959. Exec comm, Isr Mfrs Assn. Home: 121 Rothschild Blvd, Tel Aviv, Isr. Office: 84 Arlozoroff St, Ramat Gan, Isr.

FROMM, Alfred, US, business exec ; b. Ger, Feb 23, 1905; s. Max and Mathilda (Maier); in US since 1938; att Viticultural Acad, 1921; m. Hanna Gruenbaum, July 5, 1936; c: David, Carolynn. Pres, dir, Fromm & Sichel Inc, since 1944. Dir WJC; United HIAS Service; St Mary's Coll, Assos; Temple Emanu-El; vice-pres, JNF; vice-chmn, Cal Med, Clinic for Psychotherapy, trustee, SF Conservatory Music; clubs: Commonwealth; Concordia. Contbr to trade jours. Home: 850 El Camino del Mar, San Francisco, Cal. Office: 1255 Post St, San Francisco, Cal.

FROMM, Herbert, US, composer; b. Kitzingen, Ger, Feb 23, 1905; s. Max and Mathilde (Maier); in US since 1937; MA, State Acad of Music, Munich, 1930; hon, DHumL Lesley Coll, Mass, 1966; m. Leni Steinberg, Jan 22, 1942. Music dir, Temple Isr, Boston, since 1941; conductor: Civic Theatre: Bielefeld, 1930-31; Würzburg, 1931-33. Composer: works for: orch; organ; liturgy for syn; songs; chamber music; cantatas; choral cycles; recordings: The Crimson Sap; Organ Partita; String Quartet. Mem: AJComm; Amer Guild Organists; fmr, music dir, Temple Beth Zion, Buffalo, NY. Author: The Key of See, travel jours of a composer, 1966. Recipient: Ernest Bloch Award, Ernest Bloch Soc, 1945. Spec interest, lit. Home: 94 Addington Rd, Brookline, Mass. Office: 270 Riverway, Boston, Mass.

FROMM, Paul, US, business exec; b. Kitzingen, Ger, Sep 28, 1906; s. Max and Lea (Stiebel), in US since 1938; m. Erika Oppenheim, July, 1938; c: Joan Greenstone. Pres: Greeting & Fromm, since 1939. Pres, Fromm Music Found; bd mem, Chgo Inst for Psychan; secy, Ill Arts Council; bd dirs: Ill Mh Planning Bd, J Children's Bur; mem: citizens' comm, U of Ill; visiting comm Harvard U; Carnegie Inst; adv council, Princeton U; visiting comm, U of Chgo; gov bd, chgo Sym; Boston Sym; bd, Family Inst of Chgo. Hobby: music. Home: 5715 S Kenwood Ave, Chicago, Ill. Office: 1028 W Van Buren St, Chicago, Ill.

FROSH, Stanley B, US, attorney; b. Denver, Colo, Jan 9, 1919; BS, Northwestern U, 1939, JD, 1942; m. Judith Wirkman, May 7, 1943; c: Brian, Robin, Wendy. Partner, law firm Frosh, Lane, Edison, since 1970; chmn bd, State Natl Bank, since 1970; with bank since 1958; mem, Law Firm, Camalier, Frosh, Sperling, and Dorsey, 1943-70; chief rent atty, Chgo Regional Off, OPA, 1942-43; practiced law in: Wash DC, 1945; Montgomery Co, Md, 1949; fmr lectr: intl law, Amer U, Wash DC, 1945-47; for USIA, Dept of State in Ethiopia, Sierra Leone, Kenya, Nigeria, Korea, Formosa, Vietnam, Philippines. US Army, 1942-45, adj, 400th Armored Field Artillery Batallion, 1942-43. Pro-tem, Montgomery Co Council, 1961-62; Independent Lodge, Metrop Council, B'nai B'rith, 1950-52; vice-pres: State Natl Bank, Bethesda, Md, since 1959; bd regents, The Bridge, Intl U, 1966-68; mem: Natl Panel

Arbitrators, Amer Arbitration Assn; Montgomery Co Council, 1958-62; Montgomery Co and DC Bar Assns; Metrop Wash Council of Govts; Natl Assn Co Officials, 1958-62; Masons; mem, bd dirs: Comty Chest and Council, Wash Metrop Area, 1948-57; J Comty Cen of Gtr Wash, since 1958; Gibraltar Bldg and Loan Assn, 1962-68; Wash Housing, Planning Assn, 1962-66; gen counsel, Intl Club of Wash DC Inc, since 1962; Montgomery Co C of C, 1962-66; Montgomery Co Chap, ACLU, since 1967. Home: 6100 Bradley Blvd, Bethesda, MD. Office: 1430 K St, NW, Washington, DC; Natl Bank Bldg, Bethesda, Md.

FRUCHTER, Benjamin, US, educator; b. NYC, Aug 31, 1914; s. Nathan and Fannie (Freilich); BA, Bklyn Coll, 1936; MA, U of S Cal, 1946, PhD, 1948; m. Dorothy Sewell, Sep 18, 1944; c: Jonathan, Judith, David. Prof, educ, psych, research sci, U Tex, since 1949; cons, Psych Research Service Inc, since 1956; teaching f, lectr, guidance counselor, research worker, dept psych, U of S Cal, 1945-48; asso dir, research, USAF Hum Resources Research Cen, San Antonio, Tex, 1948-49; cons, NASA, 1964-66. USAAF, 1942-45. Pres: SW Psych Assn, 1965-66; Soc of Multivariate Experimental Psych, 1966-67; f: Amer Psych Assn; AAAS; mem: Intl Assn Applied Psych; Psychometric Soc; Psychonomic Soc; Assn for Computing Machinery; Amer Educ Research Assn; Sigma Xi. Author: Introduction to Factor Analysis, 1954; contbr to psych books, profsl jours. Home: 2704 Valley Springs Rd, Austin,Tex. Office: Bridgeway Hall, 301 U of Tex, Austin,Tex.

FRUHAUF, Henry, US, admn exec; b. NYC, Jan 24, 1923; s. Henry and Belle (Sohmer); att: U of Va, 1939-41; Columbia U, 1939; F Temple Admn, Bd of Cert of Temple Admns, 1964; m. Frances Falk, July 3, 1943; c: William. Comptroller, Cong Emanu-el of NYC, since 1950; spec asst, Fgn Funds Control, Off Secy of Treasury, 1942; trainee, Underwriters' Trust Co, 1941-42. US Army, 1942-45. Vice-pres, NY Chap, AJComm; vice-chmn, Comty Council; secy, Benjamin N Cardozo Lodge, B'nai B'rith, 1959; mem, exec bd, AJComm; mem: Natl Assn Temple Admns; Natl Assn Church Bus Admnr. Author: Temple Finance and Reserve Funds, 1968. Home: 310 E 70 St, New York, NY. Office: 1 E 65 St, New York, NY.

FRUMKIN, Jacob, US, organization exec, attorney; b. Kovno, Russ, Oct 1, 1897; s. Gregory and Gitla (Rapaport); in US since 1941; first class law deg, US St Petersburg, 1903; att U Berlin, 1899; 1901; U Heidelberg, 1902; m. Helene Natanson, Nov 3, 1908; c: Nina, Gregory. Dir, NY off, World ORT Union, since 1948; mem, ORT, Russ, since 1906, head control comm, 1911-12, chmn, Berlin comm, 1920; vice-pres, World OSE Union, 1924; Jt ORT-OSE Comm, 1926, Fr, 1939-41, NY, 1941-45; pvt law practice, St Petersburg, 1904-1918; asso, Pravo, law weekly, 1904-18; mem, political adv comm to J Deps of the Fourth Duma, 1914-18; mem exec, Ulstein Publ House, Berlin, 1922-35; hon legal adv, J Comty, Berlin, 1937-39. Chmn, Union of Russ J, NY, mem, exec comm,1956; mem: Amer ORT Fed. Co-ed, Set of essays,Russian Jewry,1860-1917; Russian Jewry, 1917-67. Home: 50 W 77 St, New York, NY.

FRUMKIN, Jacob, US, urologist; b. N Adams, Mass, Feb 20, 1905; s. Max and Katie (Greenberg); AB, Union Coll, 1927; MD, Albany Med Sch, 1931; m. Dolores Haley, Oct 3, 1953; c: Maxine, Kim, Daniel. Chief, urol, Ellis Hosp; att urol: St Clare Hosp; Northeastern Orthopedic Hosp; cons: Saratoga Hosp; Schenectady City Hosp. US Army, 1941-45. F: Amer Coll Surgs; Intl Coll Surgs; Intl Acad Med; dipl, Amer Bd Urol; mem: Amer Urol Assn; Northeastern Urol Assn; Elks. Contbr to med jours. Home: 1220 Lexington Ave, Schenectady, NY. Office: 1005 Union St, Schenectady, NY.

FRUMKIN, Yadin, Isr, business exec; b. Rehovot, Isr, June 15, 1911; s. Gad and Hanna (Eisenberg); BA, Trinity Coll, Cambridge U, 1931, Dipl Agric, 1932, MA, 1934; m. Esther Nathan, Jan 1, 1953; c: Naomi, Raphael, Ron, Daphna. Exec, Electro-Vista Ltd, since 1966; secy, Pal Cold Storage and Supply Co, 1936-40; mission to It for UNNRA 1946; head quartermaster dept, Isr Police Force, 1948-53; mgn dir, Delta Trading Co Ltd, Tel Aviv, 1953-66. Maj, Brit Army, 1940-46. Bd dirs, BBB; mem Isr Consumer Council; club, Rotary, pres, 1953-54. Recipient: Mention in Despatches. Home: 5 Hagefen St, Neve David, Tel Aviv, Isr. Office: 10 Shefa Tal St, Tel Aviv, Isr.

FRYDMAN, Avraham, Isr, business exec; b. Pol, May 23, 1918; s. Josef and Sheva (Librader); in Isr since 1938; att: Haschola U Warsaw, Heb U Jerusalem; m. Irka Levartowski, Sep 30, 1948; c: David, Ruth. Head, admn and org div, Isr Ports Auth, since 1963; personnel mgr, Hamashbir Hamerkazi, 1957-63. Staff off, IDF, 1948-57. Hobbies: sport, photography.

Home: 2 Maoz Aviv, Tel Aviv, Isr. Office: 74 Petah Tikva Rd, Tel Aviv. Isr.

FRYE, Peter, Isr, theatre, film dir, educator; b. Montreal, Can, May 8, 1914; s. Yaakov and Celia (Schildkraut) Prebluda; in Isr since 1953; div; c: Michal; m. 2nd. Found, dir, theatre workshop, Tel Aviv U since 1957; produc, dir, Peter Frye produc Ltd, since 1958; writer, produc, dir for CBS, NBC; actor, scripter, dir, NY Theatre, Radio, TV; dir, CBS TV series, Lamp Unto My Feet, 1950-51; produc, Kol Israel, 1956-66; artistic dir, Ohel Theatre, 1964-65, 1967-69; produc, dir, films: I Like Mike; The Hero's Wife; screenwriter, produc, Hill 24 Doesn't Answer; playwright, If I Die; produc, dir, adaptations: Ibsen's Ghosts, 1965; Lessing's Nathan the Wise, 1966; Shalom Aleichem's Napoleon's Treasure, 1968; dir, produc, designer, numerous plays. Recipient: Tchemerinsky Award for best dir, Habima Theatre, 1959; Klausner Award, 1961. Home: 11 Zeitlin St, Tel Aviv, Isr. Office: 45 Weizmann St, Tel Aviv, Isr.

FUCHS, Abram Moshe, Isr, author; b. Jezierna, Aus, Oct 17, 1892; s. Chaim and Feiga; in Isr since 1950; m. Sonia Poltun, 1915 (decd); c: Lola Carr. Co-ed, lit critic, various Yiddish lit periodicals and newspapers; corresp, NY J Daily Forward, Vienna, Cen Eur, 1915-38. Hon pres, Yiddish Writer's Assn in Isr; mem, PEN Club. Author: Einzame, 1912; Bergel; Unter Brik, 1924, 1928; Begoim, 1946; Tehom Pevar, 1954. Recipient: lit awards, world J leading cultural orgs. Home: 209 Hadar Josef St, Tel Aviv, Isr.

FUCHS, Lawrence H, US, political sci, educator; b. NYC, Jan 29, 1927; s. Alfred and Frances (Fuchs); BA, NYU, 1950; PhD, Harvard U, 1955; m. Natalie Rogers, June 5, 1950; c: Janet, Frances, Naomi. Prof, Amer Civilization and politics, Brandeis U, since 1963, on leave as dir, Peace Corps, Philippines, 1961-63, dean fac, 1960-61, chmn, dept politics, 1959-60, on fac since 1952; vice-pres, Educ Devl Cen, 1966-68. Served, USNR. Mem: adv bd, Inst for Study of Mediterranean Affairs, since 1956; comm on law and social action, AJCong since 1955; ACLU; NAACP; United World Federalists; Amer Political Sci Assn. Author: John F Kennedy and American Catholicism, 1967; Those Peculiar Americans, 1967; Amer Ethnic Politics, 1968; The Political Behavior of American Jews, 1956; Hawaii Ponoi: A Social History, 1961; contbr to profsl jours. Recipient: sr grant in Amer Govt Processes, Social Research Council, to dir research in racial conflicts and accommodation in Hawaiian politics, 1958-59. Home: Ellis Rd, Weston, Mass. Office: Brandeis U, Waltham, Mass.

FUCHS, Yehuda, Isr, actor; b. Rumania, Nov 15, 1919; s. Martin and Margaret (Kish); in Isr since 1940; m. Nina Weshler; c: Ofra Manor, Edna. Actor, Cameri Theatre, since 1958; mem mgmt, since 1968. Mem, Isr Artists Union. Home: 44 Basel St, Tel Aviv, Isr. Office: Cameri Theatre, Tel Aviv, Isr.

FUCHSBERG, Jacob D, US, attorney; b. NYC, June 14, 1913; s. Max and Gussie (Stern); LLB, NYU 1935; m. Shirley Cohen, Oct 31, 1937; c: Rosalind, Susan, Janet, Alan. Partner, law firm: Fuchsberg and Fuchsberg, since 1952; Cohen and Fuchsberg, 1937-50; pvt practice, 1950-52. Pres: J Comty Cen, Harrison, 1957-62, hon pres, since 1962; Amer Trial Lawyers Assn, 1963-64; Amer Trial Lawyers Found, since 1964; NY State Assn Trial Lawyers, 1957-59; NYU Law Rev Alumni Assn, 1956-58; chmn: Comm 100 for Dem Party, since 1965; Trial Lawyers Div, FJP, NY, since 1958; Speakers' Bur, FJP, 1964-66, since 1968; Public Employees Bd, NY State, since 1968; Natl War Fund, 1943-45; ARC Dr, NY State, 1943-45; UJA, NYC, 1950, 1952; natl publs comm, Natl Assn Claimants Counsel of Amer, 1961-63; grand chancellor, KP; vice-pres, ZOA, White Plains, NY, 1952-53; dir: St Agnes Hosp, since 1966; 92nd St Y, since 1967; Amer Arbitration Assn, since 1966; John F Kennedy Libr for Minorities, since 1967; Intl Syn John F Kennedy Intl Airport, NY, since 1962; fmr bd mem, Presbyterian Lab Temple; mem: Amer Bar Assn; NY State Bar Assn; NY Co Lawyers Assn; Bar NYC; Metrop Trial Lawyers Assn; adv bd, Legal Services Prog, OEO, since 1966; club, Mamaroneck Yacht. Ed, NY Ency of Damages, 3 vols. Recipient, Awards: Benjamin N Cardozo; B'nai B'rith Torch of Freedom. Home: 60 Sutton Place S, New York, NY. Office: 250 Broadway, New York, NY.

FUERST, Harold T, US, physician; b. NYC, May 21, 1909; s. Sigmund and Edith (Guenzberg); BA, Cornell U, 1929; MD, Jefferson Med Coll, Phila, 1933; MPH, Columbia U, 1958; m. Edith Wiener, June 14, 1940; c: Barbara. Prof, preventive med, asso prof ped, NY Med Coll; chief, preventive med service, Metrop Hosp; asso att ped, Metrop Hosp; Flower-Fifth Ave Hosp, both NYC. US Army MC, 1942-46.

Dipl, Amer Bd Preventive Med; mem: Soc for Epidemiologic Research; AHA Council on Epidemiology; Amer Public Health Assn; AMA; AAAS; NY Acad Sci; Phi Epsilon Pi; Phi Delta Epsilon. Contbr to profsl jours. Home: 45 Kew Gardens Rd, Kew Gardens, NY. Office: Dept of Health, 125 Worth St, New York, NY.

FUKS, Alexander, Isr, educator; b. Wolclawek, Pol, May 30, 1917; s. Abraham and Mindla (Linke); in Isr since 1935; MA, Heb U, Jerusalem, 1942; PhD, 1946; post-doc studies, Oxford U, 1952; m. Bela Judelowicz, Nov 12, 1943; c: Gideon, Rachel, Abraham. Prof, ancient hist, classics, Heb U, Jerusalem, since 1962, on fac since 1949. Lt, IDF, 1948-49. Vice pres, Inst Cultural Relations, Isr-Greece; mem: Mosad Bialik; Isr Hist Soc; Brit Sch of Archaeol, Athens. Author: The Ancestral Constitution, 1953; The Athenian Commonwealth, 1957; co-author, Corpus Papyrorum Judaicarum, I II, III, 1957-64; contbr to profsl jours. Home: 6 Alkalai St, Jerusalem, Isr. Office: Hebrew U, Jerusalem, Isr.

FUKS, Lajb, Netherlands, librarian; b. Kalisz, Pol, Dec 29, 1908; s. Joel and Hinda (Wolkowicz); att: Rabb Sem, Tachkemoin, Warsaw; U Liege; U Nancy; U Brussels; PhD, U Amsterdam; m. Gertrud Manfeld; c: Nadja, Simon. Keeper, Bibliotheca Rosenthaliana, Libr, U Amsterdam, since 1949; lectr, U Amsterdam. Author: The Oldest Known Literary Documents of Yiddish Literature, 1382, pub, 1957; The Medieval Yiddish; Epos Melokiun Buk, 1965; De Seven Provincies in beroering. Ust de Yiddische Krouiek van Abraham Chaim Braatbard, 1740-1752, pub 1960; Anthol, Meesters der Yiddische vertelkunst, 1959; Posthumous ed of Felix Falk, Das Semuelbuch, 1961; ed, Studia Rosenthaliana, bi-annual jour for J Culture and Hist. Office: Singel 425, Amsterdam, Netherlands.

FULD, James J, US, attorney; b. NY, Feb 16, 1916; s. Gus and Banche (Weill); BA, Harvard, 1937, LLB, 1940; m. Elaine Gerstley, Sep 14, 1942; c: Joan, James, Nancy. Partner, Proskauer, Rose, Goetz & Mendelsohn, since 1952. US Army, 1942-46. Chmn, corp law comm, NY Co Lawyers Assn; trustee: FJP, NY; Fed Employment and Guidance Service; mem, exec comm AJComm, NY chap; Phi Beta Kappa; club, Sunningdale Country, pres, 1956-59. Author: American Popular Music, 1955; A Pictorial Bibliography of First Editions of Stephen C Foster, 1957; The Book of World-Famous Music, 1966; contbr to legal jours. Recipient: Commendation Medal, US Army. Hobbies: bibliography and collecting first ed printed music. Home: 1175 Park Ave, New York, NY. Office: 300 Park Ave, New York, NY.

FULD, Stanley H, US, jurist; b. NYC, Aug 23, 1903; s. Emanuel and Hermine (Frisch); BA, CCNY, 1923; LLB, Columbia U, 1926; hon LLD: Hamilton Coll, 1949; Columbia U, 1959; Union Coll, 1961; Yeshiva U, 1962; NYU, 1963; JTSA, 1964; Syracuse U, 1967; m. Florence Geringer, May 29, 1930; c: Hermine Nessen, Judith Miller. Chief Judge, State of NY and chief judge, Court of Appeals, State of NY, since 1967; asso judge, since 1946; pvt practice, 1935-55; asst dist atty, NY Co, 1935-44. Mem: NYC, Amer Bar Assns; Amer Law Inst; trustee, Cent Syn chmn, bd, JTSA; trustee, Sara Delano Roosevelt House; bd dirs, B'nai B'rith; Phi Beta Kappa; NY Practicing Law Inst. Contbr to law jours. Home: 30 Park Ave, New York, NY. Office 36 W 44 St, New York, NY.

FULDHEIM, Dorothy Ulmer, US, author, news analyst; b. Passaic, NJ; d. Herman and Bertha (Wishnev) Snell; tchrs cert, Milw Coll, Milw, Wis, 1912; m. William Ulmer; c: Dorothy. New analyst, WEWS-TV, since 1947; bradcaster eds, Brotherhood RR Trainmen, 1946-47. Mem: League Women Voters; Womens' Sym; Hadassah; clubs: Natl Press; Cleveland Press. Author: I Laughed, I Cried, I Loved, 1965; Where Were the Arabs? 1967. Recipient: Angel Award, 1957; George Wash Hon Medal, 1955; Awards: Civic, 1958; Aftra, for outstanding personality, Amer Fed of TV, 1959; Natl Headliner, Theta Sigma Phi, 1965; Taylor Conway, for Fearless Reporting, 1965; Isr Freedom Medal, Bonds for Isr, 1968; Ment Award for fearless Bc; O State Fed of Women's clubs; Overseas Press Club Award for fgn corresp. Home: 2480 Kenilworth St, Cleveland Heights, O. Office: 3040 Euclid Ave, Cleveland O.

FULOP, Leslie Simha, Isr, business exec; b. Deregske, Hung, June 4, 1922; s. Alexander and Ilona (Benedek); in Isr since 1944; licence de droit, U Law, Debrecen, Hung, 1942; m. Miranda Volpi, Nov 20, 1952; c: Guy. Gen mgr, Beged-Or Ltd, since 1958; repr, Intercontinental Forwarding Co, Budapest, Zurich, 1946-47; vice-pres, Fukaraw Italiana, Milano, 1950-53; mgr, Afacom Ltd, 1953-56. Lt, IS, IDF, 1947-50.

Recipient: Grand Prix Semain de Boutique, Paris, 1964; Intl Fashion Award, Las Vegas, 1965. Home: 5 Derech Habeer, Kfar Shmariyahu, Isr. Office: Migdal Haemek, Isr.

FUNKE, Lewis B, US, drama editor; b. Bx, NY, Jan 25, 1912; s. Joseph and Rose (Keimowitz); BA, NYU, 1932; m. Blanche Bier, July 5, 1938; c: Phyllis, Michael. Drama ed, NY Times, since 1944. Mem: Newspaper Guild; Cong Emanuel, Mt Vernon. Co-author: Actors Talk About Acting; Max Bordou Presents; A Gift of Joy; contbr to periodicals. Office: NY Times, 229 W 43 St, New York, NY.

FURMAN, John, Isr, investment banker; b. London, Eng, July 16, 1915; s. William and Fanny (Hurwitz); in Isr since 1958; att London U; f, Inst of CAS, London, 1931-36; m. Sonia White, Dec 18, 1938; c: Dina, Roger. Chmn, mgn dir, Furman Asso Ltd, Investment Bankers; since 1968; pres, PEC Isr Econ Corp, 1963-68; exec vice-pres, 1958-63; Isr Amer Devl Bank, 1955-58; comptroller-gen, Zim-Isr Navigation Co, 1949-56; group secy, Charterhouse Group, London, 1946-48; partner, Sinclair Furman and Co, 1937-46. Lt Col, Brit Army, 1939-46; Rav-Seren, Intelligence br, IDF, 1948-49. Vice-pres, Isr Cancer Assn; mem: bd: govs and exec comm, Tel Aviv U; dirs: Isr-Amer C of C; Isr-Amer Soc; mem: CPAs of Isr; clubs: Caesaria Golf; Naval and Mil, London. Author: Be Not Fearful, 1959. Home: 55 David Hamelech Blvd, Tel Aviv, Isr. Office: POB 29305, Tel Aviv, Isr.

FURMAN, Norman Benjamin, US, business exec; b. Rachev, Russ, 1900; s. Mordechia and Ethel (Smargow); in US since 1909; att J Tchrs Sem, 1916-18; m. Helen Weir, Dec 11, 1960. Gen mgr, radio sta, WEVD, since 1963; found, mem, Feiner Advt Agcy, since 1935; found; owner, mgr, sta WKNY, 1939-43; gen mgr, sta WBMS, 1952-57. Hon chmn, PR, UJA; vice-chmn, treas, HIAS Council of Orgs; bd dirs, Histadrut; mem: Intl Radio and TV Soc, NYC; Yiddish Theatrical Alliance, NYC; club, Amer-Isr, found, pres. Recipient, Cavaliere, It Legion of Merit, 1967. Home: 60-11 Broadway, Woodside, NY. Office: 1700 Broadway, New York, NY.

FURST, Milton, US, rabbi, organization exec; b. Bklyn, NY, Sep 16, 1922; s. Adolph and Anna (Steiner); BA, magna cum laude, Yeshiva Coll, 1943; ordained rabbi, Rabbi Isaac Elchanan Theol Sem, 1946; m. Beatrice Bick, Oct 29, 1946; c: Zev, Malka, Aryeh. Asst to dean, Rabbi Isaac Elchanan Theol Sem, Yeshiva U since 1965, dir alumni activities, 1959-65; dir comty org, comty service div, 1954-58; rabbi, Young Isr, Malden, Mass, 1947; prin, Yeshiva, Spring Valley, NY, 1948; exec dir, Gtr NY Hapoel Hamizrachi, 1949-52; natl dir, League for Rel Lab in Isr, 1952-53. Vice-pres, Rel Zionists of Amer, 1964-66; natl exec bd, RabCA, fmr co-chmn, Isr comm; exec comm, AZC; fmr: natl bd dirs, JNF; comm on org, AZC; vice pres, Hapoel Hamizrachi of Amer. Fmr ed, J Horizon. Home: 2208 Woodhull Ave, Bronx, NY. Office: Yeshiva U, Amsterdam Ave at 186 St, New York, NY.

FURST, Sidney Selig, US, physician; b. NYC, Sep 21, 1921; s. Isidore and Goldie (Kreiger); BS, O State U, 1943; MD, Yale U Sch of Med, 1951; m. Ina Hodes, Sep 11, 1949; c: Jonathan, Daniel, Seth. Prof dir, Psychoanalytic Research and Devl Fund, since 1963; visiting prof, pastoral psycht, JTSA, NY, since 1961; att phys, Montefiore Hosp, NY, since 1965; spec research f, Natl Inst of Mh, 1954-56; fac mem, Dept of Psycht, Coll Phys and Surgs, Columbia U, 1954-65. USN, 1944-46. Mem: Amer Psycht Assn; Amer Psychanalytic Assn; NY Psychanalytic Soc; Group for Advancement of Psycht; Cen for Advanced Psychanalytic Studies, Princeton; AAAS; Isr Psychanalytic Soc; Amer Phys F, IMA. Author: Psychic Trauma, 1967; contbr numerous papers in biochem, neurochem, psycht jours. Recipient: Borden Award, med research, Yale U Sch of Med, 1951. Home and office: 4670 Waldo Ave, New York, NY.

FUSHAN, Louis Marcus, attorney, bus exec; b. Pittsburgh, Pa, Feb 26, 1902; s. Peter and Rena (Gilberg); BS, 1923; LLB, U Pittsburgh, 1925; JD, U Pittsburgh, 1969; m. Rena Meth, Apr 25, 1943; c: Nancy, Peter, Paul (decd). Secy, counsel, Fed Drug Co, since 1937; vice-pres, secy, counsel, Fed-Rice Drug Co, since 1951; pvt practice, 1925-37. Exec council, Amer J Hist Soc; natl pres, Phi Epsilon Pi Frat, 1931-32, 1934-37; pres, Cap and Gown Club, U Pittsburgh, 1933-34, secy since 1936; Cent Club; U of Pittsburgh; B'nai B'rith; hon, Omicron Delta Kapp Hon Soc since 1945; Pa and Allegheny Co Pharm Assn; Pa and Allegheny Co Bar Assn. Co-author: Musical Play Books for Cap & Gown Club; lyricist of musical compositions, 1921-47. Home: 618 Morewood Ave, Pittsburgh, Pa. Office: 947-49 Penn Ave, Pittsburgh, Pa.

G

GAATHON (Gruenbaum), Arye L, Isr, economist; b. Eisenach, Ger, Dec 24, 1898; s. Arnold and Philippine (Stettauer) Gruenbaum; in Isr since 1934; DRerPol, summa cum laude, U Berlin, 1934; m. Tamar Jungerman, Oct 18, 1938; c: Ariel. Sr econ, Bank of Isr, since 1955; fmr: research econ, lab dept, Econ Research Inst of JA for Pal; dir, dept econ research, PMs off; sr econ, econ adv staff, headed by Oscar Gass; UN f for econ research in US. Ger Army, 1916-19. Charter mem, Isr corresp, Intl Assn of Research in Income and Wealth. Author: National Income and Outlay in Palestine, 1936; Outline of a Development Plan for Jewish Palestine, 1946; Four Year Development Plan, 1950-53, in Heb, 1951; Survey of Israel, 1950, in Heb, 1951; Survey of Israel's Economy, 1951, in Heb, 1959; Capital Stock, Employment and Output in Israel, 1950-59, in Heb and Eng, 1961; contbr to Isr, fgn publs. Recipient: Bar-Ely Prize, Histadrut, 1961. Home: Beit Levy, Shkhunat Ben Zion, Jerusalem, Isr. Office: Bank of Isr, Jerusalem, Isr.

GABA, Morton J, US, organization exec; b. Chgo, Ill, Feb 27, 1912; s. Herman and Rose (Gaba); BA, U of Cal, 1934, MA, 1935; m. Thelma Kahn, Oct 9, 1937; c: Jeffrey, Hal, Joelle Lawson. Exec dir, JWF of New Orleans, since 1966; asso prof, Tulane U Sch of Social Service, since 1969; bd dirs, Natl Assn J Communal Service Officials, since 1969; SF J Vocational Guidance Bur, 1937-40; dir, USO—JWB, 1940-42; comty services dir: War Relocation Auth of Cal and Ariz, 1941-42; Vallejo Housing Auth, 1943-44; regional dir, CJFWF, 1944-48; exec dir, JCC of Norfolk, 1948-58; exec dir, JCF, Long Beach, Cal, 1958-66. Pres, Cal state council, Natl Assn Social Workers, 1964-65; mem: Acad Cert Social Workers; Natl Conf J Communal Service, bd dirs since 1969; B'nai B'rith; Pi Lambda Phi. Home: 3301 State St Dr, New Orleans, La. Office: 211 Camp St, New Orleans, La.

GABEL, Hortense W, US, attorney, public official; b. NYC; d. Reuben and Bessie (Goldberg) Wittstein; BA, Hunter Coll; LLB, Columbia U Law Sch; m. Milton Gabel; c: Julie. Urban cons since 1966; admnr, NYC Rent and Rehab Admn, 1962-65; research atty, NY State C of C, 1935; mem, law firm, Wittstein and Wittstein, 1936-41; asst corp counsel, NYC, 1942-44; dir, NY State Comm Against Discrimination in Housing, 1948-54; gen counsel, Temporary State Housing Rent Commn, 1955-56; dep state rent admnr, 1956-59; asst to dep mayor, 1959; asst to mayor, 1960-62; delg, NY State Constitutional Conv, 1967. Mem: Natl Gov Council, AJCong; Natl Housing Conf; Citizens Housing and Planning Council; NY Bar Assn. Contbr to profsl jours. Home and office: 210 E 68 St, New York, NY.

GABER, Irena, Isr, artist; b. Lwow, Pol; d. Isser and Regina (March) Silberman; in Isr since 1958; att Music Inst; studied painting, both Cracow; studied with: Prof Fenkowicz, Prof Schorr, both Tel Aviv; m. Leon Gaber, Dec 25, 1925. One-man shows: Yad leBanim House, 1968; Beit Mania Bialik, 1968; exhb, Alharizi Festival, 1969; fmr: worked with Mrs St Domanska and K Dejanek, Natl Theatre, Jehenia G ra, 1946-56; exhbs in Pol. Mem: Isr Painters Org. Home: 20 Gotlieb St, Tel Aviv, Isr.

GABRIEL, Kuno Ruben, Isr, educator; b. Berlin, Ger, Mar 24, 1929; s. Ernst and Ilse (Saaro); in Isr since 1935; BSc, econ, LSE, 1950; PhD, Heb U, Jerusalem, 1957; postdoc, U of NC, 1957-58; m. Ayala Langerman, July 16, 1965; c. Orna, Osnat. Chmn dept, prof, stat, Heb U, since 1968; asso prof since 1967; fmr: acad stat tchr, Heb U; research asso, visiting prof: U of NC; U of Kan; Princeton U. Sgt maj, IDF, 1950-53. Prin contribs: research work, stat; cons to Isr artificial rainfall experiment. F: Amer Stat Assn; Royal Stat Soc; Inst of Math Stat. Author: Nuptality and Fertility in Isr, 1961; contbr to profsl jours. Home: 23 Hechalutz St, Jerusalem, Isr. Office: Heb U, Jerusalem, Isr.

GABRIEL, Mordecai L, US, biologist, educator; b. NYC, Mar 18, 1918; s. Joseph and Bertha (Fram); BA, Yeshiva U, 1938; MA, Columbia U, 1938; PhD, 1944; m. Elinor Rosenstein, Nov 11, 1945; c: Alisa, Jessica. Chmn, biol dept, Bklyn Coll, since 1965, prof since 1963; asst, lectr, zool, Columbia U, 1938-42, visiting asso prof, zool, 1956; instr, genet, U of Conn, 1943-45; f, Ford Found, 1954-55; Fulbright prof, U of Tel Aviv, 1959-60. Mem: NY Acad Sci; AAAS; Amer Assn Anats; Amer Soc Zool; Soc for Study of Evolution; Sigma Xi. Co-author: Great Experiments in Biology; contbr to profsl jours. Home: 120 Old Mill Rd, Great Neck, NY. Office: Bklyn Coll, Brooklyn, NY.

GABRILOVE, Jacques Lester, US, physician, educator; b. NYC, Sep 21, 1917; s. Benjamin and Pauline (Levine); BS, magna cum laude, CCNY, 1936; MD, NYU Med Coll, 1940; m. Hilda Weiss, May 19, 1946; c: Sandra, Janice. Att phys, Mt Sinai Hosp, since 1968, fmr: resident, med, 1943-44, Blumenthal f, 1946-48, research asst, 1949-51, asst att phys, 1952-60, asso att phys, 1960-68; asso clinical prof, med, Mt Sinai Sch Med, since 1966; clinical prof, med, SUNY, since 1966, on staff since 1957; cons, endocrinology: VA Hosps, E Orange, Bx; Elizabeth A Horton Memorial Hosp, Middletown, NY. Mem, panel on metabolic and rheumatoid diseases, US Pharmacopeia XVL, since 1956; f: Amer Coll Phys; NY Acad of Med; dipl, Amer Bd of Internal Med; mem: NY Co Med Soc; AMA; NY Acad of Sci; AAAS; NY Diabetes Assn; Harvey Soc; Endocrine Soc; Amer Diabetes Assn; hon mem, Peruvian Endocrine Soc; Phi Beta Kappa; Alpha Omega Alpha; rel sch bd, brotherhood bd, Cen Syn; club: Lotos. Author: Diseases of the Endocrine Glands, 1951, 2nd ed, 1956; The Human Adrenal, 1961; mem ed bd, Jour of Mt Sinai Hosp; contbr to sci jours. Hobbies: music, art. Home: 25 E 86 St, New York, NY. Office: 79 E 79 St, New York, NY.

GADIESH, Falk, Isr, business exec; b. Berlin, Ger, June 27, 1921; s. Max and Ilse (Hahn) Grunfeld; in Isr since 1935; BSc, dipl ing, Isr Inst of Tech, 1945; MSc, MIT, 1954; m. Pnina Margalit, Sep 18, 1947; c: Orit, Talya. Mgn dir, Isr Chem Fibres Ltd, since 1965; asst to pres, Bradley Container Corp, Mass, 1954-55; gen mgr, United Saran Plastic Co, 1955-60; exec, Isr Cen Trade and Inves Co, 1961-62. Col, IDF, 1952. Chmn, Ind Mgmt Comm, Isr Mfrs Assn; exec comm: Isr Productivity Inst; Isr Mgmt Cen, 1960-67. Home: 23 Ehud St, Zahala, Isr. Office: Isr Chem Fibres Ltd, Ashdod, Isr.

GAER, Joseph, US, author, organization exec; b. Rum, Mar 16, 1897; s. Solomon and Naomi (Scholnick); in US since 1917; m. Fay Ratner, Mar 14, 1923; c: Elsa Luce, Paul. Exec dir, J Heritage Found LA, Cal, since 1958; ed, quarterly, Recall, since 1959; lectr, contemporary lit, U of Cal, 1930-35; ed-in-chief, Fed Writers Project, WPA, 1935-39; cons to admnr, Farm Security Admn, 1939-41; spec asst to US Secy, Treas, 1941-43; publs dir, CIO political action comm, 1941-44; found dir, Pamphlet Press, div of Reynal & Hitchcock, 1945-46; pres, Gaer Asso Publ Co, 1946-49. Author: numerous books between 1926 and 1963 inclu_ing: How the Great Religions Began, 1930; The Wisdom of the Living Religions, 1956; The Jewish Bible for Family Reading, 1957; co-author, Our Jewish Heritage, 1957; ed, Our Lives: American Labor Stories, 1948; contbr: natl and c's mags; Schaff-Herzog Ency of Rel Knowledge; The Universal J Ency. Life mem, Intl Inst of Arts and Letters; mem, Screen Writers' Guild. Spec interest: folklore. Home: 201 San Vicente Blvd, Santa Monica, Cal.

GAFNI, Abraham J, US, attorney; b. Bklyn, NY, June 29, 1939; s. Reuben and Betty; att Heb U, 1959; BHL, Yeshiva U, Tchrs Inst, NY, 1960; AB, Yeshiva Coll, NY, 1960; JD, Harvard Law Sch, 1963; m. Miriam Stern, Aug 6, 1961; c: Jonathan, Rachel. Pvt practice: NY, Pa, since 1963; law asst, Superior Court, Pa, 1965; gen atty, sec, 1963-65. Vice-pres, C W Henry Home & Sch Assn; dir: Germantown J Cen, sch chmn; bd, J Educ, both Phila; mem: Phila, Pa, Amer, NY State Bar Assns; clubs: Lawyers, Phila; Harvard Law

Sch Alumni. Home: 6605 Wayne Ave, Philadelphia, Pa. Office: Bankers Securities Bldg, Philadelphia, Pa.

GAFNI, Israel, Isr, business exec; b. Bessarabia, Rum, July 3, 1926; s. Zevulun and Malvina (Perelmuter); in Isr since 1933; MA, econ, Heb U, Jerusalem; m. Edna Amador, 1955; c: Eran. Gen mgn dir: Isr Loan and Savings Bank Ltd, since 1968; Ind and Commerce Bank Ltd, since 1969; dep dir, Natl Savings Auth, 1950-60. Fmr: vice-pres, C of C; chmn, mgmt cen, both Jerusalem. Hobbies: tennis, skin-diving. Home: 8 Kaf Tet Benovember St, Tel Aviv, Isr. Office: Israel Loan & Savings Bank, Tel Aviv, Isr.

GAFNI, Shlomo Simcha, Isr, business exec; b. Jerusalem, Isr, Jan 5, 1932; s. Pinchas and Miriam (Diskin); att Heb U, Jerusalem, 1950-53; m. Chana Zelnik, Jan 17, 1952; c: Yael, Ruth. Gen mgr, Jerusalem Pub House Ltd, since 1956; fmr dir to dep min, Min of Ind and Commerce; repr: Isr Ind Ltd; cultural mission to Latin Amer, JA. IDF, 1947-48. Home: 3 Sokolov St, Jerusalem, Isr. Office: 17 Abravanel St, Jerusalem, Isr.

GAFNY, Arnon, Isr, economist, business exec; b. Tel Aviv, Isr, July 14, 1932; s. Simha and Shoshana (Lifschitz); BA, Bard Coll, NY, 1952; MSc, econ, Heb U, Jerusalem, 1956; m. Mira Arshavski, Aug 6, 1953; c: Ron, Nili, Shlomit. Port mgr, Port Ashdod, since 1967; research worker, econ, Falk Found, 1954-57; chief asst, budget div, Min of Finance, 1958-61; head, commercial and econ dept, Isr Ports Auth, 1961-67. Lt, IDF, 1952-54. Mem, Rotary, Ashdod. Home: 6 Silver St, Ashdod, Isr. Office: Port of Ashdod Mgmt, Isr.

GAGUINE, Maurice, Eng, minister; b. Cairo, Egypt, Mar 9, 1919; s. Shemtob and Rosa (Blattner); in Eng since 1919; BA, U of Manchester, 1944, PhD, 1965; m. Alma Azriel, 1945; c: Denise Myers, Linda. Min, Withingtons Cong Span and Port Jews, since 1946; asst min, Ramsgate Syn, 1939-40; acting min, Withington Cong, 1941-46. Pres, Withington J Lit Soc; chmn, Manchester J Hosp Visitation Bd; mem: Chaplaincy Commn, NW Regional Hosp Bd; Worshipful Master, Menorah Freemasons, 1968-69. Author: The Falasha Version of Testaments of Abraham, Isaac and Jacob. Hobbies: carpentry, landscaping, electronics. Home: 32 Sandileigh Ave, Manchester, Eng. Study: Queen's Rd, Manchester, Eng.

GAIFMAN, Haim Zvi, Isr, mathematician; b. Rovno, Pol, Sep 26, 1934; s. Mordechai and Sofia (Singer); in Isr since 1936; MSc, with hons, Heb U, Jerusalem; PhD, with hons, U of Cal, Berkeley, 1962; m. Hana Arieh, June 25, 1969. Asso prof, math, Heb U, Jerusalem, since 1968, on staff since 1963; Ritt instr, Columbia U, 1962-63; visiting asso prof, UCLA, 1967-68. IDF, 1952-54. Prin contribs: research with Prof Carnap, foundations of probability; with Prof Tarski, math logic and Boolean algebras; set theory. Author: Infinite Boolean Polynomials, 1964; Pushing up Measurable Cardinals, 1967. Home: 23 Habanai St, Jerusalem, Isr. Office: Math Dept, Heb U, Jerusalem, Isr.

GAINES, Samuel, US, surgeon; b. Russ, Aug 20, 1896; s. Joel and Ada (Spector) Ginzburg; in US since 1905; BA, Columbia Coll, 1918; MD, Columbia Coll of Phys and Surgs, 1920; m. Adeline Rosen, June 19, 1932; c: Linda Kaufman, Julie. Surg, Trafalgar Hosp, since 1960; Grand Cen Hosp, 1930-62; Hosp and Home, Daughters of Isr, since 1940. Pres, NY Phys Soc, 1950; mem, Natl Gastroealerological Assn. Home: 1025 Fifth Ave, New York, NY. Office: 81 E 79 St, New York, NY.

GAIS, Elmer S, US, physician; b. Syracuse, NY, Oct 30, 1900; s. Reuben and Hannah (Manson); BS, med, Syracuse U, 1922, MD, 1924; m. Olga Fab, Feb 25, 1943; c: Ruth. Asso prof, clinical med, NYU; visiting phys, Bellevue Hosp; cons phys, Knickerbocker Hosp; asso att phys: U Hosp; Montefiore Hosp, NYC; research f, path, Michael Reese Hosp, Chgo, 1924-26; house phys, Mt Sinai Hosp, NY, 1926-28, research asst, biochem, Inst for Veg Physiology (Prof Embden), Frankfurt-am-Main, Ger, 1928-29. Col, US Army MC, 1942-46. F, Amer Coll Phys; mem: AMA; AAAS; NY Acad Med; NY Acad Scis; ADA; Endocrine Soc; Phi Kappa Phi; Alpha Omega Alpha; Phi Delta Epsilon. Home: 200 E 71 St, New York, NY. Office: 923 Fifth Ave, New York, NY.

GAISON, Nathan, Can, advertising exec; b. Montreal, Can, Aug 14, 1906; s. Hyman and Dora (Geller); m. Sadie Kert, June 7, 1932; c: Daniel. Advt exec, Herald Woodward Press Inc, since 1944. Chmn, E region, Can J Cong; mem: Shaar Hashomayim Syn, fmr pres, Men's Assn; Montefiore Club; fmr: hon secy, ZOC; dir, United Talmud Torahs of Montreal,

1964-68. Recipient: Centennial Medal, Can Govt, 1967. Home: 4885 Montclair Ave, Montreal, Can. Office: 970 McEachran Ave, Montreal, Can.

GALAI, Benjamin, Isr, author, poet, publicist, playwright; b. Russ, Apr 10, 1921; in Isr since 1926; m. Rachel Yishuvi, 1947; c: Shaul. Columnist, Ma'ariv newspaper. Author: poetry: Im haRuach; Shiva Shlishit; Armonim, 1968; Mishte Aramilus, 1969; prose: Atalefei Acco, 1962; Masa'i le'Eretz haGmalim, 1963; Maim Gnuvim, 1964; Divrei Yemei Gemini, 1968; publicist, Al Kafe Hafuch; playwright: Mahazot, 1960, plays performed: Sipur Uriya, Actors' Stage, 1967; Sdom City, Haifa Munic Theatre, 1968; HaBetula miRoma, Kameri Theatre, 1969. RAF, 1940-46; IDF, 1948-56. Recipient: awards: Brenner, Lamdan, Ramat Gan Munic; Anne Frank; Fichman. Home: 111 Hatishbi St, Haifa, Isr.

GALBAR, Emmanuel, Isr, diplomat; b. Vienna, Aus, 1917; s. NM and Sara (Wischnitzer) Gelber; in Isr since 1934; MA, Heb U, Jerusalem, 1946; m. Carmela Kipper, July 2, 1942; c: Yoav, Michal. Isr ambass, Sierra Leone, since 1967; fmr: Isr ambass to Rep of Nigeria; dir: admn, El Al Airlines; Ouman Inds, Devl Corp, Tel Aviv; mgn dir, Isr Plywood Plant. J Brigade, Brit Army; col, chief supply off, IDF; dep controller, Min of Defense. Hobbies: hist, music. Home: 15 Gonen Tet St, Jerusalem, Isr.

GAL-EDD, Israel, Isr, civil servant; b. London, Eng, Apr 23, 1920; s. Samuel and Ann (Mandel) Greenstein; in Isr since 1949; BA, Birkbeck Coll, London U, 1940; assn, chartered inst of secys, N Poly, London, 1949; dipl, intl taxation, Harvard U, 1960; m. Pearl Markovitch, Jan 9, 1944; c: Ann, Jonathan. Dir gen, Min of Devl, since 1966; sr ext lectr, Heb U, Jerusalem, since 1963; chmn: Dead Sea Works Ltd; Dead Sea Bromine Co; Chems and Phosphates Ltd; Tovala Ltd; Rogosin Enterprises of Isr Ltd; vice-chmn, Isr Chems Ltd; bd mem: Arad Chem Inds Ltd; Isr Elec Co Ltd; fmr: HM Insp of Taxes of Inland Revenue, UK; asst to commn of income tax, State of Isr; chief insp of taxes, Haifa; prin dep commn of income tax; dep commn of State revenue; dep dir gen, Min Commerce and Ind, all Govt of Isr. Staff sgt, Royal Elec and Mech Engrs, 1942-46. Chmn, adv comm, Assn Brit Immigrants to Isr, past chmn, adv council; comm mem, Isr br, Intl Fiscal Assn; mem, Inst of Acctnts of Isr; fmr mem world exec, Intl Fiscal Assn. Contbr to profsl jours. Recipient, Sir Enoch Hill prize, second place, world examination competition, 1949. Hobby, choral music. Home: 34 Alharizi St, Jerusalem, Isr. Office: Min of Devl, 38 Keren Hayesod St, Jerusalem, Isr.

GALGUT, Oscar, S Afr, jurist, Supreme Court Judge; b. Pretoria, S Afr, July 29, 1906; s. Philip and Freda (Rutowitz); BA; LLB; m. 1st, Rose Glasser, div, c: Brian, Glenda Cleaver; m. 2nd, Helen Cooper, 1963. Judge, Supr Court of S Afr since 1957; fmr: atty, notary, conveyancer, pvt practice; patent and trade mark agt; barrister-at-law. Lt col, pilot, S Afr Air Force, 1940-46. Fmr: chmn, Pretoria Bar Council; exec mem, Gen Council of Bar of S Afr; chmn: Young Isr Soc; S Afr Air Force Assn; clubs: Pretoria Golf, fmr capt; Pretoria; Pretoria Country; Zwartkops Country; Harlequin; Wanderers; Pretoria HS Old Boys. Recipient: OBE; mentions in dispatches, WW II. Hobby, sports. Home: 110 Lawley St, Waterkloof, S Afr. Office: Palace of Justice, Pretoria, S Afr.

GALILI, Israel, Isr, government official; b. 1911; in Isr since 1914. MK; minister without portfolio since 1965; fmr: head, Haganah command, until 1948; dep min of defense, 1948-49; secy, Ahdut HaAvoda. Home: Kibbutz Naan, Isr.

GALINSKY, Mailen, US, rabbi; b. Hartford, Conn, May 19, 1936; s. Judah and Leah (Halpern); ordained rabbi, Rabbi Jacob Joseph Theol Sem, 1957; att Bklyn Coll; MRE, Yeshiva U, 1960; m. Sonia Intrator, Aug 14, 1963; c: Adina, Judah, Dov, Devora, Ephraim. Rabbi, Sea Gate Sisterhood Talmud Torah Cong Sharei Zedek since 1957; dean, Yeshiva Sharei Zedek Heb Acad since 1957; asst dir, JA, Amer sect since 1969; chaplain, Kings Co Council of JWV; weekly radio prog, Tales of Yore, WEVD, NY. Asst dir, Torah Education and Culture Dept JA, Amer Sect, since 1969; natl exec bd, Rel Zionists of Amer; exec bd mem: Rabb Alliance, fmr vice-pres; Rel Observance Comm, RC; RabCA. Home: 4491 Surf Ave, Brooklyn, NY. Study: 2301 Mermaid Ave, Brooklyn, NY. Office: 515 Park Ave, New York, NY.

GALITZER, Philip, US, attorney; b. Novoselitz, Russ, Apr 20, 1901; in US since 1907; s. Hyman and Breine (Shutzberg); dipl, acctnt, CCNY, 1924; LLB, NY Law Sch, 1927; BS, educ, Fordham U Tchrs Coll, 1938; JSD, Bklyn Law Sch, 1939; CPA, St Lawrence U, 1940; m. Rose Rolnick, Feb 21,

1932; c: Bernice Cohen, Sylvia Goldstein, Sidney. Pvt law and CPA practice; admitted to practice, NY State, and Fed courts; Supr Court, 1964; lectr, dept acctnt, CCNY, since 1929. Dir, J Cen of Kings Hwy, Inc; trustee, Unity Friendship League, fmr: pres, vice-pres; fmr, chmn, bd dir, trustee, Cong Z'Chor L'Abraham; mem: NY Co Lawyers Assn. Author: Actuarial, Depreciation and Bonus Problems, 1941; Consolidation Principles & Techniques Briefed, 1945; Bonus Problems and Solutions; also numerous articles on J topics; contbr to legal jours. Recipient: Medal in penmanship; merit award, Remington Typewriter; gold medal award, shorthand championship team. Home and office: 1514 E 10 St, Brooklyn, NY.

GALLICO, Edoardo A, It, physician, educator; b. Mantua, It, Nov 26, 1920; s. Isacco and Diana (Castelfranchi); MD, U of Lausanne, 1945; post-grad studies, U of Milano, med radiology, 1948, chest diseases, 1950. Asst prof, Milan U since 1950; staff mem, Natl Cancer Inst since 1951; chief, radiological dept, Mil Hosp, Milan, 1949; British Council Scholarship at Royal Cancer Hosp, London, 1950; It Scholarship for Cancer Research, La Tumor Inst, Cal, 1954; researcher, Beilinson Hosp, Isr, 1956. Mem: Société Vaudoise des Sciences Naturelles; Società Italiana di Biologia Sperimentale; Società Italiana di Radiologia Medica; Biochem Soc; J Cmty of Mantua. Author, Cancerologia, 1961; contbr to med jours. Hobby, fencing, fmr, Swiss and British U fencing champion. Home: Via Boccaccio 24, Milan, It.

GALLILY, Ruth, Isr, biologist; b. Tel Aviv, Isr, June 19, 1927; d. Isaac and Branka (Turteltaub) Dror; MS, Heb U, Jerusalem, 1952; PhD, 1955; m. Isaiah Gallily, Dec 6, 1953; c: Yael, Ofra, Tamar. Research f, chem since 1967; research asso, Weizmann Inst since 1959; research f, Sloan Kettering Inst, 1956-57; research asso: U of Ill, 1957-58; Johns Hopkins U, 1962-64. IDF, 1957-59. Prin contribs: studies, genet and chemotherapeutic aspects of cancer; cellular studies of the immune response. Mem: Sigma Xi, Cal Inst of Tech. Co-author, Germinal Center in Immune Responses, 1967; contbr to profsl jours. Office: Weizmann Inst of Sci, Rehovot, Isr.

GALLINGER, Joseph S, US, rabbi, editor, publisher; b. Wittelshofen, Ger, Mar 13, 1912; s. Louis and Bertha (Lindo); in US since 1938; ordained rabbi, Yeshiva, Frankfurt/M, Ger, 1937; BAE, U of Fla, 1940, MA, 1943; DLitt, Burton Coll, Colo, 1957; m. Anne Schellenberg, Oct 22, 1936; c: Laura Denaburg, Lynn Rosemore. Found, ed, publisher, The Jewish Monitor since 1948; rabbi, Temple B'nai Isr, Florence, Ala, since 1957; rabbi: Valdosta Heb Cong, Ga, 1940-48; Temple Beth-El, Bessemer, Ala, 1948-57. Dir, US Army Sch for Interrogators of Prisoners of War, 1942-43. Pres: B'nai B'rith, Ala State Assn, 1961-62, fmr: lodge pres, state secy; pres, Ala State Alumni Assn, U of Fla; mem: ZOA; AJComm; Mh₁ Assn; Hum Relations Council; club, Kiwanis. Author: Militaerwissenschaftliche deutsche Sprachslehre, 1942; Der Jude in den Werken Gustav Freytags, 1943; The Pulpit Club, 1957. Home: 4133 Montevallo Rd, POB 9155, Birmingham, Ala. Study: 201 Hawthorne St, POB 448, Florence, Ala.

GAL-OR (Galler) Benjamin, Isr, educator; b. Afula, Isr, Aug 8, 1933; s. David and Atarra (Kanderor); BSc, Technion, Haifa, 1959, MSc, 1961, PhD, 1964; m. Leah Schulwolf, Sep 1958; c: Amir, Gillad. Asso prof: Technion since 1968; U Pittsburgh since 1966, sup research, teaching, grad schs, both insts; fmr: asst prof, post-doc f, Johns Hopkins U, Baltimore. Lt, IDF, 1951-53. Prin contribs: in field of gas-liquid; two-phase flows with mass heat transfer; boundary-layer theory; non-equilibrium thermodynamics; foundations of classical and relativistic thermodynamics. Session chmn, Engr Founds Research Conf, mixing oprs, Proctor Acad, NH, 1969; participant in intl confs on chem, aerospace engr; mem: Sigma Xi; Amer Acad Arts and Scis; past chmn, Isr Students and Scholars Org, Pittsburgh. Author: sect in book, Advances in Chemical Engineering, 1968; contbr to sci jours. Spec interests: phil of Spinoza; gen relativistic thermodynamics; theory of knowledge. Home: 72 Pinsker St, Haifa, Isr. Office: Technion, Haifa, Isr.

GAL-OR, Leah, Isr, engineer; b. Bucovina, Rum, Sep 6, 1936; d. Herman and Jetty (Sonnenschein) Schulwolf; in Isr since 1950; BSc, Technion, Haifa, 1959, MSc, 1964, DSc; m. Benjamin Gal-Or, Sep 1958; c: Amir, Gillad. Corrosion engr since 1968, Technion, 1961-64; research asst, Johns Hopkins U, Baltimore, Md, 1964-66; research asso, U of Pittsburgh,

1966-68. Lt, IDF Navy, 1959-61. Mem, Isr Chem Soc. Home: 72 Pinsker St, Haifa, Isr. Office: Technion, Haifa, Isr.

GALSTON, Arthur W, US, biologist, educator; b. NYC, Apr 21, 1920; s. Hyman and Freda (Saks) Goldstein; BS, Cornell U, 1940; MS, U of Ill, 1942, PhD, 1943; hon MA, Yale U, 1955; m. Dale Kuntz, June 27, 1941; c: William, Beth. Prof, plant phys, Yale U since 1955; asso prof, Cal Tech, 1951-55, fac mem since 1947. USN, 1944-46. Pres: Amer Soc Plant Phys; Botanical Soc Amer; chmn, comm on meetings, AAAS; past: secy-treas, Intl Assn Plant Phys; exec bd, Fed Amer Sci; mem, Amer Soc Biol Chems. Author: The Life of the Green Plant; The Green Plant; co-author, Principles of Plant Physiology, 1952; contbr to sci jours. Spec interest, woodwind instruments. Home: 307 Manley Hts, Orange, Conn. Office: Yale U, New Haven, Conn.

GALUN, Aryeh Baruch, Isr, chemist; b. Katovitz, Pol, Feb 4, 1924; s. David and Erna (Markus); in Isr since 1933; att Heb U, 1942-47; MSc, PhD, Ill U, 1952-55; m. Rachel Rabinovitch; c: Eyal, Merav. Chief chem, dir, Zion, Chemical Products since 1960; chem, Defence Min, 1948-50. I/c research, IAF, 1950-57. Author of articles on polymers and organic syntheses in fields of diphenylmethanes, fluorocompounds, indole derivatives. Home: 29 Ben-Zvi Blvd, Ramat Gan, Isr. Office: POB 51, Yavneh, Isr.

GALUN, Ezra, Isr, scientist; b. Leipzig, Ger, Apr 7, 1927; s. David and Erna (Markus); in Isr since 1933; MSc, Heb U, 1953, PhD, 1959; m. Margalit Katz, May 3, 1953; c: Eithan, Ehud. Asso prof, Weizmann Inst of Sci, sr sci, 1962-67, on staff since 1953; research f: Cal Inst Tech, 1960-62; Harvard U, 1967-68. Capt, IDF. Chmn, Isr Genet Soc, 1964-67; mem: Amer Soc Plant Phys; Sigma Xi. Contbr to sci jours. Home: 12 Hankin St, Rehovot, Isr. Office: Weizmann Inst, Rehovot, Isr.

GALUN, Margalith, Isr, educator, biologist; b. Vienna, Aus, Feb 21, 1927; s. Arie and Amalia (Teitelbaum) Katz; in Isr since 1939; MSc, Heb U, Jerusalem, 1953, PhD, 1960; m. Ezra Galun, May 3, 1953; c: Eithan, Ehud. Sr lectr, Tel Aviv U, since 1969; fmr: researcher, Isr Min of Defense; research asso, Cal Inst of Tech. Prin contrib, in field of lichen biol and floristics. Mem: Brit Lichen Soc; Amer Soc of Lichen; Isr Soc of Botany. Contbr to profsl jours. Home: 12 Hankin St, Rehovot, Isr. Office: 155 Herzl St, Tel Aviv, Isr.

GAMS, Andrija, Yugo, attorney, educator; b. Subotica, Yugo, 1911; s. Aleksander and Julia (Klopfer); LLD, U of Belgrade, 1938. Prof, law fac, U of Belgrade, mem fac since 1948; pvt practice until 1941. Fmr, mem: gen comm, Fed J Comtys, Yugo; Zionist Youth orgs; Hashomer Hatzair. Author: Responsibility for the Acts of Third Persons in Civil Law, 1940; Introduction to Civil Law, 6 eds; Elements of the Law of Property, 5 eds; Familial Patrimonial Law, 1966; contbr to legal and social sci jours. Home: Nevesinjska 17, Belgrade, Yugo. Office: Fac of Law, Blvd Revolucije 67, Belgrade, Yugo.

GAMSO, Hyman W, US, attorney, public official; b. Bklyn, NY, Feb 8, 1906; s. Nathan and Mary (Shubitz); LLB, Bklyn Law Sch, 1927; m. Blanche Kaye, Aug 30, 1942; c: Marjorie, Jeffrey. Chief clerk, Appellate Div, NY Supr Court, First Jud Dept since 1965; law clerk, Watson, Harrington & Sheppard, 1924-28, mgn atty, 1928-36, partner, successor firm, 1936-38; dep co clerk and acting counsel, NY Co, 1938-65; lectr: Practicing Law Inst; NYU Law Sch; St Johns Law Sch; Pohs Inst; law assns; legal adv, Selective Service Bd No 21, WW II; mem, evacuation div, NYC Off of Civilian Defense, 1946-65. Pres, NY State Assn of Commnr of Jurors, 1954-55; judge, J Conciliation Bd of Amer since 1950; dir, chmn, forum comm, NY Co Lawyers Assn, 1955-61; mem: Assn of Bar, NYC; Amer Bar Assn; NY State Bar Assn; NY Law Inst; Amer Judicature Soc; Inst of Judicial Admn; Civil Service Reform Assn; ZOA; J Chautauqua Soc; pres, Cong Shaaray Tefila; Grand St Boys Assn; Masons, then mem, Grand Lodge of State of Isr; mem, NY Golden Jubilee Comm, 1948; club, Men's of Shaaray Tefila, pres, 1960-63. Asst ed, NY Law Jour, off publ since 1957, asst ed, 1932-57; contbr to legal publs. Home: 175 W 93 St, New York, NY. Office: 60 Centre St, New York, NY.

GAMZU, Haim, Isr, museum curator; b. May 19, 1910; att Sorbonne; Inst d'Art, Paris; PhD, Vienna U; m. Hava Schwartz; three children. Dir, chief curator, Tel Aviv Mus since 1962; theater critic, Haaretz, Heb daily. Author: Painting and Sculpture in Israel; Ten Israeli Painters; Life and Work of Chana Orloff; The Sculptor Ben Zvi; The Song of the Quetzal. Home: 22 Hamarganit St, Ramat Gan, Isr. Office: Tel Aviv Mus, Helena Rubenstein Pavilion, Tel Aviv, Isr.

GANG, Irving Lloyd, US, attorney; b. Passaic, NJ, Oct 13, 1922; s. Solomon and Jennie (Rosenberg); BA, Amherst Coll, 1943; LLB, Yale Law Sch, 1949; m. Ruth Jacoby, Mar 28, 1950; c: Stephen, Meredith, Laura. Partner, Sullivan and Sullivan, Gang, and Woods, 1960-63; pvt practice, 1951-55; partner, Gardner and Williams, 1956-57; pvt practice, 1958-60. USAAF, 1943-46, lt, USAF Res, 1949-52. Chmn: Montclair Planning Bd, 1962-68; pres, Passaic Valley Citizens Planning Assn, 1957-60; pres: Aheka Council, Boy Scouts of Amer, 1961-64; trustee: Family and Children's Soc, Montclair, 1960-62; Essex Co Chap, AJComm since 1960; bd dirs: Passaic Chap, ARC, since 1968; YM-YWHA, Passaic, Clifton, 1954-58; Appalachian Highlands Asso, 1969; mem: Amer Bar Assn; NJ Bar Assn; Passaic Co Bar Assn; NJ State Commn to Study Meadowland Reclamation, 1965-67; Comm on Second Regional Plan, 1967-68; pres, Passaic Co Legal Aid Soc, 1963-67; clubs: Shelter Island Yacht; Pennington; Amherst, NY; Yale, Montclair; Rotary. Home: 4 Greenview Way, Upper Montclair, NJ. Office: 174 Gregory Ave, Passaic, NJ.

GANNES, Abraham P, US, educator; b. Winograd, Ukraine, June 10, 1911; s. Harry and Libba (Antonoff) Ganepolsky; in US since 1921; BA, CCNY, 1933; MA, Columbia U, 1938; PhD, Dropsie Coll, 1952; m. Miriam Jacobson, Aug 29, 1936; c: Judith Fleisig, Howard. Dir, dept educ and culture, JA since 1968; exec dir: Bur J Educ, Miami, 1944-49; Phila Council on J Educ, 1949-56; Heb tchr: Marshaliah Heb HS, NY; U of Miami, 1947-49; chmn, admn comm, fac mem, Gratz Coll, 1949-56. Pres: Natl Council for J Educ, 1967-69; Histadrut Ivrit, Phila, 1954-56; Alumni Assn, Dropsie Coll, 1956-58; vice-pres: Marshaliah Heb HS of NY; treas, Natl Conf J Communal Service, 1958-60; mem: ZOA. Author, Central Community Agencies for Jewish Education; ed, Selected Writings of Leo L Honor. Contbr to J and educ publs. Hobby, camping. Home: 110-35 72 Rd, Forest Hills, NY. Office: 515 Park Ave, New York, NY.

GANOR, David, Isr, attorney; b. Tel Aviv, Aug 6, 1919; s. Abraham and Simha (Romano) Mizrachi; family on father's side in Isr more than 300 yrs; dipl, law, Govt Law Sch, Jerusalem, 1947; m. Shulamith Elkana, Tel Aviv, Jan 1, 1953; c: Ephrat, Boaz. Pvt practice, notary, lawyer. Capt, info dept, mil prosecutor, IDF. Secy gen, Isr Numismatic Soc; mem: Chamber of Advocates; Isr Natl Mus. Author, Criminal Law and Procedure in Israel, 1957. Hobbies: antiquities, glass, coins. Home: 12 Byron St, Tel Aviv, Isr. Office: 21 Lillienblum St, Tel Aviv, Isr.

GANS, Fritz (Bedrich), Isr, obstetrician; b. Trautenau, May 20, 1898; s. Julius and Josefine (Zeissl); in Isr since 1940; MD, Ger U, Prague, 1923; m. Ilse Benzian, May 30, 1949; c: Walter. Ret, fmr: head, dept obstet and gyn, Public Hosp, Trautenau; phys i/c, pvt practice, Hadera; head, dept obstet and gyn, Cen Emek Hosp, Afula; head, dept obstet and gyn, Beilinson Hosp, Petach Tikvah; pvt practice, specializing in obstet and gyn, Tel Aviv; clinical asst prof, obstet and gyn, Heb U, Jerusalem. Lt, Aus-Hung Army, 1916-1918. F, Intl Coll Surgs; mem: Intl Fertility Assn; IMA; Isr Soc of Obstets and Gyns. Contbr to profsl jours. Home: 22 Zahal St, Petach Tikvah, Isr.

GANS, Jerome A, US, physician; b. Cleveland, O, Dec 24, 1915; s. Arthur and Annette (Mansky); AB, O State U, 1934; MD, W Reserve U, Cleveland, 1938; m. Bernice Gold, May 16, 1948; c: Beverly, Lawrence, Richard. Chief, dept ophthal, Mt Sinai Hosp of Cleveland since 1958; pvt practice since 1946; instr, eye surg, U of Chgo, 1941-43; sr clinical instr, eye surg, W Reserve U, 1953-62. US Army MC. Prin contribs: automatic visual field apparatus, 1960; holder of 3 US patents in med elecs. Chmn, ophthal sect, O State Med Assn; trustee, Cleveland Found; found pres, Tower Lodge, B'nai B'rith; mem: Sci Rev Bd, Med Research Engr; Amer Bd Ophthal; Amer Acad Ophthal and Otolaryngology; Assn for Research in Ophthal; Amer Coll Surgs; Pan Amer Assn Ophthal; Cleveland Acad Med; AMA; Mt Sinai Hosp of Cleveland Med Soc; Phi Delta Epsilon; clubs: Amer Legion; Masons; Cleveland Ophthal. Contbr to profsl jours. Home: 22500 S Woodland Rd, Shaker Heights, O. Office: 1020 Huron Rd, Cleveland, O.

GANY, Lydia Pincus, Isr, stage designer; b. Bucharest, Rum, March 24, 1929; d. Joseph and Bertha (Leibovitz) Pincus; in Isr since 1960; att Acad of Fine Arts, Bucharest; m. Pesach Gany, Oct 19, 1956; c: Yael, Iayr. Stage designer for Isr Theatres since 1960; designed sets and costumes: for Habimah, Cameri, Ohel, Godik theatres and Purim Festival, dance festivals; Army Theatre; Natl Theatre, Rum; Dance Ensemble Carmen, Olympia, Paris. Mem, Intl Theatre Inst. Home: 4 Irith St, Tel Aviv, Isr.

GANY, Pesach, Isr, archivist, publicist; b. Panciu, Rum, July 29, 1921; s. Simon and Emilia (Gany) Schechter; in Isr since 1960; att hist fac, Bucharest, 1944-47; BA, Museography Inst, Bucharest; grad, Heb U, Jerusalem, 1964; m. Lydia Pincus, Oct 19, 1956; c: Yael, Iayr. Archives mgr, Jabotinsky Inst since 1964; active in Council of Isr Archives, in comm for profsl training of archivists; fmr: hist tchr, Alpha Sch. Arrested for Zionist activities, spent 6 1/2 yrs in prison. Mem cen comm, Herut Party, chmn, Jaffa dist; gen secy, Rum Betar Vets; mem: Archivist's Assn of Isr; Hist Soc of Isr; fmr: mem exec comm, Zionist Revisionist Party, Rum; gen secy, Union of Zionist Students, Rum. Ed, Libertatea, monthly; trans; contbr to press, periodicals. Home: 4 Irith St, Tel Aviv, Isr. Office: 38 Hamelech George St, Tel Aviv, Isr.

GAON, Yakov, Yugo, physician; b. July 14, 1914; s. Avram and Beja; MD, med fac, Belgrade, 1938; sci of med deg, 1944; m. Marta, Oct 1, 1945; c: Avro, Regina. Prof, epidemiology, head, Epidemiological Inst, med fac, Sarajevo; dist phys, Gorazde, 1945-47, asst lectr, 1947-54, prof, 1960. War prisoner, Ger, 1941-45. Pres, council of med, Health Cen, Bosnia and Herzegovina; corresp mem, Acad of Sci and Arts, Bosnia and Herzegovina; mem: J Comty, Sarajevo; Royal Soc of Med, London; Intl Epidemiological Assn; contbr to Yugo and intl jours. Home: Sutjeska 34/1, Sarajevo, Yugo.

GARB, Benjamin Harry, US, accountant; b. Poland, Dec 6, 1903; s. Charles and Fanny (Lavine); in US since 1907; BS, U of Pa, 1924; m. Bella Saunders, Dec 16, 1925. CPA since 1924. Pres: NJ Soc of CPA s, 1955-56; mem of council, Amer Inst of CPA s, 1956, 1958-61; pres: Adath Isr Syn, 1960-63, financial secy, 1931-34; dir, J Fed, 1959-63; comm chmn, bd of govs, State of Isr Bonds, since 1961; trustee, NJ Masonic Home and Charity Found since 1966; bd dirs: Trenton Trust Co since 1962; J Fed of Trenton; mem, Masons. Home: 777 W State St, Trenton, NJ. Office: Trenton Trust Bldg, Trenton, NJ.

GARBACZ, Bernard, Eng, accountant; b. Westcliff-on-Sea, Eng, Dec 30, 1932; s. Aryeh and Sura (Gladstlin); f, Inst Chartered Acctnts; m. Vera Shebson, Dec 30, 1955; c: Esther, Adrian, David. Acctnt, sr partner, Landau, Merley, Scott since 1959. Treas: B'nai B'rith, London; Kingsbury JNF, JPA Comm; Kingsbury Syn Bldg Fund; United Syn, London; chmn, Kingsbury Mizrachi Soc; financial rep, Kingsbury Dist Syn; exec mem, Dist Syn; choirmaster: Kingsbury Dist Syn, Hay-Reader Cen; chmn, Southend Dist Weizman, 1950-56; treas, Fed Zionist Youth, 1953-55; council mem, Southend Heb Cong, 1955-57; exec mem, ZF, 1953-55. Hobby: music. Home: 263 Salmon St, Kingsbury, London, Eng. Office: 13 Marylebone Rd, London, Eng.

GARBER, Leah Lev, US, teacher, communal worker; b. Ludza, Latvia, Feb 7, 1885; d. Isaak and Hannah (Borov); tchr dipl, Normal Sch, Cleveland, O, 1910; BA, MA, W Res U, 1923-32; m. Moses Garber, June, 1911 (decd); c: Alice Wyner. Hon natl vice-pres, JNF, found, first pres, women's div; hon life mem, bd: Cleveland Heb Schs; Hadassah; Park Syn Sisterhood, past pres; co-found: Bur J Educ, Cleveland; Cleveland chap, Hadassah; mem: AJCong; Cleveland Orch; Inst Of Art; Technion and Brandeis U Orgs; Reconstructionist Found; fmr: educ chmn, Hadassah; pres, Histadrut Ivrit, Cleveland; chmn: J affairs, Council J Women; Heb U Comm; vice-pres, cultural chmn, Cleveland Zionist Dist; mem, natl bd, Hadassah; org, 1st bd, Bonds for Isr; delg, ZC s. Author, short stories in Heb. Recipient, Leah Garber Forest, Jerusalem, 1952. Spec interests: theater, reading hist, phil, fiction. Home: 13400 Shaker Hgts Blvd, Cleveland, O.

GARBER, Michael, Can, attorney, QC; b. Lith, May 10, 1892; s. Simchah and Gittel (Garmaise); BA, McGill U, 1914, BCL, 1917; m. Isabel Yohalem, July 23, 1923. Pvt practice since 1919. Mem, Montefiore Club; fmr: pres, Can J Cong, chmn, natl exec; natl pres, ZOC. Home: 4338 Montrose Ave, Westmount, Quebec, Can. Office: 1010 St Catherine W, Montreal, Can.

GARBER, Nathan, S Afr, surgeon; b. Lith, June 2, 1902; s. Joel and Sara (Efroiken); in S Afr since 1904; BS, U Witwatersrand, 1922, BCh, MB, 1925; m. Ida Orkin, Dec 25, 1939 (div); c: Carol, Lindsay. Pvt practice since 1939; lectr, surg, U Witwatersrand; house surg: nose and throat dept, Gen Hosp, Birmingham, 1931, casualty dept, 1931, surg unit, 1932; orthopedic dept, N Staffordshire Royal Infirmary, Stoke-on-Trent, 1933; res surg off, Essex Co Hosp, 1933; surg and gyn unit, Royal Berkshire Hosp, Reading, 1934; Eastham Memorial Hosp, London, 1937, all Eng; mem, surg staff, Gen and Non-Eur Hosp; surg, Varicose Vein and Rectal Clinic, Gen Hosp, both Johannesburg, 1939-45; cons surg, Discoverer's Hosp, Florida, Transvaal, 1941-44. FRCS; f, Intl Coll of Surgs. Contbr to med and sci jours. Home: 38 Harrow Rd, Yeoville, Johannesburg, S Afr. Office: 616 Harley Chambers, Jeppe St, Johannesburg, S Afr.

GARDOSH, Charles (Dosh), Isr, cartoonist; b. Budapest, Hung, Apr 15, 1921; s. Alexander and Margarit (Shnurmacher); in Isr since 1948; att: Szeged U, Hung, 1944-45; Sorbonne, Paris, 1946-47; m. Suzanne Roman, July 31, 1945; c: Daniella, Michael. Ed cartoonist, under pen name Dosh, for Maariv, Heb daily, since 1953; held several cartoon exhbs in Isr; Overseas Press Club, NY, 1961; cartoons reprinted in NY Times; The London Times; Le Figaro; Jerusalem Post. Mem, Journalists Assn of Isr. Author: books of cartoons; 220, cartoons of Dosh, 1956; The Sinai Story, 1957; Chronicles, 1960; To Israel with Love, in US, 1960; What Happened, 1963; Plots, 1966; co-author: So Sorry We Won, 1967; Woe to the Victors, 1969. Recipient, Nordau Prize for Ed Cartooning, 1961. Home: 8 Berliner St, Ramat Aviv, Isr.

GARFEIN, Jack, US, theater dir; b. Mukacevo, Czech, July 2, 1930; s. Herman and Blanka (Spiegel); in US since 1946; grad, New Sch for Social Research, NY, 1949; att Amer Theatre Wing, 1949-51; studied with Lee Strasberg. Tchr, film dir, U of S Cal; fmr: apprentice, Tanglewood Playhouse, Falmouth, Mass; actor, dir, off-Broadway produc s; initiator, UCLA play series; dir: sketch, Kate Smith TV show, 1951; End as a Man, Broadway, 1954; The Marriage, TV show with Jessica Tandy, Hume Cronyn, 1954; The Strange One, film, 1956; on stage, Broadway: Girls of Summer, 1956; The Sin of Pat Muldoon, 1957; The Shadow of a Gunman, 1959; wrote, dir: Something Wild, film; How Tall is Toscanini, 1967; Don't Go Gentle, 1968. Found, fmr exec dir, Actor's Studio W, LA. Recipient, Show Bus Award, best direction, End as a Man, 1954. Office: c/o Actor's Studio, 432 W 44 St, New York, NY.

GARFEIN, Stanley J, US, rabbi; b. Louisville, Ky, Nov 15, 1937; s. Maurice and Louise (Mayer); BA, U of Pa, 1959; MHL, ordained rabbi, HUC-JIR, 1964; m. Vivian Feist, Jan 23, 1966; c: Rebecca. Rabbi, Temple Isr, since 1966; asst rabbi, Temple Isr, St Louis, 1964-66. Fmr: pres, Hillel Found, U of Pa; treas: St Louis RA; Synanon, St Louis; mem: CCAR; Alpha Epsilon Pi. Home and study: 1110 Lasswade Dr, Tallahassee, Fla.

GARFIELD, Maurice, Eng, communal official; b. London, Eng, Oct 2, 1932; s. Alfred and Rebecca (Myers); m. Adrienne Lazarus, Mar 15, 1960; c: Andrew, Rachel, Judith. Asst financial secy: Anglo-J Assn, since 1955; ZF Educ Inst; Soc Friends of J Refs; J Philanthropic Assn for Isr. Office: Rex House, 4/12 Regent St, London SW 1, Eng.

GARFIN, Louis, US, actuary; b. Mason City, Ia, June 7, 1917; s. Sam and Etta (Larner); BA, State U of Ia, 1938, MS, 1939, PhD, 1942; m. Clarice Fagen, Apr 11, 1943; c: Eugene, Erica. Vice-pres, chief actuary, Pacific Mutual Life Ins Co, since 1965, with firm since 1952; instr: USAF Communications Sch, Scott Field, Ill, 1942-43; math, Ill Inst of Tech, 1943; math dept, U of Minn, 1943-44; actuary, Ore Dept of Ins, 1946-52. Pres: Mr and Mrs chap, City of Hope, 1960-61, treas, 1959-60; pres: Actuarial Club of the Pacific States, 1967-68; LA Actuarial Club, 1959-60; mem: Phi Beta Kappa; Soc of Actuaries; Amer Math Soc; Sigma Xi; Amer Risk and Ins Assn; Town Hall of Cal; Actuarial of Pacific States Club; Amer Acad Actuaries. Hobbies: clarinet, painting. Home: 11436 Kingsland St, Los Angeles, Cal. Office: Pacific Mutual Bldg, Los Angeles, Cal.

GARFINKEL, Marvin, US, attorney; b. Phila, Mar 23, 1929; s. Simon and Theresa (Brier); BA, Pomona Coll, Cal, 1951; LLB, magna cum laude, U Pa, 1954; LLM, taxation, NYU, 1962; m. Marian Schwartz, Apr 6, 1963; c: Simon. Partner, law firm, Goodis, Greenfield, Narin & Mann since 1956;

admitted to Pa Bar, 1955; law clerk: to Curtis Bok; Gerald F Flood; Louis E Levinthal, Phila, 1954-55; W H Kirkpatrick, Phila, 1957-58; dep atty gen, Pa, 1955-57. Mem: gov council AJCong; Amer, Fed, Phila, Pa Bar Assns; Intl Law Assn; Order of Coif; club, Locust, Phila. Home: 15 Merion Rd, Merion Station, Pa. Office: 1315 Walnut St, Philadelphia, Pa.

GARFUNKEL, Jack D, US, insurance underwriter; b. Jersey City, NJ, Oct 31, 1903; s. Charles and Esther (Zryl); BCS, NYU, 1924; m. Lillian Manzo, Mar 7, 1943. Chartered life underwriter since 1941; lectr, U of Conn. Life mem, Million Dollar Round Table; mem, Garfunkel-Manzo Assos; bd dirs: Life Underwriters Assn NY, 1952-55; NY chap, Amer Soc Chartered Life Underwriters, 1955-58; found, mem, Estate Planning Council of NY; bd dirs, UJA, Gtr NY, since 1960; natl council, JDC; YMHA and YWHA, Mt Vernon, 1955-60; B'nai B'rith activities: mem, NY regional bd, ADL; NY Bd Vocational Service; pres, Mt Vernon Lodge, 1951-53; vice-pres, Metrop Council, 1955-57; bd govs, dist 1, 1959-63; delg to Intl Conv, 1959, 1962, 1965; mem, Sinai Temple, Mt Vernon; ind chmn, life ins: ADL; UJA; FJP. Recipient: honored by ADL, FJP, UFA, in Mt Vernon; life ins divs, NYC; elected to Hall of Fame, Westchester-Putnam B'nai B'rith. Home: 58 Oregon Ave, Bronxville, NY. Office: 527 Lexington Ave, New York, NY.

GARFUNKEL, Leib, Isr, attorney; b. Kovno, Lith, Mar 15, 1896; s. Hirsh and Fanny (Chazan); in Isr since 1948; att U s: Petersburg, Kiev; MJ, U of Kovno, 1925; m. Dora Rabinovich, Sep 29, 1936; c: Zvi. Ret govt official; registrar of coop socs, adv on coop, since 1962; mem, adv bd, Yad VaShem, since 1959; fmr: rep bar practice; chmn, council, J People's Banks; chmn, KH; mem, Poalei Zion-Hitachdut movement; vice-chmn, J Natl Council; mem Lith Parl, 1923-27; vice-chmn, J Comty, Kovno Ghetto, 1941-44, all in Lith; in Dachau Concentration camp, 1944-45; chmn, Comm of J Refs, It, 1945-48. Author: Jewish Natl Autonomy in Lithuania, 1920; The Destruction of Kovno's Jewry, 1959. Home: 24 Jehoshua Bin Nun St, Greek Colony, Jerusalem, Isr.

GARNER, Gerald J, US, attorney; b. NYC, Dec 17, 1936; s. Louis and Anne (Marx); BS, Queens Coll, 1957; LLS, JD, Bklyn Law Sch, 1960; m. Joan Becker, Aug 10, 1963; c: Robin, Scott, Craig. Pvt practice since 1961; fmr, sr partner, Garner, Kreinces, Mega & Sipress. Pres, Lake Louise Marie Asso; sec, B'nai B'rith, Harrison chap; dir: J Comty Cen, Harrison; Crescent Hill Comty Cen; spec council, Upper Park Ave Comty Assn; gen counsel, Upaca Boys Club of Amer Inc; mem: NY Trial Lawyers Assn; NY State Bar Assn; cons, Upper Park Ave Comty Cen and NY Fed of Reform J. Home: Sunnyridge Rd, Harrison, NY. Office: 225 Broadway, New York, NY.

GARON, Herbert Julian, US, attorney; b. New Orleans, La, Aug 16, 1925; s. Harry and Leah (Blitz) Goldstein; att U of Houston, Texas (Navy), 1944; BS, La State U, 1946; att Cornell U, NY, 1947; JD, Tulane U, La, 1949; m. Margot Strauss, June 9, 1948; c: Kathleen, Kenneth, Robert. Atty, Garon, Brener, McNeely and Hart, since 1966; asst dist atty, 1950-53; asst city atty, 1954-65. USN, 1943-45. Pres, JWF, New Orleans; dir, Amer-J Comm; natl committeeman, Amer-Isr Public Affairs Comm; mem: exec comm, UJA; bd dirs: Conservative Cong New Orleans; Amer Friends Tel Aviv U; Natl Council JWF; comm on bar admissions, La State Bar Assn; natl council, JDC; exec bd trustees, ADL, adv bd, S region; exec bd: Communal Heb Sch; Tulane-Newcomb Hillel Found; mem: New Orleans, La State, Amer Bar Assns; Amer Judicature Soc; Amer Trial Lawyers Assn; Acad Trial Lawyers; campaign cabinet, JWF; Temple Sinai Reform Cong; Gtr New Orleans Negligence and Compensation Lawyers Assn, Inc; fmr: chmn: comm on ethics and grievances, munic court comm, New Orleans Bar Assn; pres, Sertoma Intl Civic Club; gov, La dist, Sertoma Intl; natl chmn, young leadership cabinet, UJA; chmn: men's div, JWF campaign; 1966 Young Leadership Mission; mem, bd dirs, Temple Sinai Brotherhood; delg: PM's Econ Conf, 1968; Isr's Conf on Hum Needs; repr, Intl Youth Leadership Cabinet, Weizmann Inst, 1968. Recipient, Gov Lehman Award, for outstanding J lay leadership. Hobbies and spec interests: public speaking, aid to needy, philately, health club. Home: 314 Audubon Blvd, New Orleans, La. Office: 1034 NBC Bldg, New Orleans, La.

GARRET, Maxwell R, US, educator, author; b. NYC, Apr 18, 1917; s. Harry and Esther (Lieber) Goldstein; BEduc, CCNY, 1939; MS, U of Ill, 1942; att Wash and Lee U, 1943, 1945;

m. Diana Rosen, Apr 3, 1943; c: Roger, Roberta, Esther, Bruce. Asso prof, recreation, U of Ill since 1958, fencing coach since 1946, fmr: instr, asst prof, phys educ, phys fitness research asst; camp dir, Camp Illini, since 1954; tchr, health educ, NY Bd of Educ; lab asst, phys educ, CUNY. USAF, 1942-46. Prin contribs, devl total body reaction timer, U of Ill Phys Fitness Labs, 1947-49. Mem: bd dirs, Hillel Found, U of Ill; AAUP; Amer Camping Assn; Amer Assn of Health, Phys Educ and Recreation; NEA; Amer Youth Hostels; Phi Epsilon Kappa; Phi Delta Kappa; Alpha Epsilon Pi; Chi Gamma Iota; USAF Res; clubs: Optimists; Moose Lodge; fmr: pres: Natl Fencing Coaches Assn; B'nai B'rith, Cen Ill council, Grand Prairie lodge, jr past mem, bd govs, dist 6. Author: How to Improve Your Fencing; Fencing; Fencing Instructors' Manual; Handbook of Activities for Recreation Leaders; Boating Know-How for Kids; A Study of Current Recreation Internship and Field Training Programs at Selected Educational Institutions and Public Agencies; co-author, Physical Fitness of Champion Athletes, 1951; ed: Swordmaster's Bull; First Annual Midwest Fencing Clinic, 1948; contributing ed, American Fencing, 1950-52; mem, ed bd: Physical Educator; The Mentor; contbr to educ jours. Recipient: Fred K Moskowitz Award; Cert of Merit, Amateur Fencers League of Amer; B'nai B'rith Man of the Year, 1959. Hobbies: athletics, carpentry, camping, dancing. Home: 910 W Hill, Champaign, Ill. Office: U of Ill, Champaign, Ill.

GARSEK, Isadore, US, rabbi; b. Russ, Nov 30, 1914; s. Joseph and Ida (Feintech); in US since 1921; att Lewis Inst, 1933-37; ordained rabbi, Heb Theol Coll, Chgo, 1939, hon DHL, 1960; m. Sadye Carshon, June 16, 1940; c: David, Edward, Elliot, Barbara. Rabbi, Cong Ahavath Sholom, since 1946; chaplain, USPHS Hosp; rabbi, Cong Shaarith Isr, 1934-44; instr, Amer hist, Tex Tech Coll, 1943-44. Chaplain, US Army, 1944-46. Bd dirs, RabCA; vice-pres, Tarrant Co Assn for Mh; chmn, Comty Relations Commn: dir: ARC; Amer Cancer Soc; Masons, Knight Cdr, Court of Honor since 1961; bd dirs: J Fed of Fort Worth; Fort Worth Sym Assn; vice-chmn, SW region, ZOA; bd trustees, United Comty Services; mem: Gen Assn; disaster comm, Harris Hosp; J Social Agcy; J U of Amer. Home: 2208 Hawthorne, Fort Worth, Tex. Study: 1600 W Myrtles, Fort Worth, Tex.

GARTNER, Donald L, US, communal leader; b. Ambridge, Pa, July 10, 1934; s. Martin and Violet (Wallach); BS, U of Pittsburgh, 1956, MSW, 1961; m. Marilyn Litman, Aug 20, 1960; c: David, Jessica. Exec dir, JWF, since 1967, asst dir, Dallas, 1961-63; asst campaign dir, United J Fed of Pittsburgh, 1963-67. US Army, 1956-62. Bd dirs: Natl Assn Social Workers Comm, cen Ia, Dallas, Tex; Natl J Comty Org; Small Cities Council, JWF; prog comm, Natl Assn J Communal Workers; mem: Acad Cert Social Workers; Omicron Delta Kappa; Phi Epsilon Pi. Spec interests: golf; experiment in intl living. Home: 3907 Fordham Dr W, Baltimore, Md. Office: 319 W Monument St, Baltimore, Md.

GARTNER, Lloyd P, US, historian; b. NYC, June 3, 1927; s. Hyman and Betty (Miller); dipl, Herzliah Tchrs Inst, 1945; BA, Bklyn Coll, 1948; MA, U of Pa, 1949; PhD, Columbia U, 1957; m. Ruth Hagler, Oct 8, 1961. Asso prof, CUNY since 1967; research asso, Amer J Hist Cen-JTSA since 1958; asst prof, 1963-67; instr, Tchrs Inst, Seminary Coll, 1958-63; lectr, Heb, contemporary civilization, Queens Coll, 1953-57; asst prof, semitic langs, lit, Wayne State U, 1957-58. Mem: Amer Hist Assn; Amer Acad for J Research; Amer J Hist Soc. Author: The Jewish Immigrant in England, 1870-1914, 1960; Rumania, America and World Jewry, 1968; Documentary History of Jewish Education in the United States, 1970; co-author: History of the Jews in Milwaukee, 1963; History of the Jews in Los Angeles, 1969; ed: Americana; Ency Judaica; contbr to profsl jours. Home: 45 Fairview Ave, New York, NY. Office: CUNY, New York, NY.

GARTNER, Samuel, US, ophthalmologist; b. NYC, Dec 3, 1901; s. Joseph and Julia (Prince); att CCNY, 1919-21; MD, LI Coll, 1925; m. Bessie Gersten, Aug 22, 1936; c: Irene Oppenheim, Jerome. Att ophthal, Montefiore Hosp; asst ophthal surg, path, NY Eye & Ear Infirmary; asso prof, Albert Einstein Coll of Med. Pres, med bd, Montefiore Hosp, 1959. Fmr pres, NY Soc for Clinical Ophthal; f: Amer Coll Surgs; Amer Acad Ophthal and Orl; NY Acad Med; mem: Assn Research in Ophthal; Pan Amer Cong Ophthal; NY State Med Soc; AMA. Contbr to med jours. Home and office: 1749 Grand Concourse, New York, NY.

GARVETT, Morris, US, attorney; b. Pittsburgh, Pa, Nov 22, 1893; s. Elihu and Dora (Mazer); LLB, Detroit Coll of Law,

1915; m. Gladys Warren, June 10, 1919; c: Charles. Sr mem, Levin, Levin, Garvett and Dill, since 1941. Mem: comm on probation and parole, Mich State Bar Assn since 1956; comm on estate and trust law, Detroit Bar Assn since 1950; Amer Bar Assn; Amer Judicature Soc; bd dirs, JWF since 1944, past chmn exec comm, educ div; bd dirs, Round Table of Catholics, J and Prot; pres, Sinai Hosp, Detroit; mem: adv, sub-comms on leg, Detroit Comm on Children and Youth; bd dirs, Comty Action for Detroit Youth; bd dirs, Midrash Coll of J Studies; hon mem, bd trustees, Temple Isr, past pres; hon mem bd govs, J Comty Cen, all Detroit; chmn, comm on comty org, mem, comm for natural study, CJFWF; bd trustees, J Hist Soc of Mich; life mem, Sixth Judicial Conf, US Courts; club, Lawyers of U of Mich. Recipient, Awards: Edward Rosenberg, CJFWF, 1958; Fred F Butzel Memorial, 1966. Home: 16500 N Park Dr, Southfield, Mich. Office: 1250 Penobscot Bldg, Detroit, Mich.

GASNER, Meyer W Can, manufacturer; b. NYC, June 10, 1906; s. Jacob and Minnie (Kanholz); in Can since 1927; att Yeshiva Coll, NYC, 1923-24; m. Goldie Sigal, Aug 9, 1928; c: Leon, Stanely. Pres, Intl Parts Ltd, Toronto, since 1945. Pres: Shaarei Shomayim Syn, 1951-53; Mizrachi, Toronto, 1957-61; Young Isr, Toronto, 1928-35; Revisionist Org, Toronto, 1946-48; campaign chmn, bd, United J Wfr Fund, Toronto, since 1953; bd trustees: Can J Cong; Yeshiva U; Bar Ilan U, Isr; vice-pres, Asso Heb Schs; bd govs, YMHA; New Mt Sinai Hosp; bd mem: B'nai B'rith; JDC; Masons; KP. Home: 32 Strathearn Rd, Toronto, Can. Office: 763 Warden Ave, Scarboro, Toronto, Can.

GASS, Oscar, US, consulting econ; b. Portland, Ore, Jan 1, 1914; s. Joseph and Celia; att: Reed Coll, Portland, 1930-34; Oxford U, 1934-37; m. Edna Sugihara, 1944. Cons econ. Home: 4000 Massachusetts Ave, NW, Washington, DC. Office: 1908 Que St, NW, Washington, DC.

GASSNER, Mordi, US, artist, designer, educator; b. NYC, May 27, 1899; s. Leopold and Sarah (Newman); att NY Sch of Fine and Applied Arts; Art Students League; Bklyn Inst of Art and Scis, all 1916-19; m. Augusta Klausner, May 30, 1925; c: Judith Schlosser. Free-lance artist, designer since 1919; art tchr, J Bd of Guardians, 1924-27; sup, design, Natl Youth Admn, 1939-41; art dir, produc mgr, US Armed Forces Training Prog, 1942-45; art dir, Westchester Playhouse, Mt Kisco, NY, 1946; lectr: New Sch for Social Research, Dramatic Workshop, 1949-50, art hist, 1962; Fordham U, 1949-51; TV Workshop, NYC, 1949-51; Pratt Inst, 1950; guest lectr: Litchfield Co Art Assn; Conn Comty Coll, Winsted; Five Towns Cultural Cen, LI; scenic artist: Metrop Opera Co since 1950; films: Funny Girl; For Love of Ivy; The Incident. Exhbs: Bklyn Mus, 1932; Mus of Modern Art, 1934; Corcoran Gal, Wash, DC, 1935; Whitney Mus, 1938-39; Richmond Acad of Arts and Scis, 1955. Murals: Ohrbach's exec offices, 1928-35; Bklyn J Cen, 1928; Guggenheim Found, 1928-31; DuPont's, 1933-39; Consumer Bldg, Communications Bldg, NY World's Fair, 1939; PO, Wash State and NY State, 1939; Ruby Foo Bldg, Wash, DC, 1941, NY, 1942; Arthur Darman Woonsocket estate, RI, 1946. Portraits: Nathan and Jerome Ohrbach; John Shelton Horsley, Justice Burt Jay Humphrey; Justice Henry W Holt; Myrtle Ehrlich; Louis Vorhaus; Judge Harry A Hollzer. Dir, cons, prog prod, Metrop Area Circle, NY; mem: adv council, NY HS of Art and Design, Bd Educ; United Scenic Artists, fmr chmn, examinations comm, exec bd, contract negotiations comm; fmr: chmn: comm on current work, Architectural League, NY; vice-pres, mem, exec bd, United Scenic Artists, local 829. Author, schematic plan for founding Fed Culture Centers; chap on Stage Production Design in Producing the Play, 1953. Recipient: Guggenheim f, 1928, 1930; 1st prizes: US Govt mural competition, 1939; US Army Water Command mural competition, 1948; two scholarships, NYU, 1943, 1944; exhb mural-Homage to Leonardo, IBM, 1959. Home: 200 W 86 St, New York, NY. Studio: 36 W 26 St, New York, NY.

GASTER, Joseph, US, surgeon, educator; b. NYC, Apr 14, 1911; s. Isidor and Ethel (Pecker); BA, Cornell U, 1932; MD, Cornell Med Coll, 1936; m. Tobe Pecker, Feb 6, 1944; c: Ronald, Wendy. Asst prof of surg, Coll of Med Evangelists, LA since 1950; res in surg: Harlem Hosp, 1936-38; Michael Reese Hosp, Chgo, 1942-43; Blain Hosp, Detroit, 1948; att surg: White Memorial Hosp; Temple Hosp; LA Gen Hosp; cons, surg, Daniel Freeman Hosp. Dipl, Amer Bd Surg; f, Intl Coll Surgs; mem: AMA; Cal Med Assn; LA Co Med Assn; AAAS; Assn Amer Med Colls. Author and produc, med motion pictures; contbr: Christopher's Textbook of Surgery; surg jours. Home: 613 N Alta Dr, Beverly Hills, Cal. Office: 6360 Wilshire Blvd, Los Angeles, Cal.

GASTER, Theodor Herzl, US, orientalist, folklorist; b. London, Eng, July 21, 1906; s. Moses and Leah (Friedlaender); MA, U London, 1936; PhD, Columbia U, 1943; m. Lotta Schmitz; c: Corinna. Prof rel: Barnard Coll; Columbia U; visiting prof, comparative rel, Dropsie Coll; fmr: chief, Hebraic Sect, Libr of Cong, Wash, DC; Fulbright prof: hist rels, U Rome; Bibl and Semitic studies, U Melbourne; Guggenheim F, 1954, 57. Mem: Amer Oriental Soc; Archaeol Inst of Amer; Soc for Bibl Exegesis; Soc for Old Testament Study; NY Oriental Club, fmr pres; bd dirs, YIVO. Author: Thespis: Ritual Myth and Drama in the Ancient Near East, 1950, 1960; The Oldest Stories in theWorld, 1952; Festivals of the Jewish Year, 1953; The Holy and the Profane: The Evolution of Jewish Folkways, 1955; The Dead Sea Scriptures, in Eng trans, 1956; Myth, Legend and Custom in the Old Testament, 1969; contbr ed, Universal J Ency; contbr to: Ency Britannica; Interpreters Dict of the Bible; Standard Dict of Folklore; Mythology and Legend; to Amer and fgn periodicals. Offices: Barnard Coll, Columbia U, New York, NY.

GATT, Shimon, Isr, biochemist; b. Lublin, Pol, Sep 29, 1926; s. Zadok and Bathsheba (Haurowitz) Greenwald; in Isr since 1936; MSc, Heb U, Jerusalem, 1950; PhD, Columbia U, 1955; m. Hanna Greenwald, Mar 28, 1950; c: Orna, Lihi, Moshe. Asso prof, biochem, Hadassah Med Sch, Jerusalem since 1968; research asso, Public Health Research, Inst of NYC, 1955-57; asst prof, Albert Einstein Coll of Med, 1963-64; asso prof, U of Cal, 1968-69. Lt, IDF, 1948-49. Prin contribs: Isolation and Characterization of Hydrolytic Enzymes of Glycolipid and Phospholipid Metabolism. Mem: Sigma Xi; Isr Chem, Biochem socs. Contbr numerous publs to sci jours. Home: 60 Hechalutz St, Jerusalem, Isr. Office: Hadassah Med Sch, Jerusalem, Isr.

GAVIS, Gustave, US, pediatrician; b. Vienna, Aus, Sep 23, 1922; s. Leopold and Bertha (Rubinstein), in US since 1938; BA, Ind U, 1948; MD, SUNY Coll of Med, Bklyn, 1952; m. Helen Schracter, May 25, 1952; c: Wendy. Pvt practice of ped and allergy since 1955; instr, dept ped, Columbia U since 1961; chief, dept ped: Comty Gen Hosp; Hamilton Ave Hosp, both NY; med dir, SC Health Clinic, Liberty, NY. Lt, US Army, 1943-46; govt trans, It and Ger; Army Reserve, 1955. Asso F, Amer Coll Allergists; trustee, Amer Phys F; dipl, ped and F, Amer Acad Ped; mem: AMA; Kings Co, NY State, Sullivan Co Med Socs; Bklyn Acad Ped; Mid-Hudson Ped Soc; NY Allergy Soc. Contbr to med jours. Recipient: Army Commendation Ribbon; Man-of-the-Year, Amer Phys F of IMA, 1967. Spec interests: public health, admn in med affairs. Home: Varnell Rd, Monticello, NY. Office: 410 Broadway, Monticello, NY.

GAVISH, Yshayahou, Isr, ret army off; b. Tel Aviv, Isr, Aug 31, 1925; s. Elchanan and Bela (Shklar); Command and Staff Coll, Isr, adv studies Ecole de Guerre, Paris; m. Gita Taube; c: Uzi, Giora. Dir, Koor Metal Works, since 1970; appt, commanding off, Command and Staff Coll; sr post, gen staff; command oprs off; serving since 1966 as commanding off of S Command. Office: Koor, Ben Yehuda St, Tel Aviv, Isr.

GAVSE, Fajvel, Isr, economist, executive; b. Pol, 1910; s. Jehoshua and Shandel; in Isr since 1934; BA, Sch of Law and Econ, Tel Aviv, 1959; MA, Heb U, Jerusalem, 1962; m. Franka Konstantinovska; c: Uri, Tamar, Edit. Gen secy, cons, Ind Devl Bank of Isr, Tel Aviv since 1961; mem, Kibbutz Messilot, 1934-55; employee, Agric Bank, Tel Aviv, 1955-60. Fmr, mem: Mapam cen comm, dir info dept; Hashomer Hatzair leadership. Home: 17 Lipski St, Tel Aviv, Isr. Office: 9 Achad Ha'am St, Tel Aviv, Isr.

GAYER, Zelig, Isr, police off; b. Dawid-Grodek, Pol, 1910; s. Osher and Rivka (Rabinovitch); in Isr since 1936; att HS, Wilno, Pol; m. Yaffa Maister, 1941; c: Ilan. Asst cdr, Isr Police, chief inves br, S dist; fmr: i/c Temporary Police, Jerusalem; chief Mil Police I Jerusalem, during Independence War, 1948. Mem, Intl Police Assn; fmr mem, Censorship Bd. Recipient decorations: Defense Medal, War Medal, both 1939-45; Independence War; Sinai Campaign; Six Day War. Home: 52 Hantke St, Jerusalem, Isr.

GAZIT, Mordechai, Isr, diplomat; b. Istanbul, Turkey, Sep 5, 1922; s. Efraim and Zippora (Schustermann) Weinstein; in Isr since 1933; MA, Heb U, Jerusalem, 1946; m. Rina Zelvianski, Oct 16, 1948; c: Avner, Orna. Counsellor, Min for

Fgn Affairs since 1967; fmr: acting dir, dept of research, adv, Min for Fgn Affairs; first secy, Isr Emb, London; political secy to Min of Fgn Affairs; Min Plen, Isr Emb, Wash; asst dir gen i/c ME affairs. Haganah, 1936-47; capt, IDF, 1947-49. Fmr secy, Isr Exploration Soc. Home: 1 Rashba St, Jerusalem, Isr.

GEALEL, Abraham, Isr, metallurgist; b. The Hague, Netherlands, May 27, 1935; s. Joel and Mitiam (Anisfeld) Grajower; in Isr since 1953; dipl, Tech Coll, The Hage, 1952; AIM, Sir John Cass Coll, London, 1967; USC, U Aston, Birmingham, 1968; m. Zehava Stahl, Apr 7, 1957; c: Zeev, Miriam, David. Head, materials application engr, Isr Aircraft Ind, Ltd, since 1968; head, metallurgical lab, 1960-66, materials engr, 1959-60; designer, Weizmann Inst, 1954-56. Cpl, IDF, Mem, Inst of Metallurgists, London; fmr, leader, B'nei Akiva, Netherlands. Recipient: John Hitchcock Prize, Sir John Cass Coll, 1968. Spec interests: reading; rel; Judaica; hist; sociol. Home: 167 Aluf David St, Ramat Gan, Isr. Office: Lod Airport, Isr.

GEBER, Hana, US, sculptor, teacher, lecturer; b. Czech, Feb 14, 1910; d. Max and Olga (Gans) Kraus; in US since 1945; tchrs dipl, Tchrs Coll, Prague, 1928; att Art Student's League, NY, 1945-50; m. Walter Geber, 1930. One-man shows: E Hampton Gal, NY; UHC, NYC; Fordham U; Phila Art Alliance; Montclair Art Mus, NJ; Silvermine Guild, Conn; Chautauqua Art Assn, NY; J Comty Cen, New Haven, Conn; traveling shows: Chapter of Our Time, Amer Fed; The Holidays, J Mus around US; USAL S Amer Show; Buenos Aires Mus; Amer Women Artists; natl shows: Pa Acad; J Mus, NYC; Riverside Mus, NYC; Baltimore Mus, Md; Montclair Art Mus; Mus of Fine Arts, Boston; Norfolk Mus of Arts and Scis; Mus of Fine Arts, Montgomery, Ala; Crafts Mus, NYC; Audubon Artists, NYC; repr in collections: J Mus; Mus of U of Amherst, Mass; Montclair Art Mus; Norfolk Mus, Va; Riverside Mus; Fordham Mus, NY; Lowe Art Mus, Miami, Fla; Mills Coll, NY; Intl Syn, LI Kennedy Airport; Free Westchester Syn, NY; Cannan Found, Chgo; Mural Memorial, Verona HS, NJ. Recipient: F grant for liturgical sculpture, Memorial Found of J Culture, 1968-69; Gold Medal, NAWA; First Prize, ASCA; several awards by Audubon Artists. Home: 140 Cabrini Blvd, New York, NY. Studio: 168 W 225 St, New York, NY.

GEETTER, Isidore S, US, hospital admnr, anesthetist; b. Aus, Dec 31, 1902; s. Heyman and Adella (Stolper); in US since 1905; BS, Trinity Coll, Hartford, Conn, 1925; MD, Jefferson Med Sch, Phila, Pa, 1929; m. Rebekah Meranski, June 16, 1929; c: David, Albert, Thalia, Harold, Suzanne. Dir, Mt Sinai Hosp, Hartford, Conn since 1946, dir dept anesthesiology, 1946-54; dir, dept anesthesiology, New Britain Gen Hosp, 1932-43, med dir, 1935-43. USNR Med Corps, 1943-46. F: AMA; Amer Coll Anesthesiology; Intl Anesthesia Research Soc; Amer Coll Hosp Admnrs; fmr pres: NE Hosp Assembly, 1960-61; Conn Hosp Assn, 1950; mem: Amer Hosp Assn; Emanuel Syn. Home: 92 Fern St, Hartford, Conn. Office: Mt Sinai Hosp, Hartford, Conn.

GEFEN, Aba, Isr, diplomat; b. Mariampol, Lith, May 31, 1920; s. Meir and Ruhama (Rubinstein) Weinstein; D Pol Sci, U Rome, It, 1955; m. Frida Szmulowicz, Oct 21, 1947; c: Ruhama, Meir, Yehuda. Consul gen of Isr, Toronto, Can since 1967; fmr: attache, Isr Emb, Rome; dep dir dept, Fgn Min, Jerusalem; counsellor, Isr Emb, Arg; leader, Briha, Aus, clandestine org, transp J survivors of the Nazis across frontiers of different countries on their way to Pal. Haganah. Mem, Histadrut. Author: Portzey haMachsomim, 1961; Los Que Rompieron Las Barredas, 1966. Hobbies: reading, chess. Home: 20 Beth Hakerem, Jerusalem, Isr. Office: 200 Bay St, Toronto, Can.

GEFFEN Abraham, US, radiologist; b. Atlanta, Ga, Sep 22, 1916; s. Tobias and Hene (Rabinowitz); BS, Emory U, 1937; MD, Columbia U, 1941; m. Ethel Petegorsky, Mar 28, 1948; c: David, Robert, Sara. Dir, radiology, Beth Isr Hosp since 1954, asso radiologist, 1949-54; prof, clinical radiology, Mt Sinai Sch of Med since 1968; asst clinical prof, radiology, NYU Med Sch since 1959. Maj, US Army MC, 1942-45. Mem: NY, Co, State Med Soc; AMA; NY Roentgen Soc; Radiological Soc of N Amer; Beth-El Syn, vice-pres since 1966; Phi Beta Kappa; Alpha Omega Alpha. Contbr to med jours. Home: 28 Disbrow Lane, New Rochelle, NY. Office: 10 Nathan D Perlman Pl, New York, NY.

GEFFEN, Joel S, US, rabbi; b. Kovno, Lith, Aug 7, 1902; s. Tobias and Hene (Rabinowitz); in US since 1903; BA, Emory

U, 1922; MHL, ordained rabbi, JTSA, 1926, hon DD, 1959; MA, NY State Tchrs Coll, 1938; m. Sylvia Mintz, July 27, 1926; c: Lisa Schlesinger, Rela Monson. Research asso, Amer J Hist Cen since 1959, dir, field activities and comty educ dept since 1944; exec mem, natl leaders training F commn, JTSA, Natl Fed Men's Clubs; found, rabbi: Temple Beth El, Harrisburg, Pa, 1926-29; Temple Beth El, Troy, NY, 1929-44; spiritual adv, Natl Fed J Men's Clubs since 1944; cons, Metrop Region, United Syn of Amer, dir, 1963-65. Civilian chaplain to naval cadets, Rensselaer Poly Inst and Russell Sage Coll, Troy, NY, WWII. Mem: bd govs, Natl Acad for Adult J Studies, natl council, jt commn on social action, United Syn of Amer; exec comm, bd overseers, dir, Ambass Group, JTSA; Isr comm, RA; Temple Isr, Gt Neck, NY; Natl J Commn on Scouting; ZOA; B'nai B'rith; AJCong; NY State Citizens; fmr: pres, NY State Zionist Region; mem: exec bd, Beth Hayeled Sch; delg, Amer Syn Council of Amer. Author: A Survey of the Status of Jewish Education in the Capital District of NY State, 1938; America in the First European Hebrew Daily, Ha-Yom, 1886-1888, pub, 1962; co-ed: Roads to Jewish Survival, 1968; Torch Mag, since 1945. Recipient: spec citation, for outstanding services to Amer J Comty, B'nai B'rith, 1952; spec award, NY State Off of Civil Defense, 1945. Hobbies: tennis, photography, hiking, music, travel. Home: 11 Riverside Dr, New York, NY. Office: 3080 Broadway, New York, NY.

GEFFEN, Louis, US, attorney; b. NYC, Nov 1, 1904; s. Tobias and Hene (Rabinowitz); BA, Emory U, Atlanta, Ga, 1923; LLB, Columbia U, 1927, JD deg, 1969; cert, Mil Govt Sch, Ft Gordon, Ga, 1951, 1957; m. Anna Birshtein, Dec 26, 1934; c: David. Pvt practice, law since 1928; chief, governmental and legal sects, 310th Mil Govt Group, 3rd Army since 1947; off, US Army, since 1937, ret, lt-col, US Army Res, 1965; capt to lt-col, Judge Advocate Gen's Corps, 1941-46; assisted, preparation of charges and specifications against Japanese war criminal, Gen Homma, 1945; chief, prosecution sect, War Crimes Br, Supr Allied Command, Manila and Japan, 1945-46; chief prosecutor, war crime trial, Yokohama, 1946. Pres, S Young Judean Assn, 1921-22; vice-pres, Atlanta City Bd Educ, 1935-37; secy, Shearith Isr Syn, 1934-40; mem, bd dirs since 1947, supt, Sunday sch, 1935-40; chmn, fund raising campaign in Manila to rebuild syn destroyed by Japanese, 1945; mem, exec comms: Atlanta dist, ZOA, 1950-55; and adv bd, JWV, since 1948, post cdr, 1948-49. Mem: Amer, Atlanta and Ga Bar Assns; Res Offs Assn; Mil Govt Assn, both Wash, DC; J Comty Cen; Home for Aged; Alpha Epsilon Upsilon, all Atlanta. Author: Manual of Procedures and Rules Governing Prosecution of War Criminals in Japan, 1945; Legal Manual for Military Government, 1954. Recipient: Amer Defense Medal, 1941; Army Commendation, 1942; Asiatic Pacific Medal, 1945; Victory Medal, 1946; Res Officers Medal, 1956. Club, Progressive. Home: 1435 N Highland Ave, NE, Atlanta, Ga. Office: 1002 Atlanta Fed Savings Bldg, Atlanta, Ga.

GEFFEN, M David, US, rabbi; b. Atlanta, Ga, Jan 11, 1938; s. Louis and Anna (Birshtein); BA, Emory U, Ga, 1959; MHL, ordained rabbi, JTSA, 1965; PhD, Columbia U, 1970; m. Rita Feld, Dec 29, 1962; c: Avram, Elissa. Asso rabbi, Temple Beth Shalom. Capt, chaplain, US Army, 1965-67. Prin contrib, discovery of Shalom Aleichem Oil Field. Mem: Phi Beta Kappa; Pi Sigma Alpha; Alpha Epsilon Pi; fmr intl pres, Student Zionist Org. Trans, Behinat haDat by Elijah del Medigo; contbr to J publs. Recipient: Bronze Gavel, B'nai B'rith, 1958; Woodrow Wilson Natl F, 1959-60; spec f, Memorial Found of J Culture, 1968-69; dissertation f, Natl Found for J Culture. Hobby, collection of Isr first day covers. Study: Cong Beth Shalom, 18th and Baynard Blvd, Wilmington, Del.

GEFFEN, Tobias, US, rabbi, author; b. Kovno, Lith, Aug 1, 1870; s. Joseph and Kuna (Strauss); in US since 1903; ordained rabbi, Slobodka Yeshiva, 1903; m. Hena Rabinowitz, Aug 14, 1898; c: Joel, Louis, Samuel, Abraham, Lottie, Annette, Bessie, Helen. Rabbi, Cong Shaerith Isr since 1911. Chmn, S dist, Union of Orthodox Rabbis in US and Can since 1912; mem, bd, Atlanta JWF; past pres, Mizrachi, Atlanta. Author: Leiv Yosef, 1923; Karnei haHod, 1934; Memory Inscripteulogy to Harold Hirsch, 1940; Hadras Yosef, 1941; Nachlath Yosef, 1946; Fifty Years in the Rabbinate, autobiography, 1951; Nazer Yosef, 1958, part II, 1963. Recipient, citation, JWB, 1946. Home and study: 1121 Zimmer Dr, NE, Atlanta, Ga.

GEFFNER, Theodore, US, attorney; b. Bx, NY, May 24, 1919;

s. Abraham and Sadie (Siegel); BA, NYU, 1940; LLB, Bklyn Law Sch, 1947; post-grad, NYU Law Sch; m. Helen Katz, Nov 3, 1945; c: Daniel, Judith Osband. Sr partner, Wasserman, Chinitz, Geffner & Green since 1962; secy, Lake Success Capital Corp since 1961; counsel, Ind & Comm Brokers since 1965. Maj, mil intelligence, 1940-63. Secy, Solomon Schechter Sch; trustee: Beth-El Syn; Beth Sholom Syn. Home: 114 The Intervale, Roslyn Estates, New York, NY. Office: 5000 Brush Hollow Rd, Westbury, NY.

GEIGER, Sydney Jr, US, engineer, business exec; b. Jacksonville, Fla, Dec 21, 1923; s. Sydney and Bertha Helen (Jacobs); BS, The Citadel, 1948; m. Joan Nirenberg, Dec 21, 1947; c: Helen, Susan, Steven, Mindy. Pres, Delta Steel Co Inc since 1955. Lt, US Army, 1943-46. Pres, Beth Isr Cong, Jackson, Miss; mem: natl bd, UAHC; bd, N Jackson Citizens Goodwill Inds; Urban League, Jackson; B'nai B'rith; Council on Hum Relations; Amer Inst of Steel Construction; Amer Soc of CE; Amer Soc of Profsl Engrs; Boy Scouts of Amer; fmr: pres: Jackson JWF; B'nai B'rith Lodge 202; mem bd, Jackson Urban League. Hobbies: boating; swimming; jogging. Home: 2246 Greenbriar Dr, Jackson, Miss. Office: POB 9966 Jackson, Miss.

GEIS, Bernard, US, publisher; b. Chgo, Ill, Aug 30, 1909; s. Harry and Bessie (Gesas); BA, Northwestern U, 1931; m. Darlene Stern, Mar 18, 1940; c: Peter, Stephen. Pres, Bernard Geis Asso Inc, since 1958; pres, subsidiary, Ampersand Press Inc, since 1963; fmr: asst ed, Esquire Mag, 1941-43; ed-in-chief, vice-pres, Grosset and Dunlap Pub Co, 1943-55; ed, Prentice-Hall Pub Co, 1956-57; war corresp, 1942-43. Chmn: NY Heart Assn annual campaign, since 1966; NYC Salvation Army, pubs group, annual appeal, 1960-66; bd dirs, ADA. Home: 2 Sutton Pl, S, New York, NY. Office: 128 E 56 St, New York, NY.

GEIS, Manfred Moshe, Isr, journalist, theater critic; b. Berlin, Ger, Dec 17, 1906; s. Isador and Erica (Loeb); in Isr since 1933; att Hildesheimer Rabb Sem; Lessing and Humbolt HS; student of actor Paul Lange; m. Louise Shamai, June 6 1950. Ed, gen secy, Moadim, play publishers and lit agts since 1942; fmr: broadcaster and reciter of poetry and lit, Ger; theater critic, reporter on cultural events to local, fgn press, several Eur stas; broadcaster Kol Yerushalim, Kol Yisrael; lit adv, Ohel Theatre. Hon secy, Isr Cen, Intl Theatre Inst, 1955-61, delg, vice-pres cong, Vienna; comm, mem's org, Isr Philharmonic Orch since 1960. Author, monograph for Heb ed, Richard Beer-Hoffman's Jacob's Dream; numerous other essays. Home: 74 Keren Kayemeth Blvd, Tel Aviv, Isr. Office: 144 Hayarkon St, Tel Aviv, Isr.

GEISLER, Febus, Isr, surgeon; b. Lwow, Pol; s. Moses and Maria (Nicker); in Isr since 1949; m. Ruth Keller, 1948; c: Dan, Ariela. Head, surg dept, med dir, Donolo Hosp. Mem: Intl Coll of Angiology; Isr Surg Soc; B'nai B'rith; fmr pres, Rotary club, Tel Aviv-Jaffa. Home: 51 Rupin St, Tel Aviv, Isr. Office: Donolo Hosp, Tel Aviv-Jaffa, Isr.

GEISMAR, Maxwell D, US, author; b. NYC, Aug 1, 1909; s. Leon and Mary (Feinberg); BA, Columbia U, 1931, MA, 1932; m. Anne Rosenberg; c: Katherine, Peter, Elizabeth. Author: Writers in Crisis, 1941; The Last of the Provincials, 1945; Rebels and Ancestors, 1952; American Moderns: A Midcentury View of Contemporary Fiction, 1958; Henry James and the Jacobites, US, Henry James and His Cult, Eng, 1963; Mark Twain and His America, 1970; ed: Thomas Wolfe Portable, 1946; The Whitman Reader, 1955; The Ring Lardner Reader, 1962; Sherwood Anderson Short Stories, 1962; contbr to periodicals; fac mem, Sarah Lawrence Coll, 1933-45. F, Boston U Libr, 1966. Home: Winfield Ave, Harrison. NY.

GELB, Charles T, US, merchant, communal worker; b. St Louis, Mo, Dec 26, 1908; s. Samuel and Annie (Thaler); LLB, St Louis Law Sch, 1931; m. Ruth Susman, Sep 2, 1930; c: George, Joy White, Richard. Owner, ATA Stores since 1949; fmr pres, Gelb Fisheries Inc. Natl chmn, S Cal Council since 1957, mem exec bd, dist grand lodge; natl commnr; gen chmn, Armed Forces Day Project; mem exec bd, LA Hillel Council and B'nai B'rith Record; fmr: pres: S Cal Council, Mid-Valley Lodge, all B'nai B'rith; mem exec: LA Youth House Corp; LA Comty Relations Conf; San Fernando J Fed; fmr: co-chmn, Inst of Judaism; pres: men's div, Natl Home for J Children, Denver; Mid-Valley Bowling League; Fish Inst, St Louis, Mo; vice pres, Valley JCC; co-chmn, Van Nuys div, United JWF. Recipient: Chain Makers Award, 1957;

Man of the Year, Mid Valley, 1958; S Cal Council Award, 1961, pres citation, 1962, all from B'nai B'rith; dist service award, Men's Club, Natl Home for J Children, St Louis Br, 1943; dist service award, VA, 1958; awards from United JWF; inducted into Hall of Fame, Mid-Valley B'nai B'rith, 1968. Spec interest, VA Hosp wfr. Home: 5008 Hazeltine Ave, Sherman Oaks, Cal. Office: 6261 Van Nuys Blvd, Van Nuys, Cal.

GELBART, Abe, US, mathematician, educational admnr; b. Paterson, NJ, Dec 22, 1911; s. Wolf and Pauline (Landau); BS, Dalhousie U, NS, Can, 1938; PhD, MIT, 1940; m. Sara Goodman, July 2, 1949; c: Carol, Judith (decd), William, Stephen. Dean, Belfer Grad Sch of Sci, Yeshiva U, since 1958; Dist U Prof, math, Yeshiva U, since 1968; fmr: grad asst, MIT; asst to Prof Norbert Weiner; instr, NC State Coll; research asst, Brown U, also, cons, research projects; asso physicist, NACA; prof, Syracuse; mem, Inst for Advanced Study; lectr, Sorbonne; visiting prof, U of S Cal; Fulbright lectr, Nor; guest lectr: Cambridge U, Eng; Stockholm; Copenhagen; Valiron Sem Henri Poincaré Inst, Paris; Prague; dir research projects sponsored by: NSF; Off of Naval Research; Off of Sci Research. Mem: Math Assn of Amer; Amer Math Soc. Prin contribs: co-devl theory of pseudo-analytic functions. Contbr to sci research jours and US Printing Off. Home: 140 West End Ave, New York, NY. Office: Yeshiva U, 601 W 183 St, New York, NY.

GELBART, Meir, Isr, government official; b. Lodz, Pol, Oct 21, 1908; s. Nahum and Margalith (Diamantstein); in Isr since 1932; MA, hum, U of Warsaw, 1932; m. Rachel Dreihorn; c: Nahum, Edith. Dep dir gen, Min of Devl since 1956; fmr: mem bd dirs: Timna Copper Mines; Negev Ceramic Materials Ltd; Geological Inst, Negev Phosphates; Tovala Transp Co; Egged Transp Co, Tel Aviv; dep dir gen, Min of Health; mem, cen control comm, Histadrut, judge high court, Histadrut. British Army, 1942-45; IDF, 1948-49. Recipient, Medals: ME, Paiforce RE, WW II, all British Army; Liberation War, Haganah; 6 Days War, all IDF. Home: 50 Arlosoroff St, Holon, Isr. Office: 38 Keren Hayesod St, Jerusalem, Isr.

GELBER, Anna D, Isr, physician; b. Safed, Isr, July 10, 1907; d. Jacob and Esther (Segal) David; DSc, U of Paris, 1929; MD, U of Toronto, 1934; m. Edward Gelber, Mar 18, 1930; c: Edna, Lynn, David. Cons phys, clinic C, Heb U Hadassah Hosp, Jerusalem since 1954; fmr: sr asst, med dept, Toronto Women's Coll Hosp. Natl chmn, Fed of U Women, Isr; chmn, child wfr dept, World WIZO, mem: presidium, WIZO; exec, Jerusalem Acad of Med; Youth Alyiah Bd. Author: Recherches Experimentales sur un Hématozoaire du Genre Leishmania. Home: 15 Ben Maimon Ave, Jerusalem, Isr. Office: Heb U Hadassah Hosp, Jerusalem, Isr.

GELBER, Arthur E, Can, business exec; b. Toronto, Can, June 22, 1915; s. Louis and Sara (Morris); m. Esther Salomon, June 17, 1941; c: Nancy, Patricia, Judith, Sara. Pres, Can Conf of the Arts since 1960; mem bd, Amer-Isr Cultural Found since 1955. Chmn bd mgmt, St Lawrence Cen for the Arts, Toronto; mem: Province of Ontario Council for the Arts; bd, Natl Found for J Culture; New Mt Sinai Hosp; J Home for Aged and Baycrest Hosp; Dominion Drama Festival; YMHA; CJC; United JWF; bd: Natl Theatre Sch of Can; Natl Ballet Sch; fmr: pres: Toronto ZC; Cen Ont Drama League; Natl Ballet Guild of Can; vice-pres, CJFWF; chmn, UJA; clubs: Primrose; Arts and Letters. Home: 166 Roxborough Dr, Toronto, Ont, Can. Office: 205 Richmond St, W, Toronto, Ont, Can.

GELBER, Edward E, Isr, communal leader; b. Toronto, Can, Nov 6, 1903; s. Moses and Sophie (Sperber); in Isr since 1954; BA, U Toronto, 1925; MA, Columbia U, 1929; ordained rabbi, MHL, JTSA, 1930; admitted, Ontario Bar, Osgoode Hall, 1934; m. Anna David, Mar 18, 1930; c: Edna, Lynn, David. Vice chmn, bd govs, fmr, chmn exec council, Heb U, Jerusalem; vice chmn, Yad VaShem, official memorial auth since 1956; chmn, bd trustees, Jerusalem Acad Music since 1960. Chmn exec, Intl Cultural Cen for Youth in Jerusalem; exec bd, Bezalel Natl Mus Art; Natl Hillel Commn, chmn adv council, Isr Hillel Found, natl council, JDC; exec bd, Har El Lib Cong, Jerusalem; fmr: pres: ZOC; Assn Heb Schs of Toronto; Toronto United JWF; hon vice-pres, Can J Cong; vice-pres, Amer Fund for Isr Insts; hon pres, Heb Cultural Org Can; found co-chmn, Isr Bond Campaign of Can. Home: 15 Ben Maimon Ave, Jerusalem, Isr.

GELBER, Marvin, Can, business exec; b. Toronto, Nov 1, 1912; s. Louis and Sara (Morris); BA, U Toronto, 1934. Fmr: MP; head Can delg to ECOSOC, Geneva; mem, Can delg to UN Gen Assembly. Lt, Can Army, WW II. Hon vice-pres, UN Assn, Can; mem: natl exec, chmn, jour adv comm, Can Inst of Intl Affairs; bd dirs: YM-YWHA; Natl UNICEF Comm; Soc Plan Council, Toronto; Empire Club; Toronto Sym Orch; trustee, Art Gal of Toronto; chmn, Old Masters Comm. Contbr articles on econ and intl affairs. Home: 131 Bloor St W, Toronto, Can. Office: 203 Richmond St W, Toronto, Can.

GELBER, S Michael, US, educator; b. Toronto, Can, Mar 1, 1918; s. Louis and Sara (Morris); BA, Columbia Coll, 1942; MA, NYU, 1963, PhD, 1967. Instr, NYU Dept of Heb Culture, since 1965. Dir, Bergen Belsen Camp for JDC, 1945-46; mgr, Pal Econ Corp, NY, 1948-50; mem: speakers bur, UJA; Royal Can Mil Inst. Author: Does the Jewish Past have a Future, 1959; The Failure of the American Rabbi, 1961; contbr to Anglo-J publs. Recipient: medals: Overseas Service, Voluntary Service. Home: 300 E 71 St, New York, NY.

GELBERG, Frederick, US, attorney; b. NYC, Sep 21, 1919; s. Henry and Sophia (Schenk); BSS, CCNY, 1939; LLB, Columbia U, 1947; m. Terie Isaacs, June 30, 1948; c: Barbara, Steven Jonathan. Pvt practice since 1947; partner: Kaye, Scholer, Fierman, Hays & Handler; Silverson & Gelberg, 1952-66; research asst, income tax project, Amer Law Inst, 1951-52; lectr, tax law: Practicing Law Inst; NYU; Colby Coll. US Army, 1943-46. Pres, Roslyn lodge, B'nai B'rith, 1957; mem: Amer and NYC Bar Assns; Tau Delta Phi. Contbr to profsl jours. Home: 17 Clover Lane, Roslyn Hts, NY. Office: 425 Park Ave, New York, NY.

GELBERG, Geoffrey Harold, Eng, solicitor; b. London, Eng, Dec 24, 1934; s. Lionel and Lilian (Finfer); LLB, LSE, 1955; m. June Schama, Sep 21, 1965; c: Miriam. Sr partner, G H Gelberg, Parkus & Co since 1968. Gov, Clapton J Day Sch; dir, Zioni Review Ltd; pres, Dalston and N London Zionist Soc, chmn, 1959-65; vice-pres, Hackney JNF Commn, chmn, 1964-67, hon secy, 1959-64; jt chmn, PR and info comm, Natl Council for Younger JNF, 1965-66; asst hon secy, ZF, 1964-67, hon off, 1967, jt vice-chmn; Org and Propaganda Comm, 1964-67, vice-chmn, Constitution Comm, 1964-67; hon secy, Hackney JPA Comm, 1960-64; vice-pres, JNF, 1960-67; ed bd, Younger JNF Rev, 1965-66; mem: Law Soc; John Carpenter Club, Old Citizens Assn. Home: 86 Ossulton Way, London, N 2, Eng. Office: 67/68 Jermyn St, St James, London, SW1, Eng.

GELBRUN, Artur, Isr, musician; b. Warsaw, Pol, July 11, 1913; s. Menahem and Hana (Warszawiak); in Isr since 1949; MA, State Conservatory, Warsaw, 1936; perfection course: Acad of Music, Rome, 1938; Siena, 1938; m. Eugenia Marshak, Nov 5, 1920. Tchr: Rubin Acad of Music, Tel Aviv U, since 1960; guest conductor, various orchs: It; Switz; Aus; Belgium; Greece. Mem: Isr League of Composers; ACUM. Composer: works for orch: Lider der Madchen (Rilke), 1945; Suite pour Orchestre, 1947; Hedva, ballet, 1951; Chant des Lamentations, 1952; Preludio, Passacaglia e Fuga, 1954; Variations pour piano and orch, 1955; Prologue Symphonique, 1956; Cinque Capricci, 1957; Symphonie No 1, 1957-8; Song of the River, 1959; Symphonie No 2, 1961; chamber music: Sonatine pour deux violons, 1944; Sonatine pour Piano, 1945; Trio à Cordes, 1945; Esquisses pour flute et harpe, 1946; 5 Caprices pour piano, 1958; Sonatine (Studio) pour violon seul, 1958; 4 Preludes pour piano, 1959; Cinque pezzi per violoncello solo, 1962; choeurs a capella: Deux Choeurs a 3 voix, 1945; 3 Choeurs mixtes, 1946; Psaume pour choeur mixte, 1951; Ricercare pour Choeur Mixte, 1958; chante et piano: Drei Lieder, 1944; Trois Melodies, 1945; Deux Berceuses, 1945; Une Longue Reflexion Amoureuse; Cycle de 10 chants pour tenor; Deux Chants, 1947; Deux Chants de la Nuit, 1951; Tre Preghiere, 1959. Recipient: composition prizes, 1965-1968, ACUM; intl prizes for performances, Geneva, 1941-42. Home: 3 Karni St, Ramat Aviv, Isr.

GELD, Solomon, US, institution exec; b. Lopatin, Tarnopol, Pol, July 15, 1911; s. Joseph and Miriam (Laszczowen); in US since 1938; PhD, U of Breslau, 1937; ordained rabbi, Theol Sem, Breslau, 1937; att: JTSA, 1938-39; Training Sch, J Comty Services; NYU; m. 2nd, Marion Ostrow, Dec 1, 1956; c: Gary, Roger, Tony. Exec dir: Daughters of Miriam Home, Infirmary for Aged, since 1939; JCC, Paterson, NJ, 1942-48; tchr, gymnasium, Ger, 1934-38; lectr, confs concerning care for the aged, on local, state and natl levels.

Fmr pres: NJ Natl Assn, J Homes for the Aged; treas: Amer Assn of Homes for the Aging; fmr, Natl Assn of J Homes for the Aged; past chmn: Admnrs Conf of Cen Bur for J Aged, NYC; prog, session of the aged, Natl Conf J Communal Service, 1961; prog, Insts on Inst Mgmt, Medicare, Natl Assn of J Homes for the Aged, Grossingers, 1962, 1966; cons, US Govt, on standards of extended care facilities and Medicare; delg, White House Conf on Aging; f, Amer, Gerontological Soc since 1954; mem: Temple Emanuel; ZOA; YWHA, Amer Hosp Assn. Contbr numerous papers on med and geriatics. Spec interests: lit, langs, golf. Home: 599 Broadway, Paterson, NJ. Office: 155 Hazel, Clifton, NJ.

GELEHRTER, Menachem Emanuel, Isr, organization exec; b. Galicia, Pol, 1900; s. Iaacov and Rachel (Karpel); in Isr since 1920; grad, U Vienna, 1926. Secy, presidium, Zionist Gen Council; fmr: mem, Hashomer Org, Vienna, co-found, Hashomer Hatzair, Stanislavov; mem, supr council, Hashomer Hatzair, Galicia; prin co-found, Hechalutz, asst in establishment of Hechalutz training farm; worked in lab camp, Yavneh; mem, Hapoel Hatzair; participant, found conf, Histadruth; delg to ZCs; gen secy, mem cen comm, Zionist Lab Party; established, Barzel, iron workshop for pioneers; co-found, Gordonia, youth movement, Galicia; tchr, Bible, J hist, Tarbut Sch, Wolinya; hon secy, KH comm, mem, territorial council, KH, Pol; with Tnuva head off; mem, JNF delg to Pol; secy, gen council, Cen Council for Spread of Heb Lang in Yishuv; dir, Latin Amer sect, Zionist exec, visited J comtys in Latin Amer. Author: The Jewish Community in Stanislavov, 1953; Jewry in a Tempestuous Continent, pamphlet; Moses Hess and His Period, in Span, 1964; Chaim Weizmann, in Span, 1968; contbr numerous articles in various langs to mags. Home: POB 7238, Jerusalem, Isr. Office: POB 92, Jerusalem, Isr.

GELFAND, Maxwell L, US, physician, educator; b. Russ, Apr 27, 1905; s. Morris and Ethel (Sheiner); in US since 1909; BS, CCNY, 1925; MD, St Louis U, 1929; m. Grace Albert, Dec 24, 1933; c: Martin, Charles. Pvt practice since 1931; asso prof, clinical med, NYU Sch of Med; dir of med, NY Infirmary; att phys: Bellevue and U Hosps; cons phys: Knickerbocker and Columbus Hosps. F: Amer Coll Phys; NY Acad Med; Amer Coll Chest Phys; Amer Coll of Card; AHA. Dipl, Amer Bd Intl Med; mem: Amer Fed for Clinical Research; NY Heart Assn; NY Acad of Scis. Contbr: to sci jours; book, Bronchopulmonary Diseases. Recipient: Merit Cash Award for med essay, Med Soc NY State, 1960. Hobby, music. Home: 45 Gramercy Pk, New York, NY. Office 60 Gramercy Park N, New York, NY.

GELFAND, Michael, Rhodesia, physician, educator; b. Wynberg, Cape Town; s. Louis and Ethel (Salkow); MB-ChB, Cape Town U, 1936, MD, distinctions, 1948; D Public Health, distinctions, Rand U, 1950; m. Esther Gelfand, Jan 26, 1937; c: Joy Phillips, Isabelle Wapnick, Anne. Prof, med, with spec reference to Afr, U Coll of Rhodesia and Nyasaland since 1962; specialist phys, Health Service, Fed of Rhodesia and Nyasaland since 1939. FRCP, London. Author: Medicine in Tropical Africa; Schistosomiasis; Tropical Victory; Livingstone the Doctor; Northern Rhodesia in the Days of the Charter; The Sick African; contbr to Shona Rel, Shona Ritual; ed, Cen Afr Jour of Med since 1955. Recipient, CBE. Home: 11 Lawson Ave, Salisbury, Rhodesia.

GELFAND, Morris A, US, librarian; b. Bayonne, NJ, June I, 1908; s. Joseph and Sadie (Schneider); BS, NYU, 1933, MA. 1939; BS, Columbia U, 1934; PhD, NYU, 1960; m. Beatrice Traube, Feb 1, 1948; c: James, Lisa. Prof and libr, Queens Coll, Flushing, NY since 1946; fmr: sup res reading room, Wash Sq Libr, NYU; libr cons, Ford Found, Brazil; libr asst, Queens Coll; spec examiner, libr positions, NY State Civil Service Dept; visiting prof, libr cons, U Delhi, India; Fulbright lectr, libr cons, U of Rangoon, Burma; UNESCO Libr adv, Min of Educ, Govt of Thailand; mem visiting comms, Middle States Assn, Colls and Secondary Schs since 1949. Maj, USAAC, 1942-46. Chmn, council of librs, CUNY since 1953; mem: Bibliographical Soc of Amer; Sigma Soc, fmr mem; Alpha Lambda Phi, past chancellor; Phi Delta Kappa; trustee: NY Metrop Reference and Research Libr Agcy; Council on Research in Bibliography; Bryant Libr, Roslyn, NY; fmr: chmn, comm on Wilson Indices, Assn of Coll and Reference Librs; pres, AAUP, Queens chap; clubs: NY Libr; Grolier. Author, University Libraries for Developing Countries, 1968; contbr to profsl jours. Hobbies; woodworking; photography; gardening. Home: Stone House,

RFD 40, Roslyn Harbor, LI, NY. Office: Queens Coll, Flushing, NY.

GELFMAN, Robert W, US, attorney; b. NYC, Jan 22, 1932; s. Irving and Lillian (Meltzer); BS, U of Pa, 1953; LLB, Harvard U Law Sch, 1956; m. Phyllis Trustman, Dec 18, 1955; c: Lisa, Peter. Partner, Wien, Lawe & Malkin since 1965. Capt, USAF, 1957-60. Trustee: J Bd of Guardians; Hawthorne Cedar Knolls Sch; mem: Amer Bar Assn; Assn of Bar, NYC; NY Co Lawyers Assn; exec bd, FJP, new leadership div, 1962-64; clubs: Harvard, NYC; Metropolis Country. Home: 17 Eton Rd, Scarsdale, NY. Office: 60 E 42 St, New York, NY.

GELFOND, Abraham, US, psychologist, educator; b. Elizabeth, NJ, June 17, 1915; s. Philip and Jennie (Bernstein); BS, Rutgers U, 1938; MA, NYU, 1947, PhD, 1952; m. Sylvia Osheroff, Dec 22, 1940; c: Joan, Peter. Pvt psych practice since 1952; prof, psych, educ, Montclair State Coll since 1963, on fac since 1954. US Army, 1943-46. Vice-pres: Cong Anshe Chesed, 1956-57; ZOA, 1955-59; mem: Amer Psych Assn; NEA; Amer Personnel and Guidance Assn; VFW; Phi Beta Kappa. Spec interest, phil. Home: 1126 Debra Dr, Linden, NJ. Office: Montclair State Coll, Linden, NJ.

GELLEI, Bela Baruch, Isr, physician; b. Piszke, Hung, Sep 14, 1913; s. Daniel and Rosa (Weichszer); in Isr since 1938; MD, U of Bari, It, 1937; m. Shoshana Weiss, Oct 23, 1935; c: Meira, Orna. Head, dept path, Rambam Hosp, Haifa, since 1948; sr lectr, Heb U, Jerusalem, since 1959; head, dept path, Munic Hosp, Haifa, 1944-51; sr path, Singapore Hosp; lectr, forensic med, U of Singapore, both 1961-64. Vice-pres, Haifa Med Assn; pres: Govt Doctors Soc; Path Soc, both 1957-60; hon treas, Singapore Med Assn, 1961-62; mem, Intl Acad Path; club, Rotary, Haifa. Contbr to profsl jours. Hobbies: chess, bridge, philately. Home: 27 Vine St, Haifa, Isr. Office: Rambam Hosp, Haifa, Isr.

GELLER, Abraham N, US, jurist; b. NYC, May 15, 1899; s. Nathan and Belah (Schwartz); LLB, Fordham U Law Sch, 1920; m. Dorothy Friedlander, Nov 19, 1929; c: Bruce, Susan Platt, Judith Warner. Justice, Supr Court, NY State, since 1962; practiced law, NYC, 1920-52; justice, court of Gen Sessions, NY Co, 1953-62. USN, WW I. Vice-pres, UJA since 1950; mem, bd of trustees, YM-YWHA, Bx; bd of trustees, Park Ave Syn; mem: NY Co Lawyers Assn; Amer Judicature Soc; Amer and NY State Bar Assns; AJComm; ZOA; Grand St Boys' Assn; Amer Legion; club, N Shore Country. Hobby, making furniture. Home: 150 Central Park S, New York, NY. Office: 100 Centre St, New York, NY.

GELLER, Abram Lewis, US, insurance underwriter, educator; b. Galveston, Tex, July 18, 1898; s. Jacob and Sara (Wittis); BA, Rice U, 1920; grad, life underwriters training council course, U of Houston, 1950; m. Libby Yellen, June 17, 1923; c: Reba Swiff, Devora Rubin, Golda Baker, Jacob. Life ins underwriter, Pacific Mutual Life Ins Co, since 1928; tchr, math, Houston HS, 1920-22; salesman, secy, Leff Bros Dry Goods Co, 1922-28; tchr, life underwriters training council course, U of Houston, 1953-55. Served WW I. Mem: speakers comm, Natl Assn of Life Underwriters, educ comm since 1958; hon life pres, United Orthodox Syns, Houston; fmr: pres: Houston chap, Amer Assn of Retired Persons; org, pres, Beth Jacob Cong, hon pres since 1945; chmn, bldg comm, mem, bd; chmn: Chevra Kadisha, Houston; JNF, Tex, chmn Houston JNF; treas, Herzl Lodge, B'nai B'rith, fmr vice-pres; secy, Houston Independent Heb Sch; 1st secy, charter mem, cultural and natl service agcys, JCC, Metrop Houston; mem: bd dir, Houston Assn Life Underwriters, pres; Amer Assn U Tchrs of Ins; bd dirs: ZOA, Houston Dist, pres southwest region, mem bd, vice-pres, Tex region, chmn, Houston Zionist Council, mem, natl admnr Council; mem: Ins Econs Soc Amer; Rice U Alumni Assn; Amer Legion; Tex Assn Life Underwriters; Masons; Shriners; YMCA; clubs: life: Leaders Round Table, Tex; Million Dollar Round Table; Lions; Houston Ins; life, Pacific Mutual Million Dollar; top star mem, Big Tree Leaders, Pacific Mutual, fmr, pres, vice-pres. Contbr to: book, How to Multiply Your Life Insurance, 1950; profsl jours. Recipient: numerous quality awards, Natl Assn Life Underwriters, 1948-68. Home: 3602 Underwood, Houston, Tex. Office: 2701 Fannin St, Houston, Tex.

GELLER, Bruce, US, writer, producer, director; b. NYC, Oct 13, 1930; s. Abraham and Dorothy (Friedlander); BA, Yale U, 1952; m. Jeannette Marx; c: Catherine, Lisa. Writer:

screenplay, Sail A Crooked Ship, 1962; created TV series: Mission Impossible, produced, exec produc; devl, Mannix, produced, exec produc; TV produc and dir: The Dick Powell Show; Kaiser Aluminum Hour; Dr Kildare; The DuPont Show; The Westerner; Rawhide; Hunter; theater: book and lyrics: All in Love, Martinique Theatre, NYC, 1961-62, Mayfair Theatre, London, 1964; Livin the Life, Phoenix Theatre, NYC, 1957. Mem: Dirs Guild; Dramatists Guild; Writers Guild; BMI. Recipient: awards: Writers Guild Award nominations: Best Anthol Script, 1959, 1963; Best Adaptation, 1960; Best Episodic Script, 1961-1968; Produc Guild Award nomination, 1962; Silver Gavel Award, Amer Bar Assn, 1963; Two W Heritage Awards, produc, lyricist, 1964; Emmy: writer, Mission Impossible, 1966, produc, 1966, 1967, exec produc, 1967, 1968; exec produc, The Execution, 1968; Golden Globe, Mission Impossible, 1967; Image Award, NAACP, 1967; Produc-of-the-Year Nomination, 1968. Home: 707 N Arden Dr, Beverly Hills, Cal. Office: Paramount Pictures, 780 N Gower, Hollywood, Cal.

GELLER, Michell D, US, rabbi; b. Houston, Tex, May 29, 1925; s. Max and Sadye (Sondock); BA, Yeshiva U, 1946; ordained rabbi, Isaac Elchanan Theol Sem, 1950; att Bernard Revel Grad Sch m. Helen Lesser, Mar 29, 1951; c: Abram, Samuel, Sara, Tova. Rabbi, Cong Brothers of Jacob, since 1953; chaplain, Norwich Hosp, since 1960. Maj, chaplain, USAF, Res, since 1951. Secy, Norwich Redevl Agcy; pres, ZOA, Norwich, 1955-66; mem: Assn of J Chaplains; Assn of Mental Hosp Chaplains; RabCA. Contbr to J periodicals. Home: 18 Pearl, Norwich, Conn. Study: 2 Broad, Norwich, Conn.

GELLER, Philip S, US, surgeon; b. Newport, RI, May 16, 1907; s. Charles and Clara (Bazel); BS, Tufts Coll, 1928, MD, cum laude, 1931; m. Jeanne Morris, Apr 21, 1951; c: Charles, Phyllis, Marry Winnick; m. 2nd, Judith Rennie, July 9, 1966. Sr surg, Sequoia Med Group, Redwood City, Cal, since 1946; staff mem, Stanford U Hosp, Palo Alto; chief of surg, Sequoia Hosp, 1950-55, chief of staff, 1956-57. Maj, US Army, 1941-46. Mem: Cal State Bd of Med Examiners, since 1967; Amer Coll of Surgs; Intl Coll of Surgs; AMA; Alpha Omega; Phi Delta Epsilon. Home: 88 Mercedes Lane, Atherton, Cal. Office: 90 Birch St, Redwood City, Cal.

GELLER, Usi, Isr, farmer, chess player; b. Haifa, Isr, Jan 27, 1931; s. Israel and Sima (Brun); m. Shoshana Chavis, Mar 14, 1954; c: Amir, Ziv, Ravit, Tal. Mem: Kibbutz Givat Hayim; active, Hakibbutz Hameuchad. Capt, IDF, 1948. Recipient: first place: chess tournament, Isr, 1958, 1965; inter-kibbutz tournament champion, 1968; Isr Open Tournament Champion, 1968; 9th place, Netanya Intl, 1969. Hobby, classical music. Home: Hakibbutz Hameuchad, Givat Hayim, Isr.

GELLER, Yonah Harry, US, rabbi; b. Houston, Tex, Aug 15, 1920; s. Max and Sadye (Sondock); BA, Yeshiva U, 1940; ordained rabbi, Isaac Elchanan Theol Sem of Yeshiva U, 1944; MA, Tex A & I Coll, 1954; m. Elizabeth Wishnia, Mar 5, 1944; c: Ivan, Markham, Suretta. Rabbi: Cong Shaarei Torah, since 1960; Bnai Isr Syn, Corpus Christi, Tex, 1944-60. Chaplain, USN, 1944-45. Found, Hillel Acad, Portland, Ore; pres: Ore Bd Rabbis; J Family and Child Service, Portland; Kallah of Tex Rabbis, 1957-58; panel mem, Challenge, Weekly TV Prog; mem: Mayor's Comm on Decent Lit; RabCA; B'nai B'rith. Home: 2463 NW Overton St, Portland, Ore. Study: 920 NW 25 Ave, Portland, Ore.

GELLES, Bernard, US, cotton broker; b. Dobromil, Aus-Hung, 1894; s. Leo and Sabina (Ehrenpreis); in US since 1913; BCS, Acad of Commerce, Vienna, 1913; m. Dorothy Sauberlich, 1917. Ret; WR Grace & Co, 1913-35; mgn dir, Grace Cotton Co, Ltd, Liverpool, 1935-37; partner, Bernard Gelles and Co, cotton exporters, NY, 1939-56; adv comm, cotton export, Commerce Dept, Off of Intl Trade, Wash, DC, 1951; mem: NY Cotton Exch, 1926-51, rep stockholders at corp meetings and activities. Foreman, Fed Grand Jury, 1963-64; exec council, Free Syn; bd, NYC Amer United for Separation of Church and State, since 1958; mem: Acad Political Sci, Columbia U, since 1956; Amer Cotton Shippers Assn; Tex Cotton Assn; Dems for Rockefeller, 1958. Contbr to profsl jours. Home: 201 E 77 St, New York, NY.

GELLIS, Isaac, US, journalist; b. NYC, Jan 5, 1908; s. Samuel and Sarah (Marder); m. Kathleen Dwyer, Mar 19, 1938; c: Harry, Dorothy, Nancy. Sports ed, NY Post since 1949; reporter, sports, 1926-49. Home: 147-58 77 Ave, Flushing, NY. Office: NY Post, 75 West St, New York, NY.

GELLMAN, Charles, US, hospital exec, industrial mgmt engr; b. Bklyn, NY, Dec 18, 1916; s. Louis and Sophie (Weisler); BS, Columbia U, 1938, MS, 1942; m. Ruth Westrich, Feb 22, 1948; c: Tessa, Margot. Exec dir, J Memorial Hosp, NYC since 1963; fmr: ind specialist, chief, fuse and pyrotechnics, War Dept, NY Ordnance Dist; cons engr, works mgr: Para Equipment Co Multi Plant Oprs; Heppe Hudson Corp, Ozone Pk, NY; tech adv and exec purchasing off, supply mission, Govt of Isr; tech dir, Isr Inst of Tech, Haifa; exec dir, Grand Cen Hosp. Bd dirs: League of Voluntary Hosps and Homes; Hosp Credit Exch; Union Mutual Savings and Loan Assn; mem: exec comm and off, Gtr NY Hosp Assn; Green Acres Civic Assn; Amer Ordinence Assn; Amer Hosp Assn; Amer Coll of Hosp Admnrs; Brith Milah Bd of NY Inc; Masons. Contbr to public health jours and to Isr health mags. Recipient, Meritorious Award Civilian, NY Dist Ordinance, 1945. Hobbies: collecting fine art, music. Home: 12 Birch Lane, Valley Stream, NY. Office: 196 St and Broadway, New York, NY.

GELMAN, Joseph Martin, US, attorney; b. Olshunka, Russ, Mar 16, 1910; s. Dave and Bella (Dries); in US since 1912; BA, U of Pittsburgh, 1930; LLB, Sch of Law, 1933; JD, U of Pittsburgh, 1968; m. Tillie Calig, Oct 12, 1932; c: Saralee Fine. Pvt practice since 1933; spec asst Atty Gen, Commonwealth of Pa since 1963; head, Pittsburgh Off, Bur of Consumer Protection, Pa Dept of Justice since 1966; fmr: counsel of Commonwealth, State of Pa. USN, 1944-46. Mem: exec bd, Pittsburgh chap, AJComm since 1956, domestic affairs and intl orgs since 1958; State Vets Employment Comm since 1956; Allegheny Co Bar Assn; Amer Legion; Disabled War Vets; JWV; Masons; VFW; fmr: mem bd trustees, Temple Sinai; bd dirs, United Vocational and Employment Service; pres: Joseph Cohen lodge, B'nai B'rith; Pa Jt Vets Council; vice pres, Commonwealth of Pa Vets Comm; gen chmn, Pittsburgh comm, Employment of the Handicapped; bd trustees, Natl Service Found; delg, World Vets Fed Assembly, Vienna. Recipient: Purple Heart; State Citation, 1949; meritorious service, Pa Jt Vets Council, 1950; natl cert of merit, AMVETS, 1949, natl citation for achievement 1953, natl cdr's spec achievement, cert, 1960; natl meritorious, conspicuous service citation, Mil Order of Purple Heart, 1955. Home: 6417 Landview Rd, Pittsburgh, Pa. Office: Frick Bldg, Pittsburgh, Pa.

GELMAN, Manuel, Australia, educator; b. London, Eng, Sep 8, 1910; s. Abraham and Rebecca; in Australia since 1912; MA, dipl Educ, U Melbourne; dipl, Sorbonne, Paris; m. Sylvia Benn, 1950. Head, langs dept, Melbourne U Secondary Tchrs Coll, since 1950, lectr, methods of teaching, U Conservatorium of Music; guest lectr: Toronto; London; Hobart; Adelaide; Brisbane. Found pres, Austr Fed of Mod Lang Tchrs Assn, since 1965; chmn, main group, Triennial Cong of Fed Intl des Profs de Langues Vivantes, Swed, 1965; fmr: hon secy, Victorian Inst of Educ Research; pres, Modern Lang Tchrs Assn; pres, Asso Judean Athletic Clubs; bd govs, chmn educ comm, Mt Scopus Coll. Author: The Teaching of French in Victoria, 1958; Practical Problems in the Teaching of Modern Languages, 1959; contbr to educ jours in Austr and abroad. Recipient, Chevalier dans l'Ordre Natl du Merite. Home: 125 Milford St, Elwood, Victoria, Australia. Office: Swanston St, Parkville 3052, Melbourne, Australia.

GELTNER, Eliezer (Luzer), Isr, physician; b. Buczacz, Dec 26, 1909; s. Juda and Rachel (Goldhirsh); in Isr since 1935; MD, Charles U, Prague, 1935; m. Lola Becher, May 30, 1957; c: David, Judith. Dir, Asaf Harofe Govt Hosp, since 1950; head, dept for geriatric diseases since 1954; fmr: dist med health off, Rehovot. Brit Army, 1941-46; IDF, 1947-48. Mem cen comm, IMA; exec bd, Magen David Adom, Isr. Author: Preliminary Report of Chronic Diseases in Israel, 1956; contbr to med jours. Hobby, gardening. Home: 65 Chen Blvd, Rehovot, Isr. Office: Asaf Harofe Hosp, Zerifin, Isr.

GELVAN, Richard, Den, business exec; b. Dvinsk, Latvia, Aug 16, 1902; s. Josua and Deborah (Unterschlak); in Den since 1905; att U of Copenhagen, 1945-49; m. Guta Kviatkowsky, Nov 21, 1926. Head mgr, Beckett & Meyer, since 1948, with firm since 1916. Monitor, Den lodge, B'nai B'rith, fmr pres; mem: bd, J Comty, Copenhagen, since 1960; Danish ORT and OSE commns; fmr: pres, Danish ZF; pres, Scandinavian J Youth Fed; chmn, J Youth Soc, Copenhagen; mem: bd of trade soc, Merchants Guild of Copenhagen. Recipient: King David Order, Nor; Danish King's Medal, 1966. Home: 49 Rebekkavel, Copenhagen, Hellerup,

Den. Office: Beckett & Meyer, Peder Skramsgade 14, Copenhagen, Den.

GENACHOWSKI, Dov, Isr, economist, author; b. Tel Aviv, Isr, Nov 27, 1933; s. Eliahu and Gita (Nachimowski); BA, Yeshiva U, 1954; BA, NYU, 1954; m. Esther Feuchtwanger, Jan 16, 1958; c: Arieh, Tama, Asher. Sr econ since 1967; i/c relations with intl financial insts since 1964, both Bank of Isr. Gov, chmn, financial comm, Shaare Zedek Hosp, Jerusalem; bd, financial comm, Horev Sch Sys, Jerusalem; Isr Political Sci Assn; Union of Acad Workers in Isr; Soc for Intl Devl; Isr Numismatic Soc; Amer Numismatic Soc; Isr Intl Numismatic Soc; fmr chmn, Bank of Isr Employees Union. Author: R S Z Hirshowitz and His Commentary to the Talmud, 1956; Tosaphot of Rabbi Isaac HaLavan to Tractate Yoma, 1958; Rabbi Eliakim Commentary to Tractate Yoma, 1964; The External Debt of Israel, 1964; contbr to encys; jours; periodicals. Recipient: f, Econ Devl Inst, World Bank, Wash, DC; judge, Kadman Prize in Numismatics, Tel Aviv. Home: 6 Magnes Sq, Jerusalem, Isr. Office: Bank of Isr, Jerusalem, Isr.

GENACHOWSKI, Eliahu Moshe, Isr, publisher, business exec, author; b. Grajewo, Russ, 1903; s. Shlomo and Tema (Tetenbaum); in Isr since 1931; m. Gita Nachimowski, 1929 (decd); c: Dov, Abraham. Partner, Genachowski Bros Ltd, Tel Aviv; mgn dir: El Hamekoroth Pub; Meoroth Pub; Alumoth Pub; Mazkereth Gita Pub; fmr: co-found: Tseirei Mizrachi Org, W Eur; Hecalutz Hamizrachi, Pol; found, League for Hapoel Hadati, Belgium; co-found: Mizrachi Fund; Yeshivat Hayishuv Hahadash; Rabbi Kook Prize, Tel Aviv Munic. Mem: various orgs of Hapoel Hamizrachi since 1933; Friends of Tel Aviv U; comm, Arieh Levin Yeshiva, Jerusalem; exec comm Otzar Pirushim; fmr: MK; vice-pres, United ZF of Belgium; mem, exec, World Mizrachi Org, Belgium; found mem, Reshet Hachinuch Hatalmudi; JCC, Jerusalem; hon secy, B'nai B'rith lodge, Jerusalem; delg to WZCs. Publisher: first Talmud pub in Isr with punctuation; Gt Jerusalem ed; Szyk Haggadah; Sarajevo Haggadah; Menorot ed: Maimonedes; Mishna; Shulchan Aruch; Tur; pub works: Ki Tavou el Haaretz, 1936, eds in: Eng, Fr, Span, Ger; Rabbi Mordechai Eliasberg, 1939, Eng ed, 1967; ed: Works of Rabbi Isaac Nissenbaum, 1948; Compendium of Commentaries on Tractate Horayoth; contbr to encys. Spec interests: ancient Heb books, Judaica. Home: Givat Rokach, Bnei Braq, Isr. Office: Menoroth Pub Co, 23 Kalisher St, Tel Aviv, Isr.

GENDZIER, Harry, US, merchant; b. NYC, Nov 5, 1897; s. Moses and Dora (Tunis); m. Belle Finkelstein, Nov 5, 1925; c: Rita, Sheldon. Partner, Fla Rag Co, since 1937. Chmn, UJA and Isr Emergency Dr, 1967; hon pres: JCC, since 1958; River Garden Home for Aged, since 1955; pres, Jacksonville J Cen, 1942-45; natl exec council, United Syn of Amer, since 1946; mem, Intl Platform Assn, since 1967. Recipient: Medal, Isr Govt, 1967; comty affair, for 50 years service, 1968. Home: 2125 Myra St, Jacksonville, Fla. Office: POB 2666, Jacksonville, Fla.

GENSLER, Walter Joseph, US, educator, chemist; b. Minneapolis, Minn, Feb 24, 1917; s. Oscar and Faye (Selovitz); BCh, with high distinction, U of Minn, 1938, MS, 1940, PhD, 1942; m. Kinnereth Dushkin, Jan 12, 1945; c: Orin, Daniel, Gail. Prof, chem, Boston U, since 1949; asso dir, antimalarials prog, Columbia U; instr, Harvard U. Chmn, comm grad educ, Arts and Sci, Boston U; Weizmann f, Weizmann Inst; spec f, USPHS; mem: Amer Chem Soc; Sigma Xi; Amer Profs for Peace in ME; Academic Comm on Soviet J; Northeastern Assn of Chem Tchrs; AAUP; AAAS. Co-author, Writing Guide for Chemists, 1961; asst ed, Jour of Amer Chem Soc, 1967-69; contbr to chem jours. Home: 45 Gale Rd, Belmont, Mass. Office: Boston U, Boston, Mass.

GENTILLI, Joseph Hefetz, Australia, educator, author; b. San Daniele del Friuli, It, Mar 13, 1912; s. Giulio and Elisa (Jona); in Australia since 1939; dipl acctnt, Tech Inst, Udine, 1929; D Rer Pol, U of Venice, 1934; m. Eliana Ricci, 1935, div; c: Leone, Cinzia; m. 2nd, Melva Smith, Apr 21, 1950; c: Neil. Lectr, geog, U of W Australia, since 1941, stat methods, 1940-46; asst, Geog Inst, U of Florence, 1934-35; visiting research f, climatology: Johns Hopkins U, 1952; Instituto di Selvicultura, Florence, It, 1959. Author: Atlas of West Australia Agriculture, 1941; The Raw Materials of the World, 1946; Australian Climates and Resources, 1947; Foundations of Australian Bird Geography, 1949; Die Klimate Australiens,

1956; Geography of Climate, 1958; Quaternary Climate of the Australian Region, 1961; I Climi del Friuli, 1963; Sun, Climate and Life, 1968; Geography of Vegetation, 1970; Climates of Australia, 1970; ed, Westralian Judean, 1942-44. F: Royal Geog Soc; Amer Geog Soc; Royal Meteorological Soc; delg, Touring Club Italiano; mem: Società Geografica Italiana; Amer Meteorological Soc; corresp mem, Accademia di Udine; W Australian Naturalists Club, past pres; fmr: found pres, W Australian Youth Hostel Assn; chmn, Australian Assn Sci Workers; secy: Alliance Française de Perth; Council J Affairs; Dante Alighieri Soc. Home: 65 Bruce St, Nedlands, Australia. Office: U of W Australia, Nedlands, Australia.

GENTILY, Anne Marie, Fr, editor; b. Paris, Jan 5, 1909; d. Maxime and Clementine (Volterra); licenciée és lettres, Faculté de Paris, 1931. Ed, gen secy, Paris WIZO since 1945; ed, secy, La Terre Retrouvée, 1946-67. Office: 24 rue du Mont Thabor, Paris 1, Fr.

GERBER, Albert B, US, attorney; b. Phila, Pa, July 10, 1913; s. Jacob and Jennie (Suffrin); BS, U of Pa, 1934, LLB, 1937; MA, George Wash U, 1940; LLM, U of Pa, 1941; m. Rhona Posner, Nov 22, 1939; c: Jack, Gail, Lynne. Partner, Gerber & Galfand, since 1947; instr, U of Pa Law Sch, 1937-38; asst counsel, Rural Electrification Admn, 1938-40; chief, state law sect, Dept of Agric, 1940-42. US Army, 1942-45. Secy, mem, bd of trustees, Franklin D Roosevelt Endowment Found, 1958; mem: bd of trustees, Beth Or Cong since 1961; ACLU; Amer Bar Assn; Phila Bar Assn, mem, intl law comm; Order of the Coif. Author: Life of Adolf Hitler, 1961; Life of Herbert Hoover, 1963; Sex, Pornography & Justice, 1965; Bashful Billionaire, 1967; contbr to profsl jours. Home: 7145 Crittenden St, Philadelphia, Pa. Office: 1512 Walnut St, Philadelphia, Pa.

GERBER, Heinz Joseph, US, business exec; b. Vienna, Aus, Apr 17, 1924; s. Jacques and Bertha (Spielman) Ossias; in US since 1940; BAE, Rensselaer Poly Inst, NY, 1947; m. Sonia Kanciper, Dec 19, 1952; c: David, Melissa. Pres, dir, The Gerber Sci Inst, since 1948; dir: Gerber Garment Tech Corp, Hartford; Boston Digital Corp, Ashland, Mass; Applied Programming Tech, Hudson, Mass; Phoenix Mutual Fund, Hartford; Beta Engr & Devl Ltd, Beersheba, Isr; asso dir, Conn Bank & Trust Co; adv bd, engr, mgmt, Rensselaer Poly Inst; engr, U Aircraft Corp 1947-51. Prin contrib, Gerber variable scale; holder of numerous US and fgn patents. Org, Amer-Isr C of C; mem: UJA, sci sect; Conn Soc of Profsl Engrs, Inc; Numerical Control Soc, Hartford chap. Recipient: Hartford's Outstanding Man-of-the-Year, 1951; One of Amer's Ten Outstanding Young Men-of-the-Year, 1952, both Hartford Jaycees. Home: 34 High Wood Rd, W Hartford, Conn. Office: 83 Gerber Rd, S Windsor, Conn.

GERBER, Israel J, US, rabbi, educator, psychologist, author; b. NYC, July 30, 1918; s. Max and Sadie (Shuster); BA, Yeshiva U, 1939; MS, CCNY, 1940; PhD, Boston U, 1950; licensed psychol, State of NC; m. Sydelle Katzman, Jan 9, 1943; c: Barbara, Sharon, Wayne. Prof, Livingstone Coll, Salisbury, NC, since 1960, Old Testament since 1961; lectr: Old Testament, U of NC, Charlotte, since 1968; psych, Johnson C Smith U, Charlotte since 1969; rabbi: Temple Beth El, Charlotte since 1959; Beth Jacob Syn, Plymouth, Mass, 1943-44; Cong Agudath Achim, Fitchburg, Mass, 1944-53; Temple Emanu-El Dothan, Ala, 1953-59; cons psychol, SE A Gen Hosp, Dothan, 1956-59. US Army, 1951-52. Mem: NC Council of Natl Council on Crime and Delinquency; NE Zionist Region, 1949; exec comm, Mh Assn of Charlotte and Mecklenburg Co; chmn, Charlotte chap NCCJ; mem: Amer, SE, NC, Ala, Psych Assns; Natl Assn of Bibl Instrs; J Chaplains Assn; Masons; Acad of Rel and Mh; hon, Intl Mark Twain Soc; clubs: Rotary; Kiwanis. Author: The Psychology of the Suffering Mind, 1951; Man on a Pendulum, 1956; Immortal Rebels, 1963; contbr to rel publs. Home: 5727 Riviere Dr, Charlotte, NC. Study: 1727 Providence Rd, Charlotte, NC.

GERBER, Leon, US, physician; b. Russ, May 27, 1913; s. Simon and Judith (Cogen); in US since 1919; MD, George Wash U Med Sch, 1936; m. Rosalie Borisow, Oct 2, 1933; c: Richard, Robert, Linda Klein. Asso prof, surg, George Wash since 1969; sr att surg, Wash Hosp Cen since 1959, fmr sr surg. Chmn, natl cabinet, UJA, Wash, DC; bd trustees, Wash Sch Psycht; mem: Smith Reed Russel, George Wash U Med Sch chap; fmr pres, Jacobi Med Soc, 1950; chmn, trustees, Isr Bond Org, 1968. Contbr to: sect on Vascular

Phys in Nash's Surg Phys; sci jours. Home: 4724 32 St, NW, Washington, DC. Office: 1800 Eye, Washington, DC.

GERBER, Rosalie B, US, attorney, author; b. Russ, 1913; d. George and Mary (Perkofsky) Borisow; in US since 1921; BA, George Wash U, Wash DC, 1933, JD, 1935; m. Leon Gerber, Oct 2, 1933; c: Linda Klein, Richard, Robert. Staff atty, Legal Aid Bur, since 1937; lectr, Amer Civilization and political sci, study groups, sponsored by Brandeis Comm, since 1964. Regional pres, Washington Women's ORT, since 1958; natl prog chmn, Natl Women's ORT; prog chmn, Women's Comm of Brandeis U, Wash, DC; bequest chmn, natl bd, Women's Amer ORT Fed; vice-pres, Wash sect, Natl Council of J Women; mem, bd: J Comm Centennial George Washington J Service Agcy; mem: Phi Sigma Sigma; Order of the Coif; DC Bar Assn. Author, The Responsibilities of Man, 1962; contbr to legal jours. Home: 4724 32 St, NW, Washington DC.

GERBER, William, US, retired government official, author; b. Phila, Pa, July 12, 1908; s. Samuel and Fanny (Kramer); BA, U of Pa, 1929; MA, George Wash U, 1932; att Johns Hopkins U, 1932-33, 1935-36; PhD, Columbia U, 1945; m. Sylvia Wigdor, Aug 6, 1933; c: Louis. Writer, fgn affairs, Ed Research Reports, Wash, DC since 1968; lectr: phil, U of Md since 1964; Amer U, Wash, DC, 1962; research and publ worker, State Dept, 1930-57, fgn service off, 1957-60; columnist, San Antonio Express, 1955; acting head, humanities div, Wash Hall Jr Coll, 1959-60; asst chief, div of fgn lab conditions, Lab Dept, 1962-68. Mem: Amer Phil Assn; Phi Beta Kappa; fmr mem, Avukah; clubs: Natl Press; Wash Phil, secy-treas since 1958. Author: The Department of State of the United States, 1942; The Domain of Reality, 1946; The Mind of India, 1967; ed, natl jour, Eta Sigma Phi, 1927-29; contbr to phil jours. Home: 4307 38 St NW, Washington, DC.

GERLA, Morton, US, engineer; b. Bklyn, NY, July 11, 1916; s. Harry and Jennie (Levy); BME, CCNY, 1937; att George Wash U, Wash, DC, 1941-42; Cal Inst of Tech, LA, 1944; New Sch for Social Research, NY, 1953-58; NYU, 1954; m. Miriam Kleeger, Oct 14, 1939; c: Harry, Seymour, Lisa. Mgr, machine design, Anaconda Wire and Cable Co since 1965; cons engr, 1946-56; ordnance engr, US Naval gun factory, 1939-45; asst chief engr, Industromatic Corp of Amer, 1945-47; cons engr, Superior Devl Corp, 1947-50; plant mgr, Screw Corp of Amer, 1950-52; design engr mgr, W L Maxon, 1952-55; pres, Lalin Construction, 1954-65. Dir, Jamaica Estates Assos; mem: Natl, NY State Socs Profsl Engrs; council, New Sch for Social Research Assns; Hillcrest J Cen, adult educ comm; Masons; prog comm, NY sect, Amer Soc for Metals; fmr: pres, dir, NY sect, Amer Rocket Soc; dir, Wash sect, Amer Soc Mech Engrs; vice-chmn, Instruments and Regulators Tech Sub-comm; mem, adult educ comm, NY Metrop region, United Syn of Amer. Spec interests: phil, psychol, aprapsych, space flight. Hobby painting. Home: 179-16 80 Rd, Jamaica Estates, NY. Office: 605 Third Ave, New York, NY.

GERSH, Harry, US, author, journalist; b. NYC, Dec 1, 1912; s. Solomon and Dvora (Lampert); att: Drexel Inst of Tech, 1930-34; Brookwood Coll, 1934-35; NYU, 1937; U of Paris, 1938; m. Violet Eberil, Oct 21, 1939; c: John, Ruth. Author: reporter: NYC, Phila newspapers; ed, lab jours; USN, 1943-45; asst, dir of educ, Textile Workers' Union, 1946-52; asst dir of info, Amer Newspaper Guild, 1952; dir of info: J Family Service, 1953-56; NY State, 1956-59; radio script writer, The Eternal Light, NBC documentaries; contbr to: Commentary, The Reconstructionist, New York Times, New Leader. Author: These Are My People, 1959; Minority Report, 1961; Women Who Made America Great, 1962; The Story of the Jew, 1964; Sacred Books of the Jews, 1968. Mem, Overseas Press Club, NY. Home: 204 Dante Ave, Tuckahoe, NY. Office: 730 Fifth Ave, New York, NY.

GERSH, Isidor, US, anatomist, educator; b. Bklyn, NY, Oct 6, 1907; s. Charles and Rebecca (Kaplan); BA, Cornell U, 1928; PhD, U of Chgo, 1932; m. Eileen Sutton, Dec 4, 1944; c: Frank, Ilona. Research prof, anat, U of Pa, since 1962; asso, Johns Hopkins Med Sch, 1933-43; asso prof, U of Ill Med Sch, 1946-49; prof, anat, U of Chgo, 1950-62. Lt cdr, chief of experimental path, Naval Med Research Inst, 1943-46. F: Julius Stieglitz Research in Chem Applied to Med, 1930-32; John Simon Guggenheim Memorial Research, 1939; Fulbright, 1956; mem: Sigma Xi; Amer Assn of Anats; Soc of Experimental Path; hon mem: Chilean Soc of Normal and Path Anat; Biol Soc of Concepcion, Chile. Contbr to sci

jours. Home: 4037 Baltimore Ave, Philadelphia, Pa. Office: U of Pa, Philadelphia, Pa.

GERSH, Richard B, US, business exec; b. Chgo, Ill, Oct 9, 1927; s. William and Bryde (Gore); att Nottingham U, 1949; BA, Syracuse U, 1950; m. Arlene Isaacs, June 17, 1956; c: Debra, Lewis. Pres, Richard Gersh Assos Inc, pr, since 1954; asst ed, Cash Box Mag, 1950-51; acct exec, Buddy Basch Assos, 1951-53; partner, Gersh and Wecht, 1953-54; guest lectr, Publicity Club of NY educ course, 1967-68. Mem, counselors sect, PR Soc of Amer; clubs: Tennis of Orange, NJ. Contbr of articles on financial pr. Hobbies: tennis, horseback riding. Home: 183 Forest Ave, Glen Ridge, NJ. Office: 200 W 57 St, New York, NY.

GERSHENFELD, Louis, US, bacteriologist, scientific cons, educator; b. Phila, Pa, Dec 23, 1895; s. George and Jennie (Stupe); BSc, Phila Coll Pharm and Sci, 1917, PhM, 1920, DSc, 1950; att: Jefferson Med Coll; U of Pa; m. Bertha Miller, Nov 17, 1918; c: George, Marvin. Dir em, Sch of Bact, Phila Coll of Pharm, and Sci, since 1968, dir 1917-18, prof em, bact and hygiene, since 1968, prof, 1920-68, hon life chmn, fac, since 1968, chmn, fac council, 1959-68, chmn, exec and grad comm, 1959-68; dir, Gershenfeld Lab, since 1919; cons: Mellon Inst; Council Pharm and Chem, AMA; Upper Darby Township Dept Health, 1930-66; instns; ind firms. Scia dv, US Govt, World War I, II. Chmn: clinical lab preparations, Natl Formulary IX, 1936-46; bact and serology comm, Pharm, Syllabus, 1932; comm on bact and immunology, Natl Council Pharm Research, 1934-39; chmn, publs comm: Amer Journal of Pharmacy; Natl Biol Stain Comm, since 1958; vice-pres: Mikveh Isr Cong, 1940; United Hebr Schs and Yeshivoth, 1946-49; hon mem, Carl Neuberg Soc for Intl Sci Relations; mem: B'nai B'rith; mem em for life, Dropsie Coll; mem bd govs, secy, 1943-68; bd govs, trustees, Erie Orphans Home; bd dirs, N Liberties Hosp; bd dirs, co-found, Akiba Acad. Author: Bacteriology and Sanitary Science; Biological Products; Bacteriology and Allied Subjects; Urine and Urinalysis; The Jew in Science; co-author, Jews in the World of Science; asso ed: US Dispensatory XXII, XXIII; Remington's Practice of Pharmacy IX, X; collaborator; Merck's Index V; Ency of Chemic Technology; Emergency Disinfections; Reddish's Antispectics; contbr to sci and lay jours. Recipient: Phila Coll Pharm and Sci Alumni Award, 1957; man of year, Rho, Pi Phi, 1958; dist service award, student council, Phila Coll Pharm and Sci, 1968. Home: 1101 N 63 St, Philadelphia, Pa. Office: 43rd and Kingsessing Ave, Philadelphia, Pa.

GERSHFIELD, Edward Morris, US, rabbi, educator; b. Winnipeg, Can, Aug 10, 1933; s. George and Lilly (Kelner); in US since 1953; BA, U of Man, 1953; MA, Columbia U, 1959, MA, Tchrs Coll, 1961; ordained rabbi, MHL, JTSA, 1958; DPhil, Oxford U, 1965; m. Toby Helman, Aug 23, 1953; c: Charles, James. Asso prof, rabb, reader, comparative law, JTSA, since 1960, TV prog ed, Eternal Light, 1965-69. Cons, comm on J law and standards, RA; mem, Can Classical Assn. Author, The Jewish Law of Divorce, 1968; contbr to theol and scholarly jours. Home: 501 W 123 St, New York, NY. Office: JTSA, 3080 Broadway, New York, NY.

GERSHMAN, Isadore, US, pediatrician; b. Providence, RI, July 12, 1913; s. Benjamin and Rose (Cohen); BA, Brown U, 1934; MD, Jefferson Med Coll, Phila, Pa, 1938; m. Helen Brosofsky, June 18, 1947; c: Sherry, James. Pvt practice since 1942; staff mem, hosps: RI; CV Chapin; Providence Lying-in; Miriam; St Joseph's; Roger Williams Gen. Med off, ground troops, 1942-46. Licentiate, Amer Bd of Peds; f, Amer Acad of Peds; mem: Providence Med Soc; RI Med Soc; Redwood Lodge; Temple Beth El. Home: 161 Waterman St, Providence, RI.

GERSHOM, Nahum, Isr, diplomat; b. Russ, Dec 27, 1909; s. Herzl and Sara (Rozovsky) Gershonovits; m. Jeannie Muraour, Dec 26, 1948. Ambassador to Congo-Brazzaville, since 1968; dir, complex of cotton gin factories, Isr, 1954-65; ambass to Guinea, 1965-67; repr, Min Fgn Affairs, Gaza area, 1967-68. Office: Min for Fgn Affairs, Jerusalem, Isr.

GERSHON, Karen, Isr, author; b. Ger, Aug 29, 1923; d. Paul and Selma (Schoenfeld) Loewenthal; in Isr since 1968; m. Val Tripp; c: Christopher, Anthony, Stella, Naomi. Author: The Relentless Years, 1959; Selected Poems, 1966; We Came As Children, 1966; Post-script, 1969. Recipient: Poetry Award, Brit Arts Council, 1967; Book Prize, J Chronicle, 1967; Poetry Award, Pioneer Women, 1968. Home and office: Jerusalem, Isr.

GERSHONI, Haim, Isr, educator; b. Chgo, Ill, Jan 2, 1922; s. Robert and Tillie (Hoodwin) Gershenow; in Isr since 1962; m. Marilyn Golinko, Nov 2, 1946; c: David, Jonathan, Judith. Sr lectr, Technion, Haifa, since 1965; chief ind engr: Joseph H Cohen and Sons, 1953-57; Richman Bros, 1957-62; gen mgr, Klil, Isr Non-Ferrous Inds, 1962-65. Lt, USN, 1943-46; lt cdr, Isr Navy, 1948-49. Contbr to profsl jours. Home: 40 Vitkin St, Haifa, Isr. Office: Technion, Haifa, Isr.

GERSHTENSON, Jack, US, social worker, administrator; b. NYC, July 12, 1909; s. Joseph and Minnie (Kalish); BS, Fordham U, 1931; att: Fordham Law Sch, 1931-33; NY Sch of Social Work, 1933-34; m. Beatrice Greenblatt, June 20, 1937; c: Sheila, Michael. Admnr, J Natl Home for Asthmatic Children, Denver, Colo since 1951; exec dir: Dallas J Comty Cen, 1942-45; B'nai B'rith Youth Org, 1945-46; Juvenile Camp and House, 1946-51. Mem: Natl Assn Social Workers; Acad Cert Social Workers; Natl Assn J Communal Workers; all hon soc of YM-YWHA, Bx, NY; charter mem, Amer Acad Med Admnrs; past pres, Westlake Comty Council. Author, A Case Study of a Group, 1935. Recipient, elected to Denver Post Gal of Fame, 1959. Home and office: 3447 W 19 St, Denver, Colo.

GERSHWIN, Ira, US, lyricist; b. NYC, Dec 6, 1896; s. Morris and Rose (Bruskin); att: CCNY; Columbia U; DFA, U of Md, 1966; m. Leonore Strunsky, Sep 14, 1926. Lyricist with brother, composer George Gershwin, and others. For stage: A Dangerous Maid, 1921; Lady, Be Good, 1924; Primrose (with D Carter), 1924; Tell Me More (with BG DeSylva), 1925; Tip Toes, 1925; Oh, Kay, 1926; Funny Face, 1927; Rosalie (with PG Wodehouse), 1927; Treasure Girl, 1928; Strike Up the Band, 1929; Show Girl (with G Kahn), 1929; Girl Crazy, 1930; Of Thee I Sing, 1932; Pardon My English, 1932; Let 'Em Eat Cake, 1933; Porgy and Bess (with DuBose Heyward), 1935. Films: Delicious, 1930; Shall We Dance? 1936; A Damsel in Distress, 1937; Goldwyn Follies, 1937; The Shocking Miss Pilgrim, 1946; An American in Paris, 1952. Lyrics for stage: Two Little Girls in Blue, 1921; Be Yourself (with Kaufman and Connelly), 1924; That's A Good Girl, 1928; Life Begins at 8:40 (with Harburg and Arlen), 1934; Ziegfeld Follies, 1936; Lady in the Dark, 1940; North Star, 1943; Cover Girl, 1943; Where Do We Go From Here? 1944; Firebrand of Florence, 1945; Park Ave, 1946; The Barkleys of Broadway, 1948; Give a Girl a Break, 1952; A Star is Born, 1954; The Country Girl, 1954; author, Lyrics on Several Occasions, 1959. Mem: ASCAP; Dramatists Guild. Recipient: Pulitzer Prize, 1932. Home: 1021 N Roxbury Drive, Beverly Hills, Cal.

GERSON, Menachem, Isr, educator; b. Frankfurt/Oder, Ger, Mar 20, 1908; s. Philipp and Betty (Lasker); in Isr since 1934; PhD, Humboldt U, Berlin, 1932; att Tchrs Acad, Berlin, 1926-34; m. Hava Schlamm, 1946; c: Jishai. Dir: Sem Hakibbutzim Oranim, Inst of Research on Kibbutz Educ. Mem educ comm, Kibbutz Arzi, fmr mem secretariat. Author: Fascism (Heb), 1939; The Tender Age in Kibbutz Education, 1947; On Education and the Family in Kibbutz, 1968. Recipient: prize for research project, Tchr's Fed, Isr, 1967. Home: Kibbutz Hasorea, Isr. Office: Sem Hakibbutzim Oranim, Kiriat Tivon, Isr.

GERSON, Nathaniel C, US, researcher, physicist; b. Boston, Mass, Oct 15, 1915; s. Benjamin and Julia (Blumenthal); BS, magna cum laude, U of Puerto Rico, 1943; MS, NYU, 1948; m. Sareen Epstein, Aug 26, 1945; c: Donald, Stanton, Richard, Martha, Stephanie. Cons physicist since 1956; asst chief, tech inves, US Weather Bur, 1944-46; asst on propagation, Watson Labs, 1946-48; chief, ionospheric physics lab, Air Force Cambridge Research Cen, 1948-56; secy, US natl comm, Intl Geophysical Year, 1953-57. Ed, Radiowave Absorption in the Ionosphere, 1962; contbr author: Advances in Geophysics, vols 1, 5, 1952, 1958; Reports on Progress in Physics, vol 14, 1951; Geophysics and the International Geophysical Year, 1957; Arctic Communications, 1964; Propagation Below 300 kc/s, 1963; The Arctic Basin, 1963; contbr: Yearbook, Ency Americana; sci jours. Club: Cosmos. Home and office: Trapelo Rd, RFD, S Lincoln, Mass.

GERSON, Stanley, US, physician; b. NYC, May 7, 1911; s. Bernard and Julie (Sprinz); AB, Harvard Coll, 1932; MD, LI Coll of Med, 1936; m. Dora Joelson, Aug 26, 1947; c: Benjamin, Bernita. Att urol, Barnert Hosp, Paterson, NJ since 1956; clinical asso, NY Med Coll since 1961; clinical instr, 1958-61; pres med bd, Barnert Hosp since 1968; surg, JWV, NJ, 1956-57. Capt, US Army MC, 1941-45. Dipl, Amer Bd

Urol; f: Amer Coll of Surgs; Intl Coll of Surgs; mem, bd, men's club, Barnert Temple; Masons; club: Harvard, NJ. Home: 570 Park Ave, Paterson, NJ. Office: 297 E 35 St, Paterson, NJ.

GERSTEIN, Israel, US, rabbi; b. Lodz, Pol, Aug 4, 1904; s. Mordecai and Esther (Weissfeld); in US since 1921; BA, Crane Coll, 1926; MA, U of Denver, 1932; ordained rabbi, Heb Theol Coll, 1927, DHL, 1958; m. Anna Swirsky, May 15, 1930; c: Hadassah Feder, Mordecai. Rabbi: Passaic Park J Cen, since 1946; Oheb Zedek, Denver, 1927-29; Agudath Achim, Shreveport, 1930-34; B'nai Zion, Chattanooga, 1934-46; columnist, Chattanooga Times, 1937-40. Chaplain, US Army, 1939-44. Pres: Rabb Council, NJ, 1954-57, hon pres since 1957; Zionist dist, Denver, 1927; Mizrachi Org, Chattanooga, 1934-46; USO, Chattanooga, 1940-46; mem, exec comm, RabCA, since 1944, chmn, natl conv, 1952; commnr, Passaic Co Mh Bd, 1964-66; bd govs: NY Bd of Rabbis; Passaic Local Assistance Bd. Author, Reveille or Taps, 1943; ed: Ohel Moed, Heb Theol Coll, Chgo, 1928; Jewish Life, 1947; Sermon Manual, RabCA, 1947. Home: 147 Van Houten Ave, Passaic, NJ. Study: 181 Van Houten Ave, Passaic, NJ.

GERSTEIN, Louis Coleman, US, rabbi; b. NYC, Mar 25, 1918; s. Solomon and Rachel (Zisser); BS, NYU, 1937, MA, 1938, PhD, 1942; MHL, JTSA, 1942, ordained rabbi, 1942; m. Amy Levinson, 1942; c: Jared, Abigail. Rabbi, Cong Shearith Isr since 1955, asso rabbi, 1942-55; lectr, JTSA: Sch of J Studies, 1942-51, Cantorial Sch, 1952-55, Women's Inst since 1958; chaplain, Civil Defense Corps, NYC since 1950; chmn, Heb Arts Comm, NY, 1939-41; chaplain, J Tchrs Assn since 1958; lectr, phil and rel, NYU since 1965; adj asso prof, CW Post Coll, 1963-65. Mem: exec council, RA, 1943-48, vice-chmn, placement comm, 1946-50, mem chmn, 1950-52; exec bd, NY Bd Rabbis, 1943-53, since 1964, mem chmn, 1951-53; exec bd, Rel in Amer Life since 1950; exec bd, Amer Friends of Touro Syn since 1960; vice-chmn, Rabbinic Cabinet of ORT since 1967; Cen Sephardic Comm. Author: Metaphysical Foundations of Bergsonian Ethics, 1938; Influence of Maimonides on Thomas Aquinas, 1943; Faith in Our Time, 1947. Recipient: A Ogden Butler Phil F, NYU, 1937-40. Home: 99 Central Park W, New York, NY. Study: 2 W 70 St, New York, NY.

GERSTEIN, Reva A, Can, psychologist; b. Toronto, Mar 27, 1917; d. David and Diana (Kraus) Appleby; BA, U Toronto, 1938, MA, 1939, PhD, 1945; m. Bertrand Gerstein, June 5, 1939; c: Irving, Ira. Natl dir, prog planning, Can Mh Assn since 1950, research, Ont div since 1953; coord, Mh Week of Can since 1949; fmr: instr, dept psych, U Toronto, 1938-50; psychol cons to: Leaside-E York Schs; J Family and Child Service, both Toronto. Pres, Hincks Treatment Cen, 1966-69; natl vice-pres, Can J Cong since 1953, mem, research comm; mem: Natl Council of J Women since 1942; Comty Chest, Toronto; Can Fed of U Women; Can Wfr Council; Can, Ont, Amer Psych Assns; Jt Planning Commn; World Fed Mh; Can Mh Assn; Holy Blossom Temple; Delta Epsilon Phi; ORT comm on U affairs, comm on educ; hon life f, Ont Psycht Assn; hon f of Founds Coll, York U; fmr: mem: organizing comm, 5th Intl Cong on Mh; bd dirs, Toronto Wfr Council. Contbr to profsl jours and mags. Office: 78 Bridle Park, RR 1, Don Mills, Ont, Can.

GERSTEL, Dan U, US, biologist; b. Berlin, Ger, Oct 23, 1914; s. Alfred and Else (Gerstal); in US since 1938; BS, U of Cal, 1940, MS, 1942, PhD, 1945; m. Eva Krojanker, Feb 13, 1938; c: David, Naomi. Wm Neal Reynolds prof, crop sci, genet, U of NC, since 1963, fac mem since 1950; kibbutz, Pal, 1935-38; asso geneticist, Stanford Research Inst, 1946-47; geneticist: US Dept Agric, 1948-49; visiting prof, plant genet, Weizmann Inst of Sci, Isr, 1961-62. Mem: Botanical Soc Amer; Genet Soc Amer; Genet Assn; Soc for Study of Evolution; NC Acad Sci; Sigma Xi. Contbr to profsl jours. Home: 1314 Crabapple Lane, Raleigh, NC. Office: Dept of Crop Sci, U of NC, Raleigh, NC.

GERSTL, Stephen John, Australia, organization exec; b. Czech, Jan 1, 1923; s. Adolph and Elizabeth (Weiss); in Austr since 1948; BA, econ, U Sydney, 1954; m. Rita Horshitz, Nov 21, 1946. Fed dir, hon secy, JNF, Austr and NZ since 1962, fmr gen secy; fmr: ed, Vestnik, Prague. Guerilla forces, Yugo, 1944-45. Found mem, Austr J Quarterly Found; mem: exec, Zionist Fed of Austr, NZ; State Zionist Council; B'nai B'rith, Sir John Monash Lodge; Tatersalls, Sydney; ed bd, The Bridge; fmr: chmn, PR dept, UIA, NSW; exec mem bd, J Mus Prague. Home: 174 Military Rd, Dover Hgts, NSW, Australia. Office: 140-146 Darlinghurst Rd, Sydney, Australia.

GERSTLE, Mark L, US, psychiatrist; b. SF, Cal, Oct 3, 1897; s. Mark and Hilda (Hecht); BA, Harvard U, 1918; BA, Stanford U, 1924; MD, 1925; m. Martha Graham, Feb 12, 1940; c: Mark, Marcia, Cynthia, Joyce, Douglas. Chief psycht, Youth Auth of Cal, since 1958; asst prof, neuropsycht: U of Cal, 1927-35; NY Postgrad Hosp, 1945-48; asso att psycht: Mt Sinai, NY, 1945-58; Hillside Hosp, 1951-58. USN, WW I and WW II. F: Amer Coll Phys; Amer Psycht Assn; NY Acad Med; Cal Acad Med; dipl, Amer Bd Psycht and Neur; mem: Mil Order of WWs; clubs: Harvard, NY and Boston. Contbr to med jours. Home: 2010 Pacific Ave, San Francisco, Cal.

GERSTMANN, Josef, US, psychiatrist, educator; b. Semberg, Aus, July 17, 1887; s. Joachim and Bertha (Zucker); in US since 1938; MD, U of Vienna, 1912; m. Martha Stein, Aug 24, 1920. Fmr: prof, psycht, neur, U of Vienna, 1928-38; dir, Inst for Nervous and Mental Disorders, Maria-Theresien Schlossel, 1930-38; neuro-psycht cons, acting research dir, Springfield State Hosp, Md, 1938-40; neur cons, research asso, St Elizabeth, Wash, DC, 1940-41; research asso, NY Neur Inst, 1941-45; visiting neuro-psycht, Goldwater Memorial, 1941-48; att neur and psycht, outpatient dept, Postgrad Hosp, 1941-49. F: Amer Psycht Assn; Acad of Neur; mem: NY State and Co Med Socs; AMA; Soc of St Elizabeth Hosp, Wash DC; Soc of Psycht and Neur, Rosario, Arg (hon). Author: Malaria Treatment of General Paresis, 1925, 1928; Gerstmann's Syndrome, 1924, 1927. Contbr to sci jours. Home and office: 240 Central Pk S, New York, NY.

GERSTNER, Robert, US, anatomist; b. NYC, Nov 7, 1906; s. Hyman and Fannie (Kanner); AB, cum laude, Wash Sq Coll, NYU, 1946; MS, Grad Sch of Arts and Scis, 1948, PhD, 1953; m. Clara Greenberg, Sep 21, 1940. Prof, anat, NYU, since 1967, fac mem since 1946; research asso, Guggenheim Inst, NYU, since 1955. F: Royal Microscopic Soc, Eng; AAAS; mem: Amer Assn Anats; AAUP; Amer Soc for Cell Biol; NY Acad Scis; Research Soc of Amer; Tissue Culture Assn; Beta Lambda Sigma; Sigma Xi. Contbr to profsl jours. Home: 5133 Surf Ave, Brooklyn, NY. Office: NYU, 339 E 25 St, New York, NY.

GERSTNER, S Berton, US, oral surgeon; b. NYC, July 4, 1900; s. Hyman and Frances (Kanner); DDS, U of Pa, 1919; m. Dorothee Cohen, July 1, 1922; c: Heywood, Elaine Wolf, Harold. Asso clinical prof, dept dent surg, Albert Einstein Med Coll, Yeshiva U, since 1955; dir, dent dept, chief oral surg service mem, med bd dirs, Bx Lebanon Med-Cen, since 1944; lectr, clinician, tchr, oral surg, at med and dent socs throughout East. F: Amer Coll Dents; Intl Coll Dents; NY Acad Dent; asso f, Brit Soc Oral Surgs; mem bd dirs, Bx Dent Soc, since 1932; chmn, dent div, Bx Co: FJP; UJA; Isr Bond Drive; mem: Amer Soc Oral Surgs; natl panel Amer Arbitration Soc; J Cen, Atlantic Beach, LI; NY Inst Clinical Oral Path; Sigma Epsilon Delta, past master, NY grad, chap; fmr: pres: mem bd dirs, chmn, ethics comm, Dist Dent Soc; N Dent Soc; Allied Dent Council; chmn, Oral Hygiene Comm of Gtr NY; Metrop Conf of Hosp Dent Chiefs; mem: house of delgs, Amer Dent Assn; council of ethics, Dent Soc State of NY. Recipient: medal, US Cong, for dist service as mem of draft bd: William Weinstein Memorial Medal for outstanding service as mem of draft bd; William Weinstein Memorial Medal for outstanding service to dent, Bx County Med Soc, 1959; testimonial dinner and awards; FJP, UJA, Isr Bond Drive. Home: 55 Park Ave, New York, NY. Office: 384 E 149 St, New York, NY.

GERTZ, Elmer, US, lawyer, author, communal leader; b. Chgo, Ill, Sep 14, 1906; s. Morris and Grace (Grossman); PhB, U Chgo, 1928; JD, 1930; m. Ceretta Samuels, Aug 16, 1931, (decd); c: Theodore, Margery Hectman; m. 2nd, Mamie Laitchin Friedman, June 21, 1959; c: Jack Friedman. Pvt practice since 1930; asso, McInerney, Epstein & Arvey; asst to masters in chancery Jacob Arvey, Samuel Epstein, 1930-41; atty for Nathan Leopold in successful parole proceedings, 1957-58; atty various censorship litigations since 1961; atty for Jack Ruby, successfully setting aside death penalty. Prin contrib: defense of individual rights and freedom of expression. Chmn: legal educ comm, Chgo Bar Assn; Bill of Rights comm, Sixth Ill Constitutional Conv, 1969-70; dir, pr, Ill Police Assn, 1934; mem: exec comm, Ill Comm Equal Job Opportunity; natl, Chgo adv bd, comm on legal action, AJCong;

chmn, soldier vote comm, Profsl and Bus People, 1944; mem, law and order comm, Commn on Human Relations, since 1945; vice-pres, Ill Freedom to Read Comm; chmn, Vets Housing Comm, 1945-47; mem, Mayor's Housing Comm, 1946-48; adv comm, Chief Justice Munic Court, Chgo, 1950-51; pres, Gtr Chgo Council, AJCong, 1959-63; mem: bd dir, Jackson Park Hosp; trustee, Bellaire; natl bd, City of Hope; mem: Public Housing Assn (found, counsel, pres, 1943-49); Civil War Round Table (found, exec comm, pres, hon life mem); Adult Educ Council, Chgo, (secy, pres); Amer Friends Heb U; Shaw Soc (found, pres); Chgo Law Inst; Amer, Fed, 7th Circuit, Chgo Bar Assns; Chgo Hist Soc; Decalogue Soc; Soc Midland Authors; clubs: Chgo Lit; Cliff Dwellers; Caxton; Boswell; City. Author: Frank Harris: A Study in Black and White, 1931; The People vs Chicago Tribune, 1942; American Ghettos, 1946; Books and Their Right to Live, 1965; A Handful of Clients, 1965; Moment of Madness: The People vs Jack Ruby, 1969; contbr to various periodicals. Recipient: Chgoland honor roll, Chgo Council Against Discrimination, 1946; Gold Key Award, City of Hope, 1966; award, Ill Div, ACLU, 1963. Spec interests: public affairs, Amer Pres, Eng authors. Home: 6249 N Albany Ave, Chicago, Ill. Office: 120 S LaSalle St, Chicago, Ill.

GERTZ, Samuel, Isr, rabbi; b. US; BA, ordained rabbi, DD, all Yeshiva U, NY, grad, Tchrs Inst; m. Sylvia Bauman. Dir, Moadon Haoleh, Tel Aviv; fmr: rabbi: Cong Agudath Achim; B'nai Jacob, Bklyn, NY; asst dean, Mesifta Tifereth, Jerusalem Rabb Sem. Vice pres, Natl Council of Young Isr; mem, RabCA. Ed, Integration, monthly for new immigrants. Home: 15 Bezalel St, Tel Aviv, Isr. Office: 109 Hayarkon St, Tel Aviv, Isr.

GERY, Ig'al, Isr, scientist, educator; b. Tel Aviv, Isr, Sep 15, 1932; s. Ozer and Dina (Shilevitch); MSc, Heb U, Jerusalem, 1958; PhD, 1963; m. Miriam Mayer, Jan 2, 1962; c: Ron, Yoav. Lectr, Med-Ecology Dept, Heb U Med Sch since 1966; Helen Hay Whitney research f, Yale U; cancer research sci, Roswell Park Memorial Inst, 1963-64. IAF, 1950-52. Contbr to sci jours. Office: Heb U Med Sch, Jerusalem, Isr.

GERZON, Maurice J, Isr, business exec; b. Groningen, Holland, 1895, s. Josef; in Isr since 1934; m. Alisa Levy, 1936; four c. Co-found, gen mgr: Frutarom Ltd, since 1934; Electrochem Inds Ltd, since 1953; commercial counsellor, Isr Legations, Fr, Benelux, 1949-50. Pres, BBB, since 1964. Home: 16 Kidron St, Mt Carmel, Haifa, Isr. Office: POB 1929, Haifa, Isr.

GESENSWAY, Louis, US, composer, violinist; b. Dvinsk, Latvia, Feb 19, 1906; s. Solomon and Sarah; in US since 1926; att: Toronto Conservatory, Can, 1916-26; Curtis Inst of Music, Phila, Pa, 1926-29; studied with Zoltan Kodaly, Budapest, Hung, 1929-31; m. Mary Kramer, Sep 19, 1929; c: Daniel, Judith Skoogfors. First violinist, Phila Orch, since 1926; toured Can at age 12. Composer: Three Movements for String and Percussion, 1945; Concerto for Flute and Orch, 1946; Four Squares of Philadelphia, a symphonic tone poem, 1955; Commemoration Sym, for large orch, 1968; Suite on J Themes; Five Russ Pieces; duos; string quartets; tone poems; sonatas; concertos; works performed world-wide by maj orchs, including: Phila Orch, under Eugene Ormandy; NY Philharmonic Orch, under Dimitri Mitropolous; State Radio Orch of Finland, under Paavo Berglung; Chgo Sym Orch, under Hans Schmidt-Isserstedt; chamber music compositions performed at: Natl Gal, Wash, DC; Acad of Music Foyer, Phila; recorded by Columbia Records. Prin contribs, devl of Color-Harmony, new form of musical expression. Mem, ASCAP. Recipient, C Hartman Kuhn Award, Phila Orch, 1945. Hobbies: swimming, painting, violin varnishes, outdoor recreation. Home: 433 Sedgwick St, Philadelphia, Pa. Office: Phila Orch, Broad and Locust Sts, Philadelphia, Pa.

GESZTES, Thomas Moshe, Isr, physician; b. Komarno, Czech, Jan 4, 1926; s. Zoltan and Irma (Politzer); in Isr since 1949; att Charles U, Prague, 1946-49; MD, Heb U, Jerusalem, 1955; m. Dinah Kerekes, Tel Aviv, Oct 28, 1954; c: Yael, Ariela. Chief anaesthesiologist, Negev Cen Hosp, since 1960; fmr, anaesthesiologist, Hadassah Hosp, Jerusalem; lectr, U Inst of Post Grad Med Training. Capt, MC, IDF, 1957-60. Fmr pres, Lions Intl, Beersheba Br; mem, Isr Assn of Anaesthesiologists; fgn asso, Royal Soc of Med. Author: Sodium Thiopenthone Supp in Paediatry, 1958; Suxamethonium Apnoea with Eye Drops, etc, 1966. Spec interests: anthropology of rel, archaeol, photography. Home: 17 Barak St, Beersheba, Isr. Office: Negev Cen Hosp, Beersheba, Isr.

GETRY, Irena, Isr, dancer, choreographer; b. Cracow, Pol, May 13, 1924; d. Leon and Felicia (Singer); in Isr since 1946; grad, Acad of Art, Vienna; att Conservatorium of Music, Cracow; div; c: Nana. Choreographer: Habimah Theatre; Ohel Theatre; Isr Opera; works choreographed: Concerto for Organ; The Barrier; Silent Dances; Majorca; Dispute with God; The Sick Village. Author: wrote, dir, produc, film, The Invited One, 1966; booklet, What is Ballet, 1960. Spec interests: film making, jazz. Home and studio: 6 Hapardess St, Tel Aviv, Isr.

GETTES, Charles N, US, surgeon; b. Kiev, Russ, Mar 23, 1902; s. Nathan and Rose (Goldenberg); in US since 1905; BA, Temple U, Phila, 1922, MD, Med Sch, 1926; post-grad study: U of Vienna, 1928-29; Harvard U Med Sch, 1931; m. 1st, Edith Hurwitz, Mar 24, 1928 (decd); c: Norton, Leonard, Eleanor Sax; m. 2nd, Gladys Cohen, Nov 1, 1964. Surg, otolaryngology, Mt Auburn Hosp, Cambridge, Mass, since 1932; cons, Waltham Hosp, Mass, since 1931; instr, otolaryngology, Tufts Med Sch, Boston, 1930-52; asst surg, otolaryngology, Boston City Hosp, 1929-52. Lt, US Army MC Res, 1929-32; capt, instr, civil defense, Watertown, 1941-45. Pres: Beth-El Temple Cen, 1936-38; Constitution lodge, B'nai B'rith, 1950; Cambridge Med Improvement Soc; Medford Med Soc; AMA; Mass Med Soc; Amer Acad of Ophthal and Otolaryngology; NE Orl Soc; Amer Orl Soc for Advancement of Plastic and Reconstructive Surg; Pan-Amer Soc of Ophthal; Pan-Amer Soc of Otolaryngology; Phi Delta Epsilon; Masons; club, Indian Ridge Country. Contbr to med jours. Home: 5 Stonehill Drive, Stoneham, Mass. Office: 51 Brattle St, Cambridge, Mass.

GETZLER, Zvi, Isr, civil engr; b. Amsterdam, Holland, Jan 14, 1919; s. Zev and Amalia (Lever); in Isr since 1938; civil engr dipl, Technion, Haifa, 1942, MSc, 1956; m. Sarah Markowich, Feb 26, 1946; c: Tirzah, Avraham. Asso prof, civil engr, Technion since 1967, fac mem since 1950, head comm for hum relations, student adv; fmr: secy, fac civil engr; mem sub-comm for grad studies in structures, all Technion; fmr: in pvt practice; structural designer, Pal Elec Co; pvt cons; visiting asst prof, MIT, US. Prin contribs: research in transmission towers; machinery found; spec found problems; soil mechs; buried structures; underground structures; differential settlements in bldgs; founds of tall bldgs. Mem: Engrs and Architects Assn, Isr; Intl Soc of Soil Mechs and Found Engr; Sigma Xi; Amer Soc of Civil Engrs. Contbr to profsl jours. Recipient: Structural Sect Award, Boston Soc of Chem Engr, 1963-64; Clemens Herschel Prize, 1966-67. Home: 71 Pinsker St, Haifa, Isr. Office: Technion, Haifa, Isr.

GEVA, Reuven, Isr, government official, jurist; b. Oswiecim, Pol, Oct 10, 1927; s. Samuel and Yochevet (Landau) Grubner; in Isr since 1945; LLB, Heb U, Jerusalem, 1961; att Natl Defense Coll; m. Sarah Milshtein, Mar 25, 1957; c: Yoav, Yael, Michal. Dep dir gen, Min of Lab since 1968; insp gen, manpower, Min of Lab, 1960-68; responsible for civil manpower mobilization, Six Days War. Maj, IDF, 1948-57. Home: 4 Afner St, Givatayim, Isr. Office: Min of Lab, Jerusalem, Isr.

GEVA, Yosef, Isr, retired army officer, business exec; b. Vienna, Aus, 1924; in Isr since 1939; att Heb U, 1955-56; m. four c. Gen mgr, Supersol supermarkets, since 1970; fmr: dir, gen, Min of Absorption, 1968-1970; major gen, IDF, cdr, cen command; mem, Haganah; co-cdr, IDF, battalion cdr, chief of staff duties br, head of training br, gen staff; defense attache, US, Can. Office: 18 Hashomer St, B'nai B'rak, Isr.

GEVIRTZ, Yitshak, Isr, government official; b. London, Eng, Aug 30, 1907; s. Aharon and Puah (Lerman); in Isr since 1921; att Whitechapel Found Sch, Etz Hayim Yeshiva, both in London; m. Malka Issaharoff, Nov, 1928; c: Oved, Aharon, Rahel, Amos. Staff off, Internal Affairs, Mil Govt, Gaza and Sinai since 1967; fmr: head, dept regional councils, Min of Interior; chmn, regional council, Hof Hasharon. IS, Haganah; IDF. Mem: Agric Workers Org (Histadrut); haKibbutz Hameuchad. Author: Rural Local Government in Israel, 1962; Local Government in Israel, 3 vols, 1962. Spec interest, ME Affairs. Home: Kibbutz Shefayim, Isr. Office: Yarmuk St, Gaza, Isr.

GEWIRTZ, Leonard B, US, rabbi; b. Bklyn, NY, Jan 25, 1918; s. Henry and Leah (Greenberg); BSS, CCNY, 1941; ordained rabbi, Heb Theol Coll, 1946; m. Sarah Kerstein, Nov 21, 1948; c: Isaac, Joseph. Rabbi: Adas Kodesh Shel Emeth Syn, since 1947; Or Chodosh Cong, Chgo, 1946-47. Exec comm, social activities comm, RabCA; bd dirs, Del Mh Assn; mem: Citizens Conf on Zoning, Housing, Planning; NCCJ; Del Ind Council for Ind Peace; B'nai B'rith; Rel Zionists Amer; Bd Rabbis of Gtr Phila; World Federalists; ACLU. Author: The Authentic Jew and His Judaism, 1961; contbr to Anglo-J jours; found, radio prog, "The Rabbi Speaks," WDEL, since 1948. Home: 127 W 37 St, Wilmington, Del. Study: Washington Blvd and Torah Way, Wilmington, Del.

GEZARI, Temima, US, artist, sculptor; b. Pinsk, Russ, Dec 21, 1907; d. Israel and Bella (Cohen); in US since 1908; dipl: Tchrs Inst, JTSA, 1925; Master Inst of United Arts, 1930; att NY Sch of Fine and Applied Arts; Art Students League; Columbia U; New Sch for Social Research; Taos Sch of Art, NM; m. Zvi Gezari, 1938; c: Daniel, Walter. Dir, art educ, J Educ Comm, NY, since 1940; lectr, art and art educ in maj cities of US; instr, arts: Tchrs Inst since 1935; fmr: Master Inst of United Arts; Clinic for Gifted Children, NYC; chmn art comm, Riverside Neighborhood Assembly, NY; mem, comm art educ, Modern Mus. One-man shows: NY; Phila; Cleveland; Wash, DC; Jerusalem; one-man sculpture shows: Retrospective, Suffolk Mus, 1965, 1966, 1967; Loeb Cen, NYU, 1965, 1968; NY Hilton; House of Living Judaism. Prin works: mural: Syn of Soc for Advancement of Judaism; Syn in Cejwin Camp, Port Jervis, NY; Children's dining room, Mishmar Haemek, Isr; illus: Children of the Emek; Gateway to Jewish Song; Hillel's Happy Holidays. Mem: Intl Soc of Educ Through Art; Natl Art Assn; Natl Comm on Art Educ; f, Intl Inst of Arts and Letters; established Art Workshop for Tchrs, NYC, 1940; Jr Gal, J Mus, NYC, 1947; Temima Gezari Sch of Art for Adults and Children, 1952. Author: Footprints and New Worlds, 1957; co-author: The Jewish Kindergarten, 1944; pub filmstrips: Growing Through Art, 1955; Art and the Growing Child, 1956; Art of Israeli Children and Miniature Stone Sculpture, 1963; contbr to educ and art periodicals. Recipient: award, Film Council of Amer, 1956; scholastic award, 1957. Home: 211 Central Park W, New York, NY.

GHEESTA, Jemmy M, India, dental surg; b. Karachi, India, Jan 29, 1904; s. MN and Diana; dipl, Bodee Dent Sch, NY, 1925; m. Mozelle Sopher, Oct 6, 1953 (decd). Pvt practice since 1923. Dent surg, British Navy personnel, Karachi, 1926-29; Capt, Civic Guards, Bombay, 1939-46. Chmn, Bombay Zionist Assn since 1962, pres since 1968, hon secy, 1959-61; mem: exec comm, Maharashtra State Govt Dent Council, 1967-72; cen council, All India Dent Assn, fmr vice pres, pres, Bombay br; exec, United Isr Appeal; Cen J Bd of India since 1965; fmr: mem exec comm, Bombay State Dent Council; asst secy, Council on Dent Health. Home: 5 Auburn House, Forjett St, Cumballa Hill, Bombay, India. Office: Princess Bldg, Corner of J J Hospital, Bombay, India.

GIAT, Aaron, US, educator; b. Sanaa, Yemen, Apr 15, 1907; s. Yichyah and Afia (Mizrachi); in US since 1928; ordained rabbi, Yeshivath Hahayim V'haShalom; PhD, Dropsie Coll, 1955; hon Rabb deg, Acad of J Rel; m. Sylvia Lipkowitz, Jan 7, 1942; c: Leona Schneider, Aaron, Steven, Daniel. Prof, Heb: Acad J Rel since 1960; People's U and J Tchrs Sem, since 1941; fac mem, Grad Sch, Yeshiva U summer sessions since 1958; instr: JTSA, 1946-51; HUC-JIR, 1946-56; Heb Union Sch, Educ and Sacred Music, 1948-56; Bklyn Coll, 1962-66; asst prof, Heb Tchrs Coll, Brookline; asso prof, libr, Baltimore Heb Coll. Mem: CCAR; Natl Assn Prof Heb; AAUP; Acad Heb Lang of Isr; Isr Exploration Soc; Dropsie Coll; JWB. Home: 205 E 94 St, New York, NY.

GICHNER, Isabelle, US, civic worker; b. NYC, Sep 1, 1908; d. Philip and Flora (Kaiser) Saloman; BA, Cornell U, 1929; m. Henry Gichner, June 1, 1930; c: Susan, Bette, David, Flora. Chmn, Mid-Cent White House Conf on Children and Youth, 1950; pres: Adas Isr Sisterhood, 1940-42; Cornell Women's Club, 1946-48; vice-pres: JCC, 1948-52; United Comty Services, 1950-52; co-chmn, women's div, NCCJ, 1958-68; parliamentarian, Natl Women's League of United Syn Amer, 1958-68; chmn: DC Commn on Status of Women, 1967-69; mem: B'nai B'rith; Hadassah; League Women Voters; Brandeis U; Alpha Epsilon Phi. Home: 5160 Linnean Terr NW, Washington, DC.

GICHON, Mordecai, Isr, army officer, educator, author; b. Berlin, Ger, Aug 16, 1922; s. Hahum and Charlotte (Salomon) Gichermann; in Isr since 1934; MA, PhD, Heb U; m. Chava Goldberg, 1950; c: Arion, Eran, Eyal. Sr lectr, mil hist, Tel Aviv U, since 1961. J Brig, Brit Army, 1941-46; rescue, relief, and immigration work in Europe, 1945-46; full-time Haganah service, 1947; command, staff, training missions, IDF, since 1948, lt col, res. Author: Carta's Atlas of Palestine; Military History, 1969; contbr to profsl jours. Mem: bd dirs, Assaf Simhoni Assn for Mil Hist; council, Isr Exploration Soc; Isr Oriental Soc; Isr Hist Soc; Isr Soc for Classical Studies; Isr Fgn Policy Assn. Recipient: Sukenik prize, archeol, Heb U, 1960. Home: 14 Assael St, Zahala, Tel Aviv, Isr. Office: Tel Aviv U, Isr.

GIDEON, Miriam, US, composer, educator; b. Greeley, Colo, Oct 23, 1906; d. Abram and Henrietta (Shoninger); BA, Boston U, 1926; MA, musicology, Columbia U, 1946; m. Frederic Ewen, Dec 19, 1949. Mem, music fac: Manhattan Sch of Music, since 1967; Cantors' Inst, JTSA, 1955-67; Bklyn Coll, 1944-54; CCNY, 1947-55. Composer: String Quartet, 1946; Woodwind Quartet, 1948; Sonata for Viola and Piano, 1948; Symphonia Brevis, 1953; Fortunato, opera, 1957; Sonata for Cello and Piano, 1961; songs; piano suites; chamber settings: Hound of Heaven, 1945; Shakespeare's Sonnets, 1951; Millay's Sonnets, 1953; choral works: Habitable Earth, cantata; Questions on Nature; Spiritual Madrigals; Rhymes from the Hill. Mem, bd govs: Amer Composers Alliance; Intl Soc Contemporary Music; League of Composers. Recipient: Bloch Prize for choral work, 1948. Home: 410 Central Park W, New York, NY. Office: 3080 Broadway, New York, NY.

GIDWITZ, Joseph L, US, business exec; b. Memphis, Tenn, Jan 16, 1905; s. Jacob and Rose (Wolff); PhD, U Chgo, 1928; m. Emily Klein, Sep 11, 1930; c: Alan, Ralph, Betsy. Chmn Consolidated Packaging Corp since 1963; John Strange Paper Co since 1956; dir: Natl Paperboard Assn since 1964; Harmony Co; Paperboard Group, Amer Paper Inst since 1966; vice-pres, dir, mem exec comm, Helene Curtis Ind Inc; dir, vice chmn, Continental Materials Corp; trustee, Federated Mortgage Inves; dir, Fibre Box Assn; adv comm, War Produc Bd. Chmn, Gerontological Council, Chgo; mem: natl council, JDC; natl comm, UJA; Chgo Assn of Commerce and Ind; Ill C of C; NAM; Pres Assn, Inc; Chgo Council on Fgn Relations; clubs: Harmonie, NY; Standard, Chgo; fmr: found, chmn, dir, Container Ind Conf; adv bd, U Mo Sch of Forestry; pres, dir, Allocation Fund; dir, vice pres, CJA; dir, pres: Comty Council of J Charities; Divs Fund, Chgo; J Children's Bur, Chgo; J Fed of Metrop Chgo; dir, vice-pres, CJFWF, NY; trustee, Chgo U Cancer Research Found. Home: 950 Dean Ave, Highland Park, Ill. Office: 72 W Adams St, Chicago, Ill.

GIFTER, Mordecai, US, rabbi, educator; b. Portsmouth, Va, Nov 4, 1916; s. Israel and Mae (Luria); att Rabbi Isaac Elchanan Theol Sem, 1930-33; ordained rabbi, Telshe Yeshiva, 1938; m. Shoshana Bloch, Dec 29, 1941; c: Benjamin, Shlomith, Luba, Chasya, Zalmen, Israel. Pres, Telshe Yeshiva, Cleveland, O, since 1964, dean since 1945, prof, Talmud, rel, ethics since 1945; instr, Rabbi Isaac Elchanan Theol Sem, NYC, 1939-40; rabbi: Cong Lubawitz Nusachari, Baltimore, 1940-42; Orthodox J Comty, Waterbury, Conn, 1942-45. Author: Novellae to Talmud; Pirkei Emvnoh, 1969; Essays in Religion and Ethics; contbr to Talmudic jours, J periodicals. Home: 28570 Nutwood Lane, Wickliffe, O. Office: 28400 Euclid Ave, Wickliffe, O.

GIL, Avimar, Isr, civil engineer; b. Tel Aviv, Isr, Jan 6, 1929; s. Aba and Rachel (Schick); dipl ing, Technion, Haifa, 1952; m. Tova Jochnowitz, Apr 11, 1954; c: Dahlia, Elana. Dist engr, N dist, PWD, Isr since 1961. Mem, Engrs and Architects Assn, Isr. Home: 22 Megiddo St, Nazareth Elite, Isr. Office: Nazareth Elite, Isr.

GIL, Benjamin Z, Isr, statistician; b. Pol, July 13, 1911; s. Chaim and Amalia (Benkendorf) Freilichmann; in Isr since 1929; D, political sci, U Rome, 1936; m. Jania Hammer, July 31, 1944; c: Avishai, Adith. UN population census expert, adv to Ghana Govt since 1959; fmr: dir, div of demographic and social stat, Cen Bur of Stat, Isr; lectr, stat, Tel Aviv U; Intl Lab Org Expert in Malawi. British Army, 1942-46; Haganah, IDF, 1939-50. Mem: Intl Stat Inst; exec bd, Intl Inst of Sociol; Intl Union of Sci Study of Population; Amer Stat Assn; Stat Assn of Paris; Sociol Soc of Ghana. Author: Thirty Years of Jewish Immigration to Israel, 1919-49, 1950; co-author: Registration of Population (8.xi, 1948) Isr, 2 Parts, 1955, 1956; Population Census of Ghana, 8 vols, 1964. Offices: Census Office, Box 1350, Accra, Ghana; UNDP, Box 1423, Accra, Ghana; Cen Bur of Stats, Jerusalem, Isr.

GILADI, Dan, Isr, social sci, educator; b. Tel Aviv, Isr, Nov 25, 1932; s. Nachum and Yocheved (Yelin); PhD, Heb U, Jerusalem, 1961; m. Ora Ardon, Aug, 1954; c: Nachum, Yoav. Lectr, Dept of Lab Studies, Tel Aviv U, since 1966; prin: Bet Berl, regional comprehensive secondary sch, 1961-66; Sdeh Boker, tchrs training coll, 1968-69. IDF, 1950-51. Author: Hityashvut Ovedet, 1966; The Fourth Aliya Period, 1968. Recipient: Shenkar Award, Histadrut, 1968; War Veteran. Hobbies: swimming, music. Home: 12 Moledet St, Kfar Saba, Isr. Office: Tel Aviv U, Tel Aviv, Isr.

GILAT, Aharon, Isr, mechanical engr; b. Vilna, Pol, Mar 27, 1910; s. Gershon and Rachel (Kessel) Glizer; in Isr since 1934; dipl, mech ing, Tech U, Warsaw, 1932; m. Agnes Rubinstein, June 4, 1933; c: Ariela, Moshe. Dir, Standard Insts of Isr, since 1968; fmr: dep dir gen, Min of Commerce and Ind; gen adv to city mgmt, Tel Aviv-Jaffa Munic; dir, Inves Cen, Govt of Isr; found, head, Productivity, Jt Productivity Councils div, Histadrut; co-found, Productivity Inst of Isr; lectr, fundamentals of produc mgmt, Heb U. Maj, IDF, 1948-49. Mem: exec comm, Histadrut; cen comm, Engrs and Architects Assn, Isr; directorate, Productivity Inst of Isr. Contbr to jours. Home: 13 Meggido St, Tel Aviv, Isr.

GILAT, Gideon, Isr, physicist, educator; b. Berlin, Ger, Mar 6, 1929; s. Haim and Shoshana (Nussbaum) Goldberg; in Isr since 1933; MSc, Heb U, Jerusalem, 1956; PhD, 1962; m. Edna Cohen, Mar 23, 1955; c: Ittai, Sharon. Asso Prof, Physics Dept, Technion, Haifa since 1969; postdoc f, AECL, Can, 1963-64; physicist, ORNL, Oak-Ridge, Tenn, 1964-67; sr research asso, CNEN, It, 1967, 1968; visiting prof, AB Atomenergi, Swed, 1969. IDF, 1948-50. Mem: Isr, Amer, Eur Phys Socs. Recipient: Hagana, War of Independence, Sinai decorations. Hobbies: music, bridge. Home: 21 Elhanan St, Haifa, Isr. Office: Technion, Haifa, Isr.

GILAT, Yitzhak Dov, Isr, educator; b. Lith, Sep 22, 1919; s. Haim and Devora (Rosing) Gitelson; in Isr since 1935; MA, Heb U, Jerusalem, 1953, PhD, 1965; m. Ruth Horn, 1947; c: Israel, Jacob, Ariel. Head, Talmud dept, Bar Ilan U since 1968; prof, Talmud, Bar Ilan and Tel Aviv U's; insp, acting head, Rel Youth Aliyah, 1947-50; insp of schs, instr, tchrs sem, Min of Educ, 1951-58. Judge on conferring Rabbi Kook Award for J Studies by Tel Aviv Munic. Author, Mishnato Shel Rabbi Eliezer Ben Horkanos uMekoma beToldot haHalacha, 1968; dep ed, Talmud Div in Ency Judaica; contbr to scholarly publs. Recipient, Kugel Award for J Studies, Holon Munic, 1969. Home: 15 Ben Sira St, Tel Aviv, Isr.

GILATH, Irith, Isr, chemical engr; b. Arad, Rum, May 10, 1939; d. Aladar and Martha (Havas) Vigh; in Isr since 1960; BSc, Technion, Haifa, 1962, MSc, 1966; m. Chaim Gilath, July 18, 1962; c: Yael, Dan. Chem engr, Weizmann Inst since 1967; lab mgr, Isr Wine Inst, 1962-67. Research: Wine Stabilization by Ion Exchangers, Separation of Xenon Isotopes by Thermal Diffusion. Delg, Tel Aviv Council of Engrs. Home: 21 Beeri, Rehovot, Isr. Office: Weizmann Inst, Rehovot, Isr.

GILBERT, Arthur N, US, rabbi, organization exec; b. Phila, Pa, June 4, 1926; s. Harry and Esther (Glaser); BA, NYU, 1947; ordained rabbi, MHL, HUC-JIR, 1951; cert, Natl Psych Assn for Psychan, 1955; hon DD, Ia Wesleyan Coll, 1967; m. Jean Kroeze; c: Karen, Amy, Lisa, Hillary. Dean, Reconstructionist Rabb Coll, Phila, since 1968; asst to pres, J Reconstructionist Found, since 1967; staff cons to project, rel freedom and public affairs, NCCJ since 1961; fmr: dir, natl dept of interrel coop, B'nai B'rith; asst rabbi, Temple B'nai Jeshurun, Newark, NJ. Fmr chmn, J Peace f; mem: N Amer Acad of Ecumenists; Rel Educ Assn; Assn of J Comty Relations Workers; NY Bd of Rabbis; Natl Assn of Intergroup Relations Officials; CCAR. Author: The Vatican Council and the Jews, 1968; A Jew in Christian America, 1966; co-author, Your Neighbor Celebrates, 1957; contrib author, American Catholics: A Protestant-Jewish Viewpoint, 1960; asso ed, Jour of Ecumenical Studies since 1966; contrib ed, Reconstructionist, since 1958; fmr: dept ed, CCAR Jour; ed: Chr Friends Bull; J Peace F Tidings; contbr to rel jours. Hobby, sculpture. Home: 145 W 79 St, New York, NY. Office: 43 W 57 St, New York, NY.

GILBERT, Jennie Z, (pen name, Jennie Z), Ir, barrister-at-law, voluntary communal leader; b. Dublin, Ir; d. Marks and Chyariva Rubinstein (Cowan); barrister-at-law, U Coll, King's Inn, Dublin; m. Gerald Gilbert, Apr 20, 1939; c: Ruth Bernstein, Michael. Barrister-at-law, first J woman to be called to the Ir Bar; peace commn. Pres: Mizrachi Women of Ir; pr off, Ir-Isr Friendship league; hon treas, Home for Aged J, ladies comm; life hon pres, Talmud Torah, ladies comm; vice-pres, secy, Heb Speakers' Circle; hon auditor, J Repres Council, Ir; intl comm mem, Ir housewives assn; repr for Ir: Mizrachi, Hapoel Hamizrachi Eur Council; life gov, Dublin Talmud Torah; hon vice-pres, Torah Ve'Avoda; past: hon secy, hon treas, vice-chmn, ZC of Ir; vice-chmn, hon treas and secy, Dublin J Debating Soc; Ir's delg, 26th ZC, Jerusalem; mem: Royal Dublin Soc; Ir Housewives Assn. Spec interests: music, intl affairs, Zionist affairs, social wfr. Home: 40 Merton Rd, Rathmines, Dublin 6, Ir.

GILBERT, Nathan, US, chemical engr, educator; b. NYC, Sep 27, 1913; s. Sam and Goldie (Rabinowitz); BS, U of Cal, Berkeley, 1936; PhD, U of Wis, 1942; m. Hilda Kessler, June 30, 1940; c: Miriam, David. Prof, chem engr, U of Cincinnati since 1953; research f, Manchester Coll of Sci and Tech, sr travelling f, OEEC, 1961-62; project leader, chem engr, TVA, 1942-53. Prin contrib, discovered process for fixation of atmospheric nitrogen, 1942. Sr vice-pres, Temple Sholom, 1960; State chmn, Ala Assn of B'nai B'rith lodges, 1952, pres, AM Cohen lodge, 1958; mem: Amer Inst Chem Engrs; Amer Chem Soc; Amer Soc for Engr Educ; JWF; Cincinnati UA. Contbr to profsl jours. Spec interests: rel; anthropology. Home: 1729 Northampton Dr, Cincinnati, O. Office: U of Cincinnati, Cincinnati, O.

GILBERT, Robin M, Eng, educator, social worker; b. London, Oct 13, 1929; s. Joseph and Carmel (Epstein); MA, hons, Balliol Coll, Oxford, 1954. Dir, dept of Org and Fund raising, World ORT Union, Geneva since 1965; dir ORT, and repr, JDC, India, 1961-63; headmaster, Selim Sch, Aden, 1954-60. Home: 10 bis Chemin Frank Thomas, Geneva, Switz. Office: World ORT Union, Centre Intl, Geneva, Switz.

GILBERT, Samuel M, US, physician; b. Newark, NJ, Nov 26, 1907; s. Morris and Rose (Robinson); BA, U of Pa, 1927, MD, 1930; postgrad study, Columbia U Coll of Phys and Surgs, 1931-40; m. Helen Robinson, May 27, 1930; c: Muriel Craner, Donald. Gastroenterologist since 1935; cons gastroenterologist, Irvington Gen Hosp since 1955; asso att in med and gastroenterology, Newark Beth Isr Hosp since 1957. F: Amer Coll Gastroenterology; Natl Gastroenterological Soc. Dipl, Amer Bd Internal Med and Gastroenterology; pres, NJ Gastroenterological Soc, 1957-58; mem: AMA; Essex Co Med Soc; Acad of Med, N NJ; Alpha Omega Alpha; Phi Lambda Kappa; B'nai B'rith; clubs: Intl Lions, Newark chap pres, 1950-51; Aliumn of N NJ-U of Pa, pres, 1956-57; Cedar Hill Country. Contbr: chap in Intl Book on Gastroeneterology; articles on med jours. Recipient: Alpha Omgea Alpha. Hon Med Soc award; Specner Morris Prize, U of Pa. Home: 142 Wyoming Ave, Maplewood, NJ. Office: 640 Valley St, Maplewood, NJ.

GILBOA, Abraham, Isr, diplomat; b. Geneva, Switz, Dec 10, 1905; att U of Lausanne; licencé en econ, U of Geneva, 1932; m. Lucie Chaikin, 1930; c: Yael. Min Plen since 1963; fmr: with Intl Lab Off, Geneva; dir intl relations dept, Histadrut; with immigration dept, JA, Paris; Isr Consul in Paris; dep, chief of protocol, Isr Min for Fgn Affairs; Consul Gen: Istanbul, Lisbon. Author, International Labor Organization, 1943; contbr articles on social problems. Home: 2 Masaryk St, Jerusalem, Isr. Office: Min for Fgn Affairs, Jerusalem, Isr.

GILBOA, Akiva, Isr, educator; b. Boryslaw, Pol, Dec 27, 1916; s. Israel and Gitel (Jekel) Blauaug; in Isr since 1938; MA, Heb U, Jerusalem, 1941, PhD, 1958; att Brasenose Coll, Oxford, 1953-54; m. Nehama Landau, Mar 6, 1947; c: Nurith, Mihal. Sr lectr, ancient hist, Haifa U Coll since 1967; tchr, Latin, classics dept, Heb U, Jerusalem, 1952-63; head, hist dept, Haifa U Coll, 1963-68. J Brigade, Brit Army, 1941-46; IDF, 1948-49. Contbr: commentaries on Tacitus' works; various articles on Roman hist. Recipient, Goodenday Scholarship for Advanced Studies at Oxford, Heb U, 1953. Home: 19 Oren St, Haifa, Isr.

GILBOA, Moshe, Isr, economist; b. Warsaw, Pol, May 17, 1922; s. Meir and Sara (From); in Isr since 1925; MA, Heb U, Jerusalem, 1952; m. Menuha Ben-Shlomo, 1946; c: Meir, Erel, Tal. Econ adv, dir, coop dept, Hevrat Haovdim' gen holding co of Isr Labor Fed since 1961; chmn, academic org, Lab Party; fmr: econ adv, Isr Min of Commerce and Ind; asst to dir gen, Min of Finance. IDF, 1948-49. Chmn, Social Scis Assn, 1952. Author: The Sociology of Democracy, 1948; Added Value in Israel, 1958; Six Years, Six Days, 1968; contrb

to econ and sociol publs. Home: 1 Alumin St, Afeka, Tel Aviv, Isr. Office: POB 303, Tel Aviv, Isr.

GILBOA, Yehoshua A, Isr, journalist; b. Pinsk, Russ, May 13, 1918; s. Isaak and Rachel (Futerman) Globerman; in Isr since 1949; m. Danuta Fürstenberg, 1948; c: Shuvit, Avishai. Columnist, Maariv daily, since 1956; fmr: researcher, hist of Soviet J, Brandeis U, 1939-53; ed, Zmanim daily, 1954-55. Author: Gehalim Lochashot, 1954; Al Horvot haTarbut haYehudit leBrit haMoetzot, 1959; Lishmor laNetzah, 1963; Uhuru-Days and Nights in Africa, 1965; A Hebrew Bookshelf, 1965; Confess! Confess!, 1968; contbr to local and fgn periodicals. Home: 12 Professor Shor St, Tel Aviv, Isr. Office: Maariv, Carlebach St, Tel Aviv, Isr.

GILD, Albert, Australia, surgeon; b. Adelaide, Australia, Jan 25, 1912; s. Louis and Gertrude (Adelson); MB, BS, U of Adelaide, 1934; m. Lily Rosenbaum, Dec, 1939; c: Lawrence, John, Geoffrey. Surg, Royal Perth Hosp; sr surg, Princess Margaret Hosp. Maj, RAMC. Pres, W Australian J bd deps, since 1961; vice-pres, exec council Australian J, since 1961; FRCS, 1940; Royal Australasian Coll of Surgeons, 1947. Home: 270 A Walcot St, Mt Lawley, Australia. Office: 242 St George's Terr St, Perth, Australia.

GILDESGAME, Leon L, US, business exec; b. Pol, Jan 27, 1895; s. Abraham and Deborah (Hildesheim); att cheders and yeshivas, Pol; LSE, 1919-22; Guildhall Sch of Music, London, 1922-24; BA, Antioch Coll, O; MA, S Ill U; m. Ruth Oppenheimer, June 27, 1940; c: Daniel, Myron. Found, pres, Gildesgame Corp, NY, since 1941; found chmn, Gildesgame Bros, Ltd, Eng, 1930-38; Argee Co Ltd, Eng, 1928-58. British Army: Zion Mule Corps with Trumpeldor's Legion in Gallipoli, 1915; Royal Field Artillery and Royal Flying Corps, 1917-19. Found, pres, The Gildesgame Found, NY; chmn: found, Anglo-Pal Club, London, 1920-40; adult educ comm, Temple Beth-El, N Westchester, 1948; UJA, N Westchester, since 1952; Isr Bonds Campaign, since 1951; and treas, Issachar Ryback Mus, Bat Yam, Isr; scholarship comm, Herzliya Heb Tchrs Inst, People's U; org, hon secy, Poalei-Zion Party of Gt Brit, 1919-26; hon life pres, Heb Circle of Manhattan, Histadrut Ivrit, since 1942; found: Amer-Isr Cultural Found, NY; sponsor: Isr Mobile Music Club, Tel Aviv, since 1957; Amer-Isr Music Alliance; sponsor, N Westchester Dance and Music Group; vice-pres, Intl Cultural Cen for Youth, Jerusalem, 1953-67; treas, Eng and Ir, WJC, 1930-36; trustee: J Cultural Found, NYU, since 1963; Amer Histadrut Cultural Exch Inst; delg, Bd of Deps of Brit Js, London, 1937-40; dir: Amer Friends of Heb U, NY, since 1949; AJComm, since 1958; mem: natl council of overseers, Dropsie Coll for Heb and Cognate Learning, since 1967; rel worship commn, soc of hon, UAHC; Amer Arbitration Assn, since 1958; gov council, AJCong; Vets of J Batallions, Eng; Hagdud Haivri, Eng; Royal Geog Soc, Eng. Recipient: Victory Medals, WW I; Gallipoli Star; Citation for bravery on the battle field from commanding off. Home: Millwood Rd, Mt Kisco, NY. Office: 475 Fifth Ave, New York, NY.

GILEAD, Mordehai, Isr, meteorologist, government official; b. Luckenwalde, Ger, Apr 10, 1906; s. Max and Louise (Simonis) Guttfeld; in Isr since 1935; att Us: Berlin; Freiburg; Frankfurt/M, Tchrs Dipl, 1932; m. Ellen Ephraim, June 6, 1934; c: Michael, Yohanan. Dir, Isr Meteorological Service since 1948, with Service since 1937; fmr tchr, It; perm Isr repr, World Meteorological Org, since 1951; mem: Amer Meteorological Soc; Royal Meteorological Soc, UK; club: Rotary. Contbr to profsl jours. Home: 80 Yahalom St, Ramat Gan, Isr. Office: POB 25, Bet Degan, Isr.

GILEAD, Shlomo, Isr, architect; b. Tyczyn, Pol, Apr 18, 1922; s. Gromet and Sarah (Hollander) Shimshon; in Isr since 1933; tchr dipl, Tchrs Sem, Jerusalem, 1940; dipl ing architect, Technion, Haifa; m. Aliza Shonfeld, Haifa; c: Eyal, Amira. Owner, architect, planning off since 1955; asso prof, fac of architecture, town planning since 1966; fmr partner, planning group; planned: Haifa Munic Theatre; Technion City Master Plan; Haifa U, co-planner with Prof Oscar Neimeyer, Brasil. Pvt, IDF, 1948-49. Mem: Engrs and Architects Assn, Isr; Haifa Architects. Recipient, several prizes in architectural competitions, AEIA. Home: 6A Ehud St, Haifa, Isr. Office: 3 Pevsner St, Haifa, Isr.

GILEAD, Zerubavel, Israel, poet, author, editor; b. Russia, 1913; s. Haim and Haya (Birbrayer) Glass; in Isr since 1922; att Heb U, 1953-54; m. Shoshana Kellner, 1941 (decd); m. 2nd, Dorothea Krook, 1968; c: Tirza, Hanna, Eilla. Mem ed bd, Kibbutz Hameuchad Pub Co, since 1952; ed, Mibifnim since 1955. Off, IDF, 1949. Author: Neurim, 1936; El haEin, 1939; Mareot Gilboa, 1943; Nigunim baSaar, 1946; Himnon haPalmach, Shibolet Playim, 1949; Prihat haOranim, 1950; Sicha al ha Chof, 1953; Nahar Yarok, 1956; Eigel Tal, 1958; Afar Noher, collected poems, 1960; Sicha shelo Tama, Im Morim ve-Reiim, 1965; Yam shel Mala (poems), 1966; ed: Magen baSeter, 1948; Pirkei Palmach, 1951; Sefer Hapalmach, 1953. Mem, Kibbutz Ein Harod, since 1922. Recipient, Holon Award for Lit, 1961. Home: Kibbutz Ein Harod Meuhad, Isr. Office: 27 Soutine St, Tel Aviv, Isr.

GILEADI, Eliezer, Isr, chemist, educator; b. Budapest, Hung, Apr 15, 1932; s. Alexander and Sara (Wienberger); in Isr since 1940; MSc, Heb U, Jerusalem, 1956; PhD, U of Ottawa, Can, 1963; div; c: Ofer, Ido, Uzi. Asso prof, chem, Tel Aviv U, since 1966; sr inves, U of Pa, Phila, 1963-66. Lt, IDF, 1956-60. Contrib, research in fundamental electrochem. Contbr to sci jours and books. Home: 77 Frishman St, Tel Aviv, Isr. Office: Tel Aviv U, Tel Aviv, Isr.

GILLIS, Joseph, Isr, educator; b. Sunderland, Eng, Aug 3, 1911; s. David and Fanny (Jaffe); in Isr since 1948; MA, PhD, Trinity Coll, Cambridge; m. Olga Kirsch, July, 1949; c: Michal, Ada. Prof, applied math, dean, grad sch, Weizmann Inst, since 1958, asso prof, 1948-58; lectr, Queen's U, Belfast, N Ir, 1937-47; mem, Inst for Advanced Study, Princeton, NJ, 1954-55. Mem: London Math Soc; Amer Math Soc; Cambridge Phil Soc. Contbr to profsl jours. Home: Shikun Neven Weizmann, Rehovot, Isr. Office: Weizmann Inst, Rehovot, Isr.

GILLON, Baruch, Isr, impresario; b. Ekaterinoslav, Russ, Sep 7, 1901; s. Isaac and Batia (Viminitz) Goriatshikov; in Isr since 1923; att Mines Engr Coll, Ekaterinoslav; dipl econ, Inst of Social Sci and Econ, Tiflis, 1923; m. Sara Model, 1924, (decd); m. 2nd, Bela Finkelstein, 1944; c: Zvi, Batia. Impresario, Tel Aviv, since 1924, presented many famous fgn artists in Isr; fmr: dir, dramatic studio, Politprosvet, Ekaterinoslav; libr, Hapoel Hatzair; agric worker; admnr, Pal Opera; co-found, co-dir, Pal Sym Orch and Pal Oratorio Soc; mgn dir, Hamatateh Theatre. Haganah, 1923-48, participated in battle of Huldah settlement, 24 defenders against over 2000 Arabs; civil defense cdr, Dizengoff dist, Six-Day War. Found, dir, Intl Bur of Concerts; co-found, Kofer Hayishuv; chmn, Union of Impresarios of Isr. Contbr to local press. Home and office: 14 Gordon St, Tel Aviv, Isr.

GILSHON, Aharon, Isr, economist; b. Jerusalem, Feb 2, 1928; s. Israel and Malka (Melnizer) Gladstein; tchrs cert, Tchrs Coll, Jerusalem, 1948; at Heb U, Jerusalem, 1949-52; postgrad studies, Us: Nebraska; Oxford; Wageningen; m. Naomi Sohlberg, Sep, 1952; c: Ella, Sarel. Chief econ, research dept, Bank of Isr, since 1964; fmr, asst to dir gen and econ adv, Min of Agric. Served J Brigade, Brit Army, 1945-46; sgt maj, IDF, 1948-49. Mem, Intl Org of Agric Econs. Ed, reports of comm on Situation of Agric; co-author, Natl Budgets, 1964-67; contbr: to Bank of Isr annual reports; articles to periodicals. Home: 11 Hasatat St, Jerusalem, Isr.

GINGOLD, Josef, US, musician, educator; b. Brest-Litovsk, Pol, Oct 28, 1909; s. Mayer and Nechama (Leizerovitch); studied with Eugene Ysaye; m. Gladys Anderson; c: George. Prof, music, Ind U, since 1960; fmr fac mem: W Reserve U; Cleveland Music Sch Settlement; visiting prof: Colo Coll; U of the S, Tenn; Utah State Coll; Meadowmount Sch of Music, NY; concerts: Belgium, US, Fr, Holland; mem: NBC Sym Orch under Toscanini; sym soloist and concertmaster, Detroit and Cleveland Sym Orchs; mem, Quartet; first violinist, June Music Festival, Albuquerque; repr,US mem of juries: Queen Elizabeth Competition, Brussels; Wieniawski Competition, Pol; Paganini Competition, Genoa. Compiled, ed: Three Vols of Orch Studies; works of classical and modern repertoires; recording artist; Columbia RCA-Victor. Recipient: Dist Service Prof, Ind U, 1964. Home: 903 Maxwell Terrace E, Bloomington, Ind.

GINGOLD, Kurt, US, information sci; b. Vienna, Aus, 1929; s. Isidor and Berta (Kleinberg); in US since 1949; BS, Tulane U, 1950; PhD, Harvard U, 1953; m. Alice Saltzman, Nov 24, 1957; c: Betty, David. Research info sci, Amer Cyanamid Co, since 1956; lit sci, Ethyl, 1953-54. US Army, 1954-56. F, Inst of Ling, London, Eng. Pres, Amer Trans Assn, 1963-65; vice-pres, Intl Fed of Trans, 1963-66; mem: Amer Chem Soc; B'nai B'rith. Trans, asso ed, Methods in Microanalysis, 4 vols; contbr articles, book reviews to profsl jours. Recipient,

Alexander Gode Medal, Amer Trans Assn, 1966. Hobbies: langs, theater, motion pictures, bridge. Home: 34 Pleasant St, Cos Cob, Conn. Office: 1937 W Main St, Stamford, Conn.

GINIEWSKI, Paul, Fr, editor, author; b. Vienna, Aus, Feb 18, 1926; s. Joseph and Sarah (Kessler); in Fr since 1940; licencie es lettres, U of Paris; m. Pesca Zonensein, Feb 2, 1946; c: Isabelle. Ed, La Terre Retrouvee, since 1951; pr mgr, El Al since 1962. Fr Resistance, 1943-45. Author: Quand Israel Combat, 1957; Israel devant l'Afrique et l'Asie, 1958; Le Bouclier de David, 1960; Bantustans: A Trek Towards the Future, 1961; Une autre Afrique du Sud, 1962; The Two Faces of Apartheid, 1965; Die Strijd om Suid Wes Afrika, 1966; Les Complices de Dieu, 1963; Le Neo-Judaisme, 1966; Le Sionisme, 1969. Chmn, mem, exec comm, Press Comm, ZF, Fr. Home: 24 Blvd des Capucines, Paris, Fr. Office: 12 rue de la Victoire, Paris 9e, Fr.

GINOR, Fanny, Isr, economist; b. Ottynia, Aus; d. Yehoshua and Rosa (Rosenrauch) Dulberg; att U of Munich; D Rer Pol, U of Basel; m. Yehoshua Ginor. Econ adv, Gov Bank of Isr since 1953; sr lectr, Dept of Devl Countries, fac of Social Scis, since 1966; research worker, econ dept JA, 1943-48; econ adv: Finance Min, 1949-53, Isr Perm Mission to UN, NYC, 1962-64. Author: Der Imperialismus im Lichte seiner Theorien, 1936; The Economy and Agriculture of Israel, 1959; Uses of Agricultural Surpluses, 1963; Reparations and their Impact on the Israel Economy, 1966; contbr to jours. Mem, Isr Assn of Graduates in Social Scis and Hums, Tel Aviv. Home: 11 Katzenelson St, Tel Aviv, Isr. Office: 37 Lilienblum St, Tel Aviv, Isr.

GINOSSAR, Rosa, Isr, attorney, communal leader; b. Gomel, Russ, June 14, 1890; d. Mordechai and Shifra (Pevsner) Hacohen; ir Isr since 1908; LLB, U Paris, 1911; m. Shlomo Ginossar, 1917. Pvt practice since 1932; first woman atty in Pal, obtained women's right to practice law in Pal by winning against Govt in High Court, 1929. Pres, World Wizo, since 1963, fmr chmn, world exec, mem exec since 1933, chmn, admn bd of training farms; mem presidium, Zionist Gen Council; org, rehab of abandoned J orphan children, WW II; mem: U Women's Assn; Equal Rights for Women Assn. Home: 6 Ussishkin St, Jerusalem, Isr.

GINOSSAR, Shalev, Isr, jurist, educator; b. Antwerp, Belgium, June 20, 1902; s. Henri and Mania (Grunzweig); in Isr since 1939; LLD, U Brussels, 1925, agrégé de l'enseignement supérieur, 1938; m. Mical Kohn, June 23, 1926; c: Dalia Sommer. Prof, law, Heb U, Jerusalem since 1962, mem fav since 1951, fmr: dean, law fac; in pvt practice, Antwerp; Tel Aviv; judge, Dist Court, Tel Aviv; visiting prof, Sorbonne, Paris. British Army, 1941-44. Mem: Fondation Universitaire, Brussels; Rotary Intl, Jerusalem. Author: L'Assistance Judiciaire et la Procédure Gratuite, 1929; Le Fonds de commerce et son passif propre, 1938; Annotated Laws of Palestine, vol 5, 1946; Din veDiyun, 1953; Droit Réel, propriété et créance, 1960; Liberté contractuelle et respect des droits des tiers, 1963. Hobby, music. Home: 44 Gaza Rd, Jerusalem, Isr. Office: Hebrew U, Jerusalem, Isr.

GINSBERG, Allen, US, poet; b. Newark, NJ, June 3, 1926; s. Louis and Naomi (Levy); AB, Columbia Coll, 1948; m. Ganesh Orlovsky, 1953. Author: Howl & Other Poems, 1956; Kaddish, 1960; Reality Sandwiches, 1963; Yage Letters, 1963; Empty Mirror, 1961; Planet News, 1968; Indian Journals, 1970; works trans into: Fr; Ger; It; Span; Finnish; Russ; Japanese; Czech; Bengali; recorded, tuned, Songs of Innocence and Experience, by W Blake, MGM Records, 1970; co-found, ed: Big Table; Black Mt Rev; Evergreen Rev. Home: 416 E 34 St, Paterson, NJ. Office: 261 Columbus Ave, San Francisco, Cal.

GINSBERG, Edward, US, attorney; b. NYC, May 30, 1917; s. Charles and Rose; BA, hons, U of Mich, 1938; LLB, Harvard U, 1941; m. Rosalie Sinek, Aug 11, 1941; c: William, Robert. Partner, Gottfried, Ginsberg, Guren and Merritt since 1941; trustee, exec vice-pres, US Realty Inves. Served USAAC. Trustee, Cleveland JCF; bd dirs: First Isr Bank and Trust of NY; Sanitas Service Corp; gen chmn, UJA, since 1968, natl campaign cabinet since 1963; bd trustee: JDC; vice-pres: United HIAS; JTA; mem: Phi Kappa Phi; Phi Sigma Delta. Home: 18000 Shaker Blvd, Shaker Hgts, O. Office: 65 Terminal Tower, Cleveland, O.

GINSBERG, Harold L, US, Bible scholar, author; b. Montreal, Can, Dec 6, 1903; s. Mendel and Golda (Levinson); in US since 1936; BA, U of London, 1927, PhD, 1930; m. Anne Gelrud, Nov 7, 1937 (decd). Prof, Bible, JTSA, since 1941, fac mem since 1936; visiting prof: Heb U, Jerusalem, 1957, 1962; U of Pa, 1957-58, 1968-69; Yale U, 1967. F, Amer Acad for J Research, vice pres, 1969; hon pres, E sect, Soc Bibl Lit and Exegesis, 1960, pres, 1959-60; treas, Amer Friends of Isr Exploration Soc, since 1949; trustee, Kohut Found, since 1954; mem: council, World Union of J Studies; publ comm, J Publs Soc, since 1959; Amer Schs Oriental Research; Amer Friends Heb U; Acad for Heb Lang, Jerusalem. Author: The Ugarit Texts, 1936; The Legend of King Keret, 1947; Studies in Daniel, 1948; Studies in Koheleth, 1950; A New Commentary on Koheleth, 1961; co-author: new J translation of the Torah; ed: The Five Megilloth and Jonah, 1969; The New Jewish Translation of the Prophets; division of Bible, Ency Judaica; contrb to scholarly jours. Home: 280 Riverside Dr, New York, NY. Office: 3080 Broadway, New York, NY.

GINSBERG, Harold S, US, physician, educator; b. Daytona Beach, Fla, May 27, 1917; s. Jacob and Anne (Kalb); BA, Duke U, 1937; MD, Tulane U Sch of Med, 1941; m. Marion Reibstein, Aug 4, 1949; c: Benjamin, Peter, Anne, Jane. Prof, chmn dept, microbiol, U of Pa, Sch of Med, since 1960; cons: NIH, USPHS, since 1949; adv, US Army; fmr: res, Mallory Inst of Path, Boston City Hosp, 1941-42; intern, Harvard, 1942-43; phys, Rockefeller Inst and Hosp, 1946-51; asst prof med, W Reserve U, 1951-60. US Army MC, 1943-46. Chmn, virology div, Amer Soc for Microbiol, 1961-62; councillor, Amer Soc for Clinical Inves, 1959-61; mem: Amer Assn Immunologists; Amer Fed Clinical Research; Harvey Soc; Soc for Experimental Biol and Med. Contbr: chaps to med books; papers to med pubs; mem, ed bd, Proc, Soc Experimental Biol and Med; jours: Bact; Immunology; Virology; Experimental Med; Bact Reviews. Recipient: Legion of Merit, 1946. Home: 254 Forrest Ave, Merion, Pa. Office: Sch of Med, U of Pa, Philadelphia, Pa.

GINSBERG, Louis, US, poet, teacher; b. Newark, NJ, Oct 1, 1895; s. Peter and Rebecca (Schectman); BA, Rutgers U, 1918; MA, Columbia U, 1924; m. Naomi Levy, 1920 (decd); c: Eugene, Allen; m. 2nd, Edith Cohen, Mar 25, 1950. Tchr, Eng, Cent HS, Paterson, 1921-61, ret. Mem, Poetry Soc of Amer. Author: poems: The Attic of the Past, 1920; The Everlasting Minute, 1937; Morning in Spring, 1970; contrb of poetry to: Atlantic Monthly, New Yorker, Saturday Review, The Nation, Poetry, NY Times; poems in anthol: Modern American and British Poetry; Yesterday and Today; Poetry, Its Appreciation and Enjoyment; Doorways to Poetry; The Third Book of Modern Verse; Contemporary Verse; The Music Makers; This is America; Discovery I; contrb: weekly corner of puns, Paterson Eve News; daily, Newark Star Ledger. Home: 416 E 34 St, Paterson, NJ.

GINSBERG, Martin David, US, attorney, educator; b. NYC, June 10, 1932; s. Morris and Evelyn (Bayer); AB, Cornell U, 1953; LLB, JD, Harvard Law Sch, 1958; m. Ruth Bader, June 23, 1954; c: Jane, James. Partner, Weil, Gotshal & Manges, NYC since 1963, asso, 1958-63; adj prof of law, NYU since 1967, mem fac since 1965; lectr, Practising Law Inst; NYU Annual Tax Inst; and numerous other tax insts. Lt, USArmy, 1954-56. Chmn, mem: exec comm, Comm on Personal Income Taxation, Tax Sect, NY State Bar Assn, co-chmn, both since 1969, mem, policy comm since 1970. Author: Tax Consequences of Investments, 1969; Tax and SEC Consequences of Corporate Acquisitions, 1970. Hobby: golf. Home: 150 E 69 St, New York, NY. Office: 767 Fifth Ave, New York, NY.

GINSBOURG, Benjamin, Fr, pathologist; b. Valensole, Fr, Feb 5, 1897; s. Simon and Sophie (Weinberg); MD, Faculté de Médecine, Paris, 1924; m. Jane Witemberg, Aug 30, 1924; c: Eve, Elie, Anne, Michele, Ariel. Path, pvt lab of clinical biol, since 1937; asst, Pasteur Inst, 1922-24; path, Reims, 1927-37; lab, chief: Rothschild Hosp, Paris, 1942-44; Bichat Hosp, 1945-53. F, Rockefeller Found, Boston, 1924-25; found, gen secy, Fr J Med Assn since 1948. Author: Données Recentes sur les Anaérobies, 1927; Manuel de Pathologie Expérimentale, 1937; Les Plaies Septiques, 1947; ed, AMIF, J Med Rev, since 1952. Recipient: Croix de Guerre, 1918; Chévalier de la Legion d'Honneur, 1935. Home and office: 2 rue Pigalle, Paris 9, Fr.

GINSBURG, David, Isr, chemist, educator; b. NYC, Sep 5, 1920; s. Simon and Tybel (Abramowitz); in Isr since 1948; BSc, CCNY, 1941; MA, Columbia U, 1942; PhD, NYU, 1947; f, Harvard U, 1952-53; m. Hemda Ber, 1940; c: Jonina, Simona. Prof, chem, Technion, Haifa, since 1954; fmr: head,

dept chem; head, dept chem engr; vice-pres for research; acting pres, all at Technion; visiting prof: Harvard U; Brandeis U; U Zurich; NYU; U Sask; McGill U; Weizmann Inst; produc chem, Pa Ordinance Works; research chem, NY Quinine and Chem Works, 1943-48; sr research chem, Weizmann Inst of Sci, Isr, 1948-54. Chmn, Isr Council for Research and Devl; mem: Isr Chem Soc, fmi chmn; Amer Chem Soc; Swiss Chem Soc; Chem Soc, London; Japanese Chem Soc; Sigma Xi; NY Acad Arts and Scis; bur, Intl Union of Pure and Applied Chem. Author, The Opium Alkaloids, 1962; ed, Non-Benzenoid Aromatic Compounds, 1960; Concerning Amines, 1967; contbr of publs in the field of organic chem. Recipient: Weizmann Prize, 1954; Tel Aviv Munic, 1954; Rothschild Prize for chem, 1965. Hobbies: art, architecture. Home: 80 a Hatishbi St, Mt Carmel, Haifa, Isr. Office: Technion, Haifa, Isr.

GINSBURG, David (Charles), US, attorney; b. NYC, Apr 20, 1912; s. Nathan and Rae (Lewis); BA, W Va U, 1932; LLB, Harvard Law Sch, 1935; m. Christina Esslay, June 1950; c: Jonathan, Susan, Mark. Pvt practice, Wash, DC since 1946; partner, law firm, Ginsburg and Feldman; adj prof, intl law, Georgetown U Grad Sch Law since 1959; law secy, Justice Wm O Douglas, 1939; legal adv, Price Stabilization Div, Natl Defense Adv Comm, 1940-41; gen counsel: OPA, Civilian Supply, 1941-42, OPA, 1942-43; dep dir, econ div, Mil Govt, Ger, 1945-46; dep commn,delg, Aus Treaty Commn, Vienna, 1947; adv delg, Council of Fgn Mins, London, 1947; adm asst, Sen M M Neely, W Va, 1950. Capt, US Army, 1943-46, ret. Exec dir, Natl Adv Commn on Civil Disorders, 1967; mem: Presidential Emergency Bd, number 166, 1966, chmn, number 169, 1967; commnr, Pres Commn on Postal Org, 1967; bd trustees, Weizmann Inst of Sci, Rehovot; bd mem, Natl Sym Orch Assn; mem, Amer Soc of Intl Law; Phi Beta Kappa, Dem; clubs: Harvard, Fed City, Army and Navy. Author, The Future of German Reparations, 1950; contbr to legal jours. Recipient: Legion of Merit, 1946; Presidential Cert of Merit, 1947. Home: 1688 31 St, NW, Washington, DC. Office: 1700 Pennsylvania Ave, NW, Washington, DC.

GINSBURG, Haim, Isr, biologist; b. Jerusalem, Isr, May 13, 1933; s. Zeev and Lea (Goldberg); MSc, cum laude, Heb U, Jerusalem, 1959; PhD, Weizmann Inst, Rehovot, 1962; m. Shulamit Steinberg, Nov 15, 1956; c: Abiathar, Jephta. Research asso, Dept of Cell Biol, Weizmann Inst since 1965, staff mem since 1962; Eleanor Roosevelt research f, Public Health Research Inst, NYC, 1963-64; researcher, dept of path, U of Wash, Seattle, 1964-65; f, St Mary's Hosp, Med Sch, London, 1969-70. Sgt, IDF, 1951-53. Prin contribs: developing techniques for growth, differentiation of blood, lymphoid cells in tissue culture; means for producing immunological reactions in cell culture; mechanism of immunological rejection of cells tissues in transplantation; immunological function of lymphocytes. Author, The Function of the Delayed Sensitivity Reaction, 1970; contbr to sci jours. Recipient: Sara Leedy Memorial Award, Weizmann Inst, 1963; travel grant, Intl Union against Cancer, 1966. Hobbies: Isr flora and fauna, hist, geog, music. Home: Meonot Wolfson, Rehovot, Isr. Office: Weizmann Inst, Rehovot, Isr.

GINSBURG, Hyman M, US, surgeon; b. NYC, June 4, 1905; s. Louis and Mollie (Sarnoff); MD, U of Colorado, 1928; m. Clara Feldesman, Mar 18, 1928; c: Brian, Bettylee Wapner. Pvt practice, Fresno, since 1946; staff member of all Fresno hosps; fmr: med dir, supt, chief surg, Fresno Co Gen Hosp, 1931-46. Phys i/c, Nutritional Home, since 1934; f: Amer Coll of Surgs; Amer Gastroscopic Soc; Intl Acad Proctology; mem: Ind Med Soc; Fresno Surg Soc, pres, 1963; Amer Coll of Hosp Admns; Pan Amer Surg Soc; Fresno Co Med Soc, pres, 1968, bd govs; Amer and Calif Med Assns; pres, St Agnes Hosp, 1963; mem, B'nai B'rith: Fresno lodge, pres, 1939; past grand pres, life mem, exec bd, 1949; natl commnr, Youth Org, 1957-61, natl treas, past pres, dist 4; natl commnr, Hillel Found, 1961-69; Intl Council, 1968-1971; mem: Men's Club and Temple Beth Isr, pres, 13 years; contrb, Cong Beth Jacob; pres, JWF, 14 years, exec bd; state chmn, Jt Defense Appeal, chmn, Fresno pr comm; 33 deg Mason, 1967; charter mem, Teheran Temple, 1949, divan, potentate, trustee, 1963-1968; Scottish Rite, 1933-34; Islam Temple, Shrine, 1934; service to bds: ARC; Natl Found for Infantile Paralysis; Soc for Crippled Children; TB Assn; Amer Cancer Soc; Fresno Co and City C of C; Bulldog Found; Gtr Fresno Youth Org; mem: Fresno: Police Commn; Bd of Health; Bd of Educ, pres since 1969; Fresno Co Grand Jury, 1957, 1963; mem of pres' council, Brandeis U; clubs: mem, Fresno

Lions, past pres, 1937-38, 4-c dist gov, 1944-45; intl counsellor, Lions Intl, since 1945. Recipient: Akiba Award, B'nai B'rith, 1936; Helm Athletic Found award, 1954, 1961; Breitbard Found award, 1956. Home: 3124 Van Ness Blvd, Fresno, Cal. Office: 1215 Del Mar Ave, Fresno, Cal.

GINSBURG, Joseph Michel, US, educator, biochemist; b. Tarascha, Russ, Jan 5, 1895; s. Menaseh and Tauba (Medvin); in US since 1911; BS, Pa State U, 1922; MS, Rutgers U, 1923, PhD, 1925; m. Mollie Rubin, Feb 8, 1932; c: Miriam Hyams, Melvin. Prof em, entomology, Rutgers U since 1959, on staff since 1925; research inves, NJ Agric Experimental Sta since 1925; adv to Isr Min of Agric, plant protection and toxicology; Research Found, SUNY, sponsored by Intl Coop Admn, 1956-58. Mem: AAAS; Amer Chem Soc; Amer Entomological Soc; Amer Mosquito Control Assn; local Comty Cen. Contbr to profsl jours. Home: 252 Lincoln Ave, Highland Park, NJ. Office: Rutgers U, New Brunswick, NJ.

GINSBURG, Nathan, US, physicist, educator; b. Casey, Ill, Aug 25, 1910; s. Louis and Dora (Brachman); BA, O State U, 1931, MA, 1932; PhD, U of Mich, 1935; m. Ruth Ostrow, Aug 25, 1942; c: Susan. Chmn, dept of physics, Syracuse U since 1965, prof since 1952, fac mem since 1946; instr, engr sci, Johns Hopkins U, 1941-42; asso, Carnegie Inst, 1941-42; asst prof, U of Tex, 1942-46. F: Amer Phys Soc; Amer Optical Soc. Contbr in fields of atomic and molecular spectral biophysics. Home: 989 James St, Syracuse, NY. Office: Syracuse U, Syracuse, NY.

GINSBURG-LURIE, Yehudith, Isr, communal worker; b. Russ, Mar 26, 1905; d. Menachem and Nechama (Chlenow); RN, Nursing Sch, Jerusalem; m. Ben-Zion Lurie; c: Arnona Paices, Talmona Orian, Menachem. Mem, Jerusalem City Council since 1950; fmr: mem, Lab Council, Histadrut; secy govt employees; nurse, org of nurses in Isr. Haganah, 1936-48. Mem bd: Pioneer Women Org; Kupat Holim; High Court, Lab Party; 1st delg to nurses conv, Atlantic City, NJ. Home: 11 Hirshenberg St, Jerusalem, Isr.

GINSBURY, Philip Norman, Eng, rabbi; b. London, Eng, Mar 26, 1936; s. Alec and Beatrice (Wolman); att Jews Coll, London, 1953-58; MA. U Coll, London, 1958; ordained rabbi, Merkaz Harav Kook Yeshiva, Jerusalem, 1959; m. Helen Frohwein, June 28, 1959; c: Montagu, Karen. Rabbi, Brixton Syn since 1966; min, Streatham Syn, 1959-66. Chmn, educ comm, Council of Mins of United Syn; mem: Publ Comm, J Marriage Educ Council; rel adv comm, Assn for J Youth. Hobby: modern jazz. Home: 146 Downton Ave, London, Eng. Office: 49 Effra Rd, London, Eng.

GINZBERG, Eli, US, economist, educator, author; b. NYC, Apr 30, 1911; s. Louis and Adele (Katzenstein); att: Heidelberg U, 1928-29; Grenoble U, Fr, 1929; BA, Columbia U, 1931, MA, 1932, PhD, 1934; m. Ruth Szold, July 14, 1946; c: Abigail, Jeremy, Rachel Hepburn. Prof, econs, Grad Sch of Bus, Columbia U, mem staff since 1935; chmn, Natl Manpower Adv Comm since 1962; cons, Lab Dept, since 1954; mem, natl adv council: Allied Health Personnel since 1968; Mh, 1959-63; cons, State Dept, Defense Dept, since 1965; dir: conservation of hum resources project, Columbia U since 1950; staff studies, Natl Manpower Council, 1951-61, hum resources, 1939-42, 1948-49; cons: personnel, Secy of Army, 1951-61; Surg Gen's Office, Dept of Army, since 1946; dir, research, UJA, 1941; spec asst, chief stat, War Dept, 1942-44; dir, resources, analysis div, Surg Gen's Office, War Dept, 1944-46; repr, US to Five Power Conf on Reparations for Non-repatriable Refs, 1946; mem, med adv bd, Secy of War, 1946-48; med coms, Hoover Commn, 1946-48; chmn, on Function of Nursing, 1948; dir, NY State Hosp Study, 1948-49; cons, State Dept, 1953; chmn, comm on studies, White House Conf on Children and Youth, 1960; cons, Govt of Isr, 1961. F, AAAS; mem: bd of govs, Heb U, Jerusalem, 1955-60; bd of dirs, Amer Friends of Heb U, 1946-60; NY State adv comm to US Commn on Civil Rights since 1962; Amer Econ Assn; Acad Political Sci; Ind Relations Research Assn; AAUP; Med Consultants WW II (hon); Phi Beta Kappa; Beta Gamma Sigma. Author: Economics of the Bible, 1932; House of Adam Smith, 1934; Illusion of Economic Stability, 1939; Grass on the Slag Heaps, 1942; Report to the American Jews, 1942; The Unemployed, 1943; The Labor Leader, 1948; A Program for the Nursing Profession, 1948; A Pattern for Hospital Care, 1949; Agenda for Military Jews, 1950; Occupational Choice, 1951; Psychiatry and Military Manpower Policy, 1953; The Uneducated, 1953; What Makes an Executive, 1955; The Negro Potential, 1956;

Effecting Change in Large Organizations, 1957; Human Resources: The Wealth of a Nation, 1958; The Ineffective Soldier, 3 vols, 1959; Planning for Better Hosp Care, 1961; Manpower Utilization in Israel, 1962; The Optimistic Tradition and American Youth, 1962; The American Worker in the Twentieth Century, 1963; The Rights of Management in a Democracy, 1963. Ed: Values and Ideals of American Youth, 1962; The Nation's Children, 3 vols, 1961; The Troublesome Presence, 1964; Talent and Performance, The Negro Challenge to the Business Community, 1964; The Pluralistic Economy, 1965; Keeper of the Law: Louis Ginzberg, 1966; Life Styles of Educated Women, Educated American Women-Self Portraits; The Development of Human Resources, all 1966; Manpower Strategy for Developing Nations, 1967; The Middle-Class Negro in the White Man's World, 1967; Manpower Strategy for the Metropolis, 1968; Business Leadership and the Negro Crisis, 1968; contbr to jours. Recipient: War Dept exceptional civilian service medal, 1946; medal, Intl U of Social Studies, Rome, 1957; research award, Ind and Personnel Assn, 1961. Home: 845 West End Ave, New York, NY. Office: Columbia U, New York, NY.

GIPS, Walter F, Jr, US, business exec; b. NYC, May 24, 1920; s. Walter and Louise (Klee); BA, Yale U, 1941; MBA, Harvard Bus Sch, 1943; m. Ann Arenberg, June 19, 1948; c: Walter F III, Robert, Donald, Ellen. Pres: Luminator Inc since 1960; chmn, Luminator-Harrison since 1964; vice-pres, Gulton Inds since 1968; asst to vice-pres, US Plywood, 1949-50; vice-pres, Harrison Wholesale Co, 1950-60. Capt, US Army, 1943-46. Pres, Ravina PTA, 1961-62; exec bd, AJComm since 1955; mem: Young Pres Org; clubs: Lake Shore Country; Yale; Downtown; Mid-Amer; Harvard Bus Sch. Home: 1185 Beach Lane, Highland Park, Ill. Office: 500 N Orleans St, Chicago, Ill.

GIRER, Irvin, US, pharmacist; b. Phila, Pa, Feb 24, 1920; s. Nathan and Ida (Fox); BS, Wayne U, Detroit, Mich, 1947; m. Dorothy Schumansky, Jan 6, 1952; c: Joanne, Pharm, Arnold's, Farmington, 1967; pharm, mgr, Cunningham Drug, 1947-53. US Army, 1942-44. Int pres, Soc of Isr Philatelists, dir, pr, 1964-66, first vice-pres, 1966-68; exec secy, org, World Philatelic Cong of Isr; Holy Land and Judaica Socs; commnr, Tabira, Isr Natl Philatelic Exhb; mem, Judaica Hist Philatelic Soc. Co-author: Jews on Stamps; ed staff mem: The Israel Philatelist; Judaica Philatelic Jour; contbr to J jours. Hobbies: Holy Land stamps and ancient coins. Home: 27436 Aberdeen, Southfield, Mich. Office: 33322 W 12 Mile Rd, Farmington, Mich.

GITAI, Munio, Isr, educator, architect; b. Szumlany, Russ, Mar 16, 1909; s. Pinchas and Fruma (Felner) Weinraub; in Isr since 1934; grad, Bauhaus, Dessau, Hochschule fur Gestaltung; m. Margalit Efratia, Oct 22, 1936; c: Gideon, Amos. Sr lectr, prof, fac of Architecture & Town Planning, Technion, Haifa since 1952, lectr, 1949-52; pvt practice, architecture, town planning, ind design, interior design; practised architecture with Mies van der Rohe's Atelier, Berlin, 1931-33; with Raefeli, Moser, Steiger, architects, Zurich, 1933-34; designed, supervised J Colonization Pavilion, Levant Fair, Tel Aviv, 1936; partnership, Munio (Weinraub) and A Mansfield, Haifa, 1937-59; head, Dept of Architecture, Min of Lab and Planning, 1949. Works and projects, 1937-59; housing: numerous designs, Haifa, Tel Aviv; educ bldgs: Maizer Inst of J Studies, Heb U, Jerusalem and others; public bldgs: libr and archives, Yad Vashem, Jerusalem and others; monuments: Yad Vashem; War of Independence Heroes, Beit-Shean, Kiryat-Haim; numerous commerce and ind bldgs: Haifa, Tel Aviv; numerous town planning projects: Haifa and other townships; naval ships, Zim Lines, Isr. Lectr: AEAI Symposium, Haifa, Tel Aviv, 1951-54, 1963, 1964, 1965; Fac of Architecture, U of Teheran, 1960; Akademie der bildenden Kunste, Vienna, 1963; exhbs: Decima Trienale di Milano, It, 1954; New Towns, UIA Cong, Moscow, 1958; Bauhaus world exhb, 50 years jubilee, 1967. Mem: numerous juries for architectural competitions, Isr; Assn of Engrs and Architects, Isr; Union Intl de Architects; fmr: chmn, Engrs Club, Haifa; Architects Union, Isr; mem: comm for qualifying examinations, architectural registration, Isr; cen comm for cultural activities, AEAI; planning comm: Architects Union, Haifa, Hadar-Hacarmel comm, Haifa; cen competitions comm, AEAI; Inst for Bldg and Tech Research, Gen Lab Fed, Tel Aviv; fmr participant: Congres Intl d'Architecture Moderne, Yugo,, 1956; World Design Conf, Tokyo, 1960; Technion positions: mem: comm: student admission; Faculti-Syllabi; curriculum, Inst of Ind Design; Technion Senate; coord comm, grad studies; adv, research. Author: introducing chap, The Architectural Department, 1949; Wohnungsbau, 1957; Raumliche Tragwerke, 1960; contbr to numerous Isr and fgn architectural jours, periodicals, books. Recipient: numerous 1st and 2nd prizes for civic, educ, syn, hosp, cen, libr designs in Haifa, Jerusalem, Tel Aviv. Home: 5 David Pinsky, Haifa, Isr. Office: 135 Hanassi Ave, Haifa, Isr.

GITIN, Joseph, US, rabbi, b. Rochester, NY, May 8, 1906; s. Rabbi Samuel and Minnie; BA, U of Cincinnati, 1929; BHL, HUC, 1930, ordained rabbi, 1932; hon DD, HUC-JIR, 1959; m. Rosalie Carl, 1936; c: David, Judith. Rabbi: Temple Emanuel, San Jose, since 1950; Temple Emanu-El, Buffalo, NY, 1932-35; B'nai Isr, Butte, Mont, 1935-42; dir, Hillel Found, U of NC, Duke U, U of Cal; fmr lectr, Coll of Pacific. Pres, Bd of Rabbis of N Cal, 1960-61; pres, W Assn of Reform Rabbis; chmn, adv comm to Police Dept; exec bd: Santa Clara Co Heart Assn; TB Soc; Assn for Infantile Paralysis; mem, adv comm on children and youth; trustee, Agnew State Hosp; exec bd, Good Samaritan Hosp; Red Cross; Community Chest; judge, bicycle court; chaplain, Fire Dept—all of San Jose. Mem: CCAR, Rotary. Recipient: dist citizen award, San Jose, 1955, KXRX award. Home: 1475 Emory St, San Jose, Cal. Study: 1010 University Ave, San Jose, Cal.

GITTELSOHN, Roland B, US, rabbi; b. Cleveland, O, May 13, 1910; s. Reuben and Anna (Manheim); BA, W Reserve U, 1931; BH, HUC, 1934, ordained rabbi, 1936; grad studies, Columbia U, 1937-39; hon DD, HUC-JIR, 1961; hon ScD, Lowell Tech Inst, 1961; m. Ruth Freyer, Sep 25, 1932; c: David, Judith Levine. Rabbi: Temple Isr, Boston, since 1953; Cen Syn of Nassau Co, 1936-53; network preacher: Church of the Air (CBS); Message of Isr (ABC). Chaplain, USNR, 1943-46; natl chaplain, JWV, 1947. Pres: JCC of Metrop Boston, 1961-63; Mass Bd Rabbis, 1958-60; chmn: placement comm, CCAR, 1949-52, comm on justice and peace, 1950-54, mem, exec bd, 1949-51, vice-pres, 1967-69; chmn, comm on J educ, UAHC, 1959-68, mem, bd trustees, exec comm, comm on social action; Mid-Cent Comm for Children and Youth, 1952; exec bd, Nassau Co Mh Assn, 1951-53; Pres Truman's Comm on Civil Rights, 1947; Gov's Comm to Survey Mass Courts, 1955; Mass Comm on Abolition of Death Penalty, 1957-58; Phi Beta Kappa; Delta Sigma Rho; Phi Sigma Delta. Author: Modern Jewish Problems, 1943; Little Lower than the Angels, 1952; Man's Best Hope, 1961; Consecrated Unto Me, 1965; My Beloved Is Mine, 1969; asso ed, Reconstructionist Mag, 1949-53. Recipient: award, Freedoms Found, 1952; Navy Commendation Ribbon; Navy Unit Citation; Pres Unit Citation as J Chaplain, campaign of Iwo Jima. Home: Jamaicaway Tower, Boston, Mass. Study: Temple Isr, Boston, Mass.

GITTELSON, Bernard, US, public relations cons; b. NYC, June 13, 1918; s. Sam and Gussie (Lefand); BA, St John U, Bklyn, 1939; m. Rosalind Weinstein, Mar 1, 1945; c: Louise, Steven. Pres: Time Pattern Research Inst since 1966; Roy Bernard Co, Inc, 1946-64; gen dir, NY State Employees Fed Credit U, 1937-40; analyst, NY State War Council, 1940-41; cons, NY State Comm on Ind and Lab Relations, 1941-42; dir, NY State Leg Comm on Discrimination, 1943-45; asso coord, Comm on Comty Interrelations, 1945-46. Cons: USAF; Cerebral Palsy Assn; Muscular Dystrophy Assn; Amer and WJC; Stephen S Wise Free Syn; ORT; Hadassah; mem: PR Soc of Amer; NY Acad Political Sci; AJCong; B'nai B'rith. Contbr to specialized publs. Home: 212 Cedar Ave, Hewlett Bay Park, LI, NY. Office: 507 Rockaway Ave, Valley Stream, NY.

GITTER, Moshe Benno, Isr, banker, business exec; b. Amsterdam, Holland, May 8, 1919; in Isr since 1957; m. Alice Rosenberg; three c. Gen mgr, Isr Devl and Mortgage Bank, Tel Aviv, since 1959; chmn, bd of dirs, since 1966; dir, various ind and commercial cos, Buenos Aires, 1942-57; co-found, gen mgr, CLAL, Isr Inves Co, 1962-64. Chmn, bd of dirs, Arpalsa SA, Promocion del Intercambio Argentino-Israeli, Buenoe Aires; dir, vice-chmn, Isr Discount Bank, Isr Discount Bank Inves Corp; vice-chmn: Delek Oil Co; bd of dirs, Isr Ind Devl Bank. Home: 18 Maharal St, Tel Aviv, Isr. Office: 16 Simtat Bet Hashoeva, Tel Aviv, Isr.

GITTER, Simon, Isr, physician; b. The Hague, Netherlands, Dec 9, 1915; s. Nathan and Jeanette (Fischler); in Isr since 1950; MD, U of Amsterdam, 1940; m. Lea Neubauer, 1940; c: Adina, Danela Leibowitz. Prof, pharm, dean fac of med, Tel Aviv U since 1969, chmn, dept phys, pharm since 1968; dep head, Rogoff-Wellcome Med Research Inst, Beilinson Hosp since 1954. Prin contribs: research on biochem, pharm,

toxicological problems. Hon treas, Isr Founds Trustees; found mem, Intl Soc for Toxinology. Author: Venomous Animals and Their Venoms, 1968; contbr to profsl jours. Home: 19 Beth Hillel, Ramat Gan, Isr. Office: Tel Aviv U, Tel Aviv, Isr.

GITTLEMAN, Morris, US, consulting metallurgist; b. Zhidkovitz, Russ, Nov 2, 1912; s. Louis and Ida (Gorodietsky); in US since 1920; BS, cum laude, Bklyn Coll, 1934; post-grad, Poly Inst of Bklyn, 1947-48; m. Clara Konefsky, Apr 7, 1937; c: Arthur, Michael. Cons metallurgist since 1958; reg profsl engr, Cal, chem and metallurgical engr; cons: Hollywood Alloy Casting Co; Overton Foundry; Familian Pipe and Supply; Universal Cast Iron Pipe Mfg Co; instr, chem, W States Coll of Engr, 1961-68; metallurgical engr, NY Naval Shipyard, 1942-47; metallurgist, tech, produc mgr, Pacific Coast Iron Pipe and Fitting Co, S Gate, Cal, 1948-58; cons: Valley Brass, Inc, 1958-61; Spartan Casting Corp, 1961-67; Commercial Enameling Co, 1963-68; instr, physics, LA Harbor Coll, 1958-59; Vulcan Foundry, Haifa, 1958-65. Prin contrib, MG Coupling. Fmr: bd trustees, Fairfax Temple; pres, Muse Soc. Mem: Amer Soc for Metals; Amer Foundrymen's Soc; AAAS. Contbr to tech jours. Home and office: 8232 Blackburn Ave, Los Angeles, Cal.

GITTLER, Joseph Bertram, US, educator; b. NYC, Sep 21, 1912; s. Morris and Toby (Rose); BS, U of Ga, Athens, 1934, MA, 1936; PhD, U of Chgo, Chgo, 1941; m. Susan Wolters, Sep 15, 1966; c: Josephine. Dean, Ferkauf Grad Sch, prof, sociol, Yeshiva U, since 1966, mem fac since 1961; dir, Cen for Study of Minority Groups; instr, asst prof, asso prof, sociol, U of Ga, 1936-43; research asso, Va State Planning Bd, 1942-43; research cons, USAF, 1943; prof, sociol, head of dept, Drake U, 1943-45; asso prof, prof, Ia State U, 1945-54; ed, Midwest Sociologist, 1945-48; dir, research project, Intergroup Relations in Rural Areas, Ia State U, 1952-55; various positions, U of Rochester, 1954-61; dean fac, Queensborough Comty Coll, City U, NY. Mem: Amer Sociol Assn, F; E Sociol Soc; Soc for Study of Social Problems; NY Acad of Scis; E Assn, Coll Deans, Advs of Students; Amer Assn, Jr Colls; NEA; Natl Council for Social Studies; Higher Educ Group, Deans in NY Metrop area; NY State Tchrs Assn; Amer Educ Research Assn; council of Fs, Upland Inst Crozer Found, Chester, Pa; Phi Beta Kappa; bd trustees, Cen for Urban Educ; adv bd, Rose F Kennedy Cen for Mental Retardation; Comm on U Relations, Off of Mayor, NYC. Author: Social Thought Among the Early Greeks, 1940; Virginia's People, 1944; Social Dynamics, 1952; Understanding Minority Groups, 1964; co-author, Your Neighbor Near and Far, 1955; ed, contbr, Review of Sociology: Analysis of a Decade, 1957; contbr to profsl jours. Home: 57 Fifth Ave, New York, NY. Office: 55 Fifth Ave, New York, NY.

GITTLIN, A Sam, US, industrialist, banker; b. Newark, NJ, Nov 21, 1914; s. Benjamin and Ethel (Bernstein); BSc, Rutgers U, 1936; m. Fay Lerner, Sep 18, 1938; c: Carol Franklin, Regina Gross, David, Steven. Chmn bd: Gittlin Bag Co since 1963, dir since 1954; Pines Shirt and Pajama Co since 1960; Pottsville Shirt and Pajama Co, Pa since 1960; Wall-co Imperial, Miami; Wall coverings by Zins, NJ; and chmn exec comm, Packaging Products and Design Corp; Barrington Ind, NY since 1936; Levin and Hecht, NYC; Barnes and Goldsmith, Inc, NYC since 1966; Brunswick Shirt Co, NYC, since 1966; Fleetline Ind, NC since 1966; All State Auto Leasing and Rental Corp; dir and financial cons: Realty Equities Corp of NY; partner and investors cons, Mission Pack, Inc; pres, Covington Fund, NYC, since 1963; dir, Harris Paint and Wallcovering Super Marts, Miami since 1967; mem, Comm to Review Dept of Banking and Ins, State Commn of NJ on Efficiency and Econ in State Govt, since 1967; fmr: dir, vice pres, Abbey Record Mfg; partner, Benjamin Mission, LA; pres, dir: Falmouth Supply, Montreal; Ascher Trading, NJ; Aptex; chmn exec comm, Peninsula Savings and Loan Assn; chmn bd, First Pa Cal. Pres, trustee, Temple Isr, Charlotte, NC; trustee, Hillel Found, Rutgers U; mem, club, Greenbrook Country; fmr: chmn, Hillel Comm, NC; treas, pres, Fed of B'nai B'rith Lodges, NC; trustee, Temple B'nai Abraham, Newark and S Orange, NJ; trustee, Benjamin Gittlin Charity Found, Newark. Home: 59 Glenview Rd, S Orange, NJ. Office: 666 Fifth Ave, New York, NY.

GITZELTER, Eliahu, Isr, attorney; b. Vilna, Pol, June 16, 1921; s. Abraham and Lipsha (Ratner); in Isr since 1935; att Balfour Coll, Tel Aviv; dipl, math, Heb U, Jerusalem, 1942; att law classes, Jerusalem, 1939-44; m. Margalit Sasson, Oct 8,

1946; c: Arnon, Amiram, Oron. Atty since 1947; lectr, civil procedure, Tel Aviv U, since 1955; fmr: tchr, math, physics. Maj, IDF, mil police, judge advocates dept, 1948-50, off, Irgun Zvai Leumi, 1939-45. Mem, Isr Bar Assn, fmr chmn; pres, Provident Fund. Hobby, math. Home: 16 Dubnov St, Tel Aviv, Isr. Office: 2 Har Sinai St, Tel Aviv, Isr.

GIVELBER, Samuel H, US, engineer, business exec; b. Satonov-Podolsk, Russ, Aug 25, 1901; s. Harry and Sarah (Melamud); in US since 1913; BS, Case Inst of Tech, 1923; att Carnegie Ist of Tech; m. Myrtle Waintrup, Apr, 1933, (decd); c: Harlan, Sherryl; m. 2nd, Esther Shapira, 1962. Chmn bd, The Reliance Co, since 1959; power plant engr, Duquesne Light Co, 1923-26; pres, Reliance Heating & Air Co, 1933-59. Pres: natl alumni assn, Case Inst of Tech, 1966-67; Mech Contractors Assn, 1950-53; bd dirs: Cleveland Engr Soc, 1967-70; The Temple, since 1955; Amer Soc for the Technion, 1956-57; bd overseers, Case W Reserve U, Cleveland, O, 1968-70; assembly delg, Cleveland J Comty, since 1957; mem: Engr Soc; Citizen's League; C of C; Amer Scc of Heating and Refrigeration Engrs; Natl Soc of Profsl Engrs; clubs: City; Commerce; Michelson. Home: 19601 Van Aken Blvd, Shaker Heights, O. Office: 4975 Hamilton Ave, Cleveland, O.

GIVEN, Herbert M, US, business exec; b. El Paso, Tex, July 12, 1912; s. Charles and Deborah (Trogman); att: Tex W Coll, 1930-32; U of Tex, 1932-33; m. Audrey Levy, Jan 19, 1935; c: Yvonne Colton, Charlene Spielvogel. Pres, Given Bros, Inc, 1962-69. Trustee: JCC, since 1950, past pres; El Paso Sym Assn, since 1950; mem: bd dirs, El Paso United Fund since 1961; fmr: pres, Temple Mt Sinai, El Paso; chmn, J Wfr Dr; clubs: Masons; Shriners; Rotary. Hobbies: art, music. Home: 1005 Singing Hills Dr, El Paso, Tex. Office: 225 S Mesa St, El Paso, Tex.

GIVEN, Louis E, US, business exec; b. Joliet, Ill, Feb 23, 1896; s. Morris and Esther (Lessersohn); BS, EE, Armour Inst of Tech, 1917; m. Esther Trackman, Aug 26, 1917; c: Sherman, Robert, James. Vice-pres, Given Bros Inc, El Paso, Tex, 1920-61, ret; elec engr, Commonwealth Edison, Chgo, Ill, 1917-20; chmn, Co Parole Bd. Pres, B'nai B'rith, 1929; JCC, 1942; Temple Mt Sinai, 1949-51, all of El Paso, Tex; club, Kiwanis. Hobby, philately. Home: 706 Blacker St, El Paso, Tex.

GIVEON, Raphael, Isr, egyptologist; b. Elberfeld, Ger, Feb 8, 1916; s. Louis and Sophie (Mendel) Grueneberg; in Isr since 1945; att Heb U, Jerusalem, 1947-48; D en etudes orientales, Sorbonne, 1962; m. Jehudith Genzer, Nov 3, 1944; c: Adaya, Dorit. Sr lectr, egyptology, Tel Aviv U, since 1969; part-time lectr: Haifa U; Heb U, since 1962; Oranim, kibbutz tchrs sem, 1958; tchr: Bruce Court Sch, Eng, 1942-45; HS, Mishmar Haemek, Isr, 1945-54; chargé de cours, Inst Intl d'Etudes Hebraiques, Paris, 1959-60. Prin contrib, research into relations between ancient Egypt and Pal. Miembro correspondiente, Inst de Estudios Avanzados, Arg. Author, Les Bedouins Shoson des Documents Egyptiens, 1970; contbr on archaeol, egyptology, to Eng, Heb, Fr jours. Home: Kibbutz Mishmar Ha'emek, Isr. Office: Tel Aviv U, Ramat Aviv, Isr.

GIVNER, Isadore, US, physician, ophthalmologist, educator; b. Charleston, SC, Jan 21, 1903; s. Louis and Jeanette (Morris); BS, Coll of Charleston, 1925; MD, SC Med Coll, 1926; m. Martha Barbe, Aug 9, 1938; c: Joan, Louis, Barbara, Eileen. Dir, ophthal, NY City Hosp, 1953; asso clinical prof, ophthal, NYU, since 1949; cons, ophthal: City Hosp, Elmhurst, 1941; U Hosp, 1949; Grand Cen Hosp, 1941; Correction Hosp, 1953; Manhattan Eye and Ear Hosp, 1966; asst ophthal surg: NY Eye and Ear Infirmary, 1935; Bellevue Hosp, 1935. Pres, NY Soc Clinical Ophthal, 1943; secy, eye sect, NY Acad of Med, 1948-49. Co-author, Prevention of Disease in Everyday Practice, 1954. Contbr to med jours; chap on bact studies in textbook, Ophthalmology. Home: 50 W 96 St, New York, NY. Office: 108 E 66 St, New York, NY.

GJEBIN, Rafael, Isr, physician; b. Tiflis, Ger, Jan 16, 1909; s. Abraham and Henrietta (Flit); in Isr since 1935; MD, U of Berlin, 1934; m. Helena Rosenfeld, Sep 8, 1933; c: Daniela, Tamar, Michal. Dir-gen, Min of Health, 1963-71, dep dir gen, 1953-55; fmr: dir, Rambam Govt Hosp, Haifa, 1948-63; asst dir, Hadassah Munic Hosp, Tel Aviv, 1946-48. Lt-col, RAMC, 1941-46. Fmr: chmn: IMA; Assn Govt Med Offs; mem, comm, Hosp Dirs Assn. Hobby: music. Home: 29 Keren Hayesod St, Jerusalem, Isr. Office: Min of Health, Jerusalem, Isr.

GLADSTEIN, Zvi Grisza, Isr, radio engr; b. Stara Siensava, Pol, May 11, 1910; s. Feivish and Henia; in Isr since 1948; dipl ing, U of Lwow, 1936; m. Henora Satinger; c: Aya Krovand, Abraham. Found, chief engr, i/c, Radio Communications, Min of Posts, since 1948; asst insp, wireless, Pal Min of Posts, 1936-48. Hon chmn, Tel Aviv sect, Inst of Elec and Radio Engrs; mem, selection comm, Engrs and Architects Assn in Isr, past chmn, Tel Aviv sect; past chmn, Inst Elec and Radio Engrs, Isr sect. Recipient: award for conversion of DSB Transmitters into ISB Emitters, Min of Posts, 1969. Home: 1 Haifa Rd, Tel Aviv, Isr. Office: Min of Posts, 34 Haganah St, Tel Aviv, Isr.

GLADSTONE, Abraham I, US, business exec; b. Pol, Jan 27, 1893; s. Jacob and Sarah (Bass); in US since 1894; BCS, NYU, 1913; LLB, Bklyn Law Sch, 1928; m. Fannie Shapiro, Nov 25, 1915 (decd); c: Mark, Arthur, Gloria (decd). Chmn, secy, dir, Marryatt, Lane & Co Inc since 1957; pres, dir, Affiliated Bus Machines Inc, since 1967; practicing public acctnt since 1913; CPA since 1924, atty since 1931; trustee, Amer Chain Ladder Corp Employees Trust Fund; owner, partner, pres, secy, asst treas, treas, dir in various orgs; fmr: secy, dir, Typographic Service Co, 1919-28; vice-pres, dir, Own Your Home Exposition, 1919-29; asso mem, New Sch for Social Research, 1925; vice-pres, dir, Republic Fire Proofing Co, 1944-52. Mem: life, Masonic, Menorah Lodge; fmr, mem: NY Co Lawyers Assn; NY State Soc CPAs; NY Assn of Attys-CPAs. Hobby, book collecting. Home and office: 4512 Kings Highway, Brooklyn, NY.

GLADSTONE, Arthur A, US, surgeon, educator; b. Burlington, Vt, July 7, 1907; s. Elchanan and Kerana (Brown); BS, U of Vt, 1928, MD, 1931; att Grad Sch of Surg, U of Pa, 1937-38; m. Esther Dinner, Oct 18, 1939; c: Miriam, Kerana, Judith, Tamar, David. Prof, chmn, dept of coloproctology, U of Vt, since 1965, on fac since 1945; cons surg: Porter Hosp, since 1950; Waterbury State Hosp, since 1948; Fanny Allen Hosp, since 1945; att surg, Med Cen Hosp of Vt; res, surg, Mt Sinai Hosp, 1938-39; chief, surg, Bishop Degoesbriand Hosp, 1945-65, dir, med educ, 1954-65; att surg, Mary Fletcher Hosp, 1944-65. F: Amer Coll Surg; Amer Proctological Soc; NE Proctological Soc; dipl, Amer Bd of Surg; hon life pres, Vt J Council; mem, NE Surg Soc. Contbr to med jours. Home: 354 S Union St, Burlington, Vt. Office: 217 S Union St, Burlington, Vt.

GLANZ, Rudolf, US, historian; b. Vienna, Aus, Dec 21, 1892; s. David and Regine (Graeber); in US since 1938; att Beth Hamidrash, Vienna, 1910-14; LLD, U Vienna, 1918; m. Rose Levi, Nov 29, 1921 (decd); c: Ruth; m. 2nd, Charlotte Brandes, Apr 16, 1950. Free-lance writer; research asso, YIVO, NYC since 1938; fmr: mem, adv research council and bd dirs, YIVO; ed, Der Jüdische Arbeiter; mem bar, Vienna; chmn law comm, mem exec comm, bd dirs, Vienna J Comty; research grant, Comm for Displaced Scholars. Mem: LZOA; Poalei Zion; fmr, Intl Mark Twain Soc. Author: Yiddish Elements in German Thief Jargon, 1928; Lower Classes of German Jewry in 18th Century, 1932; Immigration of German Jews up to 1880, 1947; Source Material, History of Jewish Immigration to US, 1951; Jews in Relation to Cultural Milieu of Germans in America, 1947; Jews in American Alaska, 1953; Jews and Chinese in America; The Rothschild Legend in America; German Jews in New York City in the 19th Century; The Jews of California, 1960; The Jew in the Old American Folklore, 1961; German Jewish Names in America, 1961; Jew and Mormon, 1963; Jew and Irish, 1966; Geschichte des Niederen Jüdischen Volkes in Deutschland, 1968; The German Jew in America; contbr to publs in Eng and Yiddish. Home: 620 W 171 St, New York, NY.

GLASBERG, Oscar S, US, journalist, editor; b. NYC, May 29, 1923; s. Bernard and Fannie (Fishbein); BS, summa cum laude, O U, Athens, O, 1947; m. Ida Odessky, Feb 26, 1956; c: Anne, Eve. Ed, publisher, Glass Digest and Glass/Metal Directory since 1959; news dir, Radio Sta WNBH, New Bedford, Mass, 1947-51; spec writer, Standard Times, New Bedford, 1949-51; news ed, Radio Sta, WMGM, NYC, 1951; ed, Post Exchange mag, NYC, 1953-59. Lt, US Army, 1943-46. Mem: Sigma Delta Chi; Kappa Tau Alpha; Masons; Toastmasters. Recipient: Jesse H Neal Award, Asso Bus Publs, NY, 1962; Bronze Star; Purple Heart with Oak Leaf Cluster. Home: Stonehenge Rd, Weston, Conn. Office: 15 E 40 St, New York, NY.

GLASER, Elmer S, US, business exec; b. Canton, O, Apr 8, 1908; s. Simon and Rose (Kohn); att Mt Union Coll, 1927; m.

Miriam Levy, June 9, 1935; c: Donald. Pres: Elm's Inc, since 1936; Oceanside Natl Bank, since 1963; Tri-City Savings and Loan Assn, 1961-63; owner-devl, Mission Square Shopping Cen, since 1960; mem bd, Oceanside Fed Savings and Loan Assn, 1949-60. Pres em, N Co Concert Assn since 1959, pres, 1958-64; pres: C of C, 1939; Oceanside-Carlsbad HS and Coll Dist, 1953-55; bd mem, Oceanside-Carlsbad Sym Assn; Boys Club; Temple Beth Isr, 1966-68; NCCJ, since 1968; mem: Oceanside Hum Relations Comm, since 1968; Mil Affairs Comm, since 1955; Oceanside Harbor Comm, 1962; B'nai B'rith; Elks; Masons; Shriners; clubs: El Camino Country; Oceanside-Carlsbad Country; Rotary. Recipient: golden man and boy award, Boys Club of Amer, 1953; silver keystone, 1960; award of merit, Daughters of Amer Revolution, 1956; dad of year, 1957; UJA Award, 1957; outstanding citizen, Jr C of C, 1960. Home: 420 S Horne St, Oceanside, Cal. Office: 1028 Mission Ave, Oceanside, Cal.

GLASER, Herman B, US, attorney; b. NYC, Dec 25, 1915; s. Abraham and Jennie; att Fordham Coll, NYC; LLB, Bklyn Law Sch; m. Lorraine, Sep 17, 1950; c: Jan, Lynne. Pvt practice. Dir, NY Acad of Trial Lawyers; fmr, pres, NY Trial Lawyers Assn. Home: Pleasant Ridge Rd, Harrison, NY. Office: 2 Lafayette St, New York, NY.

GLASER, Jerome, US, physician, educator; b. Sayre, Pa, May 22, 1898; s. Simon and Bertha (Allenstone); BA, Cornell U, 1919, MD, Med Sch, 1923; m. Frances Kauffmann, Oct 11, 1931; c: Frederick, John. Clinical prof em, peds, U of Rochester, Sch of Med and Dent, since 1960, fac mem since 1948; ped-in-chief em, Genesee Hosp; cons ped, Genesee Hosp; Rochester Gen Hosp; St Mary's Hosp; sr att ped: Strong Memorial Hosp; Munic Hosp. US Army, WW I. Exec comm, Allergy Found Amer; pres, Rochester Acad Med, 1950-51; mem: AMA; Amer Acad Peds; Amer Acad Allergy; Alpha Omega Alpha; Sigma Xi. Author: Allergy in Childhood, 1956; contbr to med jours, relating mostly to allergic diseases of children. Recipient: Albert D Kaiser award, Rochester Acad Med, 1958; citation for services in the field of ped allergy, Amer Acad of Peds, 1960; first Bret Ratner Memorial Award in Allergy, 1961. Home: 85 San Gabriel Dr, Rochester, NY. Office: 300 S Goodman St, Rochester, NY.

GLASER, Leon, US, attorney; b. NYC, July 22, 1914; s. Conrad and Gussie (Hirschberg); BA, cum laude, CCNY, 1934; LLB, Columbia Law Sch, 1937, JD, 1969; m. Dorothy Helfand, 1942; c: Joan, Gary. Dep chief counsel for decisions, Off, Solicitor of Lab, US Dept of Lab, since 1962, chief, appeals sect, div of employees compensation, 1955-59, chief, br of spec services, and alternate mem of employees' compensation appeals bd, 1959-62, staff mem, Off of Solicitor, since 1943. Mem: fac, Temple Isr, Silver Spring, Md, 1957-68; legislation comm, Allied Civic Group, Montgomery Co, 1962-63; delg from Northwest Br Estates Civic Assn, mem, exec council and chmn, comm on constitution and by-laws, 1963; Montgomery Sym Orch; B'nai B'rith; Phi Beta Kappa; Columbia Law Sch Alumni Assn; fmr pres, Cong B'nai Jeshurun chap, NYC, and natl chmn comm on interfaith coop, Young People's League, United Syn Amer. Home: 10713 Meadowhill Rd, Silver Spring, Md. Office: US Dept of Lab, 14 and Constitution Ave, Washington, DC.

GLASER, Simcha, Isr, educational admnr; b. Aus, Oct 6, 1921; s. Bernhard and Nura (Jakobovits); in Isr since 1939; att Heb U; m. Bertha Smith, Sep 11, 1949; c: Sara, Dov, Amihud. Dir, Natl Service for Rehab of Youth; fmr: dep chief, Min of Social Wfr; probation, immigration off, JA; dep dir, Youth Protection Auth, Min of Social Wfr. Served IDF, 1948. Hobbies: painting, philately. Home: 61 Hebron Way, Jerusalem, Isr. Office: Min of Social Wfr, Jerusalem, Isr.

GLASER, Sioma, US, impresario, composer, author, producer; b. Odessa, Russ, Aug 5, 1919; s. Arie and Miriam (Kreitman); desc of Toseffot Yom Tov; in US since 1942; att NYU; musical educ: Isr; Paris; NY; m. Muriel Goldstein. Music, theatrical cons, casting dir, produc: Broadway Artists Mgmt; Cultural Talent Exch; 3-D Records; Isr Motion Pictures and Newsreel Co; tchr-lectr, Opera-tunity Workshop; mgr: operas, concert tours, variety shows, US and abroad; music, drama critic, for various publs; co-publisher, ed, J World Mag; ed-in-chief, J World News Service and publishers; played leading role: Sabra; Hodedd-Hanoded, first Pal motion pictures; actor, Oriental Film Corp. Author, books and scenarios, including: My Born Enemy; My Experience as a War Correspondent; The Song of the American Jew; My Father the Commissar; To Conquer the Hebrew Language

without Trying; The Anatomy of Israel; Tamboo; Liar-Loafer; songs: My Mother's Lullaby; Caro Amor; The Gondolier's Love Call; Your Wedding Day; An American in Napoli; When Christmas Comes; America, My Wonderland. Cdr, Haganah; served US Army. Mem: Free Sons of Isr; FDR Lodge 3; Royal Lodge; ASCAP; Amer Fed of Musicians, US & Can; clubs: Maccabi Sport; Natl Showmen's; Grand Street Boys; Intl Artists, pres. Recipient, Pal Film Star Award, 1933. Hobbies: painting, inventing, sports, collecting rare books and old masters. Address: POB 1145, FDR Sta, New York, NY.

GLASNER, Abraham, Isr, chemist, educator; b. Cluj, Rum, Mar 3, 1910; s. Simon and Sarah (Hoffman); in Isr since 1924; BSc, London, 1935; PhD, Heb U, Jerusalem, 1940; m. Leah Shapira, 1937; c: Jael, Moshe, Simon. Prof, inorganic and analytical chem, Heb U, since 1967, on fac since 1937; visiting lectr, Princeton U, NJ, 1961-62. Home: 9 Gaza Rd, Jerusalem, Isr. Office: Heb U, Jerusalem, Isr.

GLASNER, Juda, US, rabbi; b. Hanusouce, Czech, May 19, 1918; s. Akiba and Hermina (Blum); in US since 1948; att: Rabb Sem & Presem, Czech, 1931-34; Sem, Montreux, Switz, 1934-36; Chatam Sofer Sch, Cluj, Rum, 1936-38; m. Deborah Deutsch, June 10, 1941; c: Moses, David. Rabbi, Cong Mishkan Yicheskel, since 1964; dep chief rabbi, dean, Chatam Sofer, 1939-44; rabbi, Temple Beth Moshe, NY, 1950-52; spec cons, repr kosher food law, State of Cal, 1957-64; participated in rescue work, Swed, 1945-48; gave gen assistance to J refs, Stockholm. Vice-pres: United Orthodox Rabbinate, Gtr LA; Chrs and Js for Law and Morality; chmn, Interfaith Comm for Release Time Rel Inst; fmr: vice-pres, Rabb Council, Cal; hon chmn, B'nai B'rith, City Terrace; mem: Union of Orthodox Rabbis, US & Can; Dist Atty's Adv Council, LA. Presented spec holiday progs: The Road to Freedom is Costly; The Perennial Struggle for Freedom; Time for Spiritual Reawakening; Return to God; contbr to various jours. Recipient: For Services to Comty, Country, Mankind, City Council of LA, 1965; Loyalty Day Award, VFW, 1969. Spec interests: hist, political sci. Home: 9431 Haines Canyon, Tujunga, Cal. Study: 10137, Commerce St, Tujunga, Cal.

GLASS, David, Isr, government official; b. Tel Aviv, Isr: s. Jacob and Rahel; LLM, Heb U, Jerusalem; m. Bracha Abella, Mar 29, 1960; c: Refael, Adiel, Daniel. Dirgen, Min for Rel Affairs; head of dept: Hechal-Shlomo 1959-62; Min for Rel Affairs, 1962-68; head, min office, Min for Rel Affairs, 1966-68. Mem exec, Natl Rel Party, chmn, Jerusalem br. Mem: Free Masons; Elizur. Home: 5 Rotenberg St, Jerusalem, Isr. Office: 30 Jaffa St, Jerusalem, Isr.

GLASS, Martin Joseph, Isr, attorney; b. Berlin, Ger, May 22, 1912; s. Michaelis and Clara Dessau; in Isr since 1936; att Friedrich Wilhelms U, 1930-33; Licence en Droit, fac de droit, Paris, 1934; m. Nora Kaufmann, Tel Aviv, Feb 6, 1941; c: Jonathan, Emanuel, Orith. Off i/c, dept of leg, Min of Justice, Isr since 1959; fmr: asst legal draftsman, Min of Justice; jr counsel, Smoira, Rosenblueth, Krongold, Bar-Shira, attys. Pvt, judge advocate off, IDF, 1948-49. Dep chmn, Jerusalem dist com, Isr Bar; mem: Soc for Protection of Nature; Intl Council for Planning and Bldg; Civil Service Disciplinary Tribunal; fmr: chmn, comm, Har El Syn. Spec interest: hist. Home: 8 Masaryk St, Jerusalem, Isr. Office: 21 Jaffa St, Jerusalem, Isr.

GLASS, Myron E, US, business exec; b. Manchester, Eng, Aug 1, 1900; s. Nathan and Ettie (Mendelsohn); in US since 1906; att Cleveland Marshall Law Sch; m. Rose Bartow, Oct 17, 1926; c, Herbert. Pres: Texby Co, Cleveland, O, since 1946; Painesville, O Shopping Cen, since 1952; fmr: Tex Distributing Co, Cleveland; mgr, Ohio, State div, Texaco. Fmr: bd, J Fed and wfr Funds; pres and life trustee, J Cmty Fed of Cleveland; pres: League for Hum Rights; and life trustee, Park Syn; Mt Sinai Hosp, also treas, chmn, devl fund campaign, life trustee; asst treas, div chmn, Cmty Chest, all Cleveland; clubs: Petroleum; Oakwood; Tamarisk Country. Recipient, awards: Dist Service, United Appeal of Gtr Cleveland, 1957; Eisenman, 1965; JCF, 1965. Home: 1 Bratenahl Pl, Cleveland, O, Office: 740 Leader Bldg, Cleveland, O.

GLASSER, Bernard, US, attorney; b. Norfolk, Va, Jan 28, 1910; s. Moses and Rachel (Salsbury); LLB, U of Va, 1932; m. Rose Levinson, June 14, 1938; c: Stuart, Richard, Jane, Michael. Bd dirs: Glasser Inves Corp since 1938; Va Natl Bank since 1951; Atlantic Perm Savings & Loan Assn since

1968; secy, Roosevelt Memorial Park, since 1957; commn in chancery: Corp of Court, City of S Norfolk; since 1953; Circuit Court of Norfolk, 1935; bus mgr, Va Law Review, 1930-32. Chmn, UJA, Norfolk, 1965; past pres, Norfolk B'nai B'rith; past master, Masons; mem: Amer, Va State, Norfolk and Portsmouth Bar Assns; Beth El Temple; Shriners; Scottish Rites; Phi Alpha; clubs: Gold Band; Unity; Lafayette Yacht; Cavalier Beach. Home: 7306 Woodway Lane, Norfolk, Va. Office: 504 Plaza One, Norfolk, Va.

GLASSER, Bess G, US, hotel operator, civic worker; b. NYC, Mar 7, 1907; d. Morris and Nina (Bockstein) Siegel; BA, cum laude, Hunter Coll, 1928; m. Louis Glasser, Oct 10, 1936; c: Phyllis Hodges, Sonia, Mona. Hotel operator, since 1935; sch tchr, NYC, 1928-30. Natl vice-pres, women's div, AJCong, since 1948, found, pres Fla women's div, since 1944, pres, Miami chap, since 1939; co-chmn, Albert Einstein Med Sch Comm, since 1952; pres; Gtr Miami USO Council, Dade Co, since 1968; mem: UN Speakers Bur, since 1950; Fla State Wfr Bd, since 1954; Temple Emanu-El; fmr: chmn, Miami Beach Cancer Dr; pres: Urban League; Conf J Womens Orgs Dade Co; Mt Sinai Auxiliary; chmn: Metrop Comty Chest, United Fund; Gtr Miami, State of Isr Bonds; armed services comm, JWB; Gtr Miami chap, Amer Soc for Technion; gen chmn, Combined J Appeal, women's div, also chmn, comty assembly; secy, Gtr Miami J Fed, also trustee; co-chmn, Truman Libr; mem, Quarter Cent Club of Natl Urban League 1968. Recipient, awards: US Treas Dept, 1945 NCCJ, 1950; State of Isr, 1954; Albert Einstein Med Sch, 1955, 1961; Woman of the Year, B'nai B'rith, 1955, 1968; Dade Co Lamplight Award, Fla Memorial Coll, 1968. Home: 3168 Prairie Ave, Miami Beach, Fla. Office: 203 W Flagler St, Miami, Fla.

GLASSER, Melvin A, US, union exec, educator; b. NYC, Sep 6, 1915; s. David and Rae (Startz); BSS, CCNY, 1935; att: Grad Sch for J Social Work, NY, NY Sch for Social Work: both, 1937-39; LLD, Adelphi U, NY, 1951; m. Esther Kron, June 25, 1939; c: Stephen, Amy, Robin. Dir, social security dept, Intl Union, United Automobile Workers, since 1963; lectr: Yale Med Sch, Sch of Public Health, U of Mich; exec dir, Mid-Cent White House Conf on Children and Youth, 1949-51; exec vice-pres Natl Found for Infantile Paralysis, 1959-61; dean of U resources and visiting prof, social wfr, Brandeis U, 1961-63; trustee: The Natl Found, Tuskegee Inst, Salk Inst for Experimental Biol, Ga Warm Springs Found. Chmn: exec comm, Natl Health Council, 1957-60; co-chmn, cabinet on social policy and action; Amer Assn of Social Workers; Amer Public Wfr Assn; Amer Public Health Assn; trustee, Natl Accreditation Council of Agcs Serving the Blind; mem: adv comm, Alcoholism, HEW; mem, comm for NIH; Mich Public Health Adv Council; Mich State Comprehensive Health Services Planning Comm; trustee, Comty Health Assn of Detroit; Group Health Assn of Amer; Gtr Detroit Hosp Planning Council; pres comm, 1960 White House Conf on Children and Youth, 1959-60; Natl Assn of Social Workers, Contbr to mag and jours. Recipient: Red Cross award, Finland; Order of White Lion, Czech; Order of Orange-Nassau, Netherlands; Den and Arg govt decorations; Home: 837 Moorland Dr, Grosse Pointe Woods, Mich. Office: 8000 E Jefferson Ave, Detroit, Mich.

GLASSER, Morris, US, certified public acctnt; b. Chgo, Ill, Apr 24, 1901; s. Meyer and Rachel (Olswang); LLB, DePaul U, 1929; m. Beatrice Drues, July 1, 1928; c: Robert, Charlotte Drucker, Jacqueline Gilbert. Mem, Altschuler, Melvoin, & Glasser, since 1925; fmr, acctnt, The Barrett Co, 1919-25. Exec comm, UJA, since 1965; co-chmn, CJA, metrop Chgo, 1962-67; chmn, J United Fund, metrop Chgo, 1970, co-chmn, 1968-69; chmn, Large City Budget Conf, 1967-69; pres, JWF, 1962-66, chmn, Ad Hoc comm on J Educ, 1967-68; dir: Chgo Med Sch, since 1965; Mt Sinai Hosp, 1958-68, pres, 1967-68; The Chgo Med Sch, since 1965; Oak Park Temple, since 1959; vice-pres, CJFWF, 1968-69; club: Standard. Home: 203 N Kenilworth Ave, Oak Park, Ill. Office: 69 W Washington St, Chicago, Ill.

GLASSMAN, Bernard S, US, business exec; b. Wash, DC, June 13, 1921; s. Herbert and Dorothy (Nussbaum); att Duke U, BS, Harvard U, 1943; m. Audrey Lavine, Sept 25, 1947; c: Laurel, Darci, Brian. Pres: GLY Construction Corp, since 1956; Metrop Leasing; Asher Ins Agcy Inc; The Stanborn Construction Co, 1948-59; Natl Mutual Insurance Co, 1958-61, vice-pres, Sun Cab, since 1950. USAF, 1943-46. Pres: Wash chap, Young Pres. Org; bd mgrs; Adas Isr Cong, since 1956; mem: Amer Mgmt Assn; Japan-Amer Soc of

Wash; Amer-Isr Soc; J Hist Soc; DC Regional Adv Council, Small Bus Admn; bd govs, Solomon Schechter Sch; clubs: Woodmount Country, Harvard. Hobbies: calligraphy. Bonsai culture, collecting chess sets, Japanese calendars, ceramics. Home: 1637 Montague St, NW, Washington, DC. Office: 1500 Massachusetts Ave, NW, Washington, DC.

GLASSMAN, Oscar, US, obstetrician, educator; b. Evanova, Pol, Sep 9, 1901; s. Moss and Anna (Bentich); in US since 1902; BA, U of Utah, 1923; MD, NYU, 1925; m: Jeanette Bitterbaum, June 5, 1926; s, George. Pvt practice since 1929; clinical asso prof, Cornell Med Coll, since 1954; cons, obstet, gyn: NY Hosp, NY Lying-in Hosp, Sydenham Hosp; courtesy staff: Mt Sinai Hosp, Drs Hosp. Lt col, US Army, 1942-46. F: Amer Coll Obstet and Gyn; Amer Coll Surgs; Intl Coll Surgs; AMA; NY Acad Med; NY Obstet Soc; dipl, Amer Bd Obstet and Gyn: mem: NY Co and State Med Socs; AAAS; Park Ave Syn; State Soc for Med Research; NY Acad Sci; Amer Geriatric Soc; Sigma Alpha Mu. Contbr to med jours. Hobby, music. Home: 1349 Lexington Ave, New York, NY. Office: 936 Fifth Ave, New York, NY.

GLATSTEIN, Jacob, US, author, poet, journalist; b. Lublin, Pol, Aug 20, 1896; s. Itzchak and Ita (Yungman); in US since 1914; att NYU Law Sch; hon deg, Baltimore Heb Coll, 1967; m. Nettie Bush, Oct 13, 1919; c: Shaul, Naomi, Gabriel. Columnist, Prost und Poshet, Day-Journal; ed, Folk un Velt, organ of WJC. Author, poetry: Yonkev Glatstein, 1921; Freie Ferzen, 1926; Credos, 1929; Yiddishteitchen, 1937; Gedenklieder, 1943; Shtralendike Yiddn, 1946; Dem Tatns Shotn, 1953; Yossel Loksh; Fun Mein Ganzer Mi, 1956; Die Freid fun Yiddischen Vort, 1961; novels: Emil un Carl, 1938; Ven Yash is Geforn, 1938; Ven Yash is Gekumen, 1940; In Tokh Genumen, 1947, 1956, 1960; Mit Meine Fartog Bicher, 1963; Eu Si, poems, trans into Span, 1967; Mikol Amali, poems, trans into Heb; A Yid from Lublin, 1968; Ch'tu demoren, 1968; Oif Greite Temes, essays, 1968; Homecoming at Twilight, 1967; Homeward Bound 1969. Co-found and co-ed, Insich, movement in Yiddish poetry. Recipient, awards: LaMed, 1941; LaMed and Kovner, JWB, 1956; Leivick, 1967; Kovner 1967; Bimko, 1967. Chmn, World Council, J Culture Cong; Yiddish Writers Union. Home: 82-15 Britton Ave, Elmhurst, NY. Office: 15 E 84 St, New York, NY.

GLATZER, Marshall M, US, cantor; b. Bx, NY, Nov, 19, 1926; s. Edward and Matilda (Spindel); BSacred Mus, HUC-JIR, 1962; m. Ann Hershenson, Nov 25, 1951; c: Judith, Lisa, Robert. Fac mem, sch of sacred music, HUC-JIR since 1966; cantor: Har Sinai Heb Cong since 1953; Temple Emanu-El, Westfield, NJ, 1949-51; Temple Beth Sholom, Bayside, NY, 1952-53. Pres, Amer Corf of Cantors, 1963-65, corresponding secy, 1953-58, exec secy, 1958-61, 1st vice-pres, 1961-63. Home: 1121 Roelofs Rd, Yardley, Pa. Office: 491 Bellevue, Ave, Trenton, NJ.

GLATZER, Nahum N, US, educator, author; b. Lemberg, Aus, Mar 25, 1903; s. Daniel and Rosa (Gottlieb); att Yeshiva Frankfurt/M, 1920-22; PhD, U Frankfurt, 1931; m. Anne Stiebel, 1932; c: Daniel, Judith Wechsler. Prof, J hist, chmn dept, Near E and Judaic studies, Brandeis U, since 1956, fac mem, since 1950; fmr: lectr, Freies Juedisches Lehrhaus, Frankfurt; dozent, J phil and ethics, U Frankfurt, 1932-33; instr: Bible, Beth Sefer Reali, Haifa, Pal; J hist, Heb Theol Coll and Coll of J Studies, Chgo, Ill, 1938-43; prof: rabb lit, Heb Tchrs Coll, Boston, Mass, 1943-47; J hist, Yeshiva U, NYC, 1948-50; Guggenheim F, 1959-60; visiting prof: hist, & UCLA, 1967; J hist, HUC, LA, 1967,69. Author: Sendung und Schicksal, 1931; Untersuchungen zur Geschichtslehre der Tannaiten, 1932; Moshe Ben Maimon, 1935; Gesprache der Weisen, 1935; Geschichte der Talmudischen Zeit, 1937; Maimonides Said, 1941; Torat Hanevuah Batalmud, 1942; Kitzur Toldot Yisrael, 1943, 5th ed, 1957; Talmudic Interpretation of Prophesy, 1946; In Time and Eternity, 1946, rev ed, 1961; Language of Faith, 1947, rev ed, 1967; Hammer on the Rock: A Midrash Reader, 1948, new ed, 1962; Franz Rosenzweig; His Life and Thought, 1953, rev ed, 1961; Hillel the Elder, 1956, 3rd ed, 1959; Zunz-An Account in Letters, 1958; Rosenzweig Hayyav u Maassav, 1959; Jerusalem and Rome: The Writings of Josephus, 1960; The Rest is Commentary: A Source Book of Judaic Antiquity, 1961; Zunz Letters, 2nd vol, 1963; Faith and Knowledge, 1963; Dynamics of Emancipation, 1965; Anfaenge des Judentums, 1966; The Way of Response: Martin Buber, 1966; The Dimensions of Job, 1968; chief ed, Schocken Books, since 1945; mem, ed bd: Judaism, since 1952; Bitzaron, since 1957; ed: Days of Awe, by Agnon, 1948; Commentary on the Passover Haggadah, by Gold schmidt, 1953; Understanding the Sick and the Healthy, by Rosenzweig, 1954; On Jewish Learning, by Rosenzweig, 1955; A History of the Jewish People, by E Schuerer, 1961; F Kafka, Parables and Paradoxes, 1961; On Judaism, by Martin Buber, 1967; On the Bible, by Martin Buber, 1968; contbr to: Ency Britannica; Ency Judaica. Mem: bd dirs, Leo Baeck Inst, since 1956; Amer Hist Assn; Amer Soc for Study of Rel; publ comm. J Publ Soc, since 1956; f, Intl Inst Arts and Letters. Home: 379 School St, Watertown, Mass. Office: Brandeis U, Waltham, Mass.

GLAZER, Harry B, US, foreign service off; b. Wash, DC, Sep 8, 1923; s. Morris and Dorothy (Cramer); BA, George Wash U, 1950; m. Carol Kane, July 21, 1956; c: Deborah, David. Secy of US Emb, Malta since 1967; intl relations off, US Dept of State, 1951-55, US Vice-Consul, Munich, 1955-60, consular off, Geneva, 1960-63, acting US Consul Gen, Geneva, 1962-63, office-i/c, Irish, Bahamian and Bermudian Affairs, 1963-67. US Army, 1943-46. Exec comm, Eng speaking J Comty of Geneva 1960-63; instr, Sunday Sch, 1961-62; bd, Amer Educ Found, Geneva, 1962-63; secy, Amer Men's Club, Geneva, 1962-63; mem: Phi Beta Kappa; Pi Gamma Mu; Phi Eta Sigma; Fgn Service, Assn; charter mem: JFK lodge; B'nai B'rith; clubs: Malta Union; Lions Intl. Recipient: Bronze Star medal; three battle stars, WW II. Office: US Dept of State, Washington, DC.

GLAZER, Mildred, US, librarian; b. Houston, Tex, Feb 7, 1909; d. Morris and Fannie (Antin) Lasser; BA, U of Mich Sch of Educ, 1932; BS, Simmons Coll, Libr Sch, 1943; m. Samuel Glazer, June 2, 1952. Head, tech and bus dept, Bridgeport Public Libr, since 1949; libr, sci and tech dept, Boston Public Libr, 1937-44; tech libr, Stamford Public Libr, 1944-46; br libr, Enoch Pratt Free Libr, Baltimore Md, 1946-49. Mem: Amer Libr Assn; Spec Librs Assn; Conn Librs Assn; Home: 97 Geneva Terr, Fairfield, Conn. Office: 925 Broad St, Bridgeport, Conn.

GLAZER, Nathan, US, sociologist, writer; b. NYC, Feb 25, 1923; s. Louis and Tillie (Zacharevich); BSS, CCNY, NY, 1944; MA, U of Pa; PhD, Columbia U, 1962; div; c: Sarah, Sophie, Elizabeth; m. 2nd, Sulochana Raghavan, Oct 4, 1962. Prof, Educ, Social Structure, Harvard U, since 1969; on staff, Commentary mag, 1944-53; ed, ed adv, Doubleday Anchor Books, 1954-57; visiting lectr, U of Cal, Berkeley, 1957-58; instr, Bennington Coll, Vermont, 1958-59; ed adv, Random House, 1958-62; visiting lectr, Smith Coll, 1959-60; f, Jt Cen, Urban Studies, Harvard-MIT, 1960-61; urban sociol, Housing and Home Finance Agcy, Wash DC, 1962-63; prof, U of Cal, Berkeley, 1963-69. Prin contribs, researches, urban social policy, ethnic, race relations. Author: American Judaism, 1957; The Social Basis of American Communism, 1961; co-author: The Lonely Crowd, 1950; Faces in the Crowd, 1952; Beyond the Melting Pot, 1963; co-ed, Studies in Housing and Minority Groups, 1960. Mem: Amer Sociol Assn; Amer Acad of Arts and Scis. Contbr to periodicals. Recipient: Guggenheim f, 1954-55; Anisfield-Wolf Award, 1964. Home: 12 Scott St, Cambridge, Mass, US. Office: Harvard U, Cambridge, Mass.

GLAZIN, Jacob Joseph, US, dentist; b. Boston Mass, Feb 13, 1899; s. Max and Aida (Lesnick); DMD, Harvard Dent Sch, 1918; m. Abigail Mekelburg, Nov 1, 1921; c: Allan, Janice Grossman. Ed, E Middlesex Dent Soc Bull, since 1950; chmn, Mass Dent Soc Commn for Study of Illegal Dent; E Middlesex Dist Illegal Dent Comm. USN, WW I; mem, Selective Service Bd, WW II. Dir: Middlesex Health Assn, 1955-60; Temple Tifereth Isr since 1930; Gtr Boston Dent Soc; Boston Dent Soc; Boston chap, Alpha Omega, supr vice-chancellor, 1929; adv bd, Jackson Assn for Cancer Research; found, Alpha Omega, Hadassah Dent Sch, Isr; mem: Amer Dent Soc; NE Mass Dent Soc; Harvard Odontological Soc; Pan-Amer Dent Soc; adv bd to Dean of Harvard Sch of Dent Med; E Middlesex Dent Soc, past pres; fmr dir: Malden Red Cross; Salvation Army; Malden Health Assn; past chmn, J Philanthropies, Malden; Masons, hon grand marshal; Grand Lodge of Isr, past dist dep, grand master Masons; clubs: Kiwanis; Malden; New Cent, pres, 1951. Author: X-rays in Dentistry, 1923; Pregnancy Gingivitis, 1925. Recipient, Medal of Merit, Grand Lodge of Masons, State of Isr. Home: 84 Appleton St, Malden, Mass. Office: 1 Salem St, Malden, Mass.

GLENN, Jacob Benjamin, US, physician, author; b. Merkinie, Lith, May 2, 1905; s. Moshe and Treine (Szerbakoff) Glembocki; in US since 1923; BS, U of Pitt, 1929; MA, Columbia

U, 1931; MD, U of Zurich, 1942; m. Elizabeth Hampel, Dec 12, 1938; c: Melvyn, Gabriel, David. Internist since 1951; dir med affairs, Greenpoint Hosp, Bklyn; fmr: Heb tchr; phys: Isr Zion Hosp; Heb Convalescent Home, Bx; Cumberland Hosp, Bklyn. Mem, B'nai Zion, Farband; fmr pres, Heb Alliance Cong; secy, Histadrut, Pittsburgh. Author: Neonatal Death, 1943; Hospitals, 1953; Bible and Modern Medicine, 1958; Impression of a Visit to Israel, 1967-68; Zu Gesunt und Zu Leben; mem ed staff, contbr, Synagogue Light, NY; columnist, J Press, Bklyn, fmr contributing ed, J Forum; contbr to profsl jours. Recipient, Maimonides Award, Chgo, 1968. Home: 140 Jaffray St, Brooklyn, NY. Offices: Kings C Hosp Brooklyn, NY; 201 Brighton 1 Rd, Brooklyn, NY.

GLENN, Menahem G, US, lecturer, educator, author, editor; b. Merkine, Lith, Dec 27, 1900; s. Moses and Treine (Szerbakoff) Glembocki; in US since 1914; att Yeshivot; BS, Columbia U, 1929; PhD, Dropsie Coll, 1945; m. Ilse Heidelberger, 1945; c: Uri, Anna. Ret; fmr: sr ed, Maurice Jacobs, Inc, Phila; tchr, Rabbs, Bible, Heb lit, Graetz Coll, Phila; prin, Heb HS, Trenton, NJ; dir, Heb Inst, Waterbury, Conn. Author: Jewish Tales and Legends, 1927; Al Gdot-haNeyeman, Heb, 1937; Rashi der Folklerer, Yiddish, 1940; haMilon haMa'asi, Heb-Eng Dict, vol I, 1947, vol 2, 1960; Rabbi Israel Salanter-Religious Ethical Thinker, 1953; asso ed, The J Book Annual since 1952; fmr mem, ed staff, New Yorker Wochenblat; columnist, The J Exponent, Phila, since 1951; contbr to Heb, Yiddish, Anglo-J press; writes under pen names: G Menahem; M Gershon; M Ben Yehezekel; M Ben Moshe; Gershon Ben Moshe; Kore Pashut; M Gimmel; M Gan Magen; M Treinin; M Bunin. Mem: Amer Acad for J Research; Natl Assn of Heb Profs; Histadrut Ivrith; Sons of Zion; PEN; Alumni of Dropsie Coll; Temple Isr, Wynnfield, Mass; fmr, J Comty Cen. Home: 5665 W Diamond St, Philadelphia, Pa.

GLENN, Morton B, US, physician; b. NYC, Mar 21, 1922; s. Harold and Mimi (Steinberg); BA, U of Pa, 1942; MD, NYU Coll of Med, 1946; div. c: Wendy, Valerie, John. Pvt practice, internal med, nutrition, since 1952; phys i/c: Kips Bay Obesity Clinic, since 1959; Morrisania Nutrition Clinic, since 1956; asst prof, clinical med, NYU Post Grad Sch of Med, since 1952; asst prof, preventative, environmental med, Albert Einstein Coll of Med since 1958; asst att phys: U Hosp, since 1952; Misericordia Hosp, 1958-59; asst visiting phys, Bellevue Hosp, since 1952; asst adjunct in med, Hosp for Jt Diseases, 1952-54; med cons, UN, 1954-56; att phys, outpatient, dept, White Plains Hosp, 1956-59. Lt, jr grade, USNR, 1943-45, 1947-49. Chmn: Inst for Nutrition Services for Puerto Ricans, 1962; mem, exec bd, since 1956; pres, Food and Nutrition Council, Gtr NY, Inc, 1962-64; comm mem: nutrition, public health, NY Co Med Soc; NY Heart Assn; AHA; f: Clinical Soc of NY Diabetes Assn; Amer Coll of Nutrition, pres, 1964-66; NY Acad of Sci; mem: Phi Delta Epsilon; AAAS. Author: How to Get Thinner Once and For All, 1965; contbr to med jours. Spec interests: research in weight control, nutrition. Home: 1070 Park Ave, New York, NY. Office: 110 E 63 St, New York, NY.

GLESINGER, Lavoslav, Yugo, physician, historian of med; b. Zagreb, Feb 6, 1901; s. William and Sharlotte (Korican); MD, Fac Med, Vienna, 1925; DSc, 1960; Dipl of Hon, Cuban Acad of Sci, 1965; m. Vera Fischer, Oct 7, 1946. Prof, hist of med, fac med, Zagreb since 1948; fmr: head, med-hist dept, Inst of Hist of Scis, Yugo Acad of Scis and Arts; pvt phys. War prisoner, 1941-45, Ger; mem, Yugo People's Army. Councillor, J Cmty, Zagreb since 1935, exec mem since 1940; exec mem, Hevra Kadisha; councillor, J Natl Soc, Zagreb; delg to perm comm, Intl Soc of Hist of Med since 1950; fmr mem: B'nai B'rith; Omanut, J Cultural Soc; exec, Intl Acad of Hist of Med; fmr mem, Intl Paracelsus Soc; corresp mem: Soc Fr d'Hist de la Med; Union Intl d'Hist de Sci. Author: Amatus Lusitanus, 1940; William Harvey and Discovery of Blood Circulation, 1949; Medicine Through the Ages, 1954; Doctors and Quacks, 1955, all in Yugo; collaborator on lexicons and encys, past secy, Medical Ency; numerous sci papers; contbr to mags and newspapers. Recipient: Order of Merits for the People, III deg, 1947; Order of Lab with Red Star, 1968. Home: Lopasicéva No 6, Zagreb, Yugo. Office: Demetrova 18, Zagreb, Yugo.

GLICK, Arnold J, US, educator; b. Bklyn, NY, Nov 7, 1931; s. Jack and Elsa (Zimmer); BA, Bklyn Coll, 1955; PhD, U of Md, 1961; m. Sydell Breslow, June 21, 1953; c: Jody, Jeri, Ora. Asso prof, physics, U of Md, since 1967, fac mem since 1961; NSF f, U of Paris, Orsay and Centre d'Etude Nucleare de

Sachay, Fr, 1967-68; NSF f, Weizmann Inst of Sci, Isr, 1959-61. US Army, 1952-54. Mem: Fed of Amer Scis; Amer Phys Soc; Sigma Pi Sigma; Pi Mu Epsilon; Sigma Xi. Contbr to: Lecture Notes on the Many Body Problems, 1961; 1962; profsl jours. Spec interests: archaeol of the ME, photography. Home: 9321 St Anderws Pl, College Park, Md. Office: U of Md, College Park, Md.

GLICK, David, US, biochemist, histochemist, educator; b. Homestead, Pa, May 3, 1908; s. Max and Anne (Lasday); BS, U of Pittsburgh, 1929, PhD, 1932; cert, Amer Bd of Chem; m. Ruth Mueller, Sep 16, 1929; c: David, Peter; m. 2nd, Annette Zelzer, Aug 9, 1941; m. 3rd, Irena Ross, Sep 2, 1945; c: Jonathan, Jeffrey. Prof, path, head div histochem, Stanford U, since 1961; cons, VA Hosp, Palo Alto, since, 1961; research f: Mt Sinai Hosp, NYC; Carlsberg Lab, Copenhagen, 1933, 1936-37, 1958; Karolinska Inst, Stockholm, 1949, 1959; Stazione Zoologica, Naples, 1959; chief, chem lab: Mt Zion Hosp, SF, 1934-36; Beth Isr Hosp, Newark, 1937-42; war research for OSRD, Mt Sinai Hosp, NYC, 1942-43; head, vitamin enzyme research, Russell Miller Milling Co, Minn, 1943-46; cons: toxicity lab, U of Chgo, 1945-46; VA Hosp, Minn, 1946-47; prof, phys chem, U of Minn, 1950-61. Mem: AAAS, Amer Chem Soc; Amer Soc of Biol Chems; Soc for Experimental Biol and Med; Histochem Soc, past pres; NRC, fmr mem, cytochem panel, comm on growth; Amer Soc Cell Biol; Intl Soc Cell Biol; AAUP; Sigma Xi; Phi Lambda Epsilon; Beth Am Syn. Author: Black and White and other poems, 1946; Techniques of Histo and Cytochemistry, 1949; Quantitative Chemical Techniques of Histo and Cytochemistry, vol I, 1962, vol II, 1963; ed, Methods of Biochemical Analysis; mem, ed bd: Jour of Histo- and Cytochemistry since 1956, asso ed; Proceedings of Soc of Experimental Biol and Med, 1957-58; spec cons, Jour of Inves Dermatology, 1968; contbr to profsl publs. Home: 680 Foothill Rd, Stanford, Cal. Office: Stanford Med Sch, Palo Alto, Cal.

GLICK, Philip M, US, attorney, b. Kiev, Russ, Dec 9, 1905; s. David and Rebecca (Sussman); in US since 1912; AA, Crane Jr Coll, 1926, PhB, U of Chgo, 1928, JD, Law Sch, 1930; m. Rose Rosenfeld, May 13, 1933. Asst dir, policy, legal adv, Fed Water Reources Council, since 1967; gen counsel, Fed Subsistence Homesteads Corp, 1933-34; asst; solicitor, US Dept of Agric, 1934-42; solicitor, dep dir, War Relocation Auth, 1942-46; gen counsel, Public Housing Admn, 1946-48; gen counsel, Inst of Inter-Amer Affairs and Tech Coop Admn, US Dept of State, 1948-53; partner, Dorfman and Glick, attys-at-law, 1955-67. USN, 1944-45. Author: The Administration of Technical Assistance, 1957; A Standard State Soil Conservation Districts Law, 1937; Standard State Soil Conservation Districts Law, enacted by all State Legs in US. Mem: Amer Bar Assn; DC Bar Assn; Amer Legion; Soc for Intl Devl. Hobby, swimming. Home: 116 E Melrose St, Chevy Chase, Md. Office: 1025 Vermont Ave, NW, Washington, DC.

GLICK, Seymour Michael, US, physician; b. Paterson, NJ, June 30, 1932; s. Zalman and Helene (Lichtenstein); AB, NYU, 1951; MD, SUNY, 1955; m. Brenda Rubenstein; c: Sorah, Menachem, Yitzchok, Yaakov, Yehudah. Chief, med services, Coney I Hosp, since 1967, chief, div of endocrinology, 1964-67; asso clinical prof, SUNY Downstate Med Cen, since 1968; clinical inves, VA Hosp, Bx, 1963-64. Capt, US Army, 1957-59. Chmn, Assn Orthodox J Sci. Home: 1272 E 5 St, Brooklyn, NY. Office: 2601 Ocean Pkwy, Brooklyn, NY.

GLICKMAN, Maurice, US, sculptor; b. Jassy, Rum, Jan 6, 1906; s. Solomon and Sara (Mosk); in US since 1920; att Alliance Art Sch, 1921-25; Art Students League, 1929-31. Found, dir, Sch for Art Studies, 1945-54. One-man shows: Morton Gals, NY, 1931; U of NC, 1941; Babcock Gal, NY, 1946; Lewison Gal, NY, 1961, 1967, 1968; Albany Inst of Hist of Art, 1963; natl exhbs: Corcoran Gals, Wash, DC, 1934; Mus of Modern Art, NY, 1935; Rockefeller Cen Intl Sculptor Exhb, 1937; Bklyn Mus, 1938; Whitney Mus, annually since 1938; Phila Mus, 1940, 1950; Pa Acad of Fine Arts, 1939, 1950, 1960; Metrop Mus, NY, 1941; Natl Acad of Design, NY, 1937, 1949; J Mus, NY, 1951; Sculptors Guild Annuals, since 1938; O'Hana Gal, London, 1962; perm collection: Mus of Art, Isr; Robertson Memorial Cen, Binghamton, NY; US Dept of Interior, Wash, DC; S River PO, NJ; Northampton, Pa; pvt collections. Mem: Sculptors Guild, exec secy, 1954-55; Natl Sculpture Soc. Contbr to profsl jours. Recipient: competitive awards, sect of fine arts, US

Treas, 1938, 1940, 1944. Hobby, chess. Home: 165 E 66 St, New York, NY. Studio: 2231 Broadway, New York, NY.

GLICKMAN, Stanley, Irwin, US, urologist; b. NYC, Aug 14, 1917; s. Joseph and Victoria (Miller); BA, Columbia U, 1937; MD, Coll Phys & Surgs, 1941; m. Ruth Kaiser; c: Randolph, Robin. Att urol: Mt Sinai Hosp since 1948; Bx Munic Cen, since 1954; clinical prof, Mt Sinai Sch of Med, since 1968; sr instr, urol, U Hosp, Ann Arbor, 1947-48, on staff since 1945. F. Amer Coll Surgs; NY Acad Med; dipl Amer Bd Urol; mem: Amer Urol Assn; NY Sect, Amer Urol Assn; AMA; Phi Beta Kappa; Alpha Omega Alpha. Contbr to med jours. Recipient, Meierhof Prize for path, 1938. Home: 181 Lyncroft Rd, New Rochelle, NY. Office: 45 E 85 St, New York, NY.

GLICKSBERG, Abraham Abba, US, educator; b. Warsaw, Pol, Jan 27, 1909; s. Alter and Chavah (Krugman); in US since 1940; BA, NYU, 1949, MA, 1950, PhD, 1962. Instr, Heb lang, Bklyn Coll, Adult Educ, since 1963; libr, Judaica-Hebraica, NYU; fmr: instr: Heb lang, Cen Yeshivah HS for Girls, Bklyn; NYU Sch of Educ, 1949-65; supr, student tchrs in romance langs, New Sch for Social Research, NYC, 1953-1965. US Army, 1943-45. Mem, Amer Assn Profs of Heb; Phi Delta Kappa. Compiler, Dict of Heb Stenography; author of one-act plays. Recipient, awards: Mitchel, 1949; B'rith Abraham, 1952; Shai Agnon, 1953. Home: 1120 Ave K, Brooklyn, NY. Office: Brooklyn Coll, Brooklyn, NY.

GLICKSBERG, Charles I, US, educator, author: b. Warsaw, Pol, 1900; s. Isidore and Helen (Lifschitz): in US since 1908; BS, CCNY, 1923; MA, Columbia U, 1924; PhD, U of Pa, 1932; m. Dorothy Kapernick, 1928; c: Paul, Stephanie Neuman. Prof, Eng, Bklyn Coll, since 1946; prof, creative writing, New Sch for Social Research, since 1947; dir, Vt Fiction Writers Conf, Windham Coll, 1953-56; Fulbright scholar, Isr, 1958-59. Mem: AAUP, Amer Humanist Assn; AJCong. Author: Walt Whitman and the Civil War, 1933; American Vanguard, 1950; American Literary Criticism, 1951; Writing the Short Story, 1953; New Voices, 1958; Literature and Religion, 1960; The Art of Creative Writing, 1961; The Tragic Vision in Twentieth-Century Literature, 1963; The Self in Modern Literature, 1964; The Death of God, 1966; The Ironic Vision in Modern Literature, 1968; co-author, American Vanguard, 1953; contbr articles on Amer lit, semantics, Judaism, educ. Home: 210 101 St, New York, NY. Office: Brooklyn Coll, Brooklyn, NY.

GLICKSTEIN, Howard Alan, US, attorney; b. NYC, Sep 4, 1929; s. Samuel and Fanning (Greenblat); BA, Dartmouth, 1951; LLB, Yale U, 1954; LLM, Georgetown U, Wash, DC, 1963. Staff dir, US Comm on Civil Rights, since 1968, gen counsel, 1965-68; atty: US Justice Dept, 1960-65; Proskauer, Rose, Goetz & Mendelsohn, 1956-60. Sgt, US Army, 1956. Home: 1304 4 St, Washington, DC. Office: 1405 I St, Washington, DC.

GLICKSTEIN, Joseph M, US, attorney; b. Jacksonville, Fla, Feb 26, 1899; s. Harry and Fannie (Shorr); LLB, Wash and Lee U, Lexington, Va, 1920; m. Myra Grunthal, Jan 8, 1924; c: Joseph, Hugh. Pvt practice, since 1920; admitted to practice: Supr Court, Fla, 1920; US Supr Court, 1933; dir, Barnett First Natl Bank of Jacksonville, since 1964; mayor, City of Neptune Beach, 1945-47, councilman, 1937-45. US Army, WW I; registrants adv bd, Jacksonville, WW II. Pres, Temple Ahavath Chesed, 1937-47, trustee, since 1924; trustee, Jacksonville Baptist Hosp, since 1950; mem: Omicron Kappa Delta; Robert E Lee Assos; Zeta Beta Tau; Amer Judicature Soc; Amer, Fla, Jacksonville, Bar Assns; Amer Legion; Natl Geographic Soc; C of C; Dem J Org; clubs: Beauclerc Country; River; Ponte Vedra; U. Hobbies: fishing, photography. Home: 1008 Ocean Front, Neptune Beach, Fla. Office: 1205 Universal Marion Bldg, Jacksonville, Fla.

GLID, Nandor, Yugo, sculptor; b. Subotica, Yugo, Dec 12, 1924; s. Armin and Emma (Hajduska); att, Applied Arts Acad, Belgrade, 1948-51; m. Gordana Stovanović; c: Daniel, Gabriel. Sculptor. Works include: monuments in Mauthausen, 1957; Subotica, 1967; Intl Monument in Dachau, 1968. Partisan Army, machine gunner, 1944-45. Vice-pres, Artist Assn Serbia, since 1957; gen secy, Assn Plastic Artists, Yugo, 1961-65; fmr: mem council: Army Gal; Mus of J Hist; mem commn: Monuments of Serbia; Art of Serbia. Mem: Assn Artists, Yugo; Communist Party, Yugo. Recipient: 1st prizes: for Students, 1948; Belgrade U, 1950; Mauthausen monument, 1957; 3rd prizes: Kragujevac, 1960; Kosmaj,

1969; 1st Intl prize for Dachau 1959-65. Hobbies: music, travelling. Home and studio: 68a B V Putnika St, Belgrade, Yugo.

GLOBE, Leah Ain, US, communal leader, author; b. Narevke, Russ, Mar 14, 1900; in US since 1906; d. Wolf and Sarah (Cohen) Ain; Tchrs Cert, JTSA Tchrs Inst, 1920; att: Hunter Coll; Bklyn Mus Art Sch; Columbia U; m. Jacob Globe, Aug 9, 1925; c, Rena Quint. Heb tchr, Heb Inst, Boro Park 1920-30; pres, Batya chap, Mizrachi Women's Org; chmn, natl cultural comm, 1946-49. Author: Bas Mitzvah Treasury, 1965; The Secret Weapon, 1966. Sabra stories, 1970. Hobby, art. Home: 164 Lincoln Rd, Brooklyn, NY.

GLOBERSON, Arye, Isr, educator; b. Pol, Mar 11, 1925; in Isr since 1938; BA, hons, Sch of Law and Econ, Tel Aviv, 1947; grad, Manpower and Personnel Mgmt, Mil staff Coll, 1948; MA, Paris U, 1951; grad, Sch of Social Research, Versailles, Fr, 1951; PhD, fac law, econ, Paris U; ILO f, Productivity and Mgmt Training, Eur U's, research cens, public and pvt undertakings; m. two c. Asso prof, org behaviour personnel mgmt, chmn, dept Lab Studies, both Tel Aviv U; cons to Govt and corps on policy making, org analysis; fmr: dir, efficiency control service State Comptroller of Isr; UN Expert on Public Admn and Staff Devl, to Govt of Dahomey; asst prof, public admn and personnel mgmt, Heb U, Jerusalem; pedg dir, Isr TA Mission to Niger on staff devl. Dep chmn, Isr Ind Relations Research Assn; chmn, manpower sect, Isr Mgmt Cen; chmn, research and public admn, Inst of Mgmt; mem council, Isr Inst of Applied Social Research. Author: L'Etat d'Israél et le Peuple Juif, 1951; Joint Consulation in Israel Industry, 1955; Principles of Personnel, Management, 1960; The Organizational Structure; Analysis and Improvement, 1968; Probationary Employment, 1968; Objectives and Effectiveness, 1968; Labor Management Conflicts; Ten Research Cases in Industrial Relations in Israel, 1968; contbr to jours. Home: 34 Arlosoroff St, Ramat Gan, Isr. Office: Tel Aviv U, Ramat Aviv, Isr.

GLOVER, Nathan, US, physician; b. Maine, Feb 23, 1918; s. Israel and Annie (Rozinsky) Glousky; AM, chem, Boston U, 1943; PhD, U of Rochester, 1948; MD, U of Vt, Burlington, Coll of Med, 1952; m: Lotte Landau; c: Joan, Alan, Jeffrey. Pvt practice, anesthesiologist, since 1954; clinical asst prof, U of Miami Med Sch, 1970; att anesthesiologist, Boston City Hosp, 1955-56. Civilian research asso, AEC, Manhattan Project, 1944-48. Bd trustees, Beth David Syn; mem: Fla Soc Anesthesiologists, Patient Care Committee; AMA; Amer Soc Anesthesiology; Fla Med Assn; Intl Anesthesiologist Research Soc. Author, chapt in: Pharmacology and Toxicology of Uranium Compounds, 1953; contbr to sci jours. Home: 42 Samana Drive, Miami, Fla. Office: 1150 NW 14 St, Miami, Fla.

GLOVSKY, Abraham, US, attorney; b. Volkovisk, Russ, Dec 10, 1896; s. Meyer and Sadie (Bromberg); in US since 1901; LLB, Boston U, Law Sch, 1917; m. Ruth Slotnick, June 27, 1917; c: Henry, William, Bertram, Sylvia. Partner, law firm, Glovsky and Glovsky since 1917; mem, Bd of Aldermen, 1923-24; city solicitor, 1925-31; trustee, Beverly Savings Bank since 1933, vice-pres, since 1967. Pres: C of C, 1941-43; B'nai B'rith, Dist, 1946-47, chmn, natl finance council, 1950-53, bd of govs, 1950-56; Intl Rotary, 1938-39; club, Mass Rep. Home: 25 Ober St, Beverly, Mass. Office: 8 Washington St, Beverly, Mass.

GLÜCK, Emil T, Swed, veterinary surg, army off; b. Lund, Swed, June 6, 1895; s. Aron and Ida (Epel); grad, Vet HS, Stockholm, 1918; m. Salka Epstein, 1921; c: Dan, Mirjam Zielnoy. Lt-col, vetr surg, Swed Army, ret. Hon pres, Swed Youth Aliyah Comm, since 1968; pres, KH-UIA, and vice-pres, J comty, Stockholm, both since 1950; initiator and leader of pioneer training in Swed, 1933-48. Contbr to Swed and Ger vetr jours. Recipient: Swed Vasaorden; Finnish Lion; Danish Liberty Medal. Homes: Wittstockgatan 7, Stockholm, Swed; 62/22 Neve Sharet, Tel-Aviv, Isr.

GLUCKLICH, Joseph, Isr, educator; b. Jerusalem, Isr, June 23, 1921; s. Samuel and Sarah; BSE, hons, U of London, 1950; DSc, Technion, Haifa, 1958; postdoc, U of Ill, 1962; m. Rachel Benshachar, Jan 18, 1952; c: Ariel, Avner, Sarah. Prof, mech, Technion, since 1963, head dept, 1966-68, mem fac, since 1955; fmr: design engr, Tahal Inc; site engr, Mekorot. Capt, J Brigade, Brit Army, 1941-46. Prin contrib, research in field of mech properties of materials. Contbr sci papers to intl sci jours. Recipient: King's Badge; Arnan Prize,

Assn of Engrs and Architects, Isr, 1961. Home: 12 Hashkedim St, Tivon, Isr. Office: Technion, Haifa, Isr.

GLUCKMAN, Earl C, US, physician, hospital planner; b. Poughkeepsie, NY, Mar 29, 1909; s. Max and Mollie (Weisberger); BA, Columbia Coll, 1931; MD, U of Paris, 1937; att Inst of Public Health, Columbia U, 1939-40; m. Lillian Auerbach, Sep 15, 1932; c: Jeffrey, Roberta. Ret as VA Cen Off, Wash DC, 1961-69; pvt practice, Yonkers, 1937-40; chief-of-staff, VA Hosp, Bx, 1946-47; dir, VA Hosp, Coral Gables, Fla, 1957-61. Lt-col, US Army MC, 1940-45; US Army Res since 1945, col, 1960-69. Mem: AMA; Amer Public Health Assn; Amer Hosp Assn. Contbr to med jours. Home: 11386 Acropolis Dr, Yucaipa, Cal.

GLUCKMAN, Henry, S Afr, business exec, legislator, physician; b. 1893. Chmn, Rapp and Maister Holdings; MP, Yeoville, Johannesburg, 1938-58; chmn, Natl Health Services Comm 1942-44; Min of Health, Govt of S Afr, 1945-48; MP, Johannesburg, 1938-58. Col, S Afr Army MC. LRCP, London; mem, Royal Coll Surgs, Eng; pres, Natl War Memorial Health Found; exec mem, S Afr Inst Intl Affairs; exec trustee, S Afr Found; chmn, Gen Smuts War Vets Found. Office: POB 6360, Johannesburg, S Afr.

GLUCKMAN, Lillian A, medical writer, editor; b. NYC, Feb 20, 1911; d. Morris and Minnie (Goldenberg) Auerbach; BA, Barnard Coll, 1931; att Sorbonne, Paris, 1932-34; m. Earl Gluckman, Sep 15, 1932; c: Jeffrey, Roberta. Free-lance med • writer; writer with USPHS, 1962-67; med ed, NYC, 1931-37; mgn ed, Amer Jour Surg, NYC, 1937-40; dir women's div, JWB, 1949-57; dir, med news bur, U of Miami, 1957-62. Mem: Natl Assn Sci Writers; Phi Beta Kappa. Home: 11386 Acropolis Dr, Yucaipa, Cal.

GLUCKSMAN, Joe, Eng, educator; b. Leeds, Eng, Oct 15, 1912; s. Morris and Mary (Cansevick); mem, Royal Soc of Tchrs, Leeds Training Coll; m. Sybil Harris, June 7, 1942; c: Hazel, Valerie. Headmaster, Coldcotes Co Secondary Sch. Chmn: Leeds J Educ Bd; St Lane Gardens Syn; exec, Leeds Rep Council; hon secy, Yorkshire Fed of Sch Sports; life mem, Leeds Sch Football Assn; fmr natl chmn, Schs Amateur Boxing Assn; mem, Leeds Civic Trust; chmn, Hist Panel Cen Secondary Educ. Recipient, MBE, 1966. Spec interest: sch sport activities. Home: 118 Street Lane, Leeds, Yorkshire, Eng.

GLUSKOTER, Morley, US, business exec; b. Chgo, Ill, Apr 7, 1905; s. Max and Olga (Kaplan); att Crane Coll; m. Mary Bramson, Jan 26, 1930; c: Gloria Golbart, Noreen Gilden, Mildred. Pres, St Louis Shower Door Co since 1953; vice-pres, Container Mfr Co since 1943; dir, Home Builders Assn, St Louis, Mo; fmr: pres, Superior Products Co; mgr, Furst and Furst. Dist chmn, B'nai B'rith Youth Org Comm, treas, Dist Grand Lodge 2; mem: bd, Health and Wfr. Council, Metrop St Louis; Traditional Cong of Creve Coeur; exec comm, Lawrence E Goldman Inst of Judaism; J Fed, Cmty Campaigns; fmr: pres, Mo Lodge 2, B'nai B'rith; B'nai B'rith Council War Bond Chmn; pres, St Louis BBYO Comm; org, 1st dir, Deborah Boys Club of Chgo; workshop and discussion leader, Whitehouse Conf for Children and Youth, Jefferson City, Mo. Recipient: Silver Medallion, for outstanding service during WW II, Treas Dept; 25 Year Jewel, Nobel Grand Independent Order of Odd Fellows; Natl Youth Service Gold Key, 1965; Natl New Lodge Founds Award, 1968; Benny Award, 1968. Hobby, softball. Home: 15 Bon Hills Dr, Olivette, Mo. Office: 8310 Olive Blvd, St Louis, Mo.

GODFREY, Bert, Can, business exec, communal worker; b. Toronto, Can, June 1, 1908; s. Solomon and Minnie (Reisman); m. Ruth Grossman, Jan 26, 1934; c: Corinne, Sheldon. Pres, S Godfrey Co Ltd, Toronto, fmr secy. Pres: J Public Libr of Toronto since 1958; fmr: Bur of J Educ of Toronto; Goel Tzedek Syn; hon pres, Beth Tzedec Syn, since 1956; found pres: Ont region, United Syn of Amer, fmr natl vice pres; found chmn, United Syn Day Sch of Toronto; chmn, Beth Tzedek Isr Bond comm; vice-pres, World Council of Syns, since 1959; mem: admn comm, Can J Cong, cen region; exec comm, Can Council Chrs and Js; Can Camp Ramah; B'nai B'rith: bd overseers, JTSA; bd dirs: New Mt Sinai Hosp Toronto; J Home for Aged; Baycrest Hosp; United JWF of Toronto; Assn Heb Schs of Toronto; co-chmn, Toronto Brotherhood Week, 1954; fmr: gen campaign chmn, Isr Bonds of Toronto; mem, Toronto Citizen's Centenary Comm; clubs: Primrose; Can; Oakdale. Recipient, awards: Louis Marshall,

JTSA, 1961; Natl Human Relations, Can Conf of Chrs and Js, 1964; honoree, Negev Dinner, JNF, 1966. Home: 325 Glenyr Rd, Toronto, Can. Office: 49 Front St E, Toronto, Can.

GODINE, Morton Robert, US, business exec, b. Montreal, Can, May 28, 1917; s. Nathan and Anne (Denenberg); in US since 1939; BA, MA, McGill U, Montreal, 1939; PhD, Harvard, 1948; m. Bernice Beckwith, Aug, 10, 1941; c: David, Louis, Amy. Vice-pres, Market Forge Co; fmr: teaching f, tutor, instr, govt, Harvard U, 1946-48. USNR, 1943-46. NE chmn, ADL; mem, steering comm, Combined J Philanthropies, Boston, 1960-62; chmn Comm on Town Org, Brookline, Mass, 1960-62; mem, Town Meeting, Brookline, Mass; mem, Mass Bay lodge, B'nai B'rith, past pres; club: Everett Rotary, past pres. Author: The Labor Problem in the Public Service, 1950. Home: 9 Cary Rd, Chestnut Hill, Mass. Office: 35 Garvey St, Everett, Mass.

GODINSKY, Samuel, Can, attorney; b. Montreal, Can, Aug 12, 1906; s. Ely and Millie (Gussman); BA, McGill U, Montreal, 1927, BCL, 1930; m. Vera Raphael, Jan 5, 1946; c: John, Paul, Jeffrey. Pvt practice, since 1930; named Q.C, 1962 Asst judge, advocate gen, RCAF, 1942-46. Mem: Que, Can Bar Assns; and chmn, finance leg comm, Prot Sch Bd of Gtr Montreal; fmr pres, YM-YWHA, Montreal. Home: 731 Upper Belmont Ave, Westmount, Can. Office: 1255 University St, Montreal, Can.

GOEBEL, Harry H, US, attorney; b. Bklyn, NY, Sep 27, 1905; s. William and Ray (Levy); BA, Columbia Coll, NYC, 1926; LLB, Columbia Law Sch, 1928; m. Maxine Hamburger, June 4, 1941; c: William, Gail Wasserman. Pvt practice since 1928; sch atty, Hicksville Sch Dist, NY, since 1970, 1956-57; atty, various trade assns, 1930-40; referee, NY State Dept of Lab, Unemployment Div, 1943-44. Pres, Metrop Region, Natl Fed of J Men's Club; vice-pres, Hicksville J Cen since 1965; Glenbrook Civic Assn; mem: grand chancellor, Theta Delta Mu; F and A Masons, Flushing, NY; adv: Assn Painters & Decorators; Assn Sign Hangers; Greenpoint Barbers Assn; Monument Dealers Assn, all of NY; fmr: pres: Cong Beth-El, Greenpoint, NY; Cong Shaarai Zedek, Hicksville, NY; vice-pres, Hicksville J Cen; secy, Manhattan Beach J Comty Cen; mem: Flushing J Cen; Greenpoint Civic Assn. Spec interest, psycht. Home: Glenbrook Rd, Hicksville, NY. Office: 150 Broadway, New York, NY.

GOELMAN, Elazar, US, educator; b. Jedwabno, Pol, Dec 15, 1913; s. Judah and Raizl (Janushevsky); in US since 1926; att: Tchrs Inst, Rabbi Isaac Elchanan Sem, NY, 1927-29; BA, W Reserve U, Cleveland, O, 1940; PhD, Dropise Coll, Phila, 1953; m. Rose Belkin, Aug 20, 1939; c: Don, Elana, Hillel. Dean, Gratz Coll, Phila, dir J Educ, since 1959; registrar, Heb Tchrs Sem, Cleveland, 1935-43; exec-dir: Intercoll ZF of Amer, 1946; Har Zion Temple, Phila, 1947-49; Buffalo Bur of J Educ, 1949-59; lectr, U of Buffalo, 1957-59. US Army, 1943-46. Pres: Natl Council for J Educ, 1963-65; Assn JA Execs, Phila; chmn, Inter-Faith Rel Educ Comm, Buffalo, NY; mem: Amer Assn Prof of Heb; Rel Educ Assn; Natl Conf of J Communal Service. Mem, ed bd, J Educ, since 1967; contbr to J publs, weekly column in Buffalo J Rev. Hobbies: music, carpentry. Home: 622 W Mt Airy Ave, Philadelphia, Pa. Office: 10 St at Tabor Rd, Philadelphia, Pa.

GOETZ, Norman, S, US, attorney; b. NYC, Mar 7, 1887; s. Samuel and Julia (Marx); AB, Columbia U, 1906, LLB, 1909; m. Mildred Blout, Feb 12, 1925 (decd); m. 2nd, Beatrice Lane, Jan 12, 1956. Partner: Proskauer, Rose, Goetz & Mendelsohn, and predecessor firms, since 1925; law firm, Leventritt, Riegelman, Carns & Goetz, 1912-24. Pvt to capt, non-flying air service, 1917-19. Dir, Gtr NY Fund since 1942, fmr pres and chmn bd; chmn bd since 1961, hon trustee, since 1948, FJP, NY; fmr: pres, chmn: lawyers div, legacy comm, city-wide campaign and communal planning comm; mem: Assn of Bar, City of NY, fmr vice-pres, mem exec comm; NY Co Lawyers Assn, past chmn, bankruptcy comm; Intl, Amer, NY, Bar Assns; fmr: dir: and pres, Hosp Council Gtr NY; United Hosp Fund; Hillside Hosp; Wfr Council, NYC; CJFWF; mem: exec and admn comms, AJComm; bd trustees, SUNY, also chmn, comm on med educ; clubs: Ocean Beach; Manhattan. Home: 480 Park Ave, New York, NY. Office: 300 Park Ave, New York, NY.

GOFFIN, Sherwood, US, cantor; b. New Haven, Conn, Sep 17, 1941; s. Hermann and Judith (Shapiro); regents dipl, Torah Vodaath, Bklyn, NY, 1958; BA, Yeshiva U, NY, 1963;

Cantorial Cert, Cantorial Inst, Yeshiva U, 1966; m. Batya Goldberg, May 5, 1964; c, Nisa. Cantor, Lincoln Sq Syn, NYC, since 1964; Heb Sch Dir, Heb Folk Singer, concert artist, guitarist, since 1961; mus dir: Yeshiva U Youth Sems, since 1965; Utopia J Cen, Flushing, NY, since 1968; Day Camp, Heb Acad, Nassau Co, 1966-67; cantor-Heb Sch tchr, Cong Anshe Amas, Bx, NY, 1963-65. Secy, Cantorial Council of Amer, 1966-68; mem, Student Struggle for Soviet J. Contbr, article on rehab, "For Those Who Need", Conn Med, 1962. Recipient: Thirteenth Anniversary Youth Leadership Citation, Youth Bur, Yeshiva U, 1967; Outstanding Service Award, Union of Orthodox J Congs of Amer, 1968. Spec interest: sketching in charcoal; composition of cantorial recitations. Home: 140 West End Ave, New York, NY. Study: 150 West End Ave, New York, NY.

GOITEIN, Shelomo Dov, US, orientalist, educator, author; b. Burgkunstadt, Ger, Apr 3, 1900; s. Edward and Frida (Braunschweiger); in US since 1957; PhD, U of Frankfurt/M, 1923; m. Theresa Gottlieb, July 16, 1929; c: Ayala Gordon, Ofra Rosner, Elon. Prof of Arabic, U of Pa, Phila since, 1957; prof of Islamics, Heb U, Jerusalem, 1928-57, em, dir, Sch of Oriental Studies, Heb U, 1949–57; sr educ off; Govt of Pal, 1938-48. F, Amer Acad for J Research; bd dirs, Conf on J Social Studies; mem: Amer Oriental Soc; Isr Oriental Soc, found, 1st pres; Mediaeval Acad of Amer; fmr, found, 1st chmn, Heb U bd for overseas examinations. Author: Pulcellina, 1927; Jemenica, 1934; Baladhuri, Arabic Historiography, 1936; Travels in Yemen, 1941; Modern Ways of Bible Teaching, 1942, 1957; Teaching Hebrew to Hebrews, 1945, 3rd ed, 1957; Tales from the Land of Sheba, 1947; Jews and Arabs, 1955, 1964; Introduction to Muslim Law, 1957; Bible, Studies, 1957, 1963; Jewish Education in Muslim Countries, 1962; Studies in Islamic History and Institutions, 1966-68; A Mediterranean Society: The Jewish Communities of the Arab World, as portrayed in the Documents of the Cairo Geniza, Vol I, Economic Foundations, 1967; Vol II, The Community, 1970; numerous papers on Cairo Geniza documents, 1950-68; trans from Arabic to Heb, The Responsa of Abraham Maimonides, 1937; The Travels of Hayyim Habshush, 1939; Hobbies: hiking, calisthenics. Home: 6035 North 12 St, Philadelphia, Pa. Office: U of Pa, Philadelphia, Pa.

GOLAN, David, Isr, government official; b. Jerusalem, 1926; s. Jacob and Zila; MA, econ, Heb U, Jerusalem; m. Ziona Goldman, Sep 14, 1948; c. Orna, Chemda, Nachum. Dir. gen, Isr Min of Commerce and Ind, since 1966; fmr: with Cen Bur of Stat; asst to Min of Commerce and Ind; dir, import-export, Min of Finance; econ attache, Isr Emb: Turkey, Yugo; Charge d'Affairs, Isr Emb, Philippines; dep controller, fgn exch dept, Min of Finance; dir, intl coop div, Min for Fgn Affairs; first adv, Bank of Isr. Home: 4 Nayot St, Jerusalem, Isr. Office: 30 Agron Bld, Palace Bldg, Jerusalem, Isr.

GOLAN, Menahem, Isr, film dir; b. Tiberias, Isr, May 31, 1929; s. Noah and Dvora (Goldman) Globus; Dipl, LAMDA, London Acad Music and Drama, 1952; Dipl, Old Vic Sch Dirs, London, 1953; att City Coll Film Inst, NY, 1960–61; m. Rachel Fishman, Mar 30, 1952; c. Ruth, Naomi, Yaeli. Dir, Noah Films Ltd and Hashdera Theater since 1962; dir, plays, musicals, Isr Theater, 1953-69. Pvt, IAF, 1948-50. Dir of films: Queen of the Road, 1971; My Love in Jerusalem, 1969; What's Good for the Goose, 1968; Tevye and His Seven Daughters, 1968; La Fille De La Mer Morte (Fortuna), 1967; Trunk to Cairo, 1965; El Dorado, 1964; produc, Sallah, 1964. Mem, bd dirs, Isr Film Producs Assn. Recipient, award for best dir of the year, Harp of David 1964, 1965, 1966, 1967. Home: 25 Haalumim St, Afeka, Isr. Office: 68 Pinsker St, Tel Aviv, Isr.

GOLAN, Michael, Isr, civil engr; b. Warsaw, Pol. March 23, 1914; s. Moses and Sarah (Shpeizman) Goldberg; in Isr since 1934; BCE, Technion, Haifa, Isr, 1939; m. Eva Hamersmith, 1936; c, Sarah. Dep dir, Public Works dept, Min. of Lab since 1957, on staff since 1940; lectr, Govt Coll of Surveyors, Holon, Isr. Lt, IDF, 1948-49. Chmn, Technion Alumni Assn; mem, cen comm, Assn Engrs and Architects of Isr. Home: 69 LaGuardia Rd, Tel Aviv, Isr. Office: 3 Lincoln St, Tel Aviv, Isr.

GOLD, Alex E, US, psychiatrist; b. NYC, Aug 24, 1906; s. Benjamin and Anna (Messing) MD, NY Med Coll, 1932; postgrad; Cert in Comprehensive Psychan, 1948; m. Mae Klein, June 21, 1936; c: Samuel, Susan. Pvt practice since 1948; sr psycht, NY Consultation Cen, Post-Grad Inst for Psychotherapy,

1946-49. Capt, US Army, 1942-46. Founding f, mem, Nassau Acad of Med; charter mem, Nassau Neuropsycht Soc; mem: Soc of Med Psychan; NY State and Nassau Co Med Socs; AMA; World Med Assn; NY Acad of Sci; NY Soc Clinical Psycht; Phi Delta Epsilon; LI Grad Club; World Fed Mh; Nassau Co Phys Guild; NY State Assn of Profs; f: Amer Psycht Assn; Amer Acad Psychan; Acad of Psychosomatic Med; Assn for Advancement of Psychotherapy; AAAS; found, postgrad sems psycht, for: phys, clergy, Mh movement Home and office: 131 Hilton Ave, Hempstead, NY.

GOLD, Baron H, US, attorney; b. Cincinnati, O, Dec 3, 1920; s. Henry and Sarah (Baron); AB, LLB, U of Cincinnati; m. Harriet Neurman, Feb 11, 1945; c: Thomas, Richard, Andrew. Partner, Kondritzer, Gold and Frank since 1963. Master sgt, USAAC, 1942-45. Secy, Isaac Wise Temple; chmn, Cincinnati ADL Council, mem natl commn; mem: bd, J Fed, Cincinnati; Cincinnati, O State Bar Assn; exec comm, Cincinnati J Comty Relations Comm; fmr pres, Dist Grand lodge 2, B'nai B'rith; club: Hills Country. Home 1344 Westminster Dr, Cincinnati, O. Office: 414 Walnut St, Cincinnati, O.

GOLD, Bert Joseph, US, business exec, TV producer; b. NYC, Aug 18, 1917; s. Jacob and Augusta (Spalter); att, Cooper Union, NYC; m. Laura Chesluk, Jan 28, 1964; c: Jack, Ruth. Owner: Park S Art Gal; TV Graphic Arts; producer: film, The Painting; 600 local TV shows; produc cons, six TV stations in US. Sgt, USAAF, 1942-46. Mem: ASCAP; Intl Mensa. Author, Dogface Soldier, song of 3rd div, US Army. Home: 180 W 58 St, New York, NY. Office: 885 Seventh Ave, New York, NY.

GOLD, Bertram H, US, communal leader; b. Toronto, Can, Oct 3, 1916; s. Harry and Fannie (Rosnick); in US since 1937; BA, U of Toronto, 1937; MSW, W Reserve U, 1939; m. Sylvia Rubin, Sep, 1938; c: Judith, Daniel, Arna. Exec vice-pres, AJComm, since 1967; asso prof, U of Toronto, 1945-47; exec dir: J Comty Cen, Essex Co, 1947-54; LA, 1954-67. Lt, US Army, 1942-45. Prin contrib, leader in establishing J role in urban crisis; help devl metrop patterns for J Comty Cens. Pres: Natl Assn J Cen Workers; Natl Conf J Communal Service; exec bd; Natl J Com Relation Admn Inc; mem, bd, JWB. Contbr to J publs. Home: 1080 Fifth Ave, New York, NY. Office: 165 E 56 St, New York, NY.

GOLD, Doris Bauman, US, editor, author; b. NYC, Nov 21, 1919; d. Saul and Gertrude (Reiss) Bauman; att Pratt Inst, Bklyn, 1937-38; BA, Bklyn Coll, 1946; MA, Wash U, St Louis, Mo, 1955; m. Bernard Gold, Aug, 1953; c: Michael, Bert. Ed, Young Judean Mag, NY since 1963; instr, Eng, U of Kan, 1946-48; SUNY, Farmingdale, LI, NY, 1958-59; prog aide: United J Social Services, KC, 1948-49; St Louis YM-YWHA, 1949-50; asst dir, women's div, Albert Einstein Coll of Med Fund Campaign, 1951-53; tchr, rel sch's, NY, midwest, 1945, 1954-59; tchr, art, Eng, HS, NYC, 1953, 1959-61; ed, women's page, LI Citizen, Nassau Co, 1957; instr, writing workshop, Adult Educ Prog, Levittown, LI, 1958; instr, Eng, NY Assn for New Amers, 1962. Author, Stories for Jewish Juniors, 1967; contbr of revs, poetry, essays to mags, press. Adv, space-age stargazers, Hall of Sci, NYC; mem: Amer J Hist Assn; hon, Amateur Observer's Soc; found, Mid-Island YM-YWHA, Wantagh, LI; fmr, publicity dir, Self-Survey of Levittown Comty Attitudes. Recipient: Sr Award in Poetry, Bklyn Coll, 1946; Alexander Carruth Poetry Award, U of Kan, 1947. Hobbies: art, astronomy, choral singing. Home: 89-25 187 St, Hollis, Queens, NY. Office: 116 W 14 St, New York, NY.

GOLD, Emanual Richard, US, attorney, b. Bklyn, NY, Aug 25, 1935; s. Jack and Lillian (Lissak); BA, Cornell U, 1957; LLB, Cornell Law Sch, 1959; m. Judith Silberfein, Dec 21, 1958; c: Steve, Susan. Assemblyman, NY State, since 1970. Home: 68-59 136 St, Flushing, NY. Office: 1 Liberty St, New York, NY.

GOLD, Harry, US, cardiologist, educator; b. Bialystock, Russ, Dec 25, 1899; s. Samuel and Naomi (Katz); in US since 1903; BA, Cornell U, 1919, MD, 1922; m. Bertha Goldman, Aug 26, 1926; c: Naomi, Stanley, Muriel. Prof em, clinical pharm, Cornell U Med Coll; att i/c cardiovascular research unit, Beth Isr Hosp, NYC, cons card since 1965; att card, Hosp for Jt Diseases, NY, cons card since 1965; cons, Seaview Hosp since 1939. F: NY Acad of Med; NY Acad of Sci; mem: bd dirs, NY Heart Assn; Harvey Soc; Amer Pharm

Soc; AAAS; fmr, Comm on Revision of US Pharmacopoeia; hon mem: Card Soc of Brazil; Soc of Pharm and Therapeutics of Arg. Author, Quinidine in Disorders of the Heart, 1952; mgn ed, Cornell Confs on Therapy, 1945; asso ed, Amer Jour of Med, 1947-57; mem ed bd: Amer Jour of Med Scis; Jour of Clinical Pharm; contbr to sci jours. Home: 7 E 82 St, New York, NY. Office: 1300 York Ave, New York, NY.

GOLD, Herbert, US, author; b. Cleveland, O, Mar 9, 1924; s. Samuel and Frieda (Frankel); BA, Columbia Coll, 1948; MA, Columbia U, 1949; div; c: Ann, Judith; m. 2nd, Melissa Dilworth, 1968. Novelist, critic, short story writer; visiting prof: Cornell U; U of Cal; Harvard U; Brandeis U. US Army, 1943-46. Author: Birth of a Hero, 1951; The Prospect Before Us, 1954; The Man Who Was Not With It, 1956; The Optimist, 1958; Love and Like, 1959; Therefore be Bold, 1960; The Age of Happy Problems, 1962; Salt, 1963; Fathers, 1967; Recipient, awards: O'Henry; Natl Inst of Arts and Letters; Hudson Rev f, 1956; Longview Found, 1959; Guggenheim f, 1957. Home and office: 1051-A Broadway, San Francisco, Cal.

GOLD, Hugo, Isr, editor, publisher, author; b. Vienna, Aus, Oct 14, 1895; s. Adolf and Fanny (Hickl); in Isr since 1940; PhD, Deutsche U, Brünn, 1928; m. Miryam Pikkel, April, 1948; c: Abraham, Amalia. Publisher, Olamenu, since 1943; fmr: ed, Jüdische Volksstimme; pub; Jud Buch und Kunstverlag; found, Zvi Perez Chajes Inst. Author: Die Juden und Jüdengemeinden Mährens in Vergangenheit und Gegenwart, 1929; Die Jüden und Jüdengemeinde Pressburgs in Vergangenheit und Gegenwart, 1932; Die Jüden und Jüdengemeinden Böhmens in Vergangenheit und Gegenwart, 1934; Geschichte der Jüden in Der Bokovina, 1962; Geschichte der Jüden in Wein, 1966; ed, publisher, Zeitschrift für die Geschichte der Jüden, since 1964. Recipient: Theodor Körner prize for lit, 1967. Home: 17 Frishman St, Tel Aviv, Isr. Office: POB 3002, Tel Aviv, Isr.

GOLD, IRWIN H, US, communal worker; b. Toronto, Can, Mar 6, 1919; s. Aaron and Fannie (Rosmick); in US since 1941; BA, U of Toronto, 1941; MSW, U of Pittsburgh, 1943; m. Beverly Shapiro, June 6, 1947; c: Donna, Lawrence, Lisa. Exec-dir, United JCC, SF, since 1960; lectr prof, SF State Coll, since 1965; asst exec-dir, Chgo JCC, 1949-54; spec lectr, U of Ill, 1952-54; exec-dir, Denver JCC, 1954-60; guest lectr, W Reserve U; Denver U; U of Cal, Berkeley, since 1948. Prin contribs: helped organize: SF State Sch of social Work, 1962; N Lawndale Citizens Council, Chgo, 1949-54; cons, numerous childrens' summer camps. Pres: W States section, Natl Assn of J Cen Workers, 1963-65; Chgo chap, Amer Assn of Group Workers, 1950-53; chmn; president's comm, SF State Coll Sch of Social Work; several comms, Wfr Planning Councils, Chgo, Denver and SF; mem: exec comm, Natl Assn J Social Workers; Natl Assn Social Workers; Natl Assn Cen Workers. US Army, 1944-46. Contbr to profsl jours. Recipient: Purple Heart. Home: 25 Irving Drive, San Anselmo, Cal. Office: 3200 California St, San Francisco, Cal.

GOLD, Jerome Jacob, US, dentist; b. Chgo, Ill, Feb 25, 1921; s. Samuel and Ruth (Goldfarb); BA, U Ill, Champaign, 1942; DDS, Loyola Dent Coll, Chgo, 1945; m. Betty Abrahams, June 21, 1945; c: Harriet, Nancy, Terry. Pvt practice since 1945. Lt-cdr, USNR, 1945-67. Mem: ethics comm, Chgo Dent Soc; Phi Epsilon Pi, U of Ill chap; Master Mason, Fortitude lodge 1003; Chgo; Scottish Rite 32, Valley of Chgo; Shriner Medinah Temple, Chgo; Natl Sojourners, Chgo chap; Amer Legion Fed Post No 437; Chgo Dent Soc; Ill State Dent Soc; Amer Dent Assn. Hobbies: photography, sailing, golf, books. Home: 1338 McDaniels, Highland Pk, Ill. Office: 25 E Washington, Chicago, Ill.

GOLD, Martin R, US, attorney; b. NYC, Dec 4, 1937; s. Samuel and Martha (Roth); BA, Amherst Coll, Mass, 1958; LLB, Columbia U, 1961; m. Billie Rosenhouse; c: David, Jonathan. Partner, Steel, Cohen, Gold, Farrell, & Marks, since 1970; asst US Atty, S Dist of NY, US Govt, 1962-65; assoc, Paul, Weiss, Goldberg, Rifkind, Wharton & Garrison, 1965-68; pvt practice, 1968-69. Staff sgt, US Army, NY Natl Guard, 1961-67. Mem: Assn of the Bar of NYC; Park Ave Syn; Amer Bar Assn; NY State Bar Assn; Fed Bar Council; Delta Upsilon, Amherst chap; fmr: comm mem: admn law comm, young lawyers comm, Assn of the Bar of NYC. Home: 8 Peter Cooper Rd, New York, NY. Office: 745 Fifth Ave, New York, NY.

GOLD, Marvin Chaucer, US, attorney, business exec; b. New Haven, Conn, Oct 15, 1912; s. Herman and Minnie (Chaucer); BA, Yale U, 1933, LLB, 1936; m. Annette Pessin, Dec 23, 1938; c: Jacqueline, Patricia, Lindalee, Lauren. Partner, law firm, Gold, Gold and Rosenbloom since 1936; pres: Markay Realty Co; Security Homes, Inc; Continental Realty, Inc; Fidelity Realty, Inc; Colony Homes, Inc; Lemar Realty, Inc; Instnl Properties, Inc; Commercial Properties, Inc; Queens Trading Co; Williams Trading Co; Horizon Towers, Inc; Westrock Gardens, Inc; Exec House of New Haven; partner: Roger Pigcon Assos; Blvd Assos; Houlton Assos; Branford Assos; specialist, devl gasoline stas for maj oil cos, apt complexes, shopping cens; devl, maj realty projects. Mem: Amer, Conn, New Haven Bar Assns; Conf Fed Bar; Bar, US Court of Appeals, Fifth Dist; Phi Beta Kappa; pres, Camp Laurelwood; vice-pres, New Haven J Comty Cen; mem: Temple Mishkan Isr; B'nai B'rith Horeb Lodge; New Haven J Home for Aged; New Haven Home for Children; clubs: vice-pres, Woodbridge Country; Yale of New Haven. Home: 650 Ellsworth Ave, New Haven, Conn. Office: 152 Temple St, New Haven, Conn.

GOLD, Solomon, Can, physician; b. Annopol, Russ, Dec 28, 1897; s. Harry and Rachel (Goldberg); in Can since 1914; MD, CM, McGill U, 1923; att U's: Berlin, 1932; Paris, 1932; licensed to practice med, surg, State of Pa, 1924; m. 1935; c: Walter, Lauraine; m. 2nd, Edith Batist, Jan 6, 1945; c: Leon, Jacob. Obstet, Gyn, pvt practice, Montreal, since 1928; mem staff, obstet and gyn, J Gen Hosp, Montreal, since 1938; prin, J Peretz Schs, Montreal, 1921. Mem: lecturing staff, YIVO J Public Libr, since 1952; Montreal Clinical Soc; Coll of Phys and Surgs; J Writers Assn; fmr: chmn: and org, People's Comm Against Anti-Semitism and Racism; Biro-Bidjan comm. Contbr to periodicals and profsl jours. Home: 817 Dunlop Ave, Outremont, Can. Office: 6000 Cote des Neiges Rd, Montreal, Can.

GOLDBERG. Abraham, Isr, educator; b. Pittsburg, Pa, Jan 22, 1913; s. Morris and Fanny (Sachs); in Isr since 1946; att U of Pitt, 1932-34; BSS, CCNY, 1937; MHL, ordained rabbi, JTSA, 1941; PhD, Heb U, Jerusalem, 1952; m. Rebecca Abrahamowitz, Oct 3, 1946; c: Meira, Mauria, Shulamit, Shira. Sr lectr, Heb U since 1955; fmr rabbi, Brookline, Mass; secy, Inst of J Studies, Heb U. Capt, chaplain, US Army. Author: The Mishnah Treatise Ohaloth Critically Edited, 1955; contbr to Tarbitz; jours. Recipient: Rabbi Kook Prize, Tel Aviv Munic, 1957. Home: 35 Harav Berlin Street, Jerusalem, Isr. Office: Heb U, Jerusalem, Isr.

GOLDBERG, Albert L, US, music critic; b. Shenandoah, Ia, June 2, 1898; s. Abraham and Minnie (Levi); MMus, Gunn Sch of Music, Chgo, 1927; att U of Neb, 1915-16; Chgo Musical Coll, 1924-26; Critic em, LA Times, since 1967, music ed, 1947-67; corresp, Musical Amer, since 1927; tchr: Gunn Sch of Music, 1922-33; Chgo Musical Coll, 1933-36; asst music critic, Chgo Herald and Examiner, 1925-35; state dir, Ill Fed Music Project, 1936-43; music critic, Chgo Tribune, 1943-47; lectr in music, UCLA, 1948-69. Contbr to musical publs. Office: 202 W First St, Los Angeles, Cal.

GOLDBERG, Alexander, Isr, administrator, engineer; b. Vilna, Lith, 1906; s. Boris and Bertha; in Isr since 1948; BSc, Royal Sch of Mines, Eng; postgrad studies, London U; m. Rosalie Schalit; c, Mark. Pres, chmn, bd of govs, Technion, Haifa, since 1965. Mem, bd dirs: Dead Sea Works; Electro-Chem Ind; fmr, mgr dir, Chems and Phosphates, Ltd, Haifa, Isr. Home: 109 Panorama Rd, Haifa, Isr. Office: Technion, Haifa, Isr.

GOLDBERG, Alfred, US, historian, educator; b. Baltimore, Md, Dec 23, 1918; s. David and Jeannette (Goldstein); AB, W Md Coll, 1938; PhD, Johns Hopkins U, 1950; m. Gertrud Kannova, June 28, 1949; c: Paul, Alan, Marian. Sr socical sci, The Rand Corp, since 1965; lectr: U of Md, since 1953; UCLA, U of S Cal, 1967-69; chief, current hist br, USAF Hist Div Liaison Off, 1950-62, hist, 1946-50; visiting Amer f, Kings Coll, U of London, 1962-63; staff mem, Warren Commn, 1964. Col, USAFR; US Army, 1942-46. Mem: Amer Hist Assn; Amer Mil Inst. Co-author: The Army Air Forces in World War II, 7 vols, 1948-57; ed, A History of the US Air Force, 1957. Recipient: Bronze Star; Commendation Medal; US Govt Meritorious Service Award, 1955, 1958, 1962. Home: 3842 N 26 St, Arlington, Va. Office: 2100 M St, NW, Washington, DC.

GOLDBERG, Arthur J, US, jurist attorney; b. Chgo, Ill, Aug 8, 1908; s. Joseph and Rebecca (Perlstein); att, Crane Jr Coll; BSL, Northwestern U, 1929, JD, 1930; m. Dorothy Kurgans, July 18, 1931; c: Barbara Cramer, Robert. Pvt practice, sr partner, Paul, Weiss, Goldberg, Rifkind, Wharton and Garrison, since 1968; admitted to practice before Ill bar, 1929, US Supr Court, 1937; pvt practice, Chgo, 1929-48; mem, law firm, Goldberg, Devoe, Shadur and Mikva, Chgo, 1945-61; gen counsel: CIO, 1948-55, United Steel Workers, 1948-61; spec counsel, AFL-CIO, 1955-61; legal adv to lab unions; mem, law firm, Goldberg, Feller & Bredhoff, Wash, DC, 1952-61; Secy of Lab, US Govt, 1961-62; asso justice, US Supr Court, 1962-65; US repr to UN, 1965-68. spec asst, maj; off of Strategic Services, WW II. Author: AFL-CIO: Labor United; Defenses of Freedom; contbr to legal and other publs. Office: 345 Park Ave, New York, NY.

GOLDBERG, Ben Zion Waife, US, author, journalist; b. Olshani, Russ, Jan 9, 1894; s. Moses and Chiena (Margolis) Waife; in US since 1907; BS, Columbia U, 1918, MA, 1919; m. Marie Rabinowitz, Dec 23, 1917; c: Sholom Waife, Mitchell Waife. Daily columnist, Day-J Journal, since 1922; Bklyn Daily Eagle, 1932-34; weekly columnist, Al Hamishmar, Tel Aviv, Isr; ed: J Digest, 1943; Einikeit, 1943-46; corresp: St Louis Post-Dispatch, Toronto Daily Star, New Republic, since 1946. Pres, Amer Comm of J Writers, Artists, and Scis, 1943-45; acting dir, J Tchrs Sem, 1920-22; mem, J Writers Union; club: Yiddish PEN. Author: The Sacred Fire, 1930, 1958, paper-back, 1962; The Jewish Problem in the Soviet Union, 1961 Home: 375 Riverside Dr, New York, NY. Office: 183 E Broadway, New York, NY.

GOLDBERG, Bernard I, US, physician; b. Boston, Mass, Dec 21, 1896; s. Max and Celia (Cooperman); BS, Tufts Coll, 1918; MD, Harvard U, 1922; m. Ethel Rich, Mar 2, 1924; c: Karl Gilmont, Ernest Gilmont. Cons, Boston City Hosp, phys-in-chief, ret; asso prof of med, em, Boston U, 1962; asst prof of med, Tufts Med Coll, 1932-45. Pres, Gtr Boston Med Soc, 1947-48; mem: Mass Med Soc; Amer Coll of Phys; AAAS. Contbr to med jours. Home: 160 Elgin St, Newton Centre, Mass. Office: 479 Beacon St, Boston, Mass.

GOLDBERG, Dan Shlomo, Isr, educator, engineer; b. Jerusalem, Isr, Oct 23, 1915; s. Arieh and Miriam (Schechter); BSc, U of London, Eng, 1936; MS, U of Cal, 1939; m. Miriam Karsenti, Nov 27, 1942; c: Oded, Amir, Ariela. Cons: TAHAL, Govt Water Auth; Min for Fgn Affairs; on missions on behalf Isr Fgn Min, to: Latin Amer; India; Korea; Nepal; prof, irrigation, head dept irrigation, Heb U Fac Agric, since 1964; chief irrigation engr, Settlement Dept, 1946-52; head, desert agric lab, Yotvata, Arava, Isr, 1968; irrigation design projects for Isr in: Afr; ME; Latin Amer; Far E, i/c several groups of sci teams. Isr Natl Service, 1939; maj, British Army, cdr engr co, 1940-46. Prin contribs, prin engr projects designed: sugar irrigation scheme, Cassequel, Angola, 1960; Kilobero Sugar Project, Tanzania, 1959; Maljobhai Madvani Sugar Project, Uganda, 1960; Hatai Valley Irrigation Project, Turkey, 1959; irrigation schemes: Phillipines; Siam; India; Iran; Turkey; Cyprus; Spain; Port; Kenya; Tanzania; Uganda; Mozambique; Senegal; Panama; Peru; Venezuela; Mexico; numerous settlements in Isr; co-designer of numerous projects. Contbr to profsl publs. Home: 14 Haoranim St, Kfar Shmaryahu, Isr. Office: Fac of Agric, Heb U, Rehovot, Isr.

GOLDBERG, David, US, business exec; b. Newport News, Va, Feb 14, 1908; s. Isaac and Ida (Rosenfeld); Att: Wm and Mary Coll, 1926-27; U of Va, 1927-30; m. Sara Levy, Dec 27, 1932; c: Stanley, Ivan. Pres: Goldkress Corp; Second Goldkress Corp; Goldberg Realty Corp; chmn bd, Bedding Supply Co, Inc, since 1932; fmr: realtor; with postal dept, Fed Govt. Mem: Va Mfg Assn; Alpha Mu Sigma; Elks; ZOA; B'nai B'rith; Adath Jeshurun Syn; Rodef Shalom Temple; clubs: Cosmopolitan, past secy; Newport News Chess, past pres. Hobbies: music, boating. Home: 6923 Huntington Ave, Newport News, Va. Office: 123 26 St, Newport News, Va.

GOLDBERG, Edward D, US, geologist, educator; b. Sacramento, Cal, Aug 2, 1921; s. Edward and Lillian (Rothholz) BS, U of Cal, 1942; PhD, U of Chgo, 1949; m. Betty Anderson, Feb 23, 1945; c: David, Wendy. Prof, chem, Scripps Inst of Oceanography, U of Cal, San Diego, since 1960, on fac since 1949. Usn Res, 1942-46. Vice pres, sect of volcanology, petrology, geochem, Amer Geophys Union; mem: Geochem Soc; Sigma Xi. Contbr to sci jours. Recipient: f to Physikalisches Institut, U of Berne, Switz, 1961. Home: 2614 Ellentown Rd, La Jolla, Cal. Office: U of Cal, San Diego, Cal.

GOLDBERG, Eliezer, Isr, scientific editor and translator; b. Moscow, Russ, Sep 21, 1918; s. Saadia and Sophia (Zaslavsky); desc of Baal Shem Tov; Nahman of Bratzlav; Shneor Zalman of Lady; in Isr since 1924; BSc, dipl, chem tech, Technion, Haifa, 1940. Sci ed, i/c ed and trans office, since 1963, mem academic staff, since 1957, all Technion; ed and trans of research publs for Technion staff, ed for local and intl confs held at Technion, adv in Heb sci terminology. Mem, judiciary comm, Technion Fac Assn; sr mem, Soc of Tech Writers and Pubs, Isr chap. Home: 8 Hashmonayim St, Haifa, Isr. Office: Technion, Haifa, Isr.

GOLDBERG, Emanuel, US, public relations counsel, journalist; b. Lynn, Mass, May 7, 1920; s. Benjamin and Lena (Young); BS, cum laude, Boston U, 1942; MA, U of Wis, 1947; att Harvard U; m. Paula Masicov, Aug 15, 1954; c: Betsy, Daniel. Pres, Arthur Monks Assos Inc, Boston, since 1969; book reviewer for Boston Herald-Traveler since 1954; Wash corresp, Newsweek, 1949; columnist, ed writer, Lynn Daily Evening Item, Mass, 1950-51; asst press secy to Gov Herter, Mass, 1952-56; dir, publicity, Boston U, 1957-64; asso dir, U planning and devl, Brandeis U, 1964-67; asst dean of U planning, Brandeis U, 1967-69. Capt, US Army, WW II. Chmn, Mayor's Comm for Civic Unity, City of Boston; dir, Citizens Scholarship Fund Amer; trustee, Inst Contemporary Art, Boston; mem: bd, Ford Hall Forum, Boston; exec comm, regional bd, ADL, since 1958; scholarship comm, NE region, NCCJ, since 1958; Amer Acad Political and Social Sci; PR Soc Amer; Sigma Delta Chi; Kappa Tau Alpha; Fair Housing, Inc; fmr: vice-chmn, United Fund of Gtr Boston Campaign; dir, NE dist, Amer Coll PR Assn; mem, Mass Commn Against Discrimination; club, Publicity. Recipient: Spec Citation, Gtr Boston United Fund, 1960; Bronze Star Medal. Home: 85 Hyde Ave, Newton, Mass. Office: 232 Bay State Rd, Boston, Mass.

GOLDBERG, Gil Moshe, Isr, pathologist; b. Tel Aviv, Isr, Apr 9, 1924; s. Arie and Miriam (Schechter); MD, U of Geneva, Switz, 1950; m. Sara Briskman, Sep 12, 1947; c: Orna, Arie, Yael. Dir, Inst of Path, Negev Cen Hosp, Beersheba, since 1961; fmr: research f, coord, Michael Reese Hosp, Chgo, Ill; asst prof, path, U of Ill, Chgo; asso prof, Albert Einstein Coll of Med, NY. Segen, IDF MC, 1951-52. Prin contribs: research in lymphovascular and lympho-proliferative diseases; DL-Ethionine effect on germinative tissues; heat and salt loading effect on experimental animals, Chmn, Isr-Amer Friendship Soc, Beersheba br; mem: IMA, Beersheba br, Isr Assn of Path; Amer Assn of Path and Bact; Amer Soc of Clinical Path; Isr Soc of Clinical Path. Contbr to Isr, fgn med jours. Home: 5 Barak St, Beersheba, Isr. Office: Inst of Path, Negev Cen Hosp, Beersheba, Isr.

GOLDBERG, Harold Maurice, S Afr, business exec; b. Cape Town, S Afr, Nov 1, 1916; s. Abraham and Janie (Sevel); BComm, U of Witwatersrand, 1938; m. Naomi Ribakoff, Oct 16, 1940; c: Rosalind, Sheila, Lorraine, Jeffrey. Dir: Barnett's Ltd, asso co's, since 1944, with firm since 1936; Currie Motors, and asso co's, since 1969. Staff sgt, S Afr Corps, Signal and Air Force, 1940-43. Hon life pres, S Afr Furniture Traders Assn; chmn, audio-visual comm, mem exec, S Afr ZF; mem: council, Johannesburg C of C; council, United Zionist Assn; exec, Johannesburg Zionist Assn; comm, Soldiers' Assistance Comm; Temple Isr; J Guild; clubs: Transvaal Automobile Assn; Killarney Golf; Old Edwardian Soc. Home: 18 Currie St, Oaklands, Johannesburg, S Afr, Office: 130 Market St, Johannesburg, S Afr.

GOLDBERG, Harold S, US, electrical engr; b. NYC, Jan 22, 1925; s. David and Rose (Maslow); BEE, Cooper Union, 1944; MEE, Poly Inst of Bklyn, 1949; m. Florence Meyerson, May 29, 1949; c: Lawrence, Irene. Ops mgr, Orion Research Inc since 1968; asst produc mgr, Allen B DuMont Labs, 1950-56; engr, fabrication mgr, Emerson Radio, 1956-57; chief engr, Consolidated Avionics Corp, 1957-59; engr, mgr, EPSCO Inc, 1959-62; vice-pres, Lexington Instruments Corp, 1962-66; prin research engr, AVCO, 1966-68. US Army, 1945-47; fmr Vice-pres, IEEE, Boston sect; mem: Inst Radio Engrs; Tau Beta Pi. Ed, IEEE Mag Reflector, 1967-69; contbr in fields of automatic instrumentation, telemetry, elecs. Home: 10 Alcott Rd, Lexington, Mass. Office: 11 Blackstone St Cambridge, Mass.

GOLDBERG, Herschel J, US, naval off; b. Highland, Kan, May 4, 1913; s. Abraham and Sarah (Berman); BS, US Naval Acad, 1935; MBA, Grad Sch of Bus Admn, Harvard U, 1949; att, Ind Coll, Armed Forces, 1953-54; m. Helen Goldstein, June 5, 1938; c: Michael, Alan. Spec asst, pres, Levi Strauss, and Co, SF, since 1968; purchasing off, Naval Supply Depot, Seattle, Wash, 1941-42; fmr: supply off, Naval Base, Guadalcanal, 1943; cdr, Naval Supply Depot, Noumee, New Caledonia, 1944; supply off, Naval Shipyard, Charleston, SC, 1945-47; logistics planning off, Supr Hdqr Allied Powers, Eur, 1951-53; asst chief, naval materiel, supply prog, 1954-56; commanding off, USN Elec Supply Off, Great Lakes, 1951-59; asst chief, Bur of Supplies and Accts, supply mgmt, 1960-61; vice-chief, naval materiel, 1961-62; rear adm, dep chief, Bur of Supplies and Accts, 1962-65, chief, 1965-1966, commr, 1966-67. Exec, Natl Alliance of Businessman; fmr: bd mem: Chcgo chap, Armed Forces Communication Electronics Assn; pres, Brotherhood, Beth-El Heb Cong, Alexandria, Va. Home: 400 E Arroyo Rd, Hillsborough, Cal. Office: 98 Battery St, San Francisco, Cal.

GOLDBERG, Jack Roy, US, organization exec; b. NYC, July 22, 1921; s. Herman and Rose (Perlman); BA, Bklyn Coll, 1942; MA, NYU, 1948, EdD, 1964; m. Sally Sandler, Jan 17, 1943; c: Ned, Peter, Beth. Commn, NYC Dept Social Services, since 1968; exec dir, Wel-Met Inc, 1948-68. Lt, US Army, 1942-45. Pres, Natl Assn J Cen Workers, NYC, since 1955; chmn, Assn Social Workers, since 1963; mem: Natl Social Wfr Assembly; Acad Cert Social Workers. Recipient: Founders Day Award, NYU, 1965. Home: 15 Black Birch Lane, Scarsdale, NY. Office: 250 Church St. New York, NY.

GOLDBERG, Jacob, US, physician; b. Mar 4, 1896; s. Herman and Frieda (Eisen); BA CCNY, 1917; MD, NYU, Med Sch, 1923; m. Helen Fischer. Chief, dept, phys and rehab service, VA Hosp, Castle Point, NY, since 1950; lectr, phys med dept, Hadassah Med Cen, Jerusalem, Isr. Capt, USN, MC, 1941-46, combat area, Asia Pacific Zone, Guadalcanal, Okinawa, Nagasaki, Japan. Mem: comms, ZOA, since 1947; exec, Beacon Heb Alliance Syn; mem: B'nai B'rith; JWV. Contbr to med jours. Home and office: 142 West End Ave, New York, NY.

GOLDBERG, Jacques Joseph, Isr, physicist, educator; b. Boulogne, Fr, May 6, 1935; s. Shlomo and Esther (Rottenberg); engr, Poly Sch, Paris, 1960; BSc, PhD, U of Paris, 1960-66; m. Danielle Galpgrin, Sep 28, 1958; c: Alain, Claire. Asso prof, Dept of Physics, Technion, since 1968; physicist, Poly Sch, 1958-69. Maj, Fr Army, 1957-69. Author, Nuclear Physics, 1969. Contbr to profsl jour. Home: 21 Antwerpen St, Haifa, Isr. Office: Technion, Haifa, Isr.

GOLDBERG, Joel, Isr, psychologist; b. Haifa, Isr, Mar 12, 1938; s. Jacob and Shoshana; BA, Heb U, Jerusalem, 1962; PhD, W Reserve U, 1966; m. Michal Noy, June 2, 1963; c: Yaron, Edith. Lectr, Bar-Ilan U, since 1968; guest lectr, dept educ, Tel-Aviv U, since 1967; psychol, SUNY, Stony Brook, NY, 1966-67; dir, guidance and counseling dept, Min of Educ, Isr, 1967-68; IDF, 1956-58. Exec secy, Isr Psych Assn; mem, Assn for Advancement of Behavior Therapy, NY; pres, Isr Student Org, 1962-63; vice-pres, Heb U Student Org, 1960-61. Home: 11 Ha'ari St, Jerusalem, Isr. Office: Dept of Psych, Bar Ilan U, Ramat Gan, Isr.

GOLDBERG, John Edward, US, educator, engineer; b. Seattle, Wash, Sep 29, 1909; s. Max and Ida (Hanock); BS, Northwestern U, 1930; CE, 1931; PhD, Ill Inst of Tech, 1950; m. Dorothy Long, June 16, 1944; c, Jane. Prof, civil engr, Purdue U, since 1950; asst prof, Ill Inst of Tech, 1947-50; civil aeronautical engr, Waco Aircraft Co, Convair, 1931-47. Mem: Amer Soc of Civil Engrs; Intl Assn for Bridge and Structural Engr; Sigma Xi; Tau Beta Pi; Chi Epsilon. Contbr to profsl jours. Home: 1805 Western Dr, W Lafayette, Ind. Office: Purdue U, Lafayette, Ind.

GOLDBERG, Joseph; US, attorney, jurist; b. Russ, April 29, 1903; s. Ludwig and Lena (Rappaport); in US since 1903; BA, Clark U, 1923; LLB, Boston U Law Sch, 1927; m. Nell Russin, Aug 20, 1944. Judge, Cen Dist Court, Worcester, Mass, since 1953; pvt law practice, 1927-53; mem: Mass Jud Council, since 1951; Bd of Immigration Appeals, Immigration & Naturalization Service, since 1951. Pres, mem, bd of govs, Amer Financial and Devel Corp for Isr Bonds, since 1951; chmn, Mass UJA, since 1951, NE co-chmn since 1951; natl vice-pres, ZOA, 1950-54; natl chmn, mem comm, 1948-52, mem, natl admn comm, 1936-46, natl exec comm, 1940-49; delg, 23rd WZC, Jerusalem, 1951; dep mem, WZAC, since 1951; mem, bd of dirs, Beth Isr Syn; mem, bd of dirs, United Pal Appeal, 1946-49; Worcester AJCong, 1944-46; mem, natl bd of dirs, KH, 1944-45; exec comm, NE region, JDC, 1944-45; bd of dirs, Natl Assn of Brandeis U, 1938-55; vice-pres, NE Comm to Aid Yemenite Js, 1942-44; mem: NAACP;

Worcester Council Against Discrimination; Worcester Co and Mass Bar Assns; clubs: Econ, pres; Brandeis U, pres; both Worcester. Home: 15 Surrey Lane, Shrewsbury, Mass. Office: 390 Main St, Worcester, Mass.

GOLDBERG, Joshua L, US, chaplain, rabbi; b. Bobruisk, Russ, Jan 6, 1896; s. Boruch and Chaya (Shapiro); in US since 1916; ordained rabbi, MHL, HUC-JIR, NY, 1926, DD, 1951; m. Eleanor Rothman, Nov 20, 1919; c: Josephine Fried, Naomi Stephanie; m. 2nd, Henrietta Davis, Aug 22, 1948. Ret capt, Chaplain Corps, USN; columnist, Wisdom of the Heart, Newhouse Publs; cons, USIA, State Dept, appd mem, comm on moral and spiritual resources, 1953; rabbi em, Astoria Cen of Isr, LI since 1950; fmr: chaplain: NYC Dept of Hosps; on staff of cdr, E Sea Frontier and Atlantic Res Fleet, USN; dist chaplain, 3rd Naval Dist; spec cons, Armed Forces Chaplains Bd. US Army, 1917-20. Trustee, Queensboro Public Libr; mem exec, Queens council, Boy Scouts of Amer; fmr: grand chaplain, Masons Grand Lodge; natl secy, AJCong; vice-pres, Queens Coll Assn; mem: adv bd, NY auxiliary, Navy Relief Soc; bd mgmt, Bklyn YMCA; co-org, WJC, Geneva, Switz; active participant in goodwill movement between Js and non-Js. Author: Jews and the Sea, 1943; Ministering to Jews in the Navy, 1944. Recipient, 5 stars on ribbon, WW I; citation with recommendation ribbon, Secy of Navy; Legion of Merit. Home: 170 N Ocean Blvd, Palm Beach, Fla.

GOLDBERG, Leo, US, astronomer, educator; b. Bklyn, NY, Jan 26, 1913; s. Harry and Rose (Ambush); BS, Harvard U, 1934, MA, 1937, PhD, 1938; m. Charlotte Wyman, July 9, 1943; c: Suzanne, David, Edward. Higgins prof, astronomy, Harvard U, since 1960, chmn, dept astronomy, since 1966, mem fac, since 1934, dir, Harvard Coll Observatory, since 1966; chmn, Astronomy Missions Bd, since 1967; fmr: instr, Wilson Coll, Pa; research asso, McMath-Hulbert Observatory, U Mich, 1941-46, asst prof, astronomy, 1945-46, asso prof, chmn, astronomy dept, 1946-60; mem, Smithsonian Astrophys Observatory, 1960-66. F, Amer Acad Arts and Scis; mem: sci and tech adv comm, manned space flight, since 1964; Natl Acad Sci, past mem, space sci bd; Intl Acad Astronautics; Astronomical Union; Amer Phil Soc; Amer Phys Soc; Amer Astronomy Soc, past pres; and dir, Amer Us for Research in Astronomy Inc; Sigma Xi; fgn asso, Royal Astronomical Soc; fmr: chmn, US Natl Commn, Intl Astronomical Union, chmn, US Delg to Gen Assembly, Moscow; mem: sci bd, USAF; defense sci bd, Defense Dept, 1962-65; solar physics sub-comm, NASA, 1962-65; trustee, Asso Us Inc; dir, Benjamin Apthrop Gould Fund, 1959. Co-author, Atoms, Stars and Nebulae, 1943; ed, Rev of Astronomy and Astrophysics, since 1961; collaborating ed, Astrophysical Jour, 1949-51, chmn, ed bd, 1954; contbr to profsl publs. Recipient: Bowdoin Essay Prize, Harvard, 1938; Navy Award, 1946. Home: 33 Ledge Wood Rd, Weston, Mass. Office: 60 Garden St, Cambridge, Mass.

GOLDBERG, Leo G, US, physician; b. NYC, Apr 22, 1904; s. Saul and Sadie (Sockin); att Columbia U, 1923; MD, LI Coll of Med, 1927; m. Marion Sokolovsky, June 19, 1931; c: Janet, Anita. Dir, dept of urol, Jamaica Hosp; cons urol: Creedmoor State Hosp, since 1950; Queens Hosp Cen; res urol, LI Coll Hosp, 1929-31. F: Intl Coll of Surg, 1949; pres, Bklyn Urol Assn; dipl, Amer Bd of Urol, 1936; mem: NY Urol Soc; Queensboro Surg Soc; Amer Urol Soc; Intl Fertility Assn. Contbr to med jours. Home: 15 Chester Dr, Great Neck, NY. Office: 90-05 153 St, Jamaica, NY.

GOLDBERG, Martin L, US, rabbi; b. Paterson, NJ, Aug 5, 1925; s. Morris and Bella (Bachrach); BSc, Syracuse U, 1949; BHL, HUC, Cincinnati, 1951, ordained rabbi, 1953; MEduc, U of Cincinnati, 1952; PhD, U of Pittsburgh, 1955; m. Claire Zeligman, July 25, 1954; c: Deborah, Joel, David. Rabbi, Temple Beth Zion, Buffalo, NY, since 1954; chaplain, police and fire depts, Buffalo; mem, Theol Dept, Canisius Coll. Mem: exec bd, clergymen's adv comm, Planned Parenthood Center; CCAR; Rel Educ Assn; Amer J Hist Soc. Recipient, Brotherhood Award, NCCJ, 1967; outstanding citizen of Buffalo, Buffalo Evening News, 1967. Study: Temple Beth Zion, 805 Delaware Ave, Buffalo, NY.

GOLDBERG, Michael, US, mathematician, ordnance engr; b. NYC, Nov 13, 1902; s. Harry and Sarah (Pastor); BS, U of Pa, 1925; MA, George Wash U, 1929; m. Goldie Back, Aug 15, 1930; c: Jeremy, Susan Wax. Cons, Bur of Naval Weapons, USN Dept, since 1963; engr, Bur of Ordnance, USN Dept, 1926-1963. Mem: AAAS; Amer Math Soc; Wash

Acad Sci; Math Assn Amer; Sigma Xi. Contbr to math and engr jours. Home: 5823 Potomac Ave NW, Washington, DC.

GOLDBERG, Milton D, US, business exec; b. Chgo, Ill, Nov 27, 1914; s. Isadore and Mollie (Feinberg); att: St Johns Mil Acad, 1927-31; Loyola U, 1931-33; BPh, U of Chgo, 1935; m. Madeline Levine, Nov 26, 1936; c: Lee, Kay. Pres, Isgo Corp, Chgo, Ill, since 1956, vice-pres, 1936-56; dir, Cen Natl Bank, Chgo, since 1963. USN, 1943-46. Pres: Wallcovering Wholesalers Assn; Young Men's J Council; mem, Pi Lambda Phi; f, Brandeis U; fmr: dir: J Fed, Metrop Chgo; JWF, Chgo; Mt Sinai Research Found; club: Northmoor Country. Home: 1087 Bluff Rd, Glencoe, Ill. Office: 2121 W 21 St, Chicago, Ill.

GOLDBERG, Minnie B, US, physician, educator; b. San Francisco, July 11, 1900; d. Jacob and Sarah (Katz) Berelson; AB, U of Cal, 1921, MD, Med Sch, 1925; m. Walter Goldberg, 1928; c: Warren, Jacqueline Feinstein, Richard. Ret, 1967; fmr: clinical prof, em, med, U of Cal, 1965-67, fac mem since 1925; hon att staff, Children's Hosp, since 1955, staff mem since 1935; cons, med, Mt Zion Hosp, since 1955. Mem, bd dirs: Co Med Soc, 1935-38; Public Health League of Cal, 1934-36; mem: SF Co, Cal State, and Amer Med Assns; SF, Cal, and Amer Socs of Internists; Endocrine Soc; Amer Med Women's Assn; Public Health League of Cal; Phi Beta Kappa; Alpha Epsilon Phi; U of Cal Alumni Assn; Council of J Women; club: SF Women's Phys, pres, 1939-41. Author: Medical Management of the Menopause, 1959; contbr to med jours. Home: 550 Battery St, San Francisco, Cal.

GOLDBERG, Morton, US, rabbi; b. Bialystok, Pol, Sep 18, 1903; s. Pinchas and Chya (Roggin); in US since 1905; att U of Pittsburgh, 1919-23; BS, NYU, 1925; ordained rabbi, MHL, JTSA, 1925; MA, Brown U, 1935; PhD, Webster U, 1937; m. Doris Radovsky, May 10, 1931; c: David, Paula Rosenbloom. Rabbi: Cong B'nai Isr, Toledo, O, since 1937; Temple Beth-El, Fall River, Mass, 1925-37. Pres, Zionist dist, 1940-43; B'nai B'rith, 1945-46; JCC, 1946-47; Mental Hygiene Clinic, 1948-59; chmn, lab-mgt, citizens comm; pres, Toledo Bd of Educ, 1963; Comty Relations, since 1959, all in Toledo, O; natl comm, The People Act of Ford Found, 1952-53; Masons; Consistory; clubs: Rotary; Torch. Home: 3424 Goddard Rd, Toledo, O. Study: 2727 Kenwood Blvd, Toledo, O.

GOLDBERG, Norman Lewis, US, art historian, critic, lecturer, ret physician; b. Nashville, Tenn, Feb 10, 1906; s. Samuel and Theresa (Cronstine); BS, U of Toledo, O, 1926; MD, Vanderbilt U, Tenn, 1930; m. Roselea Jonas, Feb 17, 1946. Ret phys; art critic, hist, since 1960; fmr: org 1st exhb of paintings and watercolors, Norwich Sch of Painting, displayed: Fla; Tenn; La; lectr: Vanderbilt U; Victoria and Albert Mus, London; Castle Mus, Eng; Metrop Mus of Art, NYC. Capt, US Army MC, 1942-45. Area chmn, Vanderbilt U; mem, bd dirs, ARC. Contbr to jours. Home: 721 Brightwaters Blvd, St Petersburg, Fla.

GOLDBERG, Percy Selvin, Eng, rabbi; b. Sunderland, Mar 26, 1917; s. Jack and Dora (Jacobius); att: London U, 1935-38; Jews' Coll, London, 1935-38; MA, U of Manchester, 1951; DD, HUC, Cincinnati, 1965; m. Frimette Yudt, Mar 20, 1938; c: David, Jonathan, Sandra Levi. Sr rabbi, Manchester Reform Cong, since 1941; Kingsbury Heb Cong, London, 1939-41. Hon chaplain, Amer J Forces, 1941-56. Vice-chmn: Manchester Council Chrs and Js; Manchester Save-The-Children Fund; patron, Sue Ryder Found; chaplain, Brit Legion; chmn, Mins Assembly, 1950-52; hon chaplain, Manchester Prisons, 1941-60; mem: United Grand Lodge of Eng, fmr asst grand chaplain. Contbr to J periodicals. Recipient: citation, JWB. Home: 99 Dene Rd, Manchester, Eng. Study: Jacksons Row, Manchester, Eng.

GOLDBERG, Philip J, US, business exec; b. NYC, Dec 20, 1921; s. Nathan and Mollie (Sabato); att Pace Coll; NYU; Blackstone Sch of Law, all NYC; m. Ruth Dickler, June 2, 1941; c: Ronald, Robert, Richard. Head, Philip J Goldberg Assos Estate & Financial Planning since 1969; chmn, bd, Inst for Financial Planning, Inc, since 1960; co-chmn, bd, Hamilton Life Ins Co, 1961-65; chmn, bd, First Natl Life Ins Co, 1965-67; chmn, bd, Financial Security Life Ins Co, 1967-69. US Army, 1941-46. Chmn: SW area, Isr Bonds; Found Comm on Legacies and Bequests, Amer Friends of Heb U; bd govs, Phoenix United JWF; trustee, NY Law Sch; mem: found, Truman Cen for Peace, Heb U, Jerusalem; fac, Purdue U, Life Ins Marketing Inst; JWV, LA; life, Natl chap, Million Dollar Round Table; NY Bd, Natl Safety Council; hon consul, Dominican Rep for Ariz; fmr: vice-pres, Assn Advanced Life Underwriters; chmn, Legacy Devl Comm, Natl Urban League; vice-pres, Assn Chanukah Festival; dir: US Comm for Refugees; Pioneer Bank; United HIAS Service; gov, JTS; bd govs, AJComm; spec econ asst, US Ambass to UN; mem: Ariz Adv Council, Small Bus Admn. Author: Estate Planning, 1960; Tax Planning for Today and Tomorrow, 1961; How to Use Life Insurance for Charitable Endowment in Estate Planning, 1962; contbr to legal jours. Recipient: awards: Intl Sr Citizens; United Shareholders Amer; Natl Council for Sr Citizens; Hum Relations, AJComm; Citation of Milligan Coll, Tenn. Home and office: Los Angeles, Cal.

GOLDBERG, Richard A, US, attorney; b. Bklyn, NY, Oct 25, 1930; s. Miles and Laura (Ganz); BBA, CCNY, 1951; JD, Columbia Law Sch, 1954; att NYU Grad Sch of Bus, 1956-57; m. Rosalyn Sheinfeld, Mar 25, 1961; c: Glenn, Evan. Pvt practice since 1954; vice-pres, Suburban Playwear Inc, 1958-59; delg, Jud Conf, NY State, 1967-69; admitted to: Treas Dept, 1959; US Tax Court, 1961. Pvt, US Army, 1954-56. Pres, City Coll Sch Bus Alumni Soc; chmn, HiRise War on Narcotics; trustee, Baruch Coll Fund; bd dirs, Baruch Coll Alumni Assn; mem: NY State Assn Trial Lawyers; Mason, Midian Lodge; fmr: pres, Trump Village Housing Coop, chmn, adv council; vice-pres, 46 AD Dem Club; dist cdr, JWV, post cdr, Post 183. Recipient: Insignium Award, CCNY, 1951; Alumni Service Medal, CCNY Alumni Assn, 1970; Plaque, UJA, 1970. Home: 460 Neptune Ave, Brooklyn, NY. Office: 16 Court St, Brooklyn, NY.

GOLDBERG, Romayne M, US, civic worker; b. Scranton, Pa, Jan 19, 1907; d. Adolph and Anna Marcus; att Sorbonne and Ecole Politique, 1926-27; BA, Wellesley Coll, 1928; m. Harold Goldberg, Dec 14, 1930; c: Martha Schimberg, Ezra, Emily Steiner, Edward. Vice-pres, Boston chap, AJComm; natl bd, Haddassah, 1948-58, pres: Boston chap, 1948-51, NE region, 1956-58; women's div, CJA, 1953-55; natl women's comm, Brandeis U, 1960-62, trustee, 1960-62, f, 1962; exec comm, Bonds for Isr; bd, women's comm, J Family and Children's Service; life trustee, Combined J Philanthropies; mem: Natl Isr Comm; AJComm; JCC; club: Belmont Country. Home: Jamaicaway Tower, Boston, Mass.

GOLDBERG, Samuel L, US, surgeon; b. Chgo, Ill, Sep 21, 1905; s. Joseph and Dora (Cohen); BS, U of Chgo, 1924; MD, Rush Med Coll, 1927; MS, U of Minn, 1932; m. Gertrude Marks, Dec 24, 1934; c: Louise, Alice. Pvt practice since 1932; att surg, Michael Reese Hosp since 1947, with hosp since 1932; clinical asso prof, surg, Chgo Med Sch, since 1954; f, surg, Mayo Found, 1929-32; chief, surg clinic, Mandel Clinic, 1932-47. Pres, Chgo Grad Club, Phi Delta Epsilon Med Frat, 1945; chmn, doctors div, CJA, 1953; hon dir, BMZ Orthodox Home for the Aged, mem, bd of dirs, 1934-52; mem: Ill State and Chgo Med Socs; AMA; N Cen Clinical Soc; Amer Coll of Surgs; Amer Bd of Surg; Chgo Surg Soc; Inst of Med of Chgo; Phi Beta Kappa; Alpha Omega Alpha; Alumni Asso of Mayo Found; KAM Temple; club, Standard of Chgo. Contbr to med jours. Recipient: Rush prize, Rush Med Coll, 1927. Hobbies: photography, travel, fishing. Home: 701 N Michigan Ave, Chicago, Ill. Office: 104 S Michigan Ave, Chicago, Ill.

GOLDBERG, Seymour, US, business exec; b. Newark, NJ, Sep 3, 1922; s. Abraham and Clara (Reimer); m. Janet Weinstock, Apr 17, 1947; c: Jerome, Judith, Robert, Karen. Co-owner: Westminster Cleaners; Capri Cleaners; Westminster Trading Co; Westminster Laundries Inc, all since 1947. USAF, 1944-47. Fmr pres, N NJ region, United Syn of Amer; chmn, Isr Bond Drive, Linden since 1959; vice-pres, Natl Ramah Comm; mem: Natl Inst of Dry Cleaning, Md; Masons; JWV; B'nai B'rith; ZOA; NJ State adv council, AJComm; bd trustees, Linden Public Libr, elected secy, 1968; hon mem, bd trustees, Suburban J Cen, Temple Mekor Chayim, Linden, since 1958, fmr pres; clubs: Craftsmen's Suburban Sq, past pres; Tenth Ward Dem; fmr: chmn, UJA dinner; chmn, Natl Camp USY; mem: bd govs, E Union Co J Council; bd overseers, JTSA; natl conv comm, United Syn. Recipient: Isr Bar Mitzvah Award Plaque, 1961; two pres unit citations; Eleanor Roosevelt Hum Award, 1965; Spec Service Award, Isr Bonds, 1968; Cert of Appreciation, United Syn of Amer, 1968. Home: 2417 DeWitt Terrace, Linden, NJ. Office: 1 St Georges Ave, Roselle, NJ.

GOLDBERG, Sidney, Eng, communal leader; b. London,

Feb 21, 1920; s. Reuben and Rachel (Cohen); att Poly, London; m. Masha Yaffe, Aug 22, 1943; c: Reuben. Gen secy, Poale Zion, Eng; Brit gen secy, Lab Friends of Isr; vice-chmn, World J chap, political dept, London. Author: Labour Studies Israel; Youth in The Garment Trades; Israel, Africa and Asia; Borochov; The Jews, The Facts. Home and office: 2 Bloomsbury Pl, London, Eng.

GOLDBERGER, Edward, US, business exec; b. Providence, RI, Nov 15, 1905; s. Samuel and Bertha (Steiner); AB, Brown U, Providence, 1927; LLB, Harvard Law Sch, 1931; m. Marjorie Lowenstein, Dec 19, 1935; c: Ann, Susan. Treas, M Lowenstein & Sons, Inc, since 1945, secy, dir, since 1936; mem, law firm, McGovern & Slattery, 1931-36; admitted to: RI Bar, 1931; NY Bar, 1938. Dir, NY Bd of Trade, 1961, mem, exec comm, textile sect, since 1949, chmn, 1951; dir, Amer Cotton Mfrs Inst, Inc, 1961; mem: bd dirs, Textile Fabrics Distributors; of mgmt, Lab Textile Adv Comm and Export Textile Adv Comm, Dept of Commerce; natl commn, secy, natl exec comm, ADL; clubs: Weavers; Metropolis Country, White Plains, NY; City; Athletic; Brown. Homes: 30 E 71 St, New York, NY; 1367 Flagler Dr, Mamaroneck, NY. Office: 1430 Broadway, New York, NY.

GOLDBERGER, Gustav, US, attorney; b. Troppau, Oppava, Czech, Apr 28, 1934; s. Eugene and Helene (Berkovitz); in US since 1957; BA, Sir George Williams U, Montreal, 1957; LLB, Rutgers U, 1961; JD, 1961; m. Betty Friedman, July 7, 1957; c: Earl, Emanuel, Elana. Dir, Neighborhood Legal Services, OEO, since 1967; asso gen counsel, Legal Aid Soc, since 1967; mem, Erickson, Sheppard & Goldberger, since 1966; chief city prosecutor, Akron, O, 1963-66; asst co-prosecutor, Summit Co, O, 1966-67. Cantor, Anshe Sfar Cong, Akron, 1961-64. Pres, Hillel Acad of Akron, 1967-69; chmn, ADL, Akron, 1966-67; mem: B'nai B'rith; Masons; Judicature Soc; Amer Trial Lawyers Assn; Amer, O and Akron Bar Assns. Recipient: Found Cert, Hillel Acad, 1968; Public Service Award, Summit Co, O, 1968. Hobbies: singing, piano. Home: 516 Moreley Ave, Akron, O. Office: 300 Wooster Ave, Akron, O.

GOLDBERGER, Marvin Leonard, US, educator; b. Chgo, Ill, Oct 22, 1922; s. Joseph and Mildred (Sedwitz); BS, Carnegie Tech, Pitt, Pa, 1943; PhD, U of Chgo, 1948; m. Mildred Ginsburg; c: Joel, Samuel. Higgins prof, physics, Princeton U, since 1957; prof, U of Chgo, 1950-57. Staff sgt, US Army, 1944-46. Mem: Natl Acad Scis, 1963; AAAS, 1964; Cosmos Club, 1965. Author, Collision Theory, 1964; contbr to profsl publs. Home: 125 Fitz-Randolph Rd, Princeton, NJ. Office: Palmer Physical Laboratory, Princeton U, Princeton, NJ.

GOLDBLATT, Harry, US, physician, educator; b. Muscatine, Ia, Mar 14, 1891; s. Philip and Jennie (Spitz); BA, McGill U, Montreal, Can, 1912, MD, MC, 1916; Beit Memorial F, Lister Inst and U Coll, London, Eng, 1921-24; hon DSc, W Reserve U, 1966; m. Jeanne Rea, June 25, 1929; c: David, Peter. Dir, Beaumont Memorial Research Lab, Mt Sinai Hosp, Cleveland, O, since 1953; asso dir, Inst of Path, prof em, experimental path, W Reserve U; fmr: path i/c, Lakeside Hosp, 1919-21; asso prof path, W Reserve U, 1924-27; dir, Inst for Med Research, Cedars of Leb Hosp, LA, Cal, 1946-53. 1st lt, US Army MC, 1917-19. Hon F, Amer Coll of Card; hon mem, Brazilian Soc of Card; mem: Assn of Amer Phys; Amer Assn of Paths and Bacts; Path Soc of Gt Brit and Ir; Phys Soc of Gt Brit; Cen Soc for Criminal Research; Fed of Amer Socs for Experimental Biol; Soc for Experimental Biol and Med; AHA; Amer Soc of Clinical Paths; Amer Cancer Soc; Intl Assn of Med Mus; AMA; Acad of Med of Cleveland. Contbr to med jours. Recipient: awards: John Phillips, Amer Coll of Phys, 1936; Alvarenga, Coll of Phys, Phila, 1937; Cert of Merit, 1st Class, AMA, 1937; Annual Sci, Phi Lambda Kappa, 1939; Ward-Burdick, Amer Soc of Clinical Paths, 1939; New Orleans Trophy, Zeta Beta Tau, 1941; Charles Eisenman, Cleveland, O, 1944; Charles Mickle f, Toronto U, 1948; Amory, Amer Acad of Arts and Scis, 1962; Ferdinand C Valentine, NY Acad of Med, 1964; Research Achievement, AHA, 1966; Stouffer Prize, 1966; Gold-Headed Cane Award, Assn of Paths and Bacts, 1966. Home: 2743 N Park Blvd, Cleveland Hgts, O. Office: Mt Sinai Hosp, 1800 E 105 St, Cleveland, O.

GOLDBLATT, Maurice, US, business exec; b. Stashov, Pol, Dec 17, 1893; s. Simon and Hannah (Diamond); m. Sylvia Gottstein, June 22, 1924 (div); c: Noel, Gloria; m. 2nd, Bernice Mendelson, Jan 7, 1936; c: Merle, Stanford. Chmn: bd, Goldblatt Bros Inc, Dept Stores, Chgo, since 1945, with firm since 1914; bd of trustees, Goldblatt Bros Found; bd, U of Chgo Cancer Research Found; Cancer Research Found; Heart Research Found; La Rabida Jackson Park B'nai B'rith; fmr exec dir, Amer Cancer Soc; hon f, Amer Coll of Hosp Admnrs; fmr mem: natl adv heart council, natl adv cancer council, both USPHS; hon mem, Amer Hosp Assn; mem: Citizens f, Inst of Med, Chgo; mem, citizens bd: Loyola U, U of Chgo; clubs: Standard; Bryn Mawr Country; Chgo. Recipient, Rosenberger medal. Home: 1040 Lake Shore Dr, Chicago, Ill. Office: 333 S State St, Chicago, Ill.

GOLDBLATT, Sidney, S Afr, artist; b. Johannesburg, Dec 20, 1919; s. Bernard and Sarah (Miller); att: Anglo-Fr Art Sch, St John Cass Art Sch, London, 1949-51; studied with: André Lhote, Fernand Léger, both Paris, 1951; m. Wendy Webster, Apr 17, 1957; c: Lisa, Paula, Amanda, Simon. Profsl painter and art tchr, since 1949; held one-man shows regularly since 1949; exhb with S Afr groups: Holland, Belgium, Ger, Yugo, Isr, Eng; represented S Afr at Venice and Sao Paulo Biennales. Mem, S Afr Arts Council. Home and studio: 34 Second St, Abbotsford, Johannesburg, S Afr.

GOLDBLITH, Samuel A, US, educator; b. Lawrence, Mass, May 5, 1919; s. Abraham and Fannie (Rubin); BS, MIT, 1940, MS, 1947, PhD, 1949; m. Diana L Greenberg, 1941; c: Judith, Errol (decd), Jonathan. Prof, food sci and exec off, dept, MIT, since 1959, dep dept head, since 1967, fac mem since 1949; vice-pres, tech dir, United Fruit and Foods Corp, Boston, Mass, 1960-64. US Army, 1941-45. Chmn, NE Section, Inst Food Technologists, 1956-57; pres sci adv comm, Panel on World Food Supply, 1966-67; Phi Tau Sigma, 1958; mem: Natl Research Comm on Radiation Preservation of Foods, Natl Acad Sci, 1963; J US-Arg Commn on Foot and Mouth Disease, since 1962; Spec AEC to Jap, 1961; White House Sci Mission to Arg, 1962; Masons, fmr lodge master; clubs: New Cent, Boston, pres, 1962-63; Chems, NY. Co-author: An Introduction to the Thermal Process of Foods, 1961; Milestones in Nutrition; contbr of numerous articles to food sci and tech jours. Recipient: Silver Star; Monsanto Presentation Award, Inst of Food Tech, 1953; one of ten outstanding young men of Boston, Jr C of C, Boston, 1954. Home: 6 Meadowview Rd, Melrose, Mass. Office: MIT, Cambridge, Mass.

GOLDBLOOM, Maurice J, US, journalist; b. Bklyn, NY, July 28, 1911; s. Simon and Betty (Jackson); BA, Columbia Coll, 1930; MA, Columbia U, 1931. Free-lance since 1951; research, publ dir, US Comm for Democracy in Greece, ed, News of Greece since 1968; ed, fgn affairs dept, AJComm, 1946; asso and asst ed, Common Sense mag, 1944-46; exec secy, Amer Assn for a Dem Ger, 1946-50; lab info off, US Fgn Service, ECA-MSA, 1950-51. Author: American Security and Freedom, 1954; asso ed, Current Mag, 1960-61; contbr: articles, book reviews, to periodicals. Home: 305 W 28 St, New York, NY.

GOLDBURG, Ariel L, US, rabbi; b. St Louis, Mo, Oct 24, 1903; s. Burt and Julia (Posnansky); BA, U of Cincinnati, 1927; ordained rabbi, HUC, 1929, DHL, 1955; DD, Morris Harvey Coll, 1936; m. Fanny Levin, June 14, 1927; c: Bette Levy, Linda Stern. Rabbi, Temple Beth Ahabah, Richmond, Va since 1945; Va St Temple, Charleston, W Va, 1929-45. Chmn, adv bd, Dept of Public Assistance: State of W Va, 1939-45, Richmond Va, 1956-59; co-found, Comty Chest; Fed J Charities, both of Charleston; mem: exec bd, CCAR; Min Assn; Salvation Army civilian chaplain, Fort Lee, Va; mem: J Cen; JCC; Open Forum, all of Richmond, Va; Libr Bd; Sym Bd; Civic Music Assn; ARC; War Fund; Comty Forum; J Chautauqua Soc, all of Charleston, W Va; club, Rotary, chmn, prog comm. Home: 2701 Park Ave, Richmond, Va. Study: 1117 W Franklin St, Richmond, Va.

GOLDEN, Alfred, US, physician, educator; b. NYC, Aug 4, 1908; s. Bernard and Rheba (Dryer); BS, U of Wis, 1930; m. Libby Siegel, 1965; c: from previous m, David, Frederick. Dir, labs: Jennings Memorial Hosp, since 1955; Alexander Blain Memorial Hosp, since 1955; path, Army Inst of Path, 1941-45, exec off, 1943-44; cons path, Wash Sanitorium and Hosp, Wash, DC, 1942-46; lectr: Army Med Sch, Wash, DC, 1942-45; George Wash U Sch of Med, Wash, DC, 1944-45; asso prof, path: U of Tenn Coll of Med, 1946-50; U of Buffalo Sch of Med, 1950-55; Wayne State Coll of Med, 1955-56; visiting prof, U of Miss Coll of Med, 1948-49; chief, lab service, VA Hosp, Buffalo, NY, 1949-55; cons: Buffalo Eye Bank and Research Soc, 1949-55; Memorial Hosp, Niagara Falls, NY, 1953-55. Lt col, Tropical Disease Inves Unit,

US Army, 1941-46. FACS; f: Amer Coll Paths; Amer Soc Clinical Paths; dipl, Amer Bd Path; mem: Amer Soc Experimental Path; Amer Soc Paths and Bacts; AMA; State of Tenn Soc Paths, fmr pres; Wash Soc Paths, fmr pres; AAAS; Amer Soc Clinical Paths; Sigma Xi; NY Acad Sci; fmr: pres, Cass Assn, Detroit, Mich; mem: Boy Scout Council, Buffalo, NY; med div, Civil Defense org, Buffalo, NY. Contbr to med jours. Recipient: Alexander Berg Prize in Bact, 1938; Army Commendation Award, 1945. Home: 26764 York Rd, Huntington Woods, Mich. Office: 7815 E Jefferson Ave, Detroit, Mich.

GOLDEN, Harry L, US, editor, author; b. Aus-Hung, May 6, 1903; s. Leib and Nuchama (Klein); BA, CCNY, 1924; m. Genevieve Gallagher, Apr 11, 1926; c: Richard, Harry, William, Peter (decd). Ed, publisher, The Carolina Israelite, since 1941; reporter: NY Post, 1932-36; NY Daily Mirror, 1936-38; Charlotte Observer, 1939-40; Hendersonville Times-News, 1940-41. Author: Jews in American History, 1950; Only in America, 1958; For 2 cents Plain, 1959; Enjoy, Enjoy, 1960; Carl Sandburg, 1961; You're Entitle', 1962; Forgotten Pioneer, 1963; Mr Kennedy and the Negroes, 1964; A Little Girl is Dead, 1965; The Best of Harry Golden, 1967; Autobiography of Harry Golden, 1969; co-author, Five Boyhoods, 1962. Mem: Shakespeare Assn; Dem Co Comm; NC Ed Writers Assn; Temple Isr. Hobby: music. Home and office: 1312 Elizabeth Ave, Charlotte, NC.

GOLDEN, Herbert H, US, educator; b. Boston, Mass, Nov 1, 1919; s. Max and Minnie (Turetzky); AB, magna cum laude, Boston U, 1941, AM, 1942; AM, Harvard U, 1947, PhD, 1951; m. Hilda Lazerow, June 13, 1943; c: Robert, Barry, Steven. Prof, romance langs, Boston U, since 1962, exec asst, dept fgn langs, since 1961. US Army, 1942-45. Chmn, It listening comprehension test, classroom testing project, MLA, since 1960; mem: Dante Soc of Amer; Amer-It Soc; Amer Assn of Tchrs of Fr; AAUP; Masons; Phi Beta Kappa, secy, Boston U chap; Phi Sigma Iota; Modern Hum Research Assn; fmr: secy-treas, pres, Amer Assn of Tchrs of It; mem exec comm, Natl Fed of Modern Lang Tchrs Assn; mem, steering comm, fgn lang prog, natl coord for It, MLA; mem, adv comm on fgn langs, Commonwealth of Boston; pres, vice-pres, NE chap, Assn Alumni and Friends, It Sch, Middlebury Coll; admn secy, pres, brotherhood, chmn, inst of adult educ, Cong Kehillath Isr, Brookline, Mass; secy, NE Conf Teaching of Fgn Langs. Co-author: Modern French Literature and Language, 1953; Modern Iberian Language and Literature, 1958; Modern Italian Language and Literature, 1959, all three, A Bibliography of Homage Studies; Studies in Honor of Samuel M Waxman, 1969; contbr to educ jours. Recipient: Purple Heart Medal; Bronze Star Medal; Medaglia d'Oro al Merito Culturale, It Govt, 1961; Fulbright lectr, U of Rome, 1962-63. Home: 29 Thorndike St, Brookline, Mass. Office: Boston U, Boston, Mass.

GOLDEN, Herbert L, US, business exec; b. Phila, Pa, Feb 12, 1914; s. Horace and Amelia (Cohen); BS, Temple U, Phila, 1936; m. Gertrude Fisher, July 15, 1938. Pres, Lexington Intl Inc, financial cons since 1962; motion picture ed, Variety, 1939-52; vice-pres, Bankers Trust Co, NY, 1952-58; vice-pres, dir, United Artists, 1958-62; dir: Cinecom; Music Markers Group; Diversities; asst to dir, motion pictures div, US Coord, Inter-Amer Affairs, 1941-42. Lt, USN, 1942-45. Mem: Radio TV Exec Soc; Acad of TV Arts and Scis; clubs: Variety; City Athletic; Corinthians. Contbr of articles on motion pictures, TV, show bus finance. Hobby, soiling. Home: 410 E 57 St, New York, NY. Office: 655 Madison Ave, New York, NY.

GOLDEN, Morris, Rhodesia, dental surg; b. Memel, Lith, Mar 9, 1922; s. Leib and Resy (Judelman); in Rhodesia since 1939; BDS, U of Witwatersrand, 1945; m. Helen Sack, Jan 2, 1949; c: Neville, David, Corinne. Pvt practice since 1945; fmr, hon dent off, Bulawayo Heb-Eng Nursery Sch. Chmn, bd govs, Carmel Sch; mem: Rhodesian J Bd of Deps since 1960; Rhodesian Dent Assn; Rhodesian Maccabi Council; Bulawayo J Guild; Bulawayo Chovevei Zion Soc; Philatelic Soc; clubs: Lions of Bulawayo; Sports, fmr mem, gov body; fmr: pres, Rhodesian ZC; vice chmn, Cen Afr ZC; chmn: Bulawayo Zionist Youth; Zionist Youth Exec; secy, Skuder Landsmannschaft Soc. Hobbies: philately, photography. Home: 28 Fitch Rd, Kumalo, Bulawayo, Rhodesia. Office: 207 Bradlow Bldgs, Abercorn St, Bulawayo, Rhodesia.

GOLDEN, Morris, US, educator, author; b. Kishinev, Rum, June 29, 1926; s. Haim and Sarah (Lieberson) Goldenbroit;

in US since 1928; BA, CCNY, 1948; MA, NYU, 1949, PhD, 1953; m. Hilda Hertz, Apr 11, 1954; c: Daniel, Olivia. Prof, Eng, U of Mass, since 1965, asso prof, 1962-65; instr, NYU, 1951-56; instr, asst prof, Bowling Green State U, 1956-62. USNR, 1944-46. Author: In Search of Stability; The Poetry of William Cowper, 1960; Richardson's Characters, 1963; Thomas Gray, 1964; Fielding's Moral Psychology, 1966; contbr to profsl jours. Recipient: Guggenheim f, 1968-69; mem: AAUP; MLA; Phi Beta Kappa. Home: 49 Ridgecrest Rd, Amherst, Mass. Office: U of Mass, Amherst, Mass.

GOLDEN, Nathan D, US, attorney, economist; b. Bellaire, O, July 4, 1895; s. Herman and Rose (Landau); att Emerson Inst, Wash, DC, 1927-30; LLB, Wash Coll of Law, Amer U, 1933; m. Rose Glueck, Dec 24, 1926. Dir, sci motion picture and photographic products div, bus and defense services admn, US Dept of Commerce, since 1951, chief, motion picture sect, bur of fgn and domestic commerce, 1933; cons, Golden Gate Intl Exposition, SF, Cal, 1939; mem: motion picture div, War Produc Bd, Off of the Coord of Inter-Amer Affairs, WW II; ind intelligence br, Jt Chiefs of Staff, 1945-46, headed mission to Ger to secure formulae of Agfa color sys; dir, motion picture, sci and photographic products div, Natl Produc Auth, 1950-53. F, Soc of Motion Picture and TV Engr; US repr, Intl Exhb of Cinematographic Art, Venice, 1953, 1960, 1961; mem: US delg, Contracting Parties on Tariffs and Trade and the Tariff Negotiations, 1949; Fr-Amer Film Quota Negotiation Comm, Paris, 1952; Motion Picture Pioneers: Projection Adv Council; Amer U Alumni Assn; Amer Legion; VFW; clubs: Natl Press, Variety; Variety Intl. Contbr to jours and govt publs. Recipient: Gold Medal Award, Projection Adv Council, 1930; cert of appreciation, Jt Chiefs of Staff, US Army, 1951; Silver Medal, 1954; Chevalier, Legion of Honor, Fr, 1956; Order of Merit, 1st Class, Fed Repub of Ger, 1961. Home: 4000 Cathedral Ave, NW, Washington, DC. Office: Warner Bldg, 501 13 St, NW, Washington, DC.

GOLDEN, William T, US, business exec; b. NYC, Oct 25, 1909; s. Herbert and Rebecca (Harris); AB, U of Pa, 1930; att Harvard Grad Sch of Bus Admn, 1930-31; m. Sibyl Levy, May 2, 1938; c: Sibyl, Pamela. Chm, bd: Fed Mortgage Inves; United Ventures, Inc since 1952; City U Construction Fund since 1967; asst to pres, Cornell, Linder & Co, 1931-34; asst to commn: Loeb, Rhodes & Co, 1934-41; AEC, 1946-50. Lt cdr, USNR, 1941-45. Dir, Asso Hosp Service, NY; trustee: U Corp for Atmospheric Research; Mt Sinai Sch of Med, Mt Sinai Hosp; NYC-Rand Inst; Riverside Research Inst; Inst for Educ Devl; Inst for the Future; Heb Free Loan Soc; Mitre Corp; NY Found; Natl Inst Public Affairs; Amer Mus Natural Hist; Carnegie Inst of Wash; Marine Biol Lab, Woods Hole, Mass; f, treas, AAAS; public mem, Hudson Inst; mem: Soc of Protozools, NYC; fmr: chmn, Sys Devl Corp; trustee: United Neighborhood Houses; Home for Aged & Infirm Heb in NY; clubs: Cosmos; Army and Navy, all Wash, DC; City Midday, NYC. Home: 730 Park Ave, New York, NY. Office: 40 Wall St, New York, NY.

GOLDENBERG, Albert, Isr, writer, journalist; b. Bucharest, Rum, Apr 26, 1934; s. Osias and Jenny (Zoller); in Isr since 1965; m. Anette Simon, July 31, 1953. Journalist since 1966; fmr: active, cultural, folkloristic instns, Bucharest. Pvt, IDF. Mem: cen comm, Union of Rum Js in Isr; B'nai B'rith; Natl Fed of Journalists in Isr. Author, I Seek the Sources, poems, 1967; contbr of short stories, poems, articles. Spec interest, cultural lectures in Rum lang. Home: Har Hatsofim St, Holon, Isr. Office: 52 Harakevet St, Tel Aviv, Isr.

GOLDENBERG, George, US, physician; b. Chgo, Ill, July 24, 1906; s. Harris and Tillie (Lebow); BS, Coll of Med, U of Ill, 1928, MD, 1932; m. Elizabeth Goldberg, Jan 4, 1942; c: Harris, David, Barry, Alan. Mem, med staff, Jackson Park Hosp; coroner's phys, Cook Co. Maj, US Army MC, WW II. Pres: Phi Lambda Kappa Alumni; mem: bd of dirs: Cong Rodfei Sholom Oir Chodesh; B'nai B'rith; mem: AMA; Chgo and Ill Med Socs; Amer Friends of Heb U; Guardian of Isr. Hobbies: boxing, swimming. Home: 9256 S Bennett Ave, Chicago, Ill. Office: 1525 E 53 St, Chicago, Ill.

GOLDENBERG, George, US, business exec; b. NYC, Feb 12, 1929; s. Gersh and Rose (Kolpacci); BS, Bklyn Coll Pharm, 1951; m. Arlene Yudell, May 22, 1955; c: Steven, Heidi, Jeffrey. Pres, dir, Ormont Drug & Chem Co Inc, since 1966; exec vice-pres, 1964-66; dir, secy, Goldleaf Pharm Co, since 1965; pres asst, Syntex Labs Inc, 1956-61; gen sales mgr, Panray-Parlam Corp, 1961-64. Vice-pres, Fed of Alumni Assn

LIU; trustee, Bklyn Coll of Pharm, LIU; fmr: pres: Bklyn Co Pharm Alumni Assn, 1966-67; Delta Sigma Theta, 1950-51; mem: B'nai B'rith, N Valley; Young Pres' Org, NJ; Amer Pharmaceutical Assn; Jr C of C; Amer Mgmt Assn; Drug, Chem & Allied Trades Assn. Home: 62 Walker Ave, Closter, NJ. Office: 520 S Dean St, Englewood, NJ.

GOLDENBERG, H Carl, Can, attorney; b. Montreal, Can, Oct 20, 1907; s. Maurice and Adela (Gradinger); BA, 1st class hons, McGill U, 1928, MA, magna cum laude, 1929, BCL, 1st class hons, 1932; hon: LLD, U of Montreal, McGill U, U Toronto; m. Shirley Block, Feb, 1945; c: Edward, Ann. Partner, Goldenberg, Yelin and Golt, since 1932; appd QC, 1952; lectr, econ, political sci, McGill U, 1932-36; in munic govt, 1944-45; adv on munic finance, Royal Commn on Dominion-Provincial Relations, 1937-38; chmn, Royal Comn on Finances and Admn, Winnipeg, 1938-39; Commn, Man Govt Commercial Enterprises Inquiry, 1939-40; dir-gen, econ and stats br, Dept of Munitions and Supply, Can Govt, 1940-45; chmn, Ind Produc Bd; mem, Natl Selective Service Adv Bd, Can Govt; exec asst to chmn, Can sect, War Produc Comm of Can and US; lab adv to Min of Reconstruction and Supply, 1945-46; Royal Commn on Provincial-Munic Relations, BC, 1946-47; spec commn to inquire into alleged: Bread Combine in W Can, 1948; combine in Wire and Cable Ind, 1952-53; spec council for BC at Fed-Provincial Conf on Taxation and Constitutional Amendment, 1950-52; Royal Commn on Lab-Mgmt Relations, Construction Ind of Ont, 1961-62; mem, Commn on Real Estate Taxation, Montreal, 1962-63; adv on munic and sch taxation, Govt of Alberta, 1960-61; Royal Commn on Munic Govt in Metrop St John, 1962-63; spec council for NF at Fed-Provincial Fiscal Confs, since 1957; counsel for NF at Fed-Provincial Confs on Constitutional Amendment, 1960-62; chmn: Commn on Enquiry into Sugar Ind of Jamaica, W Indies, 1959-60; bd of enquiry, Trinidad Sugar Ind disputes, 1962; Fed mediator, Natl RR Strike, 1966. Mem: McGill Fac; Can Soc; Can Political Sci Assn; Royal Econ Soc, London, Eng; Can Bar Assn. Author: The Law of Delicts under the Quebec Civil Code, 1935; Municipal Finance in Canada, 1940; Government Commercial Enterprises in Manitoba, 1940; Provincial-Municipal Relations in British Columbia, 1947. Recipient: OBE, 1946; Medal of Service, Order of Can, first Can Hons List, 1967. Home: 566 Roslyn Ave, Westmount, Que, Can. Office: 804 Dominion Sq Bldg, Montreal, Can.

GOLDENBERG, Kalman S, US, business exec; b. Chisholm, Minn, Dec 2, 1911; s. Jacob and Esther (Rosenfield); BA, U of Minn, 1932; m. Maxine Shapiro, Jan 1, 1938; c: William, Elizabeth, Jacob. Gen mgr, Old Peoria Co Inc ince 1947. Vice-pres, chmn exec comm, Temple of Aaron, St Paul; natl campaign cabinet, UJA; bd overseers, JTSA; pres: United J Fund and Council, 1950-52; w cen region CJFWF; secy, Minn Wine and Spirits Inst; bd dirs, Talmud Torah J Cen. Recipient, awards: Man of the Year, St Paul JWV, 1952; Louis Marshall, JTSA, 1959; PM's Medal, Bonds for Isr, 1966. Home: 19 S First St, Minneapolis, Minn. Office: 701 Stinson Blvd, Minneapolis, Minn.

GOLDENBERG, Nathan, Eng, chemist; b. Boguslav, Russ, Sep 4, 1911; s. Solomon and Rachel (Lurie); in Eng since 1921; BS, Birkbeck Coll, U of London, 1933, MS, 1935; m. Edith Dee, June 6, 1937; c: Philip. Tech exec, food group, Marks & Spencer Ltd, since 1948; fmr research chem, Messrs Lyons and Co. F: Royal Inst of Chem; Royal Soc of Health; Inst of Food Sci and Tech; fmr: chmn, food trade comm, JPA, dep chmn, vice-chmn, Wembley br; mem, mgmt comm, Soc of Chem Ind; pres, vice-pres, hon secy, Fed of Zionist Youth, Gt Brit; chmn, Hakerem, Young Zionist Soc; mem: exec council, ZF, Gr Brit; food group comm, Soc of Chem Ind; comm, Technion Soc of Gt Brit. Mem ed bd, J Observer and ME Rev; contbr: pamphlets on Zionist topics; articles to sci and trade jours. Home: 128 Bickenhall St, London, W1, Eng. Office: 67 Baker St, London, W1, Eng.

GOLDENWEISER, Alexis, US, attorney, author; b. Kiev, Russ, Nov 27, 1890; s. Alexander and Sofia (Munstein); in US since 1937; DJur, Kiev U, 1912; att: U of Berlin; U of Heidelberg; NYU; m. Eugenie Ginsburg, July 26, 1912. Fmr: atty, Kiev; prof law, political sci, Kiev U; mem, Ukranian Rada; atty, Berlin, Ger; legal expert, Nansen Off for Refugees, Geneva, Switz; surveyor of legal positions of refugees in Eur, Royal Inst of Intl Affairs, London. Pres, Assn of Russ Lawyers in NY, since 1942; co-chmn, J Teitel Comm since 1944. Author: Evolution of Moral Ideas in the Law, 1920; Jacobins and Bolsheviks—Psychological Parallels, 1922; Memoirs of the

Revolution in Kiev, (1917-21), 1922; In Defense of the Law, 1952; Impressions of a Russian Lawyer in America, 1954; co-ed: Russian Jewry: (1860-1917), 1961; (1917-1967), 1969; contbr to press, profsl jours. Home: 523 W 112 St, New York, NY.

GOLDFARB, Alvin I, US, psychiatrist; b. NYC, Apr 28, 1914; s. Louis and Celia (Friedman); AB, Brown U, Providence, RI, 1935; MD, Johns Hopkins U, Baltimore, Md, 1939; cert, psychan med, Columbia U, 1953; m. Jenny Borak, May 28, 1945; c: Jeffrey, Alison, Martha. Pvt practice; cons: Services for the Aged, NY State Dept of Mental Hygiene, 1956-68; Visiting Nurses Service of NY; chief neuropsycht and clinical researcher, Hosp and Home for Aged and Infirm Hebs; asso prof: NY Sch of Psycht; NY Med Coll, all since 1956; asso att psycht, Mt Sinai Hosp since 1963; fmr: sr phys, psycht service, Fairfield State Hosp, Newton, Conn, also chief, male admitting service; asso, Columbia Psychan Clinic; neuropsycht, Beth Isr Hosp; asst psycht, asst phys, Columbia Presbyterian Hosp. F: Amer Coll of Psycht, 1968; Amer Psycht Assn; Amer Acad of Neur; chmn, Comm on Aging, Group for Advancement Psycht since 1957; mem: AMA; NY Co Med Soc; Amer Psychosomatic Soc; Assn for Psychan Med; Amer Public Health Assn; Amer Psychan Assn; Schilder Soc. Home: 214-15 33 Ave, Bayside, NY. Office: 7 W 96 St, New York, NY.

GOLDFARB, Jack A, US, manufacturer; b. Warsaw, Pol, June 15, 1895; s. Aaron and Sarah; att CCNY; m. Bertha Leventhal, Sep 14, 1930; c: Robert, Ruth Lese, Betty Medalie, Miriam Cahners. Bd chmn, Union Underwear Co; adv, bd dirs, Phila and Reading Corp; pres, Goldfarb Investing since 1955; chmn bd, CFC since 1958; dir, Sterling Stores, Little Rock. US Army, WW I. Vice-pres, NYU J Culture Found; dir: Underwear Inst; treas: AJComm, Inst of Hum Relations Fund; Brandeis U; dir, UJA; trustee: FJP; mem: B'nai B'rith; Temple Emanu-El; Masons; clubs: Harmonie; Men's; Metropolis Country. Home: 895 Park Ave, New York, NY. Office: 1290 Ave of Americas, New York, NY.

GOLDFARB, Solomon D, US, rabbi, author; b. Sokolow, Galicia, Apr 15, 1902; s. Moses and Bracha (Katz); in US since 1904; BS, NYU, 1929; MHL, ordained rabbi, JTSA, 1932, DD, 1966; att Columbia U, 1941-43; m. Sophia Rabinowitz, Aug 16, 1929; c: Sharon. Rabbi: Temple Isr, since 1947; Sons of Isr, Albany, NY, 1935-40; Cong B'rith Shalom, Charleston, SC, 1943-47; fmr, prof, Herzliya Inst. Life mem, ZOA; mem, RA. Author: To Stand Alone, 1957; Windows in Heaven, 1960; Zramim, uRemazim, 1961; Ready Reference Jewish Ency, 1963; The Listening Heart, 1963; Torah for our Time, 1965; Lev veLashon, 1968; contbr to Hadoar, and Bull, NY Bd of Rabbis. Home: 234 E Walnut St, Long Beach, NY. Study: 70 Park Ave, Long Beach, NY.

GOLDFEDER, Anna, US, cancer researcher; b. Pol, June 25, 1897; d. Harry and Tauba (Friedman); in US since 1931; DS, Karl's U, Prague, 1923; med studies, Masaryk U, Brno, Czech, 1928-31. I/c, cancer research, cancer div, Dept of Hosps in asso with biol dept, NYU, since 1940, cancer research f, 1934; reasearch asst, dept of experimental path, Masaryk U, 1923-25, asso researcher, phys dept, 1925-27, head, cancer research lab, 1927-31; research fs: Vienna, 1928-29; Lenox Hill Hosp, NYC, 1931-33; researcher: biol chem dept, Harvard Med Coll, 1933-34; bact and immunology dept, Columbia U Coll of Phys and Surgs, 1934; guest lectr: Weizmann Inst of Sci and Heb U, both Isr, 1958, 1968; Cambridge U, 1958. F: AAAS; NY Acad of Sci; asso f, NY Acad of Med; mem: Royal Soc of Med, London; Radiological Soc of N Amer; Amer Assn for Cancer Research; Soc for Experimental Biol and Med; Amer Phys Soc; Radiological Research Soc; Harvey Soc; Soc of Cell Biol. Contbr to sci jours in US and Eur. Recipient: Radiological Soc of N Amer award, 1948; cash award, Damon Runyon Fund for Cancer Research, 1949. Home: 920 Riverside Dr, New York, NY. Office: 99 Fort Washington Ave, New York, NY.

GOLDFIEN, Irving, US, civil engr; b. Bialystock, Pol, May 12, 1893; s. Samuel and Socha-Beit (Pat); in US since 1900; BCE, Valparaiso U, 1915; BS in CE, U Wis, 1916, CE, Grad Sch, 1930; m. Rose Forman, Oct 19, 1919; c: Benjamin, Mathon, Sylvia Browne. Cons engr, engaged in research engr; fmr: research engr, City of Milw; with engr dept: Chgo, Milw, St Paul, and Pacific RR Co; div engr, city sewerage comm, sr research engr, design, construction, water construction div, Milw Water Works; engr i/c construction, sewer engr div, sewer construction div, Bur of Sewers. US

Army, 1918-19. Holder, various patents and copyrights in sewer engr. F, Amer Soc of CE, since 1929; mem: leg comm, pension study comm, Milw Govt Service League, since 1938; civic affairs comm, libr comm, Engrs Soc of Milw; Amer Soc for Public Admn; Cen States Water Pollution Control Assn; Wis Soc Profsl Engrs; Assn Grad and Reg Engrs of Milw; Munic Engrs Soc; Amer Legion; Masons; fmr, bd dirs, Talmud Torah, Milw. Recipient, Comty Service Award, Milw radio sta, WMIL, 1962. Home and office: 6885 Byron Ave, Miami Beach, Fla.

GOLDFINE, David C, US, business exec; b. Chgo, Ill, Apr 28, 1907; s. Jake and Sarah (Leichenger); att Northwestern U, 1926-29; m. Frances Tobias, Oct 7, 1926; c: Debra Borodkin, Sabra Klein. Pres, Cidco Inc; sales mgr, Reuben H Donnelly Corp, 1946-51. Mem, natl commn, ADL, since 1961; admn chmn, dist lodge 6, B'nai B'rith, since 1962, pres, 1959-60, pres, Chgo council, 1949-50. Home: 7009 Cornell Ave, Chicago, Ill. Office: 43 E Ohio St, Chicago, Ill.

GOLDFINGER, Paul, Belgium, scientist; b. Szaszregen, Rum, Jan 10, 1905; s. Oscar and Régine (Haiman); DSc, chem engr, Ecole Polytechnique Fédérale, Zurich, Switz, 1929; m. Kate Deppner, 1931; c: Marianne. Prof, phys chem, Free U of Brussels, since 1946; research asst, Kaiser Wilhelm Inst, Berlin, 1929-33; asst, U of Liege, 1933-35; chem, Gasparcolor SA, Brussels, 1935-40; head, research, Centre National de la Recherche Scientifique, 1946-48. Belgian partisans, 1940-44. Mem: Soc Chimique de Belgique; Faraday Soc; Amer Soc for Testing Materials; Union des Anciens Etudiants de l'Universite libre de Bruxelles; Fed gen des Travailleurs de Belgique; Amer Phys Soc; Sigma Xi. Contbr to sci publs. Hobby, hiking. Home: 79 ave des Chênes, Brussels, Belgium. Office: Universite Libre de Bruxelles, Brussels, Belgium.

GOLDFRANK, Esther S, US, anthropologist; b. NYC, May 5, 1896; d. Herman and Matilda (Metzger) Schiff; BA, Barnard Coll, NY, 1918; m. Walter Goldfrank, 1922, (decd); stepsons: Max, Alexander, Thomas; c: Susan; m. 2nd, Karl Wittfogel, 1940. Staff anthropologist, Chinese Hist Project, U of Wash, in coop with Columbia U, since 1943; field work: Amer Indian Pueblos, NM, 1920-22, 1924; Blackfoot Indians, Alberta, Can, 1939. Secy-treas, Amer Ethnological Soc, 1945-47, pres, 1948, ed, 1952-56; f, Amer Anthropological Assn; NY Acad of Sci; mem: Amer Folklore Soc; Soc for Applied Anthropology; Amer Political Sci Assn. Ed: Isleta Paintings, Bur of Amer Ethnology, Smithsonian Inst, 1962; The Artist of Isleta Paintings in Pueblo Society, Smithsonian Inst; contbr to Amer Anthropology, vol 5, 1967; author of monographs; contbr to social sci and anthropological jours. Home and office: 420 Riverside Dr, New York, NY.

GOLDHABER, Gertrude S, US, physicist; b. Mannheim, Ger, July 14, 1911; d. Otto and Nelly (Steinharter) Scharff; in US since 1939; PhD, summa cum laude, U of Munich, Ger, 1935; m. Maurice Goldhaber, May 24, 1939; c: Alfred, Michael. Sr physicist, Brookhaven Natl Lab, Asso Us Inc; research asso, Imperial Coll, London, 1935-39; research physicist, 1939-48, spec research asst prof, U of Ill, 1948-50; cons, Brookhaven Natl Lab, 1948-50, asso physicist, 1950-58, physicist, 1958-67. F, Amer Phys Soc; mem, Sigma Xi. Contbr to physics jours. Home: 91 S Gillette Ave, Bayport, NY. Office: Brookhaven Natl Lab, Asso Us Inc, Upton, NY.

GOLDHABER, Jacob K, US, mathematician, educator; b. Bklyn, NY, Apr 12, 1924; s. Joseph and Zirel (Heller); BA, Bklyn Coll, 1944; MA, Harvard U, 1945; PhD, U of Wis, 1950; m. Ruth Last, Dec 25, 1941; c: Doreet, David, Aviva. Chmn, dept of math, U of Md since 1968, prof since 1961; instr: U of Conn, 1950-53; Cornell U, 1953-55; asso prof, Wash U, St Louis, Mo, 1955-61. Mem: Amer Math Soc; AAUP; Amer Math Assn; Sigma Xi; Pi Mu Epsilon. Contbr to math jours. Home: 5517 39 St NW, Washington, DC. Office: U of Md, College Park, Md.

GOLDHABER, Richard F, US, attorney; b. Bklyn, NY, Mar 2, 1941; s. Max and Betty (Chatow); BS, Bklyn Coll, 1961; JD, NYU Sch of Law, 1966; m. Myrna Watnick; c: Mark, Robert, Matthew. Partner, Rosenthal & Goldhaber since 1962; secy, treas, Metal & Roofing Distributors Assn since 1967; secy, Natl Metal Spinners Assn since 1969. Chmn, Metal & Roofing, Sheet Metal Div, FJP; asso chmn, Metal & Roofing, Sheet Metal Div, UJA; fmr vice-pres, secy, Contello Towers No 3 Corp, 1968-69; life mem, Alpha Epsilon Pi, Phi Theta Chap; mem: Amer, NY State, and Kings Co Bar Assns. Office: 44 Court St, Brooklyn, NY.

GOLDHAMMER, Bernard, US, government official, economist; b. Portland, Ore, July 26, 1915; s. Harry and Elizabeth (Herman); BA, Reed Coll, 1937; MA, Colo Coll, 1938; att: Ia State Coll, 1938-39; U of Cal, 1939-42. Power mgr, Bonneville Power Admn, since 1961; commercial oprs off, Bonneville Power Admn, 1958-61; econ customer service off, 1943-58; research asst, Ia State Engr Experiment Sta, Ia State Coll, 1938-39; teaching f, U of Cal, 1939-42. Mem: bd of dirs, J Comty Cen, Portland, Ore, since 1956, pres, 1960-62; bd, Ore J Wfr Assn, bd, 1960; Amer and W Econ Assns; B'nai B'rith, Portland; club, City, Portland. Contbr to econ and bus publs. Home: 6820 SE 39 Ave, Portland, Ore. Office: 1002 NE Holladay St, Portland, Ore.

GOLDIN, Bennie, Rhodesia, jurist; b. Aug 5, 1918; s. Laizer and Braine (Shmerkowitz); BA, LLB, Cape Town U, 1942; m. Hannah Kaplan; c: Robert, Jonathan, Barbara. Judge, High Court, Rhodesia, since 1965; QC; pres: Valuation and Army Pension Appeal Courts, 1960-65; Income Tax Court, 1964-65. S/Sgt, Army Intelligence, 1941-45. Recipient: campaign medals, It, Afr. Hobbies: gardening, reading biographies. Home: 15 Bertram St, Salisbury, Rhodesia. Office: Vincent Bldgs, Salisbury, Rhodesia.

GOLDIN, Harry, US, physician, educator; b. Minsk, Russ, July 19, 1898; s. Gershon and Rachel (Robkin); in US since 1913; BS, CCNY, 1920; MD, Coll of Phys and Surgs, Columbia U, 1924; m. Anna Eskolsky, July 1, 1928; c: Gurston, Jessica Stern, Harrison. Ret, sr phys, NY, Maritime Coll; em, asso phys, Montefiore Hosp; cons phys, Morrisania City Hosp, fmr asst clinical prof, NY Med Coll. Chmn, hosp comm, Bx Co Med Soc; pres, Ivrith Med Soc, 1947-48; f: Amer Geriatric Soc; Amer Coll of Gastroenterology; NY Acad of Med; Natl Gastroenterological Assn; mem, AMA. Recipient: Presidential Citation, selective service, 1946. Home and office: 1749 Grand Concourse, New York, NY.

GOLDIN, Judah, US, educator, author; b. NYC, Sep 14,1914; s. Gerson and Rachel (Robkin); BS, CCNY, 1934; MA, Columbia U, 1938; MHL, JTSA, 1938, DHL, 1943, HLD, 1968; MA, hon causa, Yale U, 1958; m. Grace Aaronson, June 21, 1938; c: Robin, David. Prof, classical Judaica, Yale U since 1958; lectr, visiting asso prof, J lit and hist, Duke U, 1943-45; asso prof, rel, U of Ia, 1946-52; dean, asso prof, Agada Sem Coll, JTSA, 1952-58. F: John Simon Guggenheim; Amer Acad of J Research. Author: The Period of the Talmud, 1949; The Grace After Meals, 1955; The Fathers According to Rabbi Nathan, 1955; Living Talmud, 1957; trans, Shalom Spregal MeAggadot HaAkedah, The Last Trial, 1967; numerous other studies. Recipient: Amer Phil Soc award, 1957; Fulbright award, 1958, 1964. Hobby: music. Home: 103 Milbrook Rd, Hamden, Conn. Office: Yale U, New Haven, Conn.

GOLDIN, Leon, US, artist, teacher; b. Chgo, Ill, Jan 16, 1923; s. Joseph and Bertha (Metz); BFA, Art Inst of Chgo, 1948; MFA, State U of Iowa, 1950; m. Meta Solotaroff, July 30, 1949; c: Joshua, Daniel. Asst prof, painting, Columbia U: fmr: tchr: Cal Coll of Arts and Crafts; Phila Coll of Art; Queens Coll; instr, Cooper Union. US Army, 1943-46. One man shows: Oakland Art Mus, 1955; Felix Landau Gal, LA, 1956, 1957, 1959; Gal L'Attico, Rome, 1958; Krushaar Gal, NY, 1960, 1964, 1968; repr in perm collections: Bklyn, St Louis, LA Co, Santa Barbara Mus; Oakland Art Mus; Pa Acad of Fine Arts; Worcester Mus; Addison Gal of Amer Art; Cincinnati Mus of Art; Johnson Collection, Smithsonian Inst; Munson Proctor Inst; Va Mus of Fine Arts; Everson Mus; Speed Mus, Louisville, Ky. Recipient: Louis Comfort Tiffany Grant, 1951; Fulbright Scholarship, 1952; Prix de Rome, 1955; Guggenheim f, 1959; Jennie Sesnan gold medal, Pa Acad of Fine Arts, 1966; Natl Inst of Arts and Letters Grant, 1968. Home: 438 W 116 St, New York, NY.

GOLDING, Elizabeth Bass, US, jurist, attorney; b. NYC; d. William and Dora (Blinkow) Bass; LLB, NYU Law Sch; m. Samuel Golding, Nov 26, 1931. Judge, Family Court of NY State for Nassau Co, since 1963; State Commnr of Correction, since 1961. Found, pres, Natl Women's Forum Inc, since 1946; hon pres, Women's Forum of Nassau Co, since 1950; mem, natl exec comm, bd dirs, United HIAS Service, since 1945; legal adv, Wayside Sch for Girls, since 1949; regional dir, Natl Assn of Women Lawyers; chmn: juvenile law comm, Intl Fed of Women Lawyers, delg to UN Commn on Hum Rights; family law comm, Amer Bar Assn; mem bd dirs: Family Counseling Panel of LI Fund; Heb Acad of Nassau Co; Mh Assn; Family Service Assn; Correction Comm of

Health and Wfr Council; Amer Cancer Soc, all of Nassau Co; chmn, inter-profsl disciplines, NY State Wfr Conf; mem: Hadassah; Amer Assn of U Women; B'nai B'rith; AJComm; fmr: bd dirs, exec comm, Natl Council of J Women; chmn legal clinic, Nassau Co Women's Bar Assn; pres, org, JWB, Nassau Co; vice-chmn, USO; regional chmn, Civil Defense; chmn, Servicemen's Legal Aid Comm, Mitchell Field, NY. Author: Don't Underestimate Womanpower; Health of the Nation. Recipient: Nassau Co Award for Leadership, 1950; Amer Bar Assn Award of Merit to Nassau Co Bar Assn as Chmn of Youth Conf, 1959. Home: 312 E Shore Dr, Massapequa, NY. Office: 266 Fulton Ave, Hempstead, NY.

GOLDMAN, Aaron, US, business exec, civic worker; b. Wash, DC, June 8, 1913; s. Hymen and Sadie (Cohen); BS, Georgetown U, 1934; m. Cecile Saloman, Nov 26, 1939; c: Phyllis Weiner, Michael. Pres, Macke Vending Co, since 1939. Lt cdr, USN, 1942-45. Pres: Natl Automatic Merchandising Assn, Chgo, Ill, 1951-53; JCC Gtr Wash, 1953-56; chmn: Natl Comty Relations Adv Council; Commns Council on Hum Relations, Wash, DC; advance gifts, UJA, since 1959; co-chmn, Wash region, NCCJ, 1952-57; mem: AJCong, Amer Vets Comm; JWV; Urban League; clubs: Woodmont Country; Army-Navy. Recipient: Pres Citation, 1944. Home: 2801 New Mexico Ave, NW, Washington, DC. Office: 1 Macke Circle, Cheverly, Md.

GOLDMAN, Alex J, US, rabbi; b. Drohitin, Pol, June 8, 1917; s. Julius and Sarah (Rubinstein); LLB, De Paul U, Coll of Law, 1939; ordained rabbi, Heb Theol Coll, Chgo, 1944; m. Edith Borovay, Mar, 1941; c: Robert, Pamela. Rabbi, Temple Beth El, Stamford, Conn; dir, Hillel Found: Beaver Coll, Jenkintown, Pa, since 1953; Pa State Ogontz Cen, Abington, Pa, since 1953; rabbi: Temple Isr, Tallahassee, Fla, 1944-46; W Oak Lane J Comty Cen, Phila, 1954-66; dir, Hillel Found: Fla State Coll for Women, 1945-46; Temple U, Phila, 1946-54; civilian chaplain. Chmn, Brotherhood Week, Tallahassee, 1945-46; pres, found, Council of Rel Advs, Temple U; vice-pres, Rel Educ Assn, Phila, 1952-53; secy, Zionist Youth Commn, Phila, 1951-52; mem, RA. Author: A Handbook for the Jewish Family, 1958; Blessed Art Thou, 1961; A Dictionary of Symbols for the Jewish Child, 1963; Giants of Faith, 1965; John F Kennedy, the World Remembers, 1968; Power of Bible, 1969. Home: 564 Hunting Ridge Rd, Stamford, Conn. Study: Temple Beth El, Stamford, Conn.

GOLDMAN, Alma J, US, communal worker; b. Malden, Mass, Apr 2, 1918; d. Benjamin and Emily (Cohn) Shoolman; BA, Wellesley Coll, 1939; m. Morris Goldman, Nov 11, 1945; c: Louise. Office mgr, Beacon Products Corp, Needham, Mass, 1941-45. Mem, natl exec comm, Natl Council J Women, since 1969, chmn, natl overseers comm, 1963-67, vice-chmn, 1957-61, chmn, natl nominating comm, 1962-63, mem natl bd, since 1957, pres, NE region, 1961-63, pres, Boston sect, 1953-54, vice-pres, 1949-53, hon dir, since 1954; fmr: chmn, women's speakers bur, Boston Tercentenary Comm, Amer J Tercentenary; mem: exec comm, United Service for New Amers; natl council, United HIAS Service; speakers bur, women's div, CJA, Gtr Boston; natl corp, Women in Comty Service; bd: Boston Service for New Amers; JCC, Metrop Boston. Hobbies: Photography, bridge, golf. Home: 94 Longwood Ave, Brookline, Mass.

GOLDMAN, Ben J, US, jurist, attorney; b. Bialystock, Russ, July 16, 1904; s. Joseph and Rachel (Lebenhaft); in US since 1907; BA, U of Toledo, 1924; LLB, U of Mich, 1927. Judge, court of common pleas, Springfield, O, since 1957; pvt practice, 1927-32; judge, munic court, Springfield, 1954-57. US Army, 1942-43. Mem: Masons; Elks; B'nai B'rith; ZOA; Amer Legion; VFW. Home: 1590 E High St, Springfield, O. Office: Clark Co Court House, Springfield, O.

GOLDMAN, Benjamin P, US, attorney; b. NYC, Jan 25, 1894; s. Louis and Anna (Sapir); ME, Cornell U, 1914; LLB, St Lawrence U, 1925; m. Babette Schorsch Leiter, Mar 22, 1962. Practicing atty, since 1926; partner, Weit & Goldman, 1939-45; lectr, Practicing Law Inst since 1941. Dir, Amer Friends of Heb U since 1958; mem: Amer Bar Assn; NY Co Lawyers Assn; Sigma Alpha Mu, pres, 1920-22, 28, 33. Author: Examination Before Trial in a State Court, 1955, 1960; contbr to law jours. Home: 303 E 57 St, New York, NY. Office: 55 Liberty St, New York, NY.

GOLDMAN, Bernard L, US, business exec; b. Cleveland, O, July 17, 1908; s. Jacob and Anna (Shanman); BA, U Mich,

1929; LLB, W Reserve U, 1932; m. Pearl Lieberman, Jan 7, 1942; c: Jonathan, Laurence. Pres: Wright Dept Stores, since 1966; Council on Hum Relations, since 1968; Forest City Hosp, since 1968; bd mem: AJComm; B'nai B'rith; mem: Tau Epsilon Phi; Cleveland Bar Assn; United World Federalists; Masons. Hobby: gourmet cookery. Home: 3694 Stoer Rd, Shaker Heights, Cleveland, O. Office: 1400 W 6 St, Cleveland, O.

GOLDMAN, Douglas, US, psychiatrist, educator; b. NYC, Jan 22, 1906; s. Bernard and Gisela (Goldstein); BS, U of Cincinnati, 1926, MD, 1928, MS, 1929; m. c: Susan Abel, Douglas, Grace Mesel, John; m. 2nd, Evelyn Kerchner, Dec 30, 1948; c: Donald, Constance. Asst clinical prof, U of Cincinnati, since 1952; phys, J and Good Samaritan Hosps, since 1940; clinical dir, Longview State Hosp, 1937-62. Mem: AMA; Amer Psycht Assn; Amer, Cen, E Electroencephalographic Assns; Amer Soc Clinical Path; Amer Acad Forensic Sci; Assn Research Nervous and Mental Disease; Acad Med, Cincinnati; Amer Coll Neuropsychoparm; Collegium Internationale Neuropsychopharmacologicum. Co-author, Practical Psychiatry for the Internist, 1968; contbr to med jours. Hobby, photography. Home: 7000 Fair Oaks Dr, Cincinnati, O. Office: 179 E McMillan St, Cincinnati, O.

GOLDMAN, Eric F, US, educator, author; b. Wash, DC, 1915; PhD, Johns Hopkins U, 1938; hon degs: LLD; DLitt; DHumL. Rollins Prof, hist, Princeton U, since 1962, fac mem, since 1940; auth on 20th cent Amer hist; fmr: lectr: Eur; India, both under auspices of State Dept; appeared on natl TV and radio; moderator, NBC, The Open Mind, 1959-67; appd by Pres Johnson, Spec Cons to the Pres, 1963-66. Author: Rendezvous With Destiny: A History of Modern American Reform; The Crucial Decade, America, 1945-55, best seller, 1956; The Crucial Decade and After, America, 1945-60; The Tragedy of Lyndon Johnson, 1969, best seller; other books; reviewer, NY Sunday Times Book Sect; fmr, writer, Time Mag; contbr to mags and scholarly publs. Fmr pres, Amer Hist Soc. Recipient: Bancroft Prize for Rendezvous With Destiny; Best Lectr,12 consecutive years, sr class, Princeton U; McCosh L, highest scholarly award for fac mem, Princeton U, 1962. Home: 70 Washington Rd, Princeton, NJ. Office: Princeton U, Princeton, NJ.

GOLDMAN, Esther, US, social worker; b. Baltimore, Md; d. Max and Sophie (Badian) Lazarus; PhB, U Chgo, 1926; MSW, U of Pa, 1938; DSW hon, 1959; m. Albert Goldman, Nov 29, 1932. Dir, Dept of Public Wfr, City of Baltimore since 1953; fmr: caseworker, J Social Service Bur; probation off, Juvenile Court, Baltimore; planned and implemented public assistance progs, VI. Mem: Md Commn for Children and Youth, since 1956; Baltimore Commn on Aging, since 1956; Md Adv Comm on Foster Care, since 1961; Md Adv Comm on Adoption, since 1959; Jail Bd, Baltimore City, since 1953; bd, Metrop Baltimore Assn for Mh; bd, Md Assn for Mental Hygiene; bd, Health and Wfr Council, Baltimore; Natl Assn of Social Workers, fmr chmn: Md chap, prog comm, comm on social work educ; Amer Public Wfr Assn; Natl Conf on Social Work; Md State Conf on Social Work, past pres; fmr: Prisoners' Assn, Baltimore; bd, J Family and Children's Bur Inc; bd, J Social Wfr Bur, Baltimore. Contbr to profsl jours. Hobby, raising violets. Home: One Warranton Rd, Baltimore, Md. Office: 1500 Greenmount Ave, Baltimore, Md.

GOLDMAN, Henry M, US, dentist, educator; b. Boston, Mass, Dec 9, 1911; s. Joseph and Rebecca (Levy); att Brown U; DMD, Harvard Dent Sch, 1935; m. Dorothy Alter, June 7, 1936; c: Richard, Gerald. Prof, chmn stomatology dept, Boston U Sch of Med, Mass, since 1958, dean, Sch of Grad Dent, since 1963, mem exec comm; chief, stomatological service, Mass Memorial Hosps, Boston, since 1958, mem exec and policy comms; head, Reisman dent clinic, Beth Isr Hosp, Boston, since 1948, mem, exec comm; prof, chmn, dept periodontology, Grad Sch of Med, U of Pa, Phila, since 1955; lectr, dent, Columbia U, since 1952; fmr: research f, oral path, Harvard U; instr, oral path, cons: periodontology, Natl Inst of Dent Research, since 1957; Chelsea Naval Hosp; USPHS Hosp, Boston; mem, Ivory Cross Expedition. Cons to Surg Gen, Dent Corps, US Army; served, chief dent, path sect, US Army; path dent registry, Armed Forces Inst of Path, Wash, DC, cons, dent and oral registry, 1943-45. F: Amer Coll of Dents; AAAS; Amer Acad of Dent Service; dipl: Amer Bd of Periodontology; Amer Bd of Oral Path; mem: Amer Dent Assn; Amer Acad of Periodontology; NY Acad Scis; NE Soc Path; Omicron Kappa Upsilon; Sigma Xi; fmr: dir, pres, Amer Bd, Oral Path; dir, Amer Bd, Periodonto-

logy; pres, Amer Acad, Oral Path; mem: sub-comm on periodontia, NRC; council on dent research, Amer Dent Assn; ad hoc comm, periodontology, Natl Inst of Dent Research. Author, Atlas of Oral and Dental Pathology, 1944; co-author: Oral Diagnosis, chap, 1943; Oral Pathology, chap, 1950; Periodontia, 4th ed, 1957; Introduction to Periodontia, 1959; Treatment Planning in the Practice of Dentistry, 1959; Periodontal Therapy, 2nd ed, 1960; contbr to profsl jours. Recipient: Hinman Award, 1952; Army Commendation Ribbon and Pres Citation, 1945; Gold Medal Award, Amer Acad Periodontology, 1968; Alpha Omega Award, 1968. Home: 45 Beverly Rd, Chestnut Hill, Mass. Office: 1163 Beacon St, Brookline, Mass.

GOLDMAN, Israel M, US, rabbi; b. Pol, Feb 13, 1904: s. Morris and Anna (Rosen); BA, CCNY, 1924; MA, Columbia U, 1926; ordained rabbi, JTSA, 1926, DHL, 1937, hon DD, 1950; hon DD, Brown U, 1949; m. Mildred Gandal, Jan 31, 1943; c: Anna, Tobie. Rabbi: Chizuk Amuno Cong, Baltimore, Md, since 1948; Temple Emanuel, Providence, RI, 1923-48; lectr: McCoy Coll, Johns Hopkins U, 1952-53. Pres, Zionist dist, Providence and Baltimore; mem, natl admn comm, ZOA; fmr: natl pres, RA; natl dir, Natl Acad for Adult J Studies, JTSA; vice-chmn, Md Comm on Interracial Relations. Ed, textbooks on adult J educ; contbr to periodicals. Home: 7912 Winterset Ave, Baltimore, Md. Office: 8100 Stevenson Rd, Baltimore, Md.

GOLDMAN, Joseph, US, physician, educator; b. Russ, Oct 1, 1897; s. Louis and Celia (Honigman); BA, Harvard Coll, 1919; MD, Harvard Med Sch, 1922; m. Clara Greenberg, May 31, 1962; c: Dorothy Sparrow, Theodore. Instr, med, Tufts Coll, Sch of Med, 1924-50; visiting phys: Mass U Hosp, 1925-49; Beth Isr Hosp, 1929-53; asst prof, bact and immunology, Boston U Sch of Med, 1932-46, preventive med, 1936-49. Trustee, Temple Sinai, Brookline, Mass; mem: AMA; Mass and Gtr Boston Med Soc; NE Soc of Allergy; Phi Beta Kappa; Phi Lambda Kappa. Contbr to med jours. Home: 80 Gardner Rd, Brookline, Mass. Office: 483 Beacon St, Boston, Mass.

GOLDMAN, Joseph L, US, physician, educator; b. Bklyn, NY, Jan 16, 1904; s. Louis and Anna (Sapir); AB, Columbia U, 1924; MD, LI Coll Hosp Med Sch, 1927; m. Florence Green, Nov 16, 1941; c: Elizabeth Sevin, Barbara Steinbach, James. Prof, chmn, Dept of Otolaryngology, Mt Sinai Sch of Med since 1966; dir, since 1954, on staff since 1929; pvt practice since 1932; asst asso surg, otolaryngology, Bellevue Hosp, 1935-54; asst asso clinical prof, NYU, 1946-51; asso prof, clinical otorhinolaryngology, NYU Post Grad Med Sch, 1951-55; clinical prof, Columbia U, 1955-67. Col, US Army MC, 1942-46; chief, otolaryngology, AAF Regional Hosp, Fla, 1942-44, William Beaumont Gen Hosp, 1945-46. Pres, Amer Laryngological, Rhinological and Otological Soc, 1969-70, vice-pres, 1958-59; f: Amer Coll Surg; mem: Amer Bronch-Esophagological Assn; Amer Soc Ophthal and Otolaryngologic Allergy; Amer Acad Ophthal and Otolaryngology, vice-pres, 1964; Amer Bd Otolaryngology; Amer Laryngological Assn; Amer Otological Soc; Amer Soc Head and Neck Surg; U Otolaryngologists; AMA, chmn, sect, Laryngology, Otology and Rhinology, 1963; NY Acad of Med; Sigma Alpha Mu. Contbr to med jours. Recipient, Army Commendation Ribbon, 1946. Home: 1185 Park Ave, New York, NY. Office: 1050 Park Ave, New York, NY.

GOLDMAN, Leon, US, surgeon, educator; b. San Francisco, Feb 14, 1904; s. Samuel and Lily (Kalfin); BA, U of Cal, Berkeley, 1926, MD, 1930; MS, Northwestern U, 1939; m. Betty Rosenburg, June 19, 1931; c: Dianne Feinstein, Yvonne Banks, Lynn Klippsten. Chmn, dept of surg, prof, surg, asso dean, U of Cal, since 1956, on fac since 1935; chief, surg service, SF Hosp, 1939; lectr at mil hosps; i/c, mil surg courses, SF, 1942-45. First vice-pres, Amer Coll of Surgs; fmr pres, SF Surg Soc; mem: Soc of U Surgs; AMA; Pacific Coast and W Surg Assns; Amer Gastroenterological Assn; Amer Goiter Assn; Howard C Naffziger Surg Soc; Alpha Omega Alpha; Sigma Xi; Temple Emanuel; Masons. Asst ed, W Jour of Surg, Gyn, and Obstets, since 1952; contbr to med and surg jours. Home: 1050 N Point, San Francisco, Cal. Office: U of Cal Med Cen, San Francisco, Cal.

GOLDMAN, Max, US, attorney; b. Auburn, NY, July 8, 1904; s. Israel and Bella (Freedman); att: O State U, Columbus, 1925; Syracuse U, Syracuse, NY, 1929; m. Lillian Kanter, Nov 14, 1937; c: Carole, Robert, Richard. Mem, law firm, Goldman and Goldman, since 1929; JP, Auburn, NY, 1930-

35; asst dist atty, Cayuga Co, NY, 1937-40; spec co judge, Cayuga Co, NY, 1962; hearing referee, NY State dept motor vehicles, 1967-68. Dir: J Home Cen NY at Syracuse, since 1950; Auburn Wfr Fund, since 1950; mem, bd trustees, Auburn Comty Coll, since 1953; pres, Cong B'nai Isr, Auburn, since 1929. Mem: natl panel of arbitrators: Amer Arbitration Assn; Amer Judicature Soc; jud sect, NY State Bar Assn; NY State and Cayuga Co Bar Assns, pres, 1953; NY State Dist Attys Assn; NY State Assn Magistrates; C of C; clubs: Auburn Gold and Country; Elks; Masons; Shriners. Home: 9 N Marvine Ave, Auburn, NY. Office: 141 Genesee St, Auburn, NY.

GOLDMAN, Nathan C, US, business exec; b. Bialystok, Pol, July 4, 1894; s. Joe and Rachel (Lebenhoff); in US since 1907; m. Helen Bolarsky, Sep 10, 1916; c: Stanford. Chmn, bd, Commercial Elec Co, Toledo, O, since 1968. Capt, US Army Signal Corps, 1942-43. Chmn: UJA, Toledo, 1942; Fla Region, 1950-54; SE region, Technion, 1950-52; gen campaign chmn, Fed J Charities of Palm Beach Co, Fla, 1948-54, pres, 1948-49; mem: natl bd, JDC; J Fed of Palm Beach Co; Amer Legion; Temple Isr, W Palm Beach; Masons; B'nai B'rith. Home: Palm Beach Towers, Palm Beach, Fla. Office: 3300 Summit St, Toledo, O.

GOLDMAN, Paul L, US, attorney; b. Wisoko-Mazowieck, Pol, July 1, 1904; s. Abraham and Esther (Zaremsky); in US since 1920; LLB, St John's U; m. Ruth Katcher, Sep 11, 1928; c: Phyllis Lerner, Tamar Mazor. Pvt practice since 1930. Natl secy: United Lab Zionist Party, Left Poale Zion, 1938-68, world bur since 1950; vice-pres, Poale Zion, United Lab Zionist Org, since 1968; mem exec, J Lab Comm; secy, Natl Comm for Lab Isr, 1945; mem: exec bd, AZC, 1941; Natl Comty Relations Adv Council; presidium, actions comm, WZO, 1951; admn comm, Cong for J Culture, 1948; bd of dirs, J Educ Comm, 1951. Co-ed, Unzer Veg, Poale Zion, NY. Home: 2160 Caton Ave, Brooklyn, NY. Office: 305 Broadway, New York, NY.

GOLDMAN, Philip, US, attorney, jurist; b. Miami, Fla, Nov 10, 1921; s. Nathan and Ida (Fine); BA, U of Fla, 1942; postgrad, O State U, 1943-44; LLB, Harvard U, 1948; m. Sue Searcy, Dec 27, 1953; c: James, Janice, Richard, Robert. Mem, Scott, McCarthy, Steel, Hector & Davis, since 1962; asst atty gen, Fla, 1949-60; gen counsel, Inter-Amer Cen Auth, 1954-60; spec counsel, Dade Co, 1957-58; circuit judge, 1960-62; mem, Fla, State Bd Examiner; vice-pres, Dade Co Bar Assn, USAAC, 1942-46. Pres, Harvard Law Sch Assn of Fla, 1967-68; bd dirs: Family and Children Service; Natl Conf of Bar Examiners; AJComm; pres, Key Biscayne Civic Assn, 1956; mem: Phi Delta Phi; Tau Epsilon Phi; club: SW Kiwanis. Contbr to legal publs. Home: 7730 SW 52 Court, Miami, Fla. Office: 1414 First Natl Bank Bldg, Miami, Fla.

GOLDMAN, Ralph, US, physician, educator; b. NYC, June 11, 1919; s. Henry and May (Hoffman); AB, U of Cal, Berkeley, 1939, MD, 1942; m. Helen Wolfson, Jan 15, 1941; c: Paul, Richard, Elizabeth. Prof, med, UCLA Med Cen, since 1958, cons in med, since 1958; chief, med services, VA Hosp, Sepulveda, 1955-58; chief, metabolic sect, VA Cen, LA, 1951-55. Lt, USNR, 1944-46. Home: 10501 Wilshire Blvd, Los Angeles, Cal. Office: UCLA, Med Sch, Los Angeles, Cal.

GOLDMAN, Ralph I, US, organization exec; b. Russ, Sep 1, 1914; s. Max and Anna (Matzer); in US since 1925; BJE, Boston Heb Coll, 1936; BS, Boston U, 1937, Harvard U, 1938; MS, Boston U, 1941; m. Helen Goldberg, June 30, 1943; c: Judith, David, Naomi. Asso dir gen, Jt Distribution Comm, Malben, since 1969; exec dir, Isr Educ Fund, UJA; publisher, Israel Speaks, NYC; fmr dir, J Comty Cens in Boston, Mass; Canton, O; asso with Isr Consulate Gen, NYC; dir tech assistance dept, PM's Off, Govt of Isr, Jerusalem; cons, Amer Comm for Isr 10th Anniversary, 1957-58; exec vice-pres, Amer-Isr Cultural Found, Inc; exec dir, Isr Educ Fund, 1964-69. US Army, WW II. Offices: 12 Kaplan St, Tel Aviv, Isr; 60 E 42 St, New York, NY.

GOLDMAN, Richard N, US, business exec; b. San Francisco, Apr 16, 1920; s. Richard and Alice (Wertheim); m. Rhoda Haas, Apr June 20, 1946; c: Richard, John, Douglas, Susan. Pres: Richard N Goldman & Co, since 1957; Sierra Capital Co, since 1960. Dir, Grad Theol Union, Berkeley; mem, exec comm, AJComm, since 1961; chmn, JWF drive, 1961; mem: bd dirs, JWF, SF, Marin, and Peninsula; Public Utilities Commn, city and co of SF; vice-pres, Cong Emanu-El, SF,

1961; clubs: Concordia-Argonaut; Lake Merced Golf; Menlo Circus; Stock Exch. Home: 3700 Washington St, San Francisco, Cal. Office: 1 Maritime Plaza, San Francisco, Cal.

GOLDMAN, Robert D, US, artist, teacher; b. Phila, Pa, Jan 24, 1908; s. Moses and Ann (Schumsky); grad, Phila Sch of Ind Art, 1929; BS, Rutgers U, 1933; MA, Columbia U, 1939; att Art Students League, NY, 1934; doctorate courses completed, Temple U; m. Jane Ackerman, Dec 2, 1945; c: Hedva, Michael. Asst dir, div secondary sch, art educ, Phila Public Schs, since 1960; mem, staff, Cheltenham Township Art Cen, since 1940; art tchr: Cleveland Jr HS, Elizabeth, NJ, 1929-35; Barnett Jr HS, 1935-36; Simon Gratz HS, 1936-51; Adult Sch, 1939-45, all Phila; head, dept, fine and ind art, Abraham Lincoln HS, Phila, 1951-60; paintings in numerous collections. Mem: bd mgrs, Art Tchrs Assn, Phila, past pres; bd dirs, Ind Arts Assn of Pa, fmr pres; bd govs, Cheltenham Township Arts Cen; Artists Equity Assn; Phila Art Alliance; Amer Council Ind Art Suprs; Assn for Supervision Curriculum Devl; Amer Assn Ind Arts; Pa Acad Fine Arts; Phila Tchrs Assn; Pa State Tchrs Assn; NEA; Amer, Pa Vocational Assns; Intl Soc for Educ Through Art; Amer Assn Sch Admnrs; Phi Delta Kappa; fmr: mem, council, E Arts Assn; chmn: Sr HS Group Meetings, Natl Art Educ Assn; Comm on Art Educ; HS Group for Research, E Arts Assn, and chmn, research comm; judge, Intl Art Project, ARC, 1961, 1962, 1963. Author: Study, Child Art and Total Growth; ed, Ind-Arts Assn of Pa Newsletter, 1958-59; adv ed, Sch Art Magazine, 1953-65; contbr to profsl publs. Recipient: plaque, Phila Art Tchrs Assn, 1953, 1956; 1st prize, profsl div, Regional Council of Comty Art Cens, 1952; Mary E Marshall Prize, Phila Art Tchrs Assn, 1952, 1954; hon by Phila Art Tchrs Assn with one man shows, Phila Art Alliance, throughout the 60's. Home: 817 Rowland Ave, Cheltenham, Pa. Office: Admn Bldg, Phila Public Schs, 21 and The Parkway, Philadelphia, Pa.

GOLDMAN, Robert P, US, attorney; b. Cincinnati, O, May 17, 1890; s. Louis and Rose (Frohman); AB, Yale U, 1911; LLB, Harvard Law Sch, 1914; att Faculte de Droit, U of Paris, 1919; m. Therese Wolfstein, Oct 16, 1921; c: David, Agnes, Barbara Cohen. Mem, law firm, Paxton & Seasongood since 1923, with firm since 1914; govt appeal agt, Draft Board, Hamilton Co, O, 1940-47; dir: US Shoe Corp; Wolf Machine Co; Merry Mfg Co; Famous Surplus Stores Inc; Hi-Code Trading Corp, and others. Pvt, US Army, WW I. Mem: Cincinnati, O State and Amer Bar Assns; Assn of Bar of NYC; Amer Law Inst, ed bd on uniform commercial code, comm on continuing legal educ; fmr: pres: Cincinnati JCC; Isaac M Wise Temple; Cincinnati Bar Assns; Proportional Representation League; UAHC, trustee; vice-pres, dir, Fgn Policy Assn; chmn: Cincinnati Charter Rev Commn; dir: bd: City Charter Comm; legal aid comm, O State Bar Assn, comm on banking and commercial law; U Sch of Cincinnati; Cincinnati Council on World Affairs; HUC-JIR, chmn bd, mem, bd govs; co-chmn, NCCJ; trustee: Cleveland Orphan Home; O State Archaeol & Hist Soc; Legal Aid Soc; clubs: Losantiville Country; U; Cincinnati Lawyers; Yale, NY. Co-ed, Anderson's Ohio Corporation Desk Book, 1951, 1956; contbr to legal jours. Home: 5300 Hamilton Ave, Cincinnati, O. Office: Central Trust Tower, Cincinnati, O.

GOLDMAN, Rose S, US, communal worker; b. St Joseph, Mo, Jan 28, 1893; d. Herman and Anna (Horwitz) Saferstein; m. Samuel Goldman, Jan 11, 1925; c: Janice Cohen, Zelda Rich. Bd mem, United J Fund, since 1960; exec secy, Fed J Charities, 1944-60; organized: Hadassah, 1916, pres, 1916-18, 1920-22, 1926-29; ZOA, 1918, vice-pres, mem, exec comm, 1920-23; delg, Mo and Kan, first AJCong, Phia, Pa, 1918; firt pres: SW region, Hadassah, 1926; dist capt, ARC drives, WW I and II. Mem: Temple B'nai Sholem Sisterhood; Hadassah; B'nai B'rith Women; Temple Adath Joseph Sisterhood; Mo Assn for Social Wfr. Home: 2208 Francis St, St Joseph, Mo.

GOLDMAN, Simon, US, radio exec; b. Carthage, NY, Jan 18, 1913; s. Isaac and Ida (Slavin); BS, magna cum laude, Syracuse U, 1935; m. Meurice Finer, Jan 4, 1948; c: Richard, Gail, Paul. Gen Mgr, Station WJTN, WJTN-FM, since 1940; pres: James Bc Co, since 1955; Lake Shore Bc, Dunkirk, NY, since 1957; WGGO Radio, Salamanca, NY, since 1959; WERC, Eric-Pa, since 1961; WVMT, Burlington, Vt, since 1963; WTOO, Belle Fontance, O, since 1968; Job Operations; merchandising mgr, WSYR, Syracuse, 1936-37. Chmn, bd trustees, Jamestown Comty Coll; Fenton Hist Soc; mem: bd dirs: Comty Broadcasters Assn; Jamestown Devl, Natl Assn of Broadcasters; radio-TV adv comm, NY State Dept of Commerce; adv bd, ABC; fmr pres, Cong Temple Hesed Abraham; pres, Syracuse U Alumni; bd dirs: C of C; Concert Assn; Little Theatre; Chautauqua Co Fair Assn; YMCA; Chautauqua council, Boy Scouts of Amer; ADL, W NY, NY State; mem, AM radio com, 1950, chmn, 1951; dir, Radio Advt Bur 1951-58, finance comm, 1956, chmn by-laws comm, 1957-58, bd dirs, membership comm, both 1959; mem: Legion Mt Moriah Lodge; Jamestown Consistory, Ishmailia Temple; Citizens Comm; Chautauqua Co Heart Comm; clubs: Jamestown Shrine; Chautauqua Lake Yacht; Moonbrook Country; Kiwanis; Advt and Sales, vice-pres. Hobbies: golf, badminton, sailing, Home: 71 Gordon St, Jamestown, NY. Office: Hotel Jamestown Bldg, Jamestown, NY.

GOLDMANN, Nahum, Isr, statesman, communal leader; b. Wisnewo, Pol, July 10, 1895; s. Salomon and Rebecca (Kwint); att: U Marburg, 1914; U Berlin, 1915; JD, U Heidelberg, 1920; PhD, 1921; m. Alice Gottschalk, Dec 19, 1934; c: Michael, Guido. Pres, WJC; mem, Zionist Actions Comm since 1927, fmr acting chmn, mem Zionist exec, repr of JA for Pal to L of N; Pres, WZC since 1951; fmr co-found, chmn exec; pres, World Zionist Org 1956-68; fmr: negotiator with British Fgn Off and US Dept of State; repr to UN; chmn, Amer sect, JA for Pal; one of two chmn, Exec of World Zionist Org, and JA for Pal since 1951; pres: Conf of J Material Claims Against Ger, since 1951; chmn, J Claims on Aus, since 1953; fmr: org, World J Conf, Geneva; initiator: and signatory of J-Isr agreement with W Ger Govt, Luxembourg, 1952; Law of Status for Zionist Movement adopted by Knesset, 1952. Hon pres, Ency Judaica, NYC since 1960; pres, Judaica Found, Geneva since 1960; co-found, Eshkol Publ Co, Berlin, 1922-34. Author: Reisebriefe aus Palaestina, 1913; N.G. Autobiography, 1969; contbr essays and articles to Ger, Heb, Yiddish, Eng periodicals. Recipient, Officier de la Legion d'Honneur, Fr. Homes: 18 Ahad Ha'am St, Jerusalem; 12 Ave Montaigne, Paris, Fr.

GOLDMANN, Sidney, US, jurist; b. Trenton, NJ, Nov 29, 1903; s. Samuel and Stella (Reich); BS, magna cum laude, Harvard Coll, 1924; LLB, Harvard Law Sch, 1927; m. Beatrice Corosh, Nov 20, 1938; c: Donald. Sr judge, Appellate Div, Superior Court of NJ, since 1951; city atty, acting city mgr, Trenton, 1935-39; exec secy to Gov Charles Edison, 1942-44; state libr, 1944-47; state archivist and hist, 1947-49, all in NJ. Mem: natl exec and admn bds, AJComm; mem, natl exec bds; JWB, CJFWF; bd of dirs, fmr pres: Council on Hum Relations; Council of Social Agcys; J Family Ser; J Fed; Hist Soc, all Trenton; bd, J Comty Cen; Har Sinai Temple, chmn, Centennial celebration, both Trenton; Supr Court Rules Comm, NJ Comm on Rev of Statutes, 1950-51; Mercer Co, NJ State and Amer Bar Assns; Inst of Judicial Admn; Amer J Tercentenary Comm; Amer J Hist Soc; NJ Hist Soc; NJ Constitutional Conv Assn. Author: The Organization and Administration of the New Jersey Highway Department, 1942; Proceedings of the NJ Constitutional Convention of 1947, pub, 1951; contbr to Hist of Trenton, 1929. Home: 101 Renfrew Ave, Trenton, NJ. Office: State House Annex, Trenton, NJ.

GOLDNER, Bernard Burton, US, educator, consultant; b. Phila, Pa, Aug 1, 1919; s. Samuel and Katherine (Kline); BA, U of Pa, Phila, 1940, MA, 1943, PhD, 1949; m. Isabelle Frankel, July 6, 1924; c: Lawrence, Wendy. Prof, cons, chmn, ind dept, LaSalle Coll, Phila, since 1948; dir, Sch of Creative Thinking; teaching asst, U of Pa, 1941-43; training sup, VA, 1946-48; cons: US Depts: Agric; HEW; Signal Corps; Civil Service Commn; Natl Inves Council; Health, State of Pa. Capt, US Army, quartermaster corps, 1943-46. Chmn: Pa Small Bus Adv Council; Amer Arbitration Assn; Soc for Advancement of Mgmt; AJA; mem, Alpha Epsilon; hon mem, Pi Gamma Mu; fmr mem, Natl Inventors Council. Author, Strategy of Creative Thinking, 1962; records, creative thinking in ind; contbr to ind jours. Hobbies: gardening, philately. Home: 4026 MacNiff Drive, Lafayette Hill, Pa. Office: 20 St & Olney Ave, Philadelphia, Pa.

GOLDNER, Martin G, US, physician, medical sci, educator; b. Berlin, Ger, July 1, 1902; s. Salo and Seraphine (Cohn); in US since 1938; MD, U of Frankfurt/M, 1927; m. Elisabeth Baumann, 1932; c: Andrew. Dir, med, J Hosp and Med Cen, Bklyn, NY; prof, med, SUNY Downstate Med Cen; asst phys, U of Berlin, II Med Clinic Charite, 1927-33; dir, Waldpark Sanitarium for Metabolic Diseases, Baden-Baden, Ger,

1934-38; asst prof, med, U of Chic, 1943-47; clinical asst prof, U of Colo, Sch of Med, 1947-50; dir, med research, Fort Logan, Colo, 1947-50; chief, med service, VA Hosp, Bklyn, 1950-52; dir, med, J Chronic Disease Hosp, 1952-61. Capt, US Army MC, 1944-46. Pres, NY Diabetes Assn; f: Amer Coll of Phys; AAAS; Amer Diabetes Assn; dipl, Amer Bd of Internal Med; mem: AMA; Endocrine Soc; Soc Experimental Biol and Med. Author: two books, contbr to med jours. Recipient: Johann-Wolfgang Goethe Prize, U of Frankfurt/M, 1962; hon prof of med, U of Puebla, Mex, 1954. Spec interests: J philosophy, med history. Home: 350 Central Park W, New York, NY. Office: 555 Prospect Place, Brooklyn, NY.

GOLDOFTAS, Movsas, US, educator; b. Visoka Ruda, Lith, Mar 25, 1892; s. Meyer and Freide (Bellman); in US since 1940; ordained rabbi, Knesset Beth Yitzchak Sem, Slabodka, and Heb Real Gymnasia, Kaunas, both in Lith, 1917; tchrs dipl, Tchrs Sem, Vilna and Lith Tchrs Coll, Mariampole, both in Lith, 1919-1927; m. Sulamis Chwoles, Oct 8, 1920; c: Tobi. Instr, Heb, Midrasha Coll for J Studies, Detroit, since 1967; secy, city comm, Farband Lab Zionist Order, since 1967; tchr: Heb-Yiddish Sch, Rokishkis, Lit, 1920-21; Yiddishe Gymnasia, Wilkomiz, Lith, 1921-28; Tarbut Sch, Kybartai, Lith, 1925-29; secy-gen, Union Zionist, Brussels, Belg, 1933-40; instr, Haim Greenberg Heb-Yiddish Sch, Detroit, 1941-66. Pres, Farband Br 114, Detroit, 1943-47; secy, Farband Lab Zionist Order, Detroit; treas, ZC, Detroit, 1966-68; mem: Comty Council, Metrop Detroit; JNF, 1941-69; LZOA; Heb Tchrs Union; public lectr, J and Heb Lit, Bible and Hist. Author: Jewish Life in Lithuania; contbr to profsl jours. Recipient: Sabbatical Year in Isr, Haim Greenberg Heb-Yiddish Sch, 1966; Medal from Pres of Lith. Home: 18041 Schaefer St, Detroit, Mich. Office: 19161 Schaefer St, Detroit, Mich.

GOLDOWSKY, Seebert Jay, US, physician; b. Providence, RI, June 6, 1907; s. Bernard and Antoinette (Lotary); BA, summa cum laude, Brown U, 1928; MD, Harvard U Med Sch, 1932; m. Gertrude Nisson, June 25, 1942. Pvt practice, gen surg, since 1936; cons, surg: Miriam Hosp, Providence, RI, fmr, surg-in-chief; RI Hosp, Providence, past dir, peripheral vascular clinic; Charles V Chapin Hosp, Providence, RI; Roger Williams Gen Hosp. Capt, US Army, 1942-45. F, Amer Coll of Surgs; cert, Amer Bd Surg; pres council, New Eng State Med Socs; mem: bd dirs: Blue Shield, RI; League of RI Hist Socs; house delgs, RI Med Soc; Providence Surg Soc; and alternate delg, AMA; RI Med Soc; Providence Med Assn; Med Hist Soc; RI Hist Soc; RI J Hist Assn; Intl Cardiovascular Soc, N Amer chap; med adv, RI Blue Cross; fmr: pres: Miriam Hosp Staff Assn; Providence Surg Soc. Ed-in-chief, RI Medical Jour; ed, RI J Hist Notes; contbr to med and gen publs. Recipient: SW Pacific ribbon, with 3 combat stars; Unit Citation. Spec interests: RI med and J hist. Home: 458 Wayland Ave, Providence, RI. Office: 209 Angell St, Providence, RI.

GOLDRING, Gvirol Benjamin, Isr, physicist; b. Frankfurt/M, Ger, Feb 6, 1926; s. Pessah and Dora (Seligman); in Isr since 1933; MSc, Heb U Jerusalem, 1949; PhD, DSc, Imperial Coll of Sci and Tech, London, 1953; m. Hanna Kohn, Mar 25, 1950; c: Alon, Pessah, Noa. Head, Heinemann Accelerator Lab, since 1964, prof physics, Weizmann Inst of Sci, since 1965. IDF, 1948-49. Contbr to profsl jours. Hobby, piano playing. Office: Weizmann Inst of Sci, Rehovot, Isr.

GOLDSCHEIDER, Calvin, US, educator; b. Baltimore, Md, May 28, 1941; s. Albert and Minnie (Kessler); BA, cum laude, Yeshiva U, 1961, BRE, cum laude, Tchrs Inst, 1961; MA, Brown U, Providence, RI, 1963, PhD, 1964; m. Barbara Grossman, Aug 27, 1961; c: Judah, Avigaiyil. Asst prof, sociol: U of Cal, Berkeley, since 1966; U of S Cal, 1964-66; Natl Defense f, Brown U, 1961-64; f, Intl Union for Sci Study of Population, 1967. Mem: bd offs: Beth Isr Cong, Berkeley; Cong Mishkan Tfilch, 1962-64; Planned Parenthood, Alameda Co, 1966-68; Amer Sociol Assn; Pacific Sociol Assn; Population Assn of Amer; Phi Beta Kappa. Author: Jewish Americans, 1968; ed bd: Demography; Sociology and Social Research; Jours of Gerontology; Social Problems; Marriage and the Family; contbr to profsl jours. Recipient, Valedictory Award, Tchrs Inst, Yeshiva U, 1961. Home: 1343 Carlotta Ave, Berkeley, Cal. Office: Dept of Sociol, U of Cal, Berkeley, Cal.

GOLDSCHMIDT, Alexis B H, Belgium, attorney; b. Brussels, Belgium, Dec 31, 1910; s. Alfred and Marguerite (Brodsky);

D en droit, licencié en sci financières, Free U, Brussels; m. Karoline Von Ferstel, June 14, 1938; c: Pierre, Antoinette. Atty, Court of Appeals, since 1933; pres: Ateliers Demoor; Anciennes Usines Montefiore, both since 1953; active mem, Lib Party; fmr, cabinet chief to vice-pres, Council of Mins. Belgium Army, 1930-31; POW, 1940-45. Pres: Belgium sec, WJC; Action Comm for Isr; fmr pres: Friends of Fr Lang; Fonds des Prets D'Etudes. Author: under pen name Pierre Algaux: Nuits Sur Les Branches, 1948; De L'Art Moderne, from Paul Klee, 1948; co-found, Fr review, Romain, 1951; ed, Progres, quarterly, 1965-68. Recipient, Croix de Guerre, 1945. Hobby: theatre. Home and office: 26 Du Regent Blvd, Brussels, Belgium.

GOLDSCHMIDT, Alfredo Salomon, Arg, rabbi; b. Buenos Aires, Arg, Aug 4, 1945; s. German and Elsa (Rosenfelder); ordained rabbi, Neir Isr, rabb coll, MEd, Loyola, 1968; m. Raquel Fresco, Mar 14, 1965; c: Deborah, Azriel. Prin, Colegio Integral Rav José Caro, youth rabbi, Asociacion Religiosa since 1968; youth dir, Pirchei of Baltimore, 1965-68; perm contbr on J problems: Seminario Israelita; Raices, since 1969; mem bd, Educ Material, Arg J Comm; spokesman, Amer J Comm for Orthodox Judaism. Home: 2532 Monroe St, Buenos Aires, Arg. Study: 2449 Moldes St, Buenos Aires, Arg.

GOLDSCHMIDT, Daniel, Isr, librarian, author; b. Konigshutte, Ger, Dec 9, 1895; s. Salomon and Rahel (Fraenkel); in Isr since 1936; att Breslau U, 1914-15; PhD Berlin U, 1924; m. Hannah Steinfeld, 1928; c: Emilie Weil, Eva Fraenkel. Ret, fmr: libr: Natl and U Libr, Jerusalem, 1936-62; libr, Prussian St Libr; served Ger Army, 1916-18. Author: Studia Aeschinea, 1924; Haggada shel Pesach, with commentary in Ger, 1936; in Heb, 1948; History of Haggada, 1960; Selihot, Lith rite, with Heb commentary, 1965; Selihot, Polish rite, with Heb commentary, 1965; Kinot l'Tisha beav, with Heb commentary, 1968; ed, S D Luzzatto, Mavo l'Mahzor Roma, with annotation, 1966; contbr to local and fgn publs. Spec interest: J lithurgy. Home: 3 Ha'ari St, Jerusalem, Isr.

GOLDSCHMIDT, Hermann Levin, Switz, author; b. Berlin, Ger, Apr 11, 1914; s. Robert and Irene (von Goldschmidt) Levin; PhD, U of Zurich, 1941; m. Mary Bollag, 1962. Dir, Jüdisches Lehrahaus, Zurich, public courses devoted to J learning. Author: Des Geist der Erziehung bei Jeremias Gotthelf, 1939; Der Nihilismusim Licht einer kritischen Philosophie, 1941; Ein Jahrhundert Ringen um Jüdische Wirklichkeit; Hermann Cohen und Martin Buber, 1946; Philosophie als Dialogik, 1948; Veroffentlichungen des Jüdischen Lehrhauses Zurich, vols I-IX, 1951-61; Das Vermachtnis des deutschen Judentums, 1957, 3rd ed, 1965; Dialogik, Philosophie auf dem Boden der Neuzeit, 1964; Abschied von Martin Buber, 1966; Die Botschaft des Judentums, 1960. Recipient, Leo Baeck Award from Zentralrat der Juden in Deutschland, 1957. Home: 9 Balgristotr, 8008, Zurich Switz.

GOLDSCHMIDT, Leontine, US, scientist; b. Arad, Aus, Mar 9, 1913; s. Maximillian and Anna (Michel); in US since 1939; PhM, U of Vienna, 1935, PhD, 1937. Sr research sci, biochem labs, Creedmoor Inst of Psychobiol Studies; asso research sci, NY State Dept of Mental Hygiene since 1965; dir, biochem research since 1954; research asst, Boston U Sch of Med, 1942-45; research biol, USN Radiological Defense Lab, SF, Cal, 1947-50. Prin contribs: study of effects of irradiation and biol aging on red blood cells; biochem of mental illness. F: Amer Chem Soc; AAAS; NY Acad of Scis; Amer Assn of Clinical Chems. Contbr to profsl jours. Hobby, hist of art, especially Byzantine. Home and office: POB 40, Station 60, Creedmoor State Hosp, Queens Village, Ny.

GOLDSCHMIDT, Martin J, Isr, engineer, hydrologist; b. Hamburg, Ger, Nov 26, 1893; s. Levy and Johanna (Heinemann); in Isr since 1923; grad, Tech HS, Braunschweig, Ger, 1916; dipl ing, Tech HS, Munich, Ger, 1920; m. Gertrud Kochmann, Feb 1, 1924; c: Shulamit Blumenthal, Ya'aqov. Hon sci adv to Water Commn of Isr since 1959; fmr: structural engr, Tel Aviv, Jerusalem; water supply engr, Tel Aviv Munic; cons engr; irrigation insp, Dept of Devl, Govt of Pal; irrigation off, Water Commnr's Off; dir, hydrological service, Water Commn, Isr Min of Agric, ret 1958; hydrometeorology expert, World Meteorological Org, assigned to Turkish St Meteorological Service; lectr, hydrology: Technion, Haifa; Heb U; Jerusalem; MEU, Turkey; seminar on groundwater hydrology, Servicio Geologico, Ministerio de Obras Públicas, Madrid; hon adv for hydrology, Water Commnr, Isr Min of Agric.

Prin contrib: found, hydrological research of Pal, 1925-26. Hon secy, Isr intl comm for Intl Hydrological Decade, mem Isr natl commn; mem: Assn of Engrs and Architects in Isr; Intl Union of Geodesy and Geophysics, past off of Union, past pres; Isr Geol Soc; Isr Oriental Soc. Contbr on hydrological subjects. Hobbies: archaeol, music, violin, gardening, walking. Home: 34 Ha'bannai St, Jerusalem, Isr.

GOLDSCHMIDT, Robert, Switz, educator; b. Cologne, Ger, Apr 3, 1902; s. Albert and Elisabeth (Schoenbeck); in Switz since 1933; att U Cologne, 1920; dipl ing, Polytech Sch, Karlsruhe, 1924; m. Elsy Schoemann, Dec 27, 1934; c: Annette Rochaix, Mariette Boyle. Prof, telecommunications, Ecole, Polytechnique, Fédérale, Lausanne, since 1947; engr cons, S A des Câbleries et Trefileries Cossonay (Gare), since 1933; engr, Telefunken, Berlin, 1924; asst chief, lab telecommunications, AEG, Berlin, 1924-33. Prin contbr: invention of new magnetic materials. Mem: profsl Swiss socs; Amer Inst EE; past mem, presidential comm, J Comty of Lausanne 1956-62. Contbr to profsl publs. Home: 115 Ave CF Ramuz, Pully, Lausanne, Switz. Office: Ecole Polytechnique Fédérale, Lausanne, Switz.

GOLDSCHMIDT, Stefan, W Ger, organic chem, educator; b. Nurnberg, Mar 26, 1889; s. Issy and Ida (Levi); PhD, U of Munich, 1912; m. Maria Eisenmenger, July 31, 1920; c: Eleonore Theil, Helga Hose, Ursula Paul. Ret, 1957; prof chem, dir, Inst of Organic Chem, Technische Hochschule, Munich; fmr: privat-dozent, U of Wuerzburg, 1919; prof: Technische Hochschule, Karlsruhe 1923-35; Pharmaceutical Ind in the Netherlands, 1938-47. Mem: Gesellschaft Deutscher Chemiker; Bayer, Akademie der Wissenschaften; Akademie der Wissenschaften, Heidelberg. Contbr on organic and biol chem. Home: Verdistrasse 24, Munich, W Ger.

GOLDSCHMIED, Alexander, Isr, physician, educator; b. Cracow, Pol, 1906; s. Yaacov and Frimet; in Isr since 1957; MD, Cracow U, 1930; m. Miriam Czarny. Dir, rehab, geriatr cen, Tel Aviv U; fmr: rector, Med Acad, Lodz, Pol; prof, Med Acad, Warsaw; dir, Hadassah Hosp, 1957-70. Contbr of articles on internal diseases. Home: 3 Reiness St, Tel Aviv, Isr. Office: Tel Aviv U, Tel Aviv, Isr.

GOLDSHMIDT, Bertrand L, Fr, atomic scientist; b. Paris, Nov 2, 1912; s. Paul and Marcelle (Dreyfus); ChemE, Sch of Physics and Chem, Paris, 1933; DS, U of Paris, 1939; m. Naomi de Rothschild, Feb 27, 1947. Chief, external relations and gen planning, Fr AEC, since 1959, chief, chem div, 1946-59, asst, Curie Lab, Paris, 1934-40; mem staff, Dept Sci and Ind Research, Gt Brit, 1942-46; head, chem div, British-Can Atomic Energy Project, Montreal and Chalk River, Can, 1946; tech adv, Fr delg to UN AEC, 1946-48; prof, Inst of Political Studies, U of Paris, 1960. Mem, UN Sci Adv Comm, 1955; Fr repr, bd govs, Intl Atomic Energy Agcy, 1957. Home: 11 Blvd Flandrin, Paris, Fr. Office: 29 rue de la Fédération, Paris, Fr.

GOLDSMITH, Edward I, US, surgeon; b. Far Rockaway, NY, Nov 13, 1927; s. Abraham and Gertrude (Epstein); AB, Cornell U, 1947; MD, 1950; m. Gene Louise French, Aug 29, 1952; c: Joel, Jeremy, William, David (decd), Daniel. Clinical asso prof surg, Cornell U, since 1966, on staff since 1954; asso att surg, NY Hosp since 1964, on staff since 1950; asst surg, U Colo Med Sch, 1957-58; chief, Organ Transplantation Prog, NY Hosp, 1963-68. US Army MC, 1952-54. Prin contrbs: research in blood flow, open heart surg, x-ray visualization of blood vessels; organ transplantation; surg treatment of Schistosomiasis by extracorporal hemofiltration. Bd dirs, Nassau Cen for Emotionally Disturbed Children, pres since 1961; chmn, comm for Sci for Use of Primates in Med Research; chmn, Utilization Bd, Lab for Experimental Med and Surg in Primates, NYU Med; dipl, Amer Bd Surg; Med Soc Co of NY; AAAS; NY Acad of Scis; NY Acad of Med; adv comm to Jt Leg Comm on Mental Retardation and Phys Handicaps of NY State; mem: Amer Coll Surgs; NY Surg Soc; NY Soc Cardio-Vascular Surg; AMA; AHA; Amer Soc for Artificial Internal Organs; The Transplantation Soc; Intl Primatological Soc; Amer Soc of Tropical Med and Hygiene; Royal Soc of Tropical Med and Hygiene. Honors: Merit Medal of Philippines, 1968. Contrb to profsl jours. Recipient: sr research f, NY Heart Assn, 1959-60. Home: Ridge Rd, Katonah, NY. Office: 525 E 68 St, New York, NY.

GOLDSMITH, Eli D, US, educator, b. NYC, Apr 10, 1907; s. Morris and Rose; BS, CCNY, 1926; MA, Harvard U,

1928; PhD, 1934; MS, NYU, 1930; m. Gertrude Alper; c: Cathy. Prof, histology, NYU Grad Sch of Arts and Sci and the Coll of Dent, since 1948, acting dir, Off of Research Services, NYU; lab instr, 1929-31, asst prof, anat, 1945-47; asst prof, histology, 1947-48; asso prof, 1948-51; training dir, Research-Teacher Grad Training Prog, USPHS since 1959; asst, zool, Harvard U, 1928-29, 1931-33, Austin teaching f, 1933-34; instr, CCNY, 1934-45, i/c sci survey courses, Sch of Bus, 1935-40; instr, chem, Army Spec Training Prog, 1942-44; bio-med research coord, Off of Naval Research, NY, 1951-53; cons, Surg Gen, USPHS; mem: Prog-Project Comm, Natl Inst, Dent Research; Research Career Comm, Natl Inst Gen Med Scis, USPHS; F and grants: Harvard U; Marine Biol Lab, Woods Hole, Mass, 1932; Bermuda Biol Sta, 1934; Commonwealth Fund, 1944; Elizabeth Thompson Fund, 1944, 1946; USPHS since 1947; Amer Cancer Soc, 1951-56. Secy treas: Intl Assn Dent Research, NY sect since 1955; f: AAAS; Gerontological Soc; NY Acad Scis; Amer Coll of Dents, Royal Microscopial Soc, Eng; asso f, NY Acad Med; hon mem, Amer Acad Dent Med; mem: The Harvey Soc; Entomological Soc Amer; Aero Assn Cancer Research; Amer Assn Anats; Amer Soc for Zools; Amer Microscopical Soc; Amer Soc for Naturalists; Amer Phys Soc; Amer Chem Soc; Endocrine Soc; Soc Experimental Biol and Med; Soc for Study of Devl and Growth; Bermuda Biol Sta; Amer Inst, NYC; Phi Beta Kappa, Sigma Xi; Beta Lambda Sigma. Co-author, Laboratory Directions in Histology, 1948; co-ed, monograph, Influence of Hormones on Enzymes, NY Acad Scis, 1951; contbr to med and sci jours. Office: NYU, 421 First Ave, New York, NY.

GOLDSMITH, Lee Selig, US, attorney; b. NYC, Nov 18, 1939; s. Isadore and Elsie (Friedman); BS, NYU, 1960; MD, NYU Sch of Med, 1964; LLB, NYU Sch of Law, 1967; m. Arlene Applebaum, Oct 6, 1962; c: Ian. Pvt practice since 1970; asso, Speiser, Shumate, Geoghan, Krause & Rheinfold, 1967-70. Chmn: legal comty, Amer Coll of Legal Med; sub comty Med Mal, Assn of the Bar of NYC; mem, AMA, NY St & Co Med Socs, Aerospace Med Assn; Amer Trial Lawyers Assn. Author, Hospital Liability Law, 1970; med legal ed, Phys Mgt Mag; contbr to legal jours. Hobby: writing, tennis. Home: 316 Lantana Ave, Englewood, NJ. Office: 11 E 44 St, New York, NY.

GOLDSMITH, Ledter M, US, consulting engineer; b. Pottsville, Pa, July 1, 1893; s. George ans Sarah (Rohrheimer); EE, Drexel Inst of Tech, 1914, DS, 1942; m. Florence Frankel, June 26, 1921; C: George, Richard Yohn. Gen mgr, engr and construction dept, Atlantic Refining Co, 1951-58, with co since 1916; dir, vice-pres, chief engr, Atlantic Pipe Line Co, since 1929; hief engr; Keystone Pipe Line Co, Buffalo Pipe Line; Phila Tankers Inc. Expert cons, US War Dept, 1943; presently cons to US Army. F: Amer Inst of Elec Engrs; Amer Soc of Mech Engrs; mem: Amer Petroleum Inst; Amer Soc of Naval Engrs; Amer Welding Soc; Soc of Automotive Engrs; Soc of Naval Architects and Marine Engrs, Brit Inst of Mech Engrs; C of C; Franklin Inst; Amateur Cinema League; bd of trustees, Natl Agric Coll; Pi Tau Sigma; clubs: Engineers, Phila. Contbr to profslsmags. Recipient Melville Medal, 1939; exceptional civilian service medal, US War Dept, 1947; Pres Cert of merit, 1948; Meritorious Civilian Service Medal, 1957. Hobby, photography. Home: 1012 W Upsal St, Philadelphia, Pa. Office: 846 Land Title Bldg, Philadelphia, Pa.

GOLDSMITH, Raymond W, US, economist, educator; b. Brussels, Belgium, Dec 23, 1904; s. Alfred and Camilla (Marcus); in US since 1930; PhD, U of Berlin, 1927; att LSE, 1933; m. Selma Fine, May 17, 1939 (decd); c. Jane, Donald, Paul. Prof, econ, Yale U, since 1960; mem, research staff. Natl Bur Econ Research, since 1952; chief, research, sect, US SEC, 1938-41; econ, War Production Bd, 1942-44; dir, planning div, 1944-47; mem, US Govt Mission, Ger Currency Reform, 1946; US Econ Adv, Aus Treaty Negotiations, 1947; NYU, 1958-60; vice-pres, OECD Devl Cen, Paris, 1963-65. Author: Kapitalpolitik, 1933; Changing Structure of American Banking, 1933; A Study of Saving in the US, 1955; Financial Intermediaries, 1958; The National Wealth of the US, 1962; Studies in the National Balance Sheet of the US, 1963; Flow of Capital Fund in Post War Economy, 1965; Financial Structure and Development, 1969. Home: 111 Park St, New Haven, Conn. Office: Yale U, New Haven, Conn.

GOLDSMITH, Stanley, US, business exec; b. Charleston, SC

Dec 30,1915; s. Edward and Lillian (Maas); att Geo Wash U, Wash, DC, 1941-42; BS, U of Ala, 1948; m. Irma Brown, Aug 23, 1946; c: Stanley, Henry. Controller, Ajax Hardware Mfg Corp since 1959; controller, Wesco Merchandise Corp, 1931-39. Maj, US Army, 1942-64. Mem: CPAs, Cal; Elks, Selma, Ala; Masons, Demopolis, Ala; C of C, City of Industry, Cal. Recipient, Bronze Star. Spec interest: Athletics, woodworking. Home: 1111 E Woodcrest Ave, La Habra, Cal. Office: 825 S Ajax Ave, City of Industry, Cal.

GOLDSMITH, Werner, US, educator, engineering cons; b. Dusseldorf, Ger, May 23, 1924; s. Siegfried and Margarete (Grunewald) Goldschmidt; in US since 1938; BS, ME, U of Tex, 1944; MS, ME, 1945; att: U of Pittsburgh, 1945-46; U of Pa, 1946-47; PhD,U of Cal, 1949; m. 1961; div. c: Stephen, Andrea. Engr cons, prof applied mech, U of Cal, since 1960, instr, 1947-49, asst prof, 1949-55, asso prof, 1955-60; cons, US Bur of Mines; mech engr, US Naval Ordnance Test Station, China Lake since 1951; engr, Westinghouse Elec Corp, 1945-47; lectr, U of Pittsburgh, 1945-46; instr, U of Pa, 1946; cons, Army Corps of Engrs, 1951-53; Guggenheim f, 1953-54. Chmn, head injury model construction comm, Natl Inst of Neur Diseases and stroke; mem: Amer Soc ME; Soc for Experimental Stress Analysis; Hillel Found; Amer Contract Bridge League; Tau Beta Pi; Sigma Xi. Author: monograph, Impact, 1960; contrb to profsl jours. Home: 450 Gravatt Dr, Berkeley, Cal. Office: U of Cal, Berkeley, Cal.

GOLDSTAJN, Alexander, Yugo, jurist, educator; b. Vinkovci, July 15, 1912; s. Armin and Rosa (Veinmann); LLD, U of Zagreb 1938; m. Sep 23, 1934; c: Ruth, Milivoj. Prof, dean fac law, U of Zagreb; pres, court of Honor, Federal C of C; mem: Constitutional Court of Croatia; state Legal Council; fmr: pres, Supr Court, Yugo; legal expert for intl trade. Pres, legal comm, Fed C of C; vice-pres, Fed Fgn Trade Arbitration; arbitrator, Court of Arbitration, Intl Chamber of Trade, Paris; pres, Fed Assn U Profs of Yugo; mem, exec comm, World Assn of Judges; fmr pres, Supr Econ Court, Yugo. Author: Compendium of Decisions of the Federal Arbitration Court with Comments, 7 vols, Administration of Economie Organizations, 1959; The New Law Merchant, 1961; International Conventions and Standard Contracts as Means of Escaping from the Application of Municipal Law, 1962; Law on International Sale of Goods, vol 1, 1963, vol II, 1965; Commercial Contracts, 1967; State Acts and Foreign Trade Contracts; mem, ed bd, Jour of Business Law, London; contbr to profsl publs in Yugo, to fgn jours. Office: Marsala Tita 14, Zagreb, Yugo.

GOLDSTEIN, Aaron, Isr, contractor; b. Russ, Dec 19, 1902; in Isr since 1921; m. Miriam Matz. Contractor, mgn dir, Goldstein Bros, bldg contractors; cen comm, Lib Party; MK, natl comm. Pres, Fed Bldg Contractor Assns in Isr; past chmn, local comm, Borochov Qtr; mem, KH. Contbr of articles on educ, munic topics to Heb press. Home: 1 Bet Ha'shoeva St, Givatayim, Isr. Office: 18-20 Mikve Israel St, Tel Aviv, Isr.

GOLDSTEIN, Aaron M, US, business exec; b. NYC, Dec 28, 1887; s. Moses F and Gertrude (Neuberger); hon PhD, Paul Grimm Coll; m. Leonore Hirschberg, Nov 15, 1916; c: Stephen. Pres, chmn bd, Goldstein-Migel Co since 1946, past secy, secy-treas, vice pres, dir; dir, First Fed Savings and Loan Assn since 1942; City Commnr since 1932, past Mayor Pro-tem, both Waco, Tex; dir, Fed Res Bank of Dallas, Pres, J Fed since 1961; dir, YMCA since 1950, trustee since 1952, all Waco, Tex; mem, Masons, 33 deg; Shriners; Scottish Rite Bodies; fmr: dir: Gtr Waco United Fund; Waco C of C; pres: adv bd, Salvation Army; Tex Retail Dry Goods Assn; Temple Rodef Shalom; gen chmn, expansion campaign, Hillcrest Hosp; chmn: ARC; Navy League, WW II, both McLennan Co; dir, Waco Boys Club; mem budget comm, United Comty Funds and Councils of Amer; trustee, Waco Comty Chest; clubs: Rotary, Ridgewood Country; City, Waco. Recipient: Keystone Award of Boys Club of Amer, 1949; citation, City of Waco, 1964. Home: 1824 Austin Ave, Waco, Tex. Office: Amicable Bldg, Waco, Tex.

GOLDSTEIN, Abe, US, merchant; b. Atlanta, Ga, Aug 28, 1898. Chmn bd: Prior Tire Co; Delta Air Conditioning and Heating; pres Atlanta Tire Dealers. Hon pres: Southeast Bd, ADL; Atlanta J Home for Aged; Gate City Lodge, B'nai B'rith; pres, Atlanta J Wlf Assn; mem: Gov's Staff, under past three govs; bd of overseers, JTSA; vice-pres, J Children's

Service; life mem, Elks; hon life mem, Alpha Epsilon Phi; hon life commnr, Natl ADL; hon life mem, Jr C of C; past pres: J Cmty Council; clubs: Standard; Progressive; Commerce. Recipient: Man-of-the-Year, B'nai B'rith; Eternal Light Award, JTSA; Isr Bond Award; Man-of-the-Year, JWV; Brotherhood Award, NCCJ; in 1966, Annual Abe Goldstein Humanitarian Award, ADL. Home: 1621 Harvard Rd, NE, Atlanta, Ga. Office: 458 Peachtree St, NE, Atlanta, Ga.

GOLDSTEIN, Abraham C, US, attorney; b. New York, NY, Nov 15, 1896; s. Max and Mary (Goldman); LLB, Albany Law Sch, Union U; m. Satie Grotsky, June 17, 1923; c: Donald, Marjorie Lindy. Police justice, City of Troy, NY, 1962. Pres: Beth El Cong Brotherhood, 1939-42; Beth El Cong, 1952-54; Rensselaer Co Bar Assn, 1940-42; treas: Troy Council of Social Agencies, 1937-39; mem-at-large, bd delgs, AJComm; mem: Amer, NY State, Rensselaer Co Bar Assns; Amer Cancer Soc; Elks; Amer Legion. Home: head of Joseph St, Troy, NY. Office: 5 State St, Troy, NY.

GOLDSTEIN, Abraham S, US, attorney, educator; b. NYC, July 27, 1925; s. Isodore and Yetta (Crystal); BBA, CCNY, 1946; LLB, Yale U Law Sch, 1949, hon MA, 1961; hon MA, Cambridge U, 1964; m. Ruth Tessler, Aug 31, 1947; c: William, Marianne. William N Cromwell Prof of law, Yale U Law Sch, since 1961, asso prof, 1956-61; asso, law firm, Cook & Berger, Wash, DC, 1949; law clerk, US Circuit Judge David L Bazelon, 1949-51; partner, law firm, Donohue & Kaufman, Wash, DC, 1951-56. US Army, 1943-46. Vice-pres, bd trustees, Hamden Hall Country Day Sch, 1961-65; f, Branford Coll, Yale U; Christ's Coll, Cambridge, 1964-65; visiting f, Inst of Criminology; mem: comm to revise Conn Criminal Code, since 1966; Gov's Planning comm on Criminal Admn, since 1967; cons, Pres comm on Law Enforcement, 1966-67; Conn Bd of Parole, 1967-68; adv bd, div of comty services, Conn Dept of Mh, 1961-66; New Haven JCC, 1966-68; Beta Gamma Sigma; AAUP. Author, The Insanity Defense, 1967; contbr to legal jours. Home: 545 Ellsworth Ave, New, Haven, Conn. Office: Yale Law Sch, New Haven, Conn.

GOLDSTEIN, Albert Sanford, US, rabbi, educ; b. Cleveland, O; Jan 6, 1908; s. Max and Pauline (Fruchthandler); BA, U of Cincinnati, 1929; ordained rabbi, HUC, 1932; DD, HUC-JIR, 1959; m. Hesse Hoffner, Aug 11, 1935; c: Micah, Tamara, Paula. Sr rabbi, Temple Ohabei Shalom, since 1955; dean, Acad of J Studies, since 1966; rabbi: Temple Judah, Cedar Rapids; Temple Emanuel, Davenport, 1933-35; Tri-City J Cen, 1935-36; United Heb Cong, Joplin, Mo, 1936-38; Temple Emanuel, Sioux City, 1939-42; Tremont Temple, NYC, 1945-55. Chaplain, capt, USAAF, 1942-46. Pres, Assn Reform Rabbis of NY, 1943-45; Assn of J Mil Chaplains; chaplain: Vets Hosp, Bx Co; Amer Legion; chmn: NY Bd Rabbis; NY Fed Reform Syns; NY Youth Bd; NY Planned Parent-hood Assn; fac mem: Baptist Educ Cen, NY, 1948-53; Crane Theol Sch, Tufts U, 1959-64; dean, Acad of J Studies, Boston, 1965-66; past exec bd: Syn Council of Amer; Boston J Comty Council; Asso Syns of Mass; Planned Parenthood League of Mass; Boston United Chaplaincy Comm; Boston J Wfr Bd, Boston J Philanthropies; UAHC Commn on Educ, Mass Bd Rabbis; Mass Commn on Children and Youth; NE Region, UAHC; NE ADL; CCAR Comm on Unaffiliated and Conf Org; White House on Youth and Aging. Author: Passover Haggadah, 1952; Standard Haggadah, 1954; American Jewish Tercentenary Service, 1954; contbr to educ and rel jours. Home: 271 Dean Blvd, Brookline, Mass. Study: 1187 Beacon St, Brookline, Mass.

GOLDSTEIN, Bertha, Isr, communal worker; b. Keeseville, NY, July 22, 1895; d. Morris and Dora (Rosenberg) Markowitz; BA, Hunter Coll, 1915; MA, Columbia U, 1918; JD, NYU Law Sch, 1931; m. Dr Israel Goldstein, July 21, 1918; c: Avram, Vivian Olum, Natl bd, Pioneer Women, since 1937; natl adv bd, since 1951, past mem, natl presidium, past pres; hon chmn, women's div, UJA, since 1945; hon chmn, JNF since 1954; mem, World Zionist Action Comm, since 1951; exec bd, prog chmn, Jerusalem br, U Women; chmn, Jerusalem Women's Comm; found, chmn, Jerusalem Garden and Terrace Club; council mem: Council of Women's Orgs in Isr; Working Women's Org; mem: LZOA; fmr: natl chmn, Child Rescue Fund, natl bd, JNF, chmn women's div; chmn, leg comm, NY sect, Natl Council of J Women; pres, NY chap Hadassah; delg, WZO Congs. Home: 12 Pinsker St, Talbieh, Jerusalem, Isr.

GOLDSTEIN, David S, US, rabbi, b. Bklyn, NY, May 28, 1937; s. Meyer and Helen (Axinn); BA, Miami U, Oxford, O, 1959; att Heb U, Jerusalem, 1963; BHL, MAHL, HUC-JIR, NYC, 1965; m. Shoshanah Lightman, June 21, 1964; c: Ari. Rabbi, Baltimore Heb Cong, since 1968; asst dir, Hillel Found, CCNY, 1965-68, res. Mem: bd: HIAS; ZOA. Home: 2211 Rogene Dr, Baltimore, Md. Study: 7401 Park Heights Ave, Baltimore, Md.

GOLDSTEIN, E, Ernest US, attorney, educator; b. Pittsburgh, Pa, Oct 9, 1918; s. Nathan and Annie (Ginsburg); AB, cum laude, Amherst Coll, Mass, 1939; att: U Chgo Law Sch, 1940-42; LLB, Georgetown U Law Sch, Wash, DC, 1947; SJD, Wis U Law Sch, 1956; m. Peggy Rosenfeld, June 22, 1941; c: Susan, Frank. Fmr: asst counsel, spec crime commn, US Sen; gen counsel, anti-trust sub-comm, comm on judiciary, US House of Reprs; adv on anti-trust law to Secty of Commerce and Secty of Justice, Comm of Puerto Rico; trade practice specialists, Mutual Security Agcy, Off of US Spec Repr, Paris, Fr; mem law fac, Salzburg Sem in Amer Studies; prof law, U Tex; counsel, Coudent Frères, Paris; spec asst to Pres of US, 1967-69. Master sgt, US Army Security Agcy, 1942-46. Mem: Amer, Tex, DC Bar Assns; Natl Planning Assn; Amer Soc of Intl Law; Brit Inst of Intl and Comparative Law; Amer Judicature Soc. Author, Cases on Patents, Trademark and Copyright Law, 1959; contbr to legal jours. Recipient: Legion of Merit, 1946; Mil Intelligence Citation, 1946; Eur Productivity Agcy Commendation, 1953; Ford Found Intl League Studies f, 1959-60. Hobbies: philately; music; orchids; bromeliads. Home: 6 Sq Emmanuel Chabrien, Paris, Fr.

GOLDSTEIN, Edith S, US, attorney; b. Buffalo, NY, Mar 27, 1903; d. Max and Annie (Friedland) Silverman; LLB, U of Buffalo, 1924; m. David Goldstein, July 9, 1933; c: Shelley Feinberg, Toby-Lee Bulan. Pvt practice since 1926; city court clerk, head marshals dept, City Court of Buffalo, 1929-40. Chmn, membership, Buffalo Hadassah, since 1966; bd dirs, Buffalo State Hosp; mem: Rosa Coplon Home and Infirmary; Buffalo World Hospitality; Temple Beth Zion Sisterhood; Family Service of Erie Co; Camp Lakeland Assn; Brandeis U Alumni; clubs: Westwood Country; Montefiore; Rotary. Home: 58 Hallam Rd, Buffalo, NY. Office: 10 Lafayette Sq, Buffalo, NY.

GOLDSTEIN, Eli, US, physician, educator; b. Minsk, Russ, May 21, 1897; s. Julius and Yente (Komschutz); in US since 1906; MD, LI Med Coll, 1922; BS, Columbia U, 1926; post-grad med and path, U of Vienna, 1926; m. Hertzliah Zamereth; c: Judith Minowitz; Naomi Feldman. Prof, clinical med, NY Med Coll, since 1961, on fac since 1939; dir med, att phys, Heb Home for the Aged, NYC; att phys, Flower-Fifth Ave Hosp; visiting phys: Bird S Coler Memorial Hosp; cons phys, Metrop Hosp; asso att phys, Sydenham Hosp, 1939-40. US Army, WW I. F: Amer Coll of Phys; NY Acad of Med; Amer Geriatrics Soc; dipl, Amer Bd of Internal Med; mem: AMA; Med Soc Co of NY; NY State Med Soc; Metrop Med Soc; Intl Soc of Internal Med; Rudolph Virchow Med Soc; AAAS; Amer Acad J Research; NY Acad of Scis; Fgn Policy Assn; adv bd, NY Coll of Music; bd dir, Herzliya Heb Tchrs Inst and J Tchrs Sem; clubs: Lions (Yorkville); Harmonie. Contbr of articles on cardiology and hematology to med jours. Home and office: 150 E 94 St, New York, NY.

GOLDSTEIN, Estelle, Belgium, literary adv, author; b. Antwerp, Feb 18, 1902; d. Avrom and Salome (Krugel); att U of Brussels, 1921-26; div; c: Judith Weiss. Dir, Service des Lettres et de l'Art Dramatique, Ministère de l'Education Nationale et de la Culture. Journalist during the war. Author: Croquis de Correctionnelle, 1946; Promesse de Bonheur, 1947; Contre le Vent, 1947; Des Femmes Pareilles aux Autres, 1957; Lycéennes, 1959; Madame le Bourgmestre, 1962; D'Hier et d'Aujourd'hui, Mémoires, 1967; essays. Mem: Gen Fed Belgian Zionism; Assn Journalists; Assn Ecrivains Belges; PEN. Recipient, Commandeur de l'Ordre de la Couronne de Belgique. Home: 164 Ave du Diamant, Brussels 4, Belgium.

GOLDSTEIN, Gladys H, US, artist, teacher; b. Newark, O, Dec 11, 1920; d. Samuel and Dorothy (Isaacson) Hack; att: Md Inst of Art; Art Students League; Pa State U; Columbia U; m. Edward Goldstein, Mar 12, 1941; c: William. One-man shows: Baltimore Mus of Art, 1956; W Md Coll, 1957; Duveen-Graham Gal, NY, 1957; Goucher Coll, 1958; Paris, Fr, 1959; Little Gal, Phila, 1961; Playhouse, Baltimore, 1955,

1959; IFA Gal, Wash, DC, 1962; Studio N, 1963; Johns Hopkins U, 1963; exhbs: Phila Art Alliance; Rochester Memorial Art Gal, NY; Dallas, Tex Mus; Chgo Mus; Cleveland Mus; Albright Art Gal, NY; Corcoran Gal, Wash, DC; Natl Gal, Wash, DC; Peale Mus, Baltimore; Riverside Mus, NY; Pa Acad of Fine Arts; Toledo Mus; Wash Lee U; Butler Art Inst, Youngstown, O; Soc of Four Arts, Palm Beach, Fla; Columbia, SC Biennial; Morgan State Coll; Sarasota Art Assn; repr in perm collections: Pa State U; U of Ariz; Baltimore Mus of Art; Gallagher Collection; Blankford Martenet and pvt collections in US and Eur. Art tchr: Coll of Notre Dame of Md, since 1964; J Comty Cen since 1960; fmr: Forest Park Evening Cen; Metrop Sch of Art; Md Inst of Art. Recipient: purchase prize, Pa State U, 1954; Berney Memorial Award, Baltimore Mus of Art, 1956; Rulon-Miller Award, 1957; 1st prize, Natl League of Amer Pen Women, 1956. Home and studio: 2002 South Rd, Baltimore, Md.

GOLDSTEIN, Harold Israel, US, economist, b. NYC, Sep 30, 1914; s. Charles and Susan (Garman); BA, U of Ill, 1934; MA, U of Chgo, 1936; m. Sara Saltzman, Mar 18, 1938, c: Martha, Carola. Asst commn, Bur of Lab Stats, since 1959, econ, 1942-59; econ: Cen Stat Bd, 1938; wage & hour div, US Lab Dept, 1938-42; tech cons: Govt Isr, for ILO, 1961; Org for Econ Coop and Devl, 1958. Mem: Amer Econ Assn, Ind Relations Research Assn; Amer Personnel and Guidance Assn; fmr: pres, Wash Stat Soc; mem, Natl Council Amer Stat Soc. Recipient: Dist Service Award, US Lab Dept, 1961; f: Amer Stat Soc; AAAS, both in 1963. Hobby, sailing. Home: 7012 Wilson Lane, Bethesda, Md. Office: Bur of Lab Stat, US Lab Dept, Washington, DC.

GOLDSTEIN, Harry S, Australia, business exec; b. Sydney, Austr, Sep 2, 1910; s. Louis and Rebecca (Goldstein); att Sydney Tech Coll; m. Ann Green, June 30, 1936; c: Laurel, Linda. Dir, Dover Pty Ltd, merchants, since 1946; fmr: Link Belt Co. Capt, Austr Imperial Forces, 1940-46. JP, NSW; pres, Austr Fed of J Ex-Service Assns since 1962, fmr hon treas, sr vice-pres; J War Memorial since 1963, treas since 1957; J Bd Deps since 1969; fmr vice-pres, hon treas, chmn pr comm, hon secy; hon secy, King David J Day Sch since 1960; mem comm of mgmt, Exec Council of Austr Jewry, fmr sr vice-pres; mem: Returned Soldiers League; NSW Justices Assn; chmn, Joint J Communal Appeal; mem exec, Moriah Coll since 1967; fmr pres: Heb Friendly Soc; J Ex-Servicemen and Women's Assn, all of NSW; clubs: Combined Services RSL; E Subs League; dir, Shalom Ltd. Home: 20 Rivers St, Bellevue Hill, NSW, Austr. Office: 146 Darlinghurst Rd, Darlinghurst, NSW, Austr.

GOLDSTEIN, Hyman Edward, US, attorney; b. Monticello, NY, Nov 7, 1913; s. Philip and Dora (Goldsmith); att Fordham, NY; LLB, Bklyn Law Sch; m. Bessie Farber, June 6, 1935; c: Ann Alekman, Gary, Neil. Partner, Goldstein & Goldstein, since 1938; fmr, vice-pres, counsel, Gtr Flatbush Civic League. US Army, 1941-45. Vice-pres, counsel: J Cen of Kings Hwy; Gold-Kraft Family Circle; chmn, Isr Bond Drives; fmr: pres: Men's Club, J Cen of Kings Highway; Fighting 69th Infantry Div Assn; Boy Scouts of Amer; mem: Fed Lodge, KP; JWV, Meyer Levin Post; Amer Bar Assn; NY State Bar Assn; Amer Judicature Soc; NY State Trial Lawyers. Hobby, philately. Home: 1529 E 13 St, Brooklyn, NY. Office: 217 Broadway, New York, NY.

GOLDSTEIN, I Ely, US, business exec, communal leader; b. St Louis, Mo, July 21, 1897; s. Jacob and Sarah (Dubinsky); att Benton Coll of Law, 1924; m. Mary Moskow, Mar 7, 1920; c: Joyce Lewin, Elaine Berger. Pres, organizer, United Lumber Co; fmr chmn bd, United Bank and Trust Co; mem, bd, Mercantile Trust. Fmr pres, J Fed; first pres, Children's Research Found, 1945-47; pres, United Heb Congs, 1939-50, life mem, bd; Orthodox Old Folks Home, life mem, bd; JF; United Heb Cong; Children's Research Found; natl UJA Comm; mem: Natl cabinet, Bonds for Isr; exec council, CJFWF; special comm, mission to Eur and Isr to study DP problems, UJA, 1948; hon f, Brandeis U; f, Bd of J Educ, St Louis, Mo, 1951; clubs: Westwood Country, Columbian; Mo Athletic; Media. Home: 200 S Brentwood Blvd, Clayton, Mo. Office: 1401 S Hanley, St Louis, Mo.

GOLDSTEIN, Ira E, US, business exec, realtor; b. NYC, Nov 12, 1897; s. Louis and Lillian (Hirschfeld); BS, Columbia U, 1919; m. Irene Hall, Aug 18, 1959 (decd); m. 2nd, Ruth Miller, Mar 14, 1969; vice-pres, dir, L V Hoffman and Co, since 1938; secy, Hoffman Nash Co, since 1946; fmr: dir,

secy, treas, Daytona Cabana Motel Corp; real estate exec: Benenson Realty Co; Fox Theatres Corp; treas, Amer shareholders comm, Gen Aniline and Film Corp; mem fund raising comm: FJP since 1926; UJA since 1945; JWB since 1945; patron, Grand Cen Hosp; mem: Real Estate Bd of NY; Beta Gamma Sigma; Temple Emmanuel; clubs: City Athletic; Natl Real Estate; Plaza Beach. Home: Hyde Park Hotel, 25 E 77 St, New York, NY. Office: 62 W 45 St, New York, NY.

GOLDSTEIN, Irving H, US, dentist; b. Pol, Mar 1, 1905; s. Abraham and Anne (Kaufman); in US since 1906; DDS, Emory U Sch of Dent, 1926; m. Helen Mendel, July 21, 1929; c: Ronald, Elsa. Chief-of-Staff, Morris Hirsh Dent Clinic, since 1926; att dent, Home for Aged, since 1950; chief of staff, Ben Massell Dent Clinic, since 1955; mem visiting staff, Grady Memorial Hosp, all Atlanta, Ga. State chmn, employment of handicapped, B'nai B'rith, chmn, metrop comm, Gtr Atlanta, past pres: Ga State Assn; Gate City, both B'nai B'rith; pres, Children's Service Bur; mem bd, Ahavath Achim Cong, past pres; chmn, JWF, Atlanta; mem bd: Cmty Council, Gate City of B'nai B'rith; Home for Aged; Atlanta J Children's Service Fed; mem: Pierre Fauchard Acad; Amer Acad of Dent Med; Acad of Gen Dent; Amer Dent Assn; Ga Dent Assn; BBB; Atlanta C of C; AJComm; UJA; Bonds for Isr; J Cmty Cen; NCCJ; fmr: natl pres, Alpha Omega; pres, Amer Dent Interfrat Council; gen chmn, Ga State Dent Conv; mem, Fulton Masonic Lodge. Contbr to dent jours. Recipient: Dist Service Award, B'nai B'rith, 1960; Man-of-the-Year, JWV, 1956; Alpha Omega Meritorious Award, 1946. Home: 659 Peachtree NE, Atlanta, Ga.

GOLDSTEIN, Israel, Isr, rabbi, communal leader; b. Phila, Pa, June 18, 1896; s. David and Fannie (Silver); in Isr since 1961; BA, U of Pa, 1914; MA, Columbia U, 1917; ordained rabbi, JTSA, 1918, DHL, 1927, hon DD, 1945; hon: DHL, Brandeis U, 1959; DHL, Chgo Coll J Studies, 1961; LLD, NYU, 1961; m. Bertha Markowitz, July 21, 1918; c: Avram, Vivian Olum. Ret, 1961; rabbi em, Cong B'nai Jeshurun, NYC, since 1961, rabbi, 1918-61; world chmn, KH-United Isr Appeal, Jerusalem, since 1961; mem, JA Exec, since 1948; pres, J Restitution Successor Org, since 1950; mem: presidium, Conf of J Org on Material Claims against Ger, since 1951; exec bd, Comm on J Claims on Aus, since 1952; chmn W hemisphere exec, WJC, 1949-60, hon vice-pres, since 1960; pres, AJCong, 1951-58, hon pres, since 1958; pres, World Confed of Gen Zionists, since 1946; mem, bd govs, Isr Bond Drive, since 1951, chmn, NY exec comm, 1951-61; mem, natl cabinet and co-chmn, NY campaign, UJA, since 1951, natl co-chmn, 1947-48; hon pres, JNF, since 1944; mem, bd govs, Heb U, Jerusalem, since 1950, chair in Zionism; mem, exec comm, Amer Friends of Weizmann Inst of Sci, since 1950; mem council, Natl Bank of Isr, since 1953; pres, World Heb Union, since 1963; pres, J Conciliation Bd of Amer, since 1929; hon vice-pres, Amer Lib Party, since 1950; mem, bd dirs, Isr Philharmonic Orch; chmn: Jerusalem Council, Isr-Amer Friendship League; Friends of Jerusalem Artists House. Fmr: pres: Young Judea; NY Bd of J Mins; Syn Council Amer; ZOA; treas, WZO and JA, Jerusalem; pres, Amidar, natl housing co for immigrants, Isr; chmn, UPA; treas, Gtr NY Inter-faith Comm, co-chmn, commn on rel org, NCCJ, mem inter-faith team visiting army and navy stas; delg to Oxford for Org, Intl Conf of Chrs and Js, chmn, J sect, Interfaith Comm for Aid to Democracies; asso cons, Amer delg at UN Conf, SF; co-chmn, interim comm, Amer J Conf; asso chmn, Amer J Tercentenary Comm; visiting prof, contemporary J affairs, U of Judaism, J Theol Sem; found, Brandeis U, Waltham, Mass; mem: comm on immigration and naturalization, Dept of Lab; Citizens Comm on Unemployment Relief; NLRB; public repr, US Dept of Lab, wages and hours, div meat, poultry, dairy and dairy ind. Author: A Century of Judaism in New York, 1930; Towards a Solution, 1940; Mourners Devotions, 1946; Shana b'Yisrael (A Year in Israel), 1949; Brandeis University-Chapter of its Founding 1951; American Jewry Comes of Age, 1955. Contbr to: Ency Britannica Yearbook, 1947, 48; Universal Jewish Ency; Ency Hebraica. Named in hon of Dr. Goldstein: syn, Heb U campus, Jerusalem; Children's Nursing Home, by British War Relief Soc, Eng; Children's Home, Lyon, Fr; Immigrants' Hostel, Tel Aviv; Youth Village, Jerusalem; tract of land in Isr, by JNF org of Amer; Chair in Practical Theology, JTSA; Two Generations in Perspective, 1957, book sponsored by communal leaders, was dedicated on occasion of Dr Goldstein's 60th birthday. Home: Pinsker St, Talbieh, Jerusalem, Isr. Office: Keren Hayesod, Jerusalem, Isr.

GOLDSTEIN, Jerome, US, editor; b. Jersey City, NJ, Aug 5, 1931; s. David and Lillian (Greenfield); att Rutgers U, New Brunswick, 1948-52; m. Ina Pincus, Aug 23, 1952; c: Rill, Nora, Alison. Exec ed, exec vice-pres, Royer & Roger, since 1953, tech ed, 1952-53; ed, writer: Organic Gardening; Compost Sci, Quinto Lingo; circulation dir, Rodale Press mags. Trustee, Allentown, Pa NAACP Scholarship Fund; fmr, pres, Ennaus Public Libr, Pa. Author, Garbage As You Like It, 1969. Hobby, tennis. Home: 812 N 2 St, Emmaus, Pa. Office: Rodale Press, Inc, Emmaus, Pa.

GOLDSTEIN, Julius, US, business exec; b. Brockton, Mass, Dec 29, 1907; s. Joseph and Goldie (Labovitz); BS, cum laude, Wash and Lee U, 1928; MBA, Harvard Grad Sch Bus Admn, 1932; m. Amy Behrend, May 7, 1935; c: Sue Levy, Joan Cooper. Vice-pres, i/c commercial sales, Natl Mortgage Corp; bd dirs, First Natl Bank of Wash. Col, USAAC, 1942-67, ret; asst dir, Data Sys and Stat, HQ, USAF, 1961-66, maj-gen. Pres: Wash Heb Cong, 1947-48; J Comty Cen of Gtr Wash, 1959-61; chmn, Amer J Tercentenary of Gtr Wash, 1954; bd dirs: Child Guidance Clinic; Health and Wfr Council, United Comty Services; mem: Shriners; Phi Epsilon Pi Frat; Amer Legion; 32 deg Mason. Recipient: Legion of Merit. Hobbies: photography, sports. Home: 4100 Cathedral Ave, NW, Washington, DC. Office: 1701 Pennsylvania Ave, NW, Washington, DC.

GOLDSTEIN, Leon, Isr, biochemist; b. Rousse, Bulgaria, June 1, 1928; s. Jacob and Bertha (Melamed); in Isr since 1944; MSc, Heb U, Jerusalem, 1955, PhD, 1963; m. Ruth Sheinman, Feb 10, 1965; c: Daphna. Research asso, Weizmann Inst of Sci, Rehovot, since 1966. IDF, 1948-49. Mem: Isr Biochem Soc; Isr Chem Soc; Isr Biophys Soc. Author: chaps in: Methods in Enzymology; Biochemical Applications of Reactions on Solid Supports, both 1970; contr to profsl jours. Hobbies: music, hist, driving. Home: 12 Weizmann St, Rehovot, Isr. Office: Weizmann Institute of Science, Rehovot, Isr.

GOLDSTEIN, Louis, US, physicist; b. Hung, Mar 25, 1904; s. Morris and Josephine (Stern); in US since 1939; Licencie es Sciences, U of Paris, 1926, DSc, 1932; m. Ella Trammer; c: John. Physicist, on staff Los Alamos Sci Lab, since 1946; research asso, Institut Henri Poincare, Paris 1932-39; research, NYU, 1939-41; instr, physics, CCNY, 1941-44; staff, Off Sci Research and Devl, 1944-46; physicist, Fed Telecommunication Lab, Nutley, NJ, 1946. F: Amer Phys Soc. Home: 1300 Canyon Rd, Los Alamos, NM. Office: Los Alamos Sci Lab, POB 1663, Los Alamos, NM.

GOLDSTEIN, Louis B, US, obstetrician, gynecologist; b. NYC, April 23, 1909; s. David and Mary (Goodman); BS, NYU, 1929; MA, Columbia U, 1930; MD, U of Cal Med Sch, SF, Cal, 1935; m. Alice Jewel, July 6, 1936; c: Mary, Michael. Pvt practice, obstets and gyn, since 1938; asso clinical prof, U of Cal Med Sch, since 1961, on staff since 1938; asso chief, obstets and gyn, Mt Zion Hosp, SF, since 1958; mem, courtesy staff, Childrens, French Hosps, since 1946. Col, US Army MC, commanding off, 346 Gen Hosp, SF, 1955-58. F, Amer Coll of Surgs; founding f, Amer Coll of Obstets and Gyn; diplomate, Bd of Obstets and Gyn; mem: bd dirs: Aid to Visually Handicapped; SF Co Med Soc; AMA; Pacific Coast Fertility Soc; Masons; Shriners. Home: 7935 Geary Blvd, San Francisco, Cal. Office: 450 Sutter St, San Francisco, Cal.

GOLDSTEIN, Louis Eli, US, banking exec; b. NYC, Apr 19, 1896; s. Solomon and Anna (Kellner); dipl, Tchrs Inst, JTSA, NY, 1914; BS, CCNY, 1916; DJ, NYU Sch of Law, 1919; dipl, Grad Sch of Banking, Rutgers U, 1937; m. Syd Scher, Sep 24, 1969; c: Cora Furman, Alan Garen, Hilda Lubart. Ret; cons, Natl Bank of N Amer, 1966-70; limited partner, Cohen, Simonson & Rea, Inc, 1968-70; asst vice-pres, trust off, Public Natl Bank & Trust Co, NY, 1924-37; pres, Natl City Bank, Long Beach, NY, 1946-55; chmn of bd, Bank of N Amer, 1955-58; fmr: chmn, Rassco Isr Corp; dir, Citadel Life Ins Co, NY. Chmn, Camp Vacamas Assn; dir: Long Beach Memorial Hosp; hon pres, Long Beach C of C, fmr, pres; fmr: chmn, Nassau Co Clearing House Assn; mem, Natl Adv Council, Small Bus Admn; grand treas, Independent Order B'rith Abraham. Author, Investment of Trust Funds, 1938; contr to banking and financial jours. Home: 240 Central Park S, New York, NY.

GOLDSTEIN, Marcus S, US, anthropologist; b. Phila, Pa, Aug 22, 1906; s. Morris and Bessie (Silberman); AB, George Wash U, Wash, DC, 1930, MA, 1932; PhD, Columbia U,

1937; m. Leah Diamond, 1945; c: David. Grants prog spec, Natl Inst of Mh, USPHS, since 1961, public health analyst, 1946-61; research asso and anthropologist; NYU Dent Coll, 1933-39; U of Tex, 1939-43; OSS, 1944-46. F: AAAS; Amer Public Health Assn; Amer Anthropology Assn; mem: exec comm, Amer Assn of Phys Anthropologists. Contbr to profsl jours. Home: 1112 Osage St, Silver Springs, Md. Office: USPHS, Washington, DC.

GOLDSTEIN, Martin, US, educator; b. Pol, Feb 15, 1911; s. Hyman and Lena (Haber); in US since 1920; BA, MSE, CCNY, 1933, 1934; PhD, NYU, 1949; m. Frances Hoffs, Oct 18, 1936; c: Judith Rubenstein, Edward. Dean, Cleveland Coll J Studies since 1968; prin, Ohev Zedek Rel Sch, Wilkes Barre, 1936-49; educ cons, Bur J Educ, Boston, 1949-51; educ dir, Temple Emanuel, Newton, 1951-65; dir, co-found, Solomon Schechter Day Sch, Newton, 1961-68; prin, Prozdor of Heb Tchrs Coll, Boston, 1965-68. Pres: B'nai B'rith lodge; Educ Assembly, United Syn Amer, 1961-63; exec comm, Natl Council for J Educ; natl bd, Cons of United Syn Commn on J Educ; mem: ZOA; Histadrut Ivrit. Bd eds, Dorenu; Our Age, 1959-60; contbr to educ jours and texts. Hobby: painting. Home: 13995 Superior Rd, Cleveland, O. Office: 2030 S Taylor Rd, Cleveland, O.

GOLDSTEIN, Marvin C, US, dentist, educator; b. Atlanta, Ga, Mar 25, 1917; s. Avrom M and Anne (Kaufman); DDS, Emory U, 1938; att U Mich, 1938-39; Columbia U, 1940; U Detroit, 1946; Northwestern U, 1952; m. Rita Atlas, June 10, 1956; c: Armand, Aleta, Andrew, Ann, Adam. In pvt practice of orthodontia since 1939; chief of orthodontics, Ben Massell Dent Clinic and Aidmore Hosp; pres, Atlanta Americana Motor Hotel Corp, since 1962; vice-pres: Peach Tree Manor Hotel since 1947; Ga Terr Hotel since 1961; dir, Downtown Motel since 1958; fmr: visiting prof, Nihon U of Japan. Maj, USAAC, 1942-46. Chmn: Project of Hope, Ga; Atlanta armed services comm, JWB since 1959, past chmn, S region; vice pres, USO, Atlanta since 1961; f: Brandeis U; Amer Coll of Dents; dipl, Amer Bd of Orthodontics; mem: Masons; Alpha Omega, past intl pres, co-found Heb U Hadassah Sch of Dent founded by Alpha Omega; bd: Amer Friends of Heb U; B'nai B'rith since 1949; Comty Cen since 1956; Comty Council since 1955; Ahavath Achim Syn since 1954; clubs: Standard Town and Country; Mayfair; Progressive; fmr: cdr Atlanta post, JWV; chmn profsl div, JWF; pres: 5th Dist Dent Soc; Atlanta Lodge, B'nai B'rith. Contbr to dent jours. Recipient: award for outstanding service, B'nai B'rith Atlanta Lodge; Atlanta JWF Award; 6 Battle Stars; Presidential Unit Citation; Dist Service Medal, Alpha Omega, 1967; USA Award, 1968. Home: 3470 Riverly Rd, Atlanta, Ga. Office: 950 W Peachtree St, Atlanta, Ga.

GOLDSTEIN, Max F, US, attorney; b. Birmingham, Ala, July 17, 1886; s. David and Sarah (Fullmore); BL, U of Ga, 1906; LLB, cum laude, Yale U, 1909; m. Sara London, Dec 29, 1914; c: Elliott, Grace Goldstein. Partner, Powell, Goldstein, Frazer and Murphy. Pres, Heb Benevolent Cong, 1933-38; vice-chmn, JWF, 1925; mem, Atlanta and Amer Bar Assns; club, Standard. Contbr to legal publs. Home: 2520 Peachtree Rd, Atlanta, Ga. Office: 1130 Citizens and Bank Bldg, Atlanta, Ga.

GOLDSTEIN, Melvin S, US, organization exec; b. NYC, Nov 28, 1918; s. Louis and Rose (Weinus); BA, NYU, 1942; m. Lolita Eschborn, Oct 31, 1941. Asst to vice-pres, Isr Bond Org, since 1962; asst secy, Eur exec council, JDC, 1941-51; admn vice-chmn, UJA, 1951-61. Home: 5123 Post Road, New York, NY. Office: 215 Park Ave S, New York, NY.

GOLDSTEIN, Milton I, US, attorney; b. St Louis, Mo, Nov 19, 1914; s. Joseph and Dora (Hamburg); MA, Wash U, St Louis, 1936; LLB, Harvard Law Sch, 1939; m. Merle Kramer, Aug 10, 1949; c: Deborah, Joel, Kenneth, Alan. Partner: Goldstein and Price, since 1957. Lt, USCG, WW II. Vice-chmn, Natl Comty Relations Adv Council 1968; J Comty Relations Council of St Louis, pres, 1953-56; state chmn, bill of rights comm, Mo, Bar; co-chmn, jud comm, St Louis Bar Assn, chmn, profsl ethics, comm, 1959-61; pres, bd trustees, St Louis J Light, 1963-66; mem: Amer Bar Assn; Harvard Law Sch Assn; B'nai Amoona Cong; bd mem, J Fed, 1955-58; secy, J Comty Cen Assn, 1961-63; chmn, Lib Forum, 1956-59. Contbr to legal jours. Home: 7153 Kingsbury, University City, Mo. Office: 1830 Boatmen's Bank Bldg, St Louis, Mo.

GOLDSTEIN, Moritz, US, author, editor; b. Berlin, Ger, Mar 27, 1880; s. Wilheim and Sophie (Knopf); in US since 1947;

PhD, Berlin U, 1906; m. Toni Schlesinger, July 30, 1910 (decd); c: Thomas. Ed, Goldene Klassiker-Bibliothek, 1907-14; contbr and ed, Vossische Zeitung, Berlin, 1918-33; admn dir, Landschulheim Florenz, It, 1933-36. Author: Dutschjüdischer Parnass, 1912; Der Wert des Zwecklosen, phil treatise, 1920; Die Gabe Gottes, play, 1920; under pseudonym Michael Osten: Die zerbrochene Erde, short stories 1928; Katastrophe, short stories, 1928; Der verlorene Vater, play, 1932; Fuehrers Must Fall, Political sci treatise, 1942; contbr to newspapers and mags, partly under pseudonym, Inquit. Home: 895 West End Ave, New York, NY.

GOLDSTEIN, Morris, US, rabbi, author; b. Phila, Pa, Dec 2, 1904; s. David and Fannie (Silver); att Graetz Coll; Dropsie, Coll, both Phila; MA, U of Cincinnati, 1927; ordained rabbi, BHL, HUC, 1927, DHL, 1949, DD, 1958; m. Adeline Baer, May 20, 1927; c: Joyce Watson. Rabbi, Cong Sherith Isr, SF, Cal, since 1932; fmr: rabbi: Cong Beth Isr, Nigara Falls, NY; Lib J Syn, Liverpool, Eng; lectr, Old Testament, Pacific Sch of Rel, Berkeley, Cal. Fmr: pres: Bd of Rabbis of N Cal; JNF, SF Council; Assn of J Orgs, SF; Assn Reform Rabbis; chmn, JWF Appeal; grand chaplain, grand orator, Cal Grand Lodge, Masons. Author: Talmudic Appraisals of Occupations, 1927; Social Welfare Activities of the Synagogue, 1927; Thus Religion Grows: Story of Judaism, 1936; Jesus in the Jewish Tradition, 1950; Lift Up Your Life, 1962. Hobby: painting. Home: 2090 Broadway, San Francisco, Cal. Study: 2266 California St, San Francisco, Cal.

GOLDSTEIN, Moshe, Isr, public official; b. Pol, Aug 17, 1908; s. Aron and Sara; in Isr since 1933; grad, Tchrs Coll, Vilna; att U of Vilna; m. Sarah Milchiger, 1933; c: Amos. Dep mayor of Tel Aviv since 1958; fmr: prin, HS of Commerce, Vilna; mem ed bd, Baderech, weekly, Pol; head youth dept, JNF; head, public info off, Min of Interior; mem ed bd, T'murot, monthly; ed, pub, Mi uMa ba'Kalkala ha' Ysraelite, 1957. Mem: cen comm, exec council, Lib Party; secretariat, Ha'oved Hazioni; adv council, JA for Isr; bd dirs, KH, JNF; delg to ZCs; fmr secy, Progressive Party. Home: 21 Weizmann St, Tel Aviv, Isr. Office: Tel Aviv City Hall, Isr.

GOLDSTEIN, Noah, US, jurist; b. Providence, RI, Oct 5, 1907; s. Jacob and Anna (Thaler); att Fordham U, 1925-27; LLB, St Lawrence U, 1930; m. Sylvia Chervin, July 3, 1932; c: Eileen, Rice, Loretta Lewis. Judge, Civil Court, NYC, since 1969; atty since 1931; referee small claims, Civil Court, 1953-63; assemblyman, 1963-67; NY State Committeeman, 1966-68; chmn, Speakers Bur, Kings Co Dem Party; law secy, Supr Court Justice McLaughlin, 1967-68. Mem: ZOA, B'nai B'rith; B'rith Sholom; Bklyn, NY State Bar Assns; J Cen Nachlath Zion, found, past pres; KP, past chancellor; Boy Scouts, past commn; Muscular Dystrophy Assn, hon chmn; Bklyn Trial Lawyers Assn; Comty Adv Bd, Coney I Hosp; Comty Hosp, Bklyn, NY, bd dirs; club, Kiwanis, Recipient: Francis Salvatore Award, Natl Bur for J Life, 1966. Home: 2150 E 23 St, Brooklyn, NY. Office: Judge's Chambers, 120 Schermerhorn St, Brooklyn, NY.

GOLDSTEIN, Philip R, US, organization exec; b. Pol, Jan 19, 1891; s. Max and Gute (Rachelsky); in US since 1900; BA, Cornell U, 1913; MA, U of Pa, 1916, PhD, 1921; m. Sarah Schrank, May 1, 1926; c: Marjorie Kalinsky. Ret. Cons, admn secy, Natl JWB, 1950-61, fmr, field secy, dir campaigns and fund raising since 1921; dir, educ and rel activities, J Chautauqua Soc, S Jersey, 1914-20; field secy Natl Council, YMHA, 1920-21; asso dir, United J Campaign, NYC, 1930. Pres, Isr Craft Educ Soc and Julian W Mack Sch, Jerusalem; chmn: Libr and adult educ, Ft Tryon J Cen; Alumni Heb Educ Soc; found, Beta Chap, Sigma Alpha Mu Frat; mem: adv bd, Amer Fund for Isr Instns; Amer-Isr Cultural Found; Amer J Hist Soc; Natl Assn J Cens; exec: Natl Conf of J Soc Service; Masons. Author: The Social Aspects of the Jewish Colonies of South Jersey, 1921; Centers in My Life: A Personal Profile of the Jewish Center Movement, 1964. Home: 200 Cabrini Blvd, New York, NY.

GOLDSTEIN, Rose B, US, communal worker; b. Minneapolis, Minn, Mar 17, 1904; d. Alexander and Sarah (Cohen) Berman; BA, U of Minn, 1924; MA, Columbia U, 1925; m. David Goldstein, June 19, 1927; c: Jonathan, Jeremy, Alexander, Nason. Mem, natl bd, Natl Women's League of United Syns of Amer, since 1946; vice-pres, 1950-54; mem: Hadassah; Mizrachi Women; Amer Friends Hebrew U. Author: Songs to Share, 1949; Light from Our Past, 1959. Spec interest:

adult J educ. Home and office: 411 Latches Lane Apts, Merion Station, Pa.

GOLDSTEIN, Samuel, US, physician; b. Pittsburgh, Pa, May 5, 1896; s. Isaac and Bella (Giverts); BS, U of Pittsburgh, 1918, MD, 1920; m. Adeline Vatz, Aug 14, 1932 (decd); c: Joyce, Rosenbach, Nancy Sampliner; m. 2nd, Laura Adolph, Dec 27, 1961. Chief em, div of obstet and gyn, Montefiore Hosp, since 1967, chief since 1937, pres staff, 1953-55. F: Amer Coll Surgs; Intl Coll Surgs; Amer Coll Obstet and Gyn; cert bd mem, Obstet and Gyn; mem, Phi Delta Epsilon; clubs: Westmoreland Country; Concordia. Contbr to profsl jours. Home: 4601 Fifth Ave, Pittsburgh, Pa. Office: 4136 Jenkins Arcade, Pittsburgh, Pa.

GOLDSTEIN, Sydney, US, educator, scientist; b. Hull, Eng, Dec 3, 1903; s. Joseph and Hilda (Jacobs); in US since 1955; BA, Cambridge U, Eng, 1925, MA, 1926, PhD, 1928; hon f, St Johns Coll, Cambridge, Eng, 1965; hon DEng, Purdue U, 1967; hon DSc, Case Inst, 1967; m. Rosa Sass, 1926; c: David, Ruth. Gordon McKay prof, applied math, div of engr and applied physics, Harvard U, since 1955; fmr: Rockefeller research f, U of Gottingen, 1928-29; lectr math: Manchester U, 1929-31, Boyer prof, applied math, 1949-50; Cambridge U, Eng, 1931-45; f, St Johns Coll, 1929-1932, 1933-1945; Leverhulme research f, Cal Inst of Tech, 1938-39; staff mem, aerodynamics div, Natl Physical Lab, 1939-45; chmn, Aeronautical Research Council, 1946-49; vice-pres, Technion, Isr, 1950-54, chmn, aeronautical engr, prof, applied math, 1950-54. F: Royal Aeronautical Soc; Amer Inst Aeronautical Sci; fgn mem, Royal Netherlands Acad of Sci. Author: Lectures on Fluid Mechanics, 1960; ed, co-author, Modern Developments in Fluid Dynamics, contbr of papers on math, math physics, especially hydrodynamics and aerodynamics. Recipient: Tomoshenko Medal, Amer Soc of ME's, 1965. Home: 28 Elizabeth Rd, Belmont, Mass. Office: Harvard U, Cambridge, Mass.

GOLDSTEIN, Thomas E, US, historian; b. Berlin, Ger, June 23, 1913; s. Moritz and Toni (Schlesinger); in US since 1941; att U of Berlin, 1931-33; PhD, U of Florence, 1936; m. Helga Nathan, Sep 5, 1952. Asst prof, dept of hist, CUNY, since 1965; policy adv, info specialist, Bur of Ger Affairs, US State Dept, 1945-51; political commentator, Ger Service, VOA, 1951-53; chief, Cen Eur Sect, intelligence service, US, OWI, 1944-45. Pres, Soc for Hist of Discoveries 1960-63; mem: Amer Hist Assn; Renaissance Soc of Amer; club: Medieval, NY. Co-author: Journal of World History, 1960; Actas do Congresso Internacional de Historia dos Decobrimentos, 1960; Merchants and Scholars, 1965; Renaissance News, 1967; contbr to profsl jours. Hobby: creative writing. Home: 10 E 85 St, New York, NY.

GOLDSTEIN, Walter Benjamin, Isr, author, farmer; b. Breslau, Ger, May 19, 1893; s. Leo and Elise (Hainauer); in Isr since 1934; att: U Breslau, 1913-20, PhD, 1932; DJur, J Freiburg, 1914; m. Eva Herrnstadt, June 24, 1928; c: Steffi Harris; Judith Goldstein, Miriam Stern. Ret; farmer; share registrar Pal Potash, Jerusalem, 1942-48; mem, financial sect, JA, 1945-58. Ger Army, 1915-18. Mem: Internationaler Schutzverband; Deutschsprachiger Schriftsteller; Phil Soc, Heb U, Jerusalem. Author: Wassermann, 1929; Carl Hauptmann, 1931; Studien Zur Entwicklung der Psychischpysischen Probleme, 1932; Jakob Wassermann, 1933; Der Juedisch Gottesgedanke in der Entwicklung der Menschheit, 1938; Agonie des Glaubens? 1941; In Memoriam Hermann Cohen, 1942; Begegnung mit Martin Buber, 1943; Das Philosophische Werk Hermann Cohens, 1945; Gottes Witwer und Gottes Boten, 1948; Die Botschaft Martin Bubers, 1952-58; Chronik Des Herzel-Bundes, 1962. Home: 18 Bialik, St, Jerusalem, Isr.

GOLDSTEIN, Yoine Jonah, Can, attorney; b. Montreal, May 11, 1934; s. Sam and Sheiva (Melamedman); BA, McGill U, 1955, BCL, 1958; D de l'U, U of Lyon, Fr, 1960; dipl d'études comparatives de droit, Inst de Droit Comparé, Lyon, Fr, 1960. Partner, Meyerovitch, Levy and Goldstein, since 1964, active in commercial and corp law, litigations, corp reorgs. Co-chmn, finance, mem natl exec, JNF of Can: hon counsel, Can Friends of Yeshiva U; exec, legal comm, Baron de Hirsh Inst, Can; mem: Can Friends of Heb U; YMHA; Lord Reading Soc; Alliance Isr Universelle, Que. Ed, Canadian Bankruptcy Reports. Spec interests: Zionist, local music activities. Home: 6505 Cote St Luc Rd, Cote St Luc, Que, Can. Office: 1225 University St, Montreal, Can.

GOLDSTINE, Herman H, US, mathematician; b. Chgo, Ill, Sep 13, 1913; s. Isaac and Bessie (Lipsey); MS, U of Chgo, 1934, PhD, 1936; m. Adele Katz, Sep 15, 1941; c: Madlen, Jonathan; m. 2nd, Ellen Watson, Jan 8, 1966. Perm mem, Inst for Advanced Study, Princeton, since 1951; f, IBM-Thomas J Watson Research Cen; adv council: math dept, Princeton U; biomath dept, Cornell Med Coll; visiting prof, Yeshiva U, 1959-60; f, Coll of Quantitative Studies, Wesleyan U; chmn, Math and Phys Sci Comm, NSF. US Army, 1942-46. Bd dirs, Commn Engr Educ; bd trustees, Hampshire Coll; mem: Amer Math Soc; Math Assn Amer; Phi Beta Kappa; Sigma Xi. Contbr to math jours. Recipient: Meritorious Service Unit Plaque; Army Commendation Medal. Home: 18 Hayrake Lane, Chappaqua, NY. Office: Thomas J Watson Cen, POB 218, Yorktown Heights, NY.

GOLDSTON, Eli, US, business exec; b. Akron, O, Mar 8, 1920; s. Issachar and Gertrude (Robins); AB, Harvard Coll, 1942, ind admnr, wartime deg, 1943; MBA, Harvard Bus Sch, 1946; LLB, Harvard Law Sch, 1949; hon LLD, Babson Inst, 1969; m. Elaine Friedman, Oct 20, 1943; c: Dian Smith, Robert. Chief exec off, trustee, Eastern Gas and Fuel Assos, since 1963, mem, exec and oprs comms, pres, exec vice-pres; chmn, dir, subsidiaries of parent co; dir: Bels Holding Co; Forest Dell Realty Co; Park Franklin Corp; The Robins Enterprises Co; dir: affiliations: Algonquin Gas Transmission Co; First Natl Bank, Boston; John Hancock Mutual Life Ins Co; Arthur D Little, Inc; Raytheon Co; partner, law firm, Hahn, Loeser, Freedheim, Dean & Wellman, 1955; pres, Midland Enterprises, Inc, 1961. Lt, USN, Supply Corps, WW II. Chmn, Kyoto Sister City Comm, Boston; dir: Transp Assn Amer; Natl Coal Policy Conf; Council on Founds; Gtr Boston C of C; Intl Cen of NE, Inc; Natl Bur Econ Research, Inc; trustee: Boston Urban Found; NE Aquarium; World Peace Found; bd trustees, Combined J Philanthropies, Gtr Boston Inc; bd, overseers, E Asian Civilizations Visiting Comm, Harvard Coll; f, AAAS; mem: Amer, Mass, Cleveland and O Bar Assns; Amer Law Inst; visiting comm; Jt Cen for Urban Studies, MIT-Harvard; Asiatic Dept, Mus of Fine Arts; bd govs, HUC; adv comm of finance, Harvard Grad Sch of Bus Admn; gen tech adv comm, Office of Local Research, Interior Dept; finance comm, Elma Lewis Sch of Fine Arts; Comm on the Urban U; exec bd comm, Boy Scouts of Amer, Boston Council; bd overseers, Boys Club of Boston, Inc; clubs: Cambridge Boat, Skating and Tennis; Harvard, Boston; St Botolph. Home: 7 Acacia St, Cambridge, Mass. Office: 2900 Prudential Tower, Boston, Mass.

GOLDWASSER, Abraham Majer, Isr, business exec; b. Warsaw, Pol, May 1, 1919; s. Zvi and Sara (Nisenkern); in Isr since 1924; att Heb U, 1964-66; m. Judith Goldwaser, July 30, 1950; c: Joshua. Mgn dir: Oxidon Isr Oxidation Co Ltd, since 1954; Supra Paper Mills Ltd, 1952-54. Maj, IDF, 1948-50, Haganah, 1934-48. Chmn: World Comty Service Comm, Rotary Intl; Financial Comm, Mfrs Assn Isr; chem div, Mfrs Assn of Isr, since 1962. Recipient: Cavaliere Dell Ordine Al Merito Della Republica Italiana, 1967. Home: 6 Hanof, Savyon, Isr. Office: 6 Hanapach, Holon, Isr.

GOLECKI, Josef Jerzy, Isr, educator; b. Cracow, Pol, Aug 10, 1929; s. Boleslaw and Irena; in Isr since 1968; BSc, Fac of Math, Physics; MSc, Mech Engr Fac, Tech U, 1952; DSc, Acad of Mining, Metallurgy, 1956, all Cracow; m; c: Roman. Prof, Mech Dept, Technion, Haifa, since 1968; asst, sr asst, lectr, Acad of Mining, Metallurgy, Cracow, 1952-55; sr research f, Pol Acad of Scis, 1956-58; sr lectr, asso prof, Acad of Mining, 1956-62; dean, 1962-64; head, Strength of Materials Dept, 1962-68; visiting prof: Russ: Poly Inst, U of Leningrad, 1961; Acad of Sci, Minsk, 1965; Bulgaria, Sofia Poly Inst, 1960, 1966; Czech, Tech U, Ostrava, 1961-62; Eng, U Newcastle, 1967; Vienna, Tech U, 1968. Fmr: mem found, Pol Theoretical, Applied Mech; ME; Metallurgical Engr Socs. Contbr to sci publs. Recipient: sci awards, Acad of Mining, Metallurgy, Cracow. Office: Technion, Haifa, Isr.

GOLLIN, Pearl R, US, pediatrician; b. Chgo, Ill, May 25, 1924; d. Michael and Ethel (Zwick) Reiffel; BS, U of Ill, 1945, MD, 1947; m. Harvey Gollin, Oct 9, 1947; c: Susanne, Joan, Roberta. Pvt practice since 1951; att staff, Columbus Hosp and Frank Cuneo Hosp; mem faculty, Chgo Med Sch, 1952-56. Cert, Amer Bd of Ped, 1953; f, Amer Acad of Peds; mem: AMA; Amer Women's Med Assn; Chgo Med Soc; Chgo Ped Soc; Phi Beta Kappa; Sigma Delta Tau; Alpha Omega Alpha Med Soc; Assn Family Living. Hobbies:

gardening, golf. Home: 6510 N Keating, Lincolnwood, Ill. Office: 6120 N Lincoln Ave, Chicago, Ill.

GOLLOP, Harold Hillel, Rhodesia, attorney; b. Southend, Eng, Mar 29, 1915; s. Mark and Pearl (Sharotski); in Rhodesia since 1953; solicitor, Law Soc, London, 1936; LLB, U of London, 1937; m. Enid Livingston, July 5, 1940; div; c: Celia Kremer, Jessica Levy; m. 2nd, Tania Baron, Feb 9, 1969. Solicitor since 1937; atty, sr partner, Gollop & Blank, since 1953; partner, Montagu's and Cox & Cardale, London, 1946-53. Maj, British Army, 1939-46; off, J Lads' Brig, 1933-39. Vice-pres, chmn, Rashanaland Regional Comm, J Bd Deps; mem comm, Heb Cong, Salisbury, past pres; bd govs, Sharon J Day Sch, past chmn; exec, Rashanaland Regional Comm, Zionist Org; various other J communal activities, in Eng and Rhodesia. Spec interests: J educ, J communal work. Home: 44 Alfred Rd, Greendale, Salisbury, Rhodesia. Office: POB 262, Salisbury, Rhodesia.

GOLOFF, Joseph Marshall, US, business exec; b. Bridgeport, Conn, Feb 21, 1919; s. Zelig and Elizabeth (Zeitlin); BS, Wharton Sch of Econ, U of Pa, 1940; MS, Sch of Retailing, NYU, 1947; att Grad Sch of Bus Admn, NYU; m. Dorothy Spector, July 2, 1943; c: Carol, Marc Spector. Pres, Spector Jewelers, since 1950; fmr: instr, NYU; public acctnt, Milton H Friedberg and Co. Capt, finance dept, US Army, WW II. Pres: United J Council, Gtr Bridgeport; AJComm, Bridgeport; Retail Jewellers Assn, Gtr Bridgeport; dir: AJComm, NE region, natl exec bd; Action for Bridgeport Comty Devl; United Fund of E Fairfield Co; trustee: Park City Hosp; J Family Service, both Bridgeport; vice-pres, Conn Retail Jewellers Assn; mem: bd assos, U of Bridgeport; hon frats: Eta Mu Pi; Delta Pi Sigma; vice-pres, dir, Bridgeport Area C of C; trustee, Cong B'nai Isr; mem exec bd, Pomberaug Council, Boy Scouts of Amer. Contbr to retailing jours. Hobbies: sailing, music, reading. Home: 180 Linley Dr, Fairfield, Conn. Office: 1545 Post Rd, Fairfield, Conn.

GOLOMB, Abraham Isaac, US, educator, author; b. Vilna, Pol, July 18, 1888; s. Leib and Sarah (Jakobson); in US since 1964; att Yeshiva, Vilna; Sem, Grodno; U of Kiev; m. Ryvka Savitch; c: Berl. Ret; fmr: teacher: Vitebsk, 1909-12, Galta, 1912-16, Kharkov, 1916-17; dir: J Tchrs Sem, Vilna, 1921-31; biol instr, Mikve Israel and Ben Shemen agric schools, Isr, 1932-38; prin, I L Peretz Schools: Winnipeg, Can, 1938-44, Mexico, 1944-64. Author: Psychologia; Botanik; Die Sossne; Vasser Geviksen; Naturwissenshaftliche Derzeilungen für Kinder; Praktishe Arbet oif Natur-Limud; Geografie; Natur-Limud in Yiddishe Shulen; Umvegn un Oisveg; Yidn un Yiddishkeit in America; Maaselech für Kinder; Geklibene Shriften, 6 vols; Oif di Vegn fun Kium; Undzer Gang tswishn Felker; Seifer Tevie; Integrale Yidishkait, 1962. Contbr to to lit, profsl publs. Home: 1241-2 N Harper St, Los Angeles Cal.

GOLOMB, Barry, US, attorney, insurance cons; b. NYC, Sep 28, 1924; s. Joseph and Rose (Sigal); AB, Harvard, 1948; JD, cum laude, 1951; m. Barbara Meisner, June 17, 1948; c: Wesley, Ruth. Partner, Shagan, Edwinn & Golomb, since 1962; asso, Wasserman, Behrt & Shagen, 1951-60; partner, Wasserman & Shagan, 1960-62; asst dist atty, Westchester Co, NY, 1959-64; govt appeals agt, US Selective Service Supt, 1951-53. Cpl, US Army, 1942-45. Treas, Bx Tremont Heb Sch, Inc; col, NYC Auxiliary Police, Civil Defense, since 1951; fmr, pres, Ardsley Rep Club; chmn, Ardsley-Secor Volunteer Ambulance Club; corporate counsel, Village of Ardsley, NY; Westchester Co Rep Committeeman; mem: Amer Judicature Soc; NY Co Lawyers Assn; Bar Assn NYC; Westchester Co Bar Assn; NY State Trial Lawyers Assn; NY State Bar Assn. Contbr to legal jours. Recipient: Oprs Medal, Eur Theater, WW II. Home: 21 Overlook Road, Ardsley, NY. Office: 275 Madison Ave, New York, NY.

GOLOMB, David, Isr, economist, executive; b. Isr, Feb 4, 1933; s. Eliyahu and Ada (Shertock); BA, econ, Heb U, Jerusalem, 1957; m. Miriam Levenstein, 1954; c: Eliyahu, Shaul. Head: planning and devl div, sci-based inds, Koor Ind, since 1970; fmr head, econ, social research inst; dir, planning cen, both Histadrut, 1965-1970; MK, 1969. Home: 91 Ha'universita St, Ramat Aviv, Isr. Office: Koor, 99 Ben-Yehuda, Tel Aviv, Isr.

GOLOMB, Joseph, US, pediatrician; b. NYC, Apr 19, 1895; s. Isaac and Rose (Gutman); MD, LI Coll Hosp, 1917; m. Rose Sigal, Sep 4, 1923; c: Barry, Sarai Zitter, Mira. Pvt practice since 1929; fmr: dir, ped, Fordham Hosp, Bx, NY, 1946-60; visiting ped, Bx Maternity Hosp, 1936-49; cons ped, Seton Hosp, NYC, 1952-56. Lt, WW I. Dep chief, Bx, Emergency Med Field Service, chmn, Fordham Hosp, Draft Bd Examining Teams, WW II. Pres: Tremont Heb Sch, since 1950; Bx Ped Soc, 1935-36; Bx Co Med Soc, 1940-41; dir, TB and Health Assn, NY, 1936-59, mem, exec comm, 1953-59; chmn, Bx TB and Health Assn, 1946-50; public health comm, Bx Co Med Soc, since 1941; mem: coord council, five NYC, Co, med socs, 1934-58; Mayor La Guardia's Comm on Child Health, 1939-40; bd dirs, Taft Youth and Adult Cen; NY Comm on Study of Hosp Internships and Residencies; mem: Regimental Quarter; Dr's Quarter; club: Dr's of Bx, pres, 1930. Contbr to med jours. Hobbies: music, soccer, phys to soccer clubs. Home and office: 1840 Grand Concourse, New York, NY.

GOLOMB, Michael, US, mathematician, educator; b. Munich, Ger, May 3, 1909; s. Moritz and Miriam (Margolis); in US since 1939; att U Wurzburg, 1928-30; PhD, U Berlin, 1933; m. Dagmar Racic, Feb 19, 1939; c: Miriam, Deborah. Prof, math, Purdue U, since 1950, asso prof, 1946-50; cons math, Argonne Natl Lab since 1960; research engr, head, analysis sect, Franklin Inst, Phila, Pa. 1944-46; with Off of Sci Research and Devl, 1944-46; visiting prof, Math Research Cen, US Army, U of Wis, 1957-58, 1970, summers, 1959, 1967. Prin contribs: in fields of functional analysis; of functional analysis; differential and integral equations; theory of servomechanisms; approximation theory. F, AAAS, mem: Amer Math Soc; Math Assn of Amer; Ind Acad Sci; AAUP; Oester Math Gesellschaft; Soc and Applied Maths; Sigma Xi; Soc for Natural Phil. Home: 1407 Woodland Ave, W Lafayette, Ind. Office: Purdue U, Lafayette, Ind.

GOLOMBOK, Ezra, Scotland, editor; b. Glasgow, Scotland, Aug 22, 1922; s. Zvi and Rosa (Teitelman); BSc, U of Glasgow, 1943, PhD, 1947; postgrad research, Tech Sch, Zurich, Switz, 1949; m. Susan Heimler, June 8, 1958; c: Michael, Ruth. Ed, Jewish Echo, since 1954; research asst, lectr, Royal Tech Coll, Glasgow, 1943-48. Press off, Glasgow J Repr Council, Contbr to jours, newspapers, radio, TV. Hobbies: music, theatre. Home: 252 Crown St, Glasgow, Scotland.

GOLTZ, Philip, US, attorney; b. Boston, Mass, Oct 11, 1911; s. Isaac and Dora (Cohen); AB, Tufts Coll, 1933; LLB, Harvard Law Sch, 1937; m. Lenora Grozen, Sep 5, 1943; c: Barbara Sheer, Edward. Pvt practice since 1938; currently asso with Horvitz and Horvitz, Fall River, Mass. US Army, 1942-46. Pres: Fall River JCC, 1959-60, 1960-62; Fall River Dist, ZOA, 1950-51; vice-pres: UJA, Fall River, 1962; NE Zionist Region, 1956-57, 1968; Temple Beth El, 1956-57; secy, Fall River Little League, 1960-63; chmn: Isr Bond Comm of Fall River, 1954; dir, Adas Isr Syn since 1967, mem: Bristol Co Bar Assn; Fall River Bar Assn; B'nai B'rith; Phi Epsilon Pi; clubs: Men's; Gallon. Home: 710 Rock St, Fall River, Mass. Office: 7 N Main St, Fall River, Mass.

GOLUB, Leib J, US, obstetrician, gynecologist, educator; b. Bessarabia, Rum, Sep 8, 1904; s. Jacob and Jennie (Green); in US since 1921; BS, LaSalle Coll, 1927; MD, Jefferson Med Coll, 1930; m. Dorothy Weber, June 20, 1934 (decd); c: Franchot; m. 2nd, Evelyn Richman, 1968. Asst prof, obstets and gyn, Jefferson Med Coll and Hosp, 1960-69, asso gyn, 1950-57; asso prof, obstets and gyn, Hahnenmann Hosp, 1947-50; asso att gyn, St Luke's and Children's Med Cen, all Phila. F: Amer Coll Surgs; Intl Coll Surgs; Amer Coll Sports Med; Phila Coll Phys; dipl, Amer Bd Obstets and Gyns; mem: bd, Cancer Soc, Dade Co, Fla; comms, Pelvic Cancer and Breast Cancer, Phila; Pa Hist Soc; Sigma Xi; F House, Phila; Histadrut. Contbr to profsl jours. Recipient: award, Amer Bd Obstets and Gyn, 1944. Hobbies: collecting Oriental ivories, painting. Home: 801 Bayshore Dr, Miami, Fla.

GOLUB, Lionel, US, attorney; b. London, Eng, Mar 14, 1900; s. Solomon and Rose (Rubinowich) Golubowski; in US since 1908; att Clark U; LLB, NYU, 1922, LLM, 1923; m. Mollie Feit, Nov 29, 1928; c: Robert, Judith Singer. Gen counsel: Assembly of Orthodox Rabbis of Amer and Can, since 1930; Mizrachi Women's Org of Amer, since 1948; asst atty-gen, State of NY, 1945. Pres: Young Isr of Flatbush, 1949-50; Mizrachi org of Flatbush, 1943-45; chmn, law comm, Bklyn Lib Party, 1946-48; delg, Bklyn JCC; mem, state leg comm, Lib Party; mem, Tau Kappa Alpha. Home: 915 E 17 St Brooklyn, NY. Office: 261 Broadway, New York, NY.

GOLUB, Mollie F, US, attorney, communal worker, b. Bklyn, NY, Sep 11, 1901; d. Israel and Fannie (James) Feit; grad, Sem Sch of J Studies; LLB, Bklyn Law Sch, 1927; m. Lionel Golub, Nov 29, 1928; c: Robert, Judith Singer. Practicing atty since 1928; prin, rel sch, Emanuel Brotherhood, 1935-44. Natl pres, Mizrachi Women's Org of Amer, 1949-51, 1956-57; hon chmn, JNF, mem, actions comm, WZO, 1951-68; mem: bd dirs, United Israel Appeal; exec comm, AZC; delg,WZC's, 1946, '51; mem: Young Israel Syn; Women's div of Yeshiva U; Hartman Homecrest Orphan Asylum. Home: 915 E 17 St, Brooklyn, NY. Office: 261 Broadway, New York, NY.

GOLUB, William, US, business exec; b. Schenectady, NY, June 30, 1904; s. Lewis and Mathilda (Gurkin); BA, U Mich, 1926; m. Estelle Ginsberg, Apr 6, 1930; c: Paul, Neil, Meta. Pres: Golub Corp, since 1968; Cen Markets; Cen Market Operating both since 1943. Mem: bd dirs, fmr vice-pres, Natl Assn Food Chains; and fmr dir, Supermarket Inst; bd, fmr exec comm, Capitol Dist and Daughters of Sara J Home for Aged; J Comty Cen; B'nai B'rith; YMCA; C of C; Tau Epsilon Rho; bd dirs: Sunnyview Hosp; Benedict Products, Inc; fmr: mem: adv bd, Pan Amer Coffee Bur; adv bd, Educ TV; bd trustees, Temple Gates of Heaven; exec comm, Comty wfr Council; club, Kiwanis. Recipient: Citation, City of Schenectady; Man of the Year, B'nai B'rith, 1962. Hobbies: sculpture, golf, travel, collecting antique ivory, humor, speaking. Home: 1929 Union St, Schenectady, NY. Office: 501 Daunesburg Rd, Schenectady, NY.

GOLUB, William W, US, attorney; b. Bklyn, NY, Oct 7, 1914; s. Joseph and Sarah (Resnek); AB, Columbia Coll, 1934, JD, 1937; m. Barbara Lewis, 1942; c: Joan. Mem, law firm, Rosenman, Colin, Kay, Petschek, Freund and Emil, since 1969; fmr: McGoldrick, Dannett, Horowitz and Golub, 1953-69; staff mem, Atty Gen Comm on Admn Procedure, 1939-40; cons: OPA, 1943; Justice Dept, 1944-45; Hoover Commn, 1948; Gov Rockefeller on RR problems, 1959; NYC Bd of Educ, 1966; counsel, LI Transit Auth, NY, 1952-55; receiver, Hudson and Manhattan RR Co, 1954; spec counsel, NY Moreland Commn on Alcoholic Beverage Control Laws, 1964. Mem: Mayor Lindsay's Task Force on Transp, 1966; council, Admn Conf of US, 1968; Fed Bar Council; Amer Law Inst; Phi Beta Kappa; Beta Sigma Rho; FCC; NY State, Amer, NYC Bar Assns. Home: 1148 Fifth Ave, New York, NY. Office: 3 E 54 St, New York, NY.

GOMBERG, Bernard, US, obstetrician, gynecologist; b. Chicago, Ill, June 10, 1917; s. Sam and Bella (Mitchell); BS, U of Ill, 1939; MS, Coll of Med, Chgo, Ill, 1941, MD, 1941; m, Geraldine Sunderhauf, May 19, 1957; c: Beryl, Sheldon. Pvt practice since 1950; res phys: Johns Hopkins Hosp, 1947-48; Michael Reese Hosp, 1948-50; USAF, 1943-46. Mem: Amer Bd Obstets and Gyn; Amer Coll Obstets and Gyn; AMA; Seattle Gyn Assn; Wast State Obstets and Gyn Assn; Pacific Northwest Obstets and Gyn Assn; B'nai B'rith. Home: 4107-83 SE Mercer Island, Wash. Offices: 33 Stimson Med Cen, Seattle, Wash; 1011-116 NE, Bellevue, Wash.

GOMBERG, Ephraim R, US, organization exec, social worker; b. Duluth, Minn, Dec 16, 1904; s. William and Bertha (Roos); BA, U of Mich, 1927, JD, 1932; m. Lenore Fain, Aug 22, 1933; c: William, Sharon. Exec vice-pres, Crime Commn of Phila; cons, chmn, adv comm on prisons and corrections, Pa State Leg since 1961; writer, reporter: Duluth News Tribune, Minn, 1919-23; Detroit Times, Mich, 1924-32; Chgo Tribune, Paris, 1928-30; reorg, Mich State Admn of Public Wfr, Mich State Dept Corrections, 1934-36; on fac, Wayne State U Grad Sch, 1934-39; dir resettlement, comty org, Natl Ref Service, 1939-45; exec dir: Allied J Appeal, Phila, 1945-55; White House Conf on Children and Youth, 1958-60. Pres, Natl Assn of Citizen Crime Comms, since 1968; co-org, Jr sec, Amer Bar Assn, 1932-33; mem: bd trustees: Intl House; Amer for Competitive Enterprise Sys; B'nai B'rith, ADC; Phila, Amer Bar Assns; clubs: Overseas Press, NY; Locust. Home: 1032 Lindsay Lane, Rydal, Pa. Office: 12 S 12 St, Philadelphia, Pa.

GOMBERG, William, US, educator, arbitrator; b. Bklyn, NY, Sep 6, 1911; s. Alexander and Marie (Shuloff); BS, CCNY, 1932; MS, NYU, 1941; PhD, Columbia U, 1946; m. Adeline Wishengrad, Sep 24, 1939; c: Paula. Prof of ind, Wharton Sch of Finance, U of Pa, Phila, since 1959; dir, mgt engr dept, ILGWU, AFL, 1941-56; visiting lectr, U of Wis, Ind Mgt Inst, 1954-57; prof, ind engr, Wash U, St Louis, 1956-57; visiting prof: U of Cal, 1957-58; Grad Sch of Bus

Admn, Columbia U, 1958-59; ind eng, Stanford U, Cal, 1959; labor comms, arbitrator, mediator. Mem: Amer Arbitration Assn; Amer Soc of ME; Amer Inst of Ind Engr; Tau Beta Pi; Sigma Xi; Alpha Pi Mu; bd, Aspen Inst Humanistic Study; Natl Acad Arbitrators; Amer Econ Assn; AAAS. Author: A Labor Union Manual on Job Evaluation, 1948, 1955; co-author: Blue Collar World, 1964; New Perspectives on Poverty, 1965; contbr to jours. Home: 392 E Montgomery Ave, Wynnewood, Pa. Office: Wharton Sch, U of Pa, Philadelphia Pa.

GOMBOS, Stjepan, Yugo, architect; b. Sombor, Mar 10, 1895; s. Ignaz and Ilona (Liebmann); dipl, Tech Sch, Budapest; m. Susane Gabor; c: Klara Dusanovic. Head, dept architecture, tech off, Min of Construction, in liberated Croatia; dept, chief, Min of Construction, 1945; tech head, Natl Inst Architecture, 1946-51; hon prof, U of Zagreb, 1949-53. Austro-Hung Army; interned in It, 1941-43; tech off, Natl Liberation Army, 1943-45. Works include: Town Café, Dubrovnik (in collaboration); ind and residential bldgs. Mem: Assn Architects of Croatia; Assn Applied Artists, Croatia; Yugo delg to UN Econ Comm; delg to intl architects congs; past pres, Assn Architects of Zagreb. Home: Tomasiceva 13, Zagreb, Yugo.

GOMMA, Haim, Isr, diplomat; b. Breslau, Ger, Apr 5, 1924; s. Max and Ella (Abramowitz); in Isr since 1935; att Sch of Admn, Jerusalem; course for training offs and O & M offs; m. Alisa Hanon, 1954; c: David. First secy and consul, Isr Emb, London, since 1969; internal auditor, org and methods off, Jerusalem, since 1968; prin asst, civil service commn, 1950-56; asst, consular affairs, Isr mission, Cologne, 1956-58; 1st secy, Isr Emb, Addis Ababa, vice consul, 2nd secy, 1960-64; prin asst, personnel off, Min for Fgn Affairs, 1964-68. IDF, 1948-50. Recipient: Ot Hakomemiut. Special interests: lab affairs, personnel mgmt, photography. Home: 34 haLamed Heh St, Jerusalem, Isr. Office: Min for Fgn Affairs Jerusalem, Isr.

GONDELMAN, Sidney, US, attorney, business exec; b. Russ, July 28, 1897; s. Meyer and Rachel (Krisoff); in US since 1902; LLB, St Lawrence U, 1921; m. Rae Schonfeld, Sep 9, 1923; c: Herbert, George. Chmn bd: Mutual Factoes Inc, since 1940; Herbert Lee Corp, real estate and finance co, since 1946; pres Cen Foundry Co, cast iron, pipe and fittings since 1966; and pres: Essex Foundry, Newark, NJ, since 1959; Cross Country Leasing Co, Tuscaloosa, Ala, since 1964; Buffalo, NY, since 1968; Krupp Foundry, Quakertown, Pa, since 1968. Chmn, FJP; found: Albert Einstein Coll Med; Kingsbrooke Med Cen; Peninsula Hosp; mem: pres' council, Amer Inst Mgmt; Amer Foundrymen's Assn; bd dirs: UJA; Isaac Albert Research Inst; and exec comm, Kingsbrooke J Med Cen; NJ C of C; US C of C; Cast Iron Soil Pipe Inst; bd trustees, William and Mary Coll, Educ Fund; appd La Colonel by Gov Kenyon, 1954; fmr: chmn, bd trustees: Pineland Coll, Edwards Mil Acad; mem, bd dirs, Assn Commercial Finance Co's of NY; clubs: Masons; Shriner; Excelsior, bd dirs; Lake Success Golf, Gt Neck. Recipient: guest of honor and citations by: UJA; Fed J Charities; Albert Einstein Coll Med; Yeshiva Torah Vadaath. Home: 92 Merrivale Rd, Great Neck, NY. Office: 932 Broadway, New York, NY.

GOODE, Conrad Herman, US, dentist; b. Detroit, Mich, July 24, 1930; s. Isadore and Ida (Sendrofsky); AB, U of Mich, 1951, DDS, 1956; m. Lois Thal, July 3, 1960; c: Judith, Robert. DDS since 1956; mem, prosthetic staff, Sinai Hosp of Detroit. Capt, USAF, 1956-58. Pres, Temple Emanu-El, Oak Pk, Mich; secy, Metrop Detroit Fed of Reform Syns; mem: Alpha Omega, past treas, Detroit chap; Amer Prosthodontic Soc; Detroit Dist Dent Soc; Amer Dent Assn; Mich State Dent Assn; Oakland Co Dent Assn; club, Northern Dental, fmr pres. Hobby: golf. Home: 15619 Addison Ave, Southfield, Mich. Office: 1200 W 9 Mile Rd, Ferndale, Mich.

GOODFRIEND, Arthur, US, journalist, author, illustrator; b. NYC, June 21, 1907; s. Samuel and Fannie (Weiss); BS, CCNY, 1928; m. Edith Del Mar, 1951; c: Arthur, Bret, step-d, Jill Heffernan. Cons: State Dept since 1950; USIA since 1953; spec asst to chancellor, East-West Cen, Honolulu, HI; travel writer: NY Herald Tribune, 1935; NY Times, 1936-40; ed-in-chief, Stars and Stripes, Eur, China, 1944-46; ed cons, Life Mag, 1946-47; cons, Jt Commn on Rural Reconstruction, China, 1949-50; public affairs off, New Delhi, India, 1958-60; spec asst to USIA, 1960-61; fed exec f, Brookings Inst, 1961-62. Lt-col, US Army, 1940-46. Author: The Ger-

man Soldier, 1943; The Japanese Soldier, 1944; If You Were Born in Russia, 1951; The Only War We Seek, 1952; What Can a Man Believe, 1953; What Can A Man Do, 1953; Picture Story of the United States, 1952; What is America? 1954; Something is Missing, 1954; Rice Roots, 1958; Stand Fast in Liberty, 1959; The Twisted Image, 1963. Mem, Soc of Illus. Recipient: Croix de Guerre, 1944; Combat Infantry Badge, 1944; Bronze Star, 1944; Legion of Merit, 1945; Mil Commendation Medal, 1945; Hobbies: boating, fishing. Home and office: 3787A Diamond Head Rd, Honolulu, Hawaii.

GOODFRIEND, Milton J, US, physician; b. NYC, Mar 27, 1897; s. Samuel and Minnie (Friedman); att CCNY, 1913-15; MD, Columbia U, 1919; m. Rose Soman, June 22, 1930; c: Marvin. Dir: med educ, Leb Hosp, since 1960, att obstet gyn, 1922-60; obstet gyn, J Memorial Hosp, 1950-60; cons obstet gyn, Seton and Bx Maternity Hosp, 1950-58; clinical prof, NY Med Coll, 1950-60. Dir: Assn Hosp Service, 1933-66; Phys Home, since 1959; chmn, bd trustees Bx Co Med Soc, 1945-66, pres, 1939; comm on public health, NY Acad of Med, since 1959; pres, Bx Obstet and Gyn Soc, 1939; dir, United Med Service; dir, AJCong, since 1957; chmn, bd, Temple Adath Isr, 1938; exec comm, FJP, Bx divs since 1955; vice-pres, YM-YWHA, 1956; f: Amer Coll Surg; Amer Coll Obstet and Gyn; Acad Med; mem: NY Acad Sci; AAAS; hon chmn, phys comm, UJA, Bx. Hobbies: philately, print collecting. Home: 1501 Undercliff Ave, New York, NY. Office: Lebanon Hosp, Mt Eden Ave and Grand Concourse, New York, NY.

GOODHARTZ, Abraham S, US, educator; b. Bklyn, Oct 14, 1910; s. Jacob and Ida (Dudowitz); BA, CCNY, 1932; MA, Columbia U, PhD, NYU, 1951; m. Zena Frank, Dec 29, 1934; c: Natalie, Dorothy, Sima. Dean of Studies, CUNY, Bklyn, since 1960, fmr: dir, grad studies, asso dean, asst to dean, to registrar, all CUNY, Bklyn; tchr, Eng, Townsend Harris HS; visiting prof, higher educ, NYU. Chmn, bd dirs: Hillel Found, Bklyn Coll, since 1968; Natl Hillel Commn, Wash, DC, since 1964; mem: bd dirs, Pride of Judea Children's Service, since 1963; exec bd, Amer Prof for Peace in ME, since 1967; Kappa Delta Pi; MLA; AAUP. Ed: Commitment to Youth, 1960; contbr to educ jours. Recipient: Hillel Gold Service Key, 1958. Hobbies: painting, music. Home: 711 Montauk Ct, Brooklyn, NY. Office: CUNY, Brooklyn, NY.

GOODMAN, Abraham, US, business exec; b. Russ, Apr 1, 1890; s. Henry and Anna; BCS, NYU Sch of Commerce, 1917; m. Mollie Frishberg, Dec 20, 1925 (decd); c: Leonard, Philip, Morris; m. 2nd, Anna Frishberg, Feb 15, 1966. Pres, H Goodman & Sons Inc since 1925; chmn, bd dirs, Foster Grant Co, Inc, Leominster, Mass since 1929. Prin contrib: first to introduce in US injection molding opr. Pres, Brandeis Youth Found, Santa Susana, Cal; chmn, bd dirs, Tarbuth Found, NYC; treas, JA for Isr, NYC; chmn, Isr projects, ZOA, and treas, ZOA; treas, Mt Sinai Hosp, Miami Beach, Fla. Home: 112 Avon Drive, Essex Fells, NJ. Office: 606 Newark Turnpike, Kearney, NJ.

GOODMAN, Abram Vossen, US, rabbi; b. Boston, Mass, Feb 10, 1903; s. Samuel and Emma (Greenfield); BA, Harvard U, 1924; MHL, 1928; PhD, U of Tex, 1948; DD, HUC-JIR, 1950; m. May Friend, 1933; c: Gail Schulhoff, Judith Richter. Rabbi em, Temple Sinai, since 1967, rabbi since 1952; rabbi: J Comty Cen, White Plains, NY, 1929-30; Cong B'er Chayim, Cumberland, Md, 1930-35; Cong Beth Isr, Austin, Tex, 1935-41; Hillel Found, U of Tex, 1935-41; Temple Emanuel, Davenport, Ia, 1941-52. Pres, Amer J Hist Soc; fmr: pres, Alumni Assn, HUC-JIR; treas, CCAR; chmn, comm on justice and peace. Author: American Overture: Jewish Rights in Colonial Times, 1947. Home: 1 Rose St, Cedarhurst, NY. Study: 131 Washington Ave, Lawrence, NY.

GOODMAN, Andrew, US, business exec; b. NYC, Feb 13, 1907; s. Edwin and Belle (Lowenstein); att U of Mich; m. Maria Manach, Sep 29, 1935; c: Vivien Malloy, Mary Taylor, Edwin, Pamela. Pres: Bergdorf Goodman; 754 Fifth Ave Real Estate Corp; Bergdorf Goodman Fur; dir: Guardian Life Ins Co; Aurora Plastics; H & M Rayne; trustee, Central Savings' Bank. Pres, Uptown Retail Guild; chmn bd, trustee, Natl J Hosp, Denver; vice-pres, AJComm; dir: Fifth Ave Assn, fmr chmn, bd; BBB; asso chmn, NYC campaign, UJA; trustee, Fashion Inst of Tech; adv bd, Mfg Hanovers Trust Co; trustee at large, mem, exec comm, FJP; club: Country, bd govs. Recipient: Star of Solidarity from It Govt, 1957; Tobe Award, 1961; Natl Pres Trophy, Zeta Beta Tau, 1961; City of Hope Award, 1968. Home: Hilltop Place, Rye, NY. Office: 754 Fifth Ave, New York, NY.

GOODMAN, Benjamin, US, attorney; b. Memphis, Tenn, Jan 18, 1904; s. Ben and Leah (Hirsch); BA, Princeton U, 1904; s. Ben and Leah (Hirsch); BA, Princeton U, 1924; LLB, Harvard Law Sch, 1927. Mem: law firm, Armstrong, Allen, Braden, Goodman, McBride & Prewitt, since 1932; Tenn Law Revision Comm since 1963. Lt col, USAF, 1942-46. mem, natl bd govs, ARC, 1955-61; pres, JWF, 1952; Memphis Acad Arts, 1958-60; chmn, Memphis Art Commn, since 1961; mem: Memphis, Shelby Co, Tenn and Amer Bar Assns. Home: 115 S Rose Rd, Memphis, Tenn. Office: Commerce Title Bldg, Memphis, Tenn.

GOODMAN, Bertram, US, artist; b. NYC, Sep 21, 1904; s. Saul and Rose (Kantrowitz); m. Marie Caputa, Aug 18, 1928. Free-lance artist since 1937. Works in: Bklyn Mus, Metrop Mus of Art; Libr of Cong; Mus of City of NY; print collection, NY Public Libr; Butler Art Inst; Tenn Wesleyan Coll; Pa State Coll; NBC; Norfolk M; one-man exhbs: Midtown Gals; Julien Levy Gals; Laurel Gals; Butler Art Inst, O; Isaac Delgado Mus, New Orleans; Artisans Gal; and others; works in pvt collections. Pres, Bklyn Soc Artists, 1957; vice-pres, Original Graphics, Inc since 1949; mem: bd dirs, Artists Equity Assn, 1956; Amer Soc Graphic Arts; club, print, Phila. Recipient: first prize, Jo and Emily Lowe Award, 1956; Screen Publicists Guild, 1946; purchase prize, Abraham Lincoln Gal, 1947. Home and Studio: 299 W 12 St, New York, NY.

GOODMAN, Elaine L, US, psychologist; b. Huntington, W Va, Dec 12, 1905; d. William and Lillian (Broh) Loeb; BA, O State U, 1927; MA, Columbia U, 1929; m. Leonard Goodman, June 18, 1930; c: Leonard, Thomas. Pvt practice since 1941; cons psychol, Md State Dept of Public Wfr, since 1946; instr, psych, Marshall Coll, 1927-30; psychol, Baltimore City Dept of Educ, 1930-36; J Children's Soc, 1931-40; cons psychol: J Family and Children's Bur; Family and Children's Soc; Children's Aid Soc of Baltimore Co, all 1941-58; Bd of Child Care of Methodist Church, 1957-61; mem: Amer, Md Psych Assns; Sigma Delta Tau, pres, 1926-27. Home and office: 3511 Bonfield Rd, Baltimore, Md.

GOODMAN, Estelle, US, sculptress; b. NYC; d. Max and Bertha (Arbus) Weinstein; BA, Barnard Coll, NYC; m. Herman Goodman; c: Adam, Paul. One-man shows: Selected Artist Gals, 1962, 1964; Natl Design Cen, 1965; Sloane's Fifth Ave, 1966, all NYC; exhibited with: Audubon Artists; Allied Artists; Artists Equity; Knickerbocker Artists; League of Present Day Artists, all NYC; Painters and Sculptors of NJ; Yonkers Art Assn; represented: Norfolk Mus, Va; collections throughout US. Hon vice-pres, Guild Home and Hosp Daughters of Jacob; mem: Artists Equity; Knickerbocker Artists; League of Present Day Artists; Painters and Sculptors, NJ; Yonkers Art Assn; past mem, comm: UJA; J Mus; Post-grad Cen; club, Woman Pays. Recipient, awards: Mahopac Art Assn; Chr Art Assn; Painters and Sculptors of NJ, 1965, 1967; Yonkers Art Assn. Home and studio: 115 Central Park W, New York, NY.

GOODMAN, Herman, US, physician, educator, author; b. NYC, May 5, 1894; s. Barnet and Celia (Klein); BS, Columbia U, 1915, MD, Coll Phys and Surgs, 1917; m. Ruth Berlfein, June 1, 1916. Asso clinical prof, dermat and syphilology, NYU Med Coll since 1947, mem staff since 1938; asst visiting dermat and syphilologist, Bellevue Hosp since 1942, mem staff since 1920; off asst, to Drs Walter Brooks Brouner and Frederic Sylvestre Mason, 1915-18; off asso, to Dr Leo Michel, 1920-24; mem staff: NY Skin and Cancer Hosp, 1919-35; Beth Isr Hosp, 1920; W Side Clinic and Hosp, 1920-34; dir, cosmetology, Bklyn Coll Pharm, 1938-41; asst dir i/c educ and epidemiology, Bur of Social Hygiene, Dept Health, NYC, 1938-45 and 1948-63. Lt, US Army MC, WW I. Prin contribs: weight and girth control; novocain; hypoglycemia. Author: Care of the Skin in Health, 1926; Basis of Light in Therapy, 2 eds, 1926, 1927; Cosmetics and Your Skin, 1932; The Physics and Physiology of Infrared Radiation, 1932; Treatment of Common Skin Diseases, 2 eds, 1932, 1937; Story of Electricity, 1933; Sanitation, Hygiene, Bacteriology and Sterilization, 1935; Bernardino Ramazzini and Silk Handler's Disease of the Skin, 1935; Cosmetic Dermatology, 1936; Principles of Professional Beauty Culture, 1937; Contributors to the Know-

ledge of Syphilis, 1943; Venereal Disease Control as Part of the War Effort, 1945; Cosmetic Recipe and Laboratory Manual, 1947; One Hundred Dermatologic Formulas, 1947; Your Hair, 1950; Notable Contributors to the Knowledge of Dermatology, 1953; Diseases of Nails, 1956; Identification of Newlyborn, 1957; Prof Dr Anna Aslan, Her Work, 1961; Your Golden Years, 5th ed, 1963; contbr to profsl jours. F: NY Acad Med; AMA; dipl, Amer Bd Dermat and Syphilology; mem: Alumni Assn, NY Skin and Cancer Hosp; Soc Med Jurisprudence; hon mem: Swed Dermat Soc; Amer Med Soc, Vienna; fmr, secy: sect on cultural and hist med, NY Acad Med; NY Soc Med Hist. Hobby: travel. Home: 18 E 89 St, New York, NY.

GOODMAN, Irwin A, US, business exec; b. Chgo, Ill, July 1, 1910; s. Manuel and Lydia (Neff); BS, U of Ill, 1932, LLB, 1934; m. Virginia Block, Apr 14, 1940; c: Robert, Judith. Pres, dir, Natl Bank of Albany Park, since 1962; pvt practice, 1934-36; trust off, Liberty Natl Bank, 1936-48; vice-pres, trust off, Exch Natl Bank, 1949-62. Vice-pres, dir, N River Comm; trustee, Ill Found for Asthma; treas, Chgo Sch of Architecture Found; mem: Land Trust Council, Ill, fmr pres; Albany Park Action Conf, fmr pres, trustee; Ill, Chgo Bar Assns; Amer Inst Banking; B'nai B'rith Wilmetta, chap 2117; clubs: Execs, Chgo; Northside Bankers, fmr pres. Hobbies: golf, bridge, theatre, sports, music. Home: 444 Sunset, Wilmette, Ill. Office: 3424 Lawrence, Chicago, Ill.

GOODMAN, Isaac Norman, Austr, executive secy; b. Yorkshire, Eng, Dec 13, 1915; s. Max and Rosie (Furman); in Austr since 1952; att HS, Manchester, Eng; m. Hannah Toberman, Oct 21, 1942; c: Maxine, Dianne. Exec secy, since 1960; exec secy: S Manchester, 1945-52; Southport Heb Cong, 1949-52. Chmn, educ, NSW Bd of Deps; hon secy, Bondi Judean Scouts; hon treas, GSY Youth Org; mem: Masons; B'nai B'rith, both Sydney. Office: 166 Castlereach St, Sydney, Australia.

GOODMAN, Julius, US, merchant; b. Troy, NY, May 30, 1902; s. Joseph and Leah (Friedman); att Wharton Sch, U of Pa, 1924; m. Dorothy Luria, Mar 3, 1925; c: Richard, Robert. Pres, Union Fern, Inc, 1949-67; fmr mem, bd dirs, Natl City Bank. Chmn, City of Troy Commn on Human Rights, 1965-68; JWF, 1954; pres, Natl Retail Furniture Assn, 1949, chmn bd, 1950; Comty Chest, 1950, gen chmn, 1948-49, mem, bd dirs; campaign dir, United Negro Coll Fund, 1962; mem, bd dirs: Rensselaer Co Mh Bd; J Comty Cen; J Home for Aged; State Council Against Discrimination in Employment; Council Social Agcys; Samaritan Hosp; Temple B'rith Sholom; YMCA; C of C; mem, exec comm, Amer Retail Fed; mem: Masons, Elks, Rotary. Home: 1 Park Lane, W, Menands, NY. Office: 4 Interstate Ave, Albany, NY.

GOODMAN, Leo A, US, statistician, educator; b. NYC, Aug 7, 1928; s. Abraham and Mollie (Sacks); BA, summa cum laude, Syracuse U, 1948; MA, Princeton U, 1950, PhD, 1950. Prof, stats and sociol, U of Chgo, since 1955, fac mem since 1950; research asso, Population Research Cen, U of Chgo, since 1967; lab asst, stats, Syracuse U, 1948; research asst, math stats, Princeton U, 1948-49, research training f, Soc Sci Research Council, Princeton U, 1950; advanced research scholar, Fulbright, and hon research training f, Soc Sci Research Council Award, Cambridge U, Eng, 1953-54; sr postdoc f, NSF; f, John Simon Guggenh im Memorial Found, Cambridge, U, U of London, 1959-60; visiting prof, math stats, sociol, Columbia U, 1960-61. Chmn, comm on stat, div of math, Natl Acad Sci, NRC, 1963-64, mem, comm, 1961-64; f: Inst Math Stats; Amer Stat Assn; Amer Sociol Assn; Royal Stat Soc; AAAS; mem: council, Inst of Math Stats, 1955-57; Amer Math Soc; Econometric Soc; Biometric Soc; Sigma Xi; Phi Beta Kappa; contbr to profsl jours and books. Recipient: MacLaren Adv Research Award, Can Adv Research Found, 1966; R A Fisher Memorial Lecture, Comm, Pres of Stat Socs, 1968. Home: 1126 E 59 St, Chicago, Ill.

GOODMAN, Nerida J, Austr, barrister; b. Sydney, Jan 15, 1913; d. Lionel and Eva (Levy) Cohen; BA, U Sydney, 1932, LLB, 1935; m. Bernard Goodman, May 1, 1946; c: Jonathan, Paul. Pvt practice, NSW Bar, first woman, 1935-42; legal off: Dept Lab and Natl Service, Commonwealth Govt, 1942-44; Dept of Lab and Ind, State Govt, NSW, 1944-46. Vice-pres, Friends of Heb U, since 1955, hon treas, 1937-49, pres, 1952-54, fed hon secy, 1966-68; hon legal adv, State council, WIZO, since 1954; hon treas, Friends of Isr Philharmonic Orch, since 1961, fed hon secy, 1968-69; fmr: pres, Council for Women in War Work, 1942-45; found pres, Women

Lawyers Assn, 1952-53; hon secy, Bd J Educ, 1940-44, all NSW. Home: 1 Holt St, Double Bay, NSW, Austr.

GOODMAN, Paul, US, author; b. NYC, Sep 9, 1911; s. Barnet and Augusta (Goodman) Shatz; AB, CCNY, 1931; PhD, U of Chgo, 1953; m. Sara Duckstein; c: Susan, Mathew, Daisy. Author: The Facts of Life, 1945; Communities, 1947; Kafka's Prayer, 1949; The Structure of Literature, 1953; Gestalt Therapy, 1953; The Empire City, 1959; Growing Up Absurd, 1960; Utopian Essays, 1961; The Community of Scholars, 1962; Drawing The Line, 1962; Making Do, 1963; The Society I live in is Mine, 1963; The Lordly Hudson and Other Poems, 1963; The Young Disciple Faustina, Jonah, 1964; People or Personnel, 1966; Five Years, 1967; Hawkweed, 1967; Adam and His Works, 1958; North Percy, 1969; New Reformation, 1970; asso ed, Liberation, since 1961; adv bd, Radio Station WBAI, 1960-62. F: Inst for Policy Studies, Wash, DC, since 1963; Inst for Gestalt Therapy, NY, Cleveland, 1952; asso, Columbia U seminars, since 1958; mem, W Side Manhattan Bd Educ, 1962-63. Home: 402 W 20 St, New York, NY.

GOODMAN, Percival, US, architect, illustrator, educator; b. NYC, Jan 13, 1904; s. Barnet and Augusta (Goodman); att Inst of Design, NYC; Ecole des Beaux Arts, Paris, 1925, 1928; Amer Sch, Fountainebleau, 1923, 1926-27; m. Naomi Ascher, Sep, 1945; c: Rachel, Joel. Architect, pvt practice, since 1929; prof, Sch Architecture, Columbia U, since 1945. Prin building designs: Dept of Hosps, NYC; Bd Educ, NYC; Syns, temples in: Providence, RI; Detroit, Mich; Tulsa, Okla; Denver, Colo, Queenboro Comty Coll. F: Amer Inst Architects and Coll of Fs; Intl Inst Arts and Letters; mem, Soc of Beaux Arts and Architects. Author: Communitas, 1947; illus, Golden Ass of Apuleius, 1932; contbr to architectural jours. Recipient: Paris, prize, Beaux Arts Inst, 1925. Home: 40 W 77 St, New York, NY. Studio: 2114 Broadway, New York, NY.

GOODMAN, Philip, US, rabbi, organization exec; b. NYC, Sep 6, 1911; s. Harry and Molly (Epstein); att: Tchrs Inst, Yeshiva U, 1930; CCNY, 1930; ordained rabbi, Yeshiva of Rabbi Kook, 1932; m. Hanna Caspi, Aug 14, 1943; c: Abraham, Judith Rubin. Cons, small comtys, JWB, since 1968, dir, J educ, J cen div, 1944-68, staff, armed services div, 1942-44; exec secy, JBCA, since 1944; rabbi, Instn Syn, NYC, 1934-42; exec secy, Amer J Hist Soc, 1948-53; admn secy, World Fed of YMHA's, J Comty Cens, 1956-68. Mem: Natl Assn J Cen Workers; Natl Council J Educ; Cong Mt Sinai; NY Bd Rabbis; Rabb Alumni Assn, Yeshiva U. Author: The Habanoth Manual, 1938; The Purim Anthology, 1949; American Jewish Bookplates, 1946; Rejoice in Thy Festival, 1956; The Passover Anthology, 1961; co-author: The Jewish Marriage Anthology, 1965; ed: mgr ed, Jewish Book Annual, since 1944; asso, In Jewish Bookland, since 1945. Recipient: Mordecai Ben David Award, Yeshiva U, 1955; 1st Horeb Award, Yeshiva U Tchrs Inst Alumni, 1960. Hobby: bookplate collecting. Home: 100 Overlook Terr, New York, NY. Study: 15 E 26 St, New York, NY.

GOODMAN, Philip Henry, US, attorney; b. Kolk, Pol, Nov 26, 1915; s. Harry and Sarah (Schnizer); in US since 1920; LLB, U of Baltimore, 1934; m. Bertha Wolowitz, May 26, 1938; c: Gilbert. Pvt practice since 1937; chmn, Baltimore Civic Cen Comm, since 1968; pres, Baltimore City Council; Mayor, Baltimore City, 1962-63. Home: 100 W Cold Spring Lane, Baltimore, Md. Office: 15 N Guilford Ave, Baltimore, Md.

GOODMAN, Randolph, US, author, educator; b. NYC, May 29, 1908; s. Philip and Bertha (Kahn); BS, NYU, 1931; MFA, Yale U, 1946; PhD, Columbia U, 1951; cert, drama, London U, 1950. Prof, Bklyn Coll, since 1946; adj prof, Theatre Arts, grad div, Columbia U, since 1967; prof: Hunter Coll, 1947; New Sch, 1950-55. Author: A Long Way From Home, 1948; I, Walt Whitman, 1953; Drama On Stage, 1961; Introduction to Shakespeare's Merchant of Venice, 1966; Modern Drama on Stage, 1970; contbr articles on drama, Enciclopedia dello Spettacolo, 1954-60; Collier's Ency, 1956-61; Playwatching with a Third Eye, Columbia U Forum, 1967. Mem: Amer Soc Theater Research; Beta Gamma Sigma; club: Classical. Recipient: scholarships and grants: Yale U; Inst for Intl Educ, London U; Salzburger Landesregierung, Salzburg, 1962. Home: 1164 Cromwell Ave, New York, NY. Office: Bklyn Coll, Brooklyn, NY.

GOODMAN, Richard Merle, Isr, physician; b. Cleveland, O, July 31, 1932; s. Edwin and Florence (Grossman); in Isr since 1969; BS, U Cincinnati, 1954; MD, O State U, 1958; f in med, Johns Hopkins U, Baltimore, Md, 1961-64; m. Audrey Rosenberg, June 26, 1955; c: Jeff, Daniel, David. Dir, clinical genet, Tel Hashomer Govt Hosp, since 1969; asst prof, med, O State U, 1964-69. Prin contrib, research in genet diseases of man. Mem, Isr Exploration Soc. Author: Genetic Disorders of Man, 1970; The Face in Genetic Disorders, 1970; contbr numerous research papers. Spec interest: Isr archaeol. Home and office: Tel Hashomer Govt Hosp, Isr.

GOODMAN, Roy M, US, legislator; b. NYC, Mar 5, 1930; s. Bernard and Alice (Matz); AB, cum laude, Harvard Coll, 1951; MBA, with distinction, Harvard Grad Sch of Bus Admn, 1953; m. Barbara Furrer; c: Claire, Leslie, Randolph. NY State Senator, chmn, Sen Housing Comm; mem, comms: NYC Taxation; Civil Service and Pensions; Roads and Public Works; fmr: finance admnr, NYC; asso with Kuhn, Loeb & Co, inves bankers; pres, group of drug co's. Off, USN, Korean War. Trustee, chmn, exec comm, Brotherhood-in-Action; Mem, Man Borough Comty Planning Bd No 8; mem: NYC Banking Commn; bd trustees: NYC Police Pension Fund; Fire Dept Life Ins Fund; bd: Carnegie Hall Corp; Dalton Schs; LI Coll Hosp; Columbia U Coll of Pharm Sci; ADL; Tel Aviv U; Amer Parents Comm; NY Comm of Young Audiences; mem: Harvard 1951 Perm Class Comm; Young Pres Org; clubs: Wall Street; Harvard of NY and Boston; Cent Century; fmr: treas, Rep Party of NY Co; vice-chmn, Lindsay-for-Mayor Comm; treas, New Yorkers for Lindsay. Recipient: Dist Service Award and Mah of the Year, Jr C of C, 1966; hon mem, Omicron Delta Epsilon; Mt Scopus Citation, Heb U, Jerusalem, 1968. Home: 1035 Fifth Ave, New York, NY.

GOODMAN, Saul L, US, educator, writer; b. Bodzanow, Pol, Dec 1, 1901; s. Jacob and Brana (Gips); in US since 1921; grad, JTSA, 1928; BS, Boston U, 1932; att Harvard U, 1934; grad fac, New Sch for Social Research, 1952-53; MA, Columbia U, 1954; m. Sarah Glassman, 1926; c: Eli. Asst prof, J phil and educ, Herzliya J Tchrs Inst, JTSA, since 1962; exec dir, Sholem Aleichem Folk Inst, since 1949. Mem: Natl Council J Educ; YIVO; Cong for J Culture; Yiddish PEN. Author: Traditsye un Banayung, 1967; ed, Derekh, Yiddish and Eng; co-ed, Bieter for Yiddisher Dertsiung; contbr to encys, gen, profsl and Yiddish jours. Recipient: Zvi Kessel Literary Prize for best book of year, 1968. Home: 124 Gale Place, New York, NY. Office: 41 Union Sq, New York, NY.

GOODMAN, S Oliver, US, journalist; b. Cleveland, O, May 5, 1910; s. Louis and Kate (Korngut); m. Sylvia Posner, June 12, 1932; c: Donald, Abby, Linda. Bus ed, The Washington Post, since 1940; state ed, 1937-40. Dir, Wash Post Fed Employees Credit Union, since 1942; mem: Wash Newspaper Guild; Soc Inves Analysts; clubs: Metrop Wash Advt; Bond Wash. Contbr to mags. Home: 6404 Wilson Lane, Bethesda, Md. Office: 1515 L St, NW Washington, DC.

GOODRICH, Morris D, US, business exec; b. Russ, Mar 17, 1902; s. Louis and Rachel (Elgort); att Cooper Union, NYC, 1922; LLD, HC, U of San Diego; m. Sara Ferer, May 10, 1936; c: Rochelle. Owner, M D Goodrich & Co, San Diego, Cal, since 1945. Regional chmn, comm natl bd, NCCJ; pres, Health Found, San Diego; co-found, Heb Home for Aged; dir: Boys' Club; Girls' Club; chmn, Natl J Hosp, Denver; vice-pres, San Diego Heart Assn; hon life pres, Temple Beth Isr, San Diego, past pres; mem: state bd, Pilot Commns for San Diego; natl bd, Small Bus Admn; natl council, Jt Defense Appeal; clubs: B'nai B'rith; Masons; Shriners. Recipient: Mr San Diego, 1959; testimonial dinner, City of Hope, LA, Cal; regional award, NCCJ; Boys' Club Golden Man of the Year, 1966; Mr Brotherhood, SW, J Press. Home: 2215 Juan St, San Diego, Cal. Office: 1930 Main St, San Diego, Cal.

GOODSIDE, Samuel, US, educator; b. NYC, Oct 15, 1908; s. Moses and Sophie (Epstein); BA, CCNY, 1930, MS, 1939, DEd, 1951; m. Sylvia Mehlman, Feb 21, 1931; c: Susan Katz, Morris. Supervising prin, Heb Inst of LI, since 1963; tchr, sup, NY Pub Sch, 1930-43; tchr, Rabbi Jacob Joseph Sch, 1930-44; camp dir, admnr, N Star Camps, 1952-57; sup, Ramaz Sch, 1943-65, visiting asst prof, educ, Grad Sch Educ, Yeshiva U, 1952-63; instr, Bklyn Coll Sch of Gen Studies, since 1963. Pres: Young Isr, Belle Harbor, NY; Yeshiva Eng Prins Assn; vice-pres: Beth David Gershon Talmud Torah, 1951-65; Natl Assn for Yeshiva Educ, 1950-60; mem: Hapoel Hamizrachi; Natl Soc for Study of Educ; Dept Elementary Sch Prins; Dept Secondary Sch Prins; Natl Council Soc

Studies; Natl Assn Curriculum Devl; Amer J Hist Soc; Rel Educ Assn; Kappa Delta Pi. Co-author: Jews in American History, 1955. Recipient: hon awards, Isr State Bonds. Spec interests: scouting, camping, Home: 504 Beach 139 St, Belle Harbor, NY. Office: 1742 Seagirt Blvd, Far Rockaway, NY.

GOODSTEIN, Jacob, US, certified public acctnt; b. Newark, NJ, Feb 15, 1905; s. Julius and Fanie (Friedman); BS, NYU, 1926; LLB, NJ Law Sch, 1929; m. Evelyn Tepperman, Aug 25, 1929; c: Judith Kleitman, Claire Gering, Daniel. Partner, SD Leidesdorf & Co, NY, since 1947, staff mem, 1927-47; treas, dir, Natl JWB, since 1966, chmn, budget comm, since 1962, chmn comm, J Cen admn, dir, mem exec comm, NJ sect; pres, J Comty Centers, Essex Co, 1962-65; dir (life), Suburban YM & YWHA, pres, found, 1948-53; mem, bd trustees, budget and planning comm, JCC, Essex; chmn, W Essex, UJA, 1956, co-chmn, Millburn, 1958; mem, bd trustees, Temple B'nai Abraham, Newark, 1947-61; mem, various comm, NJ Soc of CPA's since 1963, mem, bd trustees, 1950-52. Mem: Amer Inst CPA's; NY Soc of CPA's; Amer Accounting Assn; finance and budget comm, Natl USO; club, NYU. Home: 885 Ridgewood Rd, Millburn, NJ. Office: 125 Park Ave, New York, NY.

GOODSTEIN, Leonard D, US, psychologist, educator; b. NYC, Jan 11, 1927; s. Moe and Stella (Warshar); BS, CUNY, 1948; MA, Columbia U, 1948, PhD, 1952; m. Ruth Einhorn, Dec 18, 1948; c: Richard, Steven. Prof, psych, dir, profsl training in psych, U of Cincinnati, since 1964; instr, Hofstra Coll, 1948-51; instr, prof, psych, State U of Ia, 1951-64, dir, U Counseling Service, 1957-64. F: O Psych Assn; Midwestern Psych Assn; Amer Psych Assn; dipl, Clinical Psych, Amer Bd Examining Prof of Psych; pres, Ia Psych Assn, 1957-58; chmn, Gov's Profsl Adv Comm on Mh, 1958-61; mem: N Hills Cong; Alpha Epsilon Pi. Hobby: duplicate bridge. Home: 373 Compton Rd, Cincinnati, O. Office: U of Cincinnati, Cincinnati, O.

GOOR, Amihud, Isr, forester, UN official; b. Mikveh Israel, Isr, Aug 16, 1898; s. Yehuda and Rachel (Neiman) Grasovsky; grad, Tchrs Sem, Jerusalem, 1918; BS, U of Cal, 1924, MS, 1925; PhD, Yale U, 1928; DF, Oxford U, 1933; m. Shifra Smilansky; c: Dan, Dina Nathan. Ret; asst conservator of forests, Pal Govt, 1928-45, conservator, 1945-48; conservator of forests, Isr, 1948-54; cons, forestry div, Food and Agric Org of UN Missions to: India; Chile; Arg; Uruguay; Turkey; Greece, 1954-68; Regents lectr, U of Cal, Berkeley, 1967. Prin contribs: research in arid zones of: Nigeria; Sahara; Algeria; Morocco; Japan; Australia; Russ; Java; Malaya; Ceylon; Spain; India; Yemen; W US; Mexico; Ven; Ecuador; Peru; Arg; Chile; Uruguay; Cuba; ME; Ethiopia. Delg: World Forestry Cong; Intl Union Forest Research: Budapest; Nancy; Helsinki; New Delhi; official guest, World Forestry Cong: Seattle, Wash, 1961; Madrid, 1966. Hon life mem: Amer Soc Forestry; Arg Soc Forestry; Pan-Hellenic Soc Forestry Engrs; mem, Sigma Xi, 1928; past chmn: Eur Forestry Co Afforestation; Eur Eucalyptus Comm; Arid Zone World Forestry Cong, India, 1915; dir, Sem Latin Amer Conifers, Mexico, 1960. Home: 10 Huberman St, Tel Aviv, Isr.

GOOR, Joel S, US, rabbi, educator; b. NYC, Feb 2, 1933; s. Benjamin and Anne (Schwartz); BS, U of Cal, 1954; BHL, MA, HUC-JIR, 1959; m. Stephanie Multer, Dec 26, 1954; c: Richard, Donald, Carolyn. Rabbi, Cong Beth Isr, since 1961; visiting lectr, U San Diego, since 1966; rabbi Putnam Co Temple and J Cen, 1956-59. Chaplain USAF, 1959-61. Chmn, social action comm, Pacific Assn of Reform Rabbis; vice-pres, U Rel Conf, U of Cal; bd mem: NCCJ, co-chmn, 1963-65; Bur J Educ; steering comm, San Diego Urban Coalition; chmn: San Diego Clergy Comm for Fair Housing, 1966; hon co-chmn, Amer Comm, 1967-68; chaplain, Navy League of San Diego, 1966-67; exec comm, United J Fed, San Diego, 1963-64; mem: HUC-JIR Alumni Assn, bd overseers; UAHC-CCAR comm on Syn Admn; Young Leadership Cabinet, UJF; CCAR; AJComm; Cal Adv Bd, ADL; Natl Council, JDC. Contbr to J press. Recipient: Hum Relations Award: ADL, 1964; B'nai B'rith, 1967. Home: 3211 Freeman St, San Diego, Cal. Study: 2512 Third Ave, San Diego, Cal.

GOOR, Shai Yeshaayahu, Isr, veterinary surg; b. Jaffa, Isr Oct 12, 1904; s. Yehuda and Rahel (Niman); att Royal Vetr Coll, Edinburgh, 1924-28; London Sch of Tropical Med, 1929; m. Zilla Miller, Nov 25, 1934; c: Rama, Flint David, Gill, Bruna. Dir, vetr services, chief vetr off, Min of Agric; fmr: asst vetr off; dist vetr off; poultry disease off, all Pal Govt. IDF. Delg,

Off Intl des Epizooties, Paris; Isr repr, Perm Comm, World Vetr Cong's; fmr: chmn, Isr Vetr Assn; mem, British Vetr Assn; scout master: Pal; 9th Edinburgh Judeans; Sea Scout, Tel Aviv; mem, Maccabi Sports Org, football team; vetr adv, food control, State of Isr, chief, vetr field services. Home: 54 Menuha Venahala St, Rehovot, Isr. Office: Min of Agric, Vetr Services, Bet Dagan, Isr.

GORDIS, Enoch, US, physician, educator; b. NYC, Feb 21, 1931; s. Robert and Fannie (Jacobson); AB, Columbia U, 1950; MD, 1954; m. Lucille Sapirstein, Apr 20, 1958; c: Deborah, Joshua. Asso prof, Rockefeller Inst, NY; fmr: chief res, internal med, Mt Sinai Hosp, NY. US Army MC, 1955-57. Dipl: Natl Bd Med Examiners; Amer Bd Internal Med. Contbr to med jours. Hobby: music. Home: 382 Central Park W, New York, NY. Office: Rockefeller U, New York, NY.

GORDIS, Leon, Isr, physician; b. NYC, July 19, 1934; s. Robert and Fanny (Jacobson); in Isr since 1969; AB, Columbia Coll, 1954; MD, Downstate Med Cen, NY, 1958; MPH, Johns Hopkins U, Baltimore, Md, 1966, DPH, 1968; m. Hadassah Cohen, June 14, 1955; c: Daniel, Elihu, Jonathan. Visiting prof, dept med ecology. Heb U, Hadassah Med Sch, since 1969; fmr: chief, dept comty med, Sinai Hosp, Baltimore, Md; asst prof, ped, Johns Hopkins U Med Sch; surg, USPHS. F: Amer Acad Ped; Amer Public Health Assn; mem: council on rheumatic fever, AHA; NY Acad Sci; Assn Tchrs of Preventive Med; Soc Epidemiological Research. Contbr numerous articles to profsl jours. Home: Shikun San Simon, Ramat Gonen, Jerusalem, Isr. Office: Hebrew U-Hadassah Med Sch, Jerusalem Isr.

GORDIS, Robert, US, rabbi, author; b. Bklyn, NY, Feb 6, 1908; s. Hyman and Lizzie (Engel); BA, cum laude, CUNY, 1926; PhD, Dropsie Coll, 1929; ordained rabbi, MHL, JTSA, 1932, DD, 1940; m. Fannie Jacobson, Feb 5, 1928; c: Enoch, Leon, David. Rabbi em, Temple Beth El, Rockaway Pk, NY, since 1968, rabbi since 1931; prof: Bible, JTSA, since 1937; rel, Temple U, since 1968; cons on rel, Fund for the Rep, since 1957; adj prof, rel, Columbia U, 1950-58; lectr: old Testament, Protestant Union Theol Sem, 1954; on radio and TV; conducted survey, rel needs of armed forces: Hawaii; Philippines; Japan; China, for US War and Navy Depts, 1946. Author: Biblical Text in the Making - A Study of the Ketib Qere, 1933; The Jew Faces a New World, 1941; Conservative Judaism - An American Philosophy, 1945; Wisdom of the Ecclesiastes, 1945; Wisdom of Koheleth, 1950; Koheleth - The Man and His World, 1951; The Song of Songs, 1954; Judaism for the Modern Age, 1955; The Ladder of Prayer, 1956; Conservative Judaism - A Modern Approach to Jewish Tradition, 1956; A Faith for Moderns, 1960; Politics and Ethics, 1961; The Root and the Branch: Judaism and the Free Society, 1962; The Book of God and Man - A Study of Job, 1965; Judaism in a Christian World, 1966; Leave a Little to God, 1967; Sex and the Family in Jewish Tradition, 1968; ed: Max L Margolis - Scholar and Teacher; From the Wells of Hasidism, Hebrew essays by A Silverstone; co-ed, Jewish Life in America; found, mem, bd eds, quarterly jour, Judaism, since 1951; contbr to rel, scholarly and other jours in US, Gt Brit and Isr. Mem, exec bd, RA, past pres; trustee, Church Peace Union, since 1958; chmn, educ comm, ZOA; mem: exec bd, Natl Hillel Commn, since 1960; exec bd, J Publ Soc; J Comm on Scouting; Boy Scouts of Amer; bd: NY Bd Rabbis; Soc Bibl Lit; natl admn council, JDC; United Syn Amer; bd govs, Natl Acad Adult J Studies; J Book Council, Amer; Phi Beta Kappa; chmn, Jt Prayerbook Comm of RA and United Syn, 1944-46. Home: 150 West End Ave, New York, NY. Office: 3080 Broadway, New York,NY.

GORDON, Alvin J, US, physician; b. NYC, Jan 26, 1915; s. Isaac and Jennie (Perla); AB, Columbia, Coll, 1934, MD, Coll of Phys and Surg, 1938; m. Elaine Isaacson, Dec 1, 1939; c: Melissa, Todd. Head, cardiac catheterization team, Mt Sinai Hosp, NY; asso att phys; pvt practice of Card and internal med since 1946. USN, 1943-46. F, Amer Coll Phys; dipl, Amer Bd Internal Med, subspecialty, cardiovascular disease; mem, Phi Beta Kappa. Co-author: Hemodynamics of Aortic and Mitral Valve Diseases, 1961; contbr to med jours. Recipient: Navy Unit Commendation, 1945. Hobbies: photography, fishing. Home: 229 E 79 St, New York, NY. Office: 815 Park Ave, New York, NY.

GORDON, Barnett D, US, business exec; b. Vilna, Lith, Sep 28, 1894; s. Abraham and Anna (Lewis); in US since 1905;

BS, MIT, 1916; hon DSc, Lowell Tech Inst, 1956; m. Ruth Myers, May 6, 1920; c: Gene, Malcolm. Pres, treas, dir: MKM Knitting Mills Inc; MKM Hosiery Mills since 1941; pres, dir, Darlene Knitwear; exec vice-pres, dir, Columbian Purchasing Group; treas, dir, Manchester Dyeing and Finishing Co, all Manchester, NH; chmn, bd dirs, Gordonshire Knitting Mills; V Cayey, PR; mem, firm, A Gordon & Son, Boston, Mass, 1916-18; treas, Mass Knitting Mills, 1918-41. Bd trustee, Lowell Tech Inst 1945-65; found: and f, Brandeis U; Albert Einstein Coll of Med; bd, NH Council on World Affairs; mem: Med Approving Auth, 1948-56; Amer Chem Soc; 32 degree Mason; clubs: New Cent; Manchester Country. Home: 173 Woodland Rd, Chestnut Hill, Mass. Office: 38 Chauncy St, Boston, Mass.

GORDON, Benjamin H, US, government official; b. Riga, Latvia, Feb 12, 1886; s. Elias and Bertha (Neihaus); in US since 1887; BA, Harvard U, 1908, LLB, 1910; att Ind Coll of Armed Forces, 1953; m. Miriam Zirinsky, 1939; c: Robert, Eliot. Coord, Civilian Defense Fed Agcys, NY, since 1950; fmr: chief, offs record div, Adjutant Gen's Dept, 1917-18; owner, Reliance Co, Phila, Pa, 1920-25; natl advt mgr, newspaper div, Curtis Pub Co, 1925-30; mgr, Barron Collier Org, 1930-40; coord, Jt Mission to Japan and China, US Depts of War and Commerce, 1947; cons, econ, Govt of Isr, 1947-68; bus cons, liaison off, foreign trade missions, US Dept of Commerce, 1942-57; liaison off to UN, 1947-57; prepared econ survey after 6-Day War, 1967, at request of Isr Govt, with coop of US Govt. Mem, bd govs, Boy Scouts of Amer; mem: NY Defense (regional) Mobilization Comm; co-found, Menorah Soc; Amer Econ Assn; Amer Marketing Assn; Trade Assn Execs; Amer Arbitration Assn; Commerce and Ind Assn; Civic Execs Conf of NY; liaison off, Jt Council of State Govts, Mid-Atlantic Region; club: Harvard. Hobby: world travel. Home: 162 W 56 St, New York, NY.

GORDON, Bernard, US, dentist, b. Kingston, NY, Mar 1, 1921; DDS, Baltimore Coll of Dent Surg, Dent Sch, U of Maryland, 1948; att U of Pa, Dent Sch; m. Letitia Zuskin, Apr 29, 1923; c: Ann, David. Ed, Jour Md State Dent Assn, since 1966; pvt practice, dent, since 1949. US Army, 1943-46. Mem: Baltimore City Dent Soc, fmr chmn, PR Council, exec bd, nominating council, since 1970; Md State Dent Assn, fmr bus mgr, Jour of State Assn, bd govs since 1966, exec bd since 1970, chmn, audit comm; Amer Dent Assn; Amer Assn Dent Eds, fmr chmn, sci manuscript comm; Alpha Omega, Baltimore Alumni chap, life mem, secy, grad dep, fmr, exec bd; Md Soc Dent for Children. Contbr to dent jours. Hobbies: fishing, philately. Home: 6606 Park Hgts Ave, Baltimore, Md. Office: 1924 Wilkens Ave, Baltimore, Md.

GORDON, Cyrus H, US, orientalist, educator; b. Phila, Pa, June 29, 1908; s. Benjamin and Dorothy (Cohen); grad, Gratz Coll, Phila, 1926; AB, 1927; MA, U of Pa, 1928; PhD, 1930; m. Joan Kendall, Sep 22, 1946; c: Deborah, Sarah, Rachel, Noah, Dan. Prof, Near Eastern studies, chmn, dept, Mediterranean studies, Brandeis U, since 1956; instr, U of Pa, 1930-31; archaeol, Amer School Oriental Research, Jerusalem and Baghdad, 1931-35; research f, instr, Johns Hopkins U, 1935-58; f: Amer Acad Arts and Sci, since 1968; Explorers Club, since 1968; staff mem: Smith Coll, 1938-41; Inst for Advanced Study, 1939-42; prof, Assyriology and Egyptology, Dropsie Coll, 1946-56. Col, USAF, Res, Ret, 1961-68, US Army, 1942-46. Trustee, Boston Heb Tchrs Coll, since 1965; mem: Amer Oriental Soc; Soc of Bibl Lit; Amer Philol Assn; Archaeol Inst of Amer; Amer Hist Assn. Author: Nouns in the Nuzi Tablets, 1936; The Living Past, 1941; Ugaritic Handbook, 1947; Ugaritic Literature, 1949; Smith College Tablets, 1952; Introduction to the Old Testament Times, 1953; Ugaritic Manual, 1955; Hammurabi's Code, 1957; Adventures in the Nearest East, 1957; The World of the Old Testament, 1958; Before the Bible, 1962; Ugaritic Textbook, 1967; The Ancient Near East, 1965; The Common Background of Greek and Hebrew Civilizations, 1965; Ugarit and Minoan Crete,1966; Evidence for the Minoan Language, 1966; Forgotten Scripts, 1968; first to write detaild grammar, dictionary, corpus of texts and comprehensive translation, Ugaritic tablets; deciphered the Minoan and Eteocretan inscriptions; numerous monographs and articles to learned jours. Home: 130 Dean Rd, Brookline, Mass. Office: Brandeis U, Waltham, Mass.

GORDON, Eddy S, Isr, jurist; b. Warsaw, Pol, 1897; d. Isaak and Zippora; LLB, fac law, Warsaw U; m; c: Carmela Turell, Yaron. Hon pres, WIZO, Jerusalem, since 1969, past pres; fmr mem: World WIZO Exec; WIZO Isr Fed; mem: Natl

Ins Inst, Isr; exec, Social Service Council, Isr. Home: 32 Gaza Rd, Jerusalem, Isr. Office: WIZO, 21 Keren Hayesod, Jerusalem, Isr.

GORDON, Ernst F, US, physician; b. New Haven, Conn, June 4, 1905; s. Israel and Anna (Goldstein); BA, Yale U, 1926; MD, Johns Hopkins Med Sch, 1930; m. Florence Oppenheim, Aug 16, 1931; c: Paul, Daniel. Att ped: St John's Riverside Hosp; Yonkers Gen Hosp; asst in med, Vanderbilt Clinic, Columbia Coll of Phys and Surgs, all since 1939; fmr: asst res, ped, New Haven Hosp, 1931-33; clinical asst, ped, Yale Med Sch, 1933-38, clinical instr, 1938-39. Prin contrib: described first case of malaria in child who had been transfused with blood from blood bank, 1940. Licenciate, Amer Bd Ped; f, Amer Acad Ped; chmn, Natl Alumni Sch Comm for Westchester Co representing Johns Hopkins U; mem: bd trustees, Family Service Soc, since 1947, past pres; NY Allergy Soc; Hudson Hills Golf Club; fmr: pres, Yonkers Acad Med; fmr mem, med bd, Yonkers Gen Hosp; vice-pres, mem, bd trustees, Temple Emanu-El; delg, J Fed. Contbr to med jours. Recipient: Family Service Soc Award, 1962. Home: 72 Highview Terr, Yonkers, NY. Office: 27 Ludlow St, Yonkers, NY.

GORDON, Everett J, US, surgeon; b. Wash, DC, July 23, 1914; s. Solvin and Freda (Weiss); BA, George Wash U, 1933; MA, Catholic U, 1937; MD, Jefferson Med Coll, 1937; m. Marian Kressin, Dec 23, 1951; c: Solvin, Stuart, Elissa. Orthopedist since 1946; clinical asso prof, orthopedic surg, Georgetown U, since 1965; Sr att surg, Dr's Hosp; chief, Orthopedic surg, Jefferson Memorial Hosp, Alexander, Va; mem: adv bd, United Bank and Trust Co of Md; bd dirs, Seaborb Land Co; chief orthopedic surg, Natl Homeopathic Hosp, 1948-58; vice-chief, orthopedic Surg, att surt, Childrens Hosp, 1967-68, cons orthopedist: crippled children's clinic, DC Health Dept; Natl Found for Infantile Paralysis; FTC; chief and dir, orthopedic appliance and prosthetic clinic. VA, Middle Atlantic States, asso chief, orthopedic aueg, Sibley Hosp; instr, orthopedic surg, U of Cincinnati, 1946; Maj, US Army. Dipl, Amer Bd Orthopedic Surg; f: AMA; Intl Coll Surgs, 1948; FACS, Amer Acad Orthopedic Surg; mem, regional bd, ADL, hon mem, Soc Pecuana de Ortopedia y Traumatologia; mem: exec bd, J Comty Council; Metrop Police Boys Club, med dir since 1950; fmr vice-pres, Argo lodge, B'nai B'rith. Clubs: Wash Orthopedic; Woodmont Country; Army and Navy; Wash Figure Skating, past pres. Contbr to med jours and medico-legal encys. Home: 2961 Ellicott Terr, NW, Wash, DC. Office: 2007 Eye St, Wash, DC.

GORDON, Harold H, US, rabbi; b. Minneapolis, Minn; s. Jacob and Nellie (Kronick); att Heb Theol Coll, Chgo, 1925-28; BA, U of Minn, 1929; ordained rabbi by Chief Rabbi Kook, and Hebron Yeshiva, Pal, 1934; DHL, JTSA, 1949, hon DD, 1966. Exec vice-pres, life tenure, NY Bd Rabbis, since 1960, chaplaincy coord since 1946, world traveler on behalf of bd; exec secy, B'rith Milah Bd of NY, since 1950; rabbi, Cong Sons of Jacob, Waterloo, Ia, 1935-42; dir, USO, Aberdeen and Laurel, Md; chaplain, JWB, 1942-43. Chaplain, maj, USAAF, 1943-46. Co-found, Intl Syn, NY Kennedy Intl Airport; co-chmn, Comm of Rel Leaders of NY; chmn, NY State Interfaith Comm on Chaplaincy; spiritual adv, Council of J Orgs in Civil Service, since 1956, secy, comm rel and educ participation, Amer J Tercentenary, 1954; mem: first delg of rabbis to Soviet Union and other Iron Curtain countries, 1956; delg: WJC, Stockholm, 1959, Brussels, 1965; WZC, Zurich, 1937, Jerusalem, 1960, 1965, 1968; White House Conf on Children and Youth, 1960; mem: adv council, Amer J Correctional Chaplains' Assn; Amer Correctional Chaplains' Assn; bd dirs, Cen Bur of J Aged; coord comm, Govs Comm on Scholastic Achievement; natl exec, Rel Zionists of Amer; mem: RA; JWV; Mil Chaplains Assn of US; Assn of J Chaplains in Armed Forces, Natl Chaplain, JWV, 1964-6; dir, B'rith Milah Sch, Mount Sinai Hosp, NY, 1968. Recipient: honored, FJP, 1959, 1966; man of the year award, council of J Orgs, 1960; citation for intl rel leadership, NYC, 1960; Avodah award, J Tchrs Assn, 1961; Interfaith Movement award, 1963; citation for moral and spiritual leadership, NYC, 1966. Study: 10 E 73 St, New York, NY.

GORDON, Hirsch L, US, neuropsychiatrist, author; b. Vilna, Lith, Nov 26, 1896; s. Elijah and Malkah (Katzenelenbogen); in US since 1915; att Acad Higher J Learning, Odessa, 1911-14; PhD, Yale U, 1922; LHD, Catholic U, 1923; MA, Amer U, 1924; MA: Columbia U, 1926, Tchrs Coll, 1927; DHL, JTSA, 1928; MA: NYU, 1928; U Berlin, 1931; DLitt, U

Rome, 1931; DSc, 1934, MD, 1934; m. Tamara Liebowitz, 1947. Asso, psycht, NY Med Coll, sinee 1953; asso visiting psycht: Metrop Hosp; Bird S Coler Hosp; Flower Fifth Ave Hosp, all since 1953; adj, neuropsycht, Beth Isr Hosp, since since 1953; prof, psycht, grad sch, Yeshiva U, since 1959; lectr, Alfred Adler Inst Individual Psycht, since 1954; mem, NY State Selective Service Appeal Bd, since 1951; neuro-psychiatric cons, NYC Dept Wfr, since 1950; psycht i/c, Psychosomatic Clinic, Wfr I Dispensary, since 1950; sr psycht, NYC Dept Mental Hygiene, since 1952; lectr: Talmud, Collegio Rabbinco, Florene, It, 1915; hist, archaeol, Talmud, Heb Sem, NYC, 1920-27; instr, phil, NJ Normal Sch, Newark, 1926-27; supt, United Heb Schs, Newark, 1926-29; phys, outpatient dept, Mt Sinai Hosp, NYC, neur, 1935, skin and syphllis clinic, 1937-40, surg, 1937-40, surg, 1940-41; phys, gyn, Harlem Hosp, 1939-41; mem, neuropsychiatric staff: Pilgrim State Hosp, 1941-42; Cornell Div, Bellevue Hosp, 1943; Kings Co Hosp, Bklyn 1943; Bellevue Psychiatric, 1944; lectr: NYC Cancer Comm, 1935-41; NYC Health Dept, 1937-41. Zion Mule Corps, Brit Expeditionary Force,1915; sgt, Amer-Pal Legion, 1918-20; maj, US Army, i/c shock therapies, Northport, NY, 1944-46; chief neuropsycht, VA, Jacksonville, Fla, 1947; mem, neuropsycht cons div, Off Surg Gen, US Army, Wash, DC, 1947-58; sr surg, cdr, USPHS, chief, neuropsycht div, US Marine Hosp, Staten I, 1948-50. Dipl; Royal Inst Legal Med, Rome; Natl Bd Med, It; f: AMA; Amer Psychiatric Assn; Amer Geriatric Assn; NY Acad Med; pres: Northport Army Med Soc, 1946; Amer Ivrith Med Soc, since 1942; mem: Amer Group Psychotherapy Assn; NY Soc for clinical Psycht; Bx Soc for Neur and Psycht; Electro-Shock Research Assn; Assn for Advancement Psychotherapy; Amer Soc for Research in Psychosomatic Problems; Assn Mil Surgs; NY Acad Sci; Hist Sci Soc; Medieval Acad of Amer: Amer Oriental Soc; Phi Delta Kappa; Amer Pal J Legion; Amer Legion; JWV; M8l Order WW; Ret Off Assn; ZOA; natl adv council, OSE; Masons. Author: The Basilica and the Stoa, 1931; L'Emofilia 1934; Mattia Ben Haresh, Medico Romano Del Primo Secolo, 1934; L'Omicidio, 1935; Plays, 1939; Objectors to Electric Shock, 1946; Fractures in Electric Shock, 1946; Fifty Shock Therapy Theories, 1946; The Maggid of Caro, 1949; New Chemotherapy in Mental Illness, 1958; Preservation of Youth, 1959; Psychiatric Concepts in Bible and Talmud, 1960; J Preuss, Med Historian, 1962; Morbus Cardiacus, 1963; co-found, co-ed, Hadoar Daily, 1921; since 1922; mgn ed, Hatoren, 1921-22; asso ed, Svilei ha Chinuch monthly, 1922-24; ed: med dept, J Amer Weekly, 1935-42; rev dept, J Morning Journal, 1935-52, contbr weekly psychiatric column, Med Leaves Yearbook, 1937; med ed, Universal Jewish Ency; mem, ed staff: Amer Jour of Psychiatry; since 1952; Amer Jour of Psychotherapy, since 1952; NY State Jour of Med; Post-Grad Jour of Med; contbr lit and sci monographs, articles to publs. Recipient: Maimonides award, Michael Reese Med Cen and Coll for J Studies, Chgo, 1967; alumni recognition award, Amer U, 1968. Home and office: 239 Central Park W, New York, NY.

GORDON, Ira J, US, educator, psychologist; b. NYC, Jan 15, 1923; s. Herman and Esther (Feltenstein); BBA, CCNY, 1943; MA, Tchrs Coll, Columbia U, 1947, EdD, 1950; m. Esther Goldberg, Aug 4, 1949; c: Gary, Bonnie. Prof, educ, U of Fla, since 1960; dir, Inst Devl of Hum Resources, since 1966, chmn, founds dept, 1964-67; asst prof, psych, 1948-49, asso prof, psych, Kan State Coll, 1949-51; asso prof, Inst for Child Study, U of Md, 1954-56; cons, USAF, Hum Resources Research Lab, 1952-54. Lt, US Army, 1943-46. Mem: Assn for Sup and Curriculum Devl; Amer Psych Assn; Amer Personnel and Guidance Assn; Amer Educ Research Assn; B'nai Isr Cong; Alpha Phi Omega; Beta Gamma Sigma; Phi Delta Kappa; Kappa Delta Pi. Author: The Teacher as a Guidance Worker, 1956; Children's Views of Themselves, 1959; Human Development, 1962, rev ed, 1970; Human Development Readings in Research, 1965; Studying The Child In School, 1966; Readings in Developmental Psychology, 1970; contbr to profsl jours. Home: 2900 SW Court, Gainesville, Fla. Office: U of Fla, Gainsville, Fla.

GORDON, Mark Samuel, US, dentist, b. Pittsburgh, Pa, Jan 20, 1937; s. Manny and Sara (Love); DDS, U of Pittsburgh, Sch of Dent, 1965; m. Nancy Wesoky, Aug 30, 1964; c: Michael. Pvt practice since 1961. Vice-pres, Rotary; mem: Alpha Omega Omicron. Home: 5411 Beacon St, Pittsburgh, Pa. Office: 757 Warrington, Pittsburgh, Pa.

GORDON, Michael Robert, US, educator; b. Chgo, Ill, July 16, 1939; s: Gordon and Bertha (Marcus); BA, Stanford U, Cal,

1961; BA, MA, Oxford, 1963; MPA, PhD, Harvard, 1967; m. Nancy Van Schreeven, 1965. Prof, political sci, U of Cal, Santa Barbara, since 1965. Author: Conflict and Consensus in Labour's Foreign Policy, 1914-1965, pub 1969. Recipient: Rhodes scholar, 1961; Littauer f, Harvard. Home: 812 de la Guerra Terr, Santa Barbara, Cal. Office: Dept Political Sci, U of Cal, Santa Barbara, Cal.

GORDON, Michel M, Fr, chemical engr; b. Wilno, Lith, Nov 12, 1902; s. Elijah and Malkah (Katznelenbogen); in Fr since 1924; att Hochschule für die Wissenschaft des Judentums, Berlin, 1922-23; U Berlin, 1922-24; U Strasbourg, Fr, 1925-26; dipl, CE; m. Mery Nirke, Apr, 1933; c: Annie Baslaw. Bus exec, dealing in chems and essential oils, since 1946; cons to chem ind; fmr: chief chem engr, gas factory, Paris, 1927-30; research chem engr, organic chem 1930-45. Fr Army, 1939-40. Vice-pres, Youth Aliyah, since 1959; secy, Aschkenazic Syn, since 1955, past vice-pres; found, first pres, J Comty of Grasse; vice-pres, Union of Importers and Exporters; pres, Zionist Fed of Nice; mem exec, UJA; asso hon mem, l'Accademia Teatine per la Scienza à Roma, It; mem: B'nai B'rith, past pres; comm, Bonds for Isr; Chem Soc of Fr; Assn ChemE; Soc pour l'encouragement des recherches et invention; active, League Against Antisemitism. Author: La Nicotine, 1945; Decoloration in Perfumery, 1945; L'industrie d'Agrumes en Israël, 1953; Description des principales essences d'Eucalyptus, 1955; Maimonide, percurseur de la médecine moderne, 1959. Recipient: Chevalier de l'ordre du mérite pour la recherche et invention, Fr. Home: 38 rue Dabray, Nice, Fr. Office: POB 28, Grasse, Fr.

GORDON, Monte J, US, security analyst; b. NYC, Aug 19, 1923; s. Louis and Geraldine (Halpern); BA, Bklyn Coll, 1947; MA, Columbia U, 1948; att NYU, 1949-56; m. Arline Bobrick, Mar 23, 1946; c: Dale, Margery. First vice-pres, dir, research, Bache & Co, Inc, since 1956; lectr: Bklyn Coll, 1948-59; Baruch Sch, CUNY, 1959-62; New Sch of Social Research, 1962-63. Staff sgt, USAAC, army airways communications, 1943-45. Bd dirs: NY Council of Econ Educ; Bklyn Coll Alumni Fund; fmr pres, Bklyn Coll Alumni in Finance; mem: Soc of Security Analysts, NY chap; Amer Econ Assn, natl chap. Hobbies: reading, horseback riding. Home: 220 Mimosa Dr, Roslyn, NY. Office: Bache & Co, 36 Wall St, New York, NY.

GORDON, Murray Abraham, US, attorney; b. NYC, Apr 22, 1920; s. Philip and Rose (Charmoy); BSS, CCNY, 1941; LLB, Columbia, 1944; m. Beatrice Hennes, Sep 24, 1944; c: Kenneth, Daniel. Atty since 1944. Natl vice-pres, AJCong; bd dirs, City Coll Alumni Assn; mem: Civil Rights and Bill of Rights Comm, Bar Assn of City of NY; Bx Co Bar Assn. Author: The Trial of the Future, 1963; The Wall Between Church and State, 1964. Recipient: Alumni Service Award, CCNY, 1941. Home: 51-51 Post Rd, Riverdale, NY. Office: 401 Broadway, New York, NY

GORDON, Nathaniel Louis, Scotland, executive; b. Edinburgh, July 28, 1944; s. Maurice and Sarah (Lukeman); personnel mgr dipl, U of Strathclyde, Glasgow, 1969. Cons, Personnel Mgmt Services, Edinburgh; internal auditor, Edinburgh Corp, 1964-67; acctnt, Graham, Smart and Annen, CA, 1967-68. Chmn: Scottish League of Young Libs; Edinburgh Assn of Zionist Youth; mem, exec comm, Scottish Lib Party; fmr instr, B'nei Akivah. Home: 14 Arden St, Edinburgh, Scotland. Office: 6 Castle St, Edinburgh, Scotland.

GORDON, Noah, US, novelist; b. Worcester, Mass, Nov 11, 1926; s. Robert and Rose (Melnikoff); BS, Boston U, 1950, AM, 1951; m. Lorraine Seay; c: Lise, Jamie, Michael. Ed, pub, Psychiatric Opinion, bi-monthly, since 1964; mem, ed bd, Omega, jour for study of dying, death, lethal behavior; reporter, Worcester Telegram, 1957-59; sci ed, Boston Herald, 1959-63. Author: The Rabbi, 1965; The Death Committee, 1969; contbr of fiction and articles to leading periodicals. US Army, 1945-46. Trustee, Temple Beth Sholom, Framingham, Mass, fmr, chmn, social actions comm; mem: natl adv council, Cen for Psych Study of Dying, Death and Lethal Behavior, Wayne State U, Detroit, Mich; Sigma Delta Chi; Natl Assn Sci Writers; Author's Guild; Author's League; B'nai B'rith. Recipient: Dist Achievement Citation, Boston U, 1966. Hobbies: fishing, tennis, gardening. Home: 29 Savoy Rd, Framingham, Mass. Office: 39 Cochituate Rd, Framingham, Mass.

GORDON, Peretz, Isr, executive; b. Bialystok, Pol, Feb 9 1923; s. Eliahu and Tova (Sunshine); in Isr since 1924; BA cum laude, W Reserve U, Cleveland, O, 1953; MA, U of Chgo, 1954; m. Yael Carmi, Nov 2, 1954; c: Tal, Gilad. Gen mgr, Isr Ins Assn, since 1966; fmr: Isr consul to India; Chargé d'Affairs, Ceylon. Seren, IDF, 1948-49. Author: Treaties of the Middle East, 1957. Home: 7 Noah St, Tel Aviv, Isr. Office: 113 Allenby St, Tel Aviv, Isr.

GORDON, Samuel S, US, obstetrician, gynecologist, educator; b. Pol, Oct 3, 1908; s. Morris and Miriam (Modes); in US since 1912; BA, U of Louisville, 1930, MD, 1932; m. Sophie Wice, Mar 7, 1943; c: Linda, James, Robert. Asso prof, obstet and gyn, U of Louisville Sch of Med, since 1952, fac mem since 1936; teaching staff, Gen Hosp, since 1936; chief, dept obstet and gyn, J Hosp, Louisville, 1950-58, pres, staff, 1956, secy, 1950; courtesy staff: Kentucky Baptist; St Joseph; Red Cross; Norton; Methodist hosps. Maj, US Army MC, 1942-46. Vice-pres, Adath Isr Cong, Louisville, 1967-71; pres, Louisville Obstet and Gyn Soc, 1949, secy, 1947-48; f: Amer Coll Surg; Amer Coll Obstet and Gyn; dipl, Amer Bd Obstet and Gyn; mem: Cen Assn Obstet and Gyn; Phi Delta Epsilon. Contbr to med jours. Recipient: Pres Unit Citation, 1944. Hobbies: golf, woodwork. Home: 609 Riverwood Pl, Louisville, Ky. Office: Heyburn Bldg, Louisville, Ky.

GORDON, Theodore Herzl, US, rabbi; b. Minneapolis, Minn, Sep 29, 1908; s. George and Sophie (Weinberg); BA, cum laude, U of Minn, 1929; BHL, ordained rabbi, HUC, 1933, DD, 1958; m. Beryl Berman, June 8, 1930; c: David, Judith, George. Rabbi, Main Line Reform Temple, suburban Phila, Pa, since 1953; dir, Hillel Founds, Pa State, 1937-40; U of Cal, 1940-42; U of Wis, 1942-48; U of Pa, 1948-53; mem, CCAR. Home and study: 650 Revere Rd, Merion Station, Pa.

GORDON, Wilfred, Can, QC, business exec, attorney; b. Toronto, Can, Aug 21, 1909; s. Jacob and Lena (Sobol); BA, McMaster U, 1931; PhD, U of Chgo, 1931; barrister, solicitor, Osgoode Hall, 1935; ordained rabbi, Heb Theol Coll, Chgo, Ill, 1932, MHL, 1963; m. Balfoura, June 30, 1947; c: Jared, Daniel, Phyllis. Pres: Brown's Line Inves Ltd, since 1954; 100 Simcoe St, Ltd, since 1953; 27 Wellington W Ltd, since 1951; Cloverdale Park, since 1950; Islington Park, since 1954; Bellgor Mgmt, since 1958; vice-pres: Cloverdale Shopping Cen, since 1953; Abgor Inves, since 1954; Mountain Theatres, since 1953; partner, Gordon, Keyfetz, Hall and Baker, barristers and solicitors, since 1959; mem, adv comm, Metrop Trust Co; rabbi, McCaul St Syn, 1935-36, 1942-44. Chaplain, RCAF, 1945-46. Vice-pres, Toronto ZC; dir: Joseph Wolinsky Charitable Found, since 1959; Harry Abramsky Charitable Found, since 1957; J Barney Goldhar Charitable Found, since 1960; vice-capt, capt, 3 natl campaigns, div B, Victory Loan Campaigns, Toronto; mem: natl council, ZOC; exec, Cen Fund for Traditional Instns; bd govs: Can Friends Yeshiva U, since 1966; YMHA; State of Isr Bonds; Ont Housing Adv Comm; exec, United JWF of Toronto, since 1954, fmr; bd, Hillel Found, since 1958; natl exec, Mizrachi Org of Can; exec, Ont Zionist Region; United ZC Toronto; B'nai B'rith; Gen Wingate br, Can Legion; Forest Hill Anshei Lida; Beth Tzedec; Shaarei Shomayim; fmr: pres, chmn bd, Asso Heb Schs, Toronto; pres: Camp Massad, Ont; Young Isr, Toronto; Heb Day HS; vice-pres: Bur J Educ, Toronto; chmn, campaign chmn, Toronto Heb Day Sch; chmn: Toronto Found, JNF, mem, natl exec; chmn, exec bd, Ner Isr Yeshiva Coll, Toronto; regional chmn, Can Friends, Bar Ilan U; div chmn, UJA; zone chmn, Red Feather Campaign; mem: natl council: Can J Cong, mem, cen region exec; bd govs, Can Isr Securities Ltd; exec, Keren Hatarbuth; bd trustees, Emet Rabbi Herzog World Acad; clubs: Reading Law; Can of Toronto. Home: 200 Dunvegan Rd, Toronto, Can. Office: Natl Bldg, 347 Bay St, Toronto, Can.

GORDON, William, US, physician; b. Phila, Pa, Oct 21, 1899; s. Samuel and Anna (Jacobson); AB, U of Pa, 1921, MD, Sch of Med, 1925, MSc, 1932; m. Lillian Goldstein, June 28, 1927; c: Joseph. Asso, otolaryngology, U of Pa Hosp, since 1933, instr, otolaryngology, since 1933, asso, Grad Sch, 1930-57; asso, otolaryngology, Phila Gen Hosp, 1947-57. Corresp secy, Cong Bnai Abraham, since 1939; f, Coll of Phys, Phila; Amer Coll Surgs; Intl Coll Surgs, life f, Amer Acad Ophthal and Otolaryngology; mem: Phila Co Med Soc; Phila Laryngology Soc; Pa State Med Soc; AMA. Book reviewer, Archives of Otolaryngology, 1937-57; contbr: chaps on Eustachian Salpingitis and treatment and prevention of deafness to Jackson & Jackson, Nose, Throat and Ear, 1945, 1959; to med publs. Home and office: 5345 Spruce St, Philadelphia, Pa.

GOREN, Howard Joseph, Can, research sci; b. Ukraine, Apr 9', 1941; s. Morris and Brucha (Nissenbaum); BSc, U Toronto, 1964; PhD, SUNY, Buffalo, 1968; m. Frances Moran, Sep 18, 1965; c: Robyn. Postdoc researcher, Weizmann Inst of Sci, since 1968. Mem, Rho Chi, hon pharm soc. Contbr to profsl publs. Recipient: Grad Sch f, SUNY, 1967; postdoc F, NRC, Can, 1968. Hobbies, sports, basketball. Home: 81 Palm Dr, Downsview, Ont, Can. Office: Weizmann Inst of Sci, Rehovot, Isr.

GOREN, Shraga, Isr, organization and business exec; b. Makarov, Russ, July 25, 1897; s. Aaron and Chaya (Burman) Gorochovsky; in Isr since 1921; m. Esther Klioner, 1920; c: Michal, Avigail. Vice-pres, Alliance Rubber and Tire Co, Ltd; vice-chmn, Delek, Isr Fuel Corp; dir, Workers Bank; fmr: MK; vice-pres, bldg workers; mgn dir, Solel Boneh; mgr, Cen Off Transp Productive and Service Corp; chmn bd, mgn dir, Devl of Areas Industrialization, Ltd. Mem: exec comm, Histadrut; natl comm, JNF; delg, WZC, 1937; missions to Eur, US. Contbr to local press. Home: 18 Zeitlin St, Tel Aviv, Isr. Office: POB 1831, Tel Aviv, Isr.

GORESS, Josef, Isr, agriculturist; b. Mainz, Ger, Apr 22, 1911; s. Max and Tilly (Stern) Gochsheimer; in Isr since 1935; m. Tirz Adania, 1947; c: Noemi, Arnon. Mem, Kibbutz Ma'ayan-Zvi; mgn dir, Isr Fruit Produc and Marketing Bd, since 1956; pres, Hof ha'Carmel Reg Munic Council, 1950-52; delg, Agrexco Agric Export Co in Fr, 1962-65. Haganah, 1939-47. Delg, Ihoud Habonim, 1962-65; Eur bur, Ihoud Olami, 1947-49; delg, Chever Hakwuzot for Eng, 1939-40; exec mem, Hechaluz, Ger, 1938; mem, World Exec Makabi Hazair, 1935-38. Contbr to profsl jours. Home: Ma'ayan-Zvi, Hof ha'Carmel, Isr. Office: 119 Hahashmonaim St, Tel Aviv, Isr.

GORFINKLE, Bernard L, US, attorney; b. Boston, Mass, Oct 29, 1889; s. Harris and Sarah (Millionthaler); LLB, Boston U, 1911; m. Frieda Edinberg, June 7, 1921; c: Herbert, Ruth Roberts, Sarah. Pvt practice, law, since 1911, col, US, Army; mil aide to Gov Volpe since 1962; pvt, Mass Cavalry, 1913; sgt, Mexican Border Service, 1916; 2nd lt, Asmer Expeditionary Forces, 1917; Fr, wounded twice; promoted on battlefield to capt, judge advocate, 1918; acted as J chaplain; created formula for Amer Expeditionary Forces payment. Fr and civilian claims; trial judge advocate, Eur, 1919; US delg: Amer Peace Commn; Comm on Ger; secy, mil aide, Bernard Baruch, raw materials sect, Supr Econ Council; Paris repr, Rhineland Commn; aide, bodyguard, Pres Woodrow Wilson, Peace Treaty, 1919; judge advocate, Maritime Affairs, NY, 1919; State Dept Judge Advocate, JWV, 1932; appd NE field sup, War Manpower Commn, 1942-45; col, mil aide to Gov Herter, Mass, 1953-57. Dir: Heb Home for Aged; Multiple Sclerosis Soc; Brandeis U Assn, Boston, fmr secy; charter mem, Mass Bay chap, US Army Assn; hon trustee: Beth Isr Hosp; Gorfinkle Found; org: YMHA of France; and treas, Chestnut Hill Improvement Soc; and secy, Newton Civic Soc; found, past cdr, Newton Post, JWV; mem: Temple Ohabei Shalom; Friends of Heb U; Amer J Hist Soc; Amer Legion; Disabled Amer Vets; Masons; clubs: co-org, first pres: NE Grad of Zeta Beta Tau; Newton Squash and Tennis, now hon pres and dir; New Century, past pres. Recipient: US Service Medal, seven stars; Purple Heart; Belgian Order of the Crown, all WWI. Home: 170 Ivy St, Brookline, Mass. Office: 44 School St, Boston, Mass.

GORMAN, Pauline, US, communal worker; b. Detroit, Mich, Nov 22, 1916; d. Joseph and Anna (Yancher) Gorman; att U of Mich, 1934-36; m. Gerald Gorman, Dec 20, 1936; c: Stuart, Karen. Mem, Mich regional bd, ADL, since 1958; exec secy, B'nai David Syn Sch, since 1960; delg, natl B'nai B'rith Women, since 1956, mem, Hillel Commn, 1962-64; bd, B'nai David Sisterhood, 1958-60. Home: 2000 N Woodward, Royal Oak, Mich.

GORNEY, Uriel, Isr, attorney; b. Riga, Latvia, June 10, 1921; s. Israel and Nina (Berlin) Gornitsky; m. Ruth Dunkelblum, Oct 30, 1951. Mem, law firm, I Gornitsky and Co, since 1946; fmr: dist atty, Tel Aviv, 1951-55; lectr, fac law, Tel Aviv U, 1952-59. Vice-pres, Automobile and Touring Club, Isr; bd govs, Herzlia Coll, Tel Aviv. Author: Digest of Criminal Law, 2nd ed, 1957; contbr to law jours. Home: 24 Hagderot St, Savyon, Isr. Office: 13 Ahad Ha'am St, Tel Aviv, Isr.

GORSON, Cyrus S, US, business exec; b. Phila, Pa, Jan 4, 1895; s. Myer and Elka (Garb); LLB, Dickinson Coll, Carlisle,

Pa, 1917; m. Ida Steinberg, June 4, 1922; c: Shirley Milgrim. Pres, Equitable Credit and Discount Co, Phila, since 1953, off of co, since 1920. Pres, Pa Ind Bankers Assn, 1960; trustee, Fed of J Charities; dir, Allied J Campaign; Phila Psycht Cen, since 1937, secy since 1953; div chmn, Comty Chest, 1949-53; patron: JTSA; YW-YMHA; mem: Temple Har Zion; Salvation Army; ARC fund raising; Natl Consumer Finance Assn; B'nai B'rith; ZOA; Phi Epsilon Pi; Masons; J Publ Soc; Phila Mus Art; Chelsea Heb Cong; Drama Guild; Fleisher Art Memorial; clubs: Golden Slipper Square; Thirty-two Carat; Locust; Green Valley Country; Linwood Country. Contbr to trade and org jours. Home: 544 Greystone Rd, Merion Station, Pa. Office: 674 N Broad St, Philadelphia Pa.

GORSON, Joseph N, US, attorney, banker; b. Phila, Pa, Oct 13, 1897; s. Myer and Elka (Garb); LLB, Dickinson Sch of Law, 1919; m. Nettie Goldenthal, Aug 9, 1918; c: Marshall, Claire Axelrod. Pres, Fidelity Bond & Mortgage Co, since 1940; chmn bd, Equitable Credit & Discount Co; fmr, treas, Gen Finance Co, 1920-40; Dept Public Assistance, State of Pa, 1935-39. Pres, Phila Psycht Cen; vice-pres: bd of City Trusts, City of Phila; Home for J Aged; mem: bd dirs, chmn, natl planning comm, JTSA; bd trustees, Fed of JA's of Gtr Phila; exec comm, Fed J Charities; bd dirs, Har Zion Temple; clubs: Locust; Green Valley Country; past pres, Mortgage Bankers Assn of Phila. Home: 429 N Highland Ave, Merion, Pa. Office: 16 & Walnut Sts, Philadelphia, Pa.

GOSHEN-GOTTSTEIN, Moshe H; Isr, orientalist, Biblical scholar; b. Berlin, Ger, Sep 6, 1925; s. Paul and Ilse (Grand) Gottstein; in Isr since 1939; MA, Heb U, Jerusalem, 1947, PhD, 1951; m. Esther Hepner, July 27, 1953; c: Alan, Jonathan. Prof, semitic langs, Bibl phil, Heb U, since 1950; visiting prof, Hebraic, Bible studies: JTSA; grad sch, NYU; Dropsie Coll, Phila, Pa; lectr at various coll's. Pres, Isr Soc Semitic Studies; mem: Soc Bible Lit of Amer; Eur Ling Soc. Author: Tahbira u'Milona shel Halashon Ha'ivrit Shebithum Hashpa'ata shel Ha'aravit, 1951; Hadikduk Ha'ivri Hashimushi, 1954; Hakonkordanitzia la Tanach le Mendelkern, rev ed, 1956; She'elot Balashon Uvadikduk, 1957; Tirgumei Hamikra Ha'aramiim, 1958; Sefer Hamitzvot le Harambam Ba'arichat Tirgum Hadash, 1958; Megilot Kumran Uma'amadan Haleshoni, 1959; Text and Language in Bible and Qumran, 1960; Textim Ivriim Meshuabarim Mimei Habenayim, 1964; Sefer Yisha'ayahu, Prakim Ledugma Im Mavo, 1965; Halashon Ha'ivrit Vehaleshonot Hashemiot-Kavim Lamavo, 1965; Sefer Chochmat Achikar-Surit Ve'aramit, 1966; Lemad Ivrit, 1968; Milon Halashon Ha'ivrit Hahadasha A, Mavo Lemilonaut Shel Ha'ivrit Hahadasha, 1969; A Syriac-English Glossary with Etymological Notes, 1969; gen ed: Heb U Bible Project; Heb Dict Project. Recipient: Bialik Prize, Warburg Prize, both Heb U. Home: 17 Jabotinsky Rd, Jerusalem, Isr. Office: Heb U, Jerusalem, Isr.

GOSS, Leonard Cecil, UK, journalist; b. London, Eng, May 19, 1925; s. Jack and Sophie (Lewis); att Raine's Found, London; m. Marion Goldstone, Mar 20, 1950. News ed, S Wales Evening Post, Swansea, since 1968, with firm since 1958; gossip columnist, specialist on rel and intl issues, travel, youth, TV critic. Hon ed, intl and natl jours; hon PR off, dir, vice-chmn: Intl Friendship League; Glamorgan Scout Council; Swansea Lions Club; Swansea Council of Chr-J; life pres, Swansea J Jr Club; comm mem, Swansea Citizens' Advice Bur; many charitable groups; comm repr for W Wales, Cen J Lecture; secy, J anti-defamation comm; adv, Welsh Assn of Youth Clubs on intl understanding; fmr: leader, Scout Movement; secy, vice-pres, pres, British Jr C of C; hon secy: JPA; Zionist Soc; Heb Cong; JCC; JNF, all of Swansea; club, Lions, Swansea. Recipient: Life mem of sen, Jr Chamber Intl, 1963; Local Jr C of C, 1965; Medal of Merit, Scout Movement, 1968. Spec interest: promotion of intl, inter-rel understanding. Home: 19 Ernald Pl, Uplands, Swansea, Wales. Office: POB 14, Swansea, Glam, Wales.

GOSS, Michael, M, US, attorney, b. Phila, Pa, Dec. 26, 1942; s. Albert and Betty (Letbowitz); AB, Pa State U, 1964; JD, Villanova Law Sch, Pa, 1967; m. Marlene Kohn, Aug 20, 1967. Pvt practice since 1967; arbitrator for Amer Arbitration Assn; vice-pres, B'nai B'rith, William J Blitman Lodge, fmr treas; mem, Pi Sigma Alpha. Hobbies: tennis, reading. Home: 240 Buckboard Rd, Willow Grove, Pa. Office: 1000 Penn Square Bldg, Philadelphia, Pa.

GOTH, Trudy, US, journalist; b. Berlin, Ger, May 31, 1913; d. Ernst and Gisella (Selden); in US since 1939; att U of Florence,

It, journalism, 1934-36; various courses, music, theatrical mgmt, press relations, NY, 1939-42, 1943-48. Free-lance journalist, reporter, critic, for various Eur and US publs, since 1950; personal repr, tour mgmt, conductor Dimitri Mitropoulos, 1951-60; chief, fgn corresp dept, music and drama festivals: Salzburg; Florence; Vienna; Berlin, 1963-68. Mem, bd dirs, Universal Ed, Vienna, Aus; cons, Intl Festival Org; mem: Associazione Stampa Estera, Rome, It; Overseas Press Club, NYC. Contbr series of articles in Ger, It, Amer, Mexican, Greek publs. Hobbies: music, theatre, langs. Home: 159 W 53 St, New York, NY.

GOTHELF, Ephraim Louis, US, attorney, b. NYC, July 25, 1907; s. Morris and Rose (Levinson); LLB, NYU, 1928; m Charlotte Hoskwith, Sep 26, 1939; c: Michael, Sara, Rebecca, Roseann. Pvt practice since 1929; arbitrator for the Amer Arbitration Assn. Pres, Temple Beth Emeth of Flatbush, Bklyn; dir, Bklyn Hgts Youth Cen; speaker, FJP; mem: UJA; Cancer Care, Inc. Spec interests: Heb lang, J studies and lit. Home: 495 Rugby Rd, Brooklyn, NY. Office: 565 Fifth Ave, New York, NY.

GOTHELF, Yehuda L, Isr, journalist; b. Warsaw, Pol, Nov 19, 1903; s. Yehoshua and Zelda (Sorgenstein); in Isr since 1929; m. Hela Mozes, 1929; c: Uri. Ret; fmr: ed, Davar daily, since 1965. Author: Torat ha-Ma'ase, 1932; Sefer ha'Shomrim, 1933; Socialism: Demokratigmul Diktatura, 1958; Tmuroth Hevratiot, 1960; Medina-Chevra-Histadrut, 1961; The Israel Society; Significance of Democracy and Socialism in our Time, 1960. Home: 5 Epstein St, Tel Aviv, Isr.

GOTLIEB, Calvin Carl, Can, mathematician; b. Toronto, Can, Mar 27, 1921; s. Israel and Jenny (Sherman); BA, U of Toronto, 1942, MA, 1946, PhD, 1948; hon DMath, U of Waterloo, Ont; m. Phyllis Bloom, June 12, 1949; c: Leo, Margaret, Jane. Dir, Inst of Computer Sci, prof, dept computer sci, spec lectr, dept math, U of Toronto, since 1962. F, Royal Soc of Can; mem: educ and cultural comm, research comm, CJCong, cen region; sch bd, Adath Isr Cong, Toronto; Assn for Computer Machinery, past chmn, natl, conv; British Computer Soc; Amer Math Soc; Can Info Processing Soc; Computer Soc of Can, past pres; Soc of Ind and Applied Math; group which established Computation Cen, Toronto, 1948; Can repr, Intl Fed for Info Processing, past chmn, admission comm. Co-author: High Speed Data Processing; ed-in-chief: Communications, Assn for Computing Machinery, 1962-65, assn jour, 1965-68; contbr to profsl publs. Home: 29 Ridgevale Dr, Toronto, Can. Office: U of Toronto, Toronto, Can.

GOTS, Joseph S, US, microbiologist, educator; b. Phila, Pa, Oct 12, 1917; s. Solomon and Lillian (Shlomoff); AB, Temple U, Phila, Pa, 1939; MS, U of Pa, 1941, PhD, 1948; m. Selma Sheinbeck, Jan 24, 1941; c: Ronald, Lynne. Prof, microbiol, Sch of Med, U of Pa, since 1963, on fac since 1946; bact, US Dept Agric, 1941-42. Maj, US Army, 1942-46, lt col, Res. F, NY Acad Scis; mem: Amer Soc Microbiols; Soc Amer Bacts, pres, E Pa br, 1959-61; Soc Gen Microbiol; Amer Assn Biol Chems; Soc Experimental Biol and Med; Genet Soc Amer; Sigma Xi, pres, U of Pa chap, 1964-65; John Morgan Soc; Soc Gen Phys; Amer Assn Cancer Research; AAAS. Contbr to profsl jours. Home: 1209 Greenhill, Flourtown, Pa. Office: Sch of Med, U of Pa, Philadelphia, Pa.

GOTSMAN, E Asher, Isr, physicist; b. Krugersdorp, S Afr, Oct 21, 1934; s. Abraham and Ethel (Rasswell); in Isr since 1963; BSc, hons, U of Witwatersrand, Johannesburg, S Afr, 1958; PhD, U of London, Imperial Coll, 1963; m. Lesley Targowsky, Dec 15, 1957; c: Aviva, Ilan, Yaron. Sr lectr, Tel Aviv U, since 1965; visiting asso prof, U of Cal, since 1969; research asst, CSIR, S Afr, 1957-59; sr research off, AEC, Isr, 1963-65. Repr of sr lectrs, Acad Sen, Tel Aviv U; secy, Habonim, S Afr, 1954-56; mem: Amer Physical Soc, US; Inst Physics and Physical Soc, Eng. Contbr to physics jours. Home: 12 Aliyah, Neve Rassco, Ramat Hasharon, Isr. Office: Dept of Physics, Tel Aviv U, Tel Aviv, Isr.

GOTTESMAN, Esther, US, communal worker; b. NYC, Dec 5, 1899; d. Aaron and Sarah (Lubetkin) Garfunkel; BS, NYU, 1921; m. Benjamin Gottesman, 1921; c: Milton, David, Alice Bayer (decd). Ed, Hadassah Magazine; chmn, Hadassah Isr Educ Services; fmr: natl treas, Hadassah, Hadassah repr on bd of United Pal Appeal; KH; Amer ZC; bd mem: Amer Assn J Educ; Bd of J Educ, Comm of NYC; delg: WZC, 1961; World Zionist Actions Comm, 1962. Responsible for publ of Great Ages and Ideas of the Jewish People. Home: 45 E 85 St, New York, NY. Office: 65 E 52 St, New York, NY.

GOTTESMANN, Leopold, Isr, business exec; b. Smolnik, Czech, Jan 4, 1913; s. Israel and Selma; m. Adina Brickman, Jan 10, 1968; c: Gabriela. Gen mgr: Kadimah Ins Co Ltd, since 1957; Samson Ins, since 1961; fmr: hon consul, Aus; delg to Zionist Cong. Chmn: Isr Art Collecting Club; Vets Tennis Assn; co-found, Zionist Revisionist Party, CRS. Leader, revisionist underground, Budapest, WW II. Mem: membership comm, Budapest Zionist Org; B'nai B'rith, Theodore Herzl lodge, Rotary. Contbr to jours and press. Hobbies: art collecting, tennis, sports. Home: Herzliya Pituach, Isr. Office: 27 Montefiore St, Tel Aviv, Isr.

GOTTESMANN, Maryan, Isr, manufacturer; b. Galicia, Aus, Sep 22, 1912; s. Noa and Sala (Sternhell); in Isr since 1935; DEcon, U of Florence, 1934; m. Hinda Seelenfreund, Dec 25, 1934. Partner, mgn dir, Elanit Ltd, knitting mills, since 1949; fmr, mgr: Zedak Ltd, Rishon le'Zion; Aled Ltd, B'nei Brak. Mem: exec council, Mfrs Assn; fmr: mem, Pal off; secy, Hechalutz, Vienna; exec, Blau-Weiss, Vienna; found: Fashion Cen, Export Inst; Tel Aviv Fashion Week. Contbr to profsl publs. Hobby: tennis. Home: 18 Soutine St, Tel Aviv, Isr. Office: 11 Massad St, Tel Aviv, Isr.

GOTTFARB, Inga, Sweden, social worker; b. Torsang, Swed, July 17, 1913; d. Leon and Sara (Pagrotsky); att U of Stockholm, 1933-41; MSc, Columbia Sch of Social Work, NY, 1951. Chief of bur, Swed Immigration and Naturalization Service, since 1969; social worker: Jt Distribution Comm, 1944-54; comty intl spec service, 1948-63; cons, Council for Swed Info abroad, 1963-69; bd mem, Magbit, Stockholm; volunteer work with refugees since 1933. Author: books for immigrants to Swed; articles on immigration to Swed; on Isr, to Swed jours. Home: 3 Östermalmsgat, Stockholm, Swed. Office: 7 Birger Jarlstorg, Stockholm, Swed.

GOTTGETREU, Eric, Isr, journalist; b. Chemnitz, Ger, July 31, 1903; s. Adolph and Elsbeth (Baswitz); in Isr since 1933; att Berlin U; m. Sara Reznik, June 23, 1934. Contbr to Ger lang newspapers: Switz; Aus; W Ger; fmr: corresp, AP, 1942-68; free-lance journalist, cen Eur dailies; asst ed: Volksbote, Leubeck; Sozialdemokratischer Pressedienst, Berlin; corresp, La Bourse Egyptienne, Cairo. Author: Haben Sie gelesen dass?, 1929; Drittes Reich Geheim, 1932; Das Land der Soehne—Palaestina Nahegerueckt, 1934; essay, Maximilian Harden—Ways and Errors of a Publicist, 1962. Home and office: 3 Pinsker St, Jerusalem, Isr.

GOTTLIEB, Abraham M, US, physician, educator; b. Chgo, Ill, Feb 22, 1909; s. Michael and Freda (Mantis); BS, U of Ill, 1930, MD, 1933; m. Florence Handelman, May 23, 1934; c: Joel, Judith Givelber. Hosp dir, VA Hosp, Palo Alto, Cal, since 1968; prof, internal med, Stanford Univ Med Sch, since 1968; hosp dir, VA Hosp, Madison, Wis, 1959-68; asso prof, internal med, U of Wis Med Sch, 1959-66; chief card, VA Hosps 1937-42, chief, staff, 1946-59; instr, asso prof, internal med, Wayne State Coll of Med, 1946-59. Col, US Army, 1942-45. Dipl, Amer Bd Internal Med; FACP; vice-pres, Amer Physicians Art Assn, since 1968; mem: AMA; AHA; Dane Co and Wis State Med Soc; Madison Heart Assn; Phi Delta Epsilon; Omicron Alpha Tau; club: Rotary. Contbr to med jours. Recipient: Pres Citation. Hobbies: book collecting, oil painting. Home: 611 Willow Rd, Menlo Park, Cal. Office: VA Hosp, Palo Alto, Cal.

GOTTLIEB, Adolph, US, artist; b. NYC, Mar 14, 1903; s. Emil and Elsie (Berger); att Art Students League; m. Esther Dick, June 12, 1932. One-man shows, pvt gals, since 1930; exhbs, Sidney Janis Gal, since 1961; Ten Year Retrospective, Bennington Coll, Williams Coll, 1954; retrospective show, J Mus, 1957; designer: Ark Curtains, Cong B'nai Isr, Millburn, NJ; Cong Beth El, Springfield, Mass; stained glass façade, Park Ave Syn, NYC; works repr in: Mus Modern Art; Guggenheim Mus; Metrop Mus; Bklyn Mus; Whitney Mus; Butler Art Mus; Detroit Art Inst; Addison Gal; Phillips Gal; Tel Aviv Mus; Isaac Delgado Mus; Soc of Four Arts; U of Ill; Yale U Art Gal; Smith Coll Mus; Ball St Coll Mus; San Jose Libr; U of Neb; U of Miami; Cornell U Art Gal; Albright-Knox Art Gal; Carnegie Inst; Va Mus Fine Arts; simultaneous exhbs at Whitney Mus of Art and Solomon R Guggenheim Mus, 1968; completed 1300 sq ft stained glass façade for 5-storey Milton Steinberg House, NYC; fmr instr, Pratt Inst. Mem, NYC Art Commn. Recipient: winner: Dudensing Natl

Competition, 1929; Govt sponsored mural contest for Yerrington, Nev, Post Off, 1939; first prize, Bklyn Mus, 1944; purchase award, U of Ill, 1951; 3rd prize, Carnegie Intl, 1961; Grand Prix, Biennale de Sao Paulo, Brazil, 1963. Home: 27 W 96 St, New York, NY. Studio: 190 Bowery, New York, NY.

GOTTLIEB, Gilbert, US, psychologist; b. NYC, Oct 22, 1929; s. Leo and Sylvia (Sherman); AB, U of Miami, 1955, MS, 1956; PhD, Duke U, 1960; m. Nora Willis, Feb 28, 1961; c: Jonathan, David, Aaron, Marc. Clinical psychol, Dorothea Dix Hosp, since 1962, 1959-61; research sci, NC Dept of Mh, since 1961; grad fac mem, NC State U, since 1961. US Army, 1951-53. F, NC Psych Assn; mem: exec comm, Animal Behaviour Soc; Amer Psych Assn; Psychonomic Soc; AAAS. Contbr to profsl jours. Hobbies: water skiing, boating. Home: Box 232, Rt 5, Raleigh, NC. Office: Dorothea Dix Hosp, Raleigh, NC.

GOTTLIEB, Jacques S, US, psychiatrist, educator; b. Trinidad, Colo, Feb 2, 1907; s. David and Sara (Sanders); att U of Colo, 1923-25; BS, Harvard U, 1928, MD, 1933; m. Helen White, Dec 19, 1934; c: Marilyn Lee, Jacquelyn, David. Dir, Lafayette Clinic, Detroit, Mich, since 1955; prof, chmn, dept psycht, Wayne State U, since 1961; prof, psycht, State U of Ia Med Sch, 1947-53, on fac since 1940; chmn, prof, U of Miami, 1953-55; dir, Inst, Jackson Memorial Hosp, Miami, Fla, 1953-55. Dir, Amer Bds Neur and Psycht, Inc, since 1959, vice-pres, 1965, pres, 1966; mem: Amer Psycht Assn; AMA, mem, res rev comm, council on educ and hosps, 1962-66; Amer Psychosomatic Soc. Contbr to med publs. Home: 1712 Lafayette Towers, W Detroit, Mich. Office: Lafayette Clinic, 951 E Lafayette, Detroit, Mich.

GOTTMANN, Jean, US, geographer, author; b. Kharkov, Russ; Oct 10, 1915; s. Elie and Sonia (Ettinger); in US since 1941; licence ès lettres, Dipl D'Etudes Supérieures, U of Paris, Sorbonne, 1937; MA, Oxford, 1968; hon LLD, Wis, 1968; m. Bernice Adelson, Aug 11, 1957. Prof, geog, U of Oxford, f, Hertford Coll, Oxford, since 1968; prof, Ecole des Hautes Etudes, U of Paris, 1959-68; prof, Institut D'Etudes Politiques, U of Paris, 1949-55; research asst, Sorbonne, 1937-1940; mem, Inst for Advanced Study, Princeton U, 1942-61; asso prof, Johns Hopkins U, 1945-48; cons, Bd Econ Warfare, Fgn Econ Admn, Wash, DC, 1942-44; adv, planning, Fr govt, Paris, 1945-46; research dir, 20th Cent Fund, NY, 1956-61; dir, studies and research, UN, NYC, 1946-47. Mem, bd trustees, Inst Mediterranean Affairs, NY; hon f, Amer Geog Soc, NY; mem, council, Remp, The Hague; mem: Assn Amer Geog; Assn de Geographes Français; Royal Geog Soc, Inst of Br Geog; Société de Géographie de Paris; Regional Plan Assn, NY. Author: Les Relations Commerciales de la France, 1943; L'Amérique, 1949; A Geography of Europe, 1950, 1954, 1962; La Politique des Etats et leur Géographie, 1952; Virginia at Mid-Century, 1955; Marches de Matières Premiers, 1957; Megalopolis, 1961. Recipient: medals and prizes of Concours Général, Fr, 1931; Institut de Fr, 1953; Société de Géographie, Paris, 1950, 1962. Homes: 19 Belsyre Ct, Oxford, Eng; 7 Rue Lenotre, Fontainebleau, Fr. Office: Sch of Geog, Oxford U, Eng.

GOTTSCHALK, Alfred, US, rabbi, educator; b. Oberwesel, Ger, Mar 7, 1930; s. Max and Erna (Trum-Gerson); in US since 1939; AB, Bklyn Coll, 1952; MA, ordained rabbi, HUC, 1957, PhD, 1965; hon STD, U of S Cal, 1968; m. Jeannie Schrag, June 28, 1952; c: Marc, Rachel. Dean, HUC-JIR, since 1959, prof, Bible and J rel thought. Vice-pres, S Cal J Hist Soc; mem: Amer Acad Rel; Natl Educ Assn; exec comm, AJComm, LA; Comty Relations Council; Natl Fed J Educators, Rabb Placement comm; Pres' Comm on Equal Employment Opportunity; Gov's Job Support Corps; CCAR; Comm on Educ; Soc for Bibl Lit and Exegesis; ACLU; Amer Acad Political and Social Sci; AAUP; Delta Sigma Rho. Contbr to jours, author of books. Recipient: US, Dept Study Grant 1963; Helen Guggenheim Grant, 1967, 1969. Home: 10563 Holman Ave, Los Angeles, Cal. Office: 8745 Appian Way, Los Angeles, Cal.

GOTTSCHALK, Louis, US, educator, historian; b. Bklyn, NY, Feb 21, 1899; s. Morris and Anna (Krystall); BA, Cornell U, 1919, MA, 1920, PhD, 1921; DLitt, Augustana Coll, Ill, 1954; DHC, U Toulouse, Fr, 1957; m. Fruma Kasdan, Dec 16, 1930; c: Alexander, Paul. Prof, hist, U of Chgo, since 1935, Gustavus F and Ann M Swift Dist Service prof, hist, since 1959, mem fac since 1927, chmn, dept hist, 1937-42; fmr: asst, hist, Cornell U, visiting asst prof, 1924, class 1916 visiting prof,

1961-62; instr, hist, U of Ill; asso prof, U of Louisville, Barry Bingham visiting prof, 1968-69; visiting asso prof, U of Minn, 1926; Guggenheim F, 1928-29; visiting prof: Centro de Estudios Pedagogicos, Mexico City, 1938; U of Cal, 1942, 49; Newberry Libr F, 1946; Walker-Ames visiting prof, U of Wash, 1948; exch prof, U of Frankfurt, Ger, 1950; visiting prof, Stanford U, 1952. Mem, USAAF Comm Historians, 1943-44. Chmn, natl commn, B'nai B'rith Hillel Found, since 1963; mem: exec comm, Amer Friends of Lafayette, since 1932; AAAS; Amer Phil Soc; Société des Etudes Robespierristes; Société d'Hist Moderne; Inst Français de Wash; Council on J Relations; Phi Beta Kappa. Author: Jean Paul Marat, 1927, rev ed, 1967; Era of the French Revolution, 1929, 6 vols on life and times of Lafayette, pub during 1935-50; Understanding History, 1950; author-ed, Vol IV, UNESCO Scientific and Cultural History of Mankind, since 1953; collaborator: Use of the Personal Document in History, Sociology and Anthropology, 1945; Theory and Practice in Historical Study, 1946; Europe and the Modern World, vol I, 1951, vol II, 1951; asst ed, Jour of Modern Hist, 1929-43, acting ed, 1943-45; mem bd eds, Amer Hist Rev, 1953-58. Recipient: Medal of Merit of Union Fédérale des Anciens Combattants de France, 1938; Princeton Bicentennial Medal, 1946; U of Louisville Sesquicentennial Medal, 1948; James Hazen Hyde Prize, 1948; Chevalier, Legion of Honor, 1953; award for dist scholarship, Amer Council of Learned Soc, 1959. Home: 5551 University Ave, Chicago, Ill. Office: U of Chgo, 1126 E 59 St, Chicago, Ill.

GOTTSCHALK, Max, Belgium, educator, sociologist; b. Liège, Belgium, Feb 9, 1899; s. Samson and Mina (Moses); LLD, U of Liège, 1911; post-grad studies: Berlin; Paris; m. Stephanie Goldschmidt, Dec 24, 1923; c: Guy, Robert. Research prof, Inst of Sociol, U of Brussels, since 1923; fmr: legal adv, Interallied Rhineland High Commn, 1919-21; sect chief, ILO, Geneva, 1921-23, repr in Belgium, 1923-40; unemployment commn, Brussels, 1934-35; pres, Social Security Bd, Belgium, 1935-40; dir, research inst for peace and postwar problems, AJComm, NY, 1940-49. Pres: Inter -U Cen of High J Studies, Brussels; Amis de l'Alliance Universelle; Cen of Regional Econ, U of Brussels, since 1951; hon pres: Centrale Oeuvres Sociales Juives (UJA), Brussels; Intl Council of Regional Econ; Amis de l'ORT, Brussels, mem, exec comm, Geneva; vice-pres: ICA, since 1929, mem, bd dirs, ICA, Isr and Can; Belgian League for Hum Rights, since 1952; mem bd dirs: Agric Soc for J in Morocco; Alliance Israélite Universelle, Paris; fmr: pres: Consistoire Cen Israélite, Belgium; Intl Assn Social Progress; Comm for Refugees; HICEM; mem, bd dirs, PICA. Contbr publs on social scis, econ and J topics. Recipient: War Medals, 1914-19, 1940; Croix de Guerre (4 Palms); Croix de Feu; Croix Volontaire de Guerre; Croix Civique première classe; Off, Legion d'Honneur, Fr; Off, Ordre de Léopold, Belgium; Off, Couronne de Chêne, Luxemburg; Cdr, Ordre Léopold II; Off, Order of Merit, Fr. Home: 19 Place Communale, Ohain, Belgium. Office: 44 Ave Jeanne, Brussels, Belgium.

GOTTSCHALK, Rudolf, Isr, attorney; b. Bernburg, Ger, Oct 6, 1901; s. Friedrich and Agnes (Frölich); in Isr since 1934; att Us: Freiburg; Munich; Berlin; DJur, U of Leipzig, 1925; LLM, U Coll, London, 1935; barrister-at-law, Grey's Inn, London, 1936; m. Malka Field, 1935; c: Michael, David. Pvt practice since 1936; fmr partner, Friedrich Gottschalk & Dr Rudolf Gottschalk, law firm. Mem, Isr Bar, since 1936; titulary mem, Comité Intl Maritime; fmr: mem: Law Council; Bar Comms; pres, Isr Maritime Law Assn. Author: Spitteler, biography, 1928, 1946; Impossibility of Performance in Contract, 1938, 1946; The Devil Knoweth Not, 1948; The Mountain of Moab, short stories, 1956. Hobbies: writing, swimming, skiing. Home: 22A Vitkin St, Haifa, Isr. Office: 26 Ibn Sina St, Haifa, Isr.

GOUDEKET, Maurits, Netherlands, educator; b. Amsterdam, Aug 11, 1912; s. Joseph and Rachel (Vintura); PhD, U of Amsterdam, 1941; m. Hendrika Kats, Mar 20, 1940; c: Joost. Rector, Spinoza Lyceum, since 1960; asst, Van-der-Waals Lab, U of Amsterdam, 1937-41; tchr, physics and chem, Peter Stuyvesant Coll, Curaçao, Netherlands Antilles, 1946-60; lay min, Temple Emanu-El, reform cong, Curaçao, 1946-60. Pres, Union of Progressive J Congs in Netherlands, since 1961; chmn, Liberal J Cong, Amsterdam, since 1963. Contbr to sci jours. Home: Stadionweg 214, Amsterdam, Netherlands. Office: Peter van Anrooyastraat 8, Amsterdam, Netherlands.

GOUDSMIT, Samuel A, US, physicist, educator; b. Hague,

Netherlands, July 11, 1902; s. Isaac and Marianne (Gompers); in US since 1927; att U Amsterdam; PhD, U Leiden, 1927; m. Jaantje Logher, Jan 19, 1927, div; c: Esther; m. 2nd, Irene Rothschild, 1960. Dep dept chmn, Brookhaven Natl Lab, 1960-67, sr sci, 1948-52, chmn, dept, physics, 1952-60; visiting lectr, Rockefeller Inst, NY; instr, asso prof, prof, physics, U of Mich, 1927-46; mem fac, Northwestern U, 1946-48. Mem, radiation lab, MIT, WW II, on mission to Eng, 1943; civilian chmn, mission to Eur, 1944. Prin contrib: co-discoverer of electron spin theory, 1925. F: Amer Phys Soc; Netherlands Physics Soc; Natl Acad Sci. Author: Alsos 1947; co-author: Structure of Line Spectra, 1930; Atomic Energy States, 1932; ed-in-chief, Amer Phys Soc; ed, Phys Rev Letters, since 1958. Recipient: Rockefeller f, 1926; Guggenheim f, 1938. Medal of Freedom, 1945; OBE, 1949. Spec interest: Egyptology. Office: Brookhaven Natl Lab, Upton, NY.

GOUGENHEIM, Georges, Fr, philologist, educator; b. Paris, July 20, 1900; s. Leon and Jeanne (Schwab); att Superior Normal Sch, 1920-23; Practical Sch of High Studies, 1920-25, PhD, 1929; m. Marie Gendronneau, June 23, 1945. Prof, hist of Fr lang, Fac Letters, U of Paris, since 1957; tchr, Lyceum Amiens, 1925; lectr: U of Clermont-Ferrand, 1929-31; U of Strasbourg, 1931-35, prof, 1935-55; prof, U of Lille, 1955-57. Mem: Ling Soc, Paris; Assn Pour la Traduction Automatique et la Linguistique Appliquée; Soc of Ancient Fr Texts. Author: Etude sur les périphrases verbales de la langue française, 1929; La langue populaire dans le 1er quart du XIXe siècle, 1929; Eléments de phonologie française, 1935; Système grammatical de la langue française, 1939; Grammaire de la langue française du XVIe siècle, 1951; Dictionnaire fondamental de la langue française, 1958; Les Mots Français dans l'Histoire et dans la Vie, vol I, 1962, vol II, 1966; ed, Cortebarbe, les trois aveugles de Compiègne, 1932; co-ed, Trois essais de Montaigne. Recipient: Officier de la Légion d'Honneur; Officier des Palmes Académiques; Chevalier du Mérite Militaire. Office: U of Paris, Sorbonne, Paris, Fr.

GOULD, Benjamin Z, US, attorney; b. Chgo, Ill, July 27, 1913; s. Samuel and Fanny (Tendrich); JD, U of Chgo Law Sch, 1937; AB, U of Chgo, 1953; m. Shirley Handleman, Nov 22, 1942; c: Edward, Fredrick, Barbara. Sr partner, law firm, Schradzke, Gould and Ratner, since 1937; dir, secy, gen counsel: Henry Crown and Co; Central Cold Storage Co, mem, exec comm; Century-Amer Corp; Burton-Dixie Corp; Exch Building Corp; The LaSalle Corp; Santa Barbara Research Park, Inc; Standard Forgings Corp; vice-pres: U Exch Corp; U Village Golf Course, Inc; Thoma B Bishop Co; Henry Crown and Co, Ill; gen council: Utah Marblehead Lime Co; Sioux City and New Orleans Terminal Corp, secy; Sioux and New Orleans Barge Lines, Inc, secy; Freeman Cold Mining Corp; Material Service Corp. USCGR, WW II. Dir: Chgo Loop Syn; Cong Beth Sholom of Rogers Park; Heb Theol Coll, both Chgo; mem: Amer, Ill Bar Assns; Amer Arbitration Assn, natl panel; Amer Soc Corp Secys; Amer Judicature Soc; Chgo Bar Assn; Chgo Council Fgn Relations; Phi Beta Kappa; clubs: Exec; Standard. Home: 1170 Michigan Ave, Wilmette, Ill. Office: 300 W Washington, Chicago, Ill.

GOULD, Bernard S, US, biochemist, educator; b. Boston, Mass, Oct 15, 1911; s. Charles and Dina (Ulin); BS, MIT, 1932; PhD, U of London, 1934; m. Sophie Ginsberg, Sep 8, 1938; c: Michael, Jonathan, David. Prof, biochem, MIT, since 1941; visiting prof, research prof, research cons: grad sch, Boston U; food, pharmaceutical and research labs; traveling research f, U of London, 1932-34; Commn for Relief in Belgium, educ found; f, U of Louvain, Belgium, 1936; med research, MIT, WW II. Fmr pres, Amer Friends of Heb U; vice-pres, Heb Tchrs Coll, since 1960, all Boston; vice-chmn, Council on J Educ, Boston; trustee, Cong Kehillath 1sr; Combined J Philanthropies, Boston; comm, B'nai B'rith Hillel Found; mem: Amer Soc Biol Chems; Soc Amer Bact; NY Acad Sci; Sigma Xi; Delta Omega; club, New Cent, fmr pres. Contbr to biochem and med jours. Home: 25 Cotswold Rd, Brookline, Mass. Office: 77 Massachusetts Ave, Cambridge, Mass.

GOULD, Edward J, US, business exec; b. New Castle, Pa, Dec 23, 1897; s. Joseph and Malvin (Rosenfeld); BS, O State U, 1920; m. Sadie Edlis, Apr 14, 1940 (decd); stepchildren: Joseph Browar (decd), Henrietta Ruekberg. Ret; fmr pres, The Steel Stamping Co, Lorain, O, 1943-65. Pres: Lorain Found, since establishment, 1949; Lorain J Fed since 1934;

United Comty Services, bd mem since 1947; Comty Chest, 1949, chmn, 1948, bd mem since 1947; St Joseph Hosp since 1952; trustee, Agudath B'nai Isr Cong, since 1928; chmn, Citizens Comms for study of civic problems, 1948, 49, 53; mem: bd, Social Agencies, since 1952; Masons; Amer Legion; B'nai B'rith, pres, 1924; club, Rotary. Recipient: award, Lorain Man of the Year, 1948. Home: 3266 E Erie Ave, Lorain, O.

GOULD, Gertrude E, US, artist; b. Rum, Mar 6, 1898; d. Samuel and Elizabeth (Hoffman) Black; in US since 1900; att: Worcester Art Mus Sch, 1949; Columbia U, 1950-51; Art Students League, NYC, 1951-54; Accademia Belle Arte, Florence, It, 1954; Sarasota Sch of Art, Fla, 1955; Hofmann Art Sch, Provincetown, Mass, 1956; m. Herman Gould (decd); c: Beatrice Green. One man shows: Barnard, Summer and Putnam's Dept Store, Worcester, Mass, 1967; exhbs: Allied Artists, NYC; ACA Gal, Tanglewood, Mass; Tyringham Gal, Lee, Mass; Carnegie Hall; City Cen, NY; Art Students League, NY; Columbia U; Gloucester Art Assn; Worcester Art Mus; perm collections: St Vincent's Hosp; Clark U, both Worcester, Mass; pvt collections: US, Can, Eng, Isr. Owner, Gould Furniture Co, 1920-30; estimator, Malden Supply Co, 1931-49. Charter mem, Gallery 15, NY, 1958-59; life mem, Art Students League, NY; mem: Eastern Star, Boston; Sarasota Art Assn, Fla; Provincetown Art Assn; Cape Cod Art Assn. Recipient: prize, Sarasota, Fla, 1955. Hobbies: opera, theatre, swimming, hiking, travel. Homes: Broadmoor Hotel, 235 W 102 St, New York, NY; 18 Tahanto Rd, Worcester, Mass.

GOULD, Harry E, US, industrialist; b. NYC, July 12, 1898; s. John and Julia (Asch); m. Lucille Quartucy, Sep 23, 1937; c: Harry, Peter, Robert. Chmn bd: Universal Amer Corp; Gould Paper Corp; dir: Pepsi Cola; Gulf & Western Inds; Brown; 795 Fifth Ave; Amron; Livingston Rock & Gravel; Young Spring & Wire; Daybrook-Ottawa. Bd govs, Club of Printing House Craftsmen of NY; past pres, Grand Cen Hosp; mem: Citizens Comm Intl Devl, Wash, DC; Boys Club Amer; AJComm; Albert Einstein Coll of Med, Yeshiva U; clubs: City Athletic; Friars; Lambs; Rockrimmon Country. Home: 2 E 61 St, New York, NY. Office: 200 Park Ave, New York, NY.

GOULD, Morton, US, composer, conductor; b. Richmond Hill, NY, Dec 10, 1913; s. James and Frances (Arkin); studied: piano with Abby Whiteside; composition with Dr Vincent Jones; played piano at age of four; composed first waltz at age six. Mem staff: Radio City Music Hall; NBC; guest conductor and soloist with major orchs; recording artist with RCA Victor; performed in US and abroad; conducted and arranged weekly series radio orchestral progs for WOR, 1934, his Pavane, American Salute and Latin American Symphonette were originally introduced on these progs. Compositions include: three Syms; Foster Gallery; Cowboy Rhapsody; Spirituals for Orch; Interplay for Piano and Orch; Concerto for Orch; Fall River Legend Ballet; Serenade of Carols; Symphony for Band; Tap Dance Concerto; Dance Variations for Two Pianos and Orch; Declaration; Jekyll and Hyde Variations; wrote musical score for: Billion Dollar Baby, Broadway musical comedy; Arms and the Girl, Theatre Guild produc; movies: Delightfully Dangerous; Cinerama Holiday; Windjammer; commissioned works include: Inventions for Four Pianos, Winds, Brass and Percussion for Steinway Centenary; Declaration, WRC-NBC, Wash, DC, for Natl Sym Orch; St Lawrence Suite, Power Auth of State of NY; Dialogues for Piano and Rhythm Gallery, Little Orch Soc; Venice for Two Orchs, Seattle Sym; Columbia, Wash Natl Sym; Troubador Music; Vivaldi Gal; currently engaged in writing full-length ballet with George Balanchine. Mem: Natl Assn Composers and Conductors; bd dirs: Amer Sym Orch League; ASCAP. Recipient: Grammy Award, 1966. Office: 609 Fifth Ave, New York, NY.

GOULD, Sylvester E, US, physician, educator; b. Detroit, Mich, July 31, 1900; s. Jude and Sarah (Stolarsky); BA, U of Mich, 1920, MD, 1924, MS, 1939, DSc, 1942; m. Minna Blumenthal, July 22, 1936; c: Joyce Rothstein, Carol Leon (decd), Mark. Hon mem, med staff, Wayne Co Gen Hosp, since 1963; dir, path, 1932-63; prof em, Wayne State U Coll of Med, since 1964; prof, since 1951; adj prof, path, U of Miami, since 1966; visiting prof, 1963-66; research asso: path, U of Mich, 1951-59; Mich Memorial Phoenix Project, 1951-61; prof, chmn, dept path, U of Detroit Sch of Dent, 1956-62; visiting prof, path, Cen U of Venezuela, 1958; lectr, U of Mich Med Sch, 1959-63;

Claude Bernard prof, U of Montreal, 1960; chief, research, path, Atomic Bomb Casualty Comm, Hiroshima, Japan, 1966-67. Lt, Med Reserve, 1930-35. Prin contribs: co-inventor, method of sterilization of trichinae by treatment of pork with ionizing radiation. Dipl, clinical path, anat path, Amer Bd Path, 1938; chmn, Natl Continuing Comm on Trichinosis, since 1954; pres, Intl Commn on Trichinellosis; mem, natl trichinosis eradication comm, Livestock Conservation, Inc; fmr: trustee, treas, Detroit Inst Cancer Research; gov, Coll Amer Paths; trustee, chmn, OA Brines Scholarship Fund; chmn: Mich 5th Selective Service Adv Bd; 1st and 2nd Natl Confs on Trichinosis. Author: Trichinosis, 1945, Span, 1952; co-author, ed: Pathology of the Heart, 1953. Span, 1956, 2nd ed, 1960, 3rd ed, Pathology of the Heart and Blood Vessels, 1968; Microscopic Pathology, 1964; Trichinosis in Man and Animals, 1970; co-author: The Acute Abdomen, 1966; ed: Amer Jour Clinical Path, 1946-55; Bull, Coll Amer Pathologists, 1957-60; Bull of Path, Amer Soc Clinical Paths, 1965-69; Laboratory Medicine, since 1970. Home: 801 Venetian Way, Miami, Fla. Office: U of Miami, Jackson Memorial Hosp, Miami, Fla.

GOULD, Valerie Gudilla, Eng, communal worker; b. Manchester, Eng, May 19, 1905; d. Bernard and Leah (Brown) Steel; att Guildhall Sch of Music and Drama, 1924-30; m. Frank Gould, Nov 9, 1930; c: Juliet Froomberg. Hon off, Fed of Women Zionists of UK and Ir, Birmingham; life pres, JNF, Gt Brit, fmr vice-pres; pres: WIZO Regional Council; Edgbaston Women Zionists Soc; vice-pres: JPA; Birmingham ZC; mem: Repr Council, Birmingham and Midland J; Council Birmingham Progressive Syn; chmn, Birmingham J Womens Luncheon Club; fmr: provincial vice-pres, ZF; chmn; Womens Appeal Comm, Youth Aliyah; JNF, Birmingham; mem, admn comm, JNF, Gt Brit and Ir. Hobbies: music, lit, art, theatre. Home: 29 Rotton Park Rd, Birmingham, Eng.

GOULDMAN, Myer Dennis, Isr, attorney; b. Manchester, Eng, Feb 25, 1935; s. Abraham and Kathleen Lizar; in Isr since 1961; LLB, U of Manchester, 1955; solicitor of Supr Court, Eng, 1958; admitted Isr Bar, 1962; m. Yvette Shalom, July 19, 1959; c: Daniel, Esther, Gidon. Sr asst to Atty Gen of Isr since 1967; fmr, sr asst to legal adv, Min of Interior, 1963-67. Mem, Eng Law Soc. Author: Legal Aspects of Town Planning in Israel, 1966. Home: 4 Ha'aderet St, Jerusalem, Isr. Office: Min of Justice, Jerusalem, Isr.

GOURGEY, Percy Sassoon, Eng, communal leader, journalist; b. Bombay, India, June 2, 1923; s. Saul and Hannah (Nissim); in Eng since 1953; att LSE, 1958-59; m. Brenda Abulafca, July 3, 1957, div; c: Jonathan. Free-lance journalist, lectr; asso ed, Jewish Advocate, Bombay, 1948-51; corresp in India, Davar, Isr, 1949-53; chmn, ed bd, Kol Sepharad, London, 1965-67. Royal Naval Indian Volunteer Res, 1943-46. Hon treas, WJC, British sect; vice-pres: London off, ZF, Gt Brit; Poale Zion, Gt Brit, past natl chmn; mem: Royal Inst Intl Affairs, Chatham House, London; Richmond UN Assn; Richmond Syn; fmr: dep mem, Zionist Gen Council, actions comm; tutor, Workers' Educ Assn, London; contested Gen Election, Mar 1966, as Parliamentary candidate, Southgate, London; mem: B'nai B'rith, First Lodge, Eng; club, Royal Navy Vet. Author: The Jew and His Mission, 1943; Ideals, India, Israel in Asia, 1950. Recipient: MBE, for political and public services, 1965. Hobbies: chess, swimming, walking, reading. Home: 4 Poplar Court, Richmond Road, E Twickenham, Middlesex, Eng. Office: 3 Essex Court, London, Eng.

GOUSMAN, Efraim, Isr, business exec; b. Tel Aviv, Isr, Aug 15, 1911; s. Shmuel and Zipora (Kornfeld); m. Batia Tennenbaum; c: Miriam Levin, Oded. Mgn dir, S Gousman & Sons Ltd; dir, S Gousman Tech Supplies. Chmn, Isr-Swed C of C; vice-chmn: Anglo-Isr C of C; Assn of Bi-Natl C of C with Isr; vice-pres, Commercial and Ind Club; mem, presidium, Tel Aviv-Jaffo C of C; past pres, Shimon Rokach B'nai B'rith Lodge. Home: 30 King David Blvd, Tel Aviv, Isr. Office: 16 Hakishon, Tel Aviv, Isr.

GOUSSINSKY, Bezalel, Isr, mechanical engr; b. Pol, 1901; att Sch N Amer YMCA; Poly, Liège; m. Rivka Jacoby; c: Naomi Krigsman, Doron. Owner, mgn dir, B Goussinsky Engr and Mfg Co Ltd, Madek, Haifa; contractor for civilian, mil supplies; mfr, material handling equipment. Chmn, metal, elec br, Mfr Assn, Haifa; mem, Council and Dist Mfr Assn. Home: 35 Hatishbi St, Haifa, Isr.

GOVRIN, Akiva, Isr, legislator; b. Szpikov, Russ, Aug 12, 1902; s. Mordechai and Adele Globman; in Isr since 1922; att U of Berlin, 1924; m. Malka Belman, 1930; c: Shlomo, David. MK since 1949; fmr: Min without portfolio, 1963; chmn, lab comm; chmn: Mapai Lab Party; govt coalition, all at Knesset; mem exec, Histadrut, since 1942; fmr: mem secretariat, Mapai; laborer, Haifa Port; construction worker, Jerusalem; mem, Lab Council, Jerusalem; gen secy, Employees Union, Histadrut; head dept, Trade Unions Council; delg to: Intl Trade Union Congs; WJC s; missions to US, Eur, on behalf of Histadrut; Min of Tourism. Haganah, chmn, high court. Contbr to the press. Hobby: archaeol. Home: 28 Mapu St, Tel Aviv, Isr. Office: Knesset, Jerusalem, Isr.

GRABER, Joseph Nathan, Isr, actor; b. Tel Aviv, Isr, Nov 2, 1933; s. Benzion and Zipora (Kaufman); dipl, Royal Acad of Dramatic Art, London, 1958; div. Actor, Cameri Theatre, Tel Aviv; fmr, actor, org, shows for Zionist Cen, Johannesburg, S Afr; prin roles in: The Birthday Party; A Man for All Seasons; A Shot in The Dark; The Fire Raisers, all S Afr; Mother Courage; A Midsummer Night's Dream; A Servant of Two Masters; The Royal Hunt of the Sun; Diary of a Scoundrel; Frank V, all Haifa Munic Theatre; Romeo and Juliet; The Birthday Party; Hamlet; Homecoming; The Beaux Stratgeme; Henry IV; Treasure Island; Mary, Mary, all Cameri Theatre; The King and I, Giora Godick Theatre; appeared: Isr TV, radio; BBC; He Walked Through the Fields, Isr film. Intelligence br, IDF, 1952-54. Hobbies: lit, painting. Home: 145 Ben Yehuda St, Tel Aviv, Isr. Office: Cameri Theatre, Tel Aviv, Isr.

GRABLI, Izhak, Isr, attorney; b. Tiberias, Isr, July 13, 1928; s. Samuel and Ziva (Bahlul); LLB, Nottingham U, Eng, 1950; m. Alegra Toledano, Feb 5, 1957; c: Avi, Sami, Uri, Iris, Ilan. Dist atty, Haifa and northern dist, since 1969; fmr: tchr, Degania Sch, 1946-47; mil atty, 1950-52; atty, Min of Justice, 1953-69. Capt, legal br, IDF, 1950-52. Secy, Rotary, Tiberias Br; mem, Isr Bar Assn. Hobby: photography. Home: 41 Golomb St, Haifa, Isr. Office: Govt House, Haifa, Isr.

GRABMAN, Abe, S Afr, business exec; b. Liverpool, Eng, Feb 16, 1920; s. Chaim and Chana (Gamplowicz); m. Zena Goldblatt, Nov 6, 1949; c: Adrianne, Michael, Julian. Jt mgr, World Tours Ltd, S Afr. RAF, 1940-46. Chmn, JNF, S Afr, mem world council, Jerusalem; natl chmn, Assn of S Afr Travel Agts; vice-chmn, S Afr ZF; mem: S Afr Bd Deps, chmn, chaplaincy comm; council, S Afr Maccabi Assn; Isr-S Afr Comm; S Afr Found; fmr: vice-pres, United Zionist Assn, S Afr; chmn, S Afr Zionist Youth Council; pres, Fed Zionist Youth, Gt Brit and Ir; provincial secy, JNF, Gt Brit and Ir; mem exec, British ZF; dep speaker, Brit Youth Parl; grand councillor, Order of Ancient Maccabeans. Home: 17 Hagen Rd, Greenside Ext 1, Johannesburg, S Afr. Office: 1 Phila Corner, Jeppe/Von Wielligh Sts, Johannesburg, S Afr.

GRABOIS, Aryeh, Isr, historian; b. Odessa, Russ, July 9, 1930; s. Eliezer and Judith (Lorberblatt); in Isr since 1948; MA, Heb U, Jerusalem, 1961; PhD, U of Dijon, Fr, titulaire des hautes études, U of Paris, 1963; m. Carmela Langleben, Apr 20, 1966; c: Shirli. Sr lectr, medieval hist, head, dept hist, mem exec comm, Haifa U Coll, since 1963. Sgt, IDF, 1948-51. Studies in Fr medieval hist; intellectual hist of W Eur in the middle ages; J-Chr relations in medieval Eur. Mem: Isr Hist Assn; Isr Exploration Soc; Eng Hist Assn; Société de Civilisation Médiévale. Contbr articles to hist publs. Home: 17 Oren St, Haifa, Isr. Office: Haifa U Coll, Haifa, Isr.

GRAD, Bernard, Can, educator; b. Montreal, Can, Feb 4, 1920; s. Hyman and Rose (Rabinovitch); BS, hons, McGill U, 1944, PhD, magna cum laude, 1949; m. Lottie Dainoff, June 20, 1948; c: Roland, Willis. Asso prof, dept psycht, McGill U, since 1965; fmr: research asst, gerontologic unit, lectr, dept psycht, 1955-61, asst prof, dept psycht, 1961-65. Mem: Gerontological Soc; Intl Assn Gerontology; Amer Assn Cancer Research; Can Phys Soc; Parapsych Assn; Sigma Xi. Contbr to profsl jours; fmr, mem, ed bd, gerontology and geriatrics sect, Excerpta Medica, 1958. Recipient: award for studies in problems of aging, Ciba Found, 1955. Spec interests: music, art, writing verses for children. Home: 4936 Kent Ave, Montreal, Can. Office: 1025 Pine Ave W, Montreal, Can.

GRADENWITZ, Peter Emanuel, Isr, musicologist, author; b. Berlin, Ger, Jan 24, 1910; s. Felix and Charlotte (Mendel); in Isr since 1936; att U of Berlin; U of Freiburg/Breisgau; Poly, London; PhD, U Prague, 1936; m. Rosi Wolfson, 1933 (decd); c: David (decd), Judith; m. 2nd, Ursula Mayer-Reinach, 1967. Co-found, exec dir, Isr Music Publs Ltd, since 1949; lectr, musicology, Tel Aviv U. Author: Johann Stamitz, 1936; History of Music, Heb, 2 vols, 1939, 45; Concert Guide, Heb, 3 vols, 1945, 8 eds; The Music of Israel, 1949, Span ed, 1949; Music and Musicians in the Land of Israel, 1959; Die Musikgeschichte Israels, 1961; Music of the Nations, Heb, 1962; Wege zur Musik der Gegenwart, 1963; contbr to: intl radio progs; intl publs. Home: 35 Nordau Blvd, Tel Aviv, Isr. Office: POB 6011, Tel Aviv, Isr.

GRADOW, Alexander G, US, physician; b. Warsaw, Pol, May 24, 1897; s. Gregor and Sofia (Rosenthal); in US since 1937; MD, Moscow Med Inst, 1926; att Berlin U, 1927-28; m. Betty Shapiro, Dec 19, 1934; c: George. Chief, dermat clinic, Homeopathic Clinic, SF, Cal, since 1941; mem: cons staff, Hahnemann Hosp; courtesy staff, Mt Zion Hosp, since 1943; Hosp St Louis, Paris, France, 1934-35. Mem: AMA; Cal Med Assn; Pacific Coast Dermat Assn; SF Med Soc; SF Dermat Soc; Amer Acad Dermat; ZOA; B'nai B'rith. Recipient: Selective Service Medal, 1946. Home: 65 San Pablo Ave, San Francisco, Cal. Office: 857 Phelan Bldg, San Francisco, Cal.

GRAEF, Irving, US, physician, educator; b. NYC, Mar 21, 1902; s. Arthur and Fannie (Crystal); BA, Cornell U, 1923, MD, 1926; m. Gretchen Waterman, Aug 25, 1931; c: Roger, John. Private med practice since 1946; cons phys, Lenox Hill Hosp; Monmouth Med Cen, since 1964; visiting phys: Bellevue; U Hosps; asso prof, clinical med, NYU Coll of Med, since 1948, asst prof, path, 1931-34, asso prof, 1934-36. US Army, 1943-46. Co-found, Natl Comm for Resettlement of Fgn Phys, 1939, chmn, 1949-56; dir, Natl Med F, since 1948, pres, 1953; vice-pres, Amer Council for Emigres in the Professions, 1969; mem, AJComm. Ed, Jour of Diabetes, 1961-67, asso ed, 1955-61; contbr of numerous articles in fields of path, rheumatic fever, diabetes and heart disease. Home: 25 E 86 St, New York, NY. Office: 791 Park Ave, New York, NY.

GRAF, Louis Gerhard, UK, rabbi; b. Berlin, Ger, Mar 28, 1912; s. Max and Margarete (Warschauer); in Eng since 1939; ordained rabbi, Hochschule fuer die Wissenschaft des Judentums, Berlin; PhD, U of Berlin, Bonn, Leeds; m. Eve-Inge Lippmann, Sep 4, 1939; c: Barbara, Michael. Rabbi: Cardiff New Syn, since 1949; Berlin J Comty, 1936-39; Sinai Syn, Leeds, found, 1948-49; Bradford Reform Syn, 1940-48. Vice-pres, Cardiff Council Chr and J; dir, Cardiff Samaritans; comm mem, Cardiff J Bd Guardians. Author: The Development of Religion According to Wilhelm Wundt and Rudolf Otto. Hobbies: music, psychology. Home: 86 Heol-y-Forlan, Whitchurch, Cardiff, UK. Study: Cardiff New Synagogue, Meira Terrace, Cardiff, UK.

GRAFMAN, L Elliot, US, rabbi; b. Jersey City, NJ, Nov 8, 1896; s. Saul and Belle (Rosen); BA, U Cincinnati, 1924; ordained rabbi, BHL, HUC, 1924; DJ, John Marshall Law Coll, Chgo, 1937; m. Florence Herst, June 30, 1925; c: Rosemary Kaplan. Mem fac, Inst J Studies, Cong Emanu-El, SF, since 1964; interim sr rabbi, 1968; rabbi, Temple Isr, Long Beach, Cal, 1938-56. USMCS, 1917-19; capt, US Army Chaplains Corps, 1942-46; Off Res Corps. Pres, S Cal Assn Lib Rabbis, 1952-53; dir: SF Chap, Amer ORT Fed; JCC, Long Beach, 1938-56; treas, W Assn Reform Rabbis, 1952-53; mem: Bd Rabbis, N Cal, since 1956; J Comty Relations Council, SF; perm J spokesman, Tri-Faith radio prog, Station KGO, SF, since 1965; CCAR; JWV; club, Rotary, chmn intl service comm, 1953-54. Recipient: Man of Year Award, 1949. Home: 1250 Jones St, San Francisco, Cal.

GRAHM, Ruth Lillian, US, songwriter; b. Phila, Pa; d. Louis and Mary (Horn) Herscher; att UCLA, 1942-45; NYU; m. Alan Grahm, July 13, 1949; c: Randall, Robert, Isabelle. With New Ideas Dept, Columbia Bc Sys, 1947-49; secy to Red Barber, sports ed, CBS, NY, 1947; worked in over 250 motion picture producs. Songs: Where Were You, 1944; Jumpin' Down at Carnegie Hall, 1945; He's Mine All Mine, from picture, The Fighting Texan, 1946; What Can I Do (I Love Him), from picture, Bowery Bombshell, 1946; Elmer The Knock-Kneed Cowboy, 1946; Mama Never Said A Word About Love, 1946; The Best Years in Our Lives, 1947; Honey Dew, 1947; Moonlight in Montevideo, 1948; My Sweetheart's Wedding Day, 1948; I Didn't Believe I'd Fall in Love, 1948;

Fifty Games of Solitaire, 1949; In the Park, 1949; Brazilian Pavilion, 1950; Orange Blossoms, 1954; Chic A Chic Dee, 1963; Baby I'm the Greatest, 1964; Break the Chain, 1964. Mem: ASCAP; Amer Guild Authors and Composers, NY; exec bd, women's div, United JWF; Sinai Temple, W LA, Cal. Recipient: ASCAP awards, for songwriting. Hobbies: swimming, reading, scrabble. Home and office: 623 N Roxbury Dr, Beverly Hills, Cal.

GRAIVER, Manuel, Isr, organization exec; b. Santiago, Chile, May 1, 1900; s. Isaac and Eva (Charmes); in Isr since 1953; att HS, Buenos Aires; m. Fanny Brunstein, 1921; c: Levi. Promoter of tourism from S Amer; exec dir: Latin Amer Dept, JNF, Jerusalem, since 1953; JNF, Arg, 1921-29, 1942-53; KH repr, S Amer, 1935-40. Hon pres, Irgun Olei Amer Latinit, Tel Aviv; hon secy, Camara de Comercio, Isr-Latino Amer, Tel Aviv. Hobbies: PR, voluntary social work. Home: 7 Klonimus St, Tel Aviv, Isr. Office: Express Tours, 9 Mendele St, Tel Aviv, Isr.

GRAJEK, Stefan Shalom, Isr, organization exec; b. Warsaw, Pol, Dec 15, 1915; s. Israel and Haya (Wandel); in Isr since 1959; dipl law, Tel Aviv U, 1957; m. Utra Wargon, 1946; c: Ora, Itzhak. Mem bd dirs, Kupat Holim, since 1956. Active, J Underground, 1939-45, Warsaw Ghetto Uprising; IDF, 1950-51. Pres, Combattants and Ghetto Fighters Org, since 1963; vice-pres, World Fed Pol J, since 1961; secy gen, Zionist Lab Movement, Pol, 1945-49; mem, exec, Cen comm Pol J, 1946-49; mem: Histadrut Council; exec comm, Yad Vashem; WZC, 1946-55. Recipient: Medal of Nazi Fighters; decoration, Fighters for Isr. Home: 5 Hankin St, Tel Aviv, Isr. Office: POB 16250, Tel Aviv, Isr.

GRAND, Samuel, US, author, producer; b. NYC, Aug 28, 1912; s. Meyer and Rose (Bronstein); BA, CCNY, 1932; MA, Columbia U, 1933, PhD, 1958; BJP, JTSA; Lena Socolow f, Heb U, Jerusalem, 1938; m. Tamar Slavin, June 14, 1942; c: Deborah, David. Tchr: Heb schs, 1931-36; public HS, NYC; prin: Forest Hills J Cen, 1936-37; Park Ave Syn, 1938-41; exec secy: Amer Assn J Educ, 1941-42; Civilian Public Service, 1942-46; cons, J Educ Comm, 1946-52; dir, dept experimental educ and audio-visual aids, UAHC, 1952-64. Prin contrib: pioneer in produc of audio-visual materials for J rel educ. Author: Palestine in the Jewish Schools, 1948; First Steps in Audio-Visual Education in the Jewish Religious School, 1952; The Jews Settle in New Amsterdam—1645, a picture book, pub 1955; A History of Zionist Youth Organizations in the United States, 1958; Hebrew Prayer Skills, 1966; co-author: Hebrew, The Audio-Lingual Way, 1962; Baderech, an audio-lingual textbook for intermediate students, 1966; dir, produc, numerous film strips in series: Jews in Distant Lands; Famous Jewish Hist Personalities; Holidays and Festivals; Israel: The Land and Its People; Art in Judaism; A Study Tour of Israel; Modern Jewish History; Jewish Religion; Archeology of the Holy Land; produc of record albums for J schs; lectr; participant in educ surveys; contbr to educ and rel mags. Mem: exec bd, Natl Council on J Audio-Visual Materials, since 1949; LZOA; J Peace F; Educ Film Libr Assn; Film Council Amer; Metrop Syn, NYC; fmr: vice-pres, Natl Conf J Communal Service; secy, Natl Council J Educ. Hobby: photography. Home and office: 90-59 56 Ave, Elmhurst, NY.

GRANEK, Solomon D, Can, organization exec; b. Dombrowa, Pol, Sep 11, 1910; . Abraham and Rose (Topf); in Can since 1923; m. Gertrude Lveine, Mar 31, 1935; c: Eleanor, Yvonne, Natl dir, United Isr Appeal, since 1961; pres, Niagara Motive Supply Co, 1938-61. Natl vice-pres, ZOC, 1956-60, chmn, natl exec bd, 1960, pres, cen region, since 195A; dep mem, actions comm, WJC, 1960; pres: B'nai B'rith, 1947; United J Wfr, St Catharines, 1940-44; mem: Dominion council, Can J Cong; natl council, JDC, exec, Natl Conf for Isr and J Rehabilitation; exec, CJFWF; Masons. Hobbies: collecting art, philately, numismatics. Home: 5160 Macdonald Ave, Cote St Luc, Montreal, Can. Office: 2025 University St, Montreal, Can.

GRANT, Bess Myerson, US, government official; b. NYC, July 16, 1924; d. Louis and Bella (Podolsky); BA, Hunter Coll, 1945; m. Arnold Grant, Jan 5, 1952; c: Barbara. Commn, NYC Dept of Consumer Affairs, since 1969; piano soloist, Carnegie Hall, NYC, 1946; MC moderator, Sta WOR-TV, 1947-1951; The Big Payoff, CBS-TV, 1951-59; commercial hostess: Philco Playhouse, NBC-TV; Jackie Gleason Show, CBS-TV, 1954-55; TV commentator: Miss Amer Pageant, ABC, 1954-68; Tournament of Roses, 1960-68; I've Got a

Secret, 1958-68; news staff: Mutual Bc Co, 1961-62; CBS radio; lectr. F, Metrop Mus Art; trustee: Friends of Music, NYC Jr HSs; League Sch Seriously Disturbed Children; fmr, NY chmn, Bonds for Isr, 1965-70; chmn, Centennial Fund. Recipient: Woman-of-the-Year, ADL, 1965; Presidential Medal, 1970; 1970 Freedom Cup Award, Women League for Isr. Home: 25 Sutton Pl, New York, NY. Office: 80 Lafayette St, New York, NY.

GRASS, Alexander, US, business exec; b. Scranton, Pa, Aug 3, 1927; s. Louis and Rose (Breman); JD, U of Fla, 1949; m. Lois Lehrman, June 30, 1950; c: Linda, Martin, Roger, Elizabeth. Chmn, bd, chief exec off, Rite Aid Corp, Amex, since 1969, mem staff since 1953; mem, bar: Fla, 1949; Pa, 1953. Seaman, USN, 1945-46. Vice-pres, Harrisburg J Comty; mem: natl cabinet, UJA; bd dirs, Ohev Sholem Temple; Rotary; fmr, gen chmn: Harrisburg, UJA and Emergency UJA. Home: 1161 Baldwin Lane, Harrisburg, Pa. Office: POB 3165, Harrisburg, Pa.

GRAUBARD, Baruch, Ger, teacher; b. Skole, Pol, Sep 17, 1900; s. Alter and Hudie (Schächter); att U Vienna; U Lemberg; m. Hanna Dunkelblum, 1927; c: Jadwiga, Alina. Lectr: Wissenschaft des Judentums, U of Marburg, Ger, since 1951; tchr: Gymnasium Konin, Pol, 1923; Gymnasium Bedzin, Pol, 1924-26; Gymnasium Sosnowice, Pol, 1926-27; Gymnasium Kielce, 1927-39; dir: Kulturamt beim Zentralverein, US Zone, Ger, 1946-49; Heb Gymnasium, Munich, 1949-51. Mem: Zentralrat der Juden in Deutschland. Author: Gelesen in den Büchern Moses, 1965; Festung ohne Mauer, play performed, Staatstheater, Tübingen, 1965; weekly commentator on Bible, Bavarian Bc; contbr to Ger mags. Home: 104 Hohenzollernstrasse, Munich, Ger.

GRAUBARD, Seymour, US, attorney; b. NYC, Mar 8, 1911; s. John and Edna (Kiesler); att Columbia Coll, NYC, 1928-31; Columbia Law Sch, NYC, 1933; m. Blanche Kazon, Aug 24, 1941; c: Katherine Calvin. Sr partner, Graubard, Moskovitz, McGoldrick, Dannett & Horowitz, since 1969; fmr: law secy, comptroller, NYC, 1937-41; secy, Supr Court Justice, 1942, 1945-46; sr partner, Graubard & Moskovitz, 1949-69. Maj, US Army, 1942-45. Natl chmn, ADL, fmr natl vice-chmn, mem, bd dirs; mem, bd dirs: Fund for City of NY; Intl Sch Services; bd trustees, New Lincoln Sch; trustee, NYC Public Events Comm, Inc; mem: NY State Bar Assn; NY Co Lawyers Assn; City Club of NY. Author: Building Regulation in New York City, 1944. Home: 993 Park Ave, New York, NY. Office: 345 Park Ave, New York, NY.

GRAUBART, David, US, rabbi, author; b. Staszow, Pol, April 6, 1907; s. Judah and Esther (Liebschuetz); in US since 1924; 1924; BS, Ill Inst Tech, 1927; rabbi, Heb Theol Coll, 1929, JTSA, 1934; DD, Cen U of Ind, 1948, PhD, 1949; m. Eunice Morris, 1933; c: Gale, Judah. Presiding rabbi, Beth Din, RA, Chgo, since 1944; prof, Talmud, Coll J Studies, since 1946. Fmr pres, Chgo region, RA; club, Covenant. Author: Beyond This Present, 1940; Attitude of Judaism to Non-Jews, 1950; contbr ed: Collier's Ency, 1951; Ency Britannica, 1954; ed, Maimonides, 1951; co-ed, The Jewish Family Bible, since 1957; Yiddish ed, Britannica World Language Dictionary, 1954. Home: 5718 N Drake Ave, Chicago, Ill. Office: 72 E 11 St, Chicago, Ill.

GRAUER, Benjamin F, US, broadcaster; b. NYC, June 2, 1908; s. Adolph and Ida (Goldberg); BS, CCNY, 1930; m. Melanie Kahane, Sep 25, 1954. With NBC since 1930, radio and TV reporter, master of ceremonies. Pres: Natl Music League; Corresps Fund, Overseas Press Club; mem: bd govs, Acad TV Arts and Scis; Radio and TV Corresps Assn; Amer Inst Graphic Arts; Bibliographic Soc of Amer; Lab of Anthropology; Tau Delta Phi; clubs: Overseas Press, mem, bd govs, 1954-58; Grolier. Ed, NBC News Picture Book of the Year, 1967, 1968, 1969; contbr to Bouillabaisse for Bibliophiles, 1955. Recipient: HP Davis Announcers Award, 1954; Alumni Service Medal, 1949; US Army Civilian Service Citation, 1951; Crusade for Freedom Citation, 1953; Man of Year award, Natl Fed Temple Brotherhoods, 1955; Chevalier, Legion of Honor, 1956; NY Emmy Nominee, TV Acad, 1962; Dist Service Award, Broadcast Pioneers, 1969. Hobbies: Mexican archaeol; book collecting. Home: 29 E 63 St, New York, NY. Office: NBC, 30 Rockefeller Plaza, New York, NY.

GRAUER, Murray, US, rabbi; b. NYC, May 20, 1921; s. Julius and Rebecca (Gold); BA, Yeshiva Coll, 1941; MA, Columbia U, 1945; ordained rabbi, Yeshiva U, 1945; m. Francine Eisinger, Feb 17, 1946; c: Sheri, David, Joshua

Deborah. Rabbi: Heb Inst of White Plains, since 1951; Cong Beth El, Miami, 1946-51. Pres, Westchester Council of Rabbis, 1964-67; vice-pres, Rabb Alumni of Yeshiva U, 1960-62; secy, NY Bd Rabbis, since 1968; bd govs, Gtr Miami J Fed, 1946-51; exec comm, RabCA; mem: Mizrachi Org of Amer; ZOA. Author: The Social Role of the Orthodox Priest in Greece, Roumania and Bulgaria, 1954. Home: 32 Vermont Ave, White Plains, NY. Study: Heb Inst, White Plains, NY.

GRAUMAN, Yaakov I, Isr, economist, editor; b. Ger, June 5, 1918; s. Naftali and Sarah; in Isr since 1924; att HS of Commerce, Tel Aviv, Brit Inst, Jerusalem; m. Malka Derdickmann, 1941; c: Leah, Devora. Dir, Jaysour Mortgage Bank Ltd, since 1959; fmr: dir, info dept, econ adv, Min of Commerce and Ind; mem, ed bd, Haboker, Heb daily, 1936-55. Mem, natl comm, Lib Party; mem, bd govs, Kfar Silver Agric Sch; chmn, cen bd, Gen Zionist Sick Fund; found, first chmn, Isr br, Intl Press Inst; gov, Rotary clubs in Isr, 1964-65. Home: 1 ha'Armonim St, Ramat Gan, Isr. Office: Jaysour Bank Ltd, 113 Allenby St, Tel Aviv, Isr.

GRAUPE, Daniel, Isr, engineer, educator; b. Jerusalem, Isr, July 31, 1934; s. Moshe and Hella (Neumann); BSc, elec, Technion, Haifa, 1958; BSc, ME, 1959; PhD, U of Liverpool, 1963; m. Dalia Smilanski, July 9, 1968; c: Menahem. Sr lectr, Technion, Haifa, since 1967; control engr, Min of Defense, 1959-60; lectr, U of Liverpool, 1963-67. Radar tech, IAF, 1952-55, sgt. Mem: Inst Math and Applications, Eng; Inst Elec Engrs, Eng; Brit Nuclear Energy Soc. Contbr to sci publs. Recipient: Anna Frank Award, Technion, 1960. Home: 11 Oren St, Romema, Haifa, Isr. Office: Technion, Haifa, Isr.

GRAUPE, Heinz Moshe, Ger, philosopher, Judaist; b. Berlin, Ger, Apr 22, 1906; s. Paul and Dora (Melchiker); PhD, U of Berlin, 1930; post-grad work, Heb U, Jerusalem, 1930-31; grad, HS for Sci of Judaism, Berlin, 1932; m. Hella Neumann May 14, 1933; c: Daniel. Dir, Inst for Hist of Ger J, U of Hamburg, lectr, hist, intellectual hist, Ger J, since 1964; tchr, Judaism, HSs, Berlin J Comty, 1932-33; secy, Mishpat Hashalom Haivri, Vaad hakehilah, Haifa, 1943-48; off, Haifa Munic, 1949-61. Mem: Phil Soc, Heb U, Jerusalem; B'nai B'rith. Author: Die Stellung der Religion im systematischen Denken der Marburger Schule, 1930; Die Entstehung des modernen Judentums, Geistesgeschichte der deutschen Juden, 1650-1942, pub 1969; ed, H J Schoeps, 1966; co-ed, Salomon Ludwig Steinheim zum Gedenken; trans, Bialik, 1935; contbr numerous articles, book reviews, essays to various publs; participant, Inter-Faith Round-table Discussions, under title: Glauben alle an denselben Gott?—Antworten der Religionen, 1969. Home: 36 Grindelallee, Hamburg, Ger. Office: Hamburg U, Hamburg, Ger.

GRAY, Milton H, US, attorney; b. Chgo, Ill, Dec 2, 1910; s. Jacob and Fannie (Hefter); BA, Northwestern U, 1931, JD, with distinction, 1934; m. Florence Subin, April 12, 1937; c: Roberta Katz, James. Sr partner, Altheimer, Gray, Naiburg, Strasburger and Lawton, since 1960; dir: Blackstone Mfg Co; Alloy Mfg; NOMA-World Wide; asso, partner, Gardner, Carton and Douglas, 1934-43; pvt practice, 1943-60; commn, Supr Court of Ill, 1959-62, 1966-68. Chmn: region VII, Boy Scouts of Amer, since 1968, mem, natl exec bd; comm on state regulation of securities and comm on fed regulation of securities, Amer Bar Assn, since 1961; comm on corporate law, Chgo Bar Assn, 1948-50, comm on securities laws, 1951-53; sect on corporate and security laws, Ill State Bar Assn, 1945; pres: N Shore Area Council, Boy Scouts of Amer, 1957-59; Ramah Lodge, B'nai B'rith, 1941-43; mem, bd mgrs, Chgo Bar Assn, 1966-68; mem: Chgo, Ill, Amer Bar Assns; Judicature Soc; Order of the Coif; club, Standard. Lectr on securities laws; contbr to legal publs. Recipient: Silver Beaver, Boy Scouts of Amer, 1959, Silver Antelope, 1963; Dist Eagle Citizens Award, 1969. Home: 420 Lakeside Pl, Highland Park, Ill. Office: 1 N LaSalle St, Chicago, Ill.

GRAY, Warren, US, dentist; b. Newark, NJ, Nov 21, 1931; s. Leonard and Miriam (Wagner); BS, U of Pa, 1953, DDS, 1957; m. Marilyn Dorflaufer, Aug 1, 1953; c: Lennie, Scott. Pvt practice since 1959. Lt, USN Dent Corps, 1957-59. Pres, N NJ Council, B'nai B'rith; chmn: Young Builders of B'nai B'rith Dist; commn, Recreation Dept, Millburn; chmn: H st Landmarks Commn, 1964; Natl Children's Dent Health Week, 1963-66; mem: Amer, NJ, Essex Co Dent Socs; Cong B'nai Isr; Citizens Comm on Youth. Home: 76 Cypress St, Millburn, NJ. Office: 116 Millburn Ave, Millburn, NJ.

GRAYZEL, David M, US, pathologist; b. Russ, June 3, 1897; s. Aaron and Rebecca (Kachon); in US since 1905; BA, Columbia Coll, 1918, ChemE, Columbia U, 1921, PhD, 1927, MD, 1931; m. Sara Gross, Dec 25, 1926; c: Arthur. Path, J Hosp of Bklyn, NY, since 1936; instr: biochem, Columbia U Coll of Phys and Surgs, 1924-27; path, Yale U, Sch of Med, 1932-36. Mem: AMA; NY State and Co Med Soc; Coll Amer Path; Amer Assn Paths and Bacts; NY Paths Soc; AAAS; NY Acad Scis; Amer Acad Forensic Scis; Sigma Xi. Contbr to profsl jours. Home: 205 West End Ave, New York, NY. Office: The J Hosp of Bklyn, Brooklyn, NY

GRAYZEL, Harold G, US, pediatrician; b. Kharkow, Russ, Apr 30, 1899; s. Aaron and Rebecca (Kachon); in US since 1905; BS, CCNY, 1920; MD, NYU Med Coll, 1924; m. Ruth Weingard, Jan 29, 1935; c: Rhoda, John. Cons ped, J Chronic Disease Hosp, since 1967, dir, 1959-67; cons ped, J Hosp of Bklyn; asso prof, clinical ped, SUNY, Downstate Med Cen, since 1935; att ped, Neponsit Beach Hosp for Sick Children, NYC, 1928-42. Mem: Amer, NY, Diabetes Assns; Amer Acad Peds; NY Ped Soc; Amer, NY State Med Assns; Kings Co Med Soc; SUNY Med Coll Research Soc. Contbr to med jours. Home: 62 Midwood St, Brooklyn, NY. Office: J Chronic Disease Hosp, E 49 St and Rutland Rd, Brooklyn, NY.

GRAYZEL, Solomon, US, editor, educator; b. Minsk, Russ, Mar 1, 1896; s. Dov-Behr and Eta (Kashdan); in US since 1908; BA, CCNY, 1917; MA, Columbia U, 1920; ordained rabbi, J Theol Sem, 1921, hon DHL, 1948; PhD, Dropsie Coll, 1927; m. Sophie Solomon, June 18, 1932. Ed em, J Publ Soc of Amer, ed since 1939; prof, hist, Dropsie U; rabbi, Cong Beth El, Camden, NJ, 1921-26; registrar, instr, hist, Gratz Coll, Phila, Pa, 1928-45. Hon pres: Bd Educ, br of United Syn, Phila, past pres; J Book Council Amer, past pres; fmr: recording secy, Amer J Hist Soc; pres, bd overseers, Gratz Coll. Author: The Church and the Jews in the XIIIth Century, 1933; A History of the Jews, 1947; A History of the Contemporary Jews, 1960; contbr to: Universal J Ency; scholarly periodicals. Home: Garden Court Apts, 47 and Pine Sts, Philadelphia, Pa. Office: 222 N 15 St, Philadelphia, Pa.

GREEN, Abel, US, editor, author; b. NYC, June 3, 1900; s. Seymour and Berta (Raines); att NYU, 1918-19; m. Gracelyn Fenn, June 3, 1921. Ed, Variety, since 1933, Eur ed, 1929-30; co-author, produc, Philco-Variety Hall of Fame, Blue Radio Network, 1941-43; author: film plays: Mr Broadway, 1947; April Showers, 1948; The Spice of Variety, 1952; Tin Pan Alley, 1955; co-author: Show Biz, Vaude to Video, 1951; Outward Bound and Gagged, 1954; ed, Variety Musical Historical Song Cavalcade, 1952, rev, 1962; Songwriter; contbr of articles on the theater. Mem: Motion Picture Pioneers; The Skeeters; ASCAP; club, Variety, NY. Home: 55 Central Park W, New York, NY. Office: 154 W 46 St, New York, NY.

GREEN, Alan S, US, rabbi; b. Chgo, Ill, Dec 6, 1907; s. William and Malvine (Singer); BA, W Reserve U, Cleveland, O, 1929, MA, 1935; att: Columbia U, 1930; Heb U, Jerusalem, 1935-36; ordained rabbi, HUC, 1934, DD, 1938, hon DDL, 1959; m. Frances Katz, May 22, 1934; c: Jonathan, David. Found, rabbi, Temple Emanu-El, Cleveland, O, since 1947; rabbi, Temple Berith Shalom, Troy, NY, 1937-44; first rabbi, Temple Emanu-El, Houston, Tex, 1944-47; chaplain, Crile VA Hosp, Cleveland, 1948-55. Pres: Zionist dist, Troy, 1938; Min Assn, 1944; Council of Soc Agcys, 1944; chmn, UJA, 1942; co-chmn: religious comm, Bonds for Isr, Cleveland, since 1958; J co-chmn, Cleveland Conf of Rel and Race, 1963-67; bd, Cleveland Council on Econ Opportunities, 1965-67; treas, CCAR, since 1967; mem, Alumni Bd Overseers, HUC, since 1968; mem: Church Commn on Housing, Houston, Tex, 1945-46; Phi Beta Kappa; Delta Sigma Rho; Zeta Beta Tau. Author: Facing the Issues of Contemporaneous Jewish Life, 1935; Modern Jewish History Taught Through Fiction, 1939; co-author: A Short History of the Jews, 1942; ed: Liberal Judaism; Natl Reform Magazine, 1942-44, columnist, 1938-44; contbr to Universal J Ency. Home: 21949 Byron Rd, Cleveland, O. Study: 2200 S Green Rd, Cleveland, O.

GREEN, David, US, attorney, business exec; b. NYC, Mar 31, 1899; s. Joseph and Sarah (Rosenstein); LLB, Rutgers U Law Sch, 1926; naval engr, Lehigh U, 1922; m. Jeannette Katchen, Mar 25, 1926; c: Alice Fried, Joan Miron (decd). Pres, dir: Motor Club of Amer; Motor Club of Amer Ins Co; Garden State Life Ins Co; Motor Club Fire and Casualty Co, all since 1926; engr, Fed Shipbuilding Co, US Steel, 1923;

partner, law firm, Green & Green, 1926-42. US Army, 1918; lt cdr, USNR, 1942-45. Dir, exec comm, Daughters of Isr Pleasant Valley Home, W Orange, NJ, 1957-64; pres, Natl Assn of Independent Insurers, 1962-63, vice-pres, mem, bd govs; secy-treas, Fed of Ins Counsel, 1962-63, pres, 1964-65; mem: Ins Soc, NY; Essex Co, NJ State, Amer, (vice-chmn, auto comm ins sect), Intl and Inter-Amer Bar Assns; Amer Soc Naval Engrs; NJ and Natl Soc Profsl Engrs; Pi Lambda Phi Council and Endowment Fund, chmn, bd trustees; Masons; Salaam Temple; clubs: Advt of NJ, bd govs, 1959-61; Kiwanis, Newark, pres, 1962. Contbr to profsl jours. Home: 15 Lowell Pl, W Orange, NJ. Office: 449 Central Ave, Newark, NJ.

GREEN, David E, US, biochemist, educator; b. NYC, Aug 5, 1910; s. Herman and Jennie (Marrow); BS, NYU, 1931, MA, 1932; PhD, Cambridge U, 1934; m. Doris Cribb, Apr 15, 1935; c: Rowena Matthews, Pamela Baldwin. Prof, enzyme chem, co-dir, Inst for Enzyme Research, U of Wis, since 1948; head, enzyme lab, Columbia U Sch of Med, 1941-48. Chmn, div biol chem, Amer Chem Soc, 1960-61; mem, Natl Acad Sci; Amer Acad Arts and Scis. Author: Mechanisms of Biological Oxidations, 1939; contbr of articles on biol oxidations, multi-enzyme sys, to profsl publs. Recipient: Paul Lewis award in enzyme chem, Amer Chem Soc, 1946. Home: 1525 Sumac Dr, Madison, Wis. Office: U of Wis, Madison, Wis.

GREEN, Gerald, US, rabbi; b. Bklyn, NY, July 27, 1928; s. Harry and Pearl (Nadel); BA, CUNY, 1949; ordained rabbi, MHL, JTSA, 1953; MA, hist, Rutgers U, 1965; m. Esther Green, Dec 27, 1953; c: Dov, Shira, Rona. Rabbi, Cong Adath Isr, since 1967; visiting lectr, Rutgers U, Hebraica dept, since 1968; asst rabbi, Flatbush J Cen, 1953-55; rabbi, Cong Poile Zedek, New Brunswick, 1955-61. Bd trustees, NJ Mh Research Devl Fund; mem: Natl Acad Rel and Mh; Natl Assn Mentally Retarded Children; RA: NY Bd Rabbis. Home: 20 Belmont Circle, Trenton, NJ. Study: 715 Bellevue Ave, Trenton, NJ.

GREEN, H Kermit, US, attorney; b. NYC, Dec 9, 1902; s. Emanuel and Frances (Aranofsky); BA, Cornell, 1924; LLB, Yale, 1926; m. Sarah Phillips, Sep 9, 1905; c: Kermit, Frederic. Sr partner, Green, Lasly and Cohen, since 1964; sr partner, Green and Yanoff, 1945-68. Maj, surg gen, Renegotiation and Termination Divs, 1943-45. Pres, commercial sect, NJ State Bar Assn, em mem; fmr, commn, chmn, N Jersey Dist Water Supply Commn; mem: Essex Co Bar Assn; Amer Bar Assn; B'nai B'rith, past pres; AJC; Pi Lambda Phi, Delta chap. Home: 320 S Harrison, E Orange, NJ. Office: 17 Academy, Newark, NJ.

GREEN, Howard Irwin, US, financier; b. NYC, Feb 6, 1924; s. Julius and Elizabeth (Greenberg); grad, Wharton Sch, U Pa, 1943; m. Ina Goldberg, Mar 26, 1950; c: Stacy, Clayton. Pres, dir: Fidelity Amer Financial Corp, found, since 1953; Fidelity Amer Small Bus Inves Co, since 1963, found; owner, Green Realty Co, since 1958; chmn, bd: Servo/Tech Corp, since 1968; Penn Consultants, Inc, since 1968; Steward & Romaine Mfr Co; The Rugdon Co; gen mgr, vice-pres, dir, Fidelity Machine Co, Inc; co-found, pres, dir, the Small Bus Inves Co of Pa. USNR, 1943-46. Pres, Commercial Finance Div, Credit Mgmt Assn, Del Valley; dir, Natl Commercial Finance Conf, Inc; co-found; mem, pres' council, bd govs, exec comm, Natl Assn Small Bus Inves Cos, fmr treas; Middle Atlantic Regional Assn Small Bus Inves Cos, past pres; fmr: chmn, Finance Div, March of Dimes; dir: Phila Grand Opera Co; regional, UJA; United Comty Campaign; clubs: Pa Athletic; Phila Art Alliance. Contbr to financial mags and periodicals. Home: 113 S 21 St, Philadelphia, Pa.

GREEN, Irwin, US, business exec; b. Russ, Feb 18, 1910; s. Anna Rozlovsky; in US since 1924; BA, LLB, Wayne State U, 1934; m. Bethea Raepe, Feb 22, 1939; c: Margo Shell, Richard, Don. Pres: St Clair Metal Products, since 1952; Century Metal Moulding Co, 1944-52. Chmn, Allied J Campaign, 1964-66; vice-pres, United J Charities; trustee: Sinai Hosp; Cong Shaarey Zedek; mem, bd: J Comty Cen, 1963-65; ADL, 1965-68; mem, Masons; clubs: Standard City; Franklin Hills Country. Hobbies: golf, boating. Home: 1520 Lincolnshire, Detroit, Mich. Office: 2727 W 14 Mile Rd, Royal Oak, Mich.

GREEN, Isadore, US, neuropsychiatrist; b. Boston, Mass, Sep 14, 1899; s. Jacob and Dora (Wigot); att Mass Coll of Pharm, 1916; MD, cum laude, Tufts Coll, 1922; m. Gertrude Flink, 1920; c: Irwin, Roberta. Neuropsycht: Soldiers Home Hosp; J Memorial Hosp; asso neur, Beth Isr Hosp; psycht cons: Heb

Ladies Home for Aged; Dept of Child Guardianship, Common wealth of Mass; lectr, neur, Tufts Coll Med Sch; prof, neuropsycht, Middlesex U, Waltham, Mass, 1935; guest lectr, dept of psych, Boston U, 1948; lectr, psycht and sociol subjects. Regimental surg, US Army, 1943-46, lt col; psycht, Boston Vets Service, 1944-48. F, Amer Psycht Assn; mem: Phi Iota Mu, hon; Phi Lambda Upsilon, hon; Phi Delta Epsilon; Amer Acad Neur; AMA; Mass Med Soc; Gtr Boston Med Soc; NE Psycht Soc; Masons; Amer Zionist Group; J Comty Cen of Brookline, Allston, Brighton and Newton; Amer Legion; JWV. Contbr to profsl and J jours. Home: 132 Naples Rd, Brookline, Mass. Office: 483 Beacon St, Boston, Mass.

GREEN, Leslie C, Can, educator; b. London, Nov 6, 1920; s. Willie and Raie (Goldberg); LLB, hons, U London, 1941; m. Lilian Meyer, Sep 1, 1945; c: Anne. Prof, intl law and land org, U Alberta, since 1965; rapporteur, intl comm on asylum, Intl Law Assn, since 1961; fmr: prof intl law, U Singapore; asst lectr intl law, U Coll, London; visiting prof: Holland; Ger; Switz; Yogo; Ethiopia; Austr; US; S Amer; India. Maj, British Army, 1941-46. Mem: Amer Soc Intl Law; British Inst Intl and Comparative Law; Intl Law Assn; London Inst World Affairs, fmr secy and org tutor; Can Inst Intl Affairs; natl council, Can Hum Rights Found; fgn affairs comm, CJC; fmr, natl council, WJC, British sect. Author: International Law Through the Cases; ed, Chen's International Law of Recognition, 1951; asst ed, Libr and Yearbook of World Affairs, London, 1948-60. Recipient: Grotius Medallist, 1954; Barou Memorial Lectr, 1960; George J Cohen Memorial Lectr, 1961. Hobbies: philately, reading, squash. Home: 7911-19 SE, Edmonton 61, Alberta, Can. Office: U of Alberta, Edmonton, Alberta, Can.

GREEN, Melville Saul, US, educator; b. Jamaica, NY, Sep 6, 1922; s. Maurice and Ella (Prichep); att Columbia U, 1941-44; Princeton U, 1944-47; m. Vivian Grossman; c: Aliza, Joel. Prof, physics, Temple U, since 1968; asst prof, natural scis, U of Chgo, 1947-51; research asso, U of Md, 1951-54; physicist, thermodynamics sect, Natl Bur Standards, Wash, DC, 1954-68. Dir, Lower Merion Syn; fmr, mem, bd educ, Heb Acad, Wash, DC. Contbr to sci jours. Recipient: gold medal for dist achievement in Fed Service, Commerce Dept, 1964. Home: 2345 N 52 St, Philadelphia, Pa. Office: Temple U, Dept of Physics, Philadelphia, Pa.

GREEN, Meyer H, US, dentist; b. Kolno, Pol, Mar 22, 1917; s. Louis and Bessie (Fellander); att Wayne State U, Detroit, 1935-40; DDS, U of Detroit, 1943; m. Hilda Rosenberg, Sep 30, 1944; c: Marc, Janice. Pvt practice since 1943; asso att, Sinai Hosp, Detroit. Capt, US Army, 1944-46. F, Royal Soc Health; dipl, Amer Bd Oral Med; cert, Amer Bd Clinical Hypnosis in Dent; bd trustees: Amer Acad Oral Med, since 1960, past pres; Young Isr Cen of Oakwoods, past vice-pres, past mem, bd educ; Mich Soc Psychosomatic Dent, past pres; mem: B'nai B'rith, Louis Marshall Lodge; Masons, Mosaic Lodge; Amer Dent Assn; Mich State Dent Assn; Detroit Dist Soc Research Found; U of Detroit, Sch of Dent Alumni; Alpha Omega, U of Detroit. Contbr to dent jours. Recipient: Amer Acad Oral Med, for service, 1955, natl meeting, for service; award for service, Grosse Pointe Kiwanis, 1967; Allied J Campaign, 1968. Spec interests: rel phil, J hist. Home: 24331 Eastwood, Oak Park, Mich. Office: 14110 Gratiot, Detroit, Mich.

GREEN, Michael B, US, attorney, public official; b. NYC, Mar 17, 1903; s. Jacob and Elsie (Rappaport) Greenberg; LLB, St John's Sch of Law, 1928; m. Sonia Gordon, Feb 22, 1937; c: Ellen Bank. Chief clerk, estate tax dept, Surrogates Court, NY Co, since 1962; staff mem, Surrogates Court, NY Co, 1923-28; pvt practice, 1928-38; various tax affairs duties, State NY, 1938-39; mortgage tax examiner, NY State Tax Commn, 1939-41; legal div, Transfer and Estate Tax Bur, 1941-46, sr estate tax examiner, 1946-62. Dir: Talmud Torah, Gan Eden Temple, 1936-37; Temple Zion, 1937-47; mem: Surrogates Court and Tax Comm, chmn; Bx Co Bar Assn; Bialystoker Home for Aged; KP. Author: Pocket Manual on Law of Wills and Inheritance, 1939; ed, Kombinet, 1935-38. Home: 2185 Valentine Ave, Bronx, NY. Office: 321 Broadway, New York, NY.

GREEN, Nathan, Can, jurist; b. Glace Bay, NS, Feb 22, 1913; s. Morris and Annie (Diamond); BA, Dalhousie U, 1934, LLB, 1936; m. Pinnie Rosenhek, July 25, 1945; c: Keile, David. Provincial magistrate, Halifax, NS, since 1959; asso lectr, Dalhousie Law Sch, since 1958; mem adv comm, Inst of Criminology, U of Toronto; mem, bd govs, Dalhousie U; fmr practicing atty. Gov, Isr Bond Comm, since 1960; mem: NS Barrister's Soc; Can Bar Assn; Halifax Memorial Libr; Bd of Trade; past pres: Can J Cong, maritime sect; Shaar Shalom Syn; Dalhousie Alumni Assn; Can Libr Trustees Assn; clubs: Can; Commercial; Halifax; Waegwoltic; Oakfield Golf and Country. Author: Divorce Practice and Procedure in Province of Nova Scotia, section in Divorce Rembrancer, 1962. Home: 864 Robie St, Halifax, NS, Can. Office: Law Courts, Spring Garden Rd, Halifax, NS, Can.

GREEN, Samuel, US, business exec; b. Newark, NJ, Feb 10, 1894; s. Ignatz and Hannah (Goldberger); ME, Bklyn Poly Inst, 1922; m. Elizabeth Mondson, May 10, 1923; c: Edward, Robert. Ret, 1959; fmr: sr vice-pres, Bklyn Union Gas Co, 1957-59, vice-pres, chief engr, 1953-57. Mem: Amer Gas Assn; Soc Gas Lighting; club, Bklyn. Home: 1776 NE 191 St, N Miami Beach, Fla.

GREEN, Sidney S, US, public acctnt; b. NYC, Nov 14, 1908; s. Barnett and Kate (Cohen); BCS, NYU, 1932; CPA, SUNY, 1932; m. Cele Frankel, June 10, 1934; c: Edith Nelson, Gerald. Partner, Green, Strocker & Co, since 1932; practicing public acctnt since 1927; pres, Isr Hotels Intl, owners, Tel Aviv Hilton; financial adv: United Pal Appeal-UJA, since 1941, comptroller, 1943-48; JA since 1941; State of Isr since 1948; State of Isr Bonds since 1951, also mem, bd govs, finance and exec comms; Commercial Bank of N Amer since 1951. Gov, Heb U, Jerusalem; asso treas, Amer Friends Heb U; dir: Amer Assos; United Assos; Intercontinental Assos; Atlantic Assos; vice-pres, Glen Oaks Club; mem: NY State Soc CPA; treas, Isr's Tenth Anniversary Comm, 1958; fmr, trustee, Concourse Cen of Isr; clubs: NYU; Men's, Concourse Cen, past pres. Home: 1 Larch Dr, Great Neck, NY. Office: 850 Third Ave, New York, NY.

GREENBAUM, Aaron, US, rabbi, educational cons; b. Czech, Oct 15, 1913; s. Philip and Anna (Klein); in US since 1921; BA, Yeshiva Coll, 1936; ordained rabbi, Isaac Elchanan Theol Sem, 1939; DHL, Bernard Revel Grad Sch, Yeshiva U, 1945; m. Miriam Kasher, Dec 27, 1942; c: Adina, Tamar, Ephraim. Educ cons, JDC, in Isr, since 1955; rabbi: Cong Williamsport, Pa, 1939-41; J Comty, Portland, Me, 1941-45; Cong Sons of Isr, Yonkers, NY, 1945-55; lectr, Bible and Talmud, Yeshiva U, 1946-55. Mem: RabCA. Contbr to Anglo-J publs. Home: 49 W Maple Ave, Monsey, NY. Office: JDC, 60 E 42 St, New York, NY.

GREENBAUM, Edward S, US, attorney, army off; b. NYC, Apr 13, 1890; s. Samuel and Selina (Ullman); BA, Williams Coll, 1910, hon LLD, 1946; LLB, Columbia Law Sch, 1913; m. Dorothea Schwarcz, Oct 21, 1920; c: David, Daniel. Mem, law firm, Greenbaum, Wolff and Ernst, since 1913; chmn, Alcohol Control Co, Wash, DC, 1933; spec asst to atty gen, 1938. US Army, 1917-19, 1940-46, brig-gen, 1943-46; exec off, off of Under Secy of War, 1943-46. Dir, NY Found; trustee, Inst for Advanced Study, Princeton, NJ; mem: J Bd Guardians; AJComm; Fed Settlement; Surprise Lake Camp; NYC, NY State, Amer, Bar Assns; NY Co Lawyers Assn; fmr, mem exec comm, armed services div, JWB; clubs: Army and Navy; Williams; Nassau. Co-author: The King's Bench Masters, 1932; A Lawyer's Job. Recipient: Dist Service Medal, 1945. Home: 104 Mercer St, Princeton, NJ. Office: 437 Madison Ave, New York, NY.

GREENBAUM, J Victor, US, pediatrician; b. Cincinnati, O, Sep 7, 1885; s. Simon and Bertha (Victor); BA, Harvard Coll, 1908, MD, Med Sch, 1911; hon DHumL, HUC-JIR, 1955; m. Fanny Frank, Nov 23, 1914; c: Victor, Frank (decd). Pvt practice, ped; dir, ped, J Hosp, 1921-48; att phys, Children's Hosp; visiting phys, Gen Hosp; fmr mem, staff, Child Guidance Home, chmn, comm which organized Home, all Cincinnati; asso prof, U Cincinnati Med Sch. Prin contribs: research in prevention of rickets; first to demonstrate diphteria prevention methods in Cincinnati, 1922. Pres, Babies Milk Fund Assn, 1951-53; mem, bd govs, HUC-JIR, 1935-59, hon mem since 1959, organized its hygiene dept, 1915; mem: exec comm, United J Social Agcys; admn comm, council of social agcys, Comty Chest; bd trustees: Rockdale Ave Temple; J Publ Soc; J Hist Soc; mem: Cincinnati Ped Soc, fmr pres; comms, Cincinnati Acad Med; chmn, comms, Amer, O State Acads of Ped; Mental Hygiene Soc; fmr delg, O State Med Assn; mem, two White House Confs on Child Wfr; clubs: U; Torch; Losantiville; Fac. Contbr to med jours. Hobbies: golf, book and stamp collecting. Home: 719 Vernon Manor, Cincinnati, O. Office: 3530 Reading Rd, Cincinnati, O.

GREENBAUM, Leonard Aaron, US, writer, educator; b. Boston, Mass, Sep 30, 1930; s. Noah and Sarah (Hookness); BA, U of Mich, 1952, MA, 1953, PhD, 1963; att U of Cal, Berkeley, 1952-53; m. Judith Levine, June 22, 1952; c: Daniel, Joshua, Sara, Susannah. Asst dir, Mich Memorial Phoenix Project, U of Mich, since 1964, producer, writer, U of Mich TV, 1958-60, asst prof, Coll Engr, 1963-68. Author: The Hound & Horn, 1966; Out of Shape, 1969. Vice-pres, Assn for Children with Social and Learning Dificulties; mem: AAUP; Natl Council Tchrs of Eng; AAAS; Conf on Coll Composition and Communication, NEA; Council for Exceptional Children; fmr: mem, found comm, Conf on Rel and Race; exec bd, Beth Isr Cong, Ann Arbor, Mich. Recipient: Asso, Danforth Found, 1969. Spec interests: spec educ, U student relations, civil rights. Home: 374 Hilldale Dr, Ann Arbor, Mich. Office: Phoenix Memorial Laboratory, Ann Arbor, Mich.

GREENBAUM, Morris A, US, attorney; b. Pol, Oct 15, 1898; s. Max and Rachel; ordained rabbi, Rabb Sch, Pol, 1918; LLB, NY Law Sch, 1936; JSP, Bklyn Law Sch, 1938; BBA, CUNY, 1951; m. Betty Yusim, Oct 15, 1929; c: Eli, Terry. Pvt practice since 1929; auditor, Amalgamated Bank, 1926-28. Secy, Far Rockaway JCC; adv atty, Queens JCC; fmr: pres, Wavecrest Civic Assn; secy, LI Zionist Region; mem: ZOA; NY Co Lawyers Assn; B'nai B'rith. Home: 526 Grassmere Terr, Far Rockaway, NY. Office: 401 Broadway, New York, NY.

GREENBAUM, Steffi R, US, artist; b. Berlin, Ger, Feb 28, 1928; d. Max and Alice (Flieg) Rosenberg; in US since 1940; BS, BFA, Tyler Coll of Fine Art, Temple U, MFA, 1967; m. Robert, Jan 1, 1950; c: Marcia, Paula. Tchr: Norristown Art League, since 1958; fmr, Whitemarsh Comty Art Cen; one-man show, Cheltenham Art Cen, 1963; participant in numerous group shows; repr in many collections in US. Mem: Phila Water Color Club; Woodmere Art Gal; Phila Art Tchrs Assn; Norristown Art League. Recipient: 1st prize for watercolor, Tyler Alumni Show, 1952; Strassburger Memorial Prize for portrait, 1961, 68; Van Sciver Memorial Prize for painting, 1962, for sculpture, 1962, 67; 1st prize for print, Phila Art Tchrs Assn, 1964; 2nd prize, painting, Regional Council of Art Cens, 1965; 1st prize for sculpture: Allen Lane Annual Juried Show, 1966, 67, 69; Phila Art Tchrs Assn, 1966, 68; Norristown Annual Juried Show, 1968; 3rd prize, sculpture, ADVAC Showcase, Phila Civic Cen, 1966; Woodmere Art Gal Prize for jewelry in silver or gold, 1968; mem prize, sculpture, Old York Rd Art Guild, 1968; 2nd prize, sculpture, Norristown Art League Annual Award Show, 1969. Home: 800 Germantown Pike, Norristown, Pa.

GREENBERG, Abraham Louis, US, dental surg; b. Russ, Feb 15, 1901; s. Louis and Shendle (Wasserman); in US since 1914; DDS, U of Minn, Minneapolis, 1925; m. Rose Reisman, June 24, 1906; c: Richard, Lawrence. Pvt practice, dent surg; found of Heb U Sch of Dent Med, Jerusalem. Lt-col, US Army, Dent Corps, 1953-58; chief dent surg, Bklyn Army Terminal, NYC. Fmr: pres: AJCong, St Paul Chap; J Educ Cen, Workmen's Loan Assn; St Paul Zionist Dist; cdr, JWV, Post 162, St Paul; secy, Temple of Aaron; found, alumni, Isr Dent Soc; mem: life, ZOA, northwest region, past pres, past natl admn, natl exec; life, Alpha Omega, past pres; bd: St Paul Talmud Torah; Herz Camp Assn; Capital City Mason Lodge 217; Heroes of 76; Natl Sojourners; life mem: Amer Dent Assn; Minn Dent Assn; St Paul Dist Dent Soc. Contbr to dent jours. Home and office: 2115 Juno Ave, St Paul, Minn.

GREENBERG, Arthur N, US, attorney; b. Detroit, Mich, Oct 4, 1927; s. Nat and Eva (Magid); att Stanford U, 1945; AB, hons, UCLA, 1949, LLB, 1952; m. Audrey Wittert, Aug 14, 1955; c: Jonathan, Daniel, Robert. Partner, Greenberg & Glusker, since 1961. US Army, 1945-46. Vice-pres, Leo Baeck Temple, LA, since 1967; chmn, AJComm, LA chap, since 1966, mem intl delgs; natl vice-chmn, jr bar conf, Amer Bar Assn, 1955-56; mem: Amer, LA, Beverly Hills Bar Assns; State Bar of Cal; Phi Beta Kappa; Pi Kappa Delta; Pi Sigma Alpha; Pi Gamma Mu; Order of Coif; clubs: Standard; Beverly Hills. Contbr to legal jours. Home: 223 N Carmelina Ave, Los Angeles, Cal. Office: 9720 Wilshire Blvd, Beverly Hills, Cal.

GREENBERG, Bernard G, US, educator; b. NYC, Oct 4, 1919; s. Samuel and Lillie (Kidansky); BS, CCNY, 1939; PhD, NC State Coll, 1949; m. Ruth Marck, Apr 7, 1946; c: Stanley, Frances, Raymond. Kenan prof, chmn, dept biostats, U of NC, since 1949; cons, USPHS, since 1949; cons, pres comms; stat clerk: Brookings Inst, 1938-39; Census Bur, 1940; asst stat, NY State Dept of Health, 1940-41, 1946; chmn, stats sect, Amer Public Health Assn, 1958-59, comm on evaluation and standards, 1959-60. F: chmn, training sect, Amer Stat Assn, 1959; Royal Stat Soc; pres, Beth-El Cong, Durham, NC, 1964-67; mem: B'nai B'rith; Biometric Soc; Inst Math Stat; Intl Stat Inst; Phi Beta Kappa; Sigma Xi; Delta Omega. Contbr: Order Statistics, 1962; profsl jours. Recipient: Bronfman award, Amer Public Health Assn, 1966. Home: 425 Brookside Dr, Chapel Hill, NC. Office: U of NC, Chapel Hill, NC.

GREENBERG, Carl, US, journalist, editor; b. Boston, Mass, Aug 19, 1908; s. Harry and Fannie (Herman); att UCLA, 1927; m. Gladys Bilansky, July 12, 1930; c: Howard. Political writer, LA Times, since 1962, mem, ed bd, since 1962; political ed, LA Examiner, 1943-62, staff mem, since 1933; reporter, LA Evening Express, 1926-28; City News Service of LA, 1928-33. USCG Res. Mem: Greater LA Press Club; Coast Guard League; Kappa Tau Alpha; Sigma Delta Chi. Recipient: Victory Medal, 1946; first prize, best story among S Cal newspaper writers, from LA chap, Theta Sigma Phi, 1944, second award, best comty service story, 1946; commendation by Cal Leg for contribs to journalism, 1957; silver award, Cal-Nevada AP Writing Contest, 1957. Hobby: stamp collecting. Home: 6001 Canterbury Drive, Culver City, Cal. Office: Times Mirror Sq, Los Angeles, Cal.

GREENBERG, Clement, US, author, artist; b. NYC, Jan 16, 1909; s. Joseph and Dora (Brodwin); BA, Syracuse U, 1930; m. Edwina Ewing, Apr, 1934; c: Daniel; m. 2nd, Janice Van Horne, May, 1956. Free-lance art writer; clerk: US Civil Service Commn, NYC, 1936-37; US Customs Service, 1937-42; ed, Partisan Review, 1940-43; mgn ed, Contemporary J Record, 1944-45; art critic, The Nation, 1945-50; asso ed, Commentary, 1945-57. Mem: Phi Beta Kappa; Sigma Alpha Mu. Author: Juan Miró, 1948; Matisse, 1953; Art and Culture, 1961; Hofmann, 1961. Home: 275 Central Park W, New York, NY.

GREENBERG, David L, US, rabbi; b. Stockton, Cal, Jan 6, 1905; s. Julius and Sofy (Barron); BA, U of Cal, 1927; MHL, ordained rabbi, JIR, 1931; hon DD, Coll of the Pacific, Stockton, 1947; DD, HUC-JIR, 1960; reg social worker, Cal, 1931; m. Estelle Rochells, June 28, 1931; c: Rochelle Anixter. Rabbi, Temple Beth Isr, Fresno, Cal, since 1931; bc, Radio Forum of Better Understanding, 1938-55; asst field dir, mil wfr, ARC, 1942-44. Mem: Gov's adv comm, Youth and Child Wfr; adv comm, Rosenberg Found, SF, 1950-52; B'nai B'rith; Masons, 32 deg; Shrine; Elks; life mem, Demolay Legion of Honor; clubs: Commonwealth; Academy; Kiwanis. Home: 740 E Vassar Ave, Fresno, Cal. Study: 2336 Calveras Ave, Fresno, Cal.

GREENBERG, David M, US, biochemist, educator; b. Boston, Mass, Sep 15, 1895; s. Samuel and Ida (Cooperman); BA, U of Cal, 1921, PhD, 1924; m. Shena Berkowitz, May 20, 1918; c: Lenore Dickstein, Joan Moises. Prof em, biochem, U of Cal, Berkeley, since 1943, dept chmn since 1946, prof, 1941-63, on fac since 1924; Guggenheim Memorial Found F, 1929-30; mem, panel on isotopes, comm on growth, NRC, Wash, DC, 1946-48; chmn, Cancer Research Coordinating Comm, U of Cal, 1948-54. Prin contrib: pioneer in use of isotopes, 1938. F: AAAS; Cal Acad Sci; mem: comm, Amer Cancer Soc; Amer Assn Biol Chem; British Assn Biol Chem; Amer Chem Soc; Amer Assn Cancer Research; Sigma Xi; B'nai B'rith; Soc Experimental Biol and Med, fmr chm, Cal sect, 1950-52. Author: Amino Acids and Proteins, 1951; Chemical Pathways of Metabolism, 1954; Metabolic Pathways, 1960, 3rd ed, 1969; ed proceedings, Soc of Experimental Biol and Med, 1946-51; contbr to sci jours. Recipient, research grants: Natl Cancer Inst; Amer Cancer Soc; Damon Runyon Memorial Found; NSF. Home: 2969 24 Ave, San Francisco Cal. Office: U of Cal, Sch of Med, San Francisco, Cal.

GREENBERG, Eliezer, US, author, poet; b. Lipkani, Russ, Dec 13, 1896; s. Ezekiel and Ethel (Haselov); in US since 1913; m. Eva Brown, Dec 12, 1926. Dir, Yiddish press relations, AJComm, since 1948; co-ed, Getseltn, 1946-48. Author: Gassen un Avenues, 1928; Foon Oometum, 1934; Fisherdorf, 1938; M L Halpern, 1942; Die Lange Nacht, 1946; Banachtiker Dialog, 1953; Tsentrale Motivn in H Leivik's Shafn, 1961; Jacob Glatstein's Di Freid Fun Yiddishen Wort, 1964; Eybiker Dorsht, poetry, 1968; co-ed: A Treasury of Yiddish Stories, 1954; The Zukunft. Vice-pres, NYC Yiddish PEN; mem: I L

Peretz Yiddish Writers Union; Workmen's Circle. Recipient: Harry Kovner Award for Yiddish Poetry, J Book Council, for Banachtiker Dialog, 1953; J Book Council of Amer Award for Poetry, 1954; Jacob Fichman Poetry Prize in Isr, Union of Bessarabian J in Isr, 1967. Home: 455 E 14 St, New York, NY.

GREENBERG, Irving, US, rabbi; b. Bklyn, NY, May 16, 1933; s. Elias and Sonia (Rabinowitz); BA, summa cum laude, Bklyn Coll, 1953; ordained rabbi, Beth Joseph Rabb Sem, Bklyn, 1953; MA, Harvard U, 1954; PhD, Harvard U, 1959; m. Blu Genaver, June 23, 1957; c: Jeremy, Deborah, Judith, David, Jonathan. Rabbi, Riverdale J Cen, since 1965; asso prof, hist, Yeshiva U, since 1964; fmr: rabbi, Young Isr, Brookline, Mass, 1954-56; lectr, near E Judaic studies, Brandeis U, 1957-68; asst prof, hist, Yeshiva U, 1959-64; visiting Fulbright lectr, Tel Aviv U, 1961-62. Found, Yavneh Natl Rel Students Assn; bd dir, Rel Educ Assn; mem: Amer Acad Rel; Amer Hist Assn; Amer J Hist Soc; RabCA. Contbr to rel and hist jours. Recipient: f's, grants: Knopf, Shackford Research, Harvard U, 1953-57; Natl Found J Culture, 1962-63; Littauer Found, 1963; Memorial Found J Culture, 1967-68. Home: 4618 Independence Ave, Riverdale, NY. Study: 3700 Independence Ave, Riverdale, NY.

GREENBERG, Irving Lawrence, US, surgeon, educator; b. Bialystock, Pol, Feb 12, 1911; s. Charles and Hannah (Esral); in US since 1913; MD, Emory U Sch of Med, 1935; postgrad study: U of Ill, 1945; Brompton Hosp for Chest Diseases, London, Eng, 1944; George Wash Med Sch, 1946; m. Regina Gabler, Aug 27, 1938; c: Leonard, Ira. Pvt practice, surgeon, Atlanta, since 1940; asso, surg, Emory U Sch of Med, since 1947, fmr, asst, dept anat; mem, surg staff: Ga Baptist Hosp, since 1940; Crawford W Long Memorial Hosp, since 1940; Grady Memorial Hosp, since 1946; Sheffield Cancer Clinic, since 1940; St Joseph's Infirmary, since 1958, all Atlanta; fmr, cons, surg, Tuskegee VA Hosp, Ala. Capt, US Army MC, 1941-46. Mem, exec comm, ARC, Atlanta, since 1952, past pres, med adv comm; hon pres, Heb Acad of Atlanta, past vice-pres; cdr, Atlanta Post, JWV; f: SE Surg Cong; FACS; Intl Coll Surgs; dipl, Amer Bd Surgs, 1955; mem: bd trustees, JWFs; bd dirs: Fulton Co chap, Amer Cancer Soc; Atlantic J Comty Cen, past pres; mem: Pres' spec study comm, Natl Blood Prog, Wash, DC; JDC; UJA; J Home for Aged; clubs: Breakfast; Grad, Phi Delta Epsilon, past pres; fmr: chmn, JWF Campaign; consul, Phi Delta Epsilon; vice-pres: local chap, ZOA; Fed for J Social Services; JCC; pres, Atlantic JCC. Contbr to med jours. Recipient: Aven Citizenship Award, Fulton Co Med Soc, 1958; Dist Service Award, B'nai B'rith, 1952; Brotherhood Award, NCCJ, 1965. Home: 1730 Doncaster Dr, NE, Atlanta, Ga. Office: 950 W Peachtree St NW, Atlanta, Ga.

GREENBERG, Joseph, US, physician, educator; b. NYC, Oct 6, 1926; s. Morris and Ruth (Milman); BA, NYU, 1947, MD, Coll of Med, 1951; m. Barbara Brodoff, Sep 12, 1954; c: Paula, Janis. Dir, dept, nuclear med, endocrinology, Med Arts Cen, since 1962; cons: US Naval Hosp, St Albans; chief, radioisotope lab, 1954-56; Oak Ridge Natl Lab; f, Natl Cancer Inst, 1952-54; chief div nuclear med, LI J Hosp, 1956-60; prof, dir, dept nuclear med, endocrinology, NY Polyclinic Med Sch and Hosp, 1960-63. Lt, USN MC, Korean War. Prin contribs: original work, chelation chem, rare earth, radio-yttrium metabolism, 1954-62. Pres, Gtr NY chap, Soc Nuclear Med, 1959-62; med adv, Leukemia Soc; f: AAAS; mem: Amer Nuclear Soc; Amer Phys Soc; Amer Assn Cancer Research; NY Cancer Soc; NY Acad Sci; Nassau Acad Med; AMA; NY State Med Soc. Contbr to: Trace Metal Metabolism in Med, 1959; Tumors of the Somatic Tissues and Bone, 1963; numerous research papers in profsl jours. Recipient: prize, Peoples Hosp Research Found, 1951. Spec interests: art, music, elec. Home: 106 Clover Drive, Great Neck, NY. Office: Med Arts Cen, 57 W 57 St, New York, NY.

GREENBERG, Joseph Emanuel, US, painter; b. Bx, NY, Sep 5, 1926; s. Max and Rose (Glasser); m. Maria Russo, Mar 26, 1949; c: Rachel, Amelia. One-man shows: Coeval Gal, 1954; Harry Salpeter Gal, 1957; Bernard Crystal, 1960; Merrill Gal, 1962; Phila Art Alliance, 1957; group shows: Berlin Acad Fine Arts, 1954; City Cen Art Gal, 1958, 59; Roko Gal; Natl Acad Annual, 1963; Butler Inst Biannual, 1963; Mary Wash Coll; Amer Artists Painting in Holland, 1968. Life mem, Art Students League. Recipient: 3rd prize, Butler Inst Biannual, 1963; 2nd prize, City Cen Art Gal, 1958. Hobby: classical music. Home: 332 E 18 St, New York, NY.

GREENBERG, Marian G, US, communal worker; b. Phila, Pa, Mar 31, 1897; d. Frederic and Regina (Levy) Gerber; BA, with honors in hist, Cornell U, 1919; m. David Greenberg, Mar 22, 1922; c: Joan Freilich, Frederic, Jonathan. Hon council, Hadassah, Women's ZOA, since 1950, natl bd since 1928, 1st chmn, Natl Youth Aliyah Comm, 1935-41; gen council, WZO, 1946-51; mem: Phi Beta Kappa. Co-author: Shopping Guide to Europe, 1954; Shopping Guide to Mexico, Guatemala and the Caribbean, 1955; ed, bull, Citizens Housing and Planning Council of NY, 1940-45; ed bd, Jewish Reconstructionist, since 1968. Home: 111 E 56 St, New York, NY. Office: 15 W 86 St, New York, NY.

GREENBERG, Max, US, labor union official; b. NYC, Aug 6, 1907; s. Isaac and Mollie (Beigel); m. Billie Garfinkle, Sep 21, 1929; c: Martin, Marsha. Intl pres, retail, wholesale, dept store union, AFL-CIO, since 1954, vice-pres: exec council, Ind Union dept; pres em, retail union, NJ local 108, since 1954, past pres, 1936-54; lab mem, regional bd, War Lab Bd, 1942-46; mem: NJ State Bd of Mediation, 1949-54; lab adv council, Pres: Equal Employment Opportunity, 1964; OEO, 1965; lab mem, Natl Lab Mgt Manpower Policy Comm, 1967; mem, Fed Adv Council, Employment Security, 1967. Bd dirs: Inst Collective Bargaining and Group Relations; Natl Found for Consumer Credit; Natl Comm for Lab Isr; Amer Trade Union Council for Histadrut; bd govs, Intl Union Food and Allied Workers Assn; mem: admn comm, AFL-CIO comm on political educ, civil rights comm, intl affairs comm, econ policy comm. Home: 47 Stanford Ave, West Orange, NJ. Office: 101 W 31 St, New York, NY.

GREENBERG, Maximilian Ely, US, attorney; b. NYC, May 9, 1894; s. Meyer and Lillian (Silverman); BA, CCNY, 1916; JD, NYU, 1919; m. Fil D'Agostino, Jan 30, 1920. Head, law firm, Max E Greenberg, Trayman, Harris, Cantor, Reiss & Blasky, since 1968; fmr, law firm, Max E Greenberg, 1919-67. Off, Field Artillery Offs Sch, 1919. Dir, City Coll Fund; bd govs, NYU Vanderbilt Assos; chmn, region 2, public contracts sect, Amer Bar Assn, comm on state and munic law; fmr: pres: City Coll Alumni Assn; master, Citizens Lodge F & AM 628; mem: B'nai B'rith, NY, fmr pres; Masons, Lodge 1, NY; NY Co Lawyers; Inst of Jud Admn; NY State Bar Assn, ins sect, comm on construction and surety law, ed, newsletter. Contbr to legal jours. Home: 911 Park Ave, New York, NY. Office: 30 Vesey, New York, NY.

GREENBERG, Maxwell E, US, attorney; b. Mar 11, 1922; s. Abe and Annette (Friedman); AB, cum laude, U of Cal, 1941; LLB, magna cum laude, Harvard Law Sch, 1949; m. Marcie Caplan, Mar 27, 1945; c: Jan, Richard. Partner, Greenberg, Shafton & Bernhard, since 1950; chmn bd: Gtr Ariz Savings & Loan Assn, Rural Devel Corp. Lt, US Army, WW II. Mem: ADL; LA Co Dem Cen Comm, 1954-57; Cal State, LA, Ill, Amer Bar Assns; Amer Judicature Soc; club, Beverly Hills Dem, found, pres. Home: 707 N Walden Dr, Beverly Hills, Cal. Office: 3540 Wilshire Blvd, Los Angeles, Cal.

GREENBERG, Meyer, US, rabbi, educator; b. NYC, Jan 11, 1914; s. Aaron and Blanche (Bernzweig); BA, magna cum laude, Yeshiva Coll, 1934; ordained rabbi, MHL, JIR, 1944; PhD,U of Md,1956; m. Evelyn Levow,June 15, 1941; c:Saadia, Jeremiah, Bryna, Dvora. Dir, B'nai B'rith Hillel Found, U of Md, since 1945, dir, Heb prog, asst prof, Heb; dir, Hillel Found: Yale U; Queens Coll, both 1944-45. Pres: Amer Alumni of Heb U, 1939-41; Wash Bd Rabbis, 1958-60; chmn: Heb Acad of Wash, bd educ, since 1951; Juvenile Court Adv Comm, 1951-55; UJA, 1950-51; exec comm: JCC, Gtr Wash; Natl Assn Hillel Dirs; f, Amer Sociol Assn; hon mem: Alpha Kappa Delta; Eta Beta Rho; mem: RA; Rel Zionists of Amer; B'nai B'rith; Phi Kappa Phi. Contbr to profsl jours. Home: 1631 Jonquil St NW, Washington, DC. Office: U of Md, 7505 Yale Ave, College Park, Md.

GREENBERG, Milton, US, business exec; b. Carteret, NJ, Apr 21, 1918; s. David and Eva (Salzer); att NYU, 1943; MS, Air Force Tech Cen, Michigan, 1943; MPA, Harvard U, 1954; ScD, hon, Canaan Coll, 1961; m. Maxine Baer, June 30, 1948; c: Eve, David, Alan. Pres, GCA Corp, Bedford, Mass, since 1958; dir, geophysics research directorate, Air Force Cambridge Research Labs, Bedford, 1954-58. Maj, USAAC, 1943-47. Trustee, Temple Emanuel, Lowell, Mass; f, AAAS; asso f, Amer Inst Aeronautics and Astronautics; mem, Masons, Frank Thompson lodge, Bedford. Home: 46 Sagamore Dr, Andover, Mass. Office: GCA Corp, Burlington Rd, Bedford, Mass.

GREENBERG, Oscar W, US, educator; b. NYC, Feb 18, 1932; s. Joseph and Betty (Sklower); BS, Rutgers U, 1952; MA, Princeton U, 1954, PhD, 1947. Prof, physics, U of Md, since 1967. Mem: AAUP; Amer Phys Soc; ACLU; Sigma Xi; Phi Beta Kappa. Contbr to profsl jours. Home: 1616 18 St NW, Washington, DC. Office: Dept of Physics and Astronomy, U of Md, College Park, Md.

GREENBERG, Reynold H, US, realtor; b. Baltimore, Md, Apr 3, 1899; s. Bernard and Ray (Pimes); att Baltimore City Coll; m. Dora Wiel; c: Reynold, Robert, Lois. Pres, Joseph J and Reynold H Greenberg Inc. Fmr: dir, Trust Co of NJ, Jersey City; secy, treas, Architects Bldg Corp; pres, Wilkie-Buick Co. Charter mem: Inst Real Estate Mgmt; Natl Assn Real Estate Bds; Phila Real Estate Bd; Phila C of C; hon pres: Cong Rodeph Shalom; United HIAS service, bd mem; Council Migration Service of Phila; trustee, Phila Coll for J Studies; co-chmn, Phila Allied J Appeal drive, 1942, chmn, allocation comm; mem bd: Fed of J Agcys; J Employment and Vocation Bur; natl JWB; natl exec, UAHC; clubs: Locust, Philmont, fmr mem, bd govs, both clubs. Office: Architects Bldg, 17 and Sansom Sts, Philadelphia, Pa.

GREENBERG, Sidney, US, rabbi, author; b. NYC, Sep 27, 1917; s. Morris and Sadie (Armel); BA, Yeshiva U, 1938; ordained rabbi, JTSA, 1942, DHL, 1947; m. Hilda Weiss, Oct 31, 1942; c: Shira, Reena, Adena. Rabbi, Temple Sinai, since 1942. Author: A Treasury of Comfort, 1954; Adding Life to Our Years, 1959; The Bar Mitzvah Companion, 1959; A Modern Treasury of Jewish Thought, 1959; Sidduraynu, 1961; A Treasury of the Art of Living, 1963; Finding Ourselves, 1964; Children's Prayerbook—For The High Holidays, 1968. Pres, Phila br, JTSA, since 1952, mem, rabb cabinet, since 1950; exec mem: RA, since 1957, pres, Phila br, 1954-56; Technion; United Syn of Amer; Bd of J Educ, Phila. Home: 300 Old Farm Rd, Wyncote, Pa. Study: Washington Lane and Limekiln Pike, Philadelphia, Pa.

GREENBERG, Simon, US, rabbi, educator; b. Horoshen, Russ, Jan 8, 1901; s. Morris and Bessie (Chaidenko); in US since 1905; att U of Minn, 1920-21; BA, CUNY, 1922; att Amer Sch for Oriental Research, Jerusalem, 1924-25; Heb U, Jerusalem, 1925; ordained rabbi, JTSA, 1925, hon DD, 1950; PhD, Dropsie Coll, Phila, 1932; m. Betty Davis, 1925; c: Moshe, Daniel. Prof, homiletics, J educ, vice-chancellor, vice-pres of fac, JTSA, NYC, since 1951, mem fac since 1932, provost, 1946-51, acting pres, 1948-49; chancellor, U of Judaism, JTSA, LA, since 1963, pres, 1958-63; rabbi, Har Zion Temple, Phila, 1925-46; exec dir, United Synagogue of Amer, 1950-53; pres, RA, 1937-39; pres, Phila ZOA, 1941-44, chmn, natl educ comm, 1943-45. Mem: Chaplains Rel Council, U of Pa; Conf of Sci, Phil and Rel. Author: Living as a Jew Today, 1939; The Ideals of the Jewish Prayer Book, 1940; The First Year in Hebrew School, A Teacher's Guide, 1945; Harishon, series of texts for study of Heb in first two years of Hebrew School, 1940; The Teachings of Judaism on God, Men, Torah and Israel, 1957; Foundations of a Faith, 1968. Home: 420 Riverside Dr, New York, NY. Offices: 3080 Broadway, New York, NY; 6525 Sunset Blvd, Los Angeles, Cal.

GREENBERG, Sydney N, Jr, US, realtor; b. New Haven, Conn, Nov 22, 1916; s. Sydney and Helen (Solomon); m. Jessie Stewart, Mar 6, 1941, div; c: Charles, John; m. 2nd, Renee Landy. Partner, Strouse, Greenberg & Co, realtors, since 1939. USAC, 1941-45. Bd dirs: Elkins Pk Free Libr; Comm of "70"; AJ Comm; Citizens Council on City Planning, 1955-61; bd trustees: Abington Memorial Hosp; Intl Council Shopping Cens; mem: Natl Assn Real Estate Bds; clubs: Philmont Country; Locust Midcity. Home: 8368 Fisher Rd, Elkins Pk, Pa. Office: 1525 Locust St, Philadelphia, Pa.

GREENBERG, Uri Zvi, Isr, poet; b. Bielkaman, Aus-Hung, 1897; in Isr since 1924. Fmr: MK; leader, Zionist-Revisionist Party. Author: Eyma Gedola veYareah, 1925; HaGavrut haOla, 1926; Anakreon al Kotev haIzavon, 1928; Hason Ahad haLigyonot, 1928; Klapey Tish'im veTishah, 1928; Kelev Bayit, 1929; Esor haMagen uNeum Ben haDam, 1930; Sefer haKitrug vehaEmuna, 1937; Rehovot haNahar, 1951, all in Heb; In Zaitens Roish, 1919; Farnachtengold, 1921; Mephisto, 1922; Krik oif der Erd, 1928, all in Yiddish; co-author: Zeeve Jabotinsky; ed: Albatross, Yiddish mag, 1922-23; contbr to daily, lit press. Mem, Heb Lang Acad. Recipient: awards: Talpir; Bialik; Neuman, NYU. Home: 13 Marganit St, Ramat Gan, Isr.

GREENBLATT, Ida M, US, attorney; b. Russ, Dec 25, 1903; d. Max and Goldie (Klugman) Schechtman; in US since 1904; LLB, St Lawrence U, Bklyn Law Sch, 1923; att Adelphi Coll, Sch of Social Work; m. Harold Greenblatt, June 27, 1925; c: Walter, Carol Corbin. Pvt practice since 1923; admitted to practice, US Mil Court of Appeals. Vice-pres for US, Intl Fed Women Lawyers, past pres; chmn, comm on Amer affairs, Hadassah; conf chmn, Natl Assn Women Lawyers; chmn, civic participation, Bus and Profsl Women; mem: Pres Kennedy's Comm on Civil Defense; Pres Kennedy's Comm on Status of Women; chmn, legal rights of mentally ill; vice-pres, Equal Rights for Women; delg to conf, Iran, 1969, Natl Assn of Women Lawyers; mem: Dallas Council for World Affairs; Dallas UN Assn; intl hospitality comm, Council of J Women; fmr: chmn, legal services to Armed Forces, WW II; pres, Town N Bus and Profsl Women's Club; official observer, UN Conf on Hum Rights, Mex. Contbr of articles to legal jours. Recipient: Natl Award, Natl Assn of Women Lawyers, 1968. Home: 7916 Royal La, Dallas, Tex. Office: 5925 Forest La, Dallas, Tex.

GREENBLATT, Irving Jules, US, biochemist; b. NYC, Sep 15, 1912; s. Samuel and Sada (Schneider); BA, NYU, 1938; MS, Georgetown U, 1939, PhD, 1941; m. Augusta Pecker, Apr 28, 1940; c: Richard, Laurence. Adj asso prof, occupational med, Columbia U, Coll of Phys and Surgs, Sch of Public Health, since 1964; dir, clinical, toxicological labs, Brookdale Hosp Cen, since 1958. Mem: AAAS; NY Acad Sci; Soc Experimental Biol and Med; Kings Co Med Soc; Amer Soc Study Arteriosclerosis; Assn Clinical Scis. Contbr to med jours. Home: 511 Allen Rd, Woodmere, NY. Office: Rockaway Pkwy, Brooklyn, NY.

GREENBURG, Dan, US, author; b. Chgo, Ill, June 20, 1936; s. Samuel and Leah (Rosalsky); BA, U of Ill, 1958; MA, UCLA, 1960; m. Nora Ephron, Apr 9, 1967. Author: How to Be a Jewish Mother, 1964; Kiss My Firm But Pliant Lips, 1965; How to Make Yourself Miserable, 1966; Chewsday, 1968; Philly, 1969; Jumbo the Boy and Arnold the Elephant, juvenile, 1969; Porno-Graphics, 1969; play, Arf and the Great Airplane Snatch, 1969; contbr to: Esquire; Playboy; Saturday Review of Literature. Advt writer, Carson/Roberts, 1960-62; mgn ed, Eros Mag, 1962-63; advt writer, Papert, Koenig, Lois, 1963-65. Mem: Authors League Amer; Amer Fed TV and Radio Artists. Home and office: 9 E 67 St, New York, NY.

GREENBURG, Samuel, US, artist, teacher; b. Uman, Ukraine, June 23, 1905; s. Isaac and Nadia (Antonow); in US since 1911; grad, Bezalel Art Sch, Jerusalem, 1927; BA, U Chgo, 1944, MA, 1946; m. Leah Rozalsky, July 3, 1929; c: Daniel, Naomi. Dist sup, art, Chgo Bd Educ, since 1962; art instr, Chgo Public HS, 1932-62. Exhibiting artist since 1929. One-man shows: Delphic Studios, NYC, 1934; Room of Chgo Art Inst, 1947; Creative Gal, NYC, 1951, 53; Hillel Found, Northwestern U, 1960, 66. Exhibited: NY World's Fair, 1939; Pa Acad Fine Arts; Phila Print Club; Libr of Cong, Wash, DC; art mus: Seattle, Cleveland, Birmingham, SF, Cincinnati. In perm collections: Libr of Cong; Bezalel Mus of Art, Jerusalem; Ein Harod Art Mus, Isr; Chgo Coll J Studies. Mem: Chgo Art Educ Assn; Renaissance Soc; Chgo Soc of Artists; Phi Beta Kappa. Author: Making Linoleum Cuts, 1947; co-author: Arts and Crafts in the Jewish School, 1952. Recipient: OCD War Poster Prize, 1942; 1st prize for painting, 1954, 2nd prize, 1956, Amer J Arts Club; 2nd prize for oil painting, Ill State Fair, 1956; 2nd prize for print, Chgo Soc of Artists, 1960, 1st prize, 1961; Midwest Glass Award, Amer J Arts Club, 1961; Murray Auerbach Memorial Award, 1968. Home: 929 W Argyle St, Chicago, Ill. Office: Chgo Bd of Educ, 228 LaSalle St, Chicago, Ill.

GREENE, Earle I, US, surgeon, educator; b. Chgo, Ill, Sep 10, 1897; s. Maurice and Rose (Fiedler); BS, U of Chgo, 1920; MD, Rush Med Coll, 1922; MS, U of Minn, 1928. Pvt practice since 1929; prof, head dept, surg, Chgo Med Sch, since 1946; f, surg, Mayo Clinic, 1924-28; instr, asst asso prof, asso prof, surg,, Northwestern U Med Sch, 1929-46; att surg: Mt Sinai Hosp; Cook Co Hosp, 1944-58; prof, surg, Cook Co Hosp, Med Sch, 1943-58. Col, US Army MC, 1942-46. Dipl, Amer Bd Surg; mem: Amer, Ill, and Chgo Med Assns; Chgo Surg Soc; Cen Surg Soc; Amer Coll Surgs; Intl Coll Surgs; Assn Res and Ex-res Mayo Clinic. Contbr to med jours. Home: 6200 N Kenmore Ave, Chicago, Ill. Office: 25 E Washington St, Chicago, Ill.

GREENE, Harry J, US, physician, educator; b. NYC, Sep 1, 1902; s. Isidor and Fanny (Wolansky); BS, Colby Coll, 1924;

MD, Cornell Med Coll, 1928; m. Lola Yokel, 1931. Cons, gyn and obstet, Kings Co Hosp, since 1959; cons: on cancer: Dept of Health, NYC; Bklyn Women's Hosp; frm, dir, gyn cancer, coord, cancer services, J Hosp of Bklyn. Dir: New Cancer comm, Amer Cancer Soc; Bklyn Cancer Comm; FACS, 1940; first vice-pres, Cong Beth Elohim; mem: Amer Coll Clinical Pharm and Chemotherapy; Bklyn Gyn Soc; NY Acad Med; NY Acad Sci; Amer Coll Gyn and Obstet; bd obstet and gyn, Amer Assn Cancer Research; NY Cancer Soc; NY Gyn Soc. Home: 855 Ocean Ave, Brooklyn, NY.

GREENE, Irving L, US, business exec; b. NYC, Feb 20, 1908; s. Abraham and Goldie (Schlesinger); att Columbia U, 1925-26; m. Harriet Altschul, Apr 2, 1933; c: Andrew. Pres, J Wfr Chest, Joliet, Ill, 1956-57; mem, Friars Club. Home: 200 E 58 St, New York, NY. Office: 527 Madison Ave, New York, NY.

GREENE, Jerome G, US, attorney; b. NYC, June 7, 1919; s. Emil and Ann (Sommers); AB, NYU, 1939; LLB, Harvard Law Sch, 1943; m. Isabelle Marshall, Oct 15, 1955; c: Adrienne Forrest. Mem, law firm, Botts and Greene, since 1954; atty: Greenbaum, Wolff & Ernst, NY, 1943-44; Myer, Weiss & Rosen, Miami, 1949-50; Price, Zaring & Florence, Miami, 1950-52; exec: CBS, NY, 1944-46; MBS, NY, 1946-47; partner, Pallot, Silver and Malloy, Miami, 1942-54. Pres, Miami Beach Taxpayers Assn, since 1962; vice-chmn, Govt Research Council of Dade Co, since 1961; pres, Research Council of S Fla, since 1969; mem, adv bd: Fla Cen and S Flood Control Dist, since 1961; League Women Voters, since 1961; mem: Housing and Urban Devl Bd, since 1969; fmr: vice-chmn, Urban Renewal Agcy, Dade Co; exec bd, AJComm, since 1957; regional bd, ADL, since 1960; bd govs: Gtr Miami J Fed, since 1959; Fla Fed B'nai B'rith Lodges, chmn bd, since 1960, pres, 1960; dir, J Vocational Service, since 1961; arbitrator, Fed Mediation and Conciliation Service, since 1962; mem: natl panel lab arbitrators, Amer Arbitration Assn, since 1955; ethics comm, Dade Co Bar Assn, since 1961; probate and real property comm, Fla State Bar Assn, since 1958; NY Bar; Fla Bar; Surpr Court of US Bar, since 1959; Dade Co Youth Council, since 1962; KP; spec dep, Atty Gen, NY State, 1947; spec hearing off, NY Rent Commn, 1948; fmr mem, Mayor's Safety Comm, Miami Beach; dir: Miami Beach Jr C of C; Brotherhood, Temple Beth Sholem; city committeeman, Boy Scouts of Amer; fmr chmn: Conv SE Temple Brotherhoods; div, Red Cross; Miami Beach Botanical Garden Campaign; mem, bd govs, dist 5, B'nai B'rith, 1959-61; mem, Harvard Law Sch Assn, Fla, 1959; club, Harvard, Miami. Recipient: comty service awards: B'nai B'rith, Fla; ARC; Miami Beach Taxpayers' Assn; Jr C of C. Hobby: sailing. Home: 1188 Marseille Dr, Miami Beach, Fla. Office: 319 Biscayne Blvd, Miami, Fla.

GREENE, Leon N, US, physician; b. Bklyn, May 1, 1910; s. Max and Fannie (Kaplan); AB, Columbia U, 1931, MD, Coll of Phys and Surgs, 1935; m. Gloria Kaufman, 1962. Att obstet and gyn: Mt Sinai Hosp, Miami; Jackson Memorial Hosp; instr, obstet and gyn, U of Miami Sch of Med; mem, att staff: Mt Sinai Hosp; Beth Isr Hosp; Bellevue Hosp, all NY, 1946-49; instr, obstet and gyn, NYU Coll of Med, 1946-49; fmr, dir, dept obstet and gyn, Mt Sinai Hosp of Gtr Miami, Fla. Maj, US Army MC, 1943-46. FACS; dipl, Amer Bd Obstet and Gyn; mem: AMA; Fla, Dade Co, Med Assns; Fla Obstet and Gyn Soc; Phi Beta Kappa; Alpha Omega Alpha; fmr, pres, Dade Co Obstet and Gyn Soc. Contbr to med jours. Hobby: painting. Home: 1200 W 21 St, Miami Beach, Fla. Office: 1431 N Bayshore Dr, Miami, Fla.

GREENEBAUM, Werner Joseph, US, dentist; b. Miltenberg, Ger, Apr 15, 1924; s. Henry and Rosi (Gutmann); in US since 1939; att: Loyola U, 1946-48; Northwestern U, 1948; DDS, Loyola U, Sch of Dent, 1952; m. Vera Baumann, Aug 11, 1953; c: Charles, James. Pvt practice since 1952; chief, Dent Clinic, Chgo Child Care Soc, since 1954; pres, St James Hosp, dent staff, 1965-66; dent cons, Ford Motor Co, Stamping Plant, Chgo Hgts. US Army, 1943-46. Prin contribs: instrumental in setting up free childrens dent clinic, St James Hosp; org dent prog, Chgo Child Care Soc. Pres, Temple Anshe Sholom, Olympia Fields, Ill, fmr, vice-pres, trustee; fmr trustee, Cong Habonim, Chgo; mem: Chgo, Ill Dent Socs; Amer Dent Assn; Alpha Omega. Hobby: boating. Home: 961 Elm, Flossmoor, Ill. Office: 316 Dixie Hwy, Chicago Heights, Ill.

GREENFELD, Elliot Monroe, US, oral surg; b. Bklyn, NY, Dec 31, 1934; s. Solomon and Evelyn (Aaronson); att Bklyn Coll, 1952-53; BA, O State U, 1956; DDS, NYU Dent Coll,

1960; postgrad, NYU Post Grad Dent Sch, 1961-62; m. Barbara Kronick, June 7, 1959; c: Jennifer, Abby. Pvt practice, oral surg, since 1963. Pres, J Comty Cen, fmr vice-pres; chmn: Clinic Comm of Dent Soc; Profsl Rev of Dent Soc; dipl, Amer Bd Oral Surg; mem: Mass Council Dent Care; Amer Dent Assn; Mass Dent Soc; Amer Dent Soc, Oral Surgs; NE Soc Oral Surgs; Mass Soc Oral Surgs; Masons, Crescent Lodge. Contbr to dent jours. Hobbies: golf, skiing. Home: 241 Dawes Ave, Pittsfield, Mass. Office: 74 N Street, Pittsfield, Mass.

GREENFIELD, Arthur A, US, attorney; b. NYC, May 26, 1919; s. Morris and Frieda (Miller); BA, cum laude, CUNY, 1938; LLB, Columbia U Law Sch, 1941; m. Beatrice Kriegstein, Aug 14, 1941; c: Deborah. Partner, law firm, Otterbourg, Steindler, Houston & Rosen, NYC, since 1961; atty, 1956-61; admitted to practice, NY State, 1941; US Dist Court, S Dist, NY, 1947; US Court of Appeals, 2nd Circuit, 1958; Blumberg, Singer & Aberman, 1946-50; asso gen counsel, Hudson & Manhattan RR, 1950-56. USAAC, 1943-46. Secy, The Village Temple, 1949-50; mem: CUNY Alumni Assn; Columbia Law Sch Alumni Assn; Phi Beta Kappa. Contbr to legal journals. Recipient: Deans Scholarship List, Columbia U Sch of Law, 1938-41. Home: 5 W 86 St, New York, NY. Office: 230 Park Ave, New York, NY.

GREENFIELD, Arthur Judah, Isr, physicist, educator; b. Oil City, Pa, Oct 3, 1934; s. Eugene and Julia (Frankfurt); in Isr since 1967; BSc, Wayne State U, 1956; MSc, U Chgo, 1956, PhD, 1963; m. Betty Eisenberg, Aug 25, 1958; c: Shimshon, Miriam, Shulamith, Dvora. Asso prof physics, Bar Ilan U, since 1967; mem tech staff, Bell Telephone Labs, 1964-67; research asso, U Chgo, 1963-64. Secy, Isr Physical Soc; mem: Isr comm: Intl Union Pure and Applied Physics; Eur Physical Soc; fmr: pres: NJ br, Assn Orthodox J Sci; Mizrachi-Hapoel Hamizrachi, Chgo Negbah Br; mem sci adv bd, JEC, Elizabeth, NJ. Contbr numerous original research publs. Home: 52 Rehov Maimon St, B'nai B'rak, Isr. Office: Bar Ilan, U, Ramat Gan, Isr.

GREENFIELD, Irving, US, physician; b. New York, NY, Jan 22, 1906; s. Meyer and Goldie (Welkowitz); att Columbia U, 1922-25; MD, LI Coll of Med, 1929; m. Bernice Low, Aug 15, 1935; c: Alice Tannenbaum, Jo Ann Abraham. Pvt practice since 1932; cons phys: Brunswick Gen and Meadowbrook Hosps, since 1959; Mercy Hosp, Rockville Cen, NY. US Army MC, 1942-45. Cons, Leukemia Found; trustee, Temple Beth El, Cedarhurst, NY; Pan-Amer Med Assn; NY Acad Scis; Nassau Acad Med; Amer Coll Phys; NY Acad Med; dipl, Amer Bd Internal Med; mem, Amer Comm, WHO. Contbr to med jours. Recipient: cert of merit, Civil Defense Forces, NY State. Home: 31 Oak St, Woodmere, NY. Office: 799 Central Ave, Woodmere, NY.

GREENFIELD, Irving H, US, attorney, business exec; b. Russ, Nov 15, 1902; s. Hyman and Fannie (Yawitz); in US since 1904; LLB, Bklyn Law Sch, 1924; m. Ethel Rudaw, Mar 19, 1944; c: Collin, Lois. Secy, atty, MGM Inc, 1954-58; asst secy, 1958-69; key chmn, motion picture and amusement ind div, UJA, since 1962, chmn, 1959-61. Pres, Cinema Lodge, B'nai B'rith, 1942; fmr mem, comm: on pr, NY Co Lawyers Assn; FJP; Joint Defense Appeal; mem, bd dirs, Men's Club of Cong B'nai Jeshurun. Home: 275 Central Park W, New York, NY. Office: 310 Madison Ave, New York, NY.

GREENFIELD, Jacob B, US, insurance exec, banker; b. Pal, Apr 14, 1896; s. Eliezer and Rachel (Nathan); in US since 1912; att Rice U, Houston, Tex, 1942-43; m. Edith Weinberger, May 2, 1923; c: Annette Strauss. Pres, chmn bd, Continental Amer Life Ins Co, since 1952; chief dep co clerk, Harris Co, 1919-32; found, chmn bd, Continental Bank & Trust Co, 1955; dir bd, Houston Natl Bank; Southern Title Co. US Army, 1917-18. Found, pres, B'rith Abraham Assn, Houston, Texas, 1922; co-found, Technion, Isr; bd, Cong Beth Yeshurun; B'nai B'rith, pres, 1922; life, ZOA; Scott & White Memorial Hosp; clubs: Brandeis U, Houston. Spec interest: study of Talmud. Home: 2212 Calumet, Houston, Tex. Office: Continental Bldg, Houston, Tex.

GREENFIELD, Murray S, Isr, business exec; b. NYC, Sep 11, 1926; s. Herman and Sarah (Milgrim); in Isr since 1947; att Pa State Coll, Pa, 1944; NY State Maritime Acad, 1944-45; m. Hana Lustig, Sep 5, 1954; c: Meira, Dror, Elan. Pres, Murray S Greenfield Ltd, since 1967; owner, dir, Greenfield Isr Art Gal, NYC and Tel Aviv, since 1954; sales repr, Pal Econ Corp, 1951-56. US Merchant Marine, 1944-47; IDF,

1947. Co-found, PR Assn, Tel Aviv; found, fmr chmn, Assn Amer and Can in Isr, exec dir, 1954-64, 1969-70, hon chmn, 1970; mem bd: Kupat Cholim Maccabi: Assn Amer and Can in Isr Mortgage Bd. Contbr of articles and lectures on Isr Art to various subjects. Special interests: art, lecturing for UJA, helping new immigrants in Isr. Home: 2 Shamir St, Tel Aviv, Isr. Office: El Al Bldg, Ben Yehuda St, Tel Aviv, Isr.

GREENHILL, Jacob P, US, surgeon, educator; b. NYC, Feb 28, 1895; s. Charles and Fanny (Pearl); BS, CUNY, 1915; MD, Johns Hopkins U, 1919; m. Olga Baumgartl, Mar 16, 1929. Prof, gyn, Cook Co Grad Sch Med, since 1932; sr att obstet gyn, Michael Reese Hosp, since 1932; att gyn, Cook Co Hosp, since 1925. F: Amer Coll Surgs, 1927; Intl Coll Surgs, 1956; hon dipl, Amer Bd Obstet and Gyn; vice-pres, Intl Fertility Soc, 1953; chmn, ed, adv bd, Standard Nomenclature of Diseases and Oprs, 1947-53; bd dirs, Amer Assn for Study of Sterility, 1953-55; AMA; Ill State and Chgo Med Socs; Amer Assn Anats; AAAS; Chgo Gyn Soc; Johns Hopkins Surg Assn; Ill State Acad Sci; Amer Public Health Assn; Cen Assn Obstet and Gyn; Amer Assn of Obstet, Gyn and Abdominal Surg; Venereal Disease Assn; Amer Soc for Control of Cancer; Socs for Study of Sterility and Internal Secretions; Amer Geriatric Soc; Fr Gyn Soc; hon mem: numerous sci socs in Cen and S Amer, Asia and Eur. Author: Obstetrics for the General Practitioner, 1935; Obstetrics in General Practice, 4th ed, 1948; Surgical Gynecology, 4th ed, 1969; Office Gynæcology, 8th ed, 1965; Obstetrics, 13th ed, 1965; Analgesia and Anesthesia in Obstetrics, 2nd ed, 1962; ed, Year Book of Obstet and Gyn, since 1931; contbr articles to med jours. Recipient: Chevalier, Fr Legion of Honor, 1957. Home: 190 E Pearson St, Chicago, Ill. Office: 55 E Washington St, Chicago, Ill.

GREENHOUSE, Barnett, US, physician; b. Russ, May 2, 1895; s. Louis and Esther (Rodman); in US since 1906; PhB, Yale U, 1918, MD, Sch of Med, 1921; m. Donah Cohen, June 22, 1927 (decd); c: Henry. Pvt practice since 1923; cons, med, Yale-New Haven Hosp and Yale Med Cen, since 1965; cons, Griffin Hosp, since 1945. Fmr: intern, Mt Sinai Hosp, Cleveland, O, 1921-22; res, SF City and Co Hosp, 1922-23. US Army MC, WWI. Fmr dir, Greenhouse Diabetic Clinic, Grace-New Haven Comty Hosp. Gov, Amer Diabetes Assn, since 1954; found and first pres, Conn Diabetes Assn, 1948; mem: B'nai Jacob Cong; Amer Coll Phys; Sci Research Soc of Amer; Amer, Conn and New Haven Med Assns; Conn Pharm Assn, hon; Phi Lambda Kappa, natl grand superior, 1940-51; Masons; asst concertmaster, New Haven Civic Orch; clubs: Woodbridge Country; Colony Beach; J Phys of New Haven, found, pres, 1924. Fmr, ed staff, Diabetes; contbr to profsl jours. Recipient: service award, Conn State Med Assn and Conn Pharm Assn, 1953. Hobby: music. Home: 1687 Boulevard, New Haven, Conn. Office: 129 Whitney Ave, New Haven, Conn.

GREENLAND, Leo, US, business exec; b. NYC, Mar 4, 1920; s. Jack and Ida (Abrams); att New School for Soc Research, NY, 1945-47; m. Rita Levine, June 29, 1955; c: Seth, Andrew. Pres, Smith/Greenland Co, Inc, advt agcy, since 1959; pres, Sherwood Producs, TV prog, 1949-52; exec, various advt agcys, 1952-59. Intelligence div, PR div, US Army. Arbitrator, Amer Arbitration Assn; mem: steering comm, chmn, urban affairs, Westchester Co, ADL; bd, Waldemar Med Research Found; Young Pres Org, Fairchester, Metrop NY chaps; Natl Businessmen's Council; Fgn Policy Assn; Interracial Businessmen's Council; Fed UJA; NY Bd Govs, Assn Amer Advt Agcys; guest lectr: Fordham U Sch of Communication Arts; Amer Mgmt Assn, mem; clubs: Sierra; Friar's. Hobbies: sports, photography, snorkeling. Home: 20 Dolma Rd, Scarsdale, NY. Office: 1414 Ave of the Americas, New York, NY.

GREENLEAF, Joseph W, US, business exec; b. Bklyn, NY, Jan 25, 1912; s. Samuel and Bertha (Whiteman) Greenblatt; BS, NYU, 1933; m. Fruma Winer, June 7, 1938; c: Jonathan, Wendy, Joyce. Pres, Greenleaf Textile Corp, since 1932; pres, Greenleaf Assos Inc, 1965-68. Fmr: pres: Philharmonic Soc Westchester; Mt Vernon Sym Soc; Westchester Zionist region, ZOA; chmn, Natl Found for Infantile Paralysis, textile div; bd dirs, UJA; sponsor, Music for Westchester, Inc; exec, World Confd Gen Zionists, Westchester Co. Mem: YMHA; B'nai B'rith; Free Syn; Beth Shalom Syn, White Plains; bd dirs: B'nai Zion, 1968; Genesis Heb Cen, 1967-68; club: Grand. Home: 6 Black Birch Lane, Scarsdale, NY. Office: 225 Park Ave S, New York, NY.

GREENSPAN, Alan Marshall, US, rabbi; b. Bridgeport, Conn, Aug 12, 1937; s. Nathan and Josephine (Weiss); BA, Yeshiva Coll, 1958; ordained rabbi, Yeshiva U, 1961; MHL, Bernard Revel Grad Sch, Yeshiva U, 1969; m. Gala Morgenstern, Dec 23, 1961; c: Ari, Dena. J chaplain, asst army chaplain, Hqr US Army, S Command, Fort Amador, Canal Zone, since 1967; J chaplain: Fort Knox, Ky, 1962-63; Korea, 1963-64; Fort Benning, Ga, 1964-66; Vietnam, 1966-67; Fort Dix, NJ, 1967; Yeshiva U repr, 1st World J Youth Conf, Jerusalem, 1958. Exec comm, Canal Zone Boy Scout Council; fmr: pres, Shimshon Youth; regional vice-pres, Yeshiva Rabb Alumni; mem: RabCA; Assn J Chaplains; Mil Chaplains Assn. Recipient: Mortimer Kogen Award, Yeshiva U, 1958; Chaplain of the Year, RabCA, 1967. Spec interest: educ magic. Home and office: Hqr, US Army, Office of Chaplain, Fort Amador, Canal Zone, APO New York 09834.

GREENSPAN, Edward B, US, physician, educator; b. Newark, NJ, June 15, 1905; s. Adolph and Sara (Weinrab); BS, U of Mich, 1927, MD, 1930; m. Norma Endel, May, 1946; c: Barbara, John, stepson, John Neuberger. Adj phys, Mt Sinai Hosp, since 1941; asso prof, clinical med, NY Med Coll, 1956-64. F: NY Acad Med; AAAS; mem: AMA; NY State and Co Med Socs; Amer Coll Phys; Chevalier du Tastevin; club, Harmonie. Contbr to profsl jours. Home: 1010 Fifth Ave, New York, NY. Office: 110 E 80 St, New York, NY.

GREENSPUN, Herman Milton, US, editor, publisher; b. Bklyn, NY, Aug 27, 1909; s. Sam and Anna (Fleischman); att St Johns Coll, 1930-32; LLB, St Johns Law Sch, 1934; m. Barbara Ritchie, May 21, 1944; c: Brian, Susan Fine, Jane, Daniel. Owner, pres, publisher, ed, Las Vegas Sun, since 1950; owner: Colo Springs Sun; Sun Outdoor Advt Co, both since 1970; pvt law practice, NYC, 1936-46; pub, Las Vegas Life, 1946-47; owner, KLAS-TV, Las Vegas, 1954-68. Maj, US Army, 1941-46. Mem: bd dir, Sun Youth Found; Amer Newspaper Publishers Assn; Amer Legion; VFW; clubs: Friars; Variety; Nev Press; Natl Press; Overseas Press; DAV. Author: Where I Stand, autobiography. Recipient: Croix de Guerre with Silver Star, WW II; Amer Legion Auxiliary award, 1969; spec Golden Press Award, 1968; S Nev Firemen's Good Fellow Award; Nev State Press Award, 1970; Amer Legion Award, comty service, 1969; Israel Medal, Isr Min Defense. Hobbies: golf, tennis. Home: 545 Griffith, Las Vegas, Nev. Office: 121 S Highland, Las Vegas, Nev.

GREENSTEIN, Harry, US, social worker; b. Baltimore, Md, Oct 31, 1895; s. Abraham and Fannie (Levinstein); LLB, U of Md, 1918, hon DSS, 1950; hon DHL, Baltimore Heb Coll, 1965. Exec vice-chmn, legacy and endowment fund, Asso J Charities of Baltimore, since 1965; fmr: State Relief Admn of Md; admnr, Md Civil Works Admn; org, Natl Refugee Service of NY, merged into present United HIAS Service Inc; org, pres, YM-YWHA of Baltimore; org, exec dir, JWF, Baltimore; US Regional Evacuation Off for Md, Pa, Va, DC; dir, wfr, UNRRA, ME mission. Mem, bd overseers, Florence Heller Grad Sch for Advanced Studies in Social Wfr, Brandeis U; found, pres, Baltimore Council of Social Agcys; natl pres: Natl Conf J Communal Service; Amer Assn Social Workers. Recipient: dist service medal, JWV of USA; award, NCCJ, 1963; dist service award, U of Md Sch of Social Work, 1967. Home: 101 W Monument St, Baltimore, Md. Office: 319 W Monument St, Baltimore, Md.

GREENSTEIN, Jesse L, US, astronomer, educator, author; b. NYC, Oct 15, 1909; s. Maurice and Leah (Feingold); BA, Harvard Coll, 1929, MA, 1930, PhD, 1937; m. Naomi Kitay, Jan 7, 1934; c: George, Peter. Prof, astrophysics, exec off, Cal Inst Tech, since 1949; staff mem, Mt Wilson and Palomar Observatories, since 1948; fmr: Natl Research f, 1937-39; instr, U Chgo, 1939, asst prof, 1942, asso, 1947. Chmn: commn on spectroscopy, Intl Astronomical Union, 1952-58; panel of consultants on astronomy, Natl Sci Found, 1952-55, chmn, divisional comm, 1957-59; vice-pres, Amer Astronomical Soc, councillor, 1945-48, and since 1966; mem, bd overseers, Harvard Coll, since 1966; mem: Amer Phil Soc; Natl Acad Scis. Author: The Upper Atmosphere Studied from Rockets, in Atmospheres of the Earth and Planets, 1947; Interstellar Matter, in Astrophysics, 1951; Astrophysics, in Modern Physics for the Engineer, 1954; Stellar Atmospheres, 1965; ed: The Hertzsprung-Russell Diagram, 1959; Stellar Spectroscopy, 1960; fgn ed: Annales d'Astrophysique, 1952-60; Astrophysical Letters, 1967; contbr to sci jours. Home: 2057 San Pasqual, Pasadena, Cal. Office: Cal Inst Tech, Pasadena, Cal.

GREENWALD, Edmund M, US, attorney; b. Nov 19, 1904; LLB, Bklyn Law Sch; m. Emily Liebman; c: Diana, Alice. Practicing atty since 1929; real estate, life, casualty ins broker, since 1933; chief clerk, Dist Court, Nassau Co, Lawrence, NY, 1938-58. Maj, US Army Amphibian Command, 1942-46. Village clerk, treas, assessor, registrar of vital stat, Traffic Violations Bur of Inc Village of Cedarhurst, NY, since 1958; org: Nassau Co Police Boys Club, Inwood, LI; and charter mem, local chap, B'nai B'rith; peninsula lodge, KP; secy-treas, atty, Nassau Co Village Clerks and Treas Assn; chmn, publicity comm, Nassau Co Village Officials Assn, also mem, civil service comm; mem, Five Towns Comty Chest, United Fund, i/c annual solicitation of funds; hon mem, Lawrence-Cedarhurst Fire Dept; charter mem, atty, Nassau Co Assessor's Assn; fmr: vice-pres, Lawrence-Cedarhurst Young Rep Club, dir, Sr Rep Club; civil defense dir, presently, chief of supplies, Five Towns Civil Defense Area 112; cdr: Post 1515, VFW; Post 339, Amer Legion; pres, Five Towns Kiwanis Club; trustee. dir, men's club, Temple Sinai, Lawrence; mem: Nassau Co Mounted Guard of JWV; and instr, US Power Squadron, local unit. Recipient: Silver Star; Bronze Star; Purple Heart; Amer Theatre; Asiatic-Pacific Theatre; Philippine Liberation; NY State Conspicuous Service Award. Hobby: sports. Home: 234 Washington Ave, Cedarhurst, LI, NY.

GREENWALD, Harold, US, attorney; b. Yonkers, NY, Apr 2, 1907; s. Louis and Rose (Schwartz); att Wash Sq Coll, NY; NYU Law Sch; m. Dorothy Nass, June 26, 1943. Partner, Greenwald, Kovner & Goldsmith; asso, Waldo Grant Morse, 1928-34; counsel, NY State Prisoner of War Farm Service Prog, 1943-45. Trustee, Wall St Syn; repr, ZOA to UN; conferee, Leg Comm for Revision of Corps Laws; mem: Court of Honor, ZOA; Conf of Pres of Major J Orgs; Amer Judicature Soc; Amer Acad Political and Social Sci. Mem, ed bd, contbr: Synagogue Light; Zionist Monthly; contbr, Letters from Israel. Home: 345 W 58 St, New York, NY. Office: 170 Broadway, New York, NY.

GREENWALD, Isidor, US, bio-chemist, educator; b. NYC, July 7, 1887; s. Jacob and Mary (Bieber); BA, U of Mich, 1909; PhD, Columbia U, 1911. Prof em, chem, NYU Coll of Med, since 1952, asso prof, 1930-49, prof, 1949-52, on fac since 1929. Fmr, asso prof, Bellevue Hosp Med Coll, 1930-35. Prin contribs: chem and metabolism of calcium and phosphorus; hist of goiter, mortality from exophthalmic goiter. F: NY Acad of Sci; NY Acad of Med; AAAS; mem: Amer Chem Soc; Soc Biol Chems; Amer Inst of Nutrition; Endocrine Soc; Soc Experimental Biol and Med; hon mem, Thyroid Soc. Home: 127 W 79 St, New York, NY. Office: NYU—Bellevue Med Cen, 550 First Ave, New York, NY.

GREENWALD, Jack, US, attorney; b. Columbus, O, June 14, 1928; s. Leopold and Gisela (Horowitz); BSL, Denver U, 1950, LLB, 1952; m. Barbara Sharoff, June 30, 1959; c: Debbie. Pres: Hillel Acad, Denver; Vaad Hoir; Columbine Toastmasters; vice-pres, Beth Joseph Cong; chmn, B'nai B'rith Inst Judaism; mem: B'nai B'rith; ADL. Home: 725 S Glencoe, Denver, Colo. Office: 32 S Broadway, Denver, Colo.

GREENWALD, Norman David, Isr, educator; b. Boston, Mass, June 8, 1925; s. Moses and Bessie (Rosen); in Isr since 1968; BA, George Washington U, 1949; MA, Columbia U, 1951, PhD, 1956; m. Simha Sofer, Aug 10, 1965; c: Yifat, Michal, Moses, Assaf. Pres, Amer Coll, Jerusalem, since 1967; fmr: lectr, CCNY; dir, Hiatt Inst in Isr; lectr, Near E studies, Brandeis U. USAF, 1943-46. Fmr chmn, Council for Constitutional Reform in Mass. Author: The ME in Focus, 1959; Portraits of Power, 1960; Higher Education in Massachusetts, 1963. Home: 3 Shikun Harel, Jerusalem, Isr. Office: 14 Bet Hakerem St, Jerusalem, Isr.

GREER, Daniel, US, attorney; b. NYC, June 15, 1940; s. Moses and Angele (Sapriel); AB, Princeton U, 1960; LLB, Yale Law Sch, 1964; att Yeshiva U Grad Sch. Dep commn, NYC Dept of Ports and Terminals, Econ Devl Admn, since 1969; counsel, NY Dept of Inves, 1966-69; asso, Simpson, Thacher & Bartlett, 1964-66. Dir: Natl J Commn on Law and Public Affairs; Union of Orthodox J Congs; fmr: vice-pres, Yavneh, Natl Rel J Students Org; pres, Young Isr Kosher Kitchen, Yale U; mem: Phi Beta Kappa. Recipient: Woodrow Wilson f, 1960. Home: 110 Riverside Dr, New York, NY. Office: Battery Marine Bldg, New York, NY.

GREIDI, Shimon, Isr, educational admnr, editor, author; b. Dhamar, Yemen, 1913; s. Yehya and Nema (Asta); MA, Heb

U, Jerusalem, 1937; m. Segoulah Nehora, Aug 31, 1949; c: Saadia, Nourit, Yehiel. Prin, official Rel Elem Sch, since 1960; secy, Agoudath Yesha, for Mutual Assistance and Cultural Enterprises, since 1964; fmr: MK; mem exec, Rel Natl Party; mem social council, Min of Wfr. Pvt, IDF, 1950-61. Mem: Org of Grads of Heb U; Oriental Soc of Isr; World Org for J Sci; fmr: gen secy, Cen of Yemenites; active, Drive for J of Yemen, US. Author: Yehudej Teyman Vehinuch Banejhem Baaretz, 1942; Merkaz Hitahduth Hateymanim Be'eretz Israel, 1943; Miginzej Hayehudim Bateyman, 1948; Perush Ivri of Lawa for Ritual Slaughter of the Rambam for a Forgotten Writer; Shoshanat Hamelekh, 1967; Mitsefunot Yehudei Teyman, 1962; lit ed: Hamizrach, 1938; Miteyman le'Zion, 1938; for Ha'aretz, Heb daily; Searat Teyman; contbr to ency Yezreel, press. Spec interests: ancient Yemenite writing; old Yemenite art, handicraft. Home: 19 Zerubabel St, Tel Aviv, Isr.

GREIDINGER, B Bernard, US, accountant, educator; b. NYC, Mar 30, 1906; s. Max and Fannie (Oster); BBA, CCNY, 1928; MS, Columbia, 1932; PhD, 1939. Sr partner, Greidinger, Hoffberg & Oberfest,CPAs; prof, acctnt,NYU Grad Sch of Bus Admn, since 1948; fmr: sr partner, B Bernard Greidinger & Co, 1945-70; sr partner, Beame & Greidinger, 1933-45; fmr prof, acctnt: Rutgers U; U Cal; CCNY; fmr dir, mem exec comm, US Hoffman Machinery Co; repr dir gen UNRRA at inception Intl Ref Org, 1946; financial adv, chief financial opr, UNRRA, 1946-47; cons, budget advisory comm, Army-Air Force Post Exch Service, 1948; cons, chief ordance dept, Army, NY Dist, since 1952; mem, Renegotiation Bd, 1952; spec cons to comptroller, NY, 1955; cons, intl coop admn, US State Dept, 1956; coord, NYU, US Opr Mission, Isr, 1956; mem, temp commn, city finances, NYC, 1965-66; served with finance dept, AUS, 1942-44; maj to 1t col, USAAF, 1944-46; USAF Res since 1950. Dir, J Comty House of Bensonhurst; financial adv, independent auditor, Yeshiva U, Bar Ilan U; mem: Amer Inst CPAs; NY State Soc CPAs; Amer Acctnt Assn; Natl Assn Cost Acctnts; Acad Political Sci; Masons; clubs: Columbia, NYU Fac. Author: Accounting Requirements of the Securities and Exchange Commission, 1941; Preparation and Certification of Financial Statements, 1950; Filings with the Securities and Exchange Commission; contbr to Big Business Methods for Small Business, 1952. Recipient: Townsend Harris Award, CUNY, 1965; Dist Achievement Award, Baruch Coll, CUNY, 1968. Spec interests: music, golf. Home: 1 Washington Square Village, New York, NY. Office: 888 Seventh Ave, New York, NY.

GREIDINGER, Coleman Kenneth, Isr, business exec; b. London, Eng, Jan 1, 1924; s. Moshe and Rebecca (Chissick); in Isr since 1929; BComm, Witwatersrand U, 1944; m. Dahlia Katz, Oct 31, 1950; c: Moshe, Rebecca, Israel, Merav. Mgn dir: Isr Theatres Ltd, since 1946; Isr Lighterage & Supply Co, since 1950. Capt, IDF, 1948-50. Chmn, dist scholarship comm, Rotary Intl; vice-pres, Cinema Owners Assn; hon Nor Consul Gen for Haifa and N Isr; mgmt comm, Mt Carmel Water Supply Assn; hon treas, Haifa Home for Needy Immigrants; past chmn, Haifa Maccabiah Org Comm; exec comm: Variety Club of Isr; Maccabi Sports Cen. Home: 98 Hatishbi St, Haifa, Isr. Office: 20 Hanamal St, Haifa, Isr.

GREIFER, Julian Leon, US, educator; b. Minsk, Russ, Oct 16, 1901; s. Solomon and Anna (Warshall); in US since 1910; BS, NYU, 1927; MA, Columbia U, 1933; PhD, Tchrs Coll, NYU, 1948; m. Adeline Molotin, 1922; c: Paul, Judith Benjamin. Prof, sociol, dir, inst comty affairs, Lincoln U, since 1966; fmr: coord, State of Pa Dept Comty Affairs; exec dir, Neighborhood Crusaders of Phila; instr, Gratz Coll; lectr: Beard Coll; Temple U. Chmn: Intl Social Work Comms; comms on health and wfr agcys, on city capital budget, Citizens Council on City Planning, Phila, past vice-pres; mem: AJComm; AAUP; Phila City Policy Comm; Natl Sociol Assn; fmr, pres, Assn J Cen Workers. Author: Time to Celebrate; contbr to J publs. Recipient: dist service award, N City, Phila, 1952. Home: 1901 Walnut St, Philadelphia, Pa. Office: Lincoln U, Oxford, Pa.

GREIFINGER, Marcus H, US, physician; b. Rahway, NJ, Mar 25, 1900; s. Bernard and Rachel (Steinberg); MD, U of Md, 1924. Pvt practice since 1926; chief surg, Newark Police Dept, since 1943. US Army, 1918. Secy, Med Soc of NJ; past pres, Essex Co Med Soc. Home: 657 Mountain Dr, S Orange, NJ. Office: 31 Lincoln Park, Newark, NJ.

GREILSAMMER, Marcel, Fr, business exec; b. Paris, Nov 26, 1902; s. Alphonse and Camille (Lévy); engr dipl, Ecole

Nationale Supérieure des Mines, Paris, 1922; m. Denise Lévy-Bauer, Nov 24, 1935; c: Jacques, Daniel, Alain, Claude. Ret since 1968; fmr mgr, domestic sales, ARMCO, Paris, 1935-68; sales agent, Sullivan Machinery Co, 1927-33; engr, SA Andre Citroen, 1933-34. Fr Army, 1939; prisoner of war, 1940-45. Pres, Union Libérale Israélite, since 1948; chmn, World Union of Progressive Judaism; mem exec, Fr J Social United Fund. Home: 23 rue des Longs Prés Boulogne, Seine, Fr. Office: Union Libérale Israélite, 24 rue Copernic, Paris, Fr.

GRIES, Robert Dauby, US, business exec; b. Cleveland, O, May 15, 1929; s. Robert and Lucille; BA, Yale U, 1951; m. Joan Selig, Oct 16, 1955; c: Robert, Peggy, Donald. Pres, Gries Inves Co, since 1964; vice-pres, Cleveland Browns Inc. Chap chmn, mem, natl exec bd, AJComm; trustee: J Comty Fed, Cleveland, endowment fund comm, comty relations comm, public wfr comm, found, adv council, all J Comty Fed; Mt Sinai Hosp; J Family Service Assn; off, trustee, numerous non-J orgs. Home: 18200 S Woodland Rd, Shaker Hgts, O. Office: 1236 Natl City Bank Bldg, Cleveland, O.

GRIESMAN, Bruno L, US, otolaryngologist; b. Nuremberg, Ger, July 17, 1888; s. Louis and Lina (Kohnstam); in US since 1936; MD, U of Heidelberg, 1912; m. Hilde Hirsch, Mar 16, 1931; c: Henry, Trude. Research asso, otolaryngology, Mt Sinai Hosp, NYC, since 1962, chief, eustachian tube research, hearing clinic, since 1960. Prin contrib: inventor of audiometer for testing of hearing. Dipl, Amer Bd Otolaryngology; mem: Amer Acad Ophthal and Otolaryngology. Author: New Methods of Testing Hearing Acuity, 1919; contbr to med publs. Home: 251 W 89 St, New York, NY. Office: 11 E 68 St, New York, NY.

GRINBERG, P Irving, US, attorney, organization exec; b. NYC, June 11, 1887; s. Paul and Rose (Hanlein); LLB, NY Law Sch, 1917; m. Herma Levy, Feb 12, 1916; c: Carol Lederer, Marion Preston, Paul; m. 2nd, Sadie Rosenburg, Jan 19, 1947. Ret; fmr: exec vice-chmn, Jewelers Vigilance Comm; owner, P Irving Grinberg, pearl importers, 1915-42; with WPB, Wash, DC, 1942-45. Pres: Pearl Assos, 1942; NY Trade Assn Execs, 1955; hon pres, J Comty Cen, White Plains, NY, found, first pres, 1922-47; charter mem, NY Chap, UJA; mem: mgmt comm, AJComm adv council, JDC; fmr pres: Manhattan lodge, B'nai B'rith; White Plains YM-YWHA. Contbr to trade jours. Home: 37 E 64 St, New York, NY. Office: 15 W 44 St, New York, NY.

GRINKER, Roy R, Sr, US, psychiatrist; b. Chgo, Ill, Aug 2, 1900; s. Julius and Minnie (Friend); BS, U of Chgo, 1919; MD, Rush Med Sch, 1921; m. Mildred Barman, 1924; c: Roy. Dir, Inst Psychosomatic and Psycht Research Training, Michael Reese Hosp, since 1945, chmn, dept psycht, since 1936; training and supervisory analyst, Chgo Psychan Inst, since 1945; mem, psycht council, Ill State, since 1950; instr, Northwestern U, 1924-27; att neur, Cook Co Hosp, 1926-28; att staff, Billings Memorial Hosp, 1927-36; asso prof, neur, U of Chgo, 1931-35, mem fac since 1929, head div, asso prof,psycht, 1935-36; lectr, psycht, Social Service Admn, 1936-50; att psycht, Chgo Psychopathic Hosp, 1946-48; clinical prof, psycht, U of Ill Med Sch, 1951-65; chmn: State of Ill Psycht Training and Research Auth, 1957-64; pharm study sect, NIH, 1961-65; psycht cons, Ill Dept Mh, since 1956. Col, US Army MC, 1945; cons, Surg 5th Army, 1955-61. F: AAAS; NY Acad Sci; Amer Coll Neuropsychopharm; mem: AMA; Cen Neuropsycht Assn, past vice-pres; Amer Psycht Assn; Amer Neur Assn; Amer Psychan Soc; Amer Assn Neuropaths; Amer Assn Research in Nervous and Mental Diseases; Natl Comm for Mh; Chgo Inst Med; Sigma Xi; fmr: pres: Chgo Neur Soc; Chgo Analytic Soc; Amer Psychosomatic Soc; Ill Psycht Soc; chmn: bd dirs, Assn Psycht Facs, Chgo; Comm for Devl of Unified Theory of Behavior; comm on research, Group for Advancement of Psycht; clubs: Standard; Ravisloe Country. Author of numerous books; chief ed, Archives of General Psychiatry (AMA), since 1956; ed, neuropsycht sect, Tice's Practice of Medicine, 1930-61; mem, ed bd: Jour of Psychosomatic Med, since 1962, asso ed, 1939-62; Family Process since 1962; fmr, mem ed bd, Jour of Amer Psychan Assn; contbr: chaps in med books; Ency Britannica Year Book; papers to profsl jours. Home: 910 Lake Shore Dr, Chicago, Ill. Office: 29 and Ellis, Chicago, Ill.

GRINSTEIN, Hyman B, US, educator; b. Dallas, Tex, Nov 15, 1899; s. Henry and Rebecca (Saxia); BS, Columbia U, 1927; MA, 1935; PhD, 1944. Prof, Amer J hist, Yeshiva U, since 1951, on fac since 1944, Tchrs Inst, 1947-68; headmaster rel school, Cong Shaarey Tefilah, Far Rockaway, NY, 1929-44. Mem: NY Hist Soc; AAUP. Author: The Rise of the Jewish Community of New York, 1945; contbr to scholarly periodicals. Home: 41 W 86 St, New York, NY. Office: Yeshiva U, 186 St and Amsterdam Ave, New York, NY

GRIZER, Leon, US, business exec; b. Warsaw, Pol, Oct 15, 1898; s. Eliezer and Hanna (Pergament) Grajcer; in US since 1920; Sch of Bus Admn, Warsaw, Pol, 1915-19; deg, lab relations, 1938; m. Isabel Belarsky; c: Esther, Martin, Leonard. Exec dir, Gtr NY Retail Merchants Assn, since 1935; pres, Metrop Employers Assn, since 1954; exec dir, Fed of Retail Merchants, since 1960; owner, wholesale firm, Miami Sportswear, 1923-35. Mem: B'nai B'rith; ZOA; Amer Soc Assn Execs; C of C; NY State Council Retail Merchants; lectr, bus econ and lab relations; arbitrator. Author: The Future of the Independent Store; Rules for Better Retailing; ed, The Retail Digest Mag. Office: 132 Madison Ave, New York, NY.

GROB, David, US, physician; b. NYC, Feb 23, 1919; s. Hyman and Fannie (Baumwall); BS, CCNY; MD, Johns Hopkins U, 1942; m. Elizabeth Nussbaum; c: Charles, Emily, Susan, Philip. Dir: med services, educ research, Maimonides Hosp; prof med, SUNY, since 1958. Capt, US Army MC, 1943-45. Chmn, med adv bd, Myasthenia Gravis Found, 1961; treas, Bklyn Soc Internal Med, 1962; cons to: Natl Cancer Inst, 1951-54; US Army Chem Corps, 1959; Bur of Med, FDA, 1967; surg-gen, US Army; f, Amer Coll Phys; mem: AMA; Baltimore City Med Soc; Amer Soc Clinical Inves; Amer Fed Clinical Research; Amer Phys Soc; Amer Soc Pharm. Home: 20 Fern Dr, Roslyn, NY. Office: 4802 Tenth Ave, Brooklyn, NY.

GRODSKY, Michael Edward, US, attorney; b. Wash, DC, July 8, 1941; s. Ben and Sally (Cooper); BA, UCLA, 1963; JD, Hastings Coll of Law, SF, 1967; m. Marcia Gilner, Sep 8, 1963. Pvt practice since 1968. Regional dir, Young Dem Clubs of Amer; fmr: vice-pres, Cal Fed of Young Dems; chmn, Gtr SF Dem Forum; mem: LA Co Bar Assn; Natl Lawyers Guild, LA chap. Spec interest: aviation. Home: 1443 S Reeves St, Los Angeles, Cal. Office: 6600 Sunset Blvd, Los Angeles, Cal.

GROLLMAN, Arthur, US, physician, educator, author; b. Baltimore, Md, Oct 20, 1901; s. Simon and Bessie (Karu); AB, Johns Hopkins U, 1920, PhD, 1923, MD, 1930. Prof, experimental med, Southwestern Med Coll, U of Tex, since 1946, prof, med, 1944-50, prof, pharm, chmn, dept phys, pharm, 1946-50; att phys: Parkland Hosp, since 1944; St Paul's Hosp, since 1959; Gaston Hosp, since 1957, all Dallas, Tex; cons: internal med, Baylor Hosp, Dallas, since 1950; Shannon W Tex Hosp, San Angelo, since 1956; VA Hosp, since 1946; USPHS Hosp, 1958; natl civilian to Surg Gen, USAF, since 1958; Lackland Hosps, since 1957; instr: chem, Johns Hopkins U, 1923-24, phys, 1924-26, asso in phys, 1926-30, asso prof, pharm and therapeutics, 1932-41; Guggenheim f, U of Berlin, London, Heidelberg, 1930-31; prof, med, research, Bowman Gray Sch of Med, Winston-Salem, NC, 1941-44; hon prof, U of Guadalajara, Mexico, 1948; lectr: U of Ala, 1944; U of Okla, 1952; U of Minn, 1953; Soc of USAF Internists, 1947; inves, Off of Sci Research and Devl, 1942-44; surg, USPHS, 1944-49; f, Amer Coll Phys; dipl, Amer Bd Internal Med; mem: study sect, endocrinology and metabolism, NIH, 1946-51; corresp, Port Endocrinological Soc, 1950; rev comm, US Pharmacopoeia, 1965, ed bd, Clinical Pharm and Therapeutics; council for study of high blood pressure, AHA; Phi Beta Kappa; Sigma Xi; Alpha Pi Alpha; Alpha Omega Alpha. Author: The Cardiac Output of Man in Health and Disease, 1932, 1933; The Adrenals, 1936, 1937; Essentials of Endocrinology, 1941, 1947, Span, 1951; Pharmacology and Therapeutics, 1950, 1953, 1957, 1960, 1962, 1964, Span, 1954; Acute Renal Failure: Pathogenesis and Treatment, 1953; Clinical Endocrinology and its Physiologic Basis, 1965; co-author: Zeitvolumen der Gesunden und Kranken Menschen, 1934; Cushny's Pharmacology and Therapeutics, 13 ed, 1947. Recipient: George Peabody prize, Baltimore City Coll, 1918; Marchman award, Dallas S Clinical Soc, 1948. Home: 3501 Princeton, Dallas, Tex. Office: 5323 Harry Hines St, Dallas, Tex.

GROLLMAN, Jerome Winston, US, rabbi; b. Baltimore, Md, Mar 25, 1922; s. Gerson and Dorah (Steinbach); BA, U of Md, 1942; MHL, ordained rabbi, HUC, 1948; m. Elaine Braff, Dec 27, 1953; c: Sara, Alan, Lisa. Rabbi, United Heb Temple, since 1958; asst prof, U of Mo, since 1966. Chmn:

St Louis Reform Rabbis; Subvention Comm, CCAR; J Comty Cens Assn Lib Forum; adv comm, ADL; bd overseers, HUC-JIR; bd dirs: Urban League; J Comty Cens Assn, St Louis; J Family and Children's Service; J Fed Students; CCAR Church-State Exec Comm; NH Comm Relations Adv Comm; mem: Phi Eta Sigma; Phi Kappa Phi. Home: 9841 Countryshire Pl, Creve, Mo. Study: 225 S Skinker, St Louis, Mo.

GROLLMAN, Sigmund S, US, psychologist, educator; b. Stevensville, Md, Feb 12, 1923; s. Ellis and Ray (Kristal); MS, U of Md, 1949, PhD, 1952. Prof, zool, U of Md, since 1966, fac mem since 1952; lectr, Montgomery Jr Coll, 1951-55. US Army, 1943-46. F: Amer Coll Sports Med; mem: AAAS; Soc Experimental Biol and Med; NY Acad Sci; AAUP; AJCong; Hillel Found; Cross of Lorraine Soc; Sigma Xi; clubs: Scuderia X Sports Car; British Racing; Meadowridge Saddle; Judo-Jiujitsu Inst of Md. Contbr to profsl jours. Recipient: Diamond award, outstanding prof of year, 1959. Home: 4203 N Charles St, Baltimore, Md. Office: U of Md, College Park, Md.

GROLNICK, Max, US, allergist, educator; b. Bklyn, NY, May 17, 1903; s. Samuel and Dora (Hefter); att Columbia U, 1920-22; MD, LI Coll of Med, 1926; m. Ruth Egert, June 10, 1928; c: Simon, Lawrence. Cons allergist: SUNY Coll of Med, since 1957; Huntington Hosp, since 1949; Deepdale Gen Hosp, since 1962; Caledonian Hosp, Bklyn, since 1968; fmr, att phys, SUNY; att phys i/c allergy div and lab, Bklyn J Hosp, since 1955, past instr, allergy, Sch of Nursing. F: Amer Acad Allergy, past vice-pres, mem exec comm; Amer Acad Compensation Med; Amer Coll Allergists, past postgrad instr; asso trustee, E Midwood J Cen, since 1940; mem: NY Allergy Soc, past pres; Soc Inves Dermat; NY Acad Sci; AMA; NY State Med Soc; Kings Co Med Soc; Ocean Med Soc; JTSA; ZOA; Heb Educ Soc; club, Phi Delta Epsilon, Bklyn. Adv ed, Allergy Abstracts, Amer Acad Allergy, since 1955; contbr to med jours. Recipient: research prize in allergy, Bklyn J Hosp, 1938. Hobbies: gardening, painting, photography. Home: 1096 E 29 St, Brooklyn, NY. Office: 555 Ocean Ave, Brooklyn, NY.

GRONER, Oscar, US, rabbi, organization exec; b. Chgo, Ill, Sep 30, 1922; s. Max and Beatrice (Lehrfeld); BA, U Chgo; MA, Northwestern U; ordained rabbi, Heb Theol Coll, Ill; m. Mildred Shapiro, Dec 30, 1945; c: Jonathan, Judith, Jeremey. Asst natl dir, B'nai B'rith Hillel Found, since 1960; fmr: dir, Hillel; lectr, Northwestern U; dir, ADL, NJ off. Mem: B'nai B'rith; Wash Bd Rabbis; past secy, Natl Assn Hillel Dirs. Contbr to J publs. Home: 8701 Jones Mills Rd, Chevy Chase, Md. Office: 1640 Rhode Island Ave NW, Washington, DC.

GROPPER, William, US, artist; b. NYC, Dec 3, 1897; s. Harry and Jenny (Nidel); att Natl Acad of Design, 1914; NY Sch of Fine and Applied Arts, 1916-19; m. Sophie Frankle, 1925; c: Gene, Lena. One-man shows: NY; Detroit; Cold Spring Harbor; Miami Beach; LA Heritage Gal; SF; Coral Gables; Chgo; Mexico City; London; Coventry; Paris; Prague; Warsaw; Moscow; Sofia; Retrospective, U Miami; repr in mus collections: Metrop Mus, NYC; Modern Mus, NYC; Whitney Mus, NYC; Chgo Art Inst; Phillips Memorial Gal, Wash, DC; LA Co Mus; St Louis Mus; Newark Mus; Fogg Art Mus; Phila Mus of Art; Walker Art Cen; Libr of Cong; U Ariz; Wadsworth Mus; Buttler Inst Amer Art, Youngstown, O; Pa Acad Fine Art; Ency Britannica Collection; Abbott Art Collection; Paul Sachs Collection; Mus of W Art, Moscow; City Mus of Sofia; Natl Gal of Prague; Tel Aviv Mus, Isr; Kharkov Mus, Russ; Biro-Bidjan Mus; murals: New Interior Bldg, Wash, DC; PO Bldgs: Freeport, LI; Detroit, Mich; Schenley Corp Bldg, NY; stained-glass windows for W Suburban Temple, Har Zion, River Forest, Ill. Publs: The Golden Land, cartoons; Alay Oop, novel in drawings; Gropper, drawings; 56 drawings USSR; Amer Folklore Lithographs; Caprichios; The Little Tailor, Portfolio; Caucasian Studies, lithographs; William Gropper: Retrospective. Recipient: Guggenheim F; Young Isr Prize; Collier Prize; Wanamaker Prize; Carnegie Intl Award; 1st prize Lithography, Metrop Mus and John Herron Art Inst; LA Co Award; elected to Natl Inst of Arts and Letters, 1968. Fmr staff artist: NY Sunday Tribune; Sunday World; American; paints memorial to victims of Warsaw Ghetto annually. Home and studio: Mt Airy Rd, Croton-on-Hudson, NY.

GROSBERG, Percy, Eng, educator; b. Cape Town, S Afr, Apr 5, 1925; s. Gershon and Pearl (Gelbard); in Eng since 1955; BSc, MSc, PhD, Witwatersrand U, Johannesburg, 1943-50; postgrad dipl, textile ind, Leeds U, Eng, 1951; m. Queenie

Fisch, Sep 3, 1951; c: Alan, Gillian, David. Research prof, textile engr, Leeds U, since 1961; sr research off: S Afr Wool Research Inst, 1950-55; ICI; research f, Leeds U, 1955-56. Chmn, Leeds Friends of Bar-Ilan U; gov, Selig Brodetsky J Day Schs, Leeds; mem: AMI Mech E; FTI, Chem Eng. Author: An Introduction to Textile Mechanisms, 1968; contbr to sci and tech jours. Recipient: Warner Memorial Medal, The Textile Inst, 1968. Hobby: music. Home: 101 King Lane, Leeds, Yorks, Eng. Office: The University, Leeds, Yorks, Eng.

GROSMAN, Ladislav, Isr, author; b. Czech, Feb 4, 1921; s. Jakub and Ester (Sommer); in Isr since 1968; att Political and Social Sci U, Prague; PhD, fac psych, Charles U, Prague, 1958; m. Edita Friedman, Dec 3, 1949; c: Jiri. Research asso, Bar Ilan U, since 1969; fmr: ed, lit adv, State Publ House; chief ed, Magazin Učebni pmucky; scenarian, dramatist, Barrandov St Film Studio, Prague. Mil working service, Slovak State, 1941-43. Author: The Shop on Main Street, 1965; The Bride, 1969; numerous short stories. Recipient: Hollywood Academy Award, for The Shop on Main Street, screenplay; Blue Ribbon Award, both 1966; Musa Melphoeme lit award; award of film critics, both Prague, 1967. Home: 13 Hameginim St, Haifa, Isr. Office: Bar Ilan U, Ramat Gan, Isr.

GROSS, Abraham, US, rabbi; b. Bklyn, NY, June 29, 1928; s. Joseph and Tillie (Lauer); desc of Ari Hakadosh; BA, CUNY, 1951; ordained rabbi, Chsan Sofer Rabb Sem, 1952; MA, Yeshiva U, NY, 1958; profsl cert, Hunter Coll, NY, 1965; m. Hannah Stern, Dec 18, 1952; c: Israel, Eliyahu, Vitel, Adel, Hinda, Shlomo. Rabbi since 1954; asst prin, NYC Bd Educ, since 1966; exec dir, Beth Jacob schs, 1952-54. Pres, Rabb Alliance of Amer. Home: 2720 Ave J, Brooklyn, NY. Office: 2815 Farragut Rd, Brooklyn, NY.

GROSS, Ben S, US, journalist, critic; b. Birmingham, Ala, Nov 24, 1891; s. Adolph and Sarah (Kaufman); att Tulane U, 1911-12; LLB, U of Ala, 1914; admitted to Ala bar, 1915; m. Kathleen Cotter, Dec 31, 1921. TV-radio ed and critic, NY Daily News; free-lance writer, lectr, news commentator; ed, World Traveler Mag, 1919-21; feature writer: NY Morning Telegraph, 1921-22; NY Amer, 1922-23. US Army, WWI. Mem: Overseas Press Club of Amer; Natl Press Club, Wash. Author: I Looked and I Listened, 1956. Hobbies: drama, music. Home: 360 E 55 St, New York, NY. Office: 220 E 42 St, New York, NY.

GROSS, Chaim, US, sculptor, painter, teacher; b. Kolomea, Aus, Mar 17, 1904; s. Moses and Leah (Sperber); in US since 1921; att Beaux Arts Inst; Educ Alliance Art Sch; Art Students League, all NYC; hon DFA, Franklin & Marshall Coll, Pa; m. Rene Nechin, Dec 13, 1932; c: Yehudah, Mimi. Instr: Educ Alliance Art Sch; New Sch of Social Research; fmr tchr, sculpture: Bklyn Mus Art; Mus Modern Art; Amer Sch Art; Five Towns Music and Art Found. Numerous one-man and group shows throughout US and in Moscow, 1959; in perm collections throughout US and in Isr; individual works: portfolio, lithographs in color, of major J holidays, 1969. Mem: Natl Inst Arts and Letters; pres, Sculptors Guild; bd, Artists Equity Assn; Architectural League, NY; Provincetown Art Assn; Profs Assn; Alumni Assn, Hall of Fame, Educ Alliance; Fed Modern Painters & Sculptors; Audubon Artists; AJCong. Author: A Sculptor's Progress, Autobiography, 1938; Fantasy Drawings, 1956; Technique of Wood Carving, 1957; illus c's books; contbr to Mag of Art. Recipient: natl competition prize, Sect of Fine Arts, Wash, DC, 1936; silver medal, Paris Intl Exposition, 1937; 2nd prize, Metrop Mus of Art, 1942; first prize, Cape Cod Art Assn, 1951; first mention, Natl Acad, Phila, 1954; anonymous prize, Audubon Soc, 1955; grant, Natl Acad of Arts and Letters, 1956; hon mention, Audubon Soc, 1957; award of merit, Amer Acad Arts and Letters, 1963; first prize, sculptor, Boston Arts Festival, 1963; Isr Freedom Award, 1965; citations: Cong Adath Jeshurun, 1966; Heb Tchrs Coll, Brookline, Mass, 1967; Brandeis U, 1968; Pres' Award, Audubon Artists, NYC, 1970; Marion Award, visual arts, J Tchrs Assn, Bd Educ, NYC, 1970. Home and studio: 526 LaGuardia Pl, New York, NY.

GROSS, Charles H, US, business exec; b. Mar 5, 1922; s. Louis and Rose (Mendel); BA, NYU, 1942; m. Norma Sherry, 1945; c: Laurie, Deborah, Amy. Mgn partner, Inves Banking Firm, since 1969; mgn partner, Gross & Co, 1949-68. Lt, USAAC, 1942-45. Pres, J Inst Geriatric Care; fmr: vice-pres, N Shore Comty Art Cen; numerous sch dist comms. Hobbies: tennis, politics, theatre. Home: 32 The Intervale, Roslyn Estate, NY. Office: 5 Hanover Square, New York, NY.

GROSS, David Arie, Venezuela, educator; b. Oleszyce, Lvov, Pol, Apr 6, 1912; s. Chaim and Golda (Zwiebel); in Venezuela since 1946; MA, U Rome, It, 1938; PhD, Dropsie Coll, Phila, Pa, 1943; m. Josephine Sungolowsky; c: Claudine, Goldye, Elana. Prin, Herzl-Bialik Sch, Caracas, since 1946, found largest J sch in S Amer; prof, U Caracas; asso prof, UCLA; asst prof, U of Judaism, LA, Calif; taught at Herzliah Tchrs Sem, NYC. Pres: Jordania, Phila, Pa; Brit Ivrit Olamit, Caracas; mem: AAUP; J Hist Soc. Contbr to educ jours. Recipient: award for merit in educ, Venezuelan Min of Educ, Caracas. Hobbies: writing, lecturing on mysticism, chess. Office: Apartado 3030, Caracas, Venezuela.

GROSS, Earl Herbert, US, oral surg; b. Phila, Pa, Nov 15, 1931; s. Philip and Esther (Rosenthal); att U of Pa, Phila, 1949-51; DDS, U of Pa Sch of Dent, 1955, study of oral surg, Grad Sch of Med, 1957-58; m. Ina Canady, Apr 3, 1955; c: Teri, Andrew. Pvt practice, oral surg, since 1958. Lt, USNR, 1955-57. Vice-pres, Oxford Hosp bd dirs, fmr secy; chmn: Disaster Med, Oxford Hosp; Motion Picture Comm, Phila Co Dent Assn; mem: Amer Dent Assn; E Dent Assn; Phila Co Dent Assn; Masons, Lodge Rising Star 126; Consistory, New Bern, NC; Shriner, Crescent Temple; clubs: Lions; Radnor Valley Country. Recipient: Matthew Cryer Hon Soc, 1954; Omicron Kappa Upsilon, 1955. Home: 365 Sprague Rd, Narberth, Pa. Office: 6740 Torresdale Ave, Philadelphia, Pa.

GROSS, Feliks, US, sociologist, educator; b. Krakow, Pol, June 17, 1906; s. Adolf and Augusta (Alexander-Silbiger); in US since 1941; MJ, U of Krakow, 1929; DJur, 1930; m. Priva Baidaff, 1937; c: Eva. Prof, sociol, Bklyn Coll and Grad Cen, CUNY, since 1947. Fmr: secy gen, Cen and E Eur Planning Bd, 1941-45; ed, New Eur, 1945-52; visiting prof, dir Inst of Intl Relations, U of Wyo, 1945-52; adj prof, dept of govt, NYU Grad Sch, 1945-68; visiting prof, U of Va, 1950-56; prof, fgn policy, U of Vt, 1957; Fulbright prof, U of Rome, 1957-58, 1964-65; cons, Natl Comm on Causes of Violence, 1968; asso, fgn policy, Research Inst, U of Pa, since 1968. Mem: Amer Sociol Soc; Amer Acad of Political Sci; Intl Acad of Political Sci; E Sociol Soc; Pol Inst of Arts and Sci; NY Acad of Sci; Institut Intl de Sociol, Rome; Authors League; Alpha Kappa Delta; Sigma Xi. Author: Nomadism, 1937; Proletariat and Culture, 1938; The Polish Worker, 1945; Crossroads of Two Continents, 1945; ed and author, European Ideologies, 1948; Foreign Policy Analysis, 1954; Seizure of Political Power, 1958; On Social Values, in Pol, 1961; World Politics of Tension Areas, 1967; Saggi Su Valori Sociali E Stouttura. 1967; ed: Struggle for Tomorrow, 1953; contbr to profsl jours. Home: 310 W 85 St, New York, NY. Office: Bklyn Coll, CUNY, Brooklyn, NY.

GROSS, Irma H, US, educator; b. Omaha, Neb, July 21, 1892; d. David and Addie (Gladstone); BS, U of Chgo, 1915, MA, 1924, PhD, 1931. Prof em, home mgmt, Mich State U, since 1959, mem fac, head, dept home mgmt and child devl, 1934-59; tchr, Cen HS, Omaha, Neb, 1915-21; field sup, US Bur Hum Nutrition and Home Econ, 1936, regional sup, 1942; cons, home mgmt: U of the Ryukyus, Okinawa, 1959; Provincial U of Taiwan, Taipei, 1959; U of India, 1959; visiting dist prof, Penn State U, 1964; visiting lectr: NY State Coll Home Econ, Cornell U, 1964; San Diego State Coll, 1966; U of Wis, 1969. Mem: Amer Home Econ Assn; Natl Council on Family Relations; AAUP; League of Women Voters; Hadassah; Phi Beta Kappa; Phi Kappa Phi; Omicron Nu, past natl pres; fmr: pres: Mich Home Econ Assn; Lansing br, Amer Assn U Women. Co-author: Home Management with Special Reference to the College Home Management House, 1938; Home Management in Theory and Practice, 1947; Management for Modern Families, 1954, rev, 1963; author of tech bulls; contbr to profsl jours. Spec interest: travel. Home: 8522 Lemon Ave, La Mesa, Cal.

GROSS, Isidor Marc, US, business exec; b. Rum, May 31, 1903; s. Marcu and Florette (Blanc); m. Daisy Eskowitz, Jan 4, 1928; c: Nancy. Pres, chmn, Multi-Amp Corp, Cranford, NJ since 1951. US Army, 1942-43. Vice-pres, Temple Sinai, Summit, NJ; fmr: pres: C of C, Cranford; Suburban Sym Soc of NJ; mem: Rotary Intl, Cranford. Home: 175 Prospect, E Orange, NJ. Office: 61 Myrtle, Cranford, NJ.

GROSS, Jack, Isr, physician, educator; b. Montreal, Can, Mar 29, 1921; s. Maurice and Pauline (Lefson); in Isr since 1951; BSc, MD, CM, PhD, magma cum laude, McGill U, Montreal, 1941-49; m. Helga Kahane, Aug 1, 1944; c: Vicki, David, Daniel. WHO visiting prof of experimental med and cancer research, head dept, Heb U Hadassah Med Sch, Jerusalem since 1957; sci adv to Min of Commere and Industry; fmr: teaching f, McGill U; lectr, asst prof, asso prof, dept of anat, all SUNY. Royal Can Army MC. Prin contrib, discovery of triiodothyronine. F, NY Acad of Sci; mem: med comm, Natl Council for Research and Devl since 1960; profsl comm, bd dirs, Isr Cancer Assn since 1960; Amer Assn of Anats; Amer Assn for Cancer Research; Amer Chem Soc; Amer Phys Soc; Histochem Soc; Biochem Soc; Soc for Endocrinology, both Gt Brit; Endocrine Soc; Sigma Xi; Soc for Experimental Biol and Med. Contbr to sci jours. Recipient: first honorable mention, Van Meter Prize, 1948; Merck post doctoral fellowship, 1950-52, for study at Natl Inst for Med Research, London; Chilean Iodine Educ Bur Award, Amer Pharm Assn, 1954; CIBA Award of Endocrine Soc, 1955; Zondeck Prize in Endocrinology, 1968. Special interest, archaeol. Home: 24 Ahad Ha'am St, Jerusalem, Isr. Office: POB 1172, Jerusalem, Isr.

GROSS, Joseph H, Isr, attorney; b. Tel Aviv, Isr, Feb 28, 1934; s. Wolff and Mali (Timberg); LLB, Tel Aviv U, 1955; LLM, 1958; PhD, London U, 1962; m. Zvia Armon, July 21, 1959; c: Raz, Eyal. Legal adv, secy, Discount Bank Investment Corp, since 1963; sr lectr: Tel Aviv U, since 1964; Bar Ilan U, since 1963; fmr: lectr, Heb U. Capt, gen atty of Army, IDF, 1954-57. Mem comm, Isr Bar. Author: Forms and Precedents, 1960; Company Law, lectures, 1966; Privileged Holding Companies, 1968; The Israel Mercantile Law; ed, various legal publs; co-ed Hapraklit, Isr Bar Assn Jour; contbr articles on legal, econ topics. Recipient: Mif'al Hapais Prize, Tel Aviv U, 1968; Rotary Prize, Tel Aviv U, 1955. Home: 2 Hevra Hadasha St, Tel Aviv, Isr. Office: 16 Beth ha'Sheva Lane, Tel Aviv, Isr.

GROSS, Leon, Isr, educator; b. Lvov, Pol, Apr 1, 1911; s. Samuel and Adela (Rosenes); in Isr since 1957; dipl ing, Tech U of Lvov, 1941; MSc, Tech U of Silesia, 1950; DSc, Tech Bauman U, Moscow, 1954; m. Taisa Guigin, Oct 31, 1944; c: Jair, Zvi. Prof, mech engr, Technion, Haifa, since 1968, head, combustion engr lab, since 1966; fmr: sr tech, Automotive Factory of Tiflis, Russ; tech mgr, State Road Transp, Pol; research f, Bauman Tech U, Moscow; sr lectr: Tech U of Warsaw; Tech Mil Acad, Warsaw; research asso: Tech U of Delft, Netherlands; Queen Mary Coll, U of London. Off, Pol Mil Forces, 1943-45. Mem: bd, Assn for Parents of Road Accident Victims; comm for tech educ, Isr; Patent Comm, Isr; Amer Soc Mech Engrs; Combustion Inst, US; Combustion Engine Soc, Automobile Club; Union of WW II Vets. Contbr to local and fgn profsl jours. Hobby: photography. Home: 62 Haviva St, Ramoth Remez, Haifa, Isr. Office: Technion, Haifa, Isr.

GROSS, Ludwik, US, physician; b. Crakow, Pol, Sep 11, 1904; s. Adolf and Augusta (Alexander); in US since 1940; MD, Iagellon U, Crakow, 1929; m. Dorothy Nelson, 1943; c: Augusta. Chief, cancer research unit, VA Hosp, Bx, NY, since 1946; fmr: cancer research: Pasteur Inst, Paris, Fr; Christ Hosp, Cincinnati, O. Maj, US Army MC, 1943-46. Prin contribs: transmission of mouse leukemia by filtrates, 1951; isolation from leukemic mouse tissues of an oncogenic virus causing parotid gland tumors, 1953; isolation of a transmissible leukemia virus from radiation-induced leukemia in mice, 1958. FACP; f: NY Acad of Sci; AAAS; Intl Soc Hematology; dipl, Amer Bd Internal Med; mem: AMA; Bx Co, NY State Med Socs; Soc Experimental Biol and Med; Amer Assn Cancer Research; Amer Soc Hematology; Assn Mil Surgs of US. Author: Oncogenic Viruses; contbr to med jours. Recipient: Prix Chevillon, Acad of Med, Paris, 1937; R R de Villiers Found Award for leukemia research, 1953; Walker Prize, RCS, Eng, 1961; Lucy Wortham James Award, James Ewing Soc, 1962; Pasteur Silver Medal, Pasteur Inst, 1962; WHO UN Prize for virus research in cancer, 1962; Albert Einstein Med Cen Centennial Medal, 1965; Bertner Found Award, U Tex, 1963. Hobby: music. Office: VA Hosp, Bronx, NY.

GROSS, Meyer Alvin, US, attorney; b. Liberty, NY, May 21, 1936; s. Emanuel and Grace (Appel); BME, Coll of Engr, Cornell U, NY, 1959; JD, Sch of Law, Columbia U, 1961; m. Karen Charal, Aug 16, 1964; c: Dana, Jennifer, Pamela. Pvt practice, patents and trademarks, since 1963; asso: J B Felshin, 1961-67; Blum, Moscovitz, Friedman, Blum & Kaplan, 1962-63. Secy, treas, Cornell Council for the Performing Arts; treas, 83 St Block Assn; fmr: mem: bd dirs: Howard City Bank, Mich; Indit Corp; exec comm, Eastside Dem Club; mem: AJCong; NY State Bar Assn; NY Patent

Law Assn; NY Co Lawyers Assn; club, Yorkville Dem. Contbr to legal jours. Home: 500 E 83 St, New York, NY.

GROSS, Reuben E, Isr, business exec, attorney, communal leader, author; b. NYC, Aug 6, 1914; s. Samuel and Regina (Herskovitz); in Isr since 1968; BA, CCNY, 1935; DJur, Harvard U, 1938; MA, Wagner Coll, 1954; m. Blanche Fisher, Sep 12, 1951; nine c. Atty since 1938; banking and finance exec since 1961. US Army, 1944-45; IAF, 1948-49. Fmr: natl chmn, Amer Vets of Isr; natl secy, Union Orthodox Cong; pres, found, Natl J Comm on Law and Public Affairs. Contbr to J Life; J Observer. Hobbies: amateur radio, chess. Home: 21 Shachal St, Jerusalem, Isr. Office: 280 Broadway, Staten Island, NY.

GROSS, Sarah Gluzman, Isr, author; b. Russ; d. Ben-Zion and Chajka-Klara (Weinrub) Gluzman; in Isr since 1915; att Tchrs Sem, Tel Aviv; m. Ben-Zion Gross, Dec 22, 1943; c: Ephraim, Ret; fmr: with Dept of Educ and Culture; secy: Off of Sch Inspecs, Va'ad Leumi; Dept of Educ and Culture. Author: Al Saf ha'Mavet, 1936; El Ha'Gvul, 1938; Homot ha'Barzel, 1940; Gad ve'Dag ha'Zahav, 1943; Pa' amonim, 1951; Parpar ha'Zahav, El ha'Bait ha'Rahok, 1960; Mistarei ha'Goral, 3 vols, 1966. Mem: Heb Writers Assn, Isr. Home: 196 Arlosoroff St, Tel Aviv, Isr.

GROSS, Sidney, US, artist, teacher; b. NYC, 1921; s. Morris and Esther; att Art Students League, NY, 1939-42; m. Kay Kranther, 1944; m. 2nd, Elaine, August, 1969. Art tchr: Art Students League since 1958; Columbia U since 1961; asso prof, art, U of Md, since 1967; one-man shows: 14 at Rehn Gal, NYC; Contemporary Arts Gal, NYC; Tirca Karlis Gal, Provincetown, Mass; repr in perm collections: Whitney Mus Amer Art; Butler Art Inst; Cornell U; U of Ga; Brandeis U; Riverside Mus; Chrysler Mus; U of Omaha; Mt Holyoke Coll; Baltimore Mus of Art; Columbia U; Corcoran Gal of Art; Krannert Mus; U of Ill; Morgan State Coll; Wash Gal of Modern Art; Standard Financial Corp; Lempert Found; Childe Hassam Found; U of Tex; Colby Coll; Allentown Mus; U of Rochester; Oklahoma Art Cen. Recipient: Louis Comfort Tiffany f, 1949; Hallmark Art Award, 1949; grand prize, Art USA Exhb, 1958. Home: 255 W 23 St, New York, NY. Studio: 5 W 21 St, New York, NY.

GROSS, Sidney W, US, neuro-surgeon, educator; b. Cleveland, O, Aug 28, 1904; s. Joseph and Frieda (Weiss); BA, W Reserve U, 1925, MD, 1928; m. Molly Harr; c: Samuel. Chmn, prof neurosurg, Mt Sinai Sch of Med; sr cons, Bx VA Hosp; dir: neurosurg, Mt Sinai Hosp, NYC since 1937; City Hosp, Elmhurst since 1936; attending neurosurg, Manhattan State Hosp. US Army, 1942-46; chief neurosurg sect, Halloran Gen Hosp; maj, US Army MC, overseas. Pres, NY Neurosurg Soc; f, Amer Coll Surgs; dipl, Amer Bd Neur Surg; corresp mem, NE Soc Neurosurg; mem: Amer Neur Soc; NY Acad Med; NY Neur Soc; Harvey Cushing Soc; NY Co Med Soc; Phi Beta Kappa; Alpha Omega Alpha. Co-author, Diagnosis and Treatment of Head Injuries, 1940; contbr numerous papers to med jours. Home and office: 44 E 81 St, New York, NY.

GROSS, Walter S, US, dentist; b. NYC, Feb 22, 1900; s. Joseph and Isabel (Grusser); DDS, Columbia U, 1922; m. Nadine Musler, 1926; c: Hyath, Walter. City dent, Schenectady, NY Dept of Health; mem, dent staff, Ellis Hosp. Trustee: B'nai B'rith; J Comty Cen; Health Comm; C of C; all Schenectady, NY; mem: pres' council, Brandeis U; bd dirs: United Fund Amer Assn Homes for Aging; Schenectady Comty Wfr Council; fmr: pres: NY State sect, JWB; J Comty Cen; JCC; Dent Soc; B'nai B'rith; Daughters of Sarah J Home for Aged; chmn: NY State White House Conf on Aging; USO; treas, mem exec comm, Council Social Agcy; mem: natl comm on aging CJFWF, also mem, exec comm, bd dirs; exec comm: Brandeis U Assn; State of Isr Bonds; club: Torch. Recipient: Man of the Year Dist Service Award, B'nai B'rith, 1955; Schenectady Patron, 1965. Hobbies: painting, fishing, gardening. Home: 939 Vrooman Ave, Schenectady, NY. Office: 613 State St, Schenectady, NY.

GROSSBERG, David, US, attorney; b. Bklyn, NY, Sep 14, 1925; s. Meyer and Ethel (Isaacson); BSS, CUNY, 1947; LLB, Harvard Law Sch, 1950; m. Miriam Weissner, Mar 22, 1959; c: Amy. Partner, Cotten, Grossberg. Staff sgt, US Army, 1944-47. Mem: AJComm; Court Lawyers Assn. Home: 501 E 87 St, New York, NY. Office: 505 Park Ave, New York, NY.

GROSSMAN, Allan, Can, public official, insurance underwriter; b. Toronto, Dec 25, 1910; s. Morris and Sarah (Pilsmaker); deg, Chartered Life Underwriter, Harbord and Jarvis Collegiates; m. Ethel Starkman, Jan 12, 1936; c: Susan, Larry, Denise Davis. Mem, Ont Leg, since 1955; Min of Correctional Services, Ont Provincial Govt, since 1963; fmr: Min Without Portfolio, Govt of Ont, 1960-63; chief commn, Liquor Control Bd of Ont, 1961-63; one of original mems of Metrop Council; alderman, City of Toronto. Mem: Can CCJ; exec, Can J Cong; United JWF; J Home for Aged, New Mt Sinai Hosp; U Settlement; St Alban's Boys Clubs; Conservative Bus Men's; Canadian; Primrose; Variety; fmr: pres, B'nai B'rith, Toronto Lodge; natl pres, J Immigrant Aid Services of Can. Hobbies: philately, numismatics. Home: 325 Rosemary Rd, Toronto, Can. Office: Parliament Bldgs, Toronto, Can.

GROSSMAN, Bernard David, US, business exec; b. Boston, Mass, Oct 18, 1917; s. Joseph and Esther (Loitman); AB, Harvard Coll, 1939; MBA, Harvard Grad Sch, 1941; m. Grace Swig, Feb 21, 1943; c: Richard, Betsy. Dir: Norfolk Co Trust Co; Home Owners Fed Savings & Loan Assn; Cramer Electronics Inc; treas, L Grossman Sons. Capt, US Army, 1942-45. Pres, Combined J Philanthropies of Gtr Boston; past: Temple Shalom; B'nai B'rith; dir: United Fund; Nantucket Theatre Workshop; bd govs, Harvard Bus Sch Assn; trustee: J Memorial Hosp; Temple Isr; Nantucket Cottage Hosp; Beth Isr Hosp; mem, Harvard Club. Home: Polpis Rd, Nantucket, Mass. Office: 200 Union, Braintree, Mass.

GROSSMAN, Edward B, US, physician; b. NYC, Apr 3, 1911; s. William and Frances (Schonfeld); BA, summa cum laude, Harvard U, 1931; MD, Johns Hopkins U, 1935; div; c: Ann; m. 2nd, Helen Thumm, July 8, 1962. Ret; fmr: asst chief, med service, VA Hosp, Bx, NY, 1954-66, with hosp since 1948; resident phys, Vanderbilt U Hosp, 1937-38; research asst chem, sr clinical asst phys, Mt Sinai Hosp, NYC, 1938-47. Lt-col, US Army MC, 1942-46. F: Amer Coll Phys; NY Acad Med; AAAS; dipl, Amer Bd Internal Med; mem: NY Acad Scis; Amer Fed Clinical Research; Phi Beta Kappa; Sigma Xi. Contbr to med jours. Home: 145 E 16 St, New York, NY.

GROSSMAN, Harry, US, attorney; b. NYC, Oct 30, 1911; s. Isaac and Anna (Hoffman); BS, NYU, 1933; LLB, Columbia Law Sch, 1936; m. Anne Rafsky, Aug 6, 1950; c: Patricia, Sandra, Ilene. Partner, Grossman & Grossman, 1950-63; Grossman, Grossman & Feigen, since 1964; admitted to practice, US Supr Court, 1944; instr: Columbia U, 1938-41; Practising Law Inst, 1940-42; Delehanty Inst, 1940-52; Collegiate Inst, 1946-47; cong candidate, NY Dem and Lib parties, 1952. Maj, US Army, 1942-46; lt col, Adjutant Gen's Corps Res. Pres: B'nai B'rith Cardozo Lodge, 1958-59; Atlantic Beach Property Owners Assn, 1956-58; dir, Harry and Jane Fischel Found for J Talmudic Studies; NY Co commn, JWV, 1948-49, repr to Natl Comty Relations Adv Council, 1949-50; mem: Natl Panel Arbitrators, Amer Arbitration Assn; Amer Bar Assn, taxation and admn law sect; NY State Bar Assn; Assn of Bar, NYC; NY Co Lawyers Assn; Fed Bar Assn, NY, NJ, Conn; Amer Judicature Soc; Amer Acad Political and Social Scis; Trade Assn Execs in NYC; Res Off Assn; Zeta Beta Tau; Natl Dem Club; George W Thompson Dem Assn, Inc; Affiliated Young Dems, Inc; Soc of Tammany; Amer Legion; Mil Order of WWs; Elks; delg, First Judicial Conv, Dem Party, 1950-58; spec referee, NY Cen Railroad Litigation, appd by NY State Supr Court, 1954. Contbr to legal jours. Recipient: Army Commendation Medal, 1946; NY State Conspicuous Service Award. Home: 25 Sutton Place S, New York, NY. Office: 551 Fifth Ave, New York, NY.

GROSSMAN, Isidore, US, manufacturer; b. Lasztoez, Hung, Sep 24, 1887; s. Leopold and Hana (Greenstein); in US since 1903; att CUNY; Columbia U, both 1908-14; Cooper Union, 1908-12; m. 2nd, Theresa, Apr 8, 1945; c: Irwin, William. Sr mem, Grossman Clothing Co, NYC; trustee, Amalgamated Life Ins. Cons to Quartermaster Gen, US Army, 1944-48. Pres: NY Clothing Mfrs Exch; Peoples Hosp, Research Found, 1937; Tomche Torah Soc, 1934; mem: men's and boy's clothing ind adv comm, War Produc Bd, 1942-46; Amer Arbitration Panel; bd of trustees, Cong Ohab Zedek, NYC; hon pres, Beth Hillel Inst; secy, org, Peoples Hosp, 1910-37; cofound, FJP, NY, 1925; mem, bd of trustees, Beth Isr Hosp, 1950; Sidney Hillman Health Cen, 1950; Sidney Hillman Found, Fashion Inst of Tech, 1952; mem, Kehillath Jeshurun Syn; club, Elmsford Co. Home: 1016 Fifth Ave, New York, NY. Office: 79 Fifth Ave, New York, NY.

GROSSMAN, James Heinz, US, business exec; b. Berlin, Ger, July 22, 1914; s. Heymann and Else (Bursch); in US since 1939; att U of Berlin, 1932-34; m. Esther Alexander, Oct 1, 1939; c: David, Edward. Pres, Jay-Gro Fabrics Inc, since 1939. Pres, United J Fund, Englewood; bd govs, Isr Bonds; natl adv bd, UJA; mem, NY Credit and Financial Mgmt Assn. Home: 269 Broad Ave, Englewood, NJ. Office: 76 Franklin St, New York, NY.

GROSSMAN, Joseph, US, physician, educator; b. Russ, May 15, 1910; s. Harry and Sophie (Nadell); in US since 1911; BA Temple U, 1931, MD, 1935; m. Claire Freedland, 1937, c: Robert, Karen. Chief and dir, ped services, St Joseph's Hosp, Phila, Pa since 1942; dep chmn, Dept of Ped, Albert Einstein Med Cen since 1959, att ped since 1955; att ped, St Christopher's Hosp for children since 1955, staff mem since 1937; asst prof, ped, Temple U since 1950; intern, Atlantic City Hosp, 1935-36; res phys, Roxborough Memorial Hosp, 1936-37. Found and chmn, Amer Med Cen; dir, Lea Assos (Med Market Research); dipl, Amer Bd of Ped; f, AMA. Mem: inves comm, Albert Einstein Med Cen; Phila Co Med Soc; Phila Ped Soc; Pa Med Soc; SE Pa Heart Soc; AAUP; AAAS; The U Mus; B'nai B'rith; Temple Judea; Phi Lambda Kappa; AJCong; F Commn; club, Med of Phila. Recipient: Leadership Award, Allied J Appeal, 1954, citation for meritorious service, 1957. Home and office: 5127 N Broad St, Philadelphia, Pa.

GROSSMAN, Joseph B, US, business exec; b. Quincy, Mass, July 15, 1892; s. Louis and Hia Pearl (Sherad); hon LLD, Nasson Coll, 1962; m. Esther Loitman, June 28, 1914 (decd); c: Bernard, Everett, Pearl Goldberg; m. 2nd, Esther Starr, Dec 22, 1963. Pres, Home Owners Fed Savings, Boston, Mass, since 1933; vice-pres, L Grossman Inds Properties Sons, Inc, since 1958; vice-pres: NE Sinai Hosp, since 1959; J Memorial Hosp, since 1956; Temple Beth El, Quincy, since 1959; dir, Quincy C of C, since 1947, pres, 1949; hon dir, Brandeis Assos, since 1960; mem: bd trustees; Combined J Philanthropies of Boston, since 1960; adv bd of Rehab, Commonwealth of Mass, 1962; Masons, B'nai B'rith. Home: 86 Monroe Rd, Quincy, Mass. Office: 130 Granite St, Quincy, Mass.

GROSSMAN, Kurt R, US, public official, author; b. Berlin, Ger, May 21, 1897; s. Hermann and Rachel (Freundlich); in US since 1939; m. Elsa Mekelburger, 1925; c: Walter. Cons, JA, 1952-66; secy-gen, Ger League for Hum Rights, 1926-33; dir, Dem Ref Relief Comm, 1933-39; exec asst, WJC, 1943-50. Author: The Jewish Refugee, 1944; Germany's Moral Debt, 1953; The Unsung Heroes, 1957; Ossietzky, A German Patriot, 1963; The Debt of Honor, Albert Schweitzer Book Award; Flight, History of Hitler Refugees, 1935-45, 1968; contbr numerous articles and essays to jours. Hobby: music. Home: 82-46 Lefferts Blvd, Kew Gardens, NY.

GROSSMAN, Louis I, US, dentist, educator; b. Russ, Dec 16, 1901; s. Harry and Rachel (Musicant); in US since 1905; DDS, U of Pa, 1923; DMD, U of Rostock, Ger, 1928; m. Emma MacIntyre, 1928; c: Clara, Richard. Prof, oral med, U of Pa, since 1954. Pres: Amer Assn Endodontists, 1949; Acad Stomatology, 1954; Dental Alumni Soc, 1954; f, AAAS: hon mem: Brazilian Dent Assn; Belgian Dent Assn; clubs: Montreal Endodontic Study: Vancouver Study. Author: Endodontic practice, 7th ed, 1970, trans into Span, Port, It, Ger; Dental Formulas, 1952; Handbook of Dental Practice, 3rd ed, 1958. Recipient: citation, Boston U, Grad Sch of Dent, 1959. Hobby: gardening. Home: 6822 Mower St, Philadelphia, Pa. Office: 2203 Med Tower Bldg, Philadelphia, Pa.

GROSSMAN, Marc J, US, attorney; b. Cleveland, O, Sep 1, 1892; s. Louis and Lillie (Meyers); BA, Harvard U, 1913; att Harvard Law Sch, 1914-15; m. Carolyn Kahn, 1916; c: Marcia Goodfried, Carole Honigsfeld. Partner, Grossman, Familo, Cavitch, Kempf and Durkin. Chmn: Jt Bar Comm on Law Enforcement; Cleveland Bar Assn Comm on Civil Rights under Law; f: Amer and O Bar Assns; mem: Amer Judicatur Soc; past pres, Cleveland Bar Assn, Council of Educ Alliance; J Family Service Assn; City Club of Cleveland; fmr mem: House of Delg, Amer Bar Assn; hon life mem, Asso Charities Cleveland; past dir, Amer Judicature Soc; trustee, Mt Sinai Hosp. Home: 16950 S Woodland Rd, Shaker Heights, O. Office: 1401 E Ohio Bldg, Cleveland, O.

GROSSMAN, Max R, US, government official; b. Odessa, Russ, Apr 21, 1904; s. Abraham and Celia (Tocman); in US since 1906; BBA, Boston U, 1926, Med, 1929, MBA, 1930; att Harvard U; m. Manya Kaufman, Mar 22, 1931; c: Lysbeth, Michael. Fgn affairs off, USA, since 1957; forum ed, VOA; fmr: reporter, Pawtucket Times, RI; feature writer, Boston Sunday Post; instr, Boston U, later prof, head, dept journalism; dean, sch journalism, Biarritz Amer U; ed, Biarritz Banner; mem, writers div, OWI; roving corresp, Stars and Stripes; provost, Brandeis U, Mass; public affairs off, Frankfurt, Ger; cultural affairs planning off, Wash; cultural affairs off: US Emb, Quito, Ecuador and London. Mem: AAUP; Amer Assn Tchrs of Journalism; Mass Press Assn; Temple Ohabei Shalom, Mass, until 1951; Masons, 32 deg; Beta Gamma Sigma, past pres, Alpha chap; clubs: Overseas Press; Natl Press; Saville, London; Eng-Speaking Union, Wash and London; past natl pres: Amer Assn of Sch and Depts of Journalism; Kappa Tau Alpha. Office: 1776 Pennsylvania Ave,NW, Washington, DC.

GROSSMAN, Morton I, US, physician, educator; b. Massillon, O, May, 4, 1919; s. David and Jeanette (Feingold); BA, O State U, 1939; MD, Northwestern U, 1944, PhD, 1944; m. Dorothy Armstrong, Nov 26, 1957. Sr med inves, VA Cen, LA since 1962; prof, med and phys; U of Cal, LA, since 1959; asso prof, phys: Northwestern U, 1945-46; Ill U, 1946-51; prof, clinical sci, U of Ill, 1951-53; head, phys div, US Army Med Nutrition Lab, 1951-55. Mem: Amer Soc for Clinical Inves; Amer Gastroenterological Assn; Soc for Experimental Biol and Med; Amer Phys Soc; AAAS; Cen and W Soc for Clinical Research. Co-author: Peptic Ulcer, 1950; ed, Gastroenterology Jours 1959-65; contbr to profsl jours. Home: 420 S Westgate, Los Angeles, Cal. Office: VA Cen, Los Angeles, Cal.

GROSSMAN, Ronald, US, attorney; b. Utica, NY, June 30, 1926; s. Edward and Gisella (Silverstein); att NYU, 1943; Union Coll, Schenectady, NY, 1944-45; Notre Dame U, Ind, 1945; JD, Albany Law Sch, NY, 1949; m. Doris Sherman, June 20, 1948; c: Gwen, Brad, Lynn, Fern. Partner, Blaugrund, Grossman & Polefsky, since 1949. Lt, US Army, 1943-46; 1952-54. Pres, Temple Beth El, Utica, NY; dir, Oneida Co Bar Assn; mem, NY State Bar Assn. Hobbies: skiing, golf, tropical fish. Home: 169 Proctor Blvd, Utica, NY. Office: 1215-21 First Natl Bldg, Utica, NY.

GROSSMAN, Samuel, US, business exec; b. Phila, Pa, Dec 6, 1897; s. Mayer and Goldie (Klempner); att Amer Bus Inst, 1914-15; CCNY, 1919-20; m. Doris Boxer, Aug 21, 1932; c: Judith Erber, Lucille Schwartz, Lawrence. Pres, Grossman Stamp Co, Inc, since 1929; pres, publisher, Longacre Publ, since 1956; acctnt, NY Times, 1915-18; pres, S Grossman, 1927-29. Pres, Amer Stamp Dealers Assn, 1966-67; mem, exec comm, co-chmn, stamp dealers div, UJA, since 1955; mem: Grand St Boys Assn; Assn Amer Stamp Exhbs; Amer Philatelic Soc; Amer Numismatic Assn; King Co Grand Jurors Assn. Author: Superior Stamp Album, 1950; Paramount Stamp Album, 1951; Monarch Stamp Album, 1952; Coronet De Luxe Stamp Album, 1954; Stamp Collector's Handbook, 1957; Gazetteer for Stamp Collectors, 1957; Regent Stamp Album, 1957; Aristocrat Stamp Album, 1957; Academy Stamp Album, 1958; Victory US Album, 1958; Capitol US Stamp Co, 1959; US Plate Block Album, 1961; Space Age World Stamp Album. Home: 10 W 16 St, New York, NY. Office: 895 Broadway, New York, NY.

GROSSMANN, Hans S, US, attorney; b. Berlin, Ger; s. Eugen and Gertrud (Dewitz); in US since 1946; DJ, Berlin U, 1923; LLB, Bklyn Law Sch, 1952; m. Erika Busse, Nov 22, 1947; c: Atina. Pvt practice, jurisprudence: in Ger since 1927; in NY since 1953; partner: Donig & Grossmann, 1927-30; Badrian & Grossman, 1930-37; sole owner, Exporter, Teheran, Iran, 1936-41. Prin contribs: first to trans the total Iranian law into Ger; helped J refugees to obtain financial restitution. Fmr dir, Israelitische Union, Berlin; mem: NY Co Lawyers Assn, NYC chap; Social Soc for Inter-Cultural Relations, NYC chap. Home: 215 W 78 St, New York, NY. Office: 225 Broadway, New York, NY.

GROSSMAN-ORKIN, Chayka, Isr, communal leader; b. Bialystok, Pol, Nov 20, 1919; d. Mordecai and Leah (Applebaum) Grossman; in Isr since 1948; att Vilna, 1941; Tel Aviv U, 1962; m. Meir Orkin, 1948; c: Yosefa, Leah. Gen secy, World Union of Mapam parties. since 1965; mem, exec: Hakibbutz Ha'artzi, Hashomer Hatzair; Mapam Party, both since 1949; Hashomer Hatzair, Hechalutz, Kovno, Lith and Pol, 1939-41; Org of ghetto fighters in Pol, 1941-44; partisan fighter against the Nazis, Cen J Comm, Pol, 1944-48. Mem: Kibbutz Evron since 1948. Author: Ansheh ha'Mahteret, 1949; Sefer ha'-Partisanim Hayehudim, 1958. Recipient: Grunwald Cross, Pol Govt, 1946. Home: Kibbutz Evron, Isr.

GROSSOWICZ, Nathan, Isr, bacteriologist, educator; b. Grodno, Pol, 1914; MSc, PhD, Heb U, Jerusalem, 1944. Prof, chmn, dept bact, Hadassah Med Sch, Jerusalem, on fac since 1944. Author: Fundamentals of Bacteriology and Immunity, vol. I, 1964; vol II, 1968; contbr to sci jours. Office: Hebrew University-Hadassah Medical School, Jerusalem, Isr.

GROSSWIRTH, Marvin, US, editor, author; b. Bklyn, NY, Aug 5, 1931; s. Isidore and Ida (Katsofi); BBA, CUNY; m. Marilyn Siegmann, Sep 7, 1969. Ed-in-chief, Pageant Press Intl Corp, since 1969. Sr ed: Amer-Isr Honorarium; Biographical Ency of US; Christmas: A Pictorial Pilgrimage; Easter: A Pictorial Pilgrimage; syndicated columnist, Courier-Life Publs. Mem, bd and fac, Workshop in Bus Opportunities; NY chmn, Mensa. Recipient: awards for service and leadership, Baruch Coll, CUNY. Spec interests: photography, music, J culture, Yiddish. Home: 344 W 72 St, New York, NY. Office: 101 Fifth Ave, New York, NY.

GROUF, Meyer, US, attorney; b. Russ, Nov 15, 1900; s. Joseph and Jennie; in US since 1904; BS, CCNY, 1921; LLB, Fordham U Law Sch, 1924; m. Betty Yarchoan, Apr 14, 1940; c: Jon. Partner, Wachtell, Manheim and Grouf, NYC, since 1926. Pres, Uptown Torah Assn, since 1943; hon pres, Brandeis Sch, Woodmere, LI since 1956, past pres; mem, bd dirs, Downtown Talmud Torah, since 1935; fmr: trustee, FJP of NY; mem, munic court comm, NY Bar Assn, 1938-48, secy, 1945-48. Home: 465 Park Ave, New York, NY. Office: 30 Rockefeller Plaza, New York, NY.

GROVER, Norman Bernard, Isr, scientist; b. Montreal, Can, Aug 19, 1933; s. Arthur and Anne; in Isr since 1955; BSc, McGill U, 1951-55; PhD, Heb U, 1955-62; m. Rita Benzakein, July 17, 1959; c: Ron, Michal. Lectr, biophysics, Heb U, since 1965; research asso, Rockefeller U, 1962-65; lectr, Poly Inst of Bklyn, 1965. IDF, 1965. Mem: Can Assn of Physicists, biophys and health physics chap; Isr Phys Soc. Author: Semiconductor Surfaces, 1965. Home: 44 Nayot, Jerusalem, Isr. Office: Hadassah Medical School, Hebrew University, Jerusalem, Isr.

GROZIN, Maurice, US, pediatrician, educator; b. Kamenetz, Lith; s. Isaac and Pearl (Zuchowic); in US since 1906; BA, W Reserve U, 1917; MD, Yale U, 1922; postgrad studies: Munich, 1924; Vienna, 1926; m. Ann Armstrong, June 29, 1962. Cons, Queens Med Center Gen Hosp, chief children's chest clinic, since 1940, asso ped; asst clinical prof, ped, NY Med Coll. Chmn, Flushing campaign comm, United HIAS Service, 1959; f: AAAS; NY Acad Med; Royal Soc of Med, London; mem: Amer Med Writers Assn; AMA; Queens Ped Soc; Queens Med Soc; clubs: Yale, NYC; Yale, Queens. Contbr to med jours. Hobby: music. Home and office: 36-19 Bowne St, Flushing, NY.

GRUBER, Abraham R, Can, organization exec; b. NYC, Dec 20, 1914; s. Joseph and Lean (Rohr); in Can since 1954; BA, McGill U, 1936; m. Peggy Schnall, Apr 19, 1940; c: Steven, Susan. Dir: State of Isr Bond Org, Montreal, since 1954, Jacksonville, Fla, 1951-52, Cleveland, O, 1952-54; sales mgr, food mfr, Amer Dietaids Inc and Twin Gabel Food Co, 1937-51. USAAF, 1941-45. Vice-pres, Lyric Opera Soc of Can; mem: Pi Lambda Phi; B'nai B'rith. Home: 4117 Beaconsfield, Montreal Can. Office: 2025 University St, Montreal, Can.

GRUBER, Irving M, US, attorney; b. NYC, Feb 12, 1917; s. Samuel and Anna (Raucher); BA, CUNY, 1936; LLB, Columbia U, 1939; m. Leanora Schwartz, May 10, 1945; c: Judith, Samson. Partner, Gruber & Gruber, since 1963; pvt practice, 1948-63; chief, meat enforcement br, OPA, 1946-47; chief of lit, Off Housing Expediter, 1947; asst to Atty Gen of US, 1948; visiting prof, Kan U Law Sch, 1947. US Army, 1942-46. Mem: NYC, Amer Bar Assns; NY Co Lawyers Assn. Contbr to legal jours. Home: 1160 Park Ave, New York, NY. Office: 1 E 42 St, New York, NY.

GRUBER, Ruth, US, foreign corresp, author, lecturer; b. NYC; d. David and Gussie (Rockower); BA, NYU; MA, U of Wis, La Frentz f; PhD, U of Cologne, Inst of Intl Educ f; m. Philip Michaels, Feb 4, 1951 (decd); c: Celia, David. Spec fgn corresp, NY Herald Tribune, since 1947; columnist, Hadassah Mag; lectr, Grad Sch, Hunter Coll, fgn corresp, NY Post, 1946; field repr for Alaska, Interior Dept, spec asst to Secy of Interior, 1941-46; govt envoy to It to bring 1000 refugees offered haven by Pres Roosevelt, 1944. Co-chmn, women's div, UJA, Gtr NY, mem: Arctic Inst of N Amer;

Writers Guild of Amer E Inc; Soc for Advancement of Judaism; club, Overseas Press. Author: I Went to the Soviet Arctic, 1939; Destination Pal, 1948; Israel Without Tears, 1950; Israel Today, 1958, rev ed, 1963; Puerto Rico, 1960; Science and the New Nations, 1961, trans into numerous langs; Israel on the Seventh Day, 1968; contbr: Look Mag; Commentary; The Nation; New Republic; Readers Digest; Saturday Review; contbr to book: I Can Tell It Now, 1964; The Generations of Israel, 1968; contbr to anthol, The American Judaism Reader, 1967; contbr, The Eternal Light Prog. Home: 300 Central Park W, New York, NY.

GRUENEWALD, Max, US, rabbi: b. Koenigsheutte, Ger, Dec 4, 1899; s. Moritz and Klara (Ostheimer); in US since 1939; PhD, U's of Breslau, Heidelberg, 1926; ordained rabbi, J Theol Sem, Breslau, 1926; hon DD, JTSA, NY; m. Hedwig Horovitz, 1926; c: Ruben. Rabbi: Cong B'nai Isr, Millburn, NJ, since 1944; J Comty, Mannheim, Ger, 1925-37. Pres, Amer Fed of J, Cen Eur 1952-62, hon pres since 1962; vice-pres, Cultural Reconstruction, 1951; mem: exec bd, cultural dept, WJC, 1942-45; exec, NY Bd Rabbis; co-chmn, Gustav-Wurzweiler Found; pres, Leo Baeck Inst, US chmn, 1956; pres, J Comty, Mannheim, 1934-37; mem, exec bd, Council of Ger J, 1936; club: Theodor Herzl, NY, pres, 1940-43. Contbr to jours. Home: 18 Haran Circle, Millburn, NJ. Study: 160 Millburn Ave, Millburn, NJ.

GRUMBACH, Arthur S, Switz, bacteriologist, educator; b. Zurich, June 25, 1895; s. Jacques and Bertha (Rothschild); MD, U of Zurich, 1921; att: Inst Pasteur, Paris, 1921; Path Inst of Geneva, 1922-25; Rockefeller Inst, 1925; m. Dagmar Curti, Sept 27, 1939. Prof em, U of Zurich, 1965, prof bact and hygiene since 1950, staff mem since 1928. Corresp and hon mem, natl and intl sci orgs. Contbr to med and sci jours. Home: Rutistrasse 20, Zurich, Switz.

GRUNBAUM, Adolf, US, educator; b. Cologne, Ger, May 15, 1923; s. Benjamin and Hannah (Freiwillig); in US since 1938; BA, summa cum laude, Wesleyan U, 1943; MS, Yale U, 1948, PhD, 1951; m. Thelma Braverman, June 26, 1949; c: Barbara. Andrew Mellon Prof Phil dir, Cen for Phil of Sci, U Pittsburgh, since 1960; physicist, div research, Columbia U, 1943-44, 1946; instr to prof, phil, Lehigh U, 1950-56, W W Selfridge Prof, 1957-60; visiting research prof, Cen for Phil Sci, U Minnesota, 1956-57. Mil IS, US Army, 1944-46. Pres, Phil of Sci Assn, 1965-70; vice-pres, AAAS, 1963; exec comm, Amer Phil Assn; mem: Phi Beta Kappa; Sigma Xi. Author: Philosophic Problems of Space and Time, 1963; Modern Science and Zeno's Paradoxes, 1967; Geometry and Chronometry in Philosophical Perspective, 1968; mem, ed bd: Jour of the Phil of Sci, since 1959; Ency of Phil, since 1960; Amer Philosophical Quarterly; The Philospher's Index; contbr to scholary books, and jours. Recipient: f: Amer Council Learned Soc, 1947-50; Ford Found, 1954-55; J Walker Tomb Prize, Princeton U, 1958; Alfred Noble Robinson award, Lehigh U, 1913; honor citation, scholarship convocation, Wesleyan U, 1959; research grants, Natl Sci Found, 1955-57, 1957-59, 1959-60, 1965-69. Hobby: music. Home: 2270 McCrea Rd, Pittsburgh, Pa. Office: U of Pittsburgh, Pittsburgh, Pa.

GRUND, Benjamin, US, certified public acctnt; b. Warsaw, Pol; s. Harry and Goldie (Kalina); LLB, Bklyn Law Sch of St Lawrence U, 1925; LIM, St John's U Sch of Law, Bklyn, 1934; m. Ruth Zelmanovitz, June 19, 1927; c: Bruce, Betty Goodman. Partner, Seidman and Seidman, CPA's, since 1944, staff mem since 1920; fmr: asst to pres, Consolidated Cigar Co, 1942-44. Pres, NY State Soc of CPA's, 1960-61; chmn: acctnts comm, NYC, for: UJA of Gtr NY, 1954; Isr Bond Drive, 1956; Jt Defense Appeal, 1958; special gifts comm, FJP of NY, 1957; trustee: Temple Beth-El, Cedarhurst, LI, 1956-62; Educ Alliance, since 1967; mem: bd govs, Lawrence Assn, 1950; governing council, Amer Inst of CPA's, 1958-64. Recipient: award, NY State Soc of CPA's, 1954. Contbr to profsl jours. Home: 870 Fifth Ave, New York, NY. Office: 80 Broad St, New York, NY.

GRUNDFEST, Dave, US, business exec; b. Cary, Miss, Sep 11, 1901; s. Morris and Mollie (Bernstein); att Miss State Coll, 1917-18; m. Maurine Frauenthal, June 22, 1926; c: Dave, Barbara Bauman. Pres: Sterling Stores Co, Inc, since 1941; Cash Wholesale Co, since 1941; vice-pres, Ark Livestock Show Assn; dir, Variety Stores Assn. Vice-pres, Leo N Levi Memorial Hosp, Hot Springs, Ark; found, Grundfest Found for Educ of Youth, Little Rock; mem, bd dirs: C of C, Little Rock, past pres; Hosp for Crippled Adults, Memphis, Tenn; Ind Devl Commn; past pres and past dir, YMCA; past dir:

Children's Hosp, Little Rock; ARC, Pulaski Co chap; NCCJ; hon life mem: Future Farmers of Amer; 4-H Club; mem: trade mission to Fr for Commerce Dept, 1957; trade mission to It, 1959. Mem: Masons, 33rd deg; Cong B'nai Isr, past vice-pres; mem, bd dirs; Rotary, past pres; clubs: Top of the Rock, Little Rock. Home: 12 River Oaks Circle, Little Rock, Ark. Office: 6500 Forbing Rd, Little Rock, Ark.

GRUNEBAUM, Erich Otto, US, investment banker; b. Essen, Ger, Mar 26, 1926; s. Ernst and Agatha (Hirschland); in US since 1941; att U of Munich, 1920-23; LSE, London, 1923-24; NYU, 1925-27; m. Gabriele Newman, Oct 21, 1921; c: Ernest, Eva Koppel, David. Chmn, bd dirs, NY Hanseatic Corp, since 1959; on staff since 1942. Pres, Cong Habonim, NYC, since 1965; mem since 1948; co-treas, Combined Campaign for Victims of Nazi Oppression, since 1964; dir, Costwold Assn, 1960-69; life mem, ZOA. Hobbies: art, music, sport. Home: 11 Costwold Way, Scarsdale, NY. Office: 60 Broad St, New York, NY.

GRUNEBAUM, Kurt H, US, business exec; b. Essen, Ger, Aug 11, 1905; s. Ernst and Agathe (Hirschland); in US since 1941; m. Anneliese Eichwald, Dec 27, 1929; c: Peter. Pres, dir, NY Hanseatic Corp, since 1959, vice-pres, 1942-48, exec vice-pres, 1948-59; dir, Nyhaco Credit Corp; vice-chmn, bd dirs, Canal-Randolph Corp; partner, Simon Hirschland, Ger, 1936-38; asst to gov, Bank of Can, 1939-40. Dir: United Stockyards Corp; Titan Group; Security Title and Guaranty Co; Standard Intl Corp; Gtr NY Mutual Ins Co; Ins Co of Gtr NY; mem, bd dirs, exec comm, Amer Fed of J from Cen Eur; mem, bd dirs Self help of Emigres from Cen Eur Inc. Hobbies: art, horseback riding. Home: 100 Muchmore Rd, Harrison, NY. Office: 60 Broad St, New York, NY.

GRÜNEWALD, Hans Isaak, W Ger, rabbi; b. Frankfurt/Main, Mar 15, 1914; s. Edmund and Julie (Rothschild); att U and Yeshiva of Frankfurt, 1932-36; Heb U, Jerusalem, 1936-39; ordained rabbi, Jews' Coll, London, 1960; m. Martha Nebenzahl, Nov 19, 1940; c: Jaakow, Eliezer, Joseph. Communal rabbi, Israelitische Kultursgemeinde, Munich; vice-pres, Conf of Ger Rabbis; mem, Standing Comm, Conf of Eur Rabbis; chief rabbi, N Ger, 1960-63. Pres, B'nai B'rith Bialik Lodge, Tel Aviv; mem, B'nai B'rith Mentor "Hebraica" Lodge, Munich. Contbr to J press in Ger Bavarian Bc; lectr, Munich Volkshochschule Chr-J Assn. Home: Kolosseumstr 6, Munich, W Ger. Study: Reichenbachstr 27, Munich, W Ger.

GRÜNFARB, Josef M, Swed, violinist; b. Stockholm, Aug 27, 1920; s. Moschko and Helena (Hexelman); att Royal Music Acad, Stockholm; studied with Ernst Glaser, Oslo; Tibor Varga, London; m. Gertrud Meyer, 1948; c: Eva, Anita. Leader, Royal Opera, Stockholm since 1964; tchr, Royal Music Acad, since 1965; first violinist, Stockholm Philharmonic Orch, 1943-61, alternate leader, 1949-61; leader, Stockholm Philharmonic Orch, 1961-64. Home: Vanadisplan 3, Stockholm, Swed. Office: Royal Opera, Stockholm, Swed.

GRUNFELD, Isaiah Isidore, Eng, rabbi; b. Bavaria, Ger, Oct 27, 1900; s. Joseph and Caroline (Fromm); in Eng since 1933; cert tchr, Tchr Training Sem, Wurzburg; LLD, U's: Marburg, Frankfurt; ordained rabbi, Yeshivot; Frankfurt, Hamburg; m. Judith Rosenbaum, 1932; c: Anneruth Cohn, Naomi, Joseph, Alexander, Raphael. Ret as dayan, mem, Chief Rabbis Ecclesiastical Court, London; barrister-at-law, Wurzburg, until 1933. Pres: Sabbath Observance Employment Bur; Sabbath League of Gt Brit; vice-pres, London Council of Social Service; vice-chmn, Commn of Status of J War-Orphans in Eur; trustee, Intl Amnesty Movement for Victims of Rel Persecution and Prisoners of Conscience; mem: exec, educ comm, London Bd J Educ; exec comm, Kosher Sch Meals Service; adv panel, Wyndham Place Trust; rel adv comm, Natl Assn Boys Clubs; Cen Brit Council for J Relief and Rehab; allocation comm, J Trust Fund for Victims of Nazism; council, Anglo-J Assn; hon lectr: Natl Marriage Guidance Council; Home Office Courses for Probation Officers. Author: The Sabbath, 1954; Judaism Eternal, 2 vols, 8 eds, 1956; Three Generations, 1958; Eng trans, Hirsch's Horeb; contbr to mags and jours in Isr, Eng, US. Home: 214 Green Lanes, London, Eng.

GRUNSFELD, Ernest A, US, architect, artist; b. Albuquerque, NM, Aug 25, 1897; s. Ernest and Thersa (Nusbaum); BS, MIT, 1918; att: Ecole des Beaux Arts, Paris, 1920-22; Amer Acad, Rome, 1921; m. Mary Loeb, 1921; m. 2nd, Maurine Gahagan, Apr, 1945; c: Ernest, Esther Klatz. Practicing architect since 1924; asso, Friedman, Altschuler, Sincere and

Grunsfeld, since 1948; cons, US Housing Auth, 1933-37; mem, Ill Housing Commn, 1936-38; lectr: U of Ill, 1947; Stanford U, 1951-53; U of Chgo, 1930. USN, 1917; cons, Chem Warfare Service, 1944. Architect of housing projects, public bldgs, throughout US, including J Peoples Inst, 1925; Infirmary, MIT, 1927; Mich Blvd Gardens, Chgo, 1928; Adler Planetarium, 1930; Bc Studio, WGN, 1935; Chgo Bar Assn, 1936; gal and residence for Lessing Rosenwald, Phila, Pa, 1939; Max Strauss Cen, 1940; temples: Chgo, 1947; Muskegon, Mich, 1947; Dayton, O, 1953; libr, HUC, Cincinnati, O, 1934; exhibited paintings, Paris Salon d'Automne, 1956, 1957, 1959. F: Amer Inst Architects; delg, Intl Union of Architects, 1950-53; found, pres, Ernest A Grunsfeld Fund, intl awards and scholarships in architecture and city planning; comptroller, Intl Union of Architects; club, Tavern, Chgo. Co-author: A Plan for Chicago, 1954. Contbr to profsl jours. Recipient: student medal, Amer Inst Architects, 1918; Rotch Prize, MIT, 1919; gold medal, Société des Architectes Diplomes par le Gouvernement Français, 1919; gold medal, Amer Inst Architects, Chgo br, for Adler Planetarium; silver medal diploma, Pan-Amer Architectural Congress, 1939; 2nd grand prize 1946; Chevalier Legion of Honor, 1959; gold medal, Merite Civique, 1958, both Fr. Homes: 105 E Delaware Pl, Chicago, Ill; 157 Blvd St Germain, Paris, Fr.

GRUNWALD, Joshua, US, rabbi; b. Hung; s. Emanuel and Sara (Kramer); in US since 1939; ordained rabbi, Rabb Sch, Ordenburg, Presburg and Frankfurt, Ger, 1914; m. Kathe Rubens. Rabbi, Adath Machsike Hadath, since 1940; chief rabbi, Provinz alto Adige, Bolsano, Merano, It, and Provinz Venezia Tridentin, 1920-39; Asst army chaplain, It Army, 1917-18. Mem: NY Bd Rabbis; Mizrachi; Bd Rabbis, It. Contbr to Talmud Halacha jours. Home: 240 W 98 St, New York, NY. Study: 310 W 95 St, New York, NY.

GRUNWALD, Tibor, Fr, physician; b. Reni, Rum, Oct 3, 1910; s. Ferdinand and Josefa (Schönzweig); in Fr since 1928; deg, Med U, Paris, 1937; m. Huguette Beaupère, June 17, 1938; c: Françoise, Catherine, Ivan, Isabelle, Sylvie. Pvt practice since 1937. Fr Army, WW II. Mem: IMA, Médecins, Pharmaciens, Dentistes Amis d'Israel. Recipient: Croix de Guerre, 1939-45; Hon Medal, Mil Health Service. Hobbies: painting, poetry, tennis, sailing. Home and office: 33 Rue Balinière, Rezé-les-Nantes, Fr.

GRUSD, Edward E, US, editor, journalist; b. Cincinnati, O, June 15, 1904; s. Moses and Rose (Morris); BS, O State U, 1926; att HUC Tchrs Inst, 1930-31; m: Elizabeth Franklin, July 8, 1932; c: David, Dulcy. Fmr ed, The Natl J Monthly of B'nai B'rith, 1928-70. Pres, Cincinnati Youth Temple, 1928-29; B'nai B'rith, Arlington, Va, 1940; mem: Sigma Alpha Mu; Sigma Delta Chi. Author: B'nai B'rith, Story of a Covenant, 1966. Home: 3707 Morrison St, Washington, DC. Office: B'nai B'rith Bldg, 1640 Rhode Island Ave, NW, Washington, DC.

GRUSKIN, Alan D, US, art dealer, author; b. Manorville, Pa, Dec 28, 1904; s. Arthur and Jennie (Pollock); att, Harvard, 1926; m. Mary Bovio, July, 1940; c: Richard, Robert. Owner, dir, Midtown Gals, contemporary Amer art, since 1932. Adv, Natl Art Mus of Sport; bd dirs, Art Dealers Assn of Amer; club, Harvard. Author: Painting in the USA, 1946; The Painter and His Techniques, William Thon, 1964; radio: Art Appreciation for All, NBC; The Story Behind the Picture, WOR. Home: RD 1, Stockton, NJ. Office: 11 E 57 St, New York, NY.

GRUSS, Noe, Fr, librarian; b. Sep 2, 1902; Kulikow, Galicia; s. Samuel and Adele (Stein); in Fr since 1952; prof, U Carcovie 1927; PhD, 1964; m. Elizabeth Lokshina, Sep 17, 1945. Libr, service Hebraique, Bibliotheque Nationale, chief, service Yiddish; chief, service Yiddish et hebraique, Ecole Nationale des Langues Orientales Vivantes, Paris; libr, Centre de Documentation Israel Moyen Orient, Comite de Coordination, Organizations juives de France; dir, HS: Bialystock, 1934-36; Tel Aviv, 1948-52. Kinder Martology, 1946; Zvishen Freund, 1953. Home: 50 rue de la Bidassoa, Paris, 20e, Fr. Office: 58 Richelieu, Paris, Fr.

GRYN, Hugo Samuel, Eng, rabbi; b. Czech, June 25, 1930; s. Geza and Bella (Neufeld); in Eng since 1964; MA, U of Cincinnati, 1952; MHL, HUC, Cincinnati, ordained rabbi, 1957; m. Jaqueline Selby, Jan 1, 1957; c: Gabrielle, Naomi, Rachelle, David. Sr rabbi, W London Syn, since 1964; rabbi, J Rel Union, Bombay, India, 1957-59; exec dir, World Union for Progressive Judaism, 1959-62; sr exec, JDC, 1962-64. Lt

cdr (ret), US Navy, 1957-58. Chmn, Mins Assembly, Reform Syns of Gt Brit; dir, Leo Baeck Coll, London; mem, B'nai B'rith, 1st lodge, Eng. Study: 33 Seymour Pl, London, Eng.

GRYN, Nathanel Tony, Isr, editor; b. Lublin, Pol, Feb 20, 1921; s. Icek and Rywka (Wacholder); in Isr since 1957; PCB cert, Sorbonne, Paris, 1940; m. Charlotte Hausmann, Mar 20, 1949; c: Robert, Elizabeth. Chief ed, found, L'Information D'Israel daily, since 1960; fmr: ed, Unser Wort daily, Paris, found, 1944. Leading mem, J Fighting Org, Fr, 1941-44; Haganah; IDF. Pres, Union de Juifs de Fr et D'Algerie, Isr, since 1966; mem, Isr Lab Party, since 1957; delg to WZC since 1946, asst delg, 26th Cong, Jerusalem; fmr: gen secy: Po'alei Zion, Hitachdouth, Paris, Fr; mem: bur, Socialist Youth Intl; Council for Integration, Isr; Comité d'Action de la Résistance, Fr. Recipient: Citation Order, Fr Interior Forces, 1944; Liberation Medal, Fr, 1957; Diplôme D'Honneur, Union Intl de la Résistance, 1963; Combattants Medal for the J State, 1968; Medal Combattants Against Nazis, 1967; Chevalier de L'Ordre National, Rep Haute Volta. Home: 10 Urim St, Holon, Isr. Office: 52 Harakevet St, Tel Aviv, Isr.

GRZYWACZ, Baruch, Isr, business exec; b. Lodge, Pol, Jan 8, 1908; s. Israel and Pessa (Ash); in Isr since 1939; grad, Textile Coll, 1926; m. Lea Levin, June 25, 1937; c: Ilana Gad, Nily Giora. Mgn dir since 1941; Goldlust, 1927-35. Chmn, bd, Isr Textile Sch; mem: Mfrs Assn Isr; Commercial and Ind Club; Lodge of Commerce; Kfar Jechezkel, Labait Velayeled. Home: 6 Huberman St, Tel Aviv, Isr. Office: 9 Herzl St, Tel Aviv, Isr.

GUBAR, Leonard, US, attorney; b. Jersey City, NJ, Apr 22, 1937; s. Jacob and Beatrice (Miller); BA, Cornell U, NY, 1958; LLB, hons, Cornell Law Sch, 1960; m. Sandra Silverman, May 26, 1963; c: Justine. Partner, Roth, Carlson, Kwit, Spengler & Mallin, since 1969; atty: Stein, Abrams & Rosen, 1960-65; Marshall, Bratter, Greene, Allison & Tucker, 1965-68. Capt, US Army Res, 1960-68. Mem: Amer Bar Assn; NY State Bar Assn; Assn of Bar, NYC. Home: 145 E 16 St, New York, NY. Office: 280 Park Ave, New York, NY.

GUBIN, Selma, US, artist; b. Kiev, Russ, Jan 1, 1903; d. Benjamin and Dora (Ostreich); in US since 1908; att Hunter Coll; Art Students League; NYU; m. Meyer Zisling, June 3, 1923, div. One-man shows: Gal de Peridistas, Mex, 1963; Rockland State Coll, NY, 1964; B'nai B'rith Mus, Wash, DC, 1968; Glass Gal, NYU, 1968; ACA Gal, NYU, 1942; Norlyst Art Gal, NY, 1948; Arthur Brown Gal, NY, 1952; Tamiment Art Gal, Pa, 1956; Capri Gal, Mex, 1959; group exhbs: City Cen; Contemporary Art Gal; Kipnis Art Gal, NY; World's Fair; Art, USA; Silvermine Guild of Artists; Painters and Sculptors Soc of NJ; Riverside Mus; Natl Assn of Women Artists; repr in collections: Albert Einstein Coll of Med, Yeshiva U; Rockland State Coll; B'nai B'rith Org, Wash, DC; Libr of Cong; NY Public Libr; Treas Dept; Mus of Art, Ein Harod, Isr; Mus of Art, Tel Aviv; Mus of Art, Jerusalem; pvt collections; traveling groups: Graphics to India, 1968; Watercolors, USA; Oils to Fr and Can, 1969; org group exhb sponsored by Artists Equity Assn; Mem: NY chap, Artists Equity Assn; Natl Assn Women Artists; Woodstock Art Assn; Art Students League of NY. Recipient: scholarship, Art Students League, 1928; Lilly Javitz Award, Silvermine Guild of Artists, 1959; J M Kaplan Award, Painters and Sculptors Soc of NY, 1960; F W Weber Award, Natl Assn Women Artists, 1961. Home and studio: 170 W 181 St, New York, NY.

GUBOW, Lawrence, US, jurist; b. Detroit, Mich, Jan 10, 1919; s. Jacob and Dora (Rubin); AB, U Mich, 1940, hon cert in real estate, LLB, Law Sch, 1950; m. Estelle Schmalberg, June 27, 1948; c: David, Mona, Janey. US Dist Judge, E dist of Mich, since 1968; fmr US Atty, practicing atty; fmr: dir of inves, Mich Corp Securities Commn, later appd commnr; chmn, Inves Securities Co; N Amer Securities Admnrs Assn. Capt, US Army, 1941-48. Natl vice-cdr, 5th region, JWV; vice-pres, Fed Exec Assn; legal adv, Allied Vets Council of Wayne Co, chmn, leg comm; pres, JCC of Metrop Detroit; co-chmn, Urban Affairs Comm, JWF, mem, comty relations div; dir: JNF; Detroit Service Group; mem: Mich, Amer, Detroit, Federal Bar Assns; Detroit Bar Assn Corp Law Comm; Judicature Soc; Amer Acad Political and Social Sci; Econ Club of Detroit, adv and prog comms; Comm to Revise Mich Criminal Code; Policy Comm, JWV; Learned Post, Amer Legion; Post 105 AMVETS; Tutro Post, VFW; Chap 1, DAV; Disabled Offs Assn; Ret Offs Assn; bd govs, JWF; Cong Shaarey Zedek, chmn prog comm; hon mem, Real

Estate Alumni of Mich; fmr: mem, various gov task forces and comms; chmn: 17th Dist, Young Dem Club; Dem Housing Comm. Recipient: 1959 Civic Award, E Detroit Realty Assn; Dist Service Award, Detroit Real Estate Brokers Assn, 1961; Women's Army Corps Vets Assn, 1967; Bronze Medal Award, JWV, 1960; St Cyprian's Comty Award, 1963; Allied Vets Council Golden Award, 1959, 67; Fed Admnr of the Year, Fed Exec Assn, 1967; Man of the Year, JWV, 1967. Home: 20100 Braile St, Detroit, Mich. Office: 213 Fed Bldg, Detroit, Mich.

GUDEMAN, Edward, US, investment banker; b. Chgo, Ill, Oct 9, 1906; s. Edward and Clara (Asher); AB, Harvard Coll, 1927; m. Frances Alschuler, 1932; c: Jon, Stephen. Dir: Marcor, Inc; Montgomery Ward & Co; Esquire; Sears, Roebuck & Co, 1948-60; partner, Lehman Bros, since 1963; Under-Secy of Commerce, Commerce Dept, 1961-63. Bd dirs: Lenox Hill Hosp, NYC; Blythedale Children's Hosp, Valhalla, NY; Natl Council on Crime and Delinquency. Home: 142 E 65 St, New York, NY. Office: 1 William St, New York, NY.

GUDMUNDSEN, Per, (PG), Den, journalist, author; b. Copenhagen, Den, Sep 5, 1900; s. Johann and Lauretta (Christensen) Gudmundsen-Holmgreen; m. Inger Heine, Apr 26, 1935; c: Nanna, Ulla. Chief ed, Isr Mag, since 1962; journalist, Social Demokraten, 1945-67. Author: Angelo; The Flute; Jonas; The Slave; The Gay One-Act. Found, mem of honor, League for Tolerance; mem: exec, Journalist Org; Zionist Org; Avodah; comm, Danish Isr Soc; Org of Critics; Danish Lab Party. Home: 34 Rudersdalsvej St, Holte, Den.

GUELFAT, Isaac, Isr, economist, educator, author; b. Novo, Ukraine, Aug 11, 1900; s. Joseph and Debora (Zaslavsky); in Isr since 1922; att U Libre, Brussels; dipl, Grad Inst of Intl Studies, Geneva; m. Sylvia Reich, 1948. Prof, social sci, Heb U. Author: Essays in Cooperative Economics, 1939; Socialism and the Agrarian Problem in our Time, 1941; New Currents in Economic Thought, 3 Vols, 1943-51. Contribs, 1958: Doctrines Economiques et Pays en voie de Developement, 1961; La Coopération devant la Science Economique, 1966; Economic Thought in the Soviet Union—Concepts and Aspects, a Comparative Outline, 1968; co-author: The Arab Economy in Palestine and in the Countries of the Middle East, 1944; ed, Consumer's Cooperation, 1946. Home: 11 Epstein St, Tel Aviv, Isr. Office: Hebrew U, Jerusalem, Isr.

GUERON, Meir, Isr, shipping exec; b. Lodz, Pol, Aug 7, 1913; in Isr since 1933; m. Shoshana Sternberg; two d. Mgn dir, Zim Navigation Co Ltd, since 1966; fmr: exec, Solel Boneh Ltd; mgn dir, Koor Inds; dep dir, mgn dir, Haifa Refineries. Home: 45 Gilboa St, Haifa, Isr. Office: Zim Navigation Co, Ha'atzmauth Rd, Haifa, Isr.

GUERON, Moshe, Isr, physician; b. Sofia, Bulgaria, Mar 20, 1926; s. Isaac and Sarah (Kastro); in Isr since 1949; MD, Heb U, Jerusalem, 1952; m. Sophie Levy, May, 1950; c: Elia, Isaac. Dir, card lab, Negev Cen Hosp, since 1963; research f, AHA, 1960-61. Contbr to med publs. Home: 319/15 Shikun Daleth, Beersheba, Isr. Office: Negev Central Hospital, Beersheba, Isr.

GUERY, Levi, Isr, government official; b. Balti, Russ, June 15, 1911; s. Itzhak and Miriam (Hitelman) Grinspun; in Isr since 1932; dipl, agron, U of Nancy, Fr, 1939; F of UN for Public Admnrs, US and Can, 1961; m. Shifra Bogoslavsky, May 15, 1935; c: Zohar, Micha, Dita. Dep dir gen, chmn, bd film censorship, dir, spec duties dept, all Min Interior, since 1956; tchr, agric, Nahalal Coll, 1942-48; secy to min, 1948-50, dir, N region, 1950-56, both Min Agric. Haganah, 1940-45; civil defence, 1945-59. Mayor, Tivon Township, voluntary, 1950-56. Contbr to agric mags, daily jours. Mem, Variety club, Isr. Home: 8 Frankel St, Tel Aviv, Isr. Office: Min of Interior, Jerusalem, Isr.

GUGGENHEIM, Karl Yehiel, Isr, nutritionist; b. Frankfurt/M, Ger, Jan 12, 1906; s. Theodor and Rosa (Rapp); in Isr since 1933; att Us: Munich, Leipzig; MD, U of Frankfurt, 1929; m. Irene Muhlfelder, 1936; c: Ruth, David, Amnon. Prof, nutrition, Heb U, Hadassah Med Sch, since 1965; adv, nutrition, Min of Health, since 1954. Hon mem, Amer Inst Nutrition; mem: IMA; Isr Soc Food and Nutrition Scis. Author: Torat Hatzuna, 1954; Tzunat ha'Adam, 1964; contbr numerous articles on phys of nutrition and public health nutrition. Recipient: Henrietta Szold Award, Tel Aviv Munic, 1955. Home: 41 Gaza St, Jerusalem, Isr. Office: Dept of Nutrition, Hadassah Med Sch, Jerusalem, Isr.

GUGGENHEIM, Kurt, Switz, author; b. Zurich, Switz, Jan 14, 1896; s. Hermann and Frieda (Ris); m. Gerda Schlozer. Author: Entfesselung, 1935; Sieben Tage, 1937; Reidland,1938; Wilder Urlaub, 1941; Die Heimliche Reise, 1945; Wir waren unser Vier, 1949; Alles in Allem, vol I, 1952, vol II, 1953, vol III, 1954, vol IV, 1955; Der Friede des Herzens, 1957; Sandkorn für Sandkorn, 1959; Die Wahrheit unter dem Fliessblatt, 1960; Das Offenbare Geheimnis, trans from Souvenirs entomologiques by Fabre, 1961; Heimat oder Domizil? 1961; Die frühen Jahre, 1962; Salzdes Meeres Salz Der Tränen, 1964; Das Ende Von Seldwyla, 1965; Tagebuch Am Schanzengraben, 1966; Der Goldene Würfel, 1967; Warum Gerade Ich? 1968; Minute Des Lebens, 1969; dramas, scripts for movies and radio. Mem: PEN; Union of Swiss Authors; Ger Acad Speech and Poetry. Recipient: lit prize, City of Zurich, 1956; Schiller Found Prize, 1960. Home: Merkurstrasse 64, Zurich, Switz.

GUGGENHEIM, Paul, Switz, jurist, educator, author; b. Zurich, Sep 15, 1899; s. Hermann and Leone (Nordman); JD, U Berlin, 1924; DHC, U's Louvaine and Dijon, 1962, Kiel, 1966, Paris, 1966, Rome, 1967; m. Helene Sachs, Mar 14, 1931; c: Thomas, Daniel. Prof, intl law, Grad Inst of Intl Studies, Geneva, since 1930; fmr: lectr: U Geneva, prof, Law Fac; Acad of Intl Law, The Hague; judge ad hoc, Intl Court of Justice; chmn: Fr-It, Anglo-It, Amer-It, Dutch-It conciliation commns by virtue of article 83 of Treaty of Peace with It, 1957-69; mem, Perm Court of Arbitration, The Hague; agt or counsel for Switz, India, Honduras, Spain, before Intl Court of Justice; mem, Arbitral Tribunal between Switz and CERN; legal adv, Bio-molecular Conf; chmn, It-Finnish Conciliation Commn; mem, Aus-Swed Conciliation Commn. Mem, Inst Intl Law, since 1948; fmr: mem bd, Coll for Eur, Bruges, Belgium; chmn, cen comm, Fed of J Comtys, Switz. Author: L'imposition des Successions en Droit International et le Probleme de la Double Imposition, 1928; Les Mesures Conservatoires dans la Procédure Arbitrale et Judicaire, 1933; Völkerbund, Dumbarton Oaks und die Schweizerische Neutralität, 1945; Lehrbuch des Völkerrechtes, vol I, 1948, vol II, 1951; Traité de Droit International Public, vol I, 1953, vol II, 1954, 2nd ed, vol I, 1967. Home: 1 Route du Bont-du-Monde, Geneva, Switz. Office: 132 Route de Lausanne, Geneva, Switz.

GUGGENHEIM, Richard E, US, business exec; b. Cincinnati, O, Jan 5, 1913; s. Eli and Eva (Stransky); BA, U of Mich, 1934; LLB, Harvard Law Sch, 1937; m. Carol Rice, Sep 14, 1942; c: Jane, Polly, Richard; m. 2nd, Alice Joseph, Feb 27, 1967. Vice-pres, The US Shoe Corp, since 1951; dir, Fed Home Loan Bank of Cincinnati, since 1966; atty, civil, antitrust div, Justice Dept, 1946-50; dep gen counsel, Econ Stabilization Agcy, 1950-51. Maj, US Army, 1942-46. Chmn, O Civil Rights Commn, 1959-62; bd trustees: Public Health Fed; AJComm, Cincinnati; Avondale Comty Council; O League for Good Govt; Isaac M Wise Temple, 1957-58; mem: Amer, O, Cincinnati Bar Assns; B'nai B'rith; LZOA; Hist and Phil Soc of O; Miami Soc. Home: 1846 Keys Crescent, Cincinnati, O. Office: The US Shoe Corp, Cincinnati, O.

GUGGENHEIM, Willy, Switz, journalist, author; b. Zurich, Switz, Dec 28, 1929; s. Henri and Florence (Grünberg); att Sorbonne, Paris, 1950-51; Heb U, Jerusalem, 1951-52; PhD, U Zurich, 1953; m. Raymonde Niddam, Feb 24, 1957; c: Abraham, Salomon. Secy-gen, Swiss Fed J Comtys, since 1971; fgn ed, Die Weltwoche, 1964-69; fmr: press liaison off, JA, Jerusalem, 1956-61; fgn corresp, Swiss radio and press, 1961-64. Chmn, Vereinigung für religiös-liberales Judentum, Zurich sect; mem: Swiss Journalists Assn; Fgn Policy Assn; fmr, exec, Swiss Union J Students; World Union J Students. Author: Jerusalem, 1968. Hobby: astrology. Home: Salomon Voegelinstr 33, Zurich, Switz.

GUGGENHEIM-GRUENBERG, Florence, Switz, pharmacist, folklorist, historian; b. Berne, Switz, Aug 30, 1898; d. Adolf and Doris (Willstaedt) Gruenberg; DScNat, Swiss Fed Inst of Tech, Zurich, 1928; m. Henri Guggenheim, 1928; c: Willy. Practicing pharm, St Gall and Zurich, 1923-28. Author: Die Arbeit der Tuberkulose-Fürsorge in der Stadt Zürich, 1928; Die Sprache der Schweizer Juden von Endingen und Lengnau, 1950; Aus einem alten Endinger Gemeindebuch, 1952; Pfarrer Ulrich als Missionar im Surbtal, 1953; Die ältesten jüdischen Familien in Lengnau und Endingen, 1954; The Horse Dealers' Language of the Swiss Jews in Endingen and Lengnau, 1954; Der Friedhof auf der Judeninsel im Rhein bei Koblenz, 1956; Die Juden auf der Zurzacher Messe im 18 Jahrhundert, 1957; Zur Phonologie des Surbtaler Jiddischen,

1958; Die ältesten Grabsteine des Friedhofes Endingen-Lengnau, 1958; Die Juden in der Schweiz, 1961; Gailinger Jiddisch, 1961; Les Juifs en Suisse, 1963; Surbtaler Jiddisch, records with accompanying texts, 1966; Judenschicksale und "Judenschuol" im mittelalterlichen Zürich, 1967; Die Torawickelbänder von Lengnau, Zeugnisse jüdischer Volkskunst, 1967; ed, Beiträge zur Geschichte und Volkskunde der Juden in der Schweiz; contbr to periodicals. Pres, Jüdische Vereinigung, Zürich since 1950; fmr: gen secy, Swiss WIZO; pres: Bund der Israelitischen Frauenvereine in der Schweiz; Brith Ivrith Olamit, Switz. Home: 23 Kurfirstenstr, Zurich, Switz.

GUGGENHEIMER, Elinor C, US, city planner, civic worker, author; b. NYC, Apr 11, 1912; d. Nathan and Lillian (Fox) Coleman; BA, Barnard Coll, 1933; att: Vassar Coll; Columbia U Tchrs Coll; Pratt Inst; m. Randolph Guggenheimer, June 2, 1932; c: Charles, Randolph. Spec asst, Bx Borough Pres, NYC, since 1969; fmr, commn, city planning, NYC, 1960-68. Chmn bd: NYC Day Care Council; Natl Comm for Day Care of Children, 1966-68; dir, film div, NY Civil Service Commn, 1942-45; vice-pres: Educ Alliance, 1950-55; Child Wfr League of Amer, 1956-59; FJP, 1960, chmn, women's div, 1958-61; bd mem: Council, Comty Service Soc; Citizens Comm for Children; Natl Recreation and Parks Assn; clubs: Cosmopolitan; Women's. Author: Recreation Planning for Urban Areas, 1968; contbr to profsl jours. Home: 1095 Park Ave, New York, NY. Office: Borough Pres, Bronx, NY.

GUGGENHEIMER, Ernst, Ger, architect; b. Stuttgart, Ger, July 27, 1880; s. Samuel and Therese (Rosenfeld); Regierungsbaumeister, Tech HS, Stuttgart, 1902; m. Susanne Peter, May 21, 1946. Pvt architect since 1909; fmr: lectr, architect, Staatliche Bauschule, Kassel. Erected: Jüdisches Schwesternheim, Stuttgart, 1911; Israelitic orphanage, Wilhelmpflege, Esslingen, 1913; Schwäb-Gmünd Syn, 1925; Ulm Syn, 1925; Memorial to Dead of WWI, Pragfriedhof, 1928; J Sch, Stuttgart, 1933; Steinhalden cemetery, Bad Cannstatt, 1937-39; reconstruction of war-damaged J cemeteries: Pragfriedhof, Steigfriedhof, Hoppelaufriedhof, all 1945-47; new syn, Stuttgart, 1951-52; interior decoration of syn, Kassel, 1954; J Temple, Freiberg/M, 1957; J Temple, Neustadt, 1957. Custodian, Property Control Off; active in reconstruction of J comty life; mem, Bund Deutscher Architekten. Author: Historische Betrachtungen ueber den Synagogenbau, 1952. Recipient: gt medal of merit, 1954; title of prof, 1959. Home: Gustav Sieglestr 6, Stuttgart, W/Ger.

GUILDEN, Ira, US, banker; b. Mar 20, 1896. Chmn bd: Trade Bank and Trust Co; Title Guarantee ; Beco Industries; Ramco Enterprises; dir, chmn exec comm, MGM; pres, dir, Baldwin Securities; dir: Atlas, Cartier; N River Securities; Stetson; chmn, fmr mgr, Gen Foster Wheeler. Pres, Boys Town of Jerusalem; natl chmn, Isr Bond Drive, chmn, Gtr NY campaign. Office: 595 Madison Ave, New York, NY.

GULKO, Harris David, Can, organization exec; b. Toronto, Oct 30, 1927; s. Morris and Nancy (Berkowitz); m. Blanche Stoll, June 12, 1949; c: Rosalind, Evelyn, Miriam, Judith, Sharon. Exec vice-pres, JNF of Can, since 1963, fmr, Ont exec dir; mem: Shaare Zion Syn of Montreal; Montefiore Club of Montreal; fmr: secy, Toronto UJA Campaign; sup, Toronto Young Judea; natl vice-pres, Zionist Men's Assn of Can; pres: Ajalon Lodge; Zionist Youth Council of Toronto; secy, JNF Council of Toronto; mem: bd dirs, Asso Heb Schs of Toronto; J Public Libr of Toronto. Home: 8251 Guelph Rd, Cote St Luc, Quebec, Can. Office: 1247 Guy St, Montreal, Quebec, Can.

GUMBINER, Joseph Henry, US, rabbi, administrator; b. Pittsfield, Ill, Sep 4, 1906; s. Louis and Jennie (Van Baalen); BA, U of Cinn, 1930; ordained rabbi, HUC, 1931, DD, 1959; MA, U Ariz, 1948; DHL, HUC-JIR, 1961; m. Sylvia Tierstein, Aug 29, 1939; c: Abigail. Dir, B'nai B'rith Hillel Found, U of Cal, Berkeley, Cal, since 1955; rabbi: Cong Mishkan Isr, Selma, Ala, 1931-38; Temple Beth Or, Reno, Nev, 1939-40; Temple Emanu-El, Tucson, Ariz, 1942- 47, and dir, Hillel Found, U of Ariz, 1942-47; Temple Beth Hillel, N Hollywood, Cal, 1947-49; dir, Hillel Found, Yale U, 1949-55. Pres, Natl Assn Hillel Dirs, 1953-55; mem: CCAR; Bd Rabbis of N Cal; ACLU; club, Rotary. Author: Isaac Mayer Wise: Leaders of our People, Vols I and II; contbr to periodicals. Home: 210 Canon Dr, Orinda, Cal. Office: 2736 Bancroft Way, Berkeley, Cal.

GUMPERT, Sanford R, US, mortician; b. NYC, Jan 29, 1898; s. Julius and Annie (Tobias); grad Renouard Training Sch

for Embalmers, Bellevue Hosp, 1918. Funeral dir, Service of Gumpert, since 1921; insurance and prearrangements cons since 1953; columnist: J Funeral Dir; NY Amer; Vital Notices of the Air. Pres: NYC J Funeral Dirs Assn, 1932-35; Men's League in Aid of Crippled Children, 1937; mem: J Funeral Dirs of Amer; Masons, past master, Truth lodge, 1931; KP, Sanford lodge; Free Sons of Isr; Fort Wash Syn, 1st vice-pres. Author: Prayers, 1928-36; contbr to profsl mags. Office: 180 W 76 St, New York, NY.

GUMPLER, Isac B, Finland, business exec; b. Turku, Finland, July 24, 1897; s. Mordechai and Eva (Pergament); EE, Poly, Konstanz, Ger, 1923; m. Itele Kjisik, July 3, 1928. Mgn dir, OY Interco, AB, since 1947; engr, elec powerplant, Ger, 1923-24; Schorch-Werke, Ger, 1925-26; mgn dir, IB Gumpler and Silkki - Keskus, 1926-46. Treas, deputy chmn, KH Magbit, Helsinki, 1959, chmn since 1968; secy, J Comty, Turku, 1927-30; chmn, J Sports Club, Makkabe, 1926-30. Home: Fredsgatan 11B, Helsinki, Finland. Office: Laivurinrinne 1A, Helsinki, Finland.

GUNDERSHEIMER, Herman S, US, art historian, educator, author; b. Wurzburg, Ger, Apr 25, 1903; s. Samuel and Sophie (Salzer); in US since 1940; att: U Munich, 1921; U Wurzburg, 1922; U Berlin, 1923-24; PhD, U Leipzig, 1925; m. Frieda Siegel, May 21, 1935; c: Werner, Ann. Prof, hist of art, Temple U, Phila, since 1947, mem fac since 1941; dir, Temple U art study tours in Eur, since 1952; dir, Temple U br, Rome, It, since 1970; dir, Rothschild Mus, Frankfurt, Ger, 1931-38; lectr, art hist, Amer U, Wash, DC, 1940-41. Hon mem: Cambridge U Art Soc; Pi Delta Phi; Delta Phi Alpha; mem: Coll Art Assn of Amer; AAUP; Renaissance Soc; Phila Mus of Art; Cong Rodef Shalom, Phila, chmn, art comm. Author: Matthias Gunther, Die Freskomalerei im suddeutschen Kirchenbau des 18 Jahrhunderts, 1930; co-author: Frankfurter Chanukkahleuchter in Silber und Zinn, 1936; contbr to profsl jours; Dict of the Arts; Ency Judaica. Home: 532 Laverock Rd, Glenside, Pa. Office: Temple U, Beech and Penrose Aves, Philadelphia, Pa.

GUNSBERGER, Fritz, Yugo, physician; b. Tuzla, Aug 27, 1903; s. Max and Ida (Flesch); MD, U of Padua, It; MD, U of Zagreb, 1928; dipl, internal med and radiology, Zurich and Vienna; m. Magda Fischgrund, July 7, 1935. Ret, 1970, as head dept of radiology, Med Cen, Sarajevo; fmr: head, inst radiology, clinic, Fac of Med, Sarajevo since 1947; lectr, radiology; phys, State Hosp, Belgrade, 1928-41; fmr, head, dept radiology, Nis and Banja Luka. War prisoner, WW II. Mem, Assn of Phys, Bosnia and Herzegovina. Author: Textbook on Diagnostic Radiology, 1953; contbr to profsl mags. Offiice: Jug, Nar Amije No 37, Sarajevo, Yugo.

GUNZBERG, Arthur, US, business exec; b. Buffalo, NY, Dec 24, 1911; s. Benjamin and Jeannette (Wile); BS, U of Pa, 1934; m. Aline DuBin, June 3, 1936; c: Guy, Lynn. Pres, M Wile & Co; dir, Hart, Schaffner, and Marx, 1969; Trustee, Clothing Mfgs Assn; chmn: ind sect, Comty Chest, 1948; spec gifts div, United Negro Coll Fund, 1951; gen chmn, UJA, 1950; mem bd, United J Fed, 1948-54, all Buffalo; club: Westwood Co, pres, 1948. Home: 71 The Common, Williamsville, NY. Office: 77 Goodwell St, Buffalo, NY.

GUNZBURG, Nico, Belgium, attorney, educator; b. Riga, Latvia, Sep 2, 1882; s. Sylvain and Amelia (Zeitlin); LLD, U Brussels, 1906; c: Jose; m. 2nd Martha Krainer, Sep 2, 1963. Atty, Antwerp Bar, since 1906; prof em, law, dean fac, secy of U, Ghent U; prof: Antwerp Sem, 1912-52; Syracuse U, 1942-44; U of Djakarta, 1953-56; legal adv, Govt of Brazil, 1940-41; found, pres, Inst of Criminology, Ghent, 1939-52. Served WW I; UNRRA off, 1944-45. Found, pres, Cen de Bienfaisance Juive, Antwerp, since 1921, hon pres since 1953; fmr: pres, Pedg Inst, Ghent; pres: Council of J Assns of Belgium; Belgium sect, Comité Tombeau Martyr Juif, Paris; mem: Assn Flemish Authors; PEN club. Author: L'Enfance en Justice, 1907; You Must Not Judge, 1913; History of Law in Flanders, 1914; Protection of Women and Children, 1933; Against Terrorism, 1935; Endocrinology and Criminology, 1935; Les transformations du droit penal, 1938; La Trajectoire du Crime, 1941; Le Code Pénal du Brésil, 1941; A Democracy in Action, 1945, 1954; Matrimonial Contract, 1925, 3rd ed, 1947; lit works: Van ziel en zenuw, 1902; Jong Vlaanderen, 1906; Het boek Ruth, 1962. Recipient: chevalier, officier, cdr and grand officier, Ordre Couronne de Belgique; chevalier, officier, Ordre Léopold; King Albert Medal; Cdr, Crown of Rum; Officier d'Instrn Publique. Home: 27 Generaal Lemanstraat, Antwerp, Belgium.

GURALNIK, David B, US, lexicographer; b. Cleveland, O, June 17, 1920; s. Julius and Rose (Chanes); BA, W Reserve U, 1941, MA, 1947; m. Shirley Nashkin, June 14, 1942; c: Eve. Vice-pres, The World Publ Co, since 1964, mem, ed staff, since 1941; gen ed, Webster's New World Dict: coll ed, 1953, concise ed, 1956; elem ed, 1961. US Army, 1943-45. Trustee: YIVO Inst for J Research, since 1967; J Comty Cen, since 1960; mem: Natl Council Tchrs of Eng; Names Soc; ACLU, Council on Hum Relations. Author: The Making of a New Dictionary, 1954; contbr to profsl jours. Recipient: Bronze Star Medal, 1945; award, Ohioana Library Assn, 1954. Hobbies: music, little theatre. Home: 3189 Scarborough Rd, Cleveland Hgts, O. Office: 2231 W 110 St, Cleveland, O.

GURDUS, Luba, US, artist; b. Bialystock, Pol, Aug 1, 1914; d. Tewja and Anna (Bryskier); in US since 1948; att: Art Sch, Switz, 1930-31; Kunstakademie and Reimann Sch, Ger, 1931-33; Acad of Arts, Warsaw, 1936-39; Inst of Fine Arts, NYU, 1949; MA, 1952, PhD, 1962; m. Jacob Gurdus, Sep 17, 1936. Head: Frick Art Reference Libr, NY, since 1968; fmr: art designer, Reimann Sch, Berlin; art ed: Bluszuz Pub House; L'Isha mag, Tel Aviv, also NY corresp, head of research, French and Co, Inc. Prin works: They Didn't Live to See, portfolio of ghetto and concentration camp drawings, 1949; illus articles for: Haaretz, Tel Aviv, 1947; The Story of Jewish DP, 1948; The Congress Weekly, 1953; London Connoisseur; Needle and Bobbin, NY; Martyrs and Fighters, 1954; exhbs: WJC; one-man shows: J Mus; Bezalel Mus, Jerusalem; Enzio Sereni House; Givat Brenner; Katz Gal, Tel Aviv; ACA Gal, Barbizon Plaza Gal; Stephen Wise House; repr in collections: Isr consulate; J Mus; UN Isr delg; all NYC; Howard U, Wash, DC; Tel Aviv Munic; Yad VeShem, Jerusalem. Mem: NYU Alumni Assn; Students Club; Inst of Fine Arts, NYU. Home: 180 W 58 St, New York, NY.

GUREASKO, Esther, US, teacher, communal worker; b. NYC, Oct 8, 1907; d. Abraham and Sarah (Kroch) Freden; grad, Jamaica Tchrs Training Sch, 1928; m Edward Gureasko, July, 1930; c: Linda, Stephan. Tchr, NYC elem schs, since 1929. Natl vice-pres, exec comm, AJCong, since 1953, AJCong delg, White House Conf, Intl Coop, 1965; fmr: natl chmn, UJA, women's div, 1953-56; mem: exec bd: Council of J Orgs for Isr Bonds, 1952-55; Bklyn JCC, div natl UN chmn, repr US mission to UN, 1963-68; AJCong delg to UN Commn on Hum Rights, 1962. Home: 1297 Old Nassau Rd, Rossmoor, Jamesburg, NJ.

GUREL, Arie Shlomo, Isr, government official; b. Warsaw, Pol, Nov 20, 1918; s. Moshe and Cyla (Rosen) Groskopf; in Isr since 1935; MIEE, chartered elec engr, Inst Elec Engr, London; m. Miriam Lukatz, 1949; c: Noa, Orith, Rivka Iris. Dir gen, Min of Lab, since 1968; engr, Haifa radio, PTTR, 1950-68, div engr, Haifa and N, 1959-68. Served Haganah, off, War of Independence. Mem: exec comm, Histadrut, trade union dept, 1965-68; secretariat; Lab Party; Civil Servants in Isr, 1949-68; cen comm, Rngrs Fed, 1965-68. Home: 16 Hahashmonaim St, Haifa, Isr. Office: Hakirya, Haifa, Isr.

GUREN, Myron, US, business exec; b Cleveland, O, Feb 29, 1896; s Samuel and Bessie (Cunisa); AB, Harvard U, 1917, AM, 1917; m. Adeline Mendelsohn, June 15, 1924; c: David, Elinor Polster. Pres: Union Oil Co of O, since 1956; Parker Refining Co, since 1945; treas, Universal Oil Inc, since 1953. Pres: Cleveland Bur J Educ, 1964-65; Cleveland Comm for Isr Bonds, 1963-64; USO, since 1961; J Comty Cens, 1957-61; Park Syn, 1954-57; J Young Adult Bur; bd dirs: social agcy comm, J Comty Fed; Bur J Educ; Council Educ Alliance, natl JWB; chmn: Cleveland J Chaplaincy Service; Natl Recovery Admn Commn; Petroleum Adv Comm; mem: O Petroleum Marketers Assn; Phi Beta Kappa; club: Cleveland Petroleum. Home: 13700 Shaker Blvd, Cleveland, O. Office: 265 Jefferson Ave, Cleveland, O.

GUREWICH, Vladmir, US, physician; b. Bern, Switz, Sep 24, 1901; s. Aron and Maria (Markowitz); in US since 1940; MD, U of Heidelberg, 1927; m. Marie Révész, Jan 10, 1928; c: Victor, Anne Gordon. Asso visiting phys: Bellevue Hosp, NY, since 1941; Metrop Hosp since 1941; internal med, asst in med, neur, U Hosp, Berlin, 1928-35; specialist, internal med, London, Eng, 1935-40; guest lectr, Postgrad, Inst of Psychotherapy, London, 1936. LRFPS, Edinburgh, 1948; mem: Amer Psychosomatic Soc; Amer Geriatrics Assn; AMA. Spec interest: hist of art and sci. Home: 333 Central Park W, New York, NY. Office: 55 Central Park W, New York, NY.

GUREWITSCH, Anatol, Isr, artist; b. Moscow, Russ, Mar 26, 1916; s. Alexander and Rachel (Blimowitsch); in Isr since 1934; grad, Reiman Acad, Berlin, 1934; att Miro Sima Art Sch, Jerusalem, 1939; m. Rifka Yarhi, Jan 17, 1961; c: Michael, Eyal. Commercial artist, painter, since 1936; owner, commercial studio, since 1957; fmr: stage designer, Theatron Ivri; stage and costume designer: Gertrud Kraus Ballet; Ohel Theatre; Habima Theatre. Cpl, Royal Engrs, 1940-41; sgt, IDF, 1948-49. One-man shows: Sauer Gal, Tel Aviv, 1939; Gal del Arte Moderne Pierre, Siena, It, 1945; Artist House, Tel Aviv, Jerusalem, 1956, 58; group shows: Tel Aviv Mus, 1954, 55, 56, 58, 60, 62, 65; repr in pvt collections: Yonathan Blumenthal, Isr; Alexander Margulis, London; pub, Help, linoleum cuts, 1938. Recipient: 1st, 2nd prizes for pen drawings, oil painting, British Army Artists Exhb, It, 1944; 1st prize, costume design, Va'ad Hapoel Competition, Tel Aviv, 1952. Home: 9 Mazeh St, Tel Aviv, Isr. Office: 20 Bloch St, Tel Aviv, Isr.

GURFEIN, Murray I, US, attorney; b. NYC, Nov 17, 1907; s. Louis and Rose (Feld); AB, Columbia Coll, 1926; LLB, magna cum laude, Harvard Law Sch, 1930; m. Eva Hadas, Aug 16, 1931; c: Abigail Hellwarth, Susan Rosett. Partner, Goldstein, Gurfein, Shames and Hyde, and predecessor law firms, since 1946; fmr: law secy, US Circuit Judge, Julian W Mack; asst US Atty, S Dist, NY; pvt practice, NY; chief asst to Hon Thomas E Dewey, inves of organized crime; asst Dist Atty, NY Co; asst to Robert E Jackson, US Chief Counsel, Nuremberg Trials; adv, intl law, JA, UN Hearings on Partition. Lt-col, chief of intelligence, psych warfare div, Supr Hqr, Allied Expeditionary Force, WW II. Pres: United HIAS Service; Intl Council J Social Service Orgs; mem: admn comm, AJComm; bd dirs, UJA of Gtr NY; trustee, Citizen's Budget Comm; f, Amer Coll Trial Lawyers; mem: NY Co Lawyers Assn; Amer Bar Assn; NY State Bar Assn; Assn of Bar, NYC; Council on Fgn Relations; Phi Beta Kappa; clubs: Columbia U; Harmonie; Lawyers; fmr mem, NY State Temp Comm on Courts. Recipient: Legion of Merit; Hon Off, OBE; Croix de Guerre, Fr. Home: 530 Park Ave, New York, NY. Office: 655 Madison Ave, New York, NY.

GURFEIN-UCHMANI, Riwka, Isr, teacher, author; b. Sanik, Pol, 1908; d. Itzhak and Faidja (Steinmetz); in Isr since 1932; tchr, Cracow U; m. Azriel Uchmani; c: Rachel Hillel. Mem, Kibbutz Ein Shemer; HS tchr. Author: Yadi Yotze la'Avoda, 1943; Ma she'Kara be'Tzel ha'Alon, 1951; Smadzia beEretz ha'Pla'ot; Kohavim me'Al la'Gan, 1963; mi'Karov ume'-Rahok, 1964; Hevenu Boker Tov, 1964; Im Shir, 1967; le'Or Panasim Dolkim, 1968; bi'Kri'a Keshuva, 1969; ed bd, Dvar haPo'elet. Recipient: Yosef Aharonovitz lit award, 1963; Ussishkin award, 1965. Home: Kibbutz Ein Shemer, Isr.

GURIN, Maurice G, US, fund-raising counsel; b. Phila, Pa, July 12, 1911; s. Adolph and Rena (Gilberg); BA, U of Pittsburgh, 1933. Partner, Bowen, Gurin, Barnes, Roche & Carlson Inc, fund-raising counsel, since 1959; vice-pres, Leonard Finder and Assos, 1946-49; pres, Maurice G Gurin Assos, PR, 1949-59. Lt-Col, USAF, WW II. Natl pres, Phi Epsilon Pi, 1947, secy, 1939-40. Recipient: Bronze Star, WW II. Home: 300 E 51 St, New York, NY. Office: 801 Second Ave, New York, NY.

GURNY, Max, Switz, jurist, legislator; b. Zurich, July 17, 1899; s. Jacob and Hannah (Gelassen); DJ, U of Zurich, 1922; m. Sylette Kleiner, Oct 18, 1925; c: Peter, Liselotte. Judge, Supr Court, Canton Zurich, 1944-67, vice-pres, pres; MP, Canton Zurich, 1935-53, pres financial comm, 1947-51. Pres, cen comm, Swiss J Comty Union, 1950-55; vice-pres, Swiss-Isr Assn, since 1957; mem exec comm, ORT Union. Contbr to legal, political jours. Home: 43 Morgentalstr, Zurich, Switz. Office: 13-15 Hirschengrabben, Zurich, Switz.

GUROCK, Noah David, US, journalist; b. Bx, NY, Sep 30, 1946; s. Jack and Leah (Lerner); att Cooper Union, NYC, 1964-66; BA, CUNY, 1969; m. Peggy Schloss, June 29, 1969; Ed, Young Isr Viewpoint, since 1967; copy ed, Hartford Times, since 1969. Mem: Blue Hills Civic Assn, Hartford, Conn; Sigma Kappa Tau. Hobby: radio bc. Home: 46 Hebron St, Hartford, Conn. Office: 3 W 16 St, New York, NY.

GURON, Moshe, Isr, diplomat; b. Brno, Czech, Aug 2, 1916; s. David and Rachel (Antmann) Unger; att Heb U; Isr Defence Coll, Jerusalem; m. Rachel Schreiber; c: Yair, Ruth, David. Consul gen, Isr Consulate Gen, Switz, Liechtenstein, since 1968; mem: Kibbutz Ga'aton, later Ne'ot Mordechai,

1940-55; 1st Isr Legation, Prague, 1947-49; commercial dir, Chevrat Hashilumim, 1954-56; commercial secy, Isr Emb, Rio de Janeiro, 1956-60; counsellor, Isr Legation, Belgrade, 1960-64; asst dir, Min for Fgn Affairs, Jerusalem: Latin Amer Dept, 1966-67; Dept for Intl Coop, 1967-68. Office: Min for Fgn Affairs, Jerusalem, Isr; Isr Consulate Gen, Stampfenbachstr 3, Zurich, Switz.

GURVITZ, Abraham, US, dentist; b. Pol, Aug 10, 1901; s. Joseph and Lena (Maybush); in US since 1902; DMD, Tufts U, Sch of Dent, 1922; m. Ethel Fink, Jan 10, 1904; c: Nancy, Joan. Pvt practice dentistry. Lay chaplain, JWB; pres, Boston Alumni Alpha Omega; chmn, service comm: WW II, Korean War; secy, Class of '22, Tufts Dent Sch; mem: Masons, Shamut Lodge. Home: 38 Kenmore, Newton, Mass. Office: 120 Boylston, Boston, Mass.

GURWITSCH, Aron, US, educator; b. Vilna, Russ, Jan 17, 1901; s. Meyer and Eva (Bloch); in US since 1940; att U of Berlin, 1919-21; U of Frankfort/M, 1921-28; PhD, U Goettingen, Ger, 1928; m. Alice Stern, Apr, 1929. Dist service prof of phil, grad fac, political and social sci, New Sch for Social Research, since 1971; on fac since 1959; asst to Prof Mortiz Geiger, U of Goettingen, 1928-29; research f, Prussian min of sci, arts and public instrn, Berlin, 1929-33; lectr, Sorbonne, Paris, 1933-40; research f, Caisse Nationale de la Recherche Scientifique, Paris, 1939-40; visiting lectr, Johns Hopkins U, 1940-42; instr, Harvard U, 1943-46; lectr, Wheaton Coll, 1947-48; asst prof, math, Brandeis U, 1948-51, asst prof, phil, 1951-58; Fulbright prof, U of Cologne, 1958-59. Mem: council, Intl Phenomenological Soc, since 1940; ZOA; AAUP; Amer Phil Assn; Hist of Sci Soc; Metaphys Soc of Amer. Author: Théorie du Champ de la Conscience, 1957; The Field of Consciousness, 1964; Studies in Phenomenology and Psychology, 1966; mem, ed bd, Philosophy and Phenomenological Research, since 1940; contbr to Ger, Fr, Eng sci publs. Home: 820 W End Ave, New York, NY. Office: New Sch for Social Research, 65 Fifth Ave, New York, NY.

GUSS, Benjamin R, Can, QC, attorney; b. Dorbian, Lith, July 15, 1905; s. Morris and Celia (Hahns); BA, Dalhousie U, 1928; LLB, 1930; m. Mildred Bassen, Dec 2, 1938; c: Keren, Judith, Faith, Jonathan. Master of Supr Court of NB; pvt practice since 1933; fmr: mem, Baxter, Lewin and Carter; read law with hon JBM Baxter, fmr Chief Justice of NB; chmn, Jr Bar of Can. Secy: Citizens Plebiscite Comm; Citizens Comm on Vet Rehab; Ezra lodge, Zionist Order of Habonim; natl chmn, munic law sect, Can Bar Assn; trustee, mem exec f, Can Found for Legal Research; pres: St John Law Soc; Fed of Can Music Festivals; Comty Concerts Assn; natl chmn, legal aid, Can Bar Assn; co-found, chmn, St John chap, Can Friends of Heb U; vice-pres: NB Sym Orch Assn; TB Assn; mem: provincial exec, Progressive Conservative Assn; Provincial Youth Commn, Citizen's War Services Comm; council, ZOC; council Can Bar Assn; Masons; Rotary, vice-pres, pres, gov for NB, NS, NF and part of Me, counselor, mem of 8 mem prog planning comms, world dir, Intl; fmr: natl chmn: Young Conservatives; radio and publicity, Conservative Assn, City and Co of St John. Home: 70 Orange St, St John, NB, Can. Office: 50 Princess St, St John, NB, Can.

GUSSOW, Don, US, editor, publisher; b. Lith, Dec 7, 1907; s. Samuel and Anna (Lurie); in US since 1920; att Maxwell Training Sch for Tchrs, Bklyn, 1926-27; NYU, 1930-32; tchr training dipl, U of Vt, 1929; m. Betty Gussow, Oct 19, 1929; c: Alan, Melvyn, Paul. Pres, treas, found: Don Gussow Pubs Inc, since 1944; Mags for Ind, since 1959; dir, Cowles Communications, since 1966; pres, Cowles Bus and Profsl Mags, since 1966; ed, pub: Candy Ind, since 1944; Soft Drink Ind, since 1946; ed-in-chief, Inside Ind, since 1964; fmr: ed: Butcher's Advocate; Confectionary Ice Cream World; Intl Confectioner. Found, Amer Assn Candy Techs, 1947; sponsor, Kettle Award, 1946; mem: Soc Bus Mag Eds; Natl Conf Bus Paper Eds; bd dirs, Amer Bus Press; trustee, Packaging Found. Author: Fifty Years of Candy Progress, 1950; A 75 Year History of the Candy Business, 1958; contbr to Ency Britannica. Home: 50 Sutton Pl S, New York, NY. Office: 777 Third Ave, New York, NY.

GUTENBERG, Arthur W, US, educator, management cons; b. Darmstadt, Ger, Nov 10, 1920; s. Beno and Hertha (Dernburg); in US since 1930; B Applied Sci, U of Cal, 1944, BS, 1947; PhD, Stanford U, 1955; m. Natalie Shapiro, Feb 9, 1947; c: Arlan, Jeffrey, Lee, Susan, Dianne. Asso prof, mgmt, U of S Cal, Grad Sch of Bus Admn, since 1960, dir of publ,

Bur of Econ and Bus Research, 1969-70, dir, Pakistan Project, 1960-66; owner, mgmt cons firm, since 1954; fmr: head, econ research sect, Pan-Amer Airways, 1947-48; instr, bus, Fresno State Coll, 1948-51; dir, Bur of Bus Services, Ariz State U, 1951-57, asst prof, mgmt, 1957-60. Mem: Amer Stat Assn; Amer Econ Assn; AAUP. Author: Profitable Studio Management, 1962; Dynamics of Management, 1968; contbr to profsl jours. Home: 1428 Santa Margarita Dr, Arcadia, Cal. Office: University Park, Los Angeles, Cal.

GUTERMAN, Abraham S, US, attorney; b. Scranton, Pa, Aug 10, 1912; s. Henry and Lena (Hurwitz); BA, Yeshiva U, NY, 1933; LLB, Harvard Law Sch, 1936; m. Irene Eisenberg, Dec 24, 1933; c: Florence. Sr partner, law firm, Hess, Segall, Guteman, Pelz & Steiner; legal secy, Chief Justice George W, Maxey, Supr Court of Pa. Pres: Weschester J Cen, Mamaroneck, NY; Hillcrest Zionist Dist, Jamaica, NY; vice-pres, Hillcrest J Cen, Jamaica; fmr: chmn: Alumni Council, Yeshiva U; UJA; FJP; ADL; B'nai B'rith; mem: Assn of Bar, NYC; Amer Bar Assn; NY Co Lawyers Assn, comm on taxation; fmr: Practising Law Inst; NYU Inst on Fed Taxation; Egypt Exploration Soc, London, Eng; Archaeol Inst Amer. Spec interest: Egyptology. Home: 742 Cove Road, Mamaroneck, NY. Office: 230 Park Ave, New York, NY.

GUTERMAN, Simeon L, US, educator; b. NYC, Dec 25, 1907; s. Henry and Lena (Hurwitz); BA, Harvard Coll, 1930; MA, Harvard U, 1932; PhD, 1944; att U of Paris, 1933-34; m. Bette Adler, Sep, 1952. Prof, hist, Grad Sch of Humanities and Social Sci, Yeshiva U, since 1959, dean of coll, prof hist, Yeshiva Coll, 1953-59; prof hist, political sci, O Northern U, 1945-46; hist, Pa State Tchrs Coll, 1946-53. Bd dirs, Riverdale J Cen, 1953-60; mem: Amer Hist Assn; Medieval Acad Amer. Author: Religious Toleration and Persecution in Ancient Rome, 1951. Home: 511 W 232 St, New York, NY. Office: Yeshiva U, 55 Fifth Ave, New York, NY.

GUTH, Hans, Switz, statistician, banker, educator; b. Zurich, Apr 18, 1913; s. Lucien and Clementine (Ortlieb); D publ, U of Zurich, 1944; m. Katia Dreyfus, Feb 19, 1951; c: Mathys, Andreas, Nadia. Pres, Dreyfus Sohne & Co, since 1967, on staff since 1956; prof, stat, U of Basle, since 1957, docent, 1956; fmr: asst, adjoint dir, Stat Off, Kanton Zurich, 1945-51; dir, Stat Off, Kanton Basle, 1951-62. Swiss Army. Pres, mem, various communal orgs. Home: 23 Malzgasse, Basle, Switz. Office: 14/16 Aeschenvorstadt, Basle, Switz.

GUTMAN, Alexander B, US, physician, educator; b. NYC, June 7, 1902; s. Jacob and Rebecca (Dogin); MA, Cornell U, 1924, PhD, 1926; MD, U of Vienna, 1928; m. Daisy Rieger, Apr 25, 1949. Prof med, Mt Sinai Sch Med, since 1968; cons phys, dir em, Mt Sinai Hosp, since 1968, on staff since 1951; fmr: teaching and research, dept med, Columbia Presbyterian Med Cen, NYC, 1929-47; prof, med, Columbia U, 1949-67; dir, Columbia Research Service, Goldwater Memorial Hosp, NYC, 1947-50; cons, USPHS, 1947-49; spec cons, NIH, 1953-57, adv council 1964-68. Maj, US Army, MC, 1941-42. F, Amer Coll Phys; NY Acad Med, pres, med sect, 1950; mem: bd govs, Arthritis and Rheumatism Found, since 1954; NY Rheumatism Assn, fmr pres, 1956-57; AMA; AAAS; NY State and Co Med Socs; Amer Soc Clinical Inves; Assn Amer Phys; Soc Experimental Biol and Med; Amer Soc Biol Chems; Sigma Xi; Alpha Omega Alpha. Found, Amer Jour Med, ed-in-chief since 1946; asso ed, Cecil and Loeb's Textbook of Med, 1950-60; contbr to sci jour. Recipient: cert, USAAF, 1946; Francis Amory award, Amer Acad Arts and Scis, 1948; dist service award in med journalism, 1954; Gairdner Found intl award, 1960; Valentine award, 1967; Columbia U Bicentennial Medallion, 1967; Holbrook Memorial Lectureship award, Arthritis and Rheumatism Found, 1964. Home: 535 E 86 St, New York, NY. Office: Mt Sinai Hosp, New York, NY.

GUTMAN, Daniel, US, attorney, educational admnr; b. NYC, July 1, 1901; s. Wolf and Theresa (Brody); LLB, cum laude, Bklyn Law Sch, 1922; LLD, Siena Coll, 1956; m. Rosamond Lease, Dec, 1954. Dean: NY Acad of the Judiciary, since 1968; NY Law Sch, since 1959; fmr: asst US Atty, E dist, NY State; spec asst to US Atty Gen; asst Dist Atty, Kings Co, NY; NY State Assemblyman; NY State Senator; justice, Munic Court, NYC; counsel to Gov of NY. Hearing referee, NYC Transit Auth, since 1959; mem: lab panel: Amer Arbitration Assn; NJ State Mediation Bd; Amer Judicature Soc; Assn of Bar, NYC; NY Co Lawyers Assn; Amer Acad Political Sci; past pres: Fed Bar Assn, NY, NJ, Conn; NE states region, Amer Soc Legal Hist. Recipient: Knight, Order of Merit, Rep of It; Order Elroy Alfaro, Rep of Panama. Homes: 1 Fifth Ave, New York, NY; Canton Cen, Conn. Office: 33 Washington Sq W, New York, NY.

GUTMAN, David, Isr, educator; b. Mlinov, Pol, June 17, 1925; 1925; s. Gregoir and Luba (Szerzon); in Isr since 1948; DDS, Ecole de Chirurgie Dentaire et de Stomatologie, Paris, 1948; postgrad studies: NYU, 1953-54; Pittsburgh U Med Cen, 1955-57; m. Rita Dworman, Dec, 1959; c: Michael, Daniel. Head, dept oral and maxillo facial surg, Rambam Govt Hosp, since 1958, sr clinical lectr, since 1967; chef de clinique, Ecole de Chirgurie Dentaire et Stomatologie, Paris, 1950. Lt, IDF, 1948-50. Found, Isr Pres, Isr Soc and Oral Maxillo-Facial Surg; mem: council, Intl Assn Oral Surgs; Intl Coll Dents; Alpha Omega; IMA; Isr Dent Assn. Ed, Isr Jour of Dental Med; contbr to profsl publs. Recipient: medal, J Freedom Fighters. Home and office: 8 Panorama Rd, Haifa, Isr.

GUTMAN, Israel, Isr, author; b. Warsaw, Pol, May 20, 1923; s. Benjamin and Sara; in Isr since 1948; att Heb U, Jerusalem; m. Irith Edelstein, 1951; c: Nimrod, Dita, Tamar. Dir Moreshet Anilevitch Memorial Inst. Active in Warsaw Ghetto uprising, mem J Fighting Org; mem, resistance movement, Auschwitz Concentration Camp. Author: Anashim Va'Efer, 1956; Mered Ha'Netzurim, 1963. Recipient: Avraham Shlonsky Prize for Lit. Home: Kibbutz Lehavoth Habashan, Isr. Office: 7 Ibn Gvirol St, Tel Aviv, Isr.

GUTMAN, Yehuda Abraham, Isr, physician; b. Radom, Pol, Dec 7, 1930; s. Chaim and Ziva (Ehrlich) Tovi; in Isr since 1931; att U of Lausanne, 1950-52; MD, Heb U, 1958; m. Alisa Bachrach, Nov 29, 1956; c: Tamar. Asso prof, pharm, Heb U, since 1968; house phys: Hadassah U Hosp, 1959-60; Cen Negev Hosp, 1960. Lt, IDF, 1948-50. Chmn, pharm comm, Natl Bd for Research and Devl; secy, Isr Soc Phys and Pharm, 1966-68; mem: IMA; Isr Soc EEG and Neurophys. Contbr to profsl jours. Recipient: Lachmann Award for Nystamus Research, 1968. Spec interests: hist, phil. Home: 12/20 Ramat Dania, Jerusalem, Isr. Office: Dept of Pharm, Med Sch, Heb U, Jerusalem, Isr.

GUTMANN, James, US, educator; b. NYC, Apr 11, 1897; s. Carl and Lilly (Liebmann); MA, Columbia U, 1919, PhD, 1936; m. Jeanette Mack, Feb 3, 1920; c: Barbara, Carl, Alice. Prof em, phil, Columbia U, since 1962, prof, 1946-62, fac mem, 1920-62; asso leader, Soc for Ethical Culture, 1928-30. Bd dirs: Encampment for Citizenship; Conf on Method in Phil and the Scis; mem: E-W Phil Conf, Hawaii; Amer Phil Assn; Phi Beta Kappa. Author: Schelling: Of Human Freedom, 1936; The Philosophy of E Cassirer, 1949; Spinoza's Ethics, 1950; Personal Integrity, 1961; Horizons of a Philosopher, 1962; co-author: Introduction to Reflective Thinking, 1923; Aspects to Ethical Religion, 1926; ed: Philosophy From A to Z, 1963; Marcus Aurelius Meditations, 1964. Home: 39 Claremont Ave, New York, NY.

GUTMANN, Joseph, US, educator, rabbi; b. Ger, Aug 17, 1923; s. Henry and Selma (Eisemann); in US since 1936; BS, Temple U, Phila, Pa, 1949; MA, NYU, 1952; ordained rabbi, PhD, HUC, 1960; m. Marilyn Tuckman, Oct 7, 1953; c: David, Sharon. Prof, art hist, Wayne State U, since 1969; fmr: Charles Friedman lectr, phil, rel, Antioch Coll, 1964; research, medieval illuminated Heb manuscripts, Amer Phil Soc Grant to Eur, 1965; assoc prof, J Art Hist, HUC-JIR, Cincinnati, 1960-69; adj prof, art, U Cincinnati, 1961-69. Interrogator, research analyst, US Strategic Bombing Survey, Eur, 1943-46. Participant: World Cong J Studies, Jerusalem, 1965; Intl Cong Rel Architecture, Visual Arts, 1967; mem: CCAR; Beta Gamma Sigma Hon Soc; Coll Art Assn of Amer; AAUP. Author: Judische Zeremonialkunst, 1963; Jewish Ceremonial Art, 1964; Images of the Jewish Past, An Introduction to Medieval Hebrew Miniatures, 1965; The Darmstadt Passover Haggadah; Make No Graven Images; Studies in Art and the Hebrew Bible; contbr to rel and educ jours, art encys. Recipient: Henry Morgenthau Traveling f, HUC, 1957, 1958; traveling f, Amer Phil Soc, 1965. Home: 14615 Ludlow, Oak Park, Mich. Office: Dept of Art History, Wayne State U, Detroit, Mich.

GUTMANN, Max, US, business exec; b. Neiderwerrn, Ger, July 12, 1922; s. Selli and Ida (Zeilberger); in US since 1940; att Commercial Sch, Ger, 1936-38; m. Dorothy Ginsburg, Apr 30, 1945; c: Sharon, Suzanne, Jay. Exec vice-pres, The Elder Beeman Co, Dayton, O, since 1961, bd dirs; vice pres:

Bee Gee Shoe Corp; Everybody's Office Outfitters; exec, Bus Furniture, Inc; bd mem, El Bee Realty & Inves Corp; El Bee Charge Co; mgr, Dan Cohen Shoe Co, 1940-53. Sgt, Mil Intelligence Service, 1943-46. Mem: bd dirs, Beth Abraham Syn; adv bd, Sinclair Coll. Hobbies: bridge, golf. Home: 3100 Marlay Rd, Dayton, O. Office: 153 E Helena, Dayton, O.

GUTNICK, Chaim H J, Austr, rabbi; b. Russ, Sep 21, 1921; s. Mordechai and Chaya (Braverman); in Austr since 1941; ordained rabbi, Yeshivah Telz, Lith; m. Rose Chester, Jan 28, 1945; six c. Chief min, Elwood Syn, since 1957; dean, rabb coll, Australia; rabbi, Mizrachi Syn, Sydney, 1946-57. Chaplain, Australian Forces. Pres, Rabb Council of Victoria; fmr pres, JNF; vice-pres, UIA; bd govs, Mt Scopus Coll; mem: B'nai B'rith; Masons. Home: 24 Milton St, Elwood, Melbourne, Austr. Study: 39 Dickens St, Elwood, Melbourne, Austr.

GUTTELMAN, Adeline S, US, orthodontist, educator; b. NYC, Sep 21, 1917; d. Morris and Vera (Pockrose); AB, NYU, 1937, DDS, Coll of Dent, 1941; cert in orthodontics, 1945; m. Irwin Gertz, Aug 21, 1937; c: Richard, James. Pvt practice since 1945; asst prof, orthodontics, NYU, Coll of Dentistry, since 1958, lectr, orthodontics, post-grad, 1969; att chief orthodontist, NY Polyclinic Med Sch and Hosp; Guggenheim f, 1941-42. Dipl, Amer Bd Orthodontics; mem: Acad Dent Med; Amer Med Writers Assn; NY Acad Sci; Soc for Children's Dent; Northeastern Orthodontic Assn; Amer Dent Assn; Women's Dent Assn; Assn U Women; Sci Research Soc of Amer; Fac Women of NYU; Research Assn of Amer; fmr pres, NYU Orthodontic Soc. Contbr to dent jours. Hobbies: theatre, music, hand crafts. Home: 2 Washington Square, Village, New York, NY. Office: 11 Fifth Ave, New York, NY.

GUTTMACHER, Alan F, US, obstetrician, educator; b. Baltimore, Md, May 19, 1898; s. Adolf and Laura (Oppenheimer); BA, Johns Hopkins U, 1919, MD, 1923; m. Leonore Gidding, July 22, 1925; c: Ann, Sally, Susan. Pres, Planned Parenthood Fed of Amer, since 1962; clinical visiting prof, Einstein Med Sch, since 1961; prof em, Mt Sinai Sch of Med; instr, asso prof, Johns Hopkins Med Sch, 1928-52; chief, obstet dept, Sinai Hosp, Baltimore, 1943-52; lectr, maternal and child health, Harvard Sch of Public Health; clinical prof, Columbia U, 1962-66. F, NY Acad Med; mem: Amer Acad Obstet; Amer Soc Study of Sterility; Amer Fertility Soc; AMA; Amer Assn Anats. Author: Life in the Making, 1933; Into This Universe, 1937; Babies By Choice or By Chance, 1961. Recipient: Lasker Award, 1947. Home: 1185 Park Ave, New York, NY. Office: 515 Madison Ave, New York, NY.

GUTTMAN, Louis, Isr, social sci; b. Bklyn, NY, Feb 10, 1916; s. Solomon and Udell (Bloch); in Isr since 1947; MA, U of Minnesota, 1939, PhD, 1942; m. Ruth Halpern, Oct 21, 1943; c: Adi, Nurit, Daphna. Prof, social and psych measurement, Heb U, since 1955; sci dir, Isr Inst of Applied Social Research, since 1947; asso prof, Cornell U; visiting prof, Harvard U; f, Cen for Advanced Study in Behavioral Scis, Ford Found; dist visiting prof, Mich State U; cons to US Secy of War, WW II; devl of Guttman Scale. Maj, IDF. Chmn, PM's Commn on Job Evaluation; mem: Public Commn on Salaries; natl exec, AACI; Amer Sociol Assn; Psychometric Soc; Amer Stat Assn; World Assn of Public Opinion Research; Isr and Amer Psych Assns; Ind Relations Research Assn of Isr; Inst of Differing Civilizations; AAAS. Recipient: Rothschild Prize for Social Sci, 1960. Home: 58 Nayot St, Jerusalem, Isr. Office: Inst for Applied Social Research, POB 7150, Jerusalem, Isr.

GUTTMAN, Nahum (Nathan), US, editor, org exec; b. Guttenberg, NJ, July 29, 1913; s. Solomon and Udel (Bloch) Gittleman; BS, U of Minn, 1934; postgrad studies, New Sch for Social Research, 1946-47; m. Miriam Heller, July 8, 1936; c: Joshua, Naomi. Dir, pr, Natl Comm for Lab, Isr, since 1940; ed, Histadrut Foto News, since 1948; natl secy: Habonim Lab Zionist Youth, 1935; Hechalutz Org of Amer, 1937-40. US Army, 1943-46. Mem: cen comm, LZOA; Poale Zion; past cdr, Enzo Sereni Post, JWV; chmn, Natl Comm for Lab, Isr chap; comty and Social Agcy Employees Union, AFL-CIO. Recipient: Bronze Star; award for script, documentary on Histadrut, 1954. Home: 585 West End Ave, New York, NY. Office: 33 E 67 St, New York, NY.

GUTTMAN, Ruth, Isr, geneticist; b. Vienna, Aus, May 24, 1923; d. Samuel and Jula (Hasten) Halpern; in Isr since 1947; BS, Cornell U, NY, 1945, MA, 1947; PhD, Heb U, Jerusalem, 1952; m. Louis Guttman, Oct 21, 1943; c: Adi Gamon,

Nurit, Daphne. Research asso, Isr Inst of Applied Social Research, since 1960; research f, dept psych, Heb U, since 1962; fmr: research asso: dept genet, U of Cal, Berkeley; Hadassah Med Sch; spec f, human genet, U of Michigan, Ann Arbor. Prin contribs: research in cytogenet, behavioral genet. Secy, Botanical Soc of Isr; mem exec, Isr Assn U Women, mem: Isr, Amer, Genet Socs; Amer Soc Human Genet; Amer Eugenics Soc; Animal Behavior Soc. Contbr to genet jours. Recipient: two research prizes, Heb U. Home: 58 Nayot St, Jerusalem, Isr. Office: Isr Inst Applied Research, 19 Washington St, Jerusalem, Isr.

GUTTMAN, Samuel A, US, psychiatrist; b. NYC, Sep 13, 1914; s. Morris and Ida (Goldberger); AB, Cornell U, 1934, MA, 1935, PhD, 1937, MD, 1940; m. 2nd, Alice Burrier; c by previous m: Elizabeth, Samuel. Pvt practice, psycht, psychan and neur cons since 1945; instr, dept psycht, U of Pa Med Sch, since 1946; training analyst, Phila Assn for Psychan, since 1954; prof, clinical psycht, psychan, Jefferson Med Coll, since 1962; asst neur: Columbia U Coll Phys and Surgs, 1942-44; Presbyterian Hosp, NYC, 1942-44; Pa Hosp, Phila, 1944-46; J Hosp Phila, 1944-47; sr clinical asso, Phila Inst of Psychan, 1944-48; lectr, neur, Phila Sch Occupational Therapy, 1944-45; psycht cons: dept psych, U of Pa, 1945-47; Southwark Neighborhood Cen, Phila, 1946-47; Shoemarker Sch, Elkins Park, 1947-48; Family Service, Wilkes-Barre, 1948-52; Family Service, Scranton and Dunmore, 1948-55; Wilkes Coll, Wilkes-Barre, 1948-55; dir, Child Guidance Cen, Lackawanna Co, 1947-55; sr clinical asso, lectr, Phila Inst of Psychan, 1948-49; chief, psycht div, Wilkes-Barre Gen Hosp, 1948-55. Mem: AMA; NJ State and Mercer Co Med Socs; Amer Psychan Assn, mem various comms; Intl Psychan Assn; Phila Assn for Psychan, past pres, training analyst since 1954; Amer Psycht Assn; Assn Research in Nervous and Mental Disorders; AAAS; NY Acad Sci. Mem, ed bd, Psychan Quarterly, since 1958; cons ed, Bull, Phila Assn for Psychan, since 1959, chief ed, 1950-59; contbr to profsl jours. Home and office: Hunter's Green, Pennington, NJ.

GUTTMANN, Alexander, US, educator; b. Budapest, Hung, Nov 16, 1904; s. Michael and Camilla (Schnurer); in US since 1940; att Budapest U; PhD, Breslau U, 1924; ordained rabbi, Breslau J Theol Sem, Hattarat Hora'ah, 1927; research in Orientalia, Berlin U, 1927-28; m. Manya Kampf, Aug 17, 1937; c: Ariel, Naomi, Esther, Judith. Prof, Talmud and rabb, HUC-JIR, Cinn, since 1940; tchr: Jacob Freimann Yeshivah, Berlin, 1931-32; Talmud, sponsored by Berlin J Cong, 1927-35; lectr, hist and archeol, Jüdisches Lehrhaus, 1931-36; fac mem, Berlin J Tchrs Coll, 1932-36; prof, Lehranstalt für die Wissenschaft des Judentums, Berlin, 1935-40. Author: Das Redaktionelle und Sachliche Verhältnis zwischen Mischna und Tosephta, 1928; Enthüllte Talmudzitate, 1930-31; Dezisionsmotive in Talmud, 1938; Essays on the History of the Halakha, Heb, Eng, and Ger, 1938-68. Home: 960 Lenox Place, Cincinnati, O. Office: HUC, Clifton Ave, Cincinnati, O.

GUTTMANN, Herman Zvi, W Ger, architect; b. Bielitz, Schlesien, Sep 13, 1917; s. Chiel and Esther (Draenger); in W Ger since 1945; att: U Jagiellonski, Crakow, fac phil, 1938-39; Poly, Lwow, fac architecture, 1939-41; dipl ing-architect, Tech HS, Munich, 1948-51; m. Gitta Torenberg, Apr 3, 1953; c: Rosa. Pvt practice since 1953; chief engr, UNRRA-IRO, 1945-48. Prin contribs, J sacral bldgs; planned and completed: Syn and parish cen: Offenbach Main, 1954-55; Düsseldorf, 1958; Hannover, 1963; Osnabrück, 1969; reconstructions: Syn Augsburg and Cemetery Hall; Syn Fürth, Bayern; constructed: Cemetery Hall, Hannover-Bothfeld, 1960; J commemorative in fmr concentration camp, Dachau, 1967; Mikwah München, 1967; Mikwah Hamburg; Parish house and Mikwah, Frankfurt/M; J old people's home, Hamburg, all 1956. Author: descriptions of sacral edifices constructed in: Syns in Eur, NY; Ency of Judaism (Lexikon des Judentums) 1967; Den Opfern der Gewalt, by Adolf Rieth; Stone Mason and Stone Sculptor, Jan, 1969; Leben und Schicksal, Hannover, 1963; and in various jours. Pres, Gemeinderat, J comty, Frankfurt/Main; mem: presidency, Zionistische Organisation Deutschlands; B'nai B'rith, Frankfurt/Main; Bund Deutscher Architekten. Home: Eppsteinerstrasse 45, Frankfurt, W Ger. Office: Bergenstrasse 40-42, Frankfurt, W Ger.

GUTTMANN, Karl, Netherlands, actor, director, producer, theatre-pedagogue; b. Bielitz, Pol, July 30, 1913; s. Leonard Frieda (Parnes); in Netherlands since 1950; studied theatre. Reinhardt Sem, Vienna; m. Luisa Treves, Sep 16, 1949; c: Barbara, Jan-Felix. Head, dramatic dept, Staatliche Hochschule f Musik u Darstellend Kunst, Stuttgart; fmr: actor,

music dir, Chamber Theatre, Tel Aviv; produc: Royal Theatre, The Hague; Rotterdams Toneel, Rotterdam; mgn dir, producer, Ensemble Theatre and TV Co. Principal producs: The Diary of Anne Frank, by Goodrich and Hackett; Requiem for a Nun, by Faulkner; The Tenth Man, by Chayefsky; Two for the Seesaw, by Gibson; O What a Lovely War, by Chilton and Littlewood; The Caretaker, by Pinter; The Price, by Miller; The Case of Robert J Oppenheimer, by Kipphardt; Curtmantle, by Fry; Liebelei, by Schnitzler; The Lonely Way, by Schnitzler; Tiger at the Gates, by Giraudoux; The Trojan Woman, by Euripides; Maria Stuart, by Schiller; Don Carlos, by Schiller; The Merchant of Venice, by Shakespeare; Heartbreak House, by Shaw; As You Like It, by Shakespeare; Pygmalion, by Shaw; Henry IV, by Pirandello; Figaro, by Beaumarchais. Principal parts with Chamber Theatre, Tel Aviv: Insect Play, by Capek; Blood Wedding, by Lorca; Jacobovsky and the Colonel, by Werfel; Antigone, by Anouilh; An Inspector Calls, by Priestley. Home: 40 Schubert St, Amsterdam, Netherlands. Office: Stuttgart, 2 Urbansplatz, W Ger.

GUTWIRTH, Charles, Fr, industrialist; b. Antwerp, Belgium, June 22, 1918; s. Chiel and Rosa Chantal (Kohane); in Fr since 1940; m. Paulette Dreyfus, Oct 17, 1944; seven c. Pres, Representative Council Traditional Judaism, France; vice-pres, UJA, Fr; mem: Consistoire Isr de Paris; B'nai B'rith; Fr sect, JWC. Home: 54 La Bruyere St, Paris, Fr. Office: 9 Buffault St, Paris, Fr.

GUTWIRTH, Samuel William, US, author, educator, dentist; b. Aus, Mar 10, 1903; s. Henry and Regina (Wachsberger); in US since 1910; DDS, Loyola U, Sch Dent, 1925; att Chgo Coll of Dent Surg; m. Sarah Fonstein, Oct 6, 1901. Author, educ, sci of tension control, since 1944; pvt practice, dent, 1925-50. Author: How to Free Yourself from Nervous Tension, 1955; You Can Stop Worrying, 1957; How to Sleep Well, 1959; You Can Learn to Relax, 1961. Mem: Amer Dent Assn; Ill State, Chgo Dent Socs. Recipient: mem, f, Royal Soc of Health, Eng, 1960, 1965. Hobbies: classical music, chess. Home: 6730 S Shore Dr, Chicago, Ill.

GUY, Yehuda, Isr, government official; b. Frauenkirchen, Aus, June 10, 1921; s. Oskar and Katharina (Karlburger) Lowenthal; in Isr since 1939; att Hohere Lehranstalt Fur Maschinenbau; Technishe Hochschule, Vienna; m. Thalia Feldman, June 27, 1943; c: Dorith Moor, Lydia. Head, road safety dept, Min of Transp, since 1967; chmn, Interim Comm for Road Safety, since 1964; fmr: road transp, Min of Transp; col, head, traffic and patrol dept, Isr Police. Capt, Royal Engrs, British Army, 1942-46; IDF. Mem, bd dirs: Technion Road Safety Research Cen; Natl Safety Council; mem, IACP; club, Tel Aviv Country. Author: Road Accidents — Causes and Preventions. Recipient: Afr Star, It Star, War Medal; Fighters for the State; hon citizen of Texas, 1955. Hobbies: polo, tennis, skin diving. Home: 22 Josef Hagili, Ramat Gan, Isr. Office: 9 Helena Hamalka, Jerusalem, Isr.

GUZIK, Leo, US, attorney; b. NYC, July 13, 1904; s. Mendel and Fanny (Stavisky); att NYU, 1924-26; LLB, Fordham U Law Sch, 1926; m. Pearl Robbins, Dec 25, 1930; c: Michael, Tamara. Partner, Guzik and Boukstein; mem, bd govs, Heb U, Jerusalem, since 1959; mem, bd dir, Amer Friends Heb U, Jerusalem, since 1957, vice-pres, 1957-1962; treas, Intl Assn of J Lawyers and Jurists; US legal counsel for Isr corps and orgs; natl exec comm, ZOA, 1944-46, admn comm 1936-44; mem: bd dir, J Natl Fund of Amer, 1941-46; KH, 1942-46; trustee, J Pub Soc of Amer, 1962-68; vice-pres, 1965-68, publs comm; bd dir, J Reconstructionist Found, 1940-1942; exec comm, J Book Council, NY; counsel: Hosiery Wholesalers Natl Assn; Woolen Wholesalers Natl Assn; Woolen Jobbers Assn; Rel Dry Goods Assn; ind rep, War Lab Board Panel, 2nd Region; mem: Assn of the Bar of NYC, chmn, 1940-42; NYC Lawyers Assn; clubs: Bankers, Oriental. Home: 75 Central Park W, New York, NY. Office: 37 Wall St, New York, NY.

GVATI, Chaim, Isr, government official; b. Pinsk, Pol, Jan 29, 1901; s. Shmuel and Esther (Zeitman) Switacz; in Isr since 1924; att Tarbut Inst, Vilna, 1922-24; m. Liuba Laskov, 1925; c: Ruth. Min of Agric since 1964; bd dirs: Isr Bank of Agric since 1952; Mekorot since 1951; mem, Kvutzat Gvat, 1924-54, Kvutzat Yifat since 1954; coord, gen econ, comm, Hakibbutz Hameuhad movement, 1942-45; agric cen, 1946-49; dir gen Isr Min of Agric, 1950-58; secy: Ihud Hakvutzot veHakibbutzim, 1960-63; Brit Hatnua Hakibutzit, 1963-64; mem Mapai, Isr Lab Party; Agric Cen Histadrut. Contbr to newspapers and Kibbutz publs. Home: Kvutzat Yifat, Isr. Office: Min of Agric, Jerusalem, Isr.

H

HAAS, Fritz, US, zoologist, curator; b. Frankfurt/M, Ger, Jan 4, 1886; s. Benjamin and Clara (Gruenebaum); in US since 1938; PhD, U Heidelberg, 1909; m. Helen Ganz, Mar 30, 1922; c: Ernst, Edith Cornfield. Ret since 1968; curator em, lower invertebrates, Chgo Natural Hist Mus, 1959-68, curator, 1938-58; curator, Senckenberg Mus, Frankfurt, 1909-34. Mem: Malacological Soc, Gt Brit and Ir; Conchological Soc, Gt Brit and Ir; Amer Malacological Union; Deutsche Malakozoologische Gesellschaft; hon mem: Sociedad Malacológica Carlos de la Forre, Cuba; corresp mem: Senckenbergische Naturforschende Gesellschaft, Frankfurt; Institucio Catalana d'Historia Natural, Barcelona; Real Academia de Ciencias, Madrid; Peking Soc Natural Scis, Phila, Pa. Author: Bivalvia, 2 vols, 1929, 1955; Bau und Bildung der Perlen, 1931; Unionacaea, 1969; contbr numerous papers on zool subjects. Home: North Ocean Dr, Hollywood, Fla.

HAAS, Walter A, US, business exec; b. San Francisco, May 11, 1889; s. Abraham and Fannie (Koshland); BA, U of Cal, 1910, LLD, 1958; LLD, Mills Coll, 1968; m. Elise Stern, Oct 18, 1914; c: Walter, Peter, Rhoda Goldman. Hon chmn, Levi Strauss & Co, since 1970, bd chmn, 1955-70, pres and dir, 1928-55; cashier, Haas Bros, wholesale grocers, 1911-1917; pres: Iris Securities Co, since 1927; Levi Strauss Realty Co; dir: Pacific Gas & Elec Co; Pacific Intermountain Express Co; fmr dir: Crocker Citizens Natl Bank; Haas Baruch & Co; SF Bank; Cal Pacific Title Co; Natl Ice & Cold Storage Co; Tide Water Associated Oil Co. Lt, Field Artillery, World War I. Vice pres, Mills College; dir: Adv Council, Sch of Bus Admn, U Cal, Save-the-Redwood League; mem: Blyth-Zellerbach Comm; fmr pres: Recreation and Park Commn, SF City and Co; JWF; SF C of C; SF War Chest; fmr vice pres, Mt Zion Hosp; fmr dir: SF Fed Fund, SF United Bay Area Crusade Exec Comm; clubs: Concordia-Argonaut; Family; SF Yacht; Stock Exch, Bankers. Home: 2100 Pacific Ave, San Francisco, Cal. Office: 98 Battery St, San Francisco, Cal.

HABER, Mendel, US, business exec; b. Mielec, Pol, Aug 11, 1887; s. Abraham and Beile (Kanner); in US since 1941; att Yeshiva Radomysher Rabbi Gaon, Mielec, 1902-04; m. Marjem Geldzahler, Mar 17, 1910; c: Berthe Abry, Mina de Lange. Pres, M Haber Inc, since 1947; head, M Haber, Antwerp, Belgium, 1909-40. Hon pres, Herzliah, Heb Tchrs Inst, fmr pres; treas, Amer-J League for Isr; mem: natl bd, JDC; life, ZOA; FJP; active: State of Isr Bonds; UJA; found, trustee, Moryea Cong, NYC; fmr: pres, Gen Zionists, Belgium; found, vice-pres, La Centrale de Bienfaisance Juive; treas, Communauté Israélite. Recipient: award, FJP, 1951; Weizmann Medalion, Weizmann Inst of Sci, 1966; award for outstanding service to Heb culture, Herzliah Heb Tchrs Inst, 1967. Home: 666 West End Ave, New York, NY. Office: 2 W 47 St, New York, NY.

HABER, William, US, economist, educator; b. Rum, Mar 6, 1899; s. Leon and Anna (Stern); in US since 1909; BA, U Wis, 1923, MA, 1926, PhD, 1927; grad study, Harvard U, 1924-25; m. Fannie Gallas, Aug 31, 1924; c: Ralph, Allan. Dean, Coll of Lit, Sci and Arts, U Mich, since 1963, fac mem since 1936; chmn, Fed Adv Council on Employment Security, since 1948; cons, manpower, to Secy of Lab and Defense Manpower Admn, since 1950; mem: public adv comm, Area Redevl Admn, Commerce Dept, since 1961; Pres's Task Force on Distressed Areas, 1960; lab mgr, Hart, Schaffner and Marx, 1923; instr, econ, U Wis, 1926-27; asso prof, econ, Mich State Coll, 1927-36; dep dir, Mich Works Progress Admn, 1935-36; cons, Mass Commn on Public Expenditures and Taxation, 1937; exec dir, Natl Ref Service, NY, 1939-41; mem, Fed Adv Council, Soc Security, US Sen Finance Comm, 1939-40; cons, Natl Resources Planning Bd, 1939-42, chmn, comms on long range work, and relief policies, 1939-42; asst exec dir, War Manpower Commn, 1942-44; spec asst, Dir of Budget, 1942; adv on manpower, lab relations to dir, Off War Mobilization and Reconversion, 1944-45. Chmn: Acad Affairs Adv Council, Amer Friends of Heb U, since 1968; Mich State Emergency Relief Admn,

1934-36; Mich Soc Security Study Comm, 1936; cen bd, World ORT Union, since 1955; B'nai B'rith Hillel Commn, since 1945; pres, ORT, US, since 1950; mem, bd govs, Heb U, Jerusalem, since 1968; mem, bd dirs, United Service for New Amers, since 1947; mem: Mich Unemployment Compensation Commn, 1936-37; panel Amer Arbitration Assn, since 1941; Natl Acad of Arbitrators, since 1955; comm on econ security, Soc Sci Research Council, 1941-43; exec comm, AJComm, since 1949; adv, J affairs, Gens Clay and Keys, 1948. Author: Industrial Relations in the Building Industry, 1931; Unemployment, A Problem of Insecurity, 1931; Unemployment Relief and Economic Security, 1936; co-author: Unemployment and Relief in Michigan, 1935; How Collective Bargaining Works, 1942; Social Security, Principles, Policies, Problems, 1962; co-ed: Readings in Social Security, 1948; Cost of Planning Unemployment Insurance, 1951; contbr to sociol mags; Post-War Economic Reconstruction, 1945. Home: 530 Hillspur Rd, Barton Hills, Ann Arbor, Mich. Office: U of Mich, Ann Arbor, Mich.

HABERMAN, Jacob, US, rabbi, business exec, author; b. Zurich, Switz, Sep 14, 1930; s. Alexander and Esther (Leibowitz); in US since 1941; BA, magna cum laude, Yeshiva U, 1950; ordained rabbi, Rabbi Isaac Elchanan Theol Sem, 1954; att Union Theol Sem, 1953-54; PhD, Columbia U, 1954; DJur, with distinction, NY Law Sch, 1970; m. Henryka Korngold, 1955; c: Sinclair, Brook. Pres, Adams Park Construction Corp, since 1955; vice-pres, Pacifica Bldg, since 1960; pres, Henryka Construction, since 1968; asso rabbi, Cong Ramath Orah, 1954-57; rabbi, part-time, Cong Torei Zohov, NYC, since 1964. Pres, Beth Isr J Cen, 1957-64; mem: Amer Acad for J Research; Amer J Hist Soc; Amer Phil Assn; Assn of Orthodox J Sci; Conf on J Social Studies; Hist Soc of Isr; Home Builders Assn; Medieval Acad Amer; RabCA; Rel Research Assn; Soc of Bibl Lit and Exegesis; Soc for Psychan Study and Research; ZOA. Author: The Microcosm of Joseph Ibn Zaddik, 1954; Studies in Judaeo-Arabic Metaphysics, 1957; Bethulin Chozrin, in Heb, 1957; The Synthesis of Systems in Medieval Philosophy, 1960; Das Problem des Reichtums im Talmud und Midrasch, 1960; The Binding of Isaac and the Crucifixion; the Background of the Pauline Doctrines of Atonement, Redemption, Forgiveness and Reconciliation, 1963; The Parallel Beteeen Rabbinic Exegesis and Modern Legal Interpretation, 1965; Psalm 110 and the Enigmatic Figure of Melchizedek According to the Interpretation of the Old Synagogue, monograph, 1966; From Credulity to Faith and Other Sermons, 1968; The Negative Golden Rule as a Maxim of the Modern Law of Property, 1969; Abraham Ibn Daud on the Existence and Attributes of God; co-author, Die Khasene fun dem Novi Hoshea mit a Zoyne in Baleichtung fun der Psikhoanaliz, Yiddish, 1966; contbr articles to: Ency Judaica; scholarly jours. Recipient, Awards: Eranos for classical studies, 1950; Amer Legion for studies in Amer hist, 1950; sch bearing his name built in Isr, 1962. Hobbies: reading, walking. Homes: 315 Central Park W, New York, NY; 180 Valley Rd, Hampton, NJ. Office: 765 Shore Rd, Long Beach, NY.

HABERMAN, Joshua O, US, rabbi; b. Vienna, Aus, Apr 2, 1919; s. Isser and Berta (Berger); in US since 1938; att Israelitisch-Theologische Lehranstalt, Vienna, 1937-38; U Vienna, 1937-38; BA, U Cincinnati, 1940; MHL, HUC, 1944, ordained rabbi, 1945; DHL, HUC-JIR, 1965; m. Maxine Rudin, Aug 27, 1944; c: Deborah, Judith, Daniel, Michael. Rabbi: Wash Heb Cong, Wash, DC, since 1969; Har Sinai Temple, Trenton, NJ, 1951-69, on leave for study in Jerusalem, 1963-64; visiting prof, Rutgers U, dept Hebraic Studies, 1969; rabbi: Shaarai Shomayim Cong, Mobile, Ala, 1944-46; asst rabbi, Temple Beth Zion, Buffalo, NY, 1946-51; dir, Hillel Found, U Buffalo, 1946-57. Mem: exec, bd Alumni Assn, HUC-JIR; exec bd, CCAR; Interfaith Commn, UAHC; exec bd, AJComm, Wash chap; chmn, comm on unaffiliated, CCAR, 1960-63; mem bd: NJ State ADL, 1960; J Fed, Trenton; Trenton Council on Hum Relations; natl council, JDC, since 1960; pres, Bd of Rabbis, Cen NJ, Del Valley, 1953; chmn, J Comty Relations Comm, Trenton, 1955-57; NJ State delg, White House

Conf on Children and Youth, 1960; mem, adv interfaith comm, NJ Tercentenary Comm, 1963; chmn, Isr Bond Campaign, Trenton, 1964-67; mem: ACLU; B'nai B'rith; ZOA; People to People; clubs: Torch, Trenton, pres, 1961; Rotary. Author, Holiday Sermons, 1955; contbr to rel jours. Hobbies: skiing, swimming, tennis. Home: 8604 Fenway Dr, Bethesda, Md. Study: 3935 Macomb St, NW, Washington, DC.

HABERMANN, Abraham Meir, Isr, librarian, author, educator; b. Zurawno, Pol, Jan 7, 1901; s. Shraga and Sara (Bratspiess); in Isr since 1934; att U Wurzburg; libr deg, libr schs, Leipzig and Berlin; m. Bilha. Libr, Schocken Libr, Jerusalem, since 1934, Ger, 1923-34; prof, Heb lit, Tel Aviv U, since 1958; sr lectr, Grad Libr Sch, Jerusalem. Author: Tefilot min Shemone Esre, 1933; haMadpisim Benei Soncino, 1933; leRon Yahad, 1945; Gezerot biKenaz veZarfat, 1946; Mishlei Shualim, 1946; Nitzotzot Geula, 1949; Megilot Midbar Yehuda, 1959; Ateret Renanim, 1967; haSefer haIvri leHitpathuto, 1968; Shaare Sefarim Torim, 1969. Home: 5 Gaza Rd, Jerusalem, Isr. Office: Tel Aviv U, Ramat Aviv, Isr.

HACKER, Andrew, US, educator, author; b. NYC, Aug 30, 1929; s. Louis and Lillian (Lewis); AB, Amherst Coll, 1951; BA, Oxford U, Eng, 1953; PhD, Princeton U, 1955; m. Lois Wetherell, June 17, 1955; c: Ann. Prof, govt, Cornell U, since 1966, fac mem since 1955; research f: Social Sci Research Council, 1954-55; Ford Found, 1962-63. Mem, Phi Beta Kappa. Author: Politics and the Corporation, 1958; Political Theory; Philosophy, Ideology, Science, 1961; The Study of Politics, 1963; Congressional Districting, 1963; contbr to jours. Home: 602 N Cayuga St, Ithaca, NY. Office: Cornell U, Ithaca, NY.

HACKER, Louis M, US, educator, author, editor; b. NYC, Mar 17, 1899; s. Morris and Celia (Waxelbaum); MA, Columbia U, 1923; hon: MA, U of Oxford, 1948; LLD, Hawaii U, 1953; m. Lillian Lewis, June 26, 1921 (decd); c: Andrew, Betsy Dexheimer; m. 2nd, Beatrice Larson, June 17, 1953. Prof, econ, Columbia U, since 1948, fac mem since 1935, dir, Sch of Gen Studies, 1949-52, dean, 1952-58; Harmsworth prof, Amer Hist, U of Oxford, f, Queen's Coll, 1948-49; visiting lectr, prof: U Wis, 1937; O State U, 1939; Utah State Agric Coll, 1945; Cambridge U, 1952; Army War Coll, 1952-61; Natl War Coll, 1953, 54; Yeshiva U, 1959-61; Pa State U, visiting dist prof, 1959-60; fac mem: New Sch for Social Research, 1940, 1943-48; Amer Inst of Banking, 1940-43; Guggenheim f, 1948, 1959; lectr for USIA in Eur countries. Author: The Farmer is Doomed, 1933; Short History of the New Deal, 1934; The United States: A Graphic History, 1937; American Problems of Today, 1938; Triumph of American Capitalism, 1940; Shaping of the American Tradition, 1947; England and America: The Ties that Bind, 1948; Alexander Hamilton in the American Tradition, 1957; American Capitalism, 1957; Larger View of the University, 1961; Documents in American Economic History, 2 vols, 1961; The World of Andrew Carnegie, 1865-1901, pub, 1968; co-author: United States since 1865, pub, 1932; New Industrial Relations, 1949; Government Assistance to Universities in Great Britain, 1952; United States in the 20th Century, 1952; Capitalism and Historians, 1953; ed and co-author, The United States and Its Place in World Affairs, 1943; ed: Amer Econ Hist Series, since 1945; Amer Cent Series, 1956-58; Modern World Series, 1936-38; New Intl Ency, 1923-25, 1928-29; contbr to Amer, Brit jours. Exec secy, Academic Freedom Project, 1953-55; mem: bd dirs, ACLU; exec comm, Amer Assn for ME Studies; trustee, New Lincoln Sch. Mem, NY Grand Jury; Amer Hist Assn; Amer Econ Assn; Econ Hist Soc; Econ Hist Assn; Soc of Amer Hists; Phi Beta Kappa; clubs: Athenaeum, London; Columbia U Fac, NY; PEN. Home: 430 W 116 St, New York, NY. Office: Columbia U, New York, NY.

HACOHEN, Mordechai, Isr, rabbi, author, editor; b. Jerusalem, Dec 10, 1906; s. Haim and Feige (Wider); att Heb U; ordained rabbi; m. Rifka Shorr; c: Shmuel, Pinchas, Menachem, Tova, Sarah, Yehudith, Amiramah. Mgr, research and info dept, Min of Rel Affairs; fmr: secy, Beth Din Hassidim; ed, publisher, Neroth Shabbat Jour. IDF, 1947, 1954-57, 1957-60. Author: Al haTorah, 5 vols; Beth haKnesset beIsrael, 1956; Agadath Ze Hayom, 1954; Zeher leMitzvot haKalah, 1953; Toharat haMishpaha beIsrael, 1953; Al haTfila, 1960; Erchei Midot beTorat haRambam, 1957; Dinei Imutz Yeladim beHalacha, 1961; Inyanei Lashon beTosafot Yom Tov, 1961; Pirkei Sho'a, 1950; Har haZetim beMasoret Israel, 1962; Bereshit Zuta, 1963; haKotel haMa'aravi, 1968; Al haRishonim, 1969; ed: Yedion Misrad Hadatot, 1950-52; contbr to

periodicals. Home: 37 David Yellin St, Jerusalem, Isr. Office: Min of Rel Affairs, Jerusalem, Isr.

HACOHEN, Mordecai, US, economist; b. Vienna, Aus, June 9, 1919; s. Israel and Batya (Guttmann-Rosenbaum); in US since 1950; att: Heb U, Jerusalem, 1939-42; Columbia U, 1951-52; dipl, ME Coll of Public Admn, Jerusalem, 1948; MA, New Sch for Social Research, NY, 1955, PhD, 1957; m. Hoshana Eliovson, Nov 1, 1953; c: Israel, Ariel, Naomi, Yael. Mgr, Amer Bank and Trust Co, NY, since 1966; importer, fashion accessories from Fr, repr, textile firms, 1939-42; asst head, stat sect, War Supply Bd; import-export licensing examiner, Dept Commerce and Ind; chief registrar, Dept Custodian Enemy Property, all Pal Govt, 1942-48; co-found, ME Coll Public Admn, 1944, secy, 1944-48; asst secy gen, Jerusalem Civil Guard, 1947-48; co-found, secy gen, Inst for Public Admn, Isr, 1948-51; mem, rapporteur gen, UN Inaugural Comm on Public Personnel Mgmt; research F, public admn, both UN, NYC, 1950-51; coord, Isr summer progs, JA for Pal, NYC, 1952-53; dir gen, Ozar Hatorah Inc, Soc J Youth Educ in ME and N Afr, NYC, 1953-66. Mem: bd overseers, Yeshiva HS, Queens; Alumni Assn, New Sch for Social Research; Amer Acad Political and Social Sci; Amer Political Sci Assn; Natl Geog Soc; hon mem, Amer Automobile Assn; guest speaker: UJA; Isr Bonds Org. Author: Some Aspects of the Jordan Valley Regional Development Projects, 1955; The Administrative Aspects of a Proposed Jordan Valley Development Project for Israel-The Jordan Valley Corporation, 1957; ed, The Concise Biography of the Hebrew Sages, 1965; contbr to profsl jours. Recipient: Ann Shofar Award, Natl Council Young Isr, 1965. Home: 84-50 117 St, Kew Gardens, NY. Offices: 70 Wall St; 526 Fifth Ave, both New York, NY.

HADANI, Arieh, Isr, veterinarian; b. Tel Aviv, Aug 24, 1927; s. Aharon and Hemda (Stern); BSc, Heb U, Jerusalem, 1950; DVM, Vetr Sch, Toulouse, Fr, 1954; DTVM, Tropical Vetr Sch, Alfort, Fr, 1955; m. Ilana Danieli, Sep 20, 1954; c: Amos, Ofer. Dir, Kimron Vetr Inst, since 1965. IDF, 1947-49. Mem: Soc for Conservation of Nature; Isr Vetr Assn; Soc Tropical Med, Hygiene. Contbr articles to profsl jours. Recipient, vetr of year, Isr Vetr Assn, 1969. Home: 9 Aisenberg St, Rehovot, Isr. Office: Kimron Vetr Inst, Bet Dagan, Isr.

HADANI, Dan, Isr, business exec; b. Lodz, Pol, Aug 24, 1924; s. Kalman and Lea (Bauman) Zloczewski; in Isr since 1948; att: Maritime Sch, It; off sch, Isr; m. Ester Ashkenasi; c: Ron, Gil. Gen mgr, Ippa Ltd, Isr press and photo agcy; fmr off, Isr Navy. Picture ed, Portrait of Dayan, 1968. Hobby: philately. Home: 6 Mane St, Tel Aviv, Isr. Office: 3 Itamar Ben Avi St, Tel Aviv, Isr.

HADAR, David, Isr, historical researcher; b. Leningrad, Russ, Nov 15, 1916; s. Zwi and Sarela (Perl) Pomeranz; in Isr since 1934; tchrs dipl, Techrs Sem, Jerusalem, 1954; MA, Heb U, Jerusalem, 1960, PhD. Researcher, Inst of Contemporary Jewry, Heb U, since 1964; mem, Kibbutz Alonim, 1936-52; archivist, Yad Vashem, 1960-67; ed, Tel Aviv U, 1964-66. IDF, 1948-65. Prin contribs: compilation material for Eichman Trial. Lectr, 5th World Cong J Studies, 1969; mem: Hist Soc, Isr; World Union J Studies. Contbr: essays in Molad; to Yad Vashem Bull; Pinkas Hakehilot. Home: Ramat Rachel, Jerusalem, Isr. Office: Heb U, Jerusalem, Isr.

HADDAD, Ezra Yehezkel, Isr, labor official, educator, author; b. Baghdad, Iraq, Sep 9, 1903; s. Yehezkel and Farha; in Isr since 1951; att Tchrs Sem, Baghdad, 1919-23; m. Naima Mizrahi, Nov 20, 1924; c: Abraham, Violet Ron, Blanche, David. Dir, absorption and devl depts, Histadrut, since 1960, mem, Arabic publs dept, 1955-60; mem: cen comm, since 1960, actions comm, since 1955; Cen Comm, Isr Lab Party, since 1959; councillor, Ramle Munic, Lab Council, chmn comm for educ and culture, 1951-59; tchr, Arab public schs, 1923-27; prin, primary, secondary schs, J comty, both Baghdad, 1927-50. F, Royal Asiatic Soc, London, since 1945; delg, ZCs; mem, Zionist Actions Comm, since 1951. Author: Itinerary of Rabbi Benjamin of Tudela, 1945; History Round the Clock, 1951; textbooks on hist for Arab schs in Isr; contbr articles hist, lit of Arabs, Islam to local and fgn periodicals. Home: 23 David Shim'oni St, Ramat Aviv, Isr. Office: 93 Arlosoroff St, Tel Aviv, Isr.

HAETZNI, Eljakim, Isr, attorney; b. Kiel, Ger, June 22, 1926; s. Shamai and Chana (Fraenkel) Bombach; in Isr since 1938; MJ, Heb U, 1954; m. Zipora Weismann, 1955; c: Boas, Nadav, Tamar, Tishai. Atty since 1958. IDF, 1948-49. Secy, found,

Shurat Hamitnadvim, 1953-57. Contbr to profsl jours. Spec interest: politics. Home: 13 Har'el St, Ramat Gan, Isr. Office: 10 Mikve Israel, Tel Aviv, Isr.

HAEZRAHI, Yehuda, Isr, author; b. Jerusalem, Feb 11, 1920; s. Samuel and Bella (Temkin) Brisker; MA, Heb U, Jerusalem, 1946; m. Pepita Perlzweig, 1943, (decd). Author, all in Heb: Al Miftan haHayim; keTzel Over; Ananim baSa'ar; Alva; Eretz haMahapecha haShketa; Im Shahar; Shlosha Mahazot; haTelefon Nutak; baHalon haMuar; Panim uMasecha; Ir Even veShamaim; lectr Heb lit, J Coll, London, 1950-53; ed, Hauniversita, Heb U, Jerusalem. Home: 17 Rahel Imenu St, Jerusalem, Isr.

HAFER, Henry M, US, business exec; b. NYC, Aug 25, 1917; s. Henry and Sarah (Barth); m. Phoebe Levy, Sep 12, 1946; c: Carol, Sara. Dir, vice-pres, treas, Chamberlin Co of Amer, since 1956; La Salle Wine, since 1958; dir, vice-pres: Sioux Falls Paint and Glass Co since 1961; dir, vice-pres, Universal Cigar Corp. USAC, 1942-45, US Army Res, 1954. Home: 26 E 81 St, New York, NY.

HAGIN, Josef, Isr, chemist, educator; b. Sisak, Yugo, Oct 30, 1921; s. Dragutin and Regina (Katic) Hönig; in Isr since 1939; MSc, Heb U, Rehovot br, 1944, PhD, 1949; m. Hanna Gumpert, May 8, 1947; c: Iris, Yaron, Anat. Prof soil chem, dir, Technion Research and Devl Found, since 1967; head, Fertilizer Devl Lab, Technion, 1963-67. Pres, Isr Soc of Soil Sci. Contbr to intl sci jours. Home: 19 Eder St, Haifa, Isr. Office: Technion, Haifa, Isr.

HAHAMOVIC, Julije, Yugo, educator; b. Sarajevo, Nov 24, 1897; s. Avram and Sarafina (Weizen); D, Tech Sc, U Prague, 1930; m. Helena Singerova, Feb 7, 1932. Prof, civil engr fac, U Sarajevo, dean, Fac Technics, head, Inst for Testing Materials and Structures, 1954-56; mem, Councillor Min of Construction, dept dir, since 1945; civil service engr, 1923-30; with Min of Construction, Belgrade, 1930. Air Command engr-in-chief, 1931-41; mem, Natl Liberation Army, 1943-45. Yugo delg to perm commn, Intl Org for Testing Research Materials and Structures; pres, RILEM, Intl Union of Lab for Testing and Research, Paris; vice-pres, Natl Org for Testing and Research of Materials and Structures; mem: in ordinary, Sci Soc for Bosnia and Herzegovina; Acad Sci and Arts. Author, Knowledge and Testing of Materials, in Yugo; profsl publs. Home: Obala 6/II, Sarajevo, Yugo. Office: Inst for Testing of Materials and Structures, Sarajevo, Yugo.

HAHN, Harold Daniel, US, rabbi; b. Phila, Pa, May 24, 1928; s. Maurice and Katherine (Weitzman); BS, Temple U, Phila, Pa, 1949; MHL, ordained rabbi, HUC-JIR, 1955; m. Nancy Cohen, Dec 16, 1962; c: Melanie, Barbara. Rabbi: Ohef Sholom Temple, since 1964; Temple Sholom, Broomall, Pa, 1957-60; asso rabbi, Temple Beth El, Detroit, 1960-64. Chaplain, USAF, 1955-57. Exec bd, AJComm; adv bd, ADL; chmn: City-wide Anti-Poverty Prog, Project Enable; J Family Service; J Comty Cen; bd mem, Child and Family Service Assn; mem: Comty Relations Commn, JCC, Norfolk; Council Social Agcys; bd, Tidewater Mh Assn; CCAR; Comm on Psycht and Rel; Soc Bibl Lit and Exegesis; Amer Sociol Assn; Acad Rel and Mh. Ed, Rabbinic Essays; contbr to J Digest, rel jours. Home: 206 Granby Park Dr, Norfolk, Va. Study: Raleigh Ave at Stockley Gardens, Norfolk, Va.

HAHN, Leo J, US, surgeon, educator; b. New Haven, Conn, Nov 10, 1892; s. Henry and Caroline (Schoenberger); PhD, Yale U, 1914; MD, 1918. Ret; fmr: cons surg, Beth David Hosp, NYC; asst clinical prof surg, NY Med Coll; adj surg, Mt Sinai Hosp, NYC. Lt col, US Army, 1942-46. Dipl, Amer Bd Surg, 1941; mem: Sigma Xi; Phi Rho Sigma. Contbr to med jours. Home: 585 West End Ave, New York, NY.

HAHN, Sanford H, US, rabbi; b. NYC, Mar 18, 1927; s. Isidor and Helene (Hausman); AB, Queens Coll, NYC, 1950; MHL, ordained rabbi, JTSA, 1954; m. Carol Westheimer, Dec 24, 1950; c: William, Daniel, Laurie. Rabbi: Cong Rodeph Shalom, since 1965; Bet Torah, Mt Kisco, NY, 1953-65. Chaplain, US Navy, 1954-56. Pres, Bardosport Bd Rabbis since 1964; mem, RA. Home: 180 Woody Lane, Fairfield, Conn.

HAHN, Viktor, Yugo, engineer, educator; b. Budapest, Aug 21, 1912; s. Desider and Camilla (Löwy); in Yugo since 1920; dipl, Chem Engr, Fac of Tech, Zagreb, 1934; DS, Inst Pasteur, Paris, 1938; m. Branka Nemet; c: Mirjana. Prof, Fac of

Tech, Zagreb, dir, Inst of Organic Chem, since 1949, volunteer asst, 1935, lectr, organic chem, 1946-49; chem engr, research lab, Kastel, factory of medicaments, Zagreb, 1936-46. Mem: Assn Engrs; Croat Assn Chems; Socialist Alliance, Yugo; Swiss Chems Assn; Amer Chem Soc; Assn U Profs. Contbr to sci and profsl jours. Home: Goljak 48, Zagreb, Yugo. Office: Chem Dept, Fac of Technics, Marulicev trg 20, Zagreb, Yugo.

HAILPERIN, Celia Moss, US, social work admnr, educator; d. Charles and Bessie (Shoop) Rosenblatt; BS, U Pittsburgh, 1939, MS, 1943; m. Nathan Moss, June 15, 1928, (decd); m. 2nd, Herman Hailperin, 1966; c: Gaile Kurren, Richard Moss. Dir, Depts of Social Service and Home Care, Montefiore Hosp Assn of W Pa, since 1945; adj prof, U Pittsburgh Grad Sch of Social Work; cons: social service admn and home care; VA; dir, Regional Inst Prog, Natl Assn Social Workers, 1959-61. F, Amer Public Health Assn; Amer Public Wfr Assn; Amer Gerontological Soc; Natl Conf Social Wfr; Intl Conf Social Wfr; mem: Acad Cert Social Workers; Natl Assn Social Workers. Author, Administration of Social Service Department, 1953; ed, Hospital Services for the Child at Home, 1968; contbr to profsl jours. Home: Gateway Towers, Pittsburgh, Pa. Office: Montefiore Hospital Assn of W Pa, Pittsburgh, Pa.

HAILPERIN, Herman, US, rabbi, educator; b. Newark, NJ, Apr 6, 1899; s. Baer and Sarah (Gutkin); BA, NYU, 1919; MHL, ordained rabbi, JTSA, 1932, hon DD, 1955; MA, U Pittsburgh, 1925, PhD, 1933; m. Harriet Silverman, July 4, 1922; c: Cyrus, Sarah; m. 2nd, Celia Moss, Dec 4, 1966. Dist adj prof, medieval hist, Duquesne U, since 1965; rabbi em, Cong Tree of Life, Pittsburgh, since 1968, rabbi from 1922; prof, J hist, U Pittsburgh, 1926-27, 1942-45. Exec comm, commn on J law, RA. Author: A Rabbi Teaches, 1939; Works on Rashi and Christian Biblical Interpretation, 1940-54; Rashi and the Christian Scholars, 1963; ed, Gentile Reactions to Jewish Ideals, 1953. Home: Gateway Towers, Pittsburgh, Pa. Office: Duquesne U, Pittsburgh, Pa.

HAIMI-COHEN, Avinoam, Isr, journalist; b. Berlin, Ger, Sep 9, 1920; s. Jacob and Rachel (Rosenberg); in Isr since 1935; MA, Heb U, Jerusalem, 1945; m. Giza Appel, Feb 26, 1952; c: Raziel, Yishhai. Chief trans, archaeol and hist corresp, Ha'aretz, Heb daily. Cpl, IDF, 1948-49. Author: Archaeology of the Ancient East, 1963; The Dead Sea Scrolls, 1965; Massada of Josephus Flavius, 1967, all in Heb; contbr: to Heb Ency; book revs, articles, sci trans to periodicals. Spec interests: archaeol, hist. Home: 9 Olifam St, Tel Aviv, Isr. Office: 56 Mazeh St, Tel Aviv, Isr.

HAIMOVIC, Issachar, Isr, business exec; b. Orhay, Bessarabia, July 16, 1919; s. Ben Zion and Hanna (Weinberg); in Irs since 1941; m. Esther Dlugatz, 1943; c: Batsheva, Yaakov, Alexander. Gen mgr, Amer Isr Paper Mills, Hadera, since 1961; mem bd dirs: Ind Devl Bank, Isr, since 1960; Isr Aircraft Ind, since 1966; chmn, bd dirs, Ind Finance Co, since 1968; gen secy, Hechalutz Movement, Rum, 1939-41; mem, Kibbutz Hanita, 1941-57; head, delg for resettlement of ref: Egypt, 1943; It, 1946-48; head, devl enterprises, Min of Defense, 1957-61; mgr: Devl and Trust Co; It-Isr Bank, both 1961. Home: 7 Barak St, Zahala, Tel Aviv, Isr. Office: POB 142, Hadera, Isr.

HAITOVSKI, Yoel, Isr, economist; b. Kovno, Lith, May 13, 1933; s. Moshe and Bella (Goldberg); in Isr since 1934; BS, high hons, NC State Coll, Raleigh, NC, 1963; AM, Harvard U, Cambridge, Mass, 1965, PhD, 1967; m. Dalia Sharfson; c: Tsippora, Michal. Sr lectr, Heb U, since 1969; research f, Natl Bur Econ Research, NY, since 1967; teaching f, Harvard U, 1961-65; lectr, Technion, 1965-67. Gen secy, Isr Boys, Girl Scouts Assn, 1957-59; mem: Econometric Soc, Isr; Amer Stat Assn, Isr. Author: Missing Data in Regression Analysis, 1967; Regression Analysis and Differently Grouped Observations, 1968; contbr to econ, stat jours. Recipient, C Oswald George Annual Award in Applied Stat, Inst of Stat, Eng, 1968. Hobbies: music, chess, photography. Home: 165 West End Ave, New York, NY. Office: National Bur of Economic Research, 261 Madison, New York, NY.

HAKHAM, Amos, Isr, biblical expert and advisor; b. Jerusalem; BA, Heb U, Jerusalem; m. Deborah Attas, 1960; c: Noah. Sci worker, Bible Pub Org, Jerusalem; fmr, writer, Maariv, Heb daily. Judge, World Bible Contest. Recipient: 1st World Hatan Hatanch, 1958. Home: 7 Rabinovitch St, Jerusalem, Isr.

HALBRECHT, Yizhak Gedaliahu, Isr, obstetrician; b. Radautz, Rum, June 11, 1906; s. Shimon and Rachel (Katz); in Isr since 1934; MD, Strasburg, 1931; m. Lea Migdali, Aug 13, 1943; c: Edo, Daniel, Zvi. Chief, dept obstet and gyn, Hasharon Hosp, since 1953; prof, chmn, dept obstet and gyn, Tel Aviv U Med Sch since 1964; cons, reproduc, WHO, since 1968; research asso, Mt Sinai Hosp, NYC, 1960-61. Pres: Isr Soc for Study of Fertility; Isr Family Planning Assn; Intl Cong, Tel Aviv, 1968; vice-pres, Intl Fertility Assn; chmn: Child and Maternal Wfr Comm, Min of Health; Sci Prog Comm, VII Cong on Fertility and Sterility, Tokyo, 1971; mem, Intl Coll Surgs. Contbr to sci and med jours. Recipient awards: Mayer, Kupat Holim, 1956; Siegler, Amer Fertility Soc, 1968. Home: 20 Hagilgal St, Ramat Gan, Isr. Office: Hasharon Hosp, Petah Tikva, Isr.

HALEVI, Emil Amitai, Isr, educator, chemist; b. Bklyn, NY, May 22, 1922; s. Mordechai and Rose (Taran); in Isr since 1946; AB, hons, U Cincinnati, 1943; MSc, Heb U, Jerusalem, 1950; PhD, U Coll, London, 1952; m. Ada Rauch, Jan 29, 1947; c: Jonathan, Dahlia. Prof, chem, Technion, Haifa, since 1964, dean, grad sch, since 1969; instr, lectr, Heb U, 1952-55; research asso: Cornell U, 1959-60; Brookhaven Natl Lab, summer, 1966; Argonne Natl Lab, summer, 1967; visiting prof: Swiss Fed Inst of Tech, summer, 1964; Ore State U, 1966-67; U of Ore, spring, 1967; Purdue U, summer, 1969. Cpl, USAAC, 1944-46; Segen Mishne, IDF, 1948-49. Mem: Isr; Amer Chem Socs; Chem Soc, London; Faraday Soc. Contbr to natl and intl chem jours. Hobby, chamber music. Home: 24 Sderoth Ha'Zvi, Haifa, Isr. Office: Technion, Haifa, Isr.

HALEVI, Haim Shalom, Isr, demographer, civil servant; b. Brest Litovsk, Russ, Mar 6, 1908; s. Shlomo and Bella (Ettinger) Gordin; in Isr since 1926; MA, Heb U, Jerusalem, 1932, PhD, 1961; m. Zila Kook, 1935; c: Shlomo, Herzl (fell in battle of Jerusalem, Six-Day War, 1967), Miriam. Asst dir gen, Min of Health, since 1951; fmr, asst dir, Hadassah. Prin contribs: org stat service, Hadassah; started Unit for Med Econ, Stat, Min of Health. Author: Influence of World War II on Jewish Demography, 1963; Hospitalization of Ophthalmic Patients in Israel, 1968; contbr to Heb, Eng profsl jours. Home: 3 Narkiss St, Jerusalem, Isr. Office: 20 Keren Hayesod St, Jerusalem, Isr.

HALEVI, Mordecai, Isr, educator; b. Kiev, Russ, Apr 15, 1890; s. Abraham and Matel (Pockrass) Levitsky; in Isr since 1956; tchrs dipl, Tchrs Coll, Jerusalem, 1914; BSc, Columbia U Tchrs Coll, MA, sup dipl, 1939; att Dropsie Coll, Phila; m. Rose Taran (decd); 2nd m. Yehudith Yoshpe; c: Amittai, Nadav. Ret; prin, Heb Sch, Bklyn J Cen, 1920-38; dir: Bur J Educ, Cincinnati, 1939-45; United Heb Schs, Phila, 1948-56. Pvt, J Legion, 1915; Zion Mule Corps; Amer J Legion, 1918. Mem: Poalei Zion of Amer; Heb Tchrs Fed; Histadruth Ivrit of Amer; fmr, dir, Heb Org of Amer. Author, Insights into the Bible and Midrash, 2 vols, 1966. Home: 33 Razif Pinchas St, Bat Galim, Haifa, Isr.

HALEVY, Avraham Hayim, Isr, educator; b. Tel Aviv, July 17, 1927; s. Naftali and Henia (Ginzburg); MSc, Heb U, 1955, PhD, 1958; m. Zilla Horngrad, Aug 20, 1952; c: Avishag, Noa, Itai. Asso prof, head dept, floriculture, Fac of Agric, Heb U, since 1966, on fac since 1958; research f, ornamental sect, Plant Ind Sta, US Dept of Agric, Beltsville, Md, 1958-59; visiting prof, horticulture, Mich State U, 1964-65; participant: 15th Intl Horticultural Cong, Nice, Fr, 1958; 16th Cong, Brussels, Belgium, 1962, symposium, 17th Cong, Md, 1968; symposium: on growth retarding chems, Geneva, Switz, 1964; Intl Soc for Horticultural Sci, Oslo, Nor, and Copenhagen, Den, 1968; 5th Intl Photobiol Cong, NH, 1968. Contbr to sci jours. Recipient: Alex Laurie Award, Amer Soc Horticultural Sci, 1960, 1963. Home: 2 Struck St, Tel Aviv, Isr. Office: Heb U, Rehovot, Isr.

HALEVY, Haim David, Isr, rabbi; b. Jerusalem, Jan 24, 1924; s. Moshe and Victoria; att Yeshivat Porat-Yosef, Jerusalem; m. Miriam Veknin; c: Rafael, Nizhia, Ronit, Gila. Chief rabbi, Rishon le Zion, since 1950; mem, Chief Rabb Council of Isr, since 1964. Haganah, War of Independence. Author: Bein Israel la'Amim, 1954; Dvar haMishpat, 3 vols, 1963-65; Mekor Haim, 2 vols, 1967-68; Dat uMdina, 1969. Recipient, Award for Dvar haMishpat, Munic of Jerusalem, 1964. Home: 5 Hagdood Haivri, Rishon leZion, Isr. Office: 5 Dror St, St, Rishon le Zion, Isr.

HALÉVY, Jacob, Eng, organization exec; b. Rishon le Zion, Isr, Aug 3, 1898; s. Isaiah and Shulamit (Rochlin) Levin-

Halévy; in Eng since 1920; MSc, Manchester U, 1925. Exec dir, vice-chmn cultural dept, WJC, since 1968, chmn Brit sect; fmr, found, headmaster, Whittingehame Coll, Brighton, Eng. Co-found, J Regiment, Pal, 1917. Chmn, Eur Shnat Sherut, ME Rev Org; mem, bd deps, Fgn Affairs, Isr Comms; co-found, Inter-U ZF; found: Haivri Sch, first sch in Gt Brit, Heb taught with Sephardic pronunciation; Shnat Sherut, one year service on Kibbutz; fmr, chmn, ZF of Gt Brit and Ir. Contbr on organic, metallic chem to Jour of Chem Soc. Home: 55 Pembroke Crescent, Hove, Sussex, Eng. Office: Congress House, 55 Cavendish St, London, Eng.

HALEVY, Meyer Abraham, Fr, rabbi; b. Piatra Neamt, Rum, Mar 21, 1900; s. Abraham and Simha (Jacobson); in Fr since 1963; dipl, Ecole des Hautes Etudes, Paris, 1923; docteur ès lettres, Sorbonne, 1925; ordained rabbi, Séminaire Israélite de France, 1925; m. Rebecca Landau, Nov 26, 1926; c: Simon, Joseph. Grand rabbi consistory, Tournelles comty, Paris; prof, J hist, Séminaire Israélite de France; chief rabbi: J Comty, Jassy, 1925-26; Span comty, Bucharest, 1926-27; Great Syn Comty, 1928-35; Holy Unity Temple, 1935-40; Choral Temple, 1940-45; Spiritual Union Cong, 1946-63, all Rum; prof, J studies: Jassy, 1925-26; Libros Coll, Bucharest, 1927-35; J Comty Coll, 1926-48; U Coll for J Students, 1940-45; prof, oriental, classic and numismatic studies, Rum Acad, 1950-63; lectr, hist of med, Rum Soc of Hist Med, Bucharest, 1955-63. Chaplain, Rum Army, 1939-45. Author: books, studies, monographs on J comty and insts, Rum; Aggada research; critical studies of old Heb and Yiddish manuscripts; fmr: ed: Heb U Bull, Bucharest; Bull, Cen Libr, Mus and Hist Archives, Bucharest; ed, dir: Sinai; Dapim. Found, gen secy, Rum Soc for J Studies, pres, 1926-63; found, mgr, Amis de la Bibliothéque Nationale et Universitaire, Paris, 1923-25; mem: council, JA for Pal, Prague, 1933; B'nai B'rith, Fr. Recipient: Order of Culture Merit, Rum; Order of Academic Palms, Fr. Home: 5 rue J Moreas, Paris 17, Fr. Study: 9 rue Vaupuelin, Paris 5, Fr.

HALEVY, Moshe, Isr, theatrical dir, actor; b. Mastislav, Russ, Feb 26, 1895; s. Zeev and Shoshana (Velikovsky) Gurevitch; in Isr since 1925; att Tech Coll, Moscow, 1914-17; m. Leah Deganit, 1927; c: Ohela. Dir, Moshe Halevy Group Theatre, Tel Aviv, since 1960; co-found, Habimah Theatre, Moscow, 1917; actor and dir, 1918-25; found, dir, the Ohel Theatre, 1925-53; dir: Tel Aviv Purim festivals, 1931-35; Shavuot festivals, Haifa, 1933-34; Yemenite Studio; Dan The Watchman, opera by M Lavry; Pal Folk Opera, 1945; Moshe, by Menachem Boreysho; pageant, Song of Songs, Kibbutz Maabarot, 1945; The Wellspring of the Sheep, Lope de Vega, Habimah, 1952; found, Beresheet, dramatic stud o, Jerusalem; directed plays, by Goldfaden, Stefan Zweig, Tolstoy, Gorki, Shakespeare, Molière. Mem: adv comm, Isr Min of Educ and Culture; presidium, Intl Theatre Inst, 1950-52; delg, congs, Intl Theatre Inst, Zurich, Paris. Contbr to theatrical jour. Recipient: Yehoshua Gordon Award for direction, The Witch. Home and office: 9 Dov Hoz St, Tel Aviv, Isr.

HALEVY, Simon, US, physician; b. Bucharest, Rum, June 5, 1929; s. Meier and Rebeca (Landau); in US since 1963; MD, U Bucharest Med Sch, 1953. Asst prof, anaesthesiology, Mt Sinai Sch of Med, NY since 1967; instr, anaesthesiology, Post-Grad Inst, U Hosp Coltzea, Bucharest, 1955-57; chief, lab, Post-Grad Inst of Med, Bucharest, 1957-60. F, Amer Coll Anaesthesiology; dipl, Amer Bd Anaesthesiology; mem: Amer Assn Anaesthesiologists; Assn des Anaesthésiologistes Français, Paris. Contbr to profsl jours. Hobbies: classical music, reading, traveling. Home: 125-10 Queens Blvd, Kew Gardens, NY. Office: 1600 Tenbroeck Ave, Bronx, NY.

HALEVY-LEVIN, Isaac, Isr, editor; b. Johannesburg, S Afr, Jan 27, 1914; s. Benzion and Sarah (Katz) Levin; in Isr since 1938; dipl, accountancy, Witwatersrand Tech Coll, Johannesburg, 1931; att Heb U, Jerusalem, 1952-55; m. Ahuva Cycowicz, Mar 9, 1942; c: Riva, Aviezer (fell in action, IDF, 1969), Benzion. Ed, Ariel, rev of arts and scis in Isr, pub by cultural and sci relations dept, Fgn Min, since 1959; ed, Eng lang publs, Zionist Org Youth and Hechalutz Dept: Igeret Lagolah, 1944-48; Hagesher, 1947-48; Pioneer, 1949-50; Focus, Isr Argosy, 1951-66; ed, vols of prose and poetry, mainly trans from Heb. Served, Haganah, 1938-48. Home: 7 Metudela St, Jerusalem, Isr.

HALKIN, Abraham S, US, educator; b. Novo-Bykhov, Russ, June 12, 1903; s. Hillel and Hannah (Paritzki); in US since 1914; MA, Columbia U, 1926, PhD, 1936; m. Shulamith Berlin, Dec 25, 1930; c: Miriam Och, Hillel. Prof, Heb,

CUNY, since 1950; prof, hist, JTSA, since 1929; lectr, Semitics, Columbia U, 1928-50; asst prof, Heb, Bklyn Coll, 1939-45. F and secy, Amer Acad J Research, since 1948; mem: exec, comm, World Union J Studies; Amer Oriental Soc; Soc Bibl Lit; Medieval Soc of Amer; ZOA. Author: Muslim Schisms and Sects, 1936; Maimonides' Epistle to Yemen, 1952; Zion in Jewish Thought, 1959; Ibn Aknin's Arabic Commentary on the Song of Songs, 1963; contbr to profsl and learned jours. Home: 895 West End Ave, New York, NY. Office: JTSA, 3080 Broadway, New York, NY.

HALKIN, Shimon, Isr, author, educator; b. Dovsk, Russ, Oct 30, 1899; s. Hillel and Hannah; in Isr since 1949; BA, NYU, 1926, MA, 1928; DHL, Columbia U, 1947. Prof em, Heb U, Jerusalem, since 1969; prof, Heb lit, 1949-68; instr, Heb and Heb lit, HUC Sch for Tchrs, NYC, 1924-32; tchr, Geulah HS, Tel Aviv, 1932-39; lectr, Bible, J sociol, modern Heb lit, Coll J Studies, Chgo, 1940-43; prof, Heb lit, JIR, NYC, 1943-49; visiting prof: UCLA, 1954-55; JTSA, 1965-66. Pres, Isr PEN; mem, Acad Heb Lang. Author: Arai vaKeva, essays, 1942; Ad Mashber, novel, 1945; Al ha Iy, poems, 1945; Modern Hebrew Literature: Trends and Values, 1951; Walt Whitman, 1954; Mavo la Sipporet ha Ivrit, 1953; Ma'avar Yabbok, poems, 1965; Littérature Hébraique Moderne, 1957; Literatura Hebrea Moderna, 1968; Collected Literary Essays and Studies, 3 vols, 1969; trans into Heb: Before Adam, The Sea Wolf, by Jack London; The Bluebird, by Maeterlinck; A Defense of Poetry, by Percy B Shelley; Amok, by Stefan Zweig; King John, The Merchant of Venice, by Shakespeare; Jewish Pioneers in America, by Lebensohn; Green Mansions, by Hudson; Nations, World and Country, by Solomon Goldman; Leaves of Grass, by Whitman. Recipient: Tchernichovsky Prize, 1953; Bialik Prize, 1968. Home: 5 Radak St, Jerusalem, Isr. Office: Heb U, Jerusalem, Isr.

HALLER, Arthur A, Kenya, accountant, public servant; b. Nairobi, Mar 3, 1914; s. Simon and Lily (Block); dipl, chartered accountant, Eng, 1939; m. Iris Barrett, Sep 1, 1949; c: Susan, Stephen, Anthony. Chmn, gen mgr: Maize Marketing Bd, Kenya, since 1959; controller, Maize and Produce, Kenya, 1944-59. Capt, E Afr Infantry Brig, 1939-44. Secy, Bd for Kenya Jewry, since 1962, chmn, 1959-61; pres, Nairobi Heb Cong, 1959-61; mem: Inst CAs, Eng and Wales; FSAA. Hobbies: tennis, swimming. Recipient: OBE. Home: 8 Boundary Rd, Marlborough Estate, Nairobi, Kenya. Office: POB 921, Nairobi, Kenya.

HALLO, William W, US, assyriologist, educator; b. Kassel, Ger, Mar 9, 1928; s. Rudolf and Gertrude (Rubensohn); in US since 1940; BA, Harvard Coll, 1950; MA, Rijks U, Leiden, Netherlands, 1951, MA, U Chgo, 1953, PhD, 1955; asso f, Columbia U Sem on Heb Bible; m. Edith Pinto, June 26, 1952; c: Ralph, Jacqueline. Prof, Assyriology, Yale U, since 1965, fac mem since 1962; curator, Babylonian Collection, Yale U, since 1963, asst curator, 1962-63; research asst, Oriental Inst, U Chgo, 1954-56; instr, HUC, Cincinnati, 1956-58, asst prof, Bible and Semitic Langs, 1958-62. Cons, Lib Torah Commentary; mem: Commn on J Educ, UAHC; Amer Oriental Soc; Soc of Bbl Lit; Phi Beta Kappa; delg: 3rd World Cong J Studies, Jerusalem, 1961, 4th Cong, 1965. Author: Early Mesopotamian Royal Titles, 1957; co-author: The Exaltation of Inanna, 1968; asso ed, Amer Oriental Soc, since 1965; ed comm, Yale Near Eastern Researches; ed, Essays in Memory of E A Speiser, 1968; contbr to profsl learned jours. Recipient: Fulbright grant, 1950-51; Gussenhein F, 1965-66; Amer Phil grantee, Leiden, 1961. Spec interests: Bibl archaeol; cuneiform texts; Mesopotamian background of J and W culture. Office: Yale U, New Haven, Conn.

HALMANN, Martin Mordehai, Isr, chemist; b. Danzig, Mar 24, 1923; s. Mendel and Regina (Eckstein); in Isr since 1938; MSc, Heb U, 1949, PhD, 1952; m. Mirjam Kucinski, 1957; c: Michal, Menahem. Sr sci, Weizmann Inst of Sci; sci, Salk Inst, Cal, 1967-68. IDF, 1948-49. Prin contrib: research on organophosphorus compounds. Mem: Isr Chem Soc; Amer Chem Soc; The Chem Soc, London. Contbr to sci jours. Office: Weizmann Inst, Rehovot, Isr.

HALPER, Sam, US, journalist; b. NYC, Aug 18, 1916; s. Sam and Anne (Halpern); BA, U Kan, 1937; grad study, Columbia U, 1938-40; m. Helen Corbett, Sep 19, 1936, div, c: Susan. Staff writer, Time-Life Books, 1963-67, and since 1969; instr, hist, econ, Kan State Tchrs Coll, 1937-38; research asst, Columbia U, 1938-40; ed dept, NY Post, 1940-47; asst ed,

Newsweek Mag, 1947-50, acting bus ed, 1949-50; contrib ed, Time Mag, 1950-61, chief Caribbean corresp, 1961-63; adv to Gov of Puerto Rico, 1967-68. Office: Pine Grove Condomium, Isla Verde, Puerto Rico.

HALPERIN, Abraham, Isr, educator; b. Vitebsk, Russ, June 27, 1915; s. Mordecai and Chava (Sheinson); in Isr since 1925; att Yeshiva, Tel Aviv and Jerusalem; MSc, Heb U, Jerusalem, 1946, PhD, 1950; m. Sarah Rostovsky, July, 1945; c: Mordecai, Chava. Prof, physics, Heb U, since 1966, mem acad staff, since 1946; fmr: visiting prof: Carnegie Inst of Tech and Mellon Inst, 1960-62; Poly Inst, Bklyn, 1966-67. Sci corps, IDF, 1948-49. Mem: Phys Soc of Isr; Assn Orthodox J Scis. Contbr numerous publs on spectroscopy and solid state physics to local and intl jours. Recipient, F: UNESCO, 1953; Humanitarian Trust, London, 1954. Home: 11 Ibn Ezra St, Jerusalem, Isr. Office: Heb U, Jerusalem, Isr.

HALPERIN, Asher Berkeley, Isr, economist, banker; b. Tel Aviv, July 29, 1925; s. Moshe and Ester (Manzon); BA, hons, Tel Aviv U, 1947; MA, U of Cal, 1952; PhD, Princeton U, 1955; m. Bellha Lanztman; c: Idit, Naama, Orit. Mgn dir, Bank Hapoalim, Tel Aviv, Isr, since 1968; lectr, money and banking, Grad Sch of Bus Admin, Tel Aviv U; dir gen, Otzar Lata'asiya, 1967-68; chief econ adv, dir, econ research dept, Bank Leumi Le'Israel, 1956-67; mem, fgn exch dept, Isr Treasury, 1950. IDF, 1948-49. Mem: profsl advancement and training comm, Assn Banks in Isr; bd dirs: Tel Aviv Stock Exch; Isr Mgmt Cen. Author: essay, Interest and Savings; Banking in Israel; chap in book, Comparative Banking, ed by H W Auburn. Hobby, sports. Home: 13 Kikar Malchey Israel, Tel Aviv, Isr. Office: 50 Rothschild Blvd, Tel Aviv, Isr.

HALPERIN, Gertrude Gray, US, business exec; communal worker; b. Chgo, Ill; d. Jacob and Fanny (Hefter) Gray; m. Carl Halperin, Aug 22, 1920, (decd); c: Wilfred (decd), Myron, Edwin. Vice-pres, dir: AIC Corp; ME Ind; My-Ed Corp; Halperin Ind. Mem adv bd, Chgo chap, Hadassah, since 1951, fmr pres, mem: natl bd, natl service comm, Natl Youth Aliya Comm; bd: women's council, Bd J Educ; Brandeis U Women's Comm; council of trustees, Anshe Emeth Sisterhood; chmn: CJA; women's div, J Fed of Chgo; AZC; active during WW II: USO; ARC; Chgo and Cook Co, Ill Victory Loan Comm; Women's Defense Corps of Amer; guarantor, Lyric Opera Co, Ravinia Pk Festival; clubs: Standard; Bryn Mawr Country. Home: 3180 Lake Shore Dr, Chicago, Ill.

HALPERIN, Harold A, US, attorney; b. Bx, NY, Oct 19, 1930; s. Meyer and Goldie (Kalkstein); BA, NYU, 1951; JD, NYU Law Sch, 1954; m. Faith Hornstein, Oct 23, 1954; c: Mallory, Stacey. Partner, Elson & Halperin, since 1960; admitted to NY, Fed Bars and US Supr Court. US Army, 1954-56. Trustee, S Baldwin J Cen; co committeeman, Dem Party; fmr Pres, Oakwood Civic Assn; mem: Amer, NY State Bar Assns; Masons. Contbr to legal jours. Home: 3494 Daniel Crescent, Baldwin Harbor, NY. Office: 40 Exchange Place, New York, NY.

HALPÉRIN, Horace B, Fr, banker; b. June 25, 1916; s. Salomon and Anna (de Gunzburg); att: Ecole Libre des Sciences Politiques, Paris, 1934-37; U Geneva, 1944; m. Janine Goetschel, 1944; c: Jacques, Béatrice, Hélène. Dir: Samuel Montagu and Co; Cie Industrielle des Piles Electriques; other cos. Fr Army, WWII. Treas, Caisse Israélite de Démarrage Economique; mem: cen comm, Alliance Israélite Universelle; natl council, Fonds Social Juif Unifié; comm dir, UJA, Fr; Conseil du Consistoire Cen Israélite de Fr; comm, Fr ORT. Recipient: Chevalier de la Légion d'Honneur; Croix de Guerre. Spec interests: Judaica, Balzaciana, memoirs. Home: 115 Ave Henri Martin, Paris 16, Fr.

HALPERIN, Samuel, US, education admnr; b. Chgo, Ill, May 5, 1930; s. Herman and Bertha (Kleban); AB, AM, Wash U, St Louis, Mo; att Columbia U, 1953-54; PhD, Wash U, 1956; m. Marlene Epstein, Aug 29, 1954; c: Elan, Deena. Dir, educ staff sem, George Wash U, Wash DC since 1968; research asst, comm on educ and lab, House of Reprs, 1960-61; leg asst, House of Reprs, 1961; cons, subcomm, educ. comm on lab and Public Wfr, US Sen, 1961; specialist, dir, Leg Services Br, Off of Educ, 1961-64; Asst Commn, Educ for Leg, dir, Off of Leg and Congressional Relations, Off of Educ, 1964-66; dep asst secy, leg, HEW, 1966-69. Lt, US Army, 1950-52. Prin contrib, co-devl of most fed aid to educ, 1963-68. Pres, Pi Sigma Alpha; mem, Phi Beta Kappa; cons: Carnegie

Found Study of Fed Govt and Higher Educ; White House Conf on Educ. Author: The University in the Web of Politics, 1960; The Political World of American Zionism, 1961; contbr to political sci jours; Dict of Political Sci; Ency Judaica. Recipient: numerous scholarships and fs at Ill Inst of Tech; Wash U; Columbia U; AFL-CIO; Wayne State U; Amer Political Sci Assn Congressional F, 1960-61; HEW Superior Service Awards, 1964, 1967, dist service award, 1968; Award of Merit, Natl Assn for Public Sch Adult Educ, 1966; Alfred N Whitehead F for Advanced Study in Educ, Harvard U. Home: 6812 6 St, Washington, DC. Office: 2000 L St, NW, Washington, DC.

HALPÉRIN, Vladimir Seev, Switz, historian, organization exec; b. Wiesbaden, Ger, Feb 26, 1921; s. Salomon and Anne (de Gunzburg); grad, Political Sci Sch, Paris, 1942; LLD, Sorbonne, Paris, 1949; m. Noemi Spierer, 1947; c: Michel, Daniel, Miriam. Dir, World ORT Union, since 1957, exec secy, 1946-57; chargé de cours, U Geneva; chmn, cen comm, Swiss Fed J Comtys; trustee, Memorial Found for J Culture. Author: Joseph Chamberlain, 1942; L'Angleterre en 1897, 1948; Lord Milner and the Empire: The Evolution of British Imperialism, 1952; Les efforts de reconstruction juive après le Hourban in "D'Auschwitz à Israël", 1968. Home: 13 Ave Bertrand, Geneva, Switz. Office: World ORT Union, Cen Intl, Geneva, Switz.

HALPERN, Abraham B, US, business exec; b. Itchnya, Ukraine, Aug 15, 1908; s. Isaac and Esther (Rodniansky); in US since 1923; att NJ Law Sch, 1933; m. Blanche Silverstein, Aug 31, 1933. Gen mgr, Bond Clothing Factory, New Brunswick, NJ, since 1945. Co-chmn, comty-wide comm, J Fed, Raritan Valley to protest treatment of J in Soviet Union; chmn, PR comm, Isr Bond Campaign, New Brunswick, Highland Park area, since 1957; mem: natl council, USO, since 1957; exec comm, J Cen div, since 1949, adv comm, lecture bur, since 1943, natl council, since 1947, natl exec, since 1951, bd dirs, since 1951, exec comm, armed services div, since 1952, fmr, mem, fund raising div, chmn, NY State Adult Educ Comm, NJ sect; chmn, sub-comm on clothing, disaster preparedness comm, ARC, since 1950, fmr mem, bd dirs; mem: bd dirs, J Comty Cen, since 1933, fmr pres; bd trustees, Anshe Emeth Temple, since 1953, fmr pres, chmn, constitution comm; Optimists; B'nai B'rith; ZOA; Natl Urban League; fmr: chmn, NJ State chap, secy, natl bd dirs, Myasthenia Gravis Found; chmn, NJ region, JWB Council on J Cultural Arts; co-chmn, comty-wide comm, J Fed, Raritan Valley to commemorate Warsaw Ghetto Uprising; pres, NJ Fed YM-YWHA and Comty Cens; chmn, United; Educ Comm; vice chmn, bd dirs, United Fund; chmn, camp comm, NJ Y Camps; mem, bd dirs, chmn, PR comm, vice pres, Comty Chest; mem, bd dirs, Salvation Army; vice pres, Comty Wfr Council; vice chmn, UJA campaign. Co-author: series, The Literary Capsule, 1950; The Halpern Journeys; co-ed and co-pub: Israel's War for Peace, by Herbert Ben-Adi; Private Letters of an Israeli Newspaper Correspondent, 1968; contbr to J jours. Home: 19 Brookfall Rd, Edison, NJ. Office: 260 Remsen Ave, New Brunswick, NJ.

HALPERN, Benjamin, US, educator; b. Boston, Mass, Apr 10, 1912; s. Zalman and Fannie (Epstein); BJE, Heb Tchrs Coll, Boston, Mass, 1932; AB, Harvard U, 1932; AM, 1933; PhD, 1936; m. Gertrude Gummer, Nov 26, 1936; c: Elkan, Joseph. Prof, Brandeis U, since 1968; research asso, Harvard Cen for ME Studies, since 1956; dir, educ, info depts, JA for Pal, NY, 1949-56; natl secy, Hechalutz Org, Amer, 1936-37; ed, Inst J Affairs, WJC, 1941-45; mgn ed, Jewish Frontier. Mem: bd trustees, Heb Tchrs Coll, Boston; bd govs, Tel Aviv U; exec, JA for Isr. Author: The American Jew, A Zionist Analysis, 1956; The Idea of the Jewish State, 1961; contbr to J jours. Recipient, Guggenheim F, 1961-62?. Home: 187 Mason Terr, Brookline, Mass. Office: Brandeis U, Waltham, Mass.

HALPERN, Bernard Naftali, Fr, physician; b. Tarnoruda, Russ, Nov 2, 1904; s. Eisig and Debora (Gelbard); licencié ès sciences, Fac of Sci, Paris, 1935, MD, Fac of Med, 1936; m. Renée Nysenholz, Sep 3, 1932; c: Georges, Françoise, Marie. Prof, experimental med, Collège de France, Paris. Prin contribs, discovered and introduced antihistaminic drugs into clinics, 1942. Mem: Brit Pharm Soc; Natl Acad Sci, Paris; Royal Acad Med, Belgium; Natl Acad Sci, Belgrade; Acad Med, Rome. Contbr to sci jours. Recipient, prizes: Acad Sci, 1945; Acad of Med, 1946, 1949; Médaille au Service de la Pensée Française, 1948; Officier de la Légion d'Honneur, 1964; Off of Natl Merit. Home and office: 197 Blvd St Germain, Paris, Fr.

HALPERN, Efraim, Isr, physician; b. Lwow, Pol, Feb 4, 1910; s. Berish and Netti (Lifschutz); in Isr since 1946; att Med Sch, Prague; MD, Med Sch, Bologne, It, 1938; postgrad studies, Paris, Fr; m. Esther Chary, Dec 17, 1939; c: Nina, Eliahu. Dep dir, Assaf Harofe Hosp, since 1952; pvt phys, J Hosp, Lwow, 1938-39; phys: Policlinic, Lwow, 1939-41, dep dir, 1945-46; J Policlinic, 1941-42; phys, dir, hosp, head dept, Ein Shemer Hosp, 1949-52. Repr, Min of Health, bd dirs, Tel Aviv Munic Hosps; mem: IMA; Isr Internal Med Soc; Isr Public Health Assn; fmr, Min of Health repr, new immigrant doctors absorption comm. Contbr articles to profsl publs. Recipient, specialist: internal diseases; public health, both sci council, IMA. Home: 9 Slonimsky St, Tel Aviv, Isr. Office: Assaf Harofe Govt Hosp, Zerifin, Isr.

HALPERN, Harry, US, rabbi; b. NYC, Feb 4, 1899; s. David and Dora (Seratchek); BA, CCNY, 1919; ordained rabbi, Rabbi Isaac Elchanan Theol Sem, 1919-22; MA, Columbia U, 1925; LLB, Bklyn Law Sch, 1925, DJur, 1926; ordained rabbi, JTSA, 1929, MHL, 1929, DHL, 1951, DD, 1958; m. Mollie Singer, Mar 23, 1941 (decd); c: Deborah. Adj prof, pastoral psycht, JTSA; rabbi: J Cen, Bklyn, since 1929; J Communal Cen of Flatbush, 1919-29; chmn, Eng Dept, Yeshiva, Flatbush, 1949. Natl co-chmn, Sem Planning Comm, JTSA, since 1951, fmr mem, bd dirs; chmn, social actions commn, Conservative Judaism; mem: NYC Commn on Hum Rights; fmr: bd dirs: J Sanitorium for Chronic Diseases; Pride of Judea Children's Home; Beth El Hosp; Bklyn JCC; pres: RA; Bklyn Zionist region, ZOA, mem, natl exec; Midwood Lodge, B'nai B'rith; vice-pres, Hillel Found, Bklyn Coll; chmn, Rabb Cabinet; mem, Kings Co adv comm, NY St Council Against Discrimination; pres, NY Bd Rabbis. Recipient: Colgate U Medal, 1916; Lampert Homiletics Prize, JTSA, 1930. Home: 1615 Ave I, Brooklyn, NY. Office: 1625 Ocean Ave, Brooklyn, NY.

HALPERN, Isidore, US, attorney; b. NYC, July 1, 1901; s. David and Dora (Seratchek); LLB, NYU Law Sch, 1924; m. Lillian Niman, June 6, 1930. Trial lawyer; lectr: postgrad courses, medico-legal jurisprudence, Practicing Law Inst, since 1949, chmn, advanced course med study, spec trial counsel, NYC, Bklyn-Manhattan Transit; trial counsel: King Features Syndicate; NY Daily Mirror; NY Evening Jour; Loew's Theatres; Consolidated Taxpayers Inc, Co; spec lectr: Yale U; Harvard U; Columbia U; Stetson U; hypnotist, Grad, Intl Inst of Hypnosis. Comm of Public Info, WW II. F: Amer Coll Trial Lawyers; Intl Acad Trial Lawyers; mem: Soc Med Jurisprudence; Fed of Ins Counsels; Amer Bar Assn; NY State Assn Plaintiff Lawyers; Metrop Trial Lawyers Assn; Bklyn and Manhattan Trial Lawyers; Assn Bar, NYC; NY Co Lawyers Assn; hon, life mem, Ind Bar Assn. Author: An Attorney's Guide to Medical Terms; contbr to legal jours; asso ed, NACCA. Home: 128 Willow St, Brooklyn, NY. Office: 26 Court St, Brooklyn, NY.

HALPERN, Israel, Isr, historian; b. Pol, 1910; s. Shlomo and Hana; in Israel since 1934. Asso prof, modern J hist, Heb U, since 1955. Author: Pinkas Vaad Arba Aratzoth, 1945; ha-Aliyot haRishonot shel haChassidim leEretz Israel, 1947; Sefer haGvura, 1950; Takanoth Medinath Mehrin, 1952; Yehudim veYahaduth beMizrach Eropa, 1968; co-ed, Zion quarterly for research in J hist. Home: 36 Hapalmach St, Jerusalem, Isr. Office: Heb U, Jerusalem, Isr.

HALPERN, Israel Isaac, US, rabbi; b. Montreal, Can, Aug 18, 1914; s. Elias and Liba (Adelstein); att Rabbi Isaac Elchanan Theol Sem; Mirer Yeshivah, Mir, Pol; ordained rabbi, Raduner Yeshivah, Radun, Pol; MA, U Detroit; m. Hinda Rabinowitz, Sep 18, 1938; c: Samson, Rella Peskowitz, Eliezer. Rabbi: Cong Beth Abraham, since 1949; Greenfield Heb Cong, Mass; Heb Cong of Kirkland Lake, Ont. Chaplain, capt, Can Army, 1942-44. Natl exec mem, RabCA; adv bd, Bagley Comty Council, Detroit; bd mem: Beth Yehudah Schs; United Heb Schs; Akiva Heb Day Sch, Detroit; fmr pres, Bus and Profsl Chap, AJCong; fmr chaplain, JWV; mem: Council Orthodox Rabbis of Detroit; counselling staff, Lawrence Inst of Tech; Detroit Service Group of JWF; Comm on Aged, J Family and Children's Service; Mizrachi. Home: 19526 Cranbrook Dr, Detroit, Mich. Study: 8100 Seven Mile Rd W, Detroit, Mich.

HALPERN, Jack, US, chemist, educator; b. Pol, Jan 19, 1925; s. Philip and Anna (Sass); in US since 1962; BSc, McGill U, Montreal, 1946, PhD, 1949; m. Helen Peritz, June 30, 1949; c: Janice, Nina. Prof, chem, U Chgo, since 1962; visiting prof: U Minn, 1962; Harvard U, 1966-67; Cal Inst Tech,

1968-69; NRC post doc f, U Manchester, 1949-50; prof, U of BC, 1950-62; Nuffield Found Traveling f, Cambridge U, 1959-60; Alfred P Sloan Research f, 1959-63. Mem: Amer Chem Soc; Brit Chem Soc; Faraday Soc; Sigma Xi; NY Acad Sci; fmr f: Amer Acad Arts and Sci; AAAS; Chem Inst of Can. Mem, ed bd: Catalysis Reviews; Inorganica Chimica Acta Rev; Accounts of Chem Research; Advances in Chem Series; Jour of Catalysis; contbr to profsl jours. Recipient, Prizes: Anne Molson, McGill U, 1946; young author's, Elctrochem Soc, 1953; Amer Chem Soc Award in Inorganic Chem, 1968. Home: 5630 S Dorchester Ave, Chicago, Ill. Office: U of Chgo, Chicago, Ill.

HALPERN, Joel, US, rabbi; b. Krakov, Pol, Dec 22, 1900; s. Mates and Chaje (Frankel); in US since 1948; m. Rachel Horowitz, June 27, 1947. Prin, Merkaz Chinuch Hatorah, since 1949; fmr: rabbi, Jaslo, Pol; dean, Yeshiva of Jaslo; chief rabbi, Brit Zone, Bergen Belsen, Ger. Study: 350 Lefferts Ave, Brooklyn, NY.

HALPERN, Julius, US, physicist, educator; b. Norfolk, Va, Feb 4, 1912; s. Jacob and Lena (Kanter); MS, Carnegie Inst Tech, 1935; DS, 1937; m. Phyllis Melnick, Feb 4, 1940; c: Paul, Sydney, Ann. Prof, physics, U of Pa, since 1952, fac mem, since 1947; research, nuclear physics, U Mich, 1937-40; U Cal, 1940-41; staff mem, MIT, 1941-47, asso dir, Brit br, Radiation Lab, 1944-45, researcher, Elec Lab, 1946-47; sr f, Paris NSF, 1956-57. Tech adv, USAF, 1944-45. Pres, Pa chap AAUP; natl chmn, Fed Amer Scis, 1952-53; f, Amer Phys Soc; mem: bd dirs, Phila chap, ACLU; Tau Beta Pi; Beta Sigma Rho; Sigma Xi; Brit Soc for Visiting Scis. Contbr to sci jours. Recipient: cert of merit, Defense Dept, 1947. Home: 243 S 4 St, Philadelphia, Pa. Office: U of Pa, Philadelphia, Pa.

HALPERN, Lawrence Samson, US, attorney; b. Kirkland Lake, Ont, Can, July 7, 1939; s. Israel and Hinda (Rabinowitz); BA, cum laude, Yeshiva Coll, 1960; Tchr Cert, Machon Haim Greenberg, Jerusalem, 1961; JD, Harvard Sch of Law, 1964; m. Miriam Batt, Apr 9, 1967; c: Adina. Mem, Hyman, Gurwin, Nachman, Friedman & Weingarten, since 1968; tchr, United Heb Schs, Detroit since 1968. Bd dirs: Union Orthodox J Congs; Akiva Day Sch, Detroit; J Natl Fund Found; exec bd, Natl J Commn on Law and Public Affairs; mem: NY, Mich Bar Assns; Yavneh; Amer Judicature Soc; Harvard Law Sch Alumni. Contbr to J publs. Spec interests: hist of Holocaust; Talmudic studies. Home: 15301 Joan, Oak Park, Mich. Office: 14400 First Natl Bldg, Detroit, Mich.

HALPERN, Louis J, US, pediatrician, educator; b. Chgo, Ill, Nov 8, 1897; s. Bernard and Sophia (Rosenfield); att Northwestern U, 1918-20; BS, MD, U of Ill, 1924; m. Gertrude Epstein, June 10, 1933. Prof em, U of Ill Coll of Med, since 1966, clinical asso prof, 1954-66; sr att ped, Michael Reese Hosp; asso, St Joseph Hosp; cons ped: Edgewater Hosp; Louis A Weiss Hosp; att phys: Munic TB Dispensary, 1928-29; Infant Wfr Dept, Chgo Bd Health, 1928-42; Munic Contagious Diseases Hosp, 1928-56. Mem: Chgo Ped Soc; Chgo, Ill Med Socs; Amer Acad Ped; Phi Delta Epsilon; Temple Sholom; licentiate, Natl Bd Ped. Author: How to Raise a Healthy Baby, 1945; contbr to med jours. Home: 3270 Lake Shore Dr, Chicago, Ill. Office: 4753 Broadway, Chicago, Ill.

HALPERN, Phyllis Camille, US, attorney; b. Phila, Pa, Feb 6, 1928; d. Nathan and Anna (Freilich) Schachter; AB, U of Pa, LLB, JD, U of Pa, Law Sch, 1951; m. Sidney Halpern, Dec 21, 1951; c: Baruch, Nikki. Counsel, Food Fair Stores, Inc, since 1968; atty: David Cohen, 1953-55; Gerber & Galfand, 1956-65; counsel, Plymouth Mutual Life Ins Co, 1965-68. Mem: Phila Bar Assn, corps, services chap; Pa Bar Assn, communications, bar and bench chap. Home: 1025 Friendship St, Philadelphia, Pa. Office: 101 N 33 St, Philadelphia, Pa.

HALPERN, Salmon R, US, physician, educator; b. NYC, June 24, 1907; s. Carl and Fanny (Kaplan); BS, U Mich, 1930; PhD, MD, U Colo, 1936; m. Doris Hamilton, July, 1943; c: Gigi, Patti, Steve. Pvt practice since 1946; chief, allergy clinic, Children's Med Cen, since 1947, med dir, 1940-42; prof, clinical ped, SW Med Sch, U Tex, since 1948; cons: Baylor Hosp, since 1948; Parkland Hosp, since 1947. Flight surg, USAAF MC, 1942-46. Dir: Child Research Council, 1935-37; JWF, 1954; J Comty Cen, 1952, pres, 1949-51, chmn, nutrition comm, 1941-42; mem: Dallas and Tex Ped Socs; AMA; Amer Acad of Peds; Amer Diabetes Assn; SW Allergy Soc; Sigma Xi; Amer Acad Allergy; Amer Coll Allergy; Bd of Peds; Bd

of Allergy. Contbr to med jours. Home: 6319 Bandera, Dallas, Tex. Office: 3524 Maple Ave, Dallas, Tex.

HALPERN, Sidney, US, businessexec; b. Phila, Pa, Jan 18, 1927; s. Bernard and Sophie (Swidler); AB, U of Pa, 1947, AM, 1950; att Harvard U, 1947-49; m. Phyllis Schachter, Dec 21, 1951; c: Baruch, Nikki. Pres: Plymouth Mutual Life Ins Co, since 1956, found, 1954; Mercury Books Inc, found, since 1961; vice-pres, Loyalty Life Ins Agcy, since 1954; mem, exec comm, bd dirs, Citizens and S Bank, since 1958; bd dirs, Commonwealth Financial Corp, 1958-60. Asst prof, hist, Temple U, 1967-70. Mem: bd trustees, F D Roosevelt Found since 1949; U Mus; Phi Beta Kappa. Author, The First Psychoanalyst, 1960; contbr to psychan jours. Home: 1025 Friendship St, Philadelphia, Pa. Office: 1512 Walnut St, Philadelphia, Pa.

HALPERN, Yeheskel Shraga, Isr, microbiologist; b. Cracow, Pol, Dec 4, 1926; s. Usher and Hannah (Fränkel); in Isr since 1947; MSc, Heb U, Jerusalem, 1952, PhD, 1956; research F, Harvard Med Sch, Mass, 1958-59; m. Rivka Kreppel, Jan 3, 1952; c: Yehonathan, Ohad. Asso prof, bact, Heb U, Hadassah Med Sch, since 1966, fmr chmn, microbiol teaching comm, curriculum comm, div of microbiol, on fac since 1959; visiting prof, MIT, 1967-68. Haganah Underground in Cyprus Camps, 1947-48; IDF, 1948-49. Mem: Amer Soc for Microbiol; Isr Microbiol Soc; Biochem Soc of Isr; fmr: mem secretariat, Union of Isr Students; treas, Org of Assts and Instrs, Heb U. Contbr to profsl jours in Isr, Eng, US, Netherlands. Recipient, Awards: Bialik, for Dist Students, 1951; J Aranov, for Excellence, 1953; Vera Chargot, for Excellence, 1956. Home: 30 Hechalutz St, Jerusalem, Isr. Office: Heb U Med Sch, Jerusalem, Isr.

HALPRIN, Henry Steiner, US, attorney; b. NYC, May 5, 1924; s. Abraham and Julia (Steiner); att U of Va, 1941-46, LLB, Law Sch, 1949; m. Miriam Kenet, Nov 22, 1956; c: Karen, Bruce. Partner, Halprin & Golen, since 1968; asso, Demou & Morris, 1961-63, partner, 1964; pvt practice, 1965-67; chmn, Practising Law Inst Sems on urban renewal and housing; instr: NYU; Pratt Inst, since 1970. USAAC, 1943-46. Pres, Temple Beth El, Men's Club, vice-pres, Norwalk, Conn; vice-pres, Jackson Hersht B'nai B'rith; fmr chmn, ADL, Real Estate Ind Lodge; mem: Amer, Conn, NYC Bar Assns; NY Co Lawyers Assn. Home: 8 Lowlyn Rd, Westport, Conn. Office: 60 E 42 St, NY.

HAMBERG, Daniel, US, economist, educator; b. Phila, Pa, Apr 25, 1924; s. Isidor and Sophia (Kravitz); MA, U of Pa, 1947, PhD, 1952; att Princeton U, 1947-48; m. Sylvia Kaplan, July 1, 1949; c: Kenneth. Chmn, econ dept, SUNY, Buffalo, NY, since 1966, prof since 1961; fac mem, U of Md, 1952-61; Fulbright prof, Netherlands Sch of Econ, 1956-57; Bologna Cen, Johns Hopkins Sch of Intl Studies, 1965-66; prof, U Buffalo, 1961. Mem: Royal Econ Soc, life; Amer Econ Assn; AAUP; Pi Gamma Mu; Phi Kappa Phi. Author: Business Cycles, 1951; Economic Growth and Instability, 1956; The Principles of a Growing Economy, 1961; Essays on the Economics of Research and Development, 1966; Models of Economic Growth, 1970; contbr to profsl jours. Spec interest, theatre. Home: 77 Wickham Dr, Williamsville, NY. Office: SUNY, Buffalo, NY.

HAMBURG, Lester A, US, business exec; b. Youngstown, O, Aug 23, 1916; s. Elmer and Belle (Margolis); BA, U Pittsburgh, 1938. Chmn bd, Hamburg Bros Inc, since 1967, with firm since 1939; adv bd: RCA; Whirlpool Corp. Pres: United J Fed, Pittsburgh, 1962-64, 1st chmn, young adult div, 1947; Montefiore Hosp, 1969, bd dirs; campaign cabinet, natl UJA, 1963-64; asso chmn, Isr Bonds, 1968; secy, bd dirs, Concordia Club; exec mgmt comm: DePaul Inst; Hosp Planning Assn of Allegheny Co; bd trustees, Duquesne U Found. Home: 5564 Northumberland St, Pittsburgh, Pa. Office: 40 24th St, Pittsburgh, Pa.

HAMBURGER, David Chaim, Eng, business exec; b. Salford, Eng, Feb 7, 1917; s. Isidor and Hedwig (Garfunkel); desc of Rabbi Akiva Eger; m. Blanche Sapper, Mar 16, 1948; c: Ruth, Rochelle. Cpl, Brit Army, 1940-46. Chmn: Manchester and Dist Council of Syns; Manchester Mizrachi; vice-pres, WJC, Brit sect; pres, Holy Law Cong, 1964-67; mem, B'nai B'rith. Home: 106 Scholes Lane, Prestwich, Eng. Office: Searchlight House, Middlewood St, Salford, Eng.

HAMBURGER, Ernst Emanuel, Isr, business exec; b. Ger, July 20, 1908; s. Ludwig and Bessie (Mayer); in Isr since 1935;

att HS of Commerce, Frankfurt/M; m. Margot Auskern; c: Gideon, Yona, Nurith. Gen mgr, co-owner, Hamishmar Ins Service; gen agt for Isr: Judea Ins Co, Tel Aviv; Gresham Life Assurance Soc, London; Guildhall Ins, London; F, Bolton and Co (Lloyds); Traders Ins Co, London; Alpina Ins, Zurich; chmn, Assn of Holders of Lloyds Contracts in Isr; Served Irgun Zvai Leumi. Mem: presidium, Kartell Juedischer Verbindungen; Govt Ins Council. Author, The Idea of State Zionism. Home: 96 Hayarkon St, Tel Aviv, Isr. Office: 33 Rothschild Blvd, Tel Aviv, Isr.

HAMBURGER, Robert N, US, pediatrician, educator; b. NYC, Jan 26, 1923; s. Samuel and Harriet (Newfield); AB, U of NC, 1947; MD, Yale U, 1951; m. Sonia Gross, Nov 9, 1943; c: Hilary, Debre, Lisa. Asst dean, sch of med, U of Cal, since 1965, chmn, dept of ped since 1968, prof ped since 1964; spec f, NIH, biol dept, since 1960; asst clinical prof, ped, Yale U, 1954-60; pvt practice, ped, 1954-60; chief, ped service, Milford Hosp, Conn, 1958-60. Dipl: Amer Bd of Ped, since 1958; Natl Bd Med Examiners, since 1951; f, Amer Acad Ped, since 1959; mem: Soc for Ped Research, since 1965; W Soc for Ped Research; Genet Soc of Amer; Amer Soc of Human Genet. Contbr to med jours. Recipient: Air Medal, USAF, 1944. Home: 9485 La Jolla Shores Dr, La Jolla, Cal. Office: U of Cal, La Jolla, Cal.

HAMBURGER, Sidney Cyril, Eng, merchant; b. Salford, Eng, July 14, 1914; s. Isadore and Hedwig (Garfunkle); m. Gertrude Sterling; c: Herzl, Dov, Morris. Alderman, City of Salford, since 1960; mayor, 1968-69; JP, since 1957. Capt, Brit Army, 1940-46. Pres: J Home for Aged; J Day Cen; Zionist Cen Council, 1964-68; Council of Manchester, Salford J, 1960-63; vice-pres: JPA; Mizrachi Fed; vice-chmn, natl exec, TAC; mem: Regional Hosp Bd; supplementary benefit commn, Min of Social Security. Recipient: CBE, 1966. Home: 26 New Hall Rd, Salford, Eng. Office: Searchlight House, Middlewood St, Salford, Eng.

HAMERMESH, Bernard, US, physicist; b. Bklyn, NY, Dec 25, 1919; s. Isidore and Rose (Kornhauser); BS, CCNY, 1940; MS, NYU, 1942, PhD, 1944; m. Sylvia Molberger, Sep 6, 1941; c: Judith Springer, Richard, Kenneth. Prof physics, chmn dept, Cleveland State U, since 1968; sr research adv, phys research div, TRW Space Tech Labs, 1959-68; tutor, physics, 1940-42; grad asst, NYU, 1940-43; instr physics, 1943-46; postdoc f, NRC, Cal Inst Tech, 1946-48; sr physicist, Argonne Natl Lab, 1948-49. F: Amer Physical Soc; mem: sch bd, Dist 163, Cook Co, Ill, 1949-51; sch trustee, Rich Township Schs, Ill, 1951-57; Phi Beta Kappa; Sigma Xi; Research Soc Amer. Contbr to profsl jours. Home: 18675 Parkland Dr, Shaker Heights, O. Office: Cleveland State U, Dept of Physics, Cleveland, O.

HAMERMESH, Morton, US, physicist; b. Bklyn, NY, Dec 27, 1915; s. Isidore and Rose (Kornhauser); BS, CCNY, 1936; PhD, NYU, 1940; m. Madeline Goldberg, Feb 2, 1941; c: Daniel, Deborah, Lawrence. Prof, chmn, dept physics, SUNY, Stony Brook, since 1969; prof, chmn, sch of physics, U Minn, 1965-69; asso prof, NYU, 1947-48; asso dir, Argonne Natl Lab, 1963-65, dir, physics div, 1959-65, on staff since 1948. Mem: comm on Russ trans, Amer Inst Physics, since 1956; Bd Educ, Villa Park, Ill, 1961-63; Amer Phys Soc; Research Soc of Amer; AAAS; Amer Chess Fed. Author: Group Theory, 1962; trans to Eng, Classical Theory of Fields by Landau and Lifshitz, 1951, 1962. Hobbies: chess, ling, philately. Home: 33 Pilgrim Dr, Port Jefferson, NY. Office: SUNY, Stony Brook, NY.

HAMLIN, Isadore, US, organization exec; b. Cambridge, Mass, Jan 22, 1917; s. Isaac and Anny (Freedman); BS, Cornell U, 1941; m. Helen Rosenstein, Sep 23, 1943; c: Abby, Matthew, Emily. Exec dir, JA, Amer Sect, since 1961, admn dir, JA for Isr, 1959-61. Capt, US Army, WW II. Co-chmn, UJA, Social Service Div, 1967-69; secy, Comm on Control and Authorization Campaigns, JA; bd dirs, JTA; natl exec comm, Intercoll ZF of Amer, 1940-41. Recipient: Bronze Star Medal; Natl B'nai B'rith f for advanced J study. Home: 82-34 Grenfell St, Kew Gardens, NY. Office: 515 Park Ave, New York, NY.

HAMMEL, Shimon Frederic, Isr, Kibbutz mem, educator; b. Strasbourg, Fr, Sep 8, 1907; s. Eli and Lina; in Isr since 1947; ChemE, Inst of Chem, Strasbourg, 1928; licencé ès sci, Fac of Scis, Strasbourg, 1930; DSc, Sorbonne, Paris, 1939; m. Jeanne Weil, June 7, 1934; c: Ruth Buhniq, Michael, Yael, Levanoni. Mem, Kibbutz Ein Hanatsiv, since 1948; tchr, physics-chem, Sde Eliahu Sch, since 1955; asst, Fac of Sci,

Strasbourg, 1946; commissaire général, Eclaireurs Israélites de Fr, 1944-47. Mem, Lichkat Hakesher, Fr J Scouts; fmr: shaliach, JA; found, J Scouts, Strasbourg; illegal salvage work of J youth in Fr, 1940-44. Contbr articles to J publs in Fr. Home: Kibbutz Ein Hanatsiv, Isr. Office: Sde Eliahu Sch, Beth Shean, Isr.

HAMMER, Gottlieb, US, organization exec; b. NYC, May 5, 1911; s. Louis and Ida (Gerstein); grad, LIU, 1931; m. Sarah Saltzman, June 29, 1939; c: Robert, Leah, Benjamin. Exec vice-chmn, United Isr Appeal, since 1960, on staff since 1944; pres, Amer Isr Shipping Co, 1955-67, on staff since 1949; pres, Transp Commercial Corp, since 1959; chmn, NY Adv Bd, Bank Leumi L'Israel, 1965-68; dir, mem, exec comm, First Isr Bank and Trust Co, NY; dir, JTA; asso treas, KH; bd govs, found mem, vice-pres, Amer comm, Weizmann Inst; comptroller, JNF, 1941-44; auditor, asst dir, Pal Pavilion, NY World Fair, 1939-41; hon trustee, Midwood J Cen, Bklyn, NY; clubs: Bankers; Putnam Country. Home: 310 E 57 St, New York, NY. Office: 515 Park Ave, New York, NY.

HAMON, Léo, Fr, attorney, educator; b. Paris, Jan 12, 1908; licencié es lettres, U Paris, 1927; docteur en droit, 1932; m. Suzanne Mongreville, Aug 6, 1927 (decd); c: Francis, Lucienne. Prof, constitutional law, law sch, Paris; atty, court of appeals, Paris; lectr, Institut d'Etudes Politiques, Paris. Résistance, Toulouse, 1940-44; vice-pres, Comité Parisien de la Libération, 1944. Munic councilman, budget chmn, Paris, 1945-47; pres, Commission de l'Intérieur, 1946-50; senator, Seine, 1946-58; dep, Essone, since 1968; exec, Union Démocrates Républicains. Author: Thèse sur le Conseil d'Etat, Juge du Fait, 1932; De Gaulle dans la République, 1958; contbr to political sci publs, especially on Afr political life. Recipient: Croix de Guerre; Médaille de la Résistance; Officier de la Légion d'Honneur, 1952. Home: 12, rue de la Glacière, Paris 13, Fr.

HANANI, Haim, Isr, educator; b. Slupca, Pol, Sep 11, 1912; s. Michael and Sara (Lubraniecki) Chojnacki; in Isr since 1935; MA, U Warsaw, 1934; PhD, Heb U, Jerusalem, 1938; m. Esther Bogatin, 1938; c: Michael, Abraham, Nizza. Prof, math, Technion, Haifa since 1962, on fac since 1954; fmr financial secy, Heb U. Chmn, Isr Math Union. Contbr numerous sci papers. Home: 63 Hanassi Ave, Haifa, Isr. Office: Technion, Haifa, Isr.

HANANI, Josef, Isr, author, educational admnr; b. Russ, Dec 8, 1909; s. Menachem and Rivka (Hadash) Hanowitz; in Isr since 1925; tchrs dipl, Tchrs Coll, Jerusalem; att U London; m. Hassia Weisfish, Oct 1944; c: Menachem, Uri. Insp of schs; bd educ since 1961; found schs: Naharaim; Hadera; Petah Tikva; fmr, agric worker, Petah Tikva. Haganah; segen, IDF. Author: BiNtiv haYisurim; Be'Ol haKibush; Anan Zahov; Shalosh Etzbaot; Et Kavu ha'Ovot; Me'arat haPlaim; Bait Malbin baPardess; Mazal; Kad Heress; haMehalel mi'Mea Shearim; Shelosha Haverim veHaver; book on teaching the short story; ed, Katif, annual of authors and poets of Petah Tikva. Mem, PEN club; fmr mem, Heb Authors Org. Hobbies: music, painting. Home: 29 Meonot Ovdim, Petah Tikva, Isr. Office: Hadar Daphna Bldg, Tel Aviv, Isr.

HANAU, Richard, US, physicist, educator; b. NYC, Aug 1, 1917; s. Leo and Stella (Bloch); SB, MIT, Mass, 1939; MS, U Mich, 1940, PhD, 1947; m. Laia Pearlmutter, Jan 2, 1941; c: Loren. Prof, U of Ky since 1960, fac mem since 1947; research asso, U Mich, 1944-46; visiting prof, U Puerto Rico, Mayaguez, 1953-54; visiting asso prof, U Conn, summers, 1954-55; prof, U Indonesia, Bandung, 1956-58; research asst, optics, U Rochester, 1958-59, summers, 1959-62; sup, coll physics insts, India, summer, 1966. Mem: Amer Phys Soc; Optical Soc, Amer; Amer Assn Physics Tchrs; Sigma Xi; Sigma Pi Sigma. Contbr to profsl jours. Office: U of Ky, Lexington, Ky.

HANDEL, Alexander F, US, executive social worker; b. St Joseph, Mo, Dec 15, 1910; s. Harry and Ethel (Krugman); PhB, U Chgo, 1931; MA, Sch of Social Service Admn; att Cen for Hum Relation Studies, NYU, 1950-52; m. Margueritte Wilks, Jan 15, 1944; c: Richard, Jeffrey, Todd. Exec dir, Natl Accreditation Council for Agcys Serving Blind and Visually Handicapped, NYC, since 1967; dir, Comty Service div, Amer Found for the Blind, NYC, 1954-67; social caseworker: Chgo Relief Admn, 1932-34; J Chdren's Bur, Chgo, 1934-37; J Social Service Bur, Detroit, Mich, 1937-38; state sup: Child Wfr, Mich Dept Social Wfr, 1938-43, Civilian

War Assistance, 1942-43; dir, Health and Wfr Services, UNRRA, 1945-46, liaison off, Anglo-Amer Commn on Pal, 1945; dir, rehab services, United Service for New Amers, 1946-49; dean, prof, Sch of Social Work, Adelphi Coll, 1949-53; lectr, cons, Cen for Hum Relations Studies, NYU, 1953-59. US Army, 1943-45. Delg, Mid-Cent White House Conf on Children and Youth, 1950; mem: bd dirs, Social Work Vocational Bur; Natl Assn, Social Workers; Intl Conf Social Work; Natl Rehab Assn; Council on Social Work Educ; Amer Public Wfr Assn; Temple Sinai, Summit, NJ. Contbr to profsl jours. Home: 14 Rahway Rd, Millburn, NJ. Office: 84 Fifth Ave, New York, NY.

HANDELMAN, Sholom Israel, US, educational admnr; b. Phila, Pa, July 24, 1934; s. Mendel and Celia (Frumer); att U of Pa; BHL, Gratz Coll, 1955; MA, Sch of Social Work, U of Pa, 1958; PhD, Dropsie Coll, 1969; m. Pauline Pincus, July 10, 1956; c: Miriam, Abbi, Joseph, Judith. Prin, Sch of Observation and Practice, Gratz Coll, since 1968, coord, inter-high activities, div comty services, instr, hist, HS dept, both since 1968; ed dir, Camp Galil, Phila, 1958; supr: adult activities, YM-YWHA, 1958-62; teen activities, J Comty Cen, 1962-64; prin, Solomon Schecter Day Sch, 1964-66. Mem: Phi Beta Kappa; Natl, Phila Councils for J Educ; Natl Council for J Communal Service; Natl Assn J Social Workers. Recipient, cert of distinction, Pi Gamma Mu, U of Pa, 1955. Hobbies: stamps, sports, meteorology. Home: 2320 Vista St, Philadelphia, Pa. Office: Gratz Coll, 10th and Tabor Rd, Philadelphia, Pa.

HANDELSMAN, Jacob, C, US, surgeon, educator; b. Elizabeth, NJ, Jan 20, 1919; s. Morris and Eve (Haberman); AB, Johns Hopkins U, 1940, MD, Med Sch, 1943; m. Shirley Silverberg, Aug 22, 1943; c: Stephen, Bruce, Walter, Jane. Pvt practice; asso prof, surg, Johns Hopkins Med Sch since 1963. Capt, US Army MC, 1946-47. Mem: AMA; Md Med Soc; Amer Coll Surgs; Soc U Surgs; Baltimore Acad Surg; med div, Asso J Charities. Contbr to profsl journals. Home: Logan Rd, Owings Mills, Md. Office: 220 W Cold Springs Ave, Baltimore, Md.

HANDLER, Arieh Leon Eng, business exec; b. Brno, Czech; s. Ephraim and Helena; att: LSE; Rabb Sem, Berlin; m. Henny Prilutzky, Jan 14, 1921; c: Daniel, Gabriel. UK dir, Intl Credit Bank, Geneva; chmn, London and Geneva Ins Co; fmr: UK dir, Migdal Ins Co. Chmn: Mizrachi Hapoel Hamizrachi Fed, treas, dir, World Hapoel-Hamizrachi Fed; Bachad F and Youth Aliya Org, dir; vice-chmn, WJC, Brit sect; council, Friends Bar Ilan U; bd deps, World Zionist Actions Comm; bd dirs, Youth Aliyah; J Colonial Trust; vice-chmn, Boys Town, Jerusalem; mem: B'nai B'rith; Inst Bankers; club, Overseas Bankers. Ed, J Rel Lab Organ; contbr to jours. Home: 24 Wellington Rd, London, NW8, Eng. Office: 15 St Swithins Lane, London, EC4, Eng.

HANDLER, David, US, economist, foreign service off; b. NYC, Apr 16, 1918; s. Harry and Toby (Topol); BBA, CCNY, 1939; MA, Amer U, Wash, DC, 1946; m. Claire Labbie, June 1, 1947; c: Beryl. Cons econ, owner, operator, plastic foam factory, Guat, since 1962; intl econ, State Dept, 1944-56, 1958-59; fgn service off, 1955-62; 1st secy, Amer Emb, Guat, 1956-58; spec asst to dir, Amer Reps div, Bur Fgn Commerce, 1959-60; commercial attache, Amer Emb, Buenos Aires, 1960-62; ret. Mem: Amer Fgn Service Assn; Diplomatic and Consular Offs Ret. Home: Apartado Postal 85, Guatemala City, Guat. Office: 13 Avenida 14-51, Zona 1, Guatemala City, Guat.

HANDLER, Maurice Samuel, US, business exec; b. Dukla, Aus, May 8, 1896; s. Nathan and Sarah (Leff); in US since 1905; m. Cecile Kleinman, June 3, 1924 (decd); c: Jerry, Shirley Horodas. Pres: Handro Corp, since 1950; Handler Realty, since 1937; mem, bd dirs: Royal State Bank of NY, since 1962; pres: Smart Maid Coat Co, 1932-50; Colleen Coats, 1937-52; mem, bd dirs, Crestwood Natl Bank, 1937-52. Trustee: Handler Found; W Side J Cen; J Memorial Hosp; Genesis Heb Cen, 1936-50; ADL, 1965-69; dir: Amer Cancer Soc; UJA, 1960-69; clubs: Grand St Boys; NYU chap, Cent. Recipient: hons from: UJA; Albert Einstein Coll of Med; Fed J Charities; ADL; Genesis Heb Cen; Cong Sons Isr, Ossining, NY; Bonds for Isr; award, Golden Fleece. Home: 754 Kitchawan Rd, Ossining, NY. Office: 151 W 40 St, New York, NY.

HANDLER, Milton, US, attorney; b. NYC, Oct 8, 1903; s. George and Ray (Friedman); AB, Columbia U, 1924, LLB,

1926; LLD, HC, Heb U, 1965; m. Marion Kahn, Dec 21, 1932 (decd); c: Carole Schoenbach; m. 2nd, Miriam Adler Cooper, Feb 3, 1955. Partner, Kaye, Scholer, Fierman, Hays and Handler; prof, law, Columbia U, on staff since 1927; gen counsel, NLRB, 1933-34; pres, NY Majestic Corp, spec counsel, Fgn Econ Admn, ass public mem, Natl War Lab Bd, 1944; adv, Amer Law Inst, Restatement of Torts; fmr lab counsel: UJA; United Service for New Amers and HIAS; Amer Financial and Devl Corp; arbitrator, lab and commercial disputes; Mitchell lectr, Buffalo Law Sch, 1956-57; lectr, U Leyden, Holland, 1963; fmr mem, Atty Gen's Natl Comm on anti-trust laws. Mem: Amer Friends Heb U; J Acad Arts and Scis; bd trustees, Cong B'nai Jeshurun; bd dirs, Conf on J Social Studies; fmr mem, Amer Zionist Emergency Council; fmr chmn, Pal comm, AJCong; mem: Amer, Fed, NY State, NYC Bar Assns; Amer Coll Trial Lawyers; Amer Bar Found; clubs: Men's Fac Columbia U; Lawyers; Harmonie. Author: Antitrust in Perspective, 1957; Cases and Materials on Trade Regulation, 4th ed, 1967; co-author: Basic Equities of the Palestine Problem, 1947; ed, Columbia Law Rev, 1924-26; contbr to legal jours. Recipient: Ordronaux Prize; bicentennial silver medallion, Columbia U, 1954; Scopus award, 1963. Home: 625 Park Ave, New York, NY. Office: 425 Park Ave, New York, NY.

HANDLER, Philip, US, biochemist, educator; b. NYC, Aug 13, 1917; s. Jacob and Lena (Heisen); BS, CCNY, 1936; MS, U Ill, 1937, PhD, 1939; m. Lucille Marcus, Dec 6, 1939; c: Mark, Eric, James. Pres, Natl Acad Sci; chmn, Natl Sci Bd, since 1966; Duke prof biochem, Duke U Sch of Med, 1961-69, fac mem since 1939; cons: comm on growth, NRC; AEC; VA; NIH, USPHS, chmn biochem sect, NIH; mem, natl adv health council, USPHS, mem, comm on environmental health; bd dirs, Squibb-Beechnut. F: NY Acad Sci; AAAS; mem: div comm for biol and med, NSF, since 1960, mem natl sci bd since 1962; Amer Soc Biol Chems, past secy, pres; exec comm of bd, Fed Amer Soc Experimental Biols; Amer Chem Soc; Amer Inst Nutrition, fmr councilor; Soc for Experimental Biol and Med, fmr secy, pres, SE sect; Amer Phil Soc; Amer Acad Arts and Scis; bd trustees: Rockefeler U; Cen for Info Amer; Found for Advancement in Sci; bd govs, Amer Friends Heb U; bd visitors: Yale U; U Notre Dame; Kettering Found; Scripps Clinic and Found; fmr: mem: Pres Sci Adv Comm; Pres Commn on Heart Disease, Cancer and Stroke; Task Force 20, Inst for Defense Analysis; Unitarian Med Mission to Japan; club, Cosmos. Co-author, Principles of Biochemistry; ed, Geriatrics; mem, ed comm: Jour of Comparative Biochem and Phys; Jour of Theoretical Biol; contbr to sci jours. Homes: Watergate W, Washington, DC; Nobaka Rd, Woods Hole, Mass. Office: 2101 Constitution Ave, Washington, DC.

HANDLIN, Oscar, US, historian, educator, author; b. NYC, Sep 29, 1915; s. Joseph and Ida (Yanowitz); AB, Bklyn Coll, 1934; MA, Harvard, 1935, PhD, 1940; hon: LLD, Colby Coll, 1962; LHD, HUC, 1967; DHum, Oakland U, 1968; m. Mary Flug, Sep 18, 1937; c: Joanna, David, Ruth. Dir, Charles Warren Cen for Studies in Amer Hist, Harvard U, since 1965, Charles Warren Prof hist, since 1965, prof, hist, 1954-62, Winthrop Prof hist, 1962-65, dir, Cen for Study Hist of Liberty in Amer, 1958-67, on fac since 1939; instr, Bklyn Coll, 1938-39. Chmn, US Bd Fgn Scholarships, 1965-66, vice-chmn, 1962-65; mem: Colonial Soc of Mass; Mass Hist Soc; Amer Acad Arts and Scis; Hist Assn; Amer J Hist Soc; S Hist Assn; Miss Valley Hist Assn; AJComm; Phi Beta Kappa. Author: Boston's Immigrants: A Study in Acculturation, 1941; This Was America, 1949, 1964; The Uprooted, 1951; Positive Contributions by Immigrants, 1953; Adventures in Freedom, 1954; American People in the Twentieth Century, 1954; Chance or Destiny, 1955; Race and Nationality in American Life, 1957; Al Smith and his America, 1958; The Newcomers, 1959; Immigration as a Factor in American History, 1959; John Dewey's Challenge to Education, 1959; The Americans, 1963; Firebell in the Night, 1964; A Continuing Task, 1964; Children of the Uprooted, 1966; Popular Sources of Political Authority, 1966; History of the United States, 1967; America as History, 1968; co-author: Commonwealth: A Study of the Role of Government in American Economy, 1947; The Dimensions of Liberty, 1961; ed, Libr of Amer Biography; co-ed, Harvard Guide to American History, 1954, 1967; contbr to scholarly jours and popular mags. Recipient: Sheldon Traveling F, 1937-38; prize, Union League Club, 1934; J H Dunning Prize, Amer Hist Assn, 1941; award of hon, Bklyn Coll, 1945; Pulitzer Prize, hist, 1952; Guggenheim F, 1954; Christopher Award, 1958; alumni award, Bklyn Coll, 1958. Home: 18 Agassiz St,

Cambridge, Mass. Office: Widener 783, Harvard U, Cambridge, Mass.

HANFT, Benjamin, US, public relations exec; b. NYC, Dec 18, 1906; s. David and Rose (Scheinman); m. Esther Berenson, Feb 25, 1933; c: Helen, Sara, Alice. PR dir, CJFWF, since 1968, dir, campaign and comty interpretation dept, 1945-48; publicity dir, US Employment Service, NY State, 1932-35; asso publicity dir, JDC, 1936-39; dir, comty campaigns, UJA, 1939-41; publicity dir: UJA, NYC, 1942-45; AJComm, 1948-51; AJCong, WJC, 1951-54; Amer Friends Heb U, 1954-56; UJA comty devl dept, 1956-61. Fmr pres, Amer-J PR Soc. Author: Building the Successful Campaign, 1947. Home: 341 W 24 St, New York, NY. Office: 315 Park Ave S, New York, NY.

HANKIN, Leonard J, US, business exec; b. Bklyn, NY, Apr 25, 1917; s. Harry and Jennie (Rubin); BBA, CCNY Sch of Bus Admn, 1936; att Cornell U, 1942; m. Kathleen Keane, Mar 14, 1952; c: Kim, Lyn. Exec vice-pres, Bergdorf Goodman since 1954, with firm since 1936; exec dir, fashion ind presentation, US Govt Exhb, Moscow, 1959. Off of Strategic Services, WWII. F, Amer Council Learned Socs; trustee, vice-pres, Educ Alliance, chmn, personnel, youth activities comms, since 1958. Recipient: Bronze Star Medal; 3 battle stars, WWII. Home: 5927 Independence Ave, Riverdale, NY. Office: 745 Fifth Ave, New York, NY.

HANTGAN, George, US, social worker; b. NYC, Mar 29, 1916; s. Nathan and Eva (Dubraminsky); BA, Bklyn Coll, 1940; MPA, NYU, 1943; MSW, Columbia U, 1948; m. Ida Meyer, Nov 27, 1949; c: Jeffrey, Roberta, Richard. Exec-dir: J Comty Cen; UJF; UJA, all Englewood, since 1950; dir, USO Mobile Service, NYC, 1943-46; regional dir, S Region, Small Comty Div, JWB, Atlanta, 1946-47; prog dir, Hecht House, Boston, 1948-50; exec-dir, JCC, since 1950; fac field adv: Boston U, 1948-50; Columbia U, 1950-56; Yeshiva U, since 1956. Chmn: Englewood Citizens Award Comm, 1966-67; project evaluation comm, OEO, 1966-67; treas, Natl Assn J Comty Workers, 1964-66; mem, bd: Moria Sch, Englewood, 1965-67; Natl Assn J Cen Workers, since 1949; official City of Englewood repr, Bergen Co, OEO, 1966-67; NJ repr, World Fed YMHA's, since 1965; mem: Natl Assn Social Workers; recreation commn, Englewood, 1968; Englewood Bd Educ, since 1967; Bergen Co Health and Wfr Agcy. Home: 158 St Nicholas Ave, Englewood, NJ. Office: 153 Tenafly Rd, Englewood, NJ.

HARAMATI, Shlomo, Isr, educator; b. Jerusalem, Isr, Mar 20, 1928; s. Samuel and Sara (Mirkin); dipl, Tchrs Coll, Jerusalem, 1946; MA, Heb U, Jerusalem, 1952; postgrad work, Tchrs Coll, Columbia U, 1956-57; PhD, Heb U, Jerusalem, 1963; m. Rivka Kurzgur, Nov 24, 1953; c: Orya, Ronit. Lectr, Sch of Educ, Heb U, since 1969; elem sch tchr, Jerusalem, 1947-51; head, adult educ, IDF, 1951-54; tchr, Yeshiva of Flatbush, NY, 1955-60; lectr, Yeshiva U, NY, 1958-60; chief insp of adult educ, Min of Educ and Culture, 1961-65, 1968; educ cons, JA of J Educ Comm; lectr, Ferkauf Grad Sch of Educ, both NYC, 1965-67. Capt, chief educ off, IDF, 1951-54. Prin contrib, new method to teach reading to illiterates. Mem: Intl Reading Assn; Adult Educ Assn. Author: Reshit, A Practice Book of Elementary Hebrew, 1954; Medinat Israel, reader, 1960; Ulpani, 1961; Games and Drills, 1962; Nivon, 1963; Teaching Hebrew to Adults, 1963; Teaching Hebrew to Illiterates, 1964; laKita veLabait, 1965; Education for Reading, 1967; laMore Series, 1967-69; Writing Simple Reading Material, a guide, 1968; Sachek uLmad, 1969; Abraham—A Father of a Nation, reader, all in Heb; An Introduction to Literary Education, 1963; Teaching Illiterates to Read, 1965, both in Eng; School Comes to Adults, in Eng and Fr, 1965. Home: 9 Marcus St, Jerusalem, Isr. Office: Heb U, Jerusalem, Isr.

HARAN, Menahem M, Isr, educator; b. Moscow, Russ, Dec 4, 1924; s. Moshe and Fani (Dulitzky) Dyman; in Isr since 1933; MA, PhD, Heb U; postgrad, Dropsie Coll, 1947; m. Raya Twersky; c: Moshe, Tali. Yehezkel Kaufmann prof, chmn, dept of Bible, Heb U, since 1968; sr lectr, chmn, dept Bible, U of Tel Aviv, 1957-62; visiting asso prof, U of Cal, Berkeley, 1963-64. Maj, IDF, 1948-50. Author: Between Rishonot and Hadashot, 1963; other books; contbr to jours. Home: 37 Alfasi, Jerusalem, Isr. Office: Heb U, Jerusalem, Isr.

HARAN, Rosa, Isr, nurse; b. Bialystock, Pol, Mar 17, 1915; d. Aizik and Etka (Jewnin) Sokolsky; in Isr since 1935; att Heb U, Jerusalem, 1935-37; Hadassah Sch of Nursing, Jerusalem,

1946-48; m. 1953. Matron, Rambam Govt Hosp, Haifa, since 1964; evening and night sup, Hadassah Hosp, Jerusalem, 1948-50; matron, Beersheba Hosp, 1950-51. Cpl, Haganah, 1942-46. Mem: Isr Nurses Assn; Magen David Adom. Hobbies: philately, collection of bells. Home: 28 Margalit St, Haifa, Isr. Office: Rambam Hosp, Haifa, Isr.

HARAP, Louis, writer, editor, librarian; b. NYC, Sep 16, 1904; s. Moses and Yetta (Karp); BA, Harvard Coll, 1928; MA, Harvard U, 1929, PhD, 1932; m. Evelyn Mann, Aug 17, 1957. Independent scholar, since 1969; libr, Phil Libr, Harvard U, 1934-39; mgn ed: J Survey, 1941-42; J Life, 1948-58; libr, New Lincoln Sch, NYC, 1960-69. US Army, 1942-45. Author: Social Roots of the Arts, 1949; mem, ed bd, J Currents, since 1958; contbr to popular and learned jours. Home: Belmont, Vt.

HARAR, George, Isr, author; b. Morocco, 1917; s. Baruch and Rachel (Danino); in Isr since 1964; dipl, ordained rabbi, Morocco; PhD, hum, U Casablanca; prof, hum, Paris, Fr. Author: Levana, 1945; Casablanca, Ir Plaim; Doctor Alexander be'Ginea; Mistorei haNefesh; Mistorei haNevua; Igeret haChoze; Adam veChava; Edward Heriot; David haMelech Chai; Sviv ha'Olam; haTslav shel Lorna; Ma'alot haShemesh. Adv: to King Muhamed, 1955-60; to King Hassan, 1960-62, both of Morocco. Fr underground, 1942. Mem, Writers Assn, Fr; hon mem, It Spiritual Academic Inst. Home: 18 Ha'avoda St, Holon, Isr.

HARARI, Ishar, Isr, attorney, legislator; b. Jaffa, Isr, July 16, 1908; s. Haim and Yehudit (Eisenberg); att: U Sorbonne; L'Ecole des Sciences Politiques, Paris; L'Ecole de Journalisme, Paris, 1926-28; Jerusalem Law Sch, 1928-31; Sch Econ, U London, 1932-33; m. Dina Neumann; c: Haim, Thalia. Pvt law practice since 1934; MK since 1949; fmr: legal comm, fgn affairs and security comm, chmn, house comm, 1st Knesset; mem, Isr delg to UN, 1953-58, 1960, 1962; constitution comm, Isr Provincial Govt Council, 1948; dep Min of Interior, 1948; Isr delg to: Brit Parl; Swed; Nor; Den; Uruguay; Chile; Arg; Brazil; Burma; Thailand; spec delg to pres: Guinea; Liberia; Ivory Coast; Upper Volta; inter-parl union cong: Istanbul; Bern; Wash, DC; Helsinki; Tokyo; Ottawa; legal adv: munic councils; Haganah Hqrs; atty gen, Haganah; active, Aliyah Bet. Lt col, IDF; pres, mil supr court, 1948. Mem, cen comm, Isr Bar Assn; found, chmn, Isr Fgn Policy Assn; mem: Intl Soc Pol Sci; cen comm, UN League in Isr; Zionist Action Comm; presidium, Gen Zionist Party; co-found: Progressive Party, 1948; Lib Party, 1961, head, party group in Knesset; pleaded for unification of parties after June 1967 war. Contbr to press. Home: 85 Ben Yehuda St, Tel Aviv, Isr. Office: 12 Bialik St, Tel Aviv, Isr.

HARBURGER, Peter Fritz, Isr, government official; b. Munich, Ger, Mar 28, 1911; s. Sigmund and Helene (Kahn); in Isr since 1935; att U Munich, 1930-34; m. Rose Heller, Nov 11, 1934; c: Shlomith, Mayan Lowenthal, Yoram. Head, Dept for Youth and Vocational Educ, Min of Lab, since 1965, head, div for adults' training, 1950-52, asst dir, 1960-62; repr, State of Isr, Intl Confs, Man Power Policy and vocational educ, ILO-UNIDO, since 1948; mechanic and electrician, 1935-40; secy, Haifa Metal Workers, 1940-46; mem: Secretariat Gen, 1946-48; experts on vocational educ, Burma, 1954-55; spec assignment to ILO, 1967; Experts' Mission to Cyprus, 1968. IDF, 1936-58. Mem: Secretariat, Vocational Guidance Org of Isr; Assn Adult Educ, Isr; Assn Political Sci, Isr; fmr mem: Chamber of Delgs; chmn, Interministerial Comm for Vocational Education in Isr, 1967; Technological Education in Developing Countries, 1969. Hobby: music. Home: 18 Radak, Jerusalem, Isr. Office: Bldg "B" Hakirya, Jerusalem, Isr.

HAREL, Samuel, Isr, chemist; b. Ramat Gan, Isr, March 15, 1938; s. Shlomo and Sara; BSc, Heb U, Jerusalem, 1962, MSc, 1963; BBA, 1964; m. Bilha, Aug 31, 1961; c: Erez, Galit. Dir, Govt Inst for Tech Educ, Min of Lab since 1968, dir, Dept for Practical Engrs and Techs, 1965-68; lectr, chem tech, Technion, Haifa, 1960-69; asst, Tel Aviv U, 1964-65. IDF, 1956-59. Chmn, Techs Comm, Isr Chem Soc, Tel Aviv. Author of numerous textbooks; contbr to sci jours. Home: 7 Hehayal Haalmoni, Rishon L'Zion, Isr. Office: 19 D, Hakirya, Tel Aviv, Isr.

HARELI, Shoshana, Isr, communal worker; b. NYC, Jan 28, 1908; d. Mordecai and Sarah (Stampfer) Bension; desc of Yehoshua Stampfer, found Petah Tikvah; in Isr since 1931; BA, Hunter Coll, NY, 1931; div; c: Yael Ishai. Pres, Intl

Council J Women; recruiting off, Pal Auxiliary Territorial Service, WWII; exec secy, Imahot Ovdot, 1948-54; delg, Pioneer Women, on missions to US, Can, Brit, Mexico; pres, Isr Council Women's Org, 1961-64; dir, Overseas Dept, Moetzet Hapoalot, 1962-68; official guest of Brit Govt, Cen Off of Info, 1968. Home: 3 Lotus St, Mt Carmel, Haifa, Isr. Office: Rothschild Community Cen, Mt Carmel, Haifa, Isr.

HARELL, Arieh, Isr, physician; b. Kiev, Russ, Oct 18, 1911; s. Boris and Vera (Rosenblith) Steinberg; in Isr since 1937; MD, U Berlin, 1937; m. Rachel Van-Den-Berg; c: Yehuda, Miriam, Nimrod. Head: med cen, Tel Aviv-Yaffo, since 1962; endocrine dept, Ichilov Hosp, Tel Aviv; Isr Min to Rum, 1956-58; Ambass to Moscow, 1958-62. Capt, RAMC, 1942-46; lt col, IDF, 1947-56. Mem: cen comm, Ha'avodah; council, haHistadrut ha'Refuit; Isr Hosp Bd; fmr mem, Isr Health Council. Author: The Conflict Between the USSR and China (Heb); contbr to profsl and gen publs. Recipient, Of of Order of Merit, Madagascar. Home: 7 Mishmeret St, Afeka, Isr.

HAREUVENI, Nogah, Isr, author; b. Jerusalem, Isr, Jan 22, 1924; s. Ephraim and Hannah (Radovilski); MSc, Heb U, Jerusalem, 1946; m. Drora Mirkin; c: Alumim, Maayan. Dir gen, Neot Kedumim, since 1965; Isr repr, mission to US, Amer-Isr Cultural Found, 1950-65; estab: educ br for IDF, teaching soldiers to use wild plants during stay in field; Field Educ Cen. Capt, IDF, 1950-58. Author: Or Hadash Al Sefer Yirmiahu, 1950; beSod Ilan uFerach, 1956; Chinuch Sade; Living Symbols of the Bible; contbr to periodicals in Heb and Eng. Home: 6 Havazelet St, Kir'on, Isr. Office: POB 299, Kiriat Ono, Isr.

HAR-EVEN, Judith, Isr, artist, painter; b. Haifa, Isr, May 1, 1926; d. Haim and Mina (Weinstock) Harnik; att: St Martin Sch of Art, London, Eng; Art Student's League, NY; c: Reuven. Artist, painter, tchr of art, Vocational HS; one-man shows, group, annual shows, since 1957; research, study tours in Spain, It, Netherlands, Russ; works in various media, in mus, pvt collections, in Isr, abroad. Mem: Painters, Sculptors Assn, Isr. Home and studio: 98 Ussishkin St, Tel Aviv, Isr.

HAR'EVEN, Shulamith, Isr, writer, poet; b. Warsaw, Pol, Feb 14, 1931; d. Abraham and Natalie (Wiener) Ryftin; in Isr since 1940; att Heb U, Jerusalem; m. Eliahu Hareven, 1953; c: Ithai, Gail. Author: Yerushalaim Dorsanit, 1962; baHodesh ha'Aharon; Mekomot Nifradim, 1967; Reshut Netuna, 1969; trans, Konrad Wallenrod by Mickiewicz; trans for Habima, Cameri, Ohel, Zavit theatres; contbr to newspapers. Lt, IDF, 1950-52. Home: 16 Moholiver St, Neve Magen, Isr.

HARGIL, Dory, Isr, business exec; b. Tel Aviv, Jan 14, 1936; s. Moshe and Fruma (Raider) Hurgel; att: Heb U, Tel Aviv br; Roosevelt U, Chgo; Chartered Ins Inst, London; m. Israella Harnik, July 28, 1958; c: Tal, Yael, Michal. Dir, Hassneh Ins Co, since 1967; mem, Kibbutz Sdeh Boker; secy, Gmul Inves Co, 1959-64; asst secy gen, Gen Fed of Lab, Histadrut, 1964-66. Home: 22 Bnei Efraim St, Maoz Aviv, Isr. Office: 19 Rothschild St, Tel Aviv, Isr.

HARKABI, Yehoshafat, Isr, army officer, government official, researcher; b. Haifa, Sep 21, 1921; s. Zidkiya and Haya (Stamper); MA, Heb U, Jerusalem, 1946; MPA, Harvard U, US, 1960; PhD, Heb U, 1968; m. Miryam Manzon, Mar 24, 1953; c: Irit, Dan. Ret: head, Strategic Research Dept, Min of Defense, 1963-68; J Brig, 1943-45; comm, students co, IDF, in defence of Jerusalem, Ramat Rachel, 1948; mem, delg, armistice conf with Egypt, Rhodes, 1949; mil secy to Min for Fgn Affairs on Arab armistice affairs, 1949-50; off i/c Mixed Armistice Commns, 1950-51; Brig Gen, chief, IS, IDF, 1955-59; dep dir-gen, PM office, 1961-62. Author: Milchama Gar'init ve Shalom Gar'ini; Bein Israel le'Arav; Emdat Israel beSichsuch Israel-Arav; Emdat ha'Aravim beSichsuch Israel-Arav; Keitzad Husberor ha'Emda ha'-Aravit Neged Israel batzava ha Mitzri. Home: 35 King David Blvd, Tel Aviv, Isr. Office: Heb U, Jerusalem, Isr.

HARKAVY, Bernard, US, attorney; b. NYC, Aug 1, 1914; s. Isaac and Rose (Levy); BA, CCNY, 1932; LLB, Bklyn Law Sch, St Lawrence U, 1935; DJur, Bklyn Law Sch, 1967; m. Judith Wishnack, Aug 11, 1946; c: Ira, Roy. Pvt practice since 1936; admitted to bar, US Supr Court, 1961; master, Civil Court, NYC, 1968. US Army, 1943; US Maritime Service, 1944-45; field repr, US War Shipping Admn, 1945-46. Chmn: admn bd, WJCong, Amer Sect, 1969; natl admn bd, Amers for Progressive Isr, since 1966; exec bd, NY J Conf,

since 1959; natl comm on comty relations, AZC, since 1960, mem, natl exec comm, since 1962; vice-pres, Bx Co br, NAACP, 1956-57, chmn, legal redress comm, 1955-57; hon natl vice-chmn, JNF, since 1962; mem, natl exec, co-chmn, Amer Activities comm, B'nai Zion, 1962-66; chmn, local sch bd, Manhattan, 1939-49; natl adm bd, AJCong, 1946-48; natl council, Amers for Haganah, 1948; judge-advocate, post of JWV, 1950-51; mem, Amer Trial Lawyers Assn; secy, equal rights comm, NY State Trial Lawyers Assn; mem, NY Co Lawyers Assn. Mgn ed, Bklyn Law Rev, 1935; contbr to legal and J jours. Recipient: Atlantic War Zone Bar, US Merchant Marine, 1945. Home: 3977 Sedgwick Ave, New York, NY. Office: 310 Madison Ave, New York, NY.

HARKAVY, Ira Bear, US, attorney; b. Bklyn, NY, Apr 13, 1931; s. Morris and Esther (Brown); BA, Bklyn Coll, 1951; JD, Columbia U, 1954; m. Roberta Firsty, Aug 11, 1957; c: Steven, Daniel, Elliot. Atty, Delson and Gordon, since 1970; partner, Harkavy & Tell, 1954-67; partner, Harkavy, Tell & Mendelson, 1967-70. Pres, Parents Assn, PS 222K; vice-pres, Bklyn Coll Fund; chmn: Comty Dist Planning Bd 14, Bklyn; ADL, Bklyn Council; fmr: pres, Kings Co Lodge, B'nai B'rith; vice-pres, Bklyn Coll Alumni Assn; mem: Amer Bar Assn; Phi Alpha Delta, NY Alumni Chap. Recipient: Awards of Merit: ADL, 1966; B'nai B'rith, 1967. Home: 1784 E 29 St, Brooklyn, NY. Office: 230 Park Ave, New York, NY.

HARKAVY, Zvi, Isr, publisher, biographer, writer; b. Yekaterinoslav, Russ, Feb 1, 1908; s. Yehuda and Rashe (Karpas); in Isr since 1926; att: Inst for Bibliography, Russ, 1926; Technion, Haifa, 1926-27; Tchrs Sem, Jerusalem, 1927-30; Heb U, 1935-40; ordained rabbi, Yeshivat Petach Tikvah, 1943; BA, MA, ThD, Cen Sch of Rel, US, 1954; m. Dina Katz, 1944; c: Yehuda. Dir, Cen Rabb Libr of Isr, Hechal Shlomo, since 1953; ed, Hasefer, bibliographical rev, since 1954; head, Hotzaat Sfarim Eretz-Israelit, pub co, since 1936; found, rel sch, Maale, Jerusalem, 1930; Mizrachi repr: Greece, 1931-32; Latvia, 1933-34; Bulgaria, 1934-35; delg to numerous countries; lectr, Yeshiva U, NY, 1958-59. Active mem, Haganah since 1926; mil chaplain, IDF, 1948-49. Cofound: Yavneh, rel academicians assn; Isr Assn Rel Authors, chmn; Magen, Soc help Russ J; Assn Russ Immigrants in Isr; natl bd, Brith Rishonim; mem secretariat, Libr Assn; cen exec comm, Brith Ivrit Olamit; cen comm, Hapoel Hamizrachi; Isr Comm for Cultural Relations with Russ, on mission to Russ: Lenin Libr, Moscow; Govt Libr, Leningrad; lectr on research in Judaica in Isr, Russ Acad Sci. Author: Shomrei haGahelet; Tshuvat haGeonim; numerous books; participated in numerous researches and articles in forums in Heb, Yiddish, Ladino, Russ; ed: Katrinoslav Dnyeproptovsk; Ency Israel; Matat Yah. Home: 7 Haran St, Jerusalem, Isr. Office: Hechal Shlomo, Jerusalem, Isr.

HARLAN, Norman R, US, business exec; b. Dayton, O, Dec 21, 1914; s. Joseph and Anna (Kaplan); Commercial Ing, U Cincinnati, 1937; m. Thelma Katz, Sep 4, 1955; c: Leslie, Todd. Pres: Amer Construction Corp, since 1949; Main Line Inves; Harlan, Inc, Realtors; Starlighter Bldg, all since 1951. Mem: Dayton and O Real Estate Bds; Natl Assn Home Builders; C of C; Phi Lambda Phi. Home: 933 Garrison Ave, Kettering, O. Office: 2451 S Dixie, Kettering, O.

HARMAN, Avraham, Isr, diplomat; b. London, Eng, 1914; s. Israel and Zippora (Hoffman); in Isr since 1940; att Wadham Coll, Oxford; BA, 1935; hon DHL, JTSA, 1959; m. Zena Stern, 1940; c: David, Naomi, Ilana. Pres, Heb U, Jerusalem, since 1968; Isr Ambass to US, Wash, DC, 1959-68; staff mem, S Afr ZF, 1939-40; head, Eng sect, youth dept, JA, Jerusalem, 1940, head, info dept, 1942-48; dep dir, press info div, Isr Min for Fgn Affairs, 1948-49; Isr Consul-Gen, Can, 1949-50; dir, Isr Off of Info, counselor to Isr delg to UN, both 1950-53; consul gen, NY, 1953-55; asst dir gen, Min for Fgn Affairs, Jerusalem, 1955-56; mem, exec, JA, Jerusalem, 1956-59. Home: 3 Disraeli St, Jerusalem, Isr. Office: Hebrew U, Jerusalem, Isr.

HARMAN, Zena, Isr, communal worker; b. London, Eng; d. Solomon and Clara Stern; in Isr since 1940; grad, LSE, Eng; att Morley Coll; m. Avraham Harman, 1939; c: David, Naomi, Ilana. Chmn, Comm for Population Planning, PM's Off, Jerusalem; chmn: exec bd, UNICEF, 1964; Fourteen Nation Prog Comm, UNICEF; exec comm, Szold Found, Jerusalem, 1955-57; vice-pres, Intl Council of Women, since 1960; dir, div of intl orgs, Min for Fgn Affairs, 1957-59; rapporteur, UN Comm on Status of Women, 1952; dep-dir, Tech Assistance Dept, PM Off, 1955-57; head, children's sect, Social Wfr Dept, Munic of Jerusalem, 1939; mem: Isr Perm Mission to UN, 1951-55; exec comm, Intl Conf Social Work, 1958-68, 1968-72; staff, J Assn for Protection of Girls, Women and Children, London. Author: Adventure in Education; Women in Israel; Immigration and Absorption of Refugees; ed, Henrietta Szold letters, covering Youth Aliyah Period; contbr to publs. Recipient: Mother of the Year, 1960; Woman of the Year, various orgs. Home: 3 D'Israeli St, Jerusalem, Isr.

HARMAT, Zoltan Shimshon, Isr, architect; b. Huszt, Hung, Aug 29, 1900; s. Jenö and Karolina (Stern); in Isr since 1925; dipl architecture, Royal Joseph Tech U, Budapest. Pvt practice, 1929-51, and since 1953; dir, Town Planning Dept, Jerusalem Dist, 1951-53; works executed: Masonic Hall, Ramallah; Potash House, Beth Shalom, Beth Hillel, Beth Yeladim, Holyland Hotel, all in Jerusalem; Botanical Labs OBDAT; apt houses; schs; ind bldgs. Hobby: piano playing. Home and office: 20 Hatibonim St, Jerusalem, Isr.

HAR-MATZ, Joseph, Isr, organization exec; b. Lith, Jan 23, 1925; s. Abraham and Dvora (Baron); att: U Vilna; Sch Law and Econ, Tel Aviv; m. Regina Kirshenfeld, June 28, 1951; c: Zvi, Ronel, Ephraim. Dir gen, ORT, Isr, since 1967; comptroller, 1960-67; head: machinery dept, agric settlement dept, JA, 1951-53, exec dir, supply and equipment dept, 1953-55, reprfor Eur, N Afr, 1955-60. Haganah, War of Independence, 1948-49. Recipient: Fr Order of Merit, Fr Govt. Home :24 Haoranim St, Kfar Shmariyahu, Isr. Office: 39 King David Blvd, Tel Aviv, Isr.

HAROUCHE, Albert, Fr, organization exec; b. Alexandria, Egypt, Nov 21, 1913; s. Isaac and Savina (Azar-Cohen); in Fr since 1948; m. Victorine Cohen, June 12, 1938; c: Isaac, Roger, Sarine. Dir gen, Consistoire Central Israelite de France et d'Algerie, since 1964. Fr Army, 1939-40. Fmr pres, B'nai B'rith, Fr Lodge, Paris; secy gen, Conseil Representatif des Juifs de France; treas, Assn Zadoc-Kahn, scholarship fund; fmr mem: ZO; Maccabi, both in Egypt; club, Masons, Grand Orient de France. Home: 15 rue du Dessous des Berges, Paris 13e, Fr. Office: 17 rue St Georges, Paris 9e, Fr.

HARPAZ, Ephraim, Isr, educator; b. Warsaw, Pol, Oct 14, 1920; s. Abraham and Zipora (Bernstein); in Isr since 1921; MA, Heb U, 1942; PhD, Sorbonne, 1950; m. Louise Tenenbaum; c: Nahum. Prof, Fr civilization, Heb U; insp, Fr schs, Min of Educ, 1954-57; councillor of cultural affairs, Isr Emb, Paris, 1960-63. Haganah, 1939-48. Author: Le Censeur Européen, 1964; L'ecole Litérale sous la Restauration, 1968; contbr to profsl jours. Home: 16 Achad Haam, Jerusalem, Isr. Office: Heb U, Jerusalem, Isr.

HAR-PAZ, Hayim, Isr, economist; b. Bucharest, Rum, Mar 8, 1926; s. Menashe and Elcka (Michel) Goldenberg; in Isr since 1948; D Law, Econ Sci, U de Lyon, Fr, 1963; BEcon, Tel Aviv U Sch of Law and Econ, 1958; MEcon, Heb U, Tel Aviv br, 1960; m. Sarah Pancer, Nov 16, 1947; c: Israel, Yeshayau, Yuval. Dir, research, stat dept, Tel Aviv-Jaffa Munic, since 1961; lectr, econ, Afro-Asian Inst for Lab Studies and Coop, Tel Aviv, since 1960; econ adv to PM of Congo, lectr, econ, Ecole Natl de Droit et d'Administration, Congo, 1964-66; prog specialist, econ planning, Ford Found, NY, 1964-66; dir, research, stat dept, Workers Health Ins Inst, Tel Aviv, 1956-61. Capt, IDF, 1949-56. Mem: Intl Assn Munic Stats; Natl Comm on Stat, Isr; research comm, Isr Assn Georontology; fmr, mem staff: Gordonia; Hasmoneya, both Zionist movements, Rum. Contbr numerous articles to profsl publs. Home: 32 Hankin St, Holon, Isr. Office: Tel Aviv-Jaffa Munic Bldg, Isr.

HARPAZ, Isaac, Isr, entomologist; b. Tel Aviv, Isr, Dec 5, 1924; s. Yekutiel and Hasha (Erster); MSc, Heb U, 1947; PhD, 1953; m. Jocheved Levy, Sep 1, 1953; c: Sheenan. Prof, chmn, dept entomology, Heb U, since 1965, dean, fac of agric, 1963-64. Lt, IDF, since 1948. Mem: Intl Panel Experts on Integrated Pest Control; Royal Entomological Soc of London; Isr Entomological Soc. Co-author, Plant Pests of Israel; contbr to profsl jours. Home: 13 Shimoni, Rehovot, Isr. Office: Heb U, Fac of Agric, Rehovot, Isr.

HARPAZ, Yoav, Isr, hydrologist, engineer; b. Tel Aviv, Isr, Sep 15, 1927; s. Nuté and Haya (Perlman); att: Agric Coll, Mikveh Isr; Wayne U, Detroit; BSc, CE, Technion, Haifa; m. Shulamith Lichtental, Jan 20, 1949; c: Ailat, Eidan, Shirry. Head: dept water resources, Water Planning for Isr, since 1967, Dept Negev Hydrology, 1960-64; mgr: Tahal

Cons Engrs Intl, since 1968; UN Devl Projects and Govt of Isr Jt Projects Underground Water Storage, since 1963; head, dept environmental safety, Isr AEC, 1959-61; mgr, coastal collector works, Tahal, UN Project, 1965-66; chief hydrologist: water resources devl mission: Cen Iran, 1960; Peru, 1962. Haganah; Maj: Palmach; Haganah; IDF, 1945-50. Prin contribs: devl of water resources in Isr deserts; devl of concept of underground water storage; sci methods for tracing water and waste effluents in the ground; establishing advanced water resources, research engr group in Isr. Mem: natl secretariat, Natl Fed Engrs; Natl Water Research Commn; safeguard comm, Isr AEC; Natl Comm for Oceanography and Lymnology; Intl Assn of Geodesy and Geophys, fmr gen secy, Isr br; Intl Assn Sci Hydrology; Assn Engrs and Architects in Isr; Natl Fed of Engrs; fmr: delg, Habonim, Hashavim Movement, ZOA; mem academic comm, Rafi, political party. Author: Water Resources in the Negev, 1960; Radio-active Isotope Methods in Groundwater Research; Water Resources in Israel New Territories, 1967; Underground Water Storage Study, 1968; Underground Water Storage for the National Water System, 1962; Use of Radio Isotope Tracers in Large Scale Recharge Studies, 1965; Mixing of Waters in Underground Storage Operations, 1963; New Methods of Ground Water Studies, 1967. Home: 13 Be'eri St, Tel Aviv, Isr. Office: 54 Ibn Gvirol St, Tel Aviv, Isr.

HARPUDER, Karl, US, physician; b. Munich, Ger, Apr 11, 1893; s. Samuel and Pauline (Reiser); in US since 1934; MD, U Munich, 1917; m. Augusta Knoesing, Sep 22, 1923. Chief att phys, i/c phys med and rehab, Montefiore Hosp, Bx, NY, since 1934, presently ret; sr cons, VA Hosp, Bx, since 1946; instr with prof rank, NY Med Coll, since 1952; asst clinical prof, med, Columbia U, since 1937, presently ret; U Hosp, Munich, 1919-20; U Hosp, Kiel, 1920-25; chief, Munic Hosp for Rheumatism, Wiesbaden, 1925-33, all Ger; research F, Guys Hosp, London, 1933-34; visiting Horowitz Prof, phys med and rehab, NYU, 1959. Dipl, Amer Bd Internal Med; sr mem, Intl Soc for Angiology; mem: NY State and Co Med Soc; AMA; hon, Amer Paraplegic Soc; fmr: pres: NY Soc Phys Med; E Sect, Amer Cong Phys Med. Mem, ed bd, Amer Jour of Phys Med; contbr to profsl jours. Recipient, Gold Key Award, Amer Cong Phys Med and Rehab, 1957. Home: 3390 Wayne Ave, Bronx, NY.

HARRIS, Abraham J, attorney; b. St Paul, Minn, Aug 8, 1908; s. Lazer and Annie (Schwartz); AB, U Minn, 1930; LLB, Harvard U, 1933; m. Harriet Goldfine, June 17, 1937; c: Kathryn, Jeremy. Pvt practice; asst Solicitor Gen, US, 1950; asst Atty Gen, US, 1950-51; chmn, Pres Emergency Fact Finding Bd, 1952-53. Vice-chmn, exce comm, Comty Council, Gtr Wash, since 1968; mem: natl exec bd, AJComm, 1953-65; Wash Heb Cong; DC and Amer Bar Assns; club, Natl Capitol, Dem. Home: 8314 Meadowlark Lane, Bethesda, Md. Office: 888 17 St, NW, Washington, DC.

HARRIS, Annie, Austr, civic worker; b. London, Eng, Aug, 1877; d. Louis; m. May 3, 1904; c: Elias, Isadore. Ret; fmr: pres, Melbourne Heb Ladies Benevolent Soc; life gov: all Melbourne Metrop Hosps; Inst for Blind; Melbourne J Philanthropic Soc; Orphans and Children's Aid Soc; Francis Backman's Children's Home; hon secy, women's comm, St Kilda Heb Cong; hon org secy for 40 years, Bachelor and Hosts Ball of Melbourne J Comty; hon secy, fund raiser, Pal Infant Wfr Cen, Tel Aviv. Recipient: MBE, 1941. Home: 61 Balaclava Rd, E St Kilda, Melbourne, Australia.

HARRIS, Benjamin R, US, chemical engr; b. Lodz, Pol, Feb 19, 1896; s. Eli and Sarah (Raczkowska); in US since 1906; BS, CCNY, Ward Medallist, 1917; MS, U Ill, 1921; m. Gertrude Epstein, 1926; c: Elihu, Akiba. Owner, Epstein, Reynolds and Harris, cons, chem and engrs, since 1923; chmn, exec comm: Ampal-Amer Isr Corp, 1949-65; Isr Devl, 1953-64; treas, Kress Products, 1943-47; vice-pres, later pres, Emulsol, Chgo, 1926-55. Chem Warfare Service, US Army, 1917-18. Pres, Akiba Found, since 1958; vice-pres, ZOA, 1953-64; chmn, exec comm, Bd J Educ, Chgo, 1940-65; co-chmn: United Isr Appeal, since 1941; J United Fund, Chgo, 1968-69; bd dirs: JWF, Chgo, 1940-51; N Suburban Syn Beth El, Highland Park, Ill; Amer Comm for Weizmann Inst; Found for Graphic Hist J Lit; natl council, JDC; bd trustees, Coll J Studies, Chgo; F, Amer Inst Chems; mem: AAAS; Amer Chem Soc; Amer Oil Chems Soc; Inst Food Technologists; Assn Cons, Chems and Chem Es; Assn J Orthodox Scis; Amer Assn J Educ; United Syn of Amer; Amer Technion Soc; United HIAS Service; ORT; Solomon Goldman Memorial Found; Amer Friends Heb U; YIVO; JTSA; NY Philharmonic Soc;

Dropsie Coll for Heb and Cognate Learning; Histadruth Ivrith; Bitzaron; JNF; CJA, Chgo; J Publ Soc of Amer; Asso Talmud Torahs of Chgo; B'nai B'rith; AJCong; Amer J League for Isr; Chgo Crime Comm; Heb Theol Coll; Citizens Sch Comm; Natural Hist Mus; Chgo Found for Rel Action; Halevi Choral Soc; Roosevelt U; Amer Music Libr in Isr; Chgo Loop Syn; Sigma Xi; Phi Lambda Upsilon; Orch Assn; Art Inst; Amer Isr Culture Found; Chgo Catholic Interracial Council; World J Bible Soc Found; US Comm for Sports in Isr; Chgo Yiddish Theater Assn; Natl Found for J Culture; Telshe Yeshiva; Amer Isr Pub Affairs Comm; Planned Parenthood Assn; Chgo Council on Fgn Relations; Hadassah; Soc Friends Touro Syn; club, Chemist, NY. Contbr to sci and tech jours. Home: 885 Elm Pl, Glencoe, Ill. Office: 5 S Wabash Ave, Chicago, Ill.

HARRIS, Bruria Kaufman, Isr, mathematician; b. NYC, Aug 21, 1918; d. Yehuda and Fruma (Selenger) Even-Shmuel; in Isr since 1960; PhD, Columbia U, 1949; m. Zellig Harris, Dec 29, 1941; c: Tamar. Asso prof, math, Weizmann Inst Sci, since 1961. Contbr to profsl jours. Hobby: music. Home: Kibbutz Mishmar HaEmek, Isr. Office: Weizmann Inst, Rehovot, Isr.

HARRIS, Donald W, US, social worker; b. Cincinnati, O, Feb 22, 1917; s. Isidore and Sara (Wittstein); att HUC, 1936-39; BA, U Cincinnati, 1939, MEd, 1959; att O State U Grad Sch of Social Admn, 1939-41; m. Dorothy Botwin, Aug 31, 1941; c: Jerald, Judith, Ellen. Exec vice-pres, Dist Grand Lodge No 2, B'nai B'rith, since 1947; chief, case-work sup, Child Wfr Bd, 1942-46. Psycht social worker, research cons, US Army, 1943-46. Vice-chmn, spec gifts div, JWF, Cincinnati; mem, bd: Leo N Levi Memorial Hosp; O-Ky, ADL; mem: B'nai B'rith, fmr pres, Alfred M Cohen Lodge; AJComm; Natl Assn Social Workers; Social Service Assn; Wise Temple. Home: 1805 Larchwood Pl, Cincinnati, O. Office: 1717 Section Rd, Cincinnati, O.

HARRIS, Elihu E, US, advertising, public relations exec; b. Cincinnati, O, Sep 16, 1908; s. Sam and Sadie (Levy); att: HUC, 1926-29; Cincinnati U and Law Sch, 1926-30; m. Joan Schaen, Sep 30, 1934; c: Martha Zielonka, Laura Harris. Asso dir, devl, WNDT/13, Educ Bc Corp, NY, since 1969; pres, Gordon Harris Org, Inc, since 1969; advt mgr, Amer Bldg Assn News, 1930-31; mgn ed, bus mgr, Radio Dial, 1931-32; dir, adv, promotion, Treas Dept, 1943-54; pres, Donall and Harman Inc, 1956-62; dir, advt, promotion, educ divs, Grolier, 1962-68; vice-pres, Surveys for Bus, 1968-69. Mem: B'nai B'rith; Sigma Alpha Mu; Big Bros Assn; club, Advt, NY. Contbr to profsl jours. Recipient: Treas Dept, Silver Medal, 1946, 1949, 1954. Home: 4555 Henry Hudson Pkway, Riverdale, NY. Office: 304 W 58 St, New York, NY.

HARRIS, Fred F, US, business exec; b. Los Angeles, Dec 13, 1909; s. Frederick and Carrie (Friendly); BA, U of Cal, 1932; m. Maxine Salomon, Aug 15, 1935, div; c: Jo Ann Lautman, Frederick; m. 2nd, Marie Daneman, 1956; step-c: Patricia Brown, Peter Finsterwald. Realtor since 1932; pres: F E Harris Co Inves securities, 1932-36; Harris Hotels, 1935-55. Pres: Wilshire Cen Assn, 1948, 1952; S Cal Hotel Assn, 1949-50, bd dirs, 1948-52; bd govs, Amer Hotel Assn, 1949-50; clubs: LA Yacht; Beverly; Trans-Pacific Yacht; Riviera Country; Cal Yacht, staff commodore; Assn of Santa Monica Bay Yacht, staff commodore; Tamarisk Country; Palm Springs. Home: 717 N Roxbury Dr, Beverly Hills, Cal. Office: 9350 Wilshire Blvd, Beverly Hills, Cal.

HARRIS, Gilbert, US, communal worker; b. St Louis, Mo, Jan 19, 1894; s. Bernard and Hulda (Nathan); att: U of Mo; Washington U; U Chgo; m. Rosalind Weil, July 21, 1930; c: Jeremy, Joel. Fac mem, Wash U, St Louis, Mo, since 1960; exec dir: YM-YWHA, 1922-58; JCC Assn, 1958-60. Pres: St Louis Grand Jury Assn; Natl Assn J Cen Workers, 1927; acting chmn, St Louis Land Clearance Auth, 1964; secy, St Louis Award Comm, since 1930; mem, bd dirs: J Hist Soc, since 1960; St Louis USO, 1940-55; mem: Natl Assn Social Workers; B'nai B'rith; JWV; Adult Educ Soc. Author: Day in the Life of a Center Executive; The Art of Being a Jew; A Study of the Boards of St Louis Agencies; short stories. Spec interests: people, comty wfr. Home: 5290 Waterman St, St Louis, Mo. Office: S Kinker and Lindell Blvd, St Louis, Mo.

HARRIS, Homer I, US, attorney, author; b. NYC, June 8, 1902; s. Arthur and Minna (Adams); BS, NYU, 1923, IE, 1924, JD, 1926; m. Evelyn Freedman, Aug 31, 1938; c: Andrea, Marsha. Pvt practice since 1926; lectr, Practicing Law Inst, 1954-68. Pres, Freeport Union Reform Temple, 1953-55; chmn, dece-

dent estate law comm, 1955-60; dir, Nassau Bar Assn, 1959-62; mem: B'nai B'rith; ADL. Author: Estates Practice Guide, 1968; Family Estate Planning Guide, 1957; Why Family Estate Planning, 1957; New York and Federal Estate Taxes, 1959; Handling Estate and Gift Taxes, 1959. Home: 160 West End Ave, New York, NY. Office: 217 Broadway, New York, NY.

HARRIS, Hugh, Eng, editor, educator; b. Liverpool, Eng, Sep 19, 1897; s. John and Edith (Michaelson); BA, King's Coll, U London, 1922; MLitt, Emmanuel Coll, Cambridge, 1928; m. Florence Beriro, Apr 10, 1934. Lit ed, J Chronicle, 1937-67; ed, J Year Book, 1951-68, both London; headmaster, W Hampstead Day Sch, 1933-38; Heb tutor, Harrow Sch, 1933-36; classics master: Perse Sch, Cambridge, 1926-28; Dulwich Coll, 1943; City of London Sch, 1945; lectr, classics, Eng lit, J Coll, London, 1949-62. London U gov, Gt London Council secondary schs, since 1947; vice-chmn, J Peace Soc and repr on UN Assn and Natl Peace Council, since 1948; chmn, Soc for J Study, since 1960; mem: comm, J Book Council; exec comm: World Cong of Faiths; London Soc of J and Chr; Cambridge U Union Soc; chmn, hon org, Anglo-J exhb, Festival of Brit, 1951; pres, 1st lodge of Eng, B'nai B'rith, 1958-60; clubs: Reform; Intl PEN, Eng cen. Author: Bandello's Tragical Tales, 1924; The Greek, the Barbarian and the Slave, 1928; Questions in Philosophy, 1948; English Words of Hebrew Origin, 1969; contbr to: Ency Britannica; The Times; periodicals; lit revs. Home: 149 Walm Lane, London NW2, Eng.

HARRIS, Hyman H, US, communal worker; b, Granov, Russ, Oct 15, 1882; s. Zwi and Bella (Steigelberg); in US since 1913; PhG, Temple U, 1917; Pharm D, Lincoln-Jefferson U, 1925; m. Rachel Selenger, Aug 15, 1905; c: Suzanne Sankowsky, Enya Live, Zellig, Zvi. Pharm, 1917-38; rel rites performer; 1905-17; Yavne Syn; lectr on J music. Prin contrib: invented surg instruments for circumcision, 1932. Fmr, chmn, lab div, JNF, Phila; mem: exec council, ZOA, Phila; council, AJCong, Phila; Farband; B'nai Zion. Author: Hebrew Liturgical Music, 1950; contbr to med publs. Recipient: testimonial, Cantors' Assn, 1951; citation, JNF, 1957; Histadrut campaign, 1958; award, State of Isr Bonds, 1963. Home: 2222 N 53 St, Philadelphia, Pa.

HARRIS, Jerome S, US, pediatrician, educator; b. NYC, Feb 27, 1909; s. Mark and Mary (Marcus); AB, Dartmouth Coll, Hanover, NH, 1929; MD, Harvard Med Sch, 1933; m. Jacqueline Hijmans, Oct 23, 1958. Prof, ped, asso prof, biochem, Duke U Sch of Med, since 1954, chmn, dept of ped, 1954-68. Maj, lt col, US Army, 1942-46. Mem: Phi Beta Kappa; Alpha Omega Alpha; Soc for Ped Research; Amer Ped Soc; Amer Soc for Clinical Inves. Contbr to sci jours. Home: 2907 Valley Rd, Durham, NC. Office: Duke Hosp, Durham, NC.

HARRIS, Lucien, Isr, organization exec; b. Antwerp, Belgium, Sep 26, 1912; s. Elias and Bertha (Stern); in Isr since 1948; Somerset Iver Scholar, Brasenose Coll, Oxford, 1930, BA, hons, 1934; m. Marie Polinsky, Aug 18, 1937; c: David, Mira, Pinhas. Dir, info services in Isr, Hadassah Med Org, since 1955; mem, Hadassah Med Org mgmt, since 1952; info, JA, London, 1941-42, 1946-48; asst, Controller of Manpower, Isr Min Lab, 1948-50; parl asst, Isr Min Trade and Ind, 1950-51; dep dir, personnel dept, Civil Service Commn, PM off, 1951-52. Flight lt, RAF, 1942-46. Mem: exec, Independent Lib Party; adv council, Hitachdut Olei Britannia; Isr Inst PR; fmr: pres, Oxford U Zionist Soc; vice-pres, U ZF, Gt Brit and Ir; vice-chmn, Manchester Zionist Assn; exec council, ZF, Gt Brit, Ir; natl chmn, British Patwa; club, Jerusalem Rotary, pres. Spec interests: lecturing; conf interpreting; served simultaneous interpreter, Heb-Eng, Eichmann trial. Home: 20 Harav Berlin St, Jerusalem, Isr. Office: POB 499, Jerusalem, Isr.

HARRIS, Milton, US, researcher, chemist; b. Los Angeles, Mar 21, 1906; s. Louis and Naomi (Granish); att U of Wash, 1925; BS, Ore State Coll, 1926; PhD, Yale U, 1929; hon DSc, Phila Coll Sci and Tech, 1955; m. Carolyn Wolf; c: Barney, John. Cons, Panel on Environment, Pres Sci Adv Comm, since 1968; cons corresp, Natl Acad Sci, Comm on Sci and Tech Communication, since 1967; mem: Agric Dept's Utilization Research and Devl Adv Comm, since 1966; NSF, Comm for Planning, since 1968; observer-cons, Task Group on Natl Sys for Sci and Tech Info, Fed Council for Sci and Tech, since 1968; Cen Comm, Intl Council Sci Unions and UN Educ, Sci and Cultural Org, Jt Project on Communication of Sci Info, since 1969; visitors comm, Research Found Wash Hosp

Cen, since 1967, exec comm, Weizmann Inst Sci, since 1967; adv comm, dept of chem, George Wash U, since 1968; ind adv group, dept chem, U of Cal, San Diego, since 1968; trustee-at-large, Dermat Found since 1969; chmn, bd dirs, Amer Chem Soc, since 1966; exec comm, Sealectro Corp, since 1966; mem bd dirs: Sealectro, since 1964; Warner-Lambert Pharmaceutical, since 1968; researcher, Cheney Bros, 1929-31; research asso, Natl Bur of Standards, 1931-38; dir, Textile Found, 1938-45; pres, Harris Research Labs, Wash, DC, 1945-61; dir, research, Gillette Co and subsidiaries, vice-pres, 1957-66. F: Textile Inst; NY Acad of Sci; mem: Amer Soc Biol Chems; AAAS; Amer Assn Textile Colorists and Chems; Amer Oil Chems Soc; Soc of Cosmetic Chems; Fiber Soc; Amer Chem Soc; Amer Inst Chems; Soc Chem Ind; Wash Acad Sci; Sigma Xi; Tau Beta Pi; Phi Lambda Upsilon, Phi Kappa Phi; Gamma Alpha; fmr: pres, Yale Chem's Assn; dir at-large, Amer Chem Soc; mem: Yale Alumni Bd; Yale U Council; Yale Devl Bd; exec comm, Yale Grad Sch Alumni Assn; bd dirs: Orbit Inds; Hazelton Labs; trustee, Textile Research Inst; chmn, comm on textiles and cordage, Army-Navy Natl Defense Research Comm, tropical deterioration project; with NRC: secy: comm on clothing; comm on degradation; natl adv comm for aeronautics, subcomm on wood and plastics; chmn, wool conservation bd; fmr mem: panel on clothing, Research and Devl Bd; subcomm, FAO, UN; chmn, panel civilian tech, Pres Sci Adv Comm; cons, exec office of Pres; chmn, Wash sect, Amer Inst Chems; with Amer Chem Soc: chmn: cellulose div; comm on natl meetings and div activities; clubs: Cosmos, Wash DC; Chem, NY. Author, Handbook on Textiles, 1954; contbr to profsl jours; adv bd, advances in chem series; sect ed, Dyes and Textile Chem, Chemistry Abstracts, adv bd, Jour of Polymer Sci, asso ed, Textile Research Jour; ed, Natural and Synthetic Fibres, both since 1944. Recipient: award, Wash Acad Scis, 1943; Olney M medal for research in textile chem, 1955; Awards: Harold DeWitt Smith Memorial Medal, 1966; dist service, Oregon State U, 1967; Perkin Medal, 1970. Home: 4101 Linnean Ave, NW, Washington, DC. Office: 3300 Whitehaven St, NW, Washington, DC.

HARRIS, Milton E, US, attorney; b. Pittsburgh, Pa, Nov 15, 1904; s. Harry and Lillian (Browarsky); BS, U Pittsburgh, 1926, DJ, 1929; m. Ruth Kerstein, July 18, 1946; c: Milton, Richard. Pvt practice since 1929; pres, Continental Transp Lines Inc, 1953-68; chmn, bd, Werner Continental, 1968-70. Pres: Natl Fed Temple Brotherhoods; J Chautauqua Soc; trustee, Rodef Shalom Cong; fmr, natl pres, Phi Epsilon Pi; mem, bd dirs, UAHC; club, Rotary, Pittsburgh chap. Home: 5365 Darlington Rd, Pittsburgh, Pa. Office: 415 Oliver Bldg, Pittsburgh, Pa.

HARRIS, Sydney M, Can, attorney; b. Toronto, June 23, 1917; s. Samuel and Rose (Geldzaeler); BA, U Toronto, 1939; Barrister-at-Law, Osgoode Hill, 1942; m. Enid Perlman, Nov 9, 1949; c: Stuart, David. Pvt practice since 1942; partner, Harris and Rubenstein, since 1950; QC, since 1963. Chmn, cen region, Can J Cong, since 1968, mem, natl exec since 1950; mem: natl exec, B'nai B'rith; Law Soc of Upper Can; fmr: pres: Can Council Reform Congs; Upper Can Lodge, B'nai B'rith; J Vocational Service; chmn, natl and cen region, comty relations comms: Can J Cong; B'nai B'rith; secy, Holy Blossom Temple. Home: 52 Avenal Dr, Toronto, Can. Office: 133 Richmond St W, Toronto, Can.

HARRISON, Donald William, US, business exec; b. New Haven, Conn, Apr 27, 1925; s. Nathan and Minnie (Chaucer); att Brown U; m. Diane Lee, Oct 4, 1953; c: Richard, Susan. Pres, Conn Distributors Inc, since 1948; dir, Lafayette Bank and Trust Co. US Army, 1943-46. Dir: Cong Rodeph Shalom; United J Council, Bridgeport; Park City Hosp, Bridgeport; fmr: dir, J Comty Cen; co-chmn: UJA Campaign, Gtr Bridgeport Area; UJA Campaign, 1969; State of Isr Bonds; gen chmn, UJA Campaign; club, Rolling Hills Country. Hobbies: golf, skiing. Home: 240 Jennie Lane, Fairfield, Conn. Office: 16 Avon St, Stratford, Conn.

HARRUS, Elias, Morocco, educator; b. Béni-Mellal, Morocco, Sep 19, 1919; s. Simon and Hanina (Assouline); att: Inst Agricole d'Algérie, 1946; Ecole Normale Supérieure de St Cloud, 1959; m. Sarah Israel, Apr 17, 1940; c: Michel, Gabriel, Daniel, Nicole. Delg to Ittihad-Maroc, Morocco, since 1960; a found and dir, Ecole Agricole Israélite, Marrakesh; insp, primary educ; chmn, dept educ, J Youth; natl commn, Eclaireurs Israélites du Maroc. Prin contribs: helped establish agric sch for J under auspices of JCA and Alliance Israélite Universelle, instrumental in realization of film, Ils

Seront des Hommes, on contribs of Alliance to Morocco. Home: 17 bis rue Boileau, Casablanca, Morocco. Office: 13 rue Eléonore Fournier, Casablanca, Morocco.

HART, David Joseph, US, attorney; b. Feb 7, 1936; s. Samuel and Charlotte (Merson) Hartstein; BA, Cornell U, 1957; JD, Cornell Law Sch, 1962; MIA, Columbia U, Sch of Intl Affairs, 1962; postgrad, NYU, 1968-69; m. Leny Basha, Mar 12, 1969. Atty, adv, US Dept of Housing and Urban Devl, since 1965; instr, econs, Pace Coll since 1965; adv, US Sen John Sherman Cooper, 1962; asso, Kelley, Drye, Newhall, Maginnes & Warren, 1963; atty, in assn with Robert Daru, 1963-65. Fmr: delg chmn, Cornell U, Model UN; hon chmn, Mirror Youth Forum; mem: NY Co Lawyers Assn; NY State, Amer, Phila, Bx Co Bar Assns. Spec interests: econs, intl relations, finance, world travel. Home: 107-40 Queens Blvd, Forest Hills, New York, NY. Office: 26 Federal Plaza, New York, NY.

HART, Desmond Adolph, Eng, organization exec; b. Westcliff-on-Sea, Eng, Feb 6, 1912; s. Alfred and Julia (Siegenberg); m. Lillian Davis, Feb 6, 1938; c: Roger, Anthony. Exec dir, Friends of Magen David Adom in Gt Brit, since 1962; dir, appeals and comms, British Technion Soc, 1952-62. Royal Artillery, 1940-45. Org: Accordion Times, Dist & All-Eng Championships; Natl Fed Accordion Clubs; ed, Accordion & Harmonica: Melody Maker; Rhythm, all 1937-39; found, org secy: British Assn of Accordionists; Intl Accordionists Assn, 1952; found, ed, Accordion Review, 1946-52; dist comm, Sr Scouts, Wembley & Dist, 1958-60, co commn, 1960-62. Recipient, Croix de Chevalier, Paris, 1949. Hobbies: photography, record collecting, travel and biographical books. Home: 42 Lawns Court, Wembley Park, Middlesex, Eng. Office: 1-2 Hanover St, London WI, Eng.

HART, James D, US, educator; b. San Francisco, Apr 18, 1911; s. Julien and Helen (Neustadter); AB, Stanford U, 1932; MA, Harvard U, 1933; PhD, 1936; m. Ruth Arnstein, June 14, 1938; c: Carol Field, Peter. Prof, Eng, U of Cal, Berkeley, since 1951, fac mem since 1936, chmn, dept of Eng, 1955-57, 1965-69, vice-chancellor, 1957-60. Mem: MLA; Philol Assn, Pacific Coast. Author: The Oxford Companion to American Literature, 1941; The Popular Book, 1950; America's Literature, 1955; ed: Dana, Two Years Before the Mast; Parkman, The Oregon Trail; Stevenson, From Scotland to Silverado; contbr to periodicals. Recipient: CBE. Home: 740 San Luis Rd, Berkeley, Cal. Office: U of Cal, Berkeley, Cal.

HART, Sidney, Eng, fire off; b. London, Eng, Sep 11, 1914; s. Samuel and Amelia (Coutinho) Hartz; att J Free Sch, London; m. Edith Bernstein, Feb 25, 1940; c: Rona. Station off, Essex Co Fire Brig, since 1958, fire brig since 1940. Council mem, Southend and Westcliff Heb Cong; youth leader, Southend and Dist Youth Club; mem, Southend Youth Adv Comm; chmn: Fire Brigs Union, Midland and Wales Dist, 1944-48; Colwyn Bay and Landudno Trade Council, 1947-58; Asso Inst of Fire Engrs N Wales, 1956. Hobbies: cricket, table tennis. Home: 244 Carlton Ave, Westcliff-on-Sea, Essex, Eng.

HARTH, Bernhard Dov, Isr, advocate; b. Yacobeni, Rum, Mar 28, 1907; s. Yehuda and Yite (Goldschläger); in Isr since 1948; advocate, U Cernautz, Rum; m. Edith Lang, June 26, 1932; c: Berenice Resch. Dep, Official Receiver, since 1967; advocate, since 1928. Mem, B'nai B'rith Lodge Hashlosha, Holon, Isr, pres, 1954-55. Hobby, chess. Home: 50 Shenkar St, Holon, Isr. Office: 39 Nahlat Benjamin St, Tel Aviv, Isr.

HARTMAN, Paul, US, attorney; b. Czech, Sep 10, 1905; s. Gustav and Martha (Schanzer); in US since 1948; DJur, Ger U Law Sch, Prague, 1927; LLB, hons, London U, 1943; m. Marianne Lichtenstern, Dec 7, 1935; c: Martin, Michael. Asso dir, law dept, ADL, since 1948; fmr: expert on Czech law before courts in Eng, US; atty, Prague. Maj, Czech Mil Justice; pres, Mil Court, Eng. Prin contribs, expert on laws against racial and rel discrimination. Mem: bd, Soc for Hist of Czech J; fmr vice-pres, Joseph Popper Lodge, B'nai B'rith. Author: Die Politische Partei in der Tschechoslowakischen Republik: Eine Juristische Studie, 1931; contbr to profsl jours. Recipient, Rockefeller Traveling f, 1928-29. Hobbies: traveling; hunting. Office: 315 Lexington Ave, New York, NY.

HARTOGENSIS, Harold, US, business exec; b. NYC, Aug 18, 1907; s. Maurice and Martha (Greenbaum); att NYU, 1925-27; m. Ruth Greenberg, Feb 1, 1928; c: Deborah, Harold (decd). Ret; pres, Hartogensis Advt Co, 1950-68;

publisher, Dance Mag, 1936-38; acct exec, Williams & Saylor, 1938-39; cons to admnr, Rural Elec Admn, 1941-47; acct exec, Olian Advt Co, 1947-49. Bd trustee, The Light, publ, J Fed of St Louis, 1962-66; bus mgr, St Louis Comty Playhouse, 1947-49; secy, Advt Agcy Affiliates; chmn, Stevenson for Pres Comm, 1952; publ chmn, St Louis Comm for McCarthy, 1968; natl delg, Bus Exec Movement for Vietnam Peace. Contbr to profsl jours; author of short stories, radio scripts. Home: 1380 Lark Ave, Kirkwood, Mo.

HARTSTEIN, Abraham Louis, US, rabbi, psychotherapist; b. NYC; s. Nathan and Lea (Harris); dipl, cum laude, Heb Tchrs Inst, Yeshiva U, 1942; BA, magna cum laude, Yeshiva Coll, 1944; ordained rabbi, Isaac Elchanan Theol Sem, 1948; PhD, Yeshiva U, 1970. Rabbi: Garment Cen Cong, since 1969; United Syn, Hoboken, NJ, 1950-54; Cong Beth Isr and Temple Ashkenaz, Cambridge, Mass, 1954-59; cons to co dist atty, on juvenile delinquency; lectr: Mh care of rel patients, Nurses' Sch, Cambridge City Hosp; under Hillel Found auspices: Harvard U, Brandeis U, Boston U, Lesley Coll, Mass Inst of Tech. Life mem, Rel Zionists of Amer; mem: bd govs, NY Bd Rabbis; cabinet, Isr Bonds Org, Manhattan; comm on syn relations, FJP, NY; Amer Soc Group Psychotherapy and Psychodrama; Acad Rel and Mh; Beth Din of Amer, family counselor; fmr: pres, Middlesex Zionist dist, life mem, ZOA; bd: Mental Assn, repr to Red Feather Org; Guidance Clinic for Disturbed Children and Young Adults; Bd J Educ; ARC, fmr, vice-chmn; Boy Scouts of Amer, chaplain and adv; exec bd, Civic Unity Comm, chmn, annual clergy sem; hon bd mem, J Comty Cen, all Cambridge, Mass; Orthodox Rabb Council, Gtr Boston, chmn, radio-TV comm; RabCA, family counselor, rel court; Rabb Alumni Yeshiva U; Cambridge Min Assn; AJCong; natl commn, Rel Orgs of Chrs and Js; clergy commn, Northeast region, NCCJ; Amer J Hist Soc; Amer Inst Family Relations; Adult Educ Assn; Masons, past chaplain; B'nai B'rith. Recipient: Man-of-the-Year award, Jr C of C, 1958; awards from: Ivriah Women; Yeshiva U; Bonds for Isr Govt. Home: 160 E Third St, New York, NY. Study: 205 W 40 St, New York, NY.

HARTSTEIN, Jacob I, US, educational admn, psychologist; b. Stary Sambor, Aus, Sept 10, 1912; s. Nathan and Lea (Harris); in US since 1920; BA, Yeshiva Coll, NY, 1932; MS, CCNY, 1933; MA, Columbia U, 1936; PhD, NYU, 1945; hon LHD, Yeshiva U, 1962; m. Florence Waldman, Aug 16, 1942; c: Kalman, Norman. Pres, Kingsborough Comty Coll, prof, educ, CUNY, since 1964; dean, grad sch, LIU, 1953-64, fac mem since 1946; secy, Tchrs Inst, Yeshiva U, 1929-37; registrar, Yeshiva Coll, 1936-44, prof educ, 1945-53, dean, grad div, 1948-53; supt of schs, Bd Secular Educ, United Yeshivas, 1945-49. Pres, Natl Assn J Day Sch Prins, 1951-54; vice-chmn: Natl Comm on Educ in Public Arts; Gov's Comm on Scholastic Achievement, State of NY; f, AAAS; mem: bd govs, J Acad Arts and Sci; acad adv council, bd trustees, Bar Ilan U, Isr; Amer Assn Sch Admnrs; AAUP; Amer Educ Research Assn; Amer, E, NY State, and Bklyn Psych Assns; Educ Research Assn of NY State; Metrop NY Assn for Applied Psych; Natl Council of J Educ; Natl Conf J Communal and Social Affairs; Natl Soc for Study of Educ; Rel Educ Assn of US; Soc for Advancement of Educ; Phi Alpha Theta; Phi Delta Kappa; B'nai B'rith; Mizrachi Org of Amer; Masons. Author: Jewish Education in New York City, 1933, 1936, 1938; State Regulatory and Supervisory Control of Higher Education in New York, 1945; A Guide to General Psychology, 1947, 1948, 1950; co-author, Education Abstracts, 1942-44; contbr to prof jours. Recipient: awards: Abraham Freda, 1954; Yeshiva of Flatbush, 1954; dist service, LIU Grad Student Council and Educ Soc, 1958; Bernard Revel Memorial, Yeshiva Coll Alumni Assn, 1959; Man of Year in Educ, elected to the Hall of Fame, Better Bklyn Comm, 1965. Home: 1125 Virginia St, Far Rockaway, NY. Office: CUNY, New York, NY.

HARTSTEIN, Sam, US, public relations dir; b. NYC, Aug 6, 1921; s. Nathan and Lea (Harris); tchr dipl, Yeshiva U, 1941; BA, Yeshiva Coll, 1943; m. Rachel Zimmerman, June 23, 1963; c: Gila, Jonathan. PR dir: Yeshiva U, since 1943; NY Times, 1940-43. Fmr pres, Metrop Coll PR Council; exec comm: Tchrs Insts Asso Alumni; Mt Sinai J Cen; mem: Amer Coll PR Assn; Assn for Higher Educ; NEA; PR Comm; Council Higher Educ Instns in NYC; Natl Sch PR Assn; Coll Sports Info Dirs of Amer; Educ Writers Assn; Amer J PR Soc; Radio-TV Film Comm; Syn Council Amer; Health & Wfr PR Assn; Justice Lodge, Masons; HIAS; Menninger Found; Yeshiva Coll Alumni Assn. Contbr to jours. Recipient:

Cert of Merit, ACPRA, 1959, Citation of Hon, 1960, Citation for Dist Achievement in PR, 1962. Home: 66 Overlook Terr, New York, NY. Office: Amsterdam Ave and 186 St, New York, NY.

HARTZMAN, Robert, US, physician; b. NYC, May 2, 1929; s. David and Estelle (Friedman); BS, CCNY, 1950; MD, SUNY, 1954; m. Ruth Berkman, Apr 17, 1955; c: Steven, Craig, Fred. Phys, internal med, since 1960. Capt, USAF, 1958-60. Pres: Cong B'nai B'rith, since 1966; B'nai B'rith Lodge, 1964-65; mem, Masons. Recipient: Man-of-Year, Santa Barbara ADL, 1969. Home: 4585 Via Maria, Santa Barbara, Cal. Office: 2320 Bath, Santa Barbara, Cal.

HARUSSI, Emmannuel Yinon, Isr, poet; b. Nikolaiev, Russ, Aug 19, 1903; in Isr since 1924; att med fac, U Odessa; m. Hana Feldman, 1926; c: Avner, Yaniv, Yael. Author: Shirim uFizmonot, 1930; Mo'adimu Mazalot, 1966; contbr: articles, poems, stories, plays to press, mags. Fmr: i/c, Info and PR Depts, Min of Defense; dir info depts, various natl insts. Found, Hamatateh Theatre. Recipient, Lit Award, Davar newspaper, 1946. Home: 46 Hanassi St, Herzliya, Isr.

HASHIMSHONY, Zion, Isr, town planner; b. Segera-Galilee Isr, Oct 10, 1905; s. Shmuel and Zehava (Sheidman); dipl ing, U Ghent, Belgium, 1929; m. Esther Shapiro, July 7, 1935; c: Gideon, Shmuel, Ihiam. Pvt practice, head agcy, architecture and town planning; fmr: city engr, Munic of Petah Tikvah, 1935-48; head dept, town planning min, Interim Govt of Isr, 1948-53; adv, Min of Devl, 1953-58. Home: 6 Baron Hirsch St, Tel Aviv, Isr. Office: 19 Helsinky St, Tel Aviv, Isr.

HASKEL, Benjamin, US, labor econ; b. NYC, Aug 9, 1910; s. Max and Ida (Heimowitz); BBS, CCNY, 1929; AM, Columbia U, 1930, postgrad studies, 1930-36; att New Sch of Social Research, 1933-34; m. Doris Reich, Jan 30, 1943; c: Peter, Ellen. Regional lab adv, Agcy for Intl Devl, Near E-S Asia Bur; instr, hist, Bklyn Coll, 1932-39; ed, research dir, United Textile Workers, AFL, 1944-52; dep dir, lab manpower div, US Mission to NATO, Regional Org of Eur, 1957-60. Mem: Workmen's Circle; Amer Fed Govt Employees. Hobbies: music, art, archaeol, gardening. Home: 8402 Whitman Dr, Bethesda, Md. Office: Agcy for Intl Devl, Washington, DC.

HASKELL, Benjamin, US, proctologist, educator; b. Norfolk, Va, Apr 27, 1901; s. Jesse and Fannie (Saks); att Temple U, 1917-19; MD, Jefferson Med Coll, 1923; m. Gertrude Haskell, June 30, 1929; c: Jean Feinberg, David, John. Clinical prof em, proctology, Jefferson Med Coll, since 1966, clinical prof, 1952-66, fac mem since 1932; head, proctology sect, Jefferson Med Coll Hosp, since 1952; chief, proctological service, Albert Einstein Med Cen, 1947-57. Exec comm, med div, Amer Friends Heb U since 1951; co-chmn, phys div, Allied J App, 1948; f: Amer Coll Surgs; Amer Proctologic Soc; AMA; FACP. Contbr numerous articles to med jours. Hobbies: woodworking, fishing. Home: 226 W Rittenhouse Sq, Philadelphia, Pa. Office: 1427 Spruce St, Philadelphia, Pa.

HASKIN, Itzhak, Isr, organization exec; b. Krakinova, Lith, June 20, 1905; s. Moshe and Hanna (Rabinowitz); in Isr since 1925; att Tech Inst, Kiev; m. Nehama Korban, 1928; c: Yigal, Hannah, Ephraim, Nurit. Mem, exec comm, Histadrut, since 1949, dir, munic dept, 1942-49. S dist command, Hagana, 1930-40. Mem: cen comm, Mapai party, 1936. Contbr to local press. Home: 36 Komemiyut St, Afeka, Tel Aviv, Isr. Office: 93 Arlosoroff St, Tel Aviv, Isr.

HASLETON, Alfred, Eng, dental surg; b. Limerick, Ir, Aug 21, 1894; s. Simon and Leah (Cohen) Hesselberg; in Eng since 1897; LDS, Liverpool U, 1917; m. Bella Black, May 5, 1943; c: Simon, Evelyn Little, Henry, Carol Isaacs, Susan. Rét. Hon life pres, Merseyside JPA comm, vice-chmn, 1942-69, co-found, fmr United Pal Appeal, 1942; fmr: chmn: Zionist Cen Council, Liverpool and Southport; vice-chmn, JNF commn, hon treas, KH, both Liverpool; mem, Merseyside J Repr Council. Home: 5 Beechtree Close, Marsh Lane, Stanmore, Middlesex, Eng.

HASSAN, Alexander, US, civil engineer; b. Nova Scotia, Can, July 8, 1904; s. Nathan and Fanny (Zarch); in US since 1923; CE, Rensselaer Poly Inst, Troy, NY, 1927; m. Sylvia Schwartzman, Aug 15, 1933; c: Lois Raphling. Pres, owner, Loisdale Utilities Corp. Mem: natl bd, Amer Technion Soc; exec bd: UJA; Heb Acad; bd: Heb U, Weizmann Inst, both DC; treas:

J Comty Cen; Adas Isr Cong; Zionist Org, Brandeis Dist; trustee, Rensselaer Poly Inst; mem: B'nai B'rith; AJComm; hon mem, Zeta Beta Tau Frat; fmr, UJA mission to Isr. Home: 2510 Virginia Ave NW, Washington, DC. Office: POB 293, Springfield, Va.

HASSENFELD, Merrill L, US, business exec; b. Providence, RI, Feb 19, 1918; s. Henry and Marion (Frank); BSE, Sch of Finance, U of Pa, 1938; m. Sylvia Kay, Oct 15, 1940; c: Stephen, Alan, Ellen Block. Pres, Hasbro Ind Inc, 1943. US Army, 1944-45. F, Brandeis U; mem, cabinet, UJA, since 1960; pres, Gen J Comm, Providence, 1963-66; mem, bd dirs, CJFWF; fmr mem, bd dirs, Toy Mfrs Assn; Alpha Epsilon Pi. Home: 4 Woodland Terrace, Providence, RI. Office: 1027 Newport Ave, Pawtucket, RI.

HASSID, Sami, US, educator, architect; b. Cairo, Egypt, Mar 19, 1912; s. Joseph and Isabelle (Israel); in US since 1957; dipl, Sch of Engr, Egypt, 1932; B Arch, hons, U London, 1935; M Arch, U Cairo, 1943; D Arch, Harvard U, 1956; m. Juliette Mizrachi, June 29, 1941; c: Fred, Muriel. Prof, architecture, U of Cal, Berkeley, since 1964, on fac since 1957; architect since 1947; prof, architectural theory and design, U of Ein-Shams, Cairo, 1957; asst prof, U Cairo, 1934-57. Pres, Temple Beth El; commn, Cal State Bd Architectural Examiners; mem: Amer Inst of Architects; Brab Bldg Research Inst; Assn of Collegiate Schs of Architecture; chmn, comm responsible for inst of PhD prog in architecture at Berkeley. Author: The Sultan's Turrets, 1939; Architectural Construction Details, 1954; Development and Application of a System for Recording Critical Evaluations of Architectural Works, 1964; Architectural Education in USA, 1967; Innovations in Housing Design and Techniques as Applied to Low-Cost Housing, 1969. Recipient: Fulbright Study-Travel Grant, 1954; Ist prize hgrs competition, Amer Inst Architects, 1963. Home: 976 Oxford St, Berkeley, Cal. Office: 15 Shattuck Sq, Berkeley, Cal.

HASSID, William Z, US, biochemist, educator; b. Jaffa, Pal, Oct 1, 1897; s. Mordecai and Esperanza; in US since 1920; BA, U of Cal, 1925, MS, 1930, PhD, 1934; m. Lila Fenigston, Jan 21, 1936. Biochem, agric experiment sta, U of Cal, since 1959, prof em since 1965, fac mem since 1927. Brit Army, 1918-20. F: Amer Acad Arts and Scis; Amer Soc Biol Chem; mem: AAAS; Natl Acad Sci; Chem Soc, London; Amer Soc Plant Phys; Amer Soc Biol Chem; Amer Chem Soc. Co-author, Manual of Plant Biochemistry, 1939; contbr to profsl jours. Recipient: Sugar research award, Natl Acad Sci, 1946; Guggenheim f, 1955, 1962; Charles Reid Barnes hon life mem award, Amer Soc Plant Phys, 1964; C S Hudson Award, Amer Chem Soc, 1967. Hobbies: photography, music. Home: 20 Northgate Ave, Berkeley, Cal. Office: U of Cal, Berkeley, Cal.

HASSIDOFF, (Albert) Abraham, Isr, banker; b. Jerusalem, Apr 14, 1898; s. Daniel and Yochevet; m. Gracia Hadaya; c: Geula, Sara, Shimcha, Daniel, Joseph. Dir: Isr Discount Bank, Ltd; Mercantile Bank Isr; Isr Devl and Mortgage Bank; Isr Inves and Finance; Discount Bank Inves; Cyprus Pal Plantations; Cyprus Olive Plantations; pres: Neti'ot Hadarom; Property and Bldg; hon consul of Panama, Jerusalem. Home: 3 Rashba St, Jerusalem, Isr. Office: Isr Discount Bank, Ltd, ll Ben Yehuda St, Jerusalem, Isr.

HASSINE, Eliahu, Isr, diplomat; b.Tiberias, Isr, Aug 23, 1916; s. Joseph and Vida (Elhadeff); LLB, Law Sch, Jerusalem, 1948; m. Renata Busso, June 10, 1952; c: Tamar, Rimona. Charge d'affaires, Isr Emb, Malta, since 1966. Sgt, RASC, 1941-46. Club: Lions. Hobbies: filming, tape recording. Home and office: Villa Mon Reve, Ta'xbiex, Malta.

HASSOUN, Mordechai Pinhas, Isr, banker; b. Hebron, Pal, 1894; s. Hanoch and Clara; m. Suzanne Aboutboul, 1928; c: Lea, Hanoch, Miriam, Dan. Ret; fmr: asst gen mgr, adv for fgn bus, Bank Leumi Le'Israel; dir gen: Mortgage Bank; Tel Aviv Stock Exch. Vice-pres, Isr-Latin Amer C of C; clubs: Isr Forex, pres; Commercial and Ind, vice-pres. Home: 55 King David Blvd, Tel Aviv, Isr.

HATALGUI, Theodore, Isr, organization exec, journalist, author; b. Warsaw, Pol, Nov 19, 1917; s. Karol and Felicja (Ferszt) Sznejberg; in Isr since 1947; MA, U Warsaw, 1939; m. Neomi Halpern, 1942; c: Ron. Ed, Am veadmato; dir, Info, PR and Tourism; exec mem JNF, since 1961. Author: The Other City, 1962; short stories in Heb lit mags; trans of 19th and 20th cent Fr and Pol lit; corresp to Eur newspapers.

Mem: Yad Vashem Council; bd, Isr Periodicals Press Assn. Home: 18 Lincoln St, Jerusalem, Isr. Office: POB 283, Jerusalem, Isr.

HATZOR, Shmuel, Isr, kibbutz mem; b. Cologne, Ger, Sep 16, 1924; s. Leo and Else (Loewenstein) Koenigshoefer; in Isr since 1947; dipl, farm mgmt, Midrashat Ruppin, Isr; m. Debora Rees, Mar 21, 1944; c: Esther, Ruth. Dir, communal activities, gen secy, fmr, farm exec, Kibbutz Kfar Hanassi; mgn dir, Habonim Metals Ltd, 1965-67. Pvt, IDF. Mem, Ihud Habonim World Movement, fmr: gen secy, cen repr, Eng. Spec interests: youth activities, Isr's social problems. Home and office: Kibbutz Kfar Hanassi, Isr.

HAUER, Benjamin, Can, rabbi, organization exec; b. Rum, Sep 18, 1927; s. Moses and Gitta (Wagner); in Can since 1948; ordained rabbi, Torah im Derech Eretz, 1948; semicha, Torath Chaim, Toronto, 1953; BA, U Toronto, 1953, postgrad studies; m. Miriam Weiss, June 8, 1958; c: Gittele, Leah, Adina, Moshe. Natl exec dir, Mizrachi, Hapoel Hamizrachi of Can, since 1965; rabbi: Beth Jacob Cong, 1953-62; Beth Torah Cons, 1962-65, both Toronto. Secy, RabCA, Can region; mem: bd dirs, Can J Cong, fmr chaplain; exec, Fed Zionist Org of Can; Montreal Bd Mins; fmr, lectr, Natl Lecture Bur. Contbr numerous articles, essays in Eng, Heb, Yiddish; appeared regularly on radio; lectured on behalf Zionist Org. Home: 2597 Bedford Rd, Montreal, Can. Office: 5497 Victoria Ave, Montreal, Can.

HAUER, Yitzchak, Isr, eye surg; b. Czech, Feb 13, 1905; s. Josef and Ethel (Glatter); in Isr since 1939; MD, U Prague, 1928; m. Gitta Nürnberg, Oct 28, 1931; c: Esra, Chayim. Chief, eye dept, Donolo Hosp, Jaffa; asst prof, Tel Aviv U, since 1967. Contbr to sci jours. Hobby: bridge. Home: 15/A Josef Haglili St, Ramat Gan, Isr. Office: 15/A Chisin St, Tel Aviv, Isr.

HAUPTMAN, Harry, US, physician; b. Hoboken, NJ, Jan 7, 1911; s. William and Pauline (Taub); att NYU, 1928-30; BA, U Mich, 1932; MD, Wash U, St Louis, Mo, 1936; m. Gladys Rosenman, Aug 10, 1941; c: Arlene, David. Obstet and gyn, pvt practice, Jersey City, NJ, since 1940; att phys, Fairmount Hosp, since 1946; att obstet, 3rd div chief, Margaret Hague Maternity Hosp, since 1946; asso, surg, Christ Hosp, 1949. Cdr, USN, 1941-46. F: Amer Coll of Surg, 1949; Amer Coll of Obstets and Gyns, 1963; dipl, Amer Bd Obstet and Gyn, 1945; mem: Hudson Co, NJ State Med Socs; Temple Beth-El, Jersey City. Contbr to profsl jours. Home and office: 44 Gifford Ave, Jersey City, NJ.

HAUSMAN, Louis, US, neuropsychiatrist, educator; b. NYC, Apr 30, 1891; s. Joseph and Fannie (Dalmatz); MD, Cornell U, 1916; m. Esther May, Jan 14, 1925. Prof em, clinical med, neur, Cornell U Med Sch, NYC, since 1957, prof, 1945-56, fac mem since 1924; dir, neur service, second med div, Cornell, Bellevue Hosp, 1950-56, asso visiting phys, 1933-49; asso att phys, NY Hosp, since 1945; clinical prof, neuropsycht, NYU Coll of Med, since 1945; cons, psycht, VA, since 1946. Prin contrib, inventor of motor plate for the reconstruction of brain, 1948. Pres, NY Neur Soc, 1961-62; dipl, Amer Bd of Psychts and Neurs; mem: AMA; AAAS; Amer Neur Assn; Assn for Research in Nervous and Mental Diseases; Amer Psycht Assn. Co-author: Nervous and Mental Disorders from Birth Through Adolescence, 1926; Atlases of the Spinal Cord and Brainstem and Forebrain, 1951; Atlas II: Consecutive Stages in the Reconstruction of the Nervous System, 1953; Atlas III: Illustrations of the Nervous System, 1961; Atlas IV: Photographs of Microscopic Sections of the Human Spinal Cord and Brain; Photographic Supplement to Atlas I, 1969; textbook: Clinical Neuroanatomy, Neurophysiology and Neurology With A Method of Brain Reconstruction, 2nd ed, 1969. Home: 1100 Park Ave, New York, NY. Office: 140 E 54 St, New York, NY.

HAUSMAN, Samuel, US, manufacturer, business exec; b. Bolechow, Aus, Nov 14, 1897; s. Morris and Bertha (Hoffman); in US since 1907; m. Vera Kuttler, May 4, 1924; c: Bruce, Merna Miller, Alice Davidson. Pres, Weldon Mills Inc, since 1939; dir, chmn: exec, mgmt comms, bd, Belding Hemingway; chmn bd: Belding Hausman Fabrics; Va Dyeing, since 1946; dir: LI Lighting, since 1957. Vice-pres: natl UJA, since 1953, hon chmn bd, Gtr NY, since 1946; and trustee, FJP; exec vice-pres, Beth Isr Med Cen; exec chmn, Amer comm, Heb U, fmr pres, Amer Friends Heb U; active: Amer Technion Soc; Weizmann Inst of Sci; mem: bd trustees, SUNY; Yeshiva U; bd, NY State Commn Against Discrimination; hon mem, JWV of Amer; fmr mem: adv council, Urban Devl Corp; NY State Manpower Adv Council; clubs: Fresh Meadow Country; City Athletic. Home: 930 Fifth Ave, New York, NY. Office: 10 E 32 St, New York, NY.

HAUSNER, Gideon M, Isr, legislator, attorney; b. Lwow, Pol, Sep 26, 1915; s. Bernard and Ema (Lande); in Isr since 1927; grad: Heb U, Jerusalem, 1940; Govt Law Sch, Jerusalem, 1941; m. Yehudith Liphshitz, Dec 16, 1944; c: Tamar, Amos. MK since 1965; pvt practice, 1946-60, and since 1963; lectr, bus law, Heb U, 1956-60; Isr Atty Gen, 1960-63; chief prosecutor, Eichman trial; chmn, Yad Vashem, memorial council auth. Served Haganah; maj, IDF, fmr pres, Jerusalem Mil Court. Mem: B'nai B'rith; Isr Political Sci Assn; delg, ZCs on behalf Progressive Party; fmr chmn, Statutory Tribunals. Hobbies: photography, gardening. Home: POB 2277, Jerusalem, Isr. Office: 15 Shamai St, Jerusalem, Isr.

HAVDALA, Henri Salomon, US, physician; b. Minia, Egypt, Apr 12, 1931; s. Jacques and Regine (Levy); in US since 1957; att St Mark Coll, Alexandria, Egypt, 1944-49; MD, Alexandria Med Sch, 1956; m. Sandra Abrams, Sep 12, 1963; c: Jack, Debra, EHen. Chmn, dept, anaesthesiology, Mt Sinai Hosp, Chgo, since 1965, att anaesthesiologist, 1960-65; asso prof, Sharrman Div, Chgo Med Sch since 1968; anaesthesiologist, J Hosp, Alexandria, Egypt, 1957. Mem: B'nai B'rith, Lincolnwood Lodge, 1965; Chgo Med Soc, N Shore chap; Chgo Anaesthesia Soc; AMA; Ill Med Assn; Ill Soc Anaesthesiologists; Amer Soc Anaesthesiologists; Intl Anaesthesia Research Soc; Soc Acad Chmn Anaesthesiology in Med Sch. Home: 4408 Morse, Lincoln, Ill. Office: 2750 W 15, Chicago, Ill.

HAVIN, Reuben, Austr, editor; b. Melbourne, Vic, Oct 4, 1913; s. Boris and Ada (Sher); BJour, Melbourne U, 1944; m. Miriam Davis, June 29, 1954; c: David, Michael. Publs ed, Monash U,since 1961; ed-in-chief: Austr J Herald; The J Post, both 1944-61. Home: 139 Centre Rd, E Brighton, Austr.

HAVIV, Israel, Isr, government official; b. Istanbul, Turkey, Jan 20, 1927; s. Salomon and Suzanne (Ojalvo); in Isr since 1949; att Istanbul U; BA, Heb U, Jerusalem, 1956; m. Yvette Carillo, Sep 29, 1949; c: Shlomo, Daniel. Dir, dept overseas works of inves, fgn exch div, Min of Finance, since 1967; asst, Min for Fgn Affairs, 1953-56; vice consul, Consulate Gen of Isr, Addis Ababa, 1956-59; first secy, charge d'affairs, Isr Legation, Bucharest, 1960-64. First sgt, intelligence br, IDF, 1950-52. Hobbies: hist, reading, music. Home: 29 Keren Hayesod St, Jerusalem, Isr. Office: Min of Finance, Hakiryah, Jerusalem, Isr.

HAVIV, Ram, Isr, civil servant; b. Rishon leZion, Isr, Feb 5, 1925; s. Zrubavel and Shulamit (Levin);MA,Heb U,Jerusalem, 1951; m. Aviva Barouch, Aug 20, 1951; c: Amnon. Dir, Econ Div, Min of Devl, since 1968; dep secy, PM Off, Jerusalem, 1954-60; dir, JNF, Eng, Ir, 1960-62; econ adv, Min of Devl, Jerusalem,1963-66; consul, dir, Isr Info Services, NY, 1966-68. Cpl, Royal Engrs Corp, Brit Army, 1943-46; lt, IDF, 1948-49. Hobbies: political, mil hist; classical, brass band music. Home: 14 Abarbanel St, Jerusalem, Isr. Office: 38 Keren Hayesod St, Jerusalem, Isr.

HAVRON, Chanan Izhak, Isr, architect; b. Stuttgart, Ger, Mar 11, 1931; s. Edgar and Anna (Rothschild) Heilbronner; BSc, Technion, Haifa, 1953, dipl ing, architecture, 1954; m. Ilana Gelernter, April 6, 1954; c: Ram, Omer, Inbar. Chief architect, Kibbutz Planning Dept, since 1965, architect, 1954-64; architect, YMR, London, 1964-65. Pvt, Palmach, 1945-49. Designer: Natl Libr, Jerusalem; Ilan Hosp for Disabled Children, Jerusalem. Fmr secy, Kibbutz Reim. Hobbies: painting, photography. Home: Kibbutz Reim, Isr. Office: 27 Soutine St, Tel Aviv, Isr.

HAY, Jacob, Isr, engineer; b. Baghdad, Iraq, July 9, 1925; s. Meir and Shoshana (Sasson); in Isr since 1933; BSc, Heb Tech Coll, Haifa, 1950; m. Leah Landau, Dec 14, 1949; c: Itzhak, Yigal, David, Jonathan. Cons engr since 1954; regional devl engr, Min of Housing, 1950-54; fmr cons,WHO, UN, in various countries. Capt, engr corps, IDF Res, since 1949. Prin contribs: surveys and master plans for water and sewer sys for various towns in Isr. Mem: Architects and Engrs Assn, Isr; Assn of Sanitary Engrs, Isr. Home: 4/B Freud St, Haifa, Isr. Office: 29 Tchernihovsky St, Haifa, Isr.

HAYES, Saul, Can, attorney, organization exec; b. Montreal, Can, May 28, 1906; s. Benjamin and Sara (Kaplansky); BA, McGill U, 1927, MA, 1929, BCL, 1932; m. Beatrice Rosen-

baum, Sep 2, 1934; c: Marilyn. QC; exec vice-pres: Can J Cong, fmr natl exec dir; United J Relief, Agcys of Can,since 1940; natl exec dir, SF Conf on Intl Security, 1945; repr: united J delgs, Second Conf, UNRRA, 1944; Can Jewry, Paris Conf on Peace Treaties, 1946; dir: Natl Film Soc, 1950-51; Can-Isr Securities Ltd, 1952; Can-Isr Corp, 1953; co-dir: Natl Conf for Isr, 1951; J Film Soc, 1951; chmn: coord comm, Natl Sem on Citizenship; Jerusalem Emergency Conf, both 1953; mem, bd dirs: United Restitution Org,1953; Conf on J Claims Against Ger; Comm for J Claims on Aus, both 1952; mem, Can Found; clubs: Montefiore, Can. Author: The Economic and Social Factors in Immigrant Integration; The Nature of the Community; The Communities, all 1953. Recipient, medals: Coronation, 1953; Can Centennial, 1967. Home: 5668 Notre Dame de Grace Ave, Montreal, ,Can. Office: 493 Sherbrooke St W, Montreal, Can.

HAYMAN, Julius, Can, publisher; b. Winnipeg, Can, Dec 2, 1907; s. Michael and Luba (Lichtenstein); BA, U Man, 1928; LLB, Man Law Sch, 1933; m. Sofee Freedman, Oct 23, 1938; c: Michael. Publisher: J Standard, since 1937; Can Clothing Jour, 1950. Pres, ZOC; mem: natl educ comm, Can J Cong; Toronto J Public Libr; J Hist Soc of Toronto; Beth Tzedec Cong. Home: 2500 Bathurst St, Toronto, Can. Office: 44 Wellington St E, Toronto, Can.

HAYMAN, Robert Charles, US, business exec; b. Niagara Falls, NY, Oct 16, 1915; s. Adam and Marie (Desbecker); BA, cum laude, Cornell U, 1937; LLB, Harvard Law Sch, 1940; m. Joan Lerner, Jan 12, 1969; c: Jonathan, Katherine, Bonnie, Amy, Richard. Vice-pres, treas, Rand Capital Corp, since 1969; treas, Cataract Theatre, 1940-69; exec vice-pres, Exch Leasing, 1963-68. Pres, United J Fed, Buffalo; dir, CJFWF; mem, natl cabinet, UJA; fmr: pres, J Cen, Buffalo; dir: Natl JWB; United HIAS Service. Home: 151 Deerhurst Blvd, Buffalo, NY. Office: 2205 Main Pl, Buffalo, NY.

HAYMES, Stephen Denis, US, business exec; b. NYC, Mar 2, 1937; s. Morice and Beatrice (Glick); BS, U of Pa, Wharton Sch of Finance and Commerce, 1957; LLB, Harvard Law Sch, 1960; m. Gail Lowe, June 20, 1965; c: Evan, Pres, dir, P Ballentine & Sons, Newark, NJ, since 1969; vice-pres, prin, Morice Haymes & Co, NY, 1961-64; vice-pres, Inves Funding Corp, NY, 1964-69. Dir, Men's Club, Temple Emanu-El, NYC; trustee, Essex Co Blood Bank, E Orange, NJ; mem: Amer, NY Bar Assns; Masons; clubs: Harvard; Lone Star Boat. Hobbies: golf, boating, skiing. Home: 945 Fifth Ave, New York, NY. Office: 57 Freeman, Newark, NJ.

HAYS, David Arthur, US, stage and theater designer; b. NYC, June 2, 1930; s. Mortimer and Sarah (Reich); AB, Harvard U, 1952; att Old Vic Sch, London, 1952-53; MFA, Boston U; m. Leonore Landau, Dec 28, 1954; c: Julia, Daniel. Theatrical designer, since 1955; dir, found, Natl Theatre for the Deaf,since 1966;designer,numerous Broadway Shows,theaters. Vice-pres, Eugene O'Neil Memorial Theatre Found; mem: bd overseers, comm on visual and performing arts, Harvard U; Phi Beta Kappa. Contbr to profsl publs. Recipient: Critics Poll, best set, No Strings, 1962; Outer Circle Award, for Natl Theatre of Deaf, 1969. Hobby: sailing. Home: 118 E 64 St, New York, NY.

HAYWOOD, Charles, US, musicologist, folklorist, educator; b. Grodno, Russ, Dec 20, 1904; s. Nathan and Dora (Blume); in US since 1916; BS, CCNY, 1926; artist dipl, Juilliard Sch of Music, 1931; MA, Columbia U, 1941, PhD, 1949; m. Frances Dillon, May 24, 1928; c: John. Prof, music and folklore, Queens Coll, Flushing, NY, since 1952; lectr, voice, folklore, Juilliard Sch of Music, since 1939; dir, Dici Music Sch, LI, 1929-33; soloist, tenor, appeared in opera, oratorio, since 1930; soloist with: NY Philharmonic Orch, 1930-35; Chautauqua Opera Co, 1930-35; Cincinnati Sym Orch, 1933; Phila Sym Orch, 1934-37; Free Syn, 1935-45; on staff of: radio sta: WOR, 1928-38; CBS, 1932-39; NBC, 1935-43; lectr, Harvard U, 1947; fs: Juilliard Sch of Music, 1933-35; Folger Shakespeare, 1952; Henry Huntington Research, 1953-54; Fulbright Research Scholar, Aus, 1961-62. Pres, US natl comm, Interfolk Music Council; mem: Amer Folklore Soc; Amer Musicological Soc; fac comm, AJCong; Phi Beta Kappa; exec comm: Amer Anthropological Soc; AAUP. Author: Spoken Drama and Lyric Theater, 1942; Gentile Note in Jewish Music, 1945; Russian Art Songs, 1946; Cervantes and Music, 1947; A Bibliography of North American Folklore and Folksong, 1951, new and enlarged ed, 2 vols, 1961; Gentile Attitudes to Jew in Musical Historiography, 1952; The Mock Tempest, 1955; Masterpieces of Sacred

Song, 1958; William Boyce and Garrick's Romeo and Juliet, 1960; World Treasury of Folksongs, 1960; Shakespeare and Music, 2 vols, 1960, 1961; Whitman and Music, 1961; Folksongs of the World, 1967; Negro Mistrelry and Shakespearian Burlesque, 1968; Revelations of an Opera Manager in 19th Century America, 1968; George Bernard Shaw on Incidental Music in Shakespearian Theater, 1969; contbr to folklore and music jours. Hobby, philately. Home: 145 E 92 St, New York, NY. Office: Queens Coll, Flushing, NY.

HAZANI, Michael Jacob, Isr, legislator; b. Bendzin, Pol, June 27, 1913; s. Israel and Frouma (Freiberg) Kantorowitz; in Isr since 1932; ordained rabbi, Tahkemony Rabb Sem, Warsaw, 1930; att Heb U, Sch of Econ, 1957-58; m. Hannah Rubin, 1933; c: Elizur, Moshe, Israel. Min, Social Wfr, since 1970; MK since 1951, mem, finance comm, since 1955, chmn, sub-comm; chmn, State Comptroll Commn; vice-pres, Mizrachi Bank, since 1956; vice-chmn, Bank of Isr, since 1962; chmn, Bar Ilan Finance Comm, since 1952. Org, rel workers settlement movement; chmn, settlement commn, 23rd ZC; dir, agric cen comm, Hapoel Hamizrachi, 1945; bd trustees: Bar Ilan U; Isr Opera Co; Isr Philharmonic Orch. Contbr to local press. Home: 69 Yehosha Bin Nun St, Tel Aviv, Isr. Office: Knesset, Jerusalem, Isr.

HAZAZ, Haim, Isr, author; b. Russ, 1898; s. Arie and Zivia; in Isr since 1931. Author: Rehaim Shvurim, 1942; haYoshevet baGanim, 1944; Avanim Rotchot, 1946; Ya'ish, 1947; beKetz haYamim, 1950; Zel Hafuch, 1955; beYishuv Shel Yaar; Chagorat Mazalot, 1958; Daltot Nechoshet, 1955; be-Kolar Echad, 1963; Ofek Natui; Chatan Damim, 1961; Al haMedina vehaSafrut, 1962; numerous vols of collected works, 1968. Mem, Heb Lang Acad. Recipient: awards: Bialik, for Rehaim Shvurim, 1942; Isr, for Ya'ish, 1952; Ussishkin, 1950; Habima, 1954, both for beKetz ha-Yamim; Davar-Berl Katznelson, for Daltot Nehoshet, 1955; Irving and Bertha Neuman Lit, NYU Inst of Heb Studies, 1966. Home: 18 Hovevei Zion St, Talbieh, Jerusalem, Isr.

HEARST, Ernest, Eng, editor; b. Berlin, Ger, Dec 1, 1912; s. Emanuel and Gabriele (Berl); in Eng since 1933; m. Flora, Mar, 1949; two c. Ed, Wiener Libr Bull, since 1966. Pvt, Brit Army, 1939-43. Contbr book revs to J press. Home: 25 Woodway Crescent, Harrow, Eng. Office: 4 Devonshire St, London, Eng.

HEBALD, Milton E, It, sculptor; b. NYC, May 24, 1917; s. Nathan and Eva (Elting); in It since 1955; att: Natl Acad, NYC, 1930-31; Beaux Arts, NYC, 1931-35; m. Cecille Rosner, June 10, 1938; c: Margo. One-man exhbs, Amer Contemporary Artists Gals, NYC, 1937-40; one-man shows: Schneider Gale, Rome, 1957, 1963; Nordess Gal, 1939, 1960, 1963. Commns: sculpture for PO, Toms River, NY, 1941; 16-ft bronze group, Albert Einstein Memorial Hosp, NYC, 1953; 20-ft aluminium light sculpture, Isla Verde Airport, Puerto Rico, 1954; designed Albert Gallatin Medal, NYU, 1957; 220 ft bronze Pan Amer sculpture screen, JFK Airport, NY, 1959; 2 bronze reliefs, Cen Queens Libr, 1965; statue, James Joyce, Zurich, 1966; Marshall Field IV Memorial, Chgo, 1966; eternal lights and menorahs, Adas Isr Temple, Wash, DC, 1969; works in collections: Whitney Mus, NYC; Phila Mus Art; Ein Harod, Tel Aviv Mus, both in Isr; Yale U; Acad Arts and Letters, NYC; U NC; U Ariz; Notre Dame; Joyce Mus, Dublin, Ir; Little Rock Mus, Ark; Richmond Art Mus, Va; Nashville Art Mus. Juror, Fulbright Comm, fine arts, since 1952; fmr: tchr, sculpture, Cooper Union. US Army, 1944-46. Recipient: first award, Artist Cong, 1937; 2nd prize, Social Security Competition, 1940; 2nd prize, Artists for Victory, 1942; Shilling Prize, 1947; 1st prize: sculpture, Bklyn Mus, 1949; TB Hosp Competition, NYC, 1952; Prix de Rome. Home: 60 Viale Trastevere, Rome, It. Studio: 60 Vie Orti d'Alibert, Rome, It.

HECHINGER, Fred M, US, editor; b. Nuremberg, Ger, July 7, 1920; s. Julius and Lilly (Niedermaier); in US since 1936; AB, CCNY, 1942; att U London, 1945-46; hon LLD: Kenyon Coll, Ohio, 1955; Bard Coll, NY; Bates Coll; Knox Coll; Wash Coll; Notre Dame U; Wilkes Coll; m. Grace Bernstein, Jan 5, 1958; c: Paul, John. Educ ed, NY Times, since 1959; corresp, London Times Educ Supplement, 1946-48; columnist, fgn corresp, The Wash Post and Overseas News Agcy, 1948-50; educ ed, NY Herald Tribune, 1950-56; asso pub, exec ed, Bridgeport Herald, 1956-59. Mil intelligence, 1943-46. Mem: Educ Writers' Assn, fmr pres; Century Assn. Author: An Adventure in Education, 1956; The Big Red Schoolhouse, 1959, rev 1962; Pre-School Education Today, 1966; co-author:

Teen-Age Tyranny, 1963; The New York Times Guide to New York City's Private Schools, 1968; contbr to lit mags. Recipient awards: Educ Writers Assn, 1948, 1949; George Polk memorial, 1950, 1951; Brit Empire medal; US Army citation. Clubs: Coffee House; Overseas Press. Home: 415 E 52 St, New York, NY. Office: 229 W 43 St, New York, NY.

HECHT, Abraham B, US, rabbi; b. Bklyn, Apr 5, 1922; s. Samuel and Sarah (Auster); ordained rabbi, Rabb Coll Tomchei Tmimim Lubavitz; BA, MS, Grad Sch, Yeshiva U; DD, Philathea Coll, Can; m. Lillian Greenhut, 1944; nine c. Rabbi, Cong Shaare Zion since 1958; found, prin, Yeshivah Achei Tmimim Lubavitz, Dorchester, Mass, 1943-45; rabbi: B'nai Magen David Cong, 1945-51; Magen David Comty Cen, 1951-58; dir: syn relations dept, Union Orthodox J Congs of Amer, 1956-58; Keren Hashmitah-Isr, 1958-59. Chmn exec bd, Rabb Alliance of Amer fmr pres; vice-pres, Rabb Bd of Flatbush, fmr pres; gave opening prayer, US Sen, 1966, US Cong, 1968. Author: Spiritual Horizons, collection of essays, sermons, articles; contbr to Anglo-J, Yiddish, Heb periodicals. Recipient, citations: Isr Bonds; Yeshiva Magen David; hon award: State of Isr Bonds, 1962; UJA, 1967-68. Home: 2110 Ocean Parkway, Brooklyn, NY. Office: 2030 Ocean Parkway, Brooklyn, NY.

HECHT, George J, US, publisher; b. NYC, Nov 1, 1895; s. Meyer and Gella (Stern); BA, Cornell U, 1917; hon DHL, Temple U, Phila, Pa, 1956; m. Freda Epstein, Jan 6, 1930; c: Susan Cramer, George. Pres, Parents Mag Enterprises, since 1925, chmn, since 1964; hon pres, publisher: Parents' Mag; Baby Care Manual; Your New Baby; Children's Digest; Humpty Dumpty Mag; Calling All Girls; The New Wonder World Cultural Libr; found ed, Better Times, 1919-31. Head, bur of cartoons, US Comm on Public Info, WW I; US Army, 1918. Found: Comty Council of NY, fmr, Wfr Council, NYC, secy, dir, 1926-45; Gtr NY Fund, 1938-44; chmn, Amer Parents Comm, since 1947; hon pres, Intl Fed Periodical Press, Paris, 1963; dir, Natl Assn Mag Publishers; mem, Ethical Culture Soc. Ed: Above Cayuga's Waters, 1916; The War in Cartoons, 1921. Home: 730 Park Ave, New York, NY. Office: 52 Vanderbilt Ave, New York, NY.

HECHT, Isaac, US, attorney; b. Baltimore, Md, Dec 28, 1913; s. Lee and Miriam (Dannenberg); BS, Johns Hopkins U, 1936; LLB, U of Md, 1938; m. Catherine Straus, Mar 26, 1941; c: Eleanor Yuspa, Henry, Marjorie Kaplan. Pvt practice since 1938; admitted to bar: Court of Appeals, Md; Supr Court of US; US Court of Appeals for Fourth Dist; US Dist Court, Dist of Md; Tax Court of US; Md Court of Appeals. Mem exec, Baltimore Estate Planning Council, fmr pres; perm mem, Jud Conf of Fourth Circuit; mem: Bar Assn, City of Baltimore, fmr chmn; orphan's court comm, comm on rev of by-laws; Md State Bar Assn; fmr repr to Conf of Lawyers, Comm on World Peace Through Law; Amer Bar Assn; Clients Security Trust Fund, Bar of Md, fmr treas; Phi Epsilon Pi; Oheb Shalom Cong, fmr pres; Bd of J Educ; bd dirs, Baltimore chap, AJComm; JWF. Home: 11 Slade Ave, Baltimore, Md. Office: 10 Light St, Baltimore, Md.

HECHT, Jacob, Switz, shipping exec; b. Ger, June 25, 1879; s. Simon and Johanna (Rosenberg); m. Ella Mohr, Nov 8, 1908; c: Ruben, Werner. Chmn, co-found: Rhenania Rhein-schiffahrts Group, Mannheim, since 1908; Rhenania Allge-meine Speditions AG, Duisburg, since 1909; chmn, found, Neptun Transport-und Schiffahrts, AG, Basle, since 1920; with Employee Shipping Co, Mannheim, 1897; in shipping bus, Antwerp and Rotterdam, 1899-1918; found, Société Belge de Navigation Fluviale SA, Antwerp, 1909; partner, mgr, Gebrüder van Uden and Co, Antwerp, 1913; co-found, dir, Neder-landsche Elevator Mij, Rotterdam, 1914; co-found: Cornelis Swarttouw Stevedoring, Mij, Rotterdam, 1914; Navex, Société d'Expédition et de Navigation SA, Antwerp, 1920; Münchener Lagerhaus-und Transport-Gesellschaft MBH, Mu-nich, 1920; Le Rhin, Société Générale de Navigation et d'Entre-pots SA, Strasbourg, 1920; Asabel Shipping, Antwerp, 1921; Bayrische Schiffbaugesellschaft, Erlenbach/M, 1921; Rhenania Wormser Langerhaus-und Speditions AG, Worms, 1923; Kohlenumschlags AG, Basle, 1924; Rheinische Umschlags-und Lagerungs AG, Basle, 1924; AG für Schiffahrt, Basle, 1925; CANAL, Strasbourg, 1927; Neptune, Société Belge de Transports et de Navigation SA, Antwerp, 1946; found, Cargo SA, Basle, 1948; vice-chmn, Ludwigshafener Walz-mühle, Ludwigshafen o/Rh, 1948; dir, Dagon Ltd, warehous-ing, Haifa, 1949; found, co-found, several other enterprises for interior navigation, seashipping interests, trans shipment, warehousing, stevedoring in: Holland; Belgium; Ger; Fr;

Switz. Pres, forwarding agts on Rhine, Antwerp. Home: Benkenstr 50, Basle, Switz.

HECHT, Jacob Judah, US, rabbi, b. Bklyn, NY, Nov 3, 1923; s. Samuel and Sadie (Auster); ordained rabbi, United Lubavitcher Yeshivos; m. Elaine Lasker, Jan 28, 1945; c: Sholom B, Channa, Basya, Ben Zion, Fraida, Sholom Y, Yosef, Yehoshua, Rivka, Rachel, Levi, Shimon, Chaye, David, Gershon. Rabbi, Cong Yeshiva Rabbi Meyer Simcha Hacohen of E Flatbush, since 1947; exec vice-pres, Natl Comm for Furtherance of J Educ, since 1946. Pres, Camp Emunah for Girls; chmn, Natl Council of Mesibos Shabbos; dir, Home of Sages of Isr; vice-pres, Rabb Bd of E Flatbush; mem: B'nai Zion, UJA. Author: tchr guide books, articles on intermarriage. Lectr: US, Eur, Isr, Australia, radio and TV. Hobby, politics. Home: 180 E 54 St, Brooklyn, NY. Study: 289 E 53 St, Brooklyn, NY. Office: 824 Eastern Parkway, Brooklyn, NY.

HECHT, Reuben R, Isr, economist, business exec; b. Antwerp, Belgium, Aug 15, 1909; s. Jacob and Ella (Mohr); in Isr since 1936; dipl, econ, U Heidelberg, 1931; DRerPol, 1933; m. Edith Zilzer, Jan 16, 1941. Found, pres, chmn bd, Dagon Batey Mamguroth le-Isr Ltd, grain elevators, affiliated cos, Haifa, since 1951; found, chmn bd, Shikmona Pub Co, Haifa, since 1965; found, dir, Archaeol Mus, Dagon, Haifa; chmn bd, Neptune Transp and Navigation Co, Basle, since 1963; mem bd, Rhenania, Rhine Shipping group of cos since 1948; mgn dir, Neptune Société Belge de Transp et de Navigation SA, Antwerp, since 1946; bd, N V Nederlandsche Elevator Maatschappij, Rotterdam, since 1962; engaged, transp, shipping enterprises, Basle, Antwerp, since 1934; chmn bd, Moledeth Devl Co, Haifa, since 1958. Mem, Irgun Zvai Leumi, 1936-48, on mission to Eur to org clandestine immigration to Pal. Mem, sub comm, Archaeol Council, Min Educ; trustee: Haifa Munic Mus Ancient and Modern Art; Mus Japanese Art; Mus of Prehist; bd: Haifa City Sym Orch; Amer Isr Cultural Found; chmn art sub-comm, planning comm, Bank of Isr, for banknotes, coins, medals; bd govs, Technion, Haifa; bd: Otzar Hityashvuth Hayehudim; J Colonial Trust; mem: comm for improvement of landscape and preservation of hist sites, PM off; fine arts sect, Natl Council of Culture, Min Educ; Heb Comm for Natl Liberation; Eur exec, Amer Va'ad Hahatzala; world exec, Revisionist Org, New Zionist Org; repatriation commn, Amer League for a Free Pal; fmr mem: Blau Weiss, Basle and KJV. Author: Die Preisbildung in der Rheinschiffahrt, 1933; contbr to econ, political jours. Recipient, Kaplan Prize, Isr Govt Efficiency Award, 1960. Hobbies: painting, archaeol, numismatics. Homes: 3 Hayovel St, Mt Carmel, Haifa; 50 Benkenstrasse, Basle, Switz. Office: POB 407, Haifa, Isr.

HECHTKOPF, Henry, Isr, artist; b. Warsaw, Pol, Apr 5, 1910; s. Isaac and Ida (Rosenman); in Isr since 1957; M, U Warsaw, 1933; m. Alice Zielinski, June 7, 1956. Bd dirs, art studio, Lodz, Pol, 1946-50; stage mgr, art counsellor, film studio, Lodz, Pol, 1956-57. Chmn, art sect, J Culture Org, Pol, 1947-50; mem, Isr Painters and Sculptors Assn. Author: Warsaw, 24 paintings, 1960; My Israel, 1964, 1965. Home: 12 Hapoel St, Bat Yam, Isr.

HECKER, Zvi, Isr, architect, educator; b. Cracow, Pol, May 31, 1939; s. Wilhelm and Leontyna (Finder); dipl, architecture, Technion, Haifa; m. Dvora Hoochman; c: Ronnie, Ela. Pvt practice, Hecker and Neumann, since 1959; visiting prof, sch of architecture, U Laval, Que, since 1968. IDF, 1955-57. Contbr to profsl publs. Recipient: first awards, competitions: City Halls; Bat Yam; Netanya; Mil Camp, Negev. Office: 34 Bloch St, Tel Aviv, Isr.

HECTOR, Morris, Can, business exec, communal worker; b. Cochrane, Alberta, Can, Mar 24, 1912; s. John and Hanna (Levy); m. Hilda Fishman, Oct 27, 1940; c: Barbara, Debbie, John. Vice-pres, Hector's Ltd, since 1932; pres: JCC, since 1962; J Comty Cen, 1952-58; JWF, 1955-57, all Calgary; chmn: ZOC Dr, since 1958; UJA Dr, 1968; Isr Bond Campaigns, 1954-56, 1960; Talmud Torah Day Sch, 1958-59; dir: W Region, Isr Bond Commn, since 1956; Beth Isr Syn, since 1962; mem: Rotary Intl, since 1964; Ind Comm, City of Calgary. Recipient: testimonial dinner for Isr Bond Dr, Calgary J Comty, 1957; Negev Dinner, 1961. Home: 53 Massey Place, Calgary, Alberta, Can. Office: 2020 17 Ave SE, Calgary, Alberta, Can.

HEFER, Hayim Baruch, Isr, author, journalist, translator, theater producer; b. Sosnowice, Pol, Oct 29, 1925; s. Isachar

and Rivka (Hertzberg) Feiner; in Isr since 1936; m. Ruth Morhy-Levy, c: Miryam. Weekly columnist, Yediot Ahronot; trans plays for: Habimah, Cameri, Li-La-Lo, Haifa, music theaters. Author: Hayo Hayu Lemanim; Yalkut haKzavim; Milim leManginot; Misdar haLohamim and others. Mem, Heb Writers Assn; Acum. Contbr, articles, trans, lyrics. Home: 53 Arlosoroff St, Tel Aviv, Isr.

HEFFER, Ernst T, US, pediatrician; b. NYC, Oct 11, 1910; s. Jacob and Yetta (Heffer); att NYU, 1927-29; BA, U Mich, 1931; MD, NYU, 1935; m. Zelda Rubinstein, Feb 14, 1937; c: Karen, Michael. Cons ped; dir, cystic fibrosis clinic, att ped, LI Coll Hosp, fmr asst dir ped; asso ped, J Hosp, 1956-69; asst clinical prof, NY State Med Coll, Downstate Div, fac mem since 1940; student health phys, NY Med Coll, 1941-42; instr, children's med, U Alberta Med Coll, 1944-45; att ped, J Sanitorium, Hosp for Chronic Diseases, 1953-58. Maj, US Army MC, 1942-46. F, Amer Acad Ped; mem: AMA; Kings Co Med Soc; Bklyn Acad Ped. Home: 1801 Dorchester Rd, Brooklyn, NY.

HEFTERMAN, Abraham, US, rabbi; b. Nemirov, Russ; s. Leiber and Sarah-Leah (Linetsky); in US since 1926; ordained rabbi, Yeshivat Kishinev, Bessarabia; m. Bertha Pruss, Feb 15, 1921; c: Rachel. Rabbi: Bikur-Cholim-Shevet Achim Syn, New Haven, Conn, since 1960; Floresti, Bessarabia, 1921-25; Manchester J Comty, NH, 1926-60. Mem, Union Orthodox Rabbis. Author: Pages of an Ex-Lunatic, (Heb), 1928; Anthology of Homiletics, (Heb), 1930; A New Life, (Yiddish), 1947; Such is Jewish Life, (Yiddish), 1960; columnist, J Forward; contbr to Seven Arts Syndicate. Home: 315 Winthrop Ave, New Haven, Conn. Study: 278 Winthrop Ave, New Haven, Conn.

HEFTLER, George, US, attorney; b. NYC, Apr 11, 1910; s. Harry and Edith (Aswal); BA, Rutgers U, 1931; LLB, Fordham U, 1934; m. Frances Haynig, Apr 19, 1935; c: Thomas. Partner, Platoff, Heftler & Harkeri, since 1950; gen counsel, bd dirs: Beaunit Corp, since 1950; First Natl Bank, N Bergen, since 1969. Mem: bd dirs, Heb Home and Hosp, Jersey City, since 1962; bd trustees: Temple Emeth, Teaneck, 1958-67; Bergen Philharmonic Inc, 1968-69; bd govs, Town and Gown Soc, Fairleigh Dickenson U, 1961-65; Hudson Co Ethics Comm, 1957-60; Bd of Adjustment, Teaneck, NJ, 1962-67, chmn, 1966-67; Teaneck Comty Chest Org; JCC; Amer, NJ, Hudson Co Bar Assns; Tau Delta Phi; Phi Beta Kappa; club, Rutgers. Home: 1206 Sussex Rd, W Englewood, NJ. Office: 400 38 St, Union City, NJ.

HEIBER, Maurice, Belgium, manufacturer; b. Stryj, Pol, Jan 4, 1908; s. Joseph and Jetti (Krieger); m. Estera Fajerstein, Aug 13, 1934. Pres, bd dirs: J Loan-Kassa, Service Social Juif; bd dirs, Centrale des Oeuvres Sociales Juives, Brussels; natl treas, Memorial National aux Martyrs Juifs de Belgique; J Resistance Org, head children's dept, 1942-44. Recipient: medals: Armed Resistance; political prisoner; Civil Resistance. Home: 149 Blvd Brand Whitlock, Brussels, Belgium. Office: 119 Ave Louise, Brussels, Belgium.

HEIDELBERGER, Michael, US, chemist, immunologist, educator; b. NYC, Apr 29, 1888; s. David and Fannie (Campe); BS, Columbia U, 1908, MA, 1909, PhD, 1911; att Fed Poly Inst, Zurich, Switz, 1911-12; John Simon Guggenheim f's, 1934, 1935, 1936; hon degs: U Bordeaux, 1947; U Paris, 1949; U Uppsala, 1950; U Strasbourg, 1952; U Oslo, 1956; U Aix-Marseille, 1959; U Nancy, 1960; Rutgers U, 1961; NY Med Coll, 1968; m. Nina Tachau, 1916, (decd); c: Charles; m. 2nd, Charlotte Rosen, 1956. Prof em, immunochem, Columbia U, since 1956, prof, Coll Phys and Surgs, 1948-56, on fac since 1928; adj prof, path, immunology, NYU Sch of Med, since 1964; visiting prof, immunochem, Inst of Microbiol, Rutgers U, 1955-64; staff mem, Rockefeller Inst for Med Research, 1912-27; chem: Mt Sinai Hosp, 1927-28; Presbyterian Hosp, NY, 1928-56. Lt, US Army Sanitation Corps, 1917-18; cons, Secy of War, WW II. Chmn, research council, NYC Public Health Research Inst, since 1953; pres: Amer Assn Immunologists, 1946-49; Harvey Soc, 1952-53; mem: Amer Chem Soc; AAAS; Soc for Ethical Culture; Metrop Mus of Art; Amer Assn for UN; ACLU; Sigma Xi; Natl Acad Sci; Amer Phil Soc; Amer Soc Biol Chems; Soc for Microbiol; hon mem, Royal Danish Acad Soc; fgn mem, Academia Nazionale dei Lincei, Roma; delg, commemoration 50th anniversary of Pasteur's death, Fr, 1946. Author: An Advanced Laboratory Manual of Organic Chemistry, 1923; Lectures in Immunochemistry, 1956; contbr to profsl publs. Recipient: Ehrlich silver medal, shared

Belgian award for Afr sleeping sickness cure, 1953; Albert Lasker Award, 1953; von Behring award and medal, 1954; Pasteur Medal, Swed Med Soc, 1960, 1961; Legion d'Honneur, 1949; Order of Leopold II, 1953; Duckett-Jones Memorial Award, 1964; Natl Medal for Sci, 1967; Medal, NY Acad Med, 1968. Hobbies: music, philately. Home: 333 Central Park W, New York, NY. Office: NYU Sch of Med, New York, NY.

HEIFERMAN, Solomon, US, business exec; b. NYC, Feb 5, 1908; s. Samuel and Mary (Grief); att CCNY, 1928-30; m. Celia Friedman, 1931; c: Esther Signet; Ruth Prenner. Secytreas, Wreckers and Excavators Inc since 1938; pres: Brookwell Construction; Solburt Realty; Ind Packing; secy-treas, Bonded Packaging; off i/c of other corps. Pres: Solomon Schechter Sch, Queens; Alumni Friends of U Settlement, 1957-59; Independent Willawczer Bukowiner Benevolent Verein, 1938-50; vice-pres: Assn Solomon Schecter Schs; Zionist Dist, 1953-55; sch assn, United Syn of Amer, since 1958; Heb HS Assn, since 1958; chmn: sch bd, Forest Hills J Cen, since 1955; spec gifts, UJA, since 1957; Fed J Charities, 1954-55; bd trustees: Bard Coll; U Settlement, since 1958; mem: B'nai B'rith; Masons; KP; Grand St Boys; House of Isr, Hot Springs, Ark; clubs: Natl Realty; Real Estate Sq; Tam-O-Shanta Golf. Recipient: service awards, JTSA, 1956, 59; Fed J Charities, 1955; AJComm Jt Defense Appeal, 1961. Home: 97-15 71 Ave, Forest Hills, NY. Office: 58-58 Grand Ave, Maspeth, NY.

HEIFETZ, Benar, US, cellist, teacher; b. Russ, Dec 11, 1899; s. Efim and Chassia (Spielman); in US since 1939; att Conservatory of Music, Leningrad, 1911-17; m. Olga Band, July 7, 1937; c: Susanne Finman. Mem, Albeneri Trio, since 1944; tchr, Manhattan Sch of Music, NY, since 1960; mem, Kolisch String Quartet, 1927-39; first cellist, Phila Orch, 1939-43; tchr, Temple U, Phila, 1939-43; first cellist, Toscanini Orch, 1943-45; tchr, Aspen Inst, 1950-51; visiting prof, U Ind, 1957-58; lectr, U Kan, 1960-61; concert tours: US; Eur; Asia. Home: 30 Deepdale Dr, Great Neck, NY. Office: Manhattan Sch of Music, New York, NY.

HEIFETZ, Milton D, US, neurosurgeon, educator; b. Hartford, Conn, Feb 7, 1921; s. Oscar and Molly (Fuchsman); BS, U of Ill, 1941, MD, 1945; m. Betty Baron, Dec 26, 1943; c: Lawrence, Daniel, Ronnie, Deborah. Asst prof, neurosurg, Loma Linda U, since 1955; chief, dept neurosurg, Cedars of Leb-Mt Sinai Hosps, since 1958; sr att surg, LA Co Hosp, since 1956. Capt, US Army, 1947-48. F, Inst Nervous Diseases, 1949-50; dipl, Amer Bd Neurosurg, 1955; mem: Harvey Cushing Soc; Amer Acad Neur; S Cal Neurosurg Soc; Amer Friends Heb U; Amer J Phys Comm; club, Explorers. Contbr to sci jours. Home: 704 N Bedford Dr, Beverly Hills, Cal. Office: 9735 Wilshire Blvd, Beverly Hills, Cal.

HEIFETZ, Vladimir Ephim, US, musician; b. Russ, Mar 28, 1883; s. Ephim and Chassia (Spielman); in US since 1921; dipl, Conservatory, Petersburg, 1918; m. Pearl Schapiro; c: William. Musical dir, organist, Temple Anshet Chesed, NY, since 1967; accompanist, arranger: TV; radio; motion pictures; piano tchr; dir, choirs; fmr: accompanist for Feodor Chaliapin; conductor orch, Schenly Theatre, Pittsburgh; chorus master, Farband; ensemble, Heifetz Singers, broadcast progs on TV, toured US. Composer: The New Era, sym, 1939; Pharaoh, opera; The Golem, oratorio; Le Mizele Maizele, children's comic opera; A Biblical Suite, for piano; cantatas: Yiddishe Legende; President Roosevelt's Message; Ani Yehudi; Lerern Mire; Babi Yar; Funvanen iz a Yid, 1967; In Midbor, 1968; Der Shoifer, 1969, and others; music for motion pictures: Potemkin; Green Fields; Mirele Efros; The Last Chapter; music for Anna Frank; Sabbath Services for various temples; conductor: festivals, Isr; orch, choir, recording for Sidor Belarsky, others; arranged compositions for Don Cossak Chorus. Home and study: 351 W 24 St, New York, NY.

HEIFETZ, Yaacov, Isr, army off; b. Jerusalem, Oct 30, 1923; s. Aron and Haya; att Teachers' Sem, Tel Aviv; Mil Acad, Isr; m. Naomi Shriber, July 23, 1947; c: Rami, Yoav, Michal. Dir, Budget Dept, Min of Defense, since 1964; financial adv to chief of staff, IDF, since 1964; asst mil, air attaché, London, 1959-62; chief, Mil Training Command, 1962-64. Palmach, 1942-48; Tat Aluf, IDF. Office: Hakirya, Tel Aviv, Isr.

HEILBRUNN, Madeleine S, US, organization exec; b. NYC, Feb 9, 1896; d. Adolph and Belle (Block) Stiefel; att: NY Training Sch for Tchrs, 1916-19; Columbia U Tchrs Coll, 1919; m. Robert Heilbrunn, Nov 25, 1920 (decd); c: Robert,

Louise van Heyst, Margot Brauer. Exec-asst, AJComm, since 1958; mem: bd dirs: Friends Rochester Libr; Memorial Art Gal; Brandeis women's comm; Natl Council J Women, fmr pres; Council Social Agcys; mem, Amer Assn U Women; fmr: pres: B'rith Kedal Sisterhood; Visiting Nurse Service; vice-pres, Bada St Settlement; bd mem, TB and Health Assn; chmn, camp and hosp service, ARC, NY, 1943-45; club, Flower City Garden. Home: 1060 Park Ave, Rochester, NY.

HEILIGMAN, Harold A, US, chemical engr; b. Reading, Pa, Jan 8, 1900; s. Samuel and Bertha (Fidler); ChemE, Lehigh U, 1921; m. Marion Bailey, Mar 15, 1933. Refractories cons, Lavino Inc, since 1965, vice-pres, research and devl, 1961-65, on staff since 1922. Holder of patents: basic refractories; metallurgy; prosthetic dent. Chmn: E Norriston-Plymouth Townships Jt Auth, since 1959; f: Amer Inst Chems; Amer Ceramic Soc; mem: Amer Soc for Testing and Materials; Amer Inst Mining, Metallurgical and Petroleum Engrs; Can Ceramic Soc; Brit Iron and Steel Inst; Brit Ceramic Soc. Contbr to sci jours. Home: 2203 Coles Blvd, Norristown, Pa. Office: POB 29, Norristown, Pa.

HEIMAN, Leo, Isr, journalist; b. Warsaw, Pol, June 30, 1925; s. Boris and Elka (Lachozwianski); in Isr since 1948; att U Munich, 1945-58; m. Nana Tenenbaum, Dec 20, 1955; c: Amir, Orit. Ed, ME News and Features; corresp: Mil Rev; J Digest; Newsday, NY; contbr ed, Intl Aviation and Marine Rev. Author: Secret Operations of World War II, 1956; I Was a Soviet Guerrilla, 1959; People's War, 1961; Sabotage, 1962; Top Secret, 1963; Blood and Gold, 1965. Home: 7 Oren St, Haifa, Isr.

HEIMAN, Marcel, US, psychoanalyst; b. Vienna, Aus, Aug 17, 1909; s. Salomon and Julia (Steiner); in US since 1938; MD, U Vienna, 1934; m. Silvia Gabor, May 14, 1933; c: Peter. Clinical prof, psycht, Mt Sinai Sch Med, CUNY, since 1962, on staff since 1951; mem, neuropsychiatric dept, Vienna U Med Sch, 1935-38; sr asst, State Hosp, Mt Pleasant, Ia, 1940-41, clinical dir, 1942-43; psycht, Vanderbilt Clinic, NY, 1945-47; asst visiting neur, Morrisania Hosp, NY, 1946-47. F: Amer Psycht Assn; NY Acad Sci; mem: AAAS; AMA; Amer Psychoanalytic Assn; Amer Psychosomatic Assn; Assn for Research, Nervous and Mental Diseases; NY Co Med Soc; NY Neur Assn; NY Psychoanalytic Soc; NY Soc Clinical Psychts; Rudolf Virchow Soc. Contbr to med jours in US, Aus and Switz. Hobbies: sailing, skating, skiing, sculpture. Home and office: 1148 Fifth Ave, New York, NY.

HEIMANN, Hugo Chaim, Isr, chemical engr; b. Duisburg, Ger, May 12, 1896; s. Moritz and Helene (Paradies); in Isr since 1933; PhD, U Bonn, 1923; m. Frieda Reiss, 1921; c: Shoshanah Heimann, Miryam Traub. Ret; fmr: prof em, ind chem, Technion, Haifa, since 1964, prof, 1936-64; chem, dir, research, Bayerische Stickstoffwerke AG, Berlin, 1922-33. Ger Army, 1914-18. Mem: Isr Chem Soc; Intl Soc for Soil Sci. Contbr to profsl jours; holder of several patents. Spec interest, agric sci. Hobby: gardening. Home: 41 Keren Keyemet St, Kiryat Bialik, Isr.

HEIMANN, Shoshana, Isr, artist; b. Ger, Jan 5, 1923; d. Chaim and Frieda (Reiss); in Isr since 1933; studied; Bezalel Sch of Arts, Jerusalem, 1939-41; with sculptor Rudolf Lehmann, 1939-44; Accademia di Belle Arti, Florence, 1946-48; on Fr Govt scholarship, Ecole des Beaux Arts, Paris, 1956; m. Carmi Charny, 1951, div; c: Gad. Sculptress since 1945; participant, Forma Viva, intl symposium for sculpture, Yugo, 1953, 1955, 1956; one man shows: sculpture and painting, Jerusalem Artist's House, 1953; woodcuts, Carmel Studio, Haifa, 1955; color lithographs, Beit Zvi, Merhavia, 1958; drawings, Beit Zvi, Ramat Gan, 1962; regular participant, annual exhbs: Isr Artists and Sculptors Assn since 1949; Ein Hod collective shows, since 1953; works in perm collections: Tel Aviv Mus; Haifa Mus Modern Art; Heb U, Jerusalem; Yad Labanim House, Petach Tikvah; in pvt collections: Isr; Switz; Paris; NY; decorative wood panels: ss Zion, 1955; ss Theodor Herzl, 1956; Nahal Memorial Room, Pardess Hannah, 1958; illus children's books, vols of poetry; participated in: Mostra Intl di Bianco e Nero, Lugano, 1958; Intl Graphic Exhb, Yugo, 1961; collective exhbs in Isr, abroad. Mem: Isr Artists and Sculptors Assn; Ein Hod Artists Village. Recipient: Dizengoff Sculpture Prize, 1951, 1967; Grand Prix Intl Pour l'Art Moderne, Monacco. Home and studio: 12 Mevoh Ze'ev St, Ramat Gan, Isr.

HEIMLICH, Henry J, US, surgeon; b. Wilmington, Del, Feb 3, 1920; s. Philip and Mary (Epstein); MD, Cornell Med Coll,

1943; m. Jane Murray, June 3, 1951; c: Peter, Philip, Janet, Elizabeth. Dir, surg, J Hosp, Cincinnati, O, since 1969; att surg, Montefiore Hosp, 1950-69; sr clinical asst surg, acting adj surg, Mt Sinai Hosp, 1950-55; asst visiting thoracic surg, Triboro and Queens Hosp, 1950-53; asso in surg, Seton Hosp, 1950-53. Lt, USN, 1944-46. Prin contrib: devised four surg operations, inventor, Heimlich Drainage Valve. F: Amer Coll Surg; Amer Coll Chest Phys; Amer Coll Gastroenterology; vice-pres, Westchester chap, Amer Coll Surg, since 1962; bd trustees, Cancer Care, since 1960; dipl: Amer Bd Surg; Amer Bd Thoracic Surg; mem: comms on pulmonary surg and postgrad med educ, Amer Coll Chest Phys; NY Soc for Thoracic Surg; Westchester Co, NY State Med Socs; AMA. Author: Postoperative Care in Thoracic Surgery, 1962; contbr to med jours. Recipient: Medaglione Di Bronzo Minerva, Fourth Intl Medico-Sci Film Festival, Turin, It, 1961; award, Chinese Nationalist Govt; commendation, Coast Artillery Battery Cdr, US Army. Hobby: boating. Home: 3850 Clifton Ave, Cincinnati, O. Office: J Hosp, Cincinnati, O.

HEIMLICH, Philip, US, social worker; b. NYC, Apr 28, 1890; s. Max and Lottie (Geiger); BS, CCNY, 1909; grad study, Columbia U, 1941-46; m. Mary Epstein, Feb 17, 1912; c: Henry, Cecelia Rosenthal. Ret; city-wide dir, Youth Counsel Bur, dist atty's off, NYC, 1941-58; instr, comty org, Yeshiva U, 1946-47. Chmn, social service dept and trustee, Stephen Wise Free Syn; bd dirs, secy, Youth Counsel Bur; found: Span-Amer Youth Counsel Bur; Amer J Correctional Chaplains Assn; hon life mem, exec comm, Amer Correctional Chaplains Assn; charter mem, Amer Prot Correctional Chaplains Assn; mem: bd, Womens Prison Assn; fmr bd mem: Upton YMCA; Feds Comm on Syn Relations; bd mgrs, Riverside Hosp, NYC; cons, Puerto Rican Bd Guardians; a found, Narcotics Anonymous; dir, Natl Assn for Prevention of Delinquency; exec bd, Dysphasia Found. Recipient, Man-of-Year, Uptown YMCA, 1963. Home: 321 Ave C, New York, NY.

HEIMOWITZ, Irwin Yitzhak, Isr, attorney; b. NYC, Nov 31, 1934; s. Benjamin and Bella (Dunaetz); in Isr since 1968; AB, CCNY, 1955; JD, Columbia Law Sch, 1958; BHL, JTSA, 1958; MIA, Columbia Sch of Intl Affairs, 1959; m. Phyllis Goodman, June 14, 1959; c: Daniel. Atty, mem, Heruti, Heimowitz, Goldenzweig, Tel Aviv, since 1969; asso, Handler & Kleiman, 1959-64; pvt practice, 1964-68; atty, law clerk, Firon, Shapiro & Karni, 1968-69. World coord, Zionist mem dr, Brit Herut-Hatzohar, world exec mem; fmr: natl pres, Betar Brit Trumpeldor; natl chmn, Emergency Action Comm for Isr; natl secy, United Zionist Revisionists, Amer; mem: exec, Isr Zionist Council; Isr Bar Assn, Tel Aviv; NY Co Lawyers Assn, NYC; Amer Soc Intl Law; Amer Fgn Law Assn. Home: 6 Havazelet St, Kiron, Isr. Office: 64A Shenkin St, Tel Aviv, Isr.

HEINEMAN, Bernard Jr, US, business exec; b. NYC, Nov 29, 1923; s. Bernard and Lucy (Morgenthau); BA, Williams Coll, Mass, 1947; m. Ruth Kress, Nov 14, 1953; c: Deborah, Matthew, Stephen. Partner, Heineman and Co, since 1949. Sgt, US Army, 1943-45. Treas, asso mem, NY Mus Natural Hist; volunteer, St Vincents Hosp; mem: Mil Order of WW's; fmr, trustee, Henry Kaufman Campground Inc; bd mem, Madison Sq Church House; exec bd mem, Village Independent Dems; clubs: Lambs; Williams. Recipient: Silver Star; Bronze Star and Cluster; Croix de Guerre; NY State Medal for Valor. Hobby: art. Home: 15 Bank St, New York, NY. Office: 1430 Broadway, New York, NY.

HEINEMAN, Lucy M, US, communal worker; b. Chgo, Ill, Oct 19, 1894; d. Julius and Regina (Rose) Morgenthau; BA, Barnard Coll, 1915; m. Bernard Heineman, Dec 8, 1921; c: Bernard, William, Andrew. Secy, Natl Council J Women, 1953-57, natl hon vice-pres, since 1961; personnel mgr, Manhattan's Civilian Defense Voluntary Org, 1942-45; mem, bd dirs, visiting housekeeper service, J Family Service, 1924-53. Home: 115 Central Park W, New York, NY. Office: Natl Council of J Women, 1 W 47 St, New York, NY.

HEINEMANN, Joseph, Isr, educator; b. Munich, Ger, Apr 15, 1915; s. Jacob and Malwine (Cohn); in Isr since 1949; ordained rabbi, Yeshiva Mir, Pol, 1935; MA, U Manchester, 1947; PhD, Heb U, Jerusalem, 1963; Judith Bronner, May, 1969; c: Naomi, Ruth. Sr lectr: Dept of Heb Lit, Heb U, Jerusalem, since 1966; Bar Ilan U, Ramat Gan. Author: Tfila biTkufat haTanaim veHa'amoraim, 1966. Home: 13 Ben Labrat St, Jerusalem, Isr.

HEINISH, Noa, Can, merchant; b. Suczawa, Aus, July 4, 1893; s. Mechel and Bruche (Bacher); in Can since 1913; m. Sarah Saffron, Oct 7, 1934; c: Ruth, Blanche, Cecelia, Morton (decd). Pres, N Heinish and Co Ltd, since 1935. Natl hon vice-pres, Can J Cong, since 1943, fmr pres, maritime sect, co-found, war efforts comm for Halifax, Maritime Provinces; Halifax repr, JIAS, since 1947; mem, natl council, JDC, since 1940; found pres, hon life pres, Shaar Shalom Cong, Halifax; co-chmn, Atlantic region, Can Council Chr and J; fmr: chmn; treas, United J Relief comm; règional dir, Reception for War Orphans Movement to Can; treas, mem bd, Children's Aid Soc of Halifax; club, Halifax Progressive. Home: 5900 Inglewood Dr, Halifax, NS, Can. Office: 233 Gottingen St, Halifax, NS, Can.

HEINS, Maurice H, US, educator; b. Boston, Mass, Nov 19, 1915; s. Samuel and Rose (Golbert); AB, summa cum laude, Harvard U, 1937, AM, 1939, PhD, 1940; m. Hadassah Wagman, Aug 25, 1940; c: Sulamith, Samuel. Prof, math, U of Ill, since 1958; asst, Inst for Advanced Study, 1940-42; asst prof, Ill Inst of Tech, 1942-44; math, US War Dept, 1944-45; prof, Brown U, 1947-58. F, Amer Acad Arts and Scis; council mem, Amer Math Soc. Author: Selected Topics in the Classical Theory of Functions, 1962; Complex Function Theory, 1968; co-author, Analytic Functions, 1960; mem, ed bd, Proceedings, 1962-67. Home: 603 W Ill, Urbana, Ill. Office: U of Ill, Urbana, Ill.

HEISZER, Morris, US, rabbi; b. Southhampton, Eng, Feb 14, 1944; s. David and Sabina (Luftman); in US since 1949; att Yeshiva E Pkwy, Bklyn, 1950-58; ordained rabbi, Ner Isr Rabb Coll, Baltimore, Md, 1962; DD, Bklyn Coll, 1968; att Grad Sch, Duquesne U, Pittsburgh, Pa, 1969; m. Zipora Lendzin, Dec 14, 1968; c: Chana. Chaplain, Ft Carson, Colo, since 1969; tchr, head, hist dept, Yeshiva Jesoda Hatorah, 1966-68; rabbi, Homestead Heb Cong, 1968-69. Capt, US Army, since 1969. Mem: Colo Springs Comty, Colo; Agudath Isr; Pittsburgh Rabb Bd, Pa. Home: 7717A, Ft Carson, Colo. Study: Ch 12, 6033, Ft Carson, Colo.

HEISZ-TIMAR, Magdolna, Scotland, educator; b. Budapest, Hung, Apr 29, 1916; d. Joseph and Serene (Timberger) Reiner; in Scotland since 1967; MA, PhD, Pazmany Peter U, Budapest; dipl, langs, Lenin U; m. Herman Heisz, Feb 5, 1967. Headmistress, grammar sch, Budapest, 1965-67; lectr, Pazmany Peter U, 1965-67; essayist; lectr, world, Hung lit. Author: Songs of Letters; My Little Sister; Light in the Night; cantata dedicated to Anne Frank; poem in memory of crew of Isr submarine Dakar. Spec interests: poetry; modern lit; fgn lit. Home: 31 Prince Edward St, Glasgow, Scotland.

HEKMAT, Shamsi Moradpour, Iran, educational dir; b. Teheran, Iran, July, 1917; d. David and Farha (Ghattan) Moradpour; dipl, Amer Sch, Teheran, 1936; BA, Sage Coll, Teheran, 1940; m. Abdullah Hekmat, May 5, 1943; c: Fery, Zadeh, Farhad, Kamyar. Prin, Hekmat Intl Sch, since 1950. Pres, found, J Ladies Org of Iran; bd mem, Women's Org of Iran; vice pres, Intl Council J Women, since 1966; mem, Women's Intl Club of Iran; fmr: mem, bd: J Cen Comm; High Council of Women's Assns; Iranian Assn of World Brotherhood; repr to: Conf of Intl Council of Women, Teheran; UN Conf on Status of Women, Teheran; Intl Conf of OMEP, Paris; Conf of Intl Schs, Geneva; WJC, Brussels; UN Conf on Hum Rights, Teheran; Intl Conf on Social Wfr, Helsinki, speaking tour, UJA, USA. Home and office: 10 Soraya, Mohamad Reza Shah Ave, Yusefabad, Teheran, Iran.

HELD, Albert E, US, surgeon; b. Montreal, Can, Aug 7, 1904; s. Max and Sarah (Tanenbaum); in US since 1930; BA, McGill U, 1926, MD, CM, Sch of Med, 1930; m. Wilma Marotzke, Sep 8, 1936; c: Robert. Otolaryngological surg, J Hosp, Bklyn, 1934; otolaryngological surg: Cumberland Hosp, 1935-59; Kingston Ave Hosp, 1946-59. Ltcol, US Army, 1942-46. F: Amer Acad Otolaryngology, 1930; Amer Coll Surgs, 1951; Mem: found, Jerusalem Acad Med, 1958; Kings Co, NY State Med Socs; Amer Coll Surgs; Union Temple, Bklyn; Pi Lambda Phi. Hobbies: philately, golf. Home and office: 1286 President St, Brooklyn, NY.

HELD, Julius Samuel, US, art historian, educator; b. Mosbach, Ger, Apr 15, 1905; s. Adolf and Nannette (Seligmann); in US since 1934; PhD, U Freiburg, 1930; m. Ingrid Nordin-Pettersson, Oct 31, 1936; c: Anna Audette, Michael. Prof, art hist, Barnard Coll, since 1954, chmn, dept art, since 1967, fac mem since 1937; cons: Mus of Art, Ponce, Puerto Rico, since 1958; Staatliche Mus, Berlin, 1931-33; visiting lectr:

Bryn Mawr Coll, 1944; New Sch for Social Research, 1946-47; Yale U, 1954, 1958; Robert S Clark prof, art, Williams Coll, 1969. Mem: Inst for Advanced Study; Coll Art Assn; Medieval Acad Amer; Renaissance Soc Amer. Author: Dürer's Einfluss auf die Niederländische Kunst, 1930; co-author: Rubens in America, 1947; Flemish Painting, 1953; Rubens, 1954; Rubens, Selcted Drawings, 2 vols, 1959; contbr to art jours. Recipient: Guggenheim F, 1966-67. Home: 21 Claremont Ave, New York, NY. Office: Barnard Coll, Columbia U, New York, NY.

HELLER, Abraham Z, Isr, rabbi, author, educator, communal leader; b. Safed, Isr, Jan 25, 1894; s. Zeev and Zipora; desc of: Rabbi Yom Tob Lippman Heller, author of Tosefot Yom Tob; Maharal of Praag and Rashi; att Yeshiva Ridbaz; ordained rabbi, Yeshiva Hotam Sofer, 1912-18; Rabb degs conferred by Rabbis: Kook, Frant, Melzer, Klazin; m. Frieda Bazsel, 1914; c: Leah Schor, Sara Wilensky, Ziporah, Yehudit Peled, Miriam Swerdlow. Rabbi, dean em, Yeshivah Hotam Sofer; dean, Yeshiva Hotam Sofer Ribbaz, 1925-55. Prin contrib: educ whole generation of rabbis and tchrs in Isr. Trustee, Rabb Coll, Safed; mem, exec comm, Mus of Safed; fmr: chmn: Defense Comm of Safed; mobilization comm of Safed; chmn: Rel Council of Safed; Vaad lemaan Hehayalvelection comm, Munic of Safed; Zofiah Assn; Mizrachi Assn of Safed; security comm, Safed, War of Liberation; mem, exec comm, Kofer Hayishuv. Author: addition to History of Safed, by Pres Ben-Zevi, vols 56, 1965; Rabbi Shemuel Shulman of Safed, vols 58-59, 1966; responsa on legal matters in various jours. Recipient, Decorations: Hakomemiyuth, 1958; Aleh, 1968; Hahaganah, 1968; Maginei Safed; Hapalmach, in 1968; Hahaganah, 1969. Home: 20 Israel Beck St, Safed, Isr.

HELLER, Albert C, US, attorney; b. Milw, Wis, June 12, 1910; s. Henry and Adele (Buxbaum); BA, U Wis, 1932, LLB, 1934; m. Barbara Meissner, Aug 28, 1946; c: Henry, Ann, Martha. Pvt practice since 1934. US Army, 1942-45. Pres: Wis Soc for J Learning, 1965-66; Jr Milw Bar Assn, 1941-42; chmn: Whitefish Bay Equal Housing Commn, 1968-69; AJComm, 1954-55; comm on courts, Comty Wfr Council, 1952-54; bd dirs, Family Service, 1948-54; mem: Fed and Wis Bar Assns; Temple Emanuel; AJComm; Wis Soc for J Learning; Milw Art Soc; Milw Mus. Contbr to profsl jours. Home: 4524 N Murray Ave, Milwaukee, Wis. Office: 622 N Water St, Milwaukee, Wis.

HELLER, Charles K, US, business exec; b. Hostka, Czech, Sep 26, 1897; s. Theodore and Hermine (Kahn); in US since 1939; att: Commercial Acad, Prague, 1914; Export Acad, Vienna, 1919; div; c: Ray, Ruth, Peter, James. Pres: Empire Dehydrated Products Inc, NYC, since 1948; Empire Dehydrated Products, Montreal, since 1951; Empire State Trading, NY, since 1940; 40 Hudson St, NYC, since 1942; Belmont Products, since 1948; fmr: co-owner, Otto Mahn, Hamburg, Ger; dir: Fruitimex, Rotterdam, Holland; Jaffa Citrus, Tel Aviv. Home: 102-55 67 Dr, Forest Hills, NY. Office: 60-05 37 Ave, Woodside, NY.

HELLER, Elliot Maurice, Can, physician; b. Sarnia, Ont, Can, Oct 15, 1912; s. Abraham and Rose (Lampel); MD, U Toronto, 1937; postgrad: St Mary's Hosp, St Louis; U Pa; U Rochester; U Edinburgh, Scotland; U Mich; m. Barbara Friedman, 1961. Chief card, NW Gen Hosp; att phys, New Mt Sinai Hosp, since 1953; asso phys, Drs Hosp, since 1960, all Toronto. Maj, Can Army MC, 1942-45. FRCP, Edinburgh, 1953; f: Amer Coll Chest Phys; Amer Coll Card; FACP, 1957; mem: exec, cdn div, ZOC, Ontario, since 1958; Beth Tzedek Syn; fmr: exec, JNF; natl council, ZOC; exec, Toronto Zionist Council; secy-treas, Isr Med Soc, Toronto; bd dirs, United JWF; club; Phi Delta Epsilon Grad, Toronto, fmr pres. Contbr to med jours. Home: 9 Berkindale Dr, Willowdale, Can. Office: 99 Avenue Rd, Toronto, Can.

HELLER, Jacob W, US, attorney; b. Bklyn, NY, June 12, 1934; s. Elias and Elsie (Wachtelkoenig); BA, Yeshiva Coll, NYC, 1956; BRE, Yeshiva U Tchr's Inst, 1956; LLB, Yale Law Sch, 1959; m. Esther Rubinfeld, June 12, 1956; c: Ira, Alan. Partner, law firm, Weiss, Rosenthal, Heller & Schwartzman, NYC since 1969; law secy to Judge C E Froessel, NY State Court of Appeals, 1959-61. Trustee: Young Isr, Woodmere, NY; The Hillel Sch; United HIAS Service; fmr, vicepres, Natl Council of Young Isr; mem, Order of Coif. Home: 386 Longacre Ave, Woodmere, NY. Office: 295 Madison Ave, New York, NY.

HELLER, Lisa, Isr, educator; b. Vienna, Aus, July 20, 1926; d. Isidor and Hedwig (Herrmann) Weissmann; in Isr since 1953; BChem, U Oxford, 1948; PhD, U London, 1951; widowed; c: Alon. Asso prof, dept geol, Heb U, Jerusalem, since 1968; X-ray crystallographer, Geol Survey, 1955-68. Mem: Isr Soc for Clay Research; Isr Crystallographic Soc; Mineralogical Soc, Gt Brit; Clay Minerals Group, Gt Brit; Amer Mineralogical Soc; Amer Clay Minerals Group. Ed-inchief, Assn Intl Pour l'Etudes des Argiles; contbr to sci jours. Home: 32 Palmach St, Jerusalem, Isr. Office: Heb U, Jerusalem, Isr.

HELLER, Max M, US, manufacturer, civic worker; b. Vienna, Aus, May 28, 1919; s. Israel and Lea (Hirschl); in US since 1938; m. Trude Schontal, Aug 2, 1942; c: Francie, Susan, Steven. Pres: Trumax Inc, since 1957; Williamston Shirt Co, 1946-47; Maxon Shirt Corp, 1948-68; mgr, Piedmont Shirt Co, 1938-45; bd mem: First Piedmont Bank and Trust, since 1968. Mem, Greenville City Council, since 1969; pres, Greenville, Housing Found, since 1969; vice-pres, Greenville Co Health Planning Council; chmn: bd trustees, St Francis Hosp; bd, Cong Beth Isr, since 1961, pres, 1949, 1957-59; bd mem: ZOA, since 1950, pres, 1950, 1954; B'nai B'rith, since 1951, pres, 1951; FJP, since 1952; C of C; Cerebral Palsy; Rehab of Youthful First Offenders; NCCJ; adv bd mem, Furman U; vice-pres,Comty Council, 1960-62,vice-pres, Greenville Symphony Assn; mem: Elks; Masons; club, Greenville City. Home: 36 Pinehurst Dr, Greenville, SC. Office: First Piedmont Bank and Trust, Greenville, SC.

HELLER, Meyer, US, rabbi; b. NYC, Dec 28, 1921; s. Moses and Fannie (Appel); BA, Yeshiva Coll, NYC, 1941; grad engr, U of Mo, 1943; MHL, HUC, 1950; m. Judith Freedman, Sep 3, 1967; c: Marc, Joel, Diane, Judy, Sherri, David, Daniel. Rabbi: Temple Emanuel, Beverly Hills, Cal, since 1969, Temple Emanuel, SF, 1950-63; Temple Solael, Woodland Hills, 1963-64; Temple Isr, Hollywood, 1964-68. Lt, US Army, 1942-46. Chmn, rabb div, JWF; pres, S Cal Assn Lib Rabbis; vice-pres, bd rabbis, S Cal; fmr pres: W Assn Reform Rabbis; bd rabbis, N Cal; N Cal Friends Heb U; mem: YMCA; Min Assn; C of C; all Beverly Hills. Home: 8844 Burton Way, Beverly Hills, Cal. Study: Temple Emanuel of Beverly Hills, Beverly Hills, Cal.

HELLER, Milton, US, research chem; b. Newark, NJ, May 18, 1921; s. David and Ethel (Raskin); BS, U Mich, 1942, MS, 1947, PhD, 1952; m. Dorothy Paul, Apr 7, 1946; c: Douglas, Daid, Suzanne, Jeri. Sr research chem, Lederle Labs Div, Amer Cyanamid Co, NY, since 1957; instr, U Mich, 1950-51. USN, 1942-1946. Prin contbr: invention triamcinolene for rheumatoid arthritis, 1956. Pres, Citizens Comm for Better Schs; trustee, bd educ, Ramapo 2, Spring Valley, NY, 1962-1968, pres, 1966-1968; mem: Amer Inst of Chems; Amer Chem Soc; chem Soc, London. Home: 7 Highview Ave, New York, NY. Office: Amer Cyanamid Co, Pearl River, NJ.

HELLER, Philip B, US, certified public acctnt, attorney; b. Chgo, Ill, May 20, 1906; s. Aaron and Goldie (Karen); LLB, John Marshall Law Sch, 1932; dipl, commerce, Northwestern U, 1928; m. Elsie Eckhaus, July 10, 1929; c: Louise Panitch, Carol Shubert. Pvt practice since 1932; counsel, Fischel, Kahn, Weinberg, Diamond and Brusslan, 1969; sr partner, Heller, Strauss and Moses, CPAs, 1926-69. Pres: Bd J Educ, 1965-69; Isaiah Isr Brotherhood, 1948-50; Temple Isaiah Isr, 1952-55; Chgo Fed of Reform Syns, 1958-60; chmn,bd trustees, Coll J Studies, Chgo, 1965-67; mem: Amer Inst CPAs; Ill Soc CPAs; Chgo Bar Assn; Decalogue Soc; trustee, UAHC, 1957-68. Hobbies: art, fishing. Home: 1640 E 50 St, Chicago, Ill. Office: 208 S LaSalle St, Chicago, Ill.

HELLER, Simon, S Afr, business exec; b. Ponevez, Lith, Mar 1, 1910; s. Tevel and Chae (Greenstein); in S Afr since 1922; m. Sonia Davidoff, Sep 9, 1939; c: Yona, David. Dir: Jackson Properties; Carbon Inves; Oakmain Inves; Greenview Inves; Progress Construction Co, all pty Ltd; fmr mgn dir: mfr; inves; wholesale foods; textiles; packaging bus. Fmr: chmn, Zionist Youth Soc; vice-chmn, Worcester Heb Cong. Home: 51 The Albany, Oak Ave, Kenilworth, Cape Town, S Afr. Office: 403-404 NBS Bldg, 98 St George St, Cape Town, S Afr.

HELLER, Zipora, Isr, civil servant, poet; b. Safed, Isr, Sep 22, 1926; d. Abraham and Aliza (Barzel); desc of Rashi; MA, Heb U, Jerusalem, 1948. Sr official, State Comptroller Off, since 1951. Author: It haHar veha'Or; Shirei Midbar ve-Nachash; contbr poetry, articles to various publs. Pres,

Ahavat Zion Lodge, B'nai B'rith. Home: 117 Ibn Gvirol St, Tel Aviv, Isr.

HELLERSTEIN, Alvin K, US, attorney; b. NYC, Dec 28, 1933; s. Max and Rose (Lichtenstein); AB, Columbia Coll, 1953; JD, Columbia U, Sch of Law, 1956; m. Mildred Markow, June 3, 1962; c: Dina, Judith, Joseph. Partner, Stroock & Stroock & Lavan, NYC, since 1969, with firm since 1960; law clerk, US Dist Judge E L Palmieri, 1956-57. Capt, US Army, Judge Advocate Gen Corps, 1957-60. Mem of various orgs; Bar Assns; Syns; communal activities. Home: 115 W 86 St, New York, NY. Office: 61 Broadway, New York, NY.

HELLERSTEIN, Jerome R, US, attorney, educator; b. Denver, Colo, July 30, 1907; s. Meyer and Ida (Hellerstein); BA, U Denver, 1927; MA, U of Ia, 1928; LLB, Harvard U, 1931; m. Pauline Lefkowitz, Aug 25, 1935; c: Judith, David, Walter, Cindy. Mem, Hellerstein, Rosler & Brudney, since 1946; prof, taxation, NYU Law Sch, since 1959; asst corp counsel, NYC, 1938-40. Mem: comm on law and social action, AJCong; Assn Bar, NYC. Author: Cases and Materials on State and Local Taxation, 3rd ed, 1969; Taxes, Loopholes and Morals, 1963. Home: 285 Central Park W, New York, NY. Office: 80 Pine St, New York, NY.

HELLMAN, C Doris, US, educator, author; b. NYC, Aug 28, 1910; d. Alfred and Clarisse (Bloom) Hellman; BA, Vassar Coll, NY, 1930; MA, Radcliffe Coll, Mass, 1931; PhD, Columbia U, 1943; m. Morton Pepper, Aug 10, 1933; c: Alice Cooper, Carol Cooper. Prof, hist, Queens Coll, CUNY, since 1967, visiting prof, hist, 1966-67; instr, lectr, adj prof, Pratt Inst, 1951-66; adj prof, hist, NYU, 1965-66; asso, Columbia U, Sem on Renaissance; f: Vassar Coll; Columbia U; sr postdoc, NSF. Secy: 10th Intl Cong, Hist of Sci, 1962, delg, Natl Acad Sci, NRC to congs, 1959, 1962; council mem, Hist of Sci Soc, 1949-51, 1954-56, 1957-59, 1964-66, secy, 1956-58, chmn, 1958-59, 1965-67, metrop NY sect; secy, US Natl Comm for Intl Union of Hist and Phil of Sci, 1958-60; mem, bd; Educ Found for J Girls, since 1942, mem, scholarship comm; George Sarton Memorial Fund, 1958-65; f: Royal Astronomical Soc, London; AAAS, acting secy, Sect L, 1957, Sec L comm mem, 1957-60, 1968-70; mem, adv council, Renaissance Soc of Amer, 1954; mem: Intl Astronomical Union; Amer Hist Assn; Amer Astronomical Soc; Phi Beta Kappa. Author: The Comet of 1577: Its Place in the History of Astronomy, 1944; trans, ed, Caspar's Kepler, 1959; contbr to sci jours. Home: 176 E 77 St, New York, NY. Office: Queens College, CUNY, Flushing, NY.

HELLMAN, Lillian, US, playwright; b. New Orleans, La, June 20, 1905; d. Max and Julia (Newhouse); att NYU, 1922-25; Columbia U, 1925; MA, Tufts Coll, 1940; LLD, Wheaton Coll; m. Arthur Kober, 1925, (div). Writer since 1925; scenario writer since 1935; with Horace Liveright Inc, publishers, 1924-25; book reviewer, Herald-Tribune, 1925-28; theatrical play reader, 1927-30. Author: The Children's Hour, 1934; Days to Come, 1936; The Little Foxes, 1939; Watch on the Rhine, 1941; The Searching Wind, 1944; Another Part of the Forest, 1946; adapted: Roble's Montserrat, 1949; The Autumn Garden, 1951; Toys in the Attic, 1960; An Unfinished Woman, memoir, 1969; dramatized for motion pictures: The Dark Angel, 1935; These Three, 1936; Dead End, 1937; The Little Foxes, 1940; The North Star, 1943; The Searching Wind, 1945; Candide, 1957; My Mother, My Father and Me, 1963; author, motion picture, The Chase, 1965; ed: The Letters of Anton Chekhov, 1955; musical version of Voltaire's Candide, 1956; The Lark, by Anouilh, 1955; Author of Short Novels and Stories of Dashiell Hammett, 1966; contbr to mags. F, Natl Inst Arts and Sci; mem: Natl Inst Arts and Letters, Dramatists Guild. Recipient, gold medal, Natl Inst Arts and Letters, 1964. Home: 63 E 82 St, New York, NY.

HELLMANN, Maximilian, W Ger, merchant; b. Kalusch, Galicia, June 25, 1895; s. Abraham and Lea (Mayer); in W Ger since 1949; att HS, Vienna; m. Genia Vogel (decd); c: Bernhard, Siegmund, Luise Heppner. Pres, Zionist Org, vice-pres, J Comty, both Munich; fmr: mem, presidium, Jt J Comms, Bavaria; pres comm, Isr Bonds; pres, J Moadon; vice-pres, Loan Inst IWRIA; Askan of Magbit. Spec interest, social, political work for Isr. Home: 43 Grillparzer St, Munich, West Ger.

HELPERN, Beatrice L N, US, civic worker; b. NYC, July 23, 1907; d. Abraham and Hannah (Weinberg) Liebovitz; BA, NJ Douglass Coll for Women, 1928; m. 2nd, Lester Nightingale (decd); c: William, Stuart; m. 3rd, Milton Helpern,

Jan 1, 1955; step-c: Nanncy Moldover, Susan Nettler, Alice. Volunteer secy, Off, Chief Med Examiner, NYC, since 1961; mem bd, NY chap, AJComm, since 1952, fmr: co-chmn, mem comm, delg; hon chmn, hospitality comm: 1st World Meeting on Med Law; 3rd cong, Intl Assn on Accident and Traffic Med; mem: ladies org comm, 2nd, 3rd, intl meeting, Forensic Path and Med, 1960, 1963; Phi Beta Kappa; fmr: mem bd, NY chap: League for Emotionally Disturbed Children; Hemophilia Found; women's div, Jt Defense Appeal. Recipient: Alliance Francaise medal, 1928. Home: 303 W 57 St, New York, NY. Office: 520 First Ave, New York, NY.

HELPERN, Milton, US, physician, medical examiner, educator; b. NYC, Apr 17, 1902; s. Moses and Bertha (Toplon); BS, CCNY, 1922; MD, Cornell U Med Coll, 1926; m. Ruth Vyner, July 10, 1927 (decd); c: Nancy Moldover, Susan Nettler, Alice Feinberg; m. 2nd, Beatrice Nightingale, Jan 1, 1955; step-c: William, Stuart. Chief med examiner, NYC, since 1954; prof, chmn, Dept Forensic Med, NYU Post-Grad Med Sch, since 1954; visiting prof, path, since 1966; asst prof, clinical med, lectr, path and legal med, Cornell U Med Coll, 1932-66; cons path, Hosp for Spec Surg, since 1958; dir labs, 1941-58; spec cons, War Dept, 1943-46. F: Coll Amer Paths; NY Acad Med; Amer Acad Compensation Med, pres, 1961-63; dipl: Amer Bd Path, 1938, forensic path, 1959; Natl Bd Med Examiners, 1929; fmr pres: Med Soc; NY, Co, 1962-63; Intl Assn Traffic and Accident Med, 1966-69; Natl Assn Med Examiners, 1968; Soc Alumni; Bellevue Hosp, 1964; Amer Acad Forensic Scis; 2nd Intl Meeting, Forensic Path and Med, 1960; vice-pres, Intl Acad of Legal Med, 1961-64; trustee: Soc of Med Jurisprudence, 1965-66; Milton Helpern Libr of Legal Med, 1962; Park Ave Syn, since 1958; adv bd. Heb U Hadassah Med Sch, Isr, since 1958; mem: Amer Acad Paths and Bacts; Amer Soc Clinical Paths; Phi Beta Kappa; Alpha Omega Alpha Co-author, Legal Medicine, Pathology and Toxicology, 2nd ed, 1954; contbr to med and medico -legal jours. Recipient, Medals; Townsend Harris, alumni assn, CCNY, 1958; gold and citation, Law Sci Inst and Found, U Tex, 1958; Redway, Med Soc State of NY, 1967; Chapin, RI State Med Soc, 1968; Order of Leopold, Belgium, 1968. Hobby: photography. Home: 303 E 57 St, New York, NY. Office: 520 First Ave, New York, NY.

HELSTEIN, Ralph L, US, labor leader; b. Duluth, Minn, Dec 11, 1902; s. Henry and Lena (Litman); BA, U Minn, 1929, LLB, 1934; m. Rachel Brin, Jan 2, 1939; c: Nina, Toni. Spec counsel, vice-pres, Amalgamated Meat Cutters & Butcher Workmen of N Amer, since 1968; exec council, AFL-CIO, since 1965; vice-pres, ind union dept, since 1961; pres, United Packinghouse Workers of Amer, 1946-68; visiting commn, social sci and citizens bd, U Chgo; gen counsel, Minn State CIO Council, 1939-43. Dir, KAM Temple, Chgo, 1945-59. Home: 5806 S Blasckstone Ave, Chicago, Ill. Office: 2800 N Sheridan Rd, Chicago, Ill.

HEMING, Henry L, US, investment banker; b. NYC, June 9, 1898; s. Joseph and Harriet (Liebmann); Blitt, Princeton U, 1918; m. Kate Sidenberg, Apr 29, 1920; c: Nancy Kramer, Susan Hecht. Partner, L F Rothschild & Co, since 1929. Col, USMCR, since 1952. Vice-chmn, J Bd Guardians; fmr pres, First Marine Div Assn; trustee, FJP, NY; fmr bd mem: Camp Ramapo; Hawthorne Cedar Knolls Sch; clubs: Princeton; Bankers; Cent Country; Army and Navy, Wash, DC. Home: Armonk, NY. Office: 99 William St, New York, NY.

HEMLEY, Samuel, US, orthodontist, educator; b. NYC, Feb 8, 1898; s. David and Hanna (Brunner); DDS, Columbia U, 1918; att CCNY, 1928-30; m. Clara Bernstein, Nov 24, 1920. Pvt practice, 1918-67; prof em, NYU Coll of Dent, since 1966, fac mem since 1929; asst surg, LI Coll Hosp, 1924-26. US Army, 1919; USN, 1951; F, Amer Coll Dents; dipl, Amer Bd Orthodontists; mem: Amer Dent Assn; Amer Assn Orthodontists; Northeastern Soc Orthodontists; Amer Soc Dent for Children; Intl Assn Dent Research; Research Soc Amer; Omicron Kappa Upsilon. Author: Fundamentals of Occlusion, 1944; Orthodontic Theory and Practice, 1953; contbr to profsl jours. Homes: 636 N Island, Golden Beach, Fla and Lake George, NY.

HENCHEL, Charles, US, jurist, attorney; b. New Haven, Conn, May 28, 1904; s. Benjamin and Lena (Nodelman); LLB, Fordham U, 1930; m. Frances Yudkin, Nov 26, 1936; c: James, Arthur. Judge, Probate Court, Dist of New Haven, since 1965; secy, Bd Zoning Appeals, 1938-45; asst statute rev commn, Conn Gen Assembly, 1941; mem, Lower House Gen Assembly, 1945-49; minority leader, spec sessions, 1946;

judge, Munic Court, 1949-51, 1955-60; asst corp counsel, New Haven, 1953-54. Vice-pres, JCC; mem: B'nai B'rith; Dem Town Comm; Conn, Amer, Co Bar Assns; Tau Epsilon Phi. Home: 149 Whittier Rd, New Haven, Conn. Office: 205 Church St, New Haven, Conn.

HENDEL, Gershon, Isr, journalist; b. Ostrolenka, Pol, May 13, 1914; s. Elieser and Rivka (Segal); in Isr since 1939; att: Yeshiva, Radzymin; Tchrs Sem, Warsaw, 1929-33; m. Lea Handelman; c: David, Esther. Journalist, Yediot Ahronot, since 1970; head, ed staff, Hayom, Heb daily, 1966-70, mem, ed bd, Haboker, 1949-65; mem staff, Hamashkif, daily, 1939-49. Mem natl council, Herut Movement; fmr comm mem, Tel Aviv Journalists Assn. Home: 14 Narkissim Blvd, Ramat Gan, Isr. Office: 38 King George St, Tel Aviv, Isr.

HENDEL, Yehudit, Isr, author; b. Warsaw, Pol, 1927; d. Akiva and Nehama; in Isr since 1930; att Levinski Sem, Tel Aviv; m. Zvi Mairovich, 1948; c: Dorit, Joshua. Author: Hem Shonim, 1950; Rehov haMadregot, novel, 1956, Eng ed, 1963; heHatzer Shel Momo haGadol, 1969. Recipient, Asher Barash Lit Prize, for Rehov haMadregot. Home: 5 Jerusalem St, Haifa, Isr.

HENDLER, Samuel I, US, attorney; b. NYC, Mar 4, 1922; s. Aaron and Molly (Okun); BA, NYU, 1942, LLB, 1948; m. Marjorie Rosenblum, Nov 5, 1950; c: William, James, Elizabeth. Pvt practice, NYC, since 1949; vice-pres, dir, Isr Wines Ltd, since 1960; dir: Aceto Chem Co Inc, since 1961; Haolim Financial Corp, since 1956, secy, Computer Exch, since 1968. USAAF and Mil Intelligence, 1941-45. Pres, Pkwy Village Comty Assn, 1959-61; natl secy, dir, Keren-Or, Jerusalem, Inst for the Blind, since 1960; mem: NY Co Lawyers Assn; Cong Sons of Isr; NY State Bar Assn; Amer Judicature Soc; Jamaica J Cen. Hobby: painting. Home: 147-15 Village Rd, Jamaica, NY. Office: 475 Fifth Ave, New York, NY.

HENIG, Philip E, US, physician, educator; b. NYC, Mar 9, 1913; s. David and Anna (Grundt); BS, NYU, 1933, MD, 1937; m. Carolyn Chessen, Aug 9, 1940; c: Peter, Andrea. Pvt practice since 1946; prof med, NY Med Coll, since 1967; visiting phys: Metrop Hosp, since 1952, dir, ambulatory care, since 1957; Bird S Coler Hosp, since 1952; Flower-Fifth Ave Hosp; phys, NYC Domestic Relations Court, 1946-67. Lt col, US Army, 1942-46. Dipl, Amer Bd Internal Med; FACP; mem: AMA; NY Co Med Assn; NY Heart Assn; NY Card Soc; NY Diabetes Assn; NY Acad Sci; Amer Mus Natural Hist; Phi Beta Kappa; Alpha Omega Alpha. Home: 201 E 79 St, New York, NY. Office: 134 W 58 St, New York, NY.

HENIS, Yigal, Isr, microbiologist; b. Tel Aviv, Nov 27, 1926; s. Uri and Mina (Bruckenstein); PhD, Heb U, Jerusalem, 1959; m. Ahuva Shulman, Mar 17, 1949; c: Yoav, Ilan. Head, dept phytopath, microbiol; asso prof, both Heb U; lectr, fac of agric, Rehovot, since 1969, on fac since 1959; asst, dept of microbiol, Heb U, Jerusalem, 1954-58, instr, 1958-59. IDF, 1947-49. Mem: Amer, Eng, Isr Microbiol Socs; Amer Phytopath Soc; Isr Biochem and Soil Sci Socs. Contbr to sci jours. Home: 19 Ben Zion St, Rehovot, Isr. Office: POB 12, Rehovot, Isr.

HENKIN, A Hillel, US, educator; b. Russ, Sep 15, 1911; s. Yoseph and Frieda (Kreindel); in US since 1923; att: Rabbi Isaac Elchanan Theol Sem; Tchrs Inst, Yeshiva U; BA, Yeshiva Coll, 1934; MA, Columbia U, 1935; DE, Dropsie Coll, Phila, 1965; m. Anne Dobris, June 20, 1937; c: Gil (decd), Judah. Educator, Herzliah J Tchrs Sem, NY, since 1969; exec dir, Bur J Educ, Conn, 1946-68; educ cons, J Fed, Waterbury, 1955-60; prin, asst dir, J Cen, Allentown, Pa, 1944-46; tchr, educ dir, Kesher Zion Heb Sch, Pa, 1937-44. Mem: Natl Comm on Testing in J Educ; J Prins Cert Comm; hon, bd dirs, New Haven J Comty Cen; ZOA; Young Isr Syn, both New Haven, Conn; fmr: chmn personnel comm, Amer Assn for J Educ; dir, Educ Summer Sems in Isr; mem: United Syn Commn on J Educ; ed staff, The Syn Sch; pres: Natl Council for J Educ; Rel Educ Assn, Gtr New Haven chap; chmn comm, Natl Orgs J Educs. Author, Courses of Studies for Three Day Hebrew Schools, 1960. Recipient, First Horeb Award for Distinction in J Educ, Assn Tchrs Inst Alumni, Yeshiva U, 1960. Home: 207 Colony Rd, New Haven, Conn. Office: 1184 Chapel St, New Haven, Conn.

HENKIN, Louis, US, jurist, educator; b. Smolyan, Russ, Nov 11, 1917; s. Yoseph and Frieda (Kreindel); in US since 1923;

AB, Yeshiva Coll, 1947; LLB, Harvard Law, Sch, 1940; hon DHL, Yeshiva U, 1963; m. Alice Hartman, June 19, 1960. Hamilton Fish prof, intl law, diplomacy, Columbia U, since 1963; mem: US, group, Perm Court of Arbitration, 1963-69; State Dept Adv, Panel on Intl Law, since 1967; cons, US Natl Council on Marine Resources; law clerk: US Court of Appeals Judge Learned Hand, 1940-41; US Supr Court Justice Felix Frankfurter, 1946-47; cons, UN Legal Dept, 1947-48; fgn affairs off, US Dept of State, 1948-57; prof, U of Pa, 1957-62. US Army, 1941-45. Mem: NY, US Supr Court Bars; Amer Soc Intl Law; Council on Fgn Relations; Assn Bar, NYC; Amer br, Intl Law Assn; AAUP; Amer Soc for Political and Legal Phil; Amer Political Sci Assn. Author: Arms Control and Inspection in American Law, 1958; The Berlin Crisis and the United Nations, 1959; Disarmament: The Lawyers Interest, 1963; How Nations Behave, 1968; Laws for the Seas Mineral Resources, 1968; ed, Arms Control: Issues for the Public, 1961; contbr to law jours. Home: 460 Riverside Dr, New York, NY. Office: Columbia U, New York, NY.

HENRIQUES, Samuel Cohen, Jamaica; b. Kingston, Jamaica Sep 17, 1916; s. Vernon and Gladys (Simons); att Munroe Coll, Jamaica, 1928-33; m. Genevieve Lyons, Jan 18, 1939; c: Erica, Norma, Sandra, Victoria. Dir: Kingston Ind Agcys Ltd, since 1946; Monex; Kingston Ind Garage; Belmont Dry Docks; New Yarmouth; Henriques Bros; W Indies Paper Products; W Indies Glass Co; mgr and dir, Kingston Ind Works, 1949-55. Pres: United Cong of Israelites; Jamaica Paraplegic Assn; chmn: Jamaica Polio Found; Natl Savings Comm; vice-chmn, Polio Tech Comm; mem: Kingston Hosps Mgmt Bd; Jamaica Rehab Soc; past pres, Rotary, Kingston; fmr: found mem, Cayman Lodge; mem: U Lodge of W Indies; St Johns Lodge. Recipient: CBE, 1967; JP, 1957. Hobbies: collecting lighters; photography. Home: 19 Hillcrest Ave, Kingston, Jamaica. Office: 381 Spanish Town Rd, Kingston, Jamaica.

HERBERT, Gilbert, Isr, architect; b. Johannesburg, S Afr, June 22, 1924; s. Benjamin and Sophia (Miller); in Isr since 1968; BArch, Witwatersrand U, 1947, MA, 1955, dipl, town planning, 1951; m. Valerie Ryan, June 18, 1953; c: Barry, Margaret. Asso prof, architecture, Technion, Haifa, since 1968; lectr, Witwatersrand U, reader in architecture and town planning, Adelaide U, 1961-68. Works executed: Cinerama Theater, Johannesburg; John Mofat Bldg. Mem: Inst S Afr Architects; Austr Planning Inst; asso, Royal Aust Inst Architects; f, Royal Inst of Brit Architects; fmr: chmn, comm, Transvaal Provincial Inst of Architects; vice-pres, architecture and engr, Austr and NZ Assn for Advancement of Sci; mem: zc of S Afr; exec, Fed Bd of Educ; housing and publs comm, Royal Austr Inst of Architecture; United Appeal, S Afr; hon architect, Adelaide Heb Cong. Author: The Synthetic Vision of Walter Gropius; contbr numerous articles to profsl jours. Recipient: Sir Herbert Baker Scholar, Inst of S Afr Architects, 1957; Meyer Found Award, 1967, 1968. Home: 8 Eder St, Haifa, Isr. Office: Technion, Haifa, Isr.

HERBSTEIN, Frank Herzl, Isr, crystallographer; b. Cape Town, S Afr, July 3, 1926; s. Joseph and Betty (Policansky); in Isr since 1965; MSc, U Cape Town, 1947, DSc, 1967; PhD, Heb U, 1956; m. Jessica Liebson, Oct 2, 1952; c: Ruth, Judith. Prof, chem, Technion, since 1965, chmn, dept chem, since 1968; jr sci, Weizmann Inst, 1949-52; research asso, MIT, 1952-55; chief sci off, Council for Sci and Ind Research, 1956-65. IDF, 1948-49. Contbr to sci jours. Home: 7 Eder St, Haifa, Isr. Office: Technion, Haifa, Isr.

HERBSTEIN, Joseph, Isr, judge; b. S Afr, Sep 29, 1897; s. Moritz and Annie (Nurick) Isaac; in Isr since 1963; BA, Rhodes U, 1915; LLB, cum laude, Cape Town U, 1921; m. Betty Policansky; c: Frank, David, Moritz, Nina Selbst. Ret; QC, since 1939; judge, Supr Court, S Afr, 1946-63. Vice chmn, S Afr ZF in Isr; gov: Technion, Haifa; Heb U, Jerusalem; hon life pres, found, Keurboom Sports Club, Cape Town; mem, Isr Bowling Assn; fmr: pres, KH, UJA; found, first J Students org, Rhodes U. Author: Supreme Court Practice in South Africa; Magistrates Court Practice. Recipient: Elizabeth II Coronation Medal; Key to City, Cape Town, 1962. Spec interests: educ, public work. Home: 9 Hadarom St, Savyon, Isr.

HERCZEG, Rosa, Arg, certified public acctnt; b. Budapest, Hung, Aug 18, 1916; d. Jaime and Fanny (Diamant) Schwarz; in Arg since 1931; BCom, State Commercial HS, Buenos Aires, 1936; CPA, DEcon, Arg State U, Buenos Aires, 1954;

m. Esteban Herczeg, Sep 24, 1942. CPA, Arg Court of Justice and Lab Court, since 1947; exec secy, Ins-ud SA, 1935-42; vice-pres: Arg Council J Women; Intl Council J Women; chmn, Ext and Field Service Comm; auditor: Liga Amas de Casa; Asociacion Arg de Entidades de Bien Comun. Spec interest: social wfr activities. Home: 2699 Malabia, Buenos Aires, Arg.

HERFORT, Robert A, US, surgeon; b. NYC, May 10, 1919; s. Paul and Elizabeth (Fertel); BS, CCNY, 1938; MD, NYU Coll of Med, 1942; m. Jane Punzelt, Sep 7, 1956; c: John, David, Steven, Robert, Deborah. Pvt practice since 1950; att surg: St Agnes Hosp; Grasslands Hosp; White Plains Hosps; cons surg, St Barnabas Hosp; res surg: Montefiore Hosp, 1946-48; Mt Sinai Hosp, 1948-49. US Army, 1943-46. F, Amer Coll of Surgs; dipl: Amer Bd of Surg; Natl Bd of Med Examiners; mem: Amer Rheumatism Assn; Gerontological Soc. Recipient: purple heart with oak leaf cluster; Silver Star Medal; Pres unit citation. Home: 35 Vermont Ave, White Plains, NY. Office: 5 Old Mamaroneck Rd, White Plains, NY.

HERLITZ, Esther, Isr, diplomat, politician; b. Berlin, Ger, 1921; d. Georg and Irma (Herzka); in Isr since 1933; grad, Heb Tchrs Coll, Jerusalem, 1941. Repr, UJA mission to Austr, since 1971; resettlement off, i/c vocational training, higher studies for servicemen and women, Pal Govt, 1946; secy, div for Arab affairs, political dept, JA for Pal, 1947-48; acting head, US div, Isr Min for Fgn Affairs, 1948-50; adv, Isr delg, UN Gen Assembly, 1949; first secy, Emb of Isr, Wash, DC, 1950-54; Isr consul, NY, 1954-57; intl secy, Mapai, 1958-62; dir, dept of PR and info, Isr Fgn Min, Jerusalem; ambass, Den, 1966-71. Dep cdr, CHEN, Women's battalion, IDF, Jerusalem, 1948. Mem: Tel Aviv City Council. Home: 188 Hayarkon St, Tel Aviv, Isr. Office: Min Fgn Affairs, Jerusalem, Isr.

HERMAN, David A, US, public relations exec; b. Marion, O, Oct 14, 1910; s. Henry and Jennie (Schadel); BA, Harvard Coll, 1932; m. Jean Saltzstein, Nov 16, 1941; c: Mary, Thomas, John. Partner, PR firm, Barkin, Herman and Asso since 1952. Maj, USAAF, 1941-46. Chmn, Milw chap, AJComm, 1952-53, mem, exec comm, since 1953; trustee, Milw Art Cen; mem, bd dirs: Temple Emanu-El; B'ne Jeshurun; Children's Arts Prog; Milw JWF, 1955-58; Wis chap, Natl Soc for Prevention of Blindness; Civic Concert Assn, all Milw, Wis; mem, PR Soc of Amer; clubs: Brynwood Country; Harvard, Milw. Home: 2607 N Wahl Ave, Milwaukee, Wis. Office: 735 N Water St, Milwaukee, Wis.

HERMAN, Floyd Lehman, US, rabbi; b. Jackson, Miss, Dec 13, 1937; s. Julius and Phyllis (Lehman); att Tulane U; BA, U Cincinnati, 1959; BHL, MHL, ordained rabbi, HUC-JIR, 1964; m. Barbara Stricker, June 19, 1960; c: David, Beth. Asst rabbi, Cong EmanuEl since 1966. Chaplain, USAF, 1964-66. Vice pres, Gtr Houston Clergy Assn; secy, Houston Rabb Assn; mem: Zeta Beta Tau; B'nai B'rith; CCAR. Hobby, golf. Home: 5726 Alvarado St, Houston, Tex. Office: 1500 Sunset Blvd, Houston, Tex.

HERMAN, George E, US, journalist; b. NYC, Jan 14, 1920; s. Sydney and Tessie (Dryfoos); BA, cum laude, Dartmouth Coll, 1941; MS, Columbia U, 1942; m. Patricia Kerwin, Feb 11, 1955; c: Charles, Scott, Douglas. Corresp, CBS News, Wash DC since 1953, joined CBS, 1944, bur mgr, Tokyo, 1951-53. Home: 3115 O St, NW, Washington, DC. Office: CBS News, Broadcast House, Washington, DC.

HERMAN, Jack, US, rabbi; b. New York, NY, Aug 19, 1922; s. Harry and Mollie (Levitt); BA, Yeshiva U, 1942; MHL, ordained rabbi, JTSA, 1945; m. Shoshana Barness, Aug 10, 1958. Rabbi: Beth Am Syn, since 1947; Temple Anshe Emeth, Youngstown, 1944-46; Beth Isr Cong, Warren, 1946-47. Pres: Gtr Cleveland Bd Rabbis; AJCong, 1952-55; chmn: ZC, 1957-58; Rabb Assn, 1953-55; rel comm, State of Isr Bonds, since 1958; mem, bd dirs: J Family Service; Fed J Comty Cen; JNF Council; JWF; mem: RA; Masons; KP. Home: 14165 Washington Blvd, Cleveland, O. Study: 3557 Washington Blvd, Cleveland Heights, O.

HERMAN, Morris, US, psychiatrist, educator; b. NYC, Oct 3, 1906; s. Jacob and Bertha (Farber); BS, CCNY, 1926; MD, NYU Coll of Med, 1930; m. June O'Brien, May 19, 1932; c: Joan Lepik, Henry. Prof, clinical psycht, NYU Coll of Med, since 1949, prof, psycht since 1951, mem of fac since 1938; att psycht, U Hosp; visiting psycht and neur, Bellevue Hosp;

sr cons, VA, NYC; cons, AEC, since 1957. Pres, NY Soc for Clinical Psycht, 1954; councilor, Amer Psychopath Assn, chmn, mem comm; f: NY Acad Med, chmn, 1957-58; Amer Psychiatric Assn, chmn, comm on cons, mem comms: med educ, liaison with gen practitioners, nominating; dipl, Amer Bd Psycht and Neur; mem, NY Psycht Soc; Soc of Med Jurisprudence; Amer Neur Assn; Harvey Soc; NY Co Med Soc; Phi Beta Kappa; Alpha Omega Alpha; Sigma Xi; Jt Leg Comm to Study Narcotics, appd by Gov Harriman, 1956; club, Vidonia. Co-ed, textbook, Psychiatric Treatment, vol XXI, 1953; contbr to med publs. Home: 3556 88 St, Jackson Heights, NY. Office: 30 E 40 St, New York, NY.

HERMAN, Oskar, Yugo, artist; b. Zagreb, Mar 17, 1886; s. Daniel and Josipa (Landesmann); dipl, Acad of Art, Munich, Ger; m. Mira Svjezic, Apr 26, 1947. Painter; custodian, Modern Gal, Zagreb, 1945-49. Natl Liberation Army, 1943-45. Mem, Assn Plastic Artists, Yugo. Home: Marticeva 14-b, Zagreb, Yugo.

HERMANNS, Heida, US, concert pianist, teacher; b. Wiesbaden, Ger; d. Moritz and Alice (Metzger) Goldschmidt ;att City Lyceum, Wiesbaden, 1914-22; grad, Staatlich-Akademische Hochschule fuer Musik, Berlin, 1925; m. Artur Holde, Dec 22, 1932 (decd). Mem: fac, schs of music: "Y", NYC, since 1937; Manhattan, since 1960; Westport, 1951-61; fac mem, Dr Hochs Konservatorium, Frankfort/M, 1931-33; Chatham Sq, 1938-42. Concert debut at age of 14; concerts throughout Ger, Holland, Belgium, Amer; recitals, NY Town Hall, 1942, 1945, 1946; Carnegie Hall, 1949; mem, violin and piano sonata team, since 1955; recorded on Contemporary Records. Recipient: Bluethner grand piano, intl contest of the Staatliche Hochschule, Berlin, 1925; Prussian govt award for outstanding success as a music pedg, 1927. Home: 2 Cross Highway, Westport, Conn.

HERMON, Erika Lydia, Isr, physicist; b. Arad, Rum, May 27, 1935; d. Oscar and Magdalena (Schwartz) Weisz; in Isr since 1965; BSc, U Bucharest, 1955, MA, 1957; PhD, Weizmann Inst Sci, 1966; m. Uri Hermon, Jan 4, 1958; c: Orly, Physicist: Weizmann Inst, since 1965; Inst Atomic Physics, Bucharest, 1957-58. Mem: Isr Physicists Org. Contbr articles to profsl jours. Home: 185 Oshiot St, Rehovot, Isr.

HERRMAN, Louis, S Afr, historian, educator; b. Southampton, Eng, Oct 11, 1883; s. Isaac and Bertha (Silverman); in S Afr since 1907; att Hartley U Coll, Southampton, 1905; MA, U Cape Town, 1929; PhD, U London, 1933; m. Ethel Friedlander, 1918; m. 2nd, Lea Friedlander, 1961. Lit secy, Intl U Soc; asst research, dept social biol, LSE, 1931-33; prin, Cape Town HS, 1933-43. Author: History of the Jews in South Africa, 1930; In the Sealed Cave—A Scientific Fantasy, 1935; ed, Travels and Adventures of Nathaniel Isaacs, 2 vols, 1936; collaborator: Study of Twins in London Area, 1931-33; A Centenary History of the Cape Town Hebrew Congregation, 1941; co-ed, Janus, a Bilingual Anthology, 1962. Clubs: PEN, Owl. Home: Queenswood, Rhodes Ave, Newlands, Cape Town, S Afr.

HERSCH, Alexander, US, business exec; b. Kosice, Czech, May 21, 1909; s. Joseph and Rosa (Mandel); in US since 1954; att Kosice Gymnasium; m. Ida Keisler, Feb 3, 1935; c: Ruth Malach, Rachel Meyerhoff. Owner, cafeteria concession since 1954; fmr: chief steward messman, second steward, purser at various periods for: Amer Pacific Steamship Co; Pacific Tankers Inc; US Petroleum Carriers; Shoham Shipping Co; M Dizengoff & Co, 1945-53. Czech Army, 1931. Treas, B'nai Zion, Kosice chap; exec mem, Nordau Circle; fmr off, Betar Zion Movement. Recipient: Award from Rabbinate for services to illegal Aliyah, 1940; for assistance, Isr Bond Drive, 1964; B'nai Zion, 1968. Home: 81-06 34 Ave, Jackson Hgts, NY. Office: Yardney Electric Corp, 40-50 Leonard, New York, NY.

HERSCH, Henry H, US, lawyer; b. Columbus, O, June 1, 1925; s. Henry and Ella (Beren); AB, Princeton, 1949; LLB, Yale Law Sch, 1952; m. Florette Bloomberg, Oct 19, 1952; c: Frederick, Henry. Partner, Dolle, O'Donnell, Cash, Fee & Hahn, since 1958. Sgt US Army Infantry, 1943-46. Mem, bd gov, HUC-JIR; trustee: J Hosp, Rockdale Temple, J Fed, all Cincinnati; fmr: pres: Rosedale Temple; chmn, JWF; pres, J Family Service; mem, Queen City Assn; club, Losantiville Country. Home: 4051 Rosehill Ave, Cincinnati, O. Office: 920 Central Trust Tower, Cincinnati, O.

HERSCHER, Louis, US, songwriter, music publisher; b. Phila, Pa, Apr 19, 1894; s. Elias and Hudis (Bodner); m. Mary

Horn, Feb 28, 1923; c: Selma, Daniel, Ruth Grahm. Songwriter since 1911; found, Bell Song Pub Co; owner, Acadia Music Co since 1958. Composer: There are Just Two I's in Dixie, 1919; Nestle in Your Daddy's Arms, 1921; Dream Daddy, 1923; Wake Up Little Girl, 1923; Are You Lonely, 1923; Down Home Blues, 1924; On My Ukelele, 1924; You're Just a Great Big Baby Doll, 1928; One More Kiss Then Good Night, 1931; I'm Free From the Chain Gang Now, 1933; When Jimmy Rogers Said Good-Bye, 1933; Mahalo, 1941; Music to Rudyard Kippling's poem, If, 1953; Don't, 1954; You're Free to Go, 1955; Como se Vienne Se Va, 1959; Happy Go Lucky, 1962; Chic-A-Chic-A Dee, 1963; Swanee River Sue, 1965; Candlelight Kisses, 1963; Tokyo Taxi, 1963; in collaboration with Ruth Grahm: Where Were You, 1944; Orange Blossoms, 1954; co-composer, Psalms, A Song of David, 1953; music for motion pictures: Edgar Guest's Poetic Gems, with Frank Loesser, 1935; Selznick produc, Adventures of Tom Sawyer, 1938; Paramount Studios, Little Orphan Annie, 1938; Universal Studios, Rhythm of the Islands, 1943; Monogram Studios, Sarong Girl, 1943; Republic Pictures, A Song for Miss Julie, 1944; The Grasshopper, 1961; John Ping Pong, 1961; I Just Happened to Be Passing By, 1962. Mem: ASCAP; Amer Guild of Authors and Composers; Amer Soc Disc Jockeys; Songwriters Protective Assn; Music Publishers Contact Employees, Gtr NY; Songwriters Hall of Fame; Music and Performing Arts Lodge, B'nai B'rith; Sinai Temple, LA. Author: Practical Songwriting, 1935; The Magic Key to Tin Pan Alley, 1953; Successful Songwriting, 1963. Home and office: 9962 1/2 Durant Dr, Beverly Hills, Cal.

HERSCHFUS, Jechiel A, US, physician; b. Rotterdam, Holland, April 19, 1918; s. Chuna and Sarah (Feigenblum); in US since 1939; BS, Rotterdam Gymnasium, 1938; BA, U Wis, 1940, MD, 1944; m. Reva Weinstein, Sep 9, 1951; c: Marvin, Judith, Lynne, Michele. On teaching staff, asst med: Tufts Coll Med Sch, since 1951; Beth Isr Hosp, Boston; staff phys: Faulkner Hosp, Boston; Norwood Hosp, Norwood; NE Sinai Hosp; outpatient phys, Beth Isr Hosp. USAAC, WW II. Pres, Sharon Zionist dist, 1955-58; chmn, Red Cross Home Nursing; 1952-55; f, Coll Chest Physicians; mem: Amer Coll Allergists; Amer Fed for Clinical Research; AMA; Mass Med Soc; Norfolk Co Med Assn; IMA; Phi Delta Epsilon; ritual comm, Temple Isr. Contbr to Amer and intl med jours. Home: 17 Robin Rd, Sharon, Mass. Office: 62 E Main St, Sharon, Mass.

HERSH, Joseph H, US, otolaryngologist; b. NYC, July 26, 1909; s. Samuel and Minnie (Gurfein); BS, NYU, 1931, MD, 1935; m. Lilian Berk, June, 1934; c: Stephen, Marc. Clinical prof, NYU Post Grad Med Sch; co-dir, head, neck surg, Fr Hosp, att otolaryngologist, chmn of dept; asso surg, head, neck service, Bx-Leb Med Cen; asso att otolaryngologist, U Hosp; asst laryngologist: Seaview Hosp, 1939-52; Kingston Ave Hosp, 1939-52; certified specialist, Amer Bd Otolaryngology. F, Amer Soc Head and Neck Surg; mem: Amer Coll Surgs; NY Co Med Soc; Amer Acad Ophthalmology and Otolaryngology; AMA. Home and office: 121 E 69 St, New York, NY.

HERSHAFT, Alex, US, research scientist; b. Warsaw, Pol, July 1, 1934; s. Joseph and Sabina (Kalina) Herszaft; in US since 1951; BA, U Conn, 1955; PhD, Ia State U, 1961; m. Eugenie Crystal, Oct 1, 1962; c: Monica. Research planner, Grumman Corp, since 1968; sci, Avco Space Sys, 1966-68; analyst, Cen for Naval Analyses, 1963-65; research asso, Technion, Haifa, 1961-62. Prin contribs in: materials sci; x-ray crystallography; mil oprs analysis; anti-submarine warfare; oceanology; air and water pollution control; waste disposal. Exec dir, Amer Friends Rel Freedom in Isr; treas, Amer Humanist Assn; dir, Amers United; mem: Amer Chem Soc; Amer Acad Political and Social Scis; Amer Men of Sci; Sigma Xi; AAAS; ACLU; J Vegetarian Soc; fmr: found, Haifa, Jerusalem regions, League for Abolishment of Rel Coersion in Isr; pres, Hillel, Ia State U; student sen, U Conn. Contbr to sci jours. Home: 97 Jerusalem Ave, Massapequa, NY. Office: Grumman Corp, Bethpage, NY.

HERSHCOVICI, Florentina, Isr, author; b. Rum; d. Iancu and Eva (Falik) Leibovici; in Isr since 1948; att HS, Rum; m. Mordechai Hershcovici, Jan 6, 1934; c: Eva Bercovici. Author: Viata Unei Vaduve, 1930; Versuri, 1931; Romanul Unei Orfane, 1966; Rătăcitorul, 1968; Incestul, 1969. Active mem, Menora, authors' org. Home: 9 39 St, Jaffa, Isr.

HERSHENSON, Edward, US, attorney; b. Chgo, Ill, Jan 23, 1903; s. Israel and Lizzie (Nimz); LLB, DJ, Chgo Kent Coll of Law, 1924; m. Bertha Stein, Apr 2, 1928; c: Lawrence. Sr partner, Hershenson & Kessler; partner, Hershenson & Her-

shenson, 1924-1953. Mem: Chgo, Ill, Cal, Fed Amer Bar Assns; Decalogue Soc of Lawyers; Judicature Soc; club, El Rio Country. Home: 3750 Lake Shore Dr, Chicago, Ill. Office: 111 W Washington St, Chicago, Ill.

HERSHLAG, Zvi Yehuda, Isr, economist, educator; b. Rzeszow, Pol, June 23, 1914; s. Eliezer and Leah (Penzak); in Isr since 1938; att U Lvov, 1937-38; PhD, Heb U, 1952; m. Mania Portman, Feb 2, 1947; c: Leorah, Avner. Prof, econ hist, econ devl, head, dept of devl countries, Tel Aviv U; dean, social scis, Tel Aviv U, 1964-65; lectr, Heb U, 1950-62. Haganah; IDF, 1948-49. Pres, Isr Inst for Intl Problems; chmn, Isr Assn of Political Sci, Tel Aviv br; fmr pres: Heb U lectrs Assn; Heb U Students Assn; mem: Isr Bc Auth; Intl Hist Assn; Intl Econ Assn; fmr gen secy, Hashomer Hatzair, Galicia. Author: Turkey, an Economy in Transition, 1960; Modern Economic History of Middle East, (also in Heb) 1964; Turkey, the Challenge of Growth, 1968, and numerous papers. Recipient: dipl with spec distinction in econ, planning, Inst of Social Studies, Holland, 1958; Ford Found F, 1965-67. Home: 7 Hillel St, Jerusalem, Isr. Office: Tel Aviv U, Tel Aviv, Isr.

HERSHMAN, Samuel I, US, business exec; b. New Haven, Conn, Oct 5, 1892; s. Israel and Sophia (Schwartz); LLB, JD, U Mich Law Sch, Ann Arbor, 1913; m. Esther Goodman, June 25, 1925; c: James. Ret; fmr, chmn bd, I Hershman & Co Inc, 1963; pres, treas: Alsa Paper Co, 1925-63; Polyxor Chem Co, 1947-69. Ensign, USNR, WWI. Pres, Sara and E J Hershman Found; vice-pres, J Home for Aged, New Haven; bd dirs, J Cen; bd trustees: Cong Mishkan Isr, fmr pres; SF Raphael Hosp; fmr: pres, JCC, New Haven; co-chmn: Isr Bonds; UJA; mem: bd: Neighborhood Music Sch; Cerebral Palsy; United Fund, all New Haven; Correction Comm, State of Conn; JNF, exec comm; Citizens Action Comm, New Haven; sponsor, New Haven Redevl project, non-profit housing; mem: bd, JCC; JWF, all of New Haven; Zeta Beta Tau, Phi chap; clubs: charter, Woodbridge City; Graduate; Union League, all New Haven. Hobbies: boating, sports, fishing. Home: 187 Armory, Hamden, Conn. Office: 50 New St, New Haven, Conn.

HERSKOVITZ, Herbert H, US, psychiatrist; b. Turtle Creek, Pa, Oct 14, 1904; s. Henry and Anna (Zimmerman); BS, U Pittsburgh, 1927; MD, Temple U, 1931; m. Gertrude Rosenbloom, 1934; c: Robert. Pvt practice since 1946; asst clinical prof, Jefferson Med Coll, since 1957; cons, psychan, Devereux Schs; training analyst, Psychan Inst; teaching staff, Phila Psycht Cen, since 1955, dir, child unit, since 1963; sr phys, clinical dir, asst supt, Norristown State Hosp, 1937-46; dir, Guidance Cen Reading, Pa, 1946-50; cons, Family Service, Reading, 1946-50; asst prof, psycht, Hahnemann Med Coll 1951-53; cons, psycht, Selective Service Sys, WW II. F: Amer Psycht Assn; Amer Orthopsycht Assn; Pa Psycht Soc; Phila Psychoanalytic Soc; council mem, Amer Psychoanalytic Assn, since 1961; hon vice-pres, Deveriux Found; mem: AMA; Amer Assn Mental Deficiency; AAAS. Contbr to profsl jours. Home: 132 Buck Lane, Haverford, Pa. Office: 191 Presidential Blvd, Bala Cynwood, Pa.

HERST, Jerome P, (pen name—music, **Jerry Herst**), US, attorney, hearing off, composer, author; b. Chgo, Ill, May 28, 1909; s. Abraham and Dora (Schwartz); att: Northwestern U, Evanston, Ill, 1926-28; U of Cal, Berkeley, 1928-30; LLB, Hastings Coll of Law, SF, Cal, 1934; Conservatoire de Musique, Paris, 1949-50; studied musical composition with: Mario Castelnuovo-Tudesco, Beverly Hills; Alexandre Tasman, Paris; Ernst von Dohnanyi, SF; m. Jeanne Taylor, Dec 24, 1947; c: Charles. Hearing off i/c, SF Off Admn Procedure, State of Cal, since 1951, with off since 1948; practicing lawyer, Faulkner & O'Connor, attys at law, SF, 1935-42; referee, asst counsel, Cal Dept of Employment, 1947-48. USNR, 1943-46, cdr ret; Judge Advocate, Sr Judge Advocate, Gen Courts-Martial, Naval Dist. Composer: songs including: Call of Tarzan, 1934; So Rare, 1937; We'll Get a Bang Out of Life, 1938; scores for revs, produced in SF: The Black and Blue Eagle, 1933; Friskiana, 1945; Dance, Anyone?, 1953; ballets performed in SF: Pedestrians; Emporium; Schooldays; Merry-go-round; Wind Quintet, 1956-57; suite for sym orch, A Child's Garden of Verses, 1958-59. Life F, Intl Inst Arts and Letters; mem: State Bar, Cal; ASCAP; SF Bar Assn; life mem, Amer Fed Musicians, local 47, LA; clubs: The Family; SF Press. Home: 5735 Clover Dr, Oakland, Cal. Office: State Bldg, 455 Golden Gate, San Francisco, Cal.

HERSTEIN, Israel Nathan, US, educator; b. Lublin, Pol, Mar 28, 1923; s. Jacob and Mary (Lichtenstein); in US since

1946; BSc, U Man, Can, 1945; MA, U Toronto, 1946; PhD, U Ind, 1948; m. Marianne Deson, June 16, 1946. Prof, math, U Chgo, since 1962; instr, U Kan, 1948-50; visiting lectr, O State U, 1950-51; asst prof, U Chgo, 1951-53; asso prof, U of Pa, 1953-57; prof, Cornell U, 1957-58; visiting prof: Yale U, 1956-57; Stanford U, 1959, 1963; U Rome, 1961-62, 1963, 1964, 1966, 1967, 1968; IMPA, Rio de Janeiro, 1969; cons: Ramo Wooldridge, 1956; Lincoln Labs, 1957-58; Gen Elec, 1958-62. Mem exec comm: Amer Math Soc; Math Assn Amer. Author: Topics in Algebra, 1964; Non-Commutative Rings, 1968; Rings with Involution, 1967; Topics in Rings, 1969; fmr cons ed, Harper and Row; contbr to jours. Recipient: Guggenheim F, 1961-62, 1968-69; Fulbright Award, 1969. Home: 5000 Cornell St, Chicago, Ill. Office: U of Chgo, Chicago, Ill.

HERTZ, David Ralph, US, attorney, jurist; b. Cleveland, O, July 21, 1898; s. Aaron and Bertha (Lichtman); BA, U Mich, 1919; LLB, Columbia U Law Sch, 1921; m. Marguerite Rosenberg, Aug 27, 1922; c: Willard, Harlan. Pvt practice, 1922-29 and since 1939; admitted to Bar, 1921; commn, Cleveland City St Railway, 1932-34; judge, Court of Common Pleas, 1934-39; chmn, Bur of Employment Problems, 1940-42; impartial umpire, lab disputes, Cleveland Transit Sys, 1945-49. Pres, Cleveland Zionist dist, 1928-29; Cleveland Mental Hygiene Assn, 1946-47, 1960-63; mem: bd trustees: Cleveland Legal Aid Soc; fmr: J Cen; Mt Sinai Hosp; Bur J Educ; bd, JWF, 1924-51; JCC, 1950-52; grievance comm, Cleveland Bar Assn, 1953-57, exec comm, 1946-48; O State Bar Assn; exec comm, Cuyahoga Co Dem Comm; clubs: City of Cleveland; Commerce; The Temple. Contbr of bookrevs to natl magazines. Home: 2835 Drummond Rd, Shaker Heights, O. Office: 1020 Leader Bldg, Cleveland, O.

HERTZ, Richard C, US, rabbi, author; b. St Paul, Minn, Oct 7, 1916; s. Abram and Nadine (Rosenberg); BA, U Cincinnati, 1938; BHL, HUC, 1938, MHL, ordained rabbi, 1942; att: U Chgo, 1942; Harvard U Chaplains Sch, 1944; PhD, Northwestern U, 1948; m. Mary Mann, Nov 25, 1943; c: Nadine, Ruth. Sr rabbi, Temple Beth El, Detroit, since 1953; asst rabbi, N Shore Cong Isr, Glencoe, Ill, 1942-47; asso rabbi, Chgo Sinai Cong, 1947-53; spec White House mission to Russ to investigate status of J and Judaism behind Iron Curtain; study mission to Isr; first Amer rabbi recd in pvt audience by Pope Paul VI. Capt, chaplain, US Army, 1943-46. Author: The Rabbi Yesterday and Today, 1942; This I Believe, 1952; Education of the Jewish Child, 1953; Our Religion Above All, 1953; Inner Peace for You, 1954; Positive Judaism, 1955; Wings of the Morning, 1956; Impressions of Israel, 1956; Prescription for Heartache, 1958; Faith in Jewish Survival, 1961; Jewish Life Today, 1962; The American Jew in Search of Himself, 1962; What Counts Most in Life, 1963; What Can A Man Believe, 1967; lit critic, Best Books of Year for Democracy, list of NCCJ; contbr to scholarly and popular J and secular jours; made regular appearances, TV prog, The Pulpit, 1950-53. Vice-chmn, Detroit chap, AJ Comm, mem, natl exec bd; chmn, bd overseers, HUC-JIR; secy, Detroit United Comty Service; treas, Chgo Rabb Assn, fmr mem exec bd; fmr natl chmn, comm on J in Soviet orbit, mem, chaplaincy comm, comm on church and state, CCAR; mem: bd dirs: J Comty Cens, JWB; United Found; United Comty Services; Detroit Inst Tech; Boys Club; Mich Soc for Mh; Detroit Hist Soc; JWF; JCC; J Family and Children's Bur; Interfaith Action Council; Gov Romney's Comm on Ethics and Morals; natl adv comm, UJA; natl bd: JDC; Rel Educ Assn; chaplaincy commn, Natl JWB; Mich adv bd, ADL; exec bd, alumni assn, HUC-JIR; mem: Interfaith Comm, UAHC; lectr, J Chautauqua Soc; fmr: dept chaplain: State of Mich, Amer Legion; JWV; pres, Hyde Park and Kenwood Council Churches and Syns; rabb chmn, combined Ill campaign, UAHC, HUC-JIR; mem, educ comm, Mayor's Comm on Hum Relations, Chgo; delg, intl confs, World Union for Progressive Judaism; clubs: Econ, bd dirs; Rotary; Wranglers', fmr pres. Home: 18215 Parkside Ave, Detroit, Mich. Study: 8801 Woodward Ave, Detroit, Mich.

HERTZBERG, Benjamin, US, business exec; b. Richmond, Va, Aug 29, 1910; s. Louis and Annie (Yelen); BA, Cornell U, 1931; MBA, Harvard U, 1933; m. Lilian Steiner, Sep 30, 1945; c: Michael, Mark. Pres: Champale, Inc, since 1942; The Champale Products Corp, since 1953. Clubs: Cent Country; The Bohemians; Harvard. Home: 812 Park Ave, New York, NY. Office: 16 W 46 St, New York, NY.

HERTZBURG, Arthur, US, rabbi; b. Lubacaow, Pol, June 9, 1921; s. Zvi and Anna (Alstadt); in US since 1926; BA, Johns

Hopkins U, 1940; ordained rabbi, JTSA, 1943; grad work in hist: Columbia U; Harvard U; m. Phyllis Cannon, May 19, 1950; two c. Rabbi, Temple Emanu-El, Englewood, NJ, since 1956; lectr hist, grad fac, Columbia U since 1961; Hillel dir, Smith Coll, 1943-44; rabbi: Ahavath Isr Cong, Phila, 1944-47; W End Syn, Nashville, Tenn, 1947-56; visiting asso prof hist, Rutgers U, 1966-68; lectr rel, Princeton U, 1968-69. Chaplain, USAAF, 1951-53. Author: The Outbursts that Await Us, 1963; The Zionist Idea; The French Enlightenment and the Jews, 1968; co-author, Judaism, 1959; pres, Conf J Social Studies; cons ed, Ency Judaica; contbr to jours; speaker, radio and TV; columnist, Natl Catholic Reporter. Recipient: Amram Award, 1967. Study: 147 Tenafly Rd, Englewood, NJ.

HERWITZ, David R, US, attorney, educator; b. Lynn, Mass, Dec 8, 1925; s. Harry and Sarah (Shapiro); BS, MIT, Mass, 1946; LLB, Harvard Law Sch, 1949; m. Carla Barron, Jan 22, 1960; c: Andrew. Prof, law, Harvard Law Sch, since 1957, asst prof, 1954-57; asso, Mintz, Levin and Cohen, 1951-54; cons, Treas Dept, 1960-63. USNR, 1944-46. Sup, Harvard-Brandeis-Isr legal studies, 1957-59. Author: Business Planning, 1966; co-author, Cases and Materials on Accounting, 1959; contbr to legal jours. Home: 44 Philips Beach Rd, Swampscott, Mass. Office: Harvard Law Sch, Cambridge, Mass.

HERZ, Naftali, Isr, physician; b. Cologne, Ger, June 1, 1910; s. Josef and Becka (Bucki); in Isr since 1935; att U Cologne, 1929-1930; U Berlin, 1931-32; MD, U Cologne, 1935; m. Irene Wertheimer, 1956; c: Hagit Tal, Ada, Daniel, Ronnie. Head: Biochem Lab, Rambam Hosp, Haifa, since 1951; Isr Poison Info Cen; gen practitioner, 1941-46; asst, Biochem Dept, Hadassa U Hosp, Jerusalem, 1946-51. Capt, IDF, MC. Mem, IMA. Ed, Isr Poison File. Home: 24 Louis Pasteur St, Haifa, Isr. Office: Rambam Hosp, Haifa, Isr.

HERZBERG, Mala, Isr, biochemist; b. Lodz, Pol, May 6, 1913; d. Yehiel and Lea (Berger) Szatan; in Isr since 1949; BSc, U Poznan, 1936; MSc, U Warsaw, 1939; PhD, U Lodz, 1949, all Pol; m. Fischel Herzberg, Nov 9, 1939; c: Victor, Matityahu. Head, dept clinical biochem, Ichilov Govt Munic Hosp, Tel Aviv, since 1962; clinical sr lectr, chem path, Tel Aviv U Med Sch; first asst, dept phys chem, Acad of Sci, Lodz, 1946-49. Prin contribs: nutritional surveys of Isr, of food habits of different J comtys, 1950-56; study of phys response to injury. Mem: Isr Biochem Soc; Clinical Path Soc; IMA; AAAS. Contbr to profsl jours. Home: 14/6 Iftah St, Tel Aviv, Isr.

HERZBERG, Mendel, US, educator, researcher; b. San Francisco, Nov 26, 1920; s. Samuel and Eva (Radinsky); BS, U of Cal, Berkeley, 1948, MA, 1950, PhD, 1953; m. Shirley Levine, Mar 3, 1946; c: Steven, Lawrence. Prof microbiol, U Hawaii, since 1967; asso prof, bact, U Fla, 1966-67, on fac since 1959; asso research bact, U of Cal, 1953-54. US Army, 1942-46. Councillor, Hawaii br, Amer Soc for Microbiol, pres, secy-treas, SE br; mem: Amer Assn of Immunologists; Amer Soc for Microbiol; AAAS; Gamma Sigma Delta; Soc of Sigma Xi; AAUP. Contbr to med jours. Home: 1460-4 Hunakai St, Honolulu, Hawaii. Office: U of Hawaii, Honolulu, Hawaii.

HERZBERGER, Maximilian J, US, researcher; b. Charlottenburg, Ger, Mar 7, 1899; s. Leopold and Sonja (Behrendt); in US since 1935; BS, Schiller Real Gymnasium, 1917; MS, PhD, Berlin U, 1922; att Jena U, 1923-24; m. Edith Kaufmann, May 31, 1925; c: Ruth Rosenberg, Ursula Bellugi, Hans. I/c, geometrical optical research, Eastman Kodak Co, Rochester, NY, since 1935, sr research asso, since 1958; lectr, ETH, Zurich, since 1965; cons prof, La State U, New Orleans, since 1969; lens designer: Emil Busch, Bathenow, Ger, 1923-25; Scophony TV Co, London, Eng, 1935; head, lens computing dept, Leitz Wetzlar, Ger, 1925-27; math, personal asst to dir, C Zeiss, Jena, Ger, 1927-34; lectr, optics, Delft U, 1934; mem, Inst for Advanced Study, Princeton U, 1946; lectured in Ger, It, Spain, Fr, Holland, Switz. Prin contribs: developed: spot diagram method, 1940; Superachromat, 1959. F: Optical Soc of Amer; AAAS; mem: bd dirs, J Wfr Council, 1942, 1953, 1954-57; bd trustees, Temple B'rith Kodesh, 1940-43; Sigma Xi; Amer Math Soc; Deutsche Optische Gesellschaft; Ger Optical Soc; Swiss Optical Soc; Council of Swiss Optical Soc; Bavarian Acad Sci; clubs: City of Rochester, bd govs, 1947-49; NY State Chess Assn, vice-pres since 1949; Chess of Rochester, vice-pres, 1952-53. Author: Strahlenoptik, 1932; Modern Geometrical Optics, 1958; ed, Vol VIII, 3rd Series of Euler Opera Omnia; asso ed, Jour of Optical Soc of Amer, 1947-62; contbr to profsl and sci jours. Recipient: Cressy Morrison prize, NY Acad of Scis, 1945; Ives medal, Optical

Soc of Amer, 1962. Home: 186 Augustine St, Rochester, NY. Office: Research Labs, Eastman Kodak Co, Rochester, NY.

HERZMARK, Maurice H, US, surgeon; b. Memphis, Tenn, June 15, 1896; s. David and Freda (Jaffe); BA, George Wash U, 1918; MD, 1921; m. Doris Kagan, May 27, 1928; c: Zita, Fredda. Practicing phys since 1924; mem, fac, George Wash U Med Sch, 1924-28; staff: Hosp for Ruptured and Crippled, 1928-34; Hosp for Jt Diseases, 1928-46. Lt col, US Army MC, 1942-46, chief, orthopedic surg, Southwest Pacific, 1944-45. Dipl, Amer Bd Orthopedic Surg, since 1927; first pres, Wash chap, Amer Friends Heb U; mem: AMA; Dist and Jacobi Med Socs; Amer Acad Orthopedic Surgs; Phi Delta Epsilon; Phi Alpha, found, 1914. Contbr to med jours. Home: The Watergate East, Washington, DC. Office: 1616-18 St, NW, Washington, DC.

HERZOG, Chaim, Isr, lawyer, army off, business exec; b. Belfast, N Ir, Sep 17, 1918; s. Isaac and Sarah (Hillman); in Isr since 1935; att: Talmudical Sem, Jerusalem, 1935-37; Cambridge U; LLB, London U; grad, Royal Mil Coll, Eng; m. Aura Ambache, May 8, 1947; c: Joel, Michael, Isaac, Ronit. Mgn dir: Gus-Rassco Ltd; Gus-Isr Ltd; dir: Gus Export Corp, London; Isr Ind Bank, Tel Aviv; numerous other cos; pvt law off, Tel Aviv, entered Isr Bar, 1950; fmr barrister, London; head, security dept, JA, 1947-48; mil, naval and air attache, Isr Emb, Wash, 1950-54; commanding off, Jerusalem dist, 1954-57; chief of staff, S Command, 1957-59; dir, IS, IDF, 1952-62; first mil gov, W Bank, 1967. Served Haganah; maj, Brit Army, WW II; gen staff, occupation forces in Ger. Pres, ORT Isr, since 1968; mem: Isr Lawyers Assn; Lab Party; Israel-Brit Commonwealth Assn; fmr pres, Variety Club. Author: Israel's Finest Hour, 1967; radio and tv commentator; contbr to Isr and fgn publs. Home: Zahala, Tel Aviv, Isr. Office: Shalom Tower, Tel Aviv, Isr.

HERZOG, Jacob, Isr, diplomat; b. Dublin, Ir, 1921; s. Isaac Halevi and Sarah (Hillman); att Heb U, Jerusalem; U of London. Ambass of Isr to Can, since 1960; fmr dir, USA div, Isr Min for Fgn Affairs; fmr, Min of Isr to Pol. Offices: Emb of Isr, 45 Powell Ave, Ottawa, Can; Min for Fgn Affairs, Jerusalem, Isr.

HERZOG, Jerome Morris, US, rabbi; b. NYC, Nov 12, 1931; s. Hyman and Zlota (Corn); BA, Bklyn Coll, 1953; ordained rabbi, Yeshiva U, 1957; att Dropsie Coll, Phila, Pa, 1958-61; m. Hedda Bukspan, Aug 23, 1959; c: Zehava, Uri, Avram, Hillel, Barry. Rabbi: Kenesseth Isr Cong, since 1961; Lower Merion Syn, Phila, Pa, 1957-61. Pres, Minn RA; natl adv bd, JDC; bd of dirs: Torah Acad; J Comty Cen; natl admin bd, B'nai Akiva of N Amer, 1951-53; exec bd: Hapoel Hamizrachi, 1951-52; RabCA, 1964-67; mem, Rel ZOA. Contbr to J jours. Home: 2620 Huntington Ave S, Minneapolis, Minn. Study: 4330 W 28 St, St Louis Park, Minneapolis, Minn.

HERZOG, Myron E, US, insurance broker; b. Chgo, Ill, Sep 7, 1911; s. Emanuel and Laura (Newhouse); BS, U of Ill, 1932; cert, Chartered Property and Casualty Underwriters, 1947; m. Celia Roth, June 16, 1937; c: Myron, Kay. Ins broker since 1935; vice-pres, Eliel & Loeb, Chgo. Hon natl chmn, B'nai B'rith Found of US, natl chmn, 1961-68, trustee since 1959, mem, bd govs, B'nai B'rith, since 1968, chmn, admn comm, dist 6, since 1953, fmr vice-pres, Chgo Council; mem: Natl Hillel Commn, since 1963, fmr mem, natl vocational service comm; bd dirs, J Vocational Service of Chgo, since 1956; N Shore Cong Isr, Glencoe, Ill; Brandeis U Assos; Chartered Property and Casualty Underwriters; clubs: Standard; Briarwood Country. Home: 444 Sheridan Rd, Highland Park, Ill. Office: 175 W Jackson Blvd, Chicago, Ill.

HES, Jozef Philip, Isr, psychiatrist; b. Culemborg, Holland, May 5, 1925; s. Meyer and Henriette (Wyzenbeek); in Isr since 1955; MD, State U Med Sch, Holland, 1954; m. Hindle Swartenberg, Mar 6, 1955; c: Judith, Uri, Haggai. Dir, psychiatric out-patient clinic, Kupat Holim, Jerusalem, since 1965; staff, Talbieh Hosp, 1961-65; visiting asst prof, Cornell Med Sch, 1968. IDF, 1948-49. Hon secy, Isr Soc for Med Psychotherapy; mem: Royal Isr Neuro-Psych Assn. Contbr to profsl jours. Recipient: Meir Prize, Med Sci, Kupat Holim, 1967. Spec interests: Yemenite folk psycht, hist of J psycht, study of social and comparative psycht. Home: 6 Ahad Haam, Jerusalem, Isr.

HESKY, Olga, Isr, author; b. London, Eng; d. Lewis and Rachael (Franks) Cowen; in Isr since 1949; att London U, 1930-31; m. Moshe Hesky, 1954; c: by previous m, Adam, Gabrielle. Author: The Painted Queen, 1961; The Purple Armchair, 1961; Number the Dust, 1963; Say Not Goodnight, 1964; The Serpent's Smile, 1966; Time for Treason, 1967; The Sequin Syndicate, 1969. Fmr reporter, sub ed, film theatre critic for Eng, S Afr newspapers; author of numerous plays broadcast by S Afr Bc Corp, several documentary films shown in Isr. Home: 124 Hayarkon St, Tel Aviv, Isr, and Hope House, Hedserly, Buckinghamshire, Eng.

HESS, Moshe Gerhard, Ger, business exec; b. Berlin, Ger, Sep 16, 1918; s. Arthur and Erna (Hirsch); tchrs cert, Heb Tchrs Coll, Jerusalem; ext exams, US London, Cambridge; m. Ann Hubner, Dec 22, 1967; c: Zipora Paster, Ilana Makov, Cyrille, Miriam. Exec dir, Deutsche Gesellschaft zur Forderung der Wirtschaftsbeziehungen mit Isr (Ger-Isr C of C), since 1967; mem, cen secretariat, Bank fur Gemeinwirtschaft AG, Frankfurt/M, since 1964; fmr: tchr, 1940-46; educ off, Dept of Educ, 1946-48; dipl, Min for Fgn Affairs, Govt of Isr, 1950-64. Lt, IDF, 1948-50. Mem: bd, Friends Heb U, Frankfurt/M; council, Ger-Isr Friendship Soc. Recipient: Ky Col, 1957; Officier de l'Ordre du Merite, Rep du Senegal, 1967. Home: 96 Hammarskjold-Ring, Frankfurt/M, Ger. Offices: 1 Rusterstrasse, Frankfurt/M, Ger; 16-24 Mainzer Landstrasse, Frankfurt/M, Ger.

HESS, Seymour L, US, educator; b. Bklyn, NY, Oct 27, 1920; s. Morris and Rose (Brumer); BS, Bklyn Coll, 1941; MS, U Chgo, 1945, PhD, 1949; m. Jeanne Carter, Dec 18, 1966; c: Stephen, Robert, Barbara. Asso dean, Coll of Arts and Sci, Fla State U, since 1966, head, dept of meteorology, 1958-63, asso prof, 1950-58; civilian instr, US Army, 1941-42; research asst, instr, U Chgo, 1946-48; research meteorologist, Lowell Observatory, Flagstaff, Ariz, 1948-50; visiting prof, NYU, 1956-58. Lt, USAC, 1942-46. Mem: Amer Meteorological Soc, fmr chmn, adv comm on meteorological educ; Amer Geophys Union; Amer Astronomical Soc; Sigma Xi; AAUP; B'nai B'rith; trustee, U Corp for Atmospheric Research; fmr, secy, trustee, Temple Isr, Tallahassee, Fla. Author, Introduction to Theoretical Meteorology, 1959; contbr to sci jours. Home: 3507 Westford Dr, Tallahassee, Fla. Office: Fla State U, Tallahassee, Fla.

HETH, Meir, Isr, attorney; b. Isr, Sep 24, 1932; s. Nahum and Michal (Levin); BA, Econ, Heb U, 1952, MJ, 1959; LLM, Harvard U, 1967; m. Rina Zmirin, 1958; c: Hadas, Noam, Hovan. Examiner banks, Bank of Isr, since 1969, sr econ, research dept, 1962-68; pvt practice, 1960-62. Pvt, Nahal, 1950-52. Author: Banking Institutions in Israel: 1950-1961, Heb 1963, Eng ed, 1966; The Legal Framework of Economic Activity in Israel, 1967; Flow of Funds in Israel Economy, Bank of Israel, 1968. Recipient: Peretz Naphtali Award, 1963. Home: 6 Tel Hai, Jerusalem, Isr. Office: Bank of Isr, POB 780, Jerusalem, Isr.

HETSRONI, Gad, Isr, educator; b. Haifa, Oct 10, 1934; s. Isaac and Kate (Pick); BSc, cum laude, Technion, Haifa, 1957; MSc, Mich State U, 1960, PhD, 1963; m. Ruth Gurevitz, Jan 5, 1960; c: Anath, Orli, Yael. Sr lectr, Technion, Haifa, since 1965; sr engr, Westinghouse, US, 1963-65. Lt, Isr Navy. Mem: Sigma Xi; Phi Kappa Phi; ASME. Contbr numerous papers to sci publs. Home: 17 Shwedia St, Haifa, Isr. Office: Technion, Haifa, Isr.

HETTELMAN, Phillip, US, investment banker; b. Baltimore, Md, June 17, 1899; s. Jacob and Lida (Hettelman); BA, U of NC, 1921; MS, Columbia U, 1923; m. Evelyn Harris, 1926, (div); m. 2nd, Elizabeth Stern, 1933 (div); c: Thomas, Nancy; m. 3rd, Ruth Rea, Nov 16, 1946; c: Jane, Linda, Phillip. Owner, Hettelman Co, inves, since 1954, sr partner, 1938-53; dir, Canal Assets Inc, New Orleans, La, since 1951; bond salesman, Ames Emerich and Co, 1922, sales mgr, 1922-28; mgr, bond dept, DH Silverberg and Co, 1928-33, gen partner, 1933-37. Pres: Alumni Assn, Sch of Bus, Columbia U, since 1959; NY Alumni U of NC, since 1959; chmn: alumni student aid fund, Columbia U Grad Sch of Bus, 1959-60; Jt Wall St div, FJP Insts, NY, 1948; gov, Natl Assn Security Dealers; mem: Wall St Comm: Boy Scouts of Amer, 1947; UJA of Gtr NY, 1946; Tau Kappa Alpha; clubs: Harmonie; NY Stock Exch Luncheon; Southampton Golf; Westhampton Yacht; Bankers. Contbr to consumer publs. Recipient: Columbia U Alumni Medal, 1961; Columbia U Sch Bus Alumni Medal for dist services. Home: 1085 Park Ave, New York, NY. Office: 61 Broadway, New York, NY.

HEWITT, Norman, US, attorney; b. NYC, Jan 4, 1928; s. Morris and Anna (Perlman); BBS, CCNY, 1948; LLB, Harvard Law Sch, 1951; m. Ginette Arouete, Sep 18, 1964. Atty since 1951; mem, State Sen, Conn, chmn, public health and safety comm; atty, adv, FCC, Wash, DC, 1944-45. Counter-Intelligence Agt, Ger, 1951, 1952; liaison between Ger and Mil Govt Courts. Pres, Abraham lodge, B'nai B'rith; state legal counsel, Conn Jaycees; pres, Gtr Bridgeport Mh Assn; chmn, banking and leg comms, Bridgeport Bar Assn; pres, Gtr Bridgeport Mh Council; asso mem, Natl Council Juvenile Court Judges; mem, Bridgeport C of C; fmr: chmn: comty relations comm, United J Council, council pres, 1966-68; Mh Fund Dr, N Fairfield Co. Contbr to legal jours. Recipient: Fairfield's Outstanding Young Man of 1961; Bridgeport's Outstanding Young Man of 1962; Key Man Award, Conn Jr C of C; B'nai B'rith Man of Year, 1966. Home: 126 Margemere Dr, Fairfield, Conn. Office: 945. Main St, Bridgeport, Conn.

HEXTER, Jack H, US, educator, historian; b. Memphis, Tenn, May 25, 1910; s. Milton and Anna (Marks); BA, U Cincinnati, 1931; MA, Harvard U, 1933; PhD, 1937; DLitt, Brown U, 1964; m. Ruth Mullin, 1942; c: Christopher, Eleanor, Anne, Richard. Charles J Stille prof hist, Yale U, since 1967, prof, hist, 1964-67; instr, hist, MIT, 1937-38; asso prof, Queens Coll, NY, 1951-57, on fac since 1939; prof, Wash U, St Louis, Mo, 1957-64, chmn, dept hist, 1957-60; f, Cen for Advanced Study in Behavioral Scis, 1966-67. Lt, US Army, 1942-45. Mem: Amer Hist Assn; Econ Hist Assn; Econ Hist Soc, Gt Brit; Renaissance Soc of Amer; AAUP; Conf on Brit Studies; Columbia U Sem on Renaissance. Author: Reign of King Pym, 1942; More's Utopia: The Biography of an Idea, 1952; Reappraisals in History, 1962; The Judaeo Christian Tradition, 1966; mem, bd eds, Jour of Modern Hist, 1950-53; contbr to hist jours. Recipient: Guggenheim f, 1942-47; Fulbright grant, 1950, 1959; award, Ford Found, 1954. Home: 455 Orange St, New Haven, Conn. Office: Dept of Hist, Yale U, New Haven, Conn.

HEXTER, Maurice B, US, organization exec; b. Cincinnati, O, June 30, 1891; s. Max and Sarah (Beck); BA, U Cincinnati, 1912; MA, Harvard U, 1922; PhD, 1924; hon: PhD, U Dominican Rep, 1955; LHD, Brandeis U, 1961; LHD, Yeshiva U, 1961; m. Marguerite Mock, Aug 11, 1921; c: Marjorie Cohen. Cons, FJP, since 1967, with org since 1938; exec dir, Milw Fed J Charities, 1915-17; supt, United J Charities, Cincinnati, 1917-19; exec dir, Fed J Charities, Boston, 1919-29; instr, tutor, social ethics dept, Harvard U, 1921-29; lectr, Sch of Social Work, Simmons Coll, 1921-29; secy, Jt Pal Survey Commn, 1927-29; dir, Pal Emergency Fund, 1929-38; non-Zionist mem, exec, JA for Pal, 1929-38; mem, comm, negotiations with Brit Cabinet, 1930-31; JA repr, Pal Royal Commn, 1936-37. Pres: Natl Conf Social Work, 1924; Amer J Jt Agric Corp, since 1942; Dominican Rep Settlement Assn, since 1948; Amer Mem ICA; mem: bd trustees, Brandeis U; Natl Assn Social Workers; cen coord comm, Comm Council, Gtr NY, since 1956; cen admission, distributing commn, Gtr NY Fund, 1939, 1957, and since 1959; Temple Emanu-El, NYC. Author: Social Consequences of Business Cycles, 1925; Cyclical Fluctuations in Juvenile Labor Market, 1926. Recipient: Order of Duarte, Dominican Rep, 1954. Home: 480 Park Ave, New York, NY. Office: 32 E 57 St, New York, NY.

HEYMAN, Israel, Isr, pediatrician; b. Detroit, Mich, May 17, 1919; s. Leo and Fanny (Openheim); in Isr since 1930; MD, Amer U, Beirut, 1944; m. Lea Freidinov, June 15, 1948, (decd); m. 2nd, Hanna Goldman; c: Samuel, Ehud, Eliahu. Chief, cons ped, clinic, Hadassah Munic Hosp, Tel Aviv; cons ped, Munic Health Services, Tel Aviv; on fac, Tel Aviv U Med Sch. Mem: IMA; chmn: Ped Clinic Soc, 1958-59; Tel Aviv chap, Ped Soc of Isr, 1966-67; B'nai B'rith. Home and office: 25 Arnon St, Tel Aviv, Isr.

HEYMAN, Moses D, US, engineer; b. Newark, NJ, Aug 27, 1896; s. William and Lena (Waldman); att: Heb Tech Inst, NY, 1914; LaSalle Ext U, Chgo, 1922; m. Irene Kashdan, May 21, 1924; c: Sidney, Alice. Pres, dir of research, Integrated Mica Corp, since 1946; cons, NASA, Houston, Tex; pres, Quiche Mining, 1924-26; pres, chief engr, Heyman, 1930-45. Prin countribs: inventor: the mechanical hand, 1938, and various machines used in metal workings; reconstituted mica, 1940, and was the first person to make continuous sheets of synthetic mica; holder, numerous US and fgn patents. Vice-pres, Amer Technion Soc, 1942-51, mem, bd dirs, since 1939; org, tech and engr comm, Amer Technion

Soc, 1945; vice-pres, ZOA, Far Rockaway br, 1943; co-chmn, bldg comm, Cong Sons of Isr, 1945-50, mem, bd dirs, 1941-50; treas, jt boycott council, AJCong, J Lab Comm, 1934-41; alternate mem, bd govs, Haifa Technion, 1957; f: AAAS; NY Acad Sci; mem: Amer Inst Mining and Metallurgical Engrs; Electro-Chem Soc; Faraday Soc of Eng; Amer Soc for Testing Materials. Contbr to tech mags. Recipient: dipl, Comm of Sci Research Personnel, 1945, War Metallurgy Comm, 1942; citation, Gen Yaakov Dori, 1949. Home: 14 Rivers Dr, Lake Success, NY. Office: 202 Franklin Pl, Woodmere, NY.

HEYMANN, Ezra, Uruguay, educator; b. Czernowitz, Rum, Oct 17, 1928; s. Moses and Frieda (Rubin); in Uruguay since 1953; att Us: Bucharest, Vienna, Heidelberg; m. Sara Pignolo, Jan 25, 1968; c: Elisa. Prof, hist of modern and contemporary phil, since 1958; phil of lang, since 1962; on staff, Instituto de Profesores Artigas, since 1956; visiting prof, U Cordoba, Arg, 1962-63, 1964-65. Contbr studies on ethical theory, phil of lang to various jours. Home: 951 Juan Paullier, ap 4, Montevideo, Uruguay. Office: Facultad de Humanidades, Cerrito 73, Montevideo, Uruguay.

HEYMANN, Rudolf Eduard, Isr, educator; b. Breslau, Ger, Oct 14, 1901; s. Bruno and Martha (Cohn); dip ing, Technische Hochschule, Berlin, 1926; m. Eleonore Wallach, July 15, 1933; c: Uriel. Sr lectr, fac mech engr, Technion, Haifa, since 1952; engr. Fritz Werner AG, Berlin, 1927-39. Hon secy, dept hist c tech, Intl Cong for Hist of Sci, Jerusalem, 1953; mem, Deutsche Gesellschaft fur die Geschichte der Medizin; participated in Work of Mus of Sci and Tech, Tel Aviv; fmr: active mem, Hist Circle, Technion; participated in erection of Maritime Mus, Haifa. Contbr papers to profsl jours. Spec interests: hist of sci and tech; mus for hist of tech. Office: Technion, Haifa, Isr.

HIAT, Philip, US, rabbi; b. NYC; grad, cum laude, Tchrs Inst, Yeshiva U; ordained rabbi, HUC-JIR; DD, Philathea Coll, 1968; m. Sylvia Tischler; three c. Rabbi, Mt Neboh Cong, NYC, since 1966, tenure for life, since 1968; exec vice-pres, Syn Council of Amer, until 1965; dir, public affairs, NY Bd Rabbis, 1952-61; rabbi, J Comty Cen, Princeton, 1949-52. USN, WW II. Adv, NY State Commn Against Discrimination; co-chmn, Mayor's Comm of Rel Leaders; adv council, Housing for Elderly, Fed Housing Auth; mem, Bus Ethics Adv Council. Recipient, Awards: Sylvania; Freedom Found. Home: 568 Grand St, New York, NY. Office: 235 Fifth Ave, New York, NY.

HIATT, Jacob, US, manufacturer; b. Obeliali, Lith, July 1, 1909; s. Joshua and Lea (Klass); in US since 1935; BA, Heb Coll, Lith, 1927; DJ, U Lith, 1931; MA, Clark U, 1946; m. Frances Lavine, May 31, 1937; c: Myra, Janice. Pres: Estey Inves Corp; Rand-Whitney; Jacob and Frances Hiatt Charitable Found; dir, Guaranty Bank & Trust Co, Worcester; Circuit judge, Court of Lith, 1934-35. Found and patron, Jacob and Frances Hiatt Inst; life trustee, Clark U; trustee: Worcester Found for Experimental Biol; Brandeis U; Holy Cross Coll; bd govs, HUC-JIR; mem: exec council, Amer J Hist Soc; Amer Antiquarian Soc; club, Mt Pleasant Country. Home: 20 Woodhaven Lane, Worcester, Mass. Office: 5 Barbara Lane, Worcester, Mass.

HIBSHMAN, Eugene Emanuel, US, rabbi; b. Cleveland, O, Oct 6, 1904; s. William and Elizabeth (Kohn); BA, U Cincinnati, 1925; BHL, ordained rabbi, HUC, 1928; m. Julia Sickel, June 10, 1941; c: Jonathan. Rabbi: Mt Zion Temple, since 1953; Temple Beth Isr, Altoona, Pa, 1928-40; B'nai Jeshurun Cong, Leavenworth, 1941-43; Sons of Isr Cong, Colo, 1943; Temple Isr, Uniontown, Pa, 1943-46; Temple Isr, Paducah, Ky, 1946-48; Ohev Shalom Cong, Huntington, W Va, 1948-52; Beth Isr Cong, Hamilton, O, 1952-53; civilian chaplain: Ft Leavenworth, 1941-43; Colo Springs, 1943; J chaplain, US Penitentiary, Leavenworth, 1941-43; acting dir, Hillel Found, U of W Va, 1944-45. Mem: CCAR; Midwest Assn Reform Rabbis; B'nai B'rith, Sioux chap; club, Kiwanis. Home: 2109 S Jefferson Ave, Sioux Falls, SD. Office: 523 W 14 St, Sioux Falls, SD.

HIGHMAN, Benjamin, US, physician; b. Russ, July 13, 1909; s. Max and Mary (Landis); in US since 1912; BS, hons, U of Ill, 1930, MS, 1932, MD, hons, 1933; m. Helen Wienshienk, May 7, 1939; c: Barbara, Lawrence, Marshall. Med dir, USPHS, since 1954, on staff since 1936, NIH since 1941; USPHS liaison off and chief, Radiopath Div, Armed Forces Inst of Path, Wash, DC, since 1965; instr, path, U of Ill Coll of Med, 1936; chief, sec on path, anat, lab of experimental path, Natl Inst of Arthritis and Metabolic Diseases, NIH, 1960-65. Assemblyman, Coll Amer Path, 1968-71, found f; pres, Wash Soc of Path, since 1968; dipl, path, anat and clinical path, Amer Bd Path; mem: Amer Assn Path and Bact; Alpha Omega Alpha, hon med soc; Amer Soc for Experimental Path; Intl Acad of Path; Biol Stain Commn; Histochem Soc; Md and Wash Socs of Path; Assn Mil Surg of US; AMA; Electron Microscopy Soc of Amer; Radiation Research Soc. Contbr to med jours. Hobbies: fishing, gardening. Home: 5202 W Cedar Lane, Bethesda, Md. Office: NIH, Bethesda, Md.

HILBORN, Walter Stern, US, attorney; b. Boston, Mass, Sep 11, 1879; s. Jacob and Matilda (Stern); BA, Harvard U, 1901, LLB, 1903; m. Aimee Gallert, Jan 1, 1908. Sr partner, Loeb & Loeb; dep asst dist atty, NY Co, 1914-15; spec asst, US Atty Gen, 1920-21. Pres, Wfr Council Metrop LA, 1952-53; trustee, Fed J Wfr Orgs; hon chmn, LA Chap, AJComm; life mem, Wfr Planning Council, LA; mem: NYC, LA, Amer Bar Assns; clubs: Hillcrest; Harvard of S Cal. Co-author: Small Loan Legislation, 1940. Home: 716 N Alpine Dr, Beverly Hills, Cal. Office: 1 Wilshire Bldg, Wilshire Blvd at Grand Ave, Los Angeles, Cal.

HILL, Irving, US, jurist; b. Lincoln, Neb, Feb 6, 1915; s. Nathan and Ida (Ferder); BA, U Neb, 1936; LLB, cum laude, Harvard Law Sch, 1939; m. Maydee Taylor, June 23, 1939; c: Lawrence, Steven, Richard. Judge, Superior Court since 1961; US Dist Judge since 1965; spec asst, US Atty Gen, Justice Dept, 1942-46; legal adv, US Delg, UNESCO, 1946; sr partner, law firm, Hill, Greenberg, and Glusker, 1948-61. Pres, J Fed Council, LA, 1961-64; vice-pres, CJFWF, 1961-64; mem, Phi Beta Kappa. Ed, Harvard Law Rev, 1938-39. Hobbies: numismatics, deep sea fishing. Home: 10508 Wyton Dr, Los Angeles, Cal. Office: US Court House, 312 N Spring St, Los Angeles, Cal.

HILL, Moshe, Isr, educator; b. George, S Afr, June 7, 1930; s. Leon and Bertha (Friedland); in Isr since 1968; BSc, U of S Afr, 1960; MA, city planning, U of Pa, 1962, PhD, 1966; m. Judith Brenner, Feb 7, 1960; c: Batsheva, Eliezer. Asso prof, regional and town planning, Technion, Haifa, since 1968; research asso, Regional Sci Research Inst, 1964-66; visiting asso prof, U of NC, 1966-68. Prin contrib: devl methods for plan evaluation. Mem: Amer Inst Planners; Regional Sci Assn; Regional Studies Assn, UK; Environmental Planning Assn, Isr; Peace Research Soc; fmr: secy, Habonim, S Afr; S Afr repr, World Habonim Exec. Contbr articles to profsl publs. Home: 25 Dalya Rd, Haifa, Isr. Office: Technion, Haifa, Isr.

HILLEL, Arie, Isr, aeronautical engr; b. Tel Aviv, Mar 19, 1922; s. Yaacov and Mina; BSc, London U, 1950; dipl, Coll of Aeronautics, Cranfield, UK, 1956; DSc, Technion, Haifa, 1962; m. Shulamit Gur-Arie, Feb, 1951; c: Orly, Itzhak. Dir, procurement and produc, Min of Defense, fmr project engr, head, Engr Dept, Directorate of Eng and Logistics, IAF. Col, IAF. Author: Paper on Stress Concentration Around Cut Outs. Recipient: Design Prize, Coll of Aeronautics; Sinai, Six Day War decorations. Home: 14 Arats St, Afeka, Tel Aviv, Isr. Office: Hakirya, Tel Aviv, Isr.

HILLEL, Shlomo, Isr, government official, diplomat; b. Baghdad, Iraq, Apr 23, 1923; s. Aharon and Hana (Shemtov); att Heb U, Jerusalem, 1956-59; m. Tmima Rosner, Aug, 1952; c: Hagit, Aharon. Min of Police, since 1969; MK, 1953-59, and since 1969; mem: Histadrut, since 1945; Kibbutz Maagen Michael, 1941-58; Isr Ambass to: Guinea, 1959-61; Ivory Coast, 1961-63; dir, Afr Dept, Min for Fgn Affairs, Jerusalem, 1963-64; mem, Isr mission to UN, 1965-67; asst dir gen, Min for Foreign Affairs, Jerusalem, 1967-69. Active in org of Aliyah Bet, illegal immigration, to Pal, 1946-48; IDF, 1948-49. Recipient, awards: Commn of Natl Order: Rep of Upper Volat, 1961; Rep of Dahomey, 1961; Rep of Ivory Coast, 1962. Home: 13 Ramat Dania, Jerusalem, Isr. Office: Min of Police, Jerusalem, Isr.

HILLER, Robert I, US, social work exec; b. Grand Rapids, Mich, Sep 26, 1921; s. William and Anne (Wepman); BA, U Mich, 1942, MSW, Inst of Social Work, 1948; m. Marianne Silver, Mar 9, 1946; c: Karen, Barbara, Joshua. Exec vice-pres; Assn Charities; JWF; lectr, instr, U of Md Sch of Social Work. Vice-chmn, personnel services comm, Council of JWF; bd dirs: The Park Sch; Health and Wfr Council, Baltimore; Md chap, Natl Assn of Social Workers; J Hist Soc;

CJFWF; bd overseers, Lown Inst for Contemporary J Studies, Brandeis U; tech adv comm, HUC-JIR, Sch of J Communal Service; prog comm, comty org sect, Natl Conf Communal Service; mem, Baltimore Heb Cong; club, Men's. Home: 3507 Overbrook Rd, Pikesville, Md. Office: 319 W Monument St, Baltimore, Md.

HILLMAN, David, Eng, artist; b. Riga, Lith, Aug 20, 1895; s. Samuel and Sanar (Porkempner); in Eng since 1908; dipl, Glasgow Sch of Art, Scotland; att St Johns Wood Acad Sch, London; deg, fine arts, Royal Acad, London; m. Annie; c: Ellis, Harold, Mayer. Stained glass artist; commns for: windows in Syns throughout London; Hechal Shlomo, Isr; Bar Ilan U, Ramat Gan, Isr. Hon lectr, syns, London; fmr: hon tchr, Maccabi Assn, London; art lectr, London Co Council. Hobby: portrait painting. Home and studio: 91 Priory, W Hampstead, London NW 6, Eng.

HILLMAN, Ruth, Isr, pianist; b. Moscow, Russ, Nov 3, 1917; d. Arieh and Sarah (Friedman); in Isr since 1921; grad, Music Acad, Vienna; m. Israel Hillman; c: Etan, Irit Fein. Dir, found, Conservatory of Music, Beersheba, since 1961; tchr, piano, theory: Dunya Conservatory, Haifa, 1938-41; Netanya, Ramat Gan, both 1941-61; org of concerts, lectures for youth and adults. Served Haganah. Vice-pres, Soroptimist Cub,l Beersheba; mem: League of Music Tchrs and Artists; Intl Chamber Music Club; fmr, head cultural dept, WIZO, Ramat Gan. Home: 8 Sokolov St, Beersheba, Isr. Office: 13 Basle St, Beersheba, Isr.

HILP, Harry H, US, contracting and business exec; b. San Francisco, Aug 1, 1888; s. Henry and Emma (Greenberg); att U of Cal, 1910-12; m. Adelaide Wollenberg, Sept 3, 1916; c: Barbara Smith, Marjorie Rhodes, Harry. Ret; gen partner, Barrett & Hilp, 1913-53; pres, Hilp & Rhodes, 1953-61; gen partner, Prospect Farms; pres: Terminix of N Cal; Selectograph. Fmr pres, mem, bd trustees, Cal Sch of Mech Arts; exec vice-pres, Cen Overland Pony Express Trails Assn; trustee, Coll of Phys and Surgs, SF, f, since 1961; fmr pres, mem, Assn Gen Contractors of Amer; f: Amer Soc CEs; Soc Cal Pioneers; Cal Hist Soc; Employers Council SF, mem, bd govs, 1939-41; clubs: Condordia-Argonaut; Lake Merced Golf and Country; Engrs, SF; Commonwealth of Cal; Meadow Golf and Country; O'Donnell Golf, Palm Springs; Merchants Exch of SF. Spec interests: hist research, photography. Home: 1070 Green St, San Francisco, Cal. Office: 615 Battery, San Francisco, Cal.

HIM, George, Eng, designer; b. Lodz, Pol, Aug 8, 1900; s. Jacob and Henriette (Kipper) Himmelfarb; in Eng since 1937; PhD, U Bonn, 1924; att: U Moscow; State Acad, Leipzig; m. Shirley Rhodes, Nov 9, 1968. Free-lance designer; cons designer, EL-AL Isr Airlines, since 1961. Work, all fields of graphic design; chief designer: Isr Pavilion, Expo 67; Massada Exhb, NY, Wash, London, Paris, 1966-70. Author: Stones of Israel, 1957; 25 Years of Youth Aliyah, 1959. Mem, Publicity Comm, Youth Aliyah, Gt Brit; fmr mem, Exec Brit ORT. Mem profsl orgs: FSIAD; FSTD; AGI. Spec interest, Isr. Home and office: 37B Greville Rd, London NW 6, Eng.

HIMES, Irving L, US, accountant; b. NYC, May 7, 1918; s. Sam and Rose (Portenoy); BS, magna cum laude, NYU, 1939; LLB, S Law U, Memphis, Tenn, 1953; c: Lloyd, David, Lesley. Practicing CPA since 1951; prof, acctnt, U Tenn, since 1951, chmn, dept, since 1957; asst to pres and comptroller, Powers-Chemco, Glen Cove, NY, 1946-51; instr, NYU, 1947-50, fac mem, 1946-51. Warrant off, US Army, 1942-45. Vice-pres, fund raising chmn, Memphis chap, Arthritis Org; chmn, continuing educ, comm, Tenn Soc of CPAs, since 1961; mem: bd trustees, Baron Hirsch Cong, 1953-55; bd dirs, B'nai B'rith, 1954-56; Tenn, La, NY State Socs of CPAs; Amer Inst of CPAs; Amer, Tenn Bar Assns; Temple Isr, various comms; Natl Assn Acctnts; Masons; Beta Gamma Sigma; club, Ridgeway Country. Author: Principles of Accounting, 1957; Intermediate Accounting, 1958. Contbr to profsl jours. Home: 3639 Galloway Dr, Memphis, Tenn. Office: Sterick Bldg, Memphis, Tenn.

HIMMEL, Ira Kenneth, US, attorney; b. Newark, NJ, Aug 26, 1938; s. Emanuel and Charlotte; BS, Wilkes Coll, Wilkes Barre, Pa, 1960; LLB, U Baltimore Law Sch, 1965; m. Sydney Fisher, Apr 6, 1962. Asso atty, Hooper, Kiefer, Sachs, Talber & Cornell, Baltimore, since 1965; instr, mgmt, Baltimore Coll of Comm, 1966-70. US Army Res, 1959-63. Vice-pres, Baltimore City Jr Assn of Commerce; exec comm, Jr Bar of Baltimore City; mem: Md State, Amer, Baltimore City, Baltimore City Jr Bar Assns; Phi Alpha Delta; KP. Home: 7525 Marston Rd, Baltimore, Md. Office: 10 Light St, Baltimore, Md.

HIMMELFARB, Milton, US,editor, research dir;b. NYC,Oct 21, 1918; s. Max and Bertha (Lerner); BA, CCNY, 1938, MS, 1939; DHL, JTSA, Coll J Studies, 1939; att: U Paris, 1939; Columbia U, 1944-48; m. Judith Siskind, Nov 26, 1950; c: Martha, Edward, Miriam, Anne, Sarah, Naomi, Dan. Dir, Info and Research Services, AJComm, since 1955; ed, Amer J Year Book, since 1967; cons ed, The Religious Situation, since 1968; contributing ed, Commentary, since 1960; visiting prof, JTSA, 1967-68. Home: 294 Fisher Ave, White Plains, NY. Office: 165 E 65 St, New York, NY.

HIMMELMAN, Alex, US, attorney, accountant; b. Russ, May 1, 1898; s. David and Minna (Auz); in US since 1906; BA, U Minn, 1922; CPA, U Wis, 1931, LLB, 1945; m. Mildred Hoffman, Oct 2, 1926; c: Estar Lakritz, David. Pvt law practice; tax adv, Joseph Schlitz Brewing Co, since 1953; US Treasury agt, 1922-53; lectr, acctnt, Marquette U, 1947-51. US Army, 1918. Secy, dir, Mt Sinai Hosp, Milw, since 1940; pres, NW Zionist Region, ZOA, 1956-60, mem, natl admn council; found, Milw JWF Inc; mem: Amer Legion; Milw, Wis Bar Assns. Recipient: Albert Gallatin award, US Treasury Dept, 1953. Home: 924 E Juneau Ave, Milwaukee, Wis. Office: 622 N Water St, Milwaukee, Wis.

HINCHIN, Martin I, US, rabbi; b. Phila, Pa, Jan 30, 1919; s. Aaron and Dora (Pavolotsky); BA, Yeshiva Coll, NYC, 1940; ordained rabbi, MHL, HUC, Cincinnati, 1946; m. Blossom Kalin, Dec 10, 1944; c: Phyllis Selber, Carolyn. Rabbi: Cong Gemiluth Chassodim, Alexandria, La, since 1958; Temple Emanuel, Dothan, Ala, 1946-48; Albany Heb Cong, Albany, Ga, 1948-58. Chaplain, USNR, since 1951. Mem, bd: ARC; Rehab Cen; mem: Rapides United Givers; B'nai B'rith; Masons; Elks; rabb adv, S Fed of Temple Youth; pres: Alexandria-Pineville Min Assn, 1960-61, all Alexandria; fmr: Marriage Counselling Bur, co-founder, pres, Albany Min Assn,1953-54;comm chmn, USO,1953-54; treas,Comty Council, 1953; chap chmn, ARC; state bd, Mh Assn, 1953-54; Libr bd, 1954, all Albany, Ga; clubs: Kiwanis; Rorary. Home: 4511 Wellington Blvd, Alexandria, La. Study: POB 863, Alexandria, La.

HINDUS, Milton H, US, educator, author; b. NYC, Aug 26, 1916; s. Meyer and Minnie (Slutsky); BA, CCNY, 1936, MS, 1938; att: Columbia U, 1938-39; U Chgo, 1947-48; m. Eva Tenenbaum, Aug 30, 1942; c: Myra. Prof, Eng, Brandeis U, since 1962, fac mem since 1948; lectr: Hunter Coll, 1943-46; New Sch for Social Research, 1944-46; asst prof, hum, U Chgo, 1946-48. Mem: publs comm, J Publ Soc of Amer; MLA; AAUP; vice-pres, Kehillath Isr. Author: The Crippled Giant, 1950; Celine tel que je l'ai vu, 1951; The Proustian Vision, 1954; Leaves of Grass, One Hundred Years After, 1955; A Reader's Guide to Marcel Proust, 1962; F Scott Fitzgerald, 1968; ed, The Old East Side, anthol, 1969; Ency Judaica, Amer Lit Sect; contbr, articles, book revs, to periodicals. Recipient, Walt Whitman prize, Amer Poetry Soc, 1959. Hobby: chess. Home: 24 Stiles Terr, Newton Center, Mass. Office: Brandeis U, Waltham, Mass.

HINENBURG, Morris, US, hospital cons; b. Russ, Feb 20, 1902; s. Abraham and Sarah (Henes); in US since 1906; BS, Yale U, 1922, MD, 1926; m. Rose Becker, Nov 11, 1928; c: Charlotte Kowal, Paul. Med care cons, FJP, NY, since 1950; asst dir, Montefiore Hosp, NYC, 1928-36; exec dir, J Hosp, Bklyn, 1936-50. Pres: Amer Assn of Hosp Cons, 1961; Hosp Assn, NY State, 1947-48; Gtr NY Hosp Assn, 1944-45; Hosp Council of Bklyn, 1942-43; vice-pres, Hosp Credit Exch, 1946-47; f, Amer Coll of Hosp Admnrs; mem: bd dirs: Health and Hosp Planning Council, S NY, since 1963; Health Ins, Plan, Gtr NY, since 1967; NY State Hosp Planning Council, since 1966; Asso Hosp Services, NY; NY State adv council, Jt Hosp Survey and Planning commn; Amer Hosp Assn. Contbr to profsljours. Hobby: fishing. Home: 535 E 86 St, New York, NY. Office: 130 E 59 St, New York, NY.

HINERFELD, Norman M, US, business exec; b. NYC, May 17, 1929; s. Benjamin and Anne (Blitz); AB, Harvard U, 1951, MBA, 1953; m. Ruth Gordon, Dec 25, 1952; c: Lee, Thomas, Joshua. Exec vice-pres, dir, Kayser-Roth Corp, since 1967, with firm since 1958; vice-pres, mfg, Catalina Inc, since 1957, dir, since 1956; asst to pres, Julius Kayser & Co, 1955-56. Lt, US Army, 1953-55. Pres, Amer Apparel Mfrs Assn, 1970-71. Co-author, Automation—Challenge to Management,

1953. Home: 11 Oak Lane, Larchmont, NY. Office: 640 Fifth Ave, New York, NY.

HIRAM, Dan, Isr, business exec; b. Prague, Czech, May 12, 1924; s. Otto and Hedda (Herrmann) Klepetar; in Isr since 1939; BA, U Tel Aviv; att Ecole de Guerre, Paris; m. Esther Kriger, Aug 21, 1951; c: Ron, Dorith. Export mgr, Citrus Marketing Bd, Isr, since 1968; defense attache, Emb of Isr, London, 1961-64. Asst dep min of defense, Min of Defense, 1964-66; i/c civil,econ affairs for all areas under mil occupation, 1967-68. Col, IDF, 1948-59; dir artillery, 1957-61. Home: 6 Kalanit, Ganei Yehuda, Isr. Office: 69 Haifa Rd, Tel Aviv, Isr.

HIRSCH, Abraham, Isr, organization exec; b. Duisburg, Ger, Sep 3, 1913; s. Avigdor and Gitel (Sprey); in Isr since 1933; m. Mirjam Kanarek, Jan 27, 1937; c: Daniel, Eliahu, Zehava, Chanah. Secy gen, Agudath Isr World Org, since 1942, mem exec since 1954; mem secretariat, Cen Agudath Isr in Isr, since 1954; mem secretariat, Kibbutz Noar Agudathi, Kfar Saba, 1933-40. Fmr mem, ed bd, Hamodj'a, Heb daily. Home: 11 B'nai B'rith St, Jerusalem, Isr. Office: POB 326, Jerusalem, Isr.

HIRSCH, Carl, Swed, surgeon,educator; b. Stocholm, Swed, July 10, 1913; s. Josef and Lina (Luft); m. Anna Ikelberg, Apr 10, 1938; c: Georg, Monica, Jan. Prof, orthopedic surg: U Karolinska Inst, Stockholm, since 1969; U Uppsala, 1957-60; U Gothenburg,1961-69. Home:Odengatan 32, 113 51 Stockholm, Swed. Office: Karolinska Hosp, Stockholm, Swed.

HIRSCH, Edith, US, economist; b. Berlin, Ger; d. Adolph and Flora (Bernheim) Jarislowsky; in US since 1943; att:U Frankfort/M; U Heidelberg; U Berlin; MSS, New Sch for Social Research, 1943; m. Julius Hirsch, Apr 8, 1927; c: Rudolph. Cons econ, lectr, since 1943; econ adv to bus firms, since 1946; lectr: econ of commodities, New Sch for Social Research, 1950-56; Inst of Finance, NY Stock Exch; adv: Forschungstelle für den Handel, Berlin, 1930-33; Standard Figures for Bus, Intl C of C, 1934-35. Mem: bd, Leo Baeck Inst, NY; Amer Econ Assn; Stat Assn; Amer Farm Assn. Co-author, Berufliche Eingliederung und Wirtschaftliche Leistung der Deutsch-Juedischen Einwanderung in Die Vereinigten Staaten, 1935-60; ed, Hermann Tietz, Geschechte einer Familie und ihrer Warenhauser; contbr articles on commodity problems to mags. Home: 57 E 88 St, New York, NY.

HIRSCH, Foca, Isr, engineer; b. Rum, Feb 6, 1908; s. Samuel and Paulina (Honig); in Isr since 1934; DEng, Reggia Scuola d'Ingegneria, Turin, It, 1932. Owner, mgn dir, CIDEV Commercial and Devl Co, Tel Aviv; liaison repr: Vickers-Armstrong Ltd; other leading Brit, Fr, It, Amer, mfrs. Pres, Irgun Yotzei Rum ,Tel Aviv. Hobbies: golf, cooking. Home: POB 2024, Tel Aviv, Isr. Office: 8 Ben Ami St, Tel Aviv, Isr.

HIRSCH, Herman, Isr, physician; b. Trier, Ger, June 30, 1905; s. Henri and Minna (Frank); in Isr since 1949; att Us: Hamburg; Munich; MD, U Freiburg, 1928; m. Rita Neumann, Oct 6, 1931; c: Elizabeth, Rachel, Hannan. Head, dept gyn, obstet, Assaf Harofe Govt Hosp, Tzrifin, since 1949; lectr, med sch, postgrad med sch, Tel Aviv U; asst sci, U clinic, gyn, obstet, Freiburg, 1928-33; chief phys, dept gyn, obstet, J Hosp, Berlin, 1933-39, dir, Polyclinic, 1934-39; prof, gyn, Cen U, Sucre, Bolivia, 1939-48; found, Inst of Cancer Research and Treatment. F, Intl Coll of Surgs; co-found, mem presidium, Isr Soc for Clinical and Experimental Hypnosis; mem presidium: Isr Soc for Gyn and Obstet; Isr Soc of Fertility; chmn, Isr Soc for Marital and Sexual Advice; mem, Intl Soc of Sterility and Fertility; fmr: pres, United ZF, Bolivia; found, f, Bolivian Soc for Gyn and Obstet; club, Roraty. Recipient: official hon distinction for merits, public health, Munic of Sucre, Bolivia. Hobby: music. Home: 22 Hameasfim St, Tel Aviv, Isr. Office: Assaf Harofe Hosp, Tel Aviv, Isr.

HIRSCH, Jakob, Isr,attorney; b. Halberstadt, Ger, June 23, 1924; s. Salli and Edith (Henschel); in Isr since 1935; Law Dipl, Govt Law Classes, Jerusalem, 1950; att Princeton U, 1965-66; m. Shoshana Bilski, Mar 20, 1957; c: Gideon, Jehudith, Orly. Dir gen, State Comptroller's Off, since 1967, staff mem since 1950. Brit Army, 1943-46; lt, IDF, 1948-50. Mem: Isr Bar Assn; Isr Mgmt Cen. Hobbies: music, camping. Home: 7 Magnes Sq, Jerusalem, Isr. Office: 66 Rashi, Jerusalem, Isr.

HIRSCH, Joseph, Isr, artist; b. Beuthen, Ger, July 12, 1920; s. Martin and Recha (Jacobsohn); in Isr since 1939; att Bezalel

Art Sch, Jerusalem, 1939-42; m. Shoshana Lifschiz, Mar 30, 1923; c: Timna Eisenboim, Dorith. Tchr, Bezalel Art Sch, Jerusalem, since 1964; exhbs, Isr, abroad. Brit Army, 1942-46. Pres, Artists Assn, Jerusalem, 1967-68. Home: 6c Katzenelson St, Jerusalem, Isr.

HIRSCH, Lawrence, US, consulting engr; b. New York, NY, Sep 20, 1929; s. Irving and Jennie (Friedman); BCE, Syracuse U, NY, 1951; MCE, U Tex, 1955; m. Marjorie Mazur; c: Gregory, David. Pres, Hirsch & Koptionak, cons engrs, since 1968, vice-pres, 1966-68; intl auth on water devl for arid lands, water waste reclamation, sewage treatment and disposal. Capt, USAF, 1952-55. Chmn: water sub-comm, San Diego C of C; San Diego, Water Pollution Control Assn; sanitary div, San Diego, Amer Soc Civil Engrs; mem: Amer Public Works Assn; Technion Soc; fmr: dir, San Diego sect, Soc Amer Mil Engrs. Contbr to profsl publs. Recipient: Cal Outstanding Young Civil Engr, Amer Soc Civil Engrs, San Diego chap. Hobbies: fishing, skiing, tennis, swimming. Home: 766 Galt Dr, El Cajon, Cal. Office: 5106 Federal Blvd, San Diego, Cal.

HIRSCH, Leon Victor, US, business exec; b. NYC, May 17, 1931; s. Benjamin and Jeanette (Weisbrod); att Dartmouth Coll, 1948-50; BA, Cornell U, 1952; MBA, distinction, Harvard Bus Sch, 1954; att LSE; Sch for Oriental and Afr Studies, London, 1954-55; DBA, Harvard Bus Sch, 1960; m. Sharlene Pearlman, July 12, 1968. Project mgr, New Ventures, Xerox Corp, Stanford, Conn, since 1969; asso, Harbridge House, 1960-61; sr asso, vice-pres, sr vice-pres, United Research Inc, 1961-69. Mem: adv bd, Black People's Cultural Arts Festival; fmr, gov's adv comm on econ devl, Mass; mem: AJComm; Amer Marketing Assn; Amer Public Health Assn, all Boston; club, Harvard, Boston. Author: Marketing in an Underdeveloped Economy, 1961; chaps: The Social Responsibilities of Marketing, 1962; Comparative Marketing, 1963; co-author: The Impact of Highway Investment on Development, 1966; Combining Public Health Nursing Agencies, 1967; Television Station Ownership: A Case Study of Federal Agency Regulation, 1970. Recipient: Fs: Charles A Smith, Harvard U, 1953; Carnegie Found, 1954; Fgn Area Training, Social Sci Research Found, Amer Council Learned Socs, 1954; Rockefeller Found, 1957; Guest of the Inst, Cen for Intl Studies, MIT, 1958; doctoral F: Ford Found Prog on Bus Admn and Econ Devl, 1958; Harvard Bus Sch, 1959; doctoral dissertation award, Ford Found, 1960. Spec interest: primitive art, Afr sculpture. Home: 113 Commonwealth Ave, Boston, Mass. Office: Xerox Corp, Stamford, Conn.

HIRSCH, Maurice L, US, business exec; b. NYC, Aug 7, 1905; s. Jacob and Caroline (Michel); att Columbia U, 1922-24; m. Barbara Messing, June 26, 1933; c: Gay Lieberman, Maurice, Carolyn. Vice-pres, World Color Press Inc, since 1955; pres, Hirsch, Tamm and Ullmann Inc, 1953-59; chmn of bd, Ridgway, Hirsch and French, 1959-63. Bd dirs: J Hosp, since 1962; BBB, since 1957; Asolo Theater Festival; exec comm, AJComm, since 1955; bd trustees: Temple Isr, since 1956; Fla State Theater; publicity chmn, J Fed, 1948-52; clubs: Westwood Country; St Charles, St Louis; Longboat Key Golf, Sarasota. Home: 46 N Polk Dr, Sarasota, Fla. Office: 44 Amer Industrial Dr, Maryland Heights, Mo.

HIRSCH, Menachem, Isr, radiologist; b. Arad, Rum, Jan 1, 1926; s. Izidor and Fanny (Grieshaber); in Isr since 1949; att med schs: Cluj, Rum, 1944-47; Budapest, 1947-49; MD, Hadassah Med Sch, Jerusalem, 1952; m. Shoshana Zuckermann, Aug 21, 1951; c: Orly, Amos, Boaz. Dir, radiology dept, Negev Hosp, since 1960; fac mem, Tel Aviv U, since 1968; asst, Tel Hashomer Hosp, 1954-59. Lt, IDF, MC, 1951-54. Author: Angiography in Diagnosis of Hydatidiform Mole, 1967; Blast Injury of the Lung, 1969. Mem: Isr Radiological Soc; IMA. Home: 321 Shikun D, Beersheba, Isr. Office: Negev Hosp, Beersheba, Isr.

HIRSCH, Milton Baruch, US, orthodontist; b. Cleveland, O, Jan 12, 1923; s. Nathan and Freda (Greenberg); BSc, O State U, 1947; DDS, Reserve U, Cleveland, O, 1951; MSc, O State U, 1963; m. Jane Fowler, Dec 1, 1951; c: David, Steven, Lawrence. Pvt practice since 1963. US Army, 1943-46. Treas: Temple Emanuel, Cleveland, bd dirs; fmr, pres, Temple Emanuel Brotherhood; mem: Masons, Forest City, O; B'nai B'rith, Shaker Hgts, O; Cleveland Dent Assn, treas, bd dirs; O and Amer Dent Assns; Cleveland, Gt Lakes, Amer Orthodontic Assns; JWF; Alpha Omega; bd dirs: Akivah HS; Shaker One Hundred; club, Hawthorne Valley Country. Hobby, golf. Home: 23978 Wimbledon Rd, Shaker Heights,

Cleveland, O. Office: 20475 Farnsleigh Rd, Shaker Heights, Cleveland, O.

HIRSCH, Nathaniel D, US, psychotherapist, psychologist; b. Nashville, Tenn, Oct 13, 1897; s. Joseph and Carrie (Bamberger); AB, Harvard U, 1917; AM, Columbia U, 1920; PhD, Harvard U, 1924; m. Lucille Frenza, Oct 16, 1958. Pvt practice since 1945; tchr, psych, Harvard U, 1924; research f: NRC, 1924-26; Natl Council on Rel in Higher Educ, 1926-27; instr, psych, Duke U, 1927-28, research f, 1928-29; chief psychol, Wayne Co Clinic for Child Study, 1929-33, dir, 1933-35; state dir, Natl Health Inventory, NJ, 1935-36; pvt practice, mental hygiene, Wash, 1936-37; sr social path, Social Security Bd, Wash, 1937-40; psychotherapist, USPHS, 1940-45. US Army, 1918. Mem: Amer Psych Assn; Amer Population Assn; Soc for Rel in Higher Educ; Masons. Author: A Study of Natio-Racial Mental Differences, 1926; An Experimental Study of the Eastern Kentucky Mountains, 1928; Twins, Heredity and Environment, 1930; An Experimental Study of 300 Children Over a Six Year Period, 1930; Genius and Creative Intelligence, 1931; Dynamic Causes of Juvenile Crime, 1937; Mental Deviants in the Population of the US, 1941; contbr to profsl jours. Spec interests: eugenics; genets; population; racial differences. Home and office: 50 E 83 St, New York, NY.

HIRSCH, Walter, US, educator, sociologist; b. Stuttgart, Ger, May 12, 1919; s. Eugene and Fanny (Wormser); in US since 1933; BA, Queens Coll, 1941; MA, Northwestern U, 1954, PhD, 1957; m. Lotte Landman, Jan 26, 1947; c: Martin, Judith, Janet, Daniel. Prof, Purdue U, since 1966, fac mem since 1947. US Army, 1942-45. Bd dirs, Asso J Charities of Lafayette; mem: Amer Sociol Assn; O Valley Sociol Soc; AAUP; AAAS. Author: The Sociology of Science; Explorations in Social Change; Scientists in American Society; contbr to profsl jours. Home: 514 Dodge St, W Lafayette, Ind. Office: Purdue U, Lafayette, Ind.

HIRSCH, Warren M, US, educator; b. NYC; s. George and Frances (Herman); BA, summa cum laude, NYU, 1947, MS, 1948, PhD, 1952; m. Gail Glavin, Jan 26, 1960. Prof, math, research math, NYU, since 1952; research asst, instr, Inst of Maths and Mechs, 1948-52; f, Rockefeller Found, 1950-51; lectr, Columbia U, 1952-53; cons, math: Rand Corp, since 1953; control sys lab, U of Ill, 1953. Maj, USAF, 1941-46. Mem: Amer Math Soc; AAAS; Math Assn of Amer; Inst Math Stats; Amer Stat Assn; Phi Beta Kappa; Sigma Xi; Pi Mu Epsilon; Sigma Pi Sigma. Contbr to profsl jours. Home: 29 Washington Sq, New York, NY. Office: NYU, 25 Waverly Pl, New York, NY.

HIRSCHBERG, Haim Zeev, (JW), Isr, rabbi, educator; b. Tarnopol, Pol, Oct 2, 1903; s. Jacob and Regina (Barbasch); in Isr since 1943; PhD, U Vienna, 1925; ordained rabbi, J Theol Sem, Vienna, 1927; m. Malka Mohl, Dec 25, 1927; c: Eliyahu. Prof, J hist, Bar Ilan U, since 1960; rabbi, Czestochowa, Pol, 1927-39; research f, J hist in Mohammedan countries, Heb U, Jerusalem, 1947-56; mem, Pol Acad of Sci. Author: The Relations of the Halacha to the Agada, 1929; Der Diwan des as Samau'al ibn Adiya, 1931; Jüdische und christliche Lehren im vor-und frühislamischen Arabien, 1939; Israel in Arabia, 1946; Stories of R Nissim, 1954; Inside Magreb, 1957; History of the Jews in North Africa, 1965; The Oriental Jewish Communities, 1968; co-ed: Eretz Kinnarot; Eretz Israel; Bar Ilan Annual. Home: 13 Shammai St, Jerusalem, Isr. Office: Bar Ilan U, Ramat Gan, Isr.

HIRSCHBERG, Nell, US, microbiologist; b. Cincinnati, O, Sep 20, 1907; d. Sylvan and Alma (Yondorf); AB, Smith Coll, 1928; MA, U Colo, 1933; PhD, U of Ill, 1937. Prof, biol, NC Central U, since 1963; microbiol: Michael Reese Hosp, 1928-37; Cook Co Hosp, 1937-39; Kellogg Fund, U of Ill, 1939-42; USPHS, 1942-45; NC State Bd of Health, 1945-63. Past pres, Family Service Soc, Raleigh; vice-pres, Natl Fed Temple Sisterhoods; dipl, Amer Bd Microbiol; f, Amer Public Health Assn; secy, Temple Beth Or, fmr choir dir; mem: Amer Soc for Microbiol; AAAS; Sigma Xi; Phi Beta Kappa; YWCA; Chamber Music Guild. Contbr to profsl jours. Home: 1500 Park Dr, Raleigh, NC. Office: NC Central U, Durham, NC.

HIRSCHFELD, Albert, US, artist, author; b. St Louis, Mo, June 21, 1903; s. Isaac and Rebecca (Rothberg); att: Natl Acad, NYC; Julienne's, Paris; m. Dolly Haas, May 8, 1943; c: Nina. Repr in perm collections including: NYC Public Libr; Fogg Mus; Musee d'Art Populaire Juif, Paris; Metrop

Mus; Whitney Mus of Amer Art; Mus of Modern Art; murals: Fifth Ave Playhouse; Eden Roc Hotel, Miami; Manhattan Hotel; theatre caricaturist, NY Times; theatre corresp, NY Herald Tribune, Moscow. Author: Manhattan Oasis, 1932; Harlem, 1942; Sweet Bye and Bye, 1946; Show Business is No Business, 1951; The American Theatre As Seen by Hirschfeld, 1961; co-author: Westward Ha! 1948; contbr to mags. Home and studio: 122 E 95 St, New York, NY.

HIRSCHFELD, Charles, US, educator; b. Bklyn, NY, Feb 9, 1913; s. Harry and Rose (Fensterblau); PhD, Johns Hopkins U, 1939; m. Miryiam Levin, Mar 28, 1941; c: Dina. Prof, hist: Richmond Coll, CUNY, since 1967; Mich State U, 1947-67. Capt, US Army, 1942-46. Mem: Amer Hist Assn; AAUP. Author: Baltimore 1870-1900: Studies in Social History, 1941; The Great Railroad Conspiracy, 1953; contbr to profsl jours. Home: 201 Milford Ave, Staten Island, NY. Office: Richmond Coll, CUNY, Staten Island, NY.

HIRSCHHORN, Harry J, US, mathematician, engineer; b. Frankfurt/M, Ger, Aug 7, 1922; s. Martin and Frieda (Gans); in US since 1948; BS, first class hons, Manchester U, 1944; MS, Columbia U, 1951; m. Ellen Feldblum, Nov 3, 1946; c: Susan, David, Michael. Asst prof, math, Chgo City Coll, since 1964; research engr, Ill Inst of Tech, 1956-64; engr, Crossley Bros, Eng, 1944-48; asso, elec engr, Manchester Coll of Tech, 1948; engr: Foster Wheeler, NYC, 1948-51; Burns and Roe, cons, NYC, 1951-54. Mem: comm, Yaar Hazikoron, JNF; J Publ Soc; Mizrachi; Cong Eretz Isr; fmr treas, Cong Ahavath Torah; Inst of Mech Engr, Eng; Amer Soc of Mech Engr. Author: Mah Mishtana, 1964; Correlation Between Catalogue Numbers of the Passover Hagaddah; Studies in Bibliography, 1965; co-author: Thermophysical Properties of Solids, 5 vols, 1961. Hobby: collecting Passover Hagaddahs. Home: 2951 W Jarlath St, Chicago, Ill. Office: 3400 N Austin St, Chicago, Ill.

HIRSCHHORN, Isidor Solomon, US, business exec; b. Prague, Czech, Oct 25, 1915; s. Ephraim and Amelia (Kornfeld); in US since 1922; AB, Montclair State Coll, 1936; att NYU, 1937-38; MA, Columbia, 1940; att U of Wis, 1945; m. Ellen Stein, Apr 2, 1947; c: Susan, Robert. Vice-pres, Ronson Metals Corp, since 1959, gen mgr, 1950-59; instr, Madison HS, 1937-42; chem engr, Hercules Powder Co, 1944-45; instr, chem, Drew U, 1945-49; tech dir, New Process Metals Inc, 1949-50. Sup, USAAC, tech training command, 1942-44. Fmr pres, Dorot Zion, LZOA; club, Chems, NYC. Contbr: to Ency of Electrochemistry; various chem jours. Recipient: Gen Elec F, Union Coll, 1946. Hobbies: sailing, photography. Home: 56 Greenwood Ave, West Orange, NJ. Office: Ronson Metals Corp, 55 Mfrs Pl, Newark, NJ.

HIRSCHMANN, Ira A, US, business exec; b. Baltimore, Md, July 7, 1901; s. Adolph and Jennie (Potts); att Johns Hopkins U, 1918-20. Pres, TV Sys of Amer Inc; chmn bd, Gotham Bank, NY; instr, NYU, 1930-36; vice-pres: Saks Fifth Ave, 1935-38; Bloomingdale Bros, 1938-46; spec repr, War Ref Bd, US Emb, Ankara, Turkey, 1944; spec insp gen, UNRRA, 1946. Found, pres, New Friends of Music, 1936; mem, bd trustees: Bd Higher Educ, NYC; New Sch for Social Research, co-found and chmn bd, U in Exile; bd govs, Heb U, Jerusalem. Author: Lifeline to Promised Land, 1946; The Embers Still Burn, 1949; Caution to the Winds, 1962; co-author, Reflections on Music, 1937; contbr, articles on Nazism, an Assault on Civilization, 1934. Home: 1075 Park Ave, New York, NY. Office: 767 Fifth Ave, New York, NY.

HIRSHAUT, Julien, US, author, accountant; b. Drohobycz, Pol, Sep 2, 1908; s. Sindel and Malka (Gottdenker); in US since 1951; DJ and DEcon, U Lwow, 1932; m. Hanna Warhaftig, July 22, 1939; c: Vivian, Betty. Writer, journalist, J newspapers and mags in US and Isr; acctnt since 1951; ed, weekly mag: Ichud, Pol, 1945-46; Unzer Weg, Paris, 1946-51. Author: Finctere Necht in Paviak, 1947; Yiddishe Napht Magnaten, 1945; Five Historical Works, 1947-54; Dr Yitzhak Schipper, His Life and Works, 1954; Dr Meier Balaban, The Polish Jewish Historian, 1959; Dr Joshua Thon, 1962; Dr Joshua Gottlieb, 1962. Recipient: Mordechai Stolar lit award, Yiddishe Cajtung Found, Buenos Aires, 1955. Club, Yiddish PEN. Home: 1875 University Ave, Bronx, NY.

HIRSHAUT, Yashar, US, physician; b. Berlin, Ger, Feb 27, 1938; s. Herman and Fannie (Rosenblueth); in US since 1946; BA, Yeshiva U, 1959; MD, Albert Einstein Coll of Med, Yeshiva U, 1963; m. Perle Katz, June 21, 1964; c: Tzvi, Aviva. Research asso, div of cell biol, Sloan-Kettering

Inst for Cancer Research, since 1968; clinical asso, Natl Cancer Inst, 1965-68; res, internal med, Montefiore Hosp, 1964-65. Lt cdr, USPHS, 1965-68. Chmn, natl bd, Raphael Soc, Med-Dent Sect, Orthodox J Scis; vice-pres, Summit Hill Cong, 1967-68, secy, 1966-67; mem, bd govs, Assn Orthodox J Scis; mem: Young Isr; NY Acad Sci; Alpha Omega Alpha. Contbr to med jours. Home: 10-11 Nameoke Ave, Far Rockaway, NY. Office: Sloan-Kettering Inst, 440 E 68 St, New York, NY.

HIRSHBERG, Saul Morton, US, dentist; b. Boston, Mass, Sep 4, 1925; s. David and Pauline (Florence); DMD, Tufts U, Boston, 1948; m. Joyce Blune, Feb 22, 1948; c: David, James, Cathie. Asst prof, restorative dent, Tufts U Sch of Dent, Boston, since 1964; guest lectr, Northwestern U, 1967-70; tchr, lectr, clinician in post-grad prosthodontics; cert, prosthetics, Tufts U Sch of Dent. Lt, JG, US Navy, 1951-53. Fmr pres, Boston Endodontic Study Club; mem: Amer Soc Prosthodontists; Acad, Dent Sci, Boston chap. Home: 54 Clements Rd, Newton, Mass. Office: 907 Park Sq Bldg, Boston, Mass.

HIRST, Eugen, NZ, business exec, communal leader; b. Budapest, Hung, Mar 16, 1911; s. Edmund and Franciska (Stahler) Hirschberger; in NZ since 1939; m. Jana Tanzer, Oct, 1938; c: Yvonne. Mgn dir: Prosthethic Processes, since 1939; Mortimer Hirst Optician Ltd, since 1950; Hirst Contact Lenses, since 1958; NZ Contact Lenzs Supplies, since 1961; fmr with Prague Dent Clinic, Czech, 1931-35. Hon instr, Royal NZ Navy Dent Corps. Pres: ZC of NZ; NZ Dent Lab Org; vice-pres, Auckland Zionist Soc, fmr chmn; commn, KH of NZ; mem, B'nai B'rith; hon mem, NZ Contact Lens Soc. Home: 80 Almoran Rd, Epsom, Auckland, NZ. Office: POB 2184, Auckland, NZ.

HITZIG, William M, US, physician, educator; b. Aus, Dec 15, 1904; s. Maier and Jeanette (Kreisberg); in US since 1914; BA, Columbia U, 1926; MD, Cornell U, 1929; m. Candis Hall, Mar 9, 1934; c: Candis Stormont-Darling, Rupert, Saartje, Pietr, William, Myron, Elizabeth. Pvt practice since 1932; asst clinical med prof, Columbia U, since 1950; med off, NY Fire Dept, 1942-43; phys, NY Police Dept, since 1943; phys, atomic bomb tests at Bikini, 1946. Prin contbrs: co-sponsor Hiroshima Maidens Project which brought 25 Japanese girls disfigured by atom bomb to US for plastic surg; Lapina project, Ravensbrueck Lapins brought to US for moral and physical rehab. F: Amer Coll Phys; NY Acad Med; dipl, Amer Bd of Internal Med; mem: Amer Fed for Clinical Research; Phi Betta Kappa; Mu Sigma; Phi Sigma Delta; Phi Delta Epsilon; Alpha Omega Alpha. Contbr to Saturday Review. Recipient: citation and alumni medal, Columbia U; hon mem, Honor Legion, Police Dept, NYC. Home: 15 Central Park W, New York, NY. Office: 787 Park Ave, New York, NY.

HOCH, Moshe, Isr, musician; b. Lvov, Pol, Sep 12, 1918; s. David and Sabina (Liberman); in Isr since 1948; att Acad of Music, 1948; m. Lia Goldfarb; c: David, Arie. Dir, Jeunesses Musicales of Isr, since 1963; stage mgr, Opera Israelit, 1954-60; tchr, Acad of Music, Tel Aviv, 1960-63; dir, Chamber Opera, Tel Aviv, 1960. Prin contrib: found, vocal ensemble Bat-Kol and Tel Aviv Chamber Opera. Author: found, vocal ensemble Bat-Kol and Tel Aviv Chamber Opera. Author: Omanut haBama haOperait, 1963; texts on the playing of the melodica, 1959; composer of chamber opera for children, compositions for cello, violin, piano. Home: 179 Ibn Gvirol, Tel Aviv, Isr. Office: Heichal Hatarbut, Tel Aviv, Isr.

HOCHBAUM, William, US, otolaryngologist, educator; b. NYC, Feb 25, 1903; s. Benjamin and Josephine (Neudorfer); BA, Columbia U, 1924, MD, 1927; m. Rosalind Cherr, 1939. Clinical prof, NYC Bellevue Post Grad Sch; pvt practice since 1933; chief, ear, nose, throat dept, Hosp for Jt Diseases, since 1959; asso otolaryngologist: Bellevue Hosp; U Hosp; Goldwater Memorial Hosp; Kings Co Hosp, 1934-45; Seaview Hosp, 1934-46; bronchoscopist, Manhattan State Hosp, 1951. US Army, 1942-46. F: Amer Coll Med; Amer Coll Surgs; mem: comm for hard of hearing sch children, NY Bd Educ, 1935-37; med bd, Heb Convalescent Home, 1938-47; bd, Fed of Handicapped; Amer Acad Facial Plastic and Reconstruction Surg; Amer Bd Otolaryngologists; AMA; NY State, NY Co Med Socs; Masons; Phi Delta Epsilon. Office: 123 E 83 St, New York, NY.

HOCHBERG, Alvin S, US, attorney; b. Paterson, NJ, Dec 5, 1920; s. Harry and Ida (Stave); att: NYU, 1938-41; LLB, Harvard U, 1948; m. Estelle Broude, May 23, 1948; c: Nancy, Betsy, Ann, William. Pvt practice since 1948. Capt, USAAC,

1942-45. Vice-pres, Boston chap, AJComm, 1952-56; vice-chmn, Newton Mass Dem City Comm, 1952-56; exec comm, Boston Arts Festival, 1960-63; exec council, Mass Comm to Abolish Capital Punishment; state bd, Mass Chap, ADA, 1952-60; Amer, Mass and Boston Bar Assns; Harvard Law Sch Assn; clubs: Newton Squash and Tennis; Sandy Bay Boat; Bass Rocks Golf. Recipient: Air Medal with seven Oak Leaf Clusters. Home: 12 Solon St, Newton Highlands, Mass. Office: 75 Federal St, Boston, Mass.

HOCHBERG, Donald Harry, US, business exec; b. Portland, Ore, July 9, 1922; s. Harry and Helene (Adler); att Princeton U, 1943-44; BA, U Wash, 1947; m. Joanne Howe, July 15, 1951; c: Marjorie, Daniel, William, Frank. Prin, Women's Sportswear Mfg Co, since 1950. US Army, 1943-45. Fmr pres: NW Needlecraft Assn; Cong Temple de Hirsch; fmr chmn, AJComm, Seattle. Recipient, Purple Heart. Home: 4148 Boulevard Pl, Mercer Island, Wash. Office: 500 E Pike St, Seattle, Wash.

HOCHBERG, George Stuart, US, attorney; b. Newark, NJ, Mar 18, 1924; s. Benjamin and Rose (Finkel); BA, Yale U, 1946; JD, Rutgers Law Sch, 1951; m. Jane Kruger, June 18, 1950; c: David, James, Louise. Partner, Waldor & Hochberg, Newark, NJ, since 1963; practising atty in: NJ; United Dist Court; US Supr Court. Lt, USMC, 1942-45. Pres, Comty Service Council of Orange and Maplewood; vice-pres, United Comty Fund and Council Essex and W Hudson Cos, all NJ; mem: Amer, Essex Co Bar Assns. Hobby: tennis. Home: 12 Grandview Ave, West Orange, NJ. Office: 1180 Raymond Blvd, Newark, NJ.

HOCHBERG, Nethanel, Isr, agronomist; b. Nes Ziona, Isr, Dec 20, 1897; s. Zevi and Haya (Nayman); agric ing dipl, Ecole Natl Agron, Montpellier, Fr, 1923; PhD, Heb U, Jerusalem, 1960; m. Hana Rosanski (decd); c: Dan (fell in action, Isr War of Independence), Nathan. Prof, viticulture, Mikveh Isr, agric sch; viticulture adv, Isr Min of Agric. Fmr: Isr delg, Intl Cong of Vine and Wine. Author, Viticulture in Israel, 2 vols, 1955; contbr to sci publs. Recipient: Isr Prize in Agric, 1954; Merite Viticole, Fr, 1965. Home and office: Mikveh Isr Agric Sch, Holon, Isr.

HOCHBERG, Philip R, US, attorney, broadcaster; b. Wash, DC, Oct 18, 1940; s. Abraham and Freida (Fajgenbaum); BS, Syracuse U, NY, 1961; LLB, George Wash U Law Sch, Wash, DC, 1965; att Amer U Grad Sch; George Wash U Grad Sch of Law. Atty with Smith, Pepper, Shack and L'Heureux, since 1969; fmr: admn asst, Westinghouse Bc Co, NY, 1968-69; atty, FCC, Wash, DC, 1965-68; news corresp, Radio Press Intl, Wash, DC, 1962-64; sports announcer, Wash Senators, 1962-68. Mem: Order of Coif; Phi Delta Phi; Alpha Epsilon Rho; Phi Epsilon Pi. Home: 3300 Shirley Lane, Chevy Chase, Md. Office: 1101 17 St, NW, Washington, DC.

HOCHENBERG, Moshe, Eng, accountant, administrative exec; b. Lodz, Pol, Dec 6, 1937; s. Abram and Mary (Himmelhoch); in Eng since 1969; CA, U S Afr, 1964; m. Rita Becker, Dec 23, 1962; c: Yael, Atalia, Braham. Financial, acctnt, admn exec, Peltours, London, since 1969; secy, admnr, Montays Furnishers Factor Finance, 1963-65; org secy, Sea Point Syn, Cape Town, 1965-68; acctnt, S Afr ZF; Isr UA, 1968-69; financial ed, The J Herald, Johannesburg, 1969. Vice-chmn, Bernard Patley Heb Sch PTA; treas: Young Tel'Hai, Johannesburg; Tnuat Aliya, S Afr; fmr: publicity off, B'nai B'rith, Sea Point; treas: Zionist Revisionist Org; S Amer Span Dance Assn; Cape Province Ballet Club; life mem, Old Herzli ns Assn, Cape Town; mem, Cape and Transvaal Socs of CA. Hobbies: philately, cantorial music, opera, reading. Office: Peltours, 7 Wigmore St, London W 1, Eng.

HOCHMAN, Abraham, Isr, physician; b. Lodz, Pol, Oct 18, 1910; s. Yehuda and Mina (Hershkovitz); in Isr since 1924; MD, Jerusalem; m. Shoshana Levy; c: Asa, Mina. Prof, head, dept of oncology, Hadassah Hosp, Jerusalem. Maj, IDF, 1948-50. Vice-chmn, Isr Cancer Soc; mem: Brit Inst of Radiology; Intl Club Radiotherapy. Home: 6 Marcus St, Jerusalem, Isr. Office: Hadassah U Hosp, Dept of Oncology, Jerusalem, Isr.

HOCHMAN, Daniel, US, business exec; b. Boryslaw, Pol, Jan 1, 1923; s. Henryk and Genia (Koch); in US since 1949; dipl ing, Technische Hochschule, Stuttgart, Ger, 1949; MEE, U of Pa, 1956; AMP, Harvard Bus Sch, 1965; m. Natalia Blum, Aug 9, 1944; c: Anna, June, Jerome. Pres, Dacom Inc, Sunnyvale, Cal, since 1966; engr: Allis Chalmers Mfg Co, 1950-52;

RCA, 1953-57; mgr, Lockheed Missile and Space Co, 1957-66. Mem, Inst of Elec and Electronic Engrs; Research Adv Comm, NASA. 1963. Contbr to sci jours. Home: 14157 Squirrel Hollow Lane, Saratoga, Cal. Office: 1060 Morse Ave, Sunnyvale, Cal.

HOCHSTEIN, Philip, US, journalist; b. Radishkovetz, Russ, Sep 5, 1901; s. Morris and Rose (Isaacson); in US since 1907; m. Leah Greenhouse, Oct 5, 1929; c: Ruth, Joseph, Judith, Deborah. Publisher, Jewish Week; reporter: NY Call, 1919; Bayonne Times, 1920, ed, 1922-23, 1925-26; ed: NY American, 1924; Staten Island Advance, 1927-30; LI Daily Press, 1931-35; fmr: ed, Newark-Star Ledger; ed adv, Newhouse Newspapers; pres, Advance News Service, Wash, DC. Mem, Amer Soc Newspaper Eds. Home: 91 Central Park W, New York, NY. Office: 747 National Press Bldg, Washington, DC.

HOCHWALD, Werner, US, economist; b. Berlin, Ger, Jan 21, 1910; s. Moritz and Elsa (Stahl); in US since 1938; BA, U Freiburg, 1929; LLB, U Berlin, 1932; PhD, Wash U, St Louis, Mo; m. Hilde Landenberger, Jan 28, 1938 (decd): c: Miriam, Eve. Tileston prof, political econ, Wash U since 1950, dir, intl econ research, 1947-50; legal counsel, coom on aid and reconstruction, Berlin, 1933-38; instr, US Army specialized training prog, 1940-44; lectr, US Army Finance Sch, 1945-47; cons: Fed Res Bank, St Louis, 1947-58; US Off of Educ, 1967. Mem: Amer Econ Assn; Econ Hist Assn; Econometric Soc; Amer Farm Econ Assn; Ind Relations Research Assn; Natl Conf on Research on Income and Wealth; fmr: pres, S Econ Assn; vice-pres, Midwest Econ Assn; mem exec council, Amer Stat Assn. Author: Twentieth Century Economic Thought, 1950; Conceptual Issues of Regional Income Estimation, 1957; Local Impact of Foreign Trade, 1959; Design of Regional Accounts, 1960; Essays in Southern Economic Development, 1964; An Economist's Image of History, 1968; contbr to profsl jours. Home: 6910 Cornell Ave, University, Mo. Office: Washington U, St Louis, Mo.

HOD, Mordechay, Isr, military officer; b. Kibbutz Degania, Isr, Sep 28, 1926; s. Yosef and Menucha (Kulliner) Fine; att: IDF Staff and Command Sch, 1953; Heb U, 1959-69; Sr Air Force Offs Course, US; m. Penina Alter, Mar 26, 1953; c: Yosef, Yuval, Nurit. Maj gen, cdr, IAF, since 1966, squadron cdr, 1955-56, base cdr, 1957-59, head, dept air, 1962-66, in Palmach, IAF since 1947; Brit Army, 1944-47. First Isr pilot to fly jet aircraft. Address: IDF, Isr.

HODES, Barnet, US, attorney; b. LaSalle, Ill, May 13, 1900; s. Simon and Ruth (Mansfield); LLB, Northwestern U, 1921; m. Eleanor Cramer, Apr 23, 1936; c: Simon, Kay. Atty, Chgo, since 1921; asst corp counsel, City of Chgo, 1923-27; pvt practice, 1927-33; alderman, 7th Ward, 1931-33; mem, Ill State Tax Commn, 1933-35; corp counsel, 1935-47; lectr, munic corps, Northwestern Law Sch, 1936-40. Lt cdr, US Coast Guard Res, 1944-47. Established: Barnet Hodes collection on local govt at Northwestern U Law Sch, 1960; Barnet and Scott Hodes annual prize for best essay on phases of local govt, 1963. Pres, Adult Educ Council, Gtr Chgo, 1958; mem, bd dirs, secv-treas: William and Noma Copley Fund; Intl Inst Contemporary Arts; chmn: Patriotic Fund of Chgo, 1941; City of Chgo flying mission to London for UN Capital, 1946; appd chmn, State of Ill Inter-Faith Comm, 1945; chmn: civil liberties comm, Natl Inst Munic Law Offs, 1944, pres, 1938-40; Chgo's Redevl Commn since 1944; Natl Jefferson Jubilee, 1950; State of Ill Protection of Amer Heritage, 1949; vice-pres, Ill Munic League, 1936-42; mem: US Civilian Defense Volunteer Participation Comm, appd by Pres Roosevelt, 1942; asst to US Coord of Civilian Defense, Chgo Metrop area, 1941-45; impartial arbitrator, Ladies Dress Ind; fmr mem: Chgo Planning Comm; Chgo Zoning Bd of Appeals; mem: Amer, Ill State, Chgo, Fed, Intl Bar Assns; Delta Sigma Rho; Nu Beta Epsilon, found; Masons; Elks; B'nai B'rith; club, Standard. Author: It's Your Money, 1935; Essay in Illinois Taxation, 1935; Law and the Modern City, 1937. Recipient: civic merit award, Jr Assn of Commerce, Chgo, 1934; Chgo Civil Liberties Comm award, 1939; Decalogue Soc of Lawyers award, 1941; Cross Chevalier of Légion d'Honneur, Fr, 1948; service award, Northwestern U Alumni Assn, 1961. Home: 555 Everett Ave, Chicago, Ill. Office: One N LaSalle St, Chicago, Ill.

HODES, Horace L, US, pediatrician, educator; b. Phila, Pa, Dec 21, 1907; s. Morris and Anna (Jacobson); BA, U of Pa, 1927, MD, 1931; m. Anne Reber, June 10, 1931; c: Ruth, David. Ped-in-chief, Mt Sinai Hosp since 1949; prof, chmn ped dept, Mt Sinai Sch of Med, since 1965; clinical prof,

Columbia U, since 1949; asst path, bact, Rockefeller Inst, 1936-38; dir, dispensary, Johns Hopkins Hosp, 1935-36, on staff until 1949; med dir, Sydenham Hosp, Baltimore, 1938-49; cons, US Secy of War, 1940-42. Lt cdr, USN, 1942-46. Pres, Soc Ped Research, 1951-52; med adv bd, Heb U; mem: Amer Ped Soc; Amer Acad Ped; Soc Experimental Biol and Med; NY Acad Sci; NY Acad Med; Sigma Xi; club, Ped Travel. Co-author, Common Contagious Diseases, 1956; contbr to med jours. Recipient, Mead Johnson award for research, Amer Acad Ped, 1946. Home: 41 Sutton Crest, Manhasset, NY. Office: Mt Sinai Hosp, New York, NY.

HODES, Lionel Harris, S Afr, communal exec; b. Somerset E, S Afr, Mar 17, 1924; s. Leon and Sarah (Glatt); BA, U Witwatersrand, Johannesburg, 1946; LLB, U of S Afr, Pretoria, 1953; m. Ruth Levin, Apr 11, 1956; c: Sarah, Jeremy, Amanda, Robin. Secy gen, S Afr ZF, since 1968; demonstrator, psych, U Witwatersrand; atty, pvt practice, 1954-63; PR off, legal adv, S Afr J Bd Deps, 1963-66; secy, intl affairs comm, WJC, 1966-68. S Afr Artillery-Armored Brig, 1944-66; IDF, 1948-49. Mem: Johannesburg Lodge B'nai B'rith; Mahal Assn, JEx-Service League; fmr: secy, Students Repr Council, U Witwatersrand; council mem, S Afr J Hist and Sociol Soc; mem, natl council: S Afr J Ex-Service League; League for Haganah; United Zionist Assn; Zionist Socialist Party, S Afr; Polei Zion, Gt Brit and Ir; chmn, Student Zionist Assn, U Witwatersrand. Ed, J Affairs; contbr to publs. Recipient: It star; Afr Service Medal. Home: 128 St George St, Observatory, Johannesburg, S Afr. Office: 84 de Villiers St, Johannesburg, S Afr.

HODES, Philip J, US, radiologist, educator; b. Apr 15, 1906; s. Jacob and Rose (Cohen); BS, U of Pa, 1928, MD, 1931, DSc, Grad Sch of Med, 1940; m. Natalie Lansing, May 21, 1936; c: Barton, Maisie; m. 2nd, Helen Auerbach, Mar 12, 1967. Prof, head, radiology dept, Jefferson Med Cen, since 1958; cons lectr, US Naval Hosp, Phila, since 1949; cons: VA Hosps: Phila; Wilminston, Del; E Orange, NJ, all since 1949; M D Anderson Hosp, Houston, Tex, since 1968; research asst, Pa Hosp, 1929-31; radiology, Hosp of U Pa, 1933-35; asst prof: U of Pa Med Sch, U Pa Grad Sch of Med, both 1941-47, on facs since 1935; cons lectr: Armed Forces Inst of Path, Wash, DC, 1949-62; Walter Reed Army Hosp, Wash, DC, 1949-62; US Naval Hosp, Phila, since 1959; chief cons, VA area III, 1949-62; cons, Jeanes Hosp, Phila, 1952-58; visiting guest lectr, U Minn, 1954; Russell Carmen Hon Lectr, St Louis Med Soc, 1956; visiting prof: Louisville Coll of Med, 1960; U of Cal, SF, 1962; W Reserve U, 1966; U Puerto Rico, 1955; visiting guest lectr, Kansas U, 1957; Leo Rigler Lectr, Isr, 1963; 1st Everett L Pirkey Memorial Lectr, Ky, 1967; 1st Gilbert W Heublein Memorial Lectr, Conn, 1968; Cultural Exch Prog, Vienna, 1968. Col, US Army MC, 1942-46. F: Amer Coll Radiology; Phila Coll Phys; mem: N Amer Radiology Soc, past vice pres; Amer Roentgen Ray Soc, fmr vice pres; Phila Roentgen Soc, past pres; AMA; Pa State, Phila Co Med Socs; Pa State Radiology Soc; Inter-Amer Coll of Radiology; New Eng Roentgen Ray Soc; John Morgan Soc; Trudeau Soc; Laennec Soc; Mil Order of WWs; Assn of Mil Surgs; AAAS; AAUP; Amer Assn U Radiologists; Pan Amer Med Assn; trustee: Phila Chamber Orch; Amer Cancer Soc; Main Line Reform Temple; Long Beach I Found of Arts and Sci; hon mem: Tex Radiology Soc; Puerto Rican Radiological Soc; Radiological Soc of: Cuba; Peru; Venezuela; Mex; Chile; Colegio Inter-Americano de Radiologia, Arg; hons: Phil Lambda Kappa; Alpha Omega Alpha; Sigma Xi; fmr: secy, Fifth Inter Amer Cong of Radiology; chancellor, Amer Coll of Radiology; disaster chmn, ARC; trustee, B'nai B'rith. Co-author, Head and Neck in Roentgen Diagnosis of Diseases of the Bone, 1966; ed-in-chief, Atlas of Tumor Radiology, 1966; sect ed, Ency of Med, 1939; asso ed, Penrose Cancer Sem, 1953; guest ed, Radiological Clinics of N Amer, 1964; contrib ed, Gastroenterology, vol III, 1964; contbr to sci jours. Recipient: Gold Medal Award: Inter-Amer Coll of Radiology, 1968; Amer Coll of Radiology, 1969. Office: Jefferson Med Coll Hosp, Philadelphia, Pa.

HOENICH, Paul Konrad, Isr, artist; b. Cernauti, Aus, Mar 13, 1907; s. Osias and Friderike (Sychrowski); in Isr since 1935; att: Graphische Lehr und Versuchsanstalt, Vienna; Acad de Belle Arti, Florence; Fac des Lettres, Paris; m. Ruth Grieshaber, 1935; one c. Asst prof, architecture and town planning, Technion, Haifa, since 1950; works: Robot-Art, Technion, 1962, Design with Sunrays, 1965, and others; conducted art-tech research. Hagana, Isr Army. Home: 4 Achad Haam, Haifa, Isr. Office: Technion, Haifa, Isr.

HOENIG, Moses H, US, attorney; b. NYC, Sept 18, 1898; s. Joseph and Lena (Goldfarb); tchrs dipl, Tchrs Inst, JTSA, 1918; LLB, cum laude, Bklyn Law Sch; St Lawrence U, 1919; m. Hannah Goldberg, Feb 22, 1928; c: Pearl Jetter, D Bernard, Samuel. Pvt practice since 1920. Pres: Natl Council Young Isr, 1926-57; Goldfarb Soc, 1940-50; E Pkwy JCC, 1952-54; dir, Bklyn JCC; Yeshivah Tora Vada'ath; Isr Bonds, 1959; rel dir, Children's Aid Soc; mem, exec: Mizrachi Org; AJCong, 1932-45; mem: NY Lawyers Fed of J Charities, trustee since 1950. Ed, Viewpoint, Natl Council Young Isr, 1928-50; contbr to mags. Homes: 225 Eastern Pkwy, Brooklyn, NY; 669 Shore Rd, Long Beach, NY. Office: 170 Broadway, New York, NY.

HOENIG, Sidney B, US, educator, rabbi, author; b. April 6, 1907; s. Joseph and Lena (Goldfarb); BSS, 1927; ordained rabbi, Yeshiva U, 1931; PhD, Dropsie Coll, 1934; m. Ann Whitehorn, March 28, 1939; c: Hava, Joseph (decd), Herschel, Fredda, Jacob. Prof, J hist, Grad Sch, Yeshiva U, since 1951, chmn, dept J studies, 1952, dir, adult educ, since 1954, fac mem since 1934; chaplain, Bklyn House of Detention, since 1947; prin, Tchrs Training Sch for Girls, 1940-50; rabbi, Young Isr of Bklyn, 1947, educ dir, 1940; sup, Heb Tchrs Coll sem, JA, Isr, 1952. Mem: RabCA; Natl Council J Prison Chaplains; Soc for Old Testament Study, Eng. Author: Guide to the Prophets, 1942, 2nd ed, 1958; Jewish Beliefs and Creeds, 1944; Jewish Family Purity, 1945; Supplement to the Passover Haggadah, 1950; The Great Sanhedrin, 1953; The Duty of the Woman, 9th ed, 1958; Jewish Identity, 1965; The Scholarship of Dr Bernard Revel, 1968; ed: Prayer Book for Jewish Personnel in Armed Forces of US, 1958; High Holiday Prayer Book, 1969; Israel Haggadah; Manual, commn on Jewish chaplaincy, JWB, 1952; contbr to: Jewish Quarterly Review; Interpreters Bible; Ency Britannica. Home: 125 Beach 126 St, Rockaway Park, NY. Office: Yeshiva U, Amsterdam Ave and 186 St, New York, NY.

HOEXTER, Werner J, Isr, philatelic expert and author; b. Treysa, Hessen, Ger, Mar 18, 1907; s. Abraham and Margarete (Lichtenstein); in Isr since 1935; att U Heidelberg, 1925-26; U Köln, 1926-27; U Frankfurt, 1930; 2nd law examination, Prussian High Court, Berlin, 1930-33; m. Elisabeth Makower, May 10, 1936; c: Miriam. Philatelic expert, author since 1940; dealer in vintage stamps since 1938, philatelic auctioneer. Haganah, 1935-49. Dir, research, World Philatelic Cong of Isr, Holy Land, Judaica Socs, since 1968; mem: exec comm: Fed Isr Philatelic Soc; Fed Intl de Philatelie; Intl Juries at intl philatelic exhbs: Palermo, 1959: Warsaw, 1960; Budapest, 1961; Prague, 1962; Istanbul, Luxembourg, 1963; Paris, 1964; Vienna, 1965; Wash, DC, 1966; Amsterdam, 1967; natl exhbs in Isr, 1945-68; Assn Intl des Experts Philatelistes; Ger Philatelists. Author: The Stamps of Palestine, in Eng, Heb, 1946, 1959; contbr to profsl mags. Recipient: E Ascher Medal for dist philatelists, 1946. Home: 4 Achad Haam St, Haifa, Isr.

HOFF, Syd, US, artist, author; b. NYC, Sep 4, 1912; s. Benjamin and Mary (Barnow); m. Dora Berman, May 30, 1937; c: Susan, Linda, Bonnie. Free-lance cartoonist since 1931; creator, daily newspaper panel, King Features syndicate, Laugh It Off. Author: Danny and the Dinosaur; Julius; Oliver; Sammy the Sea; Stanley; Where's Prancer; Little Chief; Lengthy; Mrs Switch; Baseball Mouse; Jeffrey at Camp; Roberto and the Bull; Grizzwold; Chester; Upstream; Downstream and Out of My Mind; Twixt the Cup and the Lipton; The Better Hoff; From Bed to Nurse; Oops! Wrong Party; Oops! Wrong Storeroom; So this is Matrimony!; Feeling No Pain; Okay You Can Look Now; Irving and Me; Herschel the Hero; The Litter Knight; Mahatma; Slithers; contbr to natl jours. Mem, Authors Guild. Home and office: 4335 Post Ave, Miami Beach, Fla.

HOFFBERGER, Jerold C, US, business exec; b. Baltimore, Md, Apr 7, 1919; s. Samuel and Gertrude (Miller); att U of Va; m. Alice Berney, June 10, 1946; c: David, Richard, Carol, Charles. Pres, chmn, Natl Brewing Co, since 1947; chmn, Baltimore Baseball Club; pres, Divex; mem, exec comm, Fairchild-Hiller; dir: Maryland Natl Bank; Merchants Mortgage Co; Real Estate Holding Co; Merchants Terminal Corp. Capt, US Army, WW II. Chmn, Amer Isr Public Affairs Comm, Baltimore, mem, natl bd; mem, natl cabinet, UJA, since 1963; treas: Baltimore JWF, asso, mem bd; Sinai Hosp; pres, Baltimore Heb Cong, 1961-63; mem, exec comm, Gtr Baltimore Comm; bd trustees: Mercy Hosp; Johns Hopkins Hosp; Goucher Coll; dir, JTA; clubs: Suburban Cen; Baltimore Advt. Home: Sunset Hill, Riderwood, Md. Office: 3720 Dillon St, Baltimore, Md.

HOFFERT, Paul W, US, surgeon; b. NYC, Feb 22, 1923; s. Charles and Rose (Isaacs); AB, hons, Columbia Coll, 1942; MD, cum laude, Yale Med Sch, 1945; m. Rosolyn Sheiman, Apr 20, 1947; c: Marvin, Renee, Deborah. Asst clinical prof, surg, Albert Einstein Sch Med, NY, since 1957; pvt practice since 1953; asst, surg, gyn and obstet, Yale Med Sch, 1945-46; instr, radiology, U Pa Med Sch, 1948-49. US Army MC, 1946-48. F: NY Acad Med; Clinical Soc; NY Diabetes Assn; Amer Coll Surgs; Amer Soc of Abdominal Surgs; dipl: Amer Bd Surgs; Amer Bd Abdominal Surgs; mem: AMA; Phi Beta Kappa; Alpha Omega Alpha; Phi Delta Epsilon; fmr: pres: ZOA, Lincoln Park dist, Yonkers, NY; Westchester chap, Amer Coll Surgs. Contbr to med jours. Home: 1050 Nautilus Lane, Mamaroneck, NY. Office: 27 Ludlow St, Yonkers, NY.

HOFFMAN, Anna M Rosenberg, US, public and industrial relations cons; b. Budapest, Hung, June 19, 1902; d. Albert and Charlotte (Backsai) Lederer; in US since 1912; hon: DHumL, Columbia U; LLD, Tufts Coll; MHumL, Russell Sage Coll; m. Julius Rosenberg, Oct 12, 1919; c: Thomas; m. 2nd, Paul Hoffman. Sr partner, Anna M Rosenberg Assos, public and ind relations cons, since 1946; mem: adv bd, Ency Britannica Films Inc; public, lab, and personnel relations cons, since 1924; fmr: regional dir: Natl Recovery Admn; Social Security Admn; War Manpower Commn; mem: Adv Commn on Universal Mil Training; comm on mobilization policy, Natl Security Resources Bd; adv bd, Off of War Mobilization and Reconversion; US Natl Commn on UNES CO; NYC Bd of Educ; personal repr of Pres Roosevelt and Pres Truman, Eur Theater, WW II; asst sec of Defense, 1950. Mem: adv council, Natl Conf on Intl Econ and Social Devl; Health Research Council of NYC; bd of dirs: NY World's Fair; Amer Heritage Found; Council on World Tensions; US Comm for the UN; mem bd: Founds: Albert and Mary Lasker; Franklin D Roosevelt; George C Marshall; Eleanor Roosevelt; Natl Fund for Med Educ. Recipient: medals: Freedom, 1945; Merit, 1947; award, Amer Schs and Colls Assn, 1949. Home: 8 Sutton Sq, New York, NY. Office: 444 Mddison Ave, New York, NY.

HOFFMAN, Arthur M, US, physician, educator; b. Chgo, Ill, Mar 14, 1898; s. Herman and Sary (Weiss); BA, Reed Coll, Portland, Ore, 1918; MD, Harvard Med Sch, 1922; m. Rose Lewis, 1924 (decd); c: Anne Rolston; m. 2nd, Elizabeth Burke, 1949. Chief, med service, Santa Fe Coast Lines Hosp, since 1959; clinical prof, med, U of S Cal Sch of Med, since 1953; sr att phys, LA Co Hosp, since 1925; chief-of-staff, Cedars of Leb Hosp, 1953-73. FACP; mem: bd trustees: Fed of J Wfr Orgs; JCC, both LA; Amer Bd Internal Med; Amer Trudeau Soc; AMA; AHA; Cal Med Assn; club, Hillcrest Country. Contbr to profsl jours. Hobby: music. Home: 317 N Las Palmas Ave, Los Angeles, Cal. Office: 240 S La Cienega Blvd, Beverly Hills, Cal.

HOFFMAN, Benjamin, Isr, publisher, editor; b. Radautz, Rum, Apr 24, 1923; s. Jacob and Recha (Schlesinger); in Isr since 1954; att Heb Tchrs Sem, Yeshiva, U NY; BA, Tel Aviv U; m. Hanna Brodman, Aug, 1957. Head, Binyamin Hoffman Publs, Tel Aviv, since 1961; fmr ed: Isr Export and Trade Jour; Isr Cyprus Mag; publisher, ed, MDA Quarterly, since 1965; pub booklets, Isr govt bodies; co-publisher, Isr Tourist Guide, annual; trans: Giants of the Spirit; Our Finest Year; contbr to jours. Found, Brith Hanoar, Manhattan, NY; vice-chmn bd, Yeshiva, HS, Tikvat Yaacov, Isr; mem, AACI, Tel Aviv. Hobbies: arts, sport, architecture. Home: 3 Wilson St, Tel Aviv, Isr. Office: 148 Ben Yehuda St, Tel Aviv, Isr.

HOFFMAN, Isidor B, US, rabbi, student counselor; b. Phila, Pa, Aug 4, 1898; s. Charles and Fanny (Binswanger); BA, Columbia U, 1920; ordained rabbi, MHL, JTSA, 1924; grad study: Amer Sch for Oriental Research, 1924-25; Heb U, 1925, both Jerusalem; Cornell U, 1932-34; hon DHL, Columbia U, 1954; m. Hilda Burstein, May 12, 1925; c: Daniel, Richard. Exec dir, J Peace F; counselor to J students, Columbia U, 1934-67; rabbi, Temple Beth El, Utica, NY, 1925-28; dir, Hillel Found, Cornell U, 1929-33. Mem: bd dirs, Rel and Lab Found, since 1939, past chmn; bd, Sane, since 1962; bd dirs, Amer J Soc for Service, since 1950; adv bd, Comm on World Devl and World Disarmament, since 1962; active in comms and intl relations insts of Amer Friends service comm; repr, Syn Council of Amer on bd dirs, Natl Service Bd for Rel Objectors; club, Fac, Columbia U. Home: 420 Riverside Dr, New York, NY.

HOFFMAN, Nathan Joseph, US, scientist; b. Independence, Ia, Nov 20, 1933; s. Morris and Margaret (Goldfarb); metal-lurgical ing, Colo Sch Mines, Golden, Colo, 1955; MSc, Technion, Haifa, Isr, 1961, DSc, 1969; m. Sara Rabbani, Oct 31, 1960; c: Faith, Jordan. Mem, tech staff, research dept, Rocketdyne, since 1969, engr, Liquid Rocket Engines, 1955-60, sr engr, research, 1961-66; instr, metallurgy, Technion, Haifa, 1966-69. Prin contribs: helped select materials of construction for rocket engines, Apollo launch to moon; to liquid metal corrosion theory. Found secy, Soc for Growth of Crystal & THW Films, Isr br; mem: Amer Inst Metal and Mining Engr; Amer Inst Aeronautics & Astronautics. Contbr to books and sci jours. Recipient: Engrs' Day Scholarship, Colo Sch of Mines; Rocketdyne F, 1967-69. Hobbies: writing novels, studying Semitic langs, geog of Isr. Home: 22431 Michale St, Canoga Park, Cal. Office: 6633 Canoga Ave, Canoga Park, Cal.

HOFFMAN, Philip E, US, attorney, business exec; b. NYC, Oct 2, 1908; s. David and Hildegarde (Eisinger); BA, Dartmouth Coll, 1929; LLB, Yale Law Sch, 1932; m. Florence Lehman, Sep 9, 1933; c: David, Lynn Manshel. Pvt practice since 1933; partner, Hoffman and Tuck; chmn, dir, US Realty and Inves Co, Newark, NJ; dir, various bus corps; asst gen counsel, War Produc Bd, Wash, DC, 1942-45; hearing commnr, Natl Produc Auth, 1950-52; chmn, Jewelry Ind Coord Comm, 1954-57. Natl chmn, bd govs, AJComm, fmr natl vice pres; chmn, natl domestic affairs comm, vice chmn, natl comty affairs comm, mem, natl admn, exec bds, all AJComm, hon chmn, Essex Co chap, AJComm; mem exec comm, natl comty relations adv comm, Essex Co, NJ; mem: Bipartisan Conf on Civil Rights; NJ Adv Comm to US Commn on Civil Rights; chmn, housing comm, Comm of Concern, NJ; hon chmn, Appeal for Hum Relations; trustee: E Orange Gen Hosp; Jt Defense Appeal Employees Pension Trust; fmr: chmn, initial gifts, Essex Co UJA; trustee: JCC, Essex Co; Temple B'nai Jeshurun, Short Hills, NJ; presently mem: Amer Bar Assn; Assn Bar, NYC; NY Co Lawyers Assn; Phi Beta Kappa; clubs: Downtown, Newark; Mt Ridge Country, Caldwell, NJ. Fmr mem, bd eds, Yale Law Jour. Recipient: numerous awards in hum relations. Home: 218 N Woods Dr, S Orange, NJ. Office: 917 Broad St, Newark, NJ.

HOFFMAN, William S, US, medical admnr, educator; b. Baltimore, Md, July 5, 1899; s. Louis and Lena (Miller); BA, Johns Hopkins U, 1918, PhD, chem, 1922; MD, Rush Med Coll, U Chgo, 1930; m. Miriam Berliner, July 26, 1928; c: Paul, Nancy. Professorial lectr: med, U of Ill Coll of Med, since 1953, phys, 1948-53; med dir, Sidney Hillman Health Cen, Chgo, 1953-68; asst, phys chem, instr, Johns Hopkins Med Sch, 1922-27; f, NRC, Rush Med Coll, 1931-32; prof, head, biochem dept, Chgo Med Sch, 1932-44; acting dir, Hektoen Inst for Med Research, 1944-45; dir, biochem, Cook Co Hosp and Hektoen Inst, 1945-53. F, Amer Soc for Clinical Paths; mem: ZOA; AMA; Soc for Experimental Biol and Med; Cen Soc for Clinical Research; Chgo Soc Internal Med; Chgo Diabetes Assn, trustee since 1946; Amer Diabetes Assn; Ill Soc of Paths; Amer Coll Phys; Ill, Chgo Med Socs; Inst of Med of Chgo; Amer Soc of Biol Chems; AAAS; Amer Public Health Assn; Phi Beta Kappa; Alpha Omega Alpha; Sigma Xi; natl adv, Allied Health Profsl's Council, since 1968. Author: Photelometric Clinical Chemistry, 1941; The Biochemistry of Clinical Medicine, 1954, 4th ed, 1969; asso ed, Amer Jour of Clinical Path, 1952-66; contbr to sci and profsl jours. Hobbies: photography, gardening. Home and office: 6101 N Sheridan Rd, Chicago, Ill.

HOFFMANN, Akiba, Isr, attorney; b. Kostel, Aus, Sep 27, 1911; s. Jacob and Recha (Schlesinger); in Isr since 1936; att: U Frankfurt/M; U Vienna; U Munich; DJ, U Basel, 1934; m. Hilde Kaufman, 1944; c: Gabrielle. Pvt law practice since 1941; legal adv, NV Agricola, Rotterdam and the Hague, 1934-35; mem, bd dirs, Lafayette SA, Paris; legal asst, Anglo-Pal Bank Ltd, Tel Aviv, 1939-41. Mem, exec, Lib Party, Isr, since 1961, chmn, Gtr Tel Aviv-Yaffo br, since 1961; mem: Court of Hon, WZC, since 1960; munic council, City of Tel Aviv-Yaffo, 1965-69; bd dirs: Amer, Isr Prospects Corp; Shikun Ezrahi Corp; mem: United Isr Appeal, since 1938; missions to: Far E, Cyprus, Ger. Author: Das Depositum nach Talmudischen Recht, 1935; contbr to Isr, Eur, Amer press. Home: 6 Adam Hacohen St, Tel Aviv, Isr. Office: 46 Lilienblum St, Tel Aviv, Isr.

HOFFMANN, Banesh, US, educator; b. Richmond, Surrey, Eng, Sep 6, 1906; s. Maurice and Leah (Brozel); in US since 1929; BA, Oxford U, 1929; PhD, Princeton U, 1932; m. Doris Goodday, July, 1938; c: Laurence, Deborah. Prof, math, Queens Coll, NYC, since 1953, on fac since 1937; research asso, U Rochester, 1932-35; mem, Inst for Advanced Study, Princeton, 1935-36. Inventor: Hoffmann Orthoepic Alphabet. Chmn, exec comm, Conf on Methods in Phil and Scis, 1952-53; cons on tests, Westinghouse Sci Talent Search, since 1944; spec cons, commn on tests, Coll Entrance Examination Bd, 1967; mem, Amer Math Soc; f, Amer Physical Soc. Author: The Strange Story of the Quantum, 1947, 1959, 1962; The Tyranny of Testing, 1962, 1964; About Vectors, 1966; ed, Perspectives in Geometry and Relativity, 1966; trans, from Fr, Precis of Special Relativity, by Costa de Beauregard, 1966; contbr research articles, including one with Albert Einstein, to profsl jours. Recipient: dist tchr of year, Queens Coll Alumni Assn, 1963; 1st prize, Gravity Research Found, 1964. Spec interest: music. Home: 43-17 169 St, Flushing, NY. Office: Queens Coll, Kissena Blvd, Flushing, NY.

HOFFNER, Dan Heinz, Isr, artist; b. Leipzig, Ger, Mar 7, 1921; s. David and Cesia (Kainer); in Isr since 1936; att Bezalel Sch; m. Eva Loewy; c: Anat, Yigal. Dir, Becalel Acad of Art and Design since 1963; asst dir, Art Tchrs Sem, 1949-55; art insp, Min of Educ, 1955-61; one-man shows: Tel Aviv, Jerusalem, San Francisco, Berlin. Author: Art Education in Israel, 1951; Methods of Art Teaching, 1953. Home: 17 Golani St, Jerusalem, Isr. Office: Bezalel Acad of Art and Design, Jerusalem, Isr.

HOFHEIMER, Richard D, US, business exec; b. Norfolk, Va, July 23, 1901; s. Benjamin and Sadie (Schwan); att U of Va, 1919-21; m. Geneva Greenwell, June 1, 1940; c: Diane, Charles. Pres, Cavalier Realty Corp; exec vice-pres, Hofheimer's; treas, Natl Realty; bd dirs, Seabord Citizens Natl Bank. Hon pres, Ohel Sholom Cong; bd trustees, UAHC, 1956; adv bd, De Paul Hosp; dir, Norfolk Retail Merchants Assn; pres: Norfolk Downtown Assn, 1962; Shoes Assn, 1957-59; clubs: Chesapeake, Cavalier Golf and Yacht. Home: N Shore Point, Norfolk, Va. Office: 325 Granby St, Norfolk, Va.

HOFMAN, Shlomo, Isr, musicologist; b. Warsaw, Pol, Apr 24, 1909; s. Shmul and Ryvka (Babic); grad: State Sem for Tchrs, Warsaw; State Conservatory for Music, Warsaw; DLitt, Sorbonne, Paris; m. Cyla Pelzman, 1933; c: Talma, Orit. Lectr, musicology, Isr Acad of Music, Tel Aviv U, since 1955; fmr lectr, methodology music educ, Heb U, Jerusalem, and State Sem for Arab Tchrs, Jaffa; guest lectr, Us in US. Pres, Isr Musicological Soc; mem comm: Isr League of Composers; Art and Psychopath Assn of Isr, since 1967. Author: L'Oeuvre de Clavecin de François Couperin, le Grande-Etude Stylistique, 1961; In Paths of Music Education; Music in Adult Education; Education Through Music; Miqra'ey Musica, 1965; Music in Talmud, 1969; New Trends in World and Israeli Music, 1967; Research in Samaritan Music, 1965, 1968; Research in Yemenite Music, 1967; Research in Karaite Music Expression, 1969; ed: Tsililey Halil, 1968; Dictionary of Musical Terms of the Hebrew Language Academy; music sect, Gen Ency Isr; music ed, Heb trans, Ency of the Great Composers and their Music; trans into Heb: Notes with Music, by Darius Milhaud; Jean Christophe, by Rolland; contbr to profsl jours. Composer: compositions for orch; chamber music; songs for voice and orch; music for theater. Recipient: award for musicological research: Heb U, 1957; Fr Govt, 1947; award, Isr song festival, Isr Bc Service, 1960; award for phonological research, Acad Heb Lang, 1967. Home: 67 Gordon St, Tel Aviv, Isr.

HOFMANN, Justin, US, rabbi; b. Koenigshofen, Ger, June 3, 1921; s. Julius and Selma (Schlorch); BA, Cen YMCA Coll, Chgo, 1944; ordained rabbi, Heb Theol Coll, 1946; MA, U Buffalo, 1951, EdD, 1955; m. Sofie Altmann, July 22, 1948; c: Selma, Rena, Hannah. Dir, B'nai B'rith Hillel Founds: U Buffalo; Buffalo State Tchrs Coll; Fredonia State Tchrs Coll, all since 1948; U W Va, 1946-48; lectr, Sch of Educ, U Buffalo, 1956-61. Pres: Va'ad Hakashruth, Buffalo, since 1962; Hapoel Hamizrachi, Buffalo, 1949-51; Buffalo Bd Rabbis, 1961-63; mem: RabCA; NY Bd Rabbis; Natl Assn Hillel Dirs; Phi Delta Kappa. Home: 12 Colton Dr, Buffalo, NY. Office: 40 Capen Blvd, Buffalo, NY.

HOFSHI, Natan, Isr, author; b. Volbrom, Pol, May, 1889; s. Yehoshua and Rivka (Narkis) Frenkel; in Isr since 1909. Trans from Yiddish: haHiba, by Hillel Zeitlin, 1953; Min haMaor sheba Yahadut, 1954; beLev vaNefesh, 1955; Medinat haShalom, 1968; contbr to books, newspapers, and mags. Co-found, Moshav Nahalal; fmr mem, Hapoel Hatzair. Home: 80 Shenkar St, Holon, Isr.

HOFSTADTER, Albert, US, educator; b. NYC, Mar 28, 1910; s. Louis and Henrietta (Koenigsberg); BS, CCNY, 1929; MA, Columbia U, 1934, PhD, 1935; m. Manya Huber, Feb 12, 1936; c: Marc. Prof, phil, U of Cal, Santa Cruz, since 1967; lectr, Columbia Coll, 1933-34; instr, asso prof, NYU, 1936-50; prof, Columbia U, 1953-67; f, Cen for Advanced Study in Behavioral Scis, 1966. Vice-pres, Amer Phil Assn, 1968-69, exec comm. Author: Locke and Scepticism, 1935; Truth and Art, 1965; co-ed: Philosophies of Art and Beauty; contbr to profsl jours. Recipient: Guggenheim Memorial Found f, 1943. Spec interests: esthetics, phil, anthropology, metaphysics. Home: 114 Spring St, Santa Cruz, Cal. Office: U of Cal, Santa Cruz, Cal.

HOFSTATTER, Osias, Isr, painter; b. Bochnia, Pol, Dec 28, s. Benzion and Frade (Biegeleisen); in Isr since 1957; att: Munic Sch for Applied Art, 1943-45; Acad for Applied Art, Vienna, 1947-48; m. Anna Sebesta, Nov 10, 1938. One-man shows: Haifa Mus of Modern Art, 1968; Mus Isr, Jerusalem, 1968; Yad Vashem; Kibbutz Lohamei Hageta'ot, drawings done in concentration camps; works: Benjamin Tammuz art in Isr, 1963, 1965; Osias Hofstatter Drawings, 1968. Mem, Isr Painters and Sculptors Assn. Recipient: art prizes: Munic of Holon, 1963; Migdal-David Jerusalem, Min of Educ and Culture, 1967. Home and studio: 14 Houthaker St, Hod Hasharon, Isr.

HOFSTEIN, Saul, US, social work cons, psychologist, educator; b. NYC, Feb 20, 1916; s. Morris and Rose (Schechtman); BS, CCNY, 1937; MS, Sch of Educ, 1938; MSW, U of Pa, 1942, DSW, 1954; NY State Cert, psychol, 1962; m. Isabelle Stone, Jan 12, 1947; c: Susan, Natalie. Asso prof, Wurzweiler Sch Soc Work, Yeshiva U since 1966; cons, pvt practice, since 1954; asso, case work, U Pa Sch Soc Work, 1957-67; supervised, devl, children's, youth services, J Comty Services, LI, 1946-56; asst dir, casework, Infants Home of Bklyn, 1956-58; instr, Yeshiva U Grad Sch, 1952-58; asst prof, Adelphi Coll, 1958-59. Lt, US Army, chief psycht social worker, Fort Monmouth Mental Hygiene Unit, 1941-43, clinical psych, army installations, 1943-46. Chmn, comms, services for children, Queensboro Council of Soc Work, 1946-56, parent educ, 1954-56; prog comm, Queens Co Mh Assn; bd: comm on diagnosis and evaluation, Queens Rehab Prog; comm educ, Mh Assn of Nassau Co since 1961; vice-pres, prog Gt Neck Sr Citizen Cen, 1963-67; mem: Amer Assn Psycht Soc Workers, Publ Comm, 1943-55; Natl Cong of J Communal Service, since 1946; natl comm on practice, psycht soc work and research sect, Natl Assn Soc Workers, since 1955; Amer Personnel Guidance Assn; Child Wfr Assn of Amer; Natl Council Soc Work Educ; Acad Cert Soc Workers; Child Study Assn of Amer; Natl Acad Rel and Mh; Temple Emanuel, New Hyde Park; U of Pa and CUNY Alumni Assns. Contbr to profsl publs. Recipient: Annual Mh Award, 1960. Home and office: 22 Kings Lane, New Hyde Park, NY.

HOHENSTEIN, Jac, US, business exec, engineer; b. NYC, May 8, 1893; s. Morris and Leontina (Altschul); BS, CCNY, 1914; m. Ruth Kleinfeld, Apr 15, 1917; c: Leontina Stiefel. Pres: Kahle Engr Co, since 1931; Kahle Europea, It; dir, Chukyo Elec, Japan. Home: 41 Kingswood Rd, Weehawken, NJ. Office: 3322 Hudson Ave, Union City, NJ.

HOHENSTEIN, W Peter, US, physical chem, educator, consultant; b. Vienna, Aus, Dec 17, 1908; s. Adolph and Sally (Balsam); in US since 1938; PhD, U Vienna, 1932; m. Selma Daniel, Dec 24, 1938; c: Gertrude. Prof, chem, Poly Inst of Bklyn, since 1946, fac mem since 1941; research chem, Milan, It, 1933-36; research asst, U Lausanne, Switz, 1937-38; acting chief chem, Glyco Products Co, NY, 1939-41. Mem: NY Acad Sci; Amer Chem Soc; Sigma Xi. Contbr to textbooks on chem of polymerization reactions; numerous articles to Amer, Brit, Fr, It, Span and Indian sci jours. Home: 84-51 Beverly Rd, Kew Gardens, NY. Office: 84 Livingston St, Brooklyn, NY.

HOLDHEIM, Rokhel, Isr, poet, kibbutz mem; b. Phila, Pa, June 10, 1935; d. Aaron and Sonia (Horwitz) Fishman; in Isr since 1954; m. Theodor Holdheim, Dec 22, 1954; c: Uri, Aaron. Author: Zun Iber Alts, 1962; Derner Nochn Regn; Shamayim Ba'esev-Himltsuishn Grozn, 1968. Mem: Kibbutz Bet Alfa; Hakibbutz Arzi Hashomer Hatzair; Yiddisher Shreiber Farein, Isr. Home: Kibbutz Bet Alfa, Isr.

HOLDHEIM, Theodore, Isr, educator, composer; b. Berlin, Ger, Dec 12, 1923; s. Gerhard and Alica (Baginsky); in Isr since 1933; att: Heb U, Jerusalem; Juilliard Sch of Music, NY; m. Rokhel Fishman, Dec 22, 1954; c: Uri, Aaron. Tchr, math, physics: Bet Alfa Regional HS, since 1947; Oranim Tchrs Sem, since 1968. Mem: Isr Composers League; Hakibbutz Ha'artzi; haShomer hatzair; fmr, JA Shaliach for Hashomer hatzair Youth Movement, US. Maj works: Haim baMidbar, 1946-47; String Quartet, 1954; Little Suite for Clarinet and Strings, 1960; Continua, opera, 1960-64; Sonata for Trumpet and Piano, 1958; Quintet for Oboe, Clarinet, Horn, Trumpet and Piano, 1968; Sonata for Two Flutes, 1968; Sonata for Trumpet and Piano, 1966; Call, Air and Dance for brass quartet, 1969. Home: Kibbutz Bet Alfa, Isr.

HOLISHER, Desider, US, author; b. Budapest, Hung, Feb 2, 1901; s. Leopold and Anna (Weiner); in US since 1938; M Econ, U Berlin, 1926; student, Berlin Photography Acad, 1927-28; m. Myra Zlatogorsky, Dec 25, 1928; c: Leo. Photographic illus, tchr photography and pictorial communication arts, since 1938; ed, Reporter Feature Syndicate, Berlin, 1929-33; Rome corresp for Eur jours, 1933-38. Author: Roma Centro Mondiale, 1937; The Eternal City, 1943; The House of God, 1946; Pilgrims Path 1947; Capitol Hill, 1952; The Synagogue and Its People, 1955; Growing up in Israel, 1963; contbr to natl mags. Hobbies: music, travel. Home: 611 W 111 St, New York, NY.

HOLLAND, Samuel C, US, executive, attorney; b. Lutzin, Latvia, July 1, 1892; s. Zalman and Chaya (Lev); in US since 1909; LLB, U Chgo, 1916; M Sup Studies, Universidad Nacional de Mexico, 1962; m.Tillie Perlman, Jan 8, 1920; c: Joshua, Ruth Waddell, Miriam Filler, Judith King. Exec vice-pres, J Hist Soc, Gtr Wash DC, since 1959; atty, Chgo, 1915-1959. Pres: N Lawdate Citizens Council, 1947-52; Workers Inst, 1915-20; chmn, Pal Labor Comm, Chgo, 1928-33; co-chmn, Chgo Anti-Nazi Boycott Comm, 1934-38; mem, bd dirs: JWF, 1939-53; Bur of J Employment Problems, 1947-50; Bd of J Educ, 1947-50; YIVO, 1947-57; mem: Chgo Bar Assn; John F Kennedy Lodge, B'nai B'rith; Chgo Gen J Council, 1931-33; Council of DC, 1942-58; Chgo Council Against Discrimination, 1945-48; Law and Order Comm, Chgo Commn Hum Relation, 1947-59; Comm on War Records, Chgo J Population Assn; Amer J Hist Soc; Amer Assn for State and Local Hist; club de las Americas. Co-ed, Medical Leaves, 1937-43; contbr to Chgo and Wash, DC jours (under pen name Sanford Hamlin), 1931-33. Home: 1314 Massachusetts Ave, NW, Washington, DC. Office: 1330 Massachusetts Ave, NW, Washington, DC.

HOLLANDER, Grace S, NZ, business exec, communal worker; b. Christchurch, Mar 25, 1922; d. Leon and Dina (Vander Molen) Goldsmith; m. Eber Hollander, Mar 11, 1947; c: Joseph, Steven. Mgr, clothing mfr, since 1957. Vice-pres, WIZO, fmr pres; pres, Union J Women for Dominion of NZ, since 1962, fmr pres, Christchurch chap for 8 years; secy, J Relief and Wfr Soc; mem: exec, Natl Council Women; comm: Zionist Soc; Primary Sch; J Soc Club. Hobbies: floral decoration, gardening, clothes designing. Home: 8 Philpotts Rd, Christchurch, NZ.

HOLLANDER, Leonard, US, psychiatrist; b. NYC, Dec 8, 1918; s. Herman and Tobye (Keresh); BS, CCNY, 1940; MA, O State U, 1941; MD, NYU, 1948; att Columbia U Psychan Inst, 1957-60; m. Susan Katz, Aug 12, 1956; c: Eric, Seth, David. Sup, family study unit, dept of psycht, Albert Einstein Coll of Med, since 1965, on staff since 1957; dir, psychiatric services, J Child Care Assn, since 1961; cons, Kennedy Child Study Cen, since 1960; dir, Lower Miami Valley Guidance Cen, Hamilton, O, 1954-55; dep chief, psychiatric services, USPHS Hosp, Lexington, Ky, 1955-57. Pres ex-officio, Council on Child Psycht; mem: Amer Assn on Mental Deficiency; Amer Psychiatric Assn; Amer Ortho-Psychiatric Assn; Assn Child Psycht. Contbr to profsl jours. Home: 115 E 82 St, New York, NY. Office: 345 Madison Ave, New York, NY.

HOLLANDER, Sherman Schiller, US, business exec; b. Cleveland, O, Mar 7, 1920; s. Herbert and Rose (Schiller); AB, W Reserve U, 1941; LLB, Franklin Thomas Bachus Sch of Law, 1946; m. Rodine Sadofsky, Oct 21, 1945; c: Michael, Judith, Jonathan. Pres: O Title Corp, since 1968; Hollander Abstract Co, since 1968, with firm since 1948. Lt, US Army, 1943-45. Pres: N O Council, AJCong; Beachwood City Bd of Educ; vice-pres, B'nai B'rith lodge; bd dirs: Cleveland Bd of Trustees; Cuyahoga Co Bar Assn; Richmond Hts Gen Hosp; fmr pres: O Title Assn; O Title Underwriters Assn; Beachwood City League; mem: Tau Epsilon Rho Law Frat; Phi Beta

Kappa; Zeta Beta Tau. Contbr to law jours. Hobby, photography. Home: 23902 Woodway Rd, Beachwood, O. Office: 118 St Clair Ave NE, Cleveland, O.

HOLLENDER, Abraham Risel, US, otolaryngologist, educator, author; b. NYC, Apr 15, 1892; s. Joseph and Mary (Koss); att U of Chgo, 1910-11; MD, U of Ill, 1915; hon MS, Natl Coll of Can, 1943; m. Anna Winsberg, Mar 1, 1916; c: Marc, Edythe Geiger. Clinical prof, otolaryngology, U Miami; prof em, otolaryngology, U of Ill; cons: Variety Children's Hosp; St Francis Hosp; Mt Sinai Hosp of Gtr Miami; club, Phi Delta Epsilon Grad. Author: Office Treatment of the Ear, Nose and Throat, 1942; The Pharynx, 1953; Physical Therapeutic Methods in Otolaryngology; co-author: Physical Therapy in Diseases of the Eyes, Ears, Nose, and Throat, 1936; Textbook of Ears, Nose, and Throat, 1942; Nursing in Eyes, Ears, Nose ,and Throat, 1946; ed, Eye, Ear, Nose,and Throat Monthly. Home: 1830 Meridan Ave, Miami Beach, Fla. Office: 605 Lincoln Rd, Miami Beach, Fla.

HOLLENDER, Charles, US, attorney; b. NYC, Jan 20, 1893; s. Moses and Sophie (Sporn); LLB, NYU Law Sch, 1913; m. Sally Jarmuth, May 24, 1917; c: Herbert. Pvt practice since 1914; mem, firm, Colby & Brown, 1920-30; dir, profsl law enforcement, NY State Educ Dept, 1943-46; mem, legal staff, NY State Comptroller, 1950. Mem: Bar Assn, NYC; Masons; hon mem: bd trustees, Temple Isr, New Rochelle; NY State Soc Physiotherapists; Pi Theta Phi, Ithaca Coll; club, Rep, New Rochelle, fmr pres. Contbr to med and other jours. Home: 221 Rose Hill Ave, New Rochelle, NY. Office: 36 W 44 St, New York, NY.

HOLLENDER, Samuel Sylvan, US, optometrist, business exec; b. Chgo, Ill, Dec 8, 1903; s. Joseph and Mary (Koss); att: Lewis Inst, Ill Inst of Tech; Northwestern U Sch of Acctnt; John Marshall Law Sch Chgo; OD, N Ill Coll of Ophthal and Otology, 1923; hon, DHL, HUC-JIR, 1956; m. Sylvia Jacobson, July 26, 1922; c: Elaine Kaplan, Caryl Sussman. Chmn, bd, Almer Coe Optical Co, Chgo, since 1955; pres, S S Hollender Inc, Chgo, since 1933; gen mgr, partner, Merryweather Optical Co, Chgo, 1936; gen merchandise mgr, The Fair, Chgo, 1930. Mem: bd govs, Opera Co, since 1941; bd dirs: JF since 1941; United J Bldg Fund, since 1946; JD since 1947, fmr treas, vice-pres, pres, Chgo; fmr: mem: bd dirs, Mt Sinai Hosp; J Vocational Service and Employment Cen, chmn, exec bd, hon chmn since 1953, 42nd biennial assembly; bd govs, HUC, Cincinnati; chmn, War Records Comm, JWB, Chgo, natl armed forces comm; bd, United Services Orgs Council of Chgo; AJComm; bd trustees, Heb Union Sch of Educ and Sacred Music; natl bd of dirs, Chgo Med Sch; bd, World Union for Progressive Judaism; pres, comty council: J Charities; Emanuel Cong, life mem, bd dirs; Fed of UAHC, all of Chgo; natl commn, combined campaign, UAHC-HUC-JIR; gen chmn, Chgo CJA, pres; mem: Mason, 32nd deg; Shriner; B'nai B'rith; hon, zeta Beta Tau; life mem, Art Inst of Chgo; clubs: Covenant, Ill, fmr pres; Bryn Mawr Country, fmr pres; Standard, Chgo, bd mgrs; Harmonie, NYC. Recipient: Man-of-Year for natl Reform Judaism, UAHC, 1955; Julius Rosenwald Memorial Award, JF, Chgo. Home: 247 E Chestnut St, Chicago, Ill. Office: 6 N Michigan Ave, Chicago, Ill.

HOLMAN, Nat, US, educator, coach; b. NYC, Oct 19, 1896; s. Louis and Mary (Goldman); BPE, Savage Sch Phys Educ, 1918; m. Ruth Jackson, Nov 2, 1945. Head basketball coach, CCNY, since 1918, prof, phys educ, since 1917; sent by US State Dept to teach basketball in: Can; Mex; Isr; Turkey; Japan; Taiwan; Korea, 1935-37. Bd dirs, US Comm for Sports in Isr; pres, Natl Collegiate Basketball Coaches Assn of Amer, 1941. Author: Scientific Basketball, 1920; Winning Basketball, 1930; Championship Basketball, 1945; Holman on Basketball, 1950. Recipient: Induction: Springfield Hall of Fame, 1961; Madison Sq Garden Hall of Fame, 1968. Hobbies: sculpture, golf. Home: 28 E 73 St, New York, NY. Office: CCNY, New York, NY.

HOLSTEIN, Lillian, US, communal leader; b. NYC, Mar 1, 1914; d. Ralph and Rose (Pickus) Solow; att Jamaica Tchr's Coll, 1930-33; Teaching Cert, Hunter Coll, 1933; m. Nathan Holstein, June 16, 1935; c: Stephen, Russell, Bruce. 1st vice-pres, B'nai B'rith Women, since 1948, natl mem chmn, since 1965, pres, Dist 3, 1955-56; youth org chmn, 1961-63; natl leadership training chmn, 1963-65; commn, natl Hillel Comm, 1963-65; vice-chmn, B'nai B'rith Natl Mem Cabinet; commn, ADL; fmr: pres: Temple Sinai Sisterhood; B'nai B'rith Women Menorah chap, W Pa Council; vice-chmn, ADL

Regional Bd; secy, Hillel Adv Bd, Pittsburgh; treas, B'nai B'rith Youth Org, W Region Bd; mem: Home for Aged, Auxilary; coll youth study comm, United J Fed; Ladies Hosp Aid Soc, all Pittsburgh. Hobbies: embroidery, needlepoint. Home: 262 N Kithridge St, Pittsburgh, Pa.

HOLTZMAN, Irving N, US, dermatologist, educator; b. NYC, Jan 19, 1909; s. David and Anna (Wilpan); MD, LI Coll of Med, 1931; m. Anna Gross, June 30, 1933; c: Neil. Pvt practice since 1938; prof, clinical dermat, NYU Bellevue Med Cen; att dermat: J Hosp Med Cen, since 1939; U Hosp, NY; Bellevue Hosp; Greenpoint Hosp; Adelphi Hosp; J Chronic Disease Hosp. Maj, US Army MC, 1942-46. Pres, Bklyn Dermat Soc, 1949-51; f: Amer Acad of Dermat; Amer Coll of Phys; treas, AJCong, Bklyn div, 1949; mem: Alumni Soc J Hosp. Home: 328 Beach 149 St, Neponset, NY. Office: 345 Schermerhorn St, Brooklyn, NY.

HOLTZMAN, Lester, US, jurist; b. NYC, June 1, 1913; s. Isidore and Rebecca (Holtzman); LLB, St John's U, 1935; m. Mae Gress, Oct 11, 1936; c: Joy, Matthew. Justice, NY State Supr Court, since 1962; pvt practice, NYC, 1936-52; mem, US House of Reprs, 1953-62; fmr partner, Holtzman, Sharf, Mackell & Hellenbrand. Fmr pres, Talmud Torah, Middle Village, LI; fmr chmn: Gtr NY Fund Campaign; TB campaign; mem: Queens Co Bar Assn; Queens Co Criminal Bar Assn; KP; Elks; club: Blackstone Lawyers. Home: 31 Merri-vale Rd, Great Neck, NY. Office: 88-11 NY. Sutphin Blvd , Jamaica,

HOLTZOFF, Alexander, US, jurist; b. Riga, Latvia, Nov 7, 1886; s. Lazarus and Mary (Holtzoff); in US since 1897; MA, Columbia U, 1909, LLB, 1911; m. Louise Cowan, June 17, 1925 (decd). US dist judge for DC, since 1945; exec asst to US Atty-Gen, 1945; spec asst, 1924-45. US Army, 1918. F, Inst of Jud Admn; mem: Amer Bar Assn, chmn, sect on jud admn, 1956-57; Wash, DC, and Fed Bar Assns; Assn Bar, NYC; Amer Legion, cdr, Justice Post, 1949; Phi Beta Kappa, Phi Delta Phi; club, Natl Press. Author: New Federal Procedure and the Courts, 1941; co-author: Federal Procedural Forms, 1941; Federal Practice and Procedure; contbr to legal jours. Recipient: Dist Civilian Medal, USN. Home: 3601 Connecticut Ave, Washington, DC. Office: Court House, Washington, DC.

HOLZMAN, Arthur D, US, attorney, journalist; b. Boston, Mass, Jan 5, 1914; s. George and Augusta (Schon); BA, Harvard Coll, 1935, LLB, 1937; m. Selma Silverman, June 27, 1935; c: Judith. Asst gen counsel, NASA, since 1961, chmn, bd contract appeals, 1961-66, mem, inventions and contribs bd, since 1966; pvt practice, Boston, 1937; fgn corresp, 1947-51: CBS; MBS; WMCA radio sta; McCraw-Hill Publs; Pathfinder Mag; Boston Daily Globe; chief, leg, research and opinions div, Off of Price Stabilization, 1952, spec asst to gen counsel, 1953; asst gen counsel, USAF, 1954-61. USN, 1942-46, cdr, USNR, since 1945. Mem: Mass, Fed, and US Supr Court Bars; clubs: Overseas Press; Fed City. Ed and narrator, documentary record: Israel is Born, 1953; actor, Paramount films documentary release, New Pioneers, 1950. Home: 4702 Dorset Ave, Chevy Chase, Md. Office: NASA, Washington, DC.

HOLZMAN, Shimshon, Isr, artist; b. Sambor, Pol, Dec 20, 1907; s. Shraga and Henena (Zuckerberg); in Isr since 1922; att Acad de la Grande Chaumiere, 1929-30. One-man shows: Galerie Belles Pages, Paris, 1935; Steimatzky Gal, Jerusalem, 1936; Marlborough Gal, London, 1947; Tel Aviv Mus, 1938, 1942, 1945, 1948; Gal Leon Marseille, Paris, 1951; Passedoit Gal, NYC, 1954; Wash Obelisk Gal, Wash, DC, 1954; Helena Rubenstein Mus, Tel Aviv, 1963; exhbs: annual, Isr Assn Painters and Sculptors, Tel Aviv; Mus Modern Art, Haifa; Biennale, Venice; Artists House, Jerusalem; Helena Rubenstein Mus, Tel Aviv; Gal Jacques, Paris; Frankfurt, Ger. Works in perm collections: Tel Aviv Mus; pvt collections in Isr, US, Eng. Recipient, prizes: Dizengoff, Tel Aviv Munic, 1936-55; Haifa Munic, 1938. Home and studio: Artists Colony, Safed, Isr.

HOLZSAGER, Theodore G, US, physician; b. NYC, Jan 28, 1903; s. Jonas and Lizzie (Meyers); BS, CCNY, 1921; MD, Cornell U, 1926; m. Toni Stein, Nov 25, 1944; c: David, Lisa Goldstein. Att ped, J Hosp, Bklyn, since 1930; ped neur, chief, convulsive disorder clinics, J Hosp, since 1935; N Shore Hosp, Manhasset, since 1960; cons ped, Cumberland Hosp, Bklyn, since 1960; asst clinical prof, ped, SUNY Med Coll, 1946-62. Cdr, USNR MC, WW II, Mem: Phi Beta Kappa; Alpha

Omega Alpha. Contributing ped ed: Ency of Med; Ency of Baby and Child Care. Home: 35 Gateway Dr, Great Neck, NY. Office: 345 Schemerhorn St, Brooklyn, NY.

HOMNICK, Yaakov I, US, rabbi; b. NYC, July 23, 1927; s. Aaron and Jennie (Glogover); BA, ordained rabbi, Yeshiva U, 1952; m. Hannah Hammer, Feb 9, 1952; c: Meir, Adina, Akiva. Exec dir, Heb Sunday Sch Soc of Phila, since 1968. Chmn, Rel div, JNF; hon pres, Mizrachi Council, Phila; vice-pres: RabCA; Rabb Alumni, Yeshiva U; mem: B'nai B'rith; Masons. Spec interest: Heb poetry. Home: 8930 Leonard St, Philadelphia, Pa. Office: 1729 Pine St, Philadelphia, Pa.

HONIG, Edwin, US, poet, educator; b. NYC, Sept 3, 1919; s. Abraham and Jane (Freundlich); BA, U Wis, 1941, MA, 1947; hon MA, Brown U, 1958; m. Charlotte Gilchrist, April 1, 1940 (decd); m. 2nd, Margo Dennes, 1963; c: Daniel, Jeremy. Chmn, Eng dept, Brown U, since 1967, prof, since 1960, on fac since 1957; libr asst, Libr of Cong, 1941-42; instr: Purdue U, 1942; NYU, 1946; Ill Inst of Tech, 1946-47; U of NM, 1947-48; lectr, Claremont Coll, 1949; f, Guggenheim Found, 1948-49, 1962-63; instr, Harvard U, 1949-52, Briggs-Copeland asst prof, Eng, 1952-57; visiting prof, Eng, U of Cal, Davis, 1964-65. US Army, 1943-46. Author: Garcia Lorca, 1944; The Moral Circus, 1955; The Gazabos, 1959; Dark Conceit; The Making of Allegory, 1959; Survivals, 1965; Spring Journal, 1968; trans, Cervantes: Interludes, 1964; plays produced: The Widow, Actors Workshop, SF; The Phantom Lady, Inst of Advanced Studies, Theatre Arts, Wash DC, Denver; Life Is A Dream, BBC radio; ed, poetry, Mexico: NM Quarterly, 1948-52; Spenser, 1968; co-ed, Major American Poets, 1962; Major Metaphysical Poets of the 17th Century, 1968; poems in anthols; contbr to gen and lit jours. Recipient: Golden Rose, NE Poetry Club, Boston, 1961; grants: Bollingen Found, 1963; Natl Inst Arts and Letters, 1966; Natl Trans Cent, 1966; RI Commn of Arts, 1967; Amy Lowell Travelling Poet grant, 1968-69. Home: 32 Fort Ave, Cranston, RI. Office: Brown U, Providence, RI.

HONIGMAN, Hinda L, US, music leader; b. Gastonia, NC, July 17, 1903; d. David and Lena (Schultz) Lebo; att Peabody Conservatory of Music, Baltimore; studied voice with pvt tchrs in NY, Charlotte, NC, and Greenville, SC; m. Maurice Honigman, June 19, 1923; c: Shirley Sarlin. Pres: NC Fed Music Clubs, 1940-44, hon pres, since 1944; Gastonia Music Club, 1935-37, hon pres, since 1950; Gatstonia Music Educ Found, since 1950; NC Fed J Women, 1938-40; Natl Fed Music Clubs, since 1967; vice-pres, Natl Music Council, since 1967; chmn, bd trustees, Found for Advancement of Music; vice-chmn, adv comm, NC Recreation Commn, since 1959; found, Gastonia Comty Concert Assn, 1937; bd dirs: US Comm to Further Amer Contemporary Music, since 1967; Amer Sym Orch League, since 1968; Brevard Music Cen, Brevard, NC, since 1967; natl adv council, Inst for Studies in Amer Music, since 1967; life mem, Hadassah; mem: Sigma Alpha Iota. Recipient: libr bldg, Hinda Honigman Libr, erected at Transylvania Music Camp, Brevard, through funds from 14 states in SE region, Natl Fed Music Clubs; Hinda Honigman Scholarship named in her honor by Natl Fed Music Clubs; citation, contrib to youth, recreation, NC Recreation Soc, 1957; spec citation of hon, Peabody Conservatory Alumni Awsn for dedicated work in field of music, 1968. Home: 1660 Westbrook Circle, Gastonia, NC.

HONIGMAN, Jason L, US, attorney; b. Russ, Oct 25, 1904; s. Louis and Sarah (Hoffman); in US since 1911; AB, JD, U Mich, 1926; m. Edith Horwitz, Mar 26, 1931; c: Daniel, Julie Levy. Sr partner, Honigman, Miller, Schwartz & Cohn; chmn, Allied Supermarkets Inc, 1961-68. Vice-pres, Mich State Bar Assn; chmn: Mich Law Rev Commn; civil procedure comm, Mich State Bar Assn; civil procedure comm, Mich Jud Conf; dir, Amer Judicature Soc; mem: Mich Jud Tenure Commn; Amer, Mich, and Detroit Bar Assns. Co-author, Michigan Court Rules Annotated, 1948, 2nd ed, 7 vols, 1964-69; contbr to legal jours. Recipient: Sesquicentennial Award, U Mich, 1967. Home: 19425 Gloucester Rd, Detroit, Mich. Office: 2290 First Natl Bank Bldg, Detroit, Mich.

HONIKMAN, Alfred H, S Afr, architect, public official; b. Cape Town, Feb 20, 1910; s. Isaac and Henrietta (Aaron); dipl, architecture, U Cape Town, 1932; m. Deena Margo, Feb 4, 1936; c: Basil, Terence. Prin, Honikman, Greshoff & Assts; reg architect, S Afr, UK, Ohio; dir, chmn of several cos; City Councillor, since 1948; mem, Provincial Council, 1952-60; mayor, Cape Town, 1961-63; JP; S Afr Army, WW II.

Chmn, bd trustees, S Afr Natl Gal; f, Royal Inst of Brit Architects. Ed, Cape Town City of Good Hope, 1966. Recipient, Medals: War; Afr Service; Queens, 1952. Spec interests: intl; race relations; urban rehab. Home: 301 Edingight, Queen Rd, Rondebosch, Cape Town, S Afr. Office: 606 Regis House, 126 Adderley St, Cape Town, S Afr.

HOOK, Sidney, US, philosopher, educator; b. NYC, Dec 20, 1902; s. Isaac and Jennie (Halpern); BS, CCNY, 1923; MA, Columbia U, 1926, PhD, 1927; hon: DHL, U of Me, 1960; LLD, U of Cal, 1965; m. Ann Zinken, May 25, 1935; c: Ernest, Susan. Prof, phil, NYU Grad Sch, since 1939, fac mem since 1927; tchr, NY pub schs, 1923-28; lectr: Columbia U, 1927-30; New Sch for Social Research, 1931-53; Guggenheim Research f, 1928-29, 1953. F: Amer Acad Arts and Sci; Amer Acad Educ; fmr: pres, E div, Amer Phil Soc, 1959; org: Cong for Cultural Freedom; Conf on Methods in Sci and Phil; NYU Inst of Phil; mem: John Dewey Soc; Intl Comm for Acad Freedom; Amer Phil Assn. Author: The Metaphysics of Pragmatism, 1927; Towards the Understanding of Karl Marx, 1933; American Philosophy—Today and Tomorrow, 1935; From Hegel to Marx, 1936; John Dewey: An Intellectual Portrait, 1939; Reason, Social Myths and Democracy, 1940; The Hero in History, 1943; Education for Modern Man, 1946; Heresy, Yes-Conspiracy, No, 1953; The Ambiguous Legacy: Marx and the Marxists, 1955; Common Sense and the Fifth Amendment, 1957; Political Power and Personal Freedom, 1959; The Quest for Being, 1961; The Paradoxes of Freedom, 1962; The Fail-Safe Fallacy, 1965; The Place of Religion in a Free Society, 1967; ed, Modern Science, 1958; Philosophy, Psychology, and Psychoanalysis, 1959; Dimensions of Mind, 1960; Religious Experience and Truth, 1961; Philosophy and History, 1963; Law and Philosophy, 1964; Art and Philosophy, 1966; Human Values and Economic Policy, 1967; Language and Philosophy, 1969; club: NY Phil. Office: NYU, Washington Sq, New York, NY.

HOOKER, Bernard, Jamaica, rabbi; b. London, Feb 4, 1922; s. Joseph and Polly (Price); in Jamaica since 1965; BA, hons, J Coll, 1944; m. Eileen Taylor, Dec 12, 1954. Rabbi, JCC, Jamaica, since 1965; min: Lib J Syn, Birmingham, 1948-42; Wembley Lib J Syn, 1962-65. Chaplain, Brit Army, 1945-46. Vice-pres, Union Lib and Progressive Syn, Gt Brit and Ir; mem, B'nai B'rith. Author: The Rabbi Speaks, 1968. Home: 1 G Manor Court, Manor Park, Kingston, Jamaica. Study: 92 Duke St, Kingston, Jamaica.

HOOS, Sidney S, US, educator, economist; b. Buffalo, NY, May 20, 1911; s. Jacob and Rose (Gerrish); AB, U Mich, 1934; AM, 1935; PhD, Stanford U, 1939; m. Ida Russakoff, June 13, 1942; c: Phyllis, Judith. Prof, agric econ, econ, bus admn, U of Cal, Berkeley, since 1950, dean acad personnel, 1963-67, on fac since 1938; econ: Cal Agric Experiment Sta, since 1950; Giannini Found, since 1950; econ stat, Works Progress Admn, Me, 1936; research f, Stanford U, 1936-38; econ, US Agric Dept, 1941-42; chief econ, US War Dept, 1942-45; US repr, comm on econ, Intl Horticultural Soc, since 1961; adv cons, Off of Experiment Stas, Agric Dept, since 1958; mem, natl adv comm, W-M 17, since 1961; cons to: Fed and other agcys; settlement dept, JA, Isr, 1960-61; Falk Project for Econ Research, Isr, 1960-61. Found mem, Syn Council of SF E-Bay, since 1955; pres, Cong Beth-El, Berkeley, Cal, 1954-57, mem, bd dirs, 1954-62; mem: B'nai B'rith; profsl and scholarly socs; club: Fac, U of Cal. Author: monographs, reports; contbr to scholarly jours. Recipient: commendation for meritorious service, US War Dept; citation of merit for contribs to marketing sci, Amer Marketing Assn. Home: 868 The Arlington, Berkeley, Cal. Office: U of Cal, Berkeley, Cal.

HORCH, Nettie S, US, museum dir; b. NYC, Nov 15, 1896; d. Elias and Shewa (Silverstein); att Hunter Coll; m. Louis Horch, Mar 8, 1917; c: Oriole Farb, Franklin. Co-found, dir: Master Inst of United Arts; Riverside Mus. Fine arts chmn, Natl Council of Women of US, 1937-50; hon, vice-pres, Natl Assn Women Artists, 1960. Recipient: Bolivarian Order of Merit, 1943; medal, Natl Assn Women Artists, 1960. Home and office: 310 Riverside Dr, New York, NY.

HORECKER, Bernard L, US, biochemist; b. Chgo, Ill, Oct 31, 1914; s. Paul and Bessie (Bornstein); BS, U Chgo, 1936, PhD, 1939; m. Frances Goldstein, July 12, 1936; c: Doris Colgate, Marilyn Neuwirth, Linda. Prof, chmn, dept molecular biol, Albert Einstein Coll of Med, since 1963; res asso, U Chgo, 1939-40; examiner, US Civil Service Comm, 1940-41; Hygiene

Lab, USPHS, 1941-47; Inst Arthritis and Metabolism Diseases, 1947-53; chief, NIH Lab, 1953-59; prof, chmn, dept microbiol, Sch Med, NYU, 1959-63. F: Amer Acad Arts and Sci; AAAS; mem: Natl Acad Sci; Phi Beta Kappa; Sigma Xi; personnel comm, Amer Cancer Soc; Amer Chem Soc; Amer Soc Biol Chems, pres, 1968-69; Amer Soc Microbiol; Japanese Biochem Soc, hon; Harvey Soc, fmr pres, 1970-71; Swiss Biochem Soc, bd dirs: Acad Press; Sci Adv Bd, Roche Inst Molecular Biol. Author: Pentose Metabolism in Bacteria, 1962; chmn ed bd, Archives Biochem, Biophysics, since 1967; ed: Archives Biochemistry, Biophysics, 1960-67; Biochemistry, Biophysics Res Comm, since 1959. Recipient: awards: enzyme chem, Paul Lewis Labs, 1952; superior accomplishment, FSA, 1952; biol sci, Wash Acad Sci, 1954; Rockefeller Public Service, 1957. Home: 340 E 64 St, New York, NY. Office: Albert Einstein Coll of Med, Bronx, NY.

HORKHEIMER, Max, Switz, educator, editor; b. Stuttgart, Ger, Feb 14, 1895; s. Moritz and Babette (Lauchheimer); PhD, U Frankfurt/M, 1922; m. Rose Riekher, Mar 26, 1926. Prof em, Inst Social Research, since 1963, prof, 1960-63; prof, social phil, dir, Inst Social Research, Frankfurt/M, 1930, 1930-34; dir: Inst Social Research, Columbia U, 1934; sci dept, AJComm, 1944-47; mem, UNESCO Conf on Social Tensions, Paris, 1948; prof, phil and sociol, Johann Wolfgang Goethe U, Frankfurt/M, 1949; reconstruction, Inst Social Research, U Frankfurt/M, 1949-50; dean, phil fac, U Frankfurt/M, 1950-51, rector, 1951-53; fgn cons, Libr of Cong, 1951; prof, sociol, U Chgo, 1954-59. Mem: Amer Phil, Sociol, and Psych Assns; other sci socs. Author: Uber Kants Kritik der Urteilskraft, 1925; Anfänge der bürgerlichen Geschictsphilosophie, 1930; Eclipse of Reason, 1947; Survey of the Social Sciences in West Germany, 1952; Zur Kritik der instrumentellen Vernunft, 1967; Kritische Theorie, 1968; co-author, Dialektik der Aufklärung, 1947; co-author, ed: Studies in Philosophy and Social Sciences, 1941; Authority and Family, 1936; ed, Studies in Prejudice, 5 vols, 1949-50; contbr to jours, mags. Recipient: hon citizen, City of Frankfurt/M, 1960. Home: 6926 Montagnola, Switz.

HORN, David, Isr, physicist; b. Haifa, Sep 10, 1937; s. Emanuel and Berta (Schachno); MS, Technion, Haifa, 1962; PhD, Heb U, Jerusalem, 1964; m. Nira Fuss, July 7, 1963; c: Yuval, Tamar. Asst prof, Tel Aviv U, since 1968, on fac since 1962. IDF, 1955-57. Contbr to profsl jours. Home: 79 Ha'universita St, Tel Aviv, Isr. Office: Tel Aviv U, Tel Aviv, Isr.

HORN, Shimon Yitzchak, Isr, business exec; b. Vienna, Aus, Aug 25, 1919; s. Elimelech and Chaya (Greenfeld); in Isr since 1937; BA, BSc, Roosevelt Coll, Chgo, 1951; MA, U Chgo, 1953; m. Alice Bugeslov, Sep 12, 1945; c: Armonit, Galia, Ud. Sr vice-pres, Isr Inves Corp, since 1961; chmn bd: Isr Tractors and Equipment; Beged Or; Isr Cen Trade & Inves; ed-in-chief, Ashmoret weekly 1946-49; econ adv, Min of Finance, 1953-57; dir gen, Govt of Isr Inves Auth, W Hemisphere, 1957-61. Home: 81 Hazorea St, Kfar Shmariah, Tel Aviv, Isr. Office: 32 Ben Yehuda St, Tel Aviv, Isr.

HORNSTEIN, George D, US, attorney, educator; b. NYC, Mar 29, 1904; s. Henry and Esther (Bloxberg); BA, CCNY, 1924; LLB, Columbia U, 1926, f, 1926-27; m. Lillian Herlands, Sep 8, 1935. Practicing atty, since 1926; Murry and Ida Becker Prof of Law, NYU Sch of Law, since 1969, prof law, grad div, 1951-69; lectr, corporate law, Heb U. Chmn: Selective Service Adv Bd, NYC, 1940-45; comm on fed leg, NY Co Lawyers Assn, 1950-57, comm on legal educ, since 1960; mem: natl panel of arbitrators, Amer Arbitration Assn; Amer Law Inst; Amer Bar Assn; Columbia Law Sch Alumni Assn; Masons, pres, masters and wardens assn, 6th Masonic dist. Author: Corporate Law and Practice, 1959; cumulative annual supplements, 1961-68; contbr to law jours. Recipient, Cong Cert of Merit, 1946. Home: 37 Washington Sq, New York, NY.

HORNSTEIN, Lillian H, US, educator; b. NYC, Mar 20, 1909; d. Jacob and Sarah (Sarason) Herlands; BS, summa cum laude, NYU, 1929, MA, 1930, PhD, 1940; m. George Hornstein, Sep 8, 1935. Prof, Eng, NYU, since 1959, fac mem since 1930; PR repr, colls, NY area, Natl Council Tchrs Eng, since 1948; spec cons, medieval lit, PMLA, since 1951. Pres: Soc for Librs, NYU, 1964-66; Eng Grad Assn, NYU, 1962-63; NY Council, Coll Tchrs Eng, 1950-51; chmn, Middle Eng Group, MLA, 1953-54, 1965-66; mem: Medieval Acad of Amer; Renaissance Soc of Amer; MLA; Natl Council Tchrs of Eng; Alpha Epsilon Phi; Eclectic; Sigma Delta Omicron; Tau Kappa Alpha; Phi Beta Kappa, secy, Beta chap, NY,

1940-43; club: Medieval, NY, pres, 1962-63. Author: Reader's Companion to World Literature, 1956; contbr ed, revised ed, Wells manual; current ed, Eng Grad Assn Newsletter, 1944-62; ed adv, Coll Eng, on world lit, 1956-59; contbr to educ jours. Recipient: Cong Cert of Merit, 1945. Home: 37 Washington Sq W, New York, NY. Office: NYU, Washington Sq, New York, NY.

HORNSTEIN, Moses, US, business exec; b. Bklyn, NY, Jan 19, 1907; s. Hyman and Helen (Taffel); hon DSc, Hofstra U; m. Gertrude Schectman, Aug 12, 1908; c: Lawrence, Judith Goldman. Pres, Horn Construction Co Inc, since 1945; mgr, Charles F Vachris, 1934-45; dir: Natl Bank of N Amer; Meadow Brook Natl Bank, since 1945. Pres: Heb Acad of Nassau Co; Gen Contractors Assn, NYC; vice-pres, Merrick Rep Club Comm; trustee, Hofstra U, since 1958; delg, NY State Constitutional Conv, 1967; mem: Sunrise Lodge, Freeport; The Moles, NYC; Munic Engrs, NYC; JTSA, Nassau and Suffolk Patron's Soc; bd ethics, Town of Hempstead; citizens adv comm for vocational educ, Cen High Sch Dist 3. Home: 207 N Hewlett Ave, Merrick, Long Island, NY. Office: 2174 Hewlett Ave, Merrick, Long Island, NY.

HOROVITZ, Oscar H, US, business exec; b. Chelsea, Mass, Dec 7, 1899; s. Israel and Bessie (Binsky); BS, MIT, Mass, 1922; m. Mary Freedman, Feb 21, 1926; c: Barbara Veaner, Isobel Kane. Pres: Lee Crane Service Inc; Lee Equipment Corp, both since 1952; pres, chief engr, Oscar H Horovitz steel erectors, 1926-50. US Army, 1918. Exec vice-pres, Amer chap, Inst Amateur Cinematographers; dir, Boston chap, Amer Technion Soc; life trustee, Temple Emanuel, Newton, Mass; fmr vice-pres, trustee, Alerton Hosp, Brookline, Mass; mem: Amer Soc Civil Engrs; alumni council, MIT; Photographic Soc of Amer; clubs: New Cent; MIT Boston Stein, fmr pres, mem, council of pres. Contbr articles on amateur movie making to photographic mags. Recipient: awards in natl and intl movie competitions in: US; Eng; Scotland; Port; S Afr; Austr; Japan. Five-Star Rating in motion picture div, Photographic Soc of Amer. Home: 31 Montrose St, Newton, Mass. Office: 33 Island St, Boston, Mass.

HOROVITZ, Samuel B, US, attorney, author, lecturer; b. Chelsea, Mass, Nov 23, 1897; s. Israel and Bessie (Binsky); BA, Harvard U, 1919, LLB, 1922; m. Sarah Levy, Aug 7, 1922 (decd); m. 2nd, Evelyn McCarthy, Nov 1, 1942; c: Paul, David. Sr partner, Horovitz, Petkun, Rothschild, Locke & Kistin; in pvt practice, Boston, since 1932; workmen's compensation atty, Mass Fed of Lab, since 1932; chief, workmen's compensation dept, Boston Legal Aid Soc, 1922-32; workmen's compensation atty, to Pres, AFL, Wash, DC, 1946-48; repr, Natl Assn Claimants' Compensation Attys Bar Assn, lectr, workmen's compensation, to law schs, bar assns, lay groups around the world, 1961-62. Vice-pres: Temple B'nai Moshe, Brighton, Mass; Roscoe Pound, Natl Assn Claimants' Compensation Attys Found; mem: Mass and US Supr Courts Bars; Amer, Mass, Boston Bar Assns; bd govs, Natl Assn Claimants' Compensation Attys Bar Assn; Phi Beta Kappa; bd mem: AJComm; clubs: New Cent; Charles River Yacht; Suburban; Sidney Hill; Brandeis U. Author: Practice and Procedure Under Massachusetts Workmen's Compensation Law, 1930; Horovitz on Workmen's Compensation, 1944; Current Trends in Workmen's Compensation, 1947; contbr to profsl jours. Hobbies: motion pictures, travel. Home: 16 Shuman Circle, Newton, Mass. Office: 6 Beacon St, Boston, Mass.

HOROWITZ, Aron, US, rabbi, educator; b. Safad, Isr, July 2, 1911; s. Isaiah and Ziporah (Lorberbaum); in US since 1926; att: Yeshivot in Safed and Jerusalem; Rabbi Isaac Elchanan Theological Sem; NYU; ordained rabbi, 1933; MA equivalent, Dept of Educ, Tel Aviv, 1951; m. Rachel Pilpel, Dec 8, 1935; c: Gad, Yigal, Asher. Dean, admnr, Herzliah Heb Tchrs Inst; prin, Histadruth Sem, Jerusalem, 1933-36; asst admnn secy, Heb U, Jerusalem, 1936-38; sup, Heb schs, W Can, 1939-42; natl dir, Can Assn for Heb Educ and Culture, 1946-49, 1955-64; dir, fgn studies dept, Katznelson Inst for Higher Learning, 1949-51; prin, HS for Excelling Students, Tel Aviv, 1951-52; i/c Heb curriculum, lectr, Bible and Modern Heb Lit, Sir George Williams U, 1961-64; exec dir, sch prin, concourse Centre, Bx, NY. Found, dir: 1st Judean Camp, W Can; Massad Camp, Can; Natl Youth Leadership Inst; pres, Anglo Amer J Assn, Isr, 1933-37; asst hon secy, Grand Lodge, B'nai B'rith, Isr, 1933-35; mem: Natl Bd of License, AAJE; comm, Heb Tchrs Colls; Natl Comm, for Jerusalem Examination of Heb U; Natl Council for J Educ. Author: Zionism

A Way of Life, 1942; contbr articles in Heb, Eng, Yiddish to newspapers, publs. Office: 314 W 91 St, New York, NY.

HOROWITZ, Ben, US, organization exec; b. NYC, Mar 19, 1914; s. Saul and Sonia (Meringoff); BA, Bklyn Coll, 1939; LLB, St Lawrence U Law Sch, 1935; att New Sch for Social Research, 1940; m. Beverly Lichtman, Feb 16, 1952; c: Zachary, Jody. Exec dir, City of Hope, since 1953, natl secy, 1948-53, E Coast dir, 1945-48; dir, council of orgs, NY FJP, 1940-45. Home: 221 Conway Ave, Los Angeles, Cal. Office: 208 W 8 St, Los Angeles, Cal.

HOROWITZ, C Morris, US, statistician; b. Bklyn, NY, Jan 28, 1915; s. Max and Fannie (Brieman); BA, Bklyn Coll, 1944; MA, grad fac, New Sch for Social Research, 1955; m. Helen Applbaum, Aug 5, 1945; c: Avery, Jay, Yafa. Asst prof, dept of bus, Queensborough Comty Coll, since 1965, instr, 1962-65; lectr, dept econ, Bklyn Coll, since 1946; stat, Amer Assn for J Educ, 1947-54; cons stat, J Educ Comm, NY, 1954-60; lectr, dept econ and sociol, LIU, 1959; dir, demographic survey comm, FJP, 1958-59; dir, survey, J population, NY area, 1958. Pres, Hapoel Hamizrachi of Flatbush Inc, since 1959; mem: Amer Econ Assn; Amer Sociol Assn: AAAS; Amer Acad for Political and Social Sci; Orthodox J Scis; Assn for J Demography and Stat; Acad of Political Sci. Author: Basic Statistics As Applied to the Social Sciences and Business, 1966; co-author, The Jewish Population of New York Area, 1900-1975, pub 1959; contbr to sci jours and J periodicals. Hobby: photography. Home: 1577 E 18 St, Brooklyn, NY. Office: Queensborough Comty Coll, Bayside, NY.

HOROWITZ, Charles, US, attorney; b. Bklyn, NY, Jan 5, 1905; s. Harry and Fanny (Mirkin); BA, magna cum laude, U Wash, 1925, LLB, summa cum laude, Law Sch, 1927; BJ, first class hons, Oxford U, Eng, MA, 1952; m. Diana Glickman, Mar 23, 1930; c: Caroline Miller, Elinor Gordy. Pvt practice since 1927; partner, Preston, Thorgrimson, Horowitz, Starlin and Ellis, since 1933; mem, bd dirs: Kiro Inc, since 1950; Seattle Trust and Savings Bank, since 1960; mem, Uniform Law Comm, State of Wash, since 1960. US Coast Guard Temp Res, WWII. Chmn, Temple de Hirsch Educ Found, since 1960, fmr pres, Temple de Hirsch; mem: Phi Beta Kappa; Order of the Coif; Amer Law Inst; B'nai B'rith; fmr mem or comm mem: Seattle Bar Assn, fmr pres; NW Memorial Hosp, fmr chmn bd; Traveler's Aid Soc; Caroline Kline Galland Home for the Aged; Friends Seattle Public Libr; Amer Assn for UN. Contbr to legal jours. Recipient: Rhodes Scholarship, 1927-29. Home: 3923 NE 38 St, Seattle, Wash. Office: Northern Life Tower, Seattle, Wash.

HOROWITZ, David, Isr, economist, banker; b. Drohobicz, Pol, Feb 1899; s. Sigmund and Fanny; in Isr since 1920; Dr HC, Heb U, Jerusalem, 1967; m. Riva Bobkoff, 1922; c: Dan. Gov, Bank of Isr, since 1954; Gov for Isr, World Bank, Intl Devl Assn and Intl Finance Corp; mem exec comm, Histadrut, 1923; free lance journalist, lectr, 1927-32; econ adv, secy, Amer Econ Comm for Pal, 1932-35; dir econ dept, JA, 1935-48; liaison off, UN Spec comm on Pal, 1946; mem, delg, UN Gen Assembly, Lake Success, NY, 1947; head: delg to UN Econ Survey Comm, 1948; Isr delg in London: financial talks between Isr and Gt Brit on Sterling releases, negotiations on econ and financial affairs in connection with termination of the Mandate, 1950; dir gen, Isr Min of Finance, 1948-52. Hon pres, Inst per le Relazione Intl, Rome; chmn, bd dirs, Kaplan Sch of Econ and Social Scis, since 1953; mem: State Council for Higher Educ; bd govs, Heb U, Jerusalem; exec council, Weizmann Inst of Sci; council, Soc for Intl Devl, repr of Asia; bd trustees, Truman Cen for Advancement of Peace. Author: Aspects of Economic Policy in Palestine, 1936; Jewish Colonization in Palestine, 1937; Economic Survey of Palestine, 1938; Palestine Jewry's Economic War Effort, 1942; Post-War Reconstruction, 1942; Prediction and Reality in Palestine, 1945; haKimum uBeayotav baOlam uveEretz Israel, 1946; haKalkala haEretz Israelit beHitpat'huta, 1948; State in the Making, 1953; Kalkalat Israel, 1954; Tzel haEtmol veEtgar haMahar, 1962; Anatomie unserer Zeit, 1964; Mivneh uMagama beKhalkalat Israel, 1964; Hemispheres North and South, 1966; The Economics of Israel, 1967; Horowitz Plan for the Financing of Underdeveloped Nations. Recipient: Isr Prize for Social Scis, 1968. Home: 4 Halamed Heh St, Jerusalem, Isr. Office: Bank of Isr, Jerusalem, Isr.

HOROWITZ, David, US, journalist, editor, author; b. Malmö, Swed, Apr 9, 1903; s. Aaron and Bertha (Chasan); in US since 1914; m. Nan Raili, Oct, 1952. UN corresp, since 1946; US,

UN corresp, Hayom daily, Tel Aviv; ed: United Isr Bull, since 1944; World-Union Press; corresp, WZC, Jerusalem, 1951; lectr, sci, Bible, Isr and UN, J Cen Lectr Bur. Fmr: pres: Fgn Press Assn, chmn, 50th Anniversary Comm; United Isr World Union; found: UN Corresp Circle; Galileans, Wilkes-Barre, Pa, secy, Wilkes-Barre dist, ZOA; Amer f, Intl Acad. Author: Thirty Three Candles, 1949; An Answer to Tom Paine's Age of Reason, 1950-51; column, Behind the Scenes at the UN, appears in US, fgn Anglo-J periodicals. Recipient: citation, Sigma Delta Chi; Deadline Club, NY. Home: 231 E 76 St, New York, NY. Offices: 507 Fifth Ave, New York, NY; Press Sect, UN, New York, NY.

HOROWITZ, Edward, Isr, rabbi, educator; b. NYC, June 1, 1904; s. Samuel and Bertha (Ehrenfeld); in Isr since 1967; BCS, BS, NYU, 1924; MA, Columbia U, 1927; ordained rabbi, MHL, DRE, all JTSA, 1946; m. Silvia Solomon, Oct 10, 1936; c: Tamar Kagan, Carmi, Hadasa Lewis, Jonathan. Lectr, Isr radio; weekly columnist, Jerusalem Post; instr, dept Heb, Thomas Jefferson HS, 1934-62; rabbi, B'nai Isr, Woodhaven, NY, 1930-33. Pres, Amer Assn Tchrs of Heb, since 1959; mem: J Tchrs Assn; ZOA; RA. Author: Sippurim Kalim, 1942; How the Hebrew Language Grew, 1960; Sippurim laTalmid; co-ed, Horowitz-Margareten Family Directory, 1954. Home: 19 Keren Hayesod St, Jerusalem, Isr.

HOROWITZ, Edward J, US, attorney; b. Milw, Wis, Feb 13, 1942; s. Aaron and Sue (Cohen); AB, UCLA, 1936; JD, Harvard Law Sch, 1966; m. Ellen Ansel, Nov 10, 1968. Partner, Goldhammer & Horowitz, since 1969; prof, law, San Fernando Valley Coll, since 1967; dep atty-gen, Cal Dept of Justice, 1966-69. Prin contribs: won two important law cases in US Supr Court regarding Mexican Americans: Cuevas va Cal; Torres va Cal. Mem: LA Co Bar Assn; Big Brothers of Gtr LA; Pi Sigma Alpha; Phi Beta Kappa. Spec interest, legal aid to the impoverished. Home: 4081 Mandeville Canyon Rd, Los Angeles, Cal. Office: 6363 Wilshire Blvd, Los Angeles, Cal.

HOROWITZ, Hannah M, US, communal worker; b. Pol, Aug 1, 1898: d. Hyman and Mollie (Lampert) Malovany; in US since 1903; att Montclair State Coll, Montclair, NJ, 1916-18; m. Oct 10, 1920; c: Zilla Sussman, Sonia Rubenstein, Judith Meltzer. Natl membership chmn, Natl Women's League, United Syn, recording secy, 1951-54, leadership instr, 1950, mem speaker's bur, pres, NJ br, 1942-45; pres, Sisterhood J League, Caldwell, NJ, 1940; chmn, women's div, UJA, Caldwell, 1943-44; mem: bd dirs, J Educ Assn, Essex Co, 1937-41; Hadassah; B'nai B'rith; ORT; Histadrut; tchr, Newark public schs, 1918-23. Asso ed, Outlook, mag, Natl Women's League, United Syn. Spec interest: conducting groups on Judaism. Home: 2 Ella Rd, Caldwell, NJ.

HOROWITZ, Itzchak Ish, Isr, civil engr; b. Moldovita, Aug 17, 1928; s. Zvi and Fani; in Isr since 1947; BSc, Heb Inst Tech, 1952; CE, 1953; Dipl, Conservatoire Natl Des Arts Et Metiers, Paris, 1955; MSc, Heb Inst Tech, 1966; m. Hana Kleiman, 1956; c: Raanan, Tal, Amnon. Dir, domestic marketing, Tahal Cons Engrs Ltd, since 1968. Served IAF. Dir bd, Engrs and Architects Assn, Isr; exec comm, Histadrut; mem: ASCE; ASPE; AFIP; MSICF. Contbr to profsljours. Home: 7 Kehilat Sofia, Tel Aviv, Isr. Office: 54 Ibn Gvirol, Tel Aviv, Isr.

HOROWITZ, Jacob, Isr, journalist, author; b. Kalush, Aus-Hung, Feb 1, 1901; s. Joshua and Hannah (Mülhstein); desc of Rabbi Halevy Ish Horowitz family; PhD, U Vienna, 1924; m. Ethel Stern, 1941; c: from 1st m, Vardanah Cogan. Free-lance writer, since 1923; agric worker, tchr, watchman, Pal, 1919-23; mem, Heb Theatre Co, 1924-25; secy, Art Theater, Tel Aviv, 1925-27; co-ed, Ketubim, Turim, weeklies, 1927-34; exec, Pal Gen Ins Co, 1934-43; cultural attaché, Isr Emb. Stockholm, Swed, 1958-59; lit ed, Ha'aretz, daily, 1943-66. Mem, bd dirs, Natl Council Culture and Art in Isr; found Milo, Isr Authors and Artists Club, chmn since 1953; fmr: chmn, Isr Journalists Assn; vice-chmn, Isr Authors Assn. Author: Until Crushed, 1925; Song of Vengeance, 1928; Light Sown, 1929; Gates of Contamination, 1930; Eshen the Executioner Transmuted, 1932; My White Kittens, 1939; World Not Yet Destroyed, 1950; But Men Are Not False, 1956; A Splendid Family Party, 1966; The Tables Were Weary, 1966; You May Even Dream, 1966; Three Forms of Death, 1966; contbr plays; short stories; articles; trans, adaptions of plays for Heb theatres. Recipient: Lit prize, Munic of Ramat Gan; Fichman Award, 1968. Home: 51 Yitzak Sadeh St, Tel Aviv, Isr.

HOROWITZ, Miriam B, US, business exec; b. New Haven, Conn, Apr 7, 1912; d. Hyman and Esther (Hirschberg) Botwinik; BA, Smith Coll, 1933; m. William Horowitz, June 25, 1933; c: Judith Katz, Daniel. Dir gen, Bank and Trust Co, since 1955; treas, City of New Haven, 1954-58. Case chmn and mem, bd, J Family Service, 1953; secy, Women's Assembly, 1935-37; secy, publicity chmn, Hadassah, 1948-51; mem, bd, B'nai Jacob Syn, 1948-50; finance comm, and bd, Dixwell Negro Comty House; bd dirs: Winthrop Trust Co; Comty Relations Council; distribution comm, New Haven Found, chmn, 1965; mem, Smith Coll Alumni Assn; club, Woodbridge Country. Home: 100 York St, New Haven, Conn. Office: General Bank and Trust Co, New Haven, Conn.

HOROWITZ, Samuel, US, rabbi; b. Aus, July 5, 1900; s. Harry and Sarah (Scharf); AB, U Rochester, 1923; ordained rabbi, MHL, JIR, 1931; att U Wash Grad Sch of Social Work and Social Research and Criminology, 1949-52; hon DD, HUC-JIR, 1962; m. Minna Cowan, June 8, 1929; c: Jonathan, Judith Kine. Rabbi: Temple Beth Aaron, since 1954; Temple Beth-El, Sunbury, 1931-35; Cong Keneseth Isr, Green Bay, 1935-38; Temple B'nai Jeshurun, Leavenworth, 1938-42; asso prof, Heb, U Wash Ext, 1948-51; visiting lectr, U Mont Sch of Rel, 1965-69. Chaplain, US Army, 1942-46. Mem: CCAR; Assn Reform Rabbis; ZOA; B'nai B'rith; ARC; Mayor's Comm on Hum Relations; Mayor's Adv Comm on Youth; clubs: Town and Gown; Gen Semantics. Contbr to rel jours. Recipient, USO award, 1946; 25-year chaplaincy award, JWB, 1967. Home: Bilg Res, 2116 Silver Sage Trail, Billings, Mont. Study: 1148 N Broadway, Billings, Mont.

HOROWITZ, Saul, US, business exec; b. NYC, May 27, 1897; s. Meyer and Minnie (Simon); BA, CCNY, 1917; grad studies, NYU, 1918; m. Miriam Ravitch, Dec 12, 1922; c: Saul, Alan. Chmn bd, HRH Construction Corp, since 1965, pres, 1925-65; constructed: apt houses: Beresford; San Remo; 993 Fifth Ave; 820 Park Ave; hosps: J Memorial; Daughters of Jacob; US Marine, Stapleton, SI; E Orange Vets; Charles H Silver Clinic; Beth Isr; Willowsbrook State; U Hosp; public bldgs: Family Court Bldg, Domestic Relations Court; Supr Court, Bklyn; Criminal Court and Prison; schs: Lafayette High; Mark Twain Jr High; admn bldg, Iona Coll, New Rochelle, NY; communal bldgs, erected without charge: Milton Steinberg House, 1954; The Whitney Mus Amer Art; libr, New Sch for Social Research; directed construction, Albert Einstein Coll Med, 1954-55, libr and auditorium, 1957-58; spec cons, Hadassah Med Cen, Jerusalem. Chmn: FJP, NY, 1952-53; builders div, United Hosp Fund; bldg and construction ind, Natl Found for Infantile Paralysis, 1955; bldg ind, NYC Cancer Comm, 1953-54; construction comm, Girl Scout Council, Gtr NY, Inc, 1956; bldg comm, Asso YM-YWHA's, Gtr NY, 1958; a found, Albert Einstein Coll Med; trustee, Park Ave Syn; mem: natl council, JDC, natl adv council, AJComm, 1958; neighborhood regional planning bd, Comty Council, Gtr NY, 1958; Sigma Alpha Mu; club, Beach Point, Mamaroneck, NY. Recipient: citation, Albert Einstein Coll Med, 1955; alumni service medal, CCNY, 1957; J Comty Cen Man of Year, Natl JWB, 1959; Sigma Alpha Mu Merit Award, 1960; f, Brandeis U, 1961. Home: 35 E 76 St, New York, NY. Office: 515 Madison Ave, New York, NY.

HOROWITZ, William, US, industrialist, banker; b. Kan City, Mo, May 6, 1907; s. Louis and Esther (Peabody); BA, Yale U, 1929; Cowles F in Govt, 1930; m. Miriam Botwinik, June 25, 1933; c: Judith Katz, Daniel. Pres, Gen Bank and Trust Co, since 1950; vice-pres: Botwinik Bros, since 1940, with firm since 1931; Radio Sta WELI, New Haven, since 1953; dir and vice-pres, Baker Inds, 1954-66; dir: Young Spring and Wire, 1957-63; Winthrop Bank Trust, since 1959. Pres: Aleph Zadik Aleph, Kan City, 1923, natl vice-pres, 1924; Purchasing Agts Assn, Conn, 1945; Jr Achievement, New Haven; The Botwinik Found, since 1958; B'nai Jacob Syn, 1946-47; found pres, Friends Yale Hillel Found, 1952-57; chmn: soc planning comm, JCC, 1952-54; distribution comm, New Haven Found, 1958; bd educ, State of Conn, 1959; trustee: Yale U, since 1965; Peabody Mus, New Haven; treas: J Cen, 1935; Dem Party, 1949-66; dir, Educ TV, since 1961; alternate delg, Dem Natl Conv, 1956, 1960; mem: Bd Educ, State of Conn, since 1955; White House Con for Children and Youth, 1960; clubs: Harmonie; Comty, pres, 1932; Yale; Woodbridge Country. Recipient, Awards: B'nai B'rith Comty Service, New Haven Horeb Lodge, 1953; Shem Tov, B'nai Jacob Syn; Sam Beber dist alumnus, Aleph Zadik Aleph, B'nai B'rith, 1962; Conn Educ Assn; B'nai

B'rith Americanism; f, Branford Coll, Yale, 1964. Home: 100 York St, New Haven, Conn. Office: 155 Church St, New Haven, Conn.

HORVITZ, Leo, US, chemist, geochemist; b. Central Falls, RI, Aug 12, 1909; s. Samuel and Pearl (Horvitz); BS, Brown U, 1931, MS, 1932; PhD, U Chgo, 1935; m. Sara Deluty, June 2, 1936; c: Philip, Sigmund, Ira. Cons chem, petroleum geochem, Horvitz Research Labs, since 1943; research chem, Femker Co, 1936-37; chief research chem and chief geochem, Subterrex, 1937-41; group leader, Natl Defense Comm, 1942-43. Mem: Amer Chem Soc; Amer Assn for Petroleum Geologists; Soc of Exploration Geophysicists; Amer Inst Mining and Metallurgical Engrs; AAAS. Home: 5207 S Braeswood Blvd, Houston, Tex. Office: 8116 Westglen Dr, Houston, Tex.

HORWICH, Arthur N, US, business exec; b. Chgo, Ill, Nov 28, 1887; s. Bernard and May (Anixter); m. Lee Sachs, May 25, 1913; c: Leonard, Jane Sherr. Chmn, bd, Gen Felt Ind. Dir: J Fed, Chgo; Temple Isaiah Isr; hon, Orthodox J Home for the Aged; asso dir, Brandeis U; fmr, dir, chmn, spec gifts div, CJA, Gtr Chgo Comm, Isr Bond Dr, both for 1960; clubs: Standard; Bryn Mawr Country; Tamarisk Country; Hillcrest Country. Home: 1000 Lake Shore Plaza, Chicago, Ill. Office: 2301 S Paulina St, Chicago, Ill.

HORWICH, Frances R, US, educator, author, TV artist; b. Ottawa, O, July 16, 1908; d. Samuel and Rosa (Gratz) Rappaport; PhB, U Chgo, 1929; MA, Columbia U, 1933; PhD, Northwestern U, 1942; hon DPedg, Bowling Green State U, O, 1954; m. Harvey Horwich, June 11, 1931. Cons, Curtis Pub Co, since 1965, dir, children's activities, 1962-63; educ dir, 1964; lectr, since 1941; writer, produc, Miss Frances-Ding Dong Sch, TV Nursery of the Air, NBC-TV, 1952-56, WGN-TV, Chgo, 1957-59, natl syndication, 1959-65; fmr: supr, Works Progress Admn Nursery Schs, Chgo; dir, jr kindergarten, Skokie Sch, Winnetka, Ill; dean, educ, Pestalozzi Froebel Tchrs Coll, Chgo; counsellor, student tchrs, Chgo Tchrs Coll; staff lectr, Chgo Public Libr; dir, Hessian Hills Sch, Croton-on-Hudson, NY; visiting prof, educ, U of NC; prof, chmn, dept educ, Roosevelt U, Chgo; cons, FSA, Puerto Rico; asso ed, Sci Research Assos; co-writer and produc, Parents Time TV prog, NBC, supr children's progs, radio prog, Parents' Time With Dr Frances Horwich; writer, produc: Time for Children With Miss Frances; Time for Parents With Miss Frances, TV progs; dir, children's programming, WFLD-TV, Chgo; mem, childcraft ed adv bd, educ cons, Field Enterprises Educ Corp, Chgo; mem, ed adv bd, Ranger Rick's Nature Mag, Natl Wildlife Fed, Wash, DC; mem, panel of judges: Koppers Design Competition for Plastic Toys, Pittsburgh, Pa; Pub Ind Maggie Awards, Chgo; mem, city-wide Head Start adv comm, Chgo; cons, Midwest prog on airborn TV instrn, Purdue U, Ind. Author: Miss Frances' Ding Dong School Book, 1953; Ding Dong School Books, 1953, 1954, 1955, 1956; Miss Frances' All-Day-Long Book, 1954; Have Fun With Your Children, 1954; Miss Frances' Story Book of Manners for the Very Young, 1955; Miss Frances' Story Book of Pets for the Very Young, 1956; The Magic of Bringing Up Your Child, 1959; Safety on Wheels, 1960; Stories and Poems to Enjoy, 1962; From Miss Frances' Desk, 1964; contbr: articles, cartoons, caricatures to mags. Dir: Chgo Unlimited; Girl Scouts, Chgo; Women's Advt Club, Chgo; mem: Natl Assn for Educ of Young Children, fmr pres; Assn for Nursery Educ; Broadcast Pioneers; Delta Kappa Gamma; Intl Platform Assn; NEA; Theta Sigma Phi; Acad TV Arts and Scis; Amer Assn for Gifted Children; Amer Fed TV and Radio Artists; Amer Women in Radio and TV; Assn for Childhood Educ; Assn for Childhood Educ Intl; Authors League Amer; Intl Reading Assn; Natl Assn for Mh; Natl Assn for Nursery Educ; Natl Assn Educ Broadcasters; Natl Council Women of US; Natl Soc for Study of Educ; US Natl Commn for Childhood Educ. Recipient: awards, citations, TV, mags, orgs; included in 1953 Woman of the Year in Educ; Peabody TV Award; Sylvania TV Award; Alumni Medal, U Chgo. Hobbies: travel, ceramics, knitting, cooking, baking. Home: 400 E Randolph St, Chicago, Ill.

HORWICH, Samuel Bernard, Isr, pediatrician; b. Toronto, Can, Apr 4, 1902; s. Ben-Zion and Rachel (Soloway); in Isr since 1962; BA, U Toronto, 1923, MD, 1926, postgrad studies in ped; m. Rivka Bronstein, June 20, 1926; c: Ethel Shaffer, Martin. Practicing ped. Vice-pres, Isr Res Distribution Comm, UIA, Can; UJRA, Can; charter mem, JNF, Can; fmr: pres: Bur of J Educ, Toronto; LZOA, Can; Histadrut

Campaign, Can; natl secy, Can J Cong. Spec interests: Zionism; J educ. Home: 49 Rambam St, Jerusalem, Isr.

HORWITZ, Edel J, S Afr, attorney; b. Lith, Aug 17, 1902; s. Moshe and Zipporah (Salaman); in S Afr since 1910; att U Cape Town, 1922-25; m. Anne Singer, May 31, 1928; c: Dennis, Joan Joffe. Partner, Singer, Horwitz & Co. S Afr Army, WWII. Vice-pres: S Afr ZF; S Afr J bd deps, both since 1967; chmn: S Afr ZF, 1959-67; S Afr J bd deps, 1951-55, pres, 1958-67. Home: 11 Waterfall Rd, Westcliff, Johannesburg, S Afr. Office: PO Box 341, Johannesburg, S Afr.

HORWITZ, Jacia C, Can, attorney; b. Ottawa, Ont, May 13, 1914; s, Max and Rebecca (Rodkin); BA, Queen's U, 1936; Barrister-at-Law, Osgoode Hall, 1939; m. Jeanne Rich, Nov 26, 1939; c: Rebecca, Dale, Mervyn. Pvt practice since 1939; partner, Horwitz and Simser; appd QC, 1950. Found perm pres, Hillel Found, Queen's U; fmr pres: Dist Grand Lodge 22, B'nai B'rith; Ottawa J Home for the Aged; Progressive Conservative Org, Carleton; Young Judea, Ottawa, 1931-32; Beth Isr Student Group, Queen's U, 1934-35; Pi Lambda Phi Kappa chap, U Toronto, 1938-39; Ottawa Zionist Soc, 1948-50; Ottawa Lodge, B'nai B'rith Conf, 1950-51; found co-chmn, NCCJ, Ottawa; vice-pres, Ottawa JCC; found: parliament and confd lodges, B'nai B'rith; Camp B'nai B'rith, Ottawa, 1945; repr Intl B'nai B'rith; mem, exec comm, ZC, Can; club, Rideau View Golf and Country. Home: 388 Island Park Dr, Ottawa, Ont, Can. Office: 1 Nicholas St, Ottawa, Ont, Can,

HORWITZ, Joseph Baxst, US, business exec; b. Russ, Dec 14, 1899; in US since 1901; m. Olyn Shaw, May 4, 1930; c: Judith. Mgmt cons since 1965; chmn, bd, treas, Kaiser-Nelson Corp, 1930. Prin contrib, devl reclaiming process ferrous from open hearth slag in steel mill oprs. Life trustee: Menorah Park, J Home for Aged; Fairmont Temple; clerk, Rotary, all Cleveland. Spec interests: J ceremonial and folk art; Judaica; lectr; writer. Home: 19424 Vanaken, Cleveland, O. Office: 22035 Chagrin Blvd, Cleveland, O.

HORWITZ, Julius, US, author; b. Cleveland, O, Aug 18, 1920; s. Samuel and Jennie (Chazin); att: O State U, 1940-42; Columbia U, 1946-48; BA, New Sch for Social Research, 1953; m. Lois Sandler, June 1, 1947; c: Jonathan, David. Author since 1949; cons: on social wfr problems to Majority Leader, NY State Sen; on problems of public health and Medicaid, NY State J Leg Comm; NYC Dept of Social Services. US Army, 1942-45. Secy, New Sch for Social Research Alumni Assn, 1958-69. Author: The City, 1953; The Inhabitants, 1960; Can I Get There by Candlelight, 1964; The WASP, 1967; contbr: New Light on Juvenile Delinquency, 1967; Patterns of Power: Social Foundations of Education, 1968; Readings in American Government, 1968; short stories to: Commentary Mag; Look Mag; Midstream Mag; J Frontier; articles to: NY Times Sunday Mag; The Reader's Digest. Recipient, Guggenheim f for creative writing, 1954, 1965. Home: 10 Stuyvesant Ave, Larchmont, NY.

HORWITZ, Louis David, Switz, social work exec; b. Cleveland, O, Nov 29, 1908; s. Max and Eva (Abrams); in Switz since 1967; BA, W Reserve U, Cleveland, O, 1931; att NY Sch of Social Work, NYC, 1932-42; m. Sylvia Laibman, June 3, 1934; c: Paul. Dir gen, JDC, since 1967; caseworker, sup, NY State, 1931-45; country dir: JDC, It, 1945-50; Tunisia, 1950-53; dir emigration dept, JDC, 1953-54; dir, Eur and N Afr, United HIAS Service 1954-57; country dir, Isr, JDC, 1957-63; dir, dept Overseas Studies-Services, CJFWF, 1963-65; cons on absorption, United Isr Appeal Inc, 1965-67. Vice-pres, Eur chap, Natl Assn of Voluntary Workers; chmn, Ref Commn, Intl Council of Voluntary Agcys; trustee, Paul Baerwald Sch of Social Work, Heb U; planning comm, Intl Conf of J Communal Service; mem: Natl Council of J Communal Work; Natl Conf of Soc Work. Author, papers: on J in Tunisia, 1953; on World Ref Situation, 1961; Care of the Aged in Isr, 1964. Home: 47 Route de Florissant, Geneva, Switz. Office: JDC, 75 rue de Lyon, Geneva, Switz.

HORWITZ, Moris I, US, radiologist; b. Chgo, Ill, May 28, 1914; s. Sol and Rose (Rice). BS, U of Ill, 1936, MD, 1938; m. Naomi Leno, Mar 2, 1952; c: Richard, Paul. Radiologist: W Valley Comty Hosp, since 1955; Mt Sinai Hosp, since 1946; Temple Hosp; cons radiologist: Cedars of Leb Hosp, LA, 1943-48; Centinella Valley Hosp, Inglewood, 1946-60; radiologist, Shelton Clinic, LA, 1946-48; att radiologist, LA Co Hosp, 1944-58. Chmn, tumor bd, W Valley Comty Hosp, since 1957; pres, LA Radiological Soc, 1948; bd dirs, LA TB

Health Assn, 1948-50; f, Amer Coll Radiology; mem: Soc Nuclear Med; Pan Amer Radiological Soc; AMA; Cal and LA Med Assns; Amer Bd Radiology; Radiological Soc of NA; Pacific Roentgen Soc; Radiological Soc of S Cal; LA Radiological Soc; clubs: Phi Delta Epsilon; Grad of LA; Ded Rey Yacht. Contbr to profsl jours. Hobbies: yachting, woodworking, photography, archery, music. Office: 5333 Balboa Blvd, Encino, Cal.

HORWITZ, Samuel, US, dental surg; b. Phila, Pa, Aug 28, 1895; s. Abraham and Anna (Goldes); DDS, U of Pa, 1919; m. Charlotte Lessy, Apr 20, 1911; c: Miles, Claire Kasser. Pvt practice since 1919. Capt, US Army MC, WWI. Mem: U of Pa Alumni; YMHA; Alpha Omega; Atlantic City Art Cen; Phila Orch Assn; Phila Mus of Art; asso with Collins & Arkman Corp in dent capacity. Recipient: Little Neighborhood Sch Award, 1970; hon class, U of Pa, 1970. Hobbies: oil painting, hist, tennis. Home: 2601 Parkway, Philadelphia, Pa. Office: 632 N 22 St, Philadelphia, Pa.

HOUGH, Ellis Isidore, Eng, educator, chemist; b. Leeds, Eng, June 9, 1896; s. Marks and Rebekah (Lipman) Hoffenberg; MSc, Leeds U, 1923; m. Miriam Sortman; c: Sheila Silcock. Ret; jr demonstrator, chem, Leeds U, 1923-24; asst master, J Orphanage, Norwood, London, 1930-41; sr chem master, Prescot Grammar Sch, Lancs, 1941-61. Pvt, Brit Army, 1910-17. Hon life pres, Liverpool Zionist Soc, past chmn; fmr: hon secy, Norwood Divisional Lab Party; pres, Leeds Student Zionists. Author, Detection of Phenol and of Formaldehyde, 1954. Hobbies: Zionism, photography, nature study. Home: 12 Wavertree Green, Liverpool, Eng.

HOVELL, Joseph, US, sculptor, artist, art teacher; b. Kiev, Russ, Oct 28, 1897; s. Isaac and Rachel (Weisrub); in US since 1923; att: Odessa Art Inst, Russ, 1917-19; Cooper Union Inst, 1924-26; Natl Acad of Design, 1927, both NY; cert, tchr of art: SUNY; Bd of Educ, NYC. Instr, art and sculpture, educ cens and pvt. US Army, WWII. Repr in various exhbs, mus, art gals, pvt collections, including: Natl Acad of Design; Soc of Independent Artists; Bklyn Mus; Allied Artists of Amer; Whitney Mus; Carnegie Hall Art Gal; Mus of Sci and Ind; J Mus; Lotos Club; others; commissioned for portrait busts and bas-reliefs of famous men and women, including: Herbert Lehman; Adm Hyman Rickover, Fairleigh Dickinson Jr. Recipient: Melvin A Block Award, 1963; Agnon Gold Medal, Amer Friends Heb U. Home and studio: 130 W 57 St, New York, NY.

HOWE, Irving, US, educator, author; b. NYC, June 11, 1920; s. David and Nettie (Goldman); BSS, CCNY, 1940; m. c: Nina, Nicholas. Prof, Eng, Hunter Coll since 1963; asso prof, Brandeis U, 1953-61; Stanford U, 1961-63. US Army, 1941-46. Author: The UAW and Walter Reuther, 1949; Sherwood Anderson, A Critical Biography, 1951; William Faulkner, A Critical Study, 1952; A Treasury of Yiddish Stories, 1954; Politics and the Novel, 1957; A World More Attractive: A View of Modern Literature and Politics, 1963; Thomas Hardy; Steady Work: Essays in Democratic Radicalism; co-author: A History of the American Communist Party, 1958; The Radical Papers, 1966; ed: Dissent; contrib ed: various periodicals. Recipient: Kenyon Rev f in lit criticism, 1955; Bollingenn f, 1959. Office: Hunter Coll, New York, NY.

HUDISH, Celia, US, communal worker; b. Vilna, Lith, July 5, 1897; d. Morris and Hannah (York) Lifschitz; in US since 1902; m. Benjamin Hudish, Nov 1, 1915; c: Florence Phillips, Shirley Ziff, Phyllis Friedlander. Life mem, Hadassah; HIAS. Home: 5312 17 Ave, Brooklyn, NY.

HUEBNER, Judith J, Isr, government official; b. Vienna, Aus, Mar 19, 1921; d. Philip and Mania Winkler; in Isr since 1939; LLB, Heb U, Jerusalem; m. Izchak Heubner, Mar 19, 1942; c: Miriam. Dep dir gen, Min of Interior, since 1967. Home: 39 Shaprut, Jerusalem, Isr. Office: Min of Interior, Ruppin Rd, Jerusalem, Isr.

HUROK, Sol, US, impresario; b. Pogar, Russ, Apr 9, 1890; s. Israel and Naomi; in US since 1905; m. Emma Runitch, 1935; c: Ruth Lief. Started career as impresario by presenting Hippodrome Concerts; among noted musicians under mgmt have been: Chaliapin; Schumann-Heink; Mischa Elman; Zimbalist; Marian Anderson; Artur Rubinstein; Gregor Piatigorsky; Jan Peerce; Isaac Stern; Patrice Munsel; Roberta Peters; Andres Segovia; Leonard Warren; Victoria de los Angeles; Mario del Monaco; Sviatoslav Richter; Emil Gilels; mgr for dancers and co's: Pavlova; Isadora Duncan;

Ballet Russe de Monte Carlo; Original Ballet Russe; Ballet Theatre; Sadler's Wells Ballet; Katherine Dunham; Martha Graham; Agnes de Mille Dance Theatre; Orchestre National de France; Warsaw Philharmonic Orch; Moscow State Sym Orch; Mazowsze from Pol, Vienna Boys Choir, Ukrainian Dance Co, Theatre National Populaire; Bolshoi Ballet; Leningrad Kirov Ballet; Moiseyev Dance Co; Comedie Française; Inbal; Kabuki; Folklorico de Mexico; The Black Watch; Scots Guards; theatrically presented: Compagnie Jean-Louis Barrault-Madeleine Renaud; Habimah Players; Emlyn Williams as Charles Dickens, Old Vic. Author: Impresario, 1946; movie, Tonight We Sing, 1953, based on book; Sol Hurok Presents. Recipient: CBE, 1950; Chevalier and Officier de la Legion d'Honneur, Fr; citations from NYC, Amer, Isr orgs. Office: 730 Fifth Ave, New York, NY.

HURVITZ, Leon N, US, educator, author; b. Boston, Mass, Aug 4, 1923; s. Benjamin and Rose (Marcus): BA, U Chgo, 1949; MA, Columbia U, 1951, PhD, 1959; m. Reiko Kobayashi, July 22, 1958; c: Hannah, Nathaniel, Philip. Prof, Japanese lang, U Wash, since 1968, asst prof, 1957-62, asso prof, 1962-68. US Army, 1943-48. Mem: Amer Oriental Soc; Assn for Asian Studies; Philol Assn of Pacific Coast. Author: Chih-i, (538-597), The Life and Ideas of a Chinese Buddhist Monk; trans, Treatise on Buddhism and Taoism, 1956. Recipient: grant-in-aid, China Intl Found, 1951-53; Rockefeller Found, 1960; advanced grad f, Amer Council of Learned Soc, 1952. Home: 941 E Allison St, Seattle, Wash. Office: U of Wash, Seattle, Wash.

HURWITZ, Albert, US, attorney; b. Moscow, Russ, Aug 30, 1884; s. Marks and Sophia (Shapira); in US since 1892; LLB, cum laude, Boston U, 1908; m. Ada Godinski, Sep 20, 1910; c: Herman, Joshua, Israel, Irene Lappin. Pvt practice, Hurwitz and Hurwitz, since 1908; auditor, trial of motor tort cases, Suffolk Co, Mass, since 1956; asst atty gen, Commonwealth of Mass, 1919-23; dist atty, Suffolk Co, Boston, 1922. Pres: JCC, Metrop Boston, 1950-52; Sons of Zion, 1901-04; ZC, Boston, 1904-06, 1909-11; NE div, AJCong, 1939-40, delg, 1st session, 1917-18; delg elect, WZC, 1905; chmn, army and navy comm, JWB, Boston, 1940-46; vicepres, Law Soc of Mass, 1948-49; mem: Mass Bar Assn; Temple Ohabei Shalom; club, New Cent, chmn. Author: Curriculum for Jewish Religious Schools, 1916; The District Courts of Massachusetts, 1946. Home: 25 Englewood Ave, Brookline, Mass. Office: 1 Court St, Boston, Mass.

HURWITZ, Archie R, US, dentist; b. St Paul, Minn, Feb 8, 1910; s. Joseph and Rae (Roe); DDS, U Minn, 1935; m. Nathalie Bernstein, Aug 18, 1939; c: Thomas, Barbara Lipschultz. Pvt practice since 1935; staff, St Paul Ramsey Hosp, since 1935. Maj, US Army, Dent Corps, 1942-46. F, Royal Soc Health, London; mem: St Paul, Minn, Amer Dent Assns; Amer Soc for Children; Med Educ and Research Found, dent chmn. Author, Dentomedical Problems—Geriatric Patient, 1966. Home: 1245 Stanford Ave, St Paul, Minn. Office: 1240 Lowry Med Arts Bldg, St Paul, Minn.

HURWITZ, Charles, US, researcher, educator; b. Springfield, Mass, Apr 1, 1913; s. Solomon and Stella (Buchman); BS, Mass State Coll, 1934; MS, U Wis, 1938; PhD, O State U, 1942; m. Jean Parker, May 14, 1950; c: Richard, David, Laure Lee, Cheryl. Chief, Basic Sci Research lab, VA Hosp, Albany, NY, since 1951; asso prof, Albany Med Coll, since 1967, fac mem since 1951; adj prof, Rensselaer Poly Inst, Troy, NY. US Army, 1942-46. Pres, Northeastern NY sect, Amer Soc for Microbiol, 1959-61; mem: AAAS; NY Acad of Sci; Sigma Xi. Contbr to profsl jours. Home: 108 Mosher, Rd, Delmar, NY. Office: Basic Sci Research Lab, VA Hosp, Albany, NY.

HURWITZ, David L, US, attorney; b. NYC, Feb 22, 1928; s. Irving and Sophie (Ruderman); AB, Bucknell U, 1947; LLB, Columbia U, 1950; m. Betty Sperling, June 29, 1952; c: Peter; m. 2nd, Sally Spencer, Sep 30, 1967. Pvt practice; pres, The Algonquin Press Inc, since 1965; spec asst, atty gen, NY, 1951-53. Co-chmn, bus and profsl men's round table, NY chap, NCCJ, since 1960; pres, Bucknell U Alumni, Gtr NY since 1967; mem, natl devl council, Bucknell U since 1962; exec chmn bd, discrimination in housing comm, AJ Comm since 1961; bd dirs, NY State Comm on Discrimination in Housing, since 1961; co-chmn, spec gifts, Bucknell U Devl Fund, 1958-59; mem: Omicron Delta Kappa; Tau Kappa Alpha; Pi Sigma Alpha; Pi Delta Epsilon. Home: 444 E 82 St, New York, NY. Office: 122 E 42 St, New York, NY.

HURWITZ, Gerald Joseph, US, attorney; b. Yonkers, NY, Oct 22, 1935; s. Benjamin and Jeannette (Rudovsky); BA, summa cum laude, NYU, 1957; LLB, Yale Law Sch, 1960; m. Norma Bornstein, July 4, 1965; c: Stuart. Asst atty gen, State of NY, since 1962. Psycht specialist, USAF Res, 1960-66. Vice-pres: Westchester Zionist Region; Cong Sons of Isr, Yonkers; mem: natl exec bd, ZOA, past pres, Brandeis Zionist dist; NY State Bar Assn; Yonkers Lawyers Assn; Dunwoodie Lodge, Masons; Yale Alumni Soc; fmr: natl pres, Sr Young Judea; mem, exec bd, J Fed, Yonkers. Home: 7 Highland Pl. Yonkers, NY. Office: 80 Centre St, New York, NY.

HURWITZ, Henry Jr, US, physicist; b. NYC, Dec 25, 1918; s. Henry and Ruth (Sapinsky); BA, Cornell U, 1938; PhD, Harvard U, 1941; m. Jean Klein, 1944; div; c: Barry; m. 2nd, Alma Rosenbaum, 1951; c: Robin, Julia, Wayne. Mgr, theory and sys br, Research and Devl Cen, Gen Elec Co, since 1968, mgr, nucleonics and radiation, Research Lab, 1957-68; physics instr, Cornell U, 1941-44; research asso, Los Alamos Sci Lab, 1944-46; research asso, mgr, theoretical group and cons physicist, Knolls Atomic Power Lab, 1946-56. F: Amer Phys Soc; Amer Nuclear Soc; NY Acad of Sci; AAAS. Contbr to profsl jours. Recipient, Lawrence Memorial Award, 1961. Office: Research and Devl Cen, General Elec Co, Schenectady, NY.

HURWITZ, Jacob, US, rabbi; b. Baltimore, Md, May 20, 1912; s. Samuel and Ida (Ellison); BA, Yeshiva U, 1934; ordained rabbi, MHL, JTSA, 1938; MA, Columbia U, 1939; m. Ruth Strenger, 1940; c: Phyllis, Sharon. Rabbi: Temple Isr, Binghamton, NY, since 1948; Har Zion, 1938-39; B'nai Aaron, 1939-44, both Phila, Pa; Beth Isr, Flint, Mich, 1944-48. Pres: Binghamton, Min Assn, 1951-53; Broome Co Mh Assn, 1957-59; Broome Co Comm on Alcoholism, 1967-69; bd dirs, NY State Mh Assn; dir: Police Athletic League; ARC since 1949; NCCJ, Binghamton, since 1948; mem: exec council, RA; Masons; clubs: Natl Dinner, pres, 1955; Kiwanis. Home: 64 Aldrich Ave, Binghamton, NY. Study: Deerfield Pl, Binghamton, NY.

HURWITZ, Paul, US, ophthalmologist, educator; b. Chgo, Ill, Aug 14, 1907; s. Max and Helen (Skoblo); MS, U of Ill, 1932, MD, 1932; m. Mildred Spiro, June 24, 1930; c: Mitchell, Roger. Pvt practice since 1950; asst prof, Chgo Med Sch, since 1950; att ophthal: Edgewater Hosp, since 1949; Cook Co Hosp, since 1952; res phys, Presbyterian Hosp, 1937-38; mem of fac: Rush Med Coll, 1938-40; U of Ill, 1945-48, all Chgo. US Army MC, 1934-37, maj, 1941-46. Vice-pres, ZOA; mem, exec bd, Bonds for Isr, Chgo; fmr natl surg, JWV; mem: bd dirs, Bd J Educ, Chgo; Chgo Med Soc; IMA; AMA; Acad Ophthal and Otolaryngology; Pan Amer Assn Ophthal; Chgo Soc of Ophthal; Amer Coll of Surgs; Sigma Xi. Club, Covenant, Chgo. Contbr to med jours. Home: 9030 Pottawattami Dr, Skokie, Ill. Office: 55 E Washington St, Chicago, Ill.

HURWITZ, Samuel J, US, educator; b. NYC, Aug 23, 1912; s. Jacob and Celia (Feldman); BA, Bklyn Coll, 1934; LLB, St Lawrence U, 1936; MA, Columbia U, 1940, PhD, 1946. Prof, hist, Bklyn Coll, since 1940; researcher, Amer Assn for Social Security, 1934-35; visiting prof: Columbia U, 1946-48, NYU, 1956-57; Syracuse U, 1957-58; U of W Indies, 1963-64; U Puerto Rico, 1960-61; U of Hawaii, 1963-64; U of Colo, 1964. Mem: Amer Hist Assn; J Hist Soc; AAUP; Conf on Brit Studies; Phi Beta Kappa, fmr pres, secy, Bklyn chap. Author: State Intervention in Great Britain, 1948, 1968; co-author: Some Modern Historians of Britain, 1951; Comparative Education, 1952; ed, A History of English History, 1952; ed, A History of Bolshevism by Arthur Rosenberg, 1967; co-ed, A Liberal in Two Worlds, 1968; ed, trans, The Two French Revolutions, 1968; contbr: encys; natl publs. Recipient: f: Ford Found, 1962, NY State and Ford Found, 1964, 1965; Huntington Libr, 1966. Home: 1380 E 13 St, Brooklyn, NY. Office: Bklyn Coll, Brooklyn, NY.

HURWITZ, Shmuel, Isr, agronomist, educator; b. Russ, Sep 12, 1901; s. Benjamin and Beila (Mehring); in Isr since 1933; att Inst of Tech, Moscow, 1921-23; MSc, Inst of Agric, Berlin, DAgr, 1932; m. Yocheved Weinstein; c: Tirza, Ruth. Head, dept field and vegetable crops, fac agric, Heb U, Rehovot, since 1953, dean, fac agronomy, Heb U, 1964-68; chief asst, Inst of Plant Sci, Berlin, Ger, 1931-32; head, dept forage crops, Agric Research Sta, Rehovot, 1933-53. Mem: Isr Agric Educ Council; Isr Higher Educ Council. Author: Principles of Agronomy, 1956-59; Agriculture in Arab Middle East, 1966; contbr to Isr and fgn jours. Recipient: Isr Prize for Agric,

1951. Home: 68 Beeri St, Rehovot, Isr. Office: Fac of Agric, Heb U, Rehovot, Isr.

HURWITZ, Siegmund, Switz, dentist, psychologist; b. Lucerne, Switz, Nov 3, 1904; s. Michael and Mirjam (Dreifuss); DMD, Sch of Dent, Zurich; studies in Ger and US; m. Lea Eisner, 1931; c: Emanuel, Noomi. Pvt practice, dent, since 1930; lectr, C G Jung Inst, Zurich. Author: Archtypische Motive in der chassidischen Mystik, 1952; The God Image in Kaballah, 1952; Die Gestalt des sterbenden Messias, 1958; Psychological Aspects in Early Chassidic Literature, 1968. Spec interest, rel psych. Home: Rigistr 54, Zurich, Switz. Office: Claridenstr 22, Zurich, Switz.

HURWITZ, Stephan, Den, educator, public official; b. Copenhagen, Den, June 20, 1901; s. Stephan and Louise (Nagler); LLD, U Copenhagen; hon LLD, Us: Stockholm, Helsinki; m. Lise Rode. Parliamentary commn: prof, U Copenhagen; chief, Ref Off, Swed, 1943-45. Author: Den danske Kriminalret; Den danske Strafferetspleje; Kriminologi. Home: 7 Dalsvinget, Copenhagen, Den.

HURWITZ, William, Can, business exec; b. Windsor, Ont, Nov 14, 1917; s. Barney and Hilda (Coppel); att: Assumption Coll, 1934; Detroit Inst of Tech; m. Ruth Brudner, Jan, 1944; c: Paul, Richard, Michael. Pres: Coronet TV Corp, since 1952; William Norman Co, Can, since 1943; dir, Electrotube Corp, Can, since 1952. Pres, E Can Conf, Aleph Zadik Aleph, B'nai B'rith, 1932, dir, 1951; dir: ZOC, 1952; Shaar Hashomayim Syn, 1952; local repr, JA Dept for Econ Devl of Isr, 1952. Home: 3409 Church St, Windsor, Ont, Can. Office: 1801 Walker Rd, Windsor, Ont, Can.

HUTLER, Albert A, US, organization exec; b. NYC, Mar 14, 1909; s. Harry and Molly (Garman); BA, U of Ill, 1931, LLB, 1933; att Grad Sch of Social Service Admn, U Chgo, 1939-42; m. Leanore Ehrlich, May 3, 1934; c: Frankee, Susanne Silber. Dir, fund raising, J Fed and CJA, Chgo, since 1958; asso exec dir: J United Fund; J Fed; JWF of Metrop Chgo; fmr: exec dir, United J Fed of San Diego, 1946-58; admn asst, J Charities of Chgo, 1939-42. Capt, US Army, chief DP sect, 7th Army, Amer Mil Govt, 1942-46. Chmn, Civic Unity Council; mem bd dirs: Urban League; Open Forum, all San Diego; mem: Gov's Commn on Discrimination in Employment, State of Cal; Natl Assn of Social Workers; Natl Conf on J Communal Service; JWV; B'nai B'rith. Contbr to social service jours. Recipient: Bronze Star; 5 Battle Stars; Netherlands Govt Order of Orange and Nassau with Swords for DP work; Citizen of Year, Urban League, San Diego, 1957; commendation, Co Bd of Sups, San Diego. Hobbies: tennis, squash, camping. Home: 320 Dell La, Highland Pk, Ill. Office: 15 Franklin St, Chicago, Ill.

HUTNER, Florence, Can, organization exec; b. NYC, Feb, 1907; d. Herman and Pauline (Cooper); BA, U Toronto, 1929; MA, Columbia U, 1930. Dir, jt natl comm, Can J Cong and Can comm, CJFWF; fmr: co-dir, UJA, Toronto, 1948-62; exec vice-pres, United J Fund, Toronto, 1953-62. Mem: bd dirs: Can Wfr Council; New Mt Sinai Hosp of Toronto; Social Planning Council of Toronto; exec comm, Intl Council on Social Work; adv comm: Ontario Wfr Council; Social Planning Council of Toronto; planning comm, Intl Conf on J Communal Services; mem: YMHA, YWHA, Toronto. Home: 2515 Bathurst St, Toronto, Ont, Can.

HUTNER, Joseph Louis, US, attorney; b. NYC, May 30, 1933; s. Edward and Anne (Grapes); BA, Yale U, 1955; LLB, Harvard Law Sch, 1958; att U Heidelberg, Ger; m. Willa Selenfriend, Feb 20, 1958; c: Laura, Susan, Amy. Partner, Rapaport, Rupino and Pincus, since 1967; partner, Hutner and Safian, 1960-62. Dir: United Fund of Westchester, White Plains; mem: bd dirs, ADL; bd trustees, Temple Emanu-El, Harrison, NY; NY St Bar Assn; Phi Beta Kappa; Assn Bar, NYC; fmr: pres, United Fund, White Plains; club, Yale, NY, dir. Contbr to legal periodicals. Recipient: Yale Club Award; Young Man of Year, White Plains Jr C of C. Home: 39 Hathaway La, White Plains, NY. Office: 110 E 59 St, New York, NY.

HUTTNER, Matthew, US, publisher; b. Baltimore, Md, July 15, 1915; s. Emil and Ella (Schrago); BS, Cal State Tchrs Coll, 1936; MLetters, U of Pa, 1937; m. Esta Greenspan, Nov 11, 1960; c: Richard, Hilary, James. Pres, publisher, Pyramid Publs, div of the Walter Reade Org, since 1969; pres, Pyramid Publs, since 1949. Capt, USAAC, WW II. Fmr chmn, Edward R Murrow Mem Fund of Overseas Press Club Found; mem:

natl bd, ADL; bd, Karen Horney Clinic, vice-pres; clubs: Overseas Press, fmr chmn; Friars. Recipient: John J Pershing Medal, WW II. Hobbies: golf, music, art. Home: 911 Park Ave, New York, NY. Office: 444 Madison Ave, New York, NY.

HUTZLER, Albert B, Jr, US, merchant; b. Baltimore, Md, Mar 1, 1916; s. Albert and Gretchen (Hochschild); AB, Johns Hopkins U, 1937; m. Bernice Levy, Sep 22, 1937; c: Elizabeth Friedman, Albert, James. Pres, gen mgr, Hutzler Bros Co, since 1954, with firm since 1938; dir, RH Macy & Co, 1937. Pres, Hutzler Fund; dir: Md Council of Retail Merchants; Goodwill Inds Inc; dir, pres: Asso Charities, 1967-68; Comm for Downtown, 1966-68; Retail Merchants Assn, 1952-54; dir, vice-pres, Natl Retail Merchants Assn; fmr dir, ARC; mem, jt fund comm, Comty Chest Red Cross United Appeal; exec comm mem: Gtr Baltimore Comm; Comty Chest; Govs Comm to Promote Employment of Handicapped; trustee, mem exec comm, Johns Hopkins U. Home: Oakwood, Pikesville, Md. Office: Hutzler Brothers Co, Baltimore, Md.

HUTZLER, Charles G III, US, business exec; b. Baltimore, Md, Mar 3, 1931; s. Charles and Elsa; att: Wash and Lee Coll; Columbia Grad Sch of Bus; m. Eleanor Kann, Nov 25, 1953; c: Barbara, Sheila. Gen merchandise mgr, Hutzler's department store, since 1966, vice-pres, 1963, with org since 1955; fmr, L S Ayres & Co. US Army, 1952-1954. Secy, Hutzler Fund, since 1965, trustee; mem bd: Sinai Hosp; Assoc Merchandising Corp; Valleys Planning Council, Inc; mem, Baltimore Assn of Commerce. Office: Hutzler Bros Co, Baltimore, Md.

HYAMS, Ario S, US, rabbi; b. NYC, Jan 20, 1905; s. Phineas and Fannie (Gold); BA, CCNY, 1927; ordained rabbi, MHL, JTSA, 1931; grad studies, Columbia U, 1932-36; DD, JTSA, 1966; m. Tess Bragin, June 29, 1930; c: Phineas. Rabbi: Temple Beth Sholom, Roslyn, LI, since 1952, rabbi em since 1969; Temple B'nai B'rith, Somerville, Mass, 1931-32; Beth David Syn, Lynbrook, LI, 1932-34; United J Cen, Bayside, LI, 1934-36; Temple Beth El, Asbury Park, NJ, 1936-48; J Comty Cen, Teaneck, NJ, 1948-52. Chaplain, US Army, 1944-46. Chaplain: Cen Bergen Co Policeman's Benevolent Assn; Intl Assn Fire Fighters Local, both NJ; chmn: Natl J Music Council, since 1962, prog comm, since 1950; mem: Commn on Phil of Conservative Judaism; Prayer Book Comm; fmr: chaplain, JWV; pres: Rabb Assn, Bergen Co; Nassau-Suffolk Assn Rabbis; Nassau-Suffolk region, RA; natl chmn, Jt Commn on J Educ, United Syn and RA. Author: Prayerbook for the Home, 1940, 1951; Ten Divrei Torah on Pirke Avot; ed, J Music Notes of JWB; contbr to J publs. Home: 59 Devon Rd, Hempstead, NY. Study: Roslyn Rd, Roslyn Heights, NY.

HYATT, Julius, US, rabbi; b. Preil, Latvia, Aug 27, 1911; s. Morris and Leah (Weinstein); in US since 1922; ordained rabbi, Rabbi Isaac Elchanan Theol Sem, NYC, 1932; LLB, Marquette U, 1936; m. Ida Byalos, Aug 27, 1939; c: Gary, David. Rabbi, Cong Agudas Achim, Peoria, since 1936; lectr, rel, Bradley U, 1951-54. Civilian chaplain, WWII. Mem: bd, JCC, since 1939; ZOA; B'nai B'rith; fmr: vice-pres, RabCA; mem bd: Child and Family Services; Co Infantile Paralysis Assn, Peoria. Author: Laws of Agency and Partnership, comparative study of Talmud and common law, 1935. Home: 600 W Richwoods, Peoria, Ill. Study: 606 W War Memorial Dr, Peoria, Ill.

HYMAN, Abraham S, Isr, organization exec, attorney; b. Sokoly, Ross, June 9, 1904; s. Schuman and Esther (Levinsky); BA, U of Ill, 1928; JD, U Chgo, 1931; m. Rina Friedman, Apr 6, 1952. Asst exec dir, Isr Educ Fund; exec staff, UJA, since 1957; asst adv, J Affairs in Ger and Aus, 1946-49, adv, 1949-50; gen counsel, US War Claims Commn, 1950-53; admn dir, WJC, 1953-57. Maj, US Army. Pres: B'nai B'rith, 1933; Anselm Forum, 1942, both Gary, Ind; mem: Phi Beta Kappa. Author: Supplementary Report on War Claims Arising Out of World War II, 1953; Education in Israel; contbr to J publs. Home: 6 Vitkin St, Tel Aviv, Isr.

HYMAN, Albert Salisbury, US, cardiologist, author, medical research educ; b. Boston, Mass, Apr 6, 1893; s. John and Caroline (Greenwood); AB, Harvard Coll, 1915; MD, Harvard Med Sch, 1918; ScD, Med, U London, 1924; cert card, U Vienna, 1925; att Rehfish Klinik, Berlin, 1925. Cons card: NYC Hosp, Elmhurst Div, Mt Sinai Hosp Med Cen; Manhattan Gen Hosp Div, Beth Isr Hosp Med Cen, 1964; att card: Beth David Hosp, NY, 1927; J Memorial Hosp, 1928; Man-

hattan Gen Hosp, 1928; Hosp of the Daughters of Jacob, 1928; cons card: Richmond Memorial Hosp, 1930; 3rd Naval Dist, NY, 1934; Yonkers Profsl Hosp, 1936; Long Beach Memorial Hosp, 1939; St Albans Naval Hosp, 1946; Valley Forge Heart Inst, Pa, 1949; VA Hosp, Castle Pt, NY, 1947; Dept of Research Phys, Springfield Coll, Mass; asso clinical prof em, med, NY Med Coll, 1960. Lt, US Army, MC, 1917-19, lt cdr, USNR, MC, 1934; instr, aviation med, 1939; card, Bklyn Naval Hosp, 1941; chief, card cons service, 3rd Naval Dist Recruiting Div; cdr, MC, WW II; capt, USNR, MC; ret, 1946. Prin contrib: inventor of the artificial pacemaker for resuscitation of the dying heart. Dir: Louis Adler Sound Research Fund, since 1938; Daitz Cardiovascular Research Fund, since 1955; FACP; AMA; NY Acad Scis; found: Amer Coll Card, fmr hon trustee; Amer Coll Sports Med, fmr pres; NY Card Soc, fmr pres; Amer Bd Internal Med, dipl; mem: NY State and Co Med Socs; Harvard Med Soc; Haarlem Med Assn, past pres; Riverside Med Soc, fmr pres; Yorkville Med Soc, past pres; World Med Assn; NY State Assn Professions; fmr: dir, Witkin Found for Study and Prevention of Heart Disease; chmn, Heart Research Unit, Police Athletic League, NY; mem: Phi Delta Epsilon, Rho chap, Harvard Med Sch, fmr pres, charter mem; Rising Star Lodge, Masons, Phila; Diadem Lodge, Masons, NY, charter mem; Master Mason Phys of Amer, fmr pres; Amer Legion, Harvard Post; Harvard Menorah Soc; B'nai B'rith; JWV, Harvard post; J Acad of Arts and Scis, med sect; Assn J Command Posts, fmr cdr; Red Mogen Dovid Ambulance Org Isr; J Phys Comm; Alumni Assn of J Navy Phys; Stephen Wise Free Syn, student charter mem; Hadassah Hosp Org in Pal; clubs: Sailboat; Gun and Rod; Outboard Motor Legion, Fairfield, Conn; Phys Sq, NY, found, fmr pres; Assn of Phys Sq Amer, fmr pres; Harvard, NYC. Author: Practical Cardiology, 1958; The Acute Syndromes and Emergencies 1959; co-author: Applied Electrocardiography, 1929; The Failing Heart of Middle Life, 1932; ed, Ency of Sports Medicine; contbr to Ency of Cardiology, sci jours. Recipient: Alfred E Smith Award, Witkin Found, 1930; Amer Coll Sports Med Citation, 1934; Insull Award, 1935; U Brussels Citation, 1936; Siemens & Halske Sci Citation, 1939; Valley Forge Heart Inst and Research Cen Citation, 1953. Hobbies: philately, photography, art, med elec. Home: 560 E 79 St, New York, NY. Office: 450 E 63 St, New York, NY.

HYMAN, Arthur B, US, dermatologist, educ; b. London, Eng, Aug 22, 1905; s. Aaron and Rachel (Abrahamson); in US since 1939; LRCP, MRCS, Guy's Hosp Med Sch, London, 1926; MB, BS, hons, London U, 1928; att NYU, 1941-44; m. Syd Stavisky, Sep 16, 1930; c: Merton, Alan. Prof, clinical dermat, NYU; dermatopath, Beth Isr Hosp; cons dermat, VA Hosp; att dermat, U Hosp. Dipl, Natl Amer Bd Dermat; hon mem, Isr, Venezuelan and Cuban Dermat Socs; mem: AMA; NY Acad Med; Amer Acad Dermat; Amer Soc Dermatopath; Dermat Soc of Gtr NY. Author: The Sources of the Yalkut Shimeoni, 1965; contbr to med and educ jours. Spec interest, Heb book collecting. Home: 205 W 86 St, New York, NY. Office: 2 W 87 St, New York, NY

HYMAN, Chester, US, educator; b. NYC, Mar 14, 1918; s. Isidore and Mollie (Silver); AB, U of Cal, Berkeley, 1938; MS, NYU, 1940, PhD, 1944; m. Ruth Lauter, July 11, 1943; c: Martha, Deborah, Rachel. Birely Prof Inves Dermat, prof, phys, U of Cal, Sch of Med since 1953; cons: LA Gen Hosp, since 1950; Huntington Memorial Hosp, Inst for Med Research, Pasadena, Cal since 1961. Chmn, sci subcomm, Cal Heart Assn, since 1961; f, ACC; mem: LA Acad of Med; Amer Phys Soc; Sigma Xi; Intl Cardiovascular Soc. Contbr to sci jours. Recipient, sr research f, NSF, 1956-57. Home: 1219 Chilten Way, S Pasadena, Cal. Office: 2025 Zonal Ave, Los Angeles, Cal.

HYMAN, Edith Ada, US, philanthropist and communal worker; b. Glasgow, Scotland, Nov 20, 1902; d. Solomon and Nellie (Williamowsky) Wolfson; sister of Sir Isaac Wolfson of Gt Brit; m. Esmond Barnett, June, 1924 (decd); c: Adele Suslak, Victor Barnett; m. 2nd, Ralph Hyman, June, 1946, (decd). Dir: J Guild for the Blind; Amer Friends Heb U; Cancer Research Lab, Weizmann Inst of Sci; life mem, JTSA, Brandeis U; trustee, FJP; contbr and sponsor: Mt Sinai Hosp; ICCY Jerusalem and Gt Brit; UJA; College for Girls at B'nai Brak, Isr; Accra Village, Isr; Childrens Resettlement Fund, Isr; Isr Bonds; AJComm; Cerebral Palsy; Eng Speaking Union; Metrop Mus of NY; J Mus; ARC; Finch Coll, Wharton Sch of Bus scholarship funds; WAIF; Boy and Girl Scouts of Amer; contbr of scholarships to Heb Arts

Sch, Collegiate Sch, Fifth Ave Syn, Metrop Opera. Home: 475 Park Ave, New York, NY.

HYMAN, Frieda C, US, teacher, author; b. NYC, July 3, 1913; d. Jacob and Mary (Brody); BA, Hunter Coll, 1932; m. Israel Hyman, June 24, 1934; c: Judith Rosenheim, Salo Hillel. Dir, Midrasha, Heb HS; prin, rel sch, Council J Women, 1941-42. Mem: Amer J Hist Soc; AJCong; Young Isr; Yeshiva, Hartford; Old People's Home; J Children's Bur; Hartford Fed. Author: play, Lord of Tiberias, presented by J Theater for Children; books: Jubal and the Prophet, 1958; Builders of Jerusalem, 1960; contbr of poetry, short stories to mags and rel jours. Home: 37 Colebrook St, Hartford, Conn.

HYMAN, Harold M, US, educator; b. NYC, July 24, 1924; s. Abraham and Beatrice (Herman); BA, UCLA, 1948; PhD, Columbia U, 1952; m. Ferne Handelsman, Mar 22, 1946; c: Lee, Ann, William. Hobby Prof, hist, chmn dept, Rice U, since 1968; prof, hist, U of Ill, 1963-68; asst prof, Earlham Coll, Ind, 1952-55; asso prof, Ariz State U, 1955-56; prof, UCLA, 1956-63. USMC, 1941-45. Mem, Amer Hist Assn. Author: Era of the Oath, 1954; To Try Men's Souls, 1959; co-author; Stanton: Lincoln's Secretary of War, 1962; ed: New Frontiers of the American Reconstruction, 1965; The Radical Republicans and the Reconstruction, 1861-70, pub 1967; Freedom and Order, 1967; Heard Around the World: The Impact Abroad of the American Civil War, 1968. Recipient, Awards: Beveridge, Amer Hist Assn, 1954; Sidney Hillman, 1959. Home: Houston, Tex. Office: Hist Dept, Riceu, Houston, Tex.

HYMAN, Harry H, US, rabbi; b. Bromberg, Ger, Apr 1, 1910; s. William and Hannah (Berg); in US since 1938; PhD, U Berlin, Ger, 1933; ordained rabbi, Hochschule fuer die Wissenschaft des Judetums, Berlin, 1935; m. Greta Steigerwald, 1938. Chaplaincy dir, LA J Fed Council, since 1957; rabbi: Cong B'nai Isr, Palisades Park, NJ, 1941-44; Huntington Park Heb Cong, Cal, 1944-57. Mem: B'nai B'rith; RA; Huntington Park Heb Cong; Acad of Rel and MH. Author: Sigmund Freud's Theory on Religion and its Critical Evaluation, 1933. Home: 4071 Broadway, Huntington Park, Cal. Office: 590 N Vermont Ave, Los Angeles, Cal.

HYMAN, Herbert H, US, sociologist, educator; b. NYC, March 3, 1918; s. David and Gisella (Mautner); MA, Columbia U, 1940, PhD, 1942; m. Helen Kandel, Sep 30, 1945; c: Lisa, David, Alex. Prof, sociol, Wesleyan U, since 1969; prof, asso dir, Bur Applied Sociol Research, Columbia U, 1951-69; research asso, Natl Opinion Research Cen, U Chgo, 1947-50; visiting prof: U Oslo, 1950-51; U Ankara, 1957-58; Fulbright lectr, 1950-51; prog dir, UN Research Inst for Social Devl, Geneva, 1964-65; f: Cen for Advanced Studies, Wesleyan, 1968-69. Pres, Amer Assn for Public Opinion Research, 1959-60; chmn, social psych sect, Amer Sociol Soc; f: Soc for Psychol Study of Spec Issues, exec council, Amer Psych Assn; Sigma Xi. Author: The Psychology of Status, 1942; Interviewing in Social Research, 1954; Survey Design and Analysis, 1955; Political Socialization, 1959. Recipient: Julian Wood-

ward memorial award, 1956. Home: 38 Woodside Ave, Westport, Conn. Office: Wesleyan U, Middletown, Conn.

HYMAN, Herbert H, US, chemist; b. NYC, Sep 27, 1919; s. Nathan and Estelle (Machinist); BS, CCNY, 1938; MS, Poly Inst of Bklyn, 1941; PhD, Ill Inst of Tech, 1960; m. Ruth Dixler, Dec 28, 1943; c: Mark, David. Sr chem, Argonne Natl Lab, since 1948, staff mem since 1944; jr asst chem, US War Dept, Huntsville, Ala Arsenal, 1941-44; Jacob Siskind Visiting Prof, Brandeis U, 1967-68; exch sci, Harwell, Eng, 1960-61. Pres, Argonne Chap, Research Soc of Amer, 1960; vice-pres, Chgo Chap, Amer Technion Soc; f, AAAS; mem: Amer Chem Soc; Amer Nuclear Soc; NY Acad Sci; Soc for Applied Spectroscopy; Inst of Nuclear Materials Mgmt; Phi Lambda Upsilon; Sigma Xi; Research Soc of Amer. Ed: Process Chemistry, vol I, 1956, vol II, 1958, vol III, 1960; Noble-Gas Compounds, 1963; contbr numerous papers to: Amer Chem Soc; Jour Phys Chem, and others. Home: 1347 Park Place, Chicago, Ill. Office: Argonne Natl Lab, Argonne, Ill.

HYMAN, Joseph M, US, theatrical producer; b. Cripple Creek, Colo, Sep 30, 1901; s. Nathan and Mary (Ittlesohn); m.2n d, Stephanie Augustine, Oct 16, 1956; c: by 1st m, Jayne Gallagher. Produc: TV play, Climate of Eden, 1960; theatrical producs: There's Always a Breeze, 1936; Dear Ruth, 1943; Winged Victory, 1943; The Secret Room, 1945; Christopher Blake, 1947; Mr Pebbles and Mr Hooker, 1947; Make Mine Manhattan, 1948; Light Up the Sky, 1948; Signor Chicago, 1951; Climate of Eden, 1952; Anniversary Waltz, 1954; Fair Game, 1957. Mem, Masons. Home: 500 E 71 St, New York, NY. Office: 101 W 55 St, New York, NY.

HYMES, Viola H, US, communal leader; b. Chgo, Ill, May 7, 1906; d. Aaron and Lena (Provel) Hoffman; BS, U Minn, 1926, grad work, 1930-31, 1955-57; m. Charles Hymes, Sep 21, 1930; c: Alan, Richard. Hon vice-pres, Natl Council J Women, since 1963, fmr pres; vice-pres, Intl Council of J Women, 1957-63; chmn: Gov's Commn, Status of Women, Minn, 1963-69; comm, natl voluntary services and service orgs, White House Conf on the Aging, 1961; comty services commn, Citizen's Comm for Educ in US, Minneapolis, 1957-58; social planning comm, Temple Isr Sisterhood; social planning, budget comms, J Fed, 1951-53; dir, Minneapolis Bd Educ, 1963-69, vice-chmn, 1967-69; bd dirs: JWB, 1959-63; Assn for Mh; bd trustees, Channel Two, Twin-City Area Educ TV Sta; bd govs, Heb U, 1959-63; natl adv comm, White House Conf on Aging, 1961; Natl Commn on Adult Literacy, 1959-63; curriculum adv comm, Minn State Bd Educ; Family and Childrens Services, Amer Assn U Women; Comty Chest; ARC; Emanuel Cohen Cen; J Family and Childrens Service; delg, White House Conf on Educ, 1955; mem: Natl Citizens' Adv Comm, Status of Women, 1963-69; pres, Commn on Status of Women, 1962-63; Delta Sigma Rho; Pi Lambda Theta; Delta Phi Lambda; Delta Kappa Gamma. Recipient: outstanding achievement award, U Minn, 1961; citation of hon, Gov of Minn, 1968. Home: 2044 Cedar Lake Blvd, Minneapolis, Minn. Office: Natl Council of J Women, 1 W 47 St, New York NY.

I

IANCO, Marcel, Isr, artist; b. Bucharest, Rum, May 1895; s. Zwi and Rachel (Juster); in Isr since 1941; studied with Iser and in Zurich, Switz; m. Clara Goldschleger; c: Josefine Kline, Dvora Kuperman. Co-found with Tristan Tzara and Hans Arp, the Dada movement in art and lit, 1917; co-found, New Horizons artists group, Pal, 1942; held one-man shows, exhbs, represented in perm collections in Isr, US, Fr and Switz. Pres, co-found, Artist's Village, Ein Hod, Isr. Illus: The Manifesto Against All Manifestos; The First Heavenly Adventure of Mr Antipirin, both by Tristan Tzara; Don Quichotte; designed scenery and costumes for, Chemical and Static Poems, by Tristan Tzara; theatrical producs, Habimah and Chamber Theaters, Tel Aviv. Recipient: Isr Prize, 1970. Homes: 9 Glickson St, Tel Aviv, Isr. Artists' Village, Ein Hod, Isr.

IANCU-HERMAN, Leiba David, Isr, physician; b. Bucharest, Rum, Apr 28, 1917; s. David and Clara (Davidson); in Isr since 1961; MD, U Bucharest, 1940; m. Sara Szoal, Oct 9, 1951. Head, dept hematology and blood bank, since 1967; sr lectr, Tel Aviv U, since 1969; exten, intern asst, Caritas Hosp, 1947-58; dir, CFR Hosp, 1948-61; chief asst, clotting lab, med sch, Bucharest, 1951-61. Pres, Med Org, Assaf Harofe Hosp. Contbr to profsl jours. Recipient: Evidentiat Munca Medico Sanitaria, Health Min, Rum, 1956. Home: 12 Hashoftim St, Tel Aviv, Isr.

IANCULOVICI, Chaim, Isr, bookkeeper; b. Galatz, Rum, Aug 15, 1912; s. Reuven and Rahel (Eisenstein); in Isr since 1950; m. Sarah Landau. Treas, Soltam Ltd, Haifa, since 1950. Mem, social sect, Haifa Munic; pres, loan bank, Ezra L'Oleh, Haifa; Aliya, Rum, cen comm, Independent Lib Party; vice-pres, Askanim; mem: cultural cen, Beit Rothschild; control commn, B'nai B'rith; fmr: head: Zionist Org, Rum; KH, UJA, Rum; found, Zionist Libr, Emunah, Rum; pres: B'nai B'rith, N Dist; Loje Franco-mason, Yacov Caspi. Recipient: Order Haganah, Zionist activity, 1967. Spec interest: social, wfr orgs. Home: 10 Geula St, Haifa, Isr. Office: Yokneam St, Haifa, Isr.

IDAN, Avner, Isr, diplomat; b. Berlin, Ger, Sep 1, 1921; s. Hans and Käthe (Freudenberg) Wollheim, in Isr since 1933; att Heb U, Jerusalem, 1939-42; m. Regina Havilio, Jan 24, 1948 (decd); c: Dorit, Orly. Min plen, Isr Emb, Bonn, since 1966; political counselor: Min of Defense, 1950-58; Emb of Isr, Wash DC, 1958-63, PM's Off, Isr, 1963-66. Maj, IDF, 1948-50. Home: Mecklenburger 1, Bad Godesberg, W Ger; Office: Embassy of Israel, Ubier 18, Bad Godesberg, W Ger; Min for Fgn Affairs, Jerusalem, Isr.

IDELSON, Beba, Isr, organization exec, legislator; b. Dnepro-petrowsk, Ukraine, Oct 14, 1895; d. Izchak and Rivka (Rezovski) Trachtenberg; in Isr since 1926; att U Kharkov, Russ, 1916-20; m. Haim Halperin; c: Rivka. Gen secy, Council of Women Workers since 1930; mem: exec, cen Comm, Lab Party; fmr: MK, dep speaker since 1954; mem: lab comm; security and fgn affairs comm, all in Isr Knesset; Provisional State Council. Delg: WZCs since 1935; interparliamentary convs: Ir; Wash, DC; on missions to: US; Eng; Fr; Mexico; Latin Amer. Contbr to local press. Home: 22 Rembrandt St, Tel Aviv, Isr. Office: Moetzet Hapoalot, 93 Arlosoroff St, Tel Aviv, Isr.

IDELSON, Benjamin, Isr, architect; b. Leningrad, Russ, May 5, 1911; s. Abraham and Frida (Shapiro); in Isr since 1925; architect, U Ghent, 1935; m. Hilda Pouchovsky, Dec 25, 1947. Sr partner, Idelson-Zippor, architects and town planners. Mem: architects forum, Tel Aviv U; Engrs, Architects Assn, Isr. Contbr to profsl jours. Recipient, Isr award for architecture, Isr govt, 1968. Home: 19 Akiva Arie St, Tel Aviv, Isr. Office: 18 Shlomzion Hamalka St, Tel Aviv, Isr.

IDELSON, Jerry, S Afr musical dir, composer; b. Libau, Latvia, Dec 12, 1893; s. Asriel and Dora (Hirshfield); in S Afr since 1912; att Sch of Music, Libau, 1906-10; U Witwatersrand, 1920-21; Coll of Music, Cape Town, 1922-23; m. Anne Sacks,

Dec 15, 1940. Ret, 1968; dir music, Union Progressive Judaism, Johannesburg, 1933-68; found, first org secy; hon dir music, S Afr Union for Progressive Judaism, 1946; viola player, Cape Town Munic Sym Orch, 1916-17, 1922-23; music dir; Consolidated Theaters, 1923, 1929, 1952; libr, prin viola player, S Afr BC Corp, 1932-46. Composer: of over 200 songs; choral; instrumental compositions; music for Lieder and Shirei, by Morris Hoffman, 1950-51; trans songs to Heb, Yiddish, Eng, Afrikaans, Ger, Bantu. Hon life mem, United J Reform Cong; found, first secy, Soc of S Afr Composers, chmn, 1952-54; clubs: Transvaal Mountain, found, first chmn, hon life mem, Transvaal Automobile. Recipient: S Afr BC Corp Prize, 1942. Home: 22 Mt Sheridan, Bellevue E, Johannesburg, S Afr. Office: POB 27719 Yeoville, Johannesburg, S Afr.

IFSHIN, Daniel Eli, US, attorney; b. NYC, Nov 27, 1907; s. William and Gussie (Daillion); att Columbia U, 1925-26; LLB, St Lawrence U, 1929; m. Beatrice Kaplan, Dec 27, 1931; c: Stephen, Ellen. Pvt practice since 1931; gen mgr, J Daily Forward 1968. Admn dir, Workmen's Circle, 1958-67; chmn: NYC comm, 1950-52, natl org comm, 1952-56, exec comm, med dept, 1956-58; natl exec comm, J Labor Comm, 1964-68; mem: Alpha Eta Phi, natl grand master; Bklyn JCC. Home: 330 West 28 St, New York, NY. Office: 277 Broadway, New York, NY.

IGNATOW, David, US, poet, editor, educator; b. Bklyn, NY, Feb 7, 1914; s. Max and Yetta (Wilkenfeld); att Bklyn Evening Coll, 1934; New Sch for Social Research, 1942; m. Rose Graubart, Apr, 1935; c: David, Yaedi. Treas, Enterprise Bookbinding Co, Inc, since 1955; adj prof, Columbia U since 1969; poet in residence, York Coll, CUNY, since 1969; author, Federal Writers Project, 1933-39; publicity writer: UJA, 1950-53; FJP, 1950-53; instr, lectr, creative writing, NY State Adult Educ Prog; poet in res: U Ky, 1965-66; U Kan, 1966-67; Vassar Coll, 1967-68. Author: Poems, 1948; The Gentle Weight Lifter, 1955; Say Pardon, 1961; Figures of the Human, 1964; Rescue the Dead, 1968; Earth Hard, selected poems, 1968; Collected Poems, 1934-69; ed: Analytic, 1937-39; Beloit Poetry Jour, 1949-59; co-ed, Chelsea, since 1968; poetry ed, The Nation, 1962-63; contrib ed: The American Scene, 1934-37; The Literary Arts, 1934-37; asst to ed, The Labor Zionist, 1948-50; contbr poetry, articles to mags. Chmn, educ comm, LZOA, Greenwich Village, 1948-50. Recipient: Awards: Natl Inst Arts, Letters, 1964; Shelley Memorial, 1966; Natl Endowment, Arts, Letters, 1969; Guggenheim f, 1965; Rockefeller Found Grant, 1968. Home: 17th St and Gardiner Ave, E Hampton, NY. Office: 270 Lafayette St, New York N.Y.

ILAN, Yeshayahu, Isr, architect, educator; b. Vienna, Aus, Apr 19, 1931; s. Moshe and Yaffa (Ilan); in Isr since 1935; MSc, Eng, Technion, Haifa, 1956; m. Ruth Kahn, Nov 13, 1951; c: Evyatar, Tamar, Abigail. Sr lectr, fac of architecture, Technion. Prin contribs: planning of many public bldgs, town planning. Author, Architectural Space Concepts in Halakhaic Thought in the Mishna and Talmud, 1962. Home and office: 73 Harav Kook St, Kiryat Motzkin, Isr.

ILANY, Jacob, Isr, biochemist, food expert; b. Yassay, Rum, June 21, 1910; s. Abraham and Lea (Novak) Feigenbaum; in Isr since 1930; att Natl Coll, Yassy, Rum; MSc, Heb U, Jerusalem, 1936, PhD, 1937; m. Ora Barzilai, 1937; c: Nitza Levy. Dir, applied research div, Min of Commerce, Ind, since 1965; research asso, biochem, sr lectr, biotech, Bar Ilan U, in Isr, since 1962; research asst, biochem, cancer div, Heb U, Jerusalem, 1937-48; dir, food ind dept, Min Commerce, Ind, 1948-52; sci, tech adv to food inds, 1952-65. Haganah, IDF, 1930-48. Prin contribs: devl of food ind in Isr; research into devl of new food producs. Mem: Isr Biochem and Chem Soc; Food Scis Assn of Isr; US Inst of Food Techs; Phi Tau Sigma; liaison off, Comm Intl Permanent de la Conserve, Paris; club, Rotary. Author: Food Industries Chemistry and Processing; Know Your Food, A Guide to Food Buying and Storing; Production of Chocolate and Sweets; Production of

Soft Drinks and Beverages; The Canning Industries; Dial Your Diet, pub in Fr, Heb, Chinese, Eng, It, Span; contbr to numerous sci and tech publs. Spec interests: J personalities and scis; philately. Home: 30 Alharizi St, Jerusalem, Isr. Office: 30 Agron St, Jerusalem, Isr.

ILSAR, Yehiel, Isr, diplomat, educator; b. Pol, Dec 20, 1912; s. Henoch and Elke (Blatt) Isler; in Isr since 1934; att U Cologne; Heb U; U Zurich; m. Miriam Badt, 1937; c: Tamar, Benjamin. Isr Ambass extraordinary and plen, Panama since 1968; found, prin, Children's Inst for Psych Treatment, Jerusalem, 1939-43; dir, Sem for Instrs, haNoar haOved, Jerusalem, 1943-44; co-org, dept dir, later, dir, dept for reuniting DP families, JA, 1944-47; secy to Golda Meir, dir, political dept, JA, 1947-48; dir of archives, documentation, courier service, Min Fgn Affairs, Jerusalem, 1948-51; first secy, consul, Isr legation, Rome, 1951-53; cons, dep dir, W Eur div, Min Fgn Affairs, Jerusalem, 1953-57; consul gen, Isr Consulate, Zurich, 1957-60; Isr Ambass Philippines, 1962-63, Min extraordinary and plen, 1960-62; Ambass extraordinary and plen, Thailand; non res Isr Ambass, Laos; non-res Min, Ceylon, 1963-65; i/c dept for Jerusalem and Ecclesiastical Affairs, 1965-68; mem: Kartel Jüdischer Verbindungen; Augustin Keller lodge, B'nai B'rith, Zurich; club, Wack Wack Golf, Manila. Contbr to jours. Spec interests: psych, phil, hist. Office: Min for Fgn Affairs, Jerusalem, Isr.

ILUTOVICH, Leon, US, organization exec; b. Odessa, Russia; s. Jacob and Leya (Plotycher); LLM, Warsaw U; m. Exec dir, ZOA, since 1964, asst exec dir, 1952-64; secy, Political Rep Pol J, 1937; secy gen, Gen Zionists, Pol, 1938-39; repr, JA, Far E, 1941-46; delg to ZCs. Exec mem: World Union Gen Zionists; exec comm, UJA; Natl Panel of Amer Arbitration Assn; exec comm, AZC; mem, Zionist Actions Comm. Home: 900 West End Ave, New York, NY. Office: 145 E 32 St, New York, NY.

IMBER, Errol Barton, US, organization exec; b. Chgo, Ill, Feb 20, 1938; s. Elmer and Dena (Leib); BA, U Ill, 1959; m. Barbara Tucker, Nov 30, 1961; c: Daniela. Dir, lodge services, dist 2, B'nai B'rith since 1964; cmty worker, Public Housing Auth, Isr, 1963; farmer, Isr, 1966-67; chaplain's asst, US Army UN Command, 1959-62. Mem: JPSA; Hollywood Pk B'nai B'rith; Lodge 4, B'nai B'rith; pres, B'nai B'rith Youth, AZA; exec bd, B'nai B'rith Hillel, U of Ill. Author: Short History of District 2, B'nai B'rith, 1965; Hobbies: J hist, collecting books. Home: 8615 DeSoto St, Cincinnati, O. Office: 1717 Section St, Cincinnati, O.

IMBER, Gerald H, US, attorney; b. NYC, Aug 7, 1924; s. Max and Jennie (Schilofsky); att NYU, 1949; LLB, Bklyn Law Sch, 1951; m. Mona Salzman; c: Wayne. Pvt practice since 1951; pres: Reefclub Ltd, since 1963; Woodmere Charcoal Pit Corp, since 1963. Cpl, US Army, 1943-45. Artistic dir, Epos Theater Group; mem: NY State Bar Assn; NY Co Lawyers Assn; NY State Trial Lawyers Assn; Amer Fed Musicians; club, Clearview Yacht, fmr commodore. Recipient: Yachtsmen of Year, Clearview Yacht Club, 1964. Spec interests: acting, producing plays, music, yachting, restaurant oprs. Home: 315 E 65 St, New York, NY. Office: 880 Third Ave, New York, NY.

IMBER, Herman, US, business exec; b. Bklyn, NY, Jan 30, 1916; s. Nathan and Sophie; m. Celia, June 26, 1966; c: Ruth. Sales mgr, Seward Luggage, Bklyn, since 1959; regional dir, ZOA, 1946-50; educ dir, World Memorial J Martyrs, 1953-54; city mgr, State Isr bonds, 1954-58; vice-pres, bd dirs, Bklyn B'nai B'rith Youth Org; chmn, fund raising cabinet, Bklyn Council B'nai B'rith, exec comm; pres: New Haven Zionist Dist, 1946-47; E NY Lodge, Bnai B'rith, 1964-66; mem: Natl Luggage Dealers Assn. Spec interest, Isr. Home: 2781 Ocean Ave, Brooklyn, NY. Office: 128 32 St, Brooklyn, NY.

IMBER, Isaac, US, business exec; b. Bklyn, NY, Aug, 1907; s. Nathan and Sophie (Weber); BSS, CCNY, 1931; m. Rebecca Schmuckler; c: Michal, Abigail. Pres: Isr Amer Diversified Fund, since 1967; Inland and Intl Co, Inc; Rassco Financial Corp, 1957-65. Helped found, Intercollegiate Zionist Fed of Amer, 1926; found, Amer Isr Financial Corp, 1949; Masada Youth, ZOA, 1932, pres, 1932-40; exec dir, Materials for Isr, 1947-49; secy, Zionist Commn of Educ and Youth Orgs, 1936; mem: ZOA; AJCong; B'nai B'rith; B'nai Zion. Contbr to Zionist jours. Home: 4 E 74 St, New York, NY. Office: 250 W 57 St, New York, NY.

IMBERMAN, Jacob, US, attorney; b. NYC, Aug 7, 1916; s. Sam and Pauline (Bleie); att: CCNY, 1933-35; St John's U, NYC, 1935-37; LLB, St John's U, Sch of Law, 1941; m. Beatrice Hertz, Aug 13, 1946; c: Joseph, Diane. Partner, Proskauer, Rose, Goetz & Mendelsohn, NYC, since 1960; spec asst, Atty Gen, NY State, 1952-53; counsel, commn of inves, NY State, 1954. Lt, US Army, Corps of Engrs, 1942-46. Pres, LI Div, AJComm; mem: Amer, NY State, NYC Bar Assns. Home: 41 Auerbach Ln, Cedarhurst, LI, NY. Office: 300 Park Ave, New York, NY.

IMMANUEL, Itzhak Moshe (pen name, **Ami**), Isr, historian, author, educator; b. Jerusalem, May 6, 1927; s. Abraham and Rivka (Levi); att: Heb U, Jerusalem, 1946-48; Sch, Law and Econ, Tel Aviv; Pedg Sem, Tel Aviv; m. Sara Bachar, June 5, 1949; c: Varda, Yardena, Eyal, Reviva. Tchr, Hs; ed, Young Israel, since 1958; chmn, Young Isr movement. Author, textbooks: Sefer Divrei haYamim, 1956, 1960; Yad'am Holon, 1961; haPoel Tveria, 1961; Yad'am Bat Yam, 1961; Toldot Israel beArtzo; haMahapecha haSfaradit, 1964; Za'akat Yehudei Maroko, 1967; Za'akat Yehudei Mitzrayim, 1967; haPa'ar, 1968; Yehudei Sefarad beEretz Israel; contbr articles to newspapers. Recipient, President Award, for haPa'ar. Spec interests: poetry, colleting newspapers, reading. Home: 30 Alharizi St, Holon, Isr.

INDELMAN, Elchanan (Chonon), US, author, poet, educator; b. Zuromin, Pol, May 22, 1913; s. Joseph and Alta (Bervikunkin); in US since 1947; grad, Tchrs Inst, Warsaw; m. Leah Krechevsky, Nov, 1951; c: Alta, Esther. Heb text writer, J Educ Comm, NY since 1947; ed, Lador, Heb Jr Libr, since 1951; instr, Heb lit, Herzliya Heb Tchrs' Inst, since 1968; tchr, Warsaw, Helsinki schs, 1932-39, 1946-47; ed: Olami, Olami Hakatan, Heb mags for youth and Children, Warsaw, 1936-39; instr, Heb lang and lit, Yeshiva U, NY, 1948-49; prin, Queens Heb HS, 1950-68. Author, ed numerous volumes of poetry, plays, essays, fiction in Heb and Yiddish; ed: Thesaurus of the Hebrew language, 1968; Udim, anthol of writers who perished in Eur holocaust, Vol I, 1960, Vol II, 1963; Olam Hadash; Heb monthly for children, since 1961. Home: 64-20 Saunders St, Forest Hills, NY. Office: 426 W 58 St, New York NY.

INSELBUCH, Dora R, US, communal worker; b. Vilna, Russ, Dec 12, 1899; d. Idel and Hadassah (Block) Idelson; in US since 1904; att Hunter Coll, 1917-20; tchrs cert, JTSA, 1918; m. Samuel Inselbuch, July 29, 1920; c: Hadassah Tannor, Froma Zeitlin. Mem, Hadassah, natl bd, 1937-53; natl chmn, chaluziut, 1942-45; natl educ comm, 1936-38; pres, found, Hadassah, Jersey City, NJ, 1926-29; vice-pres, Bklyn and NY Chaps, 1935-36, chmn, educ; JNF, 1938-47, chmn, admn comm, 1938-47; hon vice-pres, United Pal Appeal, 1942-45; ZC, Jerusalem, 1951; co-org, Sch for J Women, JTSA; mem: joint comm, JNF and KH; Amer Zionist Youth Commn, 1947-52; Soc for Advancement of Judaism, Reconstructionist movement. Contbr to publs. Home: 800 West End Ave, New York, NY.

INTRATER, Aaron, US, educator; b. Lwow, Pol, Dec 28, 1913; s. Jacob and Eshter (Mersel); in US since 1937; dipl, Heb Tchrs Sem, Lwow, 1934; BA, Butler U, 1954, MA, 1956; m. Roseline Minsky, July 1, 1949; c: Othniel. Exec-dir, Bur of J Educ, Cleveland, O, since 1960; prin, Beth Solomon Sch, Boston, Mass, 1942-49; exec-dir, J Educ Assn, Indianapolis, Ind, 1949-60. Pres, Histadrut Ivrit, Cleveland; vice-pres, Mid-W Council, J Educ; exec mem, Natl Council, J Educ; mem: Natl Assn of Profs of Heb; ZOA; J Communal Service. Author: The Voice of Wisdom, 1965; Tchrs Guides; contbr to various mags. Recipient, Tarbut Scholarship prize. Spec interest, sports. Home: 6717 Metro Park Dr, Mayfield, O. Office: 2030 S Taylor Rd, Cleveland, O.

IRELL, Lawrence Elliot, US, attorney; b. Boston, Mass, Mar 23, 1912; BA, UCLA, 1932; LLB, U of S Cal, 1935; LLM, Harvard Law Sch, 1936; m. Elaine Smith; c: Lauren, Eugene, Stephen. Partner, Irell & Manella; lectr: U of S Cal Tax Inst; U of S Cal, Sch of Law. Pres: Beverly Hills Bar Assn; J Cmty Found, J Fed Council, Gtr LA; natl vice pres, CFJWF, pres, W region; gen counsel, UCLA Found; mem bd: Hope for Hearing Research Found; Cedars-Sinai Med Cen, LA; pres: J Youth Council, LA, 1937-41; Metrop Recreation and Youth Services Planning Council, 1963-66; J Cens Assn of LA, 1956-59; W States region, Natl JWB, 1953-56; chmn: W area profsls div, United Fund, LA, 1966-67; planning dept, budget, allocations comm, J Fed-Council, Gtr LA, 1963-66; vice-pres, mem bd, Reiss-Davis Clinic for Child Guidance,

1955-58; mem bd: JWB, 1963-65; LA Hillel Council, 1954-57; mem council, Harvard Law Sch Assn, 1964-65; mem frats: Zeta Beta Tau; Order of Coif; Alpha Delta Sigma; pres, Barristers. Home: 965 Alpine Dr, Beverly Hills, Cal. Office: 1800 Ave of the Stars, Century City, LA, Cal.

IRMAY, Shragga, Isr, engineer, scientist, educator; b. Lodz, Pol, July 1, 1912; s. David and Sara (Danziger) Szeps; in Isr since 1924; dipl Eng, U of Liège, Belgium, 1935; m. Rinna Zaks, 1950; c: Ron, Amnon. Prof, fluid mechs, hydraulics, Technion, Haifa, since 1958; fac mem, civil engr since 1938, academic coord for research, since 1966, dean, grad sch, 1966-68; acting vice-pres for research, 1960-61; acting vice-pres, 1961-62; found, head, hydrotech soil mech lab, 1949-52; head, div of hydraulic engr, 1954-56; all at Technion; cons engr, lect, fac agric, Heb U, Jerusalem, 1946-50; asst, U of Liège; engr, Dept of Public Works, Pal, 1935-36; visiting prof: UC, Berkeley, Davis, 1965-66; Sorbonne, U Paris, 1964; NYU, Stanford U, Cal, 1958-59; chmn adv bd, Ashdod Harbor Devl, 1957-58; repr: Isr, Technion, intl confs. Mem, council of examiners, cons mem, Acad of Heb Lang; hon mem, Acad Royale des Sci d'Outre-Mer de Belgique; mem: Isr Assn and Intl Union of Geodesy and Geophys; Intl Assn of Hydraulic Research; Amer Geophys Union; Engrs and Architects Assn Isr; Assn des Engrs de Liège; Intl Soil Sci Soc; Intl Assn of Soil Mech and Found Engr; Isr Assn of Theoretical and Applied Mech; Govt Engrs and Architects. Co-author, ed, UNESCO book on water percolation; ed bd, Isr Jour Tech; contbr to profsl jours, encyclopedias. Spec interest: Heb philol, sci terminology. Home: 67 Einstein St, Haifa, Isr. Office: Technion, Haifa, Isr.

IRONI, Itzhak, Isr, business exec; b. Pol, Apr 10, 1922; s. Noah and Rivka (Shapiro); in Isr since 1932; BS, Columbia U, NY, 1953; m. Naomi Henkin, July 14, 1954; c: Anat, Nigal, Avinoah. Dir gen, Isr Mil Ind, since 1967; dep dir gen, 1953-66; acting dir gen, 1966-67. Haganah, IDF, 1940-50. Recipient, decorations: Fighters; War of Independence; Sinai; Six Days War. Home: 6 Him St, Tel Aviv, Isr. Office: 22 B St, Hakirya, Tel Aviv, Isr.

IR-SHAY, Steven Pessach, Isr, designer, sculptor; b. Budapest, Hung, Oct 6, 1896; s. Adolph and Hermine (Neumann) Irsai; in Isr since 1945; BA, Budapest Tech HS, 1918; MA, Royal Acad, Budapest; m. Aurelie Lefkovits, June 3, 1925 (decd); c: Robert, Marianne; m. 2nd, Hilde Stein, May 23, 1961. Free-lance artist, since 1920; adv, propaganda, PM Off, Hung, 1936-39; Lt, Hung Army, WW I; prin contrib, designed modern Heb lettering; posters reproduced in profsl periodicals throughout the world. Mem: Isr Painters and Sculptors Assn; B'nai B'rith, Nordau Lodge, Tel Aviv. Contbr articles on publicity, psych advt to profsl jours. Recipient: Valor Medal, 1919; first prize: YMCA Olympiade poster contest, 1938; poster, Mobiloil Europa contest, 1936; UN intl stamp design competition, second prize 1952, 1963, 1965, third prize 1961; Isr-Nordau Prize, 1963. Home and studio: 12 Graetz St, Tel Aviv, Isr.

ISAAC, Sol M, US, attorney; b. Columbus, O, Dec 5, 1911; s. Arthur and Bella (Loewenstein); BA, Yale U, 1933; LLB, Harvard U, 1936; m. Dorothy Durlacher, Dec 18, 1936; c: Beatrice Weiler, Frederick, Thomas. Partner, law firm, Isaac, Postlewaite, O'Brien and Oman; asso, Butler and Isaac, 1936-48; partner, Isaac and Postlewaite, 1950-59. Lt, USNR, 1944-46. Vice-pres, United Comty Council, since 1968; mem bd: Franklin Co; Riverside Methodist Hosp; O Citizens Council for Health and Wfr, fmr pres; Heritage House; Yale Club, Cen O, pres, 1965-67; Consumer Credit Counseling Service, Gtr Columbus Legal Aid, Defender Soc; Amer comm, Intl Council, Social Wfr; f, Amer Bar Found; mem: Columbus, O State, Amer Bar Assns, fmr pres, Columbus; B'nai B'rith; Amer Legion; Zeta Beta Tau; bd, Columbus Bar Found, fmr pres; Amer Coll Probate Counsel; Natl Conf, Lawyers and Social Workers, co-chmn, 1961-66; sect on family law, Amer Bar Assn, chmn, 1960-61; fmr pres: Family and Children's Bur, Columbus, O; Family Service Assn of Amer; Natl Conf on Social Wfr, 1964-65; delg, intl conf Soc Wfr, 1968; clubs: Winding Hollow Country, fmr vice-pres; Yale, Central O. Recipient, awards: Cen O chap, NASW, 1962; George Meany Comty Service, 1963. Home: 222 Ashbourne Rd, Columbus, O. Office: 88 E Broad, St, Columbus, O.

ISAACMAN, Daniel, US, educator; b. Phila, Pa, Aug 10, 1924; s. Reuben and Esther (Handelman); BA, U Pa, 1948, MS, 1951; att Dropsie Coll, 1951-55; m. Clara Heller, July 24, 1945; c: Yonathan. Registrar, prof, educ, J Hist, Gratz Coll,

since 1951; princ, tchr, United Heb Schs, 1946-51. US Army, Transp, MCs, 1943-45. Chmn: Phila Lab Z Youth Commn; Task Force, Natl Conf on J Camping; pres, Natl Council for J Educ, since 1969, mem, exec comm, Natl Conf of J Communal Workers. Contbr to: Arise and Build, 1961; Amer J Year Book, 1966. Home: 9211 Pine Rd, Philadelphia, Pa. Office: 10 Tabor Rd, Philadelphia, Pa.

ISAACMAN, Seymour, US, attorney; b, NYC, Dec 29, 1914; s. Adolph and Celia (Spivack); att NYU, 1932-34; LLB, Rutgers Law Sch, 1937; m. Florence Garbow, June 3, 1942; c: Richard, Donald, Alan. Sr partner, Isaacman and Isaacman, since 1939. Mem, Human Relations Commn, Elizabeth, NJ, 1964-66, chmn, 1965-66, legal cons, since 1966. Pres, ZOA, Elizabeth dist, since 1938, secy, 1946-48; pres, Temple B'nai Isr since 1960, vice-pres, 1959; co-chmn, Bonds for Isr, since 1951; trustee: Union Co J Council; B'nai B'rith, 1947; exec bd, UJA; mem: YMHA; Bais Yitzchok Chevrah Thilim; club, Men's, Temple B'nai Isr. Home: 519 Riverside Dr, Elizabeth, NJ. Office: 1143 E Jersey St, Elizabeth, NJ.

ISAACS, Ann F, US, educator, editor, school cons; b. Cincinnati, O, July 2, 1920; d. William and Bessie (Jacoby) Fabe; BA, U Cincinnati, 1943; MEd, Xavier U, 1950; PhD, O State U, 1960; postgrad studies: W Res U, 1945-54; U Chgo, 1957; HUC, 1965-69; m. S Isaacs, June 7, 1939; c: Marjorie, Susan. Pvt practice, psych, since 1945; exec dir, Natl Assn for Gifted Children, since 1958, found, 1st pres, 1954-57; psych: Hamilton Co Child Wfr Dept, 1944-45; Personality Testing Bur, 1945-48; dir, Personality Devl Pre-Sch, 1948-57; cons to schs; lectr, visiting prof: workshops on gifted Kan State Coll, Pittsburgh, 1960; Kan State U; Wilmington Coll, O; Mich State U; Dayton U, O; delg, White House Conf on Children and Youth, 1960. Mem: Natl Assn for Study of Educ; Wise Temple and Adath Isr Sisterhood; Amer Assn, Sch Admnrs; Natl Assn Nursery Educ; Intl Reading Assn; World Fed, Mh; Amer, O, Assns for Gifted Children; charter, Assn, Psychols in Pvt Practice; life mem: Natl Council J Women; Hadassah; Brandeis. Co-dir, Educ Press Assn of Amer; ed, The Gifted Child Quarterly since 1957; composer, music for The Book of Psalms; contbr to educ, psych jours. Recipient, Citation for Superlative Achievement, Educ Press Assn of Amer, 1969. Hobbies: gardening, painting. Home: 8080 Springvalley Dr, Cincinnati, O.

ISAACS, Betty L, US, sculptor; b. Hobart, Tasmania, Sep 2, 1894; d. Henry and Anna (Cohen) Lewis; in US since 1913; att: Art Students League, NY, 1925-27; Cooper Union Art Sch, NY, 1928-29; Kunstgewerbe Schule, Vienna, Aus, 1929; Alfred U, 1937; m. Julius Isaacs, Sep 11, 1921. Sculptor, since 1936; libr: NY Public Libr, 1915-16; 92nd St YMHA, 1916-18; asst to exec dir, Cen J Inst, NY, 1918-20; tchr, art, Cooper Union Art Sch and Greenwich House, 1930-38; designer of rugs, textiles, wallpaper, 1930-36. Exhbs: Natl Alliance of Art and Ind, NY, 1929-34; Phila Art Alliance, 1937; Clay Club, NY, 1941; Bonestell Gal, NY, 1944; Audubon Soc, NY, 1945, 1950, 1952, 1953, 1955; Cooper Union, NY, 1947, 1953; Ferargil Gal, NY, 1947; Arthur Brown Gal, NY, 1949-50; Argent Gal, NY, 1945, 1946, 1957; Contemporaries Gal, NY, 1957-58; Riverside Mus, NY, 1957, 1961; Natl Acad, NY, since 1954; Bertha Schaefer Gal, NY, 1959; one-man shows: Amymay Studios, Pasadena, Cal, 1941; Hacker Gal, NY, 1953; U of Louisville, Ky, 1955; Stamford Mus, Conn, 1964; Lever House NY, 1963, 1965, 1966, 1967; repr in perm collection, Cooper Union Mus; pvt collections. Mem: Natl Assn of Women Artists; Amer Soc of Contemporary Artists. Recipient, awards: Natl Assn of Women Artists, 1955, 1957, 1960; Amer Soc of Contemporary Artists, 1958, 1960, 1961. Home and studio: 21 E 10 St, New York, NY.

ISAACS, Edith S, US, author; b. NYC, June 18, 1884; d. Julius and Helen (Stirn) Somborn; BA, Barnard Coll, 1906; m. Stanley Isaacs, 1910; c: Myron, Helen Herrick. Writer: greeting card verses, 1922-23; skits, Grand St Follies and Hitchykoo, 1926; sketches, plays, Barnard Coll. Pres, Phi Beta Kappa, 1958-60; vice-pres, NY Service for Orthopedically Handicapped since 1956; dir, Council of Goodwill Inds, since 1952; trustee, Bank St Coll, since 1962; club, Women's City, dir, vice-pres, since 1942. Author: Love Affair with a City, 1967. Home: 14 E 96 St, New York, NY.

ISAACS, Elizabeth, US, college admnr; b. NYC, Oct 18, 1902; d. Philip and Julie (Hirsch) Klein; BA, Barnard Coll, 1923; m. Moses Isaacs, May 2, 1926; c: Philip, Nancy. Ret; dean of students, Stern Coll for Women, Yeshiva U, 1958-67; adv to students, dir, student activities, 1955-58. Hon pres: women's br, Union Orthodox J Congs of Amer, since 1951, pres, 1946-51; Sisterhood, Ohab Zedek, Yonkers, NY, since 1940, pres, 1935-40; chmn, conf comm, Natl J Women's Orgs, 1951-53. Home: 51 Woodycrest Dr, Northport, NY.

ISAACS, Harold Robert, US, educator,writer; b. NYC, Sep 13, 1910; s. Robert and Sophie (Berlin); AB, Columbia U, 1930; m. Viola Robinson, Sep 14, 1932; c: Arnold, Deborah. Prof, political sci, MIT, Cambridge, Mass since 1965, research asso, Cen Intl Studies, 1953-65; reporter: NY Times; Honolulu Advt; Shanghai Evening Post; China Press; all 1928-31; with: Agence Havas, Shanghai, NYC, 1931-40; CBS, NYC, Wash DC, 1940-43; war corresp, CBI, asso ed, Newsweek mag, Wash, China, SE Asia, NYC, 1943-50; Guggenheim f, 1950. Mem: Assn of Asian Studies; Afr Studies Assn; Assn of Public Opinion Research; club, Overseas Press, NYC. Author: The Tragedy of the Chinese Revolution, 1938; No Peace for Asia, 1947; Two Thirds of the World, 1950; Scratches on our Minds, American Images of China and India, 1958; Emergent Americans, a Report on Crossroads, Africa, 1961; The New World of Negro Americans, 1963; India's Ex-Untouchables, 1965; American Jews in Israel, 1967. Recipient: Anisfield-Wolf Award, 1964. Home: 96 Farlow Rd, Newton, Mass. Office: Cen Intl Studies, MIT, Cambridge, Mass.

ISAACS, Harry J, US, physician, educator; b. Chgo, Ill, Sep 21, 1895; s. Julius and Anna (Greenberg); BS, U Chgo, 1917; MD, Rush Med Coll, 1919; m. Edith Lippert, Jan 20, 1920; c: Julien, Robert. Chmn,em, prof, med, Chgo Med Sch, fac mem since 1939; prof, Sch of Med, Cook Co Grad Sch; att phys: Mt Sinai; Cook Co; Columbus and Weiss; Memorial, all Chgo hosps; sr att phys; chest: Michael Reese; Winfield. Maj, US Army MC Res. Mem: AMA; Chgo and Ill Med Soc; Chgo Soc Internal Med; Amer, Chgo Heart Assns; Amer Bd Internal Med; Amer Coll Chest Phys; Alpha Omega Alpha; Temple Sholom; club, Standard. Contbr to sci jours. Hobby, travel. Home: 2608 Lakeview Ave, Chicago, Ill. Office: 25 E Washington, Chicago, Ill.

ISAACS, Julius, US, attorney, jurist, educator; b. NYC, Dec 31, 1896; s. Louis and Rebecca (Rosencranz); BA, CCNY, 1917; JD, NYU Law Sch, 1924; m. Betty Lewis, Sep 11, 1921. Pvt law practice, 1925-33, and since 1947; tchr, Eng and citizenship, NYC night schs, 1921-26; asst corp counsel, 1934-38, acting 1938-45; City Magistrate assigned to Court of Spec Sessions, 1946-47; lectr, law and social disciplines, Indian U, 1956; US Army, WW I; mem, legal adv staff, Selective Service Admn, WW II. Vice-pres: Friends of Fr Opera; Manhattan chap, Izaak Walton League of Amer, since 1952; comm on Court reorg, Citizens Union; chmn, Contemporary Music Soc; dir: Clarion Music Soc; Gauthier Soc for Contemporary Song; LaGuardia Memorial Assn; chmn, leg comm on aging, Comty Service Soc; vice-pres, PEN, Amer Cen, delg, intl congs: Ger; Brazil; Nor; Yugo; NY; chmn, bd of visitors, Hart I, for NY Wfr, Health Council; dir, NY Co Lawyers Assn; chmn: comm on uniform state laws; comm on med jurisdiction; profsl ethics and nominations comm; mem: comm on criminal courts; City of NY and NY State Bar Assn; comm on public health; natl comm, Keren Beth Hanasi of Isr; US Comm for Sports in Isr; Phi Beta Kappa; pres, YMHA Alumni, 1951-54; fmr cdr, Fr Us Post, Amer Legion. Author: Oath of Devotion, 1949; contbr to legal and psycht jours. Hobbies: painting, music. Home: 21 E 10 St, New York, NY. Office: 292 Madison Ave, New York, NY.

ISAACS, Lewis M Jr, US, attorney; b. NYC, Jan 7, 1908; s. Lewis and Edith (Rich); BA, Harvard U, 1928; LLB, Columbia U Law Sch, 1931; m. Carrie Fabrikant, May 26, 1940; c: Carol Silver. Mem, law firm, M S and I S Isaacs, since 1936. Secy, mem, bd trustees, James Weldon Johnson Cmty Cen; mem: comm on housing and urban devl, Cmty Service Soc; Amer, NY State Bar Assns; Amer Council for Judaism since 1946; dir and counsel, Honest Ballot Assn, 1933-51; dir, treas, Edward MacDowell Assn, 1947-51; trustee, Cong Shaaray Tefila, 1946-49; mem exec comm, Assn of Bar, City of NY; club, Harvard. Contbr to legal jours. Hobby: photography. Home: 175 E 62 St, New York, NY. Office: 475 Fifth Ave, New York, NY.

ISAACS, Robert C, US, attorney, educator; b. NYC, July 16, 1919; s. David and Elsie (Weiss); BA, cum laude, NYU, 1941, LLB, 1943, JD, 1968; m. Doris Shapiro, Nov 20, 1943; c: Leigh. Lawyer, Nordlinger, Riegemar, Benetar & Charney, since 1946, mem, firm, since 1962; adj prof, St John's U Sch of Law, since 1961; fact-finder and mediator, NY State Pub

Employees Relations Bd, since 1968; lectr, labor law, NYU Practising Law Inst; spec legal asst, NY State Dept of Law, 1943, dep asst atty gen, 1943-44, spec asst atty gen, 1946. Capt, US Army Signal Corps, 1943-45; Judge Advocate, General Corps, 1951. Chmn: comm on labor law, NY State Bar Assn, since 1966; sect on labor law, Amer Bar Assn; secy, comm on labor and soc security legislation, Assn of the Bar of NYC, since 1955; mem: Natl Panel of Arbitrators, Amer Arbitration Assn, since 1957; NYU Law Review Alumni Assn; War Veterans' Bar Assn, 1946-48; brotherhood, Central Synagogue. Contbr to legal jours. Recipient: Marice Goodman Memorial Award, 1943. Home: 4 Peter Cooper Rd, New York, NY. Office: 420 Lexington Ave, New York, NY.

ISAACS, Roger D, US, public relations exec; b. Boston, Mass, Oct 23, 1925; s. Raphael and Agnes (Wolfstein); BA, Bard Coll, 1949; att: U Chgo; U Wis; m. Joyce Wexler, Oct 23, 1949; c: Jill, Jan. Pres, dir, The PR Bd Inc, with firm since 1949; secy, dir, The Financial Relations Bd. US Army, WW II. Mem: Chgo exec comm, ADL, since 1968; PR comm; Crusade of Mercy since 1967; trustee: Coll of J Studies, since 1968; Highland Park Hosp, since 1957, bd mgrs since 1964; mem: PR Soc of Amer; Assn of Commerce and Ind; clubs: Birchwood; Publicity. Co-author, Puzzling Biblical Laws, 1965; contbr to periodicals. Home: 2661 Sheridan Rd, Highland Park, Ill. Office: 75 Wacker Dr, Chicago, Ill.

ISAACSON, Simon Louis, US, educator, attorney; b. Lith, Dec 13, 1900; s. Isaac and Dora (Valenzig); in US since 1906; att Baltimore Tchrs Training Sch, 1919-21; LLB, U Md, Sch of Law, 1924, JD, 1969; att Johns Hopkins U, Tchrs Coll, 1933-35; m. Rose Singer, Aug 30, 1925; c: Stanley, Elaine Katzen. Pvt practice since 1924; instr, law, Baltimore City Coll Adult Cen since 1947; dean, Sch of Secular Studies, Talmudical Acad of Baltimore, 1923-54; dir, Sch of Secular Studies, Bais Yakov Sch for Girls, Baltimore, 1945-48; instr, law, Mt Vernon Sch of Law, 1961-64. Mem: Baltimore City Bar Assn; Legal Aid Panel; Lawyer Referral Panel; Natl Adult Tchrs Assn; pres, Mogen Isr Cong, 1948-69; vice-pres, Heb Young Men Sick Relief Soc, 1933-37; secy, Baltimore Youth Commn, 1945-49. Recipient: Commendation Plaque, Baltimore Isr Bonds Comm, 1963; Testimonial Scroll, Alumni Assn of Talmudical Acad, 1964. Spec interests: cartooning, educ drawings. Home: 3332 Clarks Lane, Baltimore, Md. Office: 220 E Lexington St, Baltimore, Md.

ISAACSON, Stanley L, US, business exec, statistician; b. Baltimore, Md, Jan 31, 1927; s. Simon and Rose (Singer); BA, Johns Hopkins U, 1945, MA, 1947, PhD, Columbia U, 1950; m. Annette Gendler, Aug 31, 1952; c: Rita Irving, Marcia. Vice-pres, Gendler Stone Products Co, since 1964, sales mgr since 1956; pres S & S Trucking Inc, since 1959; vice-pres, R & I Construction, since 1961; asst prof, Ia St Coll, 1950-55; visiting asst prof, Stnaford U, 1953-54; sr engr, Westinghouse Elec Corp, 1955-56; lectr, Drake U, 1956-59. Mem bd Trustees, Tifereth Isr Syn, since 1957, treas, 1964-66; vice-pres, 1958-59, 1966-67; pres, 1967-69; pres, Men's club, 1960-62; bd govs, JWF, since 1958, past exec comm; mem: Inst of Math Stat, cen regional prog chmn, 1955-56; Des Moines Bur of J Educ, since 1957; Amer Stat Assn; Amer Soc for Quality Control; AAUP; B'nai B'rith; ZOA; Masons; Phi Beta Kappa; Sigma Xi; Alpha Epsilon Pi; co-found, Baltimore chap, Intercollegiate Zionist Fed, 1945, treas, 1946-47; delg to natl conv, 1947; chmn Des Moines J Forum, 1957-59; mem, Habonim Lab Zionist Youth, 1940-50; club, Hyperion Field. Contbr to math publs. Spec interest, J hist. Home: 4706 Lakeview Dr, Des Moines, Ia. Office: 1075 Polk Blvd, Des Moines, Ia.

ISAACSON, William J, US, attorney; b. Gallitzin, Pa, Jan 10, 1913; s. Louis and Anna (Kaufman); AB, U Mich, 1935, JD, 1937; m. Bernice Kavinoky, Feb 9, 1936 (decd); c: Stephen; m. 2nd, Inge Ryfordt, Apr, 1966; c: Stig. Partner, Kaye, Scholer, Fierman, Hays & Handler, since 1960; atty, Detroit, 1937-39; reg dir, NLRB, 1939-48; gen sounsel, Amalgamated Clothing Workers of Amer, 1948-58; visiting prof, Cornell U, 1958; dep ind commn, State of NY, 1959-60. Chmn: NY State Grievance Appeals Bd; Comm: on Post-Admission Legal Educ, Sect on Lab Law, since 1967; Labor relations law, NY bar assn, 1958-59; comm, labor and social security legislation, 1963-66, both Bar Assn City of NY; mem: Amer and NY Bar Assns; Park Ave Syn. Contbr to legal jours. Home: 860 UN Plaza, New York, NY. Office: 425 Park Ave, New York, NY.

ISBAN, Samuel, US, author, journalist; b. Gostinin, Pol, Sept 26, 1905; s. Mordecai and Leah (Laks) Ishbitsky; att, Heb

U, Jerusalem, Pal. 1925-26; m. Sally Epstein, 1930; c: Joseph, Elliot, Ruth Zuckerbrod; in US since 1938. Staff writer: Day-Jewish Journal, since 1953; Jewish Morning Journal, 1942-52; dir, Yiddish and Hebrew Press; free-lance writer, since 1925. Author: Massen, 1929; Noch'n Shturm, 1929; Kyer, 1914-18, pub, 1933; Oif Rushtovanies, 1936; Tzvishen Hundert Toiren, 1942; Die 24 Shoh fun August Geiger, 1945; B'Veth Ha-Din, 1947; Umlegale Yidden Shpalten Yaman, 1948 (radio dramatization, 1949); Familie Karp, 1948; Dir Farshpetigte Yorshim, 1954; Di Kenigin Izevel, 2 vols, 1960; Israel Shteiger (play), 1961; Di Shtot fun Tzorn (short stories); Tales of New York, 1965; Rahab of Jericho; works translated into Heb, Eng, Span. Mem, I L Peretz Yiddish Writers Union; club, PEN. Recipient: Haint-Weltspiegel Prize, Warsaw, 1936; Zukunft Prize, NY, 1945; Kessel Prize, Mexico City, 1950. Home: 2475 E 22 St, Bklyn, NY. Office: 183 E Broadway, NYC.

ISENBERG, Abraham, Charles, US, business exec; b. Lynn, Mass, Feb 24, 1914; s. Louis and Alice (Lown); BS, U Pa, Wharton Sch of Finance and Commerce, 1935; m. Thelma Sissenwine, Oct 30, 1938; c: Edward, Lee, Gerald. Pres, chief exec off, Consolidated Natl Shoe Corp, since 1968, vicepres, 1964-67, exec vice-pres, 1967-68. Vice-pres, 210 Associates; vice-chmn, Shoe Div Combined J Philanthropies; dir: NE ADL; Amer Footwear Mfrs Assn; dir, Mens Assn Heb Rehab 1966-69; mem: Beta Sigma Rho, Epsilon chap; clubs: Gtr Boston Brandeis, Boston Boot and Shoe, exec comm. Hobby, golf. Home: 20 Ascenta Terr, Newton, Mass. Office: 10 American Dr, Norwood, Mass.

ISENBERGH, Maurice D, US, attorney; b. Troy, NY, Dec 31, 1898; s. Maurice and Millie (Dosenheim); LLB, Albany Law Sch, 1920; m. Edna Cosgro, Apr 26, 1944. Surrogate, Rensselaer Co, 1953-64; first asst, corp counsel, Troy, 1923-26. US Army, WW I, WW II. Bd trustees: Cong B rith Sholom, since 1923, pres, 1933-34; Rensselaer Co Bar Assn; exec comm, J Comty Cen, 1940-50; secy, Rensselaer Co Heart Assn, 1949-54; pres, Co Tuberculosis Hosp, 1940-46; vicepres, council Social Agcys, 1936-38; dir: Boy Scouts 1934-36; Co Red Cross, 1942-48; Girl Scouts, 1950-52; chmn, J Wfr Dr, 1935-36; exec secy, Rensselaer Co Civil Service Commn; mem: Amer Legion; Masons; AJComm; B'nai B'rith; ZOA; NY State Bar; Surrogates Assn. Home: 559 Pinewoods Ave, Troy NY. Office: 205 Broadway, New York, NY.

ISENBERGH, Max, US lawyer, educator; b. Albany, NY, Aug 28, 1913; s. David and Tess (Solomon); BA, Cornell U, 1934; LLB, Harvard J, 1938, LLM, 1939, MA, 1942; m. Pearl Evans, Aug 10, 1939; c: Tess, David Joseph. Prof law: Va U Law Sch 1965-66, and since 1968; spec adv on cultural affairs, State Dept since 1962; George Wash U Law Sch, Wash DC, 1963-65; Yale U Law Sch, 1966-67; research f, Harvard Law Sch, 1938-39; tutor, Chgo U Law Sch, 1939-40; legal secy to US Supr Court Justice Hugo L Black, 1941-42; spec asst to Atty Gen, dir, trading with enemy act litigation, Justice Dept, 1943-48; counsel, Eur oprs, AJComm, Paris, 1948-50; legal adv, Point Four Prog, State Dept, 1950-51; gen counsel, Pres Materials Policy Commn, Exec Off of Pres, 1951-52; dep gen counsel, cons on fgn affairs, AEC, 1952-56; spec asst for atomic energy, State Dept, US Emb, Paris, 1956-61; dep asst, Secy of State, for educ and cultural affairs, Wash, DC, 1961-62; counsel to chmn, Communications Satellite Corp, 1962-63; official delgs to intl conf, recently, chmn, US delg to UNESCO meeting on protection of cultural property, 1962. Mem: Local 161, Amer Fed of Musicians; Phi Beta Kappa; fmr pres, Cornell chap, Pi Lambda Pi; club, Cosmos. Fmr ed, Harvard Law Review; contbr articles on atomic energy, law, to publs. Recipient, Rockefeller Public Service Award, 1954. Hobby, clarinetist, concerts. Home and office: 2216 Massachusetts Ave NW, Washington, DC.

ISENBURGER, Herbert R, US, industrial radiologist; b. Frankfurt/M, Ger, July 22, 1900; s. Sally and Olga (Neumond); in US since 1925; att Technische Hochschule Charlottenburg; m. Anne Landsman, July 11, 1930. Pres, St John X-Ray Lab, since 1933, with lab since 1927; instr, Columbia U, war training courses, 1940-43. Prin contribs: pioneered in ind radiology; laid groundwork for Amer Soc Mech Engr boiler code, 1930; portable stress analysis unit, 1943. Co dep, civil defense coord i/c radiation since 1950; mem: Gov comm on radiation protection, NJ, 1954-56; safety div, Amer Soc Mech Engrs, since 1956; Tree Farm Assn. Author: Bibliography on Industrial Radiology, 1942; bibliography on X-Ray Stress Analysis, 1953; Bibliography on Filmbadge Monitoring, US AEC, 1961; co-author, Industrial Radiology, 1934, 1943; contbr

to tech jours. Hobby, organic gardening. Home: Bonis Farm, Califon, NJ. Office: St John X-Ray Lab, Califon, NJ.

ISENSTEIN, K Harald, Den, sculptor; b. Hannover, Ger, Aug 13, 1898; s. Adolf and Jenny (Meyer); att Kunstakademie, Berlin, 1917-20; m. Hildegard Eick, 1920; in Den since 1933. Owner, teacher, pvt art sch, Copenhagen, since 1935; teacher, fine arts for Scandinavian sch tchrs, since 1934, lectr art orgs, since 1936; lect, Hamburg TV, since 1966; tchr sculpture, Reimann's sch, Berlin, Ger, 1922-24; owner, pvt art sch, Berlin, Ger, 1925-33; leader Painting Club, Danish radio and Television, 1951; leader, cen for culture, Isle of Mors, 1962. War refugee in Swed. Exhbs: Ger, 1921-32, and postwar, Scandinavia, since 1935; monuments for Danish refugees, Helsingborg, Landskrona, both Swed; Danish Sch, Jerusalem, 1968; memorials, Jews of Norway, Trondheim and Oslo; major busts: Heinrich Heine monument, Cleveland, Ohio; Heinrich Hertz, Copenhagen; Wilhelm Dörpfeld; Ernst Cassirer, Hamburg; Friedrich Kayssler, Berlin; Alfred Döblin, Emil Ludwig; Pirandello; Edwin Fischer, Berlin; Edmund Husserl, Belgium; Albert Einstein, 1924: Poul Dirac; Niels Bohr; Thalia, statue, Danish Actors House. Lord Rutherford, Kansas City; busts of German presidents, Ebert and Hindenburg, 1930. Author: Kö the Kollwitz 1949; Creative Claywork; A.B.C. des Modellierens; radio plays, Denmark and Norway. Home and studio: Guldbergsgade 10, Copenhagen, Den.

ISERLES, Israel Ignacy, Isr, attorney; b. Tarnopol, Pol, Mar 25, 1912; s. Leib and Netty (Bandler); in Isr since 1957; Magister, U of Lwow, 1937; m. Gizela Swieca, Apr 9, 1946; c: Leonard. Atty, since 1960; pvt practice, 1939-48; judge, High Court, Warsaw, 1950-57; prof, Inst of Law, Warsaw, 1951-56; chief, ed bd, Od Nowa, weekly, Tel Aviv, 1958-63. Red Army, 1941-42. Mem: Mapam; Isr Bar Assn; Yiddish Authors and Journalists Assn of Isr. Author: Theory of State and Law, 1951; The Judge and His Problems, 1956; Polish Jewry After the Second World War, 1958; ed Ency Social Scis, law branch, 1962-69; contbr to profsl press in Pol and Isr. Recipient: medal, Ten Years Poland Independence. Home and office: 21 Daniel St, Bat Yam, Isr.

ISHAI, Moshe, Isr, attorney; b. Grodzisk, Pol, Sep 29, 1895; s. Meir and Sarah (Ash); in Isr since 1924; att U Warsaw; DJur, Ger U, Prague, Czech, 1922; m. Edwarda Kleiner; c: Amos, Hana Lahav. Pvt law practice, Tel Aviv, since 1933; mgr, Davar daily, 1925-30; JA delg to Iran, 1943-44; head delg, JA repr to Pol, 1945-46; Isr Min to: Yugo, 1949-51; It, 1951-52; mem: Supr Court, Histadrut; exec comm, higher educ in Tel Aviv; chmn comm, establishment of Tel Aviv U, 1952-53; hon secy, Friends of Tel Aviv U; mem: bd govs, Tel Aviv U; legal adv, Tel Aviv U; comms: for drafting new traffic regulations; new arbitration laws; vice pres, Isr Lawyers Assn, 1958-60; chmn, profsl ethics comm, mem disciplinary court, 1961; chmn, Isr-It Friendship League. Active in Haganah. Author: Tzir Belo Toar; Tohu veBohu; Minister Plenipotentiary; The Diorite Man. Recipient: Commendatore del Ordine al Merito, It. Home: 30 Haganim Rd, Kfar Shmaryahu, Isr. Office: 94 Allenby Rd, Tel Aviv, Isr.

ISHAI, Ori, Isr, educator; b. Jerusalem, Nov 2, 1929; s. Jeoshua and Genia (Nashofer); BSc, Technion, Haifa, 1957, MSc, 1959, DSc, 1962; m. Yael Hareli, Jan 14, 1953; c: Michal, Tamar, Eran, Yuval. Asso prof, mech dept, Technion, since 1969; mem fac, since 1959; visiting asso prof, Wash U, 1967-69, also research asso, Materials Research Lab, 1967. Pvt, Palmach, 1947-49. Mem: Isr Assn for Theoretical and Applied Mechs; Engrs and Architects Assn, Isr; Soc of Rheology; Amer Concrete Inst; Amer Soc for Testing Materials. Contbr numerous articles to profsl jours; holder of US Patents. Recipient, Aran Award, Engrs and Architects Assn, Isr, 1961. Home: 8 Lotus St, Haifa, Isr. Office: Technion, Haifa, Isr.

ISING, Ernest, US, physicist, educator; b. Cologne, Ger, May May 10, 1900; s. Gustav and Thekla (Loewe); in US since 1947; DrRerNat, U Hamburg, 1924; State Tchr Cert, U Berlin, 1928, 1930; hon DS, Bradley U, 1968; m. Jane Ehmer, Dec 23, 1930; c: Thomas. Prof, physics, Bradley U, since 1962, fac mem since 1948; research asst, Gen Electric Co, Berlin, 1925-26; tchr, physics, pub, pvt schs, 1927-38; asso prof, Minot State Tchrs Coll, ND, 1947-48. Mem: Amer Assn, Physics Tchrs; AAUP. Prin contrb: Ising-Model in ferromagnetism. Hobbies: travel, photography, skating, hiking. Home: 1014 N Institute Pl, Peoria, Ill. Office: Bradley U, Peoria, Ill.

ISKOWITZ, Joel Jay, US, rabbi, army chaplain; b. Pittsburgh, Pa, Aug 26, 1941; s. Harry and Ida (Shapiro); BS, U Pittsburgh, 1962; asso cantor cert, Cantorial Training Inst, Yeshiva U, NYC, 1967; ordained rabbi, Rabbi Isaac Elchanan Theol Sem, Yeshiva U, NYC, 1968; MHL, Yeshiva U, 1968; m. Shiela Gerber, Sep 8, 1965; c: Dov, Shimon, Gila. J Chaplain, US Army, Frankfurt, since 1970; capt, US Army since 1968; computer programmer, Westinghouse Elec Corp, 1962-63; Youth dir, rel instr, Cong Anshe Sholom, New Rochelle, 1965-66; cantor, rel instr, Cong Anshe Amas, Bx, NY, 1966-67; asst command chaplain, 8th Field Army Support Command, Korea, 1969-70. Mem: RaCA; Assn J Chaplains, Armed Forces; life, US Chess Fed; Yeshiva U Rabb Alumni Assn. Recipient, medals: Natl Defense Service, 1968; Armed Forces Expeditionary, 1969, both US Army. Hobbies: stamps, chess. Home: 215 E 54 St, Brooklyn, NY. Study: J Chaplain, Frankfurt, Ger, APO NY 09757.

ISLER, Jacob, Arg, business exec; b. Ropczye, Pol, Feb 7, 1902; s. Leib and Sara (Storch); in Arg since 1940; DJur, DRerPol, U's Basel, Geneva; div; c: Liliana, Gerardo. Pres: ind and commercial corps in Isr and abroad. Bd govs: Weizmann Inst, Rehovot; Technion, Haifa; vice-pres, Cong Isr, Buenos Aires. Author: Ruckkehr der Juden zur Landwirtschaft, 1929. Home: 819 Arroyo St, Baires, Arg. Office: 513 Reconquista St, Buenos Aires, Arg.

ISQUITH, Solomon Silas, US, naval off, attorney, business exec; b. NYC, Aug 25, 1896; s. Abraham and Pearl (Kitchner); BS, USN Acad, Annapolis, 1919; LLD, Bklyn Law Sch,1934; m. Sadie Collis, Aug 26, 1929. Pvt law practice, since 1947; pres, dir, Savoy Hotel Inc, Miami, Fla; dir, Isr Continental Oil Co, Ltd, Montreal, Canada; pres, Fairview Films, NYC. Pres, Amer Zebulun Assn since 1949; USN, off, 1919-47, ret with rank of Rear Adm; Fed Dist Court, Hawaiian Territory, 1944; dist legal off, 3rd Naval Dist, NYC, 1932-34; mem, Amer J Tercentenary Comm; fmr cdr, Navy Post 219; delg Natl Econ Conf for Isr, 1955; asso delg, Natl Conv Isr Bonds, 1952. Mem: VFW, natl and state delg; Navy League of US. Recipient: US Navy Cross; Purple Heart; Combat Commendation Ribbon; Medals:China Service; Natl Defense Service; NY State Conspicuous Service. Home: 215 Clinton Ave, Brooklyn, NY.

ISRAEL, Dorman D, US, engineer, business exec, cons; b. Newport, Ky, July 21, 1900; s. Charles and Emma (Linz); EE, U Cincinnati, 1923; m. Frances Murr, Apr 3, 1924; c: Betty Schwab. Pres, Dorman D Israel and Assos, Inc, since 1968; radio design engr, Crosley Radio Corp, Cincinnati, 1921-23, chief development engr, 1929-31; chief engr, radio div, 1932-36; chief engr: Clearstone Radio Co, Cincinnati, 1923-29; lectr, U Cincinnati, 1928-31; radio div, Grisby Grunow, Chgo, 1931-32; pres, dir: Radio Speakers, 1946-50; Plastimold Corp, 1946-56; chmn, bd, Granco Producs Co, 1962-63; sr vice-pres, engr, Emerson Radio & Phonograph Corp, 1967-68; mem, bd dirs, 1943-67, vice chmn, 1965-67, chief engr, 1936-42, vice pres, i/c engr, 1942-44, i/c engr, produc, 1944-47; holder, patents on radio and allied subjects. Mem: Jt Tech Adv Comm since 1952, chmn, 1955-56, 1964-67; admn comm, profsl group on Bc and TV receivers, Inst of Radio Engrs, 1953-67, chmn, 1951-53, chmn, papers procurement comm, 1942-43, gen chmn, 1944-47; receiver sect, engr dept, Radio-TV Mfrs Assn, 1939-50; chmn, gen standards comm, 1950-57; fmr mem: Natl TV Sys Comm; ind adv comm, Natl Prod Admn; spec adv groups, Defense Dept; tech adv, panel on elec; Natl Stereo Radio Comm, fmr chmn; gen ind adv comm, NY, UHF-TV project, FCC; adv bd, vocational and ext educ, NYC Radio Educ Commn; adv group, elec aids to army aviation, Off of Chief Signal Off; mem: bd, trustees, Temple Isr, New Rochelle, pres, 1950-52, hon trustee since 1952, bd dirs, 1942-52; club, Quaker Ridge Golf. Contbr to sci jours. Recipient, awards: tech assistance to Armed Services: War Dept; Navy Bur of Ships; Bur of Ordnance; Bur of Aeronautics; Off of Sci Research and Devl; OSS; spec awards: Inst of Radio Engrs, 1948, 1957; Inst Elec Engrs, 1967; Dist Alumni Award, U Cincinnati, 1969. Home: 605 Harrison Ave, Harrison, NY. Office: 14 & Coles St, Jersey City, NJ.

ISRAEL, Edmond S, Luxembourg, bank official; b. Luxembourg, May 5, 1924; s. Gustave and Erna (Lande); att U Montpellier, 1940-42; m. Raymonde Bloch, Jan 5, 1959. Mem, Central Mgmt, Banque Internationale à Luxembourg since 1968, with bank since 1946; factory worker, NY, Newark, US, 1942-45. Pres, Consistoire Israélite de Luxembourg,

since 1968, cultural dept, since 1959; mem bd:Keren Kayemet leIsr; State of Isr Bonds Comm; B'nai B'rith. Home: 48 Ave du Bois, Luxembourg.

ISRAEL, Gérard, Fr, organization exec; b. Oran, Algeria, Nov 24, 1928; s. Prosper and Alice; in Fr since 1947; licence d'enseignement de la philosophie, Sorbonne, 1951; diplômé d'études supérieures de philosophie, 1953. Asst secy gen, Alliance Israelite Universelle, since 1958. Dir, Nouveaux Cahiers, rev. French Army, 1956-60. Prin contrib, instrumental in preparation of the AIU centenary, UNESCO, Paris, 1960. Home: 85 Blvd Pasteur, Paris, 15, Fr. Office: 45 rue La Bruyère, Paris 9, Fr.

ISRAEL, Joachim, Swed, educator, author; b. Karlsruhe, Ger, Sep 6, 1920; s. Frederick and Eva Löwe); in Swed since 1938; licentiate: phil, 1952; sociol, 1956; PhD, 1956, all at U Stockholm; c: Dan, Jonas. Prof, sociol, U Copenhagen, Den, since 1968, on fac since 1956; research asso, Inst, Social Research, Oslo, Nor, 1954-56; on tech staff, Bell Telephone Lab, Murray Hill, NJ, 1958-59; visiting prof, Bar-Ilan U, Isr, 1962; asso prof, sociol, U Stockholm, Swed, 1959-68, on fac since 1956. Author: Self-Evaluation and Rejection in Groups, 1956; Psychological and Sociological Problems of Resistance to Change, 1958; Psychology of Leadership, 1961; Patients Look at the Hospital, 1962, all in Swed; contbr to profsl jours. Home: St Kannikestraede 18, Copenhagen, Den. Office: Dept of Sociol, U of Copenhagen, Copenhagen, Den.

ISRAEL, Richard J, US, organization dir; b. Chgo, Ill, Nov 5, 1929; s. Irving and Julia (Epstein); BA, U Chgo, 1950; BHL, HUC-JIR, 1954, MA, 1957; m. Sherry Feinberg, Sep 2, 1957; c: Alisa, David, Rachel, Joshua. Dir, Hillel Found, chaplain to J students, Yale U since 1959; dir, spec projects, Hillel Found since 1968; dir, J Rel Union, 1955-56; asso dir, Hillel Council, UCLA, 1957-59. Pres, Natl Assn Hillel Dirs; chmn, J Comty Relations Council, New Haven, Conn, 1963-64; mem: CCAR; RA. Home and office: 35 High St, New Haven, Conn.

ISRAELI, David, Isr, banker; b. Libau, Latvia, Jan 20, 1898; s. Mordechai and Rebecca (Israelstam) Israelstam; in Isr since 1919; m. Lela Mani, 1925; c: Rahela. Dir: Anglo-Israel Bank, London; Cifico Bank, Zurich; General Mortgage Bank; Bank Leumi Investment Co, both Tel Aviv; Gen mgr, Bank Leumi LeIsrael, 1957-64,with bank, since 1919; J Colonial Trust, London, 1917-19; dir: Anglo-Palestine Bank, London, later Bank Leumi leIsr, Isr; Cifico Bank, Zurich; Gen Mortgage Bank; Bank Leumi Inves Co, Isr. F: Inst of Bankers; Royal Econ Soc, London. Home: 98 Haeshel St, Herzliya, Isr.

ISRAELI, Joseph, Isr, organization official; b. Kiev, Russ, June 28, 1906; s. David and Chaya (Altman) Israel; in Isr since 1924; att Sch of Econ, Kiev; m. Leah Wess, Jan 1932; c: Gideon, Sara Moed. Mem, Kibbutz Afikim, since 1924, co-found; delg to ZCs 1934, and since 1948; co-found, mem, secretariat, Rafi Party, 1964-66; secy gen, Min of Defense, 1948-49; head Histadrut delg to US, 1939-45; Baltic countries, 1932-34; delg, Hashomer Hatzair, Latvia, 1928-30; instr, Histadrut Youth Org, 1925. High Command, Haganah. Mem: World Zionist Actions Comm, also perm finance comm; secretariat, World Lab Zionists org; cen comm, Isr Lab Party, asst secy, 1958-62; cen comm, Ihud Hakvutzot Vehakibbutzim, gen secy, 1952-56; Histadrut Council; Histadrut Comptroller's Bd; US-IsrFriendship League; bd dirs, Beth Gordon. Contbr to jours and daily press. Recipient: most Israeli military decorations. Home: Kibbutz Afikim, Isr.

ISRAELS, Abraham Montague, Can, barrister; b. Winnipeg, Man, Oct 8, 1904; s. Simon and Sarah (Girtle); LLB, U Man, 1926; m. Sally Kalef, 1930; c: Hester Kroft, Renée. Barrister at law, since 1927; appd, Q.C, 1955; elected bencher, Man Law Soc, 1961. Dir, bar admission, Law Soc of Man; hon counsel, Winnipeg Burns Club; pres, J Hist Soc of W Can; life gov, Winnipeg YMHA: mem; Can, Man Bar Assns; Man Law Soc. Home: 303 Queenston St, Winnipeg, Can. Office: 1002 Childs Bldg, Winnipeg, Can.

ISRAELS, Carlos L, US, attorney; b. NYC, Nov 21, 1904; s. Charles and Belle (Lindner); BA, Amherst Coll, 1925;

LLB, Columbia Law Sch, 1928; m. Irma Commanday, Sep 25, 1935, div; m. 2nd, Ruth Goldstein, Dec 13, 1941; c: Charles, Elizabeth, Michael. Partner, Berlack, Israels and Liberman, since 1946; adj prof, law, Columbia U, since 1962; lectr: corp practice, finance, Practicing Law Inst, since 1937; asso, White and Case, 1928-40; asst gen counsel, trustees, Asso Gas and Elec Corp, 1940-46. Mem: ed bd, Uniform Commercial Code, Amer Law Inst; Conf of Commns on Uniform State Laws; cons, NY Law Rev Comm; Pres, HIAS; dir: JDC; UJA; bd dirs CJFWF, since 1953, treas, since 1966; mem, bd dirs, exec comm, Natl Ref Service, 1942-46; secy-treas, United Service for New Amer, 1946-54; mem: Phi Beta Kappa; Delta Sigma Rho; Amer Bar Assn; Amer Law Inst; NY St Bar Assn; Assn Bar, City of NY; NY Co Lawyer's Assn; clubs: Amherst, NY; Lawyers; Sunningdale Country. Author: Corporate Practice, 2nd ed, 1968; co-author: When Corporations Go Public, 1962; Modern Securities Transfers, 1967; contbr to legal periodicals. Home: 5 Riverside Dr, New York, NY. Office: 26 Broadway, New York, NY.

ISRAELSTAM, Samuel S, S Afr, educator; b. Johannesburg, Aug 21, 1909; s. Isaiah and Florrie (Weinberg); Tchr's dipl, Johannesburg Coll of Educ, 1930; BS, U Witwatersrand, 1930; MS, 1931; PhD, 1950; m. Esther Zaidel, June 24, 1934; c: Lenard, Dennis, Myra, Carole, Kenneth. Asso prof, chem, U Witwatersrand, since 1958, on fac, since 1935; tchr, Transvaal, 1931-34. Mem, PMs Sci Adv Council, since 1962; chmn, Sci Adv Comm, S Afr; Leader Exch Prog, since 1964; mem, Exec Comm of Convocation, U Witwatersrand, since 1944, pres, 1956-63, chmn, Alumni Fund, since 1961, dir, Alumni Affairs, since 1963, pres, Lectrs Assn, 1946-50; mem, S Afr Chem Inst, since 1930, pres, 1954, chmn, educ comm; mem: Natl Comm Intl Union, Pure and Applied Chem, 1969; Chaim Weizmann lodge, Heb Order of David, 1950; chmn, NE JCC, Johannesburg, 1952-54. Chmn, Bd of Govs, King David Schs, 1968; mem: exec, educ comms, S Afr Bd of J Educ, 1968; S Afr J Bd of Deps, 1948-54; governing body, Parktown Boys' HS, 1958-65; chmn, sch comm, Parkview Sr Sch, 1956-59; club, Kelvin House. Contbr to sci publs. Recipient: grant, US - S Afr Leader Exch Prog and NSF, 1961; Carnegie travel grant, 1959; S Afr War Services Medal, 1939-45. Home: 102 Castlerosse, 8 St, Killarney, Johannesburg, S Afr. Office: U Witwatersrand, Johannesburg, S Afr.

ISSERMAN, Ferdinand M, US, rabbi, author; b. Antwerp, Belgium, Mar 4, 1898; s. Alexander and Betty (Brodheim); in US since 1906; BA, U Cincinnati, 1919; ordained rabbi, HUC, 1922, hon DHL, 1950; MA, U Pa, 1924; hon LLD, Douglas U, 1940; hon DD, Cen Coll, 1944; m. Ruth Frankenstein, June 6, 1923; c: Ferdinand, Irma Gertz. Rabbi, Temple Isr, St Louis, Mo, since 1929; weekly radio prog, KSD; asst rabbi, Rodeph Sholem Cong, Phila, 1922-25; rabbi, Holy Blossom Temple, Toronto, Can, 1925-29. US Army WW I; ARC overseas, WW II. Fmr pres: HUC-JIR Alumni; Rabb Assn, St Louis; J Student Found, U Mo; fmr: vice-pres, Hillel Adv Council, Mo; chmn: Combined J Campaign; JWF campaign, St Louis; Social Justice Commn; Judaism Sesquicentennial Comm; Honor Keyfitz Comm; Rosalie Tilles Nonsectarian Charity Fund; Amer J Tercentenary Comms, St Louis and Mo; New Temple Isr Bldg Fund Campaign; radio and TV comm, St Louis Rabb Assn; cofound, Amer J Soc for Service; found St Louis Nursery Found; Amer J Services in Paris, Fr; Reform Cong in NZ; creator, Town Hall of ARC; vice-chmn, NCCJ; mem: St Louis Comm for Natl Libr Week; NAACP; Pres Comm on Natl Traffic Safety; Acad of Rel and Mh; Mo Citizen's Comm, Hoover Report Findings; exec comm, March of Dimes, 1959; Citizens' Comm for City-Co Coord; comm on new congs, UAHC; Citizens' Comm for Better Law Enforcement; adv bd, Natl Assn of Negro Musicians, Inc; Bible Coll, U Mo; scholarship award comm, Hatters' Union. Author: Rebels and Saints, the Social Methods of the Prophets of Israel, 1933; Sentenced to Death, The Jews in Nazi Germany, 1933; This Is Judaism, 1944; The Jewish Jesus and the Christian Christ, 1950; A Rabbi with the American Red Cross, 1958; contbr to J jours. Recipient: citation: ARC, 1944; Metrop Church Fed, St Louis. Home: 82 Arundel Pl, Clayton, Mo. Study: 10675 Ladue Rd, St Louis, Mo.

ITELSON, Josef, Isr, physician; b. Lodz, Pol, May 27, 1895; s. Selmann and Tauba (Abkin); in Isr since 1950; MD, U Warsaw, 1921; studied hematology, endocrinology, Hosps in Vienna and Paris, 1936-37. Cons, endocrinology, Cen Clinic,

Kupat Holim, Petah Tikva, since 1950; head, dept med, Sick Fund Hosp, Pol, 1929-38, on staff since 1923; researcher, hematology, Paris, 1948-50. Mem: Intl Soc of Hematology; Isr Soc of Endocrinology; Intl Soc of Med. Author: Thyroid Disorders, Especially in Pregnancy; Infertility in Young Adults. Hobby, classical music. Home: 27 Brande St, Petah Tikva, Isr. Office: Kupat Holim, Rothschild Blvd, Petah Tikva, Isr.

ITTLESON, Blanche Frank, US, philanthropist; b. St Louis, Mo, 1875; hon: DHum, Washington U, St Louis, 1965; DHL, JTSA, 1965. Prin contribs: established: Blanche F Ittleson Chair, Child Psychiatry, Washington U Med Sch, 1956; scholarship, Amer-Isr Cultural Found, 1963. Recipient: numerous awards for contribs to Mh, med, arts, Judaism and pub service. Home: 200 E 57 St, New York, NY.

IVANJI, Ivan, Yugo, author; b. Yugo, Jan 24, 1929; s. Franja and Ida (Somlo); deg, Secondary Tech Sch, 1948. Asst gen mgr, Natl Theatre, Belgrade; tchr, tech sch, Belgrade, 1948-49; asst gen secy, Writers' Assn, Yugo, 1950; ed, youth publs, Omladina and Mladost, Belgrade, 1951-57; ed in chief: Mladost na autoputu, newspaper, 1958; pub dept, pub house, Mladost, 1959-61; other pub houses and theatres. Interned, concentration camps, Auschwitz and Buchenwald, 1944-45. Mem: Writers Assn, Yugo; Union of Newspapermen, Yugo. Author: Živeću uvek prolécem, 1950; Smešak pod taškom razno, 1951; Vozovi, 1952; Razgovor o lepom pona šanju, 1952; Véstina govornistva, 1953; Coveka nisu ubili, 1954; Jugoslovenska omladina u predratnom periodu, 1959; Reka bez obala, 1960; Usće koje tražimo, 1960; trans: Letters from Prison, by Rosa Luxemburg, 1952; Endre Adi: Poems, 1953; Volfgang Borhert: Generacija bez milosti, 1954; Antologija novije nemaćke lirike, od Nićea do Borherta, 1956; Junge jugoslavische Lyrik, anthology, from Serbo-Croat into Ger, 1961; radio plays: Krug krivice, 1954; Pred zvezdanim vermenom, 1957; Ajkula sa nežnim srcem, fairy tales, 1963; Bertholt Brecht: O sirotom BB, selection of poems, from Ger into Serbo-Croat; contbr: articles to mags and jours; texts for documentary films. Home: Popo Taškova 24, Belgrade, Yugo. Office: Natl Theatre, Francuska 3, Belgrade, Yugo.

IVZAN, Arieh, Isr, advocate; b. Kowno, Lithuania, Aug 5, 1928; s. Zwi and Kehyla (Kaplicky) Ipp; LLB, U Tel Aviv, 1956; m. Yohewed Kosowsky, Feb 27, 1951; c: David, Amir. Chief Supt, i/c N Sub-Dist, Tel Aviv Dist, Isr Police, since 1968; i/c Ramat Gan Sub Dist, 1962-63; i/c S Sub Dist, 1963-68. Pvt IDF, 1948-49. Hobbies: lit, photography. Home: 263 Modiin, Ramat Gan, Isr. Office: 221A Dizengoff, Tel Aviv, Isr.

IZAK, Gabriel, Isr, physician; b. Czech, Jan 4, 1923; s. Edmond and Lea (Scnorr); in Isr since 1949; MD, Pazmany Peter U, Budapest, 1949; m. Gretti Decalo, 1951; c: Ruth, Tamar. Prof med, head hematology service, Heb U, Hadassah Med Sch, since 1969; fmr research f, Harvard U. Prin contribs: cell maturation, differentiation; metabolism of iron. Pres: Isr Soc of Hematology and Blood Transfusion; chmn: Intl Panel of Iron; Intl Panel on Folate, Vitamin B 12, both ICSH. Contbr to profsl jours. Hobby, shoemaking. Home: 15 Jabotinsky St, Jerusalem, Isr. Office: Hadassah Hosp, Jerusalem, Isr.

IZAKSON, Eliahu, Isr, business exec; b. Jerusalem, Mar 21, 1921; s. Zvi and Margalit (Masie); deg, Govt Law Classes, Jerusalem, 1945; m. Ruth Zisl.ng, Dec 12, 1944; c: Aharon, Arbel, Miron. Hon consul gen of Nor in Tel Aviv and S Isr since 1966; chmn, Nor Trading Co, Isr, since 1966; dir, Amina Ltd; dep chmn: supr, Herzliya HS, Tel Aviv; Diners Club; Isr Ltd; chmn for trade and promotion of exports from Isr to Nor; dir: Scandinavian Supply Agcy, Tel Aviv; Pardess Citrus Producs; secy gen: Pardess Coop Syndicate, Israeli Citrus Growers, 1964-65; Chmn: Citrus Growers Org, Farmers Fed of Isr; Assn of Bi-Natl C of C; mem: Citrus Bd of Isr; Dep chmn, supervisory board, Gymnasia Herzliya; club, Rotary. Contbr to mags. Home: 50 Kaplan St, Herzliya, Isr. Office: 30 Levontin St, Tel Aviv, Isr.

IZAKSON, Ruth, Isr, communal leader; b. Tel Aviv, Isr, Dec 24, 1922; d. Isaac and Sima (Ismogik) Zisling; att Heb U, Jerusalem; m. Eliahu Izakson, 1944; c: Aharon, Arbel, Miron. Vice-chmn, WIZO Fed; chmn WIZO Herzliya Pituach Group;

mem, Zionist Comm for Youth and Educ. Home: 50 Kaplan St, Herzliya, Isr.

IZAKSON, Zvi, Isr, agriculturist; b. Cairo, Egypt, Dec 21, 1890; s. Zerach and Zippora (Mazie); in Isr since 1900; att Agric Schs: Pal, Turkey; U Nancy, Fr; m. Margalit Mazie, 1920; c: Eliahu, Ruth. Pres, Farmer's Fed, Isr, since 1948; pres, bd dirs, Pardess Syndicate, since 1940; mem, Citrus Marketing and Control Bds, mem delg to: Eng and Eur, since 1946; pres, Mediterranean Citrus Growers Assn; head, Isr delg intl cong since 1946; mem, bd dirs, Pardess Coop Soc Ltd; dir, Tel Aviv Port, 1933-53; mem, PM Econ Council, 1956-61; Pres, C of C, Isr-Brazil; co-found, vice pres, Isr Amer C of C, since 1952; Anglo-Pal C of C; fmr chmn, bd trustèes, Nathan Strauss Fund, LA; pres, Itzhak Yelin Lodge, B'nai B'rith. Ed, Heb Dict of Medical and Scientific Terms, by Dr A Mazie, 1934; contbr articles on agric subjects to local and fgn press. Home: 119 Rothschild Blvd, Tel Aviv, Isr. Office: POB 209, Tel Aviv, Isr.

IZRAELY, Yosef, Isr, educator, theater dir; b. Jerusalem, Isr, Dec 10, 1938; s. Moshe and Zipporah (Diamant); att Heb U, Jerusalem, 1959-60; hon dipl, Royal Acad of Dramatic Arts, London, 1962; BA, hons, U Bristol, 1965; PhD, Carnagie-Mellon U, Pittsburgh, 1969; m. Talma Gelman, Dec 28, 1966. Free-lance theater dir, since 1965; instr, U Tel Aviv, since 1968; Corresp, IDF, 1956-59. Dir: Ootzli Gootzli, Cameri Theatre; The Creditors; Diary of a Scoundrel; Striptease. Ish Hassid Hayah; Waiting for Godot; Night in May; Six Characters in Search of an Author. Recipient, Isr Arts Council Trophy for best produc, 1965-66. Hobby, photography. Home: 2 Mishmar Hayarden, Givatayim, Isr.

J

JABÉS, André, Switz, organization exec; b. Cairo, Egypt, Aug 27, 1903; s. Joseph and Judith (Curiel); in Switz since 1960; licence, Fac of Law, 1926; att Political Sci Sch, 1923-26, both Paris, Fr; m. Myriam Farahat, June 23, 1932; c: Haym. Asst dir, WJC, Geneva off, since 1960; lawyer, Chalom & Jabès, Cairo, 1926-51. Secy gen: Council Cairo J Cmty, 1945-51; commn: Wfr; Syns and Cemetery; Legal; Properties; all of Cairo J Cmty, 1943-51. Home: 40 rue Vermont, Geneva, Switz. Office: WJC, rue de Varembé, Geneva 20, Switz.

JACKSON, Bernard Stuart, UK, educator; b. Liverpool, Eng, Nov 16, 1944; s. Leslie and Isabel (Caplan); barrister-at-law, Gray's Inn, 1966; LLB, hons, U Liverpool, 1965; DPhil, U Coll, Oxford, 1967; m. Rosalyn Young, Nov 26, 1967; c: Iain. Lectr, Dept Civil Law, U Edinburgh, since 1969; visiting asst prof, U Ga, Sch of Law, 1968-69. Comm mem, Edinburgh J Lit Soc; chmn: J Music Club, Liverpool, 1960-64; Merseyside J Youth Council, 1962-65. Mem: Assn of U Tchrs; Soc Public Tchrs of Law; World J Bible Soc; Société Internationale, Fernand de Visscher, Histoire des Droits de L'Antiquité; fmr mem, Amer Fgn Law Assn. Author, Theft in Early Jewish Law, 1971; contbr articles to intl law jours. Spec interests: hist of J law; legal sys of antiquity. Hobby, music. Home: 47 Thomson Dr, Currie, Midlothian, Scotland. Office: Old College, South Bridge, Edinburgh, Scotland,

JACKSON, Edward Leo, Eng, minister of religion; b. Cork, Ir, Mar 19, 1936; s. Jacob and Rachel (Elyan); att Jews Coll; m. Frances Steiner, June 16, 1960; c: Deborah, Jacob, Leah. Min, Kingston Surbiton E Dist Syn, since 1961; asst min, Hampstead Syn, since 1959. Acting dir, Youth Torah Corps; org, Inter-Syn Quiz. Author, Adult Education and Quiz Handbook. Home: 47 Oakhill, Surbiton, Surrey, Eng.

JACKSON, Julius Leon, US, physicist; b. NYC, Nov 9, 1924; s. Hyman and Rose (Margolis); BA, Bklyn Coll, 1945; MA, Princeton U, 1947; PhD, NYU, 1950; m. Charlotte Alpert, June 29, 1947 (decd); c: Meyer, Mark, Irene; m. 2nd, Raya Sheveiger, Dec 20, 1960; c: Morris. Prof, chmn, chem eng, material sci dept, Wayne State U, since 1969; cons: NIH; Natl Bur Standards; United Aircraft Research Labs, Conn; Convair Labs, Cal; summer positions: N Amer Aviation Sci Cen, Thousand Oaks, Cal, 1965; United Aircraft Research Labs, 1967; Lawrence Radiation Lab, 1969; guest sci, Weizmann Inst of Sci, Isr, 1961, 1964, 1966, 1968; fmr, physicist, Natl Bur Standards; prof, physics, Howard U, Wash, DC, 1965-69. US Army, 1943. Prin contribs: theoretical research in stat mech and applications of probability theory to problems in chem physics; plasma physics; material scis; anobiophysics. F: Amer Phys Soc; Wash Acad Scis; contbr to sci jours. Recipient, Fulbright Research Prof, U of Leiden, Netherlands, 1963-64. Home: 25925 York Rd, Huntington Woods, Mich. Office: Wayne State U, Detroit, Mich.

JACOB, Itzhak, Isr, scientist; b. Tel Aviv, Isr, Mar 22, 1926; s. Zvi and Yochevet (Zucker) Jacobson; ME, Technion, Haifa, 1953; MSc, MIT, Boston, 1963; m. Shulamit Greizman, Aug 24, 1948; c: Ronie, Tali. Dep chief sci, Min of Defense since 1968. Col, IDF since 1948; battalion cdr, 1948; head: tank main workshops, 1958-61; weapons sys div, 1963-68. Prin contrib, use of quantitative methods in decision making, Isr defense establishment. Vice pres: Oprs Research Soc, Isr; Isr Astronautical Soc; mem, bd govs, Standards Inst of Isr; hon mem, Fed of Underwater Activities, Isr. Contbr to profsl publs. Home: Hashikmim, St, Ramataim, Isr. Office: Ministry of Defense, Tel Aviv, Isr.

JACOB, Kaethe, Isr, educator; b. Berlin, Ger, May 23, 1898; d. Max and Jenny (Bleichrode); in Isr since 1933; att Art HS; Dalcroze Sem, both Berlin. Co-found, bd dirs, Music Tchrs Sem, Tel Aviv, 1945; tchr, ryhthmics and improvisation; fmr: pres, Natl Rhythmics Tchrs; delg, Intl Union of Dalcroze Tchrs, Geneva, 1965; teacher; music acads; conservatories; pedg, rythmics and acting sems; kindergardens; lectr, intl music congs. Author: Children's Song Books; music-pedg

book, Heb, Ger; contbr to Heb, Ger, Eng, Fr, It pedg and musical jours. Home: 19 Gordon St, Tel Aviv, Isr.

JACOB, P Walter, Ger, actor, director; b. Duisburg, Jan 26, 1905; s. Max and Fanny (Strauch); att Staatliche Hochschule für Musik; Max Reinhardt Sem des Deutschen Theaters; Berlin U, all Berlin, 1923-28. Independent actor, dir for theater, radio, film, TV; asst, Staatstheater, Berlin, 1925-28; chief dir, lit adv, actor, munic theatres of: Koblenz, 1928-29; Lübeck, 1929-30; Wuppertal, 1930-31; Essen, Cologne, Dessau, all 1931-32; Radio Luxemburg, 1933-35; Deutsches Theater, Prague, and various Sudenten-Ger stages, 1936-38; found, dir, Freie Deutsche Bühne, Buenos Aires, 1940-50; supr, Städtische Bühnen, Dortmund, 1950-62; Dir and maj roles in: The Devil's General; Jacobowski and the Colonel; Stalingrad; Reichstags Brandprozess; dir, Dr Faust, opera by Busoni, 1953; produc, dir, Eli, 1962. Mem: Deutscher Bühnenverein; Assn Argentina de Actores. Author: Leo Blech, Biography, 1931; Felix von Weingartner, Biography, 1933; El Arte Lirico, 1944; La Opera, 1944; Zeitklänge, 1945; Rampenlichte, 1945; Richardo Wagner y su Obra, 1946; Theatre, 4 Almanacs of Freie Duetsche Bühne, Buenos Aires, 1946; Taten der Musik, Richard Wagner und sein Werk, 1952; Jacques Offenbach, 1969; Jakob Offenbach from Köln, 1969. Home and office: Hiltrowall 2, Dortmund, Ger.

JACOB, Walter, US, rabbi; b. Augsburg, Ger, Mar 13, 1930; s. Ernest and Annette (Loewenberg); in US since 1940; BA, Drury Coll, Springfield, Mo, 1950; BHL, MHL, DHL, HUC, 1955; m. Irene Loewenthal, Oct, 1958; c: Claire, Kenneth, Daniel. Sr rabbi, Rodef Shalom Cong, since 1966; asst asso rabbi, 1955-66; visiting prof, Pittsburgh Theol Sem, since 1967. Chaplain, USAF, 1955-57. Chmn, Gtr Pittsburgh Rabb F; vice-chmn, Project Equality, W Pa; convener, Pittsburgh Area Rel and Race Council; bd mem: Alumni Overseers, HUC, Cincinnati, NY, LA, Jerusalem; J Comty Relations Council; J Family and Children's Service; NCCJ; Metrop Pittsburgh ADL; United J Fed; United Cerebral Palsy; Pittsburgh Chamber Music Soc; Pittsburgh Zionist Dist; ARC; Intl Poetry Forum; all Pittsburgh; club, Variety. Author: Essays in Honor of Solomon B. Freehof, 1963; Our Biblical Heritage, 1965; co-ed, Paths of Faithfulness, 1964; contbr to jours. Home: 303 Le Roi Rd, Pittsburgh, Pa. Study: 4905 Fifth Ave, Pittsburgh, Pa.

JACOBI, Harry Martin, Eng, minister of religion; b. Berlin, Ger, Oct 19, 1925; s. Eugen and Margarete (Jacobi) Hirschberg; in Eng since 1940; BA, Birkbeck Coll, London, 1960; BA, hons, U Coll, 1963; m. Rose Solomon, Apr 7, 1957; c: Margaret, Richard, David. Min, Southgate and Dist Lib Syn since 1960; Aberdeen Heb Cong, 1952-55. Cpl, J Brig, Interpreter's Pool, BAOR, 1945-48. Found, vice-chmn, Southgate Council of Chrs and J; mem: B'nai B'rith; Leo Baeck and Southgate Men's Lodges; Assn of J Ex-Servicemen. Home: 61 Mayfield Ave, Southgate, London, N14, Eng. Study: 75 Chase Rd, London, N14, Eng.

JACOBOVITZ, Arthur A, US, rabbi, educator; b. Bridgeport, Conn, Sep 22, 1931; s. Joseph and Sonia (Magilnick); BA, Yeshiva U, 1935; ordained rabbi, Isaac Elchanan Theol Sem, 1955; att Heb U, Jerusalem, 1958-59. Dir, B'nai B'rith Hillel Found, U Wash, since 1959; guest prof, Seattle U, since 1960. Chaplain, USAAF, 1956-58; capt, USAF Res. Chmn, adult educ, B'nai B'rith, since 1962; bd mem: ADL, since 1959; Cascade lodge, since 1960; Fed J Fund and Council, since 1959; mem: RabCA; Natl Assn Hillel Dirs; Rel dirs Assn, U of Wash; Assn, J Chaplains of Armed Forces; AAUP; Amer Soc of Rel; Psi Chi. Contbr to profsl jours. Home: 5249/40 Ave NE, Seattle, Wash. Office: 4745/17 Ave NE, Seattle, Wash.

JACOBOVITZ, Dov, Isr, business exec; b. Pol, May 23, 1913; s. Jakob and Perla (Federman); in Isr since 1932; att Heb Coll, Pabianice, Pol, 1930; m. Betty Berlinski, Nov 18, 1942; c: Samy, Gila Stein, Jacob. Chmn, mgn dir, Keshet Combined

Textile Mills, since 1945; gen mgr, Arigim Ltd, 1936-45. Vice-pres, Isr Standards Inst; dir, Yerid Hamizrach Exhbs; mem: Isr Export Inst; bd, Isr Mfg Assn. Hobbies: painting; Judaica. Home: 85 Kaplan St, Herzliya Pituach, Isr. Office: 5 Menahem Yitzhak St, Ramat Gan, Isr.

JACOBOWSKY, Bernhard J, Swed, psychiatrist, educator; b. Uddevalla, Swed, Nov 9, 1893; s. Efraim and Rosa (Sim-kowsky); MD, U Uppsala, 1929; m. Birgit Söderström, Sept 8, 1907; c: Erik, Eva Gunnarsson, Bengt. Prof psycht, U Uppsala, 1932-60, em since 1960; dir, psycht clinic, Royal Acad Hosp; asst, psycht clinic, Uppsala, 1920-28; dir, Sträng-näs Hosp, 1928-30; dir, Västra Marks Sjukhus, Örebro, 1930-32; cons, Royal State Med Bd, 1935. Served Swed Army. Mem: forensic dept, Royal State Med Bd; pres, Swed Psycht Assn, 1933-35; inspector, Göteborgs Nation, U Uppsala, 1952-60; club, Rotary. Contbr books and papers; radio lectures. Recipient: Commander, Nordstjerneorden, Swed; Chevalier, Légion d'Honneur, Fr. Hobbies: horticulture, fishing. Home: St Olofsgatan 10 B, Uppsala, Swed.

JACOBOWSKY, Carl Ulf Vilhelm, Swed, librarian, author; b. Uddevalla, Swed, Apr 23, 1896; s. Efraim and Rosa (Sim-kowsky); att Uppsala U, 1926-27, PhD, 1932; m. Agda Sandberg, Dec 30, 1939; c: Olof. Chief libr: Skara State Libr, 1938-61; Östersund, 1930-38. Author: Uddevalla med omnejd i svensk litteratur, 1917; Böcker om Bohuslän, 1918; Svenska studenter i Oxford ca. 1620-1740, pub, 1928; Svenskar i frammande land under gängna tider; Andrée, both 1930; The Literature About New Sweden, 1937; Göteborgs mosaiska församling 1780-1955, pub, 1955; Gustafsberg, 1958; Boks-amlare, 1965; Svensk-judiskt herrgardsliv, 1967; contbr articles on bibliography, librarianship, Swed-J subjects, to Swed lit jours. Recipient, Carl Snoilsky Medal, for eminent achievement as book collector, Swed Natl Libr, 1965. Spec interests: collecting books, over eleven thousand works in all fields of Judaica; researcher, Swed J culture, hist. Home: Skara, Swed.

JACOBS, Arthur L, US, publisher; b. US, Feb 12, 1902; s. Ralph and Fannie (Bernstein); grad, Bkyln Law Sch; m. Ruth Weinberg, June, 1926; c: Gabriel. Gen mgr, acting publisher, The Day J Jour, since 1949; gen mgr, J Morning Jour, 1944-49; attorney, real estate investor, management. Co-chmn: UJA, Landesmanshaft Div; Isr Bonds; dir, Amer Friends of Heb U; fmr: mem exec, ZOA; trustee, Goddard Coll, Vt; clubs: Natl Arts; Baiting Hollow Country; contbr numerous articles to J Daily Jour, J Morning Jour. Spec interests: hist of art; archaeol; photography. Home: 45 Gramercy Pk, New York, NY. Office: 183 E Broadway, New York, NY.

JACOBS, Arthur T, US, organization exec, economist; b. Chgo, Ill, Aug 19, 1912; s. Morris and Laura (Abraham); BA, U Wis, 1934, MA, 1935; PhD, U Mich, 1951; m. Marcia Fox, Oct 23, 1937; c: John, Jeffrey. Exec vice-pres, JTSA, since 1965; lab arbitrator, NY State Bd of Mediation and Amer Arbitration Assn, since 1946, lab mediator and fact finder, NY Public Employment Relations bd, since 1969; admn secy, dir admn, UAHC, 1955-65; asst chief stat, Public Wfr dept, State of Wis, 1935-38; econ: US Govt Bur of Budget; US Employment Service; burs, Manpower Analysis and Manpower Utilization, War Manpower Comm, all 1940-44; dir cons, Labor Relations Asso, 1944-45; exec's Lab Service, Natl Foreman's Inst Inc, 1945-48; asso exec dir, NY Assn for New Amers, 1948-52; mgt cons, FJP of NY, 1952-53; exec dir, HIAS, NYC, 1953-55. Mem, bd dirs, exec comm, Amer Immigration and Citizenship Conf; asst secy, mem, bd dirs, Rabb Pension bd; mem: Amer Econs Assn; Temple Service Agcy, 1956-65; Amer Stat Assn; Natl Conf of J Communal Service; Overseas Press Club; natl and state bds, ADA. Author: Manual of Industrial Relations; How to Use Handicapped Workers; How to Negotiate With Labor Unions; What You Should Know About the Wage and Hour Act, Federal Labor Laws; The Supervisors' Guide to the Taft-Hartley Act, 1945-48. Hobbies: scouting, swimming. Home: Taramac Trail, Harrison, NY. Office: JTSA, 3080 Broadway, New York, NY.

JACOBS, Dan N, US, educator, author; b. Irvin, Ky, July 5, 1925; s. Robert and Yetta (Hellman); BA, Harvard U, 1949; MA, Yale U, 1951; cert, Russ Inst, Columbia U, 1953; MA, 1953, PhD, 1958; m. Janice Mintz, Aug 16, 1959; c: Margaret, Kenneth, Susan. Prof, political sci, Miami U, Oxford, O, since 1965; lectr, Hunter Coll, 1958-59; visiting prof: U Ind; SF State Coll; research asso, U Cal, Berkeley. Mem: Amer Political Sci Assn; Midwest Assn of Political Scis; Intl Poli-

tical Sci Assn; Amer Assn for the Advancement of Slavic Studies, Midwest Slavic Assn; AAUP. Author: New Com-munist Manifesto, 1961, 1965; The Masks of Communism, 1963; Chinese Communism: Selected Documents, 1963; New Communisms, 1969; contbr to: Modern Ideologies, 1961; On the Threshold of the Sixties, 1961; Dictionary of Political Science, 1963; contbr articles to revs and jours. Home: 211 Beechpoint Dr, Oxford, O. Office: Miami U, Oxford, O.

JACOBS, George, US, business exec; b. NYC, Nov 27, 1913; s. David and Fannie (Cohn); BA, NYU, 1937, postgrad studies, 1937-38; att: CCNY, 1938-40; Pratt Inst, 1940-42; m. Ethel Klaristenfeld, Dec 12, 1937; c: Phyllis Smith, Howard. Vice-pres, gen mgr, Circle Wire & Cable Corp, since 1968; with co since 1933; cons, wire and cable sect, War Produc Bd, 1940-45. Bd dirs, exec comm, Hillcrest J Cen, since 1950, pres, 1956-57; dir, campaign cabinet, Hillcrest div, UJA, since 1954, chmn: FJP, Hillcrest div, 1969; Hillcrest-Utopia, 1953-54; mem: Nat Elec Mfr Assn; Controllers Inst; Amer Mgmt Assn; KP, chancellor-commander, 1955. Home: 185-27 80 Rd, Jamaica Estates, NY. Office: 5500 Maspeth Ave, Maspeth, NY.

JACOBS, George Joseph, US, scientist; b. NYC, Aug 30, 1917; s. Joseph and Tamara (Fine); AB, U Miss, 1940; MSc W Va U, 1947; att U Mich, 1948-49; PhD, George Wash U, Wash DC, 1955; m. Joan Fischer, Aug 22, 1947; c: Tamara, Douglas, Jeremy. Chief, phys biol, NASA, since 1959; resear-cher, Brookhaven Natl Lab, since 1955; radiation biol, USN Med Research Inst, Wash DC, 1950-56; research biol, chief spec projects, Atomic Bomb Casualty Commn, Hiroshima, Japan, Natl Acad Sci; NRC, 1956-59. USAAC, 1941-45. Mem: AAAS; NY Acad Sci; Japanese Hematological Soc; Amer Soc Ichthyology and Herpetology; Biomed Engr Soc; Sigma Xi; Phi Epsilon Phi; Bethesda Chevy Chase J Comty Group; charter mem, Kennedy lodge, B'nai B'rith, Wash DC. Ed: Proc of Conf on Radiation Problems in Manned Space Flights, 1960; Theoretical Biology; contbr to sci jours. Home: 9208 Cypress Ave, Bethesda, Md. Office: NASA, Washington, DC.

JACOBS, Gerald, Eng, physician; b. Birmingham, Eng, Mar 1, 1916; s. Nathan and Dora (Rose); MB, ChB, MRCS, LRCP, Birmingham U, 1939-45; m. Hessie Hass, 1944; c: Nathaniel, Leonard, Maurice. Phys, surg, since 1946. Chmn, Birmingham Talmud Torah; hon secy, The Minyan, Birmingham; council mem, Birmingham Cen Syn; found, local Orthodox J Med Soc. Home: 148 Pershore Rd, Birmingham, Eng.

JACOBS, Harod Milton, US, business exec, communal leader b; b. Bklyn, Oct 25, 1912; s. Max and Kate (Fried); BS, St Johns U, 1934; MS, Columbia U, 1936; m. Pearl Schraub, Apr 11, 1937; c: Vivian Chill, Joseph, Paul. Pres, Precision Equities Inc; pres: Precision Metal Co, 1939-42; Precisionware Inc, 1942-69. Chmn, bd dirs, Union of Orthodox Congs of Amer; pres: Bklyn JCC; hon, Crown Hgts Yeshiva; found, Maimonides Inst for Retarded Children; chmn, UJA, Bklyn; dir: Yeshiva Torah Vodaath; Yeshiva Chaim Berlin; dir: Click-Operators of Bklyn Navy Yard, US Small Bus Admn; Pres Elector, 1968; mem, J Educ Comm of NYC. Recipient: Interfaith Rel Award of Bklyn; Man of Year, Natl Council of Young Isr. Home: 67 Sutton Pl, Lawrence, LI, NY. Office: 50 Court St, Brooklyn, NY.

JACOBS, Herman, US, social worker, marriage counselor; b. Bklyn, NY, Dec 5, 1902; s. Abraham and Huldah (Marks); BS, NYU, 1924; MA, Columbia U, 1931; MSS, Grad Sch for J Social Work, 1933; EdD, Wayne State U, 1952; m. Rachel Friedman, May 27, 1929; c: Eden. Dir em, B'nai B'rith Hillel Found, U Mich, dir, 1953-68; exec dir, J Comty House, Bensonhurst, 1927-30; club, educ dir, 92nd St YMHA, 1930-34; asst exec secy Bx YM-YWHA, 1934-36; ex dir, J Comty Cen, Detroit, 1936-51; profsl sup, Wayne State U 1936-44. Pres, Natl Assn, J Cen Workers, 1941; mem: commn on human relations, Ann Arbor, 1957-62; bd dir ARC, Washtenaw Co, 1956-62; found, bd dirs, Ann Arbor chap, NCCJ, 1954-61; mem: Acad Cert Social Workers; Natl Assn Social Workers; Natl Assn Hillel Dirs; Amer Sociol Assn; Natl and Intl Councils on Social Wfr; Mich Inter-Prof Assn on Marriage, Divorce and Family; B'nai B'rith; Phi Delta Kappa; Sigma Xi. Hobby, photography. Home: 2203 Navarre Circle, Ann Arbor, Mich.

JACOBS, Leon, US, researcher, science admnr; b. Bklyn, NY, Mar 26, 1915; s. Samuel and Evelyn (Rosenthal); BA, Bklyn Coll, 1935; MA, George Wash U, Wash DC, 1938, PhD,

1947; m. Eva Eisenberg, Nov 26, 1946; c: Jonathan, Alice, Abby. Asst dir, chief, lab, parasitic diseases; Natl Inst Allergy and Infectious Diseases; NIH, since 1969; dep asst secy for sci, HEW, 1967-69; dir, div biol studies, NIH, 1965-67, on staff since 1937; off, USPHS, 1948-59. Repr, Amer Soc of Tropical Med and Hygiene, NRC, Natl Acad of Scis, since 1959; pres, Helminthological Soc of Wash, 1951-52; mem: Amer Soc Parasitologists, comm bus mgmt, 1960-62; Tropical Med and Hygiene; Amer Soc Immunologists; Amer Soc Protozoologists; Sigma Xi. Ed, Tropical Medicine and Hygiene News, 1952-56; contbr to profsl jours. Recipient, awards: Arthur S Flemming, 1954; Wash Acad of Sci, 1955; Barnett Cohen, Md Soc Bact, 1955; Bklyn Coll Alumnus, honor, 1955; Fulbright Research Scholarship to NZ, 1960; Guggenheim f, 1960-61. Home: 3705 Morrison St NW, Washington, DC. Office: Lab of Parasitic Diseases, NIH, Bethesda, Md.

JACOBS, Marvin E, US, attorney; b. Wilkes-Barre, Pa, May 2, 1937; s. Max and Alice (Wohl) Jakubovitz; BChE, Drexel Inst of Tech, 1959; JD, George Wash U, 1962; m. Myra Radel, Dec 25, 1958; c: Todd, David. Atty, patents, Lindenberg, Freilich & Wasserman since 1967; patent examiner, US Patent Off, 1960-63; patent atty: Bacon & Thomas, 1963-66; Fowler, Knoble & Garbrell, 1966-67. Recording secy: Encino Lodge, B'nai B'rith, Saddlebrush Lodge, both ADL chaps; mem: Order of Coif, Tau Beta Pi. Home: 12126 Iredell St, Studio City, Cal. Home: 1100 Glendon Ave, Los Angeles, Cal.

ACOBS, Maurice, US, publisher; b. Lawrence, Mass, Dec 25, 1896; s. Samuel and Anna (Zukerman); BA, U Me, 1917, LLD, 1965; DHL, HUC, 1948; m. Elsa Wohlfeld, June 27, 1926; c: Elizabeth Klatzkin, Ruth Steele. Chmn, Maurice Jacobs Inc, publishers, since 1961, pres, 1950-61; exec vice-pres, J Publ Soc, Amer, 1936-50. Chief petty off USN WW I. Pres: Phi Epsilon Pi, 1945; Natl Interfrat Conf, 1946; Pa Council Union Amer Heb Congs, 1960-64; Graetz Coll, 1955-58; U Lodge, B'nai B'rith, 1934; chmn: B'nai B'rith Natl Vocational Service Comm, 1955-62, hon since 1962; trustee, Del Valley Coll, 1925-55; vice-pres, 1940-45; dir, Natl Fed Temple Brotherhoods, 1934-44; hon dir, since 1944; dir, adv bd J Students, Hillel, 1936-59; hon dir, since 1959, vice-pres, Fed Reform Syns, 1949-54; gov, Amer Assn J Educ, 1940-64; bd govs, Brandeis U, Inst Contemporary J since 1967; trustee: J Publ Soc, 1950-53; vice-pres, 1936-50; Union of Amer Heb Congs, since 1957; exec comm, since 1962; Reform Cong Knesset Isr, 1939-53, hon trustee, since 1953; FJA, 1956-62; chmn, bd trustees, Coll J Studies, 1958-60; dir: JWB, 1940-62; J Chautauqua Soc, 1939-44, hon dir, since 1944; Yivo Inst for J Research, 1940-62; J Book Council of Amer, 1940-67; J Occupational Council, 1958-62; United Heb Schs, 1940-58; Round Table Club; J Exponent, 1936-39, 1949-60; Natl Fed Temple Brotherhoods, 1957; Graetz Coll, 1958; Knesseth Isr, 1961; Phila B'nai B'rith Vocational Service, 1961; Phi Epsilon Pi Found's Medal, 1961; Beth Or, 1963; J Chautauqua Soc, 1964; Pa Council, UAHC, 1964; Amer J Hist Soc Friedman Medal, 1966. Home: 520 Rittenhouse Claridge, Philadelphia, Pa. Office: 1010 Arch St, Philadelphia, Pa.

JACOBS, Morris E, US, advertising exec; b. Omaha, Neb, Aug 7, 1896; s. Elias and Gertrude (Shaftan); att U Mo, 1914-16; hon, LLD, Creighton U, 1954; hon, LLD, St Joseph Coll, 1960; m. Rae Iseman, Sep 15, 1927; c: Susie Peebler. Pres, Bozell & Jacobs, Inc, since 1921; mem, bd dirs, Occidental Bldg & Loan Assn, since 1949; mem, bd of dirs, D A Schulte, Inc, 1950; chmn, bd dir, Omaha Transit Co, 1955-57; Omaha Ind Found, since 1953; secy, Devl Council Inc, since 1957. Bd of dirs: Children's Memorial Hosp, since 1950; natl bd of govs, USO, since 1955; bd of trustees, Amer Fund for Isr Instn, since 1956; bd of trustees, Bishop Clarkson Memorial Hosp, since 1957; dir, Bd for Fundamental Educ, since 1958; regional bd, NCCJ, since 1954; natl exec comm, AJComm, since 1952; adv bd, YWCA, since 1955; Mayor's Planning and

Devl Comm, since 1956; bd trusteee, St Joseph's Coll, Ind, since 1950; fmr pres: Omaha Comty Chest; State Bd of Educ, Neb; W Cen states, CJFWF; Fed of J Service; Temple Isr; active in local civic orgs; clubs: Omaha Advt; Standard; Harmony. Recipient: civic award, Omaha C of C; hon citizen, New Orleans; citation, Creighton U; hon citizen, Tex; award: Neb Wesleyan U; M. U Sch of Journalism; Man of Year, Assn Retailers of Omaha. Home: 23 Mt Shadows, E Scottsdale, Ariz.

JACOBS, Murray Livingston, US, attorney; b. St. Petersberg, Fla, May 3, 1890; s. Hermann and Esther (Rabin); AB, CCNY, 1910; LLB, Fordham U Sch of Law, 1911; m. Violette Seessel, Dec 24, 1921. Semi-ret since 1964; pvt practice, since 1912; partner, Jonas & Neuburger, 1912-32; referee, spec guardian, Supr, Surrogates Courts, NY; referee, Surrogates Court, Kings Co, 1964-69; Boyces Tigers, Selective Service Bd, WW I; OPA Appeals examiner, WW II. Vice-pres, bd, chmn, Sch of Nursing, J Hosp and Med Cen, Bklyn, since 1935, mem: bd trustees, FJP, NY; Cen Bur for J Aged, fmr vice-pres; Emanu-El Midtown YM-YWHA; JWB, USO; Natl Council, Amer JDC; Boy Scouts Amer, fmr dep commn, NYC; dist dep Grand Master, Masons; dist dep, grand chancellor, KP; Amer, NY State, NY Bar Assns, comm on Supr Court; Assn of Bar NYC, fmr chmn, arbitration comm. Recipient, dist service award, J Hosp and Med Cen, Bklyn. Home: 50 W 67 St, New York, NY. Office: 200 W 57 St, New York, NY.

JACOBS, Nathan, US, dentist; b. Mountaindale, NY, July 30, 1916; s. Aron and Sophie (Kotcher); att Cornell U, 1934-37; DDS, Georgetown U Sch of Dent, 1941; m. Betti Berlad, Nov 17, 1945; c: Julian, Gary, Ronald. Pvt practice since 1947. Lt, USN, Dent Corps, 1943-46. Vice-pres, Argo Lodge 413 B'nai B'rith; pres, Katz Lodge, B'nai B'rith, 1963-65; mem: Amer Dent Assn, Wash, DC; Alpha Omega. Hobbies: fishing, golf, hiking. Home: 9500 Crosby Rd, Silver Spring, Md. Office: 2906 Nichols Ave SE, Washington, DC.

JACOBS, Ralph S, US, accountant; b. Lead, S D, Apr 10, 1901; s. Louis and Sylvia (Adamsky); att La Salle U, 1923-27; m. Minnie Finkelstein (decd); m. 2nd, Ida Kruger (decd); c: Louis, Allan, Helen. CPA, Ralph S Jacobs & Co, since 1936. Chmn, regional bd, ADL, since 1961, Lake Co chmn, since 1960; trustee, Cong Am Echod, Waukegan, since 1956; pres, B'nai B'rith, 1930-31; mem: Mayor's Comm on Hum Relations; Masons; Elks; Scottish Rite; Amer Inst CPAs; Ill Soc CPAs. Recipient, James M Yard Award, NCCJ. Home: 610 Colville Place, Waukegan, Ill. Office: 641 Lorraine Ave, Waukegan, Ill.

JACOBS, Robert P, US, rabbi; b. Syracuse, NY, June 16, 1908; s. Meyer and Anne (Solomon); BA, Syracuse U, 1929; ordained rabbi, MHL, JIR, 1933; MSW, Wash U, Mo, 1956; DD, HUC-JIR, 1962; m. Mildred Lowenstein, Apr 19, 1933; c: David. Dir, B'nai B'rith Hillel Found, Wash U, St Louis, Mo, since 1946; rabbi: Cong Adas Amuno, Hoboken, NJ, 1934-38; Cong Beth Ha-Tephila, Asheville, NC, 1938-46. Pres, St Louis Rabb Assn, 1956, 1961; vice-pres, seaboard region, ZOA, 1936-38; chmn, comm on marriage, family and home, CCAR, 1957-61. Mem: B'nai B'rith; LZOA; AJCong; AJComm; Planned Parenthood Assn; Metrop Youth Comm; ACLU; clubs: Meadowbrook Country; Rotary. Contbr to periodicals. Home: 4466 W Pine Blvd, St Louis, Mo. Study: 6300 Forsyth Blvd, St Louis, Mo.

JACOBS, Rose L, US, business exec; b. Pol, Feb 22, 1904; d. Joseph and Rebecca (Friedman) Levine; att Cincinnati Conservatory Music, 1919-23; m. Jacob Jacobs, Sept 14, 1924 (decd); c: Augusta. Owner mgr, Eagle Coal and Iron Co, since 1957, asst mgr, 1946-57. Dir, Scioto Co unit, Amer Cancer Soc, since 1933, secy, 1954-56; treas, Portsmouth JWB; active, ARC drives and Blood Bank; mem: women's div, C of C; bd, Bus and Profsl Women's Club; Amer Legion Auxiliary; pres: Portsmouth Gen Hosp Auxiliary, 1956-57; Portsmouth Temple Sisterhood, 1951-53; secy, 1947-51; dir, Family and Children's Service, Scioto Co, 1962-63; vice-pres, hist, Mercy Hosp Auxiliary, 1950-53; co-chmn, Cancer Campaign, 1953-54; maj, Comty Chest Campaign, 1943-48; mem: Smith-Everett Hosp Auxiliary, 1958-60; adv bd, City of Portsmouth, 1956-57; clubs: Soroptomist; Women's City. Recipient: Ky Col Citation. Hobbies: knitting, gardening, music. Home: 2840 N Hill Rd, Portsmouth, O. Office: 1015 Washington St, Portsmouth, O.

JACOBS, Samuel, US, engineer; b. Cornwall, Ont, Can, Jan 2, 1911; s. Louis and Ida (Lash); in US since 1922; BS, Tri State

Coll, Angola, Ind, 1935; m. Mildred Kirschner, June 20, 1937; c: Lester, Lawrence. Pres, chmn bd, Adirondack Construction Corp, since 1950, found, 1937; dir, Glen Falls Contractors, since 1946; pres, Inter-Devl Sys; vice-pres, Glens Falls Inves; bd dirs, Glens Falls Savings and Loan; construction engr, Duplex Construction Corp, Glens Falls, NY, 1935-37. Lt-cmdr, USN, 1942-45, now capt, USNR. Trustee, Crandall Libr; mem, bd dirs: YMCA; Glens Falls Forum; Geriatrics Soc; Workshop for Handicapped; Sch Bd; mem: exec comm, Bldg Ind Employers NY State, since 1949; pres council, Amer Inst Mgmt since 1952; Amer Soc Civil Engrs; N NY Builders Exch; Asso Gen Contractors Amer; Tri-Co Soc Profsl Engrs; Gen Bldg Contractors NY State; Amer Technion Soc; B'nai B'rith; Masons; Elks; Kiwanis; JWV; Amer Legion; YMCA; clubs: Glens Falls Country, Stuyvesant Yacht. Recipient: USN Commendation Ribbon and Medal, with Valor, 1945; Expert Rifleman Medal, 1945; NY State Conspicuous Service Cross, 1946; USNR Medal, 1952. Hobbies: amateur radio operator, sailing, arts. Home: 34 Garrison Rd, Glens Falls, NY; E Lake George, NY. Office: 73-95 Mohican St, Glens Falls, NY.

JACOBS, Stanley R, US, stock broker; b. NYC, Sep 10, 1898; s. Ralph and Adele (Ansbacher); BA, Columbia U, 1918; m. Helene Brandstatter, Sep 16, 1947. Mem, NY Stock Exch, since 1927. Lt, US Army, 1918; maj, US Army and Mil Govt, Saar and Lower Bavaria, WW II. Trustee at large, FJP, hon trustee: Hillside Hosp; Educ Alliance, fmr chmn, bd of trustees; trustee, Eisenhower Coll, Seneca Falls, NY; mem: Columbia Coll Council; C of C, NY State; clubs: Columbia U; Harmonie; Cent Country. Recipient: Bronze Star Medal; four combat stars. Hobby, travel. Home: 1130 Park Ave, New York, NY. Office: 99 William St, New York, NY.

JACOBS, Sydney, US, physician, educator; b. New Orleans, La, Nov 23, 1907; s. Wolf and Hannah (Abramson); BS, Tulane U, 1928; MD, 1930; cert, Trudeau Sch for TB, 1937; m. Sadie Frumin, June 12, 1938; c: Alan, Jerome, Myron, Joel. Pvt practice, since 1932; chmn, Dept of Med, Touro Infirmary since 1967; prof, clinical med, Tulane U, since 1961; fac mem since 1932; radiologist, La Health Dept, since 1945; cons: chest diseases, VA regional off, since 1949; pulmonary diseases, USPHS Hosp, since 1945; sr visiting phys, Charity Hosp, La, 1932-52, cons, med since 1952; cons: internal med, Methodist Home Hosp, since 1933; med, Flint-Goodridge Hosp, Dillard U, since 1935; phys: Munic Boys Home, since 1933; J Childrens Home, since 1939. Pres: Natl TB and Respiratory Diseases Assn, 1966; S TB Conf, 1959; S Trudeau Soc, 1953; La TB Assn, 1947-51; Chevra Thilim Syn, 1959-61; vice-pres, Natl TB Assn, 1953; SE Region, ZOA, 1943; Young Judea, 1936-38; f, Amer Coll Phys; mem: Amer Bd Internal Med; Intl Union against TB; Amer Trudeau Soc; Amer Coll Chest Phys; AHA; Natl Rehab Soc; S Med Soc; La Heart Assn; New Orleans Acad Internal Med; Orleans Parish Med Soc; La State Med Soc; Phi Lambda Kappa; bd, JWF; bd educ, Communal Heb Sch; club, Saturday Night. Contbr to med jours. Recipient, awards: Bonds for Isr, 1958, 1966; S TB Conf, 1966. Home: 3704 Octavia St, New Orleans, La. Office: 3430 Med Bldg, Prytania St, New Orleans, La.

JACOBS, Ted Seth, US, artist; b. Newark, NJ, June 21, 1927; s. Maurice and Jessie (Jacobson); att Art Students League, NY, 1943-47; m. Dorris Hodgson, June 21, 1960; c: Jodiah, Caleb. Associated with: Portraits Inc, Kennedy Gal, NYC; Adelson Gal, Boston. One-man shows: Wickersham Gal; The Drawing Shop; Noah Goldowsky all Gal, NYC; Adelson Gal, Boston; Rolling Rock Estates, Ligonier, Pa; St Vincent's Coll, Latrobe, Pa; group exhbs: Portraits Inc, since 1950; Riverside Mus, 1950, 1952; ACA Gal, 1951; Springfield, Mass, 1952; Randolph Macon Coll, Va, 1953; Walker Art Cen, Minneapolis, 1954; Amer Artists Profsl League, 1958; Fairleigh Dickinson Coll, NJ, 1960; repr in pvt collections; portrait commns; mural decorations; stage decorations for off-Broadway theater. Mem, The Buddhist F, NY. Recipient: first prize: Kansas City Art Inst, 1943; John F and Anna Lee Stacey Natl Award, 1954. Spec interest, tchg Buddhist phil. Home and studio: 523 E 83 St, New York, NY.

JACOBS, Yaakov M, US, writer, editor; b. NYC, July 27, 1925; s. Morris and Jennie (Engel); ordained rabbi, Rabb Sem of Amer, 1952; m. Miriam Lassner, Apr 10, 1949; c: Moshe, Daniel, Geula, Eliahu. Ed: The Observer, since 1964; Young Isr Viewpoint, 1961-64; rabbi: Greenwich Village Syn, 1949-56; Young Isr of St Louis, 1956-61. Pres, Rabb Coun-

cil, Gtr St Louis, 1958-61; mem, Beth Din of Yaad Hoeir, St Louis, 1958-61. Home: 144 Castleton Ave, Staten Island, NY. Office: 5 Beekman St, New York, NY.

JACOBSEN, Martin, Isr, economist, business exec; b. Zwolle, Netherlands Oct 2, 1904; s. Yizhak and Sarah (Blom); in Isr since 1952; MSc, U Rotterdam, 1936; m. Justine de Jongh, Feb 9, 1934; c: Lea. Dir, Fertilizers and Chems Ltd; dept head, Phillips N V, Eindhoven, 1928-33; econ, Min of Agric and Fisheries, The Hague, 1936-38; admn, Hedeman's Textile Factory, 1938-43, 1945-46; partner, Benjamin de Jongh, Eindhoven, 1946-52, all in Holland; controller, finance mgr, Isr Chem Fibres Ltd; bd dirs Monsel Electron, both subsidiaries of Monsanto, 1954-65. Secy, Eindhoven chap, Dutch Zionist Org; mem, Natl Org of Acctnts, US. Home: 6 Simtat Hardafna, Sayon, Isr. Office: JCF, Industrial Zone, Ashdod, Isr.

JACOBSOHN, Kurt, Port, chemist, educator; b. Berlin, Ger, Oct 31, 1904; s. Paul and Gertrud (Dewitz); PhD, U Berlin, 1929; m. Liesel Maver, 1929; c: Lia, Eva Mayer. Vice-rector, prof, chem, U of Lisbon, since 1955, on fac since 1934; research chem, Kaiser Wilhelm Isnt for Biochem, Ger, 1926-29. Fmr pres, Centro Israelita de Portugal. Author, textbooks on chem; contbr to profsl jours; ed bd, Portuguese and intl sci revs. Home: Rua D João de Castro 3, Oeiras, Port. Office: Faculty of Sciences, U of Lisbon, Port.

JACOBSOHN, Max, Isr, farmer; b. Gleiwitz, Ger, June 20, 1887; s. Louis and Luise (Hamburger); in Isr since 1933; law grad, U of Munich, Berlin, 1908; m. Else Nathan (decd); c: Hannah Navar, Bathsheva Rosenfeld, Esther Theodor. Farmer, Pardess Hanna; law practice, 1913-33; notary, 1920-33. Chmn: tax comm, Bur of Coord Econ Orgs; council, Pardess Syndicate of Citrus Growers; Cen Libr for Blind; mem: Water Council; Govt Council for Coop, Soc; Govt Govt Council for Blind. Home: Meged, Pardess Hanna, Isr.

JACOBSON, Abraham Isaac, US, rabbi; b. Nelsonville, O, May 12, 1910; s. Solomon and Minna (Bubly); BA, CCNY, 1930; MHL, JIR, 1935; hon DD, HUC-JIR, 1960; m. Sonia Pavloff, Aug 18, 1935; c: Naomi, Paul, Ruth. Rabbi, Temple Emanue-El, Haverhill, Mass, since 1939; fac mem, hist, phil depts, Bradford Jr Coll; rabbi: Temple of Isr, Amsterdam, NY, 1935-38; Beth Isr Cong, Malden, Mass, 1938-39; found, chmn, Haverhill Comty Action Comm, OEO, 1964-68; pres: NYC Metrop Avukah, 1934-35; Hudson Valley Zion Reg, ZOA, 1937-38; Haverhill Comty Council, 1947-48; Haverhill Mins Assn, 1946-47. Auxiliary chaplain, Peace AF Base, since 1960; civilian chaplain, Naval Disciplinary Command, Portsmouth, NH, since 1960. Chaplain, J Scouts, Lone Tree Council, since 1944; hon chaplain, Haverhill Post, JWV; secy-treas, NE Conf Safety Council, 1940-53, Lib Rabbis, 1950-51; mem, exec comm: alumni assn, HUC-JIR, 1952; Girls Club, since 1946; Visiting Nurses Assn, 1946-52; ARC, since 1948; YMCA, since 1943; all Haverhill Mass; mem: admn comm, ZOA, 1937-38; admn council, Natl Council for Pal, since 1940; JDC, since 1940; admn comm, Haverhill Comty Chest, since 1943; B'nai B'rith; CCAR; Mass Bd Rabbis. Author: Jews in Spain, 1291-1415. Home: 78 Hamilton Ave, Haverhill, Mass. Study: 514 Main St, Haverhill, Mass.

JACOBSON, Amnon, Isr, scientist; b. Tel Aviv, Isr, July 15, 1931; s. Zvi and Yocheved (Zucker); BSc, Technion, Haifa, 1954, dipl, Ing, 1955; MSc, 1961; DSc, MIT, Mass, 1965; m. Rivka Klerman, Sep 1951; c: Anate, Michale. Gen dir, dir research, ISFRA Ltd, since 1969; dir and partner, Engr Devl for Ind, since 1968; chief engr, Hamat, 1959-62; head, product research and devl, Koor Ind, 1966-69. Lt, IDF, 1948-50. Prin contribs: applied research and engr devl; patents in Isr, US, Ger, Fr, Eng, S Afr, It, on aircraft support equipment, fuel tanks, rigid polyurathene. Elected mem: Sigma Xi; Tau Beta Pi; mem: ASTM; ACI; PCI; AAAS. Contbr numerous sci papers to profsl jours. Hobby, underwater fishing. Home: 28 Beeri St, Tel Aviv, Isr. Office: 8 Zeitlin St, Tel Aviv, Isr.

JACOBSON, Belle E, US, physician; b. NYC, Mar 12, 1901; d. Henry and Ida (Cohen); AB, Hunter Coll, 1922; MD, Boston U Med Sch 1926; m. Irving Greenwald, Oct 24, 1925; c: Edward. Pvt practice, since 1928; cons phys, New Rochelle Hosp, staff mem since 1952; asso phys, Montefiore Hosp, since 1952. F, Amer Coll of Card; Amer Coll of Phys; dipl, Amer Bd of Internal Med; mem, AMA. Home: 10 Lawrence Park Crescent, Bronxville, NY, 10708. Office: Montefiore Med Care Demonstration, 3675 Third Ave, Bronx, NY.

JACOBSON, Bernard H, US, chemical mfr; b. Baltimore, Md, Aug 28, 1895; s. William and Gertrude (Weinkrantz); EMetE, Lehigh U, 1917; m. Florence Blew, Oct 19, 1919 (decd); c: Charlene Macht; m. 2nd, Blanche Testerman, June 30, 1934; c: Emily. Cons Food Machinery and Chem Corp, since 1961, vice-pres, dir, 1951-61; dir: Carbon Fuel; Kanawha Valley Bank; research dept, Hooker Electrochem, 1917-21; E C Klipstein & Sons, 1921-33; mgr:S Charleston Works, Calco Chem, 1933-36; Ohio-Apex, 1936-51. Chmn: Bd Trustees, Morris Harvey Coll; exec comm, Regional Devl Auth; finance comm, W Va Centennial Commn; Kanawha Valley Hosp Planning Council; mem: bd advs, Salvation Army, Charleston; Amer Chem Soc; Amer Inst Chem; Electrochem Soc; Pi Lambda Phi; Tau Beta Pi; Masons; clubs: Rotary, Southmore Country, Charleston. Home: 1516 Connell Rd, Charleston, W Va. Office: 1523 Kanawha Valley Bldg, Charleston, W Va.

JACOBSON, Charlotte, US, communal worker; b. Apr 27, 1914; d. Jonas and Lena (Alexander) Stone; m. Mortimer Jacobson, May 31, 1936. Mem of exec, JA, Amer Section, since 1968; natl pres, Hadassah, 1964-68; fmr natl vice-pres, treas, secy, chmn, natl Zionist affairs, natl conv chmn and natl org chmn; Hadassah delg to WZC, 1951, 1956, 1960, 1964, 1965; mem, Hadassah delg to Actions Comm, Isr, annually; has travelled to Isr on behalf of Hadassah activities; has visited J Comtys, in Russ,S Amer, Morocco, Czech; mem: natl admn comm, Amer Zionist Council; League of Women Voters; fmr chmn, women's org, Bx Women's Red Cross and Amer Cancer Soc. Office: Hadassah, 65 W 52 St, New York, NY.

JACOBSON, David, US, rabbi; b. Cincinnati, O, Dec 2, 1909; s. Abraham and Rebecca (Sereinsky); BA, U Cincinnati, 1931; ordained rabbi, HUC-JIR, 1934; PhD, Cambridge U, Eng, 1936; hon DD, HUC-JIR, 1959; m. Helen Gugenheim, Nov 6, 1938; c: Elizabeth, Dorothy Miller. Rabbi, Temple Beth-El, San Antonio, Tex, since 1938; instr, HUC, 1933-34; rabbi, W Cen Lib Cong, London, Eng, 1934-36; rabbi, Indianapolis Heb Cong, 1936-38. Chaplain, USNR, 1944-46; auxiliary mil chaplain, San Antonio area. Pres: Torch Club San Antonio, 1961; San Antonio Soc for Crippled Children and Adults, 1963-66; Research and Planning Council, San Antonio, 1966-67; Tex Soc Wfr Assn, 1967-69; San Antonio Area Found, since 1965; San Antonio Manpower Devl Council, 1964-68; SW Region, CCAR, 1969; Kallah of Tex Rabbis, 1950-51; Comty Wfr Council, 1951-53; TB Assn, Bexar Co Chap, 1955-57; Goodwill Inds, 1956-60; natl repr, Boy Scouts of Amer, 1958; bd trustees, Our Lady of The Lake Coll since 1966; adv bd, Worden Sch of Soc Service, since 1958;chmn, CCAR Comm on Judaism and Heatlth since 1967; Regional Coord Comm for Vocational Rehab, Tex Educ Agcy, 1967-68; PR Comm, Goodwill Ind of Amer, since 1968, on bd, since 1965; bd, Florence G Heller-JWB Bd Research Cen since 1966; Natl JWB since 1964; Natl Conf Soc Wfr since 1967; USO Natl Council, 1968-69; Natl Assn of Drs of US since 1960; bd, HUC-JIR, 1966-68; Alumni Assn, HUC-JIR since 1966; bd overseers, HUC-JIR since 1966; SW Ecumenical Cen for Rel and Health, since 1967; S Region, Amer Soc Health Assn; San Antonio Lutheran Hosp since 1967; San Antonio Med Found since 1962; United Fund of San Antonio, since 1960; Children's Hosp Found, since 1964; Children's Service Bur, San Antonio, since 1966; Alamo chap, Assn of US Army since 1964; San Antonio Good Govt League; Catholic Youth Org since 1961. Author: Social Background of the Old Testmanet, 1942; The Synagogue through the Ages, 1958; contbr to: Universal J Ency; A Minute of Prayer, 1954; to profsl gen publs. Recipient: award from Catholic Coll Found, 1959; Boy Scout Silver Beaver, 1958; Golden Deeds Award, Exch club, 1959; hon, NCCJ, 1961; Keystone Award, Boys Clubs of Amer, 1962; hon, B'nai B'rith for Lifetime Achievement, 1964. Home: 510 Garrity Rd, San Antonio, Tex. Study: 211 Belknap Pl, San Antonio, Tex.

JACOBSON, Edmund, US, physician, author; b. Chgo, Ill, Apr 22, 1888; s. Morris and Fanny (Blum); BS, Northwestern U, 1908; MA, Harvard U, 1909, PhD, 1910; att Chgo U Med Sch, 1911-13; hon f, Cornell U, 1910-11; MD, Rush Med Coll, 1915; hon LLD, George Williams Coll, 1962; m. Elizabeth Silberman, Dec 16, 1925; c: Edmund, Nancy Engelsberg, Ruth Grommers. Pvt practice since 1917, psycht, since 1919; dir, Lab for Clinical Phys since 1935; exec dir, Found for Sci Relaxation, Inc, since 1954; pres, Natl Found for Progressive Relaxation, since 1951; asst, phys, U Chgo, 1911-12, asst prof, phys, 1926-36; att phys, House of Correction, 1918-1919; diagnostician, N Chgo Hosp, 1919-20; asso att phys, Michael Reese Hosp, 1919-26. Prin contribs: made first measurements of nervousness in man; devl elec instruments for measuring mental activities directly; devl new phys methods for treatment of nervous states. F: Amer Coll Phys; AAAS; Acad Psychosomatic Med; Intl Coll Angiology; hon life mem, St Louis Med Soc; hon pres, Amer Phys Soc for Tension Control; mem: AMA, Ill State Med Soc; Chgo Med Soc; Amer Phys Soc; Midwestern Psychosomatic Soc; NY Acad Med; Intl Soc Internal Med; Amer Psychosomatic Soc; Sigma Xi, Phi Beta Kappa; club, Quadrangle. Author: Progressive Relaxation, 1929; You Must Relax, 1934, rev ed, 1957; You Can Sleep Well, 1938; The Peace We Americans Need, 1944; How to Teach Scientific Relaxation, 1958; How to Relax and Have Your Baby, 1959; Tension Control for Businessmen, 1963; Anxiety and Tension Control, 1964; Tension in Medicine, 1967; Biology of Emotions, 1967; contbr to med jours. Spec interest, fgn affairs. Home: 5532 S Shore Dr, Chicago, Ill. Office: 55 E Washington St, Chicago, Ill.

JACOBSON, Gaynor I, US, organization exec; b. Buffalo, NY, May 17, 1912; s. Morris and Rose (Fleischman); BA, U Buffalo, 1937; Cert, Social Work, 1937; MSW, 1941; m. Florence Stulberg, Feb 22, 1937; c: Margot, Helen Goldstein. Exec vice-pres, United HIAS Service, since 1968; exec secy, JCC,Rochester, NY, 1937-40; exec dir, J Family and Child Care, Rochester, 1938-44; co-dir, JDC: It, 1944-45; Greece, 1945-46; Czech, 1946-47; Hung, 1947-50; exec dir: J Child Care Assn, Phila, 1950-51; Amer Technion Soc, 1951-53; Eur oprs, HIAS, 1953-54, asso exec dir Eur, N Afr, 1954-55; dir, Latin Amer oprs, 1955-61, dir, Eur and N African oprs, 1961-66, exec dir, 1966-68. Vice-chmn: Amer Council of Voluntary Agcys for Fgn Service, Migration and Ref Problems Comm; exec comm mem, Amer Immigration and Citizenship Conf; bd mem: J Occupational Council; Bur for Careers in J Service; publs comm mem, Natl Conf of J Communal Service; rep, Intl Council on J Social and Wfr Service, UN; chmn, Commn on Refs, Intl Council of Voluntary Agcys, 1963-66; regional vice-pres, NAACP, 1942-44; mem: Natl Assn Social Workers; Natl Assn J Family and Children's Health Services. Hobbies: sculpture, painting. Home: 340 E 64 St, New York, NY. Office: 200 Park Ave S, New York, NY.

JACOBSON, Harold G, US, physician, educator; b. Cincinnati, O, Oct 12, 1912; s. Samuel and Regina (Dittman); BS, U Cincinnati, 1934, BM, 1936, MD, 1937; m. Ruth Enenstein, Aug 10, 1941; c: Richard, Arthur. Chief, diagnostic radiology, Montefiore Hosp, radiologist i/c, residency training prog, radiological services, since 1955; prof, radiology, Albert Einstein Coll of Med, Bx, NY, since 1959; cons, VA Hosp, Bx, NY, since 1958, on staff since 1950; spec examiner, radiology, NY, Civil Service Commn, Dept of Hosp, 1960; f, path, research, U Cincinnati, 1938; asst,radiology,U Tex, Sch Med, chief resident, both 1941-42; asso radiologist, New Haven Hosp, New Haven, Conn, 1942; instr, radiology, Yale U, Sch Med, 1942; dir, Dept Roentgenology, Hosp for Spec Surg, 1953-55; visting prof: NY Med Coll, 1960; Ind U, 1962; Stanford U, 1962; U Cincinnati, 1959; Okla U, 1961; lectr, scholastic insts and profsl socs in US and Eur, since 1954. Maj, US Army, 1942-46. F, Amer Coll Radiology, since 1952, councilor, since 1960; pres: NY Roentgen Soc, Soc, 1959-60; Radiology Soc of N Amer, 1966-67; mem: bd chancellors, Amer Coll Radiology, 1963; spec comm, radiology, NY Co Med Soc, since 1954; AMA; NY State Med Soc; Amer Roentgen Ray Soc; Alpha Omega Alpha; adv comm, natl cancer prevention proj, USPHS, 1959. Co-author:Roentgent Aspects of the Papilla and Ampulla of Vater, 1953; Neuroradiology Workshcp, Vol 1, 1961, Vol 11; The Lower Esophagus; Cardiac Calcifications; Cholangicgraphy and Choledochoscopy. Hist, NY Roentgen Soc, 1969. Mem, ed bd, Amer Jour Digestive Diseases, 1956; contbr to profsl jours. Home: 3240 Henry Hudson Pkwy, NY. Office: Montefiore Hosp, New York, NY.

JACOBSON, Helen G, US, civic worker; b. San Antonio, Tex, Apr 24, 1908; d. Jac and Rosetta (Dreyfus) Gugenheim; BA, Hollins Coll, Va, 1928; m. David Jacobson, Nov 6, 1928; c: Elizabeth, Dorothy Miller. Pres, bd dirs, Cmty Wfr Council, San Antonio; secy, Natl Assembly for Social Policy and Devl; chmn, adv comm, Foster Grandparents Project, Bexar Co Hosp Dist; mem: bd trustees, Natl Council on Crime and Delinquency; bd dirs, Tex United Cmty Services; Tex-Oklahoma Fed of Temple Sisterhoods; Alamo Dist, Tex Fed of Women's Clubs; Tex Council, NCCD; Temple Beth El Sisterhood; San Antonio Mus Assn; Cmty Guidance Cen of Bexar Co, pres, bd dirs, 1960-63; adv comm, Adult Home and

Family Life Educ Prog, San Antonio Independent Sch Dist; Sunshine Cottage Sch of Deaf Children, 1952-54; Tex St repr, UNICEF; pres, bd trustees, San Antonio Public Libr, 1957-63; lst vice pres, San Antonio and Bexar Co Council of Girl Scouts, 1957-63; mem, spec events staff, NBC, 1933-38. Recipient: Headliner Award for Civic Work, San Antonio Chap, Theta Sigma Phi, 1958; Volunteer Woman of the Year, Express-News, 1959. Home: 207 Beechwood La, San Antonio, Tex.

JACOBSON, Henry B, S Afr, business exec; b. Johannesburg, July 19, 1921; s. Abel and Bertha (Fineberg); BA, Houghton Coll, Johannesburg, 1939; m. Maureen Donner, Oct 22, 1944; c: Alan, Lana, Sandor, Steven. Mgn dir: Jason Carpet Co Ltd, since 1946; Henmaur, since 1947; Jason Trading Co, since 1949; Linor Inves, since 1953; AHJ Inves, since 1945; Baynes Rhodesia, since 1951; Henmaur Cosmetics, since 1954; Raynes-Park, since 1957; Les Parfums Inc, since 1955; dir, Jason Inves, since 1944. Pres, Witwatersrand Heb Benevolent Soc; fmr pres, N Suburbs Heb Cong; trustee, Chasidim Cong, 1954-62; bd mem, Waverley Heb Cong; clubs: Glendower Golf; Transvaal Natl Sporting. Home: 6-16 Ave, Lower Houghton, Johannesburg, S, Afr. Office: 34 Siemert Rd, Box 1691, Johannesburg, S Afr.

JACOBSON, Larry Stanley, US, periodontist; b. Kan City, Mo, Sep 1, 1936; s. Al and Florence (Hamer); att U Kan City, 1954-57; DDS, U Mo, Sch of Dent, 1961; m. Deborah Shure, Dec 25, 1958; c: Douglas, Ann. Pvt practice, periodontics. U Mo, Sch of Dent, since 1965; cons, periodontics, USPHS, Fed Penitentiary, Leavenworth, Kan; staff mem, hosps: Baptist Memorial; Menorah Med Cen; St Mary's;, Research Med Cen; Childrens Mercy; fmr cons, periodontics, U Kan Med Sch. USN, Dent Corps, 1961-63; lt-cdr, USN Dent Corps Res. Mem: Gtr Kan City Dent Soc, bd dirs; Alumni Assn, U M Kan City; Amer Dent Assn; U Dent Study Club; Amer Acad Periodontology; Midwest Soc Periodontology; Amer Soc Periodontology; Chgo Dent Soc; Omicron Delta Kappa; Alpha Epsilon Pi; Psi Omega; clubs: Couples, Beth Shalom Syn, vice-pres; Golden Spade, U of Kan City Sch of Dent. Contbr to dent jours. Recipient, Outstanding Young Men of America, Jr C of C, 1970. Hobbies: golf, photography. Home: 9515 Cedar, Overland Park, Kan. Office: 205 E 63 St, Kansas City, Mo.

JACOBSON, Martha, Austr, communal worker; b. Pol, Feb Feb 12, 1924; d. Jacob and Pola (Abzac) Lederman; in Australia since 1927; m. Nathan Jacobson, May 12, 1945; c: Lynne, Russel. Pres, WIZO State Council, Vic, 1957-68; mem: exec, Australian Fed WIZO; Vic J bd deps. Hobbies: music, swimming. Home: 99 Balaclava Rd, Caulfield, Vic, Australia.

JACOBSON, Moses A, US, physician, educator; b. Portsmouth, Va, Feb 26, 1896; s. Isaac and Rebecca (Karp); BS, Poly Inst, Va, 1916; MS, Purdue U, 1918; PhD, U Chgo, 1927; MD, Rush Med Coll, 1932; m; c: Elise Fuente, Joseph; m. 2nd, Elizabeth Sears, Aug 6, 1950. Ret; fmr, path, VA Hosp, Downey, Ill; instr, biol, bact, Purdue U, 1916-18; asst prof, bact, clinical path, Med Coll Va, 1921-22; asst prof, bact, public health, U Tenn, 1922-24; extension instr, bact, public health, U Chgo, 1924-27; med dir, Pepsodent Co, 1932-37; part owner, Chgo Lab, Clinical and Analytical, 1927-30; owner, Medico-Pharmacal Research Clinical, Analytical Lab, 1937-41. Lt, US Army, 1918-19; capt, USN MC, 1942-46; cons, path, Commanding Off, USN Hosp, Gt Lakes, Ill, 1950-56; med off USMCR, Gt Lakes, 1956-58. F: Amer Soc Clinical Path; Amer Coll Path; mem: AMA; Amer Public Health Assn; Amer Soc Bact; AAAS; Amer Assn Blood Banks; Amer Trudeau Soc; B'nai B'rith; Shriners; Navy League; Amer Legion; Sigma Xi; Amer Echod Temple. Home: Route 5, Box 252, Waukegan, Ill.

JACOBSON, Nathan, US, mathematician, educator; b. Warsaw, Pol, Sep 8, 1910; s. Charles and Pauline (Rosenberg); in US since 1917; BA, U Ala, 1930; PhD, Princeton U, 1934; m. Florence Dorfman, Aug 25, 1942; c: Michael, Pauline. Prof, math, Yale U since 1947; asst, math, Inst for Advanced Study, Princeton, 1933-34; Procter F, 1934-35; lectr, Bryn Mawr Coll, 1935-36; Natl Research F, U Chgo, 1936-37; instr, asst, asso prof, U NC, 1937-42; visiting asso prof, Johns Hopkins U, 1940-41, asso prof, 1943-47; asso instr, Navy Pre-Flight Sch, 1942-43; Guggenheim F, 1951; Fulbright research grant, Fr, 1951; visiting prof, Tata Inst of Fundamental Research, Bombay, 1969. Mem: Natl Acad Sci; Amer Math Soc, councillor, 1943-48, ed, Bulletin, 1948, vice-pres, 1956-57,

mem, bd trustees, since 1968. Author: Theory of Rings, 1943; Lectures in Abstract Algebra I and II, 1951-53; Structure of Rings, 1956; Lie Algebras, 1962; Structure and Representations of Jordan Algebras, 1968; contbr to sci jours. Home: 2 Prospect Court, Hamden, Conn. Office: Yale U, New Haven, Conn.

JACOBSON, Nathan, US, rabbi; b. NYC, Sep 20, 1913; s. Shaye and Sophie (Rivin); BA, Yeshiva Coll, 1933; LLB, Bklyn Law Sch, 1934; DJS, St Lawrence U, 1935; ordained rabbi, MHL, JTSA, 1940; m. Claire Gottfried, May 28, 1939; c: Sue Zucker, Judith Reiff, Eli. Rabbi: Shaaray Torah Cong, Canton, O, since 1951; Hillcrest J Cen, Jamaica, NY, 1942-49. Pres, Canton Zionist dist, 1953-58; chmn, Mayor's comm for promotion of good reading habits; pres, Stark Co Guidance Cen; mem bd, ARC; found, Hillcrest Zionist dist; chmn bd of educ, Yeshiva, Cen Queens, 1945-49; mem: RA; ZOA; B'nai Zion; B'nai B'rith; J Publ Soc; Canton Urban League; NY State Bar Assn. Home: 119-31 St NW, Canton, O. Study: 432-30 St, NW, Canton, O.

JACOBSON, Nathan, Austr, attorney; b. Russ, Feb 12, 1916; s. Israel and Dora (Bloch); in Austr since 1936; LLB, Melbourne U, 1945; m. Martha Lederman, May 12, 1945; c: Lynne, Russell. Barrister, solicitor, N Jacobson, Chamberlin & Casen. Pres, ZF, Australia, NZ, since 1966; treas, Vic Council Chrs and J; mem exec: Council of Australian Jewry; Vic J Bd Deps, pres, 1958-61; dep mem, Zionist Actions Comm; delg, ZCs, 1956, 1968; State ZC, 1953-58; clubs: YMHA; Royal Automobile of Vic. Hobbies: skiing, philately, fishing, yoga. Home: 99 Balaclava Rd, Caulfield, Australia. Office: 150 Queen St, Melbourne, Australia.

JACOBSON, Niels, US, business exec; b. Copenhagen, Den, May 6, 1903; s. Diedrich and Anita (Lazarus); in US since 1929; att U in Ger; m. Fanny Cahn, Sep 16, 1930; c: Peter, Elizabeth. Retail exec, since 1961; territorial merchandise mgr, Sears Roebuck & Co, 1936-55; pres, owner, Natl Supply Corp, 1955-58. Served USCG. Mem, exec comm, Atlanta chap, AJComm; active mem, The Temple, Atlanta. Hobby: music. Home: 3536 Kingsboro Rd NE, Atlanta, Ga. Office: 451 Stephens St SW, Atlanta, Ga.

JACOBSON, Priscilla, Isr, organization exec; b. London, Eng, May 20, 1922; d. John and Nancy (Ellis) Mendoza; in Isr since 1946; m. Reuben Jacobson, Apr 18, 1948; c: Run, Ilana. Natl exec secy, Hitahdut Olei Britannia, since 1967; fmr: secy, dept for Eng-speaking countries, Ichud Olami; fmr mem: Kibbutz Kfar Hanassi; Habonim; Hecalutz. Admn worker: Israel from Within jour, and other info material; sems from Eng-speaking countries. Home: 68 Sokolov St, Ramat Hasharon, Isr. Office: 53A Hayarkon St, Tel Aviv, Isr.

JACOBSON, Sidney, US, author; b. Bklyn, NY, Oct 20, 1929; s. Reuben and Beatrice (Edelman); AB, NYU, 1950; m. Ruth Allison, July 4, 1957; c: Seth, Kethy. Ed, Harvey Publs since 1951; free-lance lyricist and record produc, since 1954; reporter, NY Morning Telegraph, 1950-51. Auhor: Dirty Son of a Witch, 1969; lyricist, song hits: At the End of a Rainbow; A Boy Without a Girl; Yogi; Warm; Thirty Days Hath September; I've Come of Age; Don't Pity Me; Wonderful You; Yen Yet Song; Anniversary of Love. Mem: B'nai B'rith; Cartoonists Soc; ASCAP. Home: 110 Woodridge Pl, Leonia, NJ.

JACOBY, Emil, US, education exec; b. Cop, Czech, Nov 30, 1923; s. Benjamin and Regina (Aneisz) Jakubovics; in US since 1949; PhD, U Budapest, 1947; MA, Tchrs Coll, Columbia U, 1951; BD, MRE, Tchrs Inst, JTSA, 1952; m. Erika Engel, Sep 24, 1950; c: Jonathan, Benjamin, Michael. Dir, educ, Valley J Comty Cen and Temple, N Hollywood, Cal, since 1953; instr, ext div, U of Judaism, since 1959; head tchr, Knesses Isr, Bklyn, 1949-53. Chmn, regional council on J educ, United Syn, Pacific Southwest, educ cons, Pacific Northwest; mem: Natl Council on J Educ; Educs Asesmbly; mem, Hapoel Hamizrahi Youth Exec, Budapest, 1943-47; active in rescue work, Cen and E Eur; secy, Eur exec, Mizrahi-Hapoel Hamizrahi, Paris, 1948-49. Contbr to educ jours. Home: 12710 Albers St, N Hollywood, Cal. Office: 5540 Laurel Canyon Blvd, N Hollywood, Cal.

JACOBY, Hanoch (Heinrich), Isr, composer; b. Koenigsberg, Ger, Mar 2, 1909; s. Siegfried and Antonia (Behrendt); in Isr since 1935; att U Berlin, 1927-28; Staatliche Hochschule fuer Musik, Berlin, 1927-30; m. Alice Kanel, Feb 19, 1937;

c: Eva Nir, Ilana Yaari, Rafael, Michal. Mem, Isr Philharmonic Orch, since 1958; mem, orch, Südwestdeutsche Rundfunk, Frankfurt/M, 1930-33; tchr, Jerusalem Acad of Music, 1935-58; dir, 1954-58. IDF, 1948-49. Composer: three syms, 1944, 1955, 1960; two string quartets, 1937-38; Viola Concerto, 1940; cantata: The Day Will Come, 1944; Israel Songs, Piano Trio, 1944; Seven Miniatures, 1945; Little Suite, 1946; Wind Quintet, 1946; Symphonic Prologue, 1948; King David's Lyre, 1948; Suite Populaire, 1950; Capriccio Israelien, 1951; Partita Israeliana, 1959; Sinfonietta, 1960; Canzona for Harp, 1961; Variations for Violin, Piano, 1962; Serio-Giocoso, 1964. Recipient, Engel Prize, Tel Aviv Munic. Home: Oliphant St 10, Tel Aviv, Isr.

JACOBY, Sidney B, US, attorney, educator, author; b. Berlin, Ger, Dec 7, 1908; s. Siegfried and Amanda (Rappaport); in US since 1934; att: U Grenoble, 1927; Heidelberg Law Sch; JurD, Berlin Law Sch, 1933; LLB, Columbia U, 1939; m. Elaine Heavenrich, Oct 17, 1942; c: Evelyn, Ann. Prof law, Georgetown U Law Cen, since 1957; research asst, Yale, Columbia Law Schs, 1934-39; atty US Govt; US RR Ret Bd, 1940-45; Interior Dept, 1945-47; with US Justice Jackson at Nuremberg war criminal trials, 1945-46; Justice Dept, 1945-57; counsel to US Govt, procs before World Court, The Hague, 1957-58; visiting prof, W Res U Law Sch, 1968-69. Mem: Fed Bar Assn; Amer Soc Intl Law; Amer Fgn Law Assn; Temple Shalom. Author: Government Litigation, 1960, 1963; Litigating with the Federal Government, 1969; contbr to law jours. Home: 5916 Anniston Rd, Bethesda, Md. Office: 506 E St NW, Washington, DC.

JACOLOW, Jerald Joshua, US, business exec, certified public acctnt; b. NYC, Mar 17, 1931; s. Henry and Eleanora (Varon); BBA, CCNY, Baruch Sch, 1952; m. Joyce Siano, Nov 19, 1966; c: Ellen, Sandford. Vice-pres, treas, Ormont Drug & Chem Co Inc, since 1964; pres, dir, Funds for Expansion, Ltd; pres: Lawton Labs; Gold Leaf Pharmacal Co; dir, vice-pres, Natural Scis; dir, Burnside Air Conditioning; acctnt, John J Fried, CPAs, 1952-55; CPA, A A Miller & Co, 1955-58; CPA, J J Jacolow, 1958-63. Treas, ed, Tau Delta Phi; mem: NY State Assn Professions; NY State Soc CPAs; Amer Inst CPAs; Natl Assn Tax Acctnts; NY Credit & Finance Mgmt. Home: 139 Co Rd, Demarest, NJ. Office: 520 S Dean Street, Bnglewood, NJ.

JAFFE, Aaron Maurice, US, business exec, attorney; b. Pittsburgh, Pa, Feb 17, 1904; s. Morris and Nellie (Williams); AB, Harvard U, 1924; JD, 1927; m. Hortense Greenberg, Nov 24, 1931; c: Elsa Bartlett, Nellie Swartz. Chmn, bd, J A Williams Co, since 1940; pvt law practice, 1927-40; asso city solicitor, Pittsburgh, 1930-34. Chmn, exec comm, Liberty Distributors, chmn, exec comm, Pittsburgh chap, AJComm, chmn, 1959-61; dir, Montefiore Hosp, 1958-61; clubs: Westmoreland Country; Concordia; Harvard-Yale-Princeton. Recipient: award, Hardware Merchandiser of Year, Hardware Merchandiser, 1969. Home: 1310 Squirrel Hill Ave, Pittsburgh, Pa. Office: 401 Amberson Ave, Pittsburgh, Pa.

JAFFE, Adrian Henry, US, educator; b. NYC, Jan 4, 1916; s. Benjamin and Rose (Barrows); AB, hons, U Mich, 1936; AM, 1937; PhD, NYU, 1950; m. Nancy Cummings, Dec 17, 1958; c: Alexandra, Christopher. Prof, Eng and comparative lit, acting chmn, comparative lit, Mich State U; on fac since 1947; chmn, hum div, Kirkland Coll, prof comparative lit, since 1967. US Army, 1943-45. Chmn, lit, Mich Acad of Sci, Arts and Letters, 1950; pres, Mich Assn of Justices of the Peace, 1957; mem: MLA; Amer Comparative Lit Assn; AAUP. Author: Bibliography of French Literature in American Magazines of the Eighteenth Century, 1950; Studies in the Short Story, 1949; The Laureate Fraternity, 1960; The Process of Kafka's Trial, 1967. Home: 14 Dwight Ave, Clinton, NY. Office: Kirkland Coll, Clinton, NY.

JAFFE, Aubrey Abram, Isr, physicist; b. Prestwich, Eng, Apr 22, 1926; s. Maurice and Riva (Behrman); in Isr since 1964; BSc, hons, U Manchester, 1949; att Heb U, Jerusalem, 1949-53; m. Meira Pshetsner, Mar 13, 1951; c: Ruth. Asso prof, Heb U, since 1964; lectr, physics, U of Manchester, 1955-63; visiting assoc prof, U Md, 1963-64; visiting prof, U NC, 1969. Mem: Phys Soc, London; Amer Phys Soc. Contbr of numerous publs in physics jours. Home: 29 Keren Hayesod St, Jerusalem, Isr. Office: Physics Dept, Heb U, Jerusalem, Isr.

JAFFE, Benjamin, Isr, Zionist worker, author; b. Jerusalem, Isr; s. Leib and Freda (Kaplan); MA, Heb U, 1942, MJur, 1955; m. Malka Kleinsinger, Feb 24, 1948; c: Leora. Dir, external relations dept, World Zionist Org, since 1960; dept ed, Ency Judaica, since 1967; bd dirs, Dvir Publ House; legal secy, Supr Court, Isr, 1952-56; repr, JA, Con, 1958-60. Haganah, 1938-48; British Army, 1942-46. Mem: Isr Commn of UNESCO; Isr Bar; exec Isr UN Assn; natl council, Lib Party; Soc for Rehab of Ex-Prisoners, 1956-67; B'nai B'rith; Lions Intl. Author: The Rabbi of Yahud, 1957; Herzl Reader, 1960; ed: B Disraeli; L Jaffe Letters and Diaries, 1964, 1968; co-ed, Sefer haKongress, 1951. Hobby, collecting books and cartoons. Home: 10 Alharisi, Jerusalem, Isr. Office: JA, Jerusalem, Isr.

JAFFE, Bernard, US, educator, author; b. NYC, Mar 5, 1896; s. Harris and Fraida (Barnett); BS, CCNY, 1916; MA, Columbia U, 1923; m. Celia Lesser, Sep 2, 1926; c: Lionel, Henry. Chmn, phys sci dept, James Madison HS, Bklyn, 1931-58; chem tchr, NYC HSs, 1924-31. Author: Chemical Calculation, 1926; Crucibles, The Story of Chemistry, 1930; Outposts of Science, 1935; New World of Chemistry, 1935; Men of Science in America, 1944; New World of Science, 1948; Chemistry Creates a New World, 1957; Michelson and the Speed of Light, 1960; co-author: Workbook Units in Chemistry, 1935; Chemistry, Science of Matter, Energy and Change, 1965; Moseley and the Numbering of the Elements, 1969; contbr to educ jours. Mem: Hist of Sci Soc; Amer Chem Soc; Amer Technion Soc; AAAS; Fed Amer Scis; Phi Beta Kappa. Recipient, Francis Bacon award for Humanizing Knowledge, 1930. Home: 25 Eastern Pkwy, Brooklyn, NY.

JAFFE, Eliezer David, Isr, welfare policy analyst, educator; b. Cleveland, O, Nov 28, 1933; s. Henry and Sarah (Zipperstein); in Isr since 1960; BA, Yeshiva U, 1955; MSW, Case W Res U, 1957; DSW, social wfr, 1960; MA, O State U, 1959; m. Rivka Schnerb, Aug 14, 1961; c: Uri, Yael, Ruth, Noemi. Sr lectr, social wfr, Sch of Social Work, Heb U, Jerusalem, since 1968; caseworker: Family Service Assn, Akron, 1956-57; Public Assistance Dept, Cleveland, 1957-58; Columbus State Psycht Hosp, 1958-59; div of Child Public Wfr, Cleveland, 1959-60; research cons, sup, Cleveland Psychiatric Inst and Social Service Dept, 1959-60; research asso, Bellefaire Regional Treatment Cen, Cleveland, 1959-60; instr, criminology, 1960-64; social path, 1960-63, both Heb U; cons: case work, research, Min of Wfr, Jerusalem, 1960-66; appt chmn, Comm on Determination of Standards of Public Assistance; research cons, Alyn Hosp for Crippled Children, Jerusalem, 1964-66; visiting asst prof, Cleveland State U, 1966-67; research cons: VA Hosp, Cleveland; Manpower Planning and Devl Commn, Cleveland Wfr Fed, both 1966-67. Mem: Amer Sociol Assn; Natl Assn of Social Workers, US; Council for Prevention of Juvenile Delinquency, Isr; fmr: mem research comm, Isr Gerontological Soc; chmn, Isr Assn of Grad Social Workers, 1962-66. Contbr numerous articles to profsl publs. Recipient: research study grant, Wfr Admn, HEW Dept, 1962-66. Home: 37 Gaza Rd, Jerusalem, Isr. Office: Heb U, Jerusalem, Isr.

JAFFÉ, Hans Ludwig, Netherlands, art historian, educator; b. Frankfurt/M, Ger, May 14, 1915; s. Franz and Olga; in Netherlands since 1933; DLitt, U Amsterdam, 1938; m. Elly Freem, Aug 16, 1947. Prof, modern art hist, U Amsterdam, since 1963; dir, J Hist Mus, Amsterdam, since 1961; dep dir, Munic Mus, Amsterdam, 1952-61. Capt, Royal Netherlands Army, 1947. Author: de Styl: The Dutch Contribution to Modern Art, 1956; Picasso, 1964. Pres, Netherlands State Commn on Acquisition of Paintings; mem: Netherlands Mus Council; Netherlands Council for TV and Radio; fmr vice-pres, Amsterdam Sch Art Commn; mem: Intl Assn of Art Critics; Assn of Art Hist, all in Holland. Hobbies: medieval art, architecture; alpinism. Home: 17 Nieuwe Prinsengracht, Amsterdam, Netherlands. Office: 2 Joh Vermeerstraat, Amsterdam, Netherlands.

JAFFE, Henry I, US, business exec; b. Poneviz, Lith, July 4, 1905; s. Solomon and Rachel (Schwartz); in US since 1900; m. Leah Cohen, Feb 28, 1932; c: Burton, Rita. Vice-pres, Town and Country, Inc, since 1949; secy-treas, Bran-O-Lax Corp, since 1951, both Suffolk, Va. Chmn: Va Beach Princess Anne Crippled Children Soc; ADL, 1941; co-chmn, NCCJ, s nce 1940; pres, org, Suffolk-Nansemond chap, Va Soc for Crippled Children and Adults, 1952; pres, Indoor Golf Corp; dir, Comty Charity Fund, 1950; mem bd: Cripped Children's Football; Agudas Achim Temple; org, Comty Hosp; charter mem: B'nai B'rith, 1940; Temple Emanuel, Va; life mem, Fathers Assn, Culver Mil Acad; mem: YMCA; AJComm; KP; clubs: Kiwanis, project chmn, chmn, underprivileged children's comm, 1950; Tidewater; Suburban Country; Portsmouth Execs; 10 Gallon Blood Donor. Visited Dr Schweitzer in Afr, on behalf of Amer Leprosy Mission, 1955. Recipient: Good Neighbor award, Suffolk Breakfast Club, 1948; first 10 gallon blood donor pin, Natl Red Cross, 1963; spec citation, Kiwanis Clubs, Capital Dist, 1963. Home: Cavalier Dr and Ocean Front, Va Beach, Va. Office: 189 E Washington St, Suffolk, Va.

JAFFE, Henry L, US, pathologist; b. NY, Sep 15, 1896; s. Meyer and Bessie (Koppel); MD, NYU, 1920; m. Clarisse Kross, May 23, 1931; c: Arthur, Henry. Path, dir, lab, Hosp for Jt Diseases, NYC, 1925-64; cons, path: Hosp for Jt Diseases; Hosp for Crippled Children, Newark; Monmouth Med Cen; US Naval Hosp; St Albans; NJ Orthopedic Hosp. Hon mem: Amer Orthopedic Assn; Brit Orthopedic Assn; NY Roentgen Soc; Royal Soc of Med; mem: Amer Assn of Paths and Bacts; Amer Soc of Experimental Path; Soc for Experimental Biol and Med; NY Path Soc; NY Acad of Med. Home: 202 Highbrook Ave, Pelham, NY. Office: 1919 Madison Ave, New York, NY.

JAFFE, Irma B, US, art historian; b. New Orleans, La; d. Harry and Estelle (Blumenthal) Levy; MA, PhD, Columbia U, NY; m. Samuel Jaffe; c: Yvonne Schwartz, Marvin Schwartz. Prof, art hist, chmn, fine arts dept, Fordham U, since 1966; research curator, Whitney Mus of Amer Art, 1964-66. Mem: Coll Art Assn; Amer Studies Assn; AAUP. Author, Joseph Stella, 1969; contbr to art jours. Home: 880 Fifth Ave, New York, NY. Office: Fordham U, Bronx, NY.

JAFFE, Irving, US, attorney; b. NYC, Aug 20, 1913; s. Max and Annie (Shill); att LIU, Bklyn, 1929-30; BS, CCNY, 1933; LLB, Fordham U, 1935; m. Alice Bein, Aug 30, 1936; c: Matthew, Daniel. Dep asst, Atty Gen, Civil Div, Justice Dept, Wash DC, since 1967; pvt practice, 1936-42; staff atty, chief trial atty, spec litigation counsel, sect chief, Off of Alien Prop and Civil Div, Justice Dept, 1942-67; partner, law firm, Wasserman & Jaffe, 1949-50; lectr, panelist; Govt Contract Sems, sponsored by Law Schs Bar Assn, Practising Law Inst. Chmn, legal comm, Temple Sinai, Wash DC, fmr vice-pres, chmn, various comms, bd mem; mem: B'nai B'rith, JF Kennedy Lodge; Amer, Fed, DC, Bar Assns; Adv Bd, Assn Immigration and Nationality Lawyers. Contbr to legal jours. Home: 9105 LeVelle Dr, Chevy Chase, Md. Office: 10 St & Constitution Ave NW, Washington, DC.

JAFFE, Jeff, US, business exec; b. Wash, DC, Dec 25, 1920; s. Henry and Mildred (Loewenberg); BS, Va Poly Inst, 1942; m. Natalie Rubin, Dec 30, 1945; c: Bonita, Holly, Pres, The Chunky Corp, Bklyn, NY, since 1950; pres, chmn bd, Schutter Candy Co, Chgo, Ill, since 1958; advt mgr, Sweets Co Amer, Hoboken, NJ, 1949-50. Interracial Council for Bus Opportunity, NY. Gen chmn, Bldg Campaign, Temple Sinai, Laurence, NY; bd dirs, Jr Achievement, NYC, 1958-61; Assn Mfrs Confectionery and Chocolate, pres, 1959-61; Jt Defense Appeal, confectionery div, 1959-61; dir, Young Pres Org, 1956-59, treas, 1962; trustee, Woodmere Acad since 1959; clubs: Inwood Country; Harmonie. Home: 1255 Veeder Dr, Hewlett Bay Park, LI, NY. Office: 595 Madison Ave, New York, NY.

JAFFE, Joseph H, Isr, physicist, educator; b. Prestwich, Eng, Nov 25, 1923; s. Moshe and Riva (Behrman); in Israel since 1948; BSc, U London; PhD, Heb U, Jerusalem; m. Halina Belchatowski, Aug 9, 1949; c: Alon, Roni. Prof, head, spectroscopy dept, Weizmann Inst, Rehovot since 1948; physicist, British optical ind, 1944-47; found, gen mgr, Rehovot Instruments Ltd, 1965. Prin contrib, established spectroscopy lab. F, Inst of Physics. Contbr articles on molecular physics to profsl jours. Recipient, Weizmann Prize, 1955. Home: Neve Weizmann, Rehovot, Isr. Office: Weizmann Inst of Sci, Rehovot, Isr.

JAFFÉ, Joshua Erwin, Isr, government official; b. Bromberg, Ger, Apr 25, 1913; s. Max and Emilie (Alexander); PhD, U Prague, 1939; m. Elisheva Hamburger, 1941. Min, econ affairs, Emb of Isr, London, since 1968; secy, KH Cen Offices, Berlin, 1939; chief clerk, British Forces, Jerusalem, 1940-44; Jerusalem Emergency Admn, 1948; official, Gov of Pal, Price Control, 1944-48; adv to Min of Commerce and Ind, Price Policy, Govt of Isr, 1948-68; controller of restrictive trade practices, Isr Govt, 1960-68; prin contbr: establishing machinery for price and cartel control. Org J sports activities, chess clubs, Ger, 1933-37. Fgn adv bd, Anti-trust Bull, USA, 1967-68; contbr to Heb jours. Hobbies: music, poetry. Home:

29 Walsingham, St John's Wood Park, London, NW8, Eng. Office: 2 Palace Green, London, W8, Eng.

JAFFE, Leonard, US, engineer, government official; b. Cleveland, O, Feb 1, 1926; s. Isidore and Anne (Spier); BEE, O State U, 1948; m. Elaine Michael, Oct 23, 1949; c: Ronald, Norman. Dep asso admr, Off of Space Scis and Application, NASA, since 1968, dir: communications sys, since 1961, space applications, since 1966, research engr, 1948-55, chief, data sys br, 1955-59, chief, communications satellites, 1959-61. USN, 1944-46. F, Amer Astronautical Soc; mem, Inst of Radio Engrs. Contbr articles to tech jours. Recipient: Arthur J Fleming Award, 1965; IEEE H and S Behne Award for Intl Communications, 1968. Home: 418 Sisson Court, Silver Spring, Md. Office: NASA, Washington, DC.

JAFFE, Leonard S, US, business exec; b. Baltimore, Md, Oct 31, 1916; s. Benjamin and Anna (Berkow); AB, Johns Hopkins U, 1937; MBA, Harvard Bus Sch, 1939; m. Marjorie Dorf; c: Carol Levinger, Ellen, Sue. Financial vice-pres, treas, Marvin Josephson Assos Inc, NYC since 1969; exec positions, asst corp controller, Jos E Seagram & Sons, 1942-58; financial vice-pres, secy, treas, Capehart Corp, NYC, 1958-62; financial vice-pres, secy, treas, Rheingold, NYC, 1962-68. Mem: bd, Temple Isr, Westport, Conn; Financial Exec Inst; Natl Assn Acctnts, both NYC; fmr vice, pres, Brotherhood of Temple Isr, 1952-56; mem: bd: Temple Adath Isr, 1952-56; JCC, 1954-56; all Louisville, Ky; club, Harvard, NYC. Home: 37 Pequot Trail, Westport, Conn. Office: 1301 Ave of the Americas, New York, NY.

JAFFE, Maurice A, Isr, attorney, rabbi, organization exec; b. Salford, Eng, 1917; s. Wolfe and Golda (Eidelman); in Isr since 1948; ordained rabbi, Manchester Talmudical Coll, 1938; LLB, hons, Manchester U, 1938; m. Ella Aronson, July 6, 1949; c: Zeev, Eliezer, Shnair. Exec vice-chmn, mem exec, Hechal Shlomo, Jerusalem, since 1953; mem, bd dirs: Hapoel Hamizrachi Bank; Israel-British Bank; Eliaz Isr Wines; fmr rabbi, N Manchester Syn; dir, external relations, World Mizrachi and Hapoel Hamizrachi, 1948-58; ed, Mizrachi News Service and Jerusalem Newsletter, 1949-58; feature writer, London and Continental Daily Mail, 1946-50. Sr J chaplain: Allied Land Forces, SE Asia, 1943; J Brig, 1945; British Forces in Eur, 1945-46. Pres, Union of Isr Syns; coord, Chief Rabbis Comm for W Wall and Holy Places; chmn: Isr Sabbath Comm; Hapoel Hamizrachi, Jerusalem, mem, natl, political comms; Free Loans Fund; mem: comm for tourism and devl, Jerusalem Munic; exec, Wolfson and Williams Founds; B'nai B'rith; Masons; Intl Lions; repr, Manchester U to Intl Student Conf, Geneva, 1938; off, Volunteer Fire Service, 1940; chmn, Jerusalem Civil Defense, 1956-59; vice-pres, Mizrachi Fed of Gt Brit and Ir; vice-chmn, Council of Manchester and Salford J, and Zionist Gen Council, 1946; hon secy, Hapoel Hamizrachi of Gt Brit and Ir; provincial chmn, Torah va-Avodah Org of Gt Brit; mem: Bd Deps, Brit, 1946-48; Friends of UN, Jerusalem br. Author: Achievements of Mizrachi and Hapoel Hamizrachi, 1951; Mizrachi and Hapoel Hamizrachi-50 Years of Endeavour, 1952. Home: 18 Ahad Ha'am St, Jerusalem, Isr. Office: Hechal Shlomo, Jerusalem, Isr.

JAFFE, Raymond, US, educator; b. Chgo, Ill, Jan 22, 1916; s. Herman and Sadie (Rudnick); AB, U Chgo, 1938; Cert Fr Studies, Dipl Fr Lit, U Besançon, Fr, 1945; MA, U Cal, 1951, PhD, 1953; m. Ruth Golden, Sep 20 1941; c: Joel, Carla, Lisa. Prof, phil, Wells Coll, Aurora, NY, since 1958, chmn, dept, since 1954; lectr: phil of med, Sch of Med, 1954; phil, U of Cal, 1954; med, U Cal Sch of Med, 1963-64; visiting prof, phil, 1964; visiting prof, Experimental Collegiate Prog, U Cal, 1967-69. US Army, 1942-46, final rank, maj. Mem: Amer Phil Assn; AAUP; ACLU; Intl League for Rights of Man. Author: The Pragmatic Conception of Justice, 1960; conbtr to mags. Home: Aurora, NY. Office: Wells Coll, Aurora, NY.

JAFFE, Rona F, US, author; b. NYC, June 12, 1932; d. Samuel and Diana (Ginsberg); BA, Radcliffe Coll, 1951. Author: The Best of Everything, 1958; Away From Home, 1960; The Last of the Wizards, 1961; Mr Right is Dead, 1965; The Cherry in the Martini, 1966; fmr asso ed, Fawcett Publs, 1952-56. Office: Ashley-Famous Agcy, 1301 Ave of the Americas, New York, NY.

JAFFE, Ruth, Isr, physician; b. Berlin, Ger, Dec 4, 1907; d. Alfons and Alice (Hollaender); in Isr since 1934; asso clinical prof, psycht, Shalvata Hosp, since 1968, med dir since 1953; social worker, Va'ad haLeumi, 1939-43. Training analyst, Intl Psychan Assn. Contbr to profsl jours. Spec interest, music, hist. Home: 4 Elimelech, Ramat Gan, Isr. Office: POB 94, Hod Hasharon, Isr.

JAFFE, Samuel A, US, surgeon, educator; b. Colchester, Conn, Nov 13, 1913; s. Abraham and Rose (Jaffe); BS, U Conn, 1934; MD, NYU Bellevue Hosp Med Cen, 1938; m. Frances Molstein, Feb 16, 1941; c: Richard, Karen, Douglas. Pvt practice since 1946; asst att surg: Grace New Haven Hosp; att surg, Rocky Hill State Vets Hosp; cons surg, Griffin Hosp, Derby, Conn; instr, surg, Yale U Med Sch, New Haven, Conn; surg, USPHS, various locations and overseas, 1943-46. Surg USCG, Res, 1943-46. F: Amer Coll of Surgs; Intl Coll of Surgs; dipl, Amer Bd of Surg, since 1949; mem: AMA; New Haven Co Med Assn; Assn of Mil Surgs, US; Conn State Med Soc; Conn delg to Assn of Amer Phys and Surgs; ZOA; Amer Legion; VFW; JWV; Masons; Tau Epsilon Phi, chancellor, 1933-34; club, Woodbridge Country. Contbr to profsl med jours. Home: 35 Rogers Rd, Hamden, Conn. Office: 235 Bishop St, New Haven, Conn.

JAFFE, Samuel Z, US, rabbi; b. NYC, Dec 15, 1922; s. Morris and Toby (Sharlin); BA, Yeshiva U, 1943; MA, Tchrs Coll, NY, 1946; MHL, ordained rabbi, HUC, 1948; ThD, Burton Sem, Colo, 1962; m. Edythe Golin, Aug 26, 1952; c: Arvin, Joshua, Michele. Rabbi, Temple Beth El, since 1958; dir, Hillel, U of Fla, 1948-52, rabbi: Temple Beth Sholom, Park Forest, Ill, 1954-58. Chaplain, US Army, 1952-54. Pres, Gtr Miami Rabb Assn; adv comm, JWF; vice-pres: Broword Bd of Rabbis, pres, 1961-62; Hollywood Clergymen, 1962-63; Amer J Comm, 1965-66. Author: What is Judaism? Home: 1316 Madison St, Hollywood, Fla. Office: 1351 S 14 Ave, Hollywood, Fla.

JAFFE, William, US, educator; b. NYC, June 16, 1898; s. Morris and Mary (Pomerantz); BA, summa cum laude, CCNY, 1918; MA, Columbia U, 1920; D en Droit, U Paris, 1924; m; c: Ghita Hardimon, David, Peter; m. 2nd, Olive Weaver, Oct 4, 1948. Prof em, econ, Northwestern U, since 1966, prof econ 1928-1966; tutor, econ and Fr, CCNY, 1924-25; asso, Columbia U, Soc Sci Research Council, 1926-28; visiting prof, U Algiers, Algeria, 1956; Fulbright lectr, U Genoa, It, 1956-57; visiting prof: U Cal, Riverside, 1965; Harvard U, 1967-68. F: AAAS, Econometric Soc; mem: Amer Econ Assn; Royal Econ Soc; ACLU; Royal Netherlands Acad Scis and Letters. Author: Les Théories économiques et sociales de Thornstein Veblen, 1924; Histoire des doctrines Walrasiennes, 1956; Correspondence of Leon Walras and Related Papers, 1965; co-author, The Economic Development of Post-War France, 1929, trans into Eng; The Elements of Pure Economics, 1954; contbr to profsl jours. Recipient: f: Social Sci Research Council, 1925-26; Fulbright, 1951, lectr, 1956; Guggenheim, 1956; Ford fac research, 1963- 64; grant, prin investigator, NSF, 1965-69. Home: 73 Salem Lane, Skokie, Ill. Office: Northwestern U, Evanston, Ill.

JAFFE, William B, US, attorney, business exec; b. NYC, Mar 11, 1904; s. Samuel and Mary (Ress); BA, Union Coll, NY, 1926; LLB, Columbia U, 1929; hon DHL, Dartmouth Coll, 1964; m. Evelyn Annenberg, May 11, 1948; c: Robert, Thomas. Sr partner, Shea, Gallop, Climenko & Gould, NYC; asso firm, Nathan Burkan, NYC, 1929-35; practiced NYC, since 1935; cons, motion picture financing to NY banks, since 1937; dir, gen cons, Allied Artists Intl Corp. Chmn, NY State for Manning Plan, War Manpower Commn, 1945. Chmn: art adv comm, Dartmouth Coll; mem adv comm, Amer Mother's Comm; patron, Mus Modern Art; benefactor, Metrop Mus, Art, NYC; bd dirs, NY Eye, Ear Infirmary; counsel, Modess Family Life Inst; trustee; Union Coll; Mt Sinai Hosp, NY; mem, bd govs, hon trustee: J Mus; mem: Amer, NY State, NYC, Bar Assns; Phi Beta Kappa; Tau Kappa Alpha; ADL; B'nai B'rith; Phi Epsilon Pi. Recipient, awards: Phi Epsilon Pi, 1964; Union Coll, 1946; Hopkins Cen Dartmouth Coll, 1961. Hobby, art collecting. Home: 640 Park Ave, New York, NY. Office: 330 Madison Ave, New York, NY.

JAFFE, William J, US, engineer, educator; b. Passaic, NJ, Mar 22, 1910; s. Elias and Ida (Rosensohn); BS, NYU, 1930; MA, Columbia U, 1941; MS, 1941; DSc, NYU, 1953. Prof, mgmt engr, Newark Coll of Engr, since 1954, fac mem since 1946; naval architect, 1941-45; adj asso prof, NYU, 1953-54. F: AAAS; and rep, Amer Inst of Ind Engrs since 1959; and mem, natl sem comm, Soc for Advancement of mgmt, since 1955; pres, Cong B'nai Isr Anshe Kadan, since 1960; vice-pres, educ and research, Amer Inst of Ind Engrs, NJ, chap, 1958; natl hum engr comm, since 1957; rep, hon comm, Engrs Jt Council,

1959; chmn, ind engr terminology, US Standards Inst; AAUP; mem: Amer Soc for Quality Control; Amer Soc Engr Educ; Maths Assn of Amer; Amer Maths Soc; Amer Stat Assn; Inst of Mgmt Sci; Soc for Applied Maths; Acad of Mgmt; Pi Mu Epsilon; Omicron Delta Kappa; Phi Delta Epsilon; Alpha Pi Mu; club, NYU. Author: LP Alford and the Evolution of Modern Industrial Management, 1957; Go to Arbitration, 1967; contbr to profsl jours. Home: 1175 York Ave, New York, NY. Office: Newark Coll of Engr, Newark, NJ.

JAFFE, Zalmon, Eng, business exec; b. Salford, Eng, Feb 15, 1913; s. Wolf and Golda (Eidleman); m. Roselyn Rosenthall, Sep 12, 1939; c: Anthony, Hilary, Lew. Dir, textile co. Served NFS. Chmn: Lubavitch Found, Manchester; Cassel Fox Sch, Salford; and pres, Kahal Chassidim Syn; pres, Manchester Shechita Bd, 1961-65; gov, King David Schs, 1960-66. Recipient, Defense Medal. Home: 105 Cavendish Rd, Salford, Eng. Office: 23 Park St, Salford, Eng.

JAFFIN, George M, US attorney; b. NYC, May 4, 1905; s. Barney and Ettie (Abeloff); AB, hons, Columbia U, 1924; LLB, 1926; m. Janet Guzy, 1929; c: David, Doris Greenberg, Lois Levine. Counsel: Jaffin, Schneider, Conrad & Rubin; Galpeer & Cooper both since 1967; pvt practice, 1926-42; partner, Jaffin, Schneider, Kimmel & Galpeer, 1942-67; fmr dir: Colonial Utilities Corp; Mangel Stores. Vice-chmn, bd, Amer-Isr Cultural Found, since 1968; exec comm, FJP, since 1944; trustee, Hosp for Jt Diseases, since 1957; mem: J Comty Cen, White Plains, since 1942; Amer Bar Assn; Assn of Bar of NYC; adv bd, Counsellor to J Students, Columbia U, since 1944; fmr pres, Columbia Coll Class of 1924, 1964-69; clubs: Columbia U; Metropolis Country. Recipient: Man of Year, Class, 1924. Home: 22 Oak Lane, Scarsdale, NY. Office: 245 Park Ave, New York, NY.

JAGLOM, Abraham, US, business exec; b. Russ, June 11, 1900; s. Moses and Natalie (Shoenberg); in US since 1939; att Tech Inst, Kharkov, Russ, 1920; m. Nehama Shoenberg, Jan 11, 1923; c: Natalie, Regina. Pres, Overseas Barters Inc, NYC, since 1939; vice-pres, NY Commodities Corp, NYC, since 1945; owner, dir, Jaglom Brothers, Rum, Danzig, 1923-39. Mem: ZOA; AJCong. Spec interest: art. Home: 146 Central Park W, New York, NY. Office: 745 Fifth Ave, New York, NY.

JAGLOM, Raya, Isr, organization exec; b. Lipkani, Rum, Apr 17, 1919; att King Carol U, Bucharest; m. Joseph Jaglom; c: Elan, Nurit Yolanda. Chmn, WIZO exec; mem: curatorium, Tel Aviv U; Council, Tel Aviv Mus; ladies comm, Isr Philharmonic Orch; mem, Isr WIZO exec, 1951; treas, world WIZO exec, 1959-61; chmn, 1963; mem, JA exec, 1964; Isr exec, WJC, 1964; leader of 1st official Zionist delg to Russ, 1964; mem, public comm for Defense Bonds, June 1967; on WIZO missions: Switz; Swed; Finland; Den, all 1950; S Amer, 1963; Belgium; Fr; It; Scandinavia, all 1965; Can, 1966; initiated Aliyah Conf WIZO Feds, Geneva, 1967; S Afr; Ger, both 1967; Eng, 1968; Mexico, for Aliyah Conf of all S Amer WIZO Feds, 1969. Home: 4 Ruppin St, Tel Aviv, Isr.

JAKOB, Karl Michael, Isr, biologist; b. Berlin, Ger, Nov 5, 1921; s. Max and Anna (Wassertruedinger); in Isr since 1953; BS, U of Ill, 1943; MS, 1948; PhD, U Cal, Berkeley, 1952; m. Ahuva Aizenstadt, Nov 2, 1954; c: Judith, Ruth. Research sci, Weizmann Inst of Sci, since 1953; lectr, cytology, Bar Ilan U, since 1963. Technician, US Army, 1945-46. Prin contribs: cytology, cytogenetics and sex expression in ricinus; radiation damage and repair in plants; metabolic changes during cell division cycle in plants. Mem, Sigma Xi. Contbr to profsl jours. Home: 10 Neveh Weizmann, Rehovot, Isr. Office: Weizmann Inst of Sci, Rehovot, Isr.

JAKOBOVITZ, Immanuel, Eng, rabbi; b. Koenigsberg, Ger, Feb 8, 1921; s. Julius and Paula (Wreschner); BA, U London, 1941; Asso Jews Coll, London, 1944; ordained rabbi, Yeshiva Etz Hayim, London, 1947; PhD, U London, 1955; m. Amelie Munk, July, 1949; c: Julian, Samuel, Esther, Jeanette, Aviva, Elisheva. Chief rabbi, United Heb Congs, Brit Commonwealth of Nations, since 1967; rabbi, Fifth Ave Syn, NY, 1958-67; min: Brandesbury Syn, London, 1941-44; SE London Syn, 1944-47; rabbi, Gt Syn, London, 1947-49; chief rabbi, J Comtys in Ir, 1949-58. Found, J Marriage Educ Council, London, 1948; mem, RabCA. Author: Order of Jewish Marriage Service, 1950, 1959; Jewish Medical Ethics, 1959, 1962; Journal of a Rabbi, 1966, 1967; ed, Irish-Jewish Year Book, 1951-58; contbr to periodicals. Study: Off of Chief Rabbi, Adler House, Tavistock Sq, London, WC1, Eng.

JAMES, Donald S, US, surgeon; b. NYC, May 23, 1912; s. Morris and Mary (Belapolski) Jurnove; att U of Kan, 1930-32; MD, NY Med Coll, 1936; m. Ruth Buchman, Nov 30, 1944; c: Mary, Sharon. Pvt practice since 1936; asst surg, Flower and Fifth Ave Hosp, since 1945; asst att surg: Metropolitan Hosp, since 1945; Heb Convalescent Home, since 1947; Yiddish Theatrical Alliance, since 1947; Theatrical Guild, since 1949; Bird S Coler Hosp, since 1952; gastroenterology section, Seaview Hosp; asso att surg, Trafalgar Hosp; att surg, Madison Ave Hosp, and chmn, med practice comm; chief med referee, Mutual Trust Life Ins Co; med dir, General Fire Ins Co; designated doctor, Swissair; med dir: USA-KLM Royal Dutch Airlines; Loews Hotels; instr, surg, NY Med Coll, since 1945. Capt, US Army, 1942. Dipl: Amer Bd Surg; Amer Bd Abdominal Surg; f: Amer Coll Gastroenterology; Intl Coll Surgs; NY Acad Med; exec vice-pres, Soc for the Establishment of Albert Einstein Coll of Med, Yeshiva U, 1950-52; mem, exec bd, Med Scholarship Fund, since 1952; mem: AMA; NYC and NY State Med Socs; Central Med Soc; NY Acad, Scis; KP; Ind Med Assn; NY Cancer Soc; Aerospace Med Soc; NY Soc of Gastroenterology; Phi Lambda Kappa; Temple Emanuel; clubs: Physicians Square; Manhattan, pres, 1953. Contbr to med publs. Home: 390 W End Ave, New York, NY. Office: 965 Fifth Ave, New York, NY.

JAMITOVSKY, Anita Schutz, Uruguay, organization exec; b. Vienna, Aus, Jan 10, 1923; d. Isaac and Helena (Presser) Schutz; in Uruguay since 1939; grad, HS, Vienna; m. Marcus Jamitovsky, Dec 13, 1942; c: Rebeca Lazovsky, Israel. Pres, Uruguay WIZO, since 1964; mem, presidium, Zionist Org. Hobbies: writing, classical music, giving speeches. Home: 1110/201 San José, Montevideo, Uruguay.

JAMMER, Max, Isr, scientist; b. Berlin, Ger, Apr 13, 1915; s. Salomon and Sarah (Markih); in Isr since 1935; tchrs dipl, physics, U Vienna, 1934; MSc, Heb U, Jerusalem, 1938, PhD, 1942; postgrad studies, Harvard U, 1951-52; m. Rachel Racover, 1952; c: Shlomit, Michael. Prorector, Bar Ilan U, fmr rector, pres, head, dept physics, since 1959, mem, U Sen, 1965-68; visiting lectr, Harvard U, 1952-53; asso prof, U Okla, 1954-56; sr sci, Elco Research Lab, Mass, 1958; research prof, Boston U, 1958-59; prof, Columbia U, 1968-69. British Army, WW II; IDF, 1948. Mem: Amer Phys Soc; Amer Assn for Phil of Sci. Author: The History of the Physical Sciences, 1953; Textbook of Mathematics,1954, both in Heb; Concepts of Space, 1954, rev ed, 1959, 2nd ed, 1969, trans into Ger, It; Foundations of Dynamics, 1957, 2nd ed, 1962; Concepts of Mass in Modern Physics, 1961; The Conceptual Development of Quantum Mechanics, 1966, rev ed,1968.Hobbies: music, astronomy. Home 22 Itamar Ben Avi St, Jerusalem, Isr. Office: Bar Ilan U, Ramat Gan, Isr.

JANNER, Barnett, Sir, Eng, solicitor, legislator, communal leader; b. June 20, 1892; s. Joseph and Gittel (Zwick); BA, Cardiff Coll, U of Wales; hon LLD, U of Leeds; m. Elsie Cohen, July 12, 1927; c: Greville, Lady Morris of Kenwood. Solicitor in pvt practice; MP for: Whitechapel and St George's, 1931-35, W Leicester, 1945-50, NW Leicester, since 1950. Pres: ZF of Gt Brit; Assn of J Friendly Socs; European council, World Confd of Gen Zionists; Bd Deps of Birt J; vice-pres: Monash br, Brit Legion; Assn of J Ex-Servicemen and Women; mem, policy comm and presidium, Conf on J Material Claims Against Ger; jt chmn, Coordinating Bd of J Orgs; mem, Council of J Trust Corp; gov, Leicester U Coll; hon rents adv, Lab Party; f, Royal Soc Arts. Home: 69 Albert Hall Mansions, London, SW 7, Eng.

JANNER, Greville Ewan, Eng, barrister, author; b. Cardiff, S Wales, July 11, 1928; s. Barnett and Elsie (Cohen); m. Trinity Hall, Cambridge, 1952; Smith Munot Scholar, Harvard Law Sch, 1952; m. Myra Sheink, July 6, 1955; c: Daniel, Marion, Laura. Barrister, since 1955. Sgt, War Crimes Group, BAOR, 1946-48. Author: The Businessman's Lawyer, 1962; Motorists, Know your Law, 1964; The Director's Lawyer; The Personnel Manager's Lawyer; The Retailer's Lawyer; The Sales Executive's Lawyer; Your Factory and The Law; Your Property and The Law; The Businessman's Guide to Public Speaking; The Lawyer and His World; All you Need to Know about The Law; You and The Law; Farming and The Law. Chmn, found, The Bridge in Britain; pres, British Friends of Alyn Hosp; hon secy, Assn for J Youth; mem: Bd of Deps of British J; vice-chmn, Working Party on Race Relations, mem, law, parl, educ comms; parl candidate, Wimbledon, 1955; mem: B'nai B'rith; Natl Union of Journalists; clubs: Cambridge Union Soc, pres, 1951; Trinity

Hall Athletic, 1952; Cambridge U, Lab, chmn, 1952; past chmn, Brady Boys. Hobby: collecting ancient glass. Home: 2 Linnell Dr, London, Eng. Office: 1 Garden Court, Temple, London, Eng.

JANOFF, Morris J, US, publisher; b. Newark, NJ, Sep 24, 1911; s. Jacob and Minnie (Rabinowitz); BA, Newark U, 1935; LLB, NJ Law Sch, 1939; m. Ruth Perlman, June 12, 1955; c: James, Beth. Publisher, mgn ed, The J Standard, since 1932. Dir: Yeshiva Hudson Co since 1939; Jersey City J Comty Cen since 1952. Mem, Amer J Press Assn, pres 1964-66; hon life mem, Shomrim Soc of NJ; vice-chmn, Jersey City UJA; exec comm, Isr Bonds; hon chmn, scholarship, Poale Zion; mem: KP; Oddfellows; Pollak Lodge, B'nai B'rith; Cong B'nai Jacob. Recipient: Man of the Year award, N Hudson AJCong, Women's div, 1962. Home: 19 Stegman Court, Jersey City, NJ. Office: 924 Bergen Ave, Jersey City, NJ.

JANOWSKY, Oscar Isaiah, US, educator, author; b. Suchowola, Pol, Jan 13, 1900; s. Aaron and Dina (Bobre); in US since 1910; BSS, CCNY, 1921; MA, Columbia U, 1922, PhD, 1933, hon DHL, JTSA, 1966; hon DHL, HUC, 1967; m. Pauline Rubin, Nov 5, 1922; c: Sylvia Barras, Melvin, Namon, Tamar Rabb. Prof em, hist, CCNY, CUNY, since 1966; dir, Grad Studies, CCNY, 1951-57; Jacob Ziskind Visiting Prof, Brandeis U, 1966-67; dir, Janowsky Report, JWB; advisor, L of N High Commnr for Refs, 1935; dir, survey, Natl JWB, 1946-47; chmn, co-dir, Commn for Study of J Educ in US, 1922-55; cons, J educ, cultural affairs, B'nai B'rith, 1961-64. Author: The Jews and Minority Rights, 1933; People at Bay, 1938; Nationalities and National Minorities, 1945; The JWB Survey, 1948; Foundations of Israel, 1959; co-author: International Aspects of German Racial Policies, 1937; ed: The American Jew, 1942; The American Jew: A Reappraisal, 1964; The Education of American Jewish Teachers, 1967; contbr to pubs; mem, ed bd: J Social Studies; M E Affairs. Chmn, acad council, and mem bd, Amer Friends of Heb U; chmn: educ adv comm, Hadassah, 1940's; Publ comm, adult educ, B'nai B'rith; hon mem, bd govs, Heb U, Jerusalem; f, Amer Assn, J Educ; mem: Amer Hist Assn; Amer-J Hist Soc; AAUP; Amer Hist Soc; Phi Beta Kappa. Recipient: Gitelson Memorial Medallion, 1939; Frank L Weil award, JWF, 1953; Myrtle Wreathe award, Hadassah, 1965. Hobbies: philately, numismatics, photography. Home: Claridge House, Verona, NJ.

JANUS, Sidney, US, psychologist; b. NYC, Nov 7, 1912; s. Louis and Rose (Becker); BSS, CCNY, 1933; MA, Columbia U, 1934; PhD, George Wash U, 1944; m. Leah Shapiro, June 17, 1935; c: Raizy, Barry, Micah. Pvt practice ind psych; cons, ind relations, since 1946; research cons, hum factors oprs research lab, USAF, since 1951; mem, occupational analyst, War Manpower Comm, 1940-43; prof, psych, Ga Inst of Tech, 1946-50. USN, 1943-46. Dipl, Amer Bd of Examiners in Profsl Psych, 1948; Amer Psych Assn; pres: Atlanta Bur J Educ, 1953; Atlanta Zionist Dist, 1952; Ga Psych Assn, 1952-53; mem: NY Acad of Scis; Exec comm, Atlanta chap, AJComm; NE chap, ZOA; exec comm, Amer Assn for J Educ; JWV; NCCJ; Brandeis U Assos; Ahavath Ahim Cong; B'nai B'rith; club, Rotary. Contbr to profsl jours. Home: 1435 W Wesley Rd NW, Atlanta, Ga. Office: 615 Peachtree St NE, Atlanta, Ga.

JAPHA, Erwin M, US, physician, educator; b. Berlin, Ger, Nov 17, 1910; s. Alfred and Vally (Reichmann); in US since 1949; MB, BS, Middlesex Hosp Med Sch, U London, 1938, DMR, 1944; m. Eva Danielsohn, Mar 30, 1935 (decd); m. 2nd, Etta Veit-Simon, Dec 7, 1952; c: Anthony, Carol, Irene. Dir, dept therapeutic radiology, Mt Sinai Hosp, Chgo, since 1956, radiotherapist, 1953-56; clinical asso prof, radiology, Chgo Med Sch, since 1963, fac mem since 1956; att cons, Tumor Bd, Hines VA Hosp, Ill, since 1967; mem, med staff, Orthodox Home for Aged, since 1954; clinical cancer research off, Middlesex Hosp, London, 1938-40; asst sr radiotherapist, 1941-45, 1947-49; asst registrar, clinical cancer research comm, British Empire Cancer Campaign, 1940-41; med off i/c, EMS, Radiotherapy Cen, Mt Vernon, Middlesex, 1943-44; dep med off i/c, radiotherapy cen, Addenbrooke's Hosp, Cambridge, Eng, 1944-46; researcher, lectr, Chgo Tumor Inst, 1949-52; lectr, Northwestern U, 1954. Mem: AAAS; Natl Geog Soc; AMA; Chgo Roentgen Soc; Amer Radium Soc; Radiological Soc, N Amer; Chgo, Ill State Med Socs; Amer Coll Radiology; Inter-Amer Coll Radiology; Brit Inst Radiology; Fac of Radiology, Eng; Royal Soc Med; past mem, bd trustees, Emanuel Cong, Chgo, Ill; club, Amer Therapeutic Radiologists. Author: chap in Radiation Dosimetry, 1956; contbr to Eng, Swed, Amer med jours. Spec interests: math, astronomy, hist, philately. Home: 462 Woodlawn Ave, Glencoe, Ill. Office: 2755 W 15 St, Chicago, Ill.

JAPHET, Ernest Israel M, Isr, banker; b. Berlin, Ger, May 8, 1921; s. Jacob and Elizabeth (Feuchtwanger); in Isr since 1933; m. Ella Gilead, Feb 24, 1948; c: Michal, Jacob, Ruth, Tamar, David. Gen mgr, Bank Leumi leIsrael, Ltd, since 1963; mem bd dirs: Ind Devl Bank of Isr Ltd; Isr Corp; Isr Chems; Union Bank of Isr; Otzar letaassiya; Bank Leumi Inves Co; Yaad, Agric Devl Bank; gen mgr: Jacob Japhet & Co, 1938-51; Union Bank of Isr, 1952-63. Sgt, Brit Army, 1941-46. Bd govs: Heb U; Technion. Home: 89 Hareshel St, Herzliya Pituah, Isr. Office: 26/28 Yehuda Halevy St, Tel Aviv, Isr.

JARACH, Guido, It, manufacturer; b. Milan, Nov 30, 1905; s. Federico and Giorgina (Rignano); dipl Eng, Poly Sch, Milan, 1928; m. Fernanda Schapira, Jan 25, 1942; c: Gaincarlo, Roberto, Federica, Andrea. Mem bd execs, mgn dir, OMCSA, mech ind, since 1945; tech mgn dir, Rubinetterie Riunite di Milano, 1930-39; chmn, admn bd, Banca Popolare di Milano. Mem bd: Mobiliare Milanses spa; Istituto di Credito Fondiario; ABI Assn of It Banks; It Constructors Assn of Textile Machines; pres, bd, J Cmty of Milan; hon pres, ANMI; Natl Assn of Navy Men, Milan sect; Croce Rosa Celeste, assn for transp and assistance for sick children; It ORT, since 1947; clubs: Rotary; Novara; Circolo della stampa, Milan. Recipient: cdr, Order, It Rep Merit; Knight, Merit of Labour. Home: Via Telesio, Milan, It. Office: Via Biondi 1, Milan, It.

JARBLUM, Marc, Isr, attorney, journalist, author; b. Warsaw, Pol, Jan 24, 1887; s. Baruch and Pesah; in Isr since 1953; licenciate, law and sci, U Paris; m. Laura Margolis, Aug 2, 1950. Ret; fmr: active, Russ Revolutionary Movement until 1907; pvt law practice, Paris, until WW II; with J underground, WW II; French corresp: Davar, Isr, Yiddish jours, US, S Amer, Pol; with political dept of Histadrut, 1953-64. Fmr: active: Lab Zionist Movement; Intl Zionist Movement; repr Histadrut: Socialist Intl; Intl Trade Union Movement; hon pres: Fr ZF; Fed of J Socs, fmr hon pres, both orgs; repr, JA for Pal, in Fr. Author: Le Destin de la Palestine Juive de la Declaration Balfour 1917 au Livre Blanc 1939, pub, 1939; Ils Habiteront en Securité du Ghetto d'Europe à la Palestine, 1947; La Lutte des Juifs contre les Nazis, 1944, 1945; Documents inédits sur les camps d'extermination, 1945; La Verité sur les Pourparlers avec l'Allemagne, 1952; Soviet Rusland unt di Yuden Frage, 1953; contbr to publs. Recipient: Off of Fr Legion of Honor; Ot Haganah; Itur Lochmei haMedina, Defense Min. Home: 17 King David Blvd, Tel Aviv, Isr.

JARCHO, Leonard W, US, physician, educator; b. NYC, Aug 12, 1916; s. Julius and Susana (Wallenstein); BA, Harvard Coll, 1936; MA, Columbia U, 1947, MD 1941; m. Ann Adams, Apr 11, 1956; c: John, Daniel, William. Chmn, dept, neur, U Utah, Coll Med, since 1965, prof, neur, since 1963, on fac since 1959; neur-in-chief, Salt Lake Co Gen Hosp, 1959-65; f, Phys Dept, on staff Johns Hopkins U Med Sch, 1946-52; asst phys, Johns Hopkins Hosp, 1948-52; asst res, med, Mt Sinai Hosp, NYC, 1947-48, asst res psychosomatic med, 1948; f, Natl Found for Infantile Paralysis, 1950-52; asst chief, med service, VA, Hosp, Salt Lake City, 1953-57, chief, med service, 1957-58, chief neur service, 1959-62. Maj, US Army MC, 1943-46. Dipl: Natl Bd Med Examiners; NY State Bd Med Examiners; dir, Salt Lake City chap, ARC, 1960-65; mem, med adv bd, Myasthenia Gravis Found, since 1961; asst examiner, Amer Bd Psycht and Neur, 1962; mem, neur sci research training comm, NIH, 1962-65; cons, Council on Drugs, AMA, 1957; mem, prog comm for psycht, neur and psych, VA Cen Off, 1960-63, mem: NY Acad Scis; AAAS; Amer Phys Soc; Salt Lake Country Med Soc; Utah State Med Soc; AMA; Utah Soc Internal Md; W Soc, Clinical Research; Utah Neur Soc; Amer Acad Neur; Amer Fed Clinical Research; Phi Beta Kappa. Contbr to profsl jours. Home: 1497 Devonshire Dr, Salt Lake City, Utah. Office: U Utah, Coll of Med, Salt Lake City, Utah.

JASON, Simon Judah, US, educator; b. Kolno, Pol, Dec 25, 1885; s. Louis and Ricca (Greenberg); in US since 1889; BA, CCNY, 1906; LLB, NYU, 1909; MA, 1917; m. Birdie Lippman, June 2, 1911; c: Harold, Ruth. Ret; admn asst, William Howard Taft HS, 1938-55; tchr, NY public schs, 1906-17; instr, acctnt: Hunter Coll NY, 1917-19; Sch of Bus, CCNY, 1917-42. Pres: First Assts in Acctnt, since 1950; Admn Assts

Assn, 1934-36, both NYC HSs; J Tchrs Assn, since 1936; org, vice-pres, Tchrs Comty Chest, since 1939; chmn, educs, div, FJP, 1930; JDC, 1932; Amer ORT, since 1933; mem, bd of dirs, 1942, exec comm, 1950, sch comm, 1945. Mem: Zeta Beta Tau; Masons. Author: Elements of Accounting; contbr articles on educ and social articles to mags. Homes: 121 Ridge Ave, Pittsfield, Mass; 402 Ohio Pl, Sarasota, Fla.

JASSER, Alfred A, US, chemist, business exec; b. Bklyn, NY, July 2, 1910; s. William and Rose (Holzer); BS, NYU, 1933; att CCNY, 1942; m. Mollie Cohen, June 30, 1932; c: Pamela, Robin. Pres, Anchor Chem Corp, since 1946; chief chem, since 1937; pres, ACP, Inc, since 1959; chem, H Strump Products, 1927-37. Chaplain, Graphic Arts Lodge, B'nai B'rith, mem, bd trustees; gen chmn, engr comm, printing and pub sect, Natl Safety Council, 1963-68, chmn since 1961; mem: Research, Engr Council Graphic Arts; Printers Supply Salesmen's Guild, NY; Lithographic Tech Found; safety comm, Printing Ind of Metrop NY Inc; KP, fmr chancellor; mem bd trustees; Temple Beth El, N Bellmore, NY, 1960; Marathon J Comty Cen, NY, 1953-55; club, bd mem, Printing House Craftsmen, NY. Contbr to profsl jours. Recipient: awards: UJA; FJP; Isr Bonds; ADL. Home: 2665 Manor L, N Bellmore, NY. Office: 500 W John St, Hicksville, NY.

JAVITCH, Lee Herschel, US, business exec; b. Carlisle, Pa, Mar 4, 1931; s. David and Jennie (Hervitz); BA, Syracuse U, 1953; att Mich State U, 1953-54; m. Beth Lebovitz, Oct 6, 1956; c: Jonathan, Lisa. Pres, Giant Food Stores Inc, since 1968, vice-pres, since 1960. Cpl, US Army. Pres, Temple Beth El, Harrisburg, Pa; mem: bd dirs, Supermarket Inst, Chgo, Ill; exec comm, UJA Young Leadership Cabinet; fmr chmn: Harrisburg Young Leadership Group; Harrisburg UJA Campaign; mem, bd dirs, JDC. Home: 1624 Mitchell Rd, Harrisburg, Pa. Office: 25 E High St, Carlisle, Pa.

JAVITS, Benjamin A, US, attorney, author; b. NYC, Oct 21, 1894; s. Morris and Ida (Littman); att CCNY, 1909-11; LLB, Fordham U Law Sch, 1918; m. Lily Braxton, Feb 12, 1926; c: Joan Zeeman, Eric. Pvt practice since 1922; sr partner, Javits & Javits, since 1927. Prin contribs: initiated movement to amend anti-trust laws, 1926; org first conf to consider natl econ planning, Wash, DC, 1929; helped draft Natl Ind Act, 1933. Found: Soc of Bus and Adv Professions, 1937; United Shareowners of Amer Inc, 1950; pres, Fair Return League, 1930; mem: Amer, NY State and NYC Bar Assns; NY Soc of Security Analysts; B'nai B'rith; Temple Emanu-El; clubs: Natl Repub; Palm Beach Country; City Athletic, NYC; Noyac Golf, Sag Harbor, NY. Author: Make Everybody Rich-Industry's New Goal, 1929; Bus and the Public Interest, 1932; The Commonwealth of Industry, 1936; Peace by Investment, 1950; How the Republicans Can Win in 1952, pub 1952. Ownerism: A Better World for All Through Democratic Ownership, 1969; contbr to mags. Recipient: dedicated law sch, downtown campus Fordham U, Benj A Javits Galls of Law, 1962. Hobbies: tennis, traveling, political sci. Homes: 980 Fifth Ave, New York, NY; 230 Palmo Way, Palm Beach, Fla. Office: 630 Fifth Ave, New York, NY.

JAVITZ, Jacob K, US, attorney, legislator; b. NYC, May 18, 1904; s. Morris and Ida (Littman); LLB, NYU Law Sch, 1926; hon LLD: Lincoln U; LIU; Hartwick Coll; Yeshiva U; HUC; Pace Coll; Ithaca Coll; JTSA; NYU; Dartmouth Coll; m. Marion Borris, Nov 30, 1947; c: Joy, Joshua, Carla. US Senator, since 1957; mem Sen Comms: Fgn Relations; Banking and Currency; Lab and Public Wfr; Govt Oprs; Small Bus, Jt Econ; mem, law firm, Javitz, Trubin, Sillcocks, Edelman, & Purcell, since 1958. Fmr: mem, Javitz and Javitz, 1926-40, 1945-47; US Congressman, 21st cong dist, 1947-54, mem, House Comm on Fgn Affairs during that term; elected, Atty-Gen, NY, 1954-56; US delg to: UN Conf on Trade and Employment, 1947; N Atlantic Assembly, chmn, 1957-68; legislated laws on civil rights, health, educ, arts, labor, econ policy, trade. Maj, US Army, asst to chief of oprs, Chem Warfare, 1940-42, served: Eur, 1943; Pacific, 1944; lt-col, 1945. Chmn: E Mediterranean Devl Inst; natl vice-chmn, ADL of B'nai B'rith; hon Natl Chmn, JWV; trustee, FJP; mem, bd overseers: Freedom House; JTSA; mem: Amer Judicature Soc; VFW; Amer Legion; NAACP; Comm for Intl U in Amer, Inc; Paderewski Fund; Boy Scouts of Amer; Amer-Isr Cultural Found; mem board: AJComm; Amer ORT; Inter-Faith Movement; ZOA; NY World's Fair Corp; Ballet Theater Found; clubs: Natl Repub; City Athletic, NY; Army-Navy, Wash DC. Author: Discrimination, USA, 1960; lectr, contbr to newspapers and periodicals. Recipient: Legion of Merit, Army Commendation Ribbon; citations: B'nai B'rith, 1948; AHA, 1949; Afr Methodist Episcopal Church, 1950; Temple of the Covenant, 1951; Honest Politician Award, Liberty Mag, 1951; Alpha Phi Alpha civil rights award, 1951; Histadrut, 1952; Isr Bonds Award, 1952; Home: 911 Park Ave, New York, NY. Office: US Senate, Washington, DC.

JEFROYKIN, Jules, Fr, editor; b. Petrograd, Russ, May 11, 1911; s. Israel and Malka (Silberfarb); licencié en droit, fac of law, Paris, 1932. Dir, La Terre Retrouvée since 1951; ed, Info and Agence Economique et Financière, 1932; dir, Renaissance, J Resistance weekly, 1944-49; dir, gen, Compagnie Française de Navigation, 1961-67. Capt, Fr Army, 1939-45; capt, Force Française de l'Intérieur, J combat org, 1944. Pres: Fed of J Socs of Fr, since 1962; Anciens de la Résistance Juive, since 1962; Union Mondiale de la Jeunesse Juive, 1937-40; mem: cen comm, JNF, Fr; Comité d'Action de la Résistance. Contbr articles on J questions. Recipient: Médaille de la Résistance, 1946; Médaille du Mérite Civique; Croix des Combattants volontaires de la Résistance. Home: 7 rue de St Senoch, Paris, Fr. Office: 4 rue de Castellane, Paris, Fr.

JELIN, Jerome K, US, engineer; b. New Brunswick, NJ, Oct 19, 1911; s. Abraham and Bessie (Slonimsky); att Rutgers U; BSE, U Miami, 1931; m. Marion Schwartz, Dec 1, 1932; c: Stephen. Pres, Baker Refrigeration Co, Windham, Me; chmn, bd dirs, Tabor Mfg, Phila, both since 1953; chmn: Fulton Inds Inc, Columbus, O, since 1958; chmn: HC Godman; Miller-Jones, chief cost engr, Pleasantville Constructors, Nassau, Bahamas, 1942-43; chief project engr, Ala Drydock, Mobile, 1943; mgn dir: Gasoline Engine, Buffalo, NY, 1946; Merrit Plywood Machinery, Lockport, NY, 1947; Fostoria Screw, O, 1948; Elkhart Machinery, Ind, 1949-50; Amer Saw Mill Machinery, Hackettstown, NJ, 1950-51. Chief, cost and price analysis div, Corps of Transp, Army Service Forces, 1944. Fmr: pres, ZOA; vice-pres: AJCong; JNF; dir: Bur of J Educ, since 1947; Talmud Torah, since 1947; J Comty Cen; JCC; Friends of Heb Culture, all since 1951; ADA, since 1945, all in Cincinnati midwest region, Amer Assn for J Educ; O region, ZOA; pres, Cincinnati chap Technion; Phi Epsilon Pi Alumni chap; mem, adv council, Dem Natl Comm. Home: 4201 Victory Pkwy, Cincinnati, O. Office: 35 E 7 St, Cincinnati, O.

JEMERIN, Edward E, US, surgeon: b. NYC, Nov 22, 1908; s. Noah and Mollie (Jemerin) Livshatz; BS, CCNY, 1928; MD, U of Bellevue Hosp Med Coll, 1932; m. Vick Bergheiser, Oct 29, 1949; c: Nicholas, John. Pvt practice, since 1936; att surg, Mt Sinai Hosp; clinical prof, surg, Mt Sinai Sch of Med; cons surg, Sydenham Hosp, visiting surg until 1968; instr, surg, NY Med Coll; asso att surg, Beth David Hosp, 1939-58. Maj, US Army, 1942-45. F, Amer Coll Surgs; dipl, Amer Bd Surg; mem: NY State and Co Med Soc; AMA; Amer Geriatrics Soc; NY Acad Med; NY Surg Soc; Phys' Forum; Amer Vets Comm; Alpha Omega Alpha. Author: Acute Infections of the Mediastinum, 1943; contbr to profsl jours. Home: 1185 Park Ave, New York, NY. Office: 1175 Park Ave, New York, NY.

JENKINS, Jack J, US, business exec; b. Gomel, Russ, Feb 25, 1910; s. Morris and Eva (Selitzky); in US since 1910; BA, Crane Jr Coll, Chgo, 1929; att U Ill, 1929-30; Furman U, Greenville, SC, 1931-32; LLB, Chicago Law Sch, 1935; m. Mina Katz, July 29, 1934; c: Marcia, Robert. Gen mgr, Kinsman Optical Co, since 1942. Dir, Natl Optical Assn, 1951; pres, dist grand lodge 5, B'nai B'rith 1962, intl vice-pres, since 1965; vice-chmn, natl membership cabinet, 1962-65; mem exec comm, JCC, Gtr Wash, since 1957, chmn, Admissions Comm; vice-chmn, Mayor's Comm on Employment of the Handicapped, trustee and mem exec comm, UJA, Gtr Wash; treas, Wash Interfaith Comm; bd mgrs, Wash Heb Cong, since 1968; mem: Masons; Wash Bd of Trade; Amateur Athletic Union; Heb Home for the Aged; J Social Service Agcy; club, Men's. Home 2801 New Mexico Ave NW, Washington, DC. Office 1320 F St NW, Washington, DC.

JENOFSKY, Abraham, US, general secy; b. Gorod Bershad, Russ, Jan 29, 1901; s. Leib and Frume (Sitkoff); in US since 1922; m. Frieda Barash; one c. Gen secy, Yiddisher Kultur Farband Inc since 1956. Mem AJ Conf; fraternal and philanthropic orgs. Contbr to Yiddish Kultur Mag. Home 3115 Brighton, Brooklyn, NY. Office: 189 Second Ave, New York, NY.

JERISON, Meyer, US, educator; b. Bialystok, Pol, Nov 28, 1922; s. Elia and Esther (Rasky) Jerusalimsky; in US since 1929; BS, CCNY, 1943; MS, Brown U, Providence, RI, 1947; PhD, U Mich, 1950; m. Miriam Schwartz, Aug 5, 1945; c: Michael,

David. Prof, math, Purdue U, since 1960, mem fac since 1951; physicist, Natl Adv Comm for Aeronautics, 1944-46; research instr, math, U of Ill, 1949-51; mem, Inst for Advanced Study, Princeton, NJ, 1958-59. Mem: AAUP; Amer Math Soc; Math Assn of Amer; Phi Beta Kappa; Sigma Xi; Cong Sons of Abraham; curriculum comm, Lafayette J Comty Rel Sch, 1957-58, 1960-62. Author: Rings of Continuous Functions, 1960; contbr to math publs. Home: 147 Pathway Lane, W Lafayette, Ind. Office: Purdue U, Lafayette, Ind.

JERUSALMI, Isaac, US, educator; b. Istanbul, Turkey, Nov 1, 1928; in US since 1963; licencie es lettres, U Istanbul, 1951; ordained rabbi, MHL, HUC, 1956; dipl, Classical Arabic, Ecole Natl des Langues Orientales Vivantes, Paris, 1962; PhD, Sorbonne, Paris, 1963; m. Neama Hananel, Sept 6, 1962; c: Stella, David, Hanna-Gracia. Asso prof, Bible and Semitic Langs, HUC, since 1967, fac mem, since 1963; instr, Inst Intl d'Etudes Hebraiques, Paris, 1958-63. Lt, anti-aircraft artillery, 1957-58. Hon Rabbi, Sephardic Beth Shalom Cong, Cincinnati, O; mem, CCAR. Author, auxiliary materials for study of Semitic languages, numbers 1-10, 1965. Home: 8500 Lynnehaven Dr, Cincinnati, O. Office: 3101 Clifton Ave, Cincinnati, O.

JERUSHALMI, Abraham (pen name, **Jorn Adamsly**), Isr, journalist; b. Warsaw, Pol, Dec 7, 1904; s. Mendel and Malka (Abramson); in Isr since 1959; att U, Warsaw, 1927; m. Ita Aizen; c: Ernestina Frenkel, Valencia Fridlender, Malvina Tal. Journalist, since 1922; with: Communist newspaper: Pol: Arg; Uruguay; 1920-37; Mapai; Arg, 1948-59; Isr, since 1959. Mem: many communal orgs in Pol, Arg, Isr. Author, Quo Vadis Moscu, 1958. Home: 19 Eilat St, Bat Yam, Isr.

JERUSHALMI, Jizchak Chaim, Isr, electrician, poet, composer; b. Lodz, Pol, Oct 7, 1907; att Yeshiva Lomza-Lublin, Lodz, 1924; m. Shoshana Weinstein, 1934; c: Aharon, Yigal. Electrician, Kaplan Hosp, Rehovot, since 1953; fmr electrician: Pol Gov Theater; and co-found, Ararat Theater, Lodz; Ohel, Habimah theaters, Isr Opera. Served Haganah. Author of poems and songs in Yiddish; record, Az Yashir Moshe; mem staff, Yiddishe Zeitung. Home: 11 Hadgani St, Rehovot, Isr.

JERUSHALMY, Zohara, Isr, scientist, educator; b. Tel Aviv, Isr, Mar 12, 1927; d. Yehuda and Miriam (Guralsky) Beith-Halachmy; MSc, Heb U, Jerusalem, 1955, PhD, 1960; m. Shmuel; c: Baruch. Sr research sci, Rogoff Wellcome Research Inst, since 1955; asso prof, Tel Aviv U Med Sch, since 1969; research sci: ARC, 1964-67; NYU Med Cen, 1964-67. IDF MC, 1948-49. Prin contrib: research on: interaction of viruses and blood cells; blood platelets; effect of snake venom on blood coagulation. Mem: NY Acad of Sci; Intl Soc of Hematology; Eur, Isr, Socs of Hematology; Isr Soc for Advancement of Sci. Contbr to profsl jours. Recipient, J Meir Award, Histadrut Sick Fund, 1962. Home: Herzliya A, Isr. Office: Beilinson Hosp, Petah Tikva, Isr.

JESSEL, George, US, entertainer, producer; b. NYC, Apr 3, 1898; s. Joseph and Charlotte (Schwartz); c: Jerilynn. Star, George Jessel Show, ABC-TV since 1953; on natl TV show, Here Come the Stars; motion picture, Yoshe Kolb; vaudeville debut, Imperial Theater, NYC, 1908; vaudeville tours, 1909-11; solo tours, 1911-23; star of: The Jazz Singer, Broadway, 1925; Sweet and Low, Broadway, 1930; and writer, The War Song, 1930; produced musical shows: Helen of Troy, Broadway 1923; Little Old NY, NY World Fair, 1939; George Jessel's High Kickers, Broadway, 1941; produced motion pictures: The Dolly Sisters, 1944; Nightmare Alley, 1947; I Wonder Who's Kissing Her Now, 1948; Dancing in the Dark; When My Baby Smiles at Me, both 1950; Wait Till the Sun Shines, Nellie, 1951; The I Don't Care Girl, 1952; Tonight We Sing, 1952; produced UJA motion picture in Isr, 1953. Extensively toured on behalf of UJA. Club, Friars. Author: plays, songs, specialty numbers; autobiography, So Help Me, 1942; Elegy in Manhattan, 1961. Home: 7629 Lindley Ave, Reseda, Cal.

JOB, Robert Raphaël, Fr, organization exec; b. Imling, Fr, Jan 31, 1907; s. Sylvain and Caroline (Baer); licencié ès sciences, U Strasbourg, 1927; diplomé d'études supérieures, Chem Sch, Mulhouse, 1929; m. Ruth Kauffmann, 1936; c: Danielle Greilsamer, Guy. Secy gen, D'oeuvre de Secours aux Enfants since 1942; physics tchr, 1928-39. Pres, bd dirs, Syn, Chasseloup Laubat, Paris. Recipient: Chevalier de la Légion d'Honneur; Croix de Guerre; Commandeur du Mérite Militaire; Officier d'Académie; Croix du Combattant. Home: 56 av de Suffren, Paris 15, Fr. Office: 23 rue de Clapeyron, Paris 8, Fr.

JOEL, Asher A, Austr, business exec, publisher, PR cons,legislator; b. Stanmore, Austr, May 4, 1912; s. Harry and Phoebe (Jacobs); m; c: Richard, David; m. 2nd, Sybil Jacobs, Apr 7, 1949; c: Michael, Susan. Dir: Royal N Shore Hosp, Sydney; Paynter & Dison Ind Ltd; Gtr Union Org Pty; mgn dir, Carpentaria Newspapers; journalist, 1928-38; publicity dir, Austr 150th Anniversary Celebrations, 1938; orgsecy: Lord Mayor's Patriotic and War Fund, 1939-42; Navy Day and Jack's Day Appeals, 1942. Lt, Royal Austr Navy, 1942-45; PR off, GHQ SW Pacific area. F: Advt Inst of Austr; Austr Inst of Mgmt; Inst of Dirs, PR Inst of Austr; vice-pres, JNF; pres, comm, Anzac, Memorial and Forest in Isr; mem: Sydney Comm, since 1956; Sydney Opera House Appeal Comm; Assn of J Ex-Servicemen and Women; Austr J Hist Soc; Austr Friends of Heb U; Technion Soc; ORT; B'nai B'rith; Friends of Magen David Adom; clubs: Amer Natl; Navy offs; Imperial Service; Masons; Austr Jockey; Sydney Turf; Tattersall's; City Tattersall's; Journalists; Retailers; Shalom. Recipient: US Bronze Star, WW II; OBE, 1956. Hobbies: fishing gardening. Home: 2 Ormiston Ave, Gordon, NSW, Austr. Office: 161 Clarence St, Sydney, NSW, Austr.

JOEL, Issachar, Isr, librarian; b. Hamburg, Ger, Apr 30, 1900; s. Julius and Golda (Jacobson); in Isr since 1924; att: yeshiva: Us, Frankfurt, Munich; PhD, U Hamburg, 1923; m. Ruth Oppenheimer, Apr 19, 1928; c: Ahuvah Shoham, Shulamit Shamir, Nehemya, Yonathan. Dir, J natl and U libr, Jerusalem, since 1968, on staff since 1927; ed, Kiryat Sefer, 1927-68. Author: Catalogue of Hebrew Manuscripts in the JNUL, 1934; Index of Articles on Jewish Studies, 1969; co-ed, Siddur Rabbi Saadja Gaon, 1941; contbr articles to Kiryat Sefer. Home: 17 Alfassi St, Jerusalem, Isr.

JOFFE, Abraham Z, Isr, educator; b. Dzisna, Russ, Mar 21, 1909; s. Zalman and Grunia (Ginzburg); in Isr since 1958; MSc, Stetan Batory U, Vilna, 1937; PhD, Botanical Inst Sci Acad, Leningrad, 1950; m. Rada Pricker, 1948; c: Boris, Gabriela. Asso prof, Heb U since 1967, sr lectr, dept Botany, 1959-67; head, mycological lab: Inst of Epidemiology and Microbiol, Russ, 1943-50; Inst of Experimental Med, Vilna, 1950-57. Prin contribs: research in: mycology and mycotoxicology; etiology of alimentary toxic aleukia and effects of aflatoxin on animals and plants; taxonomy of fusarium fungi, toxigenic fungi and soil mycoflora; initiated research in biol of fungus aspergillus flavis and its infectivity to plants and animals. Mem: Botanical Soc of Isr; Mycological Soc of Amer. Contbr to profsl jours. Hobby: music. Home: 8 Hehalutz St, Jerusalem, Isr. Office: Heb U, Jerusalem, Isr.

JOHANNES, Dov, Isr, civil servant; b. Cracow, Pol, Jan 3, 1914; s. Moses and Rosa (Kornfeld); in Isr since 1947; Tch cert, Pedagogic Inst, Cracow-Lvov, 1940; MJur, U of Lvov, 1941; MPA, with credit, Inst of Social Studies, The Haag, 1967; m. Irena Himmelblau, Sep 18, 1945; c: Daphna, Amir. Head, Dept of Culture and Profsl Educ, since 1952; head, Inst of Mgmt, since 1962; dir, Warsaw emigration bur, JA, 1946-47; dir housing, JA, Tel Aviv, 1948-52, journalist, Noviny Kurier, 1950-66. Mem: secretariat, Union of Admn and Clerical Employees; Histadrut; Assn of Grads in Social Scis and Hum; Isr Soc of Eds of Periodicals; mem exec, J Comty, Cracow, 1945; head, network of Heb Schs, Pol, 1945-47; mem leadership, Akiba Youth Org, 1933-47. Ed: quarterlies: Readings in Administration; Tamkhir; contbr to various jours. Home: 3 Yael St, Tel Aviv, Isr. Office: 93 Arlosoroff St, Tel Aviv, Isr.

JOHNPOLL, Bernard Keith, US, educator; b. NYC, Mar 6, 1918; s. Israel and Rachel (Elkin); BA, magna cum laude, Boston U, 1959; AM, Rutgers U, 1963; PhD, SUNY, Albany, 1966; m. Lillian Kirtzman, Feb 14, 1944; c: Janet Greenlee, Phyllis. Prof, political sci, grad sch of public affairs, SUNY, Albany, since 1966; copy ed, Pittsburgh Post Gazette, 1948-50; news ed, Boston Daily Record, 1950-62; psso prof, political sci, Hartwick Coll, 1963-66. Mem, fac council, B'nai B'rith Hillel Found, Albany, NY; pres, br 1068, Workman's Circle, 1966-68. Author, The Politics of Futility: The General Jewish Workers Bund, 1957; contbr to jours. Home: 19 Haddington La, Delmar, NY. Office: Grad Sch, Public Affairs, SUNY, Albany, NY.

JOKL, Ernst F, US, physician, educator; b. Breslau, Ger, Aug 3, 1907; s. Hans and Rosa (Oelsner); in US since 1950; MD, U Breslau, 1930; m. Erica Lestmann, June 2, 1933; c: Marion Ball, Peter. Prof, phys, U Ky, since 1953; chmn, Inst of Research in Med and Athletics, U Breslau, 1931-33; Witwatersrand Tech Coll, S Afr, 1936-39. Med cons S Afr Defense

Forces, 1939-44. F: Amer Assn Health, Phys Educ and Recreation; Amer Coll Card; and found, Amer Coll Sports Med; former pres: New Educ F; B'nai B'rith; pres: research comm, Intl Council of Sport and Phys Educ, UNESCO, 1960; mem: exec bd, since 1960; one of original mems of Ger Maccabi Sports Fed; mem: Rotary; Torch; Temple Adath Isr, Lexington, Ky; hon mem, Fed Intl Medico-Sportive, fmr, pres. Author: books on applied and clinical phys of exercise; contbr to med jours. Recipient: Buckston Brown Prize, 1942; British Empire Medal of Harveian Soc, London, med research, 1942; Afr War Medal; Dist Prof, 1964. Spec interest: J Hist; music; aviation. Home: 340 Kingsway, Lexington, Ky. Office: U of K, Kexington, Ky.

JONES, Jennie R, US, communal leader; b. NYC, June 3, 1909; d. Abraham and Anna (Fisher) Rothman; BS, NYU, 1929; MA, Wayne State U, Detroit, 1961; m. Harry Jones, 1930; c: Ellen Kushen, Richard. Dance instr, NYU, 1929-31. Pres Detroit Chap, Hadassah, 1946-48; Women's Div, JWF, 1953-55; treas, Detroit Cerebral Palsy Cen, vice-pres, 1965-67; natl chmn: women's div, UJA, 1967-68; United Negro Coll Fund Drive, 1962-64; educ chmn, Detroit Grand Opera Assn, 1961-65; camp chmn, Girl Scouts of Metrop Detroit, 1950-55; trustee, Merrill Palmer Sch; mem: Mayor's Comm, Employment of Handicapped; exec comm, JWF, Detroit; Sinai Hosp Guild; Detroit League for the Handicapped; Detroit Sym Orch; United Found, Detroit; Alpha Epsilon Phi. Recipient: awards: Civic, Women's Advt Club, Detroit, 1963; Natl Service, Alpha Epsilon Phi, 1964; Outstanding Alumni, Alpha Epsilon Phi, 1967; Butzel, for Comty Service, JWF, Detroit, 1968. Home: 18925 Muirland, Detroit, Mich.

JOSEPH, Asher, Isr, editor; b. Genhausen, Ger; s. Sigmund and Bertha; att Heb U, Jerusalem; m. Hannelore David, Jan 16, 1946; c: Jocheved, Penina, Pinchas. Chief of publs and instrs sect, ed of Isr Tax leg, Dept of Customs and Excise, since 1953; lab asst, Oscar Phillips Chems, London, 1939-40; costing clerk, Frutaron Chems, Haifa, 1945-48. Pvt, IDF, 1948-49. Prin contribs: design of encyclopedic set of tax publs in form of jours, manuals, guides, commodity indices. Mem: Isr Soc Eds of Periodicals, natl council, 1965-67; Assn, Sr Govt Officials; fmr mem, cmty and PTA comms. Ed: annually: Israel Tax Leg; Israel Tariffs and Fees; Customs Regulations in various langs; numerous booklets. Hobbies: travel, corresp, philately. Home: 5 Brever St, Bayit Vegan, Jerusalem, Isr. Office: 32 Argon St, Jerusalem, Isr.

JOSEPH, Barnett, Eng, rabbi; b. London, Eng, Oct 31, 1908; s. Max and Esther (Fedotin); BA, PhD, Jews Coll, London, 1928-34; att U Coll, London, 1932-34; m. Ruth Marmorstein, Aug 18, 1940; c: Nanette, Grace. Rabbi, since 1934; lectr, J Coll. Capt, Royal Army Chaplains Dept, 1941-46. Vice-chmn, N London Council of Chrs and J; exec, London Soc J and Chrs; chaplain, United J Friendly Soc; pres, N London B'nai B'rith, 1965-66; council, Anglo-J assn; mem, NCCJ. Contbr to profsl jours. Hobby: classical music, walking. Home: 22 Meynell Gardens, Homerton, London E9, Eng.

JOSEPH, Burton M, US, business exec; b. Apr 2, 1921; s. Isadore and Anna (Kantar); BA, cum laude, U Minn, 1942; m. Geraldine Mack, Apr 2, 1953; c: Shelly, Ira, Jonathan. Pres: I S Joseph Co Inc, since 1953, vice-pres, 1942-53; Growers Credit, since 1956, both of Minneapolis; Leche Pura de Puerto Rico, since 1961. Capt, USAF, 1942-45, 1950-51. Pres, bd of trustees, Temple Isr, Minneapolis, since 1969; vice-pres, bd govs, Mt Sinai Hosp, since 1963, pres, 1955-57; bd trustees, Amer Freedom from Hunger Found, Wash, DC, since 1962; commn, Duluth Port Auth, 1954-60; asst treas, ADL, since 1967, natl commn since 1964; mem: Phi Epsilon Pi, grand councilor, 1956-58; Masons; club, Oak Ridge Country, bd trustees since 1953; pres, 1960-62. Hobbies: skiing, golf. Home: 5 Red Cedar Lane, Minneapolis, Minn. Office: 800 Flour Exch Bldg, Minneapolis, Minn.

JOSEPH, Dov, Isr, barrister, cabinet min; b. Montreal, Can, Apr 27, 1899; s. Yerachmiel and Sarah (Fineberg) tin Isr since 1921; BA, BCL, McGill U, Montreal, 1921; PhD, London U, 1929; m. Goldie Hoffman, Jan, 1922; c: Amiram, Alma Shapir, Leila (killed in action, Isr War of Independence). Min of Justice, 1961-66; Min of Supply and Rationing, 1949-50; Min of Agric, 1949-50; Min of Transport and Communications, 1950-51; Min of Trade and Ind, 1951-53; Min of Justice 1951-52; Min of Devl, 1953-55; Min of Health, 1955; MK since 1949; atty, Bernard Joseph & Co; pvt law practice, Jerusalem, 1922-48; legal adv, political dept, JA, 1936-45, mem, exec, 1945-47, treas, 1957-61; chmn, voluntary recruiting bd, Jerusalem, WW II; mem, emergency comm, Jerusalem, 1947-48; mil gov, Jerusalem, 1948-49. Delg, WZCs since

1933; fmr pres,found, Young Judea, Can. Author: Nationality, Its Nature and Problems; British Rule in Palestine; The Faithful City, The Siege of Jerusalem, 1948, pub, 1962. Home: 22 Alharizi St, Jerusalem, Isr.

JOSEPH, Edward G, Isr, surgeon, educator; b. Wellington, NZ, Sep 20, 1894· s. Joseph and Ellis (Myers); in Isr since 1928; MB, ChB, U Edinburgh, 1918; MS, U Minn, 1923; m. Louise Fineman, 1924; c: Naomi, Ruth, Yohanan. Ret; fmr head, surg dept, Hadassah Hosp, Jerusalem, 1930-62; prof, surg, Heb U, Med Sch, Jerusalem, 1952-62, on staff since 1938; home surg, Royal Infirmary, Sheffield, NZ, 1919-28; pvt practice, NZ,1923-28. F, Mayo Clinic Found; LRCP; mem, Royal Coll Surgs.Contbr to med jours. Home: Kfar Vitkin,Isr.

JOSEPH, Howard Stephen, US, rabbi; b. NYC, Mar 13, 1940; s. William and Miriam (Finkelstein); BA, Yeshiva U, NYC, 1961; MHL, 1964; m. Norma Baumel, Mar 27, 1965; c: Leora. Rabbi, Cong Beth Isr; prin, Beth Isr Heb Sch, both since 1968; rabbi, prin, Traditional Syn, Rochdale Village, 1964-68. Exec comm, LI Comm of Rabbis, 1967-69; natl pres, Mizrachi Hatzair, 1961-63; secy, Queens Rabb Council, 1967-68; mem: RabCA; Capital Dist Bd of Rabbis. Spec interests: phil, photography. Home: 15 Lafayette St, Schenectady, NY. Study: 2175 E Parkway, Schenectady, NY.

JOSEPHS, Ray, US, journalist, author, counsultant; b. Phila, Pa, Jan 1, 1912; s. Isaac and Eva (Borsky); att U Pa, 1927-29; m. Juanita Wegner, Feb 22, 1941. Pres, chmn: Ray Josephs Asso Inc, and Ray Josephs PR Ltd; pres, Intl PR Co Ltd; cons to leading bus, ind cos, philanthropic, cultural and civic orgs; S Amer corresp since 1940, representing at various times: Wash Post, Chr Sci Monitor, Pittsburgh Post-Gazette, Newark Star-Ledger, Chgo Sun, PM, Variety, Natl J Monthly, Amer Heb, Pan Amer; journalist, Phila Evening Bull, 1929-39; columnist, Buenos Aires Herald, 1940-44; lectr, 1944-51; broadcaster, radio and TV: NBC, NBC-TV, CBS, MBS, ABC. Mem: PR Comm, Brandeis U; founds comm, Tobe Lecture series in retail distribution, Harvard Grad Sch, Bus Admn; AJ Comm; Soc Mag Writers; clubs: Amer, Buenos Aires; Overseas Press. Author: Spies and Saboteurs inArgentina, 1943; Argentine Diary, 1944; Latin America: Continent in Crisis, 1948; How to Make Money from Your Ideas, 1954; How to Gain an Extra Hour Every Day, 1955; Streamlining Your Executive Workload, 1949; co-author: Those Perplexing Argentines, 1953; Our Housing Jungle, 1960; The Magic Power of Putting Yourself Across with People, 1962; contbr to natl publs. Home: 415 E 52 St, New York, NY. Office: 230 Park Ave, New York, NY.

JOSEPHS, Sidney D, US, business exec; b. Phila, Pa, Feb 8, 1914; s. Isaac and Eva (Borsky); grad with cert of proficiency, Wharton Sch, U of Pa, 1934; m. Nina Warady, July 9, 1950; c: Barbara, Franklin, Robert, Michael. Pres: Repair Services Co; Safer Josephs Corp; Lake-45 Bldg; mem, exec comm, Gen Life Ins; asso, Walton Properties; dir, Gen Corp of O, 1965-68. Lt, US Army Signal Corps, 1941-43. Pres:J Children's Bur, Bellefaire; Residential Treatment Cen for Emotionally Disturbed Children; J Day Nursery, all 1961-64; vice-pres, bd trustees, Intl Prog for Youth Leaders and Social Workers; chmn, research commn, Cleveland J Comty Fed, since 1969; trustee, exec comm, since 1964, chmn, budget subcomm, chmn, social agcy comm, 1958-61, chmn, comty services planning comm, 1964-67; mem bd of trustees: Cleveland Inst Music, since 1967, Cleveland Chamber Music Soc, 1954-56; Mt Sinai Hosp, since 1969; mem: Cleveland Mental Retarded Assn, bd, 1965-68; Special Child Care comm, Cleveland Wfr Bur, since 1969; natl bd, Amer Comm on Afr; natl comm, JDC; natl comm, civil rights, Cleveland AJComm, exec bd, 1957-64; bd, Karamu House, Inter-racial Cultural Cen, pres since 1966; bd, Cleveland and O Civil Liberties Union, 1955-64, chmn, O, 1955-58; chmn, Cleveland, 1958-61; speakers bur, Cleveland United Appeal; B'nai B'rith, Amer Vet Comm; clubs: City; Contemporary Arts Soc; Print. Home: 17210 Aldersyde Dr, Shaker Heights, O. Office: 616 The Arcade, Cleveland, O.

JOSEPHSON, Brian David, Eng, physicist; b. Cardiff, Wales, Jan 4, 1940; s. Abraham and Mimi (Weisbard); BA, Cambridge U, 1960; MA, PhD, 1964. Asst dir, research, Physics Dept, Cambridge U, since 1967; f, Trinity Coll, Cambridge, since 1962; research asst prof, U of Ill, 1965-66. Prin contrib, discovery of weak superconductivity. Asso, Inst of Physics. Contbr to profsl books, jours. Recipient: New Sci Award, 1969. Hobbies: hiking, elec. Office: Cavendish Lab, Cambridge U, Cambridge, Eng.

JOSEPHSON, Louis A, US, rabbi; b. Phila, Pa, Aug 20, 1910; s. Julius and Marion (Fleishman); BA, U Cincinnati, 1934;

BHL, HUC, 1933; ordained rabbi, 1937; m. Eleanor Spitzer, Dec 26, 1937; c: Johanna, Carmine, Daniel. Ret; rabbi: Houston Cong for Reform Judaism, 1958-62; Moses Montefiore Cong, Bloomingdale, Ill, 1949-55; chaplain, state penitentiary, Pontiac, Ill, 1949-54; counsellor, Hillel Found, Ill State Normal U, Wesleyan U, 1949-54, instr, Bible, Wesleyan U, 1953-54. Pres, Houston Rabb Assn, fmr secy, treas; mem: Council on Educ in Race Relations; bd, Comm on Alcoholism; bd, cmty relations comm, JCC, all Houston; CCAR. Author, The Jewish Home, 1942. Home and study: 2331 Addison St, Houston, Tex.

JOSEPHSON, Matthew, US, author, historian, editor; b. Bklyn, NY, Feb 15, 1899; s. Julius and Sarah (Kasindorf); BA, Columbia U, 1920; m. Hannah Geffen, May, 1920; c: Eric, Carl. Author: Galimathias, 1923; Zola and His Time, 1928; Portrait of the Artist as American, 1930; Jean Jacques Rousseau, 1932; The Robber Barons, 1934; The Politicos, 1938; The President Makers: 1896-1919, publ 1940; Victor Hugo, 1941; Stendhal, 1946; Sidney Hillman, 1952; Union House, Union Bar, 1956; Edison, 1959; Life Among the Surrealists, 1962; Infidel in the Temple: A Memoir, of the 1930's, pub, 1967; co-author: Hero of the Cities: A Biography of Alfred E Smith, 1969; contrb to: natl periodicals. Ed, The Broom, intl mag of the arts, 1921-24; on ed staff, New Republic, 1931-32. Mem: Natl Inst of Arts and Letters. Recipient: Guggenheim f, 1933; Francis Parkman Prize for Hist, 1960. Home: Sherman, Conn.

JOSEPHTHAL, Senta, Isr, farmer, labor leader; b. Bavaria, Ger, Dec 5, 1912; d. Yaakov and Hedwig (Schild) Punfud; in Isr since 1938; att U of Erlangen, 1932-33; m. Giora Josephthal (decd). Secy-gen Ihud Hakvutzot Vehakibbutzim, 1960-65, and since 1967; MK, 1955-56; mem, Histadrut Exec, 1965-60. Home: Kibbutz Galed, Isr.

JOSIF, Enriko, Yugo, composer; b. Belgrade, Yugo, May 1, 1924; s. Mosha and Socca (Farhy); U lectr, deg, Music Acad, Belgrade; scholarship, Music Acad, Santa Cecilia, Rome; m. Vera Krstic, Mar 17, 1956. Prof, composition, Music Acad, Belgrade, since 1965, composer; U lectr. Secy, Yugo sect, Société Intl de Musique Contemporaine, since 1958; pres, Union of Serbian Composers, 1967-69, vice-pres, 1966-67. Composer: Sonata Brevis, 1949; Symphoniette, 1954; Symphonie Lyrique, 1956; Four Tales, 1957; Four Sketches, 1957; Concert for piano and orch, 1959; Rusticon, 1962; Three Psalms, 1963; Symphony in one movement, 1965; Sym, 1968; numerous compositions: for orch; piano; vocal-instrumental; chamber music; film scores; music for theater, radio. Recipient: awards: Republic, 1st class hons, Min of Culture, 1960; 20th Oct, 1965; Bosnia and Hercegovina, for Music for Hagada, 1962. Spec interests: Old testamental works and apocrypha, Talmud, Hist of J people. Home: Ivana Milutinovica 13/VII, Belgr de, Yugo. Office: Music Academy of Belgrade, Marsala Tito, 50 Belgrade, Yugo.

JOSLYN, Maynard, US, food technologist, educator; b. Alexandrovsk, Russ, July 7, 1904; s. Alexander and Anna (Kalutsky); in US since 1913; BS, U Cal, 1926, MS, 1928, PhD, 1935; m. Golda Fischer, Apr 19, 1947. Prof, food sci and tech, U Cal, Berkeley, since 1949, fac mem since 1927; chem, Cal Agric Experimental Sta, since 1962, biochem, 1949-62; cons, Cal State Dept, Health, since 1958; dir, research, Natl Juice Corp, Fla, 1931; adv, dir of foods, Australian Commonwealth, 1942-45; State of Isr, 1951, 1958-60, 1962, 1964, 1966; visiting prof, food tech, MIT, 1960; visiting comm, MIT, since 1966. Lt-col, US Army, Quartermaster Corps, 1942-46. Pres, SF Bay chap, Amer Technion Soc, since 1954, mem natl bd, since 1966; vice-pres, SF Bay chap, ZOA, 1954-55, bd dirs, 1966; charter mem, N Cal Sect, Inst Food Tech, chmn, 1957; f: Amer Inst Chems; AAAS; mem: Amer Friends Heb U; Amer Chem Soc; Amer Soc Microbiol; Amer Soc Biol Chems; Amer Soc Plant Phys; Soc Ind Microbiols; Soc for Cryobiol; Amer Public Health Assn; Amer Inst Nutrition; tech adv comm, Wine Inst; charter mem, W Frozen Food Processors Assn, 1946-50; hon mem, Soc of Med Friends of Wine, 1946; Sigma Xi; Phi Lambda Upsilon; Phi Sigma; Gamma Alpha. Author: Methods in Food Analysis; co-author: Laboratory Methods of Wine Analysis; Chemistry and Technology of Fruit and Vegetable Juice Production; Table Wines; Fruit and Vegetable Juice Processing Technology; Food Processing Operations; Dessert and Aperitiff Wines; mem, ed bd: Quick Frozen Foods; Advances in Food Research; Foof Technology; Biotechnology and Bioengineering; contbr to sci and tech jours. Recipient: Bronze Medal; Legion of Merit; Chinese Order; Intl Award, 1961, Babcock Hart Award, 1963; Nicholas Apport Award, 1966; all three from the Inst Food Tech; Man of Year Award,

Cal-Isr C of C, 1965. Hobby: mystery stories. Home: 1317 Spruce St, Berkeley, Cal. Office: Dept of Nutritional Scis, U Cal, Berkeley, Cal.

JOSPE, Alfred, US, rabbi; b. Berlin, Ger, Mar 31, 1909; s. Joseph and Rosa (Cerini); in US since 1939; PhD, U Breslau, 1932; ordained rabbi, J Theol Sem, Breslau, 1935; m. Eva Scheyer, Jan 27, 1935; c: Susanne, Naomi, Raphael. Natl dir, prog and resources, B'nai B'rith Hillel Founds, since 1949; dist rabbi, Schneidemuehl, Ger, 1934-36; rabbi: Neue Syn, Berlin, 1936-39; Tree of Life Cong, Morgantown, W Va, 1939-44; dir, B'nai B'rith Hillel Found: U W Va, 1939-44; U Ind, 1944-49. Mem: bd dirs, World U Service; ZOA; B'nai B'rith; CCAR; NY Bd Rabbis. Author: Religion and Myth in Contemporary Jewish Philosophy, 1932; Religion and Education, 1934; The B'nai B'rith Hillel Foundations: An Orientation Manual, 1951; Judaism on Campus, 1963; co-author: College Guide for Jewish Youth, 1959; 1969; ed: Israel as Idea and Experience, 1963; The Legacy of Maurice Pekarsky, 1965; and trans, Jerusalem and other Jewish Writings by Moses Mendelssohn, 1969; Hillel Little Books. Home: 2949 Upton St NW, Washington, DC. Study: 1640 Rhode Island Ave NW, Washington, DC.

JOSPEY, Maxwell, US, business exec; b. Bklyn, NY, Mar 30, 1914; s. Samuel and Anne (Barna); att Wayne State U, Detroit, Mich, 1930-35; m. Anne, June 6, 1938; c: Jane, Susan. Pres, Production Steel Strip Corp, since 1948; fmr mem: War Produc Bd; OPA. Chmn, UJA, Detroit; mem: JWB, Detroit; Sinai Hosp, Detroit; HUC, Cincinnati, O; clubs: Franklin Hills Country, pres, 1962-64; Great Lakes. Home: 27887 Fairway Hills Dr, Franklin, Mich. Office: 20001 Sherwood, Detroit, Mich.

JOURARD, Sidney M, US, psychologist, educator; b. Toronto, Can, Jan 21, 1926; s. Albert and Anna (Rubinoff); in US since 1948; BA, U Toronto, 1947; MA 1948; PhD, U Buffalo, 1953; m. Antoinette Hertz, June 20, 1948; c: Jeffrey, Martin, Leonard. Prof, psych, U Fla, since 1958; asst prof, psych: Emory U, 1951-56; U Ala Med Sch, 1956-57; pvt practice, Birmingham, Ala, 1957-58. Fmr pres, Amer Assn for Humanistic Psych; mem: Amer Psych Assn; SE Psych Assn; Fla Psych Assn; Amer Acad of Psychotherapists; Sigma Xi. Author: Personal Adjustment: An Approach Through the Study of Healthy Personality, 1958; The Transparent Self, 1964; Disclosing Man to Himself, 1968; contbr to profsl jours. Hobbies: water sports, music. Home: 1506SW 35 Pl, Gainesville, Fla. Office: U Fla, Gainesville, Fla.

JUCOVY, Milton E, US, psychiatrist, psychoanalyst; b. NYC, June 2, 1918; s. Abraham and Sophie (Cion); BS, NYU, 1938; MD, 1942; m. Shirley Lieman, Apr 23, 1944; c: Peter, Jon, Seth. Pvt practice since 1948; staff psycht treatment cen, NY Psychan Inst, since 1952, fac mem, bd trustees, since 1963, visiting staff psycht, Hillside Hosp, Glen Oaks, NY, since 1968; res, sr psycht, Pilgrim State Hosp, 1946-48; clinical asst prof, Psychoan Inst, Downstat Coll of Med, 1954-59. Lt, to capt, US Army, 1943-46, chief, neuropsycht, Langley Field, Va, 1946. F, Amer Psycht Assn; mem: Amer Psychan Assn; NY Psychan Soc; Intl Psychan Assn; Phi Beta Kappa. Home: 32 Old Farm Rd, Lake Success, Great Neck, NY. Office: 7 Park Ave, New York, NY.

JUDA, Walter, US, business exec, scientist, inventor; b. Berlin, Ger, Feb 16, 1916; s. Adolf and Gertrude (Futter); in US since 1939; PhD, U Lyon, Fr, 1939; MA, Harvard U, 1944; m. Renee Molino; c: Simone, Daniel, David, Benjamin. Pres, Prototech Inc; dir: Bolt Beranek and Newman; research asso, Harvard Med Sch, 1944-48; vice-pres, tech dir, Ionics, 1948-61; mem, div of ind coop, MIT, since 1948; tech dir, Pal Research Assos, since 1946; chmn, Gordon Research Conf of Ion Exch, 1953; cons, Oak Ridge Natl Lab, 1951-54. Prin contribs: active in construction and opr of demineralization pilot plant, 1947, now at Weizmann Inst of Sci, Rehovot, Isr; patented devices for fire- retardant coatings; devl commercial method of desalinizing water by electrodialysis. Mem: Amer Chem Soc; AAAS; NY Acad of Scis: Electrochem Soc; Assn of Harvard Chems; Sigma Xi; Contbr to sci publs. Recipient: John Price Wetherill Medal, Franklin Inst, 1960. Home: 12 Moon Hill Rd, Lexington, Mass. Office: 40 Moulton St, Cambridge, Mass.

JUDAH, Clarence F, US, attorney, organization exec; b. Louisville, Ky, Aug 23, 1906; s. Leon and Elsie (Popper); BA, U Louisville, 1927, LLB, 1931; m. Louise Kaufman, 1937; c: Frederick, James. Pvt practice since 1931; exec dir, Conf of J Org, since 1937; mgn dir, Louisville Public Forum, 1935-36; dir, Jr C of C, Louisville, 1936-42; chmn, div, Comty

chest, 1954-58. Home: 2544 Woodcreek Rd, Louisville, Ky. Office: 702 ME Taylor Bldg, Louisville, Ky.

JULES, Mervin, US, artist, educator; b. Baltimore, Md, Mar 21, 1912; s. Sidney and Anna (Goldenberg); att: Baltimore City Coll, 1930; Md Inst Sch Art, 1931-34; Art Students League, 1934-35; m. Rita Albers, Apr 20, 1940; c. Gabriel, Frederick. Chmn, Dept Art, CCNY, since 1969; prof, art, Smith Coll, since 1963, visiting artist, 1945; art teacher: J Educ Alliance, Baltimore, Md, 1934-37; Fieldston Sch, NYC, 1942-45; Mus of Modern Art, 1943-45; War Vets Art Cen, 1944-46; George Walter Smith Mus, Hillyer Coll Adult Ext 1953-59; lectr, U Wis, 1950. One-man shows: Munic Art Soc; Baltimore Mus Art; gals: Hudson D Walker; Garlin; Y, Baltimore; ACA; Weyhe, ACG; U NC; Muriel Latow; Frank Orschlinger; travelling exhbs: Amer Fed of Art; 1943-46; Mus Modern Art, 1947-48; exhbs: Carnegie Intl, SF World's Fair; NY World's Fair; Artists for Victory Exhb; Corcoran Art Gal; Whitney Mus; Pa Acad Fine Arts; Intl Exposition Modern Art; Mus Modern Art, Paris; perm collections: Metrop Mus Art; Mus Modern Art; Art Inst Chgo; Mus Fine Arts, Boston; Portland Mus, Ore; Libr Cong; Baltimore Mus Art; Phila Mus; Duncan Phillips Gal; Bklyn Mus; Walker Art Cen; Ency Britannica; Abbott Lab; State Dept; Tel Aviv Mus; Swiss Consulate; Brandeis U; Tryon Gal; Smith Coll; Mt Holyoke Coll; pvt collections. F: McDowell Colony, 1938, 1961; Corp of Yaddo, 1941. Trustee: Provincetown Art Assn; Cummington Sch of the Arts, mem: Artists Equity; Comm Art Educ; Audubon Artists; Boston Printmakers; Provincetown Art Assn, Springfield Art League; AAUP, adv ed, Sch Arts. Recipient: Wilson Levering Smith Medal, 1939, 1941; purchase prize: Baltimore Mus Fine Art, 1941; Mus Modern Art, 1941; Libr Cong, 1945; Bklyn Mus, 1946; 2nd prize, Amer Soc Painters, 1951; hon mention, 33rd Annual Jury Exhb, Springfield Art League, 1952, 1st prize for oil, 1955; hon mention, Cape Cod Art Assn, 1955, 1sr prize, 1957; purchase prize: E States Exhb, 1957; SAGA, prize, 1962. Homes: 50 Dryads Green, Northampton, Mass; 613 Commercial St, Provincetown, Mass. Studio: Smith Coll, Northampton, Mass.

JUNG, Leo, US, rabbi, educator, author; b. Ung Brod, Moravia, June 20, 1892; s. Meir and Ernestine (Silbermann); att Vienna U, 1910-11; Berlin U, 1911-14; U Giessen, Marburg, 1914; ordained rabbi, Hildesheimer Rabb Sem, 1920; BA, London U, 1919, PhD, 1921; MA, Cambridge U, 1924; hon DD, Yeshiva U, 1950; hon DHL, NYU, 1955; m. Irma Rothschild, Feb 28, 1922; c: Erna Villa, Rosalie Rosenfeld, Julie Etra, Marcella Rosen. Rabbi, The J Cen, NY, since 1922; prof, ethics, Yeshiva U, since 1931; prof, ethics, Stern Coll for Women, since 1956. Chmn: cultural comm, JDC, since 1940; NY State Adv Bd on Kosher Law Enforcement, since 1935; hon pres: Beth Jacob Tchrs' Training Coll, Jerusalem; Rabb comm, Ort, since 1966; pres: J Acad of Arts and Scis, since 1950; Amer comm, Shaare Zedek Hosp, Jerusalem, since 1964; hon trustee, Yeshiva U, since 1941; trustee: JWB, since 1928; J Social Service Comm; mem: Amer Soc U Profs; Comm, J Agcy. Author: Fallen Angels, 1926; Living Judaism, 1927; Mistranslations as Sources of Lore, 1934; Crumbs and Character, 1940; Rhythm of Life, 1950; Harvest, 1958; Heirloom, 1961; Essentials of Judaism, 12th ed, 1964; ed, J Libr, 8 vols, since 1928; only Amer contbr to Soncino Trans of Talmud, Tractates Yoma and Arakhim, 1937, 1949. Recipient: Cong Selective Service Medal, 1945. Hobbies: prison studies, book collecting, mt climbing. Home: 241 Central Park W, New York, NY. Study: 131 W 86 St, New York, NY.

JUNGREISS, Nathan, Isr, calculator; b. Gyöngyös, Hung, July 31, 1912; s. Alexander and Paulina (Steiner); att: Agric HSs 1926-29, 1945-46, cost acctnt, Tel Aviv, 1959-62; m. Sarah Stern, Aug 2, 1936; c: Adam, Margalith Gil-Bar, Uri, Orna. Mem, mgmt, Isr Chess Fed, sicne 1961, treas, since 1966; mgr, Isr Corresp Chess Fed. Prin contrib: introduced Swiss sys in chess tournaments in Isr. Home: Kibbutz Haogen, Isr. Office: 6 Frish St, Tel Aviv, Isr.

JUSTICE-DAYAN, Eli, Isr, business exec; b. Prague, Czech, Mar 30, 1902; s. Simon and Ottilie (Popper); in Isr since 1938; DEcon, DJ, DRerPol, U Prague, 1925; m. Bella Wittmann, Jan 15, 1933; c: Chava. Dir gen, Isr Co for Fairs and Exhbs, Ltd, since 1957, dir, Isr pavilions at exhbs, intl fairs and congs; dir, fashion dept, Mfrs Assn of Isr, 1940-57. Fmr: chmn org comm, Maccabiah; chmn, Maccabi, Prague; parl and gen secy, J Party, Czech, 1930-38; pres, Hart Lodge, B'nai B'rith, Prague; club, Rotary. Recipient: Caveliere Officiale de la Republika Italiana. Hobby: sports. Home: 116 Dizengoff St, Tel Aviv, Isr. Office: 48 Kalisher St, Tel Aviv, Isr.

K

KABAKOFF, Jacob, US, rabbi, educator; b. NYC, Mar 20, 1918; s. Solomon and Rose (Katzman); dipl, Tchrs Inst, Yeshiva U, 1935, BA, 1938; ordained rabbi, JTSA, 1944, DHL, 1958; m. Dorothy Arian, 1950; c: David, Daniel, Joel. Asso prof, i/c Heb div, Lehman Coll, since 1968; asst rabbi, Har Zion Temple, Phila, 1944-46; rabbi, Cong Bnei Isr, Olney, Pa, 1946-48; educ dir, Flatbush J Cen, 1948-50; mem, ed staff, Ency Hebraica, 1950-52; dean, Cleveland Coll J Studies, 1952-68. Mem: RA; Natl Council for J Educ. Author: Pioneers of American Hebrew Literature, 1966; ed, Heb books, In Jewish Bookland; Jewish Book Annual; contbr: Jewish Life in America, 1955; Essays in American Jewish History, 1958; publs in Isr and US. Home: 25 Longview Ave, White Plains, NY. Office: Lehman Coll, Bedford Park Blvd W, Bronx, NY.

KABAKOW, Bernard, US, physician; b. NYC, May 27, 1927; s. Harry and Etta (Weinstein); BS, magna cum laude, St Johns U, Bklyn, NY, 1948; MA, Harvard U, 1949; MD, cum laude, U of Vt, 1953; m. Celia Dores, Jan 26, 1958; c: Etta, Beth, Harry, Elias, Laurie, Sara. Research asso, Beth Isr Hosp, NY since 1958; adj att phys, Montefiore Hosp since 1958; att phys, NY Ear and Eye Infirmary; asso att phys, Beekman Downtown Hosp; fmr: post-doc research f, Natl Found for Infantile Paralysis. USN, 1945-46. Dipl, Amer Bd of Internal Med; FACP; mem: Sigma Xi; Alpha Omega Alpha; Amer Fed for Clinical Research; Amer Assn for Cancer Research. Contbr to profsl jours. Home: 322 Central Park W, New York, NY. Office: 2 Fifth Ave, New York, NY.

KABATCHNIK, Amnon, US, theatrical dir; b. Tel Aviv, Isr, May 24, 1929; s. Alexander and Channa (Zofnat); MS, Boston U, Mass, 1954; MFA, Yale U, 1957; m. Miriam Kapuano, Apr 4, 1967; c: Edan. Asst prof, theater, SUNY, Binghamton, NY, since 1968; dir: High Season, 1967; Genesis, 1962; Island of Aphrodite, 1962; all Habimah Theater, Isr; Winterset, 1966; Behind the Wall, 1961, both Jan Hus Playhouse, NY; Fiddler on the Roof, Isr, 1966; Vincent, 1960; The Buskers, 1962, both Cricket Theatre, NY; A Country Scandal, Greenwich Mews Theatre, NY, 1960; Evenings With Chekhov, Actors Playhouse, NY, 1961; The Tenth Man, Natl Road Co, US, Can, 1962; Call It Virtue, Astor Pl Playhouse, NY, 1963; A Far Country, Zavit Theatre, Isr, 1964; The Cat and the Canary, Stage 73, NY, 1962; Little Foxes; Summertree, SUNY, Binghamton, 1968-69; Black Comedy; A Streetcar Named Desire, both Playhouse by the Rivers, 1969; musical dir: The King and I; Brigadoon; Finian's Rainbow; Wonderful Town; Kiss Me Kate; Plain and Fancy; Guys and Dolls; Pajama Game; Call Me Madam; Bells Are Ringing; Bye-Bye Birdie; My Fair Lady; res dir, New London Players, New London, NH, 3 seasons, among plays directed: The Diary of Anne Frank; Inherit the Wind; A Streetcar Named Desire; Home of the Brave; The Mousetrap; Our Town; No Exit; Gigi; Tunnel of Love; The Happiest Millionaire; The Fourposter; Three Men on a Horse; The Dark At the Top of the Stairs; Two for the Seesaw; Mr Roberts; A Thousand Clowns; Auntie Mame; Arsenic and Old Lace; asst to: Tyrone Guthrie on Mary Stuart, The Makropoulous Secret, Phoenix Theatre, NY; Tony Richardson on The Chairs, The Lesson, Phoenix Theatre, NY. Contbr to profsl publs and Isr press. Mem: Soc of Stage Dirs and Choreographers; Actors Equity Assn; Amer Fed of TV and Radio Artists. Hobbies: books, sports. Homes: 400 Clubhouse Rd, Binghamton, NY; 8 Gnessin St, Tel Aviv, Isr. Office: SUNY, Binghamton, NY.

KABNICK, Stuart, US, biochemist, dentist; b. Glen Cove, NY, June 14, 1893; s. Michell and Libby (Weine); chem, Syracuse U; chem, dent, U of Pa; postgrad, Phila Gen Hosp, Byberry Hosp for Mental Diseases; cert, oral surg, Phila Gen Hosp; m. Jo Smeelow, June 21, 1922. Biochem, research, at: Lankenau Inst of Cancer Research; Lankenau Hosp; Chester Co Hosp; Jefferson Hosp; Amer Stomach Hosp; Douglass Hosp; Rush Hosp for TB; Phila Gen Hosp, all in Cabasil Research; in surg research, exposure tech: Metabolic Ward; Surgical Wards; X-Ray, Radium Ward; Wash Sanatorium and Hosp, Mt Sinai Hosp, Phila; Lenox Hill Hosp, NYC; Freedmans Hosp, Wash, DC; Gallinger Hosp, Wash, DC; Pa Health Dept, TB Sanatorium, Mt Alto, Pa. Pvt. US Army. Prin contribs: inventor: multiple-chambered ampules: pipette ampules; cartridge multiple-chambered ampules; vacuum syringes for blood chem; porcelain filters; cabasil implants; bone marrow hollow drill; hollow-drill method for bact study of teeth; in dent research: silver-iodide, barium; calcium tech for: treatment of teeth; treatment of oral tissue diseases; cytological findings: Kabnicyte; giant phagocytic cell; parasitological finding, unidentified fungus; cabasil research: burns; TB; dysentry; gastric lesions; diabetic lesions; bedsores; emphysemas, alkalinization of necrotic tissues; first to use: exposure tech, no dressings; turtle as lab animal; therapeutic implantation; hollow-drill method; pre-surg skin disinfection; pressure staining of tumors; mild germicides; mildly insoluble ointment coatings. Dir: Conseil Intl de Med et de Biol; Pa Inst of Chemurgic Therapology; f: Intl Inst Anesthesiologists; Royal Soc Health, life f; Amer Inst Chems; Inst Amer Inventors; patron, Smithsonian Inst, Wash, DC; mem: Franklin Inst, Pa; Phila Assn Scis; Phila Co Med Soc; AAAS; Inst of Bacts, Pa chap; Amer Dent Soc; 1st Dist Dent Soc; E Dent Soc; N Phila Assn Dent Surgs; Pa State Dent Soc. Recipient, 1961 Citation, NY Acad Scis for discovery of cabasil, cancer research, exposure tech. Spec interests: cancer research, flying. Home and office: Broad-Locust Bldg, Philadelphia, Pa.

KACHER, Leon, US, physician, educator; b. Phila, Pa, Jan 14, 1913; s. Abraham and Elsie (Packman); BA, U of Pa, 1932, att grad sch, 1931-32, MD, 1936; m. Hester Ziserman, Nov 27, 1935; c: Joy Tressan. Pvt practice obstet, gyn, since 1937; asso phys, obstet, gyn: Albert Einstein Med Cen, Phila; St Luke's and Children's Hosp; asst phys, obstet, gyn: PA Hosp; chief phys, gyn, Oxford Hosp; instr, obstet, gyn: U of Pa; Hahnemann Med Coll, Phila, 1945-53; med adv, US Selective Service Sys. Dipl, Amer Bd Obstet and Gyn; f: Amer Coll Surg; Amer Coll Obstet and Gyn; Intl Coll Surg; Phila Coll of Phys; mem: Obstet Soc, Phila; AMA; PA, Phila Co Med Socs; Amer Soc Abdominal Surgs; Amer Phys F-IMA; Jerusalem Acad Med; Amer Assn for Maternal and Infant Health; Amer Cancer Soc; Pan-Amer Cancer Cytology Soc; Assn Amer Med Colls; Phila F Commn; AAAS; ZOA; Natl Fed J -Men's clubs; PA Acad Fine Arts; US Chess Fed; Phi Lambda Kappa; Masons; clubs: Fac, U of Pa; Franklin-Mercantile Chess. Contbr to med jours. Hobbies: chess, music, Yiddish lit. Home and office: 2037 Pine St, Philadelphia, Pa.

KACZÉR, Illés, Isr, author, journalist; b. Szatmár, Hung, Oct 10, 1887; s. Joseph and Fanny (Roth) Stern; att Yeshiva, Szatmár; HS, Nagyvárad; div; c: Anna Zador, Jan, Peter; m. 2nd, Ara Ehrenthal. Author: The Jewish Saga, 4 vols, 1947-49, 1953, 1953-56; numerous books, short stories, plays; ed: Provincial Papers, 1907-11; daily, Budapest, 1911-19; in several Eur countries, 1920-59; Ujkelet, Tel Aviv since 1959. Chmn, Max Nordau Prize Awarding Comm, Tel Aviv since 1963; pres: Isr sect, World Fed Hung J, NY off; Hitahdut Olei Hung, Tel Aviv; Eng Cen F; Author's Soc, London; fmr: vice-pres, Fed, Hung J in London; pres, Hung Authors and Journalists in London; club, PEN, London. Recipient: Prize, City of Budapest, 1916; Prize of Max Nordau Comm, 1961. Home: 11 Ido St, Ramat Chen, Isr.

KADANE, David K, US, attorney; b. NYC, Apr 9, 1914; s. Joseph and Fanny (Kurzman); BS, CUNY, 1933; LLB, Harvard Law Sch, 1936; m. Helene Born, Oct 5, 1936; c: Joseph, Kathryn. Gen counsel, LI Lighting Co since 1950; spec counsel, asst dir, SEC, 1936-45. Chmn, Nassau Co Youth Bd; dir, Afr-Amer Inst; pres: B'nai B'rith, Justice Lodge, 1952-53; Health and Wfr Council, Nassau Co, 1960-63; Peace Corps volunteer, Tanzania, 1964-66; mem: AJComm; ADL. Home: 190 Vooritis Ave, Rockville Centre, NY. Office: 250 Old Country Rd, Mineola, NY.

KADANOFF, Leo P, US, theoretical physicist, educator; b. New York, NY, Jan 14, 1937; s. Abraham and Celia (Kibrick); AB, Harvard U, 1957, MA, 1958, PhD, 1960; m. Diane Gordon, June 8, 1958; c: Marcia, Felice, Betsy. Prof physics and U prof, Brown U, since 1969; co-dir, urban growth study, Coord Scis Lab, U of Ill, since 1967; cons, Avco Corp, 1956-65; NSF Post Doc F, Bohn Inst for Theoretical Physics, Copenhagen, Den, 1960-61; Alfred P Sloan Found f, Cavendish Lab, Cambridge U, 1964-65; prof physics, U of Ill, 1965-69, mem fac since 1961. Prin contribs, research in: theoretical solid state physics; urban growth. Author, Fundamental Principles of Physics, Electricity, Magnetism and Heat, 1967; co-author, Quantum Statistical Physics, 1962; contbr to: anthols; scholarly jours. Recipient: NSF Pre-Doctoral F, 1957, 1958, 1959; John Harvard Hon Scholarship, 1954 (twice), 1955, 1956; Sr Sixteen, Phi Beta Kappa, 1957. Home: 25 Grotto Ave, Providence, RI. Office: Brown U, Providence, RI.

KADDAR, Shelomo, Isr, ombudsman; b. Muenster, Ger, Sep 1, 1913; s. Siegfried and Selma (Weinberg) Kessler; in Isr since 1933; att U Utrecht; m. Marisa Passigli, Jan 21, 1945; c: Edna Tal, Ruth, Michal. Ombudsman, Jerusalem Munic, since 1967; political dept, JA, 1945-49; dep secy of govt, 1948-49; counsellor, Isr delg, Brussels, 1951-53; Isr min, Prague, 1953-57; insp, Fgn Service, 1957-60; dir, munic services, Jerusalem, 1960-67. Cdr, Haganah, 1938-45. Home: 27 Ben Yehuda St, Jerusalem, Isr. Office: 22 Yafo St, Jerusalem, Isr.

KADDARI, Menahem Zevi, Isr, educator; b. Hung, May 18, 1925; s. Jehoshua and Shoshanna (Ehrmann) Schwarcz; in Isr since 1947; att Pázmány Péter U, Budapest, Hung; MA, Heb U, Jerusalem, 1950, PhD, 1953; m. Leah Goldstein, Apr 7, 1954; c: Miryam, Michal, Ruth. Asso prof, head, Dept Heb and Semitic Langs, Bar Ilan U since 1966, dean fac hums and social scis since 1968; fmr: tchr, Heb U; prof, Tel Aviv U; visiting asso prof, Heb, UCLA. Haganah, 1947-49. Chmn, Parents of B'nei Akiba, educ comm, Ramat Gan; mem: B'nai B'rith; cons mem, Acad of Heb Lang; Senate, Bar Ilan U; fmr: chmn research comm, Bar Ilan U; hanhaga rashit, B'nei Akiba Youth Org; hanhalah artzit, Hamishmeret Hatzeira, Hapoel Hamizrachi; chmn, Igud Hasegel, Bar Ilan U. Author: The Grammar of the Aramaic of the Zohar, Heb, 1957; Thesaurus in Concordance of the Bible, Heb and Eng, vol 3, 1968; Semantic Fields in the Language of the Dead Sea Scrolls, in Heb, 1968; ed, Bar Ilan Volume in Humanities, 1968; contbr, trans, articles to scholarly publs. Recipient: research grants: cultural bd, Histadruth; Heichal Hasefer. Home: 7 Bet El St, Ramat Gan, Isr. Office: Bar Ilan U, Ramat Gan, Isr.

KADELBURG, Lavoslav, Yugo, jurist; b. Yugo, 1910; s. Tobijas and Johana (Ernst); LLD, Fac of Law, 1935; m. Sofija Matejič, 1945; c: Smiljana, Zoran. State counsellor, asst to Secy for Fed Budget and gen admn; dir, Yugo Inst of Public Admn, since 1959; asst to Atty Gen of Serbia, 1947-51; judge, Supr Court of Serbia, 1951-57; asst to Secy Fed Secretariat and Gen Admn, 1957-59. Pres: Fed of J Comtys in Yugo since 1964; fmr, vice-pres; Autonomous Comm for Aid, 1949-59; mem, Anti-Fascist League of Yugo War Prisoners in Ger, WW II; active, social and public worker; fmr, active in youth and students' J orgs in Yugo. Contbr articles on Yugo admn. Recipient: Order of Lab, II ed; Order of Merit for the People. Home: Generala Zdanova 27, Belgrade, Yugo. Office: Fed of J Comtys in Yugo, ulica 7 jula 71a, Belgrade, Yugo.

KADOORIE, Horace, Hong Kong, business exec; b. London, Eng, Sep 28, 1902; s. Sir Elly and Lady Laura (Mocatta); att Clifton Coll, Bristol. Jt prop, Sir Elly Kadoorie & Sons; dir: Sir Elly Kadoorie Successors Ltd; St George's Bldg; China Light and Power; Devonia Finance & Inves; Far E Commodities, (1950); Feisec; Green Island Cement; Hong Kong Carpet Mfrs; Hong Kong & Kowloon Wharf & Godown; Hong Kong Steel Products; Hong Kong & Whampoa Dock; Humphrey's Estate & Finance; Intl Trade and Inves; Jt Ventures; Peak Tramways; "Star" Ferry; Amalgamated Rubber Estates; Java Consolidated Estates; Rubber Trust; chmn: Hong Kong & Shanghai Hotels; Shanghai Gas; Shanghai Land Inves; Shanghai Kelantan Rubber Estates. Trustee, Ohel Leah Syn, Hong Kong; patron, Alumni Assn, Ellis Kadoorie Coll, Hong Kong; life mem: Soc for Protection of Cruelty to Animals; Family Planning Assn, Hong Kong; St John Ambulance Assn; Hong Kong Anti-Cancer Soc; hon mem, Rotary of Kowloon and Tsuen Wan; mem: Royal Auto-

mobile Club, London; Botanical Soc, S Afr; Kadoorie Agric Aid Loan Fund Comm; Rural Devl Comm; Horticulture Soc Hong Kong; Boy Scout Council; fmr: pres: J Sch; Shanghai Horticulture Soc; found, pres, Shanghai J Youth Assn Cen and Sch; found: Boys and Girls Camp; Summer club; comm to aid Eur refs in Shanghai; Kadoorie Agric Aid Assn; clubs: Hong Kong Country; Royal Automobile, London; Royal Hong Kong Jockey; Amer; Hong Kong. Author, The Art of Ivory Sculpture in Cathay, 7 vols. Recipient: OBE, 1956; Chevalier de la Legion d'Honneur, 1939; Ramon Magsaysay Award for Public Service, 1962; Solomon Schechter Award, World Council of Syns, 1959; Officier de l'Ordre de Léopold, 1966. Spec interests, hobbies: agric, animal husbandry, gardening, ancient Chinese ivory carvings. Home: Boulder Lodge, 19 miles Castle Peak Rd, New Territories, Kowloon, Hong Kong. Office: St George's Bldg, 2 Ice House St, Hong Kong.

KADOORIE, Lawrence, Hong Kong, business exec, legislator; b. Hong Kong, June 2, 1899; s. Sir Elly and Lady Laura (Mocatta); att: Clifton Coll, Bristol; law, Lincoln's Inn; hon LLD, U Hong Kong, 1961; m. Muriel Gubbay, 1938; c: Rita McAulay, Michael. Jt prop, Sir Elly Kadoorie & Sons; chmn: Sir Elly Kadoorie Successors Ltd; St George's Bldg; Alaska Enterprises; China Light & Power; Far E Commodities & Trading; Feisec; Intl Dress; Intl Trade & Inves; Island Dyeing & Printing; Jt Ventures; Maj Contractors; Nanyang Cotton Mill; Oxford Devl; Taipo Devl; dir numerous cos; mem cons comm: Hong Kong Fire Ins; Lombard Ins. Interested in devl of: land, hotels, elec supply, ship-bldg and engr, maj construction work, public works contracts in Far E, Hong Kong, Kowloon. Co-found: New Territories Benevolent Soc; Kadoorie Agric Aid Assn; numerous, various communal and public service activities; chmn, Portuguese Marranos Comm; F, Inst of Dirs, both London; trustee, mem, Ohel Leah Syn and J Benevolent Soc, Hong Kong; patron, Family Planning Assn; life mem: Anti-Cancer Soc; Soc for Rehab Drug Addicts; asso mem, Council Social Service; hon mem, Philharmonic Orch, all Hong Kong; clubs: J Recreation; Amer; Hong Kong; Country; Motor Sports; Kart, hon mem; Royal Jockey; Chinese Recreation, patron, all Hong Kong; Royal Automobile; Aston Martin Owners; Number Ten, all London. Recipient: Chevalier de la Legion d'Honneur, 1939; Off, Order of St John, 1946; Solomon Schechter Award, World Council of Syns, 1959; Ramon Magsaysay Award for Public Service, 1962; Officier de L'Ordre de Léopold, 1966. Hobbies: sports cars, photography, Chinese art works. Home: 24 Kadoorie Ave, Kowloon, Hong Kong. Office: St George's Bldg, 2 Ice House St, Hong Kong.

KADURY, Benzion, Isr, engineer, public official; b. Chernigow, Russ, Oct 10, 1904; s. Hilel and Henia (Shmueli); in Isr since 1906; DEng, Royal Sch of Engr, Turin, It, 1930; m. Abigail Lipschutz, 1932; c: Dalia, Esther. Dir, devl and properties dept, Tel Aviv Munic, since 1946, on staff since 1936; counsellor, Isr Legation, Rome, 1949-50. Dir, Mus Haaretz; mem, bd dirs: Isr Standards Inst; Tel Aviv Art Mus; vice-pres, Isr Fgn Policy Assn. Recipient: Cavalliere Officiale del'Ordine di Merito, Rep It, 1962. Home: 10 Ben Num St, Tel Aviv, Isr. Office: City Hall, Tel Aviv, Isr.

KADUSHIN, Alfred, US, educator; b. NYC, Sep 19, 1916; s. Philip and Celia (Wolff); BSS, CUNY, 1940; MSW, NY Sch of Social Work, 1948; PhD, NYU, 1955; m. Sylvia Lemkin, July, 1949; c: Goldie, Raphael. Prof, social work, Sch of Social Work, U Wis since 1959; asst prof, 1950-55, asso prof, 1955-59; caseworker, J Bd Guardians, NY, 1948-50; Fulbright lectr, Sch of Social Work, Groningen, Netherlands, 1957-58; cons, Paul Baerwald Sch of Social Work, Heb U, Jerusalem, 1960-61. USAAC, 1942-46. Bd dirs: JWB; ARC, chmn, home service comm; Neighborhood Cens, 1955; Legal Aid Soc, 1956, all Madison; chmn, S Cen Wis chap, Natl Assn Social Workers, 1960; mem: AAUP; Council on Social Work Educ. Author: Child Welfare Services, 1967. Recipient: Combat Medal. Home: 4933 Marathon Dr, Madison, Wis. Office: U of Wis, Madison, Wis.

KADUSHIN, Max, US, rabbi, educator; b. Minsk, Russ, Dec 6, 1895; s. Solomon and Rebecca (Mazel); in US since 1897; BA NYU, 1916; MHL, ordained rabbi, JTSA, 1920; DHL, 1932; hon DHL, 1950; m. Evelyn Garfiel, Nov 22, 1923; c: Phineas, Charles. Visiting prof, psych of rel, JTSA, since 1958; rabbi: Temple Isr, NYC, 1921-26; Humboldt Blvd Temple, Chgo, 1926-31; Conservative Syn, Riverdale, NYC,

1954-58. Author: The Theology of Seder Eliahu, 1932; Organic Thinking, 1938; The Rabbinic Mind, 1952, 1965; Worship and Ethics, 1962; contbr to J jours. Home: 90 La Salle St, New York, NY.

KAFRI, Sara, Isr, communal worker; b. Minsk, Russ, 1900; d. Meir and Fruma Kaplan; in Isr since 1920; att kindergarten tchrs' sem; Heb U, Jerusalem; widow; c: Datiya Knani, Rami, Miriam Ben-Zvi, Ruth Zur. Mem, Moshav Kfar Yehoshua; MK, 2nd, 3rd Knesset, 1951-59; mem, secretariat, Women's Worker Council, 1960-68. Prin contribs, active in: moshavim movement, mem of its insts; Histadrut and its depts, Va'ad Hapoel, Cultural and Educ Cen. Delg, ZCs; several missions abroad; mem, Zionist Exec Comm. Home: Moshav Kfar Yehoshua, Isr.

KAFRISSEN, Arthur Saul, US, attorney; b. Phila, Pa, Nov 27, 1940; s. Ancel and Tessie (Seffren); BA, Temple U, Phila, Pa, 1964, JD, 1967; m. Carole Hecht, Jan 26, 1963; c: Samuel, Terri. Pvt practice since 1967. Mem: Amer, Pa, Phila Bar Assns; Amer, Pa, Phila Trial Lawyers Assns; Tau Epsilon Rho. Office: One E Penn Sq Bldg, Philadelphia, Pa.

KAGAN, Benjamin M, US, pediatrician, researcher, educator; b. Wash, Pa, July 15, 1913; s. Alexander and Sara (Gains); AB, Wash and Jefferson Coll, 1933; MD, Johns Hopkins Med Sch, 1937; m. Katherine Hamburger, June 2, 1940; c: Christopher, Robert. Dir, dept ped, UCLA, since 1956; fmr: research f, instr, Marine Biol Labs, Woods Hole, Mass; res: contagion, Willard Parker Hosp, NYC; ped, Presbyterian Hosp; instr: ped, Med Coll of Va; St Phillips Sch for Public Health Nursing, Richmond, Va; asst ped, Coll Phys and Surgs, Columbia U; prof: ped, U Ill Med Sch; Northwestern U Med Sch; dir, ped research, chmn, dept ped, all Michael Reese Hosp, Chgo. Maj, US Army, MC, 1942-46. Fmr, mem, med adv bds: Natl Nephrosis Found; Sunair Found of Asthmatic Children; Gtr LA Nutritional Council; Herrick House for Rheumatic Fever; cons, Bd Health, State of Cal; official xaminer, Amer Bd Peds; FACP; f: Amer Acad Ped; Amer Coll Chest Phys; mem: Amer Ped Soc; Soc for Ped Research; W Soc for Ped Research; Fed Amer Soc for Experimental Biol; Amer Inst of Nutrition; Experimental Biol and Med Soc; AAAS; Cen Soc for Clinical Research; AMA; Cal, LA Co Med Socs; W Soc for Clinical Research; W Assn Phys; LA Acad Med; Phi Beta Kappa; Sigma Xi. Author; contbr to sci jours; mem, ed bd, several sci jours. Recipient, Cert of Theater Cdr for Outstanding Service, WW II. Hobbies: photography, carpentry, elec. Home: 5005 Finley Ave, Los Angeles, Cal. Office: 4833 Fountain Ave, Los Angeles, Cal.

KAGAN, Eliezer, Isr, author, educator; b. Swislotz, Russ, Apr 7, 1914; s. Nachman and Hana (Shulman); in Isr since 1935; MA, Heb U, Jerusalem, 1940; PhD, 1960; m. Zipora Mandel; c: Rachel, Pnina, Sar'el. Prin, secondary sch, Kiryat Haim since 1953; lectr, Haifa U since 1959. Author, poetry: Azut Metzach, 1946; Korban Asham, 1948; Haim uMishak, 1948; Shoshanim biShchor, 1951; Olam Katan, 1954; Pahad Ein-Eloha, 1954; Eima vaZemer, 1957; Sachish, 1970. Contbr, researches, articles in Heb prosody, criticism, theory of lit, to profsl publs, Ency Judaica. Home: 29 Yod St, Kiryat Haim, Isr. Office: 48 Gimel St, Kiryat Haim, Isr.

KAGAN, Henry Enoch, US, rabbi, psychologist; b. Sharpsburg, Pa, Nov 28, 1907; s. Alexander and Sarah (Ginsburg); BA, U of Cincinnati, 1928; ordained rabbi, HUC, 1929, DD, 1956; MA, W Va U, 1934; PhD, Columbia U, 1949; m. Esther Miller, July 16, 1939; c: Jonathan, Jeremy. Rabbi, Sinai Temple, Mt Vernon, NY, since 1937; visiting instr, psych guidance, Tchrs Coll, Columbia U, since 1950; rabbi: Temple Beth Zion, Johnstown, Pa, 1929; Hillel Found, W Va U, 1930-34; Rodef Sholom Temple, Pittsburgh, 1934-37. Chmn and originator, comm on pastoral psycht, CCAR; found: Mt Vernon Round Table, 1939; Mt Vernon Council Social Agcys, 1940; cons: on Judaism to Cong Jt Commn on Mh, 1959; to White House Conf on Youth, 1960; mem: Amer Psych Assn; Intl Soc of Group Psychotherapy; club, Rotary. Author: Changing the Attitude of Christian Towards Jew, A Psychological Approach Through Religion, 1952; Psychiatry and Religion, 1953; Rabbi as Counselor, 1961; Teaching Values to American Youth, 1961; Six Who Changed the World, 1963. Recipient, award, NY FJP, 1961. Home: 70 Burkewood Rd, Mt Vernon, NY. Study: 132 Crary Ave, Mt Vernon, NY.

KAGAN, Irving G, US, researcher, parasitologist; b. NYC, June 1, 1919; s. Harry and Miriam (Slatoff); AB, Bklyn Coll, 1940; MA, U Mich, 1947, PhD, 1950; m. Mildred Reese, June 18, 1940; c: Mila, Jule. Chief, parasitology sect, lab div, Natl Communicable Disease Cen, since 1957; cons, immunodiagnosis of bilharziasis, WHO, since 1959; asst prof, zool, U of Pa, 1952-57. Lt, USAAC, 1942-45. Prin contrib: research in immunology and serology of parasitic infections. Pres, Communicable Disease Cen Br, Sci Research Soc of Amer, 1962; mem: Amer Acad, Microbiol; Amer Soc, Tropical Med and Hygiene; Amer Soc Parasitologists; Amer Assn Immunologists; Phi Beta Kappa; Sigma Xi; Phi Sigma; Phi Kappa Phi. Contbr to profsl jours. Recipient: DFC; Air Medal; Purple Heart; Air Pacific Ribbon; all WW II; Dist Alumni Award, Bklyn Coll, 1963; Superior Service Award, HEW, 1965. Home: 1074 Oakdale Rd NE, Atlanta, Ga. Office: Natl Communicable Disease Cen, Atlanta, Ga.

KAGAN, Jehuda L, US, rabbi; b. Brest-Litovsk, Pol, Oct 15, 1899; s. Avigdor and Tziral (Kotkin); in US since 1941; att Rabb Sem: Slobdka, 1917-19; Kelim, 1919-21; Mir, 1921-29; m. Deborah Kossovsky, July 9, 1929; c: Leah Altusky, Israel, Saul. Dean, Rabbi Jacob Joseph Sch since 1955; rabbi, Antipoler Soc since 1941, both NYC; fmr: Rosh, Beit Din; dean, Rosh Yeshiva, Shaar Hatorah, both Antwerp, Belgium; rabbi: Jeshurun; Lyon, Fr; Rosh Yeshiva: Yeshiva Jacob Joseph, NY; Yeshiva Beth Medrash Latorah, Chgo, Ill; dean, Yeshiva Rabbi Isr Salantar, NYC. Mem: bd dirs: Union Orthodox Rabbis in US and Can; Rabb Council, Gtr NY; Antipoler Soc, NY; Mizrachi; Cong Morya, NY. Author, Halichot Yehuda, Part I, 1965, Parts II, III, 1967-68; contbr to rabb publs. Recipient, Moriah Prize, for best book of year. Home: 212 E Broadway, New York, NY. Study: 167 Henry St, New York, NY.

KAGAN, Louis R, US, attorney, jurist; b. Jersey City, NJ, June 26, 1905; s. Reuben and Rachel (Schachnow); LLM, NYU, 1930; m. Constance Lockman, Aug 10, 1931; c: Leonard, Suzanne. Pvt practice since 1927; commnr, Superior Court since 1945; secy to State Senator, James F Murray, Jr, 1954-57; dep commn, revenue and finance, Jersey City, 1957-59; judge, munic court, 1959-62. Chmn: Amer J Tercentenary, 1954-55; UJA, 1956-58; hon pres, J Comty Cen; pres, NYU Alumni Assn; dir, J Hosp and Rehab Cen of NJ; mem: Masons, 32 deg, fmr master; Shriners. Contbr to legal jours. Home: 125 Bentley Ave, Jersey City, NJ. Office: 921 Bergen Ave, Jersey City, NJ.

KAGAN, Martin E, US, business exec; b. Gomel, Russ, Nov 30, 1919; s. Aron and Rachel (Shapiro); in US since 1940; tchrs cert, Herzliah Heb Tchrs Inst, NYC, 1942; BEE, CCNY, 1949; m. Dorothy Pintell, June 5, 1949; c: David. Chmn, bd dirs, Douglas Communications since 1968; fmr: pres, Yardley Elec Corp. US Army, 1942-45. Natl chmn, Amer's for Progressive Isr-Hashomer Hatzair; mem: Gen Zionist Council; Amer Rocket Soc; Amer Inst of Elec Engrs. Home: 250 E 178 St, New York, NY. Office: 40 Leonard St, New York, NY.

KAGAN, Rachel, Isr, communal leader; b. Odessa, Russ, Mar 4, 1888; d. Jacob and Miriam (Berstein) Lubarsky; in Isr since 1919; att: U Petersburg; U Odessa; m. Noah Kagan, July 19, 1933; c: Eliyahu, Michael. Ret since 1965; exec mem, Vaad Le'umi, head, social wfr dept, Jerusalem, 1946-48; provisional council, State of Isr, 1948-49; MK, 1949-51, 1961-65. Prin contribs: initiator of leg, Equality of Women's Rights Law, 1951; signed Isr Declaration of Independence. Hon pres, Isr Fed, WIZO; exec mem, World WIZO Exec; found mem, Histadrut Nashim Ivriot, 1920; dir, social service dept, J Comty, Haifa, 1930-46. Recipient, Freeman Award, City of Haifa, 1961. Home: 2 Rahel St, Haifa, Isr.

KAGANOFF, Benzion C, US, rabbi; b. Talnow, Ukraine, June 9, 1924; s. David and Miriam (Drazhner); in US since 1932; BA, summa cum laude, Northwestern U, 1946; ordained rabbi, Heb Theol Coll, 1948; MTh, McCormick Theol Sem, 1955; m. Claire Chamedes, June 21, 1951; c: Aleta, Yarona, Penny. Rabbi: Cong Ezras Isr since 1956; Ohev Sholom Cong, Wash DC, 1949-51; Cong Anshe Sholom, Chgo, 1951-56; lectr J hist, Tchrs Inst, Heb Theol Coll, 1951-58. Pres, Chgo Bd Rabbis, 1964-66; chmn, Natl Assn Bds of Rabbis, 1965-67; mem, exec: RabCA; Rel Zionists of Chgo, 1952-55; JNF, 1952-56; f, Amer Name Soc; mem, Phi Beta Kappa. Contbr to J mags. Home:

2901 W Greenleaf Ave, Chicago, Ill. Office: 7001 N California Ave, Chicago, Ill.

KAGANOFF, Nathan M, US, librarian, editor; b. Gaisin, Russ, Apr 8, 1926; s. David and Miriam (Drazhner); in US since 1932; BA, Northwestern U, Evanston, Ill, 1947; ordained rabbi, Heb Theol Coll, Chgo, 1948; MA, Amer U, Wash, DC, 1956, PhD, 1961; m. Baila Wolk, 1950 (decd); c: Joshua, Jeremy, Abigail, David. Libr-ed, Amer J Hist Soc, since 1969, libr, 1962-68; libr, subject specialist, rel and Judaica, Libr of Cong, Wash DC, 1950-62. Chaplain, US Army, 1951-56. Pres, research div, Assn J Librs, since 1967; chmn, Tech Process Comm, since 1966. Contbr to profsl jours. Home: 81 Park St, Brookline, Mass. Office: 2 Thornton Rd, Waltham, Mass.

KAGE, Joseph, Can, social welfare exec; b. Minsk, Russ, Sep 21, 1918; s. Aron and Leah (Yachnes) Kagedan; in Can since 1924; BA, BS, Sir George Williams U, 1941; MSW, McGill U, 1942, both Montreal; MA, U Ottawa, 1942; PhD, U Montreal, 1958; m. Miriam Weiner, Jan 23, 1954; c: Ian, Allan, Stephen, Thomas. Natl exec vice-pres, J Immigrant Aid Services of Can; pres, J Public Libr, Montreal; fmr: head, single mens div, Baron de Hirsch Inst, Montreal; asst prin, J Peoples Schs; student sup, McGill Sch of Social Work. Chmn, bd educ, Heb Acad, Montreal; mem: Corp of Profsl Social Workers, Que, mem bd, since 1960; bd, Can Assn Social Workers, since 1943; Can Assn Political Sci; Can Wfr Council; Can Citizenship Council; Amer Acad Political and Social Sci; Can Hist Assn; Amer J Hist Soc; Can Geog Soc; B'nai B'rith; Masons. Author: The Dawn of Canadian History, 1956; Zwei Hundert Yor Yiddishe Immigrazie In Kanade, 1960; With Faith and Thanksgiving, 1962; contbr to periodicals. Home: 321 De L'Epee Ave, Outremont, Quebec, Can. Office: 5780 Decelles Ave, Montreal, Can.

KAGEN, Samuel N, US, educator; b. Russ, Aug 27, 1898; s. Charles and Gertrude (Slovess); in US since 1907; BA, CCNY, 1919; att Columbia U, 1919-21; m. Henrietta Rosenthal, 1927; c: Betsy, Ruth. Ret; prof and registrar, Bklyn Coll, 1930-68; asst, registrar, CCNY, 1919-30. Students Army Training Corps, 1918. Mem: NEA; Amer Assn Collegiate Registrars and Admission Offs; Phi Beta Kappa. Hobby, gardening. Home: 3719 Ave S, Brooklyn, NY. Office: Bklyn Coll, Brooklyn, NY.

KAHAN, Ignace, Fr, rabbi; b. Nyircsaholy, Czech, Sep 7, 1905; s. Feiwish and Malvina (Kahan) Karpfen; ordained rabbi, Yeshiva Pressburg; Des Lettres, U Pressburg; m. Magda Schwartz, 1947; c: Hélène, Evelyn, Eugène, by first m. Chief rabbi, Grenoble and region of Dauphiné. Chaplain, Fr Army. Recipient: Chevalier de la Légion d'Honneur; Médaille de la Fr Libre; Médaille de la Résistance; Croix des Combattants; Médaille des Engagés Volontaires; Commandeur de Nichan Iftikar, Tunis. Home: 9 rue Léo-Lagrange, Grenoble, Fr.

KAHAN, Maxim, Isr, police off; b. S Afr, Jan 25, 1918; s. Isaac and Pearl (Kravetsky) Meir; in Isr since 1935; dipl, Ind Ing, Heb Tech Inst, Haifa, 1940; m. Carmela Gabrilowitz, May 5, 1942; c: Roni Harari, Daniel, Nili, Amihud. Col, dep cdr, N dist, Isr Police Force since 1952; fmr: cdr: Police Training Acad; Isr Frontier Force. Maj, J Brig, Brit Army, 1940-46; lt col, IDF, 1948-49. Pres, Isr Cricket Assn; chmn: Isr Amateur Underwater Fishing and Research Assn; Partridge, Isr; Isr Amateur Line Fishing Assn; vice chmn, Isr Hunters Assn; mem: exec comm, Asian Shooting Fed; Confrerie de la Chaine des Rotisseurs; Rotary, Haifa. Home: 132 Dalia Rd, Haifa, Isr. Office: N Dist Police Hqrs, Nazareth, Isr.

KAHAN, Salomon, Mex, journalist, author; b. Bialystok, Pol, June 22, 1896; s. Israel and Helen (Horovitz); in Mex since 1921; MA, Mexican Tchrs Coll, 1934; m. Elise Pintel, Sep 13, 1933; c: Joseph, Alexander, Arthur. Mgn ed, Tribuna Israelita, monthly, since 1953; prof, hist of modern civilization, Mexican Natl Tchrs Coll, 1925-39; lectr, Workmen's Circle, US, 1940-44; ed, Der Weg, Mexico City, 1945-48; res corresp in Mexico, Musical America, NY, 1946-56; vice-prin, Colegio Israelita de Mexico; music critic since 1928. Corresp mem, J Acad Arts and Scis, NY, since 1939; mem, Assn Music Critics. Author: La Emoción de la Musica, 1936; Reflejos Musicales, 1938; Yiddish Meksikanesh, 1945; Impresiones Musicales, 1951; Mexikaner Widerklangen, 1951; Mexi-

kanishe Reflexen, 1954; Bosquejos Musicales, 1957; Literarishe un journalistishe Farzeichnungen, 1961; trans into Span, History of the Jewish People, by Graetz, 10 vols, 1942. Home: Montes de Oca 17, Mexico, DF.

KAHANA, Josef Meeir, Isr, rabbi; b. Spinke, Hung, Dec, 1909; s. Hirsh and Mirel (Rubin); in Isr since 1941; studied with father, Rabbi of Spinke, other rabbis, ordained rabbi, 1936; m. Malka Teitelbaum, June 17, 1930; c: Mordechai, Chaya Mordechay, Baruch, Alter, Rivka Stein, Moshe, Yitshak, Henje Rozenberger. Pres, Yeshivat Imrei Josef Spinke since 1946; fmr rabbi, Hung. Contbr to Otzar Haposkim Books. Home: 16 Salant St, Jerusalem, Isr.

KAHANA, Kalman, Isr, rabbi, legislator, author; b. Brody, Pol, 1910; in Isr since 1938; att Rabb Sem, Berlin; PhD, Us of Berlin and Würzburg; m. Hannah Kunstadt, 1935; c: Shifra Eckstein, Margalit Heyman, Tirtza Freedman, Sara Schoenberger, Benjamin, Abraham, Adina, Hadasa. MK, Poale Agudath Isr, since 1949; dep Min of Educ and Culture, 1952-53 and since 1962; co-found, Kibbutz Hafetz Haim; fmr: mem, Provisional State Council, Isr; tchr, dean, Yeshiva Fulda, Ger. Mem exec, Poalei Agudath Isr. Author: Seder Tanaim veAmoraim; Hilkhot Kil'aym veOrla; Taharat Bat Israel; Hilkhot Shmitat Karkaot; Sefer Shnat haSheva, 3 eds; Sefer haZikaron la'Ritba; HaIsh veHazono; leHeker Bi'ure Hagra; Heker veIyun, trans into Eng; contbr to local press. Home: Kibbutz Hafetz Haim, Isr. Office: The Knesset, Jerusalem, Isr.

KAHANA, Shmuel Z, Isr, government official; b. Warsaw, Pol, Dec 14, 1905; s. Shlomo and Esther (Kelpfish); in Isr since 1920; ordained rabbi, Tahkemoni Rabb Sem, Warsaw, 1928; grad, Liége U, Belgium, 1932. Dir Gen, curator of holy places, Isr Min for Rel Affairs since 1949; fmr, prin, Yavneh Schs, Pol. Mem: natl comm, Mizrachi; comm, Torah Veavoda movement; WJC; fmr: exec comm, Hapoel Hamizrachi, dir, educ comm. Author: Al haRambam, 1934; Derekh Ziona, 1935; leHeshbona shel Tkufa, 1959; Begilgulei haShana, 1961; Agadoth Har Zion; Legends of the Holy Places; Heaven on your Head; contbr to local press. Home: 14 Lunz St, Tel Aviv, Isr. Office: Min for Rel Affairs, Jerusalem, Isr.

KAHANE, Ariel, Isr, architect, planner; b. Berlin, Ger, Nov 29, 1907; s. Arthur and Polly (Ornstein); in Isr since 1934; Dipl Ing, Tech Hochschule, Berlin, 1934; m. Ernestyna Reis, Mar 1, 1938; c: Josiah, Gabriela Eliasaf. Pvt practice since 1968; head: div for natl, regional plans, Govt of Isr, 1948-63; town planning div, Jerusalem Munic, 1963-68; UN adv, regional planning, Turkey. Prin contribs: elaboration of the natl phys plans; regional plans; numerous town plans in Isr. Mem, Engrs and Architects Assn, Isr. Contbr to profsl jours. Spec interest, contemporary intellectual problems and futuristic studies. Home and office: Moza Ilit, Jerusalem, Isr.

KAHANE, David, Isr, farmer, organization exec; b. Brody, Pol, Aug 1, 1901; s. Levy and Chavah; in Isr since 1920; m. Mania Landau, 1929; c: Noemi Wininser, Reuven. Mgr, Agric Cen, Tel Aviv since 1960; mem: Isr Agric Planning Auth; Agric Inves Corp; bd dirs: Isr Agric Bank; Isr Cotton, Poultry Bds; fmr mgr, Hamasbir Hamerkazi; chief water auth, Water Commn of Isr. Contbr to agric periodicals and daily press. Home: Kibbutz Ramat Yochanan, Isr. Office: Agric Cen, Allenby Rd, Tel Aviv, Isr.

KAHANE, Melanie, US, interior designer; b. Sioux Falls, SD, Nov 26, 1910; d. Morris and Rose (Roth); att: Parsons Sch of Design, NYC; Paris Sch of Parsons, Paris, Fr; m. Ben Grauer, 1954; c: Joan. Pres, Melanie Kahane Asso, since 1935; fmr: advertising illustrator, 1931-33; fashion designer, 1933-35. Past pres, NY Chap, Amer Inst of Decorators; f, Amer Inst Interior Designers, past natl secy; mem: Architectural League of NY; NY Home Fashions League; Decorators Club; Illuminating Engr Soc; Munic Art Soc; design comm, for US Pavilion, Brussels World's Fair, 1958; adv bd, RCA advanced design and styling center. Author: Art in the Home; There's a Decorator in Your Doll House, 1968; contbr to Grolier Ency. Recipient: decorator of the year, 1953; career key award, Girls Club of Amer, 1961. Home: 29 E 63 St, New York, NY. Office: 251 E 61 St, New York, NY.

KAHANEMAN, Joseph, Isr, rabbi, Talmudist, educator; b. Kuly, Lith, May, 1888. Found, pres, dean: Ponevez Yeshiva, Bnei Brak, Isr, since 1944; Grodno Yeshiva, Ashdod, since

1967; head, affiliated educ insts: Batei Avot Ref Children's Settlement, Satinsky Talmudical Libr, Archives of Lith Jewry; fmr: rabbi, J comty, Ponevez, Lith; dep of Jewry, Lith Parl. Mem, Supr Council of Rel Leaders in Isr since 1944. Home and study: Ponevez Yeshiva, Kiryat Hayeshiva, Bnei Brak, Isr.

KAHANOFF, Isaac, Isr, business exec; b. Tel Aviv, Isr, June 9, 1914; s. Eliyahu and Hanna (Aberbaum); cert d'études, Alliance Isr, Tel Aviv; brevet elem, École Normale, Paris, 1930, brevet superieur, 1932; m. Rachel Mann, Oct 8, 1940; c: Yahly, Eliezer, Noga. Mgr, Mann Stores Ltd since 1962; fmr: tchr, Alliance, Jerusalem, Beirut, Egypt; merchant I Kahanoff, 1945-62; gen mgr, Mann and Berman Ltd. Mem, martial court, Fr Army, 1938-40; lt, IDF. Vice-pres, Jerusalem C of C; treas, Isr-Switz Friendship League; pres of exec, Lib Party; mem, Intl C of C. Home: 33 Shmaryahu Levin St, Jerusalem, Isr. Office: Givath Shaul B, Jerusalem, Isr.

KAHANY, Menachem, Isr, diplomat; b. Cracow, Pol, Nov 7, 1898; s. Yosef and Rebecca (Farber); LLD, Jagellonian U, 1922; att Us: Vienna; Paris, 1923-26; m. Chana Schibling, 1933. Spec adv, Delg to Eur, Off of UN, Geneva, Switz since 1961, perm delg, 1948-61, rank Min since 1959; fmr: political secy, WZO and JA for Pal, League of Nations, Geneva; mem, JA delg to UN; mem Isr delg to: UN Assemblies; Intl Red Cross Conf, Stockholm; diplomatic conf for rev of Geneva Conv, Geneva; Intl Lab Confs, Geneva; WHO confs. Ed, Informations de Palestine, 1935-46; fmr contbr to Zionist press in Pol, Pal, US. Recipient: Silver Medal, Aus, 1917; Charles Cross, 1917; Pol Legion Cross, 1919; Homes: Nahariya, Isr; 9 ave Trembley, Geneva, Switz. Office: 9 chemin de Bonvent, Geneva, Switz.

KAHLER, Erich G (von), US, educator, author; b. Prague, Czech, Oct 14, 1885; s. Rudolf and Antoinette (Schwarz); in US since 1948; att Us of Munich, Berlin, Heidelberg, Freiburg; PhD, U Vienna, 1911; m. Josephine Sobotka (decd). Prof em, Cornell U, since 1955, prof, Ger lit, 1947-55; visiting prof: U Manchester, Eng, 1955-56; O State U, 1957, 1959; Princeton U, 1960-62; f, Bollingen Found, 1947-50; mem, Inst for Advanced Study, Princeton, 1949; comm to frame world constitution, U of Chgo, 1945-50. Author: Poems; Ueber Recht und Moral, 1911; Weltgesicht und Politik, 1916; Das Geschlecht Hapsburg, 1919; Der Beruf der Wissenschaft, 1920; Israel unter den Voelkern, 1936; Der Deutsche Charakter in der Geschichte Europas, 1937; Man the Measure, 1943, Brit ed, 1944, Span ed, 1946; Die Verantwortung des Geistes, 1952; The Tower and the Abyss, 1957, Brit ed, 1958, Span ed, 1959, It, Ger ed; The Arabs and Palestine, 1944; Die Philosophie von Hermann Broch, 1962; The Meaning of History, 1964, Span ed, 1966; Der Sinn der Geschichte, 1964; Stefan George, 1964; Out of the Labyrinth, 1967; The Rallying Idea, 1967; The Jews among the Nations, 1967; The Disintegration of Form in the Arts, 1968; ed, Hermann Broch, Gedichte, 1953. Corresp mem, Deutsche Akademie fuer Sprache und Dichtung; mem, Commn Constitutionelle Mondiale. Home: 1 Evelyn Pl, Princeton, NJ.

KAHN, Arthur, US, psychologist; b. Elizabeth, NJ, Apr 8, 1917; s. David and Ella (Jacobson); BA, U of Pa, 1938, MA, 1941; PhD, Ind U, 1952; m. Florence Bernard, Dec 18, 1955. Adv psychol, Westinghouse Elec Corp, with firm since 1956, head, hum factors group, 1961-68; research psychol, Naval Research Lab, 1952-54. Mem: Amer and Midwestern Psych Assns; AAAS; B'nai B'rith; Sigma Xi. Home: 2 Cove of Cork Lane, Annapolis, Md. Office: POB 746, Baltimore, Md.

KAHN, Benjamin M, US, rabbi; b. Lowell, Mass, Nov 10, 1913; s. Gabriel and Celia (Leibowitz); BA, magna cum laude, Harvard U, 1934; postgrad, phil, Columbia U, 1934-38; ordained rabbi, MHL, JTSA, 1938; hon, LHD, Alfred U, 1962; m. Rosalind Aronson, June 26, 1938; c: Simon, Jenette. Natl dir, B'nai B'rith Hillel Found since 1959, dir, Pa State U, 1940-44, 1945-59, established found, McGill U, Montreal, 1944-45. Pres, Natl Assn Hillel Dirs, 1951-53; exec comm: RA; Natl Assn Profs Heb; bd overseers, Lown Inst for Contemporary J Studies, Brandeis U; mem: CJFWF; AAUP; ZOA; Natl Adv Council Peace Corps; acad council, Amer Friends Heb U. Author, Sabbath Eve Services in Hillel Foundations, 1954; co-author, Exploring Religious Ideas: The Great Western Faiths, 1959; ed comm: Jewish Heritage; Jewish Digest. Home: 7907 Rocton Ave, Chevy Chase, Md. Office: 1640 Rhode Island Ave NW, Washington, DC.

KAHN, Claude, Fr, pediatrician; b. Roubaix, Fr, May 1, 1937; s. Walter and Martha (Hanau); MD, U Nancy, Fac of Med, 1964; m. Nadine Finkelstein, July 4, 1963; c: Myriam. Pvt

practice since 1968. Lt, Fr Army MC, 1964-65. Bd of dirs, Ecole des Parents; treas, Union des Médecins, Dentistes, Pharmaciens, Amis d'Isr; fmr pres, J Students Union, Nancy. Mem: B'nai B'rith, Beer Isaac chap; WJC. Contbr publs to: Archives Françaises de Pédiatrie; Annales de Génétique. Home and office: 15 Blvd Joffre, Nancy, Fr.

KAHN, Edgar M, US, investment counselor, author; b. San Francisco, Nov 24, 1904; s. Ira and Marie (Clayburgh); BA, Stanford U, 1925; cert inves banking, Harvard Grad Sch of Bus, 1928; m. Anne Levin, Jan 19, 1935; c: Kenneth, Marjorie. Ret; fmr prop, inves mgt firm; repr, J Barth & Co, 1927-41. Mem: Security Analysts Assn; bd trustees, Cal Hist Soc, 1950-64; natl exec bd, AJComm, since 1952; adv comm, Salvation Army, 1957-65; budget comm, United Bay Crusade, 1937; Amer J Hist Soc, life mem; clubs: Commonwealth, Cal, life mem; Concordia-Argonaut; Engrs; Roxburghe; Chit-Chat. Author: Cable Car Days in San Francisco, 1940; Bret Harte in California, 1941; Tamalpais Enchanted Mountain, 1945; Andrew S Hallidie, California Pioneer Industrialist, 1947; Seven Pioneer San Francisco Libraries, 1948; Land's End to the Ferry, 1952; RLS, A Warm-Hearted Friend of Humanity, 1954; contbr to quarterlies. Home: 1998 Broadway, San Francisco, Cal.

KAHN, Edward M, US, social worker; b. Berestowicz, Russ-Pol, May 15, 1895; s. Moe and Deborah (Tyktin); in US since 1905; LLB, Bklyn Law Sch, St Lawrence U, 1914; att: CCNY; New Sch for Social Research; NY Sch Social Work Grad Sch Social Service Admn; U Chgo; m. Helen Schulman, June 14, 1936; c: Robert, David, Lucy. Ret; exec dir, J Social Service Fed, Atlanta, 1928-64; fac mem, Atlanta U Sch Social Work, since 1932; exec secy, J Wfr Fund, 1936-64; exec dir, JCC, 1945-64; prin, Thomas Davidson Soc, NYC, 1918; educ dir, J People's Inst, Chgo, 1921-26; mgr, W tour, Hakoah Soccer Team, of Vienna, Aus, 1926-27. Fmr mem, bd: Atlanta Urban League; Atlanta J Comty Cen; mem, bd: J Chilren's Service; J Home for Aged; Bur J Educ; exec secy, 7th dist, Manhattan, ZOA, 1918-19; pres, Natl Conf J Communal Service, 1956-57, mem, exec comm, 1951-54; fmr mem, exec comm, Natl Assn; J Cen Workers; fmr chmn, Atlanta cha Amer Assn Social Workers; charter mem, Natl Assn Social Workers; mem: Acad Certified Social Workers; first bd, CJFWF; Amer Acad Political and Social Sc; Natl Conf Social Wfr; fmr mem: gen comm, 5th dist, Grand Lodge B'nai B'rith, natl Hillel commn, fmr pres, Gate City Lodge, club, Atlanta Social Workers, fmr pres. Home: 55 Brighton Rd, Rd, NE, Atlanta, Ga.

KAHN, E J, Jr, US, author; b. NYC, Dec 4, 1916; s. Ely and Elsie (Plaut); BA, cum laude, Harvard Coll, 1937; m. Virginia Rice, Feb 14, 1945; c: E J, Joseph, Hamilton. Staff writer, The New Yorker since 1937. Author: The Army Life, 1942; McNair: Educator of An Army, 1945; The Voice, 1946; Who, Me?, 1948; The Peculiar War, 1952; The Merry Partners, 1955; The Big Drink, 1960; A Reporter Here and There, 1961; The Stragglers, 1962; The World of Swope, 1965; A Reporter in Micronesia, 1966; The Separated People, 1968; co-author, GI Jungle, 1943. Bd trustee, Scarborough Country Day Sch since 1952, pres, 1959-62; mem: Authors League of Amer; Authors Guild of Amer; Amer Vets Comm; Phi Beta Kappa; club, Harvard, NY. Recipient, Legion of Merit, 1945. Home: Truro, Mass. Office: The New Yorker, 25 W 43 St, New York, NY.

KAHN, Hannah, US, poet; b. NYC, June 30, 1911; d. David and Sarah (Seigelbaum) Abrahams; m. Frank Kahn, 1941; c: Melvin, Daniel, Vivian. Poetry rev ed, Miami Herald since 1958; poems included in: Poetry Soc of Amer Anthol, 1945; poems appeared in: Harper's Mag, Amer Scholar, Saturday Rev, NY Times, Ladies Home Jour, Voices; Eve's Daughter, book of poems, publ 1963. Bd dirs, Haven School; adv bd, Affiliated Mem, Acad Amer Poets; mem: Poetry Soc of Amer; Poetry Soc of Va; Poetry Soc of Ga; Natl Assn for Retarded Children; hon mem, Phi Lambda Pi, 1969. Recipient: Ralph Cheney Award, 1946; Jessie Rittenhouse, 1947; Poetry Soc of Amer, 1952, 1953; Borestone Mt Poetry, 1953, 1955, 1957; Norfolk Prize, 1954; Williamsburg Prize, 1956; Howard Parsons award, Poetry Soc of Gt Brit and Amer, 1957; Theta Sigma Phi Headliner, 1959; George Washington Hon Medal, Freedom Found, 1961. Home: 40 NE 69 St, Miami, Fla.

KAHN, Harry J, US, chemical engr; b. NYC, Dec 25, 1898; s. Mayer and Mollie (Rosenthal); BA, MIT, 1920; postgrad studies, Rutgers U, 1921; m. Hannah Morris, Dec 6, 1929; c: John. Ret; plant supt, Stylon Corp, Milford, Mass, 1952-65; asst dir, research, Amer Encaustic Tiling Co, Zanesville, O,

1920-21; laborer, Wheeling Tile Co, Wheeling, W Va, 1923; partner, Progressive Art Tile Co, 1925-31; pres, Tile Products Co, 1931-42, both Matawan, NJ; produc mgr, Amer Encaustic Co, Maurer, NJ, 1934-35; dir lab: Stewart Clay, NYC, 1947-49; Architectural Tiling, Keyport, NJ, 1949-52; volunteer exec, Intl Exec Service Corps, adv to tile plants: Iran, 1965; Philippines, 1967-69. Maj, US Army, 1945-46; off i/c, produc control, ceramic inds, Ger, 1945-46. Mem: NJ Ceramic Soc; NE Ceramic Soc; Amer Legion, fmr cdr, Matawan, NJ; Forty and Eight Soc; MIT Alumni Assn; Pi Lambda Phi; dir, Civil Defense, Matawan, NJ, 1950-52. Author: Drying of Paint of Mass Auto License Plates; Development of One-fire Ceramic Tile Glazes, 1952; owner of patents; White Rock Cement; mfr of artificial jade. Home: Albee Rd, Uxbridge, Mass.

KAHN, Harry H, US, educator; b. Baisingen, Ger, June 20, 1912; s. Max and Hanna (Stern); in US since 1940; att Israel Lehrerseminar, Würzburg, 1927-31; MA, Middlebury Coll, 1951; m. Irene Levi, 1941; c: Hazel, Max. Asso prof, Ger and Heb, U of Vt since 1954, instr, 1947; Hillel dir, U of Vt since 1948. Mem: B'nai B'rith; Natl Assn Hillel Dirs; MLA; Amer Assn, Tchrs Ger; Amer Assn, Profs Heb; Soc of Bible Lit; Amer Acad Rel. Home: 165 E Ave, Burlington, Vt. Office: U of Vt, Burlington, Vt.

KAHN, Henry S, US, banker; b. Chgo, Ill, Jan 12, 1917; s. Sidney and Neta (Straus); BEcon, Wharton Sch of Finance, U of Pa, 1938; research hon, Stonier Grad Sch of Banking, Rutgers U, 1952-54; MBA, Inst for Mgmt, Northwestern Grad Sch of Bus Admn; m. Doris Foreman, Jan 26, 1955; c: Robert, Peggy, Steven. Vice-pres, Harris Trust and Savings Bank since 1956, admn, Loan Div A since 1964, off since 1941; security analyst, Straus Securities Co, Chgo, 1938-40. Lt-cdr, USN, 1942-45. Dir: JWF; NCCJ, chmn, finance comm; mem, exec bd, Goodwill Inds; USO, vice-pres; mem: Comm Gtr Pa, adv panel, U of Pa; Amer-Isr C of C and Ind; Chgo Assn of Commerce and Ind, Chgo Mortgage Bankers Assn; Mortgage Bankers Assn of Amer; Zeta Beta Tau; clubs: Bankers; Execs; Econ, all Chgo. Home: 777 Greenleaf Avenue, Glencoe, Ill. Office: 111 W Monroe Street, Chicago, Ill.

KAHN, Herman, US, archivist, historian; b. Rochester, NY, Aug 13, 1907; s. Isadore and Dora (Schoenberg); BA, summa cum laude, U Minn, 1928, MA, 1931; m. Anne Suess, Sep 13, 1936; c: Michael, Melinda. Asso libr, manuscripts and archives, Yale U, since 1968; teaching asst, hist, U Minn, 1929-31; asst prof, Neb State Tchrs Coll, 1931-33; hist, Natl Park Service, 1934-36; dir, Franklin D Roosevelt Libr, 1948-6; asst archivist for pres librs, Natl Archives, 1964-68, archivist, 1936-41, chief, div of interior dept of archives, 1942-46, dir natural resources records off, 1946-48, asst archivist for civil archives, 1962-64. Vice-pres, James Archivists Soc, 1968-69; mem: Amer and Miss Valley Hist Assns; Soc of Amer Archivists. Contbr to hist and archival jours. Home: 98 Everit St, New Haven, Conn. Office: Yale U Libr, New Haven, Conn.

KAHN, Herman H, US, business exec; b. NYC, Aug 3, 1909; s. Joseph and Fannie (Gisnet); BS, NYU, 1932; m. Ruth Schulman, Mar 25, 1934; c: Sidney, Geraldine, Frederick. Partner, Lehman Bros since 1950, with firm since 1938; dir: Allied Stores Corp; Avco; Dayco; Microwave Assos; Seaboard Finance; United Merchants & Mfrs. Pres, Herman and Ruth Kahn Found Inc; dir, Fannie and John Hertz Engr Scholarship Found; bd trustees: J Comty Cen; Temple Emanu-El; govs comm, Employ the Physically Handicapped; club, Preakness Hills Country. Home: 334 Robin Rd, Englewood, NJ. Office: 1 William St, New York, NY.

KAHN, Herbert, US, attorney; b. NYC, Dec 30, 1927; s. Philip and Tillie (Feit); BA, NYU, 1949; LLB, Bklyn Law Sch, 1952; att U Aix-Marseille, Fr, 1948; m. Hildegarde Johnsen, Apr 20, 1956; c: Susan, Janet. Atty, Philips, Nizer, Benjamin, Krim & Ballon since 1968; pvt practice, 1952-68. US Army, 1942-47. Pres: Temple Beth Am; Queens Council for Better Housing & Comty Devl; leg chmn, PTA; treas, Interracial and Interfaith Housing Rehab Found, Inc; volunteer atty: Opr Open City, Urban League; Queens Lay Advocate Service; mem: charter, bd finance chmn, S Jamaica Comty Progress Cen; NAACP; Bklyn Law Sch Alumni Assn; fmr: pres: Tri-Comty Council of Rosedale, Laurelton and Springfield Gardens; vice-pres, Rosedale Civic Assn; chmn, Screening panel, Local Sch Bd 28. Spec interests: race relations, minority rights, interfaith, public educ. Home: 163-49 130 Ave, Jamaica, NY. Office: 477 Madison Ave, New York, NY.

KAHN, Joseph Jr, US, business exec; b. NYC, June 12, 1920; s. Joseph and Hazel (Potter); m. Virginia Spiegelberg, Apr 11, 1946; c: Peter, Nancy. Pres, J S Bernheimer & Bro, Inc, since 1954, with firm since 1938; mgr, converting div, Iselin Jefferson, since 1960; dep mgr, Ameritex Div of United Merchants & Mfrs, since 1965. USAAC, 1942-46. Bd dirs: Grand St Settlement, since 1949, treas, 1954-59; Textile Fabric Distributors Assn, treas, 1962-65; clubs: Lambs; Sunningdale Country. Home: 33 Blackthorn Lane, White Plains, NY. Office: 1412 Broadway, New York, NY.

KAHN, Ludwig W, US, educator; b. Berlin, Ger, Oct 18, 1910; s. Bernhard and Dora (Frischberg); in US since 1936; att U Berlin, 1928-29, 1931-33; PhD, U Berne, 1934; MA, U London, 1936; m. Tatyana Uffner, June 12, 1941; c: Andree, Miriam. Prof, Ger, Columbia U since 1967; chmn, dept Ger and Slavic Langs, CUNY since 1961, prof, comparative lit and Ger, on fac since 1947; instr: U Rochester, 1937-40, Bryn Mawr Coll, 1940-42; instr, asst prof, Vassar Coll, 1942-47; sr Fulbright lectr, 1959-61; visiting prof: Hochschule, Stuttgart, 1959-61; Yale U, 1968-69. Secy, fac chap, AJCong since 1961; sect chmn, MLA, 1958; mem, AAUP. Author: Shakespeares Sonette in Deutschland, 1935; Social Ideas in German Literature, 1939; Literatur und Glaubenskrise, 1964; contbr to jours. Spec interests: theater, travel. Home: 9 Atherstone Rd, Scarsdale, NY. Office: 507 Philosophy Hall, Columbia U, New York, NY.

KAHN, Milton, US, manufacturer; b. Latvia, Jan 25, 1890; s. Harry and Etta (Levin); BS, MIT, 1912; m. Edythe Miller, June 7, 1921; c: Betty White, Lila Musinsky, Martin H. Prop, Kahn Paper Co, Boston since 1919; fmr: apprentice, supr of produc, Amer Writing Paper Co, Holyoke, Mass. Lt, chem warfare service, US Army, 1918-19. Found, Milton Kabu Chair, Florence Heller Sch of Social Work, Brandeis U; natl chmn, Brandeis U Assos since 1950; natl secy, CFJWF since 1949; dir: Children's Hosp; Beth Isr Hosp; United Service for New Amer's; UJA; JDC; United Comty Services, Boston; hon trustee: Temple Isr; Beth Isr Hosp; Brandeis U; hon mem, Tau Delta Phi; mem: Masons; fmr: pres, AJP, Boston; vice chmn, Boston Comty Fund Campaigns; chmn, appeals resolutions comm, UJA; mem, Mass exec comm, United Services Orgs; clubs: Kernwood; Melmont Country. Home: 288 Kent St, Brookline, Mass. Office: 73 Tremout St, Boston, Mass.

KAHN, Peter B, US, scientist, educator; b. NY, Mar 18, 1935; s. Morton and Lillian (Miller); BS, Union Coll, Schenectady, NY, 1956; PhD, Northwestern U, Chgo, 1960; m. Lois Gibbs, Sep 16, 1956; c: Miriam, David, Yoav. Asso prof, physics, SUNY, Stony Brook since 1965, fac mem since 1961; research asso, State U of Ia, 1960-61; visiting sci: Brookhaven Natl Lab, 1962-65; Argonne Natl Lab, 1966; AERE, Harwell, Eng, 1967, 1968. Mem: Amer Phys Soc; AAAS; AAUP; N Shore J Cen. Ed, symposium, Stat Properties of Atomic and Nuclear Spectra, 1963; contbr to sci jours. Recipient: Intl Nickel Co F, 1959; NSF Award, prin inves, since 1962, for studies in stat theories; NY Research Found Grant, 1967; Sr Weizmann Memorial f, Weizmann Inst, Isr, 1967-68. Spec interest, adult educ in J hist. Home: 53 Christian Ave, Setauket, NY. Office: SUNY, Stony Brook, NY.

KAHN, Reuben Leon, US, microbiologist, serologist, educ; b. Kovno, Lith, July 26, 1887; s. Lazar and Lottie (Wolpert); in US since 1899; BS, Valparaiso U, Ind, 1909; MS, Yale U, 1913; DSc, NYU, 1917; hon: LLD, Valparaiso U, 1944; DSc, Inst Divi Thomae, Cincinnati, O, 1954; MD, Natl U of Greece, 1963; PhD, Far E U, Manila, Philippines, 1964; m. Dina Weinstein (decd); c: Lyra, David. Research prof, microbiol, Howard U, Wash, DC, since 1968; prof em, serology, research cons, dermat, U Mich, since 1957, on fac, Med Sch, 1928-68, dir labs, U Hosp, 1928-47, chief, serology lab, 1947-57; immunologist, Dept of Health, Mich, 1920-28. Capt, US Army, MC, 1917-19. Prin contribs: research on tissue immunity in relation to radiation, supported by US AEC, 1957-67; Kahn test for syphilis, 1920-23. Mem, numerous sci socs, including: Amer Soc for Microbiol; Amer Assn Immunologists; Radiation Research Soc; hon mem: Med Soc for Study of Venereal Disease, London; Mich State Med Soc; Washtenaw Co Med Soc; Greek Dermat Soc; Isr Microbiol soc; Philippine Path Soc; others; elected, Health Hall of Fame, Mich Health Council, 1965. Author: Serum Diagnosis of Syphilis by Precipitation, 1925; The Kahn Test—A Practical Guide, 1928; Tissue Immunity, 1936; Serology in Syphilis Control, 1942; Serology with Lipid Antigen, 1950; An Introduction to Universal Serologic Reaction in Health and Disease, 1951; contbr numerous sci articles. Recipient: citation, Mich State Leg, for work and service to humanity, 1931; established in his hon: Research Lab of Immunology, Heb U, Hadassah Med Sch, Jerusalem, by interest of Detroit phys, 1966; Kahn Lab, U of Teheran Med Sch, Iran; Kahn Research Lab, U of Isfahan Med Sch, Iran; Kahn Research Award, Incarnate Word Coll, San Antonio, Tex, all 1967. Home: 2100 Massachusetts Ave, N W Wash, DC. Office: Howard U, Dept of Microbiol, Washington, DC.

KAHN, Robert David, US, business exec; b. Indianapolis, Ind, Mar 11, 1920; s. S Carroll and Nannette (Falk); BChE, Purdue U, 1942; m. Rose Hyman, May 1, 1944; c: Carly, James. Vice-pres, corp secy, dir purchasing, Capital Paper Co since 1965, with co since 1946; treas, Consolidated Sales, Inc since 1965. Lt, USAAC, 1942-45. Mem: bd dirs: Soc Packaging and Handling Engrs, Indianapolis chap; Midwest Paper Assn; fmr: co-chmn, JWF; mem: B'nai B'rith; AJ Comm; Ind Temple Brotherhood, fmr, bd dirs. Home: 451 Wellington, Indianapolis, Ind. Office: 3333 N Franklin Rd, Indianapolis, Ind.

KAHN, Robert I, US, rabbi; b. Des Moines, Ia, Dec 12, 1910; s. Morris and Sadie (Finkelstein) Kohn; BHL, HUC, 1931, ordained rabbi, 1935, DHL, 1951, DD, hon, 1960; BA, U Cincinnati, 1932; m. Rozelle Rosenthal, Dec 29, 1940; c: Alfred, Edward, Sharon. Rabbi, Cong Emanu-El since 1944; asst and asso rabbi, Cong Beth Isr, 1935-43; both of Houston, Tex; J columnist, Houston Chronicle since 1953. Chaplain, US Army, 1942-45. Pres: Kallah of Tex Rabbis, 1941; Houston Rabb Soc, 1958; recording secy, CCAR, 1959; natl chaplain, Amer Legion, 1959-60; mem bd: Comty Council; Boy Scouts of Amer; Travelers' Aid; ARC; Mh Assn; Hodgkins Disease Research Found; Masons; Rotary. Home: 3609 S Braeswood Blvd, Houston, Tex. Study: 1500 Sunset Ave, Houston, Tex.

KAHN, Robert I, US, business exec; b. Oakland, Cal, May 17, 1918; s. Irving and Francesca (Lowenthal); BA, with distinction, Stanford U, 1938; MBA, Harvard U, 1940; m. Patricia Glenn, Feb 14, 1946; c: Christopher, Roberta. Bus counselor, Cal and Nev; controller, Smiths, Oakland, 1946-51; vice-pres, treas, Sherwood Swan and Co, 1953-56. USAAC, 1941-46; USAF, 1951-52. Dir, SF Bay Girl Scout Council, since 1969; vice-chmn, J Comty Relations Comm, E Bay, since 1969; trustee, Assn Mgmt Cons, since 1968; vice-pres, Alameda Co United Fund, since 1959, mem, exec comm since 1948; mem: Natl Budget and Consultation Comm since 1968; Phi Beta Kappa; Baker Scholars; Oakland, Cal, and Reno, Nev C of C's; fmr: gov, exec comm, treas, United Bay Area Crusade; dir: Fannie Wall Children's Home; ARC, Oakland; Boy Scouts of Amer, Oakland area; found mem, Inst Mgmt Cons. Contbr to bus jours. Recipient, Mgmt Cons Cert, 1969. Home: 3684 Happy Valley Rd, Lafayette, Cal. Office: POB 343, Lafayette, Cal.

KAHN, Shalom Jacob, Isr, teacher, author; b. NYC, Oct 5, 1918; s. Harry and Sophie (Begun); in Isr since 1950; BA, Columbia Coll, NY, 1938, MA, 1939, PhD, 1950; BHL, Sem Coll of J Studies, NY, 1950; m. Chava Gafni, Oct 11, 1951; c: Tamar, Uri. Sr lectr, Eng, Amer lit, Heb U since 1950; fmr: lectr, Sch of Gen Studies, Columbia U; instr, Bklyn Poly Inst; tutor, Queens Coll, NY. Sgt, USAAC, 1943-46. Author: Science and Aesthetic Judgment, 1953; Pioneering and Frontier Life in American Literature, in Heb, 1962; ed, A Whole Loaf: Stories from Israel; trans, Shaul Tchernichowsky: Poet of Revolt, 1968; hon fgn mem, ed bd, Jour of Aesthetics and Art Criticism; contbr numerous articles to learned publs. Mem: MLA; U Tchrs of Eng, Isr. Spec interest, trans modern Heb poetry. Home: 46 Nayoth St, Jerusalem. Office: Heb U, Jerusalem, Isr.

KAHN, Sidney, US, surgeon, educator; b. Paterson, NJ, Mar 30, 1913; s. Jacob and Bertha (Orleansky); BA, NYU, 1933, MD, 1937; m. Henrietta Berger, Aug 31, 1939; c: Barbara, Rhoda. Asso clinical prof, plastic surg, Mt Sinai Med Sch, since 1955; att plastic surg, Beth Isr Hosp, since 1946; cons, Nyack Hosp, since 1953; asst att plastic surg, Mt Sinai Hosp, since 1956; att plastic surg, Bx-Leb Hosp Cen, since 1958, plastic surg, NY State Rehab Hosp, W Haverstraw, NY, 1952-63; post-grad f, surg, NYU Coll of Med, 1939-40. Flight surg, US Army, 1942-46. F, Amer Coll Surgs, 1949; dipl: Amer Bd of Surg, 1949; Amer Bd of Plastic Surg, 1953; mem: AMA; Amer Soc for Plastic and Reconstructive Surg; NY State and Co Med Socs. Home: 361 Lewelen Circle, Englewood, NJ. Office: 102 E 78 St, New York, NY.

KAHN, Sol J, US, attorney; b. Chgo, Ill, Sep 28, 1908; s. Morris and Ida (Slate); LLB, U Wis, 1930; m. Miriam Posner, Dec 22, 1935; c: Sandra Davis, Judith Posner, Peggy. Partner, Meldman & Kahn; gen law practice since 1930. Chmn, Milw, Armed Services Council; dir: Milw JWF, since 1949, exec comm, 1952; dir, JWB, since 1955, bd of govs, exec comm, midwest div since 1956, mem, fund raising div comm, since 1958, natl chmn, biennial conv comm, 1956; pres, J Comty Cen of Milw, 1949-55; dir, NCCJ, Wis reg, 1962; mem, natl council: Pi Lambda Phi; JDC; USO and dir exec comm, Milw Co since 1955; trustee, Balzer-Schardt Scholarship Found; Cong Emanu-El B'nai Jeshurun, vice-pres; mem, regional adv, bd, ADL, 1960; mem: Navy League of US; Wis Consistory, Tripoli Temple; Milw, Amer, Wis Bar Assns; St Lawrence Seaway Celebration Comm; club, Brynwood Country, pres, 1962. Recipient: 20 yr service cert, Natl USO Council, 1962; Hon Blue Jacket citation, Gt Lakes Training Cen, 1962. Home: 7801 N Club Circle, Milwaukee, Wis. Office: 212 W Wisconsin Ave, Milwaukee, Wis.

KAHN, William, US, social worker; b. Pittsburgh, Pa, July 3, 1925; s. Joseph and Anna (Perlman); BA, U Pittsburgh, 1947, MSW, 1949; m. Shirlee Fink, Feb 25, 1951; c: Michael, Jane, Debby, Julie. Exec dir, J Comty Cens Assn since 1958, asst exec dir, Denver, 1955-58; asst prof, St Louis U Sch Social Service since 1963. Seaman, USN. Vice-pres, Natl Assn, J Cen Workers; chmn, prog, civil rights, Natl Assn, Social Workers; bd dirs: United Heb Temple; Health and Wfr Council, St Louis; Natl Conf, J Communal Service; adv bd, Sch J Communal Service; mem: AJCong; B'nai B'rith. Contbr to profsl jours. Home: 7111 Cornell, University City, Mo. Office: 11001 Schuetz Rd, St Louis, Mo.

KAHN, Wolf, US, artist, educator; b. Stuttgart, Ger, Oct 4, 1927; s. Emil and Nellie (Budge); in US since 1940; att, Hans Hofmann Sch of Fine Art, NY; BA, U Chgo, 1950; m. Emily Mason, Mar 13, 1957; c: Cecily, Melany. Instr, painting, Cooper Union, since 1960; visiting asso prof, U of Cal, Berkeley, 1960. Held numerous one-man shows; works represented in collections of many maj US mus. Seaman 1st class, USN, 1945-46. Recipient: Fulbright Grant; Guggenheim f. Studio: 813 Broadway, New York, NY.

KALB, S William, US, physician, educator; b. Newark, NJ, Nov 12, 1897; s. Morris and Bertha (Roth); BS, Valparaiso U, Ind, 1920, PhG, 1921; MD, Cincinnati Eclectic Med Sch, 1925; m. Amerlia Segal, May 2, 1926. Pvt practice since 1925; lectr and clinician, nutrition, NY Postgrad Med Sch, Columbia U, since 1938; endocrinology, since 1939; adj att phys, Beth Isr Hosp, Newark, since 1932; cons, nutrition, Clara Maass Memorial Hosp, Belleville, NJ, since 1963, chief, nutrition service, since 1957; cons: weight reducing modalities, PO Dept and Fed Trade Commn, since 1953; AMA Project, Vietnam, 1965-66; fmr: intern: Newark City Hosp, 1925; Wash Park Hosp, Chgo, 1926; Berwind Clinics, NY, 1926; res: Rotunda Hosp, Dublin, Ir, 1927; Allgemeines Krankenheim, Vienna, 1928; Frauenklinik, Berlin, 1928. Served, US Army MC, 1917-18. Pres: Amer Coll Nutrition, since 1959; Essex Co Med Soc, 1962-63; NJ Div, AJCong, 1936; chmn: comm, Future Phys Club, since 1959; communications and recruitment, AMA sub-comm; f: AMA; NJ Diabetic Assn; Natl Gastroenterological Assn; bd dirs, pres, Non-Sectarian Anti-Nazi League, 1937; mem: NJ Med Soc; Acad Med N NJ; NJ Gastroenterological Soc; Natl Eclectic Med Soc; pres, NJ Nutrition Council; The Endocrine Soc; Pan Amer Med Cong; Public Health Week for NJ, 1948; State Sect on Gastroenterology and Proctology, 1952-53; bd, Prospect Hill Country Day Sch, Newark, 1953; Marine Corps League; Amer Legion; Odd Fellows; Temple B'nai Jeshurun; nutrition adv: Newark chap, ARC, 1950; food and drug div, Natl Soc Security Agcy, 1954; comm, White House Conf on Aging, 1960; co-chmn, AMA Conf on Mh; volunteer phys, Vietnam, 1965-66; pres, Essex Co Blood Bank, 1966-68; natl surg-gen, JWV, 1937. Author: Anatomy and Nutrition, 1963; Calories to Burn, 1936; Your Future as a Physician, 1963; contbr to med jours. Home and office: 377 S Harrison St, East Orange, NJ.

KALIKOW, Nathan, US, business exec; b. Bklyn, NY, Sep 5, 1914; s. Joseph and Annie; grad, Sch of Bus Admn, NYU, 1936; DHum, Philathea Coll, Can, 1967; m. Marjorie Garfield, 1940; c: Randy, Richard. Chmn, Nassau Co Bridge Auth, since 1962; pres, Kalikow Realty and Construction Corp, since 1942. Found, Albert Einstein Coll of Med; dir: Life Line Cen for Child Devl; Home for the Aged of Riverdale; trustee, Iona Coll; mem: scholarship comm, Mayor's Comm on Scholastic Achievement, since 1966; bd advs, United Wheelchair Sports Fund, since 1966; Intl Temple, JF Kennedy Airport. Recipient: scroll of hon, Yeshiva U. Home: 201 Bay Blvd, Atlantic Beach, NY. Office: 97-45 Queens Blvd, New York, NY.

KALISH, Richard M, US, merchant; b. Kingston, NY, Sept 28, 1912; s. Morris and Lena (Affron); m. Dorothy Kaplan,1939; c: Joseph, Terry, Deborah. Gen mgr, secy, Kingston Laundry Corp, since 1935. Pres: Ulster County Safety Council, 1952-54; Temple Emanuel, 1948-50, bd trustees, 1950-54; B'nai B'rith, 1950, trustee, since 1951; bd trustees, Kingston Hosp, since 1959; chmn: UJA, 1967-68; Amer Cancer Soc, 1948, mem, bd dirs, since 1950; Bd Educ, since 1950; Red Cross Blood Bank, 1951; Cerebral Palsy, 1952, bd dirs, 1951-53; hosp campaign, Kingston Hosp; trustee, Jewish Comty Cen, since 1952; zone coordinator, B'nai B'rith, Hudson Valley, 1953-54; scoutmaster, 1940-44; mem, bd dirs: C of C, 1957-60; NY State Laundrymen Assn; mem: Northern Hosp Review and Planning Council of NY; Laundry Minimum Wage Bd, State of NY, 1953; AJComm; NY Guard, 1944; Masons; clubs: Lions, pres, 1960-61; Boys', pres, 1957-58. Recipient: Outstanding Citizen award, VFW; Man of the Year citation, Marine Corps League; Liberty Bell award, 1968; Kiwanis Layman award. Home: 45 Overlook Drive, Kingston, NY. Office: 83 Broadway, Kingston, NY.

KALJUSKI, Sima Simcha, Isr, engineer; b. Odessa, Russ, Nov 6, 1910; s. Mordechai and Anna (Kulin); in Isr since 1941; dipl, Acad of Music, Belgrade, Yugo; dipl, Ing, U Belgrade, 1934, post grad, Zurich, 1936; m. Hilda Frajer, Jan 3, 1937; c: Dan, Michal. Dir, Traffic Dept, Tel Aviv Munic, since 1951; cons engr, pvt practice, 1937-41; rd planning engr, Tel Aviv Munic, 1944-51. Prin contribs: laying fundamentals of traffic engr in Isr, Tel Aviv; traffic mgmt, planning, Tel Aviv; elec computer for regulating traffic signals; intl expert, cons. Mem assns: Engrs and Architects; Munic Engrs, Isr. Author, Traffic Engineering and Control; contbr to profsl jours. Hobby, violinist. Home: 3 Hashofet Nofech St, Tel Aviv, Isr. Office: Traffic Dept, Tel Aviv Munic, Isr.

KALLAI, Zecharia, Isr, technician, businessman, researcher; b. Vienna, Aus, June 24, 1923; s. Shalom and Ella (Herbster) Kleinmann; in Isr since 1934; NY Trade Sch, piano craft, NY, 1951-52; MA, Heb U, Jerusalem, 1954, PhD, 1963; m. Yona Yellin, 1948; c: David, Hanina, Eliezer, Thelma. Dir, shareholder, Kleinmann Pianos Ltd, since 1964; fmr partner, S Kleinmann, Pianos; fmr research f, Hebrew U; sr lectr, hist of Pal geog, Heb U, 1968-69. IDF, 1948-49. Author: The Northern Boundaries of Judah, 1960; The Tribes Of Israel, 1967, in Heb; contbr articles to sci jours, Ency Biblica. Recipient prizes: Klausner, Nathania munic, 1956; Ben-Zvi, Yad Ben-Zvi, 1968. Home: 25 Alharizi St, Jerusalem, Isr. Office: 2 Coresh St, Jerusalem, Isr.

KALLET, Arthur, US, business exec; b. Syracuse, NY, Dec 15, 1902; s. Barnett and Etta (Kaplan), BS, MIT, 1924; m. Opal Boston, Apr 27, 1927 (decd); c: Anthony; m. 2nd, Mary Renfer, Jan 28, 1954; c: Cynthia, Lisa. Exec dir, The Medical Letter since 1958; pres, Buyers Lab, Inc, since 1961; asst mgr, ed bur, NY Edison Co, 1924-27; staff mem, Amer Standards Assn, 1927-33; found, dir, Consumers Union of US, 1936-57. Author, Counterfeit, 1935; co-author, 100,000,000 Guinea Pigs, 1933. Home: 224 Broadview Ave, New Rochelle, NY. Office: 305 E 45 St, New York, NY.

KALLET, Herbert I, US, surgeon; b. Syracuse, NY, Mar 28, 1895; s. Mayer and Guila (Sakolski); BS, Syracuse U, 1915, MD, 1917; m. Mabel Bloomgarten, Oct 27, 1921; c: Maerit, Mary Kanner. Practicing proctologist since 1920; sr surg, dept of proctology, Harper Hosp, since 1945; att surg: Crittenden Gen Hosp, since 1946; Sinai Hosp, since 1953; asso prof, chmn, dept of proctology, Wayne State U, 1945, all Detroit. Capt, US Army MC, WW I. F: Amer Proctological Soc, vice-pres, 1934; Amer Coll of Surgs; Intl Acad of Med; Intl Coll of Surgs; dipl: Amer Bd of Surg; Amer Bd of Proctology; fmr pres, Temple Beth El, 1947-49, mem bd of trustees, 1939-53; mem: bd of dirs, Detroit Inst of Cancer Research, since 1952; exec bd, UAHC, 1948-50; Detroit Acad of Surg; Detroit Surg Soc; Detroit Execs Assn; clubs: Gt Lakes; The Bohemians; Circumnavigators. Ed, Transactions of Amer Proctologic Soc, 1934-37; contbr to med jours. Recipient: AB Graham award, Amer Proctologic Soc, 1952. Hobbies: gardening, photography. Home: 25845 Salem, Huntington Woods, Mich. Office: 651 Fisher Bldg, Detroit, Mich.

KALLMAN, Arthur, US, business exec; b. Reetz, Ger, Sep 17, 1893; s. Michaelis and Caroline (Ascher); in US since 1932; BS, Handels Hochschule U, Berlin, 1913; m. Sidonie Stein, Aug 15, 1920; c: Herbert, Erna; m. 2nd, Paula Nussbaum, Mar 6, 1951. Pres: Atlantis Import Distr Co since 1932; Original Beer Import Co since 1932; Ger Gen Elec, 1910-20; gen mgr, Stein Concern, 1920-32. Mem: Fgn Policy Assn; Acad Political Sci; Metrop Opera Guild; hon mem, Police Hon League. Home: 230 Riverside Drive, New York, NY. Office: 11 W 42 St, New York, NY.

KALMANOFF, Martin, US, pianist, composer, author; b. Bklyn, NY, May 24, 1920; s. Joseph and Anna (Mirin); MA, Harvard U, 1943; div. Owner, Opr Opera. Writer, composer for musical theater, including 15 operas; wrote: script, lyrics, music, The Victory at Massada, conducted World Premiere; words and music: The Four Poster; Young Tom Edison; concert songs sung: NBC and CBS TV and Radio; in concert by artists, including: Robert Merrill; Gladys Swarthout; Lucia Albanese; popular songs recorded by artists, including: Eddie Fisher; Steve Lawrence; Mario Lanza; Dean Martin; Robert Goulet; Tony Bennett; piano soloist and accompanist in numerous civic and comty concerts; numerous choral compositions, numerous piano pieces in print in field of educ music; lectr on opera. Mem, ASCAP. Contbr to music publs. Recipient, Robert Merrill Contest for Best One-Act Opera, 1950. Hobbies: tennis, squash. Home: 392 Central Park W, New York, NY.

KALNITSKY, George, US, biochemist, educator; b. Bklyn, NY, Oct 22, 1917; s. Harry and Fanny (Kalnitsky); BA, Bklyn Coll, 1939; PhD, Ia State Coll, 1943; m. Sylvia Duitch, Dec 25, 1940; c: Katherine, Carol, Robert. Prof, biochem, U of Ia Coll of Med, since 1957, fac mem since 1946; mem, Health Sci Advancement Award Rev Comm, NIH, 1967-69, 1969-71; research asso, instr: U Chgo, 1943; US Off of Sci Research and Devl, 1943-45; travelling f: Coll of Med, Oxford, Eng, 1956-57; Guggenheim f, Weizmann Inst of Sci, Isr, 1965-66. Chmn, Ia Sect, Amer Chem Soc, 1950; bd trustees, fmr pres, Cong Agudas Achim; mem: Amer Soc Biol Chem; Soc for Experimental Biol and Med; AAAS; NY Acad of Sci; Ia Acad of Sci; Sigma Xi; Phi Lambda Upsilon; Alpha Chi Sigma. Contbr to sci jours. Recipient, award of hon, Bklyn Coll, 1954. Hobby, photography. Home: 10 Lakeview Dr, RR1, Iowa City, Ia. Office: U of Ia Med Coll, Iowa City, Ia.

KALODNER, Harry E, US, jurist; b. Phila, Pa, Mar 28,1896; s. David and Ida (Miller); LLB, U of Pa, 1917; hon, DHL, Yeshiva U, 1950; m. Tillie Poliner, Dec 20, 1925; c: Philip, Howard. Judge, US Court of Appeals, 3rd Circuit, since 1946; fmr: staff mem, Phila N Amer, 1919-25; financial and political ed, Phila Record, 1929-35; secy of revenue, Commonwealth of Pa, 1935; judge: Court of Common Pleas, Phila Co, 1936-37; US Dist Court, E Pa, 1938-46. US Army, Judge Advocate Gen Dept, 1917-18. Vice-pres, Temple Beth Zion, since 1954; trustee, Yeshiva U, since 1954. Mem: Amer, Phila Bar Assns; Amer Judicature Soc; Brandeis Lawyers Soc; Amer Legion; clubs: Phila Lawyers; Socialegal. Recipient, hon mention in journalism, Pulitzer Prize Comm, 1931, 1932. Home: The Wellington, Philadelphia, Pa. Office: 2092 US Courthouse, Philadelphia, Pa.

KALTER, Albert, US, attorney, educator; b. NYC, Dec 27, 1936; s. Morris and Goldie (Wasser); BBA, CCNY, 1958; JD, magna cum laude, NY Law Sch, 1961; LLM, NYU, 1964; m. Brenda Kahane, Dec 24, 1966; d. Elana. Prof, taxation, Pace Coll, NYC since 1963; pvt practice, atty, CPA since 1963. Mem, Bd Educ, Manhattan Beach J Cen; Amer Bar Assn; Assn of Bar of NYC; NY Co Lawyers Assn; NY State Soc of CPAs; Natl Panel of Arbitrators, Amer Arbitration Assn. Contbr to legal jours. Recipient: Wessel Memorial Award, 1961; Elsberg Prize, 1961, both NY Law Sch; Award, Amer Arbitration Assn, 1970. Home: 1521 Brightwater, Brooklyn, NY. Office: 350 Broadway, New York, NY.

KALTER, Seymour S, US, researcher; b. NYC, Mar 19, 1918; s. Aaron and Jessie (Schulman); BS, St Joseph's Coll, Phila, Pa, 1940; MA, U Kan, 1943; PhD, Syracuse U, 1947; m. Gloria Verstein, Mar 3, 1946; c: Susan, Steven, Debra. Dir, div microbiol and infectious diseases, SW Found for Research and Educ, San Antonio, Tex, since 1966, chmn, dept, since 1967; adj prof, Trinity U, San Antonio, since 1966; with USPHS Res, since 1957; chief virus sect, Sch of Aerospace Med, Brooks Air Force Base, Tex, since 1960; cons: Pan Amer Sanitary Bur, WHO; Cologne U, Ger, Neur Inst; Lackland Air Force Base Hosp, Epidemiological Lab, since 1960; Natl Cancer Inst, NIH, Bethesda, Md; SW Found for Research, Educ, since 1960; lectr, dept virology and epidemiology, Baylor U Coll Med since 1960; cons, virology: U Tex Grad Sch Med; Robert Green Hosp, both since 1960; fmr: fac mem, SUNY, Upstate Med Cen, Syracuse, 1945-56; bact, chief, virology, Bur of Labs, City of Syracuse, NY, 1945-56; chief, virus diagnostic unit, Communicable Disease Cen, 1956-60; org: virus diagnostic lab, Natl Inst Hygiene, Caracas, Venezuela, 1959; diagnostic service, Neur Clinic, Cologne, Ger, 1960. Prin contrib: poliomyelitis vaccine field trials, 1954. F: AAAS; Amer Public Health Assn; mem: Boy Scouts; Little League coach; Amer Soc Microbiols; Acad Microbiol; Amer Assn Immunologists; NY Acad Sci; Soc for Experimental Biol and Med; Sigma Xi; Research Soc Amer; Amer Bd Microbiols; Tex Soc Microbiols; Tex Acad Sci; Tex Soc Electron Microscopy; Soc for Cryobiol; Resa; Wildlife Diseases Assn; bd trustees, Temple Beth El. Author: A Manual of Medical Virology, 1955; Procedures for Routine Laboratory Diagnosis of Virus and Rickettsial Diseases, 1963; contbr to profsl jours. Hobby, philately. Home: 1418 Haskin Dr, San Antonio, Tex. Office: POB 2296, San Antonio, Tex.

KALUGAI, Isaac, Isr, chemist, educator; b. Russ, Sep 20, 1888; s. Zvi and Hanna (Yourovsky) Kalujsky; in Isr since 1913; MSc, U Pittsburgh, 1922; m. Shulamith Ben Zvi, Aug 14, 1914. Prof em, Technion, Haifa; fmr: visiting prof, hist of chem, Heb U, Jerusalem; tchr, HS, Jerusalem; tchr, Reali Sch, Haifa. Turkish Army, 1916-1918; chem, Haganah. Mem: Amer Chem Soc, div of chem hist; Isr Chem Soc; Engrs and Architects Assn, Isr; Hist of Med and Natural Sci Soc, Isr. Author: Shiurey Chymiya, 1938; A Short History of Chemistry; Seven Metals; Book of Metals, 1960; contbr trans, articles, to Heb sci publs. Recipient: award, Isr Soc of Hist of Med and Sci, 1959. Spec interests: fiction, hist. Home: 41 Harlap St, Jerusalem, Isr.

KALUSIN, Carlos, Colombia, manufacturer; b. Czestochowa, Pol, Sep 15, 1908; s. Eliezer and Malka (Jakubowicz); in Colombia since 1924; m. Sarah Goldberg, Aug 29, 1940; c: Linda Szteinberg, Anita Brown. Found, Banco de la Costa, Corporacion del Norte and Exec Club, Barranquilla; found, J Comty, 1932, fmr, pres, mem bd; delg to WZCs and other J congs. Clubs: Centro Israelita Filantropico; Union; Country; Executive; Barranquilla. Home: Carrera 57 79-108, Barranquilla, Colombia. Office: POB 295, Barranquilla, Colombia.

KAMENKA, Eugene, Austr, philosopher, historian of ideas; b. Köln, Ger, Mar 4, 1928; s. Sergei and Nadja (Litvin); in Austr since 1937; BA, U Sydney, 1953; PhD, Austr Natl U, Canberra, 1957; m. Alice Erh-Soon Tay, Dec 18, 1964; c: Anat, Eri. Professorial f, Head, Hist of Ideas Unit, Research Sch of Social Sci, Austr Natl U, Canberra, since 1968, fac mem since 1962; fmr: cable sub-ed, chief fgn desk, Jerusalem Post; journalist, cable sub-ed, Sydney Morning Herald; lectr, phil, U Malaya, Singapore; visiting research worker, Fac of Phil, Moscow State U, Moscow; sr f, Research Inst on Communist Affairs, Columbia U, NY. Mem: Social Sci Research Council, Austr; Amer Soc for Legal and Political Phil; Austr Assn Phil; fmr mem, ZF, Austr and NZ. Author: The Ethical Foundations of Marxism, 1962; Marxism and Ethics, 1969; The Philosophy of Ludwig Feuerbach, 1970; The Portable Karl Marx, 1970; co-author, Marxism and The Theory of Law, 1970. Recipient, Academician, China Acad. Home: 233 La Perouse St, Red Hill, Canberra, Austr. Office: Australian Natl U, POB 4, Canberra, Austr.

KAMENY, Nat, US, business exec; b. NYC, Nov 6, 1923; s. Michel and Bessie (Sunshine); att CCNY, 1941-47; m. Ruth, Mar 27, 1942; c: Ellen, Leslie, Debra. Pres: Kameny Assos, Inc, advt/pr since 1947; Isr Communications, Inc. pr since 1968. US Army, Signal Corps, 1943-44. Vice-pres: U Haifa; found; JWC, Bergen Co; chmn: Comty Relations Council, Bergen Co; Arab Boycott Comm, ADL; mem: exec comm, ADL; Natl Civil Rights Comm; Natl PR Adv Comm, JWF Council; Boycott Subcomm, Conf of Pres of Maj Amer J Orgs; secy, Photography for Youth Found; Amer Assn Advt Agcys, natl chap; B'nai B'rith, N Valley, NJ chap; ZOA, Bergen, NJ Dist; fmr pres, League of Advt Agcys. Hobbies: photography, hist documents. Home: 85 Thames Blvd, Bergenfield, NJ. Office: 110 E 59 St, New York, NY.

KAMHI, Hajim, Yugo, economist, civil servant; b. Visegrad, Yugo, June 12, 1899; s. David and Ester (Levi); dipl, Hochschule fur Welthandel, Vienna, 1923; DEcon and Commercial Sci, U of Trieste, 1926. Head councillor, admn and legal dept, Town People's Comm, Sarajevo, since 1954; fmr: mgr, pvt import enterprise, 1938-41, head, depts, Min of Commerce

and Supplies, Min for State Procurements, Council for Educ, all People's Rep of Bosnia and Herzegovina, 1952-54. In It concentration camp 1941-43; partisan, Tito's Army, 1943-45. Exec Mem, vice-pres, J Comty, Sarajevo, since 1945, fmr pres; exec mem, Fed of J Comty Yugo, 1945-69. Author: La sistematisazione dei rapporti giuridici privati tra l'Italia e la Jugoslavia, 1926; contbr to profsl jours. Recipient: titles: econ, 1948; higher econ, 1950; councillor econ, 1953. Home: Slavise Vajnera Cice, 14/III, Sarajevo, Yugo.

KAMHI, Samuel, Yugo, jurist, educator; b. Visegrad, June 18, 1904; s. David and Ester (Levi); att U Paris, 1924-26; LLD, Law Fac, Zagreb, 1931; m. Nada Pudar, June 18, 1946; c: Ljubica, David. Prof, Law Fac, Sarajevo since 1949, fmr, pro-rector; legal adv, People's Assembly of People's Rep of Bosnia and Herzegovina since 1945; mem, comm to draw Constitution of People's Rep of Bosnia and Herzegovina, 1961, 1963; mem, educ council, Peoples Rep since 1959; fmr: court judge; head, legal dept, Presidency of Govt of Bosnia and Herzegovina. War prisoner, Ger, WW II. Vice chmn, Assn U Profs, Sarajevo; chmn, U comm, Alliance of Communists of Yugo; pres, mutual aid fund, Law Fac, Sarajevo; secy, La Benevolencija; first secy, Sloboda, J cultural and educ soc; mem clubs: U Profs, Sarajevo; Esperanza, fmr pres. Author: Civil Law Procedure, 1951, 2nd ed, 1957, 3rd ed, 1961, 4th ed, 1967; Execution Prodecure, 1963, 2nd ed, 1966; Cognito extraordinaria, 1968; chief ed, memorial volume marking 400th anniversary of arrival of Jews in Bosnia and Herzegovina; Sephardim and Sephardic Foment, pamphlet; contbr to mags. Home: Saloma Albaharija 2/1 Sarajevo, Yugo. Office: U of Sarajevo, Yugo.

KAMINETSKY, Joseph, US, educational admnr, educator; b. NYC, Nov 15, 1911; s. Simon and Fannie (Novilensky); BA, magna cum laude, Yeshiva Coll, 1932; MA, Tchrs Coll, Columbia U, 1940, EdD 1944; m. Selma Lefkowitz, June 23, 1940; c: Nehama, David, Judah, Phyllis, Susan. Natl dir, Torah Umesorah, NYC since 1946; educ dir, J Cen, NYC, 1934-46; asso prof, educ, Grad Sch of Educ, Yeshiva U, 1955-60, head, rel educ dept, 1960. Mem: educ commn, RabCA; Natl Council for J Educ; Sinai Fraternal Order, Hapoel Hamizrachi; fmr: pres, Yeshiva Coll Alumni Assn; natl vice-pres: Hapoel Hamizrachi Amer; Rel ZOA. Co-ed, The Model Program of the Talmud Torah, 1942. Recipient, awards: Mordecai Ben David, 1941; Dr Bernard Revel Memorial, 1957, both Yeshiva U; Young Isr Inst, 1958. Home: 1466 54 St, Brooklyn, NY. Office: 156 Fifth Ave, New York, NY.

KAMINI, Abraham, Isr, public servant; b. Brazlav, Ukraine, 1894; s. Moshe and Breine; in Isr since 1920; m. Rachel Paliatschik (decd); c: Ziva, Hayuta. Mem, Tel Aviv City, Council, since 1950, dir, Halva'a Vehisahon, Tel Aviv; fmr, clerk under Mayor Dizengoff, Tel Aviv Munic. Delg, Zionist Congs; mem: bd dirs: Davar, daily; Am Oved, pub co; fmr, mem: directorate, JNF; Shalom Aleichem House; Bialik House. Author: BeLev va Nefesh, 1968. Home: 11 Sderot Ben Zion, Tel Aviv, Isr. Office: POB 151, Jerusalem, Isr.

KAMINKA, Gideon, Isr, architect; b. Vienna, Aus, July 30, 1904; s. Armand and Clara (Loewi); in Isr since 1930; Ing DArch, Tech U, Vienna; m. Josefine Fischer, Jan 3, 1939; c: Michal Katznelson. Pvt practice since 1933. Maj works, design of homes for elderly people, parents homes, bldgs for aged immigrants; fmr, various functions; mem, Haifa Munic. Mem: Engrs and Architects Assn, Isr; Intl Fed for Housing and Planning. Contbr to profsl jours. Hobby, Modern Lit. Home and office: 74 Hatishbi St, Haifa, Isr.

KAMINSKY, Jack, US, educator; b. NYC, Mar 19, 1922; s. Rubin and Lena (Goldstein); BS, CCNY, 1943; MA, NYU, 1947, PhD, 1950; m. Alice Richkin, Oct 11, 1947; c: Eric. Prof, phil, Harpur Coll, since 1961, fac mem since 1953; instr, U Akron, 1950-51; instr, CUNY, 1952-53. US Army, 1943-46. Mem, Amer Phil Soc; club, Creighton Phil, pres, 1961-62. Author: Hegel on Art, 1962; Language and Ontology, 1969; co-author, Logic and Language, 1956; contbr to phil jours. Recipient: scholarship award, Amer Council Learned Soc, 1951-52; dist research f, SUNY, 1967. Home: 53 Church St, Cortland, NY. Office: Harpur Coll, Binghamton, NY.

KAMINSKY, Martin Ira, US, attorney; b. NYC, Aug 6, 1941; s. Leon and Beatrice (Bezahler); BA, Yale U, 1962; LLB, Harvard Law Sch, 1965. Partner: Pollack & Singer since 1970; Wachtell, Manheim & Group since 1965. Mem, bd govs, St Elmo Soc Inc. Home: 370 First Ave, New York, NY. Office: 111 Broadway, New York, NY.

KAMINSKY, Nathan, US, public official; b. NYC, Nov 28, 1903; s. Jacob and Anna (Sandbank); LLB, St John's U Law Sch, 1928; m. Hilda Neufeld, Apr 10, 1932; c: Seth, Merle Brown. Asst corp counsel, since 1947; i/c Bklyn, Queens and Richmond brs, condemnation div, Law Dept, NYC, since 1958; i/c, all condemnation trials, Bklyn, Queens and Richmond boroughs, since 1958; trial atty, acquisition; housing projects, schs, parks, express ways and other public improvements, since 1950; lectr, Practising Law Inst. Mem: Bklyn Bar Assn; Progressive Syn. Home: 1160 E 5 St, Brooklyn, NY. Office: Munic Bldg, Brooklyn, NY.

KAMSLER, Harold M, US, rabbi; b. NYC, Dec 10, 1911; s. Samuel and Annie (Levy); BA, NYU, 1932, MA, 1935; ordained rabbi, JIR, 1936; m. Etta Seymans, Dec, 5, 1937; c: Joel, David. Rabbi, exec-dir: J Comty Cen, Norristown, Pa since 1943; Hillside Hollis Heb Cen, LI, 1936-43; instr, sociol, NYU, 1933-37. Co-chmn, natl youth commn and mem, natl bd, United Syn of Amer; mem: RA; Natl Assn of J Cen Workers; ZOA; B'nai B'rith. Contbr to J periodicals. Home: 1800 Pine St, Norristown, Pa. Office: J Comty Center, Norristown, Pa.

KANAAN Haviv, Isr, journalist; b. Kuty, Pol. Apr 27, 1913; s. David and Malwina (Pistyner) Krumholz; in Isr since 1935; att: Sch of Journalism, Warsaw; Heb U; m. Malka Majzlic; c: Sima, David. Ed staff, Ha'aretz daily, since 1944; fmr: police off, 1936-44; press off, Isr Police, 1948-49; Author: Swastika Over Palestine, 1946; British Withdrawal, 1958; The Nazi 5th Column in Palestine, 1968; The Fighting Press, 1969. Pres, Isr sect, Intl Assn, Journalists, Writers on Tourism; chmn: profsl comm, Isr Journalists Assn; Mil Corresps Assn; exec comm, J Ex-Policemen's Assn. Home: 21 Margolin St, Tel Aviv, Isr. Office: 56 Maze St, Tel Aviv, Isr.

KANAEL, Baruch, Isr, historian, educator; b. Wiesbaden, Ger, Aug 12, 1921; s. Zvi and Ziporah (Kagan) Kanel; MA, Heb U, Jerusalem, 1949; PhD, 1967. Asso prof, J Hist, U of Judaism, LA, Cal, since 1969; dir, preliminary survey, Ancient J Rel Univ, since 1968; lectr, hist dept, Bar Ilan U, Ramat Gan, 1962-69; visiting lectr, Free U, Berlin, 1968; led expedition to explore ancient syns, Galilee, Golan Hgts. Capt, hon, Mil Govt, 1949. Mem: Archaeol Inst of Amer; Amer Numismatic Soc. Author: Die Kunst der Antiken Synagoge, 1961; Literaturbericht zur Altjudischen Munzkunde, 1967; The Macabbean Period in the Light of Coinage, 1970; contbr numerous papers, articles. Recipient: awards: 1st Klausner, Nathanya Munic, 1949; Numismatic, Oxford U; 1st Kadman, 1968; fs: Oxford U, 1952; J Comm, Upsala, Swed, 1954; U of Rome, 1959. Home: 26 Zfania St, Jerusalem, Isr. Office: Hebrew U, Jerusalem, Isr.

KANE, Irving, US, business cons, attorney; b. Kiev, Russ, Jan 24, 1908; s. Aaron and Clara (Blazar); in US since 1913; BA, W Reserve U, 1928, Law Sch, 1930; hon LHD; HUC, 1964; m. Adeline Faller, June 26, 1932; c: Kathie Kraft, Bonnie Raffel. Attorney, pvt practice, since 1930; chmn bd, Globe Capital Corp, since 1967. Pres: CJFWF, 1959-62; JCC, Cleveland, 1950-52; vice-pres: J Comty Fed; AJCong, 1956-58; chmn: Amer-Isr Pub Affairs Comm, since 1968; J Comty Relations Comm, 1947-50; Natl Comty Relations Adv Counc, 1949-53; Amer J Tercentenary, 1954; bd govs, AJ Comm; bd dirs: Amer Ort Fed; Amer Friends of Heb U; Admn Comm of JDC; bd trustees, Brandeis U, since 1960; mem: natl cabinet, UJA, since 1961; City of Cleveland Comty Relations Bd, 1950-61; Natl Comm of Voluntary Health and Wfr, 1962; exec council, Amer J Hist Soc; clubs: Oakwood; Commerce; Harmonie, NY. Recipient: dist citizenship award, Fed J Women's Orgs of Cleveland, 1954; gold cert of merit, JWV, US, 1952; Haym Solomon Award of Del, 1962; Eleanor Roosevelt Hum Award, 1964; dist citizen award, UA, Cleveland, 1968. Home: 13800 Shaker Heights Blvd, Cleveland, Ohio.

KANEE, Sol, Can, business exec; b. Melville, Sask, June 1, 1909; s. Sam and Rose (Lercher); BA, U Man, 1929; LLB, U Sask, 1932; m. Florence Barish, Apr 10, 1935; c: Stephen. Asso, Thompson Dilts and Co; pres: Soo Line Mills Ltd; Milling Producs, Chatham, Ont; dir: Bank of Can; Ind Devl Bank; Kipp Kelly; Kanee Grain Co; fmr, with law firms: Kanee and Deroche; Shinbane, Dorfman and Kanee. Maj, Royal Can Artillery, 1940-45. Chmn exec, CJC; pres, United Way of Gtr Winnipeg; chmn bd, Royal Winnipeg Ballet; fmr pres, Comty Wfr Planning Council. Club, Glendale Golf and Country. Home: 122 Ash St, Winnipeg, Can. Office: 7 Higgins Ave, Winnepeg, Can.

KANEV, Itzhak, Isr, social insurance expert; b. Melitopol, Russ, Apr, 1896; s. Abraham and Sara; in Isr since 1919; att. U Simferapol, Crimea; U Vienna; postgrad studies, Eng; MA, Sch Econs and Law, Tel Aviv, 1955. Ret; dir, Kupat Holim Health Inst until 1966; found, dir, Social Research Inst of Histadrut since 1947; fmr: agric worker, Pal; mem, Tel Hai Defense Group; lectr, Sch of Law and Econs, Tel Aviv; chmn, inter-ministerial comm on social ins, Govt of Isr; MK; chmn, inter-min planning comm for gen health ins in Isr; lectr: UNO Sem for ME countries, Athens; ILO Tech Assistance Sem for training sr social ins mgrs, New Delhi, India. Mem, Intl Comm for Social Security Experts, ILO since 1962; fmr: mem, exec vice pres, Council of Intl Social Security Assn, 1928-1967; also, chmn perm finance comm; delg, ILO Conf. Author: What is Social Insurance, 1932; Unemployment Insurance, 1933; Social Insurance in Palestine, Problems and Achievements, 1942; The Beveridge Plan, 1943; Population Problems and Social Security, 1944; Social Insurance Plan for the State of Israel, 1948; Social Insurance Plan for Israel, report, 1950; Social Insurance—From Planning to Legislation; Population and Society in the World and in Israel, 1957; The Plan for General Health Insurance in Israel, 1959; Society in Israel and Social Planning, all in Heb; in Eng: Social Insurance in Palestine and its Reconstruction, 1946; Social Policy and Social Insurance in Palestine, 1942, 2nd ed, 1944, 3rd, ed, 1947; Methods of Medical Care, 1947; Mutual Aid and Social Medicine in Israel, 1957, 3rd ed, 1960, also in Fr; Social and Demographic Development and the Shape of Poverty in Israel; contbr to local press and fgn jours. Recipient: Isr Prize for Social Scis, 1962. Home: 16 Bar Kochba St, Tel Aviv, Isr. Office: POB 16250, Tel Aviv, Isr.

KANEV, Phillip Sydney, US, dentist; b. Phila, Pa, Nov 15, 1912; s. Carl and Celia (Hochbaum); att Temple U, Phila, Pa, 1929-30; DDS, Temple U, Dent Sch, 1934; m. Rita Jacobs, June 5, 1941; c: Arthur, Donald. Pvt practice, oral reconstruction, since 1934; chief, Temporomandibular Jt Sect, Albert Einstein Med Cen since 1952; guest lectr, Temple U Dent Sch, Phila, 1952-68. Capt, US Army, Dent Corps, 1942-45. Area chmn, Cen City Dents, AJA-IEF; f, Intl Coll Dents; mem: Amer Prosthedontic Soc; Amer Equilibration Soc; SAAD Anesthesia; Phila Co Dent Soc; Pa State Dent Soc; Amer Dent Assn; E Dent Soc; Allied J Appeal; Temple Dent Alumni Assn; Brandeis Asso; Alpha Omega; Mason; clubs: Mens, Temple Beth Zion-Beth Isr, past pres; City of Hope; Sportsman, past pres; Phila Dent Study; Phila Clinic. Contbr to dent jours. Hobbies: sailing, fishing, photography. Home and office: 2029 Delancey Pl, Philadelphia, Pa.

KANFER, Irma (pen name: Irène Kanfer), Fr, author; b. Buczacz, Pol, Nov 24, 1919; s. Mozes and Gizela (Stern); in Fr since 1938; political econ deg, Political Econ Sch, Warsaw, 1937; MA: Sorbonne, 1940, U Geneva, 1945; div; c: Gisela Abrahamer. Writer, trans, journalist; fmr war corresp, Pol, J press, Pol. Author: Two Consonances; On the Milky Way; The Sleeping Sand-Glass; The Shattering Lute; Forebeing; Fr anthol of poetry of the ghettos and concentration camps; art, lit critic, Unzer Schtimme Mag; contbr to press, mags. Mem, Union des Ecrivains; fmr secy, Polonia, student org, Switz. Recipient, Prix Guillaume Appolinaire, 1966. Spec interests: hist, music, phil, theol, artistic dance. Home: 35 Gabriel Teri Ave, Vincennes, Fr.

KANIGSBERG, Robert Abe, Can, barrister; b. Hempstead, NY; July 7, 1909; s. Moses and Hannah (Simon); in Can since 1915; BA, Dalhousie U, NS, 1930, LLB, law sch, 1933; Q.C, 1950; m. Margo; c: Martin, Nordau. Pvt law practice since 1933. Vice chmn, Point Pleasant Park Commn; mem: bd, NS Coll of Art and Design; Can Bar Soc; Assn of Bar of NYC; natl exec, ZOC; Halifax Sym Soc; Bar Ilan U; Heb U; NS Bird Soc; NS Salmon Anglers Assn; fmr: pres: NS Barristers Soc; Shaar Shalom Cong; chmn, Isr Bond Campaign; vice pres, Halifax Wfr Council; clubs: Oakfield Country Golf, Halifax, found mem, Atlantic Sports Car. Contbr to legal jours. Recipient, Negev Testimonial Dinner, JNF, 1957. Home: 6137 Inglis St, Halifax, Can. Office: 106 Roy Bldg, Halifax, Can.

KANNAI, Yakar Israel, Isr, scientist; b. Tel Aviv, Oct 27, 1942; s. Gershon and Margit (Reiner); BSc, MSc, PhD, summa cum laude, Heb U, Jerusalem; m. Ruth Schlesinger, Aug 17, 1965; c: Elieser, Abraham. Lectr, math dept, Heb U since 1969; fmr: mem, Inst for Advanced Study, Princeton, NJ, 1968; visiting lectr: U of Cal, Berkeley; NY Inst for Math Scis, both 1969. Pvt, IDF, 1964-67. Contbr to math jours. Hobby, music.

Home: 36 Harlap St, Jerusalem, Isr. Office: Heb U, Jerusalem, Isr.

KANNER, Aaron M, US, attorney; b. Orlando, Fla, Dec 15, 1905; s. Harry and Rachael (Leibovitz); LLB, U of Fla, 1927; m. Marcella Seiden, Sep 29, 1929; c: Richard, Lewis. Pvt practice since 1927. USCG Res. Mem: Pres Council, Gtr Miami J Fed, fmr pres; Grand Council, Tau Epsilon Phi Frat, pres, alumni group, State of Fla; adv council, AJComm, bd trustees; trustee: Mt Sinai Hosp, Miami Beach; Temple Isr; J Home for the Aged; J Bur of Educ; campaign comm, CJA, 1954; Fla Bar Assn; Shriners; club, U Fla Alumni. Home: 32 Shore Dr, N Bay Heights, Miami, Fla. Office: 904 City Natl Bank Bldg, Miami, Fla.

KANNER, Israel Zwi, Isr, educator; b. Tlumac, Pol, June 9, 1907; s. Yehoshua and Bluma (Haber); in Isr since 1939; PhD, U Vienna, 1932; ordained rabbi, Rabb Sem, Vienna, 1933; m. Miriam Gutter, July 11, 1943; c: Dan, Yoram, Micha. Lectr, Tel Aviv U; tchr, HS. Author: Joseph Trumpeldor, 1939; Sarah Aronson, 1939; History, from Antiquity to Our Days; Curios and Anecdotes in History; other books on hist, Talmud, educ, 1956-68. Home: 10 Struck St, Tel Aviv, Isr.

KANNER, Leo, US, psychiatrist, educator; b. Klekotow, Aus, June 13, 1894; s. Abraham and Klara (Reisfeld); in US since 1924; MD, Friedrich Wilhelms U, Berlin, 1919; m. June Lewin, Feb 11, 1921; c: Anita Gilbert, Albert. Prof em, child psycht, Johns Hopkins U since 1959, fac mem since 1932; lectr, McCoy Coll, U dept, adult educ since 1949; hon cons, child psycht, Johns Hopkins Hosp since 1959, dir, children's psycht clinic, 1930-59; asst, Charité Hosp, 1920-23; pvt practice, 1921-23, both Berlin; sr asst phys, Yankton State Hosp, SD, 1924-28; Commonwealth Fund f, psycht, 1928-30; cons psycht, Juvenile Court of Baltimore, 1930-41; visiting lectr: Dalhousie U, NS, 1937; U Mich, 1945; U Minn, 1946; U of Tex, 1951; Mt Sinai Hosp, NYC, 1956; Kemper Knapp dist visiting prof, U of Wis, 1956; visiting prof, psycht: U Minn, 1959-60; Stanford U, 1961; lectured: US; Can; Mexico; Eng; Switz. Prin contribs: established first children's psycht unit in connection with a ped dept, Johns Hopkins Hosp, 1930, now a prin intl teaching cen in child psycht; was first to describe early infantile autism, 1943. F: Amer Psycht Assn, chmn, sect child psycht, 1942-43; Amer Assn Mental Deficiency; Amer Orthopsycht Assn; Amer Acad Child Psycht; hon asso f, Amer Acad Ped; asso examiner, Amer Bd Neur and Psycht, 1941-49; mem, bd dirs: J Family and Children's Soc; Child Study Cen of Med, 1937-44; League for Emotionally Disturbed Children; mem, adv bd: Woods Schs, Langhorne, Pa; Devereux Schs, Devon, Pa; Cove Sch, Racine, Wis; Amer Child Guidance Found; mem: research adv comm, Natl Assn for Retarded Children; exec comm, Children's Guild, Baltimore; corresp mem, Deutsche Vereinigung für Kinderpsychiatrie. Mem: Hist of Sci Soc; Assn for Hist of Med; AAAS; Amer Epilepsy Soc; Md and Baltimore City Med Soc; AAUP; Md Ped Soc; Johns Hopkins Med Soc; Md Psycht Soc, pres 1957-58; hon mem: Phi Beta Kappa, Alpha chap, Md; hon pres, 4th intl Cong, Child Psycht, Lisbon, 1958. Mem, ed bd: Amer Jour of Psycht; Nervous Child; Jour of Child Psycht; Quarterly Jour of Child Behavior; Jour of Clinical and Experimental Psychopath; Quarterly Rev of Psycht and Neur; Archives of Criminal Psychodynamics; Zeitschrift für Kinderpsychiatrie; Jour of Child Psycht and Psych, London. Hon lectureships: Elterich Memorial, Pittsburgh, 1957; Maudsley, Royal Medico-Psych Assn, London, 1958; Karen Horney Assn for Advancement of Psychoan, NY, 1959; Charles Lambert Memorial, NY, 1959. Author: Folklore of the Teeth, 1928; Judging Emotion from Facial Expression, 1931; Child Psychiatry, 1935, 3rd ed, 1957; In Defense of Mothers, 1941; A Miniature Textbook of Feeblemindedness, 1949; A Word to Parents about Mental Hygiene, 1957; A History of the Care and Study of the Mentally Retarded, 1964; contbr to profsl publs. Recipient: award, Assn for Help of Retarded Children, 1954; first annual award, Org for Mentally Ill Children, 1960; Stanley R Dean award, Fund for Behavioral Scis, 1965; Hillcrest Children's Cen award, 1965; named in his hon: Instituto Kanner Neuropsiquietrìa, Infantil, Porto Alegre, Brazil; Prof Dr Kanner Sch, for emotionally disturbed children, U of Leiden, Netherlands; Leo Kanner Comty Div, Devereux Sch, Devon, Pa. Spec interest, hist of med. Home and office: 4510 Wentworth Rd, Baltimore, Md.

KANOF, Abram, US, pediatrician; b. Russ, Dec 25, 1903; s. Feibe and Miriam (Weil); in US since 1904; MD, LI Coll, 1928; m. Frances Pascher, June 28, 1931; c: Elizabeth Levine,

Margaret Norden. Prof, SUNY Downstate Med Cen since 1966; att ped: U Hosp; Bklyn J Hosp; J Chronic Disease Hosp; cdr, USN MC, 1942-46. Chmn, Judaica Comm, J Mus of NY; bd overseers, JTSA; co-chmn, Civil War Centennial, Natl J Commn, 1961-65; mem, LI Hist Soc; fmr mem; Ped Adv Bd, Dept of Health, NYC; Med Adv Bd, Natl Tay-Sachs Assn. Contbr, films on research studies; articles to med and gen jours. Spec interest, J ceremonial art. Home: 500 E 77 St, New York, NY. Office: 450 Clarkson Ave, Brooklyn, NY.

KANOTOPSKY, Harod B, US, rabbi, educator; b. Bklyn, NY, Mar 3, 1923; s. Meyer and Ester (Kaminsky); BA, Yeshiva Coll, NY; ordained rabbi, Yeshiva U; m. Roslyn Wenger, June 25, 1944; c: Zipora Meier, Judith, Josef. Instr in Talmud, Yeshiva U since 1944; rabbi, Young Isr of W Hempstead; rel guidance counselor, Yeshiva U HS; fmr rabbi, Young Isr of E Pkwy. Mem: exec: RabCA; Mizrachi Org; active: Yavneh Students Org; Rabb Council of Young Isr; mem: Rel Guidance Comm of Yeshiva U; Rel Zionists, W Hempstead. Author, Rays of Jewish Splendor, 1956; contbr to J publs. Home: 692 Hempstead Ave, West Hempstead, NY. Office: 630 Hempstead Ave, West Hempstead, NY.

KANOWITZ, Leo, US, educator; b. NYC, Feb 27, 1926; s. Morris and Jennie (Tirkeltaub); AB, CCNY, 1947; JD, U of Cal, Berkeley, 1960; LLM, Columbia U, 1966, JSD, 1966; m. Elizabeth Belflower; c: Carrie. Prof, law, Sch of Law, U of NM, since 1964; atty at law, Hyman & Kanowitz, 1961-64. US Army, 1944. Author: California Civic Procedure Forms Manual, 1967; Women and the Law: The Unfinished Revolution, 1969. Home: 1731 Notre Dame, NE, Albuquerque, NM. Office: Sch of Law, U of NM, Albuquerque, NM.

KANTER, Albert L, US, business exec; b. Baronovici, Russ, Apr 13, 1897; s. Henry and Ida (Mirsky); in US since 1910; m. Rose Ehrenreich, Dec 16, 1917; c: Hal, William, Saralea Emerson. Chmn bd: Gilberton Co (Can) Ltd; Elliot Publishing, both since 1940; dir: Keyes-Urquhart, since 1957; Bank Adanim, Tel Aviv, Isr; Brager & Co since 1961. Pres, B'nai B'rith, 1958-60; treas: Boys Town, Jerusalem since 1955; Sutton Pl Syn since 1948; dir, Manhattan div, State of Isr Bonds since 1960; vice-pres, Intl Syn since 1960; mem: KP; Masons. Home: 239 E 79 St, New York, NY. Office: 101 Fifth Ave, New York, NY.

KANTER, Carl Irwin, US, attorney; b. Jersey City, NJ, Feb 17, 1932; s. Morris and Beatrice (Wilson); AB, Harvard Coll, 1953; LLB, Harvard Law Sch, 1956; m. Gail Herman, Nov 27, 1964; c: Deborah, David, Andrew. Partner, Strook & Strook & Lavan, since 1968, asso since 1959. US Army, 1956-58. Contbr to legal jours. Recipient, Detur Prize, Harvard Coll, 1950. Hobby, music. Home: 4 Green Acres Lane, White Plains, NY. Office: 61 Broadway, New York, NY.

KANTER, Isaac, US, psychiatrist, author; b. Kolomyja, Pol, Apr 18, 1908; s. Israel and Chaje (Weinraub); in US, since 1951; MD, German U of Prague, Czech, 1935; m; c: Marek. Staff psycht: Coney I Hosp, Bklyn, NY; S Oaks Hosp, Amityville, 1958-66; sr psycht, Harlem Valley State Hosp, 1951-58; fmr, sr asst, Neur Clinic, Lodz, Pol. Contbr: articles in Yiddish: The Jewish Wit; The Constitution and National Character; The German Anthropology and the Jews; The Jewish Bio-Pathological Types; The Jewish Character and the Jewish Fate; contbr on psychic aberrations in ghettos and German death camps to mags; The Delayed Type of Double-Bind, 1965. Mem: NY State Med Assn; Kings Co Med Soc; Amer Psycht Assn; Union of J Writers and Journalists, Pol; Assn of J Jounalists and Writers, Fr; club, PEN, NY. Home: 2650 Ocean Parkway, Brooklyn, NY. Office: 2320 Grand Concourse, Bronx, NY.

KANTER, Joseph H, US, real estate dev; b. Tarrant, Ala, Nov 15, 1923; s. Harry and Sylvia (Klein); att: U of Ala; Georgetown U, Wash DC; m. Nancy Reed, July 26, 1953; c: Harry, Hilary, Mary, John. Pres: Airo-Jet Ind City, Miami, Fla; BMR Inds Inc; Forest Park Realty; Hilary Farms; Intl Bancorporation, The Kanter Corp; Joseph H Kanter Found; Kanter Farms; Park Farms; Southwestern Leasing, all in Cincinnati; Kank Adv, Miami; chmn of bd: ITI, NY; Savings Financial, Livermore, Cal; vice-pres: Essex House; Essex Devl, all in Indianapolis; Forest Park; dir: Forest Park Nursing Home; Housing Corp of Amer; Keating, Inc, all in Cincinnati; partner: Cerberus Assos, NY; Towne House. Pres: Amer Friends of Tel Aviv U, since 1968; dir: AJComm, since 1961; JWB, Cincinnati, since 1963; Amer

Comm for Weizmann Inst of Sci, since 1966; O Council on Econ Educ, since 1966; Amer Friends of Heb U, 1966; fmr chmn: Christmas Seal Campaign, Anti-TB League, Cincinnati; natl Young Leadership Cabinet of UJA, 1963-65; State of Isr Bonds Dr, 1966; Cincinnati Comm, O Council on Educ, 1966; natl Isr Educ Fund, UJA, 1967; natl UJA, since 1967; leading gifts, JWF, Cincinnati, 1967; fmr post cmdr, Amer Legion; asso, Brandeis U; trustee, United Isr Appeal, since 1966; mem: Masons; Young Presidents' Assn; JWV, US; B'nai B'rith; The Pres Club; gov body, J Comty Relations Comm; exec comm, UJA, since 1964; Bus Leadership Adv Council, OEO, since 1967; adv bd, JNF Council of Cincinnati. Home: 1651 Waycross Rd, Cincinnati, O. Office: 690 Northland Rd, Cincinnati, O.

KANTER, Manuel A, US, chemist; b. Boston, Mass, Jan 18, 1924; BS, Northeastern U, Boston, 1944; PhD, Ill Inst of Tech, 1955; m. Madelyne Schaffner, June 22, 1948; c: Joel, Daniel, Joanne, Deborah. Asso chem, Argonne Natl Lab since 1949, on staff since 1946. USN, 1944-46. Prin contribs: research in solid state sci; specialties, high temperature; lattice defects; graphite; nuclear material safeguards. Pres, PTA council, Oak Park; mem: Amer Phys Soc; Sci Research Soc of Amer. Contbr to profsl jours. Hobby, scouting. Home: 900 N Lombard Ave, Oak Park, Ill. Office: POB 299, Lemond, Ill.

KANTOR, Joseph L, US, business exec; b. Wash, DC, Jan 13, 1915; s. Jacob and Dora (Caplan); att William and Mary Coll, Norfolk, Va, 1931-33; LLB, George Wash U, Wash, DC, 1936; m. Hannah Schreiber, Mar 17, 1938; c: Jacob, Myron, Rona. Pres, gen mgr, Broudy-Kantor Co Inc since 1937; fmr, pvt law practice. Mem: Masons; clubs: Lafayette Yacht; Unity; fmr: pres: Cong Beth El, Norfolk Va; Norfolk J Cmty Council; Norfolk Lodge, B'nai Brith; chmn: UJF; Isr Bond Dr; org, mem bd, Natl Candy Wholesalers Assn. Home: 511 Brackenridge Ave, Norfolk, Va. Office: 1021 E Princess Anne Rd, Norfolk, Va.

KANTOR, Samuel, Isr, engineer; b. Bialistok, Pol, Jan 15, 1923; s. Abraham and Perla (Vilenski); in Isr since 1934; dipl Ing, Technion, Haifa, 1948; m. Debora Abovitz, Nov 15, 1949; c: Abraham, Shai. Dep dir gen-engr Mekoroth Water Co Ltd since 1968, chief engr, since 1961; head planning dept, Tahal, 1952-61. Dir, mem comm, Intl Commn Irrigation and Drainage. Author: Strength of Materials, 1946; Water Installations in Buildings, 1947. Home: 31 Haveradim St, Gane-Yehuda, Isr. Office: 9 Lincoln St, Tel Aviv, Isr.

KANTOWITZ, Sam, US, chemist; b. Mountaindale, NY, Sep 17, 1915; s. Benjamin and Rose (Katzowitz); BA, Cornell U, 1937; m. Hilda Graubart, May 25, 1952; c: Robert, Jeffrey. Sup chem, Textile Piece Dyeing Co Inc since 1959; sup, chem and dyestuff div, Koppers, 1953-59. US Army, 1943-46. Pres: ZOA, 1946-53, bd dirs, Fairlawn chap since 1968; Servicemen Org, 1951-53; chmn, campaign comm, UJA, 1949; secy, C of C, 1950-53, all of Mountaindale, NY; ritual comm, Fairlawn J Cen; mem: Dirs, ZOA chapt Fairlawn, 1968. Home: 15-28 Chandler Dr, Fairlawn, NJ. Office: Textile Piece Dyeing Co Inc, Paterson, NJ.

KANTROWITZ, Adrian, US, surgeon, educator; b. NYC, Oct 4, 1918; s. Bernard and Rose (Esserman); BA, NYU, 1940; MD, LI Coll of Med, 1943; m. Jean Rosencraft, Nov 28, 1948; c: Niki, Lisa, Allen. Dir, surg services, Maimonides Med Cen since 1964, dir, cardiovascular surg, 1955-64, chmn, research comm, 1957-61; prof, surg, SUNY, Downstate Med Cen since 1964; fmr: asst res surg, Mt Sinai Hosp, NY; Surg, path, Montefiore Hosp, NY, cardiovascular research f, 1949, chief res surg, 1950, adj surg, 1951-55; USPHS f, cardiovascular phys, W Res U Med Sch, 1951-52, teaching f, phys, 1951-52; instr, surg, NY Med Coll, 1952-55; asst visiting surg: Flower Hosp, 1952-55; Morrisania Hosp, 1952-55; Metrop Hosp, 1952-55; Bird S Coler Hosp, 1952-55; asst prof, surg, SUNY Coll of Med, 1955-56. Capt, US Army MC, 1944-46. Specialist, gen surg, NY State Workmen's Compensation Rating, 1951; FACS, 1954; f, NY Acad Sci; dipl, Amer Bd Surg, 1953; mem: Amer Coll Surgs; Intl Soc Angiology; Amer Soc Artificial Internal Organs; NY Surg Soc; NY Co Med Soc; Harvey Soc; NY Soc for Thoracic Surg; NY Soc for Cardiovascular Surg; NY Acad Med; AHA; Amer Phys Soc; Pan Amer Med Assn; Card Soc of Peru; Card Soc of Colombia; Amer Coll of Card; Amer Coll Chest Phys; Bklyn Thoracic Soc, fmr pres; Bd Thoracic Surg, 1968. Mem: sci rev bd, Med Research Engr since 1964;

ed bd, Jour of Biomed Materials Research since 1966; contbr to med jours. Recipient: Henry L Moses Research Prize, 1949; 1st Prizes: sci exhb, conv, NY State Med Soc, 1952; for work in bladder stimulation, Maimonides Hosp Research Soc, 1963; Gold Plate Award, Amer Acad of Achievement, 1966; Max Berg Award, 1966; Bklyn Hall of Fame, Man of Year Award for Sci, 1966; Theodore and Susan B Cummings Hum Award, Amer Coll Card, 1967; Isr Freedom Medal, 1967; AMA Cert of Merit for intraaortic phase-shift balloon pumping exhb, 1968; Purkinje Soc of Czech Phys Medal, 1968. Home: 546 E 17 St, Brooklyn, NY. Office: Maimonides Med Cen, Brooklyn, NY.

KANTROWITZ, Arthur, R, US, physicist, educator; b. NYC, Oct 20, 1913; s. Bernard and Rose (Esserman); BS, Columbia U, 1934, MA, 1935, PhD, 1947; m. Rosalind Joseph, Sept 2, 1943; c: Barbara, Lore, Andrea. Dir, Avco-Everett Research Lab, since 1955; vice-pres, dir, Avco Corp, since 1956; mem: adv council, Dept of Aeronautical Engr, Princeton U, since 1959; fmr: physicist, NACA, 1935-46; asso prof, prof, aeronautical engr and engr physics, Cornell U, 1946-56; visiting lectr, Harvard U, 1952; Fulbright f, Cambridge U, 1954; Guggenheim f, Manchester U, 1954; visiting prof and f, Sch for Advanced Study, MIT. Prin contribs: research in reentry physics, magnetohydrodynamics, space sci, med tech, laser tech. F: Amer Acad of Arts and Sci; fmr chmn, fluid dynamics div, Amer Phys Soc; trustee, U of Rochester; mem: AAUP; AAAS; Amer Astronautical Soc; Natl Acad of Sci; Adv council, Sch of Engr, Stanford U; AIAA; Sigma Xi; Tau Beta Pi; club: Harvard, Boston. Home: 25 Spring Valley, Arlington, Mass. Office: 2585 Revere Beach Pkway, Everett, Mass.

KAPELOW, Paul, US, business exec; b. Memphis, Tenn, Sep 22, 1913; s. Abe and Yetta (Dorogovy); BS, U Tenn, 1936; m. Hester Leader, Oct 1939; c: Stephen, Terry, Carol. Pres, Shelby Construction Co Inc; Kesk, both since 1940; mgn dir, Goldberg Instruments, Tel Aviv, Isr since 1960. Chmn: B'nai B'rith Found; JWF campaign, 1959, pres, New Orleans chap, 1960; New Orleans Comm for State of Isr Bonds, 1960; S-Southwest conf, UJA, 1961, 1962, mem, natl cabinet, bd of govs, UJA; mem, bd dirs, Pal Econ Corp; mem, Phi Epsilon Pi. Home: 2100 St Charles Ave, 8-K, New Orleans, La. Office: 2100 St Charles Ave, 2-C, New Orleans, La.

KAPELUSZ, Tereza Maria, Isr, communal worker; b. Botoșani, Rum, Apr 24, 1899; d. Nuta and Bruha (Heinic) Freifeld; in Isr since 1950; att HS, Vienna; w. Found: B'noth Zion; B'noth Zion Avoda; WIZO, all chap Botoșani, Rum; pres, Hatarbut, Rum; Askanit; voluntary cultural manifestation to clubs for aged, Hadassah Hosp. Contbr Yiddish poems to Menorah, Problemen, Literatura și Istoriografie, Letzte Naies, Yiddishe Zeitung. Hobby, writing poetry. Home: 4 Miriam Hahashmonait, Tel Aviv, Israel.

KAPLAN, Abbott, US, educator, educational admnr; b. NYC, Jan 12, 1912; s. Nahum and Leah (Beilowitz); BS, Columbia U, 1933, MA, 1934, PhD, 1942; BJP, JTSA, 1933; m Beatrice Dresher, Nov 1, 1936. Pres, SUNY, Purchase, NY, theatre, arts since 1967; fmr: asso dean, coll of fine arts, prof, theatre, arts, U of Cal, LA; dir, s area, asso dean, Statewide U of Cal Ext; prof, Sch of Educ, U of Cal; prin, HS of Commerce; dir, bur of adult educ, Public Sch Sys, both Springfield, Mass; head lab-mgmt relations, Inst of Ind Relations, U of Cal; asso dir, U of Cal Ext. Cdr, USNR, 1943-46. Mem: Natl Acad of Arbitrators; AAUP; fmr: chmn, Cal State Commn on Arts; mem, Rockefeller Bros Fund Study Performing Arts in Amer; pres, Adult Educ Assn of US; vice-pres, chmn, intl affairs comm, mem, delg assembly; US repr to UNESCO intl meetings of experts on adult educ, Paris; leader, intl adult educ sem in Eur, sponsored by US, Can Eur Adult Educ Assns. Author: Adventures in Growing Up, 1941; Socio-Economic Circumstances and Adult Participation in Educational Activities, 1943; Making Grievance Procedures Work, 1950; Study Discussion in the Liberal Arts, 1960; contbr to profsl jours. Home: Beechwood, Purchase, NY. Office: SUNY, Purchase, NY.

KAPLAN, Abraham, US, educator, consultant; b. Odessa, Russ, June 11, 1918; s. Joseph and Chava (Lerner), in US since 1923; BA, Coll of St Thomas, 1937; PhD, UCLA, 1942; DhL, JTSA, w coast br, 1962; m. Iona Wax, Nov 17, 1939; c: Karen Diskin, Jessica. Prof, phil, U of Mich, since 1963; cons, RAND Corp, div of math and social sci, since 1947; research asso: experimental div for study of war time communications, Libr of Cong, 1942-43, political theory, 1943-45; instr, phil, NYU, 1944-45; chmn, dept phil, fac mem, UCLA, 1946-63; fac mem, HUC, LA, 1959-63; cons: Comm on Freedom of Press, 1944; survey of behavioral scis, Ford Found, U of Mich, 1954, visiting asso prof, 1951-52; mem, fac, summer session, phil dept: Harvard U, 1953; Columbia U, 1955. F: Guggenheim Found, 1945-46; Rockefeller Found, 1957-58; Cen for Advanced Study in Behavioral Sci's, Palo Alto, 1960-61; Cen for Advanced Studies, Wesleyan U, Conn, 1962-63; W Behavioral Sci Cen, La Jolla, Cal, 1966; Mem: bd govs, Brandeis Inst, since 1959; natl bd, JDC; mem, Hillel Ntl Commn; dir, EW Phil Conf, 1967; fmr, pres, Pacific div, Amer Phil Assn. Co-author: Power and Society, 1950-51; The New World of Philosophy, 1962; American Ethics and Public Policy, 1963; The Conduct of Inquiry, 1964; asso ed, Phil, E and W, since 1951; contbr to profsl jours. Home: 1745 Westridge Rd, Ann Arbor, Mich. Office: U of Mich, Ann Arbor, Mich.

KAPLAN, Albert S, US, researcher; b. Phila, Pa, Nov 29, 1917; s. Harry and Rose (Koussevitsky); BS, Phila Coll of Pharm and Sci, 1941; MS, Pa State Coll, 1949; PhD, Yale U, 1952; Tamar Ben Porat, Feb 14, 1959; c: Nira, Daniel. Head, Dept of Microbiol, Research Labs, Albert Einstein Med Cen, since 1958; research prof, Temple U Sch of Med, since 1963; f, Natl Found for Infantile Paralysis, 1952-54; instr, sect preventive med, Yale U, 1954-55; research asso, Dept of Bact, U of Ill, 1955-58. US Army, 1943-46. Mem: Amer Assn of Immunologists; AAAS; Amer Soc Microbiol; NY Acad Sci; Sigma Xi. Asso ed: Virology, 1966-69; Jour of Virology, 1967-70; contbr to sci jours. Home: 418 S Sterling Rd, Elkins Park, Pa. Office: Albert Einstein Med Cen, York and Tabor Roads, Philadelphia, Pa.

KAPLAN, Alfred, US, accountant; b. Denver, Colo, Jan 9, 1907; s. Max and Mollie (Smith); BCS, Northeastern U, 1927; MBA, Boston U, 1932; m. Gertrude Stavis, Nov 21, 1934; c: Louis. CPA, Boston since 1929; chief acctnt: Red Seal Pictures Corp; Out of Inkwells Films, both of NY, 1928-29. Chief warrant off, US Army, 1943-46. Pres, Malden dist, ZOA, 1950-55; Zionist Youth Commn, NE; Camp Young Judea; mem: JWV; Mass Soc of CPA's; Masons. Contbr to profsl and trade mags. Recipient, Army commendation medal, 1946. Home: 30 Glendale Rd, Newton, Mass. Office: 101 Tremont St, Boston, Mass.

KAPLAN, Alvin H, US, advertising exec; b. NYC, Aug 14, 1904; s. Jacob and Leah (Davis); AB, Columbia U, 1923, AM, 1926; m. Beti Streiff, Nov 29, 1928; c: Moreson, Thomas. Fmr, vice-pres, Newspaper Inst of Amer, Inc; mem bd trustees, Natl Home Study Council, since 1967; dir, Educor Inc, since 1968; vice-pres, chmn, home study div, Pvt Vocational Sch Assn, NY, since 1965; instr, advt, Lewis Hotel Training Sch, Wash, since 1941; fmr: space buyer and copywriter, Ruthrauff & Ryan, 1918-25; acct exec, space pres, Rose-Martin, NYC, 1926-44; found, partner, Kaplan & Bruck, NYC, 1944-46; sr Vice-pres, Lewin Williams & Saylor, NYC, 1956-59; mem, exec comm, Mogul Williams & Saylor, 1959-61; pres, Kaplan Agcy, NYC, 1962. Dir, Job Clinic, Gt Neck, NY, HS adult educ prog, 1941; chmn: adult educ comm, Gt Neck sch sys, 1941-43; 1948-49; comm on advt, NYU; comm, direct mail, Amer Assn Advt Agcys, 1962-65; pres, Sym Soc, 1960-63; chmn, pr comm, Comty Concerts Assn, 1959-61, both Gt Neck; mem: Authors League of Amer; Authors Guild. Co-author, with wife, under pen names John and Enid Wells: You Can Fix It, 1935; Living for Two, 1939; Prepare for the Army Tests, 1942; The Job That Fits You and How to Get It, 1946. Home: 124 Station Rd, Great Neck, NY. Office: 2 Park Ave, New York, NY.

KAPLAN, Benjamin, US, educator; b. Minsk, Russ, May 10, 1906; s. Joseph and Pesha (Greenman); in US since 1914; BA, Tulane U, La, 1928, MA, 1929; Phd, La State U, 1952; m. Yetive Tatar, May 14, 1933; c: Barbara. Godchaux Hon Prof, sociol, U Southwestern La since 1940; fmr: supr, La Dept Public Wfr; att, White House Conf for Children and Youth, Conf on Aging; Dep dir, ARC, 1942-45. F, Amer Sociol Soc; mem: La State Commn on Aging; adv mem, Marquis Biographical; UAHC-NFTS on Family Life; Phi Kappa Phi; Kappa Delta Phi; B'nai B'rith; Phi Epsilon Pi; fmr pres, Cong Temple Rodeph Shalom. Author: The Eternal Stranger, 1957; The Jew and His Family, 1967; contbr to Meet the American Jew, 1963. Hobbies: oil painting, writing, public speaking. Home: 216 Stephen St, Lafayette, La. Office: U of Southwestern La, Lafayette, La.

KAPLAN, Benjamin, US, attorney, educator; b. NYC, Apr 9, 1911; s. Morris and Mary (Berman); AB, CCNY, 1929; LLB, 1933, Columbia Law Sch; AM, hons, Harvard U, 1948; m. Felicia Lamport, Apr 16, 1942; c: James, Nancy. Royal prof, law, Harvard U, since 1961, prof, law since 1948; fmr: practiced law as asso, later mem of Greenbaum, Wolff & Ernst, NY; visiting prof, Harvard Law Sch; Ely visiting prof, Yale Law Sch; reporter to adv comm on civil rules, Judicial Conf of US. Lt-col, US Army, 1942-46. Mem: bd advs, NAACP; bd trustees, Copyright Soc of US; bd dirs, Assn Amer Indian Affairs; mem: Amer Law Inst; Assn Bar, NYC; AJComm. Author, An Unhurried View of Copyright, 1967, co-author: Cases on Copyright, 1960; Materials for a Basic Course in Civil Procedure, 2nd ed, 1968; contbr to legal jours. Recipient: Legion of Merit; Bronze Star. Home: 2 Bond St, Cambridge, Mass. Office: Harvard Law Sch, Cambridge, Mass.

KAPLAN, Daniel Richard, US, attorney; b. Bklyn, Aug 12, 1928; s. Sadje (Resnick); att Franklin & Marshall Coll, Lancaster, Pa, 1946-49; att Bklyn Law Sch, 1952; m. Renee Touriel, Apr 3, 1955; c: Susan, Lisa, Andrew, Amy. Partner, Tenzer, Greenblatt, Fallon & Kaplan, NYC since 1955; asst chmn, bd dirs; Barton's Candy Corp, NYC since 1951. Lt, USN, 1952-55. Dir: Leisure Dynamics Inc, Minneapolis, Minn; YM-YMHA, NYC; mem, planning counsel, NYC Youth Bd; Westchester Children's Players, dir, co-found; Dem Committeeman, Mamaroneck, NY; ZBT frat; NY Wine and Food Soc; Fgn Policy Assn; clubs: Harmonie, NYC; Beach Point. Home: 845 Claflin Ave, Mamaroneck, NY. Office: 235 E 42 St, New York, NY.

KAPLAN, Emanuel B, US, physician, educator; b. Russ, Apr 25, 1894; s. Boruch and Dina (Loadman); in US since 1924; att U Montpellier, Fr, 1911-12; Sch of Med, Paris, 1912-14; Kharkov U, Russ, 1914-16; MD; m. Virginia Smith, 1958; c: Robert, Elizabeth. Pvt practice since 1927; asso prof, clinical anat, Columbia U since 1955, fac mem since 1940; cons, orthopedic surg, hand surg dept, Hosp for Jt Diseases, NYC, since 1924; orthopedic surg, cons, Leb Hosp, NYC, since 1946. Author: Functional And Surgical Anatomy of the Hand, 1953; Surgical Approaches to the Cervical Spine and Upper Extremity; trans: Physiology of Motion by Duchenne; Syndesmology by Weitbrecht; contbr to profsl jours. Home: Teaneck, NJ. Office: 1020 Grand Concourse, New York, NY.

KAPLAN, Ervin, US, physician; b. Independence, Ia, June 19, 1918; s. Samuel and Bessie (Goldblatt); BS, U of Ill, 1947, MS, 1949, MD, 1949; m. Lucille Pick, Oct 20, 1945; c: Robert, John. Chief, radioisotope service, VA Hosp, Hines, Ill, since 1959, on staff since 1950; prof, med and phys, U of Ill Coll of Med, since 1968; asso att phys: Cook Co Hosp, since 1959; Chgo Research and Educ Hosp, since 1959; asso prof, med, U of Ill Coll of Med, 1964-68, fac mem, since 1952; asso prof, Cook Co Grad Sch Med, since 1959; cons, nuclear med, Mt Sinai Hosp, Chgo, since 1968; internship, Mt Sinai Hosp, Chgo, 1949-50; phys i/c, radioisotope lab, asso att phys, 1953-1959; phys i/c, radioisotope lab, Michael Reese Hosp, Chgo, 1956-59. US Army MC, 1941-45. Prin contrib: research in clinical application of radioisotopes in biol and med, cancer therapy. Pres, Cen Soc Nuclear Med, 1960; mem: exec comm, bd trustees, Soc Nuclear Med, 1958-66; AMA; Amer Bd Internal Med; Natl Bd Med Examiners; Sigma Xi; Soc Experimental Med and Biol; Cen Soc for Clinical Research; Chgo Soc Internal Med; Chgo Inst Med. Cons, Nuclear Med Jour; contbr to med jours. Recipient, Presidential Unit Citation. Hobbies: gardening, fishing. Home: 2600 Wilmette Ave, Wilmette, Ill. Office: VA Hosp, Hines, Ill.

KAPLAN, Eugene, US, pediatrician; b. NYC, Sep 6, 1912; s. Phoebus and Jennie (Hartman); AB, Dartmouth Coll, 1933; MD, NYU, 1937; m. Jane Markowitz, Sep 1, 1938 (decd); five c; m. 2nd, Mildred Fine, Nov 25, 1963. Chief, ped, Sinai Hosp since 1962, on staff since 1954; asso prof, Johns Hopkins Med Sch since 1958; fmr: asso prof: La State Med Sch; Wayne State U Med Sch. Contbr to ped, hematologic jours. Home: Longacre Lane, Stevenson, Md. Office: Sinai Hosp, Baltimore, Md.

KAPLAN, Eugene Harold, US, attorney; b. Worcester, Mass, Aug 23, 1921; s. Louis and Sarah (Harris); BEcon, Wharton Sch of Finance, U of Pa, 1943; LLB, U Conn Sch of Law, 1948; LLM, NYU Grad Sch of Law, 1966; m. Kitty Cantor, Dec 21, 1947; c: Kenneth, Jane. Partner, Weisman and Weisman, since 1968, in law practice since 1948; fmr: asst engrossing clerk, Conn State Leg; court clerk, City of Waterbury; corp counsel, City of Waterbury. USAAF, 1942-45. Chmn, J Fed Appeal; fmr: pres: J Fed of Waterbury; Temple Isr, treas, pres brotherhood, secy; vice-pres, NE council, UAHC; mem bd dirs, Easter Seal Soc; Cmty Council; presently: asst secy, United Council and Fund, Waterbury, Conn; mem: Amer Bar Assn; Commercial Law League; B'nai B'rith; Harmony Lodge, Masons; club, Rotary. Recipient: outstanding young man of year, Waterbury Jr C of C, 1957; outstanding young man of State, Conn Jr C of C, 1957. Hobbies: sports, music. Home: 74 Purdy Rd, Waterbury, Conn. Office: 49 Leavenworth St, Waterbury, Conn.

KAPLAN, Harold M, US, educator; b, Boston, Mass, Sep 4, 1908; s. Max and Mollie; BA, Dartmouth Coll, 1930; MA, Harvard U, 1931, PhD, 1933; m. Bernice Stone, June 15, 1935; c: Elaine, Joyce, Lee. Prof, chmn, Dept of Chem Phys, S Ill U since 1949; asst instr, zool, Harvard U, 1933-34; prof, phys, Middlesex Med and Vetr Schs, 1934-36; Brandeis U, 1946-47; asso prof, phys, U of Mass, 1947-49; chmn, animal experimentation comm, Ill Acad of Sci since 1959. Pres: Amer Assn Lab Animal Sci, 1966-67; Ill State Acad Sci; 1969-70; bd dirs, Ill Soc Med Research; dist chmn, Boy Scouts of Amer, 1947-49; mem: local scholarship screening comm, AHA, since 1962; Amer Phys Soc; Amer Soc Zool; Microscope Soc Amer; Ill Soc Med Research; Sigma Xi; Phi Eta Sigma; Phi Kappa Phi; Wildlife Disease Assn; f, AAAS. Author: Rabbit in Experimental Physiology, 1956; Anatomy and Physiology of Speech, 1960; Laboratory Exercises in Mammalian Physiology; ed, News Bull, Amer Soc, Biol Profs, 1948-54; asso ed, Proceedings of Animal Care Panel since 1960; contbr to profsl jours. Home: 106 N Almond St, Carbondale, Ill. Office: S Ill U, Carbondale, Ill.

KAPLAN, Harry Aaron, US, attorney; b. Waterloo, Ia, Apr 30, 1913; s. Isaac and Katie (Sachynin); JD, Southwestern U, 1935; m. Sylvia Bondy, Mar 6, 1935; c: Steven, Alan, Jill. Pvt practice since 1935; atty: all CIO Local Unions, 1936-41; Intl Longshoremen & Warehouse Union, Local 13; Shipyard Workers Local 9, 1941-49. Pres, B'nai B'rith, San Pedro, Cal; vice-pres, charter mem, B'nai B'rith, Torrance, Cal; Sigma Tau, southwestern chap. Home: 927 N Kings Rd, Los Angeles, Cal. Office: 3932 Wilshire Blvd, Los Angeles, Cal.

KAPLAN, Isaac, Isr, plastic surg; b. Kroonstad, OFS, S Afr, Apr 10, 1919; s. Shmuel and Annie (Yoffe); in Isr, since 1952; MB, BCh, Med Sch, Johannesburg, 1950; m. Masha Weingarten, Nov 13, 1956; c: Carmi. Head, Dept of Plastic, Maxillofacial Surg, Beilinson Hosp, Petah Tikva since 1958; asso clinical prof, Plastic Surg, Tel Aviv U since 1969; surg chief of staff, Children's Med Relief Intl, Plastic Surg Hosp, S Vietnam. Sgt, S Afr IS, 1941-43. Prin contribs: personal oprs for reconstructing of cervical oesophagus; shortening clitoris in pseudohermaphroditism. Mem: Isr Plastic Surgs Assn; Span Plastic Surgs Assn. Author: Scope of Plastic Surgery, 1969. Recipient: Cert of Appreciation, S Vietnam Govt, 1968; Dist Service, Children's Med Relief Intl, 1969; mil service medals. Home: 19 Habrosh St, Savyon, Isr. Office: 242 Hayarkon St, Tel Aviv, Isr.

KAPLAN, Jacob, Fr, author; b. Paris, Nov 7, 1895; s. Benjamin and Adele (Klein); licencié en philosophie, U Paris, 1919; ordained rabbi, Ecole Rabbinique de France, 1921; D honoris causa, JTSA, 1945; m. Fanny Dichter; c: Lazare, Francis, Benjamin, Myriam, Regine. Grand rabbi, Fr since 1955; chief rabbi, Paris, 1950-1955; rabbi: Mulhouse, 1922; Paris, 1929; Syn de la rue de la Victoire, 1933; asst to Grand Rabbi, Fr, 1939; grand rabbi, Fr, par interim, 1944; tchr, Institut d'Etudes Politiques, 1948. Delg, US Conseil Représentatif des Juifs de France, 1944-45; negotiated return of Finaly children to their family, 1953; hon Pres: Fr Mizrachi, 1950; Mahleketh Haharedim, JNF, 1948; found, pres, Ecole Yabne, 1948; co-found, Soc of J-Chr Friendship, 1947; mem, de l'Institut Academique des Sciences Morales et Politiques, 1967. Author: Le Judaisme et la Justice Sociale, 1937; Temoignages sur Israel, 1938; Racisme et Judaisme, 1940; French Jewry under the Occupation, 1945; Le Judaisme dans la Sociètè Contemporaine, 1948; Les Temps d'Epreuve, 1952. Recipient: Croix de Guerre, 1918, 1945; Medaille d'Honneur des Oeuvres Sociales, 1933; Commandeur de la Legion d'Honneur, 1962. Home: 1 rue Andrieux, Paris, Fr. Study: 17 rue Saint Georges, Paris, Fr.

KAPLAN, Jerome, US, attorney, certified public acctnt; b. Jersey City, NJ, Mar 17, 1926; s. Julius and Leah (Levy); Temple U, 1947; JD, U Mich, 1950; m. Edith Jaffy, June 9, 1953; c: Paul. Partner, Kaplan & Grodinsky, since 1961; estate tax examiner, Internal Revenue Service, 1953-55; partner, Abrahams & Lorwanstein, 1958-61. Pvt, US Army, 1944-45. Pres, AJCong, Phila, natl bd dirs; chmn, exec comm, ADA, natl bd dirs; bd trustees, Cong Rudeph Shalom; fmr pres, Cen Phila Reform Dems; mem: local bds: Pa and Phila J Comty Relations; New Dem Coalition; Phila, Bar Assn; Amer Bar Assn, tax comm. Hobbies: skiing, music. Home: 2042 Pine St, Philadelphia, Pa. Office: 226 S 16 St, Philadelphia, Pa.

KAPLAN, Joseph, US, artist; b. Minsk, Russ, Oct 3, 1900; s. Samuel and Mary (Cohen); in US since 1913; studied, Natl Acad Design, NYC; m. Virginia Haber, 1928. Repr: Butler Art Inst, Youngstown, O; Decatur Art Cen; Newark Mus; U Lexington, Ky; Mus W Art, Birobidjan, Russ; Tel Aviv Mus, Ein Harod, both Isr. Exhbs: Carnegie Inst, Natl Acad of Design; Audubon Artists; Hallmark; Boston Arts Festival; Corcoran Gal; U of Ill; Amer Water Color Soc; Natl Soc Painters in Casein; Pa Acad of Fine Arts; Cape Cod Art Assn; Provincetown Art Assn; ACA, Gal; World Alliance for Yiddish Culture; Friends of Ein Harod Mus; Amer J Tercentenary; J Mus, NYC. One-man shows: over thirty, in NYC; Youngstown, Coshocton, Massillon, Dayton, all O; Phila; Boston, Provincetown, Hyannis, all Mass; colls, mus. Mem: Audubon Artists; Natl Soc Painters in Casein; Artists Equity Assn. Recipient: Audubon Artists, gold medal, 1958, prizes, 1950, 1952, 1954, 1956; Grace Line, for best marine; Cape Cod Art Assn, 2 in 1952, 1954, 1955, 1956, 1958, 1960; Natl Soc of Painters in Casein, medal of hon, 1955, 1959; Obrig prize for oil, Natl Acad of Design, 1967; grant, Chapelbrook Found, Boston. Homes and Studios: 463 West St, New York, NY; 638 Commercial St, Provincetown, Mass.

KAPLAN, Kivie, US, business exec; b. Boston, Mass, Apr 1, 1904; s. Benjamin and Celia (Solomont); hon degs: DHL, Portia Law Sch, Boston; LLD, Wilberforce U, Ohio; DHum, Lincoln U, Pa; DHL, Cen State U, Wilberforce, O; DHL, HUC, 1968; m. Emily Rogers, 1924; c: Sylvia Grossman, Jean Green, Edward. Ret 1963; pres, gen mgr, Colonial Tanning Co, Boston. Pres, NAACP, since 1966, mem: exec comm, bd of dirs; dir for life, J Memorial Hosp, hon treas; mem: bd trustees, finance comm, Newton-Wellesley Hosp; Ntl Panel Arbitrators, Amer Arbitration Assn; mem, exec comm, UAHC, trustee, mem Social Action Commn; life trustee, co-found, Temple Emanuel, Newton, Mass; trustee, Temple Isr, Boston; mem, bd dirs, Heb Free Loan Soc; mem, exec comm, bd trustees, Combined J Philanthropies; life mem, bd, Brandeis U Associates; f, Brandeis U; treas, B'nai B'rith vocational commn; trustee, The Emily R and Kivie Kaplan Family Charitable Trust. Fmr: bd mem, fund co-chmn, Newton Comty Chest; treas, Roxbury Cemetery Assn; pres, 210 Associates, Inc; treas, CJA; mem, natl health planning comm, CJFWF; treas, Masons, Shawmut Lodge. Donor: admissions off, Newton-Wellesley Hosp; wing and bldg, J Memorial Hosp; Lincoln Hall, Brandeis U; Boston bldg, NAACP; Rel Action Cen, UAHC, Wash, DC; reception hall, Boston Dispensary; Rehab Inst. Recipient: awards: Men of Vision, Isr Bonds Comm; Hum Rights, Pittsburgh, Pa; Averell Harriman Equal Housing Opportunity, Modern Comty Devls; Temple Reyim Brotherhood Man of the Year; T Kenyon Holly, for outstanding service in civic, cultural, and philanthropic fields. Home: 75 Hammond St, Chestnut Hill, Mass.

KAPLAN, Lawrence S, US, educator; b. Cambridge, Mass, Oct 28, 1924; s. Jacob and Julia (Starnfield); BA, Colby Coll, 1947; MA, Yale U, 1948, PhD, 1951; m. Janice Eyges, Sep 5, 1948; c: Deborah, Joshua. Prof, hist, Kent State U, Kent, O since 1965, asso prof, 1960-65, fac mem since 1954; visiting Research Scholar, U London, 1969-70; hist, Defense Dept, 1951-54; Fulbright lectr: U Bonn, 1959-60; U Louvain, Belgium, 1964-65. US Army, 1943-46. Pres, Kent State U chap, AAUP, 1962; fac adv, Hillel Counselorship, Kent State U since 1955; mem, JWB, Akron, since 1968; mem: Phi Beta Kappa; Pi Gamma Mu; Phi Alpha Theta; Amer Hist Assn; Research Group, Kent; Temple Isr, Akron. Author: Jefferson and France, 1967; NATO and Its Commentators, 1968; contbr to periodicals. Home: 308 Wilson Ave, Kent, O. Office: Kent State U, Kent, O.

KAPLAN, Leon, US, attorney; Newark, NJ, Jan 8, 1908; s. Louis and Celia (Milsky); LLB, Rutgers U, 1927; m. Dorothy Rinzler, June 26, 1932; c: Linda Brickman, Rita Ginsburg, Stanley. Partner, Myers, Kaplan & Porter. Pres: Gtr Miami

KAPLAN

J Fed; Gtr Miami J Comty Cen, 1947-49; S sect, JWB, 1956-58; vice-pres, JWB, 1960-66; mem, Amer, Fla and Dade Co Bar Assns. Home: 1795 SW 12 St, Miami, Fla. Office: 1150 SW First St, Miami, Fla.

KAPLAN, Leonard Martin, US, rabbi; b. NYC, Oct 23, 1934; s. Samuel and Fannie (Lackman); ordained rabbi, Rabb Coll Mir, Jerusalem, 1956; BS, summa cum laude, U Louisville, 1961; MS, physics, U of Md, 1963; m. Tobie Goldstein, June 12, 1961; c: Joseph, Ronald, Abigail. Rabbi, Dover J Cen, since 1966; Adath Isr, Mason City, Ia, 1964-66; physicist, Natl Bur of Standards, 1961-64. Mem: RabCA; Amer Phys Soc; B'nai B'rith. Contbr to sci and rel jours. Home: 26 Legion Pl, Dover, NJ. Study: 18 Thompson Ave, Dover, NJ.

KAPLAN, Lewis D, US, meteorologist; b. Bklyn, NY, June 21, 1917; s. Joel and Annie (Epstein); BA, Bklyn Coll, 1939; MS, U of Chgo, 1947, PhD, 1951; m. Lillian Epstein, 1942; c: Rebecca. Staff sci, Jet Propulsion Lab, Cal Inst of Tech, since 1961; prof, atmospheric physics, U of Nev, since 1961; observer, US Weather Bur, 1940-45; meteorologist, 1947-54; instr meteorology: U of NM, 1948-49, U of Chgo, 1950; mem, Inst for Advanced Study, Princeton, 1954-56; guest, Imperial Coll, London, 1956-57; research asso, MIT, 1957-61; visiting prof, 1968; visiting prof: Oxford U, 1964-65; Oslo U, 1965; U Paris, 1969. Prin contrib: fields of planetary astrophysics and exploration, infrared spectra of atmospheric gases. F, Amer Meteorological Soc; mem: Amer Geophys Union; Royal Meteorological Soc, Eng; Amer Astronomical Soc; Amer Optical Soc. Recipient, NASA Exceptional Sci Achievement Medal, 1968. Home: 1202 Avoca Ave, Pasadena, Cal. Office: Jet Propulsion Lab, Pasadena, Cal.

KAPLAN, Louis, US, surgeon, educator; b. Grodno, Russ, Sep 20, 1904; s. Max and Alice (Nitzberg); in US since 1905; MD; m. Ruth Wapner, Apr 14, 1935; c: Judith, Charlotte. Chief, surg service, Albert Einstein Med Cen, S Div, since 1947; asso surg, U of Pa, 1929-49; clinical prof surg, Hahnemann Med Coll, 1949-64. Dipl, Amer Bd Surg; f, Amer Coll Surgs; mem: Phila Co Med Soc; Coll of Phys, Phila; Phila Acad Surg. Contbr to profsl jours. Home and office: 2040 Pine St, Philadelphia, Pa.

KAPLAN, Louis, US, librarian; b. NYC, Jan 27, 1909; s. Barney and Fanny (Radin); BS, U of Chattanooga, 1931; BLS, U of Ill, 1937; PhD, O State U, 1939; m. Esther Alk, Sep 3, 1939. Dir, librs, U of Wis, since 1957, mem staff since 1946. USN, 1943-46. Mem, Amer Libr Assn; secy, Wis chap, ACLU, 1962-67. Author, Bibliography of American Autobiographies, 1961. Home: 5725 Elder Pl, Madison, Wis. Office: Libr, U of Wis, Madison, Wis.

KAPLAN, Louis, US, chemist; b. Bridgeport, Conn, Oct 11, 1917; s. Sam and Rose (Knopow); BA, MA, UCLA; PhD, Stanford U, Cal, 1946; m. Bettye Grossbard, 1947; c: Ruth, David, Judith. Sr chem, Argonne Natl Lab, since 1946; jr chem, US Engr Off, 1939-42; research asso, Stanford U, 1942-46; Fulbright Research f, Weizmann Inst, Rehovot, Isr, 1959-60. Pres, Cong Etz Chaim; mem: Amer Chem Soc; AAAS. Contbr to profsl jours. Home: 528 Edson Ave, Lombard, Ill. Office: Argonne Natl Lab, Argonne, Ill.

KAPLAN, Luba, US, communal leader; b. Seltz, Pol, Apr 22, 1901; d. Beryl and Hennie (Isaalson) Ratner; in US since 1921; m. Morris Kaplan, Jan 31, 1921; c: Bella Widre, Jeanne Levin. Pres: Chaim Weizmann Folk Sch since 1954, charter mem; Seltzer Soc, charter mem; vice-pres, Pioneer Women, Gtr Wash Council; org, charter mem, Avrum Reizen Reading Circle; exec bd, UJA; fmr: pres, Pioneer Women, Club One; chmn, Isr Bond. Recipient: Woman of Valor, Gtr Wash, Pioneer Women, 1964; Woman of the Year, Pioneer Women, 1967. Hobbies: music, singing, Yiddish recitation. Home: 2213 Washington Ave, Silver Spring, Md.

KAPLAN, Malvina, Isr, painter; b. Lodz, Pol; d. Mordechai and Brajndla (Blass) Kaminer; in Isr since 1949; Dipl, Art Sch, Tel Aviv; m. Moshe Kaplan, 1940; c: Bruria. One-man show: Tel Aviv; Haifa; Eilat; Los Angeles; perm collection, Safed. Home: 60 Tet Vav St, Safed, Isr. Studio: 3 Bitzaron B, Janiv St, Tel Aviv, Isr.

KAPLAN, Max, US, educator; b. Milw, Wis, July 5, 1911; s. Henry and Sarah (Kaplan); BE, Milw State Tchrs Coll, 1933; M Mus, U Colo, 1941; MA, U Ill, 1948; PhD, 1951; m. Elizabeth Neu, Dec 31, 1934; c: Theresa, Marcia. Dir, Inst for Studies of Leisure, U of S Fla, Tampa, since 1968; social worker, relief dept, Milw Co, 1934-35; dir, research, lectr, public forums, US Off of Educ, Milw, 1935-36; research asst, US Suburban Resettlement Admn, Greendale, Wis, 1936-37; dir, music dept, Pueblo Coll, Colo, 1937-44; grad asst: sociol, U of Colo, 1944-45; Ill U, 1946-51, asst prof, music, sociol, anthropology, 1951-57; lectr, fine arts, leisure gerontology at profsl assns and socs, Us and colls; fmr violinist with U string quartets; concert master, Pueblo Civic Sym, 1940-45; academic dean, Bennett Coll Millbrook, NY, 1963-64; lectr, US and W Eur, 1964-68; dir, asso prof, music, Arts Cen, Sch of Fine and Applied Arts, Boston U, 1957-63. Found, 1st pres, Champaign-Urbana Comty Arts; Amer Sociol Assn; Instl Soc of Music Educs; hon life mem, Phi Mu Alpha; Golf Coast Sym; fac quartet, U of S Fla; fmr: cons: spec services, VA Hosps; Columbia U Art Cen; Comm on Demography, White House Conf on Aging; Lincoln Cen for Performing Arts; chmn: Music in the City, Music Educs Natl Conf; comm on adult educ, Boston U; mem: adv bd, Council on Aging; adv comm for older adult prog, Boston S End Fed of Settlement Houses; B'nai B'rith, Champaign-Urbana. Author: Music in Recreation, 1955; Art in a Changing America, 1958; Leisure in America, A Social Inquiry, 1960; Foundations and Frontiers of Music Education, 1966; Music for the Classroom Teacher, 1966; The Greater Boston Youth Symphony Orchestra, History and Meaning; mem, ed staff, Jour of Research in Music Educ; contbr to sociol and music publs. Home: 3415 Lacewood Rd, Tampa, Fla.

KAPLAN, Milton, US, curator, author; b. Newport, News, Va, Oct 10, 1918; s. Edwin and Reba (Morewitz); BA, Coll of William and Mary, 1940. Curator of Hist Prints, Libr of Cong, Wash DC, since 1942. Author: Presidents on Parade, 1948; Divided We Fought, 1952; The Story of the Declaration of Independence, 1954; The Ungentlemanly Art, 1968; Cons, Libr of Cong publs: Pictorial Americana, 1955, Charles Fenderich, Lithographer of American Statesman, 1959. Recipient: Avoda scholarship, 1936. Home: 843 Cox Ave, Chillum Terr, Md. Office: Libr of Cong, Washington, DC.

KAPLAN, Mordecai Menahem, US, religious leader, educator; b. Swenziany, Lith, June 11, 1881; s. Israel and Anna (Kowarsky); in US since 1899; BA, CCNY, 1900; MA, Columbia U, 1902; ordained rabbi, JTSA, 1902, DHL, 1929; m. Lena Rubin, June 2, 1908; c: Judith, Hadassah, Naomi, Selma. Prof, phils of rel, JTSA since 1947, fac mem, since 1910, prin, Tchrs Inst, 1909-31, dean, 1931-46; rabbi em, Soc for Advancement of Judaism since 1944, rabbi since 1922; fmr: rabbi, Cong Kehilath Jeshurun, NYC, 1903-1909; found, first rabbi, J Cen, NYC, 1917-22; lectr: Grad Sch for J Social Work, 1925-37; Columbia U, 1932-34; found, Reconstructionist Movement, 1935, chmn, ed bd, The Reconstructionist, 1935-39; visiting prof, Heb U, Jerusalem, 1935-39. Author: A New Approach to the Problem of Judaism, 1924; Judaism as a Civilization, 1934; Judaism in Transition, 1936; The Meaning of God in Modern Jewish Religion, 1937; The Future of the American Jew, 1948; Know How to Answer, A Guide to Reconstructionism, 1951; ha-Emunah vehaMussar, 1954; A New Zionism, 1955, 1959; Judaism Without Supernaturalism, 1958; The Greater Judaism in the Making, 1960; The Meaning and Purpose of Jewish Existence, 1963; Not So Random Thoughts, 1966; trans, ed, Text of Mesillat Yesharim, by S D Luzzatto, 1937; ed, Reconstructionist Papers, 1936; co-ed: The New Haggadah, 1941; Sabbath Prayer Book, 1945; High Holiday Prayer Book, 1948; Faith of America, 1951. Home: 415 Central Park W, New York, NY. Office: JTSA, Broadway & 122 St, New York, NY.

KAPLAN, Morris L, US, journalist; b. Portland, Me, Dec 16, 1908; s. Simon and Elizabeth (Travin); BLitt, Columbia U, Sch of Journalism, 1933; m. Margaret Stern, Oct 17, 1951; c: Marian. Reporter, NY Times since 1945; asso with Poughkeepsie, NY, newspapers, 1932-37; free-lance radio writer, 1939-40. Lt, US Army, 1941-44. Bd dirs, Columbia U Sch of Journalism Alumni Assn, 1953-54; mem: Sigma Delta Chi; Overseas Press Club; NY Reporters Assn; Silurians. Home: 300 W 23 St, New York, NY. Office: NY Times, 229 W 43 St, New York, NY.

KAPLAN, Morton A, US, educator, author; b. Phila, Pa, May 9, 1921; s. Lewis and Anthea (Ginsberg); BS, Temple U, Phila, 1943; att Stanford U, 1943; PhD, Columbia U, 1951; m. Azie Mortimer, 1967. Chmn, Comm on Intl Relations, U of Chgo, since 1958, prof since 1965, on staff since 1956; research staff, Hudson Inst, since 1961; pres, Cetra Music

Corp, since 1962; visiting asso: Cen Intl Studies, Princeton U, 1958-59, 1960-62; political sci, Yale U, 1961-62; instr, political sci, O State U, 1951-52; asst prof, political sci, Haverford Coll, 1953-54; staff mem, Brookings Inst, 1954-55. Served World War II. F: Cen Intl Studies, Princeton U, 1952-53; Cen for Advanced Study in the Behavioral Sci, 1955-56; Carnegie Traveling, 1959-60; Fgn Policy Research Inst, since 1967. Author: System and Process in International Politics, 1957; Some Problems in the Strategic Analysis of International Politics, 1959; The Strategy of Limited Retaliation, 1959; The Communist Coup in Czechoslovakia, 1960; Macropolitics, 1969; co-author: US Foreign Policy, 1945-55, 1956; Political Foundations of International Law, 1961; ed: The Revolution in World Politics, 1962; New Approaches to International Relations, 1968; bd eds, World Politics, since 1961; asso ed, Jour of Conflict Resolution, since 1960; adv ed, Orbis, since 1967; contbr to profsl jours. Home: 1126 E 59 St, Chicago, Ill. Office: U of Chicago, Chicago, Ill.

KAPLAN, Nathan, US, business exec; b. Alexandria, La, Dec 6, 1922; s. Meyer and Lena (Wellan); m. Nina Rusman, Feb 18, 1962. Pres, The Fair Store since 1958, on staff since 1940. Chmn: Retail Merchants Assn, 1967; vet comm, Alexandria ZOA, 1946-49; cultural series, JWF, Cen La, comty council, 1948-55; state, JWB armed services council since 1962; UJA campaign, 1957-60; Bonds for Isr, 1956-57; 1960-61; Cen La Comm for Isr 10th Anniversary Celebration, 1958; J Charity Fund since 1946; AZC, since 1954; pres: La State Zion dist, 1951-52, Alexandria Dist since 1958; La B'nai B'rith, 1958-59; JWF, Cen La and Comty Council, 1958-69; B'nai Isr Cong since 1961; mem bd: Memphis B'nai B'rith Home, 1968-69; Alexandria ZOA since 1947; La B'nai B'rith since 1954; B'nai Isr Cong since 1946; adv counc, Salvation Army, 1951-52; Alexandria Rodeo, Inc since 1957; mem: 13th UJA Isr Study Mission, 1967; Downtown Devl Comm, Natl Assn Retail Merchants of Amer, 1964; Yeshiva U Diamond Jubilee Comm, 1961; 1967 Natl Scopus Award Dinner Comm; natl council, JDC; United HIAS Service; Amer ORT Fed; Alexandria-Pineville C of C; Masons; clubs: Alexandria Lions, vice-pres since 1961; Temple Men's, treas, 1951. Home: 1255 Southampton Dr, Alexandria, La. Office: 1111 Main St, Alexandria, La.

KAPLAN, Nathan O, US, educator, biochemist; b. NYC, June 25, 1917; s. Philip and Rebecca (Uteff); BA, U of Cal, LA, 1939; PhD, U of Cal, Berkeley, 1943; m. Goldie Levine, Feb 9, 1947; c: Jerold. Prof, chem, U of Cal, San Diego, since 1968; fmr: prof, biochem, chmn, grad dept biochem, Brandeis U, 1957-68; research asso, Mass Gen Hosp, 1945-49; asst prof, biochem, U of Ill, 1949-50; asst prof, biol, Johns Hopkins U, 1955-57, on staff from 1950. Spec cons, Natl Cancer Inst; cons, Amer Cancer Soc; mem: Amer Chem Soc; Amer Soc Biochem; Amer Soc Bact; AAAS; NSF; Amer Acad Arts and Sci; AAUP; Natl Acad Scis; Sigma Xi; Amer Acad of Sci; Amer Acad Microbiol. Co-ed, Methods in Enzymology, 1955; contbr to profsl jours. Recipient, awards: Sugar Research, 1946; Eli Lilly, in biochem, 1953; NSF Travel, 1952. Home: 8587 La Jolla Scenic Dr, La Jolla, Cal. Office: Chem Dept, U of Cal, San Diego, La Jolla, Cal.

KAPLAN, Oscar J, US, educator; b. NYC, Oct 21, 1915; s. Philip and Rebecca (Uttef); AB, UCLA, 1937, MA, 1938; PhD, U of Cal, Berkeley, 1940; m. Rose Zankan, Dec 28, 1942; c: Stephen, Robert, David. Dir, prof psych, Cen for Survey Research, San Diego State Coll, since 1946, chmn, dept psych, 1950-52, 1963-66; instr, asso prof, psych, U Idaho, 1941-46; cons, gerontology, USPHS, 1946-50; visiting prof, public health, UCLA, 1965-66. Mem: W Gerontological Soc, pres, 1956-57; Gerontological Soc; Amer Psych Assn, pres, div maturity and old age, 1955-56; AAAS; AAUP; ed, Mental Disorders in Later Life, 2nd ed, 1956; mem, ed adv bd, Jour of Gerontology, since 1946; mem, intl bd eds, Gerontology and Geriatrics, Amsterdam, since 1958; ed-in-chief, The Gerontologist, 1961-66. Home: 5409 Hewlett Dr, San Diego, Cal. Office: San Diego State Coll, San Diego, Cal.

KAPLAN, Philip, US, business exec; b. Chgo, Ill, Oct 11, 1914; s. Joseph and Goldie (Stucker); att LaSalle Ext U; m. Pearl Miller, June 19, 1938; c: Sheila Pickard. Pres: Square Deal Plumbing & Heating Supply House Inc, since 1940; Sunset Memorial Lawns since 1955; dir, S Cen Bank since 1968. Pres, Philip Kaplan Found; fmr: pres, Chgo Plumbing and Heating Supply Assn; dir, Temple Sholom, chmn of house comm; mem: B'nai B'rith, Youth Org; CJA; J City of Hope; ADL; JF, Chgo; J United Fund, Metrop Chgo; clubs:

Covenant; Idlewild Country; Variety; Sportsman Lodge, B'nai B'rith. Hobbies: golf, painting, reading. Home: 1300 N Lake Shore Dr, Chicago, Ill. Office: 2115 S State St, Chicago, Ill.

KAPLAN, Philip, US, rabbi; b. Albany, NY, Dec 29, 1918; s. Abraham and Anna (Wepner); BA, Yeshiva U, 1939; MS, 1961, ordained rabbi: 1942; m. Esther Koffler, Oct 21, 1945; c: Andrea, Allan. Rabbi: Cong Agudas Achim since 1965; fmr: Sarnia, Ont until 1953; Colchester, Conn, until 1960. Bd dirs: United Fund of Attleboro; Attleboro Area Mh; Head Start; mayor's comm, Capital Improvements; fmr regional vice-pres, Rabb Alumni of Yeshiva U; exec comm, RabCA, 1957-59; regional gov council, Can J Cong, 1958-60; mem: RI Bd Rabbis; B'nai B'rith; Mizrachi Org; Vaad Harabbonim of Mass. Home: 57 Westchester Dr, Attleboro, Mass. Study: Kelley and Toner Blvds, Attleboro, Mass.

KAPLAN, Samuel, Can, journalist, publisher; b. Winnipeg, Can, June 30, 1925; s. Ralph and Sonia (Subitch); att, U Man, Can; m. Mona Rich, May 9, 1948; c: Barry, Jonathan, David. Pres, Anglo-J Publs, Ltd, pub, ed, J W Bull, weekly, since 1960; mgr, Bull Printers; fmr: reporter, Winnipeg Free Press, daily 1946-47; ed, W J News, 1947-52; sales mgr, Komar Printing Co, 1953-57; ed, Isr Press; owner, Bur of Printing and Advt, 1957-60, all Winnipeg. Royal Can Navy, 1944-45. Chmn, Pacific region, Keren Hatarbut Can, mem, natl bd; vice-chmn, bd, Beth Isr Rel Sch; first vice-pres, BC Ethnic Press Assn; mem: bd: Cong Beth Isr; Pacific region, ZOC; natl bd, United Isr Appeal Can Inc; Vancouver Lodge, B'nai B'rith; Fairview br, Royal Can Legion; J Home for Aged BC; org: adult Heb classes, Vancouver; Heb ulpan, under auspices Vancouver Public Sch Bd Adult Educ Evening Classes; fmr: co-produc, Vistas of the Jewish People, 48-week radio prog series; pres, B'nai B'rith, Man Lodge; chmn, Vancouver Isr Bond Campaign. Recipient, N Amer Award of Excellence, Govt of Isr, for J W Bull, 1968. Home: 4149 Osler St, Vancouver, BC, Can. Office: 3285 Heather St, Vancouver, BC, Can.

KAPLAN, Samuel I, US, oral surg; b. Hartford, Conn, Aug 15, 1909; s. Hyman and Sarah (Bailey); BS, U Pittsburgh, 1933; DDS, U Pittsburgh, Sch of Dent, 1933; m. Thelma Rakuslin, May 26, 1931; c: Arline Small. Pvt practice since 1945. Pres, Conn Soc Oral Surgs; mem: Amer Soc Oral Surgs; NE Soc Oral Surgs, chmn, credentials comm; Amer Dent Soc; Pierre Jauchard Acad; NY Inst, Oral Path; Amer Dent Soc Anesthesiology; Alpha Omega; fmr secy, Mt Sinai Hosp. Contbr to dent jours. Hobbies: woodworking, music. Home: 20 Westborough Dr, W Hartford, Conn. Office: 100 Constitution Plaza, Hartford, Conn.

KAPLAN, Sheldon Z, US, attorney, foreign affairs cons; b. Boston, Mass, Nov 15, 1911; s. Jacob and Lizzie (Strogoff); BA, Yale U, 1933; att, Harvard Law Sch, 1933-34; BA, hons, Brasenose Coll, Oxford U, 1937, MA, 1945; att: L'Ecole Libre des Sciences Politiques, 1945; Faculté de Droit, U of Paris, 1945; m. Megan Vondersmith, May 8, 1947; c: Eldon, Deborah, Daniel, Philip, Rebecca, Abigail. Partner law firm, Jacobs and Spedler, Wash DC, since 1969; practice of intl law; fmr: research asso, Elder, Whitman and Weyburn, Boston, 1937-39; pvt practice, specializing in Supr Court work, 1940-42; asst to legal adv, US State Dept, 1946-49; staff cons, House Fgn Affairs Comm, US Cong, 1947-57; partner, law firm, Dodd and Kaplan, 1957-58; admn asst to US Sen Thomas J Dodd, 1959; admitted, practice in Mass, 1940, Supr Court and Fed Courts, 1957. Capt, US Army, 1942-46. Mem, US Spec missions, pres appointment: Costa Rica, 1949; El Salvador, 1950; Uruguay, 1955; cons: spec cong missions to Eur, 1951; Far E, 1953; Intl Orgs and Movements, Eur, 1953; Cen Amer, 1955; Guat, 1956; mem, US delg, UN Gen Assembly, 1955. Mem: Comm on Latin Amer Law, Amer Bar Assn, since 1952; Boston and DC Bar Assns; Cong Beth El; ASCAP; Amer Soc Intl Law; Wash Fgn Law Soc; Inter-Amer Bar Assn; Harvard Law Sch Assn; Brasenose Soc; Oxford Soc; clubs: Natl Press; Yale, NY; Yale, Wash; Army and Navy; Cosmos; United Hunts; Lawyers, NY; British Schs and Univs, NY; Fed City. Recipient: La Medaille de la Reconnaissance Française, 1945; Bronze Star, 1945; Orden del Quetzal, Guat, 1960. Author of cong documents and reports on fgn affairs and intl law; contbr to intl legal publs; composer, popular songs, publ and recorded: Dominique, 1956; Red Shutters, 1957. Spec interest, Latin Amer affairs. Hobby: music. Home: 7810 Moorland Lane, Bethesda, Md. Office: 1025 15th St, NW, Washington DC.

KAPLAN, Shlomo, Isr, musical dir b. Bialystok, Russ, Mar 16, 1909; s. Gershon and Tzipa (Gluck); in Isr since 1926; att Music Sch, Bialistok; Sch for Conducting, Tel Aviv; m. Rachel Kanterovitch; three c. Music dir, Culture Dept, Histadrut, since 1948; conductor: Kol Isr Choir, 1929-59; thousand man choir, Assembly of Choirs, Ein Harod, 1945; musical dir: Hazamir Assn, intl org for choir festivals; Zimriah Festivals since 1951; bd dir, Jeunesse Musicale. Author, choir arrangements, especially Liturgy; profsl dir, ed, Chinuch Vetarbut, Pub House. Home: 75a Maze St, Tel Aviv, Isr. Office: 93 Arlosoroff St, Tel Aviv, Isr.

KAPLAN, Sollie, US, business exec; b. Chgo, Ill, July 28, 1917; s. Joseph and Goldie (Stucker); att: U of Ill, 1936-37; U Miami, 1937-38; m. Miriam Krinsky, Aug 11, 1946; c: Jill Amatai, Gary. Real estate broker, inves property div, Arthur Rubloff and Co, since 1969; treas, dir, Niles Savings and Loan Assn, since 1960; exec vice-pres, Sq Deal Plumbing and Heating Supply House, 1938-69. Lt, US Army, 1942-45. Pres: Sollie Kaplan Found, since 1950; Lake Shore Equestrian Soc, since 1960; patron, Aesculapius Soc, Chgo Med Sch; bd govs, Isr Bonds; dir, Anshe Emet Syn; mem: Chgo Educ TV Assn; Art Inst, Chgo; Amer Legion; B'nai B'rith; Lyric Opera Guild. Recipient: Bronze plaque, Isr bonds, 1958; hon citizen award, State of Md, 1958; Amer mil ribbons. Home: 3750 N Lake Shore Dr, Chicago, Ill. Office: 2115 S State St, Chicago, Ill.

KAPLAN, Solomon Marvin, US, rabbi; b. Bklyn, NY, June 9, 1929; s. Abraham and Edith (Kronstadt); BS, CCNY, 1949; BHL, Sem Coll, NYC, 1950; MHL, ordained rabbi, JTSA, 1954; m. Ruth Horowitz, June 22, 1950; c: Stephen, Eva, Judith. Rabbi: Cong Tree of Life, since 1968; Sons of Zion, 1959-68; asst prof, Mt Holyoke Coll. Capt, US Army, 1954-62. Fmr adv, Holyoke chap, NCCJ; org, mem, Holyoke Clergy Assn; fmr mem: Mayor's Comm on Civil Rights; mem, RA. Contbr to jours. Home: 5550 Darlington Rd, Pittsburgh, Pa. Study: Wilkens at Shady, Pittsburgh, Pa.

KAPLANSKY, Irving, US, mathematician, educator; b. Toronto, Can, Mar 22, 1917; s. Samuel and Anna (Zuckerman); BA, U Toronto, 1938, MA, 1939; PhD, Harvard U, 1941; hon DMath, Waterloo, 1968; hon DSc, Queens, 1969; m. Rachelle Brenner, 1951; c: Steven, Daniel, Lucille. Prof, math, U Chgo since 1956, fac mem since 1945; fmr: instr, math, Harvard U; math researcher, Natl Defense Research Comm, Columbia U; Guggenheim f. Mem: Natl Acad Sci; Amer Math Soc; Math Assn of Amer. Contbr to sci jours. Home: 1718 E 56 St, Chicago, Ill. Office: U of Chgo, Chicago, Ill.

KAPLANSKY, Kalmen, Can, labor exec; b. Bialystok, Pol, Jan 5 1912; s. Abraham and Masha (Wisotsky); in Can since 1929; m. Esther Kositsky, June 21, 1945; c: Marsha, Frances. Dir, Can br, ILO, since 1967; dir, Dept Intl Affairs, Can Lab Cong, 1957-66; dep mem, governing body, ILO, titular mem, 1960-66; substitute mem, exec bd, Intl Confed of Free Trade Unions, 1959-66; mem, Can Delg to Tenth Session of Gen Conf UNESCO, Paris, 1958, alternate mem, Can Natl Commn on UNESCO; adv to Workers' Delg of Can to 40th, 42nd, 43rd, 44th, 45th and 46th sessions, Intl Lab Conf, Geneva, 1957-62. Sgt, Can Army, 1943-45. Mem. comm on wfr of immigrants, Can Wfr Council; natl public educ comm, Can Inst Intl Affairs; exec comm, Local 176, Intl Typographical Union, 1939-42; Natl Council of Coop Commonwealth Fed, Can, 1949; vice-chmn, J Lab Comm since 1963, fmr natl dir, 1946-57; secy; jt advisory comm on lab relations, J Lab Comm and Can J Cong, 1948-57; Que Lab Party, 1936-38; chmn, Montreal City comm, Workmen's Circle, 1940-43; mem: bd of dirs, J Vocational Service, Montreal, 1951-53; YIVO. Home: 771 Eastbourne Ave, Ottawa, Can. Office: 178 Queen St, Ottawa 4, Can.

KAPLINSKY, Noah, Isr, physician; b. Slonim, Pol, Jan 6, 1909; s. Israel and Sara (Rabinovich); in Isr since 1945; MD, Med Fac, Vilna, 1933; m. Zahava Yoselevich, June 21, 1932; c: Eliezer, Yoheved Light. Asso dean, Tel Aviv U, Med Sch, since 1964; mem, Holon Munic, 1951-69. Segen, IDF. Pres, IMA since 1965; fmr pres, Sick Fund Phys of Isr. Home: 40 Sokolov St, Holon, Isr.

KAPLITZ, Sherman E, US, physician, educator; b. Chgo, Ill, Sep 28, 1918; s. Samuel and Sonia (Halperin); BS, U of Ill, 1941, MD, 1943; m. Beatrice Richman, Dec 15, 1955; c: Wendolyn, Nancy. Med dir, Julian Levinson Found for Retarded Children since 1958; asst med supt, dir, dept of neuropsycht and psych, Oak Forest Hosp since 1957; asso prof, Chgo Med Sch since 1960; att neur: Cook Co Hosp; Mt Sinai Hosp, dir, epilepsy clinic. US Army, WW II. Dipl, Amer Bd Psycht and Neur; bd dirs, Macabee lodge, B'nai B'rith; chmn, ADL comm; mem: AMA; Chgo, Ill Med Assns; Amer Acad of Neur. Contbr to med jours. Recipient: Purple Heart; Combat Med Badge; prof of year, Chgo Med Sch. Home: 609 Leamington, Wilmette, Ill. Office: 6 N Michigan Ave, Chicago, Ill.

KAPLON, Morton F, US, physicist, educator; b. Phila, Pa, Feb 11, 1921; s. Myer and Ida (Abramson); BS, Lehigh U, 1941, MS, 1947; PhD, U Rochester, 1951; m. Anita Harle, June 16, 1946; c: Keith, Bryna. Chmn, dept of physics and astronomy, U Rochester since 1964, prof, 1961-64, asso dean, Coll Arts and Scis, 1963-64, on fac since 1955; sr post-doc f, NSF, in res, Clarendon Lab, Oxford U, 1959-60. F, Amer Phys Soc; mem: AAAS; It Phys Soc; Natl Geog Soc; Sigma Xi. Contbr to sci jours. Home: 186 Clovercrest Dr, Rochester, NY. Office: U of Rochester, Rochester, NY.

KAPLOW, Herbert E, US, journalist; b. NYC, Feb 2, 1927; s. Solomon and Belle (Bernstein); BA, Queens Coll, NYC, 1948; MS, Northwestern U, Evanston, Ill, 1951; m. Betty Koplow, Aug 10, 1952; c: Steven Robert, Lawrence. Corresp, NBC. US Army. Mem: Sigma Delta Chi; club, Natl Press. Home: 211 Van Buren St, Falls Church, Va. Office: NBC, 4001 Nebraska Ave, NW, Washington, DC.

KAPLOW, Milton, US, scientist; b. Winthrop, Mass, Mar 14, 1921; s. Samuel and Sadie (Cohen); BS, MIT, 1942; MS, U Mass, 1955; m. Riena Leopold, Aug 16, 1956; c: Jonathan, Sara, Edith, Stella. Sr group leader, produc devl, Gen Foods Corp since 1958; food insp, US Dept of Agric, 1942-48; asst prof, U Miami, 1948-56; vice-pres, United Pre-Pared Producs, 1956-58. Mem: Inst of Food Techns; AAAS; Phi Tau Sigma; J Comty Cen. Contbr to profsl jours. Home: 44 Coralyn Ave, White Plains, NY. Office: General Foods Corp, White Plains, NY.

KAPLOWITZ, Paul, US, attorney; b. Atlantic City, NJ, Apr 22, 1906; s. Morris and Dora (Pollock); LLB, Wash Coll of Law, Amer U, 1928; m. Dora Berkman, Jan 24, 1938; c: Morris. Chmn, US Tariff Commn, 1966-67, staff mem since 1943; adv, US delg: 2nd meeting US Preparatory Comm, Intl Conf Trade and Employment, Geneva, Switz, 1947; meeting Contracting Parties to Gen Agreement on Tariffs and Trade, Torquay, Eng, 1951; cons, comm on Ways and Means, House of Repr, 1964-65. Mem, ZOA. Home: 5135 Linnean Ave, Washington, DC.

KAPROW, Maurice S, US, educator; b. Buffalo, NY, Nov 15, 1944; s. Gedaliah and Geraldine (Shapiro); BA, Yeshiva U, 1966, BHL, 1966. Asso natl youth dir, Natl Council of Young Isr, since 1964; tchr, NYC Bd of Educ, since 1967. Prin contribs: pub Young Isr prog service; trains youth leaders for syn youth work; org, Young Isr Kosher kitchens on coll campuses; assists J boys in armed services. Chmn, PS 890 chap, United Fed of Tchrs; troop scribe, jr scout master, Boy Scouts of Amer; mem: Natl Ass of J Cen Workers; Conf of Young Isr Youth Dirs; Metrop Assn of J Cen Workers; PS 890 chap, United Fed of Tchrs. Ed: Young Isr Prog Service; Young Isr Coll Cultural Series, both Natl Council of Young Isr. Home: 33-46 92 St, Jackson Heights, NY. Office: 3 W 16 St, New York, NY.

KARASICK, Joseph, US, communal leader; b. Russ, July 6, 1921; s. Jacob and Mary (Katzman); in US since 1923; BA, Yeshiva U, 1943; ordained rabbi, Rabbi Isaac Elchanan Theol Sem, 1945; m. Pepa Wakmann, Mar 3, 1946; c: Bernice Mandel, Mark, George. Pres, Wakmann Watch Co, since 1955; dir, Yeshiva U HSs. Pres: Union Orthodox J Congs of Amer, since 1966; Yeshiva Coll Alumni Ass, 1964-68; dir: Beth Din, RabCA, 1964-68; Boy Scouts of Amer, 1966-68; educ chmn, Rel Zionists of Amer; mem, Masons. Author: Magen Haelef. Recipient: Bernard Revel Memorial Award, Yeshiva U, 1969. Home: 470 West End Ave, New York, NY. Office: 15 W 47 St, New York, NY.

KARASU, Albert, Turkey, journalist; b. Salonika, July 16, 1897; s. Nissim and Vida (Matalon) Carasso; dipl, Ecole des Sciences Politiques, Paris; m. Angele Loreley, June 3, 1929. Ed-in-chief, political commentator, Journal d'Orient, since its founding. Recipient: Chevalier de la Légion d'Honneur; Médaille de la Reconnaissance Française; Chevalier de la Couronne

Belge; Commandeur de l'Ordre de l'Aigle, Czech; Commandeur de la Couronne d'Italie; Commandeur de l'Ordre du Mérite de la République Italienne: Commandeur de l'Ordre de St. Sylvestre, Pope Paul VI. Hobby, theater. Home: 43/4 Izzet Pasa Sokak, Ruta Han, Sisli, Istanbul, Turkey. Office: Journal d'Orient, Guven Han, Bankalar Caddessi, Galata, Istanbul, Turkey.

KARCHMER, Aaron, US, business exec; b. Paris, Tex, Nov 14, 1909; s. Isadore and Bessie (Gilbert); att Okla U, 1932; m. Gertrude Karchmer, June 30, 1940; c: Ronna, Don. Partner, Karchmer Pipe and Supply Co, since 1938. Pres: B'nai B'rith Lodge, 1948; Temple Solomon, 1949; fmr, Centralia United Fund, chmn, 1956-58, mem, bd; vice-pres, J Fed Soc of Ill, 1954-58; chmn: wfr dr, 1954-56; big gifts comm, since 1956; co-chmn, St Mary's Hosp, 1955-57, mem, bd, 1957-59; mem, bd sups, Marion Co, Ill, since 1959; mem, bd, Boy Scouts of Amer; mem: exec comm, JWF; Elks; Masons; Shriners; club, Hi-12. Recipient, Dist Service Award, City of Centralia, 1957. Home: 1604 Morrison Rd, Centralia, Ill. Office: 300 N Brookside, Centralia, Ill.

KAREL, Leonard, US, science admnr; b. Baltimore, Md, Jan 23, 1912; s. Max and Fannie (Marcus) Krulevitz; BA, Johns Hopkins U, 1932; PhD, U of Md, 1941; m. Charlotte Lockman, Oct 31, 1942; c: Martin, Jacqueline, Richard. Spec asst to asso dir, Libr Oprs, Natl Libr of Med, USPHS since 1966, chief Bibliographic Services Div, 1964-66; acting head, Sci Resources Manning Off, NSF, 1963-64; cons: Pan Amer Health Org, 1967-68; WHO, 1967-68; interim dir, Regional Med Libr for S Amer, 1967-68; asst to chmn, comm on Sci and Tech Info, Fed Council for Sci and Tech, Off Sci and Tech, Exec Off of Pres, 1968; exec secy, div of research grants, NIH, 1947-51; chief, Extramural prog, Natl Inst of Allergy and Infectious Diseases, 1951-61. Capt, US Army, 1942-46. Prin contribs, devl intl prog of support of research and training in microbiol, parasitology, allergy and infectious diseases. F: AAAS; Amer Public Health Assn; mem: Amer Soc for Pharm and Experimental Therapeutics; sci and educ council, Allergy Found of Amer. Co-author: A Dictionary of Antibiosis, 1951; The Children's Passover Service, 1962; contbr to sci jours. Recipient: Johns Hopkins trustees' grant, 1930; army commendation ribbon, meritorious research, 1945. Home: 7509 Westfield Dr, Bethesda, Md. Office: NIH, 8600 Rockville Pike, Bethesda, Md.

KARELITZ, Samuel, US, pediatrician, educator; b. Chomsk, Russ, June 15, 1900; s. Samuel and Sara (Sporovsky); in US since 1905; PhD, Yale U, 1920, MD, 1923; m. Ruth Frankenberg, Sep 5, 1929 (decd); c: Susan Ginsberg, Judith; m. 2nd, Ethel Ginsberg, Nov 22, 1959. Dir, ped, LI J Hosp since 1955; dir em, LI J Med Cen, 1969; cons ped, Mt Sinai Hosp, NY since 1955; staff mem since 1927; clinical prof, ped, SUNY Coll Med since 1957. US Army, 1918; col, chief of Med, Third Gen Hosp, US Army MC, WWII. Mem: bd: adoption comm, Free Syn since 1928; adoption comm, cons, Louise Wise Services; Amer Ped Soc; Soc for Ped Research; adoption comm, Child Wfr League of Amer; Intl Social Service; chmn, comm on ped, NYC Bd of Health; mem, fmr mem bd, Citizens Comm for Children; club, NY Ped. Author, When Your Child is Ill, 1957, new ed, 1969; contbr to med textbooks and profsl jours. Home: 145-15 Bayside Ave, Flushing, NY. Office: 270-05 76 St, New Hyde Park, NY.

KARGER, Hans, Isr, certified public acctnt; b. Görlitz, Ger, Jan 12, 1904; s. Louis and Elsa (Speier); in Isr since 1935; DJur, Us Freiburg, Leipzig, Breslau, 1925; lawyer, 1929; CPA, Isr, 1954; m. Liese Guttmann, Dec 25, 1929; c: Shoshana Kaufmann, Arieh. Pvt practice since 1933; fmr controller, Weizmann Inst of Sci. Prin contribs: devl internal auditing in Isr. Fmr pres, Isr chap, Internal Auditors, NY; clubs: Rotary, Rehovot, pres; Ilenshil, Rehovot, financial off. Contbr to jours. Home: 9 Neve Matz, Rehovot, Isr.

KARGER, Michael Howard, Eng, research chemist; b. Ely, Cambridge, Eng, Oct 14, 1942; s. Alec and Sarah (Bardonis); BS, U Bristol, 1964; PhD, U Cambridge, 1967; m. Chaya Plutitski, Aug 1969. Research f, Weizmann Inst of Sci, since 1967; research asst, labs, Glaxo Ltd, Greenford, Middlesex, Eng, 1960-61. Contbr to sci jours. Recipient: Thomas Malbin Prize, U Bristol, 1966; Matilda Kennedy f, Weizmann Inst of Sci, 1967. Spec interest, collecting medieval Eng church windows. Home: 27 Park View Rd, London, NW 10, Eng. Office: Weizmann Inst of Sci, Rehovot, Isr.

KARGMAN, Israel, Isr, legislator; b. Russ, Dec 23, 1906; s. Zvi and Malka (Balter); in Isr since 1929; m. Rifka Goltz, July, 1930; c: Guri, Adith. Chmn, Knesset Finance Comm, since 1965; MK since 1956; fmr: textile worker; agric, bldg worker. Haganah, 1929. Mem cen comm, Mapai; fmr mem: Hechalutz, Russ; Kibbutz Hachshara, Crimea. Contbr to Heb press. Home: 10 Beilinson St, Kiriat Hayim, Isr. Office: Knesset, Jerusalem, Isr.

KARGMAN, Max R, US, attorney; b. Chgo, Ill, Oct 13, 1908; s. Joseph and Bessie (Richman); LLB, Chgo Kent Coll of Law, 1929, LLM, 1930; PhB, U Chgo, 1934; PhD, Harvard U, 1952; m. Marie Witkin, July 14, 1935; c: William, Donna, Robert. Pres: First Realty Co of Boston and affiliated cos, since 1946; Alliance Realty, Chgo, 1933-34; mem, firm, Kargman and Kargman, since 1930. Judge advocate, US Army, MC, 1944-45. Pres, Kargman, Mitchell and Sargent, comty and sch planning org, 1955-60; chmn, Commonwealth Service Corps, Mass, 1966; trustee, Heb Tchrs Coll; exec dir, Kargman Family Found; dir: Comm for Cen Bus Dist, Boston; Leo Baeck HS, Haifa, Isr; mem: ADA, Mass, exec comm; Amer Bd, World Union for Progressive Judaism; Amer, Mass and Boston Bar Assns; clubs: Harvard, Belmont Country. Home: 115 Rutledge Rd, Belmont, Mass. Office: 120 Tremont St, Boston, Mass.

KARIN, Menachem Karger, Isr, journalist, publisher; b. Siemichov, Aus, Apr 15, 1906; s. Schalom and Fani (Landesman); in Isr since 1934; att Rabb Sem, Prague, Czech; m. Vera Scheer; c: Zwi. Free-lance journalist and publisher. Field dir, JNF, Cen Amer, 1954-62; delg: JNF, Eur, 1935-39; UJA, KH, 1962-69. Brit Army, 1942-45; IDF, Contbr to KH Yearbook, Ger, 1965-67; Judaica, Salzburg, Aus. Home: 7 Micha St, Tel Aviv, Isr.

KARIV, Abraham, Isr, poet, author; b. Kaunus, Lith, 1900; in Isr since 1934; MSc, U Moscow; m. Aviva Yedida; two c. Author: Shabat uMoed biDrush uveHasidut, 1926; Neratek et hashalshelet, 1925; Iyunim, 1950; Adabera ve-Irvach Li, 1951; Kol uVat Kol, 1952; Atara leYoshna, 1956; Shiv'at Amudei haTnach, 1958; Kitvei Maharal mePrag, 1960; Lita Mechorati, 1962; contbr to lit revs, poems, articles to Heb press. Mem, Heb Acad. Recipient: Ramat Gan Prize for Lit, 1951; Milo Prize, 1961; Heichal Shlomo Award; Kassel Award, Mex. Home: 7 Hanna Senesh St, Haifa, Isr.

KARIV, Benjamin Zeev, Isr, business exec; b. Szczercow, Pol, Aug 3, 1920; s. Abraham and Fajga (Wishnievska); in Isr since 1938; grad, Agric Sch, Mikveh Isr, 1940; BSc, Heb U, Jerusalem, 1960; m. Gila Laxer, Oct 7, 1945; c: Revital, Abraham, Sigal. Gen dir, Mekorath Water Co Ltd, since 1967, with firm since 1949; mem, Kibbutz Beit Akiva, 1941-49. Haganah, IDF, 1938-53. Mem, cen comm, Lab Party; fmr communal mem, Ganei-Yehuda; clubs: Golden; El Al; Cen Football Assn. Mem, bd dir, Davar, daily lab newspaper; contbr to jours. Recipient, decorations: Hagana, Komemiut, Sinai, Six-Day War. Home: 27 Havradim St, Ganei-Yehuda, Isr. Office: 9 Lincoln St, Tel Aviv, Isr.

KARIV, Izhak, Isr, physician; b. Pabjanice, Pol, Dec 7, 1907; s. Shlomo and Debora (Wisenberg) Krakowski; in Isr since 1933; att Heb Coll, Lodz, Pol, 1925; MD, Faculté de Medicine, Paris, Fr, 1933; m. Guta Bulwa, 1938; c: Oded. Chief, Inst of Card, Tel Hashomer Hosp, since 1954; asso clinical prof, internal med, since 1968. Lt-Col, IDF, 1954-65. F, Amer Coll of Chest Phys; mem: IMA; Isr Heart Assn. Contbr, papers on card to med jours. Home: 10a Ruppin St, Tel Aviv, Isr. Office: Tel Hashomer Govt Hosp, Isr.

KARLIN, Samuel, US, surgeon, educator; b. Portland, Me, Sep 7, 1908; s. Myer and Gussie (Rosoff); BA, cum laude, Harvard Coll, 1928, MD, 1932; m. Alece Geisenberger, June 27, 1938; c: Robert, Richard. Asso prof, surg, Tulane U, since 1954; chief, surg, Touro Infirmary, 1959-63. Maj, US Army, 1942-46. Pres, New Orleans Surg Soc, 1965; mem, exec comm, AJComm, New Orleans; Fed, New Orleans, 1957-62; Amer Coll Surgs; Southeastern Surg Cong; Surg Assn of La; dipl, Amer Bd Surg; mem: AMA; La State and Orleans Parish Med Soc; Temple Sinai; club, Harvard, a. Recipient: Bronze Star; Croix de Guerre Avec Palme. Home: 5418 S Miro, New Orleans, La. Office: 21 Medical Plaza, 3600 Prytania St, New Orleans, La.

KARLINER, William, US, psychiatrist, educator; b. Bolszowce, Aus, Dec 13, 1910; s. Meier and Lottie (Schorr); in US since

1935; MD, U Vienna Med Sch, 1935; m. Edith Gross, May 22, 1945; c: Phyliss. Asst clinical prof, psycht, Albert Einstein Coll of Med, since 1954; fmr att neuropsycht, Seton Hosp; att psycht, Hillside Hosp; dir, psycht, J Memorial Hosp. F: Amer Psycht Assn; Acad Psychosomatic Med; Westchester Acad Med; pres, Bx dist br, Amer Psycht Assn, 1956-57; dir, Bx Co Soc for Mh since 1954; mem: AMA; NY State Med Soc; Assn for Research in Nervous and Mental Diseases; NY Soc for Clinical Psycht; Amer Acad of Neur; Bx Soc of Neur and Psycht; Electroshock Research Assn. Contbr to profsl jours. Home: 20 Franklin Rd, Scarsdale, NY. Office: 1749 Grand Concourse, Bronx, NY.

KARMI, Nachman, Isr, business exec; b. Kopetchintse, Pol, Dec 25, 1910; s. Dov and Lea (Blaustein) Weingarten; in Isr since 1937; m. Chana Rosenberg (decd); m. 2nd, Alisa Kaplan; c: Ruth Harari, Neomi Salomon, Dov. Gen mgr, Ta'al Plywood Ind, since 1967; dir, Immigration & Absorption Dept, Ichud Hakvutzot Vehakibutzim, 1949-51; secy, treas, Kibbutz Mishmarot, 1951-67. British Army, 1939-42; lt, Haganah, IDF, 1942-49. Fmr mem: cen comm: Poale Zion Org; Hechalutz Org; mem: Isr-Fr Friendship Assn; Isr-Eng Friendship Assn; Isr Export Inst; delg, Lab Party Conv; fmr JA, Ichud Hakvutzot Vehakibbutzim missions to: Fr, It, Aus, 1957-58. Contbr to profsl jours. Home: Kibbutz Mishmarot, Isr. Office: 39 Montefiore St, Tel Aviv, Isr.

KARMON, Yehuda, Isr, educator; b. Oswiecim, Pol, Apr 17, 1912; s. Shlomo and Rachel (Erreich) Kaufman; in Isr since 1938; att, U Breslau, 1929-33; MA, Heb U, Jerusalem, 1953; PhD, 1959; m. Marianne Schmoller, Nov 19, 1954. Prof, Geog, Heb U, Jerusalem, since 1966; lectr, 1954-59; sr lectr, 1960-65; cons, water devl projects, Ghana, Nigeria. Sgt, Brit Army, 1942-46; capt, IDF, 1947-50. Prin contribs: research, econ, regional geog in Isr, ME. Author: The Northern Hula Valley, 1957; A Geography of Settlement in Eastern Nigeria, 1966; The Ceasefire Lines of Israel, 1967; Israel, A Regional Geography, 1970; co-author, Atlas of the Middle East, 1962; chief ed, Georgraphical Lexicon, 2 vols, 1966; contbr to profsl jours. Home: 60 Tchernihovski St, Jerusalem, Isr. Office: Heb U, Jerusalem, Isr.

KARNI, Joseph, Isr, educator; b. Uman, Russ, Oct 14, 1912; s. Jacob and Lea (Levin) Krasniansky; in Isr since 1922; BSc, Technion, Haifa, 1936, CE, 1937, BArch, 1948, MSc, 1964; postgrad studies, Northwestern U, Ill; m. Miriam Karasovsky, 1938; c: Avital, Eyal. Dir, ext div, Technion Research and Devl Found since 1963, fmr head, Research and Devl Found; asso prof, CE since 1960; fmr: head: bldg materials testing lab; bldg oprs research, Bldg Research Sta, dep head admn, acting head; with Pal Elec Corp. Off, Haganah, 1929-48; col, gen staff, IDF. Chmn: Haifa br, civil engrs; Engrs and Architects Assn, Isr; Technion Grads Assn; mem: Intl Union of Testing and Research Lab of Materials and Structures; Amer Concrete Inst. Contbr to sci and profsl jours. Spec interest, rationalization of bldg by developing and exploiting local bldg materials. Home: 6B Yanush Korczak St, Ahuza, Haifa, Isr. Office: Technion, Haifa, Isr.

KARP, Abraham J, US, rabbi, educator, author; b. Amdur, Pol, Apr 5, 1921; s. Aron and Rachel (Schor); in US since 1930; BA, magna cum laude, Yeshiva U, 1942; ordained rabbi, hons, JTSA, 1945, MHL, 1949; m. Deborah Burstein, June 17, 1945; c: Hillel, David. Rabbi: Cong Beth El, Rochester, NY, since 1956; fmr: Temple Isr, Swampscott, Mass, 1947-50; Beth Shalom, Kan City, Mo, 1950-56; visiting: rel; Dartmouth Coll, 1967; theol, St John Fisher Coll, 1968, 1969; asso prof, JTSA, 1968, 1969; research cons, Amer J Hist Cen, JTSA; visiting lectr, Heb U, Jerusalem, 1970. Pres, RA, mid-west region, 1955; dir, United Syn of Amer, metrop NY region, prayer book commn; asst dir, Sch of J Studies, JTSA, 1945; vice-pres, Amer J Hist Soc, exec council; mem: Mayor's adv comm; Rabb Cabinet, JTSA; bd mem, RA, J Social Service Bur, exec council. Author: When Your Child Asks About God, 1954; Our December Dilemma, 1958; The Jewish Way of Life, 1962; History of the United Synagogue of America, 1913-63; New York Chooses a Chief Rabbi; Conservative Judaism; Heritage of Solomon Schechter; The Jewish Experience in America; ed bd, Conservative Judaism; contbr to profsl jours; radio bc, From a Rabbi's Study, Rochester, since 1957. Recipient, f, Inst of Talmudic Ethics, 1958. Home: 59 Aberthaw Rd, Rochester, NY. Study: 139 Winton Rd, S, Rochester, NY.

KARP, Morris M, US, attorney; b. NYC, July 24, 1918; s. Sam

and Ida (Bloom); BSS, CCNY, 1939; LLB, NYU Law Sch, 1942; m. Dorothy Krevans, June 29, 1941; c: Peter, Anita. Pvt practice. Lt, mil govt, US Army. Secy, 6th Masonic Dist Soc, Manhattan, NY; fmr, vice-pres, Empire State Lodge, B'nai B'rith; mem: NY State, Bx Bar Assns; Masons, Shakespeare Lodge. Contbr to legal jours. Hobbies: golf, music, opera. Home: 11 Balint Dr, Yonkers, NY. Office: 509 Madison Ave, New York, NY.

KARPAS, Jack, Isr, physician; b. Loknik, Lith, Dec 28, 1908; s. Isaac and Mina (Rubin); in Isr since 1951; att S Afr Coll, Capetown; MB, ChB, U Capetown, 1931; m. Cecily Sacks, Jan 8, 1935; c: Alan, Dov, Charles. Dep dir, Hadassah Med Org, since 1952; med dir, Heb U, Hadassah Hosp, Jerusalem. Chmn, Jerusalem br, Public Health Drs Assn; fmr: mayor, Parow Cape, S Afr, 1944-45; chmn, Cape comm, S Afr J Bd Deps; pres, Parow Heb Cong. Contbr to Isr and Amer jours. Home: 42 Jabotinsky St, Jerusalem, Isr. Office: Ein Kerem, Jerusalem, Isr.

KARPINOVITCH, Abraham, Isr, author; b. Vilna, Pol, May 29, 1918; s. Moses and Rachel (Levitan); in Isr since 1950; BA, hons, hist, U London, 1968; m. Anna Goldstein, Mar 30, 1966. Asst secy, Isr Philharmonic Orch, since 1953. Author: Der Weg Kain Sdom, 1957; The Story of the Year, 1961; Baim Wilner Dutchhoif, 1967; The Story of the Year, 1968; perm free-lance writer: Letzte Naies, daily, Golden Keit, jour. Mem: Yiddish Writers and Journalists Assn, Isr; ACUM. Recipient, awards: Am Oved, 1955; Letzte Naies, 1958; Fishel Bimko, J Cultural Cong in Russ, 1959; Y Friedland, LA, 1963. Hobbies: hist, lit. Home: 84 Shlomo Hamelech St, Tel Aviv, Isr. Office: Isr Philharmonic Orch, Tel Aviv, Isr.

KARPINOVITZ, Meleh, Isr, author (pen name **Karmel**); b. Vilna, Lith, 1912; s. Moshe and Rachel; att Yiddisher Musical Inst, Vienna, Aus; m. Miriam Rosenthal, 1945; c: Fama, Moshe. Mgn ed, Die Goldene Keyt since 1952; news ed, Letzte Nayes, since 1949; fmr mgn dir: J Theatre, Warsaw; J State Theatre, Bialistok; Kiev-Yiddish Theatre. Author, The Bookkeeper of Death; trans, Exodus, into Yiddish; ed, Vilner Pinkas, rev. Mem: Fédération Nationale des Journalistes d'Isr; Intl Fed of Journalists; Fed of J Writers. Home: 7 Sd Um, Tel Aviv, Isr. Office: 14 Beeri St, Tel Aviv, Isr.

KARPMAN (Carmin), Itzhak J, US, Isr, editor, publishing exec; b. Warsaw, Pol, Apr 11, 1914; s. Abraham and Hannah (Premsky); in US since 1946; att: Bus Admn Sch, Warsaw; U of Warsaw; Heb U, Jerusalem; Tel Aviv Sch of Law and Econ; New Sch for Social Research, NY; hon PhD, Intl Acad, London, 1954, hon DHumL, 1961; m. Esther Goldfinger, Dec 22, 1939; c: Dahlia, Daniel, Diana. Chmn, Amer ed bd and gen ed, The Standard Jewish Ency, since 1957; ed, Who's Who in World Jewry, since 1951, chmn, ed bd, since 1968; exec vice-pres, Ency Judaica, 1959-67; found, dir, Ency Judaica Research Found, 1963-67; dir World Confd of Gen Zionists, 1946-52, mem, world exec, 1951-53; secy, Amer Amidar — Housing for Immigrants in Israel, Inc, 1952-58; mem, natl econ council, ZOA, 1947-50; ed, Blau-Weiss, weekly, and Hanoar Hazioni, monthly, Warsaw, Pol, 1929-36, Pal, 1936-46; secy general, Zionist Confd of Pal, 1938-42, mem natl bd, 1942-46; dir, Anglo-Pal Publ Ltd, London, Jerusalem, 1943-46. Author: Holon Development Plan, 1942; Mortgage Credit, 1945; Shikun uBeniya, 1946; World Wide Report, 1948; The Zionist World, 1951; contbr to periodicals. Homes: 16 Sanhedrin St, Tel Aviv, Isr; 88 Bleecker St, New York, NY.

KARRO, Jacob I, US, attorney, educator; b. NYC, Oct 27, 1909; s. Nathan and Betty (Haas); BA, Columbia U, 1930, Pulitzer scholar, 1926-30; LLB, 1932; JD, Georgetown U, 1938; m. Anne Elliot, Mar 6, 1937; c: David, Jill, Janet. Prof, law, U Puerto Rico, since 1967; fmr: public service with US Govt; lab, housing, mil govt of Ger, chief, Legal Affairs Div, Off of High Commnr for Ger, 1935-67; asso solicitor, Lab Relations & Civil Rights, Lab Dept, 1965-66. Office: POB 22040, U of Puerto Rico, Rio Piedras, Puerto Rico.

KARSCH, Samuel, US, business exec; b. Russ, June 4, 1899; s. David and Sarah; in US since 1907; att Yeshivot in Slonin, NYC; m. (decd); c: Daniel. Ret, fmr, mgr, Equitable Ins Soc of US, 1925-46. Vice-chmn, Isr Bond Campaign; mem: bd: ADL; UJA; JDC; active leader, FJP; fmr mem, Jewelry

Assn; fmr pres, NY B'nai B'rith; clubs: Masons: Grand St Boys Assn; Town, NYC. Spec interests: philanthropy, fundraising. Home: 2 E 86 St, New York, NY.

KARSCHON, René, Isr, agronomist; b. Düsseldorf, Ger, Nov 3, 1919; s. Grisha and Erna (Mayer); in Isr since 1949; att Institut Agronomique de l'Etat, Gembloux, Belgium, 1938-40; DSc, Fed Inst of Tech, Zurich, Switz, 1949; m. Raya Levin, 1949. Dir, Forestry dept, Volcani Inst of Agric Research, Bet Dagan, since 1961; sr research off, Forestry Dept, Min of Agric, 1949-61. Chmn, Isr Forestry Assn; mem, Swiss Forestry Assn. Contbr numerous publs to profsl jours. Home: Ilanot, Lev Hasharon, Isr. Office: Volcani Inst of Agric Research, Bet Dagan, Isr.

KARSZON, Alexander, Isr, engineer, educator; b. Olevsk, Russ, Sep 3, 1911; s. Moshe and Shendel (Halperin); in Isr since 1935; att Grand Sch, Belgium; m. Riva Mudrik, Sep 29, 1937; c: Ariela Har, Nira Livnat. Mgn dir, Vulcan Foundries Ltd, since 1953; sr lectr, Technion, Haifa, since 1946; tech mgr, Herut Ltd, 1935-53. Pres, Isr Mgmt Assn, Haifa br, since 1967; mem: Engrs and Architects Assn, Isr; Amer Foundrymen's Soc; mgmt: Isr Foundry Assn; Isr Mgmt Assn; fmr: mem, Koor Mgmt: pres, Isr Foundrymen's Soc. Author: Sanitary Installation, 1938; Sewerage, 1955. Home: 10 Ruth Hacohen, Neve Shaanan, Haifa, Isr. Office: POB 624, Haifa, Isr.

KARTAGENER, Manes, Switz, physician, educator; b. Przemysl, Pol, Jan 7, 1897; s. Lazar and Susanne (Guth); in Switz since 1916; MD, U Zurich, 1924; m. Rose Intrator, 1935; c: Susanne, Esther. Prof, internal med, U Zurich, since 1950; privatdozent, internal med, since 1935; chief phys, med Polyclinic, U Zurich, 1929-37. Contbr to med periodicals. Home: Aurorast 8, Zurich, Switz. Office: Börsenstr 18, Zurich, Switz.

KARU (Krupnik), Baruch, Isr, critic, lexicographer, traslator; b. Chernevtsy, Russ, 1899; in Isr since 1932; att: Acad of Baron Ginzburg, St Petersburg; Sem for J Studies, Berlin. Ed: lit sect and lit critic, Haboker daily, Tel Aviv, since 1942; Ency of Lit; mem, staff, Haaretz daily, 1933-42; fmr secy, Ency Eshkol, Berlin. Compiled: Practical Dictionary of the Talmud, Midrash and Targum; Milon Talmudi; Zeirufei Lashon, Heb-Ger, Ger-Heb; Milon haAramit haChaya; trans: History of the Jewish People, Dubnov, 10 vols; Toldot Sifrut Israel, Zinberg, 5 vols; Toldto haTfila vehaAvoda beIsrael, Elbogen; Shimshon, Jabotinsky; Lady Chatterley's Lover, Lawrence; haOlam shel Etmol, Stephen Zweig; Yirmiyahu, Werfel; Ganavim baLaila, Koestler; Mimesis, Auerbach; Acharon haZadikim, André Schwartz Bart; works of Charles Dickens and other trans from Eng, Fr, Russ, Ger, Yiddish. Co-found, Isr Journalists Assn; mem: exec, Heb Writers Assn of Isr; adv comm, Heb Lang Acad; Council for Culture and Art, Isr Min of Educ and Culture. Recipient, Tchernichowsky Prize for trans of Dubnov's Hist. Home: 90 Rothschild Blvd, Tel Aviv, Isr.

KARU, Israel, Isr, business exec; b. Vienna, Aus, Oct 22, 1926; s. Moshe and Miriam (Maisels); in Isr since 1939; att, Heb U, Jerusalem; MBA, Columbia U, NY; m. Shlomit Zait June 1948; c: Eran. Mgn dir, Rassco Corp, since 1967; dir, press relations, Isr Off of Info, NY, 1957-61; exec dir, Tel Aviv Stock Exch, 1961-67. Segan Aluf, IDF, 1948-57. Recipient, Decorations: War of Independence; Sinai; Six Days War. Home: 26 Bnayahu St, Tel Aviv, Isr. Office: 1 Har Sinai St, Tel Aviv, Isr.

KARZEN, Jay, US, rabbi; b. Chgo, Ill, Dec 31, 1934; s. Max and Yetta (Stick); BA, Roosevelt U, Chgo, Ill, 1956; ordained rabbi, BHL, Heb Theol Coll, Skokie, Ill, 1959; m. Ruby Ray, Dec 30, 1956; c: Tamar, Uri. Rabbi: Maine Township J Cong, since 1965; Cong B'nai Jacob, Ottumwa, Ia, 1959-62; Cong B'nai Isr, Council Bluffs, Ia, 1962-65. Secy-treas: Rabb F of NW Suburbs; Syn Council of NW Suburbs; found, pres, B'nai B'rith, 1962-64; mem: RabCA; Chgo Bd Rabbis; Chgo Rabb Council; Kiwanis; NCCJ. Recipient: Citation for Torah Service, Heb Theol Coll, 1962; Isr Bond Award, Isr Bonds, 1964. Hobbies: composing cantoral music, lead in operettas, writing playlets. Home: 9008 W Oaks, Des Plaines, Ill. Study: 8800 Ballard, Des Plaines, Ill.

KASDON, S Charles, US, physician, educator; b. NYC, Dec 19, 1912; s. David and Sara (Mirkin); BS, Yale U, 1933, MS, 1934, MD, 1938; m. Muriel Cohen, Dec 26, 1943; c: David, Madeline, Louisa. Asso prof, obstet and gyn dept,

Tufts U Med Sch, Boston since 1958, fmr asst prof; pres, Med Research Found of Boston, since 1954; dir, cytology lab, NE Cen Hosp since 1952; in practice, obstet and gyn since 1943. Lt-cdr, flight surg, USN, 1943-46. Mem: AAAS; Amer Assn for Cancer Research; AMA; Mass Med Soc; NE Soc of Obstet and Gyn; Amer Coll Obstet and Gyn; Inter-Soc Cytology Council; Amer Soc of Med Educ; Gtr Boston Med Soc; JWV; fmr: f, Amer Coll Surgs; found f, Amer Coll Obstet and Gyn; dipl, Amer Bd Obstet and Gyn. Author, Atlas of Cytology; contbr to med and research jours; chaps in books: Physiopathology of Cancer; Progress in Clinical Endocrinology. Hobby, sailing. Home and office: 127 Bay State Rd, Boston, Mass.

KASEN, Louis A, US, manufacturer; b. Nezhin, Russ, Nov 17, 1892; s. Mordechai and Channy (Bickoff) Keiley; in US since 1910; BS, Cooper Union, NYC, 1917; m. Bella Frashgang, 1918; c: Anyta La Pidus, Martin, Renee Cohen. Pres, Synthetic Plastics Corp, since 1926. Civil engr, Emergency Fleet, WWI, 1917-18. Pres, Polevski chap, LZOA, 1952-54; chmn, chem div, UJA, 1948-52, gen chmn, UJA of Essex Co, 1953; treas, Home for Aged, 1953-54; mem, bd trustees, Temple B'nai Abraham, 1954; mem, bd govs, Isr Bonds, 1953-54; club, Greenbrook Country. Home: 61 Spier Dr, South Orange, NJ. Office: 88 St Francis St, Newark, NJ.

KASHER, Menachem M, Isr, rabbi, author; b. Warsaw, Pol, Mar 10, 1895; s. Peretz and Perla (Pacholder) in US since 1927; ordained rabbi, Yeshiva, Nova-Minsk, 1913; hon DD, Yeshiva U, NY, 1947; m. Ester Fajerman, Mar 12, 1913; c: Simon, Moshe, Miriam, Bracha, Bernard. Author, ed, Torah Shelemah, bibl ency, 20 vols, 1927-61; found, Mechon Torah Shelemah, inst for research and publs of succeeding vols, Jerusalem, 1950; ed, Degel ha-Torah, Warsaw, 1920; head, Mesifta Acad, Warsaw, 1920-24; found, dean, Sefat Emet Yeshiva, Jerusalem, 1925-27; researcher in bibl texts, commentaries. Author: Maimonides and the Mekhilta of Rabbi Simon ben Yohai, 1941; Maimonides in Print and Manuscript, 1945; Aspects of the International Date Line, 1945; Encyclopedia of Biblical Interpretation; Israel Passover Haggadah, 1950; Sarei ha-Elef, millenial Bibliography, 1959; Haggadah Shelemah, 1961. Recipient: Lit Prize, Tel Aviv Munic, 1945, 1952; Isr Natl Prize for Torah Lit, 1963. Home and Study: 19 Malachi St, Jerusalem, Isr; 210 W 91 St, New York, NY.

KASHIV, Itzhak, Isr, economist; b. Kowno, Lith, Oct 17, 1922; s. Zvi and Nadia (Berkman) Kopchowski; in Isr since 1948; BA, MA, with distinction, Heb U, Jerusalem, 1954; PhD, LSE, London, 1966; m. Avivith Rudnik, Oct 26, 1950; c: Anadia, Amir, Yoav. Econ adv, mgr, Econ Research Dept, Bank Leumi L'Israel, Tel Aviv, since 1968; mem, Kibbutz Lohamei Hagetaot, 1949-60; econ, political researcher, Isr Emb, London, 1960-66; econ adv, Isr Citrus Bd, London, 1960-67. Mem, cen comm, Chalutzik Underground Org, Ghetto Kowno, 1941-44; IDF, 1948-49; 1956. Fmr mem, leadership, Dror, Chalutzik Youth Movement, Poalei Zion; mem: Pedg Council, Hamidrasha Leminhal; Isr Cen for Mgmt. Recipient, David Horowitz Award, Heb U, Jerusalem, 1959. Home: 3 Mozyr St, Tel Aviv, Isr. Office: Bank Leumi L'Israel, 24-32 Yehuda Halevi St, Tel Aviv, Isr.

KASHTAN, Aharon, Isr, architect; b. Warsaw, Pol, Nov 15, 1920; s. Yehuda and Bella (Wiernik); in Isr since 1939; att: fac of hum, U Warsaw, 1937-39; Inst of J Studies, Warsaw, 1937-39; B Arch Engr, Technion, Haifa, 1945; m. Miriam Mosbacher; c: Assaf, Nadav. Asso prof, fac of architecture, Technion, since 1951. Engrs Corps, IDF, 1948-69. Mem: bd dirs, Isr Inst of Ind Design; Commn for Preservation and Devl, Old Acre City; Engrs and Architects Assn, Isr; Centro di Studi Per La Storia Dell'Architectura, Rome, It. Designer: several bldgs on campus, Technion, Haifa; Heb U, Jerusalem; syns. Author, Synagogue Architecture, 1957; contbr to jours. Recipient: 1st prize, for bldg on Jerusalem campus; prizes in architectural competitions. Hobbies: hist, painting, photography, Mediterranean travel. Home: 35 Netiv Ofakim, Haifa, Isr. Office: Technion, Haifa, Isr.

KASLE, Abe, US, business exec; b. Russ, Mar 18, 1895; s. Hyman and Faige (Kamindsky) Kozle; in US since 1909; m. Pearl Silverstein, Feb 14, 1915; c: Esther Jones, Leonard, Ben, Robert. Pres, Kasle Steel Corp since 1935; fmr pres, A Kasle Co. Pres, Hillel Day Sch of Metrop Detroit; hon pres, United Heb Day Schs of Detroit; mem: bd dirs, Adas Shalom Syn; B'nai B'rith; Zionist Org; Wayne State U Press; natl bd, State of Isr Bonds; Amer Assn of J Educ; AJCong; Men's

ORT; JNF; JDC; fmr: chmn, UJA; vice-pres, JWF; bd trustees, Sinai Hosp, all of Detroit. Recipient, Fred M Mutzel Memorial Award for dist communal service, JWF of Detroit, 1958. Spec interest, J and Heb educ. Home: 19470 Lucerne Dr, Detroit, Mich. Office: 4343 Wyoming Ave, Dearborn, Mich.

KASLE, Louis, US, industrialist, business exec; b. Mitzk, Russ, Dec 10, 1909; s. Ephraim and Faiga (Kaminetsky); in US since 1921; att Toledo U, 1929; m. Charlotte Lewis, Apr 27, 1941; c: Franklin, Jerome, Joan, Noreen, Diana. Pres: Kasle Bros Inc, since 1939; W Steel; Genesee Discount Corp, all Flint, Mich; pres, treas, Kasle Steel Compressing, Springfield, O. Pres, Cong Beth Isr, 1954-59; dir, pres, JCC, 1954-57; chmn: UJA, 1949-50, 1953, hon, 1951-52; Bonds for Isr, 1951-56; life mem: ZOA, pres, 1944-45; B'nai B'rith; AJCong; Temple Beth El, all Flint. Home: 1121 Woodlawn Pk Dr, Flint, Mich. Office: Western Rd, Flint, Mich.

KASLOW, Arthur L, US, physician; b. Omaha, Neb, Jan 15, 1913; s. Hyman and Hannah (Cutler) Kazlowsky; BS, Creighton U, 1931, MD, Sch of Med, 1935; c: Harvey, Arthur, David, Jeremy, Harmon, Daniel. Pvt practice, med, specializing in clinical med and research, since 1935; research f, U of Cal, Berkeley, 1937-38; instr, Stanford U, 1938-41; postdoc scholar in Inst of Rel, Tex Med Cen, Houston, 1966. Maj, USAAC, WW II. Prin contribs: inventor of Kaslow Stomach Tubes, 1948; Kaslow Oxygen Mask, 1954; placement therapy, 1956; Kasocidin antibacterial compound, 1958. Mem: Amer Humanistic Psych Assn; AMA; Cal Med Assn; Amer Geriatric Soc; NY Acad of Sci's; Amer Coll of Gastroenterology; Cal Soc of Internal Med; Amer Coll of Angiology; AAAS; bd dirs, Westwood Temple, LA, 1947-55; Rotary Intl; Pi Lambda Phi. Home: Doxholm on Alamo Pintado, Solvang, Cal. Office: 795 Alamo Pintado Rd, Solvang, Cal.

KASS, Irving R, US, attorney; b. Russ, Dec 14, 1904; s. David and Bessie (Rogen); in US since 1906; BCS, NYU, 1923, LLB, 1926; m. Ida Cohen, July 2, 1932; c: David, Joseph, Bodonna. Mem, law firm, Tolleris, Kass & Tolleris, since 1939; counsel, Upholstered Furniture Mfrs Assn, since 1942. Cochmn: UJA; Histadrut, both since 1944; mem: Bonds for Isr; ARC; Amer Trade Assn Execs; NY Co Lawyers Assn; Ind Relations Research Assn; Masons; KP; Delta Mu Delta. Contbr: column, Furniture World; to trade jours. Recipient, Guest of Hon, furniture and allied divs, UJA, 1948. Home: 15 Marion Ave, Mt Vernon, NY. Office: 276 Fifth Ave, New York, NY.

KASSAL, Bentley, US, attorney; b. NYC, Feb 28, 1917; s. Hyman and Pauline (Nirenberg); BA, U of Pa, 1937; LLB, Harvard Law Sch, 1940. Pvt practice since 1940; assemblyman, NY State Leg, 1957-62. US Army, 1942-45. Dir, off, FJP since 1952, chmn, leg comm; chmn: Amer Vets Comm, W Side chap; ADA, 1965-67; natl bd: AJCong; ZOA; dist leader, W Side Dem, pres, 1952-60; bd mem, NY Young Dem. Recipient: Bronze Star Medal; Two Bronze Arrowheads; Seven Battle Stars, 1945. Home: 5 W 86 St, New York, NY. Office: 295 Madison Ave, New York, NY.

KASSAN, Shalom, Isr, judge; b. Jerusalem, Isr, 1900; s. Levi Itzhak and Frieda (Frumkin) Kazarnovsky; desc of, Rabbi Shneor Zalman miLadi; att: Tchrs Coll, Jerusalem; PhB, MA, U Chgo; m. Eva Dushkin, 1927; c: Jordan, Naomi Amir. Relieving pres, Dist Court, Haifa, since 1955; prin, HS, Chgo, 1928-33; instr, Coll of J Studies, Chgo, 1930-34; advocate, Advocate Eliash firm, Jerusalem, 1937; magistrate: Haifa, 1937-42; Tel Aviv, 1942-46; judge, Dist Court, Tel Tel Aviv, 1946-55. Pres, Hadera chap, Friends Heb U; mem: bd govs, exec comm, Heb U, Jerusalem; Yad Vashem; exec comm, B'nai B'rith; fmr: pres, B'nai B'rith Isr; vice pres, World B'nai B'rith; grand master, Masons, Isr. Author: Hapat Legomenon in the Book of Job, 1934; Convicted and Acquitted, 1960; Selected Judgements of Justice Frumkin of the Palestine Supreme Court, 1962. Hobby: philately. Home: 53 Hagalil St, Haifa, Isr. Office: Dist Court, Haifa, Isr.

KASTEN, Elihu, US, rabbi; b. Bx, NY, May 21, 1915; s. Joseph and Fannie (Saxe); BA, Yeshiva Coll, Yeshiva U, 1936, tchr dipl, Tchrs Inst, 1936, ordained rabbi, Rabb Sch, 1948; JD, Columbia U, 1939; m. Sarah Speiser, June 25, 1944; c: Avi, Tamar, Carmi. Rabbi: Cong Shaar Hasyamayin, since 1963; Cong Ezras Isr, Bx, 1942-43; J Cen, Wakefield and Edenwald, 1944-45; educ dir, Heb Inst, U Hghts, Bx, 1946-50; rabbi, Oceanside J Cen, 1950-63. Pres: LI Commn of

Rabbis, 1956-58; Judea Devl Corp; Yeshiva Coll Alumni Assn; mem: natl exec comm, Hapoel Hamizrachi, 1955-58; natl exec, RabCA, since 1961; NY Bd Rabbis; AJCong; Rabb Alumni, Yeshiva U; NY Trial Lawyer Assn, 1969. Co-ed, Rabb Council Record, since 1955; asso ed, Fed News Service; contbr to Anglo-J jours. Hobbies: philately, athletics. Home: 590 Waukena Ave, Oceanside, NY. Study: 3309 Skillman Ave, Oceanside, NY.

KASTLE, Harold D, US, rabbi; b. NYC, Sep 23, 1922; s. Morris and Rose (Kaufman); BJP, JTSA, 1943; BS, CCNY, 1944; MA, Tchrs Coll, Columbia U, 1950; ordained rabbi, MHL, JTSA, 1948; m. Ruth Ebert, Aug 12, 1944; c: Michael, Jonathan, Deborah. Rabbi, Temple Aliyah, Needham, Mass, since 1967; with personnel admn dept, Raytheon Co, Lexington since 1958; educ dir, Temple Emanuel, Newton Cen, 1948-51; rabbi: Temple Adas Isr, Hyde Park, 1959-66; Temple Reyim, W Newton, 1951-58; educ cons, Bur of J Educ, Boston, 1951-52. Mem, bd dirs, Family Service Bur, Newton, since 1951; secy, United Syn Comm on J Educ; treas, Mass Bd of Rabbis; club, Newton Boys, fmr mem, bd dirs. Author, 658 Stories, 1956. Home: 66 Commonwealth Park W, Newton Centre, Mass.

KASWAN, Jacques W, US, psychologist, educator; b. Vienna, Aus, June 14, 1924; s. Adolph and Regina (Niedermayer); in US since 1941; BA, U of Cal, 1951; MA, New Sch for Social Research, 1954; PhD, Wash U, 1955; m. Ruth Kissman, Dec 25, 1949; c: Daniel, Alice, Mark. Asso prof, psych, O State U, since 1968, asst prof, psych, U of Cal, 1958-68; instr, asst prof, Yale U, 1955-58. US Army, 1943-45. Mem: Amer Psych Assn; Sigma Xi. Contbr to profsl jours. Home: 1071 Sunny Hill Dr, Columbus, O. Office: O State U, Columbus, O.

KATCHALSKI, Ephraim, Isr, biochemist, educator; b. Kiev, Russ, May 16, 1916; s. Yehuda and Cila; in Isr since 1922; MSc, Heb U, 1937, PhD, 1941; m. Nina Gotlieb, Feb 14, 1938; c: Meir, Irith. Head, dept biophysics, Weizmann Inst of Sci, Rehovot, on fac since 1949; fac: Heb U, Jerusalem, 1937-45; Poly Inst, Bklyn and Columbia Us, 1946-48; visiting prof, Heb U, 1953-61; guest sci, Harvard U, 1957-59; sr fgn sc f, UCLA, 1964. Chief sci, Isr Defense Min, 1966-68. Mem: Isr Acad Sci and Hum; Natl Council for Research and Devl; Council for Higher Educ; Biochem Soc, Isr; Isr Chem Soc; Natl Acad Scis, US; Amer Acad Arts and Sci; Amer Chem Soc; NY Acad Sci; Biophys Soc; Amer Soc Biol Chems; AAAS; Intl Union Biochems; Leopoldina Acad Sci, Ger; Eur Molecular Biol Org. Mem, ed bds: Archives of Biochemistry and Biophysics; Biopolymers; Excerpta Medica; Eur Jour of Biochemistry. Recipient: Tchernikovski Prize, 1948; Weizmann Prize, Munic of Tel Aviv, 1950; Isr Prize, natural scis, 1959; Rothschild Prize, natural scis; 1961. Home: Neve Weizmann, Rehovot, Isr. Office: Weizmann Inst of Sci, Rehovot, Isr.

KATES, Arnold D, US, business exec; b. NYC, Oct 25, 1898; s. Abraham and Helena (Meyer) Katz; att CCNY, 1918-22; NYU; New Sch of Social Research; m. Jean Abrams, Oct 27, 1949; c: Barbara. Pres: Mailographic Co, since 1920; Arnold Kates Advt, since 1920; Tru-Tone Multilith Plate, since 1940. USNR, 1918-21. Dir: Park Assn, NY; Friends Cen; Brotherhood Syn; Stuyvesant Alumni Scholarship Assn; vice-pres, Assn of Advt Men and Women, 1925-32. Home: 14 Washington Sq, New York, NY. Office: 315 Hudson St, New York, NY.

KATES, Josef, Can, business exec, engineer; b. Vienna, Aus, May 5, 1921; s. Baruch and Anna (Entenberg) Katz; in Can since 1940; BA, MA, PhD, U Toronto, Can, 1951, att Goetherealschule, Vienna, 1938; m. Lillian Kroch, Dec 23, 1944; c: Louis, Naomi, Celina, Philip. Pres, Seta Computing Services Corp since 1954; asso, Kates, Peat, Marwick & Co, since 1967; sup, Imperial Optical Co, 1942-44; project engr, Rogers Majestic, 1944-48; research engr, U Toronto, 1948-54. Pvt, Can Offs Training Corps, 1944-45. Prin contribs: planning of maj transp projects in Can and fgn countries: airports; canals; ports; RRs; urban and regional plans. Mem: Can Opr Research Soc, fmr pres, Oprs Research Soc, Toronto; Oprs Research Comm, Can Ind Traffic League, fmr chmn; planning comm, Can Good Rds Assn; Engr Inst, Can, fmr chmn, mgmt sect; NRC, adv comm on computers; Ontario Inst Mgmt Cons, fmr vice-pres; appd to Sci Council by PM Pierre Trudeau. Contbr to profsl jours. Hobby, sports. Home: 17 Pifeshire, Willowdale 431, Ontario, Can. Office: 20 Spadina Rd, Toronto, Can.

KATHEIN, Reuven, Isr, veterinarian; b. Vienna, Aus, Feb 3, 1923; s. Bernhard and Miriam (Friedle); in Isr since 1939; BSc, DVM, U Cal, Davis; MPH, U Pittsburgh, 1964; cert, public admn, Ramat Rachel, Isr; m. Miriam Brill, June 21, 1950; c: Gila, Nurit, Doron. Controller, food from animal sources, vetr services, Min of Agric, since 1968; coord, continuous studies in vetr med, Tel Aviv U, since 1967; fmr: dist vetr, Hehaklait; research vetr, Chas Pfizer Co. Sgt, British Army, 1943-46; 1t, MC, IDF since 1945. Prin contribs: introduction in Isr of artificial insemination of beef cows with frozen semen; initiator, org, dept continuous educ in vetr med, Tel Aviv U. Dir, natl service, Rotary, Tel Aviv-Yaffo; mem: Masons Grand Lodge of Isr; comm: Isr Vetr Med Assn; parent adv comm, Ramat Gan Scouts; fmr: pres, Rotary, Kiriat Shmona; chmn: Kiriat Shmona Sick Fund Comm; Kiriat Shmona PTA. Contbr numerous articles to profsl publs. Recipient, Fgn Student Award, U Cal, Davis, 1952. Hobbies: youth guidance activities, swimming, skiing, horseback riding. Home: 8 Rama St, Givatayim, Isr. Office: Vetr Services, Bet Dagon, Isr.

KATONA, Ervin, Eng, architect; b. Brod, Czech, June 26 1903; s. Josef and Charlotte (Lebovics); in Eng since 1939; architect, High Tech Sch, Czech, 1924; dipl, Royal Inst of Brit Architects, London, 1944; m. Gertrude Steiner. Pvt practice since 1928; fmr: asst architect, Fritsch-Wuhrmann; chief architect, Lampl & Fuchs, both Prague, 1924-26. Prin contribs: designer of the Orlit sys of concrete prefabrication. Fmr: leader, J Youth Movement, Tchelet-Lavan, Czech; hon secy, Czech Scis, Technicians abroad; mem, Congrès Internationaux pour l'Architecture Moderne, 1937; clubs: J, Fritz Baum Group, Atid. Contbr articles to intl profsl jours. Hobby, J hist and phil. Home: 102 Langford Court, London NW8, Eng. Office: 23 Old Burlington St, London W1, Eng.

KATSH, Abraham I, US, educator, author; b. Pol, Aug 10, 1908; s. Reuben and Rachel (Maskilejson); father, fmr chief rabbi, Petah Tikva, Isr; in US since 1925; BS, NYU, 1931, MA, 1932, JD, 1936; att Princeton U, 1941; PhD, Dropsie Coll, 1944; hon DHL: HUHJIR, 1964; Chgo Coll J Studies, 1968; m. Estelle Wachtell, Feb 20, 1943; c: Ethan, Salem, Rochelle. Pres, Dropsie Coll, Heb and Cognate Learning, research prof, Hebraica, since 1967; dist prof of research, NYU, 1967-68, prof, Heb and Near E Studies, Grad Sch Arts and Scis, 1959-62, dir, Inst Heb Studies, 1962-67, found, curator, NYU Libr of Judaica and Hebraica, 1941-67; chmn, Dept of Heb Culture and Educ, 1937-59, Abraham I Katsh Professorship of Heb Culture, 1962-67; found, dir, NYU Summer Professorial Workshop in Isr, in coop with US Off of Educ, 1949-67. Author: Torat haYahasut Shel Einstein, 1936; Hebrew In American Higher Education, 1941; Hebraic Foundations of American Democracy, 1941; Hebrew Language and Literature in American Institutions of Higher Learning, 1951; Judaism in Islam, 1954; Catalogue of Hebrew MSS in the USSR, 1957; haYahaduth baIslam, 1958; Ginzei Russiya, 1958; Judaism and the Koran, 1962; The Antonin Geniza Collection in Leningrad, 1963; Midrash David Hanagid (Hebrew eds of a 13th century Judeo-Arabic manuscript): Bereshit, Genesis, 1964, Shemot, Exodus, 1967; Yiggal Hazon, Unpublished Heb poetry of the Golden Age of Spain, 1964; The Antonin Mishnah Geniza, 1968; The Antonin Talmudic Geniza, 1970; trans and ed, Scroll of Agony—The Ch A Kaplan Diary of the Warsaw Ghetto, 1965; Megilat Yesurin—full rendition of Kaplan's Heb Diary with Notes and Introduction in Heb, 1965; ed-in-chief, found, Heb Abstracts; co-ed, Ency Judaica; rev ed, Modern Lang Jour, Heb sect; co-ed, J Quarterly Rev; contbr: to encys; numerous articles to intl publs. Lectured at: 24th Intl Oriental Cong, Munich; 25th Intl Oriental Cong, Moscow, 1960; World Cong for J Scholarship, Jerusalem; many Us in US and Eur; delg, Tenth Cong Intl des Linguistas, 1967; found, hon pres, Natl Assn Profs Heb in Amer Us; chmn: bd govs, J Acad of Arts and Scis; MLA; natl screening comm, Inst of Intl Educ; natl chmn, bd licenses, Amer Assn for J Educ; mem: comm, Intl Exch of Persons; conf bd, Asso Research Councils, Wash; Amer Oriental Soc; Soc for Bibl Lit; Acad of Rel; Phi Delta Kappa; cons, Heb, Natl Assn on Standard Med Vocabulary; spec examiner, Bd of Educ, NYC. Recipient: grants: Amer Council Learned Socs; Rockefeller Found; Littauer Found; Matz Found; Heb Acad Amer; William Liebermann Research Fund; Inter-U Comm; Alexander Kohut Found; Memorial Found for J Culture Research; Natl Found on Arts and Hum; HEW; hons: Abraham I Katsh Endowed Chair of Heb, named by

NYU bd trustees; NYU pres citation; Mayor's Citation, NYC; B'rith Abraham Medal; J JBCA; Isr Govt; EO Malby award for hum relations, NYU; State of Ky; Dropise Coll Alumni; Natl Assn of Negro Bus and Profsl Women's Club; 1st $500 Schneiderman prize for outstanding Heb thought and original scholarship; Alumni Achievement award, Wash Sq Coll; NYU Hon Soc; Brotherhood award, Chapel of the Four Chalains; Katsh Festschrift for contribution to Heb Studies in Amer, Natl Assn Profs Heb. Home: 901 Walton Ave, Bronx, NY. Office: Dropsie Coll, Philadelphia, Pa.

KATTAN, Naim, Can, author, journalist; b. Bagdad, Iraq, Aug 26, 1928; s. Nessim and Hela (Joseph); in Can since 1954; att Sorbonne U, Paris, 1947-52; m. Gaétane Laniel, July 27, 1961. Dir, Cercle Juif de Langue Française; lectr, social sci fac, Laval U, Que; radio commentator: Can; Eur; dir, lit sect Can Council, Ottawa since 1967. Ed: Les Juifs et la Communauté Française; Juifs et Canadiens; fmr ed, Bulletin du Cercle Juif; contbr to publs in Eur, ME. Home: 4803 Mira Rd, Montreal, Can. Office: 140 Wellington St, Ottawa, Can.

KATZ, A Raymond, US, artist, b. Kassa, Hung, Apr 21, 1895; s. Morris and Anna (Altman); in US since 1910; att Art Inst of Chgo; m. Elsie Engel, Jan 15, 1924; c: Donald, Joan. Lectr, creative, mural painting, J art, Natl JWB; exhb at: Chgo Art Inst; Carnegie Inst; Pa Acad; LA Mus; SF Mus; Corcoran Gal; Natl Acad of Design, NYC; Whitney Mus, NYC; Mus of Contemporary Arts, NYC; one man shows: Mus voor Sierkunst, Ghent, Belgium; Chgo Art Inst; Milw Art Inst; Bernet Gal, NYC; J Mus, NY; Butler Inst of Amer Art, Youngstown, O; San Antonio, Tex; San Diego, Cal; Baltimore; frescoes, murals, mosaics, windows, sculptures commissioned by over 200 syns including: Stephen Wise Free Syn, NYC; Anshe Emet; Downtown Syn, both Chgo. Fmr head, arts and dept, Gt Lakes Naval Hosp, WW II. Fmr vice-pres, Chgo Art Inst Alumni Assn; mem: Natl Soc of Mural Painters; Artist-Craftsmen of NY. Author: White on Black, 1933; A New Art for an Old Religion, 1945; The Ten Commandments, 1946; Adventures in Casein, 1951; 23 Hebraic Selections, 1954; Religious Festivals, 1961; Song of Songs, 1968; The Prophets; The Mishnah; The Seven Names of God. Home: 260 Riverside Dr, New York, NY. Studio: 523 Sixth Ave, New York, NY.

KATZ, Aleph (Morris Abraham), US, editor, author; b. Miynow, Russ, May 15, 1898; s. Hyman and Anna (Hirsch); in US since 1913; att, CCNY; m. Celia Silverstein, July 5, 1930; c: Ephraim, Deborah. Ed, Yiddish dept, JTA, since 1925. Author: A Mayse Fun Yam, 1925; Oitzer Indzl, Yiddish trans of Stevenson's Treasure Island, 1927; Akertzeit, 1929; Dos Telerl Fun Himl, 1934; Fun Aleph Biz Tov, 1939; Amol Is Geven a Mayse, 1944; Good Morning, Aleph; Purim Play; Yossele, all 1950; Cholem Aleichem, 1958; Di Emesse Khassene, 1964; Der Morgenshtern. Mem: Yiddish Writers Union; Farband; Yiddish Dict Comm; YIVO; Cong for J Culture; club, J PEN. Recipient, Cong for J Culture Award, 1955. Home: 152 E 22 St, New York, NY. Office: 660 First Ave, New York, NY.

KATZ, Alex, US, artist; b. Bklyn, NY, July 24, 1927; s. Isaac and Ella (Marion); cert, Cooper Union; m. Ada Del Moro, Feb 1, 1958; c: Vincent. Painter since 1949; visiting critic, Yale U, since 1960; instr, art, Pratt Inst; Skowhegan Sch of Painting and Sculpture; Bklyn Mus, 1960; one-man shows, Gals: Roko; Pa State Coll; Tanager; Stable; Martha Jackson; Fischbach; David Stuart. USN, 1945-46. Home and studio: 435 W Broadway, New York, NY.

KATZ, Alfred, US, educator; b. Yaroslaw, Pol, Apr 15, 1938; s. Israel and Rose; tchrs cert, Tchrs Inst, Yeshiva U, 1958, BA, 1960; MA, Columbia U, 1962; PhD, NYU, 1966; m. Merrily Waxman, Dec, 1966; c: Sharon. Asst prof: political sci, Bradley U, Peoria, Ill, since 1967; social sci, NY Inst Tech, 1965-67. Adv, Hillel Found, Bradley U; mem: AAUP; Amer Political Sci Assn. Author: Bund, The Jewish Socialist Labor Party, 1965; Poland's Ghetto at War, 1969. Recipient, NYU Founds Day Award, 1967. Home: 627 Crestwood Dr, Peoria, Ill. Office: Bradley U, Peoria, Ill.

KATZ, Ascher, US, attorney; b. NYC, Apr 16, 1927; s. Morris and Tessie (Appel); BEE, CCNY, 1948; JD, Harvard Law Sch, 1951; m. Barbara Novins, Aug 17, 1957; c: Arlene, Beverly, Rochelle. Partner, Abelson, Bromberg & Katz since 1969; staff atty, Legal Aid Soc, civil br, NYC, 1952-54; law asst, NYC Corp Counsel's Off, 1954-55; pvt practice, 1955-69. USNR, 1945-46. Vice-pres, NY Metrop Council, AJCong, natl gov council; co-chmn, Rel Sch Bd, Temple Isr, White Plains, NY; treas, B'nai B'rith, Hillel Counsellorship, Westchester Comty Coll; fmr pres, Bklyn div, AJCong; vice-pres, J Comty Relation Council, NY, treas; mem: Amer Bar Assn; Amer and NY State Trial Lawyers Assns; NY State Bar Assn; JWV; Urban League; NAACP; ACLU; Masons, Joseph Warren Lodge; CCNY Alumni Assn; Harvard Law Sch Assn; club, Lawyers Sq. Hobbies: painting, philately. Home: 24 Primrose Ave W, White Plains, NY. Office: 400 Madison Ave, New York, NY.

KATZ, Bertha, (pen name, **Bracha Kopstein**), US, author; b. Kiev, Russ, Apr 15, 1909; d. Wolf and Nehoma (Shinder) Kopstein; in US since 1930; att I L Peretz Shule, Winnipeg, Can, 1924-28; J Tchrs Sem, NY, 1930-33; m. Benjamin Katz, June 24, 1932; c: William. Author: Shtark Bin Yich, 1939; Zing Mein Hartz, 1945; Dos Folk Is Do, 1951, all poems; Heb trans: miShemesh El Shemesh, poems, 1959; Yomtov Un Voch In Yisroel, reportage, 1965; Geklibene Lieder, Yiddish and Heb, including LP record, poetry readings, 1968; contbr to: Isr press; Yiddish press: London; Paris; Arg; Can. Social worker, JA, Immigrants Camp Belt, Lod, 1949-51; lectr on behalf of Isr govt; ed dept, Histadrut; participant in Isr radio, both 1950-59; mem: PEN; Yiddish Writers Org, both Isr. Hobbies: music, travel. Home: 165 W 66 St, New York, NY.

KATZ, Carl, Ger, merchant; b. Osterholz-Scharmbeck, Ger, Sep 14, 1899; s. Rudolf and Pauline (Katz); m. Marianne Gruenberg, Aug 14, 1923; c: Ingeborg Berger. Owner, Carl Katz Import-Export, since 1945. Chmn, J comty, Bremen, since 1945; bd dirs, Union of J Comtys, NW, Ger, since 1946. Home: Donandstr 18, Bremen, W Ger. Office: Industrie str 12a, Bremen, W Ger.

KATZ, Charles R, US, attorney; b. NYC, June 30, 1912; s. Jacob and Mary (Kort); BS, NYU, 1933; JD, NYU, Sch of Law, 1935; m. Edythe Kotler, Nov, 1967; c: Barbara Rosen, Jack, Janet Greenspan. Partner, Katz & Wolchok since 1945. Mem: Amer Bar Assn, lab law comm; Histadrut; NY State Bar Assn; NY Co Lawyers Assn; Teamsters Lodge 2201, B'nai B'rith. Contbr to law jours. Recipient, Kovod Award, YMHA, 1937. Home: 123 Calton Rd, New Rochelle, NY. Office: 360 Lexington Ave, New York, NY.

KATZ, Daniel, US, psychologist, educator; b. Trenton, NJ, July 19, 1903; s. Rudolph and Regina (Fleischer); BA, U Buffalo, 1925; MA, Syracuse U, 1926, PhD, 1928; m. Christine Braley, Sep 1, 1930. Prof, psych, U Mich since 1947; fmr: instr, asso prof, Princeton U, 1928-43; research dir, surveys div, OWI, 1943-44; prof, chmn, psych dept, Bklyn Coll, 1943-47; Fulbright prof, Nor, 1951-52. Pres, Soc for Psych Study of Social Issues, 1949-50; mem: comm on intl exch, Fulbright Comm; Amer Psych Assn; Amer Sociol Assn; Amer Assn for Public Opinion Research. Co-author: Student Attitudes, 1932; Social Psychology, 1938; Political Parties in Norway, 1964; Psychology of Organization, 1966; co-ed, Research Methods in the Behavioral Sciences, 1953; sr ed, Readings in Public Opinion and Propaganda, 1954; chmn, ed bd, Jour of Conflict Resolution; ed: Jour of Abnormal and Social Psych, 1962-64; Jour of Personality and Social Psych, 1965-67; ed bd: Psych Monographs; Personnel Psych, Contemporary Psych; Public Opinion; contbr to sci jours. Home: 1789 Country Club Rd, Ann Arbor, Mich. Office: U of Mich, Ann Arbor, Mich.

KATZ, Dov, Isr, scientist; b. Zloczow, Pol, Feb 24, 1922; s. Leib and Brane (Henis); in Isr since 1944; deg, chem ing, Technion, Haifa, 1947; PhD, Heb U, Jerusalem, 1960; m. Edith Geitheim, Dec 11, 1949; c: Arnon, Avishay. Sr research, chem, sci dept, Min of Defense, since 1948; adj prof, dept materials engr, Technion, Haifa, since 1968; adj prof, chem, Bar Ilan U, 1964-66; research asso, Princeton U, NJ, 1960-63; research chem, Styrene Produtcs Ltd, Manchester, Eng,1954-55. Prin contrib, in the field of polymer chem and rheology. Mem: Isr Chem Soc; Engrs and Architects Assn, Isr; Sigma Xi, US; Amer Chem Soc; Rheological Soc, US. Contbr to profsl jours. Recipient, Isr Security Prize, 1960. Home: 34 Disraeli St, Haifa, Isr. Office: POB 7063, Tel Aviv, Isr.

KATZ, Eliezer Yitzhak, US, author; b. Pol, Aug 13 ,1906; s. Shmuel and Nesheraisel (Brandenburg); in US since 1945; att

commercial courses, Jerusalem; m. Rachel Aaronson; c: Varda Abrahamson. I/c Heb affairs, J Braille Inst of NY since 1955; fmr agric worker, Pal; admn worker, Heb U Jerusalem, 1936-45; research in Midrash lit, JTSA, 1946-47. Author: The Hebrew Braille, a manual for study of basic Heb, Heb Braille, 1956; A Classified Concordance to the Pentateuch, Heb-Eng, 1964; A Classified Concordance to the Early Prophets; A Classified Concordance to the Late Prophets, Heb-Eng, 1969. Recipient, found grants to aid in pub works. Home: 788 Riverside Dr, New York, NY.,

KATZ, Emanuel, US, business exec; b. NYC, Dec 21, 1898; s. Bernhard and Bertha (Feiler); LLB, NYU, 1919; m. Rose Rothenstein, Nov 19, 1922; c: Marjorie Davis, Robert. Pres, Bio Producs Inc since 1961; exec vice-pres, Ketchum and Co, since 1959; pres, Doeskin Products, 1918-57; planner, exec sem's for paper ind: Chgo U; O St U; NYU; Syracuse U. Pvt, US Army, 1918. Chmn: UJA; Cosmetic Allied Ind; dir: UJA bd dirs; fmr: chmn: Red Cross Dr, drug div; Infantile Paralysis Dr, trustee, Stephen Wise Free Syn. Spec interests and hobbies: fund raising, music, reading. Home: 930 Fifth Ave, New York, NY. Office: 16 E 40 St, New York, NY.

KATZ, George R, US, business exec; b. San Francisco, May 21, 1873; s. Emanuel and Hannah (Gunst); att Harvard Coll, 1893-97; m. Lillian Migel, July 10, 1903 (decd); c: Eugene, Amy Kruglak; m. 2nd, Ruby Migel, Sep 18, 1942 (decd). Chmn, The Katz Agcy Inc since 1953, pres, 1912-53; vicepres, Okla Pub, since 1903. Mem, bd dirs: NY chap, NCCJ; Amer Newspapers Bur of Advt, 1941-44; pres, NY Newspaper Reprs Assn, 1941-43; clubs: Advt; Harmonie; Overseas Press. Home: 784 Park Ave, New York, NY. Office: 245 Park Ave, New York, NY.

KATZ, Harry L, US, physician, educator; b. Pol, Jan 27, 1910; s. Morris and Sarah (Hochman); in US since 1922; BA, W Res U, Cleveland, 1931; PhD, O State U, 1934, MD, 1938; m. Sara Lamport, June 14, 1942. Chief, chest sect, VA Hosp, Albany, NY, since 1961; asso prof, med, Med Coll, Albany, NY, since 1961; asst, clinical prof, NY State Med Sch, Bklyn, 1950-61. Maj, US Army, MC, WWII. Secy: Seaview Hosp Med Bd, NY; Heb Phys Soc, NY; mem: Isr Phys Assn; AMA; Amer Thoracic Soc; Amer Coll of Chest Phys; ZOA; B'nai B'rith; Sigma Xi; Alpha Omega Alpha. Contbr to med jours. Home: 203 S Allen St, Albany, NY. Office: VA Hosp, Albany, NY.

KATZ, Hilda, US, artist; b. NYC, June 2, 1909; d. Max and Lina (Schwartz); att Natl Acad Design; New Sch for Social Research, 1940. One-man shows: Bowdoin Coll Art Mus, Me, 1951; Cal State Libr, 1953; Albany Inst, 1955; Pa State Tchrs Coll, 1956; Massillon Mus, 1957; Ball State Tchrs Coll, Ind, 1957; J Mus, 1956; U of Me, 1955, 58; Miami Beach Art Cen, Fla, 1958; Art Assn of Richmond, Ind, 1959; Old State Capitol Mus, La; La Art Commn, 13 exhbs; repr in perm collections: Bat Yam Munic Mus, Isr; Peoria Art Cen, Ill; Safad Mus; Amer Artists Group collection; Print Club, Albany, NY; spec perm collections: US Natl Bus, 1965; U of Me Art Mus, 1965; Libr of Cong, 1965; Metrop Mus of Art, 1965; Natl Gal of Art, 1966; Natl Collection Fine Arts, 1966; repr in collections of: Baltimore Mus of Art; FD Roosevelt Coll; Santa Barbara Art Mus; Colo Springs Art Cen; Syracuse U; Pennell Collection; Soc of Amer Graphic Artists; U of Minn; H W Walker Collection; Cal State Libr; NY Public Libr; Pa State Libr; W Mack Memorial Collection; Metrop Mus of Art; Bezalel Mus, Jerusalem; Addison Gal Amer Art; U of Me; Pa State Tchrs Coll; Springfield Art Mus, Mo; Art Assn of Richmond, Ind; exhbs: Amer Graphic Artists; Corcoran Biennial; Phila Watercolor Club; Audubon Artists. Print Club, Albany; Albany Inst; Natl Acad Design; Conn Acad of Fine Arts; Cal State Libr, Boston Printmakers; Boston Public Libr; Bowdoin U; Bal State Coll; U of Me; Art: USA; Intl Women's Club, Eng; It Fed of Women in Art; Venice Biennial; Original Contemporaine-Graphic Intl, Fr; Ecuador; Isr; Royal Etchers and Painters Exch, Eng; Amer-It Print Exch; USIA exhbs. Mem: Audubon Artists; Soc Amer Graphic Artists; Print Council Amer; Conn Acad of Fine Arts; Phila Watercolor Club; Boston Printmakers; Amer Color Print Soc; Print Club, Albany; Soc of Wash DC Printmakers. Recipient: awards: Audubon Artists, 1944; Natl Assn of Women Artists, 1945; Miss Art Assn Intl, 1947; New Haven Paint and Clay Club; Soc Amer Graphic Artists, group prize, 1950; Miss Art Assn, 2 awards, 1951; Art Assn, New Orleans, 1951;

Art Assn Boston Printmakers, 1955; Miniature Painters, Sculptors, Gravers Soc, Wash DC, 1959; Libr of Cong Purchase Awards; Peoria Cen Purchase Awards; Print Club of Albany Purchase Award; life f, Metrop Mus, 1966; exec and profsl Hall of Fame, life mem, 1966; Plaque of Hon, Hall of Fame, 1966; cert F, Metrop Mus, 1966; cert of merit, Dict of Intl Biographies, 1966; Comty Leader Amer Award Plaque, 1969; ad mem, Marquis Biographical Libr Soc, 1969, cert of hon, 1969; purchases: U Minn; Cal Statl Libr; Metrop Mus; U of Me; State Tchrs Coll; Art Assn Richmond, Ind; Print Club, Albany; Peoria Art Cen; NY Public Libr; Newark Public Libr; Mt Margaret of Mary Sch Art Coll. Home and studio: 915 West End Ave, New York, NY.

KATZ, Ira R, US, business exec; b. NYC, Jan 26, 1921; s. Benjamin and Pearl (Markowitz); AB, U Mich, 1942; MBA, Harvard Grad Sch of Bus Admn, 1947; m. Joan Pappenheimer, Aug 26, 1947; c: Janey, Ellen, Benjamin, Peter, Andrew, Sally. Pres, Hartmann Luggage Co, since 1957, with firm since 1955; vice-pres, Gruen Watch Co, 1950-54, with firm since 1947. Lt, USNR, 1942-46. Dir, Luggage Mfrs Assn, since 1956; bd dirs, Nashville J Comty Cen, 1966; mem: natl council, Jt Defense Appeal since 1948; exec comm, AJComm since 1955; fmr: chmn, dir, J Wfr Council, Racine, Wis; dir: JWB; Big Brothers; mem, Queen City Assn, all Cincinnati, O. Home: 401 Wayside Ct, Nashville, Tenn. Office: Hartmann Luggage Co, Lebanon, Tenn.

KATZ, Irving I, US, temple exec, historian; b. Dvinsk, Russ, Mar 31, 1907; s. Michael and Rebecca (Deutsch); in US since 1926; ordained rabbi, Yeshiva, Riga, Latvia; BBA, Spencerian Bus Coll, O, 1930; BA, W Res U, 1934; m. Abigail Peres, June 15, 1934; c: Nina Isaac, Myrna Adelman. Exec secy, Temple Beth El, Detroit, since 1939; educ and exec dir: Morrison Ave Temple, Cleveland, O, 1927-36; Anshe Emeth Temple, Youngstown, O, 1936-39. Found, first pres, Natl Assn of Temple Admnrs, hon pres since 1948; exec bd, Gt Lakes Council, UAHC; fmr pres: Council of Syn Exec Dirs of Metrop Detroit; J Hist Soc of Mich; Metrop Detroit Cemetery Assn; mem: Commn on Syn Admn, UAHC-CCAR-NATA; Bd of Cert for Temple Admnrs; Natl Cabinet of Reform J App; adv bd, Wayne State U Press; Wayne State Commn on Prog Studies in Rel and Urban Culture; cultural comm, JCC of Metrop Detroit. Author: The Beth El Story, 1955; A Chronology of the History of Jewish Community Services in Detroit; The Jewish Soldier from Michigan in the Civil War, 1962; co-author, Successful Synagogue Administration, 1963; contbr on syn admn, hist of Jews in Mich. Citations: HUC-JIR; UAHC; Reform J Appeal; Mich JWV; The Irving I Katz Collection on Mich hist, established in his hon at Amer J Archives of HUC-JIR. Home: 16159 Oxley Rd, Southfield, Mich. Office: 8801 Woodward Ave, Detroit, Mich.

KATZ, Israel, US, engineer, educator; b. NYC, Nov 30, 1917; s. Morris and Sarah (Schwartz); BS, Northeastern U, 1941; Naval Architect, USN prog for grad engrs, MIT, 1942; MME, Cornell U, 1944; m. Betty Steigman, Mar 29, 1942; c: Susan, Judith, Ruth. Prof, engr scis, dean, Cen for Continuing Educ, Northeastern U since 1967, asso prof, 1963-67; engr, submarine propulsion, USN Diesel Engr Lab, Cornell U, 1942-45; asst prof, Grad Sch of Aeronautical Engr, Cornell U, 1945-48, asso prof, mech engr, 1948-56, prof i/c Cornell Aircrafts Powerplants Lab, 1945-56, cons, advanced weapons sys, 1951-56, mgr, Liaison and Cons Engr, Advanced Elec Cen, Gen Elec Co, Cornell U, 1956-63; cons engine designer, Pratt and Whitney Aircraft Co, 1946-49; lectr, heat transfer, Cornell Aeronautical Lab, Buffalo, 1946-48. Chmn, Research Comm, Amer Soc Engr Educ since 1968; fmr: pres: Temple Beth El, Ithaca, NY, 1956-58; chmn, bd trustees, 1958-61; Daniel Rothschild Lodge, B'nai B'rith, 1962; chmn: Ithaca sect, Amer Soc Mech Engrs, fac adv, Cornell Student br; UJA, Ithaca; JWB; mem: Amer Soc Mech Engrs; Inst Elec and Electronic Engrs; Amer Soc for Engr Educ; Research Soc Amer; Tau Beta Pi; clubs: Statler; Shriner, both Ithaca. Author: Principles of Aircraft Propulsion Machinery, 1949; Combustion Engines, 1952; The Mechanical Engineer in Industrial Research, 1958; The Boston Stone, for UNICEF anthol, Friends, 1966; sect Higher Continuing Education, for handbook, College and University Administration; asso ed, Klemin's Handbook of Aeronautical Engineering, 1950-1953; staff columnist, Electromech Design since 1958; contbr to sci jours. Recipient, awards: Alcott Memorial, 1941; Mark Twain Soc, 1949. Hobbies: oil painting; hist of aviation tech. Office: Northeastern U, Boston, Mass.

KATZ, Israel Joseph, Can, educator, musicologist; b. NYC, July 21, 1930; s. Meyer and Lillie (Schaeffer); in Can since 1968; BA, UCLA, 1956, PhD, 1967; m. Marcia Merchasin, June 28, 1959; c: Debra, Karen. Asst prof, Columbia U, since 1969; engr, Douglas Aircraft, Santa Monica, Cal, 1956-64; engr-sci, McDonnell-Douglas, Huntington Beach, Cal, 1967-68; asst prof, McGill U, Montreal, 1968-69; auth on Sephardic Ballad Music and works of A Z Idelshon; specialist on music of N Afr and ME. Cpl, US Army, 1953-55. Mem: council, Soc for Ethnomusicology; Amer Soc Sephardic Studies; past pres, Phi Mu Alpha-Sinfonia. Author: Judeo-Spanish Traditional Ballads from Jerusalem, 1970; contbr articles, trans to musicological jours; ed, Jour of Soc for Ethnomusicology; asso ed, Jour of Amer Soc for Sephardic Studies. Recipient: Charles Brown f, for study in Isr, LA JCC, 1959; Rockefeller Grant-in-Aid, for study in Isr, UCLA, Inst for Ethnomusicology, 1960; Frod Found Award, UCLA, Cen for Folklore Studies, to Spain and N Afr, 1962; Natl Defense Lang f, 1964-66; Academic Sen Award, 1966; Can Council Award, to Isr and Spain, McGill U, 1969. Home: 4741 Kent Ave, Montreal, Can. Office: Dept of Music, Columbia U, New York, NY.

KATZ, J Lawrence, US, physicist, educator; b. Bklyn, NY, Dec 18, 1927; s. Frank and Rose (Eidenberg); BS, Bklyn Poly Inst, 1950, MS, 1951, PhD, 1956; m. Gertrude Seidman, June 17, 1950; c: Robyn, Andrea, Talbot. Prof, physics, Rensselaer Poly Inst, Troy, NY, since 1967; hon research asst, crystallography, NSF f, U Coll, London, 1959-60; instr, math, Bklyn Poly Inst, 1952-56; research f, math, 1951-52. Electronic tech, USN, WW II. Chmn, dent-med-tech comm, Inst of Metals Div of Metallurgical Soc of AIME; co-chmn, social actions comm, Temple Gates of Heaven; f, AAAS; mem: exec comm, Schenectady Co Lib Party, NY; NY State Lib Party; engr in biol and med training comm, NIH; US Standards Inst, chmn, sub-comm on diagnostic radiology; Amer Crystallographic Assn; Amer Phys Soc; Intl Assn for Dent Research; Mineralogical Soc of Amer; Sigma Xi; Amer Math Assn; Sigma Pi Sigma; Schenectady Light Opera Co; ADL; Fed of Amer Scis; NAACP; SANE; CORE; fmr: bd, Temple B'rith Sholom; bd, Troy J Comty Cen; fac adv, Rensselaer-Russel Sage Hillel; chmn, Crystallographic Data Comm, Amer Crystallographic Assn. Contrb author: Handbook of X-Rays, 1967; An Approach to Physical Science, 1967; Proceedings of the International Symposium on Structural Properties of Hydroxyapatites and Hard Tissues, 1969. Recipient: WW II Victory Medal; Sci Fac F, NSF, 1958. Hobbies: folk singing, civic theatre, light opera, philately, travel. Home: 838 Maxwell Dr, Schenectady, NY. Office: Renesselaer Poly Inst, Troy, NY.

KATZ, Jacob, Isr, educator; b. Hung, Nov 15, 1904; s. Berta (Breznitz); PhD, W Goethe U, Frankfurt, Ger; m. Gerti Birenbaum, three c. Rector, Heb U, since 1969; prof, J Social and Educ Hist, Heb U, Jerusalem, since 1950; dir, Talpiot, tchrs sem; visiting prof, Harvard U, 1962-63; Author: Tradition and Crisis: Jewish Society at the End of the Middle Ages, 1958; Exclusiveness and Tolerance, 1962; Free Masons and Jews, Real and Imaginary Relations, 1968; Tradition and Crisis; contrb to profsl jours. Home: 5 Hapalmach St, Jerusalem, Isr. Office: Hebrew U, Jerusalem, Isr.

KATZ, Jochanan, Isr, business exec; b. Berlin, Ger, Sep 17, 1918; s. Rudolf and Grete (Pinner); in Isr since 1933; att Heb U, Jerusalem; m. Esther Ben Israel, Mar 9, 1952; c: Doron. Gen mgr: Pressure Lubricants, Isr Ltd, since 1952; Lod Metal Works, since 1964; fmr: with ind research inst, JA; head, dept, Min of Defense, 1950-52. Haganah; maj, IDF, 1948-69. Mem: Inst of Petroleum; Isr Standards Inst. Home: 11A Ramat Naftali, Tel Aviv, Isr. Office: POB 31, Lod, Isr.

KATZ, Joseph Howard, US, attorney; b. NYC, May 1, 1906; c. Heyman and Mary (Silver); att Fordham U, 1923-25, LLB, Law Sch, 1928; m. Marion Langsan, Dec 31, 1933. Atty, real property and estate law; sr partner, Katz, Robinson, Brog & Seymour. Chmn, real property lawyers div, UJA; dir, J Assn for Services for the Aged; hon pres, Park Ave Syn, since 1967, chmn, bd trustees, pres, 1957-67; bd of overseers, JTSA, since 1959; mem: comm on housing and urban devl, Assn of Bar, NYC; AJComm; Fed of J Charities; Amer Friends of Heb U; Fordham Law Alumni Assn. Contbr to real estate jours. Recipient: natl comty service award, JTSA, 1965. Home: 177 E 77 St, New York, NY. Office: 10 E 40 St, New York, NY.

KATZ, Joseph J, US, researcher; b. Detroit, Mich, Apr 19, 1912; s. Abraham and Stella (Asnin); BS, Wayne State U, 1932; PhD, U Chgo, 1942; m. Celia Weiner, Oct 1, 1944; c: Anna, Elizabeth, Mary, Abram. Sr chem, Argonne Natl Lab since 1946; Amer ed, Jour of Inorganic and Nuclear Chem, since 1956; tech adv, US Delg to UN Conf on Peaceful Uses of Atomic Energy, 1955. F, AAAS, since 1958; mem: Phi Beta Kappa; Sigma Xi; Amer Chem Soc. Author: The Chemistry of Uranium, 1951; The Chemistry of the Actinide Elements, 1947; contbr to sci jours. Recipient: dist alumni award, Wayne State U, 1955; award for nuclear applications in chem, Amer Chem Soc, 1961. Home: 5658 Blackstone Ave, Chicago, Ill. Office: 9700 S Cass Ave, Argonne, Ill.

KATZ, Julius, US, physician; b. Russ, Sep 28, 1901; s. Nathan and Rachel (Katzman); in US since 1907; BA, Columbia Coll, 1923; MD, LI Coll Hosp, 1928; m. Raye Roskin, Sep 7, 1930; c: Deborah Lieberman, Janet Fink. Dir, Bur of TB Control in State Insts, since 1947, with dept since 1937; pvt practice, 1930-37. F, Amer Coll, Preventive Med; dipl, Amer Bd of Preventive Med; mem, Temple Isr, Albany. Contbr to med jours. Home: 47 Holmes Dale, Albany, NY. Office: NY State Dept of Health, NY.

KATZ, Katriel, Isr, diplomat; b. Warsaw, Pol, Oct 16, 1908; s. Oscar and Haya (Ekroni); in Isr since 1924; att: U Warsaw, 1929-30; U Vienna, 1931-32; m. Ora Grunhut, 1931; c: Gyora, Jehudit, Efrat. Chmn, Yad Va Shem, since 1967, dir, PR dept, 1941-48; dir, political research dept, Min for Fgn Affairs, 1949-52; charge d'affaires, Isr Legation, Budapest, 1952-55; Isr min to Pol, 1955-58; secy, Govt of Isr, 1958-62; consul-gen, NY, 1962-65; ambass to Russ, 1965-67. Press off, IDF, 1949. Author: Five Years of Israel's Foreign Policy, 1956; contbr to gen jours. Home: 4 Hamaapilim St, Jerusalem, Isr. Office: Yad Va Shem, POB 84, Jerusalem, Isr.

KATZ, Kaufman Ray, US, business exec; b. Baltimore, Md, Aug 24, 1910; s. Ray and Ethel (Epstein); BS, Haverford Coll, 1931; MBA, Harvard Grad Sch of Bus, 1933; m. Monica Trythall, 1946. Cons, US Senator Jacob K Javits, since 1962; fmr: sales dept, Amer Oil, 1933-35; vice-pres, Charles Dept Stores, 1935-57. Lt col, US Army, 1942-46. Pres, Jacob Epstein Found; mem: Soc of Fr Legion of Hon; Triangle Soc; NY chap, AJComm, exec bd, fmr vice-pres; Munic Art Soc; Citizens' Union; Eng-Speaking Union; Cong Emanu-El; Metrop Opera Guild; Metrop Mus of Art; Park Ave Assn; Philharmonic Soc; clubs: Overseas Press; Harvard Bus Sch, NY; Sunningdale Country; Harmonie. Recipient: US Legion of Merit; Fr Legion of Hon; Fr Croix de Guerre. Home: 115 E 86 St, New York, NY. Office: 1142 Madison Ave, New York, NY.

KATZ, Kurt, US, chemical engr; b. Kassel, Ger, Aug 1, 1932; s. Siegfried and Blanca (Lowenstein); in US since 1938; BChE, Bklyn Poly Inst, 1954; MChE, NYU, 1955; BBA, U Pittsburgh, 1957; m. Helen Grau, June 10, 1956; c: Beverly, Mark, Rachel, Brenda. Gen mgr, water & waste treatment div, Westinghouse Elec Corp since 1968, with firm since 1956. Secy-treas, Cong Ahavas Isr; bd govs, Assn Orthodox J Sci, fmr pres; pres, Young Isr of Pittsburgh, 1959-62; bd dirs, Hillel Acad Day Schs; mem: Amer Chem Soc; Amer Nuclear Soc; Assn Naval Architects and Marine Eng; Phi Lambda Upsilon. Contbr to sci jours; holder of patents in nuclear field. Home: 6366 Alderson, Pittsburgh, Pa. Office: 3 Gateway Cen, Pittsburgh, Pa.

KATZ, Leo, US, statistician, educator; b. Detroit, Mich, Nov 29, 1914; s. Max and Mollie (Gastman); BS, Lawrence Inst, 1936; MA, Wayne state U, 1938; PhD, U Mich, 1945; att: U of NC, 1950; U of Cal, 1952-53; m. Jean Prepsky, Sep 5, 1936; c: Michael, Daniel. Prof, dir, stat lab, Mich State U since 1955; stat cons, stat: Mich Dept of Lab, 1941-42; aircraft devl sect, GM Corp, 1942-46; sci liaison off, Off of Naval Research, London, 1959-60; Ford Found visiting dist prof, U of NC, 1961-62; visiting prof: Stanford U, 1962; Alcoa Found, U Pittsburgh, 1968-69. Exec secy, Inst of Math Studies, 1967-69; f: Amer Stat Assn; AAAS; Royal Stat Soc; council mem, Inst of Math: Stat, 1958-61; mem Amer Math Soc; Math Assn of Amer; Psychometric Soc; Biometric Soc; Econometric Soc; AAUP; Sigma Xi. Contbr to profsl jours. Home: 425 Durand St, E Lansing, Mich. Office: Dept of Statistics, Mich State U, E Lansing, Mich.

KATZ, Leon, Can, nuclear physicist, educator; b. Pol, Aug 9, 1909; s. Jacob and Malka (Katz); in Can since 1921; BS,

Queen's U, 1933-34, MSc, 1936; PhD, Cal Inst of Tech, 1939-42; m. Georgina Caverly, Jan 4, 1941; c: Sylvan, Zender, David, Faye. Head, dept of physics, U Sask, since 1965, prof since 1962, dir, Electron Accelerator Lab since 1961, fac mem since 1946; fmr: research eng, Westinghouse Elec Co, 1942-46. Fmr pres: Can Friends of Heb U; Can Assn Physicists; f, Royal Soc of Can; Amer Phys Soc; mem: Sci Council of Can; Sigma Xi; Amer Inst of Physics Tchrs; Phys Soc of Eng; club, Fac; contbr to profsl journs. Home: 12 Weir Crs, Saskatoon, Sask, Can. Office: Dept of Physics, U Sask, Saskatoon, Sask, Can.

KATZ, Leon, US, rabbi; b. Pol, Aug 12, 1913; s. Reuben and Rachel (Maskilejson); in US since 1930; BA, Yeshiva Coll, 1938; ordained rabbi, Rabbi Isaac Elchanan Theol Sem, 1938; DHL, Yeshiva U, 1948; m. Rhea Herzog, Feb 17, 1946; c: Varda, Shimon, Avram. Rabbi, Cong Adas Isr, since 1939; instr: NYU, since 1962; Stern Coll for Women, since 1967; Yeshiva U, 1950-59; cons on dissertations, NYU Grad Sch of Arts and Sci; lectr, postgrad dept, Tchrs Training Sch, NY, 1942-50; chaplain, Police and Fire Dept. Pres: Rab Council NJ, since 1961; state region, Mizrachi, since 1950; Rab Alumni, Yeshiva U, 1951, 1952; bd govs, UJA; active in: Bonds for Isr; YMHA; wfr and vet comms, Police Athletic League; mem: RabCA; Mizrachi Org of Amer; World Acad in Jerusalem. Author: The Life, Times, and Works of Rabbi Moshe Sofer, 1960; contbr to: J publs; J ency; ed staff, J Horizon, since 1958. Home: 32 Laurel Ave, Clifton, NJ. Study: 565 Broadway, Passaic, NJ.

KATZ, Louis N, US, cardiologist, researcher, educator; b. Pinsk, Pol, Aug 25, 1897; s. Harry and Sarah (Rosenberg); in US since 1900; BA, W Res U, 1918, MD, 1921, MA, 1923; m. Aline Grossner, June 25, 1928; c: Arnold. Dir em, cardiovascular inst, Michael Reese Hosp and Med Cen, since 1967, dir 1930-67, att phys, since 1947; visiting prof, phys, U Chgo, since 1967, professorial lectr, 1941-67, asst prof, 1930-41; fmr: intern, asst res, Cleveland City Hosp, 1921-23; fac mem, W Reserve U, 1922-30; f, NRC, U London, 1924-25; cons card, St Luke's Hosp, Cleveland, 1928-30. FACP; f, AAAS; hon life mem, AHA, since 1952, mem bd dirs, 1942-46, 1958-61, fmr pres, chmn of sci councils, med adv bds and research comms; hon mem, Brit Heart Assn; mem, exec comm, Chgo Heart Assn, since 1941, mem bd govs, since 1933, chmn research comm, 1960-67, fmr pres, secy and chmn, sci comms; mem: Soc for Experimental Biol and Med, fmr pres, Ill br; Chgo Soc for Internal Med, fmr pres; circulation sect, Amer Phys Soc; hon life pres, Interamer Soc of Card; Amer Found for High Blood Pressure; Amer Soc for Study Arteriosclerosis, fmr pres; mem, intl council, Intl Soc of Card, since 1951; treas, mem bd dirs, Found, 1957-63; mem: bd govs, Inst of Med, Chgo, since 1961, pres, 1960-61; med adv comm, Herrick House, Sunset Camp Service League, since 1933; bd dirs, Ill Soc for Med Research, since 1952, fmr pres; AMA; Amer Soc for Clinical Inves; Assn Fr Phys; Cen Soc for Clinical Research; Chgo Med Soc; Chgo Soc for Internal Med; Phys Soc, Eng; corresp mem, Fr Soc of Cards; Ill Med Soc; hon mem, S Amer and Eur Card Socs; fmr mem, Natl Soc for Med Research; hon fac mem, U Chile; mem: Phi Beta Kappa; Sigma Xi; Alpha Omega Alpha. Author: Electrocardiography, 1941, 1946; Exercises in Electrocardiographic Interpretation, 1941, 1946; co-author: Elements of Electrocardiographic Interpretation, 1932, 1944; Experimental Arteriosclerosis, 1953; Introduction to the Interpretation of the Electrocardiogram, 1952; Clinical Electrocardiography, Part I, The Arrhythmias, 1956; Nutrition and Arteriosclerosis, 1958; ed: sect on Cardiovascular sys, Biol Abstracts, since 1941; mem ed bd: Acta Cardiologia, Belgium since 1946; Circulation since 1958; contbr numerous papers to natl and intl profsl jours. Recipient: Lasker Award, 1956; Gold Heart Award, 1961, both from AHA; hon lecture award, Albany Med Coll Union U, Albany, NY, 1959; Gold Medal, Phi Lambda Kappa, Detroit; Silver Medal and 3rd Einthoven Lecture, U of Leiden, Holland; Gold Medal, Intl Cong of Phys. Home: 601 E 32 St, Chicago, Ill. Office: Cardiovascular Research Inst, Michael Reese Hosp and Med Cen, Chicago, Ill.

KATZ, M Shakman, US, business exec; b. Baltimore, Md, July 10, 1900; s. Zadock and Florence (Shakman); att U of Pa, Wharton Sch of Finance, 1918-19; m. Amalie Sonneborn, Sep 4, 1924; c: John, Deborah Hermann, Mary Burak. Ret; vice pres, treas, K Katz and Sons, 1933-60; fmr: Bail Bond Commr, City of Baltimore; mem State Commn on the Aging. Mem: bd: AJComm, since 1945; Asso J Charities Wfr Fund; USO, since 1950; chmn, Md Regional Adv Med Prog; pres,

Natl and Local Travelers' Aid since 1946; life mem: J Family and Children's Bur, fmr pres; bd, Park Sch, fmr pres; all Baltimore. Home: 2609 Talbot Rd, Baltimore, Md.

KATZ, Matthew, US, research and development mgr; b. NYC, Mar 20, 1929; s. Benjamin and Frieda (Hausman); BA, cum laude, Yeshiva U, NY, 1949, ordained rabbi, 1955; MA, Columbia U, 1950; PhD, Bklyn Poly Inst, 1964; m. Bernice Weisberg, Oct 24, 1954; c: Henni, Pynchas. Tech dir, research and devl, since 1969; mgr, chem sect, Gen Precision, Kearfott div, 1962-64; tech dir: Sun Chem Co, electro-tech div, 1964-66; Tenneco-Gen Foam Div, 1966-69. Prin contribs: devl of new products: plastic laminating process; polymer reaction mechanism; elec instruments; electroluminescent devices; fuel cells; coated fabrics; synthetic leathers. Secy, Yeshiva of Crown Hgts, NY; f, Amer Inst Chems; mem: bd govs, Soc of Isr Philatelists; AAAS; Amer Radio Relay League; Amer Philatelic Soc; Assn Orthodox J Scis; Cong Ahavath Achim; Inst Elec and Electronic Engrs; Sigma Xi, Poly chap; Phi Lambda Upsilon, Alpha Zeta chap; Amer Chem Soc; fmr vice-pres, cultural chmn, Hapoel Hamizrachi of Crown Hgts, NY. Contbr to sci jours. Hobbies: amateur radio sta, W2VPW, philately. Home: 512 Montgomery St, Brooklyn, NY. Office: 1107 Broadway, New York, NY.

KATZ, Milton, US, attorney, educator, public official; b. NYC, Nov 29, 1907; s. Morris and Clara (Schiffman); AB, Harvard U, 1927, LLB, 1931; m. Vivian Greenberg, July 2, 1933; c: John, Robert, Peter. Dir: Intl Legal Studies, Harvard U since 1954, Intl Prog in Taxation, since 1961, Henry L Stimson Prof of law, since 1954, prof law, 1940-50; mem, anthropoligical expedition, Peabody Mus, Harvard U, 1927-28; held various posts, US Govt: solicitor, War Produc Board, 1941-43; US Exec Off, Combined Produc and Resources Bd, 1942-43; US ambass plen in Eur, 1950-51; US repr for econ commn for Eur, 1950-51; chmn, Defense Finance and Econ Comm under NATO, 1950-51; asso dir, Ford Found, 1951-54. Lt cdr, USN, 1944-46. Trustee: Brandeis U; Case W Res U; Intl Legal Cen; Interamer U Found; mem corp, Boston Mus of Sci; chmn: Comm on Life Sci and Social Policy; Natl Acad of Sci; NRC; mem: NY, Mass Bar Assns; US Super Court Bar; trustee: exec comm, Carnegie Endowment for Intl Peace; World Peace Found; Citizens Research Found; fmr mem, Comm on Fgn Affairs Personnel. Author: Cases and Materials on Administrative Law, 1947; The Things That Are Caesar's, 1966; The Relevance of International Adjudication, 1968; co-author: Government Under Law and the Individual, 1947; Law of International Transactions and Relations, 1960. Recipient: Legion of Merit, US Army, 1946; Commendation Ribbon, USN, 1946; Gold Medal of Merit, JWV of US, 1951. Home: 6 Berkeley St, Cambridge, Mass. Office: Harvard Law Sch, Cambridge, Mass.

KATZ, Morris Casriel, US, rabbi; b. Chgo, Ill, Sep 9, 1909; s. Paul and Sarah (Cohen); ordained rabbi, Heb Theol Coll, Chgo, 1932; BA, cum laude, U Minn, 1945; m. Molly Lerner, June 30, 1942; c: Paul, Stephen. Rabbi: B'nai Sholom Cong, Richmond, Va, since 1968; Cong Sons of Jacob, 1944-58; Beth Isr Cong, 1959-64; St Paul, Minn, Beth El, Endicott, NY, 1966-68. Chaplain, Can Army, 1939-44. Pres: Minn RA, 1952-53; Rabb Alumni, Heb Theol Coll, 1949-51; mem: RabCA; NY Bd Rabbis; Cen Yeshiva Bd Rabbis; Cen Va Bd Rabbis. Author, Deception and Fraud with a Kosher Front, 1968; contbr: numerous Heb and Yiddish words to Webster's Third New Intl Dict, 1961; to J and rel jours. Spec interest, collecting rare Judaica and Hebraica. Home: 6109 Bremo Rd, Richmond, Va. Study: 6209 Patterson Ave, Richmond, Va.

KATZ, Philip E, US, organization exec; b. Kisvarda, Hung, Mar 1, 1924; s. Menyhert and Theresa (Halpert); in US since 1946; ordained rabbi, Eitz-Chaim Rabb Sem, 1941; att U Zurich, 1945; m. Tagora Katz, July 3, 1955; c: Ariela, Nuri. Dir, Comm on Isr, B'nai B'rith, since 1956; exec-dir, E Pa, and LI region, ZOA, 1949-55; Amer-Isr Paul Ehrlich Med Inst, 1955-56. Found, first pres, J Self-Help Soc and Day Care Cen, Kisvarda, Hung, 1942-43; found, mem, presidium, DP camp, Feldafing, Ger, May, 1945; mem: Natl Conf J Communal Service; ZOA; Adas Isr Syn, Wash, DC. Ed, LI Zionist Herald, 1951-54. Home: 4210 Oakridge Lane, Chevy Chase, Md. Office: 1640 Rhode Island Ave, NW, Washington, DC.

KATZ, Reuben M, US, rabbi; b. NYC, Feb 22, 1919; s. Abraham and Sarah (Katz); BA, Bklyn Coll, 1941; ordained rabbi,

MHL, JTSA, 1944; m. Reba Farbman, May 1, 1945; c: Deborah, Naomi, Jonathan. Rabbi, Cong B'nai Isr, Freeport, LI, since 1950; fimr: asst rabbi, Har Zion Temple, Phila, Pa, 1943-44; instr, Bible, Sem Sch of J Studies, NYC, 1943; rabbi, Beth El Cong, Akron, O, 1945-50; instr, Comty Coll, Akron, O, 1948-49. Fmr: chaplain, lt-col, Civil Air Patrol, Northeast region; auxiliary police, Freeport; Ret Police Assn of Nassau-Suffolk; Police Benevolent Assn of Freeport. Pres: Interfaith Clergy Council of Freeport; RA, Nassau-Suffolk region; vice-pres, metrop council, 1953-54, 1961-62, mem, comms on ethics, conv, and educ, mem, natl exec and admn comms; chmn: comm on marriage and family, United Syn of Amer, 1951-56; prins council, Assn J Cong Schs of LI; mem, bd, Planned Parenthood Assn, Nassau Co, 1952-53; chmn, fac, Akiba Sch of Adult J Studies; dir, Freeport Inst of Adult J Studies. Recipient: citizenship award, VFW, 1952; Dist Service Award, Natl HQ, Civil Air Patrol, 1967. Home: 14 Delaware Ave, Freeport, NY. Study: Cong B'nai Isr, Freeport, NY.

KATZ, Samuel, US, dentist, musician; b. Kishinev, Russ, Jan 1, 1902; s. Shaika and Clara (Spritzman); in US since 1909; att Villanova U; DDS, Temple U, Sch of Dent, Phila, Pa, 1930; m. Sylvia Buzonsky, Aug 18, 1940; c: Rivi, Robert. Pvt practice since 1930; profsl musician, trumpet, 1930-70; dent mech, Climax Dent Lab, 1925. Mem: exec bd, Phila br, Intl Acad Orthodontists; Alpha Omega; Amer Heb Soc; Amer Musicians' Soc; Amer Soc Study of Orthodontics; Amer Acad Applied Nutrition; club, Mercedes Benz. Hobbies: basketball, tennis, music. Home and office: 129 Derwen Rd, Bala-Cynwyd, Pa.

KATZ, Samuel, US, social worker; b. Ft Dodge, Ia, July 17, 1911; s. Raphael and Rebecca (Rebbe); BS, Northeast Mo State Tchrs Coll, 1933; MSS, New Sch for Social Research; m. Alexandra Spertus, Mar 28, 1947; c: Ralph, Lawrence. Natl dir, comty services dept, AJComm, since 1965, with org since 1956; case worker, St Louis Relief Admn, 1934-36; instr, social studies, Northeast Mo State Tchrs Coll, 1936-38; group work sup, Christadora House, NYC, 1938-41; field repr, JWB-USO prog, 1941-43. US Army, 1943-46. Mem: exec bd, Assn J Comty Relations Workers, since 1959; Natl Assn Social Workers; Acad Cert Social Workers; Natl Assn Intergroup Relations Officials; Natl Conf J Communal Service; Amer Acad Political and Social Sci; Larchmont Temple; fmr: chmn, New Rochelle Comm, Mh Assn of Westchester Co; treas, Comty Syn, Port Wash, NY. Hobbies: Hi-fi radio, sci fiction. Home: 7 Glen Lane, Mamaroneck, NY. Office: 165 E 56 St, New York, NY.

KATZ, Samuel, Isr, publisher; b. Johannesburg, S Afr, Dec 9, 1914; s. Alexander and Luba (Breslow); in Isr since 1946; att U of Witwatersrand, Johannesburg, 1930. Mgn dir, Karni Publishers Ltd, since 1951; Megiddo Pub Co since 1962; fmr: secy, Commn of S Afr, Jerusalem, 1936-39; ed, J Standard, London, 1940-42; staff mem, Daily Express, London, 1943-45. Mem, council, Publishers Assn of Isr; mem exec comm, Land of Isr Movement. Fmr: secy, British Trumpeldor, Johannesburg, 1930; co-found, mem of exec, Hatechiya Org, Johannesburg, 1932-35; mem, first S Afr Zionist Youth Council, 1932-35; mem, world admn comm, New Zionist Org, 1940-42; high command IZL, 1947-48; co-found, Herut Movement, 1948, mem exec, 1948-51; MK, Herut Party, 1949-51. Author: Yom ha'Esh, 1966; Days of Fire, 1968; trans into Eng: Story of the Jewish Legion, by Vladimir Jabotinsky; The Revolt, by Menachem Begin. Home: 155 Dizengoff St, Tel Aviv, Isr. Office: Karni Publishers Ltd, 11 Yehuda Halevi St, Tel Aviv, Isr.

KATZ, Shimon, Isr, rabbi; b. Haslowitz, Pol, July 3, 1904; s. Reuven and Reichell; desc of Hagaon Maskil Zeitar; in Isr since 1933; att Gt Yeshiva, Grodno, 1918-1922; ordained rabbi, Gt Yeshiva, Mir, Pol, 1929; m. Hanna Shwalb, 1934; c: Yudit Vardi, Miriam Yankelewitz, Haya Salomon, Ditza Hertzberg. Dir, Rabb Dist Court, Petah Tikva, since 1950; rabbi, Staviok, Pol, 1929-33; munic councillor, Petah Tikva, 1940-55. Maj, IDF, rabb service, 1948-50. Found: Old Age Home, Rel Sem; chmn, Council of Credit Bank, all Petah Tikva; found, cdr, Rel Group in Hagana, mem dist hqr, 1934-48; activities, Isr and Overseas on Agunot; fmr mem, cen comm, wfr of J soldiers. Pres, B'nai B'rith; mem exec comm, Yeshiva, all Petah Tikva; mem gen comm, B'nai B'rith, Isr; chmn regional comm, B'nai B'rith, Dan Dist. Contbr to rel jours. Recipient: outstanding citizen, Pres of Isr, 1962; Hagana, IDF, Fighter for Isr Independence, medals.

Home: 29 Harav Blau St, Petah Tikva, Isr. Study: Montefiori St, Petah Tikva, Isr.

KATZ, Sol, US, physician, educator; b. NYC, Mar 29, 1913; s. Samuel and Bessie (Lev); BS, CCNY, 1935; MD, Georgetown Med Sch, 1939; m. Beatrice Paul, Nov 16, 1946; c: Paul, Rita, Judith. Prof, Georgetown Med Sch since 1965, Kober lectr, 1965, fac mem since 1958; chief, med service, VA Hosp, Wash DC since 1959; cons, chest diseases: NIH; Walter Reed Army Hosp; Children's Hosp; chief, pulmonary disease service, DC Gen Hosp, 1945-59; Chevalier Jackson lectr, Pa chap, Amer Coll Chest Phys, 1968. Mem: Phi Beta Kappa; Alpha Omega Alpha; AMA; Amer Coll Phys; Amer Bd Internal Med; Amer Coll of Chest Phys. Asst ed, GP since 1952; contbr to med jours. Home: 3909 Ridge Rd, Annandale, Va. Office: VA Hosp, 50 Irving St, NW, Washington, DC.

KATZ, Solomon, US, educator; b. Buffalo, NY, June 10, 1909; s. Saul and Sophia (Gelber); BA, Cornell U, 1930, PhD, 1933; att Sorbonne, Paris, 1932-33; m. Marcia Geller, Sep 6, 1931; c: Kenneth, Cynthia. Vice-pres for academic affairs, U Wash, since 1967, provost, 1965, dean, coll arts and sci, 1960-66, joined fac 1936; asst prof, Greek, U Ore, 1935-36. Maj, USAAC, 1942-46. Mem: AAUP; Amer Philol Assn; Amer Hist Assn; Medieval Acad; Archaeol Inst; Phi Beta Kappa. Author: Jews in Visigothic and Frankish Kingdoms of Spain and Gaul, 1937; Decline of Rome and Rise of Medieval Europe, 1955; contbr to hist jours. Recipient: Boldt f, 1932-33; f, Amer Coll of Learned Soc, 1934-35; Fulbright research scholar, 1952-53; Guggenheim f, 1953-54. Home: 7708-56 Pl NE, Seattle, Wash. Office: U of Washington, Seattle, Wash.

KATZ, Stanley, US, educator; b. New York, NY, 1921; s. Philip and Hannah (Heisman); BS, CCNY, 1940; PhD, NYU, 1951; m. Lillian Handman, 1948; c: Phillip, Andrew. Prof, chem engr, CUNY, since 1963; math cons, since 1963; fmr: math analyst, Hydrocarbon Research Inst, 1946-53; sr math, Electro Data Corp, 1954-55; staff math cons, Amer Cyanamid Co, 1955-63. Sgt, US Army, 1943-46. F, NY Acad Sci; mem: Phi Beta Kappa; Amer Inst Chem Engr; Amer Math Soc. Mem, ed bd, SIAM, Jour of Applied Math; contbr articles, math analysis of engr processes. Home: 309 Grand Ave, Englewood, NJ. Office: CCNY, CUNY, New York, NY.

KATZ, William, Austr, reverend; b. Ger, Dec 15, 1895; s. Kalman and Fanny (Levistein); in Austr since 1939; att J Tchrs Coll, Kassel, Ger, 1913-15, 1919-20; m. Rosalie Mann, Dec 26, 1928; c: Claude (decd), Eva. Min em, North Shore Syn, since 1960, chief min, 1940-60, headmaster, Rel Sch, 1940-60; tchr, J Day Schs, 1920-39; cantor, 1929-39, both Kassel, Ger. Chmn, cultural comm, N Shore Syn; sup, Heb cens, bd J educ, NSW; fmr: chmn, tchrs comm, JNF, NSW; mem: exec comm, JNF; mem, council, B'nai B'rith; educ comm, NSW Bd J Educ; Friends of Heb U. Author, And the Ark Rested, 1966. Home: 2/367 Pacific Hwy, Lindfield, Sydney, Austr. Study: 15 Treatts Rd, Lindfield, Sydney, Austr.

KATZ, Yerahmiel, Isr, business exec; b. Haifa, Isr, Nov 7, 1923; s. Yaacov and Etta; BSc, Dipl Ing, Technion, Haifa, 1955; MSc, MIT, 1960; m. Michaela Uriely, Nov 9, 1948; c: Ido, Assa, Orna. Mgn dir, Koor Metal Works, since 1969; head, metal working div, 1967-68; head projects, IDF, Col, IDF, 1948-67. Mem, Isr Mgmt Cen. Hobby, music. Home: 3 Gur St, Tel Aviv, Isr. Office: Koor Ind, 99 Ben Yehuda St, Tel Aviv, Isr.

KATZ, Yosef, Isr, government official; b. Haifa, Isr, Jan 20, 1927; s. Ephraim and Malka (Schreiber); MA, Heb U, Jerusalem, 1953; m. Carmella Stern, Jan 28, 1952; c: Semador, Iris, Erez. Controller, fgn exch, dir, fgn exch div, Min of Finance, since 1967, with min since 1949; fmr, with Atarot, pioneer settlement in Judean Hills. Hagana, 1936-48; J Settlement Police, 1945-48; sgt, IDF, 1948-69. Prin contrib: initiated trade agreements between Isr and other countries enabling Isr to enter world market; directed Isr's policy liberalizing fgn exch control. Hobbies: chess, woodcarving. Home: 176 Ibn Shaprut St, Jerusalem, Isr. Office: Min of Finance, Jerusalem, Isr.

KATZBURG, Nathaniel, Isr, educator; b. Budapest, Hung, July 31, 1922; s. Menachem and Rivka (Müller); in Isr since 1934; MA, Heb U, 1951, PhD, 1962; att: Yeshivat B'nai Akiva, Isr, 1939-41; London Sch of Slavic and Eur Studies,

1951-52; m. Judith Glasner, Nov 7, 1950; c: Shimon, Ruth. Sr lectr, modern J hist, Bar Ilan U, since 1965. Pvt, IDF, 1948-49. Author, Antisemitism in Hungary 1867-1914, pub 1969; contbr on hist of J in Hung and J in 19th cent Pal to jours. Home: Shikun Hamartzim, Bar Ilan U, Ramat Gan, Isr. Office: Bar Ilan U, Ramat Gan, Isr.

KATZELL, Raymond A, US, psychologist, educator; b. Bklyn, NY, Mar 16, 1919; s. Abraham and Fanny (Skoblow); BS, NYU, 1939, MA, 1941, PhD, 1943; m. Florence Goldstein, Sep 7, 1941; m. 2nd, Mildred Engberg, May 11, 1953. Prof, head, dept psych, NYU, since 1963; cons: US Dept of Lab; US Dept HEW, both since 1968; fmr: research asst, 1939-42, instr, 1942-43, adj asso prof, 1951-53, all NYU; instr, evening sch, bus admn, CCNY, 1942-45; asst prof, psych, asso prof, U of Tenn, 1945-48; asso prof, personnel psych, Syracuse U, 1948-51, dir, psych services cen, 1949-51; cons, USAF, 1951; research cons, vice-pres, Richardson, Bellows, Henry and Co Inc, 1951-54; lectr, psych, Columbia U, 1955-57; prof, mgmt engr and psych, dir, Research Cen for Ind Behavior, NYU, 1957-63; personnel psych, Adj Gen's Office, US War Dept, 1943-45. F: Amer Psych Assn; AAAS. Co-author: Testing and Fair Employment, 1968; contbr to profsl jours. Home: 1 Barry Dr, Glen Cove, NY. Office: NYU, New York, NY.

KATZEN, Bernard, US, attorney, public official; b. NYC, Jan 17, 1901; s. Abraham and Helen (Relkin); LLB, NYU, 1923; m. Florence Mallee, Dec 19, 1942. Pvt practice since 1924; counsel, NY State Pure Waters Auth, since 1967. Fmr spec dep atty-gen, 1928-32, counsel, NY State dept of agric and markets, 1935; asst dist atty, 1938-45; gen atty, NY State Ins Fund, 1945-46; arbitrator, panel, NY State Lab Mediation Bd, 1948; state committeeman since 1950; counsel, NY State J Leg Comm on Narcotic Study, 1956-59; spec cons, State Dept: dept of pr, 1956-58; mission to Isr, 1956-58; vice-chmn, NY State Commn for Human Rights, 1962-67, commn 1959-62; campaign mgr, Keating for US Sen, 1958; asst campaign mgr, Herbert Brownell Jr, pres campaign, 1948; Thomas Dewey for dist atty, 1937; div mgr, Dulles campaign for US Sen, 1949; candidate for State Senator, NY, 1932; asst to NY Co Rep chmn, 1933-35; secy, Seabury Citizens Non-Partisan Comm, 1937; div chmn, gubernatorial and pres campaigns, 1944-48; asst to Arthur Summerfield, pres campaign, 1952; const, rep Natl Comm, 1953, dir, ethnic div, 1956; lectr, NYU Workshop in Practical Politics, 1955. Sponsor, Amer-Isr Soc, vice-pres, NY chap; cabinet, campaign chmn, lawyers div, UJA; div chmn: FJP; ARC, Gtr NY Fund; trustee: Amer Comm for Bar-Ilan U; bd of dirs, United HIAS Service; chmn, law comm, Amer Assn of State Compensation Ins Funds. Mem: NY State Bar Assn; NY State Dist Attys Assn; Assn of the Bar of NYC; fmr master, Samaritan Lodge, Masons; clubs: Natl Rep, chmn, natl affairs comm, 1952, pres, 1949, 1950; Yorkville Sq, pres, 1928. Home: 360 E 55 St, New York, NY. Office: 40 Exchange Pl, New York, NY.

KATZEN, Harry Milton, US, rabbi; b. Vitebsk, Russ, June 20, 1900; s. Jacob and Ida (Falksohn); grad, U Odessa, 1920; MA, Columbia U, 1927; MHL, ordained rabbi, JTSA, 1928, DHL, with distinction, 1952, DD, honoris causa, 1966; m. Sophie Winecor, Oct 26, 1930; c: Joanna Becker, Judith Stern. Rabbi: Temple Beth El of Bensonhurst, since 1940; chaplain: J Hosp, Bklyn since 1946; Cumberland Hosp, Bklyn since 1948; Kurlander Young Men's Mutual Aid Soc; B'nai B'rith Cong, Somerville, Mass, 1928-29; Temple Beth El, Dorchester, Mass, 1929-35; Nathan Straus Cen, Bx, NY, 1935-40; chaplain, Montefiore Hosp, Bx, NY, 1936-44. Mem: RA; Amer Acad for J Research; ZOA; Amer Acad Political Sci; B'nai B'rith; NY, Bklyn Bds Rabbis; alumni assns: grad sch, Columbia U; Slobodker Yeshiva. Home: 7110 21 Ave, Brooklyn, NY. Study: 1656 W 10 St, Brooklyn, NY.

KATZENBERG, Marc J, US, insurance exec; b. Phila, Pa, Dec 19, 1892; s. Isaac and Denah (Stern); m. Helen Goldsmith, Jan 11, 1917; c: Jay, Nancy, Marjorie Sturm. Cons, S George Levi & Co, Phila, fmr partner. Pres, Neighborhood Cen, 1939-43; bd dirs: FJP; Gtr Phila; Allied J App, head, ins div, 1950-52; J Hosp, 1935-51; co-chmn, advance gifts div, Comty Chest, 1952, all Phila; clubs: Hon Ky Col; Philmont Country, fmr pres; Locust. Home: 1530 Locust St, Philadelphia, Pa. Office: 1616 Walnut St, Philadelphia, Pa.

KATZENELBOGEN, Solomon, US, psychiatrist, educator; b. Uman, Russ, Dec 3, 1890; s. Moise and Eva (Cohen); BS,

U of Geneva, Switz, 1916, MD, 1918; m. Nina Gandjoumoff, June 9, 1915; c: Eva; in US since 1928. Pvt practice since 1943; asst anat, path, otolaryngology, U Zurich, 1918-19; res, internal med, U Geneva, 1919-25, dir, lab, privatdozent, 1925-28; asso prof, psycht, Johns Hopkins Med Sch, 1936-38, staff mem since 1928; dir, lab and research, St Elizabeth Hosp, Wash, DC, 1938-53; clinical prof, psycht, George Wash U, 1939-56. Dipl, asso examiner, Amer Bd of Psycht and Neur, 1941-46. F: Psycht Assn; Amer Coll of Phys; mem: Amer Psychopath Assn; Amer Neur Assn; AAAS; Soc for Experimental Biol and Med. Author: Cerebrospinal Fluid and Its Relation to Blood, 1935; Studies in Psychoses, Neuroses and Psychosomatic Med, 1929-61; Analyzing Psychotherapy, 1958. Mem, ed bd, Quarterly Rev of Psycht and Neur, 1947. Home and office: 9305 Parkhill Terr, Bethesda, Md.

KATZIN, Herbert, US, ophthalmologist; b. Newark, NJ, Sept 20, 1913; s. Samuel and Ada (Samuels); att: Harvard Coll, 1930-33; MD, Harvard Med Sch, 1937; postgrad study, Columbia U, 1940-41; m. Annette Stollman, May 27, 1942; c: Richard, Mary. Pvt practice; dir, research, Eye Bank for Sight Restoration, Manhattan Eye, Ear, Nose & Throat Hosp, NY, since 1946; att surg, dir bd, Eye Bank, dir, Corneal Service at hosp; staff surg, Mt Sinai Hosp, 1943-46; instr, Columbia U, 1943-47; prof em, Aligarh Eye Clinic since 1951. Prin contrib: invention of surg instruments for ophthal. F: Amer Coll Surgs; Pan-Amer Soc Ophthal; NY Acad of Scis; dipl, Amer Bd of Ophthal; mem: AMA; Amer Acad of Ophthal and Otolaryngology; Phi Beta Kappa. Author: Rehabilitation of a Child's Eyes, 3rd ed, 1961; Atlas of Eye Surgery, 2nd ed, 1962; contbr to med jours. Recipient, Blue Ribbon Awards for research, Amer Acad of Ophthal and Otolaryngology. Home: 176 E 71 St, New York, NY. Office: 178 E 71 St, New York, NY.

KATZIN, Jerome S, US, business exec; b. Chgo, Ill, May 22, 1918; s. Jack and Eva (Genansky); BA, U Chgo, 1939; JD, cum laude, Law Sch, 1941; m. Miriam Manchis, July 9, 1941; c: David, Daniel, Diane. Partner, Kuhn, Loeb & Co, since 1962, with firm since 1953; dir: Atlas Corp; Colonial Pa Group; Codex; Amer Whipped Prods; Seatrain Lines; atty, US SEC, Wash DC, 1941-53. US Army, 1943-46. Dir: Gt Neck Student Aid Fund Inc, since 1960; JTSA, since 1959; mem: Supr Court of US, Ill, DC Bars; NY C of C; Lawyers of NY. Home: 23 Wensley Dr, Great Neck, NY. Office: 40 Wall St, New York, NY.

KATZIN, Leon Arthur, US, dentist, pharmacist; b. Ekaterinoslav, Russ, Dec 4, 1904; s. Abraham and Rebecca (Block); in US since 1904; RPh, Detroit Coll Pharm, 1925; att Alma Coll, Mich, 1925; att U of Mich, Lit Sch, 1927; DDS, U Mich, Dent Coll, 1930; m. Beatrice Kaplan, Feb 12, 1925 (decd); c: Lee, Aarone Premel. Prop, antique jewelry bus, since 1970, with wife, 1962-1970; ret pharmacist-dent since 1960; pres: Newell Gold Ref Co, 1952-53; St Thomas Apothecary, St Thomas, VI. Lt, US Army, Dent Corps Res, 1931-41. Pres, Club Leaders Detroit Comm Cen; fmr: vice-pres, US Handball Assn; trustee, B'nai David Syn, Detroit; mem: Amer Dent Assn; Mich State Dent Assn; Alpha Omega; club, Downtown Dent, Detroit. Author: Metal Inlay Dies, 1938; Dental Pharmacy, 1940. Home and office: 3205 Ocean Front Walk, Marina Del Rey, Cal.

KATZMAN, Lawrence, US, business exec, author, cartoonist; b. Ogdensburg, NY, June 14, 1922; s. Max and Lillian (Goldfarb); BS, U of Pa, 1944; m. Shirley Potash, Dec 18, 1955; c: Richard, Jonathan, Julie. Pres and chmn of bd: Kaz Mfg Co; Rual Mfg; Kaz Heating Products; Kaz Inc; Kax of Can; Richards, Jons & Lawrence; dir: Equi-Tronics Capital; 52 Assn; pres, Vaporizer Council since 1956. Lt, US Army Signal Corps, 1942-46. Mem: Young Pres Org; Pi Mu Epsilon; Natl Cartoonists Soc; jury, Intl Salon of Humor, Bordighera, It, 1967; author and cartoonist: Taking a Turn for the Nurse, 1956 to Nellie and the Pill, 1969, publ in US; Nellie the Nurse comic books, Nurse Nellie's Naughties, publ in Eng; Prima E Dopo I Pasti, publ in It; Sister Nellie's Meriter, publ in Den, Nor, Swed, Ger; contbr to mags. Recipient: awards, Intl Salon of Humor, It, 1959, 1966. Home: 101 Central Park W, New York, NY. Office: 614 W 49 St, New York, NY.

KATZMAN, Philip Aaron, US, biochemist, educator; b. Omaha, Neb, May 18, 1906; s. Aaron and Anna (Gerelick); BA, Kalamazoo Coll, 1927; PhD, St Louis U, Mo, 1932; m. Lillian Milder, Aug 6, 1933; c: Marshall, Aron. Prof, biochem, St

Louis U, since 1952, fac mem since 1932; visiting lectr, U Kan, 1950; Merck Sharp & Dohme visiting prof in biochem, State U of SD, 1963. Bd dirs: Social Health Assn, Gtr St Louis since 1953, bd educ, 1950-59; Shaare Emeth Temple, 1958-63; Hum Relations Commn, 1960-67; mem: Soc for Study of Reproduction; Royal Soc of Med; Soc for Experimental Biol and Med; Amer Chem Soc; The Endocrine Soc; Amer Soc of Biol Chems; AAAS; AAUP; Phi Delta Epsilon; Sigma Xi; Omicron Kappa Upsilon. Contbr to profsl jours. Home: 7612 Cornell, University City, Mo. Office: St Louis U, 1402 S Grand Blvd, St Louis, Mo.

KATZNELSON, Alexander M, Isr, orthopedic surg; b. Tomsk, Russ, Sep 23, 1919; s. Meyer and Rebecca (Senderson); in Isr since 1949; BS, St Johns U, Shanghai, China, 1942, MD, Sch of Med, 1946; m. Judith Roelam (decd); c: David, Jonathan; m. 2nd, Mariasa Bat-Miriam. Dir, dept orthopedic surg, Tel Hashomer Govt Hosp. Lt col, IDF, MC, since 1949. Chmn, Isr Soc of Orthopedic Surgs, since 1968; mem: Soc Intl de Chirurgie Orthopedique et de Traumatologie; SICOT, Isr. Home: 21 Ben Zvi Blvd, Ramat Gan, Isr. Office: Tel Hashomer Govt Hosp, Isr.

KATZNELSON, Daniel, Isr, physician; b. Tomsk, Russia, June 3, 1921; s. Meir and Rebecca (Senderson); in Isr since 1949; BS, MD, St John's U, Shanghai, China, 1937-45; m. 2nd, Michal Kaminka, July 23, 1967; c: Naomi, Raphael, Michael. Head, dept Peds "A", Tel Hashomer Hosp, Isr, since 1955; res, phys, St Andrews Hosp, Wusih, China, 1946-48. Major, IDF, MC, 1949-55. Leader, Boy Scouts, 1939-48. Home: 11 Emek Dotan St, Tel Hashomer, Isr. Office: Tel Hashomer Govt Hosp, Isr.

KATZNELSON, Gideon, Isr, educator, author; b. Baranovichi, Russ, Dec 28, 1914; s. David and Sara (Hashesman); in Isr since 1934; MA, U of Pal, 1939; m. Fela Feller, Aug 3, 1956. Lectr, Modern Heb Poetry, Tel Aviv U, since 1967; tchr, secondary sch, 1939-67. IDF, 1948-63. Author: The Polemics Between the Orthodox and Masskilim in Russia, 1954; A Cross Section of Modern Israel Poetry, 1968; contbr to lit jours and newspapers. Recipient, Klausner Award, Tel Aviv Munic, 1954. Home: 11 Netzah Israel St, Tel Aviv, Isr.

KATZOFF, Louis, US, educator, rabbi; b. NYC, Feb 21, 1908; s. Philip and Goldie (Putterman); BA, CCNY, 1930; ordained rabbi, JTSA, 1934; MS, U of Pa, 1942, PhD, 1948; m. Adina Abramowitz, July 7, 1935; c: Ranon, Jonathan. Dir, educ, N Suburban Syn Beth El, Highland Park, Ill, since 1958; rabbi, Cong B'nai Abraham, Easton, Pa, 1941-49; registrar, asst prof, educ, Coll J Studies, 1949-58. Pres, ZOA, Easton region, 1945-47; Rel Educ Assn, 1957-61, mem, natl bd dirs, since 1957; mem: Natl Council for J Educ; RabCA, pres, Chgo region, 1966-68; Phi Delta Kappa. Author: The Structure and Philosophy of the Curriculum of Conservative Congregational Hebrew School, 1948; Issues in Jewish Education, 1949. Home: 131 Cary Ave, Highland Park, Ill. Office: N Suburban Syn Beth El, Highland Park, Ill.

KAUDERS, Benzion, Isr, business exec; b. Körmend, Hung, May 27, 1907; s. Benyamin and Frida (Frim); in Isr since 1945; att Szombathely Gymnasium, 1921-25; DJur, U Budapest, 1929; m. Viola Salzer, Mar 10, 1942; c: Gabriel, Zehava. Dir, flour mills, since 1947; lawyer, 1934-40. Mil Police Res, 1945-47. Chmn, milling sect, Mfrs Assn; pres: Haifa br, Lib Party; Dist Grand Lodge, B'nai B'rith, since 1965; co-pres: Org of Hung Immigrants in Isr; World Org Js of Hung Origin; fmr: in Hung: pres: J Students in Szombathely, 1924-25; J Youth in Dist Vas, 1924-30; J Kehillah in Körmend, 1940-44; Dist Comm for Protection of Js, 1939-44, dir, legal dept, cen off, 1943-44; mem: Dist Comm of Js, 1934-44; cen comm, Zionist Org in Hung, 1935-44; vice-pres, Gen Zionist in Hung, 1942-44; delg, Cong of Hung Js, 1935; in Isr: pres: Assn Hung Js, 1954-57, Haifa br, 1948-52; Kibbutz Galuyot Lodge, B'nai B'rith, 1957-59, chmn, Haifa council, 1958-59, vice-pres, Dist Grand Lodge, Isr, 1959-65. Recipient: mil awards: partisan fighter, defense, Sinai. Home: 90 b Shoshanat Hacarmel, Haifa, Isr. Office: 31 Atzmaut, Haifa, Isr.

KAUFER, Alvin H, US, attorney; b. Nov 29, 1920; s. Joseph and Estelle (Hirschfeld); BSS, CCNY, 1939; att Harvard Law Sch, 1939-41; LLB, Columbia Law Sch, 1943; grad, piano, Julliard Sch of Music, NYC; m. Lucille Korn, Oct 16, 1952; c: Elizabeth. Asst Corp Counsel, Tax Counsel, Law Dept, NYC, since 1948; fmr: reclassified sr atty, 1956; law clerk to US Dist Court Judge Bondy, 1942-44; in pvt practice: Stroock and Stroock and Lavan, 1944-46; Phillips, Nizer, Benjamin, Krim and Ballon, 1947; asst counsel, City Housing Rent Commn, 1948; admitted to practice, US Supr Court, 1955. US Army Signal Corps, 1942-43. Mem, munic affairs comm, NYC Bar Assn since 1962, fmr mem: city court comm, 1955-58, domestic relations court comm sub-comm on leg, 1959-62; sr vice-cdr, Grand St Boy's Post, Amer Legion; vice-pres, found mem, munic lodge, B'nai B'rith; adj, judge-advocate, Midtown post cdr, NY dist, JWV, 1959-61; mem: bd trustees lawyer's chap, AJCong; Emeth Soc, Council J Orgs; exec bd, UJA; town and village div, FJP, NY; Amer Bar Assn; chmn, comm on interstate law and commerce, judiciary comm, Fed Bar Assn of NY, NJ, Conn, fmr: secy-treas, vice pres, sdist, NY; financial secy, Natl Bus and Profsl Council; dir, Interfaith Movement; club, City, chmn, munic taxation comm. Ed-in-chief, Fed Bar Assn of NY, Conn Directory 1962-63; contbr to law jours. Hobby, music. Home and office: 510 E 20 St, New York, NY.

KAUFMAN, Frank A, US, jurist, attorney; b. Baltimore, Md, Mar 4, 1916; s. Nathan and Hilda (Hecht); BA, summa cum laude, Dartmouth Coll, 1937; LLB, magna cum laude, Harvard Law Sch, 1940; m. Clementine Lazaron, Apr 22, 1945; c: Frank Jr, Peggy. US Dist Judge, Md, since 1968; in law practice since 1945. Fmr: lectr: U Baltimore Law Sch, 1946-62; U Md Law Sch, 1953; mem: Gov's commn on universal commercial code, 1961-66; chmn, Gov's commn on crime rev, 1962-66; mem: staff of gen counsel: US Treas Dept, Wash DC, 1941-42; Lend Lease Admn, 1941-42; repr in Turkey, 1942-43; spec asst to gen counsel, 1943; chief, leaflet sect, psych warfare div, Supr Hqr, Allied Expeditionary Force, 1943-45; counsel, enemy br, Fgn Econ Admn, 1945; cons, psych warfare, US Army, 1951-52; both Wash DC. Mem: natl exec bd, AJComm, chmn Baltimore br; bd: Goucher Coll, Md Inst; Baltimore Heb Cong; Sinai Hosp; Park Sch, fmr pres; Good Samaritan Hosp; fmr bd: Baltimore chaps: NCCJ, Asso J Charities Wfr Fund; mem: Amer, Md, Baltimore City Bar Assns; Phi Beta Kappa; clubs: Roundtable; Hamilton St; Cen; Wranglers; Rule Day Law; Suburban. Author: Maryland Ground Rent System, 1940. Home: 7 Clovelly Rd, Pikesville, Md. Office: 310 Post Office Bldg, Baltimore, Md.

KAUFMAN, Harry J, US, rabbi; b. Tarnopol, Pol, Jan 6, 1923; s. Uri and Rachel (Babad); in US since 1929; att CCNY; BS, Columbia U, 1945; ordained rabbi, Mesifta Torah Vodaath, 1945; m. Gittle Small, Mar 7, 1951; c: Sima, Uri, Eli. Rabbi, Cong Beth Sholom, Wash, DC, since 1947. Fmr chaplain, Natl Naval Med Cen, Bethesda, Md. Pres, Rabb Council, Gtr Wash; bd mem: United Services Org; JWB; JCC; Heb Acad, all Wash; J Found; RabCA; Rabb Alliance of Amer, vice-pres, 1952. Contbr to Anglo-J periodicals. Home: 7624 13 St, NW, Washington, DC. Study: 7930 Eastern Ave, NW, Washington, DC.

KAUFMAN, Herman S, US, chemist; b. NYC, Mar 31, 1922; s. Morris and Sarah (Bronson); BA, Bklyn Coll, 1942; MS, Poly Inst of Bklyn, 1945, PhD, 1947; m. Natalie Zuckerbraun, June 20, 1943; c: Linda Hiltzik, Mark, Joel. Asso prof, chem, Yeshiva U, NYC, since 1967; ed, Intl Jour Polymeric Materials, since 1969; research sect head, MW Kellog Co, 1949-56; asst tech dir, Minn Mining and Mfr Co, 1956-58; corp dir, research planning, Allied Chem Corp, 1958-67. Dir, research, trustee, Plastics Inst Amer, past chmn, bd trustees; mem, bd, JCC, Teaneck, NJ; mem: B'nai B'rith, Teaneck chap; Amer Chem Soc; Amer Phys Soc; dist mem, Soc of Plastics Engrs, fmr mem, engr bd; club: Mens Club, JCC, fmr bd mem. Author, Introduction to Polymer Science and Technology, 1971; contbr to sci jours. Recipient: postdoc f, Amer Chem Soc, 1947, 1948; dist mem, Soc of Plastics Engrs, 1969. Hobbies: bridge, photography, travel. Home: 152 Golf Court, Teaneck, NJ. Office: Yeshiva U, Amsterdam Ave & 185 St, New York, NY.

KAUFMAN, Irving, US, educator, artist; b. NYC, Oct 4, 1920; s. Herman and Sylvia (Leinstein); att Art Students League, NY, 1946-49; BA, MA, NYU, 1949-51; m. Mabel Goldfarb, Jan 15, 1943; c: Alan, Marc. Prof, art, City Coll, CUNY, since 1964; sup, art, New Canaan, Conn Schs, 1952-56; asso prof, art, U Mich, 1956-64; sr asso, Cen Atlantic Regional Educ Lab, 1968-69. One-man shows: six at Rehrs Gal, NY; Lowe Gal, Miami; O State U; U Mich; Airlie House; exhbs: Chgo Art Inst; Detroit Inst of Art; Pa Acad; Mus of Modern Art, NY; Boston Art Festival; Art in Our Time; others. Capt, US Army, 1942-46. Vice-pres, Inst Study Art Educ; mem: Coll Art Assn; Natl Art Educ Assn. Author: Art and Education in Contemporary Culture, 1966; The Visions of Art, 1970; ed, Education and The Imagination, U of Mich & Mus of Modern Art, 1958; contributing ed, Arts in Society; contbr to art and art educ jours. Home: 34 Corell Rd, Scarsdale, NY. Office: City College, CUNY, New York, NY.

KAUFMAN, Irving R, US, jurist; b. NYC, June 24, 1910; s. Herman and Rose (Spielberg); LLB, Fordham U and Sch of Law, 1931; hon LLD: JTSA; Okla City U; m. Helen Rosenberg, June 23, 1936; c: Robert, James, Richard. Circuit judge, US Court of Appeals, Second Circuit, since 1961; admitted to NY Bar, 1932; fmr: spec asst to Atty Gen of US, i/c lobbying inves; set up perm lobbying inves unit for Dept of Justice, served as its head; in pvt practice, NYC, mem firms: Simpson, Brady, Noonan and Kaufman; Kaufman and Eagan; US Dist Judge, S Dist of NY, 1949-61. Mem: adv council judges, Natl Council on Crime and Delinquency; US delg, 2nd UN Cong on Prevention of Crime and Treatment of Offenders; Second Circuit repr: pre-trial comm, comm on admn of criminal law, both Jud Conf of US; dir, Fordham Law Alumni Assn; sem asso, JTSA; mem: Park Ave Syn; Amer, Fed, NY State, NYC Bar Assns; Amer Judicature Soc; f, pres, Inst of Jud Admn; mem natl comm, ADL; trustee: em, Riverdale Country Sch; Amer Heritage Found; club, City Athletic. Contbr on socio-legal matters. Recipient: award, JWV; Americanism citation, Amer Legion; Man-of-the-Year, Tau Epsilon Phi; cert of hon, Va State Assn, B'nai B'rith; citation, NY State Fed of Women's Clubs; achievement in law award, Fordham Coll Alumni Assn; Chief Justice Harlan Fiske Stone award, Assn of Trial Lawyers of NYC; Encaenia award, Fordham U. Home: 1185 Park Ave, New York, NY. Office: US Courthouse, Foley Sq, New York, NY.

KAUFMAN, Israel, US, physician; b. Wollin, Russ, Nov 15, 1899; s. Isaac and Rebecca (Bachmutsky); in US since 1910; BS, CCNY, 1923; MD, U of Md, 1928; m. Pauline Bernstein, June 16, 1929; c: Theodor, Michael. Cons phys, Kings Co Hosp, U div, since 1966; visiting phys, med service, 1955-66; asst clinical prof, SUNY, downstate div, since 1955; phy i/c, chest clinic, NYC Dept of Health, since 1946; pvt practice, chest diseases, since 1938; fmr: dir, TB Service, Kingston Ave Hosp, Bklyn, 1950-55, att phys, 1945-55. Mem: Bklyn Thoracic Soc, pres, 1952; Amer Coll Chest Phys; Amer Trudeau Soc; Kings Co, NY State Med Socs; AMA; ZOA; B'nai B'rith; Phi Lambda Kappa. Contbr to med jours. Home: Cross Pound Rd, Pound Ridge, NY.

KAUFMAN, Jay, US, organization exec, rabbi; b. Cleveland, O, Sep 19, 1918; s. Hiram and Hannah (Spero); BA, W Reserve U, 1940; ordained rabbi, MHL, HUC, 1946; grad studies, Heb U, Jerusalem, 1946-48; m. Aviva Gootman, June 2, 1946; c: Gideon, Joshua, Abigail. Exec vice-pres, B'nai B'rith, since 1965; rabbi: Beth Isr, Laredo, Tex, 1941-42; Oheb Shalom, Sandusky, O, 1944-45; Beth El, Niagara Falls, NY, 1945-46; Old York Rd Temple, Phila, 1948-49; Comty Syn, Beth Am, Port Wash, LI, NY, 1952-53; dir, Phila Fed UAHC, 1948-49; asst to pres, HUC, NYC, 1949-57, vice-pres, 1957-65. Chmn, Comm on Scope, Conf Pres of Maj Amer J Orgs; cen comm, LZOA since 1952; bd mem: Amer J Comty Relations Workers, since 1952; Histadrut Ivrit; JWB, 1951-65; governing body, World Union for Progressive Judaism, 1951-65; exec bd, Syn Council of Amer, 1950-65; mem: B'nai B'rith; CCAR. Recipient, Henry Morgenthau Traveling Scholarship, HUC, 1946. Home: 4012 Oliver St, Chevy Chase, Md. Office: 1640 Rhode Island Ave NW, Washington, DC.

KAUFMAN, M Ralph, US, psychiatrist, educator; b. Beltz, Russ, Oct 5, 1900; s. Jakov and Sarah (Straker); in US since 1925; MD, CM, McGill U, 1925; m. Ida Esack, Sep 2, 1925; c: Paul, Bettina, Esther, Joseph Klingenstein. Prof, psycht, since 1968, chmn, psycht dept, Mt Sinai Sch of Med, since 1964, dean, Page and William Black Postgrad Sch of Med, since 1966; psycht-in-chief, dir, psycht dept, Inst of Psycht, since 1945, all Mt Sinai Hosp; lectr, Coll of Phys and Surgs, Columbia U, since 1965; chmn, med adv bd, Heb U, Hadassah Med Sch, Jerusalem, since 1961; fmr: res, neur, Montefiore Hosp; asst sr phys, Boston Psychopathic Hosp; Commonwealth Fund Research f, Harvard Med Sch; clinical dir, McLean Hosp, Mass; att neuropsycht, Beth Isr Hosp, Boston; instr, asso psycht, Harvard Med Sch; spec lectr, Simmons Coll,

Boston. Col, US Army MC, 1942-45. Dipl, Amer Bd Psycht and Neur, 1935; f, Council on Mh, NY Acad of Med, vice-pres since 1960; life mem, Amer Psycht Assn; mem: Amer Psychan Assn, past pres; Assn for Research in Nervous and Mental Diseases; AAAS; Amer Psychosomatic Soc; Soc of US Med Cons in WW II; NY Psychan Soc; NY Psycht Soc; Harvey Soc; NY Soc for Clinical Psycht, fmr pres; NY Neur Soc; clubs: Harvard, NYC; Boston. Asso ed: The Psycht Quarterly; The Archives of Gen Psycht; contbr to med jours. Recipient: Bronze Star with Cluster, WW II; Adolf Meyer award, 1957. Home: 1170 Fifth Ave, New York, NY. Office: 11 E 100 St, New York, NY.

KAUFMAN, Milton, US, business exec; b. NYC, Dec 2, 1921; s. David and Sadie (Abend); BS, Okla State U, 1944; m. Gita Hoytash Frazer, Mar 25, 1962; c: Linda, Cynthia, Barbara. Exec, real estate, Shubert Theatrical Enterprises, since 1964, and 1949-56; real estate exec, Stevens Devl Corp, 1956-60; vice-pres, S-M-W Devl, 1956-60; treas, dir, vice-pres, River Rds Properties, 1956-60; licensed real estate broker, NY; licensed profsl ME, Cal. Lt, USNR. Vice-pres, Bldg Owners and Mgrs Assn, Milw, 1957; mem: Real Estate Bd of NY; Natl Assn Real Estate Bds; Pi Tau Sigma; UJA; FJP; Red Mogen David; JNF. Home: 53 Shelter Lane, Roslyn Heights, NY. Office: 225 W 44 St, New York, NY.

KAUFMAN, Nathan J, US, jurist; b. Aus, Nov 20, 1908; s. David and Rose (Wagner); in US since 1913; LLB, Detroit Coll of Law, 1929; m. Beatrice Tauber, Dec 18, 1930; c: Rose Blake. Judge, Circuit Court, since 1953; asst prosecuting atty, Wayne Co, 1945-53. Vice-pres, Cong Beth Abraham, 1961; mem, bd govs, Allied J Campaign, 1960; mem, exec bd: Yeshiva Beth Yehuda; Natl Juvenile Judges Assn. Home: 17533 Freeland St, Detroit, Mich. Office: 1501 City County Bldg, Detroit, Mich.

KAUFMAN, Reuben, US, rabbi, author; b. Vyozen, Russ, June 1, 1890; s. Louis and Gertrude (Novosholsky); in US since 1893; BA, Clark U, 1911; MA, Columbia U, 1912; ordained rabbi, JTSA, 1915, DHL, 1917; m. Lillian Prigoff, Mar 27, 1921; c: Sarah Garth, Edward. Fmr rabbi: Temple Beth El, Patterson, NJ, 1948-66; Utica, NY, 1919-25; E Medwood J Cen, Bklyn, 1925-28; Temple Emanuel, Paterson, NJ, 1928-48; chaplain: N Jersey Training Sch; Paterson Fire Dept; hon chaplain, JWV post. Chaplain, WW I, Fr. Fmr pres: Rabb Assn of NJ; ZOA dist; org and chmn: J Court of Arbitration, Paterson; org, Eng dept, Yeshiva Yavne, Paterson; mem: NY Bd Rabbis; Mizrachi; B'nai B'rith; RA; ZOA; Masons; Kiwanis; Rotary; mem council, Boy Scouts of Amer; Grand Jurors Assn. Author: Ma'asiah Heb Text Book, 1935; Piano Method for Teaching Bar Mitzvah, 1936; Crisis in Jewish History, 1940; One Judaism, 1953; My Trip to Israel, 1960; The Philosophy of Judaism, 1963; Sects and Schisms in Judaism, 1967; contbr to: Universal J Ency; Ency of J Knowledge; ed and publisher, Amer J Post, since 1954. Hobbies: violinist, composer. Home: 349 E 36 St, Paterson, NJ.

KAUFMAN, Reuben R, US, business exec; b. Russ, Sep 10, 1903; s. Esidore and Clara (Ochs); in US since 1906; m. Jane Gabler, Nov 1, 1936; c: Curtis. Chmn of bd, Jayark Corp; pres: Jayark Instruments Corp; Jayark Films; Colorama Features; US Pictures. Bd of dirs: JTSA; J Hist Soc; United Syn of Amer; Natl Ramah Commn; dir, Sixty Sutton Corp, fmr pres; trustee, Park Ave Syn; club, Covenant, Chgo. Home: 60 Sutton Pl, New York, NY. Office: 10 E 49 St, New York, NY.

KAUFMAN, Rose B, US, communal leader; b. Kobrin, Russ, Apr 16, 1902; d. Abraham and Bessie (Silberstein) Berick; in US since 1904; BA, W Reserve U, Cleveland, O, 1921; m. Louis Kaufman; c: Laurence, Jack. Chmn, admn bd, Pioneer Women, since 1969, natl pres, 1965-69; hon vice-pres, JNF, 1965-69; natl vice-pres, Natl Comm for Lab Isr, 1965-69. Home: 150 West End Ave, New York, NY.

KAUFMAN, Sherwin A, US, obstetrician; b. Russ, July 2, 1920; s. Michael and Lala (Rabinowitz), grandson of Sholem Aleichem; in US since 1922; BA, Columbia U, 1941; MD, Cornell Med Coll, 1943; m. Mimmi Daniels, Sep 23, 1942 (decd); c: Kenneth, Keith; m. 2nd, Claire Zaldin, Oct 29, 1965; c: Michael. Pvt practice since 1949; asst att obstet, gyn: NYU Med Cen, since 1962; Beth Isr Hosp, 1957-62. Capt, US Army, 1947. Med dir, Planned Parenthood of NYC since 1952; dir, Family Counseling Service, since 1959; f: Amer Coll

Surgs; Intl Coll Surgs; dipl, Amer Bd Obstet and Gyn; mem: Amer Fertility Soc; Intl Fertility Assn; Amer Assn Marriage Counselors. Author: The Ageless Woman, 1967; co-author: Modern Office Gynecology, 1957; Infertility in Women, 1966; contbr author, Progress in Gynecology, 1969; contbr to profsl jours. Home: 55 E 87 St, New York, NY. Office: 4 E 88 St, New York, NY.

KAUFMAN, Sidney, US, geophysicist; b. Passaic, NJ, Aug 10, 1908; s. Jacob and Frances (Buxbaum); BA, Cornell U, 1930; PhD, 1934; m. Goldie Rosin, Jan 5, 1936; c: Martha, Susan. Dir, vice-pres, Globe Exploration Co; sr research asso, Shell Devl Co; geophysicist, Shell Oil, 1936-41. Prin physicist, Naval Research Labs, 1946; lt cdr, USNR. Cons, Advanced Research Projects Agcy, US Dept of Defense; mem: Natl Acad Sci Comm on Seismology; Geophysics Adv Panel, Air Force Off of Sci Research; Amer Phys Soc; Amer Inst Radio Engrs; Soc Exploration Geophysicists; Instrument Soc of Amer; Sigma Xi. Home: 2931 S Braeswood Blvd, Houston, Tex. Office: Shell Development Co, 3737 Bellaire Blvd, Houston, Tex.

KAUFMAN, Sidney S, US, surgeon; b. Pittsburgh, Pa, Oct 8, 1916; s. Mitchell and Reva (Morgan); BS, U Pittsburgh, 1937, MD, Sch of Med, 1941; m. Lois Sanger, Feb 11, 1948; c: Joanne, Patricia, David. Chmn, dept of surg, Montefiore Hosp, Pittsburgh, fmr: att surg, res surg, on staff since 1949; res surg, Mt Sinai Hosp, NYC, 1945-49. Capt, US Army MC, 1942-46. Dipl, Amer Bd of Surg; f, Amer Coll Surg; mem, AMA. Home: 6400 Beacon St, Pittsburgh, Pa. Office: 3600 Forbes St, Pittsburgh, Pa.

KAUFMAN, William I, US, writer, photographer, executive; b. NYC, June 8, 1922; s. John and Bella (Cooper); att: Wake Forest Coll, 1941-42; Leland Powers Sch of Drama, 1946; m. Rosamond Van Poznak, Dec 15, 1946; c: Iva, Lazarus. Free-lance writer, photographer, since 1961; pres, Food Photographers Inc, since 1966; fmr: exec, program, Sales, NBC-TV, 1948-61. Photo assignments: Status Dipl Mag; Venture; Hilton Intl Hotels; Clipper Mag; co-author: Your Career in TV, 1951; How to See Europe; How to See Caribbean and W Indies; author-ed: How to Write for TV; How to Direct for TV; How to Announce for TV, all 1954; author: cook-books, including Cooking in a Castle; 1001 Jobs for High School Graduates; Greatest Television Plays; ed: TV Prize Plays, 1951, 1952, 1955, 1957; Cooking with the Experts, 1956; The Art of Creole Cooking, 1962; Intl Cooking Series: Near E; Far E; Mexican; Caribbean and S Amer; S Eur; N Eur, all 1963; contbr to theater, trade periodicals; Broadway produc: The Pink Elephant, 1953. US Army, 1942-46. Chmn, Men's comm, J Mus; bd dirs: Vet's Hosp; Radio and TV Guild; parents assn bd of dirs, Park Ave Syn Rel Sch. Hobbies: Chinese painting, music, theater, youth activities. Home: 1361 Madison Ave, New York, NY. Office: 3 W 20 St, New York, NY.

KAUFMANN, Arthur, US, artist; b. Muelheim/Ruhr, Ger, July 7, 1888; s. Gottschalk and Emma (Meyer); in US since 1936; att Royal Art Acad, Dusseldorf, Ger; studied in Eng, Belgium, Fr, It; m. Elizabeth Musset, Nov 27, 1913 (decd); c: Miriam, Etz, Hans. One-man shows and group exhbs: Min of Educ, Rio de Janeiro, 1946; Architectural Inst, Sao Paulo, 1946; Domus Gal, Sao Paulo, 1946; Marie Sterner Gal, 1947; Norlyst Gal, 1947; Whitney Mus, US, 1948; Feigl Gal, 1949, all in NYC; Stendhal Gals, LA, 1939; Art Mus, Cincinnati, 1948; Gal Canard, Amsterdam, 1953; Kunsthalle, Dusseldorf, 1953; Muelheim/Ruhr, 1954, 1958; J Mus, NYC, 1958; New Masters Gal, NYC, 1961; NJ Montclair State Coll, 1962; Petite Gal, Sao Paulo, 1964; portraits: including Albert Einstein, Martin Buber. Triptych, a group portrait of 38 refs, perm collection of Deutsche Bibliothek, Frankfurt, Ger. Found, pres, Young Rhineland Artists Org, 1918-28; dir, tchr, Sch for Decorative Arts, Dusseldorf, 1929-33; mem: Art Assn, The Hague; Artists Equity; first hon mem, Muelheim/Ruhr Art Soc, 1958. Home and studio: 414 W 121 St, New York, NY.

KAUFMANN, Henry H, US, stockbroker; b. Frankfurt, Ger, July 23, 1908; s. Sali and Irma (Gideon); in US since 1940; att colls in: Geneva, Switz; London, Eng; Frankfurt, Ger; U of S Cal; BA, U Ariz, 1964, MA, 1966; m. 2nd, Roslyne Rubin, Sep 3, 1967; c: 1st, Susan, Wendy, John; c: 2nd, David, Paul, Robert, Judith. Mem adv bd, Hornblower and Weeks Hemphill Noyes & Co, since 1950. Vice-pres, UJA, since 1949; mem: NY Maccabi Athletic Club, hon pres, since

1946; bd, Handmaker J Nursing Home; life mem, exec bd, Tucson JCC; fmr: pres, ZOA, Tucson; chmn, Isr Bond Dr. Home: 560 Via Guadalupe, Tucson, Ariz. Office: 3777 E Broadway, Tucson, Ariz.

KAUFFMANN, Moysés, Brazil, business exec; b. Santos, Brazil, Aug 5, 1908; s. Adolpho and Ruchel (Goldemberg); att Fac of Law, São Paulo, 1931; m. Elisa Tabacow, Feb 15, 1928; c: Adolpho, Isa Schneider, Paulo. Pres, Textil Tabacow SA, since 1960, dir, 1931-60; dir, Jutafil SA, since 1967. Pres, Confd of Brazilian Jewry, vice-pres, Latin Amer J Cong, br of WJC; mem: governing council, exec, WJC; fmr pres: Philanthropic Inst Ezra, 1939-40; clubs: Circulo Israelita, pres, 1929-42; Hebraica, pres, 1953-59. Home: 949 Maranhão St, São Paulo, Brazil. Office: 131 José Tabacow St, São Paulo, Brazil.

KAUFMANN, Norman, US, attorney; b. Baltimore, Md, May 13, 1902; s. Joseph and Annette (Goldsmith); JD, U of Md, Baltimore, 1925; m. Marion Davis, Sep 30, 1950. Ret; consul, Rep Honduras, 1934-36; pvt practice, 1936-69. Lt-cdr, USNR, since 1928. Pres: Munic Bar Assn; Circulo Culturale Italiano; cdr, VFW. Author, Divorce in Maryland, 1936. Spec interests: langs, teaching. Home and office: 2310 Sulgrave Ave, Baltimore, Md.

KAVEY, Lillia Kaimdorf, US, banking exec; b. NYC; d. Isaac and Miriam (Schlimovitz) Blass; att: NYU; Columbia U; Amer Inst of Banking; m. Abraham Kavey, (decd); c: Milton, Edith, Leon. Org, owner, bank, Port Chester, NY, since 1914; org: Kavey Travel Bur, 1914; Pioneer Finance Co, 1916. Visited Falasha J in Ethiopia, 1967-68; adv bd, First Westchester Natl Bank; exec bd, Natl Women's League; trustee, Carver Cen; mem, United Syn of Amer; active in rescue of refs from Nazis. Home: 48 Elmont Ave, Port Chester, NY. Office: Liberty Sq, Port Chester, NY.

KAY, Harold, US, physician; b. Omaha, Neb, Aug 28, 1909; s. Joseph and Anna (Lesser); BA, U of Cal, 1931; MS, Creighton U, 1933; MD, U of Cal, 1936; att, U of Edinburgh, 1938-39; m. Frances Simon, Jan, 1938; c: Steven. Pvt practice, urol, since 1937; chief, dept of urol, Alameda Co Inst, 1954-59; Peralta Insts, since 1937, pres, visiting staff, 1961-62, both of Oakland; mem: active staff: Alta Bates Hosp, since 1939; Cowell Hosp, since 1948; cons, VA Hosp, Livermore, since 1948; pres, Herrick Hosp staff, since 1948, mem, active staff, since 1937, all of Berkeley. Capt, USNR, MC, 1938-62. Pres, B'nai B'rith, 1941; vice-pres, Alameda Co Med Assn, 1961-62; f: Amer Coll Surg; Intl Coll Surg; dipl, Amer Bd Urol; mem: Cal State Med Assn; AMA; Masons; Temple Sinai. Home: 50 Bonita Ave, Piedmont, Cal. Office: 411-30 St, Oakland, Cal.

KAYE, Alvin Maurice, Isr, scientist; b. NYC, Sep 18, 1930; s. Oscar and Rebecca (Schachman); in Isr since 1956; AB, Columbia Coll, 1951; AM, Columbia U, 1953; PhD, U of Pa, 1955; m. Myra Ockrent, Sep 12, 1958; c: David. Sr research sci, Weizmann Inst of Sci, since 1968, on staff since 1956. Prin contribs: research on causation of cancer, mechanism of heredity. Pres, Fed J Students Orgs of NY, 1952-53; mem: Isr Biochems Assn; Amer Soc for Cell Biol. Contbr sci papers to jours. Recipient: Pulitzer Prize Scholarship, Columbia U, 1947. Home: 11 Hazait St, Rehovot, Isr. Office: Dept of Biodynamics, Weizmann Inst of Sci, Rehovot, Isr.

KAYE, Danny (David Daniel), US, actor; b. Bklyn, NY, Jan 18, 1913; s. Jacob and Clara (Nemerov) Kaminsky; m. Sylvia Fine, Jan 3, 1940; c: Dena. Partner, Dena Productions, independent motion picture co, LA, since 1952; vice-pres, Lear Jet Corp, since 1966; ambass-at-large, UN Childrens Fund; fmr: weekly TV show, CBS, since 1963; mem La Vie Paree Co on world tour, 1934; entertainer: Dorchester Hotel, London, Eng, 1936; La Martineque, night club, NYC, 1940. Star, stage producs: The Keynote Review, 1939; Straw Hat Review, 1939; Lady in Dark, with Gertrude Lawrence, 1940-41; Let's Face it, 1942-43, all in NYC. Star, film producs: Up In Arms; Wonderman; The Kid From Brooklyn; The Secret Life of Walter Mitty; On The Riviera; Hans Christian Andersen; Knock On Wood; White Christmas; Five Pennies; On the Double; Me and the Colonel. Clubs: Hillcrest; Tamarisk. Home: Beverly Hills, Cal. Office: Paramount Studios, Hollywood, Cal.

KAYE, Josse, S Afr, radiologist, educator; b. Randfontein, S Afr, Feb 16, 1907; s. Josiah and Rebecca (Holzberg) Kaplan;

MPS, S Eng Coll of Pharm, 1927; att Lawrence Sch of Optics, London, qualified FSMC, FBOA, FIO, London, 1929; trained for med, London Hosp, MRCS, Eng, LRCP, London, 1940; dipl in med radiology, U Cape Town, DMR, 1944; m. Helga Schlessinger, July 19, 1932; c: Rea Gardy, Keith. Prof, radiology, U Witwatersrand since 1962; chief radiologist, Johannesburg Gen Hosp, 1945-61; med off, Emergency Med Service, London, 1939-42. Found, life pres, Fabella Med Club, since 1958; mem: Coll of Phys, Surgs and Gyns, S Afr, comm, fac of radiologists; fmr: pres, Radiology Soc, Transvaal. Contbr to med jours. Recipient, f, Fac of Radiologists, Royal Coll Surgs, Ir, 1964. Hobbies: painting, archaeol, photography, chess, collector of cacti. Home: 1377 Cambridge Rd, Bryanston, Sandton, S Afr. Office: U of Witwatersrand Med Sch, Johannesburg, S Afr.

KAYE, Maxwell Malcolm, US, optometrist; b. Bklyn, NY, June 2, 1907; s. Isaac and Ida (Lefkowitz) Kozinsky; OD, Mass Sch of Optometry, 1933; m. Doris Endelman, Aug 21, 1934; c: Michael, Paul Cohen, Leta Cohen. Pvt practice since 1940. Natl secy, United Syn of Amer, fmr pres, N NJ region; vice-pres, Low Cost Psycho-Therapy Plan of Essex Co, NJ; chmn, bd, Temple B'nai Isr, Irvington, NJ, fmr vice-pres; trustee, Newark Public Libr; mem: Robert Treat council, J Comm on Scouting; Masons; Amer, NJ, Essex Co, Optometric Socs; NJ Libr Trustee Assn; Amer Libr Assn; Assn to Advance Ethical Hypnosis; clinical asso, Optometric Ext Prog; fmr: chmn: camp comm, Natl Syn Youth; Newark Hum Rights Commn; pres, Beth David J Cen, Newark. Ed, The Record, newspaper of United Syn, N NJ region. Home: 49 Ivy St, Newark, NJ. Office: 889 Broad St, Newark, NJ.

KAYFETZ, Benjamin G, Can, organization exec; b. Toronto, Dec 24, 1916; s. Max and Leah (Orloff); BA, U of Toronto, 1939; Specialist's Cert, Ont Coll of Educ, Toronto, 1940; m. Eve Silver, Sep 5, 1954; c: Zena, Tamara, Rebecca. Exec dir, natl jt comty relations comm, Can J Cong and B'nai B'rith, cen region, since 1947, Can region, since 1955; fmr: instr, HS: Niagara Falls; Huntsville, Ont, 1941-43; mem, censorship br, Can Govt Service, Ottawa, 1943-45. Control Comm for Ger, Brit Zone. 1945-47. Mem: Assn J Comty Relations Workers; Can Ling Assn. Contributing author, A People and Its Faith, 1959; contbr to J periodicals. Spec interest, Yiddish philol. Home: 7 Austin Crescent, Toronto, Can. Office: 150 Beverly St, Toronto, Can.

KAYSER, Louise D, US, artist; b. Mannheim, Ger, Apr 26, 1899; d. Rudolf and Bertha (May) Darmstaedter; in US since 1938; att Acad of Art, Munich, 1921; m. Stephen Kayser, Jan 4, 1930; c: Charles. Stage designer, 1924-26; portraitist, since 1926; designer, stained glass windows, 1947-52; one-man show, M H De Young Memorial Mus, SF, Cal, 1942; participant in group shows. Home: 950 Second St, Santa Monica, Cal.

KAYSER, Stephen S, US, curator, educator; b. Karlsruhe, Ger, Dec 23, 1900; s. Siegbert and Mina (Hilb); in US since 1938; PhD, U Heidelberg, 1923; m. Louise Darmstaedter, Jan 4, 1930; c: Charles. Prof: aesthetics, U Judaism, LA, since 1963; hist of art and integrated arts, UCLA, since 1965; asso prof, JTSA, since 1947; cons to Tel Aviv U, Isr; lectr, art dept, U of Cal, 1940-44; prof, hist of art, San Jose State Coll, Cal, 1944-47; curator, dir exhbs, J Mus, NYC, 1947-63. Mem: Amer Fed of Art; Coll Art Assn. Author: The Book of Books in Art, 1956; Jewish Ceremonial Art, 2nd ed, 1960; contbr to rel and art jours. Home: 950 Second St, Santa Barbara, Cal.

KAZIN, Alfred, US, author, educator; b. Bklyn, NY, June 5, 1915; s. Charles and Gita (Fagelman); BSS, CCNY, 1935; MA, Columbia U, 1938; hon, DLitt, Adelphi U, 1965; m. Ann Birkstein, June 26, 1952; c: Michael, by previous m; Cathrael. Author and educ since 1935; Dist Prof Eng, SUNY, since 1963; lectr, New Sch for Social Research, since 1941; tutor, Eng, CCNY, 1937-41; Fulbright lectr, Cambridge U, Eng, 1952; visiting lectr, Harvard U, 1953; William Allan Neilson Prof, Smith Coll, 1954-55; prof, Amer studies, Amherst Coll, 1955-58; Berg prof, lit, NYU, 1957. Mem: Amer Acad Arts and Sci; Natl Inst Arts and Letters. Author: On Native Grounds, 1942; A Walker in the City, 1951; The Inmost Leaf, 1955; Contemporaries, 1962; Starting Out in the Thirties, 1965; ed: The Portable William Blake, 1946; F Scott Fitzgerald: The Man and His Work, 1951; The Stature of Theodore Dreiser, 1955; Melville's Moby Dick, 1956; Ralph Waldo Emerson: A Modern Anthology, 1958;

The Open Forum, 1961; introductions to books: Dostoevsky's Crime and Punishment, 1946; Dostoevsky's A Raw Youth, 1946; Selected Stories of Shalom Aleichem; The Novels of Theodore Dreiser; The Collected Works of Anne Frank. Recipient: Guggenheim f, 1940, 1947; Rockefeller f, 1945. Home: 440 West End Ave, New York, NY.

KAZIN, Louis E, US, editor, pharmacist; b. Bridgeport, Conn, Mar 22, 1913; s. Abraham and Ida (Elkin); PharmG, U of Conn, 1934; m. Alice Rebock, Mar 22, 1936; c: Stephen, Ellen. Ed, Jour of Natl Assn of Retail Druggists, since 1965. owner, pharm, 1939-50; asso prof, dir, pharm ext service, Rutgers U, NJ, 1950-53; asso ed, Drug Trade News, 1953-56, ed, 1956-65; ed, Drug Topics, 1958-65, vice-pres, 1962-65; vice-pres, Topics Pub Co, 1962-65. Mem: Curtis P Gladding Hon Soc; Rho Chi Hon Soc; Masons; chmn, Ill in Isr pharm group, Amer Friends of Heb U; fmr: chmn: drugs div, ARC campaign, 1962; drugs and toiletries div, USO, 1962; dist chmn, Boy Scouts Amer, Bridgeport, 1949-50; pack comm, Cub Scouts Amer, 1951-53; pr chmn, Oakview Homes Sch Assn, 1956, both Bloomfield, NJ. Found, N End Recreation Cen for Boys and Girls, Bridgeport, Conn, 1945-46; clubs: Torch; Pork Shank of Chgo; Execs of Chgo; contbr to pharm jours. Recipient: Rutgers Medal, 1957; Man of the Year award: Alpha Zeta Omega, 1960; Delta Sigma Theta, 1962. Home: 3950 N Lake Shore Dr, Chicago, Ill. Office: One E Wacker Dr, Chicago, Ill.

KAZIS, Abraham, US, rabbi; b. Cambridge, Mass, Apr 4, 1916; s. Jacob and Bessie (Rimmerman); BS, Boston U, 1940; ordained rabbi, JTSA, 1944, MHL, 1947; m. Eunice Pollack; c: Israella. Rabbi: Beth Isr Cong, Worcester, Mass since 1955; Temple Emanuel, Chelsea, Mass, 1945; Sons of Jacob Cong, Salem, Mass, 1947-55; chaplain: Amer Legion Post; JWV, both Salem. Chaplain, US Army, 1945-47. Mem: RA; Rabb Assn, Gtr Boston; bd, J Family Service; pres, Worcester Friends Public Libr; bd mem: Zionist Dist; Mh Assn; Ivriah Heb Sch; J Comty Cen; pres, Interfaith Housing Corp, all Worcester; ARC, Salem chap; mem: sub-comm on Minority Housing; Mins Assn; Clergy Comm on Comty, all Worcester; Salem C of C. Home: 8 Jamesbury Dr, Worcester, Mass. Study: Temple Park and Jamesburg Dr, Worcester, Mass.

KAZNELSON, Batsheva, Isr, communal worker; b. Russ, 1897; d. Israel and Pessia (Bekelman) Nagel; in Isr since 1913; licencié en lettres, J J Rousseau Inst, U Geneva, Switz, 1920; m. Reuben Kaznelson, Nov 6, 1918; c: Shmuel, Tamir, Shulamit Korn. Vice-pres, Isr Council of Womens Org, since 1954; mem: cen comm, Women of Lib Party, since 1961, fmr Gen Zionist Party, 1948-1960; fmr: tchr, 1921-48; served with Red Cross, 1940-42; MK, 1951-55. Fmr mem: cen comm, WIZO; J Women's Org; social wfr council, Min of Social Wfr; intl adv, Mouvement Mondial des Meres, Paris. Contbr to periodicals. Home: 10 Rashba St, Jerusalem, Isr.

KAZNELSON, Reuben, Isr, organization exec; b. Bobruisk, Russ, Apr 6, 1890; s. Nissan and Zelda (Rozovski); in Isr since 1920; att, Econ Inst, Kiev, 1911-14; grad, social sci fac, U Geneva, 1920; att London Sch Tropical Med, 1930; DRerPol, Naples, It, 1931; m. Batsheva Nagel, Nov 6, 1918; c: Shmuel, Tamir, Shulamit Korn. Found, pres, Sick Peoples Benefit Fund, since 1932; mem, health, social wfr councils, Govt of Isr, since 1940; fmr: asst dir, dir, Hadassah Med Org, 1920-31; lectr, social wfr schs: Jerusalem, Haifa, Nazareth, 1961-63; dep-dir, Pal Govt Census, 1921; sent by Russ Govt to Pal to report on econ relations between Russ and Syria, Leb and Pal, 1914. Russ Army, 1910-11; sgt-maj, J Legion, Zion Mule Corps, 1915. Mem, exec comm, Anti-TB League; pres, found, Isr-Switz Friendship League; chmn: Pro Familia, Isr; Brit Legion, Jerusalem; mem gen council, Intl Union of Family Orgs; KP, David and Jonathan Lodge. Author, L'immigrazione degli Ebrei in Palestina; contbr to the press. Home: 10 Rashba St, Jerusalem, Isr.

KEDAR, Benjamin, Isr, educator; b. Seesen, Ger, Aug 1, 1923; s. Felix and Gertrud (Eckert) Kopfstein; in Isr since 1939; BA, U London, 1954; MA, Heb U, Jerusalem, 1961, PhD, 1968; m. Miriam Heymann, Sep 27, 1943; c: Tamara, Daniela. Lectr, Heb U, Jerusalem, since 1966; staff mem, Bible project, since 1960; tchr, Jerusalem Inst for Students from Abroad, 1956-62, dep-dir, 1962-64; visiting lectr, JA, NY, 1964-66. Pal Police Force, 1941-44; IDF Res. Author, The Vulgate as a Translation, 1968; contbr, articles, Textus, 1964. Recipient, decorations: Hamishmar, Lohamei Hamedina. Home: 24 Oren St, Haifa, Isr. Office: Haifa U, Mt Carmel, Isr.

KEDEM, Orah, Isr, scientist, educator; b. Vienna, Aus, July 2, 1924; d. Eliahu and Sarah (Schonfeld) Katz; in Isr since 1940; MSc, Heb U, Jerusalem, 1949, PhD, 1956; m. Abraham Kedem; c: Ilana, Michael. Asso prof, Weizmann Inst, since 1965; fmr: research asso, Heb U, 1953-59; sr lectr, Harvard Med Sch, 1963-64. Lt, IDF, sci corps, 1947-49. Princ ontribs: research: basic and applied on transport through membranes; biophys; desalination. Mem, adv bd, Desalination Jour; contbr to sci jours. Recipient, Isr Sci award, 1960. Home: 11 Ben-Zion St, Rehovot, Isr. Office: Weizmann Inst, Rehovot, Isr.

KEENAN, Itzhak, Isr, diplomat; b. Russ, Mar 15, 1911; s. Haim and Lea (Pevsner) Kounin; in Pal since 1923; Dipl Ing, Sch Electricity and Ind Mech, Paris, 1930; m. Dina Goldberg, 1937; c: Raphael, Judith. Mgn dir, Inst for Planning and Devl, Tel Aviv, since 1968; Isr res repr to Intl Atomic Energy Agcy, Vienna, with rank, envoy extraordinary and min plen, since 1960; fmr: engr, Societe d'Electricite et de Transport de Force, Paris, 1930-35; mgr, Amer Near E Corp, Tel-Aviv, 1935-40; maintenance and oprs insp, Socony Vacuum Oil Co, Isr, 1940-43; mgr, Avizar Co, 1943-45; mgr, Hamegaper Rubber Factory, and Vulcan Agcy, Haifa; dir, Safed Pencil Factory, 1945-48; with Min Defense, 1948-60: head, supply dept, 1950-53, head, bldg property dept, 1955-57, mission to Europe, 1957-60, bus mgr Isr Reparations Mission, Ger, 1953-55; dep dir gen, Min Defense, 1964-66; PM personal rep-at-large, 1966-68. Hobbies: music, photography. Home: 32 Pinkus St, Tel Aviv, Isr. Office: 66 Peter Jordan St, Vienna, Aus.

KEESING, Nancy Florence Hertzberg (pen name, Nancy Keesing), Austr, author, editor; b. Sydney, Austr, Sep 7, 1923; d. Gordon and Margery (Hart); dipl, social studies, Sydney U, 1947; m. A M Hertzberg, Feb 2, 1955; c: Margery, John. Author: poetry: Imminent Summer, 1951; Three Men and Sydney, 1955; Showground Sketchbook, 1968; criticism, Douglas Stewart, 1965; By Gravel and Gum, for children, 1966; Australian Short Stories; Transition, both in preparation; regular contbr: The Bulletin; The Bridge; Southerly; ed, Gold Fever, 1967; co-ed, anthols: Australian Bush Ballads, 1955; Old Bush Songs, 1957; The Pacific Book of Bush Ballads, 1967, repub, 1968; contbr to mags and press in Australia and abroad, to radio. Clerk, Dept of Navy, 1942-44; social worker, Royal Alexandra Hosp for Children, 1948-51. Chmn, comms, Eng Assn, NSW; mem: PEN; Austr Authors Soc; Royal Austr Hist Soc; Austr J Hist Soc; exec comm, Hunter's Hill Hist Soc; Austr Assn Social Workers; N Shore Temple Emmanuel, fmr, tchr, rel sch; mem, liaison off, Friends Heb U; adv comm, NSW Cultural Grants, Lit, 1968, 1969; fmr, mem, Lyrebird Writers Group. Home and office: 3 Garrick Ave, Hunter's Hill, NSW, Austr.

KEGAN, Esther O, US, attorney; b. Chgo, Ill, June 29, 1913; d. Abraham and Ida (Segal) Oswianza; BS, Northwestern U, 1933, JD, 1936, MA, 1953; m. Albert Kegan, Jan 29, 1939 (decd); c: Judith Gardiner, Daniel, Franklin. Partner, law firm: Kegan, Kegan and Berkman, since 1957; Kegan and Kegan, 1943-57; research asst, City of Chgo law dept, 1935-41. Commn, Ill Food, Drug, Cosmetic and Pesticide Laws Study Commn, Ill Food, Drug, Cosmetic and Pesticide Laws Study Comm, since 1965; vice-chmn, Evanston Fair Housing Rev Bd, since 1968; mem: Ill Statewide Adv Council, Dept Public Health, 1968; Intl Assn for Protection of Ind Property, 1964-68; Intl Patent and Trademark Assn, 1964-68; US Trademark Assn, 1962-68; Amer Bar Assn; Chgo Patent Law Assn; Decalogue Lawyers Soc, bd mem, 1950-62; women's div, B'nai B'rith; Foster Parents Plan; bd mem: Northwestern U Law Alumni; Beth Emet Syn, Evanston, Ill; women's div, Chgo Soc for Technion; J Educ Comm, UAHC; mem: Phi Beta Kappa; Order of Coif. Contbr to legal periodicals; ed, Chgo Code of Munic Ordnances, 1939; fmr mem, ed bd, Ill Law Rev. Spec interests: J educ, career guidance, art. Home: 412 Ashland Ave, Evanston, Ill. Office: 79 W Monroe St, Chicago, Ill.

KEKST, Gershon, US, business exec; b. Peabody, Mass, Oct 12, 1934; s. Jacob and Anna (Lewensohn); BS, U of Md, 1956; m. Vivian Turner, Dec 31, 1959; c: Illana, Michele, David. Pres, Ruder and Finn Intl Inc, since 1969, on staff since 1959; news reporter, WWDC, 1958-59. US Army, specialist in psych testing, 1956-58. Mem: PR Soc of Amer; Amer Acad of Political and Social Sci; AAAS; Amer Mgmt Assn; Sigma Delta Chi. Contbr articles on communications. Home: 12 Lawridge Rd, Town of Rye, Port Chester, NY. Office: Ruder and Finn Intl, Inc, 110 E 59 St, New York, NY.

KELLMAN, Samuel, US, manufacturer; b. Wisniowczyk, Aus, Jan 23, 1910; s. Isaac and Hudes (Marder); in US since 1925; att CCNY, 1929-31; m. Claire Tepper, Apr 10, 1935; c: Ira, Martin. Pres, Washington Garter Corp, vice-pres from 1950. Dir, Hapoel Hamizrachi, 1934; chmn bd: Yeshiva E Pkwy, 1968-69, 1953-54; United Yeshivas Found, 1952-53; mem: Young Isr; Fort Lee J Comty Cen; Masons; Mizrachi; Prospect Park J Cen; Yeshiva Coll. Recipient: Negev award, Isr Bonds, 1963, 1966. Home: 1450 Palisade Ave, Fort Lee, NJ. Office: 26 W 17 St, New York, NY.

KELLNER, Elam Uri, Isr, business exec; b. Benyamina, Isr, June 5, 1928; s. Avigdor and Netty (Schlossberg); BSc, U Exeter, UK, 1952; FCA, Inst CAs, London, 1955; m. Hana Herrnstadt, Mar 4, 1958; c: Avital, Guy. Mgn dir, Tambour Paints Ltd, since 1968. Staff sgt, IDF, 1948-50. Treas, Isr Under-Sea Archaeol Soc; mem, Mgmt, Inds Org, Haifa. Home: 50 Margalit St, Mt Carmel, Haifa, Isr. Office: Tambour Ltd, Akko, Isr.

KELLNER, Sydney, US, organization exec, teacher; b. Bklyn, NY, Jan 13, 1911; s. Morris and Rebecca (Rosengarten); BFA, NYU, 1932, MA, 1936; m. Eleanor Lipskin, May 6, 1939; c: Rachel, Bonnie, Abigail. NJ dir, AJComm, on staff since 1952; field dir, United Service Org, JWB, 1942-46; exec dir: Wash Heb Cong, 1946-50; Baltimore Heb Cong, 1950-52; instr, art hist, Howard U, 1934-35; educ staff, Detroit Inst Arts, 1938; dir, Bklyn Comty Art Cen, 1940-42. Org, NJ Conf on Interfaith Dialogue, Seton Hall U; chmn, NJ Conf J Communal Service, 1969; mem: Assn J Comty Relations Workers; contbr to jours; lectr, Archaeol of Holy Land, Its Meaning for Isr Today. Recipient: scholarships: Carnegie, Inst Art and Archaeol, U of Paris, 1933; Heb U, Jerusalem, 1967. Home: 41 Montclair Ave, Montclair, NJ. Office: 10 Commerce Court, Newark, NJ.

KELMAN, Abraham, US, rabbi; b. Vienna, Aus, Jan 23, 1921; s. Hersch and Mirl (Fish); in US since 1950; ordained rabbi, Yeshiva Torah Chaim, Toronto, 1941; BA, U of Toronto, 1945, MA, 1947; m. Lea Pinter, 1946; c: Sharon, Joel, Dina. Rabbi: Prospect Park J Cen; found and prin, Prospect Park Day Sch, Bklyn, NY, since 1950; Cong Adath Isr, 1941-46; Cong Beth Yehudah, 1946-60, both of Toronto. Chaplain, Can Army, 1944-46. Pres, Gtr NY Council, Rel ZOA; mem, RabCA; fmr mem, natl exec, Can J Cong. Home: 31 Maple St, Brooklyn, NY. Study: 153 Ocean Ave, Brooklyn, NY.

KELMAN, Claude, Fr, communal worker; b. Warsaw, Pol, Oct 17, 1907; s. Menahem and Pessa (Goldstein); m. 1934; c: Josee, Menahem, Abraham. Chmn, Eur Council of J Comty Services; vice-pres: Repr Council Fr Js, since 1950; United J Social Fund, since 1950; gen secy, Fed J Soc in Fr, since 1944; treas, World Comm, Memorial to the Unknown J Martyr, since 1951. I/c J defense of Cote d'Azur during Ger occupation. Home: 19 Ave de Boufflers, Paris, Fr. Office: 112 Rue Reaumur, Paris 2, Fr.

KELMAN, Harold, US, psychoanalyst; b. Wallingford, Conn, May 23, 1906; s. Nathan and Ida (Sigdowitch); BS, Yale U, 1927; MD, Harvard U Med Sch, 1931; D Med Sci, Columbia U, 1938. Dean, Amer Inst for Psychoanalysis, 1954-67, fac mem since 1941; lectr, psychan, New Sch for Soc Research, since 1941; chief, div of neur and psycht and vascular diseases, USM Hosp, Staten Island, NY, 1936-45, cons, neur and psycht, 1945-46. Pres: Amer Acad of Psychoanalysis, 1966-69; Assn for the Advancement of Psychoanalysis, 1944-46; life fellow, Amer Psycht Assn. Author: The Process in Psychoanalysis, 1962; Karen Horney's Psychoanalytic Techniques, 1969; editor: Amer Jour of Psychoanalysis, since 1953; Advances in Psychoanalysis, 1964; New Perspectives in Psychoanalysis, 1965; Feminine Psychology by Karen Horney, 1967; contbr of numerous papers to professional publs. Hobby, travel. Home and office: 1230 Park Ave, NYC.

KELMAN, Wolfe, US, rabbi, executive; b. Vienna, Aus, Nov 27, 1923; s. Hersh and Mirl (Fish); in US since 1946; BA, U of Toronto, 1946; ordained rabbi, MHL, JTSA, 1950; m. Jacqueline Levy, Mar 2, 1952; c: Levi, Naama, Abigail. Exec vice-pres, RA, since 1951; visiting prof, homiletics, JTSA, since 1967; exec, Melton Research Cen, since 1968; non-govt rep, US Mission to UN, since 1968. RCAF, 1943-45. Study: 3080 Broadway, New York, NY.

KEMELMAN, Harry, US, author, educator; b. Boston, Mass, Nov 24, 1908; s. Isaac and Devorah (Prikezani); AB, Boston

U, 1930; MA, Harvard U, 1933; m. Anne Kessin, Mar 29, 1936; c: Ruth Rooks, Arthur, Diane Neustadter. Tchr, State Coll, Boston, since 1964; fmr: tchr: Boston Public Schs, 1935-41; evening div, Northwestern U, 1938-41; Franklin Inst, Boston, 1963-64; chief job analyst, wage admnr, Boston Port Embarkation, 1942-49; free-lance writer, 1949-63. Author: Friday the Rabbi Slept Late, 1964; Saturday the Rabbi Went Hungry, 1966; The Nine Mile Walk, 1967; Sunday the Rabbi Stayed Home, 1968; Commonsense in Education, 1970. Mem: Author's League; Mystery Writers Assn. Recipient: Edgar award for best 1st novel, 1965; Faith and Freedom Communications award, 1967. Home: 47 Humphrey St, Marblehead, Mass.

KEMELMAN, Yehoshua, Austr, rabbi; b. Jerusalem, Isr, July 19, 1921; s. Jacob and Hinda; att: Slobadka Yeshiva; Cen Universal Yeshiva, Merkaz Harav, Jerusalem; U of S Afr; grad: Yeshiva U, NY; NYU; U Cape Town; ordained rabbi, Cen Universal Yeshiva; m. Zahava Burenstein, 1947; three c. Chief Min, Cen Syn, Sydney, Austr; mem, Sydney Bet Din; dir: People's Coll; Cen Syn Heb Educ Cen; chmn, educ dept, State ZC, NSW; fmr: Rabbi: Potchefstroom Heb Cong, S Afr; E London Heb Cong; United Heb Insts of Germiston, Johannesburg. Chaplain, S Afr forces. Spiritual leader, S Afr Fed of Syn Youth; gen secy, Mizrachi Org; dir, Mif'al Hatorah, Cen Torah Found for Yeshivot in Isr; co-found, leader, Mizrachi Youth Movement; found, chmn, E London J Guild. Contbr to local, fgn jours. Home: 69 Edgecliff Rd, Bondi Junction, NSW, Austr.

KEMP, Rudy A, US, business exec; b. Emmerich, Ger, May 4, 1911; s. Max and Margarete (Steinberg) Kempenich; in US since 1937; m. Margareta Nathan, Oct 10, 1935; c: Alfred, Donald, Margaret. Pres, Tape-Craft Inc since 1945. Pres: Cong Beth El; Ala State B'nai B'rith; dir, Anniston C of C; treas, Fed J Charities; trustee, Intl House Endowment Fund; bd dirs: ARC; Cerebral Palsy; United Givers Fund; mem: Anniston Hum Relations Council; Ala Inds Assn; club, Exch. Office: POB 2027, Anniston, Ala.

KEMPER, Elise, US, TV and radio ed; b. Atlanta, Ga, Sep 27, 1894; d. Arthur and Lala (Hirsch) Weil; AB, Vassar Coll, 1915; m. Armand Kemper, Dec 28, 1915; c: Elinor Wolf, David, Marion Harris. Produc-moderator, Sta WMAR-TV, Baltimore, since 1956; author, broadcaster, Sally at the Switchboard, radio sta WFBR, Baltimore, 1934-36, syndicated, 1936-40; dir, publicity, women's div, War Manpower Commn, 1942-45; writer, broadcaster, Your Woman's Civil League, sta WBAL, 1949-52; moderator, City Council Report, WMAR-TV, 1955-58; produc-moderator, series, Passport, 1958-69. Chmn: radio publicity, Home Safety Comm, Baltimore Safety Council, 1953-56; Radio and TV Star Spangled Banner Flag House, since 1960; TV Women's Civic League, 1955-57; radio comm, 1951-53; dir: radio publicity, Citizen's Adv Comm, Admn Org of Md, 1951; publicity, women's div, Baltimore Conf Amer Inst Park Exec, 1954; radio publicity, UJA, 1948-54; mem: radio comm, Brotherhood Week, 1950; radio comm, Employment of Handicapped, 1954-56; Amer Assn U Women; League Women Voters; Vassar Alumni Assn. Recipient: radio award for best public service prog, Baltimore, 1950; McCall's Golden Mike Award, 1956. Home: 2616 Talbot Rd, Baltimore, Md. Office: Sta WMAR-TV, 6400 York Rd, Baltimore, Md.

KEMPNER, Margaret L, US, civic worker; b. St Louis, May 22, 1899; d. Carl and Adeline (Moses) Loeb; desc of Joseph Philips, who fought in Amer Revolution; att: Tchrs Coll, NYC; U Pittsburgh; m. Alan Kempner, June 1, 1920; c: Alan, Carl, Thomas. Chmn: bd, woman's div, FJP, 1961-62, vice-pres, 1958-60; bd, Mitropoulos Music Competition, 1966-69; mem: bd, Gallatin Assos, NYU; Westchester Council Social Agcys; Hosp for Jt Diseases; Home for Aged and Infirmed Hebs; Blythedale Home; Daughters of Amer Revolution. Hobbies: travel, sports, charity. Home: Kempner Lane, Purchase, NY.

KEMPNER, Robert M W, US, political sci, international atty; b. Freiburg, Ger, Oct 17, 1899; s. Walter and Lydia (Rabinowitsch); att Us: Berlin; Breslau; Pa; DJ, U Freiburg; m. Ruth Hahn; c: Lucian, Andre. Counsellor, fgn relations, intl law, admn, counsel on reparation, indemnification, nationality problems; prosecuting Nazi criminals as repr of J and other victims; mem, Ger Bar since 1950; asst to State Atty, Berlin, 1926; judge, Munic Court, Berlin, 1927; judge, civil service tribunal, 1931-33; lectr: Ger Acad of Politics; Sch of Social Work; Police Acad; recommended officially criminal prosecution and deportation of Hitler from Ger, 1931; counselor, intl law, J migration problems, 1934-35, admn pres, prof, political sci, Fiorenga Coll, Florence, It, Nice, Fr, 1936-39; research asso, Govt Inst, U of Pa, Phila, 1939-41; expert cons, Pres F D Roosevelt, 1942-45; US prosecutor on Justice Robert H Jackson's staff, Nuremberg, 1945-46; US Dep Chief-of-Counsel for War Crimes, Nuremberg, chief prosecutor of Nazi dipls and cabinet mems, 1946-49; spec research on hist of annihilation of Eur Jewry since 1949; cons, Isr Govt on war crime matters, 1951-53, cons, Eichmann case, 1960-61; lectr, instr, Us: Pa; Wis; W Point Mil Acad; Erlangen, Ger; Zurich, Switz. Mem: Acad Political and Social Sci; Amer Soc for Intl Law; Amer Political Sci Assn; Ger Bar Assn. Author: Prussian Civil Service, 1931; Twilight of Justice, 1932; c: Albanian Constitution, 1926, 1940; Blueprint of the Nazi Underground, 1945; The German National Registration System, 1946; Prussian Bureaucracy on Trial, 1946; Police Administration in Governing Post-War Germany, 1953; Eichmann and Accomplices, 1961, in Ger, Heb; SS Under Cross-examinations, 1964; Edith Stein and Anne Frank—Two of a Hundred Thousand, 1968; co-author: Code of Police Administration, 1931; Internal Security, 1933; Women in Nazi Germany, 1944; Judgment of the Wilhemstrassen Trial, 1950; contbr to profsl periodicals. Hobbies: libr on criminal cases, travel. Home: 112 Lansdowne Court, Lansdowne, Pa..

KEMPNER, S Marshall, US, business exec; b. NYC, Dec 30, 1898; s. Adolph and Addie (Oppenheimer); AB, Columbia Coll, 1919; att Harvard Grad Sch of Bus Admn, 1919-20; m. Charlotte Kempner, Nov 7, 1929; c: Charlotte Davis, Phyllis. Pres, Ind Capital Corp, SF, 1946-65; fmr: partner, Stern, Kempner and Co, mem, NY Stock Exch; Heidelboch, Ichelheimer and Co, pvt bankers. Lt col, US Army, finance dept, 1942-45. Gov, Assn Bond Brokers of NY Stock Exch; mem: bd trustees, World Affairs Council, N Cal, since 1961; bd dirs: Intl Hospitality Cen since 1952, co-found, 1952; Alliance Francaise since 1958; bd govs, Bus Adv Council since 1959, fmr chmn, finance comm; chmn, Bus Friends of Fr; fmr vice-chmn, SF chap, AJComm; fmr treas, Natl Ref Service; clubs: Harvard, SF; Harvard Bus Sch, SF; Columbia U, NYC; Commonwealth; Concordia; Stock Exch. Recipient: citation, Army Service Forces; Chevalier de la Legion de Honor, Fr; Chevalier Order of Leopold II, Belgium; Off, Natl Order of Merit, 1940-41. Home: 2 Fifth Ave, San Francisco, Cal. Office: 315 Montgomery St, San Francisco, Cal.

KENAANI, Yaakov, Isr, lexicographer; b. Bessarabia, Oct 12, 1894; s. Moshe and Pearl; in Isr since 1925; MA, Heb U, 1932; m. Yafa, 1928; c: Rivka, Amit, Nechama. Lexicographer since 1926; tchr: Bessarabia, Lita, Aus, 1924; sch dir, Isr, 1925-65. Contbr lit articles to profsl jours. Home: 28 Rehovot Habucharim, Jerusalem, Isr.

KENDLER, Howard H, US, educator; b. NYC, June 9, 1919; s. Harry and Sylvia (Rosenberg); AB, Bklyn Coll, 1940; MA, U of Ia, 1941, PhD, 1943; m. Tracy Seedman, Sep 20, 1941; c: Joel, Kenneth. Prof, psych, U of Cal, since 1963; fmr: research psychol, Off Sci Research, 1943-44; asst prof, U of Colo, 1946-48; prof, psych, NYU, 1951-63, chmn, dept, psych, 1951-61, mem fac since 1948; visiting prof, U Cal, Berkeley, 1960-61; f, Cen for Advanced Study in Behavioral Scis, Stanford, Cal, 1969-70. Pres: W Psych Assn, 1970-71; Amer Psych Assn, div one, 1967-68, div three, 1964-65; chmn, bd of govs, Psychonomic Soc, 1968; mem: Soc of Experimental Psychols; AAAS; Sigma Xi. Author: Basic Psychology, 1963, 1968; asso ed, Jour of Experimental Psych, 1963-65; contbr to profsl jours. Home: 4596 Camino Molineno, Santa Barbara, Cal. Office: U of Cal, Santa Barbara, Cal.

KENEN, Isaiah L, US, organization exec, journalist; b. St Stephen, NB, Can, Mar 7, 1905; s. Emanuel and Rebecca (Friedberg); in US since 1926; BA, U Toronto, 1925; LLB, Cleveland Law Sch, 1940; m. Beatrice Bain, Sep 4, 1927; c: Peter. Exec vice-chmn, Amer Isr Public Affairs Comm since 1954; ed, publisher, Near East Report since 1957; political writer, Cleveland News, 1926-43; dir, info, Amer Emergency Comm for Zionist Affairs, 1943; secy, Amer J Conf, 1943-47; dir, info, JA delg to UN, 1951-54. Counsel, AZC, Wash DC. Mem, Natl Press Club; Amer Newspaper Guild, co-found, fmr chmn, constitution comm, intl vice-pres; fmr: pres, Cleveland Newspaper Guild; mem, Mayor's

Commn on Housing and Transp, Cleveland; mem, exec comm, Cleveland Ind Union Council; pres, Cleveland Zionist Dist. Recipient: Heywood Broun memorial award for outstanding journalism, Amer Newspaper Guild, 1943. Home: 7222 Beechwood Dr, Alexandria, Va. Office: 1341 G St, NW, Washington, DC.

KENIN, Abel, US, surgeon; b. NYC, Feb 28, 1908; s. Mayer and Lizzie (Posner); BA, U Syracuse, 1929; MD, 1933; m. Kate Buzen, June 23, 1931; c: Michael, Lydia. Chief, orthopedic surg, Brookdale Hosp Cen; cons, orthopedic surg: J Hosp; Kings Brook Hosp Cen; att orthopedic surg: Bklyn Heb Home and Hosp for Aged, all in Bklyn. Maj, US Army MC, 1943-46. F: Amer Coll, Surgs; NY Acad of Med; dipl, Amer Bd, Orthopedic Surg; mem: Amer Acad Orthopedic Surg. Contbr to med jours. Recipient: gold medal award, Amer Acad Orthopedic Surg, 1952. Home: 175 E 62 St, New York, NY. Office: Brookdale Hosp Cen, Brooklyn, NY.

KENNER, Zvi Moshe, Isr, journalist, business exec; b. Tarnopol, Pol, Dec 21, 1915; s. Aharon and Betti (Rauer); in Isr since 1934; MA, Heb U, Jerusalem, 1940; m. Zipora Recanati, Apr 2, 1947; c: Eliezer, Avner. Dir Gen, Regie Isr Ltd, since 1964; fmr dir, News Reportage Div, Eur Repr, Dep Dir-Gen, Kol Isr, Bc, 1955-64. RAF, 1940-46. Bd dir, BBB-Truth in Advt; adv, Isr Advt Assn, mem comm. Contbr to local press and radio on political issues, current affairs. Mem, Heb U, grads' assn. Recipient: Afr Star, WWII Star. Hobby, chess. Home: 9 Mishmeret St, Tel Aviv, Isr. Office: 224 Ben Yehuda St, Tel Aviv, Isr.

KENNET, Max M, Isr, jurist; b. London, Eng, Mar 26, 1909; s. Haim and Hannah (Yaskolka); in Isr since 1919; dipl law, Jerusalem Law Sch, 1930; LLB, London U, 1940; admitted to Isr Bar, 1944; m. Tova Hayon, June 13, 1934; c: Haim, Dahlia. Relieving pres, Dist Court of Tel Aviv since 1954, judge, 1948-53; magistrate, Tel Aviv, 1937-48; chief execution off and registrar, Tel Aviv, 1939-45. Hon vice-pres, Disabled Persons Assn, Isr. Author: Digest Law of Evidence, 1944; Digest Criminal Law, 1961; lectr, criminal law, to probation offs. Home: 91 Rothschild Blvd, Tel Aviv, Isr. Office: District Court, Tel Aviv, Isr.

KEREM, Moshe, Isr, communal leader; b. NYC, May 10, 1924; s. Baruch and Pauline (Kaufman) Weingarten; in Isr since 1948; Grad, Tchrs Inst, Yeshiva U, 1942; BA, NYU, 1946, MA, 1966; m. Evelyn Cohen, May 27, 1948; c: Etan, Rahel, Miriam. Fmr secy, Kibbutz Gesher Haziv, 1968; mem, bd, Hakibbutzim Tchrs Sem, since 1967; tchr, prin, Sulam Zor Kibbutz HS, 1956-64; Amer repr, World Lab Zionist movement, 1964-66. Actions comm, WZO; world secretariat, World Lab Zionist Movement; cen comm, Ihud Hakvutzot Vhakibbutzim; fmr natl secy, Habonim, Lab Zionist Youth. Author: Life in a Kibbutz, 1956. Recipient: Henrietta Szold Award, AACI, 1965. Home and office: Kibbutz Gesher Haziv, Mobile Post, Western Galilee, Isr.

KEREN, Alisa, Isr, communal leader; b. Kalvaria, Lith, July 20, 1905; d. Aaron and Livsha (Goldstein) Pollack; in Isr since 1913; att Med Sch, U Paris, 1924-27; m. Maxim Keren, June 18, 1937. Exec mem, World WIZO, since 1962; head, WIZO Youth Club Dept, since 1962; hostess, Soldiers', Offs' club, 1940-45; wfr off, Red Cross, Magen David Adom, 1942-47; liaison off, Fr-speaking volunteers, 1948-50; secy, Isr Aviation Club, 1954-56; hostess, guide, WIZO tourist dept, 1956-62; adoption of Moshav Aviezer, WIZO scheme of adoption border settlements, 1959-69. Home: 54 Hovevei Zion St, Tel Aviv, Isr. Office: WIZO, 38 King David Blvd, Tel Aviv, Isr.

KEREN, Karl, Isr, documentalist; b. Ger, 1919; in Isr since 1933; educ: Agronomy, Botany, 1937-42; m. Leah Sagher; c: Anat, Gabriella. Dir, Cen of Sci and Tech Info, since 1965; fmr: with Agric Research Sta, Rehovot. J Brig, Brit Army, 1942-46; lt col, IDF, 1946-65. Contbr to profsl publs. Home: 8 Avner St, Zahala, Tel Aviv, Isr.

KEREN, Yehezkiel, Isr, educator, author, editor; b. Krim, Russ Oct 3, 1911; s. Shlomo and Golda (Zeidenberg) Rogelski; in Isr since 1929; BA, Heb U, 1936; m. Bosem, 1935: c: Uri, Giyora. Lingual ed, Study Prog Dept, Min of Educ, since 1969; dep dir, 1937-69; head, adult educ sect, Min of Educ, since 1958; gen secy, Students Org, 1934-36; secy, Students of Heb U, 1933-36. IDF, 1948-49. Author: Russian-Hebrew Dictionary, 1960; conversation books: Russ-Heb, 1963;

Eng-Heb, 1964; Fr-Heb, 1966; Arabic-Heb, 1968. Ed: Yalkut haAtzmaut, 1955; Yalkut pitgamim, 1954; adaptation to light Heb: Yalkut Shalom Aleichem, 1959-60; Kaze Haya, Entzo Sireni; Zichronot Al haAliya haShniya; Aliyato Shel Layish, Sh Lavie, all 1959-60; contbr articles and monographs. Spec interests: music, photography. Home: 6 Yisabraha St, Jerusalem, Isr.

KEREN, Zvi, Isr, musician, teacher; b. NYC, Aug 18, 1917; s. Charles and Sara (Samalman) Kirshenbaum; in Isr since 1952; BS, NYU, 1937; MA, Columbia U, 1946; PhD, London U, 1961; m. Renate Koplewicz, Dec 12, 1954; c: Shoshanna, Zibiah, Alona. Musicologist; tchr of composition; lectr, Isr Acad of Music, 1962-63; lectr, Bar Ilan U, 1969-70. Pres, Music Arrangers Union, Isr; mem: ed staff, League of Composers in Isr; Isr Musicological Soc; Composers, Authors and Pub Soc, Isr. Contbr to profsl jours. Spec interests: J studies, jazz. Home: 8 Derech Hatayasim, Tel Aviv, Isr.

KEREN, Zvi, Isr, business exec; b. Konigsberg, Ger, May 9, 1926; s. Jecheskel and Lea (Dugilitzsky) Kreistman; in Isr since 1933; m. Ruth Selka, Aug 17, 1951; c: Ron, Dan, Iftach. Chief, engr team, Netafim Ind, since 1965; fmr: bus mgr, Kibbutz Chatzerim. Palmach, 1944-46; lt, IDF, 1957-69. Mem natl bd, Boy Scouts of Isr, since 1954; fmr, natl commnr, J Scout Assn. Author: Twenty Years of Settlement in the Negev, 1966. Recipient: mil awards: Komemiuth, Sinai, Hagana, Sheruth Aleh, 6-Days War. Home and office: Kibbutz Hatzerim, Negev, Isr.

KERKER, Milton, US, chemist, educator; b. Utica, NY, Sep 25, 1920; s. Samuel and Sarah (Cohen); BA, Columbia U, 1941, MA, 1947, PhD, 1949; m. Reva Stemerman, June 16, 1946; c: Ruth, Martin, Susan, Joel. Dean, arts and sci, Clarkson Coll of Tech, fac mem since 1949; fmr: research asso, Columbia U; research asst, McGill U; Ford Found f; Unilever visiting prof, U of Bristol. US Army, 1942-45. Mem: Amer Chem Soc, fmr chmn, N NY sect, chmn, div colloid and surface chem; Sigma Xi; chmn, Clarkson-St Lawrence U club; Phi Lambda Upsilon; Hist of Sci Soc. Author: The Scattering of Light and Other Electromagnetic Radiation, 1969; ed-in-chief, Jour of Colloid and Interface Science; contbr to profsl jours. Recipient: Bronze Star. Home: 4 Hillcrest Dr, Potsdam, NY. Office: Clarkson Coll of Technology, Potsdam, NY.

KERNER, Fred, US, editor, author, b. Montreal, Can, Feb 15, 1921; s. Sam and Vera (Goldman); in US since 1948; BA, Sir George Williams U, Montreal, 1942; m. Sally Stouten, May 18, 1959; c: Jon (by previous m), David, Diane. Ed dir, book div, Reader's Digest Assn, Can, since 1969; pres, Centaur House Inc, since 1964; dir: Publitex Intl Corp; Personalized Services Inc; Peter Kent Inc; fmr: asst sports ed, Montreal Gazette, 1942-44; supr ed, Canadian Press, 1944-50; night city ed, AP, 1950-56; ed, Hawthorn Books, NYC, 1956-58, ed-in-chief, Fawcett World Libr, 1963-64; pres, ed-in-chief, Hawthorn Books, 1964-67; mgn dir, Fred Kerner Publ, 1967-69. Can Army, 1942. Mem: Can Soc, NY; Can Authors Assn: Mystery Writers of Amer, NY; Sigma Delta Chi; Advt Club, NY; Amer Mgmt Assn; clubs: Overseas Press; Toronto Men's Press, found, fmr mem bd govs; Dutch Treat, NY; Authors, London. Author: Love is a Man's Affair, 1958; A Treasury of Lincoln Quotations, 1965; co-author: Eat, Think and Be Slender, 1954; The Magic Power of Your Mind, 1955; Ten Days to a Successful Memory, 1956; Secrets of Your Supraconscious, 1965; Buy High, Sell Higher. Home: 400 Landsdowne Ave, Westmount, Quebec, Can. Office: 215 Redfern Ave, Montreal, Can.

KERNER, Richard Alan, US, attorney; b. NYC, Aug 19, 1933; s. Jacob and Fay (Karlson); BBA, acctnt, CCNY, Baruch Sch, 1954; LLB, NYU Law Sch, 1957, LLM, taxation, 1960; m. Deanne Hartman, Nov 20, 1960; c: Fern, Kenneth, Ira. Pvt practice since 1968; asst dist atty, Rockland Co, NY, since 1970; spec counsel, Town of Ramapo, NY, 1968-70. Pvt, US Army, 1957-63, Res. Dir, Dexter Park Civic Assn, charter mem, fmr chmn; club coord, Town of Ramapo Dem Comm; candidate, NY State Assembly, 94th AD, 1970; fmr, vice-pres, Harry S Truman Dem Club; mem: Assn Bar, NYC; NY Co Lawyers Assn; Rockland Co Bar Assn. Hobbies: music, swimming. Home: 5 Ave Aberdeen, Spring Valley, NY. Office: 30 Vesey St, New York, NY.

KERNOFF, Harry Aaron, Ir, artist; b. London, Eng, Jan, 1900; s. Isaac and Katherine (A'barbanelle); in Ir since 1914; att Metrop Sch of Art, Dublin, 1922-25. Twenty one-man shows since 1927, including two in London, one in NS, Can, 1957;

yearly exhbs, Royal Hibernian Acad since 1926; lectr on art; works exhb, gals: Dublin; Waterford; Limerick; Killarney; Galway; Belfast; Wash, DC; Natl Gal of Ir; works include: 3 Limited Editions; woodcuts; illus books; murals; stage sets; stained glass portraits; landscapes; water colors; oils; pastels; paintings of NS. Mem: Royal Hibernian Acad, since 1935; art adv council, Dublin Corp, since 1950; Haverty Trust Adv from Royal Hibernian Acad, since 1950; Royal Dublin Soc; club, United Arts, Dublin. Hobby, poetry. Home and studio: 13 Stamer St, Dublin, Ir.

KERSTEIN, Solomon, US, publishing exec, journalist; b. Antwerp, Belgium, Sep 7, 1901; s. Isidore and Esther (Meisels); att: Etz Hayim Yeshiva, London; Rabbi Jacob Joseph Yeshiva, NY; m. Beatrice Barth, Aug, 1926; c: Gladys. Vice pres, Bloch Pub Co, NYC, since 1947, ed, Bloch's Book Bull, since 1934; ed, Unzer Shtimme, 1941-59; Amer corresp, Hatzofeh, Tel Aviv daily, 1937-55. Found, vice-pres, Natl Council for Torah Educ, Mizrachi-Hapoel Hamizrachi; chmn, PR comm, Mizrachi Org, 1922-56; hon secy, Rel Zionists of Amer, since 1962; mem: bd dirs, admn comm, JNF; Adat B'nai Yisrael, NY; Amer Acad for J Research; Soc for J Bibliographies; JWB; Yeshiva of Flatbush, Bklyn; Young Isr of Flatbush; chmn libr comm, Bar Ilan U, Isr, since 1958; fmr: co-found, secy, vice pres, JBCA. Author: monographs: Jewish Libraries and Book Collections in American and Jewish Institutions and Universities in USA; The Literary and Spiritual Heritage of Rabbi Judah L Maimon; contbr to: Universal J Ency; Ency Judaica; Anglo-J and Yiddish press in US, Can, S Afr. Recipient: spec citation, JBSA, 1963; Chief Rabbi Isaac Herzog gold medal award, Rel Zionists of Amer, 1963; JNF citation for 43 years of service, 1968; spec citation, Mizrachi Women's Org, 1968. Home: 949 E 10 St, Brooklyn, NY. Office: 31 W 31 St, New York, NY.

KERTES, Aviezer Stevan, Isr, chemist, educator; b. Seged, Hung, May 11, 1922; s. Samuel and Ethel (Bernath); in Isr since 1948; MSc, chem engr, U of Belgrade, Yugo, 1948; PhD, Heb U, Jerusalem, 1952; m. Vera Hoenig, July 1949; c: Tamar, Amnon. Asso prof, chem, Heb U, Jerusalem, since 1966, fac mem since 1958; research asso, MIT, 1962-64; mem, delg to 3rd Geneva Conf on Peaceful Uses of Atomic Energy, 1964. Chmn, div of analytical chem, Isr Chem Soc; mem: Intl Union of Pure and Applied Chem; Rotary, Jerusalem; Free Masons, Ein Hashiloah lodge. Author: Ion Exchange and Solvent Extraction of Metal Complexes, 1969; Solvent Extraction Research, 1969; mem, ed bd, Jour Inorganic and Nuclear Chem. Home: 15 Rambam St, Jerusalem, Isr. Office: Heb U, Jerusalem, Isr.

KERTZER, Morris N, US, rabbi, author; b. Cochrane, Ont, Can, Oct 18, 1910; s. David and Pearl (Kroch); in US since 1930; BA, U Toronto, 1930; MA, U Ill, 1937; ordained rabbi, JTSA, 1934, DHL, 1947; m. Julia Hoffman, 1934; c: Ruth Seidman, David, Jonathan. Rabbi, Larchmont Temple since 1960; prof, rel, U of Ia; asso rabbi, Park Ave Syn, NYC, 1946-49; dir, inter-rel dept, AJComm, 1949-60. Chaplain, US Army, 1943-45. Pres, Assn J Chaplains of Armed Forces, 1952-55; chmn, commn on church and state, CCAR; mem, exec bd, NY Bd Rabbis, since 1952, secy, 1953; mem, Social Action Commn, UAHC; head, delg of rabbis to Soviet Union, 1956. Author: Faith to Live By, 1943; With an H on My Dog Tag, 1947; What is a Jew? 1953; The Art of Being a Jew, 1962; Today's American Jew, 1967; contbr to mags, syndicates. Recipient: Bronze Star, 1945; Freedom Founds medal, 1957; Gold Medal, Intl U, Rome, 1958. Home: 4545 Independence Ave, Riverdale, NY. Study: 75 Larchmont Ave, Larchmont, NY.

KESHET, Jeshurun, Isr, author, poet, critic, translator; b. Nowominsk, Pol, Nov 29, 1893; s. Menahem and Nehama (Goldstein) Koplewitz; in Isr since 1911; att: U of Rome; U of Berlin, 1920-26; m; c: Immanuel. Author: haHelech baAretz, 1932; haDerekh haNeelama, 1940; beDoro Shel Bialik; Elegies, poems, 1945; haChaim haGnuzim, poems, 1959; beDor Ole, critical essays; Maskiot, critical essays; A Monograph on Berditchewski, 1958; Ruhot haMaarav, essays on Eur authors, 1960; Havdaloth, critical essays; Shirath haMikra, 1955; Keren Hazuth, Essays in National Self-Criticism, 1966; Maharozoth, short essays, 1967; Between the Chestnut Tree and the Lilac Bush, 1967; Rashuyoth, essays in Heb lit, 1968; trans: L'âme Enchantée by Romain Roland; First Man in the Moon by HG Wells; Le Livre de Mon Ami by Anatole France; Martin Eden by Jack London; Revolt in the Desert by TE Lawrence; History of Europe by HAL

Fisher; Great Contemporaries by Winston S Churchill; Romeo and Juliet in the Village by Gottfried Keller; Joseph and His Brethren by Thomas Mann; Logic by Bosanquet; Pensées by Pascal; Essais by Montaigne; Historische Miniaturen by Strindberg; Der Prozess and short stories by Franz Kafka; Varieties of Religious Experience by William James; Golden Mirror by Jacob Wassermann; contbr lit revs, art criticism to press. Home: Hechalutz St, Givat Bet Hakarem, Jerusalem, Isr.

KESSLER, Avraham A, Isr, economist; b. NYC, Sep 11, 1924; s. William and Gussie (Laskin); in Isr since 1949; BS, CCNY, 1946; MA, PhD, U of Wis, 1949; m. Naomi Lynfield, June 3, 1954; c: Shueli, Timnah. Mgn dir, Econ Research Corp Ltd, since 1962; external lectr, Heb U, 1951-54; Bar Ilan U, since 1960; econ, econ advisory staff, Min of Finance and PM Off, 1953-55; research econ, Falk Project for Econ Research, 1956-58; independent econ cons, 1958-62, among first in Isr. Fmr, Natl pres, AACI; mem: Phi Beta Kappa; Amer Econ Assn. Author: An Economic Study of Voluntary Welfare Contributions in Israel, 1963; Terms of Trade under Israel's Clearing Agreements, 1965, Heb; Study of Fund Raising in European Jewish Communities, 1967; co-author, Investments in Industry through the Investment Centre, 1958; contbr articles to Ency Hebraica, Ency Judaica, profsl jours. Home: 18 Abrabanel St, Jerusalem, Isr. Office: POB 981, Jerusalem, Isr.

KESSLER, Bezalel, Isr, scientist, educator; b. Leipzig, Ger, June 25, 1922; s. Abraham and Sima (Bergruen) Hirsch; in Isr since 1938; MSc, Heb U, Jerusalem, 1951; PhD, 1954; att Cambridge U, Eng, 1952-54; m. Eva, July 15, 1954; c: Abraham. Head, dept, Volcani Inst of Agric Research, since 1959; sr lectr, Bar Ilan U, Ramat Gan, since 1964. Contbr to sci publs. Home: 51 Chen Ave, Rehovot, Isr. Offices: Volcani Inst of Agric Research, Beit Dagan, Isr; Bar Ilan U, Ramat Gan, Isr.

KESSLER, Jascha Frederick, US, writer, educator; b. NYC, Nov 27, 1929; s. Hyman and Roseela (Bronsweig); BA, NYU, 1950; MA, U Mich, 1951, PhD, 1955; m. Julia Braun, July 19, 1950; c: Margot, Adam, William. Asso prof, Eng, UCLA, since 1961; instr, Eng, Hunter Coll, 1955-56; dir, curriculum research, Harcourt Brace & Co, publishers, 1956-57; asst prof, Eng, Hamilton Coll, 1957-61. Author: American Poems: A Contemporary Collection, 1964; Whatever Love Declares, poems, 1966; An Egyptian Bondage and Other Stories, 1967; narrations for documentary films on Mh for US State Dept; TV film on Mh, Loved Ones, Lost Ones; contbr poems, essays, stories to jours in US and abroad. Recipient: F: U of NM; D H Lawrence in Creative Writing, 1961; Inst for Creative Arts, U of Cal, 1963-64, 1968-69; Fulbright Research Scholar in It, 1963-64; Fulbright lectr, Rome, 1970. Home: 218 16 St, Santa Monica, Cal. Office: UCLA, Los Angeles, Cal.

KESSLER, Minuetta, US, pianist, composer; b. Calgary, Can; d. Abraham and Luba (Lubinskaya) Shumiatcher; in US since 1934; dipl, Julliard Sch of Music, 1936, postgrad tchr's dipl and artists dipl, 1938; m. 2nd, Myer Kessler, 1952; c: Ronald, by 1st m; Jean. Concert pianist, since age of five; NY Town Hall Debut, 1945, 2nd concert, 1946; soloist at premiere of own composition, Alberta Concerto, Montreal, 1947; soloist with: Boston Pops Orch; Boston Civic Sym Orch; Que, Montreal and Toronto Sym Orchs; appeared in: Dist Artists Series; Master of Keyboard Series of Can Bc Corp; broadcasts to Latin Amer; numerous solo progs over radio WNYC, NY; prog of own compositions, Boston Conservatory of Music, 1961. Composer: Ballet Sonatina, for piano, 1945; New York Suite, for piano, 1946; Alberta Concerto, for piano and orch, 1947; ballet, Memories of Tevya, 1954, rev ed, 1962; Trio, for piano, violin, cello, 1957; Confirmation Prayer, 1957; Piano Suite No 1, 1959; cantata, Brotherhood and Peace Through Music, 1960; children's operetta, Kiddy City, 1961; Sonata, for cello and piano, 1962; cantata, Thought is a Bird of Space, 1962; children's songs; liturgical music: Thou Shalt Love; May The Words; 23rd Psalm; God's Canopy of Love; Victory Hora, 1968; arrangements of Yiddish songs; inventor of musical educ game, Staftonia, pub 1960. Vice-pres, NE J Music Forum, since 1958, co-found, first prog chmn; NE repr, Natl J Music Council; found, first pres, Boston Julliard Alumni Assn; fmr pres, NE Pianoforte Tchrs Assn. Recipient: Can ASCAP award for serious composition, 1945, 1946; Key to City of Calgary, 1951; composition award, Brookline Libr Music Assn, 1957. Home and office: 30 Hurley St, Belmont, Mass.

KESSLER, Stuart Alan, US, architect; b. NYC, Feb 10, 1939; s. Melvin and Mildred (Jacobson); BA, U Va, 1959; dipl, architecture, Columbia U, 1963; m. Catharina Aulin, Nov 9, 1967. Dir, S J Kessler and Sons, Architects and Engrs since 1961; pres, Claridge Co, real estate devls, since 1966; fmr construction sup, DeMatteis and Sons. Designer of over 200 bldgs including residential comtys; inventor of Phased Comty Redevl for urban redevl. Mgr, Alumni Assn, U Va; adv, Shield of David Home for Retarded Children; mem: bd dirs, Cong Emanu-El Men's Club, NY; J Chautauga Soc; Natl Fed Temple Brotherhoods; NY Bldg Cong; Bldg Research Inst; Concrete Inds Bd; Amer Concrete Inst; Urban Land Inst; Amer Soc for Testing and Materials; Natl Assn of Home Bldrs; NYC, State Bldrs Assn; Construction Specifications Inst; Va Student Aid Found; NY State Assn of Chiefs Police; Nassau Co Police Conf; Zoning Adv Council, NYC; club, City Athletic, NY. Author, "PCR" Redevelopment Without Relocation, 1967; contbr to profsl jours. Recipient: First Hon for: Residential Design, FHA, 1964; Urban Renewal Design, Urban Renewal Admn, 1964. Hobbies: writing, sports. Home: 205 E 63 St, New York, NY. Office: 598 Madison Ave, New York, NY.

KESTEN, Hermann, US, author, publisher, editor; b. Jan 28, 1900; s. Izak and Ida (Tisch); in US since 1940; att: U Erlangen; U Frankfurt, both Ger; m. Toni Warowitz, Dec 24, 1928. Publisher since 1926. Author: Ein Ausschweifender Mensch, 1929; Die Liebesehe, 1929, 1949; Josef Breaks Free 1930; Der Scharlatan, 1932, 1965; The Happy Man, 1934; Der Gerechte, Guernika, 1940, 1967; Copernicus and His World, 1944; Ferdinand and Isabella, 1945; The Twins of Nüremberg, 1945; Die Fremden Götter, 1950; Meine Freunde, die Poeten, 1953, 1959, 1964; Der Sohn des Glücks, 1955; Casanova, 1956, 1963; Dichter in Cafe, 1959; Bücher der Liebe, 1960; Der Geist der Unruhe, 1960; Die Abenteuer eines Moralisten, 1961; Filialen des Parnass, 1961; Die Dreissig Erzählungen von Hermann Kesten, 1962; Lauter Literaten, 1963; Deutsche Literatur im Exil, 1964; Die Zeit der Narren, 1966; Die Lust am Leben, 1968; Josef Sucht die Freiheit, 1968; ed, anthols: Heinrich Heine, 1943, 1944; The Blue Flower, 1946; Emile Zola, The Masterpiece, 1947; Unsere Zeit, best German stories, 1956; Joseph Roth, collected works, 3 vols, 1956; Die Schönsten Liebesgeschichten der Welt, 1957; Kurt Tucholsky: Man sollte mal..., 1957; Erich Kästner, collected works, 7 vols, 1958; Menschen in Rom, 1959; Rene Schickele, collected works, 3 vols, 1960, 1961; Heinrich Heine, prose works, 1961; Gotthold Ephraim Lessing, works, 2 vols; Europa Heute, Eur lit after 1945, 2 vols, 1963; co-ed, anthol, Heart of Europe, 1943; contbr short stories, essays to mags; fmr: chief ed: Gustav Kiepenheur Pub Co, Berlin; Allert de Lange, pub, Amsterdam. Mem: Ger Acad of Arts and Letters at Darmstadt and Mainz; clubs: PEN; Ger PEN. Recipient: Kleist Prize, 1928; lit prize from City of Nüremberg, 1957. Home and office: 499 Ft Washington Ave, New York, NY.

KESTENBAUM, Edward, US, dentist; b. New Bedford, Mass, July 27, 1898; s. Emanuel and Matilda (Levy); att Tufts U, Boston, 1916-18; DDS, U of Md, 1920; m. Sara Joslin, June 26, 1924; c: Joseph. Pvt practice since 1920. Chmn: New Bedford Recreation Comm, Mass; Council on Aging; mem: charter, New Bedford Dent Soc; Amer Dent Soc; Mass Dent Soc; Elks, 73 chap; New Bedford Moose-Eagles; bd, Tifereth Isr Syn. Home: 47 Reed, New Bedford, Mass. Office: 189 Cove, New Bedford, Mass.

KESTENBAUM, Jacob, US, business exec; b. Tarnow, Pol, Jan 30, 1893; s. Elias and Lea (Feigenbaum); in US since 1914; m. Yetta Braff, June 8, 1922; c: Shirley Schulder, Lionel, Asher, Lillian Levine. Importer-exporter, fur skins since 1914. Co-found: Yeshiva Mesifta Torah ve-Daath; Yeshiva Chaim Berlin; Lubavitcher Yeshiva; Yeshiva Flatbush; Young Isr of Flatbush; mem: Mizrachi; UJA; contbr mem: Herzliya Heb Acad; Bar Ilan U. Home: 920 E 17 St, Brooklyn, NY.

KESTER, Lenard, US, artist; b. NYC, May 10, 1917; s. Hyman and Yetta (Kalfus) Kestecher. Paintings in perm collections: Boston Mus of Fine Arts; U of Miami; Cal State Fair; pvt collections; natl exhbs: Corcoran Gal; Natl Acad of Design; Art Inst of Chgo; LA Mus; SF Mus; Oakland Mus; Bklyn Mus; Denver Mus; U of Ill; Pa Acad; Carnegie Inst; Ency Britannica; one-man shows. Commns: painting, first Nowell for Life Mag, 1947; mural, Mayo Clinic, Rochester, Minn, 1953. Mem: Amer Watercolor Soc; Soc of W Artists; asso, Natl Acad of Design. Contbr to profsl jours. Recipient: Tiffany Found grant, 1949; Natl Acad of Design, prize, 1951, 1956, gold medal, 1958, Obrig award, 1959. Home: Jovenita Canyon Dr, Los Angeles, Cal. Studio: 1117 N Genesee Ave, Los Angeles, Cal.

KETY, Seymour S, US, physician, educator, scientist; b. Phila, Pa, Aug 25, 1915; s. Louis and Ethel (Snyderman); BA, U of Pa, 1936, MD, 1940; m. Josephine Gross, 1940; c: Lawrence, Roberta. Prof, psycht, Harvard Med Sch, since 1967; dir, Psycht Research Labs, Mass Gen Hosp, since 1967; f, Natl Research Council, Harvard U, 1942-43; instr, pharm, U of Pa, 1943-45, asst prof, 1945-47, prof, clinical physiol, 1948-61; chief, lab clinical sci, Natl Inst of Mh, NIH, 1956-67, sci dir, 1951-56; Henry Phipps prof, psycht, Johns Hopkins U, 1961-62. Developed nitrous oxide technique for measurement of cerebral blood flow, 1945. Mem: Natl Acad of Scis; Amer Physiol Soc; Amer Acad of Arts and Scis; Amer Soc for Clinical Investigations; Amer Neur Assn; Amer Soc for Pharm and Experimental Therapeutics; research bd, Natl Assn for Mh. Recipient: Theobald Smith award, 1949; Max Weinstein award, 1955; Dist Service award, HEW, 1958; Stanley Dean award, Alvarenga Prize, 1962. Ed-in-chief, Jour of Psycht Research; contbr to med jours. Delivered: Mütter Lectr, 1951; Eastman Lectr, 1957; NIH Lectr, 1960; Salmon Lectrs, 1961; Wechsler Lectr, 1962. Office: Dept of Psycht, Mass Gen Hosp, Boston, Mass.

KEY, Ted, US, cartoonist; b. Fresno, Cal, Aug 25, 1912; s. Simon and Fanny (Kahn); BA, U of Cal, 1933; m. Anne Wilkinson, Sep 30, 1937; c: Stephen, David, Peter. Created cartoon character, Hazel, distributed by King Features Syndicate; TV prog, Hazel. Author: Hazel, 1946; Many Happy Returns, 1948; Here's Hazel, 1949; If You Like Hazel, 1952; So'm I, 1954; Hazel Rides Again, 1955; Fasten Your Seat Belts, 1956; Phyllis, 1957; All Hazel, 1958; The Hazel Jubilee, 1959; The Biggest Dog in the World, 1960; Hazel Time, 1962; Life With Hazel, 1965; Squirrels in the Feeding Station, 1967. Club, Players. Home: Box 735, Gulph Rd, Wayne, Pa. Office: 1694 Glenhardie Rd, Wayne, Pa.

KEYFETZ, Carl K, Can, attorney; b. Toronto, Ont, Oct 12, 1907; s. Mark and Leah (Isaacson); LLB, Osgoode Hall Law Sch, 1930. Pvt practice since 1930; partner, Gordon, Keyfetz, Hall, Baker and Goodman; QC, since 1951; mem, bd dirs, numerous corps. Off, RCAF, 1941-45. Pres, St Andrews Conservative Assn; chmn, admission comm, J Home for Aged, hon secy; vice-pres, Toronto-Hung Water Polo Team; fmr pres: Toronto Lodge, B'nai B'rith, 1939; Young People's League, U Ave Syn; chmn, Toronto Youth Aliyah Campaigns, 1940-41; UJF, speakers, barristers, nominations and arrangements comms; found, Guelph Lodge, 1941, and Empire Lodge, 1946, B'nai B'rith; co-found, first J Boy Scout Troop in Ont, 1921; bd dirs: J Vocational Service, hon; JIAS; George Brown Coll; JNF; J Family and Child Service; Beth Tzedec Syn; Can Council Chrs and J; Assn Heb Schs; legal counsel: Can Hemophilia Soc; Gen Wingate br, Royal Can Legion; Spadina Riding Conservative Assn; sponsor, Natl Ballet; sole Can repr, B'nai B'rith Natl Comm of Vets Affairs, Wash, DC, 1946-47; mem: exec comm, Young Peoples Leagues of Amer; Can Bar Assn; Royal Can Mil Inst; Pi Lambda Phi; clubs: Primrose; Island Yacht; Canadian. Office: 347 Bay St, Toronto, Ont.

KEYNAN, Alexander, Isr, executive, bacteriologist; b. Kiev, Russ, Feb 18, 1921; s. Efraim and Rachel (Dunitz) Kotznok; in Isr since 1930; MSc, Heb U, 1944, PhD, 1949; m. Malka Ben-Zvi; c: Irit, Daria. Vice-pres, Heb U, Jerusalem, chmn: research and devl auth, and Inst of Life Sci, since 1967; dir, Isr Inst of Biol, fmr, head, dept bact, 1952-62; prof, MIT, 1962-63; chmn, dir, Natl Council for Research and Devl, PM Off, 1963-67. Hagana; col, Isr Army, 1948-67. Mem: Amer Soc Microbiol; Woods Hole Inst Marine Biol, Mass; Isr Soc Microbiol; Isr Biochem Soc; Isr Soc for Advancement of Sci. Contbr to sci jours. Home: 16 Balfour St, Jerusalem, Isr. Office: Heb U, Jerusalem, Isr.

KEYSERLING, Leon H, US, consulting econ, attorney; b. Charleston, SC, Jan 22, 1908; s. William and Jennie (Hyman); BA, Columbia U, 1928, grad study, econ, 1931-33; LLB, Harvard U, 1931; DBusSci, hon, Bryant, 1966; m. Mary Dublin, Oct 4, 1940. Cons, econ and atty, since 1953; pres, Conf on Econ Progress, since 1954; asst, dept of econ, Columbia U, 1932-33; leg asst to US Sen Robert Wagner, 1933-37; cons, US Sen comms on leg concerning banking, taxation, monetary policy, public works, housing, lab relations, social security, employment, 1933-46, and since 1953; dep admnr, gen counsel, Fed housing agcys, 1937-46; chmn, Council Econ Adv to US Pres, 1950-53, vice-chmn, 1946-50; lectr on econ. Mem: Amer Econ, Amer Political Sci, Amer Bar Assns; hon mem, fac, Ind Coll Armed Forces, since 1965. Author: Inflation, Cause and Cure, 1959; Policies for Full Employment, 1962; Taxes and the Public Interest, 1963; The Toll of Rising Interest Rates, 1964; Progress or Poverty, 1964; Agriculture and the Public Interest, 1965; The Role of Wages in a Great Society, 1966; Achieving Nationwide Educational Excellence, 1968; The Economy of Israel, 1968; reports and econ revs of Council of Econ Advs, 1946-53; monographs; contbr to profsl and popular publs. Recipient, prize for essay on post-war employment, 1944. Home: 2908 Albermarle St, NW Washington, DC. Office: 1001 Connecticut Ave, Washington, DC.

KHAZANOV, Amram, Isr, agriculturist; b. Gedera, Isr; s. Yaakov and Haya (Liss); BS, MS, U of Cal, Berkeley, 1913-16; m. Esther Smilanski; c: Sara Dean, Shulamit Galli. Vine and citrus grower, since 1940; head agriculturist, PICA, 1920-40. Prin contribs: discovery of new almond varieties: Hanadiv, Habaronit, Pika, Khazanov; orange variety, Khazanov. Turkish Army, 1910. Fmr, head, local comm, Gedera. Contbr to profsl publs. Home: 15 Biluyim St, Gedera, Isr.

KHAZZOOM, Joseph Daniel, Can, economist; b. Baghdad, Iraq, Jan 6, 1932; s. Abraham and Loulou (Raby); BSc, Tel Aviv U, 1957; MA, PhD, Harvard U, 1960; m. Edythe Hicks, Nov 24, 1960; c: Aziza, Loolwa. Asso prof, McGill U; chief econometrician, Fed Power Commn; fmr: econ, Union of Operative Consumer Soc in Isr; cons, econometrics, WR Grace & Co, NY. Sgt, IAF. Adv bd, Sephardic Acad of Montreal; mem: Econometric Soc; Amer Stat Assn; Amer Econ Assn; Omicron Delta Epsilon. Author: The Currency Ratio in Developing Countries, 1966; contbr to profsl jours. Home: 2415 Ross Rd, Silver Spring, Md. Offices: Dept of Economics, McGill U, Montreal, Can; Fed Power Commn, 441 6 St, NW, Washington, DC.

KHUNER, Alfred, Austr, civil engineer; b. Austerlitz, Czech, Sep 9, 1897; s. Heinrich and Caecilil (Wachsmann); in Austr since 1940; CE, Tech U, Vienna, Aus, 1921; m. Helena Kikinis, Jan 30, 1930; c: Ellen Moray. Ret since 1969; engr i/c, Structural Steel Sect, Eclipse Mfg Co, Singapore, 1939-40; design engr, State Rivers and Water Supply Commn, Vic, 1941-62; sr lectr, Swinburne Tech Coll and Royal Melbourne Inst Tech, 1962-69. Fmr: hon secy, Technion Soc of Vic; fed counsellor, br comm mem, Assn Profsl Engrs, Austr; comm mem, Jüdischer Ingenieurverband, Vienna; mem: Inst of Engrs, Austr; Technion Soc, Vic. Hobbies: swimming, gardening, football. Home: 1/41 Milton St, Elwood, Victoria, Austr.

KIDRON, Mordecai Reginald, Isr, diplomat; b. Wynberg, S Afr, Nov 13, 1915; s. Solomon and Jane (Rosenberg); in Isr since 1933; att Heb U, Jerusalem, 1933-34; Stellenbosch U of S Afr, 1935-37; m. Nora Viterbo, Apr 12, 1949; c: Dan. Perm repr, intl orgs, Geneva, since 1966; staff, political dept, JA, 1945-48; mil gov, N Jerusalem, 1948-49; 1st secy, counsellor, Isr Emb, London, 1949-51; dir, intl orgs, Min Fgn Affairs, 1951-53; Isr dep rep to UN, 1953-58; ambass to Thailand, Laos, Cambodia, 1958-63; dir, armistice affairs, 1963-66. Served, Allied Forces, 1939-44; IDF, 1947-49. Office: Mission Permanente d'Israel, 9 Chemin Bonvent, 1216 Cointrin, Geneva, Switz.

KIEFF, Irving N, US, attorney; b. Phila, Pa, Aug 22, 1906; s. Nathan and Elizabeth (Breen); LLB, Temple U, Sch of Law, Phila, Pa, 1932; m. Florence Prussell, Nov 10, 1940; c: Nelson, Elliott. Law clerk, Orphans' Court, Phila, Pa, since 1959; atty, Commonwealth of Pa, 1939-50, dept atty-gen, 1950-55. Recording secy, Phila Flag Day Assn; bd mgrs, Cen HS Alumni Assn, fmr secy; fmr: govt appd agt, Selective Service; treas, Temple Law Alumni; vice-pres, B'nai Jeshurun Cong; bd mgrs, Strawberry Mansions Recreation Assn; ZOA; mem: Amer, Pa, Phila Bar Assns; Justice Lodge, B'nai B'rith; Montgomery Lodge, Masons, fmr master; Temple Law Alumni; club, 21 Jewel Sq. Home: 905 Plainfield St, Phila, Pa. Office: City Hall, Philadelphia, Pa.

KIESLER, Karl, Isr, engineer; b. Vienna, Aus, May 4, 1905; s. Josef and Dora (Grossmann); in Isr since 1936; MIRTE, Inst of Rd Transp Engrs, London, 1948; m. Ilse Koenigsbuch, Dec 4, 1936; c: Yoram, Uri. Mgn dir: Karl Kiesler Ltd, since 1958; Jona Kuebler Ltd, since 1951, with firm since 1939; firs hon consul, Fed Rep of Ger in Haifa, since 1958; fmr in automobile repair bus, Eur. Mem, Freemasons, Haifa. Recipient, Croix du Merite by Pres, Fed Rep of Ger. Home: 86 Moriah Ave, Haifa, Isr. Office: 35 Hameginim Ave, Haifa, Isr.

KIEV, Isaac Edward, US, librarian, rabbi; b. NYC, Feb 28, 1905; s. Nathan and Anna (Radin); ordained rabbi, MHL, JIR, NY, 1927; DD, HUC, 1957; m. Mary Nover, Dec 20, 1930; c: Ari, Aviva. Libr, HUC-JIR, since 1943; chaplain, Dept of Hosps, NYC; Sea View Hosp Syn; acting rabbi, Free Syn of Westchester, 1957; asso, Cong Habonim, since 1967. Pres, J Librs Assn, 1951-59; secy, J Cultural Reconstruction, NY, 1949-51; trustee: Alexander Kohut Memorial Found; Isr Matz Found; Nissan Touroff Found; mem: JBCA; Assn Bibl Instr; Soc of Bibl Lit & Exegesis; Vaad Halashon; Amer Acad for J Research; Amer J Hist Soc; Amer Oriental Soc; Isr Hist and Ethnographical Soc; NY Bd Rabbis; Isr Exploration Soc; Soc J Bibliophiles; Mekize Nirdamim Soc; CCAR. Author, Kafra Haggadah, Eng trans, 1949; asso ed: J Book Annual; Studies in Bibliography & Booklore; Libr Trends; contbr to Amer J Year Book, J Book Annual, Studies in Bibliography and Booklore. Home: 4 S Pinehurst Ave, New York, NY. Study: 40 W 68 St, New York, NY.

KIMCHI, Aaron Dov, Isr, economist; b. Russ, May 5, 1924; s. Josef and Tova (Rosman); in Isr since 1934; MA, Heb U, Jerusalem, 1951; m. Alisa Shneerson, May 27, 1950; c: Chana, Orit. Mgn dir, Isr Ind Bank Ltd, since 1966; dep dir, State's Revenues, Min of Finance, 1953-56, dep controller, fgn exch, 1956-59; mgn dir, Bank Feuchtwanger Ltd, 1959-65. Recipient: Mil Medal, Brit Army, 1945. Home: 18 Haoranim St, Kfar Shmaryahu, Isr. Office: POB 29179, Tel Aviv, Isr.

KIMCHI, Yechezkiel, Isr, painter; b. Stolin, Pol, Dec 17, 1918; s. Michall and Bracha (Bass); in Isr since 1947; dipl, Tchrs' Sem, Warsaw, 1939; att Art Acad, Warsaw; painting courses, Isr. Painter, graphic ed, Sifriat Poalim Publ Co, since 1954. One-man shows: gals: Tchemerinsky, 1962; Holon Munic, 1966; Hakibbutz-Lim, 1968; mus: Eilat, 1965; Yad Lebanim, Petah Tikva, 1966; group exhbs: Tel Aviv Mus, 1954,1965; Kibbutz, 1963; Jerusalem, 1965; Mus of Modern Art, Haifa, 1966; Ein Harod Mus, 1966; Isr Artists, exhb org by Min of Educ, 1967; four painters exhb, Holon, 1968; numerous stone reliefs, Yakum, Tel Aviv, Shfaim; pub works: Ruth Album, 1962; Y Kimchi Art Book, 1966; contbr, illus to numerous books and albums. Mem, Painters and Sculptors Assn, Isr. Recipient, Dizengoff Award, 1964. Home: Kibbutz Yakum, Isr. Studio: Sifriat Poalim, 73 Allenby St, Tel Aviv, Isr.

KIMMEL, Melvin, US, attorney; b. NYC, May 26, 1930; s. Samuel and Esther (Goldberg); BA, Bklyn Coll, 1959; JD, NY Law Sch, NYC, 1957; m. Irene Kaplan, June 29, 1961; c: Ira, Justice, Dean. Pvt practice since 1958; chief, pvt detective agcy, Kimmel, 1956-58; arbitrator, Civil Court, NYC since 1970. Mem: NY Co Lawyers Assn, comm on Fed Leg, since 1966, comm on State Leg, since 1970; pres, Manhattan Beach Comty Group, Inc, 1965; spec dep atty-gen, NY State, assigned to Elections Fraud Bur, 1959. Author, Legal Remedies For Medical Errors, A Guide to the Law of Medical Practice and Malpractice, 1970; contbr to medico-legal jours. Hobby: fruit growing. Home: 227 Corbin Place, Brooklyn, NY. Office: 150 Broadway, New York, NY.

KIMMELMAN, Benedict Brown, US, dentist, educator; b. Phila, Pa, July 20, 1915; s. Simon and Bertha (Brown); att Temple U, Phila, Pa, 1931-32; DDS, Temple U, Sch of Dent, 1936; m. Rita Apfelbaum, May 25, 1941; c: Mark, Simon, Berta Freedman. Clinical assoc prof, med, dir, dent med div, Hahnemann Med Coll and Hosp, Phila since 1961; co-dir, Dent Materials Scis Cen, Franklin Inst, since 1968; research asso, U of Pa Sch of Dent, 1955-57; att operative dent, Albert Einstein Med Cen, 1961-70. Maj, US Army, Dent Corps, 1941-46. Prin contribs, conducted fundamental studies in oral hygiene and caries. Mem: Amer Dental Assn. Contbr to dent jours. Recipient: Silver Star; Bronze Star; Four Chaplains Legion of Hon, 1965. Hobbies: lit, travel, photography. Home: 1204 Melrose, Philadelphia, Pa. Office: 1711 Pine, Philadelphia, Pa.

KING, Sol, US, architect; b. Pol, July 19, 1909; s. Lester and Celia (Sarna); in US since 1923; att U Detroit, 1929-31; BS, U Mich, 1934; m. Jennie Lifshitz, Apr 14, 1935; c: Phyllis Weiner (decd), Susan Roggin. Pres, Albert Kahn Assos, Inc, since

1958, dir of architecture, since 1956, with firm since 1935. Sponsor: Exhb for Mich Artists award, "A Work Suitable to an Architectural Setting," since 1958; AKA Grad Scholarship, U Mich, since 1956; fmr, Fgn Student Exch Prog, Assn Coll Schs Architecture, 1963-65, 1967-68. Dir, Engr Soc of Detroit, since 1965, pres, 1968-70, mem since 1959; bd govs, Cong Shaarey Zedek, Southfield, Mich, since 1966, mem since 1944. Fmr: chmn, sub-comm on architectural-engr responsibilities, 1968, mem, Public Adv Panel on Architectural Services, 1967-69, both with US Gen Services Admn; bd, alumni repr, United Heb Schs, Detroit, Mich, 1951; mem, bd dirs, Fed Apts Inc, 1967; mem: Amer Inst of Architects-Natl, serving on various comns; Amer Inst of Architects-Detroit chap, fmr: dir, vice-pres; Mich Soc of Architects, fmr: dir, chmn of various comms; J Cmty Cen, Detroit, fmr: dir, vice-pres; Founds Soc, Detroit Inst of Arts; Architectural Alumni Grad Scholarship Adv Comm, U Mich; Bldg Research Inst; Bldg Officials Conf of Amer; Gtr Detroit Bd of Commerce; Technion Soc; ORT; both Detroit chaps; clubs: Econ, Detroit; Pres', U Mich; Franklin Hills Country; Standard City. Contbr to profsl jours. Award-Winning Bldgs: Assembly Plant, St Louis, Ford Motor Co, 1948; Henry Ford Hosp parking bldg, Detroit, 1959; Natl Bank of Detroit, Hqrs Bldg, 1959; Physics and Astronomy Bldg, U of Mich, 1963; Lab and Off Bldg, Springdale, O, Avon Products Inc, 1965; truck plant, Springfield, O, Intl Harvester Co, 1967; Admn Off Bldg, Saginaw, Mich, GM Corp, 1968; recipient: mem, coll fs, Amer Inst Architects, 1966; Sesquicentennial Award, dist alumni, U Mich, 1967; gold medal, Mich Soc of Architects, 1967. Home: Park Towers E, 16500 N Park Dr, Southfield, Mich. Office: 345 New Center Bldg, Detroit, Mich.

KINGSBERG, Malcolm, US, business cons; b. Springfield, Mass, Oct 10, 1900; s. Julius and Fannie (Bregoff); BA, Harvard U, 1920, MBA, 1922; m. Rebecca Berkowitz, Oct 10, 1926; c: Harold. Bus cons since 1950; asso: Goldman Sachs & Co, 1922-31; M J Meehan, 1922-33; vice-chmn, Keith Albee Orpheum, 1934; vice-pres, treas, RKO, 1943-46, pres, RKO Theaters, 1946-50; vice-pres, treas, Magna Theatre Co, 1954-56; Loews, 1957. Home: 930 Fifth Ave, New York, NY.

KINGSFORD, Charles, US, composer, music therapist; b. Bklyn, NY, Aug 16, 1907; s. Israel and Fromka (Shafner) Konig; f grad, Juilliard Sch of Music, 1929. Music therapist: Music Therapy Cen, NY, since 1958; Hospitalized Vets Music Service, since 1953; musical dir, Fort Wash Syn, NYC, 1938-44; Free Syn of Westchester, Mt Vernon, NY, 1944-50; Camp Greylock, 1945-59; fac mem, piano and composition, voice coach, Amer Theatre Wing, 1947-58. Composer: And Already the Minutes, for voice and orch, 1937; Cantata, for chorus and orch; publ 25 songs; composer-arranger, Broadway produc: Boy Meets Girl, 1935; Good-Bye My Fancy, 1948. Mem: ASCAP; Amer Composers and Authors Guild; Juilliard Alumni Assn; Natl Assn for Music Therapy; NY Singing Tchrs Assn. Home: 150 W 57 St, New York, NY.

KINO, Eliahu Bezalel, Isr, chemist; b. Jerusalem, Feb 5, 1911; s. Felix and Nehama (Elbaum); grad, Herzliya Coll, 1929; dipl, engr, U Belgium, 1933; m. Gertrude Moos, Aug 29, 1945; c: Dorit. Dir: inves, chem and food ind, Isr Min of Trade and Ind, since 1968, chem ind, 1959-68; secy-gen, Engrs and Architects Assn, Isr, 1947-56; dir, mgr, Bldg Co, Liberia, 1956-58. Hagana, 1926-49; Brit Army, 1941-46; IDF, 1948-49. Home: 14 Lean St, Ramat Gan, Isr. Offices: Min of Trade and Ind Bldg, Jerusalem, Isr; Govt of Isr Inves Auth, Shalom Tower, Tel Aviv, Isr.

KINORI, Ben-Zion, Isr, engineer, educator; b. Sopron, Hung, Mar 7, 1908; s. Jacob and Regina (Rosenberg) Lantos; in Isr since 1933; Dipl, CE, Tech U, Budapest, 1933; m. Paula Lauber, Sep 17, 1968; c: Dina Dvir, Jacob. Asso prof, Technion, Haifa, since 1967; exec engr, Solei Boneh Ltd, 1945-49; head, drainage dept, Tahal, 1949-68; sr lectr, Technion, Haifa, 1960-67. Lt, Engr Corps, IDF, 1948-58. Prin contrib, devl, research methods for drainage in semi-arid conditions. Author: The Open Channel, 1965; Channel Linings, 1967; Surface Drainage Engineering, 1969. Mem: Engrs and Architects Assn, Isr; Intl Comm on Irrigation and Drainage. Home: 30 Hatichon St, Haifa, Isr. Office: Technion, Haifa, Isr.

KIPEN, Israel, Australia, business exec; b. Bialystok, Pol, Mar 21, 1919; s. Yudel and Sheina (Marantz); in Australia since 1946; att U of Warsaw, 1938-39; m. Laura Baitz, Sep 3, 1950;

c: Aviva, Doron. Chmn, mgn dir, I Kipen Knitwear; pres, Bialik Coll, Melbourne. Mem: J Bd of Deps, Vic; Mt Scopus Coll; dep mem, Zionist Action Comm, Jerusalem; pres, Gen Zionist Org, Melbourne, 1952-58; State ZC, Vic, 1958-59; vice-pres, ZF, Australia and NZ, 1958-59. Home: 11 Edinburgh Ave, Caulfield, Victoria, Australia. Office: 1 Claremont St, S Yarra, Victoria, Australia.

KIPNIS, Igor, US, harpsichordist; b. Berlin, Ger, Sep 29, 1930; s. Alexander and Mildred (Levy); in US since 1930; AB, Harvard Coll, Cambridge, Mass, 1952; dipl: Sch of Music, Westport, Conn; St Luke's Sch, New Canaan, Conn, both 1948; m. Judith Robison, Jan 6, 1953; c: Jeremy. Harpsichordist since 1959; critic, contributing ed, Stereo Rev, since 1961. US Army, 1952-54. Performed throughout US, Can; tours: Eur, S Amer, Isr. Recordings: Columbia Masterworks; CBS; Epic; Vanguard; Decca; Golden Crest; Kapp. Host, own radio prog, The Age of Baroque, WQXR, NY, 1966-68; tchr, Berkshire Music Cen, Lenox, Mass, 1964-67, chmn Baroque Dept, 1965-67. Ed, Clarke: Prince of Den's March, 1965; A First Harpsichord Book, 1970; contbr revs to: Amer Record Guide; Musical Courier; Notes; NY Post; NY Herald Tribune. Mem: Bohemians, NYC; Dolmetsch Soc; Galpin Soc. Recipient, nomination for Grammy Award: most promising new classical recording artist, 1964. Hobbies: baroque music, record collecting, photography. Home and office: 215 Dean St, Brooklyn, New York.

KIRCHNER, Leon, US, composer, performer, educator; b. Bklyn, NY, Jan 24, 1919; s. Samuel and Pauline; AB, U of Cal, Berkeley, 1942; hon AM, Harvard U, 1961; m. Gertrude Schoenberg, July 8, 1949; c: Paul, Lisa. Walter Bigelow Rosen Prof of Music, Harvard U, since 1966; prof since 1961; lectr, U of Cal, Berkeley, 1947-48; asst prof, asso prof, U of S Cal, 1950-54; Luther Brusie Marchant Prof of Music, Mills Coll, 1954-61. US Army, 1942-46. Composer: concerto for violin, cello, 10 winds and percussion; two piano concertos; piece for piano and orch; sinfonia for orch; tocata for strings, solo winds and percussion; duo for violin and piano; sonata concertante for violin and piano; three string quartets; trio for violin, cello and piano; choral music; vocal music; piano music; scenes for an opera. Mem: Natl Inst Arts and Letters; Natl Acad Arts and Scis. Recipient: grant, Natl Acad Arts and Letters, 1951; awards: NY Music Critics Circle, 1950, 1960; Naumburg, 1954; Pulitzer Prize in Music, 1967. Office: Harvard U, Cambridge, Mass.

KIRSCH, David, Can, business exec; b. Lith, Nov 23, 1885; s. Abraham and Malca (Plastolk); in Can since 1891; m. 1st, Sara Levinson, Nov 23, 1915 (decd); c: Arthur, Beatrice Salmon, Marguerite Grenadier, Judith Gottlieb; m. 2nd, Jessie Pearson, 1947. Pres: David Kirsch Ltd, since 1936; Globe Customs Brokers, since 1932; owner, Regent Shirt, 1908-33; impartial chmn, Prov of Que Clothing Ind, 1935-46. Hon pres: Fed J Communal Services, since 1953; J Gen Hosp, since 1953; Montefiore Club, since 1936; fmr pres, Inter-Fed Council, Montreal; chmn, war efforts comm, Can J Cong, 1939-47; gov, J Colonization Assn, since 1945; mem: Montreal Bd Trade, since 1919; Masons; club, Elm Ridge Golf. Hobby, trout fishing. Home: 4927 Grosvenor Ave, Montreal, Can. Office: 751 Victoria Sq, Montreal, Can.

KIRSCH, Henry Julius, Isr, business exec; b. Ceres, S Afr, May 1, 1906; s. Raphael and Lena (Ettmann); in Isr since 1951; m. Rivka Goldin, June 28, 1932; c: Arnon, Ella Jacobson, Ruth Berman. Jt mgn dir, Peltours Ltd, since 1951; dir: Migdal Binyan Ins Co, since 1960; Pal Afr Shippers Ltd, Johannesburg, since 1943; chmn and mgn dir: PJ Joubert, S Afr, 1935-50; Afr Distillers, Rhodesia, 1945-59. Chmn: S Afr Zionist Youth Council, 1930-33; Johannesburg Zionist Assn, 1943-46; mem exec, S Afr Zionist Assn, 1933-50. Home: 11 Hagderot St, Savyon, Isr. Office: 28 Ahad Ha'am St, Tel Aviv, Isr.

KIRSCH, Morris, US, business exec; b. Bklyn, NY, Oct 4, 1906; s. Hyman and Sara (Reizen); att Bklyn Tech, 1920-24; m. Bertha Cohen, Nov 13, 1927; c: Leon, David, Sara Lampert. Chmn bd: Kirsch Beverages Inc, pres, 1939-68; No Cal, pres, 1952-68; dir, Kings Co Lafayette Trust; mem adv bd, Mfrs Hanover Trust Co; appd US Commn of Jurors, E Dist, 1966. Trustee, Union Temple, Bklyn; chmn bd, Amer Cancer Soc, Bklyn unit; treas, Bklyn Philharmonia; pres: Kingsbrook Med Cen; NY League of Locality Mayors; dir: J Hosp of Bklyn; and vice-pres, Pride of Judea Children's Services; and secy, YM-YWHA of Williamsburg; Ind Home for Blind; Gtr

NY Histadrut Council; UJA; and vice chmn bd, ARC; trustee, Amer Cancer Soc of NY; natl trustee, dir, NCCJ, Kings Co; chmn, natl and city drs: Travelers Aid; YMCA; Boy Scouts, NY Council; United Hosp Fund; Gtr NY Fund; Amer Cancer Soc; USO; NY Heart Assn; Jt Defense Appeal; HIAS; UJA; ARC; Salvation Army; ADL; FJP; Natl Found of Infantile Paralysis; mem, Natl Soft Drink Assn; mem chmn, NY State Bottlers of Carbonated Beverages; dir, fmr pres: Metrop Soft Drink Bd of Trade; Natl Assn of Mfrs; vice-pres, chmn pr, Pres Council, Amer Inst of Mgmt; dir: Harvest Lodge, B'nai B'rith; mem: Planning Board 8; Elks; Shriners; Pilgrim Lodge; panel, Amer Arbitration Assn; adv bd, Gtr NY Safety Council; hon legion, Police Dept, NYC; clubs: Unity, Bklyn, dir; Kiwanis, Williamsburg; Rotary; Sales Exec, NY; Elcelsiro; Gov's; Brownsville Boys, life mem; Natl 10th A D Rep, Bklyn; Bklyn. Recipient: Williamsburg Settlement Gold Medal Award, 1961; State of Isr Historic Award; found's award, Isaac Albert Research Inst, 1954; Isr Bar Mitzvah Award, 1964; men's club honoree, Visiting Nurses Assn, 1966; citizens award, Kings Co Med Assn, 1966; NY State Mason of Year, 1967; service award, Flatbush C of C, 1967; Bklyn Hall of Fame, 1967; dist service award, Histadrut, 1968; Bklyn Man of Year, Isr Bond Dr, 1968; UJA, 1968; Ky Col, 1957; Adm, NC Navy, 1962. Home: 135 Eastern Pkwy, Brooklyn, NY. Office: 921 Flushing Ave, Brooklyn, NY.

KIRSCHENBAUM, Walter L, US, public relations exec; b. NYC, Oct 28, 1919; s. Jacob and Bessie (Popper); BA, NYU, 1941; m. Gertrude Frances, Dec 22, 1940. Asst finance admnr, NYC, since 1966; mem, Mayor Lindsay cabinet, NYC; produc, "Victor Riesel Interviews," radio prog. Vice-chmn, NY Co Lib Party, exec dir, Bx, 1946-51; pr dir, Amer Friends Heb U, 1941; research dir, AJCong, 1941-46; pr dir, J Lab Comm; produc, Barry Gray Show, 1953-62; candidate: state senate, 1952, 1965, city council, 1957. Natl exec comm, J Lab Comm; mem: J Daily Forward Assn; PR Off Soc; AFL Press Assn; Amer Vets Comm; NAACP; Workmen's Circle. Contbr to periodicals. Home: 453 FD Roosevelt Dr, New York, NY. Office: Munic Bldg, New York, NY.

KIRSCHNER, Leonard, US, attorney; b. Cincinnati, O, Mar 2, 1928; s. Saul and Dorothy (Chodash); AB, U of Cincinnati, 1948, JD, 1949; m. Yolanda Negin, Aug 28, 1960; c: Mark, Steven, Tami, Mindy, Debra, Barry. First asst prosecuting atty, Hamilton Co, since 1968, asst prosecuting atty, 1951-68; fmr: partner, Kirschner and Kraft. Vice-pres, Hamilton Co Rep Club; mem: exec comm, O, Ky reg bds, ADL; bd govs, dist 2, fmr pres; O Assn, Cincinnati Council, lodge 4, B'nai B'rith; Amer, O, Cincinnati Bar Assns; Natl Council of Juvenile Court Judges; Natl Assn of Dist Attys; Natl Assn of Defense Counsel in Criminal Cases; fmr: bd mem, Adath Isr Cong; pres, Hillel Adult Adv Bd; contbr to legal jours. Home: 1539 Shenandoah St, Cincinnati, O. Office: 10 W 9 St, Cincinnati, O.

KIRSH, Benjamin Sollow, US, attorney, author; b. NYC, Mar 15, 1898; s. Nathan and Celia (Sollow); AB, Columbia Coll, 1918; att Columbia Law Sch, 1918-19; LLB, NYU Law Sch, 1920; m. Leona Barach, Dec 22, 1926; c: Deborah Slom. Pvt practice since 1920; spec asst to US atty, NY, in Sherman Anti-Trust Cases; chmn, Natl Trucking Comm, Natl War Lab Bd, Wash, DC. US Army, Students Army Training Corps, 1918. Author: Trade Associations: Legal Aspects, 1928; National Industrial Recovery Act, 1933; Trade Associations in Law and Business, 1938; Automation and Collective Bargaining, 1964. Home: 505 West End Ave, New York, NY. Office: 253 Broadway, New York, NY.

KIRSHBAUM, Jack D, US, physician; b. Chgo, Ill, Dec 31, 1902; s. David and Rebecca; MS, MD, U Ill, 1928; m. Florence Rosen, Dec 27, 1931; c: Gerald, Robert, Richard. Dir labs, W Valley Comty Hosp, since 1959; sr path, Atomic Bomb Casualty Commn, Nagasaki, Japan, 1968-70; path, dir labs, San Bernardino Co Hosp; asso prof, Sch of Medieval Evangelists, 1952-62; path, Cook Co Hosp, 1932-41. Dir labs, Kern Gen Hosp, Bakersfield, Cal, 1947-49. Col, US Army, 1942-46; col, US Army Res, 1946. F: Amer Coll Phys; Coll of Path; cdr, Bakersfield Post, JWV, 1948; bd mem, Temple Emanu-El, 1952-53; mem: AMA; Sigma Xi. Contbr numerous articles to med jours. Home: 3710 Scadlock Lane, Sherman Oaks, Cal. Office: W Valley Comty Hosp, 5333 Balboa Blvd, Encino, Cal.

KIRSHBLUM, I Usher, US, rabbi; b. Bialystok, Pol, Nov 25

1911; s. Moshe and Feige (Hurwitz); in US since 1923; BA, Bklyn Coll, 1935; ordained rabbi, JIR; m. Selma Epstein, Dec 21, 1935; c: Eliezer, Marsha. Rabbi: J Cen Kew Gardens Hills, since 1946; Flushing J Cen, 1936-46. Pres: JNF council, LI, bd dirs, 1950-55; Queensborough Public Libr, 1960-62; chmn: rabb speakers bur, FJP; LI State of Isr Bonds; bd dirs: United Syn of Amer since 1950; RA since 1945; United Isr Appeal, 1950-51; N Shore Chap, ARC; Queens Council Social Wfr; natl mem chmn, admn vice pres, ZOA; delg, WZC, Jerusalem; mem, Zionist Action Comm. Home: 135-12 72 St, Flushing, NY. Study: 71-25 Main St, Flushing, NY.

KIRSHENBAUM, Isidor, US, researcher; b. NYC, June 22, 1917; s. Samuel and Kate (Smithkin); BS, CCNY, 1938; MA, Columbia U, 1939, PhD, 1942; m. Lucy Gutstein, 1947; c: Howard, Steven, Barbara, Kenneth. Sr research asso, head, Chem and Patent Info, Esso Research and Engr Co, NJ, staff mem since 1945; asst instr, chem, Columbia U, 1940-42, research chem, 1942-45; cons, AEC, 1947-55; civilian with Off Sci Research and Devl, 1944. Prin contrib, research in petrochems, catalysis, isotopes. F: Amer Inst Chem; mem: Amer Chem Soc; AAAS; Sci Research Soc. Home: 436 Otisco Dr, Westfield, NJ. Office: Esso Research and Engr Co, Linden, NJ.

KIRSON, Michael Wolf, Isr, physicist; b. Johannesburg, S Afr, Feb 22, 1940; s. Edwin and Rose (Fluxman); in Isr since 1967; BSc, hons, U Witwatersrand, Johannesburg, 1961; PhD, Cornell U, 1966; m. Judy Aarons, June 18, 1961; c: Karen, Ian, Eilon. Research asso, Weizmann Inst of Sci, since 1968; post doc f: Niels Bohr Inst, Copenhagen, 1966-67; Weizmann Inst, 1967-68. Mem: Phi Kappa Phi, Cornell U; Isr Phys Soc. Contbr articles to profsl jours. Home: 55 Hanassi Harishon St, Rehovot, Isr. Office: Dept Nuclear Phys, Weizmann Inst, Rehovot, Isr.

KISELSTEIN, Moshe, Isr, government official; b. Warsaw, Pol, Sep 16, 1912; s. Itzhak and Sara (Hoppenfeld); in Isr since 1935; att HS of Trade, Econ and Admn, Tel Aviv; m. Chasia Grünberg; c: Avi, Talma, Mina, Sara. Chief placement off, mem, mgn bd, State Employment Service, since 1960; mgn dir, Cen Farmer's Assn, 1939-53; dist food controller, Min Trade and Ind, 1953-60. Fmr, mem ed bd, Hameshek Hatzair, monthly. Mem, bd govs, Kfar Silver Agric HS; vice chmn, bd govs, Bank Halva'a Vehisahon. Home: 7 Struck St, Tel Aviv, Isr.

KISH, Maurice, US, artist, poet; b. Dvinsk, Latvia, Feb 19, 1898; s. Benjamin and Chanah (Barish); att: Natl Acad; Cooper Union. Rep in mus and pvt collections. Mem: Artist Equity; Audubon Artists: Allied Artists of Amer; Conn Acad of Fine Arts; NJ Painters and Sculptors Soc; Soc Contemporary Artists; fmr pres, Amer Vet Soc of Artists, 1962. Author: Di Velt Is Mein Lid, 1968. Recipient: awards, gold and silver medals. Home and studio: 70 S Third St, Brooklyn, NY.

KISNER, Jeremiah, US, dentist; b. Lynn, Mass, June 13, 1915; s. Joseph and Sarah (Brown); AB, U of NC, Chapel Hill, 1937; DMD, Tufts Coll Dent Sch, Boston, 1941; m. Alice Kancher, June 5, 1945; c: Sandra, Scott. Ret; staff mem: St Lukes Hosp, 1947-70; Union Hosp, 1960-70, both Phila. Capt, US Army, 1941-45. Fmr: cdr, JWV, Post 154; bd dirs, J Comty Cen; mem: Masons, Wamsutta Lodge; Shriners, Aleppo Temple. Hobbies: gardening, stamps, golf. Home: 273 Carroll St, New Bedford, Mass. Office: 271 Union St, New Bedford, Mass.

KISTER, Yitzhak, Isr, jurist; b. Mosciska, Pol, Oct 17, 1905; s. Yehuda and Sobe (Wohl); in Isr since 1935; MJ, DJ, U of Lwow, Pol, 1929; m. Gitl Schwimmer, Feb 22, 1935; c: Ruhama Merzbach, Eliezer, Akiva; m. 2nd, Sara Mayafith, Aug 24, 1947. Judge, Dist Court of Tel Aviv, since 1948; asst atty: Pol, 1929-34; Pal, 1937-39; pvt practice, Jerusalem, 1939-44; magistrate, Tel Aviv, 1945-48; lectr, family law and succession law, U of Tel Aviv, until 1961. Mem: Social Council of Isr, chmn, comm for social leg; Intl Law Assn. Author: Adoption of Children in Israel, 1953; contbr to profsl jours and lectures to Intl Lawyers' Conv, 1958. Home: 17 Or Hachaim St, Bnei Brak, Isr. Office: District Court, Tel Aviv, Isr.

KLABER, Isidor, Isr, physician; b. Vienna, Aus, Mar 24, 1892; s. Max and Charlotte (Preis); MD, U Vienna, 1919; m. Gerda Schwarzberg, 1935; c: Max. Phys: Kupat Cholim Cheut,

since 1938; various clinics, Vienna, 1919-38. Aus-Hung Army, 1914-18. Pres, Tel Aviv Chap, Isr-Aus Friendship League; mem, Theodore Herzl Lodge, B'nai B'rith. Author: Wiener Morgenzeitung, Jugend Beilage; Judische Jugend, 1938. Home and office: 12 Zerubawel St, Tel Aviv, Isr.

KLAJN, Hugo, Yugo, physician, author, theater dir; b. Yugo, Sep 30, 1894; s. Samuel and Sofia (Grun); MD, U Vienna, 1919; m. Stana Djuric, 1935; c: Ivan. Prof, Theatre Acad. Author: The Nervous System, 1933; Abnormalities of the Normal, 1936, with study of psychopathology of Jewry; Education, 1936; Basic Problems in Theatre Direction, 1951; War Neurosis of Yugoslavs, 1955; Two Hour Life, 1957; Yextbook for Amateur Directors, 1961; Shakespeare and Humanness, 1964; Phenomena and Problems of the Modern Theatre, 1969. Recipient, Order of Lab, I deg. Home: Jevremova 40, Belgrade, Yugo.

KLAPERMAN, Gilbert, US, rabbi; b. NYC, Feb 25, 1921; s. Louis and Frieda (Rubenstein); BA, Yeshiva U, 1940, ordained rabbi, 1941; MA, State U of Ia, 1945; DHL, Yeshiva U, 1955; m. Libby Mindlin, Aug 23, 1942; c: Judith, Joel, Frieda, Carol. Rabbi, Cong Beth Sholom, Lawrence, NY, since 1950; asst prof, sociol, Yeshiva U, since 1953; chaplain, Nassau Co Jail; lectr, Sch of Rel, State U of Ia, 1943-45; fac mem, Tchrs Inst of Yeshiva U, 1945-56; rabbi, Brith Sholom Cong, Charleston, SC, 1947-50. Res capt, Can Chaplain Service, WW II. Mem: exec comm, RabCA, since 1952, vicepres, 1956-58; pres, NY Bd Rabbis, 1968-70; exec mem, Rel Zionist of Amer, mem, rabb delg to Russ, 1956; pres, Natl J Book Council, since 1962. Author: The Story of the Jewish People, four vols, 1956; The How and Why of the Old Testament, 1964; The History of Yeshiva University, 1969; ed, RabCA quarterly, 1953-54; contbr to Anglo-J mags. Home: 64 Muriel Ave, Lawrence, NY. Study: 390 Broadway, Lawrence, NY.

KLAPPER, Arthur Michael, US, attorney; b. Bklyn, NY, Aug 26, 1938; s. Jerome and Phoebe (Cohen); BA, Alfred U, Alfred, NY, 1959; JD, NYU Law Sch, 1962; m. Arleen Rosenberg, June 6, 1960; c: Michele, Andrew, Judith. Pvt practice, NYC since 1962. Pvt, US Army, 1962-63. Treas, S Gannon Civic Assn; mem: Pioneer Lodge 778, KP, past chancellor; admissions comm, Camp Williams Charitable Org. Home: 725 Harris Ave, Staten Island, NY. Office: 401 Broadway, New York, NY.

KLAPPHOLZ, Kurt, US, rabbi; b. Berlin, Ger, July 5, 1913; s. Salo and Sophie (Weinhaus); in US since 1938; att U Berlin, 1933-37; ordained rabbi, Rabb Sem, Berlin, 1938; hon DD, Burton Coll, Colo, 1959; m. Esther Grintuch, Dec 19, 1943; c: David, Ruby, Shelley. Rabbi, Cong Tifereth Isr, Bklyn, since 1956, 1941-48; admnr, Cen Yeshiva Beth Joseph Rabb Sem, Bklyn, since 1953; rabbi: Cong Kneses Isr, Sea Gate, Bklyn, 1938-40; Shaare Zion Cong, 1948-56. Pres, Bklyn Bd Rabbis, since 1968, mem, exec bd, NY, since 1963; mem: Catholic-J Relations Comm, since 1968; bd educ, Yeshiva of Flatbush, since 1951; RabCA; natl exec bd, Rel Zionist Org of Amer, since 1955. Author: Spiritual Awakening, 1954; The Power Within Us, 1961; Living Faith, 1966. Recipient, award for service, State of Isr Bonds, 1956. Hobby, classic and liturgical music. Home: 1495 Dahill Rd, Brooklyn, NY. Study: 2025-64 St, Brooklyn, NY.

KLARMAN, Joseph L, Isr, organization exec; b. Pol, Sep 29, 1909; s. Shmuel and Bella; grad, Tchrs Training Sem; c: Bella Barkayit. Chmn, World Exec, Herut-Hatzohar; world vice pres, Intl Fed of Children's Comtys; mem, presidium, KH; world head, Youth Aliyah; mem exec: Zionist Org; JA; mem, presidium: Zionist Actions Comm, ZC; fmr: mem, Hashomer Hatzair; co-found: Revisionist Movement; Betar Youth Movement; mem, natl exec, Revisionist Movement Conf, Pol, secy gen, vice chmn, Movement, asst to Zeev Jabotinsky; participant, second conf, Natl Workers Org, Isr; chmn, New Zionist Org, Isr, mem, presidium, Eur Jewry Rescue Comm, negotiator with Bulgarian Govt on J emigration to Isr, 1944, secured permission for Zionist activity and J emigration, Rum; head, Balkan dept, mem, Shilton Betar; head, JA Political Dept, in countries behind iron curtain; elected mem, Adv Political Comm to UN, headed by Abba Eban; delg, ZCs. Irgun repr, Rum, active, Aliyah Bet; served Haganah. Fmr, chief ed, Unser Welt, organ of world exec, Revisionist Movement; contbr articles to various jours in Heb, Yiddish, Pol, Eng. Office: POB 92, Jerusalem, Isr.

KLARWEIN, Joseph, Isr, architect; b. Warsaw, Pol, Feb 6, 1893; s. Wendelin and Rahel; MA, Acad of Arts, Berlin, 1921; m. 2nd, 1948; c: Mathias. Pvt practice since 1933; won public competitions, designed, built: Biol bldg, Heb U, Mt Scopus; Theodore Herzl Memorial; Knesset; U Campus; plans for: new govt compound, Jerusalem; govt off bldgs, Kirya; many others. Corresp mem, Académie d'Architecture de France, since 1959; mem, architects org, Isr. Home and office: 7 David Marcus St, Jerusalem, Isr.

KLASS, Ann T, US, publisher, communal worker; b. Pittsburg, Pa, Mar 1, 1888; d. Philip and Rose (Englander) Traxler; m. Raymond Klass, Mar 1, 1916; c: Philip, Rosanne. Cons, Bobbs-Merrill Co Inc, publishers, Indianapolis, Ind, since 1963; fmr pres, Raymond Klass Asso (sold to Bobbs Merrill Co, 1963). Hon pres, local chap, Hadassah since 1950; second vice-pres since 1962; fmr: co-found, pres, chmn, various comms; recording secy, regional convs; conv chmn, Cedar Rapids, all Hadassah; fmr: conf chmn, hist, constitution revs chmn, Natl Fed Temple Sisterhoods; served Gov's Commn on Status of Women; co-found, local hist, Temple Judah Cong; co-found, pres, Temple Judah Sisterhood; charter org mem, Cedar Rapids Radio Council; found secy, Comty Concert Assn; pres, Arthur Sch PTA; mem: League Women Voters; Ia J Home for Aged; YMCA; Cedar Rapids chap, UN; El Kahir Shrine Auxiliary; Masons. Recipient: Woman of Region, Hadassah, 1959; Woman of Year, 1962. Home: 3121 Bever Ave, Cedar Rapids, Ia.

KLASS, Marvin J, US, attorney; b. Sioux City, Ia, Nov 6, 1913; s. Isaac and Rose (Raskin); BA, Morningside Coll, 1936; LLB, Harvard, 1939; m. Merry Gralnek, Mar 28, 1947; c: Tim, Marilyn, Susan, Kay, Kalman. Partner, Stewart, Hatfield & Klass, since 1939; clarinetist, Sioux City Sym Orch, 1931-34; instr, bus law, Morningside Coll, 1940-42, 1946-49. US Army, 1942-46. Pres, ZOA, Sioux City, dist, 1948; J Fed, 1953-55; Shaare Zion Cong, 1960-62; bd dirs: Morningside Coll; Sanford Cen; mem: Gov's Comm for Constitutional Conv in Ia, 1959; Fair Employment Practice Comm, Sioux City, 1959; Civil Service Comm; B'nai B'rith; JWV; Amer Legion; Interprofsl Men's Inst; Amer Judicature Soc; Sioux City, Ia State, Amer Bar Assns; Scottish Rite Bodies; clubs: Lawyers, Exch. Hobby, music. Home: 3937 Douglas, Sioux City, Ia. Office: 830-838 Frances Bldg, Sioux City, Ia.

KLASS, Philip J, US, writer; b. Des Moines, Ia, Nov 8, 1919; s. Raymond and Ann (Traxler); BS, Ia State U, 1941. Avionics ed, Aviation Week and Space Tech Mag, since 1952; engr, Gen Elec Co, 1941-52. Mem: Inst of Elec and Electronic Engrs; Aviation Writers Assn; club, Natl Press. Author: UFOs-Identified, 1968; contbr numerous articles to periodicals and mags. Hobbies: sailing, photography, skiing. Home: 560 N St, Washington, DC. Office: Natl Press Bldg, Washington, DC.

KLATZKER, Bert, US, merchant; b. Seattle, Wash, Nov 15, 1910; s. Herman and Anna (Leopold); m. Frances Mesher, June 10, 1938; c: Barry, Steven. Hardware store owner since 1946. Natl youth commn, United Syn of Amer since 1960, world council since 1962; exec council, United Syn Youth Camp since 1961, youth chmn, vice-pres, Pacific NW region, Camp Solomon Schechter since 1958; bd govs, Herzl Conservative Cong since 1950; mem: Cascade lodge, B'nai B'rith; ZOA; J Comty Cen; club, Ballard Exch. Home: 2040 McGilvra Blvd E, Seattle, Wash. Office: 2409 NW Market St, Seattle, Wash.

KLAUSNER, Abraham J, US, rabbi; b. Memphis, Tenn, May 8, 1915; s. Joseph and Tillie (Binstock); MA, U Denver, 1938; MHL, HUC, 1942, hon DD, 1948; m. Judith Haskell, June 26, 1951; m. 2nd, Judith Steinberg, June 26, 1966. Rabbi: Temple Emanuel, Yonkers, NY, since 1954; Temple Isr, Boston, 1949-53; lectr, Boston U, since 1959; provost, HUC, 1948-49. Chaplain, US Army, 1944-48. Org, dir, hon pres, Cen Comm, Liberated in Ger, 1945-48; mem, CCAR. Ed, CCAR Jour, since 1942. Study: Temple Emanuel, Yonkers, NY.

KLAUSNER, David M, US, attorney; b. NYC, Aug 20, 1896; s. Mayer and Sarah (Berman); BA, Columbia Coll, 1916; LLB, Columbia U, 1918; m. Mildred Miller, June 2, 1925; c: Robert, William. Pvt practice, Jersey City, since 1919; partner, Kinkead & Klausner, 1923-33; asst co counsel, Hudson Co, 1942-50; mem: NJ Lawyers and Bankers Conf Comm, fmr chmn; commn, Supr Court, NJ, 1930; spec Master in Chancery, NJ, 1936. Hon pres, J Hosp and Rehab Cen; pres: NJ State Bar Assn, 1944-45; J Hosp and Rehab Cen, Hudson Co, 1935-40; Council of Social Agcys, 1944-46; United Comty Fund, 1957-59, both Jersey City; chmn: Hudson Co Comm on Character and Fitness; ARC, 1952-55; trustee: NJ State Bar Found; NJ Law Inst; club: Mountain Ridge Country. Author: The Practice of Law, 1945. Home: 117 Kensington Ave, Jersey City, NJ. Office: 26 Journal Sq, Jersey City, NJ.

KLAUSNER, Israel, Isr, editor, author, bibliographer; b. Troki, Russ, Apr 4, 1905; s. Haim and Rachel (Kopilovitch); in Isr since 1936; MPh, U Vilna, Pol, 1931; PhD, Heb U, Jerusalem, 1941; m. Sara Avrahamy, Apr 15, 1938; c: Yakir, Sigla Millo. Dep dir, Zionist Cen Archives, Jerusalem, 1937-68. Author: Korot Bet ha'Almin haYashan beVilna, 1935; Toldot haKehila haIvrit beVilna, 1938; Vilna biTkufat haGa'on, 1942; Rabbi Haim Zvi Shneerson, 1943; Toldot ha'Aguda Ness Ziona beVolpjin, 1954; Chibat Zion be-Romania, 1958; Oppozitzya leHerzl, 1960; beHit'orer Am, 1962; miKatovitz Ad Bazel, 2 vols, 1965; Karka veRuah, 1966; ed: Sefer haYovel shel haGimnasia haIvrit beVilna, 1946; Ktavim Zioniim shel haRav Zvi Hirsch Kalisher, 1947; co-ed, beShulei haHistoria, 1967; mem, ed bd, Zramim, weekly, 1931-32; contbr numerous articles and pamphlets. Active in student movements; mem: Ansky Hist Soc; KKL; KH; Yad Vashem Council. Recipient: awards: Kugel, Holon Munic, 1958; Ussishkin, KKL, 1965. Home: 36 Metudela St, Jerusalem, Isr.

KLAUSNER, Margot, Isr, author, business exec; b. Berlin, Ger, Nov 2, 1905; d. Julius and Doro (Leiser); in Isr since 1926; att U Berlin, 1924-26; div; c: Miriam Spielman, Amos Mokady. Owner, Moadim Lit Agts since 1948; pres, Isr-Can TV Studios Ltd since 1968; mem mgmt: Habimah Theater, 1927-36; Young Circle of Habimah. Author: Sappho of Lesbos, 1941; Joseph in Egypt, play, 1943; Origin of Drama, 1945; The Wedding, 1947; Storm in Sivan, life of Chaim Arlosoroff, 1957; Jonathan and Tali, screenplay, 1963; Naked Souls, short stories, 1963; co-author, The Diary of Mrs Sabina, screenplay, 1963; chief ed, Mysterious Worlds, monthly; mem mgmt, Bamah Theatre Jour. Pres, Isr Soc Parapsych, Tel Aviv; mem, Soc Psychical Research, London; Isr Screen Writers Guild; fmr: active in Hashomer Hatzair; club, PEN. Hobbies: archaeol, mythology. Home: 2 Keren Kayemet Blvd, Tel Aviv, Isr. Office: 10 Glickson St, Tel Aviv, Isr.

KLAUSNER, Samuel Zundel, US, educator; b. Bklyn, NY, Dec 19, 1923; s. Edward and Bertha (Adler); BS, NYU, 1947; MA, Columbia U, 1950, DE, 1951, PhD, 1963; m. Madeleine Suringar, Feb 20, 1964; c: Rina Wald, Jonathan, Daphne, Tamar. Asso prof, sociol, U of Pa, since 1967; dir, Cen for Research on Acts of Men, since 1967. Lt, USAAF, 1943-47. F, AAAS; exec secy, Soc for Sci Study of Rel. Author: Psychiatry and Religion, 1964; Why Man Takes Chances, 1967. Home: 2307 N 51 St, Philadelphia, Pa. Office: U of Pa, Philadelphia, Pa.

KLAUSNER, Yehuda, Isr, scientist; b. Arad, Rum, July 11, 1926; s. Shmuel and Zirl (Englmann); in Isr since 1944; BSc, Ing, Technion, Haifa, 1953, MSc, 1957; PhD, Princeton U, US 1960; m. Yoheved Grünberg, May 17, 1949; c: David, Aviel, Meir. Dept head, asso prof, Negev Inst for Arid Zone Research, Mech of Soil and Materials Dept, since 1963; lectr, Technion, Haifa, 1952-57; research asst, Princeton U, 1957-60; asso prof, Wayne State U, Detroit, Mich, 1960-64; teaching, undergrad, grad courses in civil engr; cons, soil and found engr. Contbr numerous articles to intl jours. Mem, Isr socs: Physics; Soil Sci; Soil Mech Found Engr; Profsl Engr; mem, Amer socs: Physics; Engr Educ; mem, Intl Soc Rational Mech. Hobby, sports. Home: 19 Jarboa St, Beersheba, Isr. Office: POB 1025, Beersheba, Isr.

KLAUSNER, Yehuda Arye, Isr, author, bibliographer, librarian; b. Odessa, Russ, June 12, 1919; s. Alexander and Shlomit (Levin); desc, Rabbi Alexander Suskind of Grodno; nephew of Prof Joseph Klausner; in Isr since 1933; BA, U Vilna, Pol, 1933; MA, Heb U, Jerusalem, 1942; PhD, U London, 1968; c: by 1st m, Amos Oz; m. 2nd, Rosa Polak, Mar 22, 1954; c: Marganita, David. Ed, lit div, Ency Hebraica since 1967; libr, J Natl and U Libr, 1936-55; research worker, Inst Heb Manuscripts, 1959; staff mem, Inst for Heb Bibliography, 1961-67. Haganah, civil defense, 1934-49. Prin contrib discovered and identified unknown manuscripts including works of Peretz and Lampronti. Mem: Isr Libr Assn; Assn Heb Writers in Isr; Intl Comparative Lit Assn; club, Intl PEN. Author: in Heb: History of World Literature, vol I, 1942, 2nd ed, 1951, vol II, 1952; The Short Story in Hebrew Literature, 1947; Anthology of World Hebrew Literature, 2 vols, 1952, 1954; contbr to Heb encys; lit and profsl jours in Isr, Eng, Fr. Recipient, awards: Bialik, Heb U, 1938; Klausner, Tel Aviv Munic, 1945. Spec interests: hist, archaeol. Home: 43 Hechalutz St, Jerusalem, Isr. Office: King David St, Jerusalem, Isr.

KLAVAN, Bennett, US, periodontist; b. Baltimore, Md, Apr 7, 1921; s. Sol and Rose (Kantor); AB, Johns Hopkins, 1941; BS, DDS, U Ill, 1944; m. Doris Winter, May 20, 1945; c: Roselyn Gothelf, Bruce. Prof, head, dept periodontics, Coll Dent, U Ill Med Cen, Chgo since 1968; pvt practice since 1948; mem, Coll Dent, U of Ill since 1948; cons, VA Hosps since 1965. Capt, US Army, 1946-48. F: Intl Coll Dents; Amer Coll Dents; mem: AAAS; NY Acad Scis; Amer Dent Assn; Amer Acad Periodontology; Ill Soc of Periodontists, past pres; Midwest Soc Periodontology, past pres; Alpha Omega. Contbr to dent jours. Home: 3200 N Lake Shore Dr, Chicago, Ill. Office: Coll of Dent, U of Ill Med Cen, 808 S Wood St, Chicago, Ill.

KLAVAN, Israel, US, rabbi; b. Zazkevich, Lith, June 9, 1915; s. Joshua and Fannie (Sheiffer); BA, Yeshiva Coll, NY, 1937; ordained rabbi, Isaac Elchanan Theol Sem, 1940; att Bernard Revel Grad Sch, Yeshiva U; m. Sadie Rabinowitz, Feb 22, 1942; c: Avram, Macy, Judith. Exec vice-pres, RabCA since 1950; rabbi: Cong Agudas Achim, Fitchburg, Mass, 1940-42; Cong Ohev Shalom, Winsport, Pa, 1942-46; Cong Brothers of Isr, 1946-53; pres, Syn Council, both Mt Vernon, NY, 1951-53. Mem, chaplaincy commn, div of rel activities, JWB. Co-ed, Rabb Council Manual of Sermons. Home: 108-22 64 Rd, Forest Hills, NY. Office: 84 Fifth Ave, New York, NY.

KLAWANS, Arthur H, US, physician, educator; b. Chgo, Ill, Aug 14, 1902; s. Israel and Fannie (Klawans); BS, U Chgo, 1924; MD, Rush Med Sch, 1928; m. Hannah Stein, Mar 14, 1927; c: Dorothy Rosenblum, Arthur. Clinical prof, obstet, gyn, U of Ill, since 1962, fmr asso clinical prof; att obstet, gyn, Presbyterian-St Lukes Hosp since 1956. Dipl, Amer Bd Obstet and Gyn, 1939; mem: AMA; Ill Med Soc; Chgo Med Soc; Cen Assn Obstets and Gyns; Chgo Gyn Soc; Amer Coll Obstet and Gyn; Phi Delta Epsilon; Alpha Omega Alpha. Contbr numerous articles to med jours. Home: 215 E Chicago Ave, Chicago, Ill. Office: 30 N Michigan Ave, Chicago, Ill.

KLEEMAN, Charles R, US, physician; b. Los Angeles, Aug 19, 1923; s. Samuel and Bertha (Frankenthal); BS, UCLA, 1944; MD, U of Cal Sch of Med, SF, 1947; m. Annette Wollman, June 24, 1945; c: Karen, Dena, Maura. Dir, div of med, Cedars-Sinai Med Cen, since 1964; prof, med, U of Cal, LA, since 1964; asso chief, biochem unit, QM Climatic Research Lab, Lawrence, Mass, 1951-53; instr, metabolic sect, asst prof, med dept, Yale U Med Sch, 1953-56; asso clinical prof med, U of Cal Med Sch, LA, 1956-58; chief, metabolic sect, VA Hosp, LA, 1956-60; asso prof, med, U of Cal Med Cen, LA, 1959-64; Upjohn Scholar of Endocrine Soc, with Dr Hugh Davson, dept phys, U Coll, London, 1960-61; dir, div med, Mt Sinai Hosp, LA, Cal, 1961-64; visiting prof: Beilinson Hosp, Tel Aviv U Med Sch, 1968; Heb U, Hadassah Med Sch, Jerusalem, 1968; U Queensland, Austr, 1966. Lt, US Army MC, 1951-53. Mem: Amer Fed for Clinical Research; AMA; Amer Phys Soc; Amer Soc for Clinical Inves; Diabetes Assn of S Cal; Endocrine Soc; LA Co Med Assn; LA Soc Internal Med; Med Research Assn of Cal; bd dirs, Friends Tel Aviv U; Sigma Xi; W Soc for Clinical Research; Alpha Omega Alpha; Assn Amer Phys; W Assn Phys; cons, VA Cen, Wadsworth; mem: med adv bd, council on circulation, AHA; fmr mem, clinical card research study comm; sci adv council, S Cal Kidney Found; bd dirs, U Med Research Found; panel on nephrology of the registry of adverse reactions, AMA; UCLA Med Adv Comm; UCLA Educ Policy and Curriculum Comm; cons, kidney disease control prog, and artificial kidney, chronic uremia prog, NIH. Author: Reinhold Encyclopedia of Biochemistry, 1966; chaps in: A Decade With Diuril Chlorothiazide, 1968; The Biology of Pyelonephritis, 1960; The Parathyroids, 1961; Adrenal Corticosteroids in Clinical Practice, 1962; asso ed, Nephron, since 1963; mem, ed bd: Jour of Clinical Inves, 1958-65; Jour of Lab and Clinical Med, since 1958; co-ed, Disorders of Fluid and Electrolyte

Metabolism; contbr numerous articles to profsl publs. Hobbies: cycling, running. Home: 932 Hilts Ave, Los Angeles, Cal. Office: 8720 Beverly Blvd, Los Angeles, Cal.

KLEIGER, Barnard, US, orthopedic surg; b. Bklyn, NY, Nov 21, 1911; s. Jacob and Rebecca (Sobel); BS, U of Mich, 1932, MD, 1936; m. Estelle Fox, Dec 10, 1939; c: Miriam, Richard. Att surg, Hosp for Jt Diseases, since 1957, on staff since 1947, chmn: med adv bd, since 1967; hosp utilization comm, since 1962; clinical prof, Mt Sinai Sch of Med since 1967; visiting lectr, Albert Einstein Coll of Med, since 1966; asso surg, VA Hosp, Bklyn, 1950-59. Capt, US Army, 1942-44, maj, 1944-46. Med coord, jt prog, NYC Bd Educ, since 1959; mem: NY State Conf on Problems of Aging, 1955; U Mich Alumni Assn; Amer Acad Orthopedic Surg; Amer Coll Surg; NY Acad Med; AAAS; NY Co Med Soc; AMA; Intl Soc Orthopedic Surg and Traumatology; Men's Club of Free Syn of Westchester. Contbr to profsl jours. Home: 21 Forster Ave, Mt Vernon, NY. Office: 1150 Fifth Ave, New York, NY.

KLEIMAN, Alfred H, US, attorney; b. London, Eng, Feb 13, 1924; s. David and Esther (Blasenstein); in US since 1940; LLB, Columbia, 1947; BA, NYU, 1950; m. Edith Eisenberg, Apr 17, 1955; c: Shelley, Laura. Surrogate, NY Co, since 1967; pvt law firm, 1947-54; asst corp counsel, NYC, 1954-63; law secy to Justice Samuel Silverman, NY Supr Court, 1963-66. US Army, 1943-44. Delg, NY State Biannual Dem Convs, 1954-66; pres: 7th Zionist Dist, ZOA, 1951-52; J Cen Youth Club, 1942-43; natl vice pres, Natl Assn Mens Clubs, Yeshiva U, since 1961; chmn: Natl Young Zionist Comm since 1953; Manhattan Zionist Youth Comm, 1950-51; Dem Co Comm, 5th Assembly Dist, since 1961; vice chmn, Forum Comm, NY Co Lawyers Assn, since 1968; W Side Comm for Rev of McCarran Immigration Act, 1953-55; secy: NY Comm for Fair Immigration Policy since 1956; lawyers comm, UJA since 1958; mem: Fed Bar Assn; B'nai B'rith; NYU, Columbia Alumni Assns; W Park Council Rel Insts; John Carpenter Assn, Eng; fmr mem: Natl Admn Comm, ZOA; Vets Collegiate Assn; gov council, J Culture Found; bd, W Side Comty Cen; Comm to Cooperate with Jud Conf; club, NY Young Dem. Recipient: Man of Year award, 1966. Home: 515 West End Ave, New York, NY. Office: Hall of Records, New York, NY.

KLEIMAN, Joseph, US, business exec; b. Grand Rapids, Mich, Oct 1, 1919; s. Jacob and Bessie (Targowitch); BSEngr, MSEngr, U Mich, Ann Arbor, 1942; m. Shirley Present, Aug 30, 1942; c: Neil, Alan, Jay. Sr vice-pres, Corporate Devl, Whittaker Corp since 1967, various corp positions, 1958-67; asst to pres, Reeves Instrument Corp, 1946-51; vice-pres, gen mgr, Belock Instrument Corp, 1957-58. Lt, USN, 1942-46. Vice-pres, Amer Technion Soc; mem, bd trustees, UAHC; fmr, found pres, Stephen Wise Temple. Home: 11240 Chalon Rd, Los Angeles, Cal. Office: 9229 Sunset Blvd, Los Angeles, Cal.

KLEIN, Abraham, Isr, physician; b. Maineshti, Bacau, Rum, Nov 16, 1907; s. Haim and Frida (Schneider); in Isr since 1948; MD, U Bucharest Med Sch, 1936; m. Paula Nedler, 1936; c: Zmira Gottesman, Lavi. Phys, Kupat Cholim, since 1948. Trans, books, stories and poetry into Rum, Heb. Hobbies: poetry, painting caricatures. Home: 22 Hess St, Haifa, Isr.

KLEIN, Albert J, US, attorney, educator; b. Baltimore, Md, Aug 17, 1908; s. David and Dora (Bloom); att Temple U, 1927-30; LLB, Rutgers U, 1934; m. Jennie Kavitsky, Apr 2, 1933; c: Deborah Davis, James. Pvt law practice since 1935; asso prof, law, Rutgers U, since 1941; Munic Court Judge, Cherry Hill Township, NJ, since 1961; govt appeal agt, draft bd, Camden, WWII; enforcement atty, Camden area, OPA, 1947-49. Mem: natl council, Jt Defense Appeal; bd trustees: Camden Co Comty Chest; Civil Defense for NJ; bd govs, Camden Co Bar Assn, pres, 1969-70; Amer, NJ, Camden, Bar Assns; ZOA; Beth Isr Temple, fmr mem; Brith Shalom; Masons; Tau Epsilon Phi; fmr, pres, J Fed Camden Co. Author, Criminal Law in New Jersey, 1953; ed, The Barrister, publ of Camden Co Bar Assn; found, first ed, Voice, bimonthly Anglo-J Comty newspaper, 1943; contbr to law revs and legal publs. Home: 102 St Davids Rd, Colwick, Cherry Hill, NJ. Office: 505 Cooper St, Camden, NJ.

KLEIN, Alfred, US, attorney; b. Woloshin, Russ, Sep 28, 1887; s. Louis and Rachel (Berman); in US since 1898; LLB, Natl U, Wash, DC, 1924; m. Pearl Bellman, Oct 22, 1915 (decd). Pvt practice since 1952; mgn ed, Washington Life in collaboration with Reuben Fink, 1910-11; acctnt, USN and Treasury Depts, 1912-1919; Wash corresp, The Day, 1916-30; gen council, Civil Service Commn, 1943—51; mem, bd, appeals and rev, 1930-43. Club, Fed, Wash, DC. Home: 3636 16 St, NW, Washington, DC.

KLEIN, Arthur, US, newspaper ed; b. Phila, Pa, June 27, 1934; s. Philip and Esther (Moyerman); AB, Haverford Coll, 1955; MS, U of Pa, 1958; m. Marilyn Burnett, Mar 12, 1961; c: Joshua, Alexander, Rebecca, Judith. Ed, Philadelphia J Times, since 1958. US Army res. Pres, Phila Jr C of C, 1961-62; secy, World Affairs Council of Phila, 1962-64; dir, Jr Chamber Intl, 1960-61; secy, Temple Beth Zion-Beth Isr, since 1965; mem: Pa Soc Newspaper Eds; B'rith Sholom; Pannonia Beneficial Assn; Masons; Sigma Delta Chi; Phi Delta Kappa; Phila Art Alliance, treas since 1967; Navy League of US. Home: 2023 Pine St, Philadelphia, Pa. Office: 1530 Spruce St, Philadelphia, Pa.

KLEIN, Charles, US, jurist; b. Atlantic City, NJ, Sept 16, 1900; s. Samuel and Esther (Grun); LLB, Temple U, 1921, LLD, 1949; att, Villanova U, 1921-22; hon degrees: LLD, Franklin and Marshall Coll, 1959; LHD, Dickinson Coll, 1941; JD, St Joseph's Coll, 1961; DCL, Bucknell U, 1963; LLD, U of Pa, 1967; LLD, LaSalle Coll, 1968; m. Rosalie Benson, 1933; c: Richard. Presiding judge, Orphans' Court, Phila, since 1952, judge since 1934; special counsel, Pa Dept of Banking, 1927-31; counsel: Gov Pinchot, Pub Service Commn Inves, 1932; Jt Legislative Commn Inves Milk Ind, Pa, 1933; spec dep attorney gen, 1931-34; spec asst, OPA, 1942; spec econ adv, Rep of Cuba, 1943. Pres, J Hosp, 1948-52; vice-pres: Albert Einstein Med Cen, 1952; J Exponent, 1961; chmn of bd, Temple U, since 1960; hon dir, J Family Service; mem, bd dirs: Conwell Sch of Theol; Allied J Appeal; Fed of J Charities; HIAS; mem, UF. Contbr to legal mags. Recipient: Temple U Award, outstanding grad, 1943; B'nai B'rith Award, 1952; Amer Legion, Clair post, 1952. Clubs: Midday; Sociolegal; Caveat. Home: 6408 Overbrook Ave, Philadelphia, Pa. Office: 542 City Hall, Philadelphia, Pa.

KLEIN, Claude, Isr, educator; b. Dijon, Fr, Nov 16, 1939; s. Chaskel and Cecile (Hechel); in Isr since 1968; att, U Strasbourg, Fr, 1957-60; Dr, Law Fac, 1965; m. Siva Lieblich, Mar 27, 1960; c: Arielle, Neomie. Sr lectr, Law Fac, Heb U, Jerusalem, since 1968; charge de cours, Strasbourg, 1966-68. Author: La Police du Domaine Public, 1966; La Republique de Weimar, 1968. Home: San Simon 3, Jerusalem, Isr. Office: Heb U, Jerusalem, Isr.

KLEIN, David Ballin, US, psychologist, educator; b. NYC, Apr 15, 1897; s. Philip and Julia (Hirsch); BA, CCNY, 1918; MA, Columbia, 1921, PhD, 1930; m. Rose Schaffer, Sep 13, 1923 (decd); c: Grace, Philip, Stephen. Prof em, psych, U of S Cal, since 1960, on fac since 1948; prof, psych, U Tex, 1923-47. F: Amer Psych Assn; AAAS; Social Sci Research Council, 1930-31; mem: Sigma Xi; AAUP; fmr: pres, S Cal Psych Assn; commn, Natl Hillel. Author: Psychology: Its Facts and Principles, 1926; General Psychology, 1936; Mental Hygiene, 1944, rev, 1956; Abnormal Psychology, 1951; A History of Scientific Psychology: Its Origins and Philosophic Background, 1969; contbr to Ency Britannica. Home: 11901 Sunset Blvd, Los Angeles, Cal.

KLEIN, Edward, US, business exec; b. Duquesne, Pa, Oct 1, 1901; s. Samuel and Sally (Friedman); m. Stella Fink, Feb 28, 1935; c: Dorothy, Robert. Ret; sr vice-pres, Mogul, Williams & Saylor, advt agcy, 1956-65; exec vice-pres, partner: Charles M Storm Inc, 1929-48; Storm & Klein, 1948-56. Club: Briar Hall Golf and Country. Hobby, theater. Home: 75 Central Park W, New York, NY.

KLEIN, Edward E, US, rabbi; b. Newark, NJ, May 25, 1913; s. Benjamin and Elsa (Elkan); BA, NYU, 1934; MHL, ordained rabbi, HUC-JIR, 1940, DD, 1965; m. Ruth Strauss, Sep 11, 1941; c: Stephen, Barbara. Rabbi, Stephen Wise Free Syn, since 1949; instr, educ, Heb Union Sch of Educ since 1945; visiting lectr, homiletics, HUC-JIR, since 1966. Pres, Lincoln Sq Comty Council; f, Natl Council on Rel in Higher Educ; mem: Mayor's Adv Comm on Higher Educ; CCAR; Fair Housing Practices Panel; Phi Beta Kappa. Home: 240 W 98 St, New York, NY. Study: 30 W 68 St, New York, NY.

KLEIN, Elias L, US, physicist; b. Wilno, Pol, Jan 11, 1888; s. Menachem and Tauba (Slotsky); in US since 1902; BS,

Valparaiso U, 1911, BCE, 1912; PhD, Yale U, 1921; m. Bertha Rosenman, June 28, 1924; c: Marcia, David. Cons, Goddard Space Flight Cen, NASA, Wash, DC; instr, physics, Valparaiso U, 1912-17; teaching asst, Yale U, 1917-21; instr, U Sask, Can, 1921-22; research, U Chgo, 1922; asst prof, Lehigh U, 1922-25, asso prof, 1925-27; physicist, Naval Research Lab, Wash, DC, 1927-59. F: Amer Phys Soc; Amer Accoustical Soc; Amer Geophys Union; hon f, Inst Environmental Sci, 1962. Recipient: dist civilian service award, USN, 1945. Home: 4501 Connecticut Ave, Washington, NW, DC.

KLEIN, Esther, US, publisher; b. Phila, Pa, Nov 3, 1907; d. Louis and Rebecca (Feldman) Moyerman; BS, Temple U, 1929; Cert, U London, 1954; m. Philip Klein, Apr 26, 1930; c: Arthur, Karen Mannes. Publisher, Phila J Times, since 1953; reporter, Atlantic City Times, 1927; feature writer: Phila Public Ledger, 1928-29; Phila Evening Bull, 1932; Phila Record, 1933; PR counsellor, Phila communal orgs and hosps; ed, Art Alliance Bull, 1945-49; radio commentator, WPEN, 1949-53. Pres, J Times Inst, since 1955; vice-pres, Conf J Women's Orgs, since 1960; chmn, Isr Loan Exhb from Phila Collectors Intl House; mem: Pa Newspaper Publishers Assn; Bryn Mawr Art Cen; ORT; Hadassah; Council J Women; Betty Bacharach Home; Alumni, Temple U; Phila HS for Girls; dir, 51st Kosher Cooking Sch, Phila J Times Inst; fmr: org: women's auxiliary, n div, Phila Gen Hosp; Blockley div, 1957; Rittenhouse Sq Women's comm for Phila Orch; 1st workshop, adult residential educ for Adult Educ Assn of US; co-found, Long Beach Found for Arts and Scis. Author: A Guidebook to Jewish Philadelphia; International House Celebrity Cookbook. Recipient awards: City of Hope, 1961; Pa ladies auxiliary, JWV, 1961; one of outstanding 80 grads of Temple U, 80th Anniversary Celebration; Woman of Year, B'nai B'rith. Hobbies: collecting antique jewelry, Wedgewood china, glassware. Home: 1520 Spruce St, Philadelphia, Pa. Office: 1530 Spruce St, Philadelphia, Pa.

KLEIN, Fritz Shalom, Isr, chemist, educator; b. Erfurt, Ger, Jan 4, 1920; s. Ludwig and Elfriede (Braun); in Isr since 1933; MSc, PhD, Heb U, Jerusalem, 1938-47; m. Mussia Rotman, Sep 19, 1949; c: Shelly, Ittai. Research sci, Weizmann Inst, Rehovot, since 1950; asso prof, since 1966; asst, Heb U, Jerusalem, 1947-49; research chem, Min of Agric, 1949-50. Lt, IAF, 1947-48. Mem: Isr Chem Soc; Faraday Soc. Contbr to sci publs. Home: 1 Meonot Wolfson, Rehovot, Isr. Office: Weizmann Inst, Rehovot, Isr.

KLEIN, Georg, Swed, medical researcher, educator; b. Budapest, Hung, July 28, 1925; s. Henrik and Ilona (Engel); in Swed since 1947; att U Budapest, 1945-47; MK, Royal Karolinska Inst Med Sch, Stockholm, 1949, ML, 1950, MD, 1952; DSc, U Chgo, 1968; m. Eva Fischer, Nov 8, 1947; c: Peter, Margareta, Kerstin. Prof, head, Inst for Tumor Biol, Royal Karolinska Inst Med Sch since 1957, fmr research f, asso, asst prof; mem, sci adv bd, Swed Govt; sci bd, Swed Dept of Health and Wfr; fmr: Dunham lectr, Harvard U. Swed Army, 1955; lt, Res MC. Mem: bd trustees, research council, Swed Cancer Soc; fgn hon mem, Amer Acad of Arts and Sci, 1966; sci council, Intl Agcy for Cancer Research, WHO; council for analysis and projection, Amer Cancer Soc; Nobel Comm on Phys and Med. Contbr papers on experimental cancer and cell research. Recipient: Bertha Goldblatt Teplitz Award, co- recipient with wife, 1958; Knight, Royal Swed Order of N Star, 1961; Danish Path Soc Prize, 1967. Hobby: music, piano. Home: Kottlavagen 10, Lidingo, Swed. Office: Royal Karolinska Inst Med Sch, Stockholm, Swed.

KLEIN, Gerald J, US, rabbi; b. Canonburg, Pa, Oct 28, 1921; s. John and Tillie (Popover); BA, Wash and Jefferson Coll, Pa, 1943; MHL, HUC, Cincinnati, 1948; m. Dorothy Penner, Sep 8, 1946; c: Alan, Joyce. Rabbi, Temple Emanu-El, Dallas, since 1952; adv, Hillel, S Methodist U, since 1954; rabbi, Temple Gates of Heaven, Schenectady, NY, 1948-52. Mem: bd, Mh Soc; Amer Cancer Soc; United Cerebral Palsy; J Family Service, all Dallas; CCAR; Rotary; Acad of Rel and Mh. Home: 7017 Chipperton Dr, Dallas, Tex. Study: 8500 Hillcrest Rd, Dallas, Tex.

KLEIN, Harold C, US, gastroenterologist; b. NYC, Sep 29, 1914; s. Isidor and Minnie (Kolbrener); BA, Dartmouth Coll, 1935; MD, cum laude, Georgetown Med Sch, 1940; m. Miriam Simon, July 4, 1938; c: Melanie. Mem staff, Mt Sinai Hosp, since 1940. US Army, 1943-46. Pres, Mt Sinai Med Soc, 1959-60; mem: Amer Coll Gastroenterology; Amer

Gastroscopic Soc. Contbr articles to med publs. Hobbies: wood carving, oil painting. Home: 2957 S Park Blvd, Shaker Heights, O. Office: 2460 Fairmount Blvd, Cleveland, O.

KLEIN, Isaac, US, rabbi; b. Ruthenia, Hung, Sep 5, 1905; s. Samuel and Ella (Hershkovitz); in US since 1921; BA, CCNY, 1931; ordained rabbi, MHL, JTSA, 1934, Hatharat Hora'ah deg in J Law, 1937; MS, Mass State U, 1937; PhD, Harvard U, 1948; m. Henriette Levine, June 26, 1932; c: Hannah Katz, Miriam Shapiro, Ruth Berkowitz. Rabbi, Temple Emanu-El, since 1953; visiting asso prof, J law and practice, JTSA, since 1965; lectr, culture of ME and Medieval J phil, U Buffalo, 1955-60; rabbi, Kadimah Cong, Springfield, Mass, 1934-53. Chaplain, US Army, 1942-46. Prin contrib: helped reorg J comtys destroyed by Gers. Rel adv to High Commn for Ger, 1949-50; pres, RA, 1958-60; mem, natl Beth Din, Conservative rel movement. Author: The Ten Commandments in a Changing World, 1944; Sefer Kinyan, Book XII of the Code of Maimonides, 1951; contbr to Encys Britannica, Judaica; to jours of J law and rel. Recipient: 6 battle stars; Belgian Fourragier Decoration. Home: 268 Norwalk Ave, Buffalo, NY. Study: Temple Shaarey Zedek, Buffalo, NY.

KLEIN, Isidore, US, cartoonist; b. Newark, NJ, Oct 30, 1897; s. Yirma and Michla (Culber); att: Natl Acad Design; Art Students League; Educ Alliance, all NY; Newark Sch of Ind Design; art classes, Paris; m. Ann Rosenberg, 1932; c: Doris Hyman, Barbara Millstein. Motion picture cartoonist, dir for TV, free-lance, animation work, since 1935; animator: Screen Gems, Columbia Pictures; Walt Disney Studios; animator and story man, Terrytoons; story man, Paramount Cartoons; mag cartoonist: New Yorker. Pres: Natl Cartoonist Soc, since 1962; Screen Cartoonists, local 841, 1962-64; chmn, placement service bull, Natl Cartoonists Soc; mem: IATSE. Recipient: citation of merit, Expo 67, Montreal. Hobbies: etching, painting. Home and studio: 48-32 38 St, Long Island City, NY.

KLEIN, Jerome E, US, public relations exec; b. Phila, Pa, June 20, 1917; s. Louis and Jessie (Resnick); AB, Oberlin Coll, 1939; m. Jean Loewy, Oct 5, 1940; c: Robert, Judith. PR, sales promotion dir, Lane Bryant Inc since 1946; reporter, Atlantic City Daily World, 1939-40; publicity writer: Earl Newsom Assos, 1940-41; Gtr NY Fund, 1941-42. US Army, 1942-46. PR dir, bd mem, Temple Sinai, Roslyn, since 1952; bd mem, Educ Alliance, NYC since 1962; comm chmn, PR Soc of Amer since 1961; pres, Amer PR Assn, NY, 1951-56; educ adv comm, Roslyn Schs, 1953-55; Nassau co council, Boy Scouts of Amer, PR chmn, 1956-60; mem: Silver Anvil Awards PR Comm, 1960-63; clubs: Overseas Press; Publicity; Soc Amer Travel Writers. Author: We'll Tell the World, 1958; You are the PR Expert in Your Store, 1960; Dreams for Sale, 1961; Views to Dine By, 1962, 1963; Great Shops of Europe, 1969; Great Hotels and Resorts of Europe, 1969. Recipient: dist service cert, WWII; dist service award, Natl Retail Merchants Assn, 1962. Home: 127 Andover Rd, Roslyn Heights, NY. Office: 465 Fifth Ave, New York, NY.

KLEIN, Joel Tibor, US, rabbi; b. Megyaszo, Zemplen, Hung, Jan 1, 1923; s. Eugene and Serena (Reich), in US since 1957; PhD, U of Sci, Budapest, Hung, 1947; ordained rabbi, Theol Sem, Budapest, 1949; att Coll J Studies, Chgo, 1962-64; m. Anna Berkovits, June 28, 1949; c: Leslie, Judith. Rabbi, Manchester, NH, since 1964; chief rabbi: Baja, Hung, 1948-51; Gyor, Hung, 1951-56; asst rabbi, Cong Beth El, 1957-59; rabbi: Temple Meyer-David, 1959-62; Cong Am Echod, 1962-64. Pres, Comty Concert Assn; mem: B'nai B'rith; ZOA; RA; NY, Chgo, Mass Bd Rabbis. Hobbies: stamp collecting, ceramics, archaeol. Home: 721 Chestnut, Manchester, NH. Study: 678 Pine, Manchester, NH.

KLEIN, Joseph, US, rabbi; b. Toledo, O, Feb 25, 1912; s. Lewis and Laura (Kripke); BA, O State U, 1933; ordained rabbi, MHL, Heb Union Coll, 1939; att grad sch, Dropsie Coll, Pa, 1940-45; m. Rose Schalit, May 25, 1933; c: Benjamin, Judith Aronson, Jonathan. Rabbi: Temple Emanuel, Worcester, Mass, since 1949; Northeast J Comty Cen, Phila, 1939-40; asst rabbi, Cong Keneseth Isr, Phila, 1940-46; Temple Beth Isr, Altoona, Pa, 1946-47; Temple Beth Emeth, Bklyn, NY, 1947-49; dir, instr, J hist, Adult Inst J Studies, Gratz Coll, Phila, 1945-46. Mem: Amer Bd, World Union for Progressive Judaism; bd: ARC; Mass Soc for Prevention of Cruelty to Children; Archaeol Inst of Amer; JWF; J

Family Service; Civic Music Assn, all Worcester; mem: Commonwealth Mass Obscene Lit Control Commn; B'nai B'rith; Amer Technion Soc; Amer Friends Heb U; Natl Assn Temple Educ; Worcester Art Mus; Worcester Natural Hist Soc; Worcester Found for Experimental Biol; J Chautauqua Soc; Mass Bd Rabbis; Worcester J Home for Aged; AJComm; Amer Assn for J Educ; United World Federalists; Amer J Hist Soc; fmr: pres: Worcester dist, ZOA; Phila Bd J Mins; NE region, CCAR, mem, exec bd, prog chmn, conv ed, jour; mem: bd govs, exec, alumni assn, HUC-JIR; pres, Worcester Mins Assn; clubs: Rotary; Mt Pleasant Country. Home: 5 Montvale Rd, Worcester, Mass. Study: 280 May St, Worcester, Mass.

KLEIN, Jozef, Isr, chemist, educator; b. Rzeszow, Pol, May 15, 1916; s. Izak and Dina (Berger); in Isr since 1951; MPh, Jagellon U, Cracow, Pol, 1946; DSc, Sorbonne, Paris, 1949; m. Klara Wolf, May 19, 1948; c: Daniel. Asso prof, organic chem, Heb U, Jerusalem; research f: Imperial Coll, London, 1957; Harvard U, 1960-61. Home: 6 Disraeli St, Jerusalem, Isr. Office: Heb U, Dept of Organic Chem, Jerusalem, Isr.

KLEIN, Julius, US, business exec; b. Phila, Pa, Aug 11, 1900; s. Samuel and Minna (Daniel); m. Eleanor Aarons, Sep 2, 1923; c: Robert, LeRoy, Judy Franken. Bd mem, Caloric Corp, 1967-69, pres, 1951-67, vice pres, 1946-51, firm found by father 1890; mem, adv council, Amer Gas Assn, bd mem, 1957-59; bd mem, GAMA, pres, 1957-58; bd mem: Gas Inc; Silo Inc; Alliance Wall Corp. Pres, mem bd, Albert Einstein Med Cen, Phila; bd mem, exec comm, Phila Fed JAs; mem: Miami Shores CC; clubs: Locust; Jockey, Miami; Philmont Country. Office: Wyncote House, Wyncote, Pa.

KLEIN, Julius, US, army off, public relations counsel, journalist; b. Chgo, Sep 5, 1901; s. Leopold and Regina (Schick); att Sophien Coll, Berlin; grad, Sch Mil Govt, U of Va; m. Helene Holstein, May 11, 1928. Chmn, Julius Klein PR Inc, since 1947; war corresp, ed staff, Hearst newspapers, 1926-33; exec, RKO, Universal Pictures, Hollywood, 1934-39. Field clerk, US Mil Commn, US Army, 1918-19; joined Ill Natl Guard after WW I; col, 1941-46; spec asst to Secy of War, 1946; comm off, 623rd Group and attached troops, Ill Natl Guard; comm gen, 109th anti-aircraft artillery brig, 1948-51; brig-gen line; transferred to US Army Res, 1953, promoted to Maj-Gen, 1955; ret, Maj-Gen, 1961. Made fact-finding missions to Eur for US Sen comms, 1954. Mem: Ill State Armory Bd, since 1954; pres, Natl Shrine to J War Dead, JWV Memorial, since 1967; natl cdr, JWV, 1947-48; hon dir, Heb Theol Coll, Chgo; mem: Chgo Assn Commerce and Ind; Chgo Council Fgn Relations; PR Soc Amer; NAM; Amer Ordnance Assn; Amer Legion; Assn US Army; DAV; Amvets; Masons; clubs: Circumnavigators; Overseas Press; Army and Navy; Chgo Press. Author: Windy City Black Cargo; General Delivery; American Spy. Recipient: Decorated Soldier's Medal for Heroism; Citation for Heroism; Philippine Dist Service Star; Legion of Merit with 2 oak leaf clusters; Fr Legion of Hon; Natl Cdrs citation, Catholic War Vets; award, Amer J Lit Found, 1950; award of hon, Isr Govt; cited by US War Secy Patterson; Admirals: Nimitz, Halsey; Gens: MacArthur, Eisenhower. Home: 1040 Lake Shore Dr, Chicago, Ill. Office: 1 E Wacker Dr, Chicago, Ill.

KLEIN, Louis S, US, certified public acctnt; b. Chgo, Ill, Sep 13, 1908; s. Joseph and Lena (Groveman); CPA, U of State of NY, 1946; m. Syd Bass, June 2, 1934; c: Letty Gordon, Adele Kaplan, Walter. Partner: Klein, Hullett & Beam, CPA's since 1967; Louis S Klein and Max Bloomberg since 1937; pres, dir, Commercial and Financial Corp, since 1961; cons, First Natl Bank of Attalla, since 1954; acctnt, auditor, Federated Purchaser Inc, 1932-35; comptroller, acctnt, Ala Braid and Ribbon Co, C M Offray and Son, 1935-37. Chmn: Gadsden-Anniston Chap, Ala Soc CPA's, 1966-67; Fed J Charities, 1954; fmr: pres: Cong Beth Isr, Gadsden, Ala; Coosa Lodge B'nai B'rith; auditor, Gadsden Concert Assn; treas, Gadsden Art Series; repr, JWB; volunteer counselor, Korean Vets, Etowah Co; mem: C of C; NY State, Ala Socs CPAs; Amer Acctnt Assn; Amer, S Inst Mgmt; club, Gadsden Civitan. Hobbies: music, sports. Home: 102 Cleveland Court, Gadsden, Ala. Office: 269 College St, Gadsden, Ala.

KLEIN, Milton D, US, obstetrician; b. Bklyn, NY, Jan 25, 1908; s. Samuel and Molly (Sacks); AB, George Wash U, 1928, MD, 1932; m. Pauline Rubin, May 8, 1948; c: Ronnie, Edward. Cons, obstet and gyn, Montefiore Morrisania Hosp, NY, since 1964; att, obstet and gyn: Bx Leb Hosp Cen, NY since 1962; Bx Hosp Cen, since 1964; asst clinical prof, Albert Einstein Med Sch, NY, since 1964. US Army MC res. Mem: NYC Coord Council Maternal Mortality and Morbidity; Amer Comm for Maternal and Child Wfr; life, Mil Order of WW's; Mil Surgs Assn; NY Acad Med; Phi Lambda Kappa; f: Amer Coll Surgs; Intl Coll Surgs; Amer Coll Obstet and Gyn; Amer Bd Obstet and Gyn; AMA; NY Gyn Soc; fmr: pres: Bx Gyn and Obstet Soc; Bx chap, Amer Coll Surgs; NY obstet adv comm to commn of health, NY; pres, Hippocrates Med Soc; chmn, Bx div, UJA; maternal wfr comm, Bx Med Soc. Asso ed, Bx Co Med Soc. Recipient: achievement award, George Wash Alumni, 1946; Legion of Merit. Hobbies: music, golf. Home: 1777 Grand Concourse, New York, NY. Office: 1882 Grand Concourse, New York, NY.

KLEIN, Philip, US, educator, social worker; b. Hajdu-Dorogh, Hung, May 18, 1899; s. Bernat and Helen (Kupferstein); in US since 1902; BA, CCNY, 1911; dipl, NY Sch Social Work, 1913; PhD, Columbia U, 1918; m. Alice Campbell, May 19, 1922; c: Wells, Malcolm. Dir, research, prof em, social work, NY Sch of Social Work, since 1954; cons: Paul Baerwald Sch of Social Work, Versailles, Fr, since 1939; Pa Dept Public Wfr, since 1962; fmr: asst secy, Prison Assn of NY, 1913-1918; dir, profsl training, ARC, S div, 1919-20; spec invest, Russell Sage Found, 1921-22; exec secy, Amer Assn Social Workers, 1923-27; dir: social study of Pittsburgh, Allegheny Co, 1934-36; J Natl TB Study, 1937-38; research dir, White House Conf on Children in a Democracy, 1939-40; adv, Isr Min of Social Wfr, UN Tech Asst Admn, 1957-59; dir, Study of Pa Dept Social Wfr, 1962-63. Mem, Amer Assn Social Workers. Author: Prison Methods in NY, 1920; The Burden of Unemployment, 1923; A Social Study of Pittsburgh, 1938; Final Report of White House Conference on Children in a Democracy, 1940; co-author: Social Case Work, 1933; Some Basic Statistics in Social Work, 1933; From Philanthropy to Social Welfare, 1968; contbr to Ency of Soc Sci, social work books and jours. Home: 152 Hillair Circle, White Plains, NY.

KLEIN, Philip, US, business exec, educator; b. Phila, Pa, Dec 20, 1906; s. Sigmund and Rose (Jacoby); BA, U Pa, 1928; DMus, U of London, 1954; hon DHum, Moore Coll; m. Esther Moyerman, Apr 27, 1930; c: Arthur, Karen Mannes. Chmn, bd trustees: Harcum Jr Coll, pres, 1952-63; Intl House of Phila; Pathway Sch; pres, Junto Adult Sch, since 1949, co-dir, 1952; Phila Marina Inc, since 1959; chmn, bd, Philip Klein Advt Agcy, since 1957; treas, WHYY Educ Bc Corp; chmn, Maple Corp; ed, publisher, Phila J Times, 1947-50; delg, US Commn to UNESCO, 1955; official observer, White House Conf on Educ, 1955; State Dept repr, NATO Conf, 1960; pres, US Civil Defense Council, 1959-60, dir, Phila Council, 1955-61; commnr, Dept Public Property, Phila, 1961. US Merchant Marine, 1942-45. Fmr: natl pres, Adult Educ Assn; vice-pres: Amer-Korean Found, Phila, since 1958; Buten Mus of Wedgwood, since 1957; Muscular Dystrophy Assn, Phila br, 1954; Pa Wfr Forum, 1957-58; vice-chmn, Phila City Planning Commn, since 1958; mem: exec comm: Mary Bailey Found, since 1952; World Affairs Council, 1959-61; hon chmn, bd trustees, Long Beach I Found for Arts and Sci, since 1955; gov, Heart Assn, SE Pa, 1954; mem: Alliance Francaise; Amer-It Soc; Amer Assn Sch Admnrs; Amer Coll PR Assn; Amer Soc Public Admns; Eng-Speaking Union; Mus Council, Phila; Natl Planning Assn; club: Contemporary, Phila, vice-pres, 1950-58. Mem: ed bd, J Coll Jour, 1954-62; chmn, publ comm, Handbook of Adult Education, 1958; contbr to educ and civil defense publs. Recipient: meritorious service award, ARC, 1958; Pres citation, Adult Educ of US, 1959; meritorious service award, Off of Civil and Defense Mobilization, 1960; decoration, Brazilian Govt. Home: 1520 Spruce St, Philadelphia, Pa.

KLEIN, Richard Benson, US, attorney; b. Phila, Pa, Dec 24, 1939; s. Charles and Rosalie (Benson); BA, magna cum laude, Amherst Coll, 1961; LLB, with hon, Harvard Law Sch, 1964; m. Jacqueline Grant, Aug 16, 1964; c: Peter. Pvt practice since 1965; spec asst, Atty Gen of Pa, since 1969; lectr, estate planning, Pa Bar Inst. Chmn: Phila Rep Policy Comm; Phila Co Bd Examiners; mem: exec comm, Amer-Isr C of C, Phila Br; Phi Beta Kappa; club: Harvard, Phila. Hobby: music. Home: 1907 Wynnefield Terr, Philadelphia, Pa. Office: 420 Six Penn Cen, Philadelphia, Pa.

KLEIN, Robert H, US, business exec; b. Chgo, Ill, May 14, 1908; s. Henry and Bertha (Stein); PhB, U Chgo, 1929; m. Eleonora Laderchi, Aug 22, 1945; c: Paul, Sandra, Henry, Roberta (decd), Katherine. Dir, supply div, JDC, NY, 1946-47;

cons, Mental Hosp Service, Amer Psycht Assn, Wash, DC, 1953-59; bd mem: JDC; Menniger Found, Topeka, Kan; Stanford U Hosp; adv council, SF Psychan Inst; bd mem, Michael Reese Hosp, 1948-59; pres, div fund, distribution fund, Catholic Interracial Council, 1955-59; co-chmn, United Bldg Fund, J Fed, 1957-58, Chgo. Recipient: Cavalier of the Crown, It, 1945. Home: 100 La Sandra Way, Portola Valley, Cal. Office: 750 Welch Rd, Palo Alto, Cal.

KLEIN, Serge, US, architect; b. St Petersburg, Russ, Oct 13, 1914; s. Alexander and Elizabeth (Kaftal); in US since 1939; Dipl, Ecole Speciale d'Architecture, Paris, 1938; Dipl, Master Town Planning, Paris U, 1946; BArch, Columbia U Sch Architecture, 1947; m. Helen Feld, Feb 10, 1946; c: Dorothy, Laura. Pvt practice since 1949; partner, Samuel S Schiffer, 1949-53; with: Clarence S Stein, 1940-41; Shreve, Lamb and Harmon, 1946-47; Kelly and Gruzen, 1948-49; instr, architecture, Cooper Union, NYC, 1957-60. US Army, 1942-44. Mem: Amer Inst Architects; NY Soc Architects; Mayor's Panel of Architects, NYC. Contbr to profsl jours. Recipient: prize, NY State Housing competition for garden apartments, 1948. Home: 616 W 232 St, Riverdale, NY. Office: 157 W 57 St, New York, NY.

KLEIN, Theodore Ulmer, US, business exec; b. Cleveland, O, Dec 15, 1926; s. Joseph and Martha (Ulmer); BS, W Reserve U, Cleveland, O, 1948; m. Carole Honig, July 4, 1955; c: William, Emily. Pres: Ted Klein & Co, since 1969; Med Marketing & Distaff Inc, since 1969; vice-pres, dir, Paul Klemtner, 1955-69; pres, Comtact Corp, 1966-69. Pvt, US Army, 1945. Chmn, W Orange Council for Social Action; dir, Child Guidance and Family Service Agcy of the Oranges; mem: Amer Med Writers Assn, NY chap; Natl Assn Sci Writers. Author, The Father's Book, 1968; co-author, Nine Months To Go, 1961. Recipient, Best Book-of-the-Year, Natl Father's Day Comm, 1968. Home: 145 Forest Hill Rd, W Orange, NJ. Office: 477 Madison Ave, New York, NY.

KLEIN, Walter L, US, business exec; b. Chgo, Ill, Aug 12, 1905; s. Joseph and Lena (Goldberger); att Armour Inst Tech, 1920-24; Northwestern U, 1924-27; m. Ann Clamage, June 15, 1927; c: Gerald, Janet Glick. Chmn of bd, Hollanderizing-Kleinzway, pres since 1956; fmr: account exec, Walston and Co, Inves; pres: Kleinzway Inc, 1932-56; Waltco Products, 1946-56. Bd of trustees, life mem, S Shore Temple, pres, 1954-57; trustee, pension and wfr fund, Chgo Fur Cleaners Union; club: Idlewild Country. Author: Fur Service Handbook, 1945. Hobbies: painting, golf. Home: 4800 Chicago Beach Dr, Chicago, Ill. Office: 201 S LaSalle St, Chicago, Ill.

KLEIN, Zvi, Isr, rabbi, historian; b. Tiszafuered, Hung, 1912; s. Judah and Chaya; in Isr since 1940; MA, Heb U, Jerusalem, 1944; m. Sara Rotenberg; c: Pagit, Esther, Ayalah. Chief sup, Rel Educ, Min for Rel Affairs, Jerusalem, since 1948; prin, primary sch: Petah Tikva, 1942-45; Rishon L'Zion, 1945-48. Contbr articles to profsl publs. Home: 4 Moriya St, Jerusalem, Isr. Office: 30 Yaffo St, Jerusalem, Isr.

KLEINER, Julius M, US, business exec; b. Stolnoye, Russ, Oct 11, 1892; s. Meyer and Rebecca (Halperin); in US since 1916; BS, U Kiev, 1915; m. Emma Weinberger, Aug 1, 1919; c: Walter, Eugene. Pres: Nampa Creamery Co, Idaho; Marion Creamery and Poultry, Salem, Ore; Columbia Produce, Portland, Ore; Amer Poultry and Provision, San Diego, Cal, 1934; Ont Creamery and Poultry, Ont, Ore; owner, operator, JMK Farms, Meridian, Idaho. Chmn: UJA; ADL; vice-chmn, regional exec comm, Boy Scouts of Amer; mem: Masons; Elks; Shriners; B'nai B'rith, all Nampa and Boise, Idaho. Home: 80 Ord Blvd, Nampa, Idaho. Office: 620-624 First St, Nampa, Idaho.

KLEINER, Sanford, US, personnel exec; b. Easton, Pa, May 1, 1926; s. Joseph and Norma (Lott); BBA, CCNY, 1950; MBA, NYU, 1956; m. Sunya Swersky, Jan 25, 1953; c: Jan, Susan. Vice-pres, Manpower Planning & Devl, Chemical Bank, since 1969, personnel off, 1953-64, asst vice-pres, personnel, 1964-66, vice-pres, training, 1966-69. USN, 1944-46. Mem: bd dirs, Adoptive Parents Comm, Inc; bd trustees, NY chap, Amer Inst Banking; hon, Alumni Assn Amer Inst Banking; Amer Soc for Training and Devl. Author, Careers in Corporate Management, 1969; contbr to jours. Home: 191 E Chester St, Valley Stream, NY. Office: 20 Pine St, New York, NY.

KLEINFELD, Louis, US, physician; b. NYC, July 21, 1896; s. Isaac and Anna (Rothfeld); att CCNY, 1914-16; MD,

Columbia U, 1920; m. Frances Steinhardt, Mar 8, 1946. Cons otolaryngologist: Bx Hosp; Hosp for Jt Diseases; asso att, Mt Sinai Hosp; otologist, Lexington Sch for Deaf; lectr: Columbia U; Hunter Coll. Mem: AMA; NY Acad Med; AAAS; AAUP; Amer Coll Surgs; Intl Coll Surgs; Amer Speech and Hearing Assn; Amer Bd Otolaryngology; Amer Acad Ophthal and Otolaryngology. Contbr numerous articles to med jours. Home: 945 Fifth Ave, New York, NY. Office: 100 E 74 St, New York, NY.

KLEINHOLZ, Frank, US, artist, attorney; b. Bklyn, NY, Feb 17, 1901; s. Herman and Bessie (Saltzman); LLB, Fordham Law Sch, NYC, 1921; hon, DFA, Colby Coll, Waterville, Me, 1968; m. Leah Schwartz, 1928 (decd); m. 2nd, Lidia Brestovan, Apr 25, 1946; c: Lisa, Marco, Anna. Artist since 1946; pvt law practice, 1924-35; sr atty, NY State Ins Fund, 1936-46; art tchr: Bklyn Mus Art Sch, 1944-45; Hofstra Coll, 1953-54; one-man shows: NY Gals, Assn Amer Artists, 1943; Phillips Memorial Gal, 1943; traveling exhb, Amer Fed of Arts, Port Wash Public Libr, 1959; perm collections: Metrop Mus of Art; Bklyn Mus; Newark Mus; Phillips Memorial Gal; Ency Britannica Collection; Mus Modern Art; Tel Aviv Mus; Ala Poly Inst; U Okla; Brandeis U; pvt collections: Jose Ferrer, NYC; Alfred Hitchcock, Cal. Mem: Artist Equity Assn. Author: Frank Kleinholz, A Self Portrait, 1964. Recipient: purchase award, for Back Street, Metrop Mus Art, 1943; 3rd prize, prints, Syracuse State Fair, 1951; 1st prize, painting, Manhasset Art Annual, 1952. Home and studio: 10280 SW 164 St, Miami, Fla.

KLEINMAN, Abraham M, US, physician, hospital admnr; b. NYC, May 30, 1907; s. Sam and Sadie (Reich); BS, CCNY, 1926; MD, U of Md, 1930; m. Lillian Rabinowitz, June 24, 1924; c: Leonard, Sylvia. Dir, VA Hosp, Bx; prof, admn med, Mt Sinai Sch of Med, NYC; lectr, public health and admn med, Columbia U; asso att med, Cumberland Hosp, 1939-42; chief med services, Hallaran Army Gen Hosp, 1944-46; dir, profsl services, VA Hosp, Bklyn, 1949-57; clinical asso prof med, SUNY Downstate Med Cen, 1950-57. Dipl, Amer Bd Internal Med; FACP; f, NY Acad Med; mem: NY Acad Scis; Harvey Soc; AMA; IMA; Kingsbridge Hgts J Cen; Amer Friends Heb U; ZOA. Contbr to profsl jours on infection and nutrition. Home and office: 130 W Kingsbridge Rd, Bronx, NY.

KLEITMAN, Nathaniel, US, physiologist, educator; b. Kishinev, Russ, Apr 26, 1895; s. Nathaniel and Pessia (Galanter); in US since 1915; BS, CCNY, 1919; AM, Columbia U, 1920; PhD, U Chgo, 1923; NRC f: U of Utrecht, U of Paris, U of Chgo, 1923-24; m. Paulena Schweitzer, June 14, 1927; c: Hortense Snower, Esther. Ret, prof, phys, U of Chgo, 1950-60, on fac since 1922; tchr, chem, CCNY, 1919-20; instr, phys pharm, U of Ga, 1920-22. Hon mem, Soc of Biol Rhythm; mem: Amer Phys Soc; Sigma Xi; Phi Beta Kappa. Recipient: Harris Alumni Medal, CCNY, 1947; dist service award, Salmon Comm on Psych and Mental Hygiene, NY Acad of Med, 1966. Home: 222 Washington Ave, Santa Monica, Cal.

KLEMENTYNOVSKI, Zvi, Isr, attorney; b. Bialystok, Pol, Aug 3, 1904; s. David and Deborah (Tykocki); in Isr since 1941; MJ, U of Vilna, 1928; m. Frieda Schmukler, 1943; m. 2nd, Eileene Goodwin, c: Phillip, Adiv. I/c, hospitalization, Tel Aviv Munic, since 1969; pvt practice since 1943; legal adv, Fed Builders and Contractors in Isr, since 1947; fmr: pvt practice, Bialystok, 1933-39; dep mayor, Tel Aviv Munic Council, 1965-67. Mem: exec, Independent Lib Party of Isr; hon secy, United Hias Service; judge advocate, World Zionist Movement; Isr Bar Assn; dep advocate, WZC; fmr: mem, cen comm, Zionist Org, Pol; chmn, J Comty; munic council, both Bialystok. Home: 208 Ben Yehuda St, Tel Aviv, Isr. Office: Tel Aviv Municipality, Kikar Malchei Israel, Tel Aviv, Isr.

KLEMPERER, Edith, US, psychiatrist; b. Vienna, Aus, Aug 9, 1898; d. Charles and Marianne (Deutsch); in US since 1938; MD, U of Vienna, 1923. Pvt practice since 1940; fmr: intern, res, research asst, Inst for Psycht and Neur, Vienna, 1924-38; clinical asst, mental hygiene clinic, Rothschild Hosp, Vienna, 1936-37; Mt Sinai Hosp, NYC, 1941-42; res, Hillside Hosp, Bellerose, 1942-43; sr alienist, Bellevue Hosp, NY, 1943-46; sr psycht, Morrisania Hosp, Bx, 1952-58; cons: Workmen's Compensation Bd; Dept of Wfr, NYC; Dept of Social Wfr, State of NY; Morton Prime Clinic for Hypnotherapy; sup psycht, Inst for Research in Hypnosis. F: Amer Psycht Assn; Soc for Clinical and Experimental Hypnosis; Amer Soc of

Clinical Hypnosis; life f: Amer Soc of Clinical Hypnosis; Educ and Research Found; dipl, Bd of Med Hypnosis; mem: Acad of Med; Soc for Neur and Psycht, both Vienna; Vienna Specialists' Soc; AMA; State, Co Med Socs; Rudolf Virchow Soc; Med Virchow Circle; NY Soc for Clinical Psycht; NYC Soc for Alcoholism. Author: Past Ego States Emerging in Hypnoanalysis; contbr to profsl jours. Home and office: 315 E 77 St, New York, NY.

KLEMPERER, Emanuel, Isr, master mariner; b. Rodewisch, Ger, Feb 15, 1926; s. Josef and Chawa (Strupp); in Isr since 1933; att Nautical Sch, Haifa; extra master deg, U Southampton, Eng, 1955; att Technion, Haifa; m. Tirza Luncz, Mar 5, 1957; c: Ayala, Chava. Shipping comm, Isr Min of Transp, since 1968; UN Maritime Expert in Nigeria, 1967-68; dir, Isr Marine Training Cen, 1962-68; ships' capt, Isr Zim Lines, 1961-62; sr lectr, Isr Nautical Coll, 1956-61; found, dir, Isr Nautical Training Cen; initiator of extra masters course at Technion. Haganah; lt cdr, Isr Navy. Mem: Inst of Navigation; Rotary Intl. Author: Compass Adjusting, 1965; Nautical Astronomy, 1969. Home: 29 Levontine St, Haifa, Isr. Office: 39 Haatzmaut Rd, Haifa, Isr.

KLENICKI, Leon, Arg, rabbi; b. Buenos Aires, Sep 7, 1930; s. Isaias and Inda (Kuzewicka); PhB, U Cincinnati, 1963; BHL, 1965, MHL, hon, hist, HUC, Cincinnati, ordained rabbi, 1967; m. Ana Dimsitz, Aug 6, 1959; c: Ruth, Daniel, Myriam. Dir, Latin Amer off, World Union for Progressive Judaism, since 1967; libr dir, Sociedad Hebraica Argentina, 1957-59. Rel adv, AJComm, Latin Amer Off; J adv, Council of J and Chrs, Buenos Aires. Mem, CCAR. Contbr articles to various mags. Spec interests, S Amer art, Indian pottery. Home: Ciudad de la Paz 519, Primer Piso, Buenos Aires, Arg. Study: Ciudad de la Paz 547, Primer Piso, Buenos Aires, Arg.

KLEPFISZ, Heszel, Panama, educator, rabbi, author; b. Zyrardow, Pol, Mar 1, 1910; s. Zalman and Bracha (Friedman); in Panama since 1961; ordained rabbi, rabb sem, Warsaw, 1928; PhD, U Warsaw, 1934; DL, U Zurich, 1936; div; c: Bracha, Shulamit. Prin, Albert Einstein Inst, rabbi, Ashkenazi comty, since 1961; regent, U Panama, since 1968, prof, 1963-66; ed jours, Pol, Fr, 1931-40; lectr: Heb Coll, Glasgow, Scotland, 1950-52; Coll J Studies and Tchrs Sem, Miami, Fla, 1958-60; prin, Heb Sch, San Jose, Costa Rica, 1953-58. Sr J Chaplain, Pol Forces on W Front, 1940-49. Author: Judisher Anteil in Ofshtand Fun 1831, 1934; Die Prager Shechita, 1935; Maimonides, 1936; Kobieta Zydowska, 1937; Text Books for Pol and J Schs in Pol, 1938; Un Año en el Instituto Alberto Einstein, 1962; Realidad y Vision, 1965; Baal Shem Tov, 1967; Rabi Menajem Zemba, 1969; contbr to periodicals and mags. Hon mem, Asocicion Judeo-Cristiana, San José, Costa Rica; mem, Natl Commn UNESCO, Panama. Recipient: Medal of Liberation, for special merits, City of Ghent, Belgium, 1944; mil distinctions, Pol, Fr, Brit Armies, WWII; distinction for work as regent, U Panama, 1968. Home: Apartado Postal 7085, Panama, Panama.

KLIBANOFF, Morris, US, business exec; b. Jackson, Tenn, Jan 29, 1917; s. Hyman and Lillie (Aizenshtat); BS, Northwestern U, 1938; m. Roslyn Bookholtz, Mar 3, 1940; c: Judy Ingle, Ruth, Hank, Deborah, Daniel. Owner, mgr: The Bootery; Kaye's, both Florence, Ala, since 1938. Lt, US Army, 1946. Chmn, Florence Planning Comm; natl repr, Boy Scouts of Amer; pres: Temple B'nai Isr; B'nai B'rith Lodge; Jr C of C, all Florence, Ala; vice pres, Federated J Charities; mem: bd dirs: Salvation Army; Lauderdale Expansion Comm; Natl Shoe Retailers Assn; 210, shoemen's philanthropic org; Downtown Florence Unlimited; appd, Comty Adv Comm; Lauderdale Bi-racial Comm; fmr: mem bd dirs: C of C; ARC; chmn, Selective Service Bd 39; clubs: Turtle Point Golf and Country; Exch, fmr pres. Recipient, Silver Beaver, Boy Scouts of Amer, 1969. Hobbies: golf, water sports. Home: 733 Pleasant Dr, Florence, Ala. Office: 111 N Court, Florence, Ala.

KLIER, Avraham, Isr, chemical engr; b. Radautz, Aus, July 8, 1903; s. Israel and Toni (Rosenstreich); in Isr since 1934; ChemE, U Toulouse, Fr; m. Neimah Halbrecht; c: Shimon. Gen Mgr, partner, Argaman Textile Dye Works Ltd, since 1934. Prin contrib, devl of Isr textile ind, export of textiles. Mem bd dir, trustees, several econ and educ insts. Home: 41 Josef Zvi St, Ramat Gan, Isr. Office: Argaman Textile Dye Works Ltd, Bnei Brak, Isr.

KLINE, Bert F, US, editor; b. New Castle, Pa, Dec 6, 1915; s. Bertram and Mignon (Brash); att Duquesne U, 1934-35; U Pittsburgh, 1935-36; m. Helen Schein, Oct 13, 1940; c: Richard, Linda, Kathy. Mgn ed, Baltimore J Times since 1950; reporter, United Press Assn, 1936-38; sports ed, Homestead Pa Messenger, 1938-40; ed, Squirrel Hill News, 1940-43, advt mgr, 1946-49; bus mgr, Homestead Pa Dist Sun, 1949-50. USAAF, 1943-46. Mem, bd: Har Sinai Cong, mem, Brotherhood bd, 1956-59; Bd J Educ since 1960. Recipient, Pres Group Citation. Home: 3433 Philips Dr, Baltimore, Md. Office: 1800 N Charles St, Baltimore, Md.

KLINE, Nathan S, US, psychiatrist, researcher; b. Phila, Pa, Mar 22, 1916; s. Ignatz and Florence (Schellenberg); BA, hon, Swarthmore Coll, 1938; MD, NYU Coll of Med, 1943; MA, psych, Clark U, 1951; m. Margot Hess, June 29, 1942; c: Marna Ellen. Dir: research, Rockland State Hosp, Orangeburg, NY, since 1952; psycht services, Bergen Pines Co Hosp, NJ, since 1963; asst clinical prof, psycht, Columbia U Coll Phys and Surgs, since 1957, research asso, 1955-57, with dept, neur, 1948-55; child psycht, Union Co Mental Hygiene Soc, NJ, 1946-50; asso, Columbia Greystone, 1947-50; asso, NY State Hosp, Mass, 1950-52. USPHS, 1944-46; res off, 1946-50. Pres, Intl Comm Against Mental Illness since 1961; f: Royal Soc of Med, Eng; NY Acad Scis; NY Acad Med; AAAS; Amer Psycht Assn, chmn, research comm, 1956-57; FACP; charter f, Amer Coll Neuropsychopharm; dipl, Amer Bd of Psycht and Neur; intl dir, Inst of Social Psycht, U San Marco de Mayor, Lima, Peru; co-found, dir, research, Centre de Psychiatrie et Neurologie, Port-au-Prince, Haiti; mem, adv panel, psychopharm service cent, Natl Inst of Mh, 1957-59; temporary adv, WHO, 1957; mem: Natl Comm Against Mental Illness; asso, World Fed for Mh; Royal Med-Psych Assn; Amer Therapeutic Soc; Natl Health Educ Comm; Manhattan Soc for Mh; Amer Chem Soc; AMA; Med Soc Co of NY; Soc for Experimental Biol and Med; Amer Inst of Aeronautics and Astronautics; Soc for Biol Psycht; Assn for Research in Nervous and Mental Disease; Amer Psych Assn; Sigma Xi; asso, Amer Phil Assn; clubs: Princeton; Circumnavigator's. Contbr ed, Excerpta Medica; adv ed bd: Psychopharmacologia; Intl Jour of Social Psycht; mem, bd, Medico; contbr to sci jours. Recipient: Awards: Page One, sci, Newspaper Guild, NY, 1956; Adolf Meyer, Assn for Improvement of Mh, 1956; citation, Rockland Hosp Guild, 1956; Albert Lasker Award, for achievements in uses of rauwolfia, Amer Public Health Assn, 1957, 1964; Cdr, Order of Toussaint-Louverture; grand off, Legion d'Honneur et Merite, Haiti, 1959; Serenissine Mil Order of St Mary, 1961; Henry Wisner Muller award, Manhattan Soc Mh, 1963; Liberian Humane Order of Afr Redemption, Rep Liberia. Home: 1155 Sussex Rd, Teaneck, NJ. Office: 40 E 69 St, New York, NY.

KLINEMAN, Julia S, US, civic worker; b. Cleveland, O, Mar 11, 1904; d. Frank and Rose (Baller) Stuhlberger; tchrs deg, Jr Tchrs Coll, W Reserve U, Cleveland, 1923; m. Emery Klineman, Nov 5, 1925; c: Robert, William. Mem, admn, exec bds, AJComm since 1960; vice-pres, NY sect, Natl Council J Women since 1967; fmr: chmn, women's div, Jt Defense Appeal, NY; vice chmn, women's div, UJA; secy, Fed J Women's Orgs, Cleveland; club chmn, Cleveland War Finance Comm; first aid instr, volunteer, home service, ARC; co-chmn, treas gifts, Cleveland Comty Fund; chmn women's div, JWF; vice pres, Fairmount Temple Sisterhood; tchr, Cleveland Public Sch; mem, Henry Kaufman Campgrounds since 1958. Home: 575 Park Ave, New York, NY.

KLING, Gabriel, Isr, advocate, educator; b. Krakow, Pol, Feb 21, 1934; s. Yehezkiel and Natalia (Fabian); in Isr since 1941; MJ, Heb U, Jerusalem, 1957; BSc, 1958; PhD, U London, 1963; m. Helena Schomberg, Jan 6, 1966; c: Yehezkiel. Pvt practice since 1960; lectr, law, Tel Aviv U since 1968; instr, Heb U, Jerusalem, 1960-68. Mem, ed bd, haPraklit. Contbr articles to profsl jour. Home: 26 Peretz St, Tel Aviv, Isr. Office: 5 Bezal'el Yaffe St, Tel Aviv, Isr.

KLING, Samuel Grover, US, attorney, author; b. NYC, Feb 4, 1910; s. Morris and Mary (Schilling); att U Baltimore, 1930-33; m. Rena Levine. Pvt practice since 1933; author since 1933; feature article writer, Baltimore Sunday Sun, 1929-31; admitted to Md State Bar, 1933; book reviewer: NY Herald Tribune; Harvard Law Rev; NY Times; nationally syndicated column, Your Marriage, 1948-56; Marriage Cons, daily radio prog, Mutual Bc Sys, 1949. Author: Your Legal Rights, 1945; The Marriage Reader, 1947; For Better, For Worse, 1948; Adventures in Love, 1948; The Art of Being

Happy, 1948; Your Marriage Counselor, 1949; Handy Legal Advisor, 1949; Popular Legal Encyclopedia, 1957; The Legal Encyclopedia For Home and Business, 1959; The Complete Guide to Divorce, 1963; Complete Guide to Everyday Law, 1965; Sexual Behavior and the Law, 1965; The Legal Encyclopedia and Dictionary, 1970; How to Handle Estate, 1971; contr to: legal jours; to Ency Amer, 1968; legal ed, Jefferson Ency, 1970. Home and office: 4000 N Charles St, Baltimore, Md.

KLING, Simcha, US, rabbi; b. Dayton, Ky, Jan 27, 1922; s. Eli and Anna (Niman); BA, U Cincinnati, 1943; MA, Columbia U, 1947; ordained rabbi, JTSA, 1948, DHL, 1958; m. Edith Leeman, June 15, 1947; c: Elana, Adma, Reena. Rabbi, Adath Jeshurun, Louisville, since 1965; instr, sociol of rel, U Louisville; fmr: asst rabbi, educ dir, Cong B'nai Amoona, St Louis, 1948-51; rabbi, Cong Beth David, Greensboro, 1951-65. Pres: Ky Bd of Rabbis, 1968-69; Hug-Ivri, 1967-69; NC Assn of Rabbis, 1956-58; secy, Louisville Council on Rel and Race; bd mem, Amer Isr Public Affairs Comm; mem: RA; ZOA; B'nai B'rith; Amer J Hist Soc; NCCJ; ACLU; NC Conf for Social Service. Author: Nachum Sokolow, 1961; The Mighty Warrior: Menahem Ussishkin, 1965; contbr to scholarly jours. Home: 2240 Millvale Rd, Louisville, Ky. Study: 2401 Woodbourne Ave, Louisville, Ky.

KLINGHOFER, Joseph, Can, educational dir; b. Bukovina, Rum, Jan 14, 1903; s. Leon and Regina (Pressner); in Can since 1948; att U Vienna; MA, PhD, U Lwow, Pol; postgrad studies: Graz U, Aus; Kings Coll, London; Heidelberg U, Ger; m. Gisela Atlas; c: Irvin. Educ dir, Can J Cong, since 1948, past dir, research comm, cen region; fmr: HS tchr, Pol, 1927-33; instr, modern langs, Bd of Educ, Lublin, 1933-39; councillor, Pol Min of Educ, 1934-39; lectr, Ger lit, U of Lwow. Worker, Pol underground; lt, res, Pol Army, 1927-39. Prin contrib, methodology in teaching of modern langs. Mem, Commn on J Educ; fmr mem, Keren Hatarbut, Toronto. Ed, prepared various research papers; writer of curricula for J afternoon schs and adult educ progs; contbr to: Viewpoints, Montreal; Hebrew Education Ency, Jerusalem; profsl publs. Recipient of testimonial dinners, 1968. Home: 544 Old Orchard Grove, Toronto Can. Office: 150 Beverley St, Toronto, Can.

KLINGHOFFER, Clara, US, artist; b. Sczerzec, Austria-Hung; d. Solomon and Anna (Stark); in US since 1939; m. Joseph Stoppleman, 1926; c: Sonia, Michael. Painter, lithographer, sculptor; one-man shows: Hampstead Art Gal, 1919; Leicester Gal, 1923, 1936; 460 Park Ave Gal, 1941; New Sch for Soc Research, 1951; Juster Gal; 1958, all NY; Fairleigh Dickinson U, 1968; exhbts: London, 1920-39, 1951, 1961-63, 1968; Paris, 1929, 1938; Amsterdam, 1928, 1932; The Hague, 1933; Haarlem, 1934; Carnegie Intl Exhbt, Pittsburgh, 1935; Australia, 1937; S Afr, 1938; Toronto, 1939; NYC, 1942, 1945, 1949, 1952, 1953, 1956; perm collections: Tate Gal, London; City Art Gal; Manchester; Aberdeen Mus; Stoke-on-Trent Art Gal; Print Room, Victoria and Albert Mus; London; Brisbane Art Gal; The Queensland Natl Gal; NSW Natl Gal. Mem: Artists Equity Assn; New Eng Art Club, London, Eng. Home and studio: 800 Riverside Dr, New York, NY. London studio: Elms Ave, Hendon, London, Eng.

KLINGHOFFER, Yitzhak Hans, Isr, educator, legislator; b. Kolomea, Pol, Feb 17, 1905; s. David and Amalie (Weissmann); in Isr since 1953; DRerPol, U Vienna, 1927, DJ, 1930; m. Miriam Kohn, 1957. Prof, constitution and admn law, Heb U, since 1968; on fac since 1953; MK since 1961; fmr: legal off, Munic of Vienna, 1928-38; mgr, agric farm, Brazil, 1942-46; research asst, Inter-Amer Juridicial Comm, Rio de Janeiro, 1946-49; legal adv, Aus Emb, Rio de Janeiro, 1949-53. Asso mem, Soc Public Tchrs of Law, Eng; mem, Brazilian J Orgs. Author: Das Parlamentarische Regierungssystem, 1928; La Pensee Politique de President Getulio Vargas, 1942; Les Aspects Juridiques de L'Occupation de l'Autriche par L'Allemagne, 1943; Administrative Law, part I, 1957; Die Entstehung des Staates Israel, part I, 1962; contbr to profsl jours. Hobby: photography. Home: 8 Hattibonim St, Jerusalem, Isr. Office: Heb U, Jerusalem, Isr.

KLOPSTOCK, Alfred, Isr, physician, educator, bacteriologist; b. Berlin, Ger, Feb 5, 1896; s. Martin and Regina (Tietz); in Isr since 1933; MD, Berlin U, 1921; m. Elizabeth Scheyer, 1933, (decd); c: Ruth Bunn; m. 2nd, Ruth Klopstock, Dec, 1968. Head, dept microbiol, Tel Aviv U, since 1955, rector,

1959-64; asso prof, Heidelberg U, 1922-33; fmr: owner, dir, bact lab, Tel Aviv; sci adv, cen lab, Workers Sick Benefit Fund. Mem: sci comm, Isr Min of Health; cen comm, Isr Amer League. Contbr articles to sci jours. Home: 17 Hachashmal St, Tel Aviv, Isr.

KLOTZ, Irving M, US, chemist, educator; b. Chgo, Ill, Jan 22, 1916; s. Frank and Mollie (Nasatir); BS, U Chgo, 1937, PhD, 1940; m. Themis Askounis, Sep 11, 1947; c: Edward, Audie; m. 2nd, Mary Hanlon, Aug 7, 1966. Prof chem, Northwestern U, since 1950, on fac since 1940; Lalor f, Marine Biol Lab, Woods Hole, Mass, 1947, 1948, trustee, 1957-65. Mem: Amer Chem Soc; Amer Soc Biol Chems; AAAS; Phi Beta Kappa; Sigma Xi; Phi Lambda Upsilon; Alpha Chi Sigma. Author: Chemical Thermodynamics, 1950, rev, 1964; Energetics in Biochemical Reactions, 1957, rev, 1967; contbr to sci jours. Recipient: Army-Navy Cert Appreciation, wartime research, 1948; Eli Lilly award, Amer Chem Soc, 1949. Home: 2400 N Lakeview Ave, Chicago, Ill. Office: Northwestern U, Evanston, Ill.

KLOVSKY, Sidney Bryan, US, attorney; b. Philadelphia, Pa, Oct 29, 1922; s. Abraham and Rose (Brian); BS, Temple U, Phila, Pa, 1945, LLB, JD, 1948; m. Ruth Ruben, Apr 15, 1951; c: Alan, Bruce, Steven. Partner, Klovsky, Kuby & Harris since 1965; admitted to Pa Bar, 1949. Pres, Temple U Acres of Diamond Group; Zeta Beta Tau; mem: Phila, Pa, Amer Bar Assns; Amer Judicature Soc; Intl Acad Law and Sci; bd govs, Amer Trial Lawyers Assn; bd trustees, Comty Legal Services, Inc, OEO; fmr: pres, Phila Trial Lawyers Assn; gov, Pa Trial Lawyers Assn, found; chancellor, Tau Epsilon Rho; Midday Lodge, B'nai B'rith, past pres; clubs: Manor Country, Malvern, Pa, found and pres; Lawyers. Recipient, Sigma Pi Monroe Award. Home: 306 Penbree Circle, Bala-Cynwyd, Pa. Office: 121 S Broad St, Philadelphia, Pa.

KLUTZNICK, Philip M, US, diplomat; b. Kan City, Mo, July 9, 1907; s. Morris and Minnie (Spindler); att U Kan, 1924-25; U Neb, 1925-36; LLB, Creighton U, Omaha, Neb, 1929; hon DHL: Dropsie Coll, 1954; HUC-JIR, 1957; hon LLD: Creighton U, 1957; Wilberforce U, 1959; m. Ethel Riekes, June 8, 1930; c: Bettylu, Richard (decd), Thomas, James, Robert, Samuel. Ret; admitted to bar, 1930; US Commn, Fed Public Housing Auth, 1944-46; mem, US delg to UN, 1957, 1961, 1962; US repr to UN-ECOSCOC with rank, ambass, 1961-63; chmn bd: Urban Inves and Devl Co; Amer Bank and Trust Co; Swiss-Isr Trade Bank, Geneva, Switz; pres, Oak Brook Utility Co; mem bd, Mortgage Guarantee Ins, Milw; U Patents Inc. Vice-chmn: Afr-Amer Inst; Council on Rel and Intl Affairs; hon intl pres, B'nai B'rith; mem bd: Eleanor Roosevelt Memorial Found; Educ Facilities Lab; Creighton U; Roosevelt U; Natl Assembly for Social Policy and Devl; UN Assn, US; Metrop Housing and Planning Council; JWB; mem: exec comm, UJA; natl council; Boys Scouts of Amer; Lambda Alpha; hon mem, Phi Epsilon Pi; clubs: Highland, Omaha; Cosmos, Wash; Standard Ravisloe Country, Chgo. Home: 1325 N State Pkwy, Chicago, Ill. Offices: 401 N Michigan Ave, Chicago, Ill; 70 Wall St, New York, NY.

KNAANI, David, Isr, author, editor; b. Warsaw, Pol, Sep 18, 1919; s. Baruch and Etl (Rosenfeld) Handelsman; in Isr since 1934; m. Rahel Berman, Apr 15, 1940; c: Nuritt Hartuv, Hanna, Bilha. Chief, Ency of Social Sci, since 1953; fmr, co-ed, Sifriat Poalim; secy, educ, linotypist, Kibbutz Merhavia, since 1934. Author: leNogah Etz Rakav; Beinam le'bein Zmanam; Batei Midot. Mem, Assn Heb Writers. Recipient: awards: Shlonsky, 1958; Holon, 1961; Tel Aviv Munic, 1967. Home: Kibbutz Merhavia, Isr.

KNAPP, Arthur Alexander, US, physician; b. NYC, Jan 24, 1903; s. Mark and Bertha (Schlesinger); att NYU, 1922; MD, Bellevue Hosp Med Coll, 1926; postgrad work: NY Eye and Ear Infirmary, 1927-28; Columbia U, 1932; c: Arthur, Alexander, Ashly. Dir, eye service, Sing Sing Prison Hosp, Ossining, NY, since 1934; asst visiting ophthal: Flower Fifth Ave Hosp, 1946-67; Bird S Coler Hosp, since 1952; Doctors Hosp since 1937; asso eye surg, Hosp for Spec Surg, ophthal, arthritis clinic, 1933-49; att eye surg, Manhattan Gen Hosp, city TB div, 1947-63; mem, teaching staff, NY Med Coll, 1946-60; eye cons, USN Hosp, St Albans, NY, 1949-50; hon eye surg, NYC Police Dept since 1951; eye surg, NY World's Fair, 1939-40; guest lectr: U Santo Domingo, Dominican Rep, 1953; eye surg lectr, Havana, Cuba, 1949; eye

cons: Natl Council to Combat Blindness, since 1946; comm on PR, NY Acad Med since 1940. Capt, USN, since 1939; commanding off, Res Hosp, 1959-61. F, Amer and Intl Coll Surgs; mem: Comm on Ind Med, 1946; adv comm, Better Vision Inst, 1941-42; ind health and med adv comm, procurement and assignment service, Fed Security Agcy, 1949; NY leg comm, Co Med Soc, 1938; Draft Bd, Selective Service adv bd, both 1941-42; chmn: eye sect, Race Betterment Assn, 1942; phys comm: for election of Edward Corsi, 1949; of Mayor Robert F Wagner Jr, 1953; vice-chmn, adv comm, Ophthal, 1938-42; hon Col, staff, Gov of Ga, 1940; dir, Temple Emanuel, NY; mem: NY State Med Soc, eye and leg comm; Co Med Soc; Amer Bd of Ophthal and Otolaryngology; Pan Amer Ophthal Assn; Amer Acad of Compensation Med; Amer Geriatrics Soc; Assn for Research in Ophthal; World Med Assn; Assn Mil Surgs, Naval Res Off Med Assn; dipl, Intl Bd Surg; club, Adventurers, bd govs, 1937-51, 1967-70. Author: Corneal Graft or Tattooing with Iridectomy, motion picture of same title; Vitamin D Complex in Myopia and Kerotoconus, in Eye, Ear, Nose and Throat Year Book, 1943; contbr to med jours. Recipient: Commendation, USN, Surg Gen for paper on Ocular Path in Various Types of Dietry Deficiencies, 1943; Cong Medal for Selective Service, 1946. Home and office: 907 Fifth Ave, New York, NY.

KNISPEL, Gershon, Isr, artist; b. Köln, Ger, Nov 9, 1932; s. Chaim and Aliza (Nathan); in Isr since 1935; BA, Bezalel Sch of Arts and Crafts, 1954; m. Esther Cabiri, Jan 1, 1968. Art adv, Haifa Munic, since 1964; art dir, high sch of art, since 1958. IDF, 1950-52. Book illus: Shirei Dor, 1955; Engravings and Drawings, 1957; Shalom Aleichem's Katrielivka, Melodies, 1966; Berthold Brecht's Children Crusade, 1968. Mem, Painters and Sculptors Org, Isr. Contribs: mural works, lithographs, drawings. Home: 9 Rachel St, Haifa, Isr. Office: Haifa Municipality, Isr.

KNOFSKY, Abraham Raymond, US, business exec; b. Warren, O, Dec 27, 1903; s. Jacob and Sarah (White); att Case W Reserve U, Cleveland, O, 1921-22; m. Miriam Baskin, May 20, 1935; c: Judson, Frederick. Pres: Warren Scrap Iron and Metal Co, since 1962; Warren J Fed, since 1955. Pres, B'nai B'rith, 1933-35; mem: Kiwanis; Masonic Lodge. Hobbies: golf, bowling, coin collecting. Home: 901 Melwood Dr, NE, Warren, O. Office: Griswold St, Warren, O.

KNOOP, Hans, Holland, editor; b. Naarden, Holland, Dec 30, 1943; s. Richard and Elisabeth (v Amerongen); att U Holland; m. Aug 15, 1968. Ed, The J Weekly, since 1969; reporter, De Telegraaf, 1961-69. Author, The Six Days of Sinai, 1967. Mem, Lib J Comty Amsterdam. Home: 370 v Nyeurodeweg, Amsterdam, Holland. Office: N Z Voorburgwal 258, Amsterdam, Holland.

KNOPF, Alfred A, US, publisher; b. NYC, Sep 12, 1892; s. Samuel and Ida (Japhe); BA, Columbia U, 1912; hon LHD: Yale U, 1958; Columbia U, 1959; Bucknell U, 1959; William and Mary Coll, 1960; Lehigh U, 1960; Adelphi U, 1966; U of Chattanooga, 1966; m. Blanche Wolf, Apr 4, 1916 (decd); c: Alfred; m. 2nd, Helen Hedrick, Apr 20, 1967. Chmn bd, Alfred A Knopf Inc; dir, Random House. Corresp mem: Colonial Soc of Mass; Mass Hist Soc. Recipient: Comendador Ordem Nacional do Cruzeiro do Sul, Brazil; Alexander Hamilton medal, Assn Alumni Columbia U, 1966; Cornelius Amory Pugsley gold medal, 1960. Home: Purchase, New York, NY. Office: 201 E 50 St, New York, NY.

KNOPOFF, Leon, US, geophysicist, educator; b. Los Angeles, July 1, 1925; s. Max and Ray (Schor); BS, Cal Inst Tech, 1944, MS, 1946, PhD, 1949; m. Joanne Van Cleef, Apr 19, 1961; c: Katherine, Rachel, Michael. Prof, physics, geophys, research musicologist, UCLA, since 1950; asst prof, asso prof, physics, Miami U, Oxford, O, 1948-50; prof, geophys, Cal Inst Tech, 1962-63; visiting prof, Technische Hochschule Karlsruhe, 1966; sr postdoc research f, NSF, Cambridge U, Eng, 1960-61. Chmn, US comm, Upper Mantle Project, secy, intl comm; f, Amer Geophys Union; mem: Amer Acad Arts and Scis; Natl Acad Sci; Royal Astronomical Soc; Seismological Soc of Amer; Acoustical Soc of Amer; Amer Phys Soc. Contbr to profsl jours. Hobbies: composing music, mountaineering, archaeol. Office: UCLA, Los Angeles, Cal.

KNOX, Israel, US, educator, author; b. Russ, May 3, 1906; s. Asher and Zipporah (Madorsky); in US since 1913; BA, CUNY, 1926; MA, Columbia U, 1932, PhD, 1936; m. Sarah Rabinowitz, June, 1956; c: Samuel, Ashreth. Asso prof, phil

NYU, since 1951; asst prof, Ohio U, 1947-51. Author: The Aesthetic Theories of Kant, Hegel and Schopenhauer, 1936; Rabbi in America: The Story of Isaac Mayer Wise, 1957; co-ed, Anthology of Holocaust Lit, 1968; contbr articles on phil. Mem, Amer Phil Assn. Home: 67-76 Booth St, Forest Hills, NY. Office: NYU, Washington Sq, NY.

KOBER, Arthur, US, author, playwright; b. Brody, Aus-Hung, Aug 25, 1900; s. Adolph and Tillie (Ballison); in US since 1904; m. Lillian Hellman, 1925 (div); m. 2nd, Margaret Frohnknecht, Jan 11, 1941 (decd); c: Cathy. Press agt: Lee and JJ Shubert, 1922-25; Edgar Selwyn, Guthrie McClintic, Jed Harris, Herman Shumlin, Ruth Draper, Maurice Schwartz, 1925-30; screen-writer for Paramount, MGM, 20th Cent Fox, 1930-45; fac mem, New Sch for Social Research, 1953. Author: Thunder over the Bronx, 1935; Pardon Me For Pointing, 1939; My Dear Bella, 1941; That Man is Here Again, 1946; Bella, Bella Kissed a Fella, 1951; Ooh, What You Said, 1958; plays: Having Wonderful Time, 1937; co-author: Wish You Were Here, 1952; A Mighty Man is He, 1960; contbr short stories to The New Yorker. Mem: Dramatists Guild; Author's League; PEN Assn. Recipient, Roi Cooper Megrue prize for best comedy, Having Wonderful Time, 1937. Home and office: 241 Central Park W, New York, NY.

KOBLENTZ, Abe J, US, business exec; b. Chattanooga, Tenn, Aug 30, 1899; s. Louis and Hannah (Magrill); att W Tenn Normal U; m. Klari Lorincz, 1938; c: Louis. Pres: Koblentz Inc, since 1958; Dixie Land Co, since 1952; secy-treas: Chatanooga Devl Corp, since 1946; Diversified Inves, since 1957. US Army, WW I. Pres, Sales & Marketing Execs Intl; gen chmn, Sesquicentennial, 1965; vice-chmn, ADL; treas, Ochs Memorial Temple, since 1957; bd dirs: Boys Club, 1969, 1970; Girls Club of Chattanooga, 1969-70; Boys Choir, 1969, 1970; Sr Neighbors, 1970; B'nai Zion Cong, since 1932; Model Cities Prog; mem: Elks; Masons, hon life; clubs: Half Cent; Chattanooga Golf and Country. Home: 1054 Rivermont Circle, Chattanooga, Tenn. Office: 1120 Ham Natl Bank Bldg, Chattanooga, Tenn.

KOBLENZ, Edmund A, US, attorney; b. Albany, NY, Nov 14, 1908; s. Bernard and Hilda (Caplan); BA, U Mich, 1929; LLB, Yale U, 1932; m. Tillie Paul, Aug 27, 1929; c: Norman, Miriam. Counsel, leg bill, drafting comm, NY State Leg, since 1950; dep atty gen, NY State, 1943-44. Mem: natl exec comm, ZOA; natl admnr, comm, KH; natl bd: United Pal Appeal, 1948; UJA; chmn, JWF, Albany; AJComm; B'nai B'rith; Albany JCC; KP; club, Shaker Ridge Country, pres 1962. Home: 22 Clarendon Rd, Albany, NY. Office: 90 State St, Albany, NY.

KOBRIN, Lawrence A, US, attorney; b. NYC, Sep 14, 1933; s. Irving and Hortense (Freezer); BA, Columbia Coll, 1954, LLB, Columbia U, 1957; m. Ruth Freedman, Mar 5, 1967. Partner, Emil and Kobrin, since 1964; asso: Cahill, Gordon, Reindel and Ohl, 1958-59; Arthur D Emil, 1956-63. NY Natl Guard. Pres, Ramaz Sch Alumni Soc, 1960-64; vice-pres, Camp Morasha; chmn: Isr Commn, Union J Orthodox Congs Amer; campus commn, Union Orthodox Congs Amer, 1962-66; conv resolutions comm, 1964-66, vice-chmn, youth commn, 1965-68, committeeman, 1962-65, all NY Dem Party; resolutions comm, World Conf of Ashkenazi and Sephardi Syns, 1968; mem: bd dirs: J Educ Comm, NY; Massad Camps Inc; mem, bd govs, Amer Assn for J Educ; mem: admn comm, J Cen, NY; comm on rel affairs, FJP; natl adv bd, Yavneh Inc. Mgn ed, Tradition. Recipient: Elsberg Prize in Modern Hist, Phi Beta Kappa, 1954; Kent Scholar, Stone Scholar, Columbia Law Sch, 1957; NY Natl Award. Home: 115 W 86 St, New York, NY. Office: 32 E 57 St, New York, NY.

KOCHAVI, Moshe, Isr, archaeologist; b. Bucharest, Rum, Oct 26, 1928; s. Shmuel and Agatha (Abeles); in Isr since 1933; MA, Heb U, Jerusalem, 1960; PhD, 1967; m. Nora Shraier, Apr 8, 1954; c: Noam, Uri. Sr lectr, Tel Aviv U, since 1968; ed, Soc for Archaeol Survey of Isr, since 1968; field dir, Tel-Zeror Expedition, 1964-67; tchr, fac of Architecture, Technion, Haifa, 1966-69. Palmach, IDF, 1947-49. Prin contrib, excavations, surveys in bibl archaeol, hist geog of Isr. Mem, comm: Place Names, PM off; Isr Exploration Soc; mem, Soc for Archaeol Survey of Isr. Contbr: to archaeol reports; articles to Heb, Eng profsl, popular jours. Home: 18 Marcus St, Jerusalem, Isr. Office: Tel Aviv U, Ramat Aviv, Isr.

KODESH, Shlomo Zalman, Isr, educator, author; b. Lith, 1903; s. Meir and Chanah; in Isr since 1933; DLitt, U Kaunas; m. Hadassa Kohen, 1932; c: Chana. Dir, dept for Heb training and adult educ, Min of Educ. Author: Adam Bamoledeth;

Zoth Kupishok; Kibbutz Galuyoth; Asher Yirchash Lev; Haezrach Beistrel; Zeh El Zeh; Meinyan Leinyan, Ezlenu Bakitah; Leshon Amenu; Chanani Mimezadah; Ivrit; Israel With Lev Avot; Reshit I, II. Home: Ahad Haam St, Jerusalem, Isr. Office: 19 Jaffa St, Jerusalem, Isr.

KOENIG, Samuel, US, sociologist, educator, author; b. Monasterzyska, Aus-Hung, Mar 29, 1899; s. Berl and Rebecca (Liebster); in US since 1921; att U Minn, 1924-27; PhB, Marquette U, 1929; MA, Yale U, 1931, PhD, 1935; m. Miriam Nelson, Oct 13, 1932; c: Paul. Prof, sociol, anthropology, Bklyn Coll, since 1960, dep chmn dept, since 1948, fac mem since 1941; dir, sociol studies, State of Conn, Fed Writers Project, 1936-41; research f, sociol, Yale U, 1937-40; research asso, Study of Recent Immigration from Eur, 1947-48; book rev ed, Social Problems, 1953-56; Social Sci Research Council grant, for study of emergent cultural patterns in Isr, 1951-52; visiting prof, Fulbright grant, Bar Ilan U, Isr, 1957-58; Fulbright prof: Kartak U, India, 1964-65; Osmania U, India, 1968-69. Author: Immigrant Settlements in Connecticut, 1938; Sociology: An Introduction to the Science of Society, 1957, Heb ed, 1961, Chinese ed, 1962, Hindi ed, 1969; co-author, Studies in the Science of Society, 1937; Jews in a Gentile World, 1942; History of the Jewish Labor Movement in the United States, Yiddish, 1943; The Refugees Are Now Americans, 1945; One America, 1945, 1952; Contemporary Sociology, 1958; Readings in Contemporary American Sociology, 1961; Sociology of Crime, 1961; co-ed, co-author: Sociology: A Book of Readings, 1953; Criminology: A Book of Readings, 1953; contbr to various sociol jours; encys; periodicals. F, Amer Sociol Soc; fmr: mem: ed, publs comm, Soc for Study of Social Problems; commn for Study of J Educ in US; Fulbright student selection comm for Isr; commn on research, YIVO Inst for J Research, mem, bd dirs, since 1953, fmr chmn; mem: Amer Friends Heb U, prog comm for scholarships at Heb U, since 1958, chmn, Bklyn chap; Conf on J Social Studies; Amer J Hist Soc; E Sociol Soc; Amer Acad of Political and Social Sci; NY Acad Scis; AAUP; Alpha Kappa Delta; Sigma Xi. Home: 1890 E 21 St, Brooklyn, NY. Office: Bklyn Coll, Brooklyn, NY.

KOENIGSBERG, Benjamin, US, lawyer, communal worker; b. Limanow, Aus, June 3, 1884; s. Israel and Esther (Aftergut); in US since 1889; att: Yeshiva Etz Chaim; CCNY; JD, NYU, 1904; m. Pearl Friedman, 1904. Pvt practice since 1905. Pres, Amer sect, Colel Hibath, Jerusalem; found, fmr pres, Heb League, 1905; found, Young Isr movement, 1911, fmr pres, Manhattan br; sr vice-pres, chmn, bd, Heb Educ, Rabbi Jacob Joseph Sch; sr vice-pres, Union Orthodox J Cong Amer, chmn, membership comm; sr vice-pres, E Side C of C, chmn, sanitation comm; mem: bd dirs, secy, Downtown Talmud Torah; Mizrachi, Rel Zionists Amer, exec comm mem, found; bd govs, Bialystoker Syn; Sieniawer Cong Anshei Sfarad, fmr pres; Rel dept, JNF; delg, 1st NY Dist, AJCong; NY Co Lawyers Assn; Manhattan Borough Pres' Planning Bd for 3rd Dist; bd, Heb Tchrs Training Sch for Girls. Office: 15 Park Row, New York, NY.

KOENIGSBERG, Herschel, US, rabbi; b. Sieniawa, Pol, Feb 16, 1900; s. Chaim and Esther (Silfen); in US since 1925; PhD, U Berlin, 1925; ordained rabbi, Yeshiva U, NY, 1929; m. Rose Elfenbein, Aug 15, 1932; c: Natanlie Sterman, Mordecai, Isaiah. Chaplain, Creedmore State Hosp, since 1954; instr, Talmud, Yeshiva U, 1926-28; rabbi: Temple Kol Isr, Beaumont, Tex, 1929-33; Cong Crowning Glory of Isr Temple, Bklyn, 1934-46; B'nei Yehudah Cong, Bklyn, 1947-54. Mem: Rabb Bd, Gtr NY; RabCA; NY Bd Rabbis. Contbr articles on Halacha. Home: 35-11 85 St, Jackson Heights, NY. Study: Creedmore State Hosp, NY.

KOEPPEL, Max L, US, realtor; b. Bklyn, NY, June 3, 1899; s. Abraham and Anna (Rosenbaum); m. Minnie Lechner, May 25, 1918; c: Selma Friedman, Geraldine Adler, Bevin, Louise Feldman, Grace Gold, Alfred. Partner, Koeppel & Koeppel, realty inves since 1919; adv bd mem, Chase Manhattan Bank. Bd govs, HUC-JIR, since 1961; chmn, capital fund dr, since 1959; vice-pres, chmn bd, UAHC since 1962; pres: Devl Fund for Amer Judaism; Cong Beth Elohim, Bklyn, 1953-58; Bklyn Philharmonic; chmn: Reform J App, 1964-65; exec bd, J Hosp and Med Cen; trustee: J Hosp, Bklyn, since 1959; J Child Care Assn, since 1959; adv mem: Downtown Manhattan Assn; NY Real Estate Bd; clubs: Harmonie; Unity; Fresh Meadow. Hobbies: golf, boating. Home: 45 Sutton Pl S, New York, NY. Office: 26 Broadway, New York, NY.

KOESTLER, Arthur, UK, author; b. Hung, Sep 5, 1905; s. Henrik and Adele (Jeiteles); att Technische Hochschule, Vienna; hon LLD, 1969. Corresp: ME, 1926-29; Paris, Fr, 1929-30; Berlin, Ger, Russ, 1930-34; Spanish Civil War, 1936-38. Volunteer: Fr Army, 1940; Brit Army, 1941. Author: Spanish Testament, 1938; Gladiators, 1939; Darkness at Noon, 1941; Scum of the Earth, 1941; Arrival and Departure, 1943; The Yogi and the Commissar, 1945; Twilight Bar, 1945; Thieves in the Night, 1946; Insight and Outlook, 1949; Promises and Fulfillment, 1949; The Age of Longing, 1951; Arrow in the Blue, 1952; The Invisible Writing, 1954; The Trail of the Dinosaur, 1955; Reflections on Hanging, 1957; The Sleepwalkers: A History of Man's Changing Vision of the Universe, 1959; The Lotus and the Robot, 1961; The Act of Creation, 1964; The Ghost in the Machine, 1967; Drinkers of Infinity, 1968; co-author, The God That Failed, 1950; ed: Suicide of a Nation?, 1964; Beyond Reductionism: New Perspectives in the Life Sciences, 1969. F, Royal Soc Lit. Recipient: Sonning Prize, 1968. Address: c/o Macmillan Co, 60 Fifth Ave, New York, NY.

KOESTLER, Elsa W, US, civic worker; b. West End, NJ, July 12, 1909; d. Charles and Hulda (Mayer) Weschler; AB, Wellesley Coll, 1930; MSW, Rutgers Grad Sch Social Work, 1963; m. Melvin Koestler, Mar 1, 1931; c: Robert, Nancy Franklin (decd). Ins agt since 1938. Secy, Family and Children's Soc, Elizabeth, since 1967; mem: US Comm for Refs; bd dirs, Occupational Cen of Union Co; secy, local Anti-poverty Agcy; pres, Elizabeth sect, Natl Council J Women, 1936-38, natl coord, State Leg, 1960-61; pres: Elizabeth League of Women Voters, 1939-41; Union Co comm, White House Conf on Aging, 1959-60; bd trustees, Comty Wfr Council, E Union Co, 1951-56; mem: Natl Assn Social Workers; Amer Assn U Women; NJ Wfr Council; Consumers League; club, NJ Wellesley. Home: 571 Grant Ave, E Roselle Park, NJ.

KOESTLER, Frances A, US, writer, editor, public relations cons; b. NYC, Jan 11, 1914; d. Louis and Minna (Rinder) Adlerstein; BA, Bklyn Coll, 1936; m. Jacob Allen, 1947, div; m. 2nd, Milton Koestler, Aug 2, 1954. Ed, PR cons to non-profit agcys in health, wfr, rehab fields since 1964; publicity dir, JDC, NYC, 1938-43; dir PR, Wfr Council, NYC, 1943-46; overseas publicity dir, JDC, Paris, 1946-47; sales promotion mgr, Cornelius Products Co, 1947-52; dir PR, Natl Traveler's Aid Assn, 1952-57; dir, comty relations, J Child Care Assn of NYC, 1957-64. Mem bd dirs, Natl PR Council for Health and Wfr Services, since 1960; PR and Devl Comm, Natl Conf on Social Wfr, since 1964. Author: chaps, Public Publicity Manual for Regional Meetings in National Traveler's Aid Association, 1956; Dealing with Controversy, 1962; Careers in Social Work, 1964; Public Relations and the Client; chap in Public Relations in Health and Welfare, 1966; The Patient's Role in Overcoming Chronic Disabilities, 1968; ed: Guideposts and Roadblocks to Areawide Rehabilitation, 1965; The COMSTAC Report: Standards for Strengthened Services, 1966; Manpower Utilization in Rehabilitation, 1966; Utilization of Rehabilitation Manpower in the Community Setting, 1967; ed staff, The Amer Heb Mag, 1930-35, mgn ed, 1936-38; columnist, The Wonderful World of Women, Natl J Monthly, since 1959; contbr to profsl, gen publs; story ideas for radio, TV. Home: 135 Ashland Pl, Brooklyn, NY.

KOESTLER, Melvin J, US, lawyer; b. Elizabeth, NJ, Dec 25, 1907; s. Samuel and Selma (Weiss); BA, Cornell U, 1928; LLB, Cornell Law Sch, 1930; m. Elsa Weschler, Mar 1, 1931; c: Robert, Nancy (decd). Pvt practice, Koestler & Koestler, since 1960, partner, 1944-60. Chmn, ethics and grievances comm, Union Co, NJ, 1946-52; trustee, Temple Beth-El, Elizabeth, 1953-55; comm on unauthorized practice of law, appd to NJ Supr Court, vice-chmn since 1967; mem: Union Co, NJ State, and Amer Bar Assns; Phi Beta Kappa; Phi Kappa Phi; Order of the Coif; mgn ed, Cornell Law Quarterly, 1930; club: Cornell, Union Co, secy since 1947. Home: 571 Grant Ave E, Roselle Park, NJ. Office: 125 Broad St, Elizabeth, NJ.

KOFF, Stephen P, US, educator; b. Bklyn, NY, Jan 21, 1929; s. Herman and Sara (Westerman); AB, Ind U, 1950; MA, Columbia U, 1953, PhD, 1964; m. Sondra Zenowitz, Aug 20, 1961. Dir, Syracuse Semester in Florence, It, Syracuse U, since 1961, fac mem, since 1957; with natl defense res, Exec Off of Pres of US, since 1968; lectr, political sci: Bklyn Coll, 1956-57; Hunter Coll, 1956-57. Mem: bd visitors, Sch for Intl Training; Amer Political Sci Assn; Hansard Soc; AAUP; NAACP; fmr: bd trustees, Experiment in Intl Living; bd dirs, World Affairs Council; bd dirs, Amer Assn for UN. Hobbies: sport,

theater. Home: 126 Dorset Rd, Syracuse, NY. Office: Syracuse U, Syracuse, NY.

KOGAN, Bernard Robert, US, educator, author; b. Chgo, Ill, May 16, 1920; s. Isaac and Ida (Perlman); BA, U Chgo, 1941, MA, 1946, PhD, 1953; m. Irene Wishnewsky, Aug 19, 1962; c: Henry, Sophia, Naomi, Sara. Prof, Eng, U of Ill, since 1952; instr: Eng, Ind U, 1946-48; hum, U Chgo, 1949-51. USNR, 1941-45. Mem: Natl Council Tchrs Eng; MLA; Phi Beta Kappa; Coll Conf Composition and Communication. Author: The Chicago Hay Market Riot: Anarchy on Trial, 1959; Darwin and His Critics, 1960. Hobbies: tennis, handball, amateur printing. Home: 9034 N Bennett Ave, Skokie, Ill. Office: U of Illinois, Chicago, Ill.

KOGAN, Herman S, US, editor, author; b. Chgo, Ill, Nov 6, 1914; s. Isaac and Ida (Perlman); BA, U Chgo, 1936; m. Marilew Cavanagh, Oct1, 1950; c: Rick, Mark. Ed, Chgo Sun-Times Book Week, since 1968; reporter: Chgo Tribune, 1937-42; Chgo Sun, 1942-52; lit, drama critic, Chgo Sun-Times, 1952-58; dir, co relations, Ency Britannica, 1958-61; asst to exec ed, Chgo Daily News, 1961-65; asst gen mgr, WGLD-TV,1965-68. Author: Lords of the Levee, 1943; Bet A Million, 1948; Give the Lady What She Wants, 1952; Big Bill of Chicago, 1954; Chicago: A Pictorial History, 1958; The Great EB, 1958; The Long White Line, 1963; Lending Is Our Business, 1965. Mem: Phi Beta Kappa; U Chgo Alumni Cabinet; clubs: Chgo Press; Arts; Tavern. Recipient: Awards: Friends of Lit, 1955; Adult Educ Council, 1963. Hobbies: tennis, swimming, music. Home: 1715 Park Ave, Chicago, Ill. Office: 401 N Wabash Ave, Chicago, Ill.

KOGAN, Stanley, US, oral surg; b. Baltimore, Md, Oct 20, 1930; s. Louis and Lillian (Helprin); att Dartmouth Coll, 1948-50; DDS, U of Md, Dent Sch, 1954; att Tufts Dent Sch, Boston, 1955-56; m. Leslye Donner, May 20, 1966; c: Jill, Joshua. Pvt practice, o al surg since 1960; chief, oral surg, Baltimore Co Gen Hos,p; head, oral surg dept, Sinai Hosp, Baltimore. Capt, US Army, Dent Corps, 1956-58. Vice-pres, AJCong; f: Amer Bd Oral Surg; Amer Coll Dents; mem, pres, Alpha Omega, fmr regent; campaign cabinet, Asso J Charities, Baltimore; Amer Soc Oral Surg; fmr, treas,HIAS, Baltimore. Home: 3415 Clarks Lane, Baltimore, Md. Office: 6810 Park Heights Ave, Baltimore, Md.

KOGEL, Marcus D, US, physician, educator; b. Peczenizyn, Aus-Hung, Sep 28, 1903; s. Abraham and Rose (Jacobowitz); in US since 1913; att: CCNY, 1922; Columbia U, 1923; MD, NY Med Coll, 1927, hon LHD, 1953; hon LHD, Yeshiva U, 1952; m. Fannie Tomson, June 24, 1930; c: Isobel Pollack; Joan Roskin. Dean em, Albert Einstein Coll of Med, Yeshiva U, since 1967, dean, 1953-67, on staff since 1953; dean, Sue Golding grad div med sci, Yeshiva U, 1956-67, vice-pres, med affairs and sci, 1967-69, prof and chmn, dep of preventive and environmental med, 1954-60, Afran prof, social med, 1960-67; gen med supt, Dept of Hosps, NYC, 1946-48, sr gen med supt, dir, Bur of Med and Hosp Services, 1948-49, NY commn hosps, 1949-54; opened: Queens Gen Hosp, Jamaica, NY, first med sup, 1935; Triboro Hosp, NY, 1941. Med res,US Army, since 1927, col, since 1945, dir, dept of mil sanitation, US Army Med Field Service Sch, 1941-45, theater med insp, chief of preventative med, China Theater, 1945. Chmn: Bd of Hosps, NYC, 1950-54; Interdepartmental Health Council, 1953; coord, med emergency div, NYC Off Civil Defense; spec cons, USPHS, 1951; tech cons, Commn on Chronic Illness. F, NY Acad of Med; Amer Public Health Assn; dipl, Amer Bd Preventative Med and Public Health, 1950; fmr bd mem: Hosp Council Gtr NY; Public Health Research Inst; bd of govs, Gtr NY Hosp Assn; mem: Amer Hosp Assn; Bx Co and NY State Med Soc; NY State Jt Hosp Survey and Planning Comm; Masons, Elks. Co-author: Military Medical Annual, 4th ed, 1942; Essentials of Military Hygiene, 1942; Military Sanitation, 1945; contbr to med jours. Recipient: Legion of Merit, US Army, 1945; NY Conspicuous Service Cross, NY State, 1951. Home: North Wading River, LI, NY. Office: 55 Fifth Ave, New York, NY.

KOGEN, David C, US, rabbi; b. Rutki, Pol, Sept 19,1919; s. Meyer and Esther (Raiter); in US since 1928; BA, U Chgo, 1942; ordained rabbi, JTSA, 1946, MHL, 1949; MA, U of BC, 1951; m: Dena Rosenblum, June 18, 1947; c: Judah, Avram, Ben-Zion, Noam. Admn vice-chancellor, JTSA, since 1966, on staff since 1958; dir and instr, liturgy, Cantors Inst-Sem Coll of J Music, since 1958; rabbi, Cong Beth Isr, Vancouver, Can, 1946-55; dir, B'nai B'rith Hillel Found, U of BC, 1946-55; visiting rabbi: Park Ave Syn, NYC, 1956-57; Temple Ansche Chesed, 1957-58; dir, comty activities, United Syn Amer, 1955-58. Pres, Heb Arts Found, 1957-59; mem:

membership comm, RA, since 1955; NY bd Rabbis, since 1955; United Syn of Amer, comm on cong standards, since 1955. Contbr to rel jours. Home: 315 W 106 St, New York, NY. Study: 3080 Broadway, New York, NY.

KOHEN, Sami, (Sam Cohen), Turkey, journalist; b. Istanbul, July 14, 1928; s. Albert and Margueritte (Adjubel); att Sch of Journalism, U Istanbul, 1948-50, fac of law, 1948-50; m. Mirka Barzilai, May 29, 1960. Fgn ed, columnist on intl affairs, Milliyet, Istanbul, since 1954; corresp in Turkey for: Guardian; The Economist; The Sun; Wash Post; Newsweek; Christian Sci Monitor; NANA; Maariv; J Chronicle; fmr: asst fgn ed, Yeni Istanbul; fgn ed, columnist, Istanbul Ekspres. Turkish Army, 1951-52. Mem, B'nai B'rith; fmr mem, Istanbul City Council, 1964-68. Recipient, award from Turkish Journalists Assn, 1959, 1960, 1967, 1968. Hobbies: swimming, fishing. Office: Milliyet Gazetesi, Cagaloglu, Istanbul, Turkey.

KOHEN ERKIP, Heskiya, Turkey, physician; b. Edirne, Turkey, Apr 2, 1923; s. Albert and Lisa (Rodrigue); MD, Faculté de Médecine, Istanbul, 1946; dipl, spec, internal diseases, Faculté de Médecine, Ankara, 1951. Dir, clinic for internal diseases, Fac Med, Ankara, since 1951; pvt practice since 1952; asst, Fac of Med, Ankara, 1948-51. Turkish Army Res, 1946-48. Vice-pres, J Comty, Ankara, since 1961; mem: Chambre des Médecins d'Ankara; Masons. Contbr to med publs in Turkey, Switz, Fr. Recipient, Cavalliere Ordre, Pres It, 1963. Hobbies: bridge, music. Home: Atatürk Bulvari, 137/4, Ankara, Turkey.

KOHLBERG, Joshua, Isr, chemist, business exec; b. Kalusz, Aus, Dec 6, 1905; s. Chana Reig; in Isr since 1939; PhD, chem, U Vienna, MPharm, 1929; m. Irma Fuerst; c: Etan, Elon. Jt gen mgr, Salomon, Levin, Elstein Ltd, Tel Aviv; mem, bd dirs, Assia-Zori-Teva Pharmaceutical Mfg Cos; pres, mgn dir, Econ Enterprises of Pharms in Isr; mem bd govs, exec comm, Heb U, Jerusalem; hon pres, Pharmaceutical Assn Isr; chmn, pharm comm, Min of Health, Jerusalem; hon treas, Friends of Heb U, Jerusalem, Isr; mem council, Fédération Internationale Pharmaceutique; fmr delg to ZCs. Hon mem: J Pharmaceutical Soc of Amer; Alpha Zeta Omega. Home: 68 Achad Ha'am St, Tel Aviv, Isr. Office: 85 Nahlat Benyamin St, Tel Aviv, Isr.

KOHN, David, Isr, physician; b. Rimavska Sobota, Czech, Oct 21, 1932; s. Asher and Rosa (Engel); in Isr since 1945; MD, Zurich, Switz, 1959; m. Sarah Stern, Aug 7, 1961. Phys, internal med, Kaplan Hosp, Rehovot, since 1963. IDF, MC Res, since 1961. Home: 11 Hagalil St, Rehovot, Isr. Office: Kaplan Hosp, Rehovot, Isr.

KOHN, Emeric, Fr, organization exec; b. Oradea, Rum, Jan 22, 1913; s. Bernard and Esther (Nasch); in Fr since 1931; dipl, Conservatoire Natl des Arts et Metiers, 1936; m. Madeleine Strauss, June 19, 1947; four c. Secy gen: Consistoire Israélite de Paris, since 1964; Comité de Bienfaisance Israélite, since 1955; Eclaireurs Israélites de France (Scouts), 1946-47; dir, Service Accueil et Reclassement, 1947-49; head fund raising, Fonds Social Juif Unifé, 1949-55. Fr Army, 1939-45. Mem, bd dirs, Eclaireurs Israélites de France. Recipient: Médaille du Combattant. Office: 17 Rue St Georges, Paris, Fr.

KOHN, Henry, US, lawyer; b. St Louis, Mo, Feb 5, 1917; s. Henry and Hannah (Lederer); BA, Phi Beta Kappa, Yale U, 1939, LLB, Law Sch, 1942; m. Anne Frankenthaler, Sep 23, 1945; c: Margaret, Barbara, Alice. Sr partner, Frankenthaler and Kohn, since 1968; dir: Graphic Sci Inc; GSI Computer; Edison Bros Stores; Info Sci; atty, Bd of Econ Wfr, Wash DC, 1942; pres, dir: Fiduciary Mutual Investing, 1964-67; Mercer Fund, 1963-67. Capt, US Army, 1942-46. Pres, dir, Amer J Soc for Service; dir: J Wfr Fund; Natl J Wfr Bd, fmr treas; Commn on Youth Service Projects; J Conciliation Bd of Amer; Natl Muscular Dystrophy Assn; Lavanburg Corner House Found; 92nd St YM-YMHA; pres, dir: Ed Lee and Jean Campe Found; Sam and Louise Campe Found; bd govs, USO; mem: Assn Bar, NYC; Amer Bar Assn; NY Co Lawyers; clubs: Lawyer's; Harmonie; NY Lawn Bowling. Recipient, Army Commendation Medal. Home: 155 E 77 St, New York, NY. Office: 120 Broadway, New York, NY.

KOHN, Moshe M, Isr, journalist; b. NYC, Dec 22, 1923; s. Hersch and Leah (Sternberg); in Isr since 1957; BA, Roosevelt U, Chgo, 1951; m. Barbara Shalowitz, 1949, (decd); c: Michael, Vivian, Roni, Avraham. Lit ed, Jerusalem Post, since 1969, on staff since 1958; social group worker, J Comty

Cens Chgo, 1948-51; mgn ed, Natl J Post and Opinion, Indianapolis, Ind, 1951-54; dir, book dept, Herzl Press, JA, NY, 1954-57. US Army, 1943-46. Mem, AACI, fmr chmn, Jerusalem br; fmr: mem exec, Isr Journalists Assn; natl admn comm, Hapoel Hamizrachi of Amer. Author: A Song of Freedom, cantata, 1948; trans from Heb: House of Dolls by Katzetnik, 1955; In the Grip of Cross Currents by Ephraim Lisitzky, 1959; Piepel by Katzetnik, 1961; contbr of: poetry; book revs; articles; trans of Heb, Yiddish poetry; short stories to anthols, mags, newspapers. Recipient: Battle Star, India-Burma Campaign, WWII; Anti-Nazi Fighters Ribbon; Isr State Fighters Decoration. Hobby, archery. Home: 58 Hantke St, Jerusalem, Isr. Office: POB 81, Jerusalem, Isr.

KOHN, Paul Jacob, Isr, organization exec; b. Baden, Aus, Nov 17, 1930; s. Sigmund and Margit (Freund); grad, Davenant Found, London, 1948; m. Hannah Moshytz, Aug 30, 1960; c: Raphael, Galia. Repr, JA, London, since 1968; gen mgr, Concord PR, 1965-68; mgr, Eilat Tourism Bur, 1962-64; staff corresp, feature writer, mil corresp, Jerusalem Post, 1954-62. Mil Corresp, IDF, 1958-62. Vice chmn, Brit Settlers in Isr Assn, Tel Aviv br; fmr, mem, Isr Journalists Assn. Author, Lightning Out of Israel, 1967. Hobby, sports. Home: 6 Derech Hatayassim, Tel Aviv, Isr. Office: 39 Nachmani St, Tel Aviv, Isr.

KOHN, S Joshua, US, rabbi; b. Vilkomar, Lith, June 17, 1899; s. Isadore and Bella (Voichek); in US since 1908; att: Graetz Coll; Heb U, Jerusalem; BA, Columbia U, 1923, MA, 1926; ordained rabbi, MHL, JTSA, 1925, DHL, 1947, DD, HC, 1963; m. Priva Konowitz, July 5, 1925; c: Ezra, Y Ammi, Hedva. Rabbi: Cong Adath Isr, since 1946; Cong B'nai Jeshurun, Phila, 1925-26; W Phila J Comty Cen, 1926-29; Temple Beth El, Utica, NY, 1930-45. Chaplain, US Maritime Service, left with rank, lt cdr, 1943-45. Pres, Bd Rabbis, Trenton, since 1962; mem: natl council, JDC, since 1936; governing bd, AJCong, since 1956, vice-pres, NJ region, since 1958; chmn, comm on small comtys, United Syn of Amer; mem: admn comm, United Pal Appeal; Trenton Comm on Civil Rights; Fgn Policy Assn; Amer Acad J Research; natl council, Amer Friends Heb U; Acad of Political Sci; Council on Hum Relations; fmr: org, JCC, Utica; chmn, mem 1st natl admn comm, Avukah, NY; pres, W Phila dist, ZOA; vicepres: Phila Young Judea; Natl Youth Admn, Utica; Empire State region, ZOA, NY; pres, ZOA, Trenton, NJ; mem bd: Family Wfr Soc; J Fed; exec comm, Rabb Assembly, mem, comm on comty planning; clubs: Torch; Utica; Trenton. Author: The Jewish Community of Utica, NY, 1847-1948; Jacob Mordechai Netter, World Traveler, 1958; David Naar of Trenton, NJ, 1964; Mordechai M Noah's Ararat Project and the Missionaries, 1965; Outlines of Jewish Customs and Institutions, 1927; A Sociological Study of Jewish Sailors in the US Maritime Service, 1947. Home: 557 Bellevue Ave, Trenton, NJ. Study: Cong Adath Isr, Trenton, NJ.

KOHN, Walter, US, physicist; b. Vienna, Aus, Mar 9, 1923; s. Salomon and Gusti (Rapaport); in US since 1946; BA, MA, LLD, U Toronto, 1942-46; PhD, Harvard U, 1948; m. Lois Adams, Mar 12, 1947; c: Judith, Ingrid, Eva. Prof, physics, U Cal, San Diego, since 1960; instr, Harvard U, 1948-50; prof, Carnegie Inst of Tech, 1950-59. Cpl, Can Infantry Corps, 1944-45. Mem: bd dirs, San Diego Open Forum; Natl Acad Scis; Amer Acad Arts and Scis. Contbr numerous publs to phys jours. Recipient, Oliver Buckley Prize in Solid State Physics, Amer Phys Soc, 1960. Spec interest, population control. Home: 8631 Kilbourn Dr, La Jolla, Cal. Office: U of Cal, La Jolla, Cal.

KOHN, Zillah L, US, editor; b. Meridian, Miss, Feb 2, 1897; d. Wolff and Fannie Willner; BA, Rice U, 1917; m. Sylvan Kohn, July 7, 1921; c: Ezra, Joshua (killed in action, Korea). Ed: publications, Natl Women's League, United Syn of Amer, since 1952; asso ed, "Mrs G J", Women's Org, J Wfr Bd; tchr, Eng, Cen HS, 1917-19; registrar and vocational cons, S End HS, 1919-21, both of Houston, Tex. Mem: natl bd, exec comm, Natl Women's League; AJCong, exec bd, bus and profsl women's div, Gtr Newark chap; admn comm, JWB, women's div; ZOA; Hadassah; J Book Council; Miriam Auxiliary, Cong Oheb Shalom, S Orange, NJ; Newark Mus; club, Contemporary, Newark. Home: 259 Reynolds Terr, Orange, NJ. Office: 48 E 74 St, New York, NY.

KOHRMAN, Margery Smith, US, communal leader; b. Cleveland, O, Mar 30, 1928; d. Karl and Marian (Shapiro) Smith; BA, Wellesley Coll, Mass, 1950; MEd, W Reserve U, 1952; m. Lee Kohrman, July 20, 1952; c: Bruce, Katherine, Jonathan, Matthew. Mem: natl bd, Women's Amer ORT, fmr pres, Cleveland region, ed bd, Women's Amer ORT Reporter; bd trustees, Cleveland Coll J Studies; numerous philanthropic orgs. Home: 2889 Eaton Rd, Shaker Heights, O.

KOHS, Ellis B, US, composer, educator; b. Chgo, Ill, May 12, 1916; s. Samuel and Paula (Bonoff); att: SF Conservatory, 1926-28; Juillard Sch Music, 1928-33, grad sch, 1938-39; MA, U Chgo, 1938; Harvard U, 1939-41. Prof, theory and composition, Sch of Music, U of S Cal, head, theory dept, on fac since 1950; instr: U Wis, summer, 1940; Kan City Conservatory, summers, 1946, 1947; asso prof: Wesleyan U, 1946-48, Coll of Pacific, 1948-50; lectr, Stanford U, summer, 1950. US Army, 1941-46. Composer: Legend for Oboe and Strings, 1946; Symphony Noland No 2; Piano Variations, 1946; Chamber Concerto for Viola and Strings, 1949; Tocata, 1948; Ten Two Voice Inventions; Passacaglia for Organ and Strings, 1946; Capriccio for Organ, 1948; Three Chorale Variations on Hebrew Hymns, 1952; String Quartet No 1, 1942; Night Watch, 1943; Sonatina for Bassoon and Piano, 1944; Sonatine for Violin and Piano, 1951; XXIII Psalm; Three Songs from the Navajo; Three Greek Choruses; Three Medieval Latin Student Songs; Foreland and Scherzo, 1958; Lord of the Ascendant; Amerika (opera). Author, Music Theory, 1960. Mem: Composer's Alliance Music Libr Assn; fmr: chmn, LA chap, Intl Soc for Contemporary Music; pres, LA chap, Natl Assn for Amer Composers and Conductors. Recipient, Ditson award, Columbia U, 1946. Home: 8025 Highland Trail, Los Angeles, Cal. Office: U of S Cal, Los Angeles, Cal.

KOHS, Samuel C, US, social worker, psychologist; b. NYC, June 2, 1890; s. Louis and Fannie (Rosenfeld); BS, CCNY, 1912; MA, Clark U, Worcester, Mass, 1914; PhD, Stanford U, 1919; m. Paula Bonoff, Mar 1, 1912 (decd); c: Ellis. cons, psych and social services since 1956; chmn, dept social tech, Grad Sch Social Work, NYC, 1929-38; dir, resettlement div, Natl Ref Service, now HIAS, NYC, 1938-40; ref service comm, LA, 1940-41; admn field secy, w states sect, JWB, 1941-56; dir, Bur War Records, NYC, 1942-47. Prin contribs: inventor: IQ Slide Rule; Ethical Discrimination Test; Block Design Intelligence Test. F: Amer Psych Assn; AAAS; dipl, clinical psych, Amer Psych Assn; cert psych, State of Cal; mem: Amer Stat Assn; Natl Assn Social Workers; Acad Cert Social Workers; Natl Soc for Study Educ; Natl Conf on Social Wfr; Natl Conf J Communal Service; hon mem, Natl Assn J Cen Workers; fmr: pres, Ore Conf Social Work; vice pres, Cal Conf Social Work; chmn, bd dirs, YIVO. Author: Intelligence Measurement, 1923; The Roots of Social Work, 1966; contbr to J and profsl jours; contrib ed bd, Reconstructionist. Home: 1901 Garden Dr, Burlingame, Cal.

KOKHBA, Moshe, Isr, educational adv; b. Russ, July, 1900; s. Pinchas and Ita; BS, MA, PhD, Tchrs Coll, Columbia U, 1928-32; m. Lea Kirshner; c: Itzhak. Educ adv, Min of Educ and Culture; fmr: prin, Heb HS; sup schs; mem, pedg secretariat, Min of Educ and Culture. Fmr: head tchrs org, Jerusalem; mem, Cen Tchrs Org, Tel Aviv. Author: Theory and Practice in Education; Elements of Teaching; Teaching of Arithmetic. Home: 98 Ussishkin St, Tel Aviv, Isr. Office: Min of Educ, Tel Aviv, Isr.

KOL (Kolodny) Moshe, Isr, legislator, communal leader; b. Pinsk, Russ, May 28, 1911; in Isr since 1932; att Heb U, Jerusalem; m. Kaeta Muskat; three c. Min, Tourism since 1969; Tourism and Devl, 1965-69; mem, Govt of Natl Unity of Isr, since 1967; chmn, cen comm, Independent Lib Party; MK since 1959; mem, JA exec, since 1946, fmr: head, Youth Aliyah Dept; chmn, Lib Lab Movement; mem, cabinet of late Levi Eshkol; one of the signatories of Declaration of Independence of Isr, mem, Provisional State Council of Isr, first chmn, Comm for Fgn Affairs; missions to: Eur, Amer, Asia, Afr on behalf of JA; chmn: parl educ and culture comm; parl sports comm. Mem: presidium, KMK, Gen Zionists Constructive Fund; council, Yad Vashem; exec, Isr Archaeol Soc; vice-pres, Intl Fed of Children's Comtys, under UNESCO; chmn, comm, mutual aid, Intl Union of Child Wfr; delg to all ZCs since 1933; hon treas, Isr Exploration Soc; fmr: co-found, Zionist Youth Movement; mem, exec comm, Histadrut. Author: Arichim; The Youth Aliyah Story; Netivot BeChinuch uveShikum; Teachers and Friends, all Heb; Youth Aliyah—Past, Present and Future; Youth Aliyah, Fr, Eng; contbr on lab, educ, politics to local and fgn press. Recipient: Grand Croix de L'ordre de Leopold II;

Union Order of Merit. Home: 10 Jabotinsky St, Jerusalem, Isr. Office: Ministry of Tourism, Jerusalem, Isr.

KOLB, Felix O, US, physician, educator; b. Vienna, Aus, Nov 21, 1921; s. Leon and Hilde (Gruenwald); in US since 1938; BA, U Cal, 1941, MD, 1943. Clinical prof, med, research phys, U of Cal Med Sch, SF, since 1968; research phys, Metabolic Research Unit, since 1968; asso chief, med, Mt Zion Hosp; cons staff, Children's Hosp; fmr: research asst, clinical instr, med, both U Cal; clinical asst, U of Cal Hosp, staff phys since 1951; clinical asst, med, Mass Gen Hosp. Capt, US Army, 1944-46. Dipl, Amer Bd Internal Med; f, Amer Coll Phys; mem: Cal Med Soc; SF Med Soc; AMA; Amer Diabetes Assn; Endocrine Soc; W Soc Clinical Research; Amer Fed Clinical Research; Cal, SF Socs Internal Med; NY Acad Med; Phi Delta Epsilon; Alpha Omega Alpha, fmr secy-treas. Asso ed, Alumni-Fac Assn, U of Cal, since 1952; contbr numerous articles on edocrinology and metabolism. Hobby: music. Home: 9 Starboard Court, Mill Valley, Cal. Office: 3580 California St, San Francisco, Cal.

KOLB, Leon, US, physician, educator; b. Czernowitz, Aus, July 5, 1890; s. Berl and Ettie (Roth); in US since 1937; MD, U of Vienna, 1914, PhD, 1930; m. Hilde Grunwald, July 1, 1919; c: Ruth Globerson, Felix, Theodor. Asso clinical prof, pharm and therapeutics, Stanford U Med Sch, since 1954, research asso, 1952-54; practicing phys, co-owner, sanatorium, Vienna, 1919-37; staff mem, Inst of Pharm, 1919-37. Delg to opening of Heb U, Jerusalem, as pres, J U Assn, Vienna, 1925; bd dirs: ZOA; AJCong; natl exec, Amer F of IMA, corresp mem; sponsor, propagation J and Israeli art through JWB; corresp mem, IMA, since 1967; art collector since 1908, specializing in graphic art, donated art collection to Haifa Munic Mus, 1969. Author: Moses the Near Easterner, 1956; The Woodcuts of Jacob Steinhardt, 1959; Berenice Princess of Judea, 1959; Mission to Claudius, 1963; The Sage; The Sabbath Princess; The Vienna Jewish Museum; contbr to J press and profsl jours. Home: 1814 Pacific Ave, San Francisco, Cal. Office: Stanford U, Palo Alto, Cal.

KOLET, Ezra, India, public official; b. Calcutta, India, Jan 6, 1914; s. Benjamin and Sheba; m. Ruth Daniel, Nov 10, 1943; c: Edna, Rebecca, Uriel, Noel, Baruch. Chmn, exec comm, Gen Ins Council of India, since 1961; chief controller of chartering, Dept of Transp, Govt of India, since 1961; with Indian Treasury since 1939; fmr: dep secy, Min of Finance; financial adv, Min of Irrigation and Power. Pres: Cen Secretariat Service, Govt of India; J Assn, Ajmer; Cen Govt Employees Hire Purchase Coop Soc; found, secy: Delhi SymSoc; Delhi Sym Orch; found, treas, India Cen Social Wfr Bd; secy, J Wfr Assn, New Delhi; mem, ORT, India. Hobby: music. Home: 74 Babar Rd, New Delhi, India. Office: Dept of Transport, Government of India, New Delhi, India.

KOLITZ, Zelda, Isr, editor; b. Jerusalem, Nov 11, 1924; d. Mordechai and Jaffa (Werner) Sonnenfeld; att Heb U, Jerusalem; m. Chaim Kolitz, 1942; c: David, Josef. Asst ed, Gesher, since 1961; org convs, United Syns of Amer, 1963-64; head, PR Dept, Yad Vashem, 1960-63. Author: stories for plays: Dark and Bright, 1958; Kalum Fate and Freedom, 1959; The Professor and his Sister, 1959. Dep dir, Isr Exec, WJC, since 1966; hon secy, Friends of Jerusalem Artists' House. Home: 29 King George St, Jerusalem, Isr. Office: 1 Ben Yehudah St, Jerusalem, Isr.

KOLLEK, Theodore (Teddy), Isr, administrator, politician; b. Vienna, Aus, May 27, 1911; s. Alfred and Margaret (Fleischer); in Isr since 1934; m. Tamar Schwartz, May, 1937; c: Amos, Osnat. Mayor, Jerusalem, since 1965; educ missions to Zionist youth groups, Eur, 1938-40; i/c contacts with J underground in Eur for JA, 1942-45; head, Haganah mission to US, 1947-48; head, US desk, Isr Fgn Office, 1950; min plen, Wash, 1951-52; dir gen, PM's Off, 1952-65; head, Nuclear Desalination of Water Project, 1964-66. Chmn, bd, Isr Mus, since 1965; fmr: mem, T'helet Lavan Zionist Youth Org, Aus; instr, Hehalutz groups, Aus, Czech, Ger, Eng; fmr mem, Kibbutz Ein Gev. Co-author: Jerusalem: Sacred City of Mankind, 1969. Home: 6 Rashba St, Jerusalem, Isr. Office: Municipality of Jerusalem, Isr.

KOLLER, Israel B, US, rabbi; b. Dobrowa, Pol, Jan 10, 1936; s. Leib and Hela; in US since 1949; BA, Wayne State U, Detroit, Mich, 1958; MA, ordained rabbi, HUC, 1961; m. Margaret Sukrow, Jan 6, 1962; c: Jeremy, Shoshana. Rabbi, Hillel Counselor, U of Cal, since 1966; rabbi: Cong B'nai

B'rith, since 1966; Cong Rodef Shalom, Port Arthur, Tex, 1963-66. Chaplain, US Army, 1961-63. Mem: CCAR; Rotary Club; Elks. Home: 7668 Newport Dr, Goleta, Cal. Study: 900 San Antonio Creek Rd, Santa Barbara, Cal.

KOLODNER, Louis J, US, surgeon; b. Baltimore, Md, Dec 7, 1911; s. George and Rose (Lieberman); BA, Johns Hopkins U, 1932; MD, U Md Sch of Med, 1936; m. Lee Bressler, Feb 18, 1937; c: George, Robert. Pvt practice since 1943; asst prof, surg, Johns Hopkins Med Sch, since 1966; att surg, asso path, Sinai Hosp, Baltimore, since 1954; mem staff: Gtr Baltimore Med Cen, since 1965; Bon Secours Hosp, since 1953; fmr surg, MD State VFW. USN, Bainbridge Naval Hosp; chief surg, US Naval Hosp, Palermo, It, WWII. Prin contrbs: devised various new surgical instruments. F: SE Surg Conf; AMA; dipl: Amer Bd Surgs; FACS; chmn, med div, Asso J Charities and Wfr Fund, Baltimore; mem: Md Med and Chirurgical Fac; Baltimore City Med Soc; Johns Hopkins Med Soc; AAAS; S Med Assn; Amer Med Soc of Vienna; Inst Elec and Electronic Engrs; Assn for Advancement Med Instrumentation; Baltimore Heb Cong; fmr: mem: bd dirs: Asso J Charities, Baltimore; Alumni Exec Comm, Johns Hopkins U; clubs: Johns Hopkins; Tudor and Stuart; Johns Hopkins U; Green Valley Swimming. Home: 6107 Biltmore Ave, Baltimore, Md. Office: 2502 Eutaw Pl, Baltimore, Md.

KOLODNEY, Morris, US, metallurgist, educator; b. NYC, Sep 24, 1911; s. David and Eva (Gisses); BS, CCNY, 1932; Chem E, 1933; MS, Columbia U, 1936, PhD, 1939; m. Edith Charney, Oct 5, 1935; c: Steven, Elizabeth. Prof, electrochem, metallurgy, CCNY, since 1953, fac mem since 1934; fmr: research, Los Alamos Sci Lab, 1943-46; cons, war metallurgy comm, NRC, 1942; prin cons, metallurgy, Nepa Project, Oak Ridge, 1946-51; cons, Gen Elec Aircraft Propulsion project, 1951-58; cons, United Nuclear Corp, since 1950. Mem: Amer Soc Metals; Electro-chem Soc; Amer Inst Chem Engr; Amer Inst Mining and Metallurgic Engrs. Home: 187 Wales Ave, River Edge, NJ. Office: CCNY, Convent Ave & 139 St, New York, NY.

KOLODNEY, William, US, educational exec; b. Minsk, Russ, Oct 12, 1899; s. Nathan and Ida; in US since 1903; BS, NYU, 1921; MS, Columbia U, 1925, DE, 1950; m. Lea Rothus (decd); c: Rima, Nathan, David. Educ dir, 92nd St YM and YWHA; fmr cons, auditorium events, Metrop Mus of Art; educ dir, YM and YWHA, Pittsburgh, Pa, 1926-31. Mem, Amer Assn Psych Study of Social Issues. Hobby: poetry. Home: 118 E 93 St, New York, NY. Office: YM-YWHA, 1395 Lexington Ave, New York, NY.

KOLOMS, Robert Ruben, US, civil engr; b. Chgo, Ill, Aug 16, 1915; s. Simon and Ida (Itkov); m. Ruth Cohen, Sep 6, 1941; c: Stephen, Jerome. Chief engr, asso, Hazelet and Erdal, cons engrs, since 1947; fmr: engr, architect, Lester Geis; ME, Sanderson and Porter, 1941-47. Pres, Louisville Lodge 14, B'nai B'rith; commn, scout master, Boy Scouts of Amer; mem, Amer Soc Civil Engrs. Recipient: Silver Beaver, Boy Scouts of Amer. Home: 2718 Lakeside Dr, Louisville, Ky. Office: 405 Commerce Bldg, Louisville, Ky.

KOLONOMOS, Žamila, Yugo, social worker; b. Yugo, 1922; d. Isak and Esterina; m. Avram Sadikario, 1945; c: Mira, Samuel. Prof, fac of letters, Skopje; pres, Conseil de la Protection et de l'Education des Enfants de Macédoine; profsl political official since 1941. Pres, Assn of Women of Macedonia. Author: Les Parlers Judéo-Espagnols de Bitola et de Skopje en Macédoine. Recipient: Order for Valor; Partisan Memorial, 1941; Partisan Star, III deg; Order of Frat and Unity, I deg; Merits for the People, II deg; Order of the Rep with silver wreath. Home: Djuro Strugar 15A, Skopje, Yugo. Office: Council for Care and Educ of Children of Macedonia, Vodujanska 51, Skopje, Yugo.

KOLTHOFF, Izaac M, US, educator, research chemist; b. Almelo, Netherlands, Feb 11, 1894; s. Moses and Rosetta (Wysenbeek); in US since 1927; PhD, U of Utrecht, 1918; hon professorship, San Marcos U, Lima, Peru, 1954; hon doctorate: U of Chgo, 1955; U Groningen, Holland, 1964. Prof, head, analytical chem, U of Minn, since 1927; asst, pharmaceutical lab, U of Utrecht, 1915-18, conservator, 1918-23, privatdozent, 1923-27; dir, research project on emulsion polymerization, Reconstruction Finance Corp, 1942-46; chmn, comm on analytical chem, NRC, 1952;

mem, chem adv comm, Off of Air Research, 1949-52. F, AAAS; mem: Natl Acad Scis; Amer Acad Arts and Scis; Amer Assn for UN; World Federalists; Council Fgn Relations; Amer Friends of Heb U; hon mem: Amer Pharmaceutical Assn; Soc for Analytical Chem; Span, Finnish, Peruvian, Czech and Isr Chem Socs; fgn mem: Royal Bohemian Acad Scis and Fine Arts; Royal Flemish Acad Scis and Fine Arts; Royal Acad Scis, Amsterdam; Acad Scis, Lisbon; fmr: pres, sect analytical chem, Intl Union of Pure and Applied Chem, chmn, comm of phys chem data of analytic interest; mem, bd dirs, Natl Council of Arts, Scis, Professions; council mem, Atlantic Union Comm. Author: Konduktometrische Titrationen, 1924; Der Gebrauch von Farbenindikatoren, 1927, 1937, trans into Fr; The Colorimetric and Potentiometric Determination of pH, 1943, trans into Ger, Russ; Volumetric Analysis, vol I, 1942, vol II, 1946, vol III, 1958, trans into Japanese, Russ; co-author: Potentiometric Titrations, 1931; Textbook of Quantitative Inorganic Analysis, 1952, trans into Russ, Yugo, Span; Polarography, 2 vols, 1952, trans into Russ; Emulsion Polymerization, 1955; ed, Treatise of Analytical Chem, 1959; contbr to profsl jours. Recipient: Charles Medal, U of Prague, 1936; Nichols Medal, 1949; Fisher Award, analytical chem, 1950; Cdr in Order Oranje-Nassau, since 1947; Willard Gibbs Medal, 1964; Hanus Medal, Czech Chem Soc, 1967; Kolthoff Gold Medal, analytical chem, Acad Pharmaceutical Scis, 1967. Hobby: horses. Home: Campus Club, U of Minnesota, Minneapolis, Minn. Office: U of Minnesota, Minneapolis, Minn.

KOMAROVSKY, Mirra, US, sociologist, educator; b. Russ; d. Mendel and Anna (Steinberg); in US since 1922; BA, Barnard Coll, 1926; MA, Columbia U, 1927, PhD, 1939; m. Marcus Heyman, Oct 1940. Prof, sociol, Barnard Coll, since 1954, dept chmn, 1949-65, on fac since 1936; asso prof, Skidmore Coll, 1928-29; research asso: Yale, 1930-31; Columbia U, 1931-33. Fmr pres, E Sociol Soc; mem: council, Amer Sociol Assn, 1966-69; Friends Heb U. Author: The Unemployed Man and his Family, 1940; Women in the Modern World, Their Education and Their Dilemmas, 1953; Blue Collar Marriage, 1967; co-author, Leisure, A Suburban Study, 1933; ed, Common Frontiers of the Social Sciences, 1967; asso ed, Amer Sociol Review, 1956-59. Home: 340 Riverside Dr, New York, NY. Office: Barnard Coll, Columbia U, New York, NY.

KOMKOMMER, Jozef, Belgium, business exec; b. Amsterdam, Feb 12, 1911; s. Isaac and Henriette (Klok); att Koninklijk Atheneum, Antwerp; m. Susanne, Sep 20, 1934; c: Jeanrenaud Studer, Jacques. Chmn bd, I Komkommer & Zoon NV, diamond dealer. Pvt, Netherlands E Indies Army, 1941-46. Chmn, KH, Antwerp; pres, Belgium Friends of Heb U, Antwerp sect; co-chmn, Memorial aux Martyrs Juifs de Belgique; bd govs, Heb U; B'nai B'rith, Antwerp; fmr: chmn, J Wfr Org, Centrale, Antwerp; pres, commn on fundraising progs, Eur Council, J Comty Services, Geneva. Recipient: Off, Order of King Leopold II; Knight, Order of Solidarity, conferred by Pres of It. Home: 1 Hofdreef, Gravenwezel, Belgium. Office: 62 Pelikaanstaat, Antwerpen, Belgium.

KONFINO, Žak, Yugo, physician, author; b. Yugo, June 23, 1892; s. Lazar and Klara (Koen); MD, U of Belgrade, 1918; m. Andja Andrić. Ret; fmr practicing phys. Author: short stories; Moji opštinari, 1934; Lica i nalićja, 1935; Moj Jocko, 1938; Humoreske, 1941; Rotarijanci, 1947; 100 godina-90 groša, 1952; Nove Humoreske, 1960; novels: Moje jedinće, 1952; for children, Mamin veliki sin, 1960; Tesi li ti zazapeo Hrista, 1968; play, U sredu se registrujem, 1954; drama, Žaklinjem se, 1956; theater plays: Plagijat; Krv nije voda; Siroto moje pametno dete; Eksperiment, performed, Warsaw, 1942; comedy, Prevario sam svoju ženu, 1962; ed, Jewish Almanac. Fmr: pres: J Comty: Leskovac; Belgrade; People's U, Leskovac; mem exec, Fed of J Comtys. Recipient: Order of Albanian Memorial, 1919. Home: Lole Ribara 50, Belgrade, Yugo.

KONIKOFF, Adia, Isr, business exec; b. St Petersburg, Russ, Feb 5, 1912; s. Efim and Musser (Gurewitch); DRerPol, Us: Königsberg, Berlin-Bonn, Basel, 1930-35; advocate, Law Sch, Jerusalem, 1948; m. Carmel Abbady; c: Nurith Levy, Daniel, Ronny. Vice-chmn, bd: Banque Privée, SA, Geneva, since 1965; Isr Gen Bank Ltd, Tel Aviv, since 1968; dir, financial dept, KKL, 1951; controller, fgn exch, Isr Govt, 1952-53; mgn dir, Suisse-Israélien Trade Bank, Geneva, 1954-64; chmn bd, Fgn Trade Bank Ltd, 1963-64. Gov: Wiezmann Inst of Sci; Tel Aviv U. Author: Transjordan and Economics Survey,

1946. Homes: Chemin de Challendin 14, Geneva, Switz; Herzliyah Pituah, Isr. Office: 18 rue de Hesse, Geneva, Switz.

KONVISER, Julian Victor, S Afr, dentist; b. Salisbury, Rhodesia, Nov 29, 1941; s. Maurice and Rae; grad, U of Witwatersrand; att: Eastman Dent Inst, London; U of Groningem, Holland. Fmr: lectr, Oral and Dental Hosp, Johannesburg; found, ed, Diastema, dent jour. Home: 2 Riviera Mansions, Riviera, Johannesburg, S Afr.

KONVISER, Maurice, S Afr, rabbi; b. Bialystok, Russ, June 2, 1902; s. Jacob and Leah (Beila); att: Yeshiva Etz Chaim, London; Js Coll, 1924; BA, London U; ordained rabbi, 1927; m. Rachel Liptz, 1937; c: Pauline, Julian, Arthur. Chief min, Gt Syn, Cape Town, S Afr; fmr: sr min, Salisbury Dist Cong, Rhodesia; asst min: Gt Syn, London, 1925-27; Kimberly Cong, Rhodesia, 1927-35. Mem: cen council, Rhodesia U; Native Wfr Bd; comm, Queen Vic Libr; Rhodesia Childrens Home; Child Protection Soc; Rhodesian J Bd Deps; Rhodesian ZC. Author: The Jew in Southern Rhodesia, jubilee vol, Salisbury Heb Cong. Recipient: OBE, 1964. Study: 84 Hatfield St, Gardens, Cape Town, S Afr.

KONVITZ, Milton R, US, educator; b. Safed, Isr, Mar 12, 1908; s. Joseph and Welia (Wilowky); in US since 1915; BS, NYU, 1928, MA, 1930; JD, 1930; PhD, Cornell U, 1933; hon: DLitt, Rutgers U, 1954; DCL, U Liberia, 1962; LHD, HUC-JIR, 1966; m. Mary Traub, June 18, 1944; c: Josef. Prof, ind and lab relations, law, Cornell U, since 1946; fmr: gen counsel: Newark Housing Auth, 1938-43; NJ State Housing Auth, 1943-46; lectr, law and public admn, NYU, 1938-46; fac mem, New Sch for Soc Research, 1944-46; asst gen counsel, NAACP, 1943-46; dir, codification of laws, Liberia, since 1952; public repr, Natl War Lab Bd, 1943-46; fac mem, sem in Amer studies, Salzburg, Aus, 1952; mem, enforcement commn and hearing off, Natl Wage Stabilization Bd, 1952-53; Paley lectr, Heb U, Jerusalem, 1968; mem: NJ Bar since 1932; mediation and arbitration panels of: Amer Arbitration Assn; Fed Mediation and Conciliation Service; NY State Mediation Bd; NY State Public Employment Relations Bd. Chmn: Heb Culture Found; fmr, Commn for Study of J Educ in US; vice-pres, J Acad of Arts and Sci; trustee, U Liberia; treas and secy, Inst for Unity of Sci; mem, bd dirs: Conf on J Soc Studies; Workers Defense League; Amer J Legion for Isr; Histadrut Cultural Exch Inst; Amer Found for Tropical Med; Liberia Inst; mem, bd govs, Columbia U Cen for Research and Educ in Amer Liberties; mem: natl comm, ACLU; natl lawyers comm, NAACP; adv council, AJCong; natl comm, Natl Hillel Founds; legal comm, Natl Comm Against Discrimination in Housing; acad council, J Tchrs Inst and People's U; Commn on Reorg, WZO; acad council, YIVO Sci Inst; commn on rel and race, Syn Council of Amer; Amer Bar Assn; Amer Phil Soc; Amer Political Sci Assn; Amer Studies Assn; Ind Relations Research Assn; Phi Beta Kappa; Order of the Coif; Law and Soc Assn; Amer J Hist Soc; Intl Assn for Phil of Law and Soc Leg; Emerson Soc; Thoreau Soc; Amer Acad for J Research; Intl Afr Law Assn; Amer Soc for Political and Legal Phil; f: Amer Assn for J Educ; Afr Studies Assn. Author: On the Nature of Value, 1946; Alien and Asiatic in American Law, 1946; Constitution and Civil Rights, 1947; Fundamental Liberties of a Free People, 1957; Century of Civil Rights, 1961; Expanding Liberties, 1966; Religious Liberty and Conscience, 1967; co-ed: Freedom and Experience, 1947; Essays in Political Theory, 1948; ed: Law and Social Action, 1950; Education for Freedom and Responsibility, 1952; Bill of Rights Reader, 1954, 4th ed, 1967; Liberian Code of Laws, 1957; Aspects of Liberty, 1958; Liberian Law Reports, 1959; American Pragmatists, 1960; First Amendment Freedoms, 1963; Emerson: Twentieth Century Views; Industrial and Labor Relations Review; Cornell Studies in Civil Liberty; mem, ed bds: Judaism, Midstream, Jewish Social Studies, Jewish Heritage, Jewish Publ Soc, New Leader, Philosophy Forum, Ency Judaica, Dropsie Coll Apocrypha series; contbr to: Ency Britannica; Intl Ency of Social Sciences; Ency of Philosophy; co-trans, Latin American Legal Philosophy, 1948. Recipient: Commander, Order Star of Afr, Liberian Govt, 1957; grand band, Liberia, 1960; dist service award, NYU Wash Sq Coll Alumni, 1964; Mordecai Ben David award, Yeshiva U, 1965; f: Guggenheim, 1953; Fund for Rep, 1955; Ford Found, 1952; Inst for Advanced Study, Princeton, 1959-60; Cen for Advanced Study in Behavioral Scis, Stanford, 1964-65. Home: 16 The Byway, Ithaca, NY. Office: Ives Hall, Cornell U, Ithaca, NY.

KOOK, Shlomo Hacohen, Isr, rabbi, rabbinic official; b. Jerusalem, Isr, June 6, 1929; s. Rafael and Rachel (Mandelbaum); att: Mercaz Harav; Hebron Yeshiva; Kollel Avrechim; m. Judith Katz; c: Ziva, Yocheved, Dany. Chief rabbi, Rehovot; dean, Rabb Dist Court; dean, Montefiore Coll, Eng, 1954-57; dayan, Rabb Court, Tel Aviv, 1964-67. Maj, chaplain, IDF, 1958-64. Mem, Haganah Vets. Author: Torah and the State of Israel; contbr on Torah, rel educ, Halacha, phil, to jours. Home: 7 Peretz St, Rehovot, Isr. Study: Chief Rabbinate, Yaacob St, Rehovot, Isr.

KOPELOWITZ, Lionel, Eng, physician; b. Newcastle-upon-Tyne, Eng, Dec 9, 1926; s. Maurice and Mabel (Garstein) Kopp; MA, Trinity Coll, Cambridge, 1947; MRCS, LRCP, U Coll Hosp, 1951. Phys since 1953. Off, RAF, 1952-53. Pres: Rep Council for Newcastle Jewry; Newcastle J Wfr Soc; B'nai B'rith lodge, 1959-60; Jesmond Heb Cong, 1963-67; chmn: Brit Med Assn, Newcastle Zionist Assn, 1955-59; vice-pres: WJC, Brit sect, ZF Gt Brit and Ir; hon secy, Cen Council for J Rel Educ in UK; exec comm, Bd Deps, Brit J; mem: Chief Rabb Council; Yeoman Soc Apothecaries; Magistrates Assn. Home: 75 Montagu Court, Newcastle-upon-Tyne, Eng. Office: 18 Elmfield Rd, Gosforth, Newcastle-upon-Tyne, Eng.

KOPLOW, Freyda P, US, legislator, business exec; b. Willimantic, Conn, Oct 26, 1907; d. Nathan and Pauline (Appelbaum) Peck; BS, Boston U, 1930; MS, Simmons Coll, 1931; m. Irving Koplow, June 17, 1931; c: Richard, Michael, Kenneth. Commn, Banks of Mass, since 1967; social worker, Mass State Dept Public Wfr, 1931-33; mem, House of Repr, Mass, 1955-67, asst minority floor leader, 1961-67. Cons, Metrop Planning Conf, since 1958; mem: adv comm, Sr Living Inc, since 1958; bd dirs, Fed Women's Rep Clubs, since 1960; Brookline Comty Council, since 1963; study group leader, Hadassah, 1938-40, 1947-53; chmn, comm, Regis Coll Sem on Metrop Problems; mem: state bd, League of Women Voters, 1931-33, 1948-50, local bd, 1946-54; Brandeis Women's Comm; Beth Isr Hosp Auxiliary; Temple Isr. Contbr to gen jours. Home: 84 Alberta Rd, Brookline, Mass. Office: 100 Cambridge St, Boston, Mass.

KOPNIWSKY, Marcus D, Swed, organization exec; b. Växjö, Swed, July 6, 1908; s. Abraham and Esther (Biber); LLB, U of Lund, 1934; m. Doris Mattus, Dec 22, 1940; c: Hans, Sten, Eva. Mgn dir, J Comty, Stockholm, since 1939. Chmn, United Working Comm, Pensioners Home and Old Age Home; dir, Stiftelsen Clas Groschinskys Minnesfond; bd dirs: Clas Groschinsky Stiftelse; Friedländerska Old Age Home, all of Stockholm; mem, B'nai B'rith. Recipient: Knight of Order of Vasa. Home: Valhallavägen 61, Stockholm, Swed. Office: Wahrendorffsgatan 3, Stockholm, Swed.

KOPP, Mortimer Moses, US, surgeon; b. NYC, July 24, 1900; s. Charles and Kate (Leishen); att: Columbia U, 1918-19; NYU, 1919-20; MD, NYU, Bellevue Med Sch, 1925; m. Lilly Lux, Mar 11, 1938; c: Charles, Matta Freund. Pvt practice, plastic surg, since 1926; att plastic surg: Beth El; Maimonides; Lutheran; Samaritan Hosps. Lt, USNR, 1918. Dir, found, Amer Friends Heb U; found: Albert Einstein Med Coll-Yeshiva U; Truman Inst for Peace; pres, E NY Med Soc; f, Intl Coll Surgs; dipl, Amer Bd Plastic Surgs; AMA; mem: Masons, Stepping Stone Lodge 1141; Flatbush J Cen, Bklyn, NY. Contbr to surg jours. Home: 200 E 57 St, New York, NY. Office: 30 Central Park S, New York, NY.

KOPPELMAN, Chaim, US, artist, teacher; b. Bklyn, NY, Nov 17, 1920; s. Samuel and Sadie (Mondlin); att: Amer Artists Sch, NYC, 1939-40; Art Coll of W Eng, 1943-44; L'Ecole des Beaux Arts, Rheims, 1945; Ozenfant Sch of Fine Arts, 1946-48; studies, the phil of aesthetic realism, with Eli Siegal; m. Dorothy Myers, Feb 13, 1943; c: Ann Newman. Tchr: printmaking, Sch of Visual Arts, NYC, since 1959; art, NYU educ dept, 1947-55; adult educ div, Bklyn Coll, 1950-62; Rhodes Sch, NYC, 1952-59; State Tchrs Coll, New Paltz, NY, 1953-58. Repr collections: Mus of Modern Art; Metrop Mus; Yale U; Art Gal; Peabody Mus; Caracas Mus; Victoria and Albert Mus; exhbs: Documenta 11, Kassel, W Ger; 2nd Inter-Amer Biennial, Mex City, 1960; USIA overseas traveling print exhb, 1960; Whitney Mus annuals; Mus of Modern Art, 1963. Served, USAAC, 1942-45. Pres, Soc of Amer Graphic Artists, 1966-68; mem, Soc for Aesthetic Realism. Recipient: Tiffany Grants, 1957, 1959; Audubon Medal, 1960; Bronze Star, 4 battle stars. Home and studio: 498 Broome St, New York, NY.

KOPPELMAN, Dorothy Myers, US, painter, gallery dir, teacher; b. Bklyn, NY, June 13, 1920; d. Harry and May (Chalmers) Myers; BA, Bklyn Coll, 1942; att Art Students League, NY; Aesthetic Realism Studies, NY, with Eli Siegel, since 1942; m. Chaim Koppelman, Feb 13, 1943; c: Ann Newman. Lectr, aesthetic realism and art, since 1955; dir, Terrain Gal, since 1955; lectr, art, Bklyn Coll, since 1952; art tchr, Barnard Sch for Girls, 1955-60; Visual Arts Gal, 1960-61. Exhbs: Terrain Gal; Riverside Mus; Bklyn Mus; City Cen; Mus Modern Art, all NY; Jersey City Mus; SF Mus; Walker Art Cen; Baltimore City Mus; Butler Inst Fine Arts. Mem, Soc for Aesthetic Realism. Author: Aesthetic Realism: We Have Been There, 1968; monthly column, Art Criticism, Wash Independent, since 1966. Recipient: Tiffany Grant, painting, 1965-66. Home: 498 Broome St, New York, NY. Office: 39 Grove St, New York, NY.

KOPPETT, Leonard, US, journalist; b. Moscow, Russ, Sep 19, 1923; s. David and Marie (Dvoretskya) Kopeliovitch; in US since 1928; BA, Columbia U, 1946; m. Suzanne Silberstein, Apr 24, 1964; c: Katherine, David. Sports reporter, NY Times since 1963; sports reporter: NY Herald-Tribune, 1948-53; NY Post, 1954-63. Pvt, US Army, 1943-45. Author: A Thinking Man's Guide to Baseball, 1967; 24 Seconds To Shoot, 1968; The New York Mets, 1970. Mem, Amer Newspaper Guild, NY; fmr: pres, Metrop Basketball Writers Assn; chmn, NY chap, Baseball Writers Assn Amer. Hobbies: music, theater. Home: 3333 Henry Hudson Pkwy, Bronx, N.Y. Office: 229 W 43 St, New York, NY.

KOPPMAN, Lionel, US, public relations cons, editor, author; b. Waco, Tex, Nov 24, 1920; s. Meyer and Ethel (Siegel); AB, Baylor U, 1942; tchrs cert, HUC-JIR, 1952, MA, J educ, 1969; m. Mae Zuckerman, Dec, 5, 1948; c: Stephen, Debra. Dir, publs and PR, JWB, since 1946; mgn ed, J Digest, since 1955, contbd ed, since 1962; reporter, asst city ed, Temple Daily Telegram, Temple, Tex, 1942-43; med ed, War Dept, 1943-45; asst dir, PR, B'nai B'rith, 1945-46. Vice-pres, Amer J PR Soc, 1961-62; PR Assn Gtr NY, 1962; mem: bd, J Cen, Jackson Hgts, NY, 1959-60; PR Assn, NY. Author: Francis Salvador, Patriot, 1959; Jewish Landmarks in New York, 1964; The First Book of Jewish Etiquette; Purim, 1968; Shalom Aleichěm, a film strip, 1969; 200 Games for Jewish Groups; Christians Want to Know; co-author, A Jewish Tourist's Guide to the US, 1954. Recipient tercentenary award, JBCA, 1954. Home: 30-44 88 St, Jackson Heights, NY. Office: 15 E 26 St, New York, NY.

KOPS, Bernard, UK, playwright; b. London, Eng, Nov 28, 1926; s. Joel and Jenny (Zetter); m. Erica Gordon, Feb 9, 1956; c: Adam. Author, playwright since 1956; author: Awake for Mourning, 1958; Poems and Songs, 1958; The Hamlet of Stepney Green, 1959; An Anemone for Antigone, 1959; The Dream of Peter Mann, 1960; Enter Solly Gold, 1961; Motorbike, 1962; The World is a Weeding, autobiography, 1963; plays translated and performed throughout world; broadcaster, BBC, since 1957; res dramatist, Bristol Old Vic Theatre, 1958; lectured on drama: Eng Us: Pol; Hung; Isr. Recipient: Arts Council bursary for new drama, 1957. Home: 88 Great Titchfield St, London, Eng.

KORCHAK, Earl Israel, US, lawyer; b. Pittsburgh, Pa, May 11, 1924; s. Samuel and Esther (Korchak); BA, Yeshiva U, NY, 1945; DJur, NYU, 1948; m. Dorothy Ackerman, Dec 29, 1946; c: Nelson, Howard, Rochelle. Sr partner, law firm, Korchak & Echt, since 1965; put practice 1954-65. Pres, Union Orthodox Congs Amer, Pacific Coast region; vice-pres, Rambam Torah Inst, Yeshiva U HS, LA; chmn, bd, Shaarey Zedek Cong, N Hollywood, Cal, pres; mem: comm, J Fed Council, LA; bd, Shaarey Zedek Hosp, Jerusalem; mem: Amer Trial Lawyers Assn; Amer Arbitration Assn Tribunal; bd: Hillel Heb Acad, Beverly Hills; Emek Heb Acad, N Hollywood, Cal, past vice-pres; W Coast Talmudical Sem, LA; Beth Jacob Cong, Beverly Hills, Cal; fmr: co-chmn, Parents Org for B'nai Akiva, LA. Recipient: Comty Service Award, Union of Orthodox Congs, 1964; Alumni Award for Comty Service, Yeshiva U, 1966; first annual Man of the Year Award, Shaarey Zedek Hosp, Jerusalem. Hobbies: golf, working with children in sports and camping activities. Home: 234 S McCarty Dr, Beverly Hills, Cal. Office: 606 S Olive St, Los Angeles, Cal.

KOREN, Abram, Isr, engineer; b. Stock, Pol, Dec 21, 1937; s. Shmuel and Zelda (Lencner) Kronenfeld; in Isr since 1950; BSc, Technion, Haifa, 1966; m. Sonia Kogan, Aug 4, 1964; c: Eyal, Sigal. Research engr, Isr Desalination Engr, since 1968. Mech engr, IDF; sgt, IDF, mech instr, 1956-61. Prin contribs: frequencies in centrifugal rotating blade; elastic curve of a flexible rotating blade. Mem, Engr Histadrut. Home: 4 Hagdud Haivri St, Holon, Isr. Office: POB 18041, Tel Baruch, Tel Aviv, Isr.

KOREN, Avigdor Victor, Isr, physician; b. Vienna, Aus, June 16, 1908; s. Ferdinand and Camilla (Bergmann) Kornmehl; in Isr since 1934; MD, U Vienna, 1932; m. Hanna Spisbach, June 23, 1939; c: Hillel. Pvt practice since 1934; med dir, Maccabi Care Health Fund, since 1963; found, Assn Sports Med, Isr; co-found, Maccabi Care Health Fund. Maj, IDF MC, 1948-58. Fmr: prin master, Sharon chap, master, Aviv Free Masons lodge; pres: Maccabi-Atid Sports Club; Swimming Fed, Isr; f, Fed Intl Med Sportive; mem, Org of Phys, Isr. Author: Rehabilitation of Myocard Infarcts in Tel Aviv, 1965; Prophylaxis and Rehabilitation of Heart Diseases in Israel, 1968. Hobbies: swimming, sports med, bridge. Home: 3 Montefiore St, Tel Aviv, Isr. Office: 10a Balfour St, Tel Aviv, Isr.

KOREY, William, US, educator, author, communal leader; b. Chgo, Ill, June 16, 1922; s. Louis and Rose (Bernstein); BA, U Chgo, 1946; MA, PhD, Columbia U; att Coll J Studies, Chgo; m. Esther Student, Aug 17, 1947; c: Barbara, Eileen. Dir, B'nai B'rith, UN Off, since 1960; prof, Yeshiva U, since 1969; fmr: dir, Wash Off, ADL; prof: CCNY; LIU. US Army, 1943-46. Chmn observer progs, World Assembly on Hum Rights; mem, Acad Political Sci; fmr chmn, Conf on UN Reprs. Author: Human Rights—The Key to Implement Action, 1968; Legal Position of the Soviet Jewish Community, 1968; contbr articles on hum rights and Soviet J to mags, jours. Recipient: F: Ford Found, 1951-52; Carnegie Found, 1948-49. Home: 1940 Edward Lane, Merrick, NY. Office: 315 Lexington Ave, New York, NY.

KORFF, Norman, US, business exec; b. Chgo, Ill, Jan 19, 1915; s. Abram and Mollie (Prigozen); BA, Northwestern U, 1936; m. Shirley Goldsmith, July 28, 1938; c: Carol Fraggen, Sally, Jane, John. Owner, real estate co, since 1955; partner, Merkle Korff Gear Co, since 1936; dir: Mercantile Natl Bank; U Natl Bank; both Chgo. Pres, N Shore Cong Isr, Glencoe, Ill; mem, exec comm, Amer J Hist Soc; trustee, Coll of J Studies, Chgo; fmr pres: N Club, Northwestern U; Phi Epsilon Pi; club, Northmoor Country. Home: 1323 Asbury Ave, Winnetka, Ill. Office: 5636 N Western Ave, Chicago, Ill.

KORMAN, Milton D, US, judge; b. Wash, DC, Oct 22, 1904; s. Joseph and Ida (Keneman); LLB, JD, Georgetown U, 1925; att George Wash U, 1925-26; m. Bernice Rosensweig, Oct 20, 1940 (decd); c: James, Edward, Sharon Weiss. Asso judge, Superior Court, Wash, DC, since 1971; asst corp counsel, DC govt, 1937-56, prin asst, corp counsel, 1956-65, acting, corp counsel, 1965-66; asso judge, DC Court of Gen Sessions, 1967-71. Mem: Amer Bar Assn; DC Bar Assn, fmr chmn, Dist Court comm, fmr trustee, Research Found; Fed Bar Assn, past bd dirs, fmr delg, Natl Council, fmr chmn: comty affairs, judicial selection, natl council; Amer Judicature Soc; Jud Conf, DC Circuit; Theta Phi; Chevy Chase Citizens Assn, fmr bd dirs, fmr chmn, educ comm; Metrop Wash Bd of Trade; Assn of Oldest Inhabitants; Friendship Fire Assn; exec bd, Natl Capital Area Council, Boy Scouts of Amer; B'nai B'rith; Wash DC Heb Cong, fmr, bd dirs, pres, Brotherhood; bd dirs, Heb Home, Gtr Wash; Masons 32 deg and other lodges and grottos; clubs: Munic Offs, Wash, DC, fmr pres; Men's Club, Natl Children's Cen, vice-pres. Recipient: awards: Dist Service, Natl Inst of Munic Law Offs, 1965; Dist Service, Cen HS Alumni, 1966; Achievement, Georgetown U Law Cen Alumni, 1966. Home: 3314 Stephenson Pl, NW, Washington, DC. Office: 451 Indiana Ave, NW, Washington, DC.

KORN, Bertram W, US, rabbi, historian; b. Phila, Pa, Oct 6, 1918; s. Manuel and Blanche (Bergman); BA, U Cincinnati, 1939; ordained rabbi, MHL, HUC, 1943, grad f, 1946-48, DHL, 1949; hon: LLD, Temple U, 1957; DLitt, Del Valley Coll, 1967; DD, HUC, 1968; c: Judith, Bertram. Sr rabbi, Reform Cong, Keneseth Isr, Phila, since 1949; visiting prof, Amer J Hist, HUC-JIR, NY, since 1962; rabbi: Cong Shaarai Shomayim, Mobile, Ala, 1943-44; Temple Emanuel, Mansfield, O, 1946-48; asst prof, Amer J hist, asst to pres, HUC, Cincinnati, 1948-49; visiting prof, Amer J hist, Dropsie Coll, 1969-70. Chaplain, USN, 1944-46; capt, USNR, 1963. Mem: bd, J armed forces council, JWB, since 1950; Amer J Hist Soc, 1959-61; bd, Gratz Coll; adv council, Civil War Centennial Comm, Fed Govt; Comm on J Americana, Grand Lodge, B'nai B'rith; publs comm, J Publ Soc of Amer; natl council, Jt Defense Appeal; Phila br, Friends of Heb U; Amer sect, J Hist Soc of Isr; fmr: pres, Assn J Chaplains; councillor, Amer Antiquarian Soc. Author: American Jewry and the Civil War, 1951; Eventful Years and Experiences: Studies in Nineteenth Century American Jewish History, 1954; The Centenary Edition of Solomon Nunes Carvalho's Incidents of Travel and Adventure in the Far West, 1954; The American Reaction to the Mortara Case, 1957; Benjamin Levy: New Orleans Printer and Publisher, 1960; Jews and Negro Slavery in the Old South, 1961; Early Jews of New Orleans, 1969; The Middle Period of American Jewish History, in Heb, 1969; ed, Yearbook of Central Conf of Amer Rabbis, 1952-53; contbr ed, Jewish Exponent, Phila; mem, ed adv bd: Civil War Hist, Jewish Digest, Ia State U; contbr to jours. Recipient: award, Amer J Hist Soc. Home: 429 Wyncote House, Wyncote, Pa. Study: Keneseth Isr, Old York Rd and Township Line, Elkins Park, Philadelphia, Pa.

KORN, Hyman, US, jurist; b. NYC, June 30, 1902; s. David and Anna (Ritter); LLB, Bklyn Law Sch, St Lawrence U, 1925; m. Beatrice Rosenfeld, Nov 23, 1952. Justice, NY State Supr Court, since 1962; pvt practice, 1927-49; city magistrate, NY, 1949-57; judge, City Court, NY, 1957-60; co judge, 1960-62. Fmr chmn, philanthropic campaigns. Home: 1020 Grand Concourse, New York, NY. Office: 851 Grand Concourse, New York, NY.

KORNBERG, Arthur, US, biochemist, educator; b. Bklyn, NY, Mar 3, 1918; s. Joseph and Lena (Katz); BS, CCNY, 1937; MD, U Rochester, 1941; hon LLD, CUNY, 1960; DSc, U Rochester, 1962; LHD, Yeshiva U, 1962; DSc, U of Pa, 1964; U Notre Dame, 1965; Wash U, 1968; hon f, Weizmann Inst, 1965; m. Sylvia Levy, Nov 21, 1943; c: Roger, Thomas, Kenneth. Prof, chmn, dept biochem, Stanford U, since 1959; staff mem, NIH, Bethesda, 1942-52; sect chief, enzymes and metabolism, 1947-52; research worker: dept chem and pharm, Coll of Med, NYU, 1946; biol chem dept, Sch of Med, Wash U, 1947; plant biochem dept, U of Cal, 1951; prof, head, microbiol dept, Sch of Med, Wash U, 1952-59. Mem: Amer Chem Soc; Amer Soc Clinical Inves; Natl Acad Scis; Amer Soc Biol Chems; Harvey Soc; Sigma Xi; Phi Beta Kappa; Alpha Omega Alpha. Contbr to scholarly jours. Recipient: Paul-Lewis award, 1951; jt Nobel Prize in med and phys, 1959; Max Berg award for prolonging hum life, 1968; Sci Achievement award, AMA, 1968; Lucy Wortham James award, James Ewing Soc, 1968; Borden award, 1968. Home: 365 Golden Oak Dr, Alpine Hills, Portola Valley, Cal. Office: Stanford U, Stanford, Cal.

KORNBLUM, Nathan, US, chemist, educator; b. NYC, Mar 22, 1914; s. Samuel and Frances (Newmark); MS, NYU, 1937; PhD, U of Ill, 1940; m. Rachel Britton, Sep 8, 1947; c: Susan, Elisabeth, Joseph, Barbara. Prof, chem, Purdue U, since 1953, fac mem since 1943; research instr, Oberlin Coll, 1940-42; NRC f, Harvard U, 1942-43; sr research f, Fulbright Commn, U Coll, London, 1952-53; John Simon Guggenheim Memorial f, Eidgenossische Technische Hochschule, Zurich, 1953; NSF, sr postdoc f. Mem: Amer Chem Soc; Sigma Xi; AAUP; Phi Lambda Upsilon; Chem Soc of Gt Brit. Contbr to profsl jours. Home: 328 Hollywood Dr, W Lafayette, Ind. Office: Purdue U, Lafayette, Ind.

KORNBLUTH, Sheldon Edwin, US, electronics engr; b. Bklyn, NY, May 2, 1933; s. Harry and Sylvia (Katz); BA, cum laude, Yeshiva U, 1955; MS, Columbia U, 1959; m. Lillian Roth, June 9, 1957; c: Allan, Avery, Thea. Lab sup, Otis Elevator Co, since 1969, sr eng, 1958-66; group leader, project engr, Reflectone Inc, 1966-69; engr, Polarad Elec 1957-58; Prin contribs: designed data processor for elevator sys for UN Bldg and World Trade Cen; Elevator control sys safety arrangement. Treas, Young Agudah of Crown Hgts; bd govs, Assn Orthodox J Sci; bd trustees, Yeshiva of E Pkwy; mem, Yeshiva U Alumni Assn. Home: 301 Montgomery St, Brooklyn, NY. Office: 260 11 Ave, New York, NY.

KORNER, Asher, Eng, biochemist; b. London, Eng, Feb 7, 1927; s. Solomon and Hetty (Copeland); BA, first class hons, Cambridge U, 1950, MA, PhD, 1954; m. Shirley Austin, June 29, 1952; c: Deborah, Simon, Joseph, Jessica. Prof, chmn, dept biochem, U of Sussex, since 1967; demonstrator, 1955-60, lectr, 1960-67, both Cambridge U; f, tutor, Clove Coll, Cambridge, 1960-67. Contbr numerous papers to sci,

jours. Home: 20 King Henry's Rd, Lewes, Sussex, Eng. Office: U of Sussex, Falmer, Eng.

KÖRÖSY, Francis Dov, Isr, chemist; b. Budapest, Hung, May 20, 1906; s. Kornel and Blanka (Holitscher); in Isr since 1957; dipl, chem, Tech Hochschule, Karlsruhe, 1927; PhD, Budapest U, 1928; m. Stefi Aranyi, Dec 10, 1935; c: Gabriel, Josef. Dir, chem lab, Negev Inst for Arid Zone Research, since 1968; fmr: asst, Tech HS, Karlsruhe, Ger; adv to research in insts, Budapest; sci tour, US; dir, research lab, Vaccumtechnica; pvt dozent, applied phys chem, Budapest U; research chem, Tungsram Lamp Co, Budapest; visiting sci, Amer Chem Soc. Prin contribs: work and research on: barrier layer cells; gas filled lamps; iodides of Ta group metals; solubility of gases; buffer against gastric acidity; pharm chem; electrochem of carotinoids; ion-permselective membranes in water desalination and in phys analogies. Chmn, League Against Rel Coercion, Beersheba group; mem, council, Isr Chem Soc. Author: From the Atom Bomb to the Atomic Motor, 1945; Zionism of an Assimilated Jew, 1945; An Approach to Chemistry, 1969; contbr to sci jours. Recipient: prizes for chem: Weizmann, 1968; Nordau 1962. Hobbies: painting. photography, singing, tourism. Home: 8 Sokolov St, Beersheba, Isr. Office: Negev Inst for Arid Zone Research, Beersheba, Isr.

KORZENIK, Harold, US, lawyer; b. Bklyn, NY, Oct 2, 1903; s. Adolph and Sally (Seiden); BA, Columbia, 1925, LLB, 1927; m. Lillian Shapiro, Dec 1, 1931; c: Ruth Franklin, Diana. Pvt practice since 1928; counsel: Natl Textile Processors Guild, since 1938; Natl Knitted Outerwear Assn, since 1942; United Knitwear Mfg League since 1944; Knitgoods Workers Retirement Fund since 1950; gen counsel, Textile Workers Pension Fund; lectr: Practising Law Inst; Wharton Sch, U of Pa. Pres, E Flatbush-Rugby YM-YWHA; trustee: Natl Severance Pay Fund, ILGWU; ILGWU Retirement Fund; personnel comm, Asso YM-YWHA, Gtr NY; functional comm, FJP; adv trustee, E Midwood J Cen; mem: Assn Bar NYC; Bklyn Bar Assn, chmn, comm on lab law, since 1958; personnel comm, JWB; Masons; fmr: pres, Menorah Grad Soc; chancellor, Kappa frat. Contbr to profsl periodicals. Home: 2705 Ave J, Brooklyn, NY. Office: 51 Chambers St, New York, NY.

KOSE, Elvin I, US, rabbi; b. Newark, NJ, July 4, 1920; s. Charles and Celia (Shulman) Kosofsky; BA, Yeshiva Coll, NY, 1941; MA, Columbia U, 1944, PhD, 1953; ordained rabbi, MHL, JTSA, 1950; m. Leona Weiss, Dec 19, 1942; c: Adina, Michael, Jonathan, Judith. Rabbi, Cong Beth Shalom, Union, NJ, since 1944. Found, dir, Solomon Schechter Day Sch of NJ; pres, Union Free Libr; mem, exec bd: Hadoar. Ed, Hadoar Reader; trans from Heb, History of Jews of the Renaissance, by Moshe Shulwass. Home: 2070 Stowe St, Union, NJ. Study: Vauxhall Rd and Cedar Ave, Union, NJ.

KOSHLAND, Robert J, US, merchant, civic worker; b. Apr 30, 1893; s. Marcus and Corinne (Schweitzer); BS, U of Cal, 1914; m. Delphine Rosenfeld, Dec 8, 1920; c: Robert, Margaret Arnold, Susan Thede. Ret partner: Koshland and Co, Boston, Mass; S Koshland and Co, SF. Capt, US Army, WWI; col, USAAF, WWII. Fmr: pres: Fed of J Charities, SF; W States Region CJFWF, vice-pres, mem, natl bd dirs; Peninsula Hosp Dist; Assn of Cal Hosp Dists; Bay Area Wfr Planning Fed; Bay Area Health Facilities Planning Assn; mem: bd dirs: Comty Council, San Mateo Co; J Home for Aged; San Mateo Co, ARC; Asso J Philanthropies, Boston, JWF, SF; bd trustees: Children's Home Soc of Cal Presbyterian Hosp and Med Cen, since 1966; Natl Assembly for Social Policy and Devl, since 1967; exec comm: United Bay Area Crusade; Bay Area Social Planning Council, since 1966; chmn, San Mateo Unemployment Relief Admn; life mem, Mil Order of WW's. Recipient: Legion of Merit, WWII. Hobby: swimming. Home: 217 W Santa Inez Ave, Hillsborough, Cal. Office: 98 Battery St, San Francisco, Cal.

KOSLOFF, Israel R, Isr, business exec; b. Jerusalem, 1921; s. Haim and Judith (Piselman); MA, U of Chgo, 1945; m. Zipora Pincheveski, July 26, 1940; c: Dan, Ronnie, Michael. Mgn dir, Electrochem Inds (Frutarom) Ltd, since 1958; fmr: petroleum adv, commn, Govt of Isr; spec asst to pres, Richfield Oil Co; econ, Standard Oil, Ind. Home: 37 Panorama, Haifa, Isr. Office: POB 1929, Haifa, Isr.

KOSLOVSKY, Itshok, US, organization exec, editor; b. Bessarabia, Russ Dec, 1898; s. Moishe and Fruma; in US since 1921; widower. Secy, B'nai Yiddish, since 1966; ed, B'nai Yiddish Jour. Mem: Workman's Circle; B'nai B'rith, educ lodge. Author: Untern Cubaner Himel, 1939. Home: 387 Grand St, New York, NY.

KOSLOWE, Irving, US, rabbi; b. White Plains, NY, Jan 16, 1920; s. Morris and Anna (Shapiro); BA, Yeshiva U, 1940; ordained rabbi, Rabbi Isaac Elchanan Theol Sem, 1942; MA, NYU, 1949; DHL, Yeshiva U, 1962; m. Marly Schachter, Aug 22, 1943; c: Neil, Kenneth, Mark, Shari. Rabbi, Westchester J Cen, since 1949; chaplain, Sing Sing Prison, since 1949; adj asst prof, pastoral counseling, Iona Coll, grad div; instr, Moran Inst on Crime and Delinquency, since 1954; prof, psych, Westchester Comty Coll, since 1963; civilian chaplain, Off Civil Defense, Mamaroneck, 1944-47. Pres: Amer Correctional Chaplains Assn, 1955-56; Natl Council J Penal Chaplains, 1958-59; Westchester Council Rabbis, 1956-59; bd dirs: Zionist Emergency Council; RabCA; ADL; mem: bd govs, NY Bd Rabbis. Contbr to profsl jours. Home: 540 Prospect Ave, Mamaroneck, NY. Study: Rockland and Palmer Ave, Mamaroneck, NY.

KOSLOWSKY, Nota, US, artist; b. Poronzova, Pol, Apr 20, 1906; s. Louis and Leah (Wishnietsky); in US since 1926; att: Tchrs Inst for Arts and Crafts, Warsaw, Pol; Natl Acad of Design; Art Students League; Delehanty Engr Inst; m. Rachel Zelikowitch, Nov 22, 1958; c: Leon (by previous marriage). Artist, portrait painter, lectr on art; fmr, art tchr, schs, summer camps; one-man shows: NYC, 1935, 1941, 1948, 1954, 1955, 1957; Isr, 1952, LA, 1961; Toronto, Can, 1961, Cincinnati, O, 1962-1965; San Antonio; Houston, both 1962; Nashville, 1963; Chgo, 1963-1966; Northwestern U, 1964; St Paul, 1965; Milw, 1966; exhb: Whitney Mus; Riverside Mus; Contemporary Art Gals; Norlyst Gal, Caravan Gal, Tremont Public Libr, all NYC; Boston; U of Chgo; U of Ill, B'nai B'rith Conv, Chgo, in perm collections: Lochamei Hagetaot Mus, Isr; Martef Hashoa Mus, Jerusalem; illus over 40 children books; originator of comic strips: Chachmei Chelem; Hershele m'Ostropoli; Boxer un Pempik; Benny der Reporter; designer of new Heb alphabets; designer, word game, Zuch un Gefin. Author: Israel, Its People and Places, 1957; contbr to J publs. Mem: YIVO; Rockport Art Assn; Mass N Shore Art Assn; Farband; Cosmopolitan Artists; org, chmn, Isr Emergency Fund Project, Artists for Isr, 1967. Recipient: 1st prize, for oil painting, Amer Artists Profsl League, 1955; Amer J Arts Club Award, 1964, 1968. Home and studio: 321 Dodge Ave, Evanston, Ill.

KOSOFSKY, Sidney, US, psychologist, rabbi; b. NYC, May 22, 1915; s. Charles and Celia (Shulman); BA, Upsala Coll, 1936; MHL, ordained rabbi, JIR, 1941; PhD, NYU, 1950; m. Bernice Klestzik, Aug 28, 1938; c: Vivian Kotler, Mrs Morris Loskove, Mrs Jerome Toubin, Judith, Rena. Chief psychol, admnr, Drenk Memorial Guidance Cen, Mt Holly, NJ, since 1955; visiting lectr, psych, Trenton State Coll; in pvt practice, clinical psych. Home: 1457 Pennington Rd, Trenton, NJ.

KOSOVSKE, Howard Arnold, US, rabbi; b. Chgo, Ill, Jan 29, 1941; s. Abe and Ethel (Bartow); AB, hon, U of Ill, Chgo, Urbana, 1962; ordained rabbi, BHL, hon, MAHL, hon, HUC-JIR, Cincinnati, O, 1967; m. Barbara Falk, Dec 22, 1963; c: Raquel. J chaplain, capt, US Army, since 1967; rabbi, Frankfurt Amer J Comty, since 1968; rabbi: Cong Ohev Isr, Newark, O, 1964-65; Temple Beth-El, Anniston, Ala, 1965-67. Mem: CCAR; Phi Eta Sigma. Home: 2205-A2, Platenstr, Frankfurt M, Hessen, Ger. Study: Office of the J Chaplain; HQ, US Forces Support, District-Hessen; APO New York 09757.

KOSS, Saul H, US, Rabbi; b. Bklyn, NY, Dec 1, 1940; s. Morris and Rebecca (Steinberg); BA, Yeshiva U, 1962, ordained rabbi, 1965, MA, 1966; m. Susan Blumenthal, June 15, 1964; c: Miriam, Reuven. US Army chaplain, Baden-Wuerttemberg, Ger, since 1966; Heb tchr, Inwood J Cen, 1964-66; youth dir, Torath Emeth J Cen, 1965-66; youth dir, Heb Sch tchr, J Cen of Wakefield and Endenwald, 1965-66. Mem: RaCA; Assn of J Chaplains of Armed Forces. Recipient awards: Norman Palefski Memorial, 1961; Mortimor Kogon Memorial, for outstanding leadership in student activities, 1962, both Yeshiva U. Home: c/o Blumenthal, 700 W 176 St, New York, NY. Study: Office of J Chaplain, Baden-Wuerttemberg, Ger, APO NY 09154.

KOSSOFF, A David, US, educator; b. Hartford, Conn, Nov 9,

1918; s. Samuel and Ella (Ellin); AB, Amherst Coll, 1945; AM, Brown U, 1947, PhD, 1954; m. Ruth Horne, June 18, 1948. Asso prof, Span, Brown U, since 1961, on fac since 1951; visiting prof, U of RI, 1958. Mem, bd, RI, NE MLA; secy, Brown chap, AAUP, 1958-60; pres, RI chap, Amer Assn Tchrs of Span and Port, 1959-60; mem: B'nai B'rith; Renaissance Soc of Amer; Phi Betta Kappa; club, Brown Fac, secy, 1958-60. Author: El Vocabulario Poetico de Fernando de Herrera, publ in Spain; contbr to lit jours. Recipient: Fulbright research f, Spain, 1960-61. Home: 140 Brown St, Providence, RI. Office: Brown U, Providence, RI.

KOTLER, Milton, US, political sci, author; b. Chgo, Ill, Mar 15, 1935; s. Maurice and Betty (Bubar); BA, U Chgo, 1954; MA, U Chgo, Sch of Political Sci, 1957; m. Janet Oldt; c: Anthony, Joshua. Res f, Inst for Policy Studies, Wash, DC, since 1963; instr, Chgo City Coll, 1961-63; cons on urban affairs; lectr: Va Theol Sem; Columbia U; U of Cal; Antioch Coll; Yale U; MIT. Pvt, Ill Air Natl Guard, 1959-62. Fmr mem, Comm on Urban Affairs, AJComm. Author: Modern Political Rhetoric, 1968; Neighborhood Government, 1969. Home: 3505 McKinley St, NW, Washington, DC. Office: 1520 New Hampshire Ave, NW, Washington, DC.

KOTLER, Shimeon, Australia, solicitor; b. Tel Aviv, Isr, Oct 3, 1928; s. Mordechai and Esther (Ziman); in Australia since 1960; MJ, Heb U, Jerusalem; MA, LLB, U of Melbourne; m. Tamara Weyman, May 26, 1959; c: Aviva, Ella. Advocate since 1954; solicitor since 1963; partner, Grant & Co, since 1965. Lt, Palmach, IDF, 1946-49. Home: 5 Kinnoul, Caulfield, Victoria, Australia. Office: Grant & Co, 108 Queen St, Melbourne, Australia.

KOTLOWITZ, Raphael, Isr, advocate; b. Shebesh, Russ, Oct 1, 1917; s. Benjamin and Eida (Bar); in Isr since 1948; BA, LLB, U of Cape Town, S Afr; m. Elisheva Herscher, Jan 18, 1948; c: Edna. Vice-chmn, World Exec, Herut-Hatsohar, since 1968; councillor, Tel Aviv Munic, leader opposition, Gahal, 1965-69; on numerous missions: ref camps, Ger, Aus, 1946; on behalf Irgun Tsvai Leumi, Eng, Fr, It, 1946; spec repr to S Afr, 1947-48; after establishment of State: to S Afr; Fr; Mexico; US; Can. Mem: presidium World Zionist Org; Finance Comm, JA; cen exec, Herut Party; bd dir, KH; chmn, Shelach, Fund for Rehab of Underground Fighters; mem, Isr Bar Council. Home: 23 Smuts Blvd, Tel Aviv, Isr.

KOTLOWSKI, Henry, Eng, business exec; b. Vilna, Pol, Mar 31, 1907; s. Chajim and Braine (Rekatchinsky); in Eng since 1933; m. Marguerite Englisher; c: Howard, Bernice Swindon. Owner: Henrys, 1939-70; Heinrich Kotlowski, 1928-1933. Chmn, Assn, Friends, Hitachdut Olei Britannia; fmr: chmn, vice-chmn, secy gen, hon secy, Natl Exec, Poale Zion; mem: exec council, ZF, Gt Brit; comm, JNF; comm, JPA, both N London; found mem, chmn, Poale Zion Br Workers Circle Div 19; chmn, Young Poale Zion. Home: 39 Clifton Gardens, London, Eng. Office: 91 Stoke Newington High St, London, Eng.

KOTT, Ethel Fisher, US, artist; b. Galveston, Tex, June 7, 1923; d. Sam and Ada (Zax) Blankfeld; att: U of Houston, 1939-40; U of Tex, 1940-42; Wash U, St Louis, Mo, 1943; Art Students League, NY, 1943-46; m. Seymour Kott, Dec 4, 1962; c: (by previous m): Sandra Fisher, Margaret Fisher. Numerous one-man and group shows in US; Natl Mus, Havana, Cuba, 1958. Pres, Fla chap, Artists Equity Assn, 1958-60; secy-treas, Miami Artists Assn, 1958; mem: Fla Arts Commn, 1960; SF Art Assn. Home and studio: 42 E 22 St, New York, NY.

KOVACS, Edward J, US, lawyer; b. Tarrytown, NY, Dec 15, 1907; s. Louis and Mary (Israel); BA, Amherst Coll, 1928; LLB, Yale U, 1931; m. Hilda Rothman, Mar 31, 1946; c: Alan. Atty since 1931; asso partner, Folger & Rockwood, 1931-42; exec off, Countess Mara Inc, 1946-48; pres, His Majesty, 1948-54. Lt, US Army, 1942-45. Pres: Cong Brothers of Isr, 1960-62; Dutchess Co Bar Assn, 1969; trustee, Poughkeepsie J Cen bldg fund, since 1961; chmn, Dutchess Co Friends of Brandeis U, 1960-65; US repr, 1st intl golf tournament, Caesarea Golf Club, Isr, 1964; mem: Amer Trial Lawyers Assn; NY State Bar Assn; Elks; Amer Legion; Vassar Brothers Hosp Assn; clubs: Harding; Wiltwyck Golf and Country. Recipient: meritorious service award, 1944; golf champion, Grossinger Golf Club, 1963; NY State Bar Assn Sr Golf Champion, 1969. Hobbies: golf, music. Home: 59 Whittier Blvd, Poughkeepsie, NY. Office: 3 Cannon St, Poughkeepsie, NY.

KOVENOCK, Harry A, US, attorney; b. Ataki, Russ, Sep 21, 1903; s. Samuel and Mollie (Zienstein); in US since 1906; att Milw State Tchrs Coll, 1920-23; LLB, U of Wis, 1926; m. Esther Lerner, 1928; c: Marcia Pollak, David, Paul. Pvt law practice since 1926; asst city atty, City of Milw, 1932-36; dist price atty, OPA, 1942-45. Pres: regional bd, ADL, 1954-56, treas, 1956-57; Milw J Council, 1949-51, life mem since 1951; mem, bd dirs, J Comty Cen, Milw, 1949-55, 1956-61; mem: lab arbitration panel, Amer Arbitration Assn; Fed Mediation and Conciliation Service; Wis Employment Relations Bd; Wis State Bar Assn; Milw Bar Assn; Cong B'nai Jeshurun. Author of appellate briefs. Recipient: B'nai B'rith Award, Milw Co, for contrib to hum relations, 1953. Spec interest: hist of J thought Home: 2208 E Stratford Court, Milwaukee,Wis. Office: 606 W Wisconsin Ave,Milwaukee,Wis.

KOVETZ, Attay, Isr, physicist; b. Tel Aviv, Dec 9, 1935; s. Akiva and Martha; MSc, Heb U, Jerusalem, 1963; DRerNat, Ludwig Maximillian U, Munich, 1965; m. Judith Ben-Ari, 1958; c: Michal, Yael. Sr lectr, dept physics and astronomy, dept of environmental scis, Tel Aviv U, since 1969. Lt, IAF, 1954-59. Contbr to sci jours. Recipient: Alexander von Humboldt scholarship, 1963. Home: 6 Hashikma St, Kiriat Ono, Isr. Office: Tel Aviv U, Ramat Aviv, Isr.

KOVITZ, Arthur A, US, educator; b. Detroit, Mich, Aug 6, 1928; s. Hyman and Rose (Zuzel); BSE, U of Mich, 1950, MS, 1951; PhD, Princeton U, 1957; m. Valerie Silverman, June 30, 1957; c: Claudia, Jordan. Prof, dept mech engr and astronautical scis, Tech Inst, Northwestern U since 1969, fac mem since 1958; asst dir, project SQUID, Princeton U, 1956-58. Contbr articles on fluid mechs and related disciplines to profsl jours. Home: 2500 Jackson Ave, Evanston, Ill. Office: Northwestern U, Evanston, Ill.

KOZOL, Frank Louis, US, lawyer; b. Brezno, Russ, May 10, 1902; s. Louis and Rebecca (Schneider); in US since 1905; AB, Harvard Coll, 1923; AM, Harvard Grad Sch, 1924; LLB, Harvard Law Sch, 1927; m. Mildred Wechsler, Feb 12, 1929; c: Joel, Lee, Robert. Sr partner, Friedman & Atherton, since 1957. Pres, Brookline Citizens Comm; vice-pres, Temple Isr; f. Brandeis U; hon life pres, J Memorial Hosp; hon life trustee, Heb Tchrs Coll; mem: Mass Defenders Comm; Amer, Mass, Boston Bar Assns; Masons. Contbr to legal jours. Spec interest: 17th cent hist. Home: 117 Clinton Rd Brookline, Mass. Office: 28 State, Boston, Mass.

KRA, M Aaron, US, rabbi; b. Ciechanow, Pol, Oct 16, 1917; s. Nathan and Dina (Silberstrom); in US since 1927; BA, Yeshiva U, 1941; ordained rabbi, Rabbi Isaac Elchanan Theol Sem, 1942; att: Harvard U, Brandeis U; m. Bessie Shragowitz, Apr 8, 1946; c: Ethan, David. Rabbi, Heb Rehab Cen for Aged, Roslindale since 1966; chaplain, Metrop State Hosp, since 1953; rabbi: Temple Beth Isr, Waltham, Mass, 1949-66; Mt Kisco Heb Cong, 1943-46; Beth El, Ansonia, Conn, 1946-49. Secy, Vaad Harabonim of Mass; mem: RabCA; Boston Rabb Council; Boston Waltham Mins Assn; Middlesex Mh Assn; Assn of Mental Hosp Chaplains; Rotary; Masons; bd dirs, Waltham Family Service League; Boys Club; club: Waltham. Home: 89 Buchanan Rd, W Roxbury, Mass. Study: 1200 Center St, Roslindale, Mass.

KRAFT, Louis, US, welfare worker; b. Moscow, Russ, 1891; s. Abraham and Etta (Gellis); BS, CUNY, 1912; hon DHL, JTSA, 1963; m. Pauline Roman, July 1, 1948; c: Stephen, Arthur, Barbara. Ret, 1961; gen secy, natl council, JWB, 1947-61, natl exec dir, 1938-47; exec dir, Bx YM-YWHA, 1914-17; dir, Army, Navy wfr work, JWB, 1917-20; dir, J cen activities, 1921-37; gen secy, World Fed, 1947; found, Jerusalem br, YMHA, 1948; cons comty reconstruction and devl, Eur, JDC, 1953-61; lectr, Jerusalem Sch of Social Work, 1950-51. Pres: Natl Conf J Communal Service, 1943; Intl Conf J Social Work, 1948-52; mem, exec comm, USO, 1940-46; hon pres, Natl Assn J Cen Workshops, since 1947. Author: Aspects of Jewish Center Work: Development of the Jewish Community Center, 1967; Social Agency Administration, in Heb. Home: 225 Central Park W, New York, NY.

KRAFT, Saul, US, rabbi; b. Boston, Mass, Dec 22, 1912; s. Louis and Rose (Wilkowsky) Krafchinsky; att Boston Heb Tchrs Coll, 1926-30; BA, Harvard Coll, 1934; ordained rabbi, MHL, JTSA, 1938; m. Beatrice Sacks, 1946, div, 1962. Dir, B'nai B'rith Hillel Found, Queens Coll, Flushing, NY, since 1955; cons, Notre Dame Sem, New Orleans, established first course in Judaism for Catholic Sem; rabbi,

Beth Judah, Ventnor City, NJ, 1938-46; first dir, B'nai B'rith Hillel Found, Princeton U, 1947-48; lectr, phil, rel, Adelphi Coll, Garden City, NY, 1948-54; taught first courses in Judaism, Georgetown U, Wash, DC, 1967-68. Chaplain, USAF, 1942-46. Chmn, Atlantic City Zionist Emergency Council, 1946-47; co-chmn, Gtr Atlantic City UJA, 1946-47; pres, Natl Assn Hillel Dirs, 1961-63; mem, exec comm, RA, 1949-52. Contbr to profsl publs. Home: 6700 192 St, Flushing, NY. Office: B'nai B'rith Hillel Found, Queens Coll, Flushing, NY.

KRAICER, Peretz Freeman, Isr, endocrinologist; b. Toronto, Can, Aug 15, 1932; s. Menahem and Shirley (Freeman); in Isr since 1955; BA, hons, U of Toronto, 1955; PhD, Weizmann Inst of Sci, Isr, 1960; m. Ruth Mydansky, May 23, 1958; c: Eiran, Lior, Boaz. Asso prof, Tel Aviv U, since 1969; visiting asso prof, gyn, U of Mich, 1967-68; sr sci, Weizmann Inst, 1960-69. IAF, res, 1962. Mem: Isr Soc for Study of Fertility; Isr Endocrine Soc; Eur Soc for Comparative Endocrinology; Soc for Study of Fertility, Eng; Intl Soc for Research in Biol of Reproduction. Contbr to profsl jours. Home: 5 Ido St, Ramat Chen, Isr. Office: Dept of Zoology, Tel Aviv U, Ramat Aviv, Isr.

KRAID, Risa Propst, Isr, artist, art critic; b. Craiova, Rum, Mar 21, 1894; d. Hermann and Ottilia (Willner) Propst; in Isr since 1950; m. Julius Kraid (decd); m. 2nd, Marcel Pollack; c: Erwin, Jehouda, Nadia Goldmann. Lectr, art, Popular U, Bucharest; Haifa; Tel Aviv. One-man shows: Bucharest; Brashov; Galerie Zack, Paris; Tel Aviv; Haifa; Jerusalem; Beersheba; Petah Tikva; Afula; Munich, Ger; decorative works: Letzman Cinema, Haifa; Beit Haikarim, Tel Aviv, others in Rum and Isr. Perm collections: State Mus, Rum; Staedelijk Mus, Holland; pvt collections: Isr. Mem: Artists Syndicate, Bucharest; Isr Painters and Sculptors Assn. Journalist, Viata Noastra, Tel Aviv, Isr. Home and studio: Moshav Hayogev, Isr.

KRAINES, Samuel H, US, psychiatrist; b. Chgo, Ill, Apr 30, 1906; s. Louis and Rose (Mutterperl); BS, U of Ill, 1928, MD, 1930; m. Ruth Jaffe, May 29, 1934; c: Richard, David, Gerald. Pvt practice since 1950; staff mem: Cook Co Hosp, 1930-31; Johns Hopkins Hosp, 1931-32; Boston Psychopathic Hosp, 1932-33; Queens's Sq Neur Hosp, London, Eng, 1937-38; teaching staff, U of Ill Med Sch, 1933-50, clinical asst prof, psycht, 1947-50. Lt col, US Army, MC, 1942-46. Mem: Amer Psycht Assn; Cen Neuropsycht Soc; Ill Psycht Soc; Chgo Neur Soc; Sigma Xi. Author: Therapy of the Neuroses and Psychoses, 1939; Managing Your Mind, 1943; Managing Men, 1946; Live and Help Live, 1951; Mental Depressions and Their Treatment, 1957. Office: 30 N Michigan Ave, Chicago Ill.

KRAININ, Philip, US, physician, educator; b. NYC, May 31, 1902; s. Julius and Dora (Shifrin); BA, Columbia Coll, 1923; MD, Bellevue Med Coll, 1926; m. Stella Ornstein, June 15, 1934; c: Stefanie, James. Asst clinical prof, med, NY Med Coll, since 1945; att phys, J Mem Hosp, since 1956; cons phys: Bx-Leb Med Cen; Morrisania City Hosp. Cdr, USN, 1943-49; F: NY Acad of Med; Intl Soc Internal Med, Amer Coll Phys; dipl, Amer Bd Internal Med; mem: AMA, NY Co and State Med Socs. Contbr to med jours. Home: 3240 Henry Hudson Pkway, New York, NY. Office: 25 Central Park W, New York, NY.

KRAKAUER, Kurt, Brazil, art director, designer; b. Schoppinitz, Ger, May 7, 1902; s. Jacob and Valeska (Weiss); in Brazil since 1937; DJur, U of Breslau, 1925; m. Rose Buck, May 28, 1937; c: Ronald. Art dir; owner, publicity agcy, since 1938; fmr syndicus: Ind Orgs, Breslau, 1925-27; Berlin-Dresden sect, Breslau, 1927-36. Gen secy, Gen Zionists of Brazil; co-pres, Latin Amer Confd of Gen Zionists; mem: directorate, B'nai B'rith, Rio de Janeiro; Associação Brasileiro de Propaganda; ARI, fmr vice-pres, exec; fmr pres, council, Associação Religiosa Israelita, Rio de Janeiro; delg, 27th ZC, Jerusalem; dep delg, actions comm, JA. Co-ed, hc: Neue Jüdische Rundschau, first Brazilian Zionist monthly in Ger, 1953-54; Porvir, Gen Zionists monthly, 1959-61. Recipient: Merit Medal, 25 years service, Associação Brasileira de Propaganda, 1962. Hobby: music. Home: 32/302 Rua Barão de Icarai, Rio de Janeiro, Brazil. Office: 277 Rio Branco Ave, Rio de Janeiro, Brazil.

KRAKOFF, Louis Joseph, US, business exec; b. Columbus, O, July 28, 1917; s. Abraham and Anna (Goldman); BA, BSc, O State U, 1938; m. Beatrice David, Nov 1, 1942; c: Linda Fisher, David, Andrew. Spec project dir, Federated Dept

Stores Inc, since 1966; vice-pres, The Able Corp, 1946-60, pres, 1960-66. Maj ,US Army, Quartermaster Corps, 1941-46. Pres, Temple Isr, Columbus, O; mem: bd trustees: UJF and Council; Heritage House, Columbus; Phi Beta Kappa; Beta Gamma Sigma; fmr: pres, Hillel Adv Bd; mem, bd trustees, J Cen; club, Winding Hollow Country, fmr pres. Home: 91 S Merkle Rd, Columbus, O. Office: 21 E State Street, Columbus, O.

KRAKOWER, Gerald W, Isr, chemist, educator; b. Bklyn, NY, Nov 14, 1929; s. Hyman and Anna (Singer); in Isr, since 1968; BA, Yeshiva Coll, NY, 1951; MA, Columbia U, 1952; PhD, Wayne State U, Detroit, Mich, 1958; m. Risha Cohen, Dec 9, 1959; c: Chaya, Abraham, Chana, Eliezer. Asso prof, chem, Bar Ilan U, Ramat Gan, since 1968; sr research chem, Squibb Inst for Med Research, NJ, 1959-68. Mem, Amer Chem Soc. Contbr to sci jours. Home: 52 Maimon St, Bnei Brak, Isr. Office: Dept of Chem, Bar Ilan U, Ramat Gan, Isr.

KRAKOWSKI, Meyer, US, educator; b. Bendzin, Pol, Dec 27, 1901; s. Solomon and Cecilia (Krycler); in US since 1922; BA, cum laude, U of Cal, Berkeley, 1925, MA, gen secondary tchrs credential, 1927; att Stanford U, 1933; U of Mexico, 1941-42; U Paris, 1945. Prof em, fgn langs, LA City Coll, since 1967, chmn, 1966-67, prof, 1965-67, asso prof, 1962-65; dir, sch and cultural activities, Pasadena Temple B'nai Isr, 1927-29; instr, fgn langs, Pasadena Jr Coll, spring, 1929; mem, summer sessions staff, U of Cal, 1934, 1935, 1947. Capt, USAAC, 1942-46. Mem: Amer Friends of Heb U; B'nai B'rith; LA Bur J Educ; Philol Assn of Pacific Coast; MLA; Ling Sch of Amer; AAUP; co-found, Cal State Council, Fgn Lang Tchrs Assns; Amer Assn Tchrs of Ger, fmr secy, vice-pres, exec council, found, research council, chmn, 1968; Amer Assn, Tchrs of Span; Ivrith Merkazith; LA Co Mus; S Cal Folklore Soc; SW Anthropological Assn; SW Conf on the Renaissance; Delta Phi Alpha; Friends of U of Cal, LA, libr; fmr: pres, LA City Coll Fac Assn, vice-pres, org, student-fac comm on cultural relations, chmn; natl prof, Alpha Mu Gamma; co-found, Sarah Cecilia Krakowski Memorial Libr, Pasadena J Comty, chmn, exec bd, annual lectureship; bd govs, U of Judaism, LA, chmn, libr comm, bd overseers. Ed: Aspects Of Contemporary Civilization, 1956; contbr to profsl jours. Recipient: citation, MLA, S Cal, 1957, 1966; Order of Merit, 1st Class, Ger; life f, Intl Inst of Arts and Letters. Hobbies: hiking, photography. Home: 1628 Lyman Pl, Los Angeles, Cal.

KRAMER, Aaron, US, poet, educator; b. Bklyn, NY, Dec 13, 1921; s. Hyman and Mary (Glick); BA, Bklyn Coll, 1941, MA, 1951; PhD, NYU, 1966; m. Katherine Kolodny, Mar 10, 1942; c: Carol, Laura. Asso prof, Eng, Adelphi Suffolk Coll, since 1966, asst prof, 1963-66; lectr, Queens Coll, since 1966; asst sup, publs, War Dept, 1941-42; originator, dir, lit therapy prog, Hillside Hosp, Glen Oaks, NY, 1956-59; lectr, poetry, NY Guild for J Blind, 1955-58, dir, dramatics, 1958-59; poetry broadcaster, lectr. Author: vols of poetry: The Alarm Clock, 1938; Another Fountain, 1940; Till The Grass is Ripe for Dancing, 1943; Thru Our Guns, 1945; The Glass Mountain, 1946; The Thunder of the Grass, 1948; The Golden Trumpet, 1949; Thru Every Window!, 1950; Denmark Vesey, 1952; Roll the Forbidden Drums, 1954; The Tune of the Calliope, 1958; Moses, 1962; Rumshinsky's Hat, 1964; House of Buttons, 1968; Henry At The Grating, 1968; with others, Seven Poets in Search of an Answer, 1944; lit criticism: The Prophetic Tradition in American Poetry, 1835-1900, publ 1968; with others, Poetry As Therapy, 1969; trans: The Poetry and Prose of Heinrich Heine, 1948; Four Pioneer Yiddish Poets, 1950; Morris Rosenfeld-The Teardrop Millionaire, 1955; Mickiewicz's Concert of Concerts, 1956; Songs and Ballads: Goethe, Schiller, Heine, 1963; Rilke's Visions of Christ, 1968; works performed: Guernica, SF Palace of Legion of Hon; UN Cantata, NY Mus of Natural Hist; Emma Lazarus, NY Town Hall; Denmark Vesey, LA 1st Unitarian Church; The Lovers and Prothalamium, Berkshire Music Festival; Ballad of August Bondi, Bklyn Acad of Music; The Tinderbox, BBC, Eng; In Us Lives the Music, NY Carnegie Hall; A Garland of Song, NY Town Hall; Poems, of New York, NY Judson Dance Theatre; Chelm, Garden City Cathedral; Serenade, Folkways Record Album; other works, poems, trans, essays, book revs pub in gen mags, profsl jours, newspapers, rev, lit quarterlies. Mem: AAUP; Keats-Shelley Assn. Home: 172-20 133 Ave, Jamaica, NY. Office: Adelphi Suffolk Coll, Oakdale, NY.

KRAMER, Aaron, S Afr, pharmacist, manufacturer; b. Willowmore, Cape Province, S Afr, Oct 5, 1910; s. Suesskind and Bessie (Goldberg); dipl, pharm, 1935; m. Eve Chanoch; c: Graham, Corrinne. Mgn dir, Afr Chems Pty Ltd, since 1943; Pharmapak Co, since 1945. Mem, S Afr Pharm Bd, 1948-53, 1954-58, 1959-63, 1969-73; hon secy: Transvaal Pharm Students Assn, 1929-30, chmn, 1931; Pharm Soc, Transvaal, 1942-45; secy, Pharm Socs of S Afr, 1944-45; hon natl adv comm Pharm, Directorate of Demobilization, 1948. Co-author: Glossary of Afrakaans Pharmaceutical Terms, 1951; asso ed, S Afr Pharm Jour, 1944-59; mgn dir, Asso Pharm Socs Jour, publisher, S Afr Pharm Jour, 1946-58. Home: 46 Greenhill Rd, Greenside, Johannesburg, S Afr. Office: Afkem House, 256 Anderson St, Johannesburg, S Afr.

KRAMER, Aba, Isr, civil engr; b. Russ, Jan 3, 1902; s. Shlomo and Leah (Weigman); in Isr since 1921; civil engr dipl, Technion, Haifa, 1928; m. Mania Tuchin, 1929 (decd); c: Eitan; m. 2nd, Margalit Sherizly. Pvt practice since 1967; fmr: exec engr, Govt Public Works Dept; cons, asphalt works; engr i/c roads; dep city engr; planner of: modern roads, public gardens, modern street lighting. Served, Haganah. Pres, mgn comm, Technion Grad Assn; mem council, Isr Engrs Assn, Curatorium, Technion; mem: Natl Council for Prevention of Accidents Assn. Contbr to jours. Home and office: 1A Kish St, Haifa, Isr.

KRAMER, Amihud, US, educator; b. Aus-Hung, May 7, 1913; s. Nathan and Sabina (Puder); in US since 1921; BS, U of Md, 1938, MS, 1939, PhD, 1942; m. Diana Stevan, June 3, 1939; c: John, Mark. Prof, horticulture, food tech, U of Md, since 1949, fac mem since 1943; coop agt, Soil Conservation Service, 1939-40; food chem, Natl Canners Assn, Wash, DC, 1941-43; US Agcy for Ind Devl cons to: Isr, 1954-55; 1961; Ecuador, 1965; Thailand, 1966-68. Prin contribs: developed: series of instruments and chem-phys procedures for objective measurement of quality in raw and processed foods; fully nutritious foods acceptable to endemic population. Chmn: proceedings sect, Amer Soc of Horticulture Sci, 1949-50; MD and DC sect, Inst Food Techs, 1950-51; educ comm, Amer Soc for Quality Control, 1953-54; f, AAAS; mem: Amer Soc Plant Phys; AAUP. Author, vol on quality control, food and agric; contbr to experimental sta bulls, sci and trade publs. Recipient: Woodbury Award in food research, 1953. Home: 415 Windsor St, Silver Spring, Md. Office: U of Md, College Park, Md.

KRAMER, Earl, US, business exec; b. Boston, Mass, Jan 26, 1933; s. Hyman and Frances (Glickman); AB, Harvard U, 1953; MBA, Columbia U, 1955; m. Janet Rosenfield, Nov 19, 1961; c: Kathe, Betsy, Lucy, Tracy. Vice-pres, Intl Stretch Producs Inc, since 1966; gen mgr, knitted fabrics, Beaunit Mills, 1955-62; plant mgr, Electroknit Fabrics, 1962-66. Chmn, United Fund Drive, LI, NY. Hobby: classic cars. Home: 7 Willow Rd, Woodmere, NY. Office: 111 W 40 St, New York, NY.

KRAMER, Joel, US, educator; b. Bklyn, NY, Mar 20, 1937; s. Emanuel and Ruth (Bernstein); BA, Bklyn Coll, 1958; MS, Ed, Yeshiva U, 1961; ordained rabbi, Rabb Acad, 1963; m. Judith Unger, Mar 6, 1962. Prin, Prospect Park Yeshiva HS, since 1963; dir, Neighborhood Youth Corps, Natl Soc for Heb Day Schs, since 1966; asst prin, Kamenitzer Mesivta, Boro Park, 1960-62. Mem, bd, Maimonides Mh Cen; natl vice-pres, adv bd, Gtr NY, Natl Conf of Yeshiva Prin; mem: Natl Assn Secondary Sch Prin; Phi Beta Kappa. Contbr to educ jours. Home: 66 Parkville Ave, Brooklyn, NY. Office: 153 Ocean Ave, Brooklyn, NY.

KRAMER, Michael, Can, rabbi; b. NYC, Oct 18, 1936; s. Simon and Tirza (Nelson); in Can since 1969; BA, Yeshiva Coll, 1957; MHL, Yeshiva U, 1962, ordained rabbi, 1962; m. Phyllis Silverman, July 14, 1965; c: Mordecai, Elliot. Rabbi: Adath Isr Cong, Montreal, Can, since 1969; Cong Kadimah-Toras Moshe, Boston, 1963-66; Cong Sons of Isr, Allentown, Pa, 1966-69. Fmr: bd dirs: Allentown J Day Sch; Charles Kune Lodge, B'nai B'rith; off, Vaad Harabonim of Mass, 1965-66; mem: JCC, Boston, 1965-66; RabCA; Yeshiva U Rabb Alumni; Mizrachi; Heb Inst of U Hgts, Bx, NY; club, Rotary. Home: 406 Dunlop Ave, Montreal, Can. Study: 1500 Ducharme Ave, Montreal, Can.

KRAMER, Norman M, US, business exec; b. NYC, Dec 29, 1912; s. Jacob and Yetta (Prosansky); BBA, Rutgers U, 1933; m. Bernice Goodman, Sep 9, 1941; c: Joan Tucker. Vice-chmn, Longchamps Inc, since 1969; chmn, pres, Gen Meat Corp, since 1963. Lt, USNR, 1942-45. Mem: Sigma Alpha

Mu; clubs: Rockrimmon Country, Stamford, Conn, fmr pres; City Athletic, NYC. Hobby: swimming. Home: 983 Park Ave, New York, NY. Office: 820 Washington St, New York, NY.

KRAMER, Reuben Robert, US, sculptor; b. Baltimore, Md, Oct 9, 1909; s. Israel and Bessie (Silver); att Md Inst, post grad studies, 1932-34; m. Perna Krick, June 19, 1944. Instr: Baltimore J Comty Cen, since 1960; sculpture, pvt, since 1939; adult educ, Baltimore City Coll, 1950-52; Poly Inst, 1952-57; found, Baltimore Art Cen for Children, 1944, dir, 1944-56; org, dir Artists Equity Summer Workshop, 1956-58; i/c sculpture dept, Amer U Wash, DC, 1951-52; instr, evening sch, Md Inst, 1957-58; ind designer, US War Dept, 1942-45. One-man shows: Md Inst, Baltimore, 1937; Baltimore Mus of Art, 1939, 1951, 1959; Amer U, 1953; with wife, W Md Coll, 1954; Hagerstown Mus, Md, 1955; Goucher Coll, 1961; three-man show: Corcoran Gal, Wash DC; J Comty Cen: exhbs: Grand Cen Gals, NY; Intl Sculpture Exhb, Phila; Pa Acad Shows; Amer J Traveling Tercentenary; works in collections: Corcoran Cal, Baltimore Mus of Art; Walters Art Gal Coll; Horelick Coll; Martenet Coll; IBM Coll; Dr and Mrs Mason Lord Coll; Johns Hopkins U; Rosen Coll, Md; Perine Coll, Ore; Stern Coll, Wash DC. Mem: Alumni, Amer Acad in Rome; Artists Equity Assn. Recipient: Rinehart Eur scholarships, 1931-33; Prix de Rome, 1934; 1st prize, sculpture commn for Frederick Douglass Homes Competition, 1940; grand prize, Sculptors Guild of Md, 1947; grand prize, Md Show, 1948; 1st prize: Md Area Exhbs, 1951, 1953; Wash Sculptors Group, Smithsonian Inst, Wash DC, 1952, 1954; drawing award, Peale Mus, 1954; Baltimore Mus Purchase Prize, 1948; Corcoran Gal Purchase Prize, 1952; Elected to Hall of Fame, Baltimore City Coll, 1962. Home and studio: 121 Mosher St, Baltimore, Md.

KRAMER, Richard Ben, US, lawyer; b. Detroit, Mich, Aug 15, 1918; s. Morris and Mildred (Bersansky); BA, Wayne State U, Detroit, 1938, MSW, 1940; JD, U Chgo, 1953; m. Billie Goldberg, Sep 3, 1950; c: Ellen, Merrill. Sr mem, firm, specializing in admiralty, fire ins, warehouse law, since 1953; training dir, US Rubber Co, 1945-46; regional dir, CJFWF, 1949-50. Capt, USAAF, 1942-45; one of liberators of Buchenwald concentration camp, Ger, 1945, org rescue oprs and camp survivors comm. Secy, Lab Zionist Inst; chmn Exec Comm, Zionist Org, both Detroit; mem, Natl Exec Comm, ZOA; fmr: pres: Farband LZOA; Zionist Org, Detroit; div chmn, UJA, Detroit; asst dir, J Comty Cen, Indianapolis; exec secy, J Comty Relations Council, New Haven, Conn; charter mem, planning comm, Fair Employment Practices Commn. Mem: Amer, Detroit, Bar Assns; grievance comm, State Bar, Mich. Home: 5259 Whispering Oak, Birmingham, Mich. Office: 1774 First Natl Bldg, Detroit, Mich.

KRAMER, Rose Cohen, US, communal leader; b. Wash DC Jan 7, 1912; d. Harry and Nettie (Yuzik) Cohen; BS, DC Tchrs Coll, 1933; MA, Catholic U, DC, 1937; m. Harold Kramer, Aug 15, 1937; c: Madelyn Schaefer, Ellen, David, Kathryn. Mem, Montgomery Co Council, Md, since 1966; public sch tchr, DC Public Schs, 1933-41; mem, Sch Bd, Montgomery Co Public Schs, 1954-60. Prin contrib: leader in fight for open housing in Montgomery Co. Commn, Wash Metrop Transit Auth; fmr: pres, B'nai B'rith, Montgomery Co; bd, J Comty Cen, Gtr Wash, DC; bd, JCC; mem, Kappa Delta Pi. Recipient: Stephen Wise Medallion, AJCong, DC chap, 1969. Home: 9350 Harvey Rd, Silver Spring, Md. Office: County Off Bldg, Rockville, Md.

KRAMER, Samuel N, US, orientalist, educator, author; b. Zashkow, Russ, Sep 28, 1897; s. Benjamin and Yetta (Greenstein); in US since 1906; BS, Temple U, Phila, 1921; att Dropsie Coll, Phila, 1926-27; PhD, U of Pa, 1929; hon: DHL, HUC, 1967; Des Lettres, Temple U, 1960; m. Mildred Tokarsky, Oct 9, 1933; c: Daniel, Judith. Ret; curator, Tablet collections, Clark Research Prof, U of Pa, 1949-68, staff mem since 1942; research asst, Oriental Inst, U Chgo, 1932-35, asso 1937-39; prof, Amer Schs of Oriental Research, Istanbul and Baghdad, 1946-47; Fulbright research prof, Turkey, 1951-52; Pattern Found Lectr, Ind U, 1968; visiting prof, U Copenhagen, 1969-70. US Army, WW I. Mem: Amer Phil Soc; Amer Oriental Soc; AAAS; Archaeol Inst of Amer; Amer Anthropological Assn; Soc Bibl Lit. Author: Gilgamesh and the Huluppu Tree, 1938; Lamentation Over the Destruction of Ur, 1940; Sumerian Mythology, 1944; Sumerian Literary Texts from Nippur, 1944; Enmerkar and the Lord of Aratta, 1952; A Fulbright in Turkey, 1953; From

the Tablets of Sumer, 1956; History Begins at Sumer, 1959; Cradle of Civilization, 1967; The Sacred Marriage Rite, 1969. Recipient: Lewis Prize, Amer Phil Soc. Home: 5039 Schuyler St, Philadelphia, Pa.

KRAMER, Simon Gad, US, college pres; b. Aus, Jan 29, 1903; s. Mechel and Beila (Surkis); ordained rabbi, DHL, Heb Theol Coll, 1925; MA, U of Chgo, 1926; PhD, NYU, 1962; m. Tirza Nelson, Aug 14, 1932; c: Michael. Pres, Heb Theol Coll, since 1964; rabbi: Cong Knesseth Isr, Hammond, Ind, 1925-28; Temple Beth El, Gary, 1928-31; Heb Inst of U Hgts, NYC, 1931-64. Found, prin, Akoba Heb Acad, Bx; hon vice-pres, JNF of Amer; hon bd dirs: FJP; Bd J Educ; pres: Syn Council Amer, 1950-52; NY Bd Rabbis, 1948-50; mem, RabCA. Author: God and Man in the Sefer Hasidim, 1966; contbr to profsl jours. Home: 3180 Lake Shore Dr, Chicago, Ill. Office: 7135 N Carpenter Rd, Skokie, Ill.

KRAMER, William, Mordecai, US, rabbi, educator, journalist; b. Cleveland, O, Mar 29, 1920; s. Simon and Jeannette (Rosenbaum); BA, W Reserve U, 1940, MA, 1946; ordained rabbi, JIR, 1944; D, Judaic Art, Syn Archaeol, HUC; grad study, Ind U, 1946-48; m. Joan Oppenheim, Mar 13, 1954; c: Jonathan, Jeremy. Asso prof, J cultural hist, chmn fac, Sch of Educ, HUC, Cal, since 1966; rabbi, Temple Beth Emet, Burbank; licensed marriage and family counselor, State of Cal; lectr: Cal State Coll; LA Coll of J Studies, since 1948; fmr: asst rabbi, The Temple, Cleveland, 1944-46; rabbi: Muncie, Ind, 1946-48; Village Temple, LA, 1953-56. Pres, S Cal Assn Lib Rabbis, since 1963; vice-pres, LA Assn J Educ, since 1962; secy treas, Anytown, US, youth inter-faith prog, since 1956; fmr: mem: LA Co Conf on Comty Relations; mem: bd, Bur of J Educ; AJComm, all LA; ZOA; bd Rabbis, S Cal; CCAR; World Union of Progressive Judaism, London, Eng; Natl Assn Temple Educs; Natl Assn for J Educ; W Assn of Reform Rabbis; Natl Fed Temple Brotherhoods; NCCJ; HUC-JIR Alumni; found, Hillel Found, W Reserve U; Coll Art Assn; Phi Sigma Delta, natl chaplain; Soc of J Research; Archaeol Inst of Amer; Cal Assn of Marriage Counselors; Amer Sch of Oriental Research. Author: Do It Yourself Book of Hebrew, 1958; Jewish Bible Guide, 1959; co-author, Temple Israel Pulpit, 1957; lit ed, Heritage, since 1957; contbr to scholarly jours. Recipient: Louis Marshall prize, 1944; Hillel Key award, 1959; J Educ-of-the-Year, 1961; citations: LA City Council; LA Co; Gtr LA J Fed Council; NCCJ; UAHC. Home: 2907 Tilden Ave, Los Angeles, Cal. Study: 7300 Hollywood Blvd, Hollywood, Cal.

KRANCENBLUM, Abraham Albert, Fr, dental surg; b. Metz, Fr, Oct 7, 1927; s. Mordechai and Welka (Raab); dent surg, Ecole de Chirurgie Dentaire e: Stomatologie, Paris, 1949; m. Stella Horowitz, June 5, 1951. Prof, Ecole de Chirurgie Dentaire et Stomatologie, Paris; pvt practice, both since 1949. Fr Army, dent service, 1949-50; prisoner, Ger concentration camp, 1944. Vice-pres, Union des Médecins, Dentistes et Pharmaciens, Amis d'Isr; secy gen: Amitiés Odonto-Stomatologiques, Fr-Isr; Alpha Omega Frat, Paris chap, fmr pres; mem, med comm, Appel Unifié Juif, Fr. Spec interest: Isr. Office: 51 Rue Duhesme, Paris 18, Fr.

KRANITZ, Louis, US, attorney; b. Buffalo, NY, Dec 23, 1899; s. Abraham and Mary (Benyes); LLB, St Josephs Law Sch, 1919; m. Miriam Saferstein, June 7, 1921; c: Theodore, Jean Ferber, Morton. Mem, Kranitz & Kranitz, since 1949; legal adv bd, Selective Service Bd, 1941-44. Pres: Temple B'nai Yaakov, 1956-61; Social Wfr Bd, St Joseph, Mo, 1952-54; St Joseph Heb Sch, 1941-44; vice-pres: Intl B'nai B'rith, 1959-65; St Joseph Bar Assn, 1946-47; Leo N Levi Memorial Hosp, Hot Springs, 1945-47 and since 1969; St Joseph Housing Auth since 1968; trustee: Natl J Hosp, Denver, Colo; Bellefaire, Cleveland, O; delg, Isr PM Ben-Gurion's Econ Conf, 1953; mem: Amer, Mo State Bar Assns; Amer Judicature Soc. Home: 8 Ridgeland Rd, Country Club Pl, St Joseph, Mo. Office: 714A Francis St, St Joseph, Mo.

KRANTZ, Abraham, US, rabbi; b. NYC, Oct 2, 1921; s. Rubin and Clara (Krauthamer) Kranz; BSS, CCNY, 1941; MA, Columbia U, 1947; MHL, HUC-JIR, 1955; m. Jane Steinheimer, Dec 22, 1946; c: Deborah, Melissa, Jeremy. Rabbi, Tremont Temple, since 1966; chaplain, Rockland State Hosp, Orangeburg, NY, since 1964; rabbi: Monroe Temple of Lib Judaism, Monroe, NY, 1952-57; Temple Emanuel, Greensburg, Pa, 1958-62; Temple Isr, Nyack, NY, 1962-66. USAAF, 1942-46. Natl bd mem, AJCong; pres, Assn J Chaplains serving NY instns; bd mem, Rockland City Mh Assn, 1963-65;

mem: CCAR; Amer Sociol Assn; Acad Rel and Mh; Natl Assn Mh Chaplains. Home: 134 Strawtown Rd, W Nyack, NY. Study: 2064 Grand Concourse, Bronx, NY.

KRANZBERG, Melvin, US, educator; b. St Louis, Mo, Nov 22 1917; s. Samuel and Rose (Fitter); BA, Amherst Coll, 1938; MA, Harvard U, 1939, PhD, 1942; att Catholic U, 1942; Johns Hopkins U, 1943; Sorbonne U, Ecole Librede Sciences, Politiques, Paris, 1945; Heidelberg U, 1945; hon LHD, Denison U, 1967; hon DLitt, Newark Coll Engr, 1968; m. Nancy Fox, May 4, 1943; c: Steven, John; m. 2nd, Eva Mannering, 1956. Prof, hist, Case Reserve U, Cleveland, O, since 1958, fac mem since 1952; fmr: asso econ, OPA, Wash, DC, 1942-43; instr: hist, Harvard U, 1946; hum, Stevens Inst of Tech, 1946-47; asst prof, hist, Amherst Coll, 1947-52; cons, oprs research off, Johns Hopkins U, 1951-53. US Mil Intelligence, 1943-46. Vice-pres: Intl Coop in Hist of Tech Comm; Soc for Fr Hist Studies, 1958-59; found, chmn, Soc for Hist of Tech, 1958-59; chmn: Hist Adv Comm, NASA, since 1966; humanistic-soc div, Amer Soc for Educ Engr, 1957-58; secy, natl comm, Intl Union, Hist and Phil of Sci, 1960-61; f, AAAS; mem: Amer Hist Assn; Société d'Histoire Moderne; Newcomen Soc; Amherst Alumni Assn; Phi Beta Kappa; Suburban Temple; bd dirs, B'nai B'rith Hillel Found, Cleveland, since 1953; clubs: Lord Jeffrey Amherst; Natl Rocket. Author: The Siege of Paris, 1870-1871, 1951; 1848: A Turning Point?, 1959; Technology in Western Civilization, 1967; ed-in-chief, Technology and Culture, intl quarterly, since 1959; ed, Monograph Series History of Technology, since 1961; contbr to learned jours and encys. Recipient: Bronze Star Medal, 3 Battle Stars, 1945; research grant, Social Sci Research Council, 1951. Home: 2440 Overlook Rd, Cleveland Heights, O. Office: Case W Reserve U, University Circle, Cleveland, O.

KRASNER, Louis W, US, violinist, educator; b. Russ, June 21, 1903; s. Harry and Sarah (Lechovetzky); in US since 1908; Dipl, NE Conservatory of Music, 1922; postgrad studies: Berlin, Paris, Vienna; hon prof, Accademia Fillarmonica, Bologna, It, 1929; m. Adrienne Galimir, Oct 10, 1936; c: Elsa, Vivien, Naomi. Prof, violin and chamber music, Syracuse U, since 1949, coneuctor, Syracuse U Orch, since 1958; concert master, Syracuse Sym Orch, since 1961; musical dir, Syracuse Friends Chamber Music and Kasrner Chamber Music Ensemble, since 1950; chmn: Tanglewood String Symposia; Tanglewood Sem for Music Tchrs, 1965-66; concert tours in Eur and US; soloist with orchs: Vienna, Berlin; Paris; London BBC; Boston Sym; NY Philharmonic; Phila Sym Orch; first performances violin concertos by: Alban Berg; Schoenberg and others; concert master with Dimitri Mitropoulos, Minneapolis Sym Orch, 1944-49. Mem: Amer String Tchrs Assn, found, fmr pres, NY chap; fac, Amer Fed Musicians Cong of Strings. Ed, String Problems, Players on Paucity. 1965; contbr to jours. Home: 521 Scott Ave, Syracuse, NY. Office: U of Syracuse, Syracuse, NY.

KRASS, Hyman H, US, civil engineer, builder; b. Chgo, Ill, June 12, 1914; s. Louis and Rebecca (Blank); MS, Ill Inst Tech, 1939. Exec vice-pres, chief engr, Crane Construction Co Inc, since 1961; construction cons since 1953; registered profsl engr; pres, Constructors Co, 1953-61; chief engr, Inland Construction Co, 1955-57. F: AAAS; Natl Acad Contractors and Engrs; Amer Soc Civil Engrs; mem: Chgo Hi-Rise Comm; Amer Mil Engrs; Amer Technion Soc; Amer Concrete Inst; Natl Soc Profsl Engrs; Amer Soc Testing Materials; Ill State Acad Sci; Intl Assn Bridge and Structural Engrs, Zurich; Prestressed Concrete Devl Group of London; Intl Acad of Thin Shell Structures of Lisbon; Tau Beta Pi; Chi Epsilon; Delta Lambda Xi; Masons; Shriners; B'nai B'rith; Art Inst of Chgo; clubs: Covenant; Riviera. Hobbies: photography, painting, phys sci research. Home: 3600 Lake Shore Dr, Chicago, Ill. Office: 919 N Michigan Ave, Chicago Ill.

KRAUS, Arie, Isr, business exec; b. Berlin, Ger, Sep 19, 1909; s. Abraham and Devora (Ashkenazy); in Isr since 1933; att, HS, Berlin; m. Hannah Willig, Feb 7, 1954. Dir, Dept Projects, Legacies, Bequests, KH head off, since 1968; fmr: dir, youth activities, Working Youth, Tel Aviv; secy, Agric Sch, Yagur; ed mgr, Bamaaleh, mag for youth. Pvt, Brit Army. Fmr, active in numerous public and communal orgs; mem, B'nai B'rith, Haganah lodge, Jerusalem. Recipient: Afr Star. Home: 60 Nayot, Jerusalem, Isr. Office: KH, Jerusalem, Isr.

KRAUS, Jerome, US, management exec, economist; b. Chgo, Ill, Nov 13, 1921; s. Arthur and Anna (Wadler); BA, U

Chgo, 1942; BSEE, U Ill, 1947; att NYU, 1949-51; JD, George Wash U, 1953; MA, New Sch for Social Research, 1967; m. Shirley Dushkind, 1946; c: Terry, Gordon. Dir, bus planning, ITT; sup of sys mgmt and prog dir, Fairchild Camera and Instrument Corp, 1956-59. Chmn, Rel Affairs Comm, Jamaica J Cen, 1968-69; sr mem, Inst of Elec and Electronic Engrs; mem: NY, DC Bars; Amer Econ Assn; Natl Assn Bus Econs. Contbr to profsl publs. Home: 141-30 Pershing Crescent, Jamaica, NY.

KRAUS, Michael, US, educator; b. NYC, June 29, 1901; s. Herman and Lena (Goldstein); BSS, CCNY, 1923; PhD, Columbia, 1928; m. Vera Edelstadt, June 12, 1930. Prof em, CUNY, since 1965, prof, hist, 1950-65, on fac since 1925; fmr: lectr, Tchrs Coll, Columbia U, 1948-51, visiting prof, 1960-64. Mem: Amer Hist Assn; Miss Valley Hist Assn; Phi Beta Kappa. Author: Intercolonial Aspects of American Culture on the Eve of the Revolution, 1928; co-author: The Atlantic Civilization, 1943; The Atlantic Civilization: Eighteenth Century Origins, 1949; The Writings of American History, 1953; The North Atlantic Civilization, 1957; The United States to 1865, 1959; Family Album for Americans, 1961; Immigration: The American Mosaic, 1966; dept ed, Collier's Ency, 1960-64; contbr to profsl jours. Hobbies: book collecting, gardening. Homes: 370 Central Park W, New York, NY; Stoney Point, NY. Office: CUNY, New York, NY.

KRAUS, Philip E, US, educator; b. New York, NY, Feb 1, 1908; s. Solomon and Mollie (Mandel); BA, CCNY, 1928; MA, Columbia U, 1931; PhD, NYU, 1943; m. Martha Eckl, Dec 25, 1933; c: Lucy, Alice, Robert. Prof, educ, Hunter Coll, since 1963; fmr: psychiatric case worker, psychol, J Bd of Guardians, 1930-32; prof, educ, Yeshiva U, 1945-63, staff mem since 1933; asst dean, HUC Sch of Rel Educ, 1947-48; project dir, Bd of Educ, 1954-63. Fmr pres, Assn for Gifted; f: Amer Psych Assn; AAAS; educ, CCNY, 1927-28; mem: Phi Delta Kappa; Natl Soc for Study of Educ; Amer Assn Sch Admnrs; Amer Educ Research Assn; NY State Psych Assn; Natl Assn of Temple Educs. Home: 40 E 84 St, New York, NY. Office: Hunter Coll, 695 Park Ave, New York, NY.

KRAUS, Shirley D, US, pharmacologist, educator; b. NYC, Dec 24, 1919; d. Michael and Hannah (Gordon) Dushkind; BA, Hunter Coll, 1940; MA, Cornell U, 1942; PhD, U of Ill, 1946; m. Jerome Kraus, Sep 14, 1946; c: Terry, Gordon. Prof, pharm, Bklyn Coll of Pharm, LIU, since 1965, on fac since 1957, grad fac since 1965; physiologist, gastroenterology research lab, Mt Sinai Hosp, NY, 1947-48; biochemist, Cancer Research Found, Harlem Hosp, 1948-50; lectr, NYU Coll of Dent, 1950-51; pharm, cancer research and metabolism unit, Mt Alto Hosp, VA, 1951-53; instr, pharm, Sch of Med, Howard U, Wash, DC, 1955-56; visiting sci and asso prof, SUNY Downstate Med Sch, 1969-70. Mem: Soc for Experimental Biol and Med; Endocrine Soc; Amer Phys Soc; Amer Soc Pharm and Experimental Therapeutics; Intl Soc for Biochem Pharm; Sigma Xi; Sigma Delta Epsilon; Iota Sigma Pi; Phi Sigma; Rho Chi. Contbr to profsl jours. Home: 141-30 Pershing Crescent, Jamaica, NY. Office: Bklyn Coll of Pharm, LIU, Brooklyn, NY.

KRAUSHAAR, David I, US, lawyer, b. Bklyn, NY, Mar 27, 1918; s. Meyer and Rosalind (Baruth); BA, Cornell U, 1939; JD, Columbia U, 1942; m. Ruth Lasker, Jan 5, 1947; c: Jonathan, Rosalind, Judah. Fed trial examiner, FCC, since 1959, on staff since 1952; mem, Kraushaar & Kraushaar, 1946-51; adv, Natl Produc Auth, 1951-52. Lt col, USAF Res, ret. Pres, N Va Zionist Dist, 1954-56; chmn, Arlington-Fairfax UJA Dr, 1956; post cdr, JWV, 1948; mem: Fed Trial Examiners Conf; JFK lodge B'nai B'rith, Wash DC; club: Natl Lawyers. Home: 3810 Howard St, Annandale, Va. Office: FCC, Washington, DC.

KRAUSZ, Ernest, Eng, educator; b. Satumare, Rum, Aug 13, 1931; s. Maurice and Bertha (Gottlieb); in Eng since 1947; att Yeshiva Etz Hayim, London, 1947-51; BSc, econ, hons, U of London, 1955; MSc, sociol, LSE, 1960, PhD, 1964; m. Gillian Collins, Dec 18, 1962; c: Sara, Miriam, Zvi. Lectr, i/c sociol, dept social sci and hum, City U, London, since 1967; asst lectr, Leeds Coll of Commerce, 1955-57; research asst, UNESCO Social Sci Dict, 1960; lectr, Poly, London, 1957-61; participant, Edgware Survey, sponsored by Nuffield Found, LSE, London U and Hillel Found, 1961-64; prin lectr, W Ham Coll Tech, London, 1964-67. Secy, research comm, dept social sci, City U; convenor, social sem, Inst of J Affairs, London; mem, academic adv council, cultural dept, WJC; mem: British Sociol Assn; Assn of U Tchrs; LSE Soc; Inst of Race Relations; J Hist Soc; Inst of J Affairs; fmr, mem, adv comm, stat and demographic unit, Bd of Deps of British J. Author: Leeds Jewry: Its History and Social Structure, 1964; Sociology of Britain, 1969; chaps in: Jewish Life in Modern Britain, 1964; Sociological Data Comparability, 1970; contbr to jours, Ency Judaica. Recipient: Merit Award, City U, 1969. Home: 15, Golders Gardens, London NW 11, Eng. Office: City U, St John St, London EC 1, Eng.

KRAUSZ, Maurice Lazar, Eng, rabbi; b. Hung, Sep 23, 1890; s. Simon and Sarah (Gelb); in Eng since 1947; ordained rabbi, Pressburg Yeshiva, 1920; PhD, Budapest U, 1923; PhD, Prague U, 1925; m. Bertha Gottlieb, June 18, 1919 (decd); c: Elvira Schindelheim, Aliza Singer, Ernest. Sr dayan em, Beth Din, Fed of Syns, London, since 1960, auth in matters of marriage and divorce; communal rabbi, Beth Din, Alba-Julia, Rum, 1930-47; sr dayan, Leeds Beth Din, 1949-60. Mem: Chief Rabbi's Ecclesiastical Auth, London; Vaad Harabanim, London; fmr: examiner for official rabb cert, Min of Educ and Culture, Rum; chmn, Alba-Julia by, WJC; found mem, first secy, Union of Orthodox J Comtys in Transylvania. Author: Regel Yeshara, 1953; ed, Shtiley Zeitim, 1969. Recipient: 1st prize, for dissertation, Prague U, 1925. Home: 1 Cadoxton Ave, London N 15, Eng. Study: 64 Leman St, London, E 1, Eng.

KRAVITZ, Daniel, US, ophthalmologist; b. Russ, Jan 1, 1897; s. Louis and Rebecca (Goldberg); att NYU, 1915-17; MD, Bellevue Med Coll, 1921; m. Lillian Drexler, June 8, 1969; c: Sheldon, Paul. Sr surg, Bklyn Eye and Ear Hosp, since 1952, dir, glaucoma dept, since 1957, mem, bd dirs, since 1962; cons ophthal: Maimonides Hosp, Bklyn, NY, since 1951; Unity Hosp since 1962, mem staff since 1952; Long Beach Gen Hosp; asso, ophthal, cons, neuro-ophthal, Post Grad Hosp, NYC, 1934-52. US Army MC, 1917-19. Mem: ADL; Ophthal Soc, Manhattan, fmr pres; exec bd, Ophthal Soc, Bklyn, NY, since 1928, fmr pres; Soc Clinical Ophthal, NY since 1939, participating conf courses since 1954, past pres; Pan Amer Ophthal Soc; Amer Friends Heb U; hon, Ophthal Soc, Mexico. Contbr to profsl jours. Hobbies: music, travel. Home: 9 Prospect Park W, Brooklyn, NY. Office: 1 Hanson Pl, Brooklyn, NY.

KRAVITZ, Jacob H, US, social worker; b. Manchester, Eng, Aug 5, 1909; s. Morris and Bessie (Rosen); in US since 1911; BA, Amherst Coll, Mass, 1931; spec cert, Grad Sch J Social Work, NYC, 1933; m. Louis Elman, Dec 21, 1934; c: David, Barbara. Exec vice-pres, JWF, Dallas since 1943; dir, resettlement div, Natl Ref Service, 1937-41; reg dir, CJFWF, 1941-43. Fmr pres, Amer Assn Social Work, mem, bd dirs; vice-pres: Natl Conf J Communal Service, 1946; Dallas chap, Tex Social Wfr Assn, since 1943; mem, bd dirs: Council of Social Agencies; Vets Service Cen; Tex Social Wfr Assn; Dallas Sch for Blind Children; mem, adv comm, Tex U Sch of Social Work. Home: 4016 Shannon Lane, Dallas, Tex. Office: 1416 Commerce Bldg, Dallas, Tex.

KRAVITZ, Nathaniel, US, editor, publisher, author; b. Yaruga, Russ, Aug 2, 1902; s. Moishe and Lea; in US since 1923; ordained rabbi, Yeshiva, Odessa; m. Anna Greenberg; c: Morris. Ed, pub, J Way Publs; lectr, J hist and lit; ed: J World, daily, Phila, Pa, 1924-38; J Daily Courier, Chgo, 1939-45. Author: Out of the Storm, Yiddish, 1936; Torah-Lernen bei Yidden, 1942; Zacuta the Seer; Genesis — A New Interpretation, 1967; Sayings of the Fathers, 2 vols, 1969, in Eng, Heb, Yiddish; History of 3,000 Years of Hebrew Literature. Club, Phil, Phila, org; Bible Research Group, Chgo. Home and office: 6457 N Artesian St, Chicago, Ill.

KRAVITZ, Philip B, US, certified public accnt; b. NYC, July 13, 1916; s. Sam and Ray (Melanofsky); BBA, St John's U, 1939; CPA, SUNY, 1945; m. Dorothy Schlechter, June 15, 1940; c: Eileen Brenner, Sharon Bloom, Gail, Robin. Mem, Philip B Kravitz Co, CPA's, since 1945; asst prof, pharmaceutical econ, Columbia U; acctnt, LIU, 1947-52. US Selective Service Bd, 1952-55. Fmr chmn: ethics comm, Amer Inst CPA's; March of Dimes; fmr pres: 14th Pythian Dist; Gt Neck Rotary Club; vice-pres: Nassau-Suffolk chap, NYS Taxation; C of C, Gt Neck; dir, Asso Health Found; mem: Temple Isr, Gt Neck; ethics comm, NYS CPA's; adv comm, Town of Hempstead; adv comm, Gt Neck Public Sch Budget; Comm Suburban Preservation of N Hempstead; commercial

counsellor, Third Cong dist. Contbr to profsl mags. Home and office: 22 Glenwood Dr, Great Neck, NY.

KRECH, David, US, psychologist, educator; b. Russ, Mar 27, 1909; s. Joseph and Sarah (Rabinowitz) Krechevsky; in US since 1913; MA, NYU, 1931; PhD, U of Cal, 1933; m. Hilda Gruenberg, Sep 17, 1943; c: Richard. Prof, psych, U of Cal, since 1947. US Army, 1942-45. F: NRC; Amer Psych Assn; Amer Coll Neuropsychopharm; mem: Neur Scis Soc; Intl Brain Research Org, UNESCO; AAAS; AAUP; Sigma Xi. Author: Elements of Psychology, 1958, 2nd ed, 1969; co-author: Theory and Problems of Social Psychology, 1948; Individual in Society, 1962; contbr to tech jours. Home: 1496 Euclid Ave, Berkeley, Cal. Office: U of Cal, Berkeley, Cal.

KREEGER, Morris H, US, physician, hospital cons; b. NYC, Aug 17, 1910; s. Barnet and Laura; BA, Rutgers U, 1931; MD, Jefferson Med Coll, 1935; att U Pa Grad Sch of Med, 1936-37; m. Naomi Mayor, June 19, 1935; div; c: Charles, Lora; m. 2nd, Renee Gellman, Dec, 1964; c: Anne. Hosp cons since 1960; fmr: pvt practice, 1937-39; res, Mt Sinai Hosp, NYC, 1939-40; asst dir, 1940-46; exec dir, Michael Reese Hosp, Chgo, 1946-60; lectr, hosp admn, Northwestern U, 1947-57. Pres, Chgo Hosp Council, 1954; chmn, comm on profsl practice, 1954-56; chmn, S Side Planning Bd; mem: bd dirs, Chgo Blue Cross-Blue Shield, since 1959; bd dirs, Amer Comm on Maternal Wfr, 1957; Comty Fund, 1959-60; tech adv comm on hosp care, Ill State Dept of Health, since 1954; profsl adv comm, Ill State div, Services for Crippled Children, 1954-56; adv council on educ, Amer Hosp Assn, 1954-56; comm on vet relations, 1955-56; jt comm, Amer Assn Med Social Workers, Amer Hosp Assn, both 1956-58; council, govt relations, Ill Hosp Assn; mayor's adv comm, poliomyelitis, 1956; f: Amer Coll Hosp Admn; AMA. Contbr to jours. Hobbies: farming, sports, theater. Home: 2482 N Sheridan Rd, Chicago, Ill. Office: 111 N Wabash Ave, Chicago, Ill.

KREIELSHEIMER, Kurt S, NZ, scientist, educator; b. Kassel, Ger, May 22, 1903; s. Louis and Mathilde (Kaufmann); in NZ since 1934; dipl ing, Tech HS, Darmstadt, May 22, 1929, DEng, 1933; m. Freda Kay, May 20, 1935; one c. Asso prof, physics, U of Auckland, since 1952, sr lectr, radio physics, 1945-52; leader, Ger radio tech, polar year expedition, Heinrich Hertz Inst, Berlin, 1932-34; research f, Academic Assistance Council, London, 1934-35; sr research physicist, Neon Signs, Sydney, Australia, 1935-39. War service, i/c radio training and research, Auckland, 1939-45. Vice-pres, Friends of Heb U, Jerusalem, since 1952; mem, bd mgmt, Heb Cong, since 1955, fmr treas, both Auckland; f, Inst of Physics, London; mem, Inst of Elec Engrs. Contbr to profsl jours. Hobby: gardening. Home: 603 Sandringham Rd, Auckland, SW 1, NZ. Office: U of Auckland, NZ.

KREINDLER, Doris, US, artist; b. Passaic, NJ, Aug 12, 1901; d. Jacob and Rebecca (Levitch) Barsky; att: NY Sch Applied Design for Women; Natl Acad of Schs of Design; Art League; Hans Hofmann Sch of Abstract Art; Pratt and Antaglio Workshop; Contemporaries Graphic; m. Harry Kreindler, Feb 12, 1940; c: Rosamund Koffman, Lee. Art tchr, lectr, since 1929; one-man shows: Bklyn Mus, 1935; Montross Gal, 1936; Jacques Seligmann Gal, 1952-54, 1964, 1967, 1970; Esther Robles, LA; perm collections: Ala Mus; Rose Art Collection; Brandeis U; Mus of Modern Art; Metrop Mus Art; NY Public Libr; Bklyn Mus; Phila Mus; Fogg Mus; Boston Mus; graphic div, Smithsonian Inst; Natl Collection of Art, Wash, DC; Butler Inst of Art; Art Inst of Chgo. Chmn: patron prints, Bklyn Soc Artists, since 1962; nominating comm, Natl Soc Artists in Casein, since 1962; mem: Artists Equity; Ala Water Color Soc; Soc Amer Graphic Artists; Natl Assn Women Artists, ext comm, jury in oil; f, Royal Soc of Arts, Eng. Recipient: 1st prize, graphics, 1963; 2nd prize, casein painting, 1963. Hobbies: theater, music, dancing, knitting, bridge. Home: 75 Central Park W, New York, NY. Studio: Box 178, South Salem, NY.

KREINDLER, Lee Stanley, US, attorney, b. NYC, Mar 11, 1924; s. Harry and Doris; BA, Dartmouth Coll, 1945; LLB, Harvard U, 1949; m. Ruth Bilgrei, Sep 1, 1952; c: James, Laurie. Mem, firm, Kreindler and Kreindler, since 1950, specialist, aviation law, trials and appeals. Cpl, US Army, 1943-46. Found, 1st pres, dir, Birchwood Swimming Pool Assn, Chappaqua, NY; trustee, chmn bldg fund campaign, Temple Beth El; f, Intl Acad Trial Lawyers, chmn, aviation and space law sect; mem: Amer Bar Assn; Amer Trial Lawyers Assn, fmr chmn, aviation law sect; NY State Bar Assn; Assn Bar, NYC, mem aeronautical law comm; NY Co Lawyers Assn; Fed Bar Assn, NY, NJ, Conn; Metrop Trial Lawyers Assn; Amer Inst Aeronautics and Astronautics; natl panel arbitrators, Amer Arbitration Assn. Author: Aviation Accident Law, 1963; contbr numerous articles on air and tort law to law revs and bar assn publs. Home: 25 McKesson Hill Rd, Chappaqua, NY. Office: 99 Park Ave, New York, NY.

KREIS, Boris, France, physican, educator; b. Vinnitsa, Russ, Nov 9, 1907; s. Henri and Amelie (Sapir); att Fac of Sci, Paris; Pasteur Inst; MD, Fac of Paris, 1937; m. Flore de Mayo; c: Henri, Claude-Marie. Prof, chest diseases and TB, Fac Med, Paris since 1953; phys, Hôpitaux de Paris, since 1954; chief, laboratories, Laënnec Hosp. Mem: Soc Française de la Tuberculose; So de Panthologie Respiratoire; Soc de Micro-biologie. Author: La maladie d'Armstrong, 1937; co-author: Techniques de laboratoire en pneumologie, 1949; Tubercu-loses traitées par la streptomycine, 1949; Resistance et sur-vivance du bacille tuberculeux, 1966. Contbr to med publs. Home and office: 4 Ave Hohec, Paris 8, Fr.

KREISEL, Henry, Can, educator, author; b. Vienna, Aus, June 5, 1922; s. David and Helene (Schreier); in Can since 1940; BA, U of Toronto, 1946, MA, 1947; PhD, U of London, 1954; m. Esther Lazerson, June, 1947; c: Philip. Sr asso dean, grad studies, U of Alberta, since 1967, fac mem since 1947. Pres: Assn Can U Tchrs of Eng, 1961-62; Assn Acad Staff, U of Alberta, 1960-61; f, Intl Inst Arts and Letters; mem: bd govs, U of Alberta, 1966-69; gov-gen's award jury for lit, 1966-69. Author: The Rich Man, 1952; The Betrayal, 1964; stories reprinted in anthologies; contbr to periodicals and jours. Recipient: Reuben Wells Leonard f, U of Toronto, 1946; grad f, Royal Soc of Can, 1953; pres medal, U of W Ont, 1959. Hobby: music. Home: 12516-66 Ave, Edmonton, Alberta, Can. Office: U of Alberta, Edmonton, Alberta, Can.

KREITLER, Hans, Isr, psychologist; b. Perchtholdsdorf, Aus, Aug 5, 1916; s. Wilhelm and Eugenie (Menkes); in Isr since 1938; att U of Vienna, 1935-38; Heb U, Jerusalem, 1938-41; PhD, U of Graz, Aus, 1956; m. Shulamith Elbinger, Mar 27, 1963. Prof, psych, Tel Aviv U, since 1961; chief psychol, Govt Hosp for Mental Diseases, Beer-Yaacov, 1956-61; chmn, dept psych, Tel Aviv U, 1961-66; visiting scholar, Educ Testing Service, Princeton, NJ, 1968-69. F, Intl Council Psychols, US; mem: Intl Council Group Psychotherapy, US; Isr Psych Assn; fgn affiliate, Amer Psych Assn. Author: Die Weltanschauliche Orientierung der Schizofrener, 1965; Die Kognitive Orientierung des Kindes, 1967; contbr chaps to books, numerous articles to profsl jours. Hobby: music. Home: 8 Israels St, Tel Aviv, Isr. Office: Tel Aviv U, Ramat Aviv, Isr.

KREITMAN, Benjamin Z, US, rabbi; b. Warsaw, Pol, Dec 25, 1919; s. Jacob and Anna (Grobower); in US since 1924; BA, Yeshiva Coll, 1939; ordained rabbi, MHL, JTSA, 1943, DHL, 1952; att Yale U, 1949-51; m. Joyce Krimsky, Aug 7, 1956; c: Jamie, Jill. Rabbi, Cong Shaare Torah, Flatbush, since 1968; asst rabbi, Temple Kehillath Isr, Brookline, Mass, 1946-47; rabbi: Beth El Syn, New London, Conn, 1947-52; Bklyn J Cen, 1954, asso rabbi, 1952-54. Chaplain, USN, 1944-46. F, Herbert H Lehman Inst Talmudic Ethics; JTSA Asso, sem on relationship of rel to Mh; chmn, exec comm, NY Bd Rabbis, 1962-68; mem, exec comm, RabCA, 1956-59, chmn, 1962-66, chmn, Metrop region, 1962-66, chmn, Bklyn region, since 1968; chmn, comm on J Law and Standards, RabCA, since 1966. Home: 1612 Ditmas Ave, Brooklyn, NY. Study: 305 E 21 St, Brooklyn, NY.

KREITMAN, Julius, US, rabbi; b. Louisville, Ky, Sep 3, 1931; s. Sam and Fannie (Waterstone); BA, Yeshiva Coll, 1953; ordained rabbi, Yeshiva U, 1956; m. Chana Grossman, Aug 30, 1955; c: Nachman, Yisroel, Shalom, Sora. Prin, S Falls-burg Talmud Torah, since 1963; rabbi: S Fallsburgh Heb Assn, since 1963; Aetz Chaim Syn, Danville, Va, 1957-63. Pres: RabCA, Sullivan and Ulster Cos; mem: RabCA; Rabb Alliance; Yeshiva U Alumni Assn; Rel Zionists of Amer; B'nai B'rith. Contbr to J publs. Home: POB 457, S Fallsburgh, NY. Study: S Fallsburgh, NY.

KREKSTEIN, I H, US, certified public acctnt; b. Phila, Pa, May 4, 1900; s. Harry and Haddie (Hurwitz); BS, U of Pa, 1921; m. Ann Zeitlyn, June 15, 1924; c: Gerald, Nancy Love. Partner,

Laventhol, Krekstein, Horwath, & Horwath since 1923; dep secy of revenue, dir, bur corp taxes, Commonwealth of Pa, 1935-39. Mem: bd trustees: Albert Einstein Med Coll; Franklin Inst; Hahnemann Med Coll and Hosp, Phila; bd dirs: Robin Hood Dell; Fed J Charities; mem: Masons; clubs: Locust, dir; Philmont County; fmr: pres: Class of 21, U of Pa; Mt Sinai Hosp; Pa Inst CPA's, and Phila chap; mem, council, Amer Inst CPA's, chmn, annual meeting, 1960, mem, ed bd and tax comm. Author: chap, Tax Practice in CPA Handbook, 1952; co-author: Corporate Taxation and Procedure in Pennsylvania, 2 vols, 1940, 1942, 2nd ed, 1953; contbr to profsl jours; lectr. Home: 2601 Parkway, Phila-delphia, Pa. Office: 1528 Walnut St, Philadelphia, Pa.

KRELL, Wilhelm, Aus, organization exec; b. Zarwanica, Aug 25, 1902; s. Ullrich and Klara (Sass); att U of Vienna, 1923-28; m. Hermine Moser, Sep 2, 1947. Admn dir, Israelitische Kultusgemeinde, Vienna, since 1947, chief ed of its publ, Die Gemeinde, since 1958; gen secy, Bundesverband der Israeli-tischen Kultusgemeinden, Aus, since 1953, chief ed of its publ, Iskult-Presse-Nachrichten, IPN since 1955. Mem, curatorium, Hilfsfonds, since 1956; mem comm, Bundesministerium für soziale Verwaltung since 1949; mem, Aus commn for UNES-CO, 1961; mem, exec comm, Aus Comm for World Ref Year, 1962. Recipient: Goldenes Ehrenzeichen für Verdienste um die Republic Österreich; title, Regierungsrat, 1958. Home: Elisabethstr 6, Vienna 1, Aus. Office: Schottenring 25, Vienna 1, Aus.

KRENTS, Milton E, US, radio and TV produc; b. Springfield, Mass, Dec 22, 1911; s. Morris and Ethel (Kramer); BS, NYU, 1935; m. Irma Kopp, May 1, 1938; c: Lawrence, Harold, Elizabeth. Pres, Milton E Krents Assos, since 1944; produc, Eternal Light, radio, TV series, for JTSA, since 1943; radio, TV cons, AJComm, since 1944, radio, TV dir, 1938-44; cons to educ orgs and soc action groups; jr exec, NBC, 1935-38; dir, radio activities, Council for Democracy, WW II; TV cons, Fed Security Agcy, Wash, DC, 1949, 1950; US Commerce Dept, Wash, DC, 1962; radio, TV dir, Amer J Tercentenary Celebration, 1954. Mem: Broadcast Pioneers; PR Soc Amer; Natl Acad TV Arts and Sci; NYU Alumni Communications Comm. Recipient: award, Amer Colls Assn, 1950; Robert E Sherwood Award, 1958. Hobbies: Amer J hist, violin. Home: 21 E 90 St, New York, NY. Office: 165 E 56 St, New York, NY.

KRESH, Paul, US, publicist, writer, editor; b. NYC, Dec 3, 1919; s. Samuel and Jean (Finesilver); BA, Columbia U, 1939; att CCNY, 1938-40. Contributing ed: Amer Record Guide, since 1950; Stereo Rev, since 1962; writer, dir: CBS radio series, Adventures in Judaism, since 1962; documentary films: Hollywood; NY; Isr; script writer: TV films, publi-city writer, JWB, 1940-45; acct exec, Nathan C Beith Assn, 1946-48; publicity dir, Amer ORT Fed, 1948-49; asst publici-ty dir, UJA, 1950-59; PR dir, UAHC, ed, Amer Judaism, UAHC, 1959-67. Mem: Amer J PR Soc; Writers Guild. Contbr to jours. Recipient: O State U awards, 1940, 1941, 1964, 1965, 1966, 1967; Faith and Freedom Award in Bc, 1968. Hobby: photography. Home: 3 Washington Sq Village, New York, NY. Office: 838 Fifth Ave, New York, NY.

KRESS, William, US, dentist; b. Baltimore, Md, June 17, 1912; s. Louis and Gertrude (Jacobs); att U Md, Baltimore, 1932; DDS, U Md, sch of dent, 1936; cert, prof orthodontist, Coll U, Dent, NYC, 1937; m. Rosalyn Kahn, Jan 22, 1939; c: Lee, Richard. Pvt practice since 1937; asst prof, orthodontics, U Md, since 1954; instr, 1938-46; cert, Amer Bd Orthodon-tists. Lt col USAF, 1955-57. F, Amer Coll Dent; mem: Family and Children Soc, Assn J Charities; Alpha Omega, fmr pres; Omicron Kappa Upsilon; fmr, pres: Baltimore City Dent Soc; Mid Atlantic Soc Orthodontists. Home: 7 Slade Ave, Pikesville, Md. Office: 5441 Park Hgts, Baltimore, Md.

KRESSEL, Getzel, Isr, author; bibliographer; b. Zablotow, Galicia, June 12, 1911; s. Yehiel and Feige (Weiss); in Isr since 1930; m. Isabella Perlis, July 1, 1954; c: Iddo. Author of numerous books on: hist of Zionism and its leaders; Heb lit; gazettography; bibliography; hist of J resettlement in Isr; div ed, Zionism, Ency Judaica; fmr: mem ed staff, Davar daily; found, dir, Bibliographical Inst, Writers Assn, and Bio-Bibliographical Gnazim, 1951-65. Mem, Heb Writers Assn. Recipient: prize for lit contribs, Holon Munic, 1961; Usish-kin Prize, 1963; Bialik prize, 1969. Home: 109 Arlosoroff St, Holon, Isr.

KREUSLER, Abraham A, US, educator, author; b. Gologory, Russ, Oct 1, 1897; s. Lazarus and Bertha (Drettel); in US since 1947; att Ger U, Prague; MA, U of Cracow, 1928, PhD, 1929, MA, 1932; m. Esther Srebrnik, 1927; c: Lucy Carey. Prof, Women's Coll, Lynchburg, since 1948; dir, sch, J Comty, Wloclawek, Pol, 1936-39; councilman, City of Wloclawek; cons, Pol Min of Educ, 1936-39; ed, State Publ House, Pol, 1936-39; asso prof, Pedg Inst, Frunze, Russ, 1944-46. Author: The Teaching of Modern Foreign Languages in the USSR; A Teacher's Experiences in the Soviet Union; annotated texts of Wells, Chekhov. Pres, Aatseel of Va; mem: MLA; Amer Assn for Advancement of Slavic Studies; AAUP. Home: 210 Cleveland Ave, Lynchburgh, Va. Office: Randolph Macon Women's Coll, Lynchburg, Va.

KREUTNER, Simon Jacob, Isr, organization exec; b. Leipzig, Ger, Nov 10, 1916; s. Israel and Fanny (Bratspis); att: LSE; Heb U, Jerusalem, m. Ruth Zinner; c: Hanna Gat, Ruhama Yitzhaki. Dir gen, KH, since 1968; dir for Eur, 1962-68, for Eng-speaking countries and Scandanavia 1948-61; fmr free-lance writer, trans, journalist; on numerous missions on behalf of Zionist Exec and KH to Eur, N and S Amer; Financial adv, Brit Army, 1939-45. Secy, Herzl Memorial Comm; fmr secy; comm for fundamental problems, WZO of 23rd ZC; Zionist Goodwill Mission to Eur; 24th 25th ZCs. Author: A People in Search of a Common Basis; contbr to periodicals. Home: 14 Neve Shaanan, Jerusalem, Isr, Office: Keren Hayesod, Head Office: Jerusalem, Isr.

KRICK, Edward D, US, real estate agt; b. Atlanta, Ga, Mar 4, 1915; s. Isaac and Etta (Levin); m. Gertrude Fierman, Dec 29, 1940; c: Rosalyn, Elliott. Owner, real estate. Vice-pres, Bur J Educ, fmr treas; pres ZOA; mem: bd, Atlanta JWF, fmr co-chmn, food div; B'nai B'rith; J Home for Aged; fmr: pres: Cong Shearith Isr, fmr vice-pres; Heb Inst; Amer Zionist Assn, Atlanta chap; vice-pres, Heb Acad; chmn: youth comm, B'nai B'rith; Jt JDC-SOS Drive; cultural arts activities comm, J Comty Cen, chmn, youth activities; secy, Atlanta Zionist Dist. Home: 1714 Wildwood Rd, NE, Atlanta, Ga. Office: 556 Auburn Ave, NE, Atlanta, Ga.

KRIEGER, Leonard, US, educator; b. Newark, NJ, Aug 28, 1918; s. Isidore and Jennie (Glinn); BA, Rutgers U, 1938; MA, Yale U, 1942, PhD, 1949; m. Esther Smith, Aug 13, 1949; c: Alan, David, Nathaniel. Prof, hist, Columbia, U, since 1969; political analyst, State Dept, 1946; visiting lectr, Northwestern U, 1950; instr to prof, hist, Yale U, 1946-62; visiting prof: Brandeis U, 1958; Columbia U, 1960-61; prof, U Chgo, 1962-69; f, Behavioral Sci Cen for Advanced Study, 1963. Chmn, intl travel grant comm, Social Sci Research Council, 1961; prog comm, Amer Hist Assn, 1960; mem: Amer Acad Arts and Scis; Amer Soc for Political and Legal Phil. Author: The German Idea of Freedom, 1957; The Politics of Discretion, 1965; co-author, History, 1965; ed, Classic European Historians, since 1967; co-ed, The Responsibility of Power, 1967; contbr to profsl jours. Office: Columbia U, New York, NY.

KRIGER, Charles H, US, attorney; b. Baltimore, Md, Aug 9, 1901; s. Lewis and Lena (Schwartz); LLB, NYU, 1922; m. Henrietta Reichman, June 26, 1925. Area admnr, Small Bus Admn, since 1961; chmn, NYC Bd of Assessors, 1946-55; commn, standards and purchase, NY State, 1955-58. Secy, adv commr, Jt Leg Comm, on Rev of Assessments, 1941-42; dir, counsel, chmn tax rev and city budget comms, Bklyn Real Estate Bd, 1942-45; dir, Bklyn region, NCCJ; delg, appd by Gov Lehman, Annual Tax Conf, Natl Tax Assn, 1940. Fmr lodge pres, B'nai B'rith. Mem: NY State, Bklyn Bar Assns. Home: 72 Orange St, Brooklyn, NY. Office: 26 Federal Plaza, New York, NY.

KRIM, Arthur B, US, lawyer; b. NYC, Apr 4, 1910; s. Morris and Rose (Ocko); BA, Columbia U, 1930, LLD, 1932; m. Mathilde Galland, Dec 7, 1958. Mem, NY bar, since 1933; asso mem, Phillips, Nizer, Benjamin, Krim and Ballon, since 1932; pres, United Artists Corp, since 1951. Lt col, US Army, 1942-45. Dir: Afr Amer Inst; Weizmann Inst Sci; Lincoln U; trustee, John F Kennedy Libr Inc; spec cons to Pres of US, 1968; chmn, Dem Natl Finance Comm, 1966-68; mem: NY, Bar Assn, 1961-63; Phi Beta Kappa; UN Assn. Ed-in-chief, Columbia Law Rev, 1931-32. Home: 33 E 69 St, New York, NY. Office: 729 Seventh Ave, New York NY.

KRIM, Seymour M, US, author, editor; b. NYC, May 11, 1922; s. Abraham and Ida (Goldberg); att U of NC, 1939-40. Freelance writer since 1945; cons ed, Evergreen Review, since 1967; reporter, NY Herald Tribune, 1965-66; sr ed, Show, 1965; ed dir, Nugget Mag, 1961-65; fmr on ed staffs: New Yorker; OWI; Paramount Pictures; Popular Publ. Author: Views of a Nearsighted Cannoneer, essays, 1961; ed: Manhattan, anthol, 1954; The Beats, anthol, 1960; contbr lit criticism, articles, stories to: Commentary; Commonweal; New Republic; NY Times Book Rev; Hudson Rev; Tiger's Eye; New Directions 10 and 12; Provincetown Rev. Home: 120 E 10 St, New York, NY.

KRIMSKY, Emanuel, US, ophthalmologist, educator; b. NYC; s. Gerson and Rose (Hanchrow); MD, Columbia U Med Sch, 1921; c: Deborah, Cynthia, Beth, Doris. Pvt practice over 25 years; asso att ophthal, St Joseph Queens Hosp, NYC, cons, ophthal: Flower-Fifth Ave Hosp; Metrop Hosp, NYC; asst prof, ophthal, NY Med Coll. Col, MC Res, ret. Author: Binocular Imbalance, 1948; Children's Eye Problems, 1956; contbr articles on eye ailments. Home and office: 103-05 Seaview Ave, Brooklyn, NY.

KRINKIN, Yaffa, Isr, author; b. Merhavia, Isr, 1918; d. Dov and Grunik; att Heb U, 1937-42; div; c: Orith Roubini. Author: haBait haVarod, 1955; ha'I ha'Ehad, 1966; contbr poems, critical revs to newspapers; trans from Eng and Russ. Mem: Heb Writers Guild; Akum; club, Milo. Home: 30 Chen Blvd, Tel Aviv, Isr.

KRINSKY, Fred, US, rabbi, educator; b. Zdenciol, Pol, Feb 2, 1924; s. Jacob and Sarah (Rabinovitz); in US since 1927; BA, Bklyn Coll, 1944; MA, U of Pa, 1946, PhD, 1950; m. Marilyn Seltzer, Aug 3, 1947; c: David, Robert, Jeffrey, Glenn. Prof, political sci, U of S Cal, chmn dept, since 1966, fac mem since 1961; rabbi, Temple Adoth Eloheim, Thousand Oaks, Cal; fmr rabbi, Temple Beth Torah; asst instr, U of Cal, 1947; asso prof, Syracuse U, 1957-61, on fac since 1948; rabbi, Temple Solael, Woodland Hills, 1961-63. Mem, bd dirs: Syracuse J Comty Cen, 1956-59; Syracuse AJComm, 1955-60; mem: Pi Sigma Alpha; Tau Epsilon Phi; Blue Key. Author: The Renascent Jewish Nationalism, A Study of Its Leading Concepts and Practices; co-author: Franklin D Roosevelt and the Supreme Court, 1952; Yalta—Foundation for Peace or Dissension, 1952; The Current Defense of the US, 1954; Problems in Democratic Citizenship; The Middle East in Crisis, 1959; Summitry, 1960; Algeria, Crisis in Conscience, 1961; Theory and Practice of American Democracy, 1967; gen ed, The Insight Series, 1968-69. Home: 5518 Fenwood Ave, Woodland Hills, Cal. Office: U of S Cal, Los Angeles, Cal.

KRISTIANPOLLER, Nahum Norbert, Isr, physicist, educator; b. Baden, Aus, Sep 21, 1920; s. Alexander and Ida (Biegeleisen); in Isr since 1938; MSc, Heb U, Jerusalem, 1946, PhD, 1960; m. Bracha Fried, Mar 1, 1949; c: Alexander, Emanuel. Sr lectr, physics, Tel Aviv U, since 1964; reesarch asso, U of Rochester, NY, 1961-63; lectr, Heb U, Jerusalem, 1963; research asso, Princeton U, NJ, 1969. Haganah, IDF. Mem, Cen Exec Bd, Isr Tchr's Org, 1954-59; delg, Fed Intl des Profs de L'Enseignement Secondaire, 1959; chmn, Tel Aviv U Staff Assn, since 1968; mem: Amer Phys Soc; Isr Phys Soc; Sigma Xi. Contbr numerous articles to sci jours. Home: 6 Schlesinger St, Tel Aviv, Isr. Office: Tel Aviv U, Ramat Aviv, Isr.

KRIVINE, Jarvis David, Isr, journalist; b. Harrogate, Eng, Feb 22, 1919; s. Nathan and Enia (Ettman); in Isr since 1950; BA, hons, Christ Church, Oxford, 1940; m. Daphne Clunies-Ross; c: Yoram, Gil. Econ corresp, Jerusalem Post, since 1960; corresp in Isr, Intl Lab Off, 1953-57; dir, Tech Assistance Div, PM off, 1957-58. Lt, Brit Army, 1940-46. Ed, Fiscal and Monetary Problems in Developing States, Proc of the Third Rehovot Conf, 1967; contbr studies to: The Yearbook of World Affairs, London; Intl Lab Rev. Home: 27a He'halutz St, Jerusalem, Isr. Office: Jerusalem Post, 9 Ha'havatzelet St, Jerusalem, Isr.

KROCH, Aryeh, Isr, teacher; b. Lwow, Pol, Jan 11, 1892; s. Jacob and Peppy (Kroch); in Isr since 1920; att: Tech Sch, Lwow; Off's Sch, Aus, dipl, ing, Tech Coll, Dresden, 1928; m. Clara Falig, 1915; c: Hannah Kassel, Ilan. Asst prin, Beth Hasefer Hareali, Haifa, since 1928, head, math dept; fmr: lectr, descriptive geometry, Technion, Haifa; participated, World Cong of Math, Harvard U. Off, Aus Army, WWI. Chief Scout of Isr since 1937; mem, natl comm, Math of Isr; mem, vegetarians and naturalists village, Amirim, Galilee. Author: Solid Geometry, HS textbook; contbr articles to profsl jours. Home: 11 Nordau St, Haifa, Isr. Office: POB 4920, Haifa, Isr.

KROHN, Samuel, US, periodontist; b. Kan City, Mo, Aug 8, 1922; s. Jacob and Lina (Shetzer); att Wayne State U, 1939-41; DDS, U Mich, 1944; MS, 1957; m. Elaine Shiffman, Dec 15, 1946; c: David, Judith, Janet, Deborah. Pvt dent practice, specializing in periodontia, since 1957; gen dent, 1944-57; instr, U Detroit Sch Dent, 1964-65; Pres, Shaarey Zadek, since 1969; bd trustees, since 1956, mem, bd dirs, JCC, since 1954, pres, 1965-68; fmr, natl vice-pres, Masada; mem: Amer Acad Periodontology; Amer Dent Assn; Detroit Dist, Dent Soc; Mich State Dent Soc. Contbr to dent jours. Home: 23180 Laurel Valley Dr, Southfield, Mich. Office: 26789 Woodward, Huntington Woods, Mich.

KROLL, Bernard H, US, systems analyst-stat; b. Bklyn, NY, Sep 8, 1922; s. Simon and Ida (Nathanson); BA, Bklyn Coll, 1947; att: Columbia U; Amer U; Wash Coll of Law, 1947-57; m. Doris Weinblum, Mar 23, 1947; c: Richard, Martin, Ira. Head, Sect Sys Design and Data Processing, Off Biometry, Natl Inst of Neur Diseases and Stroke, Bethesda, Md, since 1968, on staff since 1958; air transp econ, CAB, Wash, DC, 1947-51; analytical stat, Natl Inst of Mh, 1951-58. US Army, 1943-47. F: Amer Public Health Assn, 1959; AAAS, 1962; mem: Amer Stat Assn; Assn for Computing Machinery; B'nai B'rith; Boy Scouts of Amer, troop cdr, since 1965; Royal Soc of Health; Sys and Procedures Assn. Contbr to profsl jours. Recipient: Bronze Star; five Battle Stars; Purple Heart; Belgian Fouragerre of Order of Leopold, WW II. Home: 3507 Farthing Dr, Wheaton, Md. Office: Inst of Neur Diseases, Off of Biometry, Bethesda, Md.

KROLL, Jack, US, labor union exec; b. London, Eng, June 10, 1885; s. Mark and Julia (Blumberg); in US since 1886; m. Sara Raben, Jan 19, 1920; c: Mark. Ret; vice-pres, natl org, Amalgamated Clothing Workers of Amer, since 1928, mgr, Cincinnati jt bd, since 1926; pres em, O AFL-CIO, since 1958; pres, O CIO Council, 1939-52; pres em, since 1952; dir, Amalgamated Life Ins Co, since 1943; trustee, Amalgamated Ins Fund, 1943; clothing cutter, 1901-18; lab org, 1910-18; natl staff org, 1919-26; mem, gen exec bd, 1928; mem, bd dirs, Cincinnati Charter Comm, 1928-36; subregional dir, textile workers organizing dr, 1937; asst chmn, S organizing dr, CIO, 1943; lab ad, US Off Produc Mgmt, 1942; regional dir, CIO Political Action Comm, 1940-44, asst to natl chmn, 1945, natl dir, 1946-55; co-dir, AFL-CIO comm on political educ, 1956-57. Fmr mem: lab adv comm, Natl Dem Party; policy comm, Hamilton Co Dem Party. Author: The Cincinnati Clothing Workers, 1913-38; A Quarter Century of Endeavors and Achievements, 1938; Reflections of a Union Organizer; contbr to lab publs and other mags. Spec interest, leg action. Hobby, fishing. Home: 2890 Belkay Lane, Amberley Village, Cincinnati, O.

KROLL, Martin Neil, US, attorney; b. NYC, Nov 30, 1937; s. Jack and Ruth (Strassman); BA, Cornell U, 1959; JD, U of Pa, 1963; m. Rita Grossman, Aug 14, 1964; c: Spencer, Jonathan. Partner, law firm, Rose & Kroll, since 1969; gen counsel to UJA, Gtr NY Inc, and UJA, Inc. Mem, Leadership Council, UJA, Gtr NY; club, Wm Draper Lewis Law, fmr pres. Home: 10 Glen Cove Rd, Roslyn, NY. Office: 535 Fifth Ave, New York, NY.

KROLOFF, Charles Arthur, US, rabbi; b. E Chgo, Ind, June 1, 1935; s. Max and Mary (Goldstein); BA, magna cum laude, Yale U, 1955; BHL, MA, ordained rabbi, HUC-JIR, 1960; att grad sch: Brandeis U; Columbia U; m. Theresa Klausner, July 11, 1955; c: Micah, Noah, Sarah. Rabbi, Temple Emanu-El, Westfield, NJ, since 1966; asst rabbi, Temple Isr, Boston, 1960-63; rabbi, Comty Reform Temple, Westbury, 1963-66; lectr, rel phil, Queens Coll, 1965-66. Dir, Westfield Comty Devl Corp; pres: Westfield Ministerium; Ministerium of Westbury, 1965-66; Young Judaea, & region, 1950-51, natl vice-pres, 1949-50; mem: church-state comm, CCAR; tchr educ comm, UAHC; B'nai B'rith. Contbr articles, revs to J jours. Hobbies: tennis, swimming. Home: 424 Otisco Dr, Westfield, NJ. Study: 756 N Broad St, Westfield, NJ.

KRONE, Moshe, Isr, organization exec; b. Warsaw, Pol, May 23, 1913; s. Menashe and Ruchla; in Isr since 1937; att Rabb Sem, Tachkemoni, Warsaw; U Warsaw; m. Rachel, 1939; c: Shira, Imi, David. Mem exec, JA, since 1968; secy gen, Rel Natl Party, Isr; delg, WZCs; 1st Isr consul in NY. Contbr books and articles. Home: 20 Smutts St, Tel Zviv, Isr.

KRONENBERG, Sanford, US, physician; b. Oct 30, 1915; s. Louis and Rebecca (Goodman); AB, O State U, 1937; MD,

U Cincinnati, 1941; m. Vera Amos, June 25, 1962; c: Lee, Steve, Don. Asso prof, surg, U of S Cal, since 1962; head, anesthesiology dept, Pasadena Comty Hosp, since 1968; asso prof, phys, Cal State Coll, Long Beach, 1956-58. Capt, US Army, 1942-46. F, Amer Coll Anesthesiologists; dipl, Amer Bd Anesthesiology; fmr, vice-pres, bd dirs, Guedel Memorial Anesthesia Cen; mem: Phi Beta Kappa; Alpha Omega Alpha, fmr secy, treas. Home: 1600 Milan Ave, S Pasadena, Cal. Office: 1600 Milan Ave, S Pasadena, Cal.

KRONENBERGER, Louis, US, critic, educator, author; b. Cincinnati, O, Dec 9, 1904; s. Louis and Mabel (Newwitter); att, U Cincinnati, 1921-24, hon DL, 1951; m. Emmy Plaut, Jan 29, 1940; c: John, Elizabeth. Prof: theater arts, Brandeis U, since 1951; Harvard U, Lawrence Lowell; visiting prof, Columbia U, 1950, 1961; regents prof, Eng, U of Cal, Berkeley, 1968; lectr: Oxford U, 1959; Gauss sem lectrs: Princeton, 1961; Stanford U, 1963; dir, Corp of Yaddo, since 1950. Mem, bd dirs: The Amer Scholar, during 1950s; The Johnsonians; secy, Natl Inst Arts and Letters, 1953-56; f, Amer Acad Arts and Scis; clubs: Cent Assn, NY; St Botolph, Boston. Author: Kings and Desperate Men, 1942; Grand Right and Left, 1952; The Thread of Laughter, 1953; Company Manners, 1954; The Republic of Letters, 1955; Marlborough's Duchess, 1958; A Month of Sundays, 1961; The Cart and the Horse, 1964; ed: Best Plays, annual, since 1952; Boni and Liveright, 1926-33; Alfred A Knopf 1933-34; Reader's Companion; Portable Johnson and Boswell; Selected Works of Alexander Pope; G B Shaw; A Critical Survey; Works of Sheridan, 1956; Novelists on Novelists, 1961; The Great World, 1963; Masters of World Literature series; co-ed, Viking Book of Aphorisms; drama critic; Time Mag, 1938-61; PM daily, NYC, 1940-48; adapter, trans: The Maxims, LaRochefoucauld; Mademoiselle Colombe, 1954. Recipient, Guggenheim f award, 1969. Home: 1514 Beacon St, Brookline, Mass.

KRONGOLD, Henry, Austr, business exec; b. Lodz, Pol, Dec 12, 1909; s. Naphtali and Bina (Rozmaryn); in Austr since 1941; att Sch of Arts, Warsaw; m. Dinah Shemberg, Dec 12, 1942; c: Ronald, Dennis, Paul. Bd chmn since 1954; mgn dir: Midlands Textile, 1949-53; Charmaine Hosiery, 1954-56; K H Textile, 1947-49. Mem, delg, intl econ adv council to PM of Isr, 1968, 1969. Pres: Fed KH-United Isr Appeal of Austr, Vic; fmr pres: Wfr Soc Appeal; Canberra comty cen; fmr, treas-gov, Mt Scopus Coll; mem, Masonic lodges: No 200, Melbourne; Mt Scopus Collegians. Hobby: golf. Home: 612 Toorak Rd, Melbourne, Austr. Office: 200 Little Collins, Melbourne, Austr.

KRONHEIM, Emil, Swed, rabbi; b. Guttstadt, Ger, Apr 22, 1890; s. Moses and Sara (Lewinson); in Swed since 1926; ordainned rabbi, Lehranstalt fur Wissenschaft des Judentums, Berlin, 1917; m. Ruth Kullick, May 15, 1923; c: Ingeborg, Monika. Rabbi: J Comty, Stockholm, since 1926; Dortmund, Ger, 1919-24; Frankfurt, 1925-26. Served WWI. Active in ref work, 1933-45; mem: J Comty Aid Soc; B'nai B'rith, 1st pres, 1949-52. Contbr to publs. Recipient: Vasa Order, 1954. Hobby: music. Home: Vanadisvagen 22A, Stockholm, Swed. Study: Wahrendorffsgatan 3, Stockholm, Swed.

KRONITZ, Leon, Can, educator; b. Kletzk, Pol, June 23, 1917; s. Harry and Nesia (Wilenchyk); in Can since 1938; tchrs dipl, Tarbut Sem, Vilna, Pol, 1935; BA, McGill U, 1944; EdD, JTSA, 1969; m. Faye Jospe, Nov 4, 1948; c: Reena, Naomi, Emanuel. Prin, Solomon Schechter Acad, since 1955; educ cons, United J Tchrs Sem, Can, since 1961; prin, Herzliah HS, 1945-48; natl exec dir, Can Assn Heb Culture and Educ, 1948-55. Can Off Training Corps, 1941-44. A natl vice-pres, Can J Cong, since 1968; pres, Lab Zionist Movement, Can, since 1962; mem: Jt Inner Exec of PR Comm, Can J Cong-Fed Zionist Org, Can, since 1958; Actions Comm, World Zionist Org, since 1955; natl exec, Can Assn Heb Culture and Educ, since 1942; Can Assn for Lab, Isr, since 1956; Heb Camps Massad; World Secretariat, Lab Zionist Movement; Day Sch Commn; United Syn Commn on Educ; Prot Sch Bd, Gtr Montreal. Chmn, ed bd, Viewpoints, quarterly; ed: booklets for children: Zalman Schneur, 1951; I L Peretz, 1952. Home: 5240 Rosedale Ave, Montreal, Can. Office: 5555 Cote St Luc Rd, Montreal, Can.

KRONMAN, Samuel Joseph, US, ceramic engr; b. NYC, Mar 6, 1918; s. Samuel and Isabel (Joseph); BSc, Rutgers U, 1939; m. Evelyn Darwin, June 15, 1941; c: Patricia Davidson, Marilyn Hartstein, Barry. Vice-pres: Cardinal China Co; Our Own Import Co, both since 1946; mayor, Highland Park,

NJ; mech engr, Mack Truck Inc, 1940-46. Vice-pres, bd mgrs, Roosevelt Hosp; mem, Div of Local Finance, State of NJ; mem: Highland Park Conservative Temple and Cen, fmr pres; bd, Raritan Valley YM-YHWA; club, Exch, Highland Park, NJ. Home: 320 Benner, Highland Park, NJ. Office: Cardinal China Co, POB D, Carteret, NJ.

KRONSBERG, Edward, US, business exec; b. Portsmouth, Va, Aug 1, 1903; s. Abraham and Lena (Jacobson); att Coll of Charleston; m. Hattie Barshay, Feb 10, 1934; c: Avram, Jonathan. Pres: Edward's Inc, since 1926; Tilghman's Island Realty Co, since 1949; Reynold's Men's Store, since 1953; Talbot Realty, since 1954; E Shore Realty Co, since 1955; Pinehaven Shopping Cen, since 1957; vice-pres: Edward's Realty Co, since 1946; Pendleton Realty Co, since 1951; mem, adv bd, The Citizens and S Natl Bank; bd dirs: Home Fed Savings and Loan Assn; Equitable Fire Ins; Claussen Baking. Fmr: pres: Chain Store Council for SC, 1956; Charleston C of C, 1956; Charleston Ind Assn 1950-54; JWF; Heb Benevolent Soc; B'rith Sholom Syn; Heb Orphan Soc; treas, Emanu-El Syn, since 1952; fmr: mem, bd dirs: J Comty Cen; Amer Jt J Comm; bd overseers, JTSA; chmn: Charleston Devl Bd, 1957-60; UF budget comm, SC, 1959-60; pres, Carolinas UF, 1960; mem, exec bd, Carolina Art Assn since 1951; exec bd, Coastal Carolina Boy Scout Council; bd trustees, Florence Crittenton Home; Coll of Charleston, civic adv group, CARE; adv bd: Jr League Speech Sch; bd dirs: Charleston Mus, chmn, finance comm; bd of commns, Roper Hosp; mem: B'nai B'rith; Elks; Masons; Shriner; Scottish Rite; St Andrew's Soc; clubs: Hibernian; Rifle; Charleston Country; Beaufort Yacht; Kiwanis, pres, 1954, chmn, Carolina conv, 1956. Recipient: Charleston Man-of-the-Year, 1954. Home: 12 Country Club Dr, Charleston, SC. Office: 5000 Lacross Rd, Charleston Heights, SC.

KRONSTADT, Henry L, US, public relations counsel; b. Pruszany, Pol, Feb 22, 1911; s. Nathan and Esther (Lippin); in US since 1922; att Natl U, 1936; Amer U, 1946; m. Claire Pauls, Aug 12, 1939 (decd); c: Esther, Robin. Info specialist, Small Bus Admn, Wash, DC; fmr: advt dir, Mueller's Lake Charles, La, 1930-31; asst art dir, Frederic Loeser's Dept Store, Bklyn, NY, 1932-34; art dir, Lansburgh's Dept Store, 1935-37; acct exec, Kaufman Asso, 1937-39; guest lectr, Amer U, Wash DC, 1958; sr partner, Henry L Kronstadt, advt and pr, Wash, DC, 1939-62; columnist, Wash Vignettes, Wash, DC, 1959-62. Technical writer, US Army, 1945-47. Vice-pres, Brandeis Zionist dist, 1947-48, mem, exec bd, 1936-54; mem: bd dirs, J Social Service Agcy, 1952-55; exec bd, JCC, 1950-52; bd, Colo and G Sts Corp; steering comm, Isr Bonds Devl Dist, 1960-62; mem: Natl Acad TV Arts and Scis; JWV; clubs: Natl Press; Variety; Fed Eds; Advt; Woodmont Country. Contbr to mil publs. Recipient: Natl award, Natl Fur Week, 1938. Home: 4528 Davenport St, NW, Washington, DC.

KROOG, Emanuel Thomas, US, attorney; b. NYC, Nov 13, 1912; s. Jacob and Sarah (Green); att U of Wis, 1930-33; LLB, Marquette U, 1936; m. Natalie Goldberg, Aug 31, 1961. Pvt practice since 1936; court commn, Milw Co, since 1962. USAC, 1942-46. Mem, bd dirs: Wis and Upper Mich Regional ADL; J Vocation Service; mem, exec bd, Milw chap, AJComm. Home: 639 E Lake View, Whitefish Bay, Wis. Office: 710 N Plankinton Ave, Milwaukee, Wis.

KROSS, Anna M, US, jurist, public servant; b. Russ, 1891; d. Meyer and Esther (Drasin) Moscowitz; LLB, LLM, NYU, 1910; MA, 1911; hon LLD, W Coll for Women, O, 1954; hon LLD, LIU; m. Isidor Kross, Apr 17, 1917; c: Helen Golden, Alice Frankel. Commn of Correction, NYC, since 1954; admitted to the Bar, 1912; pvt practice, 1912-18; magistrate, NYC, 1934-54; org, presiding magistrate, Home Term Court, 1946. Mem: Amer Bar Assn; Co Lawyers Assn; NYC Bar Assn; Natl Women's Lawyers Assn; Amer Law Inst; Gen Fed, Women's Clubs; Hadassah; Natl Council J Women; Amer U Women; Amer Women's Assn. Home: 124 W 79 St, New York, NY. Office: 100 Centre St, New York, NY.

KROUT, Sara G, US, dentist; b. Riga, Latvia, Oct 17, 1898; d. Mendel and Fannie (Grusin) Gdulin; DDS, Schroeder Coll of Dent, Ekaterinoslav, 1918; DSS, U Riga, 1919; att: Riga U Med Sch, 1918-20; Coll Dent, U of Ill, 1921-22; m. Maurice Krout, July 3, 1921; c: Johanna. Pvt practice, Chgo, since 1928; chmn, dent clinic, mem, med staff, Women and Children's Hosp, Chgo, since 1938. Lt, Latvian Red Cross, 1919-20; lt, dent corps, USN, 1944; lt cdr, 1950; cdr, 1955; first wom-

an dent commissioned in USNR. Hon pres, Asthmatic Children's Aid Soc, since 1940; fmr pres, Ann Mayber Research Found; found, Heb U Sch of Dent Med; f: Ill Dent Soc; sr instr, first aid, ARC; mem: Chgo Dent Assn; Assn Mil Surg of US, Ill Dent Soc; Amer Dent Soc, life; Hadassah; dent div, Isr Bonds. Author: Report on Women in Dentistry, 1942. Home: 1938 Cleveland, Evanston, Ill. Office: 55 E Washington St, Chicago, Ill.

KRUGER, Fania, US, poet; b. Sevastopol, Russ, Mar 8, 1893; d. Chaim and Sara (Shulman) Feldman; in US since 1909; m. Sam Kruger, Mar 24, 1912; c: Aaron, Bertha. Author: poems: Cossack Laughter, 1937; The Tenth Jew, 1949; poems reprinted: The Questing Spirit; The Passover Anthology; contbr poems, short stories to lit publs. Mem: Poetry Soc, Amer; Catholic Poetry Soc, Amer; Council J Women, Wichita Falls; Poetry Soc, Tex; Tex Inst Letters; Poetry Soc, Eng. Recipient: 1st prize for: Against the Stony Sky, Cheyney Memorial Contest, 1934; Wandering Child, 1940; Passover Eve, 1946, both from Poetry Soc, Amer; Blessing the New Moon, Lola Ridge Contest, 1947; Ghetto Fortitude, 1948; Son of Tomorrow, 1950, Clementine Dunne Awards of Tex Poetry Soc; Prize for Flag of Isr, Harry Kovner's Contest on Isr Reborn, 1949; poetry cited at NY Writers Conf, Wagner Coll, 1956. Home: 407 W 18 St, Austin, Tex.

KRUGER, Jerome, US, chemist; b. Atlanta, Ga, Feb 7, 1927; s. Isaac and Sarah (Stein); BS, Ga Inst Tech, 1948, MS, 1949; PhD, U of Va, 1952; m. Mollee Coppel, Feb 20, 1955; c: Lennard, Joseph. Chief, corrosion sect, Natl Bur Standards, since 1966, on staff since 1955; prof, U of Md, since 1959; phys chem, Naval Research Lab, 1952-55. Secy, Montgomery Co J Comty Inc; chmn: Natl Capitol Sect Electrochem Soc, 1960-61; Gordon Research Conf on Corrosion, 1966-67; mem: Amer Chem Soc; Natl Assn Corrosion Engrs; AAAS; Sigma Xi. Contbr numerous articles to sci jours. Home: 402 Harding Dr, Silver Spring, Md. Office: Nat Bur of Standards, Washington, DC.

KRUGMAN, Lillian D, US, lyricist, real estate broker; b. Bklyn, NY, Dec 4, 1911; d. Nathan and Minnie (Miller) Kramer; att Bklyn Coll, 1929-33; m. Joshua Krugman, Feb 13, 1943; c: Steven, Martin. Real estate broker since 1957; secy, Metrop Life Ins Co, 1933-43. Pub works: Poem, 1937; Little Calypsos, book and record; Song Tales of the West Indies, book and record; Brazilian Folk Songs for Children, book and record; Pretty, Pretty, records; Ducks on Parade, record; Animal and Bird Songs for Children, record; Ballad of Abe Lincoln; Say Auf Widersehn, record; The Willow Tree, record; TV, spec material, Dave Garroway Show; scripts for local orgs: Hadassah; B'nai B'rith; Natl Council J Women; others. Prog chmn, Hadassah; mem, ASCAP; fmr, active, UJA. Spec interests: book reviewing, poetry. Home: 154 B 133 St, Belle Harbor, NY. Office: 145-06 Neponsit Ave, New York, NY.

KRUKOWSKI, William Rymer, Uruguay, youth leader; b. Heindenheim, Ger, Mar 15, 1947; s. Henryk and Sofia (Rymer); dipl, elec, 1967. Secy: Hanoar Hazioni, fmr, Madrich Majon, British Hairgunim Hahalutzim; mem exec, Young ZF; repr: Young ZF, Hanoar Hazioni; Brit Hairgunim Hahalutzim, to 27th ZC, Jerusalem; mem: Club de Radiotécnicos del Uruguay; Comunidad Israelita del Uruguay. Contbr to Hanoar Hazioni publs. Spec interests: elec, J educ, psych. Home: 1165 Convención St, Montevideo, Uruguay.

KRULEWITCH, Melvin Levin, US, attorney; b. NYC, Nov 11, 1895; s. Harry and Ann (Levin); BA, Columbia Coll, 1916; LLB, Columbia Law Sch, 1920; m. Helen Rothstein, 1937 (decd); c: Ann, Elihu; m. 2nd, Hellen Sulzbacher, Feb 2, 1968. Mem, law firm, Goldstein, Gurfein, Shames & Hyde; admitted to practice: Supr Courts: NY State; US; spec counsel: Public Service Comm, NY State; Public Utilities Commn, NY State; chmn, NY State Athletic Commn, 1959-67; utility cons, Westchester Co; official referee, Supr Court, Appellate Dir, First Dept. Maj gen, USMC, ret, 1918, WWII, Korea. Dir, hon, YM-YWHA; trustee, FJP; hon trustee, Park Ave Syn, mem, bd trustees; vice-chmn, bd, vice-pres, USO, NYC; mem: Corp, Natl Bd Govs; cdr, Mil Order of WWs, NY; sponsor, Gen Krulewitch F, Post-Grad Students in Law, Columbia U; bd dirs, JWB. Recipient: Bronze Star Medal; Gold Star for 2nd Bronze Star Medal; Purple Heart; Individual Fourragere, Fr Croix-de-Guerre; Medaille d'Or de Verdun; 2 Pres Unit Citations; Navy Unit Citation. Home: 923 Fifth Ave, New York, NY. Office: 655 Madison Ave, New York, NY.

KRUMBEIN, Aaron D, US, physicist; b. NYC, Apr 6, 1921; s. Moishe and Frances (Dressler); BA, Bklyn Coll, 1941; att U of Pa, 1941-42; dipl, Tchrs Inst, Yeshiva U, 1943; PhD, NYU, 1951; m. Hilda Beim, Dec 24, 1950; c: Esther, David, Frances. Adv sci, reactor and nuclear physics, United Nuclear Corp, fmr, Nuclear Devl Corp of Amer, since 1956; visiting asst prof, physics, Yeshiva U since 1960; teaching asst, physics: U of Pa, 1942; NYU, 1942-45; mem, Cosmic Ray Expedition to Rockies, 1946; cons, Air Force Research Project, 1947-49; asst, prof, U of Md ,1950-56; prin investigator, Burof Ships, USN, Radiac Detector Contract, 1950-56. Pres NY chap, Assn Orthodox J Scis, since 1957; chmn, bd educ, vice-pres, Heb Inst, Rockland Co, since 1965; mem: Amer Nuclear Soc; AAAS; NY Acad Sci; Amer Phys Soc; Sigma Xi; Sigma Pi Sigma; B'nai Zion; Masons; fmr: pres: Hapoel Hamizrachi Org, Bklyn and Wash, DC; secy, natl council, Young Isr. Contbr to sci jours. Home: 1 Tower Lane, Monsey NY. Office: 5 New St, White Plains, NY.

KRUMBEIN, Abraham, US, business exec; b. Aus, Mar 24, 1892; s. Aaron and Channa (Fischler); in US since 1895! m. Sarah Milberg, Feb 11, 1917; c: Aaron, Eliezer, Judith Segal. Pres: Fair Maid Undergarment Co, since 1918; William Taube Travel Service; United Food Corp, since 1950; Voyager Tours, since 1954; first vice-pres, E Life Ins Co of NY, since 1943; vice-chmn, Bklyn Shore Army and Navy Comm, WWII. Vice-pres: and treas, Service for Isr, since 1945; Downtown Talmud Torah, since 1918; and treas, KH Pal Found Fund, since 1939; hon vice-pres: YM-YWHA, Boro Park, since 1943; J Educ Comm of NY, trustee, since 1939; Manhattan Region, ZOA, since 1946, asso treas, ZOA; fmr: mem: natl finance comm, natl exec, treas, Bklyn region; natl treas, JNF; treas: United Isr Appeal, since 1940; Kereth Isr Housing Project since 1946; found, founds soc, Albert Einstein Coll Med, NY, patron, Metrop Opera Assn; delg, WZC's: Zurich, 1937; Geneva, 1939; Basle, 1946; Jerusalem, 1955; mem: bd overseers, JTSA; bd dirs, Weizmann Inst of Sci; Temple Beth El, Boro Park; Temple Emmanuel; W Side Instl Syn; Cong B'nai Jeshurun; life mem, Masons; fmr: pres: Albert Lucas Rel Schs; Bklyn br, Tchrs Inst of Yeshiva Coll; Boro Park JCC; vice-pres: Yeshiva Etz Chaim, Boro Park; hon secy, Machzike Talmud Torah of Boro Park; chmn, Boro Park campaign: FJP; UJA; treas: B'nai Zion; Magen David Adom; treas, World Confd Gen Zionists. Recipient: Service Award, JWB; appd, Aid-de-Camp, with rank of col, staff, Gov of Ky, 1935; Comty Service Award, JTSA, 1966. Hobbies: collector of Lincolniana, fishing. Home: 316 W 79 St, New York, NY. Office: 113 W 42 St, New York, NY.

KRUPNIK, Samson, US, certified public acctnt, business exec; b. Berdichev, Russ, Jan 16, 1913; s. Joshua and Bella (Leibenstein); desc, Rabbi Levi Itzhak of Berdichev; in US since 1923; Heb tchr's cert, Coll J Studies, 1933; BS, DePaul U, 1934; grad studies: U Chgo, 1936-37; Loyola U, 1939-40; CPA, U of Ill, 1940; hon f, Heb Theol Coll, 1957; m. Lillian Miransky, Feb 3, 1935; c: Joseph, Deborah Bokor, Elia, Elissa, Rachel. Owner, S Krupnick & Co, CPA's, Chgo, Ill, since 1940; partner: Phillips Wholesale Supply, Detroit, Mich, since 1948; Holiday Bowl, Detroit, since 1961; Hoffman Lanes, since 1961; pres, hotel corps: St George; Peer Manor, both 1953-67; Waldorf; Stately, both 1952-59; Regis, 1954-67; vice-pres: Merle-Hayplaza Shopping Cen Inc, since 1960; Town & Country Shopping Cen, since 1960; MacArthur Bowl since 1961; Park Lanes, since 1961; trustee, Westgate Village Realty Trust; pres, Strikes and Spares; mem bd: Rassco Corp; Bank Adanim; Isr Housing Corp; Mizrachi Bank, all Isr; fmr: Heb tchr, Sioux City, Ia, 1935-36; acctnt, Maxwell Abbell & Co, 1937-40. Chmn, exec comm, Rel Zionists Amer, 1957-61, natl vice-pres, 1961-64, natl presidium, since 1964; pres: Hapoel Hamizrachi, Chgo, 1948-52, natl vice-pres, 1950-57; Council of Traditional Syns, Gtr Chgo, 1955-57, chmn, exec council, 1957-60; Cong Agudas Achim, 1949-54; pres, Syn Savyon, Isr, since 1966; vice-pres: JNF, 1950-54, trustee since 1954; Union Orthodox Congs since 1952; syn div, CJA, since 1952; natl vice-pres, Natl Assn PTA's of Heb Day Schs, 1956-58; treas, vice-pres, Amer ZC, 1954-63; mem, bd dirs: J Educ Comm; Asso Talmud Torahs; Histadrut Ivrit; J Comty Cen; Amer Friends Heb U; Bar Ilan U; Technion Soc; Communities Camp; Shaare Zedek Hosp, Jerusalem; Mosad Harav Kook; chmn, bd govs, Chgo J Acad; bd dirs, AKiba J Day Sch, since 1951; vice-chmn, bd trustees, J U of Amer, since 1960; mem: World Mizrachi, Zionist Actions Comm, since 1960; Isr Bonds, chmn, Amer delg to WZC, 1951; educ comm, Tercentenary Comm, J in Amer; mem: SE Commn, S Shore Commn, Amer Inst of CPA's; ZOA; AJCong; B'nai B'rith; Cong Anshei Sholom;

Cong Anshe Makariv. Homes: 26 Har Dafna, Isr; 6222 N Lawndale, Chicago, Ill. Office: 33 N LaSalle St, Chicago, Ill.

KUBIE, Eleanor G, (pen name, Nora Benjamin Kubis), US, author; b. NYC, Jan 4, 1899; d. Paul and Miriam (Rosenfeld) Gottheil; BA, Barnard Coll, 1920; att Art Students League, NY, 1921-22; div. Author: Hard Alee, 1937; Roving All the Day, 1939; Fathom Five, 1941; Make Way for a Sailor, 1948; Remember the Valley, 1951; Joel, 1952; First Book of Israel, 1953; King Solomon's Navy, 1955; King Solomon's Horses, 1956; First Book of Archaeology, 1958; Road to Nineveh, 1964; ed, house organ, United World Federalists, 1938-39. Mem: juvenile book comm, Child Study Assn; Author's League, Amer; Artists Equity; Art Students League, Amer; MacDowell Assn; Artists Village, Ein Hod, Isr; chmn, juvenile book comm, Writers War Bd, 1942-43; fmr: bd mem, women's div: UJA; Amer Friends of Heb U. Recipient: Isaac Siegel award, for best J book, King Solomon's Navy, 1955; f, Huntington Hartford Found, 1959. Homes: 111 E 56 St, New York, NY; Ein Hod, Isr.

KUBIN, Rosa, US, biochemist; b. Aus, Dec 15, 1906; d. Richard and Clara (Loewy) Lustig; in US since 1938; PhD, U Vienna, 1931; m. Ludwig Kubin, Dec 22, 1931 (decd). Dir, lab, vetr clinical path, since 1952; Waltham HS, since 1961; asso in educ, Harvard Coll, since 1968; research chem, Aus, 1938; asst prof, biochem: Middlesex U, 1941-47; U of Mass, 1947-49; asso prof, NE Coll Phar, 1951-52; lectr, Wellesley Coll, 1955-57. Mem: AAAS; AAUP; Amer Chem Soc. Contbr to profsl jours. Home and office: 19 Appleton St, Waltham, Mass.

KUBLIN, Hyman, US educator; b. Boston, Mass, Dec 29, 1919; s. Ralph and Tilly (Goschenberg); MA, Boston U, 1942; cert, USN Japanese Lang Sch, U of Colo, 1943; PhD, Harvard U, 1947; m. Pearl Baru, Dec 5, 1942; c: Michael, Barbara. Prof, hist, Bklyn Coll, CUNY, since 1961; fac mem since 1947, exec off, PhD prog in hist, 1964-66, asso dean, grad studies, CUNY, 1966-69. Bd dirs, Amer Friends Heb U, chmn, comm on study progs, mem, acad council; exec comm, Amer Profs for Peace in ME; vice-chmn, Tribute to Danes; mem: Amer Hist Assn; Assn Asian Studies, hon life; Phi Beta Kappa. Author: Aspects of Early Modern Japanese Labor History, 1959; The Rim of Asia, 1963; Asian Revolutionary: The Life of Sen Katayama, 1964; China, 1968; China: Selected Readings, 1968; India, 1968; India: Selected Readings, 1968; Japan: Selected Readings, 1968; Japan, 1969; Russia, 1969; Russia: Selected Readings, 1969; contbr to political, hist jours. Home: 288 Bay 38 St, Brooklyn, NY. Office: Bklyn Coll, Brooklyn, NY.

KUFELD, Frieda C, US, educator; b. Bklyn, NY, Apr 14,1922; d. Louis and Jennie (Feltenstein) Chesir; att Sem Coll, JTSA, 1939-43; BA, Hunter Coll, 1942; MA, NYU, 1947; m. William Kufeld, Apr 9, 1949; c: David. Prin, public sch, NYC, since 1963; NYC Jr HS, 1947-55; asst prin, Shell Bank Jr HS, 1955-59; tchr: Yeshiva, Flatbush, NY, 1943-47. Mem, natl bd, Jr Mizrachi Women, since 1958; delg, WZC, 1946; vice-pres, NY Princs Assn; bd dirs, JNF, 1946-49; mem: NEA; Council of Supervisory Assns; J Tchrs Assn. Home: 22 Hawthorne Lane, Great Neck, NY.

KUGELMASS, Isaac Newton, US, pediatrician, educator; author; b. NYC, June 28, 1896; s. Maurice and Sarah (Spirer); BS, CCNY, 1916; MA, Columbia U, 1917; PhD, Johns Hopkins U, 1921; DSc, U of Brussels, 1922; MD, Yale U, 1925; m. Ella Fishberg, 1934. Pvt practice since 1925; cons nutritionist, Dept of Health and Hosps, NYC, since 1945; att ped: Riverside Hosp, asso phys, 1925-30; Hosp for Ruptured and Crippled, chief, growth clinic, 1930-33; cons ped: Keckscher Inst for Child Health, dir, 1930-40; Manhattan Gen Hosp; Monmouth Memorial Hosp; Muhlenberg Hosp; Lynn Memorial Hosp; Northwood Sanatorium; visiting lectr: Can, SA, Japan; fmr: instr, chem: CCNY, 1916-17; Columbia U, 1917-18; Howard Coll, 1918-20; research asso, chem, U of Brussels, 1920-22; research asso, ped, Yale U Med Sch, 1922-25; dir, ped research and att ped, Fifth Ave Hosp, NY, 1928-30; ped-in-chief, Fr Hosp, 1935-38. Served, US Food Admn, chem warfare section, WW II. F: AMA; AAAS; Soc for Experimental Biol and Med; Amer Acad of Applied Nutrition; Amer Acad of Mental Med; Pan-Amer Med Assn; Amer Chem Soc; Harvey Soc; NY Acad of Sci; Amer Pub Health Assn; mem: Amer Assn on Mental Deficiency; Natl TB Assn; Amer Therapeutic Soc; Amer Assn of Vienna; NY State Med Soc; Assn of Amer Teachers of Diseases of Children; Alpha Mu Sigma; club: Yale : Author: The Story of Infancy, 1930;

Growing Superior Children, 1934; Practical Colloid Chemistry, 1935; Feeding in Infancy and Childhood, 1938; The Newer Nutrition in Pediatric Practice, 1939; Blood Disorders in Children, 1941; Changing Goals of Positive Health; Superior Children Through Modern Nutrition, 1943; Clinical Pediatrics, 1946; Mouth Conditions in Children, 1950; Principles and Practice of Pediatrics, 1955; Management of Mental Deficiency in Children, 1955; Better Health for Your Children, 1955; Maturing Children in Body and Mind, 1955; Chemistry of Blood in Health and Disease, 1958; Biochemical Diseases, 1964; ed: Amer Lectrs in Living Chem; Biochem Clinics; contbr to encys. Hobby: chess. Home: 910 Park Ave, New York, NY. Office: 1060 Park Ave, New York, NY.

KUGELMASS, Sol, Isr, psychologist; b. NYC, July 4, 1926; s. Paul and Tessie (Grossinger); in Isr since 1954; PhD, Columbia U, NYC, 1953; m. Judith Oxenhandler, June 14, 1953; c: Ronit, Oren, David. Dir, Cen for Hum Devl, dept of psych, Heb U, Jerusalem, since 1968; chmn, dept of psych, 1957-68. US Army, 1944-46. Mem, Amer Psych Assn. Contbr to sci jours. Home: 52 Nayot, Jerusalem, Isr. Office: Hebrew U, Jerusalem, Isr.

KUHN, Jack W, US, business exec; b. Nashville, Tenn, Nov 24, 1918; s. Gus and Caroline (Weil); att U of Va, 1936-39; m. Lois Hainsfurther, June 24, 1944; c: Carol, Jack, Jeffrey, Walter. Pres, Kuhn Bros Co Inc, since 1965; fmr exec vice-pres; mem, bd dirs, chmn, regional chain group, Variety Stores Assn. US Army, 1940-45, mem, fac, staff, Signal Corps Off Training Sch OTC, 1942-43. Vice-chmn, natl membership cabinet, Dist Lodge 7, B'nai B'rith since 1962, fmr pres, Maimonides Lodge, delg, supr lodge conv; mem bd: pres, Nashville JCC, since 1956; Leo N Levi Memorial Hosp, since 1961; mem: ZOA; Nashville JWF, div co-chmn, chmn advance gifts div; mem, Hillel Commn; natl council, JDC; exec, Temple; fmr: mem bd: Temple Brotherhood; B'nai B'rith Home and Hosp for Aged; J Children's Home Service; delg, gen assembly, CJWF & F; gen chmn, UJA; club, Woodmont Country. Hobbies: golf, fishing. Home: 4343 Sneed Rd, Nashville, Tenn. Office: 3040 Sidco Dr, Nashville, Tenn.

KUHN, Michael, Isr, architect, town planner; b. Rostov, Russ, 1913; in Isr since 1920; coll cert, Jerusalem, 1931; att Acad Royale de Beaux Arts, Belgium, 1931-33; Ecole Supérieure d' Architecture et des Arts Decoratifs, Abbaye de la Cambre, Belgium, 1933-36; dipl, architecte urbaniste, Beligan Govt, 1936. Pvt practice: with various architectural firms, Jerusalem, 1938-39; worked with Prof Van Hutten, Belgium, 1938-39; designer: ind bldgs; housing: Dead Sea Works; Pal Potash, 1939-42; worked in offices of A Sharon, Tel Aviv, 1942-45; pvt practice, Tel Aviv, 1945-48; Planning Dept, Govt of Isr, i/c Negev Regional Planning, 1949-51; sr lectr, Technion, Haifa, 1961-64; visiting prof, Schs of Architecture: Caracas, Maracaibo, Venezuela, 1963. Mil engr, IDF, 1948-49. Maj projects: plans for Ofakim new townships; Agric Coll Kanot; Kiryat Gat cen; Beersheva housing schemes; hotels: Ashdod; Dead Sea; various ind, public bldgs, Sports Cen for Ma'alot; Jerusalem: hotels, motels, housing; Rehab Cen, Tel Hashomer Hosp. Lectr on architecture: Eur; Isr, sponsored by Min for Fgn Affairs, Isr, and by Architectural Assn in Scandinavia and Yugo, 1962; S Amer; Stanford U, Cal, both in 1963; repr: Isr sect, Intl Union of Architects; Technion, at 1st World Meeting of Architectural Tchrs and Students, Cuba, 1953; World Cong Architects, Cuba, Mexico, 1963, Paris, 1965; commns for: The formation of The Architect, Czech, 1962; Industrialization of Bldg, Russ, 1962; Colloquiums: Delft, 1964; Belgrade, 1965; Barcelona, 1967. Contbr papers and articles on town planning, ind bldgs, hum space, aesthetics, to various fgn architectural jours. Recipient: 1st prize for Agric Coll Kanot, 1951; 2nd, 3rd, 4th prizes, 1956-61; 1st prize, town planning, town-scape for area facing Old City, Jerusalem, 1965. Spec interests: social role of architecture, new hum settlements, housing. Office: 33 Frug St, Tel Aviv, Isr.

KUKIN, Ira, US, chemist; b. NYC, Apr 4, 1924; s. William and Clara (Wachtel); BS, cum laude, CUNY, 1945; MA, Harvard U, 1950, PhD, 1951; m. Doris Liener, 1954; c: Marrick, Lori, Jonathan. Pres, Apollo Chem Corp, Clifton, NJ, since 1963; dir, Jemlo Inc, since 1967; dir, research, L Sonneborn Sons, Belleville, NJ, since 1957; instr, chem, Sampson Coll, 1946-48; group leader, fundamental research, Gulf Research and Devl Co, 1951-57; US Army. Mem: Amer Assn Textile Chems; NY Acad Scis; AAAS; Amer Chem Soc; Amer Soc Lubrication Engrs; Soc Corrosion Engrs; Sigma Xi; fmr, secy,

Pittsburgh chap, Amer Technion Soc. Contbr articles to chem jours. Hobbies: hi-fi, golf. Home: 45 Edgemont Rd, W, Orange, NJ. Office: Apollo Chemical Corporation, Clifton NJ.

KUKOFF, Arthur U, US, manufacturer; b. Kiev, Russ, Mar 24, 1892; s. Jacob and Leba (Brondorff); in US since 1912; att Tech Sch, Kiev, Russ, 1909; deg, ind chem, Cooper Union, NY, 1914; m. Celia Okun, June 8, 1921; c: Milton, Ruth (decd), Jack, Bernard. Ret; fmr pres, nine companies, NYC, for 45 years; Russ Army. Prin contrib: invented formulas in mfg processes of chem mfg. Co-found, Bar Ilan U; fmr: pres, Oceanview J Cen; chmn: FJP; UJA; Isr Bonds; JNF; bd, B'nai Yechim Ashkenazie Yeshiva; mem: ZOA; Mizrachi; HIAS; B'nai B'rith, Brighton Lodge, NY; trustee: Dem Org, Bklyn, NY; ADL. Recipient: Silver Tenacuh, Boy Scout Troop, Bklyn; plaque, contbrs in plastic ind; plaque, creating a scholarship for Sch of Aviation, Isr; forest created in hon; plaque, Rabbi Aba Hillel Silver, for contribs to K'far Silver. Home: 3100 Brighton 2 St, Brooklyn, NY. Office: 142 W 14 St, New York, NY.

KULAKOW, Rose C, US, community worker; b. Milw, Wis, Sept 5, 1908; d. Hyman and Rebecca (Adashek) Cohen; BA, Downer Coll, 1929; m. 1st, Harry Yampol, 1931; c: Audrey Schatell, Donna Moser, Neal; m. 2nd, Sam Kulakow, 1962. Pres, women's dist 6, Natl B'nai B'rith Women, 1952-53; chmn: sch comm and bd mem, Milw J Council, 1957-59; group guidance comm and bd mem, J Vocational Service Corp, 1955-61; Mh comm, Women's Court and Civic Conf, 1950-51; admissions off, Mt Sinai Hosp, Milw, 1959-62; placement and rehab counsellor, J Vocational Service, Milw, since 1964; mem: Natl Rehab Assn ;Wis Rehab Assn; comm on problems of aging, Milw JWF, 1963; cen planning council for J Agencies, 1952-56; Natl Women's Comm for Brandeis U; Milw Home for Aged Jews; J Children's Home; Hadassah; Women's Amer ORT; sisterhood, Cong Emanu-El B'nai Jeshurun; Downer Coll Alumnae Assn. Home: 5147 N 28 St, Milwaukee, Wis.

KULICK, Paul A, US, communal org exec; b. Wheeling, W Va, Aug 30, 1911; s. Julius and Miriam (Rosenson); BA, U Pittsburgh, 1932; att: Grad Sch for J Social Work, 1932-34; NY Sch Social Work, 1937-38; m. Sarah Buff, Aug 6, 1939; c: Frances, Gilbert. Exec dir: J Social Services Fed, San Antonio, Tex, since 1958; J Comty Cen: Schenectady, NY, 1934-39; Houston, Tex, 1939-41; Stamford J Cen, Stamford, Conn, 1941-45; J Educ Alliance, Savannah, Ga, 1945-50; Savannah J Council, Savannah, 1945-48; campaign dir, Savannah UJA and Fed, 1945-58. Mem: exec comm, chmn, PR comm, S Tex chap, Natl Assn of Social Workers; bd dirs; Natl Conf on J Communal Service; Ga Conf on Social Wfr; tech adv comm, J Children's Service, Atlanta, Ga; munic recreation comm, Savannah; Agudas Achim Syn; fmr: pres, S sect, Natl Assn of J Cen Workers; mem, bd dirs, Ga and Tex Assns for MH; and pres, Chatham-Savannah chap; delg, AZA of B'nai B'rith; pres, Social Workers Club of Houston. Contbr to: Amer J Yearbook; The J Cen Worker; fmr ed, Savannah J News. Home: 2406 W Kings Hwy, San Antonio, Tex. Office: 307 Aztec Bldg, San Antonio, Tex.

KULKA, Erich, Isr, author, business exec; b. Vsetin, Czech, Feb 18, 1911; s. Siegbert and Malvine (Deutelbaum) Schon; in Isr since 1968; m. Elly Kula (decd); m. 2nd, Olga Machackova, 1947; c: Lia, Otto, Thomas, Dan. Writer, publicist, since 1945; trained as expert, wood ind, 1930; in export bus, wood-working factory to 1945. Author: My Mrtvi Zalujemi, 1945; Tovarna Na Smrt, 19 eds, 1946-66; Frankfurtsky Proces, 1964; Tu Sa Koncia Stopy SS, 1965; Soudcove Zalobci Obhajci, 1966; Utek Z Tabora Smrti, 1967; Unos Ze San Fernanda, 1968; co-author: Dokumente uber die Endlosung, 1966; Die Wunder wiederhohlten sich, 1956-64; The Five Escapes from Auschwitz, in They Fought Back, Anthol of J Resistance, 1967; Das Theresienstadter Ghetto, 1968; Libertto und Szenarbuch fur die standige CSSR Exposition im Staatlichen Museum in Oswiecim; contbr to: Internationaler Wiederhall der Fluchten aus Auschwitz, 1965; Die Untergrund-Bewegung im Konzentrationslager Auschwitz, 1966; Authentische Fotodokumente uber die Endlosung in Auschwitz, 1967; Tausend Jahre der tschechischen Juden, 1968; The Fight Against the Final Solution in Auschwitz, 1969; Exodus der tschechoslovakischen Juden, 1969; Czechoslovakia Holocaust Period, Jewish Resistance in Protektorat Bohemia and Moravia, 1969. Chmn: dist, Union of Anti-Fascist Fighters in Prague 7, Czech, 1956-68; mem, Educ

Bd for J Youth, Union of J Comtys, Prague, 1966-68. Recipient: Order of Antifascist Fighter, Min of Defense, Prague, 1946. Spec interest: research, hist of holocaust period. Home: 143 Bar Yochai St, Jerusalem, Isr.

KULLMANN, Eugen, US, educator; b. Erlenbach, Ger, Mar 20, 1915; s. Moritz and Fanny (Siegel); in US since 1946; PhD, U of Basel, 1941. Prof, rel, Kenyon Coll; fmr: tchr, phil, New Sch for Social Research, 1947-68; prof, Bible Acad for Higher J Learning, 1955-68; visiting prof, Bard Coll, 1958-64; visiting prof, phil, grad fac, New Sch of Social Research, 1947-60; lectr, Greek, Latin lit, Gen Theol Sem, NYC, 1958-68; prof phil, JTSA, NYC, 1966-68; visiting lectr, J studies, Smith Coll, 1961-67. Mem, bd dirs, Fed J from Cen Eur, since 1962; secy, Cong Machane Chodosh, Bklyn, since 1951; vice-pres, Friends of Animals Inc, since 1967; fmr: dir, Home for Ref Children; chmn, Fed J Students, U of Basel. Author: Beitrage zum Aristotelischen Begriff der Prohairesis, 1943; Prophetische Geschichtsphilosophie, 1946; Alexandrian Philosophy, 1950. Spec interests: care of aged, protection of animals. Home: Gambier, O. Office: Ascencion Hall, Kenyon Coll, Gambier, O.

KUNIN, Jacob, US, business exec, communal leader; b. Russ, Aug 20, 1901; s. Gedalie and Esther (Lubin); in US since 1904; m. Kate Palounick, May 30, 1923; c: Phyllis Moorin, Harriet Herskowitz. Pres, Kays, dept store, since 1959. Fmr pres: J Comty Cen; United J Council; Temple B'nai Isr; mem: B'nai B'rith; club, Birchwood Country. Hobbies: golf, traveling. Home: 154 Skytop Terr, Fairfield, Conn. Office: 1160 Main St, Bridgeport, Conn.

KUNIN, Robert, US, chemist author; b. W New York, NJ, July 16, 1918; s. Morris and Rebecca (Herzig); BS, Rutgers U, 1939, PhD, 1942; m. Edith Mass, Aug 30, 1942; c: Anne, David. Research asso, Rohm & Haas Co, since 1946; asso chem, TVA, 1942-44; sr sci, atom bomb project, Columbia U, 1944-45; ind f, Mellon Inst, 1945-46; lectr: U of Del, 1958-59; U of Pa, 1956-60; Amer U, 1955-62; cons: US AEC, 1950-55; US Off of Saline Water, 1968-69. Vice-pres, Trenton chap, AJCong; trustee, Adath Isr Cong; mem: Amer Chem Soc; Electrochem Soc; AAAS; Amer Inst Chem Engrs; Amer Inst Chems; Franklin Inst; Amer J Hist Soc. Author: Ion Exchange Resins, 1949; Elements of Ion Exchange, 1959; contbr to chem jours. Recipient: gold medal award, Franklin Inst, 1966; JC Vaaler award, 1966. Home: 1318 Moon Dr, Yardley, Pa. Office: 5000 Richmond St, Philadelphia, Pa.

KUNITZ, Moses, US, biochemist; b. Slonim, Russ, Dec 19, 1887; in US since 1909; BS, Cooper Union, 1916; PhD, Columbia U, 1924; m. 2nd, Rebecca Shamaskin, 1939; c: Rosaline, Jacques. Mem em, Rockefeller U, NYC, since 1953, asst, physics, 1923-25, asso, 1925-40, asso mem, 1940-50, mem, 1950-53. Prin contribs: crystallization of enzymes. Mem: Natl Acad Scis; Soc Experimental Biol and Med; Soc Biol Chem; AAAS. Home: 500 E 77 St, New York, NY. Office: Rockefeller U, 66 St and York Ave, New York, NY.

KUNITZ, Stanley J, US, poet, editor, educator; b. Worcester, Mass, July 29, 1905; s. Solomon and Yetta (Jasspon); AB, summa cum laude, Harvard U, 1926, MA, 1927; hon D Litt, Clark U, 1961; m. Elise Asher, July 21, 1958; c: Gretchen. Prof, grad sch of writing, Columbia U, since 1967, fac mem since 1963; ed, Wilson Libr Bull, 1928-43; prof, Bennington Coll, 1946-49; visiting prof, NY State Tchrs Coll, 1949-50; lectr, New Sch for Soc Research, 1950-57; visiting prof: U of Wash, 1955-56; Queens Coll, 1956-57; Brandeis U, 1958-59; dir, poetry workshops, Poetry Cen, YMHA, NYC, 1958-62; Danforth visiting lectr at Amer Colls, 1961-63. US Army, 1943-45. Author: Intellectual Things, 1930; Living Authors, 1931; Authors Today and Yesterday, 1933; Junior Book of Authors, 1934; British Authors of the 19th Century, 1936; American Authors, 1600-1900, 1938; Twentieth Century Authors, 1942, supplement, 1955; Passport to the War, 1944; British Authors Before 1800, 1952; Selected Poems, 1928-58, 1958; Poems of John Keats, 1964; European Authors, 1000-1900, 1967; ed, Yale Series of Younger Poets, 1969. Mem: Phi Beta Kappa; Natl Inst of Arts and Letters. Recipient: Gerrison Medal for Poetry, Harvard U, 1926; Oscar Blumenthal Prize, 1941; Guggenheim f, creative writing, 1945-46; Amy Lowell Travelling f, poetry, 1953-54; Levinson Prize, poetry, 1956; Harriet Monroe award, U of Chgo, 1958; Ford Found grant, poetry, 1958-59; Natl Inst Arts and Letters grant, poetry, 1959; Pulitzer Prize, poetry, 1959; Brandeis Creative Arts Medal, poetry, 1965; Acad Amer Poets award, 1968. Home: 157 W 12 St, New York, NY.

KUNSTLER, William M, US, attorney, educator; b. NYC, July 7, 1919; s. Monroe and Frances (Mandelbaum); BA, Yale U, 1941; LLB, Columbia U, 1948; m. Lotte Rosenberger, Jan 14, 1943; c: Karin Goldman, Jane. Partner, Kunstler and Kunstler, since 1948; asso prof, NYU Law Sch, since 1949; adj asso prof, Pace Coll, since 1951; lectr: Eng, Columbia U, 1946-50; New Sch for Social Research, since 1966; spec counsel for Martin Luther King, Jr, Cong of Racial Equality, 1961-68; bd dirs, ACLU, since 1964; arbitrator, Amer Arbitration Assn, since 1957; moderator: The Law on Trial, 1956-57; Counterpoint, 1957-59, both sta WNEW; Famous Trials, 1959-61, WEVD; Pro and Con, WMCA, 1960-61. Maj, signal corps, US Army, 1941-46. Mem: NYC Bar Assn; Phi Beta Kappa Alumni Assn; natl council, Natl Emergency Civil Liberties Comm, since 1967; bd legal advs, Law Cen for Constitutional Rights, since 1966. Author: Our Pleasant Vices, 1941; Law of Accidents, 1953; Corporate Tax Summary, 1953; First Degree, 1960; Justice, radio plays, 1960-61; Beyond a Reasonable Doubt? 1961; The Case of Courage, 1962; And Justice for All, 1962; The Minister and the Choir Singer, 1964; Deep in My Heart, 1966; contbr to jours. Recipient: Bronze Star. Home: 210 West St, Mamaroneck, NY. Office: 511 Fifth Ave, New York, NY.

KUPER, Charles Goethe, Isr, physicist, educator; b. Johannesburg, S Afr, Dec 14, 1926; s. Israel and Cecilia (Gordon); in Isr since 1967; DSc, Witwatersrand U, Johannesburg, 1945; MA, PhD, Cambridge U, Eng, 1942-52; m. Marie Cooklin, May 31, 1953; c: Gabriel, Cecilia. Prof, physics, Technion, Haifa, since 1967; research f, U of Liverpool, 1952-56; lectr, U of St Andrews, 1956-62, sr lectr, 1962-65, reader, 1965-67. Prin contribs, theories: superfluidity of helium, negative ions in liquid helium, superconductivity. Mem: Phys Soc, London; Cambridge Phil Soc. Author: Introduction to the Theory of Superconductivity, 1968; co-ed, Polarons and Excitons, 1963; contbr to sci jours. Recipient: Royal Soc, Edinburgh. Home: 27 Ra'anan St, Haifa, Isr. Office: Technion, Haifa, Isr.

KUPER, Theodore F, US, attorney; b. Moscow, Russ, May 1, 1886; s. Abraham and Bertha (Goldman); in US since 1891; LLB, NYU Law Sch, 1904; m. Rose Rubinstein 1909; c: Terry. Cons: Leg conf, CCNY; Fash Inst of Tech; natl dir, Thomas Jefferson Memorial Found, 1922-32; counsel, Bd of Educ, NYC, 1932-43. Master, Masons, 1926, dep grand master, 1929-30. Author: Thomas Jefferson Still Lives. Home: 11810 E Broadway, Whittier, Cal.

KUPFERBERG, Herbert, US, journalist; b. NYC, Jan 20, 1918; s. Moses and Augusta (Lasserwitz); BA, Cornell U, 1939; MA, Columbia U, 1940, MS, 1941; m. Barbara Gottesman, Jan 24, 1954; c: Seth, Joel, Natalie. Asso ed, Parade Mag, since 1966; music critic, Natl Observer, since 1967; ed, writer, New Bedford, Mass, Standard Times, 1950-63, staff mem since 1941; ed for arts, NY Herald Tribune, 1963-66; staff mem since 1952. Mem, Overseas Press Club of Amer. Author: Those Fabulous Philadelphians, 1969; contbr to mags, including: Atlantic Monthly; Harpers; This Week; High Fidelity. Home: 113-14 72 Rd, Forest Hills, NY. Office: 733 Third Ave, New York, NY.

KUPFERMAN, Lawrence, US, artist, educator; b. Boston, Mass, Mar 25, 1909; s. Samuel and Rosa (Maysles); att Sch, Mus Fine Arts, Boston, 1929-31; BS, Mass Sch of Art, 1935; m. Ruth Cobb, Apr 29, 1937; c: David, Nancy. Prof, painting, Mass Coll of Art, since 1941; one-man exhbs: Gals: Boris Mirski, Boston, 1944-47; Mortimer Brandt, NYC, 1946; Phila Art Alliance; M Levitt, NY, 1948, 1949, 1951, 1953; M Jackson, NYC, 1955; V Wear, NY, 1956; Swetzoff, Boston, 1956; R White, NY, 1958; Gropper Art, Cambridge, 1958; Marblehead Art Assn, 1959; Pace Gal, Boston, 1961; Galerie Irla Kert, Montreal, 1962; paintings represented in perm collections: Whitney Mus Amer Art, NY; Mus Fine Arts, Boston; Bklyn Mus; Addison Gal Amer Art; Phillips Acad, Andover; Mus Modern Art, NY; Wadswoth Atheneum, Hartford, Conn; U of Ill Art Gal, Urbana; Mus Art, U Mich, Ann Arbor; Walker Art Cen, Minneapolis, Minn; prints in perm collections: Metrop Mus, NY; SF Mus Art, Harvard U; Carnegie Inst; Baltimore Mus Art; Mus Fine Arts, Boston; Boston Public Libr; Mus Modern Art, NY; Pa State U; painted murals for Amer Export Lines, for ships, Constitution and Independence. F, Royal Soc Arts; asso, Natl Acad Design; mem, Temple Shalom. Hobby, gardening. Home: 38 Devon Rd, Newton Center, Mass. Office: 370 Brookline Ave, Boston, Mass.

KURLAND, Itzhak, Isr, director; s. Yehoshua and Tauba (Gerberbaum); att City of London Coll; m. Irene Poliakov, 1934; c: Daniela Bravinsky, Yael. Dir, JA for Isr, since 1968, dir gen, econ dept, 1954-68; with Anglo-Pal Bank, 1924-32; dir, Pariser Tageblatt, Paris, 1935-38. Off, Haganah, 1925-33. Contbr articles to jours. Home: 8 Emanuel St, Tel Aviv, Isr. Office: 17 Kaplan St, Tel Aviv, Isr.

KURTZ, Efrem, US, conductor; b. St Petersburg, Russ, Nov 7, 1900; s. Aaron and Sima (Krestmain); att St Petersburg Conservatory; studied with: Tscherpnin, Glazunov, Vitol, Karl Schroeder, Artur Nikisch; m. Elaine Shaffer, Aug 15, 1955. Guest conductor; perm conductor: Stuttgart Philharmonic, 1924-33; Ballet de Monte Carlo, 1933-41; Kan City Philharmonic, 1941-47; Houston Sym Orch, 1947-54; Liverpool Philharmonic Orch, 1954-56; conductor for Isadora Duncan and Anna Pavlova; guest conductor: Munich, Darmstadt and Breslau Operas; NY Philharmonic; NBC Orch; Chgo Sym; Cleveland Sym; Cincinnati Sym; LA Philharmonic; Detroit Sym; SF Sym; Natl Sym of Wash, DC; Portland, Ore Sym; London Royal Philharmonic; Philharmonic Orch, London; Brussels Philharmonic; Havana Philharmonic; Monte Carlo Sym; Berlin Philharmonic; Vienna Sym; NHK Sym, Tokyo; Orch Conservatoire, Paris; Residence Orch, The Hague; La Scala Opera, Milan; Rome Opera, It; toured S Amer, Austr, Can, Eur, Isr. Recording artist, Columbia Records, His Masters Voice. Recipient: Gold Medal for conducting Berlioz Festival, Monte Carlo, 1955; Gold Pressing Plaque (three millionth record), Columbia Records, 1953; Order of Merit, Rep of It, 1959; Bruckner Soc of Amer Medal. Home: 895 Park Ave, New York, NY.

KURTZ, Emanuel, US, song writer; b. Bklyn, NY, Nov 15, 1911; s. Beckie (Greenspan); att, Bklyn Evening Coll, 1931-33; m. Camille Kyman, Mar 22, 1936; c: Normand, Marilyn. Songs: I'm Gonna Live 'Til I Die; My Dreams Are Getting Better All The Time; The Whole World Is Singing My Song; The Jones Boy; The Story of a Starry Night; In a Sentimental Mood; Let It Be Me; Anema E Core. Mem: ASCAP; Odd Fellows. Home: 503 B 133 St, Belle Harbor, NY.

KURTZ, Moshe A, Isr, government official; b. Jaworzno, Pol, Dec 22, 1909; s. Hirsh and Esther (Margulies); in Isr since 1936; PhD, U Vienna, 1935; ordained rabbi, Rabb Sem, Vienna, 1936; m. Chana Szydlowska, 1936; c: Amiyah, Elisheva, Shlomit. Dir gen, Isr Min Social Wfr, since 1960; lectr tours: Eur, S Amer, US, since 1945; fmr: HS tchr, Tel Aviv, 1936-41; co-found, youth dept, WZO, 1941-47; head, cultural, political depts, Hapoel Hamizrachi, 1947-57; head, org dept, World Cen Mizrachi-Hapoel Hamizrachi, 1957-60, mem, world exec, 1957-62; leader, Youth Movement, Workers Rel Movement, since 1931; dep chmn, cen elections comms to 2nd, 3rd, 4th Knesset; mem, actions comm, Zionist Org; lectr, Intl Conf of Social Work: Rio de Janeiro; Athens; Wash; Bangkok; Geneva; Helsinki; missions on behalf of JA, J Natl Comm in Pal to Pol, Eur for rescue work among J survivors of KZ, Underground, Russ; permanent commn on ICSW; appd by UN, mem, intl expert group on social wfr org and admn; vice-chmn, Isr delg, first UN Intl Conf of Mins responsible for social wfr; delg to UN adv bd on juvenile delinquency and prevention of crime. Govt repr, Intl Union of Family Orgs, since 1962; hon secy-gen, Intl Conf J Communal Service, since 1965. Home: 5 Shalom Aleichem St, Jerusalem, Isr. Office: Israel Ministry of Social Welfare, Jerusalem, Isr.

KURTZMAN, David H, US, educational research exec; b. Lettichev, Russ, Jan 11 ,1904; s. Morris and Hannah (Wolson); in US since 1921; BS, Temple U, 1930, MA, U of Pa 1931, PhD, 1935; hon: LLD, Temple U; LLD, U of Pittsburgh; LHD, Jefferson Med Coll; DSc, Pa Coll of Optometry; m. Celia Buchdrucker, July 24, 1927; c: Marshall, Rochelle Weinman. Supt, public instrn, Commonwealth of Pa, since 1967; chancellor em, U of Pittsburgh, since 1967, on fac since 1965; fmr instr, political sci, Temple U, 1930-33; dir research, Pa Econ League, 1938-59; secy, admn, Commonwealth of Pa, 1959-63. Mem: Amer Acad of Political and Social Sci; Amer Soc for Public Admn; Amer Technion Soc, bd trustees; Govt Research Assn; Natl Tax Assn; adv council, Tax Inst of Amer; bd trustees, Pittsburgh Sym Soc; Omicron Delta Kappa; Phi Beta Kappa; Phi Eta Sigma; Delta chap, Druids; Beta Gamma Sigma; fmr: pres, J Family and Services Bur; secy, Metrop Study Commn; chmn, Mayor's Mgmt Adv Comm; both Pittsburgh; chief of staff, Gov's Tax Adv Comm; chmn, Gov's Tax Study and Revision Comm; research

dir, Pa Constitutional Conv Prepatory Comm; club: Pa, Schoolman. Contbr to profsl publs. Home: 1021 S Progress Ave, Harrisburg, Pa. Office: 317 Education Bldg, Harrisburg, Pa.

KURZ, Norbert, Switz, international civil servant; b. Kotzman, Aus, July 8, 1904; s. Hersch and Bertha (Spitzer); in Switz since 1930; licence en droit, U of Czernowitz, 1929; DRerPol, U of Geneva, 1933; dipl, Acad de Droit Intl, 1934; m. Helene Mange, May 9, 1935; c: Evelyne, Michel. Official, ILO, since 1934; mem: dipl sect, 1934-49; ind comms div, 1949-51; head, chem and petroleum ind sect, since 1951; exec secy, periodic confs of mem states for chem and petroleum ind. Mem: Academic Soc Heatid, Tel Aviv; Cercle des Juristes Intl, Geneva. Author: Article 11 du Pacte de la Société des Nations, 1933; reports pub by ILO; contbr to profsl jours. Home: 22 Ave William Favre, Geneva, Switz. Office: ILO, Geneva, Switz.

KURZ, Otto, Eng, educator; b. Vienna, Aus, May 26, 1908; s. Maximilian and Anna (Mandel); in Eng since 1934; m. Hilde Schuller; c: Erica Barrett. Prof, hist of classical tradition, spec emphasis on Near E, Warburg Inst, London U, since 1965. Contbr to periodicals. Home: 49 Ralph Ct, Queensway, London, Eng. Office: Warburg Institue, Woburn Sq, London, Eng.

KURZWEIL, Zvi Erich, Isr, educator; b. Pirnitz, Czech, July 29, 1911; s. Abraham and Rachel; PhD, Ger U, Prague, 1936; ordained rabbi, Rabb Sem, Berlin, 1935; Hon BA, U London; m. Paula Rosner, 1938; c: Naomi, Abraham, Michael. Prof, educ, Technion since 1965, head, dept, gen studies and tchr training; insp of schs, Gen Council for J Educ in Gt Brit, 1947-58. Author: Modern Trends in Jewish Education, 1964; Education in a Technical Society, Heb, 1965; Janusz Korxzak, An Educator, Heb, 1968; Anxiety and Education, 1968. Home: 4 Aron Lane, Ahuza, Haifa, Isr. Office: Technion, Haifa, Isr.

KUSHLAN, Samuel D, US, physician, educator; b. New Brit, Conn, Feb 17, 1912; s. David and Bessie (Minc); BS, Yale U, 1932, MD, 1935; m. Ethel Ross, June 24, 1934; c: Nancy Wagner, David. Asso phys-in-chief, Yale-New Haven Hosp; clinical prof, med, Yale U Sch of Med; cons gastroenterologist: Bristol Hosp; Griffin Hosp; Meriden Hosp; VA Hosp; Hosp of St Raphael. Pres, Yale U Alumni in Med, 1957-59; bd govs, Hillel Found, Yale U; fmr, bd corporators, student loan Fund, Yale Men in Med Inc; mem: AMA; Amer Soc for Gastrointestinal Endoscopy; Amer Gastroenterological Assn; Sigma Xi; Alpha Omega Alpha. Ed bd, Conn State Med Jour, 1954-59; Contbr to profsl jours. Home: 655 Whitney Ave, New Haven, Conn. Office: 303 Whitney Ave, New Haven, Conn.

KUSHNER, Harvey David, US, research exec; b. Bklyn, NY, Dec 28, 1930; s. Morris and Hilda (Zwiebel); BA, Johns Hopkins U, Baltimore, Md, 1951; postgrad, U of Md, 1952; m. Rose Rehert, Jan 14, 1951; c: Gantt, Todd, Lesley. Pres, Oprs Research Inc, Silver Spring, Md, since 1969, on research staff since 1955, bd dirs, 1957-69, exec vice-pres, 1962-69; asso engr, USN, Bur of Ships, 1951-53; mem, tech staff, Melpar, 1953-55; corp tech dir, Leasco Data Processing Equip Co, 1969; cons, Natl Acad Scis, Comm on Undersea Warfare, 1963-64. Mem: Oprs Research Soc Amer; Inst of Profsl Orgs; Mgmt Scis; Amer Soc Mech Engrs; AAAS; Amer Mgmt Assn; Bethesda-Chevy Chase J Comty Group. Home: 4016 Ingersol Dr, Silver Spring, Md. Office: 1400 Spring St, Silver Spring, Md.

KUSNETZ, Chaim, (pen name, A Duboier), US, author; b. Duboi, Russ, Oct 12, 1904; s. Jacob and Rachel (Kusnetz); in US since 1923; m. Minnie Yazen, Apr 5, 1937; c: Fay Minkin, Suzie Chasnov. Author: Fun Einems a Togbuch, 1931; Mentsh un Mides, 1954; A Mentsh Tracht, 1957; Makhshoves un Rayoines; Toire Taitshn; contbr articles, essays, poetry to Yiddish publs. Secy, Duboier Young Mens Progressive Assn, since 1946. Home: 1909 Eastern Pkwy, Brooklyn, NY.

KUSS, Nathan I, US, business exec; b. Kowel, Pol, Mar 4, 1906; s. William and Fannie (Shiffer); in US since 1908; grad, Wharton Sch Acct and Finance, U of Pa, 1925; m. 2nd, Miriam Kline, Nov 15, 1964. Partner, Bundle O' Joy Baby Wear Co, since 1937; office mgr, Charles Guzy Mfg Co, 1922-37. Pres: Ahavas Achim Holche Yosher Syn, 1957-65;

Wilkes-Barre Heb Inst, 1947-53; E Pa Zionist Region, 1953-58; Wyo Valley J Comm, 1947-51; chmn, bd educ, since 1950; vice-pres: J Comty Cen, since 1959; Middle Atlantic sect JWB, since 1949; Pa region, CJFWF, since 1950; chmn, Isr Bond Campaign, UJA, 1946; natl campaign cabinet, UJA; bd govs, Isr Bonds; bd mem: J Wfr Agcy J Home; mem, B'nai B'rith. Home: 22 Maffett St, Wilkes-Barre, Pa. Office: 43 S Pennsylvania Ave, Wilkes-Barre, Pa.

KUTASH, Samuel B, US, psychologist, educator; b. Bklyn, NY, May 12, 1912; s. Isadore and Jenny (Kaplan); BS, CCNY, 1932, MSc, 1936; att Columbia U, 1936-37; PhD, NYU, 1944; cert in clinical psych, NJ, NY State Bd of Examiners in Psych; m. Lee Proschansky, Dec 24, 1936; c: Emilie, Irwin. Cons, VA Hosp, E Orange, NJ, since 1960, fmr, chief, psych service; prof, psych, Rutgers U, since 1954; pvt practice since 1946; chmn, NJ State Bd Psych Examiners, since 1967; fmr: psych, NY Bd Educ, 1934-38; psych case worker, NYC Dept Wfr, 1938-42; psych, Woodbourne Inst, NY, 1942-44; chief psychol, Harlem Valley State Hosp, NY, 1944-46; chief clinical psychol, VA Mental Hygiene Clinic, Newark, NJ, 1946-52; lectr: psychotherapy, Bklyn Coll, 1946-53; NYU, 1946-53. F: Amer Group Psychotherapy Assn; Amer Orthopsycht Assn; AAAS; Amer Assn on Mental Deficiency; Amer Psych Assn, mem, council, since 1956; dipl, Amer Bd Examiners in Profsl Psych; secy-treas, bd examiners, NJ Psych Assn, fmr pres, bd examiners; delg, Council of State Psych Assns; mem: Amer Assn Advancement Psychotherapy; bd trustees, Guidance Clinic for Retarded Children, E Orange; Temple Sharey Tefilo; fmr f: Soc for Protective Techs; Rorschach Inst. Author: Perceptual Changes in Psychopathology, 1961; chap in Handbook of Clinical Psychology; ed, Ency of Criminology, 1949; asso ed: Jour of Clinical Psychopath; Archives of Criminal Psychodynamics; Jour of Criminal Psychopath; mem, ed bd, Jour of Group Psychan and Process; contbr to med jours. Home: 3 Park Rd, Maplewood, NJ. Office: 2130 Millburn Ave, Maplewood, NJ.

KUTNER Alan, Eng, business exec; b. London, Eng, Mar 24, 1935; s. Ben and Mary (Berg); BSc, with hons, Sir John Cass Coll, London, 1956; PhD, Queen Mary Coll, 1960; m. Anita Schwartz, Dec 28, 1958; c: Jonathan, Rayna. Dir, AK Chems Ltd, since 1968; sales repr, Victor Blagden and Co, London, 1960-66; sales exec, Wogan Brameast Trading, 1966-68. Choirmaster: Edgware Syn; Stoke Newington Syn, 1955-59; Finchley Syn, 1959; f, Chem Soc. Hobby: philately. Home and office: 34 Freston Gardens, Cockfosters, Herts, Eng.

KUTNER, Bernard, US, social psychol; b. NYC, May 17, 1923; s. Samuel and Clara (Seigel); BSS, CUNY, 1944; MA, New Sch for Social Research, 1948; PhD, Harvard U, 1951; m. Elizabeth Silverstein, Sep 2, 1944; c: Robin, Kenneth. Asso prof, depts of preventive and environmental med and rehab med, Albert Einstein Coll Med, since 1959, on fac since 1955; sr investigator, socio-environmental aspects of aging, since 1958; research asso, AJCong, 1951-52; dir, studies in gerontology, Cornell U Med Coll, 1952-55, cons, study in obstet nursing, NY Hosp, 1953-54; lectr, social sci, Cornell U Sch of Nursing, NY Hosp, 1953-54. F: AAAS; Gerontological Soc; Amer Psych Assn; Amer Sociol Assn. Co-author: Five Hundred Over Sixty: A Community Survey of Aging, 1956; contbr to med, sociol jours. Home: 32 Pine Road, Syosset, LI, NY. Office: Albert Einstein Coll of Med, Eastchester Rd and Morris Park Ave, Bronx, NY.

KUTSCHER, Eduard Y, Isr, educator; b. Topolčany, Czech, June 1, 1909; s. Michael and Gita (Singer); in Isr since 1931; att Yeshivot: Czech; Ger; MA, Heb U, Jerusalem, 1941; m. Edit Schnuermacher, Oct 7, 1934; c: Ziona Raphael, Pinhas, Michal. Prof, Heb lang, Heb U, since 1949; tchr: elem, secondary schs, sem's, Isr, 1934-52; visiting prof: JTSA, NY, 1953-55; Dropise Coll, 1956-57; Yale U; U of Pa, 1962-63; NYU, 1967-68; prof, Heb, Bar Ilan U, 1958-69. Mem, Heb Lang Acad. Author: The Language and Linguistic Background of the Isaiah Scroll, 1959; Words and Their His-

tories, 1961; ed, Leshonenu, quarterly, Heb Lang Acad; contbr to Heb, Eng, Ger periodicals. Recipient: Isr Prize in hum, 1961. Home: 36 Palmach St, Jerusalem, Isr. Office: Hebrew U, Jerusalem, Isr.

KUTTNER, Bernard Albert, US, attorney; b. Berlin, Ger, Jan 13, 1934; s. Frank and Vera (Knopfmacher); in US since 1930; AB, cum laude, Dartmouth Coll, 1955; att U of Va, 1956-57; JD, Seton Hall U Law Sch, 1959; m. Cathy Ledner, Mar 11, 1961; c: Karen, Robert. Pvt practice, Newark, NJ since 1960; atty, Toner, Crowley & Vanderbilt, 1959-61. Lt, USN Res, since 1964. Corp Counsel, Irvington, NJ; vice-chmn, ADL, NJ Regional Bd; senator, Jr Chamber Intl; mem: Comty Relations Comm, Essex Co; Amer Bar Assn; Amer Trial Lawyers Assn; fmr: pres, Irvington Bar Assn; chmn, UJA, Irvington, NJ; club, Lions, fmr pres. Author: Municipal Ordinances, 1965; contbr to Congressional Record, 1966. Recipient: Outstanding Young Man of NJ, NJ Jaycees, 1967; Outstanding Civil Leaders of Amer, Bd Eds, 1968. Home: 321 Wyoming Ave, Maplewood, NJ. Office: 11 Commerce St, Newark, NJ.

KWALWASSER, Jacob, US, educator, music psychol; b. NYC, Feb 27, 1894; s. Louis and Lena (Greenberg); BA, BE, U of Pittsburgh, 1917; MA, U of Ia, 1923; PhD, 1925; m. Pearl Little, Dec 21, 1919; c: Edgar, Robert, Helen Wedeen. Prof em, Syracuse U, since 1954, research prof, music educ, 1926-54; head, public sch music dept, U of Ia, 1924-25; lectr: U Pittsburgh, 1920-21; U Minn, 1932; Chgo Musical Coll, 1933; Columbia U Tchrs Coll, 1926-29; U Idaho, 1939; U Ark, 1940; U Tex, 1941, 1945; Assn Amer Colls, 1946-48; visiting prof, Julliard Sch of Music, 1946-47. Mem: Sigma Xi; Phi Mu Alpha; Kappa Phi Kappa; fmr: chmn, research, Music Sups Natl Conf. Author: Tests and Measurements in Music, 1927; Two Hundred Songs for Junior and Senior High School, 1929; Two Hundred Songs, 1930; Problems in Music Education, 1932; chaps: Implications of Research for the Classroom Teacher, 1939; 35th Yearbook, Natl Soc for Study of Educ, 1936; Exploring the Musical Mind, 1954; contbr to profsl jours. Home: 4321 Parkman Ave, Pittsburgh, Pa.

KWART, Samuel, Isr, jurist; b. Lodz, Pol, 1914; s. Kopel and Sara (Feinsod); in Isr since 1934; att Heb U, 1934-35; LLB, Jerusalem Law Sch, 1942; m. Frieda Ziegler, 1937; c: Yigal, Oded. Judge, Dist Court, Tel Aviv, since 1965; asst dist atty, 1953-58; dep state atty, 1958-65. Contbr to law jours. Home: 9 Hankin St, Tel Aviv, Isr. Office: District Court, Weizmann St, Tel Aviv, Isr.

KWASS, Sidney J, US, lawyer; b. Pocahontas, Va, Nov 11, 1908; s. Joseph and Gussie (Aaron); JD, W Va U, 1931; m. Edna DeLott, Aug 12, 1933; c: Robert, Karel, Kathy. Pvt practice, Kwass and Stone, and predecessor firms, since 1931; chmn, appeal bd, W Va State Workmen's Compensation Comm, since 1962, mem since 1959; fmr: city atty, Bluefield, 1933-37; commn in chancery, Circuit Court of Mercer Co, 1938-46; referee, bankruptcy, US Dist Court, S Dist, 1941-46; US Commnr, 1946-48; commnr accts, Mercer Co Court, 1942-48, all W Va. Pres: Mercer Co Bar Assn, 1951; B'nai B'rith, 1943; Bluefield-Princeton Cong, 1945, 1951, 1952, 1959, 1963, 1967; secy, Bluefield Comty Chest, 1938-48; mem, bd govs, W Va State Bar, 1956-59; mem: perm, Jud Conf for 4th US Circuit; Pi Lambda Phi; Masons. Student ed, W Va Law Rev; clubs: U; Fincastle Country. Hobbies: golf; photography. Home: 1200 Castlewood Lane, Bluefield, W Va. Office: Law and Commerce Bldg, Bluefield, W Va.

KWILECKI, Erich (Arie), Isr, business exec; b. Berlin, Ger, 1908; in Isr since 1936; m. Hilde Wertheimer; c: Adin, Margalit. Mgn dir, Fgn Trade and Supply Co Ltd, since 1953; fmr: sales mgr, Fgn Trade Inst, Tel Aviv, 1944-48; head, export promotion dept, Min Commerce and Ind, 1948-53; mem, Isr trade delgs to Eur and Afr, 1945-53; Chmn, Ramat Gan br, Assn Immigrants from Eur; mem: exec council, Isr Export Inst; fmr, Ramat Gan Munic Council. Contbr articles on econ problems. Home: 11 Herzl St, Ramat Gan, Isr.

L

LABBY, Daniel H, US, physician, educator; b. Portland, Ore, Sep 1, 1914; s. Harry and Sonia (Goldfarb); BA, Reed Coll, Portland, 1935; MD, U Ore Med Sch, 1939; m. Margaret Selling, Dec 28, 1940; c: Joan, David, Louise. Prof med, U Ore Med Sch Hosp, since 1951. Fmr: intern, Johns Hopkins Hosp, Baltimore, Med; res, NY Hosp; research asso, Rockefeller Hosp, 1945-47; visiting prof med, Strasbourg, Fr, 1960-61. US Army, 1941-43. Trustee, Reed Coll; fmr: gov for Ore, Amer Coll Phys, 1960-66; pres, Portland Acad Med, 1966-67; contbr to med textbooks and jours. Recipient: f's Noble Wiley Jones; A Blaire Brower; Commonwealth Fund. Hobbies: art, langs, music, gardening. Home: 5931 SW Hamilton, Portland, Ore. Office: U of Ore Med Sch Hosp, Portland, Ore.

LABOV, Benjamin, US, business exec; b. Russ, Nov 24, 1896; s. Moses and Lisa (Lipshitz); in US since 1906; att Yale U; m. Rhea White, July 23, 1923; c: Richard, William. Pres, Union Ink Co Inc, since 1930; treas, Standard Coating Corp, since 1942. Fmr: chem, Fuchs and Lang, 1919-30. Trustee: Bergen Comty Coll; exec comm; Natl Comty Bank, Bergen Co, NJ; Englewood Hosp; pres: Ridgefield Mfrs Assn, 1956-58; pres, J Wfr Council, Bergen Co, 1960-68; vice-pres, Heb Home and Hosp, Jersey City; past chmn: UJA, Rutherford, Cliffside Park, Fort Lee, all NJ, mem natl cabinet, state cabinet; mem: Temple Isr, Cliffside Park; J Comty Cen, Fort Lee. Clubs: Preakness Hills Country, mem bd of govs, since 1945, pres 1956-60; Exch; Kiwanis; Masons, Boiling Springs Lodge 152. Contbr: instituted Ridgefield Mfrs Scholarships Fund, 1952; found Joseph Labov Memorial Scholarship Fund, Yale U, 1958. Recipient: Brotherhood Award, NCCJ, 1965. Hobbies: golf, philanthropic assns, travel. Home: 15 Crescent Way, Palisade, NJ. Office: 453 Broad St, Ridgefield, NJ.

LACK, Abe I, US, merchant; b. Lutzin, Russ, June 19, 1897; s. Solomon and Fanie (Rozen); in US since 1910; m. 1st, Sarah Stillman, 1920; c: Fredell, Zella, Sanford; m. 2nd, Gertrude, 1967. Chmn bd, Lack's Wholesale Distributers Inc since 1932. Capt, USAAC, 1942-43. Mem, adv bd, Salvation Army, since 1958; pres, SW reg, CJFWF, 1953-54, mem natl bd 1952-54; Temple Emanuel, 1951-52; JCC, 1945-47; chmn: SW reg, JDC; mem, ntl bd, NCCJ, 1950-54; mem: B'nai B'rith; ZOA; Shriners; clubs: Rotary, Westwood Country, Houston, Intl. Home: 1400 Hermann Dr, Houston, Tex. Office: 1315 Baker St, Houston, Tex.

LADANY, Shaul Paul, Isr, engineer, educator; b. Belgrade, Yugo, Apr 2, 1936; s. Dionis and Sofia (Kasowitz); in Isr since 1948; BSc, Technion, Haifa, 1956, MSC, 1961; dipl, bus admn, Heb U, Jerusalem, 1964; PhD, Columbia U, NYC, 1968; m. Shoshana Ahlfeld, Nov 6, 1960. Lectr, produc mgmt, oprs research, Tel Aviv U, since 1968; oprs research adv, Min of Transp, since 1968. Fmr: lectr, Columbia U; gen man, Atzmon Sewing Machine Co; supr engr, Knesset Bldg. Served IDF. Mem: Operations Research Soc of Isr; Maccabi Athletic Club, Tel Aviv; Intl Olympians Assn, Isr Chap. Recipient: Outstanding Phys Ability Award, Off's Sch, 1956; Outstanding Track and Field Athlete Award, Heb U, 1964; Award of Merit, Sports Illustrated, 1966; Outstanding Athlete Award, Metrop AAU, NY, 1967. Hobby, racewalking, Isr champion since 1964; Isr repr: Olympic Games, Mex, 1968; Maccabian Games 1965, 1969; E Reg Champion, 50 mile, USA, 1966, 1967, 1968; 1969; recipient of over 70 sports trophies, 200 medals in racewalking competitions. Home: 71 Aluf David St, Ramat Gan, Isr. Office: Tel Aviv U, Tel Aviv, Isr.

LADAR, Samuel A, US, attorney; b. Jackson, Cal, Oct 4, 1904; s. Max and Dora (Axelrod); BA, U of Cal, 1926, JD, 1928; m. Sylvia Favorman, 1926; c: Jerrold. Practising atty since 1928; mem, Steinhart, Goldberg, Feigenbaum and Ladar since 1945; visiting lectr, law, U of Cal Law Sch. Pres: SF Bd of Educ, 1962; SF Police Comm, 1965; U of Cal Law Sch Assn (Boalt Hall Alumni Assn), 1967-68; JWF of SF, Marin Co and Peninsula, 1965-66; vice-pres, dir, Cong Emanu-El, SF; dir: Infant Shelter Inc; SF chap, AJComm; N Cal Lawyers' Golf Assn; adv, Liberty Natl Bank, SF; SF chap, Amer Cancer Soc; mem, natl bd delgs, AJComm; mem: Amer, State, and SF Bar Assns; SF Crime Commn; B'nai B'rith lodge 163, SF; clubs: Commonwealth of Cal; Concordia-Argonaut, SF; Lake Merced Golf and Country, SF. Home: 1918 Vallejo, San Francisco, Cal. Office: 111 Sutter St, San Francisco, Cal.

LADEN, Hyman N, US, railway exec, management cons; b. Phila, Pa, July 26, 1915; s. Morris and Sara (Pojarsky); BA, U of Pa, 1936, PhD, 1941; MA, U of Md, 1938; BS, MS, US Naval Postgrad Sch, 1949; m. Lillian Borenstein, 1939; c: Richard, Vicki, Lisa. Chief, New Sys Devl, Chesapeake & Ohio RR Co, 1954-63; asst vice-pres, research, Chesapeake & O, since 1965, dir, Data Sys, 1963-65; cons: TV engr, communications, math biophysics, computers, bus sys, oprs analysis, since 1948; instr, dept of math, U of Wis, 1941-42; visiting lectr: Cornell U Grad Sch of Bus, US Army Ordnance Engr Mgmt Training Prog; Amer U; Case Inst; Cleveland Engr Soc; cons: Natl Computer Analysts Inc, 1961-64. Cdr, USN, 1942-54. Prin contrib: patents in elecs for communication sys, 1949; RR device patents pending. Pres, Univac Users Assn, 1957-59; mem: Amer Math Soc; Soc for Ind and Applied Math; Inst Elec and Elec Engrs; Inst Mgmt Sci; Oprs Research Soc Amer; Amer Stat Assn; Econometric Soc; Natl Planning Assn; Sys and Procedures Assn; RR Sys and Mgmt Assn; Assn for Computing Machinery; U of Pa Alumni Assn; Chizuk Amuno Temple, Baltimore; chmn, research cons comm, Assn Amer RR; Ind Adv Comm on Automation; Vita; Sigma Xi; Amer Mgmt Assn; Amer RR Engrs Assn; British Computer Soc; Transp Research Forum. Author: Bibliography on Orthogonal Polynomials, 1940; Television Engineering, 1953; System Design for Computer Applications, 1963; contbr to tech jours. Recipient: Battle Stars, Pacific Campaigns, 1944-45. Home: 9 Glencliffe Circle, Brooklandville, Md. Office: 2 N Charles St, Baltimore, Md.

LADERMAN, Ezra, US, composer; b. NYC, June 29, 1924; s. Isidor and Leah (Stock); BA, Bklyn Coll, 1949; MA, Columbia U, 1952; m. Aimlee Davis; c: Isaiah, Jacob, Rachel. Composer: String Quartet 1 and 2; Piano Sonatas 1 and 2; Duo for Violin and Cello; Stanzas; Magic Prison; Violin Sonata; Songs for Eve; Nonette; Flute Sonata; Clarinet Sonata; String Quartet No 3; A Single Voice; Double Helix; Celestial Bodies; Violin Concerto; prin commns: NY Philharmonic Orch; Minn Orch; NYC Opera; Erica Morini; Judith Raskin. Sgt, US Army, 1943-46. Mem: ZOA; ASCAP. Recipient: Three Guggenheim Awards; Rockefeller Award; Ford Found Award; Prix de Rome. Home: 279 Warwick St, Teaneck, NJ.

LADERMAN, Gabriel, US, educator, artist; b. Bklyn, NY, Dec 26, 1929; s. Isadore and Leah (Stock); BA, Bklyn Coll, 1952; MFA, Cornell U, 1957; m. Carol Ciavati, Feb 14, 1953; c: Raphael, Michael. Asst prof: art, Queens Coll, since 1968. Fmr, assoc prof: SUNY, 1957-59; Pratt Inst, 1959-68. One-man and group shows throughout US and in It. Pfc, US Army, 1953-55. Contbr to art pubis. Recipient: Louis C Tiffany Award; Fulbright Award to It; f, Cornell U; artist-in-res, La State U. Hobby, collector of early illus books. Home: 760 West End Ave, New York, NY. Office: Queens Coll, Queens, NY.

LADERMAN, Manuel, US, rabbi; b. NYC, Aug 25, 1909; s. William and Fannie (Mazelis); BS, Lewis Inst of Tech, Chgo, 1929; att Divinity Sch, U of Chgo, 1930; ordained rabbi, Heb Theol Coll, Chgo, 1932; DTh, Illiff Sch of Theol, U of Denver, 1937; m. Bess Mallin, Aug 6, 1933; c: Paul, Miriam Gita. Rabbi, Heb Educ Alliance, Denver, since 1932; fmr: Hillel counselor: U of Colo, 1940-46; U of Denver, 1944-46; Eur dir, rel activities, JDC, 1948-49; lectr: J Chautauqua Soc; Heb Theol Coll; chaplain, Vets Hosps, Denver and Grand Junction, Colo, 1945-52. Pres: Colo Council of Zionist Orgs, 1948-60; Adult Educ Council of Denver, 1958-60; Council of Orthodox Rabbis of Denver; vice-pres, Fed Council of Isr Instns; rabb adv comm, UJA; mem: Colo adv comm, US Commn on Civil Rights, 1958-60; bd trustees, Denver Sym Soc; Bd of Health and Hosp, city and co of Denver, chmn, 1966; hon bd mem, ARC; bd trustees, Amer Med Cen, since 1951; pres, Rabb Assn, Heb Theol Coll, 1941-42; vice-pres, RabCA, 1944-45;

chmn on social justice, 1946; clergy adv, Denver sect, NCCJ, 1945-46; mem: social justice commn, Syn Council of Amer; bd dirs: Denver Comty Chest, 1950; Gen Rose Memorial Hosp, 1952; vice-pres, Mizrachi Org of Amer, 1951-52; co-chmn, Allied Comty Council Drive, since 1950; clubs: Green Gables Country; Town; Soc of Bibl Lit. Home: 4300 W 17 Ave, Denver, Colo. Study: 1555 Stuart St, Denver, Colo.

LADERMAN, Paul Samuel, US, rabbi; b. Denver, Colo, Aug 23, 1934; s. Manuel and Bess (Mallin); att U of Chgo 1954-55; BA, ordained rabbi, Yeshiva U, 1957; att: Mercaz Harav Kook, Jerusalem, 1957-58; Heb U, Jerusalem, 1962-64; m. Shulamith Jackson, Mar 4, 1960; c: Zev, Ilana, Rafi. Rabbi, Cong Beth Jacob, since 1964. Chaplain, USAF, 1960-62. Secy, Bd of Rabbis of N Cal; mem, Cal RabCa. Recipient: Mazer f to Heb U, Yeshiva U, 1962-64. Home: 1224 Holman, Oakland, Cal. Study: 3778 Park Blvd, Oakland, Cal.

LAHAV, Eitan, Isr, biochemist; b. Tel Aviv, Apr 16, 1933; s. Zvi and Naomi (Stolovitch) Brandt; BSc, U of Copenhagen, 1957; MSc, 1959; PhD, Heb U, 1964; m. Ina Kendjersky, May 16, 1957; c: Alona, Galia, Ruth. Head, div biochem and bact, Volcani Inst Agric Research, since 1964; fmr: head research asst, U of Copenhagen, 1959-61; head, research lab, asso prof, Royal Vet Inst, Copenhagen, 1964-66. Lt, paratroops, IDF, 1949-52. Prin contribs: co-discoverer of a group of new immunizing substances which foster the protective mechanism of the mammalian body against severe infectious diseases. Comm mem, Standards Inst of Isr; bact and chem comm, Intl Dairy Fed; adv: Isr Dairy Bd; Danish Natl Research Bd, 1964-66; mem: Biochem Soc, Copenhagen; Isr Inst CE, Haifa; Assn Engrs and Architects in Isr. Author: Organic and Inorganic Chemistry, 1962; Immunogenic Activity of the Caseidins, 1969. Recipient: ribbons: Independence, Sinai, 6 Day War. Home: 5 Morgolin, Rishon Le Zion, Isr. Office: POB 6, Bet-Dagan, Isr.

LAKIN, Leonard, US, educator; b. NYC, July 9, 1931; s. Jack and Lena (Evans); BBA, cum laude, CCNY, 1953; JD, NYU Sch of Law, 1956; m. Rita Bialos, June 21, 1959; c. Jill. Asst prof, law, Baruch Coll, CUNY, since 1967. Fmr: partner, Levinson & Cobb, Hawaii, 1958-60; asst gen counsel, Walter E Heller & Co, Inc, 1960-62; asso gen counsel, AJ Armstrong Co, Inc, 1962-64; secy, gen counsel, Natl Car Rental Sys, Inc, 1964-65. Vice-pres, dir, Baruch Coll Alumni Assn Inc; cons: Bd Examiners, Amer Inst of CPAs; Barnes and Noble Inc; arbitrator, Natl Panel of Arbitrators, Amer Arbitration Assn; fmr: chmn, comm on continuing legal educ, Hawaii Bar Assn; co-chmn, Law Day-USA, 1960, Hawaii; secy, found, Hawaii Bar Jour; treas, bd trustees, Temple Emanuel, Hawaii, bd govs, Beta Gamma Sigma Alumni, NY; mem: Masons, Honolulu Lodge; NY Co Lawyers Assn; Hawaii Bar Assn of Commercial Finance Attys. Author, A Guide to Secured Transactions, 1970; contbr to legal jours. Recipient: Goodwill Ambass to Mexico, CCNY, 1953. Hobbies: photography, Amer hist, travelling. Home: 679 Warburton Ave, Yonkers, NY. Office: Baruch Coll, CUNY, 17 Lexington Ave, New York, NY.

LAMBERT, Abbott Lawrence, US, business exec; b. NYC, Mar 19, 1919; s. Woolf and Estelle (Wittcover); BA, Columbia U, 1940; MS, Columbia Grad Sch Bus, 1946; m. Lois Ribman; c: Nancy, Jane. Pres, Carthage Fabrics Corp since 1964; vice-pres, Chopak Mills Inc, since 1962; fmr, partner, CPA's Woolf W Lambert Co, 1946-48. Capt, US Army, 1942-46. Hon pres, Assn of J Sponsored Camps, pres, 1964-67; pres, J Vacation Assn; trustee: FJP; Assn of YM and YWHA's of Gtr NY; mem: NY State Soc of CPA's; Zeta Beta Tau, Columbia U, natl trustee, 1960-66. Hobby: photography. Home: 1025 Fifth Ave, New York, NY. Office: 469 Seventh Ave, New York, NY.

LAMDAN, Hanna, Isr, organization exec; b. Novoselitz, Bessarabia, Dec 23, 1904; d. Michael and Miriam (Rappaport) Kracushansky; isr since 1925; div; c: Michal. Mem: Histadrut exec comm; Moetzet Hapoalot; secretariat, Lab Party; fmr: MK, dep speaker, 2nd Knesset. Home: 1 Gottlieb St, Tel Aviv, Isr.

LAMDEN, Merton P, US, biochemist, educator; b. Boston, Mass, Sept 7, 1919; s. Samuel and Anne (Flanzbaum) Bornstein; BS, U of Mass, 1941; PhD, MIT, 1947; m. Bernice Levenson, Dec 23, 1942; c: Carol, Deborah. Asso prof, biochem, Coll of Med, U of Vt, since 1953, on fac since 1947. Fmr: teaching and research f, biol dept, 1941-43; research staff mem: Food Tech Labs, 1943-44; US Army Subsistence Research and Devl labs, 1944-46. Hoffmann-La Roche f, dept of food tech, MIT, 1946-47; Commonwealth Fund f, U Coll, London, 1961-

62; mem: Amer Chem Soc; Assn of Vitamin Chems; Amer Inst Nutrition; AAUP; Phi Kappa Phi; Sigma Xi; Tau Epsilon Phi; club, Men's of Ohavi Zedek Syn, pres, 1951-52. Contbr to sci jours. Hobbies: philately, gardening. Home: 17 Wildwood Dr, Burlington, Vt. Office: Med Bldg, of Vt, Burlington, Vt.

LaMED, Louis, US, business exec, communal worker; b. Novo-Ushitza, Russ, July 22, 1897; s. David and Bracha (Greenberg) Malamud; in US since 1921; att: Yeshiva of Odessa, 1912-17; Inst of Commerce, Kiev, 1920; LLB, U of Detroit, 1926; m. Esther Bookstein, Aug 27, 1927; c: Barbara Linden, Renah Bardenstein. Pres: La Med Inves, since 1952; Mich Furniture Co, 1927-54. Prins contbrs: Found: La Med Chair for J Studies, Wayne State U, Detroit: La Med Annual Awards for outstanding Master's Theses on J subjects, Natl Found for J Culture, NY, since 1960; Louis La Med Found for Advancement of Heb and Yiddish lit, 1939; La Med Prof, Wayne U, 1954. Trustee, Natl Found for J Culture; vice-pres, J Comty Cen, since 1962, fmr chmn, culture commn, 1953; chmn: educ div, JWF; bd, Midrasha Coll of J Studies; all Detroit; pres, LA Assn for J Educ, 1946-48; mem bd, natl bd of license, Natl J Book Council, 1952; mem: Bur of J Educ, LA, Cal; LZOA. Home: 19420 Silvercres, Southfield, Mich. Office: 19981 James Cousens, Detroit, Mich.

LAMM, Hans, Ger, organization exec, social worker; b. Munich, Ger, June 8, 1913; s. Ignaz and Martha (Pinczower); att: U Munich, 1932-33; Coll J Studies, Berlin, 1937-38; BA, U Kan City, 1940, MA, 1942; MSW, Wash U, 1942; PhD, Erlangen U, 1951. Dir dept,Volkshochschule, Munich since 1961; found, lit dir, Ner-Tamid Verlag, Frankfurt/M since 1957; dir research, JWF and J Cmty Council, Kan City, 1942-43; asst to dir, AJ Conf, 1945-46; court interpreter, Intl Mil Tribunal, US Court of Restitution Appeals, Nürenberg, 1946-52; dir: research, PR, Wfr Council, Cmty Chest, Scranton, Pa, 1953-54; off of hist info, Amer J Hist Soc and Amer J Tercentenary, NYC, 1954-55; cultural activities, Cen Assn of J Cmtys in Ger, 1955-61. Author of books and articles on topics. Recipient, Joseph E Drexel Prize for Journalism, 1967. Office: Emil Riedel St 8, Munich, Ger.

LAMM, Joseph Michael, Isr, jurist; b. Wigdorowka, Galicia, Dec 1, 1899; s. Simon and Sara (Naglerg; in Isr since 1939; D ur, U Vienna, 1924; m. Emmy Spielberg, Dec 16, 1928. Relieving pres, Tel Aviv Dist Court, since 1965, fmr judge; fmr: atty, in pvt practice: Aus, 1932-38; Tel Aviv, 1941-42; public prosecutor, 1942-48; legal adv, Price Control Off, 1942-48; magistrate, Tel Aviv, 1949; mem, first Knesset, 1949-51. Chmn: Supr Appeal Bd in matters of employment; Public Auth of Trans Communication; vice-pres, Supr lodge, B'nai B'rith, Wash, since 1965, vice chmn, 1962-65; fmr: pres, B'nai B'rith of Isr, 1961-63; grand master, Free Masons, 1963-65; delg to Zionist Convs before establishment of Isr; fmr mem: exec, Histadrut; Mapai Cen; Assefat Hanicharim; Va'ad Leumi; presidium, settler's Org from Cen Eur. Contbr to periodicals; perm columnist, Haaretz daily. Hobby: tennis. Home: 75 Jabotinsky St, Tel Aviv, Isr. Office: Dist Court, Tel Aviv, Isr.

LAMM, Maurice, US, rabbi, author; b. Bx, NY, Mar 20, 1930; s. Samuel and Pearl (Baumol); BA, Yeshiva U, 1951; ordained Rabbi, Rietz, 1953; PhD studies, Bernard Revel Grad Sch, 1963; m. Shirley Friedman, July 6, 1955; c: David, Judith, Dodi. Rabbi, Heb Inst, U Hgts since 1964; dean, Akiba Heb Acad; dir, Brenner Commn, J Chaplaincy, JWB; rabbi, Floral Park J Cen, 1957-63. Chaplain, US Army, 1954-56. Chmn, chaplain, RabCA; vice-pres: Yeshiva U Rabb Alumni; Natl Rabb ORT, Cong I Commn of Rabbis, 1958-68. Author: The Jewish Way in Death and Mourning, 1968; contbr to jours. Recipient: Dist Service Award, US Army, 1954-56. Home: 1889 Sedgewick Ave, Bronx, NY. Study: 1835 University Ave, Bronx, NY.

LAMM, Norman, US, rabbi; b. Bklyn, NY, Dec 19, 1927; s. Samuel and Pearl (Baumol); BA, summa cum laude, Yeshiva Coll, 1949; ordained rabbi, Rabbi Isaac Elchanan Theol Sem, 1951; m. Mindella Mehler, Feb 23, 1954; c: Chaye, Joshua, Shalom, Sara. Rabbi, The J Cen, since 1958; Erna Michael Prof, J phil, Yeshiva U; asst rabbi, Cong Kehillath Jeshurun, 1952-53; rabbi, Cong Kodimoh, Springfield, 1954-58. Bd govs, Assn Orthodox J Sci; Halakhah commn, RabCA; overseas commn, Union Orthodox J Congs Amer; chmn, NY Conf Soviet Jewry. Ed, Tradition: A Journal of Orthodox Jewish Thought, since 1957; author: A Hedge of Roses, 1966; The Royal Reach, 1969; co-ed: Hadarom, 1957-60; The Leo

Jung Jubilee Vol, 1962; A Treasury of Tradition, 1967; contbr to Heb and Eng jours. Home: 27 W 86 St, New York, NY. Study: 131 W 86 St, New York, NY.

LAMM, Shmuel, Isr, artist; b. Brody, Aust-Hung, Nov 28, 1905; in Isr since 1933; att Fine Arts Acad; m. Pnina Cohen. Painter: Isr landscapes; Isr poets, writers, other personalities; prin works: Israel Landscapes and Types, 1930; Woman Reading Bible, 1942; Corn Vendor, 1943; Children Chatting, 1944; Tired Violinist, 1945; Flute Player, 1950; Street Musician, 1952; Begel Vendor, 1955; Accordionist, 1956; Motherhood, 1957-67; Mother and Child; Hayarkon; shows: Technion, Haifa; Tel Aviv, Haifa, Mus, Art Gals; NY; Paris; semi jubilee exhib, Chagal House, Haifa; participant in intl exhbs, US, Fr; works in local and fgn pvt collections. Publ, Album of Paintings; contbr of articles and paintings to various local, fgn newspapers, books, jours, mags. Home: 32 Hashiloach St, Haifa, Isr.

LANCET, Aviva Müller, Isr, curator; b. Targo Mures, Rum, Dec 27, 1921; d. Josef and Ida (Kahana); in Isr since 1935; att: Heb U, Jerusalem; licencié es lettres, Sorbonne, Paris, 1954; m. Maximillian Müller, 1963; c: Shay. Asst curator, Dept of Ethnology, Isr Mus, Jerusalem, since 1965; curator, art dir, Mus of Folklore and Ethnology, Haifa, 1957-62. Cultural off, IDF, 1948-49. Prin contribs: ethnology of J in Yemen, Bokhara and other Islamic countries; specializes in problems of custome, embroidery, jewellery. Mem, U Women Assn. Contbr to jours and mus catalogues. Home: 60 Ben Maimon Blvd, Jerusalem, Isr. Office: Isr Mus, Jerusalem, Isr.

LANCET, Moshe, Isr, obstetrician; b. Târgul Mures, Rum, May 1, 1923; s. Joseph and Ida (Kahane); in Isr since 1925; BA, Amer U, Beirut, Leb, 1946; MD, U of Geneva, Switz, 1949; m. Shifra Ginsburg, July 9, 1946; c: Doron, Nava. Head Dept Obstet Gyn, Kaplan Hosp, Rehovot, since 1967; mem fac, Postgrad Sch of Med, Tel Aviv, U, since 1969; Maj, IDF, MC, since 1948. Author, The Birth, 1968; contbr to med jours in Isr, US, Eng. Mem: Isr, and Intl fertility assns; Isr, and Intl Feds of Obstet, Gyn. Recipient: Haganah, Independance War and Sinai Stars. Hobbies: fishing, photography. Home: 15 Weizmann St, Rehovot, Isr.

LANDA, Samuel, US, rabbi; b. Rowne, Pol, June 9, 1920; s. Hirsh and Sarah (Malowicki); in US since 1925; BA, Yeshiva Coll, 1944; ordained rabbi, Rabbi Isaac Elchanan Theol Sem, 1945; m. Hannah Delan, Feb 27, 1944; c: Janet, Saul, Philip, Seth. Rabbi, Ozone Park J Cen since 1945; chaplain: Boothe Memorial Hosp, Flushing, NY 1962-63; St Johns Episcopal Hosp; St Catherine's Hosp; Queens House of Detention for Men, all since 1963. Pres, prin council Talmud Torah Council of Queens since 1963, vice-pres, 1961-63; chmn: syn standards comm, RabCA since 1962, mem comm, 1960-62, mem, exec comm, 1957-60 and since 1961, secy, 1968-70; vice-pres, Vaad Harabonim of Queens, 1959-61; mem: NY Bd Rabbis; Yeshiva U Rabb Alumni; Rel ZOA. Home: 107-17 89 St, Ozone Park, NY. Study: 107-01 Cross Bay Blvd, Ozone Park, NY.

LANDAU, Charles Akiva, Isr, agricultural economist; b. Mar 26, 1920; s. Herman and Lea (Fellner); in Isr sine 1951; att Ruppin Agric Inst, 1959-61; m. Hanne Bernhard-Rath, Nov 7, 1948; c: Yehezkel, Shalvit. Dir, dept overall planning, Min of Agric, since 1964, with min since 1961; fmr: econ dir, Kibbutz Lavee 1952-59. Pvt, civil defense res, IDF. Trustee, Bachad f, London, Eng; vice-chmn, jt bd, Promotion of Export of Processed Food; mem: profsl directorate, council, Min of Agric; Food Comm; directorate, Agric Planning Cen, Isr; investigating comm, sugar beet ind; jt comm for promotion and produc of processed vegetables from Isr; exec, Eggs and Poultry Produc Marketing Bd; produc quota comm, Min of Agric; fmr: dir, Tnuva Agric Marketing Co; warden, Ramat Chen Syn; mem: Regional Council, Lower Galilee; exec: Mizrachi; Hapoel Hamizrachi; inter-dept comm for: forecasting water demand in Isr; promotion and planning of wine export. Author: Five Year Plan for Israel Agriculture, 1966-67, 1970-71, pub 1966; co-author for 1964-65, 1968-69, pub 1964; contbr papers and booklets on agric subjects. Hobby: pho graphy. Home: 31 Raziel St, Ramat Chen, Isr. Office: Hakiryah, Tel Aviv, Isr.

LANDAU, Jacob, US, educator, artist; b. Phila, Pa, Dec 17, 1917; s. Samuel and Deana (Kitaynick); att: Phila Coll of Art, Phila, 1935-38; New Sch, NY, 1948-49, 1952-53; Ácad de la Grande Chaumière, Paris, Fr, 1950-52; m. Frances Paul; c: Stephen, Jonas. Prof of graphic art, Pratt Inst, NY,

since 1968, on fac since 1957. One-man shows: Gal LeBar, Paris, Fr, 1952; Art Alliance, Phila, Pa, 1954; Art Cen, New Brunswick, NJ, 1957; Samuel Fleischer Memorial Gal, Phila, Pa, 1959; Asso Amer Artists Gal, NYC, 1960; U of Me, Orono, Me, 1961; Cober Gal, NYC, 1961, 63; Zora Gal, LA, Cal, 1964; Original Prints Gal, SF, Cal, 1965; Gal 100, Princeton, NJ; Bosshart Art Gal, Glassboro State Coll, NJ; Manhattanville Coll, NY, all 1966; Earlham Coll, Richmond, Ind; St Andrews Presbyterian Coll, Laurinburg, NC; Calapai Workshop, Glencoe, Ill; Inst Gen Elec, Montevideo, Uruguay, all 1967; Other Gal, Phila, Pa, 1968; Bertha Eccles Art Cen, Ogden, Utah; Art Gal, U of Notre Dame, Ind, both 1969; numerous natl, intl group shows, 1953-69; represented in collections: Mus Modern Art; Metrop Mus, both NY; Pa Acad Fine Arts, Phila; art mus: Phila; Bklyn; Norfolk; Montclair; San Antonio; Norwich, Conn; Newark; Trenton; Malmo, Swed; Nüremberg, Ger; Us: Princeton; Rutgers; Me; Minn; Syracuse; Yale; Ky; Berkeley; Libr Cong, Wash, DC; numerous pvt; illus: for advt, promotion; books; numerous lectures, symposia. Cons, educ prog devl, NJ State Mus, Trenton, NJ; mem, Graphic Arts Panel, NJ State Council on Arts. Recipient: Guggenheim Memorial F; Purchase Prize, Bradley Print Show, Bradley U & Art Guild, Lakeview Cen, Peoria, Ill; Purchase Award, Drawings USA, St Paul Art Cen, Minn; Purchase Award, Fifth Dulin Print & Drawing Competition, Knoxville, Tenn; numerous design awards, 1959-68. Home: 2 Pine Dr, Roosevelt, NJ. Office: Pratt Institute, Brooklyn, NY.

LANDAU, Jacob, Isr, political sci; b. Chrisinau, Rum, Mar 20, 1924; s. Michael and Miriam (Abeles); in Isr since 1935; MA, Heb U, Jerusalem, 1946; PhD, Sch of Oriental and Afr Studies, London U, 1949; m. Zipora Marcus, July 29, 1947; c: Ronnit, Iddo. Asso prof: Oriental studies, political sys, Heb U, since 1968; Arabic, Bar Ilan U; visiting lectr, Near E Studies, Brandeis U, Waltham, Mass; lectr, modern ME, Tel Aviv U; visiting prof: UCLA; Wayne State U; Columbia U. Author: Parliaments and Parties in Egypt, 1953; Studies in the Arab Theatre and Cinema, 1958; A World Count of Modern Arabic Prose, 1959; The Teaching of Arabic as a Foreign Language, 1961; The Israeli Communist Party and The Elections to the Fifth Knesset, 1961, pub 1965; A History of Arabic Literature, 1968; Egyptian Jews in the 19th Century, 1968; The Arabs in Israel: A Political Study, 1969; The Jews in Nineteenth Century Egypt, 1969; co-ed: Hamizrach Hachadash, quarterly, Jerusalem, 1956-61; contbr to: jours on political sci, Oriental studies; various encys. Home: 5 Mishael St, Jerusalem, Isr. Office: Hebrew U, Jerusalem, Isr.

LANDAU, Joseph, Eng, business exec; b. Sunderland, Eng, Aug 30, 1918; s. Simon and Fanny (Cohen); att Durham U, 1936-38; m. Evelyn Allberry, Feb 24, 1942; c: Ian, Barbara, Peter, Patricia. Chmn, mgn dir, F Clark Ltd since 1960. Maj, Royal Artillery, 1939-46. Councillor, Sunderland Co Borough Council; secy, Sunderland JPA Comm, 1963-66; comm mem, N East J Golfing Soc; mem: Inst of Dirs; clubs: Sunderland J Badminton, hon vice pres; Sunderland Carlton. Contbr: numerous articles to elec trade jours. Spec interest: golf, politics, wfr work with aged. Home: 201 Queen Alexandra Rd, Sunderland, Eng. Office: Olive St, Sunderland, Eng.

LANDAU, Lazare, FR, educator; b. Strasbourg, Aug 1, 1928; s. Abraham and Lea (Herbst); desc of Ezechiel Landau, Noda Be-Yehuda, Rabbi of Prague, 1752-93; licence es lettres, U Strasbourg, 1950, dipl d'Etudes Supérieures, 1951; m. Judith Calitchi, Dec 4, 1960; c: Lea, Bath-Sheba, Ziporah, Abraham. Tchr, Lycée de Strasbourg-Neudorf since 1960; fmr: tchr: Ecole Normale de la Méuse, 1956-57; Lycée de Colmar, 1957-60. Fr Army. Pres, Conseil d'Orientation; mem: Consistoire Israelite; cultural comm, Communauté Israelite, all Strasbourg; trustee of records of Jules Isaac since 1963; mem: bd dirs, Jeunesse Juive de l'Est, ed of its jours; Hevrah; Soc de Profs de Hist de Fr. Author of numerous papers on antisemitism; ed-in-chief, Unir, monthly of J Cmty of Strasbourg, since 1958; contbr to publs. Spec interest, hist of rels. Home: 15 rue de la Brigade Alsace-Lorraine, Strasbourg, Fr. Office: 2 Place Albert-Schweitzer, Strasbourg, Fr.

LANDAU, LeRoy, US, insurance counselor, real estate broker; b. Wilkes-Barre, Pa, Dec 3, 1909; s. Samuel and Sara (Michlosky); BS, U of Va, 1933, LLB, 1934; m. Malka Mittelman, Nov 25, 1937; c: Faye, Susan. With firm, Landau & Landau, insurance and real estate brokers; fac mem, real estate courses, Wilkes Coll, 1950-52; secy and vice-pres, Susquehanna Savings & Loan Assn. Secy, Temple Isr Syn since 1949; mem: B'nai B'rith, lodge pres, 1942-44; speakers' bur, ZOA, pres, 1947-51;

bldg comm, J Comty Cen; budget comm, United Fund; chmn, pres, JCC, 1951-53; asst treas, Wyoming Valley J Comm, pres, 1951-53, all in Wilkes-Barre, Pa; club, Rotary; Exch, pres, 1949-51. Hobbies: cameras, travel. Home: 220 Wright Ave, Kingston, Pa. Office: 195 Market St, Kingston, Pa.

LANDAU, Michael, Isr, attorney; b. Harlau, Rum, Jan 1895; s. Menahem and Feiga; in Isr since 1935; DJur, U Jassy, 1921; m. Miriam Abeles; c: Jacob. Chmn, Isr State Lottery, since 1951; fmr: pvt practice, Rum, 1921-25; secy gen, Fed of Rum, J, 1925-35; MP, Rum, 1928-33; secy gen, Emergency and Rescue Fund, 1938-49; exec dir, Natl Loan Fund, 1949; with Min of Finance, 1948-57. Mem, exec comm, Lib Party; delg to WCZ's since 1921; chmn, exec comm, Habimah Theatre; mem: exec, Tel Aviv Mus; presidium, UA, Isr; exec comm, WJC; chmn: Intl org of State Lotteries; Heb Writers Fund, 1969. Author: The Schwarzbard Trial, 1927; ed: Der Id, Unser Zeit, 1920-34; Erd und Arbeit Kishinev, 1921-24; contbr: on Compulsory Loan Law, 1952, research work on Natl Movement Rum J, A Manual of Lotteries, 1968; to local and fgn press; fmr corresp, Morgan Jour, NY. Home: 44 Chen Blvd, Tel Aviv, Isr. Office: 3 Heftman St, Tel Aviv, Isr.

LANDAU, Moses M, US, rabbi, educator; b. Aus, July 1, 1907; s. Joshua and Anne; in US since 1938; PhD, U Vienna, 1932; Rabbi, Israelitische Theologische Lehranstalt, Vienna, 1935; m. Frances Stern, 1941; c: Joshua, Ann. Rabbi: Adath Isr Cong since 1958; prof, Ger, world lit, Delta State Coll; rabbi: Temple Judea, Chgo, 1941-46; Mt Sinai Cong, Texarkana, 1946-50; Temple Beth David, Cal, 1950-54; Moses Montefiore Cong, Bloomington, Ill, 1954-57. Mem: CCAR; Miss Educ Soc; club, Rotary. Author of works in Heb lang. Home: 1308 College, Cleveland, Miss. Study: 201 Bolivar, Cleveland, Miss.

LANDAU, Moshe, Isr, jurist; b. Danzig, Ger, 1912; s. Isaac and Betty; in Isr since 1933; LLB, London U, 1933; m. Lea Douhkan, 1937; c: Ada, Shlomit, Tamar. Justice, Supr Court, Jerusalem, since 1953; pvt law practice, 1933-40; magistrate, Haifa, 1940-53; judge, Dist Court, Haifa, 1948-53; presiding judge, Eichmann trial, 1961. Vice-chmn, bd of govs, Technion, Haifa. Home: 10 Alharizi St, Jerusalem, Isr. Office: Supr Court, Jerusalem, Isr.

LANDAU, Sol, US, rabbi; b. Berlin, Ger, June 21, 1920; s. Ezekiel and Helene (Grynberg); in US since 1940; BA, Bklyn Coll; MA, NYU, 1955; MHL, ordained rabbi, JTSA, 1951; m. Gabriela, Jan 14, 1951; c: Ezra, Tamara. Rabbi, Beth David Cong, Miami, Fla since 1965; Whitestone Heb Cen, 1952-56; Beth Hillel, Wilmette, Ill, 1960-63; co-rabbi, Park Syn, Cleveland, O, 1956-60, 1963-65. Chmn, Metro Youth Adv Bd, Miami; vice-pres, SE Region RA; secy, Gtr Miami Ra, exec RA, 1965-68; bd govs, Natl Acad Adult J Educ; vice-chmn, S. Dade Mh Assn; Miami repr, Dade Co Comty Relations Bd; mem: ZOA; JWV; AAUP. Author: Bridging Two Worlds, 1968; Length of Our Days, 1961; Christian-Jewish Relations. Hobbies: music, art, drama. Home: 5195 W 25 Rd, Miami, Fla. Study: 2625 W Third Ave, Miami, Fla.

LANDAUER, Carl, US, educator, author; b. Munich, Ger, Oct 15, 1891; s. Abraham and Elsbeth (Feuchtwanger); in US since 1933; PhD, Heidelberg U, Ger, 1915; hon LLD, U of Cal, 1962; DHC, U Hamburg, 1966; m. Hilde Stein, Feb 16, 1916; c: Ilse (decd), Gerti Brunner, Walter, Ernest. Prof em, econ, U of Cal since 1959, mem of fac since 1934; research asst: Inst of Intl Econs, Kiel, Ger, 1915-16; Ger War Food Admn, 1916-19; staff mem, State Commissariat, S Bavaria, 1919-22; ed work, Muenchener Post, 1922-26; mgn ed, The German Economist, 1926-33; lectr, Sch of Bus Admin, Berlin, 1926-29, asso prof, 1929-33, visiting prof, Free U of Berlin, 1949-50; U Hamburg, 1962-63, 1966-67. Mem: Amer Econ Assn; Amer Hist Assn; Assn for Comparative Econs; ADA; Amer Assn for UN; Amer Council on Ger; ACLU; AAUP; JWF, Oakland; Selfhelp of Emigres from Cen Eur; Sierra Club. Author: Grundprobleme der funktionellen Verteilung des wirtschaftlichen Wertes, 1923; Das Wesen der Wirtschaft, 1928; Theory of Natl Economic Planning, 1944, 1947; European Socialism, 1960; Contemporary Economic Systems, 1964; German: Illusions and Dilemnas, 1969; contrib to symposium, The Amer Way, how it looks to an emigre from Ger (Harpers' prize essay, 1938); contbr to profsl jours. Recipient, Fulbright award, to teach at U of Frankfurt and Hamburg, 1959-60. Home: 1317 Arch St, Berkeley, Cal. Office: 119 S Hall, U of Cal, Berkeley, Cal.

LANDE, Adolph, Switz, attorney, UN official; b. Vienna, Aus, June 24, 1905; s. Isser and Adele (Halpern); in Switz since 1955; LLD, U, Vienna, 1929; BS, libr service, Columbia U, 1942, grad in intl law, 1945; m. Frances Lustmann, Jan 3, 1936; research asso, Columbia U since 1967; in pvt law practice, 1929-38; govt official, US OWI, 1942-44; chief, research unit, US State Dept Info Service, libr, 1944-47; chief of sect, div of narcotic drugs, UN, Geneva, 1952-63; secy dir, perm Cen Narcotics Bd of UN, 1963-67; social affairs off, 1947-52; legal adv, UN conf, opium producing and drug mfg countries, 1950, in charge of codification of treaty law on narcotic drugs, 1948-61; dep exec secy, plenipotentiary conf for the adoption of a single convention on narcotic drugs, 1961; legal adv, Intl Atomic Energy Agcy, 1957. Co-pres, Intl Lawyers Club, Geneva, 1959-62; mem, Amer Assn of Intl Law. Co-author: International Organization, 1955. Contbr of: articles to profsl jours; monographs. Home: 441 E 20 St, New York, NY.

LANDE, Lawrence Montague, Can, writer, composer; b. Ottawa, Can, Nov 11, 1906; s. Nathan and Rachel (Freiman); BA, McGill U, 1928; LLB, U Montreal, 1931; dipl, U Grenoble, Fr; Des Lettres, HC, McGill U, 1969; m. Helen Prentis, June 14, 1939; c: Denise Farber, Nelson. Author: Psalms, Intimate and Familiar, 1945; Toward the Quiet Mind, 1954; The Third Duke of Richmond, 1956; Old Lamps Aglow, 1957; Experience, 1963; pub: The Lawrence Lande Collection of Canadiana, 1965; Beethoven and Quebec, 1966; Check List of Confederation Pamphlets, 1967; Check List of Canadian Broadsides and Ephemera before Confederation, 1968; Check List of Early Publications Relating to Public Health in Canada, 1969; composed, 21 original compositions for piano, played and arranged by Karl du Plessis. Prin contribs: found Beethoven Manuscript; sponsor: Can Studies, Upsala U, Swed; Early Can Lit Studies, McGill Found; established Centennial F in Can Hist for post grad students at McGill U and U Montreal. Chmn, pres, J Hist Soc of Can, Can, 1968; dir: Can Writer's Found; Montreal Friends Heb U, past pres; gov, Montreal Children's Hosp; pres, Intl PEN, Can Cen; hon corresp mem for Que, Royal Soc of Arts, London, Eng, 1968; mem: St James Lit Soc; Sigma Alpha Mus; British Soc Aesthetics; clubs: Montefiore; Elm Country; Beaver, Montreal. Recipient: Service Medal, Order of Can, 1967; Centennial Medal, 1968. Hobbies: travel, music. Home: 4870 Crescent, Montreal, Can.

LANDER-ELAD, Pinhas Aharon, Isr, author; b. Ropczyce, Pol, Oct 13, 1905; s. Naphtali and Rachel (Goldman); att tchr sem; m. Warda Kunica; c: Osnath, Naphtali. Author: K'reakh Sade; Misrakh Shemesh; Al Eretz Zu; Paamonim; poetry, Shadmoth-Moledeth. Trans from Ger, Eng, Pol, Yiddish. Mem: Heb Writers Assn, Journalists Assn, ACUM. Home: 182 Ibn Gavirol St, Tel Aviv, Isr.

LANDERS, Ann, US, newspaper columnist; b. Sioux City, Ia, July 4, 1918; d. Abraham and Rebecca (Rushall) Friedman; att Morningside Coll, 1936-39; m. Jules Lederer, July 2, 1939; c: Margo Coleman. Syndicated columnist since 1955. Appd mem, AMA Adv Comm, 1968; chmn: Wis-Minn, ADL, 1945-49; League of Women Voters, Eau Claire, Wis, 1952; co chmn, Eau Claire Dem Party, 1951; life mem: Brandeis U; Hadassah; mem: JWV Auxiliary, Chgo. Author: Since You Ask Me, 1961; Teenagers and Sex, 1963; Truth is Stranger, 1968. Recipient: Natl Epilepsy Award, 1960; Best Dressed Award, Natl Fashion Soc, 1960; Best Coiffed Woman Award, Helene Curtis, 1960; Woman of the Year, JWV, 1961; Communicator of the Year Award, CJA, 1962; Adolf Meyer Award, Assn Advancement of Mh, 1963; important woman in US, Award, UPI Poll, 1967; Golden Plate Award, Acad of Achievement, 1969. Office: Chgo Sun-Times, Chicago, Ill.

LANDES, Aaron, US, rabbi; b. Chelsea, Mass, Oct 1, 1929; s. Henry and Bessie (Nyman); BA, summa cum laude, Yeshiva Coll, 1951; ordained rabbi, MHL, JTSA, 1955; m. Sora Eisenberg, 1953; c: Rena, Rebecca, Joshua, Tamar. Rabbi: Beth Shalom Cong, Elkins Park, Pa, since 1964; J Cen, Erie, Pa, 1957-64; J Chaplain, VA Hosp, Erie, 1961-64. Cdr, Chaplains Corps, US Naval Ready Res Off, Chaplain Co 4-1; dist chap, USN, 1955-57. Vice-pres, Family and Child Service; chmn, educ comm, Erie Comty Relations Commn; co-chmn, Clergy Sem on Mh, Erie; mem bd: Erie Hum Relations Commn; div of aging, Citizens and Agcys Comms; Wfr Council of Erie Co; Crippled Childrens Soc, Inc; Health and TB Assn; Civic Music Assn; J Comty Wfr Council; mem: Natl Rabb Cabinet, leader's training F, RA; Wash Trail

Council; Boy Scouts of Amer; Aces; Tri-State Zionist Region. Recipient: Young Man of the Year Award, Jr C of C, Erie; Solomon Schechter Award, 1963. Hobbies: swimming, walking. Home: 8372 Fisher Rd, Elkins Park, Pa. Study: 3207 State St, Erie, Pa.

LANDES, Bernard A, US, speech path; US; b. Chgo, Ill, Oct 3, 1929; s. Joseph and Anne (Breskow); BS, Purdue U, 1951, Ms, 1953; PhD, U Mich, 1957; m. Geraldine Steinberg, Jan 30, 1954; c: Sharon, Jo. Asso prof, speech path and audiology, Cal State Coll since 1961; asst prof, speech, psych, Tex Tech Coll, 1957-61. Pres, J Family Service of Long Beach; bd dirs: J Comty Fed of Long Beach; Comty Wfr Council of Long Beach, 1963-66; mem: Amer Speech and Hearing Assn; Acoustical Soc Amer; Amer Cong Rehab Med; Amer Cleft Palate Assn; Amer Inst Physics; Intl Assn Logopedics and Phoniatrics; Cal Speech and Hearing Assn; Sigma Delta Chi; Alpha Phi Omega; Phi Kappa Phi; Alpha Psi Omega; Sigma Alpha Mu. Contbr to profsl jours. Home: 3320 Julian Ave, Long Beach, Cal. Office: 6101 E 7th St, Long Beach, Cal.

LANDES, Morris A, US, rabbi; b. Russ, Oct 28, 1917; s. Henry and Bessie (Nyman); BA, magna cum laude, Yeshiva Coll, 1939; ordained rabbi, Rabbi Isaac Elchanan Theol Sem, 1941; att: Harvard U, 1942-43; Dropsie Coll, 1946-48; PhD, U Pittsburgh, 1954; m. Naomi Borkon, Mar 4, 1945; c: Nina, Sharon, Marc. Rabbi: Cong Adath Jeshurun, Pittsburgh, since 1948; Lynn, Mass, 1941-43; Johnstown, Pa, 1943-45; Lancaster, Pa, 1945-48. Natl vice-pres, ZOA, 1955-66, pres: Tri State Zionist region, 1961-63, Pittsburgh ZC, 1959-63 and since 1969; W Pa Zionist region, 1954-56; Pittsburgh Zionist dist, 1958-60; Gtr Pittsburgh Rabb F, since 1969; co-chmn, Pittsburgh chap, Rel and Race, 1965-67; mem, natl admn comm, AJCong, 1952, pres, Pittsburgh br, 1950-52; chmn, Pittsburgh Syn Council for Isr Bonds, since 1965; mem: B'nai B'rith; Yeshiva Coll Alumni; Yeshiva U Rabb Alumni; natl exec, RabCA, 1956-58. Author: Trends in Amer J Thought, 1954. Book rev ed, Horizon, 1953-55. Delivered Invocation, US Sen, on Isr Independence Day, 1968. Recipient, Man of the Year award: Pittsburgh Isr Bonds, 1961; Tri-State Zionist Region, 1963. Home: 5520 Wellesley Ave, Pittsburgh, Pa. Study: Cong Adath Jeshurun, Margaretta and N St Clair Sts, Pittsburgh, Pa.

LANDESMAN, Alter F, US, rabbi, organization exec; b. Lith, Dec 5, 1895; s. Levi and Zelatta (Schmuelson); in US since 1906; BA, W Reserve U, 1917; MA, Columbia Tchrs Coll, 1918; ordained rabbi, JTSA, 1922, DHL, 1948, DD, 1953. Ret; exec dir, Heb Educ Soc of Bklyn, 1922-61. Chmn: educ comm, United Syn of Amer, 1929-45; jt commn on J educ, United Syn and RA, 1945-47; pres: Metrop Assn J Cen Workers, 1942; Brownsville Neighborhood Health and Wfr Council, 1938-41, 1954; Brownsville Zionist Dist, 1929; vice pres, Natl Assn J Cen Workers; corresp secy, RA, 1927-30, mem, exec comm, 1926-34; treas, J Book Council; mem: exec comm, Natl Assn J Educ; bd of license, J Educ comm, NY, since 1929. Author: Curriculum for Jewish Religious Schools, United Synagogue of America, 1922; Brownsville: Birth, Development and Passing of a Jewish Community in New York, 1969. Recipient: first annual award for dist achievement in J social work, jt commn on syn relations, NY, 1959. Study: 1608 E 94 St, Brooklyn, NY.

LANDMAN, Leo, US, rabbi; b. Vienna, Aus, July 9, 1928; s. Bernard and Shirley (Schrenzel); BA, Yeshiva U, ordained rabbi; PhD, Dropsie Coll, 1964; m. Shirley Yurfest, Oct 15, 1950; c: Dina, Chana, David. Rabbi, Beth Emeth Cong since 1957; asst prof, Rabb, Dropsie Coll since 1965, fac mem since 1964; rabbi, Beth David Cong, 1952-57. Pres: Phila Bd Rabbis; RabCA, Phila region; vice-pres, Rabb Alumni of Yeshiva U; bd dirs: Neighborhood Cen, JYC; Health and Wfr Council, Phila; Mayor's Comm on Urban Affairs; Chaplaincy Commn; Shaarei Zedek Hosp, Jerusalem; adv commn, Talmudical Yeshiva of Phila; mem, Hapoel Hamizrachi. Author, Jewish Law in the Diaspora, 1968; contbr to rabb jours. Home: Bustleton Ave, Philadelphia, Pa. Study: 6652 Eastwood St, Philadelphia, Pa.

LANDMAN, Nathan Marx, US, rabbi; b. Madison, Wis, June 17, 1929; s. Solomon and Dorothy (Marx); BA, phil, U of Wis, 1950; BHL, MHL, HUC-JIR, Cincinnati, 1956; att Heb U, Jerusalem, 1953; MA, Eng, Trinity U, San Antonio, Tex, 1970; m. Georgina Swarz, June 1, 1957; c: Nathaniel. J chaplain, USAF since 1963; J Cadet Cen chaplain, USAF Acad, Colo since 1968; rabbi, Temple Sholom, W Covina, Cal, 1958-59; chaplain, VA, Sepulveda, Cal, 1959-63; rabbi,

Temple Beth Torah, Pacoima, Cal, 1960-62; asst rabbi, Westwood Temple, LA, 1962-63. Vice-pres, Assn J Chaplains; fmr, pres, W Covina Min Assn; mem: CCAR; J Reconstructionist Found; Mil Chaplains Assn. Contbr to J jours. Hobby, lit. Home: Quarters, 4206 I, USAF Acad, Colo. Study: USAF Acad, Colo.

LANDMANN, Heinz R, US, physician; b. Bad-Duerkheim, Ger, Jan 15, 1908; s. Simon and Emilie (Mayer); in US since 1935; MD, Sch of Med, Frankfurt/M, 1932; DMS, U Berne, Switz, 1934; m. Gertrude Stein (div); m. 2nd, Theodora Way; c: Robert. Att phys, St Vincent Hosp, Santa Fe, since 1950; cons phys: Embudo Presbyterian Hosp, since 1960; St Anthony Hosp, Las Vegas, NM; Las Vegas Hosp; Espanola Hosp; Los Alamos Med Cen, all since 1950; asst phys, U Hosp, Berne, Switz, 1933-35; staff phys: Mt Sinai Hosp; Hosp for Jt Diseases; St Elizabeth Hosp, all NYC, 1935-47; teaching staff, Meninger Sch Psycht, Topeka, Kan, 1947-50; guest lectr, Universidad de Antioquia, Medellin, Colombia, 1954; chmn, profsl adv comm, NM Soc of Mh, 1956-57. Lt col, US Army, WW II. F: Amer Coll Phys; NY Acad Sci; dipl: Amer Bd Internal Med; Pan Amer Med Assn; bd dirs, Santa Fe Opera; mem: NM Soc Internal Med, pres, 1960-61; Intl Soc Internal Med; Masons; Kiwanis. Contbr to Amer, Eur, Latin Amer med jours. Home: Camino Rancheros, Santa Fe, NM. Office: 227 E Palace Ave, Santa Fe, NM.

LANDMANN, Michael M, Ger, educator, author; b. Basle, Switz, Dec 16, 1913; s. Julius and Edith (Kalischer); desc of Rabbi Hirsch Zvi Kalischer; DPhil, U Basle, 1939; m. Salcia Passweg, Aug 16, 1939; c: Valentin. Prof phil, Free U, Berlin, since 1951; U asst, Switz, 1945-51. Author: Problematik, 1949; Elenktik und Maieutik, 1950; Das Tier in der jüdischen Weisung, 1959; Philosophische Anthropologie; Das Zeitalter als Schicksal, 1956; Der Mensch als Schöpfer und Geschöpf der Kultur, 1961; De homine, 1962; Pluralität und Antinomie, 1963; Zum platonisch-biblischen Gespräch, 1966; ed, Buch des Dankes an Georg Simmel, 1958. Chmn: Friends of Heb U, Berlin, since 1957; Kantgesellschaft, Berlin, since 1959; Philosophische Gesellschaft, Basel, 1946-50; mem, B'nai B'rith. Home: Vogelsang 5, Berlin-Dahlem, W Ger. Office: Freie Universitat, Berlin, W Ger.

LANDMANN, Salcia, Switz, author; b. Zólkiew, Pol, Nov 18, 1911; d. Israel and Regina (Gottesmann) Passweg; in Switz since 1919; D Phil, U Basel; m. Michael Landmann, Aug 16, 1939; c: Valentin. Author: Phaenomenologie und Ontologie, 1939; Der Jüdischer Witz, 1960; Iiddisch, abenteur einer Sprache, 1962; Gepfeffert und gesalzen, J anecdotes and proverbs, 1965; 3000 Jahre jüdische Weisheit, 1967; Die Juden als Rasse, 1967; West-Östlicher Divan, 1968; trans from Yiddish into Ger, Doss buch fun gan eden, by Itzig Manger, 1963, annotated. Home: I Winkelriedstr, St Gallen, Switz.

LANDO, Esmond, Can, attorney; b. London, Eng, Apr 29, 1908; s. Nathan and Sarah (Scheinman); in Can since 1912; att, U of BC; LLB, U Alberta, 1928; m. Edith Mitchell, Dec 25, 1937; c: Barry, Roberta, Barbara, Julie. Q. C, 1964; vice pres, Queen Charlotte Airlines Ltd, since 1943; in law practice since 1930; pres: British Pacific Life Ins Co; Gil Interprovincial Freight Lines Inc; Perry River Timber Co, Ltd. Natl vice-pres, Can J Cong since 1948, past chmn, Pacific div; mem: ZOC; Intl Law Assn; Can Bar Assn; clubs: Can; Richmond Golf and Country, hon life pres; Vancouver Tennis; fmr: mem, bd dirs, Vancouver Comty Chest and Council; Eng Speaking Union. Home: 1499 Angus Dr, Vancouver, BC, Can, Office: 902 W Pender St, Vancouver, BC, Can.

LANDO, Zelman, Den, economist, educator; b. Warsaw, Pol, Jan 10, 1895; s. Dan and Rivkah (Ribier); in Den since 1915; MA, PhD, U Basel, Switz, 1922; m. Gudrun vel Runa Petersen, 1919. Asso prof, bus econ, Fac Fgn Trade, dir, Research Inst for Fgn Trade, since 1933; lectr, Copenhagen Sch of Bus Econ, 1923; head fac banking, dir Research Inst for Banking, 1939-50; mem, Danish agric missions to: Gt Brit; US; Can; NZ; Australia, 1938-39; visiting prof, commerce, U Coll of Commerce, Gothenburg, Swed, 1944-45; head, FOA delg to US, 1954; guest prof, Us: Ljubljana, Sarajevo, Zagreb, all Yugo, 1956. Author: Die Organisation des daenischen Buttergrosshandels, 1923; Bankpraksis, 1926; Banking and Stock Exchange, 1928, 3rd ed, 1948; Milk Marketing in Denmark, 1938; Trading With Yugoslavia, 1954; ed-in-chief, The Struggle for the Market in the USA; ed, Danish Jour of Bus Econ, 1937-41; contbr pamphlets and articles on bus econ, agric trade, marketing, banking finance, methodology. Home: Bindesbollsvej 31, Charlottenlund, Den.

LANDSBERG, Rudolf, Isr, educator, engineer; b. Breslau, Ger, Oct 31, 1900; s. Heinrich and Martha (Heilborn); in Isr since 1936; PhD Ing, Technische Hochschule, Dresden, 1924; m. Elisabeth Staub, Sep 12, 1935; c: Joram. Asso prof, mech engr, Technion, Haifa since 1952; visiting prof, Tech U, Vienna since 1969; fmr: design engr, AEG Turbinenfabrik, Berlin, 1924-28; project engr: Brown Boveri, Baden, Switz, 1929-34; Volkhart Bros, Bombay, India, 1934-36; chief engr, Tel Aviv agcy, Carrier Corp, 1936-50; prin, Ort Vocational Sch, Givatayim, 1950-52; visiting prof, Swiss Fed Inst of Tech, 1965. Mem: Intl Inst of Refrigeration, Paris since 1959; fmr, Tel Aviv comm, Assn of Architects and Engrs. Author: Energiewirtschaft im Betrieb, 1928; Selected Topics in Engineering Thermodynamics, 1961; Special Refrigeration Processes, 1961; contbr to profsl mags. Home: 48 Hatichon St, Haifa, Isr. Office: Technion, Haifa, Isr.

LANDSBERGER, Michael, Isr, economist; b. Pol, Jan 9, 1935; s. Benjamin and Eugina (Brumer); PhD, Heb U, Jerusalem, 1968; m. Nilly Schechter; c: Yael, Boaz. Visiting prof, U of Pa, since 1969; fmr: sr econ, Bank of Isr, 1962-69. Pvt, IDF, 1954-56. Author: The Consumption Function and Windfall Receipts, 1969; contbr to jours. Office: Dept of Economics, Technion, Haifa, Isr.

LANDY, Simon, US, dentist; b. NYC, June 12, 1918; s. Sam and Pauline (Dobrow); att NYU, 1936-37; BS, LIU, Bklyn, 1940; DDS, St Louis U, 1943; m. Shirley Hendler, June 9, 1957; c: Neil, Lisa. Pvt practice, Hartford, Conn since 1943. Maj, dent cons, Gen Staff, SHAEF Hqr, US Army, 1942-46. Recording secy, Lions Intl; bd dirs: Cong B'nai Shalom, Newington, Conn, bd educ; mem: Alpha Omega, Hartford Alumni chap; Amer Dent Assn; Conn State Dent Assn. Recipient, Fr Medaille de Verdun. Hobbies: art, woodcraft, writing. Home: 140 Eddy Lane, Newington, Conn. Office: 1731 Park St, Hartford, Conn.

LANE, Richard S, US, attorney, jurist; b. Boston, Mass, July 7, 1919; s. Harold and Elsie (Shelly); BA, Harvard Coll, 1941; LLB, Harvard Law Sch, 1947. Appt judge, Civil Court of NY, by Mayor John Lindsay, 1969; law secy to Charles Wyzanski, Fed Dist Court, Mass, 1947-48; asst dist atty, NY Co, 1948-50; asso with law firms: Paul, Weiss, Rifkind, Wharton & Garrison, 1950-52; Skadden, Arps & Slate, 1952-55; partner, Shadlen & Lane, 1955-61; arbitrator, small claims part, Munic Court, NYC (now Civil Court), 1956-69. USNR, 1942-46. Vice pres, legal counsel, Natl Council to Combat Blindness, Inc; mem: bd dirs, Henry Kaufmann Campgrounds; Assn Bar, City of NY; Amer Bar Assn; AJComm; lawyers div, FJP, NY; ACLU; Amer Vets Comm; Citizens Union; Borough of Manhattan Planning Bd 8, past pres, NY Young Dem Club; dem dist leader, 9th Assembly Dist, Manhattan, 1961-69, pres Lexington Dem Club, 1958-59; fmr chmn, E Side br, ADA; clubs: Harvard, NY; Beach Point Yacht. Hobbies: sailing, skiing, philately. Home: 120 E 81 St, New York, NY; Office: 574 Fifth Ave, New York, NY.

LANGBAUM, Robert W, US, educator; b. NYC, Feb 23, 1924; s. Murray and Nettie (Moskowitz); AB, Cornell U, 1947; MA, Columbia U, 1949, PhD, 1954; m. Francesca Vidale, Nov 5, 1950; c: Donata. James Branch Cabell Prof of Eng, U of Va since 1967; instr to asst prof of Eng, Cornell U, 1950-60. Author: The Poetry of Experience, 1957; an edition of Shakespeare's The Tempest, 1963; The Gayety of Vision: A Study of Isak Dinensen's Art, 1964; ed of anthol, The Victorian Age, 1967; contbr to profsl jours. Mem adv bd: Victorian Poetry; Style; New Literary History; mem: MLA; AAUP; F, Cen for Advanced Study in the Behavioral Scis. Home: 1634 Brandywine Dr, Charlottesville, Va. Office: U of Va, Charlottesville, Va.

LANGBERG, Bernard, US, certified public acctnt; b. NYC, Oct 25, 1926; s. Philip and Fay (Zlotchin); BA, CCNY, 1948; m. Sonya Goldstein, Dec 25, 1949; c: Donald, Michael. Partner, Davidson and Langberg, CPA's since 1967; secy-treas, Tabby's Intl since 1969. Pfc, US Army, 1945-46. Dir bd, B'nai B'rith Grand Dist 5; mem: bd, Gtr Miami J Fed; exec comm, Fla ADL regional bd; NY, Fla CPA Soc's; F fmr treas, Mid-I YM-YWHA, Nassau Co, NY; club, Footlighters, Fla. Home: 1551 NE 167th St, N Miami Beach, Fla. Office: 420 Lincoln Rd, Miami Beach, Fla.

LANGE, Isaak Samson, Switz, educator; b. Frankfurt a/Main,

Ger, Dec 17, 1909; s. Marcus and Hermine (Kaufmann); in Switz since 1957; att Us of Frankfurt a/M, Berlin; Yeshiva, Frankfurt a/M; Rabb Sem, Berlin; m. Lea Rosner, May 1938; c: Elimelech. Rector, J Day Sch, Zurich, since 1957; fmr tchr, various schs in Ger and Isr, 1934-47; vice-dir, munic gymnasium, Tel Aviv, 1953-56, dir, 1956-57. Contbr of pamphlets to Kiriat Sefer, Jerusalem and Mekitze Nirdamim. Mem, Verband J tchrs and cantors, Switz, vice-pres, 1965-68. Hobby: study and editing of mediaeval J manuscripts. Home: 65, Anwandstr, Zurich, Switz. Office: 1, Freigutstr, Zurich, Switz.

LANGENAUER, Arthur Alan, US, rabbi; b. Bklyn, NY, Aug 18, 1932; s. Max and Regina (Gewirtz); BA, CCNY, 1953; att JTSA, 1958; MS, clinical psych, CCNY, 1958; m. Haviva Dolgin, Dec 26, 1954; c: Shamai, Dvora, Aliza, Yosef. Rabbi, Cong Bnai Isr since 1962; chaplain: Northampton State Hosp since 1962; VA Hosp since 1962; Heb tchr: Cliffside Park Cong, NJ, 1953-54; Forest Hills W Cong, Queens, NY, 1954; student rabbi, prin Sunday sch, J Cen, Saddle Brook and Rochelle Park, NJ, 1955-56; Heb tchr, Conservative Syn, Riverdale, 1958; rabbi, instr, Bnai Japan, 1958-61; rabbi, Cong Beth Tikva, Rockville, Md, 1961-62. Chaplain, USAF, Japan, 1958-61. Youth group leader, Beth Hillel Cong, Washington Hgts, 1952-54; youth dir, Cong Shaari Isr, Bklyn, 1954-55; field worker, United Syn Youth, 1955-56, dir: Queens, Nassau, Suffolk Co area, 1956-57, LI area, 1957-58; mem: RA; B'nai B'rith; Mass Bd of Rabbis; Northampton Clergy Assn. Hobbies: photography, music, drama, writing, physics. Home: 48 Nassasoit St, Northampton, Mass. Study: Prospect St, Northampton, Mass.

LANGER, Felix, Eng, lawyer, writer, playwright, lecturer; b. Brno, Czech, June 18, 1889; s. Abraham and Antonie (Schwartz); in Eng since 1939; LLD, U of Vienna. Pvt law practice, Aus-Hung. Lt, Aus-Hung Army, WW I. Author: Magelon, die Geschichte eines nervösen Mädchens; Münchhausens Verwandlung; Erotische Passion; Die Maschine; Sieben Tage Mr. Whiteman; Die Protokolle der Weisen von Zion; Stepping Stones to Peace; performed plays: Das böse Schicksal; Lore Ley; Banknoten; Der Obrist; Zweikampf; Die Verführung des Heiligen; Der Kümmere; Was tun Sie, wenn..?; Die Welt? Ein Theater!; numerous radio plays, broadcast by most Eur Bc Stas. Fmr: found, org, hon secy, Brünner Hilfsaktion für sibirische Kriegsgefangene; writer, lit critic: Berliner Tageblatt; Prager Tageblatt; Bohemia; Frankfurter Zeitung; Neue Freie Presse; Nationalzeitung, Basel; Neue Züricher Zeitung; mem bd: Kleistpreisstiftung; Deutscher Bühnenklub, both Berlin. Hobbies: music, painting. Home: 30 Belsize Park, London NW 3, Eng.

LANGERMAN, Aharon, Isr, government official; b. Wiesbaden, Ger, June 21, 1925; s. Moshe and Gitel (Zuskind); in Isr since 1934; att Sem of Youth Aliyah, 1945-46; BA, Heb U, Jerusalem, 1960; m. Shoshana Pinczower, July 29, 1958; c: Arye, Talya, Judith, Moshe. Dep dir-gen, Min of Social Wfr; fmr: dir, training sch for social educ workers, 1961-66; tchr, Tchrs Sem, Jerusalem, 1954-60. IDF, 1948-65. Mem: Council for Mentally Retarded Children; Council for Prevention of Delinquency; fmr dir, youth movement, B'nai Akiba. Contbr to periodicals. Spec interest: J lit in Middle Ages. Home: 7 Lloyd George St, Jerusalem Isr. Office: 8 King David St, Jerusalem, Isr.

LANGHAUS, Ulrich Uri, Isr, technical draftsman, chess player, intl chess arbiter; b. Bucharest, Rum, Nov 23, 1918; s. Jacob and Janeta (Weintraub); in Isr since 1960; att Duployen Tech Sch, Bucharest; m. Carolina Lebas, Apr 7, 1906; c: Adina, Eugen. Tech draftsman, Sonol Isr Ltd, since 1960; head projectant, Projects Inst, Min of Petroleum, Bucharest, 1949-60; intl chess arbiter, Rum, Isr; dir, Isr, intl chess championships; dep chief arbiter, Chess Olympic Games, Tel Aviv. Fmr: mem directory, Rum Chess Fed; pres, Chess Arbiters Assn of Rum. Author, Regulations of Chess Games, 1957. Recipient: Merit for Sports, 1955; Intl Chess Arbiter, Intl Chess Fed, 1956. Home: 12 Einstein St, Kiryat Ata, Isr. Office: 8 Bank St, Haifa, Isr.

LANGLEBEN, M Phillip, Can, physicist; b. Deblin, Pol, Apr 9, 1924; s. David and Charna (Shabason); in Can since 1929; BSc, McGill U, Montreal, 1949, MSc, 1950, PhD, 1953; m. Rose Cohen, May 26, 1948; c: Adrian, David, Louise. Prof of physics, McGill U since 1969, fac mem since 1957; research asso, Meteorological Off, London, 1953-54. Royal Can Navy, 1942-45. F, Royal Meteorological Soc; mem: Can Assn Physicists; McGill Phys Soc; Sigma Xi; Glaciological Soc.

Contbr of research papers to profsl jours. Home: 4753 Grosvenor Ave, Montreal, Can. Office: McGill U, Montreal, Can.

LANGSAM, Naftali M, US, rabbi; b. Frankfurt/M, Ger, Nov 7, 1928; s. Joshua and Biena (Adest); in US since 1938; ordained rabbi, Yeshiva and Mesivta Rabbi Chaim Berlin, 1950; post-grad studies, Syracuse U, 1950-51; BA, Bklyn Coll, 1953; MS, Yeshiva U, 1970; m. Avivia Gurewitz, Sep 10, 1951; c: Yedidyah, Shmuel, Nethanel, Elazar, Michal. Dean, Yeshiva of Brighton Beach and vicinity since 1966; lectr, Young Isr Inst for Adult J Studies since 1956; rabbi: Cong Tifereth Zvi, Utica, NY, 1950-51; Young Isr of Windsor Park, 1952-55; Young Isr of Prospect Park, 1955-68; dean, J Found Sch of Staten I, 1957-66. Chmn: Natl Conf Yeshiva Prins, NY Metrop Region since 1967; prinsconv, Heb Day Sch Prins of US and Can, 1963; comm on visitation, Natl Yeshiva Prin Commn, chmn NY State Region since 1967; rabb adv, ed bd, Young Isr Viewpoint; natl educ dir, B'nai Akiva Org of N Amer, 1947-48; bd dirs: Yeshiva and Mesivta Rabbi Chaim Berlin; Yeshiva of E Pkway; Natl Yeshiva Prin Assn; mem: RabCA; Elem Sch Prin Assn; Natl Yeshiva Prin Assn; Phi Beta Kappa. Contbr to Anglo-J periodicals. Spec interests: hist, phil. Home: 738 Troy Ave, Brooklyn, NY. Study: 293 Neptune Ave, Brooklyn, NY.

LANGSAM, Ralph H, US, business exec, educator; b. Newark, NJ, Feb 19, 1911; s. Isidore and Jenny (Greenberger); AB, CCNY, 1934; MBA, NYU, 1940; m. Bernice Farkas, Oct 20, 1934; c: Lawrence Diane Exec, vice-pres, dir, Masback Inc since 1962, with firm since 1932; chief, consumer durable goods unit, Off of Civilian Requirement, War Produc Bd, Wash, DC, 1942-43; adj asst prof, marketing, NYU since 1957, on fac since 1947; lectr, marketing, advt, Rutgers U, 1940-42; instr, marketing, CCNY, 1944-47. Mem: Amer Marketing Assn; Natl Wholesale Hardware Assn; Natl Ind Distributors Assn; Hardware Boosters; Masons, past lodge master; Shriners; fmr pres: Natl Toy Wholesalers Assn; Alpha Sigma Delta, NYU chap; clubs: Sales Execs, NY; Hardware Sq. Contbr of Chap in Sales Executives Handbook, 1950. Home: 67-68 Clyde St, Forest Hills, NY. Office: 330 Hudson St, New York, NY.

LANGSFELD, Anita Grossman, US, communal leader; b. Phila, Pa, July 20, 1915; d. David and Fannie (Harrison) Grossman; att, U of Pa, 1933-37; m. Morton Langsfeld, Jr, Mar 23, 1937; c: Morton, Robert. Pres: Assn for J Children; Cong Keneseth Isr PTA, 1949-51; Council on Volunteers; bd dirs, Women's Council, United Fund, 1963; bd dirs: Fed JAs; Phila Health and Wfr Council; secy, World Affairs Council; S Home for Children, 1965-68; mem, Pa Gov's Commn on Status of Women, 1964-68. Contbr to profsl jours. Home: 623 Elkins Ave, Elkins Park, Pa.

LANKIN, Eliahu, Isr, advocate, b. Gomel, Russ, Sept 25, 1914; s. Moshe and Chana; in Isr since 1933; magister juris, fac law, Heb U, 1953; m. Doris Kaplan, Aug 10, 1954; c: Lenora. Pvt practice since 1954; mem, Isr Bc, since its beginning, mgn comm, since 1968; MK, 1st Knesset, 1949-52. Mem, Irgun Zvi Leumi, 1934-48, Jerusalem cdr, 1944-48, cdr in exile and cdr ship, Altalena. Mem: cen comm, Herut; Munic Comm, Lawyers Org, Jerusalem, 1956-68; many public comms. Author: Memoirs of the Commander of the Altalena, Heb, 1952, 1966. Home: 24 Nayot St, Jerusalem, Isr. office: 9 Ben Yehuda St, Jerusalem, Isr.

LANSKY, Reuben, US, government official; b. Bx, NY, Mar 16, 1915; s. Abraham and Edith (Sandezzon); BA, George Wash U, 1938; m. Edith Sippin, 1945 (decd); c: Avram, Jessie; m. 2nd, Regina Cohn, 1960. Asst regional dir, Region II, HEW, since 1969; prin credit union examiner, Fed Deposit Ins Corp, 1945-48; regional repr, Bur of Fed Credit Unions, 1948-68. US Army, 1943-45. Mem: Pi Gamma Mu, Omicron Delta Gamma. Home: 21-25 34th Ave, Long Island City, NY. Office: HEW, 26 Federal Plaza, New York, NY.

LAOR, Eran, Switz, executive; b. Cifer, Slovakia, June 1, 1900; s. Max and Fanny (Squarenina) Landstein; in Switz since 1949; att: Bus HS, Bratislava, 1915-18; pvt studies, phil, lit, Vienna, 1920-25. Repr: for JA Treasury for Eur since 1949; for JA Exec on Eur Continent since 1955; perm repr for Govt of Isr to Intergovernmental Comm for Eur Migration since 1955; mem bd: CIFICO Bank Ltd, Zurich, since 1965; Soc Bancaire et Financiere, Paris, since 1956; gov dir, vice-pres, Hollis Financial and Commercial Corp since 1959; co-mgr, dept store, Istanbul, 1925-34; co-found, first J Passenger Shipping Line, Haifa, Pal, 1934-40; with Allied Mil Services,

Pal, Turkey, Leb, 1940-43; i/c overland ref transp through Turkey, Syria, Leb, Pal, 1943-45; i/c relief parcel dispatch to J ref, Russ, 1946; delg, JNF, Persia, 1946; Ref Rescue Relief Opr, Paris, 1947; Controller of Shipping, Gov of Isr, 1948-49; bd dirs, Swiss-Isr Trade Bank, 1951-65. Hon treas, J Trust Corp for Ger; mem bd, United Restitution Org, Frankfurt; co-found, Isr Oriental Soc; mem, Free Masons, Haifa. Author: Das Verlorene Wort, poems, 1929; Die Protokolle des Bundes der Sieben, 1930; Israel, poems, 1931; Orientalische Renaissance, essay, 1956; Achtzehn Gedichte, poems, 1956; Die Grosse Einheit, 1959; Ha-Achdut Ha-Elyona, 1962; De la Simplicité de Dieu; Unbekanntes Judentum, 1966; A New Sense of Purpose, essays, 1966; contbr of papers, revs, poems, short stories in Hung, Ger, Fr, Eng. Spec interests: geog, hist of Isr, collecting old travel books, maps of ME. Home: Jerusalem, Isr. Office: 26 route de Malagnou, Geneva, Switz.

LAPAN, Bernard, US, physician; b. NYC, Mar 4, 1914; s. Samuel and Sarah (Weinerman); BS, NYU, 1933; MD, Coll of Med, 1936; m. Claire Werner, June 22, 1935; c: Marilyn, Benjye, Francine. Practicing gyn and obstet since 1946; mem staff: Leb Hosp since 1936; J Memorial Hosp since 1939; Bx Leb Hosp Cen since 1963, fmr vice pres, med bd; Albert Einstein Coll Hosp since 1967; clinical instr, Albert Einstein Coll Med since 1967; visiting phys, Jacobi Hosp, Bx Munic Hosp Cen since 1967. Capt US Army MC, 1942-45. Dipl, Amer Bd Obstet and Gyn; found f, Amer Coll Obstet and Gyn; f: Amer Coll Surgs; NY Acad of Med; mem: Bx Gyn and Obstet Soc, past pres; alumni, Leb Hosp; Amer Fertility Soc; AAAS. Contbr of articles in the fields of: gyn; obstet; path; biochem to sci jours. Home: 535 E 86 St, New York, NY. Office: 1882 Grand Concourse, Bronx, NY.

LAPIDOTH, Arye, Isr, attorney: b. Jerusalem, Isr, Jan 28, 1930; s. Yaacov and Zehava (Hirschberg); M Jur, Heb U, 1953; PhD, LSE, 1964; m. Ruth Eschelbacher, Oct 30, 1956; c: Michael, Tamar, Amos. Lectr, law of taxation and bus law, Heb U since 1966; legal adv, Income Tax Dept, Min of Finance, 1955-60; dep state atty for fiscal matters, Min of Justice, 1960-64; dir, fiscal leg, Min of Justice, legal adv to finance comm, Knesset, 1964-66. Pvt, IDF, 1948-49. Mem: council, Isr br, Intl Fiscal Assn. Contbr to profsl jours. Home: 11 Balfour St, Jerusalem, Isr. Office: Heb U, Jerusalem, Isr.

LAPIDOTH, Ruth, Isr, attorney; b. Dueren, Ger, Oct 27, 1930; d. Oscar and Selma (Roer) Eschelbacher; in Isr since 1938; MJur, Heb U, Jerusalem, 1953; PhD, fac droit, Paris, 1956; dipl, Inst des Hautes Etudes Intl's, 1962; m. Arye Lapidoth, Oct 30, 1956; c: Michael, Tamar, Amos. Sr lectr, intl law, Heb U, Jerusalem, since 1963. Sgt, IDF MC, 1948-49. Mem: comm, Isr br, Intl Law Assn; Amer Soc of Intl Law; Isr Fgn Policy Assn. Author: Les Rapports entre le Droit International Public et le Droit Interne en Israel, 1959; La Conclusion des Traités Internationaux en Israel, 1962; contbr to law revs. Home: 11 Balfour St, Jerusalem, Isr. Office: Heb U, Jerusalem, Isr.

LAPIDUS, Morris, US, architect; b. Odessa, Russ, Apr 25, 1902; s. Leon and Eva (Sherman); in US since 1903; att, NYU, 1921-23; BArch, Columbia U, NYC, 1927; m. Beatrice Perlman, Feb 22, 1929; c: Richard, Alan. Architect, Morris Lapidus Assos, since 1963, own firm, since 1943; jr designer, chief architect, partner, various firms, 1926-43; works executed include: bldgs for residential, commercial, ind, rel, educ, recreational and public use; hotels: Sheraton Motor Inn, Howard Johnson Mid-Town Inn, Americana, all NYC, 1961; Aruba Caribbean, Netherlands, Antilles, 1956; Jamaica Hilton, 1957; Americana of San Juan, 1966; El Conquistador, Fajardo, Puerto Rico, 1968; housing devls: Trump Village, Coney Island, 1965; Fairfield Towers, 1966; others; one man exhb: Forty Years of Art and Architecture, Lowe Gal, U Miami; painting and water color, Crystal House Gal, 1968. Vice-pres, C of C, Miami Beach; mem: Amer Inst Architects; Amer Inst Interior Designers; Architectural League; Natl Inst Architectural Educ; Municiple Art Soc, NYC; Amer Artists Profsl League; adv board, Actors Studio; clubs: Footlighters; Kiwanis; Elks, all Miami Beach. Author, Architecture: A Profession and A Business, 1967; work appears in publs and text books in Amer, Eng, Ger, It. Recipient: Cert of Service, NY State Dept Commerce, 1949; Pres Award of Honor, Miami Jr C of C, 1963; Dist Service Award, Variety Childrens Hosp, 1963; Silver Menorah Club Award, Gtr Miami J Fed, 1964; others. Hobbies: photography, painting, golf. Home: 3 Island Ave, Miami Beach, Fla. Office: 1688 Meridian St, Miami Beach, Fla.

LAPIDUS, Paul W, US, surgeon, educator; b. Melitopol, Russ, Dec 27, 1893; s. Vladimir and Rose (Hoffschneider); in US since 1923; MD: State U of Odessa Med Sch, 1916; LI Coll of Med, 1926; m. Edith Stone, Nov 8, 1935; c: Andrew, Paul. Prof, orthopedic surg, NY Polyclinic Sch since 1941; asst clinical prof, NY Med Coll since 1945; lectr, Columbia U Coll Phys and Surgs since 1955; cons, orthopedic surg, Hosp for JT Diseases since 1960, on staff since 1923; visiting orthopedic surg: NY Hotel Health Cen; Hosp for Ruptured and Crippled, 1926-34; Trinity Hosp, Bklyn, 1929-34; NY Polyclinic Hosp since 1940; Metrop Hosp since 1944; Flower Fifth Ave Hosp since 1945; Bird & Coler Hosp since 1952; cons orthopedist, Workmen's Circle since 1931. Capt, MC, Russ Army, World War I; cons, US Army induction cen, WWII. F: Amer Coll Surgs; Amer Acad Orthopedic Surg; AMA; NY Acad Med; AAAS; Amer Soc Phys; Anthropologists and Anthropological Assn; dipl, Amer Bd Orthopedic Surg. Contbr to prof publs. Hobbies: outdoor life, fishing, photography. Home: 245 Rumsey Rd, Yonkers, NY. Office: 16 E 82 St, New York, NY.

LAPIN, Abraham H, S Afr, rabbi; b. Aberdeen, S Afr, Oct 26, 1912; s. Barnard and Doris (Karstaedt); ordained rabbi, Yeshiva Telshe, Lith, 1939; m. Maisie Thal, Jan 6, 1943; c: Daniel, David, Judith, Raphael. Rabbi: United Heb Cong; Yeoville Syn, both since 1941; sr rabbi, United Heb Cong, since 1967; dayan, Beth Din, Johannesburg, Transvaal, Orange Free State, since 1954; sr lectr, Talmud, Yeshiva Coll of S Afr, since 1962; mayor's chaplain, Johannesburg, 1949-50, 1968-69. Mem, country comtys comm, S Afr J Bd Deps; fmr: chmn, S Afr J Mins Assn; vice chmn, United Heb Schs, chmn, curriculum comm, mem exec, 1961. Home and study: 20 Young Ave, Houghton Estate, Johannesburg S Afr.

LAPIN, Albert W, Can, physician; b. Montreal, Can, Sep 18, 1910; s. Louis and Emma (Weinfield); BA, McGill U, 1931, MD, CM, 1935; m. Joy Smith, July 6, 1952; c: Michael, Joanne, Jonathan, Philip. Chief, dept card, J Gen Hosp, since 1960; chief of card, Queen Mary Vets Hosp, since 1958; asst prof med, McGill U, since 1967, on fac since 1950. Squadron leader, RCAF, 1940-45. FRCP; ACP; mem: AHA; Can Cardiovascular Soc; Can Med Assn; past pres, Montreal Cardiac Soc. Contbr to med jours. Recipient, mention in dispatches, 1945. Home: 3785 Vendome Ave, Montreal, Can. Office: 4119 Sherbrooke St W, Montreal, Can.

LAPINE, Milton J, US, advertising exec; b. Cleveland, O, July 28, 1911; s. Louis and Fannie (Landis); att W Reserve U, 1928-31; m. Dorothy Feld, Mar 4, 1934; c: Charles, Carolyn. PR and advt exec since 1958; reporter and sports ed, The Cleveland Press, 1929-53; public service dir, 1953-58; press secy for Mayor A. J. Celebrezze, Cleveland, 1958. Pres, Cleveland Newspaper Guild; fmr vice-pres, Amer Newspaper Guild; mem: Cleveland Engr Soc; Sigma Delta Chi; Masons; club: Press, pres, found; City. Recipient: Heywood Broun Award, Amer Newspaper Guild, 1943; Vinson citation, Defense Bond campaign; Cleveland Newspaper Guild Award for public service, 1957. Home: 12700 Fairhill Rd, Shaker Heights, O. Office: 1610 Euclid Ave, Cleveland, O.

LAPPIN, Ben, Can, educator; b. Pol, May 1, 1916; s. Louis and Khayeh (Burstyn); in Can since 1924; BA, McMaster U, Hamilton; att: Sch of Social Work, U Toronto, 1946-47; Training Bur for J Comty Communal Service, NY, 1949-50; D Social Work, U Toronto, 1965; m. Adah Auerbach, June 18, 1949; c: Sholom, Joseph, Naomi, Daniel. Prof, Sch of Social Work, U Toronto, since 1958; ed, Eng sect, Daily Heb Jour, 1942; exec secy, jt pr comm, Can J Cong and B'nai B'rith, 1943-46; asst dir, United JWF, Toronto, 1946-47; exec dir, Can J Cong, cen region, 1948-58; cons, Bar Ilan U Sch of Social Work, Isr, 1967-68. Mem: natl exec comm, Can J Cong; Can Assn Social Workers; Can Wfr Council; Farband Lab Zionist Org. Author, Redeemed Children, 1962; co-author, Community Organization: Theory, Principles and Practices; contbr to profsl jours. Home: 24 Elmridge Dr, Toronto, Can. Office: Sch of Social Work, U of Toronto, Toronto, Can.

LAQUEUR, Walter, Eng, author; b. Breslau, Ger, May 26, 1921; s. Fritz and Else (Berliner); m. Barbara Koch; c: Sylvia Graham, Shlomit. Dir, Wiener Library, London, since 1964; prof, hist of ideas, Brandeis U, since 1966; co-ed, Jour of Contemporary Hist. Author: Communism and Nationalism in the Middle East, 1956; Young Germany, 1962; Road to War, 1968; The Struggle for the Middle East, 1969;

Europe Since Hitler, 1970. Home: 8 Eastville Ave, London, NW 11, Eng.

LARON, Zvi, Isr, physician; b. Cernauti, Rum, Feb 6, 1927; s. Moritz and Rosa (Feller) Langberg; in Isr since 1948; MD, Heb U, Jerusalem, 1952; research f, Harvard U, 1956-67; m. Tova Shwisha, Sep 26, 1952; c: Avidan, Daphna. Dir, ped metabolic and endocrine service and ped endocrine res unit, Beilinson Hosp, since 1957; asso prof, ped, Tel Aviv U, since 1967. Visiting prof: Boston U, 1965; Cedar-Sinai Med Cen, LA, 1968; Lt, IDF, 1948. Pres, Eur Soc of Ped Endocrinology, 1966-67; secy, Isr Soc Experimental Biol, 1964-66; Isr Clinic, Ped Soc, 1963-65. Contbr to sci jours. Recipient: Joffe Prize for endocrinology, Kupat Holim, 1962. Home: 265 Modiin St, Ramat Gan, Isr. Office: Beilinson Hosp, Petah Tikva, Isr.

LASH, Abraham F, US, physician, educator; b. Chicago, Ill, Nov 25, 1898; s. Isaac and Faye (Saltzmann); BS, U Chgo, 1919; MD, Rush Med Coll, 1921; MS, U of Ill, 1925; PhD, 1929; post-grad studies, Vienna and Berlin, 1930; m. Ruth Perry, June 28, 1925; c: Elaine Cassidy, Ellen. Prof, gyn, Cook Co Grad Sch, since 1937; prof em, Northwestern U, Dept of Obstet and Gyn, since 1967; dir, div obstet, gyn, Cook Co Hosp since 1966, att gyn, since 1937; att gyn, Michael Reese Hosp, since 1953; sr att gyn, Mt. Sinai Hosp since 1950. F: Intl Coll of Surgs; Amer Coll of Surgs; Dipl, Amer Bd Obstet and Gyns; mem: Amer Assn Obstet and Gyns; Cen Assn Obstet and Gyns; Chgo Med Assn; Chgo Path Assn; Inst of Med; Chgo Gyn Soc; Sigma Xi; Amer Coll of Obstet and Gyns. Contbr to med jours. Home: 900 Lake Shore Dr, Chicago, Ill. Office: 30 N Michigan Ave, Chicago, Ill.

LASK, Israel Meir, Isr, translator, editor; b. London, Eng, Jan 19, 1906; s. Joseph and Eva (Taub) Cohen-Lask; in Isr since 1930; att London U; m. Luba Pevsner, Jan 21, 1932; c: Ruth Rasnic, Bella Doron. Adv, Eng Lang, Histadrut, since 1955; ed: Pal Tribune, 1945-46; Isr Yearbook, 1952-53; trans from Heb, Yiddish, Ger into Eng, prin classics, modern Heb lit. Contbr to jours. Home: 4 Hamelech Koresh St, Tel Aviv, Isr.

LASKER, Arnold A, US, rabbi; b. NYC, Dec 15, 1912; s. Philip and Sadie (Bernstein); BS, CCNY, 1931; MHL, ordained rabbi, JTSA, 1936; m. Miriam Price, June 7, 1942; c: Joseph, Judith, Daniel. Rabbi, Cong Beth Torah, since 1951; chaplain, E Orange VA Hosp, since 1952; rabbi: Cong Sons of Zion, Holyoke, Mass, 1940-48; Cong Beth Isr, Flint, Mich, 1948-51. Chaplain, US Army, 1943-46. Fmr: vice-pres, Bd of Rabbis of Essex Co, 1967-69, bd of trustees; secy, Assn of J Chaplains of the Armed Forces; mem, charter Commn, City of Orange, 1961; treas, Acad of Rel and Mh, metrop br; mem, comm on marriage and the family, RA, chmn, social, action comm, NNJ region; bd of trustees, J Family Service Assn of Essex Co. Contbr to rel jours. Recipient: James Monroe HS Hall of Fame Award, 1958. Home: 665 S Center St, Orange, NJ. Study: 270 Reynolds Terr, Orange, NJ.

LASKER, Edward, US, engineer, chess master, author; b. Kempen, Ger, Dec 3, 1885; s. Sigismund and Flora (Bornstein); in US since 1914; ME, Technische Hochschule, Berlin, 1908, EE, 1911; m. Cecile Heller (decd); m. 2nd, Hertha Fuerth (div). Cons, Engr and Financial, since 1945; fmr: asso with Ger Gen Elec Co, London, 1912-14; safety engr, Sears-Roebuck, 1915-19; inventor, elec breast pump, 1920; mfr, 1920-32; dir, sales, Lepel High Frequency Labs, 1932-39; asso with: ECCO High Frequency Labs, 1940-42; Kurman Elec Co, 1942-44. Author: Schachstrategie, 1910; Chess Strategy, 1915, 1961; Chess and Checkers, 1918, 1960; GO and GOMOKU, the Oriental Board Games, 1935, 1959; Chess for Fun and Chess for Blood, 1942, 1962; Modern Chess Strategy, 1945, 1969; Chess Secrets, 1950, 1969; The Adventure of Chess, 1950, 1960; The Game of Chess, 1970. F, NY Acad Sci, 1953; hon pres, Marshall Chess Club. Recipient: winner of chess championships: Berlin, 1909; Paris, 1911; London, 1914; NYC, 1915; Chgo, 1916; W US, 1916-18, 1920-21; NY Masters' Tournament, 1922; Mexico City, 1954. Home: 18 W 86 St, New York, NY.

LASKER, Harry, US, rabbi, organization exec; b. NYC, Aug 8, 1917; s. Meyer and Esther (Lipzer); BA, Bklyn Coll, 1940; MHL, ordained rabbi, HUC-JIR, 1940, DD, 1964; m. Florence Jassey, May 2, 1953; c: Esther, Leonard, Michael. Exec dir, Natl J Comm on Scouting, Boy Scouts of Amer, since 1943, natl dir, J Relationships since 1943; leader, Amer Scout contingent, World Jamboree, Fr, 1947; leader, 1st Amer Scout contingent to Natl Jamboree, Isr, 1958. Mem: RA; Scout Exec, Alliance; NY Bd of Rabbis. Ed: Scouting and the Jewish Boy, 1944; Jewish Religious Services for Boy Scout Camporees, 1945; Ner Tamid Guide for Boy Scouts and Explorers, 1949. Home: 856 Winchester Ave, Hillside, NJ. Office: Boy Scouts of Amer, New Brunswick, NJ.

LASKIN, Daniel M, US, surgeon, educator; b. NYC, Sep 3, 1924; s. Nathan and Flora (Kaplan); att NYU, 1941-42; BS, Ind U, 1947; DDS, 1947; MS, U of Ill, 1951; m. Eve Mohel, Aug 25, 1945; c: Jeffrey, Gary, Maria. Prof, head dept, oral and maxillo-facial surg, Coll of Dent, U of Ill, clinical asso prof, i/c grad training in oral surg, since 1955, fac mem since 1949. Served US Army. Dipl, Amer Bd Oral Surgs; f: Amer Coll Dents; AAAS; Intl Coll Dents; mem: Amer Intl Socs Oral Surgs; Amer Dent Assn; Amer Soc Experimental Path; Intl Assn Dent Research; NY Acad Sci; Soc for Experimental Biol and Med; Alpha Omega; Sigma Xi; Omicron Kappa Upsilon. Ed, Amer Soc Oral Surgs newsletter; contbr to profsl jours. Home: 3844 Enfield Ave, Skokie, Ill. Office: U of Ill, 808 S Wood St, Chicago, Ill.

LASKOV, Haim, Isr, army officer, government official; b. Borisov, Russ, Apr, 1919; s. Moshe and Yetta (Hirschfeld); in Isr since 1925; att Oxford U, 1953; m. Shulamit Hen, Feb 16, 1950. Ret; dir gen, Isr Ports Auth, 1961-70; served: Haganah, 1929-40; British Army, 1940-46, maj, J Brig, 1944; armor cdr, Isr War of Independence, 1948; found, 1st IDF off sch, 1948; dir gen, mil training, 1949-50; cdr, IAF, 1951-53; dep chief of staff, IDF, 1955; armor corps cdr, Sinai Campaign, 1956; cdr, S Command, 1957; chief of staff, IDF, 1958-61. Author: mil training manuals; essays on mil problems. Home: 75 Einstein St, Tel Aviv, Isr. Office: POB 20121, Tel Aviv, Isr.

LASKOWITZ, Isidor Bernard, US, business exec, consulting engineer; b. NYC, Oct 10, 1896; s. Simon and Fanny (Berman); BS, Cooper Union Sch Engr, 1918, ME, 1924; att grad sch: Columbia U, 1921-22; Bklyn Poly Inst, 1948-49; m. Lilian Brockow, Aug 19, 1926 (decd); c: Beatrice Goldberg. Pres, Laskowitz Helicopter Co, Inc, since 1925; cons engr, devl, since 1925; design engr, USN Dept, Bklyn, 1915-22; ME, US Gasoline Mfg Co, 1922-23; ME, Dept W Water Supply Gas and Electricity, NYC, 1923-26; sr ME, off of pres, Borough Bklyn, 1926-61. Prin contribs: firm's sci and engr contribs in research, design, devl, experimentation, testing of helicopters and vertical takeoff and landing aircraft; holder US patents for components used in helicopters, vertical takeoff and landing aircraft and other designs. Vice pres, engr sect, and mem bd govs, NY Acad Sci; f: NY Acad Sci; mem: Bklyn Botanical Garden; Bklyn Mus; Tau Beta Pi; Natl Soc Profsl Engrs; Amer Soc MEs; Amer Helicopter Soc; Munic Engrs City of NY. Author: Design for Helicopters, 1947, supplement, 1950; Helicopters: Their History, Development, Construction and Future, 1949. Recipient: Machine Design Prize, Cooper Union Sch Engr, 1916; award, NY Acad Sci, 1960; spec citation, profsl engrs, Kings Co Chap, NY State unit, Natl Soc Profsl Engrs, 1963. Hobbies: botany, ornithology. Home and office: 284 Eastern Pkwy, Brooklyn, NY.

LASKY, Moses, US, lawyer; b. Denver, Colo, Nov 2, 1907; s. Judah and Ida (Grossman); AB, magna cun laude, U Col, 1928; JD, 1928; LLM, Harvard, 1929; m. Ruth Abraham, July 6, 1933; c: Morelle Levine, Marshall. Pvt practice since 1929; partner, Brobeck, Phleger & Harrison, since 1941, with firm since 1929. F, Amer Coll Trial Lawyers; chmn, SF Comm on Crime; pres: SF Mus Art, 1963-64; Bay Area Arts Council; vice pres, SF Art Inst, 1963-64; trustee: SF War Memorial; SF Mus Art; dir, Amer Council for Judaism Philanthropic Fund; mem: natl exec comm, AJComm, 1947-65; Amer, SF Bar Assns; Phi Beta Kappa, Delta Sigma Rho. Home: 10 Mountain Spring Ave, San Francisco, Cal. Office: 111 Sutter, San Francisco, Cal.

LASKY, Victor, US, author, journalist; b. Liberty, NY, Jan 7, 1918; s. Max and Bella (Polen); BA, Bklyn Coll, 1939; m. Patricia Pratt, 1952. Free lance writer since 1950; combat corresp, Eur ed, Stars and Stripes, 1943-45; journalist: Paris Post, 1945; Chgo Sun, 1941-46; World Telegram and Sun, 1946-50; Spadea Syndicate, 1953; NY Herald Tribune, columnist, N Amer Paper Alliance. Author: The Hoaxters, full length documentary film for MGM, 1953; JKF, The Man and The Myth, 1963; The Ugly Russian, 1965; Robert F Kennedy, The Myth and the Man, 1968; co-author, Seeds of Treason, 1950; ed, The American Legion Reader, 1953; contbr to:

Today's Woman; Collier's Ency; Pageant; The New Leader; The Freeman; This Week; Human Events; The American Legion Mag; Saturday Evening Post; NEA Newspaper Syndicate. Mem: Screen Writers Guild; Amer Newspaper Guild; Author's League; clubs: Natl Press; Overseas Press; Natl Rep. Home and office: 116 Central Park S, New York, NY.

LASSAR, Emanuel, US, accountant; b. Bklyn, NY, Mar 19, 1917; s. Samuel and Anna (Katz); BBA, CUNY, 1938; m. Adele Gerbitz, June 10, 1942; c: Stephen, Hanina. Partner, E Lassar & Co since 1962; instr, Bklyn Coll, 1945-47. Cpl, US Army, 1942-43. Pres, Cong Shaaray Tefilach; bd dirs: YMHA; Heb Inst of LI; mem: UJA; Isr Bonds; Fed J Charities; CCNY Alumni Assn; NY State Soc CPAs; B'nai B'rith; JWV; Mizrachi. Home: 1144 Sage St, Far Rockaway, NY. Office: 225 W 34 St, New York, NY.

LASSER, David, US, labor exec; b. Baltimore, Md, Mar 20, 1902; s. Louis and Lena (Yaffe); BS, MIT, 1924; div; c: Daniel. Asst to pres for econ and collective bargaining, Intl Union of Elec, Radio and Machine Workers since 1965, dir, 1950-65; pres: Amer Interplanetary Soc, 1931-33; Workers Alliance of Amer, 1935-40; asst dir, US Off of Lab Produc, civilian produc admn, 1942-47; labor adv, US Secy of Commerce, 1947-49. US Army, 1918-19. Mem: ADA; Soc for Advancement of Mgmt; Disabled Amer Vet; Amer Inst IEs; Ind Relations Research Assn. Author: Conquest of Space, 1931; Private Monopoly, The Enemy at Home, 1946; Labor and World Affairs, 1950. Home: 2300 N Richmond St, Arlington, Va. Office: 1126-16 St, Washington, DC.

LASSER, Richard P, US, cardiologist; b. NYC, Dec 5, 1921; s. Louis and Dorothy (Gerler); BA, Columbia Coll, 1943; MD, Columbia U, 1945; m. Denise Levy, Aug 14, 1955; c: Daniel, Philip. Pvt practice since 1954; dir, med, J Memorial Hosp; clinical prof, med, Mt Sinai Med Sch. US Army, 1946-47. Mem: AHA; Amer Fed for Clinical Research; Alpha Omega Alpha. Home: 1160 Fifth Ave, New York, NY. Office: 1176 Fifth Ave, New York, NY.

LASSMAN, Laurance Philip, Eng, neurological surg; b. London, Eng, June 21, 1913; s. Henry and Julia (Abrahams); MRCS, LRCP, London Hosp Med Sch, 1937; MB, BS, FRCS, Royal Coll Surgs of Eng; FICA, Intl Coll Angiology; m. Marion Tournoff, Sep, 1939; c: Jonathan. Surg, Newcastle Gen Hosp since 1964, staff mem since 1951; cons neurosurg, Royal Vic Infirmary and U of Newcastle since 1964. Capt, British Army, 1940-46. Pres, Friends of Heb U, Newcastle Br; gov, Kenton Sch; vice-pres, Intl Coll Angiology, NY; past, JNF, Newcastle Br; mem: British Assn Ped Surgs; Soc Research Hydrocephalus and Spina Bifida; Council of Brit Soc Neur Surgs. Contbr of numerous articles on ped neurosurg, spina bifida and brain tumors to profsl jours. Spec interests: children's wfr. Home: 45 Clayton Rd, Jesmond, Newcastle upon Tyne, Eng. Office: Regional Neurological Centre, Newcastle Gen Hosp, Newcastle upon Tyne, Eng.

LASTER, Emanuel, US, attorney; b. Dickson City, Pa, Nov 14, 1910; s. Max and Fannie (Wiesenfeld); AB, U Scranton, Pa, 1932; LLB, U of Pa Law Sch, 1935; m. Elsa Feigenbaum, July 6, 1948; c: Mark, John. Sr mem law firm, Laster, Strohl, Kane, McDonald, Mattes and Kelleher since 1958. US Army, 1942-45. Mem: natl council, AJComm since 1958; bd trustees, Scranton-Lackawanna J Council since 1960, past pres; bd dirs: J Fed since 1955; Temple Isr, Scranton, since 1961, past pres; pres, J Home of E Pa since 1965; dir: Lackawanna Co Soc for Crippled Children since 1955; J Comty Cen, Scranton since 1946, past pres; mem: bd dirs, Lackawanna Bar Assn until 1967; Pa, Amer Bar Assns; Masons; Keystone Consistory; Shriners; JWV; Amer Legion; VFW; clubs, Pres of JWB; Purple. Recipient: F Club Award for outstanding comty service, 1949; citation of merit from Scranton Lackawanna J Council, 1946; service award, J Fed, 1962; presidential award, Temple Isr, 1962; award, Lackawanna Soc for Crippled C, 1966. Home: 623 Colfax Ave, Scranton, Pa. Office: Mears Bldg, Scranton, Pa.

LAU-LAVIE, Naphtali, Isr, journalist; b. Cracov, Pol, June 23, 1926; s. Moshe and Haya (Frankel); in Isr since 1945; HS, Yeshiva, Petach Tikva, 1945-48; m. Joan Lunzer, Nov 5, 1956; c: Haya, Samuel, Benyamin, Amihay. Political, spec corresp, news ed, Ha'aretz since 1956; spec mission for illegal aliya, Pol, Czech, Hung, Vienna, Paris, 1949-50; parl corresp, Shearim, 1951-54; nesw ed: Davar, 1954-55; Zmanim, 1955-56. IDF, 1952-69. Mem, Comm found Lions Gate Syn. Author: Piotokow, Memorial Book, 1965; Moshe Dayan, A Biography,

Amer, Swed, Nor eds, 1968. Hobby, photography. Home: 15 Mate Aharon, Ramat Gan, Isr. Office: 56 Maze, Tel Aviv, Isr.

LAUB, Morris, US, organization exec; b. Przemysl, Pol, June 23, 1909; s. Aron and Mollie (Diller); in US since 1914; BSS, CCNY, 1937; m. Eve Mordkowitz, 1933, (decd); c: Levi, Marc. Dir, World Council of Syn, since 1958; on loan to United HIAS Service for spec mission in Morocco, 1962; pres, Sholom Aleichem Memorial Found Inc; exec comm: Yiddish Inst for Research since 1968; JDC, 1944-56, on loan to UNRRA, Greece, 1944-45; dir, N It Reg Off, 1945-56, dir, Cyprus internment camps for J immigrants to Pal, 1946-49, dir, activities, Morocco, Tangier, Algeria, 1949, dir dept immigration, Isr, Paris, 1949-51, asst secy, NY, 1951-56; chmn, youth reference bd, Hadassah, since 1961. Home: 217 Haven Ave, New York, NY. Office: 3080 Broadway, New York, NY.

LAUER, Elias, US, rabbi; b. Bklyn, NY, June 2, 1934; s. Aaron and Freda (Klaristenfeld); BA, Yeshiva U, 1955; ordained rabbi, Rabb Acad, Bklyn, 1957; JD, NYU, 1961; m. Ilse Ungar, Aug 17, 1958; c: Simeon, Barbara, Andrew. Rabbi, Young Isr of Briarwood since 1957; atty, pvt practice since 1961. Secy, Queens Vaad Harabonim; chmn, youth commn, Council Young Isr Rabbis; mem: exec bd, Cen Queens Assn Orthodox Syns; rabb adv bd, Yeshiva of Flushing; bd of educ, Yeshiva of Cen Queens; Rabb Alliance of Amer; NY Co Lawyers Assn. Home: 141-31 Hoover Ave, Jamaica, NY. Study: 84-75 Daniels St, Jamaica, NY.

LAUER, Ilse Susan, US, educator; b. Vienna, Aus, Apr 23, 1938; d. David and Barbara (Katscher) Ungar; in US since 1939; BA, Yeshiva U, 1960; m. Elias Lauer, Aug 17, 1958; c: Simeon, Barbara, Andrew. Tchr, NYC Public Schs since 1961; Heb tchr, Young Isr of Briarwood. Pres: Mizrachi Women's Org of Amer, Margolit chap; rebbitzen, Young Isr of Briarwood. Home: 141-31 Hoover Ave, Jamaica, NY.

LAUFER, Maurice W, US, physician, educator; b. Bklyn, NY, May 2, 1914; s. Abraham and Martha (Wolfskehl); BA, U Wis, 1933; MD, LI Coll of Med, 1939; m. Naomi Steinberg, Sep 12, 1941; c: Susan, Marjorie, Deborah, Laura. Dir, Emma Pendleton Bradley Hosp since 1948; mem, Inst for Life Scis, Brown U since 1958; adj prof, RI Coll, 1958; cons: Butler Hosp since 1947; St Joseph's Hosp since 1953; Miriam Hosp since 1953; Roger Williams Gen Hosp since 1953; RI Hosp since 1968; instr, ped, Cornell U Med Coll, 1942-43; research asso, Fells Research Inst; asso prof, Antioch Coll, 1944-46. US Army, 1944-46. F: Amer Acad of Ped; RI Med Soc; AMA; mem: Amer Psychiatric Assn; Amer Acad of Child Psycht; Amer Orthopsychiatric Assn; Amer Coll of Hosp Admnrs; Gov's Council on Mh; Gov's Adv Comm on Mental Retardation; Sigma Xi; Amer Electroencephalographic Soc; Epilepsy League; Boston Psychoanalytic Soc and Inst; IMA; Royal Soc of Health, Eng; Temple Beth El. Contbr to med jours. Hobby: photography. Home: 15 Channing Ave, Providence, RI. Office: 1011 Veterans Memorial Pkwy, Riverside, RI.

LAUFER, Srul T, Can, physician; b. Rum, July 30, 1903; s. Jacob and Freda (Kries); in Can since 1939; MD, U Naples, 1930; cert, Internal Med, Royal Coll, 1945; m. Irmgard Friedlaender, June 21, 1936; c: Emanuel, Edward, Carla. Prof med, Dalhousie U, since 1969; chief in med, Halifax Infirmary, since 1961, asso with infirmary since 1939; med dir, Maritime Life Assurance Co, since 1958. Pres, Soc of Internal Med, since 1962; vice pres, NS Council of Arts; dir: NS Coll of Art; provincial bd, Boy Scout Assn; f: Clinical Council of Card; AHA; Amer Coll of Card; FACS; mem: NS Med and Heart Assn; BMA; Amer, Heart Assn; Halifax Sym Soc. Contbr to profsl publs in various langs and countries. Home and office: 1780 Oxford St, Halifax, NS, Can.

LAUFMAN, Sidney, US, artist; b. Cleveland, O, Oct 29, 1891; s. George and Betty (Toffler); att: Cleveland Sch of Art; Art Inst of Chgo, 1912-18; Art Students League of NY, 1919-20; m. Beatrice Ratner, Aug 27, 1916. Instr, painting, Art Students League of NY, 1938-50; visiting lectr, fine arts, Brandeis U, 1959-60; worked in Fr, 1920-34; represented in perm collections: Whitney Mus of Amer Art, NY; Metrop Mus, NY; Mus of Modern Art, NY; Cleveland Mus of Art; Art Inst of Chgo; Minneapolis Inst of Art; Toledo Mus of Art; Nelson Gal of Art, Kan City; U of Ore; John Herron Art Inst, Indianapolis; Amer Acad of Arts and Letters; Art Inst of Zanesville, O; Wash Co Mus of Fine Arts, Hagerstown, Md; Dudley Peter Allen Memorial Art Mus, Oberlin, O; City Art Mus of St Louis; Butler Inst of Amer Art, Youngsto-

wn, O; Colo Springs Art Cen; Ga Mus of Art, Athens, Ga; Chrysler Mus, Provincetown, Mass; Parrish Mus, Southampton, LI; Mus of Tel Aviv, Isr; Mus of Jerusalem. Mem, Natl Acad of Design, council, 1947-50; chmn, NY chap, Artists Equity Assn, 1949-50; Woodstock Art Conf, 1959. Recipient: Mr & Mrs Frank G Logan prize, Art Inst Chgo, 1932; 3rd prize, Carnegie Intl, Pittsburgh, 1934; 1st Natl Acad Design awards: Altman prize, 1937; spec landscape prize, 1949; Samuel F B Morse Gold Medal, 1953; Andrew Carnegie prize, 1959; Benj Altman Landscape prize, 1963; William R French Memorial Gold Medal, Art Inst of Chgo, 1941; Paintings of the Year, Pepsi-Cola, NY, 1946; hon mention, Paintings in the US, Carnegie Inst, Pittsburgh, 1946; Diamond Jubilee Purchase prize, Art Students League of NY, 1950; Jennie Sesnan Gold Medal, Pa Acad of Fine Arts, Phila, 1951; hon mention, Corcoran Biennial, Wash, DC, 1951; Ranger Fund Purchase award, NYC, 1954; 1st Prize Purchase award, Butler Inst of Amer Art, Youngstown, O, 1954; Hassam Fund Purchase award, 1954; Sally Jacobs Memorial Prize, Woodstock, 1968. Home: Woodstock, NY.

LAURENCE, William L, US, journalist, author; b. Salantai, Lith, Mar 7, 1888; s. Lipman and Sarah (Preuss) Siew; in US since 1905; att Harvard Coll, 1908-11, 1914-15; U of Besancon, 1919; Harvard Law Sch, 1921; LLB, Boston U Law Sch, 1925; hon DSc: Boston U, 1946; Stevens Inst of Tech, 1951; hon LHD: Grinnell Coll, 1951; Yeshiva U, 1957; m. Florence Davidow, Dec 19, 1931. Ret; sci corresp-in-chief, NY Times, 1930-56, sci ed, 1954-56; reporter, NY World, 1926-30; secret reporter at large, later exclusive pool corresp, Manhattan Engr Dist, top secret atomic project, Oak Ridge, Tenn, Los Alamos and Alamagordo, NM, 1945; off reporter, first atomic bomb test, Alamagordo, 1945; off corresp, Atomic Bomb Mission in Tinian, Marianas Islands, 1945; off eye witness, atomic bombing of Nagasaki, Japan, 1945; visiting prof, Grad Sch of Educ, Yeshiva U, 1959-60. US Army, Fr, 1917-19. Pres, Natl Assn Sci Writers, 1939-40; f: Amer Inst, NYC; AAAS; mem: Dramatist Guild of Authors League of Amer; Natl Assn of Sci Writers; Sigma Delta Chi; PEN; clubs: The Players; Harvard, NY; Natl Press, Wash, DC; Overseas Press; Dutch Treat; Soc of the Silurians. Author: Dawn Over Zero—The Story of the Atomic Bomb, 1946; The Hell Bomb, 1951; Men and Atoms, 1959; The New Frontiers of Science, 1964; contbr to leading periodicals. Recipient: Pulitzer Prize for reporting, 1937, 1946; Westinghouse Dist Sci Writers Award, AAAS, 1946; award from Soc of Silurians, 1946; Medal for Dist Service in Journalism, U of Mo, 1947; Lasker, George Polk, Page One Awards, 1950; Gold Medal, Amer Chem Soc, 1958; citations: Manhattan Dist, 1945; Army Surg Gen, 1945. Home: c/o Rosen, 5415 Riverdale Ave, New York, NY.

LAVEE, Shlomo, Isr, painter; b. Warsaw, Pol, Nov 5, 1928; s. Shimja and Miriam (Gingold) Wacholder; in Isr since 1950; dipl, machinery design, Tech Sch, Buenos Aires; m. Chana, Oct 25, 1952; c: Tamar, Orit, Naomi. One man shows: Periodist House, Tel Aviv; Chagal House, Haifa; fmr, machinery designer, Siam, Arg. Mem: Painters and Sculptors Org of Isr. Hobby, photography. Home and studio: Kibbutz Gazit, Isr.

LAVENTHOL, Lewis J, US, accountant; b. Camden, NJ, Aug 5, 1898; s. Joseph and Lena (Goldfeather); BS, U of Pa, 1921; m. Sadye Horwitz, Oct 12, 1924; c: Henry, Richard, Susan Druckman. Co-found, partner, Laventhol, Krekstein, Horwath and Horwath, Phila, 1923, offs in prin cities of US; Horwath and Horwath Intl Asso, throughout the world; CPA: Pa; NY; Mich; Ia; La. Dir, Fed of JAs since 1955, fmr chmn: budget comm, comm leisure time activities, planning comm, bd dir, FJC Found; mem, AJComm, publ bd natl mag, Commentary, co-found, Phila Chap; dir: Allied J App, 1947-53; Fed J Charities, 1947-53; fmr chmn, comm on bankruptcy and reorg, Amer Inst of CPAs, fmr mem, comm of profsl ethics; past chmn: comm on profsl ethics, relations with the bar, Pa Inst of CPAs, treas, Phila chap; NY State Soc of CPAs; Amer Acctnt Assn; Alpha Epsilon Pi Frat; Cong Rodeph Shalom, fmr bd trustees, fmr chmn, budget comm; clubs: Philmont Country, bd gov, 1951-57; Locust, Phila; Golden Slipper Sq, Phila; Empire State NYC; Mt Moriah Lodge No 155, Masons; Excelsior Consistory, Scottish Rite; Crescent Temple Pa Soc of NY. Home: 7101 Greene St, Philadelphia, Pa. Office: 1528 Walnut St, Philadelphia, Pa.

LAVI, Tsvi, Isr, educator; b. Secureni, Russ, Feb 10, 1912; s. Solomon and Sonya (Wiesental) Leivant; in Isr since 1934;

att Heb U, Jerusalem, 1946-48, 1966; m. Erna Lorber, 1935; c: Tamar, Chaim. Head, dept educ, Kibbutz Artzi Movement, since 1967, mem, dept, 1949-55; secy, Kibbutz Sarid, 1965-66. Served, Hagana, IDF, 1934-61. Contbr to profsl jours. Home: Kibbutz Sarid, Isr. Office: 4 Itamar Ben Avi, Tel Aviv, Isr.

LAVI, Yeshayahu, Isr, engineer, business exec; b. Berlin, Ger, June 26, 1926; s. Shlomo and Sara (Schulback) Lemberger; in Isr since 1933; EE, Columbia U, NY, 1953; m. Lea Zadikov, Aug 13, 1946; c: Zvi, Shlomit, Ilana. Dir-gen, Min of Defense, since 1970; chmn bd, Intl Telecommunications Inc, since 1965; fmr: sci counselor, Isr Embassy, Wash, DC, 1962-64; dir-gen, Isr Min of Posts, 1964-67; dir, Armament Devl Auth, 1968-70. Col, signal corps, IDF, 1948-67. Chmn, Isr sect, Inst of Elec and Elec Engrs; hon mem, Radio Amateur Club of Isr; mem, Engrs and Architects Assn in Isr. Recipient: Isr Defense Award, 1968. Hobby: amateur radio. Home: 6 Bat Yiftach St, Zahala, Isr. Office: POB 7057, Tel Aviv, Isr.

LAVIE, Michael, Isr, physician; b. Dobron, Czech, Dec 17, 1913; MD, Prague, 1938; MPH, Harvard Sch of Public Health, 1960; m. Shoshana Yaacobovitz, 1942; c: Naomi. Dir, Govt Hosp, Ashkelon, since 1961. Served Czech Army, 1941-49; prin med off, IDF, 1949-61. Comm mem: Isr Hosp Assn; Hosp Dirs Assn; Public Health Drs; mem: IMA; Natl Cancer League. Hobby, coins. Home: Afridar St, Ashkelon, Isr. Office: Govt Hosp, Ashkelon, Isr.

LAVIE, Raffi, Isr, painter; b. Tel Aviv, Isr, Feb 23, 1937; s. Herbert and Ethel (Rosteaborsky) Loewi; att Sem for Art Tchrs, 1958-60; m. Ilana Strom, Jan 7, 1964; c: Yoav, Aviv. Art tchr, Sem for Art Tchrs, since 1965; exhbs: Schrift und Bild, Amsterdam, 1963; New Horizons, Ein-Harrod, 1963; Biennale III, Paris, 1963; Mus Mod Art, NYC, 1964; Isr Mus, Jerusalem, 1965; Contemporary Isr Art, Bucharest, Rum, 1968; group shows, Isr, 1960-69. Found, "10t" group; mem, Isr Painters and Sculptors Assn. Home: 6 Yehuda St, Ramat Gan, Isr.

LAVIE, Salman, Isr, economist; b. Libaw, Latvia, Jan 31, 1922; s. Joseph and Lea (Kagan) Levinson; in Isr since 1946; att Lith State U; deg, Tel Aviv Sch of Law and Econ, 1953; postgrad work, Zurich, Switz; m. Shoshana Gamlielit, Apr 15, 1951; c: Smadar, Yoav. Gen secy, Bank Lemelacha Isr, since 1965; fmr guest lectr, Technion, Haifa, 1958; mgn dir, Helet Ltd, subsidiary of Rassco, Isr Govt, 1963-65; chief budget off, acting admnr, Tel Aviv Munic, 1961-63; dep water commn, Min of Agric, 1952-61. Served Haganah, cdr ships, Aliyah Bet, 1945-48; pvt, IDF, 1948-51. Mem bd, Tel Aviv br, Assn of Econs; chmn, Holon br, Assn Friends of Scouts Movement. Author: Report on Economical Aspects of Drainage and Flood Control in Italy and Switzerland; Budget and Financing Problems of Drainage and Flood Control Projects in Isr, both 1958. Recipient, scholarship, UN Food and Agric Org. Hobby, music. Home: 5 Leon Bloom St, Holon, Isr. Office: 9 Carlebach St, Tel Aviv, Isr.

LAVIE, Samuel, Isr, journalist, editor; b. Isr, Dec 10, 1933; s. Abraham and Osnat (Buiumovits); BSc, Heb U, Jerusalem; m. Ilana Bickels; c: Nili. Chief ed, Sha'ar, econ daily; fmr econ ed, Haboker daily. Club: Ind and Commercial. Hobby: tennis. Home: 3 Yehuda Gur St, Tel Aviv, Isr. Office: 19 Hatsfira St, Tel Aviv, Isr.

LAVINE, Irvin, US, engineer, educator; b. Mir, Russ, Dec 6, 1902; s. Louis and Mollie (Tobias); in US since 1905; BS, U Minn, 1924, PhD, 1930; m. Marion Rosenblatt, June 23, 1929; c: Elynor Losk, Burton, William. Partner, secy-treas, Ind Research service, Dover, since 1941; prof em, U of NH since 1965, cons to Dean of Tech since 1965, prof chem engr, 1949-65; dir, Clarostat Mfg Co; secy-treas, Knox Park, Inc; prof, dept head, chem engr, U of ND, 1927-41; cons, Natl Resources Planning Bd, Wash, DC, 1933-41. Hon life mem, Amer Assn Cost Engrs; mem: Amer Chem Soc; Amer Inst Chem Engrs; Amer Soc Engr Educ; AAUP; Sigma Xi; Phi Lambda Upsilon; Sigma Tau; Masons; Elks; club, Rotary. Co-author textbooks chem and ind engr, also research papers. Home: 8 Sunset Dr, Dover, NH.

LAVINE, Thelma Z, US, philosopher, educator; b. Boston, Mass, Feb 12, 1915; d. Samuel and Gussie (Pearlman); AB, magna cum laude, Radcliffe Coll, 1936, AM, 1937, PhD, 1939; m. Jerome Sachs, Mar 31, 1944; c: Margaret. Prof, phil, George Wash U since 1965; instr, asst prof, Wells Coll, 1941-46; asst prof, Bklyn Coll, 1946-52; prof, U of Md, 1962-65, fac mem from 1955. Mem: Amer Phil Assn; AAUP;

Phi Beta Kappa; clubs: Wash Phil; Wash Radcliffe. Contbr: Naturalism and the Human Spirit, 1944; Philosophy and the Social Sciences, 1963; profsl jours. Recipient: dist prof: combined sororities, U of Md, 1964-65; inter-frat council, George Wash U, 1967-68. Home: 1625 35th St NW, Washington DC. Office: George Wash U, Washington DC.

LAVON, Selig Israel, Isr, business exec; b. Pol, Apr 14, 1893; s. Joseph and Lea (Blonder) Lubianiker; att Commercial Acad, Prague, 1912-15; in Isr since 1923; m. Shoshana Havkin, 1938; c: Josef, Alexander. Dir, Housing Mortgage Bank Ltd; fmr gen mgr, Shikun Ovdim Co Ltd; co-found, Amidar, Isr natl housing co; found, Emun Co, NYC, 1950. Mem: secretariat, Hevrat Ovdim; housing comm, ICA; secy, Tel Aviv Lab Council, 1929-30. Home: 30 Hildesbing St, Tel Aviv, Isr. Office: 21 Leonardo da Vinci St, Tel Aviv, Isr.

LAWRENCE, Jerome, US, playwright, author; b. Cleveland, O, July 14, 1915; s. Samuel and Sarah (Rogen) Schwartz; BA, O State U, 1937; hon, DHumL, 1963; hon, DL, Fairleigh Dickinson U, 1968. Playwright, Lawrence and Lee, since 1942; sole playwright, US State Dept Cultural Exch Comm; reporter, ed, O newspapers, 1937; continuity ed, KMPC, Beverly Hills, Cal, 1938-39; sr staff writer, CBS, Hollywood and NY, 1939-41; master playwright, NYU; playwright in res, O State U. Author: Sparks Fly Upward, 1965; Mame, 1966; Dear World, 1968; co-author: Look Ma, I'm Dancin', 1948; Inherit the Wind, 1955; Shangri-La, 1956; Auntie Mame, 1956; The Gang's All Here, 1959; Only in America, 1959; A Call on Kuprin, 1961; Turn on the Night, 1961; one-act musi-dramas: Roaring Camp; Annie Laurie; The Familiar Stranger; Judy; They Live Forever; Hallmark Playhouse; Frank Sinatra Show; Army-Navy prog: Mail Call; Command Performance; VE Day; VJ Day; D Day progs; record albums: One God; Rip Van Winkle; A Cask of Amontillado; A Tale of Two Cities; text, radio writing, Off Mike; contbr to theatric jours. Mem bd: Amer Conservatory Theatre, Natl Repertory Theatre, Eugene O'Neill Found; Dramatic Guild; natl pres, Radio Writers Guild, 1953-54: dir, Writers Guild of Amer, 1955; mem: Phi Beta Kappa; ASCAP; Zeta Beta Tau. Recipient: Spec citation, Secy of War; Donalson award; Peabody award; Amer Playwrights Theatre and Margo Jones award; Ohiana lit award; Zeta Beta Tau's "Man of the Year," 1968. Home: 18106 Malibu Rd, Malibu, Cal Office: 449 W 50 St, New York, NY.

LAWRY, Sylvia, US, organization exec; b. NYC, June 28, 1915; d. Jack and Sonia (Tager) Friedman; BA, Hunter Coll, 1936; m. Michael Lawry, 1944, div; m. 2nd, Stanley Englander, April 7, 1957. Found, Natl Multiple Sclerosis Soc, exec dir since 1953, exec secy since 1946, secy, Intl Fed, since 1967; hearing reporter: NY State Lab Arbitrator, 1937-40; US Atty's off, NY, 1943-44; asst dir, radio produc, Civilian Defense Reporting, NYC, 1941-43. Bd dirs: Natl Health Council, 1959-62; mem: Comm on Health for Peace; Pres's Comm for Employment of Physically Handicapped; Natl Comm for Research in Neurol Disorders; Acad of Political Sci. Home: 66 Carlton Rd, Monsey, NY. Office: 257 Park Ave, S, New York, NY.

LAX, Bernard B, Can, investment cons; b. Montreal, Can, Mar 23, 1930; s. Abel and Mary (Rigler); BSc, McGill U, 1951; MBA, U Chgo, 1952; c: Andrew, Elyce. Mergers and acquisitions cons, Kippen and Co Inc, since 1962; lectr, bus mgmt, McGill U; inves counsel, Dominion Securities Corp, 1955-60; account exec, Merrill, Lynch, Pierce, Fenner, and Smith, 1960-61. Mem: inves comm, Fed J Comty Services; Royal Econ Soc; Amer Econ Assn; Amer Inst of Mgmt; Montreal Inst Inves Analysts. Home: 250 Clarke Ave, Westmount, Quebec, Can. Office: Suite 2900, 1155 Dorchester Blvd W, Montreal, Can.

LAX, Philip, US, interior designer; b. Newark, NJ, Apr 22, 1920; s. Nathan and Becky (Hirshorn); BS, NYU, 1940; att NYU Grad Sch; m. Mildred Baras, Feb 15, 1948; c: Corinne, Barbara. Interior designer since 1940. Hon pres, B'nai B'rith Cen, Rochester; exec vice pres, Rutgers-Douglas Hillel Found Bldg Corp; natl chmn, Young Builders, B'nai B'rith, vice chmn, natl mem cabinet; mem: bd trustees, profsl mem, Natl Soc of Interior Designers; Amer Arbitration Assn; Mason; Shriner; pres, admn bd, bd govs, Dist Grand Lodge 3, B'nai B'rith; bd govs, bd trustees, B'nai B'rith Found, vice pres, Supr Lodge; bd trustees, Leo N Levi Hosp, Hot Springs, Ark; exec comm, comty service comm, NJ regional bd, ADL; regional bd vocational service, B'nai B'rith; bd trustees, B'nai B'rith Camp, Pa; fmr: bd trustees, Orange Mt Council of Boy

Scouts; served two terms, Mayor's Budget Comm; vice chmn, chmn, UJA, Maplewood, NJ; pres: S Mt Lodge, N NJ Council, both B'nai B'rith; mem: bd trustees: Heb Acad of Essex Co; Essex Co Isr Bonds; natl mem champion, B'nai B'rith; club, NYU, found. Hobby, philately. Home: 35 Claremont Dr, Maplewood, NJ. Office: 70 Springfield Ave, Newark, NJ.

LAYTON, Irving, Can, author, educator; b. Niamtz, Rum, Mar 12, 1912; s. Moses and Keine (Moscowitch) Lazarovitch; in Can since 1913; BSc, Macdonald Coll, Can, 1939; MA, McGill U, Montreal, 1946; m. Betty Sutherland, 1946; c: Max, Naomi; m. 3rd, Aviva Cantor, Sep 13, 1959. Prof, Eng lit, York U; poet in res, U of Guelsh, 1969; lectr: Sir George Williams U, Montreal, since 1949; J Public Libr, 1943-59; tchr: Herzliah HS, 1945-60; JIAS, 1945-48. Lt, Royal Can Artillery, WW II. Author: Here and Now; Now is the Place; The Black Huntsman; Cerberus; Love the Conqueror Worm; In the Midst of My Fever; The Long Pea-Shooter; The Cold Green Element; Music on a Kazoo; The Bull Calf; The Blue Propellor; A Laughter in the Mind; The Improved Binoculars; A Red Carpet for the Sun; The Swinging Flesh; Love Where the Nights Are Long; Balls for a One-armed Juggler; The Laughing Rooster; Collected Poems; Periods of the Moon; The Shattered Plinths; Selected Poems; The Whole Bloody Bird; poems and stories appear in: Oxford Book of Canadian Verse; The World's Classics-Canadian Short Stories; The Book of Canadian Poetry; The Penguin Book of Canadian Verse; A Book of Canadian Stories; Recent Commonwealth Poetry; 20th Century Poetry and Poetics; American Poetry; co-ed, anthology, Canadian Poems 1850-1962; contbr to periodicals and jours. Recipient: Can Found award for poetry, 1958; Can Council award for poetry, 1959; Gov Gen's medal for, A Red Carpet for the Sun, 1960; Pres's medal for poetry, U of W Ont, 1961; Can Council sr award, 1968. Club, PEN. Home: 5731 Somerled Ave, Montreal, Can. Office: Dept of Eng, York U, Can.

LAYTON, Joe, US, director, choreographer; b. NYC, May 3, 1931; s. Irving and Sadie (Fischer) Lichtman; att HS of Music and Art, NY; m. Evelyn Russell, Oct 6, 1959; c: Jeb. Pres, Joue Enterprises; dir: Peterpat, Broadway produc, 1964; Eng produc: Sound of Music; Sail Away; No Strings; On the Town; TV produc: Mary Martins Easter Spec, 1959; Gershwin Years, 1960; Once Upon a Mattress, 1961; My Name is Barbra, 1965; Color Me Barbra, 1966; Belle of 14th St-Barbra Streisand, 1967; Flip Side, 1967; Theatre of the Deaf Spec, 1967; Androcles and the Lion, 1968; Jack Jones Spec, 1966; Debbie Reynolds Spec, 1968; Infancy, 1968; The Littlest Angel, 1969; The Lost Colony, for Roanoke Island Hist Assn; theatrical producs for Natl Theatre of the Deaf; dir, choreographer, Broadway producs: No Strings, 1962; Girl Who Came to Supper, 1963; Drat! The Cat!, 1966; Sherry, 1967; South Pacific, 1967; George M, 1968; Dear World, 1969; Scarlet, world premiere, Tokyo, Japan, 1970; choreographer: Thoroughly Modern Millie, 1967; motion picture; Broadway producs: Sound of Music, 1959; Greenwillow, 1960; Tenderloin, 1960; Sail Away, 1960; off-Broadway producs: On the Town, 1959; Once Upon a Mattress, 1959. US Army. Recipient: Antoinette Perry Award: No Strings, 1962; George M, 1969, both for Broadway theatre; award, Natl Acad of TV Arts and Scis, for My Name is Barbra, for TV, 1965. Home and office: 130 W 57 St, New York, NY.

LAZAR, Lucien, Isr, educator, organization exec; b. Strasbourg, Nov 11, 1924; s. Maurice and Renée (Weill); att: Yeshiva, Aix-les-Baines, 1945-46; licence d'enseignement histoire, U of Lyon, 1948; dipl d'Etudes Superieures, Inst des Etudes Politiques, Paris, 1951; PhD, U of Strasbourg, 1967; m Janine Hemmendinger, Mar 17, 1949; c: Daniel, Michel, Anne, Elisabeth. Dir, Gymnasia A Cremieux, secondary sch, Jerusalem, since 1968; fmr: secy gen, J Cmty of Strasbourg, 1959-68; youth councillor, tchr, hist, Ecole Yabne, Paris, 1948-51; dir, Ecole Israelite Brussels, Belgium, 1951-53. Fr Army WW II, decorated, Croix de Combattant. Fmr: secy gen, pres Strasbourg sect, l'Union des Etudiants Juifs de France; found, pres, Jeunes Menages. Author: Geographie d'Israel, 1956; A D Gordon: L'Homme et le philosophe (adapted from Prof D Bergmann) 1962; Apprendre et Enseigner (adapted from W. Chomsky) 1962; La pensée ouvriere zioniste, 1967; contbr to publs. Spec interest, Talmud. Home: 38 Ramban St, Jerusalem, Isr. Office: Alliance St, Jerusalem, Isr.

LAZAR, Mark Albert, Isr, psychiatrist; b. Rum, Nov 10, 1924; s. Samuel and Hilda (Rabinovitch); in Isr since 1950; MD,

Med Sch, Bucarest, Rum, 1949; m. Ida Rosenfeld, June 18, 1957; c: Yshayahu, Rona. Med dir, Holon Sanitarium. since 1961; house phys, asst, Geha Hosp, 1951-56; med dir, Nes Ziona Sanitarium, 1956-61. Contbr med papers, articles, lectures, on psycht, Mh. Hobbies: criminology, vocal music. Home: 52 Beeri St, Tel Aviv, Isr. Office: Holon Sanitarium, 12 Vav St, Holon, Isr.

LAZAR, Meyer, Fr, artist-painter; b. Galatz, Rum, Oct 4, 1923; s. Joseph and Sarah (Klein) Lazarovici; in Fr since 1950; att: J Art, Bucharest, 1941-44; Art Studio, Tel Aviv, 1946-48; Ecole Nationale des Beaux-Arts, Paris, 1950-54. Artist-painter, artistic councillor, Pré des Collectionnaires; different natl and intl exhbs; repr J Art. Served IDF, Navy, 1948-50. Recipient: Prix de la Jeune Peinture, Isr, 1949; Independence War, Isr. Hobby, collecting Judaica, J artists drawings. Home: 20 Rue Richer, Paris, Fr. Studio: 17 Quai Bourbon, Paris, Fr.

LAZAR, Rubin M, US; attorney; b. Montreal, Can, Nov 21, 1928; s. Isaac and Celia (Maron); in US since 1939; att UCLA, 1945-46, 1948; JD, cum laude, Loyola U, Sch of Law, 1951; m. Serene Sperling, Dec 24, 1950; c: Mark, David, Dana. Pvt practice since 1952; partner, law firm, Silver & Lazar since 1956; lectr, continuing educ of Bar series. Pvt, US Army, 1946-48. Pres, Valley J Comty Cen and Temple; F: U of Judaism; Amer Acad Matrimonial Lawyers, dir; bd dirs, United Syn of Amer, Pacific SW region; fmr, pres, LA Lodge, B'nai B'rith; fmr, vice-chmn, United JWF, attys div; mem: LA, Beverly Hills, Amer Bar Assns; J Publ Soc; Phi Delta Phi; Pi Kappa Delta; arbitrator, Amer Arbitration Assn. Recipient, Aggeler and Bur of Natl Affairs Awards, Loyola U Sch of Law, 1951. Home: 3920 Longridge, Sherman Oaks, Cal. Office: 6505 Wilshire Blvd, Los Angeles, Cal.

LAZARON, Morris S, US, rabbi, author; b. Savannah, Ga, Apr 16, 1888; s. Samuel and Alice (de Castro); desc: Isaac de Sola, Court phys to William of Orange and ibn Daud; Judah P. Benjamin, Secy of State, Confederacy; BA, U Cincinnati, 1909, MA, 1911; ordained Rabbi, HUC, 1914; post-grad studies: Johns Hopkins U; Hochschule für Wissenschaft des Judentums; hon DLitt, Rutgers U, 1934; m. Pauline Horkheimer, 1916 (decd); c: Morris, Harold, Clementine; m. 2nd, Hilda Rothschild Rosenblatt, 1945. Rabbi: Baltimore Heb Cong, 1915-49, ret; Cong LeShem Shomayim, Wheeling, W Va, 1914-15. J chaplain officiating at burial of Unknown Soldier, Arlington Cemetery, Nov 11, 1922. Natl hon vice-pres and co-found, Amer Council for Judaism; mem: CCAR; Amer Merchant Marine Libr Assn; AJComm. Author: Religious Services for Jewish Youth, 1925; Consolations of Our Faith, 1928; Seed of Abraham, 1930; Palestine and Jewish Nationalism, 1938; Common Ground, 1938; Olive Tree in Storm, 1955; Bridges not Walls, 1959; mem, ed bd, Jewish Newsletter. Recipient: Gottheil award, 1934; citation from Mil Chaplains Assn, 1958. Hobbies: golf, fishing, painting. Home: 241 W Indies Dr, Palm Beach, Fla; summer: Blowing Rock, NC.

LAZARUS, David, S Afr, chartered accountant; b. Kimberley, S Afr, Feb 1, 1902; s. Isaac and Rose (Chernak); m. Dorothy Perel, June 3, 1933; c: Sydney, Rhona Glasser. Sr partner, Lazarus Bros and Barr, chartered acctnts. Doyen, City Council of E London; mem: Cape Provincial Council since 1949, select comm on public accts; E London Sch Bd; bd mgmt Malcomess House Children's Home; Assn of Arts, hon life; Assn of Intl Acctnts; Inst of Commerce; Cape Soc of Acctnts and Auditors; admnrs nominee bd trustees, E London Mus; Royal Econ Soc; S Afr Inst for Public Admn; Tech Coll Council; Natl Thrift Org; gen comm, 1820 Memorial Settlers Assn; life, S Afr J Ex-Service League; hon life, RAF Assn; hon, Naval Offs Assn; pres, Border Aviation Club; chmn, Frere Hosp Bd; fmr: pres: Afr Legion of British Commonwealth Ex Service League; E London Dramatic Soc; first chmn, Art Gal Adv Bd; hon secy: Heb Cong; J Helping Hand and Burial Soc; Zionist Soc; clubs: Alexander Country; Comrades; E London; Rotary; Yacht. Recipient: Queen's Coronation Medal; S Afr Rep Medal; Freedom of City, E London; hosp block named in his honor. Home: 31 Botha Rd, E London, S Afr. Office: 3/5 Gladstone St, E London, S Afr.

LAZARUS, Jacques, Fr, organization exec; b. Payerne, Switz, Sep 2, 1916; s. Maurice and Marcelle (Dreyfus); m. Judith Cherqui, Jan 4, 1948; c: Eva, Nora. Mem, exec comm, WJC; chief, Paris sect, J Combat Org, 1944; secy gen: Cen Services for J Deportees, Paris, 1945-46; Algerian J Comm of

Social Studies, 1948-63; dir: Information Juive, newspaper, 1948-62; N Afr bur, WJC, 1949-62. Hon pres, found, Algerian ORT, 1947; mem, Intl ORT Union since 1965. Author, Juifs au Combat, 1947. Recipient: Croix de Guerre, 1945; Médaille de la Resistance avec rosette, 1946; Legion d'honneur, chevalier. Home: 4 Square Augustus Renoir, Paris 14, Fr. Office: 78 ave des Champs Elysees, Paris 8, Fr.

LAZARUS, Sanford S, US, business exec; b. Elmira, NY, May 27, 1899; s. Julius and Martha (Sellner); m. Gladys Fried, May 20, 1930; c: Marcia Spiro, Sandra Hertz. Pres: O Battery and Ignition Co since 1941. Org, Boy Scout Troop 7, past scout master; co-chmn, Canton Sesqui Centennial Celebration; mem: Canton Bd of Educ since 1958, past pres; bd, YMCA since 1958; adv bd, Timken Mercy Sch of Practical Nursing since 1959; adv council, United Motors Service Div since 1958; TB, Health Assns; Cmty Service Council; fmr: mem, Mayor's Housing Commn; org, charter mem, O Automobile Wholesalers Assn; mem adv bd, Malone Coll; chmn: Cmty Fund Campaign; TB Christmas Seals; 2 divs, War Rationing Bd; Crippled Children's Comm; vice pres, Stark Co TB and Health Assns; club, Rotary, fmr mem bd. Recipient, Man of Year, Canton C of C, 1959. Home: 2134 University Ave, NW, Canton, O. Office: 831 Market Ave N, Canton, O.

LAZER, David, Isr, writer, journalist; b. Cracow, Pol, Oct 7, 1902; s. Simon and Breindel (Ohrenstein); in Isr since 1941; PhD, U Cracow, 1946; m. Hanna Rakower; c: Aviva Dvir. Ret; fmr, mem ed bd, lit ed, Maariv, Heb daily. Author: Israeli Profiles, 2 vols, 1952, 1955; Voyage to Euzkadi, 1956; Encounters on Both Sides of the Iron Curtain, all in Heb. Mem: Heb Writers Assn; Journalists Assn. Recipient: UNESCO f for advanced studies in journalism, Strasbourg, 1957-63; Sokolow Prize, Tel Aviv Munic, 1960. Hobby: swimming. Home: 56 Itzhak Sadeh St, Tel Aviv, Isr.

LAZEROWITZ, Morris, US, educator; b. Lodz, Pol, Oct 22, 1907; s. Max and Etta (Plochzinski) Laizerowitz; in US since 1914; AB, U Mich, 1933; PhD, 1936; att Harvard, 1937-38; m. Alice Ambrose, June 15, 1938. Sophia and Austin Smith Prof, Smith Coll since 1964, prof, phil, since 1954, on fac since 1938; instr, U Mich, 1935-37; prof, Bedford Coll, U London, 1951-52. Mem: Amer Phil Assn; Royal Inst Phil; AAUP. Author: The Structure of Metaphysics, 1955; Metaphilosophy, 1963; Philosophy and Illusion, 1968; co-author: Fundamentals of Symbolic Logic, 1948; Logic: The Theory of Formal Inference, 1961; co-ed: G E Moore, Essays in Retrospect, 1970; Psychoanalysis and Philosophy, 1971; contbr to phil jours. Recipient: Rackham post doc travelling f, 1937-38; Fulbright lectureship, 1951-52. Home: 31 Langworthy Rd, Northampton, Mass. Office: Smith Coll, Northampton, Mass.

LAZERUS, Gilbert, US, attorney; b. NYC, June 24, 1912; s. Jacob and Bessie (Goldfein); PhB, Yale U, 1931; JD, Columbia Law Sch, 1934; m. Judith Kaplan, Dec 25, 1940; c: Bruce, June. Partner, law firm, Stroock & Stroock & Lavan since 1945; bd dirs, Morningside Hgts Inc. Mem: bd overseers, JTSA since 1951; bd trustees, Syn of JTSA. Home: 1175 York Ave, New York, NY. Office: 61 Broadway, New York, NY.

LAZRUS, Benjamin, US, business exec; b. NYC, Apr 29, 1894; s. Israel and Ella (Cohn); att Columbia U, 1912-13; m. Bessie Feldman, Feb 24, 1924; c: Natalie Goldstein, Jonathan. Ret, found, Benrus Watch Co, 1923, pres, 1923-59. Vice-pres, FJP, NY, 1950-53, trustee; treas, Amer J Tercentenary Comm, 1955; vice-pres, Cong Emanu-El, bd trustees; vice-pres, UJA of NY, bd dirs; bd trustees: AJComm; JWB; Gtr NY USO; chmn, adv council, Syn Council of Amer; vice-pres, CJFWF; mem: J Comty Cen, White Plains, NY; Natl J Hosp of Denver; J Bd Guardians; Natl Ref Service; clubs: Harmonie; Quaker Ridge Golf; Jewelers 24 Karat, past pres. Home: 150 E 69 St, New York, NY. Office: 1776 Broadway, New York, NY.

LAZRUS, Julian, US, business exec; b. Bklyn, NY, June 2, 1919; s. Oscar and Paula (Kronheim); BA, Harvard U, 1940; att Harvard Bus Sch, 1940-41; m. Miriam Roback, Dec 23, 1942; c: Deborah, Judith, Sarah. Pres, Benrus Watch Co since 1960. Pres, Bx House, Inc, 1950-53, bd mem since 1947; vice-pres, JWB, metrop sect, 1952-62; bd dirs, natl JWB, 1955-62; trustee: NCCJ, since 1965; FJP, 1951-53; mem: clubs: Harvard; Advt of NY. Office: 29 E 61 St, New York, NY.

LAZRUS, Oscar M, US, attorney; b. Jassy, Rum, July 12, 1887; s. Israel and Ella (Cohn); in US since 1899; LLB, St Lawrence Law Sch, 1909; m. Paula Kronheim, Feb 11, 1913 (decd); c: Julian, Jay; m. 2nd, Anna Leitner, 1952 (decd); m. 3rd, Rose Lazrus, 1962. Fmr, chmn bd, Benrus Watch Co. Natl secy, NCCJ; dir, JDC; life trustee, FJP, NY; vice-pres, exec bd, UAHC; mem: exec comm, AJComm; bd mgrs, Silver Hall Found; Amer Bar Assn; fmr, pres, Hosp for Jt Diseases; clubs: Harmonie; Bankers; 24 Karat. Home: 936 Fifth Ave, New York, NY. Office: 521 Fifth Ave, New York, NY.

LEAR, Maxwell, US, surgeon; b. Elizabethgrad, Russ, Aug 2, 1888; s. Samuel and Fannie (Freedman); desc of Rabbi Israel Salanter; in US since 1900; MD, Yale U, 1911, MS, 1923; m. Ida Avrutin, Oct 8, 1912; c: Pearl Levin, Lillian Newman, Norma Hays. Cons surg: Yale Med Cen since 1953; Yale New Haven Med Cen; St Raphael Hosp; Griffin Hosp, Em cons; fmr: res surg, New Haven Hosp; asst clinical prof surg, Yale U Med Sch; surg, Yale-New Haven Comty Hosp; mem US Info Agcy Med USA Team. F: Amer Coll Surg; Intl Coll Surg; pres, Friends of Hillel; mem bd dirs New Haven Free Public Libr since 1946, past pres; fmr: pres: New Haven Med Assn; J Home for Children; mem: natl bd dirs, Amer J Phys Comm; AMA; Phi Delta Epsilon; Sigma Xi; clubs: Probus, past pres; Probus Natl, past pres; Yale. Contbr of articles to sci jours. Home: 19 Beechwood Lane, New Haven, Conn. Office: 17 Chapel St, New Haven, Conn.

LEAR, Philip E, US, surgeon, educator; b. New Haven, Conn, Dec 7, 1905; s. Samuel and Fannie (Freedman); BS, Yale U, 1926; MD, LI Coll of Med, 1934; m. Dora Hersh, Sep 27, 1936; c: Elizabeth, Marion. Dir surg, LI J Hosp, New Hyde Park, NY; prof, surg, Med Coll SUNY; cons surg: Bklyn Vets Hosp; Caledonian Hosp; chief, surg, Valley Forge Gen Hosp, 1942-45. Pres: bd of mgrs, Alumni Assn, Med Coll, SUNY; med bd, U div, Kings Co Hosp, 1953-54; comm for study of internship and residencies, NYC; bd govs, candidates comm, sci comm, Amer Coll Surgs; chmn, phys and dent dr, FJP, 1958; mem: Amer Bd Surg; AMA; Phi Delta Epsilon; club, Fresh Meadow Country. Author, med studies. Home: 50 Nassau Dr, Great Neck, NY. Office: Long Island J Hosp, 270-05 76 Ave, New Hyde Park, NY.

LEAVITT, Joseph S, US, physician; b. Keene, NH, Sep 11, 1905; s. David and Gertrude (Silverman); BS, Webster U, Ga, 1931; MD, U Lausanne, Switz, 1936; post-grad studies: Paris; Vienna; Brussels, 1937; m. Rosamond Goldberg, Oct 19, 1941; c: Stephanie Ventura, Lorraine, Donald. Pvt practice since 1936; pres: United States Drug and Chem Corp since 1957; dir, Surety Bank and Trust Co, Wakefield since 1960, fmr pres. Prin contrib, donor with wife, Interfaith Memorial to Four Chaplains, Temple Emmanuel, Wakefield, 1955. F, AMA; mem: Mass Med Soc; Amer Phys F Comm of IMA; Temple Emmanuel, Wakefield, treas since 1957, past pres, past pres Brotherhood; fmr, bd trustees, Mass Lying-In and Gen Hosp; fmr, bd dirs, Webster Manor Hosp, Walden, Mass; AJCong; Natl Fed Temple Brotherhoods; bd dirs, YMCA since 1949; B'nai B'rith; Natl J Chautauqua Soc; Elks; Kiwanis Intl; Masons 32 deg; Shriners; Brandeis U; asso: Natl Geographic; clubs: New Cent; Intl High Noon. Hobbies: travel, art objects, philately. Home and office: 8 Avon St, Wakefield, Mass.

LEBENSOHN, James E, US, ophthalmologist, educator; b. Chgo, Ill, Nov 5, 1893; s. Morris and Rose (Elisberg); MS, U Chgo, 1915; MD, Rush Med Coll, Chgo, 1917; PhD, Northwestern U, 1935; m. Sara Kreloff, Aug 4, 1947. Pvt practice since 1925; prof em, ophthal, Northwestern U, since 1962, on fac since 1930; att ophthal: Mt Sinai Hosp, Chgo; Cook Co Hosp, 1937-38; US Vets Hosp; asso examiner, Amer Bd Ophthal. Prin contrib: invented: near vision chart, 1935; unlearnable chart, 1949; astigmometer, 1949. F, phys, U Chgo, 1917; mem: Amer Acad Ophthal and Otolaryngology; AAAS; Pan-Amer Assn Ophthal; Amer Coll Surgs; Chgo Ophthal Soc; Optical Soc of Amer; Inst of Physics; Inst of Med, Chgo; Soc for Med Hist; AMA; Sigma Xi; Phi Delta Epsilon. Asso ed: Amer Jour of Ophthal; Survey of Ophthal; trans from Fr, Bailart's Retinal Circulation, 1927; contbr to profsl jours. Recipient: Lyman Prize for research, 1916, 1917. Hobby, travel. Home: 6200 N Kenmore Ave, Chicago, Ill. Office: 4010 W Madison St, Chicago, Ill.

LEBESON, Anita L, US, historian, author; b. Vilna, Lith; d. Morris and Elizabeth (Oleiski) Libman; in US since 1907;

BA, U of Ill, 1918; MA, Northwestern U, 1935, PhD, 1969; grad studies, U Chgo; m. Hermon Lebeson, Aug 7, 1921; c: David (decd), Mariamne Goldstein. Free lance writer; research worker and lectr: Adult Educ Council; J Cen Lectr Bur; custodian, Ill Hist Soc, 1918-19; instr: hist dept, U of Ill, 1918-19; Amer J hist, Coll of J Studies, Chgo, 1951-52. Mem: exec council, Amer J Hist Soc since 1950; Author's League; Amer Technion Soc; Phi Beta Kappa; Kappa Delta Pi. Author: Jewish Pioneers in America, 1931; Tale of Gabriel, 1945; American Adventure, 1948; Pilgrim People, 1950; Brave Story, 1952; American Jewish Chronicle, 1950; co-ed, Standard J Ency, 1959; contbr to: Vol IV, Jewish People, Past and Present; History of the Jews in the US, 1955. Recipient: Chgo Found Lit award for outstanding non-fiction, 1950; JBCA award for contribs to lit on Amer hist, 1954; Coll of J Studies award, 1955. Home: 611 Wesley Ave, Evanston, Ill.

LEBHAR, Alfred David, Isr, advocate; b. Tel Aviv, Isr, Dec 26, 1904; s. Maurice and Esther (Levy); licencié en droit, Fac Law, Paris, 1932; att Heb U, Jerusalem; m. Régine Franco, Mar 21, 1947; c: Eliane Shoenman, Dalia Carr, Ruth, Ariella. Advocate and notary, since 1950; fmr: asst postmaster, Tel Aviv; dist off, Galilee, Haifa, both Pal Govt; asst dist commnr, Isr Govt. Chmn, Council Sephardic J, Haifa; vice chmn, Isr-It Friendship League, Haifa; mem, Isr exec bd, World Sephardic Fed; fmr pres, Alliance Fr in Isr. Contbr to lit and legal publs. Recipient: Chevalier de la Légion d'Honneur, Pres Fr Rep, 1954; Off, Order of Merit, Pres It Rep, 1959; hon citizen, Cleveland, and Tenn, both 1968. Hobbies: tennis, swimming. Home: 15 Margalit St, Haifa, Isr. Office: 3 Hassan Shukri St, Haifa, Isr.

LEBIUSH, Zalman, Isr, actor; b. Lith, Jan 30, 1908; s. Mordechai and Gitl; in Isr since 1935; att Dramatic Studio and Sch of Stage Mgn, Yale U; m. Yehudith Feinberg; c: Avishag. Mem: Chamber Theatre, since 1950; fmr: Pal Comedy Troupe, 1935-36; Hamatate Troupe, 1936-42; Ohel Troupe, 1942-47; maj roles: Ohel Theatre: Arms and the Man; The Doctor's Dilemma; For Whom the Bell Tolls; Chamber Theatre: Of Mice and Men; Desire Under the Elms; Twelfth Night; Marius; Life of Galilei. Recipient: Tel Aviv Munic Award, 1960; Milo, Artists Club Award, 1962. Home: 2 Hashoftim St, Tel Aviv, Isr. Office: Chamber Theatre, Tel Aviv, Isr.

LEBOVIC, Djordje, Yugo, author; b. Sombor, Yugo, June 27, 1928; s. Pavle and Tereza (Seidner); att U Belgrade, 1947-51; div; c: Gordana. Author: Himmel-Kommando, drama, Belgrade 1956, Bratislava 1957, Warsaw 1958, Prague 1965, Vienna 1966; Haleluah, drama, Novi Sad, Warsaw, 1964, Belgrade, Paris, 1965, Nürnberg, 1966, Moscow, Budapest, 1968; The Lights and the Shadows, radio-drama, Belgrade 1958, München 1959, Auro Hilversum, Lodz, 1960, Graz, Köln, 1961, Karlsruhe, Cracow, Budapest, Trieste, 1962, Berlin 1965, Brussels, Bucharest, 1968; Victoria, drama, Belgrade 1968; The Doll, TV drama, Belgrade 1966; other plays, TV and Radio dramas. Mem, Intl Auschwitz Comm, chap gen comm. Recipient: Yugo Theatre Festival Award: Himmel-Kommando, 1957; Haleluah, 1965. Home: M. Tolbuhina St, 61, Belgrade, Yugo.

LEBOW, Leonard Stanley, US, teacher, musician; b. Chgo, Ill, Feb 25, 1929; s. Philip and Rose (Wintergr); BMus, Roosevelt U, Chgo, 1952; deg, music educ, Northwestern U, Evanston, 1955; MMus, Chgo Musical, 1959. Tchr, public schs, LA, Cal since 1955; free-lance musician, composer, arranger since 1947. Pvt, Ill Natl Guard, 1949-50. Compositions: Suite for Brass, 1956; Popular Suite and Second Suite for Brass, 1960. Mem: ASCAP; LA Arrangers Soc; LA United Tchrs Assn. Hobbies: sound recording, photography. Home: 4411 Stern, Sherman Oaks, Cal. Office: 450 N Grand, Los Angeles, Cal.

LEBOW, Mark Denis, US, attorney; b. Harrisburg, Pa, Apr 2, 1940; s. Sylvan and Ruth (Lebowitz); AB, Yale U, 1961; LLB, Harvard Law Sch, 1964. Atty, Coudert Bros since 1965. Lt, USNR. Chmn: Henry St Settlement Camps Dr; NY ACLU Exec Panel on Mil and Draft Law; bd dirs, Men's Club, Cong Emanu-El; bus bd, NYC Cen. Home: 128 Central Park S, New York, NY. Office: 200 Park Ave, New York, NY.

LEBOW, Sylvan, US, organization exec; b. Baltimore, Md, July 23, 1912; s. Joseph and Marie (Propp); BA, Johns Hopkins U, 1932; BJ, U Mo, 1933; m. Ruth Lebowitz, 1934; c: Mark, Joy. Exec dir, Natl Fed of Temple Brotherhoods and its natl educ project, the J Chautauqua Soc since 1949; staff: Baltimore Post; Harrisburg Patriot-News; Phila Record, 1934-40; publicity dir, Commonwealth of Pa; PR dir, Pa Motor Truck Assn, 1940-41; owner, dir, Pa PR Service; publ, Harris-

burg Guide, both 1941-49. Vice-chmn: Rel in Amer Life; PR Soc of Amer. Author: War on Indifference, 1952; Brotherhood Program Guide, 1953; The Temple Brotherhood, 1963; ed, Brotherhood Mag; lectr on J-Chr relations, supervised TV pictures on Judaism; contbr to natl mags. Home: 360 E 72nd St, New York, NY. Office: 838 Fifth Ave, New York, NY.

LEBOWITZ, Abraham I, US, librarian; b. NYC, Aug 7, 1931; s. Samuel and Bathiah (Bloch); BA, Bklyn Coll, 1952; MSLS, Catholic U of Amer, 1966; m. Shulamith Waxman, Feb 1, 1953; c: Simon, Anne, Esther. Asst dir for systems devel, Natl Agric Libr since 1968; libr, Yeshiva U HS, 1950-52; reference libr, Hebraic sect, Libr of Cong, 1952-55; libr: Baltimore Heb Coll, 1955-59; USN Personnel Research Activity, 1960-62; sci specialist, Natl Referral Cen for Sci and Tech, 1963; dep libr, US AEC, 1963-68. Mem: Amer Libr Assn; Spec Libr Assn; Amer Soc for Info Sci. Home: 5818 Narcissus Ave, Baltimore, Md. Office: Natl Agric Libr, Beltsville, Md.

LEBOWITZ, J Leon, US, attorney, educator; b. Waco, Tex, Oct 18, 1921; s. David and Frances (Silevitch); AB, Baylor U, 1950; DJur, LLM, NYU, 1952; m. Elaine Ephraim, Aug 22, 1948; c: Brian, Amelia. Prof law, U Tex since 1957, on fac since 1956; atty, Austin, Tex since 1957; law libr, asst, asso prof, Baylor U, 1946-55; asso prof, La State U, 1955-56. US Army, 1943-45. Mem: adv bd, Hillel Found, U Tex; exec comm, SW reg bd, ADL; comm on securities law rev, State Bar, Tex; Amer Bar Assn; Travis Co Bar Assn; Order of Coif; Phi Delta Phi; Temple Beth Isr, bd trustees; pres, J Cmty Council, Austin; fmr: pres, Hill City Lodge, B'nai B'rith; pres, Zionist Org; mem bd trustees, Cong Agudas Jacob, both Waco, Tex. Author: Legal Biography and Research, 1957; co-author, Texas Business Corporation Act, 1955; fac ed: La Law Review, 1955-56; Tex Law Review, 1956-58, 1961-62. Recipient, Silver Star, WWII. Home: 3403 Cascadera, Austin, Tex. Office: 2500 Red River, Austin, Tex.

LEBOWITZ, Mortimer C, US, business exec; b. NYC, Mar 18, 1912; s. Henry and Esther (Roth); AB, U Pa, 1932; att NYU Law Sch, 1933-35; m. Adele Gusack, June 4, 1940; c: John, Emily, Caroline, Petrina. Pres, Morton's since 1935; buyer, The Mart, 1933-35. Pres: Commn on Human Resources, since 1962; Wash Urban League, 1960-61, bd mem since 1956; chmn: Inner City Boy Scouts, DC since 1967; Equal Opportunity Day, 1963; fund raising campaign, Heb U, 1953; exec comm, Wash Cen for Metrop Studies; bd dirs, UJA, 1947-48; vice-pres, Brandeis dist, ZOA, 1948; mem: Neighborhood Service Project Comm; Bd of Trade. Recipient: human relations award, Capitol Press Club, 1961; Afro-Amer award for superior public service, 1955; C of C merit award, 1962; Equal Opportunity Award, 1967; Silver Beaver Award, Boy Scouts, 1968. Home: 6319 Georgtown Pike, McLean, Va. Office: 312 7 St, NW, Washington, DC.

LECAR, Myron, US, astronomer; b. Bklyn, NY, Apr 10, 1930; s. Joshua and Raechel (Stoun); BS, MIT, 1951; MS, Case Inst Tech, 1953; PhD, Yale U, 1963. Astronomer, Smithsonian Astrophys Observatory since 1965; lectr, Harvard Coll since 1965; visiting prof, Tel Aviv U, since 1967; astronomer, Inst for Space Studies, NASA, 1961-65; lectr Yale U, 1963-65. Lt, USN, 1954-58. Prin contrib, established research group on study of the galaxy. Mem: Amer Astronomical Assn; Royal Astronomical Soc; Intl Astronomical Union. Contbr to sci jours. Spec interests: sci in Isr; photography. Home: 205 Mt Auburn St, Cambridge, Mass. Office: 60 Garden St, Cambridge, Mass.

LECHNER, Frederick, US, cantor, singer; b. Stettin, Ger, June 10, 1908; s. Gustav and Sophie (Gaster); in US since 1936; att: Berlin U, 1926-28; Natl Acad of Music, Berlin, 1926-30; m. Eva Loewenfeld, 1936. Cantor, Cen Syn, NY, since 1937; music cons and soloist, Message of Isr prog, ABC radio network, since 1937; soloist with: Philharmonic Orchestra, 1939; Boston Symphony, 1947; Dallas Symphony, 1952; Chicago Symphony, 1953; baritone, Metrop Opera Assn, 1943-50; guest performances, Teatro Colón, Buenos Aires, Argentina, 1946; concert tour, Australia, 1963. Study: 123 E 55 St, New York, NY.

LECHT, Leonard A, US, educator; b. Providence, RI, Oct 16, 1920; s. Harry and Sarah (Finkle); BA, U Minn, 1942; PhD, Columbia U, 1953; m. Jane Gillespie, Sep 15, 1951; c: David. Prof, chmn, dept econ, LIU since 1956, on fac since 1954; dir, Cen for Priority Analysis, Natl Planning Assn since 1963; lectr, Columbia U, 1947-49; asst prof: U Tex, 1949-53; Carleton Coll, Minn, 1953-54; fac f, Fund for Advancement of Educ, Ford Found, 1951-52. US Army, 1943-45. Mem: Amer Econ Assn; Ind Relations Research Assn; Phi Beta Kappa; f, Royal Econ Assn. Author: Experience Under Railway Labor Legislation, 1956; Manpower Needs for National Goals in the 1970's, 1969; Goals, Priorities and Dollars — The Next Decade, 1966; contbr to profsl jours. Home: 6410 Marjory La, Bethesda, Md. Office: 1250 Connecticut Ave, Washington, DC.

LEDERBERG, Joshua, US, geneticist; b. May 23, 1925, Montclair, NJ; s. Zwi and Esther (Goldenbaum); BA, Columbia, 1945; PhD, Yale, 1947, DSc, hon, 1960; DSc, hon: Wis, 1967, Columbia, 1967, Yeshiva, 1970; MD, hon, Turin, 1969; m. Marguerite Stein, Apr 4, 1968. Dir, Kennedy Labs for Molecular Med, Stanford U, since 1961, prof, chmn, dept genet, since 1959; research asst, zool, Columbia, 1945-46; research f, Jane Coffin Childs Fund for Med Research, Yale, 1946-47; prof, genet, U Wis, 1947-59, chmn, dept, med genet, 1957-59; visiting prof, bact, U Cal, 1950; Fulbright visiting prof, bact, Melbourne U, Australia, 1957. Mem: Pres Sci Adv Comm panels, NIH, NSF study sect on genet, since 1950; Natl Acad Sci, comm on space biol, since 1958; NASA comms, Lunar and Planetary Mission Bd, since 1960; NIMH, Natl Mh Adv Council, since 1967; cons, Arms Control and Disarmament Agcy, since 1970; bd gov, Weizmann Inst Sci, Rehovot, Isr, since 1969. Columnist, Sci and Man, Wash Post Syndicate, since 1966. Recipient: award, Natl Acad Sci, 1957; Nobel Prize in med for studies on org of genet material in bact. Office: Dept of Genet, Sch of Med, Stanford U, Stanford, Cal.

LEDERER, Francis L, US, surgeon, educator; b. Chgo, Ill, Sep 18, 1898; s. Jacob and Frances (Loeffler); BS, U Chgo, 1919; MD, Rush Coll, 1921; m. Anne Pollock, 1925; c: Francis. Sr otolaryngologist, Grant, Michael Reese and Columbus Hosps, all in Chgo, since 1946; prof em, U Ill Coll of Med, head, dept otolaryngology, 1933-67, on fac since 1923; chief, otolaryngological services, Research and Educ Hosp, 1925-67; dir, otolaryngology, Ill Eye and Ear Infirmary, 1946-67. USMC, 1917-19; capt, USN MC, 1942-46, cons: VA; Surg Gen, USAF. Hon F, Intl Coll of Surg; fmr pres: Amer Otolaryngological Soc; Amer Coll Surg; Amer Acad Ophthal and Otolaryngology; mem: AMA; Rhinological, Laryngological and Otological Assn; Amer Laryngological Assn. Author, Diseases of the Ear, Nose and Throat, 6 ed, 1938-53; co-author, Textbook of Ear, Nose and Throat, 4 ed, 1942-51; Atlas of Otorhinolaryngology and Bronchoesophagology, pub in six langs, 1969. Recipient: Raymond B Allen award, 1950, 1957, 1960. Home: 119 E Lake Shore Dr, Chicago, Ill. Office: 307 N Michigan Ave, Chicago, Ill.

LEDERER, Richard M, Jr, US, investment manager; b. NYC, Oct 6, 1916; s. Richard and Marguerite (Kern); BS, Yale U, 1939; att Amer Inst of Banking, NYC, 1940; m. Carol Grinberg, Sept 8, 1940; c: Barbara, Ann. Partner, Reredel Asso, since 1946; dir, Energy Fund, Inc; comptroller, Standard Natl Bank, Woodside, NY, 1940-42. Capt, US Army, 1942-45. Pres, JCC, 1949-52; trustee, JCCen, 1952-55, both at White Plains, NY; natl commnr, ADL, since 1957, treas, since 1957; club: Town, gov, 1957-61. Home: 15 Horseguard Lane, Scarsdale, NY. Office: 270 Martine Ave, White Plains, NY.

LEDERER, Leo Arye, Isr, educator; b. Bruex, Bohemia, Sep 5, 1903; s. Ludwig and Leontine (Kohn); in Isr since 1939; JUC, law fac, Masaryk U, 1938; m. Lydia Lea Winter, May 10, 1930; c: Ruth. Ret; fmr: active: admn, off org, sales mgmt, market research in Isr; clerk, vice mgr, ATA Textile Co, 1939-66; mgr, Bohemian Union Bank, Bruenn, 1920-39; tchr, dir, Sch of Dramatic Arts, 1934-39; found, Acad of Musical Arts, Bruenn. Mt infantry, Czech, 1923-26; lt, Haganah, IDF, 1940-53. Mem: B'nai B'rith; USHA, Kiriat Ata, Isr; fmr: leader, Zionist Youth Org, Maccabi Hatzair; i/c youth, Maccabi World Org. Hobbies: theatre; books; music; recitals; dramatic arts. Home: Kiriat Ata, Isr.

LEDERMAN, Leon M, US, physicist, educator; b. NYC, July 15, 1922; s. Morris and Minnie (Rosenberg); BS, CCNY, 1943; MA, Columbia U, 1948, PhD, 1951; m. Florence Gordon, Sep 19, 1945; c: Rena, Jesse, Heidi. Prof, Columbia U since 1958, fac mem since 1952, dir, Nevis Cyclotron Labs since 1960. Lt col, US Army, 1943-46. Mem: Amer Phys Soc; Natl Acad Sci; It Phys Soc; Sigma Xi. Contbr numerous articles on elem particle physics to profsl jours in US and It. Recipient: Ernest Kempton Adams f, 1961; Natl Medal of Sci, Natl Acad Sci, 1966. Home: 34 Overlook Rd, Dobbs Ferry, NY. Office: Columbia U, New York, NY.

LEE, Edward, US, attorney; b. NYC, May 4, 1908; s. Louis and Selma (Vanpraag); AB, summa cum laude, Harvard Coll, 1930; att Harvard Law Sch; LLB, Columbia Law Sch, 1933; m. Elaine Link, Apr 22, 1942; c: Donald, David. Partner: Bondy and Schloss since 1969; Eisman, Lee, Corn, Sheftel and Block, 1947-68. Capt, Mil Police. Mem: NY State Bar Assn; Assn Bar, NYC; exec bd, Natl Fed Temple Brotherhoods; bd trustees, J Comty Cen, White Plains; Amer bd, World Union for Progressive Judaism; fmr: chancellor, J Chautauqua Soc; bd trustees, UAHC. Home: 35 Eton Rd, Scarsdale, NY. Office: 6 E 43 St, New York, NY.

LEE, Malka, US, Yiddish poet; b. Monasterzyska, Pol, July 4, 1904; d. Chaim and Frieda (Duhl) Leopold; in US since 1921; att: J Tchrs Sem, 1921-23; Hunter Coll; CCNY; m. Aaron Rappaport, June 4, 1922, (decd); c: Joseph, Yvette; m. 2nd, Moshe Besser, 1966. Author: Lieder, 1932; Gesangen, 1940; Kines Fun Unser Zeit, 1945; Durch Loitere Qualn, 1950; In Licht Fun Doires, 1961; Durch Kindershe Oygen, 1955; Untern Nusnboim, 1969; Maiselech for Yoselen, 1969; text for musical score, Am Yisrael Chai, 1964; contbr to Yiddish lit periodicals; many anthols; encys; almanacs. Mem: Pioneer Women, Farband; Yiddish PEN Club. Recipient: Hayim Greenberg Lit Award, Pioneer Women, 1965. Home: 68 W 238 St, Bronx, NY.

LEE, Sidney S, US, physician, medical admnr; b. New Haven, Conn, Dec 5, 1921; s. Nathaniel and Alma (Dickstein); BS, Sheffield Sci Sch, Yale U, 1942, MD, 1950, MPH, 1952, DPH, 1953; m. Frances Zellick, Dec 11, 1959; c: Amanda, Civia, Jonathan, Michael. Asso dean, hosp progs, Harvard Med Sch, since 1966, lectr, preventive med, 1963-66; clinical prof, hosp and med care admn, Harvard Sch of Public Health, since 1966, lectr, public health practice, 1955-63; sr surg, USPHS, 1950-54; gen dir, Beth Isr Hosp, 1960-66, on staff from 1954. US Army, 1943-45. F: AAAS; Amer Public Health Assn; mem: Intl Hosp Fed; Mass Public Health Assn; Assn of Amer Med Colls. Contbr to profsl jours. Recipient: Chevalier de l'Ordre de Sante Publique, Fr, 1954. Home: 26 Chilton St, Brookline, Mass. Office: 25 Shattuck St, Boston, Mass.

LEEF, Nimrod, Isr, architect, business exec; b. Jerusalem, Nov 18, 1924; s. Zalman and Gutia (Strongin); att Heb U, Jerusalem, 1941-42; dipl, Ing, architect, town planner, Technion, Haifa, 1948; m. Mina Froumine, Jan, 1950; c: Zalman, Inaam. Dir: Photogrammetric Engr Co Ltd, since 1968; Zalman Leif Aerial Survey Ltd, since 1951; fmr: town planner, adv, Munics: Jerusalem; Rishon L'Zion. Mil engr, IDF. Prin contribs: use of photogrammetric engr for planning; land use surveys; road location and planning; geodesy. Mem: local comm, Isr Assn of Engrs and Architects; Amer Soc of Photogrammetry; Intl Fed of Housing and Planning, Isr. Hobbies: painting, playwriting. Home: 43 Rambam St, Jerusalem, Isr. Office: 25 Schoor St, Tel Aviv, Isr.

LEES, Lester, US, aeronautical engr, educator, consultant; b. NYC, Nov 8, 1920; s. Harry and Dorothy (Innenberg); BS, MIT, 1940, MS, 1941; m. Constance Morton, Aug 30, 1941; c: David. Prof, aeronautics, Cal Inst of Tech, since 1953, on fac since 1944; cons, Space Tech Labs Inc, LA, since 1953; aeronautical engr, Natl Adv Comm for Aeronautics, 1944-46; prof, aeronautical engr, Princeton U, 1946-53. USAC, 1944-46. Treas, Westside Martin Luther King Study Cen; f: Amer Inst of Astronautics and Aeronautics; Amer Acad Arts and Scis; mem, Altadena Dem Club. Contbr: chap, Recovery Dynamics-Heat Transfer in a Planetary Atmosphere, 1959; articles to sci jours. Home: 925 Alta Pine Dr, Altadena, Cal. Office: Cal Inst of Tech, Pasadena, Cal.

LEEUW, Abraham de, Isr, engineer, educator; b. Hilversum, Holland, Oct 27, 1898; s. Henry and Sarah (Garf); in Isr since 1924; MSc, Tech U, Delft, 1922; m. Mirjam Gerzon, 1925. Prof, hydraulic engr, head, hydraulic lab, Technion, Isr Inst of Tech, 1957-67; engr, public works dept, Tel Aviv, 1924-28; chief engr, Pal Potash Ltd, 1936-49; dir, water planning dept, Isr Min of Agric, 1949-57; adv to Brit Colonial Devl Corp in Swaziland, 1952; UN expert on hydraulic works, Ceylon, 1953; head, dept of engr, Technion, Haifa, 1957-60. Hon chmn, Dutch Immigration Assn; fmr mem, ZC; Pal pioneer training org, Holland. Contbr to profsl jours. Home: 93 Hanassi St, Haifa, Isr.

LEFF, Carl, US, business exec; b. NYC, Oct 23, 1897; s. Max and Sarah (Weinstein); DDS, Columbia U, 1919; m. Eleanor Wiesen, Jan 14, 1930; c: Marjorie Miller, Maxine Myers. Vice-chmn, bd: Natl Spinning Co, with firm, since 1919; Natl

Yarn Corp; Natl Worsted Mills, all since 1964; fmr, vice-pres, Kings Ransom Yarns. 1st lt, US Army, 1918. Trustee, FJP; mem: exec comm and trustee, UJA; exec comm, JDC; Masons; Metrop C of C; fmr secy, LI Coll of Med; clubs: Harmonie; Palm Beach Country; Metropolis Country. Recipient, Order of Merit, JTSA. Hobby, arts. Home: 860 Fifth Avenue New York, NY. Office: 183 Madison Ave, New York, NY.

LEFF, Philip, US, business exec; b. NYC, Oct 19, 1895; s. Max and Sarah (Weinstein); m. Lillian Wiesen, June 14, 1921; c: Joseph, Ruth Siegel. Chmn bd, Natl Spinning Co, since 1919; pres: Natl Yarn Corp since 1923; Natl Worsted Mills, since 1934. Dir: JTSA since 1956; ADL since 1930; trustee, Temple B'nai Jeshurun since 1927; clubs: Harmonie; Metrop Country; Manhattan. Home: 860 Fifth Avenue, New York. NY. Office: 183 Madison Ave, New York, NY.

LEFF, Rita, US, artist; b. NYC; d. Max and Elizabeth (Rudder) Zion; att: Parsons Sch of Design; Art Students League of NY; Pratt Inst; Grand Cen Sch of Design; m. Sydney Leff, June 6, 1928; c: Joan Miller, Gail Raab. Perm collections in US and Tokyo, one-man and group shows in US, Paris and Brussels. Mem: Audubon Artists; Natl Assn Women Artists; Amer Color Print Soc; Soc of Amer Graphic Artists; Bklyn Soc of Artists; NY Soc of Women Artists; Artists Equity; Silvermine Guild of Artists; Natl Soc of Casein Painters. Recipient: awards from: Audubon Artists; Natl Assn of Women Artists; Bklyn Soc of Artists; Bklyn Mus; Boston Printmakers; Soc of Amer Graphic Artists; Village Art Cen; Creative Art Exhb; Natl Soc of Casein Painters; Amer Soc of Contemporary Painters; Grand Prix Salon Intl, Fr, 1969; Medal of Honor, Natl Assn Women Artists, 1968. Home and studio: 125 Amherst St, Brooklyn, NY.

LEFFELL, Abraham Bernard, Can, rabbi; b. Montreal, Can, June 12, 1926; s. Jack and Marion (Richer); BA, McGill U, 1947; Rabbi, MHL, JTSA, NYC, 1954; m. Freda Deckelbaum, Sep 14, 1948; c: Jonathan, Daniel, David, Michael. Rabbi, Shaare Zedek Cong since 1954. Past pres, Bd J Mins of Gtr Montreal; vice-pres, Can Div, RA; mem, Acad of Rel and Mh; club, Montefiore. Home: 5511 Robinson Ave, Cote St Luc, Que, Can. Study: 5305 Rosedale Ave, Montreal, Can.

LEFFKOWITZ, Max, Isr, physician; b. Sensburg, Ger, Feb 22, 1901; in Isr since 1933; att Us: Berlin; Munich; MD, U Freiburg; m. Jutta Simson, 1932. Head, med dept A, Beilinson Hosp, Petach Tikvah, since 1950; asso prof, internal diseases, Heb U; chief phys, Moabit Hosp, Berlin, until 1933; dir, Afula Hosp, 1934-41; cons, cen clinic, Workers Sick Fund, Tel Aviv, 1941-45. Pres: Isr Clinical Med Cong, "Rambam", 1954; 9th Intl Cong, Life Assurance Med, 1967; f, Intl Coll of Angiology. Co-ed, Proceedings of Beilinson Hosp; guest ed, Dapim Refuiim, 1962; mem ed bd, Isr Med Jour; contbr to profsl jours. Home: 17 Shaul Hamelech Blvd, Tel Aviv, Isr. Office: Beilinson Hosp, Petach Tikvah, Isr.

LEFKO, Josef, Finland, engineer; b. Helsinki, Jan 17, 1904; s. Salomon and Sara (Guttman); ME, Tech U, Helsinki, 1927; m. Hanna Kamras, 1933; c: Harriet, Marina, Claire. Mgn dir, since 1934; bd admnr: Tarmo Ins Co, since 1962; Kaleva Life Ins, since 1962. Capt, Finnish Army. Pres: Finnish Fur Dressers Assn, since 1958; cen bd J comtys in Finland; J comty in Helsinki; mem, Eur council J comtys in Eur. Recipient: Finnish Lion Order; Finnish Liberty Cross. Hobbies: fishing, gardening. Home: Tologatan 24, Helsinki, Finland. Office: Helsingin Turkisteollisuus, OY, Malmi, Finland.

LEFKOVITS, Albert Meyer, US, dermatologist; b. NYC, June 30, 1937; s. Aaron and Muriel (Mark); AB, Cornell U, 1958; MD, NY Med Coll, 1962. Att dermat: Mt Sinai Hosp; Flower and 5th Ave Hosp; Metrop Hosp, NYC, since 1963; instr, dermat: Mt Sinai Sch of Med; NY Med Coll, both since 1963; chief res, dermat, 1965-66, research F, dermat, 1966-67, Mt Sinai Hosp. Maj, US Army Res MC, since 1969, capt, 1963-69; chief, dermat service, chief of med, 320th Gen Hosp, US Army Res. Prin contribs-research in: psoriasis; immunoflourescent studies in pemphigus and bullous diseases; uterine motility. Chmn, interfaith comm, Temple Emanu-El Men's Club; dir, Men's Club of Cong Emanu-El; mem: Harvey Soc; Soc for Investigative Dermat; Soc Tropical Dermat; Gtr NY Dermat Soc; NY Co Med Soc; NY State Med Soc; AMA; AJComm; new leadership div, FJP; Fifth Ave Syn; life mem, J Chautauqua Soc; fmr: capt, Cornell U Debating Team; mem, exec council, Hillel Org, Cornell U. Contbr of articles to profsl jours. Recipient: NY State Regents

Scholarship; Cornell State Scholarship; Class of 1886 Prize; Dr Fred Wise Memorial Prize in Dermat, all Cornell U. Home: 3530 Henry Hudson Pkwy, Riverdale, NY. Office: 12 E 86 St, New York, NY.

LEFKOVITS, David, US, jurist; b. Chgo, Ill, Mar 1, 1900; s. Jacob and Sally (Price); LLB, Northwestern U Coll of Law, 1922; m. Lilian Siegel, Aug 26, 1928; c: Natalie Skolnik, Nancy Spira. Judge, Munic Court of Chgo, since 1954; asso Judge, Circuit Court of Cook Co; head, ordinance enforcement div, Corp Counsel's off, Chgo, 1948-54; financial secy, Decalogue Soc of Lawyers; bd dir, S Side Heb Cong, fmr pres; mem: B'nai B'rith; JWV; Amer Legion; Zionist Org of Chgo; Moose; club, City of Chgo. Home: 7443 S Coles Ave, Chicago, Ill. Office: Civic Center, Chicago, Ill.

LEFKOWITCH, Stanley L, US, business exec; b. NYC, May 18, 1917; s. Henry and Sylvia (Fleischer); BS, CCNY, 1969; m. Clarice Fishman, May 30, 1962; c: Jay, Shelley, Amy. Owner, Metro Music Co since 1964, mgr, 1947-64. Exec mgr, secy, Soc J Composers, Publishers and Songwriters; mem, exec bd, Natl J Music Council. Recipient: Kavod award, Cantors Assembly of Amer. Home: 5444 Arlington Ave, Bronx, NY. Office: 54 Second Avenue, New York, NY.

LEFKOWITZ, David Jr, US, rabbi; b. Dayton, O, Aug 8, 1911; s. David and Sadie (Braham); BHL, HUC, 1932, ordained rabbi, 1937; DTh, Pike's Peak Sem, 1953; hon DD: Centenary Coll, 1956; HUC-JIR, 1962; m. Leona Atlas, July 22, 1937; c: David, Helen, Henry. Rabbi, B'nai Zion Cong since 1940; asst rabbi, Temple Emanu-El, Dallas, 1937-40; chaplain, Amer Legion, dept, 1948, natl, 1950; maj, USAAF, 1943-46, chaplain, 1t col, Air Force Res, ret since 1965. Natl chaplain, Air Force Assn, 1967, state chaplain; pres: Mil Order of World Wars, 1952-53; Res Offs Assn, Shreveport Chap, 1950; bd mem: J Fed; Symphony Soc; mem: B'nai B'rith; Safety Council; YMCA; CCAR. Home: 138 Preston St, Shreveport, La. Study: 175 Southfield Rd, Shreveport, La.

LEFKOWITZ, Jack, US, business exec; b. Lodz, Pol, June 15, 1904; s. Eliezer and Golda (Motyl); in US since 1913; att CCNY, 1926; m. Suzanne Horowitz, Feb 12, 1928; c: Jerome, Leonard, Josef, Eliezer. Pres: Textiles Assos Inc since 1934; Spencer Equities Co since 1949. Mem: AZC since 1952; natl exec bd, ZOA since 1951, fmr: natl vice pres, asso financial chmn, asso chmn admn comm, pres, Bx dist, chmn, fund raising, Bx dist since 1950; mem: World Zionist Actions Comm since 1964; Bx regional chmn, Kfar Silver Agric Sch, Ashkelon, Isr since 1958; natl bd, JNF; Amer Friends Heb U; B'nai B'rith; Heb Cong of Somers; Millinery Cen Syn; Mt Eden J Cen; Young Isr; Cong Kehilath Jeshurun; natl bd, UJA; delg to all ZCs in Jerusalem since 1951; fmr: delg, Confd of Gen Zionists, Jerusalem; asso mem, UJA drive, Bx; concourse chmn. Recipient: outstanding Zionist of the year award, ZOA conv, 1958; outstanding fund raising chmn award, ZOA conv, 1962. Home: 1025 Fifth Avenue, New York, NY. Office: 55 W 42nd St, New York, NY.

LEFKOWITZ, Sidney M, US, rabbi; b. NYC, Sep 11, 1908; s. Joseph and Freda (Scheibel); BA, U Cincinnati, 1929; BH, HUC, 1929, ordained Rabbi, 1933, DD, 1958; att: U Richmond, Va, 1939-42; Union Theol Sem, Richmond, 1941-42; m. Dorothy Sycle, Oct 23, 1938; c: Ann. Rabbi, Cong Ahavath Chesed, Jacksonville, Fla, since 1946; lectr, rel, Jacksonville U, since 1957; rabbi, Beth Ahavath Cong, Richmond, Va, 1933-42. Chaplain, US Army, 1942-46. Pres, SE assn, CCAR, since 1961, chmn, standing comm on resolutions, since 1960, past secy; mem: exec comm, Comty Chest-United Fund, since 1950; JCC, since 1946; bd trustees, Jacksonville Free Public Libr, since 1956; Amer J Hist Soc; Soc Bibl Lit and Exegesis; Soc Political and Social Sci; Mil Order of WWs; clubs: Rotary, fmr mem bd dirs; Torch. Recipient: Bronze Star; Eur Theatre Ribbon, with 6 battle stars. Home: 2220 Saragossa Ave, Jacksonville, Fla. Study: 1708 Mallory St, Jacksonville, Fla.

LEFRAK, Samuel J, US, housing and commercial developer, public official, publisher; b. NYC, Feb 12, 1918; s. Harry and Sarah (Schwartz); grad, U Md; post grad studies: Columbia U; Harvard U; LLD, Philathea Coll; m. Ethel Stone, May 14, 1941; c: Denise, Richard, Francine, Jacqueline. Pres, Lefrak Org, since 1948, designer, sponsor, builder, Lefrak City; publisher, LI Post; State Dept Spec Cons for urban affairs; pres, NYC Commercial Devl Corp, since 1967. Commn, Saratoga Springs Commn; vice-chmn-at-large,

ARC, NY; chmn: NCCJ; bldg comm, Saratoga Performing Arts; fund raising comms: Infantile Paralysis; Boy Scouts of Amer; Queens Adv Council on Econ Devl; dir: and chmn, Real Estate Div, Gtr NY Fund; USO; Sales Execs Club; hon commn, Amateur Athletic Union; J Hosp at Denver; and dir, Brookdale Hosp; natl chmn, Tau Epsilon Phi; found, Albert Einstein Sch of Med; mem: adv bd: radio sta WHLI; Chem Bank NY Trust Co; Pres' Comm on Employment of Handicapped; exec comm, NY Citizens Budget Commn; bd dirs, Citizens Planning and Housing Council, NY; finance and adv bd, Gtr NY Safety Council; NY C of C; bd dirs, Interfaith Movement; bd dirs, Beth Jacob Sch for Girls; Park Ave Assn; adv bd, Pace Coll; hon alumni comm, Heb U, Jerusalem; United Hunts Racing Assn; Masons (Shriners); fmr: mem, US comm, UN; US delg: Intl Conf on Housing and Urban Devl, 1967; Econ Commn for Eur, on air pollution, Switz, 1969; mem, Gov of NY finance and adv comms, NY State Traffic Safety Council; chmn, Gtr NY Fund Campaign; charter mem, NY Citizens Comm on Fire Prevention; dir, NY Worlds Fair Corp; Commn of Public Works, Borough of Manhattan; clubs: Lotos; Tuft and Field; Friars, NYC; Town; Woodcrest Country; Marco Polo; Nassau Yacht; Seawane Golf; United Hunt. Recipient: NYC Mayor's Award for Outstanding Citizen, 1960; Natl Boys Club Award, 1960; Amer J Lit Found Citation, 1960; Brotherhood Award, NCCJ, 1964; Chief Rabbi Herzog Gold Medal Torah F Citation, Rel Zionists of Amer, 1966; Citizen of Year, B'nai B'rith, 1963; Dist Achievement Award, 1967; JFK Peace Award, 1966. Home: NYC. Office: 97-77 Queens Blvd, Forest Hills, NY.

LEHMAN, Albert, US, communal leader; b. NYC, Oct 2, 1913; s. Abraham and Rae (Rosen); BSS, CCNY, 1937; MS, Columbia U, 1946; m. Yvette Kuhn, Aug 6, 1956; c: Adam; stepsons: Warren Franzen, Glenn Franzen. Exec dir, N Pacific Region, ZOA, since 1967; social service posts, 1935-51; exec, JWF, Oakland, 1951-59; ed, publisher, Cal J Record, 1959-67. Fmr pres, Temple Beth Hillel, Richmond; chmn, personnel bd, City of Pinole; mem, Press and Union League. Contbr to profsl jours. Home: 220 Stanford Ave, Berkeley, Cal. Office: 583 Market St, San Francisco, Cal.

LEHMAN, Eugene H, US, educator, camping specialist; b. Pueblo, Colo, Sep 5, 1879; s. Moritz and Rosa (Heitler); BA, Yale U, 1902, MA, 1911; att U of Berlin, 1909-10; post-grad study, Columbia U and Tchrs Coll; m. Elizabeth Novitsky Meyer, Sep 12, 1938; c: Eugene Jr, Godfrey, Carol Winfield, Rodger. Pres em, Monmouth Coll, since 1957, pres, 1956-57, fmr: found, Highland Manor Sch and Jr Coll, W Long Br, NJ, 1918, pres, 1918-56; cons: supervision, summer camps, since 1912; Highland Manor Summer Sch, both Naples, Me; instr, Bibl lit, Yale U, 1910-13; asst to Rabbi Stephen Wise, Free Syn, NY, 1910-13; dir, Highland Nature Camp, Naples, 1910-50; first educ to establish and instruct course for training camp dirs and councillors, Columbia U Tchrs Coll, 1922-25. Pres, Jordan lodge, B'nai-B'rith, 1916; found: Natl Assn Dirs of Girl's Camps, 1916, pres, 1919-20; Camp Dirs Assn of Amer, ed-in-chief, year book, both assns, 1928-35; mayor, Tarrytown-on-Hudson, NY, 1932-33; pres: Comty Chest, the Tarrytowns, 1933-35; Westchester Co Tax Payers Assn, 1934-39; clubs: Rotary of the Tarrytowns, pres, 1924-25; Yale of Ocean and Monmouth Cos. Author: The Jewish Teacher, 1913; How to Teach Ethics, 1914; co-author, The Junior Bible for Jewish Children (three parts), 1910-13; contbr: Ency Britannica; profsl publs. Recipient, first Cecil Rhodes scholarship awarded in US, 1904. Home: 22 Whitehall Ave, Deal, NJ. Office: Pres Em, Monmouth Coll, Box 154, Deal, NJ.

LEHMAN, Irving, US, artist; b. Kiev, Russ, Jan 1, 1900; s. Aaron and Pearl (Feller); in US since 1912; att Natl Acad, NYC; m. Martha Weingard, Jan 26, 1934. Artist, sculptor, printmaker; fmr tchr: Bklyn Coll, Adult Educ; Bd of Adult Educ, Studio Workshops. One man shows: ACA Gal, NYC, 1934; Uptown Gal, 1938-40; Harry Salpeter Gal, NYC, 1947, 1948, 1950, 1954, 1955; Phil Art Alliance, 1950; St Edmund's Hall, Eng, 1950; Columbia Mus of Art, 1958; Gal Ten, NY, 1960; Knapik Gal, NYC, 1961; Gladstone Gal, NY, 1961, 62; intl shows: Paris, Den, Belgium, It, Munich, 1950-51; Paris, 1951; Rouen, 1952; Algiers, 1953; Lyon, Toulouse, Valenciennes, Perpignan, Narbonne, 1954; It, 1955; Japan, 1955; natl shows: Albany Inst Hist and Art; Ala Watercolor Soc; Bklyn Mus; Chgo Art Inst; City Art Mus, St Louis; Davenport Munic Art Gal; Hudson River Mus; LIU; Mobile Art Assn; Natl Gal, Wash, DC; Neb Art

Assn, Natl Acad Gals, NYC; New Sch for Social Research; NYU; Norfolk Mus; Pa Acad; Riverside Mus; Sarasota Art Assn, Fla; Seattle Mus; S Bend Art Assn; J B Speed Mus, Ky; Whitney Mus; IBM Gals, NYC; Liver House, NYC; Shaker Mus, NY; Waterloo Munic Gals; Springfield Art Assn Ill; Fla State U; Charleston Art Gal, W Va; Siena Hgts Coll, Mich; Pa State U; U Ore; U Me; Panama Art Assn, Fla; in perm collections: Ein Harod; Natl Mus of Bezalel; Bat Yam, all Isr; Musee D'Art Populaire Juif, Paris; Abbey Art Gals, Pittsburgh; St Edmund's Hall, Eng; in pvt collections. Mem: Amer Abstract Artists; Audubon Artists of Amer; Amer Soc of Contemporary Artists. Included in books: The World of Abstract Art; How Paintings Happen; American Abstract Art; Syracuse U Libr of Manuscripts; House and Garden Decorating Guide. Recipient: Kate W Arms Memorial Prize, 1947; awards: Watercolor Soc of Ala, 1948; Wash Watercolor Club, 1949; Terry Art Inst, oils, 1952; Victor Wyler Found, oils, 1958; Kellner Award, sculpture, 1959; Distinctive Merit, for oils, 1961. Home: 70 LaSalle St, New York, NY; Red Rock Studio, RD 1, East Chatham, NY.

LEHMANN, Elias Ernst, Isr, physician; b. Nurnberg, Ger, June 14, 1914; s. Felix and Meta (Lewin); in Isr since 1938; att Heidelberg U, 1932-37; MD, U Berne, Switz, 1938; m. Margit Falck, 1948; c: Dan, Gad, David, Amos, Neomi. Head, dept med "A", Cen Negev Hosp, since 1960; fmr: head, postgrad training, Hammersmith Hosp, London, 1947-48; head, med dept, Army Hosp, Haifa, 1948-50; dir head, med dept, Hadassah Hosp, Beersheba, 1950-60. Maj, Brit Army, 1942-47; IDF, 1948-50. Mem, Comm for Arid Zone Research. Contbr to profsl jours. Home: 39 Gershon St, Beersheba, Isr. Office: Central Negev Hospital, Beersheba, Isr.

LEHMANN, Ernst, Isr, banker, economist; b. Berlin, Ger, Apr 29, 1902; s. Eugen and Elsa (Bacharach); in Isr since 1935; att: U Berlin, 1920-21, 1922-24; U Munich, 1921; m. Nelly Frank, 1926; c: Raphael. Gen mgr, Bank Leumi le Isr; vice-chmn, Gen Mortgage Bank Ltd; chmn; bd dirs: Tel Aviv Stock Exch Ltd; Yaad Agric Devl Bank; Afr-Isr Inves Ltd; Ihud Ins Agcys Ltd; vice-pres, Migdal-Binyan Ins Co Ltd; bd dirs: First Isr Bank and Trust Co, NY; Anglo-Isr Bank Ltd, London; bd govs, Technion, Haifa; fmr: staff mem, Mitteldeutsche Bodenkreditanstalt, Berlin; gen mgr, Deutsche Realkreditbank A G, Dessau-Berlin; mgr: FWI; Gesellschaft zur Förderung Wirtschaftlicher; Interessen Deutscher Juden bei der Reichsvertretung; Deutscher Juden, Berlin. Chmn, exec comm: Asso of Banks in Isr; Maurice Falk Inst for Econ Research. Contbr to profsl publs. Spec interests: hist, archaeol, art, music. Home: 23 Benjamin St, Ramat Gan, Isr. Office: 26-28 Yehuda Halevy St, Tel Aviv, Isr.

LEHMANN, Manfred Raphael, US, business exec; b. Stockholm, Swed, Aug 28, 1922; s. Hans and Fannie (Taub); MA, Johns Hopkins U, 1946; DHL, Yeshiva U, 1969; m. Sara Moskovitz, Apr 3, 1949; c: James, Barbara, Karen. Pres: Inter-Govt Philatelic Corp since 1957; Lehmann Trading Corp since 1957. Pres, Young Isr, Lawrence-Cedarhurst; bd dirs: Yeshiva U HS; mem: Collectors Club; Amer Philatelic Soc; Soc J Bibliphiles. Contbr numerous articles on archaeol and Bibl topics to scholarly jours. Spec interest: collecting old J coins, Maccabean through Roman periods. Home: 79 Cedarhurst Ave, Lawrence, NY. Office: 225 W 34, New York, NY.

LEHRFIELD, Louis Judah, US, rabbi; b. Chgo, Ill, Sep 15, 1901; s. Israel and Augusta; ordained rabbi, Heb Theol Coll, 1925; PhD, U of Chgo, 1935; DHL, Heb Theol Coll, 1959; m. Etta Rabuchin, Dec 29, 1924; c: Joel, David, Daniel. Rabbi: Austin J Comty Cen since 1933; Shomre Hodath, 1925-27; Bnai Isr, 1927-32; chaplain, Heines Hosp, 1942-45. Chmn: Educ Comm, Asso Talmud Torahs, Chgo; Placement Commn, Fac Relations Comm, Heb Theol Coll; pres: Alumni Heb Theol Coll, 1929-37; Chgo Rabb Council, 1944-46; vice-pres, RabCA, 1940; mem: Assn Orthodox J Scis; club, Covenant of Chgo. Home: 5561 Monroe, Chicago, Ill. Study: 116 Central, Chicago, Ill.

LEHRMAN, Alexander, US, chemist, educator; b. Bklyn, NY, Aug 31, 1896; c: Morris and Elizabeth (Rumsch); BS, CCNY, 1918; MS, Columbia U, 1920, PhD, 1925; m. Ethel Elfenbein, Aug 14, 1950; c: Elizabeth Ruben. Ret; instr, chem, asst prof, asso prof, prof, CCNY, 1918-53. USN, 1918-19. Mem: Amer Chem Soc; AAAS; AAUP; Sigma Xi; Phi Lambda Upsilon. Co-author: Introductory College Chemistry, 1931, 1941, 1950; General College Chemistry, 1940, 1951; contbr to profsl jours. Hobby, photography. Home: 210 W 101 St, New York, NY.

LEHRMAN, Edgar H, US, educator; b. New York, NY, Apr 13, 1926; s. Jacob and Frances (Wittenberg); AB, Cornell U, 1948; AM, Columbia U, 1950, PhD, 1954; cert, Russ Inst, 1956; m. Ruffa Makarova, Mar 28, 1963; c: Tanya, Ellen. Prof, chmn, Dept of Russ, Wash U, St Louis, Mo, since 1967; instr of Russ: Duke U, 1951-52; Dartmouth Coll, 1954-55; asst prof, Russ, Pa State U, 1956-59; Moscow State U, official Soviet-Amer exch, 1962-63; asso prof, chmn, dept of Russ, Emory U, Ga, 1959-67. Mem: Amer Assn for Advancement Slavic Studies; MLA; Amer Assn Tchrs of Slavic and E Eur Langs; AAUP. Author, articles on Akimov's Hamlet; Paustovsky; "Wanted: 'Handbooks' for Russ Masterpieces"; ed, trans: Turgenev's Letters: A Selection, 1961; trans, Nikolai Gorchakov's The Theater in Soviet Russ, 1957; ed, Vladimir Seduro's Hist of the Byelorussian Theatre and Drama, 1955. Office: Dept of Russ, Wash U, St Louis, Mo.

LEHRMAN, Hal, US, journalist, lecturer, author; b. NYC, Jan 7, 1911; s. Elias and Anna (Dattelbaum); BA, 1931, Cornell, grad sch, 1933; att Ecole des Chartes, Paris, 1934; m. Freda Jacobsohn, June 6, 1942; c: Fredric, Hal. Contbr to periodicals in US, Eur, ME and N Afr; asst in hist, Cornell U, 1931-33; Paris bur, AP, 1934-35; asst fgn ed, Newsweek, 1935-36; cable ed, Havas News Agcy, 1936-39; night cable ed, NY Daily News, 1939-41; chief, OWI, Istanbul, Turkey, 1942-43; chief, Cen and SE Eur, OWI Ed Bd, 1943-44; fgn ed, Argosy Mag, 1944-45. Author: Russia's Europe, 1947; Israel, the Beginning and Tomorrow, 1952; Portrait of Israel, 1958; A Language Recalled: The Story of Modern Hebrew, 1963; contbr: Inside Story, 1940; As We See Russia, 1948; Off the Record, 1953; The Middle East in Transition, 1958; Composition of the Essay, 1967; World Migration in Modern Times, 1968. Found, gov, pres, of Overseas Press Club of Amer. Recipient: Guggenheim fs, 1951, 1953; Council on Fgn Relations f, Carnegie Found, 1951; George Polk Memorial award, 1956; citation, Overseas Press Club, 1956; Amer Security Council Award, 1967. Home and office: 160 E 48 St, New York, NY.

LEHRMAN, Irving, US, rabbi; b. Pol, June 15, 1912; s. Abraham and Minnie (Dinowitiz); desc of Brocker Rebbe; in US since 1921; BS, CCNY, 1936; ordained rabbi, MHL, JIR, 1942; DHL, JTSA, 1958, DD, 1968; m. Bella Goldfarb, 1935; c: David, Rosalind. Rabbi, Temple Emanu-El, Miami Beach, Fla, since 1943, elected for life, 1951; student rabbi, Temple Shomrei Emunah, NJ, 1939-43; fmr visiting prof, homiletics, JTSA. Delg, Gtr Miami J Fed, to visit DP camps in Eur and Isr, 1947; mem, comm on rel orgs, NCCJ, to visit Russ, 1958; pres: S Fla Region, RA, since 1960, on exec since 1950; Rabb Assn, Gtr Miami, 1955; vice pres: ZOA; Syn Council of Amer; Gtr Miami J Fed; chmn, Dialogue Comm, NCCJ; trustee, Ency Judaica Research Found; mem: natl bd dirs, Amer Technion Soc; Bur of J Educ, Gtr Miami; comm, State of Isr Bonds; Dade Co Council on Comty Relations; Natl Comm on Rel Orgs; bd, United Fund, Dade Co; Amer Bibl Ency Soc; bd, natl council, United HIAS Service; ZOA; Soc Friends Touro Syn; natl council, JDC; Travelers Aid Soc; Rabb Cabinet and bd rabb visitors, JTSA; bd dirs, United Fund; bd, Intl Syn; State Comm on Comparative Rel and Bible; exec bd, S Fla Council, Boy Scouts of Amer; Mayor's Adv Comm on Juvenile Delinquency; bd dirs, Citizens Housing Found; ARC; Natl Commn on Obscenity and Pornography; Dist Wfr Bd; hon chaplain, JWV. Recipient: chair in his name established at JTSA, 1963. Home: 2925 Flamingo Dr, Miami Beach, Fla. Study: 1701 Washington Ave, Miami Beach, Fla.

LEHRMAN, Leo, US, educator; b. NYC, July 3, 1900; s. Morris and Elizabeth (Rumsch); BS, CCNY, 1921; MA, Columbia U, 1923, PhD, 1926; m. Etta Cohn, Aug 29, 1930; c: Barbara. Prof, chem, CCNY since 1954; instr: NYU, 1921, 1925-29; Columbia U, 1923-25. US Army, 1918. Prin contrib: research work in the field of fatty acids, starches, 1926-45; methods of analysis, 1930-51; corrosion studies since 1951. Mem: Amer Chem Soc; AAUP; Phi Lambda Upsilon; Sigma Xi; Tau Delta Phi. Contbr to chem jours. Hobby, sports. Home: 430 E 86 St, New York, NY. Office: CUNY, New York, NY.

LEHRMAN, Moses, US, rabbi; b. Tikocin, Pol, Dec 1, 1907; s. Abraham and Minnie (Dinowitz); in US since 1920; BS, CCNY, 1931; att Columbia U, 1931-32, MHL, ordained rabbi, JTSA, 1942, hon DD, 1968; m. Rose Cherkas, Aug 10, 1931; c: Miriam Lipshitz, Blossom Helman. Rabbi: B'nai Moshe Cong, Oak Park, Mich, since 1948; Temple Beth David, Buffalo, NY, 1943-48. Pres, ZOA, Detroit, since 1953, natl admnr, 1952-53; mem, exec bd, Comty Council, Detroit, since 1947; chmn, Coll of J Studies, Buffalo, NY, 1945; co-chmn, orgs, Allied J Campaign, Detroit, 1951, chmn, rel div, 1952-53, exec comm, rel and lab; exec mem, RA; mem: B'nai B'rith; AJCong; club, Knollwood Country. Contbr to periodicals. Recipient: recognition, Cong B'nai Moshe, 1959, life tenure, 1963, sabbatical, 1968. Hobby, travel. Home: 25220 Gardner, Oak Park, Mich. Study: 10 Mile and Kenosha, Oak Park, Mich.

LEHRMAN, Samuel R, US, psychiatrist; b. Bklyn, NY, June 21, 1912; s. Isidor and Anna (Lehrman); BS, Columbia, 1933; Eclectic Med Coll, Cincinnati, 1937; grad, NY Psychoanalytic Inst, 1951; m. Doris Rosenberg, 1935; c: Linda, Abbie, Jonathan. Pvt practice psycht and psychan since 1945; dir, psycht, LI J Med Cen since 1958; att psycht, Hillside Hosp since 1958; cons psycht, Peninsula Gen Hosp since 1961; clinical asso prof, psycht, SUNY Downstate Med Cen since 1961; sr psycht, Creedmore State Hosp, 1940-52; chief of clinic, outpatient dept, Mt Sinai Hosp, 1947-54; asso att psycht, 1956-58; cons psycht, HUC-JIR, 1949-59. Capt, US Army MC, 1942-45. F: NY Acad Med; Amer Psycht Assn; Assn Coll Phys; pres, NY State Hosps Med Alumni Assn, 1960-62; mem: AMA; NY State, Co Med Socs; NY Psychoanalytic Assn; NY Soc Clinical Psycht; Nassau Neuropsycht Soc; Amer Psychosomatic Assn; Modern Founds of Amer Psycht Assn; sect chmn, Queens-Nassau phys, UJA and FJP. Asso ed: The Psychiatric Quarterly; Jour of Hillside Hosp; contbr: numerous papers and book revs on psycht, neur, psychan to med jours. Hobby, photography. Home and office: 1045 Seawane Dr, Hewlett, NY.

LEHRMANN, Charles C, Ger, rabbi, educator; b. Stryzow, Aus, June 15, 1905; s. Chaim and Blima (Kranzler); in Ger since 1960; ordained rabbi, Rabb Sem, Berlin, 1933; PhD, U Wurzburg, 1932; licencié ès lettres,U Lausanne, 1934; scholarship, Dropsie Coll, Pa, 1948-49; m. Graziella Marc, Apr 29, 1937; c: Miriam. Chief rabbi, W Berlin since 1960; fmr: asst prof lit, U of Lausanne; prof, Wurzburg U; rabbi, Fribourg, Switz; grand rabbi, Luxembourg; guest prof, Bar Ilan U, Isr. Fmr: secy, Eur Fed of Rabbis; pres; Ganusth Korcziak Lodge; mem bd, Ger Fed of Rabbis. Author: Bergsonisme et Judaisme, 1937; L'élément juif dans la litterature francaise, 1941, 3rd ed, 1962; Die Feste Israels, 1946; L'élément juif dans la pensée européenne, 1948; La communauté juive du Luxembourg dans le passé et dans le présent, 1955; A la recherche de l'âme Luxembourgeoise, 1954; Heinrich Heine, Kaempfer und Dichter, 1957; Die jud-romanischen Beziehungen im Mittellalter, 1969; ed, Revue mensuelle pour les communautés israélites, 1950-51. Recipient, Natl Prize of Luxembourg, 1959. Homes: 139 Ave Fayencerie, Luxembourg; Sybelst 19, Berlin, Ger.

LEIBLER, Isi Joseph, Australia, business exec; b. Antwerp, Belgium, Oct 9, 1934; s. Abraham and Rachel; in Australia since 1939; BA, 1st class hons, U Melbourne, 1957; m. Naomi Porush, Dec 28, 1957; c: Tamara, Romy, Gary, Jonathan. Mgn dir: A S Leibler & Co, Diamond Importers; Astronaut Travel Service. Author: Soviet Jewry and Human Rights, 1965; Soviet Jewry and the Australian Communist Party, 1966. PR chmn, Vic J Bd of Deps; councillor, Exec Council Australian J; exec mem, ZF of Australia. Fmr: hon secy, PR chmn, Exec Council Australian J; pres: Natl Union of Australian J Students; Australian Zionist Youth Council. Spec interests: journalism, lectr, TV, radio public affairs spokesman. Home: 116 Kooyong Rd, Caulfield, Vic, Australia. Office: 340 Little Collins St, Melbourne, Australia.

LEIBOWITT, S David, US, attorney; b. Bklyn, NY, Feb 18, 1912; s. Morris and Bella (Small); BA, Lehigh U, 1933; LLB, Harvard Law Sch, 1936; m. Ethel Snyder, June 18, 1950. Pvt practice since 1937; gen counsel, pres, New Haven Watch & Clock Co, 1952-59. Bd dir, J Cen, NY; natl vice-pres, Union Orthodox J Congs of Amer, 1958-60; mem: Assn Bar, NYC; Masons; B'nai B'rith; ZOA; Phi Beta Kappa; clubs: Harvard, Rolling Hills Country. Recipient, ADL Hum Relations Award, 1969. Home: Fanton Hill Rd, Weston, Conn. Office: 2 Penn Plaza, New York, NY.

LEIBOWITZ, Joshua O, Isr, physician; b. Vilna, Russ, Apr 25, 1895; s. Alexander and Hannah (Masel); in Isr since 1935; MD, U of Heidelberg, 1922; m. Jeanette Bing, 1943. Asso clinical prof, hist of med, Heb U, Jerusalem, since 1959; fmr: hon lectr, Yale U Med Sch, 1956; f, Inst of Hist of Med, Johns Hopkins U, 1957; research f, Wellcome Inst, Eng, 1968.

Served IDF MC. Mem: bd, Isr Soc Hist of Med and Sci; effective mem, Intl Acad Hist of Med; corresp mem, Soc Hist of Med of Spain; Isr repr, Intl Soc for Hist of Med. Ed, Beer Mayim Hayim, by I Teller, 1968; History of Coronary Heart Disease, 1970; contbr to profsl jours. Recipient: Dr M Einhorn Prize, 1968. Spec interests: old Heb med books, J ceremonial art. Home: 3 Yordei Hasira St, Jerusalem, Isr. Office: Heb U, Jerusalem, Isr.

LEIBOWITZ, Sidney, US, physician; b. NYC, May 3, 1912; s. Abraham and Ida (Jacobson); BS, NYU, 1931; MD, U Rochester Sch of Dent and Med, 1935; m. Bennie Newman, Oct 21, 1943; c: Donna Elizabeth. Phys, internal med, pvt practice since 1938; med dir, NYC Bd of Educ since 1956; att phys, visiting staff, Beth Isr Hosp since 1938. Col: USAF, 1941-46; USAF Res since 1946. Pres, Alumni Assn, Beth Israel Hosp, 1949-50; f: NY Acad Med; Amer Coll Phys; dipl, Amer Bd of Internal Med; mem: Phi Beta Kappa; Alpha Omega Alpha. Author: Infectious Mononucleosis, 1953; contbr of numerous articles to med jours. Recipient: Alumni Medal Award, NYU, 1931; Commendation Medal. Home: 2 Stuyvesant Oval, New York, NY. Offices: 15 W 84 St, New York, NY. Bd of Educ Bldg, 110 Livingston St, Brooklyn, NY.

LEIFERMAN, Irwin H, US, civic worker, business exec; m. Silvia Weimer, Apr 20, 1947. Life mem: Brandeis U; Art Inst of Chgo; Miami Mus of Art; mem: Ind comm, Lab Dept; Chgo Assn Commerce and Ind; Ill Mfrs Assn; Ill C of C; adv comm, B'nai B'rith; asso U Chgo Cancer Research Found; Intl Platform Assn; Miami Beach Opera Guild Comm; Temple Emanu-El; Temple Sholom; donor with wife: Gift Shop, Fifth Floor Reception Room, Edgewater Hosp; Conf Room, Mary Lawrence J Children's Bur; Leiferman Awards under auspices of City of Hope; Waiting Room, Radiology Bldg, Mt Sinai Hosp, Gtr Miami; founder, Mt Sinai Hosp, Gtr Miami; clubs: Exec; Standard; Covenant; Intl; Green Acres; Bryn Mawr Country, all Chgo; Runaway Bay; Westview Country, both Miami Beach. Home: The Imperial House, 5255 Collins Ave, Miami Beach, Fla; The Standard Club, 320 S Plymouth Ct, Chicago, Ill. Office: 33 N LaSalle St, Chicago, Ill.

LEIFERMAN, Silvia W, US, artist, sculptor, civic worker; b. Chgo, Ill; d. Morris and Annah (Caplan) Weimer; att U Chgo, 1960-61; extensive study of design and painting in: Chgo; Mexico; Rome; Madrid; Provincetown, Mass; m. Irwin Leiferman, Apr 20, 1947. One-man shows: D'Arcy Gal, NYC, 1964; Stevens Annex Bldg, 1965; Schram Gal, Ft Lauderdale, Fla, 1966; Miami Mus of Modern Art, 1966, 1970; Contemporary Gal, Palm Beach, Fla, 1966; group shows: Bryn Mawr Country Club, Chgo, 1961-62; Riccardo Restaurant Gal, Chgo, 1961-62; Covenant Club, Chgo, 1963; D'Arcy Gal, NYC, 1965; Intl Platform Ass, 1967; Barry Coll, 1968; Westview Country Club, under Gal 99, 1968; Gal 99, Miami, Fla, 1968; Hollywood Mus of Art, 1968; Artist's Equity at Crystal House Gal, Miami Beach, 1968; Lowe Art Mus; Beau Art Gal, Lowe Mus, in U Miami; in pvt collections: Ambass Ali Esfendiary, Iran; Miami Mus Modern Art; perm collection: Jacob M Barmore; fmr gov, Haydon Burns; Jan and Alice Peerce; Jack Benny; Roosevelt U, Chgo; Dr Theodore M Zekman; William Pearlman; Lowe Art Mus, U Miami; Johann S B Ornstein; Comet Produc. Co-found, vice-pres, Silvia and Irwin H Leiferman Found; pres, Active Accessories by Silvia, Chgo, 1964; chmn: presentation comm, Ambassador's Ball, Bonds for Isr; Dior Isr Fashion Show; Salute to Med Research, City of Hope; Metrop campaign, 1959; Spec Sales and Spec Events, Chgo comm, State of Isr; opening, Edgewater Hosp; Women's Division, Edgewater Hosp; CJA, Shore Spec Gifts; Hawaiian Holiday, Nathan Goldblatt Soc for Cancer Research; Paris in the Spring, Natl Council for J Women; Alice in Fashion Land, Council for J Women; mem: bd: Nathan Goldblatt Soc for Cancer Research, trustee; George and Ann Portes Cancer Prevention Cen, Chgo, Inc; Mt Sinai Hosp; N Shore Women's Auxiliary, Mary Lawrence J Children's Bureau; Natl Council for J Women; Fox River Sanitorium; Temple Sholom; Brandeis U; Edgewater Hosp; Natl, Chgo bd govs, Bonds for Isr; ORT; charter, Women's Div, Heb U, Chgo; mem: Intl Platform Assn; Art Inst of Chgo; Intl Council of Mus; First Annual Cultural Conf of Chgo; Amer Fed of Arts; Temple Emanu-El; N Shore Women's Auxiliary, Mary Lawrence J Children's Bur; Mt Sinai Hosp, Chgo; George and Ann Portes Cancer Prevention Cen; Artist's Equity Assn, Inc; Fla State Poetry Sch; Miami Art Cen; Miami Beach Opera Guild Comm; Gtr Miami Cultural Art Cen; Sculptors of Fla, Inc; Lowe Art Mus; Royal Acad of Arts; Miami Mus Modern Art; donated: Gift Shop, Fifth Floor Reception Room, Edgewater Hosp; Conference Room,

Mary Lawrence J Children's Bur; The Leiferman Award under the auspices of City of Hope; founder, Mt Sinai Hosp, Gtr Miami, Fla; Waiting Room, Radiology Bldg of Mt Sinai Hosp, Gtr Miami, Fla; clubs: Intl; Boyer; Whitehall; Key; Covenant; Standard; Green Acres; Bryn Mawr Country, all Chgo; Westview Country, Miami Beach. Recipient: Woman-of-Valor, State of Isr, 1963; citations from: Edgewater Hosp; Comty Leaders of Amer; Treas Dept; CJA, Chgo; awards from Bonds of Isr. Home and studio: The Imperial House, 5255 Collins Ave, Miami Beach, Fla.

LEIGH, Nathan J, US, business exec; b. NYC, Jan 16, 1902; s. Israel and Martha (Abrahams); m. Jean Weiller, Dec 13, 1928; c: Jonathan, David, Josephine. Chmn, bd of dirs, Einson-Freeman Co, since 1957, with firm since 1922. Dir, Lexington Sch for Deaf, 1961-64; pres, dir, LI Hearing Soc; chmn, publicity comm, FJP, NY, 1962-65; clubs: Beach Point Yacht; Mamaroneck, NY; Purchase Riding; Sales Exec; NYC; Advt. Home: 35 E 75 St, New York, NY. Office: Einson-Freeman Co, Long Island City, NY.

LEINER, George C, US, physician; b. Vienna, Aus, Nov 20, 1907; s. Carl and Lotte (Popper); in US since 1938; MD, U Vienna, 1932. Asst prof med, Albert Einstein Sch of Med; at phys pulmonary diseases, Montefiore Hosp, Bx, since 1955, with Hosp since 1938; cons, pulmonary phys, VA Hosp, E Orange, NJ, since 1954; sr clinical asst, Mt Sinai Hosp, NY, 1948-58; instr phys, U Vienna, 1930-32; res, Heart Sta, Vienna, 1937-38. Dipl, Bd of Internal Med. Mem: Amer Coll Phys, Amer Thoracic Soc, Pirquet Soc, Virchow Soc. Author: Thoracic Diseases, 1961; contbr to profsl jours. Hobbies: mt climbing, skiing. Home: 780 West End Ave, New York, NY. Office: 123 E 83 St, New York, NY.

LEIPZIGER, Michael Hermann, Brazil, rabbi; b. Beutheu, Ger, Mar 17, 1937; s. Georg and Gertrud (Zweig); in Brazil since 1939; att Machon Lemadrichim, Jerusalem, 1955-56; Inst Intl d'Études Hébraiques, Paris, 1956-57; BS, Columbia U, 1962; MHL, Rabbi, JTSA, 1964; m. Fabia Terni, Nov 28, 1965; c: Deborah, David. Circuit rabbi in remote villages since 1964; rabbi, Cong Israelita Paulista since 1964. Mem: RA; B'nai B'rith. Contbr articles to rel jours. Recipient: Dorothy Gelgor Prize for pastoral psycht, 1968; Lamport Prize for Homiletics, 1968. Hobby: J Brazilian hist. Home: 653 R Antonio Carlos, Sao Paulo, Brazil. Study: 2055 Al Santos, Sao Paulo, Brazil.

LELYVELD, Arthur J, US, rabbi; b. NYC, Feb 6, 1913; s. Edward and Dora (Cohen); BA, Columbia U, 1933; MHL, HUC, 1939, hon DD, HUC-JIR, 1955; Edward L Heinsheimer f, 1939-41; m. Toby Bookholtz, Dec 26, 1933; c: Joseph, David, Michael; m. 2nd, Teela Storsky, Dec 5, 1964; c: Ben, Robin. Rabbi: Fairmount Temple, Cleveland, O, since 1958; Temple B'nai Isr, Omaha, Neb, 1941-44; exec dir, Comm on Unity for Pal, 1944-46, natl vice-chmn, 1946-48; asso natl dir, B'nai B'rith Hillel Found, 1946-48, natl dir, 1948-56; exec vice-chmn, Amer-Isr Cultural Found, 1956-58. Pres: AJCong since 1966; J Peace F, 1941-43; natl vice-pres, Amer J League for Isr since 1956; vice-pres, chmn, exec, World U Service, 1953, Amer vice-chmn, 1953-65; secy, Jt Rabb Conf on Conscientious Objectors, 1941-46; mem, exec bd, CCAR, 1959-61; found, Natl Fed Temple Youth, 1939; mem: publs comm, Hillel Found; chmn: Omaha Fair Employment Practice Council, 1942-44; publ panel, War Lab Bd, 1944; mem: Phi Beta Kappa; Nacoms; B'nai B'rith. Author, Atheism is Dead, 1968; contbr: book, Religion and the State U, 1958; Universal Jewish Ency; educ and J publs. Home: 19301 Fairmount Blvd, Shaker Hgts, O. Study: 23737 Fairmount Blvd, Cleveland, O.

LEMMERMAN, Mervin Norman, US, social worker; b. Newark, NJ, June 23, 1928; s. Harry and Celia (Schenkman); BA, Upsala Coll, 1949; MS, Columbia U, 1953; Tchr Cert, HUC, 1957; m. Sydelle Weiss, Sep 11, 1948; c: Alan, David, Daniel. Exec dir, J Comty Cen, Long Beach since 1963, on staff since 1963; dir, educ and youth activities: Temple Isr, Omaha, 1953-56; Temple Isr, Long Beach, 1956-63. Chmn: S sect, W States Chap of Natl Assn J Cen Workers; found pres: W Assn Temple Educs, 1957-58; found mem, Natl Assn Temple Educs, 1961-62; mem: Natl Conf J Communal Service; Natl Assn Social Workers; B'nai B'rith; ACLU. Contbr rel handbooks for parents, book revs and educ articles to profsl jours. Hobby: philately. Home: 7051 McManus, Lakewood, Cal. Office: 2601 Grand, Long Beach, Cal.

LEMPEL, Abraham, Isr, engineer, educator; b. Czeshanow, Pol, Feb 10, 1936; s. Aizik and Frieda (Weindling); in Isr since 1948; MSc, Technion, Haifa, 1965; PhD, 1967; m.

Deborah Zuch, Aug 18, 1959; c: Mordechai, Oded. Sr lectr, EE Dept, Technion, Haifa, since 1967; research staff mem, Sperry Rand Research Cen, USA, since 1969; asst, Technion, Haifa, 1963-65; instr, 1965-67; research scholar, U of S Cal, 1968-69. Lt, IDF, 1953-56. Mem, Inst of Elec and Elec Engrs. Contbr to profsl publs. Home: Kibbutz Yagour, Isr. Office: EE Dept, Technion, Haifa, Isr.

LENGY, Jacob Israel, Isr, parasitologist; b. Tel Aviv, Isr, Mar 14, 1928; s. Herman and Shulamit (Leader); desc of Solomon family of Jerusalem; BA, Colo U, 1951; MSc, Wyo U, 1957; PhD, Heb U, 1961; m. Sima Hassidoff; c: Orit, Amnon. Sr lectr, parasitology, dept human microbiol, Tel Aviv U Med Sch, since 1960; fmr: grad asst, Wyo U; research asst, Heb U. Sgt, USAF. Mem: Sigma Xi; Chi Gamma Iota; Psi Chi; Amer Soc of Parasitologists; AAAS; Amer Soc of Protozools; Soc of Clinical Path; Isr Soc of Microbiol; Isr Soc of Protozool. Hobbies: music, chess. Home: 6 Sderot Hagiborim, Ramat Gan, Isr. Office: 155 Herzl St, Tel Aviv, Isr.

LENZ, Ehud, Isr, educator; b. Czernowitz, Rum, Aug 5, 1930; s. Norbert and Rebeka (Granierer); in Isr since 1950; MSc, Technion, Haifa, Isr, 1957; DEng, Tech HS, Munich, Ger, 1962; m. Carmela Locker, Nov 3, 1954; c: Gdalia, Noam. Asso prof, Dept ME, Technion, head, material processing lab, since 1965; research engr, G Fischer, Switz, 1957-61; head, machine tool lab, ETH, Zurich, 1962-65; dean, dept, mech engr, Technion, Haifa, 1966-68. Sgt, IDF, 1950-52. Mem: CIRP, Intl Inst of Produc Engr Research; bd of dirs, Isr Metal Inst; expert: OECD, repr Isr, Switz. Recipient: Taylor medal, CIRP, 1963. Hobbies: photography, hist of civilization, rels. Home: 20 Leon Blum St, Haifa, Isr. Office: Technion, Haifa, Isr.

LENZ, Maurice, US, physician, educator; b. Kovno, Russ, Mar 23, 1890; s. Benjamin and Minna (Idelson); in US since 1906; MD, Columbia U, 1913; m. Anna Malmberg, Mar 10, 1917; c: Robert, Benjamin. Prof, clinical radiology, Coll Phys and Surgs, Columbia U, 1942-55, prof em since 1955; cons radiotherapist, Montifiore Hosp since 1942, att radiotherapist, 1926-42; in gen practice of med, NYC, 1915-17; asst dermat, Vanderbilt Clinic and Mt Sinai Hosp, 1919-21; studied radiotherapy, Eur, 1921-23; asst radiotherapist, Mt Sinai Hosp, 1923-26; radiotherapist, Presbyterian Hosp, 1930-46, chief, radiotherapy, 1934-46, cons radiotherapist since 1946; radiotherapist, Francis Delafield Hosp, NYC, 1952, cons radiotherapist since 1955; dir, Cancer Ser, Dept of Hosp, NYC, 1940-42. US Army MC, 1917-19. Dipl, Amer Bd Radiology; mem: NY Acad Med; NY Roentgen Ray Soc; Amer Radium Soc; AMA; Radiological Soc of N Amer; Amer Assn for Cancer Research; NY Cancer Commn; St Louis Med Soc (hon); Sociedad Venezelana de Radiologia; Royal Soc of Med; hon mem, Soc Radilogorum Terrarum Septentrionalium. Recipient: hon f, Natl Acad Med of Columbia. Home: 293 Central Park W, New York, NY.

LEON, Hyman Appleby, Eng, public official, business exec; b. London, Eng, May 1, 1898; s. Lewis and Leah (Russ); m. Phoebe Davis, June 15, 1921, (decd); c: Evelyn Davis, Annette Waldman. Alderman, London Borough of Richmond upon Thames, since 1965, mayor, 1965-66; mgn dir, PWL Properties Ltd since 1968; HA Leon & Co Ltd, 1930-58. Royal Artillery, 1916-19, maj, Army Wfr, 1941-46. Chmn: St Helier Hosp Group Mgmt comm since 1951; found and pres, Richmond JPA Comm; fmr pres, outer London JPA Combined Comms; fmr: warden, New West End Syn; council mem, Richmond, Surrey Syn; pres, Rotary, Richmond. Mem, B'nai B'rith. Recipient: MBE, 1946; OBE, 1967; Hon Freeman, Borough of Richmond, 1963. Home: 30 Fairacres, Roehampton Lane, London, Eng. Office: 4 Red Lion St, Richmond, Surrey, Eng.

LEONARD, Leo E, US, dentist; b. Phila, Pa, June 14, 1916; s. Abraham and Rebecca (Binderman); DDS, Temple Dent Sch, Phila, Pa, 1939; m. Cylvia Love, Jan 5, 1941; c: Barry, Carole, Rona. Pvt practice, dent surg since 1939. Capt, US Army, 1943-46. Secy, Oxford Circle, J Comty Cen; dent surg, Drizin-Weiss Post 215, JWV; mem: ZOA; Heb Culture Council, Phila; Amer Dent Assn; Equity Lodge No 59, Masons. Home: 811 Brighton St, Philadelphia, Pa. Office: 1371 Kerper St, Philadelphia, Pa.

LEOPOLD, Chester M, US, sales promotion exec; b. Rochester, NY, Jan 16, 1908; s. Charles and Blanche (Meyer); BA, Syracuse U, 1930; m. Claire Meyer, Aug 14, 1938; c: Clarles, Richard. Vice-pres, promotion dir, Wolf and Dessauer, Ft

Wayne, Ind, since 1947; advt mgr: Hickok Mfg Co, 1937; B Forman Co, 1947, both Rochester, NY. Chmn, mem bd, sales promotion div, Natl Retail Merchants Assn; mem: Sigma Alpha Mu; bd: Ft Wayne Comty Concerts, Inc; Ft Wayne Civic Theatre; Better Bus Bur; fmr pres: Downtown Ft Wayne Assn; Temple Club, Temple Brith Kodesh, Rochester; Men's Club, Temple Achdut Vesholom; J Fed; clubs: Ft Wayne Advt, pres; Ft Wayne Press; Fortnightly; Summit. Recipient, Advt Silver Medal Award, Ft Wayne Advt Club and Printers Ink, 1967. Home: 202 E Fleming Ave, Ft Wayne, Ind. Office: Wolf and Dessauer, Ft Wayne, Ind.

LEPAWSKY, Albert, US, social sci, educator, UN and US cons; b. Chgo, Ill, Feb 16, 1908; s. Morris and Rose (Devin); PhD, U Chgo, 1931; visiting f: U Hamburg, 1933; LSE, 1933-34; U Berlin, 1934; m. Rosalind Almond, Apr 17, 1935; c: Martha Barker, Michael, Susan Rosenstreich, Lucy Di-Bianca. Prof, political sci, U Cal since 1953; instr, lectr, research asso, U Chgo, 1930-42, dir, U Inst of Public Service, 1941-42; asst dir, Public Admn Clearing House, 1936-37; dir, Fed of Tax Admn, 1938-40; educ dir, S Regional Training Prog; prof, public admn political sci, U Ala, both 1945-52; admn and cons posts with Chgo, Ill, US Govt and UN since 1935. Capt to lt col, USAAF, 1942-45. Pres: W Political Sci Assn, 1963-64; Cal Conservation Council, 1957-58; vice-pres, Amer Political Sci Assn, 1956-57; mem: exec council, Amer Soc of Public Admn, 1952-53; Phi Beta Kappa. Author: The Judicial System of Metropolitan Chicago, 1932; State Planning and Economic Development, 1949; Administration—The Art and Science of Organization and Management, 1949; contbr to social sci jours. Hobbies: hiking, climbing. Home: 2570 Cedar St, Berkeley, Call. Office: U of Cal, Berkeley, Cal.

LERER, Samuel S, Mexico, rabbi; b. Jerusalem, Pal, Jan 4, 1915; s. Abraham and Sara (Russman); in Mex since 1966; ordained rabbi, Cen Universal Yeshiva, Jerusalem, 1936; grad, Intl Lang and Commerce Coll, Jerusalem, 1938; BA, Witworth Coll, Wash, 1950; MHL, JTSA, NY, 1961; m. Marguerite Katz, Nov 3, 1946; c: Adina Karp, Nathan, Jeffrey. Rabbi, Beth Isr Comty Cen, Mex, since 1968; fmr: rabbi: Beth El Syn, Akron, O, 1961-68; Temple Beth Shalom, Hollywood, Fla, 1953-61; Hillel dir, U Ia, 1965-68. Fmr: mem: steering comm, Olympic Ecumenical Council; JDC; inland-empire council, Boy Scouts of Amer; RA; B'nai B'rith; Masons; Shriner; pres: Assn of Fla Rabbis; Broward Bd Rabbis; Clergymens f, Gtr Hollywood Fla; Spokane dist, ZOA; dir: SE region, United Syn; Leadership Training Inst for SE region, SC; Auxiliary chaplain, Spokane Chr and J; treas, Council on Race Relations; repr, AJComm; presiding, J Court of N Ohio Beit Din; hon mayor, City of Hollywood, Fla. Home: Avenida Montes Carpatos 970-4, Mexico City, Mexico. Study: Boulevard de los Virreyes 1140-Lomas, Mexico City, Mexico.

LERMAN, Leo, US, editor, writer; b. NYC, May 23, 1914; s. Samuel and Ida (Goldwasser); att Feagin Sch Dramatic Arts. Contbr ed: Mademoiselle Mag since 1948; Dance Mag; ed, cons, Playbill Mag; author: Leonardo da Vinci, Artist and Scientist, 1940; Michelangelo, A Renaissance Profile, 1942; contbr, articles and revs on arts, entertainment and books; wrote: prog notes for NY Philharmonic Sym, Young People's Concerts; Nutcracker script, Playhouse 90, TV; cons to publishers and record co; lectr, NYU; fmr actor, dir, stage mgr, constume designer. Pres, costume div. Scenic Artists Union. Home and office: The Osborne, 205 W 57 St, New York, NY.

LERNER, Abba P, US, economist, educator; b. Bessarabia, Russ, Oct 28, 1903; s. Morris and Sofie (Buchman); in US since 1937; BS, London U, 1932, PhD, 1943; m. Alice Sendak, Mar, 1929 (div); c: Lionel, Marion, Levene; m. 2nd, Daliah Kaufmann, July, 1960. Prof, econ, U Cal, Berkeley, since 1965; asst lectr, LSE, 1935-37, research F, 1932-34; lectr, Columbia U, 1939-40, visiting prof 1957; asst prof, U Kan City, 1940-42; asso prof, New Sch for Social Research, 1942-46, prof econ, 1946-47, visiting prof, 1948; prof econ: Roosevelt U, Chgo, 1947-59, visiting prof, 1947; dist visiting prof, Mich State U, 1958, prof econ, 1959-65; visiting prof: U Cal, Berkeley, 1938, 1958-59; Amherst Coll, 1942; U Cal, LA, 1950; Heb U, Jerusalem, 1954-56; Johns Hopkins U, 1957-58; U Hawaii, Summer 1965; Tel Aviv U, Isr, 1965-66; cons: Rand Corp, 1949; Econ Commn for Eur, Geneva, 1950-51; Econ Adv Staff, Isr, 1953-55; adv, Isr Govt Treas and Bank Isr, 1955-56. Author: The Economics of Control, 1944; The Economics of Employment, 1951; Essays in Economic Analysis, 1953; co-author: Planning and Paying for Full

Employment, 1946; Everybody's Business, 1962; contbr to: Ency Britanica; profsl jours. Recipient, f: Leon, U London, 1934-35; Rockefeller, in US, 1938-39; Cen for Advanced Study in Behavioral Sci's, Standford U, 1960-61. Hobbies: graphic arts, wire sculpture. Office: U of Cal, Berkeley, Cal.

LERNER, Bernard J, US, consulting chem engr; b. Bklyn, NY, Apr 28, 1921; s. Morris and Dora (Viders); BChem E, Cooper Union, NY, 1943; MS, State U of Ia, 1947; PhD, Syracuse U, 1949; m. Dorothy Schenker, Sep 2, 1951; c: Douglas, Andrew, Richard. Cons engr, in pvt practice since 1959; pres, Patent Devl Asso, Inc since 1960; jr CE, Amer Cyanamid Co, 1943; instr, CE, dept, State U of Ia, 1946-47; research CE, Inst of Ind Research, Syracuse U, 1947-48; asst prof, U Tex, 1949-54; cons, Monsanto Chem, Tex City, 1952-53; group leader, Chem Engr Research Group, Gulf Research and Devl, Pa, 1954-59; tech adv to vice-pres, Dominion Gulf, 1957-59. US Army, 1943-46. Mem: Amer Inst of CEs; Amer Chem Soc; Sigma Xi; Phi Lambda Upsilon; Omega Chi Epsilon. Contbr to profsl jours. Hobbies: photography, hunting. Home: 727 Orchard Hill Dr, Pittsburgh, Pa. Office: 1312 Route 8, Glenshaw, Pa.

LERNER, Daniel, US, social scientist, educator; b. NYC, Oct 30, 1917; s. Louis and Yetta (Swiger); att, Johns Hopkins U, 1934-35; BA, NYU, 1938, MA, 1939, PhD, 1948; m. Jean Weinstein, May 16, 1947; c: Louise, Thomas, Amy. Ford prof, sociol, MIT since 1953; sci dir, Inst d'Etudes Eurs, Paris since 1954; dir, Camp Allegro-in-the-Berkshires, Pittsfield, Mass since 1946; fmr: Eur repr, Libr of Cong mission, 1946-47; research dir, intl studies project, Hoover Inst, 1947-53; prof sociol, Stanford U, 1947-53. Capt, US Army, chief of intelligence, psychol warfare div, SHAEF, 1945. Treas, Louis Lerner Young Men's Assn since 1961; fmr chmn, Comm on Intl Polling; mem: Amer Sociol Assn; Amer Psychol Assn; Amer Political Sci Assn; AAAS. Author: SYKEWAR: Psychological Warfare Against Germany, 1949; Propaganda in War and Crisis, 1951; The Nazi Elite, 1952; The Passing of Traditional Society, 1958; The Human Meaning of the Social Sciences, 1959; The Hayden Colloquium, 4 vols: Evidence and Inference, 1959; Quantity and Quality, 1961; Parts and Wholes 1963; Cause and Effect, 1965; World Revolutionary Elites, 1965; Communication and Change in Developing Countries, 1967; EURATLANTICA: Changing Perspectives of the European Elites, 1969. Recipient: Palmes Académiques, Officier d'Académie, Fr, 1945; Bronze Star; Purple Heart; four campaign medals. Home: 233 Grant Ave, Newton, Mass. Office: MIT, Cambridge, Mass.

LERNER, Henry H, US, radiologist, b. Chelsea, Mass, Feb 18, 1910; s. Jacob and Bess (Sokol); BS, Boston U, 1930, MD, 1934; m. Helen Kruger, June 2, 1935; c: Toby, Bennett, Susan. Pvt practice since 1949; radiologist: Parker Hill Med Cen, since 1949; Roslindale Gen Hosp, since 1965; cons: Bournewood Hosp; Brookline ILGWU health clinic, since 1949; impartial radiologist. Ind Accident Bd, Commn of Mass, since 1949; prof, radiology, Med Sch, U of Utah, 1946-48. Member: Amer Bd Radiology; AMA; Mass Med Soc; Phi Delta Epsilon; clubs: Brotherhood; Temple Isr; Brookline. Home: 25 Emerson Pl, Boston, Mass. Office: 416 Marlborough St, Boston, Mass.

LERNER, Max, US, journalist, educator, author; b. Minsk, Russ, Dec 20, 1902; s. Benjamin and Bessie (Podel); in US since 1907; BA, Yale U, 1923; MA, Wash U, Mo, 1925; PhD, Robert Brookings Grad Sch of Econ and Govt, Wash, DC, 1927; m. Anita Marburg, July 20, 1928, div; c: Constance Russell, Pamela Schofield (decd), Joanna Townsend; m. 2nd, Edna Albers, Aug 16, 1941; c: Michael, Stephen, Adam. Columnist, NY Post since 1949; LA Times Syndicate since 1967; prof, Amer civilization, Brandeis U, since 1949; mgn ed, Ency of Social Scis, 1927-33; mem, social sci fac, Sarah Lawrence Coll, NY, 1932-36; chmn, fac, Wellesley Summer Inst, 1933-35; lectr, govt, Harvard U, 1935-36, prof, govt summer sch, 1939-41; prof, political sci, Williams Coll, 1938-43; dean, Grad Sch, Brandeis U, 1954-56; Ford Found, prof, U Delhi, 1959-60. Author: It Is Later Than You Think, 1938, rev ed, 1943; Ideas Are Weapons, 1939; Ideas For the Ice Age, 1941; The Mind and Faith of Justice Holmes, 1943; Public Journal, 1945; Actions and Passions, 1948; America as a Civilization, 1957; The Unfinished Country, 1959; The Age of Overkill, 1962; Tocqueville and American Civilization, 1969; ed, The Nation, 1936-38; ed dir, PM, newspaper, 1943-48; ed: The Portable Veblen, 1948; Machiavelli's Prince and Discourses; co-ed, Tocqueville's Democracy in America,

1967. Home: 445 E 84 St, New York, NY. Office: 75 W St, New York, NY.

LERNER, Max K, US, attorney; b. NYC, Dec 27, 1916; s. Louis and Rebecca (Kasner); LLB, Bklyn Law Sch, 1939; m. Lila Schachner, Oct 5, 1943; c: Helen, Beth. Pvt practice; commanding off, Prisoner of War Spec Projects, Off of Provost Marshall Gen, 1946; spec asst, Att-Gen, NYC, 1948. Delg, Jud Council, 1949-67; Repub candidate, NYC Council, 1949; chmn: copyright off affairs comm, Amer Bar Assn, 1953-59; radio, TV comm, Fed Bar Assn, 1952-54; vice-chmn, comm, Hee Foster Care, Salvation Army; mem: copyright comm, Assn Bar, NYC, class of 1956; bd trustees, Fed Bar Assn; Fed Communications Bar Assn. Contbr to profsl jours. Home: 3 Stuyvesant Oval, New York, NY. Office: 625 Madison Ave, New York, NY.

LERNER, Michael Harvey, US, pedodontist; b. Huntington, W Va, Jan 19, 1943; s. Leonard and Marjorie (Cohen); AB, Marshall U, Huntington, W Va, 1963; DMD, U Ky, 1967; MSD, Ind U, 1969; m. Freda Miller, Feb 8, 1964; c: Neil, Marc. Pvt practice since 1969; instr, Coll of Dent, U Ky since 1969; clinical f, United Cerebral Palsy Found, 1967-69. Mem: B'nai B'rith; Ky Dent Assn; Amer Dent Assn; Amer Soc Dent for Children; Amer Acad Pedodontics; SE Soc Pedodontics; Acad Dent for Handicapped; Omicron Kappa Upsilon. Hobbies: photography, music. Home: 3403 Thistleton Dr, Lexington, Ky. Office: 342 Waller Ave, Lexington, Ky.

LERNER, Moshe Abraham, Isr, physician, radiologist; b. Manchester, Eng, June 1, 1927; s. Louis and Fanny (Wittler); in Isr since 1953; MB, ChB, U Manchester, 1950; m. Kleile Fluss, Dec 5, 1957; c: Ruth, Gila, Daniel. Dir, radiology, Hasharon Hosp, Petah Tikva, since 1969; sr clinical lectr, diagnostic radiology, Tel Aviv U, since 1966; fmr: radiologist, Tel Hashomer Hosp, 1955-68; lectr, Harvard U Med Sch, 1968-69. Capt, RAMC; mentioned in dispatches. Found mem, Ramat Chen Syn. Contbr to profsl jours. Home: 21 Massada St, Ramat Gan, Isr. Office: Hasharon Hospital, Petah Tikva, Isr.

LERNER, Natan, Isr, attorney; b. Krszemienice, Pol, Oct 12, 1925; s. Moises and Ester (Bitker); in Isr since 1966; advocate, DDL, law fac, Buenos Aires; m. Bertha Sztejnbok, Jan 5, 1952; c: Lidia, Rut, Ana. Isr dir, WJC, since 1967; fmr: head, Latin Amer desk, UN, 1963-66; practicing atty, Buenos Aires, 1951-66; first asst, chair of intl law, Buenos Aires, 1961-62. Mem: exec, S Amer exec, WJC; hon treas, Intl Law Assn, Isr br; mem: Isr Bar Assn; Intl Law Assn; Amer Soc of Intl Law; Procedural Aspects of Intl Law Inst, Inc; fmr: secy, Zionist Youth Confd, Arg. Author: En Defensa de los Derechos Humanos, 1958; Esquema del Derecho Israeli, 1963; The Crime of Incitement to Group Hatred, 1965; The UN Convention on Racial Discrimination; contbr to gen and specialized publs. Home: 52 Hama'agal St, Kiriat Ono, Isr. Office: 123 Yehuda Halevi St, Tel Aviv, Isr.

LERNER, Samuel, Eng, bank mgr; b. London, Eng, Feb 28, 1907; s. Jacob and Annie (Kisberg); m. Leah Fishman, Aug 27, 1935. Ret, dep mgr, Anglo-Isr Bank Ltd, London, 1963-67; London Registrar, Bank Leumi le-Isr, 1953-59; mem comm: ZF Econ Comm, London; Isr Aid Comm, Cockfosters; hon auditor, Berner Charity Assn, London, past hon treas; fmr: hon secy: Berner Old Boys' Club; Achei Brith Comforts Fund, both London; mem, United J Friendly Soc, Edgware Lodge. Hobby, philately, specialising in collection of Isr postage stamps. Home: 83 Belmont Ave, Cockfosters, Hertfordshire, Eng.

LE ROITH, Harold, H, S Afr; architect; b. Grahamstown, S Afr, Mar 24, 1905; s. Samuel and Rachel; att Rhodes U, Grahamstown, 1931-33; B Arch, U Witwatersrand, 1933; m. Lillian Greenfield, Sept, 1939; 2 c. Pvt practice since 1933; sr partner, Harold H Le Roith & Partners, 1936-61. Mem, Inst of Architects; asso, Royal Inst of British Architects; exec mem, United Progressive J Cong, since 1961, hon architect and chief cons, pres, 1959-61; clubs, Automobile. Hobbies: bowls, golf, tennis. Home: 36 Coronation Rd, Sandhurst, Johannesburg, S Afr. Office: 70/6 Washington House, Commissioner St, Johannesburg, S Afr.

LESER, Moshe, Isr, physician; b. Tarnow, Pol, Nov 7, 1908; s. Menachem and Rachel (Miller); in Isr since 1947; MD, U Krakow, 1933; MPH, Grad Sch of Public Health, U Pitt, 1959; m. Julia Eisenfeld; c: Sylvia Kanter, Rachel. Med dir

Rambam Govt Hosp, Haifa, since 1963; fmr: gen prac, Pol; chief phys, illegal emigration camps, Aliya Bet, Belgium; Immigration Camp Shaar Aliya, Haifa. Fmr pres: Assn of Public Health Drs, Haifa; Friends of Heb U; mem: IMA; Intl Hosp Fed; Anti Cancer League. Hobby: archaeol. Home: 13A Elhanan St, Haifa, Isr. Office: Rambam Govt Hosp, Haifa, Isr.

LESHEM, Moshe, Isr, diplomat; b. Aus-Hung, Sep 3, 1919; s. Armin and Paula (Badratzki) Lemberger; BA, Masaryk U, Brno, Czech, 1939; in Isr since 1949; m. 1st, c: Daniela, m. 2nd, Aliza Sperber, Oct 20, 1953; c: Matti, Miron. Ambass Extraordinary and Plen with Isr permanent mission to UN; fmr: journalist, Czech press, Isr War of Independence; expert on E Eur, acting press off, both Isr Min for Fgn Affairs; 1st secy, Isr legation, Rangoon, Burma; i/c, spec info prog, Min for Fgn Affairs, later press off, spokesman; acting commn gen, Brussels Intl Exposition; consul, Atlanta, Ga; ambass, Rep of Congo, Leopoldville; dir, Afr Affairs, Min for Fgn Affairs. Mem: Czech resistance, WW II. Author: study of communism in ME; contbr to Isr publs. Recipient: Czech order for meritorious service. Home: 26 Tschernichowski St, Jerusalem, Isr. Office: 11 E 70 St, New York, NY.

LESLAU, Wolf, US, educator, philologist, author; b. Krzepice, Pol, Nov 14, 1906; s. Henoch and Itta (Goldreich); in US since 1942; licence-es-lettres, Sorbonne, Paris, 1934, PhD, 1953; diplome, Ecole des Hautes Etudes, Paris, 1934; diplome, Ecole Nationale des Langues Orientales, Paris, 1934; m. Charlotte Halpern, Oct 29, 1938, c: Eliane, Sylvia. Prof of Heb and Semitic ling, U Cal, LA since 1955; lectr, visiting prof, Ecole des Hautes Etudes, Paris, 1936-39; visiting prof, Ecole des Langues Orientales, 1937-39; prof, Ecole Libre des Hautes Etudes, NY, 1942-51; asst prof, Asia Inst NY, 1946-51; visiting prof, New Sch for Social Research, 1948-50; mem, five sci study tours Ethiopia, 1946-47, 1950-54, 1959, 1962; f: Guggenheim Found, 1946-48; asso prof, Brandeis U, 1951-55. Mem: Amer Acad Arts and Scis; Amer Folklore Soc; Amer Oriental Soc; Amer Ling Soc; Amer Anthropological Soc; Société de Ling de Paris; Société Asiatique. Author: Lexique Sootri, 1938; Documents Tigrigna (Ethiopien septentrional), 1941; Gafat Documents: Records of a South-Ethiopic Language, 1945; Short Gramma of Tigre (N Ethiopic) 1945; Bibliography of the Semitic Languages of Ethiopia, 1946; Ethiopic Documents; Gurage, 1950; Falasha Anthology, 1951; Etude Descriptive et Comparative du Gafat (Ethiopian meridional), 1956; Coutumes et Croyances des Falachas, 1957; Ethiopic and S Arabic contributions to the Heb Lexicon, 1959; The Verb in Harari, 1959; Etymological Dictionary of Harari, 1963; Ethiopians Speak: studies in cultural background, 3 vols; co-author: The Fire on the Mountain and Other Ethiopian Stories, 1950. Spec interests: nature study, theatre. Home: 1662 Fairburn Ave, Los Angeles, Cal. Office: U of Cal, Los Angeles, Cal.

LESSE, Stanley, US, psychiatrist, neurologist; b. Phila, Pa, May 6, 1922; s. Charles and Ida (Klein); AB, U Pa, 1942; MD, Jefferson Med Coll, 1945; ScD, Columbia U, 1955; m. Margaret Ostrow, 1950. With neur dept, Columbia U since 1952; att neur, Neur Inst of NY; NY State Psychiatric Inst, 1951-52, sr research psycht, NY State Psychiatric Inst, 1953-59; cons neuropsycht, Amer Rehab Comm, 1951-56; US Public Health post-grad research F, 1952-53; capt, US Army MC, 1946-47; diplomate, Amer Bd Psycht and Neur; f: NY Acad Med; Amer Acad Neur; AMA; Amer Phys F Isr Med Assn; mem: NY Co Med Soc; Amer Psychiatric Assn; Assn for Research in Nervous and Mental Diseases; NY Neur Soc; Amer Psychosomatic Soc; Assn for Advancement of Psychotherapy, pres; World Med Assn; World Fed for Advancement of Mh; Natl Assn of Rel and Mh; Amer Ivrith Med Soc; NY Acad Scis; Electroshock Research Assn. Ed in chief, Amer Jour of Psychotherapy; asso ed, Jour of Therapeutics and Clinical Reports; co-ed, Intl Jour of Cycle Research; contbr to profsl publs. Home: 15 W 81 St, New York, NY. Office: Neur Inst of NY, New York, NY.

LESSER, Arthur J H, US, surgeon; b. Narol, Aus, Mar 9, 1908; s. Benjamin and Rosalie (Federbusch); in US since 1939; MD, U Vienna, 1932; m. Lily Meyer, Mar 12, 1943; c: Ronald, Raymond. Asso in surgery, Cedars of Leb Hosp, since 1942; att phys: Temple Hosp, since 1949, City of Hope, since 1943, Harbor Gen Hosp, since 1946; path, U Vienna, surg, first surg clinic, 1932-36, research f, U Edinburgh, 1938-45; asst prof, U of S Cal, 1942-51. Maj, US Army Res. Dipl, Intl Bd of Surgery; f, Intl Coll of Surgs; mem: Soc of Experimental Biol and Med; LA surg sect, Sigma Xi, Phi

Lambda Kappa. Contbr to sci publs. Hobby: sculpture. Home: Hollywood, Cal. Office: 465 N Roxbury Dr, Beverly Hills, Calif.

LESSER, Jeffrey Joseph, Eng, physician, dental surg; b. London, Feb 18, 1927; s. Louis and Golda (Katz); MB, BS, Middlesex Hosp Med Sch, 1950; BDS, Royal Dent Hosp; LDS, Royal Coll Surg, 1960; m. Sheila Goldstein, Nov 13, 1955; c: Adam, Jeremy. Dent adv, Norgine Ltd. Capt, RAMC, 1953-55. Council: Anglo-Continental Dent Soc; Mx & Hearts BDA, chmn Fluoridation Comm; fmr: chmn, U J Students; J Grads Assn, both London. Mem bd deps, British Dent Assn, chmn Finchley & Barnet sect. Hobbies: semantics, horology. Home: The Maverns, Hill Crescent, Totteridge, London N 20, Eng. Office: 27 Weymouth St, London W 1, Eng.

LESSER, Maurice A, US, physician, educator; b. Boston, Mass, Apr 15, 1900; s. Henry and Sarah (Day); BA, cum laude, Harvard Coll, 1922, MD, med sch, 1925; m. Ethel Berman, July 20, 1937; c: Stephen, Harriet. Visiting phys, Mass Memorial Hosp since 1926; staff mem, Beth Isr Hosp, since 1931; mem fac, Boston U Med Sch, dept, med and preventive med since 1926; fmr: lectr; US Army camps; radio WMAC, Boston, Mass. Prin contribs: discovery of and papers on use of Testosterone Propionate for treatment of angina pectoris, 1942-43, 1946. F, Amer Coll of Card, fmr Mass dep gov; mem: AMA; AHA; NE Heart Assn; Mass Med Soc; Masons, past master, chaplain; addressed Masons in Hung, Mexico. Author: and ed, Health, 1937; contbr to med jours. Recipient, citation Fireman's Friend of Year, Boston, Mass, 1962. Home: 116 Centre St, Brookline, Mass. Office: 314 Commonwealth Ave, Boston, Mass.

LESSER, Stanley Charles, US, attorney; b. Bklyn, NY, Dec 15, 1929; s. Morris and Estelle; AB, NYU, 1950; LLB, NYU, Sch of Law, 1953; m. Elaine Karpf, Nov 23, 1958; c: Karen, Susan, David. Mem, Helfand, Lesser, Moriber & Feldman since 1958; asso atty, Jaffe & Zabronsky, 1954-58. Trustee, Conservative Syn of Fifth Ave; mem: Amer Bar Assn; NY State Bar Assn; Assn Bar of NYC; clubs: Varsity, NYU, pres; NYU, secy, gov. Home: 505 LaGuardia Pl, New York, NY. Office: 2 W 45 St, New York, NY.

LESTER, Louis J, US, surgeon; b. Toronto, Can, Jan 1, 1915; s. Harry and Rose (Swarzberg); in US since 1939; BA, U Coll, Toronto, 1936; MD, U Toronto Med Sch, 1939; m. Sylvia Ziebelman, July 20, 1943; c: Robert, Diane. Att surg, LI J Hosp since 1957; asst surg, Mt Sinai Hosp since 1950. US Army, 1941-45. Mem: Alpha Omega Alpha; Amer Coll Surgs; Amer Bd of Surg; NY Acad of Med; active in UJA and Fed campaigns; club, N Shore Country. Contbr to med jours. Home: 43 Arleigh Rd, Great Neck, NY. Office: 275 Middle Neck Rd, Great Neck, NY.

LESTER, William M, US, engineer, business exec, manufacturer; b. Bklyn, NY, Jan 14, 1908; s. Nathan and Gussie (Pollack); BSE, Worcester Poly Inst, 1928; m. Betty Lubarsky, 1934; c: Kenneth, Gay. Pres, gen mgr, Pyro Plastics Corp, Union, NJ, since 1939; mem, bd dirs; Lester Castings Co, since 1961; cons, US, S Amer and Eur plastics firms, since 1949; engr, Precision Casting Co, Syracuse, NY, 1928-30; designer, Lester Engr Co, Cleveland, 1930-35; gen mgr, Commonwealth Plastics Corp, Mass, 1935-39. Holder of numerous patents. Past pres: Temple Beth-El, Cranford, NJ; Alpha Epsilon Phi; local chap, B'nai B'rith; mem, bd dirs, Hobby Ind Assn of Amer; fmr mem bd dirs: Soc of Plastics Ind, Inc; Amer Technion Soc; mem: Soc of Plastic Engrs, Inc; Amer Soc for Testing Materials; Amer Soc of MEs; Natl Soc Profsl Engrs; Profsl Engrs, State of NJ; Plastics Pioneers Assn; campaigned for: UJA, comty chmn for seven years; Natl J Hosp, Denver, Colo; ARC; USO; Comty Fund; club: Green Brook Country. Hobby, golf. Home: 8 Brayton Rd, Livingston, NJ. Office: Pyro Plastics Corp, Union, NJ.

LEV, Abraham, Isr, industrialist, business exec; b. Leningrad, Russ, Sep 13, 1911; s. Jacob and Rivka (Rivman); in Isr since 1925; att Montefiore Tech Sch, Tel Aviv; c: Nava Ron, Ella Kinreich, Irit; m. 2nd, Judith Steinberg, Dec 8, 1968. Gen mgn dir, Pal Can Co since 1951, fmr: dir; mgr, Jacob Co and Sons Ltd. Served Haganah. Chmn: and found, Isr Inst of Packaging and Ind Design; Strike Fund, Isr Mfr Assn; mem: exec, Isr Natl Comm, Intl C of C; Rotary Club, Ramat Gan; fmr chmn, Maccabi, Ramat Gan Chap. Hobbies: sports, travel, photography. Home: 36 Beeri St, Tel Aviv, Isr. Office: Jabotinsky St, Petah Tikva, Isr.

LEV, Aryeh, US, rabbi; b. Jerusalem, Isr, June 6, 1912; s. Jacob and Mollie (Garfinkel); in US since 1917; BS, Columbia U; BJP, Tchrs Inst, JTSA, 1933; ordained rabbi, MHL, JIR, 1937; hon DD, HUC, 1954; m. Hazel Bernard, 1936; c: Martin, Barbara, Deborah. Dir, commn on J chaplaincy, JWB, since 1945; adv to chief of spec services, VA, since 1946; chaplain, NY Co Amer Legion since 1949. Fmr: rabbi, Beth Isr, Leb, Pa, 1937-39; natl exec-dir, Young Judea, 1940; natl chaplain, JWV, 1948-50. Chaplain, col, US Army, 1940-45; sr chaplain, Augmentation Res, First Army, since 1946. Chmn, Rabb Pension Bd, 1963; pres, NY chap, Mil Chaplains Assn, 1950-52; bd, US Comm for UNICEF, since 1961; natl adv comm, USO, since 1952; natl council, Boy Scouts of Amer, since 1948; mem: Conf of N Atlantic Treaty Org Chaplains, 1952; pres, Council-on-Youth Fitness, 1957-60. Home: 1232 E 12 St, Brooklyn, NY. Office: 15 E 26 St, New York, NY.

LEV, Maurice, US, physician, educator; b. St Joseph, Mo, Nov 13, 1908; s. Benjamin and Rose (Lev); BS, NYU, 1930; MD, Creighton U Med Sch, Neb, 1934; MA, Northwestern U, 1966; m. Lesley Beswick, 1947; c: Peter, Benita. Dir, Congenital Heart Disease Research and Training Cen, Chgo, Ill, since 1957; prof, path, Northwestern U, since 1957; lectr, path, U of Ill Coll of Med, since 1963; cons, cardiovascular path, Children's Memorial Hosp, Chgo, Ill, since 1957; prof lectr, dept of path, U of Chgo, since 1959. Fmr: instr, path, Ill Med Sch, 1939-46; path, Chgo State Hosp, 1940-42; asst prof: Creighton U Med Sch, 1946-47; U of Ill, 1947-48, asso prof, 1948-51; path, dir of labs, Mt Sinai Hosp, Miami, Fla, 1951-57; asso prof, path, U of Miami Sch of Med, 1951-57; lt col, US Army MC, 1942-46. Dipl, Amer Bd of Path: in path, anat, 1941, clinical path, 1943; f: AMA, Amer Coll of Card; Amer Soc of Clinical Path; Coll of Amer Path; mem council: Coll Amer Path, SE region, 1956-57; Intl Acad Path, 1954-57; mem: Amer Soc Path and Bact; Amer Assn Anats; Histochem Soc; Gerontological Soc; Ill and Chgo Path Assns; NY Acad Sci, Amer Coll Chest Phys; Sigma Xi. Author: Autopsy, Diagnosis of Congenitally Malformed Hearts, 1953; co-author: Spitzer's Architecture of Normal and Malformed Hearts, 1951; contbr: secs, chaps, med books; to profsl jours. Home: 1014 Elmwood, Evanston, Ill. Office: 629-37 Wood St, Chicago, Ill.

LEVA, Marx, US, attorney; b. Selma, Ala, Apr 4, 1915; s. Leo and Fannie (Gusdorf); BS, U of Ala, 1937; LLB, Harvard Law Sch, 1940; m. Shirley Pearlman, Oct 31, 1942; c: Leo, Lloyd. Partner, Leva, Hawes, Symington, Martin & Oppenheimer since 1951; gen counsel, US Dept of Defense, 1947-49, asst-secy of defense, 1949-51. Lt, USN, 1942-45. Mem: Amer, DC, and Fed Bar Assns; AJComm. Recipient: Arthur Flemming Award, outstanding young man in govt service, Jr C of C, 1949; Bronze Star with combat dist device. Home: 7115 Bradley Blvd, Bethesda, Md. Office: 815 Connecticut Ave, Washington, DC.

LEVADI, Solomon Schoenberg, US, oral surg, author; b. Slonim, Russ, Feb 2, 1898; s. Wolf-Leib and Liebe (Shereshevsky) Schoenberg; in US since 1920; att: Yeshiva of Slonim, Yeshiva of Maltz, 1911; att Heb Tchrs Training Coll, Jerusalem, 1915; att U of Chgo, Lewis Inst, Chgo, 1920-22; DDS, Loyola U, Coll of Dent Surg, 1926; att Northwestern U Sch of Jour, 1950-53; m. Hanna Stein, Dec 24, 1924; c: David, Victor. Cons, dept, oral surg, Mt Sinai Hosp Med Cen, Chgo, since 1966, asso att oral surg, 1927-48, att oral surg, chmn, oral surg dept, 1948-66; att oral surg, N Chgo Hosp, 1938-41. Lt, Turkish Army, 1915-19; maj, US Army, MC, 1942-46. Mem: Chgo Dent Soc; Ill State Dent Soc; Amer Dent Assn; hon mem, Australian Dent Soc; Soc US Mil Surgs; Ret Offs Assn of the US; Res Offs Assn; B'nai B'rith, Chgo br. Author: Thresholds, a trilogy, in Yiddish, 1948; short stories, poems, essays, in Heb, Yiddish, Eng; contbr to profsl jours. Recipient: Turkish War Medal, 1st Class; Ger Iron Cross, 2nd Class. Spec interests: writing, bookplate designing, theatre, langs. Home: 2034 Warren St, Evanston, Ill.

LEVANON, Eliyahu Yoshua, Isr, rabbi, author; b. Jerusalem, May 5, 1903; s. Avraham and Miriam; ordained rabbi, Yeshivat Etz Haim; tchrs dipl, Tchrs Sem, Jerusalem; att Heb U, Jerusalem; m. Jaffa Shachor, 1923; c: Avraham, Jonah, Yitzchak, Jacob, Moshe (both fell in the war of Independence). Staff mem, Min of Rel Affairs, since 1948. Cultural off, IDF. Mem, Masons. Author: beMisholei haMoledet, 1934; Yalkut Hebron, 1937; Ish haTorah veHama'aseh, 1946; Sha'arei Krav, 1944; Sihim Ka'arazim, 1949; haMisdar Dom, 1956; Amud Yerushalaim, 1963; Even haBohan, 1963; Yizkor Diyerusha-

layim; Mashkof haMeorot beIr ha'Avot; contbr poems, commentaries. Hobbies: coins, stamps, agric. Home: 9 Barak St, Jerusalem Isr. Office: Min of Rel Affairs, Jerusalem, Isr.

LEVARIE, Siegmund, US, musician; b. Aus, July 24, 1914; s. Josef and Sofie; in US since 1938; PhD, Vienna U, 1938; conductors dipl, Vienna Conservatory, 1935; m. Norma Cohn, Mar 26, 1945; c: Janet. Prof, music, Bklyn Coll since 1954, chmn of dept, 1954-62; music fac, U Chgo, 1938-52; dean, Chgo Musical Coll, 1952-54; exec dir, Fromm Music Found, 1952-56; found, Collegium Musicum, U of Chgo, dir, 1938-52; conductor: orch, U Chgo Sym, 1938-52; Bklyn Comty Sym, 1954-58; Ill Sym Orch, 1939-41. Capt, US Army, 1941-46. Mem, Amer Musicological Soc. Author: Fugue and Form, 1941; Mozart's LeNozze di Figaro, 1952; Fundamentals of Harmony, 1954; Guillaume de Machaut, 1954; Musical Italy Revisited, 1963; co-author, Tone: A Study in Musical Acoustics, 1968. Home: 624 Third St, Brooklyn, NY. Office: Brooklyn Coll, Brooklyn, NY.

LEVAV, Jacov, Isr, economist; b. Kishinev, Russ, Apr 17, 1912; s. Baruch and Jahed (Goldenstein) Livov; in Isr since 1934; dipl, ESC, Montpellier, Fr, 1931; m. Carmela Halfon, June 12, 1935; c: Tamar, Margalith Yovel, Baruch. Dep dir-gen, Haifa U, since 1965; prin, HS 1963-65; secy, Solel Boneh, 1941-63; head dept, Pal Ashrai Bank Ltd, 1934-40. Haganah, 1936-49 cpl, IDF res, 1950-61. Mem: comm: Natl Assn of Social Scis; Isr-Afr League; Assn for Advancement of Druze Educ; mem: Acad Assn of Isr, econ br; club: Social and Econ, Haifa. Contbr to periodicals, profsl publs. Spec interests: intl relations, devl countries, gardening. Home: 8 Ruth Blvd, Haifa, Isr. Office: Haifa U, Haifa, Isr.

LEVAV, Shlomo, Isr, diplomat; b. Riga, Russ, Aug 1, 1906; s. Zwi and Deborah (Schalit) Leibowitz; in Isr since 1934; att: U of Berlin; LSE; m. Ayala Bunczel; c: Daphna Katz, Arnon, Naomi. Consul Gen of Isr in Milan, since 1968; fmr: dir, lumber bus, Berlin, 1928-33; vice-dir, E Eur dept, Min for Fgn Affairs, 1964-65; Isr Min in Havana, 1965-68. Hobbies: lit, music, chess, bridge. Home: 5/7 Rashba St, Jerusalem, Isr. Office: Min for Fgn Affairs, Jerusalem, Isr.

LEVAVI, Arye, Isr, foreign service off; b. Vilna, Pol, June 3, 1912; s. Hirsh and Ethel (Minikes) Lejbman; in Isr since 1932; att U of Heidelberg, 1931-32; MA, Heb U, Jerusalem, 1935; m. Rita Bodenheimer, July 14, 1938; c: Ruth, Ada. Isr Ambass to Switz, since 1967; mem, JA political dept, defense affairs, Jerusalem, 1938-48; counsellor, Isr emb, Moscow, 1948-50; min, Belgrade, 1954-57; ambass to Arg, 1958-60; dep dir-gen, Isr Min for Fgn Affairs, 1957-58, 1960-64; dir-gen, 1964-67. Pal Auxiliary Police, 1936; Haganah, 1938-48; attached to Brit Army, It, 1945. Contbr to scholarly jours. Home: 56 Palmach St, Jerusalem, Isr. Office: Min for Fgn Affairs, Jerusalem, Isr.

LEVAVY, Zvi, US, accountant; b. Jerusalem, Pal, Oct 1, 1910; s. Zeev and Esther (Shapiro) Livov; in US since 1929; BCS, NYU, 1934; m. Berenice Bardin, Nov 27, 1935; c: Bardin. Prin partner, Zvi Levavy and Co, CPAs; fmr: secy, Pal Trust Co, Tel Aviv, 1934-36; chief acctnt, Pal Brewery, Rishon le Zion, 1936-38; comptroller, ZOA, 1940-43. Sgt, Aus, WW II. Mem: Intl Council, JDC; Commn of Intl Affairs, Comty Relations Adv Council; mem-at-large, past pres, JCC, Perth Amboy; Bd of Sch Estimate, City of Perth Amboy; Middlesex Co Coll Found; trustee, Hillel Acad; fmr pres, Perth Amboy Zionist Org; mem: Amer Inst of CPAs; NY, NJ CPA Socs. Home: 148 Kearny Ave, Perth Amboy, NJ. Office: 21 E 40 St, New York, NY.

LEVE, Samuel, US, scenic designer; b. Russ-Pol, Dec 1, 1910; s. Bernard and Leah (Resnick); in US since 1920; att Tchrs Inst, JTSA; Dept of Fine Arts, Yale U; c: Teri. Theatrical designer since 1940; designed among others for: Yiddish Art Theatre; Theatre Guild; Maurice Evans; William Saroyan; David Merrick; Rodgers and Hammerstein; George Abbott; The Shuberts; Metrop Opera House, NY; Habima Theatre; Chanukah Festival, Bonds for Isr; Can Armed Forces Tattoo, 1967; Pres: Eisenhower, Kennedy, Johnson; for TV: Ford Theatre; Fred Waring; Revlon; Chrysler; spectaculars for David Susskind; cons-designer, Chgo's McCormick Place. Recipient, best scene designer award, Macbeth, 1942. Home and studio: 277 West End Ave, New York, NY.

LEVENBERG, Morris, US, printer; Wilmington, Del, Feb 10, 1914; s. David and Pauline (Frank); m. Marion Samet, Sept 24, 1939; c: Fredda Pennock, Benjamin. Owner, printing plant, since 1947. Appd, JP, State of Del, 1967; tchr, Heb sch, Temple Beth Emeth, Wilmington, Del, pres, Brotherhood; exec secy, B'nai B'rith lodge, past pres, fmr pres, B'nai B'rith SE Penn-Del; council, adv Aleph Zadik Aleph; active, J Comty Cen; chmn, munic affairs, Rep Comm; candidate for City Council, 1962. Home: 306 W 37 St, Wilmington, Del. Office: 419 Shipley St, Wilmington, Del.

LEVENSOHN, Lotta, US, writer, translator, communal worker; b. Syracuse, NY, Aug 13, 1882; d. Moshe and Eva (Dvoretzky); tchrs cert, JTSA, 1912; att, Columbia U, 1919-21. Free-lance writer, since 1923; off mgr, J Comty of NY, 1910-23; pr off: Hadassah Med Org, Jerusalem, 1929-34; Heb U, Jerusalem, 1941-48 and 1950-55. Mem: hon council, Hadassah; natl bd, ZOA, 1916-23; Natl bd Hadassah; chmn: Bur for Zionist Propaganda among Women, 1920-22; Pal Council of Hadassah, Jerusalem, 1930-36. Author: Outline of Zionist History, 1941; Vision and Fulfillment, 1950; trans, Oldnewland, by Theodor Herzl, from Ger; contbr to Eng-J press. Home: 1019 6 St, Santa Monica, Cal.

LEVENSON, Abraham Leonard, US, lawyer; b. Oct 28, 1906, NYC; s. Charles and Anna (Goldberg), father was noted violin tchr and composer; att, NYU, 1925-25; LLB, Fordham U, 1928; att CCNY, 1928-33; m. Rose Vogel, Dec 24, 1934, c: Martin, Carol Kaufman. Pvt practice since 1930; atty for many schs and colls. Co-chmn, vocational service adv bd, B'nai B'rith; past pres, Midwood Lodge, B'nai B'rith; mem: NY Co Lawyers Assn; NY State Bar Assn. Spec interest: music, theatre, Home: 551 Fifth Ave, New York, NY. Office: 599 E Seventh St, Brooklyn, NY.

LEVENSON, Eleanore, US, lecturer, educator; b. NYC; d. Herbert and Henrietta (Gerber); BA, Bklyn Coll, 1958, Ford Found Prog; MA, New Sch for Social Research, 1960; m. Louis Goldberg (decd); c: Karl. Publs dir; feature writer, Bklyn Daily Eagle, 1930-33; dir, Rand Sch Press, 1935-38; exec dir: League for Lab Pal, 1949-53; Sharon Press, 1944-51; speaker, J Cen Lecture Bur, 1959; commentator, dir, Amer-Isr Almanac, Radio Sta WLIB, 1952; dir: pr and info, Pioneer Women, 1958; educ, Women's League for Isr, 1954-56. Delg, WZCs, 1946, 1951; mem: League for Mutual Aid; Workers' Defense League; Amer Acad for Political Sci; Amer Assn U Women. Author: Lawless Judges, 1935. Home: 351 W 24 St, New York, NY.

LEVENSON, Harold A, US, business exec; b. Boston, Mass, May 2, 1919; s. Samuel and Sadie (Altman); c: Linda, Lisa; stepson, Carl Rossi. Pres, Harold Levenson Assos, life ins agcy, since 1950; vice-pres, Romer Zane Grey Produc Ltd; exec vice-pres, Springtime Camps, Colo since 1955. Maj, US Army, 1943. Treas: Natl Assn Bldg Contractors, 1952-56; chmn finance comm, Masquers Club, Hollywood since 1961; hon mem, Acad Magical Arts; clubs: Million Dollar Round, life; Kiwanis. Produc: Born Yesterday; The Pleasure of His Company; contbr to natl ins mags. Home and office: La Canada, Cal.

LEVENSON, Joseph R, US, educator, author: b. Boston, Mass, June 10, 1920; s. Max and Eva (Richmond); BA, Harvard, 1941, MA, 1942, PhD, 1949; m. Rosemary Sebag-Montefiore, Oct 5, 1950; c: Richard, Irene, Thomas, Leo. Prof of hist, U of Cal, since 1960; Sather prof of hist, since 1964. Author: Liang Ch'i-ch'ao and the Mind of Modern China, 1953, 1959; Confucian China and Its Modern Fate; The Problem of Intellectual Continuity, 1958, The Problem of Monarchical Decay, Vol II, 1964, The Problem of Historical Significance, Vol III, 1965, A Trilogy, 1968; European Expansion and the Counter-Example of Asia, 1300-1600, 1967; contbr to profsl jours. Mem: Amer Hist Assn; Assn for Asian Studies; Cong Beth Isr; Soc fs, Harvard. Recipient: Fulbright, 1954-55; Cen for Advanced Study in the Behavioral Scis, 1958-59; Guggenheim, 1962-63; ACLS, 1966-67; awarded honors, Amer Hist Assn, Pacific coast br, 1959. Hobby, piano. Home: 261 Stonewall Rd, Berkeley, Cal. Office: U of Cal, Berkeley, Cal.

LEVENSON, Minnie G, US, museum curator; b. Russ, Feb 5, 1905; d. Abraham and Rose (Rafer) Goldstein; BA, Boston U, 1926; att Harvard U; MA, Columbia U, 1938; m. Benjamin Levenson, Aug 8, 1940. Cons, music and films, Worcester Art Museum since 1966; curator of educ, 1956-66, with mus since 1933; pvt tutor 1926-32. Bd dirs: Friendly House; fmr pres: Public Sch Art League; Better Films Council; mem, Natl Comm for Art Educ. Contbr to mus publs; cons on films. Home: 8 Hawthorne Rd, Holden, Mass. Office: Worcester Art Mus, Worcester, Mass.

LEVENSON, Robert L, US, business exec; b. Pittsburgh, Pa, June 20, 1925; s. David and Eva (Wilcof); att: U of Pittsburgh, 1933-34; U of Pa, 1934-37; m. Helen Elinoff, Dec 30, 1936; c: Elaine, Betty, Linda, Robert. Pres, Reichart Furniture Co, since 1946; vice-pres, Elby Family Restaurants. USAAF, 1942-45. Vice-pres, mem bd, finance and exec comm, Wheeling Hosp, chmn, Hosp Site comm; mem: pres adv council, Jesuit Coll; Woodsdale Temple, past pres and chmn bldg comm; Wheeling Area Conf, since 1953; Wheeling Coll; Eoff St Temple, fmr, pres, dir, trustee, chmn bldg comm; Elks; Masons 32nd deg; fmr: co-chmn, Isr Bond Drive Comm, Wheeling, W Va, 1969; chmn, Urban Renewal Auth; found, pres, Downtown Wheeling Assos. Recipient, Citizen of the Month of Wheeling, Feb 1955. Home: Knox Lane, Wheeling, W Va. Office: Reichart Furniture Co, Wheeling, W Va.

LEVENSPIEL, Octave, US, educator; b. Shanghai, China, July 6, 1926; s. Abraham and Elizabeth (Greenhouse); in US since 1946; att: Aurora U, Shanghai, 1943-46; BS, U Cal, Berkeley, 1947; MS, PhD, Ore State U, 1947-51; m. Mary Smiley, July 13, 1952; c: Rebecca, Joseph, Morris. Prof, chem engr, Ore State U, since 1969; asst prof, Ore State Coll, 1952-54; asso prof, Bucknell U, Pa, 1954-58; prof, Ill Inst of Tech, Chgo, 1958-68. Mem: Amer Inst Chem Es; Amer Chem Soc. Author: Chemical Reaction Engineering ,1962, trans into various langs; co-author, Fluidization Engineering, 1969; contbr of books, booklets, tech publs. Recipient: US Natl Sci Found Sr Post Doc F to Cambridge U, Eng, 1963-64; 1966 Lectureship Award, Amer Soc Engr Educ, 1966; US Fulbright F to Cambridge U, Eng, 1968-69. Home: 1634 Crest Pl, Corvallis, Ore. Office: Ore State U, Corvallis, Ore.

LEVENSTEIN, Aaron, US, author, educator; b. NYC, Nov 11, 1910; s. Joseph and Anna (Mayers); dipl, HUC Tchrs Sch, 1930; BA, CCNY, 1930; JD, NYU Law Sch, 1934; m. Pearl Waller, 1933 (decd); c: Beth, Nora, Joseph; m. 2nd, Margery Littman Meisler, 1965. Prof, mgmt, Bernard Baruch Coll, CUNY, since 1960; lectr, hum relations, HUC-JIR, since 1956; weekly commentator and news analyst, radio sta WEVD, NYC, since 1955; pvt practice, lab law, 1934-40; dir ed, Research Inst of Amer, 1940-60; weekly commentator and news analyst, radio sta WINA, Peekskill, NY, 1952-54; adj prof, mgmt, NYU, 1959. Trustee, Freedom House; mem: natl exec bd, Workmen's Circle; League for Ind Democracy; Ind Relations Research Assn; J Lab Comm. Author: Labor Today and Tomorrow, 1945; Why People Work, 1962; Use Your Head—The Art of Problem Solving, 1965; Testimony for Man—The Story of the City of Hope, 1967; co-author: Two in Africa, 1959; Freedom's Advocate, 1965; ed, Labor Coordinator, 4 vols, 1946; contbr to political, social sci and other jours. Recipient, New Republic Prize, 1937. Hobby, photography. Home: 321 W 24 St, New York, NY. Office: Baruch Coll, CUNY, New York, NY.

LEVENTHAL, Ethel Helen, US, artist; b. Bklyn, Dec 20, 1912; d. Benjamin and Emma (Rothstein) Stoloff; att NYU, 1930-33; art deg, Bklyn Mus Art Sch, 1952; div; c: Steven. Mem: Natl Assn of Women Artists; Woodstock Art Assn; Artists Equity. Recipient: art awards for traveling art shows, US, Eng. Home and studio: 47 Plaza St, Brooklyn, NY.

LEVENTHAL, Fred R, US, business executive; b. Cleveland, O, June 22, 1921; s. Louis and Fannie (Neyer); att U of Ill, 1942-44; m. Maxine Margolis, Mar 16, 1947; c: Fern, Todd. Vice-pres, Vining Broom Co, since 1946; mfr, since 1936. Pres, Natl Assn of Broom Mfrs and Allied Inds, 1959-60; mem, bd of trustees, Springfield City Hosp, since 1959; pres, Temple Sholom, 1957-58, 1968-69; chmn, JWF, 1950; pres, B'nai B'rith, 1954-55, all Springfield; mem, Clark Co Hosp Comm and Clark Co Hosp Authority, since 1967; club: Rotary. Home: 439 Dover Rd, Springfield, O. Office: 2530 Columbus Rd, Springfield, O.

LEVENTHAL, Harold, US, jurist; b. NYC, Jan 5, 1915; s. Jules and Sadie (Wolcher); AB, Columbia U, 1934, LLB, 1936; m.Kathryn Kumler, Sep 18, 1948. Judge, US Court of Appeals, Wash, DC, since 1965; ed in chief, Columbia Law Review, 1935-36; law clerk, Supr Court Justices Harlan Stone and Stanley Reed, 1936-38; atty, US Solicitor Gen, 1938-39; asst gen counsel, OPA, 1940-43; dep chief, Aggressive War Sect, staff of Justice Robert Jackson, Nuremberg Trials, 1951-52; partner, law firm, Ginsburg & Leventhal, 1946-65; chief counsel, Off Price Stabilization, 1951-52; gen counsel, Dem Natl Comm, 1952-65; lectr, Yale Law Sch, 1956-62. Lt cdr, USCG Res, 1943-46. Contbr to legal jours. Home: 2406-44 St, NW, Washington, DC. Office: US Courthouse, Washington, DC.

LEVENTHAL, Ronald (pen name, **Ronny Lee**), US, writer, teacher; b. New York, NY, Mar 2, 1927; s. Abraham and Shirley (Edelstein); att, RCA Insts, NY, elec engr, 1945-46; studied: guitar, music theory, harmony, improvisation, 1940-50; m. Frances Rand, Aug 28, 1957. Writer, tchr, lectr, musician, since 1947; guitar soloist, Radio Sta WNEW, 1944-45; orch leader, guitar soloist, Ronny Lee Orch, 1943-57; owner, dir, guitar sch, Ronny Lee Guitar Studio, 1959-64. Written and pub works: numerous instrn books on guitar and other fretted musical instruments, sold throughout the world; numerous books, guitar arrangements of classical and popular selections; 10 chap series, articles on guitar, Christian Science Monitor, 1966; fmr: music critic, Guitar World Mag; performed: with NY Philharmonic, Lincoln Cen, NYC, spec concerts, utilizing guitar and banjo; guitar accompanist, Pilar Gomez Spanish Ballet Troupe, Carnegie Hall, NYC; lectured, adjudicated, guitar festivals and music trade shows; guitar tchr workshops, US, Can; cons: leading guitar mfrs; music publishers. Mem: ASCAP; Amer Guild Music; Amer Fed Musicians. Recipient, Popular Music Award, ASCAP, 1966, 1967, 1968, 1969. Hobbies: photography, electronics, sci, musical instruments. Home: 310 W 55 St, New York, NY.

LEVEY, Abraham S, US, business exec; b. Riga, Latvia, Aug 15, 1886; s. Louis and Dora (Selig); in US since 1902; m. Fannie Mack, Feb 4, 1909. Pres, treas, Reliable Furniture Co since 1920. Mem: natl council, JDC since 1942; found, pres: J Fed, 1942-45, hon pres since 1945; Vaad Heir, 1927-35; hon pres, Cong Shaarey Tephiloh since 1960; pres, Portland Heb Sch Syn Assn, 1955-58; hon chmn, State of Isr Bond Dr since 1951; gen chmn, bldg comm, J Comty Cen, 1938; found, hon vice-pres, Camp Lown since 1946; hon trustee, Me Med Cen; found, Fannie and Abraham Levey Charitable Found. Home: 320 Baxter Blvd, Portland, Me. Office: 353 Cumberland Ave, Portland, Me.

LEVEY, Samson H, US, rabbi, educator; b. Benton Harbor, Mich, Dec 19, 1909; s. Tobias and Sarah (Caplan); BS, Ill Inst of Tech, 1929; BHL, HUC, 1931, ordained rabbi, 1934, hon DD, 1959; PhD, U of S Cal, 1955. Prof, rabb and J rel thought, HUC-JIR, LA, chmn of grad comm since 1959; mem fac: U of S Cal Grad Sch of Theol; S Cal Sch of Theol, Claremont, Cal; fmr: rabbi, Temple B'nai Isr, Jackson, Tenn, 1934-39; lectr, J rel, Bethel Coll, 1934-39; rabbi, Temple Mishkan Isr, Selma, Ala, 1939-43; chaplain and dir, JWB, coll training prog, U of Pa, 1943-44; rabbi: Temple B'nai B'rith, Santa Barbara, Cal, 1948-49; Temple Beth Isr, Pomona, Cal, 1950-54; Temple Beth Torah, San Fernando Valley, Cal, 1954-59. Mem: CCAR; HUC Alumni Assn; W Assn of Reform Rabbis; Soc of Bibl Lit; AAUP; LA Cmty Relations Comm; fmr: pres: Bd of Rabbis of S Cal; S Cal Assn of Lib Rabbis; chmn: Coord Council on Social Wfr, Selma, Ala; Dallas Co United Service Org. Recipient, Moses Meilziner Prize in Talmud, HUC, 1932-34. Home: 1854 Heidleman Rd, Los Angeles, Cal.

LEVI, Aleksandar, Yugo, attorney; b. Yugo, July 20, 1915; s. Isak and Paula (Adler); LLD, Fac of Law, Belgrade, 1939; m. Mirjana Zivković, Jan 11, 1949; c: Mirko, Nela. Dep public prosecutor, People's Rep of Serbia, since 1954; pvt law practice, 1939-41. Dep pres, Fed J Comtys in Yugo, since 1964, mem exec, 1947-59; vice-pres, pres, J Comty, Belgrade, 1956-62. Mem, ed bd and perm contbr: J Review, since 1952; J Almanac, pub, Fed of J Comties, Yugo. Recipient: Order of Labour, twice; order of Merit for the People; Order for Mil Services. Home: Palmotićeva 3, Belgrade, Yugo. Office: Public Prosecution Office, Nemanjina 26, Belgrade, Yugo.

LEVI, Alexander A, US, surgeon; b. Vilna, Russ, Oct 12, 1902; s. Simon and Esther (Gorlin) in US since 1903; pre-med certificate, Tufts Coll, 1922, MD, 1926; m. Dorothy Hite, Oct 11, 1932; c: Sylvia, David. Sr clinical instr, gyn, Tufts Coll Med Sch, since 1952, mem fac, since 1929; sr visiting obstet, Booth Memorial Hosp, since 1932, staff mem, since 1929; surg, Mt Auburn Hosp, Cambridge, Mass, since 1929; surg cons, Metrop State Hosp, since 1952; surg, gyn dept, Boston Dispensary, since 1928; fmr: surg, USPHS, 1943-48; voting mem, Mass Hosp Service, Inc, 1948-57; sup of clinic, Charles Hayden Goodwill Inn for Boys, 1940-42. Capt, Newton Unit of Civil Defense, 1942-44; mem, adv comm, Boston Civilian Defense, 1943-50. Established Simon Levi Loan Fund, Tufts Coll Med Sch, 1946; gen chmn, phys comm, metrop div, CJA, 1948-49, chmn, comm, Norumbega Council, Boy Scouts of Amer, 1951-52. F: Amer Coll of Surgs; Intl Coll of Surgs;

Amer Coll of Obstets and Gyn; vice-pres (ex-officio), Mass Med Soc, 1954-55, mem, council, since 1926, chmn, comm on ins progs, since 1961, pres, Middlesex S dist, 1954-55, secy, 1929-54. Mem: AMA; NE Obstet and Gyn Soc; Mass and Gtr Boston Med Soc; Temple Isr, Boston; club: New Cent, pres, 1956-57, trustee, student aid fund, 1957-60. Contbr to surg jours. Recipient: awards: UJA, FJP, 1948; J Advocate carnation award, 1954. Home: 265 Ward St, Newton Cen, Mass. Office: 481 Beacon St, Boston, Mass.

LEVI, Augusto Yoel, Isr, attorney, tchr, business exec; b. Ancona, It, July 15, 1888; s. Guido and Sara (Castelli); in Isr since 1938; DJur, U Moderna, 1911; m. Lydia Bigiavi, Jan 22, 1925; c: Renato, Carla Zeldes. Lectr, pvt law: Heb U, Jerusalem, since 1961; Tel Aviv U, since 1940; fmr chmn, mem exec, Isr Mfrs Assn since 1942, chmn, financial and ind corps; pvt law practice, It, 1911-38. Off, It Army, WW I. Dep chmn, bd govs, Heb U, since 1962, mem exec bd since 1959; fmr: pres, Isr Assn Friends of Heb U; chmn, Isr Assn of It Immigrants; mem: Isr council, JNF, KH; ZF, all It; club, Rotary. Recipient: Silver Medal; two Crosses of Merit, WW I; Commn of Order of It Rep, 1958; A Levy Commercial Law Chair, Heb U, 1968. Home: 15 Maaleh Hazofim, Ramat Gan, Isr.

LEVI, Doro, It, archaeologist, educator, author; b. Trieste, It, June 1, 1898; s. Edoardo and Eugenia (Tivoli); PhD, U Florence, 1920; m. Anna Cosadino, 1928. Dir, It Archaeol Sch, Athens, Greece, since 1941, mem, 1921-23; insp, antiquities of Etruria, Archaeol Mus, Florence, 1926, dir antiquities, 1932; org, mem, It Archaeol Mission to Mesopotamia, 1930; lectr, archaeol, hist of ancient art, U Florence, 1933; prof, archaeol, hist of ancient art, U of Cagliari, 1935; dir, arts and antiquities in Sardinia, mus of Cagliari and Sassari, 1935-38; lectr: Princeton U; Harvard U, 1939-45; mem, Inst for Advanced Studies, 1939-45; Guggenheim F, 1941-43; adv, cultural relations, Min of Educ, Rome, It, 1945; org and mem, numerous field expeditions. Mem: Natl Acad dei Lincei; Istituto Italiano di Archaeol e Storia dell'Arte; Archaeologisches Inst des Deutschen Reiches; Greek Archaeol Soc; Istituto di Studi Etruschi, Florence; NY Acad of Sci. Author: books and papers on archaeol. Office: Scuola Archaeologica Italiana, Amalias 56, Athens, Greece.

LEVI, Edward H, US, educator, university pres; b. Chgo, Ill, June 26, 1911; s. Gerson and Elsa (Hirsch); PhB, U Chgo, 1932, JD, 1935; JSD, Yale Law Sch, 1938; hon: LLD: U Mich, 1958; U Cal, Santa Cruz, 1968; JSTA, 1968; U of Ia, 1968; Brandeis U, 1968; Lake Forest Coll, 1968; U Rochester, 1969; LHD, HUC, 1968; m. Kate Sulzberger, June 4, 1946; c: John, David, Michael. Pres, U Chgo since 1968, dean, law sch, 1950-62; U Provost, 1962-68, on fac since 1936. Chmn, Council on Legal Educ and Profsl Responsibility, Assn Amer Law Schs; trustee: Inst Intl Educ; Intl Legal Cen; Bd of Urban Inst; mem: White House Task Force on Educ, 1966-67; White House Cen Group on Domestic Affairs, 1964; Amer Acad Arts and Scis; Co council, Amer Law Inst; adv panel, Natl Sci Found; Social Sci Research Council; Amer, Ill, Chgo Bar Assns; J Publ Soc; Citizens Comm on Grad Med Educ; Comm on Founds and Pvt Philanthrophy. Author: Introduction to Legal Reasoning, 1949; Four Talks on Legal Education, 1952; co-ed: Gilbert's Collier on Bankruptcy, 1936; Elements of the Law, 1950; mem, ed bd, Jour of Legal Educ, 1956-58; asso ed, Natural Law Forum; contbr numerous articles trade regulations. Home: 5855 University Ave, Chicago, Ill. Office: U of Chgo, Chicago, Ill.

LEVI, Edwin K, US, attorney, business exec; b. Cincinnati, O, July 24, 1904; s. Charles and Rose (Blade); BA, U Cincinnati, 1926, JD, 1928; m. Fanny Thal, June 23, 1931; c: Kathryn Ades. Pres, SH Thal, Inc (doing bus as Rogers & Co), since 1958; pvt law practice, 1928-39. Pres, Dayton Retail Jewelers Assn, since 1952; treas, mem, bd dirs, Dayton Retail Merchants Assn, since 1965; mem, spec comm on excise and miscellaneous taxes, Amer Bar Assn; chmn finance comm, JCC, since 1952, mem, exec bd and bd govs, treas, 1953, vice-pres, 1954-56; mem, long-range planning comm, Temple Isr, chmn finance comm, 1951-53, vice-pres, 1954-55, 1957-58, treas, 1946-53, chmn cemetery comm, 1959; bd dirs, Temple Isr, Dayton, O; chmn: United J Campaign budget comm, 1950-52; finance comm, treas to build Cen-Home for the Aged; natl council, JDC, since 1950; mem, bd dirs: U Cincinnati Law Sch Alumnae Assn; Law Comm, C of C, Dayton, O; mem: natl council, CJFWF, 1950-57; natl council, United HIAS Service, 1950-56; Cincinnati Soc; Dayton and O State Bar Assns; Sigma Alpha Mu; Phi Delta Epsilon.

Sigma Sigma; Ky Col. Hobby, travel. Home: Apt 2, 540 Heather Dr, Dayton, O. Office: 33 S Main St, Dayton, O.

LEVI, Eliahu, Isr, government official; b. Ferrara, It, Jan 8, 1904; s. Salomone and Fortunata (Mordo); in Isr since 1939; PhD, ME, HS of Engr, Milan, 1926; m. Luisa Crema, Aug 4, 1931. Head, standards dept, Standards Inst of Isr, since 1945; fmr first secy, Ente Nazionale Per L'Unificazione, Milan, 1927-38. Contbr to profsl jours. Hobbies: philately, stat. Home: 65 Herzl St, Ramat Gan, Isr.

LEVI, Enrico, Isr, master mariner; b. Cremona, It, Apr 6, 1918; s. Giuseppe and Gemma (Rietti); in Isr since 1951; att: Nautical Coll, It; off deg, Navy Training Ship, It, 1937; Ecole Superiore de Commerce, Switz, 1940-1942; master mariner, Brit Merchant Marine, 1944; div Tech adv, Isr Ports Auth, since 1967; fmr: capt, Zim Lines passenger and cargo ships, 1948-51; prin, Haifa Nautical Sch, 1951-54; found, dir, Isr Nautical Coll, 1954-60, mgr: Eilat Port, 1960-64; Ashdod Port, 1964-67; found, Ghana Nautical Coll, 1956-57. Cdr: first illegal ship after WW II with immigrants to Pal, 1945-47; lt cdr, Isr Navy, 1951-68. Secy, Intl Cargo Handling Coord Assn, Isr; asso mem, US Naval Inst; life mem, Intl Assn of Navigational Congs; Intl Assn of Navigation; fmr secy, Isr Seaman's Union. Recipient, Chaveliere Officiale, It Rep. Contbr to profsl jours. Hobbies: sailing, ship models. Home: POB 24, Ashdod, Isr. Office: POB 20121, Tel Aviv, Isr.

LEVI, Herbert W, US, biologist; b. Frankfurt/M, Ger, Jan 3, 1921; s. Ludwig and Irma Hochschild; in US since 1938; att, Art Student League, NY, 1938-39; BS, U Conn, 1946; PhD, U Wis, 1949; m. Lorna Rose, June 13, 1949; c: Frances. Prof, biol, Harvard, since 1970, curator, arachnology since 1966, on staff since 1956; asst to asso prof, zool, U Wis, 1949-56. Bd gov, Nature Conservancy, 1956-62; secy Rocky Mt Biol Lab, 1959-65; councillor, Soc Systematic Zool, 1967-70; vice pres, Centre Intl de Documentation Arachnologique, 1965-68; mem: Amer Soc Zool; Soc Study of Evolution; Soc Systematic Zool; Amer Micros Soc; Wildlife Soc; Amer Inst Biol Sci; Wilson Ornithological Soc; Amer Ornithological Soc; Wilderness Soc. Co-author, Spiders and their Kin, 1968; co-ed and trans, Keastner, Invertebrate Zoology, Vol 1-3, 1967, 1968, 1969; contbr, numerous papers on systematic biol and conservation. Home: Wheeler Rd, Pepperell, Mass. Office: Mus of Comparative Zool, Harvard U, Cambridge, Mass.

LEVI, J Elliot, US, physician; b. Baltimore, Md, Aug 25, 1912; s. Abraham and Regina (Ottenheimer); BA, Johns Hopkins U, 1934; MD, 1938; m. Marjory Weinberg, Aug 12, 1940; c: Alan, Jan. Pvt practice, internal med and endocrinology since 1946; att phys, Sinai Hosp since 1951, on staff since 1938; instr, Johns Hopkins U since 1953; phys, Johns Hopkins Hosp since 1953, all Baltimore; cons: US VA Hosp, Fort Howard, Md; US VA Hosp, Perry Point; research f, Harvard U Med Sch; asso med research, Beth Isr Hosp, Boston Mass, 1941-42. US Army, 1942-46. F, Amer Coll Phys; mem: Amer Diabetic Assn; Endocrine Soc; AMA; Amer Soc Internal Med; Md Soc Internal Med, pres, 1950-60; Phi Beta Kappa, vice-pres, med and chirurgical fac of Md, 1960-61. Contbr to med jours on endocrine and metabolic disorders. Hobbies: tennis, photography. Home: 3411 Falstaff Rd, Baltimore, Md. Office: 222 W Cold Spring Lane, Baltimore, Md.

LEVI, Joseph, US, psychologist; b. Wolkowysk, Pol, Apr 10, 1908; s. Shalom and Minnie (Trunski); in US since 1921; BS, NYU, 1931, PhD, 1943; MA, Columbia U, 1934; m. Ruth Milner, Oct 22, 1933; c: Ethel, Haskel. Pvt practice: on staff, NYU Coll of Med, since 1948; prof, psych, CUNY, since 1967; fmr psychol: Homecrest, Yonkers, NY; Children's Service Bur; Bellevue Hosp, and att clinical psychol; instr, psych, CCNY, 1943-50; chief clinical psychol, Bx VA Hosp, 1946-48; prof, clinical psych, Grad Sch Educ, Yeshiva U, 1957-62, chmn dept, 1957-59; research psychol, emotional problems of physically handicapped, Commonwealth F, Inst of Phys Med and Rehab, NYU Med Cen, 1948-51; cons on the Rorschach, J Child Care Assn, Essex Co, NJ, 1947-50. Dipl, clinical psych, Amer Bd of Examiners in Clinical Psych, 1947. F: Amer Psych Assn, 1947; Soc for Projective Techniques, 1953. Author: Rorschach Patterns Predicting Success or Failure in the Rehabilitation of the Physically Handicapped, 1951; Hawthorne's Scarlet Letter—A Psychoanalytic Interpretation, 1953. Contbr articles on: psych; acting out as indicated on the Rorschach. Home: 1014 E 7 St, Brooklyn, NY. Office: 30 E 60 St, New York, NY.

LEVI, Kurt, US, banker; b. Wiesbaden, Ger, May 20, 1910; s. Josef and Martha (Hahn); in US since 1937; JD, U Frankfurt, 1931; m. Ruth Neumann, Feb 17, 1937; c: Peter. Vice pres, City Natl Bank and Trust Co, Kan City since 1956; gen merchandise mgr, Consolidated Retail Stores, 1937-56. Vice chmn, Plain States Regional Bd, ADL, natl asso f, ADL; Mo chmn legacy comm, mem: Isr cabinet, Intl Council, bd govs, Dist Grand Lodge, supr lodge delg, Natl Conf on Soviet Jewry, past pres: B'nai B'rith Council of Gtr KC; KC Lodge 184, all B'nai B'rith; gen and area chmn, United Campaign; vice pres, Downtown Kiwanis Club; chmn: finance comm, Camp Fire Girls of Amer; Mayor's Prayer Breakfast Club; hot line div, finance div, J Fed; Kan City Conf on Soviet Jewry; secy, mem exec bd, Cmty Relations Bur; pres, chmn bd, Kehilath Isr Syn; gen chmn, Gtr Kan City Bonds for Isr. Home: 1019 W 66th Terr, Kansas City, Mo. Office: POB 226, Kansas City, Mo.

LEVI, Leo, US, physicist; b. Mannheim, Ger, Jan 15, 1926; s. Joseph and Frida (Jacobson); in US since 1940; BEE, CCNY, 1952; MS, Physics, Polytech Inst, Bklyn, 1955, PhD, 1964; m. Miriam Wechsler; c: Joseph, Solomon, Meir, Hillel. Adj asso prof, CUNY, since 1965; cons physicist since 1958; sr physicist, Freed Electronics, 1951-55; head, applied physics dept, Fairchild Camera & Instrument Co, 1955-58. Prin contribs: Devl techniques for modulating light by ultrasonic waves; devl basic approach to analyzing optical image enhancement. Pres, natl, Assn Orthodox J Sci; vice-pres, natl, Agudath Isr Youth of Amer, 1952-53; mem: Optical Soc of Amer; Sigma Xi; IEEE. Author: Vistas From Mt Moria, 1959; Applied Optics, 1968; Jewish Chrononomy, 1967; contbr author: Radargrammetry, 1960; Rabbi Dr J Breuer Jubilee Volume, 1962; contbr numerous articles to sci Halakhah jours and jours of J thought and scholarship. Home and office: 435 Ft Washington Ave, New York, NY.

LEVI, Leo, Isr, musicologist; b. Casale, It, June 15, 1912; s. Yoseph and Sarah (Bolaffio); in Isr since 1935; MMus, Sch of Musical Palaeography, Parma; DSc, U Bologna; widowered; c: Jehiel, Joalà, Johanna, Jemima, Joseph. Research F, musicology, Heb U, Jerusalem, since 1964; fmr, dir, Intl Cen of Lithurgic Traditional Music, 1960-67. Mem, Centro di Musica Tradizonale Liturgica, Rome; fmr: org, Zionist activities, J schs, It; found: and dir, educ activities, relations with Isr, J youth org, It; org, Archives for Traditional Lithurgical Music, Rome; mem, It Immigrants in Isr Org. Author: Beth Israel (hist of J people), 1953; Boker; contbr of studies in J music to profsl publs. Spec interests: ME politics, Byzantinology. Home: 43 Hebron Rd, Jerusalem, Isr. Office: Hebrew U, Jerusalem, Isr.

LEVI, Livio Edmondo, Brazil, architect; b. Trieste, It, Mar 19, 1933; s. Carlos and Adele (Morpurgo); in Brazil since 1939; architect, Mackenzie U, Fac Arquitetura, 1956; grad studies, U Sao Paulo, 1965-66; m. Ita Seinfeld, June 16, 1957; c: Ricardo, Sergio, Andre. Architect, pvt off, since 1957; U prof, ind design, since 1964; tech dir, Wamex SA Ind Quim, 1961-63; architect, adv for interiors, Herman Miller, SP, 1963-65. Foremost spec in architectural lighting and design of spec fittings; main works including: lighting for: Min Fgn Relations; Cathedral, both Brasilia; Pull-Sport Show Room; Manchette Bldg, both Rio; St Mary's Sch; Parque Anhembi Exhb Cen, both Sao Paulo. Vice pres, B'nai B'rith, Horacio Lafer Lodge; mem, Congreçaao Israelita Paulista; fmr dir: Brazilian Assn for Ind Design; Inst Architects, Brazil. Recipient: Premio Roberto Simonsen, 1968; Punta del'Este Bienal, spec prize, 1968. Hobby, jewelry design, exhibited: Mus Modern Art, Rio, Bienal Sao Paulo, Osaka, Brazilian Exhb. Home: 960 Av Paulista, Sao Paulo, Brazil. Office: 1009 Av Paulista, Sao Paulo, Brazil.

LEVI, Primo, It, business exec, author; b. Torino, It, July 31, 1919; s. Cesare and Ester (Luzzati); laurea chem, U Torino, 1941; m. Lucia Morpurgo, Aug 8, 1947; c: Lisa, Renzo. Tech mgr, Siva since 1948. Author: Se questo é un nomo, 1958, personal account of capture and deportation to Auschwitz; La tregua, 1963, account of author's liberation by Red Army, both trans into most Eur langs; Storie Naturali, 1966. Recipient: Premio Campiello, 1963; Premio Bagutta, 1967, both lit awards. Home: 75 ReUmberto, Torino, It. Office: 84 via Leyni, Settimo Tor, It.

LEVI, Robert H, US, business exec; b. Baltimore, Md, Mar 27, 1915; s. Abraham and Regina (Ottenheimer); BS, Johns Hopkins U, 1936; m. Ryda Hecht, Oct 18, 1939; c: Sandra, Alexander, Richard. Chmn, exec comm, Mercantile-Safe

Deposit & Trust Co since 1968; vice-pres, The May Dept Store, since 1959; pres, The Hecht Wash-Baltimore, 1955-68; with co, 1941-68; dir, Savings Bank of Baltimore. Lt, USCG, 1942-45. Pres, Mt Pleasant Hosp since 1956; chmn: policy comm, Wash, DC Downtown. Study: Downtown Policy Comm of DC since 1958; dir: Sinai Hosp since 1963, 1956-59, chmn, planning comm, med cen; Asso J Charities since 1947, chmn, planning comm, med cen, 1954; Johns Hopkins Hosp, Baltimore since 1960; vice-pres, Natl Capital Downtown Comm, Wash, DC; Fed City Council, Wash, DC; chmn, trustees sec, Hosp Council of Md, Inc; Action, Inc; Citizens' Planning & Housing Assn; mem, adv bd: Fight Blight Fund: Amer U, Wash; mem: adv comm, Baltimore Sym Orch; bd overseers, Goucher Coll; bd, Baltimore Civic Opera Assn; exec comm, Gtr Baltimore Comm; vendor relations, Natl Retail Merchants Assn, NY; club, Cen, Baltimore, dir. Hobbies: fishing, hunting. Home: Box 478, RFD 1, Lutherville, Md. Office: Mercantile-Safe Deposit & Trust Co, 13 South St, Baltimore, Md.

LEVI, Shonie B, US, communal worker; b. NYC, Nov 7, 1907; d. Nathan and Sara (Grossbard) Biegelsen; dipl: Tchrs Inst, JTSA, 1926; Cooper Union Sch of Art, 1932; m. Gershon Levi, June 12, 1932; c: Don, Michal. Radio commentator, Today's Woman, WEVD since 1964; natl chmn, youth activities, Hadassah, 1958-61; chmn, ed and reading comm, Natl Women's League, 1948-60; prin, Temple Emanuel Heb Sch, 1926-29; interim dir, Hillel Found, 1947. Bd mem, Can Council J Women; pres, Tchrs Inst Alumni, 1954-57; life mem, Can WIZO; mem-at-large, women's div, JWB since 1964. Author: Across the Threshold, 1959; Guide to Jewish Homemaker, 1963. Recipient: Award: Youth Aliyah; UJA; Isr Bonds; Torah Fund, 1956-58; Tchrs Inst Alumni, 1959. Home: 164-11 Highland Ave, Jamaica, NY.

LEVI, Uriel, Isr, government official; b. Vienna, June 29, 1908; s. Julius and Ernestine (Snader); in Isr since 1928; m. Edith Schon, Mar 1930; c: Amnon, Tirza Levi-Mani, Gad. Dir, cattle dept Min Agric since 1948; mem: secretariat, Cattle Breeders Assn; dir, Animal Husbandry dept Eng; mem Kibbutz Beth Zera, 1928-49. Contbr to profsl jours. Home: 55 Tamar St, Ramat Hasharon, Isr. Office: Hakirya, POB 11, Tel Aviv, Isr.

LEVI, Walter, US, educator; b. Halberstadt, Ger, Mar 23, 1912; s. Gustav and Zipora (Petuchowski); in US since 1940; att: U Geneva, 1930; U Paris, 1930; U Berlin, 1930-31; U Heidelberg, 1932; U Frankfurt, 1932-33; DJ, U Fribourg, 1934; U Minn, 1943, PhD, 1944; m. Ilse Steerman, July 24, 1936; c: Antonia, Matthew. Prof, political sci: U Hawaii since 1963; U Minn, 1943-63; visiting prof: U Melbourne, 1947; Marburg, 1948; Delhi, 1950; Geneva, 1959; Hawaii, 1950, 1962; Munich, 1966. Author: American-Australian Relations, 1947; Fundamentals of World Organizatin, 1952; Free India in Asia, 1952; Modern China's Foreign Policy, 1953; Australia's Outlook on Asia, 1958; The Challenge of World Politics in South and Southeast Asia, 1968. Mem: Amer Political Sci Assn; AAUP. Recipient: Fulbright Scholarship, 1955, 1966; Amer Inst for Indian Studies, 1965; seminar specialist f, E-W Cen, 1966. Hobbies: music, carpentry. Home: 2400 Sonoma St, Honolulu, Hawaii. Office: U of Hawaii, Honolulu, Hawaii.

LEVI, Wendell M, US, attorney; b. Sumter, SC, Sep 28, 1891; s. Mitchell and Estella (D'Ancona); AB, Coll of Charleston, SC, 1912; PhB, U Chgo, 1915, JD, cum laude, Law Sch, 1915; hon, DLitt, Coll of Charleston, 1968; m. Bertha London, June 20, 1921; c: Estella Kirchheimer, Patricia Barnett, Wendell. Atty since 1915; chmn bd, Palmetto Pigeon Plant since 1956, pres, 1923-56; pres: Wen-le Corp since 1952; Levi Publishing Co since 1957. Lt, US Army, 1917-18, capt, Amer Expeditionary Forces, 1918-19. Dir, Carolinas United Comty Services; pres: Conf of Js, SC, 1931-33; Natl Pigeon Assn 1931-33; State Conf of Js, 1932-33; Amer Carneau Assn, 1942; mem: bd mgrs, Syn and Sch Ext, UAHC, 1931, exec comm, SE conf, 1931-33; chmn: natl mem comm, VFW, 1949; SC Camellia Soc, 1954; vice pres, United Fund Bd, 1955; trustee, Cong Sinai, 1961-64, secy-treas, 1925-29, pres for over 10 years; mem: Amer, SC, Sumter Co Bar Assns; Amer Genetic Assn; AAAS; World Poultry Sci Assn; Poultry Sci Assn; Masons, 32 deg, hon life mem since 1955; Shriners; Elks; Amer Legion; clubs: Amer Pigeon, hon life mem; Kiwanis. Author: Pigeon Raising, 1934, 1943, 1958; The Pigeon, 1941, 1957, 1963, 1969; Making Pigeons Pay, 1946, 1948; The Visible Pigeon, 1963; Encyclopedia of Pigeon Breeds, 1965; ed, question and answer dept, Amer Pigeon Jour since 1927; contbr to profsl jours. Recipient: Natl

Pigeon Assn Service Award, 1967; 1st man of year award, Intl Fed Amer Homing Pigeon Fanciers, 1968. Home: 417 W Calhoun St, Sumter, SC. Office: 207 N Washington St, Sumter, SC.

LEVI, William, US, business exec; b. Munich, Ger, Feb 28, 1913; s. Max and Bianca (Ambrunn); in US since 1936; att Commercial Coll, Munich. Exec vice-pres since 1969. Master sgt, mil intelligence, US Army, 1942-45. Spec interests: UJA; support of Tel Aviv U; trade relations Isr-US. Home: 306 E 86 St, New York, NY. Office: 450 W 33 St, New York, NY.

LEVIEN, A Mark, US, attorney; b. Minsk, Russ, July 19, 1899; s. Jacob and Anna (Novograd); in US since 1905; BS, CCNY, 1921; MA, Columbia U, 1923; LLB, Bklyn Law Sch, 1924; m. Rosalind Horowitz, June 14, 1923; c: Roger. Pvt practice since 1926; tchr, Bd of Educ, NYC, 1921-26; counsel to NY Tchrs Guild, local 2, AFL-CIO, 1935-55; lectr, Practicing Law Courses, 1937-39; conducted weekly radio progs on law in modern soc, 1938-40; Lib Party Candidate, Kings Co, Bklyn for judgeships, 1958-59; vice chmn Lib Party, 1956-65; counsel to City Tchrs Assn of NY, NEA, 1962-65. US Army, 1918. Mem: Amer, Bklyn Bar Assns; NY Co Lawyers Assn; Public Educ Assn; ZOA; LZOA; B'nai B'rith; AJCong; Amer Friends of Heb U; Urban League; NAACP; League for Ind Dem; Ave N J Cmty Cen, past chmn bd trustees; Masons. Author: Collection of Money Judgements, 1934; NY Supplementary Proceedings Law, 1935; co-author, Survey of Legal Profession in NY County, 1936; contbr of articles to legal jours. Hobbies: fishing, motorboating. Home: 43-10 Kissena Blvd, Flushing, NY. Office: 150 Broadway, New York, NY.

LEVIN, A Leo, US, educator; b. NYC, Jan 9, 1919; s. Issachar and Minerva (Shapiro); BA, Yeshiva U, 1939, LLD, 1960: LLB, U of Pa, 1942; dipl, Tchrs Inst, Rabbi Isaac Elchanan Theol Sem, 1939; m. Doris Feder, 1947; c: Allan, Jay. Vice pres for academic affairs, Yeshiva U since 1969; U F, law, Columbia U, 1946-47; instr, asst prof, law, U of Ia, 1947-49; prof law, vice provost, U of Pa, 1953-69; visiting prof: Northwestern U, 1949; U Colo, 1957; NYU, 1959; UCLA, 1959; Stanford U, 1960. US Army, 1942-46. Pres: J Exponent, Phila; Lower Merion Syn; mem: bd govs: Bar Ilan U; Dropsie Coll; bd, Fed of J Agcys, Gtr Phila; fmr f, Cen for Advanced Study in Behavioral Scis. Author of legal books; mem, publ comm, J Pub Soc; contbr to profsl jours. Home: 441 West End Ave, New York, NY. Office: Yeshiva U, New York, NY.

LEVIN, Abraham, US, attorney; b. Phila, Pa, Oct 22, 1903; s. Morris and Anna (Samson); BS, U of Pa, 1925, LLB, 1928; m. Roslyne Van Straaten, Nov 12, 1932; c: Donald. Sr partner, Levin and Levin; secy, The Rose Co, since 1952; asst atty gen, Pa, counsel to State Dept Hwys since 1968; mem, War Price and Rationing Bd, 1942-46. Vice chmn, B'rith Sholom Found since 1961, natl pres, 1958-60; pres, Cong Ahavas Achem Talmud Torah since 1942; mem: U of Pa Gen Alumni Soc; Prisoners' Family Wfr Assn; Police Athletic League; Phi Sigma Delta; clubs: Lawyers, Phila; Rep, mem, exec comm since 1930. Recipient: achievement cert: B'rith Sholom, 1960; Cong Ahavas Achem Talmud Torah, 1960. Home: 5955 Warrington Ave, Philadelphia, Pa. Office: 121 S Broad St, Philadelphia, Pa.

LEVIN, Alfred, US, historian, educator; b. Colchester, Conn, Nov 25, 1908; s. Michael and Anna (Schlossberg); BA, Brown U, 1931; PhD, Yale U, 1937; m. Fannie Wener, Oct 8, 1932. Prof, Kent State U since 1968; prof, hist, Okla State U, 1948-68, ed Research Bull, 1959-68; asst research analyst, US Off of Strategic Services, 1942-45; asso research analyst: US Army, 1943-45; Dept of State, 1945-46. Mem, Phi Beta Kappa. Author, Second Duma, 1940; co-author, Dynamics of Soviet Society, 1953. Recipient: Fulbright Research Prof to Finland, 1956-57; F, Cen for Intl Studies, MIT, 1951-52; Inter-U Travel Grant to USSR, 1960. Home: 386 Wilson Ave, Kent, O. Office: Kent State U, Kent, O.

LEVIN, Dov, Isr, sociologist; b. Kovno, Lith, Jan 27, 1925; s. Zvi and Bluma (Wigoder); in Isr since 1945; dipl, Sch of Social Work, Heb U Jerusalem, 1951; MA, Heb U, 1952; att U Chgo, 1962; m. Bilha Deutsch, Jan 23, 1951; c: Nitzana, Basmat, Zvi. Head, social research sect, Munic of Jerusalem, since 1963; research F, Inst of Contemporary Jewry, Jerusalem, since 1966. Served, Partisans, Vilna; sgt, intelligence, IDF, 1948-49. Participant: Conf on Manifestations of J Resistance during Holocaust, 1968; Fifth World Cong of J Studies, 1969, both Jerusalem; mem: Lith J Org; WW II Combatants Org, Jerusalem br, fmr: exec, J Workers Council; mem: cen comm, Natl Assn Social Workers; exec, Jerusalem Students Assn. Co-author: The Story of Underground, 1962; In Front of the Ninth Fortress. Recipient: Order of Partisans of Patriotic Wars; S Weis Prize, WJC, 1956; award, J Memorial Found, 1968. Hobbies: photography, hitchhiking. Home: 57 Tshernichovsky St, Jerusalem, Isr. Office: 34 Jaffa Rd, Jerusalem, Isr.

LEVIN, Harold A, US, government official; b. NYC, Oct 9, 1918; s. Milton and Rachel (Cooperman); BA, NYU, 1940; MS, U Denver, 1947; grad studies: Georgetown U, 1946-48; George Wash U, 1951-52; m. Toby Poizner, Apr 30, 1942; c: Jordan, Erica. Acting dir, Off of Commodity Import Progs, Aid Bur for Vietnam, State Dept, Wash, DC, since 1968; personnel off, Off of Emergency Mgmt, Wash, DC, 1942-43; fgn affairs off, State Dept, Wash, DC, 1946-49; requirements cons, US Aid Mission in Korea, 1949-50; intl econ, Econ Coop Admn, Wash, DC, 1950-51; fgn requirements specialist, Defense Produc Adm, Wash, DC, 1951-53; control prog dir, E-W Tradl, Intl Coop Admn, Wash, DC, 1953-57; cons, Russell Sage Found, NY 1955; dep US repr, Eur Regional Org and US delg, Intl E-W Trade Comm, Paris, Fr, 1958-61; chief: Intl Bus Practices Div, State Dept, 1961-67. Intl Trade Div, Aid Bur for Vietnam, 1967-68. Lt, USN, 1943-46. Mem: Amer Fgn Service Assn; Phi Beta Kappa; club, Intl of Wash. Home: 1601 Oaklawn Ct, Silver Spring, Md. Office: Dept of State, Washington, DC.

LEVIN, Herschel, US, rabbi; b. Baltimore, Md, July 19, 1916; Wolf and Dena (Silverman); BA, U Cincinnati, 1937; MHL, Rabbi, DD, HUC, 1942; m. Betty Tennenbaum, Aug 27, 1944; c: Joshua, Daniel, Jonathan. Rabbi: Temple Beth Sholom since 1953; Sinai Temple, Springfield, Mass; Temple Emanuel, Lawrence, Mass. Treas, NY Bd Rabbis; past pres: N Shore Clergy assn; HUC Student Body; Bayside Council of Churches and Syns; past vice-pres, RA, Queens; past exec bd mem, CCAR; mem: Comm of Isr, Comm on Affiliation, CCAR. Author: The American Jew and The State of Israel, 1953; ed: Directory of New England Liberal Congs. Recipient: Citation as comty service leader in Gtr Lawrence, local Council of Churches. Home: 41-27 171 St, Flushing, NY. Study: Northern Blvd at 172 St, Flushing, NY.

LEVIN, Israel, Isr, attorney; b. Jerusalem, Isr, Dec 1, 1904; s. Moshe and Zippora (Salomon); LLB, Liverpool U, 1927; m. Adina Shneibaum; c: Eliyahu, Ora Reifenberg, Dayana. Atty since 1931; fmr, judge, Dist Court, 1949-52. Pres, Commercial and Ind Club, Tel Aviv; vice pres, B'nai B'rith, dist 14; chmn, Court of Honor, Isr Lib Party; mem: Isr Bar Assn, fmr pres, Tel Aviv dist; Masons. Author, booklet, Israel Law Bills of Exchange, 1953. Hobbies: drawing, painting. Home: 4 Huberman St, Tel Aviv, Isr. Office: 4 Yehuda Halevi St, Tel Aviv, Isr.

LEVIN, Jack H, US, market researcher and analyst; b. NYC, Aug 19, 1898; s. Benjamin and Sarah (Siegle). Pres: Cert Inves Inc, since 1950; Jack H Levin, Assos, since 1950; Mutual Film Co, 1916; Ivan Film Co, 1918; road show, 1921; found: fact finding dept, NY Film Bd of Trade, 1922; Free Film Shows Control Sys, 1925; Copyright Protection Bur, 1928; Rotary Produms, 1936; Confidential Reports, 1945. Pres: Levin Family Tree Found, 1929-48; League for Wfr Crippled Children, Hosp Jt Diseases, 1928-36; Cinema Lodge, B'nai B'rith, 1947; Asso Licensed Detectives, State NY; chief justice, B'nai B'rith Court, 1964; natl chmn at large, B'nai B'rith Vocational Service, 1965; prog chmn, B'nai B'rith 125th Anniversary, Fla, 1968; chmn: Amer and civic affairs, Metrop Council, B'nai B'rith, 1944-46; bd govs, George Gershwin Memorial Found, 1954-58; NYC cabinet, UJA, 1948-52; fraternal bd, FJP, 1951; Metrop Adv Bd, ADL, since 1954; bd dirs, Trafalgar Hosp, 1957; natl adv bd, Amer Guild of Variety Artists, since 1960; Motion Pictures Pioneers; KP; Masonic Camp Seven; clubs: British Intl Detective Assos; Rena, pres, 1924; Avon Chickering, pres; B'nai B'rith Past Pres, pres, 1960. Co-author: Arguments Federal Registration, 1934; Marriage, Morals, and Mothballs, 1939; Marriage, Morals and War, 1943. Recipient: citations: for distributing motion pictures gratis to orgs and hosps; Mutual Wfr League and Sing Sing Prison, 1926; Hosp for Jt Diseases, 1935; citations: Food for Isr, 1949; US Victory Bond Sales, 1945; Natl Membership Award, B'nai B'rith, 1948. Home: 240 Central Park S, New York, NY. Office: 5101 Collins Ave, Miami Beach, Fla.

LEVIN, Jesse, US, business exec, economic stat, registered investment counsel; b. Montpelier, Vt, May 4, 1901; s. Simeon and Anna (Machanic); BS, NYU Coll of Engr, 1921; m. Esther Weinstein, 1923; c: Hugh. Owner: The Fashion Shop Inc, Barre, Vt, 1934-57; Flints, Newsport, Vt, 1926-57; Newport Realty Co, Newport, 1930-57; guest lectr, Coll of Bus Admn, Ariz State U, 1966-67; efficiency engr, B Altman and Co, NY, 1921. Pres, Vt J Council, 1947, chmn, PR, 1952-55; org, Beth-Isr Syn, 1938; dr to establish settlement, Nachlat Vermont in Isr, 1947; dir: Vt Council on World Affairs, 1953; NE Regional Bd, ADL; Natl Bd, Jt Defense Appeal; represented Vt at Amer J Conf, Cleveland and Chgo, 1946-47; introduced anti-discrimination law, 1958; clubs: Rotary; Newport Country; Memphramagog Outing, pres, 1955; Sunset Valley Country, Omaha. Author: Be Your Own Financial Analyst, 1969; contbr: articles to Barron's; Stock Market Magazine; Finance Magazine; Financial Analyst's Journal, 1968-70; Anglo-J periodicals and newspapers. Hobbies: boating, fishing, golf. Home: 9101 Arbor St, Omaha, Neb; 1055 N Country Club Dr, Mesa, Ariz.

LEVIN, Jules D, US, surgeon; b. Milw, Wis, Jan 14, 1915; s. Joseph and Anna (Rymeland); BA, U of Wis, 1936; MD, 1938; m. Beverly Lubotsky, June 19, 1945; c: Ronald, Ellen, Bruce. Pvt practice, neurosur since 1948; asso prof, neur surg, Marquette U Med Sch since 1957, fac since 1953; att neurosurg, Mt Sinai Hosp; att neurosurg and chmn div of neurosurg at: St Luke's Hosp; Deaconess Hosp; att neurosurg: St Francis Hosp; W Allis Hosp; St Michels Hosp; Milw Co Gen Hosp; cons neurosurg at: Johnston Emergency Hosp; Trinity Hosp, all Milw; f, neurosurg, neuropath, U of Minn, 1941-44; teaching f, neur, neurosurg, 1946-48; neurosurg, Northington Gen Hosp. Capt, US Army MC, 1944-46. F: Amer Coll of Surgs, 1952; Int Coll of Surgs, 1950; asso, Amer Acad of Neurol, 1949; dipl: Amer Bd of Neurol Surg, 1951; Intl Bd of Surg, 1950; mem: Harvey Cushing Soc; Cong Neurol Surgs; Assn for Research in Nervous and Mental Diseases; Milw Neuropsycht Soc; Cen Neurosurgical Soc; Inter-urban Neurosurg Soc; Milw Acad Med; Milw Co Med Soc; State Med Soc; AMA. Contbr to med jours. Home: 1530 W Spruce Ct, Milwaukee, Wis. Office: 161 W Wisconsin Ave, Milwaukee, Wis.

LEVIN, Louis, US, physician; b. NYC, Feb 17, 1900; s. Solomon and Mary (Mainster); BS, CCNY, 1919; MD, LI Coll Hosp, 1923; m. Marie Etkin, June 28, 1924, c: Rhoda Astrachan, Joan Rosenberg. Pvt practice, allergy diseases since 1935; asst chief, allergy clinic, LI Coll Hosp since 1929; att allergist, Swed Hosp since 1954; instr, allergy, SUNY Coll of Med since 1958; adj, allergy, Beth El Hosp, 1929-39; lectr, allergy, LI Coll Hosp Nurses Training Sch, 1946. US Army, WW I, maj, US Army MC, WW II. F: Amer Coll Allergists; Amer Acad Allergy; Intl Coll Allergology; AMA; Amer Assn Clinical Immunology and Allergy; dipl, Amer Bd Clinical Immunology and Allergy; mem: NY Allergy Soc; Med Soc Kings, pres, 1956; NY State Med Soc. Contbr to med jours. Home: The Kennedy House, 110-11 Queens Blvd, Forest Hills, NY. Office: 34 Plaza St, Brooklyn, NY.

LEVIN, Louis, US, scientist; b. Milw, Wis, May 9, 1908; s. Jacob and Rebecca (Offengenden); AB, Kalamazoo Coll, Mich, 1929; PhD, St Louis, U, 1934; att U Chgo, 1945-46; m. Esther Hurwitz, Oct 25, 1934; c: Miriam Leventhal, David. Exec asso dir, NSF since 1968, head, Off of Prog Devl and Analysis, 1964-66; asso dir, 1966-68; dean, sci, Brandeis U, 1960-64. Mem: Amer Soc Biol Chems; Amer Inst of Biol Sci; Endocrine Soc; Harvey Soc; Soc for Experimental Biol and Med; Sigma Xi; f: AAAS; NY Acad Scis; fmr, chmn, exec comm, Allied Civic Assn, Montgomery Co, Md. Contbr to sci jours. Home: 6617 Millwood Rd, Bethesda, Md. Office: 1800 G St, Washington, DC.

LEVIN, Martin Neil, US, rabbi; b. Bx, NY, Oct 31, 1941; s. Sol and Esther (Feinberg); BA, Bklyn Coll, 1964; att Heb U, Jerusalem, 1963; ordained rabbi, JTSA, 1969; m. Margo Zonana, Aug 9, 1964; c: Rachel. Capt, J chaplain for Thailand, USAF since 1969; salesman, Penn Mutual, 1965-67; rabbi, Conservative Syn of Canarsie, NY, 1966-67. Hobbies: painting, touring, Isr. Home: 26 Sei 22 Sukhamvit Rd, Bangkok, Thailand. Office: 631 Combat Support Group, Chapel, Box 10 APO, San Francisco, Cal.

LEVIN, Meyer, Isr, author; b. Chgo, Ill, Oct 7, 1905; s. Joseph and Goldie (Levin); PhD, U Chgo, 1924; m. Tereska Szwarc, Mar 1948; c: Jonathan, Dominique, Gabriel, Mikael. Author: Reporter, 1929; Frankie and Johnny, 1930; Yehuda, 1931; The Golden Mountain, 1932; The New Bridge, 1933; The Old

Bunch, 1937; Citizens, 1941; My Father's House, 1945; In Search, autobiography, 1950; Compulsion, novel, 1956, play, 1959; Eva, 1959; The Fanatic, 1964; The Stronghold, 1964; Gore and Igor, 1968; dramatization of Diary of Anne Frank, 1952, subject of long controversy. Home: Herzliya, Isr.

LEVIN, Morris, US, social worker; exec; b. Moscow, Russ, Dec 22, 1916; s. Boris and Chaia (Sherman); in US since 1921; BSSW, summa cum laude, O state U, 1947; MSSW, W Reserve U, 1949; m. Evelyn Malamud, June 7, 1949; c: Bruce, Steven, Judith. Asst gen dir, JCC, Chgo since 1966, dir, area and br ops, 1954-60, dir, Bernard Horwich JCC, 1960-66. Sgt, US Army, 1942-45. Pres, Natl Assn J Cen Workers; vice-pres, Chgo area chap, Natl Assn Social Workers; mem, Beth Emeter Syn. Contbr to J publs. Home: 9326 Kildare, Skokie, Ill. Office: 1 South Franklin, Chicago, Ill.

LEVIN, Morris G, US, business exec; b. Cincinnati, O, Mar 6, 1913; s. Hyman and Celia (Gordon); att U Cincinnati, 1930-33; m. Sylvia Euster, Oct 7, 1934; c: Harriet Cohen, Stuart, Charles, Myron. Pres, The Elmex Corp since 1962. Mem, bd of trustees, J Hosp since 1967; bd mem: JWF since 1954; Orthodox J Home for Aged since 1961; vice-chmn, AJ Comm, Cincinnati, since 1959; exec comm mem, Metrop Area Rel Coalition Comm, Gtr Cincinnati; pres, B'nai B'rith, 1952; div chmn, UA, 1957; chmn, Isr Bond campaign, 1959; vice-pres, Natl Assn Toy Wholesalers, 1958-61; bd mem, NCCJ; Masons. Home: 7303 Fair Oaks Dr, Cincinnati, O. Office: 315 W Fifth St, Cincinnati, O.

LEVIN, Moses G, Isr, business exec; b. Zaager, Lith, Sep 15, 1880; s. Joshua and Malka (Lipschitz); in Isr since 1893; att, Yeshiva, Jerusalem, 1896-1900; m. Ziporah Salomon, Mar, 1900; seven c. Ret; fmr: chmn: Salomon, Levin and Elstein; Assia Chem Labs Ltd; dir, Paca Ltd. Hon pres, Carmel Lodge, B'nai B'rith; fmr: pres, J Comty of Haifa; chmn bd, Reali Sch, Haifa; clubs: Rotary, hon mem. Recipient: Brit Crown medal, 1937; OBE, 1947. Home: 61 Moriah Ave, Haifa, Isr.

LEVIN, Nathan R, US, librarian; b. Chicago, Ill, July 11, 1892; s. Hayman anr Lena (Sklovsky); att Northwestern U, 1914; PhB, U Chgo, 1915; BLS, NY State Libr Sch, 1918; m. Henrietta Zuckerman, Aug 31, 1918; c: Stanley. Asst libr, Chgo Public Libr, 1923-66, on staff since 1907. Adv comm, Ill State Libr since 1950, chmn, 1958-64; pres: Ill Libr Assn, 1940; Chgo Libr Club, 1924; mem, Amer Libr Assn. Contbr to libr jours. Home: 1500 Bay Rd, Miami Beach, Fla.

LEVIN, Richard H, US, attorney; b. Chgo, Ill, Sep 9, 1916; s. Jacob and Charlotte (Getz); AB, U Chgo, 1935, JD, 1937; m. Bernice Goode, July 3, 1940; c: Roger, Kathryn, James. Partner, D'Ancona, Pflaum, Wyatt & Riskind, since 1945, with firm, since 1937. Mem, natl exec bd, vice-chmn, Chgo Chap, AJComm; dir: gen counsel, Highland Park Comty Concert Assn; mem: Chgo, Ill, Amer Bar Assns; clubs: Standard; Birchwood, Highland Park. Home: 2576 Sheridan Rd, Highland Park, Ill. Office: 33 N La Salle St, Chicago, Ill.

LEVIN, Richard Michael, US, business exec; b. Chgo, Ill, Apr 16, 1925; s. Jake and Marian (Berger); BS, U of Pa; m. Carol Hoffman, June 30, 1951; c: Nancy, Michael, Ann. Pres, Jake Levin and Sons, Inc, since 1958, co-found in 1949. Served, cpl, US Army, 1943-45. Pres, J Vocational Service; bd mem: J Fed; AJComm; Menorah Bd; chmn, Non-Local Budget Comm, J Fed, 1964-65; mem, Zeta Beta Tau; club: Oakwood Country. Recipient: Purple Heart, Combat Infantry, WWII; Kan City, Mo, J Fed Young Leadership Award, 1958. Home: 835 W 64 Terr, Kansas City, Mo. Office: 2820 Warwick, Kansas City, Mo.

LEVIN, Robert, Nor, pianist; b. Oslo, June 7, 1912; s. David and Marie (Scheer); studied with: Nils Larsen, Fartein Valen; m. Solveig Bernstein, Oct 20, 1938; c: Mona Sidsel. Debut, Oslo, 1932; soloist: Philharminic Orch, Oslo; Radio Orch Stockholm; radio and TV progs; accompanist: Yehudi Menuhin, in Isr, Eur; and on recordings: Elisabeth Schwartzkopf; Rita Streich; Mattiwilda Dobbs; Michael Rabin; Kim Borg; Bronislaw Gimpel; appeared: Dubrovnic Festival, 1961; Bergen Festival, annually. Mem: bd, Oslo Philharmonic Orch; Nor Musical Union; Tono, Assn of Composers; Intl Soc Contemporary Music; Fartein Valen Soc; Menorah. Recipient: Golden Cross, Nor Musical Union, 1952, Medal of Highest Honor, 1962; King's Gold Medal of Dist Service, 1962. Home: Gabelsgate 46b, Oslo, Nor.

LEVIN, Robert B, US, business exec; b. Roanoke, Va, Sep 24, 1918; s. Isaac and Belle (Weinkrants); BS, Ga Tech, Atlanta, Ga, 1940; m. Juanita Kahn, July 26, 1952; c: Susan, Carol. Pres: Standard Chemical Co, since 1946; Tripure Spring Water Co; Mop-Up; vice-pres, Aircraft Water Service, Inc, dir, Standardized Sanitation Sys, Inc. Maj, US Army, 1941-45; col, res, ret. Pres: Fla Sanitary Supply Assn, Fla Bottled Water Assn, 1960-62; dir, Natl Sanitary Supply Assn, 1959-61; mem: Phi Kappa Phi; Phi Epsilon Pi; Omicron Delta Kappa. Home: 14825 NE 8 Ct, N Miami, Fla. Office: 3355 NW 73 St, Miami, Fla.

LEVIN, Russell N, US, business exec; b. Boston, Mass, Sep 10, 1906; s. Maurice and Pauline (Rosenblatt); att Harvard U, 1924-25; BS, U of Pa, 1927; m. Isabel Elcock, June 15, 1934; c: Peter, Constance de Vries. Dir, exec vice pres, Lerner Stores Corp, 1940-56; exec, William Filenes Sons, 1927-40. Trustee: Montefiore Hosp and Med Cen; FJP; mem: NY bd govs, exec bd, AJComm; Pi Lambda Phi. Home: 25 Morris Lane, Scarsdale, NY, Office: 303 E 57 St, New York, NY.

LEVIN, Samuel M, Isr, attorney; b. Capetown, S Afr, Sep 14, 1915; s. Jacob and Bertha; in Isr since 1949; BA, U Capetown, 1933, LLB, 1935; m. Harriet Hades, 1942; c: Miriam, Dov. Sr exec, Peltours Travel Agcy, since 1962; admitted as atty, Supr Court, S Afr, 1937; off, Native Affairs Dept, S Afr Govt, 1937. Head, youth dept, S Afr ZF, 1938-39, head, Capetown off, 1939-48, gen secy, Isr off, 1949-62; dir, Patwa off, NY, 1954-55; participated in JPA, Gt Brit, 1961. Fmr Isr corresp, S Afr J Chronicle. Home: 10 Haoranim St, Kfar Shmaryahu, Isr. Office: POB 394, Tel Aviv, Isr.

LEVIN, Samuel M, US economist, educator; b. Liskovo, Pol, June 6, 1888; s. Judah and Esther (Levin); in US since 1893; BA, U Mich, 1912; MA, U Chgo, 1925; m. Lillian Keidan, Aug 25, 1914; c: Joseph, Miriam Friedman, Herbert, Judith Cantor. Prof em, econs, Wayne State U since 1958, prof, 1933-58, chmn, econ dept, 1933-53; instr, hist and econ, Detroit Jr Coll, 1915-19; head, comm to revise social sci curricula in Detroit public schs, 1920-22; prof, econs, and head social sci dept, Coll of Detroit, 1925-33. Mem: Mayor's unemployment comm, 1931; Mayor's comm on lab, 1931; budget rev comm, Detroit Comty Fund, 1936-39; pres: J Social Ser Bur, 1936-39; JNF Council, 1958-60; all Detroit; mem: bd dirs, J Vocational Service, 1943-49; Amer Econs Assn; AAUP; Amer Eugenics Soc; Mich Acad of Sci, Art, and Letters. Author: Malthus and the Conduct of Life, 1967; contbr to profsl mags and research publs. Home: Southfield, Mich.

LEVIN, Shalom, Isr, teacher, organization exec; b. Rakow, Pol, Mar 27, 1916; s. Yehoshua and Miriam (Shifrin); in Isr since 1937; att Heb Tchrs Coll, Tarbut, Vilna; MA, Heb U, Jerusalem, 1952; m. Dimona Shelli, 1944; c: Yoav, Naama. Gen secy, Isr Tchrs Union since 1955; fmr head, dept culture and book pub; tchr: Kfar Yehoshua, 1937-39; Degania, 1940-44; Jerusalem, 1945-50; hum tchr, Eshkoli Tchrs Coll, Jerusalem, 1951-52. Served, IDF. Mem: secretariat, Isr Lab Party; Histadrut; fmr pres, Intl Fed Tchrs. Ed, Heb ed, The Art of Teaching; contbr to educ jours, daily press. Home: 5 Mossinsohn St, Tel Aviv, Isr. Office: 8 Ben Saruk St, Tel Aviv, Isr.

LEVIN, Shaul, Isr, educator; b. Kiev, Russ, Oct 31, 1905; s. Samuel and Sophia (Kosteljanetz); in Isr since 1933; AB, Conradinum, Danzig, 1924; PhD, U Berlin, 1930; m. Miriam Nacht, June 26, 1933; c: Dan. Dir of educ, Tel Aviv-Yaffo Munic, since 1953; headmaster: Ben Yehuda Coll, 1940-48; Shalva HS, 1945-48; dir of educ, Munic of Nashanda, 1948-50; counsellor, Isr Emb, Paris, Isr perm delg to UNESCO, 1956-58; Min Counsellor Affairs, Isr Emb, Rio de Janeiro, 1963-65. Pres: Centro Cultural Isr Brazil; Natl Union of Dirs of Educ; Theater sect, Natl Culture and Art Counsel; Noar Lenoar; Union of Isr Educ for Youth Tourism; mem: B'nai B'rith; Rotary. Author: Die Einzige Loesung, plays, poetry; Das ist Nicht Der Weg. Recipient: Legion D'Honneur, Fr Govt; Cruzeiro De Sul, Brazilian Govt; Verdienstkreuz, Ger Govt. Home: Sd Hahayal, Yad Eliahu, Tel Aviv, Isr. Office: Municipality of Tel Aviv, Isr.

LEVIN, Stanley, Isr, pediatrician; b. Johannesburg, S Afr, Oct 8, 1921; s. Samuel and Alice (Smith); in Isr since 1948; MB, BCh, U of Witwatersrand, Johannesburg, 1944; att, Johns Hopkins U, Baltimore, 1957-59; m. Yocheved Ashkenazi, Nov 24, 1948; c: Elite, Zvi. Head, Dept of Ped, Ped Research Dept, Kaplan Hosp, Rehovot, since 1959; chmn, Ped Adv

Comm, Kupat Holim; visiting prof, U Colo Med Cen, Denver, 1966-67. Lt, Isr MC, 1948-49. Pres, found, Isr Clinical Ped Soc, since 1953; mem, Eur Ped Research Soc; various Isr socs. Contbr numerous articles to Profsl publs. Home and office: Kaplan Hosp, Rehovot, Isr.

LEVIN, Theodore, US, jurist; b. Chgo, Ill, Feb 18, 1897; s. Joseph and Ida (Rosin); LLB, U Detroit, 1920, LLM, 1924; hon LLD, Wayne State U, 1960; m. Rhoda Katzin, May 31, 1925; c: Charles, Miriam, Daniel, Joseph. US Dist Judge, E Dist, Mich, since 1946, chief judge, 1959-67; practicing atty, 1920-46, spec asst to Atty Gen, State of Mich, 1933. Mem: Selective Service Appeal Bd, Mich, 1944-46; comm on grievances, Detroit and Mich Bar Assns, 1928-46; exec comm, JWF; bd, United HIAS Service; JDC; Amer League for Isr; Amer Friends Heb U; bd trustees, JPS; adv council, Mich Wfr League; vice pres, CFJWF; fmr: vice chmn, Mich State Council Immigrant Educ; chmn, Gtr Detroit Big Brother Conf; mem, child wfr and family case work comms, Council of Social Agcys, Detroit; pres: J Social Service Bur; Resettlement Services; United J Charities; JWF; mem, budget rev comm, Detroit Comty Fund; bd mem, Natl Ref Service; vice pres, Mich Comm on DPs; bd, Sinai Hosp. Home: 2806 Cambridge Rd, Detroit, Mich. Office: US Dist Court, Detroit, Mich.

LEVIN, William, US statistician, economist; b. Albany, NY, Oct 5, 1910; s. Morris and Ray (Freedman); m. Nina Wender, Jan 14, 1945; c: Myles, Lawrence. Chief stat, US FTC, Wash, DC, since 1951. Home: 5423 33 St NW, Washington, DC.

LEVIN, Zeev, Isr, economist; b. Kovno, Lith, Aug 30, 1927; s. Reuven and Tova (Kronick); in Isr since 1932; BA, U of Minn, 1952; m. Ariela Levin-Ascher; c: Daniel, Michal. Ambass to Kenya since 1969; mem, intl dept, Histadrut, 1953-59; repr, Intl Confd of Free Trade Unions, in Cyprus, Greece, 1958-59; consul gen of Isr, Cyprus, 1959-60; ambass, 1960-62; dir, intl dept, Histadrut, 1962-66. Served, IDF. Home: 12 Frug St, Tel Aviv, Isr.

LEVINAS, Emmanuel, Fr, educator, author; b. Kovno, Lith, Dec 30, 1905; s. Iechiel and Dveirah (Gurvitch); in Fr since 1923; m. Raissa Levy, Sep 12, 1932; c: Simone Hansel, Michael. Dir, Ecole Normale Israélite Orientale, since 1946; prof, phil, Faculté des Lettres de Nanterre, Paris. Author: La Théorie de l'Intuition dans la Phénoménologie de Husserl, 1930; De l'Existence à l'Existant, 1947; En Découvrant l'Existence avec Husserl et Heidegger, 1949; Totalité et Infini, 1961; Difficile Liberte, 1963; Quatre Leçons Talmudiques, 1968. Recipient, Chevalier de la Légion d'Honneur. Home: 6 bis rue Michel-Ange, Paris 16, Fr.

LEVINE, Abe Lewis, US, detective, investigator, author, composer; b. Denver, Colo, Nov 9, 1915; s. Herman and Yetta (Kaye); m. Mollie Katz, Sep 1, 1940; c: Barry, Mrs D Neuman, Gary. Dist atty investigator, Denver, Colo, since 1966; with Denver Police Dept, 1940-66. Pub and recorded songs: Don't Say You're A Dream; Today is Your Birthday; Keep The Faith; I Ain't Gonna Worry No More; The Shadow Of The Blues; I Love To Eat Chili In Chile; The Man Behind The Badge, which became theme song for Denver Police Dept Safety Educ Prog, also to other police depts throughout US. Mem: ASCAP, NY; Denver Police Protective Assn; Denver Police Pension Assn. Recipient: Elected to Hall of Fame, for noteworthy service to Denver Comty, Denver Post, 1948; Merit Award, for exemplary service as citizen and public servant, Amer Legion, 1953. Hobby, singing. Home: 245 Fairfax, Denver, Colo. Office: W Colfax and Kalamath St, Denver, Colo.

LEVINE, Albert K, US, chemist, educator; b. Bayonne, NJ, Sep 13, 1917; s. Israel and Dora (Feldman); BS, Rutgers U, 1938, MS, 1939, PhD, 1941; m. Marilyn Wurtzel, Dec 13, 1953; c: David, Irving, Sally. Prof, natural sci, chmn, div sci and engr, Richmond Coll, CUNY, since 1966; chief research chem, P J Schweitzer, 1942-43; chief chem, Mutual Chem Co of Amer, 1944-47; mem, chem fac, Bklyn Coll, 1947-61; cons, solid state chem, research labs, Sylvania Elec Producs; lectr, Imperial Coll of Sci, U London, 1950-51; sci i/c laser research and luminescent materials research, Gen Telephone and Elec Labs, 1961-66; research in lasers, luminescent materials, growth of crystals. Mem: Amer Chem Soc; Workman's Circle; Phi Beta Kappa; Sigma Xi. Contbr on lasers, phosphors and photoconductor materials to profs jours and books. Home: 10-46 Utopia Pkwy, Beechhurst, NY. Office: Richmond Coll, CUNY, Staten Island, NY.

LEVINE, Arnold M, US, engineer: b. Preston, Conn, Aug 15, 1916; s. Samuel and Florence (Clark); MS EE, U of Ia, 1940; hon DSc, Tri-State Coll, 1960; m. Bernice Levich, Aug 31, 1941; c: Mark, Michael, Kevin. Vice-pres, gen mgr, ITT Aerospace since 1962; engr, sound dept, CBS, 1940-42; vice pres, tech dir, ITT Fed Labs, 1958-62, with Labs since 1942. Dir: Amer Rocket Soc; Northern NJ sub-chap, Amer Astronautical Soc; f, Inst of Radio Engrs; mem: Amer Mgmt Assn; missile guidance and control panel, Amer Ordnance Assn; Inst of Aerospace Sci; Inst of Navigation. Contbr to profsl jours. Hobbies: photography, woodworking, amateur radio. Home: 10828 Fullbright Ave, Chatsworth, Cal. Office: 15151 Bledsoe St, San Fernando, Cal.

LEVINE, Arthur J, US, certified public acctnt; b. Bklyn, NY, July 2, 1916; s. Louis and Esther (Goodman); BS, NYU, 1939; m. Rosalind Kopman, June 21, 1941; c: Nancy, Susan, Betty. Pvt practice since 1952; treas, Gen Sci Corp, since 1961; dir, pricing, Signal Corps engr labs, Dept of Defense, 1942-49; dep dir, Army Audit Agcy, 1949-52. Natl treas, United Syns of Amer since 1967, chmn, natl comm on syn admn, 1962, chmn, Nassau-Suffolk div since 1960, pres, NY region, 1964-66; pres: J Comty Relations Council of NY since 1967; Merrick J Cen, 1953-55; chmn: LI div, Fed J Charities since 1954; Merrick UN Week, 1952-55; LI div, UJA, 1953-56; mem: NY State Soc CPA's; Amer Inst CPA's; Amer Assn for UN. Author: Budgeting and Fund Raising for Synagogues, 1960; contbr to profsl jours. Home: 1 Overlook Dr, Great Neck, NY. Office: 192 Lexington Ave, New York, NY.

LEVINE, David B, US, surgeon; b. Russ, Dec 14, 1901; s. Mendel and Sarah (Goldstein); in US since 1916; MD, George Wash U, 1927; m. Florence Kampf, Dec 23, 1934; c: Nancy Zakim. Pvt practice; cons in surg, Barnett Memorial Hosp, pres, med staff, since 1955; dir, Tumor Clinic, 1945-59. Maj, US Army, ret lt col, res. Chmn, exec comm, Passaic Co Cancer Soc, 1959-61; pres, Passaic Co Med Soc, 1951, 1961-62; org, mem, Passaic Co chap, Amer Cancer Soc; f: AMA; Intl Coll of Surgs; Amer Coll of Surgs. Home and office: 647 Broadway, Paterson, NJ.

LEVINE, David L, US, educator; b. NYC, Aug 30, 1919; s. Harold and Caroline (Leibowitz); BS, CCNY, 1941; NSW, U of Pa, 1943; PhD, U of Minn, 1953; m. Laura Kaplan, June 5, 1942; c: Edwin, Deborah, Elizabeth, Helen. Asso dean, Sch of Social Work, Syracuse U; prof, social work, Fla State U, since 1953; asst sup, Assn for J Children of Phila, 1943-45; asst dir, Bklyn J Child Care Council, 1945-47; sup children's service, J Family and Children's Service, Minneapolis, Minn, 1947-51; research asso, Mh, Harvard Sch of Public Health, 1959-60. Mem: bd dirs, Fla Assn Mh since 1960; Leon Co Assn Mh, pres, 1961-62; Leon Co Fed Social Workers, pres, 1958-59; Natl Assn Social Workers, chmn, NW Fla chap, 1957-58; Fla Council on Aging, vice-pres, 1958-59; Natl Council on Aging; Amer Social Assn; Council on Social Work Educ; bd mem, Urban League, Onondaga Co; f: Amer Orthopsychiatric Assn; chmn, Twin City Group Vocational Guidance Assn, 1951-53. Contbr, profsl jours. Hobby: gardening. Home: 1054 Ackerman Ave, Syracuse, NY. Office: Syracuse U, Syracuse, NY.

LEVINE, Ed, US, business exec; b. Minsk, Russ, Oct 17, 1894; s. Rubin and Pearl (Iskiwitz); in US since 1911; att Cooper Union, 1911-17; m. Anne Rosenfield, Jan 23, 1917; c: Rosalind Miller, Muriel Traubner, Phyllis Ruskin (decd), L Harvey. Dir, Natl Restaurant Assn since 1940; past pres, The Brass Rail Inc. Chmn, restaurant div; Natl Found for Infantile Paralysis since 1943; United Cerebral Palsy since 1949; NY chap ARC since 1945; UJA since 1939; FJP since 1935; jt purchasing comm, Legal Aid Soc; bd trustees, LI J Hosp; mem: Weizmann Inst Sci; Grand St Boys Assn; Temple Emanu-El; J Chautauqua Soc; clubs: Fresh Meadows Country; Palm Beach country; Cong Emanu-El Men's. Home: 1 Kensington Gate, Great Neck, NY. Office: 122 E 42 St, New York, NY.

LEVINE, George L, US, organization exec; b. NYC, Feb 12, 1914; s. Leopold and Tessie (Kleinberg); MA, NYU, 1937; m. Elizabeth Lansky, May 24, 1942; c: Lisa. Dir, United Syn Book Service since 1966; field secy, FJP of NY, 1938-41; field mgr, UJA, Essex Co, Newark, 1943-45; regional dir; Northern NJ and Conn JTSA, 1951-59; Northern NJ region, United Syn of Amer, 1959-66. Home: 27 W 96 St, New York, NY. Office: 218 E 70 St, New York, NY.

LEVINE, Harris J, US, physician; b. NYC, Dec 24, 1899; s. Joseph and Anna (Paltiel); MD, LI Med Sch, 1921; m. Dorothy Podolsky, Nov 26, 1925; c: Norman, George. Pvt practice since 1921; chief med examiner, B'nai Zion since 1941. Chmn, B'nai Zion Found, pres, 1939-41; hon pres, JNF, pres, 1956-60, chmn NY region, 1943-44, finance comm, 1944-48, admn comm, 1948-49; vice-pres, Herzliah J Tchrs Sem; hon vice-pres, ZOA since 1958, mem since 1939; pres, Amer Red Mogen David, 1947-50; vice-chmn, United Isr Appeal, 1951; mem: Zionist Actions Comm; NY Co Med Soc; AMA. Recipient: Hons: Harris J Levine Blvd, Kfar B'nai Zion, Isr, 1949; village, Talmei Zvi in Negev, Isr. Home: 315 W 70 St, New York, NY. Office: 50 W 57 St, New York, NY.

LEVINE, Harry, US, manufacturer; b. NYC, Aug 1, 1895; s. Samuel and Sarah (Levine); att CCNY, 1914; m. Leona Edelstein, 1942; c: Irwin, Morton, Barbara. Chmn bd, US Plastic and Chem Co, Metuchen, NJ; treas, Superior Plastic Co, Chgo; fmr dir, Commonwealth Plastic Co, Leominster, Mass; found, dir, Serafon, plastic factory, Rehovot, Isr, 1948. Natl treas, Amer Comm, Weizmann Inst of Sci and Research, Rehovot, since 1944, world treas since 1950; natl treas, ZOA, 1945, pres, Fitchburg-Leominster dist, mem, exec comm, NE region since 1945; natl dir, Brandeis Youth Found since 1940; pres: CJFWF; B'nai B'rith Lodge 1938; JCC; vice pres, NE Zionist Chest, 1949; chmn, ARC dr, Fitchburg-Leominster, 1942; found and chmn, Pal Research Assn, 1945; co-found: Camp Young Judea, Mt Vernon, NY, 1938; Levine Found for Natl Sponsorship by Amer Zionist Youth Commn, Zionist Youth Camps, 1938; Zionist House, Boston, Mass; sponsor, Negev water experiment, Harvard U, 1945; originator, Pageant of Freedom, Diorama; active in Haganah; mem, bd dirs: Heb U, Jerusalem; Technion, Haifa; club, Belmont Country. Home: 1010 Memorial Dr, Cambridge, Mass. Office: 98 Adams St, Leominster, Mass.

LEVINE, Herman, US, merchant; b. Wilkes Barre, Pa, Sep 15, 1897; s. Wolf and Sarah (Cooper); m. Hannah Berger, June 24, 1948. Ret; fmr, partner, Union Clothing Co from 1920. Found, Pa Security League to foster social leg; chmn, UJA, spec gifts comm, 1961; mem: Fgn Policy Assn Amer, org of br in Pittsburgh; AJComm; ADA; B'nai B'rith; Elks; C of C; Temple B'nai Isr; ZOA. Home: 531 Shaw Ave, McKeesport, Pa.

LEVINE, Irving A, US, judge; b. Wash, DC, July 10, 1924; s. Benjamin and Minnie (Cohen); att: George Wash U, 1941-49, LLB, 1949; Natl Coll of State Trial Judge, U Nevada, 1967; m. Shirley Routhenstein, Sep 10, 1947; c: Susan, Karen. Asso judge, Sixth Judicial Circuit of Md; judge, Circuit Court for Montgomery Co, Md, both since 1967; practicing atty, 1950-67; judge, Md Tax Court, 1965-67. Sgt, USAAF 1942-45. Mem: Amer Bar Assn; Amer Judicature Soc; Natl Conf, State Trial Judges; Md State, Montgomery Co Bar Assns; Nu Beta Epsilon; Phi Alpha; Masons; fmr: vice-chmn, Dem State Cen Comm for Montgomery Co; delg, Md Dem State Conv. Recipient: Dist Unit Badge; Silver Campaign Star. Home: 9805 Inglemere Dr, Bethesda, Md. Office: Court House, Rockville, Md.

LEVINE, Irving R, US, journalist; b. Pawtucket, RI; s. Joseph and Emma (Raskin); BS, Brown U, 1944; MS, Columbia Sch of Journalism, 1947; hon Des Lettres, Brown U, 1969; m. Nancy Jones, July 12, 1957; c: Jeffrey, Daniel, Jennifer. Mediterranean dir, NBC since 1968, and 1959-67, Korean War corresp, 1950-53, bur chief, Moscow, 1955-59, London corresp, 1967-68; lectr, intl affairs. Lt, US Army, 1943-46. Author: Main Street, USSR, 1959; Travel Guide to Russia, 1960; Main Street, Italy, 1963; contr to natl mags. Mem, Phi Beta Kappa. Recipient: Overseas Press Club award for best radio-TV reporting, 1956; one of ten oustanding young men in US, Jr C of C, 1956. Home: 3 Piaza di Campitelli, Rome, It. Office: NBC, 18 Piaza Grazioli, Rome, It.

LEVINE, Isaac Don, US, journalist, author; b. Mozir, Russ, Feb 1, 1892; s. Don and Sarah (Maloff); in US since 1911; m. Ruth Newman, Dec 14, 1936; c: Robert. Contbr, Kan Ciy Star, 1914; fgn news ed, NY Tribune, 1917; fgn corresp: Chgo Daily News, 1919-20; Hearst newspapers, 1922-24; escorted Senatorial Commn through Soviet Union, 1923; ed, MaCaulay Drama Libr, 1927; mgn ed, Book League of Amer, 1928-29; publicity dir, Argo-Joint and non-partisan Zionist Conf, 1927-28; ed, exposes, disillusioned US Communists, 1935-36; conducted Unofficial Senatorial Commn through

Pal, 1936, columnist, 1937-38; ed, Plain Talk, 1946-50; organizer, Radio Liberation, Munich, 1951-52; contbr, Scripps-Howard newspapers, 1953. Trustee, Amer Comm for Liberation, NY. Author: The Russian Revolution, 1917; The Resurrected Nations 1919; The Man Lenin, 1924; History of Joint Distribution Committee, 1926-27; Stalin, 1931; Red Smoke, 1932; Billy Mitchell, Pioneer of Air Power, 1943; Stalin's Great Secret, 1956; The Mind of An Assassin, 1959; I Rediscover Russia, 1964; co-author: film biography of Jack London, 1944; collaborator and ed: Yashka, 1918; Kaiser's Letters to the Czar, 1920; Letters to and from the Czar and the Czarina, 1920-22; Letters from Russian Prisons, 1925; The Road to Oblivion, 1931; expose of Gen W Krivitsky, 1939; Jan Valtin's Out of the Night, 1941, expose of Victor Kravchenko, 1944; Oksana Kassenkina, Russian school teacher, 1948; contbr to natl periodicals. Club, Overseas Press, NY, found. Home and office: Waldorf, Md.

LEVINE, Israel E, US, publicist, author; b. NYC, Aug 30, 1923; s. Albert and Sonia (Silver); BS, CCNY, 1946; m. Joy Michael, June 23, 1946; c: David, Carol. Asst to pres and dir of PR, CCNY since 1954, asst dir, 1946-54; exec ed, City Coll Alumnus since 1955, mgn ed, 1952-55. Lt, USAF, 1943-45. Mem: Amer Coll PR Assn; Metrop Coll PR Council, treas, 1960; Amer Alumni Council; Second Div Assn; City Coll Alumni Assn; The Authors Guild. Author: The Discoverer of Insulin: Dr Frederick Banting, 1959; Conqueror of Smallpox: Dr Edward Jenner, 1960; Behind the Silken Curtain: The Story of Townsend Harris, 1961; Inventive Wizard: George Westinghouse, 1962; Champion of World Peace: Dag Hammarskjold, 1962; Miracle Man of Printing: Ottmar Mergenthaler, 1963; Electronics Pioneer: Lee De-Forest, 1964; Young Man in the White House: John Fitzgerald Kennedy, 1964; Oliver Cromwell, 1966; Spokesman for the Free World: Adlai E. Stevenson, 1967; Lenin: The Man Who Made a Revolution, 1969; co-author, The Techniques of Supervision, 1954; contbr to prof jours and natl mags. Recipient: Air Medal with 3 oak leaf clusters; 3 Battle Stars; Pres Unit Citation, all WW II. Hobbies: golf, music. Home: 140-41 69 Rd, Flushing, NY. Office: CCNY, Convent Ave at 139 St, New York, NY.

LEVINE, Jack, US, artist; b. Boston, Mass, Jan 3, 1915; s. Samuel and Mary (Grinker); hon DFA, Colby Coll, 1956; m. Ruth Gikow, Oct 4, 1946; c: Susanna. Works included in collections of: Metrop Mus of Art; Mus of Modern Art; Whitney Mus of Amer Art; Bklyn Mus, all NY. Monographs: Whitney Catalogue, 1957; Teachers and Kings of Israel (with foreword by Paul J Sachs), 1958; Jack Levine, 1966. F: Amer Acad of Arts and Sci; Natl Inst Arts and Letters. Recipient: grant, Natl Inst Arts and Letters, 1946; Guggenehim F, 1946, 1947. Home: 231 W 11 St, New York, NY. Studio: 95 Bedford St, New York, NY.

LEVINE, Joseph H, US, rabbi; b. Cleveland, O, June 7, 1933; s. Benjamin and Helen (Kaplan); BA, W Reserve U, 1955; BHL, MHL, HUC-JIR, 1960; att William Alanson White Inst of Psycht, 1961-62; m. Elinore Cohen, 1962. Dir, B'nai B'rith Hillel Found, Gtr Rochester Area, fmr Hillel dir, U of NC and State dir, B'nai B'rith Hillel Founds, NC; camp prog dir, Council Camp, Minn, 1955-60; counsellor, Hillel Found, U of Cincinnati, 1957-59; rabbi, Cen Syn of Nassau Co, Rockville Cen, NY, 1960-62; staff mem and coord, student relations, Natl Hillel Summer Leadership Inst, Camp B'nai B'rith, Pa; visiting lectr, rel, U of Nazareth, Rochester, 1967, 1968, chmn chaplains staff, 1959-70. Secy, Natl Assn Hillel Dirs, since 1968; rabb adv, SE Regional Assn, UAHC, Ga; Hillel dir, Natl Comm on J Coll Youth and Fac, Council of J Feds and Wfr Funds; natl grand chaplain, Phi Epsilon Pi, 1965-66, vice pres, Rochester Bd Rabbis; bd trustees, Bur J Educ; adv comms, JCC; Comm of Civic Concern, Rochester Jr C of C; Soc for Prisoners Aid; comty educ comm, NY chap, AJComm; fmr adv, LI Fed of Temple Youth; fmr mem, CCAR. Home: 72 Azalea Rd, Rochester, NY.

LEVINE, Maurice, US, psychiatrist, educator; b. Cincinnati, O, June 10, 1902; s. Louis and Esther (Goldstein); BA, U Cincinnati, 1923, MA, 1924; Johns Hopkins Med Sch, 1928; cert, neur, U Vienna, Aus, 1928; grad, Chgo Inst for Psychan, 1937; m. Diana Bailen, 1934; c: Ann, Ellen, Martha. Prof psycht, dept dir, Coll of Med, U Cincinnati since 1947, fac mem since 1933; Frank L Weil Lectureship in Rel and the Hum, HUC, 1968-69; dir, psycht service, Cincinnati Gen Hosp since 1947, on staff since 1932; dir, Cen Clinic for Mental Hygiene, Comty Chest since 1947; training analyst,

Chgo Inst for Psychan since 1942; dir, psycht service, Children's Hosp since 1947; cons: Army Surg Gen, 1948-52; USPHS, 1950-58; J Hosp; Chronic Disease Hosp; Dunham Hosp; Children's Convalescent Hosp; VA Hosp; res, psycht, Phipps Psycht Clinic, 1929-32; Dipl, Amer Bd Psycht and Neur, 1940; chmn: mental hygiene council, Public Health Fed, 1936-37; training comm, Natl Inst for MH, 1950-52; preparatory commn, Psycht Educ Conf, 1951; council, Natl Comm for Mental Hygiene, 1947-50; pres: Amer delg, 1st Intl Cong of Psycht, Paris, 1950; mem: Cincinnati Soc for Neur and Psycht, 1946-47; AMA; Amer Psycht Assn, chmn comm on med educ 1948-49; Amer Orthopsycht Assn; Group for Advancement of Psycht; Assn for Research in Nervous and Mental Diseases; Amer Psychosomatic Assn; Intl Psychoanalytic Assn; Alpha Omega Alpha; Sigma Xi. Author: Psychotherapy in Medical Practice, 1942, 18th ed 1968, trans into Swed, Span, Yugo; co-author: Twenty Years of Psychoanalysis, 1953; Recent Advances in Psychosomatic Medicine, 1955; Why You Do What You Do, 1957; chap in: Methods of Psychiatric Treatment in the Impact of Freudian Psychiatry, 1961; Advance in Psychosomatic Medicine, 1964; Comprehensive Textbook of Psychiatry, 1944; ed bd: Journal of Nervous and Mental Diseases; Journal of Amer Psychoanalytic Assn, 1951-53; co-ed, Psychiatry and Medical Education, 1952; contbr to med jours. Home: 984 Lenox Pl, Cincinnati, O. Office: Cincinnati Gen Hosp, Cincinnati, O.

LEVINE, Morris H, US, physician, educator; b. Lowell, Mass, Nov 4, 1905; s. Max and Bertha (Richard); BS, Tufts U, Medford, Mass, 1928; MD, Tufts U Med Sch, Boston, 1934; m. Frances Jacobs, 1937; c: Stanley, Marshall, Leonard, Lawrence. Asso prof, radiology, U Colo Med Sch, since 1948; dir radiology, Gen Rose Memorial Hosp, since 1952; chief radiology, Natl J Hosp, 1948-65; cons in radiology: Fitzsimons Army Hosp, since 1949; Denver Gen Hosp, since 1949; Mercy Hosp, since 1950, all Denver, Colo: VA Hosp, Grand Junction, Colo, since 1952; path, Montefiore Hosp, Bx, NY, 1935-36; asst res, chest diseases Montefiore Hosp, Bx, NY 1936-37; phys i/c out-patient dept, Green Point Hosp, Bklyn, NY, 1937-40; res in radiology; VA Diagnostic and Cen, Wash, DC, 1940-42; J Hosp, Cincinnati, O, 1946-47; radiologist, VA Hosps, Marion, Ill, Huntington, W Va, 1942-46. Maj, US Army MC, 1944-46. Prin contrib: first to use radioactive isotopes in med in Colo, 1949; established first sch for nuclear med technologists in Colo at Gen Rose Memorial Hosp, 1966. F: Amer Coll Radiology; pres: Colo chap, Nuclear Med Soc, 1959-60; Colo Radiological Soc, 1959-60; co-chmn, Allied J Comty Council, Denver, 1957-58; mem: AMA, Radiological Soc of N Amer; AAUP; AAAS; W Va Assn Paths; Wash, DC, Path Soc; ACLU; B'nai B'rith; bd trustees, Beth Joseph Syn, Denver, 1958-61. Contbr articles to med jours. Hobby: golf. Home: 1200 E Evergreen Blvd, Vancouver, Washington. Office: VA Hospital, Vancouver, Washington.

LEVINE, Mortimer, US, historian, educator; b. Bklyn, NY, Dec 19, 1922; s. Jacob and Anna (Schiller); BA, NYU, 1948; MA, U of Pa, 1949, PhD, 1954. Prof hist, W Va U since 1967, on fac since 1955; lectr, Bklyn Coll, 1954-55. Mem: Renaissance Soc of Amer; Amer Hist Assn; Conf on British Studies. Author: The Early Elizabethan Succession Question, 1558-1568, 1966; Tudor England, 1485-1603; co-ed, Archives of British History and Culture; contbr to scholarly jours. Home: 529 Woodhaven Dr, Morgantown, W Va. Office: W Va U, Morgantown, W Va.

LEVINE, Nathan, US, business exec; b. Bklyn, NY, Aug 6, 1919; s. Louis and Eva (Sloy); att Bklyn Coll, 1942; m. Charlotte Bargad, June 27, 1943; c: Ellen, Lewis, Robin, Barbara, Deborah. Pres: Eagle Beef Cloth Co since 1939; Lion Packaging Producs since 1960; mem, NY Cotton Exch. Prin contribs: invented and devl snap-off bags, 1959. Secy, fund raising comm: Cong Sons Isr, 1962-63, bd trustees since 1964; Marine Park J Cen, 1945-49; chmn, comm for econ affairs for Isr, ZOA, 1968; found mem, Young Pres Org, 1950; bd trustees, LI Zionist Found; mem: Masons; Woodman of World; club, Seawane Golf. Hobbies: art collecting, writing poetry. Home: 889 Ivy Hill Rd, Woodmere, LI, NY. Office: 15 E Beth Page Rd, Plainveiw, NY.

LEVINE, Norman G, US, insurance exec; b. NYC, Sept 14, 1926; s. Harris and Dorothy (Podolsky); att U Wis, 1948. Head, Levine Agcy, Aetna Life Ins Co since 1958. Natl pres, Bnai Zion since 1961; hon chmn, JNF of Amer since 1962; mem, admn comm, Amer ZC since 1961; active in: State of

Isr Bonds Org; UJA; chmn, Life Underwriters Training Council, local chap, 1961; past pres, NYC Life Underwriters Assn; pres, NY State Life Underwriters; bd of dirs, NYC Life mgrs; asso mem, NYC Life Sups; natl bd dirs, Life Underwriters Political Action Comm; mem: Linnaean Soc, Mus of Natural Hist; NY Club, Color Slide. Contbr to jours. Hobbies: photography, sports, wild life conservation. Home: 345 W 58 St, New York, NY. Office: 200 E 42 St, New NY, York.

LEVINE, Philip, US, physician, researcher; b. Kletzk, Russ, Aug 10, 1900; s. Morris and Fay (Zirulick); in US since 1908; BS, CCNY, 1919; MD, Cornell U Med Coll, 1923, MA, 1925; hon DSc, Mich State U, 1967; m. Hilda Perlmutter, 1938; c: Phyllis Klein, Mark, Victor. Dir, Div of Immunohematology, ORTHO Research Found since 1944; asst, Rockefeller Inst, 1925-32; instr, U Wis Med Sch, 1932-35; bacteriologist and transfusionist, Beth Isr Hosp, Newark, NJ, 1935-44. Prin contrib: co-discoverer with Dr Landsteiner of blood factors M and N, 1928; discoverer: hum RH factor, 1939, Cellano Factor, 1949, and its genetic relationship to the Kell factor, phenomenon of isoimmunization through pregnancy; methods of studying bacteriophage; described causes of erythroblastosis fetalis; author, laws on blood tests in paternity disputes in NJ and Wis. F: Amer Acad Allergy; Natl Acad Sci; Amer Coll Phys; asso, Columbia U Sem Assn on Genetics and Evolution of Man; mem: JWC, Plainfield, NJ; corresp mem, Ger Soc of Blood Transfusion. Mem, ed bd, transfusion; Vox Sanguinis. Recipient: awards: Mead Johnson, 1942; War Burdick, 1946; Lasker, 1946; Passano Found, 1951; Townsend Harris, 1956; Karl Landsteiner, 1956; merit, Netherlands Red Cross, 1959; Johnson Medal for Research and Devl, 1960; first Franz Oehlecker award, Ger Soc Blood Transfusion, 1964; medal from Ger Red Cross, 1965; Joseph P Kennedy Intl award, 1966; Clement von Pirquet Gold Medal, 7th Forum of Allergy, 1966; Edward J Ill award, 1966. Hobby, music. Home: 1068 Kenyon Ave, Plainfield, NJ. Office: ORTHO Research Found, Raritan, NJ.

LEVINE, Philip Theodore, US, educator; b. Malden, Mass, Apr 20, 1915; s. Marcus and Rose (Frye); BS, Biol, Tufts U, Mass, 1938; DMD, Harvard, 1942; m. Barbara Rudnick, Feb 24, 1946; c: Margaret, Stephanie. Prof, oral biol since 1967; asso dean since 1967; asst prof, Tufts U, 1950-60, on Fac since 1960; research inves, Mass Gen Hosp, 1960-67. Maj, US Army, 1942-46. Fmr dir, brotherhood, Temple Shalom; mem: Amer, Mass, Conn State Dent Assns; Amer Acad Dent Sci; Harvard Odontological Soc; Gtr Boston Dent Soc. Contbr to dent jours. Recipient: Purple Heart, Silver Star. Home: 11 Wintergreen Lane, W Hartford, Conn. Office: Hartford Plaza, Hartford, Conn.

LEVINE, Pincus P, US, veterinarian, educator; b. NYC, Aug 25, 1907; s. Joseph and Emma (Abel); BS, CCNY, 1927; MS, DVM, Cornell U, 1932, PhD, 1937; m. Selma Hyman, 1933; c: Joseph, Seth. Prof poultry diseases and head, Dept Avian Diseases, NY State Vetr Coll since 1943, fac mem since 1934; Guggenheim F, 1947-48; US AID Cons, Isr Project, 1961-62; FAO cons, Peru and Columbia projects, 1969. Pres, World Vetr Poultry Assn since 1969; mem: Amer Vetr Med Assn; AAAS; Poultry Sci Assn; Amer Soc Zool; Amer Soc Parasitology; Conf Research Workers in Animal Diseases in N Amer; US Livestock Sanitary Assn; Soc Experimental Biol and Med Amer Assn Avian Paths; Phi Kappa Phi; Sigma Xi; Phi Zeta; Temple Beth El, Ithaca, trustee, 1956-57. Ed: Cornell Veterinarian, 1941-44; Avian Diseases, 1957-61; contbr to prof jours. Home: 1872 Slaterville Rd, Ithaca, NY. Office: NY State, Veterinary Coll, Ithaca, NY.

LEVINE, Reeva Anna (pen name, Reeva Miller Levine), US, artist; b. Hollywood, Cal, Nov 23, 1912; d. Bernard and Rose (Schuman) Torf; att: Santa Monica City Coll, Cal; UCLA; m. Raphael Levine, Apr 20, 1959; c: David, Stuart. Profsl artist, since 1943; art tchr, lectr. Works include: stained glass windows: Temple Beth Sholom, Santa Monica, Cal; Wedding Chapel, Temple Sinai, Oakland, Cal; Jacob's Dream, Maarev Temple, Encino, Cal; Dome, Al Jolson Memorial, LA; rel paintings and portraits in public insts; designed, decorated, rel arks for various congs in S Cal; one-man exhbs: Santa Monica, 1948; W La Syn; Auto Club of Wash Gal, 1964, 1968; Grosvenor House, Seattle, 1964; Doce's Gal, 1968, 1969; group exhbs: Santa Monica J Comty Cen; Madonna Festival, Spokane, 1963; Church Epiphany, 1966; Northwest Bank, 1967; Seattle U, 1960, 1964, 1967; Seattle Art Mus, 1967; numerous lectures, demonstrations, TV progs; illustrated: Rabbi Levine's books, Holy Mountain, A Youth Hagadah. Pres, Temple Beth Sholom Sisterhood; org, 1st chap Camp Brotherhood Auxiliary, 1968. Recipient: 1st prize, Competitive Exhb, Santa Monica Art Assn, 1945, 2nd prize, 1946. Home: 2830 Cascadia Ave S, Seattle, Wash.

LEVINE, Richard Ira, US, attorney; b. Bx, NY, Mar 9, 1944; s. Frank and Isabelle (Gans); BA, U Neb, 1965; JD, Neb Law Sch, 1968; m. Linda Gross, Jan, 1968; c: Lana. Atty, E NY Savings Bank since 1969; fmr law asst, legal dept, Eastman Dillon, Union Securities Co. Secy, Amer Bar Assn; mem: Neb Bar Assn; NY State Bar Assn; Phi Delta Phi, Lincoln chap, secy. Hobbies: sports, antiques, travel, investments. Home: 150-15 72 Rd, Flushing, NY. Office: 2650 Atlantic Ave, Brooklyn, NY.

LEVINE, Samuel Z, US, physician, educator; b. NYC, Aug 8, 1895; s. Mendel and Rose (Strelitz); BA, CCNY, 1916; Md, Cornell U Med Coll, 1920; post grad training: Bellevue Hosp, Russell Sage Inst, NYC, 1923-24; m. Bella Morell, 1922; c: Tess (decd), Ted, Robert. Prof em, Cornell U Med Coll since 1961, prof ped, 1936-61, on fac since 1924; cons, NY Hosp since 1961, att ped in chief, 1936-61, on staff since 1932; house off: Mt Sinai Hosp, NYC, 1920-22; Infants' and Children's Hosp, Boston, 1922-23; cons, WHO. Mem: NYC Bd Health; tech adv comm on fluoridation of water supplies, NY State Dept Health; found: Found for Intl Child Health; mem: Amer Ped Soc, pres, 1959-60; Harvey Soc; Soc for Ped Research, pres, 1932-33; Amer Bd Ped; NY Acad Med; AAAS; Amer Inst Nutrition; Soc for Experimental Biol. Ed-in-chief, Advances in Ped, 1945; contbr: numerous sci papers to med jours. Recipient: NY Acad Med Medalist, 1966; Borden Award, Amer Acad Ped, 1944; Cornell U Med Coll Alumnia Assn Award, 1954; Townsend Harris Medal, CCNY, 1954; second annual Albert Einstein Commemorative Award, 1956; John Howland Medal, Amer Ped Soc, 1966. Hobbies: fishing, golf, travel. Home: 345 E 69 St, New York, NY. Office: 525 E 68 St, New York, NY.

LEVINE, Sidney, US, social worker; b. Syracuse, NY, Apr 15, 1925; s. Joseph and Sophie (Elkin); AB, Syracuse U, 1949; MSS, U Buffalo, 1951; m. Rita Friedlander, Sep 10, 1950; c: David. Exec dir, J Family Service since 1957, case worker, 1951-57. Cpl, US Army, 1943-46. Chmn, Toledo chap, Natl Assn Social Workers, 1960-64; mem, B'nai B'rith. Contbr to J publs. Hobbies: gardening, swimming, music. Home: 3536 Westchester Rd, Toledo, O. Office: 2247 Collingwood Blvd, Toledo, O.

LEVINE, Sol, US, engineer; b. Bentleyville, Pa, Nov 16, 1914; s. Sam and Bessie (Slesinger); BS, Waynesburg Coll, 1938; MS, NYU, 1948; m. Betty Broad, June 21, 1941; c: Richard, James. Chief engr: Navy Dept since 1967; Edo Corp, 1946-56; engr mgr, Martin-Marietta Corp, 1956-66; chief engr, Bendix Corp, 1966-67. Asso f, Amer Inst Aeronautics and Astronautics; sr mem, Inst Elec and Electronics Engrs; mem, Acoustical Soc of Amer. Ed: Your Future in Electronic Engineering; Your Future in NASA; Appointment in the Sky:The Story of Project Gemini; Handbook for Mathematics, Physics and Chemistry. Home: 549 Brook Rd, Baltimore, Md. Office: Munitions Bldg, Washington, DC.

LEVINSON, Aaron P, US, business exec; b. Pittsburgh, Pa, Nov 20, 1914; s. Samuel and Rose (Ruben); m. Sonia Zaludkowski, Aug 28, 1938; c: James, Eleanor. Pres: The Levinson Steel Co since 1950; S Side Land Co. Past pres: Iron League of Pittsburgh; Amer Steel Warehouse Assn; Pittsburgh Amer Technion Soc; B'nai B'rith Lodge; bd dirs: United J Fed; S Side Hosp; YM-YWHA; YIKC; Montefiore Hosp; Tree of Life Cong; Isr Bonds Assn; Allegheny Roundtable; Urban League; James Weldon Johnson Camp for Underprivileged Children; Natl J Hosp of Denver; mem: Engrs Soc W Pa; S Side C of C; ADL; life trustee, James and Rachel Levinson Found. Home: 5438 Forbes Ave, Pittsburgh, Pa. Office: S 20 and Wharton St, Pittsburgh, Pa.

LEVINSON, Albert, US, business exec; b. Perth Amboy, NJ, Aug 30, 1923; s. David and Julia (Klein); m. Joyce Berger, July 3, 1946; c: Daniel, Douglas. Pres, Pec Isr Econ Corp, since 1968; sr vice-pres, Hess Oil & Chem Corp, 1946-68. Sgt, US Army, 1943-45. Home: Ballantine Rd, Bernardsville, NJ. Office: 500 Fifth Ave, New York, NY.

LEVINSON, Bernard H, US, judge; b. Austin, Tex, Sep 2, 1907; s. Samuel and Rebecca (Lewin); BA, hons, U Cincinnati, 1929; LLB, Harvard Law Sch, 1932; att: Natl Coll State

Trial Judges, Reno, Nev, 1966; Appellate Judges Sem, NYU, 1968; m. Carlyn Krupp, 1940; c: Peter, Brent. Asso Justice, Supr Court, Hawaii, since 1967; asso, law firm, Grosscup, Morrow and Ambler, Seattle, Wash, 1932-39; atty: US Justice Dept, Wash, DC, 1939-42; US Interior Dept, Wash, DC, 1942-45; Surplus Property Off, Honolulu, 1945-47; dep atty gen, Hawaii, 1947; pvt law practice, Honolulu, 1947-65; partner, law firm: Levinson and Cobb, 1949-64; Levinson, Cobb, and Gould, 1964-65; judge, First Circuit Court, Hawaii, 1966-67. Pres: Hawaii chap, Natl Soc for Crippled Children and Adults, 1964-65; Hawaii Lodge, B'nai B'rith, 1961-62; Temple Emanu-El, 1950-60; chmn: psycht comm, Hawaii Territory, 1952-53; Hawaii unit, AJComm since 1961; Hawaii adv comm, US Commn on Civil Rights, 1964-65; probate study comm, Bar Assn of Hawaii, 1961-65; Hawaii JWF, off since 1956; mem: mgmt comm, Armed Forces, YMCA, 1957-64; bd delgs, AJComm, 1962-64, exec bd since 1967; law comm, HUAC since 1962; bd mgrs, Hawaii Cong Parents and Tchrs, 1957-59; liaison comm, Natl Conf Bar Examiners, since 1968; exec bd, Natl Fed Temple Brotherhoods, 1937-39; Hawaii, Amer, Wash State Bar Assns; Masons; Scottish Rite, 33rd deg; Shriners; Phi Beta Kappa; club: Rotary; Waikiki, pres, 1959-60. Home: Hilton Lagoon Apts, Honolulu, Hawaii. Office: POB 1205, Honolulu, Hawaii.

LEVINSON, Boris M, US, psychologist, educator; b. Kalvarijah, Lith, July 1, 1907; s. Moses and Rose (Lev); in US since 1923; BSS, CCNY, 1937, MS, 1938; PhD, NYU, 1947; m. Ruth Berkowitz, June 16, 1934; c: Martin, David. Prof, psych, Ferkauf Grad Sch Hum and Social Sci since 1956; chief psychol: Adult Guidance Service, NYC, 1937-40; J Memorial Hosp, 1957-59; lectr: CCNY, 1947-53; Hunter Coll, 1949-60; dir, Psych Cen, Yeshiva U, 1956-63, fac mem since 1951. Dipl, Amer Bd of Examiners in Profsl Psycht; f: Amer Psych Assn; AAAS; Soc for Projective Techniques; mem: NY, E and Inter-Amer Psych Assns; NY Soc Clinical Psych; Amer Group Psychotherapy Assn; NY Acad Sci; Phi Delta Kappa; Psi Chi. Author, A Comparative Study of Certain Homeless and Unattached Domiciled Men, 1947; contbr to educ and psych jours. Spec interests: astronomy, microbiol. Home: 39-25 47 St, Sunnyside, NY. Office: 55 Fifth Ave, New York, NY.

LEVINSON, Charles B, US, manufacturing exec; b. Youngstown, O, Dec 15, 1912; s. Al and Goldye (Davis); BS, U Cincinnati, 1934; m. Doris Mombach, Nov 10, 1940; c: Ronnie Shore, Barbara Stern, Suzanne Stern. Chmn bd: Steelcraft Mfg Co since 1969, on staff since 1945; Charbert Ind since 1966, on staff since 1964; pres, Candle-Lite Inc since 1967, vice pres, 1952-67; vice pres, secy, Oceanautic Mfg and Research Co since 1968; treas, secy, Abco Tool and Die Co since 1953; draftsman, Gulf Refining Co, 1934-35; designer, Hunt and Allan, 1935-36; pvt practice, architecture, 1936-39; partner: Al Levinson Co, 1940; Steelcraft Engr Co, 1941-44; pres, Knapp Bros Mfg Co, 1951-68, vice pres, 1949-51; vice pres, treas, Rosscraft Ind Inc, 1954-60; pres, Steelcraft Realty Co, 1953-59; vice pres, treas, Steelcraft Mfg Co, Can Ltd, 1962-65. Bd dir, Better Housing League; JCC; Home for J Aged, fmr vice pres; Cincinnati Big Brothers Assn, fmr pres; Big Brothers Amer, fmr vice pres; Cincinnati Summer Opera; pres, bd trustees, Cincinnati Ballet Co since 1968; bd trustees, J Hosp since 1968; vice chmn, Natl Comm Employment Youth, adv comm corp bd; treas, Natl Comm Children and Youth, fmr adv comm; mem: Natl Comm Educ Migrant Children; Gov Cincinnati Renewal Corp; Citizens Comm on Youth, in various offs 1957-66; fmr adv comm, young workers, US Dept Lab; Assn Soc Amer Reg Architects; Masons; B'nai B'rith; club: Losantiville Country, Queen City. Author: Why Prefabrication, 1949; Standardization versus Prefabrication, 1948; Fluoridation of the City of Cincinnati Water Supply, 1951. Home: 1400 Highland Towers, Cincinnati, O. Office: 9017 Blue Ash Road, Cincinnati, O.

LEVINSON, Charles William, US, business exec, communal leader; b. Russ, Oct 10, 1915; s. Meyer and Freda (Davis); in US since 1920; m. Bessie Anton, June 23, 1937; c: Morton. Sales mgr, Big 4 Auto Supply since 1955 prop, Cork'n Bottle Liquor Store, 1937-55; sales mgr, Standard Meat Co, 1953-55. Sgt, US Army, 1943-46. Pres: Cong Ahavath Sholom Syn; mem: Ft Worth J Fed Campaign Cabinet; B'nai B'rith; J Fed; J Comty Cen; fmr: pres: L F Shanblum Lodge, B'nai B'rith; Tex State Lodge B'nai B'rith; Ft Worth Retail Liquor Dealers Assn; Ft Worth chap, AZA; secy, Ft Worth Jr C of C; bd mem: Ft Worth Jaycees; Dist 7, Grand Lodge B'nai B'rith; Ft Worth J Fed; Cosmopolitan Club; Ahavath Sholom Cong Mens Club; Tex Liquor Dealers Assn; mem:

continuous mem comm, Ft Worth C of C. Recipient: Cert award, J Fed, 1966. Hobbies: fishing, bowling. Home: 4718 Briarhaven Rd, Ft Worth, Tex. Office: 512 S Jennings, Ft Worth, Tex.

LEVINSON, David, US, attorney; b. Chgo, Ill, July 24, 1889; s. Abraham and Sarah (Rubin); PhD, JD, cum laude, U Chgo, 1912; m. Sara Neumann, Dec 18, 1918 (decd); m. 2nd, Minnie Buzard, June 20, 1940 (decd); c: John (decd), William, David. Partner, Sonnenschein, Levinson, Carlin, Nath & Rosenthal and predecessors since 1918; asso: Felsenthal & Wilson, 1912-17; Sonnenschein, Berkson & Lautmann, 1917-18; dir, John Plain Co since 1957. Mem: citizens bd, U Chgo; Art Inst, Chgo; club, Standard. Home: 780 Bronson Lane, Highland Park, Ill. Office: 69 W Washington St, Chicago, Ill.

LEVINSON, J Gordon, US, attorney; b. Chgo, Ill, Apr 20, 1929; s. Paul and Evelyn (Gordon); BS, Northwestern U, 1951; JD, Northwestern Law Sch, 1953. Partner, law firm, Levinson & Edgeman since 1967; mem, Marshall & Marshall, Chgo, Ill, 1957-59; with VA, 1959-61; pvt practice, 1960-67. Capt, US Army, Judge Advocate, 1954-57. Mem: Amer Bar Assn; SF Bar Assn; Legal Aid Society; club, Sierra. Home: 2738 Pierce, San Francisco, Cal. Office: 150 Post, San Francisco, Cal.

LEVINSON, Jack, Eng, business exec; b. Salford, Lancs, Eng, May 24, 1901; s. Abraham and Rachel (Hulman); att George Heriots Sch, Edinburgh; m. Gittel Kibel, Apr 6, 1924; c: Rita Stern, Sheila Gore. Mem: Bd Deps British Js; Burgess, City of Edinburgh; fmr pres: B'nai B'rith; Zionist Assn; Royal Mile Assn, Edinburgh. Hobbies: music, writing, travel. Home: 86 Strathearn Rd, Edinburgh, Scotland. Office: The City Jewellers, 207 High St, Edinburgh, Scotland.

LEVINSON, Louis, US, actuary; b. Boston, Mass, Apr 5, 1904; s. Nathan and Ada (Leight); AB, Harvard Coll, 1927; m. Francis Barr, July 29, 1928; c: Sara Dale, Irene Sisk, Naomi Ossar. Ret; vice pres, chief actuary, Mass Mutual Life Ins Co, Springfield, Mass, 1965-69, with firm since 1927. Mem: B'nai B'rith; Soc Actuaries; Acad Actuaries; Intl Assn Actuaries. Contbr to acturial jours. Home: 106 Bronson Terr, Springfield, Mass.

LEVINSON, Morris Louis, US, business exec; b. Newburgh, NY, Dec 3, 1914; s. Israel and Rae (Schlossberg); BS, Wharton Sch Finance, U of Pa, 1934; LLB, Yale Law Sch, 1937; m. Eveta Weingarten, 1947 (decd); c: Judith, Joshua, Adam; m. 2nd, Barbara Salvage Machinist, July 5, 1964; step-c: John, Nancy, Robert. Chmn bd: Five Day Labs, NYC, since 1947; Rival Pet Foods, Chgo, since 1957; Hervin Sales Co, Portland, Ore, since 1964; Hygiene Inds, NYC, since 1965; pres, Asso Producs, NY, London, since 1947; dir: Pabst Brewing Co, Milw, Wis, since 1958; Heidenberg Textiles, NYC, since 1967; instr econ, Yale U, 1936-37; pvt law practice, Cook, Nathan, Lehman and Greenman, NYC, 1937-41; prin atty, Off Food Price Admn, Wash, DC, 1941-44; vice pres, gen counsel, Consolidated Foods Corp, Chgo, 1944-47. F, Brandeis U since 1965; pres, UJA, Gtr NY, 1969; vice pres, dir, Bus Careers Wfr Bd, NYC, since 1968; trustee: FJP, Gtr NY; United Isr Appeal, NYC; RI Sch Design; New Sch for Social Research; treas, Natl UJA; dir: Fund for Rep; Council J Feds and Wfr Funds, NYC; Natl Found for J Culture; Isr Educ Fund; Natl Businessmen's Council; natl governing council, Amer Assn for J Educ; JWB. Hobbies: hunting, fishing, skiing, reading. Home 48 E 65 St, New York, NY. Office: 445 Park Ave, New York, NY.

LEVINSON, Nathan P, Ger, rabbi; b. Berlin, Nov 21, 1921; s. Wolfe Lewinski; BA, U Cincinnati, 1945; BHL, MHL, ordained rabbi, HUC, 1948; m. Helga Heimberg, June 18, 1947; c: Sharon. Landesrabbiner, Baden, since 1964; rabbi: Selma, Ala, 1948-50; Berlin, 1950-53; Mannheim, 1961-64. Chaplain, USAF, 1955-61. J chmn: Ger Council Chr and J since 1965; Heidelberg Council Chr and J; chmn, Magen David Adom, Ger; mem: bd: Ger Soc Practical Psych; Help for Blind in Isr; Child Wfr, City of Heidelberg; educ bd: Land Baden; City of Heidelberg; youth commn, Cen Wfr Bd, J in Ger; CCAR; Rabbiner Konferenz der Bundesrepublik; B'nai B'rith; judges comm for Buber-Rosenzweig medal. Author: Martin Buber, 1966; Ruhe, Unruhe, Frieden, 1968; Monumenta Judaica Tonbildschau, 1965; mem ed bd, Jour of Practical Psychology; co-publisher: Antijudaismus im Neuen Testament, 1967; Emuna, jour for Chr-J coop; contbr to Ger, Amer jours. Home: Bergstrasse 23, 69, Heidelberg, Ger. Study: Kriegsstrasse 154, 75, Karlsruhe, Ger.

LEVINSON, Norman, US, mathematician; b. Lynn, Mass, Aug 11, 1912; s. Max and Gussie (Green); BS, MIT, 1933, MS, 1934, DS, 1935; m. Ziporah Wallman, Feb 11, 1938; c: Sylvia, Joan. Chmn, math dept, MIT since 1968, prof math since 1937; Proctor f, Cambridge U, 1934-35. F, Amer Acad Arts and Sci; mem: Natl Acad Sci; Amer Math Soc. Author: Gap and Density Theorems, 1940; Theory of Ordinary Differential Equations, 1955. Recipient: f: Natl Research Council, Princeton U, 1935-36; Guggenheim, Mathematics Inst, Copenhagen, 1948-49; Bocher Award, 1953. Home: 7 Humboldt St, Cambridge, Mass. Office: MIT, Cambridge, Mass.

LEVINSON, Samuel A, US, physician, educator, scientist; b. Chgo, Ill, Jan 8, 1905; s. Joseph and Dvora (Laden); BS, U of Ill, 1917, MS, MD, 1919; PhD, Northwestern U, 1940; m. Esther Linder, 1927; c: Joseph, Myra. Prof, em, path, U of Ill Coll of Med, since 1961, fac mem since 1940; cons: U of Ill Research and Educ Hosp Lab since 1955, dir, labs, 1929-55; dir, path, labs, Sch Med Tech, Weiss Memorial Hosp since 1965; professorial lectr, U Chgo, 1936-56. USNR, WWI. Dipl, Amer Bd Path, Clinical Path, and Forensic Path; f: Coll Amer Path; Amer Soc Clinical Path; Amer Coll Phys; Amer Coll Chest Phys; mem: Amer Assn Path; Amer Soc Experimental Biol and Med; Intl Acad Path; Inst of Med, Chgo; AAAS. Author: Clinical Laboratories Diagnosis, 7th Ed, 1969; several books; ed-in-chief, Jour of Forensic Sciences, 1956-65; ed, Symposium on Medicolegal Problems, Series I, 1948, Series II, 1949; Natl Corresp for US to Acta Medicinae Legalis et Socialis; contbr numerous original articles on basic research. Recipient: Medal and Cert Merit, AMA, 1952. Bronze Medal: Ill Med Soc, 1953; Miss Med Soc, 1954. Home: 3730 Lake Shore Dr, Chicago, Ill. Office: Weiss Memorial Hosp Labs, 4646 Marine Dr, Chicago, Ill.

LEVINSON, Solomon Isaac, Eng, solicitor; b. Hartlepool, Durham, Eng, Aug 19, 1918; s. Jacob and Rebecca (Kruschinski); LLB, Coll of Law, Newcastle, 1936; m. Betty Simon, June 12, 1947; c: Martin, Susanne. Partner: Levinsons, Walker and Lister since 1965; ANSI Levinson, 1946-65. Capt, Royal Artillery, 1939-46. Pres, secy, hon solicitor, Hartlepool Heb Cong; pres: Grammar School Old Boys Assn; W Hartlepool, 1950-51, Hartlepool Law Soc, 1967-68; mem, Freemasons Lodge, 1963-64. Hobby: gardening. Home: Whitegates, 256 Park Rd, Hartlepool, Durham, Eng. Office: 47 Church St, Hartlepool, Durham, Eng.

LEVINTHAL, Abraham A, US, attorney; b. Phila, Pa, May 25, 1895; s. Bernard and Minnie (Kleinberg); LLB, Temple U, 1918; m. Passie Ellis, Dec 25, 1918; c: Marvin, Deljean. Pvt practice since 1918; field worker, JWB, 1917-18; fmr: asso solicitor, Bd Rev Taxes, Phila; asst city solicitor, Phila. Pres, Phila council, Brith Abraham; hon pres, Mizrachi, Phila; exec vice pres, Brith Achim; delg, Amer J Conf; hon mem, bd, J Comty Relations Council; dir, United Heb Schs; found, mem, Har Zion Temple; mem: Phila, Pa Bar Assns; fmr: Secy, Phila council, AJCong; mem: exec bd, Brith Sholom; Dorshei Dath Soc. Home: 5322 Gainor Rd, Philadelphia, Pa. Office: 3 Pen Cen Plaza, Philadelphia, Pa.

LEVINTHAL, Cyrus, US, attorney; b. Phila, Pa, Jan 25, 1900; s Bernhard and Minna (Kleinberg); BS, U of Pa, 1922; DJ, NYU, 1926; LLB, Cambridge, U, 1928; m. Lillian Weintraub, Oct 18, 1934; c: Jay, Myrna. Pvt practice, Cal, Pa, NY Bars. Chmn, S Cal comm, J Publ Soc; secy, U Judaism since 1959, mem, bd overseers since 1961; mem, bd govs, J Comty Found; mem, bd dirs, LA J Fed Council; fmr, chmn Bur J Educ; pres, LA dist, ZOA, 1952-53. Spec interest: collecting 16th and 17th cent law books. Home: 126 N Lapeer Dr, Beverly Hills, Cal. Office: 6505 Wilshire Blvd, Los Angeles, Cal.

LEVINTHAL, Daniel H, US, surgeon, educator; b. Chgo, Ill, June 18, 1895; s. Harry and Dora (Shaffer); MD, Loyola U, Chgo, 1917; m. Gertrude Coski, Dec 19, 1920; c: Dorothy Strelitz, Marilyn Rosenman. Asst clinical prof, orthopedic surg, UCLA Sch of Med, since 1953; att orthopedic surg: St Johns' Hosp, Santa Monica; Santa Monica Hosp, since 1945; cons: St Joseph's Hosp, Burbank, Cal, since 1946; Temple Hosp, LA since 1948; mem, em, orthopedic staff, Cedars of Leb Hosp since 1945; cons, Mt Sinai Hosp since 1957, both LA; att orthopedic surg: Cook Co and Michael Reese Hosps, 1925-45; N Chgo Hosp, 1923-27; Mt Sinai Hosp, 1919-28; instr and asso orthopedic surg, Northwestern U Med Sch, 1925-35; asst prof, orthopedic surg, U of Ill Sch of Med, 1935-42; Coll of Med, Evangelist, LA, 1946-53; prof, Cook Co Grad Sch of Med. Capt, US Army, MC, WW I. Dipl, Amer

Bd Orthopedic Surg; f, Intl Coll Surgs; mem: life, Amer Coll Surgs; AMA, em; Amer Acad Orthopedic Surgs, found mem; Amer Assn for Study of Neoplastic Diseases; LA Co Med Assn; W Orthopedic Assn; Bay Surg Soc; hon mem: Orthopedic Soc, Chile; Mexico City, Mex; Med Soc, Tampico, Mex. Contbr to med jours. Office: 501 S Beverly Dr, Beverly Hills, Cal.

LEVINTHAL, Israel H, US, rabbi; b. Vilna, Lith, Feb 12, 1888; s. Bernard and Minna (Kleinberg); in US since 1891; BA, Columbia U, 1909, MA, 1910; MHL, Rabbi, JTSA, 1910, DHL, 1920, hon DD, 1920; JD, NYU, 1914; hon DJ Theol, JIR, 1940; m. May Bogdanoff, Aug 12, 1908; c: Helen Lyons, Lazar. Rabbi, Bklyn Jewish Center, since 1919; visiting prof of homiletics, JTSA, 1947-62; rabbi: Temple B'nai Sholom, Bklyn, 1910-15; Temple Petach Tikva, Bklyn, 1915-19. First pres, Bklyn Bd of Rabbis, 1929-31; pres, RA, 1930-32; first pres, Bklyn J Comty Council, 1940-44, hon pres since 1944; chmn, United Syn of Amer campaign for Syn Cen, Jerusalem, 1932-35; first pres, Bklyn Zionist reg, 1933-35, hon pres since 1935; delg, United Synagogue of Amer, at dedication of Heb U, 1925. Author: The Jewish Law of Agency, 1920; Steering or Drifting—Which? 1928; Judaism, An Analysis and An Interpretation, 1935; A New World is Born, 1943; Point of View—An Analysis of American Jewry, 1958; Judaism Speaks to the Modern World, 1963. Home: 576 Eastern Pkway, Brooklyn, NY. Study: 667-691 Eastern Pkwy, Brooklyn, NY.

LEVINTHAL, Louis E, US, jurist, author; b. Phila, Pa, Apr 5, 1892; s. Bernard and Minna (Kleinberg); BA, U of Pa, 1914, LLB, 1916, LLM, 1918; hon LHD: JTSA, 1948; Dropsie Coll, 1956; hon DJur, Heb U, 1967; m. Lenore Chodoff, Dec 5, 1916; c: Sylvia Bernstein, Cyrus. Counsel, law firm, Dilworth Paxson, Kalish, Kohn and Levy since 1959; fmr: spec counsel, Public Service Comm of Pa, 1935-37; judge, Court of Common Pleas, Phila, Pa, 1937-59; spec adv, J affairs, to Gen Lucias Clay and Eur command, 1947-48. Fmr: chmn: bd govs, Heb U, chmn; publ comm, J Publ Soc of Amer; pres, ZOA. Author: Land Laws of Turkey, 1916; Early History of Bankruptcy Law, 1918; Mayer Sulzberger, PJ, 1927; Credo of an American Zionist, 1942; Justice Louis D Brandeis, 1942. Home: John F Kennedy House, 19th and Kennedy Blvd, Philadelphia, Pa. Office: 2600 Fidelity Bldg, Broad and Samson Sts, Philadelphia, Pa.

LEVISSON, Robert Abraham (pen name, RAL), Holland, business exec, communal leader; b. The Hague, Holland, Dec 27, 1913; s. Levie and Amelia (Simons); LLM, U Leiden, 1937; m. Alberta Schoonheim. Mgn dir, Printing House Levisson. Served, capt, Royal Netherlands Army, 1943-46. Pres, Lib J Cong, The Hague; mem numerous comms, Zionist, rel, charitable insts. Contbr to publs. Home: 17 van Voorschotenlan, The Hague, Holland. Office: 10 de Bruyn Kopstraat, Ryswyk, Holland.

LEVIT, Bert W, US, attorney, educator; b. San Francisco, Feb 16, 1903; s. Morris and Fanny (Jacobs); BA, Stanford U, Cal, 1924; JD, Law Sch, 1925; m. Thelma Clumeck, May 10, 1928; c: Victor, Roger. Sr partner, law firm, Long and Levit, SF and LA since 1927; dir finance, State of Cal, 1959; chmn, Gov's comm on reorg of state govt, 1959-60; spec asst, US Atty Gen, Wash, DC, 1925-26; chief asst dist atty, SF, 1944-45; Cal chief dep atty gen, 1951; visiting lectr, Stanford U, Law Sch, 1932-57. F, Amer Coll Trial Lawyers; pres, Amer Cancer Soc, SF br; fmr: pres, Bd Educ, SF Unified Sch Dist; pres, Cal Sch Bd Assn; Cal delg, White House Conf on Educ; mem, comm on educ, US C of C; chmn: state and local affairs comm, charter rev comm, C of C, SF; statewide tax comm, C of C, State of Cal; pres, Cal State Jr C of C; pres, org, SF Rep Assembly; mem exec comm, Rep Co cen comm; charter mem, Cal Law Rev Comm, vice chmn, SF sups, Charter Rev Comm; mem: comm on admn of justice, Cal State Bar; State of Cal Coord Council on Higher Educ; mem: Amer Bar Assn; Intl Assn of Ins Counsel; Phi Beta Kappa; Delta Sigma Rho; Order of Coif; clubs: SF Commercial; Concordia-Argonaut; Commonwealth of Cal, past secy. Home: 850 Powell St, San Francisco, Cal. Offices: 465 California St, Merchants Exchange Bldg, San Francisco, Cal; 3600 Wilshire Blvd, Los Angeles, Cal.

LEVIT, Herschel, US, artist, educator; b. Shenandoah, Pa, May 29, 1912; s. Isador and Anna (Wolfe); att Pa Acad Fine Arts, 1930-34; Barnes Found, 1936-38; m. Janice Hackenburg, Dec 23, 1939; c: Lois. Prof art, Pratt Inst since 1960, on staff since 1947; painter, illustrator, photographer:

RCA Victor Records; Columbia; Epic; Vox Products; illustrator, MacMillan Children's Books since 1962; muralist, Sect of Fine Arts, Wash, DC, 1940-43; one-man shows: Phila and NY; paintings exhb: mus: Metrop, Whitney, Modern Art, all NY; Pa Acad Fine Arts; Print Club; photographs exhb: Village Camera Club; contbr photography: Horizon Book of Ancient Rome, 1966; Horizon Book of the Elizabethan World, 1967; Horizon Book of Great Cathedrals, 1968; perm collection, Mus of Modern Art, NYC; executed murals: PO, Louisville, O; Jenkintown, Pa; Recorder of Deeds Bldg, Wash, DC; designer, numerous record covers for Cardinal, 1967-68; contbr, avant-garde sect in Graphic Forms, 1949. Mem, Metrop Mus Art. Hobby: music. Home and studio: 220 W 93 St, New York, NY.

LEVIT, Robert J, US, mathematician, educator; b. San Francisco, Aug 17, 1916; s. Art and Manette (Lievre); BS, Cal Inst Tech, 1938, 1939; PhD, U of Cal, 1941; m. Jean Bernasconi; c: Linda, Arthur, Miles. Prof, math, SF State Coll, fmr dir, Computer Cen, on fac since 1957; asst prof, U of Ga, 1946-47, asso prof, 1947-55; visiting asst prof, MIT, 1954-55; with applied sci div, IBM, 1955-57. Lt cdr, USNR, 1946. Mem: Amer Math Soc; Math Assn of Amer; Assn Symbolic Logic; Sigma Xi. Home: 148 Miraloma Dr, San Francisco, Cal. Office: SF State Coll, San Francisco, Cal.

LEVIT, Victor B, US, attorney; b. Singapore, Apr 21, 1930; s. Bert and Thelma (Clumeck); BA, Stanford U, 1950, LLB, 1952; m. Sherry Chamove, 1962; c: Carson, Victoria. Partner, Long and Levit since 1955, asso, 1953-55; instr, law, Ins Underwriters Assn since 1959; asso legal counsel, US Jr C of C, 1959-60; gen legal counsel, 1960-62; guest lectr, Stanford Law Sch, 1958. Pres: SF Jr C of C, 1958; SF Young Reps, 1955; SF TB and Health Assn, 1966-68; SF Assn for Mh, 1968-70; chmn: SF Conf, 1961-63; NCCJ, 1962-64, 1968-70; campaign, Aid for Retarded Children, 1960; SF Planning and Urban Renewal Assn, 1959; Red Shield Youth Assn, Salvation Army since 1960; SF C of C, 1959; Natl Found for Infantile Paralysis, 1958; mem: ins comm, SF Bar Assn, 1962; Mayor's Osaka-SF Affiliation Comm since 1959; natl comm, Stanford Law Sch Fund since 1959; exec comm, US Jr C of C since 1959; SF Rep Co Cen Comm since 1956; Cal Rep State Cen Comm since 1956; life and sen, Jr Chamber Intl; clubs: Commonwealth of Cal; SF Commercial; Cal Tennis. Recipient: Award, Outstanding Young Man of SF, mgn eds of SF 1960. Home: 45 Beach Rd, Belvedere, Cal. Office: Merchants Exch, 465 California St, San Francisco, Cal.

LEVITAN, Harry D, Den, manufacturer; b. Copenhagen, Mar 10, 1917; s. Jacob and Sara (Cohn); att Inst Commercial Sci; m. Aina. Fur mfr and wholesaler; lectr, j music, Danish State Radio. Fmr pres, Scandinavian J Youth Fed; warden, Copenhagen Syn. Recipient: King Christian X's Memorial Medal; King David Order of Oslo, Nor. Home: Nojsomhedsvej 13, Copenhagen, Den. Office: Vester Voldgade 87, Copenhagen, Den.

LEVITAN, Samuel, Den, manufacturer; b. Copenhagen; s. Jacob and Sarah (Cohn); att Inst of Commercial Sci; m. Jeanne Schermeister; c: Jacob, Dow, Joel. Pres, S Levitan, fur mfr and wholesaler, since 1946. Pres: Friends of Midrashiah Noam, Isr, in Den; Comm for Danish Participation in Maccabiot; mem, bd dirs: J Comty, Copenhagen, past vice pres; Bd J Educ, mem, standing comm; Yeshiva; philanthropic orgs; fmr, vice pres, J Day Sch, Copenhagen; club, J Sports, vicepres. Home: Prins Constantinsvej 5, Copenhagen, Den. Office: Vester Voldgade 87, Copenhagen, Den.

LEVITAN, Selig J, US, lawyer; b. NYC, Mar 1, 1908; s. Morris and Dora (Levy); AB, CCNY, 1927; JD, Harvard, 1930; m. Estelle Adams, June 23, 1929; c: Eleanor Bloom, Herbert. Pvt practice since 1930; partner: Javits & Javit, 1946-57; Javits, Levitan & Held, 1946-57; Levitan & Camche, 1968-70. Chief, mgmt br and exec off, control div, Off Chief, Chem Warfare Service, War Dept, 1942-46; brig gen, ret, US Army Res. Dir: Levy Found for Med Research; Shimkin Found; mem: Amer, NY State, Fed, Intl Bar Assns; Assn Bar, NYC; NY Co Lawyers Assn; club: Harvard: NY, Boston. Recipient: Legion of Merit, 1945; Army Commendation Medal, 1946; Conspicuous Service Cross, NY, 1946. Home: 18 Wyndham Rd, Scarsdale, NY. Office: 630 Fifth Ave, New York, NY.

LEVITAN, Tina Nellie, US, author, lecturer; b. Boston, Mass, Dec 19, 1928; d. Julius and Bella (Rosen); BA, Hunter Coll, 1949; BHL, Herzliah Heb Tchrs Inst, 1949. Lectr: Amer J hist, Zionism, J lit, rel, public affairs, J contrib to sci, Natl J Lectr Bur, JWB, since 1952. Found, first pres, Hunter Coll Heb Speaking Club, Chug Ivri, 1948; mem: Authors League of Amer: Amer J Hist Soc; Hunter Coll Alumni Assn. Author: The Firsts of American Jewish History, 1952, 2nd ed, 1957; The Laureates: Jewish Winners of the Nobel Prize, 1960; The Islands of Compassion, 1963; A History of the Jewish Hospitals of New York, 1964; Baolam Hechadash, in Heb, 1968; Jews in American Life: From 1942 to the Space Age, 1969; contbr on J topics to Heb and Eng periodicals. Recipient: award for outstanding achievement, Hunter Coll, 1959. Home: 372 Central Park W, New York, NY.

LEVITAS, Elliott Harris, US, attorney; b. Atlanta, Ga, Dec 26, 1930; s. Louis and Ida; BA, LLB, Emory U; MA, Oxford U; att U of Mich; m. Barbara Hillman; c: Kevin, Karen, Susan. Atty, Arnall Golden & Gregory; repr, Ga House of Reprs, since 1965. Capt, USAF. Bd dirs, Atlanta J Comty Cen; mem: Amer and Ga Bar Assns. Home: 1352 Jody Lane, NE, Atlanta, Ga. Office: 1000 Fulton Fed Bldg, Atlanta, Ga.

LEVITAS, Judith Andron, US, communal worker; b. NYC, Oct 14, 1903; d. Jacob and Ida (Goldstein) Andron; desc, Rabbi Samuel Andron, co-found 1st Yeshiva in US; att, Bus Coll, Far Rockaway, NY, 1922; m. Joseph Levitas, Mar 23, 1930; c: Hanna, Miriam Kalman. Hon pres, mem bd, Westchester Mizrachi Women, past pres; mem bd: White Plains Hadassah; for Braille work, sisterhood, Temple Isr Cen, White Plains; life mem, Ladies League, Rabbi Jacob Joseph Sch, NY; B'nai B'rith, fmr, trustee, social secy, White Plains chap. Prin contrib: 7th person in US to be cert in Heb Braille; cert in Eng Braille; transcribed into Braille: Haftorahs; Heb work books; prayer books; Haggadah's; textbooks; A Practical Grammar for Classical Heb; An Anthology of Heb Lit. Recipient: Noteworthy Service Award, Natl Braille Assn; other awards for work in Braille, from: Isr Bonds; Mizrachi Women. Home: 266 Old Mamaroneck Rd, White Plains, NY.

LEVITATS, Isaac, US, educational dir, author; b. Zagare, Lith, Sep 3, 1907; s. Leib and Feige (Schmidt); in US since 1926; BA, Columbia U, 1929, MA, 1933, PhD, 1942; MHL, JIR, 1933; DEduc, Syracuse Sch of Educ, 1952; m. Tamar Schulz, 1936; c: Meron, Yehuda. Asso prof, Herzliah Heb Tchrs Inst; educ dir, Beth El Temple, N Bellmore, NY; tchr, Reali Sch, Haifa, Isr, 1937-40; researcher, Esco Found Pal Study, 1942-43; exec dir, Bur J Educ: Akron, O; Syracuse, NY; Milw, Wis, 1943-56. Author: The Jewish Community in Russia, 1772-1844, 1943; Jewish Boards of Education in America, 1952; co-author, Palestine—A Study of Jewish, Arab and British Policy, 1947. Mem: Natl Council for J Educ; Phi Delta Kappa; ZOA; YIVO; B'nai B'rith. Home: 510 Riverside Blvd, Long Beach, NY. Office: 515 Park Ave, New York, NY.

LEVITE, Theodore, Isr, journalist; b. Warsaw, Pol, June 27, 1919; s. Leon and Salomea; in Isr since 1940; att: Edinburgh U; LSE; m. Alexandra Burakinsky, Dec 4, 1949; c: Ariel, Mirit. Isr corresp: Thompson Newspapers; London Daily Mirror, since 1949; roving corresp, Maariv, Heb daily, 1945-58; war corresp: War Of Independence, Sinai Campaign, Six-Day War; dir, Catering Ltd, Lod Airport; found, mgn dir, Avia Hotel, Savyon, Isr. Hon secy, Fgn Press Assn in Isr, since 1961. Home: 5 Levite St, Tel Ganim, Ramat Gan, Isr.

LEVITEN, Paul, US, business exec; b. Falls River, Mass, Aug 6, 1928; s. Morris and Rebecca (Chervinsky); BS, U of Cal, 1950; m. Riva Shamray, Oct 15, 1950; c: Priscilla, Marcia, Peter. Pres, Gt Scott Food Markets since 1968; dir, Roger Williams Savings and Loan. Lt, US Army, 1952-55. Dir: Gen J Comm, RI; Temple Emanu-El, Providence; chmn, RI Isr Bonds Campaign, 1967-68; mem, bd overseers, JTSA; clubs: Atlantic Tuna; Brown Country. Hobby: big game fishing. Home: 280 Irving Ave, Providence, RI. Office: 70 Bacon St, Pawtucket, RI.

LEVITSKY, Joseph, US, educator; b. Russ, July 15, 1892; s. Joshua and Eva Shendel (Ulasovsky); BS, Temple U, 1925; Phd, Dropsie Coll, 1929; m. Liebe Kaufman, Aug 25, 1912; c: Fanny. Prof, Heb lang and culture, Temple U, 1948-57, ret. Mem: MLA; AAUP; Natl Assn Profs of Heb. Home: 1004 Stratford Ave, Philadelphia, Pa.

LEVITSKY, Louis Moses US, rabbi, educator; b. Kremenchug, Russ, Jan 4, 1897; s. Samuel and Freda (Wolowick); in US since 1916; BA, CCNY, 1920; att: Harvard U; Columbia U; ordained rabbi, JTSA, 1923, DHL, 1933, DD, 1949; m. Anna Levy, Nov 28, 1919; c: Barbara. Rabbi, Oheb Shalom

Cong, S Orange, NJ, since 1940; dir, Sem Sch J Study and Women's Inst, JTSA, since 1940; spec lectr; rel, Newark Coll Engr, since 1950; practical theol and visiting prof homiletics, JTSA; lectr, Douglass Coll Chapel; rabbi, Temple Isr, Wilkes-Barre, Pa, 1922-40; mem fac, div hum, Rutgers U, Newark, 1954-64; spec lectr, Judaism, Douglass Coll, 1957-58. Maj, chaplain, NJ State Guard, 1940-49. Public mem: NJ Lab Mediation Bd; NJ area Natl War Lab Bd, 1941-46; chmn, Lab-Mgmt Inst, Rutgers U, 1955, mem, 1949-55; mem: prayer book comm, RA, chmn, ethics comm; NY Bd Rabbis; Bd Rabbis Essex Co; Amer Assn for Political and Social Sci; Soc Bibl Lit and Exegesis; Amer J Hist Soc; Amer Arbitration Assn; Planned Pafenthood Fed; ZOA; Amer Acad J Research; exec comm, Natl J Conf; Wfr Fed Campaign Comm; exec comm, State Council United Defense Fund; bd dirs, Newark Comty and War Chest; adv bd, Salvation Army; fmr: pres, RA; trustee, JTSA; chmn, serveys comm, Essex Co Council JAs; bd dirs, Essex Co J Comty Cen; chmn, J War Records, Essex Co; mem: Comty Wfr Council, Newark; roundtable NCCJ; clubs; Torch; Rotary. Author: A Jew Looks at America, Social Life in Pumbaditha as Reflected in the Talmud; Story of an Awakened Community, brochure; Freedom Under Law; mem ed bd, Reconstructionist, 1941-46; contbr to J publs; participated radio progs: The Eternal Light; The Mutual Radio Chapel; extensive research studies to J comtys in all parts of world. Recipient: Rutgers U Medal, 1963; dist service medal, JTSA, 1963. Home: 32 S Munn Ave, E Orange, NJ. Study: 170-180 Scotland Rd, S Orange, NJ.

LEVITT, Alfred, US, artist, writer, lecturer; b. Aug 15, 1894; s. Hyman and Sadie (Levitt); att: Columbia U; Art Student's League; Hans Hoffman and Grande Chaumiere, Paris, Fr; m. Gertrude Horwitz, June 20, 1924. Lectr, modern and prehistoric art, Amer Prog Bur of Boston, Mass; numerous one-man and group exhbs, in Youngstown, O; Manchester, NH; Rockport, Mass, NYC; perm collection: Yad Labanim Mus, Isr; pvt collections in Eur and US. Coord chmn, Modern Artists of Cape Ann, Mass, 1947; found, tchr of painting and drawing, Ecole Moderne de Provence, St Remy de Provence, Fr, 1949-50, 1959-62; lectr, "Cave Art—The Birth of Painting", NYU, div gen educ; Cooper Union Forum, adult educ div; NY Public Libr; Archaeol Inst of Amer, Wagner Coll; Staten I, N Shore Soc, both NY; Phila Art Alliance, Pa and Fr. Mem: Archaeol Inst of Amer; La Société Prehistorique de L'Ariege, Fr; life mem: Archaeol Soc of Staten I, NY; f, MacDowell Colony, Peterboro NH, 1956. Home: 505 W Broadway, New York, NY.

LEVITT, Arthur, US, attorney, public official; b. Bklyn, NY, June 28, 1900; s. Israel and Rose (Daniels); BA, Columbia Coll, 1921; LLB, Columbia Law Sch, 1924; LLD; Siena Coll, 1966; Albany Law Sch, 1967; LHD, Yeshiva U, 1968; m. Dorothy Wolff, June 30, 1929; c: Arthur. Comptroller, NY State since 1955; pvt law practice, NYC, 1925-55. Col, Judge Advocate-Gen Corps, WWII. Pres: Bd Educ, NYC, 1952-54; chmn, commn on sch integration; Gov Harriman's comm on marketing sch bonds; dir, Natl Scholarship Fund for Negro Students; NY Acad Public Educ; fmr, Union Temple, Bklyn; chmn: Natl Campaign for Aid Retarded Children; state employees div, JWF, 1955-57; vice-chmn and dir, Bklyn chap, ARC; mem: NY State Tchrs Retirement Bd; NY State Comm for the White House Conf on Educ; bd dirs, NCCJ; past chancellor, Knickerbocker Lodge, KP; fmr cdr, Cpl Rosenberg Post, Amer Legion; Mason, 33 deg, grand lodge off and past master. Recipient: medals: US Army Legion of Merit, Army Commendation; awards: Assn for Help of Retarded Children, 1954; Brandeis U Citation, 1956; NY Daily Mirror youth, 1959; Urban League of NY, 1962; Man of Year Plaque, Amer Legion, Kings Co, NY; official guest, Isr Govt, 1959. Home: 203 E 72 St, New York, NY. Office: Alfred E Smith State Off Bldg, Albany, NY.

LEVITT, Barry, US, attorney; b. Chgo, Ill, Feb 25, 1931; s. Morris and Esther (Klein); BBA, Roosevelt U, Chgo, Ill, 1959; JD, Loyola Law Sch, 1964; m. Ethel Grush, Mar 27, 1966; c: Michael, Renee, Steven, Lisa. Pvt practice, LA, Cal since 1969; estate tax examiner, Internal Revenue Service, 1964-65; atty, Bornstein & Levitt, 1965-67; cpa, Berger, Schultz & Levitt, 1968-69; atty, Slavitt, Edelman & Weiser, 1969. Sgt, US Army, 1952-54. Dir, Cal Assn of Atty-CPAs; volunteer-cons, Interracial Council for Bus Opportunity; arbitrator, Amer Arbitration Assn; mem: Ill State Bar Assn; State Bar of Cal; LA Co Bar Assn; Amer Bar Assn; Decalogue Soc of Lawyers; B'nai B'rith, Justice Lodge, LA; Masons, Menorah Lodge; clubs: LA Lawyers. Home: 11711 Mayfield, Los Angeles, Cal. Office: 8201 Beverly Blvd, Los Angeles, Cal.

LEVITT, Eugene E, US, psychologist, educator; b. Bklyn, NY, Nov 5, 1921; s. Martin and Anna (Klein); BA, Bklyn Coll, 1948; MA, Columbia U, 1950, PhD, 1952; m. Faith Mandel, Feb 27, 1950; c: Hope, Tod, Lisa, Russell. Chief psych services and prof clinical psych, Ind U Med Cen and Med Sch since 1957; dir research, Ill Inst for Juvenile Research, Chgo, 1955-57; research asst prof, Child Wfr Research Sta, U of Ia, 1952-55; clinical psychol to Dr Maurice Friedman, Cleveland, O, 1951-52. Lt, US Army, 1941-46. F, Amer Psych Assn. Home: 5430 Hawthorne Dr, Indianapolis, Ind. Office: Ind U Med Cent, Indianapolis, Ind.

LEVITT, Norma U, US, communal leader; b. NYC, Aug 11, 1917; d. Henry and Anna (Probstein) Uttal; BA, Wellesley Coll, 1937; m. David Levitt, June 30, 1968; c: Sally Steinberg, Nancy Hoffman, Andrew. Pres, Natl Fed Temple Sisterhoods since 1967; vice pres, J Theatre for Children; dir, Gt Neck Sch of J Studies; pres, Gt Neck Nursery Sch, 1948-49; secy, Wellesley Alumnal Class of 1937, 1957-62; mem, Phi Beta Kappa. Contbr, adult J educ, Sabbath and Confirmation services articles, plays, hymns to J publs. Hobby, sailing. Home: 9 Mitchell Dr, Great Neck, NY. Office: 838 Fifth Ave, New York, NY.

LEVITTIES, Samuel Wexler, US, business exec; b. Phila, Pa, Feb 11, 1899; s. Solomon and Sheva (Wexler); BS, U of Pa, 1922; m. Rose Kahn, Mar 18, 1923; s. Marvin. Exec vice pres, Lane Bryant Inc since 1959, vice-pres, 1946-59; cons: US Natl Recovery Act, 1933-35; US Wage and Hour Div, Dept of Lab, 1938-40; dir, OPA, 1943-46. Mem: bd overseers, JTSA; bd dirs, Har Zion Temple. Spec interests: psych and social service. Home: 1606 Park Towne Pl, Philadelphia, Pa. Office: 1501, Seventh Ave, New York, NY.

LEVOVITZ, Pesach Z, US, rabbi; b. Pol, Sep 15, 1922; s. Reuben and Zlate (Kustanowitz); in US since 1923; ordained rabbi, Mesivtha Tifereth, Jerusalem, 1942; BA, Yeshiva U, 1942; m. Bluma Feder, Feb 4, 1945; c: Sivya Twersky, Yaakov. Rabbi, Cong Sons of Isr, Lakewood, NJ, since 1944; found, headmaster, Bezalel Heb Day Sch, since 1945; chaplain, Lakehurst Naval Air Sta since 1950. Chmn, RabCA, since 1964, chmn educ commn, exec bd, pres, 1966-68; chmn: Lakewood ZC; comty facilities comm, Housing Auth of Lakewood; delg to: Syn Council of Amer; adv comm, Natl Comty Relations Adv Council; mem: Union Orthodox Rabbis, US and Can; Rabb Alumni Yeshiva U; B'nai B'rith; Rel ZOA; ed adv bd, Judaism Series, B'nai B'rith Youth Org; exec bd: Torah Umesorah; Ocean Co council, Boy Scouts of Amer; fmr, vice pres, Rabb Council, NJ. Home: 631 Eighth St, Lakewood, NJ. Study: Cong Sons of Isr, Lakewood, NJ.

LEVTZION, Nehemia, Isr, educator; b. Be'er Tuvia, Isr, Nov 24, 1935; s. Aaron and Penina (Perlow) Lubetski; BA, MA, Heb U, Jerusalem, 1962; PhD, U London, 1965; m. Tirtza Gindel, May 4, 1961; c: Moshe, Osnath. Sr lectr, Afr Hist, Heb U, Jerusalem, since 1969; coord, Afr Studies Dept, since 1967; chief ed, Govt Cen of Info, 1958-60; lectr, Heb U, Jerusalem, 1965-69. Served, IDF, 1953-56. Author: Muslims and Chiefs in West Africa, 1968; The Ancient Kingdoms of Ghana and Mali, 1970. Home: Rabinowitz St, Jerusalem, Isr. Office: Hebrew U, Jerusalem, Isr.

LEVY, Albert G D, US, research exec; b. Berlin, Ger, June 6, 1920; s. Fritz and Susanna (Bergas); in US since 1937; AB, Davis Elkins Coll, W Va, 1938; PhD, intl relations, U Chgo, 1944; m. Sylvia Cohn, May 28, 1946; c: Janet, David, Robert. Pres, Albert Levy Asso, econ planning cons and oprs research, since 1968; commercial policy analyst, US Tariff Commn, 1944-46; co-author, intl dyestuff cartel study, 1945; prosecutor, off, Chief Counsel for War Crimes, Nüremberg, asst prosecutor, intl law adv to prosecution, 1946-47; with US Govt, 1951-57; mem, US negotiating teams, NATO, 1952-57; asst prof, hist, political sci dept, Hiram Coll, O, 1948-51; vice-pres, Marketers Research Service, Inc, Phila, Pa, 1957-58; mgr, prog research, computer and defense sys dept, Gen Elec Co, Wash, DC, 1958-60; rerearch prog mgr, Stanford Research Inst, Wash off, 1960-64; designer, Natl Mil Command Cens; org, Natl Communications Sys, 1964-66; cons, reorg US Civil Defense, 1961-62; sr mem, tech staff, Inst for Defense Analyses, 1964-66; asst dir, Franklin Inst Research Labs, Phila and Wash, 1967-68; org First Natl Consultation on Single Nationwide Emergency Telephone Number, 1968. F, Amer Geog Soc; pres, Forest Glen Citizens Assn; mem: Amer Soc for Public Admn; AAAS; Intl Assn Chiefs Police; exec comm, Allied Civic Group, Montgomery, Md; bldg fund comm, Temple Sinai, Wash, DC; Amer, Intl Political Sci Assns; Amer Soc Intl Law; Intl Law Assn; fmr: Dem candidate for US Reprs, 8th Cong Dist, Md, 1966; neighborhood commn, Boy Scouts of Amer, Silver Spring, Md; clubs: Men's for Heb Home for Aged, Wash, DC; Kiwanis, Garrettsville, O, past mem bd. Contbr to profsl jours. Recipient: U scholar, intl relations, 1942-43, F, 1943-44, both U Chgo. Hobbies: photography, art, music, civic affairs. Home: 9702 Forest Glen Court, Silver Spring, Md.

LEVY, Arnold, US, attorney; b. NYC, Mar 18, 1913; s. Charles and Sadie (Goodstein); BA, CCNY, 1932; LLB, magna cum laude, Harvard Law Sch, 1935; m. Clarice Leiner, Sep 1938; c: Joan Layton, Andrew, Laurie. Partner, law firm; legal positions: US Dept of Justice; Dept of Interior; Securities and Exch Commn, Interstate Commerce Comm of US Sen, 1934-45. Mem: bd, NCCJ, 1963; Wash Heb Cong; AJComm; B'nai B'rith. Home: 3301 Fessenden St, NW, Wash, DC. Office: 1730 K St, NW, Washingtin, DC.

LEVY, Arthur G, US, engineer; b. Rutland, Vt, June 26, 1893; s. Joseph and Gertrude (Peck); PhB, U of Vt, 1916; reg profsl engr, Tex and La; m. Giesella Schwartz, July 14, 1919; c: Gertrude Barnstone. Cons, petroleum and natural gas, since 1946; with Texa Co, 1919-23, 1925-37; independent drilling engr, 1923-25; cons, 1937-38; chief engr, Fohs Oil Co, 1938-46. Lt, US Army, WW I. Mem: Soc of Petroleum Engrs, AIME; Soc Amer Mil Engrs; Amer Assn Petroleum Geologists; Natl and Tex Soc Petroleum Engrs; Amer Petroleum Inst; Houston Engrs Council, 1949-51. Contbr to prof jours. Clubs: Houston; Houston Engrs. Home: 4313 Rossmoyne Blvd, Houston, Tex. Office: POB 66902, Houston, Tex.

LEVY, Azriel, Isr, mathematician, educator; b. Haifa, Mar 14, 1934; s. Shlomo and Sara (Kessman); MSc, Heb U, Jerusalem, 1956, PhD, 1958; m. Neomi Fridman, Oct 25, 1956; c: Efrat, Arnon, Hagit. Prof, chmn, math dept, Heb U, Jerusalem, since 1968, on fac since 1961; visiting asst prof, U of Cal, Berkeley, 1959-61; visiting asso prof, U of Cal, Stanford, 1965-66. Samal, IDF, 1956-57. Council mem, Assn for Symbolic Logic, 1966-69. Ed, Jour of Symbolic Logic; exec ed, Isr Jour of Math; contbr to profsl jours. Home: 25 Alharizi St, Jerusalem, Isr. Office: Heb U, Jerusalem, Isr.

LEVY, Bernard, US, educator, author; b. NYC, Aug 21, 1907; s. William and Fannie (Brody); BA, CCNY, 1925; MA, Columbia U, 1926, PhD, 1930; m. Ruth Kruger, Aug 9, 1946; c: Constance. Prof, Romance langs, CCNY since 1948, dir Sch of Gen Studies, 1948-66, on fac since 1925. Author: The Unpublished Plays of Carolet, a New Chapter on the History of the Theatre de la Foire, 1931; Quince Cuentos Populares, 1939; Present-Day Spanish, 1941, rev, 1941, 1969; A Grammar of Everyday Spanish, 1950, rev 1951; co-author, Modern Spanish Prose Readings from 1830-1930, 1936; contbr to Span and modern lang jours. Mem: AAUP; Romantic Rev; Amer Assn Tchrs of Span. Home: 200 E 71 St, New York, NY. Office: CUNY, New York, NY.

LEVY, Charles S, US, social worker, educator; b. NYC, Feb 22, 1919; s. Hyman and Mollie (Valenci); BSS, CCNY, 1941; MSW, Wayne State U, 1950; DSW, Columbia U, 1958; m. Faye Lewin, Apr 22, 1944; c: Barrie, Helena. Prof, Wurzweiler Sch of Social Work, Yeshiva U, since 1961, asso dean, 1963-66, acting dean, 1962-63; on fac since 1958; prog dir, USO, Anniston, Ala, 1944-46, exec dir, jt agcy opr, Phoenixville, Pa, 1946-47; dir: Mich region, B'nai B'rith Youth Org, 1947-52, NY region, 1952-54; prog dir, armed services div, JWB, 1955-58; visiting prof: Sch of Social Work, U Toronto, 1965-66; Cal State Coll, LA, 1968; cons: leader devl, Cooper Union Coll, 1961-62; Prog for Aged, NYC Comty Mh Bd, 1961. Mem: Sephardic J Brotherhood of Amer; Council on Social Work Educ; Natl Assn Social Workers. Contbr to profsl jours; author of profsl monographs; pub and produc plays and operas. Recipient: F, Council Social Agcys Metrop Detroit, 1948-50. Howe: 75-23 Utopia Pkwy, Flushing, NY. Office: 55 Fifth Ave, New York, NY.

LEVY, Chas, US, business exec; b. Chgo, Ill, Apr 27, 1913; s. Charles and Bertha (Friend); BS, U of Pa, 1935; m. Ruth Doctoroff, Oct 15, 1939; c: Barbara. Chmn bd, Chas Levy Circulating Co. Served, Lt col, US Army, 1942-45. Bd dirs: J Fed Metrop Chgo since 1959; Young Men's J Council, 1935-41; Temple Sholom, 1947-51; Mt Sinai Med Research Found, 1951-53; Park View Old Peoples Home, 1953-55; mem, exec comm, Chgo chap, ADL, 1957-61; pres, Mid-Amer Periodical Distributors, 1959 unit chmn, Chgo Comty Fund Dr; clubs: Bryn Mawr Country; Standard, Mid-Amer;

Exec. Home: 1000 Lake Shore Plaza, Chicago. Ill. Office: 1200 N Branch St, Chicago, Ill.

LEVY, Claude, Fr, researcher; b. Hanoi, Vietnam, Oct 7, 1930; d. Pierre and Manuelle (Brody); licenciée ès lettres, Sorbonne, Paris. I/c research, Institut National d'Études Démographiques, Paris. Co-author, Le Controle des Naissances—Histoire, Philosophie, murale, 1966; contbr, articles on demography to various jours. Mem, Racing club, Fr. Hobby: tennis. Home: 63, rue de la Faisanderie, Paris 16, Fr. Office: INED, 23 Roosevelt Ave, Paris, Fr.

LEVY, David M, US, psychiatrist, educator; b. Scranton, Pa, Apr 27, 1892; s. Benno and Sarah (Breakstone); AB, Harvard U, 1914; MD, U Chgo, 1918; m, Adele Rosenwald, June 2, 1927. Pvt practice NYC since 1933: clinical prof, psycht, Columbia U, 1944-57; att psycht, NY State Psycht Inst, 1949; att psychan, Psychan Clinic for Training and Research since 1945; cons, Henry Ittleson Cen for Child Research since 1956; res phys, Chgo Psychopathic Hosp and Cook Hosp, 1918-20; instr, criminology, U of Ill, 1920-22; acting dir, Ill Inst for Juvenile Research, 1923; lectr, psycht, U Chgo, 1923-27; att neur and dir, mental hygiene, clinic for children, Michael Reese Hosp, 1923-26; lectr, Smith Coll, 1924-30; chief, staff, NY Inst for Child Guidance, 1927-33; lectr, New Sch for Soc Research, 1928-39; instr, NY Psychan Inst, 1936-41; cons psycht in personnel, Off Strategic Services, 1944-45; dir, Infantry Control Div Screening Cen, Ger, 1945-46. Mem: Natl Adv Mh Council, USPHS, 1946-48; Inst for Advanced Study, Princeton U, 1951-53; f: NY Acad Med; NY Acad Sci; Assn for Psychan and Psychosomatic Med; fmr pres, Amer Psychoanalytic Assn; mem: Amer Psych Assn; Amer Neur Assn; Assn Research in Nervous and Mental Diseases; Natl Comm for Mental Hygiene; NY Neur Soc; NY Soc for Research in Child Devl; NY Soc for Clinical Psycht; Assn for Psychan Med, AMS. Author: Sibling Rivalry, 1937; Maternal Overprotection, 1943; New Fields of Psychiatry, 1947; Behavioral Analysis, 1958; Demonstration Clinic, 1959; contbr to prof jours. Recipient: cert, Natl Bd Med Examiners, 1920; Amer Bd Psycht, 1936. Home: 993 Fifth Ave, New York, NY. Office: 47 E 77 St, New York, NY.

LEVY, Eli B, US, attorney; b. NYC, Sep 22, 1909; s. Louis and Mary (Klode); BS, NYU, 1929, JD, Law Sch, 1932; m. Sylvia Goldstein, Nov 19, 1931; c: Lynn Zaubler. Pvt practice since 1933; lectr, dept psycht, SUNY Med Coll, since 1961; asst atty gen, State of NY, 1934. Chmn, bd trustees, Barnard Sch for Boys, since 1959; hon pres, Heb Kindergarten and Infants Home, since 1960, pres, 1956-60; chmn, exec bd, United Heb Comty of NY, since 1960; mem: Amer Bar Assn; NY Co Lawyers Assn; fmr: pres, Freedom Lodge, B'nai B'rith; chmn: W Side Sch Comty Cens; coord council, NYC Police Dept. Home: 2 Sutton Pl S, New York, NY. Office: 136 Church St, New York, NY.

LEVY, Ernest, Switz, musicologist, composer; b. Basel, Switz, Nov 18, 1895; s. Benjamin and Rosy (Dreifuss); att Basel Conservatory, Basel U; m. Else Hammerschlag, 1928; c: Matthys, Frank; m. 2nd, Mary Fassett, 1952; m. 3rd, Suzanne Loetscher, June 4, 1958. Ret; prof music, Bklyn Coll, 1959-66; piano master, Basel Conservatory, 1916-20; conductor, Paris Philharmonic Choir, 1928-40; instr: NE Conservatory of Music, Boston, 1941-45; Bennington Coll, 1945-49; profsl lectr, U Chgo, 1949-54; prof musicology and chorus conductor, Chgo Musical Coll, 1952-54; prof music, MIT, 1954-59. Composer: symphonies and other compositions; contbr to musicological mags. Mem: Schweizer Tonkünstlerverein. Home: Chemin de Joulens, 1110 Morges, Switz.

LEVY, Frank H, Australia, business dir; b. St Kilda, Vic, Aug 31, 1904; s. Alfred and Berthy (Moody); att: S Melbourne Coll, 1912-17; Wesley Coll, 1917-21; m. Lola Hannah, Dec 12, 1928; c: June, Robin, Bruce, Pamela. Dir, Sun Elec Co, Pty Ltd, Melbourne, since 1936; insp, Liverpool & London & Globe Ins Co, Ltd, Melbourne, 1922-36. Press: Australian, 1939-40, Victorian, 1937-39, Hockey Assns; St Kilda Heb Cong, 1949-50, treas, 1951-52; clubs: Melbourne Cricket; Amateur Sports of Vic; Royal Auto of Vic. Home: Flat 15, Greenways, 515 Toorak Rd, Toorak, 3142, Victoria, Australia. Office: 562 Lt Bourke St, Melbourne, C1, Victoria, Australia.

LEVY, Geoffrey, NZ, physician; b. London, Eng, Nov 9, 1915; s. Barnett and Rachel (Caplan); in NZ since 1947; att: Kings Coll and Westminster Hosp, London; MB, BS; m. Marta Mannasse, Sep 9, 1939; c: Vernon. Pvt practice. Served MC: RAF, Royal NZ Air Force. Pres, Auckland Zionist Soc; mem:

Royal Coll of Surgs; Royal Coll Phys; Med Assn of NZ; Royal Coll Gen Practitioners; exec, ZC of NZ; B'nai B'rith. Home: 170 Upland Rd, Remeura, NZ. Office: 99 Main Highway, Ellerslie, NZ.

LEVY, Harold, Eng, educator; b. Ayr, Eng, June 26, 1909; s. Morris and Eva (Hoppenstein); MA, Glasgow U, 1931; m. Hannah Silverman. Insp, Cen Council J Rel Educ since 1951; org, J Youth Study Groups since 1951; hon warden, J Coll since 1957. Author: Hebrew for All, 1950; contbr to J jours. Home: Jews Coll, 11 Montagu Pl, Eng. Office: Woburn House, Upper Woburn Pl, London, Eng.

LEVY, Harry, US, mathematician, educator; b. Boston, Mass, Jan 9, 1902; s. Philip and Jette (Levine); BA, Harvard U, 1920, MA, 1923; PhD, Princeton U, 1924; m. Lucretia Switzer, Aug 1, 1928. Prof math, U of Ill, since 1951, mem fac, since 1927; NRC F, 1924-27. Mem: Amer Math Soc; Math Assn Amer; Phi Beta Kappa; Sigma Xi. Contbr in field of geometry. Home: 712 W Nevada St, Urbana, Ill. Office: U of Illinois, Urbana, Ill.

LEVY, Harry, Isr, business exec; b. Ger, Nov 20, 1898; s. Moritz and Rosa (Leeuwarden); in Isr since 1933; m. Rose Casper; c: Kurt. Pres, Melonot Ltd, fmr Isr Hotel Mgmt Ltd, since 1948; in hotel ind, Ger, 1919-32; gen mgr, Kallia Seaside and Health Resorts, 1933-48; co-found, gen mgr, Sharon Hotels Co, 1948-68. Contbr articles on econ and hotel mgmt problems. Home: 5 Rupin St, Tel Aviv, Isr.

LEVY, Henry W, US, publicist; b. NYC, Apr 7, 1908; s. Joseph and Hattie (Wollreich); BCS, NYU, 1930; m. Mildred Nebb, Dec 16, 1940; c: Jeffrey. PR dir, JA, Isr-Amer Sect, since 1963; coll corresp, NY Post, 1927-29; theatrical publicity: Civic Repertory Theater; Provincetown Playhouse; Morris Gest, 1930-31; asst mgn ed, Amer Heb mag, 1931-33; mem, staff, publicity dept, United Artists Pictures, 1933; Amer news ed, JTA, 1933-35; publicity dir: ORT, 1935-36; JTSA, 1936-37; CJA, Boston, 1939-44; reporter, Rel News Service, 1938; mem, educ dept, AJComm, 1938-39, dir, NE regional off, 1939-44, pr dir, 1944-45; pr dir, Natl Council J Women, 1945-46; owner, Henry W Levy Assos, PR, 1946-50; dir, comty and pr, Assn J Charities and Wfr Fund, Baltimore, 1950-56; ed, Phila J Exponent, 1956-58; comty relations dir, Amer-Isr Cultural Found, 1959-62; asso dir, E and Middle Atlantic States, dept U resources, Brandeis U, 1962-63. Publicity chmn, Md Council Social Wfr, 1951-54; mem, adv comm, Gov McKeldin's Md Comm on Admn Reorg; PR Council Baltimore; pres, Amer J PR Soc, 1965-67; clubs: Quill Soc, NYU, Alpha Phi Sigma; mem, ed bd, J Social Service Quarterly, 1951-56; book rev, Baltimore Sun; contbr ed, Universal J Ency; contbr to periodicals. Recipient, excellence of achievement in TV, CJFWF, 1952, 1953. Home: 190 Duxbury Rd, White Plains, NY. Office: 515 Park Ave, New York, NY.

LEVY, Irvin, US, ophthalmologist; b. Trenton, NJ, Dec, 31· 1909; s. Isaac and Anna (Sykes); AB, U of Pa, 1930; MD, Georgetown U, 1934; c: Beth, Ellen. Pvt practice since 1938; asst ophthal, St Francis Hosp; ophthal cons: Hunterdon Med Cen; Donnelly Memorial Hosp; Princeton Hosp; Orthopedic Hosp; Trenton Gen Hosp; asst surg, Wills Eye Hosp. F: Amer Coll Surgs; Intl Coll Surgs; mem: Amer Acad of Ophthal and Otolaryngology; Pan Amer Assn Ophthal and Otolaryngology; NJ Ophthal Soc, pres 1957. Home: 34 Richley Pl, Trenton, NJ. Office: 383 W State St, Trenton, NJ.

LEVY, Isaac, Isr, singer, musician, journalist; b. Magnasia, Turkey, May 15, 1919; s. Daniel and Behora (Abastado); in Isr since 1922; att music conservatories: Tel Aviv, Jerusalem. Dir: Ladino Dept, Shidurei Isr, since 1955, Musical Folklore Dept, since 1963. Author: Chants Judéo-Espagnols, Vol 1, 1959, Vol II, 1969; Antologia de Liturgia Judéo-Española, 4 Vols, 1964-69. Numerous appearances: concert halls, radio, TV: Isr, Spain, Arg, Chile, Uruguay, Brazil, Venezuela, Curacao. Hobbies: hist, lit. Home: 31 Bethlehem St, Jerusalem, Isr. Office: Kol Isr, Heleni Hamalka St, Jerusalem, Isr.

LEVY J, Aaron, US, rabbi; b. Little Rock, Ark, Jan 7, 1904; s. Alexander and Julia (Goldman); ordained rabbi, HUC, Cincinnati, O, 1930, hon DD, 1959; m. Pauline Wise, June 15, 1932; c: Jacqueline Mayer. Rabbi: Temple Sinai, Sumter, SC, since 1949; Temple Isr, Stockton, Cal, 1930-47; Dallas, Tex, 1947-49. Chaplain, US Army, 1943-46. Bd mem, Sumte Co Mh Assn; mem, operating comm, USO; club, Rotary. Spec interest, pastoral psych. Home: 32 Frank Clarke St, Sumter, SC. Study: Temple Sinai, Sumter, SC.

LEVY, Jack H, US, radiologist, educator; b. Norwood, Ga, Aug 15, 1913; s. Samuel and Clara (Zelkin); MD, U of Ga Sch of Med, 1936; c: Sue-Robin. Asso prof, Med Coll of Ga since 1948; pvt practice since 1947; cons, Ga Regional Hosp; asst radiologist, Mt Sinai Hosp, NY, 1940-42; chmn, radiology dept, U Hosp; cons, St Joseph's Hosp; sr cons VA Hosp, all Augusta, Ga, asst prof, clinical radiology, Yale U Sch of med; chief radiologist, VA, Newington, Conn, both 1946-47; radiologist: Jefferson Hosp, 1949-52; Richmond Co Bd Health, 1950-52; Screven Co Hosp, 1952-53; Mt Sinai Hosp Unit, 3rd Gen Hosp, 1942-44; Regional Hosp, Fort McClellan and Foster Gen Hosp, 1944-46. US Army MC, 1942-46. F, Amer Coll Radiology, 1959; dipl, Amer Bd Radiology, 1940; fmr pres, Augusta Little Sym Orch; chmn, profsl educ div, Amer Cancer Soc, Richmond County Unit; mem: Radiological Soc N Amer; NY Acad Scis; Ga Radiological Soc; AMA; AHA; S Med and Ga Med Assns; Richmond Co Med Soc; Intl Soc Who's Who; Amer Phys F for IMA; contbr to med jours. Hobby, flying. Home: 3062 Hillsdale Dr, Augusta, Ga. Office: 1425 Gwinnett St, Augusta, Ga.

LEVY, Jack I, US, attorney; b. Brownsville, Pa, Aug 22, 1910; s. Morris and Belle (Wise); AB, U of Mich, 1931, JD, 1934; m. Harriet Mindich, June 11, 1943; c: Margaret, James. Dir, vice-pres, Gen Amer Transp Corp since 1959; asso, partner, Sonnenschein, Levinson, Carlin, Nath & Rosenthal, 1935-39. USAAF, 1942-45. Contbr to law and bus jours. Home: 825 Roslyn Pl, Evanston, Ill. Office: 120 S Riverside Plaza, Chicago, Ill.

LEVY, Jerome S, US, physician, educator; b. Morganfield, Ky, Sep 27, 1902; s. Phillip and Hattie (Sickles); BS, Wash U, 1923; MD, 1925; m. Marion Lee, June 15, 1946; c. Carol, Jere-Jane. Pvt practice since 1929; clinical prof, med, U Ark Sch of Med since 1950, on fac since 1929; asst surg, Wash U, 1925-26. Lt Col, US Army Res. Chmn: Regional Med Prog Adv Council since 1967; Cen Ark Comprehensive Health Planning Council since 1968; life mem, bd, Temple B'nai Isr, Little Rock since 1946; mem: Amer Gastroenterological Assn; AMA; Amer Coll of Gastroenterology; Art State Med Soc; B'nai B'rith; fmr: gov for Ark, Amer Coll Phys; natl bd, AJComm; vice-pres, JWB, Little Rock; treas, exec comm, SW States region, CJFWF; bd dirs, Natl TB Assn. Contbr to med jours. Home: 3 E Palisades Dr, Little Rock, Ark. Office: 500 S University Ave, Little Rock, Ark.

LEVY, Joe Seween, S Afr, attorney; b. Aliwal N, S Afr, Aug 10, 1912; s. Julius and Olga (Matz); m. Ethel Solomons, Dec 22, 1935; c: Shirley, David, Miriam. Atty and notary public since 1934, sworn appraiser, dir of cos; Mayor, Uitenhage 1950-52 and 1960-62, dep mayor 1948-50, 1958-59, 1968-69; chmn, finance comm, Uitenhage Council 1946-50, 1952-60 and since 1962; Pres, United Munic Exec of S Afr since 1962; Uitenhage Heb Cong 1945-49; Boy Scouts Assn since 1955; exec mem: Cape Midland Devl Assn since 1950; Rhodes U Council since 1951; J Bd Deps, 1943-49; clubs, Rotary. Home: 17 Barkly St, Uitenhage, S Afr. Office: 2 Church St, Uitenhage, S Afr.

LEVY, Joseph, Isr, actor, playwrite; b. Jerusalem, Aug 19, 1919; s. Aharon and Ester (Slotky); att Yeshiva Etz Chaim, Jerusalem; div; c: Yoav. Found, Bimat Hashnaim Theatre, now Dorot Theatre; mem, mgmt, repertory comm, Matateh Theatre; actor: Matateh, Ohel, Dorot Theatres; performed in plays: Chaiot haNegev; Al Yeladim veAnashim; Al Banot veZanchanim. Home: 28 Rosh Pinah St, Tel Aviv, Isr.

LEVY, Julius, US, attorney; b. NYC, Feb 15, 1913; s. Samuel and Esther (Pashman); AB, U Miss, 1934; LLB, Columbia Law Sch, 1937; m. Jane Frederick, Nov 7, 1940; c: Frederick, Douglas. Partner, Pomerantz, Levy, Haudek & Block since 1937. Lt jg, USNR, 1944-46. Vice-pres, dir, U Settlement House, NYC; mem: Assn Bar, NYC; NY Co Lawyers Assn. Home: 320 W 87 St, New York, NY. Office: 295 Madison Ave, New York, NY.

LEVY, Leonard W, US, historian, educator; b. Toronto, Can, Apr 9, 1923; s. Albert and Rae (Williams); in US since 1924; att U of Mich, 1940-43; MA, Columbia U, 1948, PhD, 1951; m. Elyse Gitlow, Oct 21, 1944; c: Wendy, Leslie. Dean, Grad Sch Arts and Sci, Earl Warren prof, Amer constitutional hist, Brandeis U since 1958, fac mem since 1951. US Army, 1943-46. Mem: Amer, Miss Valley Hist Assns; Amer Studies Assn; Amer Soc for Legal Hist. Author: The Law of the Commonwealth and Chief Justice Shaw, 1957; Legacy of Suppression: Freedom of Speech and Press in Early American

History, 1960; Major Crises in American History, 1962; Jefferson and Civil Liberties: The Darker Side, 1963; Judicial Review and the Supreme Court, 1967; Origins of the Fifth Amendment: The Self-Incrimination Clause, 1968; contbr to legal, hist jours. Recipient: Guggenheim f, 1957-58; Frank Luther Mott award, best research in journalism, 1961; Sigma Delta Chi prize, 1961. Hobby: philately. Home: 149 Wood St, Lexington, Mass. Office: Brandeis, U Waltham, Mass.

LEVY, Maurice L, US, business exec, engineer; b. Rochester, NY, June 28, 1902; s. Simon and Bertha (Lewis); BS, Union Coll, 1924; m. Miriam Baker, June 28, 1928; c: Richard. Vice-pres, engr, Emerson TV Corp since 1959, with firm since 1943; cons, TV lab, Philco Co, 1949-50. Sr mem, Inst of Radio Engrs. Contbr to engr jours. Holder of many patents. Home: 336 Creek Bed Rd, Mountainside, NJ. Office: 14 and Cole St, Jersey City, NJ.

LEVY, Michael H, US, business exec; b. Sep 16, 1913; s. Milton and Hannah (Gans); BS, U of Pa, 1932; MS, Columbia U, 1936, MA, 1948; PhD, NYU, 1946; m. Helen Green; c: Miles, Lora Weisman, Michele. Pres and found, Standard Security Life Ins Co of NY; found, Federated Brokerage Group Inc and all subsidiary cos; hon dep commn, borough works, Borough of Manhattan, NYC. Sponsor, NYC Public Service Awards for Profsl Achievement. Mem: Life Underwriters Assn of NY; Ins Fed of NY; Vets Assn 12th Infantry, 77th Div Assn; 12th Regiment Vets Office Assn; KP; B'nai B'rith; Better Bus Bur, NY; NY C of C; pres council, Amer Inst of Mgmt; Natl Sales Exec Club; life, US Flag Assn; Sons of Confederate Vets; Ins Soc of NY; Citizens Union, NYC; NY Soc Mil and Naval Offs WW's; Res Offs Assn; Natl Off Mgmt Assn; Natl Ind Conf Bd Inc; Metrop Mus Art; Amer Mus Natural Hist; Natl PR Council Health and Wfr Services Inc; Amer Forestry Assn; Friends City Cen; Amer Sym Orch Guild. Author: Your Insurance and How to Profit By It, 1955; A Handbook of Personal Insurance Terminology, 1968; contbr of articles to mags and jours. Recipient, spec award from Pan Amer Med Assn for devl of family cancer care ins and creation of Polio ins. Home: 300 Central Park W, New York, NY. Office: 111 Fifth Ave, New York, NY.

LEVY, Milton, US, biochemist, educator; b. St Louis, Mo, July 13, 1903; s. Herman and Jennie (Levanthal); BS, Wash U, 1925; PhD, St Louis U, 1929; m. Helen Class, Oct 26, 1924; c: Robert, Rosalyn Wood (decd). Prof, biochem, NYU Coll of Dent since 1956, fac mem since 1930; f, med sci, Harvard U, 1929-30; served Off sci Research and Devl, 1942-46; cons, Va since 1953. Chmn, Research, Educ Comm, Bx VA since 1961; selection comm, med sci f, NRC, 1960-65; mem: Amer Soc Biol Chem; Amer Chem Soc; Harvey Soc; Soc Experimental Biol Med; NY Acad Sci; Sigma Xi; Research Soc of Amer. Contbr to profsl jours. Recipient: Guggenheim f, 1956; Gt Tchr Award, NYU, 1964. Dist Alumnus, Wash U, 1967. Home: 39-95 48 St, Sunnyside, NY. Office: NYU, Coll of Dent, 421 First Ave, New York, NY.

LEVY, Milton L, US, business exec; b. La Grande, Ore, May 21, 1917; s. Gus and Gertrude (Fuchs); BS, U Ore, 1941; MJ, U Cal, 1949; m. Dorothy Cameron, Jan 18, 1943; c: David, Charles. Exec vice-pres, Cal Service Agcy; mgr: Cal Farm Network since 1954; radio stas, KLX, KLX-FM, Oakland, Cal, 1952-54; news ed, KBKR, Baker, Ore, 1945-47; advt mgr, KBKR andore Trail Network, 1947-52. Cdr, USNR; public info off, 1942-45; lt cdr, 1961-62. Pres, Golden Gators Chap, Res Offs Assn of US; dir, Baker Co Comty Chest; commanding off, Elec Warfare Platoon, Baker; mem: Sigma Delta Chi; Kappa Tau Alpha, past pres; Ore U Alumni Assn; Elks; clubs; Baker Co Knife and Fork, past pres; Commonwealth, bd govs; Baker Golf and Country; Press Union League. Ed, publisher: Honor Awards Handbook; Media Awards Handbook; contbr to profsl jours. Recipient: WW II medals: Naval Res, Victory, Pacific area, Amer Defense, Armed Forces Res; citations: Ore Advt Club, 1950; Billboard Mag, 1952; Cal State Fair, 1956; Natl Safety Council, 1960. Home: 621 Sheri Lane, Danville, Cal. Office: 2855 Telegraph Ave, Berkeley, Cal.

LEVY, Moise, Congo, rabbi, educator; b. Rhodes Island; s. Meir and Reyna (Piha); att: Rabb Coll, Rhodes, 1932-37; ordained rabbi: by Chief Rabbi Ben Zion Ouziel, Jerusalem; Chief Rabbi, Rishon-le-Zion; studied Roman law; m. Felicia Piha, Dec 12, 1937; c: Rivka, Meir, Malca, Eliezer. Chief rabbi, J Cmty of Congo and Ruanda-Urundi since 1953; prof, Inst Intl, Elizabethville since 1960; prof rel, Kiwele Coll, Lubumbashi, 1969; rel functionary, Congregation

Israelite, Katanga, 1937-53; fmr: prof, hist of rel, Inst Maria Jose and Coll St Francois de Sales; lectr, Fac de Theol Protestante and Coll St Gregorie le Grand. Mem: hon comm, Congres d'Institut Intl de Civilisations Differentes; asso, Union des Assns Intls since 1961; referee mem, Acad de Droit Intl, The Hague; 20th Cong, Nobel Inst, Oslo, Nor. Recipient: Medaille du Prince Charles, 1944; Medaille du Roi Baudouin I, 1956; Cavaliere Ufficiale al merite, Rep It; Knight Order Natal du Leopard au Merite from Pres, Rep of Congo, 1966; Commendatore nell' Ordine al Merito, It Rep, 1968. Home: 70 av Delcommune, Elizabethville, Congo. Study: BP 617, Elizabethville, Congo.

LEVY, Mordecai, US, rabbi; b. Malden, Mass May 28, 1928; s. Albert and Florence; BJ Educ, Heb Tchrs Coll, 1948; BS, Northeastern U, 1948; MHL ordained rabbi, JTSA, 1952; ThM, S Baptist Theol Sem, Louisville, Ky, 1964; m. Rana Kempler, Dec 25, 1955; c: Baruch, Ramni. Rabbi, Phila, since 1968; educ dir, Temple on Hgts, 1956-61; columnist, Las Vegas Israelite. Chaplain, USAF 1952. Pres, JNF Louisville: natl exec, ZOA since 1960; pres, Valley Region, 1962-64, vice-pres, NE Region 1965-68, pres, ZC, Cleveland, 1956-61; mem: Ky Civil Rights Commn; RA; club, Rotary. Home: 6209 N 13 St, Philadelphia, Pa. Study: York and Stenton, Philadelphia, Pa.

LEVY, Morris J, Isr, surg; b. Rousse, Bulgaria, July 23, 1925; s. Joseph and Ester; MD, U Sofia, Bulgaria, 1950; MSc, U Minn, 1963; m. Sylvia Levy; c: Alon, Joseph, Guy. Prof, surg, head, thoracic cardiovascular surg dept, Beilinson Hosp, since 1964; fmr asst prof, surg, U Minn. IDF, MC, 1952-53. Prin contrib: 1st in Isr to do hum lung transplant. Mem: IMA; Isr Surg Soc; Isr Thoracic Surg Soc; Soc Thoracic Surg, US: Amer Coll Chest Phys; Amer Coll Card. Contbr numerous sci articles. Home: 50 Beeri St, Tel Aviv, Isr. Office: Beilinson Hosp, Petah Tikva, Isr.

LEVY, Morris L, US, surgeon; b. London, Eng, July 4, 1890; s. Charles and Betsy (Cohen); in US since 1899; MD, NYU and Bellevue, 1913; postgrad studies, U Vienna, 1929-30; m. Hannah Tobias, Jan 8, 1922; c: Theodore, Allan, Gerald. Cons surg: Maimonides Hosp since 1940; att surg 1940-56; J Hosp for Chronic Diseases since 1952, att surg, 1936-52; extern, Beth Isr Hosp, NYC, 1913; mem, staff, NYC Dept of Health, 1915-18; asst surg, Beth Moses Hosp, 1920, adj, 1929, asso, 1930, att, 1940. Lt, US Army MC, 1918-19, capt, US Med Res, 1919-24. Dipl, Amer Bd Abdominal Surg, 1967; f, Amer Coll Surgs, 1934. Mem: Kings Co and NY State Med Socs; AMA; Kings Co chap, Amer Coll Surgs, Bklyn Surg Soc; Alumni, J Hosp of Bklyn; NYU Alumni; Zeredetha Masonic Lodge; club, Phys Sq. Contbr to med jours. Hobbies: boating, fishing, amateur farming. Home and office: 1 St Pauls Ct, Brooklyn, NY.

LEVY, Ori, Isr, actor; b. Tel Aviv, Isr, Oct 30, 1931; s. Meir and Bronia (Zak); att Mikve Isr Sch; m. Talila Ben Zaccai, Dec 26, 1954; c: Roni. Actor, Cameri Theatre, Tel Aviv. IDF, 1947-49. Maj roles on stage: Marius; A Man for All Seasons; Spring Fever; Hedda Gabler; in films: Noon 02; The Chairman; Before Winter Comes; Eldorado; Kol Mamzer Melech; Hu Halach baSadot. Mem: ITI, Isr; Variety 51. Hobby, collecting cartoons. Home: 16 Dafna St, Tel Aviv, Isr. Office: Cameri Theatre, Tel Aviv, Isr.

LEVY, Raphael, US, philologist; b. Baltimore, Md, Nov 4, 1900; s. Max and Dora (Pollack), 1922, PhD, 1924; Cert, U Paris, 1923; m. Helen Silverman, June 30, 1929; c: Manford, Jerome. Prof, Fr, U Tex, since 1962; on fac since 1946; instr, U Wis, 1924-29; asst prof: U Baltimore, 1931-43; La State U, 1943-46. Mem: ZOA; MLA; S-Cen MLA; Société des Anciens Textes Français; Société de Linguistique Romane; Société Romania, club, Fortnightly. Author: Astrological Works of Abraham Ibn Ezra, 1927; Recherches Lexicographiques sur d'Anciens Textes Français d'Origine Juive, 1932; Li Coronemenz Loois: Glossaire, 1932; Repertoire des Lexiques du Vieux Français, 1937; Contribution à la Lexicographie Française, 1960; Trésor Langue Juifs Français Moyen Age, 1964; contbr numerous articles, revs to phil jours. Home: 5509 Shoal Creek Blvd, Austin, Tex. Office: U of Tex, Austin, Tex.

LEVY, Raphael, US, public relations exec; b. Hartford, Conn, Apr 2, 1909; s. Albert and Charlotte (Schechter); BS, NYU, 1932; m. Florence Cooper, Dec 23, 1934; c: Frank, Joan. dir public affairs, UJA since 1968; vice-pres, Hal A Salzman Assos, 1936-39; staff writer, AJComm, 1940-41; publicity

dir, Natl Ref Service, 1941-43; news ed, master radio desk, feature writer, Eng sect, OWI, 1943-45; publicity dir, JDC, 1945-51; PR dir, UJA, 1951-68; PR assignments: Intl Conf J Relief and Rehab, Paris 1948; Jerusalem Econ Conf, 1953; annual UJA overseas missions, 1955-68; press repr, fmr Isr PM David Ben Gurion during 80th birthday visit to US, 1970. Found, Amer J PR Soc, 1957; exec comm, Natl Council J Audio-Visual Materials since 1951. Author of film scripts. Recipient: award for outstanding film of J interest, 1964-65. Home: 22 Pinecrest Pkway, Hastings-on-Hudson, NY. Office: 1290 Ave of the Americas, New York, NY.

LEVY, Rene Emil, Switz, business exec; b. Basel, Switz, Apr 30, 1932; s. Gaston and Susanne (Bollag); att, HS of Commerce; m. Doris Ulimann; c: Simone, Manuel. Mgn dir, Regent Lighting Fixtures since 1965. Pres, Lighting Assn, Switz; local leader, mem, Swiss bd dirs, UJA; mem: bd, Social Aid Service, Basel; B'nai B'rith, Basel. Spec, interests: activities connected with support of Isr; violin. Home: 15 Oberer Rebbengweg, Reinach, Switz. Office: 390 Dornacherstr, Basel, Switz.

LEVY, Robert J, US, stockbroker; b. New Orleans, La, Aug 31, 1902; s. Sylvan and Helen (Newburger); BA, cum laude, Harvard U, 1923; m. Patricia Schwartz, Mar 8, 1927; c: Ann Eliasoph. Partner, Robert J Levy & Co since 1932; chmn, pres, Standard Gas & Elec Co since 1953; chmn of bd, Standard Shares Inc; chmn, admn off, Bd Econ Warfare, 1942; chief liason off, OPA, 1943. Lt col, US Army, 1943-45, liaison off between Gen Eisenhower and Gen de Gaulle. Bd trustees: FJP; Heb Tech Inst; club, Wall St. Recipient: Legion of Honor, 1945; Croix de Guerre, 1945; OBE, Eng, 1945. Home: 1185 Park Ave, New York, NY. Office: 44 Wall St, New York, NY.

LEVY, Robert L, US, physician, educator; b. NYC, Oct 14, 1888; s. Louis and Harriet (Strouse); AB, Yale U, 1909; MD, Johns Hopkins Med Sch, 1913; m. Beatrice Straus, June 29, 1920; c: Barbara, Gerald, Jessica. Cons phys, Presbyterian Hosp, NYC, since 1954, asso att and att phys, 1922-54, dir, dept of card, 1925-54; on staff, Johns Hopkins Hosp and U, 1914-16, 1916-17; res phys, Rockefeller Inst Hosp, 1919-20, asso in med, 1919-22; cons card, Roosevelt, French, White Plains, Englewood hosps, NY; on fac, Columbia U since 1922, prof clinical med and prof em since 1954. Capt, US Army MC, 1917-19; cons in card to Secy of War, WW II. F: Amer Coll Phys; NY Acad Med, past pres; mem: AMA; NY Heart Assn, past pres; Amer Clinical and Climatological Assn, past pres; Amer Soc Clinical Inves; Assn Amer Phys; Amer Soc for Phar and Therapeutics; NY State Med Soc; Phi Beta Kappa; Alpha Omega; clubs: Grolier; Cent, NYC; Pilgrims. Co-author, Nomenclature and Criteria for Diagnosis of Diseases of the Heart, 1928; ed: Diseases of the Coronary Arteries and Cardiac Pain, 1936; Disorders of the Heart and Circulation, 1951; mem, ed bd, Amer Heart Jour; contbr to profsl jours. Home: 720 Park Ave, New York. NY.

LEVY, Robert Stanley, US, attorney; b. Scranton, Pa, June 27, 1933; s. Jacob and Mary (Feuerman); AB, U of Pa, 1955; LLB, Harvard Law Sch, 1958; m. Ceil Nagelberg, July 23, 1956; c: Jay, Sander, Mitchell. Pvt practice; admitted to: State of Fla; Pa Supr and Superior Courts; US Dist Court, S Dist, Fla. Active in J Fed, Palm Beach Co; exec comm mem: Fla Regional Bd, ADL; Palm Beach Chap, AJComm; pres, B'nai B'rith, Palm Beach, 1963-64; vice-pres, chmn bd, Temple Beth El, 1963-64, bd dirs, 1959-66; sponsored Isr Bonds, 1964-66; mem: JDC; Regional Bd, Rivergarden Home for Aged, Jacksonville, Fla; Natl Young Leadership Cabinet, UJA; Amer, Palm Beach Co, JR and SR Bar Assns; Beta Sigma Rho; Upsilon Lambda Phi; Amer Trial Lawyers Assn; Lawyers' Title Guarantee Fund; hon mem: Pi Gamma Mu; Pi Sigma Alpha. Recipient: Outstanding Leadership Award, UJA, 1967. Home: 407 Oyster Rd, N Palm Beach, Fla. Office: 302 Citizens Bldg, W Palm Beach, Fla.

LEVY, Samuel K, US, physician; b. NYC, Mar 31, 1894; s. Abraham and Ida (Kantor); MD, LI Coll Hosp, 1916; post-grad study, ped: Vienna, Berlin, Hanover, 1930; m. Florence Bloom, June 4, 1930 (decd); c: Joel, Audrey. Chief att ped, secy, med bd, Linden Gen Hosp since 1958; att ped, Bklyn Infants Home, since 1920, pres, med bd, 1942-47; asso att ped, Maimonides Hosp, Bklyn since 1931, em since 1969; Post Co and dist surg, VFW, since 1937, dept surg, 1939-42, 1966-68; chief, ped, Bushwick Hosp, 1954-57; Natl Surg Gen, VFW, 1967-68; vice-chmn, VFW Natl Hosp Comm, 1968. Lt, US, Army MC Res, WW I; examining phys, local draft bd since WW II; natl surg, Natl Assn 6th div, US Army 1941-45. Prin contribs: inventor, electrically illuminated vaginoscope, 1929; applied slip-joint principle to surg instruments. Pres: Flatbush Comty Council, 1957-66; ped sect, Kings Co Med Soc, 1947-48; delg, NY State conv, 1960-61; Natl VFW delg to Natl ARC Conv, 1968; mem, bd, Bklyn Assn Neighborhood Groups; mem: life, Med Assn of Vienna; Aus; AMA, LI Coll and Mt Sinai Hosps Alumni Assn; NY State Med Soc; ARC; Elks; Masons; Red Mogen David for Isr; Soc of Old Brooklynites; elected supr surg, MOC, VFW, 1958, delg, LA conv, 1959. Contbr to med and lay jours. Recipient, Vet of the Month for NYC. Hobby: collecting old stethoscopes and old and odd tablespoons. Home and office: 1694 Nostrand Ave, Brooklyn, NY; Country home: Island Park, NY.

LEVY, Shlomo, Isr, organization exec; b. Berlin, Ger, Aug 26, 1922; s. Jacob and Fanny (Farntrog); in Isr since 1939; m. Lea Hoenig, Mar 12, 1946; c: Etan, Jacob, Joram. Secy gen, Hakibbutz Hadati, rel kibbutz movement, since 1966; mem, bd dirs, Bank Adanim; fmr, treas, secy, Kibbutz Beerot Yitzchak. Served Haganah, IDF. Fmr mem: Zionist Action Comm, repr to N Amer. Contbr to kibbutz movement publs. Spec interests: hist, lit, Judaism. Home: Kibbutz Beerot Yitzchak, Isr. Office: 7 Dubnov St, Tel Aviv, Isr.

LEVY, Sol G, US, business exec; b. London, Eng, Aug 2, 1891; s. Morris and Sophia (Sasieni); in US since 1904; m. Sadie Shore, Aug 12, 1912; c: Leon, Sybil Tall. Pres, CAB Import and Export Co, Seattle since 1951; sr partner, mgr, Commission Co, Inc, wholesale grocers since 1918. Area chief food coord, Wash State Civil Defense since 1954; found, trustee, Wash State Intl Trade Fair; pres: World Scouting Volunteers since 1961; World Friendship Soc, 1950-62; Seattle Park Bd, 1953; Park Bd Commn, 1951-55; Temple De Hirsch, 1954, trustee, 1948-59; chmn, postwar goodwill tour to Far East, 1950; mem: exec bd, Found for Intl Understanding of Amer; entered scouting, 1921, exec bd, pres, Chief Seattle Council, Boy Scouts, 1947-48, mem, region XI exec comm and mem natl exec bd, 1954-57; found, Alpha Phi Omega, Phillippines, 1950; mem: Japan Soc; Masons, Elks; Pan-Xenia; B'nai B'rith; clubs: China, trustee, exec bd, past pres; Glendale Golf and Country. Recipient: Silver Beaver, Silver Antelope, Silver Buffalo, all from Boy Scouts of Amer; medal of appreciation, Govt of Japan, 1950; citation: Govt of Korea, 1950; sr Citizen of Year, Freedom House, 1967. Home: 1000 Eighth Ave, Seattle, Wash. Office: 4100-4 South, Seattle, Wash.

LEVY, Sol J, US, business exec; b. Merzig, Ger, Mar 28, 1885; s. Samuel and Amelia (Joseph); in US since 1892; m. Blanch Bergman, Nov 30, 1916; c: Richard, Claire, William (decd). Pres: Bergman Distributors Inc since 1948; W Bergman Co Inc since 1948, bd chmn; Solrich Assn Inc; treas, Seneva Audio-Visual Corp. Pres: Temple Beth Zion, Buffalo, NY, 1949-51; J Wfr Soc, Buffalo, 1933-36; J Fed for Social Services, Buffalo, 1936-42; Comty Fund, 1956-57; vice-pres, chmn allocations comm, United Fund of Eric Co; chmn, exec comm, Buffalo chap, AJComm, 1949-50; found, charter mem, Bur of J Educ; mem, exec bd: UAHC; Buffalo chap, NCCJ; Buffalo BBB; bd trustees, Comty Chest; mem: B'nai B'rith; Buffalo C of C; club, Montefiore, fmr pres. Home: 800 W Ferry St, Buffalo NY.

LEVY, Stella, Isr, ret army officer; b. Haifa, Isr; att HS, Haifa. Attache, Isr Emb, Wash DC, since 1970; fmr: col, cdr in chief, Isr Women's Army Corps, 1964-70; joined Brit Army, ATS, 1942; IDF, 1948, with first offs group; mem, Gen Hqr, Office: Embassy of Isr, Washington, DC.

LEVY, Tibbie, US, artist (pen name, **Lysan**); b. NYC, Oct 29, 1908; d. David and Minnie (Hoffman) Goldstein; AB, Cornell U, 1928, LLB, Law Sch, 1930; DJ, NYU Law Sch, 1931; m.; c: Lynn Zaubler. One-man shows: NYC, 1960, 1962, 1964, 1965; Pa, 1960; Madrid, 1962, 1963; London, 1963, 1965; represented in perm collections: U's: Colgate; Princeton; Rutgers; Syracuse; Fairleigh Dickinson; Brandeis; Cornell; Boston U Collection, Mass; Queens Coll, NYC; Norfolk Mus, Va; Cen Syn, NYC; Ga Mus; Swope Mus, Terre Haute; Mus Modern Art, Miami, Fla; Phoenix Mus of Art, Ariz; J Mus, HUC, Cincinnati, O; Whitte Mus, San Antonio, Tex; Evansville Mus, Ind; Ark Art Cen; Hinckhouse Collection of Contemporary Art, Coe Coll, Ia; George Peabody Mus, Nashville, Tenn; Wash Co Mus Art, Md; Mus Contemporary Art, Madrid, Spain; Mus Modern Art,

Barcelona, Bilbao, both Spain; Contemporary Art Soc of Gt Brit. Home and studio: 2 Sutton Pl S, New York, NY.

LEVY, Walter, US, physician, educator; b. NYC, Nov 23, 1899; s. Jacob and Annie (Freeman); BS, NYU, 1922, MD, Coll of Med, 1924; m. Gertrude Finkelstein, July 28, 1939; c: James. Cons, peds, Morrisania City Hosp since 1951 1950-62, dir, 1962-63; asso, 1933-50; dir em, cons, ped, J Mem Hosp since 1969, att ped, 1951-64, asso, 1926-51, dir, 1964-69; asso att ped, Riverside Hosp, 1931-42; att ped: Isr Orphan Asylum, 1944-56; Seton Hosp, 1948-50; asst prof, peds, NY Med Coll, 1948-52, asso clinical prof, 1952-62. Lt, US Army, Med Res, 1918-19. Designer, Infa Rule. F: Amer Acad of Peds; fmr: pres: med bd J Mem Hosp; NYU Coll Med Alumni Assn; Bx Ped Soc; Sigma Lambda Pi; dir, NYU Alumni Fed; mem: US Comm for Care of Eur Children; U Coll, NYU visiting comm; exec comm, NYU Med Cen campaign; a found, NYU Bellevue Hosp Med Cen; AMA; NY Co Med Soc; Milah Bd, NY; infant mortality comm, NY Co Med Soc; J Acad of Arts and Scis; Phi Epsilon Pi; Alpha Omega Alpha, NYU; perstare et praestare, hon mem, Masons; club, Medallion. Asso ed, J Memorial Hosp Bull since 1955; contbr to med jours, sci exhbs: Grad Fortnight, NY Acad of Med, 1940; State Med Soc, Wis, 1942; Recipient: AMA award, original sci inves, 1942; NYU Alumni meritorious service award, 1950; NYU pres citation, 1962. Home: 130 E 75 St, New York, NY. Office: 12 E 88 St, New York, NY.

LEVY, Walter J, US, economic cons; b. Hamburg, Ger, March 21, 1911; s. Moses and Bertha (Lindenberger); in US since 1941; LLD, U of Kiel, Ger, 1932; m. Augusta Sondheimer, Apr 11, 1942; c: Robert, Susan. Independent cons since 1949; cons: State Dept, off Under Secy and Asst Secys since 1960; asst to ed, Petroleum Press Bur, London, 1936-41; free-lance econ, NYC, 1941-42; chief, petroleum sect, Off of Strategic Services, Wash, DC, 1942-45; mem, enemy oil commn, Jt Chiefs of Staff, 1943-45; US delg, trade discussion with Swed, 1945; US world prog group on petroleum, 1945; asst, off of intelligence research, State Dept, 1945-48; mem, State Dept delg for oil discussion UK, 1946; petroleum adv, US delg, Aus Treaty Commn, 1947; cons, State Dept, Pres's Commn on Fgn Aid, 1948; fgn econ adv, Socony Vacuum Oil Co, 1948; chief, oil br, Econ Coop Admn, 1948-49, cons, 1949-51; econ cons, Natl Security Resources Bd, 1950-53; Pres's Materials Policy Commn, 1951; adv to Avere.l Harriman on mission to Iran, 1951; cons; policy planning staff, State Dept, 1952-53; Intl Coop Admn 1956-57; State Dept and Off of Civil and Defence Mobilization, 1960; Off of Emergency Planning, 1962; Oil Adv to Spec Emissary of Pres Kennedy to Pres of Indonesia, 1963; Adv to Eur Econ Comty, 1965; mem: adv council to Sch of Advanced Intl Studies, Johns Hopkins U; Comm on Social Scis of Yale U Council. Mem: Council on Fgn Relations; Amer Econ Assn. Contbr to profsl jours. Recipient, Pres Cert of Merit for WW II services, 1947. Spec Plaque, US Secy of State, 1968; Dato Setia Laila Jasa, Brunei, 1968; Order of Taj, Iran, 1969. Office: 30 Rockefeller Plaza, New York, NY.

LEVY, Willard Linz, US, business exec; b. St Louis, Mo, June 8, 1914; s. Mont and Elma (Linz); att, U of Pa; m. Alice Rudolph, Aug 7, 1964; c: Elma Lippman, Jill Petzall. Pres, Angelica Corp, since 1946, mem, bd dirs, with corp, since 1934; mem bd dirs: Commercial Bank of St Louis Co; Health Inds Assn; Bank of St Louis. Mem: bd dirs: J Hosp, St Louis; Span Intl Pavilion Found; United Fund Gtr St Louis; bd mgrs, Cen Inst for Deaf; St Louis Bd Munic Hosps; exec comm, Regional Heart, Cancer and Stroke Prog; natl exec comm, and natl vice-pres, AJComm; St Louis Port Commn; task force, Mo Emergency Planning Comm; life, bd dirs, J Fed, St Louis, past pres. Recipient: 1968 Hum Relations Award, AJComm; appt Hon Col of Mo by Gov Warren Hearnes. Home: 21 Spoede Lane, Crève Coeur, Mo. Office: 700 Rosedale Ave, St Louis, Mo.

LEVY, Yehoshua, Isr, organization exec; b. Jerusalem, 1905; att: Yeshivat, Etz Hayim, Mea Shearim; Commercial HS; m. Temima Brizman. Treas, Histadrut, since 1963, mem gen comm; secy, Hapoel Hatzair, Jerusalem, 1925-30; agric dept, JA, 1931-36; secy, mgr, PAZA, 1936-46; mem presidium, treas, Jerusalem Comty, 1936-46; on JA missions to DP camps: Ger, Aus, 1947-48; secy gen, Union of Public Service in Isr, 1949-60; on missions for Histadrut dr abroad; delg: 23rd, 24th, 25th WZCs; Intl Workers Congs. Contbr to jours. Office: Histadrut, 93 Arlosoroff St, Tel Aviv, Isr.

LEWIN, Fred, US, rabbi; b. Chgo, Ill, July 7, 1937; s. Samuel and Betty (Goldstein); att Heb Theol Coll, Chgo, Ill, 1950-56; ordained rabbi, Ner Isr Rabb Coll, Baltimore, Md, 1962; m. Bluma Yoffee, June 7, 1960; c: Samuel, Jonathan. J chaplain: Lackland Air Force Base, Tex, since 1962; El gin Air Force Base, Fla, 1962-64; asst rabbi, Beth Isr Syn, Omaha, Neb, 1965; J chaplain: Philippines, Taiwan, Thailand, 1966-68. Adv, San Antonio Hillel Counselorship; Air Force coord, J Armed Services Comm of San Antonio; mem: Assn J Chaplains, Armed Forces; Kallah of Tex Rabbis, San Antonio chap. Author: Symbolic Rituals of Judaism, 1963; film, The Air Force Rabbi, 1964. Recipient: Commendation Medal, USAF, 1965, 1968. Hobbies: travel, reading. Home: 206 Fairchild, San Antonio, Tex. Office: Lackland Air Force Base, San Antonio, Tex.

LEWIN, Herbert, Ger, physician; b. Schwarzenau, Apr 1, 1899; s. Isidor and Bertha (Wittkowski); MD, U Berlin, 1924; m. Alice Lewin, Sep 24; 1925; m. 2nd, Irma Sternberg, Apr 18, 1947; c: Margerit-Beate. U prof since 1967; fmr: chief phys: Jüdische Gemeinde Berlin, Krankenhilfe, 1935-37; Israelitische Krankenhaus, Cologne, 1937-41; prof: U of Cologne; Frankfurt/M, 1948; phys, Cologne, 1946-49; chief phys, dir, Staedtische Frauenklinik, Offenbach, 1950-67. Chmn, mem, Zentralrat der Juden in Deutschland. Author: Die Cyclushormone des Weibes, 1951: Die biologischen Schwangerschaftsreaktion Handbuchbeitrag in Biologie des Weibes, 1957. Home: 11 Tulpenhofstr, Offenbach/M, Ger. Office: Waldstr 32, Offenbach/M, Ger.

LEWIN, Itzhak M, Isr, rabbi, legislator; b. Goor, Pol, 1894; in Isr since 1940. MK (Agudath Isr) since 1949, fmr Min of Social Wfr. Chmn, world exec, Agudath Isr since 1939, co-found, pres, Pol, br; fmr mem, Rehab and Aid Comm for Eur Jewry. Home: 28 Malachi St, Jerusalem, Isr. Office: Agudath Isr, POB 326, Jerusalem, Isr.

LEWIN, Menachem, Isr, scientist; b. Sokoly, Pol, Mar 26, 1918; s. Itzchak and Fryda (Bialodvorski); in Isr since 1937; MSc, chem, Heb U, Jerusalem, 1945, PhD, 1947; m. Rachel Joachimowicz, Sep 30, 1944; c: Dorith, Itzchak, Judith. Dir, Inst for Fibers and Forest Products Research, since 1954; fmr: research asso, Heb U, 1945-49; prin research off, Research Council of Isr, 1949-54; reader, tech chem, Heb U; visiting sci, IP Stevens Research and Devl Div, Garfield, NJ. Lt, IAF, 1948-49. Prin contribs: chem, physio-chem, tech research on: halogen chem, cellulose, cotton, wool, wood, bleaching, fire retardation; obtained numerous patents; inventor: permanent flame-proofing and rot resisting of wood, wood products; shrink-proofing of wool with bromates; utilization of sisal waste and extraction of hecogenin; research in: oxidation and yellowing of cellulose; nitration of wood; bromine-chlorine chem. F, Textile Inst; mem, Isr, Amer Chem Socs; fmr: chmn, Jerusalem br, Isr Chemn Soc; mem, panel, wood chem, Food and Agric Org, UN, Rome. Mem ed bd: Cellulose Chem and Tech, intl jour: Isr Jour of Tech; contbr numerous publs to profsl jours. Recipient: prize for outstanding research on cellulose chem, U of Geneva, Switz, 1959. Home: 16 Hillel St, Jerusalem, Isr. Office: 3 Emek Refaim St, Jerusalem, Isr.

LEWIN, Michael L, US, surgeon; b. Warsaw, Pol, Nov 18, 1909; s. Leon and Rose (Maliniak); in US since 1934; MD, U Zurich, 1933; m. Berta Rabinoff, Aug 26, 1940; c: Robert, Barbara. In pvt practice since 1935. cons, plastic surg: Sydenham Hosp, NY; Morrisania City Hosp, NY; att, i/c plastic surg, Montefiore Hosp; sr att plastic surg, St Joseph's Hosp, Paterson, NJ; cons: Barnert Memorial Hosp, Paterson since 1947; Englewood Hosp, Englewood, NJ, since 1953; asst to Dr JW Maliniac, 1935-41; research asst, surg path, Mt Sinai Hosp, 1939-42; chief, plastic surg and maxillo-facial sect, Hammond Gen Hosp, Modesto, Cal, 1942-43; asst chief: Bushnell Gen Hosp, Brigham City, Utah, 1943-44; Cushing Gen Hosp, Framingham, Mass, 1944-46; att plastic surg, i/c sect, Halloran VA Hosp, Staten I, NY, 1947-57. Maj, US Army MC, 1942-46. Chmn, plastic surg sect, NY Regional Soc Plastic Surg, past pres; f: Amer Coll Surgs; NY Acad Med; Intl Coll Surgs; dipl: Amer Bd Otolaryngology; Amer Bd Plastic Surg; mem: Amer Soc Plastic Surgs; Amer Soc Surg of the Hand; Acad Ophthal and Oto-Rhino-Laryngology; Soc Mil Surgs; asso, Brit Soc Plastic Surgs; Amer Assn Plastic Surg; NY State Med Soc; Amer Cleft Palate Assn, intl abstracts ed, jour of assn; mem, med mission to Isr, 1952; hon mem, Isr Plastic Surg Soc. Contbr to med jours. Home: 40 Lydecker St, Englewood, NJ. Offices: 3353 Bainbridge Ave, Bronx, NY; 707 Broadway, Paterson, NJ.

LEWIN, Seymour Zalman, US, chemist, educator; b. NYC, Aug 16, 1921; s. Charles and Ida (Lazarov); BS, CCNY, 1941; MS, U Mich, 1942, PhD, 1950; m. Pearl Godman, Oct 17, 1943; c: David, Jonathan. Prof, chem, NYU, since 1960, research prof, conservation, 1965-68, mem fac since 1952. Prin contribs: inventor, methods for preservation of artistic, historic objects; research on molecular structure. Lt, chem corps, USAAC, 1942-46. Mem: Amer Chem Soc; AAAS. Author: Chemists' Dictionary; ed, Art and Archeology Tech Abstracts, 1966-69; contbr numerous articles to sci jours. Recipient: A Cressy Morrison prize, NY Acad Sci, 1954; K Fajans prize, U Mich, 1957. Home: 4 Washington Sq Village, New York, NY. Office: 4 Washington Pl, New York, NY.

LEWIN-COHEN, Pinchus Jacob, Isr, educator; b. Gur, Pol, Nov 30, 1900; s. Henach and Faiga (Alter) Hersh; desc of Sfat Emes, Chidushey Harim, rabbis of Gur and Reb Henech of Alexander; in Isr since 1940; m. Sarah Lewin, 1947; c: Chanoch, Simcha. Dean, Beth Jacob Tchrs Training Inst, since 1942; ed, Beth Jacob Jour, since 1959; mgr, Eretz Yisrael Dept, Agudath Isr Org, Pol, 1920-1939. Mem, exec bd, Agudath Isr World Org, since 1937. Author, educ books. Hobby: art. Home: 25 Amos St, Jerusalem, Isr. Office: Brandeis St, Jerusalem, Isr.

LEWIN-EPSTEIN, Jacob, Isr, dentist; b. Jerusalem, Jan 22, 1920; s. Samuel and Madeline (Epstein); att U Mich, Ann Arbor, 1939-42; DDS, U Pa, Phila, 1944; cert, oral surg, Columbia U, NY, 1948; m. Marian Stormwind, Feb 12, 1950; c: Noah, Eliahu, Naomi. Pvt practice since 1950; head, dept oral surg, Heb U-Hadassah Sch of Dent, Med, since 1955. Capt, US Army, 1944-46; IDF, 1948-49. Mem: Intl Coll Dents; Intl Assn Oral Surg; Intl Assn Dent Research; Amer Coll Dents; fmr: Alpha Omega frat, regent, dist 20, Isr; chmn, Jerusalem br, Isr Dent Assn. Contbr articles to profsl jours. Home: 2 Masaryk St, German Colony, Jerusalem, Isr. Office: Heb U-Hadassah Sch of Dental Med, Jerusalem, Isr.

LEWINSKY, Akiva, Isr, banker; b. Geneva, Switz, June 9, 1918; s. Mendel and Marie (Pottasch); in Isr since 1934; grad HS of Commerce, Tel Aviv, 1936; m. Ruth Rummelsburg, July 2, 1943; c: Vered, Igal. Dir, Bank Hapoalim Ltd; mgn dir, Nir Ltd, both since 1961; dir of cos; adv on workers' banks, OAS; fmr: dir, econ dept, Ihud Hakvutzot; perm repr, Intergovt Comm, Eur Emigration, Govt of Isr; Eur dir, Child and Youth Aliyah; dir: inves fund, Histadrut; Ind Services Ltd; mem, bd dirs, Intl Coop Bank, Basel; instr, Youth Aliyah, Kiriat Anavim; head, youth aliyah dept, Hever Hakvutzot; delg, Youth Aliyah, Istanbul; spec envoy, govt repr, Paris, Geneva. J Settlement Police; Haganah; IDF. Treas, mem secretariat, Zionist Lab Movement; dir, mgn dir, Fritz Naphtali Found; mem: perm comm, budget and finance, Zionist Actions Comm; Kibbutz Maayan Zvi, past treas, secy; fmr: mem exec: Gordonia Makkabi Hatzair Movement; Hever Hakvutzot; Ihud Hakvutzot Vehakibbutzim; delg to ZCs. Author: Bank Hapoalim, 1968. Home: Kibbutz Maayan Zvi, Isr. Office: 28 A Rothschild Blvd, Tel Aviv, Isr.

LEWINSON, Fritz A, Isr, publisher, business exec; b. Berlin Ger, May 24, 1906; s. Shlomoh and Agnes (Wohlfarth); in Isr since 1936; att Sch of Econ, Berlin; m. Irene Weinstock, Dec 23, 1934; c: Noemi Peltz, Edna Amir. Mgn dir, Isr Periodicals Co Ltd, since 1946; bd mem, co's of Tel Aviv Munic; lectr on econ issues. Lt, IDF. Chmn, Isr Periodicals Assn; mem, Isr Export Council; dir, Maccabiah Village Comm. Contbr to trade jours. Hobbies: sports, politics. Home: 32 Frug St, Tel Aviv, Isr. Office: 13 Montefiore St, Tel Aviv, Isr.

LEWINSON, Ruth, US, attorney; b. NYC, July 1, 1895; d. Benno and Fanny (Berliner); BA, Hunter Coll, 1916; DJ, NYU Sch of Law, 1919. Practising atty since 1920; mem, firm, Lewinson & Lewinson, 1927-35, sr mem, Lewinson, Lewinson & Fieland, 1937-57; spec examiner for Solicitor Gen of candidates of govt legal positions, WW II. Dir: Northrup Memorial Camp since 1951; and treas, NY Co Lawyers Assn, since 1935; trustee, Hunter Coll Student Social and Rel Clubs, since 1942; mem: Bd of Higher Educ of NYC, 1921-39; Hunter Coll Alumni Assn, past pres; Phi Beta Kappa. Author: Happy Days, Verses for Children, 1929; Happy Days—Happy Songs, 1957; contbr to legal jours Hobby: painting. Home: 17 W 71 St, New York, NY. Office 41 E 42 St, New York, NY.

LEWINSON, Sam, US, business exec; b. Ashburn, Ga, June 21,

1914; s. Mendel and Annie (Greenberg); AB, U of Fla, Gainesville, 1935; post-grad, S Coll Pharm, Atlanta, Ga, 1935-36; m. Alice Lewin, July 3, 1965; c: Nancy, Sally. Exec pres, Commercial Mills; pres, S & L Sales Corp since 1969; secy, treas, Antigua Mills since 1969; secy, treas, Margate Mills since 1968; treas, N Ga Ind Devl Corp since 1966; mgr, Friendly Dept Store, 1937-44; partner, Blue Ribbon Mills, 1944-45; pres, Royal Mills, 1945-67; exec, K & W Mfg Co, 1960-68; partner, Rafer Co of Alanta, 1961-63; dir, Ten Investors, Inc, 1965-68. Mem: BPOE, Lodge 1267; Masons, Scottish Rite; fmr: vice-pres, secy, Dalton Jaycees; treas, Dalton B'nai B'rith. Hobbies: tennis, chess, football, fishing. Home: 1410 Belmont Drive, Dalton, Ga. Office: POB 547, Dalton, Ga.

LEWIS, Bernard I, US, physician, educator, researcher; b. Winnipeg, Can, May 21, 1916; s. Isaac and Rose (Fields); in US since 1948; BA, Queen's U, Kingston, Ont, 1939, MD, 1943; m. Barbara Tennant, Dec 8, 1946; c: Douglas, Richard. Metabolic Sect, Dept Internal Med, Palo Alto Med Clinic, Cal, since 1956; research asso, Palo Alto Med Research Found, since 1956; asso prof, med, U Iowa, staff, U Hosp since 1955, on leave since 1956, asso in med, 1952, asst prof, 1952-55, dir, psychosomatic prog, internal med dept since 1950; asst phys, Johns Hopkins Hosp, 1948-50; asst clinical prof, med, Stanford U, 1956. Capt, Royal Can Army, MC, 1944-46. Dipl: Royal Coll Phys of Can, 1949; US Natl Bd Med Examiners, 1949; Amer Bd Internal Med, 1953; f: Royal Coll Phys, Can, 1949; Amer Coll Phys, 1952; mem: AMA; Amer, Cal Heart Assns; Council on Arteriosclerosis, AHA; Cal Med Assn; Cal Acad Med; Johns Hopkins Med Soc; Amer Fed Clinical Research; W Soc Clinical Research; Sigma Xi. Contbr to profsl jours. Home: 295 Cervantes Rd, Portola Valley, Cal. Office: 300 Homer Ave, Palo Alto, Cal.

LEWIS, David, Can, barrister at law; b. Swislocz, Pol, June 23, 1909; s. Morris and Rose (Lazarowitch); BA, McGill U, Montreal, 1931; Rhodes scholar, BA, Oxford U, 1932-35; m. Sophie Carson, Aug 15, 1935; c: Stephen, Michael, Janet, Nina. Counsel, with firm, Armstrong & MacLean; fmr partner, law firm, Joliffe, Lewis & Osler. Dep leader, New Dem Party, since 1962, elected natl vice-pres when party was formed; mem regional exec, Can J Cong; fmr: natl secy, natl pres, natl chmn, Coop Commonwealth Fed; vice-pres, Ont Woodsworth Memorial Found; elected to House of Commons, Ottawa, as mem for NY State, 1962, defeated in subsequent Fed election. Co-author: Make This Your Canada, 1943. Home: 138 Rodney Crescent, Ottawa, Ont. Office: 111 Richmond St W, Toronto, Ont, Can.

LEWIS, Emanuel P, US, business exec; b. Baltimore, Md, May 3, 1903; s. Joseph and Bertha (Westheimer); att: CCNY; NYU, both 1935; m. Frances Donner, Feb 14, 1934; c: Richard, Susan. Pres: Shapiro Bros, Factors Corp, since 1958; Factors Comm, Shapiro Factors Div, Chase Manhattan Bank; dir, Interstate Dept Stores. Mem, NY Credit Men's Assn. Hobbies: art, photography. Home: 21 E 87 St, New York, NY. Office: 1441 Broadway, New York, NY.

LEWIS, Nettie Marie, US, attorney; b. Indianapolis, Ind, Oct 19, 1919; d. Elias and Lillian (Pasvoll) Dulberger; LLB, Natl U Law Sch, 1942; m. Arthur Lewis, June 11, 1944; c: Elise, Barbara. Staff atty, Legal Aid Soc, 1958-68. Bd dir: J Social Service Agcy; J Comty Cen; Wash Heb Cong; fmr pres: Service Guild of Wash; Sisterhood, Wash Heb Cong; Murch Home and Sch Assn; mem: DC Women's Bar Assn; Dept Public Wfr Adv Comm. Hobbies: golf, bowling. Home: 4714 Linnean Ave NW, Washington, DC.

LEWIS, R Duffy, US, business exec; b. NYC, Aug 26, 1908; s. Samuel and Jennie (Bach); AB, Columbia Coll, 1929, LLB, 1931; m. Minna Margulies, 1935; c: Donald, Jane. Pres, chmn bd, McCrory Intl Corp, since1968; cons, pres, S Klein Dept Stores, 1966-67, merchandise cons, 1960-65; exec vice-pres, Alexander's Dept Stores, 1931-59; columnist: Haire Publ, since 1962; Women's Wear Daily, 1960-61; inventor, Duffy's Protector. Found, Infants & Children's Wear Buyers Assn, 1941, hon pres since 1943; bd dirs, Merchandising Natl Retail Merchants Assn; chmn, fgn relations comm, Amer Retail Fed, 1969; mem: Tau Epsilon Phi; clubs: Elwood Country; Columbia U. Author: How to Keep Merchandising Records; Lewis Merchandise Control Kit; Lewis OPA Price Control Kit; co-author: How to Build an Infant's, Girl's & Teen's Business; What Every Retailer Should Know About the Law. Recipient: commendation cert, NY State Dept of Commerce. Home and office: 1050 Fifth Ave, New York, NY.

LEWIS, Reuben R, US, physician, anesthesiologist; b. Montreal, Can, Nov 30, 1910; BSc, McGill U, 1932, MD, CM, 1937; post-grad studies: Beth Isr Hosp, Newark, NJ; St Mary's Hosp, Montreal; U of Ill Research and Educ Hosps, Chgo; cert, anesthesiology: Royal Coll Phys and Surgs, Can; Amer Bd Anesthesiology; m. Beatrice Pont; 2 c. Pvt practice; staff mem: St Vincent's Hosp; Cal Lutheran Hosp; Hollywood Presbyterian Hosp; Glendale Memorial Hosp; att asst clinical prof, dept surg, div anesthesiology, U of Cal, LA. Capt, Royal Can Army, MC, 1942-46. Prin contrib, devl of anesthesia dept of Heart Surg Prog, St Vincent's Hosp, 1957. Mem: Sinai Temple; Can Soc of LA; McGill U Grad Soc, fmr pres, S Cal br, fmr repr, W Coast; f: Amer Coll Anesthetists; Amer Coll Card; Phi Delta Epsilon; clubs: LA Rod & Reel; Profsl Men's. Office: 336 S Roxbury Dr, Beverly Hills, Cal.

LEWIS, Theodore N, US, rabbi; b. Russ, July 6, 1899; s. Nathan and Esther (Novack); in US since 1903; BA, U Cincinnati, 1924; ordained rabbi, HUC, 1924, DD, 1934; m. Dorothy Rothchild, Oct 25, 1925; c: Ruth Gelernter. Rabbi: Shaarei Zedek Syn, fmr Progressive Syn, Bklyn, NY, since 1939; Temple Adath Isr, Lexington, Ky, 1925-26; Mt Sinai Cong, Sioux City, Ia, 1926-39; chaplain, US Mil Acad, W Point, 1942-43. Mem: CCAR; ZOA; NY Reform Rabbis Assn; past pres, NY Bd Rabbis. Author: My Faith and People; contbr to: Currents and Trends in Contemporary Jewish Thought; Anglo-J press; fmr, contributing ed, The Reconstructionist. Home: 858 E 26 St, Brooklyn, NY. Study: 1395 Ocean Ave, Brooklyn, NY.

LEWISON, Edward F, US, surgeon, educator, researcher; b. Chgo, Ill, Feb 11, 1913; s. Maurice and Julia (Trocky); BS, U Chgo, 1932; MD, Johns Hopkins U, 1936; m. Elisabeth Oppenheim, (decd); c: John; m. 2nd, Betty Fleischmann, Mar 31, 1948; c: Edward, Robert, Richard. Asst prof, surg, Johns Hopkins U, since 1954, surg, chief, breast clinic, since 1949, on staff since 1936; f, surg, Beth Isr Hosp, NYC, 1939-40; asso cons, Sinai Hosp, Baltimore, 1944. Lt col, US Army MC, 1941-45. Pres, Amer Cancer Soc, Md div, 1966-68; vice-chmn, Intl Ref Comm on Breast Cancer; f: AMA; Amer Coll Surgs; Royal Soc Med; dipl, Amer Bd Surgs; bd trustees: NY Acad Sci; Park Sch, Baltimore, 1951. Author: Breast Cancer and Its Diagnosis and Treatment, 1955; contbr to profsl jours. Home: 7501 Park Heights Ave, Baltimore, Md. Office: 550 N Broadway, Baltimore, Md.

LEWITON, Jacob, US, jurist; b. Malden, Mass, Sep 25, 1908; s. Harris and Rebecca (Schriro); AB, Tufts Coll, 1930; LLB, Harvard Law Sch, 1933; m. Bernice Goldman, Dec 16, 1951; c: Marvin, Cynthia, Barbara. Judge, Boston Munic Court, since 1948; atty since 1933; spec counsel to Gov of Mass, 1947; asst atty-gen, Mass, 1941-42. Lt-cdr, USNR, 1942-45. Fmr vice-pres and trustee, Combined J Appeal, Gtr Boston; trustee: Combined J Philanthropies, Gtr Boston; J Memorial Hosp, Boston; Tufts Coll, Mass; J Family and Children's Service; mem: examining comm, Boston Public Libr; Mass, Boston, Bar Assns; ZOA. Author: Trials in Municipal Courts, 1951. Home: 92 Shaw Rd, Belmont, Mass. Office: Boston Munic Court, Boston, Mass.

LEWITTES, Mendell, Isr, rabbi, author; b. NYC, Dec 2, 1912; s. Max and Dora (Weberman); in Isr since 1969; BA, Yeshiva Coll, 1932; ordained rabbi, Rabbi Isaac Elchanan Theol Sem, 1933; MA, Harvard U, 1945; hon DD, Yeshiva U, 1963; m. Ethel Drazin, Feb 6, 1936; c: Joseph, David, Jewel, Rhona. Ret rabbi: Young Isr of Montreal, 1949-1969; Portland, Me J Comm, 1936-42; Cong Beth El, Dorchester, Mass, 1942-49. Pres, Rabb Council of Can, 1963; vice-pres, RabCA, 1943-44. Author: Vol XII, Yale Judaica Series: The Book of Temple Service; Yeshiva U Studies in Torah Judaism; The Nature of Jewish Law; ed, Rabbinical Council Sermon Manual, 1944. Home: 18 Rabbi Berlin St, Jerusalem, Isr.

LEWITTES, Mordecai H, US, rabbi, educator; b. Bklyn, NY, Apr 18, 1911; s. William and Bertha (Arm); BS, CCNY, 1931; MHL, ordained rabbi, JTSA, 1935; att Heb U, Jerusalem, 1933-34; m. Laura Cohen, 1937; c: Hedva, Don. Prin, NY Sch of Printing, since 1967; rabbi: Temple Isr, Hazelton, Pa, 1935-37; i/c Heb educ, Bklyn J Cen, 1937-60; instr, Heb, Eng, Thomas Jefferson HS, 1947-53; chmn, acad subjects, Sarah Hale Vocational HS, 1953-64; HS coord, Bur Curriculum Devl, 1962-64; lectr: Hunter Coll, 1961; CCNY, 1962-63; prin, Enrico Fermi Jr HS, Bklyn, 1964-65; dir, NYC-Ford Found Correlated Curriculum Project, 1966-67; pioneer of Heb educ in public HS. Pres, Amer Assn Tchrs of Heb, 1941-42; chmn, Solomon Schechter HS, Bklyn Bd

Educ, since 1967; mem: bd govs, J Tchrs Comty Chest; RA; NY Bd Rabbis; Natl Council J Educ; ZOA; Natl Assn Secondary Sch Prins. Author: The Student Bible, 1950, vol II, 1952, vol III, 1962, vol IV, 1965; Heroes and Highlights of Jewish History, 1952, vol II, 1953, vol III, 1955, vol IV, 1957; Alpon, My Hebrew Primer, 1962; co-author: Select Readings in Hebrew Literature, 1942; Modern Hebrew, 1946, rev, 1963; Readings to Enjoy, 1967. Hobby: golf. Home: 4555 Henry Hudson Pkwy, Bronx, NY.

LEWITUS, Zygmunt, Isr, physician; b. Tlumacz, fmr Pol, May 18, 1914; s. David and Lola (Haber) Haliczer; desc of Berl Locker; in Isr since 1944; MD, U Vienna, 1938; att Inst of Nuclear Sci, Oakridge, 1952; m. Dora Inslicht, Aug 1, 1938 (decd). Head, dept med, chmn, sect of med, Beilinson Hosp, Petach Tikva since 1955; chmn, nuclear med sect, Tel Aviv U Med Sch since 1967. Capt, MC, IDF, 1964. Prin contrib: research in phys of thyroid gland. Secy, Isr Endocrinology Soc; mem: secretariat, Assn of Phys, Histadrut; adv comm on cancer, Min of Health; Intl Soc Internal Med; NY Acad Sci; Soc Nuclear Med, US; Eur Thyroid Assn. Author: Advances in Thyroid Research, 1961; Current Topics in Thyroid Research, 1965; Life Assurance Medicine, 1968; contbr to sci, profsl jours. Recipient: Meir Prize, 1959; Zondek Prize, IMA, 1963; Lab Prize, Histadrut, 1967. Hobbies: painting, lit, theater. Home: 32 Bloch St, Tel Aviv, Isr. Office: Beilinson Hosp, Tel Aviv, Isr.

LEWKOWICZ, Nesanel Chaim, Belgium, organization exec; b. Warsaw, Pol, Feb 4, 1897; s. Jacob and Chaja (Rubin); in Belgium since 1920; att Yeshiva; studied fgn langs in pvt; m. Ruth Holcberg, June 19, 1935. Pres: Gen Zionists, Belgium; Union of Gen Zionists, Brussels; mem, Belgian exec, WJC; admnr, Friends of Youth Aliyah; fmr, pres: Belgian ZF; KH, Belgium. Delg: ZCs, 1958-68; Intl Confs, KH; fmr: org, orphanage, under Ger occupation, mem J Defense Comm; comm mem, Ecole Israélite de Bruxelles. Pub, sections of Babylonian Talmud: Baba Kamah, 1952; Baba Metziah, 1961; Brachot, 1967, all in Yiddish; trans Gmara into Yiddish. Recipient: decoration, Résistance Belge. Spec interests: J and Zionist subjects. Home and office: 44 rue de l'Est, Brussels, Belgium; 5 Zichron Ya'akov St, Tel Aviv, Isr.

LEWKOWICZ, Ruth, Belgium, accountant-secy; b. Warsaw, Pol, Aug 16, 1908; d. Moszek and Marjem (Kaufman) Holcberg; att HS, commercial, Warsaw, Pol; m. Nesanel Lewkowicz, June 19, 1935. Treas, WIZO, Brussels, with soc since 1936; active in Resistance, Belgium, 1940-45. Hobby: Zionist activities. Home: 44 rue de l'Est, Brussels 3, Belgium; 5 Zichron Ya'akov St, Tel Aviv, Isr.

LEWY, Hermann (pen names: **Eduardo Sanchez, Israel Weyl),** Ger, journalist; b. Berlin, Mar 1, 1906; s. Moritz and Anna (Fraenkel); att Gymnasium, Berlin; m. Gerda Brieger; c: Anna. Ed-in-chief: Allgemeine Unabhängige Jüdische Wochenzeitung, Düsseldorf, Berlin; Jüdische Illustrierte, Düsseldorf. Author: Die Endlösung im Spiegel des Nürnberger Prozesses, 1960; ed: Karl Marx, Brüscken schlagen, 1962; Diverse Anthologies: Max Brod-Gedenkbuch, 1969; Handbuch der deutschen Presse, 1969. Mem: B'nai B'rith, Franz Rosenzweig Lodge, Düsseldorf; Deutscher Presseclub, Bonn. Hobbies: theater, music. Home: 76 Kruppstr, Düsseldorf, Ger. Office: 50 Zietenstr, Düsseldorf, Ger.

LIBA, Moshe, Isr, diplomat; b. 1931; in Isr since 1938; BA, Tel Aviv U; D en droit intl public, U of Paris; diplômé: U Intl de Sci Comparées, Luxembourg; Intl Civil Service Training Org OFI; supérieur d'etudes Françaises modernes, Sorbonne; m. Tova Zuckerman; one c. Isr ambass to Togo since 1965; fmr: i/c fgn activities, dept intl coop, Min for Fgn Affairs; JA repr, Algeria, Fr; mem Kibbutz. Maj, IDF. Author: Les Forces d'Urgence des Nations Unies, 1962; contbr numerous articles to newspapers and reviews, Isr and abroad. Office: Lomé, Togo.

LIBAI, David, Isr, advocate, educator; b. Tel Aviv, Isr, Oct 22, 1934; s. Zalman and Sara (Jankelson) Lubovsky; LLM, Heb U, Jerusalem, 1956; att Inst of Criminology, Heb U, Jerusalem; MCL, U of Chgo, 1967, D Comparative Law, 1968; m. Nitza Shapiro, Nov 24, 1964; c: Daniel. Dep dir, lectr, Inst of Criminology, Criminal Law, Tel Aviv U, since 1969; pvt practice since 1964; head, Dept of Parole and Pardons, Min of Justice, Jerusalem, 1954-57; spokesman, 1959-61; chief asst, State Atty, 1961-64; lectr, Bar Ilan U, Ramat Gan, 1962-65. Lt, IDF, 1957-59. Mem: Isr Bar Assn; Cohen Comm

on Penal Reform, Isr. Contbr articles to profsl jours. Home: 9 Gordon St, Tel Aviv, Isr. Office: Tel Aviv U, Tel Aviv, Isr.

LIBAI, Israel, Isr, organization exec; b. Ostrowiec, Pol, Feb 13, 1907; s. Shmuel and Tova (Eizenman); in Isr since 1932; att Econ Sem, Tel Aviv; m. Dina Zilberberg, 1932; c: Raya. Mem exec: Solel Boneh Ltd, since 1958; Nativ, pension's fund; fmr mem: secretariat, Lab Party; Histadrut Council. Co-found, natl secy, Org of Perm Workers, Solel Boneh. Home: 43 Weizmann St, Tel Aviv, Isr. Office: Solel Boneh, 111 Allenby St, Tel Aviv, Isr.

LIBAN, George, Can, organization exec; b. Czech, May 8, 1911; s. Rudolph and Emma (Goldberger); in Can since 1951; D Intl Law, Karls U, Prague, 1936; m. Ann Schiff, Sep 3, 1946; c: Thomas. Exec vice-pres, Fed Zionist Org of Can since 1948; fmr: natl exec dir, WJC; asst dir, WJC, Czech Off; exec dir, Zionist Org of Can, cen div. Maj, Czech Army, 1936-1938. Mem, Zionist Men's Assn of Can. Ed, Canadian Zionist, monthly mag. Home: 3777 Cote des Neiges, Montreal, Quebec, Can. Office: 1247 Guy St, Montreal, Quebec, Can.

LIBBY, Harris B, US, business exec; b. Malden, Mass, Mar 2, 1918; s. Samuel and Ada (Baum) Lipsitz; att Worcester Acad; Tufts U; m. Natalie Morse, Oct 14, 1941; c: Robert, Bette, Patricia. Pres, Republic Pipe and Elec Supply Corp, Boston, since 1946; pres and dir, Plumbing and Heating Wholesalers of NE, since 1963. USN, 1940-46; lt cdr, Res, 1945. Pres: Mass Bay lodge, B'nai B'rith, since 1962; Amer Technion Soc, Boston chap, 1951-59; found: Amer Friends of Heb U; Brandeis U; secy, vice-chmn, businessmen's council, CJA; mem: Temple Ohabei Shalom; trustee, Assn J Philanthropies, asst treas, 1958, mem, exec bd, 1958. Recipient: six campaign ribbons; seven battle stars; Navy commendation, 1942; decorated for bravery by Admiral Halsey, 1944. Home: 21 Fairway Rd, Chestnut Hill, Brookline, Mass. Office: Box 217, Somerville, Mass.

LIBERANOME, Hulda, Isr, journalist; b. Vienna, Aus, Mar 10, 1930; d. Avraham and Sarah (Mayersohn) Brawer; BSc, econ, LSE, 1952; m. Manfredo Liberanome; c: Odelia, Daniel. Correspondent: Ha'aretz, in It, since 1955; Isr Bc, since 1969. Lt, IDF, hqr gen cdr-in-chief, 1953-55. Trans: The Theory of Monopolistic Competition, by Chamberlin; Southeast Asia—Its Historical Development, by Cady, both into It; contbr: Heb Ency; Heb and It jours. Co-found, Italo-Isr Friendship Assn. Home: 15 Via dell'Olmeto, Florence, It.

LIBERMAN, Cyrus S, US, organization exec; b. Boston, Mass, Dec 9, 1924; s. Julius and Mary (Liberman); BA, Rollins Coll, 1948; MS, Boston U, 1951; m. Marilyn Lahn, July 4, 1950; c: Kristen. Dir, devl, Albert Einstein Med Cen, Phila, since 1961; fund-raising cons, Oram & Rich, 1948-49; trade secy, Allied J Appeal, Phila, 1950-51; fund-raising cons, Ketchum Inc, 1952-56; dir, devl, Hahnemann Med Coll, Phila, 1957-61. USN, WW II. Mem: Natl Soc Fund Raisers; Natl Assn Sci Writers; PR Soc of Amer; past pres: Pa Hosp PR Soc; Del Valley Hosp PR Assn. Contbr articles on fund-raising, programming. Home: 4125 Barberry Dr, Lafayette Hill, Pa. Office: Albert Einstein Med Cen, Philadelphia, Pa.

LIBERMAN, Meyer F, US, artist; b. NYC, Aug 28, 1923; s. Louis and Alice (Beck); att Art Students League, NY, 1946-50; m. Nina Margules, Feb 12, 1956. Art instr: Adult Educ Div: Temple Emanu-El, NY, since 1966; J Cen, NY, since 1967; Art Life Craft Studios, NY, 1964-68; one-man shows: J Mus, NY, 1954; Gal Grippi, NY, 1955; UAHC, 1956; Libr of Art and Music, NY, 1960; Collector's Gal, Chgo, 1961; Ruth Sherman Gal, NY, 1961; Bklyn Coll, 1967; Herzl Inst, 1969; group shows: Lyman Allyn Mus, New London, Conn, 1947; Little Studio, NY, 1952; Kaufman Gal, YMHA, 1954; Mus City of NY, 1955; Mus of Modern Art, 1956; City Cen Gal, NY, 1955, 1957; Columbia U, 1956, 1957; Duncan Gals, Paris, 1960; Jacques LaCloche Gal, Paris, 1960; Grippi Gal, NY, 1963; Gilman Gal, Chgo, 1964; Charles Mann Gal, NY, 1965; perm collections: J Mus, NY. Served USCG, 1942-45. Hobbies: J hist, music. Home: 21 Lewis Pl, Brooklyn, NY. Studio: 24 E 21 St, New York, NY.

LIBSON, Margaret, US, communal worker, educator; b. Hung, Jan 17, 1909; d. Nathan and Rose (Klein) Segal; in US since 1914; AB, U Pittsburgh, 1930; m. Sylvan Libson, June 30, 1935; c: Franklin, Robert, Nancy. Vice-chmn, overseas comm, natl bd, Natl Council J Women, since 1961, pres, Pa region, since 1961; bd dirs, United J Fed, Pittsburgh, pres, women's div; asst secy, bd trustee, Pittsburgh J Publ and Educ Found; HS tchr, Pittsburgh Public Schs; bd dirs: J Family and Children's Service, vice-pres, 1960-62; Gov's Comm, White House Conf on Children and Youth, 1960; vice-pres, Conf J Women's Orgs, Pittsburgh, 1954-55. Home: 5870 Marlborough Ave, Pittsburgh, Pa.

LICHT, Frank, US, jurist, b. Providence, RI, Mar 3, 1916; s. Jacob and Rose (Kassed); BA, Brown U, 1936; LLB, Harvard Law Sch, 1941; hon LLD, St Francis Coll, Me, 1969; m. Dorothy Krauss, June 16, 1946; c: Beth, Carol, Judith. Gov, State of RI, since 1969; asso justice, Superior Court of RI, since 1956; tchr, law contracts, evening div, Bryant Coll, since 1958; law clerk: Mass Supr Judicial Court, 1941-42; US Circuit, 1st circuit, 1942-43; partner, law firm, Letts & Quinn, 1943-56; senator, RI State Sen, 1948-56; mem fac, Trial Judges Coll, Reno, Nev, 1967. Hon pres, Gen J Comm of RI, since 1969, past pres, vice-pres; co-chmn, NCCJ, S NE region, since 1959; mem, Amer, RI Bar Assns. Home: 640 Elmgrove Ave, Providence, RI. Office: Providence Co Court House, RI.

LICHT, Sidney, US, physician, lecturer; b. NYC, Apr 18, 1907; s. Herman and Julia (Frank); BS, CCNY, 1927; MD, NYU, 1931; m. Elizabeth Schweitzer, Mar 16, 1937; c: Vera, Phyllis, Jeffrey. Att phys, phys med, Grace-New Haven Hosp, New Haven, Conn, since 1961; asst clinical prof, med, phys med, Yale U Sch of Med, since 1957; cons, phys med, US, VA, Gaylord, and De Goesbriand Hosps, since 1959; lectr, phys med: NYU, 1936-42; Columbia U, 1937-42; Tufts Coll since 1947; Boston U since 1948; adj phys therapist, Mt Sinai Hosp, NYC, 1937-46; chief, profsl services, US VA, 1946-54. US Army, 1942-46. F, NY Acad Med, 1941; hon mem: Argentine Kinesiology Assn; Can Phys Med Assn; Brit, Danish, Fr, and It Assns Phys Med; pres, Amer Cong Phys Med, 1967-68; Fr Soc Med Hist. Author: Music in Medicine, 1946; Occupational Therapy Source Book, 1948; Orthotics, 1966; Rehabilitation and Medicine, 1968; Arthritis and Rehabilitation, 1969; co-author: Occupational Therapy, 1950; Physical Medicine in General Practice, 1952; ed: Electrodiagnosis and Electromyography, 1957, reprinted, 1961; Therapeutic Heat, 1958; Therapeutic Excercise, 1959, reprinted, 1961; Therapeutic Electricity, 1960; Massage, Manipulation and Traction, 1960; Medical Hydrology, 1963; Medical Climatology, 1963. Home and office: 360 Fountain St, New Haven, Conn.

LICHTENSTADTER, Ilse, US, Islamist, educator; b. Hamburg, Ger, Sep 10, 1907; d. Jacob and Flora (Levi); in US since 1938; PhD, U Frankfurt/M, Ger, 1931; f: U Frankfurt, 1930-32; Notgemeinschaft der Deutschen Wissenschaft, 1932; PhD, Oxford U, Eng, 1937. Lectr, Arabic, Harvard U, since 1960; lectr to prof: Arabic and Islamic Insts; The Asia Inst and Sch for Asiatic Studies, NY, dean of students, 1953; lectr: Islamic culture, NYU; dept hist, Rutgers U; libr, oriental dept, Queen's Coll, Cambridge, Eng, 1933-35; specialist, oriental langs, Oxford U Press, 1935-38; i/c Judaica collection, JTSA, 1938-45; lectr, Arabic and Islamic subjects, Pakistan, India, It, Ger, Eng and US. Mem, Amer Oriental Soc; club, NY Oriental, pres, 1945. Author: Islam and the Modern Age, 1958; ed, Arabic, Kitab al-Muhabbar, 1942; gen ed, series trans, classical Arabic lit; contbr to profsl jours. Hobbies: music, collecting oriental art. Home: 14 Concord Ave, Cambridge, Mass. Office: Harvard U, Cambridge, Mass.

LICHTENSTEIN, Arthur Wald, US, attorney; b. Jazberin, Hung, Nov 6, 1899; s. Samuel and Anna (Waldman); in US since 1904; BS, CCNY, 1921; LLB, Columbia U, 1923; m. Rena London; c: Ellen. Ret, atty. Pvt, US Army, 1918. Mem: NY Bd, ADL; Assn Bar, NYC; NY State Bar Assn; fmr pres, Cardozo Lodge, B'nai B'rith. Home: 33 E End Ave, New York, NY.

LICHTENSTEIN, Leo S, NZ, merchant; b. Doksich, Russ, Apr 2, 1889; s. Chaim and Itka (Alperovitch) Uschisof; m. Julia Ranco, May 10, 1961; c: from 1st m, David. Treas, Auckland Zionist Soc; financial secy, B'nai B'rith; mem: bd, Auckland Heb Cong; Chevra Kadisha; treas, ZC of NZ; mem, Heb Wfr Soc. Home: 35 Benson Rd, Remuera, Auckland, NZ. Office: POB 1247, Auckland, NZ.

LICHTENSTEIN, Stanley, US, public information off; b. Bklyn, NY, Sep 5, 1922; BSS, CCNY, 1944; m. Annalee Present, Feb 16, 1953; c: Lisa, Mark. Public info specialist, Natl Bur of Standards, since 1966; asst to: publicity dir, Lib Party, NY, 1945; ed, Committee Reporter, AJComm, 1946; publicity

writer, UJA, NY, 1947; press relations dir, Protestants and Other Americans United for Separation of Church and State; mgn ed, Church and State Review, both 1949-58; info specialist, writer, HEW, 1958-62; asst mgn ed, Intl Commerce, US Commerce Dept weekly, staff writer, 1962-66. Mem, ACLU. Contbr to J, Prot, Catholic and secular jours. Hobby: graphic arts. Home: 7925 Maryknoll Ave, Bethesda, Md. Office: Natl Bureau of Standards, Washington, DC.

LICHTIGFELD, Adolph, S Afr, minister, teacher, organization exec, author; b. Düsseldorf, Ger, Mar 23, 1904; s. Joshua and Chaye (Weissberg); in S Afr since 1939; DJur, U Cologne, Ger, 1931; PhD, U of S Afr, 1953; m. Renia Lipschitz, Apr 10, 1932; c: Freddie, Donnie. Supt, S Afr J Orphanage, since 1952; mem, fac phil, U of S Afr, since 1964; lectr: phil, Union Coll, Johannesburg, since 1951; dept of Ger, Wits U, since 1962; fmr: min, United Heb Instns, Germiston, 1939-52; part-time chaplain, S Afr Union Defense Forces, 1941-45. Mem, Royal Inst Phil, London. Author: Philosophy and Revelation in the Work of Contemporary Jewish Thinkers, 1937; Twenty Centuries of Jewish Thought, 2nd ed, 1938; The Day of Prayer, 1942; Jaspers' Metaphysics, 1954; Aspects of Jaspers' Philosophy, 1963, 2nd ed in prep; delivered papers to intl congs on: Leibniz; Leibniz and Whitehead; Maimonides and Jaspers' Cipher; contbr to: law publs; Library of Living Philosophers; phil jours. Home and office: 22 Oxford Rd, Parktown, Johannesburg, S Afr.

LIDA, Raimundo, US, educator; b. Lemberg, Aus, Nov 15, 1908; s. Mauricio and Sara (Lehrer); in US since 1953; MA, U Buenos Aires, 1931, PhD, 1943; hon MA, Harvard, 1954; m. Denah Levy, Dec 23, 1955; c: Clara, Fernando. Smith prof, Fr, Span, Harvard U, since 1954; secy, Instituto de Filologia, U Buenos Aires, 1931-47; prof, U Nacional de La Plata, Arg, 1936-47; dir, Centro de Estudios Literarios, El Colegio de Mexico, 1947-53. Mem: Amer Acad Arts and Sci; Medieval Acad Amer; Renaissance Soc, Amer; MLA; Intl Assn Hispanists. Author: Belleza, Arte, Poesia en Santayana, 1943; Letras Hispanicas, 1958; contbr to profsl jours. Recipient, Guggenheim f, 1939-40, 1960. Home: 351 Harvard St, Cambridge, Mass. Office: 218 Boylston, Harvard U, Cambridge, Mass.

LIDSKY, Zvi, Isr, advocate; b. Tel Aviv, Isr, Nov 21, 1934; s. Asher and Nehama (Kauffman); LLB, HS of Law and Econs, Tel Aviv, 1956; BA, political sci, Heb U, Tel Aviv br, 1958; m. Nira Soufrin, Apr 28, 1956; c: Galit, Osnat. Pvt practice. Chmn, Youth Parliament, 1964-65; mem, Academic Org of Lab Party. Hobbies: sport, swimming. Home: 101a Hame'a Ve'ehad St, Ramat Chen, Isr. Office: 60 Achad Haam St, Tel Aviv, Isr.

LIDZ, Theodore, US, psychiatrist, educator; b. NYC, Apr 1, 1910; s. Israel and Esther (Shedlin); BA, Columbia U, 1931, MD, 1936; hon MA, Yale U, 1951; m. Ruth Wilmanns, June 18, 1939; c: Victor, Charles, Jerome. Prof, psycht, Yale U Sch Med, since 1951, chmn, dept psycht, 1967-69; career inves, Natl Inst Mh grant, since 1961; asso prof, psycht, asst prof, med, Johns Hopkins Sch Med, 1947-51; psycht-in-chief, Grace-New Haven Comty Hosp, 1951-61; men, visiting comm, Cen for Behavioral Scis, Harvard U, since 1966; cons: VA Hosp, Md and Conn, since 1946; US Army since 1959; Army Med Cen, Wash, DC, 1942-56; sect on Mh, NRC, 1948-54; study sect, research grants, Natl Inst Mh, 1952-56, training grants comm, 1959-63. Lt col, US Army MC, 1942-46. F: Amer Psycht Assn; Cen for Advanced Study in Behavioral Scis, 1965-66; pres: Amer Psychosomatic Soc, 1957-58; Md Psycht Soc, 1948-50; mem: W NE Psychan Soc; Conn Soc Neur and Psycht; Conn Med Soc; Alpha Omega Alpha; Sigma Xi. Author: The Family and Human Adaptation, 1963; The Person, 1968; co-author, Schizophrenia and the Family, 1965; contbr to profsl publs. Recipient: Frieda Fromm-Reichman award, 1961; Salmon medal, 1967. Home: Orchard Rd, Woodbridge, Conn. Office: 333 Cedar St, New Haven, Conn.

LIEB, Leonard, US, artist, teacher; b. Pol, Dec 27, 1912; s. Isaac and Gertrude (Lieb); in US since 1921; att: Irene Kaufmann Settlement Art Sch; U Pittsburgh; m. Ida Schmidth, (decd); c: Joel, Lynn Helford. Art tchr: Arts and Crafts Cen since 1948; Irene Kaufmann Settlement Art Sch since 1957, both Pittsburgh; one-man shows: Creative Gal, NY, 1954; Asso Artists Gal, Pittsburgh, 1960; Westmoreland Country Club, 1960; Regent House, 1963, 1965; Ivy Sch Profsl Art, Pittsburgh, 1967; Pa State Coll, New Kensington, Pa, 1967; exhbs: Carnegie Inst, Pittsburgh, 1936-62; Butler Art Inst,

Youngstown, O, 1943-48; Pan-Amer Show, NY, 1944; Chgo Art Inst, 1946; Pa Acad Fine Arts, 1952; Creative Art Gal, 1953; Playhouse Competition Show, 1957-60; Knox, Albright Gals, Buffalo, NY, 1961; Contemporary Art Cen, Boston, 1961; drawings: US Natl Show, St Paul, Minn, 1963; The Drawing Soc Exhb, Phila Mus, 1963; Interior Dept, Wash, DC, 1967; perm collections: Ind State Tchrs Coll; Carnegie Inst, Pittsburgh; Bd Public Educ, Pittsburgh; Carville Marine Hosp, La; many pvt collections. Mem: Asso Artists, bd dirs, 1948-50, vice-pres, exhb chmn, 1953-55; Abstract Group; Water Color Soc, all Pittsburgh. Recipient: natl water color award, Fine Arts Div of US Govt, 1940; hon mention, water colors, Asso Artists, Pittsburgh, 1944; Henry Posner award in oils, 1945; Charles Rosenbloom award for best water color, 1947, 2nd prize in oil, 1954; black and white prize, 1951; purchase prize, Carnegie Inst, 1958; First Fed of Pittsburgh award for graphics, 1963. Home and studio: 409 Cato St, Pittsburgh, Pa.

LIEB, Morton, US, attorney; b. NYC, Mar 29, 1934; s. Morris and Lillian (Green); AB, NYU, 1951; LLB, Bklyn Law Sch, 1958; m. Marcia Weinkrantz, Nov 22, 1964; c: Mark, Hope. Pvt practice since 1959. Secy, Assn Criminal Lawyers, NY Co; arbitrator, Amer Arbitration Assn; fmr vice-pres, J Big Brothers; mem: J Bd Guardians, De Witt Clinton HS Alumni Assn; Alpha Epsilon Pi, fmr pres, NY Alumni club; NY Co Lawyers Assn. Home: 435 E 14 St, New York, NY. Office: 299 Broadway, New York, NY.

LIEB, Robert L, US, physician, educator; b. Newark, NJ, Nov 15, 1915; s. Joseph and Annie (Bronstein); BA, U Mich, 1936; MD, U of W Ont, 1943; m. Leatrice Chester, Sep 18, 1948; c: Beth, Melanie. Pvt practice since 1946; urol staff: Martland Med Cen; Neward Beth Isr Hosp; St Barnabas Med Cen; St James Hosp; Dr's Hosp; Amer Legion Hosp; Babies' Hosp-Coll Memorial, United Hosps of Newark; E Orange Gen Hosp; Clara Maass Memorial Hosp; St Mary's Hosp; cons, VA Hosp, Lyons; asst clinical prof, urol, NJ Coll Med & Dent; post-grad, urol: Boston City Hosp, 1943; Bayonne Hosp, 1944-46. Dipl: Natl Bd Med Examiners; Amer Bd Urol; f: Amer Coll Surgs; Intl Coll Surgs; mem: AMA; Amer Urol Assn. Home: 85 Kean Rd, Short Hills, NJ. Office: 354 South Orange Ave, South Orange, NJ.

LIEBER, Charles Donald, US, book publisher; b. Scheveningen, Netherlands, Jan 30, 1921; s. Edmund and Gabrielle (Lifczis); in US since 1941; BA, Université Libre, Bruxelles, Belgium; att New Sch for Social Research, NY; m. Miriam Levin, July 17, 1960; c: John, James, George, Anne. Pres, Atherton Press, Inc, since 1964; ed, coll dept, Alfred A Knopf, 1949-52; dir, coll dept, Random House, 1952-64. Lt, US Army, 1942-46. Co-ed: Great Events of World History, 1964. Home: 389 West End Ave, New York, NY. Office: 70 Fifth Ave, New York, NY.

LIEBER, David Leo, US, rabbi, administrator, educator; b. Pol, Feb 20, 1925; s. Max and Gussie (Jarmush); in US since 1927; BA, CCNY, 1944; BHL, MHL, DHL, JTSA; MA, Columbia U, 1950; m. Esther Kobre, June 10, 1945; c: Michael, Susan, Daniel, Deborah. Pres, U of Judaism, since 1963; vice pres, JTSA since 1968; fmr: tchr, NY Heb HS; rabbi, Sinai Temple, LA; chaplain: Harvard; U of Wash; co-found, Ramah Camps. Chaplain, USAF, 1951-53. Mem: exec comm: RA; Bd Rabbis, S Cal; mem: Natl Council for J Educ; Amer Phil Assn; Soc for Bibl Lit and Exegesis; Amer Oriental Soc. Mem ed bd, Conservative Judaism; contbr to periodicals. Spec interests: hist of thought; phil; Bible. Office: 6525 Sunset Blvd, Los Angeles, Cal.

LIEBER, Eric Eisi, Eng, physician; b. Zablotov, Pol, Dec 21, 1909; s. Benjamin and Rebecca (Haselman); in Eng since 1937; dipl, physics, Technische Hochschule, Dresden, 1933; Staatsexamen, U Berne, 1937; LMSSA, U London, 1941; m. Gertrude Diamond, Nov 11, 1947; c: Teresa, Judith. Chest phys, gen, ind med practitioner since 1946; phys, NW Regional Hosp, bd, med adv to ind, since 1951; res med off: W Hosp, 1942; May Day Hosp, Croydon, 1943-44; med supt, Croydon Borough Sanatorium, 1945-46; med staff, Battersea Gen Hosp, 1946-55. Prin contribs: research, respiratory, toxicological problems in plastics ind, work on deficiency diseases. Vice-pres, Brit F of IMA; comm mem, Emergency Med Aid Comm for Isr; mem, JPA Comm, Marble Arch, Golders Green; council mem, Med Practitioners, Union, 1956-66; comm mem, Counceller Comm, Age, Employment of OECD, 1961; mem: Soc Occupation-

al Med; BMA; f, Royal Soc Health; corresp mem, IMA. Author: The Elementary Quantum in Electricity and Applications in Biology, 1940; Principles of Nutrition, 1942; Occupational Health, 1964; contbr to med and sci jours. Spec interests: J life in Eng and Isr. Home and office: 17 Beaumont St, London, Eng.

LIEBER, Moshe, Isr, manufacturer; b. Leipzig, Ger, May 31, 1909; s. Israel and Zippora; in Isr since 1926; att HS of Commerce, Leipzig; m. Sara Levin, 1935; c: Dalia, Ruth, Haim, Leah. Owner and mgn dir, The Lieber Co Ltd, chocolate and candy factory; co-owner, Coffee Momento, Beth Shemesh. Mem, exec comm, Isr Mfrs Assn, since 1951. Home: 63 Rothschild Blvd, Tel Aviv, Isr. Office: POB 138, Tel Aviv, Isr.

LIEBERMAN, Charles, US, real estate and insurance broker; b. Newburgh, NY, Jan 11, 1907; s. Morris and Esther (Sherman); m. Anne Krouner, June 22, 1941; c: Emily. Owner, Charles Lieberman Agcy, since 1937. US Army, 1943-45. Pres: Central Ave Civic and Merchants Assn, 1945; Albany Realty Bd, Inc, 1949; Sons of Israel Syn, 1946, 1947; Temple Israel, 1949; J Comty Cen, 1960-61; J Social Service, 1958-59; gen chmn, JWF campaign, 1953-54; mem: exec comm, JCC, since 1950; mem, bd dirs, Comty Chest, 1954, all in Albany; natl cash cabinet, UJA, 1953; comm, JDC; ZOA; JWV; B'nai B'rith; AJComm; Natl Assn Real Estate Bds; NY State Soc of Real Estate Appraisers; NY State Assn of Real Estate Bds; Natl Assn of Real Estate Bds; NY State Assn of Ins Agts; Masons; clubs: Fellowcraft, Albany Colonie Country. Home: 259 S Main Ave, Albany, NY. Office: 92 Central Ave, Albany, NY.

LIEBERMAN, Elias, US, educator, author; b. St Petersburg, Russ, Oct 30, 1883; s. Nathan and Sophie (Elbaum); in US since 1891; BA, cum laude, CCNY, 1903; MA, NYU, 1906, PhD, 1911; m. Rose Kiesler, July 1, 1913; c: Amy Lowenstein, James. Asso supt of schs, NYC, 1940-54, ret since 1954; head, Eng and speech depts, Bushwick HS, 1912-24; prin, Thomas Jefferson HS, 1924-40, both Bklyn, NY; lectr, poetry, throughout US. Pres: Asso Alumni, CCNY, 1932-34; Gamma chap, Phi Beta Kappa, 1928-30; vice-pres, Poetry Soc of Amer, since 1946, life mem, gov bd; mem: The Craftsman Group; HS Prin Assn, life; Cong Beth Isr, Richmond Hill, NY; f, Poertry Soc of Amer, 1960; clubs: Town Hall; Writers. Author: American Short Story, 1912; Paved Streets, 1918; Hand-Organ Man, 1930; Man in the Shadows, 1940; To My Brothers Everywhere, 1954; poems: I am an American, 1916; Lavender, alma mater song of CCNY, 1916; Poetry for Junior High Schools, 2 vols, 1926; Poems of the Sea, 1926; Poems for Enjoyment, anthology, 1931; lit ed, The Amer Hebrew, 1916-32; contbr to lit periodicals and mags; recorded, Elias Lieberman Reads His Own Poems, 1957. Recipient: gold medallion, Natl Poetry Cen, 1940; Townsend Harris medal, CCNY Alumni Assn, 1953; award, Poetry Soc of Amer, 1960; James Joyce award, 1966. Hobbies: theater, ballet. Home: 104-75 111 St, Richmond Hill, NY.

LIEBERMAN, Henry R, US, journalist, editor; b. St Louis, Mo, Nov 24, 1916; s. Joseph and Goldie (Spector); BA, Columbia Coll, 1937; MA, Columbia U, 1950; m. Kathryn Martin, June 11, 1949; c: Peter, Linda. Dir, sci and educ news, NY Times, sci news coord, 1966-69, corresp, China, 1945-49, corresp China area, SE Asia, India, Pakistan, 1950-57, asst to fgn ed, 1957-60, asst news ed, 1960-66; reporter, PM Newspaper, 1940-42; ed, fgn news bur, OWI, 1942-44, chief news ed, China, 1945. F, Council on Fgn Relations, NY, 1949-50; pres, Corresp Club, Hongkong, 1952; Phi Beta Kappa; Over-seas Press Club. Home: 3 Medford Lane, Scarsdale, NY. Office: 229 W 43 St, New York, NY.

LIEBERMAN, Irving, US, librarian, educator; b. Newark, NJ, Jan 6, 1914; s. Samuel and Fanny (Drossman); BS, NYU, 1935; BS, libr sci, Columbia U, 1939; MA, Tchrs Coll, 1950; DE, 1955; m. Lillian Kasner, Aug 3, 1947; c: Barry, Ruth. Dir, Sch of Librarianship, U Wash, since 1956; staff mem, Public Libr: Newark, NJ, 1935-38; Detroit, Mich, 1938-41; dir, State Aid, Mich State Libr, Lansing, 1942, head, extension div, 1946-48; spec asst, Bklyn Public Libr, 1949, supt of its cen services, 1950, exec asst, 1951-52; dir, audio-visual project, Sch of Librarianship, U Cal, Berkeley, 1952-54; mem, fac, Columbia U Sch of Libr Service, 1954-56; adv dir, Inst of Librarianship, U of Ibadan, Nigeria, 1963-64; dir and lectr: two one-week workshops for Army and AF Librs, Hqrs, US Army, Eur, 1964; one-week workshop for Army, AF and Navy Librs, Hqrs, US Army, Pacific, 1968; co-dir,

NDEA Inst for Sch Librs, U Wash, grant by US Educ Off, 1965; surveyor, Public Libr, City of Lagos, Nigeria, 1963-64; mem, Survey Team for Army Libr Prog, Hqrs, US Army, Eur, 1964. US Army, 1942-46. Pres, Pacific NW Libr Assn, 1959-60; mem: dept, audio-visual instr, Natl Educ Assn, since 1952; regional bd, ADL; Amer, Wash Libr Assn; Adult Educ Assn of US; Educ Film Libr Assn. Author: Audio-Visual Instruction in Library Education, 1955; Survey of the Lagos City Library, 1964; The Use of Non-Print Media in Library School Instruction, in Library Education: An International mem, Survey, 1968; ed, Proceedings of an Invitational Conferen ceon Education for Health Sciences Librarianship, 1968; contbr to Librs and Museums, in Ency of Educ Research, 1960; profsl jours. Hobby: theater. Home: 19009 11 Ave, NW, Seattle, Wash. Office: U of Wash, Seattle, Wash.

LIEBERMAN, Jack, US, business exec; b. Wilkes Barre, Pa, Feb 4, 1914; s. Max and Mathilda (Williams); BSc, Bucknell U, 1935, MS Biol, 1938; MSc Social Work, U of Pa, 1940; m. Sylvia Meth, Apr 20, 1940; c: Mrs Howard Glatstein, Marc. Exec dir, Memphis J Service Agcy and JWF since 1948. US Army, 1944-45. Pres: Natl Assn Social Workers, Memphis br, 1954-56; Tenn Conf on Social Wfr, 1956-57; mem: Acad of Cert Social Workers. Recipient: Bronze Star, 1945. Home: 4063 Hilldale Ave, Memphis, Tenn. Office: 81 Madison Bldg, Memphis, Tenn.

LIEBERMAN, Jacob J, US, attorney; b. Palvagas, Czech, June 20, 1887; s. Joseph and Rosa (Winberger); in US since 1891; LLB, U Dnver, 1909; m. Minnie Morris, June 20, 1912; c: Mendel, Tose, William. Ret, partner, Leiberman, & Lieberman, LA, from 1952; asst city and co atty, Denver, Col, 1914-21; spec counsel, City Council, 1920-23; entered law practice, LA, 1924; admitted to US Supr Court, 1924; spec prosecutor, Imperial Co, Cal, 1927. Natl chmn, B'nai B'rith Youth Comm, 1946-49, hon life chmn; pres: Dist Grand Lodge 4, B'nai B'rith, 1937-38; Assn for J Educ, 1952-60; ZOA dist, 1932-33; Temple Emanuel, 1926-30; vice-pres, JCC, 1937, bd mem, 1937-46; chmn, Bureau J Educ, 1937-38, all LA; dir: Natl J Hosp, JCRS, now Amer Med Cen, Natl Home for J Children, all Denver; co-found, mem: Comty Relations Comm since 1937; Natl and LA ADL; Syn Council of Amer; 1937-47; trustee, JWF Orgs, 1943-47; Leo N Levi Memorial Hosp, 1949-52; fmr mem, Natl Council, JDC, bd overseers, U of J; mem: Amer Bar Assn; Amer Judicature Soc; State Bar of Cal, fmr pres, Wilshire Bar Assn; mem, Metrop Opera Guild, fmr mem, S Cal Opera Guild; U Rel Conf, Brandeis Camp Inst; Sinai Temple; Masons; Scottish Rite; Shriners; Beverly Hills Bus and Profsl Men's Assn; clubs: Temple Isr Men's, Guardians, Humanitarians, LA Breakfast. Contbr to law jours; spec writer, Rocky Mountain News, 1908-12. Home: 510 S Burnside Ave, Los Angeles, Cal. Office: 6399 Wilshire Blvd, Los Angeles, Cal.

LIEBERMAN, James, US, veterinarian, biomedical communications admnr; b. NYC, June 2, 1921; s. Elias and Rose (Kiesler); att Cornell U, 1938-40; DVM, Middlesex U, 1944; MPH, U Minn, 1947; m. Lucille Goldstein, Nov 7, 1943; c: Margaret. Asst Surg Gen, USPHS, since 1968, dir, Natl Med Audio-visual Cen, asso dir, Natl Libr of Med, since 1967, with USPHS since 1948; sr cons vetr UNRRA, 1946; cons, WHO, 1955. USN, 1944-46. Exec comm, Audio-visual Conf of Med and Allied Scis; bd trustees, Heb Acad of Atlanta; bd dirs, Ga Soc for Crippled Children and Adults; f, Amer Public Health Assn, elective councilor, 1959-62, 1966, mem, radiological health comm, 1960-62; mem: Amer Vetr Med Assn; Conf of Public Health Vetr, secy, 1953-57; NY Acad Scis; Assn Mil Surgs US; Sci Research Soc of Amer; Soc Motion Picture and TV Engrs; Council on Med TV; Commissioned Offs Assn, USPHS, treas, Atlanta br, 1956-57; chmn, Fed Adv Council on Med Training Aids, 1965-66. Co-author, Instructor's Guide, Sanitary Food Service, 1952; cons ed: Animal Disease and Human Health, 1958; Biomedical Communications: Problems and Resources, 1967; secy, bd eds, Comparative Medicine in Transition, 1960; contbr to profsl jours. Recipient: USPHS Meritorious Service Medal, 1965; commendation, Fulton Co Med Soc, Ga, 1966; Man of the Year, Bus Screen Mag, 1967; awards: Brenda, Theta Sigma Phi, 1968; Myrtle Wreath, Hadassah, 1969. Home: 1733 Noble Dr, NE, Atlanta, Ga. Office: Natl Med Audio-visual Cen, Atlanta, Ga.

LIEBERMAN, Milton M, US, accountant; b. Newark, NJ, Mar 16, 1912; s. Samuel and Fannie (Drossman); BSc, NYU, 1933; m. Jeannette Feierstein, June 6, 1937; c: David, Frances. Sr partner, acctnt firm, since 1934. Pres: J Educ Assn of Es-

sex Co, since 1960; Cong Beth El of the Oranges and Maplewood, 1954-56; overseer, JTSA, since 1959; prog chmn, mem exec, Friends of Hebraic Studies, Rutgers U; vice-chmn, Pace Setters div, UJA Essex Co; past chmn, acctnt div, Comty Chest; mem, bd, JCC; bd, Isr Pleasant Valley Home; past bd mem, YM-YWHA of Essex Co; state treas, AJCong, 1950-52; past-master: Masonic Lodge; mem: Amer Inst of Acctnts; NY State and NJ Socs of CPAs; Amer Arbitration Assn; JWB; Newark Assn of Commerce and Ind; Grand Jury Assn; Beta Gamma Sigma Alumni in NYC; AJComm; AJCong; B'nai B'rith, S Mt Lodge; NJ Audubon Soc; club: Green Brook Country. Hobbies: music, golf, comty fund raising. Home: 195 N Woods Dr, S Orange, NJ. Office: 60 Park Pl, Newark, NJ.

LIEBERMAN, Morris, US, rabbi; b. Cincinnati, O, Mar 9, 1909; s. Victor and Mary (Toby); BA, U Cincinnati, 1931; rabbi, HUC, 1934; PhD, Johns Hopkins U, 1958; hon DD, HUC-JIR, 1959; m. Lillian Tennenbaum, July 14, 1943. Rabbi, Baltimore Heb Cong, since 1937. Maj, chaplains corps, US Army, 1942-46. Pres: Baltimore J Council, 1950-51, dir, 1940-41; Baltimore Bd Rabbis, 1968; chmn: JWB commn on J chaplaincy, 1956-59; JWB Natl Armed Forces and Vet Services Comm, since 1967; chaplaincy comm, CCAR, 1950-60, mem, natl exec bd; vice-pres: JWB since 1964; bd govs, USO, chmn, personnel comm; mem: Bd of Natl Comty Relations, adv council; Civil Defense Adv Council of Md; adv comm, Md branch, ACLU; adv bd, Seton Psychiatric Inst of Baltimore; UJA delg to Isr, 1949. Recipient: Frank L Weil Award of JWB for contribs on behalf of J personnel in US Armed Forces, 1962. Home: 11 Slade Ave, Baltimore, Md. Study: 7401 Park Heights Ave, Baltimore, Md.

LIEBERMAN, Richard Raymond, US, dentist; b. Hartford, Conn, Mar 22, 1920; s. Thomas and Mary (Galinsky); BS, U Conn, 1942; DDS, U of Pa, 1945; m. Blanche Eisenberg, June 20, 1943; c: Leslie, Jerelyn, Jonathan. Pvt practice. Pvt, US Army, 1943-45. Mem: Amer Dent Assn; Conn State Dent Assn; Omicron Kappa Upsilon; Alpha Omega, Hartford alumni chap. Hobbies: tennis, golf. Home: 90 Brainard Rd, W Hartford, Conn. Office: 60 Gillett, Hartfora, Conn.

LIEBERMAN, Samuel, US, educator, author; b. NYC, Dec 11, 1911; s. Harry and Anna (Zlatkin); BA, CCNY, 1932, MS, 1935; PhD, Columbia U, 1953; m. Bertha Scholnik, Mar 12, 1938; c: Nathaniel. Prof, classical langs, Queens Coll, since 1965, asso prof, 1962-65, fac mem since 1947; tchr, NYC HS, 1934-43; lectr, Latin, CCNY, 1939-41. Lt, Japanese lang off, US Army, 1943-46. Mem: Amer Philological Assn; Amer Oriental Soc; AAUP; Amer Classical League; Amer Council on Teaching of Fgn Langs; Ancient Civilization Group of NY; Phi Beta Kappa; club, NY Classical. Author: Poems in Japan: Theme and Variations, 1959; Roman Drama, 1966; asso ed, Classical World, since 1953; contbr to scholarly jours. Recipient: service ribbons. Home: 56-57 205 St, Bayside, NY. Office: Queens Coll, Flushing, NY.

LIEBERMAN, Saul, US, author, educator; b. Motol, Pol, May 28, 1898; s. Moses and Luba (Katzenellenbogen); in US since 1940; ordained rabbi, Slobodka Theol Sem, 1916; MA, Heb U, Jerusalem, 1931; DHL, JTSA, 1942; hon PhD, Heb U, Jerusalem, 1931; hon DLitt, Harvard U, 1966; m. Judith Berlin, 1932. Prof, Pal lit and instns, JTSA, since 1940, dist service prof since 1966, dean, grad dept, since 1949, dean, rabb sch, since 1954; co-dir, Maxwell Abbell Research Inst in Rabb, since 1962; fmr: tchr, Talmud, Heb U, 1931-36; dean, Harry Fischell Inst, 1935-40, both Jerusalem. Pres, Amer Acad J Research; f: Amer Acad Arts and Scis, Boston; mem, Acad Heb Lang. Author: The Talmud of Caesarea Jerusalem, 1931; A Commentary on the Palestinian Talmud, 1934; A Commentary on the Tosefta, vols I-IV, 1937-39; Greek in Jewish Palestine, 1942; Roman Legal Institutions in Early Rabbinica and Acta Martyrum, 1944; The Martyrs of Caesarea, 1944; Hellenism in Jewish Palestine, 1950; Tosefta Kifshutah, vols I-VII, 1955-57; Siphre Zutta, 1968; ed: The Louis Ginsberg Jubilee Vol, 1945; The Laws of the Yerushalmi by Maimonides, 1947; The Alexander Marx vols, 1950; Harry A Wolfson Jubilee Vols, 1965; Tosefta, Vols I-III, 1955-57; contbr to learned jours. Home: 425 Riverside Dr, New York, NY. Office: 3080 Broadway, New York, NY.

LIEBERMAN, William, US, physician; b. NYC, Dec 1, 1904; s. Peter and Ida (Fink); BA, Columbia Coll, 1925; MD, SUNY, Downstate Coll of Med, 1928; m. Henrietta Straim, Aug 16, 1936; c: Robert, Peter. Att proctologist, Unity Hosp since 1956; asso, surg dept, Bklyn J Hosp, 1931-38; Beth

Moses Hosp, 1932-37; Coney Island Hosp, 1940-48. Prin contrib: devised several instruments used in Proctology. Pres, and f, Intl Acad Proctology, 1966; life f, Amer Coll Gastroenterology; sr mem, Kings Co Surg Soc; f, Natl Gastroenterological Assn; mem, local, state, natl med socs. Author: The History of the Enema, 1948; found ed, Amer Jour Proctology, 1950; contbr to med jours. Home and office: 198 Linden Blvd, Brooklyn, NY.

LIEBES, Ernest, El Salvador, business exec; b. Hamburg, Ger, Dec 3, 1907; s. Leon and Margarete (Henschel); in El Salvador since 1930; att Royal Gymnasium Heinrich Herz, Ger, 1916-25; m. Alice Philips, June 30, 1937; c: Raquel, Roberto, Marion. Partner, mgr, Casa Goldtree Liebes & Co, El Salvador, since 1945. Consul, ad-honorem, Isr, since 1949; mem: Coffee Exch, NY; J Comty of El Salvador; Casino Salvadoreno; Circulo Deportivo Intl; club, Internacional; hon pres, Zionist Org of El Salvador, 1952. Home: Colonia San Benito, San Salvador. Office: Consulado General de Isr, El Salvador.

LIEBESKIND, Alexander, Isr, physician; b. Krakow, Pol, Mar 30, 1907; s. Emile and Helena (Krongold); in Isr since 1940; MD, U Krakow, 1932, PhD, 1935; m. Etti Rössler; c: Arie. Phys, pvt clinic; cons, Munic Hosp, Haifa, since 1966; fmr: chief, allergy clinic, Kupat Holim, Haifa; lectr, Intl Congs of Allergy; guest lectr: U Navarra-Pamplona, Spain; U Zurich, Switz; NY Acad of Med; visitor, participant, Centraalbureau Voor Schimmelcultures, Netherlands; lectr: Haifa Med Assn; IMA. MO, Haganah, 1948. Active f, Amer Coll Allergists; mem: Amer Acad Allergy; La Sociedad Española de Alergia, Spain; Haganah Veterans Org; comm, Isr-Amer Friendship League. Contbr to profsl publs. Spec interests: biology, mycology, biochem, Bible, Talmud. Home and office: 21 Galomb St, Haifa, Isr.

LIEBMAN, Charles Seymour, Isr, educator; b. NYC, Oct 20, 1934; s. Seymour and Libbie; in Isr since 1969; BA, U Miami, Fla, 1956; att Johns Hopkins U, Md, 1956-57; MA, PhD, U of Ill, 1960; m. Carol Stickler, 1951; c: Rivkah, Aaron. Asso prof, Bar Ilan U, since 1969; asst prof: U of Pa, 1960-63; asso prof, Yeshiva U, 1963-69. Author: Orthodoxy in American Jewish Life, 1965; Suburban Differences and Metropolitan Policies, 1965; Training of American Rabbis, 1968; The Ambivalent Jew, 1970. Home: 22 Talpiot St, Ramat Gan, Isr. Office: Bar Ilan U, Ramat Gan, Isr.

LIEBMAN, Max, US, producer, director; b. Vienna, Aus, Aug 5, 1902; s. Harry and Sara (Glazer); in US since 1903; m. Sonia Veskova, Aug 10, 1932. Produc, TV progs: NBC; CBS; sketch writer, vaudeville acts, NYC, 1920-25; social dir: Log Tavern, Pa, summer 1925; Camp Tamiment, 1932-47; presented, Straw Hat Revue; introduced to Broadway: Danny Kaye, Imogene Coca, Betty Garrett, Jules Munshin, Sid Caesar; dance team, Mata and Hari; choreographer, Jerome Robbins; dialogue writer: motion pictures; theatres; night clubs; play doctor: Up in Arms, 1944; The Kid from Brooklyn, 1946; Make Mine Manhattan, 1948; Along Fifth Avenue, 1949; Tickets Please, 1950; civilian dir, sketch writer, USO Camp Shows, WW II; produc, dir, Tars and Spars, USCG, 1945; Columbia Pictures, 1946; produced: Shooting Star, 1947; From the Second City, Broadway, 1962; Chrysler Motor Corp Show, World's Fair, 1964; owner, produc, dir, Your Show of Shows, TV. Mem: ASCAP; Authors League Amer. Recipient: Variety Award, 1950; Look Award, 1950, 1951, 1952; Michaels Award, TV Acad Arts and Scis, 1952; Motion Picture Daily Award; Sylvania Award. Office: 130 W 56 St, New York, NY.

LIEBMAN, Morris, US, public accountant; b. Mogilev, Russ, Sep 15, 1899; s. Tobias and Feni (Aronson); in US since 1903; BS, U Pa, 1924; MBA, 1926; m. Pearl Zucker, June 22, 1924; c: Emmanuel, Ruth Sandrow, Alfred. Partner, acctnt firms: Morris Liebman and Co, since 1957; Magee, Liebman and O'Neill, 1929-38; pvt practice, 1938-57. Pres: ZOA, 1950-51; J Fed, 1947-49; Beth El Cong, 1941-45; B'nai B'rith, 1940-41, 1946-47, S NJ Council, 1940-41, secy, lodge, 1935-37, life mem, life delg, since 1958, all Camden, NJ; pres, NJ Tennis Assn, 1955-56; treas, Camden Co C of C, 1958-62, mem, taxation comm, 1952-53, bd mem, 1963-69; chmn, finance comm, TB Assn, 1929-59; Allied J Appeal, 1953-55; vice-chmn, Isr Bonds, 1952-54, mem, bd trustees, since 1951; natl chmn, Indoor Tennis Tournament, 1941; annual chmn, Boys and Jr Tennis Tournament, Camden City, since 1951; mem: budget comm, United Fund, 1957-62; bd trustees, Comty Chest, 1949-50; NJ Soc of CPA's; Cong Beth Sholom; Cong Beth El; NJ comm, UJA; club, Forest Hills Tennis, pres,

1953-69. Recipient: awards: Natl Savings Prog, Camden Co, 1942; J Comty, 1959; Allied Appeal Campaign, J Fed of Camden Co, 1966. Home: 200 Buckner Ave, Haddonfield, NJ. Office: Commerce Bldg, 1 Broadway, Camden, NJ.

LIEBMAN, Seymour B, US, author, historian, attorney; b. NYC, Mar 12, 1907; s. Henry and Fannie (Abend); LLB, St Lawrence U, 1929; MA, U of the Americas, 1963; m. Malvina Weiss; c: Charles. Pvt law practice, 1929-58; counsel and vice-chmn, bd dirs, Bank of Miami Beach, 1955-58; spec asst atty-gen, State of Fla, 1955-57; lectr: Brandeis U, Heb U, Universidad Ibero-Americano; U of the Americas; U of Miami; visiting prof: Latin Amer hist, Fla Atlantic U; Diaspora Research Cen, Tel Aviv U. Pres: SE region, ZOA, 1955-57; Zionist Council, S Fla, 1959-60, 1967-68; chmn, found, bd educ, Metrop Council of United Syn of Amer, 1946; secy, Bureau J Educ, Gtr Miami, 1956-59; vice-pres, Amer Friends of Heb U, S Fla chap, 1958-59; chmn, JNF Found, 1958-60; chmn, Bonds for Isr campaigns, 1955-58; vice-pres, Yeshiva of Flatbush, 1942-48; mem, bd govs, Gtr Miami J Fed, 1953-59; vice-pres, E Midwood JC, 1945-48; co-chmn, Dade Co Comty Chest, 1949-50; vice-pres, Miami Beach Taxpayers Assn, 1956-59; dir, Miami Beach Bar Assn, 1958-60; Amer Hist Assn; Amer Acad Political and Social Sci. Author: Guide to Jewish References in Mexican Colonial Era, 1963; The Enlightened, 1967; Faith and Flame: History of the Jews of New Spain, 1969; contbr to scholarly journs. Home: 1408 S Bayshore Dr, Miami, Fla.

LIEBOWITZ, Jonathan S, US, attorney; b. NYC, Sep 20, 1932; s. Sidney and Florence; BS, Cornell U, 1954; LLB, Columbia U, 1959; m. Helen; c: Robin. Pvt practice since 1960; atty, NLRB, 1960-62. US Army, 1954-56. Trustee, The Brotherhood Syn, NYC; fmr: pres, NYC chap, Cornell Ind and Lab Relations Alumni Assn; mem: NY Co Lawyers Assn; White Plains and NYC Bar Assns; Bars of: US Supr Court, Court of Appeals for 2nd Circuit, Dist Court for S Dist of NY; Natl Panel of Arbitrators, Public Employment Disputes Settlement Panel, Amer Arbitration Assn; Panel of Arbitrators, NY State Mediation Bd; Panels of Arbitrators, Factfinders and Mediators, NJ Public Employment Relations Commn; Comm on Arbitration and Conciliation; NY Co Lawyers Assn. Author: Equal Pay for Equal Work Legislation, 1954. Recipient: Knoblaugh Prize, Cornell U, 1954. Spec interest: Isr. Home: 70 Holbrook Rd, White Plains, NY. Office: 150 Broadway, New York, NY.

LIEBOWITZ, Seymour M, US, attorney; b. NYC, July 8, 1908; s. Samuel and Ida (Mannheimer); LLB, Bklyn Law Sch; m. Florence Chaykin, Dec 23, 1931; c: Suzanne Ritter, Frances Golden. Sr mem, Nachby & Liebowitz. Vice-pres, Temple Isr of Lawrence; exec bd, NY Fed Reform Syns; pres: Natl Fed Temple Brotherhoods, 1964-66; J Chautauqua Soc, 1962-64; Masons, fmr master, Prospect Lodge. Home: 141 Pine St, Woodmere, NY. Office: 521 Fifth Ave, New York, NY.

LIEBSON, Sidney H, US, physicist; b. Bklyn, NY, July 9, 1920; s. George and Rose (Gelasno); BSc, CCNY, 1939; MSc, U Mich, 1940; PhD, U Md, 1947; m. Jeanette Burman, Jan 18, 1947; c: Alice, Gail. Mgr, xerographic tech, Xerox Corp, since 1966; head, electromagnetics br, USN Research Lab, 1940-55; mgr, research, devl, Nuclear Devl Corp of Amer, 1955-59; asst dir, physics, Armour Research Found, 1959-60; mgr, phys research, Natl Cash Reg Co, 1960-66. Sr mem, Inst Radio Engrs; f, Amer Phys Soc; mem: Wash of Sci; Wash Phil Soc. Contbr to profsl jours. Recipient: meritorius civilian award, USN, 1945. Home: 19 Framingham Lane, Pittsford, NY. Office: Xerox Corp, Webster, NY.

LIEF, Joseph H, US, rabbi, chaplain; b. Cambridge, Mass, Jan 29, 1910; s. David and Clara (Bieber); BA, Yeshiva Coll, 1932; ordained rabbi, Rabbi Isaac Elchanan Theol Sem, NYC, 1934; m. Gertrude Goodman, June 3, 1941, (decd); c: Sandra Garrett, Beth. Chaplain, VA Hosp, Northport, NY, since 1946; chaplain, Hillside Hosp, Glen Oaks, NY, since 1959; rabbi, B'nai Isr Comty Cen, Bklyn, NY, 1934-41. Maj, chaplain, US Army, asst theater chaplain, Pacific Ocean areas, 1941-46. Chaplain: Police Dept; Patrolmen's Benevolent Assn; other police orgs, all Suffolk Co, NY; JWV, natl chaplain, 1958, cdr, Suffolk Co Post 488, 1956; chaplain, dept of NY, 1950-59, 1961-67, chaplain, Nassau-Suffolk Dist Council, 1954-69; mem: bd dirs, Suffolk Co Mh Assn, 1951-59; bd dirs, Legal Aid Soc, Suffolk Co; Boston Latin Sch Assn; Yeshiva Coll Alumni Assn; Yeshiva U Rabb Alumni; RabCA; NY Bd Rabbis; Assn J Chaplains of Armed

Forces; Mil Chaplains Assn; Suffolk Co Mh Assn; Masons; B'nai B'rith; VFW; Natl Sojourners; Suribachi Sq Club of Iwo Jima; mem: LI Regional Mh Planning Comm, 1962-65; youth bd, Town of Huntington, NY, 1967; Suffolk Co Narcotics Commn, 1967-68. Author: Outline for Prayer Worship, 1944; Friday Prayer Service, 1944; This is My Prayer, 1951, revised ed, 1957, 1959. Recipient: NY State Conspicuous Medal Award; UJA plaque, 1959; Four Chaplains Award, AD Goode-Ben Goldman lodge, B'nai B'rith, 1964; Brotherhood Award, JWV, 1965. Home: 105 Dumbarton Dr, Huntington, NY. Office: VA Hosp, Northport, NY.

LIEVERMAN, Arthur Robert, US, manufacturer; b. Columbus, O, Dec 12, 1921; s. Herman and Florence (Pass); BS chem engr, O State U, 1942; m. Lillian Weinrib, May 8, 1947; c: Theodore, Helen. Owner, Hampton Paint Mfg Co, since 1948; pres, Va Paint Varnish & Lacquer Assn. Lt, USN, 1942-46. Fmr chmn, Hampton-Phoebus JCC; bd trustee, Hampton Comty Chest; past pres, B'nai Isr Cong; chmn, comty relations, Newport News J Comm Council; delg, VA Dem Convention, 1967; active civil rights worker. Home: 20 Orchard Ave, Hampton, Va. Office: 228 Patterson Ave, Hampton, Va.

LIFSCHITZ, Benzion, Isr, engineer; b. Jaffa, Isr, Sep 15, 1908; s. Nathan and Sara (Rosenfarb); dipl ing, Montifiore Tech Sch, Tel Aviv, 1928; CE Free U, Belgium, 1931; m. Yaffa Chapnik; c: Almoga, Hava. Cons engr, quality surveying, mgr, Benzion Lifschitz Engr and Construction Co Ltd, since 1960; fmr: engr: Haifa Port, 1931-39; Jerusalem Water Supply, 1934-36; PWD, Jerusalem, 1936-38; regional engr, Town Planning Dept, Haifa, 1938-48; mgr, D Chapnik & L Feingold Metal Works, 1949-50. Haganah, engr corps, IDF, 1948-49. Engr with contractor: Mann Auditorium, Hilton Hotel, Tel Aviv; Atomic Plant, Dimona; maj works executed: supervision, model bldgs, Beersheba; quantity surveying, reconstruction, It Hosp; Educ Dept Off, Jerusalem; apts: Zahala, Tel Aviv, Fedja, Petach Tikvah; quantity surveying for: Solel Boneh; D Levitt Cons Engrs Ltd; Moya Bldg Co Ltd, all Tel Aviv; Recther-Zarhi Architects and Peri Engrs. Mem: Assn Engrs and Architects in Isr; Masons. Home and office: 18 Dubnov St, Tel Aviv, Isr.

LIFSCHUTZ, Emanuel L, US, rabbi; b. NYC, June 6, 1907; s. Hyman and Flora (Lewis); BA, CCNY, 1932; ordained rabbi, Yeshiva U, 1932, MA, 1969; m. Deborah Sternberg, Dec 24, 1938; c: Shulamith, David, Jonathan. Dir, J chaplaincy service, Milw JWF, since 1962; asso rabbi, W Side Instl Syn, NYC, to 1943; rabbi: United J Comty, Ottawa, Can, 1946-51; Cong Mikveh Isr, 1951-56; Cong Agudath Achim, Altoona, Pa, 1956-59; Cong Beth Hamedrosh Hagodol Bnai Sholom, Milw, Wis, 1959-62. Chaplain, USN, 1943-46. Mem: ZOA; Amer J Hist Soc; RA. Home: 2813 N 47 St, Milwaukee, Wis. Office: 948 N 12 St, Mt Sinai Hosp, Milwaukee, Wis.

LIFSET, Harvey M, US, attorney, legislator; b. Schenectady, NY, Mar 6, 1916; s. Abram and Rose (Barish); AB, Union Coll, 1937; LLB, Albany Law Sch, 1940; m. Violet Rubin, May 3, 1942; c: Marc, Reid. Pvt practice since 1946; NY State assemblyman, since 1957, chmn, assembly ways and means comm, 1966-68. Col, US Army Res. Dir: Albany JCC, 1969; Cerebral Palsy, Albany, 1958-68; pres: Albany Alumni of Union Coll, 1959; Albany Lions, 1959; mem: Masons; Elks; B'nai B'rith; Amer Legion; JWV; Res Off Assn; Albany Co, NY State Bar Assns; Temple Beth Emeth Brotherhood. Recipient: Bronze Star, Bronze Arrowhead, six battle stars. Home: 380 Albany-Shaker Rd, Loudonville, NY. Office: 90 State St, Albany, NY.

LIFSON, David S, US, author, educator; b. NYC, Dec 29, 1908; s. Louis and Sarah (Saffro); BS, Wash Sq Coll, 1931, MA, NYU, 1957, PhD, 1962; m. Dorothy Marburger, Nov 27, 1932; c: Hugh. Prof, Eng dept, Monmouth Coll, NJ, since 1964; prof: Pratt Inst, 1954-63; Jersey City State Coll, 1963-64. Dir, Bklyn Hgts Youth Cen; fmr, pres, Monmouth AAUP; mem: Actors Equity Assn; Amer Educ Theatre Assn; Pi Delta Epsilon. Author: The Yiddish Theatre in America, 1965; introduction to Separate Voices, An Anthol of NJ Shore Poets; contbr to jours, mags; chaps in History of the Theatre, ed, J in Drama and Theatre, Ency Judaica, 1966; plays produc: A Tiny Crime, 1947; The Gift of the Magi, 1957; Oh, Doctor! 1958; Mummers and Men, 1960, 1962; Children at the White House, 1962. Recipient: Otto Kahn Award, Metrop Opera, 1930; Founders Day Award, NYU, 1963. Hobbies: theatre, writing, tennis. Home: 40 E 10 St, New York, NY. Office: Monmouth Coll, W Long Branch, NJ.

LIGHTMAN, Jacob B, Can, educator; b. Boston, Mass, Apr 9, 1904; s. Meyer and Hannah (Setzer); in Can since 1952; AB, JD, George Wash U and Law Sch, 1928; MSS, U State NY, 1933; m. Esther Wecksler, June 15, 1931; c: Evelyn Falk, Robert, Richard. Asso prof, social work, McGill U, Montreal, since 1956, lectr, 1954-55; visiting spec lectr, Sir George Williams U, Montreal, since 1968; fmr: mem fac, Grad Sch for J Social Work, NY, 1931-33; asst exec dir, JDC, NY, 1933-37; dir: JCC, Metrop Houston, Tex, 1937-43; Buenos Aires off, JDC, 1943-50; comty relations, W Eur, Paris off, AJComm, 1950-51; Natl Conf, Isr, J Rehab, Can, 1952-55; A and H Bronfman Fund, Montreal, 1956-59; cons, urban comty devl, Govt of Costa Rica, US Intl Coop Admn, 1959; social work educ, Govt of India, 1960-61; visiting spec lectr, social work: St Louis U; Windsor U, Ontario. Bd dirs: Baron de Hirsch Inst; J Child Wfr Bur, Montreal; J Public Libr, Montreal; Can J Hist Soc; mem: Can comm, Intl Conf Social Work, since 1957; Can Friends, Alliance Isr Universelle; Can Conf Social Wfr; Can Wfr Council; Can Public Wfr Assn; fmr, mem exec comm, Pan Amer Conf Social Work. Contbr to gen and J publs; Universal J Ency. Home: 531 Grosvenor Ave, Westmount, Can. Office: McGill U, Montreal, Can.

LILIENFELD, Abraham M, US, epidemiologist, educator; b. NYC, Nov 13, 1920; s. Joel and Eugenia (Kugler); BA, Johns Hopkins U, 1941; MPH, 1949; MD, U Md, 1944; m. Lorraine Zemil, July 18, 1943; c: Julia, Saul, David. Prof, chmn, dept chronic diseases, Johns Hopkins Sch of Hygiene, since 1958, fac mem since 1950; cons: communicable disease cen, USPHS, since 1951, with service since 1947; Natl Cancer Inst; Natl Inst Neur Diseases; Natl Heart Inst, since 1966; epidemiologist, asso public health phys, NY State Health Dept, 1948-50; dir, S Health Dist, Baltimore, 1950-52; chief, dept stat, epidemiology, Roswell Park Memorial Inst, 1954-58; staff dir, Pres Commn on Heart Disease, Cancer and Stroke, 1964-66. US Army, 1946-47. F: Amer Public Health Assn; Amer Coll Preventive Med; NY Acad Sci; mem: Amer Stat Assn; AAAS; Amer Epidemiological Soc; Amer Soc Human Genetics. Contbr to med jours. Recipient: Bronfman prize for public health, 1968. Home: 6200 Gist Ave, Baltimore, Md. Office: Johns Hopkins Sch of Hygiene, Baltimore, Md.

LILIENFELD, Iwan, Isr, editor; b. Rybnik, Ger, June 3, 1910; s. Ludwig and Ida (Pick); in Isr since 1935; att Us: Freiburg; Munich; Berlin; m. Edith Fliess. Newspaper ed since 1938. Home: 21 Golani St, Ramat Chen, Isr. Office: 66 Harakevet St, Tel Aviv, Isr.

LILIENTHAL, David E, US, industrial cons, author; b. Morton, Ill, July 3, 1899; s. Leo and Minna (Rosenak); BA, DePauw U, 1920; LLB, Harvard U, 1923; LLD, DePauw U, 1945; hon LLD: Lehigh U, 1949; Mich State Coll, 1949; Boston U, 1952; U de Los Andes, Colombia, 1954; UCLA, 1964; U Ind, 1965; hon DPA, U Ill, 1967; m. Helen Lamb, Sep 4, 1923; c: Nancy Bromberger, David. Chmn, chief exec off, Devl and Resources Corp, since 1955; chmn, TVA, 1941-46; practiced law, Chgo, 1923-31; mem, Wis Public Service Commn, 1931; chmn: US State Dept Bd Cons on Intl Control of Atomic Energy, 1946; US AEC, 1946-50; trustee, Twentieth Cent Fund, Freedom House. Mem: Amer Acad Arts and Sci; Delta Upsilon; Delta Sigma Rho; Sigma Delta Chi; Phi Beta Kappa; club, Cent Assn, NY. Author: TVA-Democracy on the March, 1944; This I Do Believe, 1949; Big Business: A New Era, 1953; Change, Hope, and the Bomb, 1963; Journals of David E Lilienthal, Vols I and II, 1964, Vol III, 1966, Vol IV, 1969; Management: A Humanist Art, 1967. Recipient: Progressive Farmer Award, 1945; Catholic Comm of S Award, 1946; Franklin D Roosevelt Memorial Award, 1949; Page One Award, 1949; Freedom House Award, 1949; Public Wfr Medal, Natl Acad Sci, 1951. Homes: 88 Battle Rd, Princeton, NJ; Topside, Martha's Vineyard Island, Mass. Office: One Whitehall, New York, NY.

LIMON, Mordecai, Isr, business exec; b. Baranowitz, Pol, Jan 3, 1924; s. Benyamin and Rivka (Rabinowitz); MBA, Columbia U, 1956; m. Rachel Luria; c: Nili, Zvi. Business exec, since 1970; capt of ships, Aliya Beit, 1945-48; cdr in chief, Isr Navy, 1951-54; dep dir gen, Min of Defense, 1957-62; spec envoy, Min of Defense, Eur, 1962-70. Home: Tel Aviv, Isr.

LINDAU, Jules W, US, educator, business exec; b. Greensboro, NC, Aug 20, 1909; s. Jules and Betty (Tashman); ME, Rensselaer Poly, Troy, NY, 1931; m. Beatrice Perl, Feb 28, 1931; c: Betty Ustun, Jules, Susan, Bertha. Pres, Lindau Chems, Inc since 1967; vice-pres, Palmetto Radio Corp since

1951; pres, found, Capital Blue Print since 1932; pres, found: S Plastic Co, 1940-66, prof, mech engr, U of SC, 1941-46. Vice-pres, Tree of Life Syn; commn, Midlands Tech Educ Commn; fmr: pres, Family Service Agcy of Colo; vice-pres, Soc of Plastics Engrs; chmn, Polymer Educ Coord Comm; Bd, Plastics Inst of Amer; f, Plastic Inst; mem: dirs, Asso Social Agcys; Mfrs Council, Columbia, SC; Tau Beta Pi; dist, Soc of Plastics Engrs; Columbia C of C; Mayor's Comm on Civic Improvement; Amer Soc Mech Engrs; Illuminating Engr Soc; NY Acad Scis; AAAS; Soc Hist of Tech; SC Soc of Engrs. Author, Engineering Metallurgy, 1954; contbr to plastics engr jours. Recipient, Pres' Award, Soc of Plastics Engrs, 1955. Home: 445 Saluda Ave, Columbia, SC. Office: 750 Granby Lane, POB 641, Columbia, SC.

LINDAU, Mose S, US, jurist; b. Sioux City, Ia, Apr 15, 1910; s. William and Helene (Marchand); LLB, U of SD, 1933; att N State Tchrs Coll, 1949-50; U of Va, 1960-63; m. Rose Berkman, Nov 18, 1951; c: Mark. Judge, Dist Juvenile & Co Court, Eleventh Judicial Dist of SD, since 1969; pvt practice, law, 1933-50; judge: Juvenile & Co Court of Brown Co, SD, 1950-69; munic court, Aberdeen, SD, 1967. US Army, 1941-45; maj US Army Res. Pres: SD Mh Assn, 1955-56; Jr Bar of SD, 1939-40; vice-pres, SD Co Judges Assn, 1955-57; chmn: comm on unauthorized practice of law, SD State Bar, 1941-42, comm-at-large, 1955-58; Juvenile Protection, SD Cong of Parents and Tchrs since 1967; dir, NE SD Cong of Parents and Tchrs since 1967; dir, NE SD Mh Cen since 1957; master, Aberdeen Scottish Rite Bodies, 1964-67; mem: Gov's Comm on Children and Youth, 1959-61; bd govs, Metrop Dinner Club of Gt Aberdeen since 1969; exec comm, Natl Council of Juvenile Court Judges, 1968-71; regional comm on Crime and Delinquency since 1969; Amer Bar Assn; Natl Council of Juvenile Court Judges; State Bar of SD; Brown Co Bar Assn; Amer Acad of Political and Social Sci; Amer Philatelic Assn; Amer Topical Assn; Amer Legion; United Commercial Travelers; Yelduz Temple, Shrine; Masons; KP; B'nai B'rith. Co-author: Annotations to Restatements of Laws of Contracts, 1937, and of the Law of Conflict of Laws, 1940. Recipient, two combat stars. Hobbies: military hist; philately. Home: 1006 N 2 St, Aberdeen, SD. Office: Brown Co Court House, Aberdeen, SD.

LINDEMANN, Rolf, Eng, business exec; b. Berlin, Ger, Nov 7, 1917; s. Leopold and Hedda (Weissenburger); in Eng since 1936; att Sorbonne, 1934; m. Elaine Oppenheim, Mar 23, 1941; c: Stephen, Leopol, Clive. Chmn, gov dir, Frankenstein Group Ltd since 1946, with firm since 1936. Vice-chmn, Assn Brit Foam Laminators; hon treas, Manchester J Homes for Aged; mem: B'nai B'rith lodge; Zion Lodge. Home: Newtonhurst, Park Ave, Hale, Eng. Office: Culcheth Lane, Manchester, Eng.

LINDENBAUM, Arie, Isr, journalist, teacher; b. Pol, Nov 11, 1929; s. Itzhak and Antoinette (Stahl); in Isr since 1947; tchr dipl, Tchr Sem, Tel Aviv, 1951; m. Shulamit Sohar, c: Itzhak, Karnit. Philatelic ed: Davar newspaper, since 1956; Isr Philatelic Monthly; tchr, Dov Hoz Sch, Tel Aviv, since 1951. IDF, 1948. Author: Jews on Stamps, 1958; World Refugee Year, 1960; Judaica Guide, 1963. Mem: Judaica Philatelic Soc, Isr; Isr Philatelist Soc, US, pres, Tel Aviv chap. Recipient: Gold, Silver & Bronze Medals for org stamps exhbs; decorations: War of Independence; Hagana; Sinai Campaign; Six Days War. Hobbies: stamp collecting, Judaica. Home: 18 Lipsky St, Tel Aviv, Isr.

LINDENBAUM, Leo, US, business exec, realtor; b. Budapest, Hung, Dec 31, 1884; s. Jacob and Sarah (Freudiger de O-buda); in US since 1938; degree, Music and Art, 1906; DJ, U of Vienna, 1909; m. Olga de Poliakoff, July 8, 1929; c: Livia Schenker, Lionel. Pres, several realty corps, NY since 1943; real estate investor in Isr since 1925; dir, devl, co-owner, David Lindenbaum's Oilfields and Forest Estate, Pol, 1913-38; dir, co-owner, Gasteiner Hotel und Kuranstalten Gesellschaft, Bad Gastein, Aus, 1919-25; mem, bd dirs, Bitumen, Naphta AG, Pol, 1926-38. Chmn, art div, Amer J Lit Found; trustee, W Side Comty Coh, treas: Yeshiva Chofetz Chaim, NYC since 1948; Hisachdut Talmidei Yeshiva Chasam Sofer since 1952; mem: bd adv, J Forum Found, 1953; Citizens Budget Commn, 1955; Real Estate Bd of NY, 1955; AJCong; ZOA; Amer Friends of Heb U; Amer Fed of J from Central Eur; United HIAS Service; Amer Red Mogen David; ARC; W Side Instl Syn; Metrop Mus of Art; Metrop Opera Guild; UN Assn of US; Intl Platform Assn, Cleveland, O; Zwi Peretz Chates Inst; mem in Vienna: bd, Curatorium; Childs Found for Cancer

Research, 1928-29; Wiener Morgenzeitung, 1919-26, bd advs; found Soc for Research and Advancement of J Music, 1919. Composer: waltzes, marches, small pieces for violin and piano; contbr to Eur newspapers. Recipient, Citation of Merit, Amer J Lit Found, 1956; donated with family land in W Carmel, Isr, for construction of a rehab cen for polio-stricken children, in memory of parents. Spec interest, collecting art works. Home and office: 251 Central Park W, New York, NY.

LINDENFELD, Moshe, Isr, physician; b. Czernowitz, Rum, Feb 4, 1905; s. Benzion and Bertha (Altman); in Isr since 1948; MD, Fac Med, U of Vienna, 1931; m. Josephine Rones, May 12, 1935. Dir, first surg dept, Assaf Harofe Govt Hosp, since 1949. Maj, mil med service, IDF, 1948-49. Home and office: 54 Jabotinsky St, Tel Aviv, Isr.

LINDENSTRAUSS, Walter, Isr, banker; b. Berlin, Ger, Mar 12, 1904; s. Jacob and Jeanette (Rosenstein); in Isr since 1939; DJur, U Berlin, 1931; m. Margarethe Liebenau, Mar 24, 1932; c: Michael. Mgr, Isr Ind Bank Ltd, Haifa since 1946, bd dirs since 1968; cen bd, Lib Party of Isr; councillor, leader, Lib Party Sect, Haifa Munic since 1959; fmr: lawyer in pvt practice, Berlin; leading official, JA for Pal, Berlin off. Hon mem, Mfrs Assn, Haifa, since 1961. Home: 3 Kalisher St, Neve Shaanan, Haifa, Isr. Office: Isr Ind Bank Ltd, Haifa, Isr.

LINDER, Bertram N, US, business exec; b. NYC, Nov 24, 1915; s. Albert and Bess (Newman); BA, Williams Coll, 1936; att Yale U, 1936-37; Columbia U, 1937-38; m. Eleanor Jones, Jan 13, 1942. Pres and treas: Linder Bros Inc since 1965, with firm since 1941; Albert A & Bertram N Linder Found Inc since 1965; dir, Northeastern Pa Natl Bank & Trust Co since 1954; breeder of thoroughbred race-horses. Lt, US Army, 1942-45. Pres: J Fed, 1950-51; Child Psycht and Guidance Cen, 1950-56; United World Federalists, 1950-51, both of Lackawanna; Salvation Army Adv Bd, past chmn, 1949-50; vice-pres, gen chmn, United Comty Chest, 1953-54; dir: Scranton C of C, 1962; J Comty Cen; Allied Services for the Handicapped; Gov's Comm on Employment of the Physically Handicapped since 1958; pres, Lackawanna United Fund, 1960; mem: AJComm; B'nai B'rith; UJA, Lackawanna Co, past chmn; clubs: Williams, NY; Rotary. Recipient: Presidential Citation, 1945; Bronze Star; Combat Infantryman Badge; Purple Heart; Belgian Forreguerre. Home: Hickory Hill Farm, Dalton, Pa. Office: 1043 Capouse Ave, Scranton, Pa.

LINDER, Bruno, US, educator; b. Sniatyn, Pol, Sep 3, 1924; s. Elias and Feiga (Kleinman); in US since 1946; BS, Upsala Coll, NJ, 1948; MS, Ohio U, 1950; PhD, U of Cal, 1955; m. Cecelia Fahn, Feb 14, 1953; c: William, Diane, Richard, Nancy, Carolyn. Prof, chem, Fla State U since 1965, Hillel counselor since 1968, asso prof, 1961-65, asst prof, 1957-61; research asso, U of Wis Naval Research Lab, 1955-57; research participant, Oak Ridge Natl Lab, summers, 1958-59, 1961; Guggenheim f, Inst of Theoretical Physics, U of Amsterdam, 1964-65. Member: Amer Chem Soc, chmn, Tallahassee subsection, 1964, secy-treas, 1962; Amer Phys Soc; Sigma Xi; Phi Lambda Upsilon; Phi Mu Alpha, Sinfonia. Contbr to profsl journals. Home: 2226 Demeron Rd, Tallahassee, Fla. Office: Florida State U, Tallahassee, Fla.

LINDHEIM, Irma L, Isr, communal worker; b. NYC, Dec 9, 1886; d. Robert and Tillie (Morgenstern) Levy; in Isr since 1933; att: JIR, 1922-25; Columbia U, 1922-25; officially accepted as candidate for Rabb deg, JIR, NY, 1924; m. Norvin Lindheim, Apr 25, 1906; c: Norvin (decd), Donald (decd), Richard, Stephen, Hortense. Hon vice-pres, Hadassah, since 1942, fmr, natl pres. Lt, Motor Corps of Amer, WW I; dir, Volunteer Land Corps, WW II. Prin contribs: successful experiments in parent educ, leading to creation of Sch for Parent Educ, Herzl Inst. Hon life mem, Zionist Exec; fmr: pres, 7th dist, ZOA, NY, natl vice-pres; mem, actions comm, WZO; helped org, League for Lab Pal, 1932; mem, Histadrut; co-found, Guggenheimer Playgrounds, 1925; found, Progressive Pal (Isr) Projects, 1947; originator, Pal f's for Amer Coll youth, 1935, plan later adopted by jt comm of Zionist exec, Keren Kayemet and KH, chmn, 1939; head, JNF campaign, Eng, Australia, NZ. Author: The Immortal Adventure, 1928; Parallel Quest: A Search of a Person and a People, 1962. Home: Kibbutz Mishmar Ha-Emek, Isr.

LINDNER, Irving, US, attorney; b. Denver, Colo, June 14, 1906; s. Milton and Dora (Lewin); att: U Colo, 1926; Harvard U, 1930; m. Florence Radetsky, Aug 29, 1933; c: Diane

Rewler, Milton, Paula. Pvt practice; sr partner: Lindner & Shere, then Lindner, Shere & Rottman, 1953-58; Lindner, Arkin & Davis, law firm, 1959-62. Mem, bd trustees: Children's Asthmatic Research Inst and Hosp; J Natl Home for Asthmatic Children; mem: Phi Sigma Delta; Town Club, past secy, dir; fmr: vice-pres, ritual comm, Cong Micah. Home: 1109 Monaco Pkwy, Denver, Colo. Office: 110 16 St, Denver, Colo.

LINDNER, Richard, US, artist, educator; b. Hamburg, Ger, Nov 11, 1901; s. Julius and Mina (Bornstein); in US since 1941; att Acads: Munich; Berlin. Prof: art, Pratt Inst, Bklyn, since 1952; Yale U, New Haven, Conn. One man shows: Betty Parsons Gal, NY, 1954, 1956, 1959; Cordier-Eckstrom, Inc, 1961, 1963; Robert Fraser Gal, London, 1962; Cordier Gal, Paris, 1963; Mus of Modern Art, NY, 1963; exhbs: Chgo Art Inst; Walker Art Cen, Minneapolis; Yale U; U of Ill; Bklyn Mus; Pa Acad of Fine Arts; perm collections: Mus of Modern Art, NY; Whitney Mus, NY; in pvt collections: Paris; Holland; London; It; US. Served Fr Army, 1939-40. Home: 333 E 69 St, New York, NY.

LINFIELD, Ben Zion, US, mathematician, educator; b. Russ, June 20, 1897; s. Pincus and Slova (Kantzepovitz); in US since 1913; BS, U of Va, 1918, MS, 1920; PhD, Harvard U, 1923; DS, Strasbourg U, Fr, 1925; m. Libby Lintup, Sep 3, 1924; c: Dacie, Susan, Paul. Asso prof math, U of Va since 1926. Author: Integral and Matric Geometry, 1954; Structure of Functions and Covariants and the Analysis of Motions and Coordinates, 1962. Home: 1324 Hill Top Rd, Charlottesville, Va. Office: U of Virginia, Charlottesville, Va.

LINKS, Maurice Benzion, Scotland, business exec; b. Glasgow, Scotland, Dec 25, 1912; MA, Glasgow U; m. Ida Bernstein; c: Dorothy, David, Brian. Chmn, Links Warehouse Group, since 1963. Hon pres, JNF, Glasgow; pres, Brit Technion Soc, Glasgow group. Home: 217 Nithsdale Rd, Glasgow, Scotland. Office: 51 Wilson St, Glasgow, Scotland.

LINN, Louis, US, psychiatrist; b. Newark, NJ, May 14, 1914; s. Abraham and Anna (Ashinofsky); AB, U of Pa, 1934; MD, U of Chgo, 1938; m. Miriam Wechsler, Dec 14, 1941; c: Judith, Robert. Att psycht, Mt Sinai Hosp since 1962; lectr, JTSA since 1958; asso clinical prof, comty psycht, Columbia U, on staff since 1957; fmr dir, Dept of Psycht, Bx Leb Hosp Cen; capt, US Army MC, 1942-46. Mem: bd dirs, Amer J Phys Comm since 1960; Amer Friends of Heb U; Phi Beta Kappa; Alpha Omega Alpha. Author: Handbook of Hospital Psychiatry, 1955; Psychiatry and Religious Experience, 1958; Frontiers of General Hospital Psychiatry, 1961; Occupational Therapy in Dynamic Psychiatry, 1962; contbr numerous articles to profsl jours. Home: 55 E 86 St, New York, NY. Office: 9 E 96 St, New York, NY.

LINOWES, David F, US, educator, certified public acctnt, business exec; b. Mar 16, 1917; BS, hons, U of Ill, 1941; m. four c. CPA; partner, Laventhol, Krekstein, Horwath & Horwath, intl acctnt firm; chmn, bd dirs, Perpetual Invrs Co, Inc; dir: Richland Inds Corp; Chris Craft Inds, Inc; exec sem lectr, NYU; chmn: profsl adv bd, U of Ill; chmn, intl adv group, Tel Aviv U; cons: US State Dept, head, mission to Turkey, 1967; UN on UNIDO mission to: Pakistan; Iran; Turkey. Lt, US Army, 1942-46. Trustee: Amer Inst Benevolent Fund; Asso YM-YWHA's of Gtr NY; mem, trial bd, governing council, Amer Inst CPAs, past treas, vice-pres; fmr: pres, DC Inst CPAs; cons, Secy John W Gardner, Dept HEW; off delg, Ninth Intl Cong Acctnts, Paris, 1967. Author, Managing Growth Through Acquisition, 1968; contbr to profsl jours. Home: 9 Wayside Lane, Scarsdale, NY. Office: 866 Third Ave, New York, NY.

LINOWITZ, Sol M, US, attorney, business exec; b. Trenton, NJ, Dec 7, 1913; s. Joseph and Rose (Oglenskye); BA, Hamilton Coll, 1935; LLB, Cornell Law Sch, 1938; m. Evelyn Zimmerman, 1939; c: Ann, June, Jan, Ronni. US Ambass to Org of Amer States since 1966; pvt practice, Sutherland, Linowitz & Williams, 1942-57; asst gen counsel, OPA, Wash, DC, 1942-44; admitted to US Supr Court, 1943; pvt practice, Harris, Beach, Wilcox, Dale & Linowitz, 1957-66; chmn bd, gen counsel, chmn exec comm, Xerox Corp, 1959-66, with co, 1947-66. Lt, US Navy, WW II. Pres, NY State, Amer Assn for UN, 1953-66, pres, Rochester br, 1952, chmn bd dir, 1953; pres, Rochester C of C, 1958; co-chmn, org comm, Intl Exec Service Corps, 1964-66; mem, bd dir: United JWF since 1946; Vets Bc Co, 1947-66; J Young Men's and Women's Assn, 1947; Superba Cravats since 1950; Sch for the Deaf since 1951;

Rochester Savings Bank, 1955-66; trustee, U of Rochester since 1950; found and moderator, WHAM-TV discussion prog, The Court of Public Opinion, 1951-59; mem: off city delg to Rennes, Fr and to State of Isr, 1958; bd mgrs, Eastman Sch of Music since 1959; mem: Natl Comm for Intl Devl; intl affairs comm, Amer Bar Assn, 1946-66; NY State Bar Assn; Temple Beth El; Phi Beta Kappa; Order of Coif; Delta Sigma Rho; Phi Kappa Phi; clubs: Rochester City; past pres, U of Rochester. Contbr to law jours; ed-in-chief, Cornell Law Quarterly, 1937-38. Recipient: Leroy Snyder award, City of Rochester, for leadership in comty and civic affairs, 1952; several natl medal awards, Amer Freedom Found, for the TV progs. Home: 2204 Wyoming Ave, Washington, DC. Office: State Dept, Washington, DC.

LI-ON (Sandel) Arie, Isr, business exec; b. Slavonski, Yugo, Dec 5, 1911; s. Menahem and Esther (Tanenbaum) Sandel; in Isr since 1936; cert, Advanced Sch of Lab, Tel Aviv, 1954; att Agric Coop Orgs, Swed, Holland, Den, on Isr Govt F, 1958; m. Shoshana Adam, Feb 1934; c: Erela Geva, Azriel, Gideon, Michal Kaw, Doron, Daniel. Expert in coop orgs, Govt of Colombia since 1967. Fmr: coord for new settlements, colonization dept, JA; mgr, promotion, Org of Regional Coops; dir, bd mem, Hamashbir Hamerkazi, Hamashbir Lazarkan; mem, Kibbutz Afikim; served Haganah, IDF. Mem: village council, Moshav Kidron; Brener Region; secretariat, Movement of Coop Settlements; active, Thelet Lavan Movement, Yugo; dir, bd: Consumption Coop Movement; Coop Movement Comptroller. Hobby, folk music. Home: Kidron, Isr. Office: Isr Embassy, Apartado Aereo 14494, Bogota, Columbia.

LION, Aviva, Isr, social worker; b. Bucharest, Rum, Apr 27, 1929; d. Yehoshua and Friedel (Korner) Weinstein; in Isr since 1944; BA, Sch of Social Work, Jerusalem, 1953; MSW U of Wis, Milw, 1968; m. Eliezer Lion, Apr, 1953; c: Ehud, Tamar, Gad. Chief wfr off in charge of adoption, Min of Social Wfr, Jerusalem, since 1965; dist sup: Absorption Dept, JA, 1953-62; dist child wfr sup, Min of Social Wfr, 1962-65. IDF, 1948-49. Co-ed, Saad jour. Mem, exec comm, Org of Social Workers, Jerusalem. Contbr to profsl jours. Home: 49 Rachel Imenu St, Jerusalem, Isr. Office: Min of Social Wfr, 8 King David St, Jerusalem, Isr.

LIPCHIK, Harold, US, business exec; b. NYC, Apr 17, 1928; s. Samuel and Ida (Gutterman); BME, Carnegie-Mellon U, Pittsburgh, Pa, 1948; m. Elaine Greenbert, Mar 23, 1952; c: Alan, Debra. Pres, Water Treatment Corp since 1968; vice-pres, Chromalloy Amer Corp since 1966; vice-pres, Amer Machine & Foundry Co, 1955-66. Vice-pres: Pacific SW Region, United Syns of Amer; Valley Beth Shalom Temple; asso f, Amer Inst of Aeronautics and Astronautics; corp repr: Air Pollution Control Assn; Water Pollution Control Fed; mem: ground support comm, Amer Ordnance Assn; Intl Platform Assn; Tau Delta Phi. Home: 15921 Royal Oak Rd, Encino, Cal. Office: 17400 E Chestnut St, City of Industry, Cal.

LIPINSKI, Edward, Belgium, educator; b. Lodz, Pol, June 18, 1930; s. Szmul-Hersz and Gabrielle (Beghon); in Belgium since 1941; BA, Saint-Trond Coll, 1950; PhM, MDiv, U of Rome, 1957; DD, M Oriental Phil, U of Louvain, 1960, Mag Div, 1964-65; D Bible Studies, Bible Inst, Rome, 1964; m. Maria-Lorenza Moi, Nov 8, 1969. Prof, fac phil and letters, U of Louvain, since 1969. Author: Les Psaumes de la Royauté de Yahwé dans l'exégèse moderne, 1962; La Royauté de Yahwé dans la poésie et le culte de l'ancien Israel, 1965, 2nd ed, 1968; Le Poème royal du Psaume LXXXIX, 1-5, 20-38, 1967; La Liturgie pénitentielle dans la Bible, 1969; contbr to jours. Recipient, Laureate, Royal Flemish Acad of Sci, Letters and Arts, Brussels, 1963. Home: 7 rue des Aduatiques, Brussels, Belgium. Office: Instituut voor Oriëntalistiek, 17 Mgr Ladeuzeplein, Leuven, Belgium.

LIPIS, Philip L, US, rabbi; b. Tiraspol, Russ, Dec 14, 1906; s. Azriel and Lenah (Dickerman); in US since 1913; BA, CCNY, 1927; ordained Rabbi, MHL, JTSA, 1930, DD, honoris causa, 1967; att: Columbia U, 1928-29; Heb U, Jerusalem, 1930-31; Dropsie Coll, Phila, 1932-35; m. Shoshana Baron, 1936; c: Leah Steuer, Rinah Shaskolsky. Ret; fac, U of Judaism; rabbi: N Suburban Syn Beth El, Highland Park, Ill, 1951-69; Emanu-El Syn, Phila, 1932-35; Beth El Syn, Camden, NJ, 1935-47; Temple Beth Abraham, Oakland, Cal, 1947-51; chaplain, USN, 1943-46, cdr; instr, Coll J Studies, SF, 1948-50; conducted sem at Berchtesgaden, Ger for J chaplains in Eur at invitation of US War Dept, 1956. Rabb cabinet, JTSA since

1953, bd overseers since 1951; found, first pres, N Shore F of Rabbis; fmr pres: Chgo Bd of Rabbis; Chgo Region, RA; Camden Zionist Dist; vice-pres, Mil Chaplains Assn; exec council, N Cal Bd Rabbis; RA. Contbr to Best J Sermons, 1953-56, 59, 62, 64, 66. Recipient, Rabbi em, life, N Suburban Syn, Beth El, Highlands. Home: 1907 Fairburn Ave, W Los Angeles, Cal.

LIPKIN, David, US, chemist, educator; b. Phila, Pa, Jan 30, 1912; s. William and Ida (Zipin); BS, U of Pa, 1934; PhD, U of Cal, 1939; m. Shirley Douthitt, 1942, div; c: Jeffrey, Edward; m. 2nd, Virginia Brasch, 1956; stepc: John, Robert. Chmn, chem dept, Wash U since 1964; prof since 1948; fac mem since 1946; research chem, Atlantic Refining Co, Phila, 1934-36; research f, chem, U of Cal, 1939-42; research chem, radiation lab, 1942-43; group leader, Los Alamos Sci Lab, 1943-46; Guggenheim Memorial Found f, 1955-56; sr visiting f, Off for Eur Econ Coop, virus research unit, Agric Research Council, Cambridge, Eng, 1960; mem: NY Acad of Sci; AAUP; Amer Chem Soc; Tau Beta Pi; Sigma Xi; Pi Mu Epsilon. Holder of patents in petroleum chem; contbr to profsl jours. Home: 64 Arundel Pl, St Louis, Mo. Office: Washington U, St Louis, Mo.

LIPKIN, Seymour, US, musician; b. Detroit, Mich, May 14, 1927; s. Ezra and Leah (Vidaver); BMus, Curtis Inst of Music, 1947; m. Catherine Lee Bing, Dec 27, 1961; c: Jonathan. Concert pianist and conductor, since 1948; musical dir: Teaneck Sym, NJ, since 1961; Huntington Sym, NY, since 1964; NYC Cen Joffrey Ballet Co, 1966-68, prin guest conductor, since 1968; fac: Berkshire Music Cen, Lenox, Mass, 1951-65; Curtis Inst of Music, since 1969; head, music dept, Marymount Coll, Tarrytown, NY, since 1968, fac since 1963; asst conductor, NY Philharmonic Sym Orch, 1959-60; conductor, NYC Opera Co, 1958. Mem: bd of govs, Amer Guild Musical Artists, 1961-62; Amer Fed Musicians. Recipient: Rachmaninoff Piano Competition award, 1948. Home: 420 West End Ave, New York, NY. Office: c/o Barrett Mgmt, 1860 Broadway, New York, NY.

LIPKOWITZ, Irving D, US, attorney; b. NYC, Sep 23, 1899; s. Emanuel and Rose (Gluck); LLB, NYU, 1920; m. Sylvia Ravitch, Sep 1, 1933; c: John ,Elisabeth. Sr partner, Lipkowitz, Plaut, Salberg & Harris. Served US Army, 1918. Secy, United Pal Appeal, 1942-43; chmn, finance comm, ZOA, 1941-42; bd trustee: New Lincoln Sch, 1956-57; Beth Isr Hosp since 1947; Boardman Sch, 1950-53; admn comm, JNF, 1941-42; mem: B'rith Abraham; Masons; Glen Oaks and Quaker Ridge Golf Clubs. Home: 15 W 81 St, New York, NY. Office: 1290 Ave of Americas, New York, NY.

LIPMAN, Bernard Sylvester, US, physician; b. St Joseph, Mo, June 14, 1920; s. Harry and Sarah (Kross); BA, Wash U, 1941, MD, 1944; m. Leslie Garber, Apr 23, 1949; c: Lawrence, Robert, Bradford, William. Pvt practice since 1950; asso prof, clinical med, Emory U Sch of Med since 1950; cardiac cons: Grady Hosp, Atlanta, Ga since 1950; VA Regional Off since 1951; staff mem: Crawford W Long Hosp since 1950; St Joseph Hosp since 1950; Piedmont Hosp since 1952; Emory U Hosp since 1950, all Atlanta, Ga; co-dir, Glenville Giddings Cardiac Clinic; fmr: res: Barnes Hosp, St Louis, Mo; New Haven Hosp, Mo; teaching f, Wash U Sch of Med, St Louis, Mo. Capt, US Army. Mem: Alpha Omega Alpha; AMA; Phi Beta Kappa; Amer Fed for Clinical Research; Amer Coll of Phys; Amer Bd of Internal Med; AHA; Fulton Co Med Assn; Sigma Xi. Author: Clinical Unipolar Electrocardiography, 1951, 5th ed, 1965; chap, Clubbed Fingers and Hypertrophic Osteoarthropathy, in MacBryde's Signs and Symptoms, 1968; contbr to med jours. Home: 2562 Brookdale Dr NW, Atlanta, Ga. Office: 1285 Peachtree St, Atlanta, Ga.

LIPMAN, Eugene J, US, rabbi; b. Pittsburgh, Pa, Oct 13, 1919; s. Joshua and Bessie (Neaman); BA, U of Cincinnati, 1941; MHL, ordained rabbi, HUC, 1943; m. Esther Marcuson, July 4, 1943; c: Michael, Jonathan, David. Rabbi, Temple Sinai, Wash, DC since 1961; lectr, J Sch of Sacred Theol, Catholic U of Amer since 1968; rabbi, Temple Beth El, Ft Worth, Tex, 1943-44; teaching f, HUC, 1948-49; dir, Hillel Found, U of Wash, 1949-50; dir, Comm on Social Action, Comm on Syn Activities, UAHC, 1951-61; lectr, rel, The Amer U, 1961-68. Chaplain, US Army, 1944-46, 1950-51; liaison off between US Army and JA for Pal, Ger, 1947-48. Mem: Comm on Social Action of Reform J Exec Comm, JCC, Wash; CCAR; ACLU. Author, The Oral Torah, An Introduction to the Mishnah, 1969; co-author: Justice and

Judaism, 1956; A Tale of Ten Cities, 1962; co-ed, The American Synagogue, A Progress Report, 1957; contbr to rel jours. Home: 3512 Woodbine St, Chevy Chase, Md. Study: 3100 Military Rd, NW, Washington, DC.

LIPMANN, Fritz A, US, researcher, educator; b. Konigsberg, Ger, June 12, 1899; s. Leopold and Gertrude (Lachmanski); MD, U of Berlin, 1924, PhD, 1927; hon MD, U of Marseilles, Fr, 1947; hon MA, Harvard U, 1949; hon DS, U of Chgo, 1953; hon LHD, Brandeis U, 1959; hon MD,U of Chile, Santiago, 1963; hon LHD, Albert Einstein Coll of Med, Yeshiva U, 1964; hon DSc, U of Paris, 1966; hon DSc, Harvard U, 1967; m. Elfreda Hall, 1931; c: Stephen. Prof, Rockefeller U, since 1957; research asst, Kaiser Wilhelm Inst, Berlin and Heidelberg, 1927-31; Rockefeller f, Rockefeller Inst for Med Research, 1931-32; research asso, Biol Inst, Carlsberg Found, Copenhagen, Den, 1932-39; research asso, Dept Biol Chem, Cornell U Med Sch, 1939-41; research f in surg, Harvard Med Sch, 1941-43; sr biochem, Harvard Med Sch at Mass Gen Hosp, 1941-57; prof, biol chem, Harvard Med Sch, 1949-57. Prin contrib: discoverer of coenzyme A; main research in: energy metabolism; metabolic function of B vitamins; protein synthesis; biol sulfate transfer. Mem: Natl Acad Sci; Danish Royal Acad Sci; fgn mem, Royal Soc (Eng); Amer Phil Soc: Amer Soc Biol Chem; Biochem Soc; Harvey Soc. Contbr to sci jours. Recipient: Carl Neuberg Medal, 1948; Mead Johnson Award for work on vitamin B complex, 1948; Nobel Prize in med and phys, 1953; Natl Medal of Sci, 1966. Home: 150 E 18 St, New York, NY. Office: Rockefeller U, New York, NY.

LIPPERT, David I, US, attorney; b. LA, Cal, Jan 18, 1910; s. Alexander and Anna (Ferber), LLB, LA Coll of Law, 1932; m. Hannah Rosenberg, Nov 12, 1948. Referee, Workmens Compensation Appeals Bd of Cal, since 1958; pvt practice, 1932-42, 1950-58; dir, Judge Advocate Br, Fort MacArthur, US Army Res Sch, 1950-60; mem, field judiciary, Judge Advocate Gen's Corps, US Army Res, rank of lt-col, 1960-63; civilian atty, Dept US Army, Eur, 1946-49; US Army, 1942-46. Mem: Amer Bar Assn and sects: Intl and Comparative Law, Ins and Negligence Law, Jud Admn, Individual Rights and Responsibilities; LA Co Bar Assn, past chmn, sect Intl Law, past vice-chmn, Bar Bull Comm; Société Intl de Droit Pénal Mil et de Droit de Guerre; secy, ZOA W States region, 1951-52, 1954-55, vice-pres, LA dist, 1952-53; vice-pres, AJComm, LA, 1951-52, chmn, fgn affairs comm, 1952-54; mem, comty relations comm, LA J Fed Council, 1954-68; pres, LA Non-Govt Orgs Council, 1959-62; mem, bd dirs, Sinai Temple, since 1952, vice-pres, since 1964; mem: Amer ZC, 1954; Amer Assn for UN; Res Offs Assn; Judge Advocates Assn; Cal and LA Bar Assns. Author: The Eichmann Case and the Nuremberg Trials; contbr to profsl jours. Recipient, Commendation, US War Dept, 1949. Home: 916 S Hauser Blvd, Los Angeles, Cal. Office: State Bldg, Los Angeles, Cal.

LIPPITZ, Blanche Aronin, US, communal worker, attorney; b. Vilna, Russ, Nov 15, 1901; d. Simon and Rose (Markman) Aronin; in US since 1902; LLB, cum laude, Kent Coll of Law, Chgo, 1922; m. Milton Lippitz, Jan 6, 1924; c: Shari Rosen, Charles, Admitted to bar, State of Ill, 1923. Coord, natl org activities, Natl Women's League, United Syns of Amer, past chmn, natl leadership training, past vice-pres, pres, cen br; mem, Conf of J Women's Orgs; fmr: mem: natl speakers bur, cen br speakers bur, secy, women's div, J Charities; bd dirs, J Educ Bd, Chgo; pres, Anshe Emeth Sisterhood. pres, Recipient: Blanche Lippitz Libr, Camp Ramah, Wis, Natl Women's League, 1948. Home: 360 Wellington Ave, Chicago, Ill.

LIPPMAN, Alfred, Jr, US, chemical engr; b. New Orleans, La, Mar 13, 1908; s. Alfred and Belle (Levy); BChE, Tulane U, 1929; m. Dorothy Kahn, Oct 20, 1934; c: Alfred, Darryl, Tanya; m. 2nd, Carol Saunders, Nov 20, 1959, div. Gen dir, alumina research div, Reynolds Metals Co, since 1958; asst supt, chief chem, Bay Chem, Weeks, La, 1934-39, mgr, 1939-51; gen mgr, Commonwealth Engr Co of O, 1951-53; plant mgr, Godchaux Sugars, Reserve, La, 1953-56. Vice-chmn, Iberia dist, Boy Scouts of Amer, 1951; chmn, educ consolidation comm, Benton C of C, 1962; mem: Amer Inst of ChemE; Amer Chem Soc; Amer Ceramic Soc; Tau Beta Pi; Sigma Alpha Mu; clubs: Lions; Rotary; New Iberia, La, vice-pres, 1951. Contbr to engr jours. Recipient: Scherk Memorial award; La Engr Soc award. Hobbies: public speaking, bridge, hunting, fishing. Home: Summit House, 400 N University, Little Rock, Ark. Office: Reynolds Metals Co, Bauxite, Ark.

LIPPMANN, Kurt E, Australia, accountant; b. Hamburg, Ger, Dec 14, 1920; s. Franz and Olga (Hahlo); in Australia since 1939; m. Adeline van Engel, Dec 4, 1947; c: Helen, John. Public acctnt, since 1946; JP, 1966. Served Australian Defense Force, WW II. Chmn, Vic B'nai B'rith, since 1959, mem, B'nai B'rith Intl Council, since 1968, past pres, Melbourne Lodge; dir, Australian J Wfr Relief Soc, since 1959; chmn, Sheltered Workshop for J Aged and Handicapped, 1959-68; mem, bd of mgmt, Temple Beth Isr, 1950-59. Home: 13 Lygon St, South Caulfield, Victoria, Australia. Office: 436 St Kilda Rd, Melbourne, Australia.

LIPPMANN, Walter M, Australia, organization exec; b. Hamburg, Ger, Sep 19, 1919; s. Franz and Olga (Hahlo); in Austr since 1938; m. Lorna Matenson, Feb 15, 1945; c: Davina, Lenora. Co dir, since 1947. Pres: Australian J Wfr and Relief Soc, since 1960; hon treas, Australian Council Social Service, since 1965; appt mem, Commonwealth Immigration Adv Council; mem: Sociol Assn of Australia and NZ; Illuminating Engr Soc; exec, Vic J Bd Deps, chmn, immigration and social wfr comm. Author: Demography of Australia; Tasks in J Wfr Work; Melbourne Jewry—The Failure of a Generation; Marriage Trends in the Melbourne J Comty. Hobbies: photography, golf. Home: 1 Lomond St, Glen Iris, Victoria, Australia. Office: 137 City Rd, S Melbourne, Australia.

LIPSCHITZ, Chaim U, US, rabbi· b. Jerusalem, Aug 10, 1912; s. Moses and Chaya (Lichtman); in US since 1920: studied in Isr, 1930-38; ordained rabbi, 1938; hon DD: St Andrews Coll, London, Eng, 1957; Philaethea Coll, Windsor, Can; m. Rivka Bernstein, 1936; c: Beatrice, Bina, Sarah, Ziona. Rabbi, Con Ohev Shalom Anshe Mamorosh, Bklyn, NJ, since 1951· dir: Comty Service Bur, Yeshiva Torah Vodaath, and Mesvita, Bklyn, NY, since 1951; Cong Machzikai Hadaath, Phila, 1936-38; served with Amer consul gen, Isr, 1928; found, exec dir, prin, Beth Jacob, Sch, Phila, 1940-1950: founder, hon pres, Agudath Isr, Phila, 1938; vice-pres, dir, PR, Beth Medrash Kerem Shlomo, 1949-51. Opened session US Sen with prayer, 1958, 1962, 1965. Chmn: Bobov City, 1965-67: bd govs, Girls Coll, Jerusalem; 1967; pres for life, Natl Info Bur for J Life, since 1960; vice-pres, Torah Haadom Inst; hon vice-pres, RA, exec dir, 1951-57; treas: Yeshiva Chai Olom, Jerusalem, 1965; Yeshiva Leflaget Reuben, Jerusalem, 1966; Kupat Holim L'Bnai Yeshivos, 1966; Comm for Comty Health Service Assn, Bklyn, NY, 1967; charter mem, vice-pres, Friendship, Intl, 1959; charter mem, Metrop Orthodox Bd Rabbis; mem: Alumni Assn Torah Vodaath; Mayor's Comm Rel Leaders; NYC Youth Bd Rel Commn; Newspaper Inst of Amer; Adv bd, JF Kennedy Libr for Minorities; Intl Conf Weekly Newspaper Eds; Intl Platform Assn; hon patron, Upstate Council, Youth for Soviet Jewry. Author: The Shield of Israel, 1940; A Treatise on International Date Line in Relation to Jewish Law, 1956; co-author, Rabinical Alliance Torah and Sermon Manuel, 1955; ed: Thought of the Week, 1959; Jewish Press, 1959; asso ed, Orthodox Tribune, 1942-45; with Morning Journal, 1946-50; contbr to: Standard Jewish Ency: Amer Educator Ency; Wonderland of Knowledge Ency; Ency Britannica Year Book; daily and weekly radio progs, Phila, 1938-50; conducts weekly radio prog, Yeshiva Quiz Kids, WEVD, since 1962; conducted, TV prog, Lamp Unto My Feet, CBS, 1959; produc film, Building Tomorrow Today, on Heb day schs, 1939. Home: 225 Keap St, Brooklyn, NY. Study: 141 S Third St, Brooklyn, NY.

LIPSCHITZ, Kalman Joseph, Isr, civil engr; b. Lodz, Pol, Nov 1, 1900; s. Nathan and Sara (Rosenfarb); in Isr since 1905; BA, Amer U, Beirut, 1922, BSc, CE, 1922; m. Sara Goldin, Aug 1, 1930; c: Penina Kesler, Edna. Cons engr, since 1962; regional engr, Public Works Dept, Pal Govt, 1948; hydraulic engr, asst chief highway engr, Govt of Isr, 1948-60; asst dist engr, chief highway engr, Nigerson Co, W Nigeria, 1960-62. Pvt, Pal Volunteer Force, 1942-43. Fmr mem: cen comm, Assn of Engrs and Architects, Isr; cen comm and secretariat, Union of Engrs, Isr. Hobby: photography. Home and office: 14 Elchanan St, Haifa, Isr.

LIPSCHITZ, Shaul, Isr, business exec; b. Latvia, Jan 6, 1897; s. Joseph and Esther (Brenner); in Isr since 1933; D Rer Pol, U of Frankfurt, 1923; m. Rachel Maranz, Aug 10, 1949; c: Sam, Hanna. Chmn bd dirs: Pal Automobile Corp since 1934; Electra Ltd since 1946; fmr: chmn bd dirs, Kupat Am Bank; dir gen, Min of Commerce and Ind. Chmn: public comm, Magen David Adom; Assn of J from Latvia and Estonia; pres, Isr Lawn Tennis Assn; mem: Commercial Club, Tel Aviv; Maccabi; fmr pres, Tel Aviv C of C. Hobby, tennis. Home: 3 Hermesh St, Savyon, Isr. Office: 43 Hamasger St, Tel Aviv, Isr.

LIPSCHUTZ, Isidore, US, merchant. Partner, Lipschutz & Gutwirth, diamond merchants since 1909; pres: Belgian Diamond Mfrs Assn, 1923-39; Intl Commn for Diamond Trade and Ind, 1927-39; organized for Belgian govt and presided over diamond exhbs at World's Fairs; Antwerp, 1930; Brussels, 1935; Stockholm, Paris, 1937; NY, 1939-40; found, Profsl Sch for the Diamond Ind; past pres, found, Intl Fed of Diamond Orgs; past pres: Syndicate of the Belgian Diamond Ind; Belgian Commn on Econ Defense; Org of Family Allowances in Favor of Workers in Diamond Ind; Belgo-Luxembourg Clearing Bur. Co-found: Soc For Prevention of WW III Inc; Albert Einstein Coll of Med; charter day celebration, Yeshiva U; chmn: Amer br, World Memorial to J Martyrs, Inc; vice-pres, treas, Non-Sectarian Anti-Nazi League; active for: Weizmann Inst of Sci, Isr; Heb U; Yeshiva U; NY Fed of Charities; UJA; ZOA. Recipient: Knight of the Order of Leopold. Home: 630 Fifth Ave, New York, NY. Office: 1270 Ave of Americas, New York, NY.

LIPSCHUTZ, Naphtali, Isr, attorney; b. Lemberg, Aus, 1908; s. Eliezer Heir; att Tchrs Training Coll, Jerusalem, 1922-23; LLB, hons, U Coll, London, 1929; Barrister-at-Law, Grey's Inn; m. Rosalie Goldstein; c: Lea Caplan, Moshe, Rivka Frankel, Eliezer. Partner, Y Solomon Lipschutz and Co; fmr: mem comm: to recommend changes in civil procedure; to draft: law of guarantee, law of contract; communal procedure; for apptment of Dayanim. Mem bd govs: Technion, Haifa; Bar Ilan U, Ramat Gan. Home: 11 Dyalon St, Haifa, Isr. Office: 64 Hameginim Ave, Haifa, Isr.

LIPSET, Seymour M, US, sociologist, educator; b. NYC, Mar 18, 1922; s. Max and Lena (Lippman); BS, CCNY, 1943; PhD, Columbia U, 1949; m. Elsie Braun, Dec 26, 1943; c: David, Daniel, Carola. Prof, govt and social relations, Harvard U since 1966; lectr, U of Toronto, Can, 1946-48; asso prof, sociol, Columbia U, 1950-56; prof, sociol, U of Cal, 1956-66, dir, Inst of Intl Studies, 1962-66. Chmn, Comm on Intl Relations of Behavior Scis, Natl Acad of Sci since 1965; cons: J Lab Comm since 1952; Natl Comty Relations Adv Council, 1952-58; mem: council, Amer Sociol Assn, 1958-61; bd, Berkeley JCC, 1958-60; chmn, comm on political sociol, Intl Sociol Assn since 1959; f, Amer Acad of Arts and Scis since 1962. Author: Agrarian Socialism, 1950; Class, Status and Power, 1953; Union Democracy, 1956; Social Mobility in Industrial Society, 1959; Political Man, 1960; The First New Nation, 1963; Revolution and Counterrevolution, 1968; contbr to profsl jours and other publs. Recipient: f's: Social Sci Research Council, 1945-46; Cen for Adv Study in Behavior Scis, 1955-56; MacIver award, 1962. Home: 162 Washington St, Belmont, Mass. Office: 580 William James Hall, Harvard U, Cambridge, Mass.

LIPSHITZ, Arye, Isr, author, editor; b. Krakow, Pol, Nov 19, 1901; s. Jacob and Miryam (Sternberg); in Isr since 1920; att HS commerical, Krakow, Pol; m. Rivka Horowitz, 1921; c: Yair, Ilana Nir. Novelist, critic, ed; mem cen comm, Heb Writers Assn. Author: Adon leGoralo, stories; chief ed, publs in Youth Aliyah; ed, literary publs. Secy gen, Youth Aliyah, 1939-68; mem: Beit Ha'am Council, Chan theatre, Jerusalem; PEN club. Hobbies: music, painting. Home: 5 Smolenskin St, Jerusalem, Isr. Office: POB 92, Jerusalem, Isr.

LIPSHITZ, Israel Lippy, S Afr, sculptor; b. Lith, May 8, 1903; s. Solomon and Chaya; in S Afr since 1908; studied in Paris under Bourdelle, 1928-32; m. Rachel Seif, May 8, 1928; c: Leonore Bettman, Tony Caspi. Prof, head dept sculpture, Cape town U, 1962-69; exhbs: all prin cities in S Afr; London; Paris; Rome; Venice; Turin, It; Brazil; Munich; Amsterdam; Brussels; Wash, DC; among prin works: End and Beginning, Tree of Life; Jacob Wrestling with the Angel, acquired by S Afr Natl Gal; Sea Nude, S Afr Natl Gal; Moses, Rhodes Natl Gal, Rhodesia; Adam and Eve, S Afr Natl Gal. Trustee: S Afr Natl Gal; Michaelis Collection, Cape Town; exec mem, S Afr Assn of Arts; f, Royal Soc of Arts. Recipient: Cape Tercentenary Award and cert of merit for sculpture, 1953; prize for Ger Centenary Settler's Memorial erected at E London, Cape Province, 1960; Gold Medal of Honor, S Afr Acad of Arts and Sci, 1964; first S Afr artist honored by a retrospective exhib, S Afr Natl Gal, 1968-69. Home: 9 Higgo Rd, Cape Town, S Afr. Studio: Michaelis Studio of Fine Art, Cape Town, S Afr.

LIPSHITZ, Michael, Isr, business exec; b. Damascus, Syria, Aug 30, 1918; s. Joseph and Zipora (Felman); in Isr since 1919; att: Kadoori Agric Sch, Mt Tabor, 1939; Isr Produc Cen courses; m. Rachel Rosenzwige, Mar 3, 1942; c: Raanan. Mem, Pal Cold Storage and Supply Co Ltd since 1963; fmr: mgr, Tennè Co, 1950-63; mem, marketing study group to US, Eur, sponsored by US Operations Mission; tech aide, to Greece, Isr Govt, 1966. Haganah; IDF. Dir, Haifa Rotary Club, past hon secy; mem: presidium, Haifa C of C and Ind; Isr Mgmt Cen; Isr-Amer Friendship League. Author: Recommendation for the Organization and Establishment of a Central Cooperative Co for the Marketing of Fruits and Vegetables in Athens. Hobbies: sports, music. Home: 3 Elchanan St, Haifa, Isr. Office: 25 Ha'atzmaut St, Haifa, Isr.

LIPSHITZ, Sam, Can, business exec; b. Radom, Pol, Feb 14, 1910; s. Isser and Chana (Weisboro); in Can since 1927; att U of Toronto; m. Manya Cantor, Jan 20, 1930; c: May Cohen, Joseph. Exec vice-pres, Trade Typesetting Ltd. Pres, New Fraternal J Assn; fmr: mem: natl council, Can J Cong; J Communist Wing, Can, secy, natl J Comm; delg, Can J Cong to investigate extent of holocaust in Pol, post WW II. Ed: Fraternally Yours; Voice of Radom; fmr, ed, left-wing J and Anglo-J publs. Home: 11 Goldfinch Ct, Willowdale, Ont, Can. Office: 54 Wolseley St, Toronto, Can.

LIPSHUTZ, Daniel M, US, psychiatrist; b. Bklyn, NY, Jan 24, 1906; s. Samuel and Minnie (Bloushinsky); BA, Cornell U, 1927; MS, U of Cal, 1929; MD, U of Paris, 1936; m. Eva Klein, Nov 24, 1934. Psychiatric research in public schs; adj in psycht, Mt Sinai Hosp, 1939-52; chief of clinic, Lebanon Hosp, 1942-46; comm on psychiatric clinics, NYC, 1945-48. Lt, US Army, 1940-41. Treas-secy, It Friendship Comm, 1947-54; mem: Amer Psychiatric Assn; Amer Psychosomatic Assn; Med Psychan Soc; Assn for Advancement of Psychotherapy; Amer Group Psychotherapy Assn; Intl Assn of Mental Hygiene; Med Soc of Isr; Friends of Heb U; Amer Acad Psychan; NY Soc for Clinical Psycht. Contbr to med jours. Home and office: 1148 Fifth Ave, New York, NY.

LIPSHUTZ, Eva Klein, US, physician; b. Biecz, Aus, Dec 10, 1904; d. Usher and Giesela (Lemberger) Klein; in US since 1936; MD, Friborg Breisgau Sch, Ger, 1926; deg, psychan, Columbia U, 1947; m. Daniel Lipshutz, Nov 22, 1934. Asso in psycht since 1945; mem staff: Leb Hosp, Bx, NY, 1942-46; NY Med Coll, 1945-65. Found, treas, It-Amer Friendship Comm; charter mem, Amer Friends Heb U; mem: AMA; Amer Psycht Assn; Amer Group Psychotherapy Assn; NY Soc Clinical Psycht; Rorschach Inst; World Fed Mental Hygiene. Author: Comparison of Dreams in Group Therapy; Treatment of Alcoholics; Psychodynamics of Skin Disease. Hobbies: lit, travel, theater, music. Home and office: 1148 Fifth Ave, New York, NY.

LIPSIG, James, US, attorney, labor exec; b. NYC, April 1, 1910; s. Benjamin and Elizabeth (Rabinowitz); BA, CCNY, 1930; JD, Columbia U Law Sch, 1933; m. Frances Katz, 1943; c: Carla. Asst exec secy, ILGWU since 1948; gen counsel, Textile Workers Union Jt Bd, 1941-46; served US Army, 1943-45. Exec Comm, Natl J Comty Relations, adv council since 1968; mem, bd of dirs: Natl Sharecroppers Fund since 1956; League for Ind Dem since 1967; adv on civil rights, J Lab Comm, 1950-66; chmn, lab law comm, Lib Party since 1950; mem: NY Co Lawyers' Assn; Amer Vets Comm; Workers Defense League. Author, Sedition, Criminal Syndication, Criminal Anarchy Law, 1937. Home: 320 Central Park W, New York, NY. Office: 1710 Broadway, New York, NY.

LIPSITZ, Jerome Samuel, US, rabbi; b. Chgo, Ill, June 10, 1927; s. Ike and Sarah; BA, ordained rabbi, Yeshiva U, 1952; m. Naomi Rothstein, June 15, 1958; c: William, David, Joshua. Rabbi, Temple Beth El since 1964; chaplain, US Army, 1954-56. Exec vice-pres, Heb Acad of Atlantic Co; vice-pres, ZOA; mem, RabCA. Home: 331 N Gladstone, Margate, NJ. Study: 500 N Jerome, Margate, NJ.

LIPSON, Goldie S, US, artist, teacher; b. NYC, Nov 18, 1905; d. Herman and Tillie (Schroff) Goldman; att Amer Peoples Sch; Works Proj Adm Art Sch; m. Morris Lipson, July 13, 1924; c: Stanley, Adylin Rosenblatt. Dir, found, Goldie Lipson Studio Workshop, New Rochelle, NY, originally Mt Vernon Sch of Fine Arts since 1946; dir, tchr, Sculpture Cen, Orchid Springs Gardens, Winter Haven, Fla since 1969; tchr, YMCA, Bx, NY, 1938-39; mem, summer staff: Kolburn Sch for Problem Children, Norwalk, Conn,

1950; Arnold Coll, Milford, Conn, 1950-51; art classes, YM-YWHA, Mt Vernon, 1950-57; one-man shows since 1940; exhbs: Mus of Modern Art; Metrop Mus of Art; Natl Acad of Art; Riverside Mus; Audubon Soc; NY Coliseum, art, USA; Uptown Gal; Barsansky Gal; Clarksville Art Cen; perm exhb of outdoor sculpture, Winter Haven, Fla, 1968-69; reproduced in Artists Equity, Fantasia, 1957-58, 27 Contemporary Amers, 1959-60; included in traveling exhbs of Natl Assn of Women Artists, US, Can, Paris since 1949; works in pvt collections. Charter mem, mem, bd dirs, NY chap, Artists Equity since 1959; mem: Natl Assn of Women Artists, served, membership jury, 1959; New Rochelle and Mt Vernon Art Assns; ZOA; Hadassah. Author: Rejuvenation Through Yoga, 1964; Beyond Yoga, 1969; contbr to art publs. Recipient, citation medal, Tercentenary Art Prog, Mt Vernon, 1955. Home and studio: Lake of the Hills, 33853 Lake Wales, Fla.

LIPSON, Harry A Jr, US, educator; b. Wilkes-Barre, Pa, Mar 10, 1919; s. Harry and Irma (Lowenstein); BS, U of Ala, 1939; MBA, Northwestern U, 1941; PhD, U of Pa, 1955; m. Miriam Lipson, July 5, 1948; c: Harry III, Carolyn. Head, dept marketing, U of Ala, since 1960, prof, marketing, since 1948, mem fac since 1941; mgmt cons since 1948. Served USAAF, 1943-46. Mem: Amer Marketing Assn; Amer and S Econ Assns; Beta Gamma Sigma; Alpha Kappa Psi; past pres: J Federated Charities; S Marketing Assn; and secy, Temple Emanuel; B'nai B'rith, all Tuscaloosa, Ala. Co-author: Introduction to Marketiyg Administration; contbr to profsl publs. Home: 2825 Montclair Rd, Tuscaloosa, Ala. Office: Box 5021, U of Ala, Tuscaloosa, Ala.

LIPSON, Samuel L, Can, educator, engineer; b. Odessa, Russ, July 30, 1913; s. Morris and Annie (Wiser); in Can since 1924; BA, U of BC, 1936; MS, Cal Inst of Tech, 1937; m. Dena Pink, Nov 26, 1944; c: Florence, Morris, Alisa. Prof, civil engr, U of BC, since 1949, on fac since 1946; fmr: designer, Mark Falk, LA; designer, estimator, Consolidated Steel Corp, LA, chief estimator, 1941-46. Mem: council, Assn of Profsl Engrs in BC, fmr chmn, structural examining bd; Amer Soc of Civil Engrs; Engr Inst of Can; Amer Concrete Inst; bd: Vancouver UJA, past chmn bd; Beth Isr Rel Sch, past chmn; Vancouver J Family Wfr Agcy; exec comm, J Comty Cen, Vancouver; ZOC; Can J Cong, past pres, Pacific region; clubs: U; Richmond Country. Home: 1420 W 45 Ave, Vancouver, BC, Can. Office: U of British Columbia, Vancouver, BC, Can.

LIPSON, Stephen Geoffrey, Isr, physicist; b. Cambridge, Eng, Jan 1, 1941; s. Henry and Jane (Rosenthal); in Isr since 1966; MA, PhD, U of Cambridge; m. Rina Berman, Dec 29, 1966; c: Hod. Sen lectr, Technion, Haifa, since 1967. Author, Optical Physics, 1969. Hobbies: carpentry, drawing. Office: Technion, Haifa, Isr.

LIPSTADT, Erwin H, US, business exec; b. Hamburg, Ger, Dec 10, 1903; s. Gustav and Helene (Munk); in US since 1926; m. Miriam Peiman, Feb 14, 1943; c: Helene, Deborah, Nathaniel. Pres, Lipstadt Memorial Co, since 1936; dir: Union of Orthodox J Congs; Syn Council of Amer; found and past pres, Shomreh Hadath, NY, 1944. Mem: FJP; J Cen, trustee, Cong Gates of Hope, Ohab Zedek, 1941-50; Westside Inst Syn; Lincoln Cen Syn; Ramath Orah; Cong Ahavath Torah of WH; Men's Club of Cong Kehilath Jeshurun; Cong Shaare Tefilah of Far Rockaway; Memorial Inds of NY; past pres, NY State Assn of Monument Dealers; Freedom Lodge, B'nai B'rith; Queens Co Lodge of Free Sons of Isr. Hobbies: J hist, liturgical music. Home: 225 W 86 St, New York, NY. Office: 370 Amsterdam Ave, New York, NY.

LIPTON, Charles, US, public relations exec; b. NYC, May 11, 1928; s. Jack and Bertha (Lesser); AB, Harvard, 1948; m. Audrey Williams, Nov 11, 1951; c: Susan, Jack. PR exec, chmn bd, Ruder & Finn, NYC since 1969, sr vice-pres, account exec, 1953-69; advt exec, Cecil & Presbrey, Inc, 1948-49; publicist, 20th Century Fox, 1949-52; guest lectr: Boston U; The New Sch for Social Research. Asst treas, Norwalk Sym Soc since 1967; bd trustees: Norwalk J Cen, Conn since 1966; Temple Shalom, Norwalk since 1969; mem: adv council, Cen for Vocational Arts since 1966; Amer Mgmt Assn; clubs: Harvard, NYC; Harvard Varsity, NYC. Contbr to periodicals. Home: 18 Douglas Dr, Norwalk, Conn. Office: 110 E 59 St, New York, NY.

LIPTON, Joseph M, US, business exec; b. Sep 9, 1900; s. Isador and Ida (Barash); BS, U of Pa, 1922; m. Anna Abrash, Sep 24, 1933; c: Ronald, Harriet. Co-found, pres, Dade Fed Savings

& Loan Assn, since 1934; found, owner, J M Lipton Ins Agcy Inc, since 1926; chartered life underwriter. Pres, dir, Temple Emanuel; past pres, campaign chmn, Greater Miami J Fed; past pres, Fla Savings and Loan League; vice-pres, found, trustee, Mt Sinai Hosp; treas, Dade Co Red Cross, chmn fund drive, 1951; natl bd, UJA Cabinet; citizens comm, U of Miami; mem: B'nai B'rith; Masons; Shriners; Amer Legion; YMHA; Phi Lambda Phi; U of Pa Alumni Club, dir; Kiwanis. Home: 651-47 St, Miami Beach, Fla. Office: 101 E Flagler St, Miami, Fla.

LIPTON, Marcus, Eng, MP; b. Sunderland, Eng, Oct 29, 1900; s. Benjamin and Mary (Shieff); MA, Merton Coll, Oxford, 1922; widowered. MP for Brixton, London, since 1945. Lt col, Brit Army, 1939-1945. Pres, Assn of J Ex Service Men, S London br; fmr: mem, J Bd Deps; hon off: Brit ZF; JNF. Recipient: OBE, 1948, CBE. Office: House of Commons, London, Eng.

LIPTON, Robert I, US, attorney; b. NYC, Dec 11, 1920; s. Simon and Sadie (Berger); BS, U of NC, 1942, JD, 1946; m. Cecille Rosenblum, Sep 9, 1947; c: Howard, Lawrence, Stuart. Partner, Bryant, Lipton, Bryant & Battle, since 1946; visiting prof, U of NC, 1958. Pres: Durham Lodge, 1956-58; NC B'nai B'rith Assn, 1959; Beth-El Cong, 1962; chmn: div, ARC, 1953; NC, UJA, 1953-54; NC regional adv bd, ADL, 1959; bd dirs: Jt Defense Appeal, since 1956; United Fund, 1953; Durham Soc Financing Fight against Dread Diseases, 1953; delg, Intl Econ Conf, Jerusalem, Isr, 1953; mem: Natl Youth Commn; Amer, State, Durham, and Orange Co Bar Assns; NC State Bar Inc; Order of Coif; Beta Gamma Sigma; clubs: Willowhaven Country; Royal Oak Country; Natl Lawyers. Hobbies: philately, golf. Home: Country Club Dr, Durham, NC. Office: 700 First Union Bldg, Durham, NC.

LIPTON, S Dean, US, journalist, publicist; b. Detroit, Mich, Oct 3, 1919; s. Isadore and Dora Lipsitz; att SF City Coll, 1938-40; BBA, Woodbury Coll, 1948; m. Shirley Mills, Mar 13, 1944, div; c: Judy, Linda. Profsl writer since 1956; cons ed, Morrill Publ since 1967; moderator, chmn, SF Writer's Workshop since 1964; contbr to natl mags since 1956; reporter: Palmar Journal, 1936; Helena Independent, 1942; LA News, 1946-48; owner, W Cons Service, 1949-55; exec ed, Best Publ Co, 1950-52; staff writer, Jewish Star, 1951-52; publ, ed, Jewish Record, 1953-56; US Army historian, 1941-44. PR dir: SF Dem Club, 1948-52; Young Dems of SF, 1950-54; mem, Press and Union League. Author, Faces of Crime and Genius, 1970; ed: Lakewood City Graphic, 1935; Truth Newspaper, 1948-49. Home: 737 Woolsey, San Francisco, Cal.

LIPTZIN, Sol, Isr, educator; b. Satanov, Russ, July 27, 1901; s. Benjamin and Fannie (Grossman); in Isr since 1962; BA, CCNY, 1921; MA, Columbia U, 1922; att U of Berlin, 1922-23; PhD, Columbia U, 1924; m. Anna Ohrenstein, Aug 18, 1929; c: Yelva Lynfield, Karen Sitton. Prof comparative lit, Amer Coll Jerusalem since 1968; fmr, prof comparative lit, CCNY; visiting prof: Northwestern U; U of LA; Yeshiva U; Bar Ilan U; Fulbright lectr: Tel Aviv U; Technion, Haifa; chmn dept Ger, Slavic langs, CCNY. Chmn, Isr br, past pres, JBCA; mem: Phi Beta Kappa; AAUP; MLA; YIVO, fmr academic secy; Isr-Amer Soc; fmr: pres: Coll Yiddish Assn; natl pres, J St ZOA; chmn: commn on J affairs, AJCong; admn, Great Dict of Yiddish Lang. Author: Shelley in German, 1924; The Weavers in German Literature, 1926; Lyric Pioneers of Modern Germany, 1928; From Novalis to Nietzsche, 1929; Arthur Schnitzler, 1932; Richard Beer-Hoffman, 1936; Historical Survey of German Literature, 1936; Germany's Stepchildren, 1945; Peretz, 1946; Eliakum Zunser, 1950; English Legend of Heinrich Heine, 1954; Generation of Decision, 1958; Flowering of Yiddish Literature, 1966; The Jew in American Literature, 1966; ed: Jewish Book Annual, 1953-55; dept ed, Ency Hebraica; div ed, Ency Judaica; contbr: to Encys: Americana; Grolier's; Ency of Lit; Universal Jewish; Dict of Lit; YIRO Annual of Social Research; to profsl jours. Home: 21 Washington St, Jerusalem, Isr. Office: American Coll, Jerusalem, Isr.

LISHANSKY, Batya, Isr, sculptress; b. Malin, Russ, 1900; d. Meir and Shoshana (Moros); in Isr since 1910; att: Bezalel Art Sch, Jerusalem; Art Acad, Rome, 1920-21; Inst of Arts and Crafts, Berlin, 1923-25; studied sculpture, Fr, 1925-29. One-man shows and exhbs: Paris; Zurich; Cairo; Isr; repr in perm collections: wooden candelabra, League of Nations Bldg, Geneva; Histadrut Bldg, Tel Aviv; Tel Aviv Mus; Bezalel Mus, Jerusalem; pvt collections; presently working on Independence Day Memorial, Knesset. Maj works: Memorial

to the Fallen in the Isr War of Independence, Kfar Yehoshua; Ephraim Chizik Memorial, Hulda; Lord Melchett Memorial, Tel Mond; Hora, Onim Resort, Kfar Saba; Kibbutz Einat; Kadoori Sch; Kibbutz Beth Keshet; Memorial Monument of the Pogroms in the Ukraine, Shunath Borochov; Holocaust Memorial, Kibbutz Netzer Sireni; portrait busts: Y H Brenner; M Beilinson; Sara Lishansky; I Giladi; I Halperin; Pres Itzhak Ben Zvi; A Seid; Berl Katznelson; Henrietta Szold; Alexander Suesskind; I Rabinovitz; Sleeping Woman; The Blind Man. Recipient: Dizengoff Prize, 1944, for bust of Pres Itzhak Ben Zvi, 1957. Home and studio: 10 Nahum St, Tel Aviv, Isr.

LISKY, Summer Yehuda, Eng, editor, poet, author, journalist; b. Jezierna, Pol, Dec 12, 1903; s. Haim and Feige Fuchs; in Eng since 1930; m. Sonia Husid; c: Irving, Francis. Ed: The Jewish People, since 1958; Jewish Voice, 1958-67. Author: Productivisation, 1936; Songs to the Land of Israel, 1968. Mem, orgs: J Writers; exec mem, Journalists. Contbr, short stories, articles to jours. Home and office: 13 Carysfort Rd, London, Eng.

LISMAN, Henry, US, educator; b. Boston, Mass, July 3, 1913; s. David and Celia (Gersberg); BS, Boston U, 1934, MA, 1935, PhD, 1939; m. Rachel Lewit, Apr 3, 1938; c: Meira Max, Elliot. Prof math, Yeshiva U, since 1947; prin, Maimonides Sch, Brookline, Mass, 1939-42; instr, physics and math, Northeastern U, Boston, Mass, 1940-42; physicist, Signal Corps Engr Labs, 1942-47; cons physicist, US Army Elec Command, Ft Monmouth, NJ, 1947-68. Prin contrib, inventor, patented ultra-high frequency oscillator. Past pres, Cong Kehilath Isr, NY; bd dirs, Yeshiva Rabbi Moses Soloveitchik, NY. Author: Perturbation of Earth's Magnetic Field in the Vicinity of a Ferro Magnetic Prolate Spheroid, 1966; Magnetic Sensing of Vehicles, 1968; contbr to elec jours. Hobby, Talmudic Studies. Home: 1693 Selwyn Ave, Bronx, NY. Office: Yeshiva U, 500 W 185 St, New York, NY.

LISS, Norman, US, attorney; b. NYC, May 7, 1932; s. Morris and Frieda (Menchel); BS, NYU, 1952; JD, NYU, Sch of Law, 1955; m. Sandra Hirsch, Feb 28, 1959; c: Michael. Pvt practice since 1958; asso, Booth, Lipton & Lipton, 1956-57; admitted to US Supr Court; State and Fed courts. Mem: exec bd, AJCong; adv comm, NYU Law Sch Alumni Assn; Amer Bar Assn; NY State Trial Lawyers Assn; leader, Dem Reform Movement, NYC; comm chmn, to select Congressman Jonathan Bingham; reform comm for Robert Kennedy for Sen, 1964; fmr: dir of Bx Co Campaign for Hubert Humphrey, 1968; chmn, Social Action Comm, Riverdale J Cen; vice-pres, Riverdale chap, AJCong. Hobby, political activities. Home: 5800 Arlington Ave, New York, NY. Office: 200 W 57 St, New York, NY.

LISSAK, Moshe Avraham, Isr, sociologist; b. Tel Aviv, Isr, June 9, 1928; s. Gershon and Chava; BA, MA, PhD, Heb U, Jerusalem; m. Yemimah Shacked, Aug 28, 1953; c: Gad, Michael. Sr lectr, Heb U, Jerusalem, since 1968. Sgt, IDF, 1948-50. Author: Moshava, Kibbutz, Moshav, 1969; Social Mobility in Israel, 1970. Home: 4 Disraeli St, Jerusalem, Isr. Office: Hebrew U, Jerusalem, Isr.

LIST, Albert A, US, business exec; b. Fall River, Mass, May 18, 1901; s. Alter and Ethel (Moscowitz); m. Vera Glaser, Dec, 1930; c: JoAnn, Carol, Olga, Viki. Chmn of bd: Alberlist Corp; Gen Charities Found; Albert A List Found; Hammond North Corp; Emmess Assos. Chmn, bd of govs, Brotherhood-in-Action; chmn, finance comm, JTSA; co-chmn: Temple Sholom, Greenwich, Conn; Greenwich J Fed; trustee, Mt Sinai Hosp. Home: Byram Shore Rd, Byram, Conn. Office: 1740 Broadway, New York, NY.

LIST, George H, US, ethnomusicologist; b. Tucson, Ariz, Feb 9, 1911; s. Max and Mollie (Brouse); Dipl, Juilliard Sch of Music, 1933; BS, Columbia U, 1941, MA, 1945; PhD, Ind U, 1954; m. Eve Ehrlichman, July 5, 1934; c: Michael. Dir, Archives of Traditional Music, Folklore Inst since 1954; asso prof, folklore, Ind U since 1965, dir, Inter-Amer Prog for Ethnomusicology since 1966; asst prof, music, Miami U, 1946-48, asso prof, 1948-53. Councillor, Soc for Ethnomusicology since 1960; mem: Amer Folklore Soc; Amer Musicological Soc; Intl Folk Music Council; Afr Music Soc. Contbr to profsl jours; composed works for orch, chorus, band, piano; field research, Hopi Indians, Ariz, 1960, 1963, Colombia, S Amer, 1964-65, Ecuador, 1965. Home: 518 Colony Court, Bloomington, Ind. Office: Indiana U, Bloomington, Ind.

LISTOKIN, Philip, US, rabbi; b. Yanova, Pol, June 28, 1908;

s. David and Rachel (Avgustovsky); in US since 1920; BS, LIU, 1931; ordained rabbi, MHL, JTSA, 1935, DD, 1966; m. Ruth Speier, Nov, 1936; c: Berna Case, Norman, Gary. Rabbi: Beth El J Cen of Flatbush, Bklyn since 1946; Highland Park Conservative Temple, NJ, 1935-45; Temple Beth El, Lancaster, Pa, 1945-46. Mem: RA; Bklyn Bd of Rabbis; NY Bd of Rabbis; NY B'rith Milah Bd; ZOA. Spec interest, liturgical music. Home: 1977 Homecrest Ave, Brooklyn, NY. Study: 1219 Ave T, Brooklyn, NY.

LITCHFIELD, Harry R, US, physician; b. Montreal, Can, July 7, 1898; s. Nathan and Irene (Herkus); in US since 1906; BS, Columbia U, 1915; MD, LI Coll of Med, 1919; grad study: U of Vienna, 1925; Bklyn Polytech Inst, 1947-48; licentiate, Amer Bd of Peds, 1925; m. Esther Kaplan, June 14, 1924; c: Natalie Weinstein, Henry. Dir, peds: Bklyn Women's Hosp since 1956; cons, Head Start Program, OED, NY State; ENY Dispensary since 1935; cons, Rockaway Beach Hosp since 1940; sr att ped, Beth El Hosp since 1930, chmn, dept of peds, 1948-51; intern, Bklyn J Hosp, 1919-20; instr, peds, George Wash U, 1920-21; res: Children's Hosp, Wash DC, 1920-21; Willard Parker Hosp, NYC, 1922-23; Bklyn Thoracic Hosp, 1924-26, att ped, 1927-40; adjunct, peds, LI Coll Hosp, 1925-29; asst dir, educ hygiene, NYC schools, 1928-30, dir, 1930-40; ped path, Cumberland St Hosp, 1931-35. Capt, USN Med Corps, 1918-20. Pres: ped sect, Kings Co Med Soc, 1948; med bd, Bklyn Women's Hosp, 1949-50; f: Amer Coll of Phys, 1932; Amer Acad of Peds, 1934, state chmn, sect II since 1953; NY Acad of Sci, 1948; mem, bd of dirs, Bklyn TB Soc, 1947-53; mem: Bklyn Ped Soc; Amer Trudeau Soc; Temple Emanuel, NYC; Masons; Amer Legion; Sigma Alpha Mu; Mu Sigma; clubs: Chemist; Unity; Harmonie; Beach Point. Author, Care of the Infant and Child, 1930; co-ed: Therapeutics of Infancy and Childhood, 1943, 1948, 1952; Pediatric Manual for Mothers, 1951, 1959; ed: Pediatric Bulletin, 1932-34; Medicine Today, 1936-38; contbr to profsl jours. Recipient: silver plaque, Kreindler Found, 1950; Mu Sigma man of the year award, 1959. Home: 870 Fifth Ave, New York, NY. Office: 60 Plaza St, Brooklyn, NY.

LITKE, Julius Joel, US, rabbi; b. Ger, Jan 24, 1926; s. Saul and Anna (Bagno); in US since 1954; BA, U of Toronto, 1947, MA, 1953; ordained rabbi, Rabb Sem of Can, 1947; m. Miriam Fachler, Feb 26, 1948; c: David, Anna, Geliah. Rabbi: Cong Beth Hillel since 1954; Beth Isaiah, Guelph, Ont, 1948-54. Mem: RabCA; Council Rabbis of Detroit; B'nai B'rith. Contbr to J publs. Home and study: 19371 Coyle, Detroit, Mich.

LITMAN, Samuel, US, engineer, educator; b. Boston, Mass, May 11, 1910; s. David and Rosa (Chaplinski); BS, U of SC, 1935, MS, 1936; D Engr, Johns Hopkins U, 1962; att: MIT, 1936-37; U of Wis, 1940; m. Judith Greenberg, June, 1940; c: Fern, Deborah. Prof, elec engr, U of SC since 1962, fmr: adj prof; instr i/c CAA War Training, asso prof, acting head, dept elec engr, all U of SC; partner, Greenberg Litman Inves; pres, treas, Palmetto Radio Corp, radio, TV sta WNOK, WNOK-TV since 1947; cons, partner, L Greenberg and Co since 1943; pres, MGL Devl Corp since 1950; fmr: rate analyst, Fed Power Commn; cons, SC Tax Study Commn. Mem: Amer Inst of Elec Engrs; Inst of Radio Engrs; AAAS; Le Conte Sci Soc; Soc for Promotion of Engr Educ; SC Acad of Sci; Phi Beta Kappa, past pres, Alpha chap; Sigma Xi; Phi Epsilon Pi; Tau Beta Pi; Phi Epsilon Sigma; fmr: pres of trustees, B'nai B'rith, mem Hillel comm, fifth dist; House of Peace Syn; natl council: JDC; United HIAS Service; chmn, UJA, Columbia, SC; pres: Beth Shalom Syn; SC Johns Hopkins Alumni Assn. Author, Laboratory Experiments in Direct and Alternating Currents, 1938; contbr to profsl jours. Spec interest, langs. Hobbies: chess, photography. Home: 120 Saluda Ave, Columbia, SC. Office: U of SC, Columbia, SC.

LITT, Solomon, US, investment broker; b. April 12, 1904; BCS, NYU, 1925. Partner, Asiel & Co; gov, NY Stock Exch since 1967. Hon pres: World Fed of YMHAs; JWB; pres: J Comty Cens since 1964; J Bd of Guardians; natl pres, JWB, 1961-62, fmr chmn, exec comm, budget and finance comm; fmr gen chmn, Gtr NY, UJA; finance comm, NY FJP. Home: 870 UN Plaza, New York, NY. Office: 20 Broad St, New York, NY.

LITTMAN, Eugene, US, business exec; b. NYC, Apr 23, 1928; s. William and Helen (Linsenberg); BA, Cornell U, Ithaca, NY, 1948; m. Elfriede Zeiger, Jan 14, 1951; c: Robert, Sandra, Bonnie, David. Pres, Lightron of Cornwall Inc since 1965; dir,

Columbus Trust Co since 1968. Capt, USAF, 1948-50. Pres, Temple Beth Jacob, Newburgh, NY; vice-pres, NY Council, UAHC; dir, Otterkill Golf and Country Club, NY, past secy; mem: natl bd trustees, UAHC; Newburgh Rotary Club; Illuminating Engr Soc; fmr: pres, United J Charities, Newburgh, NY; vice-pres, Newburgh J Comty Cen. Spec interests: golf; travel; realty inves. Home: MD 16, Susan Dr, Newburgh, NY. Office: 195 Hudson St, Hudson on Cornwall, NY.

LITTMAN, Louis, Eng, superintendent; b. London, Eng, Sep 6, 1902; s. James and Fanny (Ober); att Grocer's Sch, London, 1915-18; m. Sadie Coberman, June 8, 1932; c: Anthony, Jeffrey. Supt, Edmonton Cemetery since 1938. Pres, Edmonton and Tottenham Syn; chmn: Tottenham and Dist Zionist Soc; Tottenham and Dist JPA Comm. Hobbies: communal and political work. Home: The Lodge, Montagu Rd, London, Eng. Office: Federation Cemetery, Montagu Rd, London, Eng.

LITTMAN, Richard A, US, psychologist, educator; b. NYC, May 8, 1919; s. Joseph and Sarah (Feinberg); AB, George Wash U, 1943; att U of Ind, 1943-44; PhD, O State U, 1948; m. Isabelle Cohen, 1941; c: David, Barbara, Daniel, Rebecca. Prof, psych, U of Ore, since 1959, head, dept, 1963-68, fac mem since 1948; instr, O Wesleyan U, 1946-47; NSF postdoc f, U of Paris, 1966-67. Visiting sci: Natl Inst Mh; USPHS; sci educ lectr, NSF. Exec comm: W Psychol Assn; Amer Psychol Assn; Ore Psychol Assn; mem: Psychonomic Soc; Amer Ecol Soc; AAUP; ACLU; Sigma Xi. Author: Social Sciences and School Curriculum, 1965; Nebraska Symposium on Motivation; contbr to profsl jours. Home: 3625 Glen Oak Dr, Eugene, Ore. Office: U of Oregon, Eugene, Ore.

LIVE, Israel, US, educator; b. Zakrzewce, Aus, April 26, 1907; s. Herman and Rose (Nagelberg); in US since 1928; VMD, U of Pa, 1934, AM, 1936, PhD, 1940; m. Anna Harris, Nov 25, 1936; c: Theodore, David. Prof, microbiol, School of Vetr Med, U of Pa since 1953, fac mem since 1934. F: AAAS; Amer Acad Microbiol; dipl, Amer Bd Microbiol; charter dipl, f, Amer Coll Vetr Microbiol; expert comm on brucellosis, WHO; member, Sigma Xi. Contbr to sci jours. Home: 2414 Bryn Mawr Ave, Philadelphia, Pa. Office: U of Pa, Philadelphia, Pa.

LIVINGSTONE, Isaac, Eng, minister of religion; b. Nottingham, Eng, Apr 4, 1885; s. Lewis and Sarah (Cohen); att: Aria Coll; U Coll; m. Henrietta Goodman, Aug 7, 1912; c: Nancie Craig, Barbara Michaels. Em min, Golders Green Syn since 1953; hon chaplain, Broadmoor Instn. Hon secy: Provincial J Min Fund and Keeling Clergy Endowment; Conf Anglo-J Preachers; chmn, cen J lecture comm, J Bd Deps; jt chmn, Golders Green and Hendon Council Chr and J; exec council, Jews Coll, Anglo-J Assn; rep: London Council Social Service; Brit Churches Housing Trust; Natl Council Social Service. Author: Jewish Life Interpreted, 1939; The Provincial Ministers Fund, 1935; Union of Anglo-Jewish Preachers, A Retrospect, 1949; Judaism and Temperance, 1954; contbr to jours. Home: 36 Eagle Lodge, Golders Green, London, Eng. Study: Golders Green Syn, Dunstan Rd, London, Eng.

LIVNEH, Eliezer, Isr, legislator, sociologist, editor; b. Lodz, Pol, Dec 2, 1902; s. Jehuda Liebenstein; in Isr since 1920; att Oxford U, 1937-38; m. Erna Weldler; c: Maya, Dola. MK since 1949; mem: Lab Party since 1968; fgn affairs and security comm since 1951; co-found, Land of Isr Movement; fmr: agric worker; secy Lab Council, Haifa; mem Kibbutz Ein Harod; co-org, legal, underground immigration activities, Nazi Ger; head, political, educ dept, Haganah; mem Mapai until 1957. Author: The New Territorialism, 1939; Zionism and Britain, 1946; Ferment of the Age, 1951; State and Diaspora, 1953; Test of Independence, 1955; American Jewry, 1968; ed: Maarahot, 1939-42; Milhamtenu; co-found, ed: Beterem since 1942; Hador daily since 1949; contbr to local, fgn press. Home: Kiryat Yovel, Jerusalem, Isr.

LIVNI, Hilel, Isr, organization exec; b. Slavonia, Yugo, Mar 8, 1906; s. Hugo and Josephine (Mahler) Wiess; in Isr since 1932; att U Zagreb, 1925-30; m. Towa Sperber, June 20, 1936; c: Osnat Paz. Treas, Sem Hakibbutzim, Oranim since 1956, gen secy; found, mem, Kibbutz Shaar Haamekim; mem munic, Emek Zvulon, 1965. Fmr: youth leader Ahdut Hazofim, Ahdut Haolim, Brith Hadut Hanoar Hayehudi, Yugo; found, Hashomer Hatzair, Yugo; delg, Hechalutz, Kibbutz Arzi, Hashomer Hatzair, Yugo; mem: ZC, Geneva; Zionist Actions Comm, Hitachduth Olei Yugo; immigration, educ comms: Hakibbutz Haarzi; Hashomer Hatzair; Alyath Hanoar; Histadrut; Mapam. Home: Kibbutz Shaar Haamekim, Isr.

Office: State Tchrs Training Coll of Collective Settlements, Oranim, Isr.

LIVNI, Itzhak, Isr, editor, business exec; s. Abraham and Haia (Lublinsky) Weiss; BA, Heb U, Jerusalem; m. Dalia Ravikovich, div. Dir, Isr Army Broadcasting Station; ed-in-chief, Army Mag, Bamahane since 1967; fmr: ed, Bamahane Nahal, army mag. Served IDF, Nahal br. Prin contribs in forming style and new structure of Isr mags and broadcasting. Home: 72 Raziel St, Ramat Chen, Isr. Office: Yehuda Hayamith St, Jaffa, Isr.

LIWSCHITZ, Chaim Yecheskel, Isr, educator; b. Vienna, Aus, June 22, 1919; s. Moshe and Amalia (Neumann); in Isr since 1940; MSc, Heb U, Jerusalem, 1950, PhD, 1952; m. Tova Baumgarten, Dec 3, 1943; c: Moshe, Zadok, Bracha, Noomi. Asso prof, organic chem, Hebrew U, Jerusalem, since 1962. Sgt, J Brig, 1941-46; capt, IDF, 1947-49. Author, Progress in Phytochemistry, Vol I, 1968; contbr sci papers to profsl jours. Hobbies: music, photography. Home: 12 Ibn Shaprut St, Jerusalem, Isr. Office: Hebrew U, Dept Organic Chem, Jerusalem, Isr.

LOBENSTEIN, Heinz Josef, Eng, business exec; b. Hanover, Ger, Apr 27, 1927; s. Julius and Rosa (Obermeyer); in Eng since 1939; att Gateshead Talmudical Coll, 1943-46; dipl, journalism, Bennett Coll, Cambridge; m. Bella Mosbacher, July 6, 1952; c: David, Michael, Eve, Benjamin, Moses, Naomi, Eli, Shulamith. Dir, Jaylow Supplies Ltd, since 1952; borough councillor, since 1962; gen secy, Agudat Isr Org, Gt Brit, 1947-51. Councillor, London Borough of Hackney; chmn, Planning and Highways comm; exec: Hackney and Dist C of C; Brit Natl Shechita Council; Union of Orthodox Heb Congs of Gt Brit; Agudat Isr World Org; trustee and gov, J Secondary Sch Movement; gov: Hasmonean Grammar Sch Boys; Avigdor Primary Sch; Yesode Hatorah Schs; Woodberry Down Sch; mem: ed bd, Jewish Tribune; bd deps, Brit J; Shechita Comm; vice-pres, Adass Isr Burial Soc; hon secy, Agudat Isr, Gt Brit. Hobbies: local govt, youth, educ. Home: 27 Fairholt Rd, London, Eng. Office: 93 Fairholt Rd, London, Eng.

LOC, Rafael, Isr, advocate, notary; b. Slonim, Pol, Sep 27, 1907; s. Yaakov and Chana (Lewin); in Isr since 1956; MJ, U of Warsaw, 1934; m. Fanny Solomian, Feb 22, 1946, (decd). In pvt practice: Isr, since 1956; Pol, 1934-37, 1953-56; adv, Pol Timber Trade Co, Warsaw, 1938; head, ME Dept, Min for Fgn Affairs, Pol, 1945-46; consul gen of Pol to Isr, 1946-49; dir, legal depts, Min for Fgn Affairs, Warsaw, 1950-53. Served Pol Army, WW II. Mem: Isr Advocates Assn; Histadrut High Court. Contbr, articles, stories. Recipient: Gold Cross of Merit, 1946; Aleh, Isr Fighters Award. Home: 214 Ben Yehuda St, Tel Aviv, Isr. Office: 11 Yehuda Halevi St, Tel Aviv, Isr.

LOCKER, Berl, Isr, Zionist leader; b. Krzywiec, Galicia, Apr 27, 1887; s. Jacob and Haya (Locker) Schattner; in Isr since 1936; att Law Sch, U of Czernowitz; m. Dina Locker, 1910. Chmn, Bialik Inst, Jerusalem since 1949; ret, JA post, 1956; found, lab Zionist movement; mem Zionist Actions Comm since 1925; mem exec, WZO since 1931; mem exec, Histadrut since 1936; fmr: org, students illegal Zionist org, Sereth, Bucovina; participated, provincial conv, Poalei Zion Org, Czernowitz, mem, provincial comm; mem, Poalei Zion, wartime world cen off, The Hague, Stockholm; delg, 1st postwar Intl Socialist Conf, Bern, Switzerland; dep mem, Socialist Intl; secy, Poalei Zion: World Union; US org; mem exec, JA for Pal, head, org dept, political adv to exec, London, mem, London exec, chmn exec, Jerusalem; mem exec, Ihud Olami Poalei Zion-Hitachduth; MP. Author: Palestine and the Jewish Future, 1942; A Stiff-Necked People, 1946; and others; contbr to world Zionist press. Spec interest, J hist. Home: 7 Alcalai St, Jerusalem, Isr.

LOCKER, Dina Malka, Isr, poet, playwright; b. Kuty, Galicia; m. Berl Locker, 1910; in Isr since 1936. Author: poems, Velt un Mentsh, 1932; Chorspiel 5696, play, 1937, performed in Vienna, London; Gedichte, Ger, 1938; Shtet, 1940; Die Velt iz ohn a Hieter, 1947, trans into Heb; Jean Arthur Rimbaud, 1950; Le Poet qui s'enfuit, Rimbaud, 1956; Romantiker, 1958; book on Baudelaire, Pnei haRomantica; trans into Heb and Yiddish from Fr manuscript, 1962. Recipient, Croix de Chevalier dans l'Ordre des Palmes Academiques, 1960, by Fr govt for activities in interest of Fr culture. Home: 7 Alcalai St, Jerusalem, Isr.

LOCKSHIN, Louis Leon, Can, engineer; b. Winnipeg, Can, Jan 21, 1916; s. Isaac and Etta (Micanovsky); m. Sylvia Freedman,

Feb 7, 1937; c: Brenda Freedman, Sherryn Lang, Martin. Tool engr, ind cons; fmr pres, found: Century Engr Co Ltd; Tubular Steel Products. Holder of numerous patents on produc equipment. Natl vice-pres, JNF of Can; hon vice-pres, J Public Libr; hon dir, March of Dimes; mem, Amer Soc Tool and Mfg Engrs. Recipient, Ben Sadowski Award, United JWF of Toronto, 1967. Home: 329 Richview Rd, Toronto, Can. Office: 157 Bentworth Rd, Toronto, Can.

LODNER, Max, Belgium, merchant, communal worker; b. Radauti, Rum, Dec 22, 1903; s. Pinkas and Fanny (Klinger); in Belgium since 1908; m. Héléne Wang, Mar 18, 1934; c: Colette Fulton. Merchant, since 1922; admnr: Commercial Union Arlon; High Tech Inst of State; State Inst of Tech and Vocational Educ; Assn des Anciens de l'Athénée Royal, all Arlon; pres, J Comty of Arlon; found: Commercial and Ind Assn, past admnr; Commercial Grouping of Upper Town of Arlon, past admnr; and vice-pres, Amitiés Judeo-Chretiennes d'Arlon; comm, Cercle Wallon d'Arlon; pres, Magbit; dir, Royal Philharmonic, all Arlon; repr, Keren Kayemeth le-Isr; found mem, Friends of ORT; asso mem, Assn Consistorial; mem: comm, Bank of Brussels; tax comm, Tax Auth; Consistoire Israélite de Belgique; Rotary; hon sgt, Infantry Sch, all Arlon; fmr delg of Min of Middle Classes, Commn of Appeal, Luxembourg. Recipient: Officier de l'Ordre de la Couronne; Décoration Industrielle de Ire Classe; Décoration Spec, pour promoteurs d'Unions Profsls; Medaille de la Reconnaissance Belge avec Croix Rouge; Medaille de la Résistance Belge en Fr; Ch.valier du Merite Social de Fr. Home and office: 7 Grand'-rue, Arlon, Belgium.

LOEB, Carl M Jr, US business exec; b. St Louis, Mo, Aug 10, 1904; s. Carl and Adeline (Moses); BS, Princeton U, 1926; MS, MIT, 1928; m. Lucille Schamberg, Jan 30, 1929; c: Constance Cohn, Carl. Pres: Ideax Corp, since 1954; Lubri-Case, since 1955; chmn, Slide-O-Chrome, since 1959; dir: Amer Metal Climax, since 1955; Kawecki Beryico Inds, since 1955; Windings Inc, since 1957; vice-pres, devl, Climax Molybdenum Co, 1937-54; mem: molybdenum ind adv comm, Fgn Econ Admn, 1945; adv comm on molybdenum, Defense Minerals Admn, 1951; tech ind disarmament comm to study post-surrender treatment of Ger iron, steel and ferro-alloys inds; visiting comm on earth scis, MIT, 1957-66. Pres, Natl Council on Crime and Delinquency, since 1967; dir, JWB, since 1942, vice-pres, 1943-52, chmn, exec comm, 1950-52; dir, Grand Jury Assn of NY Co, since 1950, past vice-pres; hon trustee at large, FJP, mem: Amer Welding Soc; Amer Soc for Metals; Amer Soc Lubrication Engrs; Amer Foundrymens Soc; Natl Social Wfr Assembly, Inc; Sons of Amer Revolution; Temple Emanu-El, NYC; fmr: pres, Comty Council of Gtr NY; chmn, Bd of Correction, NYC; dir, Friends of Touro Syn, hon trustee at large, since 1962; Natl Recreations Soc; mem: adv council, NY Sch of Social Work, Columbia U; NY State Comm of 100 for 1960 White House Conf on Children and Youth; clubs: Tower, Princeton U; Princeton, NY; Cent Country, White Plains; Natl Rep; Engrs; MIT, NY; La Quinta Country, Cal. Co-author, Molybdenum, Steels, Irons, Alloys, 1948; contbr of articles to tech jours. Recipient, Interfaith Award of JWV of US, 1954. Home: Whippoorwill Rd, Armonk, NY. Office: 137 E 57 St, New York, NY.

LOEB, John L, Jr, US, investment banker; b. NYC, May 2, 1930; s. John and Frances (Lehman); BA, cum laude, Harvard Coll, 1952, MBA, 1954; m. Nina Sundby, Apr 9, 1960; c: Alexandra. Partner, Loeb, Rhoades and Co; dir Amer Star Ins Co, Inc; Denver and Rio Grande WRR Co; Holly Sugar Corp; Intl Housing Capital Corp; MGM; Société Financière pour les Industries du Tourisme, Paris; spec asst, Gov Nelson Rockefeller. Lt, USAAF, 1954-56. Adv bd, Amer Field Services, Intl Scholarships, NYC; bd dirs, Visiting Nurse Service of NY; mem: Intl Council Mus Modern Art, NYC; comm on fgn commerce and affairs, NY C of C; Invest Assn of NY; The Pilgrims: NY chap, Sons of Amer Revolution; clubs: City Midday; The Recess; Harvard; Cent Country; St James, London; Young Rep. Home: 237 E 61 St, New York, NY. Office: 42 Wall St, New York, NY.

LOEB, Joseph P, US, attorney; b. LA, Dec 11, 1883; s. Leon and Estelle (Newmark); BA, U of Cal, 1905; m. Amy Kahn (decd), Jan 24, 1909; c: Kathleen Bernath, Margaret Soares. Ret, sr partner, law firm, Loeb and Loeb, since 1908; dir em, Union Bank. Mem: natl adv bd, Amer Council for Judaism, since 1944; vice-pres, Philharmonic Fund since 1955; adv council, Sch of Jurisprudence, U of Cal since 1947; bd of f, Claremont Grad Sch and U Cen, since 1947; dir, J Comty Council TB and Health Assn; LA chap, CJFWF; JDC; Natl

Ref Service; mem: exec comm, NCCJ; Amer, LA Co Bar Assns; State Bar of Cal; Masons; Shriners; Phi Beta Kappa; Phi Beta Kappa Assos; hon mem, Order of Coif; fmr mem, Cal State Bd Educ ; clubs: LA Athletic; Claremont Colls Fac House; Hillcrest Country, past dir, pres. Home: 450 N Rossmore Ave, Los Angeles, Cal. Office: 710 Pacific Mutual Bldg, Los Angeles, Cal.

LOEB, Louis M, US, attorney; b. NYC, July 12, 1908; s. Emil and Blanche (Pulaski); BA, Yale Coll, 1919; LLB, Columbia U, 1922; m. Janet Cook, Apr 8, 1926; c: Robert, Sue. Partner, Lord, Day & Lord since 1948; mem, Cook, Nathan & Lehman, 1927-47; dir, secy, WW Nerton & Co. Hon dir, 92 St YM-YWHA; chmn, Mayor's Commn on the Judiciary; vice-pres, bd mem, Walter E Meyer Research Inst of Law; pres, NYC Bar Assn, 1956-58; vice-chmn, Temp Commn on the Courts, 1953-56; hon trustee, FJP; bd mem, Eugene and Agnes E Meyer Found; mem: Bd of Health of NYC; Amer and NY State Bar Assns; NY Co Lawyers Assn; Cent Assn; Squadon A Ex-Mem Assn; clubs: Grolier; Yale of NYC; Recess. Home: Day & Sterling Rds, Greenwich, Conn. Office: 25 Broadway, New York, NY.

LOEB, William A, US, surgeon; b. NYC, Feb 28, 1906; s. Joseph and Fani (Gross); att Columbia U, 1924-27; MD, U State of NY Med Sch, 1931; m. Sondra Tillman; c: Howard, Erica, Steven, Bruce, Glen. Dir of surg, St Vincent Hosp, Montclair, since 1960; mem, surg staff: Beth Isr Hosp, Newark, since 1950; Mountainside Hosp, since 1951; Montclair Comty. Hosp, since 1951; med examiner to State of NJ; fmr: asst to prof clinical surg, Georgia Med Sch, Augusta, Ga, 1935-37. Chief of surg services, Army and Vet Hosp, 1942-46; lt col, US MC, WW II. Fellow: Amer Coll of Surgs; Intl Coll of Surgs; Soc Surgs of NJ; AMA; dipl, Amer Bd of Surg; chmn, Hosp-Comty Emergency Comm, since 1960. Contbr to med jours. Recipient: Bronze Star. Hobby: tennis. Home: 21 Lincoln St, Glen Ridge, NJ. Office: 585 E 27 St, Paterson, NJ.

LOEB, William J, US, physician, educator; b. Cleveland, O, May 14, 1912; s. Joseph and Elsie (Rosenberg); BA, Yale U, 1933; MD, W Reserve U, 1937; m. Sue Goldsmith, 1938; c: Jill, Peggy, Penny, Kit. Pvt practice since 1946; chief, dept otolaryngology, Mt Sinai Hosp; asst clinical prof, Case-W Reserve U. Col, US Army Res, MC, 1940-45. Mem: Amer Laryngological, Otological, and Rhinological Assn; Amer Broncho-Esophagologic Assn; Amer Acad Otolaryngology; Amer Coll Surgs; Cleveland and O Med Socs. Contbr to profsl jours. Home: 24815 Duffield Rd, Cleveland, O. Office: 11811 Shaker Blvd, Cleveland. O.

LOEBL, Jerrold, US, architect; b. Chgo, Ill, Sep 2, 1899; s. Max and Nettie (Sobel); BS, Armour Inst of Tech, 1921. MA,1922; m. Ruth Weil, Feb 25, 1926; c: James, Nancy Zuraw. Partner, Loebl, Schlossman, Bennett & Dart, architects, since 1925; dir, dept of architecture, Armour Inst of Tech, 1935-38. Pres: Chgo Bldg Cong, 1944-46; Chgo Brandeis U; chma, Architects Examining Comm, State of Ill, 1941-48; f, Amer Inst of Architects, pres, Chgo chap, 1940-43; trustee: Barat Coll, Lake Forest; Ill Inst of Tech; clubs: B'nai B'rith; Arts; Tavern; Downtown; Northmoor Country. Homes: 140 E Walton Pl, Chicago, Ill; 1060 Rancho Dr, Ojai, Cal. Office: 333 N Michigan Ave, Chicago, Ill.

LOEFFLER, Ludwig, Ger, civil servant; b. Hamburg, Sep 2, 1906; s. Siegfried and Emma (Weinthal); D Jur; att: Geneva U; Freiburg U; Hamburg U; m. Beci Loeffler; c: Renate. Leading official social dept, Free City of Hamburg, since 1954. Vice-chmn: J Communal Fund of N W Ger; J Hosp; mem, bd, J Comty; all Hamburg. Hobbies: J Affairs, music, gardening. Home: Maienweg 35, Hamburg 20, Ger.

LOEV, Bernard, US, chemist; b. Phila , Pa, Feb 26, 1928; s. Abraham and Anna (Greenberg); BSc, U of Pa, 1949; MA, PhD, Columbia U, 1952; m. Pearl Winter, July 16, 1931; c: Glen, Larry, Bruce. Asst dir, chem, Smith, Kline, French, Labs since 1968; sr chem, Pennsalt Chem Corp, 1952-57. Bd dir, Intl Cong Hetero Chem; chmn: Phila Organic Chem Club, 1966-67; Med Chem sect, Phila Amer Chem Soc; mem: NY Acad Sci; Amer Inst Chem; AAAS; Masons; B'nai B'rith. Mem, ed bd, Het Chem, Intra-Sci Research Found; contbr to sci jours; holder of numerous patents. Hobbies: reading, fishing. Home: 321 Robinson Dr, Broomall, Pa. Office: 1530 Spring Garden St, Philadelphia, Pa.

LOEVY, Theodore, Isr, journalist; b. Pol, Dec 21, 1905; in Isr since 1940; att HS, Berlin; m. Eliza Schneeberg; c: Ram,

Gabriela. Ed and publisher: Echo Economic Review, since 1948; Israel Diamonds, since 1968; fmr, fgn corresp in Eur capitals. Home: 37 Ibn Gvirol St, Tel Aviv, Isr. Office: Diamond Chambers, 3 Ahuzat Bait, Tel Aviv, Isr.

LOEW, Michael, US, artist, teacher; b. NYC, May 8, 1907; s. Samuel and Judith (Fass); att: Art Students League, NY, 1926-29; Academie Scandinave, Paris, 1930; Hans Hoffman Sch of Fine Arts, NY, 1947-49; Atelier Leger, Paris, 1950; m. Mildred Rodman, 1941; c: Jonathan. Chmn and painting instr, Fine Arts Dept, Sch of Visual Arts, NY, since 1958; visiting painting critic, Portland Mus Art Sch, Ore, 1956-57; visiting lectr, U Cal, Berkeley, 1960-61, 1966-67. One man shows: Artists Gal, NY, 1949; Rose Fried Gal, NY, 1953, 1955, 1957, 1959; Holland Goldowsky Gal, 1960; Portland Art Mus, 1956; U Cal, Berkeley, 1960, 1967; Stable Gal, NY, 1961, 1962, 1965; Tirka Karlis Gal, Provincetown, Mass, 1957; two-man show, Rutgers U, 1959, four-man show, Rose Fried Gal, 1955; maj group shows: Farnsworth Mus, Me, 1950; Stable Gal, 1951-55; Paris, Rome, Copenghagen, Tokyo, SF, NY Gals, 1950; Whitney Mus Annuals, 1950, 1961, NY Metrop Mus, 1952; Walker Art Cen, 1953; Intl Assn of Plastic Arts Eur Touring Show, 1957-59; Zabritzky Gal, NY, 1957; Fed of Arts Travelling Show, 1958, 1963; NY Coliseum,1959; Morgan State Coll, Md, 1960; Yale U Art Gal, 1960-61; Whitney Mus, 1962; Mus of Modern Art Touring Exhb, 1963: Art Inst of Chgo, 1964; Colby Coll, Me, 1964; Pa Acad of Fine Arts, 1966; U of Cal, Berkeley, 1967; perm collections: Union Carbide; Hirshhorn Mus, Wash DC; Whitney Mus; Phila Mus; Hampton Inst, Va; Sheldon Memorial Mus Gal, Lincoln, Neb; U Art Mus, U Cal; Gal of Contemporary Art, U Atlanta; Geigy Chem Corp, NY; Biria Acad of Art and Culture, Calcutta, India; murals: Hall of Pharm and Hall of Man, NY World's Fair, 1939; POs: Amherst O, 1941; Belle Vernon, Pa, 1942; USN, 1943-45. Mem: Amer Abstract Artists; Fed of Painters and Sculptors; Coll Arts Assn; Mayor LaGuardia's Comm of 100, 1937; art juror: NYC Cen Gal, 1957; US Comm for Intl Assn of Plastics Arts, 1956. Contbr to art jours. Recipient: hon mention, natl mural competition: Social Security Bldg, 1940, War Dept Bldg; Sadie A May F for Study Abroad, 1929; Ford Found Purchase Award, Art Inst of Chgo Exhb, 1964. Home: 280 Ninth Ave, New York, NY. Studio: 287 Seventh Ave, New York, NY.

LOEWENBERG, Bert James, US, historian, educator; b. Boston, Mass, Dec 24, 1905; s. Herman and Sarah (Kelson); BA, Clark U, 1926, MA, 1927; MA, Harvard U, 1930, PhD, 1934; m. Anne Cinamon, Oct 9, 1932; c: Robert, Judith, Sarah. Prof hist, Sarah Lawrence Coll, Bronxville NY, since 1942, dir, grad prog for coll teaching, since 1966, cen for continuing educ, 1965-69; visiting prof: U of Mo, 1938-39; U of Rochester, 1940-41; Cornwell U, 1944; Colegio de Mexico, 1945; Northwestern U, 1947; New Sch for Social Research, 1947; Ruskin Coll, Oxford, 1952; Heb U, 1953; Salzburg Sem of Amer Studies, 1953; U Leeds, 1960; Fulbright prof, U of Cambridge, 1961; f, Social Sci Research Council, U of London and Edinburgh, 1934-35, 1962-63; f: Royal Hist Soc; Newbury Libr; Soc for Amer Studies; chmn, Darwin anniversary comm, Amer Hist Assn; mem: Amer, Miss Valley Hist Assns; Amer Studies Assn; Hist of Sci Soc; Soc for Study of Tech; Phi Beta Kappa. Author: The US: American Democracy in World Perspective, 1947; Making of American Democracy, 1950; Darwin, Wallace and the Theory of Natural Selection, 1957; Charles Darwin: Evolution and Natural Selection, 1959; Historical Writing in American Culture, 2 vols, 1968-69; mem ed bd: American Quarterly: Sarah Lawrence Journal; contbr to hist revs. Home: 15 Center Knolls, Bronxville, NY. Office: Sarah Lawrence Coll, Bronxville, NY.

LOEWENBERG, Jacob, US, educator, author; b. Tuckum, Latvia, Feb 2, 1882; s. Moses and Betty (Blumenthal); in US since 1904; BA, Harvard U, 1908, MA, 1909, PhD, 1911; hon LLD, U of Cal, 1962; m. Katherine Turner, May 26' 1924 (decd); c: Jeannot Nyles. Prof em, phil, U of Cal, since 1952, mem fac since 1915; instr, phil, Wellesley Coll, 1912-15; visiting lectr, Harvard U, 1947-48; visiting prof: Columbia U, 1951-52; Wells Coll, 1952-53; Haverford Coll, 1954-55. Author: Hegel Selections, 1929; Dialogues from Delphia, 1949; Reason and the Nature of Things, 1959; Hegel's Phenomenology: Dialogues on the Life of Mind, 1965; Twice-born: Selected Memories of an Immigrant, 1968; co-author, Knowledge and Society, 1938; contbr to profsl jours. Mem: Amer Phil Assn; AAUP; Société Européenne de Culture; club: Harvard. Home: 2455 Hilgard Ave, Berkeley, Cal.

LOEWENBERG, Jerome L, US, military jurist; b. Bklyn, Mar 19, 1907; s. Ididor and Ida (Heidelberg); BA, Cornell U, 1929, LLB, 1931; m. Grace Luther, May 21, 1937; c: Bruce. Col, USAF, staff judge advocate, Continental Air Command since 1959; judge, Sea Cliff, NY, 1934-41; various assignments USAF during WW II; staff judge advocate: 1st Air Force, 1948-50; W Air Defense Force, 1951-52; 5th Air Force (Korea), 1953; Cen Air Defense Force, 1954-57; Air Proving Ground Command, 1957-59. Mem: Nasau Co Bar Assn; NY State Magistrates Assn, vice-pres, 1938; Sigma Alpha Mu; clubs: Cornell Alumni of LI, pres, 1937; Rotary. Recipient: Legion of Merit; Army Commendation medal; Croix de Guerre with Palm, Fr; Air Force Commendation medal. Hobbies: boating, fishing. Home: Glen Head, NY.

LOEWENBERG, William A, US, business exec; b. Memphis, Tenn, Nov 14, 1902; s. Ferdinand and Johanna (Selka); m. Ruth Friedman, Dec 11, 1929; c: Joanna Markell, Fredrika Feit, William. Secy-treas: S Leather Co since 1919; Perkins Oil Co; pres, Parts Distributors Warehouse. Pres: B'nai B'rith Home and Hosp since 1967, vice-pres, 1945-62; Temple Isr, 1951-54; Memphis J Fed, 1946; Memphis Club, 1962; bd member: comm, United Fund, JWF; mem: pres council, Southwestern U, parents comm, Vanderbilt U; B'nai B'rith; C of C; Shriners; Scottish Rite; clubs: Ridgeway Country; Rotary. Recipient: natl youth f award, B'nai B'rith. Office: 274 Monroe, Memphis, Tenn.

LOEWENGART, Arthur, US, business exec; b. Rexingen, Ger, June 8, 1899; s. Robin and Anna (Tannhausser); in US since 1937; m. Gerda Tiefenthal, Aug 13, 1931; c: Miriam, Ruth Goldmuntz. Pres: Loewengart & Co sinc 1937, in Ger, 1925-37; Puerto Rico Tanning Corp; Gotham Tanning Corp; Gahna Import and Export Corp; NC Lyon & Co Inc. Mem, presidium, Econ Conf, Jerusalem; chmn, Gtr NY Fund; vice-chmn, comm for J Brig, 1944; treas, loyalty comm, Victims of Nazi Oppression, 1941; bd dirs: Amer Friends Heb U since 1968; Tanner's Council of Amer; Leather Inds of Amer; UJA, Gtr NY, 1945; Selfhelp of Emigres from Cen Eur, 1952; adv comm: War Produc Bd; OPA, 1942; club, N Shore Country. Home: 45 E 72 St, New York, NY. Office: 443 Park Ave S, New York, NY.

LOEWENGART, Stefan, Isr, business exec; b. Fuerth, Ger, Dec 10, 1900; s. Solly and Anna (Bing); in Isr since 1925; att U's: Munich; Berlin; PhD, Tuebingen, 1924; m. Irma Heymann, Nov 21, 1926; c: Shimon (killed in action, War of Independence), Micha Lavi. Mgn dir, Ariol Ltd, since 1935; found, chem ind, printing inks, in Isr; research f, Technion, Haifa since 1958; co-found, fmr mem, Local Council, Kiryat Bialik; mem: Geochem Soc, US; past pres, Geological Soc of Isr; club, Rotary. Contbr on geology and geochem. Home: 22 Haifa Rd, Kiryat Bialik, Isr. Office: POB 1808, Haifa, Isr.

LOEWENSTEIN, Aharon, Isr, chemist; b. Verden, Ger, Jan 31, 1929; in Isr since 1934; MSc, Heb U, Jerusalem, 1956, PhD, 1958; m; c: Yael. Asso prof, chem, Technion, Haifa, since 1966. Contbr to sci publs. Home: 41A Einstein St, Haifa, Isr. Office: Technion, Haifa, Isr.

LOEWENSTEIN, Benjamin S, US, attorney; b. Atlantic City, NJ, Aug 22, 1912; s. Sidney and Cecilia (Steinberg); BA, Haverford Coll, Pa, 1934; LLB, U of Pa, 1937; m. Hattie Gruenstein, 1942; c: Sally Edward; m. 2nd, Eleanor Schieren, June 14, 1966. Partner, law firm, Abrahams and Lowenstein since 1937; secy and bd mem: Oxford Ind Corp since 1956; Oxford Finance Co; Oxford First Corp; Atlas Rug Cleaners. Pres: Health and Wfr Council, Gtr Phila since 1960; S Home for Children since 1967; hon pres, J Employment and Vocational Service since 1953; fmr pres: AJComm, Phila chap, 1957-59; Haverford Coll Alumni Assn, 1955-56; J Occupational Council, 1963; chmn, Task Force on Aging, Pa Comprehensive Mh Plan, 1966; vice-pres: J Comty Relations Council; Camp Council, 1953-55; chmn, Regional Comprehensive Health Planning, Southeastern Pa since 1909; delg, White House Conf on Aging, 1961; trustee, Comty Services of Pa; mem bd: Vocational Research Inst; Fed J Agcys, Gtr Phila; mem: natl bd govs, exec bd, AJComm; bd, United Fund, Gtr Phila; Amer, Pa, and Phila Bar Assns; clubs: Locust, Philmont Country; Lawyers of Phila. Recipient: Big Brother Assn Cert of Appreciation, 1943; Allied Jewish Appeal Comty Services Award, 1956; Phila County Med Society Cert of Appreciation, 1961. Home: 1910 Penn Tower Apts, Phila, Pa. Office: 1730 Land Title Bldg, Phila, Pa.

LOEWENSTEIN, Edward, US, architect; b. Chgo, Ill, May 10,

1913; s. James and Aline (Goldsmith); B Arch, MIT, Cambridge, 1935; m. Frances Stern, Apr 29, 1944; c: Jane, Laura, step c: Ferris Hetherington III. Pres, owner, Loewenstein, Atkinson & Wilson, architects and engrs; mem, fac, art dept, U of NC, Greensboro, NC since 1957. Maj, engrs, US Army, 1941-45; res, 1935-55. Pres: Greensboro Cerebral Palsy Assn, 1953-54; Weatherspoon Art Gal, Greensboro, 1954-62; NC Architectural Found, 1954-56; secy, treas, NC chap, Amer Inst Architects, 1951-53; mem: Bldg Research Inst; Constructions Specifications Inst; Soc Architectural Hists; Archeol Inst; Temple Emanuel; club, Greensboro Country. Contbr to profsl jours. Hobbies: boating, architectural hist. Home: 444 Cornwallis Dr, Greensboro, NC. Office: 1030 E Wendover Ave, Greensboro, NC.

LOEWENSTEIN, Egon Israel, Chile, rabbi; b. Berlin, Ger, Oct 2, 1912; s. Ernst and Jenny (Levy); in Chile since 1939; ordained rabbi, Rabb Sem, Breslau; att U Prague; m. Kaete Brauer, May 4, 1939. Rabbi, Santiago de Chile since 1939; lectr, U Chile since 1968; rabbi, J comty, Gleiwitz, Ger, 1938-39. Pres, Union de Rabinos en América Latina; dir: CENTRA, Asociación de Comunidades y Organizationes Israelitas en Latino-América; B'nai B'rith, Chile. Contbr: articles to Span jours. Home: Ave Vicuna Mackenna 265, Santiago, Chile. Study: Ave Portugal 810, Santiago, Chile.

LOEWENSTEIN, Regina L, US, statistician; b. Jersey City, NJ, Feb 10, 1916; d. Solomon and Frieda (Abelson); BA, Barnard Coll, NY, 1936; MA, Columbia U, 1937, post grad study, 1938-46, 1958-61; post grad study: Dept of Agric, Wash, DC, 1946-49; George Wash U, Wash DC, 1950; Ia State Coll, 1952. Stat, research unit, Columbia U Sch of Public Health since 1958; fmr: asst stat, Natl Ref Service, 1938-41; math, spec studies group, div of war research, Columbia U, 1941-45; stat, commn on cmty inter-relations, AJCong, 1945-46; chief: oprs dept, study of child health services, Amer Acad of Ped, 1946-48; stat sect, comm on vets med problems, NRC, 1948-54; asso, social research div, Natl TB Assn, 1954-58. F, Amer Public Health Assn; mem: Amer Stat Assn; Phi Beta Kappa. Co-author: Study of Child Health Service and Pediatric Education, 1949; Socio-Economic Conditions and Tuberculosis Prevalence, 1956; Tuberculin Testing Handbook, 1958; Community Fact Book of Washington Heights, 1960-61; contbr to profsl jours. Recipient: Kohn math prize, 1936; alternate, Rice F. Hobbies: hiking, music. Home: 165 West End Ave, New York, NY. Office: 21 Audubon Ave, New York, NY.

LOEWENSTEIN, Rudolph M, US, psychoanalyst; b. Lodz, Pol, Jan 17, 1898; s. Maurice and Charlotte (Taube); in US since 1942; MD, U of Berlin, 1923, U of Paris, 1935; m. Elisabeth Geleerd; c: Dominique, Elisabeth, Marie, Richard. Pvt practice, NYC since 1943; asst, Berlin Psychan Inst, 1923-25; asst, outpatient dept, Clinique Psychiatrique de la Faculté de Médecine, U of Paris, 1925-39; training analyst, lectr, Paris Psychan Inst, 1925-40; training analyst instr, NY Psychoanalytic Inst since 1943, vice-pres, 1948-50, pres, 1950-52; asso clinical prof, psycht Yale U Med Sch, 1948-52. Fr Army, 1939-40. Pres: Amer Psychan Assn, 1957-58; NY Psychan Soc, 1959-61; vice-pres, Intl Psychan Assn, 1965-67; found mem, Paris Psychan Soc; mem: AMA; Amer Psychan Assn; NY State, NY Co Med Socs; Intl Psychan Assn; AAAS; Intl Inst of Arts and Letters; Conf on J Social Studies; AJCong, Business and Prof Assos; corresponding mem, Isr Psychan Soc. Author, Christians and Jews: A Psychoanalytic Study, 1951; ed, Drives, Affects, Behavior, 1953; contbr to: profsl jours. Recipient, Croix de Guerre, Fr, 1940. Home: 1148 Fifth Ave, New York, NY. Office: 1100 Madison Ave, New York, NY.

LOEWENTHAL, Meinhardt, Isr, educator; b. Ger, Dec 3, 1911; s. Markus and Auguste (Wolff); in Isr since 1948; DM; att U's: Berlin; Pisa; Siena; Basel; m. Michaela Skariton; c: David, Orna. Dozent, path, Tel Aviv U; dir, Path Inst, Tel Aviv. Mem: B'nai B'rith; Rotisseurs. Contbr of numerous papers to profsl jours. Hobby, painting. Home: 1 Itamar Ben Avi St, Tel Aviv, Isr. Office: 98 Yehuda Halevi St, Tel Aviv, Isr.

LOEWINGER, Samuel D, Isr, Biblical scholar, rabbi; b. Debrecen, Hung, Feb 17, 1904; s. Mordechai and Hanny (Beck); in Isr since 1950; att: J Theol Sem of: Budapest; Breslau, 1926-27; U Breslau, 1926-27; PhD, U Budapest, 1930; ordained rabbi, J Theol Sem, Hung, 1931; m. Viorica Roth, 1952; c: Shimon. Act dir, Inst of Heb Manuscripts, Jerusalem, since 1951; secy, Shrine of the Book, Cen of Bibl

Manuscripts and Dead Sea Scrolls, since 1955, mem, dir, of mus since 1964; asso prof, Bible and Talmud, J Theol Sem, Budapest, 1931-42, libr, dir and prof, 1942-50; dir J Hung Free U, Budapest, 1931-42. Hon pres, Assn Alumni and Friends of J Theol Sem and J Tchrs Sem in Hung, Jerusalem; co-pres, Org for Talmud Illus and Oral Torah Explanation, Tel Aviv; pres: Wilhelm Bacher Lit Club; Ignac Goldziher Lit Club, J Theol Sem Students; fmr co-pres, Org of J Students in Hung U's. Author: Alphabetum Syracidis, 1926; Tractatio de punctis et accentibus, 1929; Die Handschriftensammlung des L Blau, 1929; Achikar, 1930; Két Középkori héber grammatitkáról, 1931; Jiddische Handschriften in Breslau, 1936; Zecharja Könyvenek egysége, 1941; Germania prófétaja, 1947; The Variants of DSJ, 1954; Hebrew Manuscripts in Austria and Germany, 1957; Mechqarin b-Kether Aram Zobah, 1960; Catalogue of the Hebrew Manuscripts in the Library of the Juedische-Theologisches Seminar in Breslau, Wiesbaden, 1965; Hebrew Manuscripts in the Vatican, 1968; ed, jubilee, memorial vols in hon of profs and rabbis; co-ed: Magyar Zsido Szemle, Budapest, 1931-47; Hassoker, Budapest, 1933-47. Home: 1 Katznelson St, Jerusalem, Isr. Office: J Natl and U Libr, Jerusalem, Isr.

LOEWY, Kurt Josef, Isr, educator; b. Vienna, Aus, Dec 24, 1906; s. Sigmund and Malwine (Steiner); in Isr since 1933; Dipl ME, Tech Hochschule, Vienna, 1931; m. Margit Kudelka, May 14, 1933; c: Dan, Ruth Dalin. Prof, ME, Technion since 1961; chief, tech office, Nesher Cement Works until 1960. Haganah. Contbr: papers and books in Heb on elements of machinery and machinery for material dressing. Home: 42 Hashkedim Rd, Tivon, Isr. Office: Technion, Haifa, Isr.

LOKER, Zvi, Isr, diplomat; b. Novisad, Aus-Hung, July 9, 1915; s. Wilhelm and Margita (Berger); in Isr since 1939; att: Fac Law, U Belgrade, 1937-39; BA, Heb U, 1941, att, Heb U, 1959-61; m. Rachel Vajs, Sep 21, 1941; c: Tamar. Elad. Isr ambass to: Malagasay Rep, since 1967; Mauritius, since 1968; with mem staff: Brit Info Dept, Cairo, 1944-47; political dept, JA, 1947-48; dir, intl org div, Min for Fgn Affairs, 1948-49; dir, consular div, 1949-51; 1st secy, consul, Isr Legation, Bucharest, 1951-52; Belgrade, 1952-57; councillor to Isr Ambass, Rome, 1957-58; dir, Brit Commonwealth div, Min for Fgn Affairs, 1958-60, dir, Afr div, 1960-62; consul gen, Isr Emb, Paris, 1962; minister plenipontentiary, 1965. Yugo Army, 1935-36; Brit Army, 1941-44. Mem directorate, Hashomer Hatsair, Zagreb, Yugo, 1935-37; org secy, ZF, Vojvoaina, 1937-39; mem exec, J Sport Club, Yugo, Silver medal, Paris, 1969. Home: 32 Palmach St, Jerusalem, Isr. Office: POB 886, Tananarive, Madagascar.

LONDON, Bezalel, Isr, actor; b. Pziluky, Russ, 1900; s. Meir and Esther; in Isr since 1925; att: Drama Sch, Odessa; Poly Eng Inst, Odessa; m. Matya Feldman; c: Jazon. Actor: Yiddish Theatre, Havana, Cuba, 1924-25; Heb Theatre, 1925-27; Kumkum Theatre, 1927-28; found, actor, repertory mgr, Matateh Theatre, 1928-54; actor, Ohel Theatre, 1954-69. Mem bd, Milo Club. Recipient: Abramovitz Prize from Histadrut. Home: 3 Motzkin St, Tel Aviv, Isr.

LONDON, George, US, opera singer; b. Montreal, Can, May 30, 1920; s. Louis and Bertha (Broad) Burnstein; att LA City Coll, 1937-39; m. Nora Sheldon, Aug 30, 1955; c: Marina, Mark. Artistic admnr, John F Kennedy Cen for Performing Arts, Wash, DC; opera appearances: Hollywood Bowl, 1941; LA, SF Civic Light Opera Assns, 1942-44; Rigoletto, SF, 1943; Aida, Vienna, 1949; Glyndebourne, 1950; Metrop, 1951-65; Bayreuth Festival, 1951-53, 1956-57, 1961-64; Salzburg Festival, 1952; Boris Godunov Bolshoi Theatre, Moscow, 1960. Pres, Amer Guild Musical Artists, AFL-CIO; secy, Natl Music Council, NY; bd dirs, NYC Cen. Contbr to musical jours. Recipient: named Kammersanger, singer to the court, by Aus Chancellor, 1953. Office: John F Kennedy Cen for Performing Arts, 726 Jackson Pl, NW, Washington, DC.

LONDON, Hannah R, US, author; b. Boston, Mass, Jan 2, 1894; d. Abraham and Goldie (Mickleshanski); grad, Radcliffe, Coll, 1916; m. Benjamin Siegel, June 14, 1923; c: Robert (killed in action, WW II). Lectr, early Amer art; asst, Copley Gal, Boston, 1920. Author: Portraits of Jews by Gilbert Stuart and Other Early American Artists, 1927; Shades of My Forefathers, 1941; Miniatures of Early American Jews, 1953; one-act play, Immortal Son, 1958; contbr to periodicals. Mem: J Hist Soc; Soc for Preservation of NE Antiquities; Copley Soc, Boston; N Shore Arts Assn; Cape Ann Hist Soc; Speech and Hearing Found, Mass; clubs: Boston Author's; China Students. Recipient, $1000 anonymous award

for Portraits of Jews, 1925; citation, JBCA, 1954. Home: 97 Toxteth St, Brookline, Mass.

LONDON, Irving M, US, physician, educator; b. Malden, Mass, July 24, 1918; s. Jacob and Rose (Goldstein); BJE, Boston Heb Tchrs Coll, 1938; AB, Harvard, 1939, MD, 1943; hon DSc, U of Chgo, 1966; m. Huguette Piedzicki, 1955; c: Robert, David. Prof, chmn, Dept of Med, Albert Einstein Coll of Med, NY, since 1955, dir, med services, Bx Munic Hosp Cen, NY since 1955; asso prof, med, Columbia U Coll of Phys and Surg, 1954-55; fac mem since 1947; asso att phys, Presbyterian Hosp, NY, 1954-55, on staff since 1947; cons, med dir, Montefiore Hosp and Med Cen, since 1965; research f, dept of med, NYU Coll of Med, 1944; med off, Tropical Disease Sect; Moore Gen Hosp, Swannanoa, NC, 1945. Capt, US Army MC, 1944-46; med off, staff, Chief of J Task Force 1, Bikini Atom Bomb Operations, 1946. Chmn: bd sci cons, Sloan-Kettering Inst for Cancer Research since 1960; Metabolism Study Sect, USPHS, 1961-63; pres, Amer Soc Clinical Inves, 1963-64; secy, Anti-Anemia Preparations Adv Bd of the US Pharmacopoeia, 1949-55; mem: bd, med, Natl Acad Sci since 1967; adv comm to the dir, NH since 1966; Panel on Biol Sci and the Advancement of Med, Natl Acad Sci since 1966; bd sci counsellors, Natl Heart Inst, USPHS, 1964-68; exec comm, Health Research Council, NYC, 1958-63; research council, Public Health Research Inst, NYC, 1958-63; med f bd, Natl Acad Sci, NRC, 1955-63; med adv bd, Heb U and Hadassah since 1955; med: adv comm, Unitarian Universalist Service Comm, 1963-66; med adv bd, Tel Aviv U Med Sch since 1966; subcomm on intravenous alimentation, Dept of Army, 1955-60; Alpha Omega Alpha; Amer Acad Arts and Sci; Amer Soc Biol Chem; Amer Soc for Clinical Inves; Assn Amer Phys; Harvey Soc; Intl Study of Hematology; Interurban Clinical Club; Phi Beta Kappa; Practitioners Soc; Soc for Developmental Biol; Soc for Experimental Biol and Med. Asso ed, Jour of Clinical Investigation, 1952-57; ed bd, Physiology and Pharmacology for Physicians, since 1962; Amer Jour of Med, since 1965. Recipient: Welch f in Internal Med, Natl Acad of Sci, 1949-52; Theobold Smith award in Med Sci, AAAS, 1953; Commonwealth Fund f, Pasteur Inst, 1962-63; lectureship: Jean Oliver, SUNY, 1957; Roger Morris, U Cincinnati, 1958; Stuart McGuire, Med Coll Va, 1960; Harvey, 1961; Phi Delta Epsilon, U Colo, 1962; Georgetown U, 1966; Jacobaeus, Stockholm, Swed, 1964; Alpha Omega Alpha, Yale U; Boston U; Columbia U; SUNY downstate Med Cen; U Chgo. Home: 4740 Iselin Ave, Riverdale, NY. Office: Albert Einstein Coll of Med, New York, NY.

LONGMAN, Ivor Martin, Isr, mathematician; b. London, Eng, Mar 8, 1923; s. Harry and Leah (Glassman); in Isr since 1953; BA, Emmanuel Coll, Eng, 1943; MA, 1948; DSc, Technion, Haifa, 1957; m. Rony Zur, Mar 25, 1953; c: David, Shulamith, Benjamin. Asso prof, math, U of Negev, since 1967; research asst, sr sci; Weizmann Inst, Rehovot, 1955-58, 1962-67; asst res geophys, U of Cal. Prin contribs: original research work in math techniques for solving theoretical geophys problems by computer. Mem various learned soc's, US, Brit, Isr. Contbr to profsl jours. Home: 3 Harimon St, Rehovot, Isr. Office: U of Negev, Beersheba, Isr.

LONGSTREET, Stephen, US, artist, author; b. NYC, Apr 18, 1907; s. Irwin and Sara (Beck); att Rutgers U; Harvard U, NY Sch of Fine and Applied Art; m. Ethel Godoff, 1932; c: Harry, Joan Tanney. Head, Dept Social Hist, Viewpoints Inst of Gen Semantics since 1966; staff mem, Dept Arts and Hum, UCLA since 1967; fmr: ed, Time Mag; motion picture critic, The Saturday Rev; lect, Art of the Twentieth Cen: U of Cal and Ariz; artist in black and white. Trustee, LA Art Assn, staff lectr, since 1945; mem: Natl Civil War Centennial Comm; Writers Guild of Amer W. Author: Decade, 1940; Last Man Around the World, 1941; Sound of an American, 1942; The Pedlocks, 1951; The Beach House, 1952; The World Revisited, 1953; The Lion at Morning, 1954; Boy in the Model-T, 1956; The Real Jazz, Old and New, 1956; The Promoters, 1957; The Burning Man, 1958; Encyclopedie du Jazz, 1958; The Crime, 1959; Eagles Where I Walk, 1961; A Treasury of the World's Great Prints, 1961; The Flesh Peddlers, 1962; Pedlock and Sons, 1966; The Wilder Shore, 1968; play, High Button Shoes, 1948; motion picture, The Jolson Story, 1948; co-author: Man of Montmartre, 1958; The Politician, 1958; Geisha, 1960; Young Men of Paris, 1963, motion pictures: Duel in the Sun; Greatest Show on Earth; The Helen Morgan Story; The Gay Sisters; Stallion Road; Silver River; Uncle Harry; Campaign mgr: Stevenson, Kennedy, and McCarthy TV. Hobbies: collecting Chinese and Japanese art, Cambodian stone carvings. Home and studio: 610 N Elm Dr, Beverly Hills, Cal.

LOOKSTEIN, Joseph Hyman, US, rabbi, educator; b. Russ, Dec 25, 1902; s. Jacob and Anna (Shapiro); in US since 1910; BA, CCNY, 1928; MA, Columbia U, 1929; ordained rabbi, Rabbi Isaac Elchanan Sem, 1926; hon DD, Yeshiva U, 1948; m. Gertrude Schlang; c: Nathalie Schacter, Haskel. Chancellor, Bar-Ilan U since 1966, acting pres, 1958-66; rabbi, Cong Kehilath Jeshurun, NYC since 1923; prof homiletics and J sociol, Yeshiva U since 1931; prin, Heb Tchrs Training Sch for Girls, 1929-39; found, Ramaz Sch, 1937. Adv, jt chiefs of staff, 1945. Pres: RabCA, 1941-43; NY Bd Rabbis, 1941-43; Mizrachi Natl Educ Comm; chmn, Yeshiva U Planning Comm; cons, US State Dept, UN Conf, SF, 1945; vice-chmn, div rel activities, JWB, WW II; chmn: Latin-Amer comm, JDC on comm J chaplaincy, JWB. Author: Judaism in Theory and Practice, 1931; What is Orthodox Judaism?, 1940; Courage— A Collection of Wartime Sermons, 1943; Faith and Destiny of Man, 1967. Home: 1160 Park Ave, New York, NY. Study: 125 E 85 St, New York, NY.

LOOMER, Harry P, US, psychiatrist; b. NYC, May 15, 1909; s. Pincus and Annie (Kliegman); BS, CCNY, 1932; att: U Heidelberg, 1932-35; U Berlin, 1935-36; CG Jung Inst, Switz, 1951-53; MD, U Vienna, 1938; c: Peter, Valerie, Jeffrey. Sup psycht, Manhattan Aftercare Clinic since 1960; pvt practice since 1956; Staten I Aftercare Clinic; dir psycht, Menorah Home and Hosp, NY; med dir, Menorah Geriatric Guidance Clinic; dir, profsl staff, Natl Family Council on Drug Addiction, 1959-60; org, staff of psychts, psychols, social workers, research workers to give voluntary service to drug addicts, NYC, 1959-60. Maj, aviation med examiner, flight surg, commanding off, sta hosp, USAAC, 1941-46. Exponent, mirror-microphone technique in psychotherapy. Mem: Amer Psycht Assn; AMA; NY Co, NY State Med Socs; Phi Beta Kappa. Contbr to med jours. Recipient: Isidor and Ida Straus Medal; Asiatic Pacific Theatre Ribbon with Bronze Star. Hobbies: painting, woodcarving, music, ceramics, sports. Home and office: 150 E 18 St, New York, NY.

LOOMSTEIN, Arthur, US, business exec; b. St Louis, Mo, July 27, 1939; s. Meyer and Ann (Mariam); BS, BA, Wash U, St Louis, 1961, LLB, JD, Law Sch, 1961-64; m. Frances Harris, June 11, 1961; c: David, Deborah. Secy-treas, Guild Mgmt Co, since 1962. Mem: Leadership Devl Council; J Fed of St Louis. Hobby, sports. Home: 727 Wenneker Dr, Ladue, Mo. Office: 7730 Carondelet Ave, Clayton, Mo.

LOPEZ, Guido, It, public relations, advertising exec, author; b. Milan, It, Jan 2, 1924; s. Sabatino and Sisa (Tapet); grad, Liceo Classico, Milan, 1942; m. Gigliola Colombo, Aug 22, 1949; c: Irene, Fabio. Head, PR dept, J Walter Thompson Italia, fmr, chief copywriter, group head, advt; head, press dept, Mondadori Pub House, 1945-57; mem, advt dept, Motta S P A, 1957-59. Author: novels: Il Campo, 1948; La Prova del Nove, 1954; one-act plays: Fiducia, 1947; Il Padre della Miss, 1958; non-fiction, Milano in mano, a guide to highlights of town, 1965. Mem, exec, It Zionist Org; past pres, Zionist Group of Milan. Recipient, lit prize, Bagutta Opera Prima, 1948. Home: Via Pancaldo 9, Milan, It. Office: J Walter Thompson, Via Durini 28, Milan, It.

LOPEZ, Robert Sabatino, US, educator, editor, author; b. Genoa, It, Oct 8, 1910; s. Sabatino and Sisa (Tabet); in US since 1939; DL, U Milan, It 1932; PhD, U Wis, 1942; hon LHD, HUC; m. Claude Kirschen, 1946; c: Michael, Lawrence. Prof hist, Yale U, since 1955, mem of fac since 1946; asso prof: State Tchrs Coll, Cagliari, 1933-34; Pavia, 1934-35; Genoa, 1935-36; asst prof, U Genoa, 1936-38; research asst U Wis, 1939-42; asso script ed, OWI, overseas br, 1942-43; lectr Bklyn Coll 1943-44; fgn news ed, CBS, NY, 1944-45; lectr, Columbia U, 1945-46; visiting prof, Wesleyan U, 1947-48, 1949-50; Harvard U, 1960-61. Mem: Amer Hist Assn; Mediaevel Acad of Amer; Econ Hist Soc; Friends of Heb U; Conn Acad; WJC. Author: Genoa, Marinara nel Dueccento, 1933; Studi sull'economia genovese nel medio evo, 1936; Storia delle colonie genovesi, 1938; Mediaeval Trade in the Mediterranean World, 1953; La prima crisi della banca di Genova, 1956; The Tenth Century, 1959; Naissance de L'Europe, 1962; chap in Cambridge Econ Hist, Vol II, 1952; contbr: to profsl mags; Ency Hebraica; mem: bd eds, Byzantion since 1948; Speculum since 1953. Recipient, f: Calhoun Coll, 1947; Guggenheim Memorial, 1948, 1949, 1952; Societa Liguri di Storia, 1947; Societa Alessandrina di Storia, Arte e Archeologia, 1949; Societa Pa-

vese di Storia Patria, 1953. Home: 41 Richmond Ave, New Haven, Conn. Office: Yale U, New Haven, Conn.

LORAND, Sander, US, psychiatrist, educator; b. Bodrogvecs, Hung, Feb 12, 1893; s. Joseph and Amalia (Spitz); att Hung Med Sch, 1912-18; MD, U Bratislava, Czech, 1920; m. Rhoda Leigh, June 23, 1943. Prof em, psycht, SUNY, fac mem since 1948; cons, VA; lectr: NY Psychan Inst since 1932; Columbia U, 1929-42; asso psycht, Mt Sinai Hosp, 1929-42. Hon pres, Psychan Assn of NY; bd dirs, Hillside Hosp since 1950; mem: NY Psychan Soc and Inst; Tokyo Psychan Soc. Author: Psychoanalysis Today, 1940; Technique of Psychoanalytic Therapy, 1946; Clinical Studies in Psychoanalysis, 1948; Dynamics and Therapy of Perversions. Recipient: Selective Service Medal, US Cong, 1947. Home and office: 40 Central Park S, New York, NY.

LORANT, Zoltan, Yugo, communal worker; b. Subotica, Dec 12, 1886; s. Jakov and Rosa (Singer); DJ, U Budapest, 1909; m. Jelena Kemenj, May 8, 1922; c: Tibor. Ret atty. Hon pres, J Comty of Subotica; found, B'nai B'rith Lodge, Subotica, 1st pres; grand vice-pres, Grand Lodge, B'nai B'rith, Yugo; pres, Good Deed Soc; vice pres, Red Cross Comm; hon mem, exec comm, Confd Yugo J Comtys. Author: History of the Jewish Religious Community in Subotica, 1925; History of the Jewish Women's Association in Subotica, 1926. Office: Maksima Gorkog 10, Subotica, Yugo.

LORBER, Stanley H, US, physician, educator; b. NYC, Nov 23, 1917; s. Samuel and Martha (Oberlander); BA, U of Pa, 1939, MD, 1943; m. Selma Rosen, Aug 16, 1945; c: Susan, Betty, Jeffrey. Internist, gastroenterologist since 1951; chmn, dept of gastroenterology, Temple U since 1963, prof, med since 1967, mem fac since 1959. Capt, US Army, 1944-46. Pres, Amer J Phys Comm; vice-chmn, trade council, Allied J Appeal. Author of 8 texts, contbr to med jours. Home: 908 Church Rd, Wyncote, Pa. Office: 3701 N Broad St, Philadelphia, Pa.

LORCH, Jacob, Isr, educator; b. Breslau, Ger, Apr 25, 1924; s. Max and Hannah (Wissman); in Isr since 1935; MSc, PhD, Heb U, Jerusalem; m. Ruth Blumer; c: Ronit, Yoav. Prof, botany, hist of sci, Heb U, since 1968; visiting prof: Cornell U, 1964-65; Princelon U 1965-66. Mem bd, Adult Educ Cen, Heb U. Spec interest: sci educ. Hanagid Home: Haivri St, Jerusalem, Isr. Office: Heb U, Jerusalem, Isr.

LORCH, Netanel, Isr, government official, diplomat; b. Ger, May 24, 1925; s. Max and Hanna (Wissmann); in Isr since 1935; tchr's dipl, Mizrachi Tchrs Sem, Jerusalem, 1943; MA, cum laude, Heb U, Jerusalem, 1951; m. Erika Frost, Oct 5, 1950; c: Amnon, Yahli, Yiftach. Dir, Latin Amer div, Min for Fgn Affairs, since 1968; tchr, Youth Aliyah 1943-44; script writer, Pal Bc Service, 1946-48; consul i/c info, Isr Consulate Gen, LA, Cal, 1955-58; charge d'affairs, Isr Legation, Ceylon, 1958-60; dir, Afr div, Min for Fgn Affairs, 1960-63; Isr Ambass to Peru, Bolivia, 1963-67; dir, info div, Jerusalem, 1967-68. Co cdr, IDF, 1948-50, aide to chief, gen staff, 1950-52, chief of mil hist, Gen Hqr, 1952-55. Author: Koroth Milkhemet haAtzmaut, 1958; Edge of the Sword, Israel's War of Independence, 1960; contbr to periodicals. Home: 14 Marcus St, Jerusalem, Isr. Office: Min Fgn Affairs, Jerusalem. Isr,

LORGE, Ernst M, US, rabbi; b. Mainz, Ger, May 26, 1916; s. Maurice and Hedwig (Steinweg); in US since 1936; BA, U of Cincinnati, 1938; BHL, HUC, 1939; ordained rabbi, MHL, 1942; DD, 1967; m. Eudice Goldman, June 7, 1942; c: Greta, Susan, Michael. Rabbi, Temple Beth Isr, since 1947; instr, Coll of J Studies, Chgo, since 1950, bd mem since 1955; rabbi: Temple Isr, Tallahassee, Fla; Hillel Found, Fla State U, both 1942-47; chaplain: Dept of Ill: JWV of US, 1955-63; VFW, 1957-58, 1965-66; Amer Legion, 1962-63. Served US Army, 1944-46, 1950-52. Pres: Chgo Bd of Rabbis, 1962-64; LZO of Chgo, since 1968; Chgo Assn of Reform Rabbis, 1955-57; bd mem, Bd of J Educ; mem, exec comm: conf on religion and race, ZOA, all Chgo; Union Inst, Oconomowoc, Wis. Mem: ZOA; B'nai B'rith; AJCong; JWV; Masons; club, Covenant of Ill. Author, The Teaching of Prayer, 1949. Recipient: Simon Lazarus prize, HUC, 1942; Bronze Star, 1945; certificate of merit, 1952. Home: 2637 Catalpa Ave, Chicago, Ill. Study: 4850 N Bernard St, Chicago, Ill.

LORGE, Heinz J, US, physician; b. Mainz, Ger, Aug 1, 1910; s. Maurice and Hedwig (Steinweg); in US since 1934; att U Frankfurt, 1928-33; MD, U Basle, 1934; m. Edna Berlin; Feb 5, 1939; c: Benjamin, Bernard, Barry, Bruce, Bryan. Med dir, Heb Home of Gtr Wash; communicable disease cons,

Montgomery Co Health Dept; staff, Wash Sanitorium and Hosp, since 1968; phys, St Vincent Hosp, since 1950; asst phys, State Sanatorium, Rutland, Mass, 1938-43, sr phys, 1946-50; supt, Worcester Co Hosp, 1950-68. Capt, US Army, 1943-46. Mem: Mass Med Soc; Md Med Soc; AHA; Amer Coll Chest Phys; Amer Thoracic Soc; ZOA; Temple Shalom. Contbr to profsl jours. Hobby, philately. Home: 9 Cherbourg Ct, Potomac, Md. Office: 6121 Montrose Rd, Rockville, Md.

LORIAN, Alexander, Isr, educator; b. Bucharest, Rum, Sep 9, 1921; s. Avram and Bianca (Reis); in Isr since 1941; BA London U, 1951; MA, Heb U, Jerusalem, 1955; DE, Sorbonne, Paris, 1959; m. Aniela Margalith, Dec 20, 1946; c: Asher, Hevel, Danit. Asso prof, Fr Dept, Heb U, Jerusalem, since 1955; dir, Fr Dept, Haifa U, since 1966; gen sup, Fr secondary studies, Min of Educ, Jerusalem, 1960-66. Sgt, IAF, 1948-49; J Brig, 1943-46. Author: L'Expression de L'Hypothese, 1964; La Cause, 1966. Mem: MLA; Association International des Etudes Françaises, Paris; Société de Linguistique Romane, Strasbourg, Contbr to sci jours. Recipient: Afr, It Stars, 1939-45; Isr Fighters Medal. Hobbies: music, photography, Isr philately. Home: Heb U, Jerusalem, Isr.

LORINCZ, Shlomo, Isr, rabbi, legislator; b. Budapest, Hung, Mar 5, 1918; s. Josef and Frida (Raab); in Isr since 1939; ordained rabbi, Yeshiva, Mir, Pol, 1939; m. Martha Zucker, 1945. MK since 1951; org, illegal immigration, Hung to Pal, 1939; found: Sde Chemed, Children's Village; Komemiut settlement; Merkaz Kafri Aluma-Kiriat Nachal for Yeshiva Students; Camp Sde Chemed Intl; printing sch, Petah Tikva. Pres, Zeire Agudas Isr; exec comm, Agudas Isr since 1939. Spec interest, children's wfr. Home: 81 Hashomer St, Bnei Brak, Isr. Office: Knesset, Jerusalem, Isr.

LORWIN, Lewis L, US, economist, author; b. Russ, Dec 4, 1883; in US since 1887; PhD, Columbia U, 1912; m. Rose Strunsky, Sep, 1920; c: Val, Boris, Rosalind Feierabend. Ret; research cons, New Sch of Social Research, 1955-58; prof, econ: Wellesley Coll, U of Mont, Beloit Coll, 1916-21; staff mem, Brookings Inst, 1925-35; econ adv: ILO, Geneva, 1935-40; US govt agcys, Wash, 1940-52; US delgs, UN Econ and Social Council, 1946-51. Mem bd trustees, League for Ind Dem; asso, lab seminar, Columbia U; mem: Amer Econ Assn; Ind Relations Research Assn; clubs: Columbia U Fac; NYU Fac. Author: Syndicalism in France, 1914; Mine Taxation in Montana, 1919; The Women's Garment Workers, 1924; Labor and Internationalism, 1929; Advisory Economic Councils, 1931; The American Federation of Labor, 1933; The World Textile Conference, 1937; Economic Consequences of the Second World War, 1941; Natl Planning in Selected Countries, 1941; Youth Work Programs, 1941; International Economic Development, 1942; Postwar Plans of the United Nations, 1943; Time for Planning, 1945; The International Labor Movement, 1953; co-author: The ABC of NRA, 1934; The National Recovery Administration, 1935; L'Economia Programmatica, 1933; Nuove Esperienze Economiche, 1934; Labor Relations Boards, 1935; Socialism, Fascism and Democracy, 1935; Technology in our Economy, 1940; America's Needs and Resources, 1947; New Horizons for Business, 1955; Discrimination and Low Incomes, 1958. Home: 45 Christopher St, New York, NY.

LOSS, Louis, US, attorney, educator; b. Lancaster, Pa, June 11, 1914; s. Zelig and Elizabeth (Wenger); BS, U of Pa, 1934; LLB, Yale U, 1937; hon MA, Harvard U, 1953; m. Bernice Segaloff, June 19, 1938; c: Margaret, Robert. Wm Nelson Cromwell prof, law, Harvard U, since 1962, prof, 1952-62; atty, SEC, 1937-44, chief counsel, div trading and exch, 1944-48, asso gen counsel, 1948-52; lectr, Catholic U, 1941-42; visiting lectr, Yale U, 1947-52; professorial lectr George Wash U, 1949-52; prof, summers: Faculté Internationale de Droit Compare, Luxembourg, 1958; U Witwatersrand, S Afr, 1962. Dir, Harvard Law Sch Study, State Securities Regulation, 1954-56; draftsman, Uniform Securities Act, 1956; mem, council, Sec of Corp, Banking and Bus Law, Amer Bar Assn, 1956-60; vice-pres and gen couns, Harvard Coop Soc since 1968, dir, 1961-68; mem: DC, Mass, NYC, US Supr Court bars; Amer Law Inst; asso mem: Soc of Public Tchrs of Law, Gt Brit. Author: Securities Regulation, 1951, 1961; 3-vol supp, 1969; sr co-author, Blue Sky Law, 1958; contbr to legal jours. Hobby, music. Home: 39 Meadow Way, Cambridge, Mass. Office: Harvard Law Sch, Cambridge, Mass.

LOSSOS, Jakob, Eng, business exec; b. Riga, Lith, Sep 10, 1905; s. Herman and Anna (Dror); in Eng since 1938; att

schs in Riga and Leningrad; chartered engr, Tech Coll, Ko'then, 1930; m. Helga Herrschaft, Dec 24, 1941; c: Ronald, David. Dir: M and J Lossos and Co Ltd; Kaloric Heater Co Ltd. Chmn, Assn of Baltic Jews in Gt Brit; natl council and exec comm mem, WJC, Gt Brit; mem: Repräsentanten Versammlung, Jüdische Gemeinde, Berlin, 1938; Jüdischer Volksbund, Berlin, 1935. Home: 38 Stormont Rd, Kenwood, London, Eng. Office: 29/31 Beethoven St, London, Eng.

LOTAN, Giora, Isr, social admn; b. Berlin, Ger, Mar 22, 1902; s. Eliezer and Ulrike (Heimann) Lubinski; in Isr since 1938; att US: Berlin; Frankfurt M, DJ, 1927; m. Hilda Kohn, Mar 31, 1931; c: Michael, Yehoakim. Dir gen, Natl Ins Inst, since 1954, co-found, first admnr; fmr, dir gen; Min of Social Wfr, 1959; Min of Lab, 1961. Chmn, Natl Rehab Council, since 1957; Isr repr to social commn, UN. Contbr to jours, in Isr and abroad; Juedisches Lexicon; Ency Hebraica. Home: 9 Nahum Sokolov St, Jerusalem, Isr. Office: Kiryat Moshe, Jerusalem, Isr.

LOTH, David, US, journalist, author; b. St Louis, Mo, Dec 7, 1899; s. Albert and Fanny (Sunshine); BJ, U of Mo, 1920; m. Helen Wilcox, July 19, 1942. Staff mem: NY World, 1920-31; Sydney Daily Guardian, Australia, 1925; NY Times, 1934-41; ed and publisher: Majorca Sun; Spanish Times, 1931-34; chief of publs, Off of Inter-Amer Affairs, 1941-44; mgn ed, Press Research, 1944; info dir, Surplus Property Bd, 1945; dir, public info, acting natl dir, Planned Parenthood Fed, 1946-51; cons, Nelson A Rockefeller, 1951; dir, publicity, Columbia U Bicentennial, 1953-54; asso Nieman F, Harvard U, 1957-58; info dir, instr, journalism, Finch Coll, 1961-65; sr ed, writer HS Geog Project, 1967-68. Author: The Brownings, a Victorian Idyll, 1929; Lorenzo the Magnificent, 1929; Charles II, Ruler and Rake, 1930; Philip II, Master of the Armada, 1932; Public Plunder, a History of Graft in America, 1938; Alexander Hamilton, Portrait of a Prodigy, 1939; Woodrow Wilson, the Fifteenth Point, 1941; Chief Justice, 1949; The People's General, 1951; The Marriage Counselor, 1952; Gold Brick Cassie, 1954; A Long Way Forward, 1957; Swope of GE, 1958; Pencoyd and the Roberts Family, 1961; The Erotic in Literature, 1961; Crime Lab, 1964; How Hot is Up, 1964; The City Within a City, 1966; Crime in the Suburbs, 1967; co-author: American Sexual Behavior and the Kinsey Report, 1948; The People Know Best, 1949; Voluntary Parenthood, 1949; For Better or Worse, 1952; Report on the American Communist, 1952; I Was a Drug Addict, 1953; Book of the Seven Seas, 1957; The Frigid Wife, 1962; The Emotional Sex, 1964; Ivan Sanderson's Book of Great Jungles, 1965; contbr to mags. Mem: Soc Amer Hists; Author's Guild; Mystery Writers of Amer; clubs: Silurians; Overseas Press. Home: Putnam Green 6B, Greenwich, Conn.

LOTH, Jean, US, communal worker; b. Boston, Mass, Sept 30, 1910; d. Carl and Sarah (Solberg) Sahl; m. Arnold Loth, 1935; c: Stanley. Natl parliamentarian, Women's Amer ORT since 1967, natl vice-pres since 1955, natl treas since 1959, pres, L.I. region, 1951-54, pres, Jamaica chap, 1950; mem: Cen Bd, World ORT Union; exec comm, Amer ORT Fed; comty worker, J affairs, Queens, since 1943; Hadassah. Home: 8544 Homelawn St, Jamaica, NY.

LOUCHHEIM, William S, US, business exec; b. Elkins Park, Pa, Dec 23, 1904; s. Jerome and Etta O (Lovenstein); CE, Cornell U, 1925; att: Grad Sch ME, U of Pa, 1933-34, Grad Sch Wharton, 1938-39; m. Jean Benoliel, Dec 28, 1925; c: Pat Foreman, William Jr. Pres, The Bobrick Corp, since 1947; fmr: off, Keystone State Corp, 1925-33; partner, Louchheim, Brown & MacDonough, 1933-39; asst vice-pres, Tradesmen's Natl Bank & Trust Co, Phila, 1939-46. Lt-cdr, CB Corps, USNR, 1943-49. Dir: J Family Service of LA, since 1947, treas, 1952-54, vice-pres, 1965-66; Cedars-Sinai Med Cen, since 1961; LA Child Guidance Clinic, 1947-65, vice-pres, 1957, 1960; LA J Fed-Council, 1950-63, mem, bd govs, LA United Crusade, since 1955, campaign chmn, agency div, 1958; hon dir, Big Bros Assn, Phila; gen vice-chmn, United Campaign, Phila, 1937; secy, Fed of JWOs, LA, 1954-56. Mem, Amer Soc of CEs; clubs: Engrs, NYC; Hillcrest Country; Tamarisk Country; The LA; Locust, Phila. Home: 1008 Lexington Rd, Beverly Hills, Cal. Office: 11611 Hart St, N Hollywood, Cal.

LOUVISH, Misha, Isr, author, translator, journalist; b. Bukowina, Rum, July 5, 1909; s. Nehemiah and Sara (Goldschlaeger); in Isr since 1949; MA, hons, U Glasgow, 1931; tchr dipl, Tchrs' Training Coll, Glasgow, 1932; m. Eva Bersinski, Apr 14, 1935; c: David, Jonathan, Simon. Dep div ed, Ency

Judaica, since 1969; staff trans, Isr US Press, since 1967; first ed: Facts About Israel; Israel Digest; ed: Isr Youth Horizon, 1949-52; Eng publs, Isr Govt Press Off, 1956-67. British Army, 1943-45. Author: The Challenge of Israel, 1968, 1969; trans, A Guest for the Night, by SJ Agnon, 1968; contbr to periodicals. Fmr: pres, UZF, Eng; chmn: Glasgow Poale Zion; Glasgow Tarbut Org. Home: 24 Gaza Rd, Jerusalem, Isr.

LOVIAN (Lubian), Hunia, Isr, economist; b. Dorohoi, Rum, June 10, 1910; s. Joseph and Goldina (Cuperman); in Isr since 1950; m. Leopoldina Camerman, Aug 19, 1942; c: Joana Zissu. Chief econ, Min of Agric Cen for Colonization Planning and Agric Devl, econ survey and adv dept, since 1952; fmr: dir, Wool Cen, Bucharest 1935-37; dir, econ, SORA import soc, 1938-44; econ, bus exec, Newman Fabrics, 1947-50. Admn off, Rum Army. Chmn, Histadrut comm of Isr Academicians in Social and Hum Sci, mem, gen council, found and chmn; mem: cen comm, Academicians, Lab Party; bd dir, Moadon Academicians, Tel Aviv-Yaffo Lab Council; secreteriat, Isr Lab Party, Tel Aviv Dist; comm of employees and treas, Min of Agric; exec, B'rith Rishonim; fmr: gen secy-treas, J Academicians Assn; mem comm, Assn of Econ Sci. Author: Agricultural Machines, 1962; Balance of Feed, 1963; Feeding Stuffs Balances, 1964; Input-Output in Israel Farming, 1965; Israel Livestock Farming, 1966; Feeding Stuffs Balances in Israel Farming, 1968; contbr to press, radio. Home: 21 Balfour St, Tel Aviv, Isr. Office: Hakiryah, Tel Aviv, Isr.

LOVINGER, Joseph, Greece, business exec; b. Vac, Hung, Apr, 29, 1914; s. Mor and Regina (Haar); in Greece since 1933; m. Bertha Gross, Sep 22, 1943; c: Andrew. Exec vice-pres, Chifar Pharm since 1947, with firm since 1945; merchant of veneer, 1933-43; employee, Greek Red Cross, Pal, 1944-45. Pres, Cen Bd J Comty in Greece; repr, Greek J at Standing Conf; repr, WJC; vice-pres, J Comty, Athens, 1961-63; treas, Hung Assn, Athens, 1934-37; mem: relief and protection comm for J refs from Cen Eur, 1938-40; B'nai B'rith; club, Royal Touring of Greece. Contbr to J publs. Home: 40/A Mithymnis, Athens, Greece. Office: 59 Petala, Athens, Greece.

LOW, Max M, US, business exec; b. Aus, July 2, 1901; s. Meir and Mina; att Eur U; m. Evlynne Kirschner, Oct 22, 1931; c: Robert, Barbara Savin. Chmn bd: Ipco Hosp Supply since 1960; Savin Bus Machines since 1964. Vice-pres, Amer Friends Heb U; trustee, found, Harry S Truman Cen for Advancement of Peace; first vice-pres, United Home for Aged of New Rochelle; trustee, Westchester J Cen; donor, benefactor: Evlynne and Max M Low: Med Lab Bldg, Heb U Med Sch, Jerusalem; res hall, Albert Einstein Coll of Med; patron: Lincoln Cen; Metrop Opera; active: UJA; FJP of NY; clubs: Town of NY; Hampshire Country, NY. Hobbies: piano; art. Home: 1077 Orienta Ave, Mamaroneck, NY. Offices: 161 Sixth Ave, New York, NY; 11 E 69 St, New York, NY.

LOW, William Zeev, Isr, scientist, educator; b. Vienna, Aus, Apr 25, 1922; s. Nachum and Erna (Rimalt); in Isr since 1950; BA, hons, Queens U, Ont, 1946; MA, Columbia U, 1947, PhD, 1950; m. Dvorah Lederer, Dec 14, 1948; c: Nachum, Avraham, Esther, Shimon. Prof, physics, Heb U since 1960, dir, microwave lab, on fac since 1955. Chmn: Inst for Sci and Halacha; Assn for Orthodox Sci, 1962-63; Auth for Research and Devl, 1960-63; pres, Phys Soc Isr, 1961-62; mem: NY Acad Sci; Amer Phys Soc; Isr Phys Soc; Eur Phys Soc; Sigma Xi. Author: Paramagnetic Resonance in Solids, 1960-1962; ed: Physics Letters; Solid State Communications. Recipient: Isr Prize in Exact Sci, 1962; Guggenheim f, 1963; Rothschild Prize in Physics, 1965. Spec interest: rabb lit, Halacha. Home: 4 Hatibonim, Jerusalem, Isr. Office: Heb U, Jerusalem, Isr.

LOWE, Adolph, US, economist, educator; b. Stuttgart, Ger, Mar 4, 1893; s. Alexander and Ottilie (Mayer); in US since 1940; att: U's of Munich, Berlin and Tuebingen, 1911-15; LLD, U Tuebingen, 1918; D Litt, 1964; m. Beatrice Loewinstein, 1919; c: Rachel Aubrey, Hanna Lustig. Alvin Johnson Em prof of econ, grad fac, New Sch for Soc Research, since 1941; civil servant, Ministries of Labor, Econ Affairs, Cen Stat Off, Ger, 1919-26; prof: econ and sociol, U of Kiel, 1926-31; political econ, U Frankfurt am Main, 1931-33; lectr, econ and political sci, U Manchester, Eng, 1933-40; dir, research, Inst of World Affairs, NYC, 1943-51; visiting prof, Heb U, Jerusalem, 1953. Vice-pres, Self Help for Refugees from Cen Europe, Inc, NYC; mem: Amer Econ Assn; Royal Econ Soc; Econometric Soc. Author: Economics and Sociology, 1935; The Price of Liberty, 1937; The Universities in

Transformation, 1940; Structural Analysis of Real Capital Formation, 1955; On Economic Knowledge, 1965; ed, Studies of the Inst of World Affairs, 1943-51. Contbr to collective works and prof jours, in Ger, Eng and US. Recipient: Rockefeller f, 1933-38. Spec interests: methodology of sci, music. Home: 10 Park Terrace, New York, NY. Office: 66 W 12 St, New York, NY.

LOWE, Elias Avery, US, educator, author; b. Lith, Oct 15, 1879; s. Charles and Sarah (Ragoler); BA, Cornell U, 1902; PhD, Munich U, Ger, 1907; hon: DLitt, Oxford U, 1946; LLD, U of NC, 1946; LLD, U Dublin, 1963; m. Helen Porter, Feb 8, 1911; c: Prudence, Frances, Patricia. Prof, paleography, Inst for Advanced Study, Princeton, NJ; Corpus Christi Coll, Oxford U, Eng; cons, paleography, Libr of Cong, Wash, DC; asso, Carnegie Inst, Wash, DC; Sandars reader, bibliography, Cambridge U, 1914; lectr, reader, paleography, Oxford U, 1913-48. F: Acad Arts and Sci; Medieval Acad of Amer; hon f: Corpus Christi Coll; Pierpont Morgan Libr, NY; corresp f: Brit Acad; Bavarian Acad; Socio dei Lincei, Rome, It; Academia de la Historia, Madrid, Spain; mem: Oxford Philological Soc; Phi Beta Kappa; Royal Irish Acad; Hispanic Soc of Amer; asso mem, Institut de France, Paris; clubs: Authors, London; Bezan. Author: Die Aeltesten Calendarien aus Monte Cassino, 1908; Studia Paleographica, 1910; The Beneventan Script, 1914; The Bobbio Missal, 1920; A Sixteenth Century Fragment of the Letters of Pliny the Younger, 1922; Codices Lugdunenses Antiquissimi, 1924; The Paleography of the Bobbio Missal, 1924; A Hand List of Half Unical Manuscripts, 1924; Regula San Benedicti, 1929; ed, Codices Latini, 12 vols, 1934-69; contbr to profsl jours. Recipient: Haskins Medal Award, Medieval Acad of Amer; gold medal award, Bibliography Soc, London. Home and office: Inst for Advanced Study, Princeton, NJ; Corpus Christi Coll, Oxford U, Oxford, Eng.

LOWELL, Stanley H, US, attorney; b. NYC, Apr 13, 1919; s. Isidor and Mildred (Cohen) Lowenbraun; BSS, CCNY, 1939; LLB, Harvard Law Sch, 1942; m. Vivian Abrams, Mar 29, 1947; c: Jeffrey, Darcy, Lauri. Partner, Gladstone & Lowell; asst, US Atty, Dept of Justice, 1943-47; asst to Pres, Borough of Manhattan, 1950-53; exec asst, Mayor, NYC, 1954-58; dep mayor, 1958; official repr, NYC, Amer J Tercentenary, 1954. Natl vice-pres, AJCong; chmn, NYC Comm on Hum Rights, 1960-65; exec comm, fmr chmn, UJA; bd dirs: JDC; Citizens Comm for Children; vice-pres, City Coll Alumni Assn; mem: NY State, NY Co, NYC Bar Assns; Soc for Advancement Judaism. Home: 173 Riverside Dr, New York, NY. Office: 99 Park Ave, New York, NY.

LOWENBERG, Helmuth S, Isr, jurist; b. Hamborn, Ger, June 20, 1919; s. Otto and Rosa (Emanuel); in Isr since 1935; LLB, LSE, 1942; Barrister-at-Law, Gray's Inn, London, 1942; m. Bessie Michlewitz, Mar 12, 1944; c: Miriam, Judith, Jonathan. Judge, Dist Court, Tel Aviv, since 1954; practicing barrister, London, 1943-46; magistrate, Tel Aviv, 1947-54. Found, chmn, Isr Natl Council for Prevention of Accidents, since 1954; chmn, Isr Philharmonic Orch Assn; pres, Isr Tax Inst; mem: Intl Fiscal Assn; Intl Ins Law Assn; Isr corresp, AJComm; fmr: chmn, Us ZC, Eng; secy, B'nai B'rith Grand Lodge, Gt Brit. Home: 18A Dubnov St, Tel Aviv, Isr. Office: Dist Court, Tel Aviv, Isr.

LOWENFELS, Albert, US, business exec; b. NYC, Oct 23, 1888; s. Frederick and Edith (Aaron); m. Corinne Brownold, Feb 22, 1915; c: Frederick, Emily Oppenheimer, Albert. Sr partner, Frederick F Lowenfels and Son, since 1907; pres, Hotel Bar Butter Co. Chmn, dairy div, NY Fed for many years; mem: NY Mercantile Exch; Plant Propagators Assn; club, Beach Point. Contbr to garden mags. Home: 1105 Mamaroneck Ave, White Plains, NY. Office: 16 Jay St, New York, NY.

LOWENSTEIN, Leon, US, business exec, communal worker; b. NYC, June 14, 1883; s. Morris and Elizabeth (Sloman); att CCNY, 1897; D Textile Inds, Clemson Coll, 1951; DHumL, Fordham U; m. Gloria Perry, July 29, 1937. Chmn bd, M Lowenstein and Sons Inc and subsidiaries, since 1947, with firm since 1899; chmn: Catawba Trucking Co Inc, SC; Clark-Schwebel Fiber Glass Corp, SC; Lowenstein Cotton and Storage Corp, SC; Lowenstein Intl Inc, Manila, Philippines; Olympic Textiles Intl; Yankee Export and Trading Corp, since 1949; mem: NY Stock Exch. Lt, US Army, WW I. Hon chmn: ADL; UJA; AJComm; Jt Defense Appeal; trustee, FJP, NY; hon chmn, bd, Hillside Hosp, Bellrose, LI;

dir, trustee, Gloria and Leon Lowenstein Nurses Residence, Mt Sinai Hosp, Miami Beach, Fla; mem: St Vincents Hosp, NYC; Brotherhood-in-Action; bd lay trustees, Fordham U; dedicated Leon Lowenstein Auditorium to Temple Emanu-El, 1965; pres, Leon Lowenstein Found; clubs: Metrop Country, White Plains; NY; Westview Country, Miami Beach, Fla; Weavers, NY; Arkwright, NYC. Home: 480 Park Ave, New York, NY. Office: 1430 Broadway, New York, NY.

LOWENSTEIN, Robert, US, attorney; b. NYC, June 12, 1918; s. Louis and Ralphina (Steinhardt); BSS, CCNY, 1939; LLB, Columbia Law Sch, 1942; m. Rollee Herbert, Dec 22, 1946; c: Susan, Steven, Carol, Beth, Linda. Pvt practice, Lowenstein and Newman since 1966; asso, Rosenman, Goldmark, Colin & Kaye, 1946-51; counsel, houseware br, Off of Price Stabilization, 1951-52; staff mem, div licensing and regulations, US AEC, 1952-61, dir, 1961-65; prof law, Geo Wash U Law Sch, 1965-66. US Army, 1942-46. Mem, Amer, Fed Bar Assns. Contbr to profsl publs. Home: 6601 Tulip Hill Terr, Washington, DC. Office: 1100 Connecticut Ave, Washington, DC.

LOWENTHAL, Alexander, US, business exec; b. Cincinnati, O, Jan 12, 1898; s. Philip and Jenny (Gloss); BA, Yale U, 1920, LLB, 1921; m. Anne Fineman, Dec 18, 1935; c: John, Mary. Fmr: partner, Rosenbloom & Lowenthal, inves securities, 1923-29; dir: Webster Hall Hotel Corp, 1926-30; Falk & Co, 1924-41; pres, dir, Devl Corps of Pittsburgh, 1927-50. Mem, natl exec bd: UJA, 1946-52; Amer Financial and Devl Corp for Isr since 1950; ZOA; United Isr Appeal; mem, natl bd: Amer Isr Cultural Found; ADA; bd of dirs: Amer Friends of Weizmann Inst, since 1952; Pittsburgh Council for Intl Visitors; Pittsburgh Chamber Music Soc; club, Yale, NY. Asso ed, Yale Law Jour, 1921. Home: 5100 Fifth Ave, Pittsburgh, Pa.

LOWENTHAL, Eric I, US, rabbi; b. Ternowitz, Pol, Oct 25, 1901; s. Abraham and Jenny (Kahn); in US since 1938; att: U's Marburg; Freiburg; PhD, U Berlin, 1933; grad, Rabbinerseminar, Berlin, 1935; m. Suzanne Moos, 1936; c: Abraham, Judith. Ret, Rabbi: Cong Agudas Achim, Leominster, Mass, 1944-66; Juedische Gemeinde, Berlin, 1935-39; instr, homiletics, phil, Rabbinerseminar, 1937-38. Dir, Assn Syns of Mass Chapel since 1967; exec council: RA, 1946-47, recording secy, 1948-49; Mass Bd of Rabbis, 1949-66; trustee, Public Libr, Leominster, 1946-66. Author: Johann Georg Schlosser, 1935. Home and study: 28 Park St, Brookline, Mass.

LOWENTHAL Leo, US, sociologist, educator; b. Frankfurt, Ger, Nov 3, 1900; s. Victor and Rosy (Bing); PhD, U Frankfurt, 1923; in US since 1934; m. Marjorie Fiske, June 26, 1953; c: Daniel, Carol. Prof, sociol, U of Cal, since 1956; sr research asso, Inst of Social Research, 1926-49; lectr, Columbia U, 1940-55; cons, OWI, 1943-44; dir, evaluation staff, VOA, 1949-54, spec asst, 1954-55. F: Cen for Advanced Study in Behavioral Scis, Stanford, Cal, 1955-56, 1966-67; Amer Psych Assn; mem: Amer Sociol Soc; Amer Assn Public Opinion Research; Soc for Psych Study of Social Issues. Author: Sociology of Literature, 1948; Prophets of Deceit, 1949; Literature and the Image of Man, 1957; The Controversy over Art and Popular Culture in Eighteenth Century England, 1957; Culture and Social Character, 1961; Literature, Popular Culture and Society, 1961. Contbr to profsl jours. Home: 1967 Clay St, San Francisco, Cal. Office: U of Cal, Berkeley, Cal.

LÖWENTHAL, Zdenko, Yugo, physician, medical hist; b. Graboavac, May 9, 1914; s. Bela and Rosa (Schlesinger); MD, Med Fac, Zagreb; m. 1947; c: Mario; m. 2nd, 1961. Head educ dept, Fed Inst of Health, Yugo since 1963; prof, med fac, Rijeka; phys, IV Med Clinic since 1949; specialist in internal diseases; phys, Inst of Endemic Syphilis Control, 1941-44; dir, State Pub House for Med Lit, 1947-49; research asso, hist of med, Harvard U, 1968. MC, Natl Liberation Army, 1945-47; prof, Army Med Sch, 1946-47. Mem: Société Internationale de l'Histoire de Médecine; fmr: secy gen, World Union Med Press; chief, hist, mus depts, Fed J Cmty in Yugo; found, J Hist Mus; active worker, J youth org; mem: Serbian Soc, found, sect on med hist. Secy pub bur, Yugo Med Assn, ed, Medicinski Glasnik, since 1949; ed: Crimes of the Fascist Invaders Against Yugoslav Jews; Jewish Almanac, 1954-62; med revs; contbr to: med jours; J lit mags. Home: Podgoricka 5, Belgrade, Yugo. Office: U of Belgrade, Belgrade, Yugo.

LOWINGER, Emanuel S, US, attorney; b. Montclair, NJ, Dec 18, 1908; s. Samuel and Mary (Lowy); LLB, Rutgers U,

1929; m. Mae Phillips, June 10, 1934, c: Joel, Eugene. Asst Co Counsel, Essex Co, NJ; in pvt practice: Millburn, NJ since 1959; Newark, 1930-59. Pres, 13th Ward, Newark, Civic Assn 1934-39; govt appeals agent, Essex Co draft board, 1940-47; secy, Essex Co Govt Appeals Agents Assn, 1941-47; counsel, Millburn-Short Hills C of C since 1959; pres, Cong B'nai Isr, Millburn, 1957-61; mem, bd govs, S Mt Estates Civic Assn since 1960; active in Rep, gen, and munic election campaigns; nominated, Essex Co Rep Party Bd of Chosen Freeholders, 1963; mem: B'rith Abraham; B'nai B'rith; Home for Chronic Sick; Heb Acad, Essex Co; Millburn Boosters; ZOA; Essex Co, NJ State Bar Assns; Compensation Assn of NJ; KP, chancellor, Granite Lodge, 1937; Order of DeMolay, master councillor, Essex chap, 1929; club, Rotary. Recipient, selective service medal. Home: 153 Myrtle Ave, Millburn, NJ. Office: 350 Millburn Ave, Millburn, NJ.

LOWINSKY, Edward E, US, musicologist, educator; b. Stuttgart, Ger, Jan 12, 1908; s. Leopold and Clara (Rosenfeld); in US since 1940; PhD, U Heidelberg, 1933; m. Gretel Hoffman, Aug 10, 1938; c: Naomi, Simon, Benjamin, Joshua. Ferdinand Schevill Dist Service Prof, U Chgo, since 1961; asso, U sem, Columbia U, since 1952; asst prof, Black Mt Coll, NC, 1942-47; asso prof, Queens Coll, 1949-56; mem, Inst for Advanced Study, Princeton, 1952-54; prof music, U Cal, 1956-61; found, chmn, Renaissance Sem, U Chgo, 1963-68. Mem: Amer Musicological Soc; Intl Musicological Soc; Music Libr Assn; Renaissance Soc. Author: Buch der Kindermusik, 1933; Orlando di Lassos Antwerpener Motettenbuch und seine Beziehungen zum Motettenschaffen der niederlandischen Zeitgenossen, 1937; Secret Chromatic Art in the Netherlands Motet, 1946; facsimile ed, Nicola Vicentino's treatise: L'Antica Musica, 1959; Tonality and Atonality in 16th Century Music, 1961; The Medici Codex of 1518 (Monuments of Renaissance Music III, Historical Introduction and Commentary; IV, transcription; V, Facsimile), 1968; Aspects of the 18th Century; The Renaissance Image of Man and the World; Art Science and History in the Renaissance; contbr: natl, intl jours; gen ed, Monuments of Renaissance Music, since 1964. Recipient: Guggenheim F, 1947-48; Bollingen F, 1952-54, 1956-57, 1960-61. Hobbies: chess, swimming. Home: 7440 S Constance Ave, Chicago, Ill. Office: U of Chgo, Chicago, Ill.

LOWN, Philip W, US, business exec, communal leader; b. Lith, Dec 20, 1890; s. Abraham and Louise (Shapiro); BS, U of Me, 1918, Hon LLD, 1954; m. Sally Robbins; c: Dorothy, Louise. Pres, Penobscot Shoe Co; vice-pres, Isr Inves Corp. Pres: Natl Friends of Hillel; Heb Tchrs Coll; found: Philip W Lown Sch of Near Judaic Studies, Brandeis U; Lown Cen for Contemporary J Studies, Brandeis U; treas: Natl Hillel Found; mem, UJA Cabinet; fmr pres: Amer Assn for J Educ; Me J Council; YMCA, Lewiston-Auburn; hon pres, Camp Lown Assn; chmn, CJA, 1956; trustee: Brandeis U; Beth Isr Hosp; fmr treas, World Council for J Educ; mem, Natl Hillel Commn. Recipient: awards: Lewiston Elks; Tarbuth Found; JTSA; Natl Fed of J men's clubs. Home: 15 Elizabeth Circle, W Newton, Mass. Office: 4640 Prudential Center, Boston, Mass.

LOWY, Jacob Max, Can, business exec; b. Bardejov, Czech, Mar 1, 1908; s. J Raphael and Rachel (Dereszewicz); in Can since 1951 att, Talmudical Coll, Bardejov, Czech; m. Fanny Zweigel, 1931: (decd) c: Ruth Pollack, Nellie Stavisky; m. 2nd, Clara Klein, June 23, 1968. Pres, Que corps: Pointe Claire Ind Park Inc; Progressive Holdings Inc; Westshore Hgts Inc; Parish Realties Inc; Lowy Inves Corp; Pointe Claire Leaseholds Inc; Cloverleaf Park Ltd; Dorval Leaseholds Inc; Cent Inves Ltd; Lakeshore Hgts Inc; Shoreland Realties Inc; pres: Ontario Corps; Hillside Golf Club Ltd; Intraco Ltd. Pres, United Isr Appeal, Can, since 1967; chmn bd, Heb Acad Day Sch, since 1966; co-chmn, Natl Fund Raising Comm, United Isr Appeal, United J Relief Agcy, Can, since 1962; mem: bd dirs, Council J Feds and Wfr Funds, US, Can, since 1962; bd admn, J Gen Hosp of Montreal, since 1966; B'nai B'rith, Mt Royal lodge, Montreal; fmr: pres: Zionist Org, Czech; Allied J Comty Services, Montreal; chmn bd dirs, first vice-pres, Fed J Comty Services, Montreal; clubs: Elm Ridge Country; De Sola. Home: 5760 Deom Ave, Montreal, Can. Office: 1010 St Catherine St W, Montreal, Can.

LOWY, Louis, Isr, industrialist; b. Cegled, Hung, May 18, 1916; s. Henrik and Gizella (Benedek); in Isr since 1949; att Acad of Commerce, Hung, 1932-36; m. Elizabeth Goldstein;

c: Aliza. Found, co-owner, Magam, United Rubber Works Ltd since 1950; co-owner, Gumavir Goods Co Ltd since 1957. Mem, B'nai B'rith; fmr vice-pres, Hung J Assn, Isr. Home: 53 Arlosoroff St, Tel Aviv, Isr. Office: Magam Ltd, 8 Hasharon St, Tel Aviv, Isr.

LOZOWICK, Louis, US, artist; b. Kiev, Russ, Dec 10, 1892; s. Abraham and Miriam (Tafipolsky); in US since 1906; att, Natl Acad of Design, 1912-15; BA, O State U, 1918; m. Adele Turner, 1931; c: Lee, Lori, Matt. Exhbs: Carnegie Intl; Corcoran Biennial; Butler Inst; Chgo Art Inst; Natl Acad of Design; Pa Acad; Mus Modern Art; Metrop Mus; Smithsonian Inst; Mus: Trenton; Houston; Montclair, NJ; London; Berlin; Paris; Mexico City; Moscow; Stockholm; represented in: Whitney Mus; Mus Modern Art; Metrop Mus Art; Mus of: Boston, Cleveland, Trenton, Cincinnati, Newark, Montclair, Jersey City; Michener Collection in Austin, Tex; pvt collections. Mem: Soc Amer Graphic Artists; Asso Artists, NJ; Amer Color Print Soc; Boston Printmakers; Albany Printmakers; Audubon Artists; Academic Artists Assn; Soc of Painters in Casein; club, Pa Water Color. Author: Modern Russian Art; A Treasury of Drawings from Prehistory to Picasso; One Hundred American Jewish Artists; article on Russ art, Ency Americana; contbr to periodicals. Recipient: awards; Chgo Art Inst; Phila Alliance; Intl Print Competition, Cleveland; Soc of Amer Graphic Artists, three times; Jersey City Mus; Painters and Sculptors Soc, NJ; Academic Artists Assn, twice; Bklyn Mus; Montclair Mus; Hunterdon Co Art Cen; Soc of Wash Printmakers. Home and studio: 62 Massell Terr, South Orange, NJ.

LUBAN, Marshall, Isr, physicist, educator; b. Seatte, Wash, May 29 1936; s. Joseph and Sara (Gann); in Isr since 1966; BA, Yeshiva U, NY, 1957; MSc, U Chgo, 1958, PhD, 1962; m. Rosalie Muhlstein, June 30, 1959; c: Joseph, Nahum, Amos, Tova. Asso prof, chmn, Physics Dept, Bar Ilan U, since 1967; mem, Inst for Advanced Study, Princeton NJ, 1962-63; asst prof, U of Pa, 1963-66. Mem: Amer Phys Soc; Isr Phys Soc. Recipient, Guggenheim F, 1966. Home: 30 Le'an St, Ramat Gan, Isr. Office: Bar Ilan U, Ramat Gan, Isr.

LUBAR, T David, US, attorney; b. NYC, Apr 9, 1915; s. Solomon and Taube (Rizika); BS, Bklyn Coll, 1935; LLB, St John's U, 1938; m. Muriel Alpert, Oct 15, 1939; c: Katherine, Thomas. Partner, Stroock, Stroock and Lavan, since 1942; vice-pres and secy, Warner Bros-Seven Arts Ltd, since 1960; dir, secy, Vieco Instruments Inc, since 1959; secy, Baldwin Securities Corp, since 1959; dir, Malt-Diastase Co, since 1955; dir, secy, Originola Inc, since 1961; secy, Weston's Shoppers City, since 1964; asso, Paskus, Gordon and Hyman, 1938-42. US Army, 1934-45. Vice-pres, secy, Amer Friends, Alliance Cult Israelite, since 1965; vice-pres, Maimonides Hosp, since 1966; bd dirs, Alumni Chem Soc, Bykln Coll, since 1962; NY Co Lawyers Assn; St Thomas More Soc; Iota Theta. Recipient: gold key, Bklyn Coll, 1935; Real Property Award, St John's U, 1937. Home: 1020 Park Ave, New York, NY. Office: 61 Broadway, New York, NY.

LUBASCH, Lothar, US, rabbi; b. Berlin, Ger; s. Herman and Hannchen (Joseph); in US since 1938; ordained rabbi, Hochschule fur Wissenschaft des Judentums, Berlin; PhD, U Erlangen; m. Lilly Decker; c: Inge. Rabbi, Cong Mishkan Isr, Selma, Ala, since 1959; asst rabbi, Temple, Hamburg, Ger; rabbi: Oppein, Ger; Wuppertal-Barmen; Agudas Achim, Elyria, O, 1938-46; Cong Beth Isr, E Liverpool, O 1946-48; Cong Rodef Shalom, Port Arthur, Tex, 1948-59. Contbr to jours. Home: 419 Birch Ave, Selma, Ala. Study: 503 Broad St, Selma, Ala.

LUBELL, Benedict I, US, business exec; b: NYC, Nov 26, 1909; s. Samuel and Jeanette (Sainy); AB, Columbia, 1930, LLB, 1932; m. Norma Rubenstein, Apr 11, 1937; c: Ann Margolis, John. Gen partner, Lubell Oil Co since 1965; asso, Stroock & Stroock, NYC, 1932-35; exec vice-pres, gen mgr, treas, secy, Bell Oil & Gas Co, 1938-65. Chmn, Arts, Commn, Tulsa, 1969; vice-pres, Tulsa Arts Council, since 1961; exec comm, Tulsa JCC, since 1949, pres, 1949-52; bd trustees: Tulsa Philharmonic Soc, 1954-55; Tulsa U; bd mem, Tulsa Comty Chest, 1946-49; pres: Temple Isr, 1946-47; Celebrity Series Inc, 1955-59; campaign chmn, Tulsa Fed Appeal, 1948; mem: Phi Beta Kappa. Recipient: Converse prize, 1932; Kent Scholar, 1932. Home: 1375 E 26 Pl, Tulsa, Okla. Office: 1033 Mayo Bldg, Tulsa, Okla.

LUBELL, Samuel, US, journalist, public opinion analyst; b. Pol, Nov 3, 1911; s. Louis and Mollie (Reitkop); in US since

1913; att CCNY, 1927-31; BS, Columbia U, 1933; m. Helen Sopot, Mar 22, 1941; c: Bernard, Walter. Free-lance mag writer; analyst of Amer elections since 1948; fmr reporter: LI Daily Press, NY; Wash Post, Richmond Times Dispatch; Wash Times Herald; writer, Off of Facts and Figures; gen secy, Rubber Survey Comm, 1942; asst to: James F Byrnes, dir, Off Econ Stabilization; Bernard M Baruch, adv unit on war and post-war adjustment policies, Off War Mobilization, 1942-43, all in Wash, DC; corresp: Saturday Evening Post; Providence jour; N Amer Newspaper alliance in Eur, 1946; mem: fac, Grad Sch of Jour, Columbia U, dir, Opinion Reporting Workshop, 1958-68. Author: The Future of American Politics, 1952; The Revolution in World Trade; Revolt of the Moderates; Black and White; spec commentator, NBC, CBS; contbr, surveys on public problems to newspapers. Club, Natl Press. Recipient: Pulitzer traveling scholarship, 1934; Guggenheim f, 1950; Woodrow Wilson Found Award, 1952. Home and office: 3200 N Mexico Ave, NW, Washington, DC.

LUBETZKI, Jean, Fr, physician; b. Boulogne, Fr, Oct 9, 1926; s. Jacques and Andrée (Lévy); MD, Fac of Med, Paris; m. Denise Zucman, Jan 17, 1951; c: Isabelle, Catherine, Jacques. Head dept, Hôpital Abmroise Paré, Boulogne; with Hôpitaux de Paris since 1946. Contbr to profsl publ. Home: 78 rue de la Fédération, Paris 15, Fr. Office: Hôpital Ambr ise Paré, 9 Ave Longchamps, Boulogne, Fr.

LUBIN, Isador, US, economic consultant; b. Worcester, Mass, June 9, 1896; s. Harris and Hinda (Francke); BA, Clark U, 1916; LLD, 1941; PhD, Brookings Inst, 1926; m. Carol Riegelman, Jan 31, 1951; c: Ann Buttenwieser, Alice Everitt. Cons, United Isr Appeal on progs in Isr, since 1960; cons, Twentieth Cent Fund, since 1962; dir, E Life Ins Co; fmr: stat, US Food Admn, 1918; expert, US War Ind Bd, 1918-19; asst prof, econ, U Mich, 1920-22; staff, Brookings Inst, 1922-33, teaching staff, Grad Sch, 1924-30; adv, educ and lab comm, US Sen, 1928-29; chmn, lab adv bd, Public Works Admn, 1933-36; mem, US Cen Stat Bd, 1933-37; commn, US Bur Lab Stat, 1933-45; Stat asst to Pres Roosevelt, 1941-45; US asso repr, Allied Commn on Reparations, 1945; US repr: UN Econ and Employment Comm, 1946-50; UN Commn on Reconstruction Devastated Areas, 1946; UN Econ and Social Council, 1950-53; adv commn to UN Korean Reconstruction Agcy, 1951-53; Ind commn, NY State Dept of Lab, 1955-59; Natl Commn on Money and Credit, 1958-61; prof, public affairs, Rutgers U, 1959-61; chmn, Pres Commn on RR Lab Conditions, 1962; cons, Off, Stat Standards, US Bur of Budget, 1963; delg, UN conf, 1963. F, Intl Stat Inst; bd gov, AJComm; mem, exec comm, JDC; dir, United HIAS Service; Amer ORT; trustee: Brandeis U; Weizmann Inst of Sci; New Sch for Social Research. Author: Miners' Wages and the Cost of Coal, 1924; The British Attack on Unemployment, 1934; Our Stake in World Trade, 1954; US State in the UN, 1954; co-author: Government Control of Prices during the War, 1919; The British Coal Dilemma, 1927. Spec interest: fishing, gardening. Home: 1085 Park Ave, New York, NY. Office: 515 Park Ave, New York, NY.

LUBIN, Joseph L, US, certified public acctnt; b. Bklyn, NY, Nov 14, 1899; s. Isidore and Ann; CPA, 1922; grad, acctnt, Pace Coll, 1921; LLB, NYU, 1928; hon: LLD, Syracuse U, 1952; DComm, Pace Coll, 1955; DHumL, Yeshiva U; m. Evelyn Cronson, 1926. Sr mem, Eisner and Lubin, CPA's, since 1923; fmr chmn, bd dirs: United Cigar-Whelan Drug Corp; Phoenix Securities Corp; chmn, appeals bd, NY Co Selective Service; dep chief investigator, War Prod Bd, both during WW II. Hon chmn, Soc of Founds of Albert Einstein Coll of Med; treas: UJA; JDC; bd trustees: Syracuse U, chmn of hon degs comm; Pace Coll; Albert Einstein Coll of Med; New Rochelle Hosp; Henry St Settlement; Children's Village, Dobbs Ferry; adv bd, Grad Div for Training in Public Service, NYU. Home: East Dr, Premium Point, New Rochelle, NY. Office: 250 Park Ave, New York, NY.

LUBIN, Leo Aryeh, Isr, painter; b. New York, Dec 6, 1897; s. Frederick and Lillian; in Isr since 1913; John Q Adams Scholarship, Art Inst of Chgo. Leader in beginning of modern art in Isr. Pvt, Brit Army, 1917-19; Haganah. Recipient: Ramat Gan Prize for Landscapes, 1954; Dizengoff Prize, 1957; Prize for Short Subject, 1957. Spec interests: Heb lang, hist, anthropology, archaeol; ling. Home: 196 Hayarkon St, Tel Aviv, Isr.

LUBKIN, Virginia L, US, ophthalmologist; b. NYC, Oct 26, 1914; d. Joseph and Anna (Stern); BS, summa cum laude, NYU, 1933; MD, Columbia U, 1937; m. Arnold Malkan,

1944, div; m, 2nd, Martin Bernstein, 1949; c: Roger, John. Asso surg, NY Eye and Ear Infirmary since 1944; asst att ophthal, Mt Sinai Hosp; instr, surg, ophthal, Amer Acad of Ophthal; Inst of Ophthal. Dipl, Amer Bd of Ophthal; f: Amer Coll Surgs; NY Acad Med; mem: NY Acad of Sci; AAAS; Amer Acad Ophthal and Otolaryngology; Phi Beta Kappa; Alpha Omega Alpha. Contbr to med jours. Home: 1 Blackstone Pl, New York, NY. Office: 41 Park Ave, New York, NY.

LUBLING, Miriam Leah, US, educator, b. Koinsk, Pol, Aug 6, 1917; d. Jonah and Pesia (Albert) Mandelbaum; in US since 1955; BA, Beth Jacob Tchrs Sem, Krakow, Pol, 1937, MA, 1938; grad study: Bank St Coll, NYC, 1961, Stern Coll, NYC, 1964; m. Jacob Lubling, June 13, 1941; c: Nechama Frankel, Chanoch, Pesia. Prin, Yeshiva Ohel Sarah Day Sch, NYC, since 1958; journalist, Shearim Daily, 1949-53; dir, Keren Yeladeinu, Isr, 1953-55; prin, Yeshiva Darkei Noam, 1955-58. Pres, women's div, Poale Agudath Isr of Amer, 1948-55; vice-pres Ladies Auxiliary Yeshiva S'Fath Emes, Isr, 1948-55; bd dir, Ind Kinsker Aid Soc, since 1941; chmn: women's div, Rel Sch System, Isr, 1948-55; Tel Aviv Election Bd, 1954-55; first-aid volunteer for the Haganah, 1945-48; mem: Torah Umesora, NYC; N'eshei Agudath Isr. Home: 658 Crown St, Brooklyn, NY. Office: 771 Crown St, Brooklyn, NY.

LUDWIG, Louis, US, business exec; b. Russ, Mar 9, 1899; s. David and Fanny (Swedersky) Grushevsky; in US since 1902; att Columbia U 1920; m. 2nd, Miriam Fisher, Sep 20, 1953; c: Melvin, Doris. Pres: Eagle Elec Mfg Co since 1920; Eagle Plastics Corp since 1938; 24th St Plaza Realty Co since 1940; vice-pres i/c Isr industrialization, Amer Pal Trading Corp, since 1952; secy, Isr Devl Corp since 1954. Holder, 146 patents on elec inventions. Dir, J Cen, Mohopacs, 1956; mem, exec comm: Weizmann Inst; UJA; club, Putnam Country, dir, exec vice-pres. Home: 310 E 44 St, New York, NY. Office: 23-10 Bridge Plaza S, Long Island City, NY.

LUDWIG, Robert Jay, US, educator; b. NYC, Nov 3, 1918; s. Samuel and Jennie (Altman); BS, Columbia U, 1937, MA, 1938; Cert, Social Service Admn, W Reserve U, 1947, att: U Paris; U Aix-Marseille; U Toulouse, Bordeaux; m. Dorothy Seaman, Dec 23, 1950. Chmn, Fgn Lang Dept, Mt Pleasant HS, since 1961; dir, activities, Schenectady J Cen, 1949-59. Pres: NY State Fed Fgn Lang Tchrs; Schenectady JCC; Alliance Française de Schenectady; chmn: Jt Comm of Chrs and Js, Schenectady Co; vice-chmn, Schenectady Co Comm for Educ in Hum Sexuality; bd mem: Schenectady J Cen; Daughters of Sara Home for J Aged; mem, natl comm, churchstate relationships, Natl Comty Relations Comm; mem: Acad of Cert Social Workers; MLA; NY State Tchrs Assn; NEA; Amer Council, Tchrs Fgn Langs; B'nai B'rith; contbr to fgn lang jours. Recipient: Book Award, Larousse Publishing Co, 1965; Chevalier de l'ordre des Palmes Academiques, Fr, 1967; Intl Service Award, Schenectady, Kiwanis Club, 1968. Home: 1102 Andsley Rd, Schenectady, NY.

LUFT, Gerda, Isr, economist, journalist; b. Koenigsberg, Ger, Apr 20, 1898; d. Joachim and Anna (Jampoler) Goldberg; in Isr since 1924; att: U Koenigsberg, 1916-17; U Berlin, 1917-20; m. Haim Arlosoroff, 1920 (decd); m. 2nd, Zvi Luft, 1927 (decd); c: Shalamith Gourevich, Eliezer, Aya. Free-lance journalist since 1960; Isr corresp: Neue Zeurcher Zeitung, Switz, since 1949; Reinischer Merkur, Cologne, since 1960; fmr: Economist, London, 1952-62; econ and parl corresp, The Jerusalem Post, 1949-60. Mem, Cen Eur Immigrants Assn; delg, 3rd Electoral Assembly. Home: 226 Hayarkon St, Tel Aviv, Isr.

LUFY, Arie, Isr, business exec; b. Ploesti, Rum, May 3, 1913; s. Dov and Ghitia (Shapiro) Lupescu; desc of Nisim Back, found, Tiferet Syn, Old City, Jerusalem; in Isr since 1932; m. Miriam Pelz; c: Rami, Niva Iaron, Dov. Mgr, Hatabor Transp Corp; exec, Tahbura Corp, both since 1966; produc mgr, gen dir, Camel Works, 1955-61; mgr, Hatabor Corp, 1949-55. Off, Palmach, Haganah, org illegal J immigration, Rum; Lt, RAF, 1943-44. Home: Kibbutz Sarid, Isr. Office: Kibbutz Mizra, Isr.

LUISADA, Aldo A, US, cardiologist, educator; b. Florence, It, June 26, 1901; s. Ezio and Elisa (Rignano); in US since 1939; MD, Royal U, Florence, 1924; m. Anna Passigli, Apr 12, 1931; c: Claude. Att phys, Mt Sinai Hosp; prof med and phys and dir, cardiovascular research, Chgo Med Sch, since 1960, on fac since 1949; asst, dept internal med and hosp, Royal U, Padua, It, 1927-30; asso prof, U Naples, 1933-35; prof: Royal U, Sassari, 1935-36; U Ferrara, 1936-38; asso prof pharm,

lectr med, Middlesex U, Waltham, Mass, 1939-43; research asso, Mass Gen Hosp, 1939; instr phys and pharm ,Tufts Coll, 1944-49. F: Amer Coll Chest Phys; Amer Coll Card; Amer Coll Phys; AMA; Amer Phys Soc; mem: AHA; Chgo Heart Assn; Chgo Soc Internal Med; Ill Med Soc; NY Acad Sci. Author: Ipotensione, 1929; Cardiologia, 1938; Heart, 1948; Heart Beat, 1953; Intracardiac Phenomena, 1958; Differential Diagnosis of Cardiovascular Research Diseases, 1965; From Auscultation to Phonocardiography, 1965; A Primer of Cardiac Diagnosis, 1968; Pulmonary Edema, 1970; ed, Cardiology, 1959-61; contbr: numerous articles to med jours. Home: 5000 S Cornell Ave, Chicago, Ill. Office: 2020 W Ogden Ave, Chicago, Ill.

LUKINSKY, Joseph Sander, US, educator; b. Chgo, Ill, Sep 22, 1930; s. Morris and Margaret (Sander); BA, Roosevelt U, Chgo, 1951; ordained rabbi, MHL, JTSA, 1956; EdD, Harvard U, 1968; m. Betty Weiss, Sep 7, 1952; c: Natan, Rachel, Hana. Asst prof, J educ, since 1968, dir, training prog for J educators, both Lown Cen for Contemporary J Studies, Brandeis U; instr, educ, Tchrs Inst, JTSA, since 1966; research asso in educ, Harvard Grad Sch of Educ, since 1968; fmr: educ dir, asst rabbi, Cong Kehillath Isr, Brookline, Mass, 1958-64; dir, Camp Ramah, NY, 1965-66. Author: Teaching Responsibility: A case Study in Curriculum Development, 1969. Recipient: Carl and Barbara Friedman Memorial Prize in J Educ, JTSA, 1966. Home: 50 A Russell St, Brookline, Mass. Office: Brandeis U, Waltham, Mass.

LUNCZ, Matityahu, Isr; b. Jerusalem, July 7, 1894; s. Avraham and Devorah; att, Tchrs Sem, Jerusaelm, 1913; m. Esther Bercoff; c: Debora, Tirza, Abraham, Moshe. Mgr: Bank Leumi le-Isr, BM, Haifa since 1953; Jerusalem, 1951-53; in banking since 1914; mgr: Anglo Pal Bank, Safad, 1920-30, Tiberias, 1930-36, dep mgr, Haifa, 1936-51. Hon Danish Consul for Haifa and Galilee, since 1957; pres, C of C, Haifa; mem, bd dirs, Reali Sch, Haifa; chmn: dist comm, KH, 1938-58; JCC, Tiberias, 1931-36; control comm, Hadar Hacarmel Council, 1940-53; club, Haifa Bankers' Assn, chmn. Contbr to Daily press. Home: 29 Levontin St, Haifa, Isr. Office: C of C and Industry, 53 Haatzmaut Rd, Haifa, Isr.

LUND, David Nathan, US, artist; b. NYC, Oct 16, 1925; s. Isidore and Mollie (Hershfeld) Lifshitz; BA, Queens Coll, NY, 1948; att, NYU, 1948-50; m. Sally Amster, June 17, 1961; c: Andrew, Giuliana. Instr, painting, Cooper Union, since 1955. Numerous one-man shows and group exhibs in US and abroad; works included in pvt and public collections, including: Whitney Mus, NYC; Toronto Gal Art; Chase Manhattan Bank; U Mass; Mfrs Hanover Trust; Harcourt Brace. Recipient: Fulbright Grants to Rome, It, 1957-58, 1958-59; Ford Found Purchase, 1961. Home and studio: 470 West End Ave, New York. NY.

LUNEL, Armand, Monaco, author; b. Aix-en-Provence, Fr, June 9, 1892; s. Auguste and Myriam; agrégé de Philosophie, Ecole Normale Supérieure, Paris, 1914; m. Suzanne Messiah, 1920; c: Georgette Jessula, Jacqueline Astruc. Hon Prof, Lycée de Monaco; served Fr Army, WW II. Author: L'Imagerie du Cordier, 1924; Occasions, 1926; Esther de Carpentras, 1926; Nicolo Peccavi ou L'Affaire Dreyfus a Carpentras, 1926; Noire et Grise, 1930; Le Balai de Sorcière, 1935; Jérusalem, à Carpentras, 1937; Par d'Etranges Chemins, 1946; La Maison de la Femme Peinte, 1946; Les Amandes d'Aix, 1949; La Belle a la Fontaine, 1959; J'ai vivre la Provence, 1962; Sénégal, 1966; librettist: Darius Milhaud compositions: Les Malheurs d'Orphée; Esther de Carpentras; Chansons d'Enfants; Maximilien; Barba Garibo; David; Henri Sauquet composition, La Chartreuse de Parme. Found, Collection des Provinces Françaises, Gallimard, under auspices of Natl Mus of Popular Art and Traditions, 1939; pres, assn des Amis de Jules Isaac; mem: Fr Soc of Ethnography Société Européenne de Culture; club, PEN, Monaco, pres. Recipient: 1st prize Théophraste Renaudot, 1926; Heinemann prize, London; Chevalier de la Légion d'Honneur, 1947; Grand Prix Litt de Provence, 1965. Home: Villa Bellevue, 49 rue Grimaldi, Monaco.

LUNENFELD, Bruno, Isr, physician, educator; b. Vienna, Aus, Feb 11, 1927; s. David and Esther (Hornung); in Isr since 1940; MD, U Geneva Med Sch, 1952; m. Suzanne Aron, 1952; c: Eitan, Yoram. Dir, Inst of Endocrinology, Tel Hashomer Govt Hosp, since 1964; head, dept life sci, Bar Ilan U, since 1968; head, endocrinology sect, fac continuing med educ, Tel Aviv U, since 1968. Capt, IDF, MC, 1954-60. Prin contrib: Research in fertility promotion of previously sterile women. Found mem, fmr treas, Isr Fertility Assn; mem: Brit

Endocrine Soc; Brit Fertility and Sterility Soc. Contbr to med publs. Recipient: Pliskin Prize for Med Contrib, 1962; Yaffeh Prize for Med Contrib, 1936. Hobby, mt climbing. Home: 14 Aron David St, Tel Aviv, Isr. Offices: Tel Hashomer Govt Hosp; Bar Ilan U, Ramat Gan, Isr.

LUNTZ, Abe M, US, business exec; b. Akron, O, Mar 6, 1893; s. Samuel and Rebecca; hon deg, Wilberforce U, Wilberforce, O; m. Fanny Teplansky, Oct 10, 1916; c: Richard, Robert, William, Joan Goulder, Ted. Chief exec off, treas, Luntz Corp; fmr with Luntz Iron and Steel Co; found: Canton Tin Plate Co; Canton Structural Steel Co; Davey Steel Co; Empire- Reeves Steel Corp, all O; dir, Soc Natl Bank of Cleveland, O. Pres, The Temple of Cleveland; chmn, Comty Fund Dr; natl vice-chmn, NCCJ; fmr: Canton Bd of Educ; Canton B'nai B'rith; Canton Wfr Fed; J Comty Cen; Montefiore Home for the Aged, Cleveland; Schnurmann House for the Aged; chmn, Canton J Fed; vice-chmn: Canton Boy Scouts council; adv bd, Mercy Hosp, Canton; mem: adv bd: Mt Sinai Hosp; Cleveland Art Mus; f: Amer Cancer Soc; natl bd, UAHC; St Alexis Hosp, Cleveland; Inst of Scrap Iron and Steel; JWF, Canton; Cleveland Wfr Fed; found: Canton Civic Orch; Canton Players Guild; mem: YMCA; Rotary. Recepient: Dist Service Award, Canton C of C, 1939; Natl Hum Relations Award, NCCJ, 1957; Hon Star Award, O HS Coaches Assn, 1961; Guardian of Menorah Award, Canton B'nai B'rith, 1967; Sr Citizens-of-Year Award, Cuyahoga Sr Citizens League, 1969. Home: 18975 Van Aken Blvd, Shaker Hgts, O. Office: 68 and Berdelle, Cleveland, O.

LURIA, Ben Zion, Isr, civil servant; b. Bialystok, Pol, 1905; s. Itzhak and Shoshana (Fuhrman); MA, Heb U, Jerusalem; m. Yehudit Ginzburg, Jan 7, 1930; c: Arnona, Talmona, Menahem. Dir, devl dept, Min Culture and Educ. Served, Haganah. Author, Glilot Bamoledet, 1948, 2nd ed 1957; ed, New Ed of the Bible; Shalag, New Explanation for Chronicles; contbr articles, monographs, explanations; Isr Bc: Bible explanation and commentary. Mem, bd dir, chmn natl conv, Hevra Leheker Hamikra; mem, Isr Exploration Soc. Home: 4 Gera St, Jerusalem, Isr. Office: Haneviim St, Jerusalem, Isr.

LURIA, Salvador Edward, US, educator; b. Turin, It, Aug 13, 1912; s. Davide and Esther (Sacerdote); in US since 1940; MD, U Turin, 1935; m. Zella Hurwitz, Apr 18, 1945; c: Daniel. Prof, microbiol, MIT, since 1959; F, NRC, Fr, 1938-40; research asst, Columbia U, 1940-42; Guggenheim F, 1942-43; asso prof, Ind U, 1948-50, mem fac, since 1943; prof, bact, U of Ill, 1950-59; Jesup lectr, Columbia U, 1950. Mem: Natl Acad Sci; Amer Acad Arts and Sci's; Amer Phil Soc; Amer Acad Microbiols; AAAS; Genetics Soc; Amer Soc Naturalists; Soc Gen Microbiol; Sigma Xi. Author, General Virology; contbr: numerous articles to profsl jours. Recipient, Nobel Prize in Phys Med, 1969. Home: 48 Peacock Farm Rd, Lexington, Mass. Office: MIT, Cambridge, Mass.

LURIE, Harry L, US, social worker; b. Goldingen, Latvia, Feb 28, 1892; s. Herz and Lina (Blumenthal); in US since 1898; MA, U of Mich, 1923; m. Bernice Stewart, June 20, 1922; c: Alison Bishop, Jennifer Cooke. Ed, Ency of Social Work, 1962-65; fac mem, U Mich, 1922-24; supt, Chgo J Social Service Bur, 1925-30; lectr: U Chgo, 1926-30; NY Sch of Social Work, 1931; exec dir, Bur J Social Research, NY, 1930-35; exec dir, CJFWF, 1935-37. Mem: Amer Sociol Soc; Amer Assn of Social Workers. Author: A Heritage Affirmed, 1961. Home: 325 Central Park W, New York, NY.

LURIE, Ilya Eliahu, Isr, physician; b. St Petersburg, Russ, Mar 24, 1913; s. David and Sonia (Treivush); in Isr since 1928; MD, U Lyons, 1939; m. Esther Bibring, 1949; c: Thalma, Nilly, Raziel, Orna. Head, med div, Ichilov Med Cen. Maj, IAF, 1950-63. Contbr, numerous papers to med jours. Office: 41 Rupin St, Tel Aviv, Isr.

LURIE, Jesse Z, US, journalist; b. Gloversville, NY, Dec 4, 1913; s. Jacob and Ida (Silverman); m. Irene Blayzor, Jan 15, 1938; c: Susan, Ellen. Exec ed, Hadassah Mag, fmr mgn ed, Hadassah Newsletter; Amer corresp, Jerusalem Post, since 1938, reporter, 1934-37; ed, NY J News, 1937-38; publicity dir: United Pal Appeal; UJA, JWB; AJCong, unitl 1947. US, Army, 1945. Mem: UN Corresp Assn; Fgn Press Assn. Home: Usonia Rd, Pleasantville, NY. Office: Hadassah, 65 E 52 St, New York, NY.

LURIE, Louis A, US, psychiatrist, educator; b. Salant, Lith, Feb 10, 1888; s. Hirsch and Celia (Singer); in US since 1890; MA, U Cincinnati, 1911, MD, 1911; m. Osna Bernstein, Oct

27, 1918; c: Max, Henry; m. 2nd, Henriette Jonap, July 1, 1952. Pvt practice, psycht and endocrinology, since 1919; sr cons neuro-psycht, J Hosp, Cincinnati, since 1951; asst prof psycht, U Cincinatti, 1931, instr in psych, 1908-11; found and dir, Child Guidance Home, Cincinnati 1920-49, cons since 1949; dir, Shoe Corp of Amer, since 1950; lectr on mental hygiene, HUC, 1925-48; cons in psycht, Draft Bds, Ohio, 1940-45. Lt, US Army MC, 1917-18. Appd by Pres Hoover, comm to draft Children's Charter, 1930; found, Amer Acad Child Psycht; mem: bd overseers, JTSA; bd dirs, United J Social Agcys, Cincinnati, 1932; natl and intl sci orgs; clubs: Torch; Losantiville Country. Asso ed, Amer Jour Orthopsychiatry, 1946-56; contbr: to sci jours; chap in books on child psycht and child guidance. Hobbies: bridge, golf. Home: 2401 Ingleside Ave, Cincinnati, O. Office: Doctors Bldg, 19 Garfield Pl, Cincinnati, O.

LURIE, Robert I, US, physician; b. Chgo, Ill, Feb 4, 1913; s. Sam and Sylvia (Nova); BS, Northwestern U, 1936, MD, 1937; m. Lora Spiesberger; c: Judy, Susan, Mike. Pvt practice, urol, since 1937; treas, Richmond Realty Corp; pres, Modern Cleaners, Saginaw; chief of staff, Saginaw Gen Hosp, 1964-67. Lt col, US Army MC, 1941-45. Pres: Saginaw JWF; Saginaw Co Med Soc, 1969-70; fmr pres: Saginaw J Comty Cen; B'nai B'rith; mem: natl council; J Hosp, Denver; Isr Bond Dr; UJA; mem: Alpha Omega Alpha; Phi Delta Epsilon; Tau Delta Phi; clubs: Standard; Franklin Hills Country; Saginaw Country. Contbr to med jours. Home: 58 Davis Dr, Saginaw, Mich. Office: 2525 S Washington, Saginaw, Mich.

LURIE, Sidney B, US, stockbroker; b. NYC, Dec 7, 1910; s. Louis and Tillie (Sacks); att NYU, 1928-30; m. Rosa Adler, May 1, 1941; c: Gail, Lawrence. Partner, Josephthal & Co, since 1955; mgr, research dept, Paine, Webber, Jackson & Curtis, 1942-54. Pres, NY Soc Security Analysts, 1953-54; club, Standard. Columnist: Forbes Mag, since 1954; Engineering Opportunities, since 1967. Home: Barkers Point Rd, Sands Point, NY. Office: 120 Broadway, New York, NY.

LUSTGARTEN, Ira Howard, US, attorney; b. NYC, July 31, 1929; s. Louis and Florine (Van Hindeno); AB, NYU, 1950; LLB, Columbia Law Sch, 1958; m. Rhoda Manne, Oct 24, 1954; c: Lise, Nancy. Partner, Proskauer, Rose, Goetz & Mendelsohn, since 1968. Lt, USN, 1951-55. Vice-chmn, law comm, FJP; dir: Asso Camps; YM-YWHA, Flushing, NY; Lavanburg Corner House; lectr, comm on post admission legal educ, Assn Bar, NYC, spec comm on found, fmr chmn, family comm. Contbr to law revs. Home: 200 Glendale Rd, Scarsdale, NY. Office: 300 Park Ave, New York, NY.

LUTTWAK, Edward Nicolae, Isr, educator, consultant; b. Arad-Transylvania, Isr, Nov 4, 1942; s. Josif and Clara (Baruch); BEcon, LSE, 1954. Dep dir, ME Study Group, Van Leer Found, Jerusalem since 1969; asst dir, CBS-TV, 1964-65; lectr, Bristol U, Eng, 1965-67; cons, Walter Levy SA, 1967-68. Author: Coup D'Etat; A Guide to Modern War. Office: 43 Jabotinsky, Jerusalem, Isr.

LUZ, Kadish, Isr, legislator; agronomist; b. Bobruisk, Russ, 1895; s. Zvi and Esther (Seldowich) Losinsky; in Isr since 1920; att: Tech Coll, Karlsruhe, 1913-14; Inst Agron, Odessa, 1917-19. Ret; Speaker of Knesset, 1959-70, MK, 1951-70; Agric Min, 1955-59; mem, Kibbutz Degania B. since 1921. Mem, cen comm, Mapai, since 1935; fmr mem secretariat: cen control comm, Histadrut; Tel Aviv Lab Council. Author: The Kvutza and the Youth, 1944; The Growth and Social Changes of the Kvutza, 1945; The Economic Factors of the Kvutza, 1947; The Way of the Kvutza, 1951; Avnei Derech, 1962, all in Heb; contbr to local lab press. Home: Kibbutz Degania B, Isr.

LUZ, Zvi, Isr, educator; b. Ein Harod, Isr, Jan 10, 1930; s. Kadish and Rachel (Kanteroviz); BA, MA, PhD, Bar Ilan U, 1957-68; m. Ahuva Frankel, Apr 2, 1957; c: Shira, Tehila, Yotam. Lectr, Heb and world lit, Bar Ilan U, since 1968, on staff since 1964; mem, Kibbutz Degania B. Capt, Isr Army, 1948-50. Author, Where The Rivers Go, 1965; contbr to jours. Recipient, Kugel Lit Prize, City of Holon, 1965. Home: Kibbutz Degania B, Emek Hayarden, Isr. Office: Bar Ilan U, Ramat Gan, Isr.

LUZZATI, Emanuele, It, stage designer, interior decorator; b. Genoa, June 3, 1921; s. Guido and Fernanda (Vita Finzi); dipl, Ecole des Beaux Arts, Lausanne, Switz, 1945. Stage designer: Scala Theatre, Milan, 1947; J Theatre, Milan, Rome, 1947; Valle Theatre, Rome 1949, 1952; Festival of Venice,

1951; Communale Theatre, Florence, 1953; Opera House, Rome; San Carlo Opera House; since 1962: Glyndebourne Festival, Eng; Chgo Lyric Opera; Vienna Opera; Covent Garden, London; Munich Staatsopera; Gulbenkian found, Lisbon. Interior decorations of: SS Conte Biancamano; SS Augustus; SS Andrea Doria; SS Leonardo da Vinci; SS Homeric; SS Ansonia; taught ceramics, Ein Hod artists village, Isr, 1958-60. Author: Chichibio and the Crane, 1960; contbr of articles, illustrations, covers, to profsl mags. Recipient: 1st prize for ceramics, Intl Festival, Cannes, 1955; 1st prize for antifascist propaganda, 1960; prize for film cartoon, Bergamo Festival, 1960. Home: Via Caffaro 12A, Genoa, It.

LUZZATTO, Guido L, It, author; b. Milan, It, Nov 7, 1903; PhD, U Milan, 1925; m. Matilde Luzzatto, Aug 21, 1944. Author: Dürer, 1924; Brunelleschi, 1926; Giotto, 1928; Dialoghi sulla Creazione Artistica, 1934; Rembrandt, 1934; L'Opera Grafica di Dürer, 1936; Van Gogh, 1937; Siro Penagini, 1957; contbr to lit and art mags, since 1923; lectr: Intl Cong of Hist of Art: Brussels, 1930; Stockholm, 1933; Berne, 1936; London, 1939; Intl Cong of Art Critics: Paris, 1948, 1949, 1958; Amsterdam, 1951, 1952; Venice, 1955; Intl Cong on Giotto, Florence, 1967; lectr on J problems: Ger; Fr; Switz; It, all 1928-39 and since 1945. Mem: Association Internationale des Critiques d'Art; Mouvement Universel pour une Confédération Mondiale. Home: 7 Via Canova, Milan, It.

LYON, Richard K, US, attorney; b. Wash, DC, Apr 24, 1912; s. Simon and Minnie (Kirshbaum); AB, Dartmouth Coll, 1933; JD, Georgetown Law Sch, 1936; m. Marjorie Hausman, (decd); m. 2nd, Dorothy Weisberg, Feb 7, 1960; c: Simon, Richard, Jon, step-c: Barbara, Patricia. Pvt practice since 1936; gen counsel, BBB since 1954; Johnson-Humphrey Inaugural Comm, 1965. Cdr, USNR, 1941-46. Fmr: pres, Wash House Rules Comm; vice-chmn, DC Dem Cen Comm; JCC; vice-pres, J Comty Cen; chmn, DC Commn Youth Council; mem: Amer, Fed, DC Bar Assns; Delta Kappa Epsilon; Gamma Eta Gamma. Home: 3149 Newark St, NW, Washington DC. Office: 220 Federal Bar Bldg W, 1819 H St, NW, Washington, DC.

LYONS, Eugene, US, editor, author; b. Uzlian, Russ, July 1, 1898; s. Nathan and Minnie (Privin); in US since 1907; att Columbia U; m. Yetta Siegel, Sep 6, 1921; c: Eugenie Haimes. Sr ed, Reader's Digest since 1951, on staff since 1945; fmr: reporter, Erie Pa Dispatch, 1919; free-lance corresp, It, Fr, 1920-21; ed, Soviet Russia Pictorial, 1922-23; staff, NY Bur, TASS, 1923-27; UP corresp in USSR, 1928-34; mem, pr firm, Ames & Norr, 1935-39; ed: American Mercury, 1939-44; Pageant, 1944-45. Author: Life and Death of Sacco and Vanzetti, 1927; Moscow Carousel, 1935; Assignment in Utopia, 1937; Stalin, Czar of all the Russians, 1940; The Red Decade, 1941; Our Unknown Ex-President: A Portrait of Herbert Hoover, 1949; Our Secret Allies: The Peoples of Russia, 1953; Herbert Hoover: A Biography, 1964; David Sarnoff: A Biography, 1966; Workers' Paradise Lost, Fifty Years of Soviet Communism: A Balance Sheet, 1967; ed: We Cover the World, 1936; Six Soviet Plays, 1936. Chmn, Amer Comm for Liberation from Bolshevism, 1951-52; clubs: Overseas Press; Dutch Treat. Home: 220 Madison Ave, New York, NY. Office: Reader's Digest, Pleasantville, NY.

LYONS, Harry, US, dentist, educator; b. Wash, DC, Mar 18, 1900; s. Max and Jennie (Natkin); DDS, Med Coll of Va, 1923; hon: DSc: Temple U, 1957; NYU, 1965; LLD, Manitoba U, 1960; m. Sara Wice, June 15, 1926. Mem fac, Med Coll of Va, since 1923, prof path, therapeutics and periodontia since 1931, head dept since 1931, dean, Sch of Dent, since 1951; dent cons: FDA, since 1945; VA: VA Hosp, Richmond, Va, 1947-53; Regional Off, Roanore, Va, 1950-52; Cen Off, Wash, DC, since 1953; Council on Fed Govt Dent Services, Amer Dental Asso, 1950-51; US Food and Drug Admn, since 1945; hon civilian cons to Surg Gen, USN. Pres: Va State Dental Assn 1947-48; Amer Acad of Periodontology, 1953-54; Amer Dent Asso, 1956-57; Amer Asso Dent Schs, 1963-64; Amer Coll Dents, 1964-65; vice-pres, Amer Fund for Dent Educ, since 1963; speaker, House of Delgs, Amer Dent Asso, 1952-53, 1954-55; chmn, Nomenclature comm: Amer Acad Periodontology, 1939-42; Amer Dent Asso, 1941-45; chmn: spec comm on Natl Emergency Dent Service, Amer Dent Asso, 1948-49; profsl relations, Amer Asso Dent Schs, 1953-54; comm on Educ, Amer Coll Dents, 1948-53; mem: Council on Dent Therapeutics, Amer Dent Asso, 1935-52; comm on Dent, NRC, 1952-54; Natl Adv Dent Research Council, Natl Inst Dent Research, USPHS since 1954; Natl Adv Council on Educ for Health Professions since 1964; Mil Dependents Med Care Adv Comm to Secy of Defense; Richmond Dent Soc; NC State Dent Soc, hon; Intl Asso for Dent Research; Omicron Kappa Upsilon; Sigma Zeta; Alpha Omega, hon; Rotary. Recipient, Alpha Omega Achievement Award, 1956. Home: 300 W Franklin St, Richmond, Va. Office: Med Coll of Va, Richmond, Va.

LYONS, Leonard, US, columnist; b. NYC, Sep 10, 1906; s. Moses and Bronna (Harnick) Sucher; att CCNY, 1924-25; LLB, St John's U Coll of Law, 1928; m. Sylvia Schonberger, Nov 29, 1934; c: George, Warren, Jeffrey, Douglas. Author, daily column, The Lyons Den, NY Post, syndicated since 1934; admitted to NY Bar, 1928; Fed Bar, 1929; law practice, NYC, 1928-34. Office: 75 West St, New York, NY.

M

MAASS, Richard, US, business exec; b. Baltimore, Md, May 20, 1919; s. Arthur and Selma (Rosenheim); BS, NYU, 1944; m. Dolly Lederer, Apr 4, 1943; c: Douglas, Richard. Partner, Reredel Assos, since 1943; pres, Lederer Found Inc, since 1948; underwriter, Amer Surety, 1937-42. USN, 1942-45. Chmn, Fgn Affairs Comm, AJComm, since 1967, natl vice-pres, 1962-65, pres, NY chap, 1958-59, mem, admn bd, since 1957, exec bd, since 1952, chmn, Westchester div, 1954-56; pres: Cage Teen Cen, White Plains, 1962-64; Urban League of Westchester Co, Inc, 1953-59, treas, 1950-53; The Manuscript Soc, 1954-56; JCC, Scarsdale, White Plains region, 1953-55; dir, White Plains Civic and Business Fed, 1952-53 and 1962; mem: housing adv council, State Commn on Hum Rights; NY and Westchester Co Hist Socs; Amer Assns for State and Local Hist; clubs: Grolier; Fed City, Wash, DC. Contbr to: Manuscripts; Library Trends. Spec interest: collecting Amer colonial and revolutionary manuscripts. Home: 3 Murchison Pl, White Plains, NY. Office: 270 Martine Ave, White Plains, NY.

MAAYANI, Ami Hay, Isr, architect, composer; b. Ramat Gan, Isr, Jan 13, 1936; s. Yehuda and Batia (Rabinowitz); BArch, Technion, Haifa, 1960; att Columbia U, NY; MSc, Sch of Architecture and Music, US, 1965. Composer: Concerto for harp; Concerto for percussion; Music for harp; music for orch, chamber orch, string orch; harp solo. Recipient: Engel Prize, Tel Aviv Munic, 1963; Prix Divvone, Fr, 1967. Home: 8 Nachum St, Tel Aviv, Isr.

MACCOBY, Nathan, US, psychologist, educator; b. London, Eng, Feb 17, 1912; s. Moses and Ethel (Fisher); in US since 1916; BA, Reed Coll, 1933; MA, U Wash, 1938; PhD, U Mich, 1950; m. Eleanor Emmons, Sep 16, 1938. Prof, communication, research asso, Inst for Communication Research, Stanford, Cal, since 1959, acting dir, 1962-63, acting exec head, dept communication, 1963-64; instr, psych, Ore State Coll, 1939-40; examiner, US Civil Service, 1940-42; research psychol, US Army Info and Educ Div, 1943-45; asst chief, and chief, personnel placement, OPA, 1945-47; study dir, survey research cen, U Mich, 1947-49; prof, psych, Boston U, 1949-59, Newsom prof, opinion research, 1949-55, chmn, research div, 1949-59, chmn, dept psych, 1958-59; visiting prof, psych and communication, Stanford U, 1958-59. F: Soc of Psych Studies of Social Issues; Amer Psych Assn; W Psych Assn; AAAS; mem, Amer Assn for Public Opinion Research. Home: 729 Mayfield Ave, Stanford, Cal. Office: Inst for Communication Research, Stanford U, Stanford, Cal.

MACEY, Morris William, US, attorney; b. Camilla, Ga Dec 25, 1922; s. Isadore and Freda (Berman); AB, LLB, U, of Ga, 1943; LLM, Harvard Law Sch, 1947; m. Dora Rosenfield, Dec 28, 1950; c: Morris, Jonathan, Rex. Partner, Lipshutz, Macey, Zusmann & Sikes, since 1947. Sgt, US Army, 1943-46. Bd dirs, Temple Sinai; pres, Commercial Law League of Amer, 1966-67; mem: Natl Bankruptcy Conf; Phi Epsilon Pi; clubs: Commerce; Harvard of Atlanta; Standard. Home: 4175 Conway Valley Rd NW, Atlanta, Ga. Office: 64 Pryor St NE, Atlanta, Ga.

MACHLIS, Meyer, Isr, attorney; b. Russ, Jan 29, 1904; s. Max and Esther (Moskowitz); in Isr since 1935; att CCNY, 1919-23; DJur, Columbia U, NY, 1925; m. Naomi Hirschowitz, June 16, 1929; c: Abraham, Judith Chaimoff, Rena Feinberg. Pvt practice since 1937; atty before NY, Fed Bars, 1927-35; fmr, partner, Machlis and Machlis. Sgt, IAF, 1943-45. Chmn: Isr Amer Soc, Petah Tikvah br; Intl Service Comm, Rotary Club, Petah Tikvah br; gabbai, Kfar Ganim Beth Syn; mem: natl panel arbitrators, Amer Arbitration Soc; B'nai B'rith; Masons; past pres: Rotary; Young Isr of Boro Pk. Home: 8 Pinness St, Petah Tikvah, Isr. Office: 15 Rothschild Blvd, Tel Aviv, Isr.

MACHLIS, Meyer, US, rabbi; b. NYC, Apr 24, 1910; s. Moses and Fanny (Moskowitz); dipl, Tchrs Inst, Yeshiva Coll, 1929; BSS, CUNY, 1931, MS, 1938; ordained rabbi, MHL, HUC-JIR, 1941, DD, 1966; m. Lillie Chwat, Mar 5, 1932. Rabbi, Temple of the Covenant, NYC, since 1952; tchr: Heb schs,

1930-35; public HS, 1932-35, both NYC; prin, Louisville Heb Sch, Ky, 1935-37; rabbi: Valley Stream J Cen, NY, 1941-48; YM-YWHA Syn of Wash Hgts, NYC, 1948-52. Civilian chaplain, 1942-44. Mem: CCAR; NY Bd Rabbis; NY Fed Reform Rabbis; Natl Assn Temple Educators, mem, exec bd, youth aid; ZOA; AJCong; HUC-JIR and CUNY Alumni Assns. Home: 120 Haven Ave, New York, NY. Study: 612 W 180 St, New York, NY.

MACHT, Stanley H, US, physician, radiologist; b. Crewe, Va, Sep 3, 1914; s. Harry and Jeanette (Rubin); BS, U of Va, 1934, MD, 1939; m. Naomi Newman, July 1, 1941; c: Jay (decd), Harold, Maury, Jon. Dir, dept radiology, Wash Co Hosp, Hagerstown, Md, since 1950; cons: Brooklane Hosp; W Md State Chronic Disease Hosp; f, roentgenology, Peter Bent Brigham Hosp, Boston, 1942; res, Jefferson Hosp, Phila, 1943-44, asst radiologist, 1944-46; dir, dept radiology, Baltimore City Hosps, and asst prof, roentgenology, U of Md, 1946-50. F: Amer Coll Radiology; S Med Assn; Pan Amer Med Assn; IMA; Radiology Soc N Amer; Amer Roentgen Ray Soc; Wash Co Med Soc; Phila Roentgen Ray Soc; Md Radiological Soc; Med and Chirurgic Fac, Md; FFA med examiner; dipl, Amer Bd Radiology; mem: AMA; B'nai B'rith; B'nai Abraham Cong; Amer Topical, philatelic, Soc; Pilots Org; Aircraft Owners and Pilots Assn; club, Torch Intl. Contbr to med jours. Home: 826 Rolling Rd, Hagerstown, Md. Office: Wash Co Hosp, Hagerstown, Md.

MACK, Edgar J, Jr, US, business exec; b. Cincinnati, O, Apr 26, 1909; s. Edgar Sr and Amy (May); BA, Princeton U, 1931; m. Elaine Joseph, June 27, 1931; c: Edgar III, Stephan, John. Pres, Red Top Malt Co, since 1958; vice-pres, Ulmack Corp, since 1960; partner, Seasongood & Mayer, since 1955; vice-pres, Red Top Brewing Co, 1933-55; dir, Security Savings & Loan Co. Lt col, USAAF, 1939-45. Chmn, Cincinnati W End Task Force for Urban Renewal; vice-pres, Jobs for Under-privileged; secy, Cincinnati Sym Orch, fmr pres, Men's Comm; chmn: O Higher Educ Assistance Commn, 1961-62; Green Areas and Recreational Fund of Indian Hill Village, since 1962; ADL since 1962; asst treas, Home for J Aged, since 1950; bd mem: Cincinnati Unlimited, since 1961; AJComm, since 1958; mem: Masons; Scottish Rite; Syrian Temple; clubs: Bankers'; Camargo Hunt; Queen City. Hobbies: fox hunting, polo, tennis. Home: 7805 Blome Rd, Indian Hill, O. Office: Security Savings Bldg, 4 & Vine Sts, Cincinnati, O.

MACK, Emanuel, Isr, attorney; b. Warsaw, Pol, Oct 21, 1915; s. Gershon and Deborah (Bornstein); in Isr since 1935; MA, Heb U, 1942, LLB, 1946; m. Miriam Halperin, 1939; c: Hananel, Gershon, Deborah. Pvt practice, since 1947; mem, Court of Appeal, Bituach Leumi, since 1950; judge, Magistrates Court, Jerusalem, 1951-53. IDF. Mem: bd, Bikur Cholim Hosp, Jerusalem; local and cen comms, Isr Bar Assn. Home: 5 Bruer St, Jerusalem, Isr. Office: 1 Ben Yehuda St, Jerusalem, Isr.

MACK, Irving, US, physician; b. Vilna, Pol, Apr 15, 1919; s. Meilach and Rebecca (Zelcer); in US since 1921; BS, U of Chgo, 1939, MD, Rush Med Sch, 1942; m. Jean Tarrant, Nov 8, 1959; c: Melissa, Susan. Att phys, chest dept, Michael Reese Hosp, Chgo, since 1950, chief, Thursday Chest Clinic, since 1952; chest cons, Psychosomatic & Psycht Inst, since 1950, adj att phys, 1947-55, asso att phys, 1955-59, mem staff since 1944; att phys, Winfield Hosp for Diseases of the Chest, Winfield, Ill, since 1959, mem staff since 1947; clinical asso prof, med, Chgo Med Sch, since 1961, mem fac since 1949; intern, Cook Co Hosp, Chgo, 1942-43, sr resident, med, 1944-45, f, cardiovascular research, 1945-46; card cons, Herrick House for Rheumatic Fever, Bartlett, Ill, 1948-54. Dipl: Amer Bd Internal Med; cert in pulmonary disease, Amer Bd Internal Med; Natl Bd Med Examiners; f: Amer Coll Chest Phys, chmn, electrocardiography sect, 1953-59; Amer Coll Phys; Amer Coll Card; Inst of Med, Chgo; mem: Amer Fed Clinical Research; Amer Acad TB Phys; Amer Psychosomatic Soc: Amer Acad Psychosomatic Med; AHA; Amer Thoracic Soc; AAAS; AMA; Amer Soc Internal Med; Amer Assn for Hist of Med; Chgo Soc Internal Med; Chgo Heart Assn; Chgo TB Soc; Ill Trudeau Soc; Chgo Med Soc; Ill State Med Soc; Soc of Med Hist of Chgo; Alpha Omega Alpha; Phi Beta Kappa; Sigma Xi. Contbr to med and sci jours. Home: 5490 S Shore Dr, Chicago, Ill. Office: 104 S Michigan Ave, Chicago, Ill.

MACK, William Jacob, US, attorney; b. Cincinnati, O, May 27, 1885; s. William and Rebecca (Tandler); BA, cum laude, Harvard, 1907; JD, Harvard Law Sch, 1910; m. Irma Rosenthal (decd), Dec 29, 1919. Ret; fmr: atty, Mack & Mack, Chgo, Ill; pvt practice, NYC. Ill Natl Guard, 1910; Cavalry, WW I; maj, Judge Advocate, 1919. Fmr: res and volunteer, Hull House, Chgo; chmn: Ladies Garment Ind, Cleveland; Comm on Arbitration, Bar Assn, NYC; IRT Pension Bd, NY Subway Sys; exec secy, JDC; chmn, lab mgmt problems, Associated Press and Union. Contbr to numerous mgmt jours and mags. Home: 1192 Park Ave, New York, NY.

MADANES, Edward (Eliahu) Simon, Eng, writer, economist; b.Warsaw, Pol, Dec 20, 1907; s. Efraim and Esther(Lipschitz); desc of Rema Rabbi Moshe Isserlis; in Eng since 1940; PhD, econ, Warsaw and Edinburgh Us, 1932; m. Sara Rothnie, Oct 19, 1946; c: Esther, Frances. Lectr, commentator, E Eur Affairs; research in J Econs, mem, Royal Inst of Intl Affairs; corresp, Hajnt & Nasz Przeglad, Warsaw, 1932-39; dir, Ger Dept, Pol Min of Info, 1941-45; mgr, Eur Off, J Chronicle, Paris, 1945-50; dir, Jerusalem off, Haaretz, daily, 1950-53; ed, Econ Review, Jerusalem, 1953-55, asst head, E Eur dept, WJC, London. Vice-chmn, Poalei Zion, Gt Brit, fmr hon secy; hon off, ZF of Gt Brit; exec mem, WJC, Brit sect; secy gen, Tarbuth, Czech, 1935-36; co-found, Pol repr, WJC, Geneva, 1936; hon secy, Isr Maritime League, Pol, 1938-39. Covered: Nüremberg trials; struggle for establishment of Isr; Aliya; negotiated Aliya of Pol J, 1957. Mem: Pol-J Ex-Combatants Assn; Pol J Assn. Author: Absorptive Capacity of Palestine, 1931; Professional and Social Structure of East European Jewry, 1935. Recipient: Fr Croix de Résistance Combattante; Pol War Medal; British campain and defense medals; Ger Cross of Merit 1st class, for fair reporting, 1968. Prin interests: nist of J econs, E Eur affairs and Ger. Home and office: 4B The Mansions, London SW5, Eng.

MADISON, Charles A, US, editor, author; b. Zhitomir, Russ, Apr 16, 1895; s. David and Bessie (Burakowsky) Zamattison; in US since 1906; BA, summa cum laude, U of Mich, 1921; MA, Harvard U, 1922; m. Edith Hellman, July 1, 1924; c: Jeptha Yarensky. Cons, Holt, Rinehart & Winston, since 1962, ed, 1924-52, ed-in-chief, coll textbooks dept, 1952-62; asst ed, Amer Book Co, 1922-24. Mem: Phi Beta Kappa; Authors League. Author: Critics and Crusaders, 1947, expanded ed, 1959; American Labor Leaders, 1950, expanded ed, 1962; Leaders and Liberals in 20th Century America, 1961; The Owl Among Colophons, 1966; Book Publishing in America, 1966; Yiddish Literature: Its Scope and Major Writers,1968; Jews as Eminent Americans, 1970; contbr to American Radicals, 1957, and mags. Home: 231 E 76 St, New York, NY.

MADLER, Michael, Isr, architect; b. Sofia, Bulgaria, Jan 5, 1921; s. Moshe and Leah Rotholz; in Isr since 1941; att: Fr Coll, Sofia; Technion, Haifa, 1941-45; m. Shulamith Kanev, June 6, 1946; c: Ariel. Independent architect since 1945; among bldgs designed: Natl and U Libr; Beit Elisheva; Munic Thearte, all Jerusalem; Tel Aviv U Libr. Engr corps, IDF. Mem: comm, Architects Assn in Isr; cen, Architects and Engrs Assn in Isr. Contbr to books and jours. Recipient: numerous prizes in architectural competitions. Hobby: art. Home: 16 Bar Kochba St, Tel Aviv, Isr. Office: 20 Helsinki St, Tel Aviv, Isr.

MADORSKY, Samuel Leo, US, chemist; b. Novo-Buikhov, Russ, Feb 28, 1891; s. Leo and Bessie (Galiutzin); in US since 1911; BS, U of Chgo, 1919, PhD, 1923; m. Rose Norinsky, Oct 9, 1917; c: Irving, Anabelle. Fmr: cons, Natl Bur of Standards, 1960-65, res chem, 1942-47, sr chem, 1947-51, prin chem, 1951-60; dir, research, Gathmys Research Co, Chgo, Ill, 1923-28; asso chem, US Dept Agric, 1929-42. Mem: Amer Chem Soc; Wash Acad Sci; Sigma Xi. Author: Thermal Degradation of Organic Polymers, 1964; contbr to profsl publs. Home: 5480 Wisconsin Ave, Bethesda, Md.

MAEIR, David Mordechai, Isr, physician; b. NYC, June 7, 1926; s. Maeir and Ethel (Bloch) Lifshitz; BA, Yeshiva U, NY, 1946; MD, U of Ottawa, 1952; m. Alisa, Mar, 1955; c: Aren, Joshua. Dir gen, Shaare-Zedek Hosp, Jerusalem; asso prof, path, Albert Einstein Coll of Med, 1959-69, dir, path dept, 1965-69. Capt, USAF, 1954-56. Contbr to sci publs.

Home: 21 Balfour St, Jerusalem, Isr. Office: Shaare-Zedek Hosp, Jerusalem, Isr.

MAG, Samuel E, US, business exec; b. New Britain, Conn, Mar 10, 1902; s. Nathan and Rebecca (Goldberg); att Yale U, 1924; m. Fanny Mittau, Apr 22, 1928; c: Margery Andrews, Joan Karff, Eliot. Pres, N E Mag and Sons, Inc, since 1937; secy, Magson Uniform, since 1947. Pres: 1st J Fed, 1948-52; C of C Retail Bd; Council of Soc Agcys, 1952-54; regional delg, J Fed and Wfr Bd, 1951-53; mem: Comty Council Relations comm; Comty Chest; Temple B'nai Israel, all New Britain; Temple Beth Israel, Hartford, Conn; B'nai B'rith; clubs: Yale, New Britain; Yale, NY; Rotary. Home: 61 Birchwood Dr, New Britain, Conn. Office: 160 Main St, New Britain, Conn.

MAGER, Nathan H, US, business exec, publisher; b. NYC, June 8, 1912; s. Samuel and Bertha (Hellman); BCS, NYU, 1932; m. Sylvia Kornmehl, Feb 13, 1944; c: Peter, Alison. Pres: Leader Publs Inc, since 1945; Natl Antiques Show, since 1945; Science and Govt Publs, since 1945; bus mgr, NY Daily Column, since 1968; Civil Service Leader, since 1939. Mem: bd trustees, Teaneck J Comty Cen, since 1950; Grand St Boys Assn. Author: Legal, Political and Business Guide, 1940; Practice Tests for All Jobs, 1948; New York City Almanac and Guide, 1957; co-author: American Household Encyclopedia, 1951; Put Your Money to Work for You, 1954; Office Encyclopedia, 1955; Complete Letter Writer, 1956; Guide to Better Living, 1959; Conquest Without War, 1961. Home: 1013 E Lawn Dr, Teaneck, NJ. Office: 97 Duane St, New York, NY.

MAGGAL, Moshe Morris, US, rabbi; b. Nagyecsed, Hung, Mar 16, 1908; s. David and Esther (Fulop) Gelberman; in US since 1949; ordained rabbi, Natl Rabb Sem, Budapest, 1934; att: Zurich U, 1936-37; Heb U, Jerusalem, 1937-38; m. Rachel Diamond, July 8, 1951; c: Davida, Michelle, Elana. Rabbi: Cong Ahavath Isr, since 1966; Temple Meyer David, Claremont, NJ, 1951-52; Temple Beth Aaron, Billings, Mont, 1952-54; Cong Beth Kodesh, Canoga Park, Cal, 1959-61. Pvt, IDF, 1948-50. Found, pres, Natl J Info Service for Propagation of Judaism; vice-pres, Min Assn, NH, 1951-52; bd dirs, Beverly Hills Zionist Org, 1956-57; mem: Gtr LA Press Club; ZOA; Intl Platform Assn. Author: Acres of Happiness, 1968; Prophecy and Fulfillment, 1968; asso ed, Heritage-Southwest J Press; pub, ed, Voice of Judaism; contbr to J jours. Recipient: Reward of Merit, Spiritual Mobilization, 1952; citation, Crusade for Freedom, 1952. Hobbies: travel, theater. Home and study: 6412½ W Olympic Blvd, Los Angeles, Cal.

MAGIL, Abraham B, US, journalist, author; b. Phila, Pa, Feb 19, 1905; s. Joseph and Rachel (Leshem); BA, U of Pa, 1925; m. Harriet Black, Aug 2, 1940; c: Margaret Litchfield. Fmr: free-lance writer, reporter, Phila Public Ledger, 1925-26; copy reader, Women's Wear Daily, 1926-28; ed, Auto Workers' News, Detroit, 1933-35; political writer, Daily Worker, 1935-38, Sunday ed, fgn ed, 1956-58; exec ed, New Masses, 1938-48; asso ed, Masses and Mainstream, 1952-56. Mem: ACLU; SANE. Author: The Peril of Fascism, 1938; Israel in Crisis, 1950; contbr to: Menorah Jour; Nation; New Republic; J Currents. Home: 180 Riverside Dr, New York, NY.

MAGIL, Reuben Jacob, US, rabbi; b. Phila, Pa, Jan 11, 1904; s. Myer and Rose (Groden); desc Rabbi Alexander Ziskin of Grodno; BA, Columbia U; LLB, U of Pa; MHL, ordained rabbi, hon DD, JTSA; PhD, Dropsie Coll; m. Selma Diskan, Oct 19, 1930; c: Judith Berliner, Ruth Perry, David. Rabbi: Temple Beth Zion-Beth Isr, since 1955; Kodimoh Syn, Springfield, 1931-34; Temple Beth El, Buffalo, 1934-39; Temple Beth El, Harrisburg, 1939-55. Chmn, Comm on ME, JCRC; mem: bd trustees, Phila Comty Coll; bd govs, Dropsie Coll; bd dirs, Amer Technion Soc, Phila; pres: Adult Educ Council of Phila, 1964-68; RA, Phila br, 1962-65; fmr: vice-pres, Planned Parenthood Assn, Phila, 1960-62; chmn, Cen Phila Br, ARC, 1965-67; chief of chaplains, Phila Civil Defense Area, 1957-58; mem: Phila Bd Rabbis; B'nai B'rith lodge; ZOA; Amer Isr PR Comm. Home: 1919 Chestnut St, Philadelphia, Pa. Study: 18 and Spruce Sts, Philadelphia, Pa.

MAGIL, Selma Diskan, US, communal leader; b. Phila, Pa, Jan 3, 1906; d. Samuel and Sophia (Kanevsky); m. Reuben Magil, Oct 19, 1930; c: Judith Berliner, Ruth Perry, David. Natl bd dirs: Natl Women's League, United Syn Amer; Women's div, Amer Technion Soc; chmn, Zionist Affairs,

JNF of Mid-City Hadassah; bd dirs, Women's div, Friends of Dropsie Coll; Temple Beth Zion-Beth Israel Sisterhood; chmn: UJA, 1943; First Isr Bond Campaign, Harrisburg; pres, E Pa Br, Natl Women's League, 1944-48, bd, Phila br, natl vice-pres, 1960-64; ed staff, Outlook Mag; mem: B'nai B'rith; Friends of Phila Libr Assn; Phila Bonds for Isr, bd dirs; Phila Mus Art; ORT; AJCong; Women's div, Heb U. Recipient: State of Isr Award, Israel Bonds, Phila. Home: 1919 Chestnut St, Philadelphia, Pa.

MAGNES, Gerald Donald, US, dentist; b. Chgo, Ill, Sep 27, 1933; s. Herman and Fae (Ray); BS, U of Ill, 1954; DDS, U of Ill, Sch of Dent, 1958; m. Loretta Bass, May 8, 1956; c: Scott, Craig. Pvt practice, dent surg, Chgo, Ill, since 1956; cons, sci exhibitor, Warner-Chilcott Labs, 1966-69; speaker, Amer Cancer Soc, 1969-70. Prin contrib: donation of sci exhb to U of Ill Med Cen, 1968. Mem: Amer Cancer Soc; Amer Dent Assn; Chgo Dent Soc, all Chgo chaps; Alpha Omega, natl chap. Contbr to dent jours. Recipient: cert of hon, cert of recognition, Amer Dent Assn, both 1967. Home: 3846 Jerome Ave, Skokie, Ill. Office: 1700 Lawrence Ave, Chicago, Ill.

MAGNIN, Edgar Fogel, US, rabbi; b. San Francisco, July 1, 1890; s. Sam and Lilly Fogel; AB, U Cincinnati, 1913; BH, ordained rabbi, HUC, 1914; DD, hon, 1945; LHD, Cal Coll Med, LA, 1944; DST, hon, U S Cal, LA, 1956; LLD, Wilberforce U, 1962; m. Evelyn Rosenthal, June 15, 1916; c: Henry, Mae Brussell. Sr rabbi, Wilshire Blvd Temple, since 1915; rabbi, Temple Isr, Stockton, Cal, 1914; lectr, U of S Cal, 1934-55; adj prof, homiletics, HUC-JIR; delivered prayer, inauguration Pres Richard Nixon, 1969; participated, inauguration Cal Gov Ronald Reagan, 1967, 1971. Dir: J Free Loan Assn; United Crusade; ARC, LA Chap; Cancer Prevention Soc; Cedars-Sinai Med Cen; LA World Affairs Council—Council for Intl Visitors; trustee, Cal Coll Med; chaplain, Beverly Hills Navy League; vice-pres, U Rel Conf; mem: Task Force for Venereal Disease Control, Dept Public Health, Cal; LA Forward-City Govt for the Future; adv comm, Gtr LA Chap, Natl Safety Council; charter bd, Hollywood Bowl; Mayor's Adv Comm on Hum Relations; admn bd, HUC-JIR; UN Assn, LA; found mem: LA Amigos del Pueblo; asso vice-pres, Boy Scouts Amer, LA Council; hon: pres, LA Hillel Council; chmn, Armed Forces and Vets Service Council; mem, March of Dimes, LA Co Chap; fmr: grand pres, B'nai B'rith, Dist 4; dir, J Fed Council, Gtr LA; clubs: Hillcrest Country; Beverly Hills; All-Year; Rotary. Author: How to Live a Richer and Fuller Life, 1951; columnist: LA Herald-Examiner, fmr, LA Mirror; contbr to Ency J Knowledge, articles to natl periodicals. Recipient: award of merit, LA Jr C of C; Man of Year, B'nai B'rith, LA Lodge 487; Newspaperboy Hall of Fame. Home: 615 N Walden Dr, Beverly Hills, Cal. Study: 3663 Wilshire Blvd, Los Angeles, Cal.

MAGRISH, James L, US, attorney; b. Cincinnati, O, Mar 17, 1901; s. Louis and Kate (Toby); AB, U of Cincinnati, 1922, AM, 1953, PhD, 1957; LLB, Yale U, 1924; m. Edith Krohn, Jan 30, 1930; c: Kate Foreman, Mary Stein. Pvt practice, Cincinnati, since 1925, and Wash, 1946-51; lectr, Coll of Law, dept psycht, U of Cincinnati; atty, with Alfred Bettman, 1925-42; with legal dept, War Produc Bd, 1942-45. Vice-chmn, Cincinnati chap, AJComm; secy, Alfred Bettman Found; pres: JWF; Mh Assn, both Cincinnati; Isaac M Wise Temple; vice-pres: J Family Service Bur; vice-pres, hon mem, bd trustees, Natl Fed Temple Brotherhoods; mem: bd dirs, Cincinnati chap, NCCJ; research council, May Inst for Med Research; bd trustees, vice-chmn, exec comm, J Hosp Assn; bd govs, HUC; Amer, O State, Cincinnati Bar Assns; fmr chmn: exec comm, MH Council, C'ncinnati; J Wfr Campaign; clubs: Cincinnati; Yale. Contbr to legal jours. Home: 5860 Wayside Ave, Cincinnati, O. Office: Provident Tower, Cincinnati, O.

MAHLER, Georges, Belgium, business exec; b. Antwerp, Belgium, June 5, 1910; s. Jacob and Anna (Margulies); desc, Rabbi Ephraim Margulies, Brody; att HS, Antwerp; m. Selma Lichtman, July 14, 1935; c: Charles, Nanette Rabinovitch. Master sgt, Belgian Army, WW II. Admnr, Syn Principale d'Anvers; hon secy, KH, Magbith; mem: Consistoire Israélite de Belgique; B'nai B'rith, pres, chap 1871; past hon secy, Communauté Israélite Shomreh Hadass. Recipient: Chevalier de l'Ordre des Palmes Académiques, Fr Govt; Médaille de Refractaire, for refusal to work for Germans, Belgian Govt; Médaille Commémorative 1940-45, Belgian

Govt. Hobbies: Isr philately, Judaica. Home and office: 49 Justitie St, Antwerp, Belgium.

MAHLER, Kurt, US, educator, researcher; b. Krefeld a/Rh, Ger, July 26, 1903; s. Hermann and Henriette (Stern); in US since 1968; att U of Frankfurt/M, U of Goettingen, both Ger; PhD, U of Frankfurt, 1929; DSc, U of Manchester, 1940. Prof, math, O State U, since 1968; research: U of Goettingen, 1929-33; U of Groningen, Netherlands, 1934-36; U of Manchester, Eng, 1933-34, 1937-63, mem fac, 1937-63, prof, 1952-63; prof, math, Inst of Advanced Studies, Austr Natl U, Canberra, 1963-68. F: Royal Soc; Austr Acad Sci. Author: Lectures on Diophantine Approximations, 1961; contbr to sci jours. Office: Dept of Math, O State U, Columbus, O.

MAHLER, Raphael, Isr, educator, author; b. Nowy Sacz, Pol, Aug 15, 1899; s. Isaac and Rachel (Schipper); in Isr since 1951; PhD: U Vienna, 1922; U Warsaw, 1928; m. Ella Osser, Mar 22, 1926; c: Alexandra. Prof, J hist: Tel Aviv U, since 1959; Sch of Law and Econ, Tel Aviv, 1953-59. Author: Jewish Emancipation, 1942; History of the Jews in Poland, 1946; The Karaites, 1947; History of the Jews in Modern Times (1780-1815), 4 vols, 1952-56; Statistics of the Jews in Poland in the 18th Century, 1958; Hasidim and Haskalah in the Congress Kingdom of Poland and Galicia, 1961; Historians and Guides, 1967; Jews in Poland Between Two World Wars, 1968; co-ed, Gesher, WJC quartely. Mem. exec council, Hist Soc of Isr; council: World Cong of J Studies; yad VaShem; presidium, 24th and 25th WZCs. Spec interest: J folklore. Home: 79 University St, Tel Aviv, Isr. Office: Tel Aviv U, Ramat Aviv, Isr.

MAHLER, Yona, Isr, engineer; b. Cracow, Pol, Mar 20, 1933; s. Yechezkel and Figa (Ginzig); in Isr since 1933; BS, Technion, 1957, BEngr, 1959, MS, 1964; m. Yehudit Merin, Sep 2, 1952; c: Rachel, Michael, Orit. Head, elec lab, since 1968; lectr, biol elec, Heb U, Jerusalem, since 1968; engr: Med Sch, Jerusalem, 1958-59; Inst of Arid Zone Research, Beersheba, 1959-61; lectr, med elec, Technion, Haifa, 1964-65. IDF, 1951-53. Mem, Intl Inst Med Elec and Biol Engr, Isr. Contbr on engr, biol to intl jours. Home: 4 Molcho St, Jerusalem, Isr. Office: Hadassah U Hosp, Jerusalem, Isr.

MAHRER, Josef, Isr, construction engr; b. Vienna, Aus, July 29, 1901; s. Berthold and Marie (Butschoviz); in Isr since 1932; m. Grete Goldschläger, July 28, 1931; c: Nomi Agmon. Tech adv, Rassco, since 1967; arch, engr, Lotte Coh-J Mahrer, 1932-45; city engr, Holon Munic, 1945-50; chief engr, mgr, Rassco, 1945-67. Leader, Blauweiss, Vienna, 1922-32. Contbr to profsl jours. Home: 16 Beilinson St, Holon, Isr. Office: 1-2 Har Sinai St, Tel Aviv, Isr.

MAIDENBURG, Ben, US, newspaper ed; b. Phila, Pa, Apr 28, 1910; s. David and Rose (Vinokur); att Butler U, Ind, 1927-38; hon LLD, Akron U; m. Jeanne Roskin, Apr 27, 1945; c: Benjamin, Suzan, David. Exec ed, publisher, Akron Beacon Jour, o, since 1948, Sunday ed, 1928-38; dir: Knight Newspapers, Inc, since 1956; Beacon Jour Publishing Co, since 1956; copy ed, Des Moines Register, 1928-29; Sunday news ed, Miami Herald, Fla, 1938-40; Sunday ed, Detroit Free Press, 1940-42; promotion dir, Chgo Daily News, 1946-48. Capt, USAAF, 1942-45; maj, USAF Res, 1947. Trustee: C of C; U of Akron, since 1968; vice-chmn: St Thomas Hosp; Area Progress Bd, Air Force Assn; Assn of US Army; secy, Knight Found; mem, bd: J Family Service; JWF; Rehab Cen; Council for Retarded Children; mem: Amer Soc Newspaper Eds; Inter-Amer Press Assn; Res Offs Assn; USN League; Sigma Delta Chi; clubs: Akron City; Natl Press, Wash, DC; Rosemont Country, Akron. Recipient: Philippine Independence Award, 1944; six combat area awards, 1945. Home: 2046 Wyndham Rd, Akron, O. Office: Beacon Jour, Akron, O.

MAIER, Joseph, US, sociologist, educator; b. Leipzig, Ger, Jan 24, 1911; s. Reuben and Sophie (Safran); in US since 1933; MA, Columbia U, 1934, PhD, 1939; m. Alice Heumann, July 14, 1937; c: Doris. Prof, sociol, Rutgers U, since 1947; research asst: Inst of Soc Research, Columbia U, 1935-38; radio research project, Princeton U, 1939; asst ed, Aufbau, NYC, 1940-43; propaganda analyst, US OWI, 1943-45; chief, analysis sect, Interrogation Dept, Off of US Chief of Council, Nuremberg War Crimes Trials, 1945-46; asst ed, Schocken Books, Inc, 1946-47; Fulbright prof, sociol, U of Frankfurt am Main, 1952-58; visiting prof, sociol: Columbia U, 1957, 1959, 1963; U of Conception, Chile, 1962. Pres, Theodor Herzl Soc, 1948-50, 1955-58; mem: Amer and E Sociol Assns; Amer

Acad Social and Political Sci. Author: On Hegel's Critique of Kant, 1939; Cooperative Group Living, 1950; Sociology: The Science of Society, 1953, with subsequent Brit, Ger, It, Span, Port, and Japanese eds; Intermarriage: A Survey of Unresearched Problems, 1963; Cyclical Theories of Social Change, 1964; Politics of Change in Latin America, 1964; The Notion of the Sared in Judaism, 1969. Recipient: Danforth Found F, 1954. Home: 991 Grace Terrace, Teaneck, NJ. Office: Rutgers U, Newark, NJ.

MAILER, Norman, US, author; b. Long Branch, NJ, Jan 31, 1923; s. Isaac and Fanny (Schneider); BS, Harvard U, 1943; m. Beatrice Silverman, Mar 18, 1944 (div); c: Susan; m. 2nd, Adele Morales, Apr 19, 1954; c: Danielle, Elizabeth; m. 3rd, Lady Campbell, 1962; c: Kate; m. 4th, Beverly Bentley, 1963; c: Michael, Stephen. Author: The Naked and the Dead, 1948; Barbary Shore, 1951; The Deer Park, 1955; The White Negro, 1958; Advertisements for Myself, 1959; Death for the Ladies and Other Disasters; Devil Revisited; The Presidential Papers, 1963; An American Dream, 1964; Cannibals and Christians, 1966; Why Are We In Vietnam, 1967; The Armies of the Night, 1968; Miami and the Siege of Chicago, 1968; dir movies: Wild 90, 1967; Beyond the Law, 1967; Maidstone, 1968; contbr ed, Dissent, political quartely, NYC. US Army, 1944-46. Mem: Soc of Authors, London, Eng; clubs: PEN; Signet; Harvard U. Office: c/o Charles Rembar, 521 Fifth Ave, New York, NY.

MAILLET, (Mayer) Léo, Switz, artist; b. Frankfurt a/Main, Ger, Mar 29, 1902; s. Eduard and Elisabeth (Nathan); in Switz since 1944; att Kunstschule, Frankfort, 1925-33. Freelance painter, engraver, since 1928; exhbs: with Baron James Ensor, Ostende, 1935; Paris, Amsterdam, 1950; Lausanne, Berne, Zurich, 1949-51; Sao Paulo, Munich, 1954; NY Public Libr, 1954; Milano; Torino; Florence; Rome; perm collections, mus: Frankfurt; Winterthur; Basle; Locarno; Cleveland; Gemeentemuseum, den Haag; Kunstgewerbehaus, Zurich; Mus of Modern Art, NYC; etchings displayed: Coll Public Libr, NY; Staatsbibliothek, Munich; Milan; Stuttgart. Contbr of Franz Kafka illus to various art reviews. Home: Verscio, Locarno, Switz.

MAIROVICH, Zvi, Isr, painter; b. Krosno, Pol, 1911; s. Joshua and Rachel; in Isr since 1934; att: High Inst for Judaism; High Art Sch, both Berlin; m. Jehudit Hendel, 1948; c: Dorit, Joshua. Exhbs: Gal du Siècle; Salon d'May; Salon d'Automne, all Paris, 1950; Mus Tel Aviv, 1950, 1952, 1959, 1963; Biennale, Sao Paulo, 1953, 1959; Biennale Venezia, 1956, 1958, 1962; Parma Gal, NY, 1956; Delius Gal, NY, 1956; Antoine Gal, LA, 1956; Art Council of Gt Brit, 1958; Kunstmuseum, Bern, 1958; Royal Acad, Oslo, 1958; mus: Athene, 1958; d'Art Moderne, Paris, 1960; d'Art Moderne, Sao Paulo, 1960; Carnegie Intl, Pittsburgh, both 1961; Gal Santee Landweer, Amsterdam, 1962, 1965; Cong of Art Critics, Ein Harod, 1963; Gal Scharpentier, Paris, 1963; mus: Bezalel; Modern Art, NY, both 1964. Recipient: Prize of City of Tel Aviv, 1942, 1951, 1961; Jerusalem Prize, 1942; Prize of Isr Comm for Art, 1957. Home: 5 Jerusalem St, Haifa, Isr.

MAISEL, Edwin, US, merchant; b. Toledo, O, Oct 20, 1917; s. Samuel and Sadie (Nevelson); BS, Cornell U, 1939; m. Mary Seeberg, Oct 20, 1939 (div); c: Stuart; m. 2nd, Marie Premetz, Jan 28, 1961. Prop, Ed Maisel's Furniture and Appliance Co, Buffalo, NY, since 1945. Fmr: pres: Heb Benevolent Loan Assn; Lafayette HS Alumni Assn; W NY Retail Furniture Dealers Assn; vice-pres, Humbolt Orthodox J Cen; mem: bd dirs: Natl Retail Furniture Assn; USO; Traveler's Aid Soc; bd govs, J Fed; NY State Comm on Alcoholism; capt, Comty Chest Drive; mem: Holy Land Lodge, F and AM, State of Isr; Jr C of C; Cornell U Alumni Assn; Cerebral Palsy Assn; B'nai B'rith; Masons, 32 deg, past grand lodge off, NY State, past grand master, lodge 1158; Moose; charter, Courier Express Good Fellows; asso mem, Police Athletic League; hon dep sheriff, Erie Co; hon mayor, Boys Town; clubs: Cornell, Buffalo; Gtr Buffalo Advt. Home: 78 Frontenac Ave, Buffalo, NY. Office: 911 Broadway, Buffalo, NY.

MAISELS, Israel Aaron, S Afr, jurist; b. Johannesburg, Nov 19, 1905; s. Henry and Andzia (Sieradzki); BA, U Witwatersrand, 1925, LLB, 1927; m. Muriel Freed, June 28, 1934; c: Keith, Jeffrey, Elizabeth, Helen. Judge of appeal for: Botswana; Lesotho; Swaziland; fmr: Justice of High Court, Rhodesia; advocate of Supr Court, S Afr, 1930-61; appd King's Counsel, 1948. S Afr Air Force, 1940-44. Mem: council, U Witwatersrand, since 1965; Zionist Congs Court, since

1958; fmr: chmn, S Afr Zionist Fed; gen council, S Afr Bar; Medico Legal Soc of S Afr; Johannesburg Bar Council; United Heb Cong of Johannesburg; natl chmn, IUA for S Afr; pres: S Afr J Bd of Deps; S Afr Zionist Fed; clubs: Salisbury; Johannesburg Country; Wingate. Hobby: golf. Home: 401 Glenhof, North Ave, Riviera, Johannesburg, S Afr. Office: Barclays Bank, Box 1153, Johannesburg, S Afr.

MAISELS, Misha, Isr, editor; b. Warsaw, Pol, May 15, 1903; s. Leib and Zeftle (Helfman); in Isr since 1959; att Rabb Sem, Warsaw, 1920-24; hon DHL, HUC-JIR, NY, 1957; m. Deborah Wald, Mar 2, 1930; c: Maxine, Joan. Ed, Mosad Bialik Pub Co, Jerusalem, since 1959; ed, Hadoar, Heb weekly, NY, 1954-59, asst ed, 1932-54. Mem: Heb Writers Union, Isr. Author: Thought and Truth, 1939, 2nd ed, 1961, Eng trans, 1956. Recipient: Bialik Prize, Tel Aviv, 1959. Home: Yehef Nof, 6 HaArazim St, Jerusalem, Isr. Office: POB 92, Jerusalem, Isr.

MAISEL-SCHOCHAT, Channa, Isr, educator; b. Grodno, Russ; d. Itzhak and Reisa Maisel; att: U of Odessa; Swiss and Fr Us; DSc, Fr, 1909; in Isr since 1909; m. Ret; fmr: found, prin, Girls' Agric Sch, Nahalal, 1923-60; found, first girls' farm, Kinneret, Galilee, 1911; established first cooking and agric courses for pioneering girls, Tel Aviv, 1919, which developed into Domestic Sci Sch of WIZO, now in Nahlat Itzhak; fmr mem, World WIZO Exec, since 1920; delg to 7th, 11th ZCs. Home: 4 Mapu St, Tel Aviv, Isr.

MAISLEN, George, US, attorney; b. 1902. In pvt practice, Freeport, NY. Hon pres, United Syn of Amer, pres, 1961-65, treas, vice-pres, past pres, NY Metrop region; mem, bd overseers, JTSA; co-found, Natl Ramah Commn; mem: ZOA; UJA; FJP. Home: Freeport, NY. Office: 46 W Sunrise Hwy, Freeport, NY.

MAITLIS, Yaakov J, Eng, author, lecturer; s. Joseph and Chana; PhD, Jena U, 1st hon deg, summa cum laude; m. Judith Maitlis; c: Peter. Lectr, extramural studies, U London; dir, ZF Educ Trust, London, since 1958; hon research secy, YIVO; asso mem, Inst for J Studies, U Coll, London; guest lectr: Us: Frankfurt; London; McGill, Montreal; Hendon Coll Tech, London. Author: Das Ma'assebuch, 1933; The Ma'aseh in the Yiddish Ethical Literature, 1958; The Exampla of Rabbi Samuel and Rabbi Judah the Pious, 1961; Dos Ma'sebuch, 1969; contbr: Ency Judaica; Kindlers Lexikon der Weltliteratur, Ger; contbr to periodicals. Mem: exec eomm, Brit Ivrit Olamit, Gt Brit; YIVO; Yiddish PEN Club, NY; Isr Folklore Soc. Recipient: Lit Prize, cultural sect, WJC, Paris, 1961; award, Karl Rotman Lit Found, NY, 1967. Home: 36 Hallswelle Rd, London, NW11, Eng.

MAJARO-MINTZ, Lea, Isr, artist, educator, author; b. Jerusalem; d. Leon and Hanna (Rokach) Majaro; dipl, Bezalel Art Inst, Jerusalem, 1950; LLB, Govt Law Classes, Jerusalem, 1951; m. Itzhak Mintz, Oct 5, 1951; c: Alexander, Israel. Lectr, art: Bar Ilan U, since 1968; Tchrs Sem, Jerusalem, 1965; Rel Tchrs Sem, Tel Aviv, since 1965; Bat Yam Art Acad, since 1965; Bezalel Art Sch, Jerusalem, 1963-64; art critic, Davar, daily, Jerusalem; participated in exhbs: The Six-Day-War Show, Jerusalem, Tel Aviv, 1967-68; The Affair Show, on the Lavon Affair; The Afr Impressionist Show, 1964. Prin contribs: Montefiore Memorial Decorative Wall; The Rabbi Benjamin Memorial Decorative Wall; decorative wall, RR Sta; decorative doors to Museum of Taxes, all Jerusalem. Author: Yotam and Bilam, children's illus booklet, 1966; Art and Color, 1967; The Wailing Wall, 1968; contbr on art to yearbooks. Delg on behalf of Isr Artists Assn to Intl Cong of Artists Assns, Paris, 1967; mem: comm, Jerusalem Artists Assn; cen comm, Isr Artists Assn. Spec interests: lit, music, theater, cinema, tech. Home and studio: 29a S Levin St, Jerusalem, Isr.

MAKIN, Myer, Isr, surgeon, educator; b. Birkenhead, Eng, Mar 18, 1919; s. Leon and Rebecca (Goldman); in Isr since 1946; MB, ChB, Liverpool U, 1941; m. Lily Freed, May 19, 1946; c: David, Shifra, Gideon. Dir, orthopedic dept, Hadassah U Hosp, Jerusalem, since 1955; med dir, Alyn Orthopedic Hosp, Jerusalem, since 1959; prof, orthopedic surg, Heb U, since 1968, asso prof, 1961-68; Hunterian prof, Royal Coll Surgs, Eng, 1957; Nuffield research scholar, Oxford U, 1957-58; visiting prof, orthopedic surg, Albert Einstein Med Coll, NY, 1967. Brit Army, WW II. Prin contrib: research on osteogenesis. Found, PATWA; f: Amer Coll Surgs; Brit Orthopedic Assn; Royal Soc Med; LRCP; MRCS; mem, Société Internationale de Chirugie et de Traumatologie. Contbr to profsl jours.

MAKLEFF

Recipient: Croix de Guerre; mention in dispatches, Brit, both WW II. Hobby: gardening. Home: 31 Shemariyahu Levin St, Jerusalem, Isr. Office: Hadassah U Hosp, Jerusalem, Isr.

MAKLEFF, Mordechai, Isr, army off, business exec; b. Jerusalem, Jan 19, 1920; s. Arieh and Chaya (Zimerinsky); att Technion, Haifa, 1938-39; m. Ora Papper, May 19, 1946; c: Amir, Edith. Gen mgr, Citrus Marketing Bd of Isr; fmr mgn dir, Dead Sea Works Ltd. Off, J Settlement Police, 1938-39; maj, J Brig, Brit 8th Army, WW II; head, Isr delg, armistice negotiations with Syria, Lebanon, 1948-49; dep chief, IDF, 1950-53, chief, gen staff, 1953-54. Home: 36 Hanassi St, Ramat Aviv, Tel Aviv, Isr.

MAKOVER, Henry B, US, physician, educator; b. Baltimore, Md, July 28, 1908, s. Bernard and Rose (Sworzyn); BA, Johns Hopkins U, 1929, MD, Sch of Med, 1933; m. Mildred Weinberg, July 6, 1931; c: Richard, Michael. Clinical prof, psycht, Albert Einstein Coll of Med, since 1956; supervising psycht, Bx State Hosp; att psycht, Bx Munic Hosp; asst res, Sinai Hosp, Baltimore, res, 1934-36, extern, 1936-38; pvt practice, internal med, 1936-42; asst, med, Johns Hopkins Sch of Med, 1936-42; adj, Sinai Hosp, 1936-42; instr, Sinai Sch of Nursing, 1936-40, asso med dir, Montefiore Hosp, 1946-47; health and med cons, Fed of J Charities, Phila, 1947-49; dir, med survey, Health Ins Plan, Gtr NY, 1949-50; med dir, Cen Manhattan Med Group, 1950-56; asst prof, Sch of Public Health, Columbia Sch of Med, 1951-54; res, psycht, Bx Munic Hosp, NY, 1956-61. Lt-col, 1942-44, chief, profsl services div, Wash, DC, sr surg, USPHS, 1944-46. F: Amer Public Health Assn; NY Acad Med; Amer Psycht Assn; chmn, public health comm, Comty Council, NY, 1957-59; mem: NY Acad Med, comm on special studies; dipl, Amer Bd Psycht and Neur; qualified psycht, State of NY; med adv bd: Heb U; Hadassah; bd educ, dist 7, Westchester Co, NY, 1950-53; AMA; NY Co Med Soc; club, Intl Epidemiological. Contbr to profsl publs. Special interests: oil painting, sculpture. Home: 3 Country Rd, Mamaroneck, NY. Office: Albert Einstein Coll of Med, Eastchester Rd and Morris Park Ave, Bronx, NY.

MAKOVER, Sylvan A, US, business exec; b. Baltimore, Md, Jan 28, 1914; s. Thomas and Mollie (Land); LLB, Atlanta Law Sch, 1933; m. Frances Katz, Sep 26, 1940; c: Marilyn Shapiro, Bette. Pres, Shirley of Atlanta Inc, since 1959. Pres, Ahavath Achim Cong, Atlanta; mem: Atlanta J Comty Cen; B'nai B'rith; clubs: Standard; Progressive. Home: 4200 Shirley Dr SW, Atlanta, Ga. Office: 3020 Nancy Creek Rd NW, Atlanta, Ga.

MALACHY, Yona, Isr, educator; b. Frankfurt/M, Ger, Jan 28, 1930; s. Avraham and Rivka (Gutglück) Englard; in Isr since 1945; licencié ès sci politique, U of Geneva, Switz, 1953; PhD, U of Paris, 1954; m. Therese Krol, Sep, 1959; c: Daphna. Lectr, Heb U, Jerusalem, since 1967; dep dir, Min for Rel Affairs, Chr Affairs dept, Jerusalem, 1960-69; dir, State of Isr Bonds, Belgium, 1955-57. Prin contribs: research in Chr attitudes to Zionism, State of Isr; fotsering interfaith activities, J-Chr relationship. Mem, Interfaith Comm, Rainbow group; club, Rotary, Jerusalem. Contbr of articles to yearbooks, ency, jours. Recipient: Sauman research f, 1967. Spec interests: ecumenical work, interfaith relations. Home: 8 Tchernichovsky St, Jerusalem, Isr.

MALAMAT, Abraham, Isr, educator; b. Vienna, Aus, Jan 26, 1922; s. Nathan and Lore (Garniol); in Isr since 1935; MA, Heb U, Jerusalem, 1946, PhD, 1951; m. Naama Schneidermann, Aug 15, 1951; c: Talia. Asso prof, J hist, Bibl studies, Heb U, Jerusalem, chmn, inter-dept, Bible and hist of J people, since 1964; lectr: Kibbutz Sem, 1944-49; Aliyath Noar, 1944-51; Tchrs Sem, Jerusalem, 1950-56; visiting scholar, U of Chgo, 1952-54; visiting prof: Coll of J Studies, Chgo, 1952-54; U of Pa, 1961-62. Lt, Dept Mil Hist and Geog IDF, 1948-49. Hon mem, S Afr Bible Soc. Author: The Aramaeans, in Aram Naharayim and the Rise of Their States, 1952; The Conquest of Palestine in the Time of Joshua, 1954; Jeremiah Chap 1, The Prophetic Call, 1955; Organs of State-Craft in the Israelite Monarchy, 1964; Syrien-Palästina in t der 2. Halfte des 2. Jahrt, 1966; ed: Eretz Isr, archaeol, hist, geog studies, since 1968; bull, Isr Exploration Soc, 1957-67; The Kingdoms of Isr and Judah, 1961; co-ed, Illus World of the Bible Libr, 1961; contbr to numerous scholarly jours. Recipient: Warburg Prize, Heb U, 1952; Klausner Prize, Munic Netanya, 1951. Home: 1 Rashba St, Jerusalem, Isr.

MALAMUD, Bernard, US, author; b. Bklyn, NY, Apr 26, 1914; s. Max and Bertha (Fidelman); BA, CCNY, 1936; MA, Columbia U, 1942; m. Ann de Chiara, Nov, 1945; c: Paul, Janna. Fac mem, lang, lit dept, Bennington Coll, since 1961; instr, Eng, Ore State Coll, 1949-54, asst prof, 1954-59, asso prof, 1959-61. Author: The Natural, novel, 1952; The Assistant, novel, 1957; The Magic Barrel, short stories, 1958; A New Life, novel, 1961; Idiots First, short stories, 1963; The Fixer, novel, 1966; Pictures of Fidelman, a picaresque novel, 1969; contbr short stories to mags. Recipient: Partisan Review Fiction F, 1956; Rosenthal Award, Natl Inst Arts and Letters, 1958; Ford Found Grant for Creative Writing, 1959; Natl Book Award, for The Magic Barrel, 1959; Natl Book Award, Pulitzer Prize, for The Fixer, 1967. Office: c/o Russell and Volkening, 551 Fifth Ave, New York, NY.

MALCHI, Eliezer, Isr, jurist; b. Jerusalem, Apr 13, 1917; s. Shlomo and Liuba (Grayevsky) Saltzman; LLB, hons, London U, 1939; barrister, 1940; m. Rachel Rafaeli, Nov 5, 1946; c: Schlomo. Dist judge, Tel Aviv Dist Court, since 1950; lectr, Eng legal sys, intl law, Heb U, Tel Aviv br, since 1958; pvt practice since 1968; legal adv, Controller of Light Inds, 1942-44; magistrate, 1944-49, chief magistrate, 1949-51, both Tel Aviv Court; lectr, asst dean, fac law, Sch of Law and Econ, Tel Aviv, 1946-58. Fmr pres, Profiteering Tribunal; chmn, Govt Comm for Rural Tenants Protection; fmr: chmn, intl relations world comm, Rotary, gov, Rotary in Isr; mem: Govt Comm for Revision of Criminal Law and Civil Procedure; Intl Law Soc, Isr br; Intl Assn Jurists; council Herzlia Gymnasium Alumni Assn. Author: History of Law in Eretz Israel, Heb, 3 vols, 1952; International Law, 1933; legal ed, Israel Ency; contbr to profsl publs. Home: 14 Nezah-Israel St, Tel Aviv, Isr.

MALEH, Jacques, Eng, editor; b. Cairo, Egypt, Jan 13, 1906; s. Joseph and Alice (Levy); in Eng since 1955; att U of Paris, Law Fac, 1926; m. Marcelle Hamaoui, Jan 14, 1940; c: Alice Landau, Maurice. Ed, J Chronicle News and Feature Service, London, since 1959, corresp, Cairo, 1951-53; fmr ed: L'Aurore, Fr-J weekly, 1931-43; La Menorah, 1950-53, both Cairo; Nouvelles Juives Mondiales, Paris, 1953-55. PR off, Brit Army, ME, WW II. Author: Chimères, poems, 1926; Deux Coeurs...et Dieu, novel, 1935; Siona, 1937. Fmr mem: Maccabi World Union, Egypt; Cairo J Comty. Home: 151 Cheviot Gardens, London NW2, Eng. Office: 25 Furnival St, London, Eng.

MALENBAUM, Wilfred, US, economist, educator; b. Boston, Mass, Jan 26, 1913; s. Harry and Bertha (Brandwyn); AB, Harvard U, 1934, MA, 1935, PhD, 1941; postgrad, LSE, 1937-38; Oslo Inst of Econ, 1938; m. Josephine Orenstein, Feb 26, 1950 (decd); c: Bruce, Roxanne, Ronald; m. 2nd, Helen Raffel, Mar 19, 1967. Prof, econ, Wharton Sch of Finance, U of Pa, since 1959; guest prof, U of Heidelberg, 1966; instr, Harvard U, 1938-41; chief, inves and devl staff, State Dept, 1948-52; prof, research dir, India Prog, MIT, 1953-59. OSS, 1941-45. Council mem, Grad Sch Arts and Scis, U of Pa, 1962-64; US adv, Econ Conf for Latin Amer, Mexico City, 1951; US repr, Colombo Plan Conf, Karachi, Pakistan, 1952; US delg, SEATO Conf, Baguio, Philippines, 1960. Mem: gov bd, Leonard Davis Inst of Health Econs, since 1967; Amer Econ Assn; Assn for Asian Studies; Asia Soc; Soc for Intl Devl; Phi Beta Kappa; Temple Har Zion. Author: The World Wheat Economy, 1885-1939, 1953; India and China, Development Contrasts, 1956; The East and West in India's Development, 1959; Prospects for Indian Development, 1962; mem, ed bd, Jour for Asian Studies, 1957-59; contbr to profsl jours. Home: 416 Baird Rd, Merion, Pa. Office: Wharton Sch of Finance and Commerce, U of Pa, Philadelphia, Pa.

MALER, Bertil, Swed, educator; b. Stockholm, Dec 25, 1910; s. Ruben and Ester (Orlowitz); docteur ès lettres, U Stockholm, 1949; m. Miriam Kroschewsky, 1939; c: Harriet, Mordechai. Prof, head, dept Ibero-Romance, U Stockholm, since 1964; tchr, Romance langs, since 1949; sch tchr, 1936-56; dir: Talmud-Torah, Stockholm, 1955-60; J Sch, 1955-58. Author: Synonymes Romans de l'interrogatif qualis, 1949; Orto do Esposo, 1956; Tratado de las enfermedades de las Aves de Caza, 1957; scholarly books on Span and Port; contbr to Swed and fgn publs. Mem, B'nai B'rith. Home: Banérgatan 75, Stockholm, Swed. Office: Universitet, Stockholm, Swed.

MALETZ, David, Isr, author; b. Bendin, Pol, Jan, 1900; s. Menahem and Rivka (Levkovitz); in Isr since 1920; m. Yehudit Menesh (decd); c: Ariella, Rafael (killed in action,

Isr War of Independence); m. 2nd, Ruhama Hazanov, 1933; c: Rina, Noga. Mem, Kibbutz Ein Harod, since 1921; prin, Ein Harod Sch, since 1960; fmr mem, Havurat Haemek, pioneer road builders, 1920-23; farmer, Ein Harod, 1923-52. Haganah. Mem: Isr Lab Party; Isr Tchrs Assn. Author: Maagalot, 1945; Hathatim baDerekh, 1947; haShaar Naul, 1959; contbr short stories, articles to kibbutz publs, local press. Recipient: Brenner Prize for Maagalot, Heb Writers Assn, 1946; Haganah decoration. Home: Kibbutz Ein Harod Ihud, Isr.

MALIN, Harry, US, educational dir; b. Bklyn, NY, Aug 23, 1916; s. Sam and Sarah (Rogoff); BJP, Tchrs Inst, JTSA, 1937; BS, CUNY, 1937; m. Pearl Cohen, Dec 23, 1939; c: Seth, Barry. Exec dir: Talmud Torah, St Paul, Minn, since 1969; educ dir, Cong Rodeph Shalom, Bridgeport, Conn, 1940-69; tchr, 1936-40; lectr, Heb, U Bridgeport, 1966-67. US Army, 1945-46. Mem, exec bd, United Syn Comm on J Educ, since 1952; hon pres, Educ Assembly; mem: natl bd, Educ Cons, since 1957; bd, Natl Youth Commn, since 1958; ZOA; Rel Educ Assn; fmr: pres: Natl Leaders Council of Young Judea; Educ's Assembly of United Syn; chmn, Bridgeport Heb Prins Assn; secy: Bridgeport Zionist Dist; repr, Educ's Assembly, World Conf on J Educ, Isr; mem: exec, Natl Council for J Educ; bd, Conn United Syn Camp. Co-author: Jewish Songster for Children, 1938; Purim Megillah for Children, 1946; A Model Seder, 1954. Home: 1925 Morgan Ave, St Paul, Minn. Office: 636 S Mississippi Blvd, St Paul, Minn.

MALINER, Martin M, US, physician, educator; b. Bklyn, NY, Sep 22, 1896; s. Isidor and Fannie (Stoller); MD, NY State Coll of Med, 1921; m. Celia Rosenberg, June 20, 1927; c: Jerome, Martin, Robert, Susan. Dir, ped, Cumberland Hosp, Bklyn, since 1963, att ped since 1938; att ped: Kingston Ave Hosp, since 1938, pres, med bd, 1952-55; U Hosp, since 1922, chief, children's cardiac dept, since 1930, all NYC; asso clinical prof, ped, NY State Coll of Med, Bklyn; asso clinical prof, NYU; examiner, draft bd, 1941-43; air, salvage oprs, 1942-43. F: Amer Acad Ped; Amer Coll Card; AHA; pres, Temple Sinai, Bklyn, 1942-47; chmn, UJA drives, since 1949; mem: AMA; NY State Med Assn; Kings Co Med Soc; B'nai B'rith; Phi Delta Epsilon. Contbr to med jours. Home and office: 164 Arlington Ave, Brooklyn, NY.

MALINIAK, Baruch, Isr, business exec; b. Warsaw, Pol, Apr 10, 1930; s. Gabriel and Felice (Bayer); in Isr since 1945; master mariner, Nautical Coll, Haifa, 1948; m. Claire Hood, Mar 16, 1955; c: Gabriel, Sharon. Mgr, manpower div, sea, Zim Lines, since 1969, capt, 1957-60; opr mgr, 1960-68. Lt cdr, Isr Navy. Mem, Assn of Master Mariners. Recipient: War of Independence Ribbon. Spec interests: reading, writing, lecturing. Home: 26 Hantke St, Haifa, Isr. Office: 7-9 Haatzmaut St, Haifa, Isr.

MALINO, Jerome R, US, rabbi; b. NYC, June 7, 1911; s. Wolff and Henrietta (Rosenbaum). BA, CCNY, 1931; ordained rabbi, MHL, JIR, 1935; hon DHL, Alfred U, 1958; DD, HUC-JIR, 1960; m. Rhoda Simon, June 9, 1936; c: Frances, Jonathan. Rabbi, United J Cen, Danbury, Conn, since 1935; chaplain, Fed Correctional Inst, since 1940. Civilian chaplain, Army Air Force Convalescent Cen, NY, 1942-45. Pres: Bd Educ, Danbury, for 8 terms; chmn, NE region, CCAR, delg to Syn Council; past pres, Danbury Min Assn; chmn: placement adv comm, CCAR; fmr chmn: natl exec comm, J Peace F; Syn Council Commn on Prison Wfr; mem, exec bd: Music Cen, since 1937; Danbury chap, ARC, 1952; Hum Relations Comm, Danbury; Danbury Concert Assn; mem, adv bd, Inst on Rel in an Age of Sci. Contbr to J jours. Home: 77 Garfield Ave, Danbury, Conn. Study: 141 Deer Hill Ave, Dunbary, Conn.

MALINOWITZ, Moses S, US, rabbi; b. Bklyn, NY, Dec 18, 1922; s. Alex and Mollie (Stone); BA, Yeshiva Coll, 1943; ordained rabbi, Isaac Elchanan Theol Sem, 1945; MS, U of Bridgeport, Conn, 1952; m. Ruth Scheinfeld, Oct 13, 1945; c: David, Alan. Admnr, Rabbi Dov Revel Yeshiva, Forest Hills, NY, since 1961; rabbi: Cong Sons of Isr, Yonkers, NY, since 1955; fmr: Cong Ahavath Chesed, New London, Conn, 1945-47; Cong Ahavath Achim, Bridgeport, 1947-55. Vice-pres, Natl Assn Heb Day Sch Admnrs of Amer; mem: natl exec, Union of Orthodox J Congs of Amer, since 1951; Mizrachi Zionist Org, since 1950; bd, Intergroup Council, since 1950; Family Soc since 1951; home service div, ARC, since 1951; fmr: pres, Rabb Cong of Conn; vice-pres, NE region, RabCA; secy, Rabb Alumni of Yeshiva U; club,

Oddfellows. Home: 144-12 70 Ave, Kew Gardens Hills, NY. Study: 71-02 113 St, Forest Hills, NY.

MALINOWSKI, Roman, Isr, civil engr, educator; b. Lwow, Pol, Aug 12, 1918; s. Benjamin and Sophia (Grünbaüm) Leibel; dipl ing, Lwow Poly U, 1941; MSc, Gliwice Poly U, 1948; DIng, Warsaw Poly U, 1957; m. Maria Markus, Nov, 1941; c: Eva, Joanna. Asso prof, civil engr, bldg materials dept, Chalmers U of Tech, Gothenburg; asst docent, dep prof, Warsaw Poly U, 1949-57; cons engr, dep dir, research, precast ind, Pol Min of Bldg, 1955-56; asso prof, civil engr, Technion, Haifa, 1957-64; cons engr, Min of Defense. Mem: Assn Engrs and Architects,Isr;Swed Bldg Engrs Assn;Amer Concrete Inst; Amer Soc for Testing and Materials; Swed Concrete Inst. Contbr to profsl jours. Homes: 119 Hagalil St, Haifa, Isr; Dirigentg 2, Gothenburg, Swed. Office: Chalmers U of Tech, Gothenburg, Swed.

MALKI, David, Fr, author; b. Lodz, Pol, Aug 8, 1899; s. Pinhas and Taobe (Grunberg) Weinsaft; in Fr since 1956; family perished in Nazi Holocaust. Free-lance writer; with Isr Min of Educ and Culture, 1948-56. Author: Der Talmud une seine Persönlichkeiten, 1964, 1969, translated into other langs. Mem: PEN Club; J Writers and Journalists' Org,Fr. Recipient: Joseph Milner Prize. Home: 17 Baudoin St, Paris 13, Fr.

MALKIEL, Shelomo Avraham, Isr, educator; b. Frankfurt/ Main, Ger, Dec 28, 1921; s. Elimelech and Sara (Teitelbaum) Beigel; in Isr since 1933; MA, Heb U, Jerusalem, 1950; att: U Coll, London; Theol Sem, NY; m. Zehava Orenstein, July 4, 1947; c: Avital, Ram, Serayah. Insp, mem pedg secretariat for primary educ and tchrs' training, Min of Educ and Culture, since 1962; fmr: prin, Kfar-Batya, Amer Mizrahi Women Org, 1954-56; head, J studies, Montefiore Coll, Eng, 1956-59; sup, service training, Min of Educ & Culture, 1960-62. IDF, 1948-49. Cultural activities, B'nai B'rith, Herzliya, 1953-56. Recipient: Ot Kommiut, Hagana, Hamishmar, Six Days War. Home: 13 Rav Reines St, Jerusalem, Isr. Office: 34 Shivtei Israel St, Jerusalem, Isr.

MALKIEL, Yakov, US, educator, author; b. Kiev, Russ, July 22, 1914; s. Leon and Claire (Saitzew); in US since 1940; PhD, magna cum laude, Friedrich-Wilhelms U, Berlin, 1938; LHD, U of Chgo, 1969; m. Maria Lida, Mar 2, 1948 (decd). Prof, Romance philol, ling, U of Cal, Berkeley, since 1952, on fac since 1942; instr, modern langs, U of Wyo, 1942; visiting prof, summer sessions: U of S Cal, 1949; U of Colo, 1958; U of Tex, ling instr, 1960; Ind U, 1965; UCLA, 1966; guest lectr, Us: London; Leeds;Oxford; Strasbourg;Copenhagen; Upsala; Lausanne, 1959. Mem: Ling Soc Amer, past pres; MLA; Medieval Acad Amer; Fac Club U, of Cal; Ling Circle, NY; Hispanic Soc Amer; Société de Ling Romane; past pres, Philol Assn, Pacific Coast. Author: The Substantivated Adjective in French, 1938; Development of the Suffixes antia and -entia in the Romance Languages, 1945; Three Hispanic Word Studies, 1947; The Hispanic "alguien" and Related Formations, 1949; The Hispanic Suffix iego, 1951; Studies in the Reconstruction of Hispano-Latin Word Families, 1954; Typology of Romance Historical Grammars, 1961; Essays on Linguistic Themes, 1968; found, ed-in-chief, Romance Philol, quarterly, since 1947; contbr to learned jours. Recipient: Guggenheim F, 1948-49, 1959, 1967; sr postdoc f, NSF, 1966. Home: 1 Arlington Lane, Berkeley, Cal. Office: 4333 Dwinelle Hall, U of Cal, Berkeley, Cal.

MALLACH, Aubrey, US, social worker, educator; b. Leeds, Eng, 1905; s. Ephraim and Rose (Fine); in US since 1923; BS, NYU, 1931; dipl, NY Sch Social Work, 1937; MS, Columbia U, 1942; m. Esther Dingol, Dec, 1931; c: Efrem, Alan, David. Exec dir, J Guild for the Blind, since 1970; asso secy, Fed of Social Agcys, Pittsburgh, 1943-47; asso prof, Yeshiva U, Sch Educ and Comty Admn, 1948-53; exec dir, Health Council, Gtr NY, 1948-52; dep exec dir, Wfr and Health Council, NYC, 1952-53; dep dir gen, Malben, Isr, 1954-59; dir, Prog Admn, Westchester Co Med Health Bd, 1959-69. F, Amer Public Health Assn. Author: New York Housing Studies, 1936-43; Pittsburgh Housing Studies, 1944-45; Population of Allegheny County, 1910-40, 1946; ed: Young Judean Mag, 1937-42; The Federator, 1943-47. Home: 16 Avondale Rd, White Plains, NY. Office: 1880 Broadway, New York, NY.

MALLER, Octav Joshua, Isr, physician; b. Bucharest, Rum, Apr 12, 1917; s. Adolf and Nechama (Rafailovici); in Isr since 1958; MD, State Med Inst, Russ, 1941; m. Shulamit Katz, July 18, 1940; c: Alexander. Dir, Govt Psycht, Hosp

Pardessia, since 1960; visiting lectr, psycht, Tel Aviv U since, 1965; asst clinical prof, Bucharest Fac and Postgrad Med Inst, 1949-58; dept head, Bucharest Govt Psycht Hosp, 1949-58. Secy, Group for Social Psycht, Isr Neuro-Psycht Assn; mem: Amer Ontoanalytic Assn; Intl Assn Psychopath of Expressionalism; Soc Moreau de Tours, Paris. Contbr to sci jours. Home: 59 Frishman St, Tel Aviv, Isr. Office: Govt Psycht Hosp, Pardessia, Netania, Isr.

MALLI, Moshe, Isr, communal leader; b. Minsk, Russ, Sep 5, 1897; s. Zalman and Deborah (Pessin); in Isr since 1925; att Yeshivot, Lith; tchr, Rabb Sem, Wilno, Lith, 1922; m. Atara Halperin, Jan 30, 1925; c: Uziel, Assaf. Chmn, Rel Council, Haifa, since 1964; fmr: secy, Hapoel Hamizrachi, Haifa; tchr, headmaster, Beit Eliahu, Lith, 1920-25; secy, Rel Council, Haifa, 1942-64. Chmn, Mafdal council, Haifa; fmr: co-found, Hapoel Hamizrachi; dep chmn, J Comty, Minsk, Wilno; mem: Assefat Ha'nivharim; bd dirs, Hapoel Hamizrachi Bank; mgmt, Hadar Hacarmel Comm. Home: 33 Michael St, Haifa, Isr. Office: 16 Arlosoroff St, Haifa, Isr.

MALLIN, Aaron W, US, psychiatrist, neurologist; b. Phila, Pa, Oct 16, 1913; s. William and Mary (Cohen); BA, U of Pa, 1935; MD, Sch of Med, 1939; m. Sylvia Weiss, Jan 26, 1939; c: William, Eugene. Pvt practice, neur, psycht, since 1946; asso, neur, U of Pa Sch of Med since 1946; instr, neur, psycht, Grad Sch of Med, since 1949, mem, neur staff, Hosp of U of Pa, since 1946, mem, neur and psycht staff, Grad Hosp, since 1949; chief: electroencephalography, Phila Gen Hosp, since 1961, mem, neur staff, since 1946; neur and psycht and electroencephalography, Mercy-Douglas Hosp, since 1952; neur and psycht, Amer Oncologic Hosp, since 1954; mem, staff: psycht, Phila Psycht Hosp, since 1946; neur, Albert Einstein Med Cen, N Div, 1949-68; psycht, VA Hosps, 1941-43, att psycht, VA mental hygiene clinic, 1946-52; cons psycht, Lehigh Valley Guidance Clinic, Bethlehem, Pa, 1947-53. Capt, US Army, 1944-46. Chmn, natl comty relations comm, B'rith Sholom, 1957-60; vice-chmn, comm on democratic educ practices, J Comty Relations Council, Gtr Phila, since 1956; first vice-pres, Phila Neur Soc, 1957; mem, bd dirs, J Comty Relations Council, Gtr Phila, 1959-68; f: AMA, 1950; Amer Psycht Assn, 1952; dipl, psycht, Amer Bd Psycht and Neur, 1946; mem: Phila Coll Phys; Phila Co Med Soc; Phila Psycht Assn; Pa State Med Soc; E Assn Electroencephalographers. Contbr, sect on encephalography, Medical Treatment of Mental Disease; contbr to med jours. Hobbies: stamp and coin collecting. Home: 1801 Kennedy Blvd, Philadelphia, Pa. Office: 1900 Spruce St, Philadelphia, Pa.

MALLIN, Samuel D, US, business exec; b. Russ, Sep 3, 1902; s. Emanuel and Anna (Scherr); in US since 1908; att: CCNY, 1920-22; NYU, 1922-24; m. Edyth Solott, 1925. Vice-pres, Albert Frank Guenther Law, Inc, advt agcy, NYC, since 1960; gen mgr, Frank Kiernan and Co, advt agcy, NYC, 1924-60. Past pres, Pal Lodge-Free Sons of Isr; past chmn, bd and educ comm, Cong B'nai Jacob, Bklyn; mem, bd trustees, Conservative Syn of Fifth Ave. Home: 30 E 9 St, New York, NY. Office: 131 Cedar St, New York, NY.

MALOW, Louis, US, physician; b. Chgo, Ill, Apr 24, 1916; s. Sam and Sonia (Swerdlow); BS, U of Ill, 1934, MD, Sch of Med, 1938; m. Beatrice Fine, Oct 14, 1942; c: Barbara, James. Pvt practice, colo-proctologist, since 1950; gen surg, 1945-50. Maj, US Army, 1941-45. F: Amer Coll Surgs; Intl Coll Surgs; Amer Proctologic Soc; Intl Acad Proctology, pres elect; dipl: Amer Bd Surg; Intl Bd Proctology; mem: Amer Med Soc; Ill State Med Soc; Chgo Med Soc. Co-author: Essentials of Clinical Proctology, 3rd rev ed, 1957; contbr to profsl jours. Recipient: Amer Defense Medal; Asiatic-Pacific Ribbon with Bronze Star; Amer Theater Ribbon; EAME Ribbon with 3 stars. Home: 1440 Lake Shore Dr, Chicago, Ill. Offices: 30 N Michigan Ave, Chicago, Ill; 9701 N Kenton, Skokie, Ill.

MALSIN, Raphael B, US, merchant; b. NYC, Feb 3, 1900; BA, Yale U, 1921. Pres, Lane Bryant, Inc, since 1938, with firm since 1929, merchandising dept, advt mgr; fmr, reporter, NY Jour. Vice-pres, Hosp for Jt Diseases, NYC; mem: Phi Beta Kappa; Sigma Xi. Home: Purchase St, Purchase, NY. Office: 1501 Broadway, New York, NY.

MALTZ, Albert, US, author; b. Bklyn, NY, Oct 28, 1908; s. Bernard and Lena (Sherry); BA, Columbia U, 1930; att Yale Sch of Drama, 1930-32; m. Margaret Larkin, Feb 27, 1937 (div); c: Peter, Katherine; m. 2nd, Rosemary Wylde, 1964 (decd); m. 3rd, Esther Engelberg, 1969. Author: novels: The

Underground Stream, 1940; The Cross and the Arrow, 1944; The Journey of Simon McKeever, 1949; A Long Day in a Short Life, 1957; A Tale of One January, 1968; collected short stories, The Way Things Are, 1938; films: This Gun for Hire, 1942; Destination Tokyo, 1943; Pride of the Marines, 1945; The House I Live In, 1945; The Naked City, 1948; screenplay, Two Mules for Sister Sarah, 1970; co-author, plays: Merry Go Round, 1932; Peace on Earth, 1933; Black Pit, 1935; instr, writing, playwriting, Sch of Adult Educ, NYU, 1937-40. Mem: Author's League Amer; Phi Beta Kappa. Recipient: O'Henry Memorial Award, for best Amer short story of 1938; Award, Acad of Motion Picture Arts, for film, The House I Live In, contrib to race tolerance, 1945. Office: c/o Author's League of Amer, 6 E 39 St, New York, NY.

MALTZ, Saul, US, teacher, poet; b. Grodek, Pol, June 15, 1908; s. Morris and Anna (Maltz); grad, J Tchr Sem, 1936; att Folk U; m. Judith Katz, Oct 15, 1936; c: Annette, Toby. Active as: poet, essayist, critic, lectr; contbr to Yiddish mags: Di Zukunft; Der Wecker; Friere Arbeiter Stimme; Goldene Keit, Isr publ; The Jewish Daily Forward. Author: In Shoten Fun Hunger, 1933; Lieder Fun Broit Un Zaltz, 1937; Dos Gezang Fun Job, poems, 1948; ed, Kinder Zeitung, 1945-52; contbr, The Great Dictionary of the Yiddish Language. Exec secy, Cen Sch, Workmen's Circle; fmr: cultural dir, Workmen's Circle Camp Kinder-ring and Circle Lodge; tchr, Heb, Yiddish, Workmen's Circle schs: NYC; Hammond, Ind; Albany, NY; mem, Workmen's Circle Tchrs Alliance; club, Yiddish PEN, bd. Home: 5210 Broadway, New York, NY.

MALTZMAN, Irving M, US, educator; b. NYC, May 9, 1924; s. Israel and Lillian (Mass); BA, NYU, 1946; PhD, State U of Iowa, 1949; m. Diane Seiden, Aug 14, 1949; c: Sara, Kenneth, Ilaine. Prof, psych, UCLA, since 1961, fac mem since 1949. Mem: Amer Psych Assn; AAAS; Phi Beta Kappa; Sigma Xi. Contbr to profsl jours. Home: 11124 Fairbanks Way, Culver City, Cal. Office: U of Cal, Los Angeles, Cal.

MALZ, Edward, US, attorney; b. Vienna, Aus, Aug 31, 1924; s. Leopold and Fanny (Herdan); in US since 1939; BA, Bklyn Coll, 1948; JD, Bklyn Law Sch, 1951; m. Lillian Pearlman, Mar 29, 1947; c: Barbara, Sanford. Pvt practice, NYC, since 1951; admitted to all Fed Courts, 1962, US Supr Court, 1963; small claims court arbitrator since 1965; panel of trial examiners, Bd of Educ, NYC; State of NY Legal Defense Panel for the indigent; Appeals Panel; Fed Indigent Defendents Panel and Appeals Panel. Sgt, US Army, War Crimes Br, 1943-46. Trustee, J Comty Cen, Bklyn, NY; adv comm, Boy Scouts Amer, past asst scoutmaster; fmr: dir, BCAA, exec comm, Lawyers Group; mem: Bklyn Bar Assn; Amer Legion; KP, past chancellor. Ed bd, Bklyn Bar Assn, Barrister; contbr to law jours. Recipient: Past Chancellor Plaque, KP, 1956; Past Pres Plaque, UCA, 1959. Spec interests: legal research, soccer, numismatics. Home: 1139 E 14 St, Brooklyn, NY. Office: 16 Court Street, Brooklyn, NY.

MALZBERG, Benjamin, US, statistician; b. NYC, Dec 2, 1893; s. Nathan and Anna (Elson); BA, CCNY, 1915; MA, Columbia U, 1917, PhD, 1934; m. Rose Hershberg, Aug 25, 1935; c: Judith, Ruth, Amy. Prin research sci, Research Found for Mental Hygiene, Albany, NY, since 1956; asst dir and dir, Bur of Stat, NY State Dept of Mental Hygiene, 1928-56; cons, Natl Inst of Mental Health, since 1949; stat, NY State Dept of Social Wfr, 1923-28; cons, Study of the Negro in Amer, 1939-40; stat, NY State Temp Commn on State Hosp Problems, 1940-44. F: sociol, Amer Field Service, U of Paris, 1919-21; AAAS; NY Acad Sci; Amer Sociol Soc; asso f, NY Acad Med; mem: Amer Stat Assn; Inst Math Stat; Biometric Soc; Population Assn of Amer; Amer Psychopath Assn; Soc Hum Genet; Sigma Xi. Author: Mortality among Patients with Mental Disease, 1934; Hereditary and Environmental Factors in the Causation of Manic-Depressive Psychoses and Dementia Praecox, 1939; Social and Biological Aspects of Mental Disease, 1940; Migration and Mental Disease, 1956; Cohort Studies of Mental Disease in NY State, 1958; Mental Disease Among Jews in NY State, 1959; Mental Health of the Negro, 1962; Ethnic Variations in Mental Disease in NY State, 1966; Mental Health of Jews in NY State, 1963; Mental Disease in NY State, 1910-1960, 1967; Migration in Relation to Mental Disease, 1968; contbr to profsl jours. Home: 33 Bancker St, Albany, NY. Office: NY State Dept of Mental Hygiene, Albany, NY.

MAMMON, Benjamin S, Isr, business exec; b. Samarkand, Russ,

June 23, 1927; s. Aba and Rachel (Sofieva); att: Haskala Coll, Tel Aviv, 1943-47; HS of Law and Econ, Tel Aviv, 1954-57; m. Shoshana Haimoff, Nov 28, 1955; c: Emelie, Odelia. Dir, gen mgr, Peltours Ltd, travel and tours div, since 1964, chief booking clerk, 1948-51, mgr, 1952-64. Capt, IAF. Chmn: Isr Tourist and Travel Agts Assn; Airtours, Isr; pres, Skal Clubs of Isr; mem: Rotary Club; bd, Universal Fed of Travel Agts Assn; fmr, warden, Hakochav, Lodge of Free Masons. Contbr articles on tourism to profsl pubs. Hobbies: chess, music. Home: 257 Dizengoff St, Tel Aviv, Isr. Office: 28 Ahad Ha'am St, Tel Aviv, Isr.

MAMUT, Pesach Sussia, Isr, publisher; b. Swenigorodka, Ukraine, Oct 28, 1906; s. Joseph and Rachel; in Isr since 1934; m. Bela Rosenberg, Sep 30, 1936; c: Dalia Bet-Arie, Rachel Pasternak. Dir, publ and advt office, since 1948, publisher, Who's Who in Isr, 1953-67; active, Hehaluz, JWB movement, Ger, until 1934; repr, corresp: Das Program; Das Organ, Ger; impresario, theaters and ensembles; with USO, Iraq, 1943; council mem, Pal Parents Comm, 1945-48. Hobby: bridge. Home: 18 Haam Hazorfati, Ramat Gan, Isr. Office: POB 2001, Tel Aviv, Isr.

MANA-ZUCCA, US, composer; b. NYC, Dec 25, 1894; s. Samuel and Janet (Deneau) Zuckermanov; studied piano with: Alexander Lambert; Leopold Godowsky; Feruccio Busoni; composition with: Herman Spielter; Max Vogrich; singing with Raimond von zur Muhler; m. Irwin Cassel; c: Marwin. Composer; concert pianist in US and Eur. Published numerous compositions. Hon natl mem: Sigma Alpha Iota; PEN Women's League. Home: 410 NE 17 St, Miami, Fla.

MANCHESTER, Michael Elliott, US, attorney; b. Hollywood, Cal, Sep 30, 1938; s. Francis and Patricia (Patten); AA, Menlo Coll, Menlo Pk, Cal, 1958; BA, Tulane U, New Orleans, 1960; LLB, Tulane U, Sch of Law, 1963. Sr trial atty, Mansell & Giddens, LA, Cal, since 1968; instr, Amer Inst of Banking, 1965-66; asso atty, Harris, Parke, Barnes & McEwen, 1965-67. Capt, Cal Army Natl Guard, Judge Advocate Gen Corps, since 1963. Fmr, vice-pres, Young Reps, Santa Barbara Co; mem: Amer Judicature Soc; Santa Barbara Co Bar Assn; LA Co Bar Assn; Cal State Bar Assn; Phi Alpha Delta, Francis Xavier chap. Home: 212 45 St, Manhattan Beach, Cal. Office: 525 S Virgil Ave, Los Angeles, Cal.

MANCOLL, Morris M, US, physician; b. Russ, Apr 1, 1903; s. Pinkus and Tillie (London); BS, Trinity Coll, Hartford, Conn, 1924; MD, Jefferson Med Coll, Phila, Pa, 1928; postgrad study, U of Pa Grad Sch of Med, 1929-30; m. Edith Mellamed, June 21, 1931; c: Tovia Siegel, Isadora Safner, Harry, William. Pvt practice since 1930; att otolaryngologist: Mt Sinai Hosp, Hartford, since 1930; Hartford Hosp since 1941; Conn Vets Hosp, Rocky Hill, since 1941; Newington Children's Hosp, Conn, since 1943; St Francis Hosp, since 1930. Pres, Hartford Med Soc, 1962; mem: AMA; Amer Acad Ophthal and Otolaryngology; Amer Rhonologic Soc; NE Otolaryngology Soc; Amer Soc Advancement Plastic Surg; Amer Otorhinologic Soc; Conn State Med Soc; Emanuel Syn; club, Tumble Brook Country. Contbr to med jours. Home: 285 N Quaker Lane, W Hartford, Conn. Office: 242 Trumbull St, Hartford, Conn.

MANDEL, Harry Frank, US, business exec; b. NYC, Dec 31, 1902; s. Joseph and Anna (Bauer); m. Gertrude Sachs, June 28, 1924; c: Alice Unger, Myron. Self employed; pres, RICO Theaters Corp, 1961-66. Pres, Cong Beth Sholom, Long Beach, NY; dir: Will Rogers Memorial Hosp; Motion Picture Pioneers; mem: B'nai B'rith; club, Variety. Home: 46 Dalton St, Long Beach, NY.

MANDEL, Howard, US, artist, sculptor; b. Bayside, NY, Feb 24, 1917; s. Edward and Gertrude (Orner); att: Pratt Inst, Bklyn, 1936-38; NY Sculpture Cen, 1938-41; Art Students League, NY, 1950; Atelier Fernand Leger, 1951-52; Atelier Andre L'Hote, 1952-53, both Paris, Fr. One-man shows: Asso Amer Artists, NY, 1949; Ganso Gal, NY, 1951, 53; Phila Art Alliance, 1955; Fairleigh Dickinson Coll, NJ, 1955; Roko Gal, NY, 1957; Rudolph Gal, Coral Gables, Fla, 1956; Selected Artists Gal, NY, 1960; Gloria Luria Gal, Miami, Fla, 1968; exhbs: Smithsonian Inst, 1958-59; 14th Salon Des Jeunes Peintres, Paris, Fr; Metrop Mus of Art; Whitney Mus of Amer Art; Amer Water Color Soc; Pa Acad of Fine Arts; Art Inst of Chgo; Corcoran Gal of Art, Wash, DC; Delgado Mus of Art; Norton Gal, W Palm Beach; High Mus of Art, Atlanta; Natl Acad of Design, NY; Detroit Inst of Arts; represented in perm collections: Butler Inst of Amer Art;

Whitney Mus of Amer Art; Abbott Labs Intl Co; San Antonio Mus; Clearwater Art Mus, Fla, and pvt collections; art dir, designer and graphic artist for prize-winning Parlons Francais educ films. Maj, US Army, WW II. Mem: natl bd dirs, Natl Soc Mural Painters; Woodstock Artists Assn; Artists Equity; Natl Soc Painters in Casein; NY Sculpture Cen. Recipient: Louis Comfort Tiffany f, 1939, 1949; purchase prize, Natl Competition, 1941; Hallmark Intl Award, 1949, 1952, 1955; Fulbright scholarship, 1951-52; Art Dirs Club award, 1955; Du Prix Arts NGM, Paris, 1952; 2 awards, mural competition, Munson-Williams-Proctor Inst, 1958; Bronze Star with oak leaf cluster, WW II. Home and studio: 285 Central Park W, New York, NY.

MANDEL, Hyman R, US, business exec; b. Warsaw, Pol, Jan 8, 1898; s. Solomon and Ida (Romanoff); in US since 1908; att: CCNY, 1923-27; NYU, 1928-29; m. Rose Feinberg, Mar 14, 1926; c: Paul. Chmn, bd, Abbott & Adams, Inc, since 1959, pres, 1945-59. USN, WW I. Dir, Citizens Housing and Planning Council of NY; trustee, treas, Inst Modern Art; mem: comm on profsl bldg standards, fmr, mem, acctnt exchoperating forum, ins and licence comms, Real Estate Bd, NYC; Amer Soc Appraisers, fmr regional gov; NY State Soc Appraisers; Soc Residential Appraisers; Natl Assn Real Estate Bds; Munic Art Soc; Village Art Cen, past pres; Chelsea Citizens Comm; all Day Neighborhood Schs; arbitrator, Amer Arbitration Assn; contrib mem, Mus of Modern Art. Hobbies: art, music, chess. Home: 201 W 16 St, New York, NY. Office: 292 Madison Ave, New York, NY.

MANDEL, Jack N, US, industrialist; b. Aus, July 16, 1911; s. Simon and Rose; m. Lilyan Zoler, Aug 14, 1938; c: Ellen Mandel. Chmn, bd, Premier Ind Corp, since 1952. Chmn, Isr Bond Drive, since 1955; fmr pres, Montefiore Home; vice pres, Heart of Euclid Assn, since 1950; trustee, The Temple, 1959; mem, bd govs, NCCJ, since 1954; club, Beechmont Country. Home: 3160 Courtland Blvd, Shaker Heights, O. Office: 4415 Euclid Ave, Cleveland, O.

MANDEL, Morton L, US, business exec; b. Cleveland, O, Sep 19, 1921; s. Simon and Rose (Nusbaum); att W Res U, 1940-42. m. Barbara Abrams, Feb 27, 1949; c: Amy, Thomas, Stacy. Pres, dir, Premier Ind Corp, sinve 1958, with firm since 1946. Lt US Army, 1942-46. Chmn, UA of Gtr Cleveland; comm on fed endowment fund devl, CJFWF; dir: W Res Holding Co; Cen Natl Bank; pres, Bur for Careers in J Service; adv bd, Gtr Cleveland Safety Council; trustee: Mt Sinai Hosp of Cleveland; Cleveland Comty Chest; J Comty Cen; vice-pres, JWB; visiting comm, Sch Applied Social Sci, Case W Res U; mem: Amer Mgmt Assn; Gtr Cleveland Growth Assn; clubs: Oakwood; Palm Beach Country; Harmonie; Standard; Columbia; City, Cleveland; Cleveland Advt. Home: 17250 Parkland Dr, Shaker Heights, O. Office: 4415 Euclid Ave, Cleveland, O.

MANDEL, Shmuel, Isr, scientist; b. Horn, Aus, Oct 9, 1918; s. David and Miriam (Obernik); in Isr since 1939; MSc, Heb U, 1951; DSc, Technion, 1962; m. Dina Hechter, 1957. Sr lectr, Heb U, since 1966; cons, Tahal Engr Cons, since 1966, head, dept hydrolic resources, 1958-66, on staff since 1952. Brit Army, 1942-46; IDF, 1947-48. Prin contribs: location of 1st successful borehole for groundwater near Jerusalem, 1957; groundwater inves in Isr and abroad; research on groundwater in karstic rocks; use of isotopes in groundwater inves. Vice-chmn, Isr Comm on Intl Hydrolical Decade; chmn, IASH, 1959-65; mem, AAAS. Contbr to sci jours. Home: 8 Yehezkiel, Ramat Gan, Isr. Office: Heb U, Jerusalem, Isr.

MANDELBAUM, Asher, Isr, chemist, educator; b. Cracow, Pol, Dec 27, 1934; s. Abraham and Ada (Kaminski); in Isr since 1948; MSc, Technion, 1960, DSc, 1963; m. Lea Faber, Nov 13, 1958; c: Moshe, Itzhak, Aviva, Ilana. Sr lectr, chem, Technion, Haifa, since 1966; research asso, MIT, 1966-68. Mem: Amer Chem Soc; The Chem Soc, London; Isr Chem Soc. Contbr to profsl jours. Home: 8 Eder St, Haifa, Isr. Office: Technion, Haifa, Isr.

MANDELBAUM, Bernard, US, rabbi, educator; b. NYC, Jan 12, 1922; s. Jacob and Ida (Cohen); BA, Columbia U, 1942; ordained rabbi, MHL, JTSA, 1946, DHL, 1953; m. Judith Webster, 1946; c: Joel, Dasi, David, Debra, Naomi. Pres, JTSA, since 1966, fmr provost, registrar, secy of fac, and dean of students; dir, World Brotherhood Prog; prof, homiletics, asso prof, midrash, JTSA, since 1963; ed, Eternal Light Prog (NBC), 1955-60; admnr, Isr activities, JTSA; rabbi, Bayswater J Cen, Far Rockaway, 1951-53. Commn, NYC Hum Rights

Commn, since 1969; mem: exec comm, Histadrut Ivrit; Amer Acad J Research; Brotherhood-in-Action. Author: Critical Edition of the Pesikta de Rav Kahana, 1962; ed, Assignment in Israel, 1960; Choose Life, 1968; contbr to publs; participant, Intl Conf J Scholarship, Jerusalem, 1960. Home: 709 Reads Lane, Far Rockaway, NY. Office: 3080 Broadway, New York, NY.

MANDELBAUM, David G, US, anthropologist, educator; b. Chgo, Ill, Aug 22, 1911; s. Samuel and Lena (Goodman); BA, Northwestern U, 1932; PhD, Yale U, 1936; m. Ruth Weiss, May 23, 1943; c: Michael, Susan, Jonathan. Prof, anthropology, U of Cal, Berkeley, since 1948, chmn, Cen for S Asian Studies, 1965-68, chmn, dept, 1955-57, fac mem since 1946; research asso, anthropology, Amer Mus of Natural Hist,1936; f, NRC, field work in India, 1937-38, 1958, 1968, 1969-1970; instr, anthropology, U of Minn, 1938-41, asst prof, on leave, 1941-46; dir, educ resources in anthropology project, NSF, 1959-62. US Army, 1943-46, maj, 1945-46. Chmn, soc sci comm, US Natl Commn for UNESCO, 1960; trustee, mem, exec bd, Amer Inst Indian Studies, 1962; mem: Amer Anthropological Assn; Amer Oriental Soc; Royal Anthropological Soc; Sigma Xi. Author: The Plains Cree, 1940; Soldier Groups and Negro Soldiers, 1952; The Teaching of Anthropology, 1962; ed, Selected Writings of Edward Sapir, 1949; fgn ed, Eastern Anthropologist, 1961. Home: 911 Mendocino Ave, Berkeley, Cal. Office: U of Cal, Berkeley, Cal.

MANDELBAUM, Hugo, US, geophysicist; b. Sommerhausen, Ger, Oct 18, 1901; s. Phillip and Rachel (Berlinger); MA, U of Hamburg, 1930, PhD, 1934; m. Sophie Fraenkel, 1931; c: Noa, Uriel, Shoshana, Yehuda, Rachel. Prof, geology, Wayne State U, since 1948; tchr, Talmud Tora HS, Hamburg, Ger, 1930-38; prin, Beth Yehuda Sch, Detroit, Mich. Mem: Amer Geophys Union; Soc of Exploration Geophysicists; AAAS; Assn of Orthodox J Scis; Sigma Xi; Intl Gt Lakes Res Assn. Author: Ora VeSimcha, 1927, Amer version,1945; Ora su Tora, I, 1928, II, 1932; Landscape of Palestine,1938; Shoresh VeAnaf, 1943; Solid Geometry, 1950; contbr to profsl jours. Home: 18460 Griggs, Detroit, Mich. Office: Dept of Geology, Wayne State U, Detroit, Mich.

MANDELBAUM, Maurice H, US, educator; b. Chgo, Ill, Dec 9, 1908; s. Maurice and Ida (Mandel); AB, Dartmouth Coll, 1929, MA, 1932; PhD, Yale U, 1936; m. Gwendolyn Norton, Oct 1, 1932 (div); c: Ann Cramer, John; m. 2nd, Alice Moran, Mar 21, 1949. Andrew W Mellon prof of phil, Johns Hopkins U, since 1966, prof, phil, chmn dept, 1957-66; asst instr, biography and comparative lit, Dartmouth Coll, 1931-32, prof, phil, 1947-57; instr, asst prof, asso prof, phil, Swarthmore Coll, 1934-47; visiting prof: U of Mich, 1950-51; Harvard U, 1957-58. Pres, Amer Phil Assn, 1962, chmn since 1967; mem, Phi Beta Kappa; f, Cen for Advanced Study in Behavioral Scis, 1967-68. Author: The Problem of Historical Knowledge, 1938; The Phenomenology of Moral Experience, 1955; Philosophy, Science and Sense Perception, 1964; co-ed: Philosophic Problems, 1957, 2nd ed, 1967; Phenomenology and Existentialism, 1967. Recipient: Guggenheim F, 1946. Home: 3700 N Charles St, Baltimore, Md. Office: Johns Hopkins U, Baltimore, Md.

MANDELBAUM, Moshe Yaacov, Isr, economist, educator; b. Jerusalem, Mar 3, 1933; s. Yechiel and Debora (Solomon); BA, MA, Heb U, Jerusalem; PhD, Vanderbilt U, Nashville, Tenn; m. Sara Solomon, Aug 26, 1957; c: Yechiel, Samuel, Abigale. Dir, chem and food div, Min of Commerce and Lab, since 1967, fmr econ adv; lectr econ, Bar Ilan U, since 1964. Mem, Union of Social Sci. Author: Role of Development Loans in the Process of Industrial Development in Israel, 1956-62; co-author: Principles of Economics, 1959; contbr to periodicals. Home: 25 Berlin St, Jerusalem, Isr. Office: Argon St, Jerusalem, Isr.

MANDELBROJT, Szolem, Fr, educator; b. Warsaw, Pol, Jan 20, 1899; s. Szliama and Miriam (Rabinowicz); DSc,Sorbonne, Paris, 1923; m. Gladys Grunwald, May 25, 1926; c: Jacques. Prof: Coll de France, since 1938; Rice Inst, since 1946; asst prof, U Lille, Fr, 1928-30; prof, U Clermont-Ferrand, 1930-38; mem, Fr Sci Mission, London, 1944-45. Fr Army,1939-40. Vice-pres, Friends of Heb U; mem: Société Mathématique de Fr; Amer Math Soc; Eur Soc of Culture. Author: Séries de Fourier et Classes Quasianalytiques de Fonctions, 1935; Analytic Functions and Classes of Infinitely Differentiable Functions, 1942; Séries Adhérentes Régularisation des Suites, 1952; Fonctions Entières et Transformées de Fourier, 1967; Séries de Dirichlet, 1969; dir, Monographies Internationales

de Mathématiques Modernes; contbr numerous articles to profsl jours. Recipient: Chevalier de la Légion d'Honneur, 1948; four awards, Fr Acad of Sci, Grand Prix des Sciences Mathématiques et Physiques, 1960; Officier de la Légion d'-Honneur, 1963; Médaille Emile Picard, Fr Acad Scis, 1965. Home: 20 rue Leverrier, Paris 6, Fr. Office: Collège de France, rue des Ecoles, Paris, Fr.

MANDELKER, Benjamin, US, attorney; b. NYC, Sep 11, 1908; s. Philip and Minnie (Unger); AB, Columbia U, 1928; JD, Harvard U Law Sch, 1931; m. Evelyn Ostow, Feb 8, 1942; c: Philip, Ronne. Lab law and lab relations counsel, NYC; practised law with: Edward S Silver, 1931-32; Panken and Levy, 1932-35; Hon Matthew M Levy, 1935-40. Capt, Mil IS, US Army, 1942-46. Pres: LI Region, Union of Orthodox J Congs of Amer, 1949-51, natl vice-pres, 1951-56, chmn, comty activities div, 1950-56, mem, exec bd, 1956-60; fmr pres, Heb Acad of Nassau Co, 1953-56; chmn, Nassau Co Vaad Hakashrut, 1953; found, mem bd, Cen Council of Yeshivas,1951; mem: natl council, JWB, 1960; natl council, Found for JNF, 1961; sponsor, First Intl Cong of J Lawyers and Jurists; referee: NYC Munic Court, 1954-62; NYC Civil Court, since 1962; mem: Amer Bar Assn; Assn of Bar, NYC; NC Co Lawyers Assn; Nassau Co Bar Assn; Phi Beta Kappa. Recipient: Bronze Star Medal, 1945. Home: 160 E 84 St, New York, NY. Office: 50 Broadway, New York, NY.

MANDELKERN, Emanuel, US, business exec, certified public acctnt; b. NYC, May 16, 1922; s. Harry and Esther (Carton); att CCNY, 1939-42; BBA, U of Miami, Fla, 1948; m. Bernice Gertzkis, June 5, 1949; c: Nancy, Peter. Vice-pres, secy: Amicale Inds Inc, NYC, since 1954; Woonsocket Spinning Co, Charlotte, NC, since 1954; Ameliotex, Inc, NYC, since 1960; jr acctnt, Julius W Baer, 1948-49; sr acctnt, SD Liedesdorf & Co, 1949-54. Sgt, US Army, 1942-46. Mem: KP; Jericho J Cen. Hobby: golf. Home: 131 Birchwood Park Dr, Jericho, Long Island, NY. Office: 1040 Ave of Americas, New York, NY.

MANDL, Ines, US, biochemist; b. Vienna, Aus, Apr 19, 1917; d. Ernst and Ida (Bassan) Hochmuth; in US since 1945; MS, PhD, Bklyn Poly Inst, 1945-49; m. Hans Mandl, May 31, 1936 (decd). Asst prof, biochem, Columbia U Coll of Phys and Surgs, since 1949; dir, gyn research labs, Francis Delafield Hosp, since 1959. Prin contribs, research in: connective tissue proteins; collagen; elastin; enzymes; cancer; reproduction; aging. Mem: Amer Chem Soc; Amer Soc Biol Chem; Biochem Soc, Eng; Gerontological Soc; AAAS; NY Acad Sci; Soc Experimental Biol and Med; Amer Assn Cancer Research; Sigma Xi. Contbr to profsl jours, chap in Methods of Enzymology. Home: 166 W 72 St, New York, NY. Office: 630 W 168 St, New York, NY.

MANÉ, Uri, Isr, meteorologist; b. Karlsruhe, Ger, Mar 1, 1913; s. Heinrich and Paula (Gerst); in Isr since 1934; att Erlangen U, Karlsruhe U, 1931-33; London U, 1943; meteorological courses, Isr; m. Jehudith Rothenberg, June 8, 1935; c: Gilah Mashiah, Ednah Breier. Asst dir, climatology and hydrometeorology, Isr Meteorological Service,since 1962;fmr: climatology, head, climatology div, Isr Meteorological Service. IAF, 1948-62. Prin contribs:sup of work in field of climatology, hydrometeorology. Mem: Comm for Hydrometeorology; EC panel of experts for Hydrological Decade; Working Group on Data Processing for Hydrometeorology; regional assn for Eur, all World Meteorological Org; mem: Amer, Royal, Isr Meteorological Socs; Isr Soc for Geodesy and Geophys, vice-chmn, div of meteorology. Contbr to sci jours. Hobbies: music, philately. Home: 57 Bialik St, Ramat Gan, Isr. Office: Bet Dagan, Isr.

MANELA, Zalman Leib, US, field dir; b. Ashlandger, Ger, Oct 12, 1948; s. Simon and Helen; m. Rachel Fuchs. Field dir, W Coast Talmudical Sem; youth dir, Pirchei Agudath Isr of LA; libr, Young Isr of Chgo, 1964. Home: 828½ N Sweetzer, Los Angeles, Cal. Office: 851 N Kings Rd, Los Angeles, Cal.

MANESS, Irving, US, attorney, government official; b. NYC, Jan 6, 1912; s. Abraham and Rachel (Cottler); LLB, St John's U, Bklyn, 1935, LLM, 1936; m. Ethel Snyder, Oct 14, 1948; c: Roberta, Debra. Attorney, Wash,DC, NY; dep admnr, off of procurement and tech assistance, Small Bus Admn, 1961-69; counsel, select comm on small bus,House of Reprs, 1955-61; pvt law practice, NY, 1937; attorney: War Dept, 1946-47; Justice Dept, 1948-49; attorney adv: Off of Rent Stabilization, 1949-54; War Claims Commn-Fgn Claims Settlement

Commn, 1954-55. Capt, Judge Advocate Gen Corps, 1943-46. Dir, Trade Mission to Isr and Cyprus, 1962. Home: 7316 Durbin Terrace, Bethesda, Md.

MANI, M Elyahu, Isr, judge; b. Hevron, Pal, 1907; att: Tchrs Coll, Jerusalem; U Liverpool; m. Ziporah Gamzu; two c. Supr Court Judge; hon consul of Mex in Isr, 1942-48. Home: 18 Radok St, Jerusalem, Isr.

MANISCHEWITZ, Bernard, US, business exec; b. Cincinnati, O, Dec 24, 1913; s. Jacob and Pearl (Quitman); cert, factory mgmt, Cincinnati U, 1940; BS, NYU, 1944; m. Esther Manischewitz, July 19, 1932; c: Elaine Sorki, Ruby Silbey, Edith. Pres, The B Manischewitz Co, Newark, NJ, since 1949, staff mem since 1934. Chmn: Manhattan div, State of Isr Bonds, 1960-61; NJ chap, Young Pres Org, 1960-61; official delg, 7th-11th Intl Mgmt Congs; mem, Chief Exec Forum; club, Men's Span and Port Syn, fmr pres. Home: 14 Lake Short Dr, White Meadow Lake, Rockaway, NJ. Office: 9 Clinton St, Newark, NJ.

MANISCHEWITZ, D Beryl, US, business exec; b. Cincinnati, O, Aug 19, 1914; s. Joseph and Bessie (Sagalowsky); att U of Cincinnati, 1933; m. Lillian Pushin, Feb 13, 1934; c: David, Claire. Chmn, marketing comm, The B Manischewitz Co, chmn, bd, since 1949, with co since 1934. Econ adv comm, NAM; fmr chmn, J Comty Relations Comm of Essex Co; fmr pres, NJ Region, AJCong; fmr vice-pres, Neighborhood Improvement Assn of S Orange; treas, NJ chap, J Hosp at Denver; fmr natl treas, mem, exec comm, Natl Comty Relations Adv Council; central bd mem, World ORT Fed, mem, exec comm, bd mem, Amer ORT Fed, since 1951; mem: NJ Regional Adv Bd, ADL; B'nai B'rith; JDC; AJComm; ZOA; J Educ Comm of Essex Co; Oheb Shalom Cong; dir, J News; sponsor, Good Neighbor Assn, Maplewood and the Oranges; club, Mountain Ridge Country. Recipient: Gold Key, UJA, Essex Co. Office: 9 Clinton St, Newark, NJ.

MANISCHEWITZ, Howard, US, business exec; b. Cincinnati, O, Mar 16, 1911; s. Jacob and Pearl (Quitman); att: U of Cincinnati, 1929-30; NY Inst of Photography, 1931; m. Helen Touff, Aug 18, 1932; c: Jack, Laura. Advt mgr, The B Manischewitz Co, since 1959, staff mem since 1934. Author: By Their Fruits, under pseudonym of Howard Manisch, 1958; contbr to advt jours. Home: 76 Winding Way, W Orange, NJ. Office: 9 Clinton St, Newark, NJ.

MANISCHEWITZ, William B, US, business exec; b. Cincinnati, O, Sep 13, 1915; s. Hirsch and Sarah (Rose); BS, NYU, 1939; m. Esther Ostrovsky, Apr 1, 1951; c: Leora, Ofra, Sharon. Mem, bd dirs, The B Manischewitz Co, since 1943. Chmn: Talpioth Yeshiva U; League for Hebron Yeshiva, Jerusalem; Life Members Assn of Rel Zionists of Amer, mem, natl bd and adv comm; a found, Bar-Ilan U; mem, bd dirs in US, United Aged Home, Jerusalem; mem: NY Comm, Albert Einstein Coll of Med; Natl Council of Young Isr; Union of Orthodox Congs of Amer; Cong B'nai Yeshurun, Teaneck, NJ. Home: 1739 Lilbet Rd, Teaneck, NJ. Office: 9 Clinton St, Newark, NJ.

MANKIEWICZ, Joseph L, US, motion picture dir, producer, writer; b. Wilkes-Barre, Pa, Feb 11, 1909; s. Frank and Johanna (Blumenau); BA, Columbia U, 1928; m. 2nd, Rosa Stradner, July 28, 1939 (decd); c: Eric (by previous m), Christopher, Thomas; m. 3rd, Rosemary Matthews, 1962. Motion picture dir, producer and writer since 1929; asst corresp, Chgo Tribune, Berlin, Ger, 1928-29; writer, subtitles in Eng, Ufa Film Studios, Ger, 1928-29; mem, writing staff, Paramount Pictures, 1929-33; affiliated with: MGM, 1933; Twentieth Century Fox, 1943-51. Maj motion pictures: author: screenplay, Skippy, 1930; Snooky, 1931; Million Dollar Legs, 1932; If I Had a Million, 1932; Alice in Wonderland, 1933; Forsaking All Others, 1934; produc and co-writer, The Keys of the Kingdom, 1944; writer and dir: Dragonwyck, 1945; A Letter to Three Wives, 1949; All About Eve, 1950; People Will Talk, 1951; The Barefoot Contessa, 1954; Guys and Dolls, 1955; The Quiet American, 1957; The Honey Pot, 1967; There Was A Crooked Man, 1969; co-writer and dir: Somewhere in the Night, 1946; No Way Out, 1950; dir: The Late George Apley, 1946; The Ghost and Mrs Muir, 1947; House of Strangers, 1949; Five Fingers, 1951; Julius Caesar, 1952; Suddenly Last Summer, 1959; produc: Fury, 1936; The Gorgeous Hussy, 1936; Three Comrades, 1938; The Philadelphia Story, 1940; Woman of the Year, 1941; dir, Eng version, La Boheme, by Puccini, Metrop Opera Assn, NYC, 1953. Pres, Amer Screen Dirs

Guild, 1950. Recipient: award for directorial achievement, Screen Dirs Guild, 1941; award for best Amer comedy, Screen Writers Guild, 1949; Academy Awards: best screen play and best dir, Acad of Motion Picture Arts and Scis, 1949, 1950. Office: 527 Madison Ave, New York, NY.

MANN, Basil Peter, US, patent lawyer; b. Fitchburg, Mass, May 29, 1925; s. Peter and Victoria (Tsipas); BE, hons, Yale U, 1948; MS, chem engr, Ill Inst Tech, 1951; MGas Tech, 1951; JD, cum laude, Loyola U, Chgo, 1956; m. Nancy Chioles, Aug 30, 1952; c: Georgia, Philip, Vanessa. Admitted to Ill Bar, 1956; partner, Merriam, Marshall, Shapiro and Klose, Chgo, since 1965; patent atty, Standard Oil Co Ind, Chgo, 1956-58; asso, Merriam, Smith and Marshall, Chgo, 1958-60, partner, 1961-65. USNR, 1943-46. Mem: Amer, Chgo Bar Assns; Sigma Xi; Tau Beta Pi; Phi Lambda Upsilon; club, U, Chgo. Home: 6467 Hiawatha Ave, Chicago, Ill.

MANN, Curtis Leo, US, attorney; b. Frankfurt, Ger, Mar 3, 1926; s. Otto and Martha (Löwenthal) Zuckermann; in US since 1940; AB, JD, U Mich, 1947-51; att Wash U, St Louis, Mo, 1946-47; m. Eunice Schneider, Sep 7, 1952; c: Robert, Richard, Susan. Pvt practice, 1952-57, and since 1969; partner, Love, Mann & Gerard, 1967-69. Cpl, US Army, 1944-46. Mem: Mo, Amer, St Louis Co Bar Assns; Amer Judicature Soc; B'nai B'rith; Bar Assn of St Louis; Commercial Law League; fmr: pres: Mo Lodge 22; Interlodge Council, St Louis; mem, bd govs, Dist Grand Lodge 2, all B'nai B'rith. Contbr to law jours. Home: 1 Planters Dr, St Louis, Mo. Office: 7701 Forsyth Blvd, St Louis, Mo.

MANN, Daniel, US, communal worker; b. Cincinnati, O, Feb 14, 1932; s. Jacob and Margit (Klein); att Bet Berl, Tzofit, Isr; Coll of J Studies, Chgo; BA, U of Chgo, Ill, 1952; MA, Columbia U, NYC, 1959; m. Elaine Scherr, Dec 23, 1956; c: David. Coord, adv comm, Amer ZF, since 1969, i/c comm establishing ZF in US; mem ed bd, J Frontier, contbr articles, 1962-69; natl secy, Habonim Lab Zionist Youth, 1955-58; youth, young adult dir, Fed JAs, Gtr Phila, 1959-61; natl exec dir: Poale Zion, League for Lab Isr, both 1961-69. Mem: natl comm, Amer-Isr Public Affairs Comm; bd dirs: Natl Comm for Lab Isr; JNF; United Isr Appeal; secy, N Amer Lab Zionist Conf, Isr, 1968; delg, 27th WZC, Jerusalem, 1968; mem: Natl Conf J Communal Service; New Hyde Park Hum Rights Comm. Hobbies: Amer govt, music. Home: 1751 West End Ave, New Hyde Park, NY. Office: 515 Park Ave, New York, NY.

MANN, David K, S Afr, advocate; b. Calitzdorp, S Afr, Jan 28, 1914; s. Chaim and Bertha (Berelowitz) Manaschewitz; BA, U Cape Town; LLB, U S Afr; m. Rahlyn Woolf, Dec 12, 1948; three c. Advocate, Supr Court of S Afr, since 1948. Capt, S Afr Army, 1941-45. Vice-chmn, S Afr J Bd Deps; mem: exec: United Heb Cong, Johannesburg, since 1952; S Afr Friends of Heb U, since 1967; United Zionist Assn, S Afr, since 1959; Isr comm, S Afr Found, since 1961; grand exec, Heb Order of David, S Afr, since 1951. Home: 8-15 Ave, Lower Houghton, Johannesburg, S Afr. Office: 909 Innes Chambers, Pritchard St, Johannesburg, S Afr.

MANN, Irving, US, business exec; b. Pelcowizna, Pol, Feb 2, 1900; s. Hersh-Leib and Esther (Kielewitz) Manczyk; in US since 1920; att Szkola Handlowa, Warsaw, Pol, 1914-17; Yeshivot, Novo Minsk, Warsaw; m. Ella Abramajtis, Oct 22, 1922; c: Ruth Korngold, Norton. Exec dir, Pacific Coast, B'nai Zion, since 1960; field dir, org, Farband, LZOA, 1957-60. Prin contribs: built W Coast Org, B'nai Zion; provided cultural and social activities for mem; org, found, Yiddish Folk House & Libr, Pelcowizna, Pol, 1915. Pres, org, Ben Gurion Br 333, Farband, LZOA; fmr secy: Kehilah; United Syn Amer; JTS, all Chgo; mem: ZOA; F for J Culture; Cal Hist Soc; exec comm, Amer Zionist Council, LA; fmr: vice-pres, Farband, LZOA, past pres, downtown br, Chgo. Recipient: citation of hon, Farband LZOA, 1954; testimonial, LA Bonds for Isr, 1956; project established honoring Irving and Stella Mann, JNF, B'nai Zion, 1968; Scroll of Hon, Farband LZOA, 1970. Home: 1424 N Poinsettia Pl, Los Angeles, Cal. Office: 5410 Wilshire Blvd, Los Angeles, Cal.

MANN, Kalman Jacob, Isr, physician, hospital admnr; b. Jerusalem, July 5, 1912; s. Itzhak and Haja (Isbi); MD, MRCP, dipl tropical med and health, U Coll, London, 1937; m. Sylvia Games, 1940; c: Ruth, Gideon, Yehonatan, Naomi. Dir, Hadassah Med Org, since 1951, asst med dir, 1949-51; asso prof, chmn dept, org and admn of health care, Heb U-Hadassah Med Sch; mem bd, fac med, Heb U, Jerusalem:

asst med registrar, U Coll Hosp, London, 1942; cons phys, Min of Health, Eng, 1943-46; research phys, Med Research Council, pneumoconiosis unit, 1946-49; appd expert on org of med care, WHO, 1955; mem, supr med and adv councils, Govt of Isr. Mem: Ind Phys Assn, Gt Brit and Ir; Assn Specialists for Diseases of Chest, Eng; Intl Assn Internists; Assn Public Health Phys. Contbr articles on TB, pneumoconiosis and public health. Home: 18 Eliezer Halevi St, Kiryat Moshe, Jerusalem, Isr. Office: Hadassah Med Org, Jerusalem, Isr.

MANN, Lawrence S, US, surgeon; b. Chgo, Ill, Oct 24, 1916; s. Henry and Rose (Bonner); BS, U of Ill, Coll of Med, 1937, MS, 1939, MD, 1940; m. Sylvia Kramer, June 25, 1950; c: Mark, Brian, Patricia. Pvt practice, surg, since 1948; clinical prof, surg, Chgo Med Sch, since 1969; att surg, Mt Sinai Hosp, since 1954; chmn, dept surg, Roosevelt Memorial Hosp, 1962-64; surg, AT and SF RR Hosp Assn, since 1948; f, biochem, U of Ill, 1939-40; intern, Cook Co Hosp, 1940-41; f, surg, U of Ill, Coll of Med, 1941-43; res, surg, VA Hosp, Batavia, NY, 1946-48; instr, surg, Chgo Med Sch, 1948-51; asso, surg, Chgo Med Sch, 1951-56; att surg, Hines VA Hosp, 1954-61; clinical asst prof, surg, Chgo Med Sch, 1956-63, clinical asso prof, 1963-69. Lt-maj, US Army MC, 1943-46. Chmn, safety and health, Boy Scouts of Amer, Austin dist, 1941-43; mem, bd dirs, Cong B'nai Emunah, 1959-60; mem: Public Health and Safety Skokie Caucus Party, since 1959; Skokie Bd Health, 1959-67; Amer Bd Surg; AMA; Amer and Intl Colls of Surgs; Chgo and Ill State Med Soc; Amer Assn RR Surgs; Assn Mil Surgs of US; Ind Med Assn; Sigma Xi; Phi Beta Delta; Phi Delta Epsilon; caucus delg to Evanstown Township schs, 1958-59. Author: Medical Aspects of Music, 1939; Famous Jewish Men of Science, 1940; 16-mm movie, Patent Urachus, 1960; contbr numerous articles to med jours. Recipient: 25 Year Award, Phi Delta Epsilon, 1961; life mem, U of Ill Alumni Assn; Dist Unit Citation; Pres Citation; Bronze Arrowhead; EAME Campaign Medal, 4 battle stars. Hobbies: photography, music. Home: 8934 Samoset Trail, Skokie, Ill. Office: 64 Old Orchard, Skokie, Ill.

MANN, Moshe, Isr, kibbutz official; b. Galicia, Pol, Apr 28, 1907; s. Abraham and Etia (Fleishman) Montag; in Isr since 1926; att Technion, Haifa; m. Cila Rosen (decd); c: Yoram, Yehuda, Nahum; m. 2nd, Ahuva Perle; c: Nadav, Shalev, Tor. Mem secretariat, treas, Kibbutz Merhavia, since 1969; fmr: locksmith; construction worker; kibbutz org, treas, factory mgr; mgr, constructing dept, Kibbutz Arzi; active, econ enterprises, Yezreel valley. Co-found, cdr, Golani Unit, IDF, 1948. Home: Kibbutz Merhavia, Isr.

MANN, Paul, US, composer; b. Vienna, Aus, Sep 3, 1910; s. Oswald and Vallerie (Siebenschein) Wechselmann; in US since 1937; law deg, U of Vienna, 1930; m. Yvonne Lenkway, May 3, 1947; c: Lindy, Larry. Composer, numerous songs, including Hit Parade songs: They Say; Angel in Disguise; Put Your Dreams Away; Looking Glass; Make Love to Me; The Finger of Suspicion. Hobbies: bridge, chess, photography. Home: 194-12 56 Ave, Flushing, NY.

MANNES, Udo Julius, Switz, business exec; b. Zurich, Switz, Mar 8, 1936; s. Fritz and Therese (Lewenstein); dipl ing, ETH, Zurich, 1960; MS, ing mgmt, MIT, US, 1963; m. Miriam Matzner, Aug 28, 1961; c: Daniel, Samuel, Tirzah. Exec dir, Mannes Engr Co, Zurich, since 1965; fmr mgmt cons, Hausermann and Co. Mem: Eur Comm for Sci-Based Ind in Isr; Isr-Switz C of C. Home: 248 Seestr, Zurich, Switz. Office: 54 Gotthard St, Zurich, Switz.

MANNHEIM, Bilha, Isr, sociologist; b. Köln, Ger, May 17, 1929; d. Samuel and Hudie (Stern) Friedman; in Isr since 1936; BSc, Kansas State Coll, 1952; MA, PhD, U of Ill, Urbana, 1957; m. Chaim Mannheim, Feb 1, 1951; c: Michal, Adie, Dallit. Sr lectr, sociol, Technion, Haifa, since 1965, research asso, 1958-1960, lectr, 1960-65. Sgt, IDF, 1948-49. Mem: cen comm, Isr Sociol Soc; Amer Sociol Assn; Phi Kappa Phi, U of Ill. Co-author: The Human Factor at Work, 1965; contbr to profsl jours. Spec interest: art. Home: 24a Hanassi Ave, Haifa, Isr. Office: Technion, Haifa, Isr.

MANNHEIM, Chaim Heinz, Isr, educator; b. Stettin, Ger, Oct 22, 1927; s. Georg and Aneliese Herlitz; in Isr since 1938; att Technion, Haifa, 1949-50; Kan State Coll, 1950-52; BSc, MSc, PhD, U of Ill, 1952-57; m. Bilha Friedman, Feb 1, 1951; c: Michal, Adie, Dallit. Asso prof, Technion, head, food instr adv sta, since 1966; research asst, U of Ill, 1953-57;

produc mgr, Adir Co, Tel Aviv, 1957-59; research engr, US Dept of Agric, 1965-66. Lt, IDF, 1947-50. Prin contribs: setting up food sci research and teaching in Isr; applied research in food sci and tech; adv to Isr food ind. Mem: Isr Assn Food and Nutrition Scis; Inst Food Tech; Sigma Tau; Sigma Xi; Gamma Sigma Delta. Contbr to sci jours. Recipient: scholarship, Heb Tech Inst, NY, 1955. Home: 24A Hanassi Ave, Haifa, Isr. Office: Technion, Haifa, Isr.

MANNHEIMER, Robert E, US, attorney; b. Des Moines, Ia, Mar 15, 1919; s. Eugene and Irma (Shloss); AB, Grinnell Coll, 1939; JD, U of Ia Law Sch, 1942; m. Joan Eisenberg, June 22, 1947; c: David, Steven, Robert. Partner, Dickinson, Throckmorton, Parker, Mannheimer & Raife, since 1952; pvt practice, since 1946. Pvt, US Army, 1942-46. Mem: Polk Co, Ia, Amer Bar Assns; Jr C of C, past vice-pres, bd dirs; Adult Educ Council; Des Moines Hearing Soc; Comty Drama Assn; Ia Children's and Family Services; United Comty Services, fmr bd; Cong B'nai Jeshurun, Des Moines, past pres; comty relations commn, JWF, past pres, past bd dirs; NCCJ, bd; Des Moines Civil Service Commn; Polk Co Comty Action Council, 1st pres; Alumni Assn, Grinnell Coll, Ia, past mem, adv council, bd dirs; clubs: Des Moines; Wakonda; Pow Wow. Recipient: Alumni Award, Alumni Assn, Grinnell Coll, Ia, 1969. Hobbies: music, travel, reading, interracial activities. Home: 622 Glenview Drive, Des Moines, Ia. Office: 500 Fleming Bldg, Des Moines, Ia.

MANNING, Leon A, NZ, business exec; b. Wellington, NZ, Dec 13, 1910; s. Max and Harriet (Marks); dipl, acctnt, Hemmingway Sch of Accountancy, NZ, 1939; m. Margaret Olive, May 30, 1938; c: Geoffrey, Judith. Mgn dir: Kelvin Mfg Co, Ltd; Kelvin Ind Ltd, both since 1946; chmn, bd dirs, Arthur Lowe, Auckland; dir, Asso Motels of NZ; fmr: tchr: Geelong Heb Sch, 1929-31; Dunedin Heb Sch, 1931-39; acctnt: London Mantle Mfr Co, 1931-37; Austin Motors (Dunedin), 1937-40. NZ Air Force. JP; chmn: J Day Sch Comm, since 1962; Choral Soc, since 1961; treas, Friends of Heb U, since 1952, all Auckland; mem: exec, dist grand lodge 21 of Austr and NZ; J Assn, past pres; J Aid Soc; Metrop Council; Regional Auth Comm; Suburban Local Bodies Assn, all Auckland; Maori Tribal Comm Adv Bd; Sr Citizens Bd; Advancement Assn, al Onehunga; One Tree Hill Domain Bd; Sir William Jordan Memorial Trust Bd; Masons; Austr, NZ Socs of Acctnts; Onehunga Jaycee; club, Onehunga Rotary; fmr: pres, Auckland lodge, B'nai B'rith; mayor, Borough of Onehunga, Auckland; dep chmn, Auckland Regional Auth; chmn, Kadima Kindergarten; pres, Onehunga Bus Assn. Asst ed, Hashofar, natl monthly J publ, since 1959. Hobbies: music, drama, athletics. Home: 80 Campbell Rd, One Tree Hill, Auckland, NZ. Office: 136A Queen St, Onehunga, Auckland, NZ.

MANO, Abraham, Isr, administrator; b. Thessaloniki, Greece, Mar 11, 1926; s. Michael and Fakima (Malalel); in Isr since 1934; att: Sem Madrichim, 1944-46; Peilei Histadruth, 1954-55, both Tel Aviv; m. Aliza Almoslinos, May 17, 1949; c: Michael, Ofira, Dorit. Sect mgr, personnel dept, Solel Boneh Ltd, since 1960. Adj, Haganah, 1943-47; sgt, IDF, 1947-50. Org: Yad Michael Fund, in memory of Michael Mano; Yeshivat Saloniki, for rabbis and youth; org and chmn: Greek Immigrants Assn, Haifa; Misgav LaDach Fund for Mutual Assistance; Hechal Haim Habib Syn and comty cen, for Sephardic comty, Haifa; dep chmn, Isr Greek Immigrants Assn; fmr: youth leader, org, Hanoar Haoved Movement, Haifa; mgr, Youth Lab Org. Hobbies: photography, philately. Home: 22 Hazayit St, Haifa, Isr. Office: Solel Boneh Ltd, Haifa, Isr.

MANOR, Amos, Isr, administrator; b. Moravska-Ostrava, Czech, Aug 14, 1907; s. Grete Kornbluh; in Isr since 1945; DJur, DRerPol, Vienna, Prague Us, LSE, London; m. Yehudith Rosenblum, Oct 10, 1954. Secy gen, Rehovot Conf, since 1959; mem, Kibbutz Givath Hayim, 1945-52; spec services dept, PM off, 1952; mem, Isr Mission to Köln, 1953-55. IDF, War of Independence. Home: 22 Hamea Veehad St, Ramat Chen, Isr. Office: POB 150, Rehovot, Isr.

MANOR, Aryeh, Isr, banker; b. Vienna, Aus, Oct 23, 1912; s. Alfred and Grete (Kornbluh) Menzel; in Isr since 1935; BSc, Tech Hochschule, Vienna, 1931; MSc, Berlin, 1934; m. Marianne Czempin, Apr, 1935 (decd); c: Michal, Tamar. Asst gen mgr, Bank Leumi LeIsrael, since 1964; head, Isr Defense Supply Mission, NY, 1949-50; dir, Isr Supply Mission, NY, 1951-58; min, econ affairs, Isr Emb, Wash, DC, 1958-64. Home: 7 Hakongress St, Herzliya, Isr. Office: 24-28 Yehuda Halevy St, Tel Aviv, Isr.

MANOR, Gideon, Isr, agricultural engr; b. Prague, Czech, Apr 18, 1902; s. Arthur and Sophie (Engel) Mendel; in Isr since 1922; m. Rachel Katzenstein, 1928; m. 2nd, Shlomith Saeger, 1936; c: Ayeleth, Ayah, Osnath, Zippora. Ret since 1968;fmr: mgr: Org of Field-Crop Growers, 1945-50; Dept of Agric Machinery, Min of Agric, 1950-65, asst mgr, Inst for Research in Agric, 1965-68. Home: Kibbutz Mishmar Haemek, Isr.

MANOR, Rachel, Isr, social worker; b. Berlin, Ger, Aug 13, 1908; d. Louis and Feodora (Loevinson) Katzenstein; in Isr since 1934; BA, Pedg Acad, Frankfurt, 1930; MSW, NY Sch Social Work, 1961; att Psychan Inst, Jerusalem, 1945-47; m. Gideon Manor, Jan 21, 1936. Head Kibbutz Child Guidance Clinic, since 1965; tchr, Kibbutz Tchrs Coll, since 1957; tchr, prin, sch, Kibbutz Mishmar Haemek, 1940-56; sup tchr, Bd of Educ of Kibbutz Arzi, 1950-53. Mem: educ comm, Kibbutz Mishmar Haemek; bd of educ, Kibbutz Arzi; Isr Assn Social Workers; Isr Assn for Group Therapy. Contbr of articles on educ, spec educ therapy, social psych to profsl jours. Home: Kibbutz Mishmar Haemek, Isr. Office: Kibbutz Child Guidance Clinic Oranim, Kiryath Tivon, Isr.

MANSFELD, Alfred, Isr, architect, educator; b. Leningrad, Russ, Mar 2, 1912; s. Yehuda and Sophia (Shapiro); in Isr since 1935; att Tech Coll, Berlin, 1931-33; dipl, architect, Ecole Spec d'Architecture, Paris, 1935; m. Bella Reinin, 1946; c: Michael, Yoel. Pvt practice since 1935; prof, architecture, Technion, since 1949, fmr head, dept architecture. Mem: Assn Engrs and Architects in Isr; Intl Architects Union. Contbr to profsl publs in Isr and abroad. Recipient: 1st prize: competition, Isr Natl Mus, Jerusalem, 1959; Lod Natl Airport; 2nd prize, Dublin U Libr, 1960; Isr Prize for Architecture, 1966. Hobby: photography. Home: 2A Hazvi Ave, Haifa, Isr. Office: 5 Keller St, Haifa, Isr.

MANSHEL, Milton M, US, business exec; b. Providence, RI, Mar 19, 1901; s. Charles and Ann (Bliss); BS, MIT, 1922; m. Ruth Berkowitz (decd); m. 2nd, Ruth Zirn, Nov 1, 1951; c: Milton, Anita Sloane, Lee, Susan Jackman. Pres, Intl Ticket Co, since 1960, staff mem since 1923; asst to chief engr, Amer Writing Paper Co, 1922-23. Chmn, Personnel Practices Comm, Union of Amer Heb Congs, since 1968, chmn, publs comm, 1958-68, mem, exec comm and bd, since 1955; pres: NJ Council, Union of Amer Heb Congs, 1956-58; J Vocational Service, Newark, NJ, 1942-44; Cong B'nai Jeshurun, Newark, 1950-55; vice-pres, J Child Care Assn, Essex Co, NJ, 1940-50; mem: Tech Assn Paper and Publ Ind; Zeta Beta Tau. Home: 200 E 57 St, New York, NY. Office: 50 Grafton Ave, Newark, NJ.

MANSON, Harold P, US, public affairs exec, university prog admnr, journalist, editor; b. NYC, Oct 23, 1918; s. Samuel and Rebecca (Prosky); att Yeshiva U, grad, Tchrs Inst, 1937; NYU, 1939; m. 2nd, Natanya Neumann, July 31, 1957; c: David, Jonathan. Dir: academic affairs, Amer Frinds of Heb U, since 1966; info, Amer Zionist Emergency Council, 1943-48; ME corresp, Overseas News Agcy, 1948; dir: PR, JA for Pal, 1949; Commn on Isr and ME, ZOA, 1950-53; exec vice-chmn, head, ZOA public info, 1953-59; dir, PR, Amer Friends Heb U, 1959-66. Author: Historical Sections of Vision and Victory, 1949; Abba Hillel Silber—An Appreciation, In the Time of Harvest, 1963; contbr to: American People's Ency; Overseas News Agcy Features; periodicals in US and abroad on problems of Isr and ME; found, ed, Zionist Quarterly, 1951-52. Club, Overseas Press of Amer. Home: 320 Central Park W, New York, NY. Office: 11 E 69 St, New York, NY.

MANSON, Julius J, US, public official; b. NYC, June 27, 1907; s. Tobias and Mollie (Libenson); BA, Columbia U, 1931, MA, 1932, PhD, 1955; LLB, Bklyn Law Sch, 1936; m. Elizabeth Butzner, Mar, 1947; c: Carol, David, Paul. Prof, mgmt, CUNY, since 1969; cons to Govt of Turkey, 1966-68; exec dir, dist dir, and mediator, NY State Bd of Mediation, 1942-69; visiting prof, New Sch for Soc Research, 1957-65; lectr, econ, Columbia U, 1950-65; head law clerk and sr inves, NY State Div of Minimum Wage, 1940-42; examiner, NY State Lab Relations Bd, 1940-42. US Army, 1943-46. Pres, Barger Coop Soc, Inc, 1938; secy, Natl Comm for Rural Schs, since 1950; mem: bd dirs, Heb Free Loan Soc, 1969; natl bd, League for Ind Democracy. Contbr articles on lab mediation, arbitration to profsl jours. Home: 14 Stuyvesant Oval, New York, NY. Office: Bd of Higher Educ, 535 E 80 St, New York, NY.

MANSOOR, Menahem, US, educator; b. Port Said, Egypt, Aug 4, 1911; s. Asher and Yonah; in US since 1954; BA, hons, Trinity Coll, Dublin, Ir, 1941, MA, 1942, PhD, 1944; m. Claire Kramer, Nov 29, 1951; c: Yardena, Daniel. Prof, chmn dept, Heb and Semitic studies, U of Wis, since 1955; fmr: sr educ off, Jerusalem, 1946-48; asst press attaché, Brit Fgn Service, 1949-54; mem fac, Johns Hopkins U, 1954-55. Mem: Soc Bible Lit; Amer Oriental Soc; Chgo Soc Bibl Research; Amer J Hist Soc. Author: The Thanksgiving Hymns, 1960; English-Arabic Dictionary of Political, Diplomatic and Conference Terms, 1960; Guide to the Dead Sea Scrolls, 1964; Advanced Readers In Modern Hebrew Literature, 2 vols, 1969; Duties of the Heart, 1969; contbr, Jewish Sects During the Second Commonwealth, Ency Britannica, 1963. Recipient: f: Fulbright, 1954; research, Harvard, 1962; Kohut res award, 1955. Spec interests: Dead Sea scrolls; Judeo-Arabic medieval liturgy; Semitic lexicography. Home: 1225 Sweetbriar Rd, Madison, Wis. Office: 1348 Van Hise Hall, U Wis, Madison, Wis.

MANTEL, Hugo, Isr, educator; b. Vienna, Aus, Mar 3, 1908; s. Herman and Irene (Friedman); in Isr since 1959; BA, Yeshiva U, 1932; ordained rabbi, Rabbi Isaac Elchanan Theol Sem, 1934; MA, Harvard U, 1943, PhD, 1952; m. Edith Maybush, Aug 18, 1940; c: Jonathan. Asso prof, Bar Ilan U, since 1969, sr lectr, J hist, 1960-69; visiting sr lectr, Haifa Coll, since 1964; fmr rabbi: Dubuque, Ia, 1934-35; Braddock, Pa, 1936-38; J Cen, Huntington, LI, 1938-39; exec dir, NE Council of Young Isr, 1939-40; rabbi: Temple Ashkenaz, Cambridge, Mass, 1940-50; Cong Sons of Zion, Holyoke, Mass, 1951-58; prof, J hist: Acad for Higher J Learning; NYU, 1958-60; research asso, Harvard U, 1967-68. US Army, 1944-46. Mem: Soc for Bibl Lit and Exegesis; Amer Acad J Research; Natl Assn Profs of Heb; Amer J Hist Soc; RA; ZOA; Mil Chaplains Assn; Assn J Chaplains of Armed Forces; Sons of Zion; Masons; fmr: pres, Council of Hapoel Hamizrachi of Gtr Boston; mem, admn council, NE region, AJCong. Author: Why Religion?; Why Judaism? both 1945-46; Removal of the Sanhedrin from Yabneh to Usha, 1957; Studies in the History of the Sanhedrin, 1969; co-author: Wort und Zeit, 2 vols, 1938; Mantel's Folksredner, 1948; co-author: trans Bible from Heb to Japanese, 1946; contbr to Harvard Theol Review; J Quarterly Review; Ency Judaica; Tarbiz, Ency of Educ, Jerusalem. Home and office: Faculty House, Bar Ilan U, Ramat Gan, Isr.

MANTELL, Herman P, US, attorney; b. NYC, July 17, 1904; s. Jacob and Annie (Halpern); BS, CCNY, 1924; JD, NY Law Sch, 1927; MA, NYU, 1941, PhD, 1943; DHumL, Philathea Coll, London, Ont, Can, 1966; hon LLD, Natl Police Acad, 1968; m. Pauline Schwartz, June 28, 1941. Asst dir, finance, NYC, since 1963, spec dep comptroller, NYC, 1962; prin, on leave, William T Sherman Sch, NYC sch system, since 1924; spec lectr, Sch of Educ, NYU, since 1945; pvt law practice since 1928. Pres: J Tchrs Assn of NYC, 1950-53, 1961-63, since 1967; citizens Forum of City and State of NY, Inc, 1956-57; tchrs council, Bd Educ, NYC, 1953; Council of J Orgs in Civil Service, Inc, since 1945; Beacon Civic League, since 1935; Interfaith Movement, Inc; vice-chancellor, Philathea Coll, London, Ont, since 1967; chmn, home, sch, comty sect, NY Soc for Experimental Study of Educ, 1945-60; hon secy, Wall St Syn; exec dir, Council of Civic Leagues of NYC, since 1939; dir: Home of Sons and Daughters of Isr, 1946; Intl Syn, Kennedy Airport, since 1963; mem, bd: W Side Sch Comty Cens; planning bd, W Side Comty; W Side C of C; coord comm, Tchrs Rel Orgs, NYC; mem: Stampa Internazionale; bd govs, Found for Child Mental Wfr, Inc; J Educ Survey Comm; ZOA; Span-Port Syn; Phi Delta Kappa; Alpha Tau Alpha; Natl Educ Assn; Natl Soc Study of Educ; Masons; Shriners; counsel, Fed of Negro Orgs in Civil Service, Inc; club: Optimists, NY. Ed, The Light, Wall St Syn monthly, since 1940; contbr to educ jours. Recipient: Golden Ayen award, Heb Culture Council, 1951; hon award, Histadrut, 1958; Amer Legion awards, 1959, 60; award, Boy Scouts and Girl Scouts of Amer, 1961; statuette, Interfaith Movement, 1961; man-of-the-year award, Council of J Orgs in Civil Service, Inc, 1962; honor awards: J Tchrs Assn; Knight of Malta, 1966; Knights of Malta, 1967; Isr Publishing Inst, 1968. Home: 246 West End Ave, New York, NY. Office: W 42 St, New York, NY.

MANY, Abraham, Isr, scientist; b. Jerusalem, Dec 16, 1922; s. Moshe and Lela (Ashkenazi); MSc, Heb U, Jerusalem, 1945, PhD, 1950; m. Miriam Goldenberg, Mar 4, 1947; c: Lela, Talia. Prof, physics, Heb U, since 1959, head, semiconductor div, physics dept, since 1956; fmr: research work:

MIT, US, 1949; Reading U, Eng, 1952-53; research cons, on leave from Heb U: Gen Telephone and Elec, Bayside, NY, 1957-58; RCA Labs, Princeton, NJ, 1962-63. IDF, 1947-48. Mem: Phys Soc Isr; Amer Phys Soc; MIT Alumni Assn. Contbr sci publs to books and jours. Home: 36 Palmach St, Jerusalem, Isr. Office: Hebrew U, Jerusalem, Isr.

MAOR, Zvi Shlomo, Isr, pharmacist; b. Lodz, Pol, Apr 21, 1933; s. Itzchak and Rachel (Lorenter) Mauer; in Isr since 1935; MPh, Heb U, Jerusalem, 1959; m. Rivka Merenstein, Nov 22, 1960; c: Moshe, Iris, Jehuda. Chief pharm, Ikapharm, since 1967, produc mgr, 1959-67, dep chief pharm, 1966-67. Staff sgt, MC, IDF, 1952-54. Prin contrib: galenical research and mgmt of produc. Author: Method of Separation of Ana-basine from Plants; Long Acting Oral Preparations, 1962; Excipients for Preparation of Tablets-Lubricating Agents, 1963; Excipients for Preparation of Tablets-Disintegration Agents, 1963; The Enteric Coating Process, 1963; The Use of Colors in Pharmaceutical Preparations, 1965; contbr to profsl jours. Home: 11 Chen St, Petah Tikvah, Isr. Office: 31 Jabotinsky St, Ramat Gan, Isr.

MAOZ, Benjamin, Isr, psychiatrist; b. Kassel, Ger, Apr 31, 1929; s. Hans and Anna (Rosenberg) Mosbacher; in Isr since 1937; MD, Munic U, Amsterdam, Holland, 1959; m. Elly Drukker, June 2, 1934; c: Michal, Ofra, Hagar. Head, out-patient clinic, Geha Hosp, Petah Tikvah, since 1969; lectr, Med Sch, Tel Aviv U, since 1969; gen practitioner, kibbutz, 1959-64. Contbr to profsl jours. Recipient: Histadrut Prize, 1965. Home: 93 Reuben Katz St, Petah Tikvah, Isr. Office: Geha Hosp, Petah Tikvah, Isr.

MARANS, Moissaye, US, sculptor; b. Kisinau, Rum, Oct 11, 1902; s. Solomon and Fania (Balkarey); in US since 1924; att: Tech Inst of Bucharest, 1923; U of Jassy, 1924, both Rum; Cooper Union Inst, 1925-27; Natl Acad Design, 1927, both NYC; Pa Acad Fine Arts, 1928; Cincinnati Acad Fine Arts, 1929-31; Beaux Arts Inst of Design, NY, 1932-33; NYU, 1945-46; m. Lillian Cohen, Sep 1, 1940. Sculptor; executed public commns: Bklyn Botanical Gardens; NY World's Fair; W Baden Coll, Ind; Rodef Shalom Cong, Pittsburgh, Pa; Temple Emanu El, Houston, Tex; First Presbyterian Church, Beloit, Wis; The Comty Church, NY; Public Libr, Linden, NJ; Har Zion Temple, Phila, Pa; San Jose Mus, Cal; Norfolk Mus of Fine Arts, Va; Church Cen, UN Plaza, NY; US AEC, Wash, DC; Smithsonian Inst, Mus of Natural Hist, Wash, DC; works exhb: Whitney Mus; LA Mus; Pa Mus of Art; Bklyn Mus; Mint Mus, Charlotte, NC; J Mus, NY; Cleveland Mus of Fine Arts; Detroit Inst Art; Natl Acad Design; Pa Acad Fine Arts; Natl Sculpture Soc; Architectural League of NY; Corcoran Gals; Amer Fed Arts; Sculpture Cen, NY; Carnegie Found for Intl Peace; Albright Gals, Buffalo, NY; Audubon Artists, Natl Arts Club, NY; Us: St Louis, Mo; Minn; St Thomas, Houston, Tex; lectr, Bklyn Coll, since 1955. F, Natl Sculpture Soc; vice-pres, Architectural League of NY, 1954-55; mem: Natl Acad Design; Allied Artists of Amer; Audubon Artists, Inc. Ed bd, Natl Sculpture Review. Recipient: 1st prize, Stevenson competition, Pa Acad of Fine Arts, 1928; hon mention, PO competition, Forest Hills, NY, 1938; hon mention, NY World's Fair, 1939; 2nd award, PO competition, York, Pa, 1941; award, Amer Fed of Arts, 1951; award, Architectural League of NY, 1953; hon mention, Natl Sculpture Soc, 1953, awards, 1963, 1965; Avery awards, Architectural League of NY, 1957, 1958; awards, Knickerbocker Artists, 1959, 1968; hon mentions, Natl Arts Club, 1965, 1968; hon mention, Audubon Artists, 1966; awards, Allied Artists of Amer, 1967, 1968; Daniel Chester French Medal, Natl Acad of Design, 1967. Home: 200 Clinton St, Brooklyn, NY. Studio: 127 Livingston St, Brooklyn, NY.

MARANTZ, Irving, US, artist; b. Elizabeth, NJ, Mar 22, 1912; s. Harry and Jennie (Silberman); grad, Newark Sch of Fine and Applied Arts, 1933; att Art Students League, 1933-34; studied with George Grosz; studied Chinese Art in China, 1937-40; m. Evelyn Hurwitz, June, 1937; c: Mady, Michael. Instr: Ballard Sch, NY, 1950-62; Provincetown Sch of Painting, 1948-62; Bayonne J Comty Cen, NJ, 1950-63; Newark Sch Fine and Ind Arts; CCNY; artist in res: U of Ia, 1964-65; U of Ga, 1966-67; NYU, 1967-69; dir, Art Tchrs Training Inst, Fed Arts Project. One-man exhbs: Hong Kong Working Artists Guild, 1939; Pepsi-Cola Opportunity Gal, 1948; Shore Studios, 1950; DeNagy Gal, 1959; Dartmouth Coll, 1960; Babcock Gal, 1952, 1955, 1957, 1958, 1962, 1964; Galeria Schneider, Rome, It; Mansfield State U; Ga Inst of Tech; U of Ga; exhibited at: Pa Acad Fine Arts; Corcoran

Art Gal; Audubon Artists Assn; Newark Mus; NYU; U of Ill; Whitney Mus; Carnegie Inst; Va Mus; Natl Acad Art; Toledo Mus; Butler Art Inst; Dayton Art Inst; Amer Fed of Arts; Panorama No 2 exhb; USIA Far E Exhb; Amer Artists Cong Print Show; Natl Acad of Design; perm collection: Butler Inst Amer Art; Bayonne J Comty Cen; Living Arts Found; Dartmouth Coll; Oberlin Coll; NY Public Libr; Lakeland Coll, Fla; Ein Harod Mus; Tel Aviv Mus, both Isr; Norfolk Mus; U of Ia; Wis State U; Holbrook Mus, Mansfield State Coll; Loeb Cen, NYU; Stout State U; outdoor sculpture commn, Bayonne J Comty Cen, 1968. Portfolio of prints: Series on Man, 1961. Mem: Provincetown Art Assn. Recipient: 100 prints of the year award, Amer Artists Cong, 1938; Pepsi-Cola award, 1947; 3rd prize, Cape Cod Art Assn, 1953. Home and studio: 198 Sixth Ave, New York, NY.

MARATECK, Sanford, US, attorney; b. Shenandoah, Pa, Aug 12, 1920; s. Abraham and Mary (Peril); BA, Dickinson Coll, 1941, LLB, 1943; m. Mildred Oberson, June 30, 1946; c: Arthur, Karen, David. Pvt practice since 1946; first asst dist atty, Northumberland Co, 1957-63. US Army, 1943-46. Pres: B'nai B'rith, 1950-51, 1956-57; B'nai Israel Syn, 1963-65; cdr: Amer Legion Post, 1948-50, 1961-63, 17th dist, Dept of Pa, 1961-63; mem, Phi Epsilon Pi. Home: 30 W Lincoln St, Shamokin, Pa. Office: Natl Dime Bank Bldg, Shamokin, Pa.

MARBACH, Sonia, Isr, educational admnr; b. Pol, Oct 9, 1908; d. Markus and Berta (Parnas) Okon; in Isr since 1933; m; c: Margalith Naor, Batia Itiel. Chief insp, dir, spec educ dept, Min of Educ & Culture; fmr: tchr, prin, Tel Aviv. Mem adv council: ILAN; MICHA; AKIM. Contbr on spec educ to profsl publs. Recipient: UNESCO F, 1956-57. Spec interests: phil, tourism. Home: 31 Sd Haim Hatzurfati, Ramat Gan, Isr. Office: Min of Educ and Culture, Jerusalem, Isr.

MARCH, Abraham W, US, physician, radiologist; b. E Chgo, Ind, Dec 11, 1909; s. Wolf and Buna (Herschkovitz) Marcovich; BS, U of Chgo, 1932, MC, 1936, MD, 1937; m. Jacqueline Front, Oct 7, 1947; c: Wayne, Gail. In pvt practice, radiology, Dayton, O, since 1946; asst radiologist, U of Chgo, 1939-41, asst prof, radiology, 1943-44; cons, radiology, Kellogg Found, 1941-43. Dipl, Amer Bd Radiology, 1941; mem: AMA; Amer Coll Radiology; Amer Roentgen Ray Soc; Radiological Soc of N Amer; O Radiological Soc; O State and Montgomery Co Med Socs. Contbr to profsl jours. Home: 2517 Rugby Rd, Dayton, O. Office: 440 Fidelity Bldg, Dayton, O.

MARCHANT, Michael, Eng, communal leader; b. London, Mar 12, 1892; s. Samuel and Eve (Hart). Secy, World Sephardi Fed; hon secy, Friends of Sephardi and Other J Refs; past secy: Span and Port Cong and Allied Instns, Bevis Marks, Eng; Sir Moses Montefiore Endowment, Ramsgate; Sir Moses Montefiore Endowment, Ramsgate: chmn, Stamford Hill JPA. Mem, B'nai B'rith. Hobbies: reading, golf. Home: 28 Stamford Hill Mansions, London N16, Eng. Office: New House, 67/8 Hatton Garden, London EC1, Eng.

MARCOVE, Maurice E, US, physician, educator; b. London, Eng, Mar 11, 1903; s. Peter and Katie (Werner); in US since 1906; MD, U of Colo, 1926; m. Gertrude Rosenberg, Nov 30, 1931; c: Gerald, Stanley, Alan, Phyllis. Asso prof, ophthal, U of Colo Med Sch, since 1940; pvt practice, Denver, since 1929; mem staff: Gen Rose Hosp, since 1949, past chmn, surg comm; St Joseph's Hosp, 1929; Colo Gen Hosp, 1929. Mem: Denver Co, State Med Socs; Colo Ophthal Soc; Amer Coll Surgs; Acad Ophthal; Ex-residencia Soc of Wills Hosp. Home: 955 Eudora St, Denver, Colo. Office: 526 Republic Bldg, Denver, Colo.

MARCUS, Alan David, US, attorney; b. NYC, July 23, 1905; s. Samuel and Amanda (Rothschild); att Brown U, Providence, RI, 1923-25; LLB, Fordham U, Sch of Law, 1928; m. Grace Rosenberg, Oct 27, 1942. Partner: Sulzberger, Wels & Marcus, since 1967; Moss, Wels & Marcus, 1956-67. Lt, US Army, 1942-44. Trustee, Beth Abraham Hosp; mem: Cemetery Comm, Cong Emanu-El; Amer, NY State Bar Assns; Bar Assn, NYC; clubs: Harmonie; Brown U, both NYC. Hobbies: painting, fishing. Home: 201 E 79 St, New York, NY. Office: 18 E 48 St, New York, NY.

MARCUS, Claude-Gérard, Fr, legislator, art expert; b. Paris, Aug 24, 1933; law deg, U Paris; dipl: Istitut d'Etudes Politiques, Paris; Ecole du Louvre. Dep, Natl Assembly; repr of 10th Arrondissement, Council of Paris, since 1968; elected to: Munic Council of Paris; Gen Council of Seine, both 1965;

mem, political commn, UDR, dept of Seine; mem, natl council, UNR-UDT; fmr: dep, asst secy gen, youth propaganda div, Gaullist Rally of Fr People; secy gen, natl secy, Young Social Rep, 1954-58. Commercial dir, Marcus Art Gal, since 1961; expert in certifying authenticity of works of art for Natl Syndicate Profsl Experts; mem, admn council, Natl Syndicate Antiquarians, since 1965; pres: Mus of J Art, Paris, 1966; Fr-Isr Friendship Group of Council of Paris; fmr, mem, cen comm, League Against Racism and Anti-Semitism. Author: Les Peintres de la Vie Juive; Les Paysagistes Français de la Fin du 18e Siècle; other works on art. Offices: Galerie Marcus, 20 rue Chauchat, Paris, Fr; Secretariat Politique, 93 rue du Faubourg-St-Denis, Paris, Fr.

MARCUS, Leo Hymie, Can, organization exec; b. Belleville, Can, Jan 3, 1933; s. Max and Reta (Samuels); BA, Queens U, Ont, 1956; m. Hilda Silver, Dec 25, 1953; c: Gary, Dale, Paul. Natl dir, UJA of Can, since 1969; exec dir, ZOC, 1954-69. Exec mem, ZOC; mem, B'nai B'rith; fmr, pres, BC Camping Assn. Contbr to Anglo-J press. Home: 5622 Castlewood Ave, Montreal, Can. Office: 1247 Guy St, Montreal, Can.

MARCUS, Mortimer, US, stockbroker; b. NYC, Oct 16, 1896; s. Julius and Sarah (Sheiman); m. Harriet Mindell, Nov 23, 1924; c: Jules, Wayne, Suzanne Mosby. Sr partner, Marcus & Co, stockbrokers, since 1937; mem, NY Stock Exch, since 1932; partner, Brickman, Landsberg & Co, 1923-32. Trustee: Cong B'nai Jeshurun; Albert Einstein Coll of Med; mem, bd overseers, JTSA; dir, Intl Syn. Recipient: Louis Marshall Award, JTSA, 1959. Hobbies: theater, music. Home: 90 Riverside Dr, New York, NY. Office: 61 Broadway, New York, NY.

MARCUS, Paul, US, management and engineering cons; b. NYC, Nov 9, 1930; s. Samuel and Frieda (Tiefenbruner); ME, IE, NYU, 1960; m. Sandra Brand, Dec 7, 1952; c: Cheryl, Dean, Steven. Pres, Intl Plastechnics Corp, since 1969; head, Marcus Assos, since 1961. Pvt, USAF Res, 1950-51. Prin contrib: patents in plastics extrusion, injection blow-molding; expert in both fields. Home: 85 Pascack Rd, Pearl River, NY. Office: 7 Elmwood Dr, New City, NY.

MARCUS, Robert, Isr, loss adjuster; b. Essen, Ger, Apr 1, 1901; s. Ernst and Berta (Auerbach); in Isr since 1933; dipl ing, Tech HS, Berlin, 1923; m. Hanna Herzfeld, Nov 19, 1935; c: Jona, Edna Neuberger, Nurit. Mgr, R Marcus & Co, Loss Adjusters and Valuers, since 1926; fmr adv: JA; Min of Transp. Pres, Isr Loss Adjusters Assn; bd mem, Isr Ins Inst; mem, Rotary; leader various Zionist Youth Orgs, 1918-32; transp, HAGA, Tel Aviv, 1940-45; mem: Soc Automotive Engr, US; Fire Protection Assn, Eng. Home: 95 Kaplan St, Herzlia B, Isr. Office: 3 Ben Zakai St, Tel Aviv, Isr.

MARCUS, Yitzhak, Isr, educator; b. Kolberg, Ger, Mar 17, 1931; s. Fritz and Rosa (Nelken); in Isr since 1936; MSc, Heb U, Jerusalem, 1952, PhD, 1956; m. Tova Semel, Oct 10, 1954; c: Tamar, Ruth. Prof, head, dept inorganic and analytical chem, since 1965; head, chem div, Isr AEC, Soreq Nuclear Research Cen, 1958-65. Sgt maj, IDF, 1948-54. Prin contrib: in fields of coord chem, solvent extraction, chem of transuranium elements. Chmn, comm equilibrium data, Intl Union Pure Applied Chem; exec comm, Isr Chem Soc, chmn, analytical sect, 1962-67; mem, Amer Chem Soc. Author: Ion Exchange and Solvent Extraction of Metal Complexes, 1969; contbr to jours and books. Home: 36 Palmach St, Jerusalem, Isr. Office: Hebrew U, Jerusalem, Isr.

MARCUSE, Ludwig, US, educator, author; b. Berlin, Ger, Feb 8, 1894; s. Carl and Paula (Gumpert); in US since 1939; att U of Freiberg, 1914; PhD, U of Berlin, 1917; m. Erna Reich, 1927. Prof, Ger and phil, U of S Cal, since 1949; fmr: tchr, Humboldt HS, 1919-24; theater critic, Frankfurt, 1925-32. Mem: AAUP; MLA; Ger Acad, Darmstadt, Ger; PEN Club, London, LA, Darmstadt. Author: Georg Buchner, 1922; The World of Tragedy, 1923; Strindberg: The Life of the Tragic Soul, 1924; Ludwig Borne: Revolutionary and Patriot, 1929; Heinrich Heine: A Life Between Yesterday and Tomorrow, 1932, 1951, trans into Eng, 1932; Soldier of the Church: The Life of Ignatius von Loyola, 1937, trans: Fr, Eng, Czech, Span, Port; Plato and Dionysius: A Double Biography, NY, 1947, Berlin, 1950, Paris, 1955; Philosophies of Happiness: From Job to Freud, 1949; Pessimism: A Stage of Maturity, 1953; Sigmund Freud: His Image of Man, 1956; American Philosophizing, 1959; My Twentieth Century, 1960; Obscene, 1962; Das Denkwuerdige Leben Richard Wagners, 1963; Aus den Papieren eines bejahrten Philosophie-

studenten, 1964; Argumente und Kommentare, 1967; Nachruf auf Ludwig Marcuse, 1969; ed: Gerhart Hauptmann, 1923; World Literature of Our Times, 2 vols, 1954. Home: Rupertiweg 14c, Bad Wiessee, Ger. Office: U of S Cal, Los Angeles, Cal.

MARCUSE, Philip R, US, advertising exec; b. Duluth, Minn, Nov 13, 1906; s. Robert and Julia (Weiss); BA, U of Mich, 1926; m. Barbara Gilbert, Dec 9, 1937; c: Philip, Ann. Partner, advt agcy, Stockwell and Marcuse, since 1932. Fmr: mem, chmn, Detroit chap, AJComm; pres, Temple Beth El; club, Gt Lakes, Detroit. Home: 20193 Renfrew, Detroit, Mich. Office: 23666 Southfield Rd, Southfield, Mich.

MARDER, Louis, US, educator; b. Bklyn, NY, Sep 26, 1915; s. Isidor and Clara (Freund); BA, Bklyn Coll, 1941; MA, Columbia U, 1947, PhD, 1950; m. Miriam Kugler, Aug 31, 1940; c: Daniel, Diana. Prof, Eng, U of Ill, Chgo Circle, Chgo, Ill, since 1965; asso prof, Eng, Kent State U, 1960-65, fac mem since 1956; lectr, Eng, Bklyn Coll, 1946-53; prof, Eng, chmn dept, Pembroke State Coll, Pembroke, NC, 1953-56; lectr, spec studies on Shakespeare, Antioch Coll, Shakespeare Festival, 1953. Sgt, US Army, 1943-46. Mem: AAUP; MLA; Shakespeare Assn of Amer; Renaissance Assn of Amer; Amer Soc Theatrical Research; English Grad Union of Columbia U; Alpha Epsilon Pi; President's Comm to celebrate Shakespeare's 400th Anniversary, 1964; delg, 11th and 12th Intl Shakespeare Confs, Stratford-on-Avon, Eng, 1964, 1966. Author: His Exits and His Entrances: The History of Shakespeare's Reputation, 1963; ed-publ, The Shakespeare Newsletter, since 1951; ed: Study Master Shakespeare Series, since 1964; Librarian of Shakespearean Scholarship and Criticism, since 1966; contbr to lit jours. Recipient: Gold Key, Bklyn Coll, 1941; f, Folger Shakespeare Libr, 1957; Annual Shakespeare award, Friends of Lit, 1969. Hobbies: book collecting, Shakespeare antiques, philately. Home: 1217 Ashland Ave, Evanston, Ill. Office: U of Ill, Chicago, Ill.

MARDOR, Munya Meir, Isr, organization exec; b. Kowel, Russ, Nov 21, 1913; s. Abraham and Genia (Klein) Marder; in Isr since 1933; m. Lea Spector, July 3, 1947; c: Rami, Gonny. Perm dep chmn, Supr Natl Emergency Bd, Isr, since 1968; Haganah, Pal, spec oprs; illegal immigration, Rechesh, 1943-48; dir gen, aviation, Isr Min of Defense, 1949-50, dir, sci dept, 1952-58, dir gen, Isr Weapons Research and Devl Auth, 1958-68. Col, IAF, 1948; chief of staff, Isr Navy, 1949. Author: Strictly Illegal, 1964; Haganah, 1966, trans into It, Port. Hobbies: archaeol, flying. Home: 33 Oranim St, Kfar Shmaryahu, Isr. Office: Min of Defense, Tel Aviv, Isr.

MARENOF, Martha H, US, publisher, author; b. Vilna, Pol, Nov 17, 1899; d. David and Yocheved (Karelitz) Friedman; in US since 1905; PhB, U of Chgo, 1934; m. Shlomo Marenof, Aug 9, 1928; c: Arnona Eisenberg, Yuda (decd). Owner, Dot Publications, since 1948, asso with Temple Isr, Detroit; pvt secy to pres, Heb U, Jerusalem, 1926-29; dir, rel educ: KAM Temple, Chgo, 1943-45; Temple Shalom, Newton, Mass, 1950-55. Found mem, Natl Assn Temple Educs; mem, Natl Council J Educ. Author: History Through Literature, 3 vols, 1954-57; Stories Round the Year, 1960, 2nd ed, 1969; coauthor: My Hebrew Reader; ed: Across Time and Space: Anthol of J Lit of Past Hundred Years. Home and office: 20300 Murray Hill, Detroit, Mich.

MARENOF, Shlomo, US, educator, author; b. Kaligorka, Russ, Aug 13, 1902; s. Eli and Naomi (Burstein) Marianovsky; in US since 1929; tchrs dipl, Tchrs' Sem, Jerusalem, 1928; PhB, U of Chgo, 1930; MA, 1932; m. Martha Friedman, Aug 9, 1928; c: Arnona Judith, Yuda Herzl (decd). Dir, dept of J Studies, U of Detroit, Detroit, Mich, since 1967, dean, 1958-67; fac adv, Coll of J Studies, Chgo, 1929-45; research f, U of Chgo, 1933-34; dir: J Educ Bur, Omaha, Neb, 1945-47; adult J Educ, Bur of J Educ, Boston, Mass, 1947-48; asst prof, Near E Civilization, Brandeis U, 1948-58. Pres: Midwest Fed Heb Tchrs, 1940-42; Natl Fed Heb Tchrs, 1943-44; Natl Assn Profs of Heb, 1954-56; mem: AAUP; Amer J Hist Soc; Amer Archaeol Soc; Amer Oriental Soc. Author: Am uMoadov, 2 vols, 1932-33; HaIvri, 4 vols, 1939-51; Pirhay haAretz, collection of stories, 1941; haAm veGiborav, 1951; Arabic Primer; The Hebrew Word in Russia; ed: Bitaon, 1934-38; Teurah, 1944-45; haIvri haKaton, 1936-45; Shai, collection of stories, 1937; Moadey Israel, 4 vols, 1943-45; asso ed, Heb Abstracts; contbr to mags. Home: 20300 Murray Hill, Detroit, Mich.

MARGALIT, Meir, Isr, actor; b. Ostrolenka, Pol, May 3, 1906; s. Aron and Feiga (Krolivjetzky); in Isr since 1921; m. Israela Lichtenstein, 1937. Actor, Ohel Theater, 1925-1969; stonemason, 1921-25. Co-found, Ohel Theater; creator of many of his own roles; entertained J troops in: It, Egypt, Syria, Leb; immigrant camps in Cyprus. Mem: Theater Union; Variety Club; Milo Club. Recipient: State of Isr Prize; Aharonovitz Prize; Gordon Prize; Histadrut Prize; Klausner Prize; Ramhal Prize; made hon citizen of Rehovot. Home: 12 Sderot Smuts, Tel Aviv, Isr.

MARGALIT, Shlomo, US, rabbi; b. Tiberias, Isr, Apr 30, 1914; s. Nechemiah and Bath Sheva (Kuperman); in US since 1954; ordained rabbi, Rabb Assembly Eitz Chaim, Isr; m. Dina Rivlin, Feb 8, 1938; c: Nechemiah, Yael Moses. Asst prof, Heb, Bible, Rabbinics, Gratz Coll; fmr: rabbi: Kefar Vitkin, Isr; Cong Ohel Achim; rel instr, Haifa; asso rabbi, Cong Rodeph Shalom, Atlantic City. Quartermaster, IDF. Prin contrib: introduced Ulpanim, adult Heb intensive classes, Phila. Fmr: pres: Heb Tchrs and Prins of Amer, Phila br; Histadruth Ivrith of Amer, Phila br; master, Har-Zion Lodge, Jerusalem; mem: Amer Assn J Educ; Natl Council J Educ. Contbr articles in Heb to jours in US and Isr. Hobbies: poetry, singing. Home: 1448 Devereaux Ave, Philadelphia, Pa. Office: Gratz Coll, 10 St and Tabor Rd, Philadelphia, Pa.

MARGALITH, Arnold, Isr, business exec; b. Leipzig, Ger, June 20, 1912; s. Jakob and Toba (Verständig); in Isr since 1933; att profsl, evening schs, Leipzig; m. Sarah Hecht, Oct 26, 1933; c: Nurith Bareket, Rafael. Dist mgr, N Dist, Haifa, of GOL, Global of London, since 1966; found, dist mgr, Egged Tours, 1953-66. Hagana, Independence War, 1948-49; IDF, Sinai war, 1956. Mem, council, J-Arab Culture Cen, Haifa; mem: Comty Council, Mt Carmel, Haifa; Travel Agt Assn, Haifa; clubs: Rotary; Scal; Variety. Hobbies: music, stamps. Home: 34 Hayarkon St, Haifa, Isr. Office: 104 Haatzmaut St, Haifa, Isr.

MARGALITH, David, Isr, physician; b. Russ, Sep 11, 1888; s. Shlomo and Haja (Talalajevska); in Isr since 1927; ordained rabbi, Odessa Yeshiva, Russ, 1911; MD, U Odessa, 1925; m. Gissa Gerner, July, 1914; c: Zeev. In pvt med practice, specializing in children's diseases, since 1925; lectr, hist of med, Bar Ilan U, since 1959. Hon secy, Isr Soc of Hist of Med and Sci, since 1950; mem: Isr Med Assn; Intl Org of Socs of the Hist of Med and Sci; B'nai B'rith. Ed, Koroth, quarterly jour, since 1952; contbr numerous articles to profsl jours, hist of med and sci. Recipient: prize, Soc of Hist of Med and Sci, 1958; Dr Einhorn Sold Award, Tel Aviv Munic, 1967. Home and office: 68 Shlomoh Hamelech St, Tel Aviv, Isr.

MARGALITH, Israel, Isr, communal exec, attorney; b. Lodz, Pol, June 23, 1920; s. Abraham and Pola (Waldberg); MA, Heb U, Jerusalem, 1944; D es Lettres, Sorbonne U, Paris, 1952; LLB, Heb U, 1963; m. Devorah Fortusoff, Apr 10, 1946; c: Aviram, Nitza. W Coast dir, Isr Aliyah Cen, JA, since 1967; fmr dep dir gen, Youth Aliyah Dept, JA; tchr, HS, Isr, 1944-49; educ dir, Youth Aliyah in Eur and N Afr, JA, 1949-53; repr, Youth Aliyah and Educ, N Afr, JA, 1953-55; visiting lectr, Hans Beyt Training Sch, Youth Aliyah, Jerusalem; lectr, postgrad summer courses, Heb U; youth Aliyah repr, Intl Union for Child Wfr Confs. Lt, LDF, War of Independence; Six Day War. Fmr: first dir, Intl Cultural Cen for Youth, Jerusalem, 1960-63; mem, Intl bd, Intl Fed of Childrens Comtys, 1959-60; mem, natl bd: Isr Soc Adult Educ; Isr Natl Commn for UNESCO, 1963-67; mem, bd dirs, Henrietta Szold Inst; mem, Jerusalem Munic Commn for Cultural Affairs, 1955-64. Author: Le Baron Edmond de Rothschild et la Colonisation Juive en Palestine, 1957; contbr to Isr and fgn periodicals; fgn corresp for Z'manim, 1953-55. Recipient: Joseph Klausner prize, Tel Aviv Munic, 1948; PhD Thesis Award, Centre Natl de la Recherche Sci, 1954. Homes: 141 S Swall Drive, Beverly Hills, Cal; 24 Rashba St, Jerusalem, Isr. Office: 590 N Vermont St, Los Angeles, Cal.

MARGALITH, Pinhas, Isr, microbiologist; b. Vienna, Aus, July 9, 1926; s. Zalman and Batia (Kramrish); in Isr since 1939; MSc, Hebrew U, Jerusalem, 1951, PhD, 1957; m. Ruth Hanaor; c: Shlomith, Yoav, Chava. Prof, dept food, biotechnology, Technion, Haifa; head, lab microbiol, since 1959; head, lab, ind microbiol, Lepetit, Milano, It, 1957-59. IDF, 1948-50. Author: Secondary Factors in Fermentation, 1964; Flavor and Microorganism, 1969; contbr to microbiol jours. Mem, Amer and Isr Assns for Microbiol. Recipient: medals: War of Independence; Sinai; Six Day War. Home: 10 Litanis St, Haifa, Isr. Office: Technion, Haifa, Isr.

MARGARETTEN, Morris, US, attorney; b. NYC, Jan 3, 1899; s. John and Mary (Rosenberg); LLB, NJ Law Sch, Rutgers U, 1923; m. Pauline Avchen, Dec 27, 1922; c: Judith Bronston, Beatrice Cohen. Pvt law practice since 1923; mem, State Comm on Unauthorized Practice of Law, appd by NJ Supr Court, since 1966; counsel, Perth Amboy Gen Hosp, since 1964; public sch tchr, Roselle and Perth Amboy, NJ, 1919-23. Sgt, Student Army Training Corps, Columbia U, 1918. Spec asst to NJ Atty Gen, re-condemnation of property, 1932-33; judge advocate, JWV of US, Dept of NJ, 1933; asst county prosecutor, Middlesex Co, NJ, 1951-56. Pres: Raritan Council, Boy Scouts of Amer, 1933-35, mem, exec bd, since 1925, org scout movement in Perth Amboy, 1919; J Comty Cen, 1931-33, mem, bd dirs, since 1923; Council of Social Agcys, 1936; JCC, 1952-54, mem, bd dirs, since 1939, all Perth Amboy; NJ Fed of YM-YWHA, 1937-39, mem, exec bd, since 1931; Horowitz-Margareten Family Assn, 1955-57, mem, bd trustees, since 1941; Middlesex Co Bar Assn, 1948-49; chmn, Perth Amboy UJA-YMHA Campaign, 1945; co-chmn, Round Table NCCJ, 1946-48; vice-pres, NJ Region, ZOA, 1948-49; mem, bd dirs, JWB, since 1954, bd govs, JWB Presidents' Club, since 1956; area sup, USO, 1943-46, mem, NJ Bd Trustees, since 1959; org, Perth Amboy Area Comty Chest, 1942, mem, exec bd; mem: JDC Council, since 1945; Cong Shaarey Tefiloh, Perth Amboy, pres, 1966-68, mem, exec comm, since 1959; JWV; Amer Legion; NJ and Perth Amboy Bar Assns; club, Rep, pres, 1952-53. Recipient: Silver Beaver, Boy Scouts of Amer, 1935; Bronze Plaque, JWB, 1957; Harry S Feller memorial award, NJ sect, JWB, 1957. Home: 140 Rector St, Perth Amboy, NJ. Office: 280 Hobart St, Perth Amboy, NJ.

MARGID, Harry, US, attorney; b. NYC, Oct 10, 1893; s. Abraham and Annie (Taub); LLB, U of S Cal, 1926; m. Goldie Edison, Jan 23, 1922. Pvt practice, LA, Cal, since 1926; dep city prosecutor, LA, Cal, 1926-33; prof, law, Pacific Coast Coll, 1940. Pvt, US Army, 1918-19. Mem: LA Co Bar Assn; Masons, lodge 623; Cal State Bar Assn; fmr post cdr, Amer Legion, Post 368, LA. Co-author: Habeas Corpus Manual, LA Co. Hobby: owner, breeder of thoroughbred horses. Home: 2425 St George St, Los Angeles, Cal. Office: 132 W First St, Los Angeles, Cal.

MARGO, Boris, US, artist, teacher; b. Wolotschisk, Russ, Nov 7, 1902; s. Israel and Shendla (Russman); in US since 1930; BA, Poly of Art, Odessa, 1925; att: Futemas, Moscow, 1926-27; Filonov Sch, Leningrad, 1927-28; m. Jan Gelb, June 30, 1941. Art tchr since 1935; master, Inst of United Arts, Roerich Mus, NY, 1930-35; Amer U, Wash, DC, 1946-48; U of Louisville, Ky, 1950-51; visiting prof: Art Inst, Chgo, Ill, 1957-59; Sch of Art, Syracuse U; O State U, 1968; visiting artist, U of Minn, 1962; visiting lectr, U of NC, 1963; artist in res: Mich State U, 1959-60; Bowers Mus, 1965; one-man exhbs: Roerich Mus; Grinnell Coll, Artists Gal; New Sch for Social Research; Amer U; Jacques Seligmann Gal; Betty Parsons Gal; Bklyn Mus; Research Studio; Lehigh U; Smithsonian Inst; Norton Gal; Art Cen Gal; Art Inst of Chgo; World House Gal; U of Minn; Norton Gal; Retrospective of Sculptures and Graphics, Syracuse U; U of Louisville; represented in: Mus of Modern Art; Whitney Mus Amer Art; Metrop Mus of Art; Public Libr, NYC; Bklyn Mus; Lessing J. Rosenwald collection; Delgado Mus; U ? Natl Mus; Phila Mus; Cincinnati Mus; Walker Art Cen; MIT; Albright Gal; LA Co Mus; in Us: Mich; Me; NC; Louisville; Cal; Yale; Syracuse; Brown; Cornell; Dartmouth; Corcoran Gal; Speed Mus; SF Mus; Isr Mus; São Paulo Mus; pvt collections: Rockefeller; Josepha Whitney. Prin contrib: inventor of cellocut process of fine-arts printmaking. Recipient: Mildred Boericke prize, Phila Print Club, 1946; purchase prize, Bklyn Mus, 1947, 1953, 1955, 1957, 1960, 1964, 1968; Waston F Blair purchase prize, Chgo Art Inst, 1947; purchase award, Portland Mus, Me, 1960. Home: 749 West End Ave, New York, NY. Studio: 8 E 18 St, New York, NY.

MARGOLIES, Morris Bernard, US, rabbi; b. Jerusalem, Dec 25, 1921; s. Joseph and Malka (Shmerling); in US since 1930; BA, Yeshiva U, 1943; MA, U of Chgo, 1946; m. Ruth Smith, Feb 10, 1952; c: Daniel, Jonathan, Marla. Rabbi: Beth Shalom Cong, since 1961; Hyde Park Heb Cen, 1943-48; fac mem, Coll of J Studies, Chgo, Ill, 1946-47; exec dir, AJCong, 1948-49; rabbi, Beth El, Bklyn, 1953-61. Capt, US Army, 1961-62. Dir: J Fed and Council, Kan City, Mo; JDC; pres: Chgo Rabb Council, 1945-47; RA, Kan City, 1964-66; Clergy for Peace in Vietnam, Kan City, 1965-66; mem: B'nai B'rith; Assn of J Chaplains; clubs: Oakwood Country; Meadowbrook Country. Author: Torah-Vision, 1961; Ten Turning

Points in Jewish History, 1963; Jew of the Century, 1963; conducted TV prog, Great Ideas of the Bible, since 1965; contbr to rel jours. Home: 3292 W 87 St, Leawood, Kan. Study: 3400 Paseo, Kansas City, Mo.

MARGOLIN, Boris, US, business exec; b. Russ, Apr 17, 1904; s. Isaac and Shifra (Maskowitz); in US since 1923; att: Slobodka Yeshiva, Russ: Columbia U; Grad Sch for Econ and Bus Admn, Minsk, Russ; m. Selma Levine, June 18, 1944; c: Miriam, Ira, Samuel. Pres: Tioga Silk Co, Inc, since 1928; Tioga Weaving, since 1943; chmn bd: Hazelton Weaving, since 1958; Tioga Textile Assn, since 1956. Pres, Hadoar, Heb weekly mag, since 1955; treas, Heb Cultural Found, since 1955; hon citizen, Beersheba, Isr; mem: exec, Isr Econ Corp; natl bd: UJA; Bonds for Isr; libr comm, bd overseers, JTSA; found, vice-pres, Massad Camps; trustee, Herzliah Heb Tchrs Inst; bd govs, Amer Silk Council; Pres Comm for Physically Handicapped; dir, Mt Vernon Hosp; fmr mem adv comm, to fmr PM Ben-Gurion on Isr bus affairs. Home: 21 Winfield Ave, Mt Vernon, NY. Offices: 469 Seventh Ave, New York, NY; 40 E 34 St, New York, NY.

MARGOLIN, Ephraim, US, attorney; b. Berlin, Ger, Oct 16, 1926; s. Julius and Eva (Spektor); in US since 1949; BA, Heb U, 1949; LLB, Yale Law Sch, 1952; m. Gilda Lasko, June 24, 1953; c: Alexander, Evan. Pvt practice, SF, Cal, since 1962; lectr: U of Cal Extension, since 1958; SF Law Sch, 1957-60; W Coast counsel, AJCong, 1958-62. Secy to M Begin, cdr of Irgun. Chmn, ME comm, JCRC; fmr: pres, N Cal div, AJCong; chmn, legal comm, ACLU, N Cal. Contbr to law jours. Hobby: ed, law commentary. Home: 132 27 Ave, San Francisco, Cal. Office: 445 Sutter St, San Francisco, Cal.

MARGOLIN, Juli, Isr, author; b. Pinsk, Russ, Oct 14, 1900; s. Boris and Olga (Halperin); PhD, U of Berlin, 1928; m. Eva Spektor. Author: Grundphaenomene des intentionalen Bewustseins, 1929; Idea Sjonizmei, 1939; La Condition Inhumaine, 1950; numerous books in Russ, 1950, 1952, 1958, 1960; Ueberleben ist Alles, 1965; contbr numerous articles in Heb, Russ, Fr press. Home: 16 Shenkin St, Tel Aviv, Isr.

MARGOLIN, Leo J, US, educator, educational admnr; b. NYC, Nov 24, 1910; s. Akiba and Fannie (Levin); BS, LIU, 1932; LLB, Bklyn Law Sch of St Lawrence U, 1935; m. Eve Wolf, Aug 8, 1959. Prof, bus admn, head, div bus admn, Manhattan Comty Coll, CUNY, since 1964; adj prof, public admn, NYU, since 1950; reporter: Bklyn Daily Times, 1926-29; NY Times, 1929-34; NY Herald Tribune, 1934-40; asso ed, Field Publs, 1940-43; sr ed, psych warfare br, US OWI, 1943-45; chief info off, UNRRA, Eur, 1945-46; atty, PR counsel, US mgn dir, Times of India, 1947-50; asst to chmn, NYC Planning Commn, 1950-51; PR dir, AJComm, 1951-56; vice-pres, AJ Armstrong Co Inc, 1962-64. Trustee, Brookdale Hosp Cen, Bklyn; mem: PR Soc of Amer; AJComm; Soc of Silurians; clubs: Overseas Press; Natl Press, Wash, DC. Author: Paper Bullets, 1946; Fundraising Made Easy, 1954; weekly columnist, Civil Service Leader, since 1961; contbr to newspapers and periodicals. Hobbies: radio bc, photography. Home: 215 E 68 St, New York, NY. Office: 134 W 51 St, New York, NY.

MARGOLINSKY, Julius, Den, librarian; b. Copenhagen, Den, Nov 19, 1895; s. Harry and Rosalie (Perlstein); att U of Copenhagen, 1914-20. Libr, J Comty, Copenhagen, since 1949; repr, HIAS, Copenhagen, 1945-66; antiquarian, 1921-33; gen dir, Hechalutz, Den, 1933-43; wfr off, Danish Legation, Stockholm, 1943-45; gen dir, J Post-War Secy, Copenhagen, 1945-50. Hon secy: Friends of Heb U of Jerusalem, 1946-47; JNF, 1936-67, both Den. Author: Statistical Investigation of the Jewish Population in Denmark, 1945; Genealogical Table of the Family Henriques, 1725-1948, publ 1949; The Danish Jewish Press, 1814-50, publ 1954; The Burial Places in the Jewish Cemeteries in Denmark, 1693-1957, 3 vols, publ, 1953-57; 299 Epitaphs in the Jewish Cemetery of St Thomas, Virgin Islands, 1837-1916, publ 1957; Chevra Kaddischa, Copenhagen, 1858-1958, publ 1958; Denmark Lodge IOBB No 712, 1912-1962, publ 1962; Judenakten, 1622-1850 im dänischen Reichsarchiv, Copenhagen, 1959, manuscript in J Hist Gen Archives, Jerusalem. Home: 54 Frederiksborggade, Copenhagen, Den. Office: 6 Ny Kongensgade, Copenhagen, Den.

MARGOLIS, Harry M, US, physician, educator; b. Kishinev, Russ, June 29, 1901; s. Maurice and Sarah (Klate); in US since 1914; BS, U of Pittsburgh, Pa, MD, Sch of Med, 1925; MS, U of Minn, 1930; m. Esther Urdangen, Mar 19, 1932;

c: Richard, John. Clinical asso prof, med, U of Pittsburgh, Sch of Med, since 1948; att phys: Montefiore Hosp; St Margaret Memorial Hosps, since 1946; pvt practice, internal med, rheumatology, Pittsburgh, since 1930. F: med, Mayo Clinic, Rochester, Minn, 1927-30; Amer Coll Phys, since 1935; mem: AMA; Amer Rheumatism Assn; ZOA. Author: Diagnosis and Treatment of Arthritis and Allied Disorders, 1941. Home: 6640 Forest Glen Rd, Pittsburgh, Pa. Office: 423 Jenkins Bldg, Pittsburgh, Pa.

MARGOLIS, Henry, US, educator; b. Belz, Rum, Jan 3, 1921; s. Philip and Betty (Rabinowitz) Kravitz; in US since 1921; BA, Yeshiva Coll, 1942; grad studies, NYU Grad Sch of Lib Arts; Dropsie Coll, as Louis Kahn f in J educ; m. Eleanore Eisenberg, June 25, 1947; c: Jay, Jed Kalman, Philip. Asso dir, Cleveland Bur J Educ, since 1956; lectr, Cleveland Coll J Studies; prin, United Heb Schs, 1950-51; educ dir, Adas Isr Cong, 1951-53; exec dir, St Paul Bur J Educ, 1953-56. Tech sgt, Mil Police, 1943-46. Vice-pres, Natl Conf J Communal Service, Cleveland br; chmn, Educ Dirs Council; exec comm, Natl Council J Educ; mem: Delgs Assembly; Mayfield Temple; Rel Educs Assn; Natl Soc Study of Educ. Home: 3632 Severn Rd, Cleveland Heights, O. Office: 2030 S Taylor Rd, Cleveland Heights, O.

MARGOLIS, Otto S, US, mortuary educ; b. Constantinople, Turkey, July 12, 1907; s. Herman and Cecile (Schwartz); in US since 1908; BA, W Reserve U, 1929, MA, 1930; PhD, NYU, 1934; m. Leona Weiss, Sep 9, 1930; c: James, Donald. Fmr: dean, Amer Acad Funeral Service, Inc, NYC, 1951-65; instr: biol: NYU; U of Newark, NJ, 1934-36; bact, path: Cleveland Coll Mortuary Sci, 1936-39; Pittsburgh Inst Mortuary Sci, 1939-50. Exec vice-pres, Amer Acad McAllister Inst Funeral Services, since 1965; secy-treas, Natl Assn, Coll Mortuary Sci, past pres; f, AAAS; mem: Genet Soc of Amer; Hum Genet Soc; AAUP; Sigma Xi; fmr vice-chmn, Jt Comm on Mortuary Educ. Co-ed: Funeral Service Abstracts; contbr on genet. Office: 2056 Broadway, New York, NY.

MARGOLIS, Richard Jules, US, author, poet; b. St Paul, Minn, June 30, 1929; s. Harry and Clara (Brunner) Sterling; BA, U of Minn, 1951, MA, 1953; m. Diane Rothbard, 1955; c: Harry, Philip. Free-lance writer, poet; pub, Bklyn Hgts Press, 1956-60; ed dir, Lerner Newspapers, 1960-62; cons, housing, Rosebud Sioux, SD, 1965-67. Author: Something to Build on, 1966; Only the Moon and Me, 1968; Looking for a Place, poetry, 1969; studies and reports for: Ford Found; Stern Found; Natl Comm Against Discrimination in Housing; US Off Econ Opportunity; US Civil Rights Commn; Bur Indian Affairs; Battelle Memorial Inst; contbr to periodicals. Mem, exec comm, Rural Housing Alliance; fmr, delg, State Dem Conv, Conn. Recipient: Polk Memorial Award, LIU, 1960; ed writing award, Natl Ed Assn, 1962. Home and office: RD 1, Georgetown, Conn.

MARGOLIUS, Bernard R, US, physician; b. Catskill, NY, Nov 21, 1910; s. Matthew and Augusta (Eliasberg); AB, Cornell U, 1932; MD, LI Coll of Med, 1936; m. Annette Rabinowitz, Jan 12, 1939; c: Peter. On staff, Greene Co Memorial Hosp; fmr: chief, anesthesiology, Riverside Hosp, Boonton, NJ; asso staff anesthesiologist, Montefiore Hosp, Bx, 1948-61. Maj, US Army MC, 1942-46. F: Amer Coll Anesthesiologists; mem: AMA; Amer Bd Anesthesiology; Greene Co Med Soc; NY State Med Soc; Temple Israel, Catskill, NY; club, Cornell. Contbr to med jours. Recipient: Asiatic Pacific Service Medal; India, Burma and Cen Burma campaign stars; Amer Service Medal. Hobbies: gardening, fishing, photography, sailing. Home and office: 13 Franklin St, Catskill, NY.

MARGOLIUS, Ralph Susman, US, realtor; b. Norfolk, Va, Apr 4, 1909; s. Isidor and Mattie (Rosenbaum); att U of Pa, 1926-28; m. Charlotte Feldman; c: Barry. Vice-pres, Goodman Segar Hogan Inc; owner, Waverly Hotel, Va Beach. Sgt, US Army, 1942-45. Crusade chmn, Amer Cancer Soc; state chmn, Natl Cash Comm, UJA; pres, Ohef Sholom Temple; vice-pres, Tidewater Arts Council; bd dirs: CJFWF; Norfolk JCC; Norfolk J Comty Cen; Va ADL; Norfolk Little Theater; bd trustees, UAHC; past chmn, United J Fund of Norfolk, 1962. Home: 1313 Cloncurry Rd, Norfolk, Va. Office: One Commercial Pl, Norfolk, Va.

MARGULIES, Joseph, US, artist; b. Aus, July 7, 1896; s. Elliot and Mary (Schachter); att: Natl Acad Design; Art Students League; Cooper Union, all NYC; art schs in Paris; Vienna; It, 1922-25; m. Mary Polisuk, Dec 17, 1921; c:

Herbert. Portrait painter, etcher; represented in perm collections: Metrop Mus Art; Bklyn Mus; NY Public Libr; Libr of Cong; JTSA; Smithsonian Inst; Co Lawyers Assn; Mus of Modern Art; State Capitol, Albany, NY; Bklyn Coll; Brandeis U; CCNY; Phila Mus; Carnegie Inst; Baltimore Mus; SF Mus; bibl mural, Bklyn Hosp; portraits include: Wendell Wilkie; Pres Franklin D Roosevelt; James G McDonald; Dr Nelson Glueck; Norman Vincent Peale; Senator Jacob Javits; Pres Dwight D Eisenhower; Pres Richard M Nixon; Congressman Emanuel Celler; Dr John Dewey. Mem: Amer Water Color Soc; Audubon Artists; Allied Artists of Amer; Artists Profsl League; Soc Amer Graphic Artists; Chgo Soc Etchers; N Shore Art Assn; Rockport Art Assn; Cape Ann Soc Modern Artists; Provincetown Art Assn; clubs: Baltimore Water Color; Salmagundi. Contbr to profsl publs. Recipient: Thomas E Reed first prize for oil; awards: Rockport Art Assn; Art League, LI; Digby Chandler first prize, Salmagundi Club; Louis E Seley purchase prize, 1959. Home and studio: 27 W 67 St, New York, NY.

MARGULIS, Bernard, US, attorney, business exec; b. NYC, Dec 9, 1901; s. Max and Esther (Schoenfeld); LLB, St Lawrence U, 1923; m. Eleanor Spiegelman, 1944; c: Robert, Max, John. Ret; fmr: pres, Reliable Metal Products Co, Inc, 1938-69; asst dep atty gen, NY, 1924-25. Capt, US Army, 1942-45. Mem: youth prog, B'nai B'rith, Westchester Co, NY; Guidance Cen, New Rochelle, NY; Omega Chi Law Frat; vice pres, trustee, B'nai B'rith, New Rochelle; club, Ryewood Country, pres. Recipient: Conspicuous Service Cross, NY; Army Commendation Ribbon, with pendant. Home: 90 Bon Air Ave, New Rochelle, NY. Office: 25 Elm Ave, Mt Vernon, NY.

MAR-HAIM, Hamuda Ish-Shalom, Isr, nurse; b. Jerusalem, Sep 5, 1921; d. Mordechai and Esther (Rabinovitz); RN, Hadassah, Jerusalem, 1943; m. Abraham Mar-Haim, May 1, 1946; c: Yechiam, Orit. Pres, Nurses' Assn, Isr, since 1965; secy, Nurses' Assn, Tel Aviv, 1958-65. Home: 62 Rainess St, Tel Aviv, Isr. Office: 93 Arlosoroff St, Tel Aviv, Isr.

MARIL, Herman, US, artist, educator; b. Baltimore, Md, Oct 13, 1908; s. Isaac and Celia (Maril) Becker; grad, Md Inst of Fine Arts; m. Esta Cook, June 8, 1948; c: David, Suzanne. Prof, dept of art, U of Md, since 1947; instr, painting: Cummington Sch of Art, Mass, 1935-40; Wash Workshop of Arts, 1946-48; Phila Mus Coll of Art, 1955-56. Sgt, US Army, 1942-45. One-man exhbs: Howard U Gal of Art, 1935; Marie Sterner Gal, 1936; Baltimore Mus of Art, 1937, 1946, 1967; Boyer Gal, 1937; Wells Coll, 1939; Everhart Mus, 1940; Macbeth Gal, 1941, 1943, 1948, 1951; Whyte Gal, 1944; U of Tenn, 1949; Barnett-Aden Gal, Wash, DC, 1951; Babcock Gal, NY, 1953, 1956, 1959; Phila Art Alliance, 1955; Franz Bader Gal, 1956, 1959, 1962, 1963; Castellane Gal, NY, 1961-62; Corcoran Gal of Art, 1961; Castellane Gal, Provincetown, RI, 1962; Athena Gal, New Haven, Conn, 1963; Wellfleet Art Gal, Mass, 1964, 1968; Forum Gal, NY, 1965, 1967, 1971; collections: Ala Poly Inst; Amer U; Amherst Coll; Baltimore Mus; Bezalel Mus, Isr; Cone Collection; Corcoran Gal; Del Fine Arts Cen; Ency Britannica; Howard U; Hudson Walker Collection; Metrop Mus of Art; Phillips Gal; Provincetown Art Assn; Sen Off Bldg; U of Ariz; Va Mus; Whitney Mus of Amer Art; Woodward Collection; exhbs: Boston Arts Festival; Bklyn Mus; Carnegie Inst; Chgo Art Inst; Corcoran Gal; Mus of Modern Art; Natl Acad of Design; NY World's Fair; Pa Acad; SF Golden Gate Exhb; Whitney Mus. Trustee, Baltimore Mus of Art, 1940-67; pres, Md chap, Arts Equity Assn, 1948-52; mem: AAUP; Coll Art Assn. Recipient: prize, Baltimore Mus Art; Silvermine Guild Award. Home: 5602 Roxbury Pl, Baltimore, Md. Office: U of Md, College Park, Md.

MARINOV, Uri, Isr, physiologist; b. Jerusalem, Isr, Dec 15, 1935; s. Rafael and Fania; DVM, Ia State U, 1965, MS, 1966; m. Ora Shiffman, Feb 26, 1957; c: Hila, Izhar. Research asso, Hebrew U Hadassa Med Sch, Jerusalem, since 1966. IDF, 1953-55. Mem: Isr Soc Phys and Pharm; Soc for Study of Reproduction. Home: 1 Eli Cohen, Jerusalem, Isr. Office: Heb U-Hadassa Med Sch, Jerusalem, Isr.

MARINSKY, Arie, Isr, attorney; b. Warsaw, Pol, Nov 15, 1927; s. Roman and Ida (Vinograd); in Isr since 1948; MJ, Heb U, Jerusalem, 1954; m. Ahuva Avrahami; c: Pinchas, Gideon. Pvt practice. Capt, IDF. Contbr legal articles to Yediot Aharonot. Mem, cen exec, Isr Bar Assn, chmn, courts comm. Recipient: 1948, 1967 Service Ribbon; Underground Service

Ribbon, Irgun Zvayi Leumi. Home: 8 Epstein St, Tel Aviv, Isr. Office: 103 Rothschild Blvd, Tel Aviv, Isr.

MARK, Howard Irwin, US, oral surg; b. Derby, Conn, Mar 30, 1929; s. Harry and Jean (Akabas); att Georgetown U, Wash, DC, 1946-48; DMD, Tufts U, Sch of Dent, Boston, 1952; m. Sheila Berger, June 24, 1951; c: Robin, Brian, Steven, Elliot. Pvt practice, oral surg, since 1957; cons, oral surg, Middlesex Memorial Hosp, Middletown, Conn; courtesy staff, St Francis and Hartford Hosps, Hartford, Conn; att, oral surg, Mt Sinai Hosp, Hartford; f, oral surg, U of Ala Med Cen, 1954-55. Capt, US Army, 1955-57. Pres, Conn Soc Oral Surgs; dir: Conn Hosp Planning Comm; Friends of U of Conn Sch of Dent Med; chmn comm, on hosp oral surg service, Amer Soc Oral Surgs; treas, Hartford Dent Soc; dipl: Natl Bd Dent Examiners; Amer Dent Assn; Amer Bd Oral Surg; regent, Regency 13, Alpha Omega, past pres; mem: Conn, NE, Amer, Intl Oral Surg Socs; council on Hosp Dent Service, Conn State Dent Assn; Amer Acad Oral Med; Intl Order of Odd Fellows, Jonathan Lodge 66; fmr: dir: Hartford JF; Conn Regional Med Prog; club, Probus, Gtr Hartford, fmr pres. Recipient: Robert R Andrews Hon Soc, Tufts U Sch of Dent Med, 1951; Service Award, Alpha Omega, 1962; Comty Leader of Amer, News Publ Co, 1969. Hobbies: golf, gardening, travel. Home: 101 W Ridge Dr, W Hartford, Conn. Office: 100 Constitution Plaza, Hartford, Conn.

MARK, Joseph, Isr, management cons; b. Sibiu, Rum, Oct 22, 1925; s. Avraham and Nelly; in Isr since 1944; BSc, Technion, Haifa, 1951; m. Anita Dermann, Apr 11, 1948; c: Dahlia, Iris. Found, dir, Mark Mgmt Cons Engrs, since 1962, fmr chief engr; chief, training and educ, Isr Productivity Inst, 1951-53; ind adv, Govt Singapore, 1962-64; found, org, Singapore Inst of Mgmt. Sgt, aerial photography and cartography, IDF, 1948-50. Chmn: Tel Aviv chap, Isr Mgmt Cen; training comm, Isr Assn of Engrs and Architects, chem engr br; treas, Isr Assn of Mgmt Cons; mem: Ancient and Accepted Masons, Brit Inst of Mgmt, Isr br; fmr: Isr repr, UN Econ Commn for Asia and Far E, Bangkok; chmn, gen mgmt, Isr Mgmt Cen; group leader, Haonar Hazioni, Rum. Author: Raising Productivity in Singapore, 1964; Know Your Camera, 1952. Recipient: Isr Kaplan Prize for Produc for clients, 7 times; Knight of Order of Merit, Pres of Madagascar, 1964; AMBIM, Brit Inst Mgmt, 1966. Spec interests: Judaism, world rel, Far E art, photography, sports. Home: 32 Benzion St, Tel Aviv, Isr. Office: 202 Dizengoff St, Tel Aviv, Isr.

MARK, Julius, US, rabbi, educator; b. Cincinnati, O, Dec 25, 1898; s. David and Ida (Tanur); BA, U of Cincinnati, 1921; BHL, HUC, 1917, ordained rabbi, 1922, hon DD, 1949; hon LLD, Cumberland U, 1936; DHum, U of Tampa, 1955; STD, NYU, 1959; hon DHL, LIU, 1967; m. Margaret Baer, June 30, 1924; c: James, Peggy Heller. Rabbi em, Temple Emanu-El, NYC, since 1968, sr rabbi, 1948-68; prof, homiletics and practical rabb, NY Sch, HUC-JIR, 1949-1961; rabbi: Temple Beth-El, S Bend, Ind, 1922-26; Vine St Temple, Nashville, Tenn, 1926-48. Lt-cdr, Chaplains' Corps, USN, 1942-45. Pres: Syn Council of Amer, 1961-63; Alumni Assn, HUC-JIR, 1948-50; J Conciliation Bd of Amer, since 1968; Alumni Assn, HUC, 1949-50, mem, bd govs, since 1946; chmn: bd overseers, HUC-JIR, 1964-68; commn on justice and, peace, CCAR, 1946-49; dir, NY World's Fair, 1964-65; col staffs of Govs, Ky and Tenn; mem, exec comm, 1938-42; Chgo Inst on Mgmt and Lab, 1947; St Louis Inst on Judaism and Civil Rights, 1948; hon vice-chmn, Lighthouse of NY Assn for Blind, since 1952; mem, bd trustees: FJP, NYC; UAHC, 1958-62; E regional bd, ADL; exec bd, AJComm; exec comm, NY Bd Rabbis, all since 1949; mem, bd dirs: Assn for New Amers, since 1952; bd trustees, NCCJ; mem: governing body, World Union for Progressive Judaism; bd chaplains, NYU, since 1952; Assn Reform Rabbis of NY and vicinity; Army and Navy Chaplains Assn; exec comm, Amer Comm, UNESCO; Conf on J Material Claims Against Ger; Theta Phi; Zeta Beta Tau, hon; one of three convenors, Natl Conf on Rel and Race, Chgo, 1963; clubs: Shamus; Woodmont Country, Nashville, Tenn; Harmonie, NYC. Author: Behaviorism and Religion, 1930; The Rabbi Meets Some Big Dilemmas, 1956; Reaching for the Moon, 1959; contbr ed, Observer, 1934-38. Recipient: Man of the Year Award, Zeta Beta Tau, 1959; Hum Relations Award, Methodist Church, 1963; Gold Medallion, NCCJ, 1966; Isr Bond Plaque, 1967; Isr Tower of David Plaque, 1968; Clergyman of the Year, Rel Heritage of Amer, 1969. Home: 575 Park Ave, New York, NY. Study: Temple Emanu-El, 1 E 65 St, New York, NY.

MARKEL, Lester, US, editor; b. NYC, Jan 9, 1894; s. Jacob and Lillian (Hecht); BL, Sch of Journalism, Columbia U, 1914; hon LLD, NY Sch for Social Research, 1952; m. Meta Edman, Apr 3, 1917; c: Helen. Editorial cons, NY Times, since 1968, asso ed, 1964-68, Sunday ed, 1923-64; reporter, NY Tribune, 1914-15, night city ed, night ed,1915-19, asst mgn ed, 1919-23; asso in journalism, Columbia U. Found, Intl Press Inst; mem: Amer Soc Newspaper Eds; Council on Fgn Relations. Author: Background and Foreground; contbr to: The Newspaper-Its Making and Meaning, 1945; While You Were Gone, 1945; contbr and ed, Public Opinion and Fgn Policy, 1949. Recipient: citation, Alumni Assn, Columbia U Grad Sch of Journalism, 1951. Home: 135 Central Park W, New York, NY. Office: 229 W 43 St, New York, NY.

MARKEWICH, Arthur, US, judge; b. NYC, Mar 6, 1906; s. Samuel; AB, Cornell U, 1926; LLB, Columbia Law Sch, 1928; m. May Elish, Apr 18, 1930; c: Maurice, Daniel. Justice, Appellate Div, Supr Court, NY State, 1st Judical Dept,since 1969; asst dist atty, NY Co, 1930-37; NYC magistrate, 1947-50; justice: City Court, NYC, 1951-54; NY State Supr Court, 1955-68; extraordinary term, Supr Court, Suffolk Co, NY, 1958-61. Mem: Columbia Law Sch Alumni Assn, fmr bd dirs; Amer Bar Assn; NY State Bar Assn; NY Co Lawyers Assn; Assn of Bar, NYC, fmr mem, exec comm; Legal Aid Soc, fmr mem, bd dirs; Cornell Alumni Assn, NYC, fmr vice-pres; Cornell U Council; DeWitt Clinton Alumni Assn, fmr pres; Masons, Shakespeare Lodge 750, fmr master; B'nai Zion, fmr Nassi; Beta Sigma Rho, fmr pres; BPO Elks, fmr exalted ruler; Cong B'nai Jeshurun, bd dirs, trustee; B'nai B'rith, Freedom Lodge; Air Warden Service,zone cdr. Home: 175 Riverside Dr, New York, NY. Office: 27 Madison Ave, New York, NY.

MARKHAM, Ernest P, NZ, business exec; b. Wellington, NZ, Aug 31, 1925; s. David and Rachel (Levy); m. Shirley Meltzer, July 1, 1947; c: Judith, Sally, Elizabeth. Sales dir, Nuffield Mfg Co, since 1954. Mem: bd, Heb Cong; ZC, NZ; comm, Maccabeans; Zionist Youth League; J Social Club, all Wellington; JNF Comm; Zionist Soc; Day Sch Found comm; B'nai B'rith, all Auckland. Ed, Hashofar, 1958-69. Home: 720 Remuera Rd, Remuera, Auckland, NZ. Office: POB 57002, Owairaka, Auckland, NZ.

MARKOVITZ, Eugene, US, rabbi; b. Rum, July 21, 1921; s. Isidore and Regina (Fogel); in US since 1937; BA, Yeshiva U, 1945; ordained rabbi, Rabbi Isaac Elchanan Theol Sem, 1946; MA, U of NH, 1949; DHL, Bernard Revel Grad Sch, Yeshiva U, 1961; m. Klara Weiss, Nov 10, 1946; c: Rachel, Geraldine, Heidi, Susan, Raphael. Rabbi, Clifton J Cen, since 1949; adj prof, Amer hist, Seton Hall U; instr, Amer hist, Fairleigh Dickinson U, 1961-62; rabbi, Temple Israel, NH, 1946-49. Pres, found, trustee, Family Mh Cen; trustee: Juvenile Conf Comm; Isr Bonds, Passaic, NJ; vice-pres, Rabb Alumni Assn of Yeshiva U, 1958-61; chaplain, Police and Fire Dept, Clifton, NJ; mem: NY Bd Rabbis; RabCA; Rabb Council, NJ; Hum Relations Commn. Home: 88 Sixth St, Clifton, NJ. Study: 18 Delaware St, Clifton, NJ.

MARKOWICZ, Heinrich, Isr, physician; b. Rum, Mar 14, 1896; s. Melech and Malka (Frenkel); in Isr since 1935; MD, U of Vienna Med Sch, 1922; m.Irma Pitzele, Nov 2, 1951. Clinical prof, em, ear, nose, and throat, Tel Aviv U Med Sch, since 1966; fmr: head, ear, nose, throat dept, Beilinson Hosp. Sgt maj, Aus Army, 1915-1918. Prin contrib: established and devl med speciality of head and neck surg, mainly cancer surg, in Isr. Mem: ENT Soc, Surg Soc, both IMA; f, Intl Coll Surgs; corresp f, Amer Soc Head and Neck Surg. Contbr in field of head and neck surg to profsl jours. Home: 3 Iris St, Ganei Yehuda, Isr. Office: 17 Soutine St, Tel Aviv, Isr.

MARKOWITZ, Arthur, S Afr, author, journalist; b. Mitau, Latvia, Feb 1, 1910; s. Samuel and Esther (Joelowitz); m. Zia Lewe, Oct 30, 1956; c: Stephen, Vivienne. Asst ed, S Afr J Times, since 1952; S Afr repr, Brit-Continental Press Ltd, 1930-50. Author: Ports of South Africa, 1935; In Leo's Kingdom, 1936; Facing North, 1949; Wild Life in South African Game Reserves, 1950; The Daughter, 1951; With Uplifted Tongue, 1956; Market Street, 1959. Spec interests: animal psych, dog training, wild-life photography, chess. Home: 5 Wantage Rd, Parkwood, Johannesburg, S Afr. Office: POB 2878, Johannesburg, S Afr.

MARKOWITZ, Samuel H, US, rabbi; b. Pottstown, Pa, Feb 11, 1892; s. Adolph and Rose (Schwartz); BA, Bucknell U, 1914; hon DLitt, 1959; AM, U of Chgo, 1917, PhD, 1932; ordained

rabbi, HUC, 1922, hon DD, 1959; m. Jewel Klein, Nov 25, 1922; c: Richard, Ruth. Ret; rabbi: Lafayette, Ind, 1922-24; Ft Wayne, Ind, 1924-40; Elmira, NY, 1940-47; Beth David Cong, Phila; mem fac, Gratz Coll, until ret. Fmr: chmn, planning comm, Natl J Stat Bur; secy, Phila Bd Rabbis; mem, exec bd, CCAR. Author: Leading a Jewish Life in the Modern World, 1942; Adjusting the Jewish Child to His World, 1943; The Family in Time of Crisis, 1944. Home: 3175 Cauby St, San Diego, Cal.

MARKOWITZ, William, US, astronomer, educator; b. Pol, Feb 8, 1907; s. Hyman and Rebecca (Baumstein); in US since 1911; BS, U of Chgo, 1927, MS, 1929, PhD, 1931; m. Rosalyn Shulemson, Jan 28, 1943; c: Harold. Wehr dist prof, physics, Marquette U, since 1966; dir, time service,US Natl Observatory, Wash, DC, 1953-66. Prin contribs: designed dual-rate moon camera; participated in determination of frequency of atomic clocks; studies in rotation of earth, and polar motion. Mem: Intl Astronomical Union, fmr pres, comm on time; Intl Union of Geodesy and Geophys, fmr pres, sect on geodetic astronomy; Amer Astronomical Soc; Amer Geophys Union. Contbr to sci jours; Encys: Americana; Britannica. Office: Dept of Physics, Marquette U, Milwaukee, Wis.

MARKS, Ben D, geologist; b. Omaha, Neb, July 28, 1911; s. Jacob and Mashe (Drissman); BS, U of Okla, 1933; m. Gertrude White, June 14, 1936; c: Robert, Susan, Ann. Pres, Padre I Inves Corp, since 1965; dir, exec comm, Parkdale State Bank; independent oil opr, geologist; partner, Tri-Mark Oil. Pres: Corpus Christi Sym Soc, 1965-66; JWF, 1951-53; JCC, 1953-54; chmn, big gifts comm, United Fund, 1951; vice-pres, B'nai Israel Syn, 1952-53; mem, bd: HIAS, 1956; Child Guidance Council; mem: ZOA; B'nai B'rith; Pi Lambda Phi; Sigma Gamma Epsilon. Recipient: B'nai B'rith award, outstanding J citizen of Corpus Christi, 1952; Special Citizen award, JCC, 1954. Hobby: writing. Home: 434 Delaine Dr, Corpus Christi, Tex. Office: POB 1168, Corpus Christi, Tex.

MARKS, Charles, US, jurist; b. NYC, May 16, 1894; s. Wolf and Lena (Fleishman); att CCNY; LLB, NY Law Sch, 1916; m. Pauline Unger, Feb 23, 1919 (decd); c: Howard, Lucille, Lester; m. 2nd, Beatrice Rubin, 1966. Justice, Supr Court, State of NY, since 1962; asst night librr, NY Co Lawyers, 1915-17; counsel: Fed of Tenants of NYC, 1920-32; Retail Meat Dealers Assn of NY, 1934-37; judge: Munic Court, NYC, 1937-56; Court of Gen Sessions, NYC, 1957-62. Pres: Manhattan Civic Club, 1940-46; Gad Lodge, Free Sons of Isr, 1945-46; chmn: lawyers' div, UJA; bd appeals, Free Sons Order; exec vice-pres, Wash Hgts Defense Council, 1942-46; vice-pres, YM-YWHA of Wash Heights Syn, 1940-53; dir: Interfaith Movement, Inc, since 1940; Grand St Boys Assn, adv, 1940-47; E Side Vacation Found, 1945-48; Camp Seven, 7th Masonic Dist, 1947; mem: Masons, fmr master; City Housing Commn; State Aid for Housing; JDC; Non-sectarian Anti-Nazi League to Champion Hum Rights; B'nai B'rith; FJP, NY. Wrote and directed, Great Epochs in Amer-Jewish Life, for Tercentenary of J in Amer; contbr of articles on housing. Home: 710 Park Ave, New York, NY. Office: 100 Center St, New York, NY.

MARKS, Raymond Adolph, US, banker; b. SF, Cal, Aug 19, 1916; s. Clarence and Jeanette (Morse); grad, Amer Inst Banking, 1934; grad cert, U of Cal, SF, 1954; m. Margaret Nathan, Oct 20, 1939; c: John, Ellen. Vice-pres,mgr, Market Jones Office, Crocker-Citizens Natl Bank, since 1934. Pres, SF Sr Cen; 1st vice-pres, Cong Emanu-El, SF; mem: bd: Salvation Army Red Shield Youth Assn; Cen SF Assn; SF C of C; clubs: Men's, Cong Emanu-El, fmr pres; Breakfast Optimist, fmr pres; Cub Scout Pack, fmr chmn; SF Commercial; Variety, bd mem; SF Optimist, bd mem. Hobby: art. Home: 334 El Camino del Mar, San Francisco, Cal. Office: 1098 Market, San Francisco, Cal.

MARKS, Sidney, US, business exec; b. NYC; s. Julius and Anne (Seltenwirth); att: CCNY; NY, Bklyn Law Schs; New Sch for Social Research; Columbia U; U of Chgo; LLD, Philathea Coll, London, Ont, Can; m. Fahimie Goldenberg, July 15, 1951; c: Joel. Pvt law practice, NYC; mem bar, Supr Court,US; prof, NY Law Sch; lectr, Coll of Law and Econs, Munic U; repr, US mission to UN. Exec dir: ZOA; United Cerebral Palsy Assn, Nassau Co, NY; delg, WZC, Jerusalem; observer, non-governmental orgs; mem: bd dirs: KH; JNF; Amer Friends of Munic U, Tel Aviv; NY Co Lawyers Assn; and vice-pres, B'nai Zion; PR Soc of Amer; Intl, Amer PR Assns; Fgn Policy Assn; Grand Street Boys Assn; Mus Modern Art;

Acad Political Sci; YMHA, NY; State Bar Assn; Kappa Phi Sigma; Iota Theta; Swed, 1955-57; B'nai B'rith; Rotary. Home: 300 West End Ave, New York, NY. Office: 390 Washington Ave, Roosevelt, Long Island, NY.

MARKS, Sydney, US, communal worker; b. Corsicana, Tex, Nov 12, 1886; s. Benjamin and Jennie (Levy); att U of Tex, 1914-15; m. Goldye Rosenthal, Nov 4, 1914; c: Alvin. Bd mem, Corsicana Cotton Mills. Lt, WW I. Pres: C of C, 1926; Comty Chest, 1954; Retail Merchants Assn, 1945; Beth El Cong, 1950; B'nai B'rith lodge, 1920; mem, bd: Navarro Comty Found; Libr Bd; Crippled Children's Soc, both Corsicana; club, Corsicana Lions, pres, 1926. Spec interest: interracial activities. Recipient: K Wolen Award, C of C, Man of the Year, 1964. Home: 1224 W Fourth Ave, Corsicana, Tex.

MARKUS, Moshe, Isr, banker; b. Sopockin, Pol, 1903; s. Benjamin and Rachel (Berman); dipl, U of Frankfurt/Main, Ger; DRerPol, U of Königsberg; m. Rachel Rypp; c: Ilana Shoham. Ret since 1968; fmr: gen secy, Cen Audit Union, Coop Credit Socs, 1935-44; gen mgr, Bank Zerubabel, 1944-60; dir, cen mgmt, Bank Leumi Le-Israel, 1960-68. Chmn: Control Commn, Lib Party; Isr State Party in Eretz-Isr, 1935-37; Ort Tool Supply Co, Isr; mem: B'nai B'rith; Habonim Hahofshim. Ed, Der Najer Weg, J weekly, Warsaw, Pol, 1931-33; contbr of articles to Heb and Yiddish newspapers. Home: 13 De-Haas St, Tel Aviv, Isr.

MARMORSTON, Jessie, US, bacteriologist, endocrinologist; b. Kiev, Russ, Sep 16, 1900; d. Aaron and Ethel (Wark); in US since 1906; BS, MD, U of Buffalo, 1924; m. 2nd, Lawrence Weingarten, Feb 2, 1945; c, previous m: Elizabeth, Norman. Prof, experimental med, U S Cal, since 1943, fmr, asso prof; f, comm on med research, 1943-44; mem staff: LA Co Hosp, since 1943; Cedars of Leb Hosp, since 1944; grants from USPHS for research in endocrine mechanism, since 1948; house staff, Montefiore Hosp, NY, 1924-25, research f, path and bact, 1925-31;asst experimental path, Cornell U, 1931-35, bact, 1935-38: outpatient dept, NY Hosp, 1938-41; mem staff, Drs Hosp, NY, 1938-43. F: Soc Experimental Biol and Med; Amer Assn Paths and Bacts; AMA; Amer Assn Immunologists; NY Acad Med; mem: LA Co Med Soc; AAAS; Amer Coll phys. Co-author: Spleen and Resistance, 1937; Natural Resistance and Clinical Medicine, 1941; contbr to sci publs. Recipient: LA Times Woman of the Year in Med, 1961. Home: 9190 Cordell Dr, Los Angeles, Cal.

MARMUR, Dow, Eng, rabbi; b. Sosnowiec, Pol, Feb 24, 1935; s. Maksymilian and Cecylia (Solewicz); in Eng since 1957; att U of Stockholm, Swed, 1955-57; ordained rabbi, Leo Baeck Coll, London, 1962; m. Fredzia Zonabend, May 20, 1956; c: Viveca, Michael, Elizabeth. Asso rabbi, NW Reform Syn; marriage and educ counsellor, Natl Marriage Guidance Council, both since 1969; prin, Leo Baeck Coll Evening Inst, since 1968; rabbi, SW Essex Reform Syn, 1962-69. Chmn, actions comm, Eur bd, World Union for Progressive Judaism, hon secy, 1965-67; vice-chmn, Assembly of Mins, Reform Syns, Gt Brit, hon secy, 1963-65; mem, Inst of Rel and Med, London. Ed, Living Judaism, since 1966; contbr articles to Anglo-J publs. Home: 96 Hodford Rd, London NW11, Eng. Study: NW Reform Synagogue, Alyth Gardens, London NW11 Eng.

MARMUR, Jacland, US, author; b. Sosnowice, Pol, Feb 14, 1901; s. Max and Gertrude (recknitz); in US since 1903; m. Vernita Pellow, 1921 (decd); m. 2nd, Caroline Welter, July 21, 1960. Author: Ecola!, 1928; Wind Driven, 1932; Three Went Armed, 1933; The Golden Medallion, 1934; The Sea and the Shore, 1941; Sea Duty, 1944; Andromeda, 1947; The Edge of Chaos, 1969; original stories for films: Return from the Sea; The Ship of State; works adapted for radio and TV; contbr to natl mags. F, Inst Arts and Letters; mem: USN Inst; Masons; clubs: Pen; SF Press. Office: Larkspur, Cal.

MARON, Samuel H, US, educator, research sci; b. Warsaw, Pol, May 28, 1908; s. Harry and Bertha (Sellin); in US since 1922; BS, Case Inst, 1931; MS, 1933; PhD, Columbia U, 1938; m. Pearl Weinstein, June 28, 1936; c: Linda Posner. Prof, phys chem and macromolecular sci, W Reserve U, since 1945, fac mem since 1931; dir, research project, Off of Synthetic Rubber, Reconstruction Finance Corp, 1943-55. Pres, Cleveland Zionist Dist, 1939-40; mem, bd, Hillel Found, W Reserve U and Case Inst, 1950; mem: admn comm, ZOA, 1939-40; Amer Technion Soc; Sigma Alpha Mu. Co-author: Principles of Physical Chemistry, 1965; contbr to profsl jours. Recipient: cert of merit, Chem Profession, Cleveland;

Sigma Xi research award, Case Chap. Home: 2632 Milton Rd, University Heights, O. Office: W Reserve U, Cleveland, O.

MARON, Stanley Owen, Isr, agricultural laborer, teacher; b. Bloomfield, NJ, Jan 31, 1925; s. Hyman and Florence (Goldman); in Isr since 1960; MA, U of Chgo, 1948; D, U of Paris, Sorbonne, 1951. Mem, Kibbutz Maayan Zvi, since 1962; lectr, Educ Cen, Kibbutz Movement; fmr: asso prof, Mexico City Coll; research asso, Yale U; research anthropologist,U of Cal; lectr, phil, U of Dacca; instr, phil, Fla State U. US Army, 1943-46. Contbr articles to Heb, Eng, Span jours. Home: Kibbutz Maayan Zvi, Isr.

MAROVITZ, Abraham Lincoln, US, jurist; b. Oshlosh, Wis, Aug 10, 1905; s. Joseph and Rachel (Glovitz); LLB, Chgo Kent Coll of Law, 1925; hon DHumL, Lincoln Coll, 1956; hon LLD, Winston Churchill Coll, 1968. Judge, US Dist Court, since 1963; asst State's Atty, 1927-32; in pvt law practice, 1932-50; mem, Ill State Sen, 1938-1950; judge, Superior Court of Ill, 1950-63. USMC, 1943-46. First natl chmn, Natl Conf of State Court Trial Judges; trustee: Ill State Hist Libr; Chgo Kent Coll of Law; Chgo Med Sch; mem, adv bd, YMCA, metrop Chgo; J Bd of Educ; Anshe Sholom B'nai Israel Syn, Chgo; dept cdr, JWV, dept of Ill; mem: lawyers adv council, U of Ill Law Forum; judge advocate, Marme Post, Amer Legion; Phi Alpha Delta; fmr mem, bd mgrs, Chgo Bar Assn; club, Standard. Recipient: Man of the Year: JNF, 1959; Isr Bond Org, 1968; Annual Award, Decalogue Soc of Lawyers, 1968. Home: 3260 Lake Shore Dr, Chicago, Ill. Office: US District Court for N Dist of Ill, Chicago, Ill.

MARROW, Alfred J, US, psychologist, business exec; b. NYC, Mar 8, 1905; s. Isidore and Rebecca (Green); BS, NYU, 1926; MA, Columbia U, 1928; PhD, NYU, 1937; m. Monette Courod, May 2, 1934; c: Paul, Marjorie. Dist lectr,psych, New Sch for Social Research; chmn bd, Harwood Cos; cons, US State Dept; commn, City of NY. Pres, Amer Bd Profsl Psych, Inc; chmn, Amer Council for Behavioral Sci in Kibbutz Mgmt; found f, Cen for Hum Devl, Heb U, Jerusalem; mem, bd trustees: New Sch for Social Research; Pres Assn of Amer Mgmt Assn; fmr: chmn, natl exec comm, AJCong; Amer Comm Mental Hygiene for Isr; f, Amer Psych Assn; mem: E Psych Assn; NY State Psych Assn; Amer Sociol Assn; NY Acad Scis; AAAS; Intl Soc Mh; Natl Training Lab in Group Devl; Topological Psychols Soc; Soc for Psych Study of Social Issues; Soc Ind Psychols; Authors Guild. Author: Living Without Hate, 1951; Making Management Human, 1957; Changing Patterns of Prejudice, 1962; Behind the Executive Mask, 1964; A Life in Psychology—Biography of Kurt Lewin, 1969; contbr to profsl publs. Recipient: Kurt Lewin Memorial Award. Home: 870 Fifth Ave, New York, NY. Office: 666 Fifth Ave, New York, NY.

MARSCHAK, Jacob, US, educator; b. Kiev, Russ, July 23, 1898; s. Israel and Sophie (Gorlov); PhD, U of Heidelberg, 1922; MA, Oxford U, 1935; hon PhD, U of Bonn, Ger; m. Marianne Kamnitzer, Feb 17, 1927; c: Thomas, Ann. Prof, econ: UCLA, since 1960; U of Chgo, 1943-45; Yale U, 1955-60; dir, Cowles Commn for Econ Research, 1943-48; prof, grad fac, New Sch for Social Research, 1940-42; privatdozent, Heidelberg U, Ger, 1930-33; lectr, reader, All Souls Coll, dir, Inst of Stat, Oxford U, 1933-39. Hon f, Royal Stat Soc, London; dist f, Amer Econ Assn; mem, Intl Stat Inst; fmr: pres, Econometric Soc; dir, vice-pres, Amer Stat Assn; f: Inst of Math Stat; Cen for Advanced Studies in Behavioral Scis. Co-author: Kapitalbildung, 1936; Statistical Inference in Dynamic Economics, 1950; Studies in Econometric Methods, 1953; Economic Aspects of Atomic Energy;contbr to: Archiv für Sozialwissenschaft, until 1933; Econometrics, since 1933; Mgmt Sci, since 1955; Behavioral Sci, since 1963, jt ed since 1956. Home: 968 Stonehill La, Los Angeles, Cal. Office: UCLA, Los Angeles, Cal.

MARSHACK, Martin, US, dentist, educator, musician; b. Chgo, Ill, Apr 2, 1928; s. Charles and Bertha (Antonow); BS, Roosevelt Coll, Chgo, 1951; DDS, Loyola Dent Coll, Chgo, 1955; m. Arlene Minkus, Dec 2, 1962; c: Rosanne. Pvt practice since 1957; prof, fixed prosthetics, Loyola Dent Sch, since 1961; musician, 1947-70. Capt, US Army, Dent Corps, 1955-57. Mem: Alpha Omega, fmr treas; Fed of Chgo Musicians;fmr: dir, band, own orch; asst, band dir, Ill Natl Guard. Author: Bleeding and Clotting Time, 1954; Crown and Bridge Illustrations, manual, 1967, 1969; contbr to dent jours. Hobby:

painting. Home: 1075 North Ave, Deerfield, Ill. Office: 4120 Lawrence Ave, Chicago, Ill.

MARSHAK, Benyamin, Isr, kibbutz mem; b. Kiev, Russ, Sep 16, 1913; s. Samuel and Esther; in Isr since 1929; att Sems: Kibbutz Ein Harod; Ef'al; m. Rachel, 1935; c: Mary, Alina, Yoel. Mem, Kibbutz Giv'at Hashlosha, since 1929; secy, Absorption Comm, Kibbutz Meuhad. Maj, IDF, 1942-49; Mem: secretariat, Kibbutz Meuhad; Ahdut Ha'avoda Party; Histadrut, Va'ad Hapoel. Recipient, decorations: Hagana; War of Independence; Sinai Campaign; Six Day War. Home: Kibbutz Giv'at Hashlosha, Isr. Office: Mazkirut Hakibbutz Hameuhad, 27 Soutine St, Tel Aviv, Isr.

MARSHAK, Robert E, US, physicist, educator; b. NYC, Oct 11, 1916; s. Harry and Rose (Shapiro); BA, Columbia U, 1936; PhD, Cornell U, 1939; m. Ruth Gup, Apr 18, 1943; c: Ann, Steven. Pres, CCNY, since 1970; dist U prof, 1964-70, fmr chmn, dept physics, U of Rochester, mem fac since 1939; lectr, Harvard Coll Observatory, 1940; phys: radiation lab, MIT, 1942-43; Montreal Atomic Energy Project, Dept Sci and Ind Research of Gt Brit, 1943-44; dep group leader, theoretical phys, Los Alamos Sci Lab, 1944-46; mem, Inst for Advanced Study, Princeton, NJ, 1948; visiting prof: Columbia U, 1950; U of Mich, 1952; Tata Inst for Fundamental Research, Bombay, 1953; Sorbonne, Paris, 1953-54; Fr Sch of Theoretical Phys at Les Houches, 1954; Cornell U, 1959; Eur Cen of Nuclear Research, CERN, Geneva, 1960-61; Inst for Math Sci, Madras, India, 1963; U of Tokyo, 1965; Intl Sch in Yalta, USSR, 1965; Hercog Novi, Yugo, 1967; Carnegie-Mellon U, 1968; Guggenheim f, 1953-54, 1960-61, 1967-68. F: Amer Phys Soc; AAAS; fmr chmn, comm on sci exch with Soviet Union and E Eur, Natl Acad Scis; mem: NY State Sci Adv Council; Sci Council of Intl Cen for Theoretical Phys, Trieste; Amer-Japanese Comm on Sci Coop; Amer Acad Arts and Scis; AAUP; Fed Amer Scis; Phi Beta Kappa; Sigma Xi; Phi Kappa Phi; trustee, Atoms for Peace Awards. Author: Meson Physics, 1952; co-author: Introduction to Elementary Particle Physics, 1961; Our Atomic World, 1946; Theory of Weak Interactions in Particle Physics, 1969. Recipient: A Cressy Morrison astronomical prize, NY Acad Scis, 1940. Home: 45 E 89 St, New York, NY. Office: Convent Ave and 138 St, New York, NY.

MARSHALL, David S, Singapore, barrister-at-law, legislator; b. Singapore, Mar 12, 1910; s. Saul and Florah (Guston); barrister-at-law, Middle Temple, London, 1937; LLB, London U, 1937; m. Jean Gray, Apr 5, 1961; c: Ruth, Sara, Joanna, Jonathan. Advocate, solicitor, Singapore and Fed of Malaya, since 1937; hon lectr, criminal procedure, U Singapore; first Chief Min of Singapore, 1955-56. Japanese prisoner of war, WW II. Mem: Leg Assembly, Singapore, pres, Workers' Party; org, Lab Front, 1950; Singapore Advocates and Solicitors Soc; trustee, Manasseh Meyer Talmud Torah Trust; fmr: leader, Singapore Merdeka Mission to London, 1956; pres, J Wfr Bd. Home: "Tumasek" 276 Wing Loong Rd, Singapore. Office: 8/10 Bank of China Chambers, Singapore.

MARSHALL, Frank G, US, attorney; b. Chgo, Ill, Oct 28, 1894; s. Isadore and Sarah (Leader); LLB, Northwestern U, 1917; DHL, Coll of J Studies, Chgo, Ill, 1963; m. Mary Heyman, Dec 21, 1924; c: Robert, Betty. Partner, law firm, Marshall and Marshall; admitted to Ill Bar, 1917. Capt, US Army, WW I. Pres: Cong Anshe Emet, 1954-57; Bd J Educ, 1948-54; Chgo div, Denver Sanitarium, 1935; J Council, Lake View, 1932-34; Lincoln Park Lodge, B'nai B'rith, 1928-30; Young Men's J Council, 1928; vice-pres, Amer Assn J Educ, since 1950; found, Roosevelt U, Chgo, Ill, 1961; chmn, bd trustees, Coll of J Studies, 1948-54; mem, bd dirs, J People's Inst, 1929-31; scoutmaster, troop committeeman, Boy Scouts of Amer, 1916-44; master, Chgo Lodge 437, Masons, 1926; mem: Amer, Ill State and Chgo Bar Assns; club, Men's, Cong Anshe Emet, pres, 1942. Recipient: Bernard Semel award, Amer Assn J Educ, 1960. Home: 2801 N Sheridan Rd, Chicago, Ill. Office: 10 S LaSalle St, Chicago, Ill.

MARSHALL, James, US, attorney, educator; b. NYC, May 12, 1896; s. Louis and Florence (Lowenstein); LLB, Columbia Law Sch, 1920; m. Lenore Guinzburg, Aug 20, 1919; c: Ellen Scholle, Jonathan. Counsel to law firm, Marshall, Bratter, Greene, Allison and Tucker, since 1947; adj prof, public admn, NYU, 1959-65, lectr, 1953-59; training asso, Boston U, Human Relations Lab; partner, law firm, Guggenheimer, Untermeyer and Marshall, NY, 1920-30; pvt law practice, 1930-34; mem, law firm, Marshall, Bratter, Seligson and Klein,

NY, 1934-37; mem, US Natl Comm for UNESCO, 1946-51; adv, US Delg, UNESCO Conf, Paris, 1946, Mexico City, 1947; cons, Florence, 1950. Lt, US Army, 1917-18. Pres: NYC Bd Educ, 1938-42; NY State Training Sch for Boys, 1934-35; hon vice-pres: AJComm; Amer Friends of Heb U; mem, bd govs, JDC; fmr mem: bd dirs, NAACP; bd, Trustees Inst of Intl Educ. Author: Ordeal by Glory, 1927; Swords and Symbols: The Technique of Sovereignty, 1939, rev ed, 1969; The Freedom to Be Free, 1943; Law and Psychology in Conflict, 1966; Intention in Law and Society, 1968; contbr to profsl jours. Recipient: Butler Silver Medal, for contribution to political phil and educ, Columbia, 1941; award for Dist Public Service, Educs Lodge and Chap, B'nai B'rith, 1946; Gold Medal, dist service to the NYC public schs, Public Educ Assn, 1952; Public Service award, NY region, Amer Vets Comm, 1952. Home: 30 W 54 St, New York, NY. Office: 430 Park Ave, New York, NY.

MARSHALL, Lenore G, US, author; b. NYC, Sep 7, 1898; d. Henry and Leonie (Kleinert) Guinzburg; BA, Barnard Coll, NY, 1919; m. James Marshall, Aug 20, 1919; c: Ellen Scholle, Jonathan. Writer, novels, poetry, since 1935; lit ed, Jonathan Cape and Harrison Smith, 1929-32; book reviewer, critic, 1934; poetry ed, Amer Mercury, 1938; leader, children's writing clubs, NY public sch, 1940-43. Author: Only the Fear, 1935; Hall of Mirrors, 1937; No Boundary, 1943; Other Knowledge, 1957; The Hill is Level, 1959; Short Stories, 1947, 1968; Latest Will, new and selected poems, 1969; recorded reading of poems, Spoken Arts, 1957. Bd dirs, Amer PEN, 1966-69; co-found, Sane, 1957, exec comm, 1966-69; exec comm: Post War World Council, 1940-68; Council of Correspondence; mem: Poetry Soc of Amer; Authors League; club, Pen and Brush. Hobby: gardening. Home: Hotel Dorset, 30 W 54 St, New York, NY.

MARSHALL, Richard M, US, attorney; b. NYC, Apr 4, 1925; s. Louis and Sylvia (Rosenfeld); BA, NYU, 1947; LLB, Harvard Law School, 1950; m. Elinor Marcus, Dec 12, 1958; c: Peter, James, stepsons: Anthony, Richard. Partner, law firm, Pross, Halpern, Lefevre, Raphael & Alter, since 1957; gen partner: New Furniture Mart Assos; Mara Assos; Twin Bldgs Assos; 205 Lexington Assos; Teaneck Assos; Anagram Assos. US Army, 1943-46. Bd dirs, Mh Assn, Westchester, since 1961; exec bd, NY chap, AJComm, since 1955; fmr: Rep co committeeman; candidate for NY State Sen and NYC Council; mem: Assn Bar, NYC; Westchester Co Bar Assn; Pi Lambda Phi; club, Harvard, NYC. Home: 3 Oaks, Fenimore Dr, Harrison, NY. Office: 530 Fifth Ave, New York, NY.

MARSHALL, Valerie Rosetta, Eng, civic and social worker; b. Hove, Sussex, Eng, Apr 2, 1929; d. Nathan and Beatrice (Coleman) Dancyger; dipl, youth leadership, Middlesex Educ Auth and Borough of Barnet, LEA; m. Alfred Marshall, June 9, 1948; c: Stephanie, Charisse. Exec youth leader, Herbert Wilmot Youth Cen, since 1966; found, leader, Finchley J Youth Club, since 1961; instr youth work in clubs for young trainees; lectr, youth work to schs; careers adv to young people; secy, social worker, Birmingham Boys and Girls Union, 1947-48. Fmr: capt, Girl Guide Co, Finchley Liberal Syn; hon secy, Social Comm, Finchley Lib Syn; PR off, Finchley Lib Syn; mem: J Social Workers Org; Assn for J Youth. Prin contrib: org of annual Eur J Youth Festival. Hobbies: theater, bridge, reading, writing. Home: 9 Tillingham Way, Woodside Park, London, N12, Eng. Office: Wilmot Youth Centre, Market Place, East End Rd, London, N2, Eng.

MARSO, Friedrich, Isr, architect; b. Vienna, Aus, Dec 3, 1904; s. Heinrich and Paula (Goldberg); in Isr since 1934; BArch, Acad of Applied Art, Vienna, 1925; m. Rita Schaerf, Dec 31, 1962; c: Eve. Lectr, arch, HSs, Tel Aviv; assessor and adv to Isr Govt on wooden work and architectural display. Sgt, British Army; sr off, IDF, 1941-45. Adv, Isr Consumers Council; mem: B'nai B'rith; Union of Engrs and Architects. Recipient: numerous British medals; Isr medals. Home: 23 Hayarkon St, Tel Aviv, Isr.

MARTHAN, Abraham Albert, US, educator; b. Casablanca, Morocco, Feb 4, 1933; s. Judah and Rachel (Elbaz); in US since 1948; tchr dipl, Yeshiva U 1951; BA, Boston U, 1956; PhD studies, Dropsie Coll, 1959. Chmn, dept Heb lit, Gratz Coll, since 1969, lectr since 1959. Exec bd, Histadruth Ivrit of Amer; mem, Eta Sigma Phi. Author: Shavot Ha-Sirot Im Erev, poems, 1966; co-author: Anthology of Heb Lit for Coll Students; ed bd, NIV, Heb lit quarterly. Hobbies: camping, biking, music, boating. Home: 1723 Spruce St, Philadelphia, Pa. Office: 10 St and Tabor Rd, Philadelphia, Pa.

MARTIN, Bernard, US, educator; b. Soklence, Czech, Mar 13, 1928; s. Benjamin and Helen (Herskovitz); in US since 1934; BA, U of Chgo; ordained rabbi, MHL, HUC; PhD, U of Ill; m. Nancy Platt, June 1, 1955; c: Rachel, Joseph. Abba Hillel Silver prof, J studies, Case W Reserve U, since 1966; rabbi, Sinai Temple, Champaign, 1951-57; asso rabbi, Sinai Temple, Chgo, 1957-61; rabbi, Mt Zion Temple, St Paul, 1961-65. Chmn, Comm on Theol, CCAR; mem: Amer Acad J Research; Amer Phil Assn; AAUP; Soc Bibl Lit; Amer Acad Rel; Soc for Sci Study Rel; Natl Assn Profs Heb. Author: The Existentialist Theology of Paul Tillich, 1963; Prayer in Judaism, 1968; Three Twentieth Century Jewish Philosophers, 1969; ed, Contemporary Reform J Thought; trans, Athens and Jerusalem, 1966. Home: 2593 Dysart Rd, Cleveland, O. Office: Case W Reserve U, Cleveland, O.

MARTIN, Ernest H, US, theatrical produc; b. Pittsburgh, Pa, Aug 28, 1919; s. Samuel and Cecilia (Sklar) Markowitz; AB, UCLA, 1942; m. Nancy Guild; c: Elizabeth Muller, Cecilia, Polly Day. With Feuer & Martin Producs, Inc; co-produc: Where's Charley?, 1948; Guys and Dolls, 1950; Can-Can, 1953; The Boy Friend, 1954; Silk Stockings, 1955; Whoop-Up, 1958; How to Succeed in Business Without Really Trying, 1961; Little Me, 1962; Skyscraper, 1965; Walking Happy, 1966. Office: 505 Park Ave, New York, NY.

MARTON, Michael, Isr, engineer, business exec; b. Cluj, Transylvania, Jan 10, 1909; s. Ernest and Gizella; in Isr since 1946; BChE, Technion, Haifa, 1961; dipl, bus admn, Heb U, Jerusalem, 1963; m. Ruchama Smuelevitc. Mgn dir, Ujkelet, Hung lang daily newspaper, since 1963. Lt, IDF. Mem, Hapoel, Petah Tikvah. Hobbies: pistol shooting, Isr champion, 1966-68; Olympic Medal, Mexico City, 1968. Home: 24 Eduard Bernstein St, Tel Aviv, Isr. Office: 62 Harakevet St, Tel Aviv, Isr.

MARWICK, Lawrence, US, librarian, author; b. Sopockinie, Pol, Sep 16, 1909; s. Eliezer and Helene (Mirkowski); in US since 1929; PhB, U of Chgo, 1931, MA, 1932; PhD, Dropsie Coll, 1937; att Natl U, Cairo, 1935-36; m. Claire Sklaroff, Mar, 1946; c: David, Ellen. Head, Hebraic sect, Libr of Cong, since 1948; adj prof, Arabic and Islamic studies, Dropsie Coll, since 1967; research asst to Prof SL Skoss, 1937-40; asst dir, Bd of J Educ, St Louis, Mo, 1947-48; tchr: Arabic and Islamic studies, Dropsie Coll, 1954-56; modern Heb lit and Arabic, NYU, since 1961. Spec agent i/c, Counter Intelligence Corps, US Army, 1941-45. Chmn, natl libr comm, Amer Friends Heb U, since 1958; bd govs, Dropsie Coll, Phila since 1959; mem: Amer Acad J Research; Amer Oriental Soc. Author: A Handbook of Diplomatic Hebrew, 1957; ed, The Arabic Commentary of Salmon b. Yeruham on The Book of Psalms, Chaps 42-72, 1956; ed, adv bd, J Book Annual, since 1959; co-ed, Bloch Memorial Vol, 1960; contbr to jours. Home: 3221 Brooklawn Terrace, Chevy Chase, Md. Office: Libr of Cong, Washington, DC.

MARX, Alfred, Ger, jurist; b. Cannstatt, Jan 15, 1899; s. Eduard and Babette (Rothschild); att: U Tübingen, 1919; U of Freiburg, 1920; U Munich, 1921-22; m. Johanna Eckstein, Nov 2, 1929. Ret, 1964; presently active, Rückerstattungskammer, restitution to fmr Fr and Amer Zones, Württemberg, chmn, 1948-56; law clerk, Court of Stuttgart, 1923-25; assessor, Court of Tuttlingen and Nürtingen, 1925-28; judge: Lower Court, 1928-35; Co Court, Stuttgart, 1946-48, later court dir; perm repr, Landgerichtspräsident, Stuttgart, 1956-64; judge, Supr Court. Mem bd, Israelitische Kultusvereinigung Württemberg und Hohenzollern. Home: 85 Gaensheidestr, Stuttgart, Ger.

MARX, Emanuel Erich, Isr, social anthropologist; b. Munich, Ger, May 8, 1927; s. Yitshak and Rivkah (Epstein); in Isr since 1940; MA, Heb U, Jerusalem, 1958; PhD, U Manchester, 1963; m. Dalia Fabrikant, July 28, 1953; c: Dina, Yuval, Alon. Sr lectr, dept sociol, Tel Aviv U, since 1968; asst to adv, Arab affairs, PM off, 1955-59; research asso, U Manchester, 1960-64, research f, 1964-67; lectr, Tel Aviv U, 1964-68. IDF, 1947-50. Mem: Social Anthropologists Assn; ME Studies Assn. Author: Bedouin of the Negev, 1967. Recipient: Sr Simon F, Manchester U, 1969. Home: 55 Tchernihovski St, Jerusalem, Isr. Office: Tel Aviv U, Tel Aviv, Isr.

MARX, Leopold, Isr, author; b. Bad Cannstatt, Ger, Dec 8, 1889; s. Ephraim and Babette (Rothschild); in Isr since 1939;

att Jüdisches Lehrhaus, Stuttgart, Ger, 1926-37; m. Judith Hartog, Apr 22, 1916; c: Erich (killed in action, Independence War, 1948), Ephraim. Ret settler, gardenler; mgr weaving mill, Ger, 1909-38. Ger Army, WW I. Author: Hachschara, poems, 1942; Shavej Zion, Experiment and Promise, Ger, 1953, Eng, 1958; Lied Der Lieder, lyrical trans with notes, explanations, 1964; poems, essays, in various anthols, jours. Mem, Moshav Shavej Zion; co-found, fmr secy, Jüdisches Lehrhaus, Stuttgart; mem: Schutzverband Deutscher Schriftsteller, Zurich chap; Süddeutscher Schriftstellerverband, Stuttgart. Home: POB 78, Shavej Zion, Isr.

MARX, Robert J, US, rabbi; b. Cleveland, O, Aug 17, 1927; s. Sylvester and Lucile (Kline); BA, U of Cincinnati, 1948; MHL, HUC, 1951; PhD, Yale U, 1958; m. Marjorie Plaut, Dec 20, 1948; c: Richard, David. Dir, Chgo Fed, UAHC, since 1962; found, pres, J Council on Urban Affairs; asst rabbi, Temple Beth Zion, Buffalo, NY, 1951-54; rabbi, Temple Sinai, Stamford, Conn, 1954-58; regional dir, UAHC, Cincinnati, O, 1958-62. Home: 101 Lakeview Terr, Highland Park, Ill. Office: 100 W Monroe, Chicago, Ill.

MASERITZ, Isadore H, US, orthopedic surg; b. Baltimore, Md, Dec 4, 1898; s. Louis and Clara (Cordish); att Mt Vernon Coll, 1920; MD, U of Md Med Sch, 1924; m. Gertrude Miller, June 7, 1932; c: Mildred Goldsmith, Guy. Asso att orthopedic surg, Sinai Hosp, fmr orthopedic cons, arthritis clinic, intern, mem exec comm; orthopedic cons, Levindale Aged Home; visiting surg: Mercy Hosp, since 1930; Lutheran Hosp, since 1930; Women's Hosp, since 1940; fmr: orthopedic surg-in-chief, Doctor's Hosp, mem, med exec comm; asso orthopedic surg, U of Md Med Sch, lectr, orthopedic surg, for over 30 yrs; bone tumor research, Johns Hopkins U, 1935-40. US Army, WW I, orthopedic cons, WW II. F, Amer Acad Orthopedic Surgs, past mem, bone tumor comm; dipl, Amer Bd Orthopedic Surgs; mem: AMA; Baltimore City Med Soc; Phi Delta Epsilon; Phi Alpha; club, Chestnut Ridge Country. Contbr to med jours. Recipient: Bronze Medal, Amer Acad Orthopedic Surgs, 1938, cert of honorable mention, 1939. Home: 11 Slade Apts, Pikesville, Md. Office: Temple Garden Apts, Baltimore, Md.

MASLANSKY, Manuel M, US, oral surg; b. NYC, Nov 8, 1903; s. Herman and Gussie (Lovitch); desc of Zvi Hirsch Masliansky, author, pioneer Zionist; att NYU, 1922-24; DS, Columbia U, 1928; att maxillo-facial surg Army courses, Columbia U, 1942-43; E Grimstead, Eng, 1943; div; c: Robert, Paul, Michael; m. 2nd, Ruth Hirsch, 1957. Dir, div dent, Grasslands Hosp, Westchester, NY, since 1965, mem staff since 1954; dir, oral surg, St Agnes Hosp, chief, oral surg, since 1962; chief, oral surg: White Plains Hosp, since 1966; Hawthorne Cedar Knoll Sch, Valhalla, NY, since 1951; cons, Sydenham Hosp, since 1950, visiting asst adj oral surg, 1930; asst adj oral surg: City Hosp of NY, 1933; Bellevue Hosp, 1931; visiting lectr: Intl Dent Cong, London, 1952; Heb U Dent Sch, Jerusalem, 1952; Rome, 1957; Helsinki, 1960; clinical prof, Columbia U, 1965, asso clinical prof, 1961. US Army, 1940-46, lt col, US Army Res, ret. Princ contrib: inventor and designer, plastic light-conveying instruments, 1938. F: Intl Coll Dents; Amer Coll Dents, 1959; Amer Acad Dent Hist; dipl, NY, Amer Bds Oral Surg; mem: Assn Mil Surgs; Metrop Soc Oral Surgs; US Res Offs Assn; Amer Friends Heb U; ZOA; B'nai B'rith; AJCong; Alpha Omega; Omicron Kappa Upsilon; Tau Delta Phi; Masons; fmr: pres: Ninth Dist Dent Soc; NY State Dent Soc Anaesthesiology; dent sect, Westchester Acad Med; Columbia Dent Alumni Assn; chmn, Westchester div: Amer Cancer Soc; Natl Found; natl vice-cdr, JWV. Author: The Use of Anti-Histamines in Oral Surgery, 1953; The Anesthesia Problem with the Aberrant Child, 1954; Post-Operative Problems in Oral Surgery and Their Treatment, 1954; Pioneer Oral Surgery, 1955; ed, Columni Dent Jour, 1954; contbr to profsl jours. Recipient: US Commendation Medal, 1944; Dist Alumni Medal, Columbia U, 1950. Spec interests: dent iconographica, rare profsl books. Home: Genesee Trail, Harrison, NY. Office: 125 S Broadway, White Plains, NY.

MASLIN, Simeon Joseph, US, rabbi; b. Boston, Mass, Mar 18, 1931; s. Leon and Frances (Savitz); BA, cum laude, Harvard U, 1952; MA, U of Pa, 1954; ordained rabbi, BHL, HUC, 1957; m. Judith Blumberg, Aug 22, 1954; c: Naomi, David, Eve. Rabbi: KAM Temple, since 1967; Temple of Lib Judaism, Monroe, NY, 1957-62; Cong Mikve Isr-Emanuel of Curacao, NA, 1962-67. Vice-pres, Hyde Park-Kenwood Council of Churches and Syns; bd mem: Chgo Planned Parenthood Assn; Chgo Friends of Heb U; Amers for Music Libr in Isr;

merged Sephardi Orthodox Cong Mikve Isr of Curacao and Reform Cong Temple Emanuel, 1963; org, dir, Caribbean Speakers Circuit, 1963-67; org, chmn, Assn of Caribbean Congs, 1965-67; bd mem, B'nai B'rith, Curacao, 1962-67; mem: CCAR; J Reconstructionist Found; Amer J Hist Soc; club, Rotary, Curacao, fmr mem bd. Author: Analysis and Translation of Selected Documents of Napoleonic Jewry, 1957; contbr to J jours. Home: 5333 Hyde Park Blvd, Chicago, Ill. Study: 930 E 50 St, Chicago, Ill.

MASLOW, Will, US, attorney; b. Kiev, Russ, Sep 27, 1907; s. Saul and Raeesa (Moonves); in US since 1911; BA, Cornell U, 1929; JD, Columbia U, 1931; m. Beatrice Greenfield, Dec 21, 1933; c: Laura, Catha. Adj asso prof, CUNY since 1965, lectr since 1948; lectr, New Sch for Social Research, since 1948; reporter, NY Times, 1929-31; with law firm, AG Hays, 1932-34; asso counsel, NYC Dept of Inves, 1934-37; atty and trial examiner, NLRB, 1937-43; dir, oprs, Pres Roosevelt's Comm on Fair Employment Practice, 1943-45. Exec dir, AJCong, since 1960; bd dirs, ACLU; mem, exec comm, WJC. Contbr to profsl and other jours. Home: 401 E 86 St, New York, NY. Office: 15 E 84 St, New York, NY.

MASS, Haim, Isr, journalist, translator; b. Brno, Czech; s. Oskar and Sabine (Mayer) Massaryk; in Isr since 1938; m. Ada Meyerson; c: Uri, Amir, Saviona. Fgn corresp, newspapers, Switz, Ger; trans books into Heb, Eng. Irgun Tzvai Leumi, IDF. Mem: Isr Journalists Assn; Fgn Press Assn; Isr War Disabled Servicemen's Assn; Assn Immigrants from Czech. Hobby: elec. Home: 26 Rachel Imenu St, Jerusalem, Isr. Office: POB 365, Jerusalem, Isr.

MASS, Jonathan, Isr, scientist; b. Berlin, Ger, May 17, 1922; s. Rubin and Hanna (Heimann); in Isr since 1933; ing, Technion, Haifa, 1944; DEng, U of Paris, Fr, 1963; m. Carmela Ulreich, June 30, 1946; c: Chava, Daniel, Oren. Dir, Radio Observatory, since 1963; head, research div, sci dept, Min of Defense, 1950-60. Maj, IDF, 1948-58. Author: L'Etude de L'Ionosphère à l'Aide des Satellites Artificiels, 1965. Mem, Natl Comm for Space Research; fmr vice-pres, IRE, Isr sect; fmr chmn, Astronautical Soc, Isr; mem, IEEE, Isr; Brit Interplanetary Soc. Recipient: Isr Defense Prize, 1960; It Star; 1939-45 Star; War of Independence; Sinai Campaign; Fighters for the State. Home: 111 Hagalil St, Haifa, Isr. Office: POB 4655, Haifa, Isr.

MASS, Rubin, Isr, publisher; b. Vistyten, Lith, June 10, 1894; s. Nehemia and Haya (Barkowsky); in Isr since 1933; m. Hannah Heimann, June 21, 1921; c: Jonathan, Daniel (killed in action, Isr War of Independence). Found, owner, Rubin Mass Pub House, Jerusalem, publisher Heb fiction and sci lit, since 1933, fmr Berlin, Ger, 1927-33. Mem: Yad Labanim Assn, chmn, Jerusalem br; chmn: Council for Commemoration of Soldiers, Govt of Isr; War Graves Comm; Assn of Heb Pubs; B'nai B'rith; fmr: chmn, Talbieh Local Council, Jerusalem; House of Heb Council, Berlin. Ed, Heb Lit Catalogue, since 1927. Home: 11 David Marcus St, Talbieh, Jerusalem. Office: POB 990, Jerusalem, Isr.

MASSELL, Sam, US, realtor, public official; b. Atlanta, Ga, Aug 26, 1927; s. Sam and Florence (Rubin); LLB, Atlanta Law Sch, 1949; BCS, Ga State Coll of Bus Admn, 1951, postgrad cert, selling, 1952, postgrad dipl, real estate, 1953; m. Doris Middlebrooks, Oct 25, 1952; c: Cynthia, Steven, Melanie. Mayor, Atlanta, Ga, since 1970; fmr vice-mayor, mem, bd aldermen, Atlanta, since 1962; vice-pres, Allan-Grayson Realty Co, since 1955, on staff since 1951; chief of publs, Natl Assn Women's and Children's Apparel Salesmen, Inc, 1949-51; instr, real estate, Smith-Hughes Atlanta Vocational Sch, 1956; vice-pres, Mallin Developers, Fla, 1956-65; dir: Security Fed Savings and Loan Assn of Atlanta, 1961-67; United Trust Life Ins Co, 1964-68. Pres: Atlanta Area Chap, Muscular Dystrophy Assns of Amer, 1958-60; Atlanta Humane Soc and Soc for Prevention of Cruelty to Animals, 1960-62; chmn: Mayor's UN Day Comm, 1964; Aviation Comm of Natl League of Cities, 1966; Atlanta Govt Study Comm, since 1966; Atlanta ML King Memorial Comm, since 1968; Atlanta Urban Observatory Adv Council, since 1969; vice-chmn, Comm on Transp and Communication, Aviation Comm of Natl League of Cities, since 1966; councilman, City of Mountain Park, Ga, 1950-52; secy: Atlanta City Exec Comm, 1953-61; Hum Resources Devl Comm of US Conf of Mayors, since 1964; vice-pres, Natl Alumni Assn, Ga State Coll, 1952; adjutant, Athens Mangleburg-Elrod Post, Amer Legion, 1947-48; admn sch instr, USAAF, 1946-47; chancellor, Georgia-Zeta Chap, Nu Beta Epsilon Natl Frat,

1950; Fulton Co Govt Appeal. Agt, US Selective Service Sys, 1950-58, bd mem, since 1958; commodore, Ga Gov's Staff, 1951-54; adv to dir, Ga Civil Defense, 1954-55; treas: Fulton Co Democratic Stevenson Comm, 1956; AJComm, 1960-62; trustee: Atlanta Chap, AJComm, since 1956; Atlanta Lodge 1773, B'nai B'rith, since 1959; Democratic Forum, 1960; Miss Atlanta Pageant, since 1966; grand councillor, Phi Epsilon Pi Natl Frat, 1956-59, grand recorder, 1959-60; dir: Atlanta Civic Ballet, 1957-62; Metrop Atlanta Council on Alcoholism, 1958-67; Atlanta Concert Band, 1960-62; Atlanta chap, Amer Natl Theater and Acad, 1964-65; SE Regional Adv Bd, ADL, since 1964; Atlanta Post 112, JWV, 1964-68; Hub of the South Chap, Assn of US Army, since 1964; Bus Educ Employment Services, 1965-66; Atlanta chap, Natl Cystic Fibrosis Research Found, since 1965; Atlanta chap, NCCJ, since 1965; ACLU, Ga, since 1966; mem: Atlanta Gen Depot Army Adv Comm, 1955-61; Atlanta Metrop Area Civil Defense Filter Cen Adv Council, 1956-59; Civic Adv Group, Pres Comm on Fund-Raising within the Fed Service, 1959-61; Tech Adv Comm, Econ Opportunity Atlanta, since 1965; Heb Benevolent Cong; clubs: Standard; Commerce. Recipient: Alvin B Gates silver trophy for Most Outstanding Real Estate Transaction of the Year, Ga Assn Real Estate Bds, 1955, 1957, 1959; Atlanta's Outstanding Young Man of the Year, Atlanta Jaycees, 1957; dist service award for oustanding community service, US Jaycees, 1957; elected to membership, Million Dollar Club, Atlanta Real Estate Bd, 1959, 1960; citation of merit, SE Region ADL, 1964; Phi Epsilon Pi achievement citation in Govt, 1965. Home: 2750 Wyngate, NW, Atlanta, Ga. Office: 40 Pryor St, SW, Atlanta, Ga.

MASSEY, Irving J, Can, educator; b. Montreal, Can, June 15, 1924; s. Alexander and Ida (Zukofsky); BA, McGill U, 1944; AM, Columbia U, 1945; AM, Harvard U, 1946, PhD, 1954; m. Arlene Reichenbach, Aug 30, 1946; c: Melez, Ephraim. Prof, Eng, McGill U, since 1969, asst prof, 1960-64; instr, Eng, Wayne U, 1946-50; teaching f, hum, Harvard U, 1950-54; instr, asst prof, comparative lit, Brandeis U, 1954-60, chmn, dept, 1957-60; asso prof, prof, comparative lit, Eng, SUNY, Buffalo, 1964-69. Can Offs' Training Corps, McGill U, 1943-44. Mem: MLA; Comparative Lit Assn; Keats-Shelley Assn; Can Tchrs of Eng; McGill Assn of U Tchrs. Author: Romanticism and the Object, 1970; trans with introduction and notes, Alfred de Vigny's Stello, 1963; ed, Posthumous Poems of Shelley, 1969; contbr to profsl publs. Recipient: research grants: Amer Phil Soc, 1959; Amer Council of Learned Soc, 1961. Home: c/o Duchow, 7910 Westbrooke Rd, Montreal, Can. Office: McGill U, Montreal, Can.

MASSLER, Maury, US, dentist, educator; b. NYC, Mar 24, 1912; s. Samuel and Celia (Fabricant); BS, NYU, 1932; DDS, U of Ill, 1939, MS, 1941; m. Hilde Wang, Feb 19, 1947; c: Joan. Prof, Coll of Dent, U of Ill, since 1950, mem fac since 1939, dir, child research clinic, since 1941, asso dean, postgrad and tchr educ. Cons: US Army Dent Corps; USN Research Facility; FDA; UNRRA, 1944. Mem: Amer Dent Assn; Intl Assn Dent Research; Amer Acad Pedodontics; Amer Assn Public Health. Home: 311 S Elmwood Ave, Oak Park, Ill. Office: Coll of Dent, U of Ill, Chicago, Ill.

MASUR, Norbert, Isr, business exec, consul gen; b. Friedrichstadt, Ger, May 13, 1901; s. Leser and Hanna (Levy); educ, Hamburg; m. Ella Metz; c: Kurt. Hon Consul Gen of Swed, Tel Aviv; partner, Hollander Org, Stockholm, NY; chmn bd, Hollander and Co, Ltd, Tel Aviv; bd dirs, Isr Devl and Mortgage Bank; mgn dir, AB Baltiska Skinnkompaniet, Stockholm, 1924-57. Council mem: Zionist Org; J Comty, both Swed; negotiated for WJC with Himmler for rescue of inmates of concentration camps. Author: En Jude talar med Himmler, 1945. Recipient: Fr Legion d'Honneur; Danish Liberty Cross. Home: 94 Haeshel, Herzlia Pituah, Isr. Office: 94 Allenby St, Tel Aviv, Isr.

MATALON, Aaron Joseph, Jamaica, business exec; b. St Andrew, Jamaica, Oct 30, 1919; s. Joseph and Florizel (Henriquez); att Jamaica Coll; m. Marjorie DeMercado, Jan 21, 1945; c: Joseph, Barbara, Ricardo, Janet. Chmn: Facey Commodity Co Ltd; PA Benjamin Mfg; Commodity Service; Homelectrix; Home Appliance Finance; dir: Ind Commercial Devls Ltd; Comserv Pharm; Tropicair Jalousies; W Indies Paints; W Indies Home Contractors; Conditioned Air; Redimix Concrete; Jamaica Cocoa Products. Chmn, Things Jamaican; dir: Jamaican Inst Mgmt; Jamaica Mfrs Assn; mem: United Cong Isrs; bd govs, St Hugh's HS. Home: 3 Tyndhurst Ave, Kingston, Jamaica. Office: 7-9 Harbour St, Kingston, Jamaica.

MATELES, Richard Isaac, Isr, educator; b. NYC, Sep 11, 1935; s. Simon and Jean (Phillips); in Isr since 1968; BS, MIT, Mass, 1956, MS, 1957, DSc, 1959; m. Roslyn Fish, Sep 2, 1956; c: Naomi, Susan. Visiting prof, Heb U, Jerusalem, since 1968; asso prof, MIT, since 1960; research f, Technische Hogeschool, Dclft, Holland, 1959-60. Mem: Sons of the Amer Revolution; Amer J Hist Soc; numerous sci orgs. Contbr to profsl jours. Hobbies: travel, salling. Home: 60 Hehalutz St, Jerusalem, Isr. Office: Heb U-Hadassah Med Sch, Jerusalem, Isr.

MATIS, Jacob D, US, physician; b. NYC, Sep 27, 1911; s. Joseph and Rose (Rand); BA, Cornell U, 1932; MD, LI Coll of Med, 1936; m. Rosalie Metzger, Oct 12, 1942; c: George, Nancy. Phys in pvt practice; att phys, Roosevelt Hosp, card clinic, since 1965; sr clinical asst card, Mt Sinai Hosp, since 1939; asso phys, Beth David Hosp, NY, 1939-55; att phys, Grand Cen Hosp, 1960-63. Lt col, Army MC, 1942-46. FACP; US f: Amer Coll Chest Phys; Amer Coll Card; dipl, Amer Bd Internal Med; mem: AMA; NY Acad Med; Amer Trudeau Soc; AHA; Cong Rodeph Sholem; Odd Fellows; Masons. Contbr to profsl jours. Hobby: photography. Homes: 25 Central Park W, New York, NY; Dutchess Blvd, Atlantic Beach, NY. Office: 25 Central Park W, New York, NY.

MATLIN, David Arthur, US, attorney; b. Los Angeles, Cal, Oct 24, 1910; s. Bernard and Elizabeth (Olincy); AB, UCLA, 1932; JD, U of S Cal Law Sch, 1934; m. Frances Karsh, Jan 9, 1932; c: Roger, William. Atty since 1934. Seaman, USNR, 1927-31. Dir, US Olympic Comm; exec off, Amateur Athletic Union of US, fmr pres; mem: Sigma Alpha Mu; LA, Cal State Bar Assns; Temple Emanuel, Beverly Hills; LA Athletic Club; fmr: chmn: US Olympic Weightlifting Comm; Natl AAU Weightlifting Comm; pres: S Pacific Assn, AAU; S Cal Soaring Assn; S Cal Weightlifting Assn; master, Loyalty Masonic Lodge; dir, gen counsel, Soaring Soc Amer; capt, UCLA Boxing Team; treas, LA Convalescent Home; dir, LA J Employment Agcy; mem, bd mgrs, LA YMCA; intl weight-lifting referee: Olympic Games; Macabiah Games; Pan Amer Games; World Weightlifting Championships. Hobbies: weightlifting, travel, photography. Home: 218 S Bedford Dr, Beverly Hills, Cal. Office: 606 S Olive St, Los Angeles, Cal.

MATLOFF, Maurice, US, historian; b. Bklyn, NY, June 18, 1915; s. Joseph and Ida (Glickhouse); BA, Columbia Coll, 1936; MA, Harvard U, 1937, PhD, 1956; cert, Russ ares and lang, Yale U, 1944; m. Gertrude Glickler, Oct 21, 1942; c: Howard, Jeffrey, Jody. Sr hist adv, chief, general hist br off, Chief of Mil Hist, Dept of Army, since 1965, chief current hist br, 1960-65, chmn, incentives award comm, 1961-62, chief, strategic plans sect, 1949-60, sr hist, oprs div, 1946-49; instr, hist dept, Bklyn Coll, 1939-42, acting asso prof, 1946; lectr, adult educ prog, YWCA, 1948-51; prof, lectr, hist dept, U of Md, since 1957; visiting prof, hist dept, U of Cal, 1968-69; lectr: Army War Coll; Navy War Coll; Columbia; U of Cal, San Diego; U of Wash; tchr, hist dept, SF State Coll, summer 1965. US Army, WW II. Comm mem, hist and fed govt, Amer Hist Assn, 1958-63; chmn, vocational guidance comm, Independence Lodge, B'nai B'rith, 1947-1948; mem: Phi Beta Kappa; Inst Strategic Studies, London. Author: Strategic Planning for Coalition Warfare, 1943-1944, publ 1959; co-author: Strategic Planning for Coalition Warfare, 1941-42, publ 1953; contbr to hist and mil publs. Recipient: Secy of Army study and research f, 1959-60; Superior Performance Award, US Govt, 1958; Meritorious Civil Service Medal, 1965. Spec interests: adult educ, writing, travel. Home: 4109 Dewmar Court, Kensington, Md. Office: Off Chief of Mil Hist, Dept of Army, Washington, DC.

MATLUCK, Joseph H, US, educator; b. Bklyn, NY, Nov 25, 1917; s. Max and Jennie (Lifschitz); BA, Bklyn Coll, 1940; att U of Rome, 1946-47; MA, Mexico City Coll, 1949; PhD, magna cum laude, Natl U of Mexico, 1951; m. Maria Pireti, Feb 20, 1947 (decd). Asso prof, romance langs, dir, lang lab, U of Tex, since 1955, mem, U of Tex Grad School Fac; instr, romance langs, Northwestern U, 1951-55; visiting prof: audio-visual cons, U of Puerto Rico, 1958-59; applied ling ands— modern langs, U of NM, 1960-61; applied ling, NYU, 1962; Hispano dialectology, Colegio de Mexico, 1963; Span and Portling, 2nd Inter-Amer Ling Inst, Mexico, 1967-68; Hispanic dialectology, U of Mexico, 1968; Baird Found lectr, U of the Americas, Mexico City, 1963; Fulbright advanced research scholar, Rome, It, 1963-64; ling cons to Gov, State of Oxaca, Mexico, 1969. Capt, USAAF, 1942-46. Mem: Amer Assn Tchrs of Span and Port; MLA; Ling Soc of Amer; AAUP. Author: La Pronunciation en el Espanol del Valle de Mexico, 1951;

Entonacion Hispanica, 1965; contbr to profsl jours. Recipient: Natl Found for Hum research grant, 1969-70. Hobbies: sport, classical music. Home: 3903 Bailey Lane, Austin, Tex. Office: U of Tex, Austin, Tex.

MATSAS, Minos Samuel, Greece, business exec, communal leader; b. Preveza, Greece, Dec 24, 1903; s. Samuel and Stamoula (Abraham); att U of Greece, Athens, 1922-27; m. Margaret Sarfati, 1936; c: Samuel. Chmn, Minos Matsas & Son, Ltd. Greek Army. Chmn, J Comty, Athens; fmr: chmn, Communal J Sch, Athens; mng dir, Voice of Isr, monthly rev; mem, B'nai B'rith. Home: 5 Kodrington St, Athens, Greece. Office: 48 Stadium St, Athens, Greece.

MATSDORF, Wolf Simon, Asutr, social worker; b. Berlin, Ger, Aug 9, 1907; s. Georg and Elfriede (Singer); in Austr since 1938; LLD, U of Breslau, Ger, 1930; social work, U of Sydney, 1953-56; m. Hilda Meyerowitz, 1956; c: Peter. Sr social worker, comty org, dept correctional services, since 1959; dir, sr social worker, J Welfare Agcy, since 1949; off, J Chronicle, London, since 1950; free-lance writer on J and social wfr issues. Army, 1942-45. Hon dir: Austr Natl Assn for Mh; B'nai B'rith Parents Home, Sydney; exec, Good Neighbor Council; past: dir, J aid org, Frankfurt, Ger; chmn, Overseas J Comm, exec council of Australian J; exec: Old People's Wfr Council; Sheltered Workshops org; delg, B'nai B'rith, UN sem on Police and Hum Rights, Canberra, 1963; official delg, Austr Citizenship Conv, Canberra, 1964-1969; mem, Austr delg, UN cong, Crime and Treatment of Offenders, Stockholm, 1965; leader, Austr delg, cong of World Fed for Mh, Bangkok, 1965; mem: Austr Assn Social Workers; B'nai B'rith Albert Einstein lodge, Sydney; Austr and NZ Soc Criminology. Author: Migrant Youth, 1963; Work With Migrants In Prison After-Care, 1965; author, publisher, Social Defense in Israel, 1965; mem ed bd, Australian J Quarterly Found; contbr articles on Mh. Spec interest: Mh problems, particularly concerning immigration. Home and office: 36 Shirley Rd, Roseville, NSW, Austr.

MATZNER, Mendel, Isr, business exec; b. Krakow, Pol, Nov 11, 1909; s. Salomon and Malka (Reich); in Isr since 1952; ordained rabbi, Rabb Sem, Berlin; att U of Berlin, U of Zurich; m. Rosa Goldberg, Dec 19, 1939; c: Miriam Mannes, Ori. Dir, owner, Dr Matzner Ltd, spinning mills, since 1952. Pres, Ognisko J Student Org, Pol; mem, B'nai B'rith. Spec interests: Talmud, Bible. Home: 22 Chen Ave, Tel Aviv, Isr. Office: Herzlia, Isr.

MAY, Alan M, US, business exec; b. NYC, Apr 23, 1935; s. Jack and Madeline (Mutnick); SB, MIT, Cambridge, 1957; MBA, NYU, Grad Sch of Bus, 1959; m. Marcia Wolfson, June 6, 1963; c: Alexandra. Exec vice-pres, dir, Steak and Ale Restaurants of Amer, Inc, since 1970; asst vice-pres, Bankers Trust Co, 1957-65; vice-pres, finance, treas, Elcor Chem Corp, 1965-69. Capt, US Army, Chem Corps. Dir: Midland Co United Fund; Mus of Southwest, Midland, Tex, treas; trustee, Hillander Sch; fmr: vice-pres, B'nai B'rith, Permian chap; chmn, Isr Bond Drive; vice-chmn, New Leadership Div, FJP, NYC; treas, Temple Beth El, Odessa, Tex; mem, Financial Execs Inst, Dallas; clubs: Midland Country; The, Racquet, both Midland, Tex. Home: 6 Hanover Dr, Midland, Texas. Office: 3305 Turtle Creek, Dallas, Tex.

MAY, Alfred Albert, US, attorney; b. Wash, DC, Feb 24, 1906; s. Isadore and Mina (David); BA, U of Md, 1924; LLB, George Wash U, 1929; m. Sylvia Scheer, Nov 22, 1928; c: Nancy, Alan. Atty, cons, Ford Motor Co; legal adv, Selective Service, Wayne Co Public Admn; spec agt, FBI, 1929-31; asst US Atty, 1931-33. Chief, intelligence off, USAAF, 1942-45. Chmn: Rep Comm, 1st Cong Dist; Loyalty Inves Commn, City of Detroit, 1952-60; pres, Detroit Round Table of Catholics, Js and Prots; natl bd dirs, NCCJ; natl financial comm, ADL; trustee: Marygrove Coll; Kirwood Hosp; clubs: Probus; City Detroit Hundred; Standard City; Franklin Hills Country. Home: 17610 Fairway Dr, Detroit, Mich. Office: 1150 First Natl Bldg, Detroit, Mich.

MAY, Armand, US, business exec, manufacturer; b. Marseilles, Fr, Oct 27, 1882; s. Meyer and Pauline (Levy); in US since 1883. Chmn, bd, Amer Assos Co, comprising: Amer Mills; Asso Thread; Amer Factors; mem, bd, Amer Lecithin; chmn bd, Asso Concentrates, all since 1959, pres, 1902-1959; spec adv, Export-Import Bank, Wash, DC, 1918; vice-pres, Amer Mfrs Export Assn, 1919. Chmn, bd, J Children's Service, Atlanta, since 1955; mem, Heb Benevolent Cong; club, Standard Town and Country, Atlanta. Home: 2161 Ponce de Leon

Ave, NE, Atlanta, Ga. Office: 451-475 Stephens St, SW, Atlanta, Ga.

MAY, Jean Wise, US, communal worker; b. Cincinnati, O, Feb 21, 1881; d. Isaac and Selma (Bondi) Wise; BA, U of Cincinnati, 1901; m. Albert May, Dec 11, 1906 (decd); c: Albert, Elsie Herzog. Hon pres: Natl Fed Temple Sisterhoods, since 1960; Sisterhood Rel Schs Comm; fmr, pres, Heb Women's Aid, Flushing; hon vice-pres: Natl Fed Temple Youth; NY Fed Reform Syns; NY Fed J Women's Orgs; hon mem: bd, NY sect, Natl Council J Women; JWB; Cen Syn Sisterhood; JDC; co-found: public health nursing, Flushing, Queens, NY, 1925-28; Big Sisters of Queens, 1926. Home: 420 E 86 St, New York, NY.

MAY, Karl Haran, Isr, engineer; b. Hamburg, Ger, Mar 28, 1899; s. Hugo and Elika (Samson); in Isr since 1933; att Tech U, Munich, 1919-20; dipl, ing, Tech U, Berlin, 1924; m. Kathe Lemberg, July 17, 1927; c: Alisa England. Ret; first asst of chief elec engr, engr i/c wireless communications, chief research engr, all Isr Elec Corp, 1933-64; voluntary mem, elec comm, Isr Standards Inst; lab engr, AEG, Berlin, 1924-33. Chmn, Haifa br, elec sect, Assn Engrs and Architects, Isr, 1962-68. Home: 5 Hanadiv Blvd, Haifa, Isr.

MAY, Leopold, US, educator; b. Bklyn, NY, Nov 26, 1923; s. Louis and Rose (Lutz); BChE, CCNY, 1944; MS, Poly Inst of Bklyn, 1948; PhD, 1951; m. Evelyn Spector, June 29, 1947; c: Kenneth, Ira. Asso prof, chem, Catholic U of Amer, since 1961; research biochem, Columbia U, 1950-54; lectr, chem, Bklyn Coll, 1953; instr, chem, Johns Hopkins U, 1954-57; instr, psycht, U of Md, 1954-60. USN, 1944-46. Mem: Soc of Joseph Bros; Soc Applied Spectroscopy; Amer Chem Soc; AAUP; Phi Lambda Upsilon; Sigma Xi. Ed in chief, Applied Spectroscopy, 1961-64. Home: 10217 Lorain Ave, Silver Spring, Md. Office: Catholic U, Washington, DC.

MAY, Mortimer, US, business exec; b. Laconia, NH, Dec 20, 1892; s. Jacob and Rebecca (Weingarten); BS, Columbia U, 1914; m. Gertrude Bloch, Dec 26, 1917; c: Leon, Mrs Robert Blum. Chmn, bd, May Corp, Nashville, Tenn, since 1958, pres, 1946-58. Natl pres, ZOA, 1954-56, hon pres, SE Zionist region, since 1946, pres, Nashville dist, 1937-40; bd, Miami Beach Zionist Dist, since 1960; pres: Vine St Temple, 1940-43; JCC, 1943-45, both Nashville; vice-pres: CJFWF, 1950-58; Amer Comm for Weizmann Inst, since 1945; mem bd: United Isr Appeal, since 1935; Brandeis Youth Found since 1940; HUC, 1942-48; WZ Actions Comm since 1946; Amer Assn for J Educ, 1945-55; UAHC since 1950; Amer Financial Devl Corp for Isr since 1950; JNF since 1940; ORT since 1955; AJCong, bd mem, 1936-66; mem: Comm on Fgn Relations; Barnard Astronomical Soc. Author: May, Foot Soldier in Zion. Home: 5024 Alton Rd, Miami Beach, Fla. Office: May Corp, Nashville, Tenn.

MAYBAUM, Ignaz, Eng, rabbi; b. Vienna, Aus; s. Moritz and Josephine; att Gymnasium, Vienna. Minister em, Edgware & Dist Reform Syn; co-ed, European Judaism, biannual, London; fmr: rabbi: Bingen Rhein; Frankfurt/Oder; Berlin; lectr, theol, Leo Baeck Coll, London. Lt, Aus Army, WW I. Author: Parteibefreites Judentum, 1935; Neue Jugend & Alter Glaube, 1936; Man and Catastrophy, 1941; Synagogue and Society, 1944; The Jewish Home, 1945; The Jewish Mission, 1949; Sacrifice of Isaac, 1959; Jewish Existence, 1960; The Faith of the Jewish Diaspora, 1962; The Faith of God after Auschwitz, 1963; Creation and Guilt, 1968. Spec interest: theol writing. Home: 60 Whitchurch Gardens, Edgware, Middlesex, Eng.

MAYER, Albert, US, architect, town planner; b. NYC, Dec 29, 1897; s. Bernhard and Sophia (Buttenwieser); AB, Columbia, 1917; BCE, MIT, 1919; m. Phyllis Carter, Aug 20, 1925(div); c: Stella, Kerry; m. 2nd, Marion Preminger, Mar 21, 1961. Pvt practice; lectr, architecture and planning: MIT; O State U; Columbia U; Wis U; visiting prof, Urban Design Studio, Columbia U; lectr, for USIA, Brazil, 1968; cons, Public Housing Admn, US Govt; mem, Mayer, Whittlesey & Glass, NYC, 1935-61. Lt, US Army, 1918; lt col, 1942-45. Projects include: Manhattan House, NYC; new city for Aluminium Co of Can, Kitimat, BC; housing and bldgs, Standard Vacuum Oil Co Refinery, Bombay; Ft Greene Housing Project, NYC; master plans: Gtr Bombay; New Delhi region; new Punjab capital city, Chandigarh; Gujarat U; Allahabad Agric Inst; Ashdod new seaport, Isr; Etawal Rural Devl projects, India; housing, shops, comty facilities, Bellmawr, NJ; planning adv, United Provinces, Govt of India. Dir, Natl

Housing Conf; fmr trustee: New Sch for Social Research; Lavanburg Found; f: Amer Inst Architects, chmn, comm urban design and housing, 1950-52; Soc Applied Anthropology; mem: Amer Soc Civil Engrs; Amer Inst Planners; Housing Study Guild, co-founder; Regional Devl Council of Amer; dir, Regional Plan Assn, NY; fmr dir, NY State Citizens Council; Phi Beta Kappa. Author: Pilot Project: India,1958; The Urgent Future, People, Housing, City, Region, 1967; Greenbelt Towns Revisited, 1968. Recipient: Apartment House medal, NY chap, Amer Inst Architects, 1940, 1952, medal of honor, 1952; Munic Art Soc award for design of E Harlem Plaza in Jefferson Houses, NYC; honor award, Amer Soc Landscape Architects, 1962; citation, NY chap, Amer Inst Architects, 1963; citation for Public Housing and Community Design, Natl Assn of Housing and Redevl Officials, 1963, 1964; Man of the Year award, NY Metrop Chap, 1969. Home: 550 Park Ave, New York, NY. Office: 31 Union Sq W, New York, NY.

MAYER, Alfred Max, Isr, plant physiologist; b. Halberstadt, Ger, Oct 5, 1926; s. Rudolf and Paula (Joseph); in Isr since 1950; BS , PhD, U of London, Eng. Prof, botany, Heb U, Jerusalem, since 1969. Author: Textbook of Plant Physiology, 1959; Germination of Seeds, 1963; contbr to sci jours. Home: 5 Palmach St, Jerusalem, Isr. Office: Botany Dept, Heb U, Jerusalem, Isr.

MAYER, Arthur L, US, business exec, author, educator; b. Demopolis,Ala, May 28, 1886; s. Simon and Rachel (Bernheim); BA, Harvard Coll, 1907; m. Lillie Stein, May 16, 1913; c: Peter, Michael, Nora Simon. Pres, Mayer Enterprises, since 1950; gen mgr, Great States Theaters, Chgo,Ill, 1919-22; dir, Oprs Midwest Theaters, Paramount Pictures Corp, 1922-27; dir, advt, publicity, 1927-29; owner, Rialto Theater, NYC, 1929-48; pres, Mayer-Burstyn Inc, 1929-49; asst to coord, war activities comm, Motion Picture Ind, 1941-44; chief, motion picture bur, US Forces in Ger, 1948-49; instr, Dartmouth, NYU, USC, Columbia, Stanford. Pres, Independent Distributors of Amer, 1949-54; exec vice-pres, Council of Motion Pictures Org, 1949-53; sup, educ picture project, Motion Picture Assn, 1946-47; asst to chmn, ARC, 1945-47; mem, AJComm; clubs: Pioneers; Variety; City. Author: Merely Colossal, 1953; The Movies, 1957. Recipient: US Medal of Merit, 1945. Hobbies: gardening, photography. Home: Mt Ivy, Rockland Co, NY.

MAYER, Astorre, It, industrialist; b. Milan, Mar 12, 1906; s. Sally (Salomone) and Matilda (Vita); ME, Poly, Milan, 1928; m. Elena Levi de Veali, June 21, 1936; c: Maria, Marcella, Maurizio. Pres, Vita Mayer & Co, since 1928. Lt, It Army. Pres, It ZF; hon gen consul of Isr in Milan; fmr: pres, J Comty, Milan; hon chmn: Eur Council J Comty Services; JNF, It; club, Rotary. Home: Via Bigli 5, Milan, It. Office: Via Monte Napoleone 9, Milan, It.

MAYER, Clara W, US, educator; b. NYC, June 1, 1895; d. Bernhard and Sophia (Buttenwieser); BA, Barnard Coll, 1915; att Columbia U, 1915-19; Des Lettres, New Sch for Social Research, 1948. Dean, sch of phil and lib arts, New Sch for Social Research, 1943-61, trustee, 1924-30, asst dir, 1929-36, asso dir, 1937-43, secy, bd trustees, 1931-46, vice-pres, 1950-61; dir, numerous real estate corps. Author: The Man-made Wilderness, 1964; The Great Adventure. Home: 41 E 72 St, New York, NY.

MAYER, Daniel, Fr, journalist; b. Paris, Apr 29, 1909; s. Emile and Lucie (Weill); m. Claire Leibovici-Livian, May 19, 1931. Pres, Ligue des Droits de l'Homme, since 1958; Social Service Populaire, 1933-39; mem, Conseil Natl de la Résistance; gen secy, Socialist Party, 1943-46; mem, Provisionary, Constituent and Natl Assemblies, 1944-46, 1951, 1956; Min of Lab, 1946-49; Min of Public Health and Vets Affairs, 1947; Paris dep, 1944, 58, pres, 1953-57, Fgn Affairs Comm of Natl Assembly. Fmr, ed-in-chief, clandestine Populaire. Recipient: Rosette de la Résistance, 1943; Chevalier de la Légion d'Honneur, 1947; Croix de Guerre, 1947; Commandeur de la Santé Publique, 1948; Commandeur du Mérite Social, 1950; Commandeur de la Libération Espagnole, 1952. Office: 27 rue Jean Dolent, Paris, Fr.

MAYER, Frank Jacob, Luxembourg, financial cons, exec; b. Luxembourg, June 30, 1901; s. Adolph and Jenny (Reis); att Us: Munich; Paris; PhD, U Heidelberg, 1923; m. Ida Lieben, May 24, 1924; c: Arno, Ruth Burger. Econ and financial cons; mem, bd dirs, various cos; pres: Mayer-Reis, 1923-40; Pennshire Shirt Co, 1941-58; gen mgr, SA Des

Minerais, 1959-69. Pres, Luxembourg Freinds of Heb U; secy, Amis d'Israel, Luxembourg; mem, KJV. Home: 11A Blvd Prince Henri, Luxembourg. Office: 3-5 Pl Winston Churchill, Luxembourg.

MAYER, Jane Rothschild, US, author; b. Kansas City, Mo, Dec 30, 1903; d. Louis and Nora (Westheimer); AB, Vassar Coll, 1925; m. David Mayer Jr, 1927 (decd); c: David, Philip, Mary Bezark. Author: Betsy Ross and the Flag, 1952; Dolly Madison, 1954; The Year of the White Trees, 1958: co-author: Instruct My Sorrows, 1942; These Are the Times, 1944; This Eager Heart, 1947; The Early Frost, 1952. Mem: Author's League; steering comm, women's bd, U of Chgo; bd dirs, Soc of Midland Authors; exec comm, women's bd, Field Mus; clubs: Arts, Chgo; Chgo Press. Home: 1445 N State Pkwy, Chicago, Ill.

MAYER, Kurt Bernd, Switz, sociologist, educator; b. Zurich, Switz, Sep 6, 1916; s. Anna Hirsch; MA, Brown U, 1956; PhD, Columbia U, 1951; m. Elizabeth Meyer, Mar 28, 1942; c: Charles, Eva, David. Prof, Inst of Sociol, U of Bern, since 1966; lectr, grad fac, political and social sci, New Sch for Social Research, 1947-50; instr, Rutgers U, 1948-50; prof, Brown U, 1956-66, fac mem since 1950, chmn, dept sociol and anthropology, 1957-63; visiting prof, Australian Natl U, 1963. Author: The Population of Switzerland, 1952; Class and Society, 1955; co-author: Migration and Economic Development in Rhode Island, 1958; The Ecology of Providence, vol I, 1958, vol II, 1961; The First Two Years, 1961; Metropolitanization and Population Change in Rhode Island, 1962; Population Projections, Rhode Island Cities and Towns, 1970 and 1980, 1963; The People of Rhode Island, 1960, 1963; Residential Mobility, Migration and Commuting in Rhode Island, 1963; contbr to intl jours. Home: Wyhalenstr 704D, Hinterkappelen, Switz. Office: U of Bern, Inst Sociol, Brückfeldstr 14, Bern, Switz.

MAYER, Marcel, Fr, stockbroker; b. Brodaux, Fr, Sep 7, 1893; m. Helen Jaudel, Mar 25, 1925; c: Francois. Porp: Mayer Freres, 1927-62; Marcel Mayer, 1962-65; Francois Mayer, since 1965. Jt treas, Consistoire Cen de Fr; Bordeaux delg to Cen Consistory. Home: 49 rue de Monceau, Paris, Fr.

MAYER, Michael F, US, attorney; b. White Plains, NY, Sep 8, 1917; s. Arthur and Lillie (Stein); BS, cum laude, Harvard Coll, 1939; LLB, Yale Law School, 1942; m. Janet Claster, Aug 15, 1943; c: Joan, Arthur, Aline, Shelley. Partner, law firm, Mayer & Bucher, since 1968; exec dir, Independent Firm Importers & Distributors of Amer Inc, 1959-67; staff atty, Greenbaum, Wolff & Ernst, law firm, 1946-48; instr, bus problems in entertainment world, NYU Sch of Continuing Educ, since 1969. Capt, USAAC, 1943-45. Pres, Beach Hill Edgemont Civic Assn, 1958-60; secy, Film Soc of Lincoln Cen, Inc, since 1969; mem: exec bd, AJComm, since 1958, chmn, Westchester div, 1957-59; bd dirs, Amer J Soc for Service, NY, 1951-59; Dem candidate for surrogate, Westchester Co, 1961. Author: Foreign Films on American Screens, 1965; Divorce and Annulment in the 50 States, 1967; What You Should Know about Libel and Slander, 1968; contbr to publs. Home: 9 Inverness Rd, Scarsdale, NY. Office: 111 W 57 St, New York, NY.

MAYER, René, Fr, statesman; b. Paris, May 4, 1895; dipl, Ecole Libre des Sci Politiques; D en Droit, U Paris; m. Denise Bloch. Mem, Fr Parliament, since 1945; auditor, Conseil d'Etat, 1920-25, maître des Requêtes; admnr, council, Port of Strasbourg; secy gen, suprcomm, Fr RR; prof, Ecole des Sci Politiques; commissar, head, mission to Gt Brit, Fr Min of Armament, WW II; secy of communications, Fr Liberation Comm, Algiers, WW II; mem, Gen Council, Eure Region, 1945; Min: Public Works, 1944; Finance, 1947; Natl Defense, 1948; Justice, 1949; Finance, 1951; Premier of Fr, 1953; pres, High Auth of Eur Coal and Steel Comty, 1955-58; hon chmn, Fr Council of the Eur Movement. Fr Army, WW I. Recipient: Croix de Guerre, 1918; Grand Officier, Légion d'Honneur; Médaille des Evadés; US Freedom Medal. Office: 75 Ave des Champs Elysées, Paris, Fr.

MAYER, Reuven Rudolf, Isr, psychiatrist; b. Essen, Ger, Mar 6, 1910; s. Bernhard and Elly; in Isr since 1937; MD, Us: Ger, Aus, Switz, 1928-34; postgrad studies: Boston; Topeka, 1953-54; m. Miriam Wullis; c: Ayala Lavie, Irit Eisenberg, Ram. Dir, Govt Psycht Hosp, Beer Yakov, regional psycht; sr lectr, Tel Aviv U. Maj, MC, IDF. Pres: Group Psychotherapy Soc; Med Soc, Ramat Gan, 1940-41; Neuropsycht Soc,

Tel Aviv, 1962-65. Contbr to profsl jours. Home: 8 Harakefet St, Rehovot, Isr.

MAYER, Victor, US, surgeon; b. Bklyn, NY, May 22, 1913; s. William and Esther (Onifater); BA, Lehigh U, 1934; MD, Jefferson Med Coll, 1938; grad study, Columbia U Presbyterian Hosp, 1947; m. Marilyn Marksville, Nov 14, 1945; c: Wendy, David, Nancy. Asst att surg: Hosp for Spec Surg, since 1949; NY Hosp; orthopedic cons: Bd of Health, NYC; Inst for Phys Med, NY Hosp, Bellevue; Richmond Co Cerebral Palsy Assn, both since 1953; med dir, Richmond Co Cerebral Palsy Treatment Cen, since 1954; asst prof, orthopedic surg, Cornell U Med Sch, since 1958, instr, orthopedic clinic, 1952-56; teaching f, NYU Bellevue Med Sch, 1953-55; med dir, Godmothers League, Cerebral Palsy Assn, 1952-54; chief, orthopedic service, Bx VA Hosp, 1948-50; f, children's orthopedics, Hosp for Spec Surg, 1942-48. US Army, 1941-46. FACS, 1950; f, Amer Acad Orthopedic Surgs, 1951; dipl, Amer Bd Orthopedic Surg, 1950; mem: NY Co Med Soc; Amer Assn Mental and Phys Rehab; Phi Beta Kappa; Alpha Omega Alpha. Contbr to med jours. Home: 108-40 66 Ave, Forest Hills, NY. Office: 109-20 Queens Blvd, Forest Hills, NY.

MAYERSON, Hymen S, US, physiologist, educator; b. Providence, RI, Sep 10, 1900; s. Moses and Frances (Shepper); BA, Boston U, 1922, hon DSc, 1962; PhD, Yale U, 1925; m. Caroline Wolf, June 10, 1930; c: Peter, Mary. Prof em, Tulane U Sch of Med, since 1965, prof, chmn, dept phys, 1945-65, fac mem since 1926; asso dir, Touro Infirmary, since 1965; cons in phys, 1949-65; cons, research div, Vets Hosp, since 1953; asst, biol, Brown U, 1921-22; asst, phys, Yale U, 1922-25, instr, 1925-26. Pres, Amer Phys Soc, 1962-63; chmn, adv bd, Fed of Amer Socs of Experimental Biol, 1963-64; mem: Soc Experimental Biol and Med, chmn, S sect, 1938-39; AAUP, pres, Tulane chap, 1941-42; New Orleans Acad of Scis, vice-pres, 1950-52; La Heart Assn, secy, 1955-56, vice-chmn, 1955-60; fmr, bd dir, AHA; S Soc for Clinical Research; sub-comm on shock, 1954-61; Natl Bd Med Examiners; USA Natl Comm, Intl Union of Phys Scis; Sigma Xi, pres, Tulane chap, 1943-44. Chmn, ed bd, Physiological Revs, 1956-62; contbr to profsl jours. Home: 1140 Seventh St, New Orleans, La. Office: 1400 Foucher St, New Orleans, La.

MAYERSON, Philip, US, educator; b. NYC, May 20, 1918; s. David and Clara (Feder); PhD, NYU, 1956; m. Ann Barkow, Nov 28, 1957; c: Miriam, Clare. Asso prof, classics, NYU, since 1960; vice dean, Wash Sq Coll, NYU, since 1969. USN, 1942-45. Mem: Amer Philol Assn; Archaeol Inst Amer; Amer Oriental Soc; Colt Archaeol Inst. Author: The Ancient Agricultural Regime of Nessana and the Central Negeb, 1961. Recipient: grant-in-aid, Rockefeller Found, 1956-57; f, Amer Council Learned Soc, 1961-62. Home: 610 Cathedral Pkwy, New York, NY. Office: NYU, New York, NY.

MAZAR, Benjamin, Isr, archaeologist, educator; b. Grodno, Russ, July 28, 1906; in Isr since 1928; PhD, U Giessen, 1928; hon degs: HUC; JTSA; m. Dinah Shimshi, 1932; c: Ory. Full prof, ancient J hist and archaeol of Pal, Heb U, Jerusalem, since 1951, mem fac since 1942; visiting prof, U Chgo, 1950-51; Brandeis U, 1962; i/c excavations: Ramath Rahel; Jerusalem; Tell Qasila, near Tel Aviv; Beth Searim, Galilee; Beth Yarah, Jordan Valley; Ein Gedi, Dead Sea Region, since 1931. Pres, Isr Exploration Soc; mem, admn bd, Intl Assn of Us; chmn, Archaeol Bd of Isr; mem, Isr Acad Scis; fmr chmn, Inst for J Studies. Author: Untersuchungen zur alten Geschichte Syriens und Palästinas, 1930; History of the Archaeological Excavations in Palestine, 1936; History of Palestine, 1938; Historical Atlas of Palestine, Biblical Period, 1942; Archaeological Excavations in Tell Quasila, 1951; Geographical Names of the Settlements in Eretz Israel, 1933; The Beth Shearim Excavations, 1942, 1959; chmn, ed bd, Ency Biblica; ed: ancient East sect, Ency Hebraica; Views of the Bible World; World History of the Jewish People, vol 2, 1968; contbr to Pal, Syrian hist, hist geog, archaeol, to publs. Home: 9 Abarbanel St, Jerusalem, Isr. Office: Hebrew U, Jerusalem, Isr.

MAZAR, Ory N, Isr, publisher; b. Jerusalem, Jan 21, 1932; s. Benjamin and Dinah (Shimshi); nephew of late pres Itzhak Ben Zvi; att Heb U, Jerusalem, 1951-55. Pres: Isr Pub Inst, since 1958; Unibook Inc, NY; mgn dir, ORIM, Isr book enterprises, Jerusalem; ed, Isr Army Newspapers, 1948-49; free-lance journalist, 1950-55; vice-pres, Intl Pub Co, 1956-58; gen ed, World J Ency; Heb Heritage Libr; Biographical Ency of US. Mem, cen comm, Mapai party; fmr: chmn youth div, court chmn, Lapid, political group; chmn, Lecked, political group; secy gen, Assn Isr-Brazil Cultural Relations. Author:

The Pharaohs of Egypt; Life and Time of Abraham Lincoln; Crete; contbr to jours. Home: 42 Ussishkin St, Jerusalem, Isr. Offices: Mt Scopus Rd, Jerusalem, Isr; 215 Park Aves, New York, NY.

MAZER, William, US, business exec; b. NYC, July 30, 1905; s. Abraham and Rose (Kamensky); BS, NYU, 1926; att Columbia U Law Sch, 1927; m. Helen Cohen, July 16, 1932; c: Linda Berkowitz, Frank, Robert, Pres, Hudson Pulp and Paper Corp, since 1955, purchasing agent, 1932-37, vice-pres, 1937-47, exec vice-pres, 1947-55. Pres, Muscular Dystrophy Assn of Amer, since 1953; chmn, bd, Amer-Isr Cultural Found, since 1960; trustee: Brandeis U, since 1954; Leb Hosp; J Sanitarium and Hosp for Chronic Diseases; FJP; UJA; mem, Pi Lambda Phi; club, Metrop Country. Hobby: music. Home: 944 Fifth Ave, New York, NY. Office: 477 Madison Ave, New York, NY.

MAZGAONKER, Eliezer Joseph, India, communal worker; b. Nimej, India, Mar 20, 1905; s. Joseph and Mary (Daniel); m. Esther Elijah, Apr 10, 1946. Ret; detective insp, salt revenue, Burma Salt Revenue Dept, Burma Govt, 1922-51. Pres, Poona Zionist Assn, since 1958; mem: bd trustees, Succath Shelomo Syn, since 1954, fmr pres; Free Masons; fmr mem, Rotary, Belgum, India. Recipient: shield, KH, UJA; medal, for Zionist activities, WZO. Home: 12 Todiwalo Rd, Poona, India.

MAZIN, Max, Spain, business exec; b. Cracow, Pol, June 7, 1918; s. Wolf and Sofia (Brodovka); in Spain since 1950; m. Atara Mor, Jan 6, 1960; c: Dafna, Daniel, Ariel. Pres: Compania Castellana Continental; Expansion Financiera; Inmobiliaria Torrejon; Omag; Renta Inmobiliaria. Pres, J Comty of Madrid, since 1961, vice-pres, 1955-61; found, co-pres, J-Chr, comm, Friendship Org of Spain, since 1961; vice-chmn, Eur Council J Comty Services; intl chmn, B'nai B'rith; mem: intl comm, Inst of Contemporary Judaism, Jerusalem; bd: Inst of Sephardic Studies, Madrid; Sephardic State Mus, Toledo. Home: 42 Paseo de la Habana, Madrid, Span. Office: 23 Calle de Serrano, Madrid, Spain.

MAZO, Earl, US, writer; b. Warsaw, Pol, July 7, 1919; s. Samuel and Sonia (Portugal); in US since 1921; BS, Clemson U, 1940; m. Rita Vane, June 15, 1941; c: Judith, Mark. Writer, Reader's Digest, since 1965; ed writer, Camden Courier-Post, Camden, NJ, 1945-49; natl political corresp: NY Herald Tribune, 1949-63; NY Times, 1963-65. Lt, USAAC, 1942-45, staff, Stars and Stripes, 1943-45. Mem: White House Corresps Assn; Acad Political Sci; Amer Assn Public Opinion Research; clubs: Overseas Press; Natl Press; Federal City. Author: Richard Nixon: Personal, Political Portrait, 1959; The Great Debates, 1961; co-author, Nixon, an update, 1968. Recipient: Air Medals, Bronze Star, 2 Pres Citations World War II; Dist Alumnus Award, Clemson U. Home and office: 5915 Nebraska Ave, NW, Washington, DC.

MAZOR, Adam Aharon, Isr, architect; b. Cracov, Pol, Jan 4, 1936; s. Jehoshua and Irene; in Isr since 1939; dipl, architect, Technion, Haifa, 1960; m. Elinoar Shechterman, Oct 13, 1960; c: Gadi, Dani, Keren. Dir, Isr Inst Urban Studies, since 1967; Mazor, Katz, architects, town planners, since 1967; dir, Mazor, Rozen, since 1963. Mem, Architects and Engrs Assn. Author: Town Planning and Welfare Maximization, A Methodological Approach, 1968; New Approach To Urban and Regional Planning, 1967; various papers, on architecture, town planning. Recipient: Kadman Award, Kadman Legacy and Found, 1968. Home: 32 Pituah Herzliya, Isr. Office: 10 Smuts St, Tel Aviv, Isr.

MAZOR, Moshe, Isr, physician, author; b. Racziejew, Pol, Mar 25, 1909; s. Meir and Rachel (Natanowicz); MD, U of Milan, It, 1938; m. Emily Baras, Dec 7, 1941; c: Miriam Herc. Specialist in neuropsycht, Kupath Cholim, Tel Aviv. Pres, J Comm, Lublin-Warsaw, Pol, 1944-45; mem, Isr Neuropsycht Soc. Author: On; i Ona, 1958; Dargney Yish Veyishe, 1959; inventor of psych game, Admor. Home: 66 Gordon St, Tel Aviv, Isr.

MAZUR, Albert, pen name, **Al Mazur,** US, musician, music tchr; b. Schenectady, NY, Oct 21, 1929; s. Seymour and Louise (Ettinger); m. Marion, Oct 18, 1961. Music tchr since 1947; writer, songs including: It Was Nice Loving You; Tennessee Rock; Bar Mitzvah songs. Mem: Masons; ASCAP. Home: 5715 Ave I, Brooklyn, NY.

MAZUR, Irene, Isr, communal leader; b. Cracov, Pol, June 11, 1910; d. Leon and Franziska (Reich) Braciejowski; in Isr

since 1949; m. Yehoshua Mazur, May 23, 1932; c: Rita, Gur, Adam. Chmn, WIZO Child and Youth Dept; mem: World WIZO Exec; B'nai B'rith, found, Rebecca Sieff Lodge. Home: 24 Hanviim St, Tel Aviv, Isr.

MECHOULAM, Raphael, Isr, chemist, educator; b. Sofia, Bulgaria, Nov 5, 1930; s. Moreno and Rosa (Levy); in Isr since 1949; MSc, Heb U, Jerusalem, 1953; PhD, Weizmann Inst, Rehovot, 1958; m. Dalia Borowitz, 1950; c: Roy, Dafna. Asso prof, head, natural products lab, Heb U, Jerusalem, since 1966; research asso, Weizmann Inst, Rehovot, 1958-66. Lt, IDF, 1953-56. Prin contribs: research in chem of natural products; isolation, structure, elucidation, synthesis and chem behavior of components of hashish. Mem, Amer Chem Soc. Recipient: Somach-Sachs Award, Weizmann Inst, 1964. Home: 12 Tchernihovski St, Jerusalem, Isr. Office: Heb U, Jerusalem, Isr.

MECKLENBURGER, Albert F, US, attorney; b. Okolona, Miss, Apr 2, 1888; s. Marcus and Dora (Feibelman); BS, U of Miss, 1907; JD, U of Chgo Law Sch, 1911; m. Josephine Pollak, June 2, 1917; c: Jerome, Martha Blackman, Alvin. Counsel, Pendleton, Neuman, Seibold and Williams, since 1963; asso, Jones, Addington, Ames and Seibold, 1911-19, mem of firm and successor firms, specialists in patent, trade-mark, copyright law, since 1919. Pres: and hon life mem, bd trustees, Natl Fed Temple Brotherhoods, 1938-41; North Shore Cong Israel, Glencoe, Ill, 1944-47; vice-chmn, mem, bd trustees, UAHC, since 1959; Chgo delg, AJConf, 1943; mem: Chgo, Ill, Amer Bar Assns; Bar Assn 7th Fed Jud Circuit; Patent Law Assn of Chgo; Masons; clubs: Northmoor Country; Standard. Home: 315 Windsor St, Park Forest, Ill. Office: 77 W Washington St, Chicago, Ill.

MEDAK, Herman, US, dentist; b. Vienna, Aus, Apr 26, 1914; s. Ignaz and Ella (Medak); in US since 1939; BS, U of Toledo, Ohio, 1943; DDS, Northwestern U, 1946, MS, 1946; PhD, U of Ill, 1959; m. Vivian Fried, Dec 22, 1945; c: Ruth, Joanne, Susan, Alan. Prof, chief, clinical oral path, since 1967, prof, dept preventive med, comty health, since 1966; dent staff: Lutheran Gen Hosp, Parkridge, Ill; Ill Masonic Hosp, Chgo; dent cons, Ill Research Hosp Tumor Clinic, 1948-51. Capt, US Army, 1951-53. Prin contrib: early detection of oral cancer. F: Amer Coll Dents; Intl Coll Dents; dipl, Amer Bd of Oral Path; mem: bd dirs, Chgo south Theater, Chgo; Amer Dent Assn; Intl Assn for Dent Research; AAAS; Amer Soc Cytology; Amer Acad Oral Path; Sigma Xi; Omicron Kappa Upsilon; Alpha Omega; fmr, bd dirs, bd educ, Temple Judea. Author: Atlas of Oral Cytology, 1970; contbr to cytological and dent jours. Home: 6820 Kostner St, Lincolnwood, Ill. Office: 808 S Wood St, Chicago, Ill.

MEDAN, Meir, Isr, linguist; b. Cracow, Pol, June 6, 1915; s. Barukh and Sara; in Isr since 1933; MA, Heb U, Jerusalem; m. Lea Weiss; c: Barukh, Yaakov. Sr sci secy, Heb Lang Acad, since 1948. Served in IDF. Secy, ed bd: Heb Dict of Eliezer Ben Yehuda, 1939-52; ed: Bible Dictionary by Yehoshua Steinberg, 1961; Me'alef Ad' Tav, Heb dict, 1953; Ktav Haet; Leshoneinu, laAm; Reminiscences of the Heb Lang Acad; contbr to sci publs, encys. Home: 24 Yehoshua Ben Nun St, Jerusalem, Isr. Office: Heb Lang Acad, Jerusalem, Isr.

MEDJUCK, Ben Zion, Can, merchant; b. Glubokie, Pol, May 28, 1911; s. Morris and Cipy (Milstein); m. Faye Claener, Mar 22, 1936; c: Gertrude, Marilyn, Joseph. Owner, furniture and appliance bus, since 1936. Mem: exec, ZOC; B'nai B'rith; Masons; fmr pres: YMCA; Zionist order, Habonim lodge; Sgoolai Isr Syn. Home: 147 Lynhaven St, Fredericton, Can. Office: 364 York St, Fredericton, Can.

MEDZINI, Dov, Isr, artist, educator; b. Irkutsk, Russ, Apr 23, 1915; s. Abraham and Josepha (Yrmanovitz); in Isr since 1922; MA, Art Inst, Venice, It; m. Rita Neumann, Sep 20, 1945; c: Amos, Arnon. Artist, lectr, hist of art, Reali Secondary Sch, since 1950; guest lectr, hum studies, Technion, Haifa, 1963, 1965. Numerous one-man shows, Isr and abroad, 1944-66. Cpl, Brit Army, 1942-46; lt, IDF, 1948. Mem, Isr Painters and Sculptors Assn. Recipient: It Govt Medal, 1961. Home: 32 Horeb St, Haifa, Isr.

MEGGED, Aharon, Isr, diplomat, author; b. Wloclawek, Pol, Aug 10, 1920; s. Moshe and Leah (Reichgot); in Isr since 1926; m. Eda Zirlin, May 10, 1944; c: Eyal, Amos. Counsellor for cultural affairs, Isr Emb, London; mem, Kibbutz Sdot Yam, 1938-50; ed, Massa, 1951-55; lit ed, Lamerav, 1955-68.

Lt, IDF, 1948-69. Author: books: Spirit of the Seas, 1950; Far in the Wasteland, 1951; Hedva and I, 1954; Israeli Folk, 1955; Hannah Senesh, 1958; Fortunes of a Fool, 1960; The Escape, 1962; Living on the Dead, 1965, 70; The Second Day, 1968; plays: Incubator on the Rock, 1950; Far in the Wasteland, 1951; Hedva and I, 1956; I Like Mike, 1957; Tit for Tat, 1957; Hannah Senesh, 1958; Genesis, 1962; The High Season, 1968. Mem: Heb Writers Assn, fmr mem, cen comm; Journalists Assn, Tel Aviv; fmr: mem, natl council: Habimah Theater; WJCong. Recipient: Ussishkin Lit Prize, 1955, 1966; Brenner Lit Prize, 1957; Shlonsky Lit Prize, 1963. Home: 26 Ruppin St, Tel Aviv, Isr. Office: Isr Emb, London, Eng.

MEGGED, Matti, Isr, author, educator; b. Kutno, Pol, May 1, 1923; s. Moshe and Lea (Reichgot); in Isr since 1926; MA, Heb U, Jerusalem, 1963; m. Hanna Brickman, Nov 11, 1946; c: Elad, Semadar, Amitay. Lectr, Heb and modern lit, Haifa Coll, since 1963; art adv, Munic Theater, Haifa. Lt, Palmach; IDF, 1941-49. Author: Hamigdal Halavan, 1949; Or Basoreg, 1953; Yomo H'acharon Shel Dani, 1959, 2nd ed, 1968; The Modern Drama, essays, 1966; co-ed: Sefer Hapalmach, 1955; Sefer Hashomer, 1958; trans into Heb, Happy Days by, S Beckett, 1967. Recipient: Jerusalem Prize for Lit, 1959; IIE Grant to Young Writers, NY, 1960. Home: 12 Oren St, Haifa, Isr. Office: Haifa Coll, Haifa, Isr.

MEGIDDO, Raphael, Isr, civil engr; b. Odessa, Russ, July 7, 1913; s. Jehuda and Ethel (Fogel) Magidovitch; in Isr since 1919; BSc, hons, Queen Mary's Coll, London, 1934; m. Miriam Friedmann, June 27, 1935; c: Eithan, Benjamin, Ruth. Dir, engr and contracting co, since 1956; partner, engr cons, J & R Magidovitch, architects, 1934-1954; engr, Ramat Gan Munic, 1937-1944; project engr, designer, A A Lewis & Co, Chgo, Ill, 1939-1940; city planning adv, Natanya, 1940-1945; cons, Shimshon Cement works, 1946-1948. Haganah, 1935-1948; IDF, 1948-1950. Prin contribs: designed: basic city plan, parks, Ramat Gan, Givatayim, Natanya; constructed commercial cen, Ashdod. Chmn, Isr Soc for Advancement of Engr Educ; mem: Isr Soc Engrs and Architects; Isr Contractors Assn; fmr mem, B'nei Brak City Council. Contbr to profsl publs. Hobbies: gardening, photography. Home: 8 Hagilgal St, Ramat Gan, Isr. Office: 17 Haroe St, Ramat Gan, Isr.

MEHLMAN, Benjamin W, US, attorney; b. Bklyn, NY, Aug 6, 1910; s. Henry and Lena (Bieber); AB, Pa State Coll, 1931; JD, Columbia U Law Sch, 1934; m. Evelyn Rubin, May 1, 1938; c: Lisa Robinson, Deane, Irna Gadd. In pvt practice since 1935; mem, Goodstein, Zamore, Mehlman & Krones; village justice, Village of Ocean Beach, Fire I, NY, since 1959. Mem: bd trustees: Soc for Advancement of Judaism, chmn, 1955-58; J Reconstructionist Found Inc; Heb Arts Sch for Music and Dance; pres, Fed of Reconstructionist Congs and Fellowships; bd dirs, Reconstructionist Rabb Coll; mem: Phi Sigma Delta; NY Co Lawyers Assn. Contbr articles to jours. Spec interests: music, J studies. Homes: 41 W 83 St, New York, NY; 696 Ocean Breeze Walk, Ocean Beach, NY. Office: 21 E 40 St, New York, NY.

MEHLMANN, Israel, Isr, educator, education admnr, bibiliographer; b. Olchowiec, Galicia, Mar 26, 1900; s. Michael and Miriam (Redlich); in Isr since 1935; PhD, U Vienna, 1922; grad, Tchrs Coll, Vienna, 1923; m. Miriam Chackel, 1936 (decd); c: Michael, Shelomit. Dir, dept educ and culture in diaspora, affiliated with WZO, since 1953; lectr, hist of drama, Tel Aviv U, since 1955; co-found of U, first dir, 1953; mem, sup bd: Alice Seligsberg Vocational Sch, Jerusalem; Ulpan Akiba, Natanya; prin, secondary sch, Ponevezys, Lith, 1929-35; found, tchr, People's U, Lith, 1929-35; acting prin, U HS, Jerusalem, 1937-48; prin, Heb Tchrs Coll, Jerusalem, 1948-53. Co-found, bd dirs, World J Bible Soc; mem: ed bd, Ency of Educ; ed staff, Inst for Heb Bibliography; contbr to periodicals. Spec interest: rare books. Home: 9 Hameyasdim St, Jerusalem, Isr. Office: Tel Aviv U, Ramat Aviv, Isr.

MEHULAL, Arieh, Isr, organization exec; b. Haifa, Isr, Sep 10, 1921; s. Israel and Chaya (Shaposhnik); grad, Bialik Gymnasium, Haifa; m. Nechama Bendet; c: Yaron, Daphna. Gen secy, Haifa C of C & Ind; secy, Isr Shippers' Council. Off, Irgun Zvai Leumi, 1938-48; in Brit detention and exile for 6 years; IDF, 1948-49. Mem: Misdar Jabotinsky; Rotary, both Haifa. Home: 7 Ehud St, Haifa, Isr. Office: 53 Ha'atzmaut Rd, Haifa, Isr.

MEIDAN, Israel Haim, Isr, organization exec; b. Warsaw, Pol, May 23, 1923; s. Dov and Ester (Wasermil) Mintz; in

Isr since 1932; MBA, Harvard Bus Sch, 1957; att: Off's Training Sch; Command and Staff Sch, 1947-56; Sch of Law and Econ, Tel Aviv, 1940-41; m. Shoshana Bombas, Mar 1, 1949; c: Nili, Orli, Ester. Chmn: Natl Comm for Devl of Textile Ind in Isr; Natl Comm for Direction of Ind Quality in Isr; Comm of Programming Mgmt Devl in Isr; mem: bd govs, Intl Council for Sci Mgmt; bd, Inst for Research of Earnings and Wages in Isr; bd, Isr Mgmt Cen; Natl Comm for Devl of Sys and Automation in Isr Economy; active in mgt, devl, productivity in developing countries; dir, Isr Inst of Productivity, 1961-68; registrar of shipping, Isr Govt, 1947-48. Brit Army; col, chief of logistics, IDF. Contbr of publs in fields of productivity; natl econ; mgmt; devl; comprehensive managerial approach; incentive sys in a dynamic developing society. Home: 6 Yoav St, Zahala, Isr. Office: 4 Sold St, Tel Aviv, Isr.

MEIER, Heinz, Ger, organization exec; b. Stuttgart, Jan 10, 1912; s. Joseph and Olga (Bachmann). Pres, Bayerisches Landesentschädigungsamt, Munich, since 1967, vice-pres, 1951-67; apprentice, pvt bank, 1929-31; independent gen agt, Münchener und Aachener Ins Co, 1932-38; interned by Ger, 1941-45; mgr, wfr and staff dept, Bayerisches Hilfswerk, Free Wfr Co, Munich, 1946-48, dir, bus affairs dept, 1948-51. Pres, Regional Assn of J Comtys, Bavaria, since 1955; mem, bc council, Bavarian Bc Sys, since 1953; fmr, mem bd, vice-pres, J Cong, Munich. Home: Heimstr 61, Stockdorf near Munich, Ger. Office: Prinz Ludwigstr 1-3, Munich, Ger.

MEIERS, Joseph, US, neuropsychiatrist; b. Berlin-Charlottenburg, Ger, Nov 25, 1894; s. Bernhard and Elisabeth (Neumann) Meyer; MD, U of Berlin, 1925; m. Annie Dix, Oct 14, 1950. Pvt practice, NYC, since 1951; qualified psycht, NY State, 1952; cons, Sydenham hosp, NYC; sup psycht, Alfred Adler Consultation Cen and Mental Hygiene Clinic, NYC, since 1953; pvt practice, Berlin, 1925-32; neuropsycht cons, OSE, Latvia, 1934-39; res psycht, state and pvt mental hosps, NY, 1939-50; asso visiting phys, City Hosp, NYC, 1954-62. F: Amer Geriatrics Soc; Amer Soc Group Psychotherapy and Psychodrama; Assn for Advancement of Psychotherapy; mem: Amer Psycht Assn; NY Acad Scis; Amer Sociometric Assn; Intl Soc for Gen Semantics; Inst Gen Semantics; World Fed for Mh; Amer Soc Adlerian Psych; AAAS. Contbr monographs to profsl jours. Home and office: 601 W 115 St, New York, NY.

MEIJER, Alexander, Isr, child psycht; b. Musselkanaal, Netherlands, Oct 6, 1926; s. Simon and Esther (Goudsmid); in Isr since 1956; MD: Med Sch, Groningen, Netherlands, 1954; Inst for Higher Clinical Studies, Rotterdam, 1956; m. Joan Silman, Jan 7, 1958; c: Esther, Amos, Naomi. Dir, student counseling service, Heb U, Jerusalem, since 1965; acting head, child psycht div, Hadassah U Hosp, since 1966; lectr, Heb U Med Sch, since 1966; dir, Jerusalem Marriage Guidance Clinic, 1961-63. Med off, IDF, Res. Mem: Isr Neuropsycht Soc; Isr Sci Council on Mental Deficiency; Isr Soc for Group Psychotherapy. Contbr to profsl jours. Home: 48 Bayt Vegan St, Jerusalem, Isr. Office: Hadassah U Hosp, Jerusalem, Isr.

MEIR, Golda, Isr, government official; b. Kiev, Russ, May 3, 1898; d. Moshe and Bluma (Neiditz) Mabovitch; in Isr since 1921; att Tehrs Sem, Milw; m. Morris Myerson, Dec 24, 1917 (decd); c: Menachem, Sara. PM of Isr since 1969; with Solel Boneh, 1924-26; secy, Women's Lab Council, Histadrut, 1928; mem, exec, secretariat, Fed of Lab, 1929-34; chmn, bd dirs, Workers Sick Fund; head, political dept, Fed of Lab; Mapai delg, Actions Comm, World Zionist Org, 1936; mem, War Econ Adv Council, Pal Govt, 1939; head, political dept, JA, Jerusalem, 1946-48; Ambass to Moscow, 1948-49; Min of Lab, 1949-56; Min for Fgn Affairs, 1956-66; secy gen, Mapai, 1966-68. Office: PM off, Jerusalem, Isr.

MEIROVITZ, Mordehai, Isr, engineer; b. Dorohoi, Rum, May 13, 1930; s. Aron and Rachel; in Isr since 1948, dipl, tchr, Routhenberg Sem, Cyprus, 1948; telecommunication deg, London, 1955; m. Tamar Zalmanovitz, Aug 28, 1950; c: Eliezer. Engr, PO training dept, N dist, since 1965. Cpl, communications, IDF, 1950-52. Author: Electrotechnics, 1964; Public Telephone Instruction Manual, 1966. Recipient: Kaplan Award, Min of Lab, 1969; Productivity Award, PO. Spec interest: inventions. Home: 8 Sea Rd, Haifa, Isr. Office: 152 Jaffa St, Haifa, Isr,

MEIRY, Meir Benzion, Isr, accountant; b. Briansk, Russ, Nov 15, 1905; s. Baruch and Asnah (Itin); in Isr since 1925;

CPA, Isr; m. Rivkah Reitman, 1933; c: Hagith Friedlander. Comptroller, JA, World Zionist Org, since 1962; asst acctnt gen, State of Isr, 1948-49; dir-gen, State Comptrollers Off, 1949-62. F: Assn Intl Acctnts; Corp Cert Secys, London, Eng. Vice-pres, Rokah lodge, B'nai B'rith, Tel Aviv; master, Dror lodge, Masons, Jerusalem; mem: Intl Fiscal Assn; Isr Inst of CPAs; Auditors' Council; council, Inst of CPAs; govt comm for granting auditors licenses; Comm for Appointment of Auditors to Govt Corps; Govt Supervisory Comm of Examinations for Qualification as CPA. Home: 12 Feival St, Tel Aviv, Isr. Office: 14 Hillel St, Jerusalem, Isr.

MEISEL, Blanche, US, communal leader; b. Chgo, Ill, Apr 16, 1927; d. Nathan and Minnie (Somers) Long; BS, U of Ill, 1948; m. Philip Meisel, Dec 18, 1949; c: Myron, Lee, Robert, Neil. Exec secy, bd dirs, Chem & Pollution Scis, Inc, since 1955; dietitian: Michael Reese Hosp; Syracuse Memorial Hosp; George Wash U Hosp, 1949-52; case worker, Cook Co, Ill, 1949-50. Dir, N NJ br, United Syn Youth Steering Comm; trustee, Temple Beth Ahm, Springfield, NJ; youth chmn, N NJ br, Natl Women's League, United Syn of Amer; mem, Omicron Nu; fmr: pres, vice-pres, Sisterhood, Temple Beth Ahm; vice-pres, Hadassah, Sarah Kussy Group. Hobbies: sports, theater, youth educ. Home: 45 Janet La, Springfield, NJ.

MEISEL, Max, US, bibliographer; b. Bklyn, NY, Dec 25, 1892; s. Louis and Pauline (Bergen); BS, CCNY, 1914; BLS, Columbia U, 1916; m. Blanche Gelb, Mar 28, 1926; c: Lewis. Ret; fmr: vice-pres, Hall-Mark Elec Sales Co, Inc, 1921-68; libr:sci div, NY Public Libr, 1916-1917; Amer Libr War Service Assn, 1918-1920. US Army, 1918. F, AAAS; charter mem: Hist of Sci Soc; Amer Libr Assn; fmr: pres, Bur J Educ, Miami; Temple Isr. Author: A Bibliography of American Natural History: The Pioneer Century, 1769-1865, 3 vols, 1924-1929, reprinted, 1967. Recipient: Oberly prize, Amer Libr Assn, 1925. Spec interest: bibliography of biol scis in US. Home: 4444 Post Ave, Miami Beach, Fla.

MEISELS, Andrew, Isr, author, journalist; b. Budapest, Hung, Mar 30, 1933; s. David and Margaret (Magyar); in Isr since 1963; BA, CCNY, 1955; m. Martha Miller, Jan 1, 1967; c: Tamar. Tel Aviv ed, Eng lang news, Isr Bc, since 1966; Isr Bc corresp, ABC, since 1967; reporter, Jerusalem Post, 1964-66; newman, AP, 1956-63. Author: Son of a Star, 1969; collaborator, Lightning Out of Israel, 1967; stories included in anthol, The Professional Story Writer and His Art, 1963; contbr to mags. Mem: Isr Journalists Assn; clubs: Overseas Press; Variety, Isr. Home: 160 Arlosoroff St, Tel Aviv, Isr. Office: Israel Broadcasting, Hakirya, Tel Aviv, Isr.

MEISL, Edith, Isr, painter; b. Arad, Rum, Mar 8, 1919; s. Alexander and Gizela (Samu); in Isr since 1964; att Acad of Belles Arts, Rome; m. Bernard Ton, Sep 12, 1963. Artist, painter, scenographer: State Theater, Rum; State Theater, Arad; Isr Natl Opera. Exhbs: Arad; Timisora, Bucharest; Tel Aviv; Frankfurt; Can; Chgo. Home: 7 Gordon St, Tel Aviv, Isr.

MEISSNER, Edwin B, Jr, US, business exec; b. St Louis, Mo, Dec 27, 1918; s. Edwin and Edna (Rice); BS, U of Pa, 1940; m. Nina Renard, Dec 17, 1946; c: Edwin, Wallace, Robert, Donald. Sr vice-pres, Gen Steel Inds, Inc; dir, Natl Stock Yards Natl Bank, Natl City, Ill, since 1956. Maj, US Army, WWII. Dir, Humane Soc of Mo, since 1953; bd dirs: Amer Ordnance Assn; Barnard Free Skin and Cancer Hosp; Cen Inst for Deaf, Comm for Econ Devl; Safety Council; Flood Control Assn; United Fund; fmr pres, Natl Defense Transp Assn, all St Louis; clubs: Mo Athletic; Westwood Country; Bridlespur Hunt; St Louis; Engrs of St Louis. Hobbies: shooting, fox-hunting. Home: 7 Maryhill Lane, Ladue, St Louis, Mo. Office: One Memorial Drive, St Louis, Mo.

MEISSNER, George Samuel, US, attorney; b. Berlin, Ger, Aug 6, 1929; s. Leo and Ida (Kober); in US since 1938; BSS, CCNY, 1949; LLB, Bklyn Law Sch, 1951, LLM, JD, 1955; m. Beverly Reed, Oct 28, 1951; c: Margo, Philip, Michele, Stuart. Partner, Spector, Meissner, Greenspun, Berman & Fink, since 1969; partner, Spector & Meissner, 1961-68; spec army counsel, Army-McCarthy Hearings, US Sen, 1954; chief counsel: NY State Assembly Comm on Mental Hygiene, 1966-67; NY State Jt Leg Comm on Child Care Needs, 1968-69; asso counsel, NY State Jt Leg Comm on Court Reorg, 1965; spec counsel to Congressman Frank Brasco on J and Intl Affairs; admitted to practice in: all NY State Courts; US Supr Court; US Circuit Court of Appeals; Fed Dist Courts for E and S dists of NY. Capt, US Army, Judge Ad-

vocate Gen Corps, 1952-55. Co-chmn: Intl League for Repatriation of Russ J; Zionist Cultural Soc, Bklyn; campaign chmn, exec mem, Dem Party, Bklyn; dir: Bklyn JCC; Yeshiva Ateres Yisroel; Yeshiva of Kings Bay; JNF, Mill Basin Council; chmn, local draft bd; fmr: counsel, J Friends Soc; vice-pres, Young Israel, Bensonhurst; Temple Sholom, Flatbush; dir, Flatbush Park J Cen; mem: Bklyn Bar Assn; KP; NY Trial Lawyers Assn; JWV; Bklyn Histadrut Council; Mill I Civic Assn; club, Thomas Jefferson Dem, dir. Recipient: Dist Service Award, Yeshiva of Kings Bay, 1967; Merit Award, Flatbush Park J Cen, 1967; Man of the Year Award, Intl League for Repatriation of Russ J, 1969. Spec interest: political activities. Home: 2363 E 65 St, Brooklyn, NY. Office: 16 Court St, Brooklyn, NY.

MEISSNER, Rose Eva, von, Eng, court milliner; b. Lundenburg, Aus, Nov 13, 1902; d. Julius and Helene (Donath) Werner; in Eng since 1938; master deg, millinery, hons, Vienna, Aus; m. F von Meissner (decd). Owner, chief designer, Vernier Modelhats Ltd, court milliner since 1945; designer to late Duchess of Kent, Duchess of Gloucester. Fund raising mem: ORT, Isr; Intl Refugee Comm (Corra); Friends of Heb U, Jerusalem; found mem, Asso Designers' Group. Home: 33 Gt Cumberland Pl, London W1, Eng. Office: 11 Dover St, London W1, Eng.

MEISTER, Morris, US, educator; b. Gonietz, Russ, Oct 20, 1895; s. Harris and Jennie (Koslovsky); in US since 1902; BS, CCNY, 1916; MS, Columbia, 1917; PhD, 1921; hon DSc, NYU, 1958; m. Florence Glickstein, Aug 20, 1921; c: Alton, Anna Burton. Ret; pres em, Bx Comty Coll, 1958-66; head, sci dept NY Tchr Training Coll, 1921-33; sci sup, Bd Educ, NYC, 1935-38; found prin, Bx HS Sci, 1938-58; dir, planning, Hall of Sci, 1966-70. Cons, pre-induction training courses, Pentagon, 1942-43. Prin, Albert Lucas Rel Classes; chmn, bd govs, Civic Assn of Mahopacs; vice-pres, Grand St Boys Found; mem: exec comm: ADL, NY Sect; AJComm, NY Sect; mem: AAAS; NEA; Natl Sci Tchrs Assn; fmr: pres: Natl Sci Tchrs Assn; Gamma chap, Phi Beta Kappa. Author: Looking Ahead in Education, 1945; Living with Science ,9 vols, 1933-57; ed, The Science Classroom; contbr to School Science and Mathematics; The Science Teacher. Recipient: Townsend Harris Medal, CCNY, 1956. Home: 315 Riverside Dr, New York, NY.

MEJZLER, David, Isr, mathematician; b. Polonnoye, Russ, Sept 20, 1913; s. Hersh and Rachel (Katz); in Isr since 1958; PhD, U Lvov, 1950; m. Fania Charaz, July 14, 1953; c: Giora, Gil. Asso prof, math and stat, Heb U, since 1969, on fac since 1958; tchr math, Ukraine, 1940-41; jr research f, Math Inst of Ukrainian Acad of Scis, 1947-51; asst, sr lectr, dozent, dept math, Poly Inst, Lvov, 1950-57; math, Inst for Fibres and Forest Products Research, Jerusalem, 1958-64. Red Army, 1941-42. Mem: Isr Math Soc; Oprs Research Soc of Isr; Assn for Demography and Stat of Jews. Contbr on probability theory to sci publs. Home: 41 Hapalmach St, Jerusalem, Isr. Office: Hebrew U, Jerusalem, Isr.

MEKORI-FELSTEINER, Tamar, Isr, biologist; b. Tel Aviv, Isr, Nov 21, 1936; d. Shlomo and Gusti (Katz) Mekori; MSc, Tel Aviv U, 1962; PhD, Weizmann Inst of Sci, Rehovot, Isr, 1966; m. Asso researcher, dept oncology and nuclear med, Rambam Govt Hosp, Haifa; postdoc f, U of Toronto, Can, 1966-67. Cpl, IDF, MC, 1954-56. Co-author: The Thymus: Experimental and Clinical Studies, 1965; contbr to sci jours. Recipient: Bar-Lemesdorff for Cancer Research, 1969. Hobbies: theater, music. Home: 71 Zalman Shneur St, Haifa, Isr. Office: Rambam Hosp, Haifa, Isr.

MELAMED, Abraham, US, radiologist; b. Chgo, Ill, Nov 19, 1914; s. Israel and Minnie (Kramer); BS, U Ill, 1935, MD, Coll Med, 1937; cert, radiology, Amer Coll Radiology; m. Hope Goodman; c: Abigail, Agatha Hurwitz, John. Dir, dept radiology: Evangelical Deaconess Hosp, Milw, since 1944; St Joseph's Hosp, W Bend, Wis, since 1948; asso clinical prof, radiology, Marquette U; Mt Sinai Hosp, Milw, 1942-46. F, Amer Coll Radiology; trustee, Archives of Amer Art, Detroit; mem, Govs Council on Arts; bd dirs: Wis Arts Found and Council; Amer Friends Heb U, NY; fmr pres: Roentgen Ray Soc; Wis Soc for J Learning; Milw chap, Amer Friends Heb U; chmn, sect on radiology, State Med Soc of Wis. Contbr papers on card and related subjects; numerous sci exhbs. Home: 1107 E Lilac Lane, Milwaukee, Wis. Office: 2500 N Mayfair Rd, Milwaukee, Wis.

MELAMED, Joseph Aharon, Isr, attorney, economist, business exec; b. Kaunas, Lith, June 28, 1926; s. Mordehay and Miryam (Zak); in Isr since 1948; BA, econ, Heb U, Tel Aviv, 1952, LLB, 1954, LLM, 1955; MSc, U Cal, Berkeley, 1957; m. Ziva Shachar, July 29, 1958; c: Shachar, Gill, Limor. Dir, Mutual Investment Services, gen mgr, Investors' Overseas Services in Isr, since 1966; dir, Investment Guarantee Co, since 1968; asst to mgr, absorption dept, JA, 1949-54; econ adv, Min of Agric, 1954-60; mgn dir, Investment Auth, Jerusalem, 1960-64; adv, Isr delg to UN, 1962-64. Underground movement, ghetto Kaunas, 1941-43; guerilla fighter, Russ, 1943-44; org, flight, protecting, training of DPs in Eur, 1944-48; Palmach, 1948-49. Dir, Investors' Overseas Services Found; pres, Mutual Investment Services Scholarship Fund. Contbr on econ problems to jours. Hobbies: sport, theater, music. Home: 10 Lilien St, Tel Aviv, Isr. Office: 76 Ibn Gvirol St, Tel Aviv, Isr.

MELAMED, Nissan Cohen, Isr, educator, composer; b. Shiraz, Iran, Mar 23, 1906; s. Yoseph and Ahuva (Bezalel); in Isr since 1908; att Tchrs' Sem, Conservatory, Jerusalem; m. Ester Shalgui, Mar, 1931; c: Roni, Uziel, Joseph. Dir, tchr, Sefardi Syn Music Sem, since 1968; tchr, oriental music, Music Acad, Tel Aviv U, since 1953; Music Tchrs' Acad, since 1950; prin: elem schs: Alia Alef, Tel Aviv, 1947-56; Ehad Haam, Ramat Gan, 1966-68; prin, J-Sefardi schs, Mexico City, 1956-62; educ repr, JA, Teheran, 1963-66. Author, composer: Rinati, 3 vols, 1942-53; Shirim, 1952; The War of the Maccabeans Against the Greeks, 1961; Songs of Jerusalem, 1967; research and devl: Sefaradi Cantilations; elements of oriental music, Hakamat; contbr songs, poems, to publs. Mem: Soc Composers; Acum Ltd; B'nai B'rith; Milo. Home: Kiryat Sefer St, Tel Aviv, Isr.

MELBER, Jehuda, US, rabbi; b. Berlin, Ger, May 3, 1916; s. Samuel and Dina (Hirsh); in US since 1955; ordained rabbi, Yeshivat Chachmey Lublin, Pol, 1934; MA, Tufts U, Boston, 1960; PhD, Yeshiva U, NYC, 1963; m. Esther Hendeles, 1938 (decd); c: Miriam, Samuel. Rabbi: Briarwood J Cen, since 1960; Adas Israel, Havana, Cuba, 1953-55; Kadimah, Brighton, Mass, 1955-58; U Hgts Cen, Bx, NY, 1959-60. Chaplain, IDF, 1948-50. Vice-pres, Rel Zionists of Amer, NE region; mem: RabCA; NY Bd Rabbis, chaplain, commn. Author: The Universality of Maimonides, 1960; Hermann Cohen's Philosophy of Judaism, 1967. Home: 83-40 Daniels St, Jamaica, NY. Study: 139-06 86 Ave, Jamaica, NY.

MELCHIOR, Bent, Den, rabbi; b. Beuthen, June 24, 1929; s. Marcus and Meta (Schornstein); min dipl, J Coll, London, 1961, rabb dipl, 1963; m. Lillian Weisdorff, Dec 16, 1951; c: Michael, John, Alan, Kim. Rabbi, Copenhagen J Cong, since 1963; tchr, J Comty, Den, 1949-58; secy, Zionist Fed, 1950-53. Haganah; IDF, 1947-49. Pres: KH, Den; Mizrachi; mem: B'nai B'rith; Danish Church Comm for Vietnam; Amnesty Intl; fmr: secy, Den Zionist Fed; chmn: Zeire Mizrachi; J Youth. Fmr ed, Zionist monthly, Isr; contbr to periodicals. Home: Frederiksborggade 27, 1360 Copenhagen K, Den.

MELLITZ, Samuel, US, jurist; b. Bridgeport, Conn, May 6, 1891; s. Jacob and Peppie (Hausman); LLB, Yale U, 1911; hon LLD, Yeshiva U, 1954; m. Sayde Silverman, June 18, 1916; c: Jacob, Barbara Krentzman, Beulah Levenson. Asso Justice, Supr Court of Errors, Conn, since 1958; chmn, Gov's Comm on Gambling, since 1965; judge, Conn Superior Court, 1942-58, chief judge, 1957-58; judge, Court of Common Pleas of Conn, 1936-42; pvt practice, 1912-36; chmn, Conn Jud Council, 1960-61. Chmn, Beardsley Scholarship Comm of Yale U, since 1933; co-chmn, Planning Comm on Criminal Admn, since 1967; hon pres, J Comty Council, fmr pres; mem: bd, St Vincent's Hosp of Bridgeport; bd trustees, Yeshiva U, NY; bd, Amer Assn for J Educ; Amer, Conn State Bar Assns; ZOA; Mizrachi; AJCong; B'nai B'rith; vice-pres, Union of Orthodox Heb Congs of Amer; fmr: pres, J Comty Cen; chmn, United J Campaign; charter mem, Masons; org, West End Savings and Loan Assn; bd mem, W Side Bank; pres, Cong Ahavath Achim, Bridgeport; mem, Grievance Comm, Fairfield Co; Bridgeport delg to AJConf; mem, Conn Commn on Civil Rights. Recipient: citation, Conn region, NCCJ, for contrib to betterment of group relations, 1954; Americanism Award, Conn Valley Council, B'nai B'rith, 1958. Home: 97 Argonne St, Fairfield, Conn. Office: 172 Golden Hill St, Bridgeport, Conn.

MELMAN, Myron, Isr, computer engr; b. NYC, Apr 1, 1922; s. Abraham and Pauline (Kazdan); in Isr since 1946; EE, Technion, Haifa, Isr, 1951; MEE, Columbia U, 1957; m. Shoshana Beloch, Oct 21, 1947; c: Oded, Noam, Eytan. Computer engr, sr sci, Weizmann Inst of Sci, Rehovot, since

1962; sr engr, Airborne Instruments Lab, LI, NY, 1957-60; Digital Computer Lab, U of Ill, 1960-62. Prin contribs: design and devl of Golem A and Golem B computer sys, Weizmann Inst of Sci. Sgt, US Army, signal corps, 1943-46. Mem, Inst Elec and Electronic Engrs, Isr. Home: Meonoth Wolfson C, Rehovot, Isr. Office: Weizmann Inst of Sci, Rehovot, Isr.

MELMED, David Jacob, Rhodesia, business exec; b. Queenstown, S Afr, Oct 30, 1907; s. Mayer and Dora (Kahanowitz); in Rhodesia since 1946; m. Esther Eliasov, Jan 14, 1936; c: Meir, Raphael, Judith. Co dir, Harolds Ltd, Bulawayo, since 1947; asst mgr, OK Bazaars, Johannesburg, 1940-43; mgr: Harolds, Durban, 1943-46; Morrisons, Bulawayo, 1946-47. Pres, Zionist Revisionist Org, mem, World Revisionist exec; first pres, Cen Afr Autonomous Zionist Org, all Rhodesia; speaker for J cause, S Afr and Rhodesia; chmn, United Isr Appeal, past chmn, 1967 Six Day War Emergency Appeal; club, Weizmann-Parkview Sports. Hobbies: music, bowling, walking. Home: 504 Sunningdale, Borrow St, Bulawayo, Rhodesia.

MELMED, Nathan, S Afr, pharmacist; b. Queenstown, S Afr, Mar 22, 1913; s. Mayer and Dora (Kahanowitz); grad, Queens Coll, Queenstown, 1930, dipl pharm, 1935; m. Tamara Samsonov, 1943; c: Ronni; m. 2nd, Marianne Kaiser, 1956. Mgn dir, Mells Products Distributors, Port Eliizabeth. Chmn, E Province Zionist Council, since 1953; mem exec: Port Elizabeth C of C, since 1965; S Afr ZF, since 1953; fmr, chmn, Cape Midland br, S Afr Pharm Soc. Home: 804 Granten Hgts, Humewood, Port Elizabeth, S Afr. Office: POB 1777, Port Elizabeth, S Afr.

MELNICK, Joseph L, US, virologist, educator; b. Boston, Mass, Oct 9, 1914; s. Samuel and Esther (Melny); BA, Wesleyan U, Conn, 1936; m. Sarah Chasnoff; c: Nancy; m. 2nd, Matilda Benyesh. Prof, chmn, dept virology and epidemiology, Baylor Coll of Med, since 1958, asso dean, Grad Studies, since 1968; research f, phys chem, Yale U, 1939-41; NRC f in med sci, preventive med and ped, 1941-42, instr, 1942-44, asso prof, 1944-54, prof, epidemiology, 1954-57; chief, virus labs, div biol standards, NIH, 1957-58; temp staff mem, Rockefeller Found, assigned to Virus Research Cen, Poona, India, 1956; mem, panel on virology and immunology, Comm on Growth, NRC, Wash, DC, 1952-56. Mem: Viral and Rickettsial Registry Comm, since 1951; Surg Gen's Comm on liver diseases, US Army Research and Devl Command; expert comm, virus diseases, WHO, since 1957; intl comm on cell cultures, Intl Comm on Nomenclature of Viruses; cons on adv and planning groups for NIH, Wash, DC, as: chmn, panel on entero and related virus; mem, hum cancer task force, Natl Adv Cancer Council; infectious diseases training grant comm, Natl Inst for Allergy and Infectious Diseases; bd for virus reference reagents, Natl Inst of Allergy and Infectious Diseases; secy-gen, Intl Cong for Virology, since 1968; f: AAAS; Amer-Scandinavian Found, Caroline Inst, Stockholm, Swed, 1949; Amer Public Health Assn; Amer Acad Microbiol; NY Acad Sci; mem: Amer Epidemiological Soc; Soc for Experimental Biol and Med; Amer Assn Immunologists; Amer Soc for Microbiol; hon mem, Isr Microbiol Soc, 1962; fmr: chmn: comm on echo viruses, Natl Found for Infantile Paralysis, 1955-57; comm on entero-viruses, Natl Found, 1958-61; Surg Gen's comm on live poliovirus vaccine, 1958-61. Co-author: Review of Medical Microbiology, 8th ed, 1968; ed, Progress in Medical Virology, since 1958; asso ed: Cancer Research; Amer Jour Epidemiology; Jour of Virology; Experimental and Molecular Path; Applied Microbiol; contbr to sci publs. Recipient: Wesleyan U citation for outstanding achievement as tchr and scholar, 1961; included in Polio Hall of Fame, Warm Springs, Ga, for contribs leading to a vaccine against poliomyelitis; Eleanor Roosevelt Hum Award, 1965; Modern Med Dist Achievement Award, 1966; co-recipient: Intl Gold Medal, Arg Found Against Infantile Paralysis, 1949. Home: 8838 Chatsworth Dr, Houston, Tex. Office: Baylor Coll of Med, Houston, Tex.

MELTON, Samuel Mendel, US, business exec; b. Aus-Hung, Mar 21, 1900; s. Emil and Sarah (Mendlowitz); in US since 1904; grad, O State U, Columbus, O; BSc, commerce, 1923; m. Esther Cobey, Feb, 1938 (decd); c: Minna Rehm, Michael (decd); m. 2nd, Florence Zacks, Mar, 1968. Mem, bd, Harsco Corp; hon life chmn, Capitol Mfg Co, Columbus, O; found: Capitol Mfg & Supply, Columbus, O; Chgo Nipple Mfg, Chgo & Baltimore; Capital Pipe & Nipple Mfg, Detroit, Mich, all merged with Harsco; Capitol Mfg & Supply Co of

Isr, Tel Aviv, gifted to various orgs, 1955. Hon life pres, Cong Tifereth Isr, mem, bd trustees; pres, Melton Research Cen, Tchrs Inst and Sem Coll J Studies; chmn, Columbus JWF; treas, United J Fund & Council, Columbus; mem, bd: J Cen; Heritage House; Heb Sch, all Columbus; Amer Friends Heb U; JTSA; mem, natl cabinet, UJA; elected full mem, Soc Hon Alumni, Heb U, Jerusalem; f, mem, governing council, Amer Assn J Educ; established numerous founds, endowments, grants, scholarships, in US and Isr. Home: 88 E Broad St, Columbus, O.

MELTZER, Adolph, US, surgeon; b. NYC, July 19, 1910; s. Abraham and Sarah (Seid); BS, CCNY, 1930; MD, Cornell Med Sch, 1934; m. Paula Dorfman, Sep 7, 1935; c: Naomi Rubin, Glenn. In pvt practice since 1940; surg-in-chief, Drs Hosp, Worcester, Mass, since 1960; asso surg, Beth Isr Hosp, Boston, since 1940; cons surg, tumor clinic, 1940-55; med cons, Buffington Co, Pharm Mfrs, 1940-50; mem fac: Tufts Med Sch, both 1939-41. Maj, US Army MC, 1942-46. FACS; dipl, Amer Bd Surg; mem: AMA; Phi Beta Kappa; Alpha Omega Alpha; KP; exec comm, Worcester Zionist Assn, fmr pres; B'nai B'rith; Beth Isr Syn; fmr, pres, Worcester Surg Forum. Ed, Biology in Surgery, 1969; contbr to med jours. Recipient: theater ribbons: N Afr; China; Burma; India. Hobbies: philately, Judaica. Home: 15 Southwood Rd, Worcester, Mass. Office: 20 Fruit St, Worcester, Mass.

MELTZER, Bernard D, US, educator, attorney; b. Phila, Pa, Nov 21, 1914; s. Julius and Rose (Welkov); BA, JD, U of Chgo, 1937; LLM, Harvard Law Sch, 1938; m. Jean Sulzberger, Jan 17, 1947; c: Joan, Daniel, Susan. Prof, law, U of Chgo, since 1947; atty, asst to chmn, SEC, 1938-40; asso, Mayer, Meyer, Austrian & Platt, 1940; legal cons, Natl Defense Comm, 1940-41; spec asst to asst secy of State and acting chief of fgn funds, control div, State Dept, 1941-43; trial counsel, Nuremberg War Trials, 1945-46; counsel, Vedder, Price, Kaufman & Kaminholz, 1954-55. Lt, USNR, 1943-46. Chmn, bd, U of Chgo Press, 1968-69; bd dirs, SE Chgo Commn, 1957-59; exec comm, AJComm, Chgo, 1955-58; Chgo, Ill and Amer Bar Assns; Amer Law Inst; Phi Beta Kappa; Coif. Co-author: Case and Materials on Business Corporations, 1949; The Law of Labor Relations: Cases and Materials, 1969; contbr to legal and other jours. Home: 1219 E 50 St, Chicago, Ill. Office: U of Chgo Law Sch, Chicago, Ill.

MELTZER, Hyman, US, psychologist, educator; b. Russ, Sep 1, 1899; s. Abe and Faygeth (Romanoff); in US since 1907; BA, U of Ill, 1921; MA, Columbia U, 1923, PhD, 1925. Vice-pres, Orchard Paper Co, St Louis, Mo, since 1956, dir of hum relations, 1952-62; prof, Wash U, St Louis, since 1962, mem fac since 1928; asst prof, psych, Ore State Coll, 1925-28; chief psychol, St Louis Psycht Clinic, 1928-34. Mem: Mo Psych Assn; Amer Psych Assn; Amer Orthopsycht Assn; AAAS; Gerontological Soc; World Fed for Mh; bd dirs, YMHA. Contbr to profsl jours. Home: 4510 Maryland Ave, St Louis, Mo. Office: Washington U, St Louis, Mo.

MELTZER, Jack, NZ, barrister, solicitor; b. Eng, Oct 21, 1898; att Vic U, Wellington, NZ, 1917-21; m. Anne Garshook, 1926; c: Jocelyn Lederman. Wellington city coroner, since 1966. Mem: B'nai B'rith; Intl Commn of Jurists; NZ Olympic Council; fmr: pres: Wellington Heb Cong; Wellington Youth Orch; NZ Football Assn; Wellington J Social Club; Friends of Heb U; gen secy, NZ Police Assn; mgr, NZ Empire Games Team, Cardiff. Recipient: MBE, 1957; OBE, 1966. Spec interests: criminal and med law. Home: 6 Park St, Wellington, NZ. Office: POB 5090, Wellington, NZ.

MELTZER, Julian L, Isr, author, organization exec, translator; b. London, Eng, Mar 11, 1904; s. Joseph and Regina (Siegel); in Isr since 1921. Exec vice-chmn, Yad Chaim Weizmann; dir, Weizmann Archives, Rehovot; counsellor for spec affairs, Weizmann Inst of Sci, Rehovot, 1962-66; PR adv, 1952-62; mem, ed staff: Pal Weekly, Jerusalem, 1921-25; Pal Bulletin, 1931-32; Pal Post, 1934-37; Pal corresp: Jewish Chronicle, London, 1925-48; NY Times, 1932-33, 1940-47; press secy, Heb U, Jerusalem, 1931-34; ed, Eng div, Palcor News Agcy, 1933-48; PR adv: Pal Economic Corp, NY, 1949; Weizmann Inst campaign, London, 1949-51. Trans Heb works into Eng, incl: First Jerusalem Illustrated Passover Haggadah, 1930; State in the Making, by David Horowitz; Three Days, by Zeev Sharef, 1962; contbr to local and fgn press, mags and anthols. Home: Beit Meltzer, Talpiot, Jerusalem, Isr. Office: Yad Weizmann, Rehovot, Isr.

MELTZER, M, Isr, physician; b. Cernauti, Rum, June 11,

1922; s. David and Jety (Herzig); in Isr since 1949; att Med Sch, Timisoara, Rum, 1946-47; MD, Heb U Med Sch, 1952; m. Selma Gottlieb, Aug 14, 1949. Chief phys, urology; instr, Tel Aviv Med Sch. Capt, IDF. Pres: Med Students Soc, 1950-52; Bethar, Cyprus, 1948-49; mem: Tel Aviv, Isr Med Assns; exec, Doctors' Org. Contbr to med jours. Home and office: 74 Yahalom St, Ramat Gan, Isr.

MELZER, Shimshon, Isr, editor, poet; b. Tluste, Pol, Feb 19, 1909; s. Shmuel and Sara (Ginzberg); in Isr since 1933; att Tchrs Sem, Lvov, 1926-31; m. Miriam Schechter, Sep 15, 1932; c: Aviv, Yehuda, Shmuel, Malka. Ed, Heb lang, Hasifriya Hazionit, WZO, since 1959; adv mem, Heb Lang Acad, since 1958; ed, youth monthly mag, Atidot, 1953-59; mem, ed bd, Davar, daily, 1936-52; ed, Davar le-Yeladim, 1935-47; mem, ed bd, Am Oved, publishers, 1945-47. Author: Be-Shiva Meitarim, 1938; Meir ha-Klizmar na'asa Kommissar, 1940; Lilach; Asara Shearim, 1943; Alef, 1945, 2nd ed, 1963; Sefer ha-Shirot veha-Baladot, 1951, 4th ed, 1956; Or Zarua, 1959, 2nd ed, 1966; trans books of poetry and prose from: Pol, Ger, Yiddish, including: 10 vols of works of Y L Peretz; Al Neharot, anthol of Yiddish poetry. Recipient: Tchernichovsky Prize, for trans of Peretz, 1948; Kessel Prize, Mex, for Sefer Ha-Shirot veha-Baladot, 1952, Holon Prize, for same book, 1953; Ruppin Prize, Haifa Munic, for Or Zarua, 1959; Lamdan Prize, Ramat Gan Munic, for Alef, 1963. Home: 8 Yifta St, Tel Aviv, Isr.

MENACHOVSKY, Moshe, Can, educator; b. Pinsk, Pol, Nov 15, 1893; s. Ruben and Dvora (Shifman); in Can since 1930; tchrs dipl, Warsaw, 1927; m. Esther Gurin, Aug 21, 1919; c: Brina, Zelda. Co-prin, J Folk Schs, Toronto, since 1955; prin, Borochov Sch and Kindergarten, Toronto, 1932-55; found, first J Sch in Brest-Litovsk, 1920. Mem: cen comm, co-found, Cen Yiddish Sch Org, Pol, 1921-23; cen comm, Achduth-Avodah, Poale Zion; bd dirs, YIVO; world bur for J educ, Cong for J Culture, all Can; fmr mem: Poale Zion; alderman, Brest-Litovsk City Council, both Pol. Author: Jewish Youth at the Crossroads, 1938; Ber Borochov, His Life and Works, 1959; Mixed Marriages in the Jewish Literature, 1968; Retarded Children in the Jewish Literature, 1969; ed, Proletarian Thought, now Undzer Veg, 1938-41; contbr to pedg and lit jours. Home: 174 Falkirk St, Toronto, Can. Office: 12 Viewmount, Toronto, Can.

MENAKER, Jerome S, US, physician; b. Wilkes Barre, Pa, Jan 12, 1916; s. Max and Sadye (Horowitz); AB, magna cum laude, Duke U, 1937; MD, magna cum laude, Georgetown U Sch of Med, 1941; m. Thelma Kornfeld, Aug 14, 1943; c: Michael, Howard. Chief, obstet, gyn, Wesley Hosp, since 1956; cons, obstet, gyn, McConnel Air Force Base, since 1951; chmn, obstet, gyn dept, St Joseph Hosp, since 1960; clinical instr, obstet, gyn, Kan U Med Cen. Maj, US Army MC, 1946. Pres, Mid-Kan Wfr Bd; co-chmn, Isr Bond Drive; vice-pres, Wichita Sym, 1961; mem, bd, Wichita Sym Assn, since 1959; bd dirs: Avath Achim Syn; YMCA; Mh Assn; Family Consultation Service; Amer Cancer Soc; ARC; Comty Chest; mem: Amer, Intl Coll of Surgs; Amer Coll Obstet and Gyn; AMA; IMA; B'nai B'rith; Phi Beta Kappa; club, Men's, Temple Emanuel, pres, 1953. Contbr to profsl jours. Hobbies: travel, photography, theater. Home: 120 Morningside Dr, Wichita, Kan. Office: 2703 E Central, Wichita, Kan.

MENASE, Israel, Turkey, business exec; b. Instanbul, Turkey, July 21, 1913; s. Abraham and Donna (Behar); m. Lucie Avayou, June 9, 1935; c: Becky, Albert. Partner, exec, Koc firm, since 1942; mgr, Izak Niego, 1928-41. Vice-pres, J Comty of Istanbul, since 1952; pres, council, Chief Rabbinate of Istanbul, since 1958; mem, exec comm, Istanbul C of C; mem: Masons; B'nai B'rith; Rotary; Mishne Torah, fmr chmn. Home: Cumhuriyet Caddesi Dag Apt 11, Elmadag, Istanbul, Turkey. Office: Koc Ticaret, Galata Fermeneciler 90, Istanbul, Turkey.

MENCZEL, Jacob, Isr, physician; b. Czernowitz, Rum, Apr 23, 1923; s. Moses and Blima; in Isr since 1949; att: Czernowitz U; Iassy U, 1945-49; MD, Heb U, 1951; m. Lilly Simons, Aug 15, 1950. Asso prof, med, metabolic unit for bone diseases, Heb U-Hadassah Hosp, since 1963; head, dept internal med, Shaare Zedek Hosp, Jerusalem, since 1967; visiting sci, NIH, Bethesda, Md, 1961-62; Eleanor Roosevelt Intl f, Hines VA Hosp, 1962-63; cons, Gerontological Cen, Jerusalem. Lt, IDF, 1953-55. Mem: sci council, IMA; comm, Soc Internal Med; Soc Experimental Biol and Med; Intl Assn Dent Research; Amer Geriatrics Soc; Bone and Tooth

Soc; Isr Soc Gerontology. Contbr to sci publs. Home: 30 Tchernichovsky St, Jerusalem, Isr. Office: Hadassah Hosp, Jerusalem, Isr.

MENDEL, Arthur, US, educator, musician; b. Boston, Mass, June 6, 1905; s. Phillip and Gertrude (Newman); BA, Harvard Coll, 1925; att Ecole Normale de Musique, Paris, 1925-27; m. Elsa Wissell, Aug 23, 1934. Henry Putnam U Prof, Princeton U, since 1969, mem fac since 1952; lit ed, G Schirmer, 1930-38; music critic, The Nation, 1930-33; ed: Asso Music Publishers, 1941-47; Amer Musicological Soc, 1941-44; pres, Dalcroze Sch of Music, 1947-50; conductor, The Cantata Singers, 1936-53. Mem: Intl Musicological Soc; Soc Musicologica, It; Amer Musicological Soc; Gesellschaft für Musikforschung. Trans: Paul Hindemith's The Craft of Musical Composition, Theoretical Part, 1942; Alfred Einstein's Mozart, 1945; co-ed: The Bach Reader, 1945, revised ed, 1966; ed and co-author, Studies in the History of Musical Pitch, 1880-1881, 1948-1955, 1969, mem. Herausgeberkollegium, Neue Bach Ausgabe; contbr to profsl jours. Office: Princeton U, Princeton, NJ.

MENDEL, Kurt, Isr, researcher; b. Hamburg, Ger, Nov 11, 1903; s. Max and Anna; in Isr since 1930; att Us: Hamburg, Breslau; dipl, Inst for Horticultural Instrn and Research, Berlin-Dahlem; MSc, Heb U, Jerusalem, 1942, PhD, 1949; m. Senta Weitmann, Mar 9, 1930; c: Naomi Smulian. Asso prof, horticultural plant propagation, Heb U, Rehovot, since 1965, on fac since 1942; coord, citrus research, Volcani Inst of Agric Research, since 1963, chmn, dept horticulture, 1963-68, on staff since 1932; study tour to It, Sicily, Spain, 1959; travel to W and Cen Afr on behalf of Isr Mins for Fgn Affairs, Agric, 1961; adv to Govt of Ceylon, 1962; adv on devl of citriculture, govts of: Trinidad, Columbia, Ecuador, 1965, Madagascar, 1968; guest lectr, FAO Horticultural Training Cen, Nairobi, Kenya, 1966. Participant, intl confs on citriculture; Isr repr: Intl Soc for Horticultural Sci; Cong of Assn for Advancement of Sci, Ceylon; mem: Isr Assn for Conservation of Nature; Amer Soc Horticultural Sci; Intl Plant Propagators Soc; Isr Botanical Soc, fmr pres. Recipient: Weizmann Prize for Exact Sci, 1950. Home: 23A Hanassi Harishon St, Rehovot, Isr. Office: Volcani Institute for Agricultural Research, POB 6, Bet Dagan, Isr.

MENDEL, Mendel P, Isr, accountant, author; b. Piatra Neamtz, Rum, Oct 22, 1898; s. Pinchas and Sara (Caufman); in Isr since 1945; m. Shifra Sufrin, Feb 1, 1922; c: Samuel, Sivia Indovich, Ana Lubowsky. Author: Hebrew-Rumanian Dictionary, 1932; Rumanian-Hebrew Dictionary, 1933; Hebrew-Rumanian Grammar; contbr articles on lit, hist, Zionist topics. Fmr mem, Haganah. Mem: exec, Irgun Askanim Zionim M'Rum B'Isr; B'nai B'rith; Brith Rishonim. Home: 51 Bialik St, Holon, Isr.

MENDELL, M Lester, US, banker; b. Rum, June 18, 1896; s. Abraham and Fannie; in US since 1898; att: CCNY, 1915-16; Yale U, 1918; m. Malvina Cohen, June 6, 1919; c: Edward, Oliver, Mrs Wilbur Toll. Ret; mem: bd, First Natl Bank, Palm Beach, Fla; bd and exec comm: Natl Equipment Corp; Glen Alden; Interstate Dept Stores; NY adv bd, Bank Leumi Le Isr; chmn, bd, Flushing Natl Bank, 1941-50; vice-pres, Bankers Trust Co, NY, 1950-61; fmr, prop, lumber wholesaler. Trustee, FJP, since 1948; mem: bd: Good Samaritan Hosp, Palm Beach, Fla; Comty Chest, Palm Beach; and exec comm, Pal Econ Corp; bd trustees, NYC Hosps, bd chmn, Queens Gen, since 1961; bd govs, Flushing Interfaith Soc; Intl Service Corp; Navy League; fmr: pres, J Comty Services, LI; gen chmn, NY region, UJA; chmn, NY region, JWB; hon chmn, Visiting Nurse Service, Queens; co-chmn, Queens State of Isr Bonds Dr; vice-pres, Queens Coll Speech Cen; clubs: Glen Oaks, Gt Neck, NY; Harmonie, NY; Lotos, NY; Palm Beach Country. Spec interests: golf, fishing, communal work. Homes: 25 Canterbury Rd, Great Neck, NY.

MENDELL, Theodore H, US, physician, educator; b. Phila, Pa, July 20, 1904; s. Samuel and Celia (Friedman); MD, Temple U, Phila, 1929; att U of Vienna Grad Sch of Med, 1932-33; m. Mary Scharff, Aug 16, 1933; c: Janet. Asso phys, grad hosp, U of Pa; phys em, cons, Albert Einstein Med Cen; chief, med service, Mt Sinai Hosp, 1946-52, mem staff since 1929; clinical prof, med, Hahnemann Med Coll, 1947-62, chmn, dept med, Albert Einstein Med Cen, S div, Phila, 1952-68. Col, US Army MC, 1942-46. Dipl, Amer Bd Internal Med, since 1940; FACP, f, Phila Coll Phys; mem: AMA; Pa Soc Med; Phila Co Med Soc, fmr pres; Amer Soc Internal Med; Mil Surgs Assn; Beth Zion Cong. Contbr to

med jours. Home and office: 2023 Spruce St, Philadelphia, Pa.

MENDELOWITZ, Daniel Marcus, US, educator, artist; b. Linton, ND, Jan 28, 1905; s. Ido and Clara (Reichenstein); BA, Stanford U, Cal, 1926, MA, 1927; scholarship, Art Students League, NY, 1930-31; m. Mildred Mondschein; c: Louis. Prof, art and educ, Stanford U, since 1949; with art dept, San Jose State Coll, Cal, 1927-33, asst prof, 1931-34; visiting prof: Columbia U, 1949; U of Guadalajara, Mexico, 1953; exhbs, one-man shows: Gump's, SF, 1944, 1946, 1948, 1953; Courvoisiers Gal, SF, 1940; Thomas Walton Stanford Art Gal, Stanford U, 1947, 1950, 1953, 1963, 1967, 1969; Maxwell Gals, SF, 1954, 1958, 1963; E B Crocker Art Gal, Sacramento, 1947; Cowie Gals, Biltmore Hotel, LA, 1948; Santa Barbara Mus of Art, 1948; Kenneth Slaughter Gals, SF, 1950; Breuner Gals, Sacramento, 1950; Montalvo Found, Saratoga, 1951; Lindsay Art Assn, Lindsay, 1951; all Cal; Elfstrom Gals, Salem, Ore, 1946; regular water color exhbs, Amer Water Color Soc, NY; executed mural commn, PO, Onward, Cal, 1940. Mem: Pacific Art Assn; Natl Art Educ Assn. Author: Children are Artists, 1953, rev ed, 1963; History of American Art, 1960, rev ed, 1970; Drawing, 1967; A Study Guide to Drawing, 1967. Home: 800 Lathrop Dr, Stanford, Cal. Office: Stanford U, Palo Alto, Cal.

MENDELS, Morton M, Can, attorney; b. Montreal, Can, Mar 1, 1908; s. Louis and Minnie (Silver); BA, McGill U, 1929, MA, 1930, BCL, 1932; m. Rebecca Darwin, Sep 22, 1931; c: Barbara, Michael. Secy, Intl Bank of Reconstruction and Devl, since 1946; pvt practice, 1932-39. Gen staff, Can Army, 1940-45. Mem: Bar of Montreal; Can Bar Assn. Home: 3400 Garrison St, NW, Washington, DC. Office: 1818 H St NW, Washington, DC.

MENDELSOHN, Hindley R, US, business exec; b. Newark, NJ, Aug 26, 1920; s. Mendel and Clotilda (Milwitzky); BS, Newark Coll of Engr, 1941; m. Rita Usdin, Apr 16, 1943; c: Marc, Irene. Pres, GKM Mfg Corp, since 1957; sales engr, Ferro-Co. USAAC, 1944-45. Chmn, bd trustees, Jericho J Cen, 1955-59, budget comm, 1958-69, pres, 1957. Home: 234 Halsey Ave, Jericho, NY. Office: 110 Troutman St, Brooklyn, NY.

MENDELSOHN, Irving, US, attorney; b. New Rochelle, NY, Nov 10, 1910; s. Nathan and Sophie (Goodman); LLB, NYU, Sch of Law, 1934; m. Dorothy Slavin, July 25, 1937; c: Nancy Cohen. JP, Town of Waverly, Franklin Co, since 1957, town atty, 1950-57; pvt practice, atty: St Regis Falls, NY, since 1946; New Rochelle, NY, 1935-42. US Army, 1943-45. Mem: St Regis Post, Amer Legion; Masons; Elks; St Lawrence Scottish Rites Bodies, Norwood, NY; Temple Beth El, Malone, NY; Franklin Co Bar Assn; club, Kiwanis, Brushton-Moira, pres, 1952. Hobbies: fishing, gardening. Home and office: St Regis Falls, NY.

MENDELSOHN, Isak Mendel, Nor, business exec; b. Trondheim, Nor, Nov 3, 1900; s. Aron and Thora (Paltiel); m. Ester Levin, Mar 1, 1925; c: Rita Kremer, Liv-Berit Henius. Ret, 1965; fmr: exec mgr, Trondhjems Konfektionsfabrik Co, 1923-65. Served, Royal Guard. Vice-pres, Trondelag Ind Org; chmn, Trondheim Inds Fair and Sports Hall; active worker, KH, since 1921; fmr pres, Rotary Club, Trondhjem West. Recipient: Ritter av Sankt Olavs, 1st Class; Deltager Medal. Hobbies: angling, skiing, hunting. Home and office: Sverdrupsvei 22, Trondheim, Nor.

MENDELSOHN, Leonard T, US, jurist; b. Louisville, Ky, July 19, 1907; s. Julius and Betty (Elias); BA, magna cum laude, U of S Cal, 1932, LLB, 1934; m. Ida Miller, July 10, 1927; c: Juel Janis, Bonny Langendorf, Ilene Albert. Judge, LA Munic Court, since 1966; fmr mem, law firm, Mendelsohn and Haves; fac mem, Cal Coll of Trial Judges. Pres, S Cal Golf Assn, since 1962; vice-pres: Cal Golf Assn, since 1961; Recreation and Youth Services Planning Council; Inst Judicial Sems; charter mem, bd trustees: J Fed Council, Gtr LA; J Family Service, LA; mem: State Bar of Cal; Phi Beta Kappa; Phi Kappa Phi; Conf of Cal Judges; LA Co Bar Assn; Beverly Hills Bar Assn; club, Hillcrest Co, dir, 1953-59, secy, 1953-57. Contbr to legal jours. Home: 10375 Wilshire Blvd, Los Angeles, Cal. Office: 110 N Grand Ave, Los Angeles, Cal.

MENDELSOHN, Walter, US, lawyer; b. NYC, Jan 22, 1897; s. Sigmund and Paula (Stieglitz); AB, Yale U, 1918, LLB, 1921; m. Josephine Becker, Mar 31, 1927; c: Sue, Paul. Admitted to NY Bar, 1921; partner, Proskauer, Rose, Goetz and Mendelsohn, and predecessor firms, since 1926; dir, Seligman and Latz, Inc. US Army, WW I; lt col, WW II, liaison off to Under-Secy of War. Chmn: J Bd Guardians, fmr pres; communal planning comm, FJP; hon trustee, fmr pres, Camp Ramapo; trustee: Inst Intl Educ; Henry Kaufmann Found; Edmund de Rothschild Found; mem, bd: Surprise Lake Camp; Wfr and Health Council; State Training Sch for Boys; Yale Law Sch Assn of NY; mem: exec, admn comms, AJComm; NYC Bar Assn; NY Co Lawyers Assn; Amer and NY State Bar Assns; Amer Judicature Soc; clubs: Yale; Harmonie, NY. Homes: 150 Central Park S, New York, NY; High Up, Purdy's Station, NY. Office: 300 Park Ave, New York, NY.

MENDELSON, Emanuel, US, physician; b. NYC, Dec 27, 1903; s. Jacob and Selma (May); BS, CCNY, 1922; MD, LI Coll Med, 1926; m. Florence Guelman, 1928; c: Edith. Att radiologist: Caledonian Hosp; House of St Giles; Kings Highway Hosp; LI Coll Hosp; Flatbush Gen Hosp; Coney Island Hosp. Pres, Bklyn Figure Skating Club, 1955-61; mem: B'nai B'rith; Sigma Alpha Mu; club, Unity. Contbr to med publs. Home: 27 Prospect Park W, Brooklyn, NY. Office: Caledonian Hosp, 10 St Paul's Place, Brooklyn, NY.

MENDELSON, Louis Abraham, US, insurance examiner; b. Houston, Tex, Dec 16, 1893; s. Abraham and Sarah (Hotchkiss); widower. Ins examiner sup, State of Fla, since 1961; owner, Mendelson Printing Co, 1914-40. Org, Fla J News, Jacksonville; mem: Masons; Scottish Rite; Shriners; Grotto. Home: 1102 Seminole Dr, Tallahassee, Fla. Office: J Edwin Larson Bldg, Tallahassee, Fla.

MENDELSON, Marcel L, Isr, educator; b. Berlin, Ger, June 9, 1928; s. Jakor and Frances (England); in Isr since 1958; BA, Queens Coll, NYC, 1948; MA, Yale U, 1950, PhD, 1955. Sr lectr, Bar Ilan U, Ramat Gan, since 1958; lectr, Ulpan Akiva, Natanya; art adv, ZOA House, Tel Aviv. Author: Marcel Janco, 1963; The Poems of Apollinaire, 1968. Home: 27 Reading St, Ramat Aviv, Isr. Office: Bar Ilan U, Ramat Gan, Isr.

MENDELSSOHN, Edwin, US, surgeon; b. Phila, Pa, May 30, 1913; s. Samuel and Anna (Rebock); BS, Temple U, 1934, MD, Med Coll, 1938; m. Flora Wernick, May 20, 1946 (decd); c: Marvin, Roy; m. 2nd, Etta Batt, Oct 9, 1966. Asso prof, surg, Temple Med Sch; guest examiner, Amer Bd Thoracic Surg; chief surg, div thoracic surg, Phila Gen Hosp, 1948-66; surg, N div, Albert Einstein Med Cen, since 1945. Lt, US Army MC, 1940-41. F: Amer Coll Card; Amer Coll Chest Phys; Phila Coll Phys and Surg; Amer Coll Surgs; Intl Coll Surg; dipl: Amer Bd Surg; Amer Bd Thoracic Surg; mem: AMA; Amer Assn Thoracic Surg; chmn, sch comm, Germantown J Cen, 1960-62. Contbr to surg jours. Hobby: collecting ancient Judaica coins. Home: 815 N Mt Pleasant Rd, Philadelphia, , Pa. Office: 1351 Tabor Rd, Philadelphia, Pa.

MENDELSSOHN, Heinrich, Isr, zoologist; b. Berlin, Ger, Oct 31, 1910; s. Joseph and Lucie; in Isr since 1933; att Humboldt U, Berlin; MSc, Heb U, Jerusalem, 1935, PhD, 1940; m. Tamar Pressmann. Asso prof, zool, Tel Aviv U, since 1961; zool, Biol Pedg Inst, Tel Aviv, 1935-47, head, inst, 1947-53; dean, U Inst for Sci, Tel Aviv Munic, 1953-56; head, dept zool, Tel Aviv U, 1956-66; dean, fac sci, Tel Aviv U, 1956-59, 1963-66. Chmn: Fauna Palestina Comm, Isr Acad of Sci, since 1966; Nature Conservation Comm, Intl Biol Prog, since 1967. Contbr to profsl publs. Home: 11 Oded St, Ramat Chen, Isr. Office: Tel Aviv U, Ramat Aviv, Isr.

MENDES, Abraham Piza, US, chemist, manufacturer; b. NYC, Apr 30, 1894; s. Henry and Rosalie (Piza); BS, hons, Columbia U, 1915; m. Edith Wise, Dec 12, 1920; c: Alvin, Margot Oppenheimer; m. 2nd, Mildred Strauss, 1961. Chemist: explosive sect, Fr High Commn to US, 1917; explosives research div, US Bur of Engr, 1918; Critchfield and Co, 1920; Harding and Co, 1930; Valdome, Inc, 1940. Pres, Lexington Sch for Deaf, 1966-67, trustee since 1921, secy, 1924-66; trustee, Span-Port Syn, since 1943; trustee, N Amer Relief Soc, since 1930; mem: Amer J Tercentenary Comm, Mayor's Comm, 1955; Phi Beta Kappa Alumni, NY, council, since 1966; exec comm, Judeans; club, Sunningdale Country. Home: 25 E 86 St, New York, NY. Office: 51 E 42 St, New York, NY.

MENDES, Marion de Sola, US, artist; b. NYC, June 27, 1909; d. Edmund and Alma (de Sola Mendes); att: NY Sch of Applied Design for Women, 1926-32; Natl Acad of Design, 1928-32; Naum Los Studio, 1940-41. One man shows: Argent

Gal, 1950, 1959; Clyde Mack Gal, NY; Natl Bank of Westchester, NY; West Corner Gal, Grafton, Vt; Old Mill, Chester, Vt; exhbs: Natl Assn Women Artists, since 1948; Allied Artists of Amer, since 1953; Amer Soc Miniature Painters, 1954; Amer Artists Profsl League, 1957, 1958; Academic Artists Assn, 1957; Knickerbocker Artists, since 1956; Natl Arts Club, 1959, 1961; Pen and Brush Club since 1957; Natl Soc Painters in Casein, 1960; Berkshire Art Assn, 1961; The Catherine Lorillard Wolfe Art Club; The Exposition Intercontinentale of Monaco. F, Royal Soc Art; mem: NY Soc of Women Painters; Daughters of the Amer Revolution; Allied Artists of Amer; Knickerbocker Artists; Natl Arts Club; mem, bd govs: Natl Soc Painters in Casein; The Natl Assn Women Artists; clubs: Pen and Brush, chmn, membership jury and brush sect; Catherine Lorillard Art, acting pres, 1959-60. Recipient: still life award, Catherine Lorillard Wolfe Art Club, 1956; Grumbacher medal and prize, 1962; Edith A Lehman Award, Natl Assn Women Artists, 1957; Kaymore Prize, 1960; Grumbacher Award, Amer Artists Profsl League, 1958; portrait award, Academic Artists Assn, 1958; J Spencer White Award, 1961; oil award, Pen and Brush Club, 1958, 1961; Heydenryk Prize, Allied Artists of Amer, 1959. Home: 1435 Lexington Ave, New York, NY. Studio: 150 E 93 St, New York, NY.

MENDES-FRANCE, Pierre, Fr, statesman; b. Paris, Jan 11, 1907; dipl, L'Ecole des Sciences Politiques, Paris, 1926; LLD, Fac en Droit, U Paris, 1929; m. Lily Cicurel, Dec, 1933; c: Bernard, Michel. PM, June, 1954 to Feb, 1955; MP, since 1932, chmn, finance comm, 1953-54; atty, Court of Appeals; under-secy, Treasury, 1938; Min of Finance, Fr Govt in Exile, Algiers, 1944; Min of Econ Affairs, 1944-45. Fr Air Force, 1939-43. Author of books, contbr to mags. Recipient: Officier de la Légion d'Honneur; Croix de Guerre; Médaille de la Résistance: Médaille des Évadés; Grand Officier de l'Ordre de Léopold. Address: Les Monts, Louviers, Eure, Fr.

MENDLOWITZ, Harold, US, physicist; b. NYC, Aug 23, 1927; s. Aaron and Rose (Bruder); BS, CCNY, 1947; AM, Columbia U, 1948; PhD, U of Mich, 1954; ordained rabbi, Mesifta Torah Vodaath, 1949; m. Ann Friedman, June 18, 1950; c: Judith, Abbe, Sarah. Prof, physics, Howard U, Wash, DC, since 1965; lectr, Howard U Grad Sch, since 1955; asst prin, Beth Yehudah Schs, Detroit, 1948-49; instr, research asst, U of Mich, 1952-54; physicist, Natl Bur of Standards, Wash, DC, 1951, 1954-65. Pres: Young Israel Shomrai Emunah, Gtr Wash, DC, 1963-64, and since 1969; Cong Shomrei Emunah, 1960-61; secy, Combined Congs of Wash, 1955-59; f: Amer Phys Soc; Wash Acad Sci; mem: Sigma Xi; Phi Beta Kappa; Assn Orthodox J Sci. Contbr to profsl jours. Home: 708 Lamberton Dr, Silver Spring, Md. Office: Howard U, Washington, DC.

MENDLOWITZ, Milton, US, physician, educator; b. NYC, Dec 30, 1906; s. Benjamin and Emma (Schramm); AB, CCNY, 1928; MD, U Mich, 1932; m. Muriel Chertoff, June 4, 1940; c: Judith, Susan, Benjamin. Att phys, Mt Sinai Hosp, NY, since 1959, on staff since 1932; asso clinical prof, med, Columbia U, since 1960, fac mem since 1946; f, phys, Michael Reese Hosp, Chgo, 1937; f, clinical research, U Coll Hosp, London, 1938; sr phys, NY regional off, VA, 1946-53; research f, Goldwater Memorial Hosp, 1950-62; police phys, NYC, 1950-69; clinical prof, med, Mt Sinai Sch of Med, CUNY, 1966-69. Lt col, US Army MC, 1942-46. F: AMA; Amer Coll Phys; Amer Coll Chest Phys; AAAS; NY Acad Scis; NY Acad Med; dipl, Amer Bd Internal Med; mem: NY Co Med Soc; NY State Med Soc; Fed Clinical Research; US Public Health Assn; AHA; Amer Soc Clinical Inves; Amer Phys Soc; Soc for Experimental Biol and Med; Alpha Omega Alpha; Phi Kappa Phi. Author: The Digital Circulation, 1954; Hypertension, 1961; contbr to med jours. Recipient: grants-in-aid: Dazian Fund, 1942; AHA, 1950-62; Natl Heart Inst, HEW, 1951-62. Hobby: fishing. Home: 1200 Fifth Ave, New York, NY. Office: 1136 Fifth Ave, New York, NY.

MENICKS, Samuel Yale, US, oral surg; b. Providence, RI, Aug 3, 1906; s. Solomon and Bess (King); att Tufts U, 1924-25, DMD, 1929. Pvt practice since 1929; asso, Forsythe Children Clinic; staff mem: Cen Hosp, Sommerville, Mass; Kenmore Hosp, Boston, Mass. Capt, US Army, 1942-46. Mem: Kehillath Isr Cong, Brookline, Mass; Chaim Weizmann Inst; Friends of Brandeis Inst, both Boston; Meah Sheavim; Lubovitz Yeshiva; Young Isr; Amer Dent Assn; Middlesex Dent Assn; Tufts Alumni Assn; Cambridge Civic League; Boy Scouts Amer; DAV. Contbr to dent jours. Home: 125 Allen Ave, Waban, Mass. Office: 1210 Cambridge, Cambridge, Mass.

MENKES, Jacob David, US, attorney; b. NYC, July 11, 1908; s. Samuel and Sophie; LLB, cum laude, St John's U, 1930; m. Molly Fuchs, June 4, 1932; c: Stephen, Susan Sassower, Jane Rosen. Pvt practice since 1932; atty, Home Owners' Loan Corp, 1933-45; dep sanitation commn, NYC, 1953-64; mem, Roosevelt team to organize agcy to prevent home foreclosures during depression. Pres: Lemberg Home and Geriatric Inst; Lemberger Cong; chmn bd: Beth Jacob Parochial Sch; Esther Schoenfeld HS; Heb Tchrs Coll; found, trustee: Dickstein Lodge, Munic Lodge, B'nai B'rith; mem: AJCong. Home: 457 FDR Drive, New York, NY. Office: 51 Chambers St, New York, NY.

MENUSY, Yedidia, (pen name **Didi**), Isr, journalist, author; b. Geva, Isr, May 9, 1928; s. Shmuel and Haya (Vilkovitz) Manusovitz; BA, Hebrew U, Jerusalem; m. Cyla London, Mar 25, 1959; c: Keren, Dana. Political columnist, daily newspaper, radio; UN war corresp, Korean, Indo-China wars; fgn corresp, Asia, Afr, US. Capt, IDF. Author: Shirot B'Rashit; Hufsha LeLo Tashlum; Bikurei Boker; 101 Limericks. Hobby: traveling. Home: 131 Hayarkon St, Tel Aviv, Isr. Office: 5 Moses St, Tel Aviv, Isr.

MERANZE, David R, US, physician, educator; b. Phila, Pa, Dec 25, 1900; s. Samuel and Yetta (Rotman); BS, U of Pa, 1921, MA, 1930; MD, Jefferson Med Coll, 1927; m. Yetta Kaplan, July 11, 1928; c: David, Walter. Head, research path, Korman Research Inst, Einstein Med Cen, since 1966; cons path: Fels Research Inst, Temple U Med Sch, since 1960; experimental hepatic carcinogenesis, NIH, since 1966; fac mem, biochem dept, Jefferson Med Coll, 1922-23, path dept, 1931-33, instr, bact, 1934-47; gen practice, 1928-30; dep asst path, Phila Gen Hosp, 1938-46; spec dep coroner, Phila Co, 1942; cons specialist, Selective Service Bd of Inductees, 1941-45; acting admnr, Mt Sinai Hosp, Phila, 1939-40, 1950-51; path, dir, lab and research, S Div, Albert Einstein Med Cen, 1930-65; dir, research and med educ, 1954-55; prof, path, Hahnemann Med Coll, 1947-64. Dipl, Amer Bd of Path, 1945; mem, bd dirs, J Comty Relations Council; mem: AMA; Amer Soc Clinical Paths; Amer Assn Sci; Amer Coll Paths; Phila Coll Phys; Phila Path Soc; Phila Co Med Soc; Pa Med Soc; NY Acad Sci; Alpha Omega Alpha. Contbr to med jours. Home: 412 Pelham Park Apts, 229 W Upsal St, Philadelphia, Pa. Office: Korman Research Inst, Albert Einstein Med Cen, Philadelphia, Pa.

MERARI, Tanchum, Isr, government official; b. Danzig, Ger, Dec 25, 1921; s. Siskind and Henriette (Blum) Müller; in Isr since 1933; tchr cert, Mizrachi Tchrs Training Sch, 1942; att Heb U; m. Jehudith Cohen, June 14, 1949; c: Ruhama, Naomi, Jemina, Osnat, Jishai. Dir, child and youth dept, Min of Social Wfr, since 1969; dir, Dept of Devl, Min of Social Wfr, 1957-63; commn of homes, Youth Protection Auth, 1963-69. Haganah; maj, IDF, 1940-57. Home: 19 Arbarbanel St, Jerusalem, Isr.

MERCER, Julian, Austr, barrister, solicitor; b. Warsaw, Pol, Jan 31, 1908; s. Abraham nd Frada (Glowiczower); in Austr since 1948; LLM, U of Warsaw, 1930; LLB, U of Melbourne, 1953; m. Sophie Herbst, Apr 10, 1945. Pvt practice since 1954. Mem: Gen ZC, actions comm; exec, World Union of Gen Zionists; fmr: found pres, Bialik Coll; pres, state ZC, Vic; sr vice-pres, ZF of Austr and NZ. Contbr to local press. Hobbies: Chess, music. Home: 8 Dawson Ave, Elwood, Vic, Austr. Office: 224 Queen St, Melbourne, Austr.

MEREMINSKY, Meyer, US, rabbi; b. Pol, Dec 27, 1918; s. Joshua and Rachel (Kagan); in US since 1925; BS, CCNY, 1937; BHL, ordained rabbi, JTSA, 1942; m. Arline Levendorf, Jan 30, 1956; c: Rachel, Joshua. Rabbi: West LA Syn and Adat Shalom Temple, since 1948; Beth Judah Cong, Phila, 1942; Temple Emanuel, Lawrence, Mass, 1947; instr, Bible, Heb and rel, U of Judaism, LA, 1949-55. Chaplain, USAAC, 1944-45. Cabinet mem, Bonds for Isr, Syn div; pres, W region, RA, 1954-56; vice-pres, Bd of Rabbis, S Cal, 1956-58. Contbr to J mags. Home: 1907 Fairburn Ave, Los Angeles, Cal. Study: 3000 Westwood Blvd, Los Angeles, Cal.

MERETZ, David P, Isr, government official; b. Hradiśté, Czech, Dec 26, 1894; s. Moritz and Cäcilie (Adler) März; in Isr since 1939; att U Vienna, 1913-20; DJ, U Prague, 1920; m. Tamarah Kresta-Kohn, Mav 23, 1923; c: Uri, Michael. Ret; fmr: treas, Isr Min of Interior; atty, pvt practice, Czech, 1920-39; mgr, Pal off, Prague, 1939; dir, Czech Transfer Off, 1940-43; comptroller, Haganah, 1943-48. Hon treas, Isr-Swed Friendship Assn; mem, Assn of Fmr Mems Ivria, Vienna;

delg: WZC's; United Isr Appeal to Scandinavia; fmr: chmn, Zionist Org of Czech; vice-chmn, WZC court. Contbr to Zionist press. Home: 2 Gan Rehavia, Jerusalem, Isr.

MERHAV, Menachem, Isr, civil engr; b. Leipzig, Ger, Sep 15, 1931; s. Ernst and Hilde (Wolf) Markowicz; in Isr since 1937; BS, cum laude, Technion, Haifa, 1954; MS, U of Cal, Berkeley, 1959; m. Naomi Zysmann, Sep 20, 1960; c: Tamir, Dorit. Head engnr econs research, Min of Housing, since 1968, chief research engr, 1967-68; structural engr, with firms in Cal and NY, 1959-63. Lt, IDF Res, since 1955. Mem, Engrs and Architects Soc, Isr. Home: 4 Yegia-Kapayim, Ramat Hasharon, Isr. Office: Min of Housing, Hakirya, Tel Aviv, Isr.

MERHAV, Shmuel Jacob, Isr, research engr; b. Hagen, Ger, Feb 26, 1924; s. Abraham and Atara (Szieradzky) Landsberg; EE, Technion, Haifa, 1948; PhD, U of Cambridge, Eng, 1964; m. Noemi Roifer, May 27, 1948; c: Zvi, Neri. Dir, Control Sys Div, since 1969; research engr, sci dept, Min of Defense, 1949-58, sys analysis group leader, 1958-62, tech dir, 1964-69. Capt, IDF, 1948-56. Prin contribs: devl of electronic computers, research in automatic control sys theory, grad sch courses in advanced control theory. Mem: Inst of Electronic and Elec Engrs; Intl Fed of Automatic Control, Isr sect. Contbr to profsl jours. Recipient: Ot Komemiut, Ot Sinai, Ot Sheshet Hayamim. Hobbies: gardening, painting. Home: 12A Nitzanim St, Haifa, Isr. Office: Min of Defense, Jerusalem, Isr.

MERMEY, Maurice, US, business exec; b. Hung, Sep 21, 1901; s. Israel and Hannah (Goldman); grad, Coll of Forestry, Syracuse U, 1922; m. Fayvelle Schulman, Feb 25, 1944; c: Michael, Constance, Nina. Pres, The Mermey Org, PR counsel; cable ed, United Press, 1926-28; exec secy, Retail Code Auth, NYC, 1933-34; dir, exhbs and concessions, NY World's Fair, 1939. Mem: bd dirs, exec comm, JWB, since 1942; chmn, Frank L Weil awards comm, since 1951; Commerce and Ind Assn of NY; PR Soc of Amer; Soc of Silurians; Larchmont Temple. Ed, Footnotes to Public Relations, 1945-49; co-ed, The Shopping Guide, 1937. Home: 960 Green Meadow La, Mamaroneck, NY. Office: 485 Madison Ave, New York, NY.

MERRELL, Louis Jacob, US, attorney; b. Odobesti, Rum, Dec 26, 1892; s. Israel and Golda (Schechter) Mutterperl; BA, CCNY, 1913; JD, NYU Law Sch, 1920; m. Molly Merrell, Feb 6, 1927; c: Charles. Mem, Mayor's Comm on Judiciary, NYC, since 1962; pres em, NY Leg Serivce, since 1966, pres, 1953-66; ed dept, NY Times, 1912-17; instr, bus law, CCNY, 1923-24; admitted to practice: NY State, 1920; US Supr Court, 1943. Sgt maj, US Army, 1917-18. Trustee, Cong Shaare Torah, Bklyn, NY; mem: Phi Beta Kappa; Kings Co Lib Party, fmr chmn; Bklyn Bar Assn, fmr pres. Contbr to law jours. Hobby: reading. Home: 221 Linden Blvd, Brooklyn, NY. Office: 16 Court St, Brooklyn, NY.

MERSKEY, Harold, Eng, psychiatrist; b. Sunderland, Eng, Feb 11, 1929; s. Harry and Sophie (Lieberman); att Tech Coll, Sunderland, 1945-46; MA, MD, Exeter Coll, Oxford, 1950; DPM, U Coll Hosp Med Sch, London, 1953; m. Susan Crann, Feb 21, 1965; c: Helen. Cons phys, psych med, Natl Hosp for Nervous Diseases, London, since 1967; lectr, psycht, U Sheffield, 1961-64; cons psycht, Nottingham, 1964-67. Capt, RAMC, 1954-56. Mem: Friends of Heb U; JPA Drs and Comm; fmr, pres, Oxford U J Soc. Co-author: Psychiatric Illness,1965; Pain Dents: Psychological and Psychiatric Aspects 1967; contbr to profsl jours. Hobbies: Heb lit, gardening. Home: 53 Ravenscroft Ave, Wembley, Middlesex, Eng. Office: National Hosp, Queen Sq, London, Eng.

MERTENS, Hanan, Isr, architect, town planner; Vienna, Aus, Jan 17, 1912; in Isr since 1935; dipl ing, TechU, Vienna, 1934. Head, town planning dept, i/c, urban planning, urban design, planning of new towns, Min of Housing, since 1954; with pvt architecture firms, 1935-39; Public Works Dept, Mandatory Govt, Haifa Dist, 1939-44; Iraq Petroleum Co, Haifa, 1944-48; Min of Interior, head, Haifa dist, planning div, Min of Interior, 1949-53. Lt, field engrs, IDF, 1943-49. Mem: Isr Assn Engrs and Architects; Ger Acad for Town and Country Planning, Dusseldorf; Intl Soc of City and Regional Planners; secretariat, Delft, Netherlands. Contbr to profsl jours. Recipient: UN f Tech Assistance Admn, Netherlands, 1952. Office: 139 Arlosoroff St, Tel Aviv, Isr.

MERVIS, Sanford Lee, US, attorney; b. Baltimore, Md, Mar 23, 1933; s. Julius and Sarah (Duke); LLB, JD, Mt Vernon Law Sch, Baltimore; att: U of Baltimore; Towson State Coll; m. Lisa Caplan, Aug 21, 1966; c: Shara. Pvt practice since 1959;

counsel Md Fed of Fed Employees, since 1968; dir, radio-TV, United Fund, 1958-59; counsel, US Cong, 1964-66. Pres, B'nai B'rith, Lodge 1737; fmr: pres: UN Youth of Md; Dist Young Dems; bd dir, Dolfield Dem Club; mem: Fed Bar Assn, Md chap; Amer Judicature Assn, natl chap. Hobbies: photography, sociol, hypnosis. Home: 8409 Downev Dale Dr, Baltimore, Md. Office: Equitable Bldg, Baltimore, Md.

MERZBACH, David, Isr, microbiologist; b. Frankfurt/M, Ger, June 23, 1927; s. Aron and Rivka (Feist); in Isr since 1939; MSc, Heb U, Jerusalem, 1952, PhD, 1962; m. Bella Emanuel, Sep 2, 1952; c: Channa, Aron, Yacov, Moshe, Zippora, Yemima. Head, dept bact and serology, Rambam Govt Hosp, Haifa, since 1961. Lt, IDF, MC, 1947-49. Mem: Rel Bd, Haifa; exec comm, Isr Soc Microbiol; Isr Soc of Protozool; asso, IMA. Contbr sci papers. Spec interests: Talmud, study of Judaism, sports. Home: 38 Pevsner St, Haifa, Isr.

MESCHAN, Isadore, US, physician, educator; b. Cleveland, O, May 30, 1914; s. Julius and Helen (Gordon); BA, W Reserve U, Cleveland, 1935, MA, 1937, MD, 1939; m. Rachel Farrer, Sep 3, 1943; c: David, Eleanor, Rosalind, Joyce. Prof, dir dept, radiology, Bowman Gray Sch Med, since 1955; prof, dir, dept radiology, NC Baptist Hosp, since 1955; Crile f, Reserve U, 1935, 1937-39; teaching research f, gastroenterology, 1936-37, instr, radiology, 1946-47; res in radiology, U Hosp, Cleveland, 1940-42; asso, radiology, 1946-47; spec course, radium techs, Royal Melbourne Hosp, Australia, 1942-43; prof, head, dept radiology, U Ark, 1947-55; course, methods in radiation biol, Argonne Natl Lab, 1959. Maj, US, Army, MC, 1942-46. F: Amer Coll Radiology, mem, commn on educ, 1956-59; AMA; mem: Amer Bd Radiology; Ark State Med Soc; Amer Roentgen Ray Soc; Radiological Soc of N Amer; Soc Experimental Biol and Med; S Med Assn; Teletherapy Bd of Oak Ridge Inst of Nuclear Studies; Radiation Research Soc; Soc Nuclear Med; Sigma Xi; Phi Beta Kappa; Alpha Omega Alpha. Author: Atlas of Normal Radiographic Anatomy, 1951, 1959; Roentgen Signs in Clinical Diagnosis, 1956; Synopsis of Roentgen Signs, 1962; Radiographic Positioning and Related Anatomy, 1968; contbr to med jours. Hobbies: photography, music, tennis. Home: 2716 Bartram Rd, Winston-Salem, NC. Office: Bowman Gray Sch of Med, Winston-Salem, NC.

MESCHELOFF, Moses, US, rabbi; b. NYC, June 12, 1909; s. Meyer and Bessie (Kroll); BA, CCNY, 1932; ordained rabbi, Isaac Elchanan Theol Sem, 1932; m. Magda Schonfeld, Mar 10, 1935; c: Renah Bell, Efraim, David. Rabbi: Cong KINS, W Rogers Park, since 1954; Vine St Syn, Scranton, Pa, 1932-36; Beth Jacob, Miami Beach, Fla, 1937-54. Vicepres, Chgo Bd Rabbis; bd dirs: N Town Comty Council; Chgo Zionist Org; Bonds for Isr; fmr pres: Chgo Rabb Council; Rel Zionists of Chgo; vice-pres, RabCA; chmn, JNF; mem: B'nai B'rith. Author: Jewish Laws and Customs, 1940; contbr to rel jours. Home: 6644 N Fairfield, Chicago, Ill. Study: 2800 W North Shore Ave, Chicago, Ill.

MESHORER, Yaakov, Isr, numismatist; b. Jerusalem; s. Ahraham and Zmira (Many); BA, MA, PhD, Heb U, Jerusalem; m. Adaya Weise, 1956; c: Chagit, Nitzan. Curator, numismatic dept, Isr Mus, since 1969; numismatic cons, Isr Govt, Coins and Medals Co, since 1962; cons, ancient coins, Bank of Isr, 1964. IDF, 1955-57. Author: Jewish Coins of the Second Temple Period, 1967. Mem, Isr, Swiss, Brit numismatic socs. Hobby: violin playing. Home: 8 Luria St, Jerusalem, Isr. Office: Isr Mus, Ruppin St, Jerusalem, Isr.

MESHULAM, David, Isr, artist; b. Bulgaria, May 25, 1930; s. Reuven and Zipora (Baruch); att: AVNI Inst; Sem for Art Tchrs; Surveyors Sch; Acad des Beaux Arts, Paris; studied under Dan Hoffner, Abba Fenichel; m. Jeudith, 1956; c: Korach, Noam. One-man show, Dizengoff, Mus; exhbs: Katz Gal; Paris Biennale for Young Artists; Helena Rubinstein Pavillion, Tel Aviv. Served IDF. Mem, Assn of Isr Painters; fmr mem: Zionist Hecalutz, Bulgaria; Kibbutz Eyal. Publ: Lithograph Albums, 1963, 1965, 1967, 1968; books of paintings, 1960-68. Recipient: Dizengoff Award, 1963; Kolb Prize, 1965. Home: 26 Bilu St, Tel Aviv, Isr.

MESSE, Abba A, US, surgeon; b. Cleveland, O, Nov 29, 1916; s. Morris and Sadie (Kay); BS, NYU, 1937; MD, NYU Coll of Med, 1941; m. Carolyn Fielding, Dec 18, 1946; c: Mark, Winifred, Madelyn. Pvt practice, surg, since 1950. US Army, 1942-46. F, Amer Coll Surgs, dipl, surg, Contbr to med jours. Recipient: Purple Heart; Oak Leaf Cluster; battle stars, Afr, Eur, ME theaters. Hobby: amateur radio. Home: 3240 Henry Hudson Pkwy, New York, NY. Office: 1475 Grand Concourse, New York, NY.

MESSELOFF, Charles R, US, physician; b. Lodz, Pol, Mar 15, 1903; s. Morris and Rachel (Bernstein); in US since 1904; MD, Bellevue Med Coll, 1926; m. Lillian Levinson, 1928; c: Alice Fraenkel, Reva Greenberg. Med dir, Beth Abraham Hosp, since 1967; dir, med, Lincoln Hosp, 1955-67; chief, med, Riverside Hosp, since 1957; asso card, Hosp for Jt Diseases, 1937-67; chief card, Dept of Health, 1945-53; phys, Selective Service, 1941-53; chief att phys, Beth Abraham Home, 1952-55; Frankenheimer F, Mt Sinai Hosp, 1930-31. Pres, N Bx Med Soc, 1952; dipl, Bd Internal Med; mem: Amer Coll Phys; Amer Geriatric Soc; Amer Coll Clinical Pharm and Therapeutics; Amer Soc Phys Chronic Disease Facilities; Amer Gerontological Soc; Alpha Omega Alpha; AMA; NY Heart Assn; AHA. Contbr to med jours. Home: 3725 Henry Hudson Pkwy, New York, NY. Office: 1750 Grand Concourse, New York, NY.

MESSING, Joseph Berglass, US, rabbi; b. NYC, Jan 24, 1920; s. Henry and Amelia (Berglass); AB, cum laude, Bklyn Coll, 1941; ordained rabbi, JIR, NY, 1945; MA, U of Wash, 1957; MHL. HUC-JIR, 1970; instrs' course, Judge Advocate Gen Sch, U of Va, 1957; m. Maria Michalovskis, June 5, 1947; c: Henry, Joel. Dep staff chaplain, US Army, Eur, since 1969; rabbi, Temple Beth Tefilloh, 1944-47; instr, Amer hist and Amer diplomatic hist, U of Heidelberg since 1969, 1962-65; instr, mil law, logistics, leadership, intl affairs, 1957-61; instr, Amer hist and Amer diplomatic hist, U of Louisville, 1948-49; chmn, profsl subjects comm, US Chaplains Sch, 1960-61; post chaplain, Heidelberg Post, Ger, 1962-65; dep 4th Army chaplain, Ft Sam Houston, Tex, 1965-66; instr, Amer hist and Amer diplomatic hist, San Antonio Coll, 1965-66; dir, admn, mgmt, Off Chief of Chaplains, 1966-69. Col, US Army since 1945. Mem: Assn of J Chaplains of Armed forces; Mil Chaplains Assn; CCAR; Phi Alpha Theta; Assn of US Army, Heidelberg chap. Contbr to jours. Recipient: Korean Service Medal; Korean Pres Unit Citation; UN Service Medal; Four Chaplains Award, B'nai B'rith, 1968. Home: 125 B Roemerstr, Heidelberg, Ger. Study: OSCH, HQ, USAREUR & 7th Army, APO, New York, 09403.

MESSINGER, Martin E, US, financial exec; b. Rochester, NY, Aug 15, 1928; s. David and Anne (Wakuck); BA, U of Rochester, 1949; MA, Grad Sch of Bus, Columbia U, 1950; m. Joan Frank, Dec 22, 1956; c: Daryl, Sarah, Alice, Liza. Dir, off planning and analysis, Merril, Lynch, Pierce, Fenner & Smith, since 1968, sr account exec, 1956-67; vice-pres, Messinger Co, Inc, 1950-55; dir, forensics, U of Rochester, 1954-57. Mem: Fed of Financial Analysts; fmr, mem bd: AJComm; NAACP; club, City, Rochester. Spec interests: govt and politics; public speaking, debating. Home: 38 Aspen Rd, Scarsdale, NY. Office: 70 Pine St, New York, NY.

METZKER, Isaac, US, author, journalist; b. Galicia, Pol, July 27, 1901; s. David and Fanny (Reich); in US since 1924; att J Tchrs Sem, NY, 1927-29; m. Bella Stark, July 2, 1944. Ed staff mem, J Daily Forward, since 1944; tchr, Workmen's Circle Schs, 1932-34. US Army, 1942-43. Mem: IL Peretz Writers Union; Workmen's Circle; club, PEN. Author: novels: Toiun Toby, 1936; Oifn Zeidns Felder, 1953; short stories: Erd un Zun, 1937; Gots Bashefenishen, 1958; biographical story, Don Itzchak Abarbanel, 1941; serially in J Daily Forward; Die Eibige Shtime, 1942; Beatrice un Ben, 1945; Oif Americaner Erd, 1967. Recipient: Bimko Award, for Oifn Zeidns Felder, 1953; Lamed Prize, for Gots Bashefenishen, 1958. Home: 2044 E 13 St, New York, NY. Office: 175 E Broadway, New York, NY.

METZNER, Charles M, US, jurist; b. NYC, Mar 13, 1912; s. Emanuel and Gertrude (Miller); BA, Columbia U, 1931, LLB, 1933; m. Jeanne Gottlieb, 1966. US dist judge, NYC, since 1959; pvt law practice, 1934; mem, Jud Council, State of NY, 1935-41; law clerk, NY Supr Court, 1942-52; exec asst, US Atty Gen Herbert Brownell Jr, 1953-54; mem, law firm, Chapman Walsh and O' Connell, 1954-59; Natl commn, ADL; mem: NY Co Lawyers Assn; NY State Bar Assn; Fed Bar Assn; Assn of Bar, NYC; fmr: Columbia Coll Council; Law Revision Commn, State of NY. Home: 35 Sutton Pl S, New York, NY. Office: US Court House, Foley Sq, New York, NY.

MEYER, Baron de Hirsch, US, attorney, banker: b. Prairie du Chien, Wis, Apr 12, 1899; s. John and Sarah (Jay); BA, U of Wis, 1920; LLB, Harvard Law Sch, 1923; hon LLD,

Bethune Cookman Coll; m. Polly Lux, Aug, 1951. Mem, Meyer, Weiss, Rose and Arkin, since 1942; org, pres, Miami Beach Fed Savings and Loan Assn, 1933-58; chmn, bd, Ind Natl Bank, 1948-56; pres, Fed Title and Ins Corp, 1947-56; dir, N Shore Bank, 1950-57. Cpl, WWI, maj, USAAC, 1942-46. Donor: law sch bldgs, U of Miami, 1955; co-donor: Comty Chest bldg, 1955. Mem, Miami Beach City Council, 1930-42; fmr pres: Mt Sinai Hosp, Gtr Miami, 1946-48, 1967-1970; JWB; dir: C of C, Miami Beach, since 1946; State C of C, 1955-70; natl vice-pres, AJComm, since 1957, pres, Miami Beach region; vice-pres, J Home for the Aged, since 1949; mem, bd of trustees: U of Miami, since 1955; Bethune Cookman Coll; found: Truman Inst for the Advancement of Peace in Jerusalem; Baron de Hirsch Free Loan Fund; org, first secy, Gtr Miami J Fed; mem bd: Comty Dade Co; United Fund; Beth Jacob Syn; mem, bd trustees: Temple Emanuel; Temple Isr; mem: exec bd, AJComm; Amer Dade Co, and Miami Beach Bar Assns; NCCJ; Kiwanis, life; Opera Guild; Masons; Shriners; Newcomen Soc; S Fla Hist Assn; clubs: Beverly Hills; Harmonie; Harvard; Lawyers, NY; Miami; Variety; Pioneers; Westview Country; Miami Standard. Recipient: Bronze Star; Air Medal; awards: AJComm, 1957; Miami Beach Civic League, 1955; Exch Club, 1955; Intl Rescue Comm, 1957; NCCJ, 1958; Law Alumni Assn, U of Miami, 1959; Fla State chap, Amer Inst of Architects, 1961. Home: 5255 Collins Ave, Miami Beach, Fla. Office: 407 Lincoln Rd, Miami Beach, Fla.

MEYER, Bernard S, US, jurist; b. Baltimore, Md, June 7, 1916; s. Benjamin and Josephine (Lyon); BS, Johns Hopkins U, 1936; LLB, U of Md Sch of Law, 1938; m. Elaine Strass, June 25, 1939; c: Susan (decd), Patricia. Justice, NY State Supr Court, since 1959; att with: Fisher and Fisher, Baltimore, 1938-41; US Treasury, 1941-43; Pol Amer Supply Corp, 1946-48; pvt law practice, 1948-54; partner, Meyer, Fink, Weinberger and Levin, 1954-58. Air combat intelligence off, USNR, 1943-46. Chmn: spec comm on news reporting, Natl Conf of State Trial Judges; program comm and pattern jury instruction comm, Assn of Supr Court Justices; vice-chmn, Natl Conf of State Trial Judges; vice-pres, Assn of Supr Court Justices; fmr pres, bd med, Health and Wfr Council of Nassau Co; fmr bd mem: Five Towns Comty House; Waldemar Med Research Found; fmr adv bd, Adelphi Coll Sch of Soc Work; Nassau-Suffolk Region, NCCJ; Nassau Co Council, Boy Scouts of Amer; NY Regional Adv Comm, ADL; mem: Amer Bar Assn; Amer Law Inst; Amer Judicature Soc; Inst of Jud Admn; Scribes; Omicron Delta Kappa; Order of the Coif; NY State, NY Co, and Fed Bar Assns; Bar Assn of Nassau Co, Inc; Nassau Lawyers Assn; Elks; VVW; Temple Sinai, Men's Club, Lawrence, NY. Contbr to legal jours. Recipient: Commendation Ribbon; Pres Unit Citation, WW II. Home: 298 Linwood Ave, Cedarhurst, NY. Office: Supr Court Chambers, Mineola, NY.

MEYER, David Solomon, US, attorney, editor; b. Odessa, Russ, Feb 7, 1906; s. Joseph and Rose (Rabinowitz); in US since 1906; att CCNY, 1924-27; grad, Amer Inst of Banking; LLB, Bklyn Law Sch, 1931; m. Rhoda Silverman, Dec 23, 1928; c: Renee Margulies. In pvt law practice since 1933. Mem: exec bd, Free Sons of Isr; Amer-Isr Public Affairs Comm; bd trustees, Cong Shaare Torah; natl exec council, ZOA; pres, Gad Widow and Orphan Benevolent Assn, since 1958; mem: Amer Bar Assn; Order of Foresters; KP; active: JTSA; JNF; Bonds for Isr; fmr: pres: Bklyn Zionist Region; Brandeis Zionist Dist; vice-pres, ZOA. Fmr ed: Shaare Torah Messenger; Bklyn Region Reporter; Free Son Reporter. Hobby: philately. Home: 590 Flatbush Ave, Brooklyn, NY. Office: 310 Madison Ave, New York, NY.

MEYER, Howard N, US, attorney; b. Bklyn, NY, Oct 8, 1914; s. Richard anu Minnie (Tietelbaum); AB, Columbia U, 1934, LLB, 1936; m. Sylvette Engel, Aug 30, 1942; c: Andrew, Franklin, Jonathan. Atty, O'Dwyer and Bernstien, since 1954; pvt practice since 1948; spec asst to US Atty Gen, Justice Dept, 1942-48; ed, Columbia Law Rev, 1934-36. Mem, bd trustees, Rockville Cen Comm for Better Educ, since 1954; mem, bd: PTA, 1950-60; scout comm man, Boy Scouts of Amer, 1954-57; mem: NAACP; United Fed of Tchrs; Afr-Amer Hist Comm; J Tchrs for Comty Control; NY Civil Liberties Union. Author: Let us Have Peace: the Story of US Grant, 1966; Colonel of the Black Regiment; The Life of Thomas Wentworth Higginson, 1967; ed: Higginson's Army Life in a Black Regiment, 1962; Herndon's Let me Live, 1968; Integrating America's Heritage, a congressional hearing reprinted, 1969; contbr of articles dealing with civil rights

Negro hist. Home: 76 Tarence St, Rockville Cen, NY. Office: 50 Broad St, New York, NY.

MEYER, Howard R, US, architect; b. NYC, Feb 17, 1903; s. Emile and Esthelle (Freund); AB, Columbia Coll, 1923; BArch, Columbia U, 1928; m. Schon Landman, Oct 16, 1928; c: Paul. Pvt practice since 1934; with: William E Lescaze, 1926; Bertram Grosvenor Goodhue Assos, 1929-30; sup, construction, Albanian-Amer Inst Near E Found, Kavaja, Albania, for Thompson & Churchill, Architects, 1932; partner, Morris B Sanders and Howard R Meyer, 1933-34; prin works include: 13th Church Christ, Sci, NYC, 1934; Temple Beth El, Tyler, Tex, 1938; Hillel Found, U of Tex, 1950; Red River Arsenal and Longhorn Ordinance Works, 120 bldgs, 1951-53; PHA housing projects, Dallas, 1953; Burnet Elem Sch, Dallas, 1955; cons architect, student chapel, Tex A & M Coll, 1956; 3525 Turtle Creek, Dallas, 1957; Temple Emanu-El, Dallas, 1957; Caruth Memorial Rehab Cen, 1960; Dallas Home for J Aged, 1956, 1962; Turtle Creek Village, 1960. Maj, Engrs Corps, US Army, 1942-46. F, Amer Inst Architects, 1957; trustee, Dallas Mus for Contemporary Arts, 1958-62; chmn, architecture adv comm, Dallas Hist Monuments Commn, 1959-60; mem: trustee, Cen Bus Dist Assn of Dallas, 1961; JWF, 1949; Temple Emanu-El, 1950-53; dir, Dallas chap, Amer Inst Architects, since 1942, pres, 1961; Tex Soc Architects; Zeta Beta Tau, Columbia U. Recipient: award of merit, Amer Inst Architects, 1959; medal of merit, Tex Soc of Architects, 1950, award of merit 1958, architecture of merit for the past 10 years. 1960; grand prize, Matico Competition, 1959. Home: 4433 Belclaire, Dallas, Tex. Office: 2727 Oak Lawn Ave, Dallas, Tex.

MEYER, Isidore S, US, rabbi, editor; b. New London, Conn, Nov 19, 1903; s. Max and Rachel (Ritt); BA, CCNY, 1925; MA, Columbia U, 1928; ordained rabbi, MHL, JTSA, 1929, DD, 1961; m. Hannah Myers, Sep 11, 1938; c: Jonathan. Ed em, Amer J Hist Soc, since 1969, publ ed, 1940-68; librarian, 1940-62; rabbi: J Cen of Bay Shore, 1938-43; Cong Sons of Isr, Palisades Park, NJ, 1944-48; lectr: hist, Yeshiva U, 1958-59; J hist, Bklyn J Cen Inst of Adult J Studies; ed: Early History of Zionism in America, 1958; The American Jew in the Civil War, 1961; co-ed: The Writing of American Jewish History, 1957; The Joshua Bloch Memorial Volume, 1960; The Lee Max Friedman Collection of American Jewish Colonial Correspondence: Letters of the Franks Family, 1733-1748, 1968. Contbr to periodicals. Mem, bd: J Book Council of Amer; Amer-It Hist Assn; mem: Manuscript Soc; RA; NY Bd Rabbis; corresp mem: Austr J Hist Soc. Recipient: Lee Max Friedman award, Amer J Hist Soc, 1960. Home: 90 Laurel Hill Terr, New York, NY. Office: 2 Thornton Rd, Waltham, Mass.

MEYER, Issachar Seligman, Isr, rabbi, Yeshiva dir; b. Hamburg, Ger, Feb 3, 1927; s. Jacob and Leah (Auerbach); in Isr since 1938; att Yeshivot: Lomzeh, Petah Tikvah; Ponevish, Bnei Brak; m. Judith Prager, Mar 24, 1954. Head, dir, found, Yeshivat Hanegev, since 1961; Sr Magid Shiur Yeshiva, Switz, 1951-56; head Yeshiva: Ozar Hatorah, 1956; Etz Hayim, 1959, both Morocco; Yeshiva HS, Kfar Haroeh, Isr, 1961. Head, communal org on befalf of needy in Netivot "Torah Vachesed"; mem, Agudat Achvah. Preparing new Talmud commentary. Home: 20 Abouchazera St, Netivot, Negev, Isr. Office: Yeshivat Hanegev, Isr.

MEYER, Jacques, Fr, government adv, author; b. Valenciennes, Fr, Jan 29, 1895; s. Felix and Lea (Levy); agrégé de philosophie, Ecole Normale Supérieure, 1920, docteur en droit, 1923; m. Yvonne Monier, July 7, 1942. Govt adv, since 1949; secy gen, dir, l'Intransigeant, newspaper, Paris, 1931-40; dir gen, Radiodiffusion et Télévision Françaises, 1944-50. Author: La Biffe, la guerre,...mon vieux question de confiance, 1928, 4th ed, 1948; Approche de la Mort, 1953; Vie et Mort des Français, 1914-18, pub 1959, 3rd ed, 1968; Le 11 Novembre, 1964; Vie Quotidienne des Soldats de la Grande Guerre, 1967. Pres, Assn des Combattants Evadés de France pendant l'occupation; mem: comm, Assn des Ecrivains Combattants; cen comm: Alliance Israélite Universelle, since 1956; ORT, since 1961; Fr sect, WJC, since 1961; initiator, monument for Fr Army, WW I, erected in Place du Trocadero, Paris. Recipient: Commandeur de la Légion d'Honneur; Croix de Guerre, WW I, WW II; Médaille des Evadés; Médaille de la Résistance; Médaille des Combattants Volontaires; Grand Prix de L'Académie Française, 1960, 1965, 1968. Home: 147 Blvd Malesherbes, Paris, Fr.

MEYER, Jacques, Fr, educator; b. La Walck, Fr, Aug 27, 1895;

s. Samuel and Jeannette (Sichel); dipl, Fac de Pharm et Sci, 1925, DPharm, U Strasbourg, 1927; D d'Etat, 1947; m. Marguerite Girardet, Sep 17, 1939. Prof, hygiene, microbiol, Fac de Pharm, Strasbourg, since 1949, chef de travaux, 1936; lab technician, Sanatorium Rollier & Van Bergen, Leysin, Switz, 1920; asst bact, Strasbourgh, 1925; research worker, 1928-36. War service, 1939-45. Mem: Biol Soc of Fr; Assn Fr Advancement of Scis; Societe de Pathologie Comparée; Société Biologie Pharmacie; Société de Chimie Biologique; Société Française de Microbiologie; Société Française de Ther, et Pharmacodyn Author: Influence du Radium et des Rayons X sur l'Evolution Morphologique et Reproduction d'Aspergillus Fumigatus fres, 1927; Les Mycoses Nouvelles, 1932; Les Ferments Lipolytiques du Sérum Sanguin et des Bactéries Acido-alcoolo-résistantes, 1947; Microbiologie Pratique, 1950. Recipient: Lauréat, Acad of Med, 1931; Officier d'Académie, 1932; Chevalier du Mérite Agricole et Croix des Services Militaires Volontaires, 1939; Officier d'Instruction Publique, 1946; Chevalier de la Légion d'Honneur, 1951. Home and office: 25 Blvd de la Marne, Strasbourg, Fr,

MEYER, Jerome H, US, surgeon; b. Butler, Pa, Sep 6, 1910; s. Hyman and Sarah (Shur); BA, O State U, 1933, MS, 1940, MD, 1940; m. Florence Cohen, Feb 22, 1931; c: David, Darlene. In pvt practice since 1948; chief, surg, Good Samaritan Hosp,since 1967; staff mem, St Elizabeth Hosp; Miami Valley Hosp,since 1948; asst chief, surg, Dayton State Hosp since 1948; cons surg, USAF Hosp, since 1952, all Dayton, O; intern, St Luke's Hosp, Cleveland, O, 1940-41; asst res, surg, St Luke's Hosp, 1941-42; res surg, St Joseph's Hosp, Milw, Wis, 1942-43; instr, surg, Marquette U, 1942-43; chief res surg,instr,sch of nursing,Aultman Hosp, Canton, O, 1946-47; chief, aseptic surg, VA Brown Gen Hosp, Dayton, O, 1947-48; med adv, Civil Air Patrol, rated pilot, 1950. Flight surg, USAAC, 1943-46. F: Intl Coll Surgs; Amer Coll Surgs; dipl: Amer Bd Surg; Intl Bd Surg; pres: Dayton Surg Soc,1963-64; J Home for Aged, 1960-65; instr, Amer Soc Abdominal Surgs, since 1967; trustee, Aviation Hall of Fame, since 1968; mem, bd dirs: JCC, 1955-65; Air Force Assn, 1952-63, group cdr, 1951; squadron celr, Wright Memorial Air Force Assn,1948-51; mem: AMA, Montgomery Co Med Soc; O Med Assn; O State Surg Assn; Dayton Surg Assn; C of C Aviation Sect, Dayton, O. Author: The Effect of Increased Iodine Feeding Upon the Iodine Content of Cow's Milk, 1939; Double Gallbladder, 1949; Nitrofurazone in Skin Grafting, 1950; Hereditary Spherocytic Anemia in a Negro Family, 1953; Liver Function Studies in a Case of Massive Rupture of the Liver, 1956; Primary Sclerosing Cholangitis, 1962; Obstructive Lesions of the Biliary Tract, 1968; contbr to profsljours. Recipient: Air Force Assn Award, 1949; Wright Aviation Award, 1957; Purple Heart, US Army, 1945. Home: 4237 Catalpa Dr, Dayton, O. Office: 880 Fidelity Bldg, Day on, O.

MEYER, Jerome S, US, author; b. NYC, Jan 14, 1895; s. Arthur and Jessie (Moore); att Columbia U, 1920-21; m. Tyroler, Nov 10, 1927. Author: Advice on the Care of Babies, 1927; Mind Your P's and Q's, 1927; Mental Whoopee, 1927; Fun for the Family, 1934; More Fun for the Family, 1936; The Big Fun Book, 1940; Fun with Words, 1941; Puzzle Paradise, 1943; Correctograms, 1944; ABC of Physics, 1945; Picture Book of Astronomy, 1945; Picture Book of Atoms and Molecules, 1946; Picture Book of Weather, 1947; Picture Book of Earth, 1948; Picture Book of Radio and TV, 1949; Picture Book of Electricity, 1950; Book of Amazing Facts, 1950; Picture Book of Chemistry, 1951; Picture Book of Sea, 1952; Mirror Book for Boys, 1953; Mirror Book for Girls, 1953; World Book of Great Inventions,1955; Fun with Mathematics, 1957; Elements, Builders of the Universe, 1958; Machines, 1958; Prisms and Lenses, 1959; Engines, 1961; Water at Work, 1963; First Book of Mechanical Drawing, 1963; More Fun with Mathematics, 1965; Iron and Steel, 1966; Sound and its Reproduction, 1966; Getting a Line on Mathematics, 1967; Little Accidents in Science that Changed the World, 1967; Fun for All, 1968. Copywriter, Sackheim and Scherman, NY, 1925-28; pres, Zinn and Meyer Advt Agcy, 1929-36; ed, game books, Doubleday, Doran, 1936-37; freelance sales promotion, 1937-39; mail-order cons, Crown Publishers, NY, 1949-54. US Army, WW I. Pres, Gilbert and Sullivan Soc, 1935; mem, Authors Guild; Scripta Mathematica. Hobbies: music, mathematics. Home: 135 W 79 St, New York, NY.

MEYER, Julien H, US, surgeon; b. Enfield, NC, May 7, 1914; s. Joseph and Hennye (Lehman); BS, U of NC, 1935; MD, Med Coll of Va, 1937; m. Dorothy Kahn, July 14, 1940; c: Julien, Carol. Att obstet and gyn: Roanoke Memorial Hosp, since 1940, alternate chief, obstet and gyn service; Lewis-Gale Hosp since 1940; Burrell Memorial Hosp since 1946; mem, staff, Comty Hosp of Roanoke Valley; cons, gyn and obstet, VA Hosp since 1946. Capt, US Army, MC 1943-46. F: Amer Coll Surgs; Amer Coll Gyn and Obstet; chmn, med adv comm, ARC, 1957; pres, Temple Emanuel, 1962; mem, Masons; clubs: Green Hill Country; Arrow Wood Country; Pickwick Town. Contbr to med jours. Hobbies: piano, golf. Home: 2123 Mt Vernon Rd, SW, Roanoke, Va. Office: 101 Med Cen Bldg, McClanahan St, SW, Roanoke, Va.

MEYER, Karl, US, biochemist, educator; b. Kerpen/Cologne, Ger, Sep 4, 1899; s. Ludwig and Ida (Aaron); in US since 1930; MD, U of Cologne, 1924; PhD, U of Berlin, 1927; m. Marthe Ehrlich, Apr 15, 1930; c: Robert, Janet. Prof em, biochem, Coll of Phys and Surgs, Columbia U, since 1967, fac mem, since 1932; prof, biochem, Belfer Grad Sch of Sci, Yeshiva U, since 1967; chem, Presbyterian Hosp; asst, Kaiser Wilhelm Inst of Biol, Berlin-Dahlem, 1927; Rockefeller f, chem dept, Swiss Poly Inst, Zurich, 1928-29; asst prof, experimental biol, U of Cal, Berkeley, 1930-32. F, Amer Acad Arts and Scis; mem: Natl Acad Sci; Amer Chem Soc; Amer Soc Biol Chems; Harvey Soc. Author: The Polysaccharides of Vitreous Humor and Umbilical Cord, 1936; Action of the Lytic Principle of Pneumococcus on Certain Tissues Polysaccharides,1936; Lysozyme Activity in Chronic Ulcerative Colitis, 1948; Hyaluronidases in Advances in Enzymology, 1952. Recipient: Lasker Award, 1956; Duckett Jones Award, 1959; Gairdner Award, 1960. Home: 642 Wyndham Rd, Teaneck, NJ. Office: 630 W 168 St, New York, NY.

MEYER, Leo M, US, physician, educator; b. NYC, Jan 14, 1906; s. Meyer and Sarah (Diamond); BS, CCNY, 1926; MA, Cornell U, 1927; MD, U Md, 1931; m. Lillian Berlin, 1928; Hematologist i/c, Queens Hosp Cen, since 1964; asst prof med, NYU Med Coll, since 1947; research collaborator, Brookhaven Natl Lab, since 1955; dir lab, S Nassau Comtys Hosp, 1941-64; Fulbright research scholar, Finland, 1967; exch sci to India, NSF, 1968. Mem, Sigma Xi; fmr pres, Soc for Study of Blood. Mem, ed bd, Acta Hematologica; contbr to med jours. Home: 43 S Lewis Pl, Rockville Centre, NY.

MEYER, Leonard B, US, educator; b. NYC, Jan 12, 1918; s. Arthur and Marion (Wolff); BA, Columbia U, 1940; MA, 1948; PhD, U of Chgo, 1954; hon LHD, Grinnell Coll; m. Lee Malakoff, Aug 15, 1945; c: Marion, Carlin, Erica. Prof, music, chmn dept, U of Chgo, since 1961, on fac since 1946. US Army, 1942-45. Mem: council, Amer Musicological Soc, since 1962; bd trustees, Amer Soc for Aesthetics, since 1962; AAAS; Phi Beta Kappa; Soc for Ethnomusicology. Author: Emotion and Meaning in Music, 1956; co-author: The Rhythmic Structure of Music, 1960; Music, The Arts and Ideas, 1967; contbr to music jours. Recipient: f, Cen for Advanced Study, Wesleyan U, 1960-61. Home: 5801 S Blackstone Ave, Chicago, Ill. Office: U of Chgo, Chicago, Ill.

MEYER, Leopold L, US, business exec; b. Galveston, Tex; June 21, 1892; s. Achille and Malline (Kahn); BA, cum laude, Tulane U, La, 1912; m. Adelena Goldman, June 30,1931; c: Alan. Chmn bd, Meyer Bros, Inc, since 1945; vice-pres, Foley Bros Dry Goods Co, 1925-45. Chmn, bd, Houston Civic Music Assn; chmn em, Harris Co Cen for Retarded; pres, Tex Children's Hosp; Houston Horse Show Assn; mem, bd trustees, Baylor Coll Med; Tex Heart Inst; St Luke's Episcopal Hosp; Houston Livestock Show; Houston Sch for Deaf Children; Tulane Alumni Assn; Houston Speech and Hearing Cen; Friends of Libr of U of Houston; mem: Elks; B'nai B'rith; Omicron Delta Kappa; fmr: bd: U Houston; Rice Inst Assos; Holly Hall Home for Aged, Houston Sym Soc; Houston Heart Assn; United Fund; City of Hope; Lighthouse for Blind; HUC;Child Guidance Cen;Tulane Devl Council;fmr pres: Cong Beth Isr; Houston Amateur Baseball Fed; Natl Retail Credit Assn; Houston Crime Commn; treas, UJA; clubs: Hundred, Houston, chmn bd; Houston Country, Westwood Country; Petroleum; Intl; Houston. Recipient: citations: VFW, US; Houston Police Assn; Houston Council for Retarded Children, Houston Ped Soc; Soc of Friends of Amer Judaism; Houston Civic Music Assn; Houston Peace offs Assn; Tex Assn for Retarded Children; Int Assn Chiefs of Police; Horses Harris Co; Boston Conf on Distribution, NCCJ; City of Hosp; Coronat Medal, St Edward's U; Natl J Hosp Man of the Year, Houston, 1969 Home: 216 Main St, Houston, Tex. Office: 1035 Meyerland Plaza Mall, Houston, Tex.

MEYER, Marshall Theodore, Arg, rabbi, educator; b. NYC, Mar 25, 1930; s. Isaac and Anita (Silberstein); in Arg since

1959; AB, Dartmouth Coll, 1952; MHL, ordained rabbi, JTSA, 1958; m. Naomi Friedman, June 19, 1955; c: Anne, Dodi, Gabriel. Rector, found, Seminario Rabinico Latino Americano, since 1962; Latin Amer dir, World Council of Syns, since 1961; rabbi, found, Comunidad Bet El, since 1963; dir, found, Camp Ramah, since 1960; secy commn on J law and standards, RA, 1958-59; rabbi, Cong Isr, 1959-62. Exec comm: Arg Inst MH; Arg Assn Family Planning; vice-pres, UJA of Arg; mem: B'nai B'rith; Pi Lambda Phi. Ed: Libr of Sci and Hist of Rel; first complete Sidur in Heb and Span, since the Span expulsion, 1965; Complete Mejzor in Span and Heb, 1967. Home: 1646 Zapiola, Buenos Aires, Arg. Office: 11 de Septiembre 1669, Buenos Aires, Arg.

MEYER, Maurice Jr, US, business exec; b. Newark, NJ, Feb 26, 1911; s. Maurice and Adelaide (Mendel); AB, Princeton U, 1931; m. Carolyn Buchsbaum, Feb 4, 1932; c: Maurice, Dorothy Purcell. Partner, Hirsch and Co, since 1938; chmn, trustees, Tex Pacific Land Trust, since 1961; dir: Sorg Paper Co, since 1952; Daitch Crystal Dairies, since 1952; with: Solomon Bros and Hutzler, 1931-36; Emanuel and Co, 1936-37; dir: TXL Oil Co, 1955-62; Realty and Utilities, 1959-62; Havana Lithographing, 1946-61. Mem: bd trustees, treas, Columbia Grammar Sch, since 1948; Phi Beta Kappa; clubs: Princeton, NY; Hollywood Golf; Bond, NY; Wall St; Manasquan River and Tuna; Deep Sea; Buccaneer Yacht; Brielle Marlin and Tuna, commodore; Crown Colony; Chub Cay, Bahamas. Hobbies: orchid growing, deep sea fishing. Home: 9 Garfield Rd, Elberon, NJ. Office: 25 Broad St, New York, NY.

MEYER, Michael A, US, historian, educator; b. Berlin, Ger, Nov 15, 1937; s. Charles and Susanne (Frey); in US since 1941; BA, hons, U of Cal, 1959; BHL, HUC, 1960, PhD, 1964; m. Margaret Mayer, June 25, 1961; c: Daniel, Jonathan, Rebecca. Asso prof, J hist, HUC-JIR, since 1968, fac mem since 1964. Author: The Origins of the Modern Jew, 1967; contbr to J jours. Recipient: Cohen award for book on J thought, J Book Council of Amer, 1967; Hilberry award, Wayne State U Press, 1968. Home: 1031 Avondale Ave, Cincinnati, O. Office: 3101 Clifton, Ave Cincinnati, O.

MEYER, Nathan, US, corporate secy; b. Baltimore, Md, Mar 5, 1910; s. Isidore and Nellie (Cooper); att Old Dominion Coll; m. Zelda Peck, Jan 9, 1938; c: Joyce Copleman, Ellen. Pres, JCC; chmn: Amer Cancer Campaign; UJA; comm mem, acctnt div, Inst Scrap Iron and Metal Dealers; mem: Tax Commn, Portsmouth. Hobby: athletics. Home: 505 Rockbridge Rd, Portsmouth, Va. Office: POB 100, Portsmouth, Va.

MEYER, Sigmund O, US, attorney; b. Butte, Mont, Apr 22, 1912; s. William and Hattye (Oppenheimer); BA, U of S Cal, 1934, JD, 1936; m. Claire Hochnfield, Mar 24, 1940 (decd); c: Diane Sherick; m. 2nd, Zelma Gevurtz, Feb 14, 1960; step-d Stephanie. Partner, law firm, Meyer and Meyer, since 1937. Pres: Butte J Wfr Chest, 1940-60; Dist Grand Lodge No 4, B'nai B'rith, 1951-52; dir: Butte Comty Hosp, 1956-60; St James Comty Hosp, since 1965; YMCA, 1960-66; Campfire Girls, since 1950; Rainbow Girls, 1962-64, 1965-69; mem: Dem Co Cen Comm, Butte, 1940-48; Amer, Mont, Silver Bow Co Bar Assns; Amer Trial Lawyers Assn; natl comm, ADL, since 1962; Masons; Shriners; Elks Lodge; club: Exch. Home: 3400 St Ann St, Penn Bldg, Butte, Mont.

MEYER, Werner, Switz, economist; b. Koenigsberg, Ger, June 22, 1924; s. Hans and Charlotte (Baerwald); in Switz since 1936; DRerPol, summa cum laude, U Basel, 1949; m. Ilse Abend, Feb 28, 1950; c: Brigitte, Hans. Chief, econ dept, National-Zeitung, Basel, since 1952; ed-in-chief, Schweizer Finanz-Zeitung, since 1968; sci collaborator, Handels Hochschule, St Gallen, Switz, 1950-52. Served, Swiss Army. Pres, J Mus of Switz, Basel; mem, Verein der Schweizer Presse. Author: Diss. Elemente zu einer Beschaffungstheorie des Betriebes, 1951; co-author: Der Schweizerische Kapitalmarkt, 2 vols, 1952; contbr to mags and jours. Hobby: travel. Home: 24 Lange Gasse, Basel, Switz. Office: National-Zeitung, Basel, Switz.

MEYERHOFF, Joseph, US, business exec, communal leader; b. Russ, Apr 8, 1899; s. Oscar and Hanna (Gurewitz); in US since 1906; LLB, U of Md, 1920; m. Rebecca Witten, Aug 21, 1921; c: Harvey, Peggy Pearlstone, Eleanor Kogan. Pres, The Joseph Meyerhoff Corp, and asso real-estate and bldg companies, since 1921. US Army, 1918. Gen chmn, UJA, since 1961, mem campaign cabinet, since 1951, mem special missions on behalf of UJA, since 1955, chmn, campaign cabinet, 1956-57,

natl chmn, 1958-61; chmn bd and exec comm, PEC-Isr Econ Corp, fmr Pal Econ Corp, since 1963, pres, and chmn, exec comm, 1957-63, mem, bd dirs, since 1950; mem: natl exec comm, JDC, since 1959; natl exec comm, State of Isr Bonds, since 1951, gen chmn for Baltimore, 1951, 1953, 1954; pres, Ency Judaica Press, Inc, since 1959; vice-chmn, JA for Isr, Inc; pres, Asso J Charities, Baltimore, 1959-62, vice-pres, 1954-59; pres, JWF, Baltimore, 1951-54, bd dirs, since 1946; gen chmn, Asso J Charities and Wfr Fund campaigns, 1949, 1951, 1952; mem: bd govs, Heb U, Jerusalem, since 1961; bd govs, Technion, since 1961; bd trustees, J Publ Soc, since 1952; spec Mission, invited by PM of Isr, 1950. Pres, Natl Assn of Home Builders of US, 1964-47, dir since 1943; pres, Home Builders Assn of Md, 1943-46, dir since 1942; chmn, State Planning Commn of Md, since 1957, appd mem, 1953; mem, Gov's Comm on Baltimore Metrop Area, since 1961; mem, Dept of Public Wfr, Md, 1953-57; mem and vice-chmn, Gov's Special Self Survey Commn of Md, 1946-58; dir, treas, Park Sch, Baltimore, 1946-58; chmn, Baltimore, construction div, Comty Chest — Red Cross campaigns, 1950-54; clubs: Woodholme Country, pres, 1952-53, dir since 1944; Advertising; Assn of Commerce; Center, vice-pres, and dir, since 1962. Home: 6724 Westbrook Rd, Baltimore, Md. Office: First National Bank Bldg, Baltimore, Md.

MEYEROVITCH, Philip, Can, attorney; b. Rum, Mar 15, 1899; s. Julius and Leah (Brief); in Can since 1907; BCL, McGill U, 1921; m. Queenie Klineberg, June 6, 1926; c: Perry Meyer, Mrs. Sorel Young. Partner: Meyerovitch, Levy & Goldstein, since 1963; Bernfeld & Meyerovitch, 1921-25; Meyerovitch & Batshaw, 1925-50; Meyerovitch & Levy, 1950-53; Meyerovitch, Levy & Meyer, 1953-63; counsel, lab relations, Cloak Ind, Que, since 1932; Q.C, since 1940. Pres: Mt Royal Lodge, B'nai B'rith, 1931; Reading Soc of Montreal, 1954; dir, Hillel Found, McGill U, since 1945, pres, 1950-52; hon solicitor, Shaar Hashomayim Syn, Montreal, since 1950; councillor, Que Bar Assn, 1954; secy: Can Comm, 1932-34; Can JCong; mem, perm comm, CJA; clubs: Montefiore; Elmridge Country. Home: 4850 Cote St Luc Rd, Montreal, Can. Office: 1255 University St, Montreal, Can.

MEYEROWITZ, Theresa Bernstein, US, artist; b. Phila, Pa; d. Isadore and Annette (Ferber) Bernstein; att Phila Acad; Art Students League, NY; m. William Meyerowitz. Represented: Metrop Mus; Chgo Art Inst; Boston Mus; Bklyn Mus; Libr of Cong; Natl Art Gal; Smithsonian Inst, Wash, DC. Hon dir, NY Soc Women Artists; mem: Audubon Artists; Soc Amer Graphic Artists; N Shore, Rockport Art Assns; Allied Artists Amer; Natl Assn Women Artists. Contbr of articles on current Amer art. Recipient: Bd of Educ Art Scholarship; John Sartain F; awards include: Shillard Gold Medal, Plastic Club, Phila; Portrait Prize, Phila Art Club; Natl Arts Club Prize; Phillips Prize for Original Composition; Peterson Prize; Davis Prize; Cooper Prize, 1952; Cantorella Award, Natl Assn Women Artists; Knickerboker Artists Prize; Jeanne d'Arc Medal, Fr Inst Arts and Letters; Matson Portrait Prize, Rockport Arts and Letters Assn, 1968; N Shore Arts Assn; NE Art Assn. Homes: 54 W 74 St, New York, NY; summers: 44 Mt Pleasant Ave, Gloucester, Mass.

MEYEROWITZ, William, US, artist; b. Ekaterinoslav, Russ, July 15, 1896; s. Gershon and Shendel (Mitelman); in US since 1908; att Natl Acad of Design, NYC, 1914; m. Theresa Bernstein, 1919. Paintings in perm collections: US Natl Mus; Phillips Memorial Art Gal; Libr of Cong; Boston Mus of Fine Arts; Boston U; Bklyn Mus of Fine Arts; NY Pub Libr; CCNY; Harvard Club; Natl Acad, NYC; Albany Inst of Art and Hist; Concord Arts Assn, NH; Bibliothèque Nationale, Paris; Yale U; U of Pa; Harvard Law Sch; John Herron Art Inst; U of Ky; Mus Ein Harod; Tel Aviv Art Mus, both Isr; J Mus, NY; Fitchburg Art Mus; Bezalel Mus; Mus of Modern Art; Brandeis U, Columbus Mus of Art; U of Gp; Cooaer Union, NY; Norfolk Mus of Art. One-man shows: Chase Art Gal, 1964; Columbus Mus of Arts and Crafts, 1966; U of Ga, 1966; Ga Mus of Art, 1966; Montgomery Mus of Art, 1967; Bar Harbor Art Gal, 1967; Chase Art Gal, 1968; paintings exhibited: U of Me; Smithsonian Inst; Corcoran Gal, both Wash, DC; Metrop Mus; Acad of Arts and Letters; Whitney Mus, all NYC; Baltimore Mus, Md; Dayton Art Inst, O; Carnegie Inst, Pittsburgh; Currier Art Gal, Manchester, NH; etched portraits of US Supr Court Justices; dir, summer art course, Gloucester, Mass, 1953. Asso, Natl Acad; dir, Audubon Soc of NY, 1950-54; mem: Amer Color Print Soc; Amer Soc Etchers; N Shore Artists Assn; Cape Ann Soc Modern Artists; Acad of Political Sci; Allied Artists of Amer; The Judeans; Friends of Zion; Arts Council, Gloucester,

Mass. Recipient: 1st prize, Natl Acad Design, 1914; hon mention: Amer Acad, Rome, It, 1914; Conn Acad Fine Arts, 1928; 1st etching prize, 1934; 1st prize; 1941, N Shore Art Assn; gold medal and 1st prize, Modern Jury of NE Artists, 1946; Pennell Prize, Libr of Cong, Wash, DC, 1947, 2nd prize, 1948; 1st prize, Amer Color Print Soc, 1950; prize, Audubon Artists, 1955; best painting, N Shore Arts Assn, Gloucester, Mass, 1957; prize, Allied Artists of Amer, 1958; Seton Hall U gold medal and prize, 1958; Shorewood Press Citation and contract, Audubon Artists Assn of Amer, 1958; Grumbacher award, 1958; Augunquit Art Assn prize, 1959; Hudson Painting prize, Rockport Arts Assn, 1960; Allied Artists of Amer award, 1961; Gloria Layton Allied Artists of Amer prize, 1962; best painting in exhb, W F Schraft Corp, 1966; Ellen F S Speyer prize, Natl Acad Design, NY, 1966; Rotheburg award for original and provocative painting, 1967; Rockport Art Assn prize for musical theme, The Vayana Memorial Prize, 1967; Hatfield Prize for Still Life, N Shore Arts Assn, Gloucester, Mass, 1968. Home and studio: 54 W 74 St, New York, NY.

MEYERS, Lawrence Charles, US, educational dir; b. LA, Cal, Apr 5, 1933; s. Kallman and Bettie (Abromovitz); BA, UCLA, 1954; MA, rel ed, HUC, 1956; MA, hist, Memphis State U, 1965; PhD, US Intl U, 1970; m. Reva Tackel, Mar 25, 1956; c: Nathan, Debra, Daniel. Educ dir, Temple Beth Isr, since 1967; educ cons, UAHC; educ dir: Temple Emanu-El, Birmingham, 1956-61; Temple Isr, Memphis, 1961-67. Bd dirs, W Assn of Temple Educs; mem, US Intl U Doctoral Soc. Author: Teaching in the Jewish Religious School, 1967; jour ed, Natl Assn Temple Educs; contbr to J pedg publls. Home: 5830 Adelaide, San Diego, Cal. Office: 2512 3rd, San Diego, Cal.

MEYERS, Nechemia, Isr, journalist; b. Minneapolis, Minn, June 8, 1930; s. Kallman and Bettie (Abromovitz); in Isr since 1951; att UCLA, 1948-50; BA, Heb U, Tel Aviv, 1959; m. Adeerah Mushin, Feb 3, 1959; c: Eytan, Dana, Oren. Head, PR off, Weizmann Inst of Sci, Rehovot, since 1967; secy, World Habonim, 1952-53; dep dir, publs, Govt Press off, 1959-63. IDF, 1951-53. Contbr: weekly column, Isr Mailbag, US, Brit, Australia; numerous articles to local, overseas publs; repr overseas J jours in Isr. Fmr, bd mem, AACI; mem, PR Assn, Isr. Home: 21 Spinoza St, Rehovot, Isr. Office: Weizmann Inst of Sci, Rehovot, Isr.

MEYERS, Philip M, US, business exec; b. Cincinnati, O, June 25, 1899; s. Mitchell and Bessie (Jaffe); BA, U of Cincinnati, 1922; m. Lucille Goldberg, Dec 1929; c: Philip, Lynne Gordon, Susan. Chmn, bd, The Meyers Devl Corp, since 1958; pres, Fashion Frocks, 1942-67; dir and mem, exec comm First Natl Bank of Cincinnati, since 1946; Fada Corp, since 1956, chmn, bd, Goldsmith Stores, since 1951. US Army, WW I. Pres: J Hosp, 1953-67; JCC, 1942-44; Natl Assn Direct Selling Cos, 1939-41; and co-found, JWF, 1944, chmn, 1944, all Cincinnati; chmn, finance comm and trustee, Cincinnati Zool Soc, since 1946; natl chmn, J Defense Appeal, 1953-54; chmn: J Comty Relations Comm, 1953-54; Cincinnati Comm for Amer J Tercentenary, 1955; co-chmn, NCCJ, 1946-50; vice-chmn, UAHC, 1944-52; secy, mem, bd fellows, Brandeis U, since 1956; mem, bd trustees, U of Cincinnati, since 1954; dir, Cincinnati Sch Found, 1950-45, mem, adv comm, since 1948; Bur of Governmental Research, since 1952; BBB since 1944; mem. exec bd, City Charter Comm, 1951-61; adv comm, Citizens Sch Comm, since 1948; US Tech Assistance Prog to Isr, 1956; charter mem, Cincinnati chap, AJComm, since 1950; clubs: Losantville Country; Bankers; Cincinnati. Spec interests: farming, cattle raising. Home: 230 W Galbraith Rd, Cincinnati, O. Office: 530 Maxwell Ave, Cincinnati, O.

MEYERSON, Leo I, US, merchant; b. Omaha, Neb, Mar 7, 1911; s. Samuel and May (Woolfson); att U of Neb, 1929-31; m. Helen Wolinsky, 1933; c: Larry, Darlynn. Pres, gen mgr, World Radio Labs, since 1936. Pres, Council Bluffs, Ia, chap, ZOA, since 1940; fmr pres, Ia, Neb chap, Natl Elec Distributor Assn Amateur Radio Sta WOGFQ, chmn, amateur div, Finance of Elec Ind Assn Wash, DC; Natl Defense Exec Res, US Dept Commerce; vice-pres, W Ia Music Assn, 1946; communications dir, Council Bluffs Chap, ARC, since 1951; mem: Air Force Mil Amateur Radio Sys; B'nai B'rith; Masons; Shriners; Chanticleer, Little Theater; clubs: Kiwanis, pres, 1956-57; Elks, Home: 704 Forest Dr, Council Bluffs, Ia. Office: 3415-27 W Broadway, Council Bluffs, Ia.

MEYROWITZ, Alvin A, US, business exec; b. NYC, Dec 16, 1917; s. Jacob and Annie (Bader); AB, Cornell U, 1938; MBA, NYU Grad Sch of Bus, 1941; att George Wash U Law

Sch, 1949-51; m. Ruth Liberman, Feb 1, 1942; c: Linda, Jack. Vice-pres, Kramer & Co, since 1964, and 1951-62; mem: bd dirs, Merchants Petroleum; adv bd, Mfrs Bank, LA; asso bus research, U of Newark, 1937-38; market analyst, Miller Franklin & Co, 1938-41; chief, copper br, Off of Civilian Supply, War Production Bd, 1941-46; dir, basic materials, Natl Housing Admn, 1946-49; asst dir, copper div, Natl Produc Auth, 1949-51; exec vice-pres, Cal Tech Sys, 1962-64. Mem: exec res prog, Bus and Defense Adv Service, Dept of Commerce since 1956; bd trustees, City of Hope, since 1959; fmr mem bd dirs and treas, U Syn; mem: Amer Marketing Assn; Amer Stat Assn; Amer Econ Assn; Amer Inst Mgmt; Amer Ordnance Assn; Air Pollution Control Assn; C of C; Sigma Alpha Mu; clubs: Rotary; Brentwood Country; Beverly Hills. Home: 10450 Wilshire Blvd, Los Angeles, Cal. Office: POB 7, El Segundo, Cal.

MEYSHAN, Josef, Isr, physician, author; b. Odessa, Russ, Dec 26, 1899; s. Rachmiel and Beila (Glanc) Mestshanski; in Isr sinc 1937; att: Inst of Psychoneur, Petrograd, 1916-17; MD, U Königsberg, 1930; m. Esther Sokolik, 1927. In pvt med practice, Tel Aviv, since 1937; asst Munic Hosp, Danzig, 1923-30; chief phys, OSE clinic, 1930-37. Chmn, Tel Aviv br: IMA; Numismatic Soc, since 1962; f: Royal Numismatic Soc, London, since 1960; Royal Soc of Med, London, since 1966; mem, exec comm: Isr Numismatic Soc, since 1950; Isr Exploration Fund, Tel Aviv sect; mem: Isr Sci Council; Soc Internal Med; Soc Heart Diseases; fmr chmn, Isr Soc Friends of Antiquities. Author: Treatment of Ozaena, 1923; Thymo-Thyroideae Behandlung der Psoriasis, 1923; Ueber die Brucksche Reaktion, 1924; Polycytaemia vera und acne, 1925; Paget Disease, 1927; Neurolues und Blutgruppen, 1928; The Periods of Jerusalem Coinage, 1954; Agrippa I, Jewish King and His Coins, 1954; The Legion Which Reconquered Jerusalem in the War of Bar Kochba, 1958; The Symbols on the Coinage of Herod the Great and Their Meanings, 1959; The Chronology of the Coins of the Herodian Dynasty, 1960; The Disease of Herod the Great, King of Judaea, 1957; The Death of Agrippa I, King of Judaea, 1959; Essays in Jewish Numismatics, 1968; contbr to local and fgn jours. Home and office: 39 Balfour St, Tel Aviv, Isr.

MEYUHAS, Joseph, Isr, government official; b. Jerusalem, 1906; s. Rahamim and Simcha; BA, U London, 1934; postgrad, tchrs' dipl, Inst of Educ, 1935; m. Nehama Silberstein, 1937. Dir, youth dept, Min of Educ and Culture, since 1948; dir, youth bur, educ dept, Va'ad Leumi, 1935-48. Co-found: Scout Movement in Isr; youth hostels; active in youth movement since 1935. Author: Mahanot Noar, 1941; Kaitanot Leyeladim, 1943; Hahinukh Hamashlim Bereshet Hamekomit, 1952; Hatzofiut Shitat Hinukh Lanoar, 1957; contbr to jours. Home: 1 Hapalmach St, Jerusalem, Isr. Office: Min of Educ and Culture, Jerusalem, Isr.

MEZEI, Andras, Hung, editor, author; b. Budapest, Hung, Dec 23, 1930; s. Dezsö and Emma (Duetsch) Meisler; MSc, engr, U Budapest, 1966; m. Magda Szekély, 1962; c: Gabor. Ed, Elet ès Irodálom, lit periodical, since 1962; secy, Min of Culture, until 1962. Mem: Hung Soc of Writers; PEN. Author: A Csodaterö, 1966; Kezdetben, 1970; books of poems. Recipient: Jozsef Attila Prize, Min of Culture, 1961. Home: 20 Medve, Budapest, Hung. Office: 22 Alpari Gyula, Budapes t Hung.

MEZGER, Fritz Ludwig, Isr, auditor; b. Frankfurt/M, Ger, Sep 23, 1899; s. Siegmund and Flora (Geiger); in Isr since 1936; DRerPol, Friedrich Wilhelm U, Berlin, 1922; m. Lotte Bodlaender, May 22, 1936; c: Ruth, Nordenberg, Gabriele, Daniel. Sr partner, Hesselman and Hesselman, since 1942; fmr: mem staff, M M Warburg and Co, bankers, Hamburg; econ ed, Wirtschaftsdienst, Hamburg. F: Assn Cert Corp Acctnts, Eng; Natl Assn Acctnts, US; Brit Inst of Taxation; Corp of Secys, Eng; chmn, comm, Isr Mgmt Cen; treas, mem mgmt comm, ZOA House, Tel Aviv; club, Ramat Gan Bowling and Sports. Author, Revisions programme, 1933; contbr to Amer, Heb profsl periodicals. Hobbies: music, archaeol, hist. Home: 12 Huberman St, Tel Aviv, Isr. Office: 31 Lilienblum St, Tel Aviv, Isr.

MICHAEL, Avraham, Isr, economist; b. Isr, Mar 21, 1928; s. Shlomo and Lili (Florentin); BA, Heb U, 1952; MA, New Sch for Social Research, NYC, 1955; PhD, Columbia U, 1962. Econ adv, Min of Lab, since 1968; sr lectr, Bar Ilan U, since 1967; mem, Isr delg to UN, 1956-58; asst prof, CCNY, 1962-65; head, econ div, Natl Council for Research, Devl

1966-68. Cdr, IDF, 1948-50. Mem, Amer Econ Assn. Contbr to sci quarterlies. Recipient: research f, New Sch for Social Research, 1958-60. Spec interest: music. Home: 69 Yitzhak Sadeh St, Tel Aviv, Isr. Office: Min of Lab, Hakirya, Jerusalem, Isr.

MICHAEL, Elaine, US, author, composer; b. Bx, NY, Jan 9, 1930; d. Herman and Ruth (Moss) Fisher; att: LIU, 1950-52; Bklyn Coll, 1962-64; m. 2nd, Edwin Michael, Oct 12, 1958; c: Peter White, Caryn. Songs include: They're Playing Our Song; Little Boy; Drink to a Fool; Don't Say Good-bye; Time and Time Again; Jeremy; Over and Over; album, Moonlight Magic. Mem: ASCAP Amer Guild Composers and Authors; Cancer Care; sisterhood, S Baldwin J Cen; fmr: entertainment chmn, Children's Asthmatic Research Inst and Hosp; writer, shows for Cerebral Palsy Org. Hobbies: pastels, oil painting. Home and office: 717 Arthur St, Baldwin, NY.

MICHAEL, Elton, Eng, rabbi, educator; b. Budapest, Hung, Sep 10, 1911; s. Benjamin and Jolan (Schnuermacher) Ehrntal; BA, hons, U of London, 1934; dipl of min Jews Coll, London, 1939; dipl epigraphy, Sch of Oriental Studies, London, 1950; ordained rabbi, HUC, Cincinnati, 1958; m. Vera Wolff, Aug 20, 1940; c: Howard. Rabbi, Southend Progressive Syn, since 1966; lectr: J music, Leo Baeck Coll, London, since 1967; Judaic studies, Inner London Educ Auth, since 1965; J hist, U of London, tutorial classes, since 1967; min, United Syn, 1940-54; chief libr, Jews Coll, 1947-54; sr rabbi, Temple Isr, Johannesburg, 1955-63; prin, Progressive Sem for Tchrs, Johannesburg, 1960-63; lectr, Judaism, J hist, Heb, Leo Baeck Evening Inst, 1965-67. Chmn, Cen Ecclesiastical Bd of S Afr, 1960-63; fmr exec, Johannesburg Adult Educ Council; mem, S Afr J Bd Deps, 1957-63; CCAR; Rabb Conf; B'nai B'rith. Author: Challenge of Destiny, 1961; contbr to jours. Spec interests: communal work, work for aged, journalism, J art and music, photography, audio-visual aids for educ. Home: 31a The Leas, Westcliff, Essex, Eng. Study: 851 London Rd, Westcliff, Essex, Eng.

MICHAEL, Ernest Arthur, US, mathematician; b. Zürich, Switz, Aug 26, 1925; s. Jacob and Erna (Sondheimer); BA, Cornell U, 1947; MA, Harvard U, 1948; PhD, U of Chgo, 1951; postdoc AEC f: Inst for Advanced Study, 1951-52; U of Chgo, 1952-53; mem, Inst for Advanced Study, 1956-57, 1960-61, 1968; m. Erika Goodman, 1966; c: Alan, David, Gerard, Hillary, Joshua. Prof, math, U of Wash, since 1960, on fac since 1953. Mem: Amer Math Soc; ACLU. Contbr to sci jours. Office: U of Wash, Seattle, Wash.

MICHAEL, Jakob, US, industrialist; b. Frankfurt/M, Ger, Feb 28, 1894; s. Elieser and Bertha (Kohn); in US since 1939; m. Erna Sondheimer, Aug 12, 1924; c: Ernest, Jacquelina Errera, Charles. Pres, NE Inds, NY, since 1939; chmn, exec comm, Lehigh Valley Inds, Inc, since 1954; with: Beer, Sondheimer & Co, 1910-13; EJ Michael, Radium and Uranium Corp, 1913-14, both Frankfurt/M; owner, commercial, ind corps, Eur, 1918-38. Mil service, 1914-17. Trustee: World Acad for Higher J Studies, Jerusalem; Women's Social Service, Tel Aviv; Yeshiva U; mem: bd overseers, Albert Einstein Coll of Med; natl adv comm, Syn Council of Amer; admn comm, J Cen, NY; bd dirs: J book Council Amer; JDC; Keren Yaldenu, Jerusalem; Natl J Music Council; Ozar Hatorah; United HIAS Service; UJA of Gtr NY; bd govs: Heb U, Jerusalem; Weizmann Inst of Sci; Isr Mus, Jerusalem; found, Jakob Michael Libr, Mosad Harav Kook Inst, Jerusalem; co-found: Ahawa Kinderheim, Berlin; Jüdisches Hilfswerk, Berlin; Yeshiva J Comty, Frankfurt/M; Albert Einstein Coll of Med; Harry S Truman Peace Cen, Jerusalem; Technion, Haifa; New Campus, Heb U, Jeruslaem; Boys Town, Jerusalem; donated bldgs to: Horeb Schs; World Acad for Higher J Studies; Keren Yaldenu Home, all Jerusalem; Women's Social Service, Tel Aviv; Children's Home Hapoel Hamizrachi, Pardes Hanna; Yeshiva Torah Um'lacha, Tel Aviv; Schs for Isr, Nathanya; Inst of Nuclear Sci, Weizmann Inst; donated: Syn Vittorio Veneto and Horeb Chapel; Collection of ceremonial objects and illuminated manuscripts, both to Isr Mus; collection of J music, Heb U Natl Libr, all Jerusalem; Inst of Bio-Med Research, Albert Einstein Coll of Med; Erna Michael Chair, J phil, Erna Michael Coll Hebraic Studies; Eli Michael Cen for Genizah Studies, all Yeshiva U. Spec interests: collecting J ceremonial objects, J music libr. Home: 211 Central Park W, New York, NY. Office: 120 Wall St, New York, NY.

MICHAEL, Michael T, Isr, diplomat, army officer; b. Cracow, Pol, Oct 6, 1918; s. Shimon and Varda (Goldberger) Feldblum; in Isr since 1936; att: Technion, Haifa; Sch of Law and Econ, Tel Aviv U; m. Esther Kartzovnik, Feb 14, 1949; c: Ronith, Orly. Charge d'affairs, Legation of Isr, Pretoria, S Afr, since 1969; dir, dept research, Min for Fgn Affairs, Jerusalem; fmr: ambass to Uganda; consul gen to India. Mem staff, Haganah, 1939-48; col, IDF, 1948-59. Home: 11 Ramat Dania, Jerusalem, Isr. Office: POB 180, Cape Town, S Afr.

MICHAEL, Rosi Rebecka, US, communal leader; b. Frankfurt/M, Ger; d. Eli and Bertha (Kohn); m. c: Henry, Kenneth, Lillian Shapiro. Pres, Women's Social Service for Isr, Inc; chmn, Isr Comm, Leo Baeck chap, B'nai B'rith, 1944-59; bd dirs: Bd Guardian for Refs, London, 1936-40; Home of J League of Women, Ger, 1928-33; mem, Volunteer Civil Nursing Res, London, 1939-40. Home: 265 Riverside Dr, New York, NY.

MICHAELI, Isaac, Isr, scientist; b. Riga, Latvia, July 28, 1921; s. Zevulun and Esther (Rappoport) Michelson; in Isr since 1936; MSc, Heb U, Jerusalem, 1950, PhD, 1955; m. Miriam Fodor, Mar 30, 1947; c: Daniela. Sr sci, Weizmann Inst of Sci, since 1960, sci since 1949. Author: What is New in Science, 2 vols; contbr research to profsl jours; bd mem, ed bd, Mada, Isr jour popular sci; fmr ed, sci news, Isr radio. Mem, profsl sci org. Spec interest: presentation of sci to gen public. Home: Neve Weizmann, Rehovot, Isr. Office: Weizmann Inst of Sci, Rehovot, Isr.

MICHAELI, Wilhelm, Swed, attorney, organization exec; b. Schwiebus, Ger, Mar 10, 1889; s. Wilhelm and Emma (Samson); in Swed since 1933; DJ, U of Berlin, 1911; m. Sophie Goldstein, June 28, 1919; c: Hans. Ret; fmr: dir, emigration dept & restitution off, J Comty, 1938-67; barrister, Kammergericht, Berlin, 1919-33; notary, 1926-33. Ger Army, 1915-18. Author: Private International Law in Sweden, 1948; contbr to sci and J jours. Home: Frejgatan 8, Stockholm, Swed.

MICHAELIS, Sir Archie, Austr, business exec, legislator; b. St Kilda, Melbourne, Vic, Dec 19, 1889; s. Frederick and Esther (Phillips); att Wesley Coll, Melbourne; m. Claire Hart, Jan 14, 1920; c: Mary Salek, Joan Parker, Helen Marks. Chmn, Michaelis, Hallenstein and Co, Pty, Ltd, tanners, Melbourne; fmr: chmn, Asso Leathers Ltd; repr for St Kilda, Leg Assembly, Vic, 1932-52, speaker, 1950-52, hon min, asst treas, 1945. Brit Army, 1914-19. Mem, Navy and Mil Club, Melbourne; fmr: pres, Vic J Adv Bd; chmn, Patriotic Funds Council; treas, trustee, pres, St Kilda Heb Cong. Home: 281 Williams Rd, South Yarra, Victoria, Austr.

MICHAELIS, Dolf, Isr, banker; b. Magdeburg, Ger, Feb 20, 1906; s. Max and Minni (Borchert); in Isr since 1938; m. Eva Stern, Apr, 1938; c: David R. Asst mgr, Bank Leumi leIsrael, since 1947; mgr, fgn exch, Bank Gebr, Arnold, Berlin, 1928 38; mgr, Intria Ltd, London, 1938-40; econ adv, JNF, London, 1941-45. Brit Army, 1942-44; IDF, 1950-53. Mem, bd govs, Heb U, Jerusalem; hon treas, Jerusalem Artist House; mem exec, Leo Baeck Inst; fmr: mem, Blau-Weiss Zionist Youth, Berlin; exec council: ZF, Ger; Reichsvertratung der Juden in Deutschland; F, Gt Brit mem: Political Sci Assn, Jerusalem; Masons; club. Bankers, Jerusalem. Contbr to profsl publs. Hobbies: painting, hist. Home: 6 Shlomo Molcho St, Jerusalem, Isr. Office: 21 Jaffa Rd, Jerusalem, Isr.

MICHAELY, Michael, Isr, economist, educator; b. Kinneret, Isr, Oct 3, 1928; s. Aharon and Yona (Shkolnik); MA, Heb U, Jerusalem, 1952; PhD, Johns Hopkins U, 1955; m. Ora Avny-Steiner, Mar 25, 1952; c: Ailon, Yoav, Boaz. Dean, fac social scis, Heb U, since 1968; mem, dept of econs, since 1955; visiting prof, CUNY, 1966-67. Lt, IDF, 1945-49. Author: Concentration in International Trade, 1962; Foreign Trade and Capital Imports in Israel, 1963; Balance of Payments Adjustment Policies, 1968; Israel's Exchange-Rate System, 1968; contbr to profsl jours. Home: 52 Hehalutz St, Jerusalem, Isr. Office: Heb U, Jerusalem, Isr.

MICHAELY, Uri, Isr, government official; b. Kamenetz-Podolsk, Russ, Jan 7, 1900; s. Michael and Lea (Ackerman) Pressman; in Isr since 1921; m. Hana Bronstein, May, 1921; c: Tamar Eshet, Amram-Rami. Adv, civil aviation, Min of Transp, since 1960; mem, dir gen, Natl Council Civil Aviation, since 1960; secy, immigration dept, Histadrut, 1929-40; dir, Aviron, Pal Aviation Co, 1941-48; dir, Dept, of Civil Aviation, 1948-60. Mem: bd, Haganah Vets Assn; exec comm, Isr Philharmonic Orch; council, Aero Club of Isr, fmr secy gen; chmn bd, Kamenetz-Podolsk Landsmen's Assr in Isr; repr, Govt of Isr, to intl aviation assemblies. Contbr to press, jours. Recipient: Dov Hoz Award, Munic of Tel Aviv, 1960. Spec interests: space, music. Home: 63 Maze St, Tel Aviv, Isr. Office: 9 Ahad Ha'am St, Tel Aviv, Isr.

MICHALY, Benjamin I, Isr, editor; b. Bessarabia, Rum, July 26, 1910; s. Yehiel and Hinda (Roizman) Duhovni; in Isr since 1939; m. Hadassah Goldberg, Jan, 1938. Mgr, archives and mus of J lab movement, since 1951, secy since 1942; Rum corresp for Davar daily, 1932-39 and 1947-48; secy, Kupat Milve Behisachon, Tel Aviv, 1941; on JA and Histadruth missions to Rum, 1947-48; ed, Unser Wort, Yiddish daily, Fr, delegated to Ihud Haolami, 1950-51. Mem: bd govs, for grant of creativity awards in name of PM; bd dirs: Brith Ivrit Olamit, since 1962; Lamdan Fund for Creative Works, since 1954; exec comm: Beit Bialik, since 1961; Heb Writers Assn, Isr, since 1952, fmr ed, Mozanim, assn jour; mem: Public Council for Art and Culture, since 1954; bd dirs and ed bd, Inst for Trans of Heb Lit, both connected with Isr Min of Educ and Culture; fmr: world exec, Rum exec, Dror, pioneer org; cen comm, Poalei Zion-Zeirei Zion, Rum. Author: Olamam Shel Bnei Haaretz, 1950; Yaakov Fichman, b'Shir uv'Massa, 1951; Leyad ha'Ovnayim, 1958; Pri Haaretz, 1966; Haim Hazaz, Iyunim Bitzirato, 1968; ed, Biblical Anthology, 3 vols, 1953-63; co-ed, 10 books, works of Heb authors in Bessarabia, 1946-52; selected, ed, B'Leil Ze, peoms, 1945; contbr to Heb and Yiddish lit and political publs, Isr and Eur. Recipient: Holon Prize for Lit, 1960; Milo Award for Lit, 1968. Home: 81 Ibn Gvirol St, Tel Aviv, Isr. Office: 34 Weizmann St, Tel Aviv, Isr.

MICHEL, Ernest Wolf, Fr, fund raising exec; b. Mannheim, Ger, July 1, 1923; s. Otto and Frieda (Wolf); in Fr since 1967; att Colorado Coll, 1947; m. Suzanne Stein, Aug 13, 1950; c: Laurie, Joel, Karen. Adv, UJA, Fr, since 1967; adv for Eur, KH, since 1969; w region dir, 1962-67; dir, comty devl dept, 1958-62; field repr, 1948-58, all UJA; corresp for Ger news agcy, Nuremberg Trials. Fmr: co-chmn, Auschwitz-Buna Memorial Fund; chmn, Auschwitz Memorial Dinner, 1960, first reunion of survivors in US. Contbr to periodicals. Hobby: autograph collection of J interest. Home: 26 Ave Charles Floquet, Paris, Fr. Office: 19 Rue de Teheran, Paris, Fr.

MICHEL, Howard, US, business exec; b. NYC, Jan 15, 1919; s. Albert Helen (Harris); att: Bklyn Coll, 1936-38; St Johns U, 1938-41; m. Bernice Ross, Aug 4, 1944; c: Barbara, Susan, Lawrence. Pres, Mart Furniture Inc, since 1959; asso, Ross Furniture Co, since 1945. Chmn, regional adv bd; ADL, mem: exec bd, Seattle J Fed Fund and Council, since 1951, budget comm since 1954, fmr treas; exec comm, Hillel Found, U of Wash, since 1949, fmr vice-pres, bldgcorp: exec comm, Seattle J Comty Cen, since 1949; fmr vice-pres, ZOA; Masons; Shriners; YMCA; 2nd vice-pres, Dist Grand lodge, B'nai B'rith, since 1959, fmr pres. Recipient: Dist Service award, Eur Theatre; Akiba award, Seattle lodge, B'nai B'rith, 1949, Dist Grand lodge 4, 1952. Home: 12657 NE 5 St, Bellevue, Wash. Office: 1110 E Pine, Seattle, Wash.

MICHELSON, A Elihu, US, rabbi; b. NYC, Nov 1, 1909; s. Samuel and Nellie (Jacobs); BS, CCNY, 1930; ordained rabbi, MA, JTSA, 1935; m. Leah Greenfeld, Oct, 27, 1935; c: Aaron. Dir, prog, Commn on J Chaplaincy of Natl JWB, since 1952. Chaplain, US Army, 1944-46. Mem: RA; ZOA. Home: 164-32 76 Ave, Flushing, NY. Office: 15 E 26 St, New York, NY.

MICHELSON, Edward J, US, journalist; b. Northampton, Mass, Apr 3, 1915; s. I H and Fannie (Avrach); BA, Williams Coll, 1937; m. Dorothea Pohlman, Feb 3, 1938; c: Kathleen, Paul, Emily. Wash ed, Sci and Tech Mag; contbr ed, Ocean Sci News; corresp: N Amer Newspaper Alliance; daily newspapers and gen and bus mags, since 1946; spec cons, Off of Secy of War, 1946. US Army WW II. Mem, White House Corresps Assn; clubs: Natl Press, Wash; Williams, NY. Home: 2153 Florida Ave, NW Washington, DC. Office: 1032 Natl Press Bldg, Washington, DC.

MICHELSON, George, US engineer, businees exec; b. Cedar Rapids, Ia Apr 24, 1899; s. Morris and Sophia (Lumelsky); BS, Harvard U, 1918; BS, MIT, 1919; m. Bella Slotnik, Dec 9, 1930; c: Ruth Glotzer, Joseph, Nancy Yanofsky. Vice-pres, J Slotnik Co, since 1937, with firm since 1935; engr: Underwriters Labs, 1919-22; Construction Supply Co, 1922-35. Life trustee, CJP, fmr asso treas; hon pres, dir, J Family and Children's Service, fmr pres; trustee, Heb Tchrs Coll, since 1945, fmr pres; Ist vice-pres, Asso J Philanthropies; mem: bldg commn, Town of Brookline, since 1954; Town Meeting,

since 1955; trustee: CJA; Beth Isr Hosp; dir, Amer Technion Soc; mem: bd govs, Amer Assn of J Educ; Harvard Engi Soc; Zeta Beta Tau; JCC; Kehillath Isr Heb Sch Comm; fmr: chmn, Large City Budgeting Conf; pres, NE region, CFJWF; mem, Boston Service for New Amers; club: Boston Stein, dir. Contbr to engr jours. Home: 34 Orchard Rd, Brookline, Mass. Office: 99 Chauncy St, Boston, Mass.

MICHELSON, Herman Elchanan, Eng, business exec; b. Yelgava, Latvia, Oct 18, 1908; s. Yeshayahu and Dvora (Chait); in Eng since 1939; deg, law and econ, U Riga, 1938; m. Ethel Atkin, Jan 1, 1931; c: Augusta, Dvora, Daniel. Chmn: H Henry, Textiles, since 1956; Intertrade, since 1939, both London. Chmn, Jabotinsky Inst, London; mem: World Exec, Herut-Hatzohar; exec, Assn Baltic J in Gt Brit; fmr: chmn: New Zionist Org, Latvia; Comm for Inves of Nazi Crimes in Baltic countries; mem, Council, Friends Heb U. Hobbies: Journalism, writing, reading, music. Home: 92 Regency Lodge, London NW 3, Eng. Office: 58/59 Margaret St, London W1, Eng.

MICHELSON, Morris, US, attorney; b. Boston, Mass, Jan 22, 1903; s. Benjamin and Lena (Lebov); BA, Harvard Coll, 1924; LLB, Harvard Law Sch, 1927; m. Harriet Steinberg, July 3, 1932; c: Mark, Stephan. Pvt practice since 1927; liaison between Mass Bar Assn and Mass Court to expedite trials; mem, Atty Gen of Mass commn, Civil Rights and Civil Liberties, since 1958; elected, Brookline Town Meeting mem, since 1950, mem, adv comm since 1942; co-chmn, natl gov council, AJCong, since 1964, pres, NE div, 1954-56; pres, JCC, Boston, 1957-59; chmn: NE ZC, 1946-50; jt comm, JCC and AJCong, Mass Commn Against Discrimination, 1950-53; pres: Pal Soc, 1933-35; Avukah, 1930-32, pres, NE region, 1927-29. Contbr to legal and Anglo-J periodicals. Hobbies: travel, bird-watching. Home: 78 Evans Rd, Brookline, Mass. Office: 10 Tremont St, Boston, Mass.

MICHELSON, Nicholas, US, physician; b. Riga, Russ, Dec 3, 1897; s. Abraham and Rebecka (Loewensohn); in US since 1923; MD, Hamburg U, 1922; m. Franziska Boas, 1928; c: Gertrude Pinsky; m. 2nd, Eva Schlesinger, 1944; c: Dina, Ernst. Staff phys, VA, Lyons, NJ, since 1928; phys, Castle Point, NY, 1944-58; asst med dir, Montefiore Hosp, 1927-28; research, Columbia U, dept anthropology, 1938-41; cons, Natl Ref Service, 1939; surg, USPHS, active duty, 1941-44;. specialist, internal med, Dept of Health, State of NY, 1951. F: NY Card Soc; Amer Coll Sports Med, chmn, comm for social anthropology, 1958; Amer Coll Card; Amer Coll Chest Phys; mem: Amer Assn Phys Anthropology; Assn Mil Surgs of US; NY State and Duchess Co Med Socs; Royal Soc Health; NY Card Soc; Intl Mark Twain Soc. Author: Weltwind, 1937; Abba, 1937; Esther, 1939; Bilateral Ventricular Hypertrophy Due to Pulmonary Disease, 1960; co-author: The Challenge of Chronic Diseases, 1929; contbr to med and anthropological jours. Home: 800 Valley Rd, Watchung, Plainfield, NJ. Office: VA, Box 134, Lyons, NJ.

MICHLIN, Arnold Sidney, US, business exec; b. Altoona, Pa, Sep 2, 1920; s. Mandel and Zelda (Solomon); BS, Detroit Inst of Tech, 1944; m. Florence Karbal, Aug 16, 1941; c: Leslye, Kenneth, Steven, Joan. Pres, Mich Ind Finishes Corp, since 1948; secy, Michlin Chem Corp, since 1948; secy, Dannz Land Co, since 1954. US Army, Chem Warfare Service, 1945-46. Mem: Mich Regional Adv Bd, ADL, B'nai B'rith; fmr pres: Marshall Lodge, Suburban, B'nai B'rith; mem: Detroit Soc of Paint Tech. Hobbies: bowling, hist of rel practices. Home: 31460 Stonewood Ct, Farmington, Mich. Office: 9045 Vincent, Detroit, Mich.

MICHLIN, Norman, US, business exec; b. Tyrone, Pa, June 22, 1922; s. John and Zelda (Solomon); att La State U, Baton Rouge, 1943; att Rose Poly, Terra Haute, Ind, 1944; m. Bernice Goldberg, Mar 9, 1946; c: Robert, Jeffrey, Marjorie. Pres, Michlin Chem Corp, since 1954; secy, Mich Ind Finishes Corp, since 1958; pres, Dannz Land Co, since 1958. Sgt, US Army, Signal Corps, 1943-46. Pres, Twyckingham Civic Assn; co-chmn: Isr Bonds, Marshall Lodge, B'nai B'rith, fmr pres; ADL; fmr pres, Vandenberg PTA; mem: Amer Vets Comm; B'nai B'rith, Marshall Lodge. Recipient: William B Chapman Award B'nai B'rith, 1963. Spec interests: hist, politics, stamps. Home: 28200 Bell Rd, Southfield, Mich. Office: 9045 Vincent, Detroit, Mich.

MICHMAN, (Melkman) Jozeph, Isr, government official; b. Amsterdam, Netherlands, Apr 2, 1914; s. Abraham and Duifina (Bloemendal) Melkman; in Isr since 1957; MA, U Amsterdam, 1938, PhD, 1951; m. Frederika de Paauw, Sep 22, 1940; c: Awraham, Dan. Dir, cultural div, min Educ and Culture, since 1960; ed, 1945-57; dir, Yad ve-Shem, 1957-60; lectr, U Amsterdam. Secy, Inst for Trans of Heb Lit; chmn: Cen for Public Librs; Art for People; pres, Inst for Research of Dutch Jewry; mem bd: Council for Arts and Culture; Amer Isr Cultural Found; fmr: pres, Zionist Youth Fed, Netherlands; repr, JA, Netherlands. Author: David Franco Mendes; Israel; contbr of articles on Heb Lit and Dutch Jewry. Home: 7 Alfast St, Jerusalem, Isr.

MICHMAN, Julius, Isr, dentist, educator; b. Nuremberg, Ger, Feb 5, 1909; s. Solomon and Raya (Berditchevsky); in Isr since 1935; att, U Wurzburg, 1931; DMD, U Munich, Ger, 1933; m. Gretl Stein, Nov 10, 1935; c: Michael, Hannah. Chmn, Oral Rehab Dept, Heb U, Sch of Dent Med, since 1955, asso prof, since 1963. Secy, chmn, Isr Dent Assn, Jerusalem br; mem: Amer Dent Assn; Intl Assn Dent Research; Intl Coll Dents; Amer Coll Dents; AAAS; Fed Dent Int Isrl; Dent Assn; Alpha Omega Frat; B'nai B'rith. Hobbies: music, painting. Home: 7 Tel Hai St, Jerusalem, Isr. Office: Hadassah Dent Sch, Jerusalem, Isr.

MICHTOM, Benjamin Franklin, US, business exec; b. Bklyn, NY, July 13, 1901; s. Morris and Rose (Katz); BEcon, U of Pa, Wharton Sch of Finance, 1921; m. Hadassah Feil, June 14, 1925; c: William, Mark. Chmn, bd, Ideal Toy Corp, since 1938. Dir: Amer ORT Fed; AJComm; mem: pres council, Brandeis U; Zeta Beta Tau, U of Pa; fmr, trustee: Thanks to the Danes Scholarsphip Fund; Thanks to Scandinavia Scholarship Fund; Phi Sigma Delta Found; mem, Toy Mfrs of US, Inc; clubs: Metrop Country; Advt; Sales Execs. Home: Sterling Rd, Harrison, NY. Office: 200 Fifth Ave, New York, NY.

MIDLO, Charles, US, physician, educator; b. Sosnoviec, Pol, Feb 27, 1899; s. Sabbathai and Augusta (Granatmann); in US since 1914; att U of Chgo, 1920-22; MD, Tulane U, La, 1928; m. Natalie Strauss, Dec 24, 1932; c: Maury, Kenneth, David. Clinical asst prof, neur, Tulane U, since 1951; asst visiting phys, Charity Hosp, since 1949; asst visiting surg, Touro Infirmary, since 1944; all New Orleans; admitting phys, St Charity Hosp, 1928-29; fmr: asst, instr, asso prof, anat; Johns Hopkins, Med Sch, Baltimore, Md, 1929-30; asst, gyn, La State U, asst prof, anat. Mem. Amer Assn Anats; Orleans Parish Med Soc; La State Med Soc; Alpha Omega Alpha; Phi Lambda Kappa. Author: Fingerprints, Palms and Soles, An Introduction to Dermatoglyphics, 1943, 1961; contbr to sci jours. Home: 2436 Jefferson Ave, New Orleans, La. Office: 1520 Louisiana Ave, New Orleans, La.

MIDONICK, Millard L, US, jurist; b. NYC, May 24, 1914; s. Ahraham and Ida (Lesser); AB, Columbia U, 1934; JD, 1936; m. Dorothy Rosenberg, Mav 1, 1941. Judge, Family Court, State of NY, since 1962; chmn, Constitutional Law Comm, Assn of Family Court Judges; trial examiner, trial atty, NLRB, 1937-46; partner, Polier, Midonick and Zinsser, 1951-62; justice, Munic Court, NYC, 1956; impartial arbitrator, numerous inds, 1946-62. Lt cdr, USCG Res, WWII. Vice-pres: AJComm, since 1959; AJCong since 1963; dist leader, Dem Party, NYC, 1953-61; hon mem, bd dirs, NY Urban League, since 1960; mem: NYC, Amer Bar Assns; NY Co Lawyers Assn; Beta Sigma Rho; Citizens Comm for Children of NY; J Bd Guardians; Park Ave Syn; mem, Intercollegiate Fencing Championship Team, 1935; clubs: City Athletic; Varsity C, Columbia. Ed, Columbia Law Rev, 1934-36. Home: 155 E 38 St, New York, NY. Office: 135 E 22 St, New York, NY.

MIGICOVSKY, Bert B, Can, biochemist; b. Winnipeg, Can, Mar 15, 1915; s. Samuel and Brocha (Winestock); BSA, U of Man, 1935; MS U of Minn, 1937; PhD, 1939; m. Geraldine Schnier, 1943; c: John, Janet. Dir-gen, research br, Canada Dept of Agric, since 1968, res dir, 1945-68. Maj, Can Army, overseas Can base lab, WW II. Mem: Can Biochem Soc; Can Phys Soc; Nutrition Soc of Can; Agric Inst of Can. Contbr to profsl jours. Home: 185 Patricia St, Ottawa, Can. Office: KW Neatby Bldg, Central Experimental Farm, Ottawa, Can.

MIHAIL, Negrescu Negrillo, Isr, writer, composer; b. Budapest, Rum, June 3, 1903; s. Louis and Sofia (Steinhart) Swartz; in Isr since 1964; m. 2nd, Nina Lazarovici, May 4, 1962; c,: Lia Hershkovici. Fmr: mgr, cultural dept, Budapest Town Hall; insp of librs; man, mus, all Rum. Served Rum Army. Author, in Rum: Clasul Vremii; Nuham Boiberic; Superstitions; Pleaca Ai Nostri; Vin Ai Nostri; Cei de Alta Data; Evreul

Toivi Chidale; Tolba Cu Sageti; Eroica Veaculuixx; Doamna Cli Masca; contbr: reviews, short stories, sketches to press; composer: dance and folk music; patriotic songs. Mem: Menorah Lit Circle, Jerusalem; fmr: mem, Writers Org, Composer's Org, both Rum. Home: 131/133 Ben Yehuda St, Tel Aviv, Isr. Office: Tel Aviv Munic, Tel Aviv, Isr.

MIKUNIS, Shmuel, Isr, legislator, engineer, journalist; b. Russ, Aug 10, 1903; s. Israel and Haya; in Isr since 1921; deg, civil engr, Poly, Fr, 1933; m. Slava Wielikovska. MK, secy gen, Communist Party of Isr, chmn, political bur, Cen Comm, both since 1948; co-found, Ohel Theatre; engr, Shell Oil Co, 1933-45; active in E Eur countries in support of Isr's fight for independence, 1948. Mem: Asseifat Hanivcharim; Histadrut Council; friendship leagues of Isr and socialist countries; delg, numerous convs of Communist Party abroad; mem, delg appearing before UN Commn on Pal, 1947. Author: Besa'ar Tkufot, 1948; fmr ed, Kol Ha'am, organ of Isr Communist Party; contbr to press. Spec interest: lit. Home: 13 Shmaryahu Levin St, Tel Aviv, Isr.

MIKVA, Abner Joseph, US, legistator; b. Milw, Wis, Jan 21, 1926; s. Henry and Ida (Fishman); JD, U of Chgo, 1951; m. Zoe Wise, Sep 19, 1948; c: Mary, Laurie, Rachel. US Cong, 2nd Dist, Ill, since 1969; state repr, Ill Gen Assembly, 1956-66; partner, Devoe, Shadur, Mikva & Plotkin, 1956-69. Lt, USAAC, 1944-45. Bd mgrs, Chgo Bar Assn; vice-pres, KAM Temple; bd dirs, Chgo Conf on Rel and Race; mem: ACLU; club, City, Chgo. Home: 5545 S Kenwood, Chicago, Ill. Office: 1532 Longworth House Office Bldg, Washington, DC.

MILENDER, Louis, US, business exec; b. Haverhill, Mass, Nov 23, 1906; s. William and Rose (Polsky); LLB, Boston U, Law Sch, 1926; m. Bess Feldman, June 25, 1933; c: Mrs Robert Goldwyn; Mrs Joseph Bower. Owner, Loumis Leather Co, since 1953; partner, W Milender and Sons, 1934-52. Pres, J Vocational Service of Boston, 1950-52; vice-pres: Temple Israel Brotherhood, 1947-51; Businessmen's Council, 1950-51; JCC, Gtr Boston, 1959-60; chmn: Commn on Families and Individuals, Combined J Philanthropies; Boston Chap, AJComm, 1954-56; and bd mem, Temple Comm, Temple Isr, Boston; dist div and mem, bd trustees, CJA, Boston, since 1950; mem, Masons. Home: 210 Lincoln St, Boston, Mass. Office: 85 South St, Boston, Mass.

MILESCU, Milu A, Isr, chemist; b. Bârlad, Rum, Nov 11, 1911; s. Saim and Golda (Avram) Augutstein; in Isr since 1961; PharmD, U of Bucarest, Rum, 1936; m. Sylvia Varcovici, Jan 20, 1945; c: Mariana. Arbitre Intl de la Composition, Fédération Intl d'Echecs, FIDE since 1964; mem, ed staff, Schachmat mag, since 1962; chief ed, Rum Chess Mag, 1930-43. Author: Problémes Choisis, 1948; co-author: Das 1X1 des Endspiels, 1964; contbr problems, studies to chess jours. Hobby: chess. Home: 3 Hanesiim St, Holon, Isr.

MILGRAM, Roberta Mades, US, educator; b. Everett, Mass, Aug 17, 1931; d. Abram and Esther (Landman); BA, Boston U, 1952, MA, 1957; BJE, Boston Heb Tchrs Coll, 1953; EdD, Amer U, 1969; m. Norman Milgram, Feb 21, 1951; c: Shoshana, David. Asso prof, psych, West Chester State Coll, West Chester, Pa; cons, Gratz Coll, Phila; educ dir, Montgomery Co J Cen, 1963-69; prin, Solomon Schechter Sch, Gtr Wash, DC, 1965; tchr, Boston Rel Schs, 1952-60; youth dir, Omaha JCC, 1960-61; asst prin, B'nai Isr Cong, Wash, DC, 1961-63. Exec bd, educ assembly, United Syn Amer; bd J educ, JCC, Wash, DC; mem: ORT; Hadassah; Pioneer Women. Recipient: Decalogue Honor, Solomon Schechter Sch, 1969. Home: 133 Whitemarsh Rd, Ardmore, Pa. Office: West Chester State Coll, West Chester, Pa.

MILGRIM, Franklin Marshall, US, business exc; b. NYC, Aug 24, 1925; s. Charles and Sally (Knobel); BS, hons, Wharton Sch, U of Pa, 1944, grad, 1949; m. Carol Kleinman, Sep 2, 1945; c: Nancy, Catherine. Pres, Milgrim Inc, Cleveland, O, since 1957, buyer and div merchandise mgr, 1949-52, vice-pres, dir and gen merchandise mgr, 1952-57. USN, 1943-46. Dir, Severance Cen Merchants Assn, Cleveland Hgts, fmr pres; mem: Cleveland C of C; Euclid Ave Assn; defense and inves comm, J Fed; AJComm; clubs: City; Variety; Mid-Day; Oakwood Country. Recipient: Victory Amer, Eur Theater medals. Home: 1 Bratenahl Pl, Cleveland, O. Office: 1310 Huron Rd, Cleveland, O.

MILHAUD, Darius, US, composer, conductor, educator; b. Aix-en-Provence, Fr, Sep 4, 1892; s. Gabriel and Sophie (Allatini); in US since 1940; att Conservatoire de Paris, Fr,

1909-16; hon: DHL, U of Judaism, 1954; DHL, HUC, 1955; LHD, Brandeis U, 1955; DM, Lewis and Clark Coll, 1959; DFA, U of Cal, Berkeley, 1963; LLD, Mills Coll, 1965; m. Madeline Milhaud, May 4, 1925; c: Daniel. Prof: music, Mills Coll, Cal, since 1940; Conservatory of Music, Paris, since 1947; composer since 1912; attaché to Fr Legation, Brazil, 1917-18; mem, superior council, Fr State Radio, 1935-40; concert comm, Fr Opera Comique, 1936-39; superior council, Conservatory of Music, Paris, 1937-40; pres, L'Academie du Disque Français, 1957. Mem: Natl Inst Arts and Letters, NY; Acad Arts and Letters, Boston; Accademia di Santa Cecilia, Rome; Acad of Arts, Stockholm; Bayerische Akademie der Schönen Kunste, Munich; Kunst Akademie, Berlin. Musical compositions: numerous operas; ballets; concertos; string quartets; quintets; symphonies; sonatas; chamber orch symphonies; piano scores; songs; theater and film music. Compositions include: Couronne de Gloire: Le Cycle de la Création; La Brebis Egarée; L'Homme et son Désir; La Cantate Nuptiale; The Man from Midian; La Création du Monde; Le Retour de l'Enfant Prodigue; L'-Orestie d'Eschyle; Le Boeuf sur le Troit; Le Train Bleu; Esther de Carpentras; Le Pauvre Matelot; Salade; Les Malheurs d'Orphée; Christophe Colomb; Maximilien; Bolivar; David; Fiesta. Author: Notes Without Music, autobiography. Recipient: Grand Officier de la Legion d'Honneur; Commandeur de l'Ordre des Arts et Lettres; Commandeur des Palmes Academiques; Off of the Order of the Cross, Brazil; Louis Spohr Prize, Braunschweig, 1967. Home and office: Mills Coll, Oakland, Cal; 10 Blvd de Clichy, Paris, Fr.

MILIMAN, Alfred Victor, US, attorney; b. Baltimore, Md, Nov 28, 1920; s. Samuel and Ethel (Taylor); att: Baltimore City Coll, 1935-37; Johns Hopkins U, 1937-38; LLB, JD, Eastern Coll, 1960; m. Sophie Siegel, July 23, 1942; c: Gloria Epstein, Evelyn Grodnitzky, Barbara. Pvt practice since 1961; counselor, researcher, Drug Abuse and Alcoholism, since 1963; bus mgr, chief admissions official, Taylor Manor Hosp, Ellicott City, Md, 1963-69; counselor, Project Adapt, Provident Hosp, 1969-70. Maj, US Army, 1942-60. Dir, Howard Co Council on Alcoholism; chmn, bd govs, Friends of Adapt, Provident Hosp, Baltimore, Md; mem: American Judicature Soc; Md Bar Assn; Amer Bar Assn; Amer Philatelic Soc; Amer Contract Bridge League; Intl Soc Criminology; fmr: pres, Mt Vernon Sch of Law Frat; cons: Man Alive Drug Addict Prog; Women's House of Correction, Jessup, Md. Contbr to mags, newspapers, jours. Home: 6934 Milbrook Park Dr, Baltimore, Md. Office: 430 Equitale Bldg, Baltimore, Md.

MILLENSON, Roy H, US, public official; b. Wash, DC, Oct 1, 1921; s. Joseph and Helen (Handen); BA, George Wash U, 1947; m. Charlotte Katz, May 28, 1950; c: Janet, Michael, Elliot. Minority staf dir, comm on lab and public wfr, US Senate, since 1965; participant, White House Confs on Health and Educ, 1965; Wash natl repr, AJComm, 1959-65; mem, ed staff, Bell Publs, Denver, Colo, 1948-65; leg and press asst to Senator Javits, 1957-59; alternate US delg to Atlantic Cong, London, 1959; mem, pres, inaugural comms, 1953, 1957; mem, DC Rep state comm, 1956-58; chmn, Natl Civil Liberties Clearing House, 1961-63; mem, Natl Captive Nations Week Comm, 1960. USAAC, 1942-46, capt, res. Mem: DC Political Sci Assn; Commn on Relationships between Montgomery Co, Md, Bd Educ and Co Commns, 1966. Contbr to periodicals. Home: 7013 Amy Lane, Bethesda, Md. Office: New Sen Off Bldg, Washington, DC.

MILLER, Alan Asher Wolf, US, rabbi; b. Hull, Eng, Oct 1, 1926; s. Lewis and Bessie (Champagne); in US since 1961; MA, PhD, U of London, 1948; min dipl, Jews Coll, 1948; MA, Balliol Coll, Oxford, 1951; rabb dipl, Leo Baeck Coll, London; m. Naomi Max, June 29, 1958; c: Jonathan, Susanna, David, Adam. Rabbi: Soc for Advancement of Judaism, since 1961; SW Essex Reform Syn, 1956-61; lectr, Leo Baeck Coll, 1956-61. Chaplain, capt, Brit Army, 1951-54. Author: God of Daniel S: In search of the American Jew, 1969; ed bd, Reconstructionist Mag. Home: 40 W 86 St, New York, NY. Study: 15 W 86 St, New York, NY.

MILLER, Alexander F, US, organisation exec; b. NYC, May 19, 1908; s. William and Fannie (Finn); BA, NYU, 1930; f, NY Sch of Social Work, 1934-36; m. Eleanor Fastenberg, Apr 2, 1935; c: Susan Brown, William. Dir, natl comty service, ADL, since 1954, Fla dir, 1943-45, s dir, 1945-54; parole off, NY State, 1936-41; probation off, Court of Gen Sessions, NYC, 1941-43. Pres: lodge, B'nai B'rith, 1946-47, mem, exec comm, 1947-50; Atlanta Metro Council, 1950-54; chmn, New

Rochelle Hum Rights Commn, 1963-68; vice-pres: Natl Assn Intergroup Relations Officials; New Rochelle Council of Unity; mem: ZOA; PTA; The Temple; Urban League; Assn of J Communal Workers; club, New Rochelle Tennis. Auhor: The Example of Levittown, 1957; Crisis Without Violence, 1964; co-author: Safety, Security and the South, 1948; How to Stop Violence in Your Community, 1951. Recipient: f, Southern Churchmen, 1951; B'nai B'rith Award, 1953. Hobbies: tennis, gardening. Home: 77 Rosehill Ave, New Rochelle, NY. Office: 315 Lexington Ave, New York, NY.

MILLER, Amos W, US, rabbi; b. Bklyn, NY, Apr 9, 1927; s. Joseph and Frances (Hershberg); BA, Bklyn Coll, 1947; ordained rabbi, MHL, JTSA, 1951, DHL, 1961; MA, Columbia U, 1953; m. Hannah Wiedman, Jan 25, 1953; c: Seth, Fredric, Felicia. Rabbi, Cong Beth Sholom East End Syn, Long Beach, LI, since 1954; cons, Nassau-Suffolk United Syn, since 1961. Chaplain, US Army, 1951-53. Mem: RabCA, since 1961; exec bd, NY Bd Rabbis, since 1962. Author: Understanding the Midrash, 1965. Home: 210 Greenway Rd, Lido Beach, NY. Study: 700 E Park Ave, Long Beach, NY.

MILLER, Anne, US, psychiatric social worker; b. Paxton, Ill, May 20, 1910; d. Robert and Rebecca (Klein); AB, Syracuse U, 1931; BS, Simmons Coll Sch of Social Work, 1934, MS, 1939. Chief psycht social worker, Milw Co Child Psycht Clinic, since 1947; chief social worker, Danville, Pa State Hosp, 1934-35; psycht social worker, Worcester, Mass, Child Guidance Clinic, 1935-42; case work sup, ARC, Columbus, O, 1942-44; chief psycht social worker, Buffalo Guidance Clinic, 1945-47; instr, social case work, U of Wis, 1949-54; spec instr: Milw Children's Hosp Sch of Nursing, 1954-62; St Mary's Hill Sanatorium, Sch of Nursing, 1954-62. F, Amer Orthopsycht Assn; mem: Natl Assn Social Workers; Wis Psycht Clinics for children, fmr secy-treas; Intl Assn Social Work; Natl Conf Social Wfr; Wis Wfr Council; Milw Youth Workers Assn, fmr pres; Amer Soc for Public Admn; Milw Govt Service League; Hadassah; JWF, Home for Aged, J Convalescent, all Milw. Recipient: Social Worker of Year Award, local chap, Natl Assn Social Workers. Home: 1039 N Cass St, Milwaukee, Wis. Office: 8700 W, Wisconsin Ave, Milwaukee, Wis.

MILLER, Arnold J, US, educator; b. Worcester, Mass, July 10, 1917; s. Samuel and Rae (Comp); BA, Yeshiva Coll, NY, 1939; dipl, Tchrs Inst, 1939; MA, Brown U, Providence, RI, 1941; JD, Harvard Law Sch, 1943; m. Blanche Hait, June 27, 1948; c: Sheldon, Louis. Asst dean, U of Pa Law School, since 1967; in pvt practice, Worcester, Mass, 1946-67; admitted: Mass State Bar, 1943; US Supr Court Bar, 1969; with law firm, Mintz, Levin and Cohn, Boston, 1943; prin, Ahavath Sholom Heb Sch, Providence, RI, 1940-41. US Army, 1943-46. Pres, Young Isr of Worcester, 1947-52, vice-pres, NE region, 1957; mem, exec comm, chmn, educ comm, and mem, allocations comm, Worcester J Fed; vice-pres, Ivriah Sch; treas, Chug Ivri; mem, bd dirs: J Family Agcy; J Home for Aged, all Worcester; chmn, Natl Council, mem, exec comm, Yeshiva Coll Alumni Assn, 1961-64; mem: Worcester Co and Boston Bar Assns; fmr auditor, Mass Superior Court; adv comm, Morgan State Coll, U of Pa Coop Projetc, 1967-69; research asso, Cen for Research on the Acts of Man, U of Pa. Author: Past and Present, plays, 1957; ed: The Jewish Concept of Labor, 1956; Yeshiva Coll Alumni Assn paper, 1946-47; mem, bd eds, The J Horizon, 1951-1969; contbr to law jours and J publs. Recipient: 4th Annual Bernard Revel Memorial Award, Yeshiva Coll Alumni Assn. Home: 5050 Wynnefield Ave, Philadelphia, Pa. Office: U of Pa Law Sch, Philadelphia, Pa.

MILLER, Arthur, US, playwright; b. NYC, Oct 17, 1915; s. Isadore and Augusta (Barnett); BA, U of Mich, 1938, hon DHL, 1958; m. Mary Slattery, Aug 5, 1940, (div) c: Jane, Robert; m. 2nd, Marilyn Monroe, July, 1956 (div); m. 3rd, Ingeborg Morath, Feb, 1962; c: Rebecca. Author: reportage, Situation Normal, 1944; novel, Focus, 1945; plays: All My Sons, 1947; Death of a Salesman, 1949; The Crucible, 1953; A View From the Bridge, 1955; A Memory of Two Mondays, 1955; publ Collected Plays, 1958; The Misfits, screenplay, 1960; After the Fall, 1964; Incident At Vichy, 1965; I Don't Need You Anymore, collected stories, 1967; The Price 1968; co-author, In Russia, 1969; contbr to mags. Mem, Dramatists Guild of Authors League of Amer. Recipient: Theatre Guild Natl Award, 1938; Pulitzer Prize and NY Drama Critics Award, for Death of a Salesman, 1949; Antoinette Perry Award, 1947, 1949, 1953; Donaldson Award, for All My Sons, 1947, Death of a Salesman, 1949, The Crucible, 1953;

NY Drama Critics Award, for All Mv Sons, 1948. Address: c/o ASCAP, 575 Madison Ave, New York, NY.

MILLER, Arthur William, US, attorney; b. NYC, Feb 27, 1928; s. Norman and Rose (Bayer); BA, Yale U, 1948; JD, NYU, 1952; m. Barbara Dickter, Dec 21, 1952; c: Nancy, Jane, Richard. Partner, Simon McKinsey and Miller, since 1957. Vice-pres: Temple Isr, Long Beach, Cal; J Comty Cen; mem: bd dirs, J Comty Fed, both Long Beach; Amer, Long Beach, Cal State, NY Bar Assns; fmr pres: Los Alamitos Sch Bd; J Family Service, Long Beach. Home: 11951 Wallingsford St, Los Alamitos, Cal. Office: 2750 Bellflower Blvd, Long Beach, Cal.

MILLER, Belle K, US, communal worker; b. Newport, Ky, Mar 19, 1905; d. Saul and Minnie (Chaliff) Kondritzer; att Akron U, 1923-24; reg nurse, Akron City Sch of Nursing, 1927; m. Noah Miller, Dec 14, 1926; c: Marilyn Berk, Cheryl Berk, Jessica Resnick. Pres: J Family Service, 1959-60; Child Guidance Clinic, 1953-54, 1959-60, Mental Hygiene Clinic, 1955; League of Women Voters, 1946-50; fmr pres, Sisterhood of Temple Israel; chmn, Urban Design and Fine Arts Commn, 1963-69; vice-pres: United Comty Council, 1963-67; mem, natl bd: women's communal services, CJFWF; JDC; mem, bd: JWF, chmn, 1956, 1957, 1959; natl women's div, UJA, 1958-60; Sagamore Hills Mental Hosp of Summit and Cuyahoga Co, O; United Fund of Akron, since 1966; United Fund Women, since 1966; Council J Feds and Wfr Fund, since 1967; mem: hon, Zonta; bd, Akron Council of J Women; Citizens Adv Comm to Planning Commn; clubs: Akron City, Rosemont Country. Recipient: Brotherhood Award, 1963; Dist Citizen Award, United Fund, 1966; Women of Achievement, Beacon Jour, 1968. Home: 631 Vinita Ave, Akron, O.

MILLER, David, US, physician, educator; b. Cincinnati, O; Jan 17, 1900; s. Moses and Rachel (Zeff); PhC, Cincinnati Coll of Pharm, 1921; BS, U of Cincinnati, 1926, BM, Med Coll, 1928, MD, 1929; m. Pearl Dyer, Aug, 1933; c: Steffan, Merwyn. Clinical prof, proctology, Coll of Med Evangelists, since 1959, asso prof, 1939-59. US Army MC, 1942-46. F: Amer Proctologic Soc; mem: AMA; S Cal Soc Gastroenterology; LA Co Med Assn Surg Soc. Contbr to med jours; produc, teaching med movies. Recipient: Collier, Ford, Martin Award for outstanding sci exhb, 1956. Hobby: photography. Home: 157 S Clark Dr, Beverly Hills, Cal. Office: 6333 Wilshire Blvd, Los Angeles, Cal.

MILLER, Donald S, US, physician; b. Maywood, Ill, Dec 9, 1908; s. Harry and Sarah (Cohen); BS, MS, MD, PhD, U of Ill; m. Anne Ghingold, 1934; c: Harvey, Rollie Grayson, Alice Breakstone, Prof, chmn orthopedics, Chgo Med Sch, since 1950. US Army, 1943-46. Mem: Sigma Xi; Alpha Omega Alpha; med socs. Contbr to med jours. Spec interests: photography, theatre. Home: 6626 N Sauganash, Lincolnwood, Ill. Office: 6 N Michigan Ave, Chicago, Ill.

MILLER, George Julius, US, attorney; b. Perth Amboy, NJ, Jan 15, 1895; s. Julius and Lena (Markoff); LLB, NJ Law Sch, 1918; m. Lillian Pamerantz, Dec 23, 1944; c: Carol Roth, David. Registrar, Gen Bd of Proprietors, E Div of NJ, since 1940; asst atty gen, NJ State, 1935-38; hearing off, Unemployment Compensation Div, 1938-59. Sgt maj, Coast Artillery Corps, 1919-21. Mem: Natl Council, Amer J Hist Soc; NJ Bar Assn. Author: The Middlesex County Courts, 1932; The Early Courts of Chancery in New Jersey, 1940. Home and office: 1 Kilmer Dr, Short Hills, NJ.

MILLER, Harold, Eng, insurance broker; b. London, Eng, July 21, 1917. Hon vice-pres, dep chmn, ZF of Gt Brit, chmn, 1964-67; vice-pres: Poale Zion, Gt Brit, chmn, 1958-64; WJC, Brit sect; dir, J Observer; fmr: mem actions comm, WZO; mem, Eretz Isr Comm Bd Deps. Served, Infantry and Educ Corp. Contbr articles to press. Recipient: awards for service in N Afr, It. Home: 71 Francklyn Gdns, Edgware, Middlesex, Eng. Office: Temple Chambers, Temple Ave, London EC4, Eng.

MILLER, Hyman, US, physician, educator; b. Paterson, NJ, Sep 28, 1897; s. Joseph and Kate (Grossman); AB, Stanford U, 1918; MD, Stanford U Med Sch, 1922; m. Dorothy Baruch, Feb 13, 1947 (decd); c: Mrs Vincent Eckel, Mrs Heston Wilson; m. 2nd Alathena Kasten, Sep 8, 1963. Asso clinical prof, med, UCLA Med Sch, 1951-56, and since 1961; sr cons, chief, allergy clinic, US VA Wadsworth Hosp, since 1946; pvt practice, since 1923; att phys: Children's Hosp, 1925-42; Good Hope Clinic, 1926-42; asso att phys, Cedars

of Leb Hosp, 1930-50; sr att phys, LA Gen Hosp, 1943-51; asso clinical prof, med, U of S Cal Med Sch, 1943-51. Cert: Amer Bd Internal Med, 1937; Amer Bd Allergy, 1940; F: Amer Coll Allergy, 1943; Amer Acad Allergy, 1924; Amer Group Therapy Assn, 1954; mem, AMA. Contbr to med and sci jours. Home: 1634 Gilcrest Dr, Beverly Hills, Cal. Office: 201 S Lasky Dr, Beverly Hills, Cal.

MILLER, Irving Ernest, US, attorney, real estate broker; b. New Bedford, Mass, Aug 10, 1926; BA, Brown U, 1948; LLB, Boston U, Sch of Law, 1951; m. Shirley Levine, June 10, 1950; c: Sherri, Michelle, Renee, Cary, Roger. Pres, The Miller Co, Inc, since 1958; dir, S Realty Utilities Corp, 1960-62; exec vice-pres, pres, Cong Intl, Inc, 1960-62. Air cadet, USAAC, 1944-45. Pres, Temple Beth Sholom; mem: Fund Raising Comm, Heb Acad; bldg fund comm, co-chmn, Mt Sinai Hosp; fund raising comm, Brown U Alumni Assn; dir, treas, Fla Land Assn; NCCJ; UJA; Combined J Appeal; Fla Bar Assn; Zeta Beta Tau; Pi Lambda Phi; clubs: Elks; Westview Country; Sunset I Assns, 3 & 4, fmr pres. Hobbies: boating, golf, stein collection. Home: 2305 Lake Ave, Sunset Island No. 3, Miami Beach, Fla. Office: 1674 Meridan Ave, Miami Beach, Fla.

MILLER, Israel, US, rabbi; b. Baltimore, Md, Apr 6, 1918; s. Tobias and Bluma (Bunchez); BA, Yeshiva Coll, 1938; MA, Columbia U, 1949; ordained rabbi, Yeshiva U, 1941, DD, 1967; m. Ruth Goldman, Oct 16, 1945; c: Michael, David, Deborah, Judith. Vice-pres, Yeshiva U, since 1970, fmr, asst to pres; rabbi, Kingsbridge Hgts J Cen, since 1942. Chaplain, USAAC, 1945-46. Hon pres, RabCA; pres, Amer ZF, since 1970; vice-pres, JWB, since 1969; chmn: Amer J Conf on Soviet Jewry; AZC; Commn on Chaplaincy, 1962-65; pres, Assn J Chaplains Armed Forces, 1955-56. Home: 2619 Davidson Ave, Bronx, NY. Office: Yeshiva U, Amsterdam Ave and 186 St, New York, NY.

MILLER, Jack Elius, Scotland, physician; b. Glasgow, Scotland, Mar 7, 1918; s. Maurice and Milly (Levitus); LRCP, LRCS, LRFPS, Glasgow U, 1938-43; m. Ida Warrens, Feb 22, 1944; c: Howard. Gen med practitioner since 1946; treasury med off, since 1961; JP. Capt, RAMC, 1944-46. Pres, Glasgow J Repr Council; chmn: bd govs, Scottish Physiotherapy Hosp; Gen Med Services Comm, Scotland; dep chmn, pvt practice comm, BMA; dep treas, Gen Med Services Defense Trusts; council mem: BMA, f, 1964, Scottish Council; mem, Royal Coll Gen Practitioners; chmn: WJC, Scotland, 1955-65; Assn of J Ex-Servicemen and Women of Scotland, 1956-68; Glasgow Local Med Comm, 1964-66; master, Lodge Montefiore, 1964-65; f, Royal Soc Med, 1966. Author: Glasgow Doctors' Handbook, 1963. Hobbies: social services, reading, golf. Home and office: 158 Hyndland Rd, Glasgow, Scotland.

MILLER, Jeanette, Eng, educator; b. London, Eng; s. Bernard and Rebecca (Dancyger) Goldburgh; m. Samuel Miller, Nov 14, 1937; c: Berenice Levy, Raly. Vice-chmn: Org Comm, WJC; Poale Zion; Barclay House Day Sch; chmn, Golders Green Ward, Lab Party; hon secy: J Vanguard; Hendon Anglo-Isr Assn; bd govs: Rosh Pinah and Hillel House J Day Schs; Hendon Co Grammar Sch; Whitefields Comprehensive Schs; cen lecture comm, Bd Deps; exec council, Zionist Fed; found, hon secy: Young Mizrachi Soc, 1932; Derby Zionist Soc, 1939-48; chmn, Cricklewood WIZO, 1932-37; natl chmn, Pioneer Women of Gt Brit 1950-57. Mem, ed bd, Pioneer Women's News. Spec interests, theatre. Home: 23, The Drive, Golders Green, London, Eng.

MILLER, Joseph B, US, pediatrician; b. Mobile, Ala, Sep 21, 1921; s. Abraham and Minnie (Adler); att: Spring Hill Coll, 1938-41; U of Ala, 1941-42; MD, La State U Med Sch, 1944; m. Edith Gurwitch, June 6, 1943; c: Joan, Alice, Bruce, Carol. Ped, since 1950; asso clinical prof, peds, U of Ala Med Sch; research asso, Spring Hill Coll, 1952; dir, Ped Allergy Clinic, Mobile Gen Hosp. Capt, US Army MC, 1946-48. Mem: Amer, S, Ala State and Mobile Co Med Assns; Ala State and Mobile Peds Socs; Amer Acad and Amer Bd Peds; Amer Acad Allergy; Amer Coll Allergists; Southwest Allergy Forum; Soc for Clinical Ecology; Beta Beta Beta. Contbr to med jours. Home: 101 Jordan Lane, Mobile, Ala. Office: 3 Office Park, Mobile, Ala.

MILLER, Joseph M, US, physician; b. Boston, Mass, Nov 9, 1921; s. Benjamin and Esther (Sugar); AB, Harvard Coll, 1942; MD, Harvard Med Sch, 1945; MPH, Hprvard Sch of Public Health, 1960; div; c: Beth, Keith, Eric. Res asso,

Harvard Sch of Public Health; sr asso, med, Peter Bent Brigham Hosp. US Army MC, 1946-48. Mem: Amer Fed Clinical Research; Amer Coll Phys; Amer Bd Internal Med; Phi Beta Kappa; Alpha Omega Alpha; exec bd, AJComm, Boston; fmr secy, Gtr Boston chap, Mass Heart Assn. Home: 650 Huntington Ave, Boston, Mass. Office: 110 Francis St, Boston, Mass.

MILLER, Leo F, US, surgeon; b. Chgo, Ill, July 5, 1906; s. Joseph and Sarah (Goldberg); BS, U of Ill, MD, Coll of Med, 1929; m. Mamie Katz, Oct 7, 1931; c: Luanne Murphy, Henrica Jacobs. In pvt practice since 1929; asst prof, orthopedics, U of Ill; att surg, dept orthopedics; Mt Sinai Hosp; Alexian Bros Hosp; fmr cons, orthopedics: VA Hines Hosp; Franklin Blvd Hosp; Served US Army. F: AMA; Amer Acad Orthopedic Surgs; Amer Coll Surgs; Intl Coll Surgs, US sect; dipl, Amer Bd Orthopedic Surg; mem: Amer Geriatrics Soc; Law and Sci Inst, U of Tex; Ill, Chgo Med Soc; Clinical Orthopedic Soc; Assn Mil Surgs; Hines Surg Assn VA; Sigma Alpha Mu; Phi Delta Epsilon. Contbr to med jours. Hobbies: art, philately. Home: 244 Lincoln Dr, Glencoe, Ill. Office: 116 S Mich Ave, Chicago, Ill.

MILLER, Leon Gordon, US, designer, artist, writer, lecturer; b. NYC, Aug 3, 1917; s. Harry and Dora (Garodnick); CFA, Newark Sch of Fine and Ind Arts, NJ, 1935; BS, NJ State Tchrs Coll, 1939; CME, Newark Coll of Engr, 1941; att Art Students League, NYC, 1941-42; m. Polly Gladish; c: Brandt, Scott. Pres, Leon Gordon Miller and Assos, since 1947; tchr, art and design, 1939-40; chief designer, war dept, US Govt, 1940-45; tchr, ind design, Cleveland Inst of Art, 1947-49; design cons, State of Isr, 1968-69; cons, planning and design, W Reserve U. Seven one-man shows of painting and prints, NY, Cleveland; exhbs in numerous gals and mus, throughout US; represented in perm collection of Libr of Cong and pvt collections; designed: stained-glass windows; sculpture; textiles. Engr, tech intelligence, US Army, 1945-47. Pres, chmn bd, Natl Design Soc; chmn bd, J Comty Cen; trustee, vice-pres, Ind Design Inst, found, fmr pres, O valley chap; delg to UNESCO Intl Design Cong: Swed, 1959; It, 1963; London, 1969; speaker before civic, profsl, mus groups mem: bd dirs, Ind Design Soc Amer; and fmr trustee, Inter-Soc Color Council. Author, Lost Heritage of Alaska, 1967; contbr numerous articles to jours. Recipient: 2 Bronze Stars; Annual Award fr Design in Hardwoods, 1959; Instn's Interior Award, 1959; Design Derby Honor for Space Control, 1960. Spec interests: ecclesiastical arts, sculpture, art photography. Home: 16250 Aldersyde Rd, Shaker Heights, O. Office: 1220 Huron Rd, Cleveland, O.

MILLER, Louis, Isr, psychiatrist; b. Somerset West, S Afr, Apr 9, 1917; s. Jonah and Ida; in Isr since 1948; MB, ChB, Med Sch, Cape Town, 1939; m. Joyce Gluckmann, Nov 27, 1941; c: Judith, Nomi. Chief natl psycht, Min of Health, Jerusalem, since 1969, dir, mental health div, 1949-54; dir: public health services, Hadassah Med Org, Jerusalem, 1954-59; MH services, Min of Health, 1959-69. Capt, S Afr MC, 1941-46; maj, Isr MC, 1948-49. Chmn, Isr MH Assn; mem: IMA; Isr Psychiatric Soc. Author: Community Psychiatry in Israel, 1967; Social Psychiatry in Israel; Child Rearing in the Kibbutz, 1969; mem: ed bd, Isr Annals of Psycht; dep ed, psycht, Ency Judaica. Home: Bet Barzel, Rab Berlin St, Jerusalem, Isr. Office: Min of Health, 20 Hamelech David St, Jerusalem, Isr.

MILLER, Marion, US, radio commentator; b. NYC, Sep 19, 1920; d. Harry and Ida (Sweetwine) Freed; BMusEd, cum laude, U of Miami, 1941; m. Paul Miller, Sep 3, 1944; c: Paul Jr, Betsy, Robert. Exec dir, Chr and J for Law and Morality, since 1967; radio commentator, Time for the Truth, KTYM, since 1966. Pres: Pioneer Women chap, 1947-53; B'nai B'rith Women chap, 1961-62; past off, Bus and Profsl Women's Br, Hadassah; adv comm: Mayor's Citizens; Dist Atty; adv bd, Cong Mishkan Yicheskel; mem: Amer Inst Fine Arts; Delta Phi Epsilon; Amer Women in Radio and TV; club, Gtr LA Press. Author: I Was a Spy, 1960; contbr to jours. Home and office: 10591 Cushdon, Los Angeles, Cal.

MILLER, Meyer, S Afr, rabbi; b. Bklyn, NY, July 4, 1904; s. Max and Fanny (Schachnowitz); in S Afr since 1950; BS, NYU, 1930, MA, 1950; MHL, ordained rabbi, JIR, NY, 1936; hon DD, HUC-UIR, 1961; m. Shulamith Wittenberg, Oct 20, 1933; c: Deborah, Edna, Mordecai. Rabbi: Temple David, Durban, since 1950; Greenwich Heb Inst, Conn, 1936-50. Maj, chaplain, US Army, 1942-46. Mem exec, S Afr Union for Progressive Judaism, since 1950, fmr chmn,

Cen Ecclesiastical Bd; hon pres, Isr United Appeal, since 1950; hon vice-pres, United Communal Fund, Durban, since 1950; exec mem: ZC for Natal Jewry, since 1950; S Afr Inst of Race Relations, since 1959; mem, CCAR; fmr: mem: gov body, World Union for Progressive Judaism; exec comm, Chesterville Child Wfr Assn; exec, Durban Mh Soc; S Afr Council for Progressive J Educ, fmr chmn; exec, S Afr Council for Marriage Guidance and Family Life. Home: 40 Berriedale Rd, Durban, S Afr. Study: 369 Ridge Rd, Durban, S Afr.

MILLER, Michael, S Afr, business exec; b. Lith, Jan 2, 1893; s. Samuel and Welma; in S Afr since 1911. Dir: Federated Stores Ltd, since 1951; OK Bazaars, since 1929; subsidiary cos since 1927. Home: 501 Park Ave, 3rd St, Johannesburg, S Afr. Office: POB 3171, Johannesburg, S Afr.

MILLER, Milton, US, editor; b. NYC, Dec 10, 1911; s. Harry and Minnie (Kreiner); att NYU Sch of Educ, 1931-36; m. Irma Ganz, Sep 3, 1939; c: Jeffrey, Lee. Ed: soccer news, LI Press, since 1947; Soccer News, NY, since 1952; Local 338 News, Retail, Wholesale and Dept Store Union, NY, since 1955; Local 888 Leader, RCIA, since 1963; Soccer Assn, since 1946; Frontpage, Newspaper Guild of NY, 1949-54; lab cons, Muscular Dystrophy Assn, since 1968; sports commentator, radio, TV, since 1938; radio script writer; sports writer: Bx Home News, 1931-33; NY American, 1933-36; sports ed, Wilkes-Barre Record, Pa, 1943-46; asst sports ed: PM, 1943-46; NY Post, 1946-47. Pres: Sports lodge, B'nai B'rith, 1960-62; Soccer Writers Assn since 1959; E League Baseball Writers, 1939; chmn, People to People Sports Comm, soccer div, since 1959; vice-pres: Amer Newspaper Guild, NY and Wilkes-Barre, 1940-43; mem: Sports Broadcasters Assn; clubs: Lambs; Overseas Press; Silurians. Ed, Soccer, 1944; contbr: annual soccer rev, Collier's Yearbook, 1948-67. Recipient, awards: 1959 Newspaperman's; Pa Newspaper Publishers Assn; Natl Soccer Coaches Assn; Intl Lab Press Assn; Rutgers U Lab Press Contests. Hobbies: stamp collecting,photography. Home: 2—Holly Dr, New Rochelle, NY.

MILLER, Milton A, US, physician; b. NYC, Aug 20, 1894; s. Max and Fannie (Benjamin); att NYC, 1912-13; MD, NYU Med Coll, 1917; m. c: Joan Singer, Cynthia Schneierson; m. 2nd, Edna Sager, Apr 19, 1968. Cons phys, J Memorial Hosp, NY, since 1953, att phys 1948-53, pres, med bd, 1952-53; fmr mem staff: Knickerbocker Hosp; Mt Sinai Hosp; Harlem Hosp; NY Dept of Health; Lincoln Hosp. Lt, US Army MC, 1917-18. F, NY Acad Med, 1950; dipl, Natl Bd Internal Med, 1948; mem: NY Co Med Soc; AMA; NY State Med Soc; AHA; KP; Masons. Contbr to med jours. Hobbies: music, rifle-shooting. Home: c/o Singer, 99 Willets Rd, Harrison, NY.

MILLER, Morton D, US, actuary; b. NYC, Jan 4, 1915; s. Samuel and Rhea (Loewenthal); BS, cum laude, CCNY, 1937; m. Florence Louis, Feb 14, 1949; c: Jonathan. Vice-pres, chief actuary, Equitable Life Assurance Soc of US, since 1967, with firm since 1937. Chmn: Health Ins Council, 1958-59; vice-chmn: adv council, NY State Health Planning Comm; health ins comm, Commerce and Ind Assn; pres: Soc of Actuaries, 1967-68; NY 65 Health Ins Assn, 1962-66; mem, bd dirs, Point Lookout Civic Assn; trustee, Amer Fund for Dent Educ; mem: Natl adv Council, Leonard Davis Inst of Health Econ, U of Pa; ind adv comm, Automobile Ins and Compensation Study being conducted by US Dept of Transp; actuarial adv comm, NY State Dept of Audit and Control. Homes: 35 Sutton Place, New York, NY; 128 Cedarhurst Ave, Point Lookout, Long Island, NY. Office: 1285 Ave of the Americas, New York, NY.

MILLER, Nelson J, US, business exec; b. NYC, Sep 24, 1904; s. Abraham and Mamie (Cohen); BS, Harvard Coll, 1926; m. Blanche Lesser, Sep 21, 1928; c: Marilyn Mech, Nina Wolfson. Pres and treas, The Howard and Barber Co, since 1959; adj instr, bus admn, New Haven Coll, since 1967; merchandise mgr, Abraham and Straus, 1928-48, vice-pres, 1948-49; pres, dir, Namm's, 1949-52; pres, treas, Shartenberg's-New Haven, 1952-62. Mem: ind adv comm, CPA; tech pricing comm, Surplus Property Bd; Dept Commerce Trade Mission to S Afr, 1957; Agcy for Intl Devl Mission to Mexico, 1962. Home: Branford, Conn. Office: Box 114, Parcel Post Sta, Milford, Conn.

MILLER, Oscar, US, educator; b. Chgo,Ill,Oct 1, 1920; s. Meyer and Dina (Shenfield); BA, Central Y, 1943; MA, U of Chgo, 1947; m. Esther Bromberg, June 10, 1945; c: Lauren, Sharon, Ira. Acting dean, Student Affairs, U of Ill, Chgo, 1969, asst dean, Coll of Bus Admn, since 1967, fac mem since 1948; prin, rel sch, Temple Beth Israel, 1958-68, Heb tchr, 1952-68; cons, Weekend Sch Tchrs Bd of J Educ, Chgo, since 1967; speaker on Isr and ME, Chgo Council on Fgn Relations, 1968. USN, 1943-46. Mem: ZOA; Amer Econ Assn; AAUD; Phi Beta Sigma. Recipient: Navy letter of recommendation medal; Navy Unit Citation. Spec interests: Bible criticism; archaeol. Home: 4638 W Dempster, Skokie, Ill. Office: U of Ill, Navy Pier, Chicago, Ill.

MILLER, Paul, US, business exec; b. Chgo, Ill, Mar 21, 1909; s. Abraham and Annie (Ginsberg); Grad, marine engr, US Maritime Acad; m. Marion Freed, Sep 3, 1944; c: Paul, Betsy Robert. Owner, Paul Miller Co. Lt USMC, 1939-46. Vice-pres, Selective Service Sys Draft Bd; mem, Mayor's Citizens Adv Comm; Dist Atty Adv Council; Amer Inst Fine Arts; Peace Offs Assn; Cong Mishkan Yicheskel; Wilshire Blvd Temple; Pa Chiefs of Police Assn; Intl Footprint Assn; clubs: Saints and Sinners of LA; Vikings; Masonic Press. Recipient: Gold Medal for Americanism; US JWV Certificate of Merit; USMC Merchant Marine Combat Bar for active engagement in direct action against the Nazis. Special interest: lectr on experience of posing as Communist for FBI. Home and office: 10591 Cushdon Ave, Los Angeles, Cal.

MILLER, Robert Davis, US, certified public acctnt; b. Hartford, Conn, Nov 7, 1920; s. Joseph and Anna (Davis); BBA, magna cum laude, Boston U, 1942; m. Sylvia Mindell, 1944; c: Stuart, Susan. Sr partner, Robert D Miller & Co, CPAs, since 1946; sr vice-pres, Fabrics Natl, Inc, since 1958; instr, Navy Supply Sch, Harvard Grad Sch of Bus Admn, 1944-45. USN, Supply Corps, 1942-45. Mem: Amer Inst CPAs; Conn Soc of CPAs, auditor; bd dirs: Hartford J Fed; Beth El Temple, W Hartford, Conn; corporation, St Francis Hosp; Masons, Tall Cedars of Leb; Beta Gamma Sigma; club, Cliffside Country, bd dirs, fmr pres. Home: 59 Whitehill Dr, West Hartford, Conn. Office: 3333 Berlin Turnpike, Newington, Conn.

MILLER, Robert M, US, cantor; b. Bklyn, June 23, 1923; s. Benjamin and Dorothy (Jaffe); BS, Ithaca Coll, 1943; BSM, HUC, Sch of Sacred Music, 1952, MA, 1955; m. Harriet Zacharias, 1954; c: Phillip, Terry, Jonathan, Joel, Naomi, Jeremy. Cantor: Cong B'nai Jehudah, Kan City, Mo, since 1966; Temple Emanuel, San Bernardino, Cal, 1962-66; Cong Ahavath Chesed, Jacksonville, Fla, 1952-55; Cong Beth Emeth, Albany, NY, 1955-62. Pres, Amer Conf of Cantors, 1960-62; mem: Phi Mu Alpha, Beta chap; San Bernardino Sym and Valley Coll Symphonietta. Home: 10941 Lydia, Kansas City, Mo. Office: 712 E 69 St, Kansas City, Mo.

MILLER, Salomon, Belgium, business exec; b. Lodz, Pol, Apr 23, 1904; s. Chaim and Bella (Blaustein); in Belgium since 1926; m; c: David, Isidore. Admnr: J Social Services; Oeuvres Centrales Israelites; Maison de Netroite; pres: Syn Aharot Haim; Chesseol Shel Emeth. Recipient: Médaille du Résistant; Médaille d'Or de l'Ordre de Leopold II; Officier de l'Académie; Croix du Mérite Cdr; Croix du Combattant de l'Europe; Education Civique d'Officier; Medaille d'Or, Académie Nationale de Paris. Home: 2 Albert Ave, Brussels, Belgium.

MILLER, Saul, US, editor; b. Bx, NY, Sep 23, 1918; s. Louis and Kate (Zismor); BS, NYU, 1941; m. Beatrice Elbaum, Nov 10, 1945; c: David, Kate, Judith, Jonathan. Dir, publs, AFL-CIO, since 1958; reporter, Gazette & Daily, York, Pa, 1945-48; copy ed, Richmond Times-Dispatch, Va, 1948-49; news ed, Jamestown Sun, NY, 1949-51; dir, New Newspaper Service, Wash, 1951-55; asso ed, AFL, News Reporter, 1955; mgn ed, AFL-CIO News, 1955-58. Sgt, US Army, 1942-45. Mem: exec council, Intl Lab Press Assn; Histadrut Assos, Natl Council for Lab Isr; Amer Newspaper Guild; club, Natl Press. Home: 3410 Highview Court, Silver Spring, MD. Office: 815 16 St, NW, Washington, DC.

MILLER, Simon, US, dentist; b. Hung, Sep 28, 1887; s. Samuel and Amalia (Heller); in US since 1907; DDS, NYU, Coll of Dent, 1914; m. Helen Kornfeld, Dec 8, 1914; c: Gladys. Pvt practice, dent surg; mem, staff, St Johns Riverside Hosp, 1926-28; med and dent service, Heb Natl Orphan Home, 1922-52; both Yonkers. Hon pres, Yonkers Dent Soc, since 1958; mem: Westchester Dent Soc, pres, 1937-39; Amer Dent Assn; NY State Dent Assn; Cong Ohab Zedek, pres, 1924-25; pres, ZOA, Yonkers chap, 1930-36; J Comty Cen, secy, 1927-32; Masons. Ed, Publisher, Heb monthly, Apiryon, 1924-28; pub Abraham Ibn-Ezra's commentpry to Exodus as prepared by Leopold Fleisher, 1926; contbr to periodicals.

Hobbies: stamp collecting and reading. Home: 257 Valentine Lane, Yonkers, NY. Office: 20 S Broadway, Yonkers, NY.

MILLER, Solomon, S Afr, Judge of Supr Court; b. Tweespruit, S Afr, May 6, 1916; s. Myers and Minna (Aaron); BA, hons, Rhodes U, Grahamstown, 1935; LLB, U of Orange Free State, Bloemfontein, 1937; m. Grace Fainsinger, Feb 2, 1941; c: Denis, Barbara. Judge, Supr Court, S Afr, since 1962; pvt practice, Bloemfontein, 1938-61; and QC, 1950. Capt, S Afr Army, WW II. Fmr: chmn, Orange Free State Bar Council; mem, Orange Free State comm, S Afr J Bd Deps; clubs: Ramblers, fmr vice-chmn; fmr mem, Rotary, Bloemfontein. Hobbies: lit, cricket, tennis. Home: 441A Essenwood Rd, Durban S Afr. Office: Supr Court, Durban, S Afr.

MILLER, Stanley A, US, merchant; b. Harrisburg, Pa, Aug 3, 1928; s. Sigmund and Molly (Abrams); att: Wharton Sch of Commerce and Finance, 1946-47; m. Shirley Tuck, Jan 2, 1949; c: Marlene, Sigmund, Elliott. Pres: Miller's Auto Supplies, since 1952; Stanley Distributors Co, since 1952; vice-pres, Toy Wholesalers of Amer, 1959-61. Chmn: transp, Rep Natl Comm for Pa Delg; ACES HS Comm; Harrisburg Sales Days, 1965; Commerce and Ind Div, United Fund, 1966; C of C Comty Events Comm, 1967; Harrisburg Inaugural Comm, 1967; co-chmn: Mem Drive and Finance Comm, Harrisburg Comty Theater, 1966-67, pres, 1964-66; asso chmn, JNF; former pres, and mem, bd dirs, Second Generation Club Automotive Accessory Ind; Harrisburg Reciprocity Club; Fmr vice-pres: Front of House, Harrisburg Comty Theater, 1966-67; J Comty Cen; C of C, Harrisburg Area, 1960-61; secy, Pa Hum Relations Comm, 1969; mem bd: Child Guidance Cen, 1964; United Fund; fmr, Tri-Co Mh; J Comty Cen, 1965; Tri-Co Council on Alcoholism; YABS; mem: natl council Jt Distribution Comm, 1967-70; Gov's Prayer Breakfast Comm, 1964-65; adv council: Harrisburg Hosp; Harrisburg Polyclinic Hosp; exec council, Boy Scouts of Amer; Tall Cedars of Lebanon, Forest 43, Harrisburg; C of C; SOS Comm, Harrisburg Area C of C; Dauphin C Rep Finance Comm, 1963-64; Armed Forces Day Comm; Paxton Lodge 798 F and Am; PaSoc; Intl Platform Comm; Harrisburg Sym Orch; Elks; Susquehanna Township Rep Org; Devl Adv Comm, Elizabethtown Coll; bd, ADL; State Negro Council; sect leader, Commerce and Ind Div Tri-Co United Fund Dr, 1965; clubs: Century; Rotary 23; Tuesday; Contact, Harrisburg. Recipient: Avis "We Try Harder" Award; cert of appreciation, Boy Scouts of Amer; first recipient, hon life mem, Young Rep of Dauphin Co; Humanitarian Award, B'nai B'rith, Salem Lodge No 26. Home: 3495 Green St, Harrisburg, Pa. Office: 200 S 18 St, Harrisburg, Pa.

MILLER, Uri, US, rabbi; NYC, July 19, 1905; s. Samuel and, Esther (Ingber); BS Ill Inst of Tech, 1926; ordained rabbi, Heb Theol Coll, Chgo, 1927, hon DHL, 1957; m. Rose Shafer, Oct 27, 1935; c: Bryna Fertig, Batya, Esther. Rabbi: Beth Jacob Cong, Baltimore, Md, since 1945; B'nai Abraham Cong, Terre Haute, Ind, 1927-32; United Orthodox Cong, Omaha, Neb, 1932-35; Beth Israel Syn, New Orleans, La, 1935-45; Bainbridge, Md Naval Acad, 1946-49; Aberdeen Proving Grounds, Army Chem Cen, Edgewood, Md, 1946-53. Pres: RabCA, 1946-48; Syn Council of Amer, 1963-65; Baltimore Bd of Rabbis, 1966-68; chmn: Md Commn on J Chaplaincy, since 1962; natl comm of social justice, RabCA, 1950-58; Natl Scouting Comm since 1950; co-chmn, Pres, Comm on Civil Rights, 1963; mem: Natl Comm on J Chaplaincy, JWB, 1945-58; Mizrachi Org of Amer since 1958; B'nai B'rith; Md Comm to study problems of drug addiction since 1965; bd trustees, Conf on Material Claims Against Ger, 1964-65; admn comm, Memorial Found for J Culture, 1965-66; Natl Comm on Scouting; delg and speaker at various natl confs, such as White House Conf on Children and Youth; White House Conf on Aged. Author, booklets: Your Jewish Community, 1939; For Your Happiness, 1940; Be Comforted, 1940; Essentials of Judaism, 1941; Bar Mitzvah Book, 1941; Thy Healing Shall Spring Forth, 1957, 2nd ed, 1962; contbr to med jours in field of rel. Home: 6210 Park Heights Ave, Baltimore, Md. Study: Beth Jacob Cong, 5713 Park Heights Ave, Baltimore, Md.

MILLER, Wade Norman, US, physician; b. Akron, O, July 2, 1922; s. Sylvester and Gertrude (Grossman); BS, Harvard Coll, 1943, MD, Med School, 1946; m. Miriam Turteltaub, Mar 3, 1946; c: Ellen, Gail, Theodore, Sara. Pvt practice, med, since 1946; att phys, Presbyterian Hosp, Newark, NJ, since 1956; att phys, Orange Memorial Hosp, since 1962; cons, VA Hosp, East Orange, NJ since 1962. Capt, US Army, 1947-49. Mem, bd trustees: AJComm, Essex Co, NJ, since

1957; Amer Cancer Soc, Essex Co div, 1956-60; mem: AMA; Soc of Nuclear Med; f, Amer Coll Phys. Contbr to med jours. Home: 280 Redmond Rd, South Orange, NJ. Office: 144 S Harrison St, East Orange, NJ.

MILLER, Walter A, US, attorney, civic worker; b. Bklyn, NY, Dec 23, 1904; s. Manasseh and Charlotte (Cohen); BA, Princeton U, 1925; LLB, Bklyn Law School, 1928; m. Betti Schellenberg, Sep 3, 1929; c: Ann Loewenwarter, Elizabeth Dodge, Judith Childs. Partner, law firm, Delatour & Miller, since 1932; counsel, trustee, Prudential Savings Bank, since 1936; mem, Bklyn Adv Comm, Chemical Bank NY Trust Co, since 1959. Dir, Fed Employment and Guidance Service, since 1934; pres, 1946-62; dir, NYC Wfr Council, 1944-53, vice-pres, 1950-53; trustee, Bklyn J Family Wfr Soc, 1931-46, pres, 1943-46; trustee: FJP, of NY, since 1946; J Family Service since 1946, vice-pres, 1946-51; Bklyn Fed of J Charities, 1935-46; mem: NYC Youth Bd, since 1954; NY State Council on Rehab since 1959; chmn, Mayor's Task Force on Youth and Work, 1961-66; trustee and counsel, Southside Hosp, Bay Shore, 1960-64; Cong Beth Elohim, asst trustee, since 1953. Home: 160 Columbia Hgts, Brooklyn, NY. Office: 185 Montague St, Brooklyn, NY.

MILLMAN, Herbert, US, social worker; b. Kiev, Russ, Dec 25, 1909; s. Henry and Sima (Moskowska); in US since 1914; BS, Springfield Coll, 1937; Med Harvard U, 1940; m. Susan Feinburg, Auo 18, 1940; c: Ellen, Lester. Asso exec, JWB, since 1960; field secy, NE sect, 1943-49, dir, field services, 1949-60; exec dir, Gtr Boston Council of J Cens, 1945-49. Pres, Natl Assn J Cen Workers, 1966-68; chmn, ed comm, Natl Social Wfr Forum, Natl Conf on Social Wfr, 1961-62; chmn: Boston chap, Amer Assn Group Workers, 1947; field service comm, Natl Social Wfr Assembly, 1957-59; program chmn, Mass Conf Social Workers, 1946; mem, exec bd, Comty Syn, Rye, NY,1956-58;mem: Acad Cert Social Workers, Natl Assn Social Workers, Natl Conf J Communal Service. Ed, Yearbook J Comty Cen Field, 1961-62; contbr to Amer Year Book and J Wfr jours. Home: 104 Hix Ave, Rye, NY. Office: 15 E 26 St, New York, NY.

MILLMAN, Jacob, US, electric engr, educator; b. Russ, May 17, 1911; s. Philip and Gertrude (Nachschen); in US since 1913; BS, MIT, 1932, PhD, 1935; att U of Munich, 1932-33; m. Sally Dublin, Oct 11, 1936; c: Richard, Jeffrey. Prof, elec engr, Columbia U, since 1952; asst, physics, MIT, 1935-36, staff mem, radiation lab, 1942-45; instr, asst prof and asso prof, elec engr, CCNY, 1936-51; Fulbright lectr: Rome, 1959-60; Montevideo, 1968. F: Amer Phys Soc; Inst Elec and electrical engrs; mem: AAAS; Amer Soc Engr Educ. Author: Electronics, 1941, 2nd ed, 1951, Span, 1959; Pulse and Digital Circuits, 1956, Japanese, 1960, Russ, 1961, Ger, 1962, Span, 1965; Vacuumtube and Semiconductor Electronics, 1958, Span, 1961; Pulse, Digital and Switching Waveforms, 1965, Japanese, 1967, Span, 1969; Electronic Devices and Circuits, 1967. Home: 7 Adrienne Pl, White Plains, NY. NY. Office: Columbia U, 120 St, New York, NY.

MILLO, Joseph, Isr, theater director and producer; b. Prague, Czech, May 26, 1916; s. Richard and Frieda (Pasovsky); in Isr since 1921; att Acad of Arts, Prague and Vienna; m. Yemima Persitz, 1942. Found, dir, Haifa Munic Theater; co-found, vocal impersonator, Wooden Troup, marionette theatre, 1941-42; actor, Hamatate Troup, 1942; found, dir, Cameri Theatre, 1946-58; visiting dir: Zürich Schauspielhaus; Ankara Natl Theater; Prague Natl Theater; guest dir: Theater am Kurfürstendam, Berlin, 1959; Theater in der Josefstadt, Vienna; Isr repr, UNESCO Conf of Intl Theater Inst; maj roles: Jack the Melancholy; Richard the Third; maj producs at Cameri Theater; Tartuffe; As You Like It; Romeo and Juliet; The Inspector Comes; at Hiafa Theatre: Antigone; The Taming of the Shrew; Midsummer Night's Dream; Mother Courage; Three Sisters; Andorra; Marat Sade; Three Penny Opera; producs in intl festivals: Hu Halach Basadot; The Caucasian Chalk Circle; The Good Person of Szechwan; adaptor and trans of plays from Czech into Heb. Recipient: Isr Prize, 1968. Office: 50 Pevsner St, Haifa, Isr.

MILLSTEIN, Ira Martin, US, attorney; b. NYC, Nov 8, 1926; s. Harry and Birdie (Rosenbaum); BS, Columbia U, Sch of Engr, 1947; LLB, Columbia U, Sch of Law, 1949; m. Diane Greenberg, July 3, 1949; c: James, Elizabeth. Partner, Weil, Gotshal & Manges, since 1967, asso 1951-57; adj prof, law, NYU Sch of Law, since 1965; atty Antitrust Div, US Justice Dept, 1949-51; spec asst to Atty Gen, 1951; mem, Natl Commn on Consumer Finance, 1969; lectr: Practising Law

Inst; Natl Ind Conf Bd; Amer Bar Assn. Chmn, prog comm, Antitrust Law Sect, Amer Bar Assn, fmr chmn; mem, adv bd: spec comm, Natl Conf of Commns on Uniform State Laws; Antitrust and Trade Regulations Report, Bur Natl Affairs, Inc; fmr: secy, comm on U Affairs, Alumni Assn, Columbia Coll; mem, Commn to Study Fed Trade Commn, Amer Bar Assn. Home: 3 Douglas Circle, Rye, NY. Office: 767 Fifth Ave, New York, NY.

MILLSTONE, Isadore Erwin, US, business exec; b. St Louis, Mo, Jan 6, 1907; s. Louis and Marv (Apter); BS, Architectural engr, Wash U, 1927; m. Goldie Gollin, Aug 24, 1930; c: Mary Kuhn, David. Pres, Millstone Construction Inc, since 1930; bd dirs, Mercantile Trust Co. Pres, Millstone Found; vice-pres: Natl JWB; World Fed YMHA's and J Comty Cen; bd trustees: HUC-JIR; Wash U; St Louis J Fed; United Fund, Gtr St Louis; United Heb Temple, St Louis; clubs: Mo Athletic; Engrs. Home: 801 S Skinker, St Louis, Mo. Office: 8510 Eager Rd, St Louis, Mo.

MILNER, Max, US, chemist, food technologist; b. Edmonton, Alberta, Can, Jan 24, 1914; s. Morris and Rose (Lertzman); BS, U of Sask, 1938; MS, U of Minn, 1941; PhD, 1945; m. Elizabeth Banen, Aug 9, 1942; c: Ruth, Marcia. Sr food tech, UNICEF, NY, since 1959; adj prof, nutrition sci, Columbia U; cons, Off of War on Hunger, Agcy for Intl Devl; chief, nutrition br, Off of Tech Coop and Research, Agcy for Intl Devl, State Dept, Wash, DC, 1966-67; prof, dept of grain, sci and ind, Kan State U, and chem, Kan Agric Experiment Sta, 1947-59; cons to FAO, EPTA prog, 1954, 1958; visiting inves, plant biol, Carnegie Inst, Wash, DC, 1957; research asso, dept of biochem, U of Minn, 1945-46; chem, Pillsbury Mills, Inc, Minneapolis, Minn, 1939-40; cons to ind, govts and applied sci instns. Chmn: Gordon Research Conf on Food and Nutrition, 1968; Symposium, Third Intl. Cong of Food, Sci and Tech, Wash, DC, 1970; org, numerous tech symposia and confs; mem: research adv comm, Agcy for Intl Devl; subpanel, Panel on World Food Supply, Pres's Sci Adv Comm, 1966-67; gov bd, Agric Research Inst, Natl Acad Sci, Natl Research Council; Inst Food Techs, chmn, awards comm, 1969; Amer Chem Soc; Amer Assn Cereal Chems, NY Acad Sci; participant, Workshop on Food, US Natl Acad Sci and Indonesian Inst Sci, Djakarta, 1968; f, AAAS. Ed, Protein-enriched Cereal Foods for World Needs, Amer Assn Cereal Chemist,1968; contbr to sci jours. Recipient: Intl Award, Inst of Food Techs. Hobbies: photography, music. Home: 87 Edgemont Rd, Scarsdale, NY. Office: UN Secretariat, New York, NY.

MILO (Milwidsky), Josef J, Isr, banker; b. Ber, Ger,Aug 14,1915; s. Shabtai and Henriette (Rothenberg); in Isr since 1938; att: Rabbiner- seminar, Berlin, 1937-38; Heb U, Jerusalem, 1954-55; f, Admn Staff Coll, Henley, Eng, 1954; m. Brurya Weitzen, 1953; c: Daniel, Michal, Tal. Dir, Bank of Isr, fmr: secy gen; econ counsellor, Isr Emb, Paris, 1963-65; dep chmn, Securities Auth, 1968; Brit Army, J Brig, 1942-46; col, IDF, 1950; head, org br, Gen Staff, 1951-54. Mem, Admn Staff Coll, Henley, Eng. Home: 22 Avner St, Zahala, Tel Aviv, Isr. Office: Bank of Israel, Jerusalem, Isr.

MILSTON, Alan Kaufman, Austr, consulting engr; b. Sydney, Oct 24, 1922; s. Jacob and Ada (Neshling); BSc, U of Sydney, 1943; BE, London U, Eng, 1948; m. Marcia Apte, Mpr 4, 1947; c: John, Karen, David. Partner, cons engrs, since 1957; dir, invest co, since 1954; engr, inves, NSW Irrigation Commn, 1946-51; design engr, P O Miller,1951-57. Pres, Cons Structural Engrs, NSW, fmr secy; vice-pres, NSW Friends of Heb U, Jerusalem, fmr pres; fmr treas, Austr Friends of Heb U; devl off, Rostrum Clubs, NSW; mem: Inst of Engrs, Sydney div; Lions Intl, Bondi club. Hobbies: public speaking; devl of new public speaking clubs. Home: 31 Benelong Cres, Bellevue Hill, NSW, Austr. Office: 300 Castlereagh St, Sydney, Austr.

MINCHIN, Nina Mesirow, US, concert pianist; b. Chgo, Ill; d. Elias and Rebecca (Helfand) Mesirow; studied piano with Moritz Rosenthal, Leopold Godowsky, Heniot Levy; c: Jarvis, Gloria. Pianist-found, Pro Musica Trio, musical dir, Pro Musica Soc of Chgo, since 1957; pioneered in chamber music; performed in concerts throughout US; appeared with Pro Musica Trio in annual monthly concerts in Chgo, since 1935, under auspices Chamber Music Soc; appeared in recitals; soloist with sym orchs; presents noted chamber music ensembles from all parts of the world at Orchestra Hall, Chgo. Club, Arts, Chgo. Hobbies: painting, reading. Home and office: 900 Lake Shore Dr, Chicago, Ill.

MINDEL, Barry, Eng, organization secy; b. Latvia, May 14, 1914; s. Jacob and Buna (Merson); BComm, U of Birmingham, 1937; m. Gertrude Wittler, June 15, 1944; c: Jacob, Bernice, Tessa. Gen secy, Mizrachi Fed of Gt Brit and Ir, since 1942. Hon secy, Mifal Hatorah; exec, WJC; comm mem, Isr and educ, Bd of Deps. Contbr to J publs. Hobbies: painting, chess. Home: 40 Downage St, London, NW4, Eng. Office: 345 Gray's Inn Rd, London, WC1, Eng.

MINDEL, Joseph, US, research admnr, teacher, writer; b. NYC, May 3, 1912; s. Isaac and Esther (Eventoff); BS, CCNY, 1932; MA, Columbia U, 1937; PhD, NYU, 1943; m. Lucy Wyle, Sep 23, 1934; c: Judith Efman. Off of dir, Lincoln Lab, MIT, since 1961; tchr, physics and chem, NYC, HSs, 1934-46; chmn, dept sci, 1946-61. Educ cons, US Army, 1944-46. Mem: Writers Guild of Amer; NY Acad Scis; AAAS; Natl Sci Tchrs Assn; Phi Beta Kappa; Sigma Xi. Author: numerous radio and TV plays produced on natl networks; contbr to educ and sci jours. Recipient: Best TV Play, Writers' Guild of Amer, 1958; Best Radio Play, 1961-62. Home: 222 Winslow Rd, Waban, Mass. Office: Lincoln Lab, MIT, Lexington, Mass.

MINDEL, Nissan, US, author; b. Rezekne, Latvia, Mar 20, 1912; s. Yaakov and Buna (Marson); in US since 1940; BA, MA, Manchester U, Eng; ordained rabbi, Yeshiva Tomche Tmimim, Pol, 1939; PhD, Columbia U, 1962; m. Nettie Nemtzov, 1937; c: Frida Shapiro. Dir: publs, Merkos L'Inyonei Chinuch, since 1941; Chabad Research Cen, since 1960. Author: The Commandments, 1956, 6th ed, 1966; The Complete Story of Tishrei, 1961; Complete Festival Series, 1961; Rabbi Schneur Zalman of Liadi, vol I, 1969; trans: Lubavitcher Rabbi's Memoirs, vol I, 1956, vol II, 1960; Liqqutei Amarim, Tanya, by R Schneur Zalman, 1962; ed: Talks and Tales, monthly, since 1942; Shmuessen mit Kinder un Yugnt, since 1942; contbr to short stories, plays, articles. First secy to Lubavitcher Rebbe, Rabbi Menachem M Schneerson; dir, Machne Isr, Inc. Spec interests: Hasidic phil, Heb educ. Home: 238 E Walnut St, Long Beach, NY. Office: 770 Eastern Pkwy, Brooklyn, NY.

MINDELL, Bianka G, US, communal worker; b. Czernowitz, Aus; d. Carl and Regina (Glass) Gruenberg; m. Max Mindell, May 30, 1931; c: Carl, Arnold. Mem: Americanization Council and Adv Comm, chmn, reception, new Amers; Planed Parenthood League; J Comty Cen; Hadassah; Brandeis Women; Temple Gates of Heaven; fmr: pres, chmn: service to fgn born comm, comparative rel lectures, birthday parties for residents of Troy Home for Aged, mem, natl service comm, all Natl Council of J Women; secy, United World Federalists of Schenectady, mem, bd trustees, Capitol dist; mem bd, SCAP. Hobby: sculpture. Home: 1810 Randolph Rd, Schenectady, NY.

MINDELL, Joseph, US, economist; b. NYC, Feb 9, 1909; s. Israel and Matilda (Goldsmith); BS, NYU, 1931; att Columbia Law Sch, 1933-35; m. Geraldine Lesczinski, June 14, 1936. Partner, Marcus and Co, NYC; cons, Argus Research Corp, NYC, both since 1940; guest lectr, inves, New Sch for Social Research, NYC, 1951. Mem: bd guardians, JTS, 1951-52; Author's League; Wall St Forum; NY Soc Security Analysts. Author: The Stock Market, 1948; contbr to mags. Hobbies: writing, antiques. Home: 18 W 9 St, New York, NY. Office: 61 Broadway, New York, NY

MINERBI, Itzhak Sergio, Isr, diplomat; b. Rome, It, Aug 3, 1929; s. Arturo and Fanny (Ginzburg); in Isr since 1947; BA, Heb U, Jerusalem, 1960; PhD, Sorbonne, Paris, 1967; m. Hanna Wertheimer, Aug 15, 1950; c: Tamar, Nurit, Iris. Ambass to Ivory Coast, since 1967; tchr, Inst for Instrs from abroad, JA, Jerusalem, 1956-60; corresp, It radio and newspaper, Jerusalem, 1957; asst to dir, econ dept, Min for Fgn Affairs, 1961-63; chief Isr delg, UN Intl Conf for Tourism, Rome, 1963; dep chief, Isr Mission to EEC, Brussels, 1963-67; counsellor to Isr delg, 20th session, UN Gen Assembly, 1965; participated in: negotiation of several air agreements with Afr states; negotiations of commercial treaty with EEC. Fmr: chmn, Isr Cen, World Union of J Students, chief of bc service, Jerusalem; secy, HeHalutz; It; mem, Kibbutz Ruhama; active in absorption of N Afr immigrants to Isr. Author: La Belva in Gabbia, 1962; Lo Stato d'Israele, 1963; Riva' on leKalkala, 1959; Angelo Levi Bianchini e la Sua Opera nel Levante 1918-20, 1967; Clio, 1967; La Rassegna Mensile di Israel, 1967; Asian and African Studies, vol 4, 1968; contbr to: Dapcy HeHalutz, fmr ed; Expresso, both Rome. Recipient: Arlosoroff prize, for hist research on

It policy towards Pal, 1914-1920. Hobbies: archaeol, diplomatic hist, photography. Home: 8 Neve Granot, Jerusalem, Isr. Office: Min for Fgn Affairs, Jerusalem, Isr.

MINKOFF, Isaac, Isr, educator; b. London, Eng, July 2, 1922; s. Jacob and Asna (Stralazilitz); in Isr since 1948; BSc, London U, 1943; MS, DSc, MIT, 1957; m. Rena Serkes, Jan 15, 1950; c: Yael, Gidon, Gila, Michael, Nadia. Assn prof, Technion, Haifa, since 1963; mem, bd dirs, Timna copper mines, Eilat, since 1967; cons, Battelle, Genéve, since 1969. Capt, Brit Army, 1943-47. Chmn, Isr Crystallographic Soc, 1967-69; co-chmn, Isr Soc for Crystal Growth; f, Inst of Metallurgists, Brit. Home: 83 Horeb St, Haifa. Isr. Office: Technion, Haifa, Isr.

MINKOFF, Isaiah M, US, organization exec; b. Russ, Jan 20 1901; s. Moses and Olga Knopoff); att U of Moscow, 1918-20; BA, U of Cal, 1926; m. Dussia Samson, June 3, 1926; c: Nina, Paul. Exec vice-chmn, Natl J Comty Relations Adv Council, fmr exec dir; exec secy, J Lab Comm, 1936-41; Gen J Council, 1941-44. Mem: bd dirs: J Daily Forward Assn; Frank Z Atran Found; YIVO; League for Ind Dem; fmr, Amer J Tercentenary Comm. Home: 200 Haven Ave, New York, NY. Office: 55 W 42 St, New York, NY.

MINKOWICH, Abram Selig, Isr, psychologist; b. Bezera, Pol, Mar 10, 1910; s. Yekuthiel and Sara (Shapiro); att Tchrs Coll, Pol; MA, Heb U, Jerusalem, 1952; MA, PhD, U Mich; single. Asso prof, educ and psych, Heb U, Jerusalem, since 1959; tchr, Pol, 1933-39; tchr, Isr, 1942-54; lectr, research asso, U Mich, 1958-59; counsellor: Min of Educ; educ guidance kibbutzim. Cpl, Pol Army, 1937-39; sgt, IDF, 1948-49. Prin contribs: research and counselling in areas of: personality; educ psych; psycholinguistics; curriculum construction; methods of instr. Mem: Isr Psych Assn; Sigma Xi; chmn, Cen for Advancement of Culturally Disadvantaged Children. Author: The Disadvantaged Child, 1969; mem ed comm, Megamoth, Isr socio-psych jour; contbr to profsl publs. Recipient: Racham Doctoral F, Mich Grad Sch, 1959. Special interests: archaeol; hist of ancient Isr; Bible sci. Home: 3/3 Givath Beith Hakerem, Jerusalem. Office: Heb U, Jerusalem, Isr.

MINKOWITZ, Martin, US, attorney; b. July 2, 1939; s. Jacob and Marion (Kornblau); AA, Bklyn Coll, 1960; LLB, Bklyn Law Sch, 1963, LLM, 1965, JD; m. Helen Chesler, Feb 14, 1965; c: Stuart. Partner, Minkowitz, Hagen & Rosenbluth. Mem: Amer, NY State, NYC Bar Assns; KP; NY Co Lawyers Assn; fmr, analyst, NYC Council. Home: 3655 Shore Pkwy, New York, NY. Office: 310 Madison Ave, New York, NY.

MINKOWSKI, Eugene, Fr, psychiatrist; b. Petrograd, Russ, Apr 17, 1885; s. August and Tecla (Lichtenbaum); MD, Paris, 1925; D hon causa, Facultés de Zurich et de Varsovie; m. Francoise Brockman, Apr, 1913 (decd); c: Alexander, Jeanine Pilliard. Psycht, Henri Rouselle Hosp, since 1925; phys, Fr Army, 1915-19. Pres, exec comm, Fr ORT, since 1946; hon pres, World OSE Union; fmr pres: Medico-Psych Soc; Fr Psych Soc. Author: La Schizophrénie, 1927; Le Temps Vécu, 1933; Vers une Cosmologie, 1936; Traité de Psychopathologie, 1966; ed, L'Evolution Psychiatrique, since 1930. Recipient: Croix de Guerre; Croix du Combattant Volontaire, 1918; Officier de la Légion d'Honneur, 1950. Office: 68 rue de Babylone, Paris, Fr.

MINKOWSKI, Mechislav, Switz, physician, educator; b. Warsaw, Pol, Apr 15, 1884; s. August and Tecla (Lichtenbaum); in Switz since 1911; MD, Breslau U, 1907; m. Irene Fux, Feb 18, 1936; c: Peter. Prof em, neur, Inst for Brain Anat and Clinic for Nervous Disease, U Zurich, since 1954, prof, 1928-54, mem fac, since 1911; researcher: IP Pavlov Physiological Lab, St Petersburg, Russ, 1907-08; Med Clinic, Greifswald, 1908; Neuropsycht Clinic, Berlin, Ger, 1909-11. Hon pres: Swiss Neur Soc, since 1946, fmr pres; Soc of Psycht and Neur, Zurich, since 1959, fmr pres; Swiss Friends of Heb U, Jerusalem, since 1957, fmr vice-pres, pres; non mem: Pol Acad Scis, Cracow; Société Française de Neurologie; Belgian Soc for Mental Med; Greek Med Soc; It Neur Soc; Amer Neur Assn; Amer Assn Neuropaths; Mexican Neur Soc; Neur Soc of Arg; IMA; Intl Brain Research Org; Swed Med Soc. Ed, Schweizer Archiv für Neurologie und Psychiatrie; contbr to: Encyclopédie Française; med jours. Home: 55 Freistrasse, Zurich, Switz.

MINOW, Newton N, US, lawyer; b. Milw, Wis, Jan 17, 1926; s. Jay and Doris (Stein); BS, Northwestern U, 1949, JD, 1950, hon LLD, 1965; hon LLD: Brandeis U, 1963; U Wis, 1963; m. Josephine Baskin, May 1949; c: Susan, Martha, Mary. Pvt practice, Leibman, Williams, Bennet, Baird and Mi ow, since 1965; bd dirs: Amer Computer Communications Inc; Barnaby's Inc, Berger-Kent Spec Fund Inc; Computer Transmission Corp; Dynascan Corp; FAS Intl; FCB Cablevision Inc; Intl Digisonics Corp; asso, Mayer, Brown & Platt, 1950-51; law clerk, Chief Justice Fred M Vinson, US Supr Court, 1951-52; admn asst, Ill Gov Adlai Stevenson, 1952-53; asso, Mayer, Brown & Platt, 1953-55; partner, Stevenson, Rifkind & Wirtz, 1955-61; chmn, FCC, 1961-63; exec vice-pres, gen counsel, dir, Ency Britannica Inc, 1963-65; lectr, Medill Sch Journalism, Northwestern U. Sgt, US Army, 1944-46. Bd chmn, Rand Corp; chmn, dir, Chgo Educ TV Assn; chmn, Study of Campaign Costs in Elec Era, Twentieth Cent Fund; trustee, U Notre Dame; rector, Communications Fac, Lincoln Acad, Ill; dir: Adlai E Stevenson Inst Intl Affairs; Acad for Educ Devl; Adler Planetarium; Erickson Inst for Early Educ; Natl Book Comm; Natl Civil Service League; Natl Exec Comm, AJComm; mem, natl adv council: Hampshire Coll; Mass Communications Cen, State Hist Soc, Ill; Amer Bar Found; Amer Judicature Soc; Amer Soc Intl Law; Amer, Chgo, Ill, Wis Bar Assns; adv comm, Comm on Ill Govt; Brandeis U Alumni Assn; Intl Broadcast Inst; Chgo Comm, Council on Fgn Relations; Leadership Council for Metrop Open Comtys; Midland Authors; Natl Acad TV Arts and Scis; clubs: Law; Legal; Economic; Execs; Fed City; Mid-Amer; Northmoor Country; Standard; Wayfarer's. Author: Equal Time: The Private Broadcaster and the Public Interest, 1964. Recipient: John Henry Wigmore Award, Northwestern U Law Sch, 1950; one of ten outstanding young men in Chgo, Jr C of C, 1960; one of ten outstanning young men in US, Natl Jr C of C, 1961; George Foster Peabody Bc Award, 1961; Dr Lee De Forest Award, Natl Assn for Better Radio and TV, 1962; merit award, Northwestern U Alumni Assn, 1963. Home: 375 Palos Rd, Glencoe, Ill. Office: 1 First National Plaza, Chicago Ill.

MINSK, Louis M, US, chemist; b. NYC, June 14, 1908; s. Harris and Gussie (Udelowitz); BS, Wesleyan U, 1929, MA, 1930; m. Rose Strick, June 13, 1933; c: Barbara Baskin, Marla. Sr lab head, Eastman Kodak Co, research chem since 1930. Prin contrib: adaptation of polymers to photographic ind. Mem: Amer Chem Soc; Sigma Xi; Phi Beta Kappa. Contbr to sci jours. Home: 551 Hillside Ave, Rochester, NY. Office: Eastman Kodak Co, Kodak Park, Rochester, NY.

MINTZ, Betty C, US, civic official; b. Cleveland, O, Apr 13, 1910; d. AR and Alice (Rosenwasser) Cohn; BA, U of Wis, 1932; m. Alexander Mintz, Dec 17, 1932; c: Loren, Barbara Rosenblatt, Karen Margulies. Mem, City Council of Shaker Heignts, O, since 1955, city planning commn and bd of zoning appeals, both since 1959. Mem, natl bd, Natl Council of J Women, since 1955; treas, Bellefaire J Children's Bur, since 1950; mem: Alpha Kappa Delta; Alpha Epsilon Phi. Home: 3300 Van Aken Blvd, Shaker Heights, O.

MINTZ, Edward N, US, public relations counsel; b. Chgo, Ill, Feb 1, 1916; s. Nathan and Dara (Rich); LLB, Bklyn Law Sch, 1943; att: New Sch for Social Research, 1946-47; Columhia U, 1947-48; m. Esther Kaplan, Aug 25, 1940; c: Lawrence, Barbara. PR counsel, exec secy, Kingsbrook J Med Cen, NYC, since 1947; mem, Fed Grand Jury, since 1963; mgr, Bx Sym Orch 1940-41; mem, NY Grand Jury, 1958. Trustee, Isaac Albert Research Inst; mem: PR Soc; secy, Amer Publicists Guild; Comty Agcys PR Assn; Gtr NY, Bklyn J Cen; Natl PR Council; Health and Wfr Services; Assn Fund Raising Dirs; Amer Hosp Assn; fmr: NY War Services Scholar; mem exec, Natl Expansion Comm, JWV; asso secy, Pal Histadrut Campaign Comm; found, Intercoll, Inter-scholastic Music League, NYC; clubs: PR Dirs; City, NYC. Recipient: Malcolm T MacEachern Memorial Competition Award, 1962. Home: 44 Bennett Ave, New York, NY. Office: 86 E 49 St, Brooklyn, NY.

MINTZ, Harry, US, artist, educator; b. Pol, Sep 27, 1909; s. Zysman and Sarah (Milgram); in US since 1929; MFA, Acad of Fine Arts, Warsaw, Pol, 1927; m. Rosabelle Truglio, Sep 1, 1958; c: William Sari. Prof, advanced painting, Art Inst of Chgo, since 1955; instr, lectr, advanced painting, Evanston Art Cen, Ill, since 1942; instr, painting, N Shore Art League, Winnetka, Ill, 1949-59; visiting prof, fine arts, Wash U, St Louis, Mo, 1954-55; exhb at: Art Inst of Chgo, since 1932; Mus of Modern Art, NYC; Whitney Mus, NYC; Corcoran Gal, Wash, DC; Palace of Legion of Honor, SF, Cal; LA Co Mus; U of Ill Exhb, Urbana, Ill, 1948-50, 1953, 1961, 1963;

Carnegie Intl, Pittsburgh, Pa; Mus of Cincinnati, O; Mus of Richmond, Va; NY World's Fair, 1939; Denver Art Mus, Colo; Seattle Art Mus, Wash; Sarasota Art Assn, Fla; St Louis Art Mus; The Biennale, Venice, It; paintings owned by: Art Inst of Chgo; Modern Mus of Tel Aviv, Isr; Whitney Mus, NY; Mus of Modern Art, Rio de Janeiro, Brazil; New Evansville Mus, Ind; Warsaw Acad of Fine Arts, Pol; U of Notre Dame; over 600 pvt cellections. Recipient: prizes and honorable mention, Art Inst of Chgo, 1937, 1938, 1939, 1946, 1949, 1952, 1953, 1954, 1962; silver medal, Palace of Legion of Honor, SF, 1946; cash award, Old NW Territory Exhb, Ill, 1948; first prize, Amer J Arts Club, 1948; hon mention, Terry Natl Exhb, Miami, 1952; prizes, Evanston Women's Club, Ill, 1948, 1949, 1953; cash award, Magnificent Mile, Chgo, 1955; purchase prize, Union League Art Exhb, Chgo, 1959; third prize, Sarasota Natl Art Exhb, Fla, 1959; hon mention and first prize, Old Orchard, Chgo, 1958, 1959, 1960, 1962. Hobbies: travel, music. Home and studio: 452 Belden Ave, Chicago, Ill.

MINTZ, Hymen B, US, attorney; b. Newark, NJ, Sep 12, 1909; s. Abraham and Gussie (Muskat); BA, cum laude, Upsala Coll, 1929; LLB, Rutgers U Law Sch, 1932; m. Beatrice Altshuler, Sep 6, 1942; c: Mark, Joan. Atty since 1933; mem, NJ, State Assembly, 1954-58. Chmn: middle income housing commn, mem, appropriations comm; Newark Trades and Businessmen's Council, UJA, 1962-68; pres, Upsala Coll Alumni Assn, 1965-67; vice-pres, S Ward-Newark br, Boys Club; mem, bd trustees, Temple Emanu-El, Livingston, NJ; mem, Bd of Chosen Freeholders of Essex Co, since 1967. Hobbies: sports, music, travel. Home: 70 Eastbrook Terr, Livingston, NJ. Office: 11 Commerce St, Newark, NJ.

MINTZ, Izhak Jossef, Isr, attorney; b. Warsaw, Pol, June 16, 1918; s. Nissan and Esther (Wassermil); LLB, U of London, Eng, 1946; LLM, Harvard U, 1954; in Isr since 1933; m. Lea Majaro, Oct 5, 1951; c: Alexander, Israel. Legal adv, Min of Transp, since 1950, asst legal adv, 1954-50; secy, law firm, Selig, Levitzky and Co, 1936-45; staff, Shvo and Scupak, 1945-48; repr Isr at Intl confs of maritime law, 1957-1969; expert cons, maritime and shipping leg, to Ghana, 1957; Ethiopia, 1963. Prin contbrs: Isr's merchant shipping leg; Isr's first road traffic code. Haganah, 1941-48; IAF, 1948. Chmn: Lawyers in Public Service Assn; academic profsls council, Lab Party, Jerusalem; vice-chmn, natl council, Isr Bar; mem: Supr Court of Histadrut, 1964-69; Disciplinary Court of State Civil Service, 1953-69; club, Lions Intl, Jerusalem. Author: Maritime Law, 1966; ed bd, haPraklit; contbr to legal periodicals. Recipient: Haganah Emblem; Aleh, State of Isr Fighters Decoration. Spec interests: theater, lit. Home: 29a S Levin St, Jerusalem, Isr. Office: 1 Ibn Gvirol St, Jerusalem, Isr.

MINTZER, Ida J, US, dermatologist; b. Vienna, Aus, Dec 10, 1893; d. Marcus and Zivia (Halpern); in US since 1900; MD, NY Med Coll and Hosp for Women, 1916; m. Bertram Krugman, Dec 25, 1920 (decd); c: Mitchel, Gloria Karmiohl, Joan Kornblum. Pvt practice since 1916; chief woman phys, Middletown State Hosp, 1917-19; instr, later clinical prof, dermat, Flower and Fifth Ave Hosp, 1919-30; asst att dermat: Metrop Hosp, 1930-35; Skin and Cancer Hosp, 1928; Mary Immaculate Hosp; and dir, dermat: Jamaica Hosp, 1930-59, and cons; Queens Gen Hosp, and cons; Triboro Hosp; Neponsit Hosp. FACP; f: Amer Bd Dermat and Syphilology NY Acad Med; mem: AMA; Queens Co Med Soc; LI Dermat Soc. Home and Office: 89-15 Parsons Blvd, Jamaica, NY.

MINTZER, Julius, US, organization exec; b. NYC, Aug 13, 1913; s. Hyman and Molly (Werfel); BS, NYU, 1934; MA, 1935; MS, Columbia U, 1940; grad cert, Training Bur for J Communal Service, 1950; m. Rhoda Glick, July 21, 1942; c: Susan, Amy, Kenneth. Exec dir, Richmond J Comty Council, since 1953; asst dir: DP Camp, UNRRA, Ger, 1945-46; JWF, Cincinnati, O, 1949-53. US Army, 1942-45. Secy, Cong Beth El, Richmond, Va; mem: natl comms, CJFWF; Natl Assn Social Workers; Va Council of Social Work. Recipient: dist man of the month, Amer J Times Outlook Mag, 1961. Home: 4507 Park Ave, Richmond, Va. Office: 5403 Monument Ave, Richmond, Va.

MIRMAN, Louis, US, accountant; b. Norfolk, Va, Dec 31, 1920; s. Morris and Lillian (Cooper); BS, Wharton Sch of Finance, U of Pa, 1942; m. Shirley Aron, Aug 6, 1950; c: Ina, Marc, Fay. Pvt practice since 1943. Commn, Natl B'nai B'rith Youth Org, 1962-68; chmn, adv bd, Norfolk chap, Order of De Molay, since 1961; mem: Natl Soc Public Acctnts Inc;

Masons; Shriners; bd, Beth El Temple; Southside Lions, fmr pres; fmr: pres, Temple Emanuel; Worshipful Master, Norfolk lodge 1, AF and AM; pres: Seabord chap, Va Soc Public Acctnts Inc; Acctnts Soc of Va, Inc; mem, Natl exec comm, Natl Comty Relations Adv Council; pres, Va state Assn of B'nai B'rith lodges; chmn, comty relations council, Norfolk JCC; pres, Thalia PTA. Recipient: Order of Chevalier; Legion of Honor; Cross of Honor; Order of De Molay; citation, outstanding mem, Va State Assn of B'nai B'rith lodges; Man of the Year, Arnold Gamsey lodge, B'nai B'rith, 1966. Home: 549 Holbrook Rd, Virginia Beach, Va. Office: 318 Lynn Shores Dr, Virginia Beach, Va.

MIRON, Dan, Isr, author, educator; b. Tel Aviv, Nov 13, 1934; s. Arieh and Malka (Singer); BA, Hebrew U, Jerusalem, 1957; PhD, Columbia U, NY, 1967; m. Yael Schocken, Aug 3, 1931; c: David, Menahem. Asst prof, U of Tel Aviv. IDF, 1956-58. Author: Chayim Hazaz, 1959; Arba Panim Basifrut Haivrit Bat Yameynu, 1962. Home: 42 Pincas St, Tel Aviv, Isr.

MIRON, Eliahu, Isr, attorney; b. Warsaw, Pol, Sep 18, 1921; s. Itzhak and Esther (Zolberg) Znamirowski; in Isr since 1932; att HS of Econ, Tel Aviv, 1939-41; law deg, Govt Law Classes, Jerusalem, 1946; m. Shoshana Halperin, Aug 14, 1945; c: Esther, Itzhak, Mordehai. Bd dirs, Isr Elec Corp, since 1956, chmn, finance comm, since 1964; in pvt law practice since 1954; legal adv: Munic of Tel Aviv, 1946-48; Mil Govt Hqr, 1948-49; head, local govt dept, Min of Interior, 1949-52, dir gen, 1952-53; Haganah, 1936-39; Palmach, 1940-47; maj, mil govt hqr, Six Day War; IDF, 1948-49. Mem, dist comm Isr Bar Assn, since 1961; chmn, leg comm, since 1966. Bd govs, mem, financial comm, Bar Ilan U, since 1956; bd, govs & exec comm since 1968; council, legal adv, Magan David Adom; bd dirs, exec comm, United Mizrachi Bank, since 1969; bd dirs, Maurice Pollack Found, since 1958; local govt council, since 1958; fmr Supr Court, ZC. Mem, ed bd, Psakim; contbr to jours. Home: 3 Shilo St, Tel Aviv, Isr. Office: 25A Lilienblum St, Tel Aviv, Isr.

MIRON, Issachar, Isr, composer, educator, editor, organization exec; b. Kutno, Pol, July 5, 1920; s. Shlomo and Chaya (Elbaum) Michrovsky; in Isr since 1939; m. Tsipora Tchetchik, Jan 25 1944; c: Ruth Schleider, Shlomit, Miriam. Asso prof, music, and chmn, music fac, J Tchrs Sem-People's U and Herzliah Heb Tchr Inst, NYC; head, info and spec events, Amer Friends Heb U, NYC, 1968-69; vice-pres, Star Records Enterprises, Inc, NYC, 1967-68; chmn bd, Bat Kol, Isr Music Jour, 1958-59; pres, Isr Composers League Publ, 1957-64; vice-pres: Isr Composers League, 1941-61; ACUM; Société d'Auteurs, Compositeurs et Editeurs de Musique en Isr; exec, Intl Culture Cens for Youth, NYC, 1965-67; exec vice-chmn and org, Amer-Isr Music Alliance; mus dir, Amer-Isr Cultural Found, 1961-65; Isr Min Educ and Culture, 1950-53. Brit Army, J Brig, 1940. Co-found, Amer for Music Libr in Isr; mus ed, Zemirot, JA folk music periodical, 1953-61; chief ed, Israel's first Arabic songbook, Garland of Melodies, 1953; composer of numerous songs, including: Tzena-Tzena; sym and chamber music; oratorios, arabesques for two flutes; trio for violin, cello and piano; music for horn and wind instruments; seven syncopated preludes for piano; passacaglia for moderns; liturgical music, including four complete Sabbath services for cantor, choir, organ and orchestra. Recipient: Isr Engel Prize for Music, 1959; Kavod Award, Cantors Assembly of Amer, 1956. Home: 515 W End Ave, New York, NY.

MIRON, Shabtai, Isr, business exec; b. Hislavitch, Russ, Mar 15, 1885; s. Itzhak and Faia (Prigozin) Mirenburg; in Isr since 1924; att U Saratov, 1906; m. Rebecca Ladijensky, Jan 30, 1918; c: Isaac. Mgr, Land and Loan Corp Ltd, since 1937; merchant and ind: Russ; Pal, 1925-31; found, dir, Agrobank, Ltd, 1931-59; chmn, Hamifde Haezrahi and Hashikun Haezrahi Ltd. Vice-chmn, bd govs, Heb U, since 1944, mem exec council; chmn, Friends of Heb U, Tel Aviv br, since 1935; mem: exec comm, Lib Zionists Org; exec, budget comms, Zionist Agcy in Isr; dir, Gen Zionist Club; exec comm, ZOA House, Tel Aviv. Co-found, mem exec council, Haboker, Heb daily. Home: 11 Ben Ami St, Tel Aviv, Isr. Office: 2 Pinsker St, Tel Aviv, Isr.

MIRON, Wilfrid Lyonel, Eng, solicitor; b. Llanelli, Wales, Jan 27, 1913; s. Solman and Minnie (Lyons); in Eng since 1934; m. Doreen Hill, Aug 19, 1958. Regional chmn, Natl Coal Bd, since 1967, on staff since 1946; solicitor, Shipley Collinis Ltd, 1938-46. Lt col, Brit Army, 1944-45. Chmn:

ind and trade comm, E Midlands Regional Econ Planning Council; Midland Miners Fatal Accident Relief Soc; vice-chmn, Berry Hill Hosp Mgmt Comm; JP, Co of Nottingham; trustee: Nottingham Trustee Savings Bank; Nottingham Poponir J Cong; gov comm, Nottingham U; mem: Nottingham Law Soc. Hobbies: music, cricket, rugby, football, theatre. Home: 24 Calstock Rd, Woodthorpe, Nottingham, Eng. Office: Eastwood Hall, Eastwood, Nottinghamshire, Eng.

MIRSKY, Aharon, Isr, educator; b. Nowogrodek, Pol, 1914; s. Isaak anu Rivkah (Ratner); in Isr since 1935; MA, PhD, Heb U, Jerusalem, 1952; m Itka Kirshenbaum, 1946; c: Isaak, Hananel, Nahum. Asso prof, Heb lit, Heb U, Jerusalem; tchr, Mizrachi Tchrs' Training Sch, 1946-53; ed, Bialik Inst, 1951-62. IDF, 1948-59. Mem: Heb Writers' Assn; Acad of Heb Lang. Author: Yalkut Happiyutim, 1958; Shirey Rabbi Isaak Ibn Halfun, 1961; Reshit Happiyut, 1962; Aley Siah, poems, 1966; Mahzavtan Shel Zuroth Happiyut, 1968; contbr to jours. Recipient: lit prize, Mizrachi, Mafdal, 1967. Home: 3 Ben-Labrat St, Jerusalem, Isr.

MIRSKY, David, US, educator; b. Jerusalem, Sep 7, 1921; s. Samuel and Shulamith (Solomon); in US since 1926; dipl, Tchrs Inst, Yeshiva U, 1939; BA, Yeshiva Coll, 1942; MA, Columbia U, 1948; ordained rabbi, Isaac Elchanan Theol Sem, 1945; m. Sarrah Appel, Feb 1, 1949; c: Zipporah, Moshe, Yehudah. Dean, Stern Coll, Yeshiva U, since 1968; dean, admissions, Yeshiva U, 1963-68, prof, Eng and Heb lit, since 1962, fac mem, since 1947; educ dir, Hapoel Hamizrachi, 1945-46; asst dir, NYU J Cultural Found, 1946-47; prin, Shulamith Midrasha, 1947-48; introduced achievement test in Heb lang into coll entrance examination bd, 1959. Pres, Histadruth Ivrith, since 1969; vice-pres: Hapoel Hamizrachi, 1948-58; Yeshiva Coll Alumni Assn, 1945; secy, Amer Profs for Peace in ME, since 1968; mem, Gov's Comm on Scholastic Achievement, NY; mem, exec comm, Yeshiva Coll Alumni Assn; mem: AAUP; MLA; Heb Acad; Eastern Assn of Deans B'nai Zion; NY State Assn of Deans and Guidance Personnel; Young Isr of W Side. Author: The Fictive Jew, 1948; The Jew in English Literature, 1953-54; Beginnings of Hebrew in the US, 1956; ed, J Horizon, 1945-52; contbr in Heb and Eng to mags. Home: 258 Riverside Dr, New York, NY. Office: Yeshiva U, Amsterdam Ave and 186 St, New York, NY.

MIRSKY, I Arthur, US, physician, psychiatrist, educator; b. Montreal, Can, Mar 28, 1907; s. Solomon and Esther (Shapiro); in US since 1931; BS, McGill U, Montreal, 1927, MS, 1929, MD, 1931; m. Eleanor Fels, Aug 25, 1931; c: Lynn, O'Connor, Elisabeth Goldman, U of Pittsburgh prof-at-large, dir, Lab of Clinical Sci, since 1966, prof and chmn, extern and Oliver Rhea f in experimental med, NY Postgrad Hosp, 1931-33; f, dept phys, U of Chgo, Ill, 1933-35; asst dir, dept, metabolic research, Nelson Morris Inst, Michael Reese Hosp, Chgo, 1933-35; mem staff, J Hosp, Cincinnati, O, 1935-51, dir, May Inst for Med Research, 1935-51; instr, dept of biol chem, U of Cincinnati, O, 1938-40, asst prof, 1940-46, asso prof, experimental med, 1946-51, asso prof, psycht, 1947-51; clinical research cons, Eli Lilly and Co, Indianapolis, Ind, 1946-51; cons, Cincinnati Gen Hosp, dept psycht, 1946-51, mem staff, dept med, 1946-51. Lt col, US Army, 1942-46. F: AAAS; Amer Coll Phys; Amer Diabetes Assn; Amer Soc Clinical Path; Clinical Soc of Pittsburgh Diabetes Assn; Clinical Soc for NY Diabetes Assn, hon f, 1950; NY Acad Scis; fmr pres: council on diabetes, Public Health Fed, Cincinnati, 1949-50; Amer Psychosomatic Soc, 1956-57; mem, bd dirs, Gamma of Pa, hon mem, 1954; mem: sci research comm on mental illness, Natl Assn for Mh, since 1954; sci council, AHA; council, Amer Psychosomatic Soc, 1948-50; Amer Chem Soc; AMA; Amer Phys Soc; O State Med Soc; Phila Psychan Soc; Pittsburgh Neuropsycht Soc; Amer Psycht Assn; Amer Psychan Assn; Amer Soc for Clinical Inves; Assn for Study of Internal Secretions; Assn for Research in Nervous and Mental Diseases; Cen Soc for Clinical Research; Cincinnati Soc of Neur and Psycht; Fed for Clinical Research; Soc for Experimental Biol and Med; Soc for Biol Research, U of Pittsburgh; Allegheny Co Med Soc; Pa Assn for Study of Animal Behavior; AAUP; Alpha Omega Alpha; Sigma Xi. Ed, Dibetes Abstracts and Proc of Amer Diabetes Assn, 1941-47; asso ed, Amer Jour Clinical Inves, 1941-51; mem, ed bds: Psychosomatic Med, 1948-60; Cincinnati Jour of Med, 1947-50; contbr to med and sci jours. Home: 7021 Meade Place, Pittsburgh, Pa. Office: U of Pittsburgh, Sch of Med, 3811 O'Hara St, Pittsburgh, Pa.

MIRVIS, Allan, US, rabbi; b. Baltimore, Md, Feb 17, 1918; s. Harry and Sarah (Cohen); BA, Yeshiva Coll, 1939; ordained rabbi, Isaac Elchanan Theol Sem, 1941; m. Lena Sear, Mar 12, 1944; c: David, Theodore. Rabbi, Cong B'nai Isr, Hampton, Va, since 1942; auxiliary chaplain: Ft Eustis: Kecoughtan Vet Facility; Langley, Air Force Base; E State Hosp, 1941-44, 1950-52. Secy, Hampton JCC, since 1944; mem, bd dirs: ARC; NCCJ; mem: Peninsula Zionist Dist; Rab CA; Tidewater Bd of Rabbis. Home: 158 Algonquin Rd, Hampton, Va. Study: 3116 Kecoughtan Rd, Hampton, Va.

MISCHAKOFF, Mischa, US, musician, educator; b. Proskurov, Russ, Apr 6, 1897; s. Isaac and Massia (Fishberg); in US since 1921; BA, St Petersburg Conservatory, 1912; DMus, U of E Mich; m. Hortense Moritz, Sep 30, 1937; c: Paul, Anne, Matthew. Violinist since 1918; concert master: Detroit Sym, since 1952; Chautauqua Sym, since 1924; prof: Wayne State U; Peabody Conservatory, Baltimore, Md; spec guest concert master, Baltimore Sym; head, violin dept, Chautauqua Inst, 1924; prof, Conservatory of Nighni-Novgorod, Russ, 1918-19; soloist, Bolshoi Theater, 1919-20; leader: Mischakoff Quartet, 1923; Detroit Trio, 1952; concert master: Warsaw Philharmonic, 1920-21; NY Sym, 1921-23; Phila Orch, 1927-30; Chgo Sym, 1930-37; NBC Orch under Toscanini, 1937-52; guest prof: U of Colo, 1950-51, 1954; Royal Conservatory of Toronto, 1953; Russ Army, WW I. Mem: Chamber Music Soc of Detroit; Bohemian Soc of NY; Temple Isr, Detroit; J Comty Cen. Recipient: Laureate, Gold Medal and Anton Rubenstein Prize, Imperial Conservatory of St Petersburg, 1912. Home: 18695 Fairfield, Detroit, Mich.

MISHEIKER, Aron, S Afr, secretary; b. Shavli, Lith, Nov 12, 1912; s. Maurice and Rachel (Sroliowitz); in S Afr since 1934; att U Kaunas, 1930-34; BA, U Witwatersrand, 1941; f, fac of secretaries, London; m. Beatrice Fairly, Oct 24, 1942; c: Jonathan, Ilona Guinsberg. Gen sec, S Afr Bd of J Educ, since 1943; ed, J Herald, 1940-43. Contbr short stories, articles to jours. Hobbies: writing, swimming. Home: 27 Melrose Gardens, North St, Illovo, Johannesburg, S Afr. Office: S Afr Bd of J Educ, POB 2942, Johannesburg, S Afr.

MISHEIKER, Betty, S Afr, author, songwriter, composer; b. Pretoria, June 7, 1919; d. Kalman and Yetta (Bloch) Fairly; m. Aron Misheiker, Oct 24, 1942; c: Jonathan, Ilona. Script and songwriter for radio, S Afr, since 1956; three one-hour radio musicals; dramatized David Copperfield as radio serial; author and composer: children's musical plays: Watermelons, 1962; The Old Kabobly Tree, 1966; Senor Onyon, 1966; Jack and the Turtledoves, 1968; two albums of children's songs; album of Afrikaans Children's Songs; composed lyrics and music for children's songs recorded in: S Afr; Eng; Australia; wrote numerous children's radio progs of stories and songs. Author: Strange Odyssey, 1952, US ed, Wings on Her Petticoat, 1953; books for children: Handsome Piggywig, 1963; The Bear Who Wanted the Mostest, 1963; contbr articles, short stories, book reviews. Mem: PEN Club; Performing Right Soc; Amer Guild of Authors and Composers; Songwriters Guild of Gt Brit. Hobby: cooking. Home: 27 Melrose Gardens, North St, Illovo, Johannesburg, S Afr. Office: POB 7738, Johannesburg, S Afr.

MISHKIN, Leah, US, librarian, communal worker; b. Slobodka, Lith, July 19, 1909; d. Nisson and Czippe (Klibansky) Yablonsky; in US since 1924; att Lewis Inst, 1928-31; BHL, Heb Theol Coll, 1930; m. Leonard Mishkin, Aug 4, 1931; c: Annette, Marguerite. Libr, J U of Amer, since 1938 asst, 1927-31, 1935-38. Pres, Ivriah Assn, since 1951; mem, exec: Rel Zionists Hadassah; JNF; Yeshiva Women. Bibligrapher: Heb and Yiddish publs in Chgo, 1952; Festschriften of J Educ Instns, 1961. Hobbies: ex libris, J art folkore. Home: 3530 Lake Lake Shore Dr, Chicago, Ill. Office: 7135 N Carpenter Rd, Skokie, Ill.

MISHKIN, Leonard C, US, rabbi, school system supt; b. Lith, Oct 15, 1907; s. Zalman and Sara (Silberman); in US since 1921; ordained rabbi, Heb Theol Coll, 1929; BS, Lewis Inst, 1937; PhD, Chgo Coll of Law, 1944; DHL, Heb Theol Coll, 1954; m. Leah Yablonsky, Aug 4, 1931; c: Annette, Marguerite. Supt, Asso Talmud Torahs of Chgo, since 1936; lectr, educ, practical rabbinics and hist of medieval J, Heb Theol Coll, since 1941, visiting prof, hist, since 1953; instr, Heb Theol Coll, 1930-31; rabbi, Cong Beth Israel, New Orleans, 1930-35. Pres: RabCA, 1937-39, Chgo chap, 1948-52; vice-chmn, Chgo chap, NCCJ; mem, exec bd: Natl Council of J Educ; Chgo Tercentenary Comm; Keren Hatzala of Chgo; Chgo J All-Day Sch Found; Mizrachi Org of Amer; Heb Theol Coll; J Peoples Inst; JNF; Vaad Hapoel. Author:

Life and Times of Jehajah Hapenini Bedareshi, 1929; History of the Jews in Languedoc, 1931; Responsa of Rabbenu Gershom, 1951, Heb; contbr articles on J and Judaism to World Book Ency, Yiddish and Eng publs. Recipient: Rabbi of the Year, Chgo Tribune, 1954. Home: 3530 N Lake Shore Dr, Chicago, Ill.

MISHKIN, Paul J, US, educator; b. Trenton, NJ, Jan 1, 1927; s. Mordecai and Bella (Dworetsky); BA, Columbia U, 1947, LLB, Law School, 1950; m. Audrey Johnson, 1965. Prof, law, U of Pa, since 1957, fac mem since 1950; spec cons, City Solicitor of Phila, 1953; reporter, Amer Law Inst study of div of jurisdiction between Fed and State Courts, 1960-65; visiting prof: political sci, Haverford Coll, 1960-61; law, U of Mich, 1961; law, U of Tex, 1964. USN, 1945-46. F, Cen for Advanced Study in Behavioral Scis, 1965; mem: Bar of US Supr Court; Bar of NY; Amer Law Inst; Phi Beta Kappa. Co-author: On Law in Courts, 1965; contbr to legal jours. Recipient: Rockefeller Found research grant, Eng, 1956. Home: 625 Broad Acres Rd, Narberth, Pa. Office: U of Pa Law Sch, 3400 Chestnut St, Philadelphia, Pa.

MISHKINSKY, Moshe Yehuda, Isr, educator; b. Bialistok, Pol, June 12, 1917; s. Chaim and Joheved (Fayans); in Isr since 1936; PhD, Heb U Jerusalem; m. Masha Osherovsky; c: Gavriella. Sr lectr, modern J hist: Heb U, Jerusalem; Tel Aviv U. Chmn, Students Union, Jerusalem; dir, Project on the J Lab Movement, Heb U; mem, Council of Inst for Lab Research, Beit Berl. Author of essays and contbr to jours. Home: 27 Gnessin St, Givatayim, Isr. Office: Heb U, Jerusalem; Tel Aviv U, Tel Aviv, Isr.

MISHKOVSKY, Zelda, Isr, author; b. Tchernigoff, Russ; d. Shalom and Rachel (Chein) Schneerson; att Mizrachi Tchrs Sem, Jerusalem; m. Chaim Mishkovsky. Fmr tchr. Author: Pnai, book of verse; contbr of verse and prose to mags and press. Home: 31 Zepania St, Jerusalem, Isr.

MITCHEL, Claire, US, public relations exec; b. NYC, Feb 7, 1921; d. Bernard and Yetta (Israel) Furman; att O State U; m. Arnold Mitchel, Oct 13, 1941; c: Jeffrey, Madelaine Miller. Dir, public info, comty action commn, OEO, Cincinnati area, since 1965; owner, Claire Mitchel PR since 1959; dir, PR, Schindler-Howard Advt Agcy, 1961. Contbr to profsl jours. Home: 4514 Perth Lane, Cincinnati, O. Office: 820 Linn Mall, Cincinnati, O.

MITCHEL, Philip H, US, attorney; b. Chgo, Ill, Nov 13, 1904; s. Michael and Rose (Cohen); att U of Chgo; LLB, DePaul U, 1925; m. Lillian Dulsky, June 8, 1927; c: Michael, Diane Gilbert. Master in chancery, Circuit Court, Cook Co, Ill, since 1943; pvt practice, since 1926. Pres: Dist 6, B'nai B'rith lodge, 1952-53; Intl vice-pres, commn ADL; mem, Intl Council, all B'nai B'rith; club, Covenant, Ill, pres 1958-60. Home: 2970 Lake Shore Dr, Chicago, Ill. Office: 33 N LaSalle St, Chicago, Ill.

MITCHELL, Edward D, US, business exec; b. Monosterysk, Pol, Sep 11, 1889; s. Benjamin and Kayla (Seltzer); in US since 1930; m. Anna Copp, Feb, 1914; c: Kayla, Elaine, Joseph, Edith. Hon chmn bd, Beneficial Standard Life Insurance Co, LA, Cal, chmn bd, since 1947, pres, 1940-47; chmn bd, Beneficial Standard; pres, Jackson-Mitchell Pharmaceutical, LA, since 1936. Treas, United JWF, 1953, pres, Key Men, 1951, chmn: spec gifts, 1947-50; Beverly Hills div, 1946, 1947; mem, natl council, JDC, since 1946; clubs: Hillcrest Country; Tamarisk Country; Harmonie; Cavendish; NYC Athletic. Home: 910 Benedict Canyon Rd, Beverly Hills, Cal. Office: 3700 Wilshire Blvd, Los Angeles, Cal.

MITCHELL, Joseph N, US, insurance exec; b. Winnipeg, Can, Oct 10, 1922; s. Edward and Anna (Copp); in US since 1931; att UCLA; m. Beverly Henigson, Oct 27, 1946; c: Jonathan, Jan, Karin. Pres: Beneficial Standard Corp; and dir, BIG Service, Phila, Pa; dir: Brit Pacific Life Ins, BC; Transit Casualty, St Lous, Mo; Selective Ins, Cincinnati, O; Beneficial Natl Life Ins, NY; Bank of St Louis, Mo; Gen Bancshares, St Louis; vice-pres: Ampal Amer-Isr, NY; and asst secy, Jackson-Mitchell Pharms, Cal; chmn, Beneficial Standard Life Ins; fmr: treas, dir, exec vice-pres, pres, Beneficial Fire and Casualty Ins, and Beneficial Standard Life; pres, dir, Vt Accident Ins. Fr interpreter, US Army Signal Corps, 1942-46. Mem exec comm, State of Isr Bonds; mem: bd dirs, Cedars Sinai Med Cen; trustee, secy, treas, Edward and Anna Mitchell Family Found; fmr: mem: Key Gifts Comm; Cen LA bd dirs; exec comm, United Crusade Comm, Gen Fund Raising

Comm; chmn: Govt and Educ; Profsls Div, United Way and United Crusade; mem: Amer Comm for Weizmann Inst of Sci; Young Pres' Org; Mayor's Steering Comm on Urban Coalition, LA; Dist Atty's Adv Council; bd dirs, Commerce Assos; ADL; Meninger Found Assn; US C of C; Cal-Isr C of C; Cal State, LA C of C; mgmt comm, Comty Service Comm; chmn, JWF comm; vice-chmn, maj gifts comm, JWF, vice-pres, J Fed Council of Gtr LA; bd trustees, inves comm, J Comty Found; natl campaign cabinet, UJA; exec comm, JDC; bd trustees, J Cens Assn; bd govs, Technion Soc; AJCong; clubs: Cent; Hillcrest Country, treas, mem, bd dirs; Tamarisk Country; LA. Hobbies: golf, photography, bridge. Home: 1001 N Roxbury Dr, Beverly Hills, Cal. Office: 3700 Wilshire Blvd, Los Angeles, Cal.

MITGANG, Herbert, US, journalist, author; b. NYC, Jan 20, 1920; s. Benjamin and Florence (Altman); LLB, St Johns Law Sch, 1941; m. Shirley Kravchick, May 13, 1945; c: Esther, Lee, Laura. Ed writer, mem, ed bd, NY Times, 1963-64 and since 1967, copy ed, reviewer, 1945-54, supervising ed, Sunday drama sect, 1955-62; asst to pres, exec ed, CBS News, 1964-67. Counter intelligence, USAC, 1942-43; Army corresp, mgn ed, Stars and Stripes, N Afr, Sicily, It, Corsica, Greece, 1943-45. Pres, Authors Guild of Amer, since 1971; mem council Authors League of Amer, since 1962; exec bd, PEN, Amer delg, Intl Exec Comm, London, 1969; mem: Soc of Amer Hist; Cent Assn; Temple Emanuel, Great Neck, NY. Author: Lincoln as They Saw Him, 1956, 1971; The Return, novel, 1959; The Man Who Rode the Tiger: The Life of Judge Samuel Seabury, 1963; Working for the Reader, Art War, Politics in Books, 1970; Lincoln's Long Shadow, 3 vol hist, 1971; Spectator of America, 1971; ed: Washington, DC, in Lincoln's Times, 1958, 1971; Civilians Under Arms: Stars and Stripes, Civil War to Korea, 1959; America at Random, Topics of The Times, 1970; The Letters of Carl Sandburg, 1969; TV documentary writer-produc: Carl Sandberg at Gettysburg; Lincoln's Prairie Years; Henry Moore, Man of Form; Ben Gurion on the Bible; Anthony Eden on Vietnam; D-Day Plus 20 years; Eisenhower Returns to Normandy; contbr articles and book reviews to publs. Recipient: Gavel Award, Amer Bar Assn, 1964, 1969, 1970; Broadcast Preceptor Award, SF State Coll, 1970. Home: 21 Nirvana Ave, Great Neck, NY. Office: 229 W 43 St, New York, NY.

MITLER, Milton Donald, US, business exec; b. West NY, NJ, Mar 29, 1925; s. Morris and Minnie (Hein); BS, U of Richmond, 1948; att Northwestern U, Chgo, 1943-44; m. Barbara Zuckerman, Dec 20, 1950; c: Marci, Wendi. Pres, owner Atlas-Hartley Corp, since 1962, vice-pres, 1948-62. Lt, USN, 1943-46. Mem: exec bd, Young Men's Group, Einstein Coll; Kiwanis, Ardsley, NY; head, drive, Young Men's Div, Westchester For Fed. Hobbies: walking, travel, educ. Home: 4 Agnes Circle, Ardsley, NY. Office: 261 Fifth Ave, New York, NY.

MITTLEMAN, Anna R, US, artist; b. NYC, Jan 15, 1898; d. Barnet and Rebecca (Ginsburg) Rivlin; att NYU; m. George Mittleman, Dec 30, 1917; c: Myron, Helen Laper. Artist since 1937; mental guidance lectr, women's groups, Radio Sta WBBC, 1942-45; asst ed, Modern Psychol Mag, 1942-45. Numerous one-man shows in NY; one-man mus exhbs; exhb in group shows through US, Ger, Japan; one-man touring exhb in mus thoughout US; included in perm collections of numerous mus; Archives of Amer Art. F, Royal Soc of Art, London; mem: Natl Assn Women Artists; Artists Equity; Bklyn Soc Painters and Sculptors; Mus of Modern Art; NJ Soc Sculptors and Painters; Natl Council J Women; Amer Humane League. Home and studio: 710 Park Ave, New York, NY.

MITTLEMAN, Norman Dale, US, dentist; b. Cleveland, O, July 31, 1939; s. Harry and Dorothy (Shapiro); att Adelbert Coll of W Reserve U, Cleveland, 1957-60; DDS, Sch of Dent, W Reserve U, 1964; m. Margery Millsberg, Aug 4, 1960; c: Sheryl, Harold, Howard. Pres: Norman D Mittleman & Ronald L Rhodes, Inc, since 1966; Normark Producs, Inc, since 1970; lectr, W Reserve U Dent Sch, 1967. Capt, USAF, Dent Corps, 1964-66. Mem: comms, Cleveland Dent Soc; Alpha Omega; JWF; Amer Dent Soc; O State Dent Assn; Amer Analgesia Soc; Amer Pin Implant Soc; Phi Sigma Delta; Cleveland Acad for Dent Studies; club, Hawthorne Valley Country. Hobbies: travel, golf, motorcycling. Home: 5412 Chickadee Lane, Lyndhurst, O. Office: 3104 W 25 St, Cleveland, O.

MIZAFON, Daniel, Isr, government official; b. Alexandrovsk,

Russ, Nov 10, 1918; s. Raman and Agrafin a(Nitchaiava) Yurkin; in Isr since 1923; div; c: Dan, Michael, Rafael, Dalya. Dir, road transp, Haifa and N Dist, since 1960; mgr, Port of Eilat, 1955-60. Maj, IDF, 1948-55. Recipient: Palestine Medal; Afr Star. Hobbies: painting, music. Home: 1 Dreifus St, Haifa, Isr. Office: 82 Haatzmaut St, Haifa, Isr.

MIZRAHI, Joseph, Isr, accountant; b. Athens, Grreece, Dec 23, 1923; s. Mordehai and Fanny (Goldstein); in Isr since 1945; m. Hanna Hamburger, Feb 4, 1947; c: Gila, Judith. Dept chief, Solel Boneh, since 1963. IDF, 1948-49. Gen secy: Union of Greek Jewry in Isr; Claims Comm of Greek Jewry in Isr; mem, Tel Aviv Secretariat, Lab Party. Home: 8 Aharonovitch St, Tel Aviv, Isr. Office: 111 Allenby St, Tel Aviv, Isr.

MLOTEK, Joseph, US, author, communal leader; b. Proszewice, Pol, July 25, 1918; s. Zalman and Feygl Nirenberg; in US since 1949; att: YIVO Inst for Soc Research, Vilna, Pol, 1940-41; J Tchrs Sem, NYC, 1949-51; New Sch for Soc Research, NYC, 1951-54; m. Eleanor Gordon, Aug 7, 1949; c: Zalman, Mark. Educ dir, Workmen's Circle, since 1966, exec secy, Cen Sch Comm, 1952-66; journalist, Naye Folks Tseitung, Warsaw, Pol, 1936-39; tchr Workmen's Circle Schs and HS, 1949-51; exec secy, Youth Dept, Cong for J Culture, since 1950. Author: Yiddishe Kinder-Alef, primer for J schs, 1956; records, issued by educ dept, Workmen's Circle: This, Golden Land; Lomir Zingen; Amol iz geven a Mayse; Zingt Mit Mir; Songs of the E Side; ed: Traditions and Secular Jewishness; Culture and Educ, 1966-67; Culture and Life, since 1967; Kindertzeitung, since 1963; Parents Bull, since 1960. Vice-pres: J Tchrs Sem and Herzliah Inst, NYC; Cong for J Culture, NYC; secy treas, Forward Assn, J Daily Forward and Radio Sta WEVD; secy, M Chanin Culture Found, Inc, NYC; exec mem, J Lab Comm, NYC; mem: Workmen's Circle; Amer Assn for J Educ, NYC. Home: 3605 Sedgwick Ave, New York, NY. Office: 175 E Broadway, New York, NY.

MNOOKIN, I J, US, hospital exec; b. Kansas City, Mo, Feb 23, 1913; s. Jacob and Denah (Goldman); BS, U of Ill, 1933, JD, 1935; m. Marion Sittenfeld, Dec 26, 1937; c: Robert, James. Pres, Diamant's Inc, 1959-65, with firm since 1939; mem, Charno and Drummond, attys, 1935-39. Life dir, Menorah Med Cen, 1956-65, fmr vice-pres, mem, bd councillors; mem: bd, J Fed, Kan City, since 1947; J Comty Cen, since 1954; B'nai B'rith; fmr: pres, vice pres, treas, mem, exec comm, bd govs, midcen region, CJFWF; vice-pres, J Vocational Services, Kan City; mem bd, J Family Service; regional chmn, UJA, Mo and Kan; chmn, coord comm on refs, Council of Social Agcys; mem: bd dirs, United J Social Service; bd councillors, Home for J Aged; regional adv, Sigma Alpha Mu; club, Oakwood Country. Home: 4550 Warwick, Kansas City, Mo. Office: 4949 Rockhill Rd, Kansas City, Mo.

MOAV, Rom, Isr, scientist; b. Afula, Isr, June 24, 1930; s. Abraham and Sara (Milirovich) Milstein; BSc, UCLA, 1953; MA, U Col, Berkeley, PhD, 1957; m. Jehudith Glasner, Mar 20, 1958; c: Omer, Jael. Head, genet dept, Heb U, Jerusalem, since 1968, sr lectr since 1958. Prin contribs: devl of fish genet in Isr. IDF, 1948-50. Pres, natl comm, League for Abolishment of Rel Coercion in Isr, Jerusalem chap. Exec ed, publisher, Shirei Rachel Umichtaveiha Bichtav Yada, 1969; contbr to profsl jours. Home: Ramat-Motza, Jerusalem, Isr. Office: Heb U, Jerusalem, Isr.

MOCH, Jules, Fr, statesman; b. Paris, Fr, Mar 15, 1893; s. Gaston and Alice (Pontremoli); grad: Ecole Polytechnique, 1912; Ecole des Ingénieurs de la Marine, 1919, both Paris; m. Germaine Picard, Jan 24, 1917; c: André (killed in action), Raymond. Delg to Natl Assembly, since 1928; dir, Service for Ind and Agric Rehab in Ger, 1918-20; engr, 1920-27; delg of l'Hérault, 1928-40; Undersecy of State, Blum's cabinet, 1936; Min of Public Works, 1938; mem, Consultative Assembly of Algiers, 1944; delg, Natl Constituent Assembly, Natl Assembly; Min of Public Works, 1945-47; Min of Interior, Vice-PM, 1947-50; Min of Defense, 1950-51; Min of Interior, 1958. War service, 1914-18; Fr Navy, 1939-40; imprisoned for voting against constitutional power for Pétain, 1940-41; Free Fr Navy, London, 1943. Prin works: Jean Jaurès et les Problèmes du Temps Présent; Le Rail et la Nation; Capitalisme et les Transports; L'Espagne Républicaine; Guerre aux Trusts; Arguments Socialistes; Confrontations; Yougoslavie, Terre d'Expériences; Alerte; La Folie des Hommes; Histoire du Réarmement Allemand depuis

1950; Rencontres avec Darlan et Eisenhower; contbr to press and periodicals. Recipient: Croix de Guerre, 1918, 1945, with 5 citations; Commandeur de la Légion d'Honneur; Médaille de la Résistance with Rosette. Home: 45 Allée de la Forêt, 78 La Celle St Cloud, Fr.

MOCHLY, Josef, Isr, architect; b. Bârlad, Rum, Apr 18, 1920; s. Carol and Sofia (Goldenstein) Zisman; in Isr since 1938; att: U of Rome, It; Technion, Haifa; m. Alda Delostrologo, May 18, 1946; c: Dan, Dafna, Daria, David, Dagan, Exec, J Mochly Ltd, architects, since 1959; asso prof, Technion, Haifa, since 1952; partner, Zevet architects, 1952-57. Capt, Brit Army, IDF. Prin contribs: lab design, Isr and abroad. Mem: Assn of Engrs and Architects, Isr; Illuminating Engr Soc. Contbr profsl papers on lab design. Hobbies: music, bomb disposal. Home: Shave Zion, Isr. Office: 4 Vitkin St, Haifa, Isr.

MOCKTON, Leslie, Eng, communal leader; b. Manchester, Eng, Aug 5, 1928; s. Isaac and Hetty (Forester); m. Rachel Jaswon, Aug 25, 1959; c: Elizabeth, Joyce, Isaac. Min: Bradford Heb Cong, since 1965; Barking and Becontree Heb Cong, 1955-58; asst min, W End Gt Syn, 1958-65. Wfr off, Bradford J Benevolent Soc; vice-pres, UN Assn, Bradford; comm mem, Bradford Citizens' Advice Bur; mem, B'nai B'rith. Hobbies: music, walking, handicrafts. Home: 264 Bradford Rd, Shipley, Yorks, Eng. Study: The Synagogue, Spring Gardens, Bradford 1, Eng.

MODAN, Baruch, Isr, physician; b. Krakow, Pol, Mar 16, 1932; s. Gdaliahu and Tova (Kutainer) Vagshul; in Isr since 1940; MD, Heb U, Jerusalem, 1958; MPH, Johns Hopkins U, 1962, DPH, 1964; m. Michaela Segal, Feb 26, 1959; c: Dalit, Ruth. Head, dept, clinical epidemiology, Tel Hashomer Hosp, since 1965; research f, Johns Hopkins U, 1961-64; res, hematology, Mt Sinai Hosp, NYC, 1959-61. Lt, IDF, 1950-52. Prin contribs: research in chronic disease and cancer epidemiology; evaluation of clinical and epidemiological aspects of polycythemia. F: Amer Public Health Assn; Intl Soc Hematology; mem: NY Acad Sci; Intl Assn Epidemiologists; AAAS; Amer Fed for Clinical Research; IMA; Isr Genet Soc; Isr Assn Public Health Phys. Contbr to profsl publs. Hobbies: theater, travel. Home: Emek Dotan 14, Tel Hashomer, Isr. Office: Tel Hashomer Govt Hosp, Isr.

MODAY, Yitzhak, Isr, business exec; b. Tel Aviv, Jan 17, 1926; s. Michael and Bracha Medzovitch; BS, Technion, Haifa, 1947; BA, LSE, 1953; LLB, Tel Aviv U, 1960; m. Michal Harrison, June 3, 1953; c: Harela, Boaz, Galia. Gen mgr, Revlon, Isr, Ltd, since 1961; site engr, Fertilizer Chemicals, 1953-56; opr mgr: Shell Chem 1956-58; Paz Chems, 1959-61. Lt col, IDF, 1948-53. Chmn, Technion Alumni Assn, 1959-61; exec bd mem: Isr-Amer Chamber of Ind and Commerce; Maccabi, Isr; Inds Assn; Lib Party, 1963-68; Advertisers Assn, 1966-68; mem: Soc Cosmetic Chems, US; Lions, Isr. Spec interest: politics. Home: 65a Hanassi St, Herzliya, Isr. Office: Revlon Ltd, Ashdod, Isr.

MODIANO, Sam Elie, Greece, journalist; b. Salonika, Greece, Apr 29, 1895; s. Elie and Allegra (Coen); degs in phil and Fr lit, Sorbonne, Paris; grad, journalism and advt, Milan and London; m. Nella Cenio, June 30, 1920; c: Elie, Mario. Corresp in Greece: Daily Telegraph, Sunday Telegraph, J Chronicle, all London; Chicago Tribune; mgr, chief corresp, Greece and Turkey, Reuters News Agency, 1944-68. Author: The World War I; other historical books and studies on Balkan Peninsula, 1920-40; publisher, Le Progrès de Salonique, main Fr lang J jour, 1922-41. Participated actively in rescue of Jews from Salonika during Nazi persecution. Recipient: Polish Gold Medal of Merit; It and Fr MC, WW I; off: Fr Acad; Brit Empire; Crown of It and Rum; Cdr of Royal Order of the Phoenix of Greece. Home: 39 Patriarchou Ioakim St, Athens, Greece.

MOISEEFF, Moise, US, business exec; b. Russ, Feb 5, 1905; s. Mendel and Beila (Esinovsky); in US since 1946; PhD, U of Liège, Belgium, 1929; m. Esther Ponevejsky, Aug 30, 1925; c: Gregory, Simonne. Gen mgr, Ponve Inves Co, since 1946; dist sales mgr, NV Philips, Belgium, 1929-40; co-dir, ed, Revue des Sciences Economiques, Liège, 1929-40; ed writer, Unser Lebn, Brussels, 1938-40. Mem: AJCong; Amer Econ Assn; Beth Sholom; club, Commonwealth, Cal. Contbr to publs. Spec interests: gen econ theory; Isr and intl relations. Home: 2809 Mariposa Dr, Burlingame, Cal.

MOLDAUER, Irving, US, attorney; b. Bklyn, NY, Sep 23,

1906; s. Osias and Pauline (Sinkovitz); LLB, St Lawrence U, Bklyn, 1927; m. Esther Stulman, Mar 8, 1942; c: Nancy Lehrer, Patricia Tabnik, Joan. Pvt practice; partner: Hirsh, Newman, Reass & Becker, 1933-42; Moldauer & Tepper, 1955-56; Moldauer & Katz, 1963-69. Trustee, Cong Beth Sholom, Lawrence, NY; clubs: Inwood Country; Unity, Bklyn, NY. Hobbies: golf, fishing. Home: 18 Pine St, Woodmere, NY. Office: 1501 Broadway, New York, NY.

MOLDAVSKY, Leon F, US, obstetrician, gynecologist; b. Schenectady, NY, Nov 23, 1911; s. Frank and Pauline (Poch); AB, Reserve U, 1931; MS, Grad Sch Med, U of Ill, 1932, BM, 1937, MD, 1938. Pvt practice, since 1946; chief, obstet and gyn: Citizens Hosp, Barberton, O, 1952-59, 1961-69, chief staff, 1960; Akron Gen Hosp, Akron, O, 1968-69, vice-chief staff, 1969-70; chief, staff, 1970-71; courtesy staff, obstet and gyn: St Thomas Hosp; City Hosp, both Akron, O. Maj, US Army, MC, 1942-45. F: Intl Coll Surgs, 1949; AMA, 1949; Amer Coll Obstet and Gyn, 1951; Amer Coll Surgs, 1949; Amer Geriatrics Soc, 1969; life f, Amer Soc Abdominal Surgs; dipl: Amer Bd Obstet and Gyn, 1948; Intl Bd Surg, 1949; mem: Sci Research Soc Amer; Assn Mil Surgs; World Med Assn; Sigma Xi; Phi Lambda Kappa; Summit Co Med Assn; O State Med Assn; AAAS; Soc for Study of Sterility and Fertility; O Acad of Sci; Akron Art Inst; Akron J Cen; Barberton C of C; B'nai B'rith; Amer Legion; JWV; Masons; Shriners; club, Rosemont Country. Contbr to med jours. Hobbies: medical photography, golf. Home: 143 Schocalog Rd, Akron, O. Office: 1000 Second Natl Bldg, Akron, O.

MOLDOVER, Edward David, US, attorney; b. Albany, NY, Feb 21, 1926; s. Abraham and Lilly (Sanders); AB, Cornell U, 1945, MA, 1946; LLB, Harvard Law Sch, 1949; m. Nancy Helpern, July 22, 1956. Mem, law firm, Moldover, Hauser and Strauss. Pres, NY Chap, AJComm; mem: bd govs, exec bd, Domestic Affairs Comm and Comty Services Comm, Natl AJComm; counsel to NY State Comm for Public Higher Educ and Comm for Public Educ and Rel Liberty; Amer, NY State, NYC, NY Co Bar Assns. Author: The Poll Tax as a Limitation on Suffrage in the US. Home: 2 Peter Cooper Rd, New York, NY. Office: 110 E 42 St, New York, NY.

MOLHO, Isaac R, Isr, business exec, author; b. Salonika, Greece, Aug 25, 1894; s. Raphael and Yaffa (de Botton); in Isr since 1919; att Beth Yosef Rabb Sem, Salonika; m. Simha Cohen, 1921; c: Raphael, Yaffa, Sara. Mgr, Mildand Co Ltd, since 1946; ed, Otzar Yehudei Sfarad, since 1959; fmr: mgr, Gaumont and MGM Film Co, for Pal, Trans-Jordan, Iraq, Iran; owner, Noga Film Co. Fmr: pres: Ohel Yosef Sephardic Syn; Isr-Greece Assn; Isr-Fr Assn; Isr Assn of Film Distributors; chmn: Misgav la Dakh Hosp; Sephardic Comty Council, Jerusalem; mem: Acad of Cordoba; Acad of Bogotá, Colombia; adv council, Kol Yerushalayim and Kol Zion la-Gola radio stas, org, Fr progs; gen educ council, Vaad Leumi; Beth Haam Comm; Inst Cen Ibero Amer, España y Portugal; hon collaborator, Inst Miguel Cervantes of Madrid; co-found: Rehavia Quarter; Jerusalem Inst for Blind; Ha-Hed, monthly; corresp mem, Acad de Buenas Letres, Barcelona, Spain; delg, Intl Conf of Sephardic Comtys, Amsterdam; treas, Jerusalem br, Isr Assn for UN. Author: Las Diversas Tentativas de Reformar la Nacionalidad Judia, 1912; Moshe Almosnino, 1942; Behair ha-Mizrah, 1944; Yosef Marco Baruch, 1946; Tor ha-Zahav le Toldot Saloniki, 1948; Douceur du Samedi, 1951; Yamayim Salonikayim be-Israel, 1951; Valeurs et Silhouettes Israéliennes, 1955; Rabbi Yehuda Bibas, 1957; Nekudot Hen, 1958. Recipient: Off, Ordre Phénix de Grèce, 1955, cdr, 1964; Chevalier des Palmes Académiques, 1959. Home: 22 Ibn Gvirol St, Jerusalem, Isr. Office: POB 390, Jerusalem, Isr.

MOLHO, Mordehai Moise, Greece, real estate expert; b. Salonica, May 31, 1892; s. Moise and Grazia (Tazartes); att It Lyceum, Salonica; m. Bella Koune; c: Jeanette, Laura Sard. Tvt practice since 1925; clerk, Saul Modiano Bank, 1911-20; bldg contractor, 1921-24. Hon pres, Salonica J Comty, fmr mem, bd; mem, local comm, Alliance Israélite Universelle. Spec interests, Judaism, mountain climbing. Home: 59 Fr Roosevelt St, Salonica, Greece. Office: 4 Vassileos Heracliou St, Salonica, Greece.

MOLINE, Roger, Fr, educator; b. Levallois-Perret, Fr, Dec 19, 1901; s. Fernand and Deborah (Weill); grad, Ecole Normale Supérieure de St Cloud; licence ès lettres, U of Paris, 1927; m. Juliette Lebon, Apr 17, 1924; c: Dorah, Gérard. Head, pedg research, Inst Pédagogique National, since 1957; tchr, 1925-28; dir gen, schs of J comty, Cairo, Egypt, 1928-56. Mem,

League for Hum Rights; pres, Assn of Frenchmen of Heb Faith, returned from Egypt; fmr, gen secy, B'nai B'rith, Cairo. Contbr to: Livre d'or des Instituteurs, 1962; Courrier de la Recherche Pédagogique, 1957-68; Amis de Sèvres, 1967; Hommage à Roger Gal, 1968; Histoire de l'Education, 1969; educ publs. Recipient: Commandeur Palmes Académiques. Home: 138 rue Houdan, Sceaux, Seine, Fr. Office: 29 rue d'Ulm, Paris 5, Fr.

MOLODOWSKY-LEW, Kadia, US, poet, playwright, novelist; b. Bereza-Kartuzka, Pol, May 10, 1894; d. Isaac and Itka (Katz) Molodowsky; in US since 1935; att Heb Tchrs Sem, Warsaw, 1913-15; m. Symcha Lew, 1921. Author, poetry: Cheshvendige Necht, 1927; Kinder Masselach, 1930; Dzike-Gass, 1931; Freidke, 1935; In Land fun Mein Gebein, 1937; Der Meilach David Alein is Gebliben, 1946; In Jerusholaim Kumen Malochim, 1952; selected children's poems, Heb, publ in Isr, 1945; plays: Alle Fenster Tzu der Zun, 1936; Nochn Gott fun Midbar, 1949, produced, Ohel Theater, Tel Aviv, 1956; A Hoiz oif Grand Street, 1953, produced in NY, 1953; novels: Fun Lublin biz New York, 1942; Zeides un Einiklech, 1944; Oif Eigener Erd, 1957, dramatized, radio sta, WEVD, 1958; Oif di Vegn fun Zion, hist essays, 1957; A Shtub mit Zibn Fenster, short stories, 1957; Licht fun Dornboim, poetry, 1966; Baim Toyer, 1967; Marzepanes, poems and stories for children and youth, 1970; records; films for children; ed: Heim, Tel Aviv, 1950-52; Seviva, NY, 1943-44 and since 1960; co-ed, Amol in a Yovel, Warsaw, 1932. Mem: I L Peretz Writers Union; Farband Org; Pioneer Women Org; club, Yiddish PEN. Recipient: poetry prize, Warasw J Comty and J PEN Club, 1930; Louis LaMed Prize, 1946; Hayim Greenberg lit award, Pioneer Women Org, 1958; N Chanin Poetry prize, 1966; poetry prize, J Book Council of Amer, 1967; Zvee Kessel Prize, 1968. Home: 570 Grand St, New York, NY.

MOMIGLIANO, Eucardio, It, attorney, historian; b. Monesiglio, It, Oct 18, 1888; s. Leon and Regina (della Torre); LLD, U Pavia, 1910; m. Elisa Vigna, Sep 30, 1945. Atty since 1910; mem: Comunale nella Città de Miradolo. Mem: dept hist, Accademia Nazionale di Firenze; Ordine Mazionale degli Autori e Scrittori; Mark Twain Acad; fmr: pres, Vittoriale Mus (in memory of D'Annunzio), 1944; mem, Provinciale di Milano. Author: Cromwell, 1931; Elizabeth of England, 1932; Anne Boleyn, 1934; Frederick II, 1935; Barbarossa, 1938; Tre Tribuni, 1939; Storia Grottesca e Tragica del Razzismo Fascista, 1943. Home: Via Canova 31, Milan, It.

MOND, Bertram, Austr, educator; b. NYC, Aug 24, 1931; s. Isaac and Mollie (Turk); in Austr since 1969; BA, Yeshiva, U 1951; MA, Bucknell U, Pa, 1959; ordained rabbi, Yeshiva U, NY, 1954; PhD, U Cincinnati, 1963; m. Judith Porush, July 7, 1957; c: Daniel, Michelle. Prof, math, La Trobe U, since 1969; research math, Wright-Patterson Air Force Base, 1963-64; found, rabbi, N Hills Syn, 1960-64. Chaplain, lt, USAF, 1955-56. Mem: Amer Math Soc; Math Assn Amer; Austr Math Soc, chmn, opr research meeting, Japan; RabCA; B'nai B'rith; Pi Mu Epsilon; Soc for Ind and Applied Math; fmr vice-pres, JNF, Cincinnati. Ed: Jour of Austr Math Soc; Blanch Anniversary Volume; contbr to profsl publs. Home: 22 Crotonhurst Ave, Caulfield 3161, Melbourne, Austr. Office: LaTrobe U, Bundoora 3083, Austr.

MONDOLFO, Anita, It, librarian, educator; b. Senigallia, It, Feb 9, 1886; d. Elia and Giuseppina (Terni); deg, classical philol, specialization in palaeography, U Florence ,1908. Gen bibliographic inspector, Min of Public Educ, since 1954; dir: Natl Libr, Florence; State Libr of Lucca, 1926-28; Marucelliana Libr, Florence, 1929-35; Natl Cen Libr, Florence and supt, Tuscany Librs, 1936-53; prof: U Florence, 1952-53; U of Rome, 1953-56. Mem: It Commn for UNESCO; Min Commn Index and Catalogues of It Librs; commn for Catalogo Unico delle Biblioteche It; mgn bd, J Comty, Florence; mem: J-Chr Alliance; Friends of U of Jerusalem; ADEI, J It Women's Assn; FILDIS, Intl Fed U Women. Author: Il Tiraboschi e il Bandini, 1937; Le Biblioteche d'Italia e la Guerra, 1946; La Biblioteca Landau Finaly, 1950; Biblioteche e Decentramento, 1950; Guido Biagi, 1956; Pancrazi Lattore, 1962; Ricorda di Fortunato Pintor, 1963; collaborator: Enciclopedia Italiana; Enciclopedia Minore; Dizionario Biografico degli Italiani; contbr to jours. Recipient: Commenda al Merito della Repubblica; Medaglia d'oro benemer Cultura. Home: 42 Via Tripoli, Florence, It.

MONOSSON, Fred, US, business exec; communal leader; b. Moscow, Russ, Feb 22, 1893; s. Abraham; in US since 1905;

att Northeastern U Law Sch, Boston, Mass, 1920-21; m. Minnie Poley, Dec 25, 1913; c: Alice Freedland, Ruth Savel, Adolf. Pres and treas, Cosmopolitan Mfg Co, Boston, Mass, since 1929; NE Clothing and Rainwear Mfrs Assn, since 1925; Natl Rainwear Mfrs Assn, since 1946; vice-pres, ILGWU, 1921-25, gen org, AFL, 1921-25. Found, pres, Zionist House, Boston, 1946; pres: J Archives of New Eng, Isr Projects; NE JNF, natl chmn, campaign, 1949, natl vice-pres; and co-found, Zionist Chest, NE, 1946-54; Harry S Truman Village, Isr, 1952; Freedom Forest, Isr, 1960; hon, MICHA, Soc for Deaf Mute Children in Isr; vice-pres, NE chap, Weizmann Inst of Sci; natl treas and life mem, ZOA, 1949-52; natl co-chmn, Isr Bond Campaign, 1951; co-found and chmn, ZOA House, Isr, 1949; co-found: Histadrut Comm, US, 1923; Brandeis U, 1948; Ein Gev Music Festival, Lake Tiberias, Isr, 1951; found: Amal Trade Sch, Jerusalem, 1946; and builder, Neve Monosson, Isr, 1951; mem, bd dirs: United Isr Appeal; UJA; Combined J Philanthropies, Gtr Boston; Beth Isr Hosp; Boston BBB; mem, bd trustees, Hillel House, Boston U; life mem, World Zionists Actions Comm, since 1951, delg, WZC, 1951; mem: Natl Comm for Harvard Law Sch-Isr Coop Research for Isr Legal Devl; Masons; clubs: W End House; Pinebrook Country. Home: 75 Gardner Rd, Brookline, Mass. Office: 712 Beacon St, Boston, Mass.

MONSELISE, Shaul Paul, Isr, educator; b. Milano, It, Apr 23, 1920; s. Maurizio and Pierina (Ottolenghi); in Isr since 1939; PhD, Heb U, 1950; m. Rachel Mosheyov, Feb 19, 1948; c: Nira, Edna, Dan. Asso prof, horticulture, dean, fac agric, Heb U; research asso, E Malling Research Sta, Kent, 1964; research f, Cal Inst Tech, 1956; research asso, U of Cal, 1955. IDF, 1948-49. Steering bd, Citrus Ind, Min of Agric. Contbr to sci jours. Home: 64 Yaakow, Rehovot, Isr. Office: Heb U, Rehovot, Isr.

MONTAGU, Ashley, US, anthropologist, author; b. London, Eng, June 28, 1905; s. Charles and Mary (Plot); in US since 1930; PhD, Columbia U, 1937; hon DSc, Grinnell Coll, 1968; m. Marjorie Peakes, Sep 18, 1931; c: Audrey Murphy, Barbara Johnstone, Geoffrey. Lectr, New Sch for Social Research, since 1931, sr lectr, VA postgrad training program, sinec 1946; asst prof, anat, NYU, 1931-38; asso prof, anat, Hahnemann Med Coll and Hosp, Phila, 1938-49; chmn, dept anthropology, Rutgers U, 1949-55; visiting lectr, dept social sci, Harvard U, 1945; visiting prof, U of Del, 1955; Regents prof, U of Cal, Santa Barbara, 1962; research dir, NJ Comm for Phys Devl and Health, 1953-57; family affairs ed, NBC-TV, 1954; cons, UNESCO, 1949, responsible for drafting statement on race for UNESCO, 1949-50. Chmn, Anisfield-Wolf Award Comm in Race Relations; f: AAAS; Amer Acad Psychosomatic Med; mem: Assn Human Biols; Intl Soc for Study of Race Relation; Amer Soc Study Child Growht and Devl; Amer Assn of Anats; Amer Assn Phys Anthropologists; Sigma Xi; club, PEN. Author: Coming into Being Among the Australian Aborigines, 1937; Man's Most Dangerous Myth: The Fallacy of Race, 1942; Edward Tyson, MD, FRS, 1650-1708, and the Rise of Human and Comparative Anatomy in England, 1943; Introduction to Physical Anthropology, 1945; Adolescent Sterility, 1946; On Being Human, 1950; On Being Intelligent, 1951; Statement on Race, 1952; Darwin, Competition and Cooperation, 1952; The Natural Superiority of Women, 1953; The Director of Human Development, 1955; Immortality, 1955; Biosocial Nature of Man, 1956; Anthropology and Human Nature, 1957; Man: His First Million Years, 1957; The Reproductive Development of the Female, 1957; Education and Human Relations, 1958; The Cultured Man, 1958; Human Heredity, 1959; Handbook of Anthropometry, 1960; Man in Process, 1961; Prenatal Influences, 1961; The Humanization of Man, 1962; Race, Science and Humanity, 1963; Life Before Birth, 1964; The Science of Man, 1964; The Human Revolution, 1965; Up the Ivy, 1965; Man's Evolution, 1965; The American Way of Life, 1967; Man Observed, 1968; The Anatomy of Swearing, 1968; Man: His First Two Million Years, 1969; Sex, Man and Society, 1969; co-author: Anatomy and Physiology, 1959; The Human Dialogue, 1967; The Prevalence of Nonsense, 1967; Textbook of Human Genetics, 1970; wrote, produced and directed film, One World or None, 1946. Recipient: Morris Chaim Prize, Dental Soc of NY, 1936; award, Chgo Forum lit contest, 1943. Hobby: book collecting. Home: 321 Cherry Hill Rd, Princeton, NJ.

MONTAGU, The Hon Ewen Edward Samuel, Eng, QC; b. London, Mar 29, 1901; s. Lord Swaythling and Gladys (Goldsmid); att Harvard U, Mass, 1919-20; LLB, U Cambridge, Eng, 1923, MA, 1924; m. Iris Solomon, June 14, 1923; c: Jeremy, Jennifer. QC, fmr, King's Counsel, since 1939; Master of the Bench of Middle Temple, 1949; Judge Advocate of the Fleet, since 1945; chmn, Middlesex Quarter Sessions, since 1956, asst chmn, 1951-54, dep chmn, 1954-56; dep lt, Co of Hampshire, since 1953; recorder of Southampton, of Devizes, 1951-61; chmn, Hampshire Quarter Sessions, 1951-61. Royal Navy Volunteer Res, 1939-45. Chmn, Pioneer Health Cen, since 1945; pres, J Memorial Council, since 1953; vice-pres, Anglo J Assn, since 1954, fmr pres; vice-pres, J Mus, since 1959; fmr, pres, treas, vice-pres, United Syn. Author: The Man Who Never Was, 1953. Recipient: OBE, 1944; CBE, 1950. Home: 5 Vicarage Gardens, Campden Hill, London W8, Eng. Office: 3 Pump Ct, Temple, London EC4, Eng.

MOONMAN, Eric, Eng, legislator; b. Liverpool, Eng, Aug 29, 1929; s. Borach and Leah; MSc, U of Manchester, cert, personnel mgmt; dipl, social sci, U of Liverpool, 1955; m. Jane Dillon, Sep 9, 1962; c: Daniel, Natasha. MP since 1966, chmn (parliamentary) lab party's sci and tech comm; adv, Inbucon group of cos; hum relations adv, Brit Inst Mgmt, 1956-62; sr research f, mgmt sci, U of Manchester, 1965-66. Sgt, Brit Army, 1951-53. Gov, Imperial Coll Sci and Tech; hon treas, Brit Assn Residential Settlements, 1960-63; mem: Inst Personnel Mgmt Research Comm; Natl Graphical Assn; Brit Inst Mgmt. Author: The Manager and the Organization, 1961; Science and Technology in Europe, 1968; The Press: A Case for Commitment, 1969; Communication in an Expanding Organization, 1969; Government and Industry, 1970; ed bd, Bus Admn; contbr to bus jours in US and Eng. Hobbies: art and antique collector. Home: Chalkwell Esplanade, Westcliff-on-Sea, Essex, Eng. Office: 169-171 High St, Southend-on-Sea, Essex, Eng.

MOORE, Matthew T, US, neuropsychiatrist, educator; b. Phila, Pa, Sep 12, 1901, s. Joseph and Sarah (Gottlieb); att: Pa U, 1920-21; Harvard U, 1921-23; MD, Temple U Med Sch, 1927; postgrad study: Cushing Clinic, Harvard Med Sch, 1932; Natl Hosp, London, Eng, 1937; Montreal Neur Inst, 1940; m. Stella Chalfin, Feb 2, 1927. Neuropsycht-in-chief, Doctors Hosp, Phila, since 1940; att chief psycht, Phila Psycht Hosp, since 1937; neuropath, Grad Sch of Med, U of Pa, since 1936; sr cons psycht, Phila Psycht Cen, since 1967; prof, neuropath (U of Pa Sch Med grad div), since 1960; em sr att neur, Albert Einstein Med Cen, since 1967, on staff, since 1929; psychosurg: Del State Hosp, Farnhurst, Del, since 1951; visiting neuropoath, 1952-1968; cons-neuropsycht, Home for J Aged, since 1958; asst in neur dispensary, Temple U Hosp, 1929-35, head, Convulsive State Clinic, 1929-35; clinical asst, neur, Temple U Med Sch and J Hosp, 1928-29, asst neurosurg, 1929-33; asst neurosurg, Phila Gen Hosp, 1929-33; instr, neur, Temple U Med Sch, 1929-33, demonstrator, neur, 1933-35; encephalographist, Norristown State Hosp, 1930-34; asso, neur J Hosp, 1933-54; instr, neuropath, U of Pa Grad Sch of Med, 1936-40, asso, neuropath, 1940-45, asso path, neuropath, 1945-52; asso prof, neuropath, 1952-60; med examiner, neur, Induction Bd, Phila, 1942-44; prof, clinical neur, Hahnemann Med Coll and Hosp, 1953-58; affiliate of Home for J Aged, 1953-58; cons, psychosurg, Wernersville, State Hosp, Wernersville, Pa, 1949-54; neuropsycht, Home for the J Aged, 1952-58. F: Phila Coll Phys; Pa Psycht Soc; life, Amer Coll Phys; Amer Acad Neur; Amer Psycht Assn; Amer Geriatrics Soc; dipl, Amer Bd Psycht and Neur, 1939; pres: N Med Assn, 1950; Amer Assn Neuropaths, 1958-59; Amer Soc Med Psycht, 1967-68; Phila Neur Soc, 1968; pres, Friends of Heb U in Jerusalem, 1953-58; mem: Painting and Sculpture Comm, Phila Mus of Art; Phila Co Med Soc; Phila Neur Soc; Phila Psycht Soc; Pa Med Soc; Assn for Research in Nervous and Mental Disease; Natl Comm for Mental Hygiene; AAAS; Natl Multiple Sclerosis Soc; Natl Council on Family Relations; Amer Epilepsy Soc; Electroshock Research Soc; Sigma Xi; Amer J Phys Comm; hon mem, Med-Surg Acad of Athens, Greece, since 1952; club, Phila. Mem, adv bd, staff, Jour of Neuropath and Experimental Neur, since 1961; contbr to med jours. Hobbies: collecting art, music, photography, travel. Home and office: 1813 Delancey Pl, Philadelphia, Pa.

MOOSBERG, Kurt Alexander, Isr, business exec; b. Paderborn, W Ger, June 22, 1903; s. Moritz and Ella Blank; in Isr since 1933; att Us: Leipzig; Berlin; PhD, U of Giessen; m. Rita Levis, 1931; c: Yael Schechter, Rayah Grinberg, Yehudith Bieler. Chmn, mgn dir, Nechushtan Ltd and asso cos, Isr. Chmn: Friends of Mus Haaretz, Tel Aviv; Isr-Japan C of C; Isr-Ger C of C and Ind, Tel Aviv; vice-chmn: Tel Aviv-Yafo C of C; Isr regional council, Intl C of C. Contbr to econ and bus publs. Recipient: Verdienstkreutz 1st class, Pres of Fed Rep of Ger. Hobbies: archaeol, hunting, nature protection. Home: 3A Shalag St, Tel Aviv, Isr. Office: POB 1758, Tel Aviv, Isr.

MOR, Eliyahu, Isr, chemist; b. Kirovograd, Russ, Sep 4, 1904; s. Moshe and Bracha (Zadkovetsky) Muravsky; in Isr since 1925; BChE, Caen U, Fr, 1934; m. Rachel Krawiec, Mar 10, 1935; c: Moshe. Head, dept of soils and water, Volcani Inst of Agric Research, Min of Agric, since 1967; bldg and agric laborer; male nurse, 1926-31; f, FAO, Ger, Fr, and It, on problems of sewage irrigation, 1956-57; participant: Intl Cong of Irrigation and Drainage, Madrid, 1960; Symposium on Sodic Soils, Budapest, 1964; soil chem, Agric Research Sta, 1937-48, sr soil chem, 1948-61, head, soil salinity div, 1961-69. Haganah, 1932-48. Prin contrib: influence of irrigation with water of varying degs of salinity on soil and crops; improvement of saline and alkali soils; utilization of sewage effluents for irrigation. Chmn, Lab Exch Council, Rehovot; secy, Control Bd, Kupat Cholim, Rehovot, 1940-45; mem: exec, Anti-TB League; exec, Lab Party, Rehovot, 1940-48; Intl Soc of Soil Sci; Isr Chem Soc. Contbr on soil salinity problems to sci jours. Recipient: Haganah ribbon. Hobby: philately. Home: 3 Kibovitch St, Rehovot, Isr. Office: Valcani Inst for Agric Research, Beit Dagan, Isr.

MORAG, Shelomo, Isr, educator; b. Petah Tikvah, Isr, July 7, 1926; s. Moshe and Sara (Margalit) Mirkin; MA, Heb U, Jerusalem, 1948, PhD, 1955; att Sorbonne, Paris; m. Shoshana Disenhouse, Oct 16, 1952; c: Rinat, Ariela. Asso prof, ling and Heb lang, Heb U, since 1965, fmr asst lectr, sr lectr; dir, Heb U research project in lang tradition of J comtys; fmr: visiting prof, Brandeis U. Capt, IDF. Mem: Ling Soc of Amer; Amer. Oriental Soc; adv mem, Heb Lang Acad. Author: The Vocalization Systems of Hebrew, Arabic and Aramaic, 1962; The Hebrew Language Tradition of the Yemenite Jews, 1963; mem, ed bd, Phonetica, intl jour of phonetics; contbr to sci jours. Recipient: Isr Award for J Studies, Min of Educ, 1966; Leib Yoffe Prize, KH, 1964. Home: 8 Shikun Nayoth, Jerusalem, Isr. Office: Hebrew U, Jerusalem, Isr.

MORAWETZ, Herbert, US, chemist, educator; b. Prague, Czech, Oct 16, 1915; s. Richard and Frida (Glaser); in US since 1945; BS, U of Toronto, 1943, MS, 1944; PhD, Bklyn Poly Inst, 1950; m. Cathleen Synge, Oct 28, 1945; c: Pegeen, John, Linda Nancy. Prof, chem, Poly Inst, since 1958, asst prof, 1951-53, asso prof, 1953-58; research chem, Bakelite Co, 1944-49; Natl Inst of Health research, f, 1950-51; Louis Lipsky exch f, Weizmann Inst of Sci, Isr, 1956. Mem: AAAS; Amer Chem Soc. Contbr on phys chem of high polymers. Home: 246 W 12 St, New York, NY. Office: Poly Inst of Bklyn, Brooklyn, NY.

MORDECHAI, B (M Bartana), Isr, government official; b. Podbrodz, Pol, Dec 1, 1909; s. Israel and Rachel (Kopelovitz) Brataniski; in Isr since 1935; att Takhkemoni Rabb Sem; grad, Tchrs Sem, 1933, both Warsaw; Heb U, Jerusalem, 1935-37; m. Sarah Rotman, 1947; c: Orzion. Sch insp, Tel Aviv, since 1948; fmr tchr, headmaster. IDF, War of Independence. Author, poems: Yiddish: Ofene Tirn, 1929; Shotens Oifn Weg, 1933; in Heb: Zaadim daLaila, 1939; Min ha-Mezar, 1941; Sheerat ha-Eden ha-Avud, 1947; Yom ha-Tamid, 1955; Or le-Et Erev, 1961; HaNefilim Hayu Ba-Aretz, 1964; Ha-Shaa Ha-Acheret, 1969; legends, Ilan ha-Playim, 1957; trans into Heb, works of: M Kulbak; B Pruss; S Zeromsky; contbr to educ publs. Recipient: Cassel Prize, Mexico, for poems, Yom HaTamid, 1956; Ramat Gan prize for HaNefilim Hayu Ba-Aretz, 1965. Home: 15 David Yellin St, Tel Aviv, Isr. Office: Min of Educ, 37 Shaul Hamelech Blvd, Tel Aviv, Isr.

MORENO, J L, US, psychiatrist; b. Bucharest, Rum, May 20, 1892; s. Nissim and Pauline (Wolf); in US since 1927; MD, U of Vienna, 1917; DHC, U of Barcelona, 1968; golden doctor dipl, U of Vienna, 1969; m. Zerka Toeman, Dec 8, 1949; c: Regina, Zachariah, Jonathan. Pvt practice, psycht, NYC, since 1927; found, phys-in-charge, Beacon Hill Sanitarium, now Moreno Sanitarium since 1936; off of health, Vöslau, Aus, 1919-25; pvt practice, psycht, Vöslau and Vienna, 1919-25; found, The Spontaneity Theater, 1921-25; inventor, stage adapted to spontaneity work, 1922; inventor, radio film, 1924; introduced psychodramatic work with children, Plymouth Inst, Bklyn, and spontaneity test, mental hygiene clinic, Mt Sinai Hosp, NYC, 1928; found, Impromptu Theater, Carnegie Hall, 1929-31; publ, Impromptu Mag, 1931; conducted: sociometric studies, Sing Sing Prison, 1931-32; sociometric comty work, NY State Training Sch for Girls, Hudson, NY, 1932-38; spec lect: New Sch for Social Research, 1937-38; Tchrs Coll, Columbia U, 1939-40; found: Psychodramatic Inst, Beacon, NY, 1940; Sociometric and Psychodramatic Insts, now Moreno Inst, 1942. Life f, Amer Psycht and Sociometric Assns; f: Amer Soc of Group Psychotherapy and Psychodrama; Amer Sociol Soc; Med Soc of NY State. Author: Sociometry, Experimental Method and the Science of Society, 1951; Who Shall Survive?, 1934, 1953; ed, Sociometry and the Science of Man, 1956; Psychodrama, Vol III, 1969; works trans into numerous langs. Home: 259 Wolcott Ave, Beacon, NY. Office: 236 W 78 St, New York, NY.

MORGENSTERN, David, Isr, business exec; b. Pol, Mar 24, 1902; s. Isaac anu Miriam (Engel); att U Vienna; m. Tony Herzig, Mar 6, 1931; c: Joseph. Pres: Pellon Corp, NY; Morgenstern Fabrics Devl Corp, NY; found, Yarlona Ltd, Isr. Prin contribs: first to produce non-woven fabrics in US. Fmr pres, Herzliah Heb Tchrs Sem, NY. Hobbies: theatre, music. Homes: 38 Beeri St, Tel Aviv, Isr.; 505 Park Ave, New York, NY.

MORGENSTERN, Tony, Isr, interior decorator; b. Cracow, Pol, July 19, 1910; d. David and Mariem (Matzner) Herzig; att: Rackov's Acad, Ger; Columbia U; NY Sch of Interior Design; m. David Morgenstern, Mar 6, 1931; c: Joseph. Fmr: office manager, Pellon Corp, NY; interior decorator, NY. Pres, found, Voluntary Tourist Service in Isr; vice-pres, W End Hadassah, NY, chmn, Youth Aliyah. Hobbies: art, music. Home: 38 Beeri St, Tel Aviv, Isr.

MORGENTHAU, Hans Joachim, US, educator; b. Coburg, Ger, Feb 17, 1904; s. Ludwig and Frieda (Bachmann); in US since 1937; att: U Berlin, Frankfort, Munich, 1923-27; magna cum laude, U Munich, 1927; summa cum laude, U Frankfort, 1929; LLD: Clark U, 1962; Ripon Coll, 1962; Alma Coll, 1965; U Denver, 1971; DLitt, W Reserve U, 1965; m. Irma Thormann, June 3, 1935; c: Matthew, Susanna. Albert A Michelson Dist Service Prof, political sci and modern hist, U Chgo, since 1963; dir, Cen for Study of Amer Fgn and Mil Policy, U Chgo, since 1950, on fac since 1943; Leonard Davis Dist Prof, political sci, CUNY, since 1968; asst to law fac, U Frankfort, 1931; acting pres, Lab Law Court, Frankfort, 1931-33; instr, political sci, U Geneva, 1932-35; prof, Inst of Intl and Econ Studies, Madrid, 1935-36; instr, govt, Bklyn Coll, 1937-39; asst prof, law, hist, political sci, U Kan City, Mo, 1939-43; visiting prof: U Cal, Berkeley, 1949; Harvard, 1951, 1959, 1960-61; Northwestern, 1954; Wyoming, 1955, 1958; Columbia, Yale, 1956-57; lectr: Armed Forces Staff Coll; Air, Army, Naval, Natl War Colls; Ind Coll of Armed Forces; Inter-Amer, NATO Defense Colls; cons: State Dept, 1949, 1951, and since 1963; Dept of Defense, 1963-65; mem, Inst for Advanced Study, Princeton, 1958-59; asso, Wash Cen for Fgn Policy Research, 1958-60; sr research f, Council on Fgn Relations, 1966. Mem: Amer Acad Arts and Sci; Amer Phil Soc; Amer Political Sci Assn; John Hopkins U Soc of Scholars; AAUP; hon mem, Span Inst Political Sci. Author: Die Internationale Rechtspflege ihr Wesen und ihre Grenzen, 1929; La Notion du "Politique" et la Theorie des Differends Internationaux, 1933; La Realité des Normes, en particulier des Normes du Droit International, 1934; Scientific Man vs Power Politics, 1946; Politics Among Nations, 1948, 1954, 1960, 1967; In Defense of the National Interest, 1951; Dilemmas of Politics, 1958; The Purpose of American Politics, 1960, 1964; Politics in the Twentieth Century, 3 vols, 1962; Vietnam and the United States, 1965; A New Foreign Policy for the United States, 1969; Truth and Power, 1970; co-author, The Origins of The Cold War, 1970; ed: Peace, Security and the United Nations, 1946; Principles and Problems of International Politics, 1950; Germany and the Future of Europe, 1951; The Crossroad Papers: A Look into the American Future, 1965. Home: 5542 S Dorchester Ave, Chicago, Ill.

MORGENTHAU, Robert M, US, attorney, government official; b. NYC, July 31, 1919; s. Henry and Elinor (Fatman); BA, magna cum laude, Amherst Coll, 1941; LLB, Yale U Law Sch, 1948; m. Martha Pattridge, Dec 30, 1943; c: Joan, Anne, Elinor, Robert, Barbara. Dep mayor of NY, since 1970; US Atty for S Dist of NY, 1961-69; partner, law firm, Patterson, Belknap and Webb, 1954-61. USN, 1941-45. Pres, dir, J Agric Soc; pres: Police Athletic League; NY Leg Service; treas, Jt Comm on Legal Educ; trustee: FJP; Baron de Hirsch Fund; and chmn bd, NY Sch for Nursery Years; mem: natl commn, ADL; Riverdale Lodge, B'nai B'rith; adv council, Sch of Criminal justice of SUNY; adv comm: Commn to Reform Fed Criminal Law; Bx Comty Coll; council, NY Sch of Social Work, Columbia U; NYC Bar Assn; NY Co

Lawyers Assn; Bx Co, NY State, Fed Bar Assns; Phi Beta Kappa. Home: 4725 Independence Ave, Riverdale, NY. Office: US Court House, Foley Sq, New York, NY.

MORIEL, Shlomo, Isr, business exec; b. Riga, Latvia, Nov 6, 1904; s. Zvi and Esther (Rapoport) Meerovitch; in Isr since 1924; grad, Sch of Econ, U of Moscow, 1924; LLB, Sorbonne U, 1933; att Sch of Political Sci, Paris, 1931; m. Alisa Lemberg, Feb 10, 1938; c: Evyatar. Hon consul gen of Liberia in Isr since 1958; mgn dir, vice-chmn, Utilgas, Nigerian and Overseas Gas Co Ltd, since 1961; org, vice-chmn, Dumez Construction, Nigeria, since 1957; mem, Isr Lib Party, since 1953; promoter, found, Liberian Construction, 1956; dir, lab dept, and intl relations, Isr Mfr Assn, 1940-54; dep dir gen, Isr Min of Commerce, 1955. Chmn, co-found, Isr-Afr Friendship Assn; econ affairs repr, JA, Eur; fmr mem: Russ Zionist Youth Movement; Revisionist Party; Isr delg, ILO Conf, Geneva, dep mem, gov body; clubs Commercial and Ind, Tel Aviv. Ed, Econ Life of Isr, Paris; contbr to the press. Recipient: Star of Afr, deg commn, Rep of Liberia, 1959. Home and office: 8 Meggido St, Tel Aviv, Isr.

MORINI, Erica, US, violinist; b. Vienna, Aus; d. Oscar and Amalia (Weismann); studied music with father and Prof Sevcic Master Sch, Vienna, Aus; DMus, Smith Coll, 1953; hon DMus, NE Conservatory of Music Mass, 1963; m. Felice Siracusano, Apr 28, 1928. Debut at Beethoven Festival, Leipzig Gewandhaus, under conductor Artur Nikisch at age of 9; US debut under conductor Artur Bodanzky, 1920; concert tours: US, Austr, Asia, Eur, Afr, Can, Cuba, Russ. Recording artist: Decca Records; Westminster Recording; London, FFRR. Hon mem, Sigma Alpha Iota. Home: 1200 Fifth Ave, New York, NY. Office: Columbia Artists Mgmt, 165 W 57 St, New York, NY.

MORITZ, Manfred, Swed, philosopher; b. Berlin, Ger, June 4, 1909; s. Alfred and Wally (Posner); in Swed since 1934; PhD, U Berlin, 1933; att U Gothenburg, 1935-36; PhD, U Lund, 1951; m. Britta Hasselgren, Sep 24, 1951. Prof, phil, Lund U, since 1958, docent, 1951-58, chmn, dept phil. Mem: New Soc of Letters; Intl Inst of Phil, Paris; Royal Soc of Letters, Lund. Author: Der Pflichtbegriff in Kants Kritischer Ethik; Über Hohfelds System der juridischen Grundbegriffe; contbr to phil publs. Hobbies: book collecting, travel. Home: 5C Vintergatan, Lund, Swed. Office: U Lund, Kungshuset, Lundagard, Swed.

MORO, Lina, It, autor; b. Neuilly sur Seine, Fr, July 6, 1905; d. Carlo and Pia (Ascoli); in It since 1907; laurea in lettere, U Florence, 1929; single. Author: Liriche (Ebraiche), 1952; Un'Anima, 1956; Lontana Favola, 1961; contbr of articles and poems to newspapers, mags, anthol. Mem: cultural sect, WIZO, Florence; Assn of It-J Women; Amicizia Ebraico Cristiana; FILDIS; Gruppo Sionistico, all Florence. Recipient: various prizes in poetry competitions; SpillaD'oro, 1969. Home: 36 Via Fra Bartolomeo, Florence, It.

MOROWITZ, Harold J, US, biophysicist, educator; b. Poughkepsie, NY, Dec 4, 1927; . Philip and Anna (Levine); BS, Yale U, 1947, MS, 1950; PhD, 1951; nm. Lucille Stei, Jan 30, 1949; c: Joanna, Eli, Joshua, Zachary, Noah. Prof, biophysics, Yale U, since 1968, asso prof, 1960-68; asst prof, 1955-60; physicist: Natl Bur Standards, 1951-53; Natl Heart Inst, 1953-55. F, NY Acad Scis; mem: Biophys Soc; AAAS; Sigma Xi. Author: Life in the Physical Sciences, 1963; Energy Flow in Biology 1968; contbr to sci publs: Home: Ox Bow Lane, Woodbridge, Conn. Office: J Williar Gibbs Lab, Yale U, New Haven, Conn.

MOROZ, Chaya, Isr, scientist; b. Tel Aviv, May 14, 1936; d. Israel and Zahava (Bornshtein) Perlmutter; MSc, Tel Aviv U, 1960; PhD, Heb U, Jerusalem, 1964; m. Zeev Moroz, Mar 14, 1957; c: Nir, Tal. Head: immunology unit, Rogoff-Welcome Research Inst, since 1969; dept experimental med, Tel Aviv U; research f, Weizmann Inst, 1964-65; research asst, NYU, 1966-69. Pvt, MC, IDF, 1954-56. Prin contribs: devl of antiserum for treatment of snake bite cases in Isr. Mem, sci socs in Isr. Author: Nucleic Acids in Immunology. Home: 3 Mozir St, Tel Aviv, Isr. Office: Beilinson Hosp, Petah Tikvah, Isr.

MORRIS, David, UK, attorney; b. Brynmawr, Wales, Feb 21, 1908; s. Jacob and Bessie (Ranbach); LLB, U Coll, U of Wales, 1928; m. Joyce Pappé, Mar 21, 1938; c: Anthony, Phillip. Atty since 1930; sr partner, David Morris and Co. Chmn: Bristol and Western Cos Legal Aid Comm; Newport

JNF Commn; vice-pres, Monmouthshire Inc Law Soc; pres, Newport Heb Corg 1959-61; chmn, Newport J Educ Comm, 1961-63; repr, S Wales and W of Eng Old Age Home, 1958-69; mem: B'nai B'rith; Masons, past master Lions Intl. Home: 16 Ridgeway, Newport, Wales, UK. Office: 14 Clytha Park Rd, Newport, Wales, UK.

MORRIS, George Reginald, Ir, business exec; b. London, Eng, Jan 12, 1905; s. Sydney and Sarah (Davis); in Ir since 1926; att N Poly, London; m. Julia Spiro, Nov 25, 1928; c: Joan Finkel, Alan. Co secy, dir, Newton Victor Ltd. Vice chmn, Dublin J Progressive Cong; treas, Ir Med Exhibitors Assn; trustee, Karmel Masonic Benevolent Fund; past master, Masonic Lodge; repr, Fgn Grand Lodge and Grand Chap in Ir. Hobbies: photography, bowling. Home: 10 Belmont Villas, Donnybrook, Dublin, Ir.

MORRIS, I Paul, US, pediatrician; b. Athens, Ga, Nov 15, 1904; BS, U of Ga, 1923; MD, Columbia U, 1927; m. Joan Nusbaum, 1940; c: Richard, Elizabeth. In pvt practice since 1932; cons, ped, Albert Einstein Med Cen, since 1958; chief, ped service, Mt Sinai Hosp, 1944-58; res: Chgo Munic Contagious Disease Hosp, 1930; Children's Hosp of Mich, Detroit, 1930-31; postgrad work, U Children's Clinic and Berlin City Children's Hosp, Berlin, Ger, 1931-32; instr, ped, U of Pa, 1934-52; mem, ped staff: Children's Hosp of Phila; Abington Memorial Hosp, Pa; asso prof, Hahneman Sch of Med, 1952-55. Licentiate, Natl Bd Med Examiners; cert, Amer Bd Ped; mem: Phila Coll Phys; Amer Acad Ped; AMA; Phila Ped Soc; AJ Comm; Alpha Omega Alpha; Phi Epsilon Pi; Phi Delta Epsilon; Rodeph Shalom Reform Syn; club, Round Table. Contbr to profsl jours. Home: 242 E Waverly Rd, Wyncote, Pa. Office: 1939 Cheltenham Ave, Phila, Pa.

MORRIS, Norman Harold, S Afr, communal leader; b. London, Eng, June 8, 1932; s. Ernest and Rebecca (Shernoff); m. Julia Levenson, Dec 2, 1962; c: Jonathan. Secy, E Cape ZC, since 1969; dep provincial dir, ZF of Gt Brit and N Ir, 1959-69. Sgt, RAF, 1950-53. Mem: Brit Bd Deps; natl council, British sect, WJC, fmr mem, org comm; fmr: exec and ed, Young Zionist, both Fed Zionist Youth. Hobbies: skiing, music, books, travel. Home: 413 Fernkloof Park Dr, Port Elizabeth, S Afr. Office: POB 631, Port Elizabeth, S Afr.

MORRIS, Solomon Simon, S Afr, civil engr, town planner; b. Cape Town, Mar 25, 1913; s. Max and Eva (Samuel); BSc, U of Cape Town, 1933, PhD, 1958; m. Lydia Lange, June 18, 1939; c: Sorel, Maureen. City engr, Cape Town, since 1950; pres, S Afr Instn of CEs; engr asst, 1934-36; asst sewerage engr, Munic of Krugersdorp, 1936; chief engr asst br, 1936-40; sr tech asst, structural engr, bldg survey br, 1940-41; org i/c, engr dept, Air Raid Protection, 1942-44; bldg surveyor, 1944-50. F: Amer Soc CEs; Instn of Munic Engrs; Instn of CEs and Town Planning Inst, London; Royal Soc Health; pres: S Afr dist, Instn of Munic Engrs, 1954, mem: bd examiners, 1943, 1950,1954; hon dist secy, 1943-50; chmn, bd engrs, New Cape Town Water Augmentation Scheme, since 1950; council, U of Cape Town. Office: City Engr, City Hall, Cape Town, S Afr.

MORRIS, Yaakov, Isr, diplomat; b. Belfast, N Ir, May 16, 1920; s. Samuel and Ethel (Levine); m. Sadie Cohen, 1941; c: Benjamin, Michal. Consul in Bombay, since 1969; dep dir, info, Isr Fgn Min, 1967-69; treas, JA for US, Can, Cen Amer, 1964-67; Isr Counsul, NY, 1951-61. Pvt, Haganah, 1947-48; IDF, 1948-68. Fmr: chmn, Hitachdut Olei Britania; chmn, staff comm, Isr Fgn Min. Author: Pioneers From the West, 1953; Israel's Struggle for Peace, 1960; Masters of the Desert, 1961; On the Soil of Israel, 1964. Office: Consulate of Israel, Bombay, India.

MORRISON, Samuel, US, physician, educator; b. Phila, Pa, Jan 4, 1904; s. Morris and Annie (Lipsitz); BA, Johns Hopkins U,1925; MD, 1929; m. Mary Selser, July, 1941. Asso prof, med, gastroenterology, U of Md Med School, since 1947; cons, gastroenterology: Veterans Hosp, Ft Howard, since 1946; USPHS, since 1956; Surg Gen Off, since 1946; visiting phys, hosps: Sinai, 1935; Church Home, 1934; St Joseph's, 1952; Mercy, 1930; U, 1930; Women's, now Gtr Baltimore Med Cen, 1950; Union Memorial, 1947; Lutheran, 1947; S Baltimore Gen Hosp, 1945; Bon Secours, 1956; Franklin Sq, 1956; N Charles Gen, 1956. Chief, med service, WW II. Cert, Amer Bd Internal Med and Gastroenterology; mem: Baltimore Med Soc; Med Chirurgical Fac of Md, vice-pres, 1959-1969; AMA, Amer Coll Phys; Amer Gastroenterological Assn; Alpha Omega Alpha; accreditation comm, State Med Assn;

fmr pres, Baltimore City Med Soc, 1965. Author: Secondary Gastrointestinal Disorders-Secondary Relationships, 1937; Diet in Surgery, Lewis' System of Surgery, 1958; contbr to profsl jours. Recipient: citation for med work, Camp Pickett, WW II. Home: 3799 Juniper Rd, Baltimore, Md. Office: 11 E Chase St, Baltimore, Md.

MORSE, Alan R, US business exec; b. Boston, Mass, Nov 10, 1897; s. Jacob and Rebecca (Rathesky); AB, Harvard Coll, 1919; MBA, Bus Sch, 1921; m. Theresa Jacobson, Sep 8, 1927; c: Edith Greene, Ann Cohen. Commercial banker; fmr: dir, Frank G Shattuck Co, Schrafft's pres, US Trust; Selectman, Town of Brookline. Chief petty off, USN, WW I. Bd dirs, Gtr Boston ARC; bd govs, NE Med Cen Hosps; bd trustees, Asso J Philanthropies; trustee: Boston Hosp for Women; NE Conservatory of Music; mem, natl exec comm, ADL, B'nai B'rith; fmr: natl bd govs, ARC; vice-pres: Boston C of C; JCC, Metrop Boston; mem, bd trustees, Temple Israel, Boston. Hobbies: sailing, music. Home: 32 Borland St, Brookline, Mass.

MORSE, Earl L, US, business exec; b. Milw, Wis, Mar 19, 1907; s. Benjamin and Flora (Werner); BA, U of Wis, 1927; LLB, Harvard Law Sch, 1930; m. Irene Levitt, Dec 23, 1936; c: Albert, Jonathan, Stephen. Exec vice-pres, DCA Food Inds Inc since 1947; spec counsel, FCC, Wash, DC, 1935-37. Chmn bd, UAHC; hon vice-pres, J Educ Comm; vice-pres: AJC, 1962-64; Amer Assn J Educ, NYC; bd govs, HUC-JIR since 1960; bd mem, HUC-JIR; mem: Temple Beth El. Great Neck, NY; Cen Syn, NYC; China Art Soc; Horticultural Soc of NY; club, Harmonie, NYC. Hobbies: collecting Chinese art, gardening. Home: 15 E 64 St, New York, NY. Office: 45 W 36 St, New York, NY.

MORSTEIN, Stanley Irwin, US, attorney; b. Baltimore, Md, July 2, 1930; s. David and Sophia (Weiner); BS, U of Md, 1951, LLB, JD, 1954; m. Mildred Rothberg, Mar 1, 1957; c: Susan, Ruth, Deborah. Pvt practice since 1954; owner, mgr, Morstein Jewelers, 1952-53. Cpl, US Army, 1954-56. Vice-pres, Baltimore Co Council PTA; bd govs, J Big Brother League, Baltimore; fmr pres, Fort Garrison Elem PTA; mem: Bar Assn of Baltimore City; Sigma Alpha Mu; Upsilon Lambda Phi; club, Towne Drama, fmr pres. Hobbies: educ, theater, politics. Home: 3309 Janellen Dr, Baltimore, Md. Office: 14 W Saratoga, Baltimore, Md.

MORTON, James, US, business exec; b. Jamaica, NY, May 23, 1923; s. Lawrence and Irma (Gross); BA, Union Coll, NY, 1948; div; c: Robert, Laurie, James. Holder of various offs in family real estate corps. Lt, pilot, USN, 1943-46. Pres, New Orleans Lodge 182, B'nai B'rith, chmn, comm on housing, Dist 7; treas, New Orleans adv bd, ADL; mem bd: Touro Syn; J Comty Cen; Cultural Attractions Fund; S Cen Regional Bd, ADL; mem, natl comm on admn and finance, ADL; mem exec comm, Hillel, all New Orleans; fmr, mem bd, J Comty Services, LI; club, Lakewood Country, Exec Comm. Recipient: 2 air medals, USN. Home: 2511 St Charles St, New Orleans, La. Office: 5009 Rochester Dr, Marrero, La.

MOSBERG, Falic, Isr, physician; b. Gurahomora, Rum, Aug 3, 1904; s. Aharon and Berta (Blasenstein); in Isr since 1944; DM, U of Bucarest, Rum, 1929; MPH, Yale, New Haven, 1960; m. Rachel Goldenberg June 21, 1935; c: Ronald. Sr MO, Health Dept, Haifa dist, since 1956; med dir, OSE, Morocco, 1953-55; cons, social ped, WHO, Philippines, 1963-65. Chmn, Isr-Philippines Friendship League; vice-chmn, Ilan, Isr; mem, bd dirs, Magen David Adom, Haifa; fmr mem, Org of Phys, Isr. Home: 89 Moriah St, Haifa, Isr. Office: 15 Haparsim St, Haifa, Isr.

MOSCOVITZ, Isadore, US, editor, publisher; b. Jacksonville, Fla, Sep 15, 1911; s. Joseph and Ann (Zussman); BSJ, U of Fla, 1933; m. Ethel Katz, Oct 7, 1934; c: Arlene Shainbrown, David, Howard. Ed, publisher, Soutnern J Weekly, since 1933. Capt, maj, US Army, 1941-45. PR dir, SE region, ZOA, since 1959, pres, Jacksonville dist, 1934; mem: ZOA, life; B'nai B'rith; Phi Kappa Phi; Sigma Delta Chi; Pi Lambda Phi; Tau Kappa Alpha; club, Beauclerc Country. Home: 1320 Lakewood Rd, Jacksonville, Fla. Office: POB 3297, Jacksonville, Fla.

MOSCOW, Warren, US, journalist, public official; b. Bklyn, NY, Mar 15, 1908; s. Jacob and Stella (Klass); att: Columbia U, 1925-26; Bklyn Law School, 1926-27; m. Jean Shalen, Jan 10, 1946; c: Judith Heimann, John, Katherine. Cons, governmental affairs, since 1966; City Hall reporter: Bklyn Daily

Citizen, 1926; NY American, 1928-30; political reporter, head, Albany Bur, NY Times, 1930-52; commn boro works, Manhattan, 1952-54; asst to Mayor, 1954-55; exec dir, NYC Housing Auth, 1955-57; exec asst to NYC Mayor, 1958-61; cons to NY City on intergovt affairs, 1962-63; lectr, New Sch for Social Research, 1966,1968; cons, 20th Century Fund, 1968; dir, promotion, Natl Alliance of Businessmen, 1968-69. War corresp, 1945. Mem: NY State Leg Corresps Assn, pres, 1942; Ninth Amer Assembly, 1955; clubs: Natl Press; Overseas Press. Author: Politics in the Empire State, 1948; What Have You Done for Me Lately, 1967; Roosevelt and Willkie, 1968; ed-in-chief, NY Law Journal, 1963-66; contbr to mags. Home and office: 924 W End Ave, New York, NY.

MOSCOWITZ, Grover M, US, business exec; b. Bklyn, NY, Nov 4, 1916; s. Grover and Miriam (Greenebaum); BA, Lafayette Coll, 1938; LLB, Bklyn Law Sch, 1946; m. Beatrice Lefkowitz, Jan 8, 1946; c: Grover, James. Exec vice-pres, atty, since 1956; pvt practice since 1946. Lt, US Army, Mil Police, 1941-46. Pres: NY State C of C; Civic Exec Conf of Metrop NY; chmn, Planning Bd, Bklyn, NY; mem: bd govs: LIU; Bklyn Cumberland Hosp; clubs: Rotary; Bklyn; Soc of Old Brooklynites; NYC Munic Engrs. Home: 94 Overlook Terr, Roslyn Hgts, NY. Office: 32 Court, St, Brooklyn, NY.

MOSENKIS, Matthew, US, educator; b. Ostropol, Russ, Nov 5, 1909; s. Yehudah and Chanah (Podger); in US since 1921; Heb tchrs dipl, Herzliah Heb Tchrs Sem, NY, 1929; BS, NYU, 1933; MA, Tchrs Coll, Columbia U, 1935; m. Sarah Rachlin, Feb 14, 1935; c: Robert, Daniel. Educ cons, Bd of J Educ, NYC, since 1948; lectr, educ, Herzliah Heb Tchrs Sem, NY, since 1965; tchr, prin, Heb Schs, NYC and Long Island, 1929-48; head, dept, Heb Secondary Educ, J Educ Comm, 1955-60; prin, Marshalliah HS, Gtr NY. Chmn: presidium, Natl Fed Heb Tchrs and Prins; Educ Council of NY, Dept Youth and Educ, JNF; mem: bd rev, Natl Council on J Audio-Visual Materials; Natl Council for J Educ. Contbr to educ mags; produc, award-winning film strips. Home: 968 E 10 St, Brooklyn, NY. Office: 426 W 58 St, New York, NY.

MOSER, Martin P, US, attorney; b. Baltimore, Md, Jan 16, 1928; s. Herman and Henrietta (Lehmayer); AB, The Citadel, Charleston, SC, 1947; LLB, Harvard Law Sch, 1950; m. Elizabeth Kohn, June 14, 1949; c: Martin, Deborah, Richard. Partner, Frank, Bernstein, Conaway & Goldman, and predecessor firm, since 1955; asst states' atty, 1951; 1953-55; instr, U of Baltimore Law Sch, 1954-56; mem, Md Commn on Munic Courts, 1959-68; mem, Planning Comm, Baltimore City, 1961-66; mem, Baltimore Regional Planning Council, 1963-66; delg and chmn, Local Gov Comm, 1961-68, Md Constitutional Conv; chmn, Baltimore Steering Comm, Lawyers' Comm for Civil Rights under Law. US Army, Korea, 1951-53. Fmr pres, J Big Brother League; vice-pres: Citizen's Planning and Housing Assn, 1965-66; mem: Baltimore City, Md State, Amer Fed & Plaintiffs Bar Assns; Masons. Contbr to legal jours. Hobbies: tennis, boating. Home: 2201 Cross Country Blvd, Baltimore, Md.

MOSES, Leslie, US, attorney, oil exec; b. New Orleans, La, Sep 7, 1903; s. Phineas and Carrie (Schwartz); LLB, JD, Tulane U, 1924; m. Eleanore Leipziger, Nov 11, 1929; c: William. Mgr, oil and gas properties of Ellis Rudy, Houston inves, since 1969; pvt practice, New Orleans, 1924-36; Fohs Oil Co, 1936-41, gen atty, secy, 1941-47; div atty, asst to vice-pres, Midstates Oil Corp, 1947-51; lectr, speaker: S Texas Coll of Law, S Methodist U; U Colo; U of NM; La State U; assns in oil, gas ind; tchr, Rel Sch, 1926-52; asst to vice-pres, exploration and produc, Crown Cen Petroleum Corp, 1951-68. Vice-pres, bd mem, J Home for Aged, Houston, Tex, since 1960; mem, bd dirs, Visiting Nurses Assn, 1960-66; bd mem, J Family Service, ince 1953; pres, 1956-59; bd mem, Loans Funds bd, since 1956, pres, 1962-64; fmr: bd mem, Family Service Assn Amer; bd mem, Houston chap, Petroleum Landmen's Assn; mem, bd trustees, Cong Beth Isr; mem, exec comm: J Comty Council; Houston chap, AJComm; mem bd, family and child wfr sect, Houston Comty Council; mem: La State Bar Assn; Amer Assn Petroleum Landmen; Houston Assn Petroleum Landmen; Mid-Continent Oil and Gas Assn; Temple B'nai Zion, Shreveport, La; Touro Syn, New Orleans; Sigma Alpha Mu; club, Men's, Temple Beth Isr, bd mem. Contbr to profsl jours. Recipient: Dist Service Award, Amer Assn Petroleum Landmen, 1967. Home: 2027 Addison Rd, Houston, Tex. Office: 3818 Canal St, Houston, Tex.

MOSES, Rafael, Isr, psychiatrist; b. Berlin, Ger, May 31, 1924; s. Siegfried and Margarete (Orthal); in Isr since 1937; att Heb U, 1941-42; MD, Zurich U, 1951; Jerusalem Psychan Inst, 1964; m. Karin Gruenfeld, Jan 5,1951; c: Allon, Elisha, Tamar. Sr lectr, psycht, and perm chief phys, Heb U, since 1961; visiting lectr, Albert Einstein Coll of Med, NY, 1964-65; visiting sci, Natl Inst of Mh, Bethesda, Md, 1965-66. Lt, Brit Army, 1942-46, IDF, 1948-49. Sci secy, Isr Psychoanalytic Assn; secy, Isr Neuropsycht Assn; mem: Amer Psycht Assn; Intl Psychoanalytic Assn. Contbr to profsl jours. Home: 16 Emek Refaim St, Jerusalem, Isr. Office: Heb U Jerusalem, Isr.

MOSES, Robert, US, public official; b. New Haven, Conn, Dec 18, 1888; s. Emanuel and Bella; BA, Yale U, 1909; BA, hons, jurisprudence, Oxford U, 1911, MA, 1913; PhD, Columbia U, 1914; hon degs: AM, Yale, 1936; LLD: Syracuse U, 1936; Union, 1938; Bates, 1945; Princeton U, 1947; Hofstra Coll, 1948; Columbia U, 1952; Yale 1952; Harvard, 1953; LIU, 1954; Pratt Inst, 1955; NY Law Sch, 1961; Coll of Charleston, 1969; DE: NYU, 1950; U Mich, 1953; Manhattan Coll, 1954; Poly Inst, Bklyn, 1956; St John's U, 1959; U Buffalo, 1959; LHD: Colgate U, 1954; Fordham U, 1959; DFA, Niagara U, 1961; DPA, U RI, 1964; hon f, Wadham Coll, 1960; m. Mary Sims, Aug 28, 1915; c: Barbara Olds, Jane Collins; m. 2nd, Mary Grady, Oct 3, 1966. Cons to chmn, Metrop Transp Auth, since 1968; dir em, Lincoln Cen for Performing Arts, since 1969, dir, 1960-69; chief staff, NY State Reconstruction Commn, 1919-21; pres, LI State Park Commn; chmn, State Council of Parks, 1924-63; mem, State Fine Arts Commn, 1924-27; chmn, Metrop Conf on Parks, 1926-30; NY Secy of State, 1927-28; chmn, Comm on Public Improvements, NY, 1927-28; mem, Moreland Comm to Investigate State Banking Dept, 1929; repr mem, LI Sanitary Commn, 1930; chmn, Jones Beach State Pkwy Auth and Bethpage Park Auth, 1933-63; Rep candidate for Gov, NY, 1934; NYC Park Commn, 1934-60; mem, Henry Hudson Pkwy Auth and Marine Pkwy Auth, 1934-38; cmn: Triborough Bridge Auth, 1936, consolidated, Triborough Bridge and NYC Tunnel Auth, 1946-68; exec off, NYC World's Fair Commn, 1936-40; mem, NYC Pkwy Auth, 1938; mem, NYC Planning Commn, 1942-60; chief exec off, NYC Tunnel Auth, 1945-46; NYC construction coord, 1946-60; chmn, Mayer's Slum Clearance Comm, 1948-60; chmn, NY State, Power Auth, 1954-63; coord, arterial projects, NYC, 1960-66; pres, NY Worlds Fair 1964-65 Corp, 1960-67; lectr, various Us, 1939-61. Mem: Fordham U Council, since 1967; life, NY Bldg Cong; at-large, Gtr NY Boy Scouts of Amer; comm for Govt of People, all since 1966; bd, Make NY Beautiful; natl comm, Immigration Reform, both since 1965; bd trustees, Hall of Sci, City of NY, 1964-67; exec comm, Manhattan Coll, since 1956; hon chmn: Richmondtown Restoration; Prospect Park Centennial; hon mem: Amer Inst Architects; Amer Soc Landscape Architects; Amer Public Works Assn; hon f, Natl Sculpture Soc 1960; hon mem, NY State Judges Assn, 1965; Benjamin Franklin f, Royal Soc Arts, London, 1968; mem, Electoral Coll, Hall of Fame,1969; mem, Phi Beta Kappa; clubs: Players, NYC; Southward Ho, Bay Shore, NY; Lotos, NYC. Contbr to mags and jours. Recipient: numerous awards and medals among the most recent being Medal of NYC, 1964; NY Soc Profsl Engrs; Legion of Valor Testimonial; Cdr, Order of Merit, Rep of It, all 1965; Fordham, Civic Assn; Dist Citizen, St Peter's Coll, Jersey City, both 1966; Bklyn Hgts; Construction Man of Years; Boy Scouts of Amer, Suffolk Co Council, all 1967; Nassau-Suffolk Hosp Council; Rochdale Village, both 1968; Citizens Housing & Planning Council, 1969. Homes: One Gracie Terr, New York, NY; Oak Beach, LI, NY. Office: Randall's Island, New York, NY.

MOSES, Sass, Eng, bank official; b. Bombay, India, Nov 19, 1917; s. Moses and Hilda (Kadoorie); in Eng since 1967; certified asso: Inst of Bankers: Bombay; London; m. Helen Meyer, Mar 16, 1955; two sons. Exec, Chartered Bank, London, since 1967, Bombey, 1937-67; asst, Cen Bank of India, Bombay, 1933-37. Mem: Maccabi Assn; Masons, both London; fmr: chmn, Maccabi Assn; comm, Bene Akiva; Masons, all Bombay; clubs: J; United Services. Hobby: sport. Home: 22 Hartland Dr, Edgware, Middlesex, Eng. Office: 38 Bishopsgate, London EC2, Eng.

MOSES, Shimon Walter, Isr, physician; b. Berlin, Ger, Oct 9, 1926; s. Moses and Mathilde (Rothstein), Bruno; in Isr since 1938; att Heb U-Hadassah Med Sch, Jerusalem; f, ped, Stanford Med Sch; m. Ala Winter; c: Amir, Joram. Head, dept ped "B", dir, head ped research labs, Cen Negev Hosp, since 1966; asst chief, ped, Kaplan Hosp, 1965-66; head, maternal and child care cen, Kupat Holim, 1959-62.

Cpl, J Brig, 1944-45; capt, IDF, 1949. Mem: Isr Clinical Ped Soc, fmr pres; Isr Med Org; Isr Genet Assn; Isr Hematological Assn; Isr Biochem Assn; med adv, Isr br, Familial Dysautonomia Assn; head peds' comm, Isr Lab Sick Fund. Contbr to profsl jours. Recipient: NIH Grant; US Research and Devl Grant; Histadrut Grants; Familial Dysautonomia Assn Grants. Home: 8 Yiftach St, Beersheva, Isr. Office: Central Negev Hosp, Beersheva, Isr.

MOSES, Siegfried, Isr, public servant; b. Lautenburg, Ger, May 3, 1887; s. Julius and Hedwig (Gratz); in Isr since 1936; att U Berlin; DJur, U Heidelberg, 1908; m. Margarete Orthal, 1921; c: Eli, Rafael. Ret; fmr: in pvt practice, 1912-17, 1920-23, 1929-36; org, Food Control, Danzig, 1917-19; dep mgn dir, Org of Ger Towns, 1919; Controller of Footwear Supply, 1920; public auditor, 1932-36; dir, mem bd, chmn, Schocken chain stores, all in Ger; mgn dir, Haavara, org of transfer of J property from Ger to Pal, 1937-38; State Comptroller of Isr 1949-61. Pres: Council of J from Ger, London, Jerusalem; Leo Baeck Inst, since 1955; Org of Cen Eur Immigrants, since 1953; fmr pres, Zionist Org of Ger. Author: Deutsches Kohlen-Wirtschaftsgesetz, 1920; Reform des Obligationen-Wesens, 1933; The Income Tax Ordinance of Palestine, 1942, 1946; Jewish Post War Claims, 1943. Home: 9 Shlomo Molcho St, Jerusalem, Isr.

MOSESON, David, US, rabbi; b. NYC, Oct 7, 1923; s. Chaim and Sarah (Ryshpan); BA, Yeshiva Coll, 1944; MHL, ordained rabbi JTSA, 1951; MA, Tchrs Coll, Columbia U, 1957; m. Gladyce Gerbitz, Mar 24, 1946; c: Sheryl, Deborah, Judith. Rabbi: New Hyde Park J Cen, since 1952; Temple, Emanuel, Westwood, NJ, 1948-52. Pres, RA, Nassau, Suffolk Region, 1961-67; chaplain, LI J Hosp, New Hyde Park, NY, since 1956; mem: RA, Nassau-Suffolk Assn of Rabbis; Bd of Rabbis, NY; B'nai B'rith; KP; club, New Hyde Park, Rotary Intl, bd dir, 1962. Home: 540 N 11 St, New Hyde Park, NY. Study: 100 Lakeville Rd, New Hyde Park, NY.

MOSESSON, Gloria R, US, editor; b. Bklyn NY, Dec 16, 1924; d. Louis and Regina (Greenfield) Rubin; BA, cum laude, Bklyn Coll, 1943; MS, Cornell U, 1945; m. Norman Mosesson, Aug 16, 1955; c: Eric, Neil, Roger, Carl, Carol. Sr ed, Pitman Pub Co, since 1963; juvenile ed, Meredith Press, since 1964; ed: Chem Pub Co, Inc 1947-48; Chartwell House, Inc, 1948-56; dir, teaching material, Educ Pub Corp, 1956-61; juvenile ed, Bobbs-Merrill, 1961-63. Mem: Women's Natl Book Assn; Pub Libr Promotion Group; fmr: natl pres, Jr Hadassah; vice-pres, NY Hadassah; mem, bd dirs: UJA; JNF. Author: Breeding Laboratory Animals, 1968. Hobbies: dairy farming, dressmaking. Home: 290 W End Ave, New York, NY.

MOSHEVICH, Mark, Isr, business exec; b. Russ, Aug 22, 1920; in Isr since 1940; att: Dulwich Coll, London; Jesus Coll, Cambridge; m. Judith Baumoel; 2 c. Chmn, bd, dirs, Elite Chocolate & Sweets Mfg Co, Ltd; chmn, bd dirs, Isr Ind Bank; chmn, Isr Export Inst. Pres, Isr Mfg Assn; mem comm, Isr-Amer Friendship League. Home: 7 Havakuk St, Tel Aviv, Isr.

MOSK, Stanley, US, jurist; b. San Antonio, Tex, Sep 4, 1912; s. Paul and Minna (Perl); att U of Tex, 1930; PhB, U of Chgo, 1933, JLB, 1935; m. Edna Mitchell, Sep 27, 1936; c: Richard. Justice, Cal Supr Court, since 1964; exec secy to Gov of Cal, 1939-42; mem, bd regents, U of Cal, 1940; judge, Superior Court of LA Co, 1943-59; atty-gen, Cal, 1959-64. US Army, WWII. Pres: LA JCC, 1957-58; Vista Del Mar Child Care Service, 1954-58; Beverly Hills B'nai B'rith, 1947; mem, Natl ADL Commn, 1957-58, chmn, southwestern regional adv bd, 1956; natl vice-chmn, B'nai B'rith Vets Commn, 1946-52; mem: Amer Bar Assn; Amer Arbitration Assn; Amer Legion; Elks; Eagles; Coast Guard League; Phi Sigma Delta; clubs: Big Ten; Town Hall; Town of Santa Monica; Commonwealth, SF; Hillcrest Country; Beverly Hills Tennis. Contbr to legal jours. Home: 1200 California St, San Francisco Cal. Office: State Bldg, San Francisco, Cal.

MOSKIN, John Robert, US, editor, author; b. NYC, May 9, 1923; s. Morris and Irma (Rosenfeld); BS, Harvard Coll, 1943; MA, Columbia, 1947; m. Doris Bloch, Oct 7, 1948; c: Mark, David, Nancy. Fgn ed, Look Mag, since 1966, sr ed, 1955-66; reporter, Boston Post, 1941-42; reporter, Newark News, 1947-48; asst to gen mgr, NY Star, 1948-49; ed, Westport Town Crier, Conn, 1949. Tech sgt, US Army, 1943-46. Chmn, bd trustees, Scarsdale Adult Sch; chmn, Fgn Eds Group; mem: Natl Freedom of Info Comm, Sigma Delta Chi; ed bd

adv comm, Dimensions Mag; Dana Reed Prize Comm, Harvard; Harvard Class of 1944 Comm; educ adv comm, Scarsdale Tchrs Inst; bd gov, Scarsdale Town Club; adv comm, World Press Inst; Amer Hist Assn; Authors Guild; clubs: Natl Press, Wash; Harvard, NYC; Scarsdale Town. Author: Morality in America, 1966; Turncoat, 1968. Home: 140 Fox Meadow Rd, Scarsdale, NY. Office: 488 Madison Ave, New York, NY.

MOSKOVIT, Harold R, US, public relations cons; b. Hung, Dec 1, 1906; s. Adolph and Anne (Ritter); in US since 1907; BS, St Johns Coll, Bklyn, 1929, LLB, Law Sch, 1933; m. Ruth' Breitbart, Jan 10, 1935; c: June Schneider. Public and lab relations cons, own firm, since 1945; state dir, Office of Govt Reports, NY, Conn, and RI, 1940-41, asst to natl dir, 1943-45; PR cons, NY State Commerce Commn, 1955-58. Found, state pres, Affiliated Young Dem, NY, since 1932; natl pres, Votes for Youth, since 1936; hon chmn, mem, bd trustees, Home of Old Isr, since 1947; scoutmaster, Boy Scouts of Amer, 1929-35; pres, Judge Cardozo Law Soc, 1932-34; state pres, Intercollegiate Dem League of NY, 1932-42; natl pres, First Voters League of Amer, 1936-44; vice-pres, Comty Reform Temple, 1947-49, pres, 1949-51; hon chmn, Shield of David Home, 1955-59; dir, Kings Co chap, Natl Multiple Sclerosis Soc, 1960-61; hon co: Okla and Ala, 1957; Ky, since 1959; mem: speakers Comm, Gtr NY Fund, 1954-55; St John's Alumni Assn; Colby Coll Alumni Assn; Amer Arbitration Bd, since 1955; adv bd, Aufbau, since 1949; Tau Delta Phi. Ed, publisher, The Young Dem, since 1948. Recipient: award, Judge Cardozo Law Soc, 1933; name on med bldg, Isr, Bx chap, Hadassah, 1956; plaque, Loyalty Day Parade, VFW, 1959; plaque, Home of Old Isr, 1960. Home: 400 E 17 St, Brooklyn, NY. Office: 227 W 45 St, New York, NY.

MOSKOVITCH, Samuel, Can, attorney; b. Montreal, Oct 14, 1904; s. Simon and Sonya (Gersonovitch); BA, McGill U, 1925, BCL, 1928; m. Bess Zumar, Dec 23, 1939; c: Shirley Spunt, Monna. Atty since 1928; King's Counsel, 1948; QC, 1952. Pres: Pi Lambda Phi Frat, McGill U, 1925-26; first Can to receive Frat Key for Merit, 1930; Montefiore Club, Montreal, 1948-49; found, pres, Men's Assn Cong Shaar Hashomayim, Westmount, 1949, 1950, 1951; Mayor, City of Cote Saint-Luc; chmn, CJA, Montreal, 1948; dir, Can Council Chrs & Js; secy, McGill U Law Class, 1928; hon pres, Maimonides Hosp & Home for Aged; hon secy, Can Isr Securities Ltd; mem: bd trustees: Allied J Comty Services; YM-YWHA, both Montreal; bd admn, hon, J Gen Hosp; fmr: pres: Mt Royal Lodge; E Can Council; Dist 1; vice-pres, World Order; mem, Intl Council, all B'nai B'rith; mem, bd dirs, Hillel Found, McGill U; club, Montefiore. Recipient: Maurice Memorial Award, 1958 Man of Year; Montreal Isr Bond Org, 1966 Man Year; Can Centennial Medal, 1967. Home: 5564 Alpine Ave, Cote Saint-Luc 266, Que, Can. Office: 423 Mayor St, Montreal, Can.

MOSKOVITZ, David, US, educator; b. Ungvar, Aus-Hung, Apr 1, 1903; s. Max and Regina (Weiss); in US since 1906; BS, Carnegie Inst of Tech, 1925; MS, 1927; PhD, Brown U, 1932; m. Marion Sacks, 1927 (decd) ;m. 2nd, Ruth Benjamin, 1969, c: Sema Faigen, Richard. Prof, Carnegie Inst of Tech, since 1951, fac mem since 1925; weighmaster, Pa RR Co, 1918-21; instr, Brown U, 1930-31. Mem: Amer Math Soc; Math Assn of Amer; AAUP; Sigma Xi; Tau Beta Pi; Phi Kappa Phi; Pi Mu Epsilon; B'nai B'rith; ZOA. Author: Plane and Spherical Trigonometry, 1937; Mathematical Tables, 1937; Essentials of Trigonometry, 1950; contbr to math jours. Home: 4625 Fifth Ave, Pittsburgh, Pa. Office: Carnegie-Mellon U, Pittsburgh, Pa.

MOSKOWITZ, David, US, manufacturer; b. Pol, 1900. Pres, Nova of Cal. Natl vice-pres, ZOA, hon pres, Bx region and dist, mem, World Zionist Action Comm, delg, 22nd and 23rd WZCs; secy, United Isr Appeal; chmn, KH; mem, bd dirs, JNF; fmr: pres, Kingsbridge Hgts J Cen, Bx, NY; chmn local UJA; co-chmn, State of Isr Bonds. Home: 5436 W 57, St, Los Angeles, Cal. Office: 2849 Leonis Blvd, Los Angeles, Cal.

MOSKOWITZ, George, US, attorney; b. NYC, June 10, 1907; s. Abraham and Rose (Abramovitz); LLB, Bklyn Law Sch of St Lawrence U, 1929; att CCNY, 1925-27; m. Nell Blaustein, May 8, 1947; c: Steven, Victoria. Pvt practice since 1930; counsel, Gov Workmen's Compensation Rev Comm, State of NY, sine 1962; dir, lab dept, Research Inst of Amer, 1944-56; chmn: NY State Bd of Mediation, 1959-61; NY State Minimum Wagl Bd, 1961; impartial chmn, Pubs Assn of

NYC; Newspaper and Mail Deliverers' Uonion of NYC, 1961-62; spec lab counsel to Co Westchester, NY. Mem: bd overseers, JTSA; bd dirs, NY TB and Health Assn; Cen Syn; lab law comm, City of NY Bar Assn; law comm, Amer Arbitration Assn; Amer Bar Assn. Home: 1165 Park Ave, New York, NY. Office: 347 Madison Ave, New York, NY.

MOSKOWITZ, Moses, US, organization exec; b. Aus, Dec 15, 1911; s. Israel and Miriam (Yolles); in US since 1928; BS, CCNY, 1934; att Columbia U, 1935-40; m. Lea Salvin, Mar, 1942; c: Howard, Judith. Secy gen, Consultative Council of J Orgs,since 1947. Capt, US Army, 1942-46. Mem: Amer Soc Intl Law; Res Offs Assn of USA. Author: Human Rights and World Order, 1958; The Politics and Dynamics of Human Rights, 1968; contbr to encys and profsl jours. Office: 61 Broad-way, New York, NY.

MOSKOWITZ, Seymour, US, rabbi; b. NYC, Mar 20, 1930; s. Sol and Ida (Leve); deg, phil, Yeshiva U, NYC; MHL, Boston Heb Tchrs Coll; ordained rabbi, Isaac Elchanan Theol Sem, NYC, 1956; m. Selma Watenmaker, June 23, 1957; c: Tal, Gil, Jonina. Chaplain, US Army, since 1957; Ft Sam Houston, Tex, 1957-58; Poitiers, Fr, 1958-61; Ft Devens, Mass, 1961-64; Ft Hamilton, NY, 1964-65; Ouijongbu, Korea, 1965-66; Camp Zama, Japan, 1966-70. Mem: RabCA; Vaad Harabonim, Mass; Mil Chaplains Assn; J Chaplains Assn; Masons; Sojourners. Recipient: Army Commendation Medal with Oak Leaf Cluster. Hobbies: motor cycling, oil painting, chess. Address: Off of J Chaplain HQ, US Army, Japan.

MOSKOWITZ, Shirley E, US, artist; b. Houston, Tex, Aug 4, 1920; d. Joseph and Flora (Susnitsky); BA, Rice U, Houston, 1941; MA, Oberlin Coll, O, 1942; att Morris Davison Sch of Art, NY, 1943, 1948; m. Jacob Gruber, Feb 3, 1946; c: Ruth, Frank, Samuel. Art instr, U of Tex, 1943; spec lectr, tchr, Mus of Fine Arts, Houston, 1943-46; dir of art, Oberlin Public Schs, 1947-48; one-man shows: Allen Art Mus, Oberlin, 1946; Temple U, Phila, 1948, 1956; Wolpert Gal, Springhouse, Pa, 1957; Intl House, Phila, 1961; Cheltenham Township Art Cen, 1962; Woodmere Art Gallery, Phila, Pa, 1968; three-women show, Beaver Coll, Phila, 1962; group shows: Pa Acad of Fine Arts; Detroit Art Inst; Phila Art Alliance; Akron Art Inst. Pres, Norristown Art League, 1963-64; program chmn, 1960-62; mem: Artists Equity; Woodmere Gal; Women's Intl League for Peace and Freedom; Temple Beth Zion, Beth Israel, Phila, Pa; club, Phila Water Color, secy since 1968. Recipient: prize for oil, Mus of Fine Arts, Houston, 1944; R B Strassburger prize for portraiture, Norristown Art League, 1958, 1960, 1963, 1965; 2nd prize, Cheltenham Art Cen, 1962; 2nd prize, Downtown Norristown Art Festival, 1962; 1st prize, painting, Norristown Art League, 1967; hon mention, Phila Art Tchrs, 1967. Home and studio: 2211 Delancey Place, Philadelphia, Pa.

MOSS, John I, US, business exec; b. Lodz, Pol, May 23, 1912; in US since 1912; s. Ben and Hilda; BS, Ill Inst Tech, 1936; m. Judith, June 21, 1936; c: Debbie, Barbara. Pres: Eastwood Inds Inc, since 1951; Mete-Maker, since 1958; John I Moss Inc, since 1960; tech adv on machinery and equipment, ORT; asst engr, Motorola, 1930-42; tchr, elec, Crane Tech Evening Sch, 1930-42; contract negotiator, elec div, Navy Dept, 1942-45. Pres: Kehelat Jeshurun Syn; Chgo Men's Chap, ORT; Suburban lodge, B'nai B'rith, 1967-68; bd dirs, Selective Service, since 1958; mem: MTDA for Chgo, since 1967; IEEE; AFCEA, life. Home: 6850 Lorel, Skokie, Ill. Office: 1101-11 W Armitage Ave, Chicago, Ill.

MOSS, Joseph Harry, US, business exec; b. NYC, Aug 2, 1907; s. Max and Fanny; BBA, CCNY; m. Betty Math, Dec 20, 1934. Pres, Moss Assos Advt Agcy. Secy, Metrop Geriatric Cen, Bklyn, NY; asso trustee, Cong Kehilath Jeshurun, NYC; chmn, admissions bd, Bklyn Heb Home and Hosp for Aged; mem: Masons, Criterion 907; B'nai B'rith. Hobbies: theater, J educ, geriatrics. Home: 200 E 71 St, New York, NY. Office: 415 Lexington, New York, NY.

MOSS, Leo D, US, physician, educator; b. Berlin, Ger, June 25, 1911; s. Philip and Regina (Polter) Moschkowitz; in US since 1942; att U of Berlin 1929-32 and 1933; U of Freiburg, 1929, 1932; MD, U of Berne, 1934; m. Leonore Chill, Apr 14, 1935; c: Judith, Jeffrey, Deborah. Path, dir of labs, Olean Gen Hosp and St Francis Hosp, since 1942; dir, Cattaraugus Co Labs, since 1960; dep commn of health, Cattaraugus Co, NY; voluntary asst, f, dept path, Mt Sinai Hosp, 1937-42; path, Bradford Hosp, Bradford, Pa, 1942-58; adj prof,biol, St Bonaventure U, since 1960. Chmn, UJA, Olean, 1968; f: Amer Coll Phys; Coll Amer Paths; mem: Amer Assn Paths and Bacts; Amer Soc Clinical Paths; Intl Acad Path; Amer J Phys Comm; Co Med Soc, pres, 1955; W NY Soc of Paths, pres, 1969; Co Cancer Soc, pres, 1962, both of Cattaraugus; B'nai Isr Cong; ZOA; B'nai B'rith lodge, Olean; clubs: Bartlett Country; Olean. Contbr papers in field of hypertension and arteriosclerosis. Home: 477 Vermont St, Olean, NY. Office: Olean Gen Hosp and St Francis Hosp, Olean, NY.

MOSS, Lorraine S, US, civic worker; b. Chgo, Ill, May 1, 1912; d. Lewis and Sara (Ludgin) Solomon; BPh, U of Chgo, 1933, att Grad Sch of Social Service Admn, 1933-34; m. Laurence Du Bois, May 2, 1934 (decd); c: Betsy Gelb; m. 2nd, Otto Moss, June 7, 1952. Admn vice-pres, Chgo sect, Natl Council J Women, fmr, pres, Aurora sect; mem, bd, women's div, J Fed of Metrop Chgo; fmr: secy: Ill Social Hygiene League; and pres, Chgo Women's Aid; women's bd and pres, Mt Sinai Hosp, pres, Infants Aid; pres, Evanston J Comty; asst treas, Aurora sect, Amer Assn U Women; case worker, Unemployment Relief Service; studio mgr: Du Bois-the Drake, 1936-51; Daguerre Studio, 1951-52. Home: 1331 Carl Sandburg Terr, Chicago, Ill.

MOSS, Robert Stewart, US, consultant, business exec; b. NYC, Sep 16, 1919; s. Arthur and Helen (Litzky); BBA, magna cum laude, Baruch Sch of Bus, NYC, 1944; att New Sch of Social Research; m. Doris Holzinger, Aug 15, 1954; c: Nicole, Andrea. Independent cons; vice-pres, Lightoller, 1950-62; pres, Airequipt, Inc, 1963-69. Pvt, US Army, 1943. Dir, trustee, Art Cen, Northern NJ; fmr dir, New Sch Assos. Hobbies: photography, music, art, gardening, travel, reading. Home and office: 20 Marcotte Lane, Bergenfield, NJ.

MOSSE, George L, US, educator, author; b. Berlin, Ger, Sep 20, 1918; s. Hans and Felicia (Mosse); in US since 1939; att U of Cambridge, 1937-39; BS, Haverford Coll, 1941; PhD, Harvard U, 1946. Prof ,hist, U of Wis, since 1955; council, Amer Soc of Church Hist, since 1969; lectr, U of Mich, 1944; visiting expert, US High Commn in Ger, 1951; asso prof, hist, State U of Ia, 1949-55, chmn, Core Course W Civilization, 1946-56, mem, fac of hist, 1944-46; lectures, Heb U, 1962; visiting prof, Heb U, Jerusalem, 1969-70. Pres, Amer, Soc Reformation Research, 1961-62; Ia State chmn, AAUP, 1954-55; mem: Amer Hist Soc; Amer Soc for Church Hist; Wis Soc of J Learning; Intl Commn for Hist of Repr and Parliamentary Insts; Phi Beta Kappa. Author: The Struggle for Sovereignty in England, 1950; The Reformation, 1953; The Holy Pretence: a Study of Christianity and Reason of State, 1957; The Culture of Western Europe: Nineteenth and Twentieth Century, 1961; The Crisis of German Ideology, 1964; Nazi Culture, 1966; Germans and Jews, 1969; co-author: Europe in Review, 1957; The Jewish Question at the End of the Weimar Republic, 1962; Europe in the Sixteenth Century, 1968; contbr to profsl mags; to Schaff-Herzog Ency of Rel Knowledge; New Cambridge Modern Hist; co-ed, Jour of Contemporary Hist, since 1966. Home: 36 Glenway, Madison, Wis. Office: U of Wis, Madison, Wis.

MOSSLER, Liebert I, US, business exec; b. Indianapolis, Ind, Jan 26, 1904; s Jesse and Fannie (Solomon); m. Shirley Miller, May 30, 1933; c: James, Nancy Taffel. Chmn bd, Mossler Ins Agcy, Inc, since 1938; exec, Peoples Outfitting Syndicate, 1920-38. Capt, US Army, 1943-46. Pres, JWF; mem, natl comm, AJComm, since 1948, fmr pres, Indianapolis chap; natl council, JDC, since 1955; mem, pres council, Brandeis U; dir, J Comty Cen; dir, J Educ Assn; fmr pres: Dist Golf Assn; Indianapolis Ins Agts Assn; Ind State Golf Assn; club, Broadmoor Country, fmr pres and secy. Home: 4000 N Meridian St, Indianapolis, Ind. Office: 1815 N Meridian St, Indianapolis, Ind.

MOST, Harry, US, physician, educator; b. NYC, Sep 18, 1907; s. Philip and Sarah (Abend); BS, NYU, 1927; MD, 1931, DMS, 1939; DTM and H, London Sch of Tropical Med and Hygiene, Eng, 1936; m. Rita Gold, Nov 20, 1938; c: Susan, Paul. Hermann M Biggs prof, preventive med, chmn of dept, NYU, since 1954, asst prof, med, 1941-46, asso prof, preventive med, 1946-49, prof, tropical med, 1949-50, acting chmn, dept preventive med, 1950-54; visiting phys, Bellevue Hosp, since 1938; dir, tropical diseases clinic, NYC Dept of Health, since 1949; visiting lectr, Harvard Sch of Public Health, since 1955; cons: tropical med, Marine Hosp, 1944; Kingsbridge VA Hosp, 1946; asso att phys, NYU Hosp, 1949; cons phys, Meadowbrook Hosp, 1953, cons in tropical med to Surg Gen, US Army, 1946; dep chief cons in tropical med, VA, Wash, DC, 1947; cons in schistosomiasis, USN, 1950. Maj,

US Army, MC, 1944-46. F: NY Acad Med; NY Acad Scis; dipl, Amer Bd Preventive Med and Public Health, 1950; mem: tropical med study sect, USPHS, 1947; comm on naval med research, NRC, 1952; comm on parasitic diseases. Armed Forces Epidemiological Bd, 1953; impartial spec bd, NY State Workmen's Compensation Bd, 1947; vice-pres, Amer Soc Tropical Med, 1950-51; council mem, 1948-52, mem, ed bd, since 1950; chmn, microbiol sect, NY Acad Med, 1950-51, secy, 1948-50; Royal Soc Tropical Med and Hygiene; Amer Soc Parasitologists; Natl Malaria Soc; NY Soc Tropical Med; Amer Soc Clinical Inves; Amer Public Health Assn; AMA; NY Co Med Soc; AAAS; Amer Acad Tropical Med; Amer Found for Tropical Med; Harvey Soc; Phi Beta Kappa; Beta Lambda Sigma; Sigma Xi; Alpha Omega Alpha. Contbr to profsl jours. Recipient: Legion of Merit, US Army, 1946. Home: 40 Walnut Lane, Manhasset, NY. Office: 550 First Ave, New York, NY.

MOSZKOWSKI, Steven A, US, physicist; b. Berlin, Ger, Mar 13, 1927; s. Richard and Ruth (Bamberger); in US since 1940; BS, U of Chgo, 1946; PhD, 1952; m. Lena Iggers, Aug 29, 1952; c: Benjamin, Richard, Ronald, Prof, physics, UCLA, since 1953; research asso, Columbia U, 1952-53. Pvt, US Army, 1946-47. Prin contrib: research in theoretical nuclear physics. Mem, Phi Beta Kappa. Co-author: Beta Decay, 1966. Re-, cipient: Guggenheim f, 1961. Hobby: philately. Home: 3283 Inglewood Blvd, Los Angeles, Cal. Office: U of Cal, Los Angeles, Cal.

MOTZ, Lloyd, US astrophysicist, educator; b. Susquehanna, Pa, June 5, 1910; s. Solomon and Minnie (Seltzer); BS, CCNY, 1930; PhD, Columbia U, 1936; m. Minnie Rosenbaum, June, 1934; c: Robin, Julie. Prof, astronomy, Columbia U, since 1962, mem fac since 1935; adj prof, physics, Poly Inst, Bklyn, since 1950. Pres, NY Acad of Scis, f: Royal Astronomical Soc; Amer Phys Inst; mem: Amer Astronomical Soc; AAAS; Sigma Xi; Phi Beta Kappa. Author: This is Astronomy; This is Outer Space; Essential; of Astronomy; Astrophysics and Stellar Structure; contbr to sci jours. Recipient: first prize, for theory of elem particles, Gravity Research Found, 1960. Home: 815 W 181 St, New York, NY. Office: Columbia U, New York, NY.

MOTZKIN, Arthur P, US, business exec; b. New Rochelle, NY, May 27, 1922; s. Isidore and Julia (Polansky); BS, Franklin and Marshall Coll, Lancaster, Pa, 1943; att: Texas A & M; Syracuse U; U of Ill; m. Marilyn Messinger, Aug 22, 1948; c: Nancy, Judith, Barry. Pres, Motzbro Corp, since 1947; vice-pres, Empire State Petroleum Assn; exec, Kingston Oil Supply Corp, since 1957; pres, Motzkin Bros, 1947-54; vice-pres, Rite Cleaners Dyers, Inc, 1954-55. US Corps of Engrs, WW II. Initial gifts chmn, UJA, since 1961, allocations chmn, since 1960, chmn, 1959-60; pres, Hudson Valley Oil Heat Council, since 1963, vice-pres, 1962; bd dirs: The Children's Home, Kingston, NY; Kingston Area C of C; trustee: Temple Emanuel, J Comty; mem: Masons; B'nai B'rith; Cong Ahavath Isr; ZOA; clubs: Wiltwyck Country, mem, bd dirs, since 1960; Kiwanis. Recipient: 5 battle stars; NY State Oil Man of the Year, 1968; Man of the Month, 1969. Hobby: golf. Home: Rd 5, Box 22B, Kingston, NY. Office: POB 788, Port Ewen, NY.

MOTZKIN, Leo, Finland, business exec; b. Helsingfors, Finland, June 7, 1918; s. Davis and Genia (Schwer); m. Mirjam Weitzman, Mar 9, 1941; c: Fred, Renée, Marion. Mgn dir: Oy Pukinetehdas Prima Konfektionsfabrik Ab, since 1934; Leo Motzkin Enterprise, Jaguar Products, since 1965. Bd dirs, taxation bd, J Cong; treas, Maccabi Sports Org; mem: J Comty bd; J Council Admn; KH; Magbit. Home: Risto Rytivägen 1D, Helsingfors 57, Finland. Office: Kalevagatan 28, Helsingfors 10, Finland.

MOTZKIN, Theodore S, US, mathematician, educator; b. Berlin, Ger, Mar 26, 1908; s. Leo and Paula (Rosenblum); in US since 1948; PhD, U of Basel, Switz, 1934; m. Naomi Orenstein; c: Aryeh, Joseph, Gabriel. Prof, UCLA, since 1950; visiting prof: Harvard U, 1948-49; Heb U, Jerusalem, 1962, 1968; U of Copenhagen, 1963; U of Cal, Berkeley, 1969. Mem: Amer Math Soc; Société Math de Fr; London Math Soc; Schweizer Math Gesellschaft; Math Soc of Isr, pres, 1936-48. Recipient: NSF f, 1962-63. Home: 10728 Rochester Ave, Los Angeles, Cal. Office: U of Cal, Los Angeles, Cal.

MOVITT, Eli R, US, physician; b. Kiev, Russ, Dec 24, 1907; s. Lev and Anna (Liokumovittch) Rodin; in US since 1926; att UCLA; BA, Stanford U, 1931, MD, Med Sch, 1935; m.

Jennie Kennedy, June 9, 1936; c: John. Chief, med service, VA Hosp, Oakland, since 1946; phys, VA Hosp, SF, 1939-46; clinical asso prof, med, U Cal Med Sch, since 1963. FACP; mem: AAAS; Amer Fed for Clinical Research; W Soc for Clinical Research; Amer Assn for Study of Liver Diseases. Contbr to med jours. Home: 67 Brookwood Rd, Orinda, Cal. Office: VA Hosp, Martinez, Cal.

MOVSKY, Myron B, US, rabbi; b. Rochester, NY, Aug 21, 1917; s. Philip and Rose (Gordon); att U of Rochester, 1940-41; BA, ordained rabbi; Yeshiva U, 1942; m. Hadassah Hollander, July 29, 1945; c: Peggy, David. Rabbi: Cong of Moses, Kalamazoo, Mich, since 1959; B'rith Kodesh, Rochester, NY, 1942-46; Temple Beth El, Hornell, NY, 1942-46; Shaare Zedek, Lima, O, 1946-59; lectr, Old Testament, O Council of Churches, 1946-59. Chaplain, US Army, Alfred U, 1942-45. Dir, Teenagers TV Forum, 1953-56; pres, Lima lodge, B'nai B'rith, 1954-55; Lima chap, ZOA, 1946-49; mem: natl bd, ZOA, 1950-60; J Publ Soc; Rabb Assn of Amer; O Narcotics Bd; Cerebral Palsy Bd; JDC; J Hist Soc; clubs: Torch, Optimist, med bd, 1956-58. Contrib ed, Fellowship in Prayer. Home: 2508 Aberdeen Dr, Kalamazoo, Mich. Study: 2501 Stadium Dr, Kalamazoo, Mich.

MOWSHOWITZ, Israel, US, rabbi; b. Olinko, Pol, July 10, 1914; s. Samuel and Genie (Nitzberg); in US since 1929; BA, Yeshiva U, 1935; MA, Duke U, NC, 1942, PhD, 1951; ordained rabbi, Rabbi Isaac Elhanan Theol Sem, 1937; m. Lillian, Polachek, Aug 8, 1937; c: Sylvia Orenstein, Solomon. Rabbi, Hillcrest J Cen, since 1949, awarded life tenure, 1957; rabbi: Beth El Cong, Durham, NC, 1937-43; Cong Beth Isr, Omaha, Neb, 1943-49. Found, chmn bd, Intl Syn, Kennedy Airport; chmn, natl inter-rel coop comm, ADL; pres, NY Bd Rabbis, since 1962; mem: bd: NY State Mh Soc; J Comty Services, LI; Natl TBRDA Bd; Queensboro TB and Health Assn; Queens Co chap, State Commn Against Discrimination; adv comm, City of NY Bur of Child Guidance; mem: Amer Psych Assn; ZOA; B'nai B'rith; Kiwanis; bd trustees, Dowling Coll; fmr: mem: travel and study sem, NCCJ to 13 countries; first delg of rabbis to Russ to study conditions of J; leader, student group from 45 U's in US to W Afr; asso dir, Cross Roads Afr Project; delg: Amer J Conf; WZC, Basle; found, Mayor's Hum Relations Comm; pres, Urban League, both Omaha. Contbr to: J Daily Forward; Anglo-J mags and periodicals. Recipient: award, Interfaith Movement; citations from: NCCJ; Mayor of NYC. Spec interests: intl affairs, chess. Home: 81-26 Haddon St, Jamaica, NY. Study: 183-02 Union Turnpike, Flushing, NY.

MOYER, Sidney S, US, manufacturer; b. Youngstown, O, Dec 24, 1899; s. Morris and Miriam (Simon); att U Pa; m. Helen Weil, Dec 8, 1927; c: Richard, John. Pres, Moyer Inves Co, Youngstown, O, since 1948. Pres, Comprehensive Mh Cen; mem: bd dirs, St Elizabeth's Hosp; cotton garment ind code auth, Natl Rehab Admn; ind adv comm, Quartermaster Corp; Mayor's Conciliation Panel, City of Youngstown; bd dirs, Union Natl Bank; exec, admn comms and asso treas, AJComm; regional exec comm, Boy Scouts of Amer; Mahoning Valley chap, ARC; Youngstown Area Heart Assn; regional bd, B'nai B'rith; Playground Assn; Intl Inst Rotary, fmr pres; fmr: pres, chmn bd: Intl Assn of Garment Mfrs; Assn of Pants Mfrs of Amer; mem, men's and boy's clothes comm, War Produc Bd and OPA, WW II; vice-pres, Youngstown Comty Corp; natl chmn, Jf Defense Appeal; mem, exec comm, J Fed of Youngstown; chmn, J Comty Relations Council; pres, Comty Chest. Home: 959 Ravine Dr, Youngstown, O. Office: 18-24 N Walnut St, Youngstown, O.

MOZES, Mark, Isr, surgeon, educator; b. Warsaw, Pol, Dec 3, 1909; s. Aharon and Sara (Lichtendacht); m. Anna Engel c: Martin. Prof, head, surg dept, Tel Hashomer Hosp. Lt Col, MC. Mem: Isr Surg Soc; Amer Coll of Surg; Intl Soc Cardio-Vascular Surg. Contbr to profsl jours. Recipient: Mil Cross, Pol; Monte Cassino Cross, Cross of Merit. Home: 12 Akiva Arie St, Tel Aviv, Isr. Office: Tel Hashomer Hosp, Isr.

MU'ALIM, Selim Ezra, Isr, business exec; b. Basrah, Iraq, Oct 14, 1920; s. Ezra and Naima (Zelikha); in Isr since 1956; BBA, Amer U, Beirut, Leb, 1943, MA, 1944; m. Doris Obadia, Apr 2, 1956; c: Tirzah, Ezra. Gen mgr, Arab Isr Bank Ltd, since 1959; fmr: secy to gen mgr, Rafidain Bank, Baghdad, 1944-51; found, tchr, Shamash Commercial Evening Sch; lectr, Commercial-Econ Inst, Baghdad; active in Zionist, Aliyah activities, caught by Iraqi auths, sentenced to 5 years hard lab, 1951. Home: 1 Moria St, Haifa, Isr. Office: 2 Shivat Zion, Haifa, Isr.

MUHSAM, Brouria, Isr parasitologist, educator; b. Jerusalem; d. Uria and Hanna (Weinshenker) Feldman; licence, Biol Scis, U Geneve; PhD, Heb U, Jerusalem, 1942; m. Helmut Muhsam; c: Ofrah. Asso prof, parasitology, Heb U, Jerusalem, since 1969; dir, med research, Isr Research Council, 1955-59; guest lectr, Inst of Acarology, U Md, 1958; research asso, Dept of Entomology, Parasitology, U Cal, Berkeley, 1961-62. Prin contrib, discoveries: new type symbiosis; function of areae porosae of hard ticks. Panel mem, FAO Expert Panel on Tick Borne Diseases; mem, Amer Soc Parasitologists. Recipient : Holon Marx-Kirbey f, Intl Assn of U Women, 1944; Henrietta Szold Award, Tel Aviv Munic, 1955. Contbr to sci jours; one sci motion picture. Hobbies: photography, cinematography. Home: 18 Brodi St, Jerusalem, Isr. Office: Heb U, Jerusalem, Isr.

MUHSAM, Helmut V, Isr, statistician, demographer; b. Berlin, Ger, Aug 12, 1914; s. Kurt and Alice (Freymark)Muehsam; in Isr since 1937; grad, math, U Geneva, Switz, 1934; physics, 1935, DSc, 1937; m. Brouria Feldman, 1937; c: Ofra. Asso prof, stat, Heb U, Jerusalem, since 1958; fmr: head, dept stat, ext tchr, lectr, all Heb U; stat: JA, Va'ad Leumi, 1938-44; asst stat, Govt of Pal, 1944-48; prin stat, Govt of Isr, Jerusalem, 1948-52; social affairs off, UN, NY, 1957-58; visiting asso prof, sociol, public health, U Cal, Berkeley, 1961-62; cons, UNESCO, 1968. Haganah, IDF. Vice-pres, Union Internationale pour l'Etude Scientifique de la Population; mem: Intl Stat Inst; Amer Stat Assn; Biometrical Soc. Author: The Supply of Professional Manpower, 1959; Bedouin in the Negev, 1966; contbr to jours. Home: 18 Brodi St, Jerusalem, Isr. Office Hebrew U, Jerusalem, Isr.

MÜLLER, Ladislas S, Isr, engineer; b. Szekszard, Hung, Sep 11, 1905; s. Albert and Maria (Hirschfeld); in Isr since 1936; dipl, engr, Royal Tech U, Hung, 1927; m. Irène Fischer, Mar 15, 1937. Ret: head, chief designer, structural dept, Isr Land Devl Co, 1950-68; structural engr with: B Chaikin, architect, Jerusalem, 1936-50; A Gut Tel Aviv, 1942-43; tchr, structural engr, Brit Inst of Engr Tech, Jerusalem, 1944-46; construction engr of: St John Ophthalmic Hosp, Jerusalem, 1939-40; Haifa Munic Bldg, 1940-41; Iraq Petroleum Co; Kirkuk Hosp, 1947-48. Mem: Assn Engrs and Architects in Isr; Amer Concrete Inst; fmr pres, Hung Immigrants Assn, Jerusalem. Contbr to profsl jours. Hobbies: book collecting, painting. Home: 14 Ben Yehuda St, Jerusalem, Isr.

MULLIN, Harry, US, physician; b. Olyphant, Pa, Aug 10, 1910; s. Samuel and Bertha (Rudin), BS, St Thomas Coll, Scranton, Pa, 1931; U of Cincinnati Sch of Med, 1936, postgrad work, J Hosp, Bklyn, 1937; m. Ethel Kochansky July 20, 1944; c: Brian, Robin. Allergist, in pvt practice since 1946; chief, dept allergy, Scranton State Hosp, Pa; cons, allergy: Mercy Hosp, Scranton; Wayne Co Memorial Hosp, Homesdale, Pa; fmr: allergy clinician: Queen's Gen Hosp, Gen Hosp, Jamaica, NY, 1937-40; Wyckoff Hosp, Bklyn, 1938-40; allergist, staff, Wilson Memorial Hosp, Johnson City, NY, 1953. Capt, USAAC, MC, 1942-46. Mem: Lackawanna Co Med Soc; Med Soc of State of Pa; AMA; Amer Coll Allergists; Pa Allergy Assn; Amer Acad Allergy; Intl Corresp Soc Allergists; Amer Acad Dermat and Syphilology; Soc for Inves Dermat; Phila Allerg Soc; Masons; Shriners; JWV; Heb Orthodox Cen. Hobbies: philately, antique paper-weights collecting. Home: 601 Madison Ave, Scranton, Pa. Offices: 1005 Med Arts Bldg, Scranton, Pa; 84 Oak St, Binghamton, NY.

MULLOR, (Miller), Moshe L, Isr, attorney; b. Belzec, Aust, Oct 31, 1908; s. Joseph and Goldie (Hahn) Miller; in Isr since 1934; grad, Heb Tchrs Sem, Lvov, 1929; MJur, U Lvov, 1932; m. Rivka Macht, Aug 8, 1941; c: Miryam, Chana, Josef. Pvt practice since 1940; mem, adv council for absorption of newcomers to Isr; journalist, Pal, 1934-35; magistrate, Munic Court, Tel Aiv, 1954-57. Mem: exec council, Liberal Independent Party; exec, Friends of Heb U; J Advocates Assn; Masons; vice-pres, B'nai Brith Dist, Isr; fmr: vice-pres: Assn of Pol Jews; Isr sect, Assn for UN; council, Isr State Party; world council, Brith Kanaim; Magbith Hahitgaysut. Contbr to periodicals. Home: 14 Adam Hacohen St, Tel Aviv, Isr. Office: 55 Nahlat Benyamin St, Tel Aviv, Isr.

MULTER, Abraham J, US, jurist; b. NYC, Dec 24, 1900; s. Max and Emma (Rock); LLB, Bklyn Law Sch, 1921, LLM, 1922; LLD, Yeshiva U, 1963; c: Robert, Howard. Justice, Supr Court, New York State, since 1968; pvt practice, 1923-68; mem, firm, Rayfiel & Multer, until 1947; sr mem, Multer, Nova and Seymour, 1947-68; US

congressman, 1948-68; fmr: spec asst atty gen, NY State, for election matters; spec counsel to Mayor, NYC; counsel to city, state and fed leg comms. USCG Res,WW II. Pres: Council of Yeshiva U; Amer ORT; trustee: UAHC; vice-chmn: Albert Einstein Med Coll; Bklyn JCC; vice-pres: Bnai Zion; Temple Beth Emeth; dir: JNF; Coney I YM-YWHA; Shorefront YM-YWHA; Lay Bd, NY Bd, Rabbis; FJP; Nottingham Civic Assn; Lawyers Club; Bklyn Law Sch Alumni Assn; life mem: ZOA; Heb Inst of LI; J Chautauqua Soc; mem: Inter-Amer, Amer, Fed, NY State, Bklyn Bar Assns; NY Law Inst; Amer Judicature Soc; Amer Soc Intl Law; Bklyn-Manhattan Trial Lawyers Assn; Amer Political Sci Assn; Assn of Supr Court Justices; comty adv bd, Coney I Hosp; adv bd, E Midwood J Cen; UJA; Syn Council of Amer; J Theol Soc; ADL; Boy Scouts of Amer; Police Athletic League; Boys Clubs; hon f, Archaeol Inst of Amer; hon trustee, Boys HS Alumni Assn; fmr: secy pres, Kings Hwy Dem Club; chmn, Kings Co Dem Law Comm; vice-chmn, NY State Dem Law Comm; mem, Dem Co and State Exec Comms; club, Richmond Co Country. Home: 1397 E 21 St, Brooklyn, NY. Office: Supr Court, Civic Cen, Brooklyn, NY.

MUNDEL, George, Isr, pediatrician; b. Rustenburg, Transvaal, S Afr, July 11, 1921; s. Sam and Rona (Miller); in Isr since 1949; MB, BCh, U of Witwatersrand 1943; MRCP, DCH, Royal Coll of Phys, London; MRCP, Edinburgh; att Harvard Sch of Public Health, Boston, Mass; m. Rosalie Michaelson, Aug 30, 1946; c: Alon, Shelley. Chief, ped dept, Asaf Harofe Hosp, since 1954; dir, Rehab Cen for Children, since 1959; sr phys, ped, Hadassah Hosp, 1949-51; sr ped, Hosp for Children, Rosh haAyin Immigrant Camp, 1951-54; ped adv, Min of Health, Maternal and Child Health Dept, 1954-59. Capt, S Afr MC, 1944-46. Chmn, Ilan, Isr Crippled Children Org; med adv, WIZO Maternal and Child Training Cen; mem: S Afr ZF Med Comm; fmr chmn, Isr Clinical Ped Clubs; pec mem, World Commn for Cerebral Palsy; fgn corresp mem, Amer Acad for Cerebral Palsy. Contbr to med jours. Home: 4 haYasmin St, Herzlia Pituach, Isr. Office: Asaf Harofe Govt Hosp, Zerifin, Isr.

MUNDY, Joseph, Isr, author; b. Bucharest, Rum, May 22, 1935; s. Avigdor and Roza (Rozenhapht). Playwright; plays at: Habima Theater, Tel Aviv; Cameri Theater, Tel Aviv; Manffield Theater; L'Epe de Bois Theatre; Café Theater; Royal Theater; Bombarde Theater, all Paris; repr Isr in Festival of Interdrama, Berlin; contbr to radio and press. IDF, 1954-56. Home: 85 Gordon St, Tel Aviv, Isr.

MUNITZ, Milton K, US, educator; b. NYC, July 10, 1913; s. Samuel and Anna (Blumberg); BA, CCNY, 1933; MA, Columbia U, 1935, PhD, 1939; m. Leonore Bloom, Dec 22, 1946; c: Charles, Andrew. Prof, phil, head, all-U dept of phil, NYU, since 1946; instr: CCNY, 1937-46; Queens Coll, NY, 1946; lectr, Columbia U, 1946; Ford Fac f, 1954-55; Fulbright sr research f, Cambridge U, 1960-61; Guggenheim f, 1960-61; visiting dist prof, phil, SUNY, Brockport, 1967-68. Lt, USAAC, 1943-45. F, Royal Astronomical Soc; mem: Amer Phil Assn; Aristotelian Soc. Author: The Moral Philosophy of Santayana, 1939; Space, Time and Creation, 1957; Theories of the Universe, 1957; A Modern Introduction to Ethics, 1958; The Mystery of Existence, 1965. Recipient: Nicholas Murray Butler Medal, Columbia U, 1963. Home: Marlborough Rd, Scarborough, NY. Office: NYU, New York, NY.

MUNK, Elie, Fr, rabbi, author; b. Paris, Sep 15, 1900; s. Samuel and Amélie (Strauss); PhD, U of Berlin, 1925; ordained rabbi, Hildesheimer Sem, Berlin, 1926; m. Fanny Goldberger, Apr 15, 1927; c: Amélie Jacobovits, Jacob, Ruth, Françoise, Miriam, Max, Judith. Rabbi, Orthodox Cong, Adath Jereim, Paris, since 1937. Pres: Keren Hatorah, Fr, since 1938; Eur Union Orthodox J Congs; Admn Council Yavne Sch; Conseil-Représentatif du Judaisme Traditionaliste de Fr; delg to UNESCO of Agudath Isr World Org, since 1947; vice-pres; Agudath Isr, Fr, 1939. Author: Die Welt der Gebete, 1933; Das Licht der Ewigkeit, 1935; La Justice, Sociale en Israel, 1947; Vers l'Harmonie; The World of Prayer, both 1954; commentary of Rashi in Fr, La Voix de la Torah. Home and study: 18 rue Notre Dame de Lorette, Paris 9e, Fr.

MUNTNER, Suessmann, Isr, physician, educator; b. Kolomea, Pol, Sep 17,1897; s. Jakob and Miryamne (Szobel); in Isr since 1933; MD, Friedrich Wilhelm U, Berlin, 1925; m. Nelly Taussik, 1931. Pvt practice, Jerusalem since 1933; prof, med hist, Heb U, Jerusalem, since 1959; guest lectr: Madrid; Barcelona, 1949. F, hon mem, Intl Acad Hist of Sci; secy, Isr

Soc for Med Hist and Sci; laureat, Académie Nationale de Médecine, Paris, 1967; mem: med sect, Heb Lang Acad; Jerusalem Acad of Med; co-found, Maccabi World Org. Author: Donnolo, First Medical Writer in Hebrew in Europe, 1950; Saladino di Ascoli-Pharmaceutics, 1955; Introduction to the Book of Assaph the Physician, VI Cent, 1956; ed: Maimonides Med Works with Heb commentaries, 10 vols, Heb, partly Eng, Ger; Jour of Med Hist and Sci; trans from Greek into Heb, Hero and Leander, 1936; contbr to jours. Spec interests: astronomy, archaeol. Home and office: 54 Prophets St, Jerusalem, Isr.

MUSCHAT, Maurice, US, surgeon; b. Riga, Latvia, July 30, 1898; s. Joseph and Rachel (Jacobson); in US since 1923; MD, U of Heidelburg, Ger, 1923; m. Clare Muschat, 1917; c: Mimi. Ret; fmr: chief urol surg: Einstein Med Cen; St Agnes Hosp, both Phila, Pa; mem, council on med educ and hosps, AMA; J William White f, 1925; asso, urol surg and research urol, 1928-46. Mem, life, Amer Coll Surgs; found, Amer Bd Urol Surg; mem: Amer Urol Assn; AMA. Contbr to profsl jours. Home: 1111 Ocean Ave, Brooklyn, NY.

MUSHER, Jermey I, US, physicist; educator; b. NYC, Dec 3, 1935; s. Sidney and Hadassah (Kaplan); AB, Harvard Coll, 1957; att Oxford U, 1957-58; AM, PhD, Harvard U, 1958-62; m. Evelyn Torczyner, Sep 20, 1964; c: Joshua, Raphael. Asso prof,chem, Belfer Grad Sch of Sci, Yeshiva U, NY, since 1966; asst prof, Rockefeller U, 1963-65; visiting prof: Acad of Scis, Russ, 1964-65; Heb U, 1969; U of Nottingham, Eng, 1969. Contbr profsl jours. Home: 210 W 101 St, New York, NY. Office: Yeshiva U, New York, NY.

MUSHER, Sidney, US, business exec; b. Newark, NJ, Nov 9, 1905; s. Nathan and Anna (Goldstein); BA, Johns Hopkins U, 1925; m. Hadassah Kaplan, Jan 7, 1935; c: Jermey, Daniel, David. Chmn, Isr Research and Devl Corp Ltd, since 1967; exec comm, PEC Isr Econ Corp, since 1948; bd dirs, Cooper Labs; pres, Musher Found, 1935-63; dir research, Pompeian Olive Oil, 1928-30. Holder of numerous patents. Chmn, Comm on Manpower of Isr; vice-pres, Pal Endowment, Fund; treas, J Reconstructionist Found; adv council, Soc for Advancement of Judaism; pres, Hadassah and Sidney Musher Found; adv, Isr Natl Council for Research and Devl; exec council, Amer J Hist Soc; mem: PM Council for Econ Devl of Isr; Amer Chem Soc; AAAS; Amer Oil Chem Soc; Inst Food Techs; Amer Dairy Sci Assn; World Assn Vet Parasitology; B'nai B'rith; ZOA; Amer Technion Soc. Contbr to jours. Home: 59 W 71 St, New York, NY. Office: 500 Fifth Ave, New York, NY.

MUSHKAT, Marion Max, Isr, educator; b. Suwalki, Pol, Nov 5, 1915; s. Mark and Sophie (Holberski); in Isr since 1957; MA, Inst Commercial, Nancy, Fr, 1935; DJur, Fac Law, Nancy, 1939; LLD, MA, Fac Law and Econ, Warsaw, 1947; m. Shoshana Greenfield, Oct 28, 1944; c: Miron, Silvia, Irit. Prof, intl law, intl relations, U Tel Aviv, since 1957; academic dir, Isr Inst Intl Affairs, since 1964; prof, rector, Duracz Sch Law, Warsaw, 1948-51; prof, Warsaw U, 1950-56; dir, Pol Inst Intl Affairs, 1949-51; Pol repr, UN War Crimes Commn, London, 1946-48; head, Pol Mission, Inves War Crimes, Nürnberg, 1946-48; repr at several peeace confs. Col, Pol Tank Brig, 1943-45. Pres, Isr Union WW II Vets; adv, bd dirs Acad World Studies, Ross, Cal; pres, Pol ORT, 1945-50; f, World Acad Art and Sci; mem: corresp of Fr Polemological Inst; Yad Vashem Memorial Auth; coord of Yad Vashem Studies for Eichmann Trial. Author: Nürnberg Trial, 1962; Theory and Practice of International Relations,1967; International Cooperation and International Institutions, 1967; Observations on Modern Approaches to the Study of International, Relations; The African Approach to Basic Problems of International Law; The Indian Society of International Law; The Development Assistance Machinery of the UN Family, 1968; ed, rev, Intl Problems. Recipient: mil awards: Viztuti Mil; Lenino Order; Cross of Merit; Ot Lohamey haNazim; Itur Lohamey haMedina; Minski Rapachi's prize, Min of Educ, Pol, 1952; Naftali Prize, Tel Aviv Munic, 1967. Hobby: swimming. Home: 9 Hamishna, Tel Aviv, Isr. Office: Tel Aviv U, Ramat Aviv, Isr.

MYERBERG, Michael, US, theatrical produc; b. Baltimore, Md, Aug 5, 1906; s. Nathan and Anna (deBoskey); att Johns Hopkins U; m. Adrienne Matzenauer, Mar 9, 1935; c: Edward, Paul. Producer: vaudeville, band acts, 1925-30; legitimate theater, 1930-36; asst produc, film, 100 Men and a Girl, 1938; mgr: Leopold Stokowski; Phila Ballet; other artists,1938; org,All Amer Youth Orch, with Leopold Stokow-

ski, under auspices of US State Dept, 1940; toured: SA, 1940; US, 1941; produc: Skin of Our Teeth, 1942; Stardust, 1943; Lute Song, 1945; The Barrier, 1948; Hänsel and Gretel, film, 1954; Patterns, film, 1955; Waiting for Godot, 1956; Compulsion, 1958. Recipient: Pulitzer Prize, for Skin of Our Teeth, 1942; DAR Award, for Hansel and Gretel, 1954; Christopher's Award, for Patterns, 1955. Home: 144 Beach 147 St, Neponsit, NY. Office: 1564 Broadway, New York, NY.

MYERS, A Howard, US, educator; b. Albany, NY, Aug 6, 1904; s. Nathan and Florence (Lilienstern); AB, Cornell U, Ithaca, NY, 1926; MA, Columbia U, 1932, PhD, 1933; m. Ethel Goodman, Apr 27, 1935; c: Howard, Joy Silverman. Prof, ind relations, Northeastern U, since 1954; lab arbitrator, Boston, Mass, since 1945; exec dir, Natl Recovery Admn, lab adv bd, 1933-35; regional dir, NLRB, 1935-45; lectr, Harvard U, 1946-51; regional chmn, Wage Stabilization Bd, 1951-52; asso prof, U of Mich, 1952-53. Trustee, mem Comm; Natl Temple Israel, Boston; treas: Mass Civil Liberties exec comm,Acad of Arbitrators,1956-60; chmn, Boston chap, Acad of Arbitrators, 1961-62; mem: Amer Econ Assn; Amer Arbitration Assn; Fed Mediation Service. Author: Crisis Bargaining, 1958; Labor Law and Legislation, 1962; contbr to profsl jours. Home: 64 Garland Rd, Newton Center, Mass. Office: Northeastern U, Boston, Mass.

MYERS, Allen Murray, US, judge; b. NYC, Dec 12, 1912; s. Philip and Lena (Shapiro) Meyerowitz; BA, NYU, 1933, JD, 1937; m. Roslyn Golberg, Aug 29, 1936; c: Shelley Ross. Judge, Civil Court, NYC, since 1967; atty, 1937-67. Chmn, Fgn Affairs Comm, NY chap, AJComm; hon pres, E End Temple; mem: Amer Bar Assn; Assn of Bar, NYC. Author: Could You Afford A Fair Trial? 1954. Home: 343 E 30 St, New York, NY. Office: 111 Centre, New York, NY.

MYERS, Bernard S, US, editor, author,educator; b. NYC, May 4, 1908; s. Louis and Dora (Waxenberg); BS, NYU, 1928; MA, 1929, PhD, 1933; dipl, Sorbonne, Paris, 1932; m. Shirley Levene, Aug 11 1938; c: Peter, Lucy. Ed in-chief, gen mgr, art book dept, McGraw-Hill Book Co, since 1958; lectr: NYU, 1929-43; Rutgers U, 1945-46; Art Students League, NY, 1945-47; CUNY, 1950-58; guest prof, U of Tex, 1948-50; cons ed, Ency of World Art, since 1958. Mem: Coll Art Assn; Phi Beta Kappa. Author: Modern Art in the Making, 1950, 2nd ed, 1958; Fifty Great Artists, 1954; Encyclopedia of Painting, 1955; Mexican Painting in our Time, 1955; Problems of Younger American Artist, 1956; The German Expressionists, 1957; Art and Civilization, 1957, 2nd ed, 1968; Understanding the Arts, 1958; McGraw-Hill Dictionary of Art, 5 vols, 1969. Recipient: f: Inst Intl Educ, 1932; Bollingen, 1950-51. Home: 82 Willow St, Brooklyn, NY. Office: 330 W 42 St, New York, NY.

MYERS, David, US, physician, educator; b. Phila, Pa, Sep 13, 1906; s. Charles and Sadie (Herscovici); att U of Pa, 1924-26; MD, Temple U, Sch of Med, 1930; m Rosalind Nicholas, Sep 14, 1930; c: Eugene, Susan Piver. Chief, otology, Presbyterian Hosp, Phila, since 1962, dir, Inst of otology, since 1962; prof, otolaryngology, U of Pa, Sch of Med, since 1962; prof, otorhinology, Temple U, Sch of Med, 1939-62, chmn, dept, 1955-62; preceptorship, Dr Matthew S Ersner, 1932-40. Lt col, US Army MC, 1942-46. F: Amer Otological Soc; Amer Acad Otology, Rhinology and Laryngology, Triological Soc; Amer Coll Surgs; Amer Acad Ophthal and Otolaryngology; dipl, Amer Bd Ear, Nose and Throat Examiners; mem: Amer Otosclerosis Soc; Amer Soc Mil Surgs; Phila Coll Phys; Phila Allergy Assn; Phila Co and Pa State Med Soc; Pa Acad Ophthal and Otorhinology; Phila Laryngological Soc; hon, Reading Ear, Nose and Throat Soc; Temple Judea Syn; Phila Art Alliance; Amity Lodge; Masons; clubs: Green Valley Country; Golden Slipper Sq. Contbr to med jours. Home: Philadelphian Apt 2044 C, Philadelphia, Pa. Office: 3701 N Broad St, Philadelphia, Pa.

MYERS, David N, US, business exec; b. Cleveland, O, June 22, 1900; s. Robert and Annie (Grosberg); BBA, Cleveland Coll of Bus, Cleveland, 1922; m. Inez Pink, Mar 27, 1929; c: Hal, Dieter. Pres, Byerlyte Corp, 1931-1956; bd chmn: Consolidated Paint & Varnish Corp, since 1956; Hastings Pavement, NY, since 1965; dir, Union Commerce Bank, Cleveland since 1962; chmn, exec comm, Asphalt Inst, since 1953. Pres, Menorah Park J Home for Aged, 1956-1964; treas, trustee, Mt Sinai Hosp, since 1946; trustee-at-large, J Comty Fed since 1941, pres, 1965-1968; treas, Bur of J Educ since 1942; treas, Cleveland Heb Schs, since 1939; natl trustee, Children's

Asthma Research Inst & Hosp, Denver, 1954-1969; trustee Wfr Fed, Cleveland, since 1951; life mem: Amer Ordnance Assn Cleveland Mus of Art; Mus of Natural Sci; Asphalt tech, elected life mem Assn Asphalt Techs; clubs: Oakwood; Commerce; Mid-day, Mason. Recipient: Eleanor Roosevelt Humanities Award, 1967; Dist Service Award United Appeal, Cleveland, 1967. Home: 16900 S Park Blvd, Shaker Heights, O. Office: E Ohio Bldg, Cleveland, O.

MYERS, Frank Leslie, Jamaica, solicitor; b. Jamaica, June 3, 1910; s. Alfred and Sybil (Barrow); MA, jurisprudence, Exeter Coll, Oxford U, 1931; m. Elaine Brandon, Oct 6, 1936; c: Darryl. Sr partner, Myers, Hetcher & Gordon, solicitors, since 1949, partner since 1935. Dir, United Cong of Israelites; comm mem, Inc law Soc of Jamaica; mem, The Solicitor Comm; vice-pres, Jamaica Olympic Assn, 1952-53; chmn, Banana Ind Ins Bd, 1953-60. Hobbies: track athletics, tennis. Home: 7F Manor Court, Kingston, Jamaica. Office: POB 162, 36 Duke St, Kingston, Jamaica.

MYERS, Israel, US, business exec; b. Baltimore, Md, Apr 12, 1906; s. Max and Zelda (Blumenstien); LLB, U of Md, 1927; m. Mollie Glassman (decd); c: Judith, Jonathan. Chmn, bd, Londontown Mfg Co, Baltimore, Md, since 1967. Home: 6210 Park Hgts Ave, Baltimore, Md. Office: 3600 Clipper Mill Rd, Baltimore, Md.

MYERS, Jerome, I, US attorney; b. Phila, Pa, Nov 26, 1895; s. Morris and Anna (Liebeskind); LLB, Dickinson Sch of Law, Carlisle, Pa, 1919; m. Ethel Gress, July 27, 1934, (decd); c: Marcia. Pvt practice since 1919; dir, gen counsel, Green Ridge Bank, since 1930, fmr pres; admitted to practice: US Supr Court; Circuit Court of Appeals; Pa State and local courts; pvt secy to mayor, acting police magistrate, 1920-22; city solicitor, 1934-46; dep mayor, 1942-46, all Scranton, Pa; commn, US Dist Court, Middle Dist of Pa, 1928-42. Served WWI. Mem: Scranton Post-War Planning Commn, 1945; Elks, fmr exalted ruler; Temple Isr; JWV; Vets of WWI, Inc; fmr: vice-chmn, munic sect, Pa Bar Assn, mem, comm on unlawful law practice; dir, Lackawanna Bar Assn; trustee, Natl Inst of Munic Law Offs, also chmn, taxation and torts comms; mem, comm on model banking code for states, Amer Bar Assn, also mem, comm on powers of appointment; dir: United Cerebral Palsy Bd, Lackawanna Co; and vice-pres, J Home of Friendless, Scranton; pres, Pa State and Scranton, YMHA. Contbr on taxation and civil liability of munic corp to Natl Inst of Munic Law Offs. Home: 638 Taylor Ave, Scarnton, Pa. Office: 414-415 Mears Bldg, Scranton, Pa.

MYERS, Martha, US, civic worker; b. NYC, July 23, 1908; d. Mendel and Esther (Asch) Scheinberg; att U Miami; m. Stanley Myers, June 16, 1929; c: Kenneth, Judith Gilbert. Hon natl vice-pres, Natl Council of J Women, since 1967, fmr natl vice-pres; natl pres, Women in Comty Service, Inc; hon mem, Alpha Epsilon Phi, U Miami; mem, Fla Commn on Status of Women; fmr: pres: Miami sect, S Interstate Regional, Natl Council J Women; vice-pres, Gtr Miami J Fed; mem: social planning comm, public wfr comm, CJFWF; adv comm, social work recruitment, State of Fla; bd, dist 9, State Dept Public Wfr; pres, J Family Service, Miami; chmn, volunteer services, ARC; co-chmn, women's group, S Fla Conf of Chr and J; vice-chmn, study comm on family and child care needs, Dade Co Wfr Planning Council. Recipient: comty headliner award, Gtr Miami chap, Theta Sigma Phi, 1958; brotherhood award, NCCJ, 1960. Home: 3620 Granada Blvd, Coral Gables, Fla.

MYERS, Morey M, US, attorney; b. Scranton, Pa, Aug 5, 1927; s. Samuel and Libbye (Kaplan); AB, Syracuse U, 1949; att U of Pa, 1949-50; LLB, Yale U, 1952; m. Sondra Gelb; c: Jonathan, David. Practicing atty; asst city solicitor, City of Scranton, Pa, 1957-61; dep atty gen, Commonwealth of Pa 1962; chief counsel to Milk Control Commn, Commonwealth of Pa, 1962-63. Served USN. Pres, Scranton-Lackawanna J Council, since 1967; chmn, United J Campaign; dir, mem, exec comm, Lackawanna United Fund, chmn, 1968 annual campaign; chmn, Dem Comm, City of Scranton; trustee, Scranton Public Libr; mem: Panel, Amer Arbitration Assn; Amer Bar Assn; Harvard U-Brandeis U Coop Research Project for Devl of Isr; UJA Natl Young Leadership Cabinet; bd dirs, HIAS; bd trustees, UIA. Home: 1121 Myrtle St, Scranton, Pa. Office: 700 Scranton Life Bldg, Scranton, Pa.

MYERS, Stanley C, US, attorney; b. NYC, Sep 11, 1905; s. Cecil and Martha (Schnell); LLB, Fordham U Sch of Law, 1925; m. Martha Scheinberg, June 16, 1929; c: Kenneth, Judith. Pvt law practice, since 1926; sr mem, Myers, Kaplan, Porter, Levinsen & Kenin; pres, Mt Nebo Cemetery, Inc, since 1948; secy and vice-pres, Tripure Products, and Standard Chem, since 1940; admitted to Fla Bar, 1926, and to practice in: US Dist Court for S Dist of Fla; US Circuit Court of Appeals in Fifth Dist; Supr Court of US and Tax Court of US. Ensign, USCG, 1942-45. Natl pres, CJFWF, 1945-50; pres: Gtr Miami J Cen, 1951-53; Social Service Exch, 1940-41; Council Social Agcys, 1943-45, both Dade Co; Gtr Miami J Fed, 1938-41, found, mem, bd dirs, exec comm and chmn, comty planning comm; vice-pres, United Syn of Amer, 1952; mem, bd dirs: J Social Service Bur; and mem, budget comm, and vice-pres, Dade Co Comty Chest, campaign chmn, 1946; ARC, Dade Co chap, chmn, sub-comm, disaster relief comm; appd mem: Enemy Alien Hearing Bd, S Dist, Fla, 1942-45; Children's Code Commn, State of Fla, 1942; mem: adv bd, Selective Service, 1940-47; of 50 outstanding J leaders of US to spec conf in Jerusalem, 1950; life trustee, Mt Sinai Hosp, Gtr Miami; mem: Dade Co, Fla and Amer Bar Assns. Recipient: natl service award, Phi Epsilon Pi, 1949; man of year award, Tau Epsilon Phi, 1953; annual brotherhood award, NCCJ, 1955. Home: 2451 Burkell Ave, Miami, Fla. Office: 1150 SW 1 St, Miami, Fla.

MYERSON, Albert, L, US, physical chemist; b. NYC, Nov 14, 1919; s. Myer and Deborah (Weiner); BS, Pa State U, 1941; PhD, U of Wis 1948. Research asso Corporate Research Labs, Esso Research and Engr Co, NJ, since 1969; research asst: natl defense research comm, Columbia U, 1941-42; Manhattan poject, 1942-45; sr research chem, Franklin Inst, Phila, Pa, 1948-56; mgr, phys chem, missile and space vehicle dept, Gen Elec Co, Phila, 1956-60; prin phys chem, Cornell Aeronautical Lab, Buffalo, NY, 1960-69. F, Amer Inst Chems, 1969; mem: Combustion Inst; Amer Chem Soc; Amer Phys Soc; Sigma Xi; Phi Kappa Phi; Phi Lambda Upsilon. Co-ed, Physical Chemistry in Aerodynamics and Space Flight, 1960; contbr to chem and phys jours. Home: 1529 Long Meadow, Mountainside, NJ. Office: Esso Research and Engr, Linden, NJ.

MYERSON, Moses Hyman, Can, attorney; b. Russ, May 10, 1893; s. Joseph and Sarah (Rave); BA, McGill U, 1916, BCL, 1917; QC, 1961; m. Annie Siegler, Jan 21, 1918; c: David. Pvt law practice since 1921. Can Armed Forces, 1940-45. Mem: natl exec, Can J Cong; J People's Schs; J Public Libr. Author: Germany's War Crimes and Punishment, 1944; contbr to legal publs. Home: 5235 Cote St Luc Rd, Montreal, Can. Office: 455 Craig St, W, Montreal, Can.

N

NAAMANI, Israel T, US, educator; b. Zhitomir, Russ, Nov 3, 1913; s. Peter and Sarah (Sherif) Tarkow; in US since 1929; AA, Crane Jr Coll, 1933; PhB, Marquette U, 1935; MA, 1nd U, 1942, PhD, 1945; m. Zehava Rabichow, June 30, 1940; c: Roanete, Aviv. Prof, political sci, U Louisville, Ky, since 1964; teaching f, Ind U, 1941-42; tchr and lectr, U's in US and Isr; dir, B'nai Isr Schs, Chgo, Ill, 1944-46; exec dir, J Educ Soc, SF, Cal, 1946-48; exec dir, Bur of J Educ,Louisville, 1948-66; dir, NYU and State Dept Prof Workshops in Isr, 1955, 1965; prof lectr, Ind U, Southeast Cen, 1958-59. Pres: Midwest Council of J Educs, 1954-56; Heb Prin Assn, Chgo, 1944-46; Natl Assn Profs of Heb, 1962-64; vice-pres, Natl Council for J Educ, 1955-57; mem: ME Inst; ME Studies Assn; academic honor socs; Amer Political Sci Acad; Amer J Hist Soc; Amer Hist Soc. Author: The Abandonment of Splendid Isolation by Great Britain, 1946; Nefilim Bamaarav, 1968; co-author: Hebraic Studies, 1965; ed: Omer, 1951-55; Igereth, since 1959; ed bd: Hebrew Abstracts; Sheviley Hahinuch; contbr to scholarly jours. Home: 2804 Limekiln Lane, Louisville, Ky. Office: Dept of Political Sci, U of Louisville, Louisville, Ky.

NABARRO Frank Reginald Nunes, S Afr, physicist, educator; b. London, Eng, Mar 7, 1916; s. Stanley and Leah (Cohen); in S Afr since 1953; BA, New Coll, Oxford, Eng, 1937; att Bristol U, 1938-40, 1945-49; BSc, 1940, MA, 1946; DSc, Birmingham U, 1953; m. Margaret Dalziel; c: David, Ruth, Jonathan, Mairi, Andrew. Prof, head, dept physics, U Witwatersrand, since 1953; repr of Sen, U Council, since 1967, dean, fac sci, 1968-69; sr experimental off, Min of Supply, Eng, 1940-45; Royal Soc Warren research f, U Bristol, 1945-49; lectr, metallurgy, U Birmingham, 1949-53. Mem: Royal Soc Arts; Phys Soc; fmr vice-pres, S Afr Inst of Physics. Contbr to sci jours. Recipient: MBE, 1945; Berlby Memorial Award, 1950. Hobby: gardening. Home: 32 Cookham Rd, Aukland Park, Johannesburg, S Afr. Office: U Witwatersrand, Johannesburg, S Afr.

NABATOFF Robert Allan US, cardiovascular surgeon; b. NYC, Nov 19, 1918; s. Abraham and Emma (Golden); BA, U Mich, 1939; MD, State U Coll of Med, NYC, 1943; m. Joan Herman, Sep 11, 1956; c: Diane, Richard, Ross. Research asst surg, chief, vascular clinic, dept of obstet and gyn, Mt Sinai Hosp, Sch of Med, since 1950; vascular surg, Hosp for Aged and Infirm Heb, Kingsbridge House, since 1950; att surg, chief,cardiovascular surg clinic, Beth El Hosp, 1950-66; asso vascular surg, Hosp for Jt Diseases, 1952-66; asso surg, chief, cardiovascular surg clinic, Harlem Hosp, 1950-65. US Army Res MC, 1942-44. Pres, Metrop Med Soc, 1963; f: NY Acad Med; Amer Coll Surgs; Intl Cardiovascular Soc; Pan-Amer Med Soc; NY Co, NY State, Med Socs; AMA; dipl: Amer Bd Surg; Amer Bd Med Examiners; mem: Masons; Phi Delta Epsilon; club, Phys Square of NY. Author: Complications of Pregnancy, 1960; contbr to med jours. Hobbies: violin, gymnastics. Home: 145 E 92 St, New York, NY. Office: 1020 Park Ave, New York, NY.

NABOICHECK, N Aaron, US, business exec; b. Hartford, Conn, Oct 16, 1917; s. Isidor and Rebecca (Bricker); att: Worcester Acad, 1936-37; Worcester Poly Inst, 1937-41; Yale U, 1942; Trinity Coll, 1947; m. Alfrea Salvin, Feb 1, 1948; c: Peter, Robert. Pres, Gold Bond Mattress Co. USAF, 1941-46. Mem: bd dirs, NE Bedding Assn, 1967-69; zone dir, bd trustees, Natl Assn of Bedding Mfrs; natl cabinet, UJA, since 1960; chmn bd, Hartford J Fed, 1961-63; bd dirs: J Comty Cen, J Heb Home for Aged; Amer Friends of Heb U; Amer Friends of Tel Aviv U; Amer U of Jerusalem; Hartford Sym Soc; Wadsworth Atheneum; natl pres, Young Pres Found, 1967-68; mem, pres council, Yeshiva U; incorporator, Westledge Sch, Simsbury; mem, Phi Gamma Delta. Home: 79 Ledyard Rd, W Hartford, Conn. Office: 801 Windsor St, Hartford, Conn.

NACHAMIE Irving, US, physician; b. NYC, Jan 24, 1902; s. Hyman and Anna (Baer); BA, Columbia Coll, 1923, MD, Coll of Phys and Surgs, 1926; m. Hudythe Levin, June 28,

1931; c: Henry, Benjamin, David, Rebecca. Obstet, gyn: asso, Caledonian Hosp, since 1938; affiliate, Coney I Hosp, since 1958, asso, 1932-57; att obstet, gyn, Unity Hosp, 1958-66, cons since 1966; house surg, Harlem Hosp, NYC, 1928-30. Capt, US Army MC, 1942-45, maj, Res, 1945-53. Dipl, Amer Bds Obstet and Gyn, 1949; f: Bklyn Gyn Soc; Amer Coll Surgs; found f, Amer Coll Obstet and Gyn, 1952; f, Amer Soc Abdominal Surgs; mem: AMA; NY State and Kings Co Med Soc; Assn Mil Surgs of US; Kings Co Phys Guild; Amer Phys F Comm, IMA; Res Off Assn; Amer Vets Comm; Prospect Park J Cen; Phil Delta Mu; Phi Lambda Kappa, mem, bd trustees, since 1958; club. Bklyn Alumni. Contbr to med jours. Home and office: 125 Maple St, Brooklyn, NY.

NACHMAN, Lothar E, US, attorney; b. Frankfurt, Ger, May 21, 1922; s. Frederick and Hilda (Ettlinger); in US since 1937; BSS, CCNY, 1951; LLB, NYU Law Sch, 1954, JD; m. Gabriele Levy, Dec 24, 1946; c: Dorothy, Barbara. Pvt practice since 1954. Active in numerous intl and communal orgs. Home: 121 Bella Vista St, Tuckahoe, NY. Office: 258 Broadway, New York, NY.

NACHMAN, Mordecai, US, physician; b. Lake City, SC, Feb 28, 1907; s. Henry and Annie (Rephan); MD, Med Coll of SC, 1930; m. Frances Brown, Oct 3, 1936; c: Malinda, Frances, Elizabeth. In urol practice since 1930; chief urol: Greenville Gen Hosp; St Frances Hosp, Greenville. F, Amer Coll Surgs; dipl, Amer Bd Urol; mem: Co, State and Amer Med Assns; Amer Urol Assn, SE sect: clubs: Rotary; Ponsett; Elks. Contbr to profsl jours. Home: 18 E Hillcrest Dr, Greenville, SC. Office: 413 Vardry St, Greenville, SC.

NACHT, Moshe, Isr, jurist; b. Vienna, Aus, Feb 23, 1915; s. Isaac and Rosa (Dym); in Isr since 1934; m. Tamar Bloch; c: Yair. Dir, Courts in Isr; relieving pres, Dist Court, Jerusalem; fmr: legal adv, Govt Service. Maj ,Brit Army; off, IDF. Home: 9 Hatamar St, Tel Aviv, Isr. Office: Courts of Justice, Jerusalem, Isr.

NACHTIGAL, David, Isr, scientist; b. Warsaw, Pol, June 22, 1914; s. Zeev and Sarah (Gutwiellen); in Isr since 1924; MSc, PhD, Heb U, Jerusalem, 1942; m. Sr sci, Weizmann Inst of Sci, since 1969; spec asst, Heb U, 1939-43; dir, med lab, 1948-66. Lt, IDF, 1948-50. Mem: IMA; Isr Immunological Soc. Contbr to sci publs. Hobbies: photography, rod and line fishing. Home: 9 Frug St, Tel Aviv, Isr. Office: Weizmann Inst, Rehovot, Isr.

NADAV, Mordekhai, Isr, archivist, educator; b. Yanov, Pol, Mar 27, 1920; s. Pinhas and Dobka (Shuster) Katzykovich; in Isr since 1941; PhD, Heb U, Jerusalem; m. Yael Zelikovitz, 1951; c: Jehonatan, Noam. Head, dept of manuscripts and archives, J Natl, U Libr; research f, Heb U, Jerusalem, since 1966; lectr, J hist, Inst for Higher Studies, Beersheva. Ed: Yad Lakore, since 1963; contbr to jours. Home: 14 Karmon St, Jerusalem, Isr. Office: Heb U, Jerusalem, Isr.

NADEL, Itzhak, (pen name, **Itzhak Oren**), Isr,author;b. Vierkhnieudinsк, Russ, May 8, 1918; s. Yekhezkel and Rachel (Hirshberg); att Heb U, Jerusalem, 1936-40; m. Isabella Kemblinsky, July 31, 1963; c: Timna Lilach. Dep ed, off publs, State Comptroller's Off, since 1966. Author: Somewhere,1950; Behind the Lines, 1953; The Ventures of Benjamin the Fifth, 1958; Fathers and Sour Grapes, 1964; The Portrait of a Generation as a Dog, 1968; trans, Ivan Goucharov, Oblomov, 1959; Nikolai Gogol, The Evenings in the Village Near Dikanka, 1969; Cecil Roth, The J Disraeli, 1955; Alexander Vardi, The Ice-Hole, 1964; contbr stories and articles to newspapers and jours. Home: 68a Tchernikovsky St, Jerusalem, Isr.

NADEL, Jack, US, social worker; b. NYC, Jan 10, 1893; s. Louis and Mollie (Schuss); att: Ext Sch, CCNY, 1912-15; NY Sch of Philanthropy, 1916; J Communal Sch, 1917; LLB, NYU, 1922, LLM, 1939; ACSW, 1961; m. Clare Hersch, June 3, 1917; c: Evelyn, Leonard, Melvin. Ret; exec vice-pres, YM-YWHA, 1956-58, exec dir, 1922-56, joined staff, 1906; lectr, social work, Yeshiva U, 1951-63. Pres: Metrop Assn of J Cen Workers, 1922-23; Natl Assn of J Cen Workers, 1925-26; natl chmn, Jerusalem YM-YWHA, since 1956; found, first chmn, Fed Health and Wfr Div and J Comty Cen Div; chmn, Regional Civic Council, 1948; mem, bd, JWB, since 1930; found, mem bd, Fed Employment and Guidance Service, since 1934; club, Lions, pres, 1947-48. Recipient: Natl Frank L Weil Award, 1957; UJA Award, 1966; Fed Award, 1967. Home: 152 E 94 St, New York, NY. Office: 1395 Lexington Ave, New York, NY.

NADELMAN, Alfred H, US, educator, chemist; b. Stettin, Ger, July 21, 1904; s. Hugo and Elizabeth (Russ); in US since 1938; MA, U of Berlin, 1929, PhD, 1929; m. Hilde Wolfe, Dec 31, 1944; c: Ruth, David. Pres, Nadelman and Assos, Inc, cons to pulp and paper ind, since 1961; chief chem, Milprint, 1938-40; chief research chem, Glassine Paper, 1940-44; tech supt, Intl Paper Co, 1944-48; prof, chmn, dept paper tech, W Mich U, 1948-61. Mem: Amer Chem Soc; Tech Assn of Pulp and Paper Ind; Amer Technion Soc; B'nai B'rith; Rotary Intl. Co-author: Coating Formulations- Principles and Practices, 1966; co-ed, Converting of Paper and Paperboard, 1954; contbr to profsl mags. Home and office: 1748 Waite Ave, Kalamazoo, Mich.

NADELMANN, Leo, Switz, composer; b. Bienne, Switz, Jan 16, 1913; s. Naftali and Chana (Rosbruch); att Conservatory, Basel, 1928-32; piano studies with: Rudolf Serkin; Raoul v. Koczalski; Arthur Schnabel, 1930-34; m. Rachel Ritter, Jan 2, 1958; c: Noemi. Compositions: Chassidic Suite for strings, timpani and solo piano (also for sym orch); 5 Chassidic Songs for baritone, violin and piano; Partita Hebraica for string orch; Concerto de Ballet for piano and orch; arrange- ments of Yiddish folk songs for male choir; Passacaglia for orch; Sinfonietta Americana, for orch; The Dybuk, ballet in 3 acts, for orch; for stage presentations: Lejb der Fiedler, by JL Perez; Aus dieser und aus jener Welt, 3 one-act plays by Shalom Aleichem; chamber music; vocal music with piano, or chamher orch. Conductor and artistic dir, Perez-Hasomir Zurich, since 1958; musical adv, Omanut, Zurich, since 1960. Press, Intl Music Cen of Vienna, since 1969; mem: Swiss Assn of Musicians; Swiss Assn of Writers. Hobbies: chess, sports. Home and office: Neumarkt 8, Zurich, Switz.

NADELMANN, Ludwig, US, rabbi; b. Berlin, Ger, Apr 29, 1928; s. Erich and Edith (Weinberg); in US since 1946; BA, Heb tchr's dipl, Yeshiva U, 1951; ordained rabbi, MHL, JTSA, 1955; grad studies, Dropsie Coll, Phila, Pa; m. Judith Wolpert June 21, 1953; c: Ethan, Jeremy, Daniel, Deborah. Rabbi, Genesis Heb Cen, since 1963; asso rabbi, Soc for Advance- ment of Judaism, NYC, 1955-59; rabbi, Beth Shalom Syn, 1959-63. Pres, Westchester bd of rabbis, since 1967; dir, J Reconstructionist; mem: NY Bd Rabbis; RA. Recipient: Citations, Isr Bonds, UJA. Contbr to rel jours. Home: 219, Crestwood, Crestwood, NY. Study: 25 Oakland,Tuckahoe NY.

NADICH, Judah, US, rabbi; b. Baltimore, Md, May 13, 1912; s. Isaac and Lena (Nathanson); BA, CCNY, 1932; MA, Columbia U, 1936; ordained rabbi, MHL, JTSA, 1936, DHL, 1953, DD, HC, 1966; m. Martha Ribalow, Jan 26, 1947; c: Leah Meyers, Shira, Nahma. Rabbi: Park Ave Syn, NYC, since 1957; Temple Beth David, Buffalo, NY, 1936-40; Anshe Emet Syn, Chgo, Ill, 1940-42; toured DP camps in Ger, Aus, It, JDC, 1946-47; rabbi, Cong, Kehillath Isr, Boston, 1947-57. Chaplain, US Army, 1942-46, lt col, sr J chaplain, Eur Theatre, 1942-45, adv, Gen Eisenhower, on J affairs, 1945. Pres, J Book Council of Amer, 1968, fmr dir; treas, RA, 1966; vice-pres, assn of J Chaplains of Armed Forces; dir: ARC, NY chap, since 1962; Natl Ramah Commn, 1967; Commn on J Chaplaincy of JWB; 92nd St YM-YMHA, since 1957; Natl Fed of Isr Inst, since 1954; f, Lehman Inst of J Ethics; vice-pres, J Braille Inst of Amer; mem: rabb cabinet, JTSA; RA; Assn of J Chaplains of Armed Forces; Mil Chaplains Assn; Phi Beta Kappa; Masons; Sojourners; Order of '76. Author: Eisenhower and the Jews, 1953; Yom Kippur, 1955; trans, ed, The Flowering of Modern Heb Lit, 1959; ed, Al Halakha v'Agada, essays of Louis Ginzberg, Heb, 1959; mem, exec comm, Hadoar; contbr: Universal J Ency; One Minute of Prayer; periodicals. Recipient: OBE, 1944; Croix de Guerre, 1944. Home: 993 Park Ave, New York, NY. Study: 50 E 87 St, New York, NY.

NADLER, Myron Jay, US, attorney; b. Youngstown, O, July 22, 1923; s. Murray and Jean (Davis); BS, U of Pa, 1947; JD, U Mich Law Sch, 1949; m. Alice Blue, Nov 4, 1951; c: Jed,

Wendy, John. Partner, Nadler & Nadler, since 1951. US Army, 1943-45. Vice-pres, exec budget comm, Youngstown Comty Chest, since 1967, fmr chmn; trustee, mem, exec comm, Youngstown Comty Corp; chmn: uniform state laws comm, O State Bar Assn; J Comty Relations Council of Youngstown; AJComm, Youngstown chap; mem: Natl Budget and Con- sultation Comm; Mahoning Co Planning Comm; bd trustees, J Fed of Youngstown; Mahoning Co, O State, Amer Bar Assns; Commercial Law League of Amer; Elks; Phi Lam- bda Phi; fmr pres: Anshe Emeth Cong; Squaw Creek Country Club. Co-author: Nadler on Bankruptcy, 2nd ed; contbr to profsl jours. Home: 2260 Fifth Ave, Youngstown, O. Office: 1100 Wick Bldg, Youngstown, O.

NADLER, Shulamith, Isr, architect; b. Tel Aviv, Aug 16, 1923; d. Yitzhak and Rachel (Ramis) Kanev; engr architect, Techni- on, Haifa, 1945; m. June 6, 1946; c: Ariel. Pvt practice since 1945. Major works: Natl U Libr. Munic Theatre; Bet Eli- sheva, Jerusalem; Tel Aviv U Libr, Contbr to books and jours. Recipient: numerous awards in architectural competi- tions. Home: 16 Bar Kochba St, Tel Aviv, Isr. Office: 20 Helsinki St, Tel Aviv, Isr.

NAFTALIN, Arthur, US, educator; b. Fargo, ND, June 28, 1917; s. Sandel and Tillie (Bresky); BA, U Minn, 1939, MA, 1942, PhD, 1948; m. Frances Healy July 3, 1941; c: Mark, David, Gail. Prof, public affairs, U Minn, since 1969, on fac since 1941; cons, public affairs div, Ford Found, 1960-69; ed staff, Fargo Forum, 1934-36; mem stafff Minn Daily, 1936-39; reporter, Minneapolis Tribune, 1939-41. Mayor, Minneapolis, 1961-69; commn, admn, State of Minn. 1954-60; secy to Hubert H Humphrey, 1945-47; cons, Intl Coop Admn, Mich State U Project, Saigon, Vietnam 1957; mem, bd trustees, Natl Inst Public Affairs; fmr: hon pres, vice-pres, US Conf Mayors; pres, League Minn Munici- cs; mem: Natl Steering Comm, Urban Coalition; Public Offs Adv Council, Off Econ Opportunity; exec comm, adv bd, Natl League Cities; Panel on Fed-State Relations, Pres Commn Natl Goals; Advisory Commn on Inter-govern- mental Relations; various overseas assignments to: Isr, Swed, Aus, Chile, Mexico, Ger, Vietnam. Recipient: Annual Dist Service Award, Minn Chap, Amer Soc Public Admn, 1957; C C Ludwig, League of Minn Munics, 1969. Home: 66 Seymour Ave SE, Minneapolis, Minn. Office: 3300 University Ave SE, Minneapolis, Minn.

NAGEL, Ernest, US, educator; b. Novemesto, Czech, Nov 16, 1901; s. Isidor and Frieda (Weisz); in US since 1911; BS, CCNY, 1933; MA, Columbia U, 1925, PhD, 1930; m. Edith Haggstrom, Jan 29, 1935; c: Alexander, Sidney. U prof, Columbia U, since 1967; John Dewey prof, phil, since 1954, prof, phil, since 1946, on fac since 1931; instr, phil, CCNY, 1930-31. Pres: Amer Phil Assn, E div, 1954; Assn for Sym- bolic Logic, 1946-48; Phil of Sci Assn, 1961-63; vice-pres, AAAS, sect L, 1953; f: Amer Acad Arts and Scis; Amer Phil Soc; mem, Phi Beta Kappa; club, NY Phil, Author: On the Logic of Measurement, 1930; Principles of the Theory of Probability, 1939; Sovereign Reason, 1954; Logic Without Metaphysics, 1957; co-author: Introduction of Logic and Scientific Method, 1934; Godel's Proof, 1958; The Structure of Science, 1961; ed, Jour of Phil, 1939-56; contbr to jours of sci and phil. Recipient: Guggenheim f, 1934, 1950; dist scholar- ship in hum, Amer Council of Learned Socs, 1959. Home: 25 Claremont Ave, New York, NY. Office: Phil Hall, Columbia U, New York, NY.

NAGLER, Charles Arthur, US, engineer, educator; b. Whitsette, Pa, May 10, 1916; s. Jacob and Laura (Greenbaum); MSE, U of Mich, 1939; PhD, U of Minn, 1945; m. Billie Cugell, Aug 21, 1947; c: William, Anthony. Asso prof, dept chem and metallurgical engr, Wayne State U, since 1946; pres, Metallur- gical Cons Inc, profsl cons, since 1946; instr, U Minn, 1939-46; metallurgist, Engr Research Inst, U Mich, 1938-39; chief metallurgist, Twin Cities Ordnance Plants, New Brighton, Minn, 1942-45. Mem: Amer Soc Safety Engrs; Sys Safety Soc; Intl Acad Law and Sci; highway research bd, Natl Acad Scis; NCR; Amer Soc for Metals; Amer Soc for Mining, Metallurgy and Petroleum Engrs; Soc Automotive Engrs; Amer Soc for Testing Materials; Amer Foundrymen's Soc; Amer Welding Soc; NY Acad Sci; Amer Soc Tool and Produc Engrs; Sigma Xi; Phi Lambda Upsilon; Alpha Sigma Mu. Contbr to profsl jours. Home: 16369 Melrose Ave, South- field, Mich. Office: Wayne State U, Detroit, Mich.

NAHMIAS, Joseph Jacques, Fr, business exec; b. Comotini, May 14, 1901; s. Jacques and Mathilde (Cazes); att LSE; m.

Mathilde Modiano, June 27, 1923; c: Renée Chabert. Pres, Pétrofrance. since 1934; hon pres, Association d'Industriels du Pétrole, since 1950. Pres, Union Sephardic J, Fr, since 1945; vice-pres, Fonds Social Juif Unifié. Home: 44 Ave du Président Kennedy, Paris, 16e, Fr. Office: Pétrofrance, 42 Ave Raymond Poincaré, Paris 16e, Fr.

NAHMIAS, Shlomo Abraham, Isr, diplomat; b. Jerusalem, May 2, 1917; s. Abraham and Rachel (Negrin); att: Intl Sch, Paris, 1951-53; Inst of Public Admn, Jerusalem, 1945-47; m. Haya Aknin, Aug 2, 1942; c: Nurith Pasternak, Daphna, Tamar. Consul Gen of Isr to Brazil since 1968; sr asst, Min for Fgn Affairs, 1964-68; first secy and consul, Emb of Isr: Paris, 1960-64; Rome, 1958-60. Dep front cdr, Haganah, 1934-48. Chmn, phys comm, YMCA, Jerusalem; mem, B'nai B'rith; fmr: secy gen, gov't employees; mem, Jerusalem Communal Wfr Comm. Hobbies: music, stamps, tennis. Home: 19 Radak St, Jerusalem, Isr. Office: Consulate of Isr, 19 Don Jose de Barros, São Paulo, Brazil.

NAHON, Gérard, Fr, historian; b. Paris, Fr, Jan 19, 1931; s. Sauveur and Yvette(Kenoui); dipl Heb, Sch for Oriental Langs, Paris, 1962; D es lettres, Fac des Lettres, Paris, 1969; m. Maryvonne Rouret, Dec 23, 1954; c: Myriam, Jacques, Ariel, Elisabeth. Chargé de recherches, Centre National de la Recherche Scientifique, since 1965; prof, govt schs, Maimonide sch, 1954-64; researcher: hist of J in mediaeval Fr; hist of J Port comtys in Fr; i/c confs J hist: Centre U d' Etudes Juives, Centre U des Langues Orientales, both Paris; archivist, Consistoire de Paris. Secy, Soc des Etudes Juives, Paris; mem,Assn Culturelle Israélite, Versailles.Author: Les Hébreux, 1963; contbr to Revue des Etudes Juives. Home: 28 rue de la Chabourne, 78 Le Mesnil Saint-Denis, Fr.

NAHON, Salomone Umberto, Isr, government org official; b. Leghorn, It, Oct 4, 1905; s. Leone and Giorgina (Molco); in Isr since 1939; m. Anita Levi, Nov 1, 1932; c: Lea Felber, Simcha Hazan. Dir, official publs, Org and Info Dept, Zionist Exec; coord, Govt Agcy Comm for Mt Herzl; gen secy, It ZF, 1927-39; co-ed, Israel, weekly, Milan, 1931-39. Pres: It Syn, Jerusalem; Hevrat Yehudei-Italia Lefeula Ruchanit; fmr,hon secy, Milan J Comty. Author: Sir Moses Montefiore, Eng,Fr, Span, It, Heb; ed, publisher, books in Heb, It. Recipient: Officer of Order of Merit of It Rep, 1965. Home: 3 Gan Rehavia St, Jerusalem, Isr. Office: JA, Jerusalem, Isr.

NAHSHON, Moshe Kipper, Isr, educator; b. Ukraine, Oct 1, 1888; s. Nahman and Lea (Kipper); in Isr since 1921; MSc, math Novorossisk U, Odessa, 1915; MSc, pedg, St Vladimir U, Kiev, Russ, 1919; att Inst of Psycho-Neur, Petrograd; m. Hana Bierman (decd); c: Emanuel (decd), Zipora Lubetkin, Carmela Galbar; m. 2nd, Heva Goldstein. Ret; math tchr, Tarbut Tchrs Sem, Kiev, 1918-19; schoolmaster, Tarbut HS, Pol, 1919-21; math tchr, Herzlia HS, Tel Aviv, 1921-55. Mem: Heb Writers Assn in Isr; Isr Tchrs Org; exec: Heb Educ Archives; tchrs council, JNF, fmr pres; fmr mem, exec, Brith Ivrith Olamith. Author: Tze ve-Hashev, 1937; Bepardess hamisparim, 1958; contbr of articles and trans. Spec interests: Heb lit, recreational math. Home: 25 Haifa Rd, Tel Aviv, Isr.

NAHUM, Gaston, Fr, fiinancier; b. Salonika, Greece, July 17, 1897; s. Saul and Flore (Carasso); in Fr since 1918; m. Flory Diaz, Jan 4 1919; c: Mary Frank. Pvt finance bus with intl banks, since 1945; asso with: Bank of Salonika, 1913-17; Saul Amar Bank, Salonika, 1917-18; with Bank Marmorosch, Blank & Co, 1920-24; Saul Amar & Co, 1924-41, both Paris, Secy, Fr Gen Secretariat of Natl Defense, 1940. Chmn, World Sephardi Fed, Paris; mem, Union des Israélites Sephardis de France; fmr chmn, Ozar Hatorah, Fr. Home and office: 8 rue de Varize, Paris 16, Fr.

NAHUM-LEVY, Benjamin, US, artist; b. Tel Aviv, Isr, Feb 28, 1940; s. Ovadya and Bath-Sheva (Mizrachi); in US since 1966; att: Art Sch, Haifa, 1958-59; Ecole de Mont Parnes, Paris, 1960-61; Pratt Graphic Art Cen, 1965-67; m. Hanna Vroman, Oct 10, 1962; c: Ofer. One-man shows: Dugit Gal, Tel Aviv, 1961; Tchermerinsky Gal, Tel Aviv, 1964; Isr Art Gal, NYC, 1966; Morris Gal, Woodstock, NY, 1966; Picture People Gal, NYC, 1968; group shows: Tel Aviv and Jerusalem Mus, since 1962; Demena Gal, 1966; Chgo, LI, Baltimore, 1966; LA, Baltimore, Boston, Miami Beach, 1967; gals: Waverly, Morris, Isr Art, all NY, 1967; Georgetown Gal, Wash, DC, 1969; represented in: Rome; Amsterdam; Isr; Mus of Modern Art, NYC; Eur; S Afr; Can; US; Public Libr, NYC. Pub in spec ed of Commentary Mag, etchings on Jacob and Esau. Recipient: Prize for Young Isr Artists, 1965; Norman Fund Prize, 1966; Audubon Artists Exhb, NYC, 1969. Hobbies: animals collecting antiques. Home and studio: 215 W 90 St, New York, NY.

NAIMAN, Barnet, US, educator, researcher; b. Baltimore, Md, Mar 21, 1900; s. Jacob and Annie (Marks); MS, U NC, 1922; PhD, Columbia U, 1934; m. Dorothy Neuhof, June 27, 1934; c: Barbara. Prof, chem, CCNY, since 1958, on fac since 1924; asst chem, NC Dept of Agric, 1922-24; prof, Columbia U, 1953, 1954. Chmn, Analytical Chems, 1952-53; mem, finance comm, NY sect, Amer Chem Soc, 1953-54, chmn, constitutional comm, analytical sect, 1952-53; mem: AAAS; NY Acad Sci; AAUP; Sigma Xi. Co-author: Quantitative Analysis, 3rd ed, 1951; contbr to profsl jours. Home: 1123 Cambridge Rd, W Englewood, NJ. Office: CCNY, New York,NY.

NAJAR, Amiel Emile, Isr, diplomat; b. Egypt, 1912; s. Haim and Esther (Ades); in Isr since 1947; grad, Fac of Law, Paris, 1931, dipl, Higher Studies of Public Law and Political Econ, 1933; m. Aviva Weisman. Ambass to It since 1968; fmr: dir, asst dir gen, W Eur div, Min for Fgn Affairs; observer, Suez Conf, London, 1956; Min to Japan, 1958-60; Ambass to Belgium and Lux, 1960-68; head, Isr Mission to EEC and other Eur Comtys, 1961-68; mem, delg to UN. Fmr: pres, ZF of Egypt; delg: Zionist Conf, London, WZC, Basle. Office: Israel Embassy, Rome, It.

NAJENSON, Theodore, Isr, physician; b. Buenos Aires, Arg, Nov 11, 1920; s. Leopold and Rosa (Menuhim); in Isr since 1951; MD, U of Arg; m. Theresa Ikonicoff, 1947; c: Thalma, Dina, Deborah. Dir, Loewenstein Hosp; with Rehab Cen, Kupat Holim, Health Ins Inst of Gen Fed of Labour in Isr. Mem: Intl Soc Paraplegia; Intl Soc Electromyographic Kinesiology; World Fed Occupational Therapists; Amer Paraplegia Soc; NY Acad Scis. Home: Dov-Hos St, Kfar Saba, Isr. Office: Loewenstein Hosp, Raanana, Isr.

NAJMAN, Julija, Yugo, author; b. Yugo, Oct 13, 1905; d. Aleksandar and Klara (Srenger) Klopfer; att U Lausanne, Switz, 1943-45; m. Josif Najman, July 7, 1929 (decd); c: Dragoljub, Ivanka Savic. Author: Cassou "1848",pub 1950;Nolit, 1951; Tocak u Blatu, and Zuti Kavez, 1951; Price o Ani, 1952; short story, Rodjendan; ed Sapat, short stories; play: Parastos za Sampiona; radio-plays: Godisnjice; Cetvorica u Liftu; Generalna Proba; Doktor Za Ljubav; Saslušanja; film scenario, Muskarci; pub, numerous interviews with authors and painters. Lectr, women's sect, Fed of J Comtys. Mem: Assn Dramatists of Yugo; Soc of Letters. Hobby: painting. Home: Uzun Mirkova 5, Belgrade, Yugo.

NAMER, Léon, Turkey, physician; b. Istanbul, May 24, 1924; s. Israel and Esther (Ezrati); MD, fac med, Istanbul, 1947; postgrad studies, internal med, fac med, Ankara, 1948-52. Phys: Ankara Cimento Fabrikasi since 1954; ME Tech U, since 1967. Mem, Chamber Med, Ankara. Home: Cihan Sokak 4/7, Ankara, Turkey.

NAMIR, Mordecai, Isr, legislator; b. Ukraine, Feb 23, 1897; s. Itzhak and Batya (Baumer) Nemirovsky; in Isr since 1924; att Conservatory, 1916-19; grad, U Odessa, 1924; m. Dora Groodsky, 1923 (decd); c: Yael; m. 2nd, Ora Taub. Ret; mayor, Tel Aviv-Jaffa, 1959-69; MK, 1951-69; laborer, bakery, 1924-25; circulation mgr, Davar, daily, 1925-26; secy, Ahdut Avoda Party, 1926-29; dir, stat dept, Histadrut, 1929-36, chmn, unemployment fund, 1932-49, gen secy, Lab Council, Tel Aviv, 1936-43, mem, Histadrut exec, 1944-48, gen secy, Histadrut, 1951-56, delg: World Fed Trade Unions, Prague, 1947; Histadrut campaigns, US and Can; spec envoy for Isr Min for Fgn Affairs, Bulgaria, Czech, Rum, 1948; counsellor, Isr Legation, Moscow, 1948-49; min plen in Moscow, 1949-59; min of lab and housing, 1956-59. Mem, Haganah command: Tel Aviv dist, 1933-47; natl, 1947-48. Mem, presidium, World Zionist Actions Comm, 1946-59; WJC, 1961-63; delg, ZCs, 1937, 1946; chmn, Friends of Ohel Theater, 1933-48. Author: Industry in Palestine, 1932; Yearly Economic Palestine Summaries, 1932-35; Work in Progress, 1953; ed, econ and trade union publs; contbr to local press. Home: 40 Beeri St, Tel Aviv, Isr.

NAOR, Mordechay, Isr, author, journalist; b. Tel Aviv, Isr, Aug 19, 1934; s. Meshulam and Tova (Levinhertz); BA, Heb U, Jerusalem, 1962; m. Leah Mishkowski, Oct 25, 1955; c: Neta, Amir. Ed in chief: Bamahane-Nahal, Bamahane-Gadna, Hez-Vakeshet, army periodicals, since 1961; ed, Bama'ale, 1961. Pvt IDF, 1952-55. Author: Kan Hashirionim,

1964; Al Hagova, 1965; Hashevah Lahem, 1969; co-author: Youth Movements in Israel and the World, 1963; co-ed, June Days, 1967. Recipient: Amos Lev Award, 1958. Home: 12 Sirkin St, Herzliya, Isr. Office: 17B Hakiryah, Tel Aviv, Isr.

NAOR, Pinhas P, Isr, scientist, educator; b. Vienna, Aus, Feb 26, 1923; s. Leiser and Chava (Reis) Reiss; in Isr since 1939; BSc, Technion, Haifa, 1947, dipl ing, 1948; PhD, U Birmingham, 1952; m. Nehama Kliban, Apr 22, 1948; c: Joseph, Simeon. Prof, Technion, Haifa, since 1964, on fac since 1953, head, dept ind and mgmt engr; postdoc f, U Chgo, Ill, 1952-53; Brit Council Scholar, U Birmingham, Eng, 1950-52; visiting prof: Case Inst of Tech, Cleveland, O, 1960; U of NC, Chapel Hill, 1962-64, 1966; CCNY, 1969; Stanford U, Cal, 1969. Fmr: mem, grad council, bd govs, Technion; mem, bd dirs, Isr Inst Productivity; chmn, Isr Cen for Quality Control; pres, Oprs Research Soc of Isr; mem: Natl Council on Stat; Council of Isr Bc Auth; Inst of Mgmt Scis; f, Royal Stat Soc; mem: Econometric Soc; Inst of Math Stat; Assn of Engrs and Architects in Isr. Contbr to profsl jours. Home: 13 Habroshim Ave, Haifa, Isr. Office: Technion, Haifa, Isr.

NAOR, Shmuel, Isr, attorney; b. Tarnopol, Pol, Feb 12, 1925; s. Nachum and Tova (Shapiro) Leiner; in Isr since 1937; att Pal Law Classes, 1945-48; LLB, LSE; m. Malka Ast, Dec 18, 1950; c: Shalva, Varda, Adi. Pvt practice since 1951; councillor, Ramat Gan Munic; judge, High Court, Lab Party. Capt, info and educ br, IDF. Mem sen, Jr C of C, Tel Aviv, fmr: natl pres, world vice-pres, Intl J C of C. Home: 11 Daniel St, Ramat Gan, Isr. Office: Nachlat Benjamin St, Tel Aviv, Isr.

NAOR, Uri, Isr, journalist, diplomat; b. Saaz, Bohemia, June 14, 1906; s. Richard and Clara (Weissberger) Lichtwitz; in Isr since 1939; LLD, U of Prague, 1933. Min, press and info, Isr Emb, Godesberg, Ger, since 1968; ed, Zionist Weekly, Prague, 1925-38; press attaché, Isr Legation, Prague, 1948-50; with Min of Fgn Affairs, Jerusalem, 1950-52; dir, info div, Isr Mission, Cologne, Ger, 1952-56; asst dir, info div, Fgn Min, Jerusalem, 1956-60; Isr consul, Zürich, 1960-63; ambass, Chile, Ecuador, 1963-68; dir, PR div, Min Fgn Affairs, Jerusalem, 1968. J Brig, WW II. Mem, B'nai B'rith. Author: History of the Zionist Movement, Czech, 1937. Home: 7 Hama'apilim St, Jerusalem, Isr. Office: Embassy of Israel, Ubierstr 78, 552 Bad Godesberg, Ger.

NARDI, Noah, Isr, education psychologist; b. Kiev, Russ, Oct 4, 1902; s. Abraam and Rachel (Braginsky); in Isr since 1921; att Tchrs Coll, Jerusalem, 1923-25; BSc, Tchrs Coll, NY, 1930; MA, Columbia U, 1931, PhD, 1934; m. Shulamit Schwartz, 1933; c: Eran, Meira, Zviah. Ret; dir, Pedg Cens, Isr Min Educ and Culture, 1949-69; cons, J Educ Comm, New York, 1939-49. Author: Zionism and Education in Palestine, 1933; Education in Palestine, 1945; Psychology of the Child, 1958; Psychology and Education, 1959; Technology in Education, 1968. Home: 22 Arlosoroff St, Jerusalem, Isr.

NARDI, Shulamit, Isr, educator; b. Bklyn, NY, Apr 23, 1909; d. Abraham and Fanny (Masliansky) Schwartz; BA, Barnard Coll, NYC, 1929; MA, Columbia U, 1933. Instr, Eng, contemporary J hist, Heb U, Jerusalem, since 1953; asst to Pres Shazar, since 1963. Pres, Jr Hadassah, 1931-33; dir, publs, Amer Zionist Emergency Council, 1943-51; mem, Isr delg to UN Gen Assembly, 1961, 1962; mem exec, Isr Oriental Soc. Trans, Dead Sea Scroll, A Genesis Apocrypha, 1956; ed, Hadassah Mag, 1941-43. Home: 22 Arlosoroff St, Jerusalem, Isr. Office: Off of the Pres, Jerusalem, Isr.

NAREV, Robert, NZ, attorney; b. Eschwege, Ger, Oct 6, 1935; s. Erich and Gertrud (Dalberg) Narewczewitz; in NZ since 1947; BA, U Auckland, 1956, LLB, 1959; m. Freda Malacka, Jan 22, 1959; c: Kim, Eric, Ian. Barrister, solicitor, Supr Court of NZ, since 1959. Hon treas, ZC of NZ; vice-pres, Auckland Zionist Soc; mem: bd dirs, Heb Cong; dist Law Soc, both Auckland. Home: 16 Stoneyroyd Gardens, Auckland 5, NZ. Office: POB 63, Auckland, NZ.

NARKISS, Uzi, Isr, army officer, govt official; b. Jerusalem, Isr, Jan 6, 1925; s. Itzhak and Frida (Storkhain); att: Heb U, Jerusalem, 1946-47; Ecole Supérieure de Guerre, Paris, 1953-55; m. Esther Hacohen, Oct 16, 1949; c: Itzhak, Ruth, Tamar. Dir gen, dept immigration and absorption, JA, since 1968; commanding gen, Jerusalem Brig, Six Day War, 1967; mem, Palmach, 1941-46; battalion cdr, Isr War of Independence, 1947-49; cdr, oprs div, gen hqr, Sinai Campaign, 1956; mil

attaché of Isr to Fr, 1959-62; dir, Natl Defense Coll, Isr, 1963-65; commanding gen, Cen Command, IDF, 1965-68. Contbr to mil jours. Hobby: photography. Home: 8 Bath Yftah St, Zahala, Isr. Office: JA, Jerusalem, Isr.

NAROT, Joseph R, US, rabbi; b, Lith, Apr 24, 1913; s. Morris and Grace (Rapoport) Narotsky; in US since 1920; BA, W Reserve U, 1936; MA, ordained rabbi, HUC, 1940, DHL, 1946; m. Frieda Brill, Apr 6, 1942; c: David, Ruth; m. 2nd, Helene Berg, Oct 1, 1961; c: Susan, Peter, Betsy. Sr rabbi, Temple Isr, Gtr Miami, Fla, since 1950; rabbi, Temple Beth Isr, Atlantic City, 1940-50. Chmn, AJComm; fmr: chmn, Dade Co Comty Relations Bd; pres Dade Co Wfr Planning Council; Gtr Miami RA; chmn, Liturgy Comm, CCAR, 1965-67; mem: Natl Bd, UAHC; Intl Publs Comm. Author: Why I am a Jew; For Whom The Rabbi Speaks; An Introduction to a Faith; A Primer for Temple Life; A Preface to Well-Being; contbr to rel jours. Study: 137 NE 19, Miami, Fla.

NARROWE, Morton Herman, Swed, rabbi; b. Phila, Pa, Mar 15, 1932; s. Morris and Sarah (Lisack); in Swed since 1965; BA, Yeshiva U, 1954; MHL, ordained rabbi, JTSA, 1959; m. Judith Halpren, June 15, 1958; c: Joshua, Elizabeth, David. Rabbi: J Comty, Stockholm, since 1965; Temple Beth Sholom, Satellite Beach, Fla, 1962-65. Lt, chaplain, USNR, 1959-62. Mem, bd dirs, Stockholm J Cen; rabb adv: J Day Sch; KH; vice-pres, Fla Council on Hum Relations, 1963-65; treas, Min Assn, Brevard Co, 1962-64; mem: B'nai B'rith; RA; Rabb Assn of World Union of Progressive Syns. Hobby: candlemaking. Home: Torstenssonsgatan 4, Stockholm, Swed. Study: Wahrendorffsgatan 3, Stockholm, Swed.

NASATIR, Abraham P, US, educator, historian; b. Santa Ana, Cal, Nov 24, 1904; s. Morris and Sarah (Hurwitz); BA, U of Cal, 1921, MA, 1922, PhD, 1926; m. Ida Hirsch, Sep 8, 1929. Prof, hist, San Diego State Coll, Cal, since 1928; teaching f, U of Cal, 1923-24; instr, U of Ia, 1926-27; vice-consul: Paraguay, 1940-50; Ecuador, 1942-44; Fulbright lectr, U of Chile, 1959-69. Pres: San Diego Fed J Agcys, since 1942; dist ZOA, 1947-50; Pacific W br, Amer Hist Assn; Phi Alpha Theta, 1968; vice-pres, Union of Orthodox J Congs, W Coast region, since 1958; dir: United Fund, since 1934; Social Wfr, since 1935; J Educ Comm, since 1948; Amer Assn for J Educ, W States region, since 1952; mem: AAUP; Hispanic Amer Assn; Hist Socs of Cal, La, Mo, Miss Valley, San Diego; Pi Lambda Phi; Zeta Beta Tau. Author: Anglo-Spanish Frontier in Illinois County during the American Revolution, 1928; John Evans, Explorer and Surveyor, 1931; The French in the California Gold Rush, 1934; Inside Story of the Gold Rush, 1934; French Activities in California, 1945; Government Employees and Salaries in Spanish Louisiana, 1946; Before Lewis and Clark, 2 vols, 1952; Spanish War Vessels on the Mississippi 1792-1796, 1968; hist monographs; co-author: Latin America: Political and Cultural Development, 1960, 2nd ed, 1968; Pedro Vial and the Roads to Santa Fe, 1967; French Journalist in California: Life and Letters of Derbec, 1966; contbr to profsl jours. Recipient: f: Native Sons of Golden W, 1924-25; Social Sci Research Council, 1930-31; Fulbright Research, 1950-51; Huntington Libr, San Marino, Cal, 1952. Home: 3340 N Mountain View Drive, San Diego, Cal. Office: San Diego State Coll, San Diego, Cal.

NASCHITZ, Peter Gad, Isr, attorney; b. Budapest, Hung, July 16, 1932; s. Fritz and Jenny (Hann); att Tel Aviv U, 1951-55; m. Nechama Ben-Ezer, Feb 28, 1961; c: Eytan, Anat. Atty and notary since 1957; hon consul of Iceland since 1956. IDF, 1951-54. Mem, Rotary Club, Tel Aviv-Yaffo, fmr pres. Home: 25 Liessin St, Tel Aviv, Isr. Office: 136 Rothschild Blvd, Tel Aviv, Isr.

NASS, Samuel, US, business exec; b. NYC, Sep 7, 1908; s. Max and Eva (Faden); BCS, NYU, 1928; m. Edna Kadin, June 27, 1946; c: Ruth, Henry, David, Linda, Herbert. Vice-pres, Gimbel Bros, Inc, since 1953, with firm since 1929. Vice-pres: and dir, 34 St Midtown Assn, since 1944; and trustee, J Comty Cen, Harrison, NY, since 1958; dir, Ave of the Americas Assn, since 1942; vice-pres, bd dirs, NY Assn for New Amers; club, Beach Point. Home: Stratford Rd, Harrison, NY. Office: Gimbel Bros, Inc, Broadway and 33 St, New York, NY.

NASSAU, Erich, Isr, physician; b. Reichenbach, Ger, July 25, 1888; s. Herrmann and Flora (Engel); in Isr since 1938; att Us: Freiburg; Berlin; Heidelberg; MD, 1914; m. Toni Stern, 1917; c: Gertrud Sacker, Gerhard. Cons ped, Workers Sick Fund, since 1961; chief, dept ped, Workers Sick Fund Cen

Hosp, 1938-61; Prof, Heb U, 1956. Ger Army, WW I. Mem, Isr Ped Soc. Contbr to med jours. Recipient: Henrietta Szold Prize, 1957. Home: 5 Kisch Ave, Haifa, Isr.

NATHAN, Clemens Neumann, Eng, technologist; b. Hamburg, Ger, Aug 24, 1933; s. Kurt and Else (Kanin); in Eng since 1936; ATI, M Int MSA, Scottish Coll of Textiles, 1953; postgrad research, U of Leeds; m. Barbara; c: Jennifer, Richard. Chmn, mgn dir, The Cunart Co, Ltd, since 1958; visiting lectr: Coll for Distributive Trades; Royal Coll of Art, London. Vice-chmn, Textile Inst, London sect, judge, design competitions; chmn, admn and finance comm, hon treas, Anglo-J Assn, chmn, Younger Mems Org; gov, cons council, J Orgs; mem: council, Scottish Union of Students; Textile Inst; Bow Group; Inst of Direction, J Hist Soc. Hobbies: hist of art, music, walking, swimming. Home: 2 Ellerdale Close, London NW3, Eng. Office: 231 Oxford St, London W1, Eng.

NATHAN, Edgar J III, attorney; b. NYC, June 29 1919; s. Edgar and Mabel (Unterberg); BA, Williams Coll, Mass, 1941; LLB, Yale Law Sch, 1947; m. Ruth Gottesman, Nov 7, 1948; c: Arthur, Sara, David. Partner: Karelsen, Karelsen, Lawrence and Nathan, since 1959; Marshall, Bratter, Greene, Allison and Tucker, 1956-59; Gale and Falk, 1954-56, asso, Gale, Bernays, Falk and Eisner, 1951-54; asst dist atty, NY Co, 1947-51; public mem, NY State Minimum Wage Bd, hotel ind, 1952-54; mem, NY State Bd of Mediation, 1959-66; exec comm, citizens comm, Family Court, since 1962. Capt, USAAF, 1942-46. Pres, Cong Shearith Isr, NYC, since 1968, vice-pres, 1965-68, mem, bd trustees, since 1956; mem, natl exec bd, AJComm, since 1959, bd delgs, since 1960, exec bd, NY chap, since 1959; bd dirs, J Vacation Assn, 1957-63; bd: Soc of Friends of Touro Syn, since 1966; James Weldon Cen, 1952-60; United Neighborhood Houses, 1950-52; NY State Comm Against Discrimination in Housing, 1950-53; J Mus comm, JTSA, 1955-60; chmn: Civil Court Comm, since 1968; Domestic Relations Court Comm, 1960-62; Comm on Family Court and Family Law, 1962-63, all Assn of Bar, NYC; mem: NY State Bar Assn; Amer Bar Assn; NY Co Lawyers Assn; NY State Dist Attys Assn; Amer Arbitration Assn, natl panel, since 1963, natl lab panel, since 1965; club, Yale, NY. Home: 322 Central Park W, New York, NY. Office: 320 Park Ave, New York, NY.

NATHAN, Ernest, US, business exec; b. Augsburg, Ger, June 21, 1905; s. Rudolph and Lina (Bernheim); in US since 1930; att Inst Textile Tech, Reutlingen, Ger, 1924-26; m. Pearl Glueck, May 5, 1937; c: Alan, Joan, Richard. Pres, dir, treas, Elmwood Sensors Inc since 1961; dir: Sterling Stores of Amer since 1948; PEC Isr Econ Corp since 1948; exec vice-pres, 1952-54; pres, Warwick Chem Corp, 1930-52; vice-pres, Sun-Chem Corp, 1948-52; pres, dir, Chemo Products Inc, 1954-61. Chmn, RI Council of JNF; pres, Temple Beth-El, Providence; hon vice-chmn, JNF, NY, vice-pres, NE region; mem: Amer Technion Soc; Chem Club. Home: 204 Freeman Pkwy, Providence, RI.

NATHAN, Ernst W, US, dermatologist; b. Darmstadt, Ger, May 23, 1889; s. Siegfried and Mathilde (Katz); in US since 1939; att med schs: Giessen, Munich, Berlin; MD, U of Giessen, 1912; m. Betty Levin, Sep 14, 1949. Pvt practice, dermat, NYC, since 1941; research asst, Inst of Experimental Therapy, Frankfurt-am-Main, 1913-14; asso, Frankfurt U Hosp for Skin Diseases, chief of clinic, clinical instr, asso prof, 1914-23; dir, dept dermat, Gen Hosp, Nuerenberg, 1923-33; pvt practice, dermat, Nuerenberg, 1933-39; instr, asst prof, asso prof, asst and asso dermat, NYU Hosp, Skin and Cancer United, 1941-55. Mem: AMA; NY Co Med Soc; Rudolph Virchow Med Soc; Dermat Soc, Gtr NY; Ger Dermat Soc. Contbr to profsl jours. Home: 200 E 66 St, New York, NY. Office: 133 E 58 St, New York, NY.

NATHAN, Hans, US, musicologist; b. Berlin, Ger, Aug 5, 1910; s. Jacob and Lucy (Dobrin); in US since 1936; PhD, Berlin U, 1934; att Harvard U, 1936-38; m. Jael Wahlburg, 1937. Prof, music, Mich State U, since 1964; music critic, Berlin, 1932-35; visiting asst prof, music, Tufts Coll, 1945; Fulbright prof, U Rome, 1952-53; mem, Inst for Advanced Study, Princeton, 1957-58; visiting prof, music, Tulane U, 1966. Mem, Amer Musicological Soc. Author: The Continental Harmony, 1961; Dan Emmett and the Rise of Early Negro Minstrelsy, 1962; co-author: A History of Song, 1961; contbr to musical jours; Ency Americana, 1962. Recipient: Fulbright Award, 1952-53; Guggenheim F, 1957-58; grant-in-aid, Amer Phil Soc, 1944, 1961; grant, Sonneck Memorial Fund, Libr of Cong, 1959; grant, It Govt, 1961-62. Home:

728 Elm St, E Lansing, Mich. Office: Mich State U, E Lansing, Mich.

NATHAN, Helmuth M, US, surgeon, educator; b. Hamburg, Ger, Oct 26, 1901; s. Neumann and Regina (Seligmann); in, US since 1936; MD, U Hamburg, 1925; m. Irene Nelson, Jan 17, 1927; c: Ruth Norden. Prof em, anat and hist of med, Albert Einstein Coll of Med, since 1969, mem staff since 1960; visiting att surg, Bx Munic Hosp Cen, since 1954; asst surg, U Freiburg and Hamburg, 1927-33; asso surg, J Hosp Hamburg, 1933-36; sr clinical asst, Mt Sinai Hosp, NY, 1936-46; att surg, Sydenham Hosp, NY, 1940-53; prof, surg, Hamburg U, 1950. Ger Army, 1919-20. Dipl: Ger Bd Surg; hon f, Soc Med Illustrators; vice-pres, Selfhelp Emigrées from Cen Eur, since 1948; mem: NW Ger Surg Soc; Amer Soc Hist of Med; Amer Anat Soc; NY Med Soc; AMA; Intl Coll Surgs; Intl Bd Surg; Amer Coll Gastroenterology; Amer Coll Card; Amer Soc Abdominal Surgs; Amer Soc Facial Plastic Surg; Amer Geriatric Soc; Acad of Med; Acad of Sci; Assn Amer Mil Surgs; Virchow Soc; Med Circle; life mem, Ger Surg Soc; fmr: pres: NY Phys Assn; Kameraden, Ger J youth movement; mem, bd trustees, Cen Org Ger Jews; clubs: Northshore Country, NY; Bay and Golf, Sarasota, Fla. Co-ed: Should A Patient Know the Truth?; contbr to med jours. Recipient: Deneke Medal, 1932; Salomon Heine Medal, 1936; prizes for art work. Home: 327 Central Park W, New York, NY. Office: 667 Madison Ave, New York, NY.

NATHAN, Hilel, Isr, physician, educator; b. Santa Fe, Arg, 1907; s. Isaac and Palchik (Sime) Notkovich; in Isr since 1951; MD, Rosario, Arg, 1941; postgrad studies, anat, phys anthropology: Jefferson Med Coll, Phila; U Pa, Phila; W Reserve U, Cleveland, O; m. Madeleine Goldschmidt, June 27, 1969; c: Malka, Sharona, Hana. Prof, anat, head, dept anat, anthropology, since 1966; head, sect anat, fac for continuing med educ, since 1969, all Tel Aviv U Med Sch; asst prof, anat, Heb U-Hadassah Med Sch, 1966; visiting asso prof, anat: Albert Einstein Coll of Med, Yeshiva U, NY, 1962-63; Julius Silver Inst, bio-med engr scis, Technion, Haifa; prof, anat, Sch of Communication Disorders, Speech and Hearing, Tel Aviv U; med phys, Baron Hirsch Hosp; dir, Health Dept, both Arg. MC, IDF. Pres, Zionist Youth, Arg. Contbr to med jours. Recipient: Judah Magnes F, 1955-56; co-recipient: Dr Federgreen Prize, 1964, both Heb U-Hadassah Med Sch. Home: 16 Emek Dotan, Tel Hashomer Hosp, Isr. Office: Tel Aviv U, Ramat Aviv, Isr.

NATHAN, Lawrence D, NZ, merchant; b. Auckland, Apr 18, 1910; s. David and Simone (Oulman); MA, Cambridge U, Eng, 1931; m. Anne Brendon, Dec 10, 1947; c: Sarah, Dinah, Judith, David. Chmn and mgn dir, L D Nathan & Co Ltd, since 1944. NZ Forces, 1940-43. Chmn, United Syns of NZ; pres, Auckland Beth Isr Cong; hon consul for Port; mem, Auckland Harbour Bd, chmn, 1955-57. Hobby: yachting. Home: 73 Victoria Ave, Remuera, Auckland, NZ. Office: CPO Box 190, Auckland, NZ.

NATHAN, Norman, US, educator; b. Bklyn, NY, Nov 19, 1915; s. Michael and Fannie (Levine); MA, NYU, 1938, PhD, 1947; m. Frieda Agin, July 21, 1940; c: Linda, Michele, Lois. Prof, Eng, Fla Atlantic U, since 1968; instr, CCNY, 1946-49; lectr: Rutgers U, 1947-49; Shakespeare, TV Sta WKTV, 1954-55; Bible as lit, syns and orgs, since 1952; prof, Utica Coll of Syracuse U, 1958-68, fac mem since 1949. Co-counselor, Hillel Found, Utica Coll, 1951-68; mem: MLA; Shakespeare Assn of Amer; Coll Eng Assn; Natl Council Tchrs of Eng. Author: Though Night Remains, poems, 1959; Judging Poetry, 1961; The Right Word, 1962; Writing Sentences, 1964; Short Stories, 1969; contbr of poems, short stories, articles to periodicals. Home: 1189 SW Tamarind Way, Boca Raton, Fla. Office: Fla Atlantic 4, Boca Raton, Fla.

NATHAN, Otto, US, economist, educator; b. Bingen, Ger, July 15, 1893; s. Jacob and Sara (Freiberg); in US since 1930; att U's: Brussels, London, Freiburg, Munich; PhD, U Wurzburg, Ger, 1920. Trustee, Albert Einstein's lit estate; adv to Ger Govt in stat off, trapsury, and econs dept, 1920-33; dir, intl research, Inst for Bus Cycle Research, Ger, 1926-30; fac mem, Hochschule für Politik, Berlin, 1928-33; spec econ adv, Pres Hoover's Emergency Comm on Employment, 1930-31; visiting lectr: Princeton U, 1933-35; Columbia U, 1940; asso prof, econs, NYU, 1935-58; cons, US Natl Defense Commn, 1940-41; prof, econs, Vassar Coll, 1942-44; chief econ analyst, US Treasury Dept, 1944-45; visiting prof, econs, Howard U, Wash, DC, 1946-52. F, Inst of Econs, Wash, DC, 1930-31;

mem: Amer Econ Assn; Royal Econ Soc; War Resisters League; Women's Intl League for Peace and Freedom; delg to: League of Nations and ILO, 1925-30; intl confs. Author The Nazi Economic System, 1944; Nazi Banking and Finance, 1944; ed: Die Wirtschaft des Auslandes, 1900-27; Die Wirtshaft des Auslandes, 1928; co-ed, Einstein on Peace, 1960; contbr to econ periodicals. Home: 55 E 10 St, New York, NY. Office: Estate of Albert Einstein, 55 E 10 St, New York, NY.

NATHAN, Paul, Isr, surgeon; b. St Wendel, Saar, Nov 23, 1899; MD, U Berlin; m. Eva Kallner; two c. Ret; chief, surg dept, Beilinson Hosp, 1936-69; asso clinical prof, surgery, Heb U Med Sch. Office: Beilinson Hosp, Petah Tikva, Isr.

NATHAN, Robert, US, author; b. NYC, Jan 2, 1894; s. Harold and Sara (Gruntal); att Harvard Coll, 1912-15; m. Dorothy Michaels, 1915; c. Joan; m. 2nd, Helen Kneeland, Dec 14, 1955. Author: Peter Kindred, 1919; Autumn, 1921; The Puppet Master, 1923; Jonah, 1925; The Fiddler in Barley, 1926; The Woodcutter's House, 1927; The Bishop's Wife, 1928; There is Another Heaven, 1929; The Orchid, 1933; One More Spring, 1933; Road of Ages, 1935; The Enchanted Voyage, 1936; Winter in April, 1938; Journey of Tapiola, 1938; The Barley Fields, omnibus, 1938; The Concert, 1940; Portrait of Jenny, 1940; Tapiola's Brave Regiment, 1941; They Went on Together, 1941; The Sea Gull Cry, 1942; But Gently Day, 1943; Journey for Josephine, 1943; Mr Whittle and the Morning Star, 1947; Long After Summer, 1948; The River Journey, 1949; The Married Look, 1950; The Innocent Eve, 1952; The Train in the Meadow, 1953; Jezebel's Husband, plays, 1953; The Adventures of Tapiola, 1954; Sir Henry, 1955; The Rancho of the Little Loves, 1956; So Love Returns, 1958; Color of Evening, 1960; The Weans, 1960; The Snowflake and the Starfish, juvenile, 1960; The Wilderness Stone, 1961; A Star in the Wind, 1962; The Married Man, 1962; The Devil with Love, 1963; The Fair, 1964; The Mallot Diaries, 1965; Stonecliff, 1967; Juliet in Mantua, play, 1967; poetry: Youth Grows Old, 1922; A Cedar Box, 1929; Selected Poems, 1935; The Darkening Meadows, 1940; Morning in Iowa, 1944; The Green Leaf, 1950; A Winter Tide, 1950; screen writer, MGM: The Clock; The White Cliffs of Dover; Pagan Love Song—1943-49; illustrated juvenile book, Tina Mina, 1930. Vice-pres, Natl Inst Arts and Letters, 1938-39; chancellor, Acad Amer Poets, 1950-67; mem, lit comm, Huntington Hartford Found, since 1948; mem: ASCAP; Dramatists Guild; Acad of Motion Picture Arts & Scis; Screen Writers Guild; club, PEN, charter mem, pres, 1940-44. Home: 1240 N Doheny Dr, Los Angeles, Cal.

NATHAN, Robert R, US, consulting economist; b. Dayton, O, Dec 25, 1908; s. Louis and Hannah (Schnee); BS, U of Pa, 1931, MA, 1933; LLB, Georgetown U, Wash, DC, 1938; m. Mary Tillotson, July 17, 1947; c. Richard, Ann, David. Chmn, bd, Brager and Co, NYC; pres, chmn bd, Robert R Nathan Assos, cons econs, since 1946; mem, bd dirs: B Manischewitz; Josam Mfg; DC Natl Bank; research asst, Ind Research Dept, U of Pa, 1931-33; econ, US Dept of Commerce, 1933-34; cons Pres Comm on Econ Security, 1934; asst dir, research, Pa State Emergency Relief Bd, 1934; chief, natl income div, US Dept of Commerce, 1934-40; chief, requirements div, Defense Adv Commn and Off of Production Mgmt, 1940-41; chmn, planning comm, War Production Bd, 1942-43; cons econ, 1944; dep dir, Off of War Mobilization and Reconversion, 1945; econ adv to: Fr, 1946; Burma, 1951-59; UN Korean Reconstruction Agcy, 1952-53; Columbia, 1959; Ghana, 1960; Afghanistan, 1961; El Salvador, 1961-62. Pvt, US Army, 1943. Natl chmn, ADA, 1957-59; chmn, exec comm, since 1952; chmn, regional exec comm, ADL, since 1956; vice-pres, Amer Stat Assn, 1940; trustee, Comm for Econ Devl, since 1961; mem: Natl Commn on Money and Credit, 1958-61; natl prog comm, ADL, since 1959; bd, AJCong; natl council, Amer Friends of Heb U; natl planning comm, Amer Vets Comm; DC Bar Assn; Amer Econ Assn; Pi Gamma Mu; club, Cosmos. Author: National Income, 1929-36, 1937; Mobilizing for Abundance, 1944; co-author: Unemployment in Philadelphia, 1931; A National Wage Policy for 1947, 1946; A National Economic Policy for 1949, 1949; Economic Position of the Steel Industry, 1949; Pal: Problem and Promise, 1946; contbr to profsl publs. Recipient: one of 10 outstanding young men in US, Jr C of C, 1940. Hobbies: coin collecting, fishing. Home: 7101 Crail Dr, Bethesda, Md. Office: 1218 16 St, Washington, DC.

NATHAN, Shmuel, Isr, rabbi, govt official; b. Breslau, Ger, Nov 21, 1914; s. Julius and Gertrud (Herrnstadt); in Isr since 1939; ordained rabbi, J Theol Sem, Breslau, 1939; research student, Heb U, Jerusalem, 1939-41; att: Heb U, Cornell U, 1948-59; m. Eva Kahn, Feb 24, 1943; c. Ada, Joel, Judith. Adv, chmn, adv bds, Isr Min of Tourism, since 1962, dept head since 1948; fmr: secy to pres, Va'ad Leumi, 1947-48; guide trainer, 1949-59. Sr J chaplain, RAF; Haganah; IDF. Pres, Yeshurun Org, Jerusalem; hon secy, Isr Inst of Talmudic Publs; mem: research comm, Union of Official Travel Orgs; Intl Acad of Tourism; fmr chmn: Yeshurun Cen Syn; Isr Touring Club. Contbr to Isr and fgn press. Spec interest: communal activities. Home: 8 Shmuel Hanagid St, Jerusalem, Isr. Office: 24 King George Ave, Jerusalem, Isr.

NATHANI, Izhak, Eng, lawyer; b. Bender, Russ, Mar 27,1903; s. Moshe and Rebbeca (Tiraspolsky) Natanzon; in Eng since 1931; att U Berlin, 1921-24; barrister, Council Legal Educ, London, 1939; m. Haya Rogovsky, Aug, 1929; c. Myron, Adah. Pvt practice since 1939; legal adv, GHP Group Ltd, since 1940. Chmn, Mapam, Gt Brit; mem: world exec, WJC; action comm, World Zionist Org; fmr: vice-pres, exec council, ZF, Gt Brit & Ir; mem, cen comm, Left Poalei Zion. Spec interest: social scis. Home: 4A Woronzow Rd, London NW8, Eng.

NATHANSON, Esther A, US, physician; b. Newport News, Va; d. Morris and Betty (Levy); BA, George Wash U, 1922, MD, cum laude, Med Sch, 1925. Pvt med practice since 1929; clinical instr, obstet and gyn, George Wash U Med Sch,1929-46; phys in chief, Natl Training Sch for Girls, Wash, 1930-37; cons, gyn, psycht div, DC Gen Hosp, 1935-42. Mem: AMA; S. Med Assn; Med Soc of DC, vice-pres, 1942; George Wash Med Soc, vice-pres, 1942; Natl Women's Med Assn; Women's Med Soc of DC, pres, 1956; Jacobi Med Soc, vice-pres, 1946; Amer and Can Socs for Study of Sterility; Intl Fertility Assn; Alpha Epsilon Iota. Home and office: 2500 Virginia Ave, NW, Washington, DC,

NATHANSON, Israel, US, dentist; b. Phila, Pa, Aug 26, 1907; s. Nathan and Fanny (Perlow); att Villanova U, 1926-28; DDS, U of Pa Dent Sch, 1933; m. Sophia Manstein, Nov 25, 1913; c. Melvyn Neil. Pvt practice since 1933; cons, dent, Skin and Cancer Hosp, Phila, 1955-65, staff mem, 1933-55; dent examiner, Sch Dist, Phila, since 1948. Lt, USAF, Dent Service, 1942-46. Mem: Masons, PM of Welcome Lodge 354. Contbr to dent jours. Hobby: philately. Home and office: 2711 N 11 St, Philadelphia, Pa.

NATHANSON, Joseph N, US, physician, educator; b. NYC, Apr 24, 1895; s. Benjamin and Fannie (Bach); MD, McGill U Fac of Med, 1919 m; c. Bernard, Marion Rosenberg. Prof, clinical obstet and gyn, Cornell U Med Coll, since 1957, on teaching staff since 1925; cons obstet, gyn: NY Hosp-Cornell Med Cen, since 1932; Women's Hosp div, St Luke's Hosp, since 1925; postgrad teaching at various hosps and med colls. F: Amer Coll Surgs; Amer Soc Abdominal Surgs; NY Obstet Soc; mem: Soc of J Bibliophiles; Ill State Hist Soc; Temple Rodeph Sholom, NYC. Contbr to profsl jours. Hobby: collector of Lincolniana. Office: 950 Park Ave, New York, NY.

NATHANSON, Muriel Ann, US, social worker; b. Cleveland, O, Nov 3, 1922; d. Joseph and Frances (Palevsky) Paller; MS, W Reserve U, 1946; m. Irving Nathanson, Mar 19, 1950; c. Frances, Richard. Caseworker: J Children's Bur and J Day Nursery of Cleveland, since 1964; Bellefaire, 1946-51. Pres, B'nai B'rith Women, Dist 2, 1968-69; mem: Natl Assn Social Workers; Acad Cert Social Workers. Home: 4386 Baintree, University Heights, O. Office: 21811 Fairmount Blvd, Cleveland, O.

NATIV, Nissan, Isr, stage director, educator; b, Munich, Ger, Nov 5, 1922; s. Samuel and Helena (Tuchman) Notowitz; in Isr since 1939; grad: Heb U, Jerusalem, 1942; Habimah Studio, Tel Aviv, 1942; Etienne Decroux, Paris, 1951; Guildhall Sch of Music, Drama, 1956. Found, dir, Studio of Acting, since 1963; stage dir since 1951; dir, radio plays, ed, various progs, Isr radio, since 1958; dir: The Refusal, by Yehuda Haezrachi; Tchin-Tchin, by F Billetdoux; Tamed Birds,by Benjamin Tammuz; Tzor and Jerusalem, by M Shoham; Drawings for a Theater, by Natan Zach; The Maids, by Jean Genet; The Empire Builders, by Boris Vian; Ayin Bayad, by Y Avissar; dir, Habimah Sch of Dramatic Art, 1956-58; artistic adv, Tel Aviv Munic, 1961-63. Cpl, J Brig, Brit Army; capt, IDF. Hobby: art collecting. Home: 26 Dov Hos St, Tel Aviv, Isr.

NATRA, Sergiu, Isr, composer; b. Bucharest, Rum, Apr 12, 1924; s. Benjamin and Nora (Lustgarten) Nadler; in Isr since 1961; BA, Lyceum, Bucharest, 1942; att J Art Sch, 1942-44; MA, Acad of Music, 1951, both Bucharest; m. Sonia Rosen, Dec 15, 1944; c: Daniel, Gabriel. Composer: Music for piano, 1949; Suite for orch, 1956; Sinfonia for strings, 1964; Music for violin and harp, 1962; Sonatina for harp, 1964; Variations for piano and orch, 1967; Music for Harpsicord and Six Instruments, 1965; Song of Deborah, 1968; Toccata for orch, 1963; A Symphony, 1964; Music, for oboe and strings,1965; Voice of Fire, ballet music; Commentary on Nehemia, 1968; works performed by leading orchs and soloists in Isr, Eur, Amer; repr Isr in several intl music and ballet festivals. Mem, Isr Composers League. ACUM; fmr, comm mem, Rum Composer's Union. Recipient: George Enesco prize for composition, Rum Min of Educ, 1945; State Prize, Rum Govt,1951; Milo Prize, Artists Club, Tel Aviv, 1966. Home: 10 Barth St, Tel Aviv, Isr.

NATRA, Sonia, Isr, sculptor, ceramicist, educator; b. Bucharest, Rum, Apr, 28, 1925; d. Moshe and Elsa (Sufrin) Rosen; in Isr since 1961; att: J Art Sch, 1943-44; Acad of Art, 1944-48; MA, Grigoresco Inst of Art, 1953, all Bucharest; m. Sergiu, Dec 15, 1944; c: Daniel, Gabriel. Art tchr, Hanna Yaffe Vocational HS, since 1962; tchr, sculpture: Mizrachi Tchrs Sem, 1965-68; Renanim Vocational HS, 1962-66; participant in exhbs: Bucharest; Prague; Moscow; Warsaw; Milan; Tel Aviv. Mem: Painters and sculptors Assn in Isr; Isr Ceramic Assn. Contbr on art to Rum press in Isr. Recipient: Intl Art Exhb Award for Sculpture, Moscow, 1955. Home: 10 Barth St, Tel Aviv, Isr.

NAUHEIM Ferdinand Alan, US, business exec, counsellor; b. NYC, Mar 11, 1909; s. Elias and Sadie (Rosenberger); m. Beatrice Strasburger, Aug 23, 1934; c: Gail Kaufman, Stephen. Partner, Kalb, Voorhis & Co, since 1954; professorial lectr, Amer U Sch of Bus Admn, Wash, DC; owner: Sales and Direct Mail cons, 1949-54; Plymoth Printing Co, 1936-49. US Army, 1943-45. Mem, adv bd, Salvation Army, Wash, DC; fmr: bd govs, Direct Mail Advt Assn Intl; pres, Sales and Marketing Exec Club, Wash, DC. Author: Business Letters That Turn Inquiries Into Sales; The Ferd Nauheim Nine-Day Sale Clinic; Salesmen's Complete Model Letter Handbook. Recipient: Man of the Year, Sales and Marketing Exec Club, 1959; Direct Mail Man of the Year, Mail Advt Club, Wash, DC, 1965. Home: 4201 Cathedral Ave, Washington, DC. Office: Woodward Bldg, Washington, DC.

NAVE, Pnina, (pen name P Bat shela), Isr educator; b. Berlin, Ger, Apr 3, 1921; d. Markus and Sabina (Pflanzgraben) Fass; in Isr since 1935; MA, Heb U, Jerusalem, 1945, PhD, 1952; widowed; c: Miriam Gluzman, Oded. Visiting prof, J studies, Heidelberg, Ger, since 1967; fmr, research f, Heb U, Jerusalem. Mem: liturgical bd, Hug Mevakshei Derekh; Heb Writers Assn; Schutzverband Deutscher Schriftsteller, Zürich, Switz; fmr, bd, Hugim l'Jahaduth Mitkademet. Author: Heb poems; essays on Eur, Heb lit, modern Span poets; contbr to encys, mags and jours; trans of works into Heb; fmr, secy, hum, and mem, ed bd, Ency Hebraica. Recipient: Klausner Award, Heb U, 1952; Leo Baeck Award, 1962. Hobbies: art, gardening. Home: 30 Abarbanel St, Jerusalem, Isr.

NAVEH, Menachem, Isr, economist; b. Petah Tikvah, Isr, Jan 26, 1930; s. Yehuda and Shoshana (Feigin) Neifeld; MSc, Heb U, Jerusalem, 1962; m. Nira Shechori, Aug 23, 1955; c: Gili, Yehuda, Roni. Econ counsellor, head, fgn assistance off, Min of Finance, since 1968; econ adv, Inves Cen of Isr in US, 1964-68; sr econ, Min of Commerce and Ind, 1958-64; mem, Kibbutz Erez, 1949-57. Palmach, 1947-49. Prin contrib: among establishers of econ concept "Added Value Ratio and Price of the Dollar Added". Fmr: active, secretariat, Hanoar Haoved; repr to US, Habonim. Home: 27 Habanai St, Jerusalem, Isr. Office: Min of Finance, Jerusalem, Isr.

NAVEH, Zeev, Isr, scientist; b. Amsterdam, Dec 2, 1919; s. Mosheh and Berta (Rosenkranz) Lieber; in Isr since 1935; MSc, Heb U, Jeruaslem, 1950, PhD, 1960; m. Zionah Blitzman, 1951; c: David, Semadar. Sr lectr: ecology, agronomy, since 1965, agric geog, since 1967, both Technion, Haifa; fmr: research agron, Isr Min of Agric; research f, U Cal. Sgt, MC, IDF. Prin contrib: devl of methods for improvement of natural pastures in Isr, E Afr; in applied ecology and vegetation scis. Co-author: Natural Pastures in Israel, 1959; contbr to sci publs. Hobbies: photography, Afr anthropology. Home: 8A Yohevet, Haifa, Isr. Office: Technion, Haifa, Isr.

NAVI, Eliahu, Isr, public official; b. Basra, Iraq, 1920; s. Saleh and Simha (Habusha); in Isr since 1925; att Tchrs Coll, Jerusalem; grad, cum laude, Tel Aviv Sch of Law; m. Bruria Maier, 1947; c: Yael, Tamar, Hagar. Mayor of Beersheva since 1963; atty, 1954-57; judge, 1957-63. Maj, IDF, 1948-54. Co-found, Isr Arabic Bc Service, News commentator in colloquial Arabic; mem: bd, U Negev; secretariat, Lab Party; Isr Bc Auth; mgn bd, ORT; mgmt, Cen Local Auth; Friends of Heb U. Home: 29 Barak St, Beersheva, Isr. Office: City Hall, Beersheva, Isr.

NAVON, Arieh, Isr, artist; b. Donievtzi, Russ, May 22, 1909; s. Moshe and Malka (Landau) Kliegman; in Isr since 1919; att Acad of Art, Paris; m. Etta Zipkovitz; c: David. Cartoonist, Davar daily, 1934-64; pub weekly comic strip, Davar Le' Yeladim, 1935-55; illus prose, poetry, children's books; participated in exhbs: Isr, Paris, US. Author: books of cartoons: Shahor Al Gabei Lavan, 1938; Gluyoat Min ha-Emek, 1942; BaHazit u-Va-Oref, 1945; Fun du und Dort, 1949; Alpaim Shana ve Shana, 1950; Ad Kan, 1948; Mar Yisrael, 1956; Ani Ben Eser, 1958; film, Derech Zemer Ba-Midbar, 1956; designed numerous produc for: Cameri; Habimah; Haifa Munic Theater. Recipient: Dizengoff Prize, 1941; Yerushalmi Prizes, 1943, 1945; Sokolov Prize for Journalistic Work, 1958; Lapid Prize, 1960; Kinor David Prize for set design, 1967. Home: 33 Shlomzion Hamalka St, Tel Aviv, Isr. Office: Cameri Theater, 101 Dizengoff St, Tel Aviv, Isr.

NAVON, Itzhak, Isr, diplomat; b. Haifa, Isr, 1924; s. Eliezer and Pircha (Ouannu) Tiano; att Nautical Sch, Haifa; m. Miriam, Feb, 1948; c: Eliezer, Ruth. Chargé d'affaires, Legation of Isr, Colombo, since 1968; consul, Bombay, India, since 1963; fmr: civilian head, Dept Brit Naval Hqr, Levant Area; personnel mgr, large ind concern; assigned by Fgn Min to: Cyprus; Switz; It. Haganah; maj, IDF. Home: 11 Rama Dania, Jerusalem, Isr. Office: Min for Fgn Affairs, Jerusalem, Isr.

NAVON, Shmuel, Isr, education official; b. Ukraine, Aug 16, 1904; s. Moshe and Malca (Landau); in Isr since 1919; att Us: Königsberg; Zürich; Vienna; Jerusalem; m. Ruth Kovner; c: Amos, Shaul. Sup, elem educ, since 1954; fmr: tchr, Beit Hachinuch, 1924-48, prin 1948-54. Pvt IDF, 1948-52. Prin contrib: invented new method to teach reading. Mem: Org of Sups; Org of Academics; fmr: pres, Isr Reading Assn; mem, Tchrs Council. Author: psych, educ books; contbr to profsl jours. Recipient: Ford Found Grant for comparative study of reading problems among culturally deprived children in US anu Isr. Hobby: song writer. Home: 16 Gottlieb St, Tel Aviv, Isr.

NEAMAN, Avraham Y E, Isr, economist, banker; b. Budapest, Hung, Aug 27, 1907; s. Joseph and Martha (Duschinsky) Neumann; in Isr since 1939; dipl, Coll for World Trade, Vienna, Aus, 1931; DEcon, U for Econ and Commerce, Bologna, It, 1935; CPA, Isr, 1953; m. Lea Neumann, July 5, 1936 (decd); c: Michaelah, Adiel; m. 2nd Elizabeth Sabinsky, 1966. Mgn dir, mem, bd dirs, Ind Devl Bank of Isr Ltd, since 1961; bus exec, Hung, 1938; mem, staff, financial dept, JA, 1939-48; acctnt-gen, Govt of Isr, 1952-61, with dept since 1948; guest lectr, Heb U, Jerusalem, and Tel Aviv br, 1955-61; chmn, Lapidoth Isr Oil Prospectors Corp, Ltd, 1961; mem, bd govs, Technion, Haifa. Author: Outlines of Government Accounting Systems, Heb, 1958; contbr to profsl jours. Home: 16 Yair St, Ramat Chen, Isr. Office: POB 1462, Tel Aviv, Isr.

NEAR, Henry Chaim, Isr kibbutz mem; b. London, Eng, May 23, 1929; s. Ezekiel and Leah (Segal); in Isr since 1955; BA, MA, New Coll, Oxford; PhD, Heb U, Jerusalem; m. Alisa Goldenberg, 1952; c: Yael, Shulamit, Eitan. Mem, Kibbutz Beit Haemek; fmr: educ dir, Ichud Habonim; secy, Kibbutz Beit Haemek. Served IDF. Contbr to jours. Home: Kibbutz Beit Haemek, Isr.

NEBENZAHL, Itzhak Ernst, Isr, State Comptroller; b. Frankfurt/M, Ger, Oct 24, 1907; s. Leopold and Betty (Hirsch); in Isr since 1933; att Us: Frankfurt; Berlin; Freiburg; DJur, 1929; prof ordinarius, em, U Frankfurt; m. Hilde Hollander, 1933; c: Avigdor, Plea Albeck, Ishaiah, Shulamit. State Comptroller of Isr, since 1961; partner, Hollander Concern, chmn, bd dirs, 1947-61; researcher, Roman law, 1931; asst lectr, civil law, U Frankfurt, 1932; legal adv, Japhet Bank, Jerusalem, 1934-46; dir: Jerusalem devl dept, JA for Isr, 1948-50; Bank Leumi le-Isr, Ltd, 1956-61; Jerusalem Econ Corp, 1947-61; Binyanei Haoomah Ltd, 1949-61; hon Consul Gen of Swed, 1952-62. Staff off, IDF, War of Independence. Pres, Fifth Intl Cong, Supr Audit Instns, Jerusalem, 1965; chmn, Isr-Swed C of C, mem, fiscal comm; mem: governing bd, Intl Org of Supr Audit Instns, since 1965, chmn, 1965-68; B'nai B'rith, fmr pres, Jerusalem lodge; fmr: chmn: adv comm and council, Bank of Isr; Isr PO Bank; mem: Petroleum Bd; Anti-Trust Council of Isr; Govt Inquiry Comms on book pub, Shabbat demonstrations, diamond control; chmn, Isr Comm, Hadassah Med Org; mem: council, Yad va-Shem; bd trustees, Bar Ilan U; Bezalel Natl Mus; KJV Zionist Students Org, Ger; pres, Ezra Rel Youth Movement, Ger. Author: Study in German Civil Law, 1931. Recipient: 1st Prize, Frankfurt U, for book, Study in Ger on Civil Law, 1928; Chevalier First Class, Swedish Order of Vasa, 1957. Home: 9 Rashba St, Jerusalem, Isr. Office: State Comptroller Office, Jerusalem, Isr.

NECHELES, Heinrich, US, physician, educator; b. Hamburg, Ger, July 8, 1897; s. Fabian and Rosa (Gutterman); in US since 1932; MD, Hamburg U Med Sch, 1923, PhD, 1924; grad study: Us: Berlin, Kiel, Freiburg; m. Stefanie Schlesinger, Aug 6, 1933; c: Fabian. Dir em, dept gastrointestinal research, Michael Reese Hosp, since 1932; att phys since 1946, chmn, research and labs div, 1946; prof, dept med, Chgo Med Sch, since 1960, prof lectr, phys, U Chgo, since 1944, asso prof, 1928-29, 1931-34; asso prof, Peking Union Med Coll, 1925-31. Chmn, research comm, Natl Gastroenterological Assn, 1953, council mem, 1953; mem: AAAS; AAUP; Amer Coll Phys; Amer Gastroenterological Assn; Amer Phys F Comm, IMA; Amer Phys Soc; Amer Soc for Study Arteriosclerosis; Assn for Study Liver Diseases; Cen Soc for Clinical Research; Chgo Soc for Internal Med; Chgo Inst Med; Soc for Experimental Biol and Med; Yu Wang Fu Assn; Sigma Xi. Contbr to profsl books and jours. Hobby: mech, lit. Home: 1328 E Madison Park, Chicago, Ill. Office: 2900 S Ellis Ave, Chicago, Ill.

NEDELMAN, Charles Irving, US, dentist; b. Chgo, Ill, Apr 6, 1911; s. Abraham and Sarah (Chaden); BS, DDS, U of S Cal, 1934; m. Naomi Dietch; c: Adam, Eric. Asso prof, Sch of Dent, U of S Cal, since 1960; pvt practice, prosthodontics. Cdr, USNR, 1942-68. Dipl, Amer Bd Prosthodontics; mem: asso, Amer Acad Periodontology; Alpha Omega; Alpha Epsilon Pi; fmr, pres, ZOA, Pacific region. Contbr to dent jours. Spec interests: biol photography, biol research. Home: 2255 Westridge Rd, Los Angeles, Cal. Office: 6221 Wilshire Blvd, Los Angeles, Cal.

NEDIVI, Yehudah, Isr, public official; b. Gomel, Russ, June 22, 1899; s. Shlomo and Hanna (Babovnik) Frankel; in Isr since 1913; grad, Herzliya Gymnasia, 1918; m. Rachel Weissbord-Livni, Jan 31, 1922 (decd); c: Carmela Shoulman, Uzi; m. 2nd, Aurelia Kahn, Nov 17, 1968; c: town clerk, Tel Aviv, 1924-64; admn staff, Pal Govt, Jaffa dist, 1918; dir, dept J settlements, 1921; missions for JA to London, 1930, 1935, 1947, India, Singapore, 1939; missions: Isr Bond Drive, 1951; natl instns, Kenya, Rhodesia, S Afr, 1958; Gt Brit, Ir, 1962. Capt, Brit Army, 1942-45; liaison off, J Pal troops. Found chmn, Soc Clerks of Isr Local Auths; asso mem, Intl City Mgrs Assn; life mem, Intl Inst Munic Clerks. Home: 4 Katzenelson St, Tel Aviv, Isr.

NEEMAN, Gideon M, Isr, editor; b. Halle, Ger, Jan 22, 1924; s. Wilhelm and Maha (Jacob); in Isr since 1939; m. Batya Zigelman, Mar 15, 1945; c: Nurit Azoulay, Elan. Mgn dir, mem, ed bd, Davar, Histadrut daily, since 1965; Eur repr, Histadrut, London, 1961-64; JA emissary to S Amer, 1951-54. Mem exec, Isr Newspaper Publishers Assn; fmr, co-found, mem, Kibbutz Gezer. Contbr articles on lab movement. Hobby: photography. Home: 22 Yagur St, Tel Aviv, Isr.

NEEMAN, Moshe, Isr, government official; b. Czernowitz, Russ, Jan 7, 1906; s. Nahum and Alte Lowenthal, in Isr since 1939; DJur, U of Vienna, 1931; m. Hava Schoenbach, Apr 11, 1937. Dir, fuel auth, Min of Finance, since 1968; mgn dir, Petroleum Services Ltd, since 1959; fmr fuel controller, Min of Finance. Mem bd, Isr Petroleum Inst; chmn, Isr Natl Comm to World Energy Conf. Contbr to World Energy Conf; to profsl jours. Home: 26 Ehud St, Haifa, Isr. Office: 82 Atzmauth Rd, Haifa, Isr.

NE'EMAN, Yuval, Isr, physicist; b. Tel Aviv, Isr, May 14, 1925; s. Gedalia and Tzipora (Benyaacov) BSc, Technion, Haifa, 1946; PhD, London U, 1962; DIC, Imperial Coll of Sci and Tech, London, 1962; Diplome d'Etat Major, Ecole Superieure de Guerre, Paris, 1952, DSc, HC, 1966; m. Dvora

Rubinstein, June 28, 1951; c. Anath, Tid'al. Prof, chmn, dept physics and astronomy, Tel Aviv U, since 1965, vice-pres, 1965-66; dir, Cen of Particle Theory, U Tex, since 1968; sci dir, Isr AERE, 1961-63; prof, physics, Cal Inst of Tech, 1964-65. Col, IDF, 1948-60. Prin contrib: unitary symmetry theory of elem particles. Hon pres, Nitsan org for children with devl and learning difficulties; chmn, Isr AEC research subcomm; mem, Isr Acad of Scis; Isr, Eur and Amer Phys Soc; Brit Inst of Physics; Inst of Strategic Studies, London. Author: Algebraic Theory of Particle Physics, 1967; co-author: The Eighth-fold Way, 1964. Recipient: Rothschild Prize for Natural Scis, Rothschild Found, 1968; Weizmann Prize for Natural Scis, Tel Aviv Munic, 1966. Home: 6 Ehud St, Zahala, Tel Aviv, Isr. Office: Tel Aviv U, Isr.

NEFF, Jack Henry, US, oral surg; b. Phila, Pa, Apr 30, 1934; s. Samuel and Kate (Feingold); att U of Pa, 1951-53; DDS, Temple U, Phila, 1957; att U of Pa Grad Sch of Med, 1958-59; m. Jane Segeal, Dec 23, 1956; c: Samuel, Alan. Asst prof, surg, Hahnemann Med Sch, since 1967; clinical asst prof, anat, Temple Dent Sch, since 1966; chief, oral surg, Doctors Hosp, since 1965; asst chief, oral surg, Phila Gen Hosp; asst instr, oral surg, U of Pa Sch of Dent Med 1962-65. Dipl, Amer Bd Oral Surg; mem: bd govs: Phila Co Dent Soc; Doctors Hosp, Phila; Alpha Omega; Amer Soc Oral Surgs; Amer Dent Assn; Pa Dent Assn; Del Valley Soc Oral Surgs; E Dent Soc; NY Inst Clinical Oral Path. Ed, Temple Dent Alumni Newsletter. Hobbies: music, antique clocks, art. Home: 478 Ballytore Rd, Wynnewood, Pa. Office: 230 N Broad St, Philadelphia, Pa.

NEGBI, Zeev, Isr, attorney; b. Bialystok, Pol, June 27, 1915; s. Moses and Berta (Lurie) Katznelson; in Isr since 1941; MJur, Warsaw U, 1937; LLM, Harvard U, 1958, DJS, 1962; m. Aliza Rabovsky, July 29, 1947; c: Moshe, Matti. Sr asst atty gen since 1964; asst dir, leg, Min of Justice, 1951-52; legal adv, Min of Devl, 1956-57; Cpl, RASC, 1941-45; legal service, IDF. Mem: natl comm: Isr Bar Chamber; Union of Salaried Lawyers, legal sect, Gen Fed of Lab; Harvard Club, Isr; coord comm, Profsl Academic Orgs; fmr judge, comrade's court, Gen Fed of Lab. Author: Prevention of Nuisances in Israel; The Government as Civil Law Defendant, 1962. Recipient: research f, Harvard-Brandeis Coop Research, 1957; research f in Soviet law, Russ Research Cen, Harvard, 1961. Home: 4 Mendele St, Jerusalem, Isr. Office: Min of Justice, Jerusalem, Isr.

NEGIN, Arthur William, US, attorney; b. Cleveland, Oct 3, 1913; s. Samuel and Yetta (Schwartz); att O State U, 1930-31; LLB, LLD, John Marshall U, Cleveland, O, 1933-37; m. Sylvia Zychick, Jan 25, 1936; c: Yolanda Kirschner, Miriam Halle, Gary. Pres: Ont Loan and Mortgage Co, since 1969; Ont Loan Co, since 1965; atty since 1937. Legal adv: Temple Emanuel; B'nai Jacob Cong, fmr pres, mem bd; vice-pres: Mansfield J Fed, since 1951; mem: bd, life, B'nai Jacob Cong; prog comm, Natl ADL; charter, Natl Youth Adv Bd, since 1957; Masons; Elks; Grotto; Richland Co, O State, Amer Bar Assns; B'nai B'rith, fmr pres, Mansfield Lodge; fmr: pres, O Assn, B'nai B'rith, mem, bd govs, treas, Dist Grand Lodge 2; vice-pres, O-Ky Regional Bd, ADL, chmn, admn comm for O-Ky. Home: 365 W Cook Rd, Mansfield, O. Office: 3 N Main St, Mansfield, O.

NEHER, André, Fr, educator; b. Obernai, Fr, Oct 22, 1914; s. Albert and Rosette (Strauss); ordained rabbi; docteur ès lettres, U of Strasbourg, 1947; m. Renée Bernheim, Dec 25, 1947. Head, dept, Heb lang and lit, U Strasbourg, since 1948; tchr, Sarrebourg, Lyon, Strasbourg, 1936-40, 1945-48, visiting prof, Tel-Aviv U, 1968. Head, Fr sect WJC head, Intl Cultural Commn, since 1965, head conf of J intellectuals, Paris, 1957; vice-pres, ZF of Fr, Paris, 1949; named among the Sages of Isr by PM Ben-Gurion, 1957; mem: cen comm, Alliance Israélite Universelle, since 1962; bd govs, Tel Aviv U, since 1968; exec comm, Intl Union for J Studies, Jerusalem, 1957. Author: Amos, Contribution à l'Etude du Prophétisme, 1950; Notes sur Qohélet, 1951; L'Essence du Prophétisme, 1955; Moise et la Vocation Juive, 1956; Jérémie, 1960; L'Existence Juive, Solitude et Affrontements, 1962; Le Puits de l'Exil, la Théologie Dialectique du Maharal de Prague, 1966; De l'Hébreu au Français, 1969; co-author: Histoire Biblique du Peuple d'Israël, 1962; contbr to Ency Française, Heb Ency. Home: 6 rue Ehrmann, Strasbourg, Fr.

NEHER-BERNHEIM, Renée, Fr, educator; b. Paris, Apr 4, 1922; d. André and Marguerite (Wellhoff) Bernheim; docteur ès lettres, U Strasbourg, 1961; m. André Neher, Dec 25, 1947. Tchr, lit, J Hist: École Aquiba, Strasbourg, since 1948; École Maimonide, Paris, 1946-47. Author: Les Contes de l'Arche de

Noé, 1955; Le Judaisme dans le Monde Romain, 1959; Histoire Juive de la Renaissance à Nos Jours, 1963-65; La Déclaration Balfour, 1969; co-author: Histoire Biblique du Peuple d'Israël, 1962; contbr to jours. Found, dir, Collection Classique Judaica; mem exec, Fr WIZO. Home: 6 rue Ehrmann, Strasbourg, Fr.

NEIDICH, Sol, US, physician; b. NYC, July 6, 1913; s. Morris and Rose (Levine); BS, U of SC, 1934, MD, 1938; m. Evelyn Rudowitz, Dec 25, 1938; c: Alan, Marilyn, Linda. Pvt practice since 1945; chief of staff, Beaufort Co Hosp, 1948-49, 1952-53, 1958-59. USAF MC, 1940-41, maj, 1942-45. Pres: B'nai B'rith Cen, Rochester, Minn, commnr, adult educ, natl cabinet, pres, dist grand lodge 5, 1958-59, mem, supr lodge bd govs, since 1965; pres, SC Assn of B'nai B'rith lodges, 1950-51; chmn, United Comty Fund, 1959-60; Coastal Med Assn, 1958-59; mem: Gov's Commn on Alcoholism; AMA; SC Med Assn; S Med Assn; World Med Assn; Rotary. Recipient: Man of Year Award, Rotary, 1960. Home: 2101 Simms Ave, Beaufort, SC. Office: 1112 Craven St, Beaufort, SC.

NEIGUS, Irwin, US, obstetrician; b. NYC, July 4, 1908; s. Abraham and Ida (Aidlin); BS, CCNY, 1929; MS, Creighton U, 1933, MD, 1935; m. Esther Levin, May 8, 1947; c: Nancy, David. Clinical asst prof, obstet and gyn, Downstate Med Cen, since 1966, clinical instr, 1954-65; att obstet, gyn: J Hosp of Bklyn, since 1965; Kings Co Hosp, since 1954; chief, gyn clinic, VA regional off, Bklyn, since 1948. Lt col, US Army, 1941-45. F: Amer Coll Surgs; Amer Coll Obstet and Gyn; Brooklyn Gyn Soc; mem: AMA; Amer Bd Obstet and Gyn; Kings Co Med Soc. Contbr to med jours. Recipient: Bronze Star; Combat Medic Badge; campaign stars; Unit Meritorious Service plaque; awards: Upsilon Pi; Gamma Pi Sigma. Hobby: photography. Home: 444 E 19 St, Brooklyn, NY. Office: 1705 Caton Ave, Brooklyn, NY.

NEIMAN, David, US, Biblical scholar, theologian, author; b. Novgorod-Seversk, Russ, Sep 10, 1921; s. Israel and Tzipporah (Hendlin); in US since 1923; Heb tchr, Herzliah Oriental Inst, NY, 1943; att: CCNY, 1938-43; Yeshiva Tomche T'mimim, Bklyn, 1940-44; MA, U of Chgo, 1947; PhD, Dropsie Coll, Phila, 1950; m. Shulamith Dubno, Apr 21, 1955; c: Rachel, Rina, Rebecca. Asso prof, theol, since 1966, dir, Boston Coll Inst of Archaeol, since 1967; dean, Acad for Higher J Learning, 1955-60; lectr, New Sch for Social Research, 1956-63; asso prof, Bible, Brandeis U, 1963-66. Found: Acad for Higher J Learning, NY, 1956; Boston Coll Inst of Archaeol; mem: Soc of Bibl Lit; Amer Oriental Soc. Contbr to profsl jours. Home: 1745 Commonwealth Ave, W Newton, Mass. Office: 140 Commonwealth Ave, Chestnut Hill, Mass.

NEISNER, Fred, US, business exec; b. White Plains, NY, Mar 30, 1909; s. Joseph and Hattie (Plaut); BS, U of Pa, 1931; m. Eileen Mann, Apr 23, 1936; c: Lewis, Merry. Chmn bd, Neisner Bros, Inc, since 1956, vice-pres, 1935, pres, 1942-56; dir, Lincoln Rochester Trust Co, since 1950; mem bd, Lincoln First Banks, Inc, since 1967. Mem, bd dirs: United J Wfr Fund, since 1948; J Comty Council, since 1952; Highland Hosp, since 1949; Baden St Settlement, since 1964; Urban League of Rochester, since 1965. Home: 1151 Clover St, ter, NY. Office: 49 East Ave, Rochester, NY.

NEISNER, Melvin B, US, business exec; b. Rochester, NY, Aug 19, 1914; s. Abraham and Irene (Bauer); att U Pa, 1932-34; m. Ellen Garson, Dec 16, 1947; four c. Pres, Neisner Bros, Inc, since 1956; dir, Security Trust Co, Rochester, NY. US Army, 1943-46. Dir, Comty Chest, Rochester, NY; vice-pres, Zeta Beta Tau. Home: 1090 Allens Creek Rd, Rochester, Roch NY. Office: 49 East Ave, Rochester, NY.

NELESON, Leonard, US, psychologist, researcher; b. Bklyn, NY. Oct 23, 1916; s. David and Jessie (Levoritz) Katzeneleson; MA, Tchrs Coll, Columbia U, 1956; PhD, NYU, 1962; m. Evelyn Brenner, Mar 29, 1940; c: Susan. Coord, NY State Narcotics Addiction Control Commn, since 1967; independent cons since 1941; educ researcher, 1935-47; exec dir, Amer-Isr Lighthouse, 1952-65; bur chief, Conn Dept of Educ, 1965-67; adj prof, psych, U Hartford, 1965-67. Founu: rehab cen for Isr blind, 1957; normal sch educ sys for blind children in Isr, 1958; mem: Amer Psych Assn; Kappa Delta Pi; Natl Rehab Assn; Assn of Workers for Blind. Contbr to profsl jours. Home: 73-72 194 St, Flushing, NY. Office: 30 E 60 St, New York, NY.

NELSON, Joseph, US, business exec; b. Gary ,Ind, Dec 25, 1911; s. Max and Rose (Snofsky); PhB, U Chgo, 1933, JD, 1936; m. Violet Schaffer, Feb 17, 1946; c: Jacoba, Jacob, Rohert. Pres, Schaffer Belts, Inc, since 1946; atty, 1936-41. Lt col, Gen Staff Corps, 1941-45. Pres: Yavneh Acad, Paterson, NJ. Mahopac Temple, 1950-52; chmn: UJA, Englewood, 1954-56; Isr Bond Appeal, 1954-55. Home: 281 Linden, Englewood, NJ. Office: 330 Fifth Ave, New York, NY.

NELSON, Joseph N, US, attorney; b. NYC, Oct 10, 1908; s. Nathan and Sarah (Zletz); att NYU, 1925-27; LLB, St Johns U, NYC, 1930; m. Lillian Stern, Feb 20, 1932; c: Michael, Seth. Mem, Rev Bd, FCC, since 1962, sr atty, law dept, 1946-50, chief TV br, 1950-56, chief, renewal and transfer div, Fed Communications Div, 1956-62; pvt practice, NYC, 1931-38; cons, Dept of Wfr, NYC, 1938-44; chief counsel, OPA, 1944-46; atty, NLRB, 1946. Mem: Fed Bar Assn; club, Natl Lawyers. Home: 9039 Sligo Creek Pkwy, Silver Spring, Md. Office: FCC, Washington, DC.

NELSON, Leonard Martin, US, attorney; b. Rumford, Me, Sep 23, 1935; s. Harold and Mildred (Rolnick); AB, Harvard Coll, 1957; LLB, Harvard Law Sch, 1960; m. Merle Royte, June 17, 1956; c: Judd, Eve, Julie. Partner, Bernstien, Shur, Sawyer & Nelson, since 1962; lectr, U Me Sch of Law, since 1963. Chmn: Me State Commn on Arts and Hums; Me State Bar Assn Judiciary Comm; trustee, Wayneflete Sch; trustee, fmr pres, Portland Sym Orch; mem, Phi Beta Kappa. Contbr to law jours. Home: 179 Falmouth, Portland, Me. Office: 443 Congress St, Portland, Me.

NEMEROV, Howard, US, educator, author; b. NYC, Mar 1, 1920; s. David and Gertrude (Russek); BA, Harvard, 1941; hon degs: Tufts U; Lawrence U; m. Margaret Russell, Jan 26, 1944; c: David, Alexander, Jeremy. Prof, Eng, Wash U, since 1969; mem fac, Bennington Coll, 1948-66; prof, Brandeis U, 1966-69; cons, poetry, Libr of Cong, 1963-64. Lt, RCAF, USAAF, 1941-45. Mem: Natl Inst Arts and Letters; Amer Acad Arts and Sci. Author: The Image and the Law, poems, 1947; The Melodramatists, novel, 1949; Guide to the Ruins, poems, 1950; The Salt Gardens, poems, 1954; Federigo, or the Power of Love, novel, 1955; Mirrors & Windows, poems, 1958; A Commodity of Dreams, stories, 1959; New and Selected Poems, 1960; The Next Room of the Dream, poems and 2 verse plays, 1962; Poetry and Fiction, 1963; Journal of the Fictive Life, 1965; The Blue Swallows, 1967; Stories, Fables, and Other Diversions, 1971; ed, Poets on Poetry, 1965. Recipient: Creative Arts Award, Brandeis U, 1964; grant, Natl Inst Arts and Letters, 1965; Award for poetry, St Botolphs, Club, Boston, 1968; 1sr Theodore Roethke Memorial Award for Poetry, 1968; Guggenheim F, 1969; Acad of Amer Poets, 1971. Home: 6970 Cornell Ave, St Louis, Mo. Office: Eng Dept, Wash U, St Louis, Mo.

NEMES-NAGEL, Endre, Swed, painter; b. Pécsvárad, Hung, Nov 10, 1909; s. Ignac and Elizabet (Kugel) Nagel; in Swed since 1940; att Acad of Art, Prague, 1930-34; m. Hélène Exemplaroff (decd); m. 2nd, Britt Sundell; c: Catherine, Lena. Prof, since 1968; mem: Royal Acad of Art, since 1965; Art Council of State, 1967-70. Mem, Org of Swed Artists. Recipient: Yearly Artist Award, Swed Govt, 1965; Order of Merit, City of Gothenburg, 1967. Home: 11 Drakenbergsgatan, Stockholm, Swed. Office: 71 Götgatan, Stockholm, Swed.

NEMETZ, Nathaniel Theodore, Can, jurist; b. Winnipeg, Sep 8, 1913; s. Samuel and Rebecca (Birch); BA, U of BC, 1934; King's Counsel, 1950; m. Bel Newman, Aug 10, 1935; c: Peter. Justice appeal, Court of BC, since 1968; sr partner, Nemetz, Austin, Christie & Bruk; Puisne Judge, Supr Court of BC, 1963-68; fmr dir: Expanded Metal Co of Can, Ltd; Pacific Valves Ltd; fmr counsel: Public Utilities Commn; lab relations, Corp of Dist of Burnaby, Cities of Vancouver and New Westminster; Royal Commn on Expropriation; Royal Commn, Election Irregularities, 1965; commn: Forest Ind Dispute, 1966; Lab Report on Swed, 1968; Fishing Ind Dispute, 1964. Pres: Vancouver Inst, 1960-61; Alumni Assn, U of BC, 1956-57; Vancouver Lodge, B'nai B'rith, 1948; dir: Comty Chest and Council, 1957; Festival Soc, 1962-63, both Vancouver; Can Arthritis and Rheumatism Soc, 1959-61; chmn: jt PR comm, B'nai B'rith and Can J Cong, 1942-57; chmn, sen and bd govs, U of BC, 1957-68; bd, sch trustees, U Dist, 1957-58; co-chmn, Can Council of Chr and J, Pacific region, 1962-63; delg: Intl Conf Us, Tokyo, 1965; Intl Conf of Judges, Geneva, 1967; Commonwealth Conf of Us, Sydney, 1968; mem: Can Bar Assn; Can Inst Intl Affairs; clubs U of Vancouver, pres, 1961-62; Fac, U of BC. Recipient: hum relations award, Can Council of Chr and J, 1958; Gt Trekker

Award, U of BC, 1969; Home: 5688 Newton Wynd, Vancouver, BC, Can. Office: Law Courts, Vancouver, BC, Can.

NEPPI-MODONA, Aldo, It, educator, author; b. Florence, It, Oct 20, 1895; s. Leone and Ada (Carpi); dipl, lit, U Florence, 1918, dipl, classical philol, 1920; m. Rachel Fintz, 1929; c: Leo, Lionella Viterbo. Prof, Latin and Greek antiquities and Etruscology, U Genoa, since 1940; co-dir, Studi Etruschi, Florence; vice-secy, Casa Editrice Bemporad, 1921-22; dir, sect, Inst di Studi Romani, Rome, 1935-38; prof, Latin, Greek, Licei Statali, 1935-40; Maj, WW I. Prin contrib: discovered Etruscan town walls of Cortona (Arezzo), It. Secy, Friendship Assn of Chr and J, Florence; mem: Natl Union of Fmr Offs in It; Colombaria Acad, Florence; Unione Fiorentina; Etruscan Acad, Cortona. Author: Cortona, etruscae romana, 1925; L'isola di Coo nell'antichità classica, 1933; Forma Italiae, Pisae, 1950; Inscriptiones Italiae, Pisae, 1950; Edifici Teatrali: Greci e Romani, 1961; contbr to hist and archaeol jours. Recipient: Mil Cross, 1918. Home: Via dei Banchi 5, Florence, It. Office: U of Genoa, Genoa, It.

NERLOVE, Samuel Henry, US, economist; b. Vitebsk, Russ, Dec 19, 1901; s. Max and Mary (Lissner); in US since 1905; AM, U Chgo, 1923; m. Evelyn Andelman, Mar 24, 1932; c: Marc, Harriet Mischel, Sara. Prof, econ and bus policy, U Cal, since 1963; prof, econ, U Chgo, 1943-63, fac mem since 1923; sr financial econ, Treasury Dept, 1930-31; trustee, Security Life Ins Co of Amer Trust, 1933-47. Mem: Amer Econ Assn; AAUP. Author: The Use of Wage Statistics in Arbitration of Labor Disputes, 1923; Outlines of Economic Order, 1930; A Decade of Corporate Incomes, 1920-30, 1932; Risk and Risk Bearing, 1933; Insurance,1938; An Introduction to the Economics of Business Enterprise, 1945; contbr to profsl jours. Home: 10450 Wilshire Blvd, Los Angeles, Cal. Office: U of Cal, Los Angeles, Cal.

NESSIM, Simon S, US, attorney; b. Salonica, Greece, May 31, 1896; s. Samuel and Miriam (Confino); in US since 1914; LLB, NY Law Sch, 1923; m. Lillian Wein, June 12, 1937; c: Marion, Sharon. Pvt practice; mem, Romano, Nessim & Gluckstein, 1925-30. Pres: Cen Sephardic J Comty of Amer, 1949-62; Sephardic Brotherhood of Amer, 1933-34; Amer Sephardic Council, 1932-35; Sephardic J Comty of NY, 1930-47; Kahal Kol Isr, 1925-28; Maccabee Sephardic Zionist Org, 1914-16; vice-pres, co-found, World Sephardic Fed, since 1951; dir, B'rith Shalom Cong, 1923-25; exec dir, Span and Port Settlement House, 1921-24; mem, NY Co Lawyers Assn. Ed, La Renacencia, Zionist publ in Ladino, 1917; publ, ed, La Luz, Ladino weekly, 1921-22. Home: 67-76 Booth St, Forest Hills, NY. Office: 152 W 42 St, New York, NY.

NESSYAHU, Mordechai, Isr, research worker, lecturer; b. Haifa, Isr, Sep 25, 1929; s. Naftali and Zippora (Tversky); att Heb U, Jerusalem, 1949-52; m. Jehudith, Apr 5, 1962; c: Haim. Dir, research dept, Lab Party of Isr, since 1964; fmr dir, Lab Party. Lt, hist dept, IDF, 1952-54. Author: Cosmic Science and Scientific Society, 1951; The Scientific Revolution and the Developing World, 1964; Israel As A Challenge, 1969; contbr to periodicals; fmr ed, Lab Party periodical. Home: 27 Ben Zion St, Tel Aviv, Isr. Office: Beit Berl, Kfar Saba, Isr.

NESTADT, Morris, S Afr, business exec; b. Johannesburg, S Afr, Nov 1, 1896; m. Celia Sapiro, May 30, 1920; c: Gerald, Allan, Stanley, Harry. Mgn dir, George Rennie & Co (Pty) Ltd, estate agts; mem, Transvaal Provincial Council, since 1930; commn of oaths; JP. Pres: E Transvaal Cricket Union; E Rand Cricket Union; hon life mem, Benoni Caledonian Soc; clubs: Benoni Soccer; Benoni Lake; Round Table. Recipient: Queen Elizabeth Coronation Medal, 1953; Freeman of Benoni, 1954. Home: 5 Ambleside Ave, Lakefield, Benoni, S Afr. Office: 46 Prince's Ave, Benoni, S Afr.

NETANYAHU, Benzion, Isr, editor, author; b. Warsaw, Pol, Mar 25, 1910; s. Nathan Mileikowsky; in Isr since 1920; grad, Heb Tchrs Sem, Jerusalem, 1929; MA, Heb U, 1933; PhD, Dropsie Coll, Phila, 1947; m. Cela Segal; three c. Prof, Hebraic studies, U Denver, since 1968; prof, J hist, Heb lit,chmn, dept Heb lang and lit, Dropsie Coll, 1957-68; ed in chief, Ency Hebraica, 1948-62; Ency Judaica, 1961-63. Mem, New Zionist Org delg to US, 1940; exec bd, comm for J Army, 1941; exec dir, ZOA, United Revisionist Party in Amer, 1941-48; mem, Amer Zionist Emergency Council, 1946-48; f, mem, exec comm, Amer Acad for J Research, NY; mem, adv council, Inst for Advanced Rel Studies, U Notre Dame, Ind. Author: Max Nordau, three studies, Heb, 1935, 1936, 1954; Theodor Herzl, Heb,1937; Israel Zangwill, Heb, 1938; Max Nordau

to his People, 1941; Leo Pinsker, 1944; Don Isaac Abravanel, 1953, 2nd rev ed, 1968; Anti-Semitism, Heb, 1959; Theodor Herzl as Theoretician and Statesman, 1962; The Marranos according to the Hebrew Sources, 1963; The Marranos of Spain, 1966; found, co-ed, Bethar, monthly, 1933-34; ed, Hayarden, daily, 1934-35; ed: Series of Zionist Political Writings, Heb, 6 vols, 1935-38; Nordau's Zionist Works, Heb, 4 vols, 1954-62; co-ed, J Quarterly Review, 1959-60; gen ed, The World History of the Jewish People, vol 1, 1964; contbr to Heb and Eng publs. Home: 2085 S Monroe St, Denver, Colo. Office: Dept of Hist, U of Denver, Denver, Colo.

NETANYAHU, Elisha, Isr, mathematician, educator; b. Warsaw, Pol, Dec 21, 1912; MA, Heb U, Jerusalem, 1934, PhD, 1942; m. Shoshana Shenberg; two c. Prof, math, Technion, since 1946; dean, fac of sci, head, dept of math, 1956-68. Mem, Amer Math Soc. Contbr to profsl jours. Office: Technion, Haifa, Isr.

NETTER, Zviya Zagith, Isr, choreographer, author; b. Haifa, Isr; d. Yehuda and Shoshana (Berliner) Gottleib; att: Physical Culture Tchrs Sch, Haifa; Schs of Dance and Choreography: Gertrud Kraus; Brill Morina and Taly Biaty, all Tel Aviv; m. Zvi Netter; c: Shunit. Dir, dance studio, children's theater, until 1965; lectr, fgn tchr sch, on arranging J holiday festivals, 1955-56; choreographer, Orot Theater, Jerusalem, 1954-56; org, dir, various festivals, 1950-65. Sgt, MC, IDF, 1949-50. Author: songs and radio plays for Isr radio; column in Divrei Hayamim, Women and Customs of Bible Times, 1954-57; poems; column in Dvar Hayeladim, 1967-68; poems and songs for children; contbr to press and periodicals. Mem: Phys Culture Tchrs Assn; Ein Hod Artists Village. Hobbies: painting, music. Home: Artists Village, Ein Hod, Isr. Office: 35 Nativ Ofakim St, Haifa, Isr.

NETTL, Paul, US, musicologist, educator; b. Hohenelbe, Bohemia, Jan 10, 1889; s. Karl and Johanna (Beck); in US since 1939; att U of Vienna, 1908-13; LLD, U of Prague, 1913, PhD, 1915; m. Margaret von Gutfeld, May 23, 1953; c: Bruno. Prof, musicology; Ind U since 1946; Ger U, Prague,1922-29; dir, music div, Ger radio sta, Prague, 1935-39. Mem, FM Humanitas Lodge, NY. Author of numerous books in five langs, including: Mozart in Bohmen, 1936; Story of Dance Music, 1947; Musical Documents, 1950; Other Casanova, 1950; Forgotten Musicians, 1951; National Anthems, 1952; contbr to profsl jours. Recipient: Mozart Medal, Salzburg Mozarteum, 1956. Home: 620 S Fess Ave, Bloomington, Ind. Office: Ind U, Bloomington, Ind.

NETZER, Devora, Isr, educator, legislator; b. Russ, May, 1892; d. Shimon and Pesia; in Isr since 1925; att U Harkov, Russ, 1922; m. Sheraga Netzer, July, 1920; c: Moshe, Rina Shapira. Dep speaker, Knesset, MK since 1949; prin and tchr, Evening Elem Sch, 1925-49. Head, Natl Comm Isr Soc Workers; gen secy, Working Mothers Org; mem: secretariat, Lab Party; comm, Kupat Cholim; fmr mem, Social-Zionist Political Party, Russ. Home: 9 Levi-Itshak St, Tel Aviv, Isr. Office: The Knesset, Jerusalem, Isr.

NETZER, Moshe, Isr, community exec; b. Russ, Jan 16, 1922; s. Sheraga and Devorah (Diskin); in Isr since 1925; m. Eta Anochi, Dec 28, 1943; c: Hagai, Yael, Amos, Rachel. Head, youth div, Nahal, since 1968; cdr, battalion, Palmach, 1948; col, IDF, 1950-54; gen secy, Ichud Hakibbutzim Movement, 1949-62. Secy-treas, Kibbutz Ramat Yohanan; mem: Vaad Hapoel, Histadrut; secretariat, Lab Party; secretariat, Rafi Party. Recipient, decorations: War of Independence; Sinai Campaign; Six Day War. Home: Kibbutz Ramat Yohanan, Isr. Office: Min of Defense, Tel Aviv, Isr.

NETZER, Shraga, Isr, organization exec; b. Sosnitza, Ukraine, Russ, Jan 1, 1898; s. Haim and Rachel (Rasnovsky) Nosovitsky; in Isr since 1925; m. Dvora Diskin, July 28, 1920; c: Rina Shapira, Moshe. Mem: bur, Isr Lab Party, chmn,munic, art and draft depts; chmn, bd dirs: Beth Arlosoroff, party real estate co; Union of Coop Consumers in Isr; fmr: sanitary worker; insp, dep chmn, sanitary dept, all Tel Aviv Munic. Mem exec, Histadrut; mem, bur, Tel Aviv lab council; patron, Shimshon Football Team. Contbr to lab party mag, daily press. Home: 9 Levi Itzhak St, Tel Aviv, Isr. Office: 110 Hayarkon St, Tel Aviv, Isr.

NEUBERGER, Herman N, US, rabbi; b. Ger, June 26, 1918; s. Max and Bertha (Hiller); in US since 1938; ordained rabbi, Ner Isr Rabb Coll, 1943; m. Judith Kramer, Mar 10, 1941; c: Sheftel, Isaac, Shrago, Yaakov, Ezra. Exec dir, Ner Isr

Rabb Coll. Mem: bd govs, Union of Orthodox J Congs of Amer; exec comm, RabCA; found, Council of Orthodox Congs of Baltimore. Home: 3817 Ridgewood Ave, Baltimore, Md. Office: 4411 Garrison Blvd, Baltimore, Md.

NEUFELD, Henry Nachman, Isr, physician; b. Lwow, Pol, Mar 13, 1923; s. Lipa and Bina (Seidman); in Isr since 1952; MD, Vienna, 1948; m. Julie Brumer, May 7, 1947; c: David, Bina. Chief, heart inst, Tel Hashomer Govt Hosp, Tel Aviv, since 1961; clinical asso prof, med, Heb U, Jerusalem, since 1965; head, card sect, fac continuing med educ, Tel Aviv U Med Sch, since 1965; asso prof, Tel Aviv U Med Sch, since 1967; spec appointee, Mayo Clinic, 1959-60; visiting prof, Richmond Med Coll, 1965. Pres: Isr Heart Assn, 1966; Asian Pacific Cong of Card, 1968; Asian Pacific Soc of Card, 1968; f, Amer Coll Card; hon f, U Minn. Co-author: An Atlas of Acquired Diseases of the Heart and the Great Vessels, 3 vols, 1961; Congenital Heart Disease, 2 vols, 1965; contbr to med jours; mem, ed bd, Isr Jour Med Sci. Hobbies: music, lit. Home: 25 Dubnov St, Tel Aviv, Isr. Office: Tel Hashomer Govt Hosp, Tel Aviv, Isr.

NEUFELD, Joseph M, US, architect; b. Monasterzyska, Aus-Hung, Feb 16, 1899; s. Jeremias and Anne; att Acad of Fine Arts, Rome, 1923; MA, Sch of Architecture, Vienna, Aus, 1925; MArch, Sch of Architecture, U Rome, 1926. Pvt practice, NYC, since 1943; asst architect to Erich Mendelson, Berlin, Ger, 1926-29; fmr: visiting prof: architecture, Pratt Inst, Bklyn, NY; comty health planning, Yale U, Amer Psycht Assn; cons, hosp planning USPHS; lectr, Us: New Delhi, India; Kuala Lumpur, Malaya; Tokyo, Japan; cons, med cen planning to govts of: India, Malaya, Japan, under auspices of Cultural Exchange Prog, US Dept of State, 1963; works executed include: Assutah Hosp, Tel Aviv; Agric Sch, Mishmar Haemek; admn bldg, Kupat Holim, Tel Aviv; Hadassah-Heb U Med Cen, Jerusalem; housing; comty planning. Mem: Amer Inst Architects; Amer Hosp Assn. Home: 186 Sullivan St, New York, NY. Office: 133 Fifth Ave, New York, NY.

NEUFELD, Maurice Frank, US, educator, historian, planning expert; b. Wash, DC, Oct 27, 1910; s. David and Rosa (Ornstein); BA, U Wis, 1932, MA, 1932, PhD, 1935; m. Hinda Cohen, Dec 18, 1938. Prof, ind and lab relations, Cornell U, since 1946; secy, chief asst, research and econ, NJ State Planning Bd, 1935-39; dir, div of State planning, NY State, 1939-41, dep commn of commerce, 1941-42, dir, Bur of Rationing, 1941-42, asst coord, state war plans, State War Council, 1942, chmn, Gov Comm on Post-War Employment, 1942, mem, Post-War Public Works Planning Commn, 1942; chmn, planning commn, US Fed Adv Council of Defence, Health and Wfr Services, 1941-42; exec off, regional hqr, Allied Mil Govt, Sicily, Naples, Rome, Milan, all It, 1943-45. Natl Lab Panel, Amer Arbitration Assn, since 1967; Panel of Mediators, Fact-Finders and Arbitrators, NY State Public Employment Relations Bd, since 1969; Public Employment Disputes Settlement Panel, Amer Arbitration Assn, since 1969; ACLU; Ind Relations Research Assn; Amer Hist Assn; Soc for It Hist Studies; Phi Beta Kappa. Author: Day In, Day Out, with Local 3, 1951, 1955; Labor Unions and National Politics in Italian Industry Plants, 1954; Italy: School for Awakening Countries, 1961; A Representative Bibliography of American Labor History, 1964; Poor Countries and Authoritarian Rule,1965; co-ed, The House of Labor, 1951; mem, ed bd, Labor History. Home: 25 Cornell St, Ithaca, NY. Office: Cornell U, Ithaca, NY.

NEUFELD, Siegbert, Isr, rabbi, author; b. Berlin, Ger, June 15, 1891; s. Meyer and Paula (Cohn); in Isr since 1939; att Us: Berlin; Freiburg; Acad for Sci of Judaism; PhD, Strassburg U, 1914; m. Grete Harris, Jan 22, 1919; c: Meyer, Esther Neurath. Ret, 1953; fmr: radio lectr to Eur countries; rabbi: Briesen, 1915-20; Interburg, 1920-25; Elbing, 1925-39; State of Wuertemberg, Ger, 1951-53; guest lectr, J hist of Middle Ages: Us: Frankfurt; Tuebingen, both Ger, 1958-60. Fmr pres, B'nai B'rith, Elbing. Author: Jews of Halle in the Middle Ages, 1915; The Jews of Thuringia and Saxony in the Middle Ages, I, 1917, II, 1927; The German Jews in the Middle Ages, 1924; Jüdische Gelehrte in Sachsen, 1925; Der Judenmeister Lipmann, 1928; Of Past and Present of the Jews in Wuertemberg, 1952; Die Jüdische Gemeinde Elbing, I, 1965, II, 1968; contbr to: Jüdisches Lexicon; Ency Judaica; Ency Eshkol; Universal J Ency; Ency Germania Judaica. Home: Beth Horim, Ramat Chen, Isr.

NEUGEBOREN, Benjamin, US, attorney, insurance broker; b. NYC, Dec 24, 1906; s. Jacob and Bella (Gerlich); LLB, Ford-

ham Law Sch; LLM, St John's Law Sch, Bklyn, 1929; m. Marcella Freiman, June 28, 1936; c: Jerrold. Sr partner: Neugeboren & Zuckerbrot, Peoples Brokerage Co, since 1949. Hon pres, Young Isr of E Parkway, Bklyn, NY, fmr pres, bd chmn; mem: Gtr NY Ins Brokers Assn; NY Co Lawyers Assn; Rel Zionists Amer, natl chap. Home: 701 Empire Blvd, Brooklyn, NY. Office: 19 W 44 St, New York, NY.

NEUMAN, Harold L, US, manufacturer; b. Phila, Pa, Sep 12, 1907; s. Nathan and Anna (Kaplan); att U of Pa, 1925-28; m. Sylvia Haimovitz; c: Ruth, William. Pres, Robert Bruce Inc. Pres, Knitted Outerwear Assn, 1946-53; chmn: Bonds for Isr Comm, Phila, 1965, 1966; fund raising, Beth Sholom, since 1950; knitwear div, Allied J Appeal, 1948-49, asso chmn, 1946-47, 1950-52; mem, Men's Apparel Assn. Recipient: man of the year award, Men's Apparel Assn, 1958. Home: 707 Ashbourne Rd, Elkins Park, Pa. Office: C and Westmoreland Sts, Philadelphia, Pa.

NEUMAN, Isaac, US, rabbi, educator; b. Pol, Dec 4, 1922; s. Mordchai and Sarah; in US since 1950; BA, U Cincinnati; BHL, HUC, 1958; m. Ruth Cohen, 1959; c: Ari, David. Rabbi, Temple Judah, since 1961; fac mem, dept of phil and rel, Cornell Coll, Mt Vernon, Ia; visiting prof, rel dept, Marymount Coll, Boca Raton, Fla; rabbi: Temple Emanuel, Dothan, Ala, 1961; Kol Shearith Isr, Panama; chaplain: Goose Bay, Labrador, 1963; I of Terceira, Azores, 1964. Pres, Cedar Rapids-Marion Area Council of Churches; chmn, Brotherhood Week Comm, Cedar Rapids, Marion; vice-pres, Council on Hum Relations; mem: CCAR; Rotary Club. Contbr to J jours. Home: 432 Memorial Drive SE, Cedar Rapids, Ia. Study: 3221 Lindsay Lane SE, Cedar Rapids, Ia.

NEUMAN, Janet N, US, public relations advisor; b. NYC, Oct 14, 1894; d. David and Hattie (Ballin) Nusbaum; grad: Pratt Inst, 1914; NYU, 1941; m. Lester Neuman, Feb 22, 1918; c: Robert, Alice Bessman. PR adv: Women's Intl League for Peace and Freedom, since 1950; Women Strike for Peace, since 1961; dir, orientation group for refs, Wash Heb Cong sisterhood, 1940-42. Mem: Natl Council of J Women; Sane; Women's Intl League for Peace and Freedom; Natl Women's Dem Club. Hobby: painting. Home: 2737 Devonshire Pl, Washington, DC.

NEUMAN, Zvi, Isr, plastic surgeon; b. Gladbeck, Ger, Jan 1, 1918; s. Abraham and Ella (Golda); in Isr since 1927; att Paris U, Fr, 1936-38; BSc, U Geneva, Switz, 1940; att Wash U Med Sch; training, Johannesburg, S Afr; MD, St Joseph's U, Beirut, Leb, 1944; m. Levanona David, Oct, 1940; c: Avital Davidson, Avraham, Daniel. Head, dept plastic and maxillofacial surg, Hadassah U Hosp since 1958; asso prof, Heb U Hadassah Med Sch, since 1964; fmr: second asst, first asst, house phys, dept surg; chief phys, Hadassah U Hosp; set up plastic surg, Hadassah U Hosp; cons, plastic surg: Assaf Harofe Hosp, Zriffin; Donolo Govt Hosp, Tel Aviv; cons, Gen Hosp, Emek Afula. Maj, MC, IDF. Exec mem, Sci Council of IMA; mem: Isr Surg Soc; Isr Assn Plastic Surgs; Soc Fr de Chirurgie Plastique et Reconstructive; Soc des Chirurgiens de Paris; Pan-Pacific Surg Assn; Span Plastic Surg Assn; asso mem, Brit Assn of Plastic Surgs; f, Amer Coll Surgs; affiliate mem, Royal Soc Med; Lions Intl; Misdar Jabotinsky Moriah, both Jerusalem. Contbr to profsl jours. Hobby: photography. Home: 1 Alfasi St, Jerusalem, Isr. Office: Hadassah U Hosp, Jerusalem, Isr.

NEUMANN, Alfred M, US, organization exec; b. Vienna, Aus, Dec 3, 1910; s. Jacob and Cecilia (Bandler); in US since 1938; DJ, U Vienna, 1933; MS, Columbia U, 1942; m. Johanna Seligmann, Aug 30, 1941; c: Margaret, Frank. Exec dir, J Family and Children's Service of Denver, since 1948; law clerk, Civil and Criminal Fed Court, Vienna, 1933-36; legal asst, Min of Finance, Vienna, 1936-38. Vice-pres, family and child wfr sect, Denver Area Wfr Council; mem, Gov Comm on Resettlement of Refs, 1960; Colo chmn, comm on health and well-being, White House Conf on Children, 1960; mem, bd, Council of Sr Citizens, since 1955; charter mem, Natl Assn of Social Workers; f, Gerontological Soc; mem: Acad Cert Social Workers; Acad Clinical Sociols; Natl Rehab Assn; Natl Conf Social Work; Intl Conf Social Work; Masons. Contbr to profsl jours. Home: 4940 E Vassar Lane, Denver, Colo. Office: 1375 Delaware St, Denver, Colo.

NEUMANN, Aron, (pen-name **A Ben Gad**), Brazil, journalist; b. Kempen, Ger, Nov 8, 1907; s. Leopold and Henrietta (Schacher). Publisher, ed in chief, Adonde Vamos? since 1943. Co-found, Lar Da Criança Israelita Rosa Waisman, J children home, 1938; fmr: hon secy gen, Organização Sionista do Brasil; exec mem: Confederação Sionista Gerail América Latina; Federação Sionista Gerais do Brasil. Home: 162 R Toneleros, Rio de Janeiro, Brazil. Office: 23 s/1540 Av 13 de Maio, Rio de Janeiro, Brazil.

NEUMANN, David, Isr, business exec; b. Tel Aviv, Isr, Aug 16, 1936; s. Bernhard and Mary (Steindorf); att Heb U, Jerusalem; m. Lea Weiss, Aug 20, 1962; c: Michael, Uri. Dir, PR, Isr Bc Auth, since 1968; dir, Jerusalem br, Kupat Am Bank, 1966-68; publ ed, spokesman, Cen Bur of Stat, 1957-66. PR off, Rotary Intl, dist 199, Isr; bd mem, Isr PR Assn; secy, treas, Isr Sci Film Org; mem bd, J Demographic and Stat Assn. Home: 13 Ibn Gvirol St, Jerusalem, Isr. Office: Isr Bc Auth, Jerusalem, Isr.

NEUMANN, Emanuel, US, communal leader, organization exec; b. Libau, Latvia, July 2, 1896; s. Sundel Hirsh and Danna (Esterman); BA, Columbia Coll; JD, NYU; m. Fannie Rutchick, Aug 16, 1921; c: Natanya, Gabriel. Chmn, exec, JA and World Zionist Org, since 1951, head, econ dept, 1951-53, head, info and publ, since 1953; mem, JA, Jerusalem, 1931-39, 1946-47; repr JA in final negotiations with UK, London, 1947; testified before Fgn Affairs Comm, US House of Repr in securing passage of Pal resolution; org presentation and made address before Anglo-Amer Comm of Inquiry, 1945; presented memorandum on Jordan Valley Auth Project to Anglo-Amer Comm, 1946; participated in presentation of J case before UN, leading to partition resolution, 1947; educ dir, ZOA, 1918-20, pres, 1947-49, hon pres; co-found: KH, 1921, first natl dir, pres; chmn, exec comm, United Pal Appeal, 1925; pres, JNF, 1928-30; political repr, Zionist Movement, Wash, DC, 1940-46; org: Amer Pal Comm; Comm on Pal Surveys, 1943. Contbr to newspapers and mags. Home: 749 West End Ave, New York, NY. Office: 515 Park Ave, New York, NY.

NEUMANN, Filip, Isr, veterinarian path; b. Lugos, Rum, May 8, 1921; s. Fracisc and Rosa (Beck); in Isr since 1959; DVM, Vetr Fac, Bucharest, 1949; PhD, Heb U, Jerusalem, 1969; m. Nitza Gabin, Mar 24, 1967. Sr vetr path, Vetr Inst, Bet Dagan, since 1959; asst, vetr fac, Bucharest, 1949-53; lectr, 1953-58. Pvt, IDF. Mem, Isr Vetr Med Assn. Contbr to profsl jours. Home: 67 Rothschild St, Rishon Lezion, Isr. Office: Vetr Inst, Bet Dagan, Isr.

NEUMANN, Hava Eva, Isr, chemist; b. Segesvar, Hung, Jan 15, 1920; d. Joseph and Bella (Emmerich) Beregi; in Isr since 1940; MSc, Heb U, Jerusalem, 1949; PhD, Weizmann Inst, Rehovot, 1964; m. Jeduda Neumann, Aug 18, 1941; c: Michael, Orna. Sr sci, Weizmann Inst; research asso, prof, dept biochem and biophys, Tex A and M U, 1967-68. Prin contribs: studies on proteolytic enzymes; phosphatases; covalent bonds other than peptide bonds in proteins. Hobbies: art, reading, theater. Home: 16 Haknesset Hagedola St, Tel Aviv, Isr, Office: Weizmann Inst, Rehovot, Isr.

NEUMANN, Jehuda, Isr, educator; b. Sepsiszentgyörgy, Hung, Feb 17, 1915; s. Joseph and Catherina (Bick); in Isr since 1940; att: U Budapest, 1934-38; m. Hava Beregi, Aug 18, 1941; c: Michael, Orna. Prof, head, dept meteorology, Heb U, Jerusalem, since 1969, fmr, asso prof; chief, div research and instr, Isr Meteorological Service, 1949-58. Capt: Brit Army, 1942-46; IDF, 1948-49. Prin contribs: evaporation estimates; heat balance of water bodies; rin stimulation; turbulence theory. Chmn: Reactor Safeguard Comm, Isr AEC; Artificial Ra in Comm, Isr Natl Council for RVD; div of meteorology and atmospheric phys, Isr Union of Geodesy and Geophysics; mem: Amer, Royal Meteorological Socs; AAAS; Isr Natl Comm for Space Research. Contbr to sci jours. Recipient: math prize, Budapest U, 1937. Spec interests: music,archaeol. Home: 16 Haknesset Hagedola St, Tel Aviv, Isr Office: Heb U, Jerusalem, Isr.

NEUMANN, Jirmejahu Oskar, Isr, author; b. Brüx, Czech, Oct 3, 1894; s. Adolf and Friederike (Ornstein); in Isr since 1946; att U Prague, 1914-16; LLD, U Vienna, 1920; m. Hermina Knöpfelmacher, Oct 4, 1923; c: Uriel, Margalith Sommer, Ruben. Author: Ruth, 1923; Zwischen zwei Dunkeln, 1924; Aus Dem Buche Ewigkeit, 1926; Flucht aus der Zeit, 1929; Rote Perlen, 1931; Fahrt nach Osten, 1933; Gottes Zigeuner, 1935; Im Schatten des Todes, 1956; trans into Heb: Bezel Hamavet, 1958; chief ed, Juristische Volkszeitung Bratislava, 1925-36. Chmn, Org, of Immigrants from Czech; mem, Brith Harishonim, Tel-Aviv; fmr: chmn, Zionist Org of Slovakia; delg, WZC's; pres, B'nai B'rith, Yaacov Ehrlich lodge. Spec inter-

ests: books, mineralogy, music, archaeol. Home: 5 Alexander Janai St, Tel Aviv, Isr.

NEUMANN, Julius G, US, rabbi; b. Hung, Oct 28, 1918; s. Benjamin and Sarah (Tauber); in US since 1940; DHum, Philathea Coll, 1936; ordained rabbi, Yeshiva of Benedekovice, 1937; m. Esther Rubin, Aug 15, 1943; c: Frances, Milton, Joshua, Nina. Rabbi, Cong Zichron Moshe, since 1948; vice-pres, House of Sages Inc, since 1953; chaplain, NYC Transit Police, Detective Div, since 1966; rabbi, Cong Rabbi Hillel Lichtenstein, 1940-47. Chmn, town and village comm, UJA, since 1953; hon chmn, Isr Bonds, since 1958; dir, United J Orgs of Williamsburg, since 1968; pres J-Amer Bd for Peace and Justice, Inc; chmn bd, Natl Info Bur for J Life; treas, assns of bds of visitors, Mental Hygiene Instns of NY State; commn on hum rights, NYC, 1965-67; perm vice-chmn, Manhattan div, FJP, 1954-55; mem: Union of Orthodox Rabbis of US and Can; RabCA; Rabb Bd of Gtr NY. Home: 4 Stuyvesant Oval, New York, NY. Study: 342 E 20 St, New York, NY.

NEUMANN, Robert, Switz, author; b. Vienna, Aus, May 22, 1897; s. Samuel and Josephine (Pilpel); in Switz since 1958; att U Vienna; m. 4th, Helga Heller, 1960; c: Michael. Author: Gedichte, 1918; 20 Gedichte, 1922; Die Pest von Lianora, 1927; Mit Fremden Federn, 1927, vol, 2, 1955; Jagd auf Menschen und Gespenster, 1928; Die Blinden von Kagoll, 1929; Sintflut, 1929; Hochstapler, 1930; Passion, 1930; Panoptikum, 1930; Karriere, 1931; Das Schiff Experance, 1931; Die Puppen von Poshansk, 1931; Die Macht, 1932; Unter falscher Flagge, 1932; Die blinden Passagiere, 1934; Sir Basil Zaharoff, 1935; Struensee, 1935; Eine Frau hat geschrien, 1938; By the Waters of Babylon, 1939; 23 Women, 1940; Scene in Passing, 1942; The Inquest, 1944; Children of Vienna, 1946; Blind Man's Buff, 1948; Insurrection in Poshansk, 1951; Sur les pas de Morell, 1952; Mein altes Haus in Kent, autobiography, 1957; Die dunkle Seite des Mondes, 1959; Olympia, 1961; Hitler-Aufstieg und Untergang des Dritten Reichs, 1961; Das Leben von Adolf Hitler, film, 1961; Ausflüchte unseres Gewissens, 1961; Festival, 1962; Ein leichtes Leben, 1963; Karrieren, 1966; Vielleicht das Heitere, 1968; Dämon Weib, Vorsicht Bücher, Nie wieder Politik, 3 vols, 1969. Hon pres, Aus sect, intl vice-pres, PEN Club; club, Savile, London. Home: Locarno-Monti, La Giorgica, Switz.

NEUMANN, Yaacov Bernhard, Isr, physician; b. Berlin, Ger, July 9, 1902; s. Max and Charlotte (Fraenkel); in Isr since 1933; att: U Berlin, 1920-23, 1924-25; U Vienna, 1923-24; U Freiburg, 1924; MD, U Berlin, 1927; m. Elizabeth Schnittkind, 1941; c: David. Specialist, gen surg and public health; chmn, Govt Med Bd for Indemnification Claims from Ger; med adv, Yaaroth Hacarmel Sanatorium; surg, pvt practice, Tel Aviv, 1933-48; dir, Govt Hosp, Haifa, 1948; supt of med professsions, Min of Health, 1948-56; dir, med affairs, Natl Ins Inst, Jerusalem, 1956-68. F, Intl Coll Surgs; mem: Rehab Council, Health Council, Isr Govt; Perm Commn, Intl Assn on Occupational Health; fmr: cen comm, Pal J Med Assn, chmn, Tel Aviv br. Author: Medical Education, 1953; Employment Injuries Insurance and Rehabilitation, 1961; Occupational Health, Workmen's Compensation and Rehabilitation, 1965; contbr to sci jours. Home: 14 Benjamin Metudela St, Jerusalem, Isr.

NEUMARK, Leo W, US, business exec; b. NYC, June 5, 1890; s. Julius and Pauline (Kalb); m. Marion Hart, May 29, 1925 (decd); c: Janet Fribourg, Toni Abramson. Dir, devl, Bellefaire Home for Disturbed Children; chmn, bd, Printz Biederman Co, 1927-53; cons, Tremco Mfg Co, 1961-65, with co since 1953. US Army, WW I. Vice-pres, chmn, finance, The Temple, Cleveland, since 1943; pres, J Comty Fed, 1959-61; vice-pres, BBB, 1953; trustee: J Family Service, 1947-49; Heb Free Loan Assn, 1943-53; Convalescent, Hosp, 1951-59; CJFWF, 1960-62; Wfr Fed, 1935-61; Mt Sinai Hosp, 1937-53; gen chmn, JWF Campaign, 1943-44, all Cleveland; mem, C of C; club, Oakwood Country. Recipient: award of merit, J Comty Fed, 1954; dist service award, Comty Fund, 1960. Home: 2943 S Park Blvd, Shaker Heights, O.

NEUMARK, Zvi, Isr, government official; b. Posen, Pol, Aug 11, 1913; s. Moritz and Ella (Landshut); in Isr since 1933; m. Debora Scheiner 1940; c: Chavi. Genmgr, Isr Cotton Bd, since 1953; fmr: mem secretariat, treas: Kibbutz Ein Hanatziv; regional council, Bet Sha'an. Served Haganah. Mem, Rel Party. Home: Kibbutz Ein Hanatziv, Isr. Office: 10 Carlebach St, Tel Aviv, Isr.

NEUSNER, Jacob, US, educator; b. July 28, 1932; AB, magna cum laude, Harvard Coll, 1953; MHL, ordained rabbi, JTSA, 1960; PhD, Columbia U, 1960; m. Suzanne Richter, Mar 15, 1964; c: Samuel, Eli. Prof, rel studies, Brown U, since 1968; asso prof, Dartmouth Coll, 1966-68, asst prof, 1964-66; research asso, Brandeis U, 1962-64; asst prof, U Wis, 1961-62. Pres, Amer Acad Rel, 1968-69; chmn, resolutions comm, RA; mem: adv council, Natl Found for J Culture; found comm, Coord Comm of Orgs in Field of Rel, Amer Council Learned Socs; profsl adv council, Bur J Affairs, AJComm; f, Royal Asiatic Soc; asso in council, Soc Bibl Lit; bd dirs, Natl Council on Rel in Higher Educ, 1960-62; mem: Amer Soc for Study of Rel; Amer Oriental Soc. Author: A History of the Jews in Babylonia, 5 vols, 1965-69; A Life of Rabban Yohanan Ben Zakkai, 2nd ed, 1970; ed: Religions in Antiquity: Essays in Memory of E R Goodenough, 1968; asst ed, Judaism, Chgo Ency Rel; dept ed, Babylonia, Ency Judaica; ed comm, Amer J Hist Soc; contbr ed, Rel and Theol Abstracts; contbr to profsl jours. Recipient: Fulbright Scholar, 1957-58; Kent F, Natl Council on Rel in Higher Educ, 1957-60; Lown F, Brandeis U, 1962-64; research f, Amer Council of Learned Socs, 1966-67, 1970-71. Office: 70 Vassar Ave, Providence, RI.

NEUSTEIN, Abraham, US, rabbi, attorney; b. NYC; s. Joseph and Sarah (Henig); LLB, St Lawrence U, 1936; ordained rabbi, Yeshiva U, 1940, MHL, 1948, DHL, 1953; m. Shirley Friedberg, Sep 29, 1940; c: Joshua, Frima, Amy. Rabbi, J Cen, Brighton Beach, NY, since 1958 and 1940-54; chaplain, Off of Civilian Defense, since 1957; prin, Yeshiva of Flatbush HS, 1950-53; rabbi, J Cen, Kings Highway, Bklyn, NY, 1954-58. Chaplain, USN post, 1943. Counsel, Heb Prin Assn, since 1962; pres, Mizrachi Org of Brighton Beach, 1945-50, hon pres, since 1951; vice-pres, Rabb Alumni Assn of Yeshiva U, 1948-49; chmn, Seashore dist, USO, 1941-42, org, Juvenile Delinquency Comm, Bklyn, 1944; mem: RabCA; NY Bar Assn; Natl Assn Secondary Sch Prin. Author: Life and Works of Bezalel Ashkenazi, 1948; Life and Works of Judah Ben Benjamin Anav, 1953. Recipient: citation, US Govt, for War Bond activities, 1948; plaque, J Cen of Brighton Beach, 1954; plaque, Yeshiva of Flatbush HS, 1954; plaque UJA, 1960; award, Yeshiva U, 1963. Home: 235 Dover Street, Brooklyn, NY. Study: J Cen, Brighton Beach, NY. Office: 612 Brighton Beach Ave, Brooklyn, NY.

NEUWIRTH, Benjamin, US, certified public acctnt; b. NYC, Oct 25, 1901; s. Sam and Pearl (Berger); dipl, grad, accountancy, CCNY, 1923, CPA, 1928; m. Anna Kaufman, June 28, 1931; c: Paul, Sylvia. Partner, Alexander Grant and Co, successor to Klein, Hinds and Finke, CPAs, since 1943, with firm since 1929; lectr, Bernard Baruch Sch of Bus and Public Admn, CCNY, 1938-57. Vice-pres, NY State Soc of CPAs, 1959-60; mem, bd dirs: Sch of Bus Alumni Soc, CCNY; CCNY Alumni Assn; Bx YM-YWHA, vice-pres since 1968; JWB, since 1961; Amer Inst of CPAs, mem council, since 1961; trustee, Franklin Lodge, B'nai B'rith; mem: AJComm; Congs: Zichron Ephraim; Erste Gorlitze Rudnicker; hon mem: Beta Alpa Psi; Torch and Scroll Soc. Contbr to profsl jours. Home: 401 E 69 St, New York, NY. Office: 60 E 42 St, New York, NY.

NEVAS, Leo, US, attorney; b. Norwalk, Conn, 1912: s. Morris and Ethel (Baron) Navasky; BA, U Mich 1933; LLB, Cornell Law Sch, 1936; m. Libby Joseloff, Dec 4, 1937; c: Jo Ann, Bernard, Marc. Pvt law practice since 1936; judge, Munic Court, 1943-49; secy-treas, Hydra Feed Machine Tool Corp, 1942-54. Chmn, finance comm, World Peace Through Law Cen, mem, planning comm; mem: Conn State Bar Assn; House of Delgs; adv bd, Norwalk Hosp; Amer Intl Bar Assns; Masons; fmr: pres: Westport Bar Assn; J Comty Council, Norwalk; Temple Beth-El, Norwalk; vice-pres, Conn br, AJCong; chmn: War and Finance Comm, Westport; UJA, Norwalk, Westport; club, Birchwood Country. Mem, ed bd, Cornell Law Quarterly, 1935-36. Home: 17 Quarter Mile Rd, Westport, Conn. Office: 256 E State St, Westport, Conn.

NEVIASER, Julius S, US, surgeon, educator; b. Brandywine, Md, Oct 21, 1902; s. Isaac and Eva (Edlavitch); BA, George Wash U, 1923, MD, 1927; m. Jane Gibbons, June 9, 1933; c: Jules, Robert, Thomas. Pvt practice since 1930; chief, orthopedic service, Prince George's Hosp, since 1946; sr att orthopedic surg, Children's Hosp, since 1957; sr adv orthopedic surg, Wash Hosp Cen; att orthopedic surg: DC Gen Hosp, since 1930; George Wash U Hosp, since 1932; cons orthopedic surg: Walter Reed Army Hosp; Freedmen's Hosp, since 1943; Providence Hosp; cons, lectr, orthopedic surg, USN Hosp, Bethesda, Md; clinical prof, orthopedic

surg, Howard U Med Sch, since 1943; clinical prof, George Wash U, since 1948, all Wash, DC; mem, Med Adv Bd A, Wash, 1941; examiner, Ft Myer Induction Cen, 1942-44; dir, Madison Natl Bank. F: Amer Coll Surgs; pres, Hosp for Jt Diseases Alumni Assn, 1950; fmr chmn, med adv comm, Natl Found for Infantile Paralysis, Wash; trustee, Wash Hosp Cen, 1968-69; mem: Amer Orthopedic Assn; Orthopedic Research Soc; Intl Soc for Orthopedic Surg and Traumatology; Mexican Orthopedic Soc; SE Surg Cong; jt comm on public care of crippled children, Amer Acad Orthopedic Surgs, secy, 1953-54; Wash Acad Surg; Amer Bd Orthopedic Surg; clubs: Woodmont Country; Wash Orthopedic, pres, 1943, 1952-53. Contbr to med jours. Hobbies: golf, coin and stamp collecting. Home: 550 N St, SW, Washington, DC. Office: 1918 K St, NW, Washington, DC.

NEVO, Yosef, Isr, analyst, commentator; b. Chattanooga, Tenn, Apr 12, 1919; s. Simon and Anne (Sweidelson) Levine; in Isr since 1922; dipl, Inst for Public Service, Jerusalem, 1948; dipl, staff and Command Coll, Isr Army, 1955; BA, Heb U, Jerusalem, 1967; m. Naomi Bennun, May 9, 1948; c: Yair, Gilead. Mil and political analyst, commentator; consul of Isr, NY, 1950-52; Consul gen of Isr, Montreal, Can, 1952-54; CO, Jerusalem Command, IDF, 1961-64. Pal Unit, Brit Army, 1940-46; Haganah, 1947-49, 2nd in command, Moriah Battalion; cdr, Artillery & Armour, Jerusalem Dist; cdr, Anti-Tank Battalion, IDF, 1948; IDF, 1954-65; head, planning dept, Gen Staff, 1956-59; cdr, Sarea, Sinai Campaign; chief of staff, S Command, 1959-61. Found mem, kibbutz Maoz-Haim, Beisan Valley; trustee, Bennun Sch, Alyn Hosp, Jerusalem. Contbr to mil jours and daily newspapers. Recipient: IDF Campaign Medals, Africa Star. Home: 44 Nordau St, Herzliya, Isr.

NEWBURGER, Frank L Jr, US, investment broker; b. Phila, Pa, Nov 26, 1908; s. Frank and Helen (Langfeld); BA, Cornell U, 1929; m. Dorothy Einstein, Nov 7, 1946; c: Patricia, Frank. Partner: Newburger and Co, since 1948; Newburger, Loeb, and Co, 1930-47; dir, Bankers Bond and Mortgage Guaranty Co, since 1958; pres, Phila-Baltimore Stock Exch, 1954-57, vice-pres, 1953, mem, bd govs, 1946-59; gov, NY Stock Exch, 1959-62. Fmr pres: vice-pres, Fed of J Agcys, mem, bd dirs, since 1948; treas since 1962; Neighborhood Cen; asso chmn, Comty Chest, 1960; exec comm, United Fund, 1965-67; treas: Albert Einstein Med Cen, 1957-60; J Hosp, 1938-42, 1946-48; trustee: Cong Keneseth Isr, since 1948; Acad of Natural Scis, since 1967; mem, Cornell U Council, since 1965; clubs: Philmont Country; Midday; Locust. Home: Cherry Lane, Rydal, Pa. Office: 1401 Walnut St, Philadelphia, Pa.

NEWMAN, Aubrey Norris, Eng, educator; b. London, Dec 14, 1927; s. Myer and Jean (Harrison); MA, hons, U Glasgow, 1949; BA hons, Wadham Coll, Oxford, 1953, MA, PhD, 1957; m. Bernice Gould, Dec 14, 1954; c: Sara, Deborah, Michael, Judith. Sr lectr, hist, U Leicester, since 1969, asst lectr, 1959-69; research f, Bedford Coll, U London, 1954-55; research asst, Hist of Parl Trust, London, 1955-59. RAF, 1949-51. Chmn, Hillel Educ Comm; mem comm: J Hist Soc, chmn, conf comm; Academic Advisory Comm, Cultural Sect, WJC; Scholarship Comm, J Memorial Council; fmr chmn, Friends of Heb U, Leicester br. Author: Parliamentary Diary of Sir Edward Knatchbull, 1963; Stanhopes of Chevening, 1969; Leicester House Politics, 1750-60, pub 1969; contbr to publs. Recipient: f, Royal Hist Soc. Home: 33 Stanley Rd, Leicester, Eng. Office: Dept of Hist, U of Leicester, Eng.

NEWMAN, David Bruce, US, attorney; b. NYC, Dec 6, 1940; s. Nathan and Yvonne (Luber); BS, NYU, 1962; LLB, Cornell Law Sch, 1965; LLM, NYU, 1970; m. Margot Hoffman, June 15, 1963; c: Barbara. Mem, Phillips, Nizer, Benjamin, Krim & Ballon, since 1969; mem, House, Grossman, Vorhaus & Hemley, 1965-69; lectr, Practising Law Inst. Mem: Assn of Bar, NYC; Beta Alpha Psi; Phi Alpha Kappa; J Comty Cen of White Plains. Author: Basic Income Tax Planning for Fiduciaries, 1969; contbr to taxation jours. Home: 61 Church Lane, Scarsdale, NY. Office: 477 Madison Ave, New York, NY.

NEWMAN, David E, Can, attorney; b. Turka, Aus-Hung, May 5, 1910; s. Joseph and Gertrude (Reich); in Can since 1923; BCS, U Toronto, 1932; barrister-at-law, Osgoode Hall, 1935; QC, 1957; m. Doris Miller, Nov 12, 1944; c: Tamar, Hannah, Eli. Pvt practice since 1935. Chmn, cen region, Can J Cong Educ Comm, since 1963; vice-pres, Asso Heb Schs, since 1960; chmn, Midrashah, Heb Tchrs Sem, since 1955; fmr:

vice-pres: ZOC; Keren Hatarbuth, Can; Bur of J Educ; chmn, Youth Aliyah; exec mem, YMHA, all Toronto; clubs: Can Zionist; J Jour. Co-author: Tales of the Talmud; contbr on J educ and Zionism. Home: 26 Braemore Gardens, Toronto, Can.

NEWMAN, Elias, US, artist; b. Stashow, Pol, Feb 12, 1903; s. Simon and Rebecca (Becker); in US since 1913; att: Natl Acad of Design, NYC, 1918-20; Educ Alliance Art Sch, NYC, 1920-25; Academie Chaumiere, Paris, 1929; m. Lillian Tesser, Feb 26, 1945. Free-lance artist and tchr, since 1927; corresp in Jerusalem for Bklyn Eagle, 1925-26; cons, Bialik Memorial Exhb, Tel Aviv, 1933; art curator, Pal Pavilion, NY World's Fair, 1938-40; cons, Intl Exposition, Cleveland, O, 1941; research cons, Artists Equity Fund, 1959; art instr: Educ Alliance Art Sch, 1946-47; 92 St YMHA, NYC, 1948-49. US Coast Artillery, 1942-43. Held over 100 one-man shows, including: Babcock Gals; J Mus, both NYC; Doll and Richards Gal, Boston, Mass; Baltimore Mus of Art; Md Art Inst, Baltimore; Phila Art Alliance; Maxwell Gals, SF, Cal; Werbe Gals, Detroit, Mich; Tel Aviv Mus, Isr; participated in exhbs at: Natl Acad of Design; Amer Water Color Soc; Amer Acad of Arts and Letters; Audubon Artists; Natl Soc of Painters in Casein; Rockport Art Assn; Cape Ann Soc of Modern Artists; Cape Ann Festival of Arts; Salon Brendle, Zurich, Switz. Repr in perm collections: Addison Gal of Amer Art, Andover, Mass; De Cordova Mus, Lexington, Mass; Everson Mus of Art, Syracuse, NY; SF Mus; Joslyn Art Mus, Omaha, Neb; U of Neb; Hillel House, Boston U; Butler Mus of Amer Art, Youngstown, O; Bklyn Mus; John Heron Mus, Indianapolis, Ind; J Mus; Roosevelt House, both NYC; Baltimore Mus, Md; Norfolk Mus, Va; Davenport Mus, Ia; Denver Mus, Colo; Brandeis U; Tel Aviv Mus; Haifa Mus of Modern Art, both Isr; Isr Emb, Wash, DC; Histadrut House, Tel Aviv; Prudential Bldg, Newark, NJ. Pres: Natl Soc of Painters in Casein, Inc, since 1967; Cape Ann Soc of Modern Artists, since 1958; Artists Equity Assn, 1960-62; chmn: art mission to Isr, Amer Fund for Isr Instns, 1949; natl secy, Artists Equity Assn, 1953, vice-pres, NY chap, since 1963; mem: Mayor's Comm, Cape Ann Festival of Arts, Gloucester, Mass, 1952; bd dirs, NYC dist, ZOA. Author: Art in Palestine 1939; contbr to mags and newspapers in US and Isr. Recipient: Stern Memorial Medal and Prize, Audubon Artists 18th Annual Exhb, 1960; Mayer Prize, 1966; Gramercy Prize, Natl Soc of Painters in Casein Exhb, 1968. Home: 215 Park Row, New York, NY. Studio: 32 Union Sq, New York, NY.

NEWMAN, Harry R, US, surgeon, educator; b. Russ, Sep 10, 1909; s. Abraham and Mary (Rudolph); in US since 1935; MD, U Toronto, Can, 1935; MS, U Pa, 1940; m. Lillian Lear, Aug 18, 1942; c: Nancy, Robert, Suzanne. Prof, urol, Albert Einstein Coll of Med, NY, since 1966, clinical prof, 1954-66; asst clinical prof, urol, Yale U Sch of Med, since 1949; att Yale New Haven Hosp, since 1946; dir, urol, Bx Munic Med Cen, since 1954; cons urol: St Joseph's Hosp, Stamford, Conn, since 1958; Griffin Hosp, Derby, Conn, since 1946; instr, basic sci in urol, U Pa, 1938-39; sr res, urol, NY Post-Grad Hosp, 1939-40; asst prof, clinical urol, NYU-Bellevue Med Cen, 1949-54. Maj, USAAF MC, 1942-46. Dipl, Amer Bd Urol, 1947; f, Amer Coll Surgs, 1966; mem: Masons; Temple Mishkan Isr, New Haven; Pi Lambda Phi, Sigma Xi, Yale U; clubs: Woodbridge Country; Yale Fac; Yale, New Haven. Contbr to med jours. Home: 95 Broadfield Rd, Hamden, Conn. Offices: 2 Church St, New Haven, Conn; Albert Einstein Coll of Med, New York, NY.

NEWMAN, Jacob, S Afr, rabbi, educator; b. Bratislava, Czech, July 29, 1914; s. William and Nechama (Bick) Neumann; in S Afr since 1951; ordained rabbi, Yeshiva Coll and Beth Din, Bratislava, 1936; MA, U Manchester, Eng, 1945; DL, U Pretoria, 1955; m. Zelda Myburg, Sep 10, 1952; c: Nahum, Avron, Gabriel, Hillel. Rabbi, N Suburbs Cong; prof, post-Bibl J lit, U Pretoria; head, J studies, U S Afr, 1959-64; lectr, social sci, U Liverpool, Eng, 1945-46; rabbi, Addiscombe and Dist Cong, Croydon, Surrey, Eng, 1947-51; natl rabbi of Country Comtys, Union of S Afr, 1951-57. Pres, S Afr J Mins Assn; mem, presidium, Semicha Bd, Training Coll for Rabbis, Johannesburg; pres, J Students Assn, U Pretoria. Author: Semikhah (Ordination), 1951; Judaism in the Home, 1953; With Ink in the Book, Speak Unto the Children of Israel, 1957; Lessons in Jewish History, Lessons in Jewish Heritage, 1957; Guide to Judaism for the Young, 1959; Nahmanides, 1961; The Eternal Quest, 1966; Towards Light, 1967; Halachic Sources, 1969; Halachic Treatises, 1965-67;

Handbook for Bar and Bat Mitzvah, 1967. Home: 7 Kenneth Rd, Bramley Reserve, Johannesburg, S Afr.

NEWMAN, John B, US, educator; b. Lowell, Mass, May 3, 1917; s. Max and Anna (Hochberg): BA, Bklyn Coll, 1937; MA, La State U, 1939; PhD, NYU, 1950; m. Elaine Goran, June 25, 1944; c: Jane, John. Prof, communication arts and scis, Queens Coll, CUNY, since 1946. Mem: Speech Assn of Amer; Intl Soc for Gen Semantics; Intl Phonetic Assn; AAUP. Contbr to profsl jours. Home: 146-15 20 Rd, Whitestone, NY. Office: Queens Coll, Flushing, NY.

NEWMAN, Joseph, US, attorney; b. Bklyn, NY, Sep 30, 1910; s. Emanuel and Bertha (Stein), att LIU, 1928-30; LLB, Bklyn Law Sch, 1933; m. Jennie Garelick, Dec 25, 1935; c: Elliot. Pvt practice since 1934. Mem: UJA; FJP; atty, Bd Rabbis, Cong and Talmud Torah Tifereth Isr, Ave O Syn, Bklyn, NY; fund-raiser for numerous local charities; fmr: bd dirs, J Comty House, Bensonhurst, Bklyn; master, Amos Lodge, Masons; chancellor, KP, King Solomon Lodge; pres, 3rd Kings Masonic Camp and Charity Fund; chmn, Youth Comm, Masons. Contbr to law and masonic jours. Spec interest: social service. Home: 1222 E 13 St, Brooklyn, NY. Office: 401 Broadway, New York, NY.

NEWMAN, Louis B, US, physician, physical medicine and rehab; b. NYC, Apr 5, 1900; s. Morris and Mollie (Benzuly); ME, Ill Inst Tech, 1921; MD, Rush Med Coll, 1931; m. Rose Manilow, Jan 21, 1951. Cons, rehab med, Chgo Area, and several comty hosps; prof lectr, rehab med, U of Ill Coll of Med, Chgo; prof, dept of phys med, Northwestern U, since 1946; head, dept phys med, US Navy Hosps, Oakland, Cal, and Seattle, Wash, 1942-46; chief, phys med and rehab service, VA Hosp, Hines, Ill, 1946-53; chief, phys med and rehab service, VA Research Hosp, Chgo, Ill, 1953-67; mem, adv bd: Armour Research Found, Ill Inst of Tech; Natl Parkinson Found, Inc; Amer Rehab Found; Assn for Phys and Mental Rehab; Amer Assn Rehab Therapists; rehab comm: Chgo Med Soc; Inst of Med of Chgo; Natl Multiple Sclerosis Soc; Action Research Project on Rehab, Chgo Metrop Area; Chgo Med Soc Adv Comm to Action Research Project on Rehab; cons to AMA Council on Phys Med. Cdr, USNR. Dipl, Amer Bd Phys Med and Rehab; found mem, first pres, Chgo Soc Phys Med and Rehab; fmr chmn, sect on phys med, AMA; mem: Soc of Phys Med and Rehab, fmr pres; Amer Cong of Rehab Med; Assn Mil Surgs; World Med Assn; Amer Soc Mech Engrs; Amer Soc Mil Engrs; Inst Radio Engrs, bio-med elec; Chgo and Ill Med Socs; Technion; Weizmann Inst of Sci; B'na B'rith; Amer Friends of Heb U; Jerusalem Acad of Med; ZOA; IMA; Phi Delta Epsilon; Sigma Alpha Mu. Inventor of med machines and devices. Contbr to med jours. Recipient: B'nai B'rith Award, 1952; commendation from Pres Comm on Employment of Physically Handicapped, 1956; selected for Armed Forces Med Libr, Wash, DC, 1956; John E Davis Award, Assn for Phys and Mental Rehab, 1956; dist service award, Ill Inst Tech, 1957; Civil Servant of Year Award, 1958; meritorious service award, VA, 1958; citation for public service, U Chgo, 1959; commendation, VA; Dist Service Key, Amer Cong of Rehab Med, 1963; Dist Achievement Award, Assn for Phys and Mental Rehab, 1966; Natl Rehab Citation, Natl Rehab Commn of Amer Legion, 1967; Profsl Achievement Award, Assn of Med Rehab Dirs and Coords, 1967. Home: 400 E Randolph St, Chicago, Ill. Office: VA West Side Hosp, 820 S Damen Ave, Chicago, Ill.

NEWMAN, Louis I, US, rabbi, author; b. Providence, RI, Dec 20, 1893; s. Paul and Antonia (Hecker); BA, Brown U, 1913; hon DD, 1942; MA, U of Cal, 1917; PhD, Columbia U, 1924; ordained rabbi, by Stephen S Wise, Martin A Meyer, Sidney E Goldstein, 1918; m. Lucile Uhry, June 14, 1923; c: Jeremy, Jonathan, Daniel. Rabbi, Cong Rodeph Sholom, NY, since 1930; rabbi: First Heb Cong, Berkeley, Cal, 1913-16; asst to Rabbi Stephen S Wise, Free Syn, 1916-21; asso rabbi, Temple Isr, NY, 1921-24; Temple Emanu-El, SF, Cal, 1924-30; conductor, rel prog, radio, TV, Cal, NYC. Co-found, Amer Friends of J Pal; active mem, Aliyah Beth, 1939-40; aided Irgun, 1939-40; leader, successful movement to restore J Inst of Rel, NY Sch of HUC-JIR, to full status with ordination in NYC, 1953-56; chmn, chaplaincy comm, J Bd of Guardians, NYC; org, Acad for Lib Judaism, 1955; off observer, CCAR at UN, 1946-53; dir, Amer Tel Hai Fund; trustee, NY FJP; mem: Zionist Revisionist Movement; Temple House Movement; a found, JIR, 1922. Author: plays: The Eternal Temple, 1942; The Miracle of the Scrolls, 1947; No Alternative, 1949; Son of His Generation, 1950; Daughter of the Queen, 1954;

Pangs of Messiah, 1958; The Woman at the Wall, 1958; The Little Zaddik, 1961; books: Studies in Biblical Parallelism, 1918; Jewish Influence on Christian Reform Movements, 1924; A Chief Rabbi of Rome Becomes a Catholic, 1945; Prayer in our Times, 1947; Jewish People, Faith and Life, 1965; books of poetry: Songs of Jewish Rebirth, 1921; Joyful Jeremiads, 1926; Trumpet in Adversity, 1948; co-author: anthols: Hassidic Anthology, 1934; The Talmudic Anthology, 1946; Maggidim and Hassidim: Their Wisdom, 1962; collections of sermons: Biting on Granite, 1946; Becoming a New Person, 1950; Living with Ourselves, 1952; The Search for Serenity, 1954; What does God Mean to You, 1959. Recipient: 2nd prize, B'nai B'rith Natl Play Contest, 1944; 2nd prize, ZOA Natl Play Contest, 1950. Home: 271 Central Park W, New York, NY. Study: 7 W 83 St, New York, NY.

NEWMAN, Marion Eliot, US, certified public acctnt; b. Minneapolis, Minn, Mar 2, 1917; s. Samuel and Sara (Helstein); BS, U Minn, 1938; MBA, Harvard U, 1940; m. Annette Shedorsky, Dec 21, 1941; c: Thomas, Stanley, Louis, Jane. Partner, Garfin, Launer, Newman, Peller & Salloway, since 1955. Cpl, US Army, 1942-43. Pres, United J Fund and Council, St Paul. Recipient: Humanitarian Award, Mt Zion Heb Cong, 1969. Home: 662 Mt Curve Blvd, St Paul, Minn. Office: 609 Second Ave S, Minneapolis, Minn.

NEWMAN, Melvin S, US, educator, chemist; b. NYC, Mar 10, 1908; s. Jacob and Mae (Polack); BS, Yale U, 1929, PhD, 1932; m. Beatrice Crystal, June 30, 1933; c: Anthony, Susan, Beth, Robert. Regents prof, chem, O State U, since 1966, on fac since 1936; f: Natl TB Assn, 1932-33; NRC, 1933-34; Harvard U, 1934-36; Elizabeth Clay Howard scholar, 1939-40; research, Manhattan Project, Off Sci Research and Devl, WW II. Pres, Columbus sect, Amer Chem Soc, 1941; mem: Sigma Xi; Amer Chem Soc; Natl Acad of Scis; Zeta Beta Tau. Mem, ed bd: Jour of Amer Chem Soc, 1952; Jour of Organic Chem, 1953; ed staff, Organic Synthesis, 1955-62; contbr to profsl jours. Recipient: Amer Chem Soc award for creative work in synthetic organic chem, 1961; Synthetic Organic Chem Mfrs Assn Medal for creative research in organic chem, 1961. Home: 2239 Onandaga Dr, Columbus, O. Office: O State U, Columbus, O.

NEWMAN, Peter Charles, Can, editor; b. Vienna, Aus, May 10, 1929; s. Oskar and Wanda (Neumann); BA, MA, U Toronto; m. Christina McCall. Ed in chief, Toronto Daily Star; fmr ed: Toronto Star; MacLeans Mag, both Ottawa. Author: The Distemper of Our Times; Renegade in Power; Flame of Power. Home: 122 Farnham St, Toronto, Can. Office: 80 King W, Toronto, Can.

NEWMAN, Ralph Geoffrey, US, author, business exec; b. Chgo, Ill, Nov 3, 1911; s. Henry and Dora (Glickman); att Northwestern U, 1930-31; DLitt: Milliken U, Decatur, Ill; Lincoln Coll, Lincoln, Ill; Knox Coll, Galesburg, Ill; Rockford Coll, Rockford, Ill; LLD, Ia Wesleyan, Mt Pleasant, Ia; m. Mary McCree, Aug 26, 1968; c: Maxine Brandenburg, Carol Parry. Pres: Abraham Lincoln Book Shop, Inc, since 1934; Ralph Geoffrey Newman, Inc, since 1955; Lincoln's New Salem Enterprises, since 1952; cons, White House Archives, since 1964. Found, Manuscript Soc; pres, bd dirs, Chgo Public Libr; pres: Adult Educ Council of Gtr Chgo; Ulysses S Grant Assn; Friends Chgo Public Libr; Ill State Hist Soc, 1960; chmn, Ill Sesquicentennial Commn, 1964-68; mem: Chgo Hist Soc; Amer Soc of Appraisers; Royal Soc of Arts, London; Bibliographical Soc of Amer; Bibliographical Soc, London; clubs: Arts, Chgo; Lotus, NYC; Players, NYC. Author: The American Iliad, 1947; The Civil War, 1956. Recipient: Lincoln Dipl of Honor, Lincoln Memorial U, 1953; Independence Hall Assn Amer of Year, 1963; Ill News Bcs Man of Year, 1968. Home: 220 E Walton St, Chicago, Ill. Office: 18 E Chestnut, St, Chicago, Ill.

NEWMAN, Randolph H, US, attorney; b. Berlin, July 3, 1904; s. Salomon and Else (Rubino); in US since 1939; att Berlin U, 1923-26; DJ, U of Basle, 1937; LLB, St Lawrence U, 1943; m. Eva Feilchenfeld, Jan 19, 1933; c: Thomas, Steven, Robert. Pvt law practices; asst to fac, Berlin U, 1927-33; econ adv, corps, 1932-44; prosecutor, War Crimes Trials, Nuremberg, US Dept of War, 1946-48; chief, IG Farben Control Off, Off of US High Commn, 1950-53. Mem: NY Bar. Author: Foreign Currency Restrictions and the Conflict of Laws, 1938, 1941; Wunderlichstes Buch der Buecher, Munich, Starnberg, 1960. Hobbies: collecting Nietzscheana; trans lyrics from classic and modern langs. Office: 27 Pacific St, Baldwin, NY.

NEYER, Joseph, US, educator; b. New Rochelle, NY, Mar 8, 1913; s. Louis and Tillie (Berzon); AB, Harvard Coll, 1934; AM, Harvard Grad Sch of Arts and Sci, 1935, PhD, 1942; att U Paris, 1936-37. Prof, dept phil, Rutgers U, since 1963, chmn, 1953-65; mem fac since 1947; asst in phil, Harvard U, 1937-40; instr, phil, Vassar Coll, 1940-42. US Army, 1942-46. Mem: steering and exec comms, Amer Profs for Peace in ME since 1967; Amer Phil Assn; Amer Sociol Soc; Phi Beta Kappa. Contbr to jours. Home: 55 W 11 St, New York, NY. Office: Rutgers U, New Brunswick, NJ.

NICHOLAS, Leslie, US, dermatologist, educator; b. Phila, Pa, Dec 22, 1913; s. Samuel and Esther (Trallis); BS, Temple U, 1935, MD, 1937. Pvt practice since 1946; clinical prof, dermat and syphilology, Hahnemann Med Coll, since 1959; dermat: Hahnemann Hosp, since 1952; Doctor's Hosp, since 1940; St Luke's Hosp, since 1950; Grad Hosp, 1940-65; Kensington-Maimonides Hosp, 1949-61; cons, dermato-path, VA, 1946-50. US Army, 1943-46. Mem: Amer Acad Dermat; Soc Investigative Dermat; AAAS; Phila Dermat Soc; AMA. Contbr to med jours. Home: 1919 Chestnut St, Philadelphia, Pa. Office: 255 S 17 St, Philadelphia, Pa.

NICHOLS, Fred William, US, certified public acctnt; b. Knoxville, Tenn, Mar 1, 1912; s. Adolph and Emma (Strauss); BS, U Ala, 1933; m. Jeannette Cooper, June 17, 1937; c: Judith Huizenga, Patsy Lefont, Joan Freeman, Arthur, Michael. Partner i/c, Atlanta Birmingham off, Touche, Ross & Co; fmr Birmingham off, Touche, Ross, Barley & Smart, since 1966; credit and off mgr, Firestone Service Store, 1933-35; internal auditor, Pizitz, 1935-36; acctnt, Winer and Dial, CPAs, 1936-38; sr partner, FW Nichols & Co, 1938-66. Pres: Temple Beth El Cong, 1951-52; Jefferson Co Assn for Mh, 1960-62; chmn: United J Fund of Birmingham, 1955; comm on profsl devl, Ala Soc of CPAs, since 1961, council, 1950, tax clinic, 1946-48; Select of UA of Birmingham, Ala, 1961; mem: bd: natl council, United Syn of Amer, since 1960; Jefferson Co Coord Council of Social Forces, since 1961; mem: adv comm, local practitioners, Amer Inst CPAs, 1958; SE regional comm, Amer Soc Health Assn, since 1961; natl local relations comm, CJFWF, since 1961; Natl Assn of Acctnts; Amer Acctnts Assn; Beta Alpha Psi; Beta Gamma Sigma; Omicron Delta Kappa; UJA study mission to Isr, 1958; Amer Advisory Council, Leon Recanati Grad Sch of Bus Admn, Tel Aviv U. Recipient: Delta Sigma Pi award; nomination for Man of Year; 1961. Home: 456 Glen Castle Dr, NW, Atlanta, Ga. Office: 1100 First National Bank Tower, Atlanta, Ga.

NIEDERLAND, William G, US, psychiatrist, educator; b. Schippenbeil, Ger, Aug 29, 1904; s. Abraham and Rosa (Mindes); in US since 1940; MD, U Wurzburg, Ger, 1929; MD, U Genoa, It, 1934; m. Jacqueline Rosenberg, July 20, 1952; c: James, Daniel, Alan. Clinical asso prof, psycht, SUNY, since 1961, clinical asst prof, 1956-61; public health off, Dusseldorf, 1930-32; med dir, sanatorium, Rheinburg, 1933-34, both Ger; phys, Milan, It, 1935-39; clinical instr, U Philippines, Manila, 1939-40; visiting prof, med psych, U Tampa, Fla, 1946-47. F: Amer Geriatric Assn; Amer Psycht Assn; mem: AMA; Amer Psychan Assn. Author: Seelisch-Nervöse Leiden, 1932; Man Made Plague, 1949; L'uomo Contro Se Stesso, 1952; contbr to local and fgn sci and med jours. Recipient: annual award, Ger Med Assn, 1933; medal, Intercultural Educ, U Tampa, Fla, 1948; Achievement Medal, 1952; annual award, Mich Soc for Psycht and Neur, 1969. Home: 108 Glenwood Rd, Englewood, NJ. Office: SUNY, 1143 Fifth Ave, New York, NY.

NIEDERMAIER, Curt Henri, Fr, sociologist; b. Ratisbonne, Ger; s. Max and Carola; dipl, Inst d'Études Politiques, Sorbonne. Prof, Cen U of J Studies; Gilbert Block Sch; mgr, Centre de Documentation, Israel Moyen-Orient; Partisan, Forces Françaises. Home: 153 Ordener St, Paris, Fr. Office: 19 Poissoniere St, Paris, Fr.

NIGROSH, Israel, US, architect; b. Boston, Mass, Jan 21, 1911; s. Max and Jennie (Silver); BArch, MIT, 1934; m. Frances Polak, Nov 11, 1935; c: Leon, Barry. Prin architect, owner, Israel Nigrosh Assos; architectural designs include: Temples at Belmont, Worcester, Newton and Marblehead; Cen Fire Sta, Swampscott; Heb Tchrs Coll, Brookline. Trustee, Beth El Temple Cen; mem: Town of Belmont Planning Bd and Park Commn; Mass Assn Architects; Boston Soc Architects; Amer Inst Architects. Hobby: watercoloring. Home: 90 Brighton St, Belmont, Mass. Office: 23 Miner St, Boston, Mass.

NINIO, Abraham Albert, Isr, actor, producer; b. Alexandria, Egypt, Dec 25, 1918; att Paris, NY Dramatic Studios; m. Hanna Ben Ari; one c. Actor, producer, member of Habimah Natl Theatre; productions include: Gigi; The Miracle Worker; 12 Angry Men; The Physicists; Irma la Douce; Stop the World I Want to Get Off; The Representative. Home: 13 Kaplan St, Tel Aviv, Isr.

NINIO-BEN-ARI, Hanna Judith, Isr, radio producer; b. Berlin, Ger, Aug 29, 1928; d. Max and Sonia (Raines) Silberstein; in Isr since 1938; m. Abraham, Mar 9, 1952; c: Ron. Head, documentary progs, Isr Bc Corp, since 1969, announcer, produc, 1949-58, head, drama dept, 1958-69. Staff sgt, Army Radio Sta. Mem: council, Mania Bialik House; cultural comm, Journalists Assn, both Tel Aviv. Trans and adaptions of plays; radio plays; film scripts; youth plays; book for musical drama. Hobbies: sculpture, theater, films. Home: 13 Kaplan St, Tel Aviv, Isr. Office: Hakiryah, Tel Aviv. Isr.

NIR, Akiba, Isr, business exec; b. Polhora, Czech, Apr 10, 1922; s. Ludwig and Ella (Horowitz) Neufeld; in Isr since 1948; m. Zipora Lowinger; c: Talila, Amiram, Naama. Personnel mgr since 1968; secy, Kibbutz Shomrat, 1967-68; secy, Mapam, Haifa, 1965-67; mgr, orchards, Kibbutz Shomrat, 1962-65; repr to Czech, to org J student visits in Isr, and, facilitate immigration of Jews. Partisan army, Czech; cpl IDF. Mem: cen comm, Mapam; exec comm, Kibbutz Arzi; secretariat Moreshet; fmr secy, Hashomer Hatzair, Czech. Author: Paths in a Ring of Fire, 1967. Recipient: Shlomo Harkas Award, 1969. Spec interests: collecting hist documents dealing with J Nazi fighters underground movement. Home: Kibbutz Shomrat, Isr. Office: Milouot Ltd, POB 195, Haifa, Isr.

NIR, Dov, Isr, engineer, educator; b. Jerusalem, Feb 6, 1927; s. Moshe and Shifra (Rogoswky) Wolfson; att Heb U, Jerusalem, 1945-47; BSc, U of Cal, Davis, 1948; DSc, Technion, Haifa, 1963; div; c: Doron, Oded. Sr lectr, agric engr, Technion, Haifa, since 1963; drainage engr, Tahal, 1952-54; irrigation, water-use expert, UN, 1966-68. Capt, IDF, 1948-52. Mem: Amer Agric Engr Soc; Amer CE Soc. Contbr to profsl publs. Home: 68 Horev St, Haifa, Isr. Office: Technion, Haifa, Ir.

NIR, Isaac, Isr, pharmacologist; b. Radom, Pol, June 16, 1916; s. Mendel and Gela (Zylberger) Grosfeld; in Isr since 1935; MSc, Heb U, Jerusalem, 1942, PhD, 1946, MD, 1957; m. Barbara Morrison, Nov 21, 1959. Head, dept chem pharm, prof, pharm, Heb U, since 1965; head, toxicology, WHO, Geneva, 1957-60; dir, Inst of Drugs, Isr Min of Health, 1960-61; visiting asso prof, U Chgo Med Sch, 1963-65. Contbr to profsl jours. Home: 14/1 Ramat Danya St, Jerusalem, Isr. Office: Heb U, Jerusalem, Isr.

NIRENSTEIN, Samuel, US, attorney; b. Hartford, Conn, June 3, 1899; s. Ellik and Bertha (Leavitt); BA, Trinity Coll, 1919; MA, U of Pa, 1921; PhD, Dropsie Coll, 1922; LLB, Columbia U Law Sch, 1924; m. Muriel Levine, June 29, 1936; c: Julius. Legal counsel in pvt practice, NYC, since 1925; instr, phil, HUC Tchrs Training Sch, NYC, 1927-28; law secy to Justice Philip J McCook, NY Supr Court, 1933-43; US alien property custodian, 1941-42; spec counsel, NY State Lab Dept, 1948. Hon pres, Orthodox J Congs of Amer, since 1948, pres, 1942-48; mem, exec comm: JWB; Boy Scouts of Amer; mem, Phi Beta Kappa. Author: The Problems of the Existence of God in Maimonides, Averroes and Alanus, 1922; ed in chief: Columbia Law Rev, 1924; J Life, 1946-47; contbr to profsl publs. Home: 210 E 68 St, New York, NY. Office: 8 W 40 St, New York, NY.

NISELL, Samuel, Swed, attorney; b. Malmö, Swed, Oct 2, 1892; s. Klone and Malina (Schwartzman) Nissalowitz; LLB, U Lund, Swed, 1916; m. Astrid Sterner, Oct 24, 1920; c: Ove, Göran, Harry. Pvt practice since 1921. Fmr: chmn, Chevra Kadisha, Stockholm; mem bd, J Comty, Stockholm. Home: Norr Mälarstrand 26, Stockholm, Swed. Office: Drottninggatan 14, Stockholm, Swed.

NISHRY, Varda, Isr, pianist; b. Tel Aviv, Isr; d. Emanuel and Hanna (Skolsky); cert, Shulamit Conservatory, Tel Aviv, 1950; att: Natl Conservatory, Paris, Fr, 1950-52; Claudio Arrau Sch of Music, 1954-55; U Florence It, 1959; m. Hanoch Paruz, Nov 1, 1959; c: Michal. Performances: TV, radio, concerts, recordings. Spec interests: hist of art, teaching. Home: 15 Herzog St, Givatayim, Isr.

NISSAN, Shemuel, Isr, surgeon; b. Jaffa, Isr, Feb 12, 1924; s. Abraham and Sima (Kaplan); grad, Heb U-Hadassah Med Sch, 1952; postgrad studies, Wash U, Mo; m. Yael Wind, 1955; c: Aviram, Eliv, Avital, Oriav, Avyasaf. Chief, dept surg, Cen Emek Hosp, Afula, since 1963; chief elect, dept surg, Hadassah Mt Scopus Hosp, Jerusalem, since 1969; fmr, clinical sr lectr, surg, Hadassah-Heb U Med Sch. Mem, Brit Assn Ped Surgs; FACS; mem comm: Isr Surg Assn; Isr Sci Council; Assn of Heads of Depts. Contbr to profsl publs. Home: 13 Shoshanim St, Kiryat Tivon, Isr. Office: Cen Emek Hosp, Afula, Isr.

NISSENBAUM, Sidney, US, rabbi; b. NYC, June 26, 1913; s. Samuel and Bella (Shaferman); BA, Yeshiva Coll, 1933; ordained rabbi, Yeshiva U, 1939; m. Hannah Rapoport, Oct 25, 1942; c: Deborah Beeber, Marvin. Rabbi, Temple Beth El, since 1942, life tenure since 1962; chaplain: N Hudson Hosp; Hudson Co Blvd Police Dept; Policemen's Benevolent Assn; rabbi, Hoboken J Cen, 1938-42; tchr, Eng, Jersey City HS, 1938-42. Vice-pres: N Hudson Comty Action Prog; Rabb Council of NJ, 1949-55; fmr pres, NJ ZOA; bd dirs, Hudson Co Mh Assn; bd govs, N Hudson Hosp; exec bd, ARC; mem: RabCA; NY Bd Rabbis. Home: 6600 Blvd E, West New York, NJ. Study: Temple Beth El, N Bergen, NJ.

NISSENSON, Hugh H, US, author; b. NYC, Mar 10, 1933; s. Charles and Harriette (Dolch); BA, Swarthmore Coll, 1955. Author: A Pile of Stones, 1965; Notes From The Frontier, 1968; contbr to mags. Mem: Phi Beta Kappa. Recipient: Wallace Stegner f, Stanford U, 1961-62; Edward Lewis Wallant Award, for significant contrib to Amer J Lit. Home: 333 E 34 St, New York, NY.

NISSIM, Itzhak, Isr, rabbi; b. Baghdad, Iraq, 1896; s. Rahamin and Amam; in Isr since 1925; att J Rel Acad, Baghdad; m. Victoria Ben-Yaacov; c: Bezalel, Meir, Moshe. Chief Rabbi of Isr, Rishon Le-Zion, since 1955; pres, Chief Rabbinate of Isr Council; pres, Rabb High Court; pres, Beth Hamidrash leRabbinim veDayanim, Jerusalem. Author: Kanoga Zidkah, 1933; Yain haTov, 1947. Spec interest: collector of rabb works and rare manuscripts. Home and study: 1 Brenner St, Jerusalem, Isr.

NISSIM, Nissim Ezra, Isr, biochemist; b. Diwaniya, Iraq, Oct 10, 1917; s. Ezra and Chahla (Hami); in Isr since 1951; BSc, U Mich, 1940, MSc, 1941; PhD, Heb U, Jerusalem, 1959; m. Suzette Gabbay, Apr 11, 1954; c: Uzzi. Dep mayor, Ramat Gan, Isr, since 1965, mem, city exec, since 1959; head, dept organic chem, microbiol, Volcani Inst, since 1961; fmr f: Brit research insts, 1962-63; Ohio State U, 1963. Mem exec: Israelis of Iraq Origin; Educ Advance Fund; chmn: Achava Movement; Soil Sci Soc of Isr; mem, Chem Soc of Isr; exec mem, cen comm, Engrs and Chems Assn. Author: A Textbook of General Chemistry, 1947; Elementary Physical Chemistry, 1950; contbr to sci jours. Recipient: Lord Marks Scholarship, 1962. Spec interests: Arabic lit, Iraqi folklore; travel. Home: 7 Harimmon St, Ramat Gan, Isr. Office: 35 Bialik St, Ramat Gan, Isr.

NITKIN, Robert L, US, physician; b. Torrington, Conn, Aug 18, 1909; s. Abraham and Bertha (Danziger); BS, Harvard U, 1932; MD LI Coll of Med, 1936; m. Lilyan Wolf, May 10, 1936; c: Barry, Karen. Pvt practice since 1936; att radiologist: Jamaica Hosp, Jamaica, NY; Queens Gen Hosp, Jamaica, NY, 1940-58; dir radiology, Terrace Hgts Hosp; clinical prof, radiology, Flower Fifth Ave Hosp, 1950-55; asso att radiologist, J Sanatorium and Chronic Hosp, Bklyn, 1939-44. Mem: Queens Co Med Soc; AMA; NY Med Soc; NY Roentgen Ray Soc; Queens Roentgen Ray Soc; Phys Sq Club of Queens; Masons. Contbr to med jours. Hobbies: carpentry, painting. Home: 26 Rivers Dr, Lake Success, NY. Office: 90-10 149 St, Jamaica, NY.

NITZANI, Enzo Yehuda, Isr, business exec; b. Florence, It, Mar 13, 1926; s. Hizkiahu and Tina (Calo); in Isr since 1939; MA, Heb U, Jerusalem, 1951; D es Lettres, U Strasbourg, Fr, 1954; m. Miriam Frenkel, Sep 8, 1949; c: Michael, Yoel, Yair. Mgn dir, Haifa Chem, since 1966; Eur dir, Dead Sea Works, 1960-62, vice-mgn dir. 1962-66; mgn dir, Bromine Compounds, 1962-66. Lt, IDF, 1947-50. Pres, Isr Students Fed; vice-chmn, J Students World Org. Home: 4 Hama'ayan St, Haifa, Isr. Office: Haifa Chemicals, POB 1809, Haifa, Isr.

NIV, David, Isr, editor; b. Wolkowysk, Pol, Dec 15, 1915; s. Zvi and Sheina; in Isr since 1935; MA, Heb U, Jerusalem, 1954; m. Naomi Czango; c: Nava, Michal. Ed: Divrei

Haknesset, since 1968; Ha-Umma, lit quarterly, since 1962; head, Heb press dept, JNF head off, 1949-60. J Brig, 1942-45; cdr, Irgun Zvai Leumi, 1936-48. Author: Battle for Freedom, Hist of Irgun Zvai Leumi, 3 vols, 1967. Spec interest: trans of poetry, prose. Home: 9 Itamar Ben Avi St, Jerusalem, Isr. Office: Knesset, Jerusalem, Isr.

NIZAN, Arye, Isr, statistician; b. Bessarabia, Rum, Aug 10, 1910; s. Isaac and Zipora; in Isr since 1934; MS, Heb U, Jerusalem, 1943, PhD, 1953; m. Miriam Kushnir, 1935; c: Yoram, Eli. Dir, research and stat div, Natl Ins Inst, since 1956; lectr, various instns of higher educ, since 1943; responsible for stat, research projects, JA, Pal, 1939-48; dir, div of lab and prices, Cen Bur of Stat, 1948-56. Mem: Amer Stat Assn; Demographic and Stat Assn, Isr. Author: The Standard of Living in Palestine (Israel) During the Last 20 Years, 1952; Statistics of Wages in Industry, 1953; The Economic Situation of Widows and Orphans in Receipt of National Insurance, 1959; Living Conditions of the Aged in Israel, 1963; Rehabilitation and Job Resettlement of Persons Disabled bv Work Accidents, 1965; co-author: Public Expenditure on Social Security and Social Services in Isr; An Empirical Study of Disabled Persons in Israel in Need of Vocational Rehabilitation; contbr to jours. Hobbies: reading, theater. Home: 11 Resh Lakish St, Jerusalem, Isr. Office: 13 Weizmann St, Jerusalem, Isr.

NIZAN, Yehuda, Isr, business exec; b. Mannheim, Ger, Jan 17, 1923; s. Yeshaja and Else (Wagner) Blum; in Isr since 1935; MBA, Harvard Sch of Bus, Boston; m. Klara Ambruch, Oct 10, 1947; c: Shoshana, Jehudith. Mgn dir, United Mizrachi Bank Ltd, since 1969; fmr: dep mgn dir, Rassco, 1964-69. Col, Palmach, IDF; financial adv to chief of staff, head of org dept, manpower br. Chmn, Syn of Zahala; mem: comm for gen mgmt, Isr Mgmt Cen; Zeveth, ex-army off org. Home: 8 Avishai St, Zahala, Isr. Office: 48 Lilienblum St, Tel Aviv, Isr.

NIZER, Louis, US, attorney, author; b. London, Eng, Feb 6, 1902; s. Joseph and Bella (Bialestock); BA, Columbia Coll, 1922; LLB, Columbia U Law Sch, 1924; m. Mildred Mantel, July 1939. Mem, law firm, Phillips, Nizer, Benjamin and Krim, since 1926; atty, exec secy, NY Film Bd of Trade, since 1928; gen counsel, The Motion Picture Assn of Amer, Inc, since 1966. Dir: Motion Picture Charity Fund; Film Daily Relief Fund; chmn: theatrical div, ARC; La Guardia, Dewey, political campaigns; Gtr NY Campaign, March of Dimes, 1949; Gtr NY UJA, speakers bur, 1948; adv chmn, theatrical div, Natl Draft Bd; hon mem, Amer Motion Picture Acad; mem: Amer Bar Assn; Bar Assn, NYC; Odd Fellows. Author: New Courts of Industry, 1935; Thinking on Your Feet, 1940; What to do with Germany, 1944; Between You and Me, 1948; My Life in Court, 1962; The Jury Returns, 1966; An Analysis of the Warren Commission Report on the Assassination of President John Kennedy, 1964; Legal Essays; contbr to law revs. Recipient: Curtis Oratorical Prize, twice, Columbia U. Home: 180 W 58 St, New York, NY. Office: 477 Madison Ave, New York, NY.

NIZNIK, Abram D, Can, rabbi; b. Pol, Feb 2, 1931; s. Josel and Alta (Znaida); in Can since 1953; ordained rabbi, Mirer Yeshivah; m. Zyna Segal, Sep 27, 1947; c: Hyman. Rosh Yeshiva Merkaz Hatorah, since 1953; rabbi, Cong B'nai Jacob and Cong Zeirei Dath, since 1956. Mem: Montreal Council of Orthodox Rabbis; presidium, Agudath Isr Org of Montreal. Home: 2305 Barclay Ave, Montreal, Can. Study: 4099 Esplanade Ave, Montreal, Can.

NOACH, Wilhelm M E, Holland, criminologist; b. Leiden, Holland, May 9, 1917; s. Bernard and Käthe (Riesenfeld); MA, Leiden U, 1941, LLD, 1948; m. Magdolna Renner, June 21, 1948; c: Marion. Dir, Criminological Inst, Utrecht State U, since 1958; asst prof, Leiden U, 1945-48; prof, criminology, U Indonesia, Djakarta, 1948-55, dean, law fac, 1951-53; found, inst of Criminology, U Indonesia, 1948-55. Vice-pres, J Comty, since 1960; mem: bd dirs, Cen J Orphanage, since 1958; Parole and Probation Bd, all Utrecht; Dutch Criminological Assn; Intl Soc Criminology; Assn of Sociol; Psycht Juridical Soc; Dutch Zionist Org; vice-pres, J Comty, Djakarta, 1952-55. Author: De Byzondere Rechtspleging, 1948; Criminologie-Een Inleiding, 1955; contbr to Dutch ency and periodicals. Spec interests: social work, modern political hist, photography. Home: Adr v Ostadelaan 155, Utrecht, Holland. Office: Criminological Inst, Koningslaan 10, Utrecht, Holland.

NOAH, Isidore, Greece, mechanical engr; b. Thessaloniki,

Greece, Feb 21, 1914; s. Raphael and Mazaltov (Tazartes); BS, Lycée Français, Salonika, 1931; dipl engr, Ecole Nationale Superieure d'Aeronautique, Paris, 1936; m. Mary Perez, July 12, 1943; c: Aris. Engr: spec metallic constructions, since 1966; Tech Off Mech Works, since 1948; engr off, State Aircraft Factory, 1937-48; partner: Electrotechnical Co, 1954-60; Electromechanical Ltd, 1961-66. Greek Air Force, 1936-37. Fmr mem: Cen Relief Comm; Athens Comty Bd; and pres, Cen Comty Bd. Home and office: 19 Akademias St, Athens, Greece.

NOBLE, Shlomo, US, educator; b. Sanok, Pol, July 4, 1905; s. Pinchas and Necha (Peller); in US since 1920; BA, St Thomas U, 1929; grad student, U of Zurich, Switz, 1931-32; PhD, O State U, 1939; m. Nina Peller; c: Naomi. Secy, commn on research, YIVO, since 1950, on staff since 1944; instr, Bible and hist, Sem Sch of J Studies, JTSA, since 1944; visiting prof, U of Judaism, 1949-50; instr, Bible, J Tchrs Sem and People's U, 1951, prof, hist, since 1965. Author: Khumesh-Taytsh, 1943; co-ed: YIVO Annual of J Social Sci; YIVO Bleter. Home: 3411 Corlear Ave, Bronx, NY. Office: 1048 Fifth Ave, New York, NY.

NOBLEMAN, Eli E, US, attorney, educator; b. Jersey City, NJ, Mar 8, 1916; s. Herman and Clara (Fischer); BA, NYU, 1936, LLB, 1939, LLM, 1941, JSD, 1950; grad: career course, Judge Advocate Gen Sch; US Army Civil Affairs Sch; Ind Coll of Armed Forces; m. Elaine Jacobs, Jan 4, 1942; c: Hazel, Paula. Legal and profsl staff mem, US Sen comm on govt oprs, since 1951; adj prof, Sch of Intl Service and Sch of Govt, Amer U, since 1954, adj prof, Grad Sch, since 1947; asso, law firm, House, Grossman, Vorhaus and Hemley, 1939-40; law secy, US Dist Court Judges, S Dist, NY, 1941-42; spec asst to atty gen, US Dept of Justice, 1942-48; counsel: Sen Subcomm on Relations with Intl Orgs of Sen Comm on Expenditures in Exec Depts, 1948-51. US Army, 1942-46, chief, Mil Govt Courts Br, Mil Govt for Bavaria, 1946-46; col, Judge Advocate Gen Corps, US Army, 1968, recalled to active duty in Berlin Crisis, 1961-62. Natl pres, Mil Govt Assn, 1959, dir since 1952; chmn, comm on law of occupied and extraterritorial defense areas, Amer Bar Assn, since 1949; mem: Seldon Soc; Inst Mil Law; Amer Judicature Soc; natl council, Fed Bar Assn, Judge Advocate's Assn; Amer Political Assn; Amer Acad Political and Social Sci; Cong Ohr Kodesh; Bar, State of NY, DC; Supr Court of US; US Court of Appeals, DC; US Court of Claims; US Court of Mil Appeals; Pi Sigma Alpha. Author: American Military Government Courts in Germany, 1953; articles and monographs in fields of public and intl law; contbr ed, publs of Ind Coll of Armed Forces; contbr to profsl jours. Recipient: 5 Battle Stars; Victory Medal; Mil Occupation Medal, WW II; Army citation for meritorious service; cert of achievement, 3rd Army, 1962; cert of achievement, Dept of Army, 1968. Hobby: music. Home: 3106 Brooklawn Terr, Chevy Chase, Md. Office: Sen Off Bldg, Washington, DC.

NODEL, Julius J, US, rabbi; b. Baltimore, Md, Oct 27, 1915; s. Mordecai and Sarah (King); BA, Wash U, St Louis, Mo, 1938; ordained rabbi, MHL, HUC, 1943; hon DHum, Philathea Coll, London, Ont, Can, 1966; hon DD, HUC-JIR, 1968; m; c: Lawrence; m. 2nd, Else Bohmer Voremberg, Nov 2, 1959; Sr rabbi, Temple Shaare Emeth, since 1959; asst rabbi: Euclid Ave Temple, Cleveland, O, 1943-44; The Temple, Cleveland, 1946-50; rabbi, Temple Beth Isr, Portland, Ore, 1950-59; lectr, Judaism, Fonthonne Catholic Coll, St Louis, Mo, 1967-68. Chaplain, USNR, 1944-46. Pres: St Louis Rabb Assn, 1964; St Louis ZC, 1961; St Louis ZOA Dist, 1963; ZOA, Portland, Ore, 1951-56; Portland Lodge, B'nai B'rith, 1956-57; vice-pres: mid-west region, ZOA, since 1962, W coast region, 1957-59; hon chmn, JWF, Ore, 1954-55; vice-chmn, Ore Comm for Equal Rights, 1953-54; chaplain: St Louis Police Dept, since 1963; O State, JWV, 1947-49; delg, Natl Conf, UNESCO, for Syn Council of Amer, 1949; Ore State, Amer Legion, 1953-54; mem: bd govs, HUC-JIR, since 1968, Alumni Bd of Overseers, since 1966; found, St Louis Interfaith Clergy Council, 1966; exec comm, St Louis Conf on Rel and Race, 1963; natl prog comm, ADL, 1955-59, and since 1962; adv comm, Ore Parole and Probation Survey, 1956-58; Gov Comm on Youth, 1952-59; CCAR; Masons; counsellor, Hillel Found, U of Ore, 1951-53; arbitrator, Iron Workers and Asso Employers, Portland, 1954; weekly radio and TV broadcaster, Portland, 1951-59; club, Meadowbrook Country, St Louis. Author: The Ties Between, 1958; sermons in anthols of speeches; columnist, Kaleidoscope; ed contbr, J Review and Observer, 1946-50. Recipient: Freedom Award, Amer Vet Comm, 1952. Hobbies: painting, music. Home:

10 Dumbarton Dr, St Louis, Mo. Study: 560 Trinity, St Louis, Mo.

NODEL, Sol, US, artist, illuminator; b. Wash, DC, Sep 29, 1912; s. Mordecai and Sarah (King); att: Wash U Sch of Fine Arts, 1931-34; Grand Cen Sch Art, 1939-40; studied with Edmund Wuerpel; miniatures with Leo Dubson; m. Shulamith Gold, Apr 6, 1941. Group shows: St Louis Art Mus; St Louis Artists Guild; High Mus, Atlanta; Queens Coll, NYC; NYU; Pope Pius XII Memorial Libr; St Louis U; repr in perm collections: Natl Archives, Wash, DC; Herbert Hoover Mus; Harry Truman Libr; Libr of Cong; FDR Hyde Park Libr; Eur; US; Isr; Far E; repr in pvt collections; executed 12 panel illumination of Lincoln's Gettysburg Address; commns received and illuminations exhb: Japan, Switz, Eng, Isr, Congo, Fr, It; instr, painting, St Louis Settlement House, 1937-39; asst instr, Grand Cen Sch Art, 1939-40. Master Sgt, US Army, 1942-46. Mem: fine arts comm, Mary McLeod Bethune Memorial and Educ Cen, Wash, DC; Natl Council on Art in J Life; 1st vice-pres, Cong Shaare Zedek, NYC; chmn, art commn, Intl Syn, JFK Airport, NY; hon found mem, Law Sci Found, U Tex; mem: B'nai Zion; B'nai B'rith; life f, Royal Soc Art, London. Author: Some of My Best Friends, 1942; Ketubah, 1942, 1950, 1961; co-author: Book of Grace. Recipient: 1st prize, Monsanto Chem Award; Proctor and Gamble Award; Gold Medal, US Army; award, St Louis YMHA; St Louis Artist Guild. Hobby: music, violinist. Home: 639 West End Ave, New York, NY. Office: 55 W 42 St, New York, NY.

NOGI, Henry, US, attorney; b. Wilkes-Barre, Pa, Dec 29, 1900; s. Jacob and Ida (Aronson); LLB, Cornell U Law Sch, 1924; m. Jeanette Suravitz, Sep 29, 1925; c: Judith Snyder, Ann Schneider. Sr mem, Nogi, O'Malley and Harris, since 1933; chmn, bd dirs: Parodi Cigar Mfg Co, Scranton, Pa, since 1960; Gold-Cup Bakers, since 1939; dir, W Side Bank, Scranton; spec asst dist atty, Lackawanna Co, election fraud inves, 1933; spec asst to atty-gen of US, 1953; spec hearing off, Justice Dept, 1955. Chmn: comty relations comm, Scranton-Lackawanna J Council, since 1962; exec comm, J Comty Cen, 1956; UJA, 1947; budget comm, Scranton-Dunmore Comty Chest, 1946-49; pres: Scranton-Lackawanna J Council, 1953; J Comty Cen, 1928; Scranton C of C, 1955; vice-pres: Scranton-Lackawanna Ind Devl Co, since 1947; Temple Isr, Scranton, 1932; dir, J Home of E Pa, since 1962; mem: B'nai B'rith; ZOA; club: Glen Oak Country. Recipient: F Club award, 1954; B'nai B'rith Americanism award, 1968. Home: 530 Clay Ave, Scranton, Pa. Office: 420 Miller Bldg, Scranton, Pa.

NORDAU, Maxa, Fr, artist, lecturer; b. Paris, Jan 10, 1897; d. Max and Anna (Dons); studied art with: José M López Mezquita; Jules Adler, 1915-19; m. Claude Gruenblat-Nordau, Feb 7, 1929; c: Claudy-Gabrielle. One-man shows: Paris, 1922, 1929, 1934, 1947, 1950, 1955, 1960, 1963, 1966; Budapest, 1927; Tel Aviv, 1937, 1952; NY, 1944-45; Jerusalem, 1952; Brussels and Luxembourg, 1958; London, 1964; exhbs in group shows and salons: Fr, since 1921; Brit, 1939; US, 1941-46; Mexico, 1944; works purchased by: Mus Carnavalet, Paris; Fr Govt Mus; City of Paris, 1961, 1964; Munic Mus, Tel Aviv; Ein Harod Mus, Isr. Works include: Head of A Girl, 1918; Portrait of Max Nordau, 1920; Composition, 1920; Portrait of Miguelo de Unamuno, 1924; The Holy Sepulchre, 1927, Santiago, Chile; An Iraqi Woman, 1927, Tel Aviv Mus; portraits: Gal Koenig; Jabotinsky; illus for Contes pour Maxa, by Max Nordau, 1929; The Jaffe Port, 1934; A Sephardic Girl, 1935, Ein Harod Mus; Murals at Pal Pavilion, Paris World Fair, 1937; Old House in Paris, 1939; Head of A Woman, 1948; Portrait of Justin Godart, 1953; illus work. Coauthor: Max Nordau, A Biography, 1942; contbr to mags; lectr: Max Nordau's life and works, Zionism, art, lit; travels in US, 1926, 1941-46; Morocco, 1927; Aus, Hung, Rum, Greece, 1927-28; Paris, Belgium, Switz, since 1928; instr, CCNY, adult educ courses, 1944-45. Vice-pres: Assn of J Painters and Sculptors in Fr; Union Féminine Artistique Culturelle, Salon Internationaux, Paris. Recipient: medals: Conseil Gen du Dept de la Seine, 1957; Salon Ibaia, Bayonne, 1967; prizes: Gennevilliers-Asnières, 1957; City of Asnières, 1960; Grand Prix Intl de Vichy, 1961; Syndicate of Initiative, Festival of Plastic Art, Bergerac, 1961; Intl Grand Prize, Monbazillac, 1968; Chevalier, Mérite Culturel et Artistique, 1969. Home: 3 rue Massanet, Paris, Fr.

NORDLINGER, Henry Harold, US, attorney; b. NYC, Oct 25, 1893; s. Edwin and Henriette (Bacharach); BA, Columbia U, 1912, LLB, 1914; m. Elsie Lehrburger, Nov 8, 1924; c: Eleanor

Hauser, Ruth Baylinson, Edwin. Partner, Nordlinger, Riegelman, Benetar and Charney, since 1919; dir, Music Careers, Inc. Dir, NY Co Lawyers Assn, since 1965; mem: Amer, NY State Bar Assns; Assn of Bar, NYC; NY Co Lawyers Assn; Amateur Astronomers Assn; Gilbert and Sullivan Soc of NY, fmr vice-pres; fmr: chmn, natl law comm, mem, exec comm, JWB; mem, exec comm, NYC Bar Assn; chmn, spec comm on court congestion in Metrop dist, NY State Bar Assn; mem, bd govs, Harmonie club. Contbr to legal jours. Home: 115 Central Park W, New York, NY. Office: 420 Lexington Ave, New York, NY.

NORMAN, Charles, US, biologist, educator; b. NYC, Jan 16, 1916; s. Samuel and Yetta (Saft) Numerofsky; BS, U Miami, 1948, MS 1949; PhD, State U of Ia, 1954; m. Beverley Salzhauer, Feb 24, 1945; c: Ellen, Rebecca, Samuel. Sr research f, US NIH; cons, US Agcy for Intl Devl, since 1963; prof, biol, W Va U, since 1961, on fac since 1953; instr, zool, U Miami, 1949-50; instr, biol, State U of Ia, 1951-53; visiting inves, Animal Research Sta, Cambridge, Eng, 1961; visiting prof, MIT, 1965-66. US Navy, 1943-45. Prin contrib: discovered artificial medium for vitro-maintenance of mammalian germ cells, 1958. Mem: Amer Soc Zool; NY Acad Sci; Sigma Xi; Soc for Study of Fertility. Contbr to scholarly jours. Recipient: research f, Amer Phys Soc, 1959. Home: 344 Laurel St, Morgantown, W Va. Office: W Va U, Morgantown, W Va.

NORMAN, Theodore, US, economist, organization exec; b. Cambridge, Mass, Mar 12, 1910; BA, Harvard U, 1930, 'MA, 1932, PhD, 1939; m. Jane Posner, Dec 22, 1935; c: Alice, Lucy. Mgn dir, Baron de Hirsch Fund; gen mgr, J Agric Soc, NYC; instr, Harvard U, 1935-38; econ: US Dept Agric, 1938-47; Sen Civil Liberties Comm, 1939-40; staff mem: Brookings Inst, 1947; CJFWF, 1948-49; asst exec dir, NY Assn for New Amers, 1949-50. Co-author: Economics with Applications to Agriculture, 1950; Traveler's Guide to Europe's Art, 1959; Traveler's Guide to American Art, 1968; Home: 300 Central Park W, New York, NY. Office: 386 Park Ave S, New York, NY.

NORRY, Irving S, US, business exec; b. NYC, Oct 22, 1910; s. Julius and Helen (Danishefsky); m. Ann Rabin, Sep 17, 1930; c: Neil, Deborah. Pres, Norry Elec Corp, Rochester, NY, since 1934; treas, Isr Elec Products, Jerusalem, since 1951; partner, Furman Assos, Inves Bankers, Tel Aviv, Isr; vice-pres, Slavin Engr Co, Tel Aviv; mem, bd dirs, Pal Econ Corp, since 1954. Pres, United JWF, Rochester, 1949; chmn, intl adv comm, WJC; mem, bd govs, Isr Bonds, since 1950; mem, bd dirs: Wegmen Found, Rochester; JTSA, since 1956; Amer Friends of Heb U, since 1957; Amer Financial Corp, 1951; trustee, Pal Endowment Fund, since 1969; mem: Temple Beth El; natl cabinet, UJA, since 1949; exec comm: AJCong; United Isr Appeal; US Govt-Intl Coop Admn mgmt mission to Isr, 1960. Home: 2680 Highland Ave, Rochester, NY.

NORTON, Harvey Niman, Scot, pharmaceutical chem; b. Leeds, Eng, Feb 22, 1910; s. Philip and Annie (Nayman); att U Leeds, 1928; m. Dorothy Langman, Dec 29, 1936; c: Nigel, Hazel Webber, Coral. Mgn dir, HN Norton & Co Ltd, since 1957. Pres, Glasgow Bd Shechita; B'nai B'rith, 1954-56; life pres, Glasgow Burial Bd, 1940-63; chmn, Kosher Food Distribution Comm; treas, Natl Council Shechita Bds; 1st vice-pres, Giffnock Syn; mem, Bd Deps Brit Js, 1960-69. Hobby: golf. Office: 19 Queen St, Glasgow, Scot.

NOTHMAN, Martin M, US, educator, physician; b. Katowitz, Ger, May 14, 1894; s. Max and Amalie (Wiener); in US since 1939; MD, U Breslau, Ger, 1919; m. Mia Bergmann, Dec 2, 1919; c: Evelore Poras. Asst clinical prof, med, Tufts U Med Sch, postgrad div, since 1951, on staff since 1939; mem, staff: NE Cen Hosp; Beth Isr Hosp, Boston, Mass; asst, med clinic, Breslau U, 1920-25; lectr, internal med, U Breslau, 1925, asso prof, internal med, 1930; research f, Pharm Inst, Graz U, Aus, 1926; phys in chief, med dept, J Hosp, Leipzig, Ger, 1932-38; prof, em, 1954. Mem: Mass Med Soc; Med Assn of Isr; NY Acad Sci; ZOA; AAAS; Gtr Boston Med Soc; Amer Soc for Pharm and Experimental Therapeutics. Author: Endocrine Disturbances of the Thyroid and Parathyroids, 1937; Simplified Diabetic Manual, 1947; contbr to profsl jours. Home: 94 Williston Rd, Brookline, Mass. Office: 311 Commonwealth Ave, Boston, Mass.

NOTKIN, Anne S, Can, communal worker, journalist; b. Que, May 24, 1902; d. Leon and Deborah (Ortenberg) Lerner; m.

Louis Notkin, May 28, 1930; c: Joan, Barbara. Secy, Intl Council of J Women, 1957-63, conv chmn, Basle, Switz, 1960, conv prog chmn, Cleveland, 1963, chmn, resolutions comm, 1954-57, mem, comm on legal status of women, 1951-56; mem, bd dirs, Can Assn of Consumers, Que, 1953-65; fmr: natl vice-pres, Natl Council of J Women of Can; natl secy and natl chmn, public affairs, pres, Montreal sect; treas, councillor and vice-pres, Montreal Council of Women; educ dir, Montreal Women's Club; co-natl chmn, JNF, Hadassah Org of Can; mem: women's PR comm, Can J Cong; Montreal Comty Comm for Future Canadians. Mem, ed staff: Quebec Chronicle, 1919; Montreal Daily Star, 1920-26; London Daily Express; Pal Weekly, both 1929-30; dir, press bur, ZOC, 1926-29; ed, Can Zionist, 1930-31; Montreal corresp, JTA, 1926-29; substitute London ed, JTA, Bull, 1929, PR, JNF of Gt Brit and Ir, 1929-30; contbr to Anglo-J and Eng-Can periodicals. Home: 3555 Côte des Neiges Rd, Montreal, Can.

NOTKIN, Louis J, Can, physician; b. Ekaterinoslav, Russ, Dec 8, 1893; s. Joseph and Aniuta (Spiegel); in Can since 1905; MD, CM, McGill U, 1920; m. Anne Lerner, May 28, 1930; c: Joan, Barbara. Sr phys and gastroenterologist, J Gen Hosp, 1933-60, hon att staff, since 1961; cons, Herzl Dispensary, since 1929; demonstrator, phys, McGill U, 1920-21, lectr, 1921-23; house surg, St Peters Hosp, Bklyn, NY, 1923; asso, gastrointestinal clinic, Royal Victoria Hosp, Montreal, Que, 1924-34; gastroenterologist, Women's Gen Hosp, 1927-31; radiologist, 1930-31. Mem: Coll of Phys and Surg, Que; Can Med Assn; Medico-Chirurgical Soc; Clinical Soc; Phys Soc; sr mem, Amer Gaetroenterological Assn; f, Amer Coll Gastroenterology, Montreal, Mus of Fine Arts; council mem, Montreal chap, Can Friends of Heb U; club, Montreal Camera, pres, 1946-47. Contbr to med jours. Home: 3555 Côte des Neiges Rd, Montreal, Can.

NOTKIN, Myron, Can, physician; b. Russ, Dec 25, 1894; s. Joseph and Anuta (Spiegel); in Can since 1905; MD, CM, FCCP, CRCP, CSPQ, McGill U, Montreal; m. Esther Finestone, 1934; c: Richard, Audrey. Hon att phys, Royal Edward Chest Hosp; med referee, Occidental Life Ins Co of Can, since 1934; hon att phys: Montreal Gen Hosp, since 1958; J Gen Hosp, since 1957, fmr co-chief, chest diseases dept; asst prof, med zool, McGill U, 1928-35, lectr, until 1963; cons, chest diseases, Reddy Memorial Hosp, 1930-35. F, Amer Coll Chest Phys; fmr pres: Montreal Clinical Soc; TB sect, Medico-Chirurgical Soc. Hobby: writing poems for children. Home: 18 Grenville Ave, Westmount, Que, Can. Office: 1538 Sherbrooke St W, Montreal, Can.

NOVACK, Martin, US, attorney; b. Bklyn, NY, Oct 9, 1930; s. Abraham and Bella (Mordkowitz); BA, Bklyn Coll, 1952; JD, NYU, Sch of Law, 1954; m. Fay Nazimovitz, Nov 26, 1955; c: Beth, Alan. Partner, Novack & Richter, NYC, since 1965; asso, Groban & Rava, 1956-63, mem, 1963-65. Pvt, judge advocate, US Army, 1954-56. Counsel to Govt of Isr; mem: Consular Law Soc; NY State Bar Assn; Assn of Bar, NYC; Kappa Delta Pi; Delta Sigma Rho; fmr mem: NY Reform Dems; J Lab Comm; Fair Housing Comm, Assn of Bar, NYC. Home: 1527 E 35 St, New York, NY. Office: 60 E 42 St, New York, NY.

NOVAK, Cornelius (pen name, **Dan Zacharia**), Isr, journalist, writer; b. Bucharest, Rum, Feb 24, 1928; s. Sinai and Johanna Greter; in Isr since 1959; att: Econ High Acad and Law Fac, Bucharest U, 1945-49; fac of journalism, Rum Mil Acad, 1950-51; m. Eva Rosner, Mar 21, 1953. Free-lance journalist, writer, since 1959; ed, Hashachar, Masonic monthly, Tel Aviv, since 1969; contbr to: Kol Israel; Davar; Davar Le-yeladim; Davar Hapoeleth; Hayom; Min Hayessod; Burda Verlag; Stern; ed: Youth's Fight, Bucharest, 1946-47; Geological Bull, Bucharest, 1953-55; Coop Bull, 1956-57; mgr, The Documentary Cen Ltd, Tel Aviv, 1963-64; ed, Lemaaneich Gvirti, Isr, 1967-68. Cpl, journalist, trans, Rum Army, 1949-51. Secy: Comm for New Immigrants; Heb Writers Assn; mem: Masons; Intl Fed Free Journalists; fmr: secy: J Students Assn, Bucharest; Eliezer Steinbarg Cultural Club, Tel Aviv; mem, lit found, Writers Union of Rum. Author: The Transylvanian Peasants, 1955; Two Misogynic Plays-An Adam and Eve Book, 1967; co-author: Short Plays, 1957. Home and office: 10 Soutine St, Tel Aviv, Isr.

NOVAK, Eva, Isr, journalist, critic; b. Oradea, Rum, Jan 6, 1927; d. Sigismund and Regina (Kun) Rosner; in Isr since 1959; m. Cornelius Novak, Mar 21, 1953. Journalist, critic, ed, theatre and cinema, Davar, Omer dailies since 1960; contbr to periodicals, lit trans, since 1946; journalist, The

Woman, 1948-59; gen secy, off of review, The Peasant Woman, 1949-51; writer, Rum Bc Corp, 1951-52; journalist, second ed, Red Cross Reviews, 1953-57, all Rum. Mem: Isr Fed of Journalists, since 1963, fmr mem, cinema critics comm; fmr mem: Profsl Union of Artists, Journalists and Writers; Journalists Union of Rum; lit found, Writers Union of Rum, all Bucharest. Co-author: Plays and Short Plays; Stories and Features. Recipient: Dishon Prize for Journalism, Isr Natl Fed of Journalists, 1961. Home: 10 Soutine St, Tel Aviv, Isr. Office: 45 Shenkin St, Tel Aviv, Isr.

NOVICK, Abraham G, US, social welfare exec; b. NYC, Oct 21, 1916; s. Max and Anna (Goldfarb); BA, Yeshiva U, 1937, dipl, Erna Michael Coll of J Studies, Yeshiva U, 1936; MS, Columbia U, 1939; PhD, Syracuse U, 1953; m. Matilda Davidov, Mar 22, 1941; c: Judith, Deborah, Valerie. Exec dir: Berkshire Farm for Boys; Berkshire Inst for Training and Research, since 1963; visiting prof, Moran Inst on Crime and Delinquency, St Laurence U, since 1957; supt, NY State Training Sch for Girls, 1953-63; asst supt, NY State Agric and Ind Sch, 1946-53; visiting prof, Russell Sage Coll, 1955-63; cons: Child Wfr Leage of Amer; Natl Council on Crime and Delinquency; US Children's Bur; Md State Dept of Social Wfr; Cuyahoga Co Dept of Public Wfr; Pa Dept of Public Wfr; NC Bd of Correction and Training; Cal Youth Auth; States of Del, Ga, and Okla; conducted workshops and insts on delinquency and child wfr throughout US; mem, atty gen comm on crime and delinquency, 1961; delg, UN Cong on Crime Prevention and Treatment of Offenders, Stockholm, Swed, 1965; adv, Pres Crime Commn, 1966-67. Pres: profsl council, Natl Assn of Training Schs and Juvenile Agcys, 1957-59; Hudson J Comty Cen, 1955-57; Berkshire chap, Soc Isr Philatelists; mem, bd dirs: profsl council, Natl Council on Crime and Delinquency; Abdullah chap, B'nai B'rith; Pittsfield J Comty Cen; Cong Anshe Amunim; J Wfr Bd, 1959-61; Hudson Comty Chest, 1955-57; Cong Anshe Emeth; f, Amer Orthopsycht Assn; mem: Amer Group Psychotherapy Assn; Natl Assn Soc Workers; Amer Acad Soc Workers; Amer Soc for Public Admn; Natl Assn of Training Schs and Juvenile Agcys; Natl Council on Crime and Delinquency; Intl Council on Soc Wfr; Amer Correctional Assn; Council on Social Work Educ; B'nai B'rith; Rotary; Masons; Grand St Boys Assn. Contbr to profsl jours. Recipient: two citations for developing new techniques in treatment of psycht casualties, US Army; Gov Charles E Hughes Award, Amer Soc for Pub Admn, 1959; Plaque of Recognition, NY State Dept of Social Wfr, 1963. Home: Route 295, Richmond, Mass. Office: Berkshire Farm for Boys, Canaan, NY.

NOVICK, Herbert, US, attorney; b. Bklyn, NY, Aug 13, 1908; s. Louis and Rose (Balbes); LLB, Rutgers Law Sch, 1929; m. Rose Pearlman, July 26, 1931; c: Helene, Saul. Pvt practice since 1930; exec dir, Assn of Men's Belt Mfrs; chief atty, Prosecutor of the Pleas, Passaic Co, NJ, 1931-32; counsellor-at-law, master-in-chancery of NJ, 1933; lab relations repr, 1935; park comm, City of Paterson, 1945-46; police and fire commn, 1949, educ commn, 1950-52. Hon chmn, UJA Belt Ind and Allied Trades Div; Deborah Hosp, Ind and Allied Trades Div; Histadrut, Ind and Allied Trades Div; Dem leader, fourth ward, Paterson; chmn, ladies belt div: Deborah Sanatorium, 1951-53; UJA, 1950-53; mem: Temple Emanuel, Paterson; Jacob Dineson Lodge; Passaic Co Dems; Barnett Memorial Hosp. Ed: The Beltline, newsletter; Annual Trade Directory of the Belt Industry. Home: 464 17 Ave, Paterson, NJ. Office: 300 W 40 St, New York, NY.

NOVICK, Rudolph G, US, psychiatrist, educator; b. Warsaw, Pol, Dec 16, 1910; s. Samuel and Simca (Greenwald); in US since 1920; BS, Northwestern U, 1931, MD, 1936; att Inst of Psychan of Chgo; m. Judith Topin, Feb 13, 1927; c: Laurence, Barbara. Pvt practice since 1945; med dir, Forest Hosp, since 1957; psycht cons: Ill Dept of Public Health, since 1966; Chgo TB Sanatorium, 1955-58; psycht educ cons, Ill Dept of Public Health, since 1968; mem, courtesy staff, Michael Reese Hosp, since 1954; jr phys, Jacksonville State Hosp, Ill, 1937-40; sr phys: Manteno State Hosp, 1940-41; Elgin State Hosp, 1941-43; med dir, Ill Soc for Mh, 1943-57; asso clinical prof, psycht, U of Ill Coll of Med, 1947-56, asst prof, 1941-42; psycht cons: Chgo Bd of Health, mental hygiene sect, 1948-49; Chgo State Hosp, 1955-56; tech cons, Gov Adlai Stevenson's Comm on Midcent White House Conf on Children and Youth, 1950; served on: Gov Comm to survey state prog and facilities for vets discharged on a neuro-psycht basis, 1943; comty services adv comm, USPHS, HEW, 1954. Dipl, Amer Bd Psycht and Neur; f, Amer Psycht Assn; chmn, Group for Advancement of Psycht

1954; pres, Cen Neuropsycht Hosp Assn, 1967; mem: comm on academic educ, Amer Psycht Assn; Ill Psycht Soc; AMA; Ill State Med Soc; Chgo Med Soc. Contbr to med jours. Home: 6400 Kilpatrick, Lincolnwood, Ill. Office: Forest Hosp, Des Plaines, Ill.

NOVICK, Sylvan R, US, attorney; b. NYC, June 16, 1919; s. Samuel and Rachel (Chilvsky); att: Rutgers U, 1946; CCNY; LLB, Bklyn Law Sch, 1949; m. Pearl Codner, Dec 22, 1962; c: Robert, Michael, Ronald. Pvt practice since 1949; real estate, 1946-49. Lt, US Army, 1941-46. Pres, Lower Manhattan E Dem Assn; trustee, Town & Village Syn; post cdr, JWV; mem: NY Co Lawyers Assn; Disabled War Vets. Home: 431 E 20 St, New York, NY. Office: 401 Broadway, New York, NY.

NOVIK, Meir, Isr, police officer; b. Warsaw, Pol, May 15, 1914; s. Elieser and Mina (Wintraub); in Isr since 1936; dipl, Sports Tchrs Sch, Warsaw, 1934; m. Blima Finbaum, Mar 22, 1936; c: Loya Shamir, Nimrod. Asst cdr, head, training div, Isr Police, since 1959; sports tchr, Tel Aviv Schs and Hapoel, 1936-39; group sgt, ISP, 1939-46; head: dept, Gen Security Service, 1948-50; spec div, Isr Police Hqr, 1950-59. Dist intelligence off, Haganah, 1943-48; maj, IDF, 1948-50. Off, Intl Police Assn. Home: 4 Haseren Dov St, Ramat Chen, Isr. Office: 14 Harakevet St, Tel Aviv, Isr.

NOVIKOFF, Alex B, US, pathologist, educator; b. Chernigov, Russ, Feb 28, 1913; s. Jack and Anna (Tretyakoff); in US since 1913; BS, Columbia U, 1931, MA, 1933, PhD, 1938; m. Phyllis Iaciofano, Dec 1, 1968; c: Kenneth, Lawrence. Research prof, path dept, Albert Einstein Coll of Med, since 1956; asst prof, biol dept, Bklyn Coll, 1931-48; US Army film cons, 1947-51; prof, experimental path, U of Vt Coll of Med, 1948-54, asso prof, biochem, 1948-54. Pres: Histochem Soc, 1958-59; NY Soc for Electron Microscopy, 1961-62; Amer Soc for Cell Biol, 1962-63; f: Amer Cancer Soc, U of Wis Med Sch, 1946-47; NY Acad Sci, since 1949; hon mem: Japan Soc for Cellular Chem; Société Française de Microscopie Electronique; mem: natl council, Histochem Soc, since 1953; AAAS; Amer Assn for Cancer Research; Amer Soc Biol Chem; AAUP; Amer Soc Zool; Sigma Xi. Author: children's books: Climbing Our Family Tree, 1945; From Head to Foot, 1946; films on cell chem; chaps to sci books; mem, ed bd: Cancer Research; Jour of Histochem and Cytochem; Jour of Cell Biol; Jour of Morphology; contbr to sci jours. Recipient: Most Dist Alumni Award, Columbia U, 1960; USPHS career award, 1962. Home: 51 White Oak St, New Rochelle, NY. Office: Albert Einstein Coll of Med, New York, NY.

NOVOSELLER, Sherman, US, rabbi; b. Russ, Aug 9, 1917; s. David and Freida (Berliant); in US since 1929; dipl, Gratz Coll, Phila, 1935; BA, Yeshiva Coll, 1940; ordained rabbi, Rabbi Isaac Elchanan Theol Sem, 1940; m. Rose Kauffman, June 21, 1942 (decd); c: Norman, Daniel, Amiel; m. 2nd, Hanna Roling. Rabbi: Beth Tovim, Phila, Pa, since 1964; Temple Isr, Wynnefield, 1942-64. Pres, Adas Harabonim, since 1956; exec dir, Kosher Service, since 1948; pres: Yeshiva Students Org, Rabbi Isaac Elchanan Theol Sem, 1937-39; Rabb Assn, Phila, 1946-47; secy, Bd Rabbis, Phila, 1946; mem: ZOA; Mizrachi; bd, Beth Jacob Heb Day Sch; Phila Yeshiva; J Comty Relations Council. Hobby: philately. Home: 5871 Drexel Rd, Phila, Pa. Study: Beth Tovim, 59 St & Drexel Rd, Phila, Pa.

NOVY, Jim, US, business exec; b. Pol, Mar 15, 1896; s. Eli and Chyah (Zirl); in US since 1913; m. Estelle Fishbein (decd); c: Dave, Elaine Shapiro. Pres, Producers Utilities Corp, since 1955; partner: Austin Metal and Iron Co, 1914-1943; Austin Pipe and Supply Co; pres, Northwood Terrace Inc, 1951-54; Mazel Oil and Gas Co, 1955. Hon vice-pres, Envy Judaica Research Found; hon chmn, JNF; mem: natl exec council, ZOA; Hillel Found, Austin; SW adv bd, ADL; Boy Scouts Amer; Natl Adv Comm, Scrap Iron and Steel; War Produc Bd; fmr: appd by Gov of Tex as personal repr to Isr during celebration of 10th anniversary, 1958; pres: ZOA, hon pres, SW region; Austin J Fed; SW Council of Syns; United Brotherhood for Austin Jewry; pres, life mem, bd dirs, Cong Agudas Achim, chmn, bldg comm; Austin Free Loan Fund; vice-pres, JCC, Austin; chmn: UJA Drive; Bonds for Isr; JWB; mem, bd dirs: Salvation Army, Austin, vice-chmn; Comty War Chest; C of C, Austin; secy-treas, SW region, United Syn Amer; vice-chmn: SW council, United Pal Appeal; Salvation Army Adv Bd; delg, WZC, Jerusalem, 1964; Established: Jim Novy Found for Charity, 1955; Jim Novy

Trust. Recipient: 25 year cert, B'nai B'rith, 1950; citation of honor, ZOA, 1954; cert of merit, Inst of Scrap Iron and Steel, 1954; hon plaque, VFW, 1957; bronze plaque erected in his honor, Cong Agudas Achim; citation of honor, ZOA-Kfar Silver Fund, 1960; citation of honor, USO, 1960; Herzl centennial citation of hon, ZOA humanitarian award for devoted service to Isr, 1961; cert of honor, 25th anniversary, UJA; Hon Misselman, mem, 4th Missile Battalion, Nike Hercules, 7th Artillery, 1964; ZOA Award, 1964; plaque, 1965 campaign, UJA, Gtr NY. Home: 5104 Ridge Oak Dr, Austin, Tex. Office: 3rd and Medina, Austin, Tex.

NOY, Daniel, Isr, organization exec; b. Haifa, Sep 7, 1928; s. Heinrich and Sara (Rapaport); att agric fac, Rehovot, 1952-55; m. Yehudith Galenson, 1949; c: Nira, Eyal, Orna, Vered. Head, ind dept, Hakibbutz Hameuchad, since 1969, mem, exec comm; found, educ and research auth, Inter-Kibbutz Org, 1960-63; with econ dept, Hakibbutz Hameuchad, 1959-63; farm mgr, Kibbutz Palmachim, 1949-51, 1955-59, 1965-68. Mem: Agric Council, Histadrut; Inter-Kibbutz Ind Assn Mgmt. Home: Kibbutz Palmachim, Isr. Office: 27 Soutine St, Tel Aviv, Isr.

NOY, Dov, Isr, museum dir; b. Kozomyja, Pol, Oct 20, 1920; s. Zundel and Sheindl (Wachs) Neuman; in Isr since 1938; MA, Heb U, Jerusalem, 1946; att Yale U, 1952; PhD, Ind U, 1954; m. Tamar Yizreeli; c: Yizhar, Amos, Haim. Asso prof, Heb U, Jerusalem, since 1955; dir, Haifa Munic Ethnological Mus, since 1955; prof, J and Slavic folklore, Ind U, 1953-54; dir, cultural, educ activities, Cyprus Ref Camps, 1948-49. Royal Engrs, Brit Army; educ and culture dept, IDF. Vice-pres, Intl Soc for Folktale Research; found, Isr Folktale Archives. Author: Folktales of Israel, 1963; Jefet Schwili Erzählt, 1963; Moroccan Jewish Folktales, 1966; Contes Populaires Racontés Par Des Juifsde Tunisie, 1968; ed: Israel, Folklore Archives Series; folklore and ethonology dept, Ency Judaica; pub books and papers. Recipient: Five Year Warburg F, Heb U, 1955. Home: 17 Redak St, Jerusalem, Isr. Offices: Heb U, Jerusalem; Ethnological Mus, Haifa, Isr.

NOY, Mordechai, Isr, government official; b. Frankfurt, Ger, Dec 29, 1905; s. Shimon and Fanny (Meyer); in Isr since 1933; atty, U, Frankfurt, 1926; m. Jehudith Rosenheim, Jan 15, 1934; c: Michal Goldberg. Dir, spec services dept, Min of Social Wfr, since 1950; fmr, govt official, Pal, Isr Govt. Secy, B'nai B'rith, Haganah lodge, fmr pres; vice-chmn, Chevra Kadisha Khillat Yerushalaim; mem bd, Sr Govt Offs Assn. Home: 11 Alcharizi St, Jerusalem, Isr. Office: 10 David St, Jerusalem, Isr.

NUDELL, Gerald, US, physician; b. Minneapolis, Minn, Mar 2, 1925; s. Harry and Frances (Herman); BS, MB, MD, U of Minn, 1951; m. Dorothy Schoen, June 19, 1948; c: Karen, Nancy, Bruce. Pvt practice; clinical instr, div of anesthesiology, UCLA Med Cen, since 1955; instr, dept anesthesiology, U of Minn, 1951-52. Capt, USAF, 1952-54. Pres, LA Co Soc Anesthesiologists; chmn, bd, Union Heb HS, LA; various offices, Temple Beth Hillel Cong; delg: Pacific SW Council, UAHC; World Fed Progressive Judaism; mem: Pres Adv Council, HUC-JIR; Amer, Cal, LA Socs Anesthesiologists; AMA; IMA. Contbr to sci jours. Home: 19316 Palomar Pl, Tarzana, Cal. Office: POB 1881, Beverly Hills, Cal.

NUDELMAN, Oscar M, US, attorney; b. Russ, Mar 24, 1899; s. Sam and Ida (Perlman); in US since 1906; LLB, Northwestern U, 1923; m. Fay Miller, Nov 30, 1922; c: Harold. Partner, Nudelman & Nudelman, since 1951. Co-founder, Decalogue Soc of Lawyers, 1934, asst treas since 1952; commn, adult educ, B'nai B'rith; mem: ZOA; AJCong; Amer, Ill, Chgo Bar Assns; Amer Judicature Soc. Contbr to profsl jours. Recipient: Cong Medal for service as govt appeal agent, Selective Service Sys, 1940-41, with Draft Bd, 1941-53. Hobbies: photography, hypnosis, Yiddish. Home: 1400 N Kedzie Ave, Chicago, Ill. Office: 134 N LaSalle St, Chicago, Ill.

NULMAN, Seymour, US, rabbi, educator; b. Newark, NJ, Sep 6, 1921; s. Samuel and Nellie (Feder); att Yeshiva U, 1938-42; ordained rabbi, Rabb Sem of Amer, 1943; MA, Columbia U, 1943; m. Miriam Weinberg, May 24, 1942; c: Shifra Zwick, Basheva Schreiber. Rabbi, E Side Torah Cen, since 1943; dean: Yeshiva Konvitz; Talmud Torah Jacob David, since 1945; chaplain: J Teamsters; Goodwill; Natl Slutzker Landsmanshaft Orgs. Chmn: Natl Conf of Day Sch Prin; Natl Tchrs Licensing Commn, Natl Assn of Day Schs; Jacob David Assn, 1950-53; JCC of E Side; Youth Comm,

E Side C of C; Adult Educ, E Side B'nai B'rith; Rel Instns Comm, NYC; pres, Yehudah Wolf Inst, 1939-45; vice-pres, Natl Day Sch Prin; sup, Church-Related Schs, HEW, NY State; secy: Alumni Assn, E Side B'nai B'rith; Communal Settlements Assn, 1960-61; Natl Eng Prin Assn; mem: Metrop Lodge, Odd Fellows; Tree and Life Soc; Sephardic Fraternal Order; Union of Orthodox Rabbis of US and Can; Rabb Alumni, Yeshiva U; Natl Educ Assn; Union of Orthodox J Congs of Amer; Natl Commn for Natl Conf of Syn Youth; org and ext comm, Gtr NY Councils, Boy Scouts of Amer; J Comm, Boy Scouts of Amer; planning bd, Borough of Manhattan; Assn of Orthodox J Sci; Dept of Sch Prin, NEA; mem bd: Mobilization for Youth; Lower E Side Neighborhoods Assn; Massaryk Towers; club, Grand St Boys. Author: Syllabus and Techniques for Hebrew Day School, 1953; Holiday Customs and Ceremonies, 1959; Torah Journal, 1959; The Memorial Book, 1965; articles on rel and secular educ. Recipient: Citation, March of Dimes, 1950; Citation, AHA, 1953; Cert of Merit, Boy Scouts of Amer, 1954; Cert of Merit, Girl Scouts of America, 1955; Charter of Honor Award ,Union of Orthodox J Congs, 1958; UJA Award, 1961; Brotherhood Award, B'nai B'rith, 1964; Cert of Merit, C of C, 1965; Isr Bonds, 1966; Service Award, Intl Torah Schs, 1966; Outstanding Educ, Parents' Assns, 1968. Home: 268 E Broadway, New York, NY. Study: 313 Heney St, New York, NY.

NUROCK, Max, Isr, civil servant; b. Dublin, Ir, Apr 28, 1893; s. William and Rachel (Zlotover); MA, Trinity Coll, Dublin, hon LLD; m. Bertha Roskin, May, 1918; two c. Adv on publs, Min Fgn Affairs, since 1958; personal rank of Ambass of Isr; colonial admn service, Pal, Uganda, 1920-49; with Brit Control Commn, Ger, Aus, 1945-49; financial secy, gov, Heb U, Jerusalem, 1951-52; Min of Isr to: Austr, NZ, 1953-58; chargé d'affaires, S Afr, 1959. Co-author: Fruits of the Holy Land; trans, ed, Rebirth and Destiny of Israel by David Ben-Gurion; ed, Eng ed, Isr Govt Yearbook; Eng recension, El-Am Talmud. Recipient: OBE. Spec interest: philol. Office: Min for Fgn Affairs, Jerusalem, Isr.

NUSSBAUM, Aaron, US, attorney, communal worker; b. NYC, July 9, 1910; s. Samuel and Dorothy (Biesenstock); LLB, St John's U Sch of Law, 1932, LLM, 1934; m. Helene Lew, Sep 15, 1934; c: Carol Peck, Robert. Asst dist atty, Kings Co Appeals Bur, since 1947; asso chief counsel: State Hotel Assn, 1945-47; Amer Hotel Assn, 1945-47; mem, Gov Comm on Law Enforcement, 1950-60. NY State Guard, 1945-47. Prin contrib: projecting new reform in criminology and penology. Exec bd, Manhattan Beach J Cen, since 1959; exec comm, JNF, Kings Co council, since 1947; chmn: Manhattan Beach div, ARC, since 1955; natl Shelach, Rehab of Fighters for Freedom of Isr, 1952-55; Atlantic lodge, ADL, B'nai B'rith; public action, ZOA; Manhattan Beach div, AJCong; mem: Intl Platform Assn; Natl Dist Attys Assn; NY State Dist Attys Assn; Bklyn Bar Assn; Amer Correctional Assn; Natl Council of Crime and Delinquency. Author: First Offenders—A Second Chance, 1956. Home: 2 West End Ave, Brooklyn, NY. Office: Municipal Bldg, Brooklyn, NY.

NUSSBAUM, Louis I, US, accountant; b. NYC, Nov 30, 1908; s. Mendel and Anna (Engelman); BBA, CCNY, 1930; CPA, NY, 1934; MA, NYU, 1938; m. Rebecca Rubin, Dec 26, 1931; c: Sigmund, Rhoda Kreamer. Mem, Peat, Marwick, Mitchell & Co, CPAs, since 1955; partner, Allen & Co, CPAs, 1943-55. Pres: Bur of J Educ, 1947-48; Ia Soc of CPAs, 1952; ZOA, 1950-52; vice-pres, J Fed of Des Moines, 1954; chmn: All-In-One Drive, 1953; JWF, 1956-57; fmr, natl bd, JWF; adv bd, acctnt dept, Drake U, 1959-67; mem: B'nai B'rith; Tax Club of Des Moines; bd, Temple B'nai Jeshurun; Amer Inst Acctnts; Masons; Shriners; charter mem, fmr chmn, Des Moines Estate Planning Council; clubs: Standard, Des Moines, pres, 1953; Consistory. Recipient: award, U of Miami Tax Conf, 1961; Meritorious Award, NCCJ, 1963; Meritorious Service Award, Simpson Coll, 1968; Man of Year Award,

Des Moines B'nai B'rith, 1968. Home: 4033 River Oaks Dr, Des Moines, Ia. Office: 708 Hubbell Bldg, Des Moines, Ia.

NUSSBAUM, Max, US, rabbi, communal leader; b. Suczava, Aus, Apr 4, 1910; s. Joseph and Rachel (Bittkover); in US since 1940; att U Breslau, 1929-32; PhD, summa cum laude, U Wurzburg, 1933; ordained rabbi, Breslau Theol Sem, 1934; hon DD, HUC-JIR, 1959; hon DLitt, Dropsie Coll, 1961; m. Ruth Offenstadt, July 14, 1938; c: Hannah Marsh, Jeremy. Rabbi: Temple Isr of Hollywood, Cal, since 1942; Gt J Cong, Berlin, Ger, 1936-40; Beth Ahaba, Muskogee, Okla, 1940-42; dir, Hillel Council, State U of Okla, 1941-42. Pres: Bd of Rabbis, S Cal, 1969; ZOA, 1962-65; W Assn of Reform Rabbis, 1957; S Cal Assn of Lib Rabbis, 1954; chmn: Natl Exec Council, ZOA, 1958-62; Amer ZC, LA, 1949-56; natl vice-pres, AJCong, since 1958, hon pres, S Cal dist, since 1957; LA Coll of J Studies, since 1950; vice-chmn, Natl Rabb Council, Reform J App, UAHC-JIR, since 1959; hon chmn, Amer ZC, since 1967, chmn, 1964-67; chmn, Amer sect, WJC, 1964-68, hon chmn, Amer sect, 1968; mem: Zionist Actions Comm, since 1960; rabb adv council, UJA, since 1961; exec comm, CCAR, since 1961; natl council, JDC, since 1948; bd dirs, United Isr Appeal, repr LA J Comty Council, since 1954; bd govs, Bonds for Isr, since 1959; admn bd, Cal Sch, HUC-JIR, since 1957; regional bd, NCCJ, since 1958; Cal State Comm, Food for Peace Prog, since 1962; Zionist leader in Ger until 1938. Author: Yehuda Halevi's Philosophy of Nationalism, 1933; Kantianismus und Marxismus in der Sozialphilosophie Max Adlers, 1934; Nachman Krochmal, the Philosopher of Israel's Eternity, 1942-43; Eretz Yisrael, Galut and Chutz La'Aretz, in Their Historic Settings, 1952; Temple Israel Pulpit, 1957; contbr: Marriage and Family Life by Twayne, 1959; J publs. Hobbies: music, art. Home: 1757 N Gardner, Los Angeles, Cal. Study: 7300 Hollywood Blvd, Hollywood, Cal.

NUSSBAUM, Michael, Isr, business exec; b. Czortkow, Pol, Sep 11, 1909; s. Pinchas and Mathilda (Shperber); in Isr since 1929; m. Bertha Israeler; c: Gad. Mgn dir, Hassneh Ins Co, Isr, Ltd, since 1964; mr mgn dir, Agric Mutual Funds; chmn, bd: Am Oved Pub House; Devl Areas Industrialization Ltd; mem, bd dirs, Ind Devl Bank of Isr; Citadel Ins Co, NY; exec council, Histadrut. Brit Army; capt, IDF. Chmn: Isr Ins Assn; Reinsurance Corp; mem: council, World Vets Assn; Ins Devl Bur, Stockholm. Contbr to Isr press, econ publs. Home: 25 Gonen St, Givatayim, Isr. Office: 19 Rothschild Blvd, Tel Aviv, Isr.

NUSSBAUM, Perry E, US, rabbi; b. Toronto, Can, Feb 16, 1908; s. Eisig and Adela (Newman); in US since 1926; BHL, HUC, 1930, ordained rabbi, 1933, hon DHL, 1958; BA, U Cincinnati, 1931; MA, U Colo, 1938; att U of Ottawa, 1951-52; hon DD, Burton Coll, Colo, 1955; m. Arene Talpis, Oct 15, 1936; c: Leslie Rubinstein. Rabbi: Beth Isr Cong, Jackson, Miss, since 1954; Beth Isr Syn, Melbourne, Austr, 1933-34; Temple B'nai Isr, Amarillo, Tex, 1934-35; Temple Emanuel, Pueblo, Colo, 1935-41; Temple Emanu-El, Wichita, Kan, 1941-43; Temple Emanuel, Long Beach, NY, 1947-50; Temple Anshe Amunim, Pittsfield, Mass, 1950-54. Chaplain, US Army, WW II; US Army Ready Res, since 1946; col, AUS, ret, 1968. Delg, White House Conf on Children and Youth, 1960; fmr pres: SW region, CCAR; JWF, Jackson; found, Miss Assembly of J Congs; J Educ Assn of S New Eng; Miss ADL Comm; mem, chaplaincy comm, CCAR, fmr mem, exec bd; mem bd: AJComm; JDC; Miss Assn for Mh, fmr pres; Jackson Urban League; Star, Inc, OEO agcy; Gtr Jackson Clergy Alliance, found, vice-pres; Council of Churches, fmr vice-pres, Berkshire Co; ADL Regional Comm; mem: Natl Acad for Rel and Mh; Assn for J Chaplains; HUC-JIR Alumni Assn, fmr mem, exec bd; Mil Chaplains Assn; Amer Legion, dept chaplain, Miss; Miss Res Officers Assn, dept chaplain; Masons; Shriners, chaplain; clubs: Patio; Jackson. Author: Guide for Service to Jewish Soldiers, 1944; numerous articles. Home: 5025 Wayneland Dr, Jackson, Miss. Study: POB 12329, Jackson, Miss.

O

OAKES, John Bertram, US, journalist; b. Elkins Pk, Pa, Apr 30, 1913; s. George and Bertie (Gans); AB, Princeton U, 1934; AB, AM, Queen's Coll, Oxford U, Eng, 1936; m. Margery Hartman, Oct 24, 1945; c: Andranan, Alison, Cynthia, John. Ed, editorial page, NY Times, since 1961, fmr: mem, ed bd, 1949-61; ed, rev of the week, 1946-49; reporter: Trenton State Gazette; Trenton Times, NJ, 1936-37; reporter, spec feature writer, Wash Post, 1937-41. Maj, US Army, 1941-46; lt col, US Army Res. Mem, adv bd on natl parks, hist sites, bldgs and monuments, Dept of Interior, 1955-62. Author, The Edge of Freedom, 1961; contbr of articles on conservation of natural resources to NY Times. Recipient: spec study grant, Carnegie Corp, 1959; awards: Collegiate Sch, Honor, 1963; Columbia-Catherwood, journalism; Princeton U Class of 1934, outstanding achievement, 1964; George Polk Memorial, 1966; Thomas Jefferson, Unitarian Universalist Dist of NY, 1968. Hobbies: sailing, camping, conservation. Home: 1120 Fifth Ave, New York, NY. Office: 229 W 43 St, New York, NY.

OBADIA, Meyer, Fr, business exec; b. Fez, Morocco, Feb 2, 1913; s. Jacob and Zahra (Attias); licencié ès lettres; m. Reine Elbaz, Aug 29, 1939. Engaged in textile bus. Pres, Casablanca J Comty, since 1956; secy gen, JCC, Morocco, since 1962; rapporteur général de la Commission des Finances, député à la Chambre des Représentants du Royaume, 2e Circonscription, Casablanca, 1963-65. Home: 10 Ave Deroulède, Vincennes, Fr. Office: 3a Rue des Jeuneurs, Paris 2e, Fr.

OBERDORFER, Donald, US, business exec; b. Atlanta, Ga, Nov 25, 1901; s. Eugene and Daisy (Israel); BS, U Ga, 1921; m. Dorothy Bayersdorfer, June 22, 1927; c: Eugene, Donald. Pres, Oberdorfer Ins Agcy, since 1956, vice-pres, 1926-56. Hon natl chmn, Jt Defense Appeal, chmn, natl exec comm, chmn, natl council, 1946; mem, natl adv comm, AJComm, fmr mem, natl admn and exec comms; charter mem, Natl USO; chmn, disaster relief prog, Atlanta Metrop chap, ARC, gen chmn, Atlanta Campaign, 1953; fmr: hon natl chmn, ADL; natl vice-pres, JWB; chief natl council, Hai Resh, fmr pres, Atlanta chap; pres, southeastern region, CJFWF, fmr natl bd mem; treas, chmn, group work budget comm, Comty Chest; chmn, JWF; vice-pres, J Fed; pres, JCC; mem, bd Atlanta council, Boy Scouts of Amer, all of Atlanta, Ga; mem: B'nai B'rith; Phi Epsilon Pi; Heb Benevolent Cong; Masons, 32nd degree; Shriners; clubs: Standard, Town and Country, fmr pres; Progressive; Touchdown; Varsity Football G; Burns; Commerce; pres, Futures Inc, all of Atlanta. Home: 3722 Peachtree Rd, NE, Atlanta, Ga. Office: POB 954, Atlanta, Ga.

OBERLANDER, Marek, Fr, painter, journalist; b. Szczerzec, Russ, Sep 14, 1922; s. Jacob and Rachel (Schreiber); in Fr since 1963; PhD, Acad Fine Arts, Warsaw, 1954; m. Halina Pfeffer, May 10, 1969. One-man shows: Nowa Kultura, Warsaw, 1959; Gal Wspolczesnosc, Warsaw, 1960; Cbwa, Wroclaw, 1961; Zakopane, 1962; Svea Gal, Stockholm, 1963; Gal Le Soleil dans la Tête, Paris, 1964; Gal La Veille Échope, St Paul de Vence, Fr, 1965; Svea Gal, Stockholm, 1965; Gal 6, Berlin, 1967; collective exhbs: Pol; Den; Russ; Czech; Amsterdam; Stockholm; Copenhagen; USA; Can; China; India, all 1954-64; perm collections: Natl Mus: Warsaw; Stockholm; J Mus, Warsaw; Revolutionary Mus, Warsaw; Modern Art Mus, Stockholm; Torun Mus, Pol; Mus Zielona Gora, Pol; City Mus, Lublin; Abf-Huset collection, Stockholm; Svenska Handelsbanken collection, Stockholm; pvt collections: Isr; US; Russ; Fr; Sweden; Ger; Finland; Netherlands; Switz; Brazil; Czech; contbr to arts newspapers. Pvt, Red Army, 1941-46. Recipient: Po Prostu Award, 1955. Home: 140 Cyrille Besset Ave, Nice, Fr.

OBERMAN, Morris D, US, business exec, publisher; b. Springfield, Ill, Mar 3, 1914; s. Harry and Ida Guralnik; att St Louis Coll of Pharm, 1931-33; m. Bobbye Friedman, Oct 8, 1939; c: Michael, Martin, William, Marjorie. Ed, publisher, Scrap Age Mag, since 1944; pres: Emde Realty Corp; Execs, Inc; N

Shore Inves; exec-secy, Midwest Scrap Dealers Assn; past exec dir, City of Springfield Area Devl and Tourism Comm. Pres: local B'nai B'rith, 1945-58; Ill Assn of J Cens, 1935-40; chmn, Temple Isr Bldg Comm, Isr Bond Drive; bd dirs, Jr C of C, 1941-49; mem: Addas Isr Cong, Wash, DC; ed, Cong Publs, N Suburban Syn Beth El, Highland Park, Ill. Home: 857 Stonegate Dr, Highland Park, Ill. Office: 403 Jefferson St, Springfield, Ill.

OBERMAYER, Arthur S, US, chemical exec; b. Phila, Pa, July 17, 1931; s. Leon and Julia (Sinsheimer); BA, hons, Swarthmore Coll, 1952; PhD, MIT, 1956; m. Judith Hirschfield, June 23, 1963; c: Henry, Joel. Pres, Moleculon Research Corp, since 1960; project leader, Tralerlab Inc, 1956-59; mgr, phys sci div, Allied Research Asso Inc, 1959-61. Prin contribs: research and radiation measurement and processing of polymers, use of organic materials for advance applications in physics and elecs. Chmn of bd, Research Mgmt Assn; exec council, Amer J Hist Soc; mem: Newton Dem Ward Comm; Amer Chem Soc; Amer Phys Soc; Soc Plastics Engrs; Amer Mgmt Assn; Soc of Sigma Xi; clubs: MIT Fac; Chem. Hobby: collecting sci books of hist interest. Home: 239 Chestnut St, W Newton, Mass. Office: 139 Main St, Cambridge, Mass.

OBERMAYER, Leon Jacob, US, attorney, civic worker; b. Sciota, Ill, Sept 24, 1886; s. Hermann and Veronika (Lehman); LLB, U Pa, 1908; DHL, HUC-JIR, 1954; LLD, Temple U, 1956; m. Julia Sinsheimer, 1923; c: Herman, Helen Sellers, Arthur. Sr mem, law firm, Obermayer, Rebmann, Maxwell & Hippel, Phila; mem, law firm, Edmonds, Obermayer & Rebmann, 1909-1959. F, Brandeis U, 1968; pres: Phila Bd Pub Educ, 1955-61; Law Alumni, U of Pa, 1957-60; Alumni Assn, Cen High Sch, Phila, 1954-60; YM-YWHA, Phila, 1915-26; chmn: bd govs, Phila Bar Assn, 1938-49; comm on prof guidance, Phila Bar Assn, 1938-59; bd, Woods Schs for Exceptional Children, Langhorne, Pa; comm on legal ethics and grievances, Phila Bar Assn; Natl Vocational Service Commn of B'nai B'rith, 1938-57; vice-chmn, HUC-JIR, Cincinnati, O; AHA; vice-pres: Amers for the Competitive Enterprise System; Pa Bar Assn, 1940; mem: exec comm, natl council of JWB; bd, Acad Natural Sci; World Affairs Council, Phila; natl comm on employment of youth, Natl Child Lab Comm; Heb Sunday Sch Soc; Lucien Moss Home; Rodeph Shalom Syn; J Hosp, 1917-55; United Fund, all Phila; US Natl Commn for UNESCO, 1953-60; City Housing Rent Commn; Fed Adv Rent Commn; Gratz Coll; Amer Bar Assn; Amer Law Inst; B'nai B'rith; Masons; Phi Epsilon Pi; solicitor: Phila Council, Boy Scouts of Amer, since 1944; Amer J Hist Soc, pres, 1964-67; clubs: Locust; Lawyers, life; Union League; Peale; Sunday Breakfast; Midday; Constitutional; Philmont Country; Socialegal. Recipient: Silver Beaver Award, 1941 and spec services medal, 1948, from Boy Scouts of Amer; Award of Merit, U of Pa, 1962. Home: 135 S 19 St, Philadelphia, Pa. Office: 1418 Packard Bldg, Philadelphia, Pa.

OBERNAUER, Harold, US, attorney; b. Pittsburgh, Pa, Jan 3, 1887; s. Herman and Bertha (Dinch); BA, hons, Yale U, 1910; LLB, U of Pittsburgh Law Sch, 1913. Pvt practice since 1913; spec counsel for Mercantile Appraisers, 1920-21; chmn, appeal bd, Selective Service Sys, W Fed Dist of Pa, 1940-67; chmn, Legal Adv Bd, Selective Service, WW I, Appeal Bd-1940-67. Pres: U of Pittsburgh Alumni Assn, 1935-36; Allegheny Co Bar Assn, 1938-40; pres em, U Pittsburgh Law Sch Alumni Assn, 1969, bd govs, 1940-42, 1961-65; chmn: Comm on PR, Allegheny Co Bar Assn, 1936-37, 1940-44, comm on the judiciary, 1945; Comm on PR: Amer Bar Assn, 1937-40, Pa Bar Assn, 1936-44, 1945-46; vice-chmn, Bd of Law Examiners of Allegheny Co, 1942, mem, 1935-43; trustee: Irene Kaufman Settlement, 1942-1959; Bellefield Found, 1948-53; mem: exec comm, Pittsburgh charter plan; Pittsburgh Defense Council; bd govs, Masons, dist dep grand master. 1926-50; trustee, Bellefield Lodge, since 1922; Elks; KP; Odd Fellows; Omicron Delta Kappa; Pi Lambda Phi; Acacia; Intercultural Council of Pittsburgh, 1947-60; dir: FJP, 1933-

36; Heb Free Loan Assn, 1934-37; YM-YWHA, 1929-35, 1939-42; clubs: Pittsburgh Athletic Assn; Yale, Pittsburgh; Pa Soc, NY. Home: 906 Arlington Apts, Pittsburgh, Pa. Office: 701 Arlington Apts, Pittsburgh, Pa.

OBOLER, Eli M, US, librarian; b. Chgo, Ill, Sep 26, 1915; s. Leo and Clara (Obeler); BA, U Chgo, 1941; BA, libr service, Columbia U, 1942; m. Marcia Wolf, Dec 28, 1938; c: Leon, Carol. U Libr, Idaho State U, since 1964; commentator, Books and You, Pocatello Radio Sta, since 1949; reviewer: Libr Jour, since 1953; Intermountain Observer, since 1967; asst chief, lend lease expediting unit, War Production Bd, Wash, DC, 1942-43; head, reserved book room, U Chgo, 1946-49, libr, U Coll Libr, 1947-49, lectr, Gt Books Prog, 1948-49; bibliographical cons, Great Books Found, 1947-49; libr, Idaho State Coll, 1949-63; columnist, Idaho State Jour, 1960-65. US Army, 1943-46. Prin contribs: planned new libr bldg, Idaho State U, 1953-54; org, Libr Periodicals Round Table Amer Libr Assn, 1952-53. Chmn: Adv Comm on Research and Training Projects, US Off of Educ, 1968-69; libr educ comm, Idaho Libr Assn, 1960-67; Libr Periodicals Round Table, 1953-54; coll sect, Assn of Coll and Research Librs; pres: Pocatello Chap, B'nai B'rith, 1951-53; Idaho State Libr Assn, 1950-53; Pacific NW Libr Assn, 1955-56; dir, Temple Emanuel Sunday Sch, 1952; councilor representing Idaho, Amer Libr Assn, 1954-59; mem: Intellectual Freedom Comm, ALA, 1965-71; AAUP. Ed, co-compiler, Coll and U Libr Accreditation Standards, 1957-58; ed: Pacific NW Libr Assn Quarterly, 1958-67; Libr Periodicals Round Table Newsletter, 1961-62; mem, ed bd, Coll and Research Librs, 1962-63; contbr to scholarly jours. Recipient: good conduct medal, 1945; Amer Libr Assn Periodical Award, 1964. Hobby: philately. Home: 1397 Jane St, Pocatello, Idaho. Office: Idaho State U Libr, Pocatello, Idaho.

OBST, Joseph J, US, dentist; b. Bklyn, NY, Dec 2, 1904; s. George and Augusta (Weill); DDS, NYU, 1929, BS, 1938, MA, 1940; m. Pearl Newmark, 1936; c: George, Norman. Pvt practice since 1929; examiner, NY State Bd of Dent Examiners, since 1967; dir dent, chief of endodontics, Kingsbrook J Med Con, since 1952; chmn, dent educ comm, Adv Bd for Vocational and Ext Educ, Bd Educ, NYC, since 1959; cons, endodontics: Dent Info Bur, NY, since 1960; NYC Medicaid Prog, since 1967; Oral Health Comm of Gtr NY, since 1959; 2nd Dist Dent Soc, State of NY, 1952-64. Dipl, Amer Bd Endodontics; f: AAAS; Amer Public Health Assn; Amer Coll Dent; LI Acad Odontology; Amer Assn Endodontists; NY Acad Dent; chmn: Tri-State Soc Endodontics, 1963-65; Amer Assn Endodontists; Council on Publs, NY State Dent Jour, 1952-56; publ comm, Bull of NY State Soc Dent for Children, 1950-65; comm on pub and profsl relations, NY State Dent Soc Anesthesiology, since 1960; Oral Health Comm of Gtr NY, 1948; Dent Comms: ARC, 1951; NY Chap, Amer Cancer Soc, 1950; United Hosp Fund, 1961; Isr Bond Dr, 1963-66; Boy Scouts, Amer, 1940; pres: NY State Soc of Dent for Children, 1949; 2nd Dist Dent Soc, State of NY, 1951; Metrop Conf, Hosp Dent Chiefs, 1958; Dent Guidance Council of United Cerebral Palsy, 1958; LI Acad of Odontology, 1962-64; bd dirs: Comm to Protect Children's Teeth, 1953-61; Coll of Dent Alumni Assn, NYU, 1948-60; Amer Mus of Health, 1949-52; Bklyn Philharmonic Orch, since 1956; bd govs, Isaac Albert Research Inst, 1957-64; bd sups, Inst of Continuing Dent Educ, Dent Soc of State of NY, 1957; mem: Amer Dent Assn, since 1929; Dent Soc State of NY, since 1929; comm educ, NY State Assn of the Professions, 1964; Amer Soc Dent for Children, since 1943; Amer Assn of Hosp Dent Chiefs, since 1963; dent adv comm, NYC Dept of Health, 1958-61; Dent Adv Bd, ILA Health Cen, 1961-64, 1966-67; Dent Adv Bd, A Holly Patterson Home for the Aged, since 1965; Dent Adv Bd, Local 1205 Health Cen, since 1962; dent hygiene adv comm, NYC Comty Coll, since 1966; Natl Panel, Arbitrators, Amer Arbitration Assn, since 1963; NY State Assn for Health, Phys Educ and Recreation Inc, 1963-65; Omicron Kappa Upsilon, since 1929; Kappa Delta Pi; Phi Delta Kappa; hon mem, Police Benevolent Assn, NY State Police, since 1952; delg: Bklyn Health Cen, 1945-55; Health Council Div, Bklyn Council for Soc Planning, 1942-48; Bklyn Civic Council, 1944-49; Wfr and Health Council, NYC, 1952-56; official judge, Amer Inst's Sch Sci Fair, Bklyn, 1964, 1966. Ed: jour, 2nd Dist Dent Soc, State of NY, 1940-46. Recipient: Chevalier Officier, Du Sacre Imperial Ordre Constantine Nemagnique de St Etienne, 1952; UJA Scroll for Comty Service, 1953; testimonial dinner, Isr Bonds, 1963. Home: 798 E 34 St, Brooklyn, NY. Office: 1 Hanson Place, Brooklyn, NY.

OCH, Bernard, Isr, educator; b. NYC, Aug 23, 1933; s. Abraham and Anna (Verona); in Isr since 1962; BA, Harvard U, 1954; BJEduc, Heb Coll, Boston, 1954; ordained rabbi, MHL, J Sem, 1960; MPA, NYU, 1958; m. Miriam Halkin, June 16, 1957; c: Adina, Eitan, Sharon. Dir, Hillel Org: Haifa Technion; Haifa U Coll, since 1963. Home and study: 4 Downes, Haifa, Isr.

OCHSHORN, Ariel, Isr, physician; b. Tel Aviv, Jan 3, 1938; s. Zvi and Rivka (Paletz); MD, Heb U Med Sch, Jerusalem; postgrad studies, in obstet and gyn, U Med Sch, Tel Aviv. Chief phys, lectr, obstet and gyn, Munic Govt Med Cen, Tel Aviv U Med Sch; lectr, obstet and gyn, Munic Govt Sch for Midwifery and Nursing; owner and dir: Universal Drug Co; numerous real estate firms; plantations. Fmr, news ed, UPI, Tel Aviv. Prin contrib: found and devl real estate and plantations in newly-developed areas. Served, IDF MC. Mem: B'nai B'rith; Obstet and Gyn Soc; Fertility and Sterility Research Assn. Author: Human Genetics; contbr of numerous articles to profsl jours. Hobbies: coin collecting, photography, sports. Home: 4 Biltmore St, Tel Aviv, Isr.

ODESS, Bluma, Isr, artist; b. Lith; d. Shalom and Gitta (Sacs); in Isr since 1935; att Bezalel Art Sch, Jerusalem; studied, Fr, Eng, It; m. Itzhack Ronkin; c: Emanuel, Anat. One-man shows in: Tel Aviv; Jerusalem; participated in group shows: Monaco; Fr; Switz; US. Mem: Kibbutz Kfar Masaryk; Artists Assn of Isr. Recipient: Struck Prize, Haifa Munic, 1955. Home: 27a Brodetzky St, Ramat Aviv, Isr.

OESTREICH, Mitchell, US, physician; b. NYC, Mar 26, 1910; s. Hyman and Esther (Miklowitz); BS, NYU, 1930; MD, U Vienna, 1935; m. Edith Liebling, Aug 18, 1935; c: Alan, Janet. Pvt practice, radiology, since 1945; att radiologist: Meyer Memorial Hosp. since 1948; US Vets Hosp, since 1950; St Francis Hosp, since 1959; clinical asst prof, radiology, U Buffalo Med Sch, since 1957, all Buffalo, NY. Lt col, US Army MC, 1941-46. Dipl, Amer Bd of Radiology; past pres, Maimonides Med Soc; mem: AMA; Radiological Socs N Amer, NY State and Buffalo; Amer Coll of Radiology; NY State and Erie Co Med Soc; Buffalo Acad of Med; Phi Lambda Kappa; Temple Beth Zion, Buffalo, fmr: mem, bd of trustees, chmn, sch bd; B'nai B'rith; JWV; Buffalo Chamber Music Soc; club, Buffalo Alumni, past pres. Co-trans: Roentgen Diagnostics, by Schinz, Baensch, Friedl and Uehlinger, 1953. Hobbies: photography, piano. Home: 82 Marjann Terr, Buffalo, NY. Office: 666 Colvin Ave, Buffalo, NY.

OFEK, Uriel, Isr, author; b. Tel Aviv, June 30, 1926; s. Arie and Bronia (Vogel) Popik; MA, Heb U, Jerusalem, 1951; att U Toronto, Ont, 1959-60; m. Bina Dellman, Apr 3, 1952; c: Atara, Amira. Co-ed, Davar leYeladim, since 1951; lectr, children's lit, since 1962; libr, Toronto Pub Libr, 1961-62. Sgt, Palmach Har'el, 1944-49; IDF, Sinai Campaign. Author: Maoz Etzion, 1949; beSod Yeladim, 1954; From Robinson to Lobengulu, 1963; From Cinderella to Emil, 1967; From Tarzan to Hassamba, 1969; Yaldei haOlam Sharim, 2 vols, 1963, 1968; Kochavim baGvul, 1963; Tzeadim baChol, 1966; haHatzaga Haievet leHimashech, 1967; Hey, Habbitu Lemaala, 1968; trans, children's books and poems by: G MacDonald; Mulock; O Butterworth; L Tetzner; G Brandon; Mark Twain; T Jansson; Charles Dickens; B Harte; ed: anthols: Best East Indian Stories; Israeli War Stories; Heb Children's Poems; The Dog That Flew, Eng. Councillor: Heb Writers Org; Isr Press. Hobby: collecting early children's books. Recipient: Lamdan Prize, Ramat Gan Munic, 1965; 3rd Prize, Song Festival, 1965. Home: 18 Haeshel St, Herzliya, Isr. Office: 45 Shenkin St, Tel Aviv, Isr.

OFER, Abraham, Isr, business exec; b. Pol, 1922; in Isr since 1933. Dep mayor, Tel Aviv-Yaffo Munic, since 1965; dir gen, Shikun Ovdim Ltd, since 1967; chmn, mgmt, Bank Mashkantaot leShikun, since 1969; co-found, mem, Kibbutz Hamadiya, 1941-47; co found, mgr, Poultry Council, 1958-1960; dep dir gen, Min of Agric, 1960-63, chmn: poultry council, vegetable council, agric export corp; dir gen, Ashdod Co, 1964; mem, Ashdod Town Council, 1965. Lt col, Isr Navy, War of Independence; head, manpower dept, 1st cdr, Navy base, Eilat. Co-found, Tnua haMeuhedet, 1945; natl secy, Mapai, 1945-47; co-found, dir, young circle, Mapai Party, 1950-65; secy, Tel Aviv dist, 1952-53. Home: 9 Hamishmar Haezrahi St, Afeka, Isr.

OFER, Shimon, Isr, physicist, educator; b. Jerusalem, Isr, Oct 18, 1927; s. Jacob and Sarah (Yaffe) Friedman; MSc, Heb U, Jerusalem, 1954, PhD, 1957; m. Mira Zvitov, 1952; c: Dov,

Shai. Dean, fac, math and scis, Heb U, since 1969; prof physics, since 1968; chmn, physics dept, 1966-69. Capt, IDF, 1949. Contbr to profsl jours. Home: 36 Hapalmach St, Jerusalem, Isr. Office: Heb U, Jerusalem, Isr.

OFFENBACHER, Elmer L, US, physicist, educator; b. Frankfurt/Main, Ger, Sep 29, 1923; s. Emile and Beatrice (Bondi); BA, Bklyn Coll, 1943; MS, U of Pa, 1949, PhD, 1951; m. Esther Gladstone, June, 1952; c: Nathan, Beatrice, Joseph. Prof, physics, Temple U, dir physics insts, 1959-62, dir, middle Atlantic phys sci symposia, 1960-61; visiting prof, Heb U, Jerusalem, 1962. USN, 1944-46. Pres: J Orthodox Soc, Gtr Phila; Phila chap, Assn Orthodox J Scis, natl pres, 1960-62; dir, Union Orthodox J Congs of US and Can; mem: Amer Phys Soc; Amer Assn Physics Tchrs; AAUP. Home: 44 Oakland Terr, Bala Cynwyd, Pa. Office: Temple U, Philadelphia, Pa.

OFRY, Dan, Isr, journalist; b. Budapest, Hung, Nov 20, 1929; s. Zoltán and Ilona (Hermann) Herskovits; in Isr since 1949; BSc, Heb U, Jerusalem, 1960; m. Veronica Feiler, Mar 31, 1963; c: Shay. Sr news and political commentator, Uj Kelet, Hung lang daily newspaper, Tel Aviv, since 1952, political and parliamentary corresp, 1952-61, spec fgn corresp, UN, NYC: Jerusalem corresp: Yediot Ahronot, 1956-57; Isr Bc Service, 1958-61, chief ed, Hung News Broadcasts, 1955-61. Lt, IDF. Natl delg, Assn of Isr Journalists; mem: Assn of Isr Journalists; Bnai Herzl. Author: Israel's Victorious Six Days, 1967, 1968; Twenty Years of Israel, 1968. Recipient: decoration, IDF, Sinai Campaign, 1956; Herzl Journalistic Prize, Bnai Herzl Assn, 1968. Home: 113 Yehuda Hamakabi St, Tel Aviv, Isr. Office: 52 Harakevet St, Tel Aviv, Isr.

OHANA, Jacques, Eng, business exec; b. Casablanca, Morocco, Sep 5, 1899; in Eng since 1942; s. Simon and Mazaltob (Bengio); Dipl, U of Neuchatel, Switz, 1918; att Independent U, Paris, 1918-21; m. Eugenie Pines, Apr 28, 1943. Owner, Ohana Gal, since 1945; dir, Jacques Ohana Ltd, since 1945; partner, dir, Ohana and De Cordova, NY, 1922-34; owner, Ohana Gal, Paris, 1934-39. Served, WW II. Chmn: Friends of Sephardi and other J Refugees; World Sephardi Fed, London; Mahamad, Span and Port Syn, 1965-68. Home: 9 S Bolton Gardens, London SW5, Eng. Office: 13 Carlos Pl, London W1, Eng.

OHEL, Mila Yerahmiel, Isr, author, editor; b. Vilna, Pol, March 24, 1925; s. Jacob and Chaya (Rapport); in Israel since 1935; tchr's cert, Sem Givat Hashlosha, 1951; BA, Heb U, 1956; m. Tamar Davidson, April 8, 1948; c: Eyal, Nivi, Yochay. Ed staff, Maariv newspaper, since 1964; mem, Kibbutz Hasolelim, 1946-50; asst PR off, Min of Lab, 1953-62; PR off, Mekorot Water Co, 1962-64. Sgt maj, Isr Navy, 1948-49. Mem, Isr Journalists Assn; Isr Writers Assn. Author: Hakshivu-na vaAsaper, 1951; Gesher, 1954; haMginim haZirim, 1955; Havurat haEglonim, 1958; Ish Nidham, 1960; Hut haSara, 1965; haFarfarey Minneret haLitany, 1967; Mahlaka Betzanov, 1967; Ya-Wa Oleh leOlah, 1968; contbr to newspapers and mags. Recipient: all medals of Haganah and IDF; Ussishkin Prize, JNF, 1956; ACUM Prize, 1960; Davar Daily Prize, 1957. Office: 2 Carlebach St, Tel Aviv, Isr. Home: 19 Baron Hirsch St, Rishon LeZion, Isr.

OKIN, Louis, US, attorney, public official; b. Oshipowitz, Russ, Aug 25, 1912; s. Benjamin and Zira (Dubrof); in US since 1913; BS, NYU, 1932, JD, 1936; m. Anne Rick, Sep 13, 1940; c: Steven, Elizabeth. Atty since 1936; partner, law firm: Eiber, Okin and Rafsky, since 1964; Fisher, Okin, Gleiberman & Ezrine, since 1961; Sohn & Okin, 1949-61; mem, City Council, NYC, 1957-61, dist leader, Dem Party, NY Co, 1957-61; tax commnr, City of NY, 1961-64. Mem, Kappa Nu. Home: 75 Central Park W, New York, NY. Office: 350 Fifth Ave, New York, NY.

OKO, Dorothy K, US, librarian; b. Cincinnati, O, July 22, 1896; d. Simon and Setty (Swarts) Kuhn; BA, Radcliffe Coll, 1918; BS, Columbia U Libr Sch, 1947; MA, New Sch for Social Research, NY, 1955; m. Adolph Oko, July 28, 1933 (decd); c: Joe Minster, Louise Mullin, Benjamin. Cons, lab education; exec dir, Ind Health Conservancy Labs, Cincinnati, 1921-31; lab educ specialist, NY Public Libr, 1948-61. Mem, bd of govs, Amer Assn for J Educ; asso mem, New Sch for Social Research; mem: Amer and NY Libr Assns; Adult Educ Assn; Amer Fed of Tchrs. Home and office: 545 W 111 St, New York, NY.

OLAN, Levi A, US, rabbi; b. Kiev, Russ, Mar 22, 1903; s. Max and Bessie (Leshtchinsky); in US since 1906; att U Rochester, 1921-23; BA, U Cincinnati, 1926; ordained rabbi, HUC, 1929, hon DD, 1955; hon DHL: S Methodist U; Austin Coll; m. Sarita Messer, June 9, 1931; c: Elizabeth Hirsch, Frances, David. Rabbi, Temple Emanuel, Dallas, Tex, since 1949; visiting prof, Perkins Sch of Theol, Dallas, since 1952; participant, Sun morning radio sermon, sta WFAA, Dallas; rabbi, Temple Emanuel, Worcester, Mass, 1929-49. Mem: exec bd, circle ten council, Boy Scouts of Amer, since 1951; bd, JWF, Dallas, since 1949; HUC, LA br; Tex Phil Soc; Tex chap of Natl Rehab; Dallas Sym Orch; Dallas Council on World Affairs; Area Educ TV Found; bd dirs: Dallas Civic Music Assn; Dallas Co Assn for Blind, 1952; adv council, Dallas Citizens Inter-racial Assn Inc; pres, CCAR, 1967-69; vicepres, Dallas Co Campfire Council, 1951; secy, Tex Soc for Mh, 1953; chmn publs comm, Alumni for HUC, 1950. Author: monographs: The Philosophy of Liberal Judaism, 1942; Rethinking the Liberal Religion, 1948; On the Nature of Man, 1949; Judaism and Modern Theology, 1955; Reinhold Niebuhr and the Hebraic Spirit, 1956; Judaism and Immortality. Home: 3131 Maple Ave, Dallas, Tex. Study: 8500 Hillcrest, Dallas, Tex.

OLER, Abraham N, US, rabbi; b. Warsaw, Pol ,Oct 19, 1911; s. Isaiah and Esther (Landau); in US since 1948; att Yeshivas, Pol; ordained rabbi, Pol; att: Us London; Durham; m. Ann Borenstein; c: Leah, Ruth, Charles, Norman, David. Rabbi, sch prin, Temple Beth Tefilah since 1963; rabbi: Sunderland, Eng, 1946; St John, NB, Can, 1946-48; Stapleton, Staten I, NY, 1953-56; New Flatlands J Cen, Bklyn, 1956-59; Cong Zera Kodesh, Norwalk, Conn, 1959-63. Pres, Educs Council, 1966-68; hon, pres, Mizrachi, Norwalk, Conn, 1960-63; bd mem: Yeshiva; J Fed; J Cen, all Hartford; Freemasons; B'nai B'rith. Home: 11a Rector St, East Hartford, Conn.

OLINS, Harry, US, attorney, educator; b. Boston, Mass, Nov 16, 1904; s. Abraham and Anna (Cohen) Olitzky; BA, cum laude, Harvard U, 1926, JD, 1929; m. Janice Porosky, Dec 3, 1933; c: Andrew, Robert, Nancy. Atty since 1929; mem fac, cons, Law Dept, U Coll, Northeastern U. Dir, J Comty Housing for Elderly, Inc; fmr pres: NE Council, Union of Amer Heb Congs; Brookline-Brighton-Newton J Comty Cen; pres and hon life trustee, Temple Ohabei Shalom; hon life trustee, Combined J Philanthropies, Gtr Boston; hon mem, Northeastern U Alumni Assn; mem: Brookline Town Meeting; Rep Town Comm, Brookline; Northeastern U Corp; fmr mem: Mass Bd of Educ Assistance; Adv Comm to Atty Gen on Public Charities; Brookline Adv Comm; fmr counsel quartermaster, Price Adjustment Bd; club, Harvard, Boston. Home: 333 Clark Rd, Brookline, Mass. Office: 79 Milk St, Boston, Mass.

OLITSKY, Mates, US, author, educator; b. Trisk, Pol, Nov 10, 1915; s. Nachman and Rejza (Mospanis); in US since 1949; att U Warsaw, 1934-37; m. Sonia Geller, 1946; c: Morris, Esther. Author: In Fremden Land, 1948; Freiliche Teg, 1962; Lieder Zu A Bruder. 1964; Gekliebene Lieder, 1967, all poetry; co-ed, Kinder-Zeitung. Secy, Tchrs Union; club exec comm, NY PEN. Recipient: Kessel Award for Lit, Mex, 1962; PEN Club Poetry Award, 1969. Home: 5240 Broadway, New York, NY. Office: Workmens Circle, 175 E Broadway, New York, NY.

OLITZKI, Arieh L, Isr, bacteriologist, educator; b. Allenstein, Ger, June 4, 1898; s. Mordecai Marcus; in Isr since 1924; att U Berlin; PhD, U Breslau, 1921; m. Zahava Bitan (decd); c: Tamar Naboth, Yael Pahter. Prof em; prof bact, head dept, Heb U-Hadassah Med Sch, Jerusalem, 1950-68, dean, fac med, since 1961, on fac since 1928; asst instr hygiene, U Breslau, Ger, 1921-23; gen lab, Hadassah Hosp, Safed, 1926-28; dir, serological research lab, Hadassah Hosp, Jerusalem, 1929-32; visiting sci, NIH, Bethesda, Md, 1950-51; research work: U Cal, Berkeley, 1958; Istituto Superiore di Sanità, Rome, It, 1959; visiting lectr, Pol Acad of Sci, 1958, 1962; visiting sci: Natl J Hosp for Respiratory Diseases, Denver, Colo, 1966-67; Inst of Microbiol, Rutgers State U. F: Royal Soc for Tropical Med, London; Biometric Soc; Royal Soc, Med, London; Soc for Experimental Biol and Med, NY; Amer Soc for Microbiol; chmn, Isr Microbiol Assn; mem ed bd: Excerpta Medica, Amsterdam; Pathologia et Mikrobiologia, Basel; contbr to local and fgn med jours. Home: 1 Kikar Magnes, Jerusalem, Isr. Office: Heb U-Hadassah Med Sch, Jerusalem, Isr.

OLITZKI, Leib, Isr, author; b. Trisk, Pol, 1897; att Yeshivot, Pol. Ed in chief, Yidishe Shriften; 2nd ed in chief, editor,

Dish Buch; with Yad Veshem Memorial; fmr, tchr: Bible, Yiddish, J hist. Author: In En Akupirt Shtetl, 1924; Meshalim Far Kinder Un Grois, 1929; Main Hartz-Raize; Dodya Hanapach; Yeshiva-Lait; Fun Galdenhem Krug; Tzum Zun In Zahal; trans: Hazaz, by N Sokolov; trans of Russ, Pol, Heb poetry. Fmr mem, Writers Org, Warsaw. Home: 39 Hama'avak St, Givatayim, Isr.

OLOF, Theo, Netherlands, violinist; b. Ger, May 5, 1924; s. Heinz and Elvira (Schmuckler) Wolffberg; in Netherlands since 1933; studied with Oskar Back. Concert violinist, leader, Residentie Orch of The Hague; concert tours: Eur, W Indies, US, Isr, Russ, since 1946. Home: Weteringstr 16, Amsterdam, Netherlands.

OLSHAN, Itzhak, Isr, jurist; b. Kovno, Lith, Feb 19, 1895; s. Asher and Libba (Levin) Olshansky; in Isr since 1912; BA, LLB, London U; MSS, LSE; m. Sima Amiel, 1940; c: Yoram. Ret; pres, Supr Court of Isr, 1953-65; Justice, Supr Court, 1948-53; pvt practice, Jerusalem, 1927-48; secy, Poalei Zion, Gt Brit, 1924-27; liaison off, Histadrut and Brit Lab Party, London, 1923-27. Pal, J Legion, British Army, 1918-21; co-found, mem, Hagana, 1922, cdr, Tel Aviv-Jaffa dist, 1921-23. Hon pres, Isr Press Council, since 1965; chmn, exec, Sharet Inst Oncology, Jerusalem, since 1967. Author, The Rule of Law in a Democratic System and Problems of Education in Israel; co-trans, Lessons of October, by L Trotzky, 1927; contbr to newspapers. Home: 8 Alfasi St, Jerusalem, Isr. Office: Supr Court, Jerusalem, Isr.

OLSHANSKY, Charles, US, organization exec; b. NYC, Jan 3, 1913; s. Joseph and Mary (Weinman); BS, Columbia U, 1937, MA, 1938; att NY Sch of Social Work, 1945-46; m. Belle Rothblatt, Mar 8, 1940; c: Kenneth, Norman, Edward. Exec dir, JCC and J Comty Cen, Newport News, Va, since 1947; dir: activities, Grand St Settlement, NYC, 1935-41; USO and JWB, Newport News, 1941-44; USO and JWB, Puerto Rico, 1944-45; JCC and Cen, Port Chester, NY, 1945-46. Pres: Newport News Mental Hygiene Clinic, 1963; Newport News Conf of Soc Work, 1942-43; Va Peninsula Assn of Soc Workers, 1944; chmn, comm on aging, Va Conf of Soc Work; vice-pres, Middle Atlantic Sect, Natl Assn of J Cen Workers, 1951; mem: bd dirs, Newport News Girls Club; bd, Newport News Mental Hygiene Clinic and Cancer Soc; Temple Rodef Shalom; ZOA; B'nai B'rith; Grand St Settlement Alumni; Phi Epsilon Kappa; clubs: Rotary, Torch, vice-pres, 1962. Author: Manual for Playground Directors, 1939; Inegration of Military Into Community, JWB Program Aids, 1949. Recipient: Emblem, War Dept, Civilian Service, 1947; Grand St Settlement Alumni Award, 1959. Hobby: sports. Home: 165 Yeardley Dr, Newport News, Va. Office: 2700 Spring Rd, Newport News, Va.

OMANSKY, Morris, US, chemist; b. Kiev, Russ, Dec 24, 1889; s. Robert and Bessie (Raiman); BS, MIT, 1911; m. Ricca Wies, July 10, 1917; c: Samuel, Freida Cohen. Cons chem and rubber tech, since 1921; chem, Boston Woven Hose and Rubber Co, 1911-17; chief chem: Plymouth Rubber, 1917-20, 1922-24; Needham Tire, 1920-22; expert in ind controversies and litigations for Justice Dept, customs div, 1950; lectr, prof, rubber chem and tech: Northeastern U; Mass U, 1938-46. F, AAAS; holder of numerous patents; mem: Amer Chem Soc; Amer Inst Chem Engrs; J Vocational Service, Boston; Amer Mus of Natural Hist; clubs: Boston Stein; Technion. Home: 9 Babcock St, Brookline, Mass.

OMER, Binyamin, Isr, musician; b. Warsaw, Pol, Dec 30, 1902; s. Zvi and Hana (Kalvary) Kotowicz; in Isr since 1920; 3rd class deg, Music Tchrs Acad, Jerusalem, 1944; att Trinity Coll of Music, London; studied with pvt tchrs, Isr; m. Shulamith Feldhorn, 1924; c: Hillel, Shlomo. Ret; music tchr, Mishmar Haemek, 1931-68; mgr, music educ, kibbutz movement, 1958-61. Spec constable, WW II. Composer: Shirim leFeutot; Kochav Katan; haMusica biTkufat haBarok. Contbr: song booklets; transl and adaptations of folk songs. Recipient: Award for song, Zichru Oti, 1949. Home: Kibbutz Mishmar Haemek, Isr.

OMER, Hillel, Isr, landscape architect, poet; b. Mishmar haEmek, Isr, Aug 4, 1926; s. Benjamin and Shulamit (Feldhorn); Arch, Ecole Nationale d'Horticulture, Fr, 1953; m. Zipora Levman, June 11, 1952; c: Tal, Noa. Pvt practice since 1962; landscape dir, Heb U, gardens, 1954-56; dir, gardening dept, Jerusalem Munic, 1956-60; landscape architect, Amidar Co, 1960-62. Palmach, 1948-50. Author: Eretz haTzohoraim, 1950, 5 eds; Nishra, 1960; Tarof Toraf, 1964; poetry, stories

for children: Boker Tov, 1956; Hutzla'aretz, Hutzla'aretz, 1960; Dodi Simha, 1965; Harpatka baKibbutz, 1966; Bilbul Lama Kaha, 1966; Oti Lir'ot Af Ehad Lo Yahol, 1967; Ani Pashosh, 1969; song lyrics; contbr to newspapers. Home: 87 Hauniversita St, Tel Aviv, Isr. Office: 60 Ussishkin St, Tel Aviv, Isr.

OPLER, Ascher, US, physicist; b. Bklyn, NY, Sep 5, 1916; s. Samuel and Sarah (Weinstein); att: Bklyn Coll, 1933-34; U Mich, 1934-36, 1938; BS, Wayne State U, 1944; m. Pauline Schneirla, July 1, 1936, (div); m. 2nd, Jean Cushman, May 18, 1960, (div); m. 3rd, Tamor Turin, Jan 10, 1968; c: Paul, Nora. Cons to research dir, IBM, since 1967; project leader, physics, Dow Chemical Co, 1947-57, spec cons, 1957-58; vice-pres, Computer Usage Co, 1962-67, sr analyst, 1958, dir, programming sys, 1959-67. Asso ed, Jour of Assn for Computing Machinery; mem: Soc for Ind and Applied Math; Inst for Mgmt Sci; Assn for Computing Machinery, natl lectr, 1969. Contbr to sci jours. Home: 440 E 62nd St, New York, NY. Office: Yorktown Heights, New York, NY.

OPLER, Marvin K, US, educator, author; b. Buffalo, NY, June 13, 1914; s. Arthur and Fanny (Coleman-Haas); att U Buffalo, 1932-33; AB, U Mich, 1935; PhD, Columbia U, 1938; m. Charlotte Fox, Dec 1935; c: Lewis, Ruth Perry. Chmn, dept anthropology, SUNY, Buffalo, since 1969, prof, soc psycht, dept of psycht, Sch of Med, prof, sociol and anthropology, Grad Sch, both since 1958; chmn, dept anthropology and sociol, Reed Coll, 1938-43; chief, comty, analysis, War Relocation Auth, Interior Dept, 1943-46; asso prof, anthropology, Stanford U, 1947-48; asso prof, social relations, Harvard U, 1948-51; prof, anthropology and sociol, Tulane U, 1952; prof, anthropology in psycht and prin inves, Midtown Comty Mh Research Study, Cornell U Med Coll, 1952-58. F: Social Sci Research Council; Amer Anthropological Assn; chmn, social research, LA Comty Chest; publ panel, 12th region, Natl Lab Relations Bd; fmr vice-chmn, Portland Council of Social Agencies; pres, NE Anthropological Assn; mem: Amer Sociol Assn; Soc for the Study of Social Problems; Acad of Psychan; Amer Ethnological Soc; Sigma Xi. Author: Culture, Psychiatry and Human Values, 1956; co-author: Acculturation in Seven Amer Tribes, 1940; Symposium on Preventive and Social Psychiatry, 1958; Mental Health in the Metropolis, 1962; ed: Culture and Mental Health, Cross Cultural Studies, 1959; Internatl Jour of Soc Psycht, since 1956; asso ed, American Anthropologist, since 1962; mem, ed bd: Jour of Nervous and Mental Disease; Family Process; Transcultural Psychiatric Research. Spec interests: culture and personality studies; anthropology and modern ethnic studies; social psycht. Home: 22 Summerwood Court, Buffalo, NY. Office: SUNY Sch of Med, Buffalo, NY.

OPPENHEIM, Adolph David, US, city planner; b. Hanau/M, Ger, Feb 15, 1918; s. Joseph and Malka (Oppenheim); in US since 1939; BSS, magna cum laude, CCNY, 1947; MCP, MIT, 1949; m. Julia Frankenhuis, Dec 12, 1950; c: Joseph, Aaron. Prin planner, NYC Dept of City Planning, since 1961; head, research sect, Tel Aviv Town Planning Dept, 1955-60; project chief, Pa-Jersey Transp Study, 1960-61. Vice chmn, bd of govs, Assn Orthodox J Scis; dir, Soc for Promotion of J Educ; mem: Amer Inst Planners; Amer Soc Planning Officials; Phi Beta Kappa. Home: 66 Overlook Terr, New York, NY. Office: 2 Lafayette St, New York, NY.

OPPENHEIM, Sir Alexander, Malaysia, educator; b. Salford, Eng, Feb 4, 1903; s. Harris and Fanny (Ginsberg); in Malaya since 1931; BA, Oxford U, 1924, MA, 1952, DSc, 1955; PhD, U Chgo, 1930; hon DSc, Hong Kong, 1961; hon LLD, Singapore, 1962; m. Beatrice Templer Nesbit, 1930; c: Judith Nwanodi. Vice-chancellor, U Malaya, Kuala Lumpur, since 1957, prof, math, 1949-59, dean fac, arts, 1949-50, 1954, acting vice-chancellor, 1955-57; f, Commonwealth Fund, 1927-30; lectr, U Edinburgh, 1930-31; prof, math, Raffles Coll, Straits Settlements, 1931-49. Prisoner of war, Singapore and Thailand, 1942-45. Chmn, bd of mgmt, Tropical Fish Culture Research Inst, Malacca, Fed of Malaysia; trustee, Tanglin Trust Ltd, Singapore; mem: London Math Soc; Amer Math Soc; Edinburgh Math Soc; Math Assn, Gt Brit; Malayan Math Soc, pres, 1951-55, 1957; Oxford and Cambridge Soc; life mem, Oxford Soc; clubs: Selangor; Lake; Menorah; Singapore Chess, pres, 1956-60; Amer U, pres, 1956. Contbr to math jours. Recipient: Efficiency Decoration; OBE, 1955; Knight Bachelor, 1961; Dato, Panglima Mangku Negara, 1962. Hobbies: chess, bridge, walking, swimming. Home and office: U Malaya, Pantai Valley, Kuala Lumpur, Malaysia.

OPPENHEIMER, Alice, US, editor-publisher, communal worker; b. Ger; d. Edward and Frieda (Simon) August; in US since 1938; grad, Coll of Higher Econ; m. Max Oppenheimer, June 21, 1921 (decd); c: Werner, Edith Ullmann. Ed-publisher, The J Way, since 1942; ed, Leo Baeck, B'nai B'rith Bull, 1955-67; writer for newspapers. Pres: Sisterhood, Ahavath Torah Cong Tikvah Chadashah, since 1957; Leo Baeck Chap, B'nai B'rith, 1944-56; J Friends Soc, 1952-55, hon pres; Channah Chap ,Mizrachi Women of Amer, since 1953; chmn, FJP, since 1955; found, leader, Golden Age Club Ahavath Torah Sisterhood; mem: exec bd, Gemiluth Chessed Sr Citizen Home, Palisades Garden; Women's Soc Service for Isr. Author: Cook Book, 1942; Impression of a Trip to Europe, 1956; Jewish Women in America, 1956; Impressions of a Trip to Israel, 1959. Recipient: hon cert, Leo Baeck Chap, B'nai B'rith, 1955; hon dipl, Cong Ahavath Torah, 1962; Isr Freedom Medal, 1965. Home and office: 740 W 187th St, New York, NY.

OPPENHEIMER, Chanan, Isr, horticultural scientist; b. Berlin, Ger, May 22, 1905; s. Karl and Hedwig (Troplowitz); in Isr since 1932; DAgric, Landwirtschaftliche Hochschule, Berlin, 1932; m. Maya Kloss, Jan 2, 1931; c: Vered Halamish, Yael Goshen. Head, Div of Subtr-opical Horticulture, Volcani Inst, since 1942; prof, subtropical horticulture, Heb U, since 1962. Author, books on subtropical horticulture. Recipient: Agric Research, Histadrut, 1957; Isr Prize for Agric, 1968. Spec interests: travel, hist, art, ecology. Home: 24 Ruppin St, Rehovot, Isr. Office: Volcani Inst of Agric Research, Beit Dagan, Isr.

OPPENHEIMER, Jane M, US, educator; b. Phila, Pa, Sep 19, 1911; d. James and Sylvia (Stern); BA, Bryn Mawr Coll, 1932; PhD, Yale U, 1935. Prof, biol, Bryn Mawr Coll, since 1953, acting dean of grad sch, semester II, 1946-47, on fac since 1938; visiting prof, biol, Johns Hopkins U, 1967. F: Guggenheim Found, 1942-43, 1952-53; Rockefeller Found, 1950-51; NSF, 1959-60; mem: Sigma Xi; Amer Soc of Zools; Amer Assn of Anats; AAAS; Amer Soc of Naturalists; Internal Inst of Embryology; Hist of Sci Soc; Amer Assn for Hist of Med; Soc for Developmental Biol. Author: New Aspects of John and William Hunter, 1946; Essays in the History of Embryology and Biology, 1967; co-ed, Foundations of Experimental Embryology, 1964; contbr to scholarly and med jours. Office: Bryn Mawr Coll, Bryn Mawr, Pa.

OPPENHEIMER, Jesse Halff, US, attorney; b. San Antonio, Tex, Jan 4, 1919; s. Jesse and Lillie (Halff); BA, U Ariz, 1939; LLB, Harvard Law Sch, 1942; m. Susan Rosenthal; c: David, Jean, Barbara. Lt col, US Army, 1942-46. Attorney. San Antonio chap chmn, AJComm; pres, Sym Soc of San Antonio, 1948-49; vice pres, trustee, McNay Art Inst; trustee, St Mary's Hall; mem, Amer Bar Assn. Contbr to legal jours. Home: 400 Mandalay Dr E, San Antonio, Tex. Office: 1540 Milam Bldg, San Antonio, Tex.

OPPENHEIMER, John F, US, author; b. Fürth, Ger, Nov 13, 1903; in US since 1938; educated in Darmstadt and Berlin. Pres, Wallenberg and Wallenberg, Inc; ed, Lexikon des Judentums, Gutersloh, 1967-70; official Jüdischer Central-Verein, Frankfurt, Stettin, Berlin, 1923-29, 1935-38; with Ullstein and Propyläenverlag, Berlin, 1929-35; found, co-ed Philo-Lexikon, Handbuch des jüdischen Wissens, Berlin, 1935, 1938; co-worker, Philo-Zitaten-Lexikon, Worte von Juden, Worte für Juden, Berlin, 1936; co-ed, Philo-Atlas, Handbuch für die jüdische Auswanderung, Berlin, 1938; ed, modern biography, Universal J Encyclopedia, NY, 1939-43. Secy-treas, Artur Schnabel Memorial Comm, NY, 1952-62. Home: 36-35 193rd St, Flushing, NY. Office: 10358 Park Ave, New York, NY.

OPPENHEIMER, Josef, Arg, rabbi; b. Frankfurt/M, Ger, Jan 18, 1911; s. Leopold and Félice (Weil); ordained rabbi, Yeshiva, Lith, 1938; PhD, U Zurich, 1947; m. Margarete Cahn, 1944; c: Israel, Malka Benhamu, Jehuda, Channa, Daniel, David. Rabbi: Assn Religiosa, Concordia Israelita, since 1953; Hoofd Syn, Amsterdam, 1949-53. Prin, Beth Jacob Sem; pres, Poalei Agudat Isr. Home: 2775 Cramer, Buenos Aires, Arg.

OPPENHEIMER, Martin, US, attorney; b. Burghaun, Ger, Nov 4, 1933; s. Julius and Sylvia (Haas); in US since 1936; BA, U Pa, 1953; LLB, Yale Law Sch, 1956; att U Frankfurt, Ger, 1956-1957; m. Suzanne Rosenhirsch, July 3, 1960; c: Marcy, Evan, Joshua, Alexandra. Partner, Proskauer, Rose, Goetz & Mendelsohn, since 1966. F: Fulbright,1956-57; mem:

Amer, NY State, NYC Bar Assns; AJComm. Home: 400 Claflin Ave, Mamaroneck, NY. Office: 300 Park Ave, New York, NY.

OPPENHEIMER, Reuben, US, jurist; b. Baltimore, Md, Oct 24, 1897; s. Leon and Flora (Oppenheimer) Schwab; BA, Johns Hopkins U, 1917; LLB, Harvard Law Sch, 1920; m. Selma Levy, June 26, 1922; c: Martin, Joan Weiss. Ret; asso judge, Court of Appeals of Md, 1964-67; asso judge, Supr Bench of Baltimore City, Md, 1955-64; partner, Emory, Beeuwkes, Skeen and Oppenheimer, and its successors, 1922-25; chief atty, Md State OPA, 1942-43; pub mem and co-chmn, Appeals and Review Comms, Natl War Lab Bd, Wash, DC, 1943-45; instr, admn law, fed jurisdiction, U Md Law Sch, 1947-55. USNR, WW I. Chmn: comm on reorg of the People's Court, Baltimore City, 1938; comm on additional tax revenue, City of Baltimore, 1945; Bd of Md, Dept of Correction, 1947-51; Md State Bd of Ethics, since 1969; commn on Amendments to Baltimore City charter, since 1969; pres: Bar Assn of Baltimore City, 1952-53; Md State Bar Assn, 1955-56; Harvard Law Sch Assn of Md, 1955-56; Baltimore J Council, 1940-41; JWF, Baltimore, 1942; vice-pres: Har Sinai Cong, 1923-26; mem, bd trustees: The Sheppard and Enoch Pratt Hosp; AJComm, 1922-26; mem: US Delg, Twelfth Intl Penal and Penitentiary Cong, Hague, Holl, 1950; comm, admn org of State of Md, 1951-53; comm on judicial admn, 1953-55; f, Amer Bar Found; mem: Amer Bar Assn; Phi Beta Kappa; Omicron Delta Kappa; hon mem, Order of the Coif. Author: report on admn of deportation laws of US, for Natl Comm on Law Observance and Enforcement, 1931; co-author, monographs for US Children's Bur on Juvenile and Family Courts; contbr to legal jours. Home: 3506 Bancroft Rd, Baltimore, Md. Office: Room 408, The Quadrangle, Village of Cross Keys, Baltimore, Md.

OPPENHEIMER, Selma L, US, artist; b. Baltimore, Md, Jan 13, 1898; d. William and Beatrice (Stern) Levy; BA, Goucher Coll, 1919; att Md Inst, 1920-22; m. Reuben Oppenheimer, June 26, 1922; c: Martin, Joan Weiss. One-man shows: Munic Art Soc, Baltimore, 1937; Baltimore Mus of Art, 1941; Johns Hopkins Hosp, Residence Hall, 1961; Retrospective Exhb, J Comty Cen, 1967; Notre Dame Coll, 1966; exhbs: Cannes, France, 1966; Pa Acad of Fine Arts; Va Mus of Fine Arts; Art Inst, Chgo; Corcoran Gal; Phillips Memorial Gal, both Wash, DC; Mus of Modern Art; Midtown Gal; Rockefeller Cen, all NYC; Mus of Art; Munic Mus, both Baltimore; Hagerstown Mus, Md; worked for OPA and Baltimore Ration Bd, WW II. Press, Md Chap, Artists Equity Assn, 1955-56; fmr chmn, publ comm, Md Fed of Women's Clubs; mem, bd trustees, Baltimore Mus of Art, since 1959; vice-chmn, artist comm, US, 1955; secy-trea, 1st Baltimore Outdoor Festival; mem, bd dirs: J Comty Cen, 1959-65; mem: art comm, Vagabond Theater, 1958-66; Council of J Women; J Educ Alliance; YM and YWHA; Amer Fed of Art; Natl Assn of Women Artists; Natl League of Amer Penwomen; Har Sinai Syn; clubs: Suburban of Baltimore co; Baltimore Water Color; Goucher; Hamilton St.Recipient: prize for oil paintings: Md Inst, 1933; Baltimore Mus of Art, 1935-1938; Natl Assn of Women Artists, 1952, 1960, 1965; for water color:hon mention,Natl Water Color Exhb,Baltimore Mus of Art, 1950; Baltimore Council of J Women, 1953, for ceramics, 1954; Baltimore Water Color Club, 1959, 1961; purchase award, Loyola Coll of Baltimore, 1967. Home and studio: 3506 Bancroft Rd, Baltimore, Md.

ORDMAN, Arnold, US, government official; b. Somersworth, NH, Feb 16, 1912; s. Maurice and Anna (Pierce); AB, Boston U, 1933; LLB, Harvard, 1936; m. Evelyn Sisson, Feb 5, 1939; c: Edward, Alfred. Gen counsel, NLRB, since 1963. Lt, USN, 1942-45. Dir, Intl Soc for Lab Law and Social Action; hon vice-pres, UJA; mem, Phi Beta Kappa; pres, Boston U Avukah chap, 1932-33; various positions, B'nai B'rith, 1939-42. Home: 4701 Willard, Chevy Chase, Md. Office: 1717 Pennsylvania Ave, Washington, DC.

OREN, Isaac, Isr, govt exec; b. Stepan, Pol, Feb 2, 1912; s. Tanhum and Ita (Eidelstein); in Isr since 1934; m. Sarah Kalmanovitz; c: Dan, Tanhum. Treas, Munic of Tel Aviv-Jaffa, since 1953, asst treas, 1948-53; repr Munic on bds of dirs of cos connected with Munic; co dir, Isr Natl Lottery; repr munic on missions abroad: Eur, Amer. Chmn, Union of Local Council's Treas, Isr; mem, Finance Offs Assn of US and Can. Home: 10 Danin St, Tel Aviv, Isr. Office: 69 Ibn Gevirol St, Tel Aviv, Isr.

OREN, Mordecai, Isr, journalist, organization exec; b. Podhaitze,

Aus-Hung, Mar 16, 1905; s. Moshe and Klara (Gang) Ornstein; in Isr since 1929; m. Rega Warszawiak; c: Puah, Moshe. Secy gen, World Union of Mapam, since 1960; agric worker, Kibbutz Mizra since 1929; co-ed, newspaper, Al Hamishmar, 1950-51 and since 1965. Arrested in Czech, 1951 on political charge, in connection with Slansky trial, sentenced to 15 yrs imprisonment, released 1956. Mem, world exec, WJC, since 1948; fmr mem: presidium, Vaad Leumi; exec, political comms, Mapam Party; exec comm, Kibbutz Artzi; world exec Hashomer Hatzair; exec comm, Histadrut. Author, A Political Prisoner in Prague, 1958, trans from Heb into Yiddish, Fr. Home: Kibbutz Mizra, Isr. Office: Al Hamishmar, Tel Aviv, Isr.

OREN, Oded, Isr, metallurgist; b. Haifa, Isr, Jan 25, 1930; s. Eliahu and Haia (Feldman); BSc, Technion, Haifa, 1955, MSc, 1961; m. Mina Einoch, Aug 19, 1958; c: Lior, Avital. Head, heat treatment and foundry dept, aircraft structure and process directorate, Isr Aircraft Ind, since 1967, design engr, Haargaz Ltd, 1955-58; asst, Technion, 1958-61; materials and process engr, 1961-67. Sgt, Isr Navy, 1948-50; 1t, IDF Reserve, 1958-67. Principal contrib: introducing modern tech processes. Ind repr, Min Educ comm on tech educ. Contbr to metals jours. Home: 36 Zirelson St, Tel Aviv, Isr. Office: Lod Airport, Isr.

ORENSTEIN, Leo L, US, psychiatrist, psychoanalyst, b. Penki, Russ, Dec 25, 1905; s. Eliakim and Anna (Dubin); in US since 1921; BS, Columbia U, 1931; MD, NYU Med Sch, 1934; m. Beatrice Edelman, Mar 30, 1941; c: Reed, Jane Liebman. Pvt practice since 1950; asso clinical prof, NYU Med Sch, since 1960, asst clinical prof, 1955-60; cons psycht, Beth Isr Hosp; sr psycht, Bellevue Hosp, 1939-50; i/c, psychiatric clinic, Court of Gen Sessions, 1946-50. US Army, 1941-46. Council mem, NY Co dist br, Amer Psychiatric Assn, 1959-62; chmn bd dirs, Downtown Comty School, 1951-52; f, Amer Coll Phys; life f, Amer Psychiatric Assn; mem: Intl Psychoanalytic Assn; Amer Psychoanalytic Assn; club, Grand St Boys. Contbr to med jours. Hobby: gardening. Home and office: 1225 Park Ave, New York, NY.

ORENT, Norman B, US, business exec; b. Brockton, Mass, Oct 19, 1920; s. George and Yetta (Eiferman) Orentlicher; BA, Brown U, 1942; MBA, Harvard, 1947; m. Dorothy Seidman, Mar 19, 1944; c: Jean, Rena. Pres: Hamilton-Skotch Corp, since 1958, vice-pres, 1955-58; Hampden Specialty Products Corp, since 1959; admn asst, Westover Mills, 1947-51; sales mgr: Verney Corp, 1951-54; Textron, 1954-55. US Army, 1943-46. Mem: Phi Beta Kappa; Young Pres Org; Temple Isr, White Plains, NY; clubs: Lambs; Brown U; Harvard Bus Sch. Recipient: Bronze Star. Home: 39 Lincoln Rd, Scarsdale, NY. Office: 295 Fifth Ave, New York, NY.

ORGAD, Benzion, Isr, composer; b. Ger, Aug 21, 1926; s. David and Miriam (Zuckermann) Büschel; in Isr since 1933; dipl, Isr Acad, 1947; MFA, Brandeis U, 1961; div; c: Ron, Eyal. Sup of music educ, Min of Educ and Culture, since 1950. Palmach, IDF, 1944-45, 1947-50. Composer: cantatas, The Spies' Tale; The Vision of Isiah; Building a King's Stage; Choreographic Notes, for orch; Ballad, for violin; Taksim, for harp solo; Leave Out My Name, for soprano and flute; Seven Variations on C, for piano; Monologue, for viola; Hatsvi Israel, sym; Out of the Dust; Music for Horn and Orchestra; Two Motets; Music for Orchestra; Septet; Death Came to the Wooden Horse Michael; Songs of an Early Morning; Mizmorim; Kaleidoscope, for sym orch. Recipient, prizes: Koussevitsky, UNESCO, 1952; Conquest of the Desert, Jerusalem, 1957; Isr Philharmonic Orch, 1957; ACUM, 1960, 1968; Segalyn, Tanglewood, 1961; Engel, 1961-62. Home: 14 Bloch St, Tel Aviv, Isr.

ORGEL, Samuel Z, US, psychiatrist; b. NYC, June 25, 1892; s. Simon and Pearl (Bilder); MD, Bellevue Hosp, Med Coll, 1917; dipl: U Vienna, 1925; Individual Psych Inst, 1925; Gestalt Psych Inst, Berlin, 1926; m. Esther Kitay, Aug 10, 1930; c: Stephen Kitay. Pvt practice, psychan, NYC, since 1923, gen practice, 1919-22, ped and child psycht, 1922-32; att psycht, Hillside Hosp, Glen Oaks, NY, since 1936; psycht, Isr Orphan Asylum, NYC, since 1920; cons psycht: Miriam Barnett Memorial Hosp, Paterson, NJ, since 1933; NY J Child Care Assn, since 1941; Madison Neighborhood House, NYC, since 1942; psycht, Dept Mental Hygiene, NY, since 1936; lectr, Natl Comm Mental Hygiene, NY, since 1928; out-patient dept, sr asst: ped: Lebanon Hosp, Bx, 1919-25; Mt Sinai Hosp, NYC, 1919-28; J Bd of Guardians, 1926-30; Heb Sheltering Guardian Soc, Pleasantville, NY, 1927-41;

Children's Court, Kings Co, Bklyn, 1928-30; Heb Orphan Asylum, NYC, 1929-41; lectr, psycht and law, Practicing Law Inst, NYC, 1949; perceptor, Inst of Psycht, Mt Sinai Hosp, NY, 1963; lectr, psycht, Mt Sinai Med Coll, NYC, 1967. Lt, US Army, 1917-19, psychiatric examiner, 1942-44. Dipl, Bd Neur and Psycht, 1939; f: NY Acad Med, 1927, neur and psycht, 1935; Amer Psychiatric Assn, 1937; Amer Orthopsychiatric Assn, 1928; pres, med bd, Hillside Hosp, 1949; mem: NY Co and State Med Socs; NY Soc for Clinical Psycht; NY Psychan Soc and Inst; Amer Psychan Assn; Intl Psychan Assn; AMA; Amer Phys Art Assn. Author: Psychiatry Today and Tomorrow, 1946; contbr to med jours. Recipient: prizes, Amer Phys Art Assn, 1944-53. Home: 1075 Park Ave, New York, NY. Office: 667 Madison Ave, New York, NY.

ORKIN, Lazarus A, US, physician; b. NYC, Feb 2, 1910; s. John and Anne Davidow; BS, NYU, 1930, MS, 1931, MD, 1935; m. Sylvia Holland, May 30, 1941; c: Fredrick, Stuart. Dir, urol, Beth Isr Med Cen, since 1957; clinical prof, urol, Mt Sinai Sch Med, NYC, since 1970; cons, urol: Beekman Downtown Hosp; Catholic Med Cen, Bklyn; Far Rockaway Hosp. F: Amer Coll Surgs; Amer Assn for Surg Trauma; Acad Med; NY, Amer, Can, Urol Assns; Pan Pacific Surg Assn; Intl Fertility Assn; Amer Sterility Soc; Amer Geriatrics Soc; dipl, Amer Bd Urol, 1943; mem: KP, NY; club, Town, NYC. Author: Trauma to the Ureter, 1966. Hobbies: photography, fishing. Home: 11 E 86 St, New York, NY. Office: 10 Nathan D Perlman Pl, New York, NY.

ORKIN, Louis R, US, anesthesiologist, educator; b. NYC, Dec 23, 1915; s. Samuel and Rebecca (Rish); BA, U Wis, 1937; MD, NYU, 1941; m. Florence Fine, Mar 5, 1938; c: Rita. Prof, chmn, dept of anesthesiology, Albert Einstein Coll of Med, since 1955; dir, dept of anesthesiology, Bx Munic Hosp Cen, since 1955; cons: USPHS Hosp, since 1956; US Naval Hosp, St Albans, NY, since 1957; cons anesthesiologist, Triboro Hosp, 1955-62, dir, anesthesia, WW Backus Hosp; cons: Norwich State Hosp; Uncas on Thames, all at Norwich, Conn, 1948-49; anesthesiologist, Bellevue Hosp, NY, 1950-55; asst att asso anesthetist, U Hosp, 1950-54; asst prof anesthesia, NYU, Postgrad Coll of Med, 1950-55; asst prof, oral surg, anesthesia, NYU, Coll of Dent, 1950-55; sr cons, anesthesia, Bx VA Hosp, 1958. Capt, US Army MC, 1942-45. Dipl, Amer Bd of Anesthesiologists; f: NY Acad Med; Amer Coll Chest Phys; mem: Natl Research Council, anesthesiology, since 1964; AMA; Amer and NY State Soc of Anesthesiologists; NY Acad of Scis; NY Co Med Soc; Assn U Anesthetists; Soc Pharm and Experimental Therapeutics; Sigma Xi; Alpha Omega Alpha. Asso ed: Clinical Anesthesia; Survey of Anesthesiology, since 1957; contbr to profsl jours. Recipient, Bronze Star, 1944. Home: 11 Stuyvesant Oval, New York, NY. Office: Albert Einstein Coll of Med, New York, NY.

ORLAND, Yaakov, Isr, poet; b. Russ, July 14, 1914; s. Eliezer and Batya; in Isr since 1921; att Heb U, Jerusalem; Royal Acad of Dramatic Art, London; m. Bat-El Axelrod, Aug 22, 1944; c: Shimrit, Reuel. Author: Ilan Baruach, 1939; Shirim al Ait veAl Yona, 1946; haIr haZot, 1953; Beir haTzaatzuim, 1962; Shirim meEretz Utz, 1962; Bar-Kochba, 1965; Hershele of Ostropoli, 1966; The Black Office, 1967; Alpenberg, 1967; Man of Legend, 1969; Magen Ugav, 1969; trans Brit and Amer poetry, lit works. Brit Army, WW II; IDF, Isr War Independence. Mem: JNF mission to S Afr, 1951-52; Fgn Off mission to Scandinavia, 1965; council mem, Authors Assn, Haifa; mem: ACUM; Heb Authors Assn; club, Intl PEN. Recipient: Lamdan award for lit, 1953; mil medals. Home: 79 Moriah Ave, Mt Carmel, Haifa, Isr.

ORLANS, Harold, US, sociologist; b. NYC, July 29, 1921; s. Morris and Celia (Fudalowitz) Orlansky; BSS, CCNY, 1941; PhD, Yale U, 1949; Fulbright scholar, LSE, 1949-50; m. Barbara Hughes, July, 1959; c: Claire, Andrew, Paul. Sr staff, Brookings Inst, since 1960; sr info off, The Social Survey, 1951-52; research asso, Inst for Research in Hum Relations, 1952-54; sect chief, prog analyst, NSF, 1954-59; dir, studies, White House Conf on Children and Youth, 1959-60; mem: subcomm on research and tech progs, Comm on Govt Oprs, US House of Reprs, 1966-67. Mem: Amer Sociol Assn; AAAS. Author: The Effects of Federal Programs on Higher Education, 1962; Utopia Ltd, 1953; Contracting for Atoms, 1967; ed: The Use of Social Research in Federal Domestic Programs, 1967; Science Policy and the University, 1968. Home: 7035 Wilson La, Bethesda, Md. Office: 1775 Massachusetts Ave NW, Washington, DC.

ORLINSKY, Harry M, US, biblical scholar, educator; b. Owen Sound, Ont, Can, Mar 14, 1908; s. Isaac and Elizabeth (Ardy) Orlansky; in US since 1931; BA, U Toronto, Can, 1931; PhD, Dropsie Coll, 1935; grad, Theol Union, Berkeley, 1969; m. Donya Fein, Sep 2, 1934; c: Walter, Seymour. Prof: Bible, HUC-JIR, NYC, since 1943; Bible and J Hist, Baltimore Heb Coll, Md, 1936-44; lectr, summer sessions, Dropsie Coll, since 1948; mem, staff, Heb U excavations at Ramat Gan, 1936; lectr, New Sch for Social Research, NYC, 1947-49; visiting prof: Heb U, Jerusalem, 1962. F: Dropsie Coll Phila, Pa; U of Pa, 1931-35; Amer Sch Oriental Research, Heb U, 1935-36; orientals dept, Johns Hopkins U, Baltimore, 1937-43; Guggenheim Found, 1968-69; Princeton U Council of the Hum; Amer Acad J Research; fmr asso in council, Soc of Bibl Lit; fmr asso trustee, Amer Schs Oriental Research; chmn: Amer Friends of Isr Exploration Soc; Intl org for Septuagint and Cognate Studies; bd dirs, Amer Friends of the Heb U; mem: Comité de Direction pour Littérature, pseud-épigraphique grecque d'Ancient Testament, since 1967; exec comm, Oriental Soc, 1953; natl comm, JBCA; Old Testament Soc, Amer Standard Bible Comm; mem, J Acad of Arts and Scis. Author: The Septuagint, the Oldest Translation of the Bible, 1949; The So-called "Servant of the Lord" and "Suffering Servant" in Second Isaiah, 1967; publs on Old Testament and Dead Sea Scrolls; co-trans: into Eng, five volume work of Rashi Commentary on the Pentateuch, 1949-50; Ancient Israel, 1954, Japanese ed, 1962, It ed, 1967; ed in chief, The Torah, new Eng trans of the Heb Bible, for J Publ Soc of Amer, 1963; ed, Libr of Bibl Studies, Ktav, NY; ed bd: Soc of Bibl Lit, since 1945; J Apocryphal Lit, Dropsie Coll, since 1947; Isr Exploration Soc, since 1953; Amer Schs of Oriental Research, 1948-50. Recipient: Frank L Weil award, JWB, 1959. Office: 40 W 68 St, New York, NY.

ORLINSKY, Walter Sidney, US, attorney, legislator; b. Baltimore, Md, May 19, 1938; s. Harry and Doyna (Fein); AB, Johns Hopkins U, 1960; LLB. U Md Law Sch, 1964; m. Jo-Ann Mayer, June 18, 1961; c: Eric. Pvt practice, since 1965; mem, Md House of Delgs, since 1966, chmn, Metrop Affairs Comm. Treas, Baltimore Assn for Histadrut; mem: natl bd, Amer Habonim Assn; Baltimore bd: AJCong; ADA; ACLU; club: Alpha Epsilon Pi, Johns Hopkins chap; New Dem natl bd. Home: 1530 Bolton St, Baltimore, Md. Office: 210 E Redwood, Baltimore, Md.

ORMIAN, Haim Yosef, Isr, editor, psychologist; b. Tarnow, Pol, Dec 8, 1901; s. Izak and Faige (Kapellner); in Isr since 1936; tchrs dipl, Heb Tchrs Sem, Vienna, 1922; PhD, U Vienna, 1925; m. Ruth Jarblum, June 30, 1931; c: Dalit, Aminadav. Ed, The Educ Ency, since 1951; secondary sch tchr, Assn for Heb Secondary Schs, Lodz, Pol, 1925-36; asst, lectr, U of Lodz, 1929-36; secondary sch tchr, Tel Aviv, 1936-39; lectr, Secondary Sch and Tchr Training Coll, Jerusalem, 1939-50; lectr, psych, Heb U, Jerusalem, 1945-50; insp of tchr training colls, Min of Educ and Culture, 1953, dir, tchr training div, 1956-59, 1965-66. Served, Haganah and IDF. F, UNESCO, study of tchr training colls in W Eur, 1958; mem: comm on Heb terms in psych and educ, Heb Lang Acad; publ and ed dept, Tchrs Union in Isr; Amer Psych Assn; Intl Assn Applied Psych; Isr Psych Assn, chmn, natl exec, 1954, chmn, Assn Former Haganah Mems; world exec, B'rit Ivrit Olamit, Jerusalem; chmn, Psych Assn, Lodz, 1930-36; mem, comm for psych educ, Sci Educ Assn, Warsaw, 1931-36; chmn, Heb Soc Tarbut, Lodz, 1934-36; mem: Isr comm of tchrs, Keren Kayemet leIsr, 1936-49; council on juvenile bc, Pal Bc Service, 1943-47; cons comm, juvenile leg, Isr Min, 1950-54; fmr Isr delg, to confs on psych with respect to educ. Author: The Syllogistic Thinking of Children, 1926; Testing and Evaluation of Intelligence by Teachers, 1935; Psychological Background of Youth Organization, 1937; The Educational Ideas of the Polish Jewry, 1939; Psychology of Later Childhood, 1946, 1951, 1957; Psychology of Adolescence, 1948, 1953; The Vocational Interest of Israel Students, 1953; Educational Psychology, 1969; sci ed, of Heb books on psych and educ; contbr to profsl jours; Ency Hebraica; Educ Ency; to psych abstracts. Recipient: Isr Prize Educ, Educ Min, 1971. Home: 16 Mitudela St, Jerusalem, Isr. Office: 7a Narkis St, Jerusalem, Isr.

ORNISH, Natalie Gene, US, business executive, author; b. Galveston, Tex, Feb 15, 1926; d. George and Bess (Shapiro) Moskowitz; BA, Sam Houston State Coll, Huntsville, Tex, 1943; MS, Northwestern U, Evanston, Ill, 1944; m. Edwin Ornish, Nov 6, 1949; c: Laurel, Dean, Steven, Kathy. Pres, Dallas Records Co, since 1957; dir, Natwin Co, since 1959; owner, TV show, The Sugar Plum, since 1957; ed, AP, Omaha,

1945-46; dir, publicity, Library Bond Election, Galveston, 1946; PR staff, Rogers & Smith Advt, 1947; dir publicity, Galveston Pleasure Pier, 1948-49. Author: Songs for Suburban Children, and other educ record albums; Just Twelve, play, 1963; The Third Parent; A Portrait of Rabbi Henry Cohen, 1963; The Ages of Childhood Song Book, 1968; contbr to natl mags; lectr on early Tex hist; writer, adv for children's TV shows. Mem: Dallas Motion Picture Classification Bd; ASCAP. Recipient: award, Council of Social Agencies of Dallas, 1956. Home and office: 7146 Currin Dr, Dallas, Tex.

ORNSTEEN, Abraham M, US, neurologist-psychiatrist, educator; b. Phila, Pa, Sep 30, 1894; s. Morris and Pauline (Zeckman); grad pharm, Phila Coll of Pharm, 1913; MD, U Pa, 1917; m. Hilda Kaplan, Aug 24, 1919; c: Jerome, Richard. Prof em: prof, clinical neur, U Pa Med Sch, 1952-1960, on fac since 1929; chief, neur, Phila Gen Hosp, 1930-60, hon cons, since 1960; fmr, psycht, Phila Psycht Hosp; asst prof of neur, Temple U Med Sch, 1921-29; cons, psychiatrist, E State Penitentiary, Pa, 1924-32; chief neur, Albert Einstein Med Cen, 1930-56; personnel cons, Phila Youth Study Cen, 1951. Lt, US Army MC, WW I; cons psycht, Selective Service, WW II. Dipl, Amer Bd Psycht and Neur; f: Amer Acad of Neur; Amer Coll of Phys; Phila Coll of Phys; mem: Amer Neur Assn; Amer Psychiatric Assn; Amer Assn Research Nervous and Mental Disturbances; AMA; Amer Psychosomatic Soc; Amer Neur Assn; Intl League against Epilepsy; Pa State Med Soc; Phila Co Med Soc; Alpha Omega Alpha; Intl Pictorialists Soc. Contbr to med jours. Hobby, exhb photography. Home and office: 2007 Delancey Pl, Philadelphia, Pa.

ORNSTEIN, Jacob A, US, educator, artist; b. Bklyn, NY, June 7, 1907; s. Abram and Anne (Eisner); BS, NYU, 1936, MA, 1939, DEd, 1960; m. Augusta Karlin, May 25, 1940; c: Peter, Alice. Prin, Wm Cowper Jr HS, since 1954; profsl painter since 1932, exhb in natl mus and gals, since 1939; lectr, since 1939; tchr, HS dept head, NYC Bd of Educ, 1935-54. Chmn: art sect, NY Soc for Experimental Study of Educ, 1958-64; sch bd, Temple Sinai, Queens, NY, 1955-64; educ dir, Bklyn Scout Camps, 1936-38; pres, Art Chairmen's Assn, NY, 1951-52; mem: Natl Art Comm, Mus of Modern Art; Amer Soc for Aesthetics; Jr HS Prins Assn, NYC. Author: Lettering for Fun, 1939; Paintbrush Fun, 1944; Decorating Unpainted Furniture, 1946; ed, Intercom, educ jour, 1957-64; contbr to educ jours. Spec interests: nature lore, microscopy. Home: 141-55 72nd Crescent, Flushing, NY. Office: 70-02 54 Ave, Maspeth, NY.

ORNSTEIN, Joseph G, US, dentist; b. NYC, Oct 18, 1914; s. Louis and Sadie (Rothenberg); AB, Columbia U, 1933; DDS, 1938; m. Dorothy Kamen, Aug 10, 1945; c: Marilyn, Louis. Pvt practice, since 1939; visiting staff: E Me Gen Hosp, Bangor; Kings Co Hosp, Bklyn, 1939-43; Triboro Hosp, Queens, 1940-42. Maj, US Army, 1942-46. Pres: Cong Beth Isr, since 1965; bd dir, since 1948; JCC, Bangor, 1951-52; bd dirs since 1949; secy, JWV, since 1950, cdr, 1948-50; exec comm, NE sect, JWB, 1957-66, vice-pres, 1961; life mem, Alpha Omega; mem: Amer, Me, Penobscot Valley Dental Socs; Amer Legion; Masons; Shriners; B'nai B'rith. Home: 224 Nowell Rd, Bangor, Me. Office: 209 State St, Bangor, Me.

ORODENKER, Maurie H, US, public relations exec; b. Phila, Pa, Dec 21, 1908; s. Philip and Rose (Sigesmund); BS, Franklin & Marshall Coll, Lancaster, Pa, 1932; MA, U of Pa, 1934; m. Edith Shenkman, Oct 20, 1937; c: Harriet Gurmankin, Jerry. Pres, Maurie H Orodenker Advt Agcy, since 1954; pr dir, Dropsie Coll, since 1967; asso ed, Billboard Publ Co, 1938-41; pr dir: J Comty Relations Council, Gtr Phila, 1944-69; Phila Allied J Appeal, 1952-54. Pres: Cong Emanu-El, since 1969; natl secy, Pop Warner Little Scholars, since 1963; exec comm, United Syn Amer, Phila br; vice pres, Phila chap, Amer PR Assn, 1958; mem: Lu Lu Temple, Shriners; clubs: Poor Richard; Bc Pioneers; Circus Sts and Sinners; TV and Radio Advt; Pen and Pencil; 32 Carat, pres, 1961-62; Fourth Estate Square, pres, 1950-51, both Masons. Hobby, art collector. Home: 6004 N 13 St, Philadelphia, Pa. Office: 1025 W Savings Fund Bldg, Philadelphia, Pa.

ORON, Moshe, Isr, materials sci; b. Pol, Dec 1, 1937; s. Yehoshua and Esther (Berger) Hochman; in Isr since 1950; ME, Technion, Haifa, 1960; MSc, 1964; DSc, MIT, Cambridge, 1966; m. Rachel Oppenheim, Sep 17, 1959; c: Menachem, Assaph, Hagit. Research asso, Weizmann Inst, Rehovot, since 1968; head, research group, ISPRA, Tel Aviv, since 1969; staff engr, IBM Corp, 1966-67. Lt, IAF, 1960-62.

Contbr articles to sci publs. Home: 39 Gordon St, Rehovot, Isr. Office: Weizmann Inst, Rehovot, Isr.

ORPAZ, Yitzhak, Isr, author, journalist; b. Zinkov, Ukraine, Oct 15, 1923; s. Zeev and Esther (Segal) Averbuch; in Isr since 1938; BA, Tel Aviv U, 1963; div; c: Zeev, Orna, Talila. Journalist, since 1962. Author: Skin for Skin; Ants; Wild Grass; The Death of Lysanda; The Hunting of the Doe. Maj, IDF, 1948-62. Adv council, Security Through Peace; mem: Heb Writers' Assn; Isr Journalists Assn. Recipient: Asher Barash Prize, 1962; Miriam Talpir Prize, 1968. Home: 191a Ben Yehuda St, Tel Aviv, Isr. Office: Al Hamishmar, Hamasger St, Tel Aviv, Isr.

ORTAR, Gina Rivka, Isr, educator; b. Leningrad, Russ, Jan 30, 1912; d. Simha and Elizabeth (Gliklich) Zabludowski; in Isr since 1934; PhD, Heb U, Jerusalem, 1958; m. Yohanan Ortar, 1935; c: Ada Samid, Dafna Meroz, Elisheva. Sr lectr, psych and educ, Heb U, since 1958; sci adv, Min of Educ and Culture, since 1958; psych: haNoar haOved, 1936-42; Hadassah-Brandeis Cen, 1942-46, inspector-psych, 1951-58. Prin contribs: organized 1st Vocational Guidance Inst in Jerusalem, 1936; initiated and administered annual 8th grade survey in Isr, since 1955. Pres, Isr Psych Assn, since 1966; mem, Intl Assn Applied Psych. Author, Psychological Tests, 1953; contbr articles in Heb and Eng. Home: 5 Molho St, Jerusalem, Isr. Office: Heb U, Jerusalem, Isr.

OSEAS, Israel B, US, attorney; b. NYC, Aug 10, 1901; s. Joshua and Fannie (Taxier); BSS, CCNY, 1922; JD, Harvard Law Sch, 1925; m. Hilda Nathanson, June 27, 1926; c: Jonathan. Pvt practice since 1936; spec asst: US Atty, S dist, NY, 1925-27; Atty Gen of US, 1927-31, 1934, 1944; counsel to supt of banks in liquidation of Bank of US, 1931-34; govt appeal agent, 1940-46; mem, draft bd, Selective Service Admn, WW II. Bd dirs, United Syn of Amer, 1943-69; hon dir, since 1969; pres, Park Ave Syn, since 1966, mem bd trustees, since 1943; mem: Assn Bar, City of NY; NY Co Lawyers Assn; NY State and Amer Bar Assns. Home: 115 Central Park W, New York, NY. Office: 1133 Ave of the Americas, New York, NY.

OSEN, Max N, US, attorney; b. Frankfurt/M, Ger, July 8, 1926; s. Irving and Rachel (Amster); in US since 1937; JD, NY Law Sch, 1949; m. Esther Wenger, Apr 28, 1957; c: Janet, Garson. Importer, distributor, film: theater; 16 mm; TV; films: Kapo, It; Three, Yugo; Shop on Main Street, Czech; Sweet Light in a Dark Room, Czech. US Army, Mil Govt, Berlin. Home: 3850 Hudson Manor Terr, Riverdale, NY. Office: 1414 Ave of the Americas, New York, NY.

OSGOOD, Herbert W, US, advertising cons; b. Pittsburgh, Pa, June 30, 1904; s. Samuel and Bessie (Wilkoff); BA, Princeton U, 1925; m. Elizabeth Purdy, Dec 25, 1936; c: Bessie Anderson. Advt cons. Pres: Downtown Bd of Trade, 1959-60; Rodef Sholom Cong, 1952-55; Merchants Council, 1962; chmn, Friends of Brandeis U, 1956-59; found and 1st chmn, Civic Forum, 1938-41, all of Youngstown, O; pres, Mahoning Valley Furniture Dealers Assn, 1952-55; mem: bd, J Fed of Youngstown, 1938; B'nai B'rith; club, Squaw Creek Country. Home: 466 Bradley La, Youngstown, O. Office: POB 2222, Youngstown, O.

OSHEROW, Aaron Irving, US, business exec; b. St Louis, Mo, Sep 26, 1931; s. Saul and Ruby (Ginsberg); BS, Wash U, St Louis, 1954; m. Ilene Vesper, Aug 23, 1953; c: Neal, Ruthellen, William. Exec vice-pres, Direct Mail Corp of Amer, since 1964. Lt, US Army, 1954-56. Mem: bd, J Comty Cen Assn, St Louis; Zeta Beta Tau. Home: 9500 Crockett Dr, Olivette, Mo. Office: 1533 Washington Ave, St Louis, Mo.

OSSERMAN, Kermit E, US, physician; b. NYC, June 21, 1909; s. Edward and Rose (Baumann); AB, Johns Hopkins U, 1929; MD, U of Md Med Sch, 1933; m. Dorothy Jacobs, June 2, 1935; Ruth. Asso clinical prof med, Mt Sinai Sch of Med, CUNY, since 1966; asso att phys, Mt Sinai Hosp, since 1959, phys i/c Myasthenia Gravis Clinic, since 1951, on staff since 1935; asso med, Columbia U, 1961-67; cons, med: Greenpoint Hosp, Bklyn, 1962-64; City Hosp of Elmhurst, LI, since 1964; Knickerbocker Hosp, since 1964; instr, gyn and obstet, Polyclinic Hosp and Med Sch, 1935-38; adj phys, dermat, Bx Hosp, 1935-39. Prin contrib: developed tensilon test for rapid diagnosis of myasthenia gravis, 1951. F: Amer Coll Phys; NY Acad of Med; NY Acad of Sci; NY Diabetes Assn; pres, Bentley Sch Educ Fund, since 1959; mem, exec

comm, med adv bd, Myasthenia Gravis Found, Inc, 1959-61, chmn, since 1953; chmn, diabetes detection for NYC, 1955-62; mem: Temple Emanu-El; Amer Diabetes Assn; Harvey Soc; Royal Acad of Med, London; Amer Soc for Pharm and Experimental Therapeutics; Amer Acad of Neur; Phi Lambda Kappa; Phi Sigma Delta; Kappa Alpha Tau. Author: Myasthenia Gravis, 1958; contbr to med jours. Recipient: cert of merit, AMA, 1953, 1965; hon mention, 1961. Hobbies: golf, traveling, music, arts. Home: 49 E 96 St, New York, NY. Office: 4 E 89 St, New York, NY.

OSTASHINSKY, Eliakum, Isr, business exec; b. Petah Tikva, Feb 16, 1909; s. Eliahu and Miriam (Gissin); Dipl, agronomy, U Toulouse, Fr, 1929; DAgric Scis U Portici, Naples, It, 1931; m. Shulamit Tulipman, Feb 16, 1941; c: Daphna Chelouche, Ruth. Mgn dir: Société Cooperative Vigneronne des Grandes Caves Richon-le-Zion-Zichron-Jacob Ltd, since 1953; Carmel Wine Co; Carmel Oriental; Isr Distillers Corp; mgr: Hanotaiah, 1931-40; Agric Dept, Farmers' Fed, 1940-46; Mayor, Rishon leZion, 1946-50; Isr Citrus Bd, 1950-53. Mem: presidium, J Farmers Fed, Isr; council, Bank of Isr, Jerusalem. Contbr articles on political and agric subjects to periodicals, newspapers. Home: 20 Huberman St, Tel Aviv, Isr. Office: 25 Carmel St, Rishon leZion, Isr.

OSTER, Zvi H, Isr, educator; b. Burdujene, Rum, Mar 2, 1932; s. Isaac and Shifra (Meirovici); in Isr since 1947; att Tel Aviv U, 1953-54; MD, Heb U-Hadassah Med Sch, Jerusalem, 1960; postdoc training, US, 1969; m. Blanche Marcuson, 1951; c: Michal, Adi. Asst Dean, Heb U-Hadassah Med Sch, Jerusalem, since 1967; head, Student Health Services, Heb U, Hadassah, since 1964; res, tchr, Dept of Internal Med, Hadassah Hosp, 1962-67; mem, med mission to Malawi, 1963; tchr, Hadassah Nursing Sch, 1963. Capt, Isr MC. Mem: Isr Assn for Internal Diseases; Royal Coll of Tropical Diseases. Contbr articles to profsl publs. Recipient: Halper Found scholarship, 1958; Sulke Prize, 1962; WHO Training f. Home: 8 Schiller St, Jerusalem, Isr. Office: Heb U-Hadassah Med Sch, Jerusalem, Isr.

OSTERWEIS, Rollin G, US, historian; b. W Haven, Conn, Aug 15, 1907; s. Gustav and Rose (Osterweis); BA, Yale U, 1930, MA, 1943, PhD, 1946; att: Oxford U, summers: 1929, 1931; Georgetown Fgn Service Sch, 1931-32; m. Ruth Loewenstein, Sep 27, 1932; c: Sally, Nancy, Ruth, Rollyn. Prof, hist, oratory, Yale U, since 1968, fac mem since 1943; asst prof, Navy V-12 prog, 1948-54, instr, 1943-45; sales mgr, partner, Lewis Osterweis and Sons, cigar mfr, 1933-41. Pres, New Haven Colony Hist Soc, 1962-67; mem: Amer J Hist Soc; Amer Hist Assn; Miss Valley Hist Assn; Conn Acad Arts and Scis; Delta Sigma Rho; Zeta Beta Tau; clubs: Authors, London; Yale, NYC; Mory's Assn; Yale; Elizabethan; Fac; Grad. Author: Judah P Benjamin, Statesman of the Lost Cause, 1933; Rebecca Gratz, A Study in Charm, 1935; Sesquicentennial History of Connecticut Academy of Arts and Sciences, 1949; Romanticism and Nationalism in the Old South, 1949; Santarem, Fr, 1960; co-author, Three Centuries of New Haven, 1638-1938, pub, 1953. Home: 396 Ronan St, New Haven, Conn. Office: Yale U, New Haven, Conn.

OSTOW, Mortimer, US, psychiatrist; b. Bklyn, NY, Jan 8, 1918; s. Kalman and Gertrude (Liebman); BA, Columbia U, 1937, MA, 1938; MD, NYU Coll of Med, 1941; DMedSc, Coll of Phys and Surgs, Columbia U, 1949; grad, NY Psychan Inst, 1950; m. Miriam Furst, 1942; c: Robin, Meir, Abigail, Rachel. Pvt practice, psycht, since 1948; asst att neur, Mt Sinai Hosp, since 1949; Edward T Sandrow visiting prof, Pastoral Psycht, JTSA; asst in neur, NYU Coll of Med, 1948-49; asst surg, USPHS, 1944-46; asso att psycht, Montefiore Hosp, 1960-66. F: Amer Psychiatric Assn; NY Acad of Med. Pres, Psychan Research and Devl Fund; vice-pres, Conservative Syn, Riverdale; charter mem, Amer Electroencephalographic Soc; mem: E Assn of Electroencephalographers; Bx Co Med Soc; NY Psychan Assn; Group for the Advancement of Psycht; Bx Soc for Neur and Psycht; Phi Beta Kappa; Alpha Omega Alpha; Sigma Xi. Author: Drugs in Psychoanalysis and Psychotherapy, 1962; co-author: Diagnostic Electroencephalography, 1952; The Need to Believe, 1954. Home and office: 5021 Iselin Ave, Riverdale, NY.

OSTRACH, Simon, US, educator; b. Providence, RI, Dec 26, 1923; s. Samuel and Bella (Sackman); BS, U of RI, 1944, ME, 1949; MSc, Brown U, 1949, PhD, 1950; m. Gloria Ostrov, Dec 31, 1944; c: Stefan, Louis, Naomi, David, Judith. Prof of Engr, head, Div of Fluid, Thermal, and Aerospace Scis, Case W Reserve U, Cleveland, O, since 1960; aeronautical research sci, NACA, 1944-47, chief, applied mech br, 1950-58, chief, fluid physics br, 1958-60; research asso, Brown U, 1947-50. Past chmn, heat transfer div, Amer Soc of Mech Engrs; chmn, educ comm, Park Syn, since 1957; mem: AAUP; Sigma Xi; High Sch Educ Comm, United Syn Comm on J Educ; Research Comm, J Comty Fed; asso f, Inst Aerospace Sci; club, Couples, cultural vice-pres, 1951-54 and since 1963. Contbr to research jours and books. Hobby: interscholastic and intercollegiate wrestling refereeing. Home: 2671 Green Rd, Shaker Heights, O. Office: Case W Reserve U, University Circle, Cleveland, O.

OSTROFF, Nathan, US, attorney; b. New Haven, Conn, Apr 27, 1910; s. Aaron and Sophie (Smirnoff); BA, Yale U, 1932, LLB, 1935; m. Ann Littman, Nov 21, 1940; c: Peter, Robert, Aaron. Dep gen counsel, Commerce Dept, since 1961; chmn, Appeals Bd, Dept of Commerce, since 1964; mem, Admn Conf of the US; asst to gen counsel, Bd Econ Warfare, 1941-43; Fgn Econ Admn, 1943-45; gen counsel, Off of Intl Trade, 1945-55; govt delg: to Moscow to negotiate for trade fair exch, 1958-1959; other intl trade confs, 1960. Gen counsel, Worldwide Assurance for Employees of Public Agcys; mem: Fed Bar Assn; Amer Acad Political Sci; Yale Law Sch Alumni Assn. Contbr to profsl jours. Recipient: Silver Medal, Commerce Dept, 1951. Home: 2914 Kanawha St NW, Washington, DC. Office: Commerce Dept, Washington, DC.

OSTROW, Gerald S, US, business exec; b. Phila, Pa, Apr 6, 1922; s. Charles and Essie (Wanger); BS, William and Mary Coll, 1942; m. Helen Struminger, July 1, 1945; c: William, Richard, Douglas, Carol. Pres, Clean Linen Service, since 1945. Lt, USAAF, 1942-45. Pres: J Family and Children's Service; Pa Textile Rental Service Assn; fmr, Pittsburgh Purveyors Assn; vice-pres, YM & YWHA; secy, United J Fed; bd mem, AJComm. Home: 1424 Hawthorne St, Pittsburgh, Pa. Office: 128 N Lexington Ave, Pittsburgh, Pa.

OSTROWSKI, Alexander Marcus, Switz, mathematician, educator; b. Kiev, Russ, Sep 25, 1893; s. Markus and Vera (Rashewski); att U Marburg; PhD, U Göttingen, 1920; hon PhD: U Zurich, Switz; U Besancon, Fr; U Waterloo, Can. Prof em, math, U Basel, since 1958; prof, dir, Math Inst, 1927-58; privat-dozent: U Hamburg, 1922; U Göttingen, 1923; Rockefeller f, Cambridge and Oxford, 1925-26. Mem: Hamburger Mathematische Gesellschaft; Basle Naturforschende; Gesellschaft für angewandte Mathematik; Basle Historisch-Antiquarische Gesellschaft; Swiss Math Soc; Amer Math Soc; Amer Math Assn; Berliner Mathematische Gesellschaft. Author: Studien über den Schottkyschen Satz, 1931; Vorlesungen über Differential- und Integralrechnung, vol I, 1965, vol II, 1961, vol III, 1967; Solutions of Equations and Systems of Equations, 1966; Aufagabensammlung zur Infinitesimalrechnung, vol I, 1964; contbr to sci jours. Home: Certenago, Montagnola, Ticino, Switz.

OSTROWSKY, Abbo, US, artist, teacher; b. Elisavetgrad, Russ, Oct 23, 1885; s. Frank and Rebecca (Boguslavsky); in US since 1908; att: Fine Art Sch, Odessa, 1905-07; Natl Acad of Design, NY, 1908-11. Dir em, Educ Alliance Art Sch, since 1955, found and dir, 1917-1955; head, Art Clan U Settlement, 1914. One-man shows: Women's City Club, Boston, 1916; Anderson Gals, NY, 1924; US Natl Mus, Wash, DC, 1931; Baltimore Art Mus, 1931; Keppel Art Gal, NY, 1937; represented in perm collections: Libr of Cong, Wash, DC; Amer Fed of Lab, Wash, DC; Bibliotèque Nationale, Paris; Mus of Western Art, Moscow; Natl Bezalel Mus, Jerusalem; Tel Aviv Mus, Isr; Baltimore Mus of Art; Metrop Mus of Art; exhibited at: Natl Acad of Design; Pa Acad of Fine Arts; Art Inst of Chgo; LA Art Assn; Soc of Amer Graphic Artists; Phila Print Club; Phila Art Alliance; Springfield Art Mus, Mass; Metrop Mus of Art; Natl Bezalel Mus, Jerusalem; Tel Aviv Mus, Isr; Mus of Western Art, Moscow; Bibliotèque Nationale, Paris; Victoria and Albert Mus, London; Oslo Mus, Norway. Fmr chmn, visual arts comm, Natl Fed Settlements and United Neighborhood Houses, NY; mem: Allied Artists Amer; Soc Amer Graphic Artists; Artists Equity Assn; Natl Workers Alliance. Recipient: Prize, Soc Amer Graphic Artists, 1937. Home: 9528 67 Ave, Forest Hills, NY.

OSTROWSKY, Avi, Isr, conductor; b. Petah Tikva, Isr, Aug 10, 1939; s. Michael and Yona (Tsfathman); att: Music Tchrs' Training Coll, Tel Aviv, 1956-58; Rubin Acad of Music, Tel Aviv, 1959-62; Staats-Akademie für Musik und darstellende Kunst, Vienna, 1966-68. Musical dir, perm conductor, Haifa Sym Orch, since 1969; conductor, kibbutzim orch, since 1961; perm conductor, Isr Bc Choir, 1965-66; guest conductor:

Isr Philharmonic Orch; Isr Chamber Ensemble; Orch of the Isr Bc Service; orchs abroad. Cpl, Nahal, 1958-61. Recipient: scholarships, Isr-Amer Cultural Found, 1966-68; 1st Prize, Intl Competition for Young Conductors, The Nicolai Malko Competition, 1968. Home: Kibbutz Lahav, Isr. Office: Haifa Sym Orch, POB 5270, Haifa, Isr.

OTTENBERG, Miriam, US, journalist, author; b. Wash, DC, July 10, 1914; d. Louis and Nettie (Podell); att Goucher Coll, Baltimore, 1931-33; BA, U Wis, 1933-35. Investigative reporter, Evening Star, Wash, DC since 1937; copy writer, Neisser-Meyerhoff, 1935-37; reporter, Akron Times Press, 1937. Pres, Women's Natl Press Club, 1964-65. Author, The Federal Investigators, 1962. Recipient: Pulitzer Prize, journalism, 1960; Natl Headliner Award, public service, 1970. Spec interests: exposing crime, corruption and consumer fraud, travel, ships. Home: 2939 Van Ness St NW, Washington, DC. Office: 225 Virginia Ave SE, Washington, DC.

OTTINGER, Richard Lawrence, US, attorney, comty organizer; b. NYC, Jan 27, 1929; s. Lawrence and Louise (Loewenstein); BA, Cornell U, 1950; LLB, Harvard, 1953; att Georgetown U Law Sch, 1960-61; m. Betty Schneider, Oct 3, 1953; c: Ronald, Randall, Lawrence, Jenny. Org dir, Grassroots Action Inc, since 1971; asso, Cleary, Gottlieb, Friendly & Hamilton, 1955-56; partner, with William J Kridel, 1956-60; contract mgr, Intl Coop Admn, 1960-61; dir progs, W Coast, S Amer, Peace Corps, 1961-64; mem, 89-91 US Congs, 25th Dist, NY, 1965-70; Dem candidate, NY, US Senate, 1970. Capt, USAF, 1953-55. Prin contribs: sponsored and supported conservation legislation in Cong. Bd dirs: UN Assn, US; chmn, Rogers Coll; Friends of Earth; Environmental Defense Fund; mem: Cornell U Council; natl adv council, Tuskegee Inst; Atlantic Council, US; adv comm, Natl Rivers and Harbors Cong; Natl Audubon Soc; Friends of Hudson; Temple Beth El, N Westchester; Bronxville Amer Legion Post, 464; Cortlandt Conservation Assn; Scarsdale Elks Lodge; B'nai B'rith, Saw Mill River Lodge 2126; Mahopac Grange; KP; clubs: Sierra, Golden Retriever, US. Home: 235 Bear Ridge Rd, Pleasantville, NY. Office: 2000 P St NW, Washington, DC.

OUHANNA, Alberto Elie, Isr, banker; b. Valletta, Malta, Nov 2, 1915; s. Nessim Ouhanna; att Lycée Français, Port Said, Egypt; m. Nitzhia Cohen; c: Yuval, Oded. Mgr, main br, Barclays Bank, Tel Aviv, with firm since 1935; fmr: mem, Banim Legvulam, public instn for assisting colonization of Sephardic J; with finance dept, Min of Defense, Isr War of Independence. Mem: B'nai B'rith, Jerusalem and Tel Aviv; Masons; Rotary; co-found, Egyptian Immigrants Org. Home: 23 Rembrandt St, Tel Aviv, Isr. Office: 103 Allenby St, Tel Aviv, Isr.

OUR, Helholz Menachem, Isr, trade unionist, painter; b. Pol, Mar 14, 1911; s. Yeshayahu and Sarah (Mlinek); in Isr since 1933; att U Belgium, Brussels, 1930-32; m. Esther Henig, 1947; c: Cyla. Mem secretariat, Confd Clerical Employees, Isr, since 1949, mem exec, Local Council of Haifa; RR laborer, secy, Haifa sect, Intl Assn of Post, Telegraph and RR Employees, 1933-42. Haganah, 1934-48. Mem, Assn of Painters and Sculptors in Isr; Haifa Youth Council, 1944-48; secy, leAsirenu, aid assn for prisoners, Haifa, 1946-48. Home: 4 Hadai St, Bat Yam, Isr. Office: 93 Arlosoroff St, Tel Aviv, Isr.

OVADIA, Jacques, Isr, journalist; b. Athens, Greece, Aug 1, 1919; s. Alfred and Lotti (Schmicker); in Isr since 1950; m. Fernande Amar, June 29, 1953; c: Alfred. Journalist: cinema critic, police reporter, and chief, day's info, since 1963; fmr, reporter for various weeklies and periodicals in Egypt and Fr, after WW II. Sgt, Fgn Legion, Free Fr Forces. Secy, Isr Sect, Assn de Fr Libres, Paris. Author: Clameurs rationnées, 1962; Elie Cohen, l'espion de Damas, 1967; writer of poetry for various jours. Recipient: Croix de Guerre avec Palmes; Médaille Coloniale avec Agrafes; Médaille du Levant; 1st prize for poetry, Tutti gli uomini, It, 1964. Home: 33 Arlosoroff St, Ramat Gan, Isr. Office: 52 Harakevet St, Tel Aviv, Isr.

OVADYAHU, Mordechai, Isr, author, journalist; b. Siedlce, Pol, 1909; s. David and Ita (Silberman) Gottesdiener; in Isr since 1931; att: Agric Sch; U of London; m. Henny Zisle; c: Yehudith Shachar, Zvi. Lit ed, Dapim Refuiim, Kupat Holim, since 1944; fmr: active in Halutz Hahshara, Pol; agric worker, Pal; ed staff, haOlam. Mem, Isr Authors Assn. Author: A Man in the Street, 1941; Conversations with Bialik, 1945; Essays on Literary Criticism, 1952; Day by Day,

1954; One Stop too Soon, 1960; Bialik Speaks, 1969; regular contbr to: Davar; Al Hamishmar; labor press; lit mags, in Isr, US; broadcaster, lit subjects, Kol Israel Radio. Home: 182 Ibn Gevirol St, Tel Aviv, Isr. Office: 101 Arlosoroff St, Tel Aviv, Isr.

OWEN, Arthur, Eng, business exec; b. Fürth , Ger, July 29, 1901; s. Louis and Betty (Wassermann) Offenstadt; Abitur, Reform Gymnasium, 1916; m. Rosie Friedmann, Aug 9, 1925; c: Peter. Bus exec since 1933; dir, Vision Press Publ, 1946-69. Grand vice pres, B'nai B'rith Dist Grand Lodge of Gt Brit and Ir; pres, B'nai B'rith, Leo Baeck Lodge, London, 1959-62, 1964-65. Spec interests: social service, lit. Home: 41 Barn Rise, Wembley Park, Middlesex, Eng. Office: 74a Regent St, London W1, Eng.

OZ, Amos, Isr, author; b. Jerusalem, May 4, 1939; s. Yehuda and Rivka (Mussman) Klausner; BA, Heb U, 1963; m. Nily Zuckerman, Apr 5, 1960; c: Fania, Galia. Author: Where the Jackals Howl, 1964; Somewhere Else, 1965; My Michael, 1967. Sgt, Nahal, 1958-61. Recipient: Lit Award, Holon Munic, 1966; Working Award, Amer-Isr Culture Found, 1968. Home: Kibbutz Hulda, Isr.

mie Française; two prizes, l'Académie des Sciences Morales et Politiques. Home: 4 rue Thiers, Paris, Fr.

PARDES, Markus, Belgium, attorney; b. Berlin, Ger, Dec 16, 1930; s. Moszek and Braune; in Belgium since 1939; D en droit, U Libre de Brussels, 1957; licencié en droit comparé, U Intl de Strasbourg, 1961; m. Eva Teger, Dec 22, 1957; c: David, Michel, Anne. Atty, Brussels Court of Appeals, since 1959; researcher, Intl Cen of Comparative Law, Brussels; mem, Henri Capitant Assn. Pres, Youth Cen, Brussels; admnr: Isr Sch, Brussels; Consistoire Central Israelite de Belgique. Author: Le Statut Juridique de l'Entreprise en Droit Comparé, 1967; Egalité et Discrimination en Droit Commercial Belge, 1965. Spec interests: educ, culture. Home: 77 Hettewie Blvd, Brussels, Belgium. Office: 100 Louis Schmidt Blvd, Brussels, Belgium.

PARDESS, Shlomo, Isr, public official; b. Jerusalem, Dec 8, 1925; s. Eliyahu and Zohara (Aburabiah); att: Jerusalem Tech Sch; Inst for Elec Engr; m. Dvorah Muhlbauer, Aug 4, 1960; c: Eliyahu, Zohara, Moshe. Dir, telephone services of Jerusalem and S dist, since 1961; dir off, Min of Rel Affairs, 1958-61. Lt, Signal Corps, IDF, 1948-50. Mem, secretariat, Lab Party, Jerusalem; coord, Post Off Workers, Jerusalem; fmr: mem exec: Histadrut; Sephardic Council; Rel Council. Contbr to jours. Home: 11 Arlosoroff St, Jerusalem, Isr. Office: 43 Narkiss St, Jerusalem, Isr.

PARDO, Tova, Isr, actress; b. Bulgaria; d. Angelo and Erna (Frölich) Geron; widow; c: Erel. Mem: Habimah Theater; Ohel Theatre; roles in radio plays, motion pictures; leading roles: Alice, Strindberg's Dance of Death; Blanche, Streetcar Named Desire; daughter, Pirandello's Six Characters; Marie, Ionesco's Thirst and Hunger; Helen, A Taste of Honey. Mem, Isr Actors Assn. Home: I Mapu St, Tel Aviv, Isr. Office: Habimah Theater, Tel Aviv, Isr.

PARELMAN, Samuel I, US, foreign service off, attorney; b. Wilmington, Del, Feb 11, 1916; s. Morris and Pearl (Cagan); BCS, Benjamin Franklin U, 1938; LLB, Columbia U, 1941; grad Natl War Coll, 1956; MA, Boston U, 1965; m. Anita Stephenson, Oct 13, 1941; c: Rhona, Sara. Spec asst, Off of Secy of State, since 1968; served in domestic agcys, Fed Govt, 1934-42; budget dir, Lend Lease, 1943-46; adv, US delg to UN, 1946-47; planning off on Marshall Plan, 1947-48; dep, Philippine Rehab Coord, 1948-50; spec asst to Asst Secy of State for Far E, 1949-55; consul, first secy of emb, Tokyo, 1956-58; fgn policy adv: Pres Comm to Study US Mil Assistance Prog, White House, 1958-59; US Forces, Japan, 1956-58; sr planning off, Off of Under Secy and Secy of State, Wash, DC, 1959-62; fgn service off, since 1955; first secy of Emb, Bonn, and political adv to Cdr in Chief, US Army, Eur, Heidelberg, 1963-65; acting dir and dep dir, Off of Intl Confs, 1965-68. Mem: DC Bar Assn; Amer Fgn Service Assn; Fed Bar Assn; Natl Planning Assn; Amer Soc for Intl Law; club, Natl Lawyers. Home: 10602 Bucknell Dr, Silver Spring, Md. Office: Dept of State, Washington, DC.

PARENT, Sol, US, cardiologist; b. Minsk, Russ, Nov 17, 1903; s. Samuel and Libe (Golub); in US since 1909; BS, Rutgers U, 1924; MD, NYU Bellevue Med Coll, 1928; m. Rosalie Goldberg, Aug 27, 1927; c: Samuel, Sondra Greenberg. Dir, dept med educ, Newark Beth Isr Med Cen, since 1965; cons card, Coit Memorial Babies Hosp, since 1951; adjunct att phys, Beth Isr Hosp, since 1940; att card, St Michaels Hosp, since 1956; asso phys, Presbyterian Hosp, since 1935; pvt practice 1931-65. L] col, US Army MC, 1942-46. Dipl, Amer Bd Intl Med; and treas, Acad Med of NJ; f: Amer Coll Phys; Amer Coll Cardiology; mem, bd trustees: Essex Co Heart Assn, pres, 1953-55; NJ Heart Assn; JCC of Essex Co; bd govs, Pleasant Valley Way Home for Aged; mem: Assn Mil Surgs; Temple B'nai Abraham; B'nai B'rith; Masons. Contbr to med jours. Home: 184 Wilder St, Hillside, NJ. Office: 89 Lincoln Pk, Newark, NJ.

PARKER, Albert, US, attorney, business exec; grad: Columbia U, 1919; NY Law Sch, 1921. Sr partner law firm, Parker, Chapin and Flattau; mem, bd dirs and exec comm: Interstate Dept Stores; Belding Heminway Co; Leslie Fay; vice chmn, bd dirs, exec comm, First Isr Bank and Trust Co, NY. Natl co-chmn, UJA, fmr: chmn, pres, Gtr NY, chmn, Natl study mission comm, chmn, exec comm, Gtr NY, natl co-chmn, Isr Educ Fund; dir, JDC; trustee, United Isr Appeal; trustee at large, FJP, NY; pres, Haifa U Found; dir: Amer Comm Weizmann Inst of Sci; Amer Friends of Heb U; chmn bd, Amer Trade and Ind Devl with Isr; mem: bd overseers,

Albert Einstein Coll of Med; bd dirs, CJFWF; Intl Econ Adv Comm to State of Isr; bd overseers, overseas bd trustees; Bar Ilan U, fmr, mem bd dirs, Columbia Coll Fund; clubs: Harmonie, NYC; Columbia U, NYC; Palm Beach, Country, Fla. Recipient: hon f, Bar Ilan U, 1965; f, Brandeis U, 1967; Dist Service Award, Albert Einstein Coll of Med, 1962; chmn's award, UJA of Gtr NY, 1969. Home: 785 Fifth Ave, New York, NY. Office: 530 Fifth Ave, New York, NY.

PARKER, Morris L, US, surgeon, educator; b. Kiev, Russ, Sep 25, 1896; s. Julius and Sophie; in US since 1906; BS, Northwestern U, 1919, MD, 1923. Sr att surg, Michael Reese Hosp, Chgo, since 1953; clinical asst prof, surg, U of Ill, 1927-62; em since 1962. US Army, 1918-19. Dipl, Amer Bd of Surgs; chmn, med div, CJA, since 1962; co-chmn, Chgo div, Amer Phys Comm, Heb U, since 1962; bd, J Fed, Metrop Chgo, 1964-69; bd trustees, Chgo Health Cen, ILGWU, since 1957; mem: Amer Coll of Surgs; Chgo Surg Soc; Chgo Med Soc; Intl Coll of Surg; B'nai B'rith. Contbr to med jours. Home: 400 E Randolph St, Chicago, Ill. Office: 30 N Michigan Ave, Chicago, Ill.

PARTOS, Oedoen, Isr, composer, violist; b. Budapest, Hung, Oct 1, 1907; s. Richard and Johanna (Hirsch); in Isr since 1938; dipl, Acad of Music, Budapest, 1925; studied with Hubay and Kodaly; m. Dina Raiskin, Nov, 1943. Dir: Isr Acad of Music, Tel Aviv, since 1951; Beth Daniel, chamber music sem, since 1957; asso prof, music, Tel Aviv, U, since 1961; judge: intl competitions, intl sems, courses for viola and chamber music, Holland, It; mem adv bd, Isr Min of Educ-and Culture, since 1959; first violist; soloist, Isr Philharmonic Orch, 1938-56; concertmaster, orchs: Switz, Hung, Ger, until 1938; toured: Eur, US, Can. Composer: Konzertstück, 1934; Choral Fantasia on Yemenite Themes, chorus and orch, 1946; Alu Seh beNegeb, chorus, 1948; four Israeli Melodies, for violin and piano, 1948; Yizkor, viola and orch, 1949; Song of Praise, viola and orch, 1949; Symphony, 1951; Bnei Amal, chorus; Three Fantasias on Palestinian Folksongs; String Quartet; two viola concerti, 1957; Violin Concerto, 1958; Ballad for Viola, 1957; Dmuyot, orch and two string quartets, 1960; Maquamat, flute and strings, 1960; Yltur for 12 harps, 1961; arrangements: Concerto No 1, for viola and orch, by Karl Stamitz; Arpeggiona Sonata, by Schubert; Yemenite and Oriental Folksongs. Recipient: 1st prize for string quartet, NY Music Critics Circle, 1941; Engel Prize, Tel Aviv 1948, 1951; Isr Prize, 1954. Home: 25 Tzimhei Hayehudim St, Ramat Aviv, Isr.

PARUZ, Hanoch, Isr, scientist; b. Bialystok, Pol, Feb 10, 1923; s. Jehuda and Mina (Zylberg) Pruzan; BSc, Technion, Haifa, 1947, EE, 1949, ME, 1952; DEng, U of Paris, Fr, 1963; m. Varda Nishry, Nov 1, 1959; c: Michal. Asst to Chief Sci, Min of Defense, since 1967; head of research group: Sci Dept, Min of Defense, 1953-59; Isr AEC, 1959-67. Capt, IDF, 1948-53. Contbr to sci jours. Hobbies: hist of art, archaeol. Home: 15 Herzog St, Givatayim, Isr. Office: Min of Defense, Hakirya, Tel Aviv, Isr.

PARZEN, Herbert, US, rabbi author; b. Ozorkow, Pol, Dec 23, 1896; s. Charles and Malka (Dobzinski); in US since 1907; BA, U Mich, 1919; MA, Columbia U, 1926; ordained rabbi, MHL, JTSA, 1926; m. Sylvia Goldsmith, Sep 30, 1923. Research asso, Theodor Herzl Inst, since 1957, spec lectr, J hist lit, since 1957; rabbi, 1924-29; dir: progs, United Syn Amer, 1949-55; Reconstructionist Found, 1955-59. Author: Early History of Zionism in America, 1958; Short History of Zionism, 1962; Herzl Shows His Mind on Issues, 1962; Architects of Conservative Judaism, 1964; ed: United Syn Rev, 1952-55; RA Bull, 1952-55; mem, bd eds, Conservative Judaism, 1955-57; asso, ed bd, The Reconstructionist, 1957-59; contbr to: Harvard Theol Rev; J Quarterly Rev; Herzl Yearbook; J Book Annual; Commentary; The Reconstructionist; Amer J Hist Quarterly. Mem: RA, past mem, bd dirs, ZOA. Home: 205 Pinehurst Ave, New York, NY. Office: 515 Park Ave, New York, NY.

PASCH, Maurice Bernard, US, attorney; b. Chilton, Wis, June 17, 1910; s. Jacob and Eva; att George Wash U Law Sch; JD, U Wis; m. Janet Gerhardt, 1936; c: Ellen Bortz, Robert, Suzy. Practicing atty, Maurice B Pasch and Assos, since 1940; atty: FCC, 1930-31; Wis Rural Electrification Admn, 1931-32; secy to US Sen Robert M LaFollette Jr, 1932-36; asst atty gen, State of Wis, 1936-40; fac mem, U Wis Law Sch, 1968-69. Lt-cdr, USN, 1942-46. Fmr pres: King David lodge, B'nai B'rith; S Wis Council, B'nai B'rith; Beth El Temple; Madison Navy League; Nakoma PTA; chmn, Madison JWF, secy;

State Cdr, Mil Order of WWs; dir, Commercial Law League of Amer; mem: State Coordinating Comm for Higher Educ; bd dirs, Wis Soc for J Learning; bd regents, U Wis; regional council, ADL; exec comm, AJComm; Wis Higher Educ Aids Bd; co, state, Amer Bar Assns; Masons; Elks; Amer Judicature Soc; ZOA; B'nai B'rith; Phi Sigma Delta; Civic Music Assn; Libr Assn; Gen Hosp Assn; Heb Free Loan Soc all Madison; Amer Legion; VFW; clubs: Lions; Shriners; Madison. Recipient: navy ribbons, during, WW II; State Award, outstanding service, NCCJ; citation, B'nai B'rith; citation, UJA. Home: 4834 Sherwood Rd, Madison, Wis. Office: 30 West Mifflin St,Madison, Wis.

PASCHER, Frances, US, physician, educator; b. NYC, June 5, 1905; d. Mendel and Taube (Dubester); MD, LI Coll Hosp, 1928; m. Abram Kanof, June 28, 1931; c: Elizabeth Levine, Margaret Norden. Visiting phys, Bellevue Hosp, since 1967; prof, clinical dermat, NYU Sch of Med and Postgrad Med Sch, since 1954; att phys, dermat, U Hosp NYU Med Cen, since 1948; engaged in clinical research; pvt practice, 1934-66. F: AMA; Soc for Investigative Dermat; Amer Acad Dermat; chmn: Frances Pascher Research Fund in Dermat, Hadassah Rothschild Hosp, Jerusalem, since 1958; curriculm comm, and mem, formulary comm, NY Skin and Cancer Unit, NYU Med Cen; pres, Bx Dermat Soc, 1956-57; vice-pres, Friends of NYU Med Libr; trustee, med libr, NYU Med Cen; mem: Soc for Study of Blood; Shaare Torah, Bklyn; J Mus; Modern Mus of Art; Metrop Mus of Art; Audubon Soc and Natl Parks; Dermat Found; NY Zool Soc; record room, libr, pharm therapeutics comms, NYU Med Cen; life: NY Acad of Med, since 1958; ZOA; hon, Dermat and Syphilology Socs: Cuba, since 1954; Venezuela, since 1956; Isr since 1957; Brazil, since 1958. Author, chaps in med textbooks and encys; co-author, med teaching film, Dermatologic Allergy, 1942; ed, Dermatologic Formulary, 1952, 1957; contbr to profsl jours. Hobbies: contemporary art, gerdening, travel. Home: 500 E 77 St, New York, NY. Office: 562 First Ave, New York, NY.

PASKOW, Shimon, US, rabbi; b. Newark, NJ, June 21, 1932; s. Aron and Celia (Daniels) Piaskowsky; BA, Bklyn Coll; MA, ordained rabbi, HUC-JIR, 1959; m. Carol Bauman, July 18, 1962; c: Michele. Asso rabbi, Valley J Comty Cen and Temple; intsr rel, U of Judaism; bibl tchr, Northridge Methodist Church, 1965; fmr: instr, Talmud, Houston J Tchrs Inst; Spiritual leader, Houston, Tex; conducted radio prog; rabb: Temple Sholom, Bklyn, NY; Cong B'nai Isr, Parkersburg, W Va; Chaplain, US Army, 1960-62. Found, S Cal Comm on Behalf of Soviet J; mem: Comty Adv comm, 12 dist, LA, Cal; CCAR; Assn of J Chaplains; Mil Chaplains Assn; Bd Rabbis S Cal; Soc of Bibl Lit; RA. Contbr to jours; appears: radio, TV. Recipient: Outstanding service award, NJWB; US Army, both 1962. Home: 14320 Burbank Blvd, Van Nuys, Cal. Study: 5540 Laurel Canyon Blvd, Hollywood, Cal.

PASMANTIER, David, US, business exec; b. NYC, Jan 17, 1899; s. John and Rose (Rosenberg); att Tchrs Coll, Columbia U, 1915-18; m. Anne Richman, Aug 18, 1918; c: Jean deMesquita, Paul. Owner, Pasmantier Co, since 1956, partner, John L Pasmantier & Sons, 1919-56; chmn of bd, Arcadia Export-import Corp, since 1946; pres: Call Realty, since 1951; Dadson Co since 1957; secy-treas, Pasmantier Motors, since 1950; dir, Joint Purchasing Corp, since 1952. Dir, UJA, since 1950, mem exec bd; secy and trustee, Bx Hosp, since 1943; chmn, bd, Temple Adath Israel, 1923, chmn, bldg comm, 1921; mem: council, JDC, 1952; bd, FJP, 1951; Masons; clubs: Level; Town; Housewares, China and Glass. Home: 10 Park Ave, New York, NY. Office: 224 Fifth Ave, New York, NY.

PASSAMANECK, Stephen Maurice, US, rabbi, educator; b. Pittsburgh, Pa, Dec 7, 1933; s. Herman and Dolores (Jaskol); BA, U Pittsburgh, 1955; MA, HUC, 1960; PhD, 1964; dipl, law, Oxford U, 1963; m. Majorie Blattner, Sep 2, 1962; c: Daniel, Eve, Asso prof, rabb, HUC-JIR, LA, since 1968, asso prof 1964-68. Chaplain, Phi Epsilon Pi Frat; mem, CCAR. Contbr to scholarly jours. Home: 4518 Wortser Ave, N Hollywood, Cal. Office: 8745 Appian Way, Los Angeles, Cal.

PASTERNACK, Robert Francis, US, educator; b. NYC, Sep 20, 1936; s, Jack and Sarah (Miller); BA Cornell U 1957, PhD, 1962; m. Dorothy Topken, Apr 7, 1959; c: Jennifer, Jeffrey. Prof, chem, Ithaca Coll, since 1967, mem fac since 1963; cons, NY State Dept Educ, since 1966; visiting research sci, Cornell U, since 1963; postdoc chem, U of Ill, 1962-63; cons, Natl Bur Standards, 1963, 1964, research

chem, summers; research asso, Brandeis U, summers 1965, 1966, 1967; numerous research sems, 1965-69. Prin contrib: co-found, Pasternack-McDonnel sys for nomenclature of transition metal complexes. Found, dir C P Snow lectr series; mem: Amer Chem Soc; AAAS; AAUP; Phi Beta Kappa; Phi Kappa Phi; Sigma Xi; Oracle Soc. Recipient: Cornell Scholarship; Chem Prize; Clevite Award; Gen Elec f; NIH f; research grants; educ grants. Contbr numerous papers to sci jours. Office: Ithaca Coll, Ithaca, NY.

PASTOR, Harry Bernard, US, rabbi; b. Kiev, Russ, Oct 5, 1910; s. Cecil and Dora (Chrisman); in US, since 1913; BA, U Cincinnati, 1932; BH, ordained rabbi, HUC, 1935, DD; m. Cylvia Bear, Feb 7, 1953; c: Andrea, David. Rabbi: Cong, Shalom, since 1951; Cong, Ansheai Emeth, Peoria, Ill, 1935-47; Cong Emanuel, Milwaukee, 1947-51. Fmr pres: Phi Beta Kappa, Milwaukee; N Shore Council on Hum Relations; Wis Council of Rabbis. Home: 8439 Indian Creek Pkwy, Milwaukee, Wis. Office: 7630 N Santa Monica Blvd, Milwaukee, Wis.

PATAI, Raphael, US, anthropologist; b. Budapest, Hung, Nov 22, 1910; s. Joseph and Edith (Ehrenfeld); in US since 1947; PhD, U Budapest, 1933; PhD, Heb U, 1936; c: Ofra, Daphne. Dir, research, Herzl Inst and ed, Herzl Press, NY, since 1956; prof, anthropology, Fairleigh-Dickinson U, since 1966; research, Heb U, 1937-38, 1944-47, instr, 1938-42; dir, research, Pal Inst of Folklore and Ethnology, Jerusalem, 1945-47; Viking fund f, 1947-48; visiting prof, anthropology, U of Pa, 1948-49; lectr, New Sch for Social Research, 1948; lectr, anthropology, Columbia U, 1948, 1954-56, 1960-61, research asso, Bur Applied Soc Research, 1949; prof anthropology, Dropsie Coll, 1948-57; lectr, educ, NYU, 1951; cons on ME Dept Social Affairs, UN Secretariat, 1951; visiting lectr, Princeton U, 1952-54; dir, Syria-Leb-Jordan research project, Hum Relations Area Files, New Haven, 1955-56; visiting prof, anthropology, O State U, 1956. F: Amer Anthropological Assn; chmn, Comm on Intl Relations in Folklore, 1953-55; mem, Council of Amer Folklore Soc. Author: Poems of Israel Berechia Fontanella, 1933; A Study in Palestinian Folklore, 1936; Jewish Seafaring in Ancient Times, 1938; Man and Earth in Hebrew Custom, Belief and Legend, 2 vols, 1942-43; The Science of Man, an Introduction to Anthropology, 2 Vols, 1947-48; Man and Temple in Ancient Jewish Myth and Ritual, 1947, 2nd ed, 1967; Israel Between East and West, 1953; The Hashemite Kingdom of Jordan, 1956; The Republic of Lebanon, 2 vols, 1956; The Republic of Syria, 2 vols, 1956; Annotated Bibliography of Syria, Lebanon and Jordan, 1957; Jordan, 1957; The Kingdon of Jordan, 1958; Current Jewish Social Research, 1958; Cultures in Conflict, 1958, 1961; Sex and Family in the Bible and the Middle East, 1959, 1960; Golden River to Golden Road: Society, Culture and Change in the Middle East, 1962, 3rd ed, 1969; The Hebrew Goddess, 1967; co-author, Hebrew Myths, 1964; ed: Anthology of Palestinian Short Stories, 1938, 6 eds; Edoth, communities: A Quartely for Folklore and Ethnology, Jerusalem, Jerusalem, 1945-48; Studies in Folklore and Ethnology, Jerusalem; Social Studies, Jerusalem; Studies in Biblical and Jewish Folklore, 1960; Herzl Year Book, Vols I-VI, 1958-66; Complete Diaries of Theodore Herzl, 1960; Women in the Modern World, 1967. Contbr on ME and J anthropology. Home: 39 Bow St, Forest Hills, NY. Office: 515 Park Ave, New York, NY.

PATAI, Saul, Isr, educator; b. Budapest, Hung, Aug 2, 1918; s. Joseph and Edith (Ehrenfeld); in Isr since 1938; MSc, Heb U, 1941, PhD, 1947; m. Elise Schaner, 1944; c: Irith Diklah, Michael. Asso prof, organic chem, Heb U, since 1957. IDF, 1947-48. Mem: Chem Soc, London; NY Acad Sci. Author: Textbook of Organic Chemistry, Heb; Glossary of Organic Chemistry, 1962; co-author, High School Organic Chemistry, 1960; gen ed, The Chemistry of the Functional Groups; ed: The Chemistry of the Alkenes, 1964; The Chemistry of the Carbonyl Group, 1966; The Chemistry of the Ether Linkage, 1967; The Chemistry of the Amino Group, 1968; The Chemistry of the Carboxyl Group; The Chemistry of the Azomethine Group; contbr to sci jours. Hobby, philately. Home: 28 Radak St, Jerusalem, Isr. Office: Dept Organic Chem, Heb U, Jerusalem, Isr.

PATCHAN, Joseph, US, attorney; b. Bklyn, NY, June 29, 1922; s. Jacob and Gertrude (Yalan) Pashin; BS, BA, Miami U, Ohio; att W Reserve U; JD, Cleveland Marshall Law Sch, O, 1952; m. Nancy Letaw, Jan 7, 1951; c: Reed, Judith, David. Partner law firm, Selker, Patchan and Einbund, since 1969; lectr: debtor-creditor law, Cleveland Marshall Law Sch; bar

P

PACANOWSKA, Felicia, Fr, artist; b. Lodz, Pol, Jan 15, 1907; d. Hajman and Gustawa (Roth); in Fr since 1937; att Acad of Fine Art, Warsaw, Rome; Scuola della Medaglia, Rome. One-man shows: Lodz, 1937; Mus Royan, 1938; Padova, 1949; Paris, 1953, 1958; Bezalel, Isr, 1963, 1964; group shows: mus and gals, all over the world, 1935-69; exhbs of orgs, salons: Indépendents; Le Trait; Automne; Comparaisons; Réalités Nouvelles; Mai; Art Sacré, all Fr; paintings, etchings, in collections: Govt of Fr, City of Paris; Natl Mus of Modern Art, Paris; mus: Jerusalem; Tel Aviv; Haifa; Ein Harod; Ashdot Yaacov, Rehovot, all Israel; Cabinets des Estampes: Natl Libr, Paris; U of Warsaw; Royal Libr, Brussels, Antwerp; Brit Mus; Victoria and Albert Mus, both London; Farnesina, Rome; Royal Mus, Copenhagen. Paintings and engravings reproduced in numerous books. Mem: Le Trait, since 1949; Automne, since 1950; fmr mem, Indépendents. Home and studio: 1 rue Adjudant-Réau, Paris 20, Fr.

PACANOWSKI, Moshe David, It, architect; b. Lodz, Pol, Jan 4, 1905; s. Chaim and Golda (Roth); in It since 1923; deg, Sch of Architecture, Rome, 1928; DEng architect, Poly Sch, Milan, 1928, att spec courses in reinforced concrete, 1929; m. Lidia Sterle, Apr 4, 1956; c: Ermanno, Andrea, Mirta. Pvt practice since 1937; architect: London, 1929-30; Paris, 1930-34. Among works executed: Telephone Co off Bldg, Naples; ind bldgs, Milan, Rome; stations of Roman underground; interior decoration for ships; exhb at: Afr Architectural Exhb, Rome, 1938; Intl Exhb of Architecture, Sao Paulo, Brazil, 1954. Engr, Allied Troops, WW II. Mem: Roman Architects Assn; Inst It Architects; Roman Engrs and Architects Assn; J Comty; clubs: Garden; Lions, both Rome; It Touring; Landscape and Archeol. Works pub in books and architectural mags in It and abroad. Recepient: award, garden planning, Rome Airport, 1958. Hobby: gardening. Home: 1009 Cassia St, Rome, It. Office: 859 Cassia St, Rome, It.

PACHTER, Heinz, Maximilian (Henry), US, author, journalist; b. Berlin, Ger, Jan 22, 1907; s. Emil and Helene (Streisand); in US since 1941; PhD, U Berlin; m. Hedwig Roesler, 1940; c: Renee. NY corresp, Weltwoche, Zurich, Switz; fgn corresp since 1949; lectr, CCNY; free-lance writer, lectr, Ger, 1933; researcher, newspaper writer, Paris, 1933-40; fmr asso with OWI and Office of Strategic Services; ed, Econ Trends, 1945-50; Guggenheim f, 1953. Author: Wirtschaft unterm Rutenbündel, 1932; Monopol und Nationalsozialismus, 1936; Espagne, Creuset Politique, 1938; Nazi Deutsch, 1944; Magic into Science-the Life of Paracelsus, 1952; Totalitarian Propaganda, 1954; Kennedy-Castro-Khruschev, 1963; Weltmacht Russland, 1968; co-author, Axis Grand Strategy. Mem: UN Corresps Assn; Amer Hist Soc; clubs: Overseas Press; Renaissance. Home: 310 W 106 St, New York, NY.

PACKMAN, Victor, US, attorney; b. St Louis, Mo, Dec 5, 1903; s. Alexander and Dora (Atlas); JD, Wash U, St Louis; m. Selma Coopersmith, June 16, 1928; c: Vicki, Patti. Dir: Ampal-Amer Isr Corp, since 1946, chmn, exec comm, since 1966; Amer-Isr Ind Devl Bank Ltd, Tel Aviv, since 1959; regional dir, Histadrut Campaign, since 1959. Trustee: Stizy Lewin and David Orblitt Charity Fund; Rudolph Coopersmith Found; Summer Travel Study Found; mem, B'nai Amoona Cong; fmr chmn, chaplaincy comm, treas, J Fed, Home: 7506 Wydown, Clayton, Mo. Office: 10 S Brentwood, Clayton, Mo.

PADOVER, Saul K, US, educator, political sci; b. Aus, Apr 13, 1905; s. Keva and Frumet (Goldmann); in US since 1920; BA, Wayne U, 1928; MA, U Chgo, 1930, PhD, 1932. Prof, grad fac, New Sch for Social Research, NYC, since 1949, dean, Sch of Politics, 1949-55; lectr, Ethical Culture Soc, since 1948; research asso, U of Cal, 1933-36; Guggenheim f, 1936; asst to US Secy of Interior, 1938-43; cons, Off of Facts and Figures, 1942; prin analyst, FCC, 1944; Rockefeller f, 1945; US War Dept mission to Ger, 1946; ed writer, PM newspaper, NYC, 1946-48; cons, Hoover Inst, Stanford U, 1948; visiting prof, Sorbonne U, Paris, 1949; leader, Quaker Intl Sems in Eur, 1949-51; lectr for US State Dept, SE Asian Us, 1953; visiting

prof: U Tokyo,1960; U Malaya,1960. 1962, 1968; prof, Salzburg Sem, 1966. Political intelligence off, Office of Strategic Services and US Army, 1944-45. Mem: Phi Beta Kappa. Author: Revolutionary Emperor, Joseph II, 1935; Secret Diplomacy, 1937; Life and Death of Louis XVI, 1939; Jefferson, 1942; Experiment in Germany, 1946; La Vie Politique des Etats-Unis, 1949; France: Setting or Rising Star, 1950; Psychological Warfare, 1951; Europe's Quest for Unity, 1952; Living US Constitution, 1953; French Institutions, 1954; The Genius of America, 1960; The Meaning of Democracy, 1963; ed: Democracy by Thomas Jefferson, 1939; The Complete Jefferson, 1941; Wilson's Ideals, 1942; Jefferson and the National Capital, 1946; The Complete Madison, 1953; The Washington Papers, 1955; The Mind of Alexander Hamilton, 1959; Nehru on World History, 1960; The World of the Founding Fathers, 1960; To Secure These Blessings, 1962; Thomas Jefferson and the Foundations of American Freedom, 1965; The Writings of Thomas Jefferson, 1968.Recipient: Commonwealth Silver Medal, 1935; Bronze Star, 1945; Chevalier, Légion d'Honneur, 1947; Wayne U Almuni Award, 1952; U Chgo Profsl Achievement Award, 1969. Hobby: walking. Home: 129 Amity St, Brooklyn, NY. Office: 66 W 12 St, New York, NY.

PAEFF, Bashka, US, sculptor; b. Minsk, Russ, Aug 12, 1893; d. Louis and Fannie (Kischen); grad: Mass Normal Art Sch, 1911; Boston Mus Sch of Fine Arts, 1914; m. Samuel Waxman, June 1, 1940. Prin works include: bas relief and medal of Dr. Simon Flexner, Rockefeller Inst; statue Edward MacDowell, Columbia U; Oliver Wendell Holmes, Washington, DC; Jane Addams, Hull House, Chgo; Minute Men Memorial, Lexington, Mass; Justice Brandeis, Brandeis U; bronze medal, Boston U Alumni Assn; mem: Guild of Boston Artists; Natl Sculpture Soc. Recipient: won competition: war memorial in State House, Boston; WW memorial State of Me, Kittery. Home and studio: 21 Foster St, Cambridge, Mass; summer: Greenbush, Mass.

PAGEL, Bernard Ephraim Julius, Eng, astronomer; b. Berlin, Ger, Jan 4, 1930; s. Walter and Magdalene (Koll); in Eng since 1933; BA, U of Cambridge, 1950, PhD, 1955; m. Annabel Tuby, July 14, 1958; c: Celia, David, Jonathan. Sr prin sci off, Royal Greenwich Observatory, since 1961, prin sci off, 1956-61; visiting reader, astronomy, U of Sussex, since 1967; research f, Sidney Sussex Coll, Cambridge, 1953-56; astrophysicist, Sacramento Peak Observatory, Sunspot, NM, 1960. Council mem, Royal Astronomical Soc, 1959-62, 1967-69; mem: Royal Astronomical Soc; Inst of Profsl Civil Servants, chap RGO. Ed, The Observatory, mag, 1961-62; contbr to profsl jours. Home: Red Dwarf, Western Rd, Hailsham, Sussex, Eng. Office: Royal Greenwich Observatory, Herstmonceux, Sussex, Eng.

PAGLIN, Max D, US, attorney, government official; b. NYC, May 1, 1914; s. Philip and Bella (Yellen); BSS, CCNY, 1936; LLB, Columbia U Law Sch, 1939; m. Sally Kobak, June 8, 1941; c: David, Eric (decd). Exec dir, FCC, since 1966, staff mem since 1942; vice-chmn, mem, Pres council, Admn Conf of US, 1968; pvt law practice, 1939-42, 1964-66. Chmn, law comm, Fed Bar Assn; fmr pres, John F Kennedy lodge, B'nai B'rith; mem: Phi Epsilon Pi; CCNY Alumni Assn; Columbia Law Sch Assn. Contbr to jours. Recipient: Distinguished Service Award, Phi Epsilon Pi, 1962; Exceptional Service Award, FCC, 1964. Home: 3001 Veazey Terr, Washington, DC. Office: 1919 M St, Washington, DC.

PAIS, Abraham, US, physicist, educator; b. Amsterdam, Holland, May 19, 1918; s. Jesajah and Kaatje (van Kleeff); in US since 1946; BS, U Amsterdam, 1938; MS, U Utrecht, 1940, PhD, 1941; att U Copenhágen, 1946; m. Lila Atwill (div); c: Joshuah. Prof, Rockefeller Inst, since 1963; adj prof, Columbia U, since 1963; prof, physics, Inst for Advanced Study, Princeton, NJ, 1950-63. F, Amer Phys Soc; corresp mem, Royal Acad Sci, Netherlands; mem, Natl Acad Scis, US. Home: Fricke Hall, Rockefeller U, New York, NY. Office: Rockefeller Inst, New York, NY.

PAIZER Eliahu Moses, Isr, attorney, teacher; b. Ploiesti, Rum, Apr 22, 1912; s. Moses and Ides (Jacob); in Isr since 1965; LLB, Law Fac, Bucharest, Rum, 1952; m. Ann Davidescu, 1949; c: Eliezer. Pvt tchr, music, since 1965; tchr, state schs, 1946-53; judge, Court of Ploiesti, 1953-55; atty, Court of Ploiesti, 1955-65. Recipient: decoration, State of Rum, for lit activity. Hobbies: music, drawing, lit. Home and office: Hamelech Ioshafat, Mahane David, Haifa, Isr.

PALAN, Dov Vojtech, Isr, civil engr; b. Budapest, Hung, Feb 7, 1924; s. Alexander and Helen (Politzer); in Isr since 1949; BSc, engr, Technion, 1950; m. Olivia Kostka, Aug 22, 1947; c: Ronen, Uri. Partner, Dov Palan & E Farsky, Cons Engr, Ltd, since 1966; sr partner, Weltsch & Palan, CEs, 1956-66; owner, Palan Cons Engr, 1961-66. Lt, IDF, 1951-54. Mem: Assn Engrs and Architects, Isr; Amer Concrete Inst; Concrete Inst of Gt Brit. Home: 9 Barak St, Tel Aviv, Isr. Office: 14 Bernstein St, Tel Aviv, Isr.

PALDI, Israel, Isr, artist; b. Berdiansk, Russ, Mar 14, 1892; s. Haim and Leah (Calmanovitch) Feldmann; in Isr since 1909; att: Bezalel Art Sch, Jerusalem, 1909-11; Art Acad, Munich, 1911-14; m. Miriam Padowicz, 1931; c: Raphael, Azgad, Ramon, Rachel. Painter, art tchr, illus children's books; exhbs: Jerusalem, 1922; Tel Aviv, 1941, 1944, 1946; Biennale, Sao Paulo, 1957; Venice Biennale, 1958; NY, Paris, 1958-60; Tel Aviv Mus, 1961; Isr Mus, Jerusalem, 1967. Mem: Isr Artists Assn. Recipient: Dizengoff Prize, 1941, 1959. Home and studio: 264 Hayarkon St, Tel Aviv, Isr.

PALGI, Yoel, Isr, government official; b. Cluj, Rum, Feb 17, 1918; s. Yitchak and Cecilia (Hirsh) Nuszbacher; in Isr since 1939; m. Phyllis Rabkin, 1947; c: Ilana, Anath. Mem exec, Kupat Holim; dir, dept civil aviation, Min of Transp and Communications, since 1960; Isr Ambass to Tanganyika, Zanzibar, 1963-66; fmr mem, Kibbutz Ma'agan; dep dir, oprs exec, El Al, 1949-60. Brit Army, 1941-45, parachuted into Yugo and Hung; on mission for Haganah, S Afr, 1947; cdr, IDF paratroopers, 1948. Author: The Great Storm Arises, 1946. Home: 19 Smuts Ave, Tel Aviv, Isr.

PALTI, Josef, Isr, agronomist; b. Berlin, Ger, Nov 18, 1915; s. Alfred and Margarete (Baschwitz) Peltesohn; in Isr since 1934; BSc, U Reading, Eng, 1938, MSc, 1960; PhD, Heb U, Jerusalem, 1968; m. Jeanne Orfinger, May 7, 1939; c: Naomi Bendor, Ronny, Daniel. Dir, Dept of Plant Protection, Ext Services, Min of Agric, since 1960; plant path, JA agric research sta, 1938-46; found, dir: Chimavir Ltd, 1948-52; Farms Cons, 1952-60. Prin contribs: forecasting and control of plant diseases in Isr, role of irrigation in plant protection, introduction of aircraft spraying to Isr. Author: Vegetable Diseases in Israel, 1962; contbr profsl papers to intl jours. Home: 9 Prague St, Tel Aviv, Isr. Office: Min of Agric, Hakirya, Tel Aviv, Isr.

PANCER, Oton, Yugo, agronomist, educator; b. Yugo, Mar 4, 1907; s. David and Ana (Bergmann); dipl, Fac Agric and Forestry, 1929; m. Ila Lemberger, Apr 17, 1935 c: Vladimira, Ranka. Prof, fac agric, Zagreb, since 1962; prof, 2nd Agric Sch, Krizevci, 1934-41; chief, Inst for Agric Econ, Zagreb, 1945-48; prof, fac agric, U of Sarajevo, 1948-62. Mem: Assn of Esperantists, Yugo; Assn of World Esperantists; fmr vice-pres, J Comty of Sarajevo. Author: Productivity of Work in Agriculture of Bosnia and Herzegovina in the Years 1956-60; contbr to sci jours. Recipient: Medal for Valor; Order of Merit for the People, 3rd deg; Order of Frat and Unity. Home: Zagreb. Vócarsko Naselje 10, Yugo. Office: Fac of Agric, Zagreb, Maksimir, Yugo.

PANITZ, Seymour Manuel, US, rabbi; b. Baltimore, Md, Feb 24, 1925; s. Ezekiel and Nettie (Yaniger); BA, Johns Hopkins U, 1944; ordained rabbi, MHL, JTSA, 1949; m. Barbara Reisner, June 28, 1955; c: Varda, Debra, Aliza, Ora. Rabbi: Cong Tifereth Anschai Sfard and Sons of Isr, since 1967; Cong Ezrath Isr, Malden, Mass, 1959-64; Cong Shearith Isr, Columbus, Ga, 1962-64; Cong Ahavath Achim, Detroit, Mich, 1964-67. Lt, chaplain, USAF, 1951-53. Home: 34 Yale St, Lawrence, Mass. Study: 492 Lowell St, Lawrence, Mass.

PANUSH, Louis, US, teacher, editor; b. Szczuczyn, Pol, Feb 16, 1910; s. Abraham and Rebecca (Berensztein); in US since 1929; BS, Wayne State U, Detroit, 1934, MA, 1935; m. Tillie Lipsitz, June 23, 1935; c: Elissa Benedek, Judy Michaelson, Margo Cohen, Naomi. Prin, Western HS since 1963; tchr: E Windsor Heb Sch, Ont, Can; United Heb Schs, Detroit, 1929-30, 1933-44; prin, Yeshiva Torath Emeth,

Wilkes-Barre, Pa, 1930-33; sci tchr, Cen HS. Detroit. 1936-52 researcher, Ethyl Corp, Detroit, 1946; instr, Heb, Wayne State U, 1945-58; head sci and math depts, Norteastern HS, 1952-57; H Ford HS, 1957-58; coord, Radiation Biol Inst for Tchrs, Wayne State U, 1958; co-dir, Inst for HS Sci and Math Tchrs, Mich State U, 1959-61; asst prin, Mackenzie HS, 1958-63. Pres, Cen Assn of Sci and Math Tchrs, 1957-58, dir, 1953-56, vice-pres, 1956-57; f, AAAS; exec comm, Natl Assn of Profs of Heb, 1953-56; coord, Mich Jr Sci and Hum Symposium, since 1964; vice-chmn, AAAS Coop Comm on Teaching of Sci and Math; mem: Natl Sci Tchrs Assn; Mich Sci Tchrs Assn; Org of Sch Admnrs and Sups; Phi Delta Kappa; Kvutzah Ivrit; Histadruth Ivrit; Cong Shaarey Zedek, comm on educ, 1952-66; natl exec comm, ZOA, since 1966; dir, Zionist Org of Detroit, 1953-65, vice-pres, 1965-68, pres since 1968. Ed, Metrop Detroit Sci Rev, 1942-60; contbr ed, Science Teacher, 1946-50, ed cons, 1951-53, mem adv bd, 1953-58, contbr to profsl jours. Hobbies: travel, book reviewing. Home: 24380 Lafayette Circle, Southfield, Mich. Office: Western HS, Detroit, Mich.

PANZER, Martin, US, organization exec, author; b. Paterson, NJ, June 12, 1905; s. Otto and Lena (Fortgang); m. Pauline Richman, June 21, 1931; c: Leonore, Carolyn Sobel. Spec asst to vice-pres, Isr Bonds, since 1957, dir, Eur, 1954-56; exec vice-pres, Amer Friends of Tel Aviv U, on leave, 1965-66; columnist, Pawling, NY Chronicle, 1930; ed: Psychology and Psychology Digest, 1937-38; American Heb, 1938-41; publicity dir, UJA, 1941-42, asst to exec vice-chmn, 1942-54. Author: Father Knows Better, 1940; It's Your Future, 1943; Get A Kick Out of Living, 1945; Raise Your Sights, 1947; Publicity Girl, 1947; You Can Change Your Career, 1950; Developing Your Personality, 1963; The Pink Cigar, 1964; contbr to mags and newspapers. Home: 340 E 64 St, New York, NY. Office: 215 Park Ave S, New York, NY.

PAPPENHEIM, Albert, Can, rabbi; b. Frankfurt, Ger; s. Jonas and Irma (Stern); in Can since 1940; ordained rabbi, Yeshivah Torat Chaim, Toronto, 1948; BA, U Toronto, 1947, MA, 1949; m. Rhoda Kay, Oct 5, 1945; c: Irma. Rabbi: B'nai Isr Beth David Cong, Downsview, Ont, since 1956; B'nai Isr Cong, St Catharines, Ont, 1948-53; Ohava Zion Cong, Lexington, Ky, 1953-56; prin, Basis Yehuda Talmud Torah, Toronto, 1947-48; lectr, U Ky, 1953-56. Pres: RA, Ontario region, since 1967; Toronto Rabb F, 1966-67; chmn: educ comm, Ont region, United Syn of Amer, since 1959; Syn Council, UJA of Toronto, 1969; mem: educ and cultural comm, Cen region, Can J Cong, since 1957; B'nai B'rith. Home: 145 McAllister Rd, Downsview, Ont, Can. Study: 55 Yeomans Road, Downsview, Ont, Can.

PARAF, Pierre, Fr, radio and newspaper editor, author; b. Paris, Dec 6, 1893; s. Emile and Inés (Sourdis); licencié ès lettres, diplôme d'études supérieures classiques, 1911, 1912; Ecole des Sciences Politiques, 1913; docteur en droit, Faculté de Droit, Paris, 1924; m. Anne-Mathilde Dons-Kaufmann-Nordau, June 16, 1921; c: Liliane Brissac. Ed in chief, Fr Radio-TV, asso with Fr Radio, since 1936; fmr dir, Friendship France-Israël, monthly reviews; lit dir: La République, daily, 1930-39; Combat, daily; L'Europe, monthly. Off, Fr Army, 1914-18, 1939-40; underground activities, 1940-44. Author: Sous la Terre de France, 1916; Les Métiers du Théâtre, 1922; Le Syndicalisme en France, 1924; Vie de Victor Hugo, 1925; Plus Près de Toi, 1925; Quand Israël Aima, 1928; Anthologie du Romantisme, 1930; Israël, 1931; Clartés d'Europe, 1934; Les Cités du Bonheur, 1945; L'Information, 1946; Israël dans le Monde, 1946; Rendez-vous Africains, 1953; L'Ascension des Peuples Noirs, 1958; L'Etat d'Israël dans le Monde, 1960; Les Démocraties Populaires, 1962; Le Racisme dans le Monde, 1965, 2nd ed, 1967, 3rd ed, 1969; co-author, Fr versions of Hans Christian Andersen and J V Jensen, 1927-46. Vice-pres, Intl League Against Racism; chief secy, Universal Comm of the Unknown J Martyr; pres, Mouvement contre le Racisme, l'Antisémitisme et pour la Paix; mem: council: ORT; Youth Aliyah; comm, Ligue des Droits la Paix; mem: council: ORT; Youth Aliyah; comm, Ligue des Droits de l'Homme; Société Gens de Lettres; Société Auteurs et Compositeurs Dramatiques; Assn des Ecrivains Combattants des deux Guerres: Société des Amis de Zola; Société des Amis d'Anatole France; Amis de Henri Barbusse, pres; fmr dir, Friendship Fr-Isr. Recipient: Croix de Guerre, 1916, 1918; Médaille de Verdun; Médaille de la Paix Carl von Ossietzky; Chevalier du Danebrog, 1937; Officier de l'Ordre de la Résistance, 1946; Frimedalie, 1946; Officier de la Légion d'Honneur, 1949; three prizes, l'Acadé-

Inst Tech, Pittsburgh, 1949; MA, Inst Fine Arts, NYU, 1955; m. Dorothy Cantor, Aug 20, 1950; c: William, Julia, Ellen. Asso prof, Bklyn Coll, fac mem since 1961. One-man exhbs: Tanager Gal, 1955, 1959; Peridot Gal, 1956, 1957, 1959; Frumkin Gal, 1961, 1962, 1963, 1965, 1967, 1969; Kan City Art Inst, 1962; represented in perm collections: Whitney Mus; Newark Mus; U Neb Mus; Mus Modern Art, Vassar Coll; Joseph Hirshorn Collection; James Michner Found; in pvt collections. Home: 163 W 88 St, New York, NY.

PECHENICK, Aaron (pen name, **Halevi**) Isr, rabbi, author; b. Ostrog, Pol, Mar 28, 1904; s. Nachum and Hinda (Sfard); in Isr since 1960; ordained rabbi, Yeshiva, Sarny, Pol, 1926; BA, Tachkemony, Warsaw, 1934; m. Sheiva Zuckerman, July 28, 1934; c: Shalom, Samuel. Dir info, ed publs, Hechal Shlomo, Jerusalem, since 1960; rabbi: Dombrowica, Pol, 1926-35; Cong Anshei Rashkov, NY, 1936-50; dir publs, info, Mizrachi Org of Amer, 1937-60. Author: Poems in Prose, 1932; Zionism and Judaism in Soviet Russia, 1942; ed: Or Hamizrach, 1954-60; Hadashot, 1962-69; Shana B'shana, 10 vols, 1960-70; contbr numerous articles on Judaism, Zionism, Isr, Hum Rights. Chmn: Hashomer Hadati, NY, 1936-39; mem comm, World Zionist Org, 1962-64; Circle Olim from W Countries, Jerusalem; delg, ZCs, 1939, 1961, 1965; exec mem, Merkaz Mafdal, Isr; mem natl council, World Mizrachi Org. Home: 7 Ahad Haam St, Jerusalem, Isr. Office: 58 King George St, Jerusalem, Isr.

PECHMAN, Joseph Aaron, US, economist; b. NYC, Apr 2, 1918; s. Gershon and Lena (Pechman); BS, CCNY, 1937; MA, U Wis, 1938; PhD, 1942; m. Sylvia Massow, Sep 29, 1943; c: Ellen, Jane. Dir, econ studies, Brookings Inst, since 1962, exec dir, studies of govt finance, 1960-70; stat, Natl Research Project, Phila, 1937; asst dir, Wis Income Tax Study, Wis Tax Commn, 1938-39; research asso, U Wis, 1939-41; econ, OPA, 1941-42; asst dir, tax adv staff, US Treasury Dept, 1946-53; asst prof, finance, sch ind mgmt, MIT, 1953-54; econ: Council Econ Advs, 1954-56; Comm for Econ Devl, 1956-60; Irving Fisher Research Prof, Yale U, 1966-67. Capt, US Army, 1942-45; Mem: TIA CREF Policyholders Nominating Comm; Mayor's Task Force, fiscal affairs, NYC; steering comm, Minn Experimental City Project; academic adv group, Amer-Isr Tax Found; econ bd, Time Mag; tax task force, Council Environmental Quality; adv comm, U Cal prog, research on admn of higher educ; pres, Amer Finance Assn; financial adv, Gov Mandel, Md; mem: Natl Accounts Review Comm, 1957; Gaither Comm, 1958; Samuelson Task Force, 1961; ed bd, Amer Econ Review, 1961-63; chmn, pres task force, intergovernmental fiscal coop, 1964; adv council Woodrow Wilson Sch Public Affairs, Princetown, U, 1964-66; comm taxation, Amer Council on Educ, 1965-69; econ panel, Survey Behavioral and Social Sci, 1966-70; mayor's task force on CATV, NYC; cons: Council Econ Advs, Treasury Dept, Adv Comm on Intergovernmental Affairs. Author: Federal Tax Policy, 1966, 1971; co author, Social Security: Perspective for Reform, 1968; contbr numerous articles to publs. Home: 7112 Wilson Lane, Bethesda, Md. Office: 1775 Massachusetts Ave, Washington, DC.

PEER, Shlomo, Isr, engineer; b. Riga, Latvia, June 27, 1923; s. Gedalia and Shifra (Stone); in Isr since 1947; att Latvian U, Riga, 1944-45; BSc, Technion, Haifa, 1954; CE, 1955; DEng, Techische Hochschule, Stuttgart, 1963; m. Ester Behr, June 24, 1945; c: Osnat, Joram. Head, dept of construction mgmt and econ, Technion, Haifa, since 1963, sr lectr, since 1964, research sci, 1958-60. Mem: natl council on rationalization and productivity in building ind; comm on industrialization in building ind, PM's off, 1965-66; Intl CIB working comm; RILEM; ORSA. Author: Vorfertigung auf der Baustelle, 1964. Hobby: chess. Home: 18b Nitsanim St, Haifa, Isr. Office: Technion, Haifa, Isr.

PEERCE, Alice K, US, communal worker; m. Jan Peerce; c: Lawrence, Joyce, Susan. Co-producer of The Megilla. Natl chmn, women's div, State of Isr Bonds, delg, Isr Bond Jerusalem Leaders Conf, 1961; fmr chmn, women's div, Gtr NY. Home: 370 Beechmont Dr, New Rochelle, NY.

PEERCE, Jan, US, concert tenor; b. NYC; hon DMus, NY Coll of Music; m. Alice Kaye; c: Lawrence, Joyce, Susan. Debut Metrop Opera in La Traviata; sung entire It and Fr repertory at Metrop, Chgo, SF Operas; tours US biannually; starred in Holland Festival, 1962, in La Forza del Destino; many other festivals; recitals: Nor; Swed; Holland; W Ger; tours: Isr nine times, Russ twice; Japan, S Afr, Austr, NZ; appeared in motion pictures: Carnegie Hall; Hymn of all

Nations; Something in the Wind; Tonight We Sing; Of Man and Music; Goodbye Columbus. Recordings with Toscanini, Knappertsbusch, Hermann Scherchen and others. Records of 1969: Handel Arias; Christus am Oelberg; Fidelio; Student Prince; Jan Peerce on Broadway; Victor Herbert Melodies; Cantorial Prayers and Yiddish Folk Songs; Jan Peerce Sings Hebrew Melodies; Jan Peerce in Las Vagas; Journey Through Opera. TV appearances: Ed Sullivan; Johnny Carson's Tonight Show; on: NBC, CBS, ABC, and Eurovision. Address: c/o Maurice Feldman, 551 Fifth Ave, New York, NY.

PEIERLS, Rudolf Ernst, Eng, theoretical physicist, educator; b. Berlin, Ger, June 5, 1907; s. Heinrich and Elisabeth (Weigert); in Eng since 1933; DPhil, U Leipzig, 1929; DSc, U Manchester, 1936; MA, U Cambridge, 1936; M Sc, U Birmingham, 1937; MA, U Oxford, 1963; hon DSc, Us: Liverpool, 1960; Birmingham, 1967; Edinburgh, 1969; m. Eugenia Kannegiesser, Mar 15, 1931; c: Gaby Gross, Ronald, Catherine Coppin, Joanna. Wykeham prof, theoretical physics, U Oxford, since 1963; f New College, Oxford, since 1963; research f: U Manchester, 1933-35; Royal Soc Mond Lab, Cambridge, 1935-37; prof, math, physics, U Birmingham, 1937-63. Author: The Quantum Theory of Solids, 1955; The Laws of Nature, 1955. Recipient: CBE, 1946 f, Royal Medal, Royal Soc, 1959; medals: Lorentz, Netherlands Royal Acad, 1962; Max Planck, Assn of Ger Phys Socs, 1963; Brit Crown, 1946, Knight Bachelor, 1968. Home: Farleigh, Orchard Lane, Old Boar's Hill, Oxford, Eng. Office: Dept of Theoretical Physics, 12 Parks Rd, Oxford, Eng.

PEILEN, Ellis, USA business exec; b. St Paul, Minn, Jan 26, 1910; s. Samuel and Mathilda (Debo); B, Aeronautical Engr, U Minn, 1932; m. Ruth Rauch, Jan 28, 1937; c: Samuel, Elizabeth Cahan. Owner, Peilen & Peilen, gen ins agcy, since 1933; instr, aeronauti eal engr, U Minn, 1942-46, ext dept, 1946-62. Vice-pres, Family and Children Service, since 1968, treas, 1966-68, mem bd dirs, since 1962; pres: Adath Jeshurun Syn, 1955-58; Independent Ins Agts Minneapolis, 1962-63; treas, Fed for J Service, since 1960; bd dirs: J Comty Cen Gtr Minneapolis, since 1959; mem: ACLU; Large City Budget Comm; Minn Hillel Adv Commn; Minneapolis Camping Assn; AJCong; ZOA; B'nai B'rith lodge pres, 1960; Natl Assn Independent Ins Agts; Inst Aerospace Scis; Alumni Assn, U Minn; Phi Epsilon Pi Alumni Assn,Twin Cities; clubs: Oak Ridge Country, treas, 1952-56; Standard, secy, 1946-47. Recipient: Ins Man of Year, Independent Ins Agts, Minneapolis, 1964. Home: 2901 Ewing Ave S, Minneapolis, Minn. Office: 1150 Baker Bldg, Minneapolis, Minn.

PEKERIS, Chaim L, Isr, applied mathematician, geophysicist, educator; b. Alytus, Lith, June 15, 1908; s. Samuel and Chaya (Rivel); BS, MIT, 1929, DS, 1934; m. Leah Kaplan. Prof and head, dept of applied maths, Weizmann Inst of Sci, Rehovot, since 1948; Rockefeller f, 1934-35; research, Cambridge U, 1935-36; geophys, MIT, 1936-40; mem, war research dept, Columbia U, 1940-45, dir, math phys group, 1945-47; mem, Inst for Advanced Study, Princeton, 1947-48. Mem: US Natl Acad of Scis; Isr Natl Acad Scis; Amer Phys Soc; Amer Geophys Union; Amer Seismological Soc; fgn asso, Royal, Astronomical Soc. Contbr of numerous papers on applied math and geophys. Recipient: Rothschild Prize in Math, 1966. Home: Shikun Neveh Weizmann, Rehovot, Isr. Office: Weizmann Inst of Sci, Rehovot, Isr.

PELA, David, Eng, editor; b. London, Eng, Sep 28, 1919; s. Woolf and Annie (Plaskwa); m. Lily Brown, Jan 4, 1942; s. Michael. Dep ed, travel ed, London J Chronicle; broadcaster on ME affairs. RAF, WW II. Chmn, Guild of Anglo-J Journalists; exec mem, Guild of British Travel Writers. Contbr on ME affairs to BBC. Office: 25 Furnival St, London EC4, Eng.

PELAH, Zvi, Isr, educator; b. Lomza, Pol, Aug 30, 1924; s. Moshe and Yafa (Plonsky) Pelchowicz; in Isr since 1925; MSc, Heb U, 1947, PhD, 1954; m. Rivka Krichevsky, July 29, 1956; c: Dan, Gie. Asst chief sci, Min of Defense, since 1967, head, organic chem dept, 1953-59; prof, chem, head dept, U Negev, since 1967; sci dir, chem br, Isr Inst for Biol Research, since 1965, head organic chem dept, 1959-67. Capt, sci unit, IDF, 1948-53. Mem: Isr Chem Soc; Chem Soc, London; Amer Chem Soc. Contbr to sci jours. Recipient: Isr award, Min of Defense, 1967. Home: 10 101 St, Ramat Gan, Isr. Offices: Off of Chief Sci, Min of Defense, Tel Aviv, Isr. U Negev, Beersheva, Isr.

PELAVIN, B Morris, US, attorney; b. David Horodock, Pol, Oct 26, 1906; s. Jacob and Sarah (Krikun); m. Elizabeth

Weiss, June 12, 1932, (decd); c: Michael; m. 2nd, Fannie Weissinger Mack, Aug 4, 1968. Pres, Pelavin & Pelavin; off and dir, many bus corps. Bd dirs, Amer Assn J Educ, since 1968; mem, comm on J educ, CJFWF; pres: B'nai B'rith, 1943-47; Urban League, 1947-51; J Comty Council, 1948-52; chmn, Mich region, UJA, 1951-53. Home: 1220 Beard St, Flint, Mich. Office: Phoenix Bldg, Flint, Mich.

PELAVIN, Michael Allen, US, attorney; b. Flint, Mich, Sep 5, 1936; s. Morris and Elizabeth (Weiss); att Wayne State U, 1955-57; JD, Detroit Coll Law, 1960; m. Natalie Katz, June 18, 1960; c: Gordon, Mark. Partner, Pelavin & Pelavin, since 1960. Chmn, Natl Comm Small Cities, CJFWF, natl bd dirs; natl exec comm, Natl J Comty Relations Adv Council, comm Church State and Inter-rel Activities; UJA Young Leadership Cabinet; adv bd, young Leaders CJFWF; Vice chmn, mid continent region natl bd, HIAS; vice pres, Flint J Comty Council; chmn, bd dirs COMPACT, local poverty prog coord comm, 1967-68; bd dirs, CAPE, comm to advance public Educ; treas, Gtr Flint Interfaith Action Council; bd dirs: ACLU, Flint; bd govs, Flint Comty Council; bd trustees, Temple Beth El; mem: Amer, State, Genesee Co Bar Assns; comms on crime prevention and juvenile problems; Amer Arbitration Assn; Tau Epsilon Rho; Natl Lawyers Guild. Home: 807 Maxine St, Flint, Mich. Office: 800 S Saginaw St, Flint, Mich.

PELED, Matityahu, Isr, army officer; b. Isr, Juiy 20, 1923; s. Baruch and Sara (Ruminik) Ifland; att: U London, 1946-47; Heb U, Jerusalem, 1961-62; m. Zeeva Katznelson, Aug 8 1946; c: Yoav, Nurith, Asnath, Abraham. Asst to Dep Defence Min, 1963-68; chief, logistics, IDF, 1964-68; mil gov, Gaza Strip, 1957; mil cdr, Jerusalem dist, 1957-59. Home: Ha'ela St, Motza Ilit, Isr.

PELED, Nathan, Isr, government official; b. Odessa, Russ, June 3, 1913; s. Yosef and Lea (Gavurin) Friedel; in Isr since 1933; m. Mania Perlman, 1936; c: Irit, Ora. Min of Absorption; MK since 1965; mem, Kibbutz Sarid; secy, Kibbutz HaArtzi, 1936-39, 1950-55; secy, Security Comm, Histadrut, 1939-45; Histadrut missions to US, 1946-49; secy, Mapam Party, 1956-58; ambass of Isr: Bulgaria, 1958-60; Aus, 1960-63; mem, Isr delg, UN, 1967. Served Haganah. Active, Hashomer Hatzair and Hechalutz, Rum. Home: Kibbutz Sarid, Isr.

PELED, Uzi, Isr, business exec; social researcher; b. Tel Aviv, Isr, July 10, 1937; s. Avraham and Sara (Mokotovsky) Wisenfeld; att Heb U, 1958-61; MA, Brandeis U, Waltham, Mass, 1966; m. Tsiyona Molk, Dec 11, 1958; c: Eyal, Tal. Exec dir, Isr Inst Applied Social Research, since 1969, dep dir, 1963-67; external tchr, Grad Sch of Bus Admn, Heb U, Jerusalem, since 1966; research f, Cen for Intl Affairs, Harvard U, 1965-66; dep dir, team setting up TV in Isr, 1967-69. Lt, IDF, 1955-58. Mem: research comm, Isr Mgmt Cen; World Assn for Public Opinion Research, US. Author: Managerial Climate in Israel; contr to jours. Home: 59 King George St, Jerusalem, Isr. Office: 19 George Washington St, Jerusalem, Isr.

PELEG, Alexander, Isr, actor; b. Bucharest, Rum, May 25, 1938; s. Haim and Sara (Aizic); in Isr since 1952; att Tania Balachova Drama Sch, Paris. Mem, Habimah Natl Theater Co, since 1963, major roles in: The Representative; Who's Afraid of Virginia Woolf; The Lover; Othello; The Promise; Tango; The Sea Gull. Mil entertainment group, IDF, 1956-57. Recipient, Aharon Meskin award. Amer-Isr Cultural Found and Isr Cen, Intl Theatre Inst, Home: 11 Spinoza St, Tel Aviv, Isr. Office: Habimah Natl Theater, Tel Aviv, Isr.

PELEG, David, Isr, government official; b. Nahlat Yehuda, Isr, July 27, 1923; s. Isaac and Rachel (Zaltzman) Fligelman; dipl law, Tel-Aviv U, 1956; m. Judith Puchs, Sep 22, 1953; c: Ehud, Anat. Admn dir, Isr AEC, since 1966. Lt-col, IAF, 1948-53. Home: 20 Hamishmar Haezrahi, Afeka, Isr. Office: 26 Hauniversita St, Ramat Aviv, Isr.

PELEG, Mordechai, Isr, engineer, educator; b. Boguslav, Russ, July 8, 1901; s. Moshe and Hanna (Pritzker) Polonsky; in Isr since 1922; att Inst of Mineral Engr, Yekaterinoslav, Russ, 1919-21; BSc, Technion, Haifa, 1931; m. Bunia Medovoi, 1924; c: Shmuel, Naaman. Asso prof, CE, Technion, since 1966, research asst, sr lectr, 1944-66; engr and surveyor, Haifa Port, 1931-33; cons engr, Housing Min, 1950-60. Mem: Cen Comm of Public Works Engrs, 1940-50; Assn of Architects and Engrs, Haifa comm, 1940-45; Intl Soc of Biometeorology, Intl Soc of Soil Mechs and Found Engr. Author: To-

pics on Traffic Engineering, 1964, 1968; contr to engr sci jours. Home: 11 Yerushalayim St, Haifa, Isr. Office: Technion, Haifa, Isr.

PELI, Alexander, Isr, publisher, editor; b. Kiev, Russ, June 17, 1915; s. Meir and Bracha (Kutzenok); in Isr, since 1921; MA, Heb U, Jerusalem, 1936; m. Naomi Tabachnik, 1938; c: Idith, David. Mgn, dir, Heb Ency Pub Co, Jerusalem, since 1945; mem, bd dirs, Massada Pub Co, since 1946; pres, Massada Press, since 1960, exec dir 14 affiliated pub cos; ed: UNESCO Courier, Heb, since 1968; Iton haYom, 1947-48; exec mgn ed: World Hist of the J People, 22 vols, 1966; Ency Hebraica, 32 vols; Standard J Ency. Mem, Tel Aviv comm, haBahrut haZionit, 1939-40; club, Rotary. Hobbies: music, tape recording. Home: 29 Jabotinsky St, Jerusalem, Isr. Office: 1 King David St, Jerusalem, Isr.

PELI, Bracha, Isr, publisher; b. Starowitz, Russ, Jan 1893; d. Samuel and Sara Kutzenok; in Isr since 1921; grad, Kiev U, Sch of Commerce; m. Meir Peli (decd); c: Alexander, Sara Barash; Found, chmn bd, Massadah Pub Co, and subsidiary cos, since 1932; found, chmn, bd dirs: Ever Libr, 1921; Achiever book shops, 1925; Found, Moria Book Distributors; chmn, bd of dirs, Heb Ency Pub Co, Ltd; Massada Printing Co. Home: 3 Ariel St, Givatayim, Isr. Office: 21 Jabotinsky Rd, Ramat Gan, Isr.

PELLED, Elad, Isr, business exec; b. Jerusalem, Nov 12, 1927; s. Reuven and Miriam (Rosenblum) Reisfeld; att mil schs: Isr, Fr; BA, Heb U, Jerusalem, 1955; m. Zimra Flex, June 18, 1948; c: Yuval, Yael. Mgn dir, Min Educ and Culture, since 1970; dep mgn dir, Isr Electric Co, 1968-70. Maj gen, IDF, until 1968. Home: 7 Itamar Ben Avi St, Jerusalem, Isr. Office: POB 10, Haifa, Isr.

PELLED, Haim, Isr, business exec, advertiser; b. Tel Aviv, Jan 13, 1929; s. Reuven and Hanna (Leitman) Feldman; LLB, U London, Eng, 1949; grad, Inst of Advanced Study, Isr, 1958; m. Zmira Davidson, Oct 28, 1949; c: Ori, Raz. Gen mgr, Pelled Advt and PR Ltd, since 1959. Maj, IDF: War of Independence; Sinai Campaign; Six Day War. Pres, Isr Advt Assn, since 1966; dep chmn, Cinema Owners Assn, 1952-58. Home: 6 Mordechai St, Ramat Gan, Isr. Office: 18 Hess St, Tel Aviv, Isr.

PELLER, Sigismund, US, physician; b. Tarnopol, Aus, Dec 16, 1890; s. Meshulam and Ernestine (Grossman); in US since 1936; MD, U Vienna, 1914; m. Lili Roubicek Aug 31, 1933 (decd). Pvt practice, since 1944; fmr: res, Wiener Allgemeines Karankenhus; dir, Bur of Public Health, Zionist Exec, Pal, 1926-28; public health off, Vienna Public Health Dept, 1929-33; f, Johns Hopkins U, Baltimore, Md, 1936-40; research asso, NYU, 1940-43. Aus Army WW I. F: NY Acad Med; Royal Soc Health, Gt Brit; Intl Coll Angiology; Amer Geriatrics Soc; Amer Public Health Assn; mem: AAAS; AMA; Amer Soc of Hum Genet; Rudolf Virchow Soc; Amer Stat Assn; NY Acad Scis; Med Circle; Amer Phys F Comm for IMA; B'nai B'rith; Intl Mark Twain Soc; club, Amer Automobile. Author: Fehlgeburt und Bevoelkerungsfrage, 1930; Der Geburstod, 1936; Cancer in Man 1952; Cancer in Childhood and Youth, 1962; Quantitative Research in Human Biology and Medicine, 1967; ed, Briut Haam, public health jour, Isr, 1926-27; contr to intl med jours. Hobbies: swimming, hiking, mountaineering. Home: Lakes Rd, Monroe, NY.

PELLES, Elhanan, Isr, engineer, organization exec; b. Charsznica, Pol, July 14, 1912; s. Zeev and Miriam (Feigenblat) Polski; in Isr since 1933; CE, U Caen, Fr, 1937; m. Batya Cohen, Mar 16, 1943; c: Rachel, Joseph. Dir gen, Isr Assn of Engrs and Architects, since 1952; secy, 1937-52. Lt, IDF. Club, Lions. Contr articles to profsl jours. Home: 3 Havatzelet St, Ramat Gan, Isr. Office: 200 Dizengoff St, Tel Aviv, Isr.

PELLES, Mordechai, Isr, business exec; b. Lwow, Pol, Apr 11, 1920; s. Saul and Ida (Loewi) Pillersdorf; in Isr sine 1937; att Heb U, Jerusalem, 1937-41; m. Bianca Selinger, May 27, 1948; c: Saul, Ilana, Orit. Dir, Adereth Co, Tel Aviv, since 1962; mgn dir, Shekem Co, 1950-62. Capt, Brit Army, 1941-46; lt col, IDF, 1948-50. Mem, bd of dirs, Isr Mgmt Cen, 1959-61. Home: 47 Hamazbiim St, Zahala, Isr. Office: POB 2372, Tel Aviv, Isr.

PELNER, Louis, US, physician; b. Pol, Sep 26, 1907; s. Jacob and Ida (Pietrokovski); in US since 1912; BS, NYU, 1929,

assns. Lt USN. Pres, Cong Brith Emeth; mem: Zeta Beta Tau; Phi Alpha Delta; O State, Cleveland, Cuyahoga Bar Assns. Contbr to legal jours.Hobby: sailing.Home: 14800 Co Line Rd, Hunting Valley, O. Office: 3000 Terminal Tower, Cleveland, O.

PATINKIN, Don, Isr, economist, educator; b. Chgo, Ill, Jan 8, 1922; s. Albert and Sadie (Brezinsky); in Isr since 1949; att Heb Theol Coll, Chgo, 1937-43; MA, U Chgo, 1945, PhD, 1947; m. Deborah Trossman, June 17, 1945; c: Naama, Aran, Ilana, Tmira. Prof econ, Heb U, Jerusalem, since 1957, on fac, since 1949; dir research Maurice Falk Inst for Econ Research in Isr, since 1956; asst prof: U Chgo, 1947-48; U of Ill, 1948-49. Author: Money, Interest and Prices, 1956, 2nd ed, 1965; The Israel Economy: The First Decade, 1959; contbr to sci jours. Recipient: Rothschild Prize in scis, 1959; Ruppin Prize in social scis, 1960. Home: 5 Hovevei Zion St, Jerusalem, Isr. Office: Heb U, Jerusalem, Isr.

PATISH, Yitzhak, Isr, organization exec; b. Lucenec, Czech, Jan 20, 1914; s. Martin and Alice (Pikler) Hammermueller; in Isr since 1935; deg, U Bratislava; m. Masha Gut, 1937; c: Ada Gan, Esther Ben David. Mem: cen comm: and cofound, Mapam, secy, cen comm, Mapam, 1950-60, 1964-66, political secy, 1966-69; Histadrut, and mem political dept; exec comm, secretariat, Kibbutz Arzi; exec Hashomer Hatzair, secy, Haifa br; co-found, mem, Kibbutz Kfar Masaryk; fmr: on missions to: Czech; It; Fr; Den; Japan; India; Cambodia; Rum; secy gen, Hashomer Hatzair, Czech. Pvt, Haganah, IDF, 1935-64. Author: book of poelms in Hung, 1935. Home and office: Kibbutz Kfar Masaryk, Isr.

PATKIN, Benzion, Austr, business exec; b. Tatarsk, Russ, Oct 23, 1903; s. Israel and Nehama (Bykhovsky); in Austr since 1929; att U Moscow, 1920-22; m. Hemda Shani, Jan 25, 1929; c: Michael, Nehama. Distributor in Australia representing Isr mfg firms, since 1937; mgn dir: Benpat Pty Ltd, since 1959; Patross Knitting Mills Pty, 1931-59; Austr corresp, Haboker, Heb daily, Tel Aviv, 1946-48; org, mgr, knitting factories for new immigrants, Safad, Hatzor, Isr, for Isr Min Trade and Ind, 1961. Mem, Vic J Bd Deps, since 1938, mem exec 1941-49; pres, Brit Ivrit Olamit: Vic, 1958-59, 1962-65 and 1968, Austr, since 1965; mem: Zionist Org, Ahdut Uthiah, Moscow, since 1917; Gehower, 1918; cen Maccabi Comm, Russ, 1922-24; Havurat haDarom, Nes Ziona, Pal, 1924-25; co-found: Eretz Isr Soc Ivriah, 1929; State ZC of Victoria, 1936; Vic Zionist Org, 1936, vice-pres, 1936-37, hon secy, 1938-42; found: Magen David Adom, Australia, 1940; J Day Sch, Mt Scopus Coll, Melbourne, 1947, pres, 1948-52; initiator, sponsor, Austr tour, Isr Maccabi Soccer Team, 1939; mem, Exec Council Australian Jewry, 1945-49; hon secy: Zionist Fed of Austr and NZ, 1940-45; KH, 1933-47; hon treas, JNF, 1931-32, 1939-42; pres, Kadimah, J natl cultural Org, 1955-58, vice-pres, 1951-54; vice-pres, Intl Club Vic, 1938-49; mem exec, Vic UN Assn, 1966-69. Home: 30 Williams Rd, Windsor, Victoria, Australia.

PATT, Raymond Martin, US attorney; b. Bklyn, NY, Jan 1, 1917; s. Harry and Elizabeth (Cohen); BA, Bklyn Coll, 1936; LLB, cum laude, Bklyn Law Sch, 1939; m. Edith Epstein, Mar 10, 1946; s. David. Partner, Patt & Heimowitz, since 1946. Capt, US Army, 1941-46. Natl pres, Bnai Zion; natl hon chmn, JNF; mem: natl comm, Amer-Isr Public Affairs Comm, NY comm; NAACP; NY Co Lawyers Assn; Amer Sect; WJC; bd dirs, Bklyn Coll Alumni Assn; interim bd, Amer Zionist Fed; exec, admn comms, AZC; First Armored Div Assn. Home: 2785 Bedford Ave, Brooklyn, NY. Office: 11 Broadway, New York, NY.

PATTASHNICK, Sidney, US, rabbi; b. Baltimore, Md, Sep 18, 1930; s. David and Annie (Rochkind); ordained rabbi, Ner Isr Rabb Coll, Baltimore, 1955; BA, New Eng Inst, 1957; m. Helga Sperber, Mar 22, 1959; c: Judah, Deborah, Morton. Rabbi: Cong Tikvas Isr, Dorchester, Mass, since 1956; Cong Beth Jacob, Highlandtown, Md, 1952-56; Young Isr, Dorchester, Mass, 1956. Mem: RabCA; Mass Council of Rabbis. Recipient: award, Combined J Appeal, Boston, 1959. Home: 100 Alabama St, Mattapan, Mass. Study: 114 Southern Ave, Dorchester, Mass.

PAUL, Eve W, US, attorney; b. NYC, June 16, 1930; d. Leo and Tamara (Sogolow) Weinschenker; BA, Cornell U, 1950; LLB, Columbia U, 1952; m. Robert Paul, Apr 9, 1952; c: Jeremy, Sarah. Pvt practice since 1959; asso: Hays, Sklar and Herzberg, 1952-54; Bernard D Cahn, 1954-56; research asst, Temp Commn on Courts, 1957-58; research cons, commn on inquiry, NYC Bd Educ, 1961. Mem: exec bd, Stamford

League Women Voters, 1960-61; NY, Conn, NYC, Stamford Bar Assns; Stamford Planning Bd, since 1966; NY Co Lawyers Assn. Home: 395 Janes La, Stamford, Conn. Office: 162 Bedford St, Stamford, Conn.

PAUL, Julius, US, educator; b. Cleveland, O, May 25, 1926; s. Jacob and Gertrude (Levitt); BA, U Minn, 1947; att: U Hawaii, 1947-48; Harvard Law Sch, 1948-49; PhD, O State U, 1954; m. Laura Rankin, 1952; c: Derrick, Aaron, Sara, Allegra, Brian. Research Political Sci, Walter Reed Army Inst Research, since 1964; instr, O State U, 1954-55; visiting instr, Denison U, O, 1954-55; visiting asst prof: Kenyon Coll, O, spring, 1955; Ohio U, summer, 1955; asst and asso prof, S Ill U, 1955-59; asso prof, political sci, Wayne State U, 1959-64. Vice-pres: S Ill U Chap, AAUP, 1958-59; Fitzgerald Comty Council, Detroit, Mich, 1962-64; Commn, Rockville, Md Hum Relations Comm, since 1966; mem: Amer Political Sci Assn; Eugenics Soc, London; Amer Soc for Political and Legal Phil; Intl Assn for Phil of Law and Social Phil, Amer Sect; Law and Social Assn. Author: The Legal Realism of Jerome N Frank: A Study of Fact-Skepticism and the Judicial Process, 1959; contbr to profsl periodicals Recipient: grant, Amer Phil Soc of Phila, 1958-59, 1962-63. Home: 802 Leverton Rd, Rockville, Md. Office: Dept of Psycht, Walter Reed Army Inst of Research, Walter Reed Army Med Cen, Washington, DC.

PAUL, Shalom Morton, US, educator; b. Phila, Pa, May 2, 1936; s. Samuel and Celia (Soffian); BHL, Gratz Coll, 1957; BA, Temple U, 1957; MHL ordained rabbi, JTSA, 1962; PhD, U of Pa, 1964; m. Yona Ovadia; c: Rehela, Yael, Ben-Zion. Asso prof, Bible, Grad Rabb Sch, JTSA, since 1967, fac mem since 1962; visiting lectr, Heb U; U Tel Aviv, both 1969-70. Mem: Soc Bible Lit; Amer Oriental Soc; Amer Acad Rel; World Cong J Studies; Isr Exploration Soc. Author: Studies In the Book of the Covenant in the Light of Cuneiform and Biblical Law, 1969; Asso ed, Bible, Ency Judaica; contbr to scholarly jours in US, Isr, Eur. Recipient: Cyrus Adler award, JTSA, 1962. Home: 90 La Salle St, New York, NY. Office: 3080 Broadway, New York, NY.

PAZ, Azaria, Isr, mathematician; b. Iasy, Rum, Nov 17, 1931; s. Moshe and Rachel (Feldman) Finkelstein; in Isr since 1948; MSc, Heb U, Jerusalem, 1962; DSc, Technion, 1964; m. Erela Sigal, Oct 18, 1961; c: Ephrat, David. Asso prof, Technion, since 1969, lectr: 1964-66; sr, 1968-69; visiting lectr, U of Cal, Berkeley, 1966-68; asso research engr, UCLA, summers: 1968, 1969. Sgt, IDF. Mem: Isr Math Union; Amer Math Soc. Contbr to sci jours. Home: 11 Ehud St, Haifa, Isr. Office: Technion, Haifa, Isr.

PAZ, Chanoch, Isr, educator, theater dir; b. Lith, Feb 1909; s. Pinchas and Chaya (Wingreen); in Isr since 1937; cert, Tarbuth Tchrs Sem, Lith, 1928; att U Kovno, 1928-31; Heb Studio, Lith, 1938-44; Hebrew U, Jerusalem, 1928-31; m. Liba Klapholz, 1940; c: Matyah Azulay, Shaul, Jonathan. Lectr, tchr, Oranim, govt tchrs sem, since 1958; theater dir, Intl Theater Instn, since 1931; tchr: cen boarding sch, Mishmar Haemek, 1937-45; Mizra boarding sch, 1945-49; sch insp, N dist, Isr govt, 1949-52; tchr Kibbutz Mizra, 1952-58. Res off, Lith infantry, 1931-33; pvt, Haganah, IDF, 1937-59. Mem: Cen Pedagogical Comm for Higher Educ; educ comm, Mapam; cen comm: Hechalutz, Lith; Hashomer Hatzair, Pal Off, Lith; JNF, all 1933-37; Tchrs Org, Isr, 1958-66; Amateur Theatrical Group, Trade Union, 1954-64; Isr cen comm, Intl Theater Instn. Dir plays by: Sophocles; Shakespeare; Molière; Gorky; Chechov; Brecht; Frisch; Colney; Goldfaden; Levic; Shalom Aleichem; Peretz; Halkin; Shoham; dir plays: amateur adults, children, kibbutz. Contbr to profsl jours. Recipient, special mention for dirs, Amateur Theater of Isr, 1958. Home: Kibbutz Mizra, Isr. Office: Oranim Tchrs Sem, Isr.

PAZNER, Chaim, Isr, economist; b. Kowal, Pol, Jan 14, 1899; s. Itzhak and Esther (Chaimovitz); BA, Acad Social Sci, Econs, Königsberg, 1931; DRerPol, U Basel, 1939; m. Regina Erlanger, 1936; c: Avi-Ezer, Elisha, Mikha. Repr Min of Finance on bd dirs of various govt cos and public instns, since 1964; chmn, econ and financial sect, Control Inst, Isr Lab Party, since 1964; mem, permanent budget and finance comm, JA, since 1968; fmr: Min of Econ Affairs, Isr Emb, Sweden; dir, Pal off: Danzig, 1934-35; Geneva, 1940-46; head, JA off for financial affairs in Eur, Geneva, 1945-48; Eur repr, Isr Min of Finance, Geneva, 1948-53; lectr, Sch of Interpreters, U Geneva, 1945-53; econ counsellor, Isr Embs: Arg; Uruguay, both 1957-60; dir revenue and services dept, fgn exch dir,

Min of Finance, Jerusalem, 1963-66. Mem exec bd, Yad vaShem Memorial Auth, co-chmn finance comm, since 1966; judge, ZC Tribunal, since 1966; active, Zionist activities, Danzig, 1920-38; delg to Zionist congs, since 1921; active in rescue work in Eur, as repr of Vaad haHatzala, JA, 1942-46. Author: Zur Planwirtschaft der Sowjetunion, 1946; contbr articles on econ and Zionist topics. Home: 9 Hananyah St, Jerusalem, Isr.

PAZOL, James Leslie, US, attorney; b. Cleveland, O, Oct 28, 1937; s. Sidney and Anne; BA, O State U, 1960, LLB, 1962, DJur, 1967; m. Roberta Mark, Aug 23, 1959; c: Steven, Jonathan. Partner, law firm, Waldman, Sperling & Pazol; legal aide, Off of Atty Gen of State of O, 1961-62; pvt practice, 1962-67. Vice-chmn: bd, Swanson Fresh Air Comty Camping Corp; J Comty Relations Council, Youngstown; commnr, Mayor's Hum Relations Commn; co-chmn: legal educ comm, Mahoning Co Bar Assn; vocational service comm, B'nai B'rith grand lodge 2, mem, bd govs, lodge, chmn, Youth Adv Council of Youngstown, 1967-68; trustee, Asso Neighborhood Cens, Youngstown; mem: Kent State, Hillel Adv Bd, 1966; J Family and C Service Bd, J Fed of Youngstown; Ky reg bd, ADL; Cleveland adv council, Amer Arbitration Assn; Anshe Ameth Temple; Amer Trial Lawyers Acad; O State Bar Assn; O Acad of Trial Lawyers; ACLU, Youngstown; Tau Epsilon Phi; Phi Delta Phi. Recipient: Presidential Citation, B'nai B'rith Intl. Spec interests: comty relations; adv to youth. Home: 5463 Sampson Rd, Girard, O. Office: 932 Belmont St, Youngstown, O.

PEARCE, Alexander E, US, surgeon, educator; b. Phila, Pa, Nov 2, 1913; s. Aaron and Pauline (Rapoport); BA, U of Pa, 1933; MD, Hahnemann Med Coll, 1937; m. Ruth Lilienthal, Oct 17, 1942; c: Henry, Maria, Jon, Robert, Paula. Clinical prof, sr att surg, Hahnemann Med Coll and Hosp; chmn, div of surg, W Park Hosp, Phila. Lt col, US Army, 1942-46. Dipl: Amer Bd Surg; Intl Bd Surg; f: AMA; Amer and Intl Coll of Surgs; mem: AAAS; AAUP; Phila Co and Pa State Med Assns; Phys Soc of Phila. Contbr to med jours. Home: 257 Cross Roads, Merion, Pa. Office: 1420 Race St, Philadelphia, Pa.

PEARCE, Henry, US, business exec; b. NYC, Feb 8, 1908; s. Morris and Mary (Ruffman); att Fordham U, NYC, 1926-1928; LLB, Bklyn Law Sch, 1932; m. Sarah Segal, Feb 7, 1936; c: David, Linda Rosensweig. Chmn, bd, chief exec off, Pearce, Mayer & Greer, Inc, since 1969, partner, 1928-68. Chmn, campaign, Real Estate Ind, FJP, NY, 1969-70; gen chmn, S Shore Friends of JTSA, 1969; trustee, J Assn of Services for the Aged; mem: Natl Patrons Soc, JTSA, bd of overseers; Natl Assn of Real Estate Bds; Real Estate Bds: NY; Bx; Bklyn; Amer Arbitration Assn; Natl Panel of Arbitrators; B'nai B'rith, LI Lodge 1353; fmr mem, real estate adv commn, dept real estate, NYC; club, Woodmere, LI. Home: 1050 Fifth Ave, New York, NY. Office: 41 E 42 St, New York, NY.

PEARL, Chaim H, US, rabbi; b. Liverpool, Eng, Nov 25, 1919; s. Alexander and Rebecca (Epstein); in US since 1964; att: Yeshiva Etz Hayim, Liverpool; Jews Coll, London; MA, U Birmingham; PhD, U London; m. Anita Newman, Nov 16, 1941; c: David, Jonathan, Simon, Judith. Rabbi: Conservative Syn, Riverdale, NY, since 1964; Birmingham, Eng, 1945-60; New W End Syn, London, 1960-64. Dean, Acad for J Rel; mem, Metrop Council, RA. Author: Guide to Jewish Knowledge, 1957; Guide to Shavuoth, 1959; Minor Festivals, 1962. Home: 5360 Arlington Ave, Bronx, NY.

PEARLMAN, Arthur, US, business exec; b. NYC, Feb 8, 1930; s. Harry and Martha (Drucker); CBA, Bucknell U, 1948; m. Barbara Gluck, Mar 7, 1953; c: Pamela, Gary, Michael. Exec vice-pres, secy, dir, Swanee Paper Corp, since 1961, fmr vice-pres and treas; partner, Lion Paper Sales; treas, asst secy, dir, Clearwater Tissue Mills; vice-pres, St Lawrence Paper, 1949-51. Mem: exec comm, Bonds for Israel; bd of trustees, Temple Sinai, both Tenafly, NJ; life mem, Brandeis U; mem: Masons; Shriners; clubs: Intl, Natl and NY Sales Execs; Edgewood Country; Harmonie, NYC. Home: 267 Devon Rd, Tenafly, NJ. Office: 205 E 42 St, New York, NY.

PEARLMAN, Louis Jr, US, jurist, attorney; b. Crawfordsville Ind, Sep 27, 1930; s. Louis and Beatrice (Benson); BS, U of Pa, 1952; LLB, U Mich, 1955. Pvt practice, law, since 1956; judge, W Lafayette City Court, 1962-64. Pres, Fed of J Charities, Lafayette, Ind; dir: S Side Comty Cen; Cancer Soc; Girl Scouts; Jaycees; Borinstein Home, Indianapolis; secy-

treas, Tipp Co Bar Assn, 1957-59; chmn, comm, C of C, 1958; mem: Ind State, 7th Circuit and Amer Bar Assns; YMCA; B'nai B'rith; Tau Epsilon Rho; Elks; clubs: Lafayette Country; Columbia. Home: 1428 Northwestern, W Lafayette, Ind. Office: 412 Main St, Lafayette, Ind.

PEARLMAN, Moshe, Isr, author; b. London, Eng, Mar 23; 1911; s. Lipman and Rebecca (Winegarten); in Isr since 1948; BSc, U London, 1933. Author: Collective Adventure, 1938; Mufti of Jerusalem, 1947; Adventure in the Sun, 1948; The Army of Israel, 1950; The Capture and Trial of Adolf Eichmann, 1963; Ben Gurion Looks Back, 1965; The Zealots of Massada, 1967; co-author: Historical Sites in Israel, 1964; Jerusalem, A History of Forty Centuries, 1968. Dir, Govt Press Div, chief govt spokesman, chief army spokesman, all 1948-52; dir: Isr Bc Service, 1952-55; info services and adv to PM, 1955-60; ambass on spec mission to Congo, Leopoldville, 1960; spec asst to Min of Defense, during Six Day War, 1967. Maj, Brit Army, WW II; lt col, IDF. Home: 16 David Marcus St, Jerusalem, Isr.

PEARLSON, Elias, Eng, dental surgeon; b. Kingston upon Hull, Eng, May 2, 1917; s. Gustave and Mary; att Sorbonne, Paris, 1933-34; Dipl, Hispanic Studies, U Madrid, 1936; LDS, U Newcastle, 1945; m. Blanche Mar 15, 1947; c: Godfrey, Marcia. Pvt practice, dent surg. F, Royal Soc of Arts, 1958; secy, Sunderland Isr Med Aid Comm; fmr secy, chmn, treas, Sunderland Friends Anti-TB League of Isr; chmn, Brit Dent Assn, 1960; mem, Inst of Linguists. Office: 1 Elmwood St, Sunderland, Eng.

PEARLSON, Jordan, Can, rabbi; b. Somerville, Mass, Sep 2, 1924; s. Jacob and Frieda (Spivak); in Can since 1956; BA, hons, Northeastern U, 1948, LLB, 1950; BHL, HUC-JIR, Cincinnati, O, 1954, ordained rabbi, MHL, 1956; m. Geraldine Goldstein, Jan 19, 1958; c: Joshua, Nessa, Abigail. Rabbi, Temple Sinai Cong, Toronto, since 1954. Pres, Toronto Rabb F, 1960; found mem, Can Council Reform Congs; mem: exec bd, HUC Alumni; bd alumni overseers, HUC; CJCong; J Child and Family Service; CCAR, comm on interfaith activities; Metrop Assn for Retarded Children; UA; UJA; Red Cross; Acad Northeastern U; Mass Bar; ZOC; first rabbi to sit on natl rel adv bd, Can Bc Corp. Spec interests: devl of new syn music, Mh, adult educ progs. Home: 2 Carnwath Crescent, Willowdale, Ont, Can. Study: 210 Wilson Ave, Toronto, Can.

PEARLSTEIN, Irvin Edward, US, business exec; b. Davenport, Ia, Sep 9, 1916; s. Charles and Ethel (Estes); att St Ambrose Coll, 1935; m. Annette Goodman; c: Lynn, Billie Shepard, Patricia, Carol. Pres: Arizona Land Research Corp, since 1950; Mainline Properties, since 1950; Havasu Del Sol; Townsite Devl; Complete Food Service, 1948-60; co-owner, Grand Canyon Sub-Division; owner of brokerage agencies in Denver, Colo; Chgo, Ill. Prin contrib: initiated new concepts in land devl in SW US. Sgt maj, US Army, 1942-46. Chmn: Phoenix J Fed, 1968-69; has held every important position in Phoenix JWF, UJA since WW II; mem, bd: Comty Relations Comm, Phoenix JCC; Temple Beth Isr; B'nai B'rith; Amer Legion; JWV; C of C: Flagstaff, Phoenix, Williams; assists local fed in training students in comty org, fund raising, Ariz State U Sch of Social Service Admn; speaker for J orgs; conducts leadership training prog; clubs: Ariz; Century Country. Spec interests: travel, athletics, golf, music. Home: 601 W Belmont St, Phoenix, Ariz. Office: 2727 N Central St, Phoenix, Ariz.

PEARLSTEIN, Jacob D, Can, attorney; b. Montreal, Sep 30, 1894; s. David and Anna (Bilsky); BA, U Toronto, 1916; grad, hons, Osgoode Law Sch, Toronto, 1919; m. Mary Blatt, Dec 25, 1935; c: John. QC; pvt practice; mem, ed staff, Toronto Star, 1916-22; spec writer, Toronto Star Weekly, 1916-22. Natl exec mem, ZOC; hon chmn, B'nai B'rith Hillel Commn, chmn, 1948-57; chmn, ZC, 1951, both Toronto; vice pres, Ont Zionist region, 1950-53; exec mem: Bur of J Educ, Toronto, since 1951, pres, 1964-67; Can J Cong, 1952-53; asso chmn, United JWF Service Council, 1953-54, treas, United JWF, 1956; vice chmn, UJA, 1953, asso campaign chmn, 1954, gen chmn, 1955, all Toronto; mem, natl council, JDC, 1955; chmn, bd of trustees, B'nai B'rith, 1948-53, treas, Toronto lodge, since 1954; treas, Camp Shalom, Young Judaea, Ont, 1947-53; clubs: Primrose; Holy Blossom Temple Brotherhood, Toronto. Home: 650 Briar Hill Ave, Toronto, Can. Office: 372 Bay St, Toronto, Can.

PEARLSTEIN, Philip M, US, artist, teacher; b. Pittsburgh, Pa, May 24, 1924; s. David and Libby (Kalser); BFA, Carnegie

Yeshiva, Jerusalem, 1969; m. Jiskah Feuchtwanger, July 20, 1964; c: Alexander, Shaoul, David. Tchr, secondary sch and yeshiva, since 1963; lectr, Torah Shebeal Peah Confs. Army Rabbinate, IDF, since 1961. Co-ed, Beth Hatalmud, Talmudical yearbook; contbr to rel publs. Home: 10 Kosovsky St, Jerusalem, Isr.

PERLBERG, Arye, Isr, educator; b. Vienna, Aus, Jan 16, 1926; s. Itzhak and Aviva (Firstenberg); in Isr since 1926; BA, Heb U, Jerusalem, 1954; MA, Columbia U, TC, NY, 1955, DEduc, 1958; m. Chava Zingerman, Mar 7, 1950; c: Don, Gil. Sr lectr, Technion since 1962, on fac since 1959; mem Kibbutz Hatzerim, 1944-51; tchr, youth aliyah leader, JA: 1943-44; and org, Boy Scouts, Haifa, 1944-47; repr, youth aliyah, detention camps, Cyprus, 1947; educ admnr, Inst of J Youth Leaders, Jerusalem, 1951-53; tchr Heb schs, dir summer camps, US, 1955-58; cons, training and educ, Isr Inst of Productivity, 1958; visiting research asso prof, U Ill, 1966-68; visiting asst prof, Tel Aviv U, 1968-69; lectr, cons: various orgs. Mem: Phi Delta Kappa; Kappa Delta Phi; Amer Educ Research Assn; Amer Vocational Research Assn; Amer Vocational Assn; Amer Tech Educ Assn; Histadrut Council, 1949-50, Isr Boy Scout hqrs, 1943-45. Co-author: An Anthology of Readings in Vocational Education, 1968; research reports; contbr: Ency Educ, vol III, 1964; educ jours. Recipient: UNESCO grant grad studies; Columbia U grant. Home: 15 Yotam St, Haifa, Isr. Office: Technion, Haifa, Isr.

PERLE, George, US, composer, educator; b. Bayonne, NJ, May 6, 1915; s. Joseph and Mary (Sanders) Perlman; BMus, De Paul U, Chgo, Ill, 1938; MMus, Amer Conservatory of Music, Chgo, 1942; PhD, NYU, 1956; m. Barbara Phillips, 1958; c: Max, Kathy, Annette. Prof, music fac, Queens Coll, since 1966, fac mem, since 1961; asst prof, U Louisville, 1949-57; asso prof, U Cal, Davis, 1957-61. US Army, 1943-45. Chmn, NY chap, Intl Soc Contemporary Music, since 1967; bd govs, Intl Alban Berg Soc, since 1966. Author: Serial Composition and Atonality: An Introduction to the Music of Schoenberg, Berg and Webern, 1962; 2nd ed, 1968; composer of works for orch, chamber ensemble, solo instrument, voice and chorus; recorded works: Rhapsody for Orchestra; Quintet for Strings; Monody for Flute; Monody for doublebass; Six preludes for piano; ed bd: Perspectives in New Music, since 1961; Music Forum, since 1966; contbr to scholarly jours. Recipient: Guggenheim f, 1966-67; Koussevitzky Commn, 1967-68. Home: 114 82 Rd, Kew Gardens, NY. Office: Queens Coll, Flushing, NY.

PERLEY, Maie E, US, author, communal worker; b. London, Eng, Sep 14, 1901; d. Robert and Hannah (Cohen) Clements; in US since 1938; m. Martin Perley, July 11, 1938. Author: Not By Bread Alone, 1937; Without My Gloves, 1940; freelance painter; lit critic, Louisville Times. Mem, exec bd: ACLU, Ky, since 1954; Natl Urban League, Louisville, 1948-58; chmn, women's div, United J Campaign, 1952-56; mem, natl bd, women's div, UJA, 1952-57; life mem, Louisville Conf of J Orgs. Recipient: award for comty service, Conf of J Orgs, 1958; best artist, Art Cen annual show, Louisville, Ky, 1962. Home: 507 Country Lane, Louisville, Ky.

PERLEY, Martin M, US, rabbi; b. Phila, Pa, Oct 11, 1910; s. Benjamin and Tillie (Goren) Perelmuter; BA, McGill U, 1930; MHL, ordained rabbi, JIR, 1934; hon DD, HUC-JIR, 1959; m. Maie Clements, July 11, 1938. Exec dir, Louisville and Jefferson Co Hum Relations Commn, since 1968; rabbi: Beth Isr, Melbourne, Austr, 1934-36; dir Hillel found: U of Ill, 1937-38; Ind U, 1938-41; Brith Sholom Temple, Louisville, 1946-68. Chaplain, maj, US Army, WW II. Co-chmn: mayor's civic rel adv comm, 1957-60; mayor's comm hum relations, 1958-61; vice-chmn, Louisville and Jefferson Co Comty Action Commn, 1965-68; exec bd, CCAR, 1948-50, 1958-60, vice-chmn, chaplaincy comm, 1953-60; speakers bur: Comty Chest; ARC. Home: 507 Country Lane, Louisville, Ky. Study: 400 S Sixth St, Louisville, Ky.

PERLIS, Leo, US, labor union exec; b. Bialystock, Russ, Feb 22, 1912; s. David and Anna (Gershowitz); in US since 1923; m. Betty Grantz; c: Howard, Michael. Natl dir: AFL-CIO Comty Services, since 1943, and co-found, CIO war relief comm; CIO comty services, both 1943-45, org Textile Workers Union, 1936-38, dir, Lab Non-Partisan League, 1938-41; prin lab cons, War Production Bd, 1941-43; ed: Patterson Press, NJ, 1936; Labor's Non-Partisan League News, 1940. Cons on planning, comm on social service, White House Conf on Aging, 1961; served on pres' comms under Eisenhower, Kennedy; cons to UN, 1948; asso trustee, U of Pa; co-found:

Care; US Comm for UNICEF; Natl Citizens Commn for Public Schs; mem bd dirs: United Way, Amer; Natl Cen Voluntary Action; Natl Assembly Social Policy and Devl; AHA; Legal Aid Soc; United Comty Funds and Councils of Amer; Natl Assn for Mh; pres' adv comm, NYU; adv comm, Louis M. Rabinowitz Sch of Social Work, Hunter Coll; mem, Amer Newspaper Guild. Contbr to publs. Recipient: awards: Council on Social Work Educ; Amer Newspaper Guild; NY Sch of Social Work; Natl Urban League; ARC; Columbia U; Boy Scouts Amer; Boys Clubs Amer; USO; United Fund, LI. Home: 6101 16 St, NW, Washington, DC. Office: 815 16 St, NW, Washington, DC.

PERLIS, Sam, US, mathematician, educator; b. Oak Park, Ill, Apr 18, 1913; s. Adolph and Ida (Ziskind); BS, U of Chgo, 1934, MS, 1936, PhD, 1938; m. Esther Rockoff, June 24, 1939; c: Donald, Robert. Asso prof, math, Purdue U, since 1951, on fac since 1946; instr: Ill Inst Tech, 1938-41; U Mich, 1941-42; research math, Lockheed Aircraft Corp, 1942-46. Mem: Amer Math Soc; Sigma Xi. Author: Theory of Matrices, 1951; Introduction to Algebra, 1966; contbr to profsl jours. Home: 704 Sugar Hill Dr, W Lafayette, Ind. Office: Dept Math, Purdue U, Lafayette, Ind.

PERLMAN, Anita M, US, civic worker; b. Butte, Mont, Oct 3, 1905; d. Max and Esther (Kenoffel) Morris; BA, Northwestern U, 1925; m. Louis Pearlman, Sep 9, 1925; c: Dorene Dunkleman, Theodore. Intl pres, B'nai B'rith Women, 1955-57, pres, N Shore, 1938-40, pres dist 6, 1944-45; natl chmn Pre-Natal Care Educ, Natl Found March Dimes; natl vice-chmn, ADL, 1963-69; vice-chmn: Natl Henry Monsky Found; youth commn; women's supr council 1950; women's div, YMCA, 1934-36; Rogers Park Little Theater, 1938-41; Eugene Field, PTA, 1934-36; vice-pres: Hillel Found, Ill, 1950, adv bd, Northwestern U; women's council, Bd of J Educ, 1949-52; policy chmn, Conf J Women's Orgs, 1951; secy, Mizpah Temple Sisterhood, 1936-38; trustee, Alpha Epsilon Phi Found, 1961; mem: hon life, B'nai B'rith Girls; B'nai B'rith Youth Comm; Brandeis Women's Comm; bd dirs, Natl Safety Council, 1961; Gov of Ill adv bd, div of youth and comty service, Dept Pub Welfare, 1950; charter, Beth Emet Syn and Sisterhood; speakers bur, Combined JA; cabinet and comm of 100, Bonds for Isr; hon life, Aleph Zedek Aleph; Natl Council of J Women; Hadassah; Urban League, NCCJ; J Big Sisters; Ill Assn Big Brothers and Sisters; Chgo Consumptive Aid Soc; United HIAS Service; Natl Found for Infantile Paralysis; Northwestern U Alumni Assn, Anita Perlman Scholarship Fund established for work for B'nai B'rith Girls, 1944; cons, US Treasury Dept, women's div; delg, White House Conf on Children and Youth, 1960. Recipient: Hillel Honor Key, 1942, certificate of honor, Chgo Sun Times, 1945; citation, Treas Dept, 1954; awards: Chgo Bd Health, 1967; Natl Found March Dimes, 1968-69; Natl Council Negro Women, 1957; hum relations brotherhood, N Shore Orgs, 1964; Legion of Honor, B'nai B'rith Youth Commn, 1947; Outstanding Alumni, Alpha Epsilon Phi, 1963. Home: 804 Mosely Rd, Highland Park, Ill.

PERLMAN, Florence, US, communal worker; b. NYC, July 28, 1897; d. Max and Dora (Schneck) Burman; BA, Barnard Coll, 1918; m. Nathan Perlman, June 20, 1917 (decd); c: Jack. Treas, Natl Hadassah, since 1968; mem, natl bd, since 1944, held various portfolios, fmr natl vice-pres, mem, Zionist Gen Council, fmr delg, WZC, fmr chmn, Isr Vocational Services; managed husband's political campaigns in NY including US Cong; Home: 25 E 9 St, New York, NY. Office: 65 E 52 St, New York, NY.

PERLMAN, George, US, attorney; b. NYC, Nov 10, 1908; s. Israel and Margolis (Perlis); BS, LIU, 1931; LLB, Bklyn Law Sch, St Lawrence U, 1935; JD, Bklyn Law Sch 1969; m. Sylvia, June 25, 1934; c: Marcia Meselsohn, Gail Ratto. Pvt practice. Mem: Seymour L Fass League, Med Research. Author: A Practical Guide to Social Security, 1962. Hobbies: art, antiques. Home and office: 267 Dover, Brooklyn, NY.

PERLMAN, Helen H, US, social worker, educator; b. St Paul, Minn, Dec 20, 1905; d. Lazer and Annie (Schwartz) Harris; BA, U Minn, 1926; MS, Columbia U, 1943; m. Max Perlman, Aug 16, 1935; c: Jonathan. Prof, social work, U Chgo, since 1945; social worker, Family and Child Guidance Agencies: Chgo; NY, both 1927-40; lectr, sup, NY Sch Social Work, Columbia U, 1940-45. F, Amer Orthopsychiatric Assn; mem, Phi Beta Kappa. Author: Social Casework: A Problem-Solving Process, 1957; So You Want To Be A Social Worker, 1962; Persona: Social Role and Personality, 1968. Recipient:

Distinguished Achievement award, U Minn, 1967. Home: 1321 E 56 St, Chicago, Ill. Office: U Chgo, Chicago, Ill.

PERLMAN, Ivan Elliot, US, cantor; b. Flushing, NY, June 3, 1925; s. Henry and Katherine (Glantz); grad, Sem Sch J Studies, JTSA, 1950; m. Muriel Herman, Aug 16, 1947; c: Eli, Emanuel, Richard, Josh. Cantor: Temple Emanu-El, since 1964; Lyonhurst Heb Cen and Fairlawn J Cen, NJ, 1948-51; B'nai Emunah Syn, 1951-54; Tifereth Isr Syn, Des Moines, 1954-64. Pvt, USMCR, 1943-46. Exec council, Cantors Assembly Amer; natl dep chaplain, JWV; dept chaplain, RI; bd dirs: Easter Seal Cen, Des Moines, Ia, 1960-64; Providence Heb Day Sch; RI Soc Crippled Children and Adults; mayors commn youth, chmn, problem youth, Des Moines, Ia, 1963-64; mem: KP. Author: recording, Liturgical Moods, 1967. Recipient: Bronze Star; hon f, Cantors Inst, JTSA, 1969. Hobbies: fishing, boating, working with comty orgs. Home: 35 Astral Ave, Providence, RI; 89 Horseshoe Lane, Centerville, Cape Cod, Mass. Study: 99 Taft Ave, Providence, RI.

PERLMAN, Louis Lester, US, business exec; b. Lanovitz, Russ, May 20, 1902; s. Max and Tillie (Sprecher); in US since 1907; BS, Northwestern U, Evanston Ill, 1925; m. Anita Morris, Sep 9, 1925; c: Dorene Dunkleman, Theodore. Chmn bd, Martin-Brower Corp, since 1968, pres, 1960-68; pres, Restaurant Supply Co, 1925-34; sales, Levin Brothers Paper Co, 1934-40; pres, Cent Plastics Corp, 1940-46; found, pres, Perlman Paper Co, 1950-60. Mem: Soc of Plastic Engrs; Chgo Assn of Commerce and Ind; Chgo Paper Assn, past prog chmn; natl youth commn, B'nai B'rith, pres, N Shore Lodge, 1940-42, chmn, spec events; trustee: Leo N Levi Natl Arthritis Hosp, Hot Springs, Ark; Beth Emet Syn, Evanston, Ill; allied membership chmn, Intl Franchise Assn. Recipient: B'nai B'rith Intl Pres' Medal, 1969. Hobby: music. Home: 804 Moseley Rd, Highland Park, Ill. Office: 4800 S Austin Ave, Chgo, Ill.

PERLMAN, Mark, US, educator, editor; b. Madison, Wis, Dec 23, 1923; s. Selig and Eva (Shaber); BA, U Wis, 1947, MA, 1947; PhD, Columbia U, 1950; m. Naomi Waxman; c: Abigail. U Prof, econ, U Pittsburgh, since 1965; chmn dept, since 1965; prof econ and hist, econ in health, Grad Sch of Public Health, U Pittsburgh research asso, Cen for Regional Econ Studies, since 1963; asst prof: U Hawaii 1951-52; Cornell U, 1952-55; Johns Hopkins U, 1955-58, asso prof, 1958-63, visiting prof, 1963-64; mem: survey team evaluating public health prog, Brazil, 1960, Med Manpower Team, Taiwan, 1962-64; research asso, Harvard U, 1955-57. Mem: AAUP; Amer Econ Assn; Amer Public Health Assn; Econ Hist Assn; Econ Hist Soc; Population Assn; S Econ Assn; Royal Econ Soc; Intl Union for Sci Study of Population. Author: Judges in Industry: A Study of Labor Arbitration in Australia, 1954; Labor Union Theories in America: Background and Development, 1958; The Machinists: A New Study in American Trade Unionism, 1961; Democracy in the AMI, 1962; The Methodology of Economic Investment in Public Health Programs; co-author: Health Manpower in a Developing Economy, 1967; The Future American Population Problems; A Disaggregated Cohort Analysis; ed, Human Resources in Urban Economy, 1963; co-ed, Contemporary Economics and Selected Readings, 1967; ed, Jour of Econ Lit, 1968; mem bd eds, Indus and Lab Relations Rev, 1953-55; contbr to profsl jours. Home: 5622 Bartlett St, Pittsburg Pa. Office: Dept Econ U Pittsburgh, Pittsburgh, Pa.

PERLMAN, Michael, Isr, educator; b. Hamburg, Ger, Mar 21, 1917; s. Benjamin and Elsa (Van Son); in Isr since 1939; att Yeshiva, Mannheim, Ger; m. Elisabeth Singer, Aug, 1943; c: Yigal, Benjamin, Ovadiah, Nathaniel, Jehonadav. Head, music dept, Kibbutz haDati; counselor, yearly workshop, Bnei Akiva Scholarship Inst; tchr, accents of the Bible, tchrs sems. Served Haganah. Mem: bd, Isr Inst of Rel Music; world exec, Bnei Akiva. Club, ACUM. Author: Dapim leLimud Taamei haMikra, vols I-VI, 1959-69; Madrich leMoreh, 1969; pub, ed, music of rel liturgical songs, choir and instrumental. Home: Kibbutz Yavne, Isr.

PERLMAN, Milton B, US, educator; b. NYC, Aug 14, 1894; s. Abraham and Flora (Cohen); BA CCNY, 1914; MA, Columbia U, 1916; att NYU Law Sch, 1917-18; m. Celia Cohen, Aug 17, 1922; c: Justi. Ret; prin, Public Sch 164, Bklyn, 1940-61, tchr, NYC schs, 1914-28, asst prin, 1928-40; camp dir, Pocono Camp Club, Pine Lake Camp, 1926-35; prin, B'nai Jeshurun, 1926-31. US Army, 1918-19. Chmn: accreditation comm, United Syn Schs, 1961-68; Talmud

Torah comm, E Middlewood J Cen since 1956, mem bd trustees, since 1953, vice-pres, since 1966; vice-pres: Flatbush Dist 32, Council for J Educ, since 1949; Flatbush Dist, ZOA, 1947-57, exec comm, since 1954; bd govs, J Tchrs Comty Chest, since 1940; bd educ, Solomon Schechter Day HS, Bklyn, since 1968; regional activities comm, United Syn Natl Commn on Educ; bd educ, Metrop Council, United Syn of Amer, since 1957; bd, conciliation and review, J Educ Comm, since 1958; mem: UJA since 1938; FJP, since 1940; JTSA, since 1940; NY Acad Pub Educ; NY Prins Assn; Omega Pi Alpha. Book rev ed, The Bulletin, E Midwood J Cen, since 1945; lectr, contbr to educ publs. Recipient. citations: JTSA, 1959; ZOA, 1968. Hobby: philately. Home: 585 E 16 St, Brooklyn, NY.

PERLMAN, Morris L, US, nuclear chem; b. Detroit, Mich, Aug 10, 1916; s. Samuel and Emma (Kumpinski); BS, U of La, 1937; PhD, U of Cal, 1940; m. Ilse Serlin, Oct 24, 1941; c: David, Daniel. Sr sci, Brookhaven Natl Lab, since 1949; asst chem, US bur of Mines, 1940-41; research asso, U of Cal, 1941- 43; sci, Los Alamos Lab, 1943-46; research asso, Gen Electric Co, NYC, 1946-48; asst prof, chem, U of Wyo, 1948-49. Prin contrib: effects of nuclear transition on atomic electrons, beta decay, and nuclear structure. Mem: Amer Phys Soc; Sigma Xi. Home: Snedecor Ave, Bayport, NY. Office: Brookhaven Natl Lab, Upton, LI, NY.

PERLMAN, Shalom, Isr, educator; b. Tarnopol, Pol, Nov 22, 1919; s. Karol and Klara (Kurfürst); in Isr since 1937; MA, Heb U, Jerusalem, PhD, 1960; British Council Scholar, Oxford U, Eng, 1955-57; m. Erela Bardach; c: Hana. Asso prof, Tel Aviv U, since 1967, dean, fac hum, since 1969, head, dept classics, since 1969, dean of students, 1965-67; asst, lectr Heb U, 1955-60; visiting prof, U of Mich, 1967-68. Pvt, IDF. Pres, Eranos, classical assn, Tel Aviv U; participant, Conf Deans of Students, US State Dept and U of Utah, 1966. Ed: Doron, 1966; Philip II and the Greeks; contbr to profsl periodicals in Isr and abroad. Hobby: swimming. Home: 16 Bialik St, Tel Aviv, Isr. Office: Tel Aviv U, Ramat Aviv, Isr.

PERLMANN, Moshe, US, educator; b. Odessa, Russ, Sep 28, 1905; s. Eliezer and Razia (Leigrab); in US since 1940; att U Odessa, 1921-24; MA, Heb U, Jerusalem, 1934; PhD, U London, 1941; m. Ida Brenner, April 2, 1941; c: Ari-Joel. Prof Arabic, UCLA, since 1961; lectr, New Sch for Social Research, 1945-52; prof, Dropsie Coll, 1948-55; lectr, Harvard U, 1955-61. F, Amer Acad of Research, mem: Amer Oriental Soc; Amer Hist Assn; Isr, Oriental Soc. Author: studies in Islamic and J history. Recipient: Rockefeller grant, 1959-60. Home: 2227, Malcolm Ave, Los Angeles, Cal. Office: U of Cal, RH 302, Los Angeles, Cal.

PERLMUTTER, Irwin, US, physician, educator; b. NYC, Mar 24, 1917; s. Jonathan and Bertha (Lipsky); BA, Columbia Coll, 1937; MD, Coll Phys and Surgs, 1941; m. Corinne Levine, 1946; c: Susan, Jordan, Abigail, Eliza, David. Asso clinical prof, neur surg, U Miami Sch of Med, since 1960; fac mem, since 1953; att surg, Drs Hosp, Coral Gables, Fla, since 1961; chief, neurosurg section: and cons Mt Sinai Hosp, Miami Beach, since 1949; and dir surg, Variety Children's Hosp, Miami, since 1958; Cedars of Lebanon Hosp, since 1961; sr att neurosurg, Jackson Hosp, Miami, since 1957; asso att neurosurg, Mercy Hosp, since 1961; att neurosurg, Miami Baptist, since 1961; cons: Naples Hosp, since 1952; Hialeah Hosp, since 1957. Lt cdr, USNR, 1942-46. Dipl, Amer Bd Neur Surg; Pres, Fla Neurosurg Soc, 1960-61; mem: bd trustees, Betham Cong, since 1960; Dade Co Lunacy Commn, 1951-56; Amer Coll Surgs; Amer Acad Neur; Amer Cerebral Palsy; Harvey Cushing Soc; S Neurosurg Soc; Cong Neur Surgs; Amer League against Epilepsy. Home: 5808 Michelangelo, Coral Gables, Fla. Office: 4685 Ponce de Leon Blvd, Coral Gables, Fla.

PERLMUTTER, Nathan, US, organization exec; b. NYC, Mar 2, 1923; s. Hyman and Bella (Finkelstein); att: Fgn Service Sch, Georgetown U, 1942-43; Villanova Coll, 1943-44; LLB, NYU, 1949; m. Ruth Osofsky, 1943; c: Nina, Dean. Vice-pres, Devl, Brandeis U, since 1969; dir, NY regional off, ADL, 1964-65, dir, Mich off, 1952-53, civil rights dept, Mt States div, 1949-52, exec dir, Fla off, 1956-64. Asso dir, AJ Comm 1965-69. Lt, USMC, 1943-46. Mem, NY Bar Assn. Contbr to jours. Office: Brandeis U, Waltham, Mass.

PERLMUTTER, Zoltan, Isr, painter, sculptor; b. Hung, Jan 23, 1922; in Isr since 1950; att Art Acad, Budapest; m. 2nd,

MD, 1933, postgrad studies, 1933-35, 1941, Lahey Clinic, 1942; Post Grad Hosp, 1947; m. Lillian Rosen, 1936; c: Madeleine Cosman, Ruth Donnelly, Ceil. Dir, dept of med, Swedish Hosp of Bklyn. Diplomate, Amer Bd of Internal Med; f: Amer Coll Cardiology; Amer Coll Allergy; Amer Coll Gastroenterology; Amer Psychosomatic Soc; Amer Geriatrics Soc; NY Diabetic Soc; AMA. Author: Dietherapy of Disease, 1944; Management of Obesity, 1944; Gastroenterology in General Practice, 1946; contbr to med jours. Home and office: 161 Rugby Rd, Brooklyn, NY.

PELTIN, Lawrence J, US, jurist; b. NYC, Mar 18, 1898; s. Samuel and Rose (Lande); LLB, NYU, 1917; m. Ida Sokolsky, Nov 5, 1922 (decd); m. 2nd, Rose Glasser, Aug 5, 1968. Pvt practice since 1966; asst dist atty, Bx, 1933-55, chief asst dist atty 1955-57; justice, City Court of NY, 1958-60, chief justice, 1960-66. Vice chmn, bd of dirs, Hebrew Home for Aged at Riverdale; mem: Bx Co Bar Assn; Dist Attys Assn of NY State. Home: 1001 Grand Concourse, Bronx, NY. Office: 59 E 161 St, Bx, NY.

PELTZ, Richard W, US, educator; b. Rock Island, Ill, June 27, 1927; s. Samuel and Doris (Arshack); MA, U Chgo, 1949; PhD, 1953; m. Cissie Liebshutz, Jan 1, 1952; c: Julie, David. Prof phil, U Wis, Milw, since 1965; chmn, dept, 1963-68; instr, U of Ill, 1950; asst prof, Fresno State Coll, 1956-57. Mem: Amer Phil Assn; U Chgo Alumni Assn; Wis Soc for J Learning; Phi Kappa Phi; Phi Betta Kappa; Amer Soc for Aesthetics. Author: Logic, 1951; How To Read Contemporary Philosophy, 1952; God, Faith and Reason, 1953; Introduction to Symbolic Logic, 1956; Plato and Aristotle: Art, Science and Morality, 1957; Philosophy and the Birth of Science, 1957; contbr to phil jours. Spec interest: art. Office: U Wis, Milwaukee, Wis.

PENAN, Harry D, US, attorney, jurist; b. Fitchburg, Mass, Sep 3, 1906; s. Hyman and Lena (Epstein); attended Boston U Bus Sch, 1924-26, LLB, Boston U Law Sch, 1929; m. Natalie Baron, Aug 22, 1943; c: Ellen, Victor. Special judge, Dist Court of Winchendon, since 1939; cons to Boston U, since 1959; govt appeal agent, Draft Bd, 1940-46. Pres: Zionist dist, 1940; Achdus lodge, B'nai B'rith, 1941, mem, general comm, dist 1, 1945; Agudas Achim Syn, 1944; Family Service, 1950; J Comty Center, 1951, all Fitchburg; past master, Masons; mem: Shriners; Fed Amer and Mass Bar Assns; trustee, Worcester N Savings Inst; clubs: Probus, pres, 1934; Civitan, pres, 1935. Home: 125 Lincoln St, Fitchburg, Mass. Office: 280 Main St, Fitchburg, Mass.

PENKAR, Saul S, India, railway official; b. Bombay, India; s. Samuel and Miryam; m. Leena Abigail, Sep 6, 1948; two c. Head draughtsman, W Railway since 1957. Chmn trust bd, mem mgn comm, Magen Hasidim Syn, Bombay, pres, 1954-57, 1959-61; vice-pres, Union of Orthodox Congs of India, since 1960. Home: New Readymoney Bldg, Clare Rd, Bombay 8, India. Office: Divisional Off, W Railway, Bombay, 8, India.

PENN, Harry S, US, physician; b. Russ, Oct 24, 1891; s. Solomon and Hanna; in US since 1909; MD, Tufts Med Coll, Boston, Mass, 1919; m. Ella Gales, Mar 7, 1937; c: Nathan. Pvt practice since 1919; cancer research, since 1932; research asso, oncology UCLA, 1945-48. Prin contribs: Penn seroflocculation reaction, 1951; new chemotherapeutic agt for treatment of advanced malignancies, 1963. Dipl, Intl Coll Surgs; mem: AMA; LA Co Med Assn; Soc for Cancer Research; Soc for Experimental Biol and Med; Sigma Xi. Contbr to med jours. Home: 2678 Glendower Ave, Los Angeles, Cal. Office: 9735 Wilshire Blvd, Beverly Hills, Cal.

PENN, Mordechai, Isr, artist; b. Petah Tikva, Isr, May 31, 1938; s. Matitiahoo and Miriam (Sirkis) Pinkassovich; dipl, Bezalel Art Sch, Jerusalem, 1936; att Slade Sch Fine Arts, U Coll, London, 1936-64; m. Nechama Friedman, Apr 6, 1967; c: Dalia. One-man exhbs: Yad laBanim, Petah Tikva, 1963; Katz Gal, Tel Aviv, 1965; Chemerinski Gal, Tel Aviv, 1966; Gal du Sfinx, Amsterdam, 1967; group exhbs: including Gal Mokum; Frankhuis Amsterdam, 1967; Sgt, Nahal, 1956-59 Mem: Painters, Sculptors Assn; Graphic Designers, Isr. Hobbies: lit, phil. Home and studio: 8 Michal St, Tel Aviv Isr.

PEPPER, Morton, US, attorney; b. NYC, May 28, 1906; s; George and Pauline (Goldstone); BA, Harvard U, 1927; JD, 1930; m. Doris Hellman, Oct 8, 1933; c: Alice Cooper, Carole Cooper. Partner: Pepper & Pepper, since 1958; Oseas, Pepper & Siegel, 1936-50; Pepper & Siegel, 1950-54; all NYC. Lt cdr, USNR. Pres, J Guild for the Blind, 1965-67; treas, Manhattanville Comty Cens; mem: bd overseers, JTSA; bd trustees, Temple Emanu-El; bd dirs, Mobilization for Youth and Mobilization for Youth Legal Services; chmn, comm on Taxation, NY Co Lawyers Assn, 1955-56, 1962-64; comm on admn law, comm gen income tax problems, Amer Bar Assn; comm on judiciary, chmn, comm on housing and urban devl, Assn of Bar City of NY, 1965-68, NY State Bar Assn; club, Sunningdale Country. Author: monography on income tax deductions, 1943; contbr, legal periodicals. Home: 176 E 77 St, New York, NY. Office: 55 Liberty St, New York, NY.

PEREK, Melech, Isr, veterinary educ; b. Kovno, Lith, Mar 20, 1908; s. Faiwel and Raisel (Feinberg) Perek, in Isr since 1936; att Vetr Coll, Vienna, 1927-29; DVM, U Bern, Switz, 1932; m. Shoshana Gavrielov, 1938; c: Tsafrira, Atalija, Daniel. Head, dept animal hygiene, poultry sci, Heb U fac of agric, Rehovot, since 1953; research asst, dept Vetr path and bact, U Bern, 1932-36; vetr practitioner, Binyamina, Isr, 1936-37; research f, dept bact, Heb U, Jerusalem 1937-48. Served Haganah. Mem: World Poultry Sci Assn; Isr Vetr Med Assn; Microbiol Soc, Isr; fmr mem: Hechalutz Cen Comm; Hashomer, both Lith; club, Rotary, Rehovot, pres, 1961-62. Contbr to Avian Physiology, 1938-62; profsl jours. Hobby: photography. Home: 31 Ben Zion St, Rehovot, Isr. Office: Heb U Fac of Agric, Rehovot, Isr.

PEREL, Léon, Fr, surgeon; b. Strykow, Pol, Aug 31, 1910; s. Henoch and Freda (Zylber); lauréate. Acad of Med, Paris, 1939; qualification, surg, 1948; m. Germaine Simon; c: Jean-Francois. Pvt practice; surg, Rothschild Hosp, Paris, 1945-48. Fr Résistance, 1939-44. Found, mem: Société française de chirurgie esthétique; AMIF; mem: Soc Médico-chirurgicale, des hôpitaux libres de Fr; Association française de chirurgie; Société de médecine, Paris; Société nationale de gynécologie, d'obstétrique, France; Pan Pacific Surg Assn; Société française d'histoire de la médécine; Association française, l'avancement de la science; Société médecine hébraïque; Société internationale d'histoire de la médecine; Union Mondiale des écrivains médecins. Contbr to sci, profsl and lit jours. Office: 18 rue d'Aguesseau, Paris 8, Fr.

PERELMAN, Chaim, Belgium, educator; b. Warsaw, Pol, May 20, 1912; s. Abraham and Lea (Garbownik); Docteur en droit, U Libre, Bruxelles, 1934; DPhil, 1938; hon degs, Us: Florence; Jerusalem; m. Félicie Liwer, Jan 13, 1935; c: Noémi Mattis. Fmr prof, logic and metaphysics, U Libre Bruxelles, dean fac phil and letters. Secy gen, Fédération Internationale Sociétés Philosophie; vice-pres. Belgium Friends of Heb U; mem: bd govs, Heb U; Intl Inst Phil; Intl Inst of Political Phil; fmr: pres: Menorah; Centre des Jeunes, Soc Belge de Philosophie; Soc Belge de Logique et Phil des Sciences; Magbit. Author: De L'Arbitraire dans la Connaissance; De la Justice; Rhétorique et Philosophie; Cours de Logique; Traité de l'Argumentation; The Idea of Justice and the Problem of Argument, A Historical Introduction to Philosophical Thinking; Justice, The New Rhetoric. Recipient: Officier de l'Ordre de Léopold; Officier de l'Ordre du Mérite, It; Cdr of Order of Crown. Home: 32 rue de la Pêcherie, Brussels, Belgium.

PERELMAN, Marcos, Peru, banker; b. Noua Sulita, Bessarabia, Rum, Nov 28, 1909; s. Benjamin and Brana (Coifman); in Peru since 1928; DHC, U San Marcos, Lima, 1966; m.Golda Seltzer, July 30, 1939; c: Benjamin. Chmn of bd, gen mgr, Banco del Progreso, since 1961; pres: Banco de la industria de la Construccion, since 1965; Inversiones y Finanzas Peru, SA, since 1956; Compañia de Seguros, La Universal, SA, since 1954; dir: CLAL, Isr; Isr Devl & Mortgage Bank, Tel Aviv, since 1959; pres: Peru Import Export, SA, 1930-45; Hilanderia y Tejeduria. SA, 1947-55. Prin contribs: auditorium, Leon Pinelo HS, Lima; main lectr hall, Inst Contemporary Jewry, Heb U, Jerusalem. F, Intl Bankers Assn; pres, State of Isr Bonds Comm, 1954; fmr pres, Magbit; vice-pres, Latin Amer bd govs, Weizmann Inst of Sci, pres Peruvian comm; co-pres, Sharon Cultural Assn; mem, Colegio de Economistas; repr, Peru, United HIAS Services. Home: Javier Prado 640, San Isidro, Lima, Peru. Office: 491 Ave Abancay, Lima, Peru.

PERELMUTER, Hayim Goren, US, rabbi; b. Montreal, Can, June 2, 1914; s. Benjamin and Tillie (Goren); in US since 1939; BA, McGill U, Montreal, 1935; ordained rabbi; MHL, HUC JIR, NY, 1939, DD, 1960; att Harvard U, 1939-41; m. Nancy Goodman, July 20, 1940; c: Mayer, Michael. Rabbi, Temple Isaiah Isr, Chgo, since 1957; lectr, rabb, Catholic Theol Union, Chgo, since 1969; rabbi: Temple Beth Isr, Waltham, Mass, 1939-41; Beth Zion Temple, Johnston, Pa, 1941-57. Prin contribs: shaping Reform J youth movement; pioneer in Youth Canteen Movement. Mem bd: social action commn, UAHC; mem exec, Hyde Park Council Churches and Syns, pres, 1962-64; mem: CCAR; B'nai B'rith; ZOA; pres, Chgo Assn Reform Rabbis, 1963-65; vice pres, Chgo chap, AJCong, 1957-62; life mem, Natl Fed Temple Youth. Trans: Jewish History in 1,000 Questions and Answers, Zachev, from Yiddish, 1937; The Immortal People, EB Cohen, from Ger, 1939. Home: 5000 E End Ave, Chicago, Ill. Study: 1100 Hyde Park Blvd, Chicago, Ill.

PERES, Shimon, Isr, government official; b. Pol, 1923; s. Itchak and Sara Persky; in Isr since 1934; att Harvard U, Min of Transportation and Communications; MK, since 1959; dep secy gen, Isr Lab Party, since 1968; fmr: mem, Kvutzat Alumot; secy, haNoar haOved; dir gen, Min of Defense, 1953-59, dep Min of Defense, 1959-65; mem, secretariat, Mapai Party, 1959-65; found, secy gen, Rafi Party, 1965-67. Author, The Next Step. Recipient, Legion of Hon, Fr Govt, 1957. Home: 186 Arlosoroff St, Tel Aviv, Isr. Office: Isr Labor Party, 110 Hayarkon St, Tel Aviv, Isr.

PERETZ, Aharon, Isr, physician; b. Butrimunis, Lith, Jan 1, 1910; s. Bezalel and Raschel (Romanov) Percikovitz; in Isr since 1945; MD, U Med Sch, Kovno, Lith; m. Raja Berger; c: Bezalel. Asso prof obstet and gyn, Heb U, Jerusalem; head, dept obstet and gyn, Rambam Hosp, Haifa, since 1949; head dept, Munic Hosp, Kovno, 1939-41; obstet, gyn, Kovno Ghetto, 1941-44. Dachau Concentration Camp, 1944-45; maj, IDF, MC, 1948-49. Witness in Eichmann trial; mem: IFA; Isr Soc of Obstet and Gyn. Author: baMachanot Lo Bachu; pamphlets on med subjects; contbr to med jours in Isr and US. Home: 14 Ofakim Lane, Haifa, Isr. Office: 20 Jerusalem St, Haifa, Isr.

PERETZ, Aharon M, Isr; business exec; b. Istanbul, Turkey, 1896; s. Mordachi and Ventura; in Isr since 1935; m. Victoria Agiman; real estate exec; repr fgn firms; chmn exec council, Israel Chain Co. Chmn, Council Turkish Immigrants, Isr; found, Kadima Cen; mem: Banim leGvulam, Mitbah Zol leNitzrachim; rep., Lina; mem: TB Assn; repr, Turkish J in Isr, World Sephardic Congs: Paris, Jerusalem, pres: Yehuda Levi Lodge, B'nai B'rith, Tel Aviv, mem, intl B'nai B'rith; admn chmn, Tora veHoraa, Tel Aviv; exec mem, Kadisha, sr citizen home, Recanati; fmr mem: Maccabi, Istanbul, Banim Hofshim; active J Comty, Istanbul. Home: 35 Mazeh St, Tel Aviv, Isr.

PERETZ, Don, US, educator; b. Baltimore, Md, Oct 31, 1922; s. Haym and Josephine (Lasser); BA, U Minn, 1945; MA, Columbia U, 1952, PhD, 1955; m. Janet Benson, 1962. Prof political sci and dir SW Asia-N Afr Prog, SUNY, Binghamton, NY, since 1967; asso dir, Off Fgn Area Studies, NY State Educ Dept, 1962-67; corresp, NBC, 1947-48; repr Amer Friends Service Comm, 1949; ME media evaluator, Dept of State, VOA, 1952; ME lectr, Hofstra Coll, 1954; research dir, Regional Research Analysts, 1954-56; ME cons, AJComm, 1956-58; specialist and lectr on ME: Hunter Coll, 1960; Vassar, Coll, 1959-61; LIU, 1959-62; Williams Coll, 1966; Ford Found f, 1952-54; Rockefeller Found grantee, 1962. US Army, 1942-46. F: ME Inst; ME Studies Assn; Afr Studies Assn; Inst of Strategic Studies, London; natl chmn, Amer Friends of Ihud 1952-54; mem: natl council, J Peace F; ME Inst; Amer Friends Service Comm, ME subcomm; Intl Affairs exec comm; Council on Fgn Relations; ME Adv Panel, US Dept of State, 1967-69. Author: Israel and the Palestine Arabs, 1958; The Middle East Today, 1963; The Middle East, Selected Reading, 1968; contbr to: American Jewish Year Book; Colliers Yearbook; World Scope Ency Yearbook; articles dealing with ME policy to newspapers and periodicals, US, Isr. Home: 209 Pennsylvania Ave, Binghamton, NY. Office: SUNY, Binghamton, NY.

PERETZ, ARAD, Esther, Isr, artist; b. Burgas, Bulgaria, June 17, 1921; d. Peretz and Viza (Farchy); in Isr since 1924; studied with Ahron Avini, Histadrut Art Studio, Tel Aviv, 1937-45; m. Grisha Arad, June 11, 1923; c: Atar, Ron. Exhbs: Isr Artists Assn; one man show, Helena Rubinstein Pavilion, Tel Aviv Mus. Recipient, Dizengoff Prize, Tel Aviv Munic, 1955. Home and studio: 20a Offir St, Tel Aviv, Isr.

PERFIT, Irving, US, business exec; b. Bklyn, NY, Dec 26, 1911; s. Louis and Minnie (Hoch); m. Jean Rosenberg, May 29, 1937; c: Roberta, Stephen, Helen. Vice pres, dir, Garden State Container Corp. Vice pres: Temple Emanu El of Boro Park,

since 1959; Machzike Talmud Torah since 1959; dir, YM & YWHA, Boro Park; vice chmn, Bklyn div, FJP of NY; bd trustees: Maimonides Hosp, 1961-65; Infants Home of Bklyn; mem: Masons; B'nai B'rith; KP. Home: 1517 54th St, Brooklyn, NY. Office: 27-35 Hudson Blvd, Bayonne, NJ.

PERI, Elazar, Isr, journalist; b. Galicia, Aus Hung, Feb 2, 1902; s. Shmuel and Leah Wilder; in Isr since 1926; att U Lvov, 1922-23; Heb Tchrs Seminary, Lvov, 1922; m; c: Yael; m. 2nd, Sylvia Binder, 1966. Mem: ed bd, Al Hamishmar, since 1943; Kibbutz Merhavia, since 1926; journalist: Poland, 1921-26, 1930; Isr since 1926; ed in chief, Hashomer Hatzair, weekly political mag, 1930-43; mem secretariat and exec comm, Hakibbutz Haartzi, 1928-69; mem Histadrut Council, delg Histadrut conventions; mem, Asefat haNivharim, under the Mandate; MK, 1949-55. Political comm, Mapam, since 1948; delg, ZCs. Author: political pamphlets. Home: Kibbutz Merhavia, Isr. Office: Al Hamishmar, Tel Aviv, Isr.

PERI, Eliezer, Isr, public official; b. Leningrad, Russ, Aug 19, 1894; in Isr since 1921; att: Tech Coll, Leningrad, 1917; Inst for Cooperatives, Moscow, 1918; m. Masha Nathanson; two c. Dir gen, Amidar, natl housing corp for immigrants; chmn bd, Davar, Heb daily; mem, City Council Tel Aviv, dep mayor, 1944-48; dir gen, Isr Min of Defense, 1948-50; fmr: mem, cen comm and admn dir, Workers' Sick Benefit Fund; mem, Vaad Leumi. Chmn, Amer-Isr Cultural Found; mem: bd govs, Heb U, bd dirs, Friends of Habimah Theater; chmn, Soldiers' Wfr Comm, Tel Aviv; delg WZCs. Home: 79 Gordon St, Tel Aviv, Isr. Office: Am Oved Publishers, 22 Mazah St, Tel Aviv, Isr.

PERI, Yaacov, Isr, military off, communal leader; b. Bulgaria, 1915; s. Shlomo and Sophia (Levy) Proulov; in Isr since 1925; att Isr Mil Acad; widower; c: Shlomo, Yoseph, Jonathan. Appt pres, Supr Mil Court of Appeal, IDF, 1963; chmn, Assn for Wfr of Soldiers in Isr, since 1969; fmr: mem perm establishment, Haganah, dist cdr, S Galilee; Givati Brig; appt cdr, 1949; chief gen staff oprs dept 1950; S command chief staff, 1953; gen off command, S command; chief instructional command, 1955-59; Jerusalem dist cdr; IDF Mil Attache: It, Yugo, Switz, 1961; maj general, 1964. Office: 8 Haarba St, Tel Aviv, Isr.

PERILMUTER, William Adelbert, US, attorney; b. Winnipeg, Can, Apr 2, 1902; s. Louis and Sarah (Krushen); in US since 1924; BSc, U Manitoba, Winnipeg, 1924; LLB, LA Coll of Law, 1929; hon DJS, Olympic U, LA, 1933; m. Pearl Fox, Sep 11, 1932; c: Sandra Price. Pvt practice since 1930. Pres: J Home for Wayfarers LA, since 1941; Isr Soc, Hollywood, 1957-58; trustee, Cong Mogen David, past secy; key man, UJWF; vice-pres, ZOA, W region, 1957-58; past chmn, Olympic Div; mem: B'nai B'rith, Beverly Hills, Cal; club, Men's, Temple Isr, Hollywood. Hobbies: golf, working in UJWF movements. Home: 9955 Durant Dr, Beverly Hills, Cal. Office: 6399 Wilshire Blvd, Los Angeles, Cal.

PERITZ, Edith, US, surgeon; b. Breslau, Ger, May 23, 1897; d. Max and Martha (Anspach); in US since 1936; MD, Breslau U, 1921; m. Karl von Lojewski, Jan 6, 1937 (decd). Cons surg, NY Infirmary, since 1956. Mem: AMA; AMA Med Women's Assn; Med Women's Assn of NY State; Med Women's Assn of NYC; Rudolf Virchow Soc; clubs: Wash Sq; Bus and Profsl Women; Soroptimist, found, first Ger br, 1929, mem NY br. Home and office: 152 W 58 St, New York, NY.

PERL, Arnold, US, playwright, producer; b. NYC, Apr 14, 1914; s. Louis and Ida (Reisman) Freeman; att: Cornell U; CCNY; NYU Law Sch; m. 2nd, Nancy Reals, 1956; c: Rachel, Adam, Joshua, Rebecca, Sarah. Writer and producer, since 1941; TV productions: East Side/West Side; Deadline; Naked City; The Eleventh Hour; The Nurses; Espionage; NYPD; theatrical productions: World of Sholem Aleichem, 1953; Sandhog, 1955; I Knock at the Door, 1957; Tevya, 1958; The Quare Fellow, 1959; screenplays: Friday the Rabbi Slept Late; Cotton comes to Harlem; Malcolm X; plays included in: Best One-Act Plays, 1947; Best TV Plays, 1951, 1952; anthologized in Radio's Best Plays, 1951. Mem: council, Authors League of Amer; Radio Writers Guild. Recipient: Peabody Award; Variety Award; Radio Daily Award. Home: 305 E 10 St, New York, NY.

PERL, Gideon, Isr, educator; b. Jerusalem, Dec 30, 1940; s. Alexander and Jael (Speyer); tchrs dipl, Tchrs Sem, Pehovot, 1960; dipl, Yeshiva, Jerusalem, 1964; ordained rabbi, High

Decalogue Soc of Lawyers, Chgo; cen comm: Independent Lib Party; Isr UN Assn, fmr chmn Tel Aviv; pension comm, Isr Bar Assn; public commn, Demographic Cen, PM's off: fmr: judge: Antiprofiteering Tribunal; J Court of Peace; mem, Petrograd comm, Hehaver Students Org; delg: World Advocates Conf; UNESCO Hum Rights Cong; participant, Zionist activities. Author: Israel Commercial Law, 1950, Income Tax; Cooperative Law; Israel and Human Rights; Chess Magnum, 1957; inventor, games: Triangles; chess magnum; contbr to Isr press. Hobbies: J and Isr art, chess. Home: 3 Yosef Eliahu St, Tel Aviv, Isr. Office: 109 Allenby St, Tel Aviv, Isr.

PEYSER, Eli, Isr, physician; b. Göttingen, Ger, Feb 21, 1919; s. Fritz and Alice (Nothmann); in Isr since 1932; MD, U Basel, Switz, 1943; m. Vera Kahn, Aug 21, 1945; c: Yael, Amos. Head, dept neurosurg, Rambam Govt Hosp, Haifa, since 1957; clinical asso prof, Med Sch, Jerusalem, since 1968. Lt, MC, 1948-50. Mem: IMA; Isr Surg Soc; Intl Coll Surgs. Contbr of papers to med jours. Spec interest: crafts. Home: 104 Hatishbi, Haifa, Isr. Office: Rambam Hosp, Haifa, Isr.

PEYSER, Jefferson Edwin, US, attorney; b. San Francisco, Cal, Nov 14, 1899; s. David and Gussie; BA, U of Cal, Berkeley, 1920, DJur, 1923. Atty since 1923; gen counsel: Wine Inst; Mortgage Brokers Inst, since 1934; sup, City, Co, SF, 1929-33; mem, Cal State Leg, 1935-39. Served WW I. Vice-pres: Heb Free Loan Assn, SF; J Educ Soc; Sinai Memorial Chapel; dir: Civic League of Improvement Clubs; Temple Emanuel; vice-pres, mem bd govs, Supr Lodge, past: grand pres, grand treas, Dist 4, pres, SF Lodge 21, all B'nai B'rith; mem exec comm, past: vice-chmn, natl commn, chmn, regional adv bd, all ADL; mem: Zeta Beta Tau; Delta Sigma Rho; SF Sym Found; Masons, past master, lodge 470; past wisemaster, Rose Croix, Scottish Rite; SF Post 1, Amer Legion; Castro Parlor 232, Native Sons of Golden West; charter revision commn, City and Co of SF; bd dirs, 7th Step Found; Wine and Food Soc of SF; Lawyer Friends of Wine; Council for Civic Unity; Commonwealth; Amer, Cal, SF Bar Assns; World Affairs Council; fmr pres, Asso J Orgs; chmn, J Comty Relations Council; clubs: Concordia; Lake Merced Golf and Country; Press and Union League; pres: Cal Exch, 1952-53; Golden State Exch; and fmr mem bd dirs, Kiwanis, Pacific-SF; dir, JWF; fmr dir: Temple Emanuel men's club; J Home for Aged; secy, J Comty Bulletin. Home: 1200 California St, San Francisco, Cal. Office: 220 Bush St, San Francisco, Cal.

PFAU, Alphonse, Isr, physician; b. Bucharest, Rum, Apr 17, 1925; s. Israel and Betty (Rintzler); in Isr since 1949; MD, Med Sch, State U, Bucharest, 1949; m. Lea Shalitin, Nov 22, 1956; c: Eytan, Alon, Yuval. Perm chief phys, Dep of Urol, Hadassah U Hosp, Jerusalem, since 1963; sr lectr, surg/urol, Heb U-Hadassah Med Sch, Jerusalem, since 1963. F, Amer Coll of Surgs; mem: Isr Surg Soc; Isr Urol Assn. Contbr to: Investigative Urol, US, 1963; Isr Jour of Med Scis, 1968. Home: 6 Alkalay St, Jerusalem, Isr. Office: Dept of Urol, Hadassah U Hosp, Jerusalem, Isr.

PFEFFER, Leo, US, attorney; b. Hung, Dec 25, 1910; s. Alter and Honi (Yaeger); in US since 1912; BSS, CCNY, 1930; JD, NYU, 1933; m. Freda Plotkin, Sep 18, 1937; c: Alan, Susan. Spec counsel, AJCong, since 1964, dir, commn on law, social action, gen counsel, 1957-64, asst dir, 1947-57, mem legal staff, since 1945; chmn, dept political sci, prof, constitutional law, LIU Bklyn Cen, since 1964; pvt instr, law, 1933-37; ed, Appeal News and Statute Digest, 1937-44; lectr: New Sch for Social Research, 1952-58; Mt Holyoke Coll, 1958-60; David W Petegosky prof of constitutional law, Yeshiva U, 1962-63. Pres, NYU Law Rev Alumni Assn, 1964-66, vice-pres, 1959-64; mem: Natl Assn of Intergroup Relations Offs; Soc for the Sci Study of Rel; Authors' League. Author: Church, State and Freedom, 1953; The Liberties of an American, 1956; Creeds in Competition, 1958; The Honorable Court, 1965; co-author: Religion in the State University, 1950; Cultural Pluralism and the American Idea, 1957; Religion in America, 1958; Church and State in the United States, 1964; contbr to: Colliers Ency, 1963; New Catholic Ency, 1967; mem ed bd: Jour of Church and State, since 1957; Judaism, since 1964. Recipient: awards: Rel Freedom, Americans United for Separation of Church and State, 1955; Bill of Rights, Minn JCC, 1962; Thomas Jefferson Rel Freedom, Unitarian Universalist Church of NY, 1967; Bklyn Civil Liberties, 1968; Leo Pfeffer papers established at Syracuse U, 1967. Spec interest: Bible research and Dead Sea Scrolls. Home: 191 Willoughby St, Brooklyn, NY. Office: 15 E 84 St, New York, NY.

PFEFFERMANN, Reuven, Isr, surgeon; b. Timisuara, Rum, Sep 7, 1936; s. Jona and Jehudit (Edlitz); in Isr since 1946; MD, Heb U Med Sch, Jerusalem, 1961. Surg, Hadassah Med Cen, Jerusalem, since 1964. Flight surg, IAF, 1962-64. Home: 8 Shmuel Hanagid St, Jerusalem, Isr.

PFLAUM, Hans-Georg, Fr, historian; b. Berlin, Ger, June 3, 1902; s. Fritz and Betty (Sello); in Fr since 1933; D Ivris, U Breslau, 1925; att U Berlin, 1928-33; Docteur es lettres, Sorbonne, Paris, 1936; m. Marie Heinisch, Nov 12, 1938; c: Marie Steckel. Sci dir, Natl Cen for Sci Research, since 1961. Author: Les Procurateurs Equestres sous le Haut-Empire Romain, 1950; Les Carrières Procuratoriennes Equestres sous le Haut-Empire Romain, 1962. Recipient: Korrespondierendes Mitglied, Göttingen Acad, 1964; corresp f, Brit Acad, 1967. Hobby: numismatics. Home: 8 rue Poullstier, Paris, Fr.

PHILIPPSON, Paul, Belgium, banker, business exec; b. Brussels, Belgium, Mar 27, 1910; s. Maurice and Marguerite (Wiener); grad econ, Institut de Sociologie Solvay, Université Libre de Bruxelles, 1930; c: Alain, Diane, Gérard. Bus adv, Banque Lambert; company dir. Res off Belgian Army, 1939-45. Chmn: Consistoire Central Israélite de Belgique, since 1962; Service social Juif, since 1945; Caisse de Prêts et de Crédits, both since 1945; mem: bd, JCA, London, since 1947; club, Landsdown, London. Recipient: Croix de Guerre, 1940; avec Lion de Bronze-Medaille Commémorative, 1940-44; MBE; Médaille Franco-Allemagne, 1944; Médaille Campagne, 1930-45; Médaille Defense de la Grande Bretagne; Chevalier de l'Ordre de Léopold; Officier de la Couronne. Home: 17 ave General Baron Empain, Woluwé St, Pierre, Belgium. Office: 24 ave Marnix, Brussels, Belgium.

PHILIPS, Robert Jay, US, attorney; b. NYC, Aug 20, 1917; s. Jacob and Elizabeth (Frank); AB, Harvard, 1939; LLB, Columbia, 1944; div; c: Lawrence, Risë. Trial lawyer, fmr associated with Hon Stanley H Field, Chief Judge, NY Court of Appeals. Mem: Bar Assn of NYC; Bd of Arbitrators, Amer Arbitration Assn; club, Harvard, NYC. Home: 715 Park Ave, New York, NY. Office: 565 Fifth Ave, New York, NY.

PHILIPSON, Gertrude, Swed, communal leader; b. Berlin, Ger, Oct 4, 1902; d. Simon and Selma (Karo) Mühlenthal; in Swed since 1953; att Us: Heidelberg, Berlin, Würzburg, Lausanne; m. Ivar Philipson; c: Ulrich Caro, Judith Caro. With Youth Aliyah since 1936; chmn, Swed Comm for Children and Youth Aliyah, since 1967; mem bd: J Women's Council, Stockholm, since 1956, past chmn, social comm; Judiska Pensionärshemmet; Judiska Sjukhemmet; secy, Svensk-Israeliska Fonden; Scandinavian repr, Weizmann Inst, Rehovot; treas, Israelhjälpen. Home: 21 Floragatan, Stockholm, Swed.

PHILIPSON, J Ivar, Swed, attorney; b. Stockholm, Swed, Dec 12, 1901; s. Walter and Harriet (Fränckel); LLB, U Stockholm, 1926; m. Gertrude Mühlenthal, July 10, 1953. Pvt practice since 1928. Pres: Swedish Ort; J Comty exec comm for assistance to J arrived in Swed after 1945, since 1945; mem, bd of deps, J Cong, Stockholm, since 1931; bd mem: Stockholm Concert Hall; Drottningholms Theater. Author: Das Devisenrecht Schwedens. Home: Floragatan 21, Stockholm Ö, Swed. Office: Västra Trädgårdsgatan 15, Stockholm C, Swed.

PHILIPSON, Max, US, business exec; b. Utica, NY, June 11, 1900; s. Abraham and Leba (Bauer); BS, U of Pa, 1922; m. Ruth Cain, Aug 22, 1943; c: Leba Price, Louis Dubin. Pres: Max Philipson and Co, since 1959; First Utica Corp, since 1957; dir, Mohawk Data Scis Corp, since 1964; Student Army Training Corps, 1918. Pres, J Social Service, Utica, 1958; chmn: Upper Div Coll Comm, Utica, 1966-68; Comty Devl Prog, Oneida Co, 1957; mem: Masons; B'nai B'rith; Ziyara Temple, Utica; Mohawk Valley Consistory; clubs: Harmonie, NY; Higby Hills Country, Utica; U of Pa, Mohawk Valley, pres. Home: 10 Hills Dr, Utica, NY. Office: Mayro Bldg, Utica, NY.

PHILLIPS, Jay, US, business exec; b. Minsk, Russ, Mar 22, 1898; s. Edward and Rose; in US since 1900; m. Rose Toby Ebin, Aug 7, 1917; c: Morton, Helen Levin, Paula Bernstein. Chmn bd: Ed Phillips & Sons Co, Minneapolis, pres, since 1920; Century Metalcraft, LA, since 1944; dir: Viviane Woodard, Panorama City, Cal; Natl Presto Inds, Eau Claire, Wis; N Cen Airlines, Wausau, Wis; fist Natl Bank of Minn; mem,

NY Stock Exch. Found: pres, Mt Sinai Hosp, Minn; Albert Einstein Coll of Med, NY; pres, The Phillips Found; secy, trustee, U of Minn Found; treas, Minn Rahab Cen; trustee: Natl J Hosp, Denver; Natl Soc for Crippled Children and Adults; Gtr Minn Safety Council; The Minn Found; dir: Licensed Beverage Inds, Inc; Natl Asso of Alcoholic Beverage Importers; and found, past chmn bd, Wine and Spirits Wholesalers of Amer; Minn Soc for Crippled Children and Adults; Intl Soc for Rehab of Disabled, US comm; Minn Fed J Service; Gtr Minn C of C, past pres; Jr Achievement, Gtr Minn; Orch Asso of Minn; N Star Research and Devl Inst; radio Free Eur; Boy Scouts, Viking Council; Boys Club, Minn; Sky Ranch for Boys; Camp Courage Found; and hon chmn Natl Distillers Distributors Found; dir, ex-officio, Minn Aquatennial Asso; natl men's comm, Hadassah-Heb U Med Center; exec comm, Jt Defense Appeal Natl Council; Natl adv council, JWV, US; bd overseers, Friends of JTSA; f in perperuity, Minn Soc of Fine Arts; f: Mancalester Coll, St Paul, Minn; U Minn, and trustee, Brandeis U; hon alumni, Heb U of Jerusalem; clubs: Standard, Minn, dir; Oak Ridge Country, dir; Commercial Club, Chaska, found, dir; Hillcrest Country, LA; Westview Country, Miami; Variety, NW; Minneapolis. Recipient: awards: man of year, JWV, 1946; state of Isr Org, 1952; Minn Soc Crippled Children, Adults, 1957, Natl Soc, 1961; Plaque, Minn Fed J Service, 1958; Minn Urban League, 1960; Mt Sinai Hosp, 1961; Wine & Spirits Wholesalers, 1962; City of Hope, 1962; Gtr Minn C of C, 1962; John F Kennedy Peace, 1964; Edgar ind man of year 1965. Home: 4833 E Lake Harriet Blvd, Minneapolis, Minn. Office: 2345 Kennedy St, NE Minneapolis, Minn.

PHILLIPS, Justin Percival, Isr, physician; b. London, Eng, July 26, 1940; s. Laurence and Sophie (Sourasky); in Isr since 1966; MB, BS, Middlesex Hosp, Med Sch, London U, 1964; m. Suzanne Boukadanna, May 15, 1968; c: Aryeh. Res phys, Arad, since 1969; visiting phys, Ein Gedi, since 1968; med sup Asthmatic Children's Sanatorium, Arad, since 1968; phys, Prince of Wales Hosp, London, 1965; surg, New End Hosp, London, 1965-66; phys, Hadassah Hosp, Jerusalem, 1966-67. Treas, J Youth Study Groups; chmn: London J Students Assn; U's Zionist Council; J Youth Council of Gt Brit; Inter-U J Fed; found chmn, U of London Isr Soc; leader, British delg, World J Youth Cong; co-found, Intl Grad Cen for Heb and J Studies, World Union of J Students, Arad; vice-chmn, Histadrut Olei Britania; mem bd deps, Brit Jews; delg: ZC; WZO Actions Comm; mem: IMA; Brit Med Assn. Contbr to profsl jours. Hobby, hist. Home: 24 Rehov Yehuda, Arad, Isr. Office: Kupat Holim, Arad, Isr.

PHILLIPS, Kenneth F, US, attorney; b. NYC, Aug 5, 1929; s. Daniel and Florence (Klotz); att: NYU, 1947-48; Fordham U, 1950-51; BA, Colgate U, NY, 1950; LLB, Harvard U, 1965; m. Paula Levin, Sep 2, 1951; c: Anthony, Thomas. Dir, Natl Housing Law Project, since 1968; spec asst to admn, 1962-64, asst gen counsel, Agcy for Intl Devl, 1964-65, both State Dept; partner, law firm, Feldman, Waldman & Klin, 1965-69. Lt, USAF, 1951-52. Trustee, World Affairs Council, N Cal; vice-pres, Soc for Intl Devl, Bay area, Recipient: Meritorious Services, Citation, AID, 1967. Home: 3001 Jackson St, San Francisco, Cal. Office: Earl Warren Legal Inst, U of Cal, Berkeley, Cal.

PHILLIPS, Leonard W, US, business exec; b. Cleveland, O, Sep 17, 1917; s. Joseph and Stella (Borgos); BA, U Denver, 1936; BAL, Westminster U Law Sch, 1939; m. Betty Sklar, Aug 20, 1942; c: Sandra, Fred. Pres: Bowlero, since 1956; Cen Stations Alarms, since 1960; vice-pres: Sklar & Phillips, Inc, since 1950; La Iron & Supply Co, since 1942; dir, Midwest Video Corp, since 1962. Maj, USAAF, 1941-46. Pres, Assn of La Cs of C, since 1961, Shreveport C of C, 1960; vice-pres, Independent Petroleum Assn of Amer, since 1959; mem, bd trustees, B'nai Zion, since 1961. Home: 420 Spring Lake Dr, Shreveport, La. Office: 2928 Mansfield Rd, Shreveport, La.

PHILLIPS, Nathan, Can, barrister-at-law; b. Brockville, Ont, Nov 7, 1892; s. Jacob and Mary (Rosenbloom); Barrister at Law, Osgoode Hall, Toronto, 1913; m. Esther Lyons, Mar 7, 1917; c: Howard, Madeline Brodey. QC, appd, 1929; counsel, law firm, Phillips and Phillips; mayor of Toronto, 1955-62; alderman, 1924-51, pres of Council, 1948; counsel for plaintiff in Applebaum vs Gilchrist case, 1946, won legal counsel for plaintiff in Applebaum vs Gilchrist case, 1946, won legal equality for women. Pres: Co of York Law Assn, 1957; and life mem, Law Soc Upper Canada; Ontario Mayors and Reeves Assn, 1959-60; Toronto Lodge, B'nai B'rith, 1922; hon

pres, Brotherhood, Holy Blossom Temple; found, Toronto Heb Free Loan Assn; Dir, Can Council of Chr and J; hon life mem: Intl Assn of Fire Chiefs; Navy, Army and Air Force Vets of Can; Ont Command, Royal Can Legion; hon Indian Chief, Six Nations, Mohawk Tribe; past dist dep grand master; Masons, Dist A, Toronto; mem, Can Bar Assn; clubs: hon mem: Toronto Press Club; Harmonie; Island Yacht; mem: Kiwanis; Lions; Candian; Empire; Metro Toronto Bd of Trade; Can-Austr Soc (pres); Author: Mayor of All the People, 1967. Recipient: hum relations award, Can Council of Chr and J, 1959; Fiorello LaGuardia award; Eagles, 1960, civic sq, Toronto, named Nathan Phillips Sq; Can Centennial Medal, 1967, City of Toronto award of Merit; Gold Medal of Madrid; Cdr, Order of Isabel la Catolica. Hobby: photography. Home: 4 Deer Park Crescent, Toronto, Ont, Can. Office: 111 Richmond St, W, Toronto, Ont, Can.

PIANKA, Max, Eng, organic chemist; b. Makow-Mazowiecki, Pol, Jan 5, 1916; s. Samuel and Chaja (Nejman); in Eng since 1938; BSc, hons, U London, 1948, MSc, 1950, PhD, 1956; DSc, 1971; f, Royal Inst Chem, 1954; m. Edith Kleiner, June 26, 1947; c: Helen, Jacob. Head, chem synthesis and organic research, Murphy Chem Co Ltd, since 1950; sr research chem, 1942-45, sect head, 1945-50, both Dufay. Prin contribs: new ultra-violet absorbers, new pesticides and chem processes. Warden, St Albans United Syn, past chmn, J Educ comm; mem: Chem Soc; Royal Inst Chem; Amer Chem Soc; Soc Chem Ind. Contbr to profsl jours. Spec interests: langs, music. Home: 67 Sandpit Lane, St Albans, Herts,Eng. Office: Wheathampstead, St Albans, Herts, Eng.

PICK, Josef, Isr, accountant; b. Ratibor, Ger Oct 4, 1914; s. Otto and Herta (Schwarz); in Isr since 1938; att, Breslau U; DRerPol, Munich U; FACCA, London; m. Elisabeth Kohan, Dec 6, 1942; c: Uri, Mirjam, Gideon. Sr partner, Pick, Cohn & Co, Tel Aviv, since 1951; official, Palaestina Treuhand Stelle der Juden In Dutschland, Zionist money transfer org, 1937-38; asst to bank mgr, Palestine Corp, 1943-49; export asst, fgn exch control, Isr Treas, 1949-51; treas, Isr br, mem sci comm, Intl Fiscal Assn; mem, Assn of Public Acctnts, Tel Aviv. Contbr to profsl jours. Home: 36 Yosef Zvi St, Ramat Gan, Isr. Office: 18 Rothschild Blvd, Tel Aviv, Isr.

PICK, Joseph Charles, US, business exec; b. Mlada Boleslav, Czech, Dec 21, 1891; s. Karl and Pauline (Kaufmann); in US since 1941; att: Export Acad, Vienna, 1918-19; Columbia U, 1944-45; grad, sch public admn, Harvard U, 1943; m. Ida Stern, June 15, 1922; c: Elizabeth Schnur, George. Licensed ins broker, marine and aviation adjuster, Hagedorn & Co, since 1941; dept head, Intercontinental Ltd, Prague, 1922-26; dep mgr, Moldavia-Generali Ins Co, Prague, 1927-39; fgn marine ins adv, Halifax Ins Co-Toronto, Can, 1939-40; chief Can Trade Commn in Gt Brit, organized monetary clearing between Czech and Can, 1939; Survey of Eur Experts, Harvard U, 1942; cons,War Depts, 1943. Lt, Czech Army, 1910-11, 1914-18. Vice-pres, Soc for the Hist of Czech J, NY; trustee, B'nai B'rith, Joseph Popper lodge, NY; charter mem: Natl Defense Transp Assn, Wash, DC; perm delg, Intl Union of Marine Ins, 1928-39; tech adv, Intl Civil Aviation Conf, Chgo, 1944; mem: NY Acad Scis, 1954-64; Ins Inst, London, 1932-39; 1944-45; Czech Econ Council in US, 1942-45; Amer Med Mogen David for Isr, NY; Ins Brokers Assn of NY State; club, NY Minneralogical Author: The Way Through the Panama Canal, 1914; chapter, Jews of Czechoslovakia 1968; contbr of reports to L of N; confs newspapers; jours.; Recipient: Signum Laudis Triple with Swords; Karl Truppen Kreuz. Hobbies: aviation, geology. Home: 9 Stonewall Dr, Stamford, Conn. Office: 1 Liberty St, New York, NY.

PICK, Philip Leon, Eng, surveyor; b. Bath, Eng, Feb 10, 1910; s. Gershon and Bloomah (Karneber); att Green Park Coll, Bath; f: Fac of Architects and Surveyors; Valuers Instn; Asso, Ins Inst; m. Minna Cohen, June 24, 1939; c: Vivien. Prin, P L Pick & Co, since 1945. Pres, J Vegetarian Soc, Min of Food, Emergency Feeding Off for S Wales, 1940-42; rep for H M Govt in reforestation in S Wales. Ed: The J Vegetarian. Home: 20 Denewood Ave, Highgate, London, N6, Eng. Office: 35 Queen's Ave, London N 10, Eng.

PICK, Zigmund, Eng, engineer; b. Czech, June 29, 1906; s. Jacob and Leonora (Klein); in Eng since 1939; att U Prague, 1925-30; m. Basia Beer, Nov 6, 1942; c: Michael. Cons engr, since 1947; chief engr, Orlit Ltd, 1940-47. Prin contribs: designed bldgs: schs; Us; hosps; offs; old people's homes; ind

Helen Haim; Tchr, painting, 1955-57; works exhibited: Eur, Amer, Asia, S Afr, Austr; in Isr, 1955, 1962, 1963, 1965, 1966; perm exhib, Hilton Gal, Tel Aviv; Last exhib, London, Corner Gal, 1969. Concentration camp, 1942-45. Mem, Lodge Hashachar, 32, Masons. Home and studio: 77 Sokolov St, Herzliyah, Isr.

PERLOFF, Robert, US, educator, psychologist; b. Phila, Pa, Feb 3, 1921; s. Myer and Elizabeth (Sherman); BS, Temple U, 1948; MA, O State U, 1949; PhD, 1951; m. Evelyn Potechin, Sep 22, 1946; c: Richard, Linda, Judith. Dir, mgmt research cen, grad sch bus, prof, bus admn, psych, U Pittsburgh, since 1969; research psychol, chief stat research and consultation unit, personnel research sect, Army Dept, 1951-55; dir, research and devl, Sci Research Assos, 1955-59; asso prof, psych, Purdu U, 1959-64, prof, 1964-69. Tech sgt, US Army, 1942-45. Prin contrib: pioneer in devl of consumer psych. Dipl, Ind Psych; f: Amer Psych Assn; NY Acad Sci; AAAS; Soc for Psych Study of Socia Issues; chmn, Assn Consumer Research, 1970-71; pres, div consumer psych, Amer Psych Assn, mem educ and training bd; vice-pres PTA, Burtsfield sch, W Lafayette, Ind, 1968; mem: bd dirs: Gtr Pittsburgh ACLU, 1970; Book Cen, U Pittsburgh, 1969-72; Amer Marketing Assn; Thoreau Soc. Contbr: numerous articles to profsl publs. Recipient: Bronze Star. Spec interests: philately, free-lance writing, tennis, Home: 825 Morewood Ave, Pittsburgh, Pa. Office: Grad Sch of Bus, U Pittsburgh, Pittsburgh, Pa.

PERLOFF, William H, US, endocrinologist, educator; b. Phila, Pa, May 14, 1911; s. Harry and Esther (Brenner); BA, Swarthmore Coll, 1932; MD, U of Pa, 1936; f: Coll Phys and Surgs, Columbia U, 1938-39; Henrietta Hecksher, 1942; George Keim, 1947, both U of Pa; m. Dorothy Averett, Dec 22, 1933; c: William, Carol Cooper. Pvt parctice, since 1939; chief, div of endocrinology and hum reproduction, research labs, Albert Einstein Med Cen, since 1961; lectr, grad sch of med, U of Pa, since 1949, instr, 1939-50; lectr, affiliate mem, Phila Psychan Inst, since 1950; chief, endocrine dept, Phila Gen Hosp, 1947-58; prof med, dir dept of endocrinology, Temple U Sch of Med, 1950-59; endocrinologist, Phila Psychiatric Hosp, 1953-59. US Army, 1942-45. F: AMA; Assn for the Study of Internal Secretions; Acad of Psychosomatic Med; Amer Psychomatic Soc; Phila Coll of Phys; Amer Soc for Study of Sterility; Intl Fertility Assn; hon f, Sigma Xi; pres, endocrine sect, Pan Amer Med Assn; mem: AAAS; Phila Co Med Soc; Phila Endocrine Soc, pres, 1940-41; NY Acad of Scis; hon mem: Mexican and Arg Endocrine Socs. Contbr to med jours. Home: 5450 Wissahickon Ave, Philadelphia, Pa. Office: Albert Einstein Med Cen, York and Tabor Rds, Philadelphia, Pa.

PERLSON, Edward F, US, attorney, editor; b. Passaic, NJ, Jan 15, 1906; s. William and Dora (Dworkin); LLB, U Wis, 1933; m. Ada Parelskin, Oct 24, 1936; c: Boyd, Lewis. Pvt practice since 1933; mgn ed, chief ed writer, Wis J Chronicle, since 1949. Pres: Bay Shore Lodge, B'nai B'rith, 1948-49; Pi chap, Alpha Epsilon Pi, 1930-33; mem, bd dirs: JWF; Milw J Home for Aged; Milw J Comty Cen; Bur of J Educ; J Vocational Service; J Family and Children's Service; Amer Friends of Heb U; Wis Soc J Learning; chmn, bldg comm, Cumberland Sch, Whitefish Bay, Wis; club, Men's, Temple Emanuel-El B'ne Jeshurun. Hobbies: records, theater. Home: 1631 E Chateau Pl, Milwaukee, Wis. Office: 340 N Milwaukee St, Milwaukee, Wis.

PERLSTEIN, Harris, US, business exec; b. NYC, Aug 18, 1892; s. Abram and Betsy (Cohen); BS, Armour Inst Tech, 1914; hon LLD, Ill Inst Tech, 1965; m. Anne Agazim, Mar 11, 1929, (decd); c: Betsy Cowan, Lawrence; m. 2nd, Florence Weiss, 1960. Chmn, dir, Pabst Brewing Co, since 1956, chmn, pres, dir, 1954-56, pres, dir, 1932-54; partner, Singer-Perlstein Co, 1918-24; treas, dir, Premier Malt Products Co, 1924-27, pres, 1927-32. Dir: and mem exec comm, US Brewers Assn; Pabst Breweries Found; and pres, Perlstein Found; and past pres, J Fed, Metrop Chgo; chmn, bd trustees, Ill Inst Tech, IIT Research Inst; adv bd, Lumbermen's Mutual Casualty Co; adv hosp council, Dept of Public Health, Ill; past dir: JWF, Chgo; Ill Mfrs Assn; vice-pres, Comty Fund, Chgo; mem: Amer Chem Soc; Masons 32 deg; Shriners; Pi Delta Epsilon; Zeta Beta Tau; clubs: Lake Shore Country; Exec; Northmoor Country; Standard; Chem. Home: 1440 N Lake Shore Dr, Chicago, Ill. Office: 1 Wacker Dr, Chicago, Ill.

PERLSTEIN, Meyer A, US, physician, educator; b. Apr 6, 1902; s. Moses and Rose (Silverman); BS, U Chgo, 1924; MD, Rush Med Sch, 1928; m. Minnie Oboler, May 7, 1928; c: Lee Axelrad, Ruth Stein, Paul. Asso prof, peds, Northwestern U; prof, peds, Cook Co Hosp Postgrad Sch; chief, children's neur clinic, Cook Co Hosp; dir, cerebral palsy project, Michael Reese Hosp; chmn, med adv bd, Ill Children's Hosp Sch, Chgo; cerebral palsy cons: Natl Soc for Crippled Children and Adults, Inc; Mich Soc for Crippled Children and Adults; Ind Soc for Crippled Children; Crippled Children's Sch, Jamestown, ND,; div of services for crippled children, Springfield; Children's Bur, Wash, DC. Pres, Amer Acad for Cerebral Palsy, 1954; chmn, Maurice Lamm Blatt Memorial Fund, Cook Co Hosp; bd govs, Ill Assn for the Crippled; med adv bd: Pemberton House, Inc, NYC; Julian D Levinson Research Found; Ill Epilepsy League; Cerebral Palsy Research Soc, Chgo: div of services for crippled children, U of Ill; Chgo Club for Crippled Children; Spastic Children's Cen; World Commn on Cerebral Palsy; Acad for Oral Rehab of Cerebral Palsy; mem: AMA; Ill Med Soc; Chgo Med Soc; Chgo Ped Soc; Chgo Diabetes Assn; Inst of Med, Chgo; Amer Neur Assn; Amer phys f comm; IMA; Amer Acad Ped; Intl Council for Exceptional Children; Amer League Against Epilepsy; AAAS; Ill Epilepsy League; Assn for Mental Deficiency; Phi Beta Delta; B'nai B'rith; Natl Geog Soc. Contbr of numerous articles and monographs to profsl jours; reviewed books in med jours, 1949-53; produced four movies on med subjects. Home and office: 4743 N Drake Ave, Chicago, Ill.

PERLSTEIN, Minnie O, US, physician; b. Bklyn, NY, June 18, 1905; d. Leom and Clara (Obeler) Obeler; BS U Chgo, 1925; MD, Rush Grad Sch of Med, 1928; m. Meyer Perlstein, May 7, 1928; c: Lee Axelrad, Ruth Stein, Paul. Pvt practice since 1928; mem staff, Mt Sinai Hosp, 1927-39; city phys, Juvenile Court, 1928-39; mem staff, Cook Co Hosp, 1930-38, all Chgo; cons dermat, FDA, 1938-50; asso prof of dermat, U of Ill Med Sch, 1945-47. Mem: AMA; Chgo Med Soc; Chgo Dermat Soc; Amer Acad of Dermat; Soc Inves Dermat; Miss Valley Soc of Dermat. Contbr to med jours. Home and office: 1721 Laurelwood Dr, San Jose, Cal.

PERMUTT, James L, US, attorney; b. Birmingham, Ala, Dec 10, 1910; s. Harry and Rachel (Damsky); BS, U of Ala, 1931, LLB, 1935; m. Marguerite Kessler, 1936; c: Marshall, Patricia. Mem, law firm, Sirote, Permutt, Friend & Friedman, since 1935. Mem: natl campaign cabinet, UJA, Ala state chmn; natl bd: Bonds for Isr; JWB; bd of educ, Mountain Brook, Ala; fmr pres: Temple Beth-El, 1952-54; B'nai B'rith, 1943-45; ZOA, 1942-44; J Comty Cen, 1949-54, all Birmingham; SE region, CJFWF, 1955-56. Mem: Ala and Amer Bar Assns; club, Fairmont, Birmingham, mem, bd dirs, since 1948. Home: 12 Richmar Dr, Birmingham, Ala. Office: 2030 First Ave, N Birmingham, Ala.

PERRAS, Gary G, US, rabbi; b. Baltimore, Md, June 25, 1942; s. Hyman and Freda (Schlaffer); BS, Johns Hopkins U, 1962; Dipl, Baltimore Heb Coll, 1962; MHL, att Heb U, Jerusalem, 1965-66; ordained rabbi, JTSA, 1967. Rabbi: Tree of Life, Syn, since 1967; Lake Carmel J Cen, Lake Carmel, NY, summer, 1965; Bemple Beth El, Oneonta, NY, 1966-67. Pres, Oil City Lodge, B'nai B'tith; bd mem: United Cerebral Palsy, NW Pa; Mh Assn, Venango Co, Pa; mem: RA; Oil City Min Assn. Home: 6 Reed St, Oil City, Pa. Study: 316 W First St, Oil City, Pa.

PERRY, Richard Thomas, US, dentist; b. Chgo, Ill, Apr 7, 1940; s. Robert and Gertrude (Hyman); BS, Roosevelt U, Chgo, 1963; DDS, U of Ill, Sch of Dent, 1968; m. Eleanor Bruni, Aug 21, 1966; d. Katherine, Pvt practice since 1968; staff, Schwab Rehab Hosp, Chgo since 1968. Pres, Western-Polk Neighborhood Assn; mem: Irving Sch Comty Educ Council; Amer Dental Assn; Delta Sigma Delta; Amer Soc Dent for Children; Amer Soc Geriatric Dent; Chgo Dent Soc; Ill State Dent Soc. Home: 823 S Oakley Chicago, Ill. Office: 752 W Western, Chicago, Ill.

PERRY, Ruth Magil, US, communal leader; b. Buffalo, NY, June 26, 1934; d. Reuben and Selma (Diskan) Magil; att U of Pa; m. M Milton Perry, Nov 28, 1954; c: Stephanie, Daniel. Chmn, Natl J Family Living, Natl Women's League, vice-pres, Phila br, natl speaker, cons; secy sch chmn, Temple Sinai Cong; secy, Phila Br, United Syn of Amer; exec comm, Cyrus Adler, Regional Heb HS; mem: bd dirs, J Educ, Phila; bd, Friends of Dropsie Coll; Hadassah; Women's Technion. Author: Kosher Cookery Unlimited 1960; Kosher Parties Unlimited, 1968. Home: 525 E Mt Airy Ave, Philadelphia, Pa.

PERSKY, Robert A, US, attorney; b. Louisville, Ky, Aug 12, 1908; s. Ralph and Rashel (Simon); LLB, Louisville Male High and Law U, 1929; m. Miriam Grablowsky, June 25, 1940; c: Marshall, Saradona Lefkowitz. Pvt practice since 1929; mem, Ky Leg, 1933-36. Pres, SE region, ZOA, 1951-53, vice-pres, 1949-51, mem, exec comm, natl ZOA, since 1951, hon life pres, ZOA of Ga, since 1950, chmn, regional admn council, 1947-49; delg, WZC, Jerusalem, 1951; mem: Ky, Ga, Augusta, Amer and Fed Bar Assns; admn comm, JDC, since 1950; Elks: speaker for UJA and Isr Bonds in SE US. Home: 1302 Buena Vista Rd, Augusta, Ga. Office: Marion Bldg, Augusta, Ga.

PESHKIN, M Murray, US, allergist, educator; b. NYC, May 23, 1892; s. Zelick and Goldie (Feigen); MD, Fordham U Sch of Med, 1914; m. Lillian Rapaport, Oct 9, 1921. Chief cons phys, Children's Asthma Research Inst and Hosp, Denver, 1940-62; cons allergist, Mt Sinai Hosp, since 1952, on staff since 1926; intstr, postgrad ext course, Coll of Phys, and Surgs, Columbia U, 1926-52; chief, children's Allergy clinic, Fr Hosp, 1934-36; att allergist J Memorial, Hosp, 1938-40; em clinical prof, med and ped, for allergy, Albert Einstein Coll of Med, Yeshiva U, 1954-60; visiting allergist, Bx Munic Hosp Cen, NY, 1954-60; em clinical prof, dept of ped, Mt Sinai Sch of Med, City U of NY, 1968; cons: Asthmatic Children's Treatment Cen, N Miami Beach, Fla, 1966; Asthmatic Children's Foundation of NY, 1966. Dipl, Amer Bd of Internal Med and Allergy; f: Amer Coll of Phys; AMA; Amer Coll of Allergists; Amer Acad of Allergy; AAAS; Acad Psychosomatic Med; hon pres: Music Lovers League, since 1956; Amer Soc for Crippled Children in Isr, since 1956; pres: Asthmatic Children's Found, since 1962, NY chap, 1963; phys chap, AJ Cong, 1959; Assn of Study of Allergy, 1936; Amer Coll Allergists, 1953-54; secy, Allergy Found of Amer, Inc, 1955-63; hon, mem, Fr Allergy Soc; mem: NY Allergy Soc; Isr Med Assn; Soc for Advancement of Judaism; Masons; life mem, ZOA; club, Friars. Asso ed: Jour of Asthma Research since 1963; cons ed, Psychosomatics; contbr to med jours. Homes: 450 W End Ave, New York, NY; Weston, Conn. Office: 450 W End Ave, New York, NY.

PESIN, Edward, US, attorney; b. Jersey City, NJ, Sep 23, 1924; s. Samuel and Libby (Weisman); AB, Rutgers U, 1947; LLB, Harvard U, 1950; LLM, NYU, 1957; m. Helene Rattner, June 22, 1952; c: Ella, Samuel. Counsellor, tax law, since 1949; pres, Edward Pesin, Public Account, since 1970; trial atty, Internal Revenue Service, 1951-55; tax atty, JK Lasser & Co, NYC, 1955-57; lectr, taxation: NYU; Rutgers Law Sch; chmn, NJ Supr Court comm on profsl corps. Lt, US Army, 1943-46. Delg, NJ State Bar Assn, to Mid-Atlantic Internal Revenue Regional Liaison Comm, mem, exec comm, tax sect, chmn, comm on fed taxation, 1960-63; trustee, Temple Beth El, N Bergen, NJ; vice-pres, NJ Co Traffic Coord Assn, 1960-63; chmn, N Bergen, ARC, 1963; mem: Phi Beta Kappa; tax sect, Amer Bar Assn. Author: Techniques in Proving A Tax Case, 1959; Professional Associations Doing Business As Corporations, 1963. Recipient: Loyal Sons of Rutgers U Award, 1962. Home: 5 75 St, North Bergen, NJ. Office: 17 Academy St, Newark, NJ.

PETERS, Elsa, US, communal worker; b. Berlin, Ger, Apr 27, 1916; d. Herman and Hermine (Suess) Elkan; BA, U Berlin, 1934; att Hoschschule für Wissenschaft des Judentums, Berlin, 1935; m. Stephen Sherman, 1936 (decd); m. 2nd, Charles Peters, 1960. Exec dir, dist 2, B'nai B'rith Women, Cleveland fmr dir, dist, 6, Chgv; acting dir, B'nai B'rith Hillel Found,W Reserve U, 1965-57; mem: League of WomenVoters; Brandeis; Amer Fed of TV and Radio Artists; Council of Hum Rel; Adult Educ Soc. Home: 13620 Ardoon, Shaker Heights, O. Office: 1900 Euclid Ave, Cleveland, O.

PETERS, Roberta, US, singer; b. NYC, May 4, 1930; d. Sol and Ruth (Hirsch) Peterman; studied with William Hermann; m. Bertram Fields, Apr 10, 1955; c: Paul, Bruce. Soprano, Metrop Opera Assn, since 1950; roles in: Rigoletto; Don Giovanni; The Magic Flute; Cosi Fan Tutte; Gianni Schicchi; The Barber of Seville; Lucia di Lammermoor; Die Fledermaus; Marriage of Figaro; Der Rosenkavalier; L'Elisir d'Amore; Tales of Hoffmann; Arabella; The Masked Ball; Don Pasquale; Orfeo; Ariadne auf Naxos; sung at Royal Opera House, Covent Garden, London, Eng, 1950-60; stared in motion picture, Tonight We Sing, 1952; concert tours, appeared with major sym orchs, including: NY Philharmonic; Phila; Pittsburgh; Chgo; recordings for: RCA Victor; Columbia Masterworks. Mem: NY Bus and Profsl Women's Assn; Amer

Guild Musical Artists. Author: Debut at the Met. Home: 64 Garden Rd, Scarsdale, NY. Office: Hurok Attractions Inc, 730 Fifth Ave, New York, NY.

PETKUN, Bertram A, US, attorney; b. Chelsea, Mass, Dec 6, 1906; s. James and Jennie (Rosenthal); AB, Harvard U, 1928; LLB, 1931; m. Ruth Grass, Apr 23, 1944; c: Carol, Richard. Practicing atty, since 1931; sr partner, Horovitz, Petkun, Rothschild, Locke & Kistin, specializing in workmen's compensation, since 1945. USCG Res, WW II Mem: exec bd, Mass chap, AJComm, since 1961; exec comm, Mass br, Natl Assn Claimants Counsel of Amer, since 1955; Amer, Boston and Middlesex Bar Assns; Mass Trial Lawyers Assn; Harvard Law Sch Assn; B'nai B'rith, fmr bd mem; Brandeis Assos; Temple Isr; clubs: New Century, fmr bd mem; Chestnut Hill Country. Asso ed: Law Jour of Natl Assn Claimants Counsel of Amer,.since 1955. Hobbies: travel, golf, boating, painting. Home: 73 Bonad Rd, W Newton, Mass. Office: 6 Beacon St, Boston, Mass.

PETLUCK, Ann S, US, lawyer, social work admnr; b. NYC, Apr 17, 1908; d. Joseph and Alice (Serber); BS NYU, 1928; LLM, 1930; MSS, NY Sch of Social Work, Columbia U, 1942; m. Meyer Poses, June 19, 1932. Dep regional rep, UN High Commn for Refs at UN, 1964-68; pvt law practice, 1931-33; caseworker, Natl Council J Women, 1934-36, caseworker then sup, natl coordinating comm, 1936-42; dir, migration services. Natl Ref Service, 1942-46; United Service for New Amers, 1946-51, asst exec dir, 1951-54; instr, Adelphi Sch of Social Work, 1951-60; dir US oprs, United Hias Service: 1954-64. Mem: bd: Amer Immigration and Citizenship Council, 1959-64, and since 1968; Intl League Rights Man; adv comm social work, Amer Council for Emigres in the Professions, since 1968; Intl Conf on Social Work; Natl Women Lawyers Assn, Assn Immigration, Nationality Lawyers; Conf of J Communal Service; Epsilon Phi; Tau Kappa Alpha; Eclectic; Amer Bar Assn, Intl Platform Assn. Fmr ed bd: J Social Service Quarterly; NYU Law Rev. Home: 441 E 20 St, New York, NY.

PETRUSHKA, Shabtai Arieh, Isr, composer; b. Leipzig, Ger, Mar 15, 1903; s. Yehoshua and Minna (Werber); in Isr since 1938; att Conservatory: Leipzig, 1921-23; Berlin, 1925-27; dipl, Tech U, Berlin-Charlottenburg, 1919-28; m. Miriam Schwarzer, Aug 15, 1934. Ret; fmr dir, music, Isr Bc Sys, 1958-68; on staff since 1938; orch dir, Ger Aus, theaters: including Komödie Theater/Kurfürstendamm, Berlin, Komödie Kammerspiele, Vienna, 1929-30; arranger: Universal-Film Aktien, Berlin, 1931-35; Deutsche Grammophon, Berlin, 1933-37; conductor, arranger, Lucraphone Records, Berlin, 1933-37. Served Haganah. Composer: Four Movements for Band, 1953; Five Oriental Dances, 1956; Three Movements for Orch, 1959. Mem: council, Isr Composers Assn; Natl Fed Isr Journalists; club, Jerusalem Rotary, pres, 1965-66. Recipient: Music Award, Amer-Isr Soc, NY, 1957; US State Dept travel grant, 1957; commn, Isr Composers Fund, 1969. Home: 13 Abba Hilkiya St, Jerusalem, Isr.

PETUCHOWSKI, Jakob J, US, educator, rabbi; b. Berlin, Ger, July 30, 1925; s. Siegmund and Lucie (Loewenthal); in US since 1948; BA, U London, 1947; MHL, ordained rabbi, HUC, 1952, PhD, 1955; hon FHL, Maimonides Coll, Winnipeg, Can, 1959; m. Elizabeth Mayer, Nov 28, 1946; c: Samuel, Aaron, Jonathan. Prof, rabb and theol, HUC- JIR, Cincinnati, since 1963, on fac since 1956; educ dir, Youth Assn of Syns, Gt Brit, 1946-48; rabbi: Temple Emanuel,Welch, W Va, 1949-55; Beth Isr Cong, Wash, Pa, 1955-56; visiting prof, phil and rel, Antioch Coll, Yellow Springs, O, 1961. Mem, Soc of Bibl Lit and Exegesis. Author:The Theology of Haham David Nieto, 1954; Ever Since Sinai—A Modern View of Torah, 1961; Prayerbook Reform in Europe, 1968; mem, ed bd, CCAR jour, since 1960; contbr to Ency Britannica; scholarly and gen jours. Home: 7836 Greenland Pl, Cincinnati, O. Office: HUC, Clifton Ave, Cincinnati, O.

PEVSNER, Isaiah, Isr, attorney; b. Romny, Russ, Jan 11, 1896; s. Mendel and Bella (Teoumin); in Isr since 1925; dipl: Classical Coll, Yekaterinoslav, 1914; Law Fac U, Petrograd, Kharkov, 1919; m. Stella Perper, Mar 15, 1939; c: Daniel, Mikhaela. Atty since 1927; lectr: intl law, state, 1921-24; ed, Palestine Directory and Handbook, 1926-27. Pvt, Haganah, 1939-49. Pres: Isr Hum Rights Assn; council, Premarriage Advice Assn, Isr; vice-pres: World Fed Hum Rights; Ephrat, Isr Demographic Soc; mem: council, Intl Assn J Lawyers and Jurists; mem: B'nai B'rith, fmr pres, Weizman Lodge; Haganah Vets; cen comm, UN Assn of Isr;

PINES, Kapai, Isr, author, journalist; b. Moscow, Russ, Jan 25, 1926; s. Don and Feiga (Taxa); in Isr since 1930; att Columbia U Sch of Journalism, 1947-49; m. Chana Heimann, June, 1950; c: Ori, Niri. Gen ed, Mada, Heb jour for popularization of sci, since 1962; delg to US, Hechalutz Org, 1947-49; fgn corresp, Davar daily, 1947-48; head, div of publs, Agric Research Sta, Rehovot; with dailies: Maariv, Omer; weekly, Dvar haShavua; ed: What's What in the Histadrut, 1955; Who's Who in the World, 1959; Ptach Dah, 1961; contbr of numerous articles and columns on political, econ, popular sci topics. Lt, IDF, since 1957. Mem: Intl Sci Writers Assn; Conf of Biol Ed's; Isr Assn of Amateur: Astronomers. Hobbies: classical music, plastic arts, sports, Heb lang. Home: Ramat Motza, Jerusalem, Isr. Office: POB 801, Jerusalem, Isr.

PINK, Lutka, Fr, painter; b. Warsaw, Pol, Apr 28, 1916; d. Benjamin and Faje; in Fr since 1939; att Acad des Beaux Arts. Fresco, Amer Hosp, Aix-en-Provence, Fr; one-man shows: Gal 8; Jeune Cartel; Armand, all Paris; Montreal Mus; New Vision Cen; Drian, both London; Bologna, It; Numero, Florence, It; Helene Rubinstein Mus, Tel Aviv; Gal Citadella, Ascona; Bezalel Mus, Jerusalem; represented in numerous salons, pvt collections. Contbr to various publs. Home and studio: 59 Ave de Saxe, Paris, Fr.

PINKEL, Benjamin, US, engineer; b. Gloversville, NY, Mar 31, 1909; s. Herman and Ethel (Turower); BS, U of Pa, 1930; m. Ann Abel, Jan 28, 1940; c: Sheila, Joseph. Sr staff, Rand Corp, since, 1968, asso head, aero-astronautics dept, 1956-68; physicist, Natl Adv Comm for Aeronautics, 1931-38, head, engine analysis sect, 1938-42, chief, thermodynamics div, 1942-45, fuel and thermodynamics div, 1945-49, chief, materials and thermodynamics research div, 1949-56. Asso f, Amer Inst for Astronautics and Aeronautics, mem publs comm; vicepres B'nai B'rith Balfour lodge, Cleveland, O, 1955; mem: bd dirs: Beth Sholom Temple, Santa Monica, since 1960; Santa Monica chap, NCCJ, since 1960; Amer Nuclear Soc; gas turbine comm, Amer Soc for Mech Engrs; Amer Soc for Metal; Tau Beta Pi; Pi Mu Epsilon; contbr to numerous profsl jours. Home: 726 Adelaide Pl, Santa Monica, Cal. Office: 1700 Main St, Santa Monica, Cal.

PINKERFELD-AMIR, Anda, Isr, author; b. Rzeszow, Pol, June 26, 1902; d. Yoel and Frida (Monderev); in Isr since 1923; att Us in Pol and Ger, 1921-24; m. Arie Amir, 1922; c: Amos, Zipor. Author: Yamim Dovevim, 1929; Yuval, 1931; meOlam Dmuyot miKedem, 1934; Shirey Yeladim, 1935; Dudaim, 1937; Seharhoret Peleh, 1938; HaShafan haLavan, 1939; Haruzim Alizim, 1942; Shalom Yeladim, 1945; Gadish, 1949; Ahat, 1953; Kohavim baDli, 1955; Mishpat Bnei haYaar, 1957; Gadish vaOmer, 1961; Geisha Lian Tang Shara, poem, 1964; Tehiot, 1967; prose: Bahajeyhem; Sodi im Ahi haGadol; Taaluley Ayin Ikeshet; ed, "The 35," Lamed-Heh, memorial to fallen of Isr War of Independence, 1948-49. Fmr served, volunteer social worker, DP camps, Ger. Recepient: Bialik Prize, 1935; Ruppin Prize, 1954. Home: 87 Ahad Ha'am St, Tel Aviv, Isr.

PINKERT, Joseph S, US, business exec; b. Chgo, Ill, June 2, 1908; s. Simon and Ida (Graff); PhB, U Chgo, 1930; m. Claire Bloomberg, March 1, 1936; c: Stuart, Dale, Ralph. Pres, Peoples Iron & Metal Co, since 1951; found and sr partner: Consolidated Mill Supply Co, since 1941; pres: Scrap Corp of Amer, since 1953; bd chmn, Ind Briquetting Corp, since 1944. Dir: Woodlawn Hosp, since 1968; trustee: Bd of J Educ since 1963; Coll of J Studies, since 1957; chmn, Hoffman House, since 1962, Hoffman Memorial libr; United Syn of Amer since 1956; Chicago SE Commn since 1959; natl dir, Inst if Scrap Iron and Steel, Wash DC, since 1960; past dir, Mt Sinai Hosp; past pres, Cong Rodfei Zedek; natl chmn, Scrap Political Action Comm; asso chmn, Jewish United Fund; bd govs, State of Isr Bonds, since 1960; clubs: Quadrangle, U Chgo; Illinois Athletic. Home: 5555 S Everett, Chicago, Ill. Office: 5843 S Loomis Blvd, Chicago, Ill.

PINKHAS, Jack, Isr, physician; b. Plovdiv, Bulgaria, Mar 27, 1930; s. Shlomo and Hilda (Wertheimer); in Isr since 1949; MD, Heb U, Jerusalem, 1957; m. Rachel Avritcher, Apr 26, 1960; c: Hanna, Ram. Chief phys, dept med, D, Beilinson Hosp, since 1966, on staff since 1960; lectr, med, Tel Aviv U Med Sch, since 1967, mem fac, continuing med educ, since 1969; tchr hematology, Workers Sick Fund-Hadassah Med Sch post grad inst for gen practitioners, 1965. Maj, IDF, res, MC, 1949-69. Mem: IMA; Isr Soc of Hematology; Isr Soc of Internal Med. Contbr to profsl publs. Recipient: award, Ber-

Lemsdorf Found, 1969. Home: 48 Katznelson St, Petah Tikva, Isr. Office: Beilinson Hosp, Petah Tikva, Isr.

PINNER, Hayim, Eng, organization exec; b. London, Eng, May 25, 1925; s. Simon and Annie (Wagner); att Tchrs Training Coll, U London; m. Rita Reuben, June 1956; c: Simon. Exec dir, B'nai B'rith, since 1957. British Army, 1945-48. Mem, exec council: ZF, Gt Brit and Ir; Poale Zion; WJC, British sect; J Cultural Soc; Lab Friends of Isr; mem, Bd Deps of Brit J; secy, Young Paole Zion, 1948-50. Chmn, ed bd, J Vanguard, ed 1950-60; contbr to Anglo-J and overseas press, jours. Home: 95 Millway, London NW7, Eng. Office: B'nai B'rith, Woburn House, Upper Woburn Pl, London WC1, Eng.

PINS, Jacob, Isr, artist; b. Höxter, Ger, Jan 16, 1917; s. Leo and Ida (Lipper); in Isr since 1936; studied with Jacob Steinhardt, 1941-45; m. Elsa Rothschild, Oct 13, 1966. Artist, painter; tchr Bezalel Sch of Art and Design, Jerusalem, since 1956; envoy to Japan fgn min, Isr Painters and Sculptors Assn, 1962. One-man shows: Tel Aviv, 1945, 1946, 1949, 1952, 1956; Jerusalem, 1953, 1956, 1960, 1967; Haifa, 1954, 1958; Public Libr, Boston, 1953; US Natl Mus, Wash, DC, 1954; London, 1955, 1964; NY, 1959; Zurich, 1960; Bogota, 1962; Melbourne, 1963; Sydney, 1964; San Jose, Costa Rica, 1968; group shows: Black and White Beinnale Switz, 1955; Annual Exhib of Soc of Woodengravers, London, 1957; Biennale of Graphic Art, Yugo, 1959-61; Xylon Intl Woodcut Exhb, Berlin, Gelsenkirchen, Ljubljana, 1959-62; XXX Beinnale, Venice, 1960; Isr Graphic Exhb, Tokyo, 1962; 30th Exhb of Japanese Print Assn, Tokyo, 1962; Isr Graphic: Yugo, 1962; Warsaw, Moscow, 1964-65; Melbourne, Sydney, 1965; 1st Intl Exhb of Original Drawings, Yugo, 1968; repr in collections: Isr Mus, Jerusalem; Munic Mus of Modern Art, Haifa; Mus Tel Aviv; Metrop Mus, NY; Mus of Modern Art, NY; Mus of Fine Arts, Boston; Fogg Art Mus, Mass; US Natl Mus, Wash, DC; Libr of Cong, Wash, DC; Ft Wayne Mus; Art Inst Chgo; J Mus, NY; Public Libr: Boston, Malden, both Mass; Ohara Mus, Japan; Stedelijk Mus, Amsterdam; Natl Gal of Victoria, Austr; Natl Gal of NSW, Sydney; Gal of Art, Geelong, Austr; Natl Mus, Warsaw; Mus Pushkin, Moscow. Pub: illustrations to: Michael Kohlhaas, by H v Kleist, Heb, by Chartiner, 1952; Shlomiel Matza Tzel, by Yehuda Yaari, 1947; Jacob Pins Landscapes, 1955. Co-found: Jerusalem Artists group; Jerusalem Artists' House; mem, Isr Painters and Sculptors Assn; hon mem, Academia delli Arti del Disegno, Florence. Recipient: Ohara Mus Prize, Tokyo, 1957; Jerusalem Prize, 1962. Hobby: collecting Far E art. Home: 5 Ethiopia St, Jerusalem, Isr.

PINSKER, William, US, institute exec, communal worker; b. Ukraine, Sep 12, 1896; s. Harris and Leah (Simonov); in US since 1906; m. Pauline Feinberg, Sep 23, 1920; c: Robert, Henry. Ret; exec-dir, YM-YWHA, Paterson, NJ, 1944-65; gen-secy, YM-YWHA, Wilkes-Barre, Pa, 1917-1920; found, exec dir: Educ Alliance, Savanah, Ga, 1920-1931; YM-YWHA, Brockton, Mass, 1938-41; exec dir: YMHA, Stamford, Conn, 1938-41; YMHA, Boston, Mass, 1941-44. Pres, NE sect, Natl Assn J C Workers, 1937; chmn, Conf of Big Cen Execs, 1956-59; secy, Natl Conf of J Communal Service, 1959-60; fmr PR chmn: Savanah Comty Chest; Brockton Comty Chest, 1932-35; fmr vice-pres, La Soc for the Blind, mem: B'nai B'rith; Veritans Club. Fmr ed bd, J Cen mag; contbr of numerous articles to J org mags. Recipient: Harry S Feller award, NJ Region, JWB, 1968. Spec interests: reading, gardening, sports. Home: 504 15 Ave, Paterson, NJ.

PINSKY, Abe, US, psychiatrist; b. NYC, Mar 9, 1914; s. Benjamin and Yetta (Zaretsky); BS, NYU, 1933, 1937; m. Annette Heimerdinger, July 31, 1940; c: David, Ruth. Pvt practice, psychan, since 1946; clinical asst prof, psycht, Downstate Med Cen, since 1955. Mem: Amer Psychiatric Assn; Amer Inst for Psychan; Acad of Psychan. Home: 3083 Bedford Ave, Brooklyn, NY. Office: 1 Hanson Pl, Brooklyn, NY.

PINTO, Avram (pen name **Panto**), Yugo, educator; b. Yugo, 1903; s. Hajim and Sara (Kaveson); deg, fac of phil, 1928; m. Berta Papo. Cons, pedg, Dist People's Comm, Sarajevo. Secy, pres, Sephardic Academic Soc, Esperanza, 1925-28; mem: gen comm, Benevolencija, 1928-41; exec, Profs Assn of Yugo, 1935-36; comm, J Comty, Sarajevo, 1938-41. Contbr articles on hist of Sephardic Js, J arrival in Bosnia, Sephardic folklore, culture; corresp, Jevrejski Pregled; Jevresjki Zivot; contbr to educ to profsl jours. Home: Djure Salaja 28, Sarajevo, Yugo. Office: District People's Comm, Sarajevo, Yugo.

PIORE, Emanuel R, US, physicist; b. Wilno, Russ, July 19, 1908; s. Ruben and Olga (Gegusin); in US since 1917; BA, U Wis, 1930, PhD, 1935; m. Nora Kahn, Aug 26, 1931; c: Michael, Margot, Jane. Vice-pres, chief sci, IBM, since 1965, mem staff, since 1956; research physicist, RCA, 1935-38; engr, TV lab, CBS, 1938-42; head, spec weapons div, bur of ships, USN, 1942-44; physicist, research lab elec, MIT, 1948-49; dep chief sci, Off of Naval Research, 1951-55, on staff since 1946; vice-pres, Avco Mfr Corp, NYC, 1955-56. USNR, 1944-46. F: Amer Phys Soc; Inst Elec and Electronics Engrs; corp mem, trustee, Woods Hole Oceanographic Instn; mem; Amer Phil Soc; Natl Sci Bd; visiting comm, dept physics, Harvard Coll; Phil Soc, Wash; Wash Acad Sci; Sci Research Soc Amer; Pres' Sci Adv Comm, 1959-62; clubs: Cosmos, Wash, DC; U, NYC. Recipient: Dist Civilian Service award, 1955; Ind Inst Research medal, 1967; Eta Kappa Nu Eminent Membership award, 1969. Home: 115 Central Park W, New York, NY. Office: Armonk, NY.

PIPERNO, Beer Sergio, It, attorney; b. Rome, Sep 20, 1906; s. Angelo and Rachele (Bises); DJur U Rome, 1929; m. Livia Modigliani, Mar 14, 1943; c: Giuliana, Maurizio, Gino, Bruno. Magistrate, Rome Cassazione Court, since 1968. Capt, It Army Res, 1928-29. Exec mem, WJC. Home: Via Bartolomeo Gosio 77, Rome, It. Office: Lungotevere Sanzio 9, Rome, It.

PIRON, Mordechai, Isr, rabbi; b. Vienna, Aus, Dec 28, 1921; s. Jacob and Irene (Weiss) Pisk; in Isr since 1938; ordained rabbi, Rabbi Kook Sem, Jerusalem, 1948; att Heb U, Jerusalem, 1944-48; BA, London U, 1950; m. Ahuva Gardi, 1946; c: Jacov, Tova, Orna. Head, Dept of Rel Culture, Chief Chaplaincy, IDF, Lt col, chief army chaplain, IDF; rabbi and pres, Cong for Young People, Bat Yam; lectr, Kol Isr. Vice-pres, Hashlosha Lodge, B'nai B'rith; mem, directorial bd, Yeshiva HS, Bat Yam. Contbr to articles in fields of Judaism, Halacha and phil to academic mags. Home: 5 Kedoshe Kahir St, Bat Yam, Isr. Office: IDF, Isr.

PLAFKER, Nathan V, US, dentist, lecturer; b. NYC, Oct 17, 1905; s. Jacob and Fannie (Schachner); DDS, Temple U, 1927; att Crozer Theol Sem, 1945-54; m. Pearl Fisher, May 18, 1940 (decd). Pvt practice, dent, since 1927; lectr: comparative rel, YMCA, 1952-54; Judaism, Baptist Inst for Social Workers, Bryn Mawr, Pa, 1953-54; mem, Selective Service Bd 2, 1941-47. Pres: bd of mgrs, Child Health Cens, 1954-61; J Comty Relations Council, 1954; chmn: Housing Auth, since 1958; Fair Employment Practice Commn, 1960; City Planning Comm, 1962, all Chester, Pa; mem, Del Co Dent Soc; secy, Chester Zionist dist, 1935-42; club, Phil, pres, 1949-54. Recipient: Pres cert, 1948; Selective Service Medal, 1949. Spec interests: comaparative rel, antiques, harness racing. Home: 919 Edgmont Ave, Chester, Pa. Office: Med Arts Bldg, Chester, Pa.

PLANT, Alfred L, US, business exec; b. Miami, Fla, July 22, 1912; s. Morris and Evelyn (Herstein); BS, NYU, 1938; m, Ann Stein, Nov 8, 1942; c: Kaaren, Marcia. Vice-pres, advt, Block Drug Co, since 1955; sr acct exec: Fed Advt Agcy, 1946-53; Grey Advt Agcy, 1952-55. Maj, US Army, 1942-46, Vice-pres, YM-YWHA, Emanuel Midtown; treas, Assn Natl Advts; bd trustees: E End Temple; advt div, United Fund; Intl Radio and TV Soc; Natl TV Acad Arts and Sci; local div, UJA, 1949-68; co-chmn, local dir, FJP, 1949-68. Home: 445 E 80 St, New York, NY. Office: 257 Cornelison Ave, Jersey City, NJ.

PLASKOW, Michael Lionel, Eng, minister; b. Tel Aviv, Isr, July 8, 1936; s. Solomon and Bella (Cohen); in Eng since 1937; LTSC, Curwen Coll Music; ALCM, London Coll Music; att: Tree of Life Talmudical Coll; Jews' Coll; m. Phyllis Weisfogel, June 20, 1961; c: Angela. Min reader, N Finchley and Woodside Park Syn, since 1956; surg mohel, Initiation Soc. Ed comm, Woodside Park Garden Suburb Retepayers Assn; mem, Assn Mins of Gt Brit. Recipient: Samuel Alman prize, Jews Coll, twice. Hobbies: chess, athletics. Home: 12 Singleton Scarp, Woodside Park, London N12, Eng. Study: N Finchley and Woodside Park Dist Synagogue, Woodside Park Rd, London N12, Eng.

PLATT, Harry H, US, attorney, labor arbitrator; b. Russ, May 8, 1902; s. Morris and Dora (Miller); in US since 1911; BA, U Mich, 1924, LLB, 1926; m. Evelyn Friedman, June 15, 1930; c: Elaine Binger, Catherine Kutchai. Pvt practice, since 1926; umpire: between Ford Motor Co, and United Automobile Workers, since 1950; Republic Steel Corp and United Steel Workers of Amer, 1954-59. Pres: Men's ORT, Detroit chap, vice-pres, Amer ORT Fed; Natl Acad Arbitrators, 1958-59; dir: J Family Service Assn, since 1955; Detroit Bar Assn, 1950; chmn, Pres Emergency Bd in S Pacific RR Dispute, 1961; mem, Amer Bar Assn, Contbr to legal jours and ind relations reviews. Home: 17546 Birchcrest Dr, Detroit, Mich. Office: 2080 Penobscot Bldg, Detroit, Mich.

PLAUT, W Gunther, Can, rabbi; b. Münster, Ger, Nov 1, 1912; s. Jonas and Selma (Gumprich); LLB, Berlin U, 1933, JSD, 1934; MHL, ordained rabbi, HUC, 1939, DD, 1964; m. Elizabeth Strauss, Nov 10, 1938; c: Jonathan, Judith. Rabbi: Holy: Blossom Temple, Toronto, since 1961; Wash Blvd (Oak Park) Temple, Chgo, 1939-43, 1946-48; Mt Zion Heb Cong, St Paul, Minn, 1948-61; lectr, phil, Macalester Coll, St Paul, 1952-54. Chaplain, capt, US Army, 1943-46. Pres: World Federalists of Can, 1966-68; Zionist Youth Commn, Chgo, 1941-43; Minn Rabb Assn, 1955-56; St Paul Gal, Sch of Art, 1953-59; chmn: Zionist Emergency Council, St Paul, 1953-61; Minn Tercentenary Comm, 1954; Twin Cities coord council on ME and intl affairs, 1957-61; Gov's Comm on ethics in govt, 1958-61; Forum of Rels, since 1969; delg, Midcentury White House Conf, 1951; mem bd: Toronto Sym Orch; CCAR, 1954-56; mem: interim comm, Amer J Conf, gov's interracial comm, 1949-61; gov's adv council on youth, 1951-56; clubs: Oakdale and Maple Downs Golf and Country; Primrose. Author: Ehe-Unguelgigkeit im internationalen Privatrecht, 1934; Dramalogues, a series, 1946-52; High Holy Day Services for Children; Mt Zion, the First Hundred Years, 1956; The Jews in Minnesota, 1959; Book of Proverbs-A Commentary, 1961; Judaism and the Scientific Spirit, 1962, trans into Heb; Germany Today, 1962; The Rise of Reform Judaism, 1963; The Growth of Reform Judaism, 1965; The Case for the Chosen People, 1965, Heb Fr; Your Neighbor is a Jew, 1967; Israel since the 6-Day War, 1968; contbr ed, Universal J Ency. Recipient: Bronze Star, 1945. Home: 46 Ridelle Ave, Toronto, Can. Study: 1950 Bathurst St, Toronto, Can.

PLEASURE, Hyman, US, psychiatrist; b. NYC, Mar 31, 1908; s. Joseph and Goldie (Heim); BS, NYU, 1931, MD, 1935; m, Edith Schlank, Nov 25, 1932; c: David Robert, Judith. Dep. comm local services, NY State Dept of Mental Hygiene; fmr dir, Middletown State Hosp, NY, since 1955; med dir, epilepsy project, NY State Correction Dept, Coxsackie, NY, 1960-63; chmn, Catskill regional adv council, mental hygiene, 1962-63; psycht, Dannemora State Hosp, 1937-41; sup psycht, Cen Islip State Hosp, 1941-48; asst dir, Pilgrim State Hosp, 1949-55, all NY. F, Amer Psychiatric Assn; bd dirs: Orange Co Health Assn, since 1956; Orange Co Mh Assn, since 1957; mem: Albany Co and NY State Med Socs; AMA; Orange Co Med Soc; Middletown Heb Cong; Phi Beta Kappa. Contbr to med jours. Home: 111 Greenleaf Dr, Newtonville, NY. Office: 44 Holland Ave, Albany, NY.

PLEIN, Barnabas, S Afr, appraiser, business exec; b. S Afr, Sep 25, 1898; s. Joshua and Sonia (Manthematic); att Schs of Mines and Tech, 1914; m. Anne Gootman, Dec 23, 1934; c: Joan, Justin. Owner own bus; dept mgr, Parry, Leon & Hayhoe, Ltd, since 1922. Mem, gov commn: J Helping Hand, 1924; J Aged Home, 1925; Civic Guard, 1939; mem, div council, United Party Club, 1951; found, mem: Johannesburg Reprs, 1943; S Afr Football Assn, 1951. Home: Berkeley Sq- D302 Main Ave, Riviera, S Afr. Office: Majesty's Bldg, Eloff St, Johannesburg, S Afr.

PLESSER, Pearl S, US, communal worker; b. NYC, July 7, 1906; d. Josef and Miriam (Friedman) Schreiber; att Bklyn Coll, 1929; m. Maurice Plesser, 1928; c: Zachary, Tully. Natl vice-pres, Mizrachi Women's Org, 1961-62; natl mem chmn, 1951, natl publicity chmn, 1952; natl JNF chmn for Mizrachi Women, 1957-61; natl vice-pres, JNF, 1963-66; treas, 1960-62; mem: Young Isr; Women's Div, Yeshiva U; Yeshiva of Flatbush; toured on speaking engagements for Mizrachi Women and JNF. Home: 866 E 12 St, Brooklyn, NY.

PLESSNER, Martin M, Isr, orientalist; b. Poznan, Dec 30, 1900; s. Isaac and Rosa Reisner; in Isr since 1933; att U Berlin; PhD, U Breslau, 1925; m. Dec 28, 1930, (separated) c: Yakir, Chagit Lawsky. Prof, Islamic Civilization, Heb U, Jerusalem, since 1963; libr, sch of Oriental Studies, 1951-55; asst at Us and Insts, Ger 1925-33; privatdozent, Frankfurt/Main, 1931-33, inactive prof since 1956; tchr, Isr, HSs, 1931-52. Mem: Intl Soc of Hist and Sci; Intl Soc for Oriental Research; Isr Oriental Soc; Ihud Assn for J-Arab Rappro-

bldgs. F: Inst of Civil Engr; Inst of Structural Engr; hon treas, chmn house comm, Leo Beack B'nai B'rith, London Lodge, mem council, 1967-69; mem: Inst of Civil Engrs, Fr; Assn of Cons Engr. Contbr to tech press. Hobbies: painting, sculpture. Home and office: 42 Ferncroft Ave, London, NW 3, Eng.

PICKEL, Carol, US, industrialist; b. Atu, Rum, Mar 9, 1909; s. Eugene and Rozalia (Salamon); in US since 1941; m. Rosa Biegeleisen, Mar 8, 1932; c: Renee, Anne Patt. Pres, Fancyshape Diamond Corp, since 1952. Prin contribs: pioneer of diamond ind in Isr; established 1st diamond polishing factory, Isr, 1937. Mem: bd dirs, JNF; Diamond Mfrs Assn, 1939-41; natl exec, ZOA, pres, Manhattan region, 1958-61; financial chmn, 1960-69; gen council, World Zionist Org; B'nai B'rith, Jordan Manhattan Lodge 15; clubs: Diamond Dealers, secy, 1952-54, mem, bd dirs; Edgwood Country, Riverdale, NJ; Vanderbilt Athletic; NYC. Hobbies: tennis, golf, ice-skating. Home: 650 Park Ave, New York, NY. Office: 31 W 47 St, New York, NY.

PICKHOLTZ, Isidore, US, rabbi; b. NYC, Oct 17, 1918; s. Berisch and Gussie (Pickholtz); ordained rabbi, Mesitta Torah Vodaath, 1942; BA, CCNY, 1942; att Boston U, 1960-61; m. Eleanor Schaffer, Oct 11, 1942; c: Alan, Paul, Arnold, Judah, Jeffrey. Rabbi: Sinai Syn, Cleveland, O; chaplain: Mass Correctional Instn; US Penitentiary, Lewisburg, Pa. Mem: RabCA; Cleveland Rabb Council, Egud Harabonim. Home: 3294 Beechwood Ave, Cleveland Heights, O. Study: Berkeley and Desota Aves, Cleveland Heights, O.

PICKHOLZ, Morris, US, rabbi; b. Pol, Dec 4, 1919; s. Berisch and Golde (Pickholz); in US since 1924; ordained rabbi, Mesifta Torah Vodaath, Bklyn, 1944; BS, Columbia U, 1950; M Educ, Temple U, 1954; m. Esther Tendler, Feb 2, 1947; c: Rochelle, Cheryl, Gary. Rabbi: Cong B'nai Jeshurun Ahavas Chesed, since 1957; Wash Highland Cong, Wash, DC, 1947-50; Cong B'nai Jeshurun, Phila, 1950-57. Pres, Bd of Rabbis of Gtr Phila, 1962-64; mem: RabCA; RA; Acad Rel and Mental Health. Contbr to Jewish Parents Mag. Home: 1401 E Cardeza St, Philadelphia, Pa. Study: Stenton Ave and Dorset St, Philadelphia, Pa.

PIEKARCZYK, Alexander, Isr, architect; b. Konin, Pol, May 26, 1909; s. Meir and Celina (Meilzynski); in Isr since 1948; MSc, Warsaw U, Pol, 1930; MArch, Tech U, Warsaw, 1936; m. Emmi Hamburger Feb 3, 1948; c: Michael. Dir, architectural research and standardization dept, Min of Housing, since 1963; pvt practice, architecture, Warsaw, 1936-39; U off, i/c J DP U students, US Zone, Ger, JDC, 1946-48; independent architect, PM's off, 1948-53; chief architect, Min of Housing, 1955-63. Lt, Pol Army, 1932-39; prisoner of war, Ger, 1939-45. Prin contribs: introduction of modular coordination in bldg in Isr; standardization of bldg elements; design of the Monument for the Warsaw Ghetto Revolt, erected in Martef haShoah, Mt Zion, Jerusalem. Pres: J Students Assn, Tech U, Warsaw, 1930-32; Assn of J Architects and Engrs, US Zone, Ger, 1946-48; mem: Intl Modular Group, Paris; Assn of Engrs and Architects, Isr. Author: Principles of Designing Standard Building Elements, vol I, 1963, vol II, 1967; Coordination of Units of Measures in the Bible, 1968. Recipient: Fighter against Nazis, Isr Min of Defense, 1967. Hobbies: painting, sculpture, gardening, photography. Home: 18 Olei Hagardom St, Tel Aviv, Isr. Office: Hakirya, 15 Dalet St, Tel Aviv, Isr.

PIERCE, Sydney D, Can, diplomat; b. Montreal, Que, Mar 30, 1901; s. Asher and Ella (Vineberg); BA, 1922, BCL, 1925, LLD, all McGill U; m. Jean Crombie, Dec 2, 1927; c: Deborah, Margaret, David, Judith. Chmn, Can Manpower and Immigration Council, since 1969; mem, Can Olympic Team, Paris, 1924; reporter, Montreal Gazette, 1925-26; lectr, Dalhousie U, Halifax, NS, 1926; reporter, AP, NYC, 1927; pvt interests, 1928-39; Can exec off, combined produc and resources bd, Dept of Munitions and Supply, Wash, DC, 1940-44; Jt War Produc Comm, 1943-44, dir gen, 1944; spec asst to Undersecy of State for External Affairs, Ottawa, 1944; Can Ambass to Mex, 1947-49; spec duty with Eur Recovery Prog, Paris, 1948-49; asst dep min, Dept of Trade and Commerce, Ottawa, 1949-50; min, dir, Wash, DC off, Dept of Defense, Produc, 1951-53; Ambass to Brazil, 1953-55; dep High Commn, London, 1955-58; Ambass to Belgium, Luxembourg and the Eur Econ Comtys, 1958-65; chief negotiator for Can, Kennedy Round, Geneva, 1966-67. Address: 174 Rufferin Rd, Ottawa, Can.

PIERS, Gerhart, US, psychiatrist; b. Vienna, Aus, Sep 30, 1908;

s. Hermann and Ernestine (Adler) Pisk; in US since 1939; MD, U Vienna, 1933; m. Maria Weigl, 1938; c: Peggy, Matthew. Dir, Chgo Inst for Psychan, since 1956, research asso, 1942-47, mem fac, since 1947; staff mem, Elgin State Hosp, 1940-42; acting dir, Chgo Comty Clinic, 1943; F, Amer Psychiatric Assn; mem: Amer Psychan Assn. Co-author: Shame and Guilt, 1953; contbr to Ger and Amer psychiatric jours. Home: 5811 S Dorchester Ave, Chicago, Ill. Office: 180 N Michigan Ave, Chicago, Ill.

PIKOVSKI, Miriam, Isr, biologist; b. Odessa, Russ, 1904; d. Abraham and Rachel (Baranik); in Isr since 1926; PhD, Novorossiski U, Russ, 1926; m. 1924. Clinical sr lectr, Heb-U-Hadassah Med Sch, Jerusalem, since 1959, research f, since 1952. Mem: Amer Assn for Cancer Research; Isr Immunological Soc. Contbr to sci jours: Amer; Isr; Eng. Home: 7 Abyssinian St, Jerusalem, Isr. Office: Heb U-Hadassah Med Sch, Jerusalem, Isr.

PILCH, Judah, US, educator; b. Vachnovka, Russ, Sep 8, 1902; s. Joseph and Bat-Sheba (Milstein); in US since 1923; BS, Lewis Inst, Chgo, 1932; MA, Columbia U, 1946; PhD, Dropsie Coll, Phila, Pa, 1952; m. Bernice Shapery, 1933; c: Yoseph, Ben-Zion. Dean, grad div, J Tchrs Sem, and Peoples' U, since 1968, prof educ since 1965; visiting lectr, educ, Dropsie Coll, since 1957; exec dir, J Educ Assn, Rochester, NY, 1939-45; dir, Bx Council for J Educ, 1945-47; exec dir, J Educ Assn of Essex Co, Newark, NJ, 1947-49; exec dir, Amer Assn for J Educ, 1949-61; lectr: grad sch, Yeshiva U, 1956-61; NYU, 1960-64; summer in service sems, Isr, 1959. Pres: Natl Conf of J Communal Service, 1954-55; Natl Council for J Educ, 1948-50; vice-pres: Natl Conf for J Soc Service, since 1952; Rel Educ Assn of Amer, since 1953; chmn: exec comm, Rel Educ Assn of Amer, 1958; Histadrut Ivrit of Amer, 1934-48; Natl Heb Youth Comm, 1945-48; mem: J Hist Soc; Amer Sociol Soc; Amer Acad of Rel and Mh; Soc for Sci Study of Rel. Author: Mishakim L'Votei Seifer, 1932; Hayei Hayehudim Bizmaneinu, 1935; Hakolelim Hayehudim B'America, 1938; Teaching Contemporary Jewish Life, 1944; The Heder Metukaan, 1880-1914; pub, 1949; Readings in Jewish Educational Philosophy, 1960; Basic Jewish Concepts, 1962; Fate and Faith-The Contemporary Jewish Scene, 1963; monographs: Sineat Israel B'America, 1943; Jewish Life in our Times, 1943; Changing Patterns in Jewish Education, 1959; editor: Jewish Education Register and Directory,1951; 1954, vol III, 1959; Jewish Catastrophe in Europe, 1968; Philip Low-His Life and Work, 1968; A History of Jewish Education in USA, 1968; mem, ed bd: The Reconstructionist; J Educ. Recipient: Dropsie Coll Alumni Citation, 1958; award, Book Council America, 1969. Home: 25 Earle Pl, New Rochelle, NY.

PILCHIK, Ely E, US, rabbi, author; b. Baranowicze, Pol, June 12, 1913; s. Abraham and Rebecca (Lipovitch); in US since 1920; BA, U Cincinnati, 1935; ordained rabbi, MHL, HUC, 1939; m. Ruth Schuchat, Nov 20, 1941; c: Susan, Judith. Rabbi, Cong B'nai Jeshurun, since 1947; found, dir, Hillel, U of Md, 1939-40; asst rabbi HarSinai Temple, Baltimore, 1940-41; rabbi, Temple Isr, Tulsa, 1941-47. Chaplain, USN, 1944-46. Pres: Syn Council, 1949-51; bd of rabbis, 1951-52, both Essex Co; JBCA 1954-58; Assn of Reform Rabbis of NY, 1958-59; exec bd CCAR, 1951-53, chmn, comm on Isr; exec comm NY Bd of Rabbis; mem, NJ State Scholarship Commn. Author: Hillel, 1951; Maimonides Creed, 1952; Duties of the Heart, 1953; From the Beginning, 1956; Jeshurun Sermons, 1957; Judaism Outside the Holy Land. 1964; Jeshurun Essays, 1967; The Comassion Cantata, 1968; plays: Strength, 1964; The Greatest Gift, 1966; Toby, 1968; contbr to Anglo-J Publs. Home: 320 Tillou Rd, S Orange, NJ. Study: 1025 S Orange Ave, Short Hills, NJ.

PILOT, Isadore, US, physician, educator; b. Chgo, Ill, Oct 15, 1895; s. Israel and Ida (Guss); BS, U Chgo, 1918; MD, U of Ill, 1917; m. Anna Glick, July 2, 1923; asso prof, med, U of Ill, since 1929. Lt, US Army, MC, WW I, lt Col, WW II. Mem: Alpha Omega Alpha; Sigma Xi; club, Green Acres Country. Contbr to med jours. Home: 300 N State St, Chicago, Ill. Office: 185 N Wabush Ave, Chicago, Ill.

PILPEL, Robert, US, organization exec; b. NYC, Mar 27, 1905; s. Emanuel and Cecile (Meyer); BA, Harvard Coll, 1926; LLB, NY Law Sch, 1931; m. Harriet Fleischl, June 15, 1933; c: Judith, Robert. Gen con, div on aging, Fed of Prot Wfr Agcys, since 1968; gen counsel, JDC, 1939-52; secy, Amer J Jt Agric Corp, 1945-52; vice-pres, Robert Joseph & Co, real estate brokers, 1953-63; exec asst, Hudson Guild Neighborhood House, 1963-68. Mem, bd of trustees, Educ Alliance Inc, since 1949; bd of dirs, Gen Bur for the J Aged Inc, since 1953; bd of govs, Ethical Culture Schs, 1933-44. Home: 70 E 96 St, New York, NY. Office: 436 W 27 St, New York, NY.

PIMONTEL, Abraham, US, rabbi; b. Amsterdam, Netherlands, July 6, 1908; s. Isaac and Lea (Dugue); BA, Manchester U, Eng, 1936, MA, 1937; m. Gertrude Devons, Aug 13, 1933; c: Helen, Edith. Dir, B'nai B'rith Hillel Found, U of Mo; min, Cong of Span and Port J, Manchester, Eng, 1930-40; asso rabbi, Span and Port Syn, Montreal, Can, 1946-48. Chaplain, Brit Army, 1941-46. Home: 1701 University Ave, Columbia, Mo. Study: 1107 University Ave, Columbia, Mo.

PINANSKI, Viola R, US, civic worker; b. Boston, Mass, June 24, 1898; d. Julius and Fannie (Berg) Rottenberg; BA, Wellesley Coll, 1917, MA, 1918; att Harvard Sch of Educ, 1936-37; hon DHum, Suffolk U, 1958; m. Abraham E Pinaski, Aug 10, 1920, (decd); c: Jean Dietz, Joan Morse, Jane, June Schiff. Natl chmn, council on auxiliaries, Amer Hosp Assn, 1952; chmn, Brookline Sch Comm, since 1960; pres, Jewish Women's Health Assn, 1961-62; vice-pres, United Comty Services, 1948-54; hon fellow, Amer Coll Hosp Admnstrs, since 1960; delegate: from Amer Hosp Assn to Internal Fed of Hosps, 1957; Isr, 1962; Switz, 1968; Republican Natl Convention, 1952, 1956, 1960; WHO, 1957; trustee: Peter Bent Brighman Hosp, since 1949; New Eng, Med Cen, since 1964; Beth Israel Hosp, 1942-62, hon, since 1962, hon vice-pres, since 1948; Combined J Philanthropies, since 1961; dir: Blood Research Org, 1967; Mass Comm for Prevention of Blindness, 1960; Boston Children's Service Assn, since 1926; mem: council, Natl Inst for Neur Diseases and Blindness, since1956; adv comm, Brookline Health Dept and Mass Dept of Public Health, since 1952; Gov's Commn to study Educ Facilities of Mass, 1962; natl bd, Women's Med Coll of Pa; Amer Pub Health Assn; exec comm, Mass Mental Health Assn; Royal Soc Health; Natl League Nurisng Educ. Contbr of articles to profsl jours. Recipient: Distinguished Comty Service Award, Rotary Club, 1959. Home: 283 Buckminster Rd, Brookline, Mass.

PINCHAS, Isaac Lev, Isr, rabbi attorney; b. Russ, Dec 12, 1893; s. Abram and Chaja (Kreshes); in Isr since 1920; att rabb colls, Russ, 1908-15; m. Rosa Kahn, 1914; c: Shraga. Agent: Omega, Swiza and Tissot, since 1927; rabbi, Gt Syn, Tel Aviv, 1923; fmr: judge, Tel Aviv district court; chmn, co-found, Tel Nordau; rabb lawyer, council, chief rabbi, expert on Heb law during Mandate period. Co-found, Yeshiva Tel Aviv; orphan house, Tel Aviv; fmr pres, Gt Syn, Tel Aviv; Author: Pshuto shel Mikra; contbr to publs. Home: Karl Netter 5, Tel Aviv, Isr. Office: Ben Zion Blvd, 15, Tel Aviv, Isr.

PINCHAS, Shraga, Isr, research chemist; b. Tel Aviv, June, 9 1922; s. Itshac and Zilla (Poliakevitch) Leib; att Herron Yeshiva, Jerusalem, 1939-40; MSc, PhD, Heb U, Jerusalem, 1945; m. Rachel Auerbach, June 12, 1947; c: Avraham, Tirza. Sr sci, lab for applied spectroscopy, Weizmann Inst, since 1957, research chem, 1945-57. Lt, sci corps, IDF, 1948-49. Mem: Isr Chem Soc; Chem Soc of Gt Brit. Contbr to sci jours. Spec interest: Talmudic studies. Home: 4 Peretz Hayot St, Tel Aviv, Isr. Office: Weizmann Inst, Rehovot, Isr.

PINCHASIK, Rivka Kwiatkowski, Isr, author; b. Lodz, Pol, Nov 20, 1920; d. Chil and Aliza Mayer; att Lodz U, 1947-48; m. Moshe Pinchasik, Nov 9, 1947; c: Gershon. Author: Fun Lager in Lager, 1961; Hand, 1956; beYadaim Neemanot, 1964; contbr of numerous articles in Heb and Yiddish to children's and profsl jours. Youth reporter, Maty Pozeglasd; journalist, Votum; author, Impreso En La Argentina, since 1950. Mem: Writers Union, since 1949; Yiddish Writers Union; cultural comm: Org of fmr Nazi Prisoners; Moetzat Hapoalot. Hobbies: gardening, reading. Home: 22 Hermon St, Kiryat Bialik, Isr.

PINCK, Bernard D, US, city official physician, educator; b. Passaic, NJ, Jan 21, 1916; s. Joseph and Miriam (Baker) BA, Johns Hopkins U, 1937, MD, 1941; m. Gladys Pasternack, Dec 16, 1950; c: Lawrence, Jonathon, Elizabeth. Mayor, Passaic, NJ; asso prof, urol dept, NYU, Coll of Med, since 1956, fmr instr and asst prof. US Army, 1944-46. Mem: Passaic Bd of Educ; Amer Coll of Surgs; Amer Urol Assn; Phi Beta Kappa; Order of Odd Fellows. Contbr to med jours. Home and office: 203 Passaic Ave, Passaic, NJ.

PINCK, Louis Aaron, US, chemist; b. Liskovo, Russ, June 20, 1894; **s.** Rubin and Esther (Fisher); in US since 1903; BS,

NYU, 1918, ChemE, 1927; MS, George Wash U, 1923; m. Esther Surasky, July 3, 1921; c: Dan. Ret; chemist, US Dept of Agric, 1919-64. Mem: Amer Chem Soc; NY Acad Scis AAAS; Amer Soc Agronomy; Soil Sci Soc; Geochem Soc; Intl Soil Sci Soc. ZOA, past vice-pres; mem: campaigns JNF, UJA, Isr Bonds. Author, sci papers. Home: 5805 Bradley Blvd, Bethesda, Md.

PINCUS, Joel, Rhodesia, legislator, attorney; b. Ladybrand, Orange Free State, Apr 18,1907; s. Aaron and Esther (Daleski); in Rhodesia since 1950; cert, U Witwatersrand, Johannesburg, S Afr; m. Lily Couzin, Dec 23, 1937; c: Jonathan, Gideon, Esther. MP, Rhodesia; atty: High Court, Rhodesia, since 1954; Joel Pincus, Konson and Partners; Supr Court, S Afr, 1929. Fmr: chmn: New Zionist Org of S Afr; Revisionist Party; mem of council, S Afr Zionist Org; pres, Assn of Attys, Bulawayo. Home: 5 Bentley Place, Selborne Ave, Bulaway, Rhodesia. Office: York House, 8th Ave, Bulawayo, Rhodesia.

PINCUS, Louis Abraham, Isr, attorney, public official; b. S Afr, May 21, 1912; s. Aaron and Esther (Daleski); in Isr since 1948; BA, Witwatersrand U, LLB, 1934; m. Cynthia Rabkin, Dec 13, 1945; c: David, Alon. Chmn exec, JA, and head, aliyah and absorption dept, fmr treas; lawyer, Johannesburg, 1934-48; fmr mem, law frm, Herman, Pincus, Schwartz and Peled, Tel Aviv; secy-gen and legal adv, Min of Transp, Isr, 1948-49; mgn dir, El Al, 1949-56. Chmn bd govs, Tel Aviv U; mem: exec, Tnuat haAvoda haTzionit; cen comm, Mifleget haAvoda haYisraelit; chmn: Profsl Workers Org, Mapai; S Afr Socialist Party, 1939-48; vice-chmn, Afr Zionist Fed, 1940-48; co-found, Habonim, S Afr; mem, J Bd of Deps, S Afr, 1940-48. Home: 18 Derech Haganim, Kfar Shmaryahu, Isr.

PINCUS, Louis Arye, Isr, lawyer; b. S Afr, May 21, 1912; s. Aaron and Esther (Daleski); in Isr since 1948; BA, LLB, Witwatersrand U, S Afr, 1934; m. Chassia Rabkin, Dec 13, 1945; c: David, Alon. Chmn, JA Exec, since 1966, mem exec, and treas, 1961-65; mgn dir, El Al Isr Airlines, 1949-57; pvt law practice, 1957-65. Chmn, bd govs, Tel Aviv U; mem, cen comm, Histadrut; fmr: chmn: Zionist Socialist Party, S Afr; S Afr Zionist Fed; mem, exec, J Bd Deps. Home: 18 Derech Ganim, Kfar Shmaryahu, Isr.

PINCZOWER, Felix Daniel, Isr, journalist, bookseller; G. Berlin, Ger, May 29, 1901; s. Louis and Judith (Freimann); in Isr since 1939; att HS, Berlin,Ger; m. Hilda Kamerling, Jan 31 1935; c: Shoshanah Langerman. Owner, mgr, F Pinczower, Book-shop, Tel Aviv, since 1939; fmr: sport ed, Israelitische Familienblatt, Hamburg; sport journalist. Author: Der Jüdische Läufer, 1937; Juden in Deutschen Sport, 1968; co-ed: Beck-mann Sport Lexikon, 1932; Philo-Lexikon, 1935; contbr to Isr, fgn sport jours. Hobby, rare books. Home and office: 83 Sokolow St, Tel Aviv, Isr.

PINERMAN, Eli H, US, organization and business exec; b. Baltimore, Md, Feb 6, 1907; s. Louis and Fannie (Goodman); LLB, U of Md, 1927; m. Claire Rosner, Mar 7, 1934. Exec dir, Baltimore Heb Cong, since 1958; fmr vice-pres, The Hecht Co, with co, 1922-28; partner, Harris Dept Store, 1951-58. Vice-pres, J Big Brother League, 1940-50; bd mem, Baltimore Heb Cong, 1951-54, 1955-57; mem: Amer Cemetery Assn; Natl Assn of Temple Admnrs; club, Suburban, Baltimore. Hobbies: chess, philately, collecting Amer antiques. Home: 3506 Seven Mile Lane, Baltimore, Md. Office: 7401 Park Heights Ave, Baltimore, Md.

PINES, Herman, US chemist, educator; b. Lodz, Pol, Jan 17, 1902; s. Isaac and Eugenia (Greenfield); in US since 1928; ChemE, Inst de Chimie, Lyon, Fr, 1927; PhD, U Chgo, 1935; m. Dorothy Mlotek, Aug 13, 1927; c: Judith Levin. Vladimir Ipatieff research prof, dir Ipatieff high pressure and catalytic lab, Northwestern U, Ill, since 1953, fac, mem since 1941; research coord, Universal Oil Products Co, Riverside, Ill, 1945-53; research chem, 1930-45; visiting prof: U São Paulo, Brazil, 1963; U Central, Venezuela, 1968. Numerous patents in petroleum chem. Chmn, Gordon Conf on Catalysis, 1960; mem: Amer Chem Soc; AAUP; Sigma Xi; Phi Lambda Upsilon. Co-ed: Advances in Catalysis, since 1962; contbr numerous sci papers. Recipient: awards: Fritzsche, 1956; Petroleum Research Fund, 1957; Midwest, 1963. Home: 827 Monticello Pl, Evanston, Ill. Office: Northwestern U, Evanston, Ill.

both 1968-69. Composer: 2 syms; 3 string quartets; Antigone, for soprano and strings; 3 flute sonatas; instrumental and choral chamber works. Mem: Natl Assn Amer Composers and Conductors; Phila Composers Forum; Amer Music Cen; Amer Musicological Soc; Phila Art Alliance; U Mus; Delta Omicron; Intl Musicological Soc; British Composers Guild; Bibliothèque Internationale de Musique Contemporaine. Author: Music of the Ancient Near East, 1954; Gifts of Jubal, 1954; co-author; Art and Practice of Modern Flute Technique 5 vols, contbr of articles on music. Recipient: Delta Omicron Intl Award, 1953; 1959; citations: Mannheim, Ger, 1961, Vercelli, It, 1962; Pres' Music Comm, Wash, DC. Hobbies: archeol, poetry. Home: Dragon Hill, Baird and Heath Rds, Merion Station, Pa. Office: Rutgers U, Camden, NJ.

POLIN, Milton Harold, US, rabbi; b. Chgo, Ill, Oct 7, 1930; s. Abraham and Dorothy (Blacher); MA, U Chgo, 1953; ordained rabbi, BHL, cum laude, Heb Theol Coll, 1954; m. Shainee Sachs, Aug 15, 1954; c: Kenneth, Dorothy, Rena. Gail. Rabbi: Tpheris Isr Chevra Kadisha Cong, since 1966; Mt Sinai Cong, Cheyenne, Wyo, 1954-56; Keneseth Isr Cong, Louisville, Ky, 1956-66. Exec comm, RabCA, secy, St Louis; mem, educ comm: HF Epstein Heb Acad; Torah Acad; Vaad Hoeir; St Louis Rabb Coll. Recipient: Dist Service award, Louisville, Jr C of C, 1964; Louisville Slugger, radio sta, WKLO; Kentucky Colonel. Spec interest: syn architecture. Home: 6958 Washington Ave, St Louis, Mo. Study: 6912 Delmar Blvd, St Louis, Mo.

POLITI, Maurice, Isr, author; b. Athens, Greece, Sep 21, 1925; s. Nissim and Ida (De Naar); in Isr since 1950; att U Athens, 1944-47; m. Betty Cutin, Nov 9, 1957; c: Ilana, Abigail, Yannay. Exec ed, L'Information d'Isr, Fr daily, 1957-65, and since 1968; journalist, Athens, 1945-50; mem, Kibbutz Affikim, 1950-56; accredited by Fgn Min, adv to: Pres, Cen Afr Rep, 1963; Min of Info, Dahomey, W Afr, 1965-68. Greek resistance, 1942-44. Author: Les Faubourgs d'Athènes; Les Evadés du Paradis; Maaynna, Play, 1955; contbr numerous essays, articles, to Heb, Fr, Greek press. Mem: Assn Isr Journalists; Assn Theater Critics in Isr. Hobbies: chess, bridge. Home: 25 Elat St, Holon, Isr. Office: 52 Harakevet St, Tel Aviv, Isr.

POLLACK, Benjamin, US, psychiatrist; b. Toronto, Can, July 18, 1904; s. Louis and Anna (Goldstein); in US since 1929; MD, U Toronto, 1929, LMCC, 1929; m. Helen, Janowski, 1936; c: Donald, Linda. Pvt practice, neuropsycht, since 1968; psycht, Mental Health Clinic Health Bur, since 1950; asst psycht, Strong Memorial Hosp, since 1942; asso, dept of psycht, Med and Dent Sch, since 1942, lectr, psycht, Med Sch, since 1940, both Rochester U; cons psycht, Rochester, Batavia, LeRoy, NY draft bds, since 1940; house surg and lectr in psych, Psychiatric Clinic, Barnett Memorial Hosp, Paterson, NJ, 1929-30; asst phys, Willard State Hosp, 1931, sr asst phys, 1933-36; civilian psycht: Army Induction Sta, 1942-45; VA Genesee Hosp and Gen Hosp, 1944-45; psycht: ARC Vets Clinic, 1945-48; Attica State Prison, 1947-50; asst dir, admn, Rochester State Hosp, 1951-68, on staff since 1933. Life f, Amer Psychiatric Assn; charter f, Amer Coll of Neuropschopharm; delg; Amer Psychiatric Assn, NY State Assembly of Dist Brs, councilor, past pres, Cen NY Psychiatric Soc; pres, Finger Lakes Neuropsychiatric Soc, 1952-53; chmn, speaker's bur, mem, exec, and health planning comms, neighborhood project comms of Rochester and Monroe Co Mh Assns, since 1952; mem: AMA; NY State and Monroe Co Med Socs; Natl Comm for Mental Hygiene; Monroe Co Mental Hygiene Soc; Rochester Path Soc; mem, bd dirs, med care comm and personnel comm, J Home for the Aged. Broadcaster: weekly radio progs, from State Hosp; co-author, med movie on prefrontal lobotomies; contbr to med jours. Home and office: 2800 Elmwood Ave, Rochester, NY.

POLLACK, Charles Constantine, US, business exec; b. Que,, Can, Dec 25, 1919; s. Maurice and Rebecca (Tarantour); in US since 1947; BSE, U of Pa, 1940; m. Constance Coane, June 16, 1940; c: Valerie, Susan. Gen mgr: Samuel Coane Inc; Coane Knitting Mills Inc, since 1947; Maurice Pollack Ltd 1940-43. Lt, Can Navy, 1943-45. Hon pres, Reform Cong Keneseth Isr, pres, 1964-68, lay asst rabbi; pres: Maurice Pollack Found: Home and Sch Assn, Abington Friends Sch, 1961-62; mem: bd, Camp Council, 1962-64; Beta Sigma Rho Frat; Pi Gamma Mu; club; Rydal Country. Recipient: Lt. Gov's medal, Que Province, 1936; Legion of Honor, Chapel Four Chaplains, 1968; Voluntary Service medal; Victory medal. Spec interests: rel educ for retarded children, golf.

Home: Elkins Park House, Elkins Park, Pa. Office: 248 N 11 St, Philadelphia, Pa.

POLLACK, Ervin H, US, educator; b. St Louis, Mo, Apr 19, 1913; s. Jacob and Tillie (Patratzik); att: St Louis U, 1932-35; Columbia U, 1939-41; LLB, Wash U, St Louis, 1939, JD, 1968; m. Lydia Weiss, June 12, 1940; c: Jay, Joan. Prof law, dir, research services, O State U Coll of Law, since 1947; cons, US State Dept, since 1966; secy, OPA, 1942-47; cons: Off Econ Stabilization, 1951; Libr of Cong, 1959-64, F, O State Bar Assn Found: mem: adv bd: B'nai B'rith Hillel, O State U, since 1957; rel affairs, O State U, 1962-64; bd trustees, O Legal Cen Inst, since 1961; Mo, O State, Amer Bar Assns; Amer Arbitration Assn; Amer Law Libr Assn, pres, 1958-59; O Assn of Law Librs, pres, 1949-51; Amer Soc Political and Legal Phil. Author: Ohio Court Rules Annotated, 1949; Legal Research and Materials, 1950; Ohio Unreported Judicial Decisions Prior to 1823, pub, 1952; Brandeis Reader, 1956; Fundamentals of Legal Research, 1956, 1962, 1968; contbr to profsl jours. Recipient: Order of the Coif, hon, 1949. Hobby: travel. Home: 1000 Urlin Ave, Columbus, O. Office: O State U, Coll of Law, Columbus, O.

POLLACK, Herbert, US, physician, educator; b. NYC, June 29, 1905; s. Isaac and Mary (Luntz); BA, Wash and Lee U, 1925; MD, Cornell U, 1929; PhD, U Minn, 1933; m. Ruth Hexter Brill, Nov 14, 1946; c: Jane, Constance. Prof, clinical med, George Wash U; cons: dir, defense Research and Engr; Inst for Defense Analysis; Ford Found; instr, Cornell U Med Coll, 1934-40; fmr, asso prof, clinical med, NYU; phys i/c, metabolic clinic, Sinai Hosp, 1937-51, chief, metabolic div 1946-51; lectr, med, Columbia U, 1946-54; cons to Secy of War, 1946; Mayor NYC, 1950-51; NY State Nutrition Comm, 1949-52; Surg Gen, 1951-54. Col, US Army, 1942-46. F: NY Acad Med; Amer Coll Phys; AMA; Amer Public Health Assn. Chmn, NYC Food and Nutrition Comm, 1948-49; Clinical Soc for Diabetes, 1933, vice-chmn, 1951-52, secy, 1950; spec comm on nutrition, NY Med Soc, 1948-53; councilor, Amer Diabetic Assn, 1951-54; pres, NY Diabetic Assn, 1953-54 vice-pres, Health Council, Gtr NY, 1951; adv comm: NYC Off Civilian Defense, 1950-53; Health Dept, NY State, 1951; mem, food and nutrition bd, Natl Research Council, 1950-54, comm on Quartermasters Affairs, 1947-53; sci adv, Quartermaster Food and Container Inst, 1947-53; mem: Amer Soc for Clinical Inves; Amer Inst of Nutrition; Amer Physiological Soc; Soc for Experimental Biol and Med; Sigma Phi; Phi Beta Kappa; AAAS. Asso ed: Jour of Metabolism, since 1951; mem, ed bd, Jour of Diabetes, since 1953. Home: Westview Farm, Leeburg, Va.

POLLACK, Victor S, US, business exec; b. Cleveland, O, July 13, 1912; s. Jacob and Edith (Lewis); BA, W Reserve U, 1933; LLB, 1935; m. Ruetta Bialosky, Aug 29, 1937; c: Abigail, David. Pres, Atlantic Products Corp, since 1955, vice-pres, gen mgr, 1946-55; dir, First Trenton Natl Bank, since 1956; atty, Horwitz, Kiefer and Harmel, Cleveland, 1935-40; pres, Pocono Rubber Co, Trenton, 1939-40; gen mgr, Trenton div, Natl Automotive Fibres, Detroit, 1940-43. Lt, US Navy, 1943-46. Mem, bd of dirs: Mercer Hosp, since 1954; Fed of Trenton, since 1947; trustee, Har Sinai Heb Cong, since 1949; mem: Phi Beta Kappa; Delta Sigma Rho; Order of Coif; Phi Sigma Delta; club, Trenton Rotary, dir, 1956-59. Recipient: Commendation Ribbon, US Navy, 1944. Home: River Rd, Yardley, Pa. Office: Atlantic Products Corp, Trenton, NJ.

POLLAK, Henry, US, business exec; b. NYC, Oct 22, 1922; s. Maurice and Lucille (Rosenberg); att Yale U, 1939-42; m. Jean de Beer, Aug 25, 1948; c: Richard, Thomas, William, John, Steven. Pres, Henry Pollak Inc, since 1952; vice-pres, Pollak Ind Corp, since 1952. USAF, 1942-45. Vice-pres, White Plains Hosp, since 1965, bd govs, since 1960; bd dirs: Color Assn of Amer, since 1965; White Plains Comty Chest, hintl since 1952; exec comm, AJComm, Westchester, mem, intl comm; clubs: Yale, NY; Sunningdale Country. Hobby: numismatics. Home: 3 Leith Pl, White Plains, NY. Office: 1040 Ave of Americas, New York, NY.

POLLAK, Louis H, US, attorney; b. NYC, Dec 7, 1922; s. Walter and Marion (Heilprin); AB, Harvard U, 1943; LLB Yale U, 1948; m. Katherine Weiss, July 25, 1952; c: Nancy, Elizabeth, Susan, Sarah, Deborah. Dean, Yale Law Sch, since 1965, prof, law, since 1961, fac mem since 1955; law clerk, US Supr Court, Justice Wiley Rutledge, 1948-49; atty: Paul Weiss, Rifkind, Wharton and Garrison, 1949-51; State Dept 1951-53; asst counsel, Amalgamated Clothing Workers, 1954-55. US Army, 1943-46. Bd dirs: NAACP, Legal Defense and

Educ Fund Inc, since 1960; New Haven Bd of Educ, 1962-68; mem: Bar Assn, City of NY; Conn Bar Assn. Ed: The Constitution and the Supreme Court: A Documentary History 1966; contbr to legal jours. Home: 24 Everit St, New Haven, Conn. Office: Yale Law Sch, New Haven, Conn.

POLLAK Theresa, US, artist, educator; b. Richmond, Va, Aug 13, 1899; d. Armin and Esther (Teiser); BS, Westhampton Coll, U Richmond, 1921. Prof, art, Va Commonwealth U, since 1935, fac mem, since 1928; advt artist: Metrop Engraving Co, 1919; Staples & Staples Advt Agcy, 1923-25; instr, art, Westhampton Coll, 1930-35. One-man exhbs: Delphic Studios, NYC, 1934; A A Anderson Gal, Richmond, 1936; Lynchburg Fed Art Gal, 1936; Va Mus Fine Arts, 1940; Westhampton Coll, 1940; Randolph-Macon Coll for Women, 1940; Farmville State Tchrs Coll, 1941; Mary Baldwin Coll, 1951; J Comty Cen, 1960; Wash and Lee U, 1960; group exhbs at mus, art gals and Us, since 1926; represented in perm collections: Va Mus Fine Arts; U Va; Collegiate Sch, Richmond; Va Commonwealth U; Mary Baldwin Coll; Norfolk Mus Art; Longwood Coll; Va Natl Bank, Norfolk; Fed Deposit Ins Corp, Richmond; pvt collections. Chmn, artists adv comm, Va Mus, 1943-44, 1945-46; pres, Va Art Alliance, 1941-45; vice-pres, Richmond Artists Assn, 1958-59; mem: Phi Beta Kappa; Art Students League, NY; Va Educ Assn; J Family Services; Assn for Preservation of Va Antiques; Friends of Richmond Public Libr; Alumnae Assn, Westhampton Coll; Va and Valentine Mus, Richmond. Recipient: Tiffany Found f award, 1932; Carnegie f award, 1933; first prize, painting, Studio Club, NY, 1926; awards: second, portraiture, Richmond Acad of Arts, 1931; first, painting, Va Mus of Fine Arts, 1939; artists', painting, Richmond Artists Assn, 1957, 1959, 1960; hon and purchase prize, Irene Leache Memorial Exhb, Norfolk Mus, 1960. Home: 3912 Stuart Ave, Richmond, Va. Office: Va Commonwealth U, 901 W Franklin St, Richmond, Va.

POLLECOFF, Israel, Wales, business exec; b. Holyhead, Wales, Aug 14, 1894; s. Philip and Amelia (Harris); att U Coll, Bangor; m. Bertha Jacobs, Apr 1965. Mgn dir, Pollecoffs Ltd since 1933. F, Inst of Dirs; pres, J Comty, Bangor area; mem, Bangor Chamber of Trade; clubs: Dirs, London; Bangor Golf, past pres. Hobbies: Heb U, Jerusalem, golf. Home: Swenlan, Bangor, Wales. Office: Pollecoffs Ltd, Bangor, Wales.

POLLER, H Leonard, Can, rabbi; b. Scranton, Pa, Nov 5, 1928; s. Herman and Bertha (Steckel); in Can since 1962; BS, U Scranton, 1950; att Heb Union Schs of Educ and Sacred Music, 1951-52; BHL, MHL, ordained rabbi, HUC-JIR, 1957; m. Priscilla Marks, Dec 29, 1957; c: Judith, Sharon, Elyse. Rabbi: Temple Beth Sholom, Montreal, since 1962; Temple B'nai Isr, E Liverpool, O, 1955-57; Temple Oheb Shalom, Baltimore, 1957-62. Home: 5777 Westluke Ave, Cote St Luc, Que, Can. Study: 6666 Terrebonne St, Montreal, Can.

POLLIACK, Aaron, Isr, physician; b. Cape Town, S Afr, Jan 12, 1939; s. Majrym and Ida (Kopelowitz); in Isr since 1962; MB, ChB, Med Sch, Cape Town; m. Lily Singer, Apr 3, 1963; c: Meira, Vered. Res, dept path, Hadassah-Heb U Hosp, since 1965; MO, IDF, 1963-65. Contbr to profsl publs, Recipient, Research prize, Isr Cancer Soc, 1969. Hobbies: music, theater, lit, hist. Home and office: 7 Habanai St, Jerusalem, Isr.

POLONSKY, Aron, (pen name **Apollo**), Isr, attorney, educator, editor; b. Ukraine, June, 1903; s. Yakov and Tova (Resnik); in Isr since 1922; LLB, LLM, first class hons, Leeds U, Eng, 1935; m. Pnina Yardeni, Mar 18, 1945; c: Yael, Tova. Atty; sr lectr, law, Tel Aviv U. Mem: council, Fac of Law; high court, Histadrut; cen comm, Isr Bar Assn; exec, Magen David Adom; council, Isr Opera. Author, book on specific performance, 1938; ed, haPraklit law rev; contbr to legal jours. Home: 4 Warburg St, Tel Aviv, Isr. Office: 28 Yavneh St, Tel Aviv, Isr.

POLONSKY, Arthur, US, artist, teacher; b. Lynn, Mass, June 6, 1925; s. Benjamin and Celia (Hurwitz); att Boston Heb Tchrs Coll; grad, Boston Mus Sch of Fine Arts, 1948; m. Lois Tarlow, 1953; three c. Asso prof, art, Boston U, since 1965; instr in painting, Boston Mus Sch, 1950-60; asst prof, fine arts, Brandeis U, 1955-65; lectr: Harvard U; Wheaton Coll; St Bonaventure U. One-man exhbs: Boris Mirsky Gal, Boston 1951, 1956, 1964, 1966; Brandeis U, 1959; Galleria di Bellardo, Provincetown, Mass, 1961; Durlacher Bros Gal, NY, 1965;

Mickelson Gal, Wash, DC, 1966; in exhbs: Metrop Mus, NY; Inst Contemporary Art, Boston; Carnegie Intl Exposition, Pittsburgh; Boston Mus Fine Arts; Palace of Legion of Honor, Cal; Chateau des Rohans, Strasbourg, Fr; salon des Jeunes Peintres, Paris; Stedelijk Mus, Amsterdam; repr in exhbs circulated in Amer by Smithsonian Inst, in Eur and Asia by US Info Agcy; paintings in perm collections: Fogg Mus; Harvard U; SF Mus Fine Arts; Brandeis U; Stedelijk Mus, Amersterdam; Addison Gal Amer Art, Andover, Mass; U of NH; illustrations include: Lincoln, A Big Man, 1958; children's book about the Bible; contbr to jours. Recipient: Eur traveling scholarship, Boston Mus Sch, 1948-50; Louis Comfort Tiffany grant, 1951-52; Ist prize for drawing and graphics, Boston Arts Festival, 1954. Spec interests: electronics, Fr Lit, phil. Home: 364 Cabot St, Newtonville, Mass. Office: Boston U, Boston, Mass.

POLSKY, Carl Arthur, US, attorney, educator; b. NYC, Aug 15, 1930; s. Irving and Augusta (Reckendorf); BS, U of Pa, 1952; JD, Temple U 1958; LLM, NYU, Sch of Law, 1963; m. Germaine Bender, Dec 20, 1959; c: Judith, Steven, Karen. Lectr, Wharton Sch, U of Pa, Phila, since 1956; partner Diamond, Polsky & Bauer, since 1960; acctnt, A L Diamond & Co, 1954-59; intl lectr, sponsored by AMR Intl. Cpl, US Army, 1952-54. Mem: Phila and Pa Bar Asssns; Amer Inst CPAs; Pa Inst CPAs; Amer Accounting Assn. Contbr to profsl jours. Home: 3025 David Dr, Roslyn, Pa. Office: 1530 W Savings Bank Bldg, Philadelphia, Pa.

POLSKY, Morris, US, physician; b. Kiev, Russ, Dec 19, 1908; s. Aron and Gertrude (Rosenbloom); in US since 1911; MD, U Kan 1932; f, Columbia U, 1935-36; m. Zelda Glassman, June 12, 1938; c: Sandra, Brenda, Fred. Phys, pvt practice in dermat, since 1936; att dermat: Seton Hosp; Holy Cross Hosp; St David's Hosp; Brackenridge Hosp, all Austin, Tex, since 1946; res, Kan City Gen Hosp, 1932-35, att dermat, 1936-42, chief of dermat, 1939-42; att dermat: Menorah Hosp, St Mary's Children's Mercy Hosp, Alfred Benjamin Dispensary all Kan City, Mo, 1936-42; chief, dermat, Brackenridge, Hosp, 1953-54, 1963-64. Capt to maj, US Army MC, 1942-46. Dipl, Amer Bd of Dermat, 1939; pres: Austin Hill City lodge, B'nai B'rith, 1949, vice-pres, Tex State conf, 1953-54, dist chmn for adult educ, 1956-59, mem, natl comm for adult educ, 1959-60; ZOA, Austin dist, 1951; JCC, 1956; JWF, 1953, both Austin; mem: Amer Acad of Dermat; Soc for Inves Dermat; AMA; S Med Assn; Tex Med Assn; Travis Co Med Assn; ed: Travis Co Med jour, 1962-65. Contbr to med jours and textbooks. Recipient: cert of honor, Tex State Med Assn, 1956. Home: 6408 Mesa Dr, Austin, Tex. Office: 9 Medical Arts Sq, Austin, Tex.

POMERANCE, Alan Saul, US, dentist; b. Bklyn, NY, Dec 24, 1926; s. Benjamin and Anna (Goldstein); AB, Brown U, 1946; DDS, Columbia U, 1950; m. Iris Kellner, Apr 27, 1952; c: Carol, Ruth. Dent, since 1950; asso att dent, Montefiore Hosp; att dent, Edenwald Sch. Lt, USN, 1951-53. F, Intl Assn Dent Research; dir of educ, Dent Dept, Montefiore Hosp; club, Men's Temple Emanuel, mem, bd dirs. Contbr to jours. Spec interests: writing: plays, music, short stories; acting, tennis, golf. Home: 176 E 77 St, New York, NY Office: 65 E 55 St, New York, NY.

POMERANTZ, Abraham, Isr, academic secy; b. Lukow, Pol, Oct 1, 1926; s. Zvi and Frieda (Volland); att Mizrachi Tchr's Sem, Isr, 1942-47; MJ Hebrew U, Jerusalem, 1955; m. Sarah Rosenov; c: Moshe, Tova, Michal. Academic secy, Bar Ilan U, since 1960; tchr, 1947-48; repr, 1950-51; secy, haPoel haMizrachi factions, Knesset, 1952-55. Lt, IDF, 1948-50. Home: 27 Hayarden St, Ramat Gan, Isr, Office: Bar Ilan U, Ramat Gan, Isr.

POMERANTZ, Maurice, US, rabbi; b. Tel Aviv, Mar 21, 1934; s. George and Jennie (Zelonky); in US since 1937; BHL, Baltimore Heb Coll, 1953; BA, Johns Hopkins U, 1954; MHL, ordained rabbi, JTSA, 1959; m. Kay Kantor, 1958; c: Raquel, Alisa. Rabbi: Temple Etz Chaim, 1967-69; Beth Isr Comm, Cen, Mexico DF, 1959-61; Tifereth Isr Syn, 1961-67; prof, Heb, Cotner Coll Rel; Hillel Counselor, U Neb, both 1961-67; Secy: W States Rabb Assembly, 1969; Cen States Rabb Assembly, 1966-67; chmn, Mayor's Safety Commn; ed chmn, B'nai B'rith bd dirs, Lincoln JWF; fmr exec bd, Brit Ivrit Olamit, Mex; clubs: Kiwanis; Rotary. Home: 2500 81 St, SE, Mercer Island, Wash.

POMROCK, Zvi Abraham, Isr, attorney; b. Tel Aviv, Mar 31, 1931; s. Joseph, and Simcha (Chelouche); att Tel Aviv Sch of

chement; corresp mem, Akademie der Wissenschaften, Göttingen, 1967; fmr, mem, Hadar haCarmel Reprs Assembly, Haifa. Author: Der Oikonomikos des Neupythagoreers Bryson, 1928; Die Geschichte der Wissenschaften im Islam, 1931; Medicine and Science, The Legacy of Islam, 1969; Arabic Grammar for Schools, in Heb; co-author, Ps. Magriti, Das Zeil des Weisen, 1962; contbr to: Ency of Islam; Ency Judaica; Ency Hebraica; periodicals. Hobby: music. Home: 29 Jabotinsky Rd, Jerusalem, Isr. Office: Heb U, Jerusalem, Isr.

PLISKIN, Reuben Robert, US, physician; b. NYC, Aug 23, 1907; s. Abraham and Sonia (Slavin); BSc, Akron U, 1929; MA, O State U, Columbus, 1930, MD, 1934; m. Evelyn Capp, Oct 1, 1941; c: Robert, Marilyn, Michael, David. Phys and surg, since 1934; sr surg staff; Akron Gen Hosp, 1952-67; City Hosp, 1960-68; chief, surg, Children's Hosp, 1952-69. Lt col, US Army, MC, 1941-46. F, Amer Coll Surgs pres, Temple Isr; bd of trustees, JWF; chief, staff, Akron: Gen Hosp, 1959-60; bd trustees, Akron J Cen, 1960-62; mem: Amer Bd Surg; Phi Delta Epsilon. Recipient: Purple Heart. Home: 999 Merriman Rd, Akron, O. Office: 106 Main St, Akron, O.

PLOSCOWE, Morris, US, attorney; author; b. Russ, Jan 25, 1904; s. Harry and Anna (Berezinsk); in US since 1907; BA Harvard U, 1925, LLB, 1928; m. Zelma Friedman July 1, 1931; c: Deborah, Bernard. Pvt practice, since 1953; cons: Wickersham Comm, 1930-31; Columbia Crime Survey, 1931; Mass Crime Commn, 1933; dep commn; Dept of Inves, NYC, 1938-39; chief clerk, Court of Spec Sessions, 1939-45, city magistrate, NYC, 1945-53; cons, Commn on Organized Crime, 1950-52; dir, Amer Bar Assn-AMA jt comm on narcotics; 1957-58; commn, NYC Commn on Human Rights, 1962. Hon pres, Assn, Intl de Droit Pénal, Amer sect; mem: AJComm; Amer Bar Assn; Citizens Comm on Children; Amer Prison Assn. Author: Crime and the Criminal Law, 1939; Sex and the Law, 1951; The Truth About Divorce, 1955; Cases and Materials in Family Law, 1964. Home: 125 Riverside Dr, New York, NY. Office: 60 E 42 St, New York, NY.

PLOTKIN, Albert, US, rabbi; b. South Bend, Ind, Sep 9, 1920; s. Samuel and Sophie (Novak); BA, U Notre Dame, 1942; MHL, ordained rabbi, HUC, 1948, DHL, 1961; att U Wash, 1948-49; m. Sylvia Pincus, Aug 28, 1949; c: Janice, Debra. Rabbi, Temple Beth Isr, Phoenix, Ariz, since 1955; instr, Danforth Chapel, Ariz State U, since 1956; asst rabbi, Temple De-Hirsch, Seattle, Wash, 1948-49; rabbi, Temple Emanu-El Spokane, Wash, 1949-55. Lt col, Civic Air Patrol, 1954. Pres: rels conf, Ariz State U 1959; Public info, ARC, 1959; fmr pres, Pacific Assn of Reform Rabbis; educ chmn, Brandeis Zionist Dist of Ariz, since 1958; mem: speakers comm: Amer Cancer Soc, since 1959; Isr Bonds, since 1958; exec comm NCCJ, since 1955; bd, HUC-JIR; exec bd, CCAR; lectr, Shakespeare Festival of Phoenix, 1956; mem: ADL comm, B'nai B'rith; Phoenix Civic Opera Co; W Assn of Reform Rabbis; Natl Assn of Temple Educs; JCC; case comm, J Social Service; bd, Campfire Girls; bd, Boy Scouts; combined campaign, UAHC, all Phoenix; W Assn Temple Educs; Hillel Found, Ariz State U; Phoenix Rabb Council; Kivel Phoenix J Comty Nursing Home: Ariz Rabb Council. Recipient: man of year, C of C, Spokane, Wash, 1953. Hobbies: music, opera; dramatics. Home: 930 W Catalina, Phoenix, Ariz. Study: 3310 N 10 Ave, Ariz.

PLOTKIN, Gershon, Isr, theater dir; b. Dniepropetrovsk, Russ, Mar 12, 1917; s. Nachum and Batsheva (Faber); in Isr since 1924; att Technion workshop, Haifa; The New Sch for Social Research, NY, 1947-48; m. Glilia Katinke, Sep 18, 1946; c: Nimrod, Ben Yehouda. Dir, produc, Cameri Theater, since 1949; mem, bd dirs and mgnt, since 1950; maj producs: Ever Since Paradise; Call Me Siomka; Pygmalion Marius; Mary Stuart; Man for all Seasons; Master Builder; Enrico IV; many Isr original plays by: Alterman, M Shamir, Lea Goldberg, others. Capt, IDF, 1944-49. Home: 23 Mapu St, Tel Aviv, Isr. Office: 101 Dizengoff St, Tel Aviv, Isr.

PLOTKIN, Isaac, Isr, business exec; b. Wilno, Pol, Feb 23, 1923; s. Israel and Michal; BA, Amer U, Beirut, Leb. m: Miriam Arnsberg; c: Ron, Yael, Gidon. Owner and gen mgr, Vita Co, I Plotkin and Sons, Ltd. Lt, IDF Res. Mem: Consumer Council of Isr: Isr Mgmt Advt Assn. Home: Herzliya Pituah, Isr. Office: 11 Modiin, Ramat Gan, Isr.

PLOTNICK, Alan R, Can, educator; b. Phila Pa, April 10, 1926;

s. Walter and Rachel (Soffer); in Can since 1961; BA, Temple U, Phila, 1950; MA, U of Pa, Phila, 1951, PhD, 1960; m. Rosemary Tracy, Dec 28, 1956; c: Alison; Asst prof, political econ, U Alberta, Calgary, since 1961; instr, econ: Temple U, 1955-56; U Maine, 1956-59; asst prof, econ: U of RI, 1959-60; Drexel Inst Tech, 1960-61. US Army, 1944-46. Mem: Can Inst of Intl Affairs; Amer Econ Assn; Beta Gamma Sigma; Pi Gamma Mu. Contbr to periodicals. Hobby: music. Home: 2804 Conrad Dr, Calgary, Can. Office: U Alberta, Calgary, Can.

PNUELI, Amir, Isr, mathematician; b. Nahalal, Isr, Apr 22, 1941; s. Shmuel and Henia (Thau); BS, Technion, 1962; PhD, with distinction, Weizmann Inst, of Sci, 1967; m. Ariela Pienik, June 3, 1962; c: Shira. Research f, applied math dept Weizmann Inst of Sci, since 1967; instr, computer sci, Stanford U, Cal, 1967-68. Home: 109 Arlosoroff St, Holon, Isr. Office: Weizmann Inst of Sci, Rehovot, Isr.

PNUELI, David, Isr, mechanical engr, educator; b. Vilna, Pol, Jan 14, 1933; s. Shmuel and Henia (Thau) Yeshayahu; in Isr since 1935; BSc, Technion, Haifa, 1951; MSc, 1959; PhD, Case Inst Tech, Cleveland O, 1962; m. Olga Suez, 1954; c: Yachin, Lilach. Asso prof, mech engr, Technion, Haifa, since 1966. Lt, IDF Navy, 1950-53. Mem: Sigma Xi; AAAS; AAUP. Contbr to profsl jours. Home: 2 Rabenu Tam St, Haifa, Isr. Office: Technion, Haifa, Isr.

PODELL, Bertram L, US, legislator, attorney; b. Bklyn, NY, Dec 27, 1925; s. Hyman and Henrietta (Menaker); att St John's U, Bklyn; LLB Bklyn Law Sch, m. Bernice Posen, Feb 15, 1953 c: Stephen, Ellen, Gary. US Congressman, since 1968 NY State Assemblyman, 1954-68; atty, partner, Podell and Podell, 1955-69. USN, 1944-46. Dir, Flatbush Boys Club; adv bd, Yeshiva of Flatbush; bd trustees, E Midwood J Cen; bd dirs, ADL; mem: Young Men's Philanthropic League; JWV; UJA; Isr Bonds; Fed J Charities; club, Flatbush Dem, dir. Home: 153 Rugby Rd, Brooklyn, NY. Office: 1712 Longworth Bldg, Washington, DC.

PODHORETZ, Norman H, US, editor, writer; b. Bklyn, NY, Jan 16, 1930; s. Julius and Helen (Woliner); AB, Columbia U, 1950; BHL, JTSA, 1950; BA, Cambridge U, 1952, MA, 1957; m. Midge Rosenthal, Oct 21, 1956; c: Rachel, Naomi, Ruth, John. Ed, Commentary, since 1960, asso ed, 1956-58; ed in chief, Looking-Glass Library, 1958-60; ed, The Commentary Reader, 1966. US Army, 1953-55. Author: Doings and Undoings, 1964; Making It, 1968; contbr: Commentary; Partisan Review; New Yorker; Harper's. Home: 924 W End Ave, New York, NY. Office: 165 E 56 St, New York, NY.

PODIS, Eunice, US, concert pianist; b. Cleveland, O, Jan 14, 1922; d. Louis and Malvina (Kelisky); att W Reserve U 1938-41; m. Robert Weiskopf, Mar 8, 1942; c: Bernard, Wendy. Concert pianist, since 1941; concert tours throughout US and Eur, 1945-55; NY debut, Town Hall, 1947; numerous appearances with Cleveland Orch. Trustee, women's comm, Cleveland Orch; mem: Mu Phi Epsilon; Ohio Soc for Strings; clubs: hon mem: Fortnightly Musical; Lecture-Recital. Recipient: Young Artist award, Natl Fed of Music Clubs, 1945; artist in res, Cleveland Inst of Music, 1966. Home: 2653 Ramsay Rd Cleveland, Ohio.

PODOLSKY, Abraham, US, business exec; b. NYC, Sep 14, 1909; s. Nathan and Sarah (Cezar); m. Anne Rapaport, Oct 2, 1934; c: Sanford. Owner, mgr, Penobscot Indian Trading Post, since 1940; owner, Econ Furniture Outlet, since 1956; pres, Old Town Assos, since 1954; preliminary training instr, ships terms, Maritime Training Base, Bklyn, NY, 1945. Dir: YMCA, since 1945; Dent Clinic, since 1953 Temple Isr, since 1950; trustee and chmn, HS dist, since 1951; all Old Town, Me; mem: Katahdin area council, Boy Scouts; B'nai B'rith; ZOA; AJComm; Masons; Odd Fellows; Elks; Shriners; club, Old Town Rotary, pres, 1953-54. Home: 143 Middle St, Old Town, Me. Office: 88 N Main St, Old Town, Me.

PODVINEC, Srécko, Yugo, surgeon; b. Osijek, Croatia, Yugo, Nov 23, 1899; s. Lavoslav and Ruza (Eibenschütz); att Med Fac, Zagreb, 1918-21; MD, Med Fac, Vienna, 1925; m. 3rd, Ana Rajič, July 16, 1966; c: Radojica, Mihael. Prof em, Orl U Belgrad, since 1969, titulary prof, 1954-69; clinical asst, ORL, U Zagreb, 1927-48; Dozent, 1948-51, prof, 1951-54. Capt, MC, Army of Liberation, Yugo, 1943-44. Pres: Orl Sect, Med Assn, of Serbia, 1954-69; Fr Soc of Broncho-Oesophagology, 1964. Author: textbook of otorhinolaryngology, 1964, 1969; co-author, Surgery of the Maxilla, 1936; contbr to profsl jours. Recipient: State Prize, 7th July, Exec Comm of Serbia, 1964; Merit for the Nation, with Golden Star, Pres of Rep, 1969; Merit for the Nation, 3rd class; Medal for Bravery. Hobby: artistic photography. Home: 8 Smetanina, Belgrad, Yugo.

POHORYLES, Henry, Fr, business exec; b. Strasbourg, Dec 26, 1920; s. Marc and Ida (Ginsberg); licence ès lettres, Ecole Maimonide, Paris; att:Sorbonne, Paris; U Clermont-Ferrand; m. Gilberte Cornely; seven c. Asst to pres, Eur Air Service, since 1961; mgr, Lloyd Outremer, 1948-61. Cdr, J Underground, Fr, 1942-44. Pres, Relais Juifs; bd mem: UJA; ZF. Recipient: Médaille de Résistance. Home: 24, Ave Pierre 1 de Serbie, Paris, 16, Fr. Office: 92 St Cloud, Fr.

POIS, Joseph, US, educator, b. NYC, Dec 25, 1905; s. Adolph and Augusta (Lesser); AB, U Wis, 1926; MA, U Chgo, 1927; PhD, 1929; JD, Chgo Kent Coll Law, 1934; m. Rose Tomarkin June 24, 1928; c: Robert, Marc, Richard (decd). Prof, public admn, U Pittsburgh, since 1961; cons panel, comptroller gen, US since 1966; staff mem, J L Jacobs & Co, 1929-35, partner 1946-47; gen field sup, Public Admn Service, 1935-38; chief, admn studies sect, US Bur Old Age Survivors Ins, 1938-39; chief, admn and fiscal reorg sect, US Bur of Budget, exec off of Pres, 1939-42; counsel, asst to pres, Signode Steel Strapping Co, 1947-48; treas, co counsel, 1948-49, vice-pres treas, mem, bd dirs, 1949-61; cons: Econ Coop Admn, 1948; State Dept, 1949; dir, finance, State of Ill, 1951-53; cons, US Defense Dept, 1954; mem, State Dept adv comm, intl orgs, 1962-65. Cdr, then capt USCG, 1942-46. Pres: Metrop Housing and Planning Council, Chgo, 1956-57, mem bd govs, 1953-61; Immigrants Service League, Chgo, 1960-61, mem bd, 1956-61; mem: chgo Bd of Educ, 1956-61; comm to study aid to dependent children prog, Cook Co, 1959-61; Comty Fund Chgo, 1959-61; exec comm, Tri-Co divs Ill Assn of School Bds, 1957-59; bd, S Shore Planning Comm 1955-57; exec comm, Taxpayers' Fed of Ill, 1953-59; bd dirs, Citizens Public Personnel Assn, 1954-56; U of Ill Citizens Commn, 1955-60; U Chgo Citizens Bd, since 1958; Survey Commn, munic employees, Chgo, 1953-54; adv comm, Cook Co Family Court, 1955-57; Amer, Fed, Chgo and Allegheny Co Bar Assns; Amer Acctnt Assn; Amer Political Sci Assn; Amer Acad Political and Social Sci; Amer Soc for Public Admn; Financial Execs Inst of Amer; Natl Assn Acctnts; Royal Ins Public Admn; B'nai Isr Cong, Pittsburgh; Phil Beta Kappa; Pi Lambda Phi; Phi Delta Phi; clubs: Army and Navy, Wash, DC; Econ Chgo; Fed City, Wash, DC; Author: Public Personnel Administration in the City of Cincinnati, 1936; Kentucky Handbook of Financial Administration, 1937; Financial Administration in the Michigan State Government, 1938; The School Board Crisis, A Chicago Case Study, 1964; co-author: The Merit System in Illinois, 1935. contbr to social sci periodicals. Recipient: Navy Commendation Medal, 1946; U of Chicago Alumni Citation, 1960. Home: 927½ St James St, Pittsburgh, Pa. Office: U Pittsburgh, Pittsburgh, Pa.

POKORNY, Richard Raphael, Isr, psychologist, graphologist, b. Vienna, Aus, July 16, 1894; in Isr since 1939; LLD, U Vienna; PhD, U Heidelberg, Ger; m. Elisabeth Gerö; c: Peter, Hans (fell in War of Independence, 1948). Pvt practice; guest lectr, graphology, Zurich; lawyer, Vienna, 1926-38. Prin contrib: first found of graphology of Heb handwriting. Mem: Isr Union of Psychols; profsl unions: Holland, Fr; World Acad of Art and Sci. Author: Austrian Law of Labour, 6 vols, 1926-38; Ktav Yad va Ofi, 1952, 6 ed, 1965; Die Anwendung der Modernen Graphologie auf die hebräische Handschrift, 1952; School of Death Psychology heb, 1953 Modern Handwriting-analysis, 1963; Systematic Graphology, Heb, 1968; Psychologie der Handschrift, 1968; contbr numerous papers on law, graphology, psych, in 5 langs. Home and office: 10, Smolenskin St, Tel Aviv Isr.

POLACCO, Cesare, It, actor; b. Venice, It, May 14, 1900; s. Davide and Rosa (Trevi); m. Clelia Bernacchi, Oct 23, 1947; c: Elena, Arduina, Marina. Actor, RAI TV Studios, Florence, since 1967; appeared in weekly TV shows, since 1957; worked in dubbing of films in It lang, 1935-45; acted, It films, 1945-57; actor, Piccolo Theater, Milan, 1957-67. It Army, WW I. Mem, B'nai B'rith, Rome. Recipient: Croce di Guerra. Home: Via Fratelli Rosselli 7, Rome, It.

POLACHEK, Harry, US, mathematician; b. Lida, Pol, June 1, 1913; s. Solomon and Anna (Rubinchek); in US since 1923; BA, Yeshiva U, 1934; MA, Columbia U, 1935; PhD, 1947;

hon DHL, Yeshiva U, 1964; m. Blanche Katz, Dec 21, 1940; c: Solomon, Linda. Specialist, math and computers, US AEC since 1965; tchr, math, NYC HSs, 1937-43; prin computer, Aberdeen Proving Grounds, 1941-43; math, USN Bur of Ordnance, 1943-47; research math, Naval Ordnance Lab, 1947-52; asso prof, math, U of Md, 1950-51; tech dir, Applied Math Lab, USN, 1952-65. F, Yeshiva U, 1935-36; mem: Amer Phys Soc; Amer Math Soc; Wash Acad of Sci; Wash Phil Soc; Assn for Computing Machines. Author: Fundamentals of Gas Dynamics Shock Wave Interactions, 1958; ed, Mathematics of Computation, quarterly jour, since 1959; contbr to profsl jours. Recipient: Dist Civilian Service award, USN, 1960; Bernard Revel award, Yeshiva U, 1960; Dist Civilian Service award, Defense Dept, 1961. Home: 8510 16St, Silver Spring Md, Office: David Taylor Model Basin, Washington, DC.

POLAK, Irma, Isr, communal worker; b. Czech; d. Hugo and Berta (Hochman) Lichtenstein; in Isr since 1940. Co-found, chmn, Isr Consumers Assn, since 1956; mem council, Intl Org of Consumer Unions; hon life mem: World WIZO; Isr WIZO; mem: natl bd, JNF, on mission to Eur, 1946; head J App mission to Scandinavia, 1949; fmr: vice-pres, WIZO; chmn, Tarbut, Heb cultural org; mem, council, J Party, all Czech. Home: 20 Spinoza St, Tel Aviv, Isr.

POLESCHUCK, Ida V, US, educator; b. Lynn, Mass, Dec 26, 1914; d. Harry and Rebecca (Stone); BS, Mass State Tchrs Coll, 1935. Tchr, asst prin, Cobbet Elem Sch, since 1954; tchr, Sewell Anderson Sch, 1935; prin, Aldworth Sch, 1937-54. Pres: Jr Hadassah, 1942-43, chmn: Amer affairs, NE region, 1943, educ; 1951; Cen Young Women, 1951-52; N Shore chap, B'nai B'rith, 1953, bd mem, Youth Commn NE since 1964, PR chmn, NE region vocational service, 1966, bd, mem, 1968; counselor, 1952-53; vocational guidance chmn, 1959 council off, 1960-61; women's comm, Bonds for Isr, 1944-45; vice-pres, Cen for Adults, NE region comty cens, 1950-45; bd member, Jewish Comty Cen, 1941; adv, Alpha Lambda Sorority, since 1955; chmn, Service Sci Comm for Tchrs, 1962-63. Recipient: J Hadassah f key 1941; Item Bouquet of Week, Lynn Daily Evening Item Newspaper, 1946. Home: 180 Summer St, Lynn, Mass.

POLIAKOV, Léon, Fr, historian; b. Leningrad, Russ, Nov 25, 1910. s. Wladimir and Fanny (Friedmann); in Fr since 1924; m. Germaine Rousso, Jan 8, 1952; c: Jean-Michael. With Ecole Pratique des Hautes Etudes, Paris, since 1954; head dept of research, Centre de Documentation Juive Contemporaine, Paris, 1945-54, Author: Bréviaire de la Haine, 1952; Histoire de l'Antisémitisme, 1956; De Mahomet aux Marranes, 1961; De Voltaire à Wagner, 1968. Home: 35 Av, JF Kennedy, Massy, Fr.

POLIER, Justine Wise, US, jurist; b. Portland, Ore, Apr 12, 1903; d. Stephen and Louise (Waterman) Wise; father, Amer Zionist leader; mother, found and pres, women's div, AJ-Cong; BA, Barnard Coll, 1924; studied, Intl Lab Off, Geneva, Switz, 1925; LLB, Yale Law Sch, 1928; m. Leon Tulin, June 14, 1927 (decd); c: Stephen; m. 2nd, Shad Polier, Mar 26, 1937; c: Trudy Festinger, Jonathan, Michael (decd). Judge, NY State Family Court, since 1962; first woman referee, Workmen's Compensation Div, NY State Dept of Lab, 1929-34; asst corp counsel, NYC, 1934-35; secy and counsel, Mayor La Guardia's comm on unemployment relief; counsel, Emergency Relief Bur, both 1935; spec adv to Mrs. Eleanor Roosevelt, Off of Civil Defense, Wash, DC, 1941-42; justice, Domestic Relations Court, NYC, 1935-62. Pres: Louise Wise Services, since 1941; Witwyck Sch for Boys, since 1960; natl women's div, AJCong, 1948-56; chmn, natl exec comm, 1956-60; mem, exec, WJC, since 1956; vice-pres, Citizen's Comm for Children, 1945-61; mem, NYC commn on foster care of children, since 1950; mem: Bar Assn of NYC; Stephen Wise Free Syn; Lake Placid Syn. Author: Everyone's Children, Nobody's Child, 1941; Back to What Woodshed? 1957; The Rule of Law and the Role of Psychiatry, 1968. Home: 175 E 64 St, New York, NY. Office: 135 E 22 St, New York, NY.

POLIN, Claire, US, educator, composer; b. Phila, Pa, Jan 1, 1926; d. Josef and Celia (Dolgien); att: Dropsie Coll; Gratz Coll; Temple U; BMus, Phila Conservatory Music, 1948, MMus, 1950, DMus, 1955; att Julliard Sch, NY, 1950-52; m. Merle Schaff, June 3, 1956; c: Josef, Gabriel. Prof: art and aesthetics, Rutgers U, since 1957; musicology and composition Phila Musical Acad, since 1949; flutist, spec lectr in allied arts and J music, old and new; Leverhulme Scholar to U Coll, Wales, 1968-69; lectr, scholar-performer: Gt Brit; Near East,

Inter-Faith Charity Fund, all LA; admn secy, USO, LA area, 1941-43; PR and radio cons, JWB, 1946-47; dir, J Comty relations council, Indianapolis, 1947-50; exec dir, J Comty relations comm, Cincinnati, O, 1950-63; Armed Forces Radio Service, 1943-46. Pres, F House, Cincinnati, 1952-55; vice-pres, Assn of J Comty Relations Workers, since 1958; bd mem: Natl Assn of Intergroup Relations Officials, 1949-50; cons, interreligious comm, LA Region Goals Project; adv council, div of secondary educ, LA City Schs, priority adv council, supplementary educ planning cen; citizens resource comm, LA Trade-Tech Coll; citizens resource comm, urban affairs comm, LA City Bd Educ; mem: NAACP; exec comm, Natl J Comty Relations Adv Council; treas, J Communal Execs Assn, LA; Amer J Hist Soc; Natl Conf of J Communal Service. Home: 544 Via Media, Palos Verdes Estates, Cal. Office: 590 N Vermont, Los Angeles, Cal.

POST, Joseph, US, physician, educator; b. NYC, Mar 6, 1913; s. Charles and Mollie (Post); BS, CCNY, 1932; MD, Sch of Med, U Chgo, 1936; DMedSc, Coll of Phys and Surgs, Columbia U, 1941; m. Anne Bretzfelder, Mar 1, 1942; c: David, Thomas. Pvt practice, since 1946; asso prof, clinical med, Sch of Med, NYU, since 1952, asst prof, 1947-52; asso att phys, med, U Hosp, since 1952; cons gastroenterologist, USN Hosp, Since 1947; research asso, Goldwater Memorial Hosp, since 1948; res, Columbia Research Service, 1938-42; cons in med, VA Hosp, since 1946; att phys, Lenox Hill Hosp, since 1952; med off, NY Fire Dept, since 1957; instr med, Colombia, U, 1939-46. US Army, 1942-46. Mem: exec comm, NY Alcoholism Soc, since 1960; exec comm, asst treas, NY Council on Alcoholism, since 1961; Clinical Inves; Amer Gastroenterological Assn; Amer Gerontological Soc; Soc for Experimental Biol and Med; Amer Coll Phys; Radiation Research Soc; Amer Cell Biol; Phi Beta Kappa; Alpha Omega Alpha. Contrb to med jours. Hobbies: music, art. Home: 29 Washington Sq W, New York, NY. Office: 1100 Madison Ave, New York, NY.

POSTAL, Bernard, US, organization exec, editor, journalist; b. NYC, Nov 1, 1905; s. Harry and Sarah (Roth); desc of Joseph Caro; att: CCNY, 1921-22; U Wis, 1922-25; NYU, 1925-26; m. Margaret Selikowitz, 1930; c: Anne Schott, Paul Dir, public info, Natl JWB, since 1946; ed: JWB Circle, since 1946; Jewish Digest, since 1955; reporter: scholastic news, NY Globe, 1922; NY World, 1923; feature writer, Holmes News Service, Madison, Wis, 1923-24; exch ed, NY Times, 1926-28; mgn ed: Grand Central Zone Tab, 1928-29; Seven Arts Feature Syndicate, NYC, 1933-38; Eve, mag, NYC, 1937; ed in chief: Jewish Daily Bulletin, NYC, Jewish Telegraphic Agency, NYC, both 1929-31; ed: Jersey City Jewish Standard, 1932-34; Jewish War Veteran, NY, 1934-37; B'nai B'rith News, 1939; and found, This is B'nai B'rith, 1941; asso ed and contrb, Universal J Ency, 1938-42; dir, PR, Amer Jewish Conf, 1943-44; PR cons, ARC, 1942-45; mem, PR staff, United Jewish Delegation, UN Conf, SF, Cal, 1945; cons, OSS, Wash, DC, 1943-45; chmn, Interfaith Publ Comm, War Finance Div, US Treasury Dept, 1943-45; mem: PR commn, UAHC; Amer J Hist Soc; Natl Conf of J Communal Service. Pres, Rockville Cen, NY, J Comty Council, 1950-52; chmn: PR Comm, Natl Conf of J Communal Service, 1965-69; vice-pres: and co-found, Amer J PR Soc, 1957; co-found, J Comty Cen, Montgomery, Md, 1944; mem: exec council, Amer J Hist Soc; bd, Natl Health and Wfr PR Council; bd, Bur Careers J Communal Service; PR comm, Natl Conf of Soc Wfr; PR Soc of Amer; Amer Assn of Eng-J Newspaper Publs Assn; Amer PR Assn; Health and Wfr PR Assn NY; Central Syn, Nassau County. Author: Youth and National Defense, 1940; Jewish Landmarks in NY, 1964; Best of Ten Years of Jewish Digest, 1965; co-author: A Jewish Tourist's Guide to the US, 1954; Landmarks of a People: A Guide to Jewish Sites in Europe, 1962; Change and Challenge, 1966; The Day Israel was Born, 1970. Mem, adv council, Reconstructionist, NYC, 1954; contrb to Jewish press. Recipient: citation for contribution to Amer Jewish History, Amer Jewish Tercentenary Commn. Spec interest: collecting Judaica. Home: 3459 Frederick St, Oceanside, NY. Office: 15 E 26 St, NYC.

POSTELNEK, William, US, chemist; b. Peoria, Ill, Jan 22, 1918; s. Samuel and Sara (Brodsky); BS, Ill Inst of Tech, 1942; MSc, O State U, 1954; MBA, U Chgo, 1959; m. Helen Dryfoos, Apr 11, 1945; c: Claire, Marsha, Susan. Cons, Gen Elec Co, Missile and Space Div, since 1967; Weather off, USAF, 1942-46; chief, polymer br, Materials Cen, 1951-58, chief applications lab, 1962-67, maj, 1962-67; chief materials div, Eur Off Aerospace Research, Brussels, 1959-62. Prin

contribs: research and devl of high temperature stable materials for aircraft and missiles, fluorine and polymer chem. Mem: Amer Chemical Soc; AAAS; Sci Research Soc of Amer; Soc Aerospace Materials and Process Engr. Co-author: Aliphatic Fluorine Compounds, 1958; contrb to profsl jours. Recipient: Legion of Merit, 1959. Home: 200 Clwyd Rd, Balacynwyd, Pa.

POSTER, Hermann David, US, educator; b. Hamburg, Ger, Dec 1, 1909; s. Salomon and Fanny (Pasternak) Poczter; in US since 1938; att: U Hamburg, 1928-31; U Berlin and Acad Political Scis, Berlin, 1931-32; Tchrs Coll, Hamburg, 1934-36; MA, Lehigh U, 1942; PhD, NYU, 1949; m. Pasha Deutschman, June 30, 1940. Asso prof, Romance and Germanic langs, Wayne State U, since 1969, on fac since 1950; tchr, Talmud Torah, Hamburg, 1934-38; instr: army specialized training prog: U of Pa, 1943-44, 1945; NYU, 1944; Ger, NYU, 1945-50; ed, weekly radio prog on postwar Ger, WDET, since 1956; adv on Ger-speaking films, Detroit Inst of Arts, since 1951; Mem: academicians comm, Bar Ilan U, since 1956; Allied J Campaign, since 1960; MLA, chmn, bibliography comm for 19th cent Ger lit, 1952; AAUP; Amer Assn Tchrs of Ger; Cong Beth Yehudah; study commn, Amer U Profs for study of Ger Us, 1955; educ radio dents Assn, Ger. Contrb to profsl jours. Hobbies: fgn films, hi-fi, philately. Home: 630 Merrick Ave, Detroit, Mich. Office: Wayne State U, Detroit, Mich.

POSY, Arnold, US, author; b. Mohilev, Russ, Mar 21, 1894; s. Mordecai and Miriam (Lazarev), in US since 1920; m. Bella Shapiro, Dec, 1929; c: Deena Metzger, Manuel. Dir, J Ethical Soc since 1966; ed: Heshbon, since 1966; J Daily Express, London, 1914-16; Aufbraus, Chgo, 1928-30; Milw J Life, 1931-32; Yiddishe Shriften, NYC, 1940-43; Amer J Life, 1949-50; Amer J Home, 1951-65. Author: Shalit and Tamara, 1929; Joash, 1932; Nazi Bible of Hate and the Present War, 1939; Hakenkreitz: The Crooked Cross, 1939; Israeli Tales and Legends, 1948; Holiday Night Dreams, 1953; Chains of Messiah, 1962; Mystic Trends in Judaism, 1966; H Leivick, The Poet of Martyrdom and Holiness, 1968; dramatic poems, plays, essays. Hon mem, Eugene Field Soc, since 1939. Home and Office: 1221 N Spaulding Ave, Los Angeles, Cal.

POTASH, Max, US, chemical exec; b. NYC, Nov 16, 1920; s. Isidor and Anna (Roseman); BChE, CCNY, 1941; m. Leola Russell, June 14, 1942; c: Naomi, Robert, William, Laura, Daniel, Pres, Polyvinyl Chems Inc, since 1955; engr; TVA, 1942-43; Manhattan Project, 1944; Publicker Inds, 1944-48; chief engr, Amer Polymer Div, Borden, 1950-54; chem engr, 1948-50. Mem: Amer Chem Soc; Amer Inst Chem Engrs; Home: 20 Laurel Rd, Swampscott, Mass. Office: 730 Main St, Wilmington, Mass.

POTOFSKY, Jacob S, US, labor leader; b. Radomisl, Russ, Nov 16, 1894; s. Simon and Rebecca; in US since 1908; hon: DHumL: HUC JIR, 1961; Roosevelt Coll, 1967; DCS, Villanova U, 1969; LLD, Brandeis U, 1969; m; c: Delia Gottlieb, Jacqueline Broughton, Bruce, (decd). m. 2nd, Blanche Zetland, 1951. Gen pres, Amalgamated Clothing Workers of Amer, since 1946, mem, since inception, 1914, secy-treas, Chgo jt bd, 1914-16, asst secy-treas, ACWA, 1916-34, asst pres, 1934-40, gen secy-treas, 1940; pres, Amalgamated Ins Co, chmn, ins fund; chmn, bd, Amalgamated Bank, NY; vice-pres, exec council, AFL-CIO. Prin contribs: organizing non union workers; innovations in union-mgmt relations; organizing coop labor instns. Pres: Sidney Hillman Found; Amalgamated Dwellings, Inc; United Housing Found; vice-pres, Riverbay Corp; dir: Hillman Housing Corp; Gtr NY Fund; treas, Amalgamated Housing Corp; mem: bd trustees, Harry S Truman Libr; natl council, US Comm for Refs; adv comm, Harvard Trade Union Prog, 1962; natl comm, Amer Mus of Immigration; bd dirs: Comm for Nation's Health; Amer Arbitration Assn; Natl Park Found; Inst Amer Democracy; natl council, Eleanor Roosevelt Memorial Found; cen bd, ORT; fmr: vice-pres, mem bd, Amun-Isr Housing Corp; mem: Intl Devl Point Four Adv Bd, Dept of State; Amer Assembly; Rockefeller Brothers Fund; Natl Non-Partisan Comm for Intl Econ Growth bd Govs, ARC; Natl Manpower Council, Columbia U; temporary comm on city finances; US delg to ILO tripartite tech meeting for clothing ind, Geneva, 1964. Recipient: chair, Brandeis U; Equal Opportunity award, Urban League, 1957; award, Newspaper Guild, NY, 1954, 1964; award, NCCJ, 1948; Four Freedoms award, It-Amer Lab Council, 1964; Order, Star of Solidarity, It Govt, 1966. Home: 19 E 88 St, New York, NY. Office: 15 Union Sq, New York, NY.

POTOK, Chaim, US, author, editor; b. NYC, Feb 17, 1929; s. Benjamin and Mollie (Friedman); BA, summa cum laude, Yeshiva U, 1950; MHL, ordained rabbi, JTSA, 1954; PhD, U of Pa, 1963; m. Adena Mosevitzky; c: Rena, Naama, Akiva. Ed, J Publ Soc of Amer, since 1965; mem fac, U Judaism, LA, 1957-59; scholar in res, Har Zion Temple, Phila, 1959-63; mem fac, Tchrs Inst, JTSA, 1964-65. Author, novels: The Chosen, 1967; The Promise, 1969. Lt, chaplain, US Army, 1955-57. Mem: RA; PEN. Recipient: for The Chosen: Edward Lewis Wallant Award, 1968; nomination, Natl Book Award, 1968. Hobbies: painting, photography. Home: 2281 N 51 St, Philadelphia, Pa. Office: 222 N 15 St, Philadelphia, Pa.

POUPKO, Bernard A, US, rabbi; b. Vieliz, Russ, Feb 5, 1918; s. Eliezer and Pesha (Sapir); in US since 1932; BA, Yeshiva U, 1939, ordained rabbi, 1941; att CCNY, Columbia U; PhD, U Pittsburgh, 1952; m. Gilda Twersky-Novosellor, June, 1945; c. Joel, Jacob, Debora, Rebecca, Reuben. Rabbi, life tenure, Shaare Torah Cong, Pittsburgh, since 1942; mem, Beth Din, Phila, since 1964; visiting lectr, J phil, mysticism, U Pittsburgh, since 1959. Civilian chaplain, USAAC, WW II. Chmn: Rabb Bd Gtr Pittsburgh; natl conv, Rabbi Alumni, Yeshiva U, 1963; Natl conv, RabCA, 1952, 1966, 1968, mem, exec comm, since 1947, vice pres, 1966-68; preached in central Syn, Moscow, Russ; US repr JA for Isr; natl vice-pres, Mizrachi Hapoel Hamizrachi, mem, exec comm, Mizrachi Org of Amer, since 1945, found, Mizrachi Tri-State Region, 1945; mem, World Rel Zionist Exec; co-found: Yeshiva Talmudical Coll, Pittsburgh; mem, gov bd; Hillel Acad, Pittsburgh; vice pres, world exec, Rel Zionists of Amer; mem, Union of Orthodox Rabbis, US, Can; mem exec comm, Yeshiva U Alumni Assn; mem: Agudas Harabonim of Amer. Author: Forms of Jewish Adult Religious Education in America, 1952; In the Shadow of the Kremlin; Forms of Jewish Adult Religious Education: ed: Kochov Mazhir, Yeshiva U Rabb Jour; Eidenu, Yeshiva U Rabb vol, 1941; RabCA Sermons, vol, 1955, asso ed, 1957-69, mem, ed bd, Tradition; contbr articles to J jours. Recipient: Main sanctuary of Shaare Torah Cong named as Bernard Poupko Syn, 1961. Home: 2523 Beechwood Blvd, Pittsburgh, Pa. Study: 2319 Murray Ave, Pittsburgh, Pa.

PRAG, Jehuda L, Isr, police off; b. Warsaw, Pol, June 7, 1915; s. Israel and Zivia (Smolarz); in Isr since 1934; att U Warsaw 1933-34; Govt Inst for Political Sci, Jerusalem, 1955-56; m. Sheila Cook, 1957; three c. Cdr, Isr Police Force, since 1964, commanding off, Tel Aviv dist, since 1969, head, criminal inves dept, 1950-52, commandant, Sr Offs Coll, 1956-58, head org dept, 1962-69; chief adv to commn of Imperial Ethiopian Police, 1960-62. Cdr, Haganah, 1934-48; IDF. Contbr to: Ency of Zionism and Isr; profsl publs. Home: 44 King David St, Herzliya, Isr. Office: Motzkin St, Tel Aviv, Isr.

PRAGAI, Michael John, Isr, diplomat; b. Berlin, Ger, Nov 23, 1919; s. Eugen and Gertrud (Friedlaender); in Isr since 1936; tchrs dipl, Isr Tchrs Coll, 1941; att: JA political dept Sch for Dipls, 1948; Heb U, Jerusalem; m. Dina Lozinski, Aug 12, 1943; c: Oded, Timora. I/c, ecclesiastical affairs, Min Fgn Affairs, since 1968, fmr: political secy, i/c Isr legations abroad, pol adv, Isr UN delg, 1952-55; counsel of Isr, NY, Phila, 1959-63; councilor of Emb, Rangoon, Burma, 1963-66; dep dir, armistice affairs, 1966-67. Haganah, 1936-41; cpl, RAF, 1941-45; lt, IDF, 1948. Hobbies: music, art, maps, swimming skiing, tennis. Home: 44 Hantke St, Kiryat Yovel, Jerusalem, Isr. Office: Min Fgn Affairs, Jerusalem, Isr.

PRATT, Simcha, Isr, diplomat; b. Kovno, Russ, Nov 26, 1912; s. Meier and Shulamit (Rayman); in Isr since 1926; LLB, U London, 1934; m. Malca Rokach, Dec 20, 1938. Ambass, Australia and NZ since 1967; consul gen; Chgo, 1953-57; NY. 1957-60; dir, intl orgs div, Fgn Min, 1960-61; mem, Isr delg to UN Gen Assembly, 1959, 1960, 1963; min plen, S Afr, 1961-63; ambass to Mexico, 1963-64; dir, British Commonwealth div, Min Fgn Affairs, 1964-67. Lt, IDF, 1948. Mem, B'nai B'rith. Office: Min Fgn Affairs, Jerusalem, Isr.

PREDMESKY Akiba, US, rabbi, b. Kovno, Lith, Dec 18, 1914; s. Eliezer and Esther (Smolensky); in US since 1932; ordained rabbi, Rabbi Isaac Elchanan Yeshiva, 1940; BA, NYU, 1940; LLB, Harvard U, 1943; DHL, Yeshiva U, 1946; m. Byrdie Geiger, 1943; c: Shulamith. Rabbi, J Cen, Williamsbridge, Bx, since 1943; instr, hist and govt, Stern Coll for Women, Yeshiva U, since 1956; chaplain, Meseritzer Young Mens Soc, since 1943; rabbi, Cong Agudath Sholom, Flatbush, 1940-43. Pres, Bx Mizrachi Org, 1949-53; delg, 23rd WZC, Jerusalem, 1951; co-chmn, Bx ZC, since 1949; mem: bd dirs, exec, and admn comms Mizrachi Org of Amer, since 1948; exec comm: KH, since 1950; RabCA, 1945-51; rel dept, comm, JNF, since 1950; bd dirs and bd educ: Salanter Yeshiva, Tremont Heb Sch, both Bx; Odd Fellows; Lodzer True Brothers Asso. Ed: Rabb Council Sermons Manual, 1943. Home: 2739 Holland Ave, Bronx, NY. Study: 2910 Barnes Ave, Bronx, NY.

PREGER, Andreja, Yugo, pianist, educator; b. Mar 20, 1912; s. Jakov and Adela (Hamburger); LLD, Fac of Law, 1937; m; c: Jaśa; m. 2nd, Gina Djoković, May 13, 1958; c: Eva. Prof, Music Acad, Belgrade, since 1951; found Belgrade Trio, with A Pavlović and V Jakovčić, 1963; chief ed, music prog, Radio Belgrade, 1945-51; concert tours: Yugo; Isr; Greece; Aus; It; Fr; Belgium; with Trio: Aus; It; Fr; Belgium; Den; Nor; Greece; Bulgaria; Czech; Russ; Can. Recipient: Order of Merit for the People, II degree; Oct Award of City of Belgrade, 1964. Home: Svet Markovića 22, Belgrade, Yugo. Office: Music Acad, Marśala Tita 50, Belgrade, Yugo.

PREGER, Paul D, US, business executive, financial cons; b. Corning, NY, Aug 1, 1899; s. Abraham and Pauline (Singer); att Pace Coll, 1919-20; m. Esther Hyman, 1925; c: Paul, Marianne; m. 2nd, Rachel Goodman, 1948; c: Barbara, Mitchell. Financial cons, since 1955; dir: Inter-State Dept Stores, since 1959; Frankfort Intercontinental Hotels; Union Electric Co; fmr dir, Anchor Mfg; Hevi-Duty Electric Co; Wis Elec Power; N Amer Co. US Army, WW I. Mem, Financial Execs Inst. Home: Park Kensington Apartments, Great Neck, NY.

PREIL, Gabriel, US, Heb-Yiddish poet; b. Yuriev, Estonia, Aug 21, 1911; s. Elias and Clara (Gold); in US since 1922; att: Rabbi Isaac Elchanan Theol Sem, NYC, 1923-24, Teachers' Inst, 1924-26. Freelance writer and translator, Heb Yiddish Eng poetry and prose, since 1936. Author: Nof Shemesh Uchfor, poems, 1944; Ner Mool Kochavim, poems, 1954; Israeli Poetry in Peace and War, essay, 1959; Mapat Erev, poems, 1961; Gavriel Preil; Mivhar Shirim, poems, 1965; Lieder, poems, 1966; haEsh vahaDmama, 1968; translator of Sandburg, Frost and others into Heb; poems included in anthologies; co-editor, Niv, Heb monthly, 1937-38; contbr to Heb and Yiddish periodicals. Treas, Heb PEN Club, 1943-45, 1948-50, mem, exec bd, since 1951, delg, Intl PEN congress, 1966; mem, exec comm in Amer, Writers' Cen of Isr, 1949-55. Recipient: Louis LaMed Prize for Heb lit, 1942; Kovner Memorial Heb Poetry award, Jewish Book Council of Amer, 1955, 1962; Bitzaron award for Heb lit, Haifa Munic, Isr, 1960, free residence for life, 1953; Lisa and Willy Shore grant, 1965. Hobbies: art, music Home: 1011 Walton Ave, Bronx, NY.

PREISS, Kenneth, Isr, engineer, researcher; b. Cape Town. S Afr, Aug 11, 1937; s. Benjamin and Minnie (Alper); in Isr since 1966; BSc, U Witwatersrand, Johannesburg, 1957; DIC, Imperial Coll, London, 1961; PhD, U London, 1964; m. Miriam Zolkov, Oct 29, 1968. Sr research engr, Negev Inst for Arid Zone Research, Beersheva, since 1966, sr lectr, engr, since 1968; design engr: Solel Boneh, 1959-60; Reinf Steel Co, 1960; asst prof, nuclear, civil engr, U of Ill, 1964-66. Sgt, IDF, 1958-59. Exec offs Habonim, S Afr; asso mem, SAICE; mem: ANS; ACI. Contbr to sci jours. Recipient: Commonwealth Scholarship, 1960. Home: 16 Rotam St, Omer, Isr. Office: Negev Inst for Arid Zone Research, Beersheva, Isr.

PREMINGER, Alexander Salo, US, librarian, editor; b. Berlin, Ger, July 29, 1915; s. Saly and Lea (Sprechmann-Woroner); in US since 1940; BA, NYU, 1950; MA, Columbia U, 1952; m. Augusta Friedman, Aug 7, 1960. Asso prof, chief hum div, Bklyn Coll Libr, CUNY, since 1969; on libr staff, since 1952; ed cons, Frederick Ungar Publishers, since 1965. US Army, 1942-45. Author: Eng lit section in, Bibliography; Current State and Future Trends, 1967; ed and contbr, Ency of Poetry and Poetics, now Princeton Ency of Poetry and Poetics; ed, Against the Running Tide, by Harry Gideons, 1967; contbr to lit and profsl publs. Chmn, Flushing Affiliates of Educ Bc Corp, 1963-66; dir, Columbia U Sch Libr Sci Alumni Assn, 1965-67; mem: AJCong; Fac-Hillel Assos Bklyn Coll; AAUP; MLA; Amer Comparative Lit Assn; bibliography comm, Amer Libr Assn; Phi Beta Kappa Recipient: f, Bollingen Found, 1962. Spec interest: educ. TV. Home: 1311 Decker St, Valley Stream, NY. Office: Bklyn Coll Libr, Brooklyn, NY.

Law and Econ, 1952-53; LLB, Heb U, 1957; m. Dalia Danenberg, 1960. Pvt practice, since 1964; asso, law firm, Moyal, 1960-64. IDF, 1950-52. Hobbies: art collecting, philately, tennis. Home: 3 Glizenstein St, Tel Aviv, Isr. Office: 56 Ahad Haam St, Tel Aviv, Isr.

PONVE, Anatole, US, business exec; b. Irkutsk, Siberia, Dec 25, 1899; s. Gregory and Miriam (Rosenzweig) Ponevejsky; in US since 1941; m. Gita Preisman, Feb 12, 1935; c: Tamara, Irene. Pres, A Ponve Co Inc, since 1947, owner, 1943-47; pres, Eastridge Estates. Org, J Comty, Kobe, Japan, 1937, pres, 1937-41; pres: J Comty, Tokyo, Japan, 1952; J Ref Org, Kobe, 1939-41; chmn, Temple Hollywood Beth El, since 1965; mem, founders comm, J Heritage Found, since 1959. Home: 917 Oxford Way, Beverly Hills, Cal.

POOL, Tamar de Sola, US, communal worker, author; b. Jerusalem; d. Chaim and Eva (Cohen) Hirshenson; in US since 1904; BA, Hunter Coll, NY, 1913; travelling f, U Paris, 1913-14; att Columbia U, 1914-17; m. David de Sola Pool, Feb 6, 1917; c: Ithiel, Naomi Rodstein. Tutor, Eng lang and lit, Lycée Lamartine, Paris, 1913-14; instr, Fr, Latin, Greek, Hunter Coll. 1914-17. Pres: Hudson Co Womens Suffrage Assoc, 1915-16; Hadassah, 1939-43, ed, Newsletter, 1936-46, pres, NY chap, 1930-35; co-found and chmn, Amer Mothers Comm, 1935; chmn and found, Heb U-Hadassah Med School Bldg Fund, 1948; hon chmn, JNF; dir: Natl Council of Women, US; Sisterhood, Span and Port Syn, NYC; fmr mem: bd of govs, Heb U; gen council, World Zionist Org; exec comm, AJComm; interim comm, Amer J Conf; gov bd, Youth Aliyah; exec comm, Children to Pal; presidium for world observance of Henrietta Szold centennial. Author: In the Spirit of '76', drama, 1926; Palestine and the Post War World, 1945; Israel and the United Nations, 1947; The Threefold Cord; co-author; An Old Faith in a New World, 1955; Is there an Answer? An Inquiry into Some Human Dilemmas; co-ed and trans, Passover Haggadah. Recipient: Woman of Year award, Intl Women's Expo. Home: 91 Central Park W, New York, NY. Office: 8 W 70th St, New York, NY.

POPICK, Jack S, US, business exec, communal leader; b. Rum, Aug 15, 1902; s. Abram and Rose (Probareshevska); in US, since 1904; m. Ruth Waldman, June 15, 1935; c: David Rose. Pres: Everglades Laundry Inc, since 1948; Standard Ind Laundries; Dade Rentals, both since 1954; Mechanics Uniform Service; Ace Uniform Service; Dipl Service; vice-pres: Ind Uniform and Towel supply, Tulsa, since 1956; Vinnie Tulsa, since 1960; Hunnicutt Mfg, Puerto Rico, since 1959; Mechanics Overall Service, NJ, 1922-48; bd, Isr Inves, since 1962. Pres, Fla Div, Amer Friends of Heb U, since 1962; dir, Inst of Ind launderers, 1959-61; chmn, bd govs, Gtr Miami Comm for Isr Bonds, since 1962; dir, Miami Beach Taxpayers Assn, since 1959; vice-pres: J Home for the Aged; Temple Emanu-El; co-found; Yeshiva U Grad Sch of Educ; New Campus, Heb U, Jerusalem; Technion, Haifa, mem: exec comm, ZOA since 1961; life, Brandeis U; bd, Gtr Miami J Fed, since 1959; bd, J family and Children Service, since 1963; bd, Heb Acad, since 1963; natl bd, Amer Isr Public Affairs Comm, since 1960; B'nai B'rith; Civic League of Miami Beach; Miami Dade C of C; Mediterranean Cong of Culture; patron, JWV; Pres's Comm, Aid to the Handicapped; club, Variety, asso mem. Recipient, Mark A Light Award for aid to the handicapped, 1962. Home: 20 Island Ave, Belle Isle, Miami Beach, Fla. Office: 2100 NW First Ave, Miami, Fla.

POPKIN, Zelda, US, author; b. Bklyn, NY, July 5, 1898; d. Harry and Anna (Glass) Feinberg; att: Columbia U, 1916-18; NYU Law Sch, 1945; m. Louis Popkin, Oct 19, 1919 (decd); c: Roy, Richard. PR work with husband, 1919-43; PR dir, JDC, 1943; contr ed, Coronet Mag, 1952-54; exec dir, Hadassah Org of Can, 1954-55; PR dir, Amer-Isr Cultural Found, 1957-58; dir of comty relations, Amer Friends of Heb U, 1958-60. ARC, Eur, 1945-46. Author: Death Wears a Whitet Gardenia, 1938; Time Off for Murder, 1940; Murder in the Mist, 1940; Dead Man's Gift, 1941; No Crime for a Lady, 1942; So Much Blood, 1944; The Journey Home, 1945; Small Victory, 1947; Walk Through the Valley, 1950; Quiet Street, 1951; Open Every Door, autobiography, 1956; Herman Had Two Daughters, 1968; contbr fiction and non-fiction to: The New Yorker; Harpers; McCalls; Ladies Home Jour; Readers Digest; Coronet; Amer Mag. Recipient: Samuel H Daroff fiction award, JBCA, 1952. Home: 272 First Ave, New York, NY.

POPPER, Hans, US, physician, educator; b. Vienna, Aus, Nov 24, 1903; s. Carl and Emma (Gruenbaum); in US since 1938; MD, U Vienna, 1928; MS, U of Ill, 1941, PhD, 1944; m. Lina Billig, June 4, 1943; c: Frank, Charles. Path in chief, Mt Sinai Hosp, NY, since 1957; dean for academic affairs, Given Found, prof and chmn, dept of path, Mt Sinai Sch of Med, CUNY, since 1967; asst, dept of path and med, U Vienna, 1928-38; dir, dept of path, Cook Co Hosp, Chgo, 1946-57; sci dir, Hektoen Inst Med Research, 1943-57; asst prof, prof path, North-western U, 1949-57, both Chgo; prof, path, Columbia U 1957-67. Maj, US Army MC, 1944-46. Dipl, Amer Bd of Path, f: AMA; Amer Coll of Phys; Amer Soc of Clinical Path; NY Acad Med; mem: NY Path Soc; Amer Assn for Study of Liver Diseases, pres, 1962-63; Amer Assn Path and Bact; Amer Gastroenterological Assn; Sigma Xi. Co-author: Serous Inflamation, 1935; Clinical Pathological Conferences at Cook County Hosp, 1954; Liver: Structure and Function, 1957; ed, trends in New Medical Schools, 1967; co-ed, Progress in Liver Disease, Vol I, 1961, Vol II, 1965, Vol III, 1969; contbr to med jours. Office: Mt Sinai Hosp, Fifth Ave and 100 St, New York, NY.

PORAT, Joseph, Isr, organization exec; b. Breslau, Ger, June 7, 1909; s. David and Tony (Mittwoch) Foerder; desc of Rabbi Zvi Kalischer; in Isr since 1934; att U Breslau and Berlin, 1927-31; m. Miriam Goldschmitd, Oct 4, 1934; c: Ruben, Michael. Secy: Agric Coop Soc, El-Al, Ramot Hashavim, since 1958, chief acctnt, 1948-58. Intl chess master, champion of Pal, 1937, 1940; Isr, 1953, 1957, 1959, 1963. Home: Ramot Hashavim, Isr. Office: Cooperative Society El-Al, Ramot Hashavim, Isr.

PORAT, Orna, Isr, actress; b. Cologne, Ger, June 6, 1924; in Isr since 1947; att drama Sch, Cologne, 1940-42; m. Joseph Porat, 1945; c: Yoram, Lital. Actress, mem mgmt, Cameri Theatre, Tel Aviv, since 1948; found, dir, Cameri Theatre for Children, since 1964; fmr mem theater group, Ger. Maj roles in: I remember Mama; My Sister Eileen; St Joan; Twelfth Night; Romeo and Juliet; The Good Woman of Szechuan; Mary Stuart; Two for the Seesaw; Dear Liar; O Dad Poor Dad; Bayit ve Yam; Lady From the Sea. Recipient, Ramhal award. Home: 45 Aluf David St, Ramat Hen, Isr. Studio: Cameri Theatre, Tel Aviv, Isr.

PORAT, Ovadia (pen name Ain), Isr, farmer, communal leader; b. Dvinsk, Latvia, July, 1911; s. Joseph and Sara (Zas) Yoselevitz; in Isr since 1929; m. Raya Fisher; c: Joseph, Michal Hanna. Mem: Cen Control Comm, Histadrut, since 1962, chmn, Travel Comm, dep mem, exec comm; mem, cen comm, Lab party; head, haSharon Regional Council, 1951-53; chm cen control comm, Mapai Party, 1953-58; secy, Kibbutz Einat, 1959-60. Haganah; intl dept, JA, liaison off, J police forces, 1936-37. Missions to Pol, Hehalutz, 1934-35; US, Youth and Hehalutz, JA, 1946-47. Contbr to newspapers: Davar, haPoel haZair. Home: Kibbutz Einat, Isr. Office: 93 Arlosoroff St, Tel Aviv, Isr.

PORATH, Elijahu, Isr, journalist; b. Vilna, Russ, Jan 17, 1910; s. Elchanan and Shosha (Abramowitch) Poretzky; in Isr since 1935; PhD, U Basel 1930; m. Sarah Wollach. News ed, Letzte Neies, since 1960; mem ed bd, Haaretz, daily; ed, Hadashot Haerev daily; contbr to: Davar, Yediot Ahronot, fmr contbr to publs, Warsaw. Author: The Middle East, 1956; Mizrajim, 1960; Syria, 1960; History of Jewish Labor in Russia. Home: 53a Bin Nun St, Tel Aviv, Isr. Office: 52 Harakevet St, Tel Aviv, Isr.

PORATH, Moshe, Isr, attorney; b. Bialystock, Pol, May 7, 1920; s. Israel and Zila (Kalina) Porozowsky; in Isr since 1941; law deg: U Warsaw, 1937; U Liverpool, 1939; Jerusalem law sch 1944; econ deg, Heb U, Jerusalem, 1956; m. Zila Chmilevsky, Feb 20, 1947; c: Yael, Israel. Sr partner, Porath & Haggin, attys, since 1952; dir, Am Oved, Histadrut Pub Corp; legal adv: Fed of Agric Works, Histadrut; Min of Finance, Isr Govt, 1948-52; custodian of absentee property Isr Govt, 1950-52. Haganah; IDF, 1944-49. Mem: bd govs, Herzliya HS; hon treas, Isr Bar Assn, 1953-57, mem cen comm, 1956-59. Home: 28 Ahavat Zion St, Tel Aviv, Isr. Office: 10 Carlebach St, Tel Aviv, Isr.

PORATH, Tzvi H, US, rabbi; b. Jerusalem, Dec 19, 1916; s. s. Israel and Peshe (Tiktin); in US since 1922, BA, W Reserve U, 1939; MA, U Pittsburgh, 1941; ordained rabbi, Heb Theol Sem, 1939; DHL, Yeshiva U, 1968; m. Esther Levin, Mar 11, 1942; c: Sara, Jonathan. Rabbi: Chevy Chase Md, since 1952. Brith Sholom Cong, 1948-52. Capt, chaplain, USAAF, 1942-46. Dist dir, B'nai B'rith Youth Org, 1946-48; co-chmn and found, Solomon Schehter Sch; chaplain, NIH, 1953-55; vice-chmn, Educ Council of Gtr Wash, 1954; pres: Wash Bd of, Rabbis, 1956-60; RA, Gtr Wash, 1960-63, exec comm, RA 1963-66; mem: Md Commn on Children and Youth; exec comm, JCC, Gtr Wash; Juvenile Court Comm, Montgomery Co; Govs Comm on Old Age; Pres Commn on Rehab for Handicapped; B'nai B'rith; J Chaplains Assn. Home: 8508 Freyman Dr, Chevy Chase, Md. Study: 8402 Freyman Dr, Chevy Chase, Md.

POREH, Michael, Isr, scientist; b. Tel Aviv, Oct 15, 1931; s. Nachman and Rachel (Zuckernik); BSc, Technion, Haifa, 1955, dipl engr, 1955; MS, PhD, Colo State U, 1961; m. Shoshana Schwartz, Aug 8, 1957; c: Illan, Amir. Asso prof, Technion, since 1967, asst prof, 1963-67; asst prof, Pa State U, 1962-63. Pvt, IDF, 1948-50. Mem: Intl Assn of Hydraulic Research; Sigma Xi. Author: Basic Laws of Fluid Mechanics, 1966; contbr to intl sci jours. Home: 28 Einstein St, Haifa, Isr. Office: Technion, Haifa, Isr.

PORTER, Maurice, S Afr, solicitor; b. Russ, Oct 26, 1905; s. Joseph and Jane (Edelson); in S Afr since 1914; BA, Rhodes U, Grahamstown, 1925; LLB, U of S Afr, 1927; m. Lola Hyman, June 10, 1936; c: Neil, Basil. Sr partner, law firm, since 1934. Pres, S Afr J Orphanage, 1951-53; exec mem, since 1936; chmn, exec council, S Afr J Bd of Deps, since 1965; exec mem: Witwatersrand Wfr Council, since 1952; fmr master, Masons; clubs: Houghton Golf; Johannesburg. Home: 81 Central St, Houghton, Johannesburg, S Afr. Office: 400 Surrey House, Rissik St, Johannesburg, S Afr.

PORUSH, Israel, Austr, rabbi; b. Jerusalem, Isr, 1907; s. Elias and Deborah (Jaffe); in Austr since 1940; att Rabb Sem, Berlin, Ger, 1927-32; U Berlin, 1927-31; PhD, U Marburg, Ger 1931; m. Bertha Link, Oct, 1934; c: Judith, Naomi. Chief Rabbi, The Great Syn, Sydney, since 1940; lectr, post-bibl Heb, Sydney U, since 1951; rabbi, Finchley Syn. Vice-pres, and hon dir, NSW Bd of J Educ; pres: Austr J Hist Soc, since 1948; Assn J Mins of Austr, since 1952; chmn, Beth Din, Sydney, since 1940; mem, B'nai B'rith. Collaborator: Soncino, Eng trans of Talmud, Valentine's J Ency Judaica; contbr to publs. Recipient: OBE. Home: 20 Wylde St, Potts Point, Sydney, NSW, Austr. Study: Great Syn, 164 Castlereagl St, Sydney NSW, Austr.

PORUSH, Menachem, Isr, rabbi, legislator; b. Jerusalem, Apr 2, 1916; s. Moshe and Shifra (Rivlin); m. Bracha Paksher, 1951; c: Eli Shifra, Bracha, Naftali, Meyer. MK, since 1959. Found and chmn: Children's Day Nurseries in Isr, Free Loan Founds; Nachlat Isr Building Trust; found: Spero Printing and Pub Co; Kiryat haYeled; built Shikunei Schonfeld; Cen Hotel; various J educ schs; co-found and Co-dir, Hinuch Atzmai Torah Schs since 1951; dir, Cen Agudat Isr, Jerusalem, mem, Cen Comm, Agudat Isr World Org, mem exec, Cen Agudat Isr. Ed: Kol Isr, 1936-49; haMevaser, 1950-51; corresp, fgn newspapers, 1932-38. Home: 13 Mesilat Yesharim St, Jerusalem, Isr. Office: 2 Press St, Jerusalem, Isr.

POSENER, Charlotte Yael, Isr, organization exec; b. Berlin, Ger, Apr 16, 1910; d. Heinrich and Lilly (Spiro) Neumann; in Isr since 1938; PhD, U Berlin, 1933; m. Ludwig Posener; c: Yohanan Peres, Ruth Ottolenghi. Dir, bldg sect, Min of Educ, since 1964; chmn bd, govt co for cultural, youth and sports cens, since 1969; insp, head, dept for equipment, Youth Aliya, JA, 1940-52; adv, dept of research, Fgn Off, 1952-64; Home: 22 Pinsker St, Rehovot, Isr. Office: Min of Educ, Shivtei Israel St, Jerusalem, Isr.

POSENER, Ludwig Nachman, Isr, educator; b. Berlin, Ger, Feb 20, 1902; s. Moritz and Gertrude (Oppenheim); in Isr since 1937; PhD, U Berlin, 1926; m. Charlotte Neumann, Nov 15, 1930; c: Yohanan Peres, Ruth Ottolenghi. Asso prof, Tel Aviv U, since 1961, sr lectr, 1955-61; prin: J boarding sch, Västraby, Swed, 1934-37; Rehovot Munic HS, 1942-54; visiting prof, Catholic U of Amer, Wash DC, 1965-66; Author: Introduction to Statistics, 1966; Basic Statistics and Probability, 1970; contbr to profsl jours. Mem: Isr Math Soc; Royal Stat Soc, London; Inst of Math Stat, US. Spec interests: math, music. Home: 22 Pinsker St, Rehovot, Isr. Office: Tel Aviv U, Tel Aviv, Isr.

POSEQ, Avigdor, Isr, artist; b. Krakow, Pol, 1934; in Isr since 1942; studied under Aharon Avni; att Academia di Belle Arti di Brera, Milan, 1952-56; One-man shows: Chemerinsky Gal, 1958; Gal, 220, 1963; Lim Gal, all Tel Aviv; group shows include: Young Artists Exhb; Image and Imagination, both

Tel Aviv Mus; lectr, hist of art, Bezalel Sch of Art and Design; mem, dept art hist, Heb U, Jerusalem; designed sets for Isr theatre and films, 1957-60. Home: 2 Yahalel St, Tel Aviv, Isr.

POSHTER, Asher, Isr, business exec; b. Wasiliszki, Russ, Aug 14, 1897; s. Jacob and Sonia (Shapiro); in Isr since 1933; att Us: Vilno; Berlin; DJur, DRerPol, U Jena, Ger, 1927; m. Mirjam Fejgus, Jan 2, 1924; c: Eve Berman, Ora Maoz. Dir: Bank Leumi Inves Co, Ltd, mgn dir until 1967, dep gen mgr, Bank Leumi Inves Co, Ltd, mgr dir until 1967, dep gen mgr, Bank Leumi leIsr, until 1965, with bank since 1933; PIA, Isr Trust Mgmt; Delek, Isr Fuel Corp; Post off Bank; mem: Govt Securities Auth; Govt Securities Comm; served with Ger banks; with Reichs-Kredit-Gesellschaft AG, Berlin, 1928-33; lectr, Tel Aviv Sch of Law and Econ, 1950-61; dir, Tel Aviv Stock Exch, 1961-63; Past mem exec: KH; Assn of Friends of Heb U. Author: Wesen und Recht der Konzession Verleihung in Deuthland und Sowjet-Russland, 1927; Banking Theory and Practice Heb 1960. Home: 16 Biltmor St, Tel Aviv, Isr. Office: 26-28 Yehuda Halevi St, Tel Aviv, Isr.

POSIN, Sidney, US, social worker; b. Bklyn, NY, Apr 28, 1917; s. Benjamin and Celia (Levine); BS, CCNY, 1939; MSW, Carnegie Inst of Tech, Pittsburgh, Pa, 1942; m. Renée Karpf, Apr 3, 1955; c: Barry, Lisa. Asso exec dir, J Educ of St Louis, since 1965; rel sch tchr, R Temples, LA, San Diego, San Mateo, 1944-59; prog dir, J Comty Cen LA, 1944-52; field work instr, U of S Cal, LA, 1945-52; instr, social group work, San Diego State Coll; exec dir, San Diego J Comty Cen, 1952-55; planning dir, group work and recreation; Comty Wfr Council, San Diego, 1955-59; Health and Wfr Council of St Louis, 1959-63; W regional dir, CJFWF, 1963-65. Chmn: group work and recreation secys, United Comtys Funds and Councils, 1960-61; research comm, mem bd, Comty Wfr Council, San Diego, 1953-54; S Cal Fed Settlements, 1950; comm on neighborhood services, LA Wfr Council, 1949; social services div, JWF, LA, 1948; vice-pres, Amer Assn Social Workers, LA chap, 1951; discussion leader, 1960 White House Conf on Children and Youth; mem: Natl Assn Social Workers; Natl Conf J Communal Services; recreation commn, City of Olivette, 1962; bd: Natl Fed Settlements, 1950; coord councils, San Diego and LA. Home: 9443 Laguna Dr, St Louis, Mo. Office: 611 Oliver St, St Louis, Mo.

POSNACK, Emanuel R, US, attorney; b. NYC, Oct 24, 1897; s. Aaron and Sarah (Lourie); ME, Polytech Inst Bklyn, 1918; Cost acctnt: J Lee Inst of Cost Acctnt, 1921; NYU; LLB, Bklyn Law Sch, 1928; m. Ann Bock, Aug 2, 1936; c: Alan. Pvt practice, patent law, since 1928. Prin contribs: inventor recuperator for ind furnaces; stapling machines. Trustee, Gt Neck Syn; mem: NY Patent Law Assn; NY Co Lawyers; Amer, Fed Bar Assns; Pi Tau Sigma, hon. Author: The 21st Century Looks Back, 1946; Time to Understand, 1950; World Without Barriers, 1956; contbr to profsl jours. Home: 200 S Middle Neck Rd, Great Neck, LI, NY, Office: 355 Lexington Ave, New York.

POSNANSKY, Merrick, Ghana, archaeologist; b. Bolton, Eng, Mar 8, 1931; s. Simon and Dora (Cohen); in Ghana since 1967; BA, U Nottingham; dipl archaeol, Peterhouse, Cambridge, 1953; PhD, U Nottingham, 1956; m. Eunice Lubega, Feb 10, 1961; c: Sheba, Tess, Helen. Prof, archaeol, U Ghana, since 1967; warden, prehistoric sites, Royal Natl Parks, Kenya, 1956-58; curator, Uganda Mus, 1958-62; dep dir, Brit Inst Hist and Archaeol in E Afr, 1926-64; dir, Afr studies, Makerere U Coll, Kampala, Uganda, 1965-67; visiting prof: U of Cal, 1966; Heb U; Haille Selassie U, both 1967; Syracuse U, 1969; F, Brit Inst of Hist and Archaeol in E Afr; founder, pres, U Nottingham Archaeol Soc, 1951-52; Mus Assn of Middle Afr, 1959-61, vice-pres, Mus Assn of Tropical Afr, 1961-64; pres: The Uganda Soc, 1964-65; U Nottingham J Soc; chmn, Uganda Ancient and Hist Monuments Commn, 1964-67; vice-chmn, trustees of Uganda Mus, 1965-67; mem council: Ghana Hist Soc; Ghana Mus and Monuments Bd. Author: Prelude to East African History, 1966; ed, Uganda jour, 1962-66; mem ed comm, W Africa Jour Archaeol; contbr to Afr hist and archaeol jours. Office: U of Ghana, POB 3, Legon, Ghana.

POSNER, Charles, US, organization exec; b. Denver, Colo, Mar 18, 1913; s. Max and Yetta (Gorkin); BS, UCLA, 1936, BA; att U of S Cal, Sch of Social Work; m. Bernice Benson, Apr, 1946; c: Alan, Joseph. Asso dir, comty relations comm, J Fed Council, Gtr LA; visiting lectr, HUC, Cincinnati; PR cons: Natl Boys Week; Cedars of Leb Hosp; Mt Sinai Hosp;

in US since 1937; att U Berlin, 1922-23; PhD, U Giessen, 1924; ordained rabbi, J Theol Sem, Breslau, 1925; hon DD, HUC, NY, 1959; m. Lucie Horowitz, Dec 25, 1925 (decd); m. 2nd, Hilde Goldschmidt, May 24, 1932; c: Lucie Berkowitz, Michael, Jonathan, Deborah. Rabbi: Temple B'nai Abraham, Newark, NJ, since 1939; J Comty, Berlin, Ger, 1925-37. Natl pres, AJCong, since 1958, vice-pres, 1952; dir, Conf on J Material Claims Against Ger, since 1958; vice-chmn, governing council, WJC, since 1960, mem, exec bd, 1948; dir, JCC; chmn, UJA; pres, J Educ Assn, all Essex Co NJ. Author: Heroes and Adventures of the Bible, 1929; Jewish History, 1930; Children's Bible, 2 vols, 1933-34; We Jews, 1933; Friday Night, 1935; Life in Ghetto, 1937; The Great Jewish Books, ed by S Kaplan and H U Ribalow, 1952; The Dilemma of the Modern Jew, 1962; Popes from the Ghetto, 1966. Home: 306 Elmwynd Dr, Orange, NJ.

PRINZMETAL, Isadore H, US, attorney; b. Buffalo, NY, Jan 21, 1906; s. Harry and Anna (Stein); BA, UCLA 1927; JD, U of Cal, Berkeley, 1930; m. Nancy Kaufman, Apr 22, 1942; c: Karen, Michael, Deborah, Jan, Donna, Mark. Pvt practice, since 1930; res atty, MGM, Loew's Inc; fac mem, U of Cal, econ dept; mem, law firm Lissner, Roth & Gunter, 1930-36. Pres: LA Hillel Council, since 1952; Beverly Hills Bar Assn, 1965-66; vice-pres: natl AJCong, since 1953; LA J Comty Relations Comm; J Fed Council, Gtr LA; bd overseers, U of Judaism; Order of Coif; club, Hillcrest Country. Ed, Jour, Beverly Hills Bar Assn; ed bd, Cal Law Review, 1928-31. Home: 645 Comstock Ave, Los Angeles, Cal. Office: 1800 Ave of the Stars, Los Angeles, Cal.

PRITZKER, Abram N, US, attorney; b. Chgo, Ill, Jan 6, 1896; s. Nicholas and Annie (Cohen); PhB, U Chgo, 1916; LLB, Harvard U, 1920; m. Fanny Doppelt, Sep 12, 1921; c: Jay, Robert, Donald. partner, law firm, Pritzker and Pritzker, since 1920; lectr, acctnt, Northwestern U, 1921-22. USN, 1917-18. Vice-pres Wfr Fund, since 1955; dir: Fed of J Charities, since 1957; ADL since 1950; chmn, UJA, 1954; mem, B'nai B'rith, all Chgo; club, Standard. Home: 1040 N Lake Shore Dr, Chicago, Ill. Office: 134 N La Salle St, Chicago, Ill.

PROBSTEIN, Ronald Filmore, US, educator; b. NYC, Mar 11, 1928; s. Sidney and Sally (Rosenstein); BME, NYU, 1948; MSE, Princeton U, 1950, AM, 1951, PhD, 1952; hon AM, Brown U, RI, 1957; m. Irène Weindling, June 30, 1950; c: Sidney. Prof, mech engr, MIT, since 1962; cons, since 1955; instr, mech engr, NYU, 1947-48; asst prof, Princeton U, 1953-54; mem fac, since 1948; prof engr, Princeton, U, 1959-62, mem fac, since 1954. F: AAAS, 1961; Amer Inst Aeronautics and Astronautics, 1962; corresp mem, Intl Acad Astronautics; adv to pres, Technion, Isr, since 1965; mem: Amer Phys Soc; Amer Technion Soc. Co-author: Hypersonic Flow Theory, 1959; Hypersonic Flow Theory, Vol I, Inviscid Flows, 1966; ed: and trans, Introduction to Hypersonic Flow by G G Cherny, 1961; Physics of Shock Waves and High-Temperature Hydrodynamic Phenomena, 2 vols, 1966-67; Elements of Gas Dynamics and Classical Theory of Shock Waves, both by Zel'dovich and Raizer, 1968; contbr to sci and engr jours. Recipient: f, Guggenheim Found, 1960. Home: 53 Jordan Rd, Brookline, Mass. Office: 77 Massachusetts Ave, Cambridge, Mass.

PROCACCIA, Gualtiero, Isr, lawyer, educator; b. Florence, It, Nov 30, 1913; s. Giorgio and Gina (Passigli); in Isr since 1937; DJur, U Florence; m. Miriam Abeliowicz; c: Uriel Itamar. Asso prof and dean, law fac, Tel Aviv U; pvt practice since 1942. Author: Hataagid, Mahuto viTzirato, 1965; mem: Isr Bar Assn; club, Rotary. Contbr to profsl jours. Office: Tel Aviv U, Tel Aviv, Isr.

PROPES, Aron Zvi (pen name, **Margri**), Isr, executive; b. Mitau, Latvia, May 25, 1904; s. Moshe and Feiga (Kropman); in Isr since 1939; att Tchrs Sem, Riga, 1924-25; U Prague, Czech, 1926-30; m. Maria Aronstam, Nov 3, 1929. Found, dir, Intl Harp Contest, Isr; dir: Isr Festival, Caesarea; spec events dept, Min of Tourism; Hazamir, world Assembly of Choirs; Intl Youth City; co-found, first head, Betar youth movement, Riga, 1923-26, mem world exec, 1925-50, head: Betar Latvia, 1923-26, 1928, Czech, 1927, Pol, 1929-33, 1935-39; Rum, 1934, USA and Can, 1940-48, head World exec, since 1948. Latvian Army, 1932; US Army, war corresp, 1945. Found, dir: J Aviation League, NY, 1940; Jabotinsky aviation sch, NY; mem: world exec, New Zionist Org, 1946-49; ZCs; Zionist Council. Author: The Biography of Joseph Trumpeldor; How to Organize Congresses; fmr ed, Hamedina,

Betar weekly. Home: 4 Shadal St, Tel Aviv, Isr. Office: Migdal Shalom, POB, 29874, Tel Aviv, Isr.

PROPPER, Eugen, Isr, industrialist; b. Teplice-Sanov, Bohemia, Sep 5, 1911; s. Eduard and Ottilie (Frey); in Isr since 1939; att Commercial Acad, Teplice-Sanov; m. Alice Hajek, Apr 7, 1935; c: Dan, Gad. Co-found, dir, Osem Cos, since 1942; mem, bd dirs, Ind Devl Bank of Isr, since 1969; mgn owner, Teigwarenfabrik Propper, Czech, 1932-38; dir, Hadagan Ltd, Tel Aviv, 1939-62. Mem of presidium, Isr Mfr Assn, 1965-69, chmn, food sect, 1967-69, mem, exec council; mem council, Isr Export Inst; delg, Ist, 2nd Econ Confs, 1968, 1969; club, Rotary, Tel Aviv, Home: 139 Rothschild Blvd, Tel Aviv, Isr. Office: 3 Hachashmal St, Tel Aviv, Isr.

PROSKAUER, Joseph M, US, attorney; b. Mobile, Ala, Aug 6, 1877; s. Alfred and Rebecca (Leinkauf); AB, Columbia U, 1896; LLB, 1899; LLD, 1929; hon DHL, HUC, 1946; hon LLD; Dartmouth Coll, 1953; Brandeis U, 1955; LIU, NYU, both 1956; Colgate U, 1957; Fordham U, 1967; m. Alice Naumberg, Oct 14, 1903; c: Frances, Ruth, Richard. Sr mem, law firm, Proskauer, Rose, Goetz & Mendelsohn; admitted NY Bar, 1899; judge, Appellate Div, Ist dept, Supr Court NY, 1923-39; mem, NYC, Charter Revision Comm, 1935; cons to Amer delg, UN Conf, SF, 1945; chmn, NY State Crime Commn, 1951-53. Trustee, past pres, FJP; fmr pres, hon pres, AJComm; fmr pres, YMHA, NY; mem: Assn Bar City, NY, fmr vice-pres; NY State and Amer Bar Assns; NY Co Lawyers Assn, fmr pres; Phi Beta Kappa; Phi Beta Kappa Assos; clubs: Harmonie, past pres; Lotos; Manhattan; Lawyers; Columbia U; City. Home: 205 W 57 St, New York, NY. Office: 300 Park Ave, New York, NY.

PROUJANSKY, Zeev Joseph Isr, physician; b. Semiaticha, Russ, 1896; s. Solomon and Eva (Grunberg); in Isr since 1949; MRCS, LRCP, London U, Eng, 1920; MD, Brussels U, Belgium, 1922; m. Clara Grunberg, Apr 19, 1928; c: Ruth Gold. Head clinic, Kupat Holim Histadrut Med Service, since 1955; pvt practice: Antwerp, Belgium, 1922-40; NYC, 1941-49; clinical asst, internal med, Beth Isr Hosp, NYC, 1942-49, Pres: Belgian Zionist Fed, 1925-26; vice-pres: Isr-Belgium Friendship Soc; Young Zionist Org, UK, 1917-20; chmn, NYC Council, LZOA, 1941-49; judge, highest court of Histadrut Lab Org; mem, exec: acad professions section; phys sect, both Isr Lab Party; phys sect, Histadrut Lab Org; mem, IMA; club, Maccabi Sports, pres Antwerp, Belgium, 1925-40. Home: 19 Hakalir St, Tel Aviv, Isr.

PRUPES, Moshe, Isr, artist; b. Warsaw, Pol, Oct 18, 1922; s. Shmuel and Sara (Strumfman); in Isr since 1925; cert, Max Fine Sch of Tech Design, m. Miriam Oren, Oct 1962. Jt dir, Auni Sch of Art, since 1958; fmr, tchr, public schs. IDF, 1948-49; cultural off, res. Off, Agudat Hatzayarim; club Milo, mem comm. Author: series of children's books; Pesach Haggadah. Recipient: Dizengoff Prize, 1951; Art Prize: Educ Min, 1955; Histadrut, 1958. Home: 90 Ussishkin, St, Tel Aviv, Isr. Office: Auni Sch 6 Elat St, Tel Aviv, Isr.

PRYER, Hilary H, Austr, business exec; b. Landeshut, Ger, May 8, 1906; s. Felix and Gertrud (Hammerschlag) Prerauer; in Austr since 1936; m. Betty Wolff, June 24, 1937; c: Ian, Barry. Co-found and mgn dir, Natl Chem Products Pty Ltd, since 1939. Chmn, Australasian Council, B'nai B'rith, 1960-62, charter pres, Grand Lodge of Austr and NZ, 1962-65, pres, Sydney Lodge, 1948-50, 1956-58; bd dirs, Austr J Wfr Soc, since 1941; mem, mgmt comm, exec council, Austr J, since 1968. Home: 20 Victoria Rd, Bellevue Hill, NSW, Austr. Office: POB 242, Darlinghurst, NSW, Australia.

PRYWES, Moshe, Isr, physician, educator; b. Warsaw, Pol, Jan 3, 1914; s. Yehoshua and Yenta (Zylberberg); in Isr since 1951; MD, U Warsaw, 1939; m. Isabella Bloch, July 30, 1939; c: Jenny, Vivian; m. 2nd Rachel Levy-Brzezinski, 1966; c: Amnon, Rafael. Vice-pres, Heb U, Jerusalem, since 1968, prof, med educ, since 1965, asso dean, Heb U-Hadassah Med Sch, since 1952; adv: med schs in: Guat, 1959; Singapore, 1960; Arg, 1961; mem: WHO adv comm on med research, since 1969, expert comm on med educ, since 1961; exec comm, Natl Council for Research and Devl, since 1960. Maj, IDF, 1957. Chmn, Bath-Sheva de Rothschild Found for Advancement of Research in Isr; exec-secy, OSE, Paris, 1947-51; mem: IMA; Isr Assn for Advancement of Sci; Amer Public Health Assn; Assn of Amer Med Colls. Ed in chief: Isr Jour of Med Scis, since 1964; contbr to profsl jours. Recipient: Chevalier de la Légion d'Honneur, 1962. Home: 27

Bet Hakerem St, Jerusalem. Office: Heb U-Hadassah Med Sch, Jerusalem, Isr.

PSATY, I Roy, US, construction exec; b. NYC, Sep 25, 1904; s. Max and Rebecca (Besner); BCS, NYU, 1923; m. Irene Cooper, June 8, 1937; c: Michael, Merry. Pres, Psaty & Fuhrman, Inc, since 1946, dir, since 1924, on staff since 1922; vice-pres and dir, Park Seventy-Ninth Corp, since 1952. Pres and dir, Psaty Found, Inc, since 1948; pres, Bldg Trades Employers Assn, NY, 1960-61; vice-pres, NYU Commerce Alumni Assn, 1959-60; dir: Metrop Builders Assn; Bldg Contractors and Mason Builders Assn, mem, exec comm, trade agreement comm; trustee, Psaty Employees Fund; mem, bd dirs: Citizens Housing and Planning Council, NY, Inc; Public Bldgs Contractors Assn; mem, exec comm, Cement League; mem: Temple Emanu-El; Masons; Shriners; clubs: NYU; Natl Dem. Collaborated on book: From Blueprint to Building, 1947. Home: 895 Park Ave, New York, NY. Office: 369 Lexington Ave, New York, NY.

PUCKER, Bernard Harvey, US, art dealer; b. Kan City, Mo, Oct 19, 1937; s. Joseph and Ida (Katz); BA, Columbia U, 1960; att Heb U, 1960-61; MA, Brandeis U, 1969; m. Suzanne Finkelstein, June 15, 1959; c: Michael, Kenneth, Jonathan. Owner, dir, Pucker-Safir Art Gal, since 1968. Mem bd dirs, Solomon Schecter Day Sch, Boston. Contbr to book revs to J publs. Home: 90 Clinton Rd, Brookline, Mass. Office: 171 Newbury St, Boston, Mass.

PUGACZ, Yitzhak, Isr, artist; b. Kowel, Pol, Sep 13, 1919; s. Moshe and Hana (Rojter); in Isr since 1939; att Bezalel Art Sch, Jerusalem, 1947-50; m. Ruth Tirza, July 29, 1948; c: Hana, Michal. Tchr, Bezalel Art Sch, since 1949; repr Isr at intl exhb, Tours, Fr, 1963; designed woolen tapestry, Nazareth, 1964; toured cultural cens, Fr, upon invitation of Fr Govt, 1964, exhb, 1967. Brit Army, 1940-46; J Brigade, IDF, 1947-49. Album: Tmuna vaShir, with poems by Yehuda Amichai. Mem: Artists Assn, Jerusalem; Intl Assn of Plastic Arts, Paris. Recipient: Jerusalem Prize, 1962. Home and studio: 5 Pinsker St, Jerusalem, Isr.

PUNER, Morton, Fr, editor b. NYC, Nov 11, 1921; s. Jacob and Sarah (Zuckerman); in Fr since 1969; att: NYU, 1939-42; U Alaska, 1944-45; m. Adeline Ramoni, Feb 4, 1950. Cons: Ency Britannica, since 1969; Praeger Publishers, since 1969, vice-pres, 1964-69; Dept of Defense; ed, ADL Bulletin, 1956-64; asst to Vice-Pres of US, 1968. Ed: Freedom and Public Educ, 1953; Barriers: Patterns of Discrimination, 1957;

The Cause is Mankind, 1964; contbr to: Reporter; NY Times; Coronet; Catholic Digest; New Leader; New Republic. Mil Intelligence, US Army, WW II. Fmr pres, Alumni Yeshiva of Crown Hgts. Spec interests: cryptanalysis, political sci, J affairs. Home and office: La Seraphine, La Pierre Plantée, Route des Salins, St Tropez, Fr.

PUSITZ, Manuel E, US, surgeon; b. Toronto, Can, Dec 18, 1904; s. Abraham and Nellie (Brown); in US since 1929; BA, U Toronto, 1926; MD, 1929; MS, State U Ia, 1932; m. Anne Anderson, June, 1927; c: Martha Kellerman. Pvt practice, since 1933; orthopedic surg: Kan Crippled Children Comm; Stormont Vail Hosp; St Francis Hosp; Capper Found for Crippled Children; cons orthopedic surg, Security Benefit Hosp, all Topeka, Kan, since 1933; res orthopedic surg, clinical asst, dept orthopedic surg, U Hosps, 1931-32. Lt col, US Army MC, 1942-46. Dipl, Amer Bd of Orthopedic Surg; f: Amer Acad Orthopedic Surgs; Amer Cong Phys Med; Amer Acad for Cerebral Palsy; Intl Coll of Surgs; Intl Acad of Med; mem: Clinical Orthopedic Soc; Amer Acad Neur; Shawnee Co Med Soc; AMA; Kan Med Soc; B'nai B'rith; AJComm; Kan Crippled Children Comm; C of C; Masons, 32nd degree; Temple Beth Sholom; club, Kan Orthopedic. Contbr to med jours. Hobby: travel. Home: 701 Grandview, Topeka, Kan. Office: 628 Mills Bldg, Topeka, Kan.

PUTTERMAN, Harold, US, certified public acctnt; b. Antopol, Pol, May 16, 1923; s. Oscar and Rachel (Czernuk); in US since 1929; BBA, CCNY, 1943; m. Audrey Goldsmat, May 20, 1950; c: Karen, Lanee. Partner. Putterman, Rush, Shapiro & Gassman, CPAs, since 1961; partner: Rosenstein & Putterman, 1950-55; MacAlber Bank & Co, 1955-61. Mem: Temple Isr, Gt Neck, NY; CPA Soc, comms: coop-credit grantors, coop with bankers; Masons; NY State Soc CPAs; Amer Inst CPAs. Home: 24 Bayside Dr, Great Neck, NY. Office: 350 Fifth Ave, New York, NY.

PYLAUM, Helena, Isr, diplomat, librarian; b. Lemberg, Aus, Jan 4, 1902; d. Gershon and Maria (Korngold) Zipper; in Isr since 1924; att: U Lemberg; U Prague; Ecole des Hautes Etudes, Paris, all 1919-23; PhD, Music Conservatory, Lemberg; m. Hiram Peri (Pflaum), 1927, (div). Ret: counselor, Min Fgn Affairs, until 1968, chief libr, 1953-68; libr, head depts, Heb U, 1925-42; 1st secy and chargé d'affaires, Isr legation, Warsaw, 1950-52. Contbr articles on lit subjects and libr sci. Spec interests: music, lit, cats, tennis, bridge. Home: 3 Akiba St, Jerusalem, Isr.

Q

QUASTEL, Henrietta J, Canada, organization exec; b. NYC, Nov 30, 1905; d. Markus and Pearl (Thierfield) Jungman; in Can since 1947; BA, Barnard Coll, 1927; MA, Columbia U, 1928; m. Judah Quastel, Dec 27, 1931; c: Michael, David, Barbara Glick; Exec dir, Mizrachi-Hapoel Hamizrachi Women's Org, Can, since 1958; natl recording secy, natl chmn for educ; Canadian Hadassah, 1955-58. Home: 4585, Langara St, Vancouver, BC, Can.

QUASTEL, Judah Hirsch, Can, educator; b. Sheffield. Eng, Oct 2, 1899; s. Jonas and Flora (Itcovite); in Can since 1947; ARCS, BSc, DSc, London, U, 1921; PhD, Cambridge U 1929; hon DSc, McGill U; m. Henrietta Jungman, Dec 27, 1931; c: Michael, David, Barbara Glick. Prof, neurochem, U of BC, since 1966; f, Trinity Coll, Cambridge, U, 1924-29; dir research, Cardiff City Mental Hosp, Wales, 1929-41; dir, agric research council, Unit of Soil Metabolism, UK, 1941-47; prof, biochem, McGill U, Montreal, 1947-66; spec lectureships: Leeuwenhoek Lectr, Royal Soc of London, 1954, Brian Priestman Lectr, U New Brunswick, 1956; visiting prof: India, 1957, 1966; Kearney Found Lectr, U Cal, 1958; Heb U, Jerusalem, 1966. Pvt, Brit Army, 1917-19. F: Royal Inst Chem; Royal Socs: Can, London; NY Acad Scis, 1954; hon f: Japanese Pharm Soc, 1963; Can Soc Microbiol, 1966; N Pacific Soc Neur Psychol, 1966; mem, bd govs, Heb U, Jerusalem, since 1951; pres: Montreal Phys Soc, 1952-53; Can Biochem Soc, 1965-66; mem, med adv bd, Heb U-Hadassah Hosp, Heb U, 1952-66; natl secy, Can Friends

Friends of Heb U, 1948-65; found mem, Neurochem Commn, World Fed of Neur, 1959; mem: Intl Brain Research Org, 1961; N Amer Coop Commn of Study of Alcoholism, 1958; fmr mem: Water Pollution Research Bd, Eng; Med Research Council; Forestry Commn; Agric Research Council, Dept of Sci and Ind Research. Author: Neurochemistry, 1955, 1962; Metabolic Inhibitors, 2 vols, 1963; co-author: Chemistry of Brain Metabolism in Health and Disease, 1961; ed in chief, Methods in Medical Research, vol 9; contbr to sci jours. Recipient: Meldola Medal, Royal Inst of Chem, 1927; Beit Memorial Research f, 1928; Rockefeller Traveling f, 1936; Pasteur Medal, Pasteur Inst, Paris, 1955; Home: 4585 Langara, Vancouver, BC, Can. Office: U of BC, Vancouver, BC, Can.

QUINT, Howard H, US, educator, author; b. New Haven, Conn. Jan 3, 1917; s. Louis and Bessie (Clark); BA, Yale U, 1940; MA, Stanford U, 1942; PhD, Johns Hopkins, U, 1947; m. Eleanor Dolsky, Jan 9, 1944; c: Janet, David. Prof, hist, U Mass, since 1959; asst prof, U of S C, 1947-58, asso dir, inter-U comm on superior student, U Colo, 1958-59; visiting prof: Natl U, Mex, 1956; Johns Hopkins Sch of Advanced Intl Studies, 1961. Author: The Forging of American Socialism, 1953; Profile in Black and White, 1958; co-ed: Main Problems in American History, 1964; The Talkative President, 1964; contbr to hist jours. Mem: Amer Hist Assn; Miss Valley Hist Assn; AAUP. Home: 41 Blue Hills Rd, Amherst, Mass. Office: U Mass, Amherst, Mass.

PREMINGER, Julius, Isr, educator; b. Pol, July 11, 1924; s. David and Klara (Leder); MEE, Wroclaw Inst Tech, Pol, 1950, DEE, 1953; m. Shoshana, 1963; c: Aviya, David, Asso prof, EE, Technion, Haifa, since 1966, sr lectr, 1958-66. Chmn, Isr chap Intl Fed of Automatic Control, since 1968; mem: Conf Internationale des Grands Reseaux Electriques; sr, Inst of Elec and Electronic Engrs, US. Contbr to tech jours. Home: 22 Nitzanim St, Haifa, Isr. Office: Technion, Haifa, Isr.

PRESBERG, Miriam (pen name, Miriam Gilbert), US, author, literary agt; b. NYC, Dec 1, 1919; d. Charles and Kate (Kinstler) Goldstein; BA, Hunter Coll, 1940; m. Abe Presberg, June 18, 1944; c: Andrea, Karen. Dir, Authors and Publishers Service, since 1949; secy, Robert M McBride & Co 1941-43; ed, Didier Pub Co, 1943-45; publicity dir, Arco Pub Co, 1945-46; dir Island Press, 1946-48. Author, Eli Whitney: Master Craftsman, 1956; Jane Addams: World Neighbor, 1960; Starting an Aquarium, 1961; Cross Country Adventure, 1961; Henry Ford: Maker of the Model T, 1962; The Prophet Isaiah, 1963; Shy Girl, 1965; First Party, 1966; Glory Be! 1967; This is My Country, 1968; Care and Development of Your Baby, 1969. Recipient: Brotherhood award, NCCJ, 1962. Home and office: 146-47 29 Ave, Flushing, NY.

PRESS, Frank, US, scientist, educator; b. Bklyn, NY, Dec 4, 1924; s. Solomon and Dora (Steinholtz); BS, CCNY, 1944; MA, Columbia U, 1946, PhD, 1949; m. Billie Kallick, June 6, 1946; c: Paula, William. Chmn, dept geology and geophys, MIT; bd dirs, United Electro Dynamics Corp, since 1959; mem, Pres, Sci Adv Comm, 1961-64, Lunar Planetary Missions Bd, 1968; cons: Dept of State; Defense Dept; US Geological Survey; asso prof, geophys, Columbia U, 1952-55; fmr prof, geophys, Cal Inst Tech, dir seismological lab. F, Royal Astronomical Soc; pres, Sesmological Soc Amer, 1962, vice-pres, 1959-61; mem: Natl Acad Scis; Geological Soc Amer; Amer Phys Soc. Co-author, Elastic Waves in Layered Media, 1957; contbr to profsl jours. Recipient Columbia Medal for Excellence, 1959; Cal Sci of Year, 1960; CCNY Townsend Harris Medal, 1962. Hobby: sailing. Home: 26 Spring Valley Rd, Belmont, Mass. Office: MIT, Cambridge, Mass.

PRESSER, Jacob, Netherlands, educator, author; b. Amsterdam, Feb 24, 1899; s. Gerrit and Aaltje (Stempel); PhD, U. Amsterdam, 1926; m. 2nd, Bertha Hartog, Jan 22, 1954 Prof, U Amsterdam, since 1948, lectr, 1946-48; tchr, Vossiusgymnasium, 1926-47. Author: De Tachtigjarige Oorlog, 1941; Orpheus en Ahasverus, poetry, 1945; Napoleon, 1946; Amerika, 1949; De Nacht der Girondijnen, Eng, Breaking Point, 1957; Ondergang, 1965, Eng, The Destruction of the Dutch Jews, 1969. Mem: Historisch Genootschap; Maatschappij v Nederlandse Letterkunde. Recipient: Wynaends Francken Prize, 1946; Van der Hoogt Prize, 1958; Jan Campert Prize, 1966. Hobbies: music, chess. Home: Lindenlaan 40B, Beraen, Netherlands. Office: U Amsterdam, Netherlands.

PRESSMAN, David, US, biochemist, educator; b. Detroit, Mich, Nov 24, 1916; s. Jacob and Lottie (Frankfort); BS, Cal Inst Tech, 1937; MA, UCLA, 1938; PhD, Cal Inst Tech, 1940; m. Reinie Epstein, 1940; c: Jeffrey, Adele. Asso inst dir, Roswell Park Memorial Inst, since 1967, dir, biochem research, since 1954; research prof, microbiol, Med Sch, SUNY, Buffalo, since 1968, research prof, chem, grad sch, since 1956; asso mem, head, immunochem sect, Sloan-Kettering Inst, NYC, 1947-54; asso prof, immunochem, Cornell U Sch of Med, 1952-54. F: NY Acad Sci; AAAS; mem: Amer Chem Soc; Amer Soc Biol Chems; Amer Assn Immunologists; Soc Experimental Biol and Med; Amer Assn Cancer Research. Contbr to sci jours. Home: 76 Edge Park, Buffalo, NY. Office: 666 Elm St, Buffalo, NY.

PRESSMAN, Harold B, US, business exec; b. Phila, Pa, Apr 1, 1913; s. Charles and Bessie (Balmazie); BS, Carnegie Inst Tech, 1933; m. Lillian Slater, June 18, 1939; c: Richard, Mark. Pres, Pearl-Pressman-Liberty, Inc, printers, lithographers, since 1955. Pres: Phila br, United Syn Amer, 1959-63 Cong Temple Sinai Phila, 1949-54; Graphic Arts Assn, Del Valley, 1965-67; chmn, finance comm, mem bd and exec comm, Printing Inds Amer, 1967-70; mem: trade council, Allied J Appeal, 1961-68; bd, Graphic Arts Tech Found, since 1968; exec comm, Isr Bonds. Recipient: Man-of-Year, Printing Inds of Phila, 1967. Spec interests: charitable orgs, golf, fishing. Home: Cedarbrook Hill Apts, Wyncote, Pa. Office: 5th and Popular Sts, Philadelphia, Pa.

PRESSMAN, Lee, US, attorney; b. NYC, July 1, 1906; s. Harry and Clara (Rich); AB, Cornell U, 1926; LLB, Harvard

U, 1929; m. Sophia Platnik, June 28, 1930; c: Ann, Marcia, Susan. Pvt practice, NYC and Wash DC, since 1929; participated in legal cases concerning lab unions, civil liberties and minority group rights before US Supr Court; counsel: United Steelworkers of Amer, 1936-48; Natl Marine Engrs Beneficial Assn, since 1948; asst gen council, Agric Adjustment Admn, 1933-35; gen counsel: Fed Emergency Relief Admn, 1936; Natl Youth Admn, 1936; Works Progress Admn and Resettlement Admn, 1936-37; CIO, 1936-48. Mem: Phi Beta Kappa; Bar Assn of NYC; Free Syn of Mt Vernon, NY. Contbr to legal jours. Home: 26 Forster Ave, Mt Vernon, NY. Office: 50 Broadway, New York, NY.

PRESSMAN, Lillian S, US, communal worker, editor; b. Windber, Pa, Feb 16, 1912; d. Morris and Goldie (Medow) Slutsky; BSc, Temple U, Phila, 1933; m. Harold Pressman, June 18, 1939; c: Richard, Mark. Ed, Hadassah News Bull, Phila chap, since 1954; free-lance writer: Phila J Times 1933-36, City ed, 1936-39; Phila Record, 1933-36; free-lance, publicity, 1933-41; natl ed, The Sphinx, Phi Sigma Sigma, 1933-61; dir, publicity and promotion, radio sta, WPEN, 1939-40; publicity dir, YM-YWHA, 1935-36; ed, The News, Temple Sinai, 1949-54. Pres: Phila women's div, Amer Technion Soc, since 1967; mem bd, Phila women's div, Amer Friends of Heb U, since 1958, vice-pres, 1958-60; vice-pres, Phila chap, Hadassah, 1957-60; natl chmn, PR, Phi Sigma Sigma, since 1961; mem: Theta Sigma Phi; Temple Sinai Sisterhood; club, Green Valley Country. Recipient: Gold Key, Phi Sigma Sigma, 1958; plaque, 1961; cited twice by Isr Bonds. Hobbies: music, golf. Home: 318 Old Farm Rd, Wyncote, Pa.

PRESSMAN, Mildred (pen name Mildred Phillips), US, lyricist composer; b. Phila, Pa; d. Isaac and Dora (Phillips) Goldberger; att Strayers Bus Coll, Phila, Pa; m. Harry Pressman; c: c: David. Numerous songs recorded professionally, including: Happy Holidays; Mambo Rock; If You're Not Completely Satisfied. Fmr: chmn, Blood Bank, Phila; pres, dist off, B'nai B'rith. Recipient: ASCAP award, 1964, 1965, 1966. Hobby, writing. Home and office: 3710 Conshohocken Ave, Philadelphia, Pa.

PRESTON, Ruth L, US, business exec, editor; b. NYC, July 26, 1906; d. Joseph and Augusta (Stadler) Levin; BA, Syracuse U, 1927; att: Sorbonne, 1929-30; NYU, 1930; MA, Columbia U, 1930; m. Robert Peskin, Nov 15, 1931; c: Abbey Klein, Stephen. Partner, Levin Corp, since 1937; fashion ed, columnist, New York, Post, since 1946; dir, Prudential Finance Corp, since 1958; caseworker, FJP, 1928; advt exec, Macy's NY, 1930; dist dir, Temp Emergency Relief Assn, NY State, 1932-33; asso promotion dir, Harper's Bazaar 1944-45. Exec bd, HS of Fashion Industries, NY Bd of Educ; fashion comm, FJP, since 1950; leg comm, The Fashion Group; publicity chmn, Union Temple, Bklyn, 1957-58; mem: Natl Found for Infantile Paralysis, since 1950; NY Newspaper Guild; Amer Fed TV and Radio; Phi Beta Kappa; Phi Kappa Phi; Alpha Epsilon Phi, club, NY Newspaper Womens. Hobbies: travel, music, theater. Home: 2 Fifth Ave, New York, NY. Office: 75 West St, New York, NY.

PREUSS, Walter, Isr, educator, author; b. Berlin, Ger, Jan 20, 1895; s. Eugen and Alice (Lowenherz); in Isr since 1922; DEcon, Berlin U, 1920 m. Erna Seidel, 1942; c: Reuven, Dvora. Ret; vice-dean, fac social sci, Tel Aviv U, 1960-65, on fac since 1934; dir, stat dept, Histadrut, 1922-60; lectr, econ, stats: Inst for Higher Studies, Isr Govt; Sch for Histadrut Workers; Sch for Social Work, Tel Aviv. Author: Census of Jewish Labor in Palestine, 1927, 1937; Paolei Zion, The Jewish Labor Movement in Palestine, 1928. Die Jüdische Arbeiterbewegung in Palestine, 1936; Der Ring Schielisst Sich, 1950, Heb, 1968; Thirty Years of Histadrut, 1950; Democratic Socialism, 1951; Social Policy in Israel and the World, 1952; Co-operation in Israel and the World, 1960; Der Einfluss der Jüdischen Einwanderung auf die Okonomischen Verhaltnisse Palestinas; A Statistical Survey of Jewish Workers in Palestine; Co-operative Enterprise in Israel; The Problem of Trade Unionism; The Histadrut in Numbers; The Labor Movement in Israel, 1965, Ger, 1969; Die Arbeiterbewegung in Israel, 1969; co-author: Die Theoretischen Grundlagen des Zionismus, 1922; The Economic Situation in Palestine, 1932, 1934; contbr to newspapers. Member: presidium, Ger Immigrants Assn; gen secy, Jüdisches Fürsorgeamt, Hapoel haTzair, both Ger; delg, WZCs. Home: 16 Rembrandt St, Tel Aviv, Isr.

PRICE, Julius Joseph, US, rabbi; b. Worcester, Mass, June 14, 1887; s. Abraham and Rose (Aronson); BA, U of Pa, 1908; MA, Johns Hopkins U 1910; PhD, Columbia U, 1914;

ordained rabbi, JTSA, 1914; m. Florence Cooper, June 14, 1916; c: Winston, Ira. Chaplain, Bx Co jail, since 1948; rabbi: Goel Zedek Cong, Toronto, Can, 1914-16; Temple Sholem, Plainfield, NJ, 1916-21; Sinai Temple NYC, 1921-31; chaplain: Nordacs Soc, since 1926. Pres, Natl Chaplains Assn, 1948; mem: Masons; KP; Shriners; club, Lions. Author: Yemenite Manuscripts of Megilla, 1914; Yemenite Manuscripts of Pesahim, 1914; The Laws of Barter and Sale According to the Talmud, 1915; Yemenite Manuscripts of Zebahim, 1920; Yemenite Manuscripts of Mo'ed Katon, 1920; contributing ed, Masonic Craftsman; contbr on Semitics and Greek to scholarly publs. Home: 1560 Grand Concourse, New York, NY.

PRICE, Leo, US, physician; b. Poltava, Russ, Feb 9, 1894; s. George and Anna (Kopkin); MD, Cornell U, 1931; postgrad studies, Krankenkasse, Vienna; Cardio-Renal Hosp Frankfurt/M, London Heart Hosp, all 1932; m. Harriet Goldberg, July 19, 1928; c: Linda. Ret; dir: Union Health Cen, NYC, 1937-60; em instr, card, Polyclinic Hosp and Med Sch, 1942-61; asso clinical prof em ind med, NYU; cons: health center, lithographic ind, NY; meat ind, Chgo; ind hygiene, USPHS, 1949-54; secy, med adv comm, SSA, 1955; Dir: NY Heart Assn, 1952-60; NY State Heart Assembly 1956-60; NY Heart Assn; Natl TB Assn, 1952-57; Ind Med Assn, 1951-53; mem: comty health services, Natl Council on the Aging, 1960-62; AMA, comm care of workers in ind, 1948-60; NYC Med Soc Ind Med, 1954-59; IMA. Contbr Author: Epidemiology of Health, 1953; The Handicapped and Their Rehabilitation, 1957; Worlk and the Heart, 1959 Contbr articles in sci publs. Home: 20 Oakdale Dr, Hastings-on-Hudson, NY.

PRICE, Norman A, US, business exec; b. Cleveland, O. Feb 15 1914; s. Max and Iva (Zuckerman); att: Adelbert W Reserve U, 1932-35; Cleveland Coll, 1945, 1955; m. Mildred Trattner, Aug 8, 1937; c: Maxine, Joyce. Exec vice-pres, the Colson Corp, since 1956; vice-pres: Rusco Inds Inc since 1966; Asso Mfrs Intl, SA, Chgo, since 1959; dir, LA Darling Co, Bronson, Mich, since 1960; vice-pres, dir, Colson, Can, since 1954; gen mgr, Harvard Mfg, since 1966; insp, Aro Equipment, 1943-44; insp sup, Warner Swasey, 1944-45; salesman, State Chem Mfg Co, 1945-46; pres, Norman Price & Assos, 1946-52. Pres, Material Handling Inst, 1963; seminar head, Amer Mgmt Assn, 1960; mem: Masons; Intl Sales Execs; B'nai B'rith. Contbr to sales and bus mgmt mags. Spec interests: tape books for the blind, philately, numismatics. Home: 20759 Fairmount Blvd, Shaker Hgts, O. Office: 24300 Solon Rd, Bedford Hgts, O.

PRICE, Richard Lee, US, attorney; b. NYC, Sep 19, 1940; s. Saul and Claire (Bernstein); BA, Roanoke Coll Salem, Va, 1961; LLB, NY Law Sch, 1964; m. Carolyn Small, July 10 1965; c: Lisa. Law secy to judge, since 1969; pvt practice, since 1965. Chmn, Coop Village Health Drive; co-chmn, Coop Village: UJA; Fed; sgt, 7th precinct police auxiliary, 1970; mem: NY Co Lawyers Assn; Assn of Bar of NYC. Contbr to law jours. Home: 577 Grand St, New York, NY. Office 111 Centre, New York, NY.

PRICE, Robert, US, investment trust mgr, lawyer; b. NYC, Aug 27, 1932; s. Solomon and Frances (Berger); AB NYU, 1953; LLD, Columbia Law Sch, 1958; m. Margery Wiener, Dec 18, 1955; c: Eileen, Steven. Pres: Price Capital Corp; Price Mgmt Corp, both since 1969; pvt law practice, NYC, 1958-65; law clerk, judge, US Dist Court, S Dist NY, 1958-59; asst US atty, S Dist, NY, 1959-60; partner, Kupferman & Price, 1960-65; chmn bd, pres, Atlantic States Ind Inc, 1963-66; pres, WNYV, Pensacola, Fla, 1965-66; dep Mayor, NYC, 1965-66; exec vice-pres, dir, Dreyfus Corp, 1966-69; lectr: U Conn; Natl Ind Conf Bd; U Cincinnati; Ind U. US Army, 1953-55. Chmn, NYC Port Auth Negotiating Comm for World Trade Cen, 1965-66; mem, NYC Policy Planning Council, 1966; spec counsel, NY State jt leg comm on court reorg, 1962-63; asst counsel, NY State jt leg comm on NY banking laws, 1961-62; chmn, govt and civil service div, UJA, Gtr NY, 1966; co-chmn, Metrop NY Red Cross Blood Dr, 1966; vice-pres, NY Young Reps Club, 1957-58; delg, NY State Rep Conv, 1962, 1966; campaign mgr: John Lindsay campaigns for, US Cong; Nelson Rockefeller Ore Rep Pres primary campaign, 1964; Lindsay campaign for mayor, NYC, 1965; bd dirs: New Dimensions in Educ; Amer Friends Heb U; trustee, NYC, Police Pension Fund; mem: Amer, Fed Communications; NY State, NYC Bar Assns; NY State Dist Attys Assn; Tau Kappa Alpha; club, City. Contbr articles to publs. Recipient: Yeshiva U

Heritage award, 1966; public service award, Queens Catholic War Vets, 1966; public Service award Phila, 21 Jewel Sq Club, 1967; Outstanding Young Man of Year award, NYC Jr C of C, 1967, one of America's Ten Outstanding Young Men, US Jr C of C, 1967. Home: 25 E 86 St, New York, NY. Office: 555 Madison Ave, New York, NY.

PRICE, Saul, US, jurist; b. NYC, July 8, 1902; s. Barnett and Jennie (Marshall); LLB, Fordham Law Sch, 1923; m. Claire Bernstein, June 28, 1927; c: Barbara Behr, Joyce Goodman, James, Richard. Judge, Munic and Civil Court, NYC, since 1948; pvt practice, 1925-27, 1938-48; asst dist atty, 1927-38, all NYC. Secy, bd of dirs, Amalgamated Dwellings Inc, 1938-50; mem: bd of trustees, Educ Alliance, since 1950; natl exec bd, Union Orthodox J Congs, 1948-53; chmn, sponsors comm, NY Heart Assn, 1951; dir, E Side C of C, since 1945; pres: Bialystoker Syn and Talmud Torah, 1943-53; Sunshine Circle, Heb Day Nursery, 1933-53. vice-pres, NY Civil and Criminal Bar Assn, 1945-55; mem: comms, UJA; B'nai B'rith; ZOA; Grand St Boy's Assn; Amer Bar Assn; NY Co Lawyers Assn; KP, past chancellor, trustee; Henry St Settlement Old Timers. Home: 500A Grand St, New York, NY.

PRIEL, Vivian, Isr, editor; b. NYC, Apr 11, 1934; s. Victor and Eleanor (Joffe) Ross; in Isr since 1959; BA, Barnard Coll, NY, 1954; MA, Columbia U, Tchrs Coll, 1957; m. Aaron Priel, Apr 11, 1954; c: Ethan, Adam, Sharon, Eliav. Exec ed, Isr Jour Agric Research, since 1963. Home: 41 Hish St, Rehovot, Isr. Office: Volcani Inst Agric Research, Bet Dagan, Isr.

PRIJS, Bernhard, Switz, researcher, chemist; b. Würzburg, Ger, Sep 19, 1916; s. Joseph and Bella (Horowitz); in Switz since 1934; PhD, U Basel, 1946; m. Rosalie Schwarz, 1946; c: Moses, Leo, David, Jakob, Aron, Joseph, Fanny, Rahel, Esther, Mirjam, Benjamin. Lectr, chem, U Basel, since 1959, research asst, 1946-59; Author: Kartothek der Thiazolverbindungen, 4 vols, 1952; co-author and ed, Die Basle hebräischen Drucke, 1492-1866, pub, 1964; contbr to sci jours. Home: Rudolfstrasse 28, Basel, Switz. Office: Institut für Anorganische Chemie der Universität, Spitalstr 51, Basel, Switz.

PRIMAKOFF, Mildred C, US, scientist, educator; b. NYC, July 12, 1913; d. Isidore and Bertha (Klein) Cohn; AB, Hunter Coll, 1931; PhD, Columbia U, 1938; Hon ScD, Womens Med Coll, Phila, 1966; m. Henry Primakoff, 1938; c: Nina, Paul, Laura. Prof, biophysics and phys biochem, Johnson Found, U of Pa, since 1961; career inves, Amer Heart Assn, since 1964, established inves, 1953-58; research asso: Cornell U, 1938-46; Wash U, 1946-58; asso prof, biochem, 1958-60; Harvard U, 1950-51. Mem: Amer Chem Soc; Harvey Soc; Amer Soc of Biol Chems; Amer Acad Arts and Scis; The Amer Inst of Chems; Phi Beta Kappa; Sigma Xi;. Contbr to profsl jours. Recipient: Garvan Medal, Amer Chem Soc, 1963. Home: 135 S 18 St, Philadelphia, Pa. Office: Richards Bldg, U of Pa, Philadelphia, Pa.

PRINCE, Harry M, US, architect; b. NYC, Jan 22, 1889; s. John and Susie (Simmonds); att: Cooper Union, 1909; Carnegie Inst of Tech, 1918; Amer Expeditionary Force U, Fr, 1919; m. Caroline Krooks, June 29, 1925; c: John. Sr partner, Harry M Prince Assos, since 1941; architectural cons, NY State Leg comm on housing and urban redevl, 1948-67; commn: Tenement House Dept, 1934-38; housing div, Dept of Housing and Bldgs, 1938-41; cons architect, NYC Housing Auth, 1941-45; commn of appraisals, condemnation awards Rondout water takings, 1938-48; architect for: Concourse Village; House of Living Judaism; UAHC, all NYC; Temple Kenneseth Isr, Allentown. Pa; mem, US commn to Eng to study civilian protection services, 1941; chief civilian protection adv, US Office of Civilian Defense, 1941-43; F, Amer Inst of Architects, pres, NY chap 1952-53; chmn, architects adv panel, UAHC, 1948-49; UAHC delg, Syn Council of Amer, 1942-48; pres: Ft Wash Syn, 1936-45; NY Fed of Temple Pres, 1943-44; NY State Assn of Architects; mem: Natl panel: Amer Arbitration Assn; War Emergency Bd, NYC, 1939-43; Trustee, Temple, Temple of the Covenant, 1945-49. Author: Synagogue Planning, 1950; Liturgical Architecture-The Synagogue, 1954. Recipient: architectural award, Fifth Ave Assn, 1952; Rutkins Memorial award, NY Chap, Amer Inst of Architects, 1966, public service award, NY State Assn Architects, 1969. Home: 115 Central Park W, New York, NY. Office: 101 Park Ave, New York, NY.

PRINZ, Joachim, US, rabbi, communal leader, author; b. Burkhardsdorf, Ger, May 10, 1902, s. Joseph and Nani (Berg);

R

RAAB, Menachem, US, rabbi; b. Phila, Pa, July 9, 1923; s. Feivel and Anna (Soffer); BA, Yeshiva U, 1944; ordained rabbi, Rabbi Isaac Elchanan Theol Sem, 1947; MA, Educ Admn, Columbia U, 1948; m. Sara Hammer, June 12, 1949; c: David, Moshe, Tikva, Noam, Yaron. Rabbi, Cong People of Truth, since 1965; dir, Trenton Heb Acad, since 1965; rabbi: Beth Emeth Cong, 1950-55; Beth Joseph Cen, Rochester, 1955-63; dir, Hillel Sch, 1963-65. Found, pres, Mizrachi Org of Gtr Trenton; Rabb Council of West NY, 1955-58; exec bd: RabCA; Natl Council Yeshiva Prins; bd dirs, Rel Zionists Amer; vice-pres, Yeshiva U Rabb Alumni, 1962-63. Author: Understanding the Siddur, 1957. Contbr to rel jours. Home: 27 S Westfield Ave, Trenton, NJ. Study: 1201 W State St, Trenton, NJ.

RABAU, Erwin M, Isr, physician; b. Berlin, Ger, Nov 15, 1899; s. Max and Bertha (Glas); in Isr since 1933; att U Heidelberg; MD, U Berlin, 1922; m. Ziona Katinski, Mar 3, 1936; c: Nurit Cahanski, Yael Kazir, Micha. Dir, gyn dept, Tel Hashomer Hosp, since 1951; asso clinical prof, gyn and obstet, Heb U, Med Sch, Jerusalem; prof, Tel Aviv U, Med Sch, since 1959; dir gyn and obstet dept, Beilinson Hosp, 1936-47; Hayarkon Hosp, 1947-49. Hon mem, Turkish Gyn Soc; mem: IMA; Intl Fertility Assn; corresp mem, Amer Soc for Study of Sterility; IJFL. Contbr to profsl jours. Home: 21 Levi Itzhak St, Tel Aviv, Isr. Office: Tel Hashomer Hosp, Isr.

RABB, Irving W, US, business exec; b. Boston, Mass, Feb 4, 1913; s. Joseph and Lottie (Wolf) Rabinovitz; AB, cum laude, Harvard Coll, 1935; m. Charlotte Frank, June 23, 1938; c: Betty, James. Vice-chmn of bd, Stop & Stop Inc, with firm since 1943. Pres: Beth Isr Hosp of Boston, since 1967; Hillel Found, Cambridge, 1956-58; Super Market Inst, 1963; vice-pres, Natl Assn Food Chains, 1957-58; chmn, NE Bonds for Isr, 1952, Boston, 1951; bd dirs: Newton Jr Coll, 1962-63; Mass Safety Council; Asso J Philanthropies, since 1953; BBB, since 1951; Boston J Vocational Service, 1950; Boston chap, NAACP, 1944; United Comty Service, 1955-56; Cerebral Palsy of Gtr Boston, 1959; bd trustee, Combined J Philanthropies of Gtr Boston; mem, Masons; clubs: Harvard; Belmont Country; Newton Squash and Tennis. Home: 1010 Memorial Dr, Cambridge, Mass. Office: 393 D St, Boston, Mass.

RABB, Maurice G, Zambia, business exec, legislator; b. Johannesburg, Oct 31,1910; s. Joseph and Golda (Galgut) Rabinowitz; BCom, U of Witwatersrand, 1934; m. Peggy Susman, Apr 12, 1939; c: Tessa, John, Anne. Co dir, since 1946; JP, since 1958; alderman, City of Livingstone, since 1959, mem, munic council, 1949-59, mayor, 1951-52, 1956-57; fmr: buyer, Woolworths Ltd, S Afr, 1935-46; mem, N Rhodesia Leg Council, 1959-62. Served, S Afr Defense Forces, 1941-45. Mem: exec, Livingstone Memorial Cong, since 1948, past pres; Zambia Tax Review Bd; Livingstone Comm, Natl Mus Bd of Zambia; Bd Commerce and Ind; Commonwealth Parl Assn; fmr, mem, Livingstone Hosp Adv Bd; club: Rotary. Home: Spray View, Beaufort Rd, Livingstone, Zambia. Office: POB 22, Livingstone, Zambia.

RABB, Maxwell M, US, attorney; b. Boston, Mass, Sep 28, 1910; s. Solomon and Rose (Kostick); BA, Harvard Coll, 1932, LLB, Law Sch, 1935; m. Ruth Cryden, Nov 2, 1939; c: Bruce, Sheila Weidenfeld, Emily Maltby, Priscilla. Partner, law firm, Stroock & Stroock & Lavan, since 1958; admn asst to: Senator Henry Cabot Lodge, 1937-43; Senator Sinclair Weeks, 1944; legal and leg cons to US Secy of Navy, James Forrestal, 1946; mem law firm, Rabb and Rabb, Boston, Mass, 1946-52; asso counsel to Pres of US, 1953-54; Secy to US Cabinet, 1954-58; chmn, Amer delg to UNESCO, 10th session, 1958. USNR, 1944-46. Dir Amer-Isr C of C; dir and vice-pres, J Publ Soc; pres, US Comm for Refs; chmn, govt div, UJA, 1953, 1957; mem: bd of govs, HUC-JIR; civil rights comm, natl comm on org and planning, ADL, vice-chmn, NY exec comm; natl adv bd for youth, B'nai B'rith Found; dir: J Publ Soc of Amer; Amer Friends of the Alliance Is-

raelite Universelle; clubs: Harvard; Army and Navy; Belmont Country. Recipient: commendation ribbon, USN, 1944; Commendatore Order of Merit of It Rep, 1959. Home: 145 Central Park W, New York, NY. Office: 61 Broadway, New York, NY.

RABB, Norman S, US, business exec; b. Boston, Mass, Sep 13, 1905; s. Joseph and Lottie (Wolf) Rabinovitz; BA, cum laude, Harvard Coll, 1925; hon LHD, Brandeis U, 1958; hon deg, D Laws, Northeastern U, 1967; hon Alumnus, Heb U; m. Eleanor Epstein, Aug 1, 1933; c: Hope Edison, Jan Cohen. Ret,1965; sr vice-pres, Stop and Shop Inc, since 1959, vice-pres, dir, since 1929; lt, USN, 1941-44. Vice-pres, Combined J Philanthropies, 1967, hon life trustee, mem, exec comm; bd of gov, AJComm, hon pres, NE Region; chmn, bd of overseers, Hiatt Inst, Jerusalem; mem, adv comm: public charities, comm of Mass; Citizens' Scholarship Found; Hillel adv council, Metrop Boston; trustee: Heb Rehab Cen for Aged; Boston U; Mass; Brandeis U, found trustee, chmn bd, 1961-67; United Isr Appeal, Inc; Temple Adath Isr; Children's Med Center; Perpetual Benevolent Fund; Beth Isr Hosp; dir: Newton-Waltham Band and Trust Co; Mass Assn for Mh; Amer Friends of Heb U, Gtr Boston Chap; Market Lodge; B'nai B'rith; Amer Trade and Ind Devl with Isr, Inc, found mem, 1968; mem: JWV; Amer Legion; Aleppo Temple, Shriners; Masons; life mem, NAACP; clubs: Harvard of Boston; Belmont Country. Home: 180 Beacon St, Boston, Mass. Office: 393 D St, Boston, Mass.

RABB, Sidney R, US, business exec, civic worker; b. Boston, Mass, Oct 20, 1900; s. Joseph and Lottie (Wolf) Rabinovitz; att Harvard Coll, 1920; hon: LLD, Tufts U, 1961; MA, Harvard Coll, 1962; LHD, Boston Coll, 1964; DCS, Suffolk U, 1966; m. Esther Cohn, Feb 29, 1920; c: Carol Goldberg, Helene Cahners. Chmn of Bd, Stop & Shop, Inc, since 1930, treas, 1925-65. Served USMC, WW I. Dir: Boston Edison Co; Cahners Pub Co; Civic Educ Found; Gillette Co; Heb Rehab Cen for Aged; Johnston Mutual Fund; Liberty Mutual Fire Ins Co; Liberty Mutual Ins Co; Ritz-Carlton Hotel Co, Boston; 1975 World Freedom Fair, Inc; dir, mem exec comm: Boston Coll; Boston Co; Boston Safe Deposit & Trust Co; Super Market Inst, past pres; hon life trustee: Beth Isr Hosp, mem exec comm, past pres; Combined J Philanthropies; trustee: Boston Urban Found; Boston Sym Orch; Harvard Med Cen; Mass Gen Hosp, and mem, McLean Hosp Trustee comm; Mus Fine Arts, Boston; Recuperative Cen; hon trustee, mem visiting comm, Harvard Bus Sch; vice-pres, dir, Nathan H Gordon Corp; f: Amer Acad Arts and Scis, mem commn on Future of Acad; Brandeis U,mem bd overseers, Florence Heller Grad Sch for Advanced Studies Social Wfr; vice-chmn, mem exec comm, Mass comm, Catholics, Prots and J; trustee, vice-pres, past pres, Public Educ City of Boston; overseer, Boys' Club, Boston; mem: at large of Natl Council, Boy Scouts Amer, Regional Exec Comm, region 1; comm, U Resources of Bd Overseers, Harvard U; natl bd govs, Isr Bond Org; Mass Bay United Fund, chap Plan Comm, 1966-67; regional panel of commn, White House Fs; hon alumni, Heb U, Jerusalem, 1965; trustee, Perm Life Membership Funds, Eliot lodge, Masons; dir, Kehillath Isr Syn; hon life trustee, Temple Isr; clubs: Belmont Country; Harvard, Boston; Palm Beach Country. Home: 65 Commonwealth Ave, Boston, Mass. Office: 393 D St, Boston, Mass.

RABB, Theodore K, US, educator; b. Templice-Sanov, Czech, Mar 5, 1937; s. Oskar and Rosa (Oliner) Rabinowicz; in US since 1956; BA, MA, Queen's Coll, Eng, 1958; PhD, Princeton U, 1961; m. Tamar Janowsky, June 7, 1959; c: Susannah, Jonathan. Asso prof hist, Princeton U, since 1967; fmr: asst prof hist, Harvard U, 1963-67; instr hist: Northwestern U, 1962-63. Stanford U, 1961-62. Mem: comm on quantitative data in hist, Amer Hist Assn; comm on info tech, Amer Council of Learned Soc's Conf on Brit studies; bd, Conf of J Studies; Hist Assn; Past and Present Soc; Soc for Hist of Discoveries; Hakluyt Soc; Renaissance Soc of Amer; Amer J Hist Soc; f, Royal Hist Soc. Author: The Thirty

Years War, 1964; Enterprise and Empire, 1967; ed: Action and Conviction in Early Modern Europe, 1969; Jour of Inter-Disciplinary History; ed bd: Computers and Humanities; Computer Studies in the Humanities and Verbal Behaviour. Recipient: f: Social Sci Research Council; Amer Phil Soc; Amer Council of Learned Socs; Guggenheim Found. Hobby, chess. Home: 293 Hartley Ave, Princeton, NJ. Office: Princeton U, Princeton, NJ.

RABENSTEIN, Manfred, US, reverend; b. Tann, Ger, July 13, 1911; s. Hugo and Lina (Fichtelberger) Rev, Tchrs Sem, Cologne, Ger, 1932; att, Union U of Cinn; m. Flora Plaut, Mar 31, 1936; c: Aaron, Bernard, Naomi, Jacob. Rev, New Hope Cong, since 1939. Mem, of Orthodox Congs. Home: 7866 Greenland Pl, Cincinnati, O. Study: 1625 Cresthill Ave, Cincinnati, O.

RABI, Isidor I, US, physicist, educator; b. Rymanow, Aus-Hung, July 29, 1898; s. David and Scheindl (Teig); in US since 1900; BCh, Cornell U, 1919; PhD, Columbia U, 1927; hon: DS: Princeton U, 1947; Harvard U, 1955; Williams Coll, 1958; LLD, Dropsie Coll, 1958; DHL, HUC, 1958; DSc, Technion, Haifa; m. Helen Newmark, Aug 17, 1926; c: Nancy Lichtenstein, Margaret. Prof, physics, Columbia U, since 1937, Higgins Prof, since 1950, mem fac, since 1929; chmn, gen adv comm, AEC, since 1953, mem, 1947-53; mem, Natl Research Adv Comm, since 1952; US mem, UN planning panel for Intl Atomic Meeting; tutor, physics, CCNY, 1924-27; f: Barnard, 1927-28; Intl Educ Bd, 1928-29; Ernest Kempton Adams, 1935; lectr: U of Mich, 1936; Stanford U, 1938; mem staff, asso dir, radiation labs, MIT, Cambridge, Mass, 1940-45; vice-pres, Intl Conf on Peaceful Uses of Atomic Energy, Geneva, 1955, 1958; chmn, Pres' Adv Comm on Sci, 1957; mem, NATO Sci Comm, 1958. Served, Students Army Training Corps, 1918. F, Amer Phys Soc, mem council, since 1945, past pres; US delg, UNESCO Conf, Florence, It, 1950; mem: bd trustees, Asso Us Inc, since 1947; bd govs, Weizmann Inst; UN Sci Comm; gen adv comm, Arms Control and Disarmament Agcy; Natl Acad Sci; Japanese Acad; Acad of Sci of Brazil; Amer Phil Soc; Sigma Xi. Asso ed, Physical Review, 1935, 1938, 1941-44; contbr to sci jours. Recipient: semicentennial prize, Sigma Xi, 1939; $1000 Prize, AAAS, 1936; Elliot Cresson Medal, Franklin Inst, 1942; Nobel Prize in Physics, 1944; Medal for Merit, 1948; King's Medal, 1948; cdr, Order of Southern Cross, Brazil, 1952; Commander, Légion d'Honneur, Fr; Priestly Memorial Award, 1964; named U Prof, Columbia U, 1964. Clubs: Fac, Columbia U; Cosmos, Wash, DC. Home: 450 Riverside Dr, New York, NY. Office: Columbia U, New York, NY.

RABIN, Chaim, Isr, educator; b. Giessen, Ger, Nov 22, 1915; s. Israel and Martel (Wolodarsky); in Isr since 1956; att Heb U, Jerusalem, 1933-34; BA, London U, 1937, PhD, 1939; dipl, Sch of Oriental and Afr Studies, London, 1938; PhD, Oxford U, 1943, MA, 1944; m. Batya Emanuel, 1952; c: Nechama Yemima. Chmn, Inst of J Studies, Heb U, Jerusalem, 1967-69; fac mem since 1956; Cowley lectr, post-bibl Heb, U of Oxford, 1941-56. Fmr: pres, London J Grad's Assn; ed bd: Heb U Bible Project; Ency Miqraith; sr mem, Oxford U Isr Soc; mem, Heb Lang Acad. Author: A Prelude to Modern Science, 1946; An Arabic Reader, 1947; A Hebrew Reader, 1949; Ancient West-Arabian, 1951; The Zadokite Documents, 1953, 2nd ed, 1958; Qumran Studies, 1957; co-author: Everyday Arabic, 1945; Everyday Hebrew, 1943; ed: Sifrut, 1955-56; Aspects of the Dead Sea Scrolls, 1958; Iyyunim beSefer Yehoshua, 1960; Ency Kelalit, 1960; Mehkarim baMegilot haGenuzot, 1961; Studies in the Bible, 1961; Textus, 1960. Home: 8 Keren Kayemeth St, Jerusalem, Isr. Office: POB 7158, Jerusalem, Isr.

RABIN, Samuel, US, jurist; b. NYC, Oct 12, 1905; s. Harry and Sarah (Kaufman); BA, Cornell U, 1926; JD, NYU, 1928; m. Florence Mittlemann, Feb 11, 1938; c: Robert, Jane. Asso justice, Supr Court, Appellate Div, Second Judicial Dept, since 1962; NY State assemblyman from Queens, 1945-54; judge, Supr Court, 10th Judicial Dist, 1954-67. Past pres: Queens Council for Social Wfr; trustee, J Comty Services of LI; mem, bd of founds, trustee, LI J Hosp; fmr mem, Wfr Council of NYC; club: Queens Lawyers of FJP, past pres. Home: 182-15 Radnor Rd, Jamaica Estates, Jamaica, NY. Office: Appellate Division, Supreme Court, 45 Monroe Pl, Brooklyn, NY.

RABIN, Yitzhak, Isr, diplomat, army officer; b. Jerusalem, 1922; Agric Sch, Kfar Tabor; grad, Staff Coll, Eng; hon degs: Heb U, Jerusalem; Dropsie Coll, Phila; Brandeis U, Mass; Ye-

shiva U, NYC; m. two c. Isr ambass to the US, since 1968; chief of staff, IDF, 1964-68; served WW II, Allied invasion of Syria, oprs behind enemy lines, 1941; battalion cdr, Palmach, 1944; service cdr, 1948 War of Independence; mem, Isr delg, Rhodes armistice negotiations, 1949; head: tactical oprs dept, Hqr; training dept, IDF; commanding off, N Command, 1956-59; head, Manpower Br, 1959-60; Dep Chief of Staff, head, gen staff br, 1960-64. Office: Emb of Isr, Washington, DC.

RABINER, Abraham M, US, neurologist, educator; b. Bklyn, NY, Sept 21, 1892; s. Max and Dora (Brower); MD, Albany Med Coll, 1916; m. Ella Feldman, Nov 4, 1919 (decd); c: Betty Rothfeld, Saul, Alice Dreyfuss; m. 2nd, Pauline Blum, 1964. Pvt practice since 1923; prof em, neur, SUNY, Coll of Med, since 1959, fac mem since 1934; dir of neur and clinical dir, J Chronic Disease Hosp, 1924-61; cons neur: St Catherine's Hosp; J Chronic Disease Hosp; Maimonides Hosp; Kings Co Hosp; LI Coll Hosp; Bklyn Hosp; Vets Hosps; Bklyn; NY; Northport, LI, Bklyn State Hosp; clinical studies, neuropathology: Hamburg; Berlin; London, all 1923; instr, neur, Columbia U, 1922-25; asso prof, neur and psycht, NY Postgrad Med Sch, 1924-34. Lt, US Army MC, 1917-19. Dipl, Amer Bd of Psycht and Neur; f: NY Acad of Med; Amer Coll of Phys; Bklyn Neur Soc, pres, 1934; Amer Coll Angiology, pres, 1963. Mem: Amer Neur Assn; NY Neur Soc; Assn for Research in Nervous and Mental Diseases; NY Soc for Clinical Psycht; Soc of Biol Psycht; Kings Co Med Soc, fmr: trustee, vice-pres; NY State Med Soc, chmn, sect of neur and psycht; Alpha Omega Alpha. Asso ed, Jour of Angiology. Contbr to med jours. Home: 90 Eighth Ave, Brooklyn, NY. Office: 78 Eighth Ave, Brooklyn, NY.

RABINO, Saul, US, artist; b. Odessa, Russ, July 7, 1891; s. Jacob and Malka (Gurovitz) Rabinovitz; in US since 1923; att: Imperial Art Sch, Odessa; Ecole des Arts Decoratifs, Paris; m. Eva Abracen, Oct, 1925; c: Gilda Collins. Works exhb: Yad Vashem, Jerusalem; Bezalel Mus, Jerusalem; Mus of Modern Art, Haifa; Mus Eilat; LA Co Mus; San Diego Balboa Park Mus; Palace of Legion of Honor; World's Fair, SF, 1937, works selected by a jury; Laguna Beach Art Gal; pvt collections: Eddie Fisher; Jerry Lewis; Mary Pickford; Edward G Robinson; Jan Peerce; Rothschild Collection, Paris; perm collections: UN; J Mus, NY; Libr of Cong, Wash, DC; Cen Public Libr, NY; Cen Public Libr, LA; murals at LA J Home for the Aged. Mem: Farband; Mizrachi. Home and studio: 621 N Martel Ave, Los Angeles, Cal.

RABINOR, Samuel G, US, attorney; b. Bklyn, NY, Dec 5, 1907; s. Aaron and Esther (Enteen); LLB, Bklyn Law Sch, 1929; m. Shirley Arkawy, 1941; c: Harold, Edward. Pvt practice, since 1930; fmr spec counsel: Bank of Manhattan; West Publishing Co; Bankers and Shippers Ins Co, all 1935-39. Served, US Army, 1943-45. Chmn, legal med and tort comms, Queens Co Bar Assn; co-chmn: lawyers' div, FJP, Queens, since 1939; Queens drive, Friends of Heb U, since 1959; vice-pres: Queens Lawyers Club of FJP; Jamaica Lawyers Club; gov, Queens, NY State Assn of Trial Lawyers; mem: planning bd, Village of Woodburgh, NY, since 1958; Queens Co and NY State Bar Assns; NY State Plaintiff's Trial Assn; Judge Advocates Assn; Comm on Admn of Justice, Queens; clubs: Woodmere Bay Yacht; Seawane Golf; Lake Placid Ski. Home: 825 Ivy Hill Rd, Woodmere, LI, NY. Office: 163-18 Jamaica Ave, Jamaica, NY.

RABINOV, Yehoshua, Isr, author, farmer; b. Pinsk, Pol, Apr 15, 1906; s. Itzhak and Sara (Jtoransky); in Isr since 1925; att HS, Vilna, 1921; m. Braha Dubovsky; c: Hana Drezner. Author: beShadmot Israel, 1941; Misholim laOfek, 1946; meAl Har haAkeda, 1950; Shira Amitai, 1957; Brakim baHalon, 1963. Mem, PEN. Recipient: awards: Kishon Council, 1959; Ussishkin, 1960; Holon, 1963. Home: Kibbutz Gvat, Isr.

RABINOVICH, Gutman, Isr, newspaper exec; b. Latvia, June 25, 1913; in Isr since 1936; att Inst of Law, Riga; m. Yova Buchsbaum; c: Itamar, Michal Kaplan. Mgn dir, Maariv daily, since 1947; mem bd, Itim, Isr News Agcy; personnel mgr, Pal Potash Works, 1940-48. Vice-pres, Ilan, Isr Polio Found; fmr: chmn: Avivia; Hasmonia; gen secy, Tzohar, all Latvia; Betar cdr: S and Jerusalem dists. Home: 22 Hamarganit St, Ramat Gan, Isr. Office: 2 Carlebach St, Tel Aviv, Isr.

RABINOVICH, Isaiah, US, educator, author; b. Khodorkov, Kiev, Russ, Nov 22, 1904; s. Eisik and Sheindel (Rabinovich);

in US since 1960; grad, Tchrs Sem, Kiev, 1923; AB, U of Manitoba, 1930; MA, U of Toronto, 1946; D Rel Educ, JTSA, 1950; m. Sarah Unick, Nov 14, 1924; c: Solomon. Prof, Heb Lit, Coll of J Studies, Chgo, since 1960; prin, J Folk Schs, Toronto, Can, 1935-60; dir, educ and cultural div, Can J Cong, Ont, 1940-47; lectr, Heb lit, J Tchrs Sem, 1953-60. Mem: World Union of J Scholars; Poalei Zion; Heb Schs; club: Heb PEN of Amer, exec comm. Author: Hasifruth beMashber Hador, 1947; Yezer Viziyrah, 1952; Ner Dolek, 1954; Behevley Doram, 1959; Aley Adamoth, 1963; haSipporeth haIvrit Mehappeset Gibbor, 1967; Major Trends in Modern Hebrew Fiction, 1968; contbr to Heb and Yiddish jours. Recipient: Louis Lamed Lit award, 1947. Home: 6442 N Richmond, Chicago, Ill. Office: Coll of J Studies, 72 E 11 St, Chicago, Ill.

RABINOVITZ, Samuel, Rhodesia, business exec, communal worker; b. Vasuli, Rum, May 26, 1893; s. Zeidl and Raechel; in Rhodesia since 1902; m. Rebecca Sarif, July 13, 1919; c: Raymond, Anita Abrahamson. Chmn, mgn dir, The Union Agcys Ltd, since 1913. Hon life pres, Cen Afr ZO, past found, first chmn; co-found, chmn bd govs, Carmel Sch, J Day Sch; pres, Bulawayo Heb Cong, fmr secy, treas; natl chmn, United Isr Appeal; delg to confs of: WJC; WZO; S Afr Zionist Fed; Rhodesian Zionist Conf; vice-pres, Bulawayo C of C; fmr: pres, Bulawayo Chovevei Zion Soc; club: Weizmann Country, co-found, mem exec, council. Home: 6 Edward Rd, Kumalo, Bulawayo, Rhodesia. Office: POB 2, Bulawayo, Rhodesia.

RABINOVITZ, Yehoshua, Isr, public servant; b. Vishenba, Pol, Nov 3, 1911; in Isr since 1934; tchrs dipl, Tchrs Sem, Vilna, Pol. Mayor, Tel Aviv Munic, since 1969, vice-mayor, 1959-60; mem, Tel Aviv City Council, chmn, treas comty. Mem cen comm, Lab Party, Tel Aviv zone. Contbr to the press. Office: Tel Aviv Municipality, Kikar Malchei Israel, Tel Aviv, Isr.

RABINOVITZ, Zvi Meir, Isr, educator; b. Radomsko, Pol, Jan 15, 1908; s. Itzchak and Roiza Bornstein; tchrs cert, Tchrs Sem, Jerusalem, 1937; BA, MA, Heb U, Jerusalem, 1957, PhD, 1967; m. 2nd, Debora Engelstein. Prof, U Tel Aviv; fmr: tchr, Tchrs Sem; prof, Bar Ilan U. Served Haganah. Author: Halacha veHagadah bePeeutei Yanai, 1965; Midrash haGadol baMidbar. Home: 8 Kremieux St, Tel Aviv, Isr. Office: Tel Aviv U, Ramat Aviv, Isr.

RABINOWICZ, Ernest, US, educator; b. Berlin, Ger, Apr 22, 1926; s. Leo and Fanny (Bochner); in US since 1950; BA, Cambridge U, Eng, 1947, PhD, 1950; m. Ina Feldman, Aug 23, 1953; c: Deena, Judith, Laura. Prof mech engr, MIT, since 1967, fac mem since 1944; visiting prof, Technion, Haifa, 1969. Mem sch comm, Temple Emanuel, Newton, Mass. Author: Friction and Wear of Materials, 1965; Physical Measurement and Analysis, 1963. Recipient: Hodson Award, Amer Soc of Lubrication Engrs, 1957. Home: 14 Exmoor Rd, Newton, Mass. Office: MIT, Cambridge, Mass.

RABINOWICZ, Harry Mordka, Eng, rabbi, author; b. Warsaw, Pol, July 8, 1919; s. Nathan and Sheindel (Perlow); BA, hons, City of London Coll; PhD, Jews Coll; m. Bella Grossman, June 15, 1951. Rabbi, Dollis Hill Syn, since 1952; lectr, Jews Coll, since 1968; min: St Albans Heb Comty, 1947-49; Ilford Syn, 1949-51; hon chaplain, RAF, 1947-48. Hon pres, JPA Comty Cen; examiner, London Bd J Rel Educ. Author: A Guide to Hasidism, 1960; The Jewish Literary Treasures, 1962; A Guide to Life, 1964; The Legacy of Polish Jewry, 1965. Home: 151 Anson Rd, London, Eng.

RABINOWICZ, K Aharon Moshe, Isr, jurist; b. Czech, 1915; s. Yehuda and Gennie Rosenkranz; att: Rabb Sem, Breslau, 1933-44; U Brno, 1934-39; Heb U, Jerusalem, 1940-44; PhD, U Amsterdam, 1965; M Comparative Juris, U Washington, 1965; m. Hanna Halpern, 1945; five c. Academic secy, fac law, Heb U, since 1949; fmr: fgn corresp, journalist, 1945-48; ed, Pal Digest; secy, research council, Isr PM's off; Fulbright f, US; visiting lectr, SUNY. Off, Haganah. Zone chmn, Lions Intl; mem: Intl Org of Jurists; adv, Hist Assn for J of Czech; appointing assn, Intl Assn for Authors of Law Works; and lectr, Intl Symposium for Hum Rights, Wash; intl cong, World Peace Through Law. Author: Makor Niftach, 1938; Grundlage der Bibelsprache in 1000 Bibelversen, 1939; Al haMusar wal haCherew, 1942; bEin Shkia uZricha, 1945; contbr to press and periodicals; lectrs on Isr radio. Hobbies: music; art; reading. Home: 11 Balfour St, Jerusalem, Isr. Office: Heb U, Jerusalem, Isr.

RABINOWITCH, Eugene, US, biochemist, educator; b. St Petersburg, Russ, Apr 27, 1901; s. Isaac and Zinaida (Weinlud);

in US since 1938; PhD, U Berlin, 1926; m. Anna Majersohn, Mar 12, 1932; c: Alexander, Victor. Prof, chem, biol, sr adv, Cen for Sci and Hum Affairs, SUNY, since 1968; research asso: U Gottingen, 1929-32; U Copenhagen, 1933; U Coll, London, 1934-38; MIT, 1939-46; chem, Manhattan Project, 1943-46; research prof, botany, biophysics, U of Ill, 1947-68. Author: Periodic System, 1930; Photosynthesis, three vols, 1946, 1951, 1954; Minutes to Midnight, 1950; Uranium Chemistry, 1951; Dawn of a New Age, 1964; ed: Bulletin of Atomic Scientists, since 1946; Atomic Age, 1963; contbr to profsl jours. Mem: Cen for Advanced Study, U of Ill, 1966-68; Amer Phys Soc; Amer Chem Soc; Biophysics Soc; Fed of Amer Scis. Home: 1021 W Church St, Champaign, Ill, Office: SUNY, Albany, New York.

RABINOWITSCH, Wolf Zeev, Isr, physician; b. Pinsk, Russ, Nov 28, 1900; s. Saul and Regina (Marcus); in Isr since 1933; MD, U of Koenigsberg, 1928; att Acad for J Sci, Berlin,1921-31; m. Irma Selz; c: Saul, David. Head surg, outpatient dept, Munic Hosp of Haifa, since 1933; mem, Supr Med Appeals Comm, Isr Min of Defense; fmr: phys: U of Koenigsberg Hosp, 1929-30; J Cmty, Berlin, 1931-33; Hadassah Hosp, Haifa, 1933-41; perm mem, med bd of Isr Mins of Treasury, Lab and Justice. Mem: bd, IMA, Haifa br; bd, Jews from Pinsk in Isr; Surg Soc of Isr; Hist Soc of Isr; Urol Soc of Isr; fmr: co-found, Lith and Pol J Students Org in Ger; mem bd, Munic Drs of Haifa. Author: Lithuanian Hasidim, 1961. Recipient: prize, Koenigsberg U, 1928; Leib Yaffe prize for Lithuanian Hasidim, 1961. Spec interests: J hist; Hasidim. Home and office: 34 Nordau St, Haifa, Isr.

RABINOWITZ, Aaron, US, realtor; b. Russ, Feb 22, 1884; s. Jacob and Jennie (Braudy); in US since 1884; hon degs: HUC, 1962; JTSA, 1965; Juniata Coll, Pa, 1968; m. Clara Greenhut, Dec 5, 1921; c: Betty, Susan, Alan. Chmn, bd dirs, Fred F French Inves Co, Inc, since 1937; pres, found, Spear and Co, Inc, 1903-28; pres, found, Spear Securities Corp, since 1926; bd dirs: Amalgamated Housing Corp, 1927-41; Amalgamated Dwellings, Inc, since 1929, treas, 1929-50; Hillman Housing Corp, since 1946, treas since 1946. Commn, NY State Bd of Housing, 1926-42; condemnation commr, Port of NY Auth, 1932-33; mem: NY State Ins Bd, 1935-43; Real Estate Bd of NY, gov, 1927-29; dir: Lawyers Trust Co, 1931-47; Ave of Amers Assn, since 1949; Lawyers Title Corp of NY; exec comm, 1938-43; adv comm, realty and mortgage, Mfrs Hanover Trust Co; bd trustees, Baron de Hirsch Found; finance comm, Cong Emanu-el, since 1951, trustee, 1936-59, vice-pres, 1949-56. Home: Hotel Westbury, 15 E 69 St, New York, NY. Office: 551 Fifth Ave, New York, NY.

RABINOWITZ, Ezekiel, US, journalist, organization exec; b. Zwanitz, Russ, Sept 19, 1892; s. Chaim and Rosa (Wortsman); in US since 1914; att: U of Constantinople, Turkey, 1911-14; Bklyn Law Sch, 1927; m. Anna Marantz, May 3, 1923; c: Nina Slutsky. Ed staff, The Day, since 1947, fmr mem, 1922-23; asst ed, Dos Yiddishe Folk, ZOA, 1915; managing ed, Haint, NYC, 1917; editor, Far'n Folk, 1925-27; co-founder and dir, JTA, 1918-20; delg, ZC, Carlsbad, 1921; exec secy, Amer ORT, 1930-33; co-founder and exec secy, Non-Sectarian Anti-Nazi League, 1933-35; pres, Audio Scriptions, Inc, 1935-47. Mem: Sons of Zion; J Natl Workmen's Alliance. Transl into Yiddish: Gesammelte Schriften, by Theodor Herzl, 1920. Author: Justice Louis D Brandeis, The Zionist Chapter of His Life, 1968. Home: 111-14 76 Ave, Forest Hills, NY. Office: 183 E Broadway, New York, NY.

RABINOWITZ, Isaac, US, educator; b. Bklyn, NY, July 3, 1909; s. Bezalel and Lily (Garowitz); BA, cum laude, U of Cal, 1929; PhD, Yale U, 1932; m. Alice Elson, 1946; c: Susannah, Abigail. Chmn, Dept of Semitic Lang and Lit, Cornell U, since 1966, fac mem since 1957; tchr, public schs, St Louis, 1932-33; dir, Youth Educ, UAHC, 1935-38; dir, B'nai B'rith Hillel Found: U of Mich, 1938-40; Bklyn Coll, 1940-44; U of Pa and Temple U, 1944-45; natl dir, B'nai B'rith Boys Work, 1945-46; dir, E New York YM-YWHA, 1946-55; prof, J Studies, Wayne State U, 1955-57. Served, Off of Strategic Services, 1942-45. Hellman Scholar, U of Cal, 1928-29; fs: Kohut, Yale U, 1930-31; Amer Council of Learned Socs, 1934-35; Guggenheim, 1961-62. Mem: Amer Oriental Soc; Soc Bibl Lit, Amer Schs of Oriental Research; Phi Beta Kappa. Author: Towards a Valid Theory of Biblical Hebrew Literature; contbr to profsl publs. Home: 912 E State, Ithaca, NY. Office: Cornell U, Ithaca, NY.

RABINOWITZ, Kurt, Isr, physician; b. Vienna, Aus, May 26, 1916; s. Lazar and Hanika (Thaler); in Isr since 1938; att

Vienna U, 1936-38; MSc, Heb U, Jerusalem, 1941, PhD, 1947, MD, 1956, MPH, 1961; m. Sonya-Sarah Bergner, Dec 15, 1942; c: Moshe, Alfred. Dep dir, regional health services, since 1960; fmr: dir, dist public health lab, Min Health, 1941-56; dir, Beit Shemesh Med Cen, Hadassah, Jerusalem,1951-58; family phys, Kiriat Yovel Med Cen, Jerusalem, 1958-60. Maj, med corps, IDF, 1950-67. Repr: highest council: State Drs Assn; IMA; Jerusalem Med Assn; Public Health Phys Assn; mem: Isr Assn of Microbiol. Contbr to profsl jours. Recipient: Maimonides prize, Boston Med Soc, 1955. Hobbies: gardening, sports, music. Home: 39 Hehalutz St, Jerusalem, Isr. Office: Min Health, 18-20 King David St, Jerusalem, Isr.

RABINOWITZ, Louis I, Isr, rabbi, author; b. Edinburgh, Scotland, May 24, 1906; s. Jacob; in Isr since 1962; MA, U of London, 1928, PhD, 1934; m. Tania Amiel, 1927; c: Naomi, Denise, Jacob. Asso ed, Ency Judaica; gov, Heb U; rabbi: Shepherds Bush Syn, 1926-28; S Hackney Syn, 1928-32; Cricklewood Syn, 1932-39, all in Eng; chief rabbi: United Heb Cong of Johannesburg, S Afr, 1945-61; Fed of Syns in the Transvaal, 1946-61; prof, Heb, U of Witwatersrand, 1945; lectr, homiletics, Harry Fishel Inst, Jerusalem. Chaplain, Brit Army, 1939-44. Hon pres: S Afr J Hist and Social Soc; Soc for Wfr of J Deaf; World Herut-Hazohar; S Afr SF; mem: actions comm, WZO. Author: The Social Life of the Jews of Northern France in the 12th to 14th Centuries, 1938; Soldiers from Judea, 1942; The Herem Hayyishub, 1945; Jewish Merchant Adventurers, A Study of the Radanites, 1948; Out of the Depths, 1951; Far East Mission, 1952; Sparks from the Anvil, 1955; Sabbath Light, 1960; asso ed, Ency Judaica. Home: 6 Mapu St, Jerusalem, Isr.

RABINOWITZ, Meyer A, US, physician; b. Ukraine, Apr 21, 1887; s. David and Bessie (Rabinowitz); in US since 1890; MD, Cornell U, 1907; m. Lena Post, 1908; c: Adolph, Beatrice Rabbino. Ret; fmr cons phys, J Hosp, NYC, since 1950. i/c J Hosp unit, WW II. Hon dir, Friends of Heb U, Jerusalem; mem: Amer Phys Comm; Kings Co Med Soc; f: Isr Med Assn. Contbr to med jours. Hobbies: travel, photography. Home: 200 E 71 St, New York, NY.

RABINOWITZ, Sheldon, US, certified public acctnt; b. Des Moines, Ia, Nov 19, 1932; att State U of Ia; m. Roselind Pomerantz, July 8, 1951; c: Vic, Julie, Joy, Elyse. Partner, Lybrand Ross Bros & Montgomery, since 1955. Treas, JWF, Des Moines, chmn, spec gifts; chmn, Bd of J Educ. Contbr to profsl jours. Spec interest: going to Isr. Home: 25211 Duffield Rd, Beachwood, O. Office: 1070 Union Commerce Bldg, Cleveland, O.

RABINOWITZ, Stanley S, US, rabbi; b. Duluth, Minn, June 8, 1917; s. Jacob and Rose (Zeichik); BA, State U of Ia, 1939; ordained rabbi, JTSA, 1943, MHL, 1949; MA, Yale U, 1950; m. Anita Lifson, June 24, 1945; c: Nathaniel, Sharon, Judith. Rabbi, Adas Isr Syn since 1960; acting exec dir, United Syn of Amer, 1945-46; rabbi: B'nai Jacob Syn, New Haven, Conn, 1946-53; Adath Jeshurun Syn, Minneapolis, 1953-60. Vice-chmn, natl youth commn, B'nai B'rith since 1964; natl pres, Aleph Zadik Aleph; secy, RA; pres, ZOA, New Haven, 1950-52. Home: 3115 Normanstone Terr, Washington, DC. Study: 2850 Quebec St, NW, Washington, DC.

RABWIN, Marcus H, US, surgeon; b. Eveleth, Minn, Aug 16, 1901; s. Frank and Rose (Sax); MD, U of Minn, 1925; postgrad work, U Vienna, 1926; m. Marcella Bennett, Sep 19, 1934; c: Frank, Dina, Mark, Paul. Chief of staff, Cedars of Leb Hosp; pvt practice of surg since 1930. Dipl: Amer Bd of Surg; Bay Dist Surg Soc; LA Surg Soc; mem: Beverly Hills Acad of Med, pres, 1951; Cal State and LA Co Med Assns; AMA; LA Acad of Med; Amer Coll of Surgs; chmn, med div: Comty Chest; JWF; ARC; Cedars of Leb Bldg Fund. Contbr to med jours. Recipient: Selective Service medal, WW II. Home: 856 Devon Ave, Los Angeles, Cal. Office: 9730 Wilshire Blvd, Beverly Hills.

RACINE, Emmanuel, Isr, business exec; b. 1911; s. Georges and Berthe (Orchoff); att Law Sch, Paris; m. Sara Wexler, 1938; c: Cecile Peyser, Daniella Wexler. Pres and gen mgr, Société Gazoline SA, Paris, since 1939; vice-pres, Isr Petrol Inst; gen mgr: Delek, Isr Fuel Corp, since 1951; Tanker Services Ltd, Tel Aviv; Sopetrol, Geneva; dir: Naphta Oil Prospect Co; Isratom; Isr Nuclear Engr Co, Ltd; Amisragas Ltd; Frutarom, Electrochemical Inds Ltd; Unico Ltd; all Isr; dir: Tri Continental Pipe Lines Ltd; Utilgas Ltd, Lagos, Nigeria. Pres, Fr Union; treas: Assn of Jews from Fr in Isr; J Scout Movement in Fr; Youth Wfr Org; Magbith;

vice-pres, Fr-Isr C of C; mem, exec comm, Fonds Social Juif Unifié-all orgs in Fr, until 1951. Recipient: Croix de Guerre; Médaille de Résistance; decorated: Haganah and Six-Day War. Homes: 123 Rothschild Blvd, Tel Aviv, Isr; 146 Blvd Haussmann, Paris, Fr. Office: 6 Ahuzat Beit, Tel Aviv, Isr.

RACKMAN, Emanuel, US, rabbi; b. Albany, NY, June 24, 1910; s. David and Anna (Mannescovitch); BA, Columbia Coll, 1931; JD, Columbia Law Sch, 1933; ordained rabbi, Yeshiva U, 1934, DD, honoris causa, 1961; PhD, Columbia U, 1953; m. Ruth Fischman, Dec 28, 1930; c: Michael, Bennett, Joseph. Rabbi, Fifth Avenue Syn, since 1967; asso prof, political phil, jurisprudence, Yeshiva U, asst to pres, since 1962; rabbi: Cong Tifereth Isr, Glen Cove, NY, 1930-36; Cong Beth David, Lynbrook, NY, 1936-46; Cong Shaarey Tefila and J Cen, Far Rockaway, 1946-67. Chaplain, USAAC, 1943-46; col, USAF res, since 1962. Vice-chmn, comm on J chaplaincy, JWB; mem, exec, JA; pres, RabCA, 1958-60, hon pres, member exec comm; vice-pres, Zionists of Amer; mem: Phi Beta Kappa; AAUP; Amer Assn Political Sci; Acad Political Sci. Author: Israel's Emerging Constitution; Jewish Values for Modern Man; contbr ed: Menorah Jour; Judaism; contbr to rel and law jours. Recipient: US Army Commendation Ribbon with Oak Leaf Cluster. Home: 30 E 62 St, New York, NY. Study: 5 E 62 St, New York, NY.

RACKMIL, Milton R, US, business exec; b. Feb 12, 1903; s. Isaac and Fany (Lauer); BCS, NYU, 1924; div; c: Marlene Salkin. Pres, Decca Records, Inc; Universal Pictures Co. Mem: Masons. Home: 781 Fifth Ave, New York, NY. Office: 445 Park Ave, New York, NY.

RACKOVSKY, Isaiah, US, rabbi; b. Jerusalem, Sep 14, 1907; s. Solomon and Frances (Levine); in US since 1917; att: Rabbi Isaac Elchanan Theol Sem, 1917-29; CCNY, 1925-27; NYU, 1927-29; Herzliah J Tchrs Sem, NY, 1966-68; m. Sylvia Weiner, Nov 29, 1943; c: Sholom. Rabbi: since 1961; Cong B'nai Abraham, Dayton, O; Va'ad Ha'ir, Worcester, Mass; United Orthodox Congs, Omaha, Neb; Cong Rodeph Sholom, LA, Cal. Capt, US Army, 1943-47. Mem bd: cultural affairs comm, J Comty Cen; Urban Coalition, Bridgeport, Conn; Bd of Rabbis; fmr: pres: Zionist Org, Bridgeport, Conn; Bd of Rabbis, Bridgeport, Conn; vice-pres: RabCA; Rel Zionists of America. Author: Words and Thoughts; contbr to periodicals. Home: 465 Anson St, Bridgeport, Conn. Office: 3050 Main St, Bridgeport, Conn.

RADAN, Miroslav, Isr, veterinarian; b. Belovar, Yugo, Apr 16, 1907; s. Carlo and Catherine (Schön); in Isr since 1948; DVM, U of Zagreb, 1932; DVM, U of Vienna, 1938; m. Miriam Herzl; c: Tamar. Dir, Lab for Food Inspection, since 1954, vetr inst, Min of Agric; fmr: first asst, vetr fac, Bern, 1943-45; chief, vetr lab, Belgrad, 1946-48. Mem, Free Masons. Contbr to profsl publs. Hobbies: music, stamps. Home: 4 Radak St, Ramat Gan, Isr. Office: Veterinary Inst, Bet Dagan, Isr.

RADAY, Haim, Isr, organization exec; b. Benderi, Russ, Sep 9, 1908; s. Moshe Berman; in Isr since 1924; dipl, Agric E Natl Agric Coll, Fr, 1933; m. Esther Ezrat; c: Peleg, Rivka. Ret; fmr chief lab relations div, Min of Lab, since 1955, dep dir gen, 1948-53; secy gen, Min for Fgn Affairs, 1948-53; agric worker, 1924-28; tchr, prin, Heb Sch, Can, 1929-30; secy, Zeirei-Zion Org in Can, 1929-31; co-cound, Nahariya settlement, 1934; secy, political dept: Haifa lab council and Histadrut exec, 1939-46; JA, 1947-48; on govt missions for inves projects, S Amer, 1959-60. Hobbies: collecting Bibles in all langs; collecting pipes; philately. Home: 3 Mivtza Kadesh, Jerusalem, Isr.

RADBERG, Monty, Eng, organization exec; b. London, Eng, June 22, 1917; s. David and Rose (Yukovitch) Rothberg; att Tree of Life Theol Coll, London, 1935-38; m. Dora Dunitz, Feb 11, 1940; c: Chava Cohen, David, Susan, Mark. Organizing secy, JPA, since 1946; headmaster, Brixton Syn, Heb and Rel Class, 1946-64. Served Intelligence Corps, WW II, mentioned in dispatches. Fmr: visitor, J Prisoners, H M Brixton Prison; mem, First Gedud, Habonim, Trumpeldor. Hobby: classical music. Home: 63 St Margaret's Rd, Edgware, Middlesex, Eng. Office: Rex House, 4/12 Regent St, London SW 1, Eng.

RADDAY, Yehuda Thomas, Isr, educator, author; b. Czech, July 21, 1912; s. Felix and Franziska (Budlowsky) Reichmann; in Isr since 1930; BL, Charles U, Prague, 1933; tchr dipl, Heb Tchrs Coll, Jerusalem, 1936; MA, JTSA, NY, 1959;

PhD, Heb U, Jerusalem; m. Ilse Warburg, July 9, 1941; c: Elinor Felicitas. Lectr, Bible, Heb Lang, Technion, Haifa, since 1950; tchr, Chugim Secondary Sch, Haifa, 1937-62, vice-prin, 1945-52. Capt, IDF, 1948-49. Author: Tzaad Rishon, Tzaad Tzaad, Tzaad Sheni, 1950-58; Uziyahu King of Judah, 1958; Technical Report Writing, 1964; The Unity of Isaiah, 1970; co-ed, Yair Katz Memorial Volume of Biblical Studies, 1966. Mem, Soc of Tech Writers and Publishers. Contbr to profsl publs. Recipient: decorations: Hagana; War of Independence; Sinai Campaign. Home: 38 Hillel St, Haifa, Isr. Office: Technion, Haifa, Isr.

RADDOCK, Charles, US, journalist, author; b. NYC, Apr 15, 1916; s. David and Rebekah (Shinover-Feldstein). Ed-in-chief, The J Forum, since 1961; mgn ed, fgn news ed, Trade Union Courier, 1940-60; fgn corresp, Eur, Near E, 1951, 1953. Mem: UN Corresps Assn; Authors League of Amer. Club, Overseas Press. Author: Portrait of a People, 3 vols, 1965; etc. Home: 330 E 80 St, New York, NY.

RADKOWSKY, Alvin, US, physicist; b. Elizabeth, NJ, June 30, 1915; s. Aaron and Bessie (Jacobson); BS, CCNY, 1935; AM, George Wash U, 1941; PhD, Catholic U of Amer, 1947; m. Annette Eisenberg, Sep, 1950; c: Gilliette. Chief sci, Off of Naval Reactors, AEC, since 1950; secy, AEC adv comm, reactor physics, since 1959; fmr: elec engr, USN, Bur of Ships, 1938-48; nuclear physicist, Argonne Natl Lab, 1948-50. Founder, pres, Summit Hill Cong, Silver Spring; mem, Asso of Orthodox J Scis, bd of govs, found; f: Amer Physical Soc; Sigma Xi; Natl Sci Research Honor Soc; Sigma Pi Sigma, Physics Honor Soc. Author: Physical Review, 1948; ed, Naval Reactors Physics Handbook, 1964; contbr classified publs, and to profsl and sci jours. Recipient: Civilian Service awards, US Navy Dept, 1946, 1954, 1964; citation, AEC, 1953; sci award, Catholic U of Amer Alumni, 1965; Mordecai Ben David award, Yeshiva U, 1967; spec medal, Sch of Enrg, CCNY, 1969. Home: 8502 16 St, Silver Spring, Md. Office: US AEC, Washington, DC.

RADMAN, H Melvin, US, obstetrician; b. Omaha, Neb, Nov 24, 1905; s. John and Eve (Jablanow); BS, Creighton U, 1927, MD, 1929; m. Alice Miller, June 15, 1930. Pvt practice since 1935; chief, gyn, Baltimore Co Gen Hosp; att gyn, obstet: Women's Hosp since 1950; Sinai Hosp since 1950, on staff since 1929; Hosp for Women of Md, 1947; asso visiting obstet, gyn, Church Home and Infirmary, 1935; att gyn, Levindale Home and Infirmary, 1935. Maj, US Army, MC, 1943-46. Diplomate: Bd of Abdominal Surgs; Amer Bd Gyn and Obstet, 1944; f: Amer Coll Surgs; Intl Coll Surgs; mem: Amer and S Med Assns; Amer Coll Obstet and Gyn; Phi Delta Epsilon. Contbr to med jours. Home and office: The Esplanade Apts, Baltimore, Md.

RADNER, Ephraim, US, business exc; b. Springfield, Mass, Oct 21, 1921; s. Max and Stella (Gottlieb); BA, U of Mass, 1943; MS, MIT; 1945; att Harvard Grad Sch of Engr,1945-46; MBA, Harvard Bus Sch, 1948; m. Babette Solomon, June 4, 1950; c: Judy, James, Wendy, Nancy. Dir, finance, GCA Corp, since 1970, sr vice-pres since 1967, vice-pres, treas, 1958-67, one of GCA founders. Lt, USAAC, 1943-46. Mem: AJComm; finance comm, Beth El Temple, Belmont, Mass; B'nai B'rith; town meeting mem, Belmont; finance planning council, Amer Mgmt Assn; Natl Panel of Arbitrators, Amer Arbitration Assn; Financial Execs Inst, exec devl comm; fmr: chmn, Sci Instruments Sect, Mass Bay United Fund; secy, treas, Harvard Bus Sch Assn, Boston; clubs: Treasurers, Boston; Harvard, Boston and NYC; Executives of Gtr Boston C of C; Bankers of Amer. Recipient: Campaign award, Mass Bay United Fund, 1970; Cert award, Amer Mgmt Assn. Home: 116 Douglas Rd, Belmont, Mass. Office: GCA Corp, Burlington Rd, Bedford, Mass.

RADT, Paul, Isr, physician; b. Berlin, Ger, Dec 28, 1902; s. Max and Clara (Friedenthal); in Isr since 1933; MD, U Berlin, 1926; m. Thea Herzbrunn, Oct 20, 1949; c: Dorit. Dept chief, Tel Hashomer Hosp since 1963; fmr: dept chief, Mil Hosp, 1951-54; dir, hosp med services, 1954-63; tchr, Tel Aviv U Med Sch, since 1962. Mem, IMA, defense med sect. Contbr to profsl jours. Home: 57 Hanassi St, Herzliya, Isr. Office: Tel Hashomer Govt Hosp, Isr.

RAFAEL, Gideon, Isr, diplomat; b. Berlin, Ger, Mar 5, 1913; s. Max and Frederike (Jacobowitz) Ruffer; att U of Berlin; in Isr since 1934; m. Nurit Weissburg, 1940; c: Amnon, Ruth. Dir-gen, Fgn Min, Jerusalem, since 1968, dep dir since 1960; repr to UN Gen Assemblies since 1947; agric worker,

Pal, 1933-36; liaison off for JA with Allied Forces, 1945-45; secy, JA comm for preparation of J case, Nuremberg war crimes tribunal, 1945; mem, JA delg, Anglo-Amer Commn of Inquiry, Pal, 1946; UN Spec Commn on Pal, 1947; UN Gen Assembly, 1947; mem, Isr perm delg to UN, 1951-53, perm repr, 1967; Isr repr, Pal Conciliation Commn, rapporteur, UN Peace Observation Commn, 1952; councillor, UN and ME Affairs, 1953-57; ambass to Belgium, Luxemburg and EEC, 1957-60; ambass-at-large, Jerusalem, 1966; ambass, UN Eur Off, Geneva, Switz, 1965-66. Office: Min for Fgn Affairs, Jerusalem, Isr.

RAFAELI, Alexander, Isr, industrialist; b. Riga, Latvia, July 1, 1910; s. Boris and Rosa (Kahn) Rafaelowitsh; in Isr since 1954; dipl econ, 1930, U Heidleberg, DRerPol, 1933; dipl, U of Leipzig, 1931; att: U of Frankfurt, 1931-32; Heb U, Jerusalem, 1934-35; m. Esther Shapiro, Jan 20, 1950; c: Asya-Dov, Aylon, Varda, Karni. Mgn dir: Jerusalem Pencils Ltd; Vered Tool & Dies Inds, Ltd; Graphite Ind Ltd; partner; Dura Ind Plastics, B'nei Brak, 1950; Cargal Ltd, 1953; pres, Commonwealth Intl Corp, NYC, 1946. Staff off, Irgun Zvai Leumi, 1936, head, Eur off, Paris, 1938; US Army, counter intelligence corps, 1943-46. Mem: presidium, Isr Mfrs Assn; bd: Fgn Invest Assn of Isr; Isr Co for Fairs and Exhbs Ltd; mem: lab relations bd, Isr Min of Lab; curatorium, Bezalel Natl Mus; comm, Irgun Oley Merkaz Europa; found mem: Betar Youth Movement, Riga, 1925; New Zionist Org,Vienna, 1935; vice-pres: Amer League for Free Pal, 1941; Emergency Comm to Save the J People of Eur, 1942, both in NYC. Author: Staatswirtschaft in der Krise, 1933; ed, Economic Post, Tel Aviv, 1934-36. Contbr to Eur periodicals. Recipient: Cert of Merit, US Army. Hobby: Afr sculptures, modern paintings. Home: 12 Disraeli St, Talbieh, Jerusalem, Isr. Office: Ind Cen, Mekor Baruch, Jerusalem, Isr.

RAFAL, Marjorie L, US, librarian, communal worker; b. Hartford, Conn, Mar 24, 1918; d. William and Lilyan (Tillis) Leichner; BA,Wellesley Coll, 1938; grad, St Joseph Coll, 1940; m. Sidney Rafal, Oct 3, 1941; c: Jane, John, Mary. Head libr, Metro,U of Hartford Libr; pres: auxiliary, Hartford Dent Soc; Sisterhood Temple Beth Isr; Deborah Soc, 1963-64; vice-pres: auxiliary, Mt Sinai Hosp; Hartford sect, Natl Council J Women; 1st vice-pres: NE Fed Temple Sisterhoods, 1959; Wellesley Club, since 1963; mem, Alpha Omega. Contbr poetry, feature articles to children's mags; poems to anthols; book reviews to women's groups. Home: 35 Norwood Rd, W Hartford, Conn.

RAFFEL, Burton Nathan, Isr, educator, author; b. NYC, Apr 27, 1928; s. Harry and Rose (Karr); in Isr since 1968; BA, Bklyn Coll, 1948; MA, O State U, 1949; LLB, Yale U, 1958; m. Mia Stageberg, Apr 3, 1966; c: Brian, Blake, Stefan, Kezia, Shifra. Visiting prof, Haifa U Coll, since 1968; instr, Ford Found, Eng Lang Tchrs Training Prog, Indonesia, 1953-55; atty, Milbank, Tweed, Hadley & McCloy, NYC, 1958-60; asso prof, SUNY, 1966-68. Author: Short Story 3, 1960; Poems From the Old English, 1960; Beowulf, 1963; Chairil Anwar: Selected Poems, 1963; An Anthology of Modern Indonesian Poetry, 1964; The Development of Modern Indonesian Poetry, 1967; Mia Poems, 1968; From The Vietnamese, 1968; The Complete Poetry and Prose of Chairil Anwar, 1969; Sir Gawain and the Green Knight, 1970; The Forked Tongue: A Study of the Translation Process; Some Songs of Solomon; From Peter to Trotsky; Russian Poetry Before The Revolution; co-author: Selected Poems of Yehuda Amichai, ed, Found News, NYC, 1960-63. Contbr to periodicals. Home: 24 Rehov Oren, Romema, Haifa, Isr. Office: Haifa U Coll, Haifa, Isr.

RAFFEL, Sidney, US, physician, educator; b. Baltimore, Md, Aug 24, 1911; s. Solomon and Leah (Kaplan); BA, Johns Hopkins U, 1930, DS, 1933; MD, Stanford U, 1942; m. Yvonne Fay, Apr 15, 1938; c: Linda, Gail, Polly, Cynthia, Emily. Prof, med microbiol, exec, Stanford U Sch of Med, both since 1953, acting dean, 1964-65; cons: Vets Hosp, since 1946; surg gen, USPHS, since 1955. Mem: Amer Assn of Immunologists; Amer Trudeau Soc; Alpha Omega Alpha; Sigma Xi. Recipient: Guggenheim f, 1949-50. Author: Immunity, 1953, 2nd ed, 1961. Contbr to med jours. Hobbies: painting, gardening. Home: 770 Santa Ynez St, Stanford, Cal. Office: Stanford U Sch of Med, Stanford, Cal.

RAFKIND, Israel, US, government official; b. Sheboygan, Wis, June 12, 1911; s. Max and Anna (Hootkin); att NYU, 1929-30; BA, U of Wis, 1936; m. Shirley Mullin, July 2, 1939; c: Linda Stein, Faith, Charles. Off of Dep Under Secy,

Dept of Housing and Urban Devl, since 1965; fmr: asst commn, cmty facilities admn, Housing and Home Finance Agcy, US Govt, 1961-65; official of various assns ot public officials and govt agcy, 1936-46; secy, controller, Amer Cmty Builders Inc, 1946-52; pres, Rafkind and Co Inc, Cal, 1952-59. Mem: B'nai Brith, JFK lodge; Phi Beta Kappa; Phi Eta Sigma; fmr: org, bd of J educ and new cong, Pk Forest, Ill; chmn, UJA; pres, Zionist Org, Baldwin, LI; mem bd trustees, Temple Sinai, Wash, DC; village treas, Pk Forest, Ill; mem bd, Bldg Contractors Assn of Cal; chmn, Common Public Employee Retirement. Author of books; contbr to jours. Hobbies: fishing, photography. Home: 8750 Georgia Ave, Silver Spring, Md. Office: 451 7 St, Washington, DC.

RAFSKY, Jeanne C, US, gastroenterologist; b. NYC, July 16, 1925; d. Henry and Bertha (Fischel); BA, cum laude, Brown U, 1945; MD, NYU, 1949; m. Norman Jaspan, Dec 22, 1946; c: Michael, Ronald. Phys, Sidney Hillman Health Cen, since 1966; asst adj, gastroenterology, Lenox, Hill Hosp, since 1954, on staff since 1949; staff, U Hosp, since 1954, asst att radiologist, 1958-66; gastroscopist, Grand Cen Hosp, 1956-62; clinical teaching asst, radiology, NYU, 1960-66. F, NY Acad Med; dipl: Natl Bd Med Examiners; mem: NY State Workmens Compensation Bd; adv council, Sen Comm on Health, NY State, since 1966; mem: Cong Kehilath Jeshurun; J Cen; Atlantic Beach J Cen; NY Co Med Soc; NY Acad Sci; AMA; Amer Soc Gastrointestinal Endoscopy. Contbr to med jours. Home: 993 Park Ave, New York, NY. Office: 79 E 79 St, New York, NY.

RAGINSKY, Anna, Can, communal worker; b. St Stephen, NB, Nov 2, 1891; d. Emanuel and Rebecca (Friedberg) Kenen; att Rothsey Coll, 1909; m. Abraham Raginsky, 1931 (decd); c: Leo Selick. Pres, JNF, Can; hon pres, Can Hadassah since 1947, found, Toronto org, 1916; Montreal Hadassah-WIZO; bd, trustees, YM-YWHA; natl chmn, Free Loan of Jerusalem, Can; mem: Amer Fund of Isr Instns; Heb U, intl exec council; Council of J Women; UN Assn; B'nai B'rith; hon vice-pres, Can J Cong; chmn, archives ZOC, chmn, Tourism for Eastern Region; Hadassah WIZO, Can, chmn of archives; bd dirs, Can-Isr Securities; bd dirs, Montreal Isr Bonds; fmr: pres: Heb Maternity Aid Soc; women's div, Talmud Torah; vice-pres; Montreal J Sect, Can Red Cross; women's auxiliary, J Gen Hosp; FJP, Montreal; Natl Council of Women; chmn, Vad Chalutz; mem: world exec, WIZO; exec comm, ZOC; exec comm, Can Bond Comm, WWII. Recipient: Negev dinner, a village in Isr in her name; Coronation Medal, 1937; Centennial Medal, 1967; Medal of Freedom, Isr Bond Org; JNF Medal. Home: 4250 Sherbrooke St W, Montreal, Can.

RAGINSKY, Bernard B, Can, physician; b. Ekaterinoslav, Russ, Oct 10, 1902; s. Abraham and Rena (Ratchefsky); in Can since 1905; att McGill U of Engr, 1919-21, MD, 1927; m. Helen Steinkopf, May 31, 1938; c: Nina. Asso phys in med, Montreal J Gen Hosp, since 1934; researcher, pharm, phys, conditioned reflexes, McGill U, 1929-34. F: Intl Coll Anesthesia; Amer Coll Card; AAAS; Intl Coll Angiology; Amer Med Writers Assn; Intl Coll for Clinical and Experimental Hypnosis; chmn, spec comm on hypnosis, Can Med Assn, since 1960; mem: Amer Med Eds and Authors Assn; AHA; Amer Psychosomatic Soc; Montreal Medico-Chirurgical Soc; Montreal Psycht Soc; Can Psycht Soc; Intl Anesthesia Research Soc; Inter-Amer Soc Psychol; Sigma Xi; clubs: Lord Reading Yacht; Murray's; Greystone Curling; Montefiore; fmr: pres: Soc for Clinical and Experimental Hypnosis; Intl Soc Clinical and Experimental Hypnosis; sect on clinical hypnosis, Pan Amer Med Assn; Acad Psychosomatic Med; secy-treas, Amer Bd Med Hypnosis; N Amer co-chmn, sect on clinical hypnosis, Pan Amer Med Assn; councillor, Sociedad Mexicana de Hipnologica Medica, 1967. Contrib ed, Jour of Psychosomatics; asso ed, Jour of Clinical and Experimental Hypnosis; fgn ed, Acta Hipnologica Latino Americana, Arg; contbr to profsl publs. Recipient: 1st prize, Brit Jour of Anesthesia, 1935; gold medal, Soc for Clinical and Experimental Hypnosis, 1958; bronze plaque, Acad Psychosomatic Med, 1958; Bernard B Raginsky annual award for leadership achievement, created by Soc for Clinical and Experimental Hypnosis, 1960; Jules Weinstein award, Amer Hypnodontic Soc, 1961; bronze plaque, Pan Amer Med Assn, 1962; Shirley Schneck award, 1963. Home: 220 Chester Ave, Montreal, Can. Office: 376 Redfern Ave, Montreal, Can.

RAICH, Lea, Fr, social worker; b. Paris, Fr, June 10, 1901; d. Maurice and Sophie (Rappoport) Fridmon; att Sorbonne, Paris; social asst, Red Cross, Paris, 1949; m. Michel Raich; c: Jacqueline Rubinski. Mem, Cen Commn of Aliyah, dir comm

ZF of Fr; fmr: social work for the victims of Nazism (service clandestin d'enfants de la WIZO, Résistance Juive); hon gen secy, WIZO, since 1948; mem: world exec, WIZO, since 1963; Eur exec, WJC, 1964; admn council, OPEJ, (oeuvre de protection des enfants juifs); comm mem, Mouvement Mondiale des Mères. Home: 50 rue Jeanne d'Arc, St Mandé 94, Fr. Office: 24 rue du Mt Thabor, Paris 1, Fr.

RAIDER, Joseph, US, physician; b. Troyanov, Russ, Feb 9, 1909; s. Zissie and Sarah (Rabinowich); in US since 1923; BS, U of Ill, 1935, MD, Coll of Med, U of Ill, 1935; m. Beatrice Goldsmith, June 25, 1940; c: Donna, John, Ira. Pvt practice since 1936. Lt col, US Army MC, 1941-46. Mem: AMA; Amer Acad of Gen Practice; AHA; Amer Legion; Mil Surgs of US; Amer Soc of Abdominal Surgs; B'nai B'rith; ZOA; club: Lions. Contbr to profsl jours. Home: 275 N Lake St, Mundelein, Ill. Office: 287 N Lake St, Mundelein, Ill.

RAIDER, Leonard J, US, physician, business exec; b. Phila, Pa, May 13, 1924; s. Joseph and Esther (Levin); AB, U of Pa, 1944; MD, U of Pittsburgh, Sch of Med, 1948; MBA, NYU, Grad Sch of Bus, 1958; m. Thelma Fassler, Mar 26, 1950; c: Steven, Stacey. Pres, United Med Services, since 1962; with firm since 1950. USN, 1944-45; lt, USN, 1948-49; capt, USAF, 1952-54. Dir: Comty Council of Gtr NY; NY Safety Council; Natl Assn of Blue Shield Plans; fmr: chmn, Young Pres' Org, Metrop chap; dir: Jr Achievement, NY Chap; Blue Shield Found on Health Care; mem: AMA, Amer Public Health Assn; Ind Med Assn; NY State and NY Co Med Soc; Royal Soc for Health; Phi Delta Epsilon; Amer Mgmt Assn; NY Bd of Trade; Phys Epicure Soc; Young Pres' Org; World Med Assn; NY State Assn of Professions; Empire State Health Council, Inc; comms: Med Indemnity of Amer, Inc; Chase Manhattan Bank; NY State Blue Cross and Blue Shield Plans; clubs: Advt, NY; City, NY; NYU; U of Pittsburgh; U of Pa. Spec interests: mgmt, med, sports. Home: 435 E 57 St, New York, NY. Office: 2 Park Ave, New York, NY.

RAIF, Shlomo, Isr, economist; b. Mikuliczyn, Pol, May 8, 1910; s. Samuel and Clara (Singer) Schindler; in Isr since 1933; DEcon, U of Florence, 1932; CA, Tel Aviv, 1956; m. Miriam Cholatnikow, 1934; c: Doron. Dep gen mgr, Ceasarea Textile Works Ltd, since 1967; secy, Tnuva Ltd, 1933-53; mgr, Audit Union of Provident and Pension Funds Ltd, 1953-60; gen mgr, Gmul Inves Co Ltd, since 1957; dir: Mutual Ins Dept, under jt ownership of Audit Union and Hassneh Ins Co; Cen Fund of Discharge Indemnities Ltd; mem: securities comm, Min of Finance; finance comm, Hevrat Ovdim; bd, Natl Ins Inst. Home: 55 Weizmann St, Tel Aviv, Isr. Office: POB 1177, Tel Aviv, Isr.

RAKOVER, Nachum, Isr, attorney, rabbi; b. Jerusalem, Isr, Nov 13, 1932; s. Haim and Hanna (Mandelbaum); PhD, Heb U, Jerusalem; ordained rabbi, World Cen Yeshiva of Rabbi Kook; m. Batya Berger, Jan 1, 1961; c: Benjamin, Hana, Hilla, Rachel. Adv on J law, Min of Justice; lectr, fac law, Heb U, Jerusalem; fmr: mem public comm for replacement of the Mejelle; secy, comm on Comty Property Between Spouses; J law sect, 4th World Cong of J Studies. Home: 22 Ittamar Ben Avi St, Jerusalem, Isr.

RAKSIN, Irving Jacob, US, oral surg; b. Baltimore, Md, Aug 14, 1939; s. Bernard and Rose (Kramer); BS, MD, U of Md, 1960; m. Barbara Zimring. Pvt practice since 1970; f, surg, NY Hosp-Cornell Med Cen, 1966-68; instr, phys diagnosis, Cornell Med Sch, 1966-68; chief, oral surg, Ft Eustis, Va, 1968-70. Capt, US Army, 1968-70. Mem: Amer Dent Assn; Middle Atlantic Soc Oral Surgs; Alpha Omega, Baltimore chap. Home: 3012 Fallstaff Manor Court, Baltimore, Md.

RAM, Arie, Isr, chemist, educator; b. Duisburg, Ger, July 15, 1926; s. Zvi and Debora (Gewurtz); in Isr since 1933; BSc, Chem Eng, Technion, Haifa, 1951; DSc, Chem Eng, MIT, 1961; m. Sara Baron, June 20, 1951; c: Michal, Uzi. Asso prof, chem engr, Technion, Haifa, since 1967; fmr: visiting prof, Case Inst of Tech, Cleveland, O. Prin contrib: sup of research: high shear viscometry; role of polymer additives in flow properties of lubricating oils; characterization and workability of polyethylene; instability in flow of non-Newtonian liquids; relationship between structure and phys properties of cross-linked polymers; reduction of friction in pipes by polymer additives; structure of Rheology of Polycarbonate; flow properties of PVC plastisols; shear degradation of polymers. Mem: Isr Inst of Chem Engrs; Isr Chem Soc; Amer Soc of Rheology; Amer Inst of Physics;

hon mem: Phi Lambda Epsilon; Sigma Xi. Author: Plastics Materials, chap in Rheology, Vol IV, 1968; contbr to profsl publs. Home: 8 Gilboa St, Haifa, Isr. Office: Technion, Haifa, Isr.

RAM, Gerson L, US, educator; b. Bloomfield, NJ, Oct 18, 1919; s. Max and Ida (Chayet); BA, Upsala Coll, NJ, 1941; deg, grad sanitary engr, Rutgers U, NJ, 1943, MSc, 1947; DSc, Johns Hopkins U, Md, 1953; m. Rita Wiesenfeld, Aug 7, 1947; c: Anita, Joel. Prof, chem, Newark Coll of Engr, since 1947. Served, US Army, 1942-46. Holder of 5 US patents. F: AAAS; AIC; Sigma Xi; Royal Soc of Health, Gt Brit. Home: 15 Briar Hill Rd, Cedar Grove, NJ. Office: Newark Coll of Engineering, Newark, NJ.

RAM, Moshe, Isr, engineer; b. Tatarsk, Russ, Jan 30, 1895; s. Ben-Zion and Reshe; in Isr since 1935; att U of Cal, Berkeley, 1915-17; grad, Timiriazev Acad, Moscow, 1923; m. Rebecca Kublanov, 1918; c: Miriam, Rina. Cons engr: Rolling Mills, for non-ferrous metals, Albar Ltd, Kfar Sava; Water Planning for Isr (Tahal) Ltd, 1960-65; head, soil phys dept, Cen Hydromodule Lab, Moscow, 1925; reg, eng, first Jordan power house, 1931; chief water engr, Lord Mondos Plantations, 1933; pvt practice, 1933-36; cons engr, JA, 1936-40; chief eng, Water Research Bur, JA and JNF, 1940-48; dir, water utilization div, Water Auth, Min of Agric, 1948-60. Found, mgr, country-wide field service and ext service cen at Midrasha Ruppin, 1953-60. Found, head, Isr Comm, Intl Comm on Irrigation and Drainage, 1950-57; delg: cong, Algiers, 1954; exec council meeting, Madrid, 1956. Mem: Amer Soc Civil Engrs; Assn Engrs and Architects in Isr; Intl Assn for Hydraulic Research, delg to Intl Cong, Grenoble, Fr, 1949; Intl Soil Research Assn; Assn for the Advancement of Sci, Isr; off mission: Algeria, Fr, Holland, 1950; Food and Agric Org (FAO), UN expert to Bihar State Govt, India, 1957-59; lectr, on irrigation practices in semi-arid regions, U of Holland, Wageningen, 1964; repr ICID: cong, Tokyo, 1963; Prague, 1963; Athens, 1965; club: Rotary. Author: Water and Soil; contbr to local and fgn profsl jours. Recipient: prize, Assn of Engrs and Architects in Isr. Home: 33 Borochov St, Givatayim, Isr. Office: POB 20, Kfar Sava, Isr.

RAMATI, Yohanan Joseph, Isr, government official, editor; b. Warsaw, Pol, Nov 17, 1921; s. Gustav and Pola (Tenenbaum) Rosenberg; in Isr since 1949; cert, Wycliffe Coll, Eng; MA, Lincoln Coll, Oxford U, 1942; m. Datia Kaplan, Nov 30, 1947; c: Michal, Eliora, Jonathan. Councillor, Jerusalem Munic, since 1959; mgn ed, Israel Economist, since 1951; fmr: dir gen, Negev Ceramic Materials Ltd; chmn: public works comm; assessments comm, both Jerusalem Munic; dep chmn: town planning comm; bldg permits comm; mem: exec; finance comm, tenders comm, leader, United Jerusalem Faction, all Jerusalem Munic. Capt, British Army, 1945-48. Author: Life in a Model Coal Mining Village, 1947; The Problem of Minorities, 1945. Hobbies: philately; sports. Home and office: 4 Ein Rogel St, Jerusalem, Isr.

RAMOT, Bracha, Isr, physician, educator; b. Kovno, Lith, Oct 5, 1927; d. Mordechai and Margalit (Finkelbrand) Chweidan; in Isr since 1948; MD, Med Sch, Jerusalem, 1952; m. Joshua Ramot, Dec 18, 1949; c: Arye, Orna. Dir, dept of hematology, Tel Hashomer Hosp, since 1957; sr lectr, med, Heb U, Jerusalem, since 1964; asso prof, Tel Aviv U, since 1966; asst prof, Albert Einstein Med Sch, Bx, 1958; chief, hematology, Ichilov Hosp, Tel Aviv, 1964-65. IDF MC, 1948-49. Mem: IMA; Isr Hematology Soc; cons, Isr Cancer Soc. Contbr to med jours. Recipient: f, Chgo Soc for Hematology Research; War of Independence decoration. Home: 20 Dubnov St, Tel Aviv, Isr. Office: Tel Hashomer Hosp, Isr.

RAND, Jacob, US, attorney; b. NYC, June 19, 1921; s. Morris and Rose (Schnurer); BA, NYU, 1942; LLB, Harvard, 1948. Pvt practice since 1949; teaching f, dept of public speaking, Cornell U, 1942; asst city atty, city prosecutor, 1960-66; acting city mgr of Long Branch, 1965-66. US Army, 1942-46. Fmr: pres: Long Branch chap, ZOA, 1951-53; chmn, Isr Bond Dr, 1951-53, redemption chmn, Monmouth and Ocean Cos; natl dep judge advocate, JWV, 1955, post cdr, 1953-54; trustee, Elberon Comty Assn, since 1960; vice-pres, B'nai B'rith lodge, 1951-52; pres, Cong Brothers of Isr Syn, 1952-53. Home: 859 Red Oaks Dr, Long Branch, NJ. Office: 46 Memorial Pkwy, Long Branch, NJ.

RAND, Melvin Aaron, US, clinical psychologist; b. Long Branch, NJ, Oct 9, 1934; s. Max and Sarah (Schein); BA, Monmouth Coll, NJ, 1961; MS, LIU, 1963; PhD, U of Okla-

homa, 1967; m. Daryl Harrison, Nov 22, 1962; c: Jason. Dir, chief psych, NJ State Diagnostic Cen, since 1969; cons psych: State Prison, since 1967; NJ Dept Commerce and Lab, since 1969; psychotherapist, Mh Consultation Cen, Hackensack, since 1967; adj prof, Fairleigh Dickinson U, since 1967. Served US Army, 1955-57. Mem: Amer, NJ, Psychol Assns; Amer, NJ, Socs Clinical Hypnosis; Natl Hon Soc in Psychol; B'nai B'rith. Contbr to profsl jours. Recipient: Soldiers' Commendation; Postdoc f in Clinical Med Psychol, NJ Coll of Med and Dept Instns and Agcys, 1967. Hobbies: electronics, numismatics. Home: 6040 Blvd East, West New York, NJ. Office: NJ State Diagnostic Center, Menlo Park, NJ.

RAPAPORT, Henry N, US, attorney; b. NYC, Mar 19, 1905; s. Meyer and Fannie (Relkin); BA, Columbia U, 1925, MA, 1927, LLB, 1927, JD, 1969; m. Selma Simon, 1936; c: Michael, Peter, David. Mem, law firm, Rapaport Bros, since 1929; spec dep, Supt of Ins, NY State, 1935; chief rationing atty, spec counsel, NY rent dir, OPA, 1944. Pres, United Syn Amer; chmn, Isr Found Conservative Movement; mem: bd, JTSA; Assn of Bar, NYC; Bx Co, Intl Bar Assns; past pres, Temple Isr Cen, White Plains, NY. Recipient, Eternal Light Medal, JTSA, 1968. Home: 27 Olmsted Rd, Scarsdale, NY. Office: 9 E 40 St, New York, NY.

RAPAPORT, Ionel, US, physician, researcher; b. Buzau, Rum, Mar 30, 1909; s. Florian and Elise (Goldstein); in US since 1954; MD, U of Paris Med Sch, 1937, PhD, 1945; m. Marjorie O'Brien, 1951; c: Gilberte, Pola. Supervising psycht, Willowbrook State Sch, Staten I, NY; sr research sci, NY Psycht Inst, 1961-64; lectr, New Sch for Social Research, 1962-67; dir, medico-social cen, Seine, 1946-48; pvt practice, Seine, 1946-54; lectr and prof, Fr Sch of Anthropology, Paris, 1946-54; project asso, Psycht Inst, U Wis, 1954-59, asst prof, 1959-61; prin research investigator, U Wis, 1958-62. Lt, Fr Army MC, 1944-45. Mem: Amer Soc Human Genetics; Amer Genetic Assn; Amer Eugenic Soc; AAAS; NY Acad Scis; Amer Assn on Mental Deficiency; Amer Acad on Mental Retardation; Ordre Natl des Medicins, Paris. Org first intl exhb of art by mentally retarded, since 1957. Author: Introduction a la Psychopathologie Collective, 1949; contbr to profsl jours. Recipient: prize, Natl Acad of Med, Paris, 1950; Medaille de la Ville de Paris, 1951; Chevalier, Order of Public Health, Paris, 1954. Home: 69 Sherman Ave, Staten Island, NY. Office: 20 E 9 St, New York, NY.

RAPHAEL, Eugene J, US, attorney; b. NYC, Dec 21, 1900; s. Ralph and Leah (Goldsmith); BA, Yale U, 1922; LLB, Columbia U, 1925; m. Rosalie Moyse, Sept 25, 1928; c: Peter, Susan Calman. Pvt practice since 1926; operator, Asia Plantation, Greenville, Miss, 1943-52. Pres: Heb Union Cong, 1950-51, vice-pres, 1947-49, mem, bd of dirs, since 1944; vice-pres, Delta area council, Boy Scouts of Amer, 1952-53, mem, exec bd, since 1948, dist chmn, Wash dist, 1955-56, mem, dist comm, since 1945; drive chmn, Wash County, UJA, 1948-49; an org and campaign chmn, JWF, Greenville area, 1953; mem: Amer, Miss State, Bar Assns; Wash County Bar Assn, pres, 1963, vice-pres, 1962; B'nai B'rith; Phi Beta Kappa; Sigma Alpha Mu; club: Greenville Rotary. Recipient, Silver Beaver award, Boy Scouts of Amer, 1955. Spec interest: Boy Scout work. Home: 942 Arnold Ave, Greenville, Miss. Office: Woolworth Bldg, Greenville, Miss.

RAPHAEL, Itzhak, Isr, author, legislator; b. Sassow, Aus-Hung, July 5, 1914; s. Shmuel and Esther (Horowitz) Werfel; in Isr since 1935; MA, Heb U, Jerusalem, 1939; postgrad studies, London U; PhD, JTSA; m. Geula Maimon, 1936; c: Shilo. Dep Min Health, since 1961; MK, since 1951; chmn, bd dirs, Mosad Harav Kook; fmr: secy, bd dirs, Torah veAvoda, Galicia; tchr, Ma'ale Sch, Pal; mem: Vaad Leumi, 1948; Jerusalem Comm, 1948; head: War Victims Off; immigration dept; mem, exec, JA, Jerusalem, 1948-54. Mem: exec comm, Hapoel Hamizrachi; cen comm, World Mizrachi Org; bd dirs, Idud Soc; delg, 21st and 22nd WZCs. Author: The Jews of Castille in the Times of Rabbi Asher, 1937; The Correspondence of Rabbi Kalischer, 1938; History of the Ashkenazi Community in Eretz Israel, 1939; Hassidim and Eretz Israel, 1940; Rashi in His Answers, 1942; Sassow, My Hometown, 1946; Hassidic Folklore, 1946; The Book of Hassidism, 1947; Rishonim veAchronim, 1947; ed: Amana Areshet; baMishor Libr; Profiles in Zionism and Hist of the Yishuv Libr; Ency of Rel Zionism; baMishor Weekly; Sinai monthly. Home: Achad Ha'am 24, Jerusalem, Isr. Offices: The Knesset, Jerusalem, Isr; Mosad Harav Kook, POB 642, Jerusalem, Isr.

RAPHAEL, Shilo, Isr, author, rabbi; b. Jerusalem, Nov 9, 1940; s. Itschak and Geulah (Maimon); att Hebron Yeshiva, Jerusalem, 1958-63; ordained rabbi, Beit Hatalmud Rabb Coll, Jerusalem, 1969; m. Mina Katz, Aug 5, 1963; c: Batia, Malka. Dist rabbi, Jerusalem, since 1969; lit ed, Mosad Harav Kook, since 1967; head rabb coll, Beit Hatalmud, since 1969. Author: monographs on J Rabb scholars; contbr of articles on talmudical topics, Halachic problems. Exec mem: Mosad Harav Kook; Jad Harav Maimon. Home and study: 3 Reines St, Jerusalem, Isr.

RAPOPORT, Anatol, US, educator; b. Lozovaya, Russ, May 22, 1917; s. Boris and Adel; in US since 1922; BS, U of Chgo, 1938, MS, 1940, PhD, 1941; m. Gwen Goodrich, Jan 29, 1949; c: Anya, Alexander, Charles. Prof, math biol, sr research math, Mh research inst, U of Mich, since 1955, asso prof, 1955-60; research asso, U of Chgo, 1947-49, asst prof math biol, 1947-54. USAAC, 1942-46. F: AAAS; Amer Acad of Arts and Scis; mem: Amer Math Soc; Math Assn Amer; Intl Soc for Gen Semantics, pres, 1953-55; Soc for Gen Sys Research. Author: Science and the Goals of Man, 1950; Operational Philosophy, 1953; Fights, Games and Debates, 1960; Strategy and Conscience, 1964; Two-Person Game Theory, 1968; N-Person Game Theory, 1969; co-author, Prisoners' Dilemma, 1966; contbr to sci jours. Recipient: f, Cen for Advanced Study in Behavioral Sci, 1954-55. Home: 516 Oswego, Ann Arbor, Mich. Office: U of Mich, Ann Arbor, Mich.

RAPOPORT, Azariahu, (R Azaria), Isr, TV and radio producer, editor; b. Tel Aviv, Isr, May 13, 1924; s. Eliyahu and Yocheved (Lerinman); att Heb U, Jerusalem; NYU Film Dept; m. Ruth Zakheim, Jan 27, 1952; c: Hannai, Tallie, Yael. Sr produc, Isr radio and TV, since 1961; film critic, Maariv daily, since 1953; Isr corresp, Variety, NY, since 1963; fmr: actor, Habimah, Ohel Theaters; films; Isr corresp, Billboard, NY. Palmach; British Army; mil corresp, IDF. Dep chmn, film critics sect, Isr Press Assn; mem: Tel Aviv exec, Tent 51, Variety Intl; progs comm, ZOA House, Tel Aviv. Hobbies: classical music; walking. Home: 73 Ahad Haam St, Tel Aviv, Isr. Office: Isr Bc Auth, Hakiryah, Tel Aviv, Isr.

RAPOPORT, Bernard, US, business exec; b. San Antonio, Tex, July 17, 1917; s. David and Riva (Feldman); BA, Tex U, 1940; m. Audrey Newman, Feb 15, 1942; c: Ronald. Pres, Amer Income Life Ins Co, Waco, Tex since 1960, with firm since 1951; fmr: partner, Art's Jewelry Store, 1944-48; salesman, Pioneer Amer Life Ins Co, 1950-51. Finance chmn, Bus Execs Move for Vietnam Peace, Cal; natl treas, S Comm on Political Ethics, Wash, DC; sponsor: Intl Self-Help Housing Assn; Inst for Amer Dem, Wash, DC; trustee, Paul Quinn Coll, Waco; mem: bd of overseers, Dag Hammarskjöld Coll, Wash, DC; founding mem, Cen for the Study of Dem Instns, Cal; interim exec comm, Alliance for Rural-Urban Balance; fmr, state chmn, Texans for Voter Registration. Home: 2332 Wendy Lane, Waco, Tex. Office: 609 N 25 St, Waco, Tex.

RAPOPORT, Shlomo, US, rabbi, educator; b. Des Moines, Iowa, Dec 10, 1914; s. Israel and Julia (Norenbersky); BS, Ill Inst of Tech, 1936; cert, Chgo Tchrs Coll, 1937; ordained rabbi, Heb Theol Coll, 1940, DHL, 1964; MS, Northwestern U, 1941; m. Hilda Ross, June 24, 1945; c: Gitelle, Cheryl, Ashira. Prin, Chgo J Acad, since 1945, prof math, Schurz Evening Jr Coll, 1941-48; rabbi: B'nai Isr Cong, Kankakee, Ill, 1941-42; Adas Hapoel Hamizrachi, 1942-55; Cong Achei Yavneh, 1955-64. Past pres, Rabb Group of Mizrachi Hapoel Hamizrachi; past vice-pres, cultural chmn, Rel Zionists of Chgo, 1945-1955; treas, Chgo Rabb Council, 1946-54; chmn, prins' council, Asso Talmud Torahs, Chgo, 1965-68; mem: RabCA; Chgo Rabb Council; Rel Zionist of Amer; Natl Assn Secondary School Prins; Natl Conf of Yeshiva Prins; Natl Council of J Educ. Contbr to periodicals. Home: 6338 N Whipple St, Chicago, Ill. Office: 2828 W Pratt Blvd, Chicago, Ill.

RAPP, John, US, certified public accountant; b. Wuppertal, Ger, Feb 24, 1920; s. Ernest and Anne (Rapp); in US since 1949; BSc, London U, 1945; MS, Columbia Grad Sch of Bus, 1952; m. Doris Stern, Mar 14, 1953; c: Marianne. Mgr, review and research dept, Sharlach Ress Goldrich & Co, since 1968; audit mgr, Hurdman & Cranstown, 1957-67; audit staff, Seidman & Seidman, 1967-68. Sgt, Brit Army, 1940-45. Pres, Summit J Comty Cen; dir, N NJ region, United Syn Amer; Summit area treas, UJA; mem: Amer Inst CPAs; NY State Soc CPAs; Beta Gamma Sigma. Contbr to profsl jours. Hobbies: music, lit. Home: 17 Butler Pkwy, Summit, NJ. Office: 39 Hudson St, Hackensack, NJ.

RAPPAPORT, Ben Z, US, physician, educator; b. Russ, Mar 21, 1897; s. Morris and Miriam (Drell); in US since 1908; BS, U of Ill, Coll of Med, 1920, MD, 1922; MS, 1932; m. Sally Goldberg, June 28, 1931; c: Michael. Pvt practice since 1925; prof em, med, U of Ill, Coll of Med, on fac since 1924; mem, bd on allergy, State of Ill. Selective Service, 1941-45; served, US Army, 1918. Pres: Chgo Soc of Allergy, 1938; Amer Acad of Allergy, 1952-53, secy, 1951-52; mem, bd of trustees, Amer Found for Allergic Diseases, 1953-62. Mem: Alpha Omega Alpha; Sigma Xi; Phi Delta Epsilon; N Shore Cong Isr. Contbr to med and sci jours. Recipient: Selective Service award, 1945. Club, Birchwood Golf. Hobbies: painting, art collecting. Home: 1403 Waverly, Highland Park, Ill. Offices: 55 E Washington, Chicago, Ill; 735 St Johns, Highland Park, Ill.

RAPPAPORT, Gary Burton, US, business exec; b. Minneapolis, Minn, Apr 27, 1937; s. Max and Beatrice (Berkinsky); BS, U of Pa, Wharton Sch of Finance and Commerce, 1959; m. Susan Heller, Nov 26, 1961; c: Debra, Melissa. Pres, NAPCO Inds, Inc since 1965, with firm since 1959. USAF, 1961-62. Mem: Amer Mgmt Assn; Pres' Assn, Inc; spec adv panel, fgn trade policy, US C of C; Natl Security Ind Assn; Amer Ordnance Assn; Govt Affairs Comm, Gtr Minneapolis C of C; Amer Metalworking Comm Isr Ltd; Mt Sinai Hosp Assn, Minneapolis; Temple Isr Men's Club, Challenge Comm; ADL. Hobbies: skiing, woodworking, boating. Home: 4470 Gaywood Dr, Hopkins, Minn. Office: 1600 Second St S, Hopkins, Minn.

RAPPAPORT, Hyman, US, physician; b. Kishinev, Russ, Sep 1, 1899; s. David and Esther (Polonsky); in US since 1903; att: U of Mo, 1917; U of Va, 1918; MD, LI Coll Hosp, 1923; m. Augusta Koren, Aug 16, 1925; c: Ruth Lehman, Marilyn Marsh. Ped, pvt practice, since 1924; att ped and dir, newborn service, Phys' Hosp, Jackson Hgts, NY, since 1936; cons ped: St Johns Queens Hosp; Phys' Hosp; staff ped, Blvd Hosp; med adv, local bd 56, Selective Service, since 1955; mem, emergency med team, St Johns Queens Hosp, 1941, att ped, 1953-56; asst visiting phys, Willard Parker Hosp, NY, 1955; mem, coord council, police sta, Elmhurst, LI, 1950. Served, Student Army Training Corps, U of Va, 1918; sr examining phys, draft bd 257, WW II. F: Amer Acad Ped, life mem; NY Acad of Med; mem: Soc for Adolescent Med; coord council, police dept, 110 precinct; life mem, Queens Co Med Soc; charter, Queens Ped Soc; Sr Amer Fed for Clinical Research; Assn for Endocrine Diseases; Phys' of 2nd Ward, Queens, past pres; Elks; Masons; Amer Legion; Phys Sq Club, Queens, NY. Contbr to med jours. Home: 110-11 69 Ave, Forest Hills, NY. Office: 3710 76 St, Jackson Hgts, NY.

RAPPAPORT, Lawrence, US, educator; b. NYC, May 28, 1928; s. Aaron and Elsie; att U of Idaho, 1946-50; MS, Mich State Coll, 1951; PhD, Mich State U, 1956; m. Norma Horwitz; c: Meryl, Debra, Craig. Prof, vegetable crops, U of Cal, Davis, since 1956. Research in plant phys. Sgt, US Army, 1952-53. Counselor, Hillel Found, U of Cal, Davis; mem: bd, J Fellowship of Davis; B'nai B'rith; several sci socs; fmr: pres, mem bd dirs, Davis Human Relations Council. Contbr to sci publs. Home: 637 Elmwood Dr, Davis, Cal. Office: U of Cal, Davis, Cal.

RAPPAPORT, Solomon, S Afr, rabbi, lectr; b. Lemberg, Aus-Hung, June 25, 1905; s. Samuel and Blume (Kadinsky); in S Afr since 1943; PhD, U of Vienna, 1929; ordained rabbi, J Theol Sem, Vienna, 1930; m. Elizabeth Spritzer, Jan 30, 1938; c: Carol. Ret; fmr: rabbi, Northeastern Heb Cong; prof, Heb, U of Witwatersrand, both Johannesburg; prof, rel, HS, Vienna, 1930-38; lectr, Maimonides Coll, Vienna, 1930-38. Past pres, B'nai B'rith Lodge, Johannesburg. Author: Agada und Exegese bei Flavius Josephus, 1930; Rabbinic Thoughts on Race, 1951; Jewish Horizons, 1959. Home: 28A Orchards Rd, Johannesburg, S Afr.

RAPPOPORT, Zvi, Isr, chemist; b. Jerusalem, Sep 24, 1936; s. Aryeh and Pnina (Kadishevitch); MSc, Heb U, 1959, PhD, 1962; postgrad work, U of Cal, LA; m. Sara Efrati, May 3, 1961; c: Ari, Anat. Sr lectr, Heb U since 1967; fmr: asst, lectr, both Heb U; guest lectr, phys organic chem, Tel Aviv U, Bar Ilan, both 1967; postdoctoral f, U of Cal. Mem: Chem Soc, London; Amer, Isr Chem Socs. Author: Handbook of Tables for Identification of Organic Compounds, 1967; The Chemistry of the Cyano Groups, 1969; ed, organic sect, Handbook of Chemistry and Physics; contbr of articles and reviews to sci jours. Hobby, philately. Home: 4/10 Neve Granoth, Jerusalem, Isr. Office: Heb U, Jerusalem, Isr.

RASH, Yehoshua, Isr, diplomat; b. Antwerp, Belgium, Dec 19, 1924; s. Simon and Jeanne (Lowenthal) Hirsch; att HS, Antwerp; m. Myriam Tragarz, Oct 28, 1948; c: Dina, Uri, Avishai. Isr Ambass to Niger, since 1967. Served, Fr Army; IDF. Dir: Isr-Afr Friendship League; Afro-Asian Inst, Histadrut. Recipient: Fr War Cross; Isr Anti-Nazi and Aleh Isr State decorations. Spec interest, Afr hist. Home: Kibbutz Hashonim, Isr. Office: Min for Fgn Affairs, Jerusalem, Isr.

RASKAS, Stuart Irving, US, business exec; b. Detroit, Mich, Mar 23, 1937; s. Morris and Dolly (Bachrach); att: Wayne State U, Detroit, 1954-57; Wash U, St Louis, Mo, 1957-58; m. Joann Landau, June 8, 1958; c: Julie, Sharon, Eric. Pres, Meyer-Mueller-Goodman Co & Stuart Raskas Enterprises, since 1961; acct exec, Dun & Bradstreet, 1959-61. Pres, St Louis B'nai B'rith Council; dir: Men's Tie Found; Shaare Zedek Syn; fmr: pres, Archway Lodge B'nai B'rith; comm, Land Clearance for Redevl Auth, Olivette, Mo; bd mem, ADL. Home: 1704 Wishingwell Dr, Creve Coeur, Mo. Office: 1210 Washington Ave, St Louis, Mo.

RASKIN, Joseph, US, artist; b. Russ, Apr 14, 1897; s. Naphtoly and Lea (Vaniler); att Natl Acad of Design; m. Edith Lefkowitz, Oct 30, 1936. One man shows: NYC; Boston; Miami; Tricker Gal; Schneider Gabriel Gal; Asso Amer Artists; Carnegie Inst; Corcoran Gal; Pa Acad; Natl Acad. Perm collections: Bat Yam Museum; Safed Museum; Ein Harod, all Isr; Harvard U; Dartmouth Coll; US State Dept. Author: Harvard Portfolio of Etchings, 1932; co-author: Indian Tales of the Hudson Valley, 1969. Mem: Rockport Art Assn; Audubon Artists Assn; Woodstock Art Assn. Recipient: F, Tiffany Found, 1922, 1924; Chalon prize, 1948. Home and studio: 59 W 71 St, New York, NY.

RASKIN, Melvin Newell, US, dentist; b. Boston, Mass, Oct 1, 1916; s. Louis and Esther (Rosen); att U of Ala, 1936; BS, U of NH, 1938; DMD, Tufts Dent Sch, Boston, 1943; m. Elaine Zeff, Apr 9, 1944; c: Patricia, Russell, Paul. Dent dir, Conn State Wfr Dept since 1969; pres, Conn Dent Service, 1962-70. Lt col, USAF, 1938-66. Trustee, Temple Beth Israel, mem, Men's Club; mem, Alpha Omega, past pres; fmr: pres, Hartford Dent Soc; dent leader, UJA. Hobby, boating. Home: 35 Ridgewood Rd, West Hartford, Conn. Office: 242 Trismbull, Hartford, Conn.

RASMINSKY, Louis, Can, economist, monetary specialist; b. Montreal, Can, 1908; s. David and Etta; BA, U Toronto, 1928, hon LLD, 1953; hon f, LSE, 1939; hon DHL, HUC; hon LLD, Queens U; hon DCL, Bishops U; m. Lyla Rotenberg; c: Michael, Lola. Gov, Bank of Can, since 1961; alternate gov for Can, IMF, 1962; past exec dir; fmr: mem staff, L of N; org, research and state sect, Can Fgn Exch Control Bd, later alternate chmn, exec off of bd; exec asst to govs, Bank of Can; chmn, drafting comm, Bretton Woods Conf, which approved the IMF Articles of Agreement; exec dir, Intl Bank for Reconstruction and Devl; mem, Can delg to UN Org found conf and first meetings of UN Assembly and Econ Social Council; participant: Commonwealth Finance and Econ Confs, since 1949; meetings of Jt Can-US Trade and Econ Affairs Comm; Can-UK Continuing Econ Comm; Commonwealth PMs Conf, London; Org Eur Econ Comty, Paris. Recipient: Companion of Order of Can, 1968; Outstanding Achievement Award of Public Service of Can, 1968. Home: 440 Roxborough Rd, Rockcliffe Park, Ottawa, Can. Office: Bank of Canada, Ottawa, Can.

RASOOLY, Goory, Isr, researcher; b. Imarah, Iraq, Jan 13, 1920; s. Yosef and Lulu (Sasson); in Isr since 1950; PhC, Royal Coll of Pharm, Baghdad, 1943; MSc, Heb U, Jerusalem, 1959, PhD, 1967; m. Molouk Irani, Apr 20, 1949; c: Yosef, Abraham, Raphael, Lili, Reuben, Israel. Research asst, Heb U-Hadassah Med Sch, since 1955; fmr: pharm: Baghdad; Kupat Holim. Mem, Microbiol Soc of Isr. Contbr to profsl jours. Home: 25 Antigonos St, Jerusalem, Isr. Office: Hebrew U-Hadassah Med Sch, Jerusalem, Isr.

RATNER, Sidney, US, educator; b. NYC, June 18, 1908; s. Israel and Olga (Handman); BA, CCNY, 1930; MA, Columbia U, 1931, PhD, 1942; m. Louise Rosenblatt, 1932; c: Jonathan. Prof, hist, Rutgers U, 1957-67, fac mem, since 1948; instr, Sarah Lawrence, 1938-39; instr and lectr, Cooper Union Inst of Tech, 1938-41; lectr, New Sch for Soc Research, 1940; econ, Bd Econ Warfare, 1942-44; sr econ, Fgn Econ Admn, 1944-45; prin econ, planning div, Off of Fgn Liquidation Commn, US State Dept, 1946; lectr, US Air War Coll, 1949; mem, Inst for Advanced Study, 1956-57, lectr: Us: Kyoto,

Japan, 1964; Nigeria, 1967. Chmn: Conf on Methods in Phil and Scis, 1947-48; John Dewey Centennial Exec Comm, 1959-60; adult educ comm, Princeton J Cen, 1960-61; mem: AAAS: Amer Studies Assn; Amer Hist Assn; Amer Econ Assn; Royal Econ Soc. Author: American Taxation, 1942; Taxation and Democracy in America, 1967; ed and co-author: The Philosopher of the Common Man, 1940; Vision and Action, 1953; History of Great American Fortunes, 1953; New Light on the Inquiry into Inquiries, 1954; ed: John Dewey and JF Bentley, A Philosophical Correspondence, 1964; Makers, Users and Masters, 1968; contbr to anthols and scholarly jours. Hobbies: swimming, theater, art, music. Home: 11 Cleveland Lane, Princeton, NJ. Office: Rutgers U, New Brunswick, NJ.

RATZABY, Yehuda, Isr, educator; b. Sawan, Yemen, May 11, 1917; s. Zacharia and Sarah; att Heb U, Jerusalem 1936-39; m. Rivka Keisar, 1953; c: Amitay, Mitka, Noga, Yemimah. Sr lectr, Heb, Heb-Arabic Lit, Tel Aviv U and Bar Ilan U; fmr: researcher, hist, lit, folklore of Yemenite Jewry; medieval lit; Heb-Arabic lit; with Defense Min, 1936-48. IS, Haganah, 1939-48. Author: Hagalut Vehageula, 1956; Yahadut Teiman, 1958; Har'el, 1962; Sefer Hamusar, 1965; Sichot Arav, 1957; Yalkut Shirei Teiman, 1969; ed, Boi Teiman; contbr to periodicals. Recipient: Bialik award, 1965. Home: 10 Oliphant St, Tel Aviv, Isr.

RATZKOVSKY, Nahum, Isr, banker; b. Jerusalem, Mar 2, 1902; s. Dov and Henia (Sussman); m. Menuha Slonim, 1922; c: Hanania, Shneiur. Ret; gen mgr, Kupat Am Bank, 1959-67, mgr, Haifa br, 1932-59, on staff since 1919; hon consul of Guat, since 1949; mem bd of govs, vice-treas, Technion, Haifa; chmn, bd dirs, Bosmath, vocational training HS; pres: C of C, Haifa, 1954-59; Isr Maritime League, Haifa, 1967-69; mem exec comm, chmn council, Assn of Banks in Isr; club: Rotary, Haifa. Hobbies: reading, music. Home: 25 Wedgwood St, Haifa, Isr. Office: 43 Haatzmaut St, Haifa, Isr.

RAUCH, Marshall Arthur, US, business exec; b. NYC, Feb 2, 1923; s. Nathan and Tillie; att Duke U; m. Jeanne Girard; c: John, Ingrid, Marc, Pete, Stephanie. Chmn of bd, dir, treas: Pyramid Mills Co Inc; Pyramid Dye Corp; Homeside Yarn, all Bessemer City, NC; Nile Star; Woodmere, NY; Gastonia Dyeing Corp; dir: EP Press; Gazette Publ Co; Jet Line Products; Darby Chem Co; S Inves Corp; Sedgefield Realty Co; Majestic Ins Financing Corp; Advance Inves Fund; US Army, WW II. Dir, NC UJA Cabinet, 1968-69; 1st vice-pres, NC Assn J Men, 1966; natl council, JDC, 1968-69; bd govs, NC J Home for Aged, 1968-69; dir: Planned Parenthood and World Population, NYC, 1968-69; mem, Gov's Good Neighbor Council; leg research comm on interest rates, 1968-69; NC State Sen, 1967-69. Recipient: Combat Infantry medal; man-of-the-year: Gaston Co Omega Psi Phi, 1966; NC Health Dept, 1968; citation, Natl Recreation Asso, 1965. Home: 1121 Scotch Dr, Gastonia, NC.

RAUDNITZ, Max, Isr, engineer; b. Frankfurt/M, Aug 26, 1898; s. Jakob and Emilie (Koretz); in Isr since 1934; DEng, Tech HS, Darmstadt, Ger, 1922; m. Herta Wohl, June 7, 1930; c: Jakob, Uriel. Mgn dir, Isr Scales Ltd, Tel Aviv since 1956; engr, Carl Schenk Scales Factory, Darmstadt, 1922-30; tech mgr, Franke & Heidecke, factory of cameras, Braunschweig, Ger, 1930-33. Author: Handbuch des Waagenbaus, 1936, 1956. Hobby, piano playing. Home: 9 Malachi St, Ramat Gan, Isr. Office: 114 Giborei Israel St, Tel Aviv, Isr.

RAUH, Joseph L, Jr, US, attorney; b. Cincinnati, O, Jan 3, 1911; s. Joseph and Sara (Weiler); BS, Harvard Coll, 1932, LLB, Law Sch, 1935; m. Olie Westheimer, Sep 1, 1935; c: Michael, Carl. Mem: law firm, Rauh & Silard, Wash, DC, since 1961; Rauh & Levy, 1946-61; law secy to Supr Court Justices, Cardozo and Frankfurter, 1936-39; counsel, various govt agencies, 1939-42; dep US Housing Expediter, 1946. US Army, 1942-46. Chmn, Dem Cen Comm, Wash, DC, 1964-67; natl chmn, ADA, 1955-57; gen counsel, Leadership Conf on Civil Rights, since 1964; trustee, Antioch Coll, since 1966. Mem, AJCong. Contbr to legal jours. Recipient: Legion of Merit award, 1945; Phillipine Dist Service Star, 1945. Club: DC Harvard. Home: 3625 Appleton St, Washington, DC. Office: 1001 Conn Ave, Washington, DC.

RAVEH, Jizchak Franz, Isr, jurist; b. Aurich, Ger, Nov 10, 1906; s. Heinrich and Selma (Wolff) Reuss; in Isr sinc 1933; D Jur, U of Berlin; U of Halle; m. Batya Sadovsky, 1932; c: Immanuela Moss, Achinoam Persitz. Dist court judge, since

1952. Home: 80 Rothschild Blvd, Tel Aviv, Isr. Office: Tel Aviv-Jaffa Dist Court, Isr.

RAVICH, Abraham, US, urologist; b. Bitten, Pol, June 10, 1889; s. Isadore and Ida (Karelitz); in US since 1893; BA, CCNY, 1908; MA, MD, Columbia U, 1912; m. Martha Zuckert, Sep 3, 1918; c: Robert. Hon surg, Hon Legion, NYC Police Dept, since 1934; fmr: asst, asso, att urol, Bklyn J Hosp; asso urol, Beth Moses Hosp; att urol, Isr Zion Hosp; dir, Ravich Urol Inst; asst clinical prof, urol, LI Coll of Med; chief urol, Beth El Hosp; dir, urol, Bklyn Heb Home and Hosp for Aged; cons urol, Menorah Home for Aged; att, cons urol, Adelphi Hosp; found: and exec dir, Cancer Research and Hosp Found; and pres, Inst Applied Biol; Trafalgar Hosp, NYC; mem, bd visitors, Creedmoor State Hosp. Devised: Ravich Cystoscope; Lithotriptoscope; Urethroscope; other urol instruments; instruments and methods of transurethral resection in large prostates; first to find that the incidence of cancer of prostate was greater in Gentiles than in Jews and to postulate that cancer of the prostate, cervix and bladder was a venereally transmitted viral infection from the smegma of uncircumcised males and was prevented by complete circumcision of newborn males, 1942; first to postulate the role of renal artery or vein obstruction in intra-renal type of kidneys in producing hypertension; first to discover that benign Granular Cell Myoblastoma could become malignant, 1941; first to refute long accepted fallacy that Japan had lowest incidence of prostatic cancer in the world, even lower than in Isr, 1964. Life, FACS; mem: life, Bklyn Urol Soc, past pres; sr, Amer Urol Assn; NY Urol Soc; life, AMA; NY State Med Soc; Kings Co Med Soc; Masons. Mem, ed bd, Clinical Abstracts, 1934-37; contbr to med jours. Recipient: CCNY Townsend Harris Medal for Achievement, 1950. Home: 1135 103 St, Miami Beach, Fla.

RAVID, Michael, Isr, diplomat; b. Russ, Apr 5, 1914; s. Salamon and Rebeca Rabinowitsch, dipl, agric engr, U of Algiers, 1934; m. Hanna Kliger, Jan 5, 1944; c: Dan, Dov, Shlomo. Consul Gen of Isr, Los Angeles, since 1967; mem, Kibbutz Glil-yam; fmr: worked for illegal immigration to Pal, Ger; org, Youth Aliyah groups, N Afr; Eur hqr, JA, Paris; lectr: Tchrs Sem's; Afro-Asian Inst; Isr Ambass to Guinea. Served Haganah. Home: 156 S Las Palmas St, Los Angeles, Cal. Office: 659 S Highland St, Los Angeles, Cal.

RAVIKOVITCH, Dahlia, Isr, poet; b. Ramat Gan, Isr, Nov 17, 1936; d. Levy and Michal (Houminer); att Heb U, Jerusalem, 1955-58; div. Tchr, high sch, 1959-63. Poet: Ahavat Tapuah haZahav, 1959, 2nd ed, 1964, 3rd ed, 1967; Horef Kashe, 1964, 2nd ed, 1968; haSefer haShlishi, 1969. Contbr childrens stories, trans, criticism. IDF, 1954-55. Recipient: Shlonsky award, 1965. Home: 4 Mordecai St, Ramat Gan, Isr.

RAVIN, Abe, US, physician, educator; b. Denver, Colo, Sep 9, 1908; s. Hyman and Lena (Rapkin); BA, U of Colo, 1929, MA, 1938, MD, Sch of Med, 1932; m. Rose Steed, Dec 27, 1937; c: Thomas, Lenore. Pvt practice since 1952; clinical prof, med, U of Colo, since 1950; instr, Cincinnati Gen Hosp, 1935-39, on staff since 1932; NRC f, Harvard U, 1939-40; dir, cardiopulmonary lab, Natl J Hosp, 1948-52. F: Amer Coll of Cardiology, 1958; Amer Coll of Phys, 1938; mem: AMA; AHA; Phi Beta Kappa; Alpha Omega Alpha; Sigma Xi. Contbr to med jours. Home and office: 45 South Dahlia, Denver, Colo.

RAVIN, Arnold W, US, geneticist, educator; b. NYC, Aug 15, 1921; s. Max and Rae (Levinson); BS, CCNY, 1942; MA, Columbia U, 1948, PhD, 1951; m. Sophie Brody, June 11, 1956; c: Sonia, Andrea. Prof, biol, U of Chgo, master, coll div of biol, asso dean, div biol sci, since 1968; prof, U of Rochester, 1962-68, dean, Coll Arts and Sci, 1961-62, fac mem since 1953. Lt, USAAC, 1942-46. Trustee: Bergey's Manual Trust; Amer Type Culture Collection; mem: Amer Soc for Microbiol; Genetics Soc Amer; Soc Amer Naturalists; Amer Soc Cell Biol; Soc Gen Microbiol; AAAS; Sigma Xi. Contbr to genetic publs. Recipient: postdoc f, USPHS, Lab de Genetique, Paris, 1951-53; spec research f, NIH, 1960-61. Spec interest: contemporary art. Home: 4816 S Greenwood Ave, Chicago, Ill. Office: U of Chicago, Chicago, Ill.

RAVIV, Shabtai, Isr, government official; b. Tel Aviv, Isr, Apr 11, 1926; s. David and Yehudith Rabinowitz; studied political sci, Jerusalem, 1954-55; m. Lea Silberstein, Apr 6, 1948; c: Ronit, Tal. PR off, Isr Ports Auth, since 1961; fmr: secy, Kibbutz Hassolelim; consul for press relations, Gen Consulate of Isr, NY. Haganah, chief educ off, Nahal, IDF,

since 1940. Mem, exec comm, Isr PR Assn; fmr mem natl comm, Maccabi Hatzair Youth Movement. Ed: Anu Halohamim, 1967; Yamei Rama, 1964. Home: 30 Trumpeldor St, Ramat HaSharon, Isr. Office: Isr Port Auth, 74 Petach Tikva Rd, Tel Aviv, Isr.

RAY, Gerald J, Can, business exec; b. Toronto, Can, June 26, 1926; s. Isaac and Molly (Cornfield); B Applied Sci, hons, U of Toronto, 1949; m. Esther Magerman, May 8, 1948; c: Keith, Richard, Howard. Dir, Borden Co Ltd; pres, Borden Chem Co (Can) Ltd, fmr, Amer Resinous Chems of Can Ltd, since 1957, mem staff, since 1953; compounder, Dunlop Tire Co, 1949-53. F, Chem Inst of Can; mem: Assn of Profsl Engrs of Province of Ont; Packaging Assn of Can; B'nai B'rith; Adath Isr Syn. Recipient: Hugh Gall award, 1947. Home: 4 Chieftain Crescent, Willowdale, Ont, Can. Office: POB 610, West Hill, Ont, Can.

RAYNER, John Desmond, Eng, rabbi; b. Berlin, Ger, May 30, 1924; s. Ferdinand and Charlotte (Landshut) Rahmer; in Eng since 1939; BA, MA, Emmanuel Coll, Cambridge, 1953; ordained rabbi, HUC, 1965; m. Jane Heilbronn, June 19, 1955; c: Jeremy, Benjamin, Susan. Sr min, Lib J Syn, since 1961; hon dir of studies, Leo Baeck Coll, since 1966; min, S London Lib J Syn, 1953-57. Capt, Brit Army, 1943-47. Vice-chmn, Council Reform and Lib Rabbis; chmn, Youth Sec, World Union for Progressive Judaism. Author, Toward Mutual Understanding between Jews and Christians, 1960; co-ed: Service of the Heart, prayerbook, 1967; contbr to J publs. Home: 181 Anson Rd, London, Eng. Study: 28 St Johns Wood Rd, London, Eng.

RAZ, Naftali, Isr, engineer; b. Tel Aviv, Isr, Sep 30, 1921; s. Matetyahu and Yona (Prober) Reiser; att Brit Inst, London, 1951-54; m. Hanna Back, Apr 11, 1946; c: Noga, Hela. Dep dir, engr services, Isr PO, since 1969; area gen mgr, Tel Aviv, Cen PO, 1961-69. Lt, signal corps, IDF, 1948-61. Mem: Isr Data Processing Assn; Army Pensioners Assn, Zevet, Isr. Recipient: Afr Star; War of Independence; Sinai Decorations. Home: 44 Matzbim St, Tel Aviv, Isr. Office: Shalom Tower, Tel Aviv, Isr.

RAZ, Simcha, Isr, writer; b. Jerusalem, Isr, Aug 15, 1931; s. Chaim and Chana (Mandelbaum) Rakover; ordained rabbi, Yeshiva Ha-Rav Kook, Jerusalem; att off training sch for admn Zahal; dipl, public admn, Heb U; m. Colleen Nurok; c: Esther, Chana. Author: The Face of Israel; Chapters in Israel History; The History of Rabbi Akiva; The History of Hillel; contbr to newspapers, radio. Capt, IDF. Gen secy, Brith Ivrit Olamit (Heb World Union). Home: 20 Hatibonim St, Jerusalem, Isr. Office: 18 Bezalel St, Jerusalem, Isr.

RAZILY, Haim, Isr, business exec; b. Russ, Sep 9, 1896; s. Eliezer and Rebeka (Reznik); in Isr since 1913; att LSE, 1920-33; m. Segoula Backman, 1919. Dir, Electra Ltd, since 1957; gen mgr, Egged Coop Soc, 1933-42; owner and pres, H Razily, Ltd, 1942-43; partner and dir, Even Haysesod Ltd, 1942-57; dir gen, Min of Transp and Communications, 1952-55. Turkish Army, 1917-18. Fmr vice-pres, Intl Diamond Mfrs Assn; dir, Mifalei Jovala, Ltd; mem: exec comm, Independent Lib Party, Tel Aviv; Diamond Exch; Isr bd, Friends of Heb U; clubs: Rotary; Ind and Commercial; Intl Aero, fmr pres, Isr sect. Contbr to periodicals. Hobby: photography. Home: 66 Keren Kayemeth Blvd, Tel Aviv, Isr. Office: Electra Ltd, POB 2180, Tel Aviv, Isr.

RAZIN, Benzion, Isr, banker; b. Novo-Archangelsk, Russ, Mar 14, 1907; s. Itzhak and Dina (Lobensky) Resnik; in Isr since 1927; att Gymnasium of Law and Econ, Russ; LLB, Tel Aviv, 1938; DJ, U of Caen, Fr, 1944; m. Atalia Kastenbaum, Oct 28, 1933; c: Nurit, Yael. Sr mgr, Bank Leumi le-Isr, Tel Aviv, since 1939; repr of Gen Mortgage, Jerusalem, 1941-45; repr, Bank Leumi in S Amer, 1962-66. Maj, Haganah, Zahal, 1929-48. Mem: Secretariat of the Control Comm, Lab Movement; Bar Assn, Tel Aviv; fmr: rent commn, Munic of Jerusalem and Tel Aviv; organizer, secy, V League for Russian Aid, Jerusalem, WWII; head, JA delg, Bulgarian Fair, 1947; chargé d'affaires, Isr Govt, Sofia, Bulgaria, initiated renewal of relations between Isr and Russ, 1953; UJA mission: Montevideo, Uraguay; Porto Alegra, Brazil, 1960. Home: 20 Amsterdam, Tel Aviv, Isr.

RAZIN, Shmuel, Isr, educator; b. Tel Aviv, Feb 1, 1929; s. Yehezkiel and Henia (Galante) Rosenberg; MSc, Heb U, Jerusalem, 1954, PhD, 1958; m. Yaffa Rothenberg, May 7, 1951; c: Gran, Yuval. Asso prof, microbiol, Heb U, since

1967; fmr: visiting prof, U Conn; visiting sci, NIH. Sgt, Haganah, served IDF. Secy, Isr Microbiol Soc; mem: Biochem Soc of Isr; Amer Soc of Microbiol; Soc of Gen Microbiol; Sigma Xi. Author: The Mycoplasma Membrane, 1969; Structure and Function in Mycoplasma, 1969. Recipient, Abraham Back Award for Dist Sci, 1969. Hobby, painting. Home: 2 Neve Granot St, Jerusalem, Isr. Office: Heb U-Hadassah Med Sch, Jerusalem, Isr.

RAZRAN, Gregory, US, educator; b. Czaplici, Russ, June 4, 1901; s. Zalman and Riva (Ongeybar); in US since 1927; BS, Columbia U, 1927, MA, 1928, PhD, 1933; m. Elna Bernholz, Sep 15, 1939; c: Lydia. Chmn, dept of psych, Queens Coll, since 1945; lectr, psych, Columbia U, 1930-38; stat cons, Civil Aeronautics Auth, NYC, 1939-40; psych cons, Off of Strategic Services, 1941-44; Guggenheim f, 1948-49; visiting prof, Heb U, Jerusalem, 1952. F, experimental phys, cons, gen psych, Amer Psych Assn, 1963-64; mem: Soc for Study of Psych Issues; E Psych Assn; hon mem, Fla State Psych Assn. Contbr to profsl jours; trans ed, Higher Nervous Activity, by Pavlov, 1960-62. Home: 67-15A 186 Lane, Fresh Meadows, NY. Office: Queens Coll, Flushing, NY.

REABACK, William W, US, dentist; b. Russ, Oct 17, 1900; s. Myer and Rose (Raden); in US since 1902; DDS, Temple U, Phila, 1928; m. Elenor Golder, Nov 27, 1949. Pvt practice since 1925; lectr, St Agnes Hosp, Phila, Pa. USCGR, WW II. Vice-pres, Men's Club, Beth El Cong; secy, Dent Soc, S Dist; mem: Sigma Epsilon Delta, Amer Dent Assn. Contbr to dent jours. Hobbies: painting, sculpturing. Home: 3600 Conshohocken Ave, Philadelphia, Pa. Office: 1947 W Passyunk Ave, Philadelphia, Pa.

REBHUN, Menahem, Isr, engineer, educator; b. Tarnov, Pol, Mar 12, 1929; s. Yehezkiel and Rachel (Blaser); in Isr since 1950; BSc, Technion, 1953, Ing, 1954; MSc, U of Cal, Berkeley, 1958; DSc, Technion, 1966; m. Stella Frenkel, Aug 9, 1956; c: Rachel, Arie, Uziel. Asso prof, Technion, since 1968; cons engr, since 1958; chem engr, Ayalon Water Co, 1955-57; lectr, Technion, 1958-66; sr lectr, 1966-68; visiting research, U of Cal, 1966-67. Sgt, IDF, 1954-56. Mem: Water Pollution Control Fed; Intl Water Supply Assn; Isr Chem Soc; Assn of Engrs and Architects, Isr; Isr Assn, Chem Engrs. Contbr to sci jours. Home: 6 Asher St, Haifa, Isr. Office: Tehnion, Haifa, Isr.

RECANATI, Daniel, Isr, banker; b. Salonika, Greece, Oct 25, 1921; s. Leon and Mathilde (Saporta); in Isr since 1935; m. Mathilde Carasso, 1946; c: Leon, Judith. Chmn and mgn dir, Isr Discount Bank Ltd; chmn: Discount Bank Inves Corp; Mercantile Bank of Isr; dir: Ind Devl Bank of Isr; Isr Devl and Mortgage Bank; Delek-Isr Fuel Corp; Cargo Ships El-Yam; mem adv council, Bank of Isr. Home: 29 Ben Zion Blvd, Tel Aviv, Isr. Office: Israel Discount Bank, Yehuda Halevi St, Tel Aviv, Isr.

RECANATI, Raphael, Isr, banker; b. Salonika, Greece, Feb 12, 1924; s. Leon and Mathilde (Saporta); m. Dinah Hettena, Oct 8, 1946; c: Yehuda, Michael. Pres: Maritime Overseas Corp, since 1953; Overseas Discount Corp; mgn dir: Isr Discount Bank, Ltd, NY; chmn, Cargo Ships El-Yam, Ltd; fmr: pres, Amer Isr Shipping Co; mgn dir, Isr-Amer Line. Home: 944 Fifth Ave, New York, NY. Office: 511 Fifth Ave, New York, NY.

RECHTER, Yakov, Isr, architect; b. Tel Aviv, Isr, June 14, 1924; s. Zeev and Paula; engr architect, Technion, Haifa, 1946; m. Hanna Maron, 1957; five c. Dir, Rechter, Zarhy, Architects, Peri Engr, since 1960. Maj works: Mann Auditorium, Hilton Hotel, law courts, all Tel Aviv. Lt, IDF, 1947-49. Recipient, Rokach Award. Home: 56 Hanassi St, Herzliya, Isr. Office: 8 Kikar Malchey Israel, Tel Aviv, Isr.

RECKLER, Sidney M, US, surgeon, educator; b. Denver, Colo, Dec 22, 1911; s. Joseph and Tillie (Silverberg); BA, U Denver, 1929; MD, U Colo, 1933; m. Sarah Redman, Mar 24, 1939; c: Jon, Linda. Pvt practice, surg, since 1945; cons in surg, Natl J Hosp, since 1946, mem, bd of dirs, since 1950; sr surg, Rose Memorial Hosp, since 1950; cons surg, VA Hosp, since 1950; asso clinical prof, surg, U Colo Med Sch, since 1958; att surg: U Colo Hosp, since 1941; Children's Hosp, since 1941; St Joseph's Hosp, since 1941; St Anthony's Hosp, since 1950, all Denver. Maj, US Army, 1941-45. Dipl, Amer Bd of Surg; f: Amer Coll of Surgs; SW Surg Cong. Mem: Masons; Pi Lambda Phi; Alpha Omega Alpha; clubs: Green Gables

Country; Town. Home: 1 S Dahlia St, Denver, Colo. Office: 1825 Gilpin St, Denver, Colo.

REDER, Melvin W, US, economist, educator; b. SF, Cal, May 25, 1919; s. Frank and Anna (Lipshitz); AB, U of Cal, 1939; PhD, Columbia U, 1946; m. Edna Oliker, Dec 20, 1942; c: Stephen, Lynne. Prof, econ, Stanford U, since 1949; asst, Carnegie Inst of Tech, 1946-48; asso, U of Pa, 1948-49; cons, UN, 1949; Garth f, Columbia U, 1941-42; Guggenheim f, 1954; f, Cen for Advanced Study in Behavioral Sci, 1957-58; Ford fac f, 1961-62; cons: Dept of Defense, 1964; Dept of Lab, 1967; HEW, 1968. Mem: Amer Econ Assn; Econometric Soc; Ind Relations Research Assn. Author: Studies in Theory of Welfare Economics, 1946; Labor in a Growing Economy, 1957; ed bd, American Economic Review, 1960-63; contbr to scholarly jours. Home: 830 Santa Fe Ave, Stanford, Cal. Office: Stanford U, Stanford, Cal.

REDSTONE, Louis G, US, architect; b. Grodno, Pol, Mar 16, 1903; s. Abraham and Anna (Grudski) Routenstein; in US since 1923; BS, Arch, Coll of Arch, U of Mich, 1929; MS, Arch, Cranbrook Acad of Art, Cranbrook, Mich, 1948; m. Ruth Rosenbaum, 1939; c: Daniel, Eliel. Pvt practice, Louis G Redstone, Architects, Inc, since 1937; Louis G Redstone, Isr, 1933-37. Delg: Pan-Amer Cong of Architects, Caracas, Venezuela, 1955; Conv on Reciprocal E-W Architectural Influences, Tokyo, 1956; Intl Cong of Architects, Moscow, 1958. F, Amer Inst of Architects, 1964; chmn: Urban Design Collaborative, Detroit chap, Amer Inst Architects, 1959; prof adv comm, Mich Soc Architects, 1958; Amer Technion Soc, 1948; art comm, J Comty Cen, 1960; pres, Detroit chap, Amer Inst Architects, 1965; mem: Engr Soc of Detroit; exec comm, Pan-Amer Fed of Architects, since 1955. Contbr to profsl jours. Author: Art in Architecture, 1968. Recipient: hon award: Mich Liquor Control Commn, 1955; Wonderland Shopping Cen; Mfrs Natl Bank; gold medal, Amer Inst Architects, Detroit chap, 1969. Hobby: painting. Home: 19303 Appoline Ave, Detroit, Mich. Office: 10811 Puritan Ave, Detroit, Mich.

REGELSON, Abraham, Isr, author, journalist; b. Hlusk, Russ, 1896; s. Judah and Rachel (Ozik); in Isr since 1949; m. Ida Rosen, 1922; c: Ephraim, Naomi Bar-Nathan, Leon, Sharona Tel-Oren, Tamar Ginat. Free-lance writer, journalist, since 1962; journalist: Davar, daily, 1933-36, co-found children's weekly, Davar leYeladim; Al Hamishmar, daily, 1950-62, both in Tel Aviv; ed work for publ firms: Am Oved, haKibbutz haMeuhad, Dvir, since 1949; organized: Heb Poetry Soc of Amer, NYC, 1946; Hevel Philopoesia, Tel Aviv, 1958. Author: Cain and Abel, 1931; The Dolls' Journey to Palestine, 1935; A Shawlful of Leaves, 1941; There the Crystal Is, 1942; El haAyin veNivqa, 1943; Engraved are Thy Letters, 1964; Fountain of the Horse-tales from Greek Mythology, 1967; Mighty Men of Thought, 1968; trans into Heb, works of: Blake; Whitman; Kipling; Hawthorne; Melville; Mordecai M Kaplan's The Meaning of God in Modern Jewish Religion; Solomon Goodman's The Jew and the Universe; from Heb into Eng: Jacob Klatzkin's In Praise of Wisdom; M Maisel's Thought and Truth; contbr to lit jours and periodicals, in Isr and abroad. Home: N'veh Ephraim, Isr.

REGENSTEIN, Louis, US, attorney; b. Atlanta, Ga, Feb 9, 1912; s. Louis and Venia (Liebman); AB, cum laude, Harvard U, 1933, LLB, cum laude, 1936; m. Helen Moses, July 30, 1939; c: Lewis, Jonathan. Partner, Kilpatrick, Cody, Rogers, McClatchey, Regenstein, Atlanta, Ga, since 1942. Lt col, US Army, 1941-45. Mem, bd trustees, Clark Coll; The Temple, 1948-50; Metrop Atlanta Comty Services; natl exec comm, AJComm; sect on taxation, Amer Bar Assn; pres, Atlanta Legal Aid Soc; dir, Atlanta C of C, 1955-58; pres, Atlanta chap, Multiple Sclerosis Soc, 1959; mem bd: High Mus of Art; Comty Service; for Blind; mem: Natl Planning Comm and delg, White House Conf on Aging, 1961; ACLU; Amer Judicature Soc; Atlanta Art Assn; Atlanta Comm on Fgn Relations; Atlanta Sym Guild; B'nai B'rith; comm, NCCJ; Newcomen Soc; State Cen Comm, Rep Party. Recipient, Army Commendation Medal. Hobbies: modern art, music. Home: 3691 Tuxedo Rd, NW, Atlanta, Ga. Office: 1045 Hurt Bldg, Atlanta, Ga.

REGNER, Sidney L, US, organization exec, rabbi; b. NYC, Sep 25, 1903; s. Martin and Kate (Lichtman); BA, U Cinn, 1942; ordained rabbi, HUC, Cinn, 1927, hon DD, 1954; m. Dorothy Marcus, Aug 18, 1931; c: Babette Eisenberg, James. Exec vice-pres, CCAR, since 1954, ed, CCAR Yearbook, since 1954; mem, governing body, World Union for Progressive

Judaism, since 1957; mem, exec comm, Syn Council of Amer, since 1955; rabbi, Temple Oheb Sholom, Reading, Pa, 1927-54. Mem: Assn of Reform Rabbis of NYC and Vicinity; NY Bd of Rabbis; Rabb Pension Bd, since 1954; Bd of Govs, NY Bd of Rabbis, since 1969; Phi Beta Kappa. Home: 205 West End Ave, New York, NY. Office: 790 Madison Ave, New York, NY.

REGUER, Moshe Aron, US, rabbi, educator; b. Brest-Litovsk, Pol, Nov 20, 1905; s. Simcha and Sarah (Rudensky) Ryjer; in US since 1929; att: Slobodker Yeshiva, Lith; Heb U, Jerusalem; ordained rabbi, Rabbi Isaac Elchanan Theol Sem, NY; grad, Tchrs Inst, Yeshiva U, 1935; BA, Yeshiva U, 1942, DHL, 1946; m. Anne Shabasson, Apr 3, 1936; c: Gabriel, Sara, Simcha. Asso prof, J studies, Yeshiva U, since 1968; instr, Bible, Heb lit, Tchrs Inst, Yeshiva U, 1951-68, mem fac since 1946; fmr: instr, Tchrs Training Sch for Girls, NYC, 1935-38; dir, Heb Tchrs Sem, Montreal, Can, 1946-51; secy, Beth Din, Bd of J Mins, Montreal, 1950-51; chmn, bd educ, Yeshiva Rabbi Moses Soloveichik, 1945-46. Mem: RabCA, educ and Isr comms; NY Bd of Rabbis; Bibl Soc of NY Bd of Rabbis; Rabb Alumni and Tchrs Inst Comm, Yeshiva U. Home: 666 W 188 St, New York, NY. Office: Yeshiva U, Amsterdam Ave and 187 St, New York, NY.

REHMAN, Irving, US, anatomist, educator; b. NYC, July 17, 1911; s. Louis and Elizabeth (Wachs); BS, NYU, 1933, MS, 1935, PhD, 1940; m. Sophie Shoer, Nov 23, 1938; c: Dorothea, Kenneth. Prof, anat, U of S Cal, since 1947, asst prof, 1944-47; vice-regent, Intl Coll of Surgs, since 1968; cons, anat: San Diego Naval Hosp; LA Co Gen Hosp; Chief of Naval Oprs; Naval Underwater Warfare Cen; US Naval Hosp; Camp Pendleton; Oakland; Long Beach, 1949-50; fmr: instr, anat, NYU, 1933-43; asso dir, otology lab, Cedars of Leb Hosp, LA, 1951-54. Mem: Amer Assn Anats; AAUP; Intl Coll Surgs; Sigma Xi; Sigma Tau Phi; Phi Lambda Kappa. Author: A Guide To Human Dissection, 1939; Surgical Anatomy, 1943; Functional Human Anatomy, 1944; Descriptive Atlas of Surgical Anatomy, 1965; contbr to profsl jours. Home: 5153 Tampa Ave, Tarzana, Cal. Office: U of S Cal, Sch of Med, Los Angeles, Cal.

REIBMAN, Jeanette F, US, public official; b. Fort Wayne, Ind, Aug 18, 1915; d. Meir and Pearl (Schwartz) Fichman; AB, Hunter Coll, 1937; LLB, Ind U, 1940; hon LLD, Lafayette Coll, 1969; m. Nathan Reibman, June 20, 1943; c: Joseph, Edward, James. State Senator, Pa, since 1966; atty, US War Dept and US War Produc Bd, WW II; mem, Pa House Repr, 1955-56, 1959-66. Adv comm: Tchr Educ for State Council Educ; Working Conditions for Women and Children for State Dept Lab and Ind; Lehigh Valley Hosp Planning Council; bd dirs: Forks of Del United Fund; Northampton Co Family Couns Service; citizenship couns, Del Area Council Boy Scouts Amer. Recipient: award and medal, Dist Daughter of Pa, 1968. Home: 514 McCartney, Easton, Pa. Office: 711 Lehigh, Easton, Pa.

REICH, Joseph, Fr, physician; b. Rozwadow, Pol, Jan 19, 1903; s. Abe and Cypora (Zangen); in Fr since 1923; MD, U of Strasbourg, 1932; m. Gertrude Heppenheimer, Jan 1, 1932; c: Laure, Eliane-Miriam. Stomatologist, since 1933; health service off, 1939-40. Pres: B'nai B'rith, since 1951; Magbit, since 1949; WJC; Zionist Fed, all in Lyon; vice-pres, Consistoire Israelite de Lyon; mem: Consistoire Central de Paris; WJC; natl and world execs; repr, JA. Home: 323 Cours Emile Zola, Lyon-Villeurbanne, Fr.

REICH, Nathan, US, economist, educator; b. Terszow, Aus-Hung, June 6, 1900; s. Sholem and Lea (Hartman); in US since 1932; MA, McGill U, 1926; PhD, Columbia U, 1937; m. Riva Rudy, Apr 20, 1930; c: Daniel, Judith. Prof, econ, Hunter Coll, NYC, since 1951, on fac since 1934; asso dir, jt Hunter Coll-U of Frankfurt Research Project; Guggenheim f, 1940-41; comparative study of lab relations in Fed Ger Rep and US, 1953-55; asst ed, Ency of the Social Scis, 1930-34; lectr, Columbia U, 1944-49; research dir, JDC, NY, 1944-49; mem, panel, NJ State Mediation Bd; chmn, bd of dirs, YIVO, mem, acad council. Mem: ed council, J social Studies, NY; Friends of the Heb U; libr comm, AJComm. Author: Canadian Pulp and Paper Industry, 1927; Labor Relations in Republican Ger, 1937. Home: 510 E 86 St, New York, NY. Office: Hunter Coll, 695 Park Ave, New York, NY.

REICH, Nathaniel E, US, cardiologist, educator; b. NYC, May 19, 1907; s. Alexander and Betty (Feigenbaum); BS, NYU, 1927; MD, U of Chgo, 1931; att Marguette U Sch of Med,

1927-29; m. Joan Finkel, 1943; c: Andrew, Matthew. Asso prof, clinical med, SUNY, since 1954; card: Kingsbrook J Med Cen, mem exec comm, chmn, libr comm; att card: SUNY Downstate Med Cen; cons: St Joseph's Hosp; Unity Hosp; Long Beach Memorial Hosp; visiting lectr; Heb U, Jerusalem, 1968; Afghanistan; Iran, both 1970; Surinam, 1971; fmr: asst att phys, NY Post-Grad Med Sch, 1939; cons in card, VA, 1947-52; att phys, Harbor Hosp, 1948-50; impartial specialist, Workmen's Compensation Bd, State Dept of Lab, 1952-59; visiting prof, San Marcos U Fac of Med, Lima, Peru. Major, US Army MC, 1943-47. F: Amer Coll of Phys; Amer Coll Chest Phys; Amer Coll Card; Amer Coll Angiology; Amer Coll Legal Med; dipl, Amer Bd Internal Med; chmn: exec bd, NY Card Soc; coronary disease comm, Amer Coll Chest Phys, pres, NY State chap; chest sect, Med Soc, State of NY; exec comm, Kingsbrook J Med Cen; mem, council on thrombosis, AHA; Intl and NY State Socs Internal Med; AMA; Phi Delta Epsilon; hon mem, Kappa Alpha; clubs: Temple, vice-pres, 1953-54; Bklyn Drs, vice-chmn, bd govs, 1953. Author: Diseases of the Aorta, 1949; The Uncommon Heart Disease, 1954; co-author: Chest Pain, 1960; contbr to med jours, encys. Paintings in Huntington Hartford Collection; Lowe Mus, U Miami; Wash Co Mus; Fine Arts Mus of Hagerstown, Md; Evansville Mus of Arts and Scis; seven one-man shows. Recipient: St Gaudens Medal, 1924; 3rd prize, Amer Phys Art Soc, 1949; 1st prize, Amer Phys Lit Soc, 1950. Hobbies: art, sports. Home: 1620 Ave I, Brooklyn, NY. Office: 135 Eastern Pkwy, Brooklyn, NY.

REICH, Shimon, Isr, organization exec; b. Berlin, Ger, Nov 23, 1914; s. Nissan and Sara (Herzfeld); in Isr since 1938; m. Tilly Zunder, June 2, 1946; c: Giora Eitan, Orit. Chmn, Kibbutz Ind Assn, Ltd, since 1967; mem bd dirs, KOOR, since 1965; fmr mem mgmt, Isr Export Inst; established factory for measuring instruments, pressure gauges and valves. Mem: Natl Ind Forum, chmn, SHAERF; Isr-Amer C of C; Friends of Tel Aviv U; Isi Cen for Mgmt. Hobbies: books, theater. Home: Kibbutz Afek, isr. Office: 13 Tjomkin St, Tel Aviv, Isr.

REICHAW, Meir, Isr, mathematician; b. Grodek Jagiellonski, Pol, Dec 20, 1923; s. Joseph and Klara (Podhoretz) Reichbach; in Isr since 1957; MSc, U of Wroclow, Pol, 1950; DSc, 1956; m. Halina Sawicka-Puterman, Nov 27, 1955. Asso prof, dept of math, Technion, Haifa, since 1963; asso prof, U of Wroclow, 1948-56; sr lectr, Technion, 1957-63. Contbr in topology and functional analysis; introduced polynomial mappings in gen spaces. Mem: Isr Math Union; Amer Math Soc; Polskie Towarzystwo Matematyczne; fmr secy, Isr Math Union. Author: Elements of Algebraic Topology, 1969. Home: 32 Sd Hazvi, Haifa, Isr. Office: Technion, Haifa, Isr.

REICHEL, Josephine G, US, communal worker; b. NYC, Apr 8, 1928; d. Herbert and Rebecca (Fischel) Goldstein; att Heb Tchrs Training Sch for Girls, 1945-48; BA, Hunter Coll, 1949; m. Rabbi Oscar Reichel, June 5, 1947; c: Aaron, Miriam, Hillel. Natl pres, Agudah Women of Amer, since 1961; natl bd mem, women's branch, Union of Orthodox J Congs of Amer, since 1958, natl bd secy since 1966; pres, Yeshiva U Alumni Wives, 1956-57; Sisterhood W Side Instl Syn, 1962-63. Home: 230 W 79 St, New York, NY.

REICHEL, O Asher, US, rabbi; b. Bklyn, NY, July 24, 1921; s. Benjamin and Lena (Hiltzik); BA, Yeshiva Coll, 1942; ordained rabbi, Rabbi Isaac Elchanan Theol Sem, 1944; MA, NYU, 1947; MHL, Yeshiva U, 1948, DHL, 1960; m. Josephine Goldstein, June 5, 1947; c: Aaron, Miriam, Hillel. Rabbi: W Side Instl Syn, NYC, since 1947; fmr: Young Isr of Cincinnati; Cong Zicharon Ephraim, NYC. Treas, Harry and Jane Fischel Found, since 1959, trustee since 1954; mem bd dirs, Rabbi Herzog World Acad in Jerusalem, since 1956; vice-pres, Metrop Bd of Orthodox Rabbis, NYC; mem bd, Manhattan Day Sch; chmn, hist soc, Heb Day Schs; fmr: mem: comm of citizens, Juvenile Delinquency Evaluation of City of NY; regional co-chmn, educ comm, RabCA. Author: Isaac Halevy—Spokesman and Historian of Jewish Tradition, Heb vol, R Yitzhok Isaac Halevy-Harav Verigotav; chap in Sefer Zicharon leRabbi Yitzhok Isaac Halevy, 1964; ed, West Side Instl Review, since 1947; contbr to publs. Home: 230 W 79 St, New York, NY. Study: 122 W 76 St, New York, NY.

REICHENBACH, Iizhak Bernard, Isr, physician; b. Tarnopol, Pol, June 20, 1908; s. Shevach and Clara (Prinz); in Isr since 1952; MD, U Med Schs: Vienna; Prague; Pisa, 1935; specialist in public health; m. Ida Zanni, June 26, 1943; c: Clara, Avi. Head, curative services, Isr Min of Health, since 1967; med dir: JDC for It, 1946-52; Malben Hosp, Shaar Menashe, 1952-60; Govt Hosp, Nahariya, 1960-65. Maj, MC, 1943-46. Mem: Ordine dei Medici, It; IMA. Recipient: Silver Cross of Merit; Virtuti Militari Medal; and others. Home: 16 Hatishbi St, Haifa, Isr. Office: 20 King David St, Jerusalem, Isr.

REICHENTHAL, Ferenc, (Frank), US, artist; b. Velky Leg, Aus-Hung, May 6, 1895; s. Jonas and Fanny (Weinberger); in US since 1949; att Acad of Arts: Budapest, Hung, 1915, 1922-23; Petrograd, Russ, 1919-22; m. Margaret Fleischmann, July 1, 1936; c: Mary. Prof, State Art Sch, Bratislava, Czech, 1933-39; head, ORT Art Sch, Budapest, 1939-44. One-man shows: Galerie Wuerthle-Flechteim, Vienna, Aus, 1923; Galerie Helikon, Budapest, 1924; Kunstverein, Prague, 1924; Umelecka Beseda: Prague, 1925, 1929; Bratislava, 1925, 1930, 1945; Museum Kosice, 1926, 1933, 1946; Skunpina Vytv Umelcu, Brno, 1936; Galerie Vilimek, Prague, 1947; Galerie Ehrfurt, Dresden, Ger, 1927; Galerie Aux Sacre Du Printemps, Paris, 1928; Gal Rotschink, NYC, 1966; Mus of Modern Art, Miami Mus, both 1960; NYC, 1962; Gal Internationale, NYC, 1967. Perm collections of: all leading Czech mus; Albertina, Vienna; J Mus, Chgo; J Mus, NYC; Mus of W Art, Moscow; Cultural Cen, Tel Aviv. Pres, Slovakian Art Assn, Bratislava, 1946-48. Mem: Kunstverein, Vienna; Salon d'Automne, Paris; Muveszeti Egylet, Budapest; Umelecka Beseda: Prague and Bratislava; Skupina Vytv Umelcu, Brno. Home: 197-20 89 Rd, Hollis, NY.

REICHERT, Israel, Isr, plant pathologist, educator; b. Ozorkov, Pol, Aug 5, 1891; s. Eliezer and Rohma (Kryszek); in Isr since 1908; grad, Tchrs Sem, Jerusalem, 1913; PhD, Berlin U, 1920; postgrad study, Biologische Reichsanstalt, Berlin, 1920-21; m. Nadia Eitington, 1928. Ret; fmr: found, head, div plant path, Agric Research Sta, Rehovot; prof em, plant path, fac agric, Heb U, Jerusalem; cons to Min of Agric; biol tchr, Haifa. Mem: Brit Mycology Assn; Soc Botanique de Fr; Soc Mycology de Fr; Amer Psychopathological Soc; cen comm, Intl Org for Study of Citrus Viruses. Contbr to profsl jours in Eng, Fr, It, and Heb. Recipient: State of Isr Sci Prize, 1955; Citrus Prize, Isr Citrus Marketing Bd, 1960. Home: 22 Dizengoff St, Tel Aviv, Isr.

REICHERT, Victor E, US, rabbi, scholar, educator; b. Bklyn, NY, Mar 17, 1897; s. Isidor and Miriam (Pakas); BA, CCNY, 1919; BLitt, Columbia U, Sch of Journalism, 1921; BHL, HUC, 1923, ordained rabbi, 1926, DD, 1932, hon DHL, 1955; DLitt, honoris causa, U of Cincinnati, 1965; m. Louise Feibel, Dec 22, 1928; c: David, Jonathan. Rabbi em, Rockdale Temple, Bene Isr, Cincinnati, since 1962, rabbi, 1927-62; lectr, Bible lit, McMickan Coll of Lib Arts, U of Cincinnati, since 1970; tchr, Eng dept, journalism, 1926-51; visiting lectr, HUC-JIR, Cincinnati, 1959-65. US Army, WWI. Hon dir, Children's Protective Service, O Humane Soc; mem: Cancer Control Council; CCAR; Delta Sigma Chi; Sigma Alpha Mu; Police Protective Assn; found, Honorable Order of the Ten Batlanim; preacher: Dublin, sponsorship, World Union for Progressive Judaism; Paris; Geneva, Switz; Middlebury; E Middlebury; Ripton, all Vt; Western Coll, Oxford, O; club, Lit, U of Cincinnati. Author: Highway Through Judaism, 1936; co-author: Commentary on Job; Commentary on Ecclesiastes, Soncino Books of the Bible, 1946, 1967; trans: On ben Peleh; The Fourteenth Gate of Judah Al-Harizi's Tahkemoni and Al-Harizi's other works; introductory essay and Eng trans and reproduction, Editio Princeps, Heb; poems, Tower of David, 1964; contbr to lit and Bibl jours; papers on E A Robinson, Robert Frost. Recipient: dedication of volume, Daniel, Ezra, Nehemiah, Soncino Bible Commentaries, 1951. Home: 752 Red Bud Ave, Cincinnati, O. Study: Rockdale Temple, 8501 Ridge Rd, Cincinnati, O.

REICHMAN, Hanania, Isr, author, translator; b. Grishino, Ukraine, Russ, May 6, 1905; s. Solomon and Gita (Leites); in Isr since 1926; m. Miriam Idelson, 1935; c: A Ran. Heb writer since 1945; fmr: clerk, head, shipping dept, Jaffa Fruit Co Ltd; dir, Jaffa Citrus Co Ltd, Tel Aviv, 1934-45. Author: Pitgamim, 1937; Mimishlei Ha'amim Umipi Hahamim, 1941; Bdihot Baharuzim Vesha'ashuei Lashon, 1956; Dvash Va'oketz, 1960; Hedei Hayamim, 1957; Zror Humor Litz'ir Hador, 1969; trans: Kol Mishlei Krilov, 1949; Mishlei Eliezer Shteinberg, 1954; Mishirat Haolam, 1964; Kitvei Zeev Jabotinsky, 1947-59. Mem, Heb Writers Assn in Isr. Hobby, ling. Home: 182 Ibn Gvirol St, Tel Aviv, Isr.

REICHMAN, Miriam A, US, communal worker; b. Colchester, Conn; d. Pincus and Dora (Davidson) Cutler; att Conn Bus Coll; Bacon Acad, Colchester; m. Solomon Reichman, Mar 26, 1926; c: Ephraim, Raphael. Natl hon vice-pres, women's br, Union of Orthodox J Congs of Amer since 1953, natl biennial conf and conv chmn, and natl vice-pres, 1947-53, corresp secy and prog chmn, Gtr NY council, 1935-47; found and pres, Miriam chap, Mizrachi Women's Org, since 1941, mem, regional bd and NY Council, since 1948, chmn, Bx borough; Bonds for Isr, JNF, UJA, all since 1953; vice-chmn, Bx council, JNF, since 1953; vice-pres, ladies auxiliary: Yeshiva Rabbi Israel Salanter Ahavas Torah, Bx, since 1937; Beth Hatalmud, NY, hon vice-pres, Yeshiva U, Women's Org, Bx chap, 1953, vice-pres, 1947-53, corresp secy, 1930-37; natl pres, women's league of Kamenitzer Yeshiva of NY and Jerusalem, mem, exec bd, since 1934; secy, Amer Friends of Inst for Higher Talmudic Learning and Research Atereth Shlomo, Jerusalem, since 1956; mem natl council, JWB; exec bd: Bx ZC, 1952-57; Bx Bd, FJP, since 1955; Sisterhood, Beth Jacob Beth Miriam Sch, Bx; women's league, Mirer Yeshiva; ladies auxiliary, Hebron Yeshiva, both Jerusalem; ladies auxiliary: Rabb Sem of Amer; Rabbenu Chaim Ozer Acad; Talmudic Acad, Kollel Kovno; secy, Bd of Educ, Colchester; fmr: mem: ARC; March of Dimes; leader, Young Judaea; chief, Pythian Sisters; mem: Yeshiva U Alumni Wives; AJCong; mem, Comty Syn of Monsey. Recipient, bronze plaque and citation, ladies auxiliary, Rabbi Israel Salanter Yeshiva of Bx, 1949; citation, Mizrachi Women's Org, 1951; (chap named in her honor); citation: NY chap, women's br, Union of Orthodox J Congs of Amer, 1953; women's div, FJP of NY, 1956; Miriam A Reichman groves planted in Isr, 1953. Home: Highview Rd, Monsey, NY.

REICHMAN, Solomon, US, rabbi; b. Blonia, Russ, Dec 25, 1900; s. Abraham and Liba (Arotzker) Rachmanchik; in US since 1922; ordained rabbi, Yeshivot Mir and Slobodka; grad, Rabbi Isaac Elchanan Theol Sem, Yeshiva U, 1924; D Talmudic Law, Ner Isr Rabbinical Coll, Baltimore, 1964; m. Miriam Cutler, 1926; c: Ephraim, Raphael. Rabbi emeritus, YM-YWHA, Bx, since 1954, rabbi, 1924-54; rabbi, Temple Zion, Bx, 1954-61; instr, Talmud, Rabbi Isaac Elchanan Theol Sem, 1922-24; publ, J Morning Jour, 1950-51. Chmn, exec bd, Union of Orthodox Rabbis of US and Can, since 1957; exec comm, Rabb Bd of Bx, 1953-58; mem, UJA, Bx; found and pres: Sabbath Observance Assn of Gtr NY; Inst for Higher Talmudic Learning and Research, Atereth Shlomo, Jerusalem; Bx Mizrachi region, RabCA; mem: admn bd, Rabb Bd of Gtr NY; Natl Council, JWB, since 1940; cabinet, Isr Bonds; first vice-pres, Fed Council of Isr Insts; admn comm, Vaad Hatzala; Esrath Torah; exec comm, Alumni Assn of Yeshiva U, 1952-60; delg, AJConf, 1945-47. Ed: Chiddushe Ha'Rambam on Chulin, with notes and commentaries, 1954; Chiddushe Ha'Ritba on Sabbath, 1963. Home: Highview Rd, Monsey, NY.

REICH-RANICKI, Marcel, Ger, author; b. Wloclawek, Pol, June 2, 1920; s. David and Helene (Reich) Auerbach; in Ger since 1958. Lit critic, Die Zeit weekly, Hamburg, since 1960; author: Deutsche Literatur in West und Ost, 1963; Literarisches Leben in Deutschland, 1965; Wer Schreibt, Provoziert, 1966; Literatur Der Kleinen Schritte, 1967; Die Ungeliebten Sieben Emigranten, 1968; ed: Auch dort Erzahlt Deutschland, 1960; Sechzehn Polnische Erzahler, 1962; Erfundene Wahrheit, 1945, 1965; Notwendige Geschichten, 1933-45, 1967; In Sachen Boll—Ansichten und Einsichten, 1968; Gesichtete Zeit, 1933; 1969. Mem: PEN Club. Home: 10B Ubierweg, Hamburg, Ger.

REICHSTEIN, Tadeusz, Switz, educator, chemist; b. Wloclawek, Pol, July 20, 1897; s. Isidor and Gustava (Brokmann); in Switz since 1908; D Engr, Eidgenossische Technische Hochschule, Zurich, 1922; D hon causa, U of Paris, 1947; med fac, U of Basel, 1951; U of Geneva, 1967; ETH, Zurich, 1967; U of Abidjan, 1967; U of London, 1968; m. Louise Quarles van Ufford, July 21, 1927; c: Ruth. Prof em, organic chem, U of Basel, since 1938; dir: Inst of Organic Chem, since 1946; fmr: Pharm Inst; asst to Prof Staudinger; work in pvt lab; lectr, asst, prof, Eidgenossische Technische Hochschule, Zurich. Fgn mem: Royal Soc, London; Natl Acad of Sci, Wash; hon f, Weizmann Inst, Rehovot; hon mem: Indian Acad; Royal Ir Acad; Chem Soc, London. Contbr to sci jours. Recipient: Marcel Benoit Prize, 1948; Nobel Prize in med and physiology, 1950; Cameron Prize, 1951; Copely Medal, Royal Soc of London, 1968. Home: Weissensteinstr 22, Basel, Switz. Office: St Johanns-Ring 19, Basel, Switz.

REIF, Paul, US, composer; b. Prague, Czech, Mar 23, 1910; s. Oskar and Else (Körner); in US since 1940; grad, Music Acad, Vienna; PhD, music, Sorbonne, Paris; m. Rita Murphy; c: Leslie, Timothy. Composer: song cycle: Five Finger Exercises, 1958; And Be My Love, 1962; opera: Mad Hamlet, 1962; Portrait in Brownstone; chamber works: Reverence for Life; Monsieur le Pelican, both 1960; cantata: Requiem to War, 1963; Letter from a Birmingham Jail, 1965; for chorus and brass ensemble, Triple City, 1964; score of live and electronic music, A Murderer Among Us, 1964; musical setting, Birches, 1965; chess game set to music, Philidor's Defense, 1965; Banter for Flute and Piano; 4 Songs on Words by Kenneth Koch, 1968; Pentagram, 1969. Sgt, US Army, 1942-45. Recipient: Purple Heart; Croix de Guerre. Hobbies: chess, tennis. Home: 57 W 58 St, New York, NY.

REIFF, Robert, US, psychologist, educator; b. NYC, Sep 23, 1913; s. Henry and Mae (Levine); BA, Wayne State U, 1950; MA, U of Kan, 1953, PhD, 1954; m. Marguerite Davis, June 6, 1946; c: Mark. Dir, psych div, asso prof, psycht, Albert Einstein Coll of Med, Yeshiva U, since 1963, dir, Cen for Study of Social Intervention, since 1967; dir, Mh prog, Natl Inst of Lab Educ, 1957-65; adj asso prof, psych, NYU, 1960-63; dir, educ, Inst for Research in Hypnosis, 1961; chief psychol, Chattanooga Guidance Clinic, 1954-57; visiting asso prof, Vanderbilt U, 1957; chief psychol, JBd of Guardians, 1957-63. USAAF, 1942-45. Pres, Div of Comty Psych, Amer Psych Assn, 1967-68; exec council, Soc for Clinical and Experimental Hypnosis, 1961; prog comm, Amer Orthopsychiatric Assn, 1964-65; dipl, Amer Bd of Examiners in Psych Hypnosis; mem: NY State Psych Assn; AAAS; NY Acad Sci. Co-author, Memory and Hypnotic Age Regression, 1959. Home: 15 Browning Dr, Ossining, NY. Office: Albert Einstein Coll of Med, Morris Park Ave and Eastchester Rd, Bronx, NY.

REIK, Theodor, US, psychoanalyst, author; b. Vienna, Aus, May 12, 1888; s. Max and Caroline (Trebitsch); PhD, U Vienna, 1911; m. Maria Cubelic, 1934; c: Arthur, Irene Soffer, Miriam; in US since 1938. Lectr: Vienna Psychoanalytic Inst, 1919-28; Berlin Psychoanalytic Inst, 1928-34; The Hague Psychoanalytic Inst, 1934-38. Diplomate, Amer Psych Assn, 1950. Pres, Natl Assn for Psychoanalytic Psych, since 1946. Author: From Thirty Years with Freud, 1914; The Ritual, 1915; Surprise and the Psychoanalyst, 1936; Dogma and Compulsion, 1939; Masochism in Modern Man, 1940; A Psychoanalyst Looks at Love, 1941; Listening With The Third Ear, 1948; The Secret Self, 1951; The Haunting Melody, 1953; The Search Within, 1956; Mystery on the Mountain, 1959; Of Love and Lust, 1959; Creation of Woman, 1960; The Temptation, 1961; Sex in Man and Woman, 1961; The Need to be Loved, 1963. Recipient: first intl prize for applied psychoanalysis, 1915. Home: 51 W 86 St, New York, NY.

REINER, Markus, Isr, physicist, engineer, educator; b. Czernovitz, Aus-Hung, Jan 5, 1886; s. Ephraim and Rachel (Altmann); in Isr since 1922; DTech, Tech U, Vienna, 1909; m. Rebecca Schoenfeld, July 7, 1929; c: Ephraim, Hannah, Dorit, Shlomit. Research prof, applied mech, Technion, Haifa, since 1948; fmr: chief engr, public works dept, Pal Mandatory Govt; research prof, Lafayette Coll, Easton, Pa; visiting lectr, Heb U, Jerusalem; tech adv, Pal Standards Bur; mem research council, Isr Govt. Off, Aus Army, WW I. Mem: British Soc of Rheology; Amer Soc of Rheology; Isr Acad of Sci and Hum; Ihud Assn; Natl Assn for Theoretical and Applied Mechs. Prin contrib, co-found with Prof E C Bingham of rheology as a separate br of physics. Author: Ten Lectures on Theoretical Rheology, 1943, in Russ, 1947; Twelve Lectures in Theoretical Rheology, 1949; Deformation and Flow, 1949; Lectures on Theoretical Rheology, 1960; Deformation Strain and Flow, 1960. Home: 21 Kiriat Sefer, Haifa, Isr. Office: Technion, Haifa, Isr.

REINGOLD, Haim, US, educator; b. Lodz, Pol, Mar 16, 1910; s. Shmaryahu and Esther (Rudniansky); in US since 1930; AB, U of Cinn, 1933, AM, 1934, PhD, 1938; m. Leah Jacobson, Apr 16, 1943 (decd); c: Edward, Arthur; m. 2nd, Badonna Levinson Glatt, Nov 16, 1966; c: David. Chmn, math dept, Ill Inst of Tech, since 1954; prof, math since 1956; sup, instruc, Signal Corps Training Schs, 1942-43, asst prof math, 1943-47, asso prof, 1947-56, acting chmn, math dept, 1951-54; instr, math, U of Cinn, 1935-36; prof, head dept of math, Our Lady of Cinn Coll, 1938-42. Vice-pres, S Side Heb Cong, Chgo, since 1960. Mem: Amer Soc of Engr Educ, chmn, math div, 1955-56, mem, council, 1957-59; Amer Math Soc; Math Assn of Amer; Future Engrs of Amer.

Author: Basic Mathematics for Engineers, 1944; Basic Mathematics for Science and Engineering, 1955. Home: 7541 S Clyde Ave, Chicago, Ill. Office: Ill Inst of Tech, Chicago, Ill.

REINGOLD, Martin, US, pharmacist; b. NYC, Aug 8, 1932; s. Irving and Rose (Madresh); BS, St Johns U, NY, 1953; m. Barbara Fisher, Aug 26, 1961; c: Leslie, Jonathan, Peter. Owner, Park Sheraton Pharm, since 1964; owner, Thomas Pharm, 1957-64. Served US Army, 1953-55. Pres, Empire City Pharm Soc; natl vice-chmn, young leadership cabinet, UJA; fmr, div chmn, UJA; mem, exec comm: HIAS; Amer ORT; leadership council, UJA, NY; mem, B'nai B'rith. Hobbies: golf, tennis, reading. Home: 240 Paine Ave, New Rochelle, NY. Office: 880 Seventh Ave, New York, NY.

REIS, Max Walter, Isr, business exec; b. Berlin, Ger, Nov 18, 1927; in Isr since 1956; PhD, ChemE, Imperial Coll, London, 1952; m. Michal Goren, 1958; c: David, Jonathan. Gen mgr, Miles Chem, Isr, since 1966; devl engr, Royal Dutch Shell Coop, 1952-56; chem phosphates, 1956-66. Active mem: AEC; Petroleum Inst; mem: Inst Chem Engrs, London; club: Lions, Haifa. Home: 21 Panorama St, Haifa, Isr. Office: POB 288, Haifa, Isr.

REIS, Ralph A, US, physician, editor; b. Chgo, Ill, Dec 18, 1895; s. Ignace and Nannie (Ashenheim); att U of Chgo, 1912-15; BS, Northwestern U, 1919, MD, 1919; m. Rose Kramer, Apr 11, 1922; c: Marjorie Graham, Ruth Pomaranc, Herbert. Prof em, obstet and gyn, Northwestern U Med Sch, prof, since 1948; att obstet and gyn, Passavant Memorial Hosp. F: Royal Coll Obstet and Gyn; Amer Coll Obstet and Gyn, past secy; Amer Gyn Soc; Amer Assn Obstet and Gyn; Cen Assn Obstet and Gyn, past secy-treas, pres; Chgo Gyn Soc, past treas, pres; Inst Med of Chgo; life f, Amer Coll Surgs; co-chmn, US-Pan Amer Cytology Soc; hon f: Obstet and Gyn Soc, Chile and Uruguay; Peruvian Soc of Fertility; Amer Brit Cowdray Med Soc, Mexico City; Soc Obstet and Gyn, Buenos Aires; New Eng, NW Pacific, Ind, SW, Pittsburgh, Obstet and Gyn Socs; New Orleans, N Dakota, La, Obstet Socs; Dallas Post Grad Soc; Wash State Obstet Assn; Queens Gyn Soc, Bklyn; mem, Chgo Diabetes Assn. Co-author: monograph, Diabetes and Pregnancy; ed em, Obstetrics and Gynecology, since 1948; contbr to med jours. Home: 215 E Chicago Ave, Chicago, Ill. Office: 104 S Michigan Ave, Chicago, Ill.

REISER, Morton F, US, psychiatrist, educator; b. Cincinnati, O, Aug 22, 1919; s. Sigmund and Mary (Roth); BS, U Cincinnati, 1940, MD, 1943; grad, NY Psychoanalytic Inst, 1955-60; m. Jane Lomas, Mar 18, 1945; c: David, Barbara, Linda. Chief, div psycht, Montefiore Hosp and Med Cen, since 1965; prof, psycht, Albert Einstein Coll of Med, since 1965; visiting psycht, Bx Munic Hosp Cen, since 1954; att psycht, Montefiore Hosp; professorial lectr in psycht, SUNY, Downstate Med Cen, NY, since 1959; fmr: asst lectr, NY Psychoanalytic Inst; sr asst res, internal med, instr, clinician, att phys, psycht, asst prof psycht, research f, all Cincinnati Gen Hosp, 1944-52; mem fac, Wash Sch of Psycht, 1953-55; prof, dir research, Albert Einstein Coll of Med, 1955-58; mem staff, Christian R Holmes Hosp, O; asso staff, J Hosp; research psycht, neuropsycht div, Army Med Service Grad Sch, Walter Reed Army Med Cen, cons neuropsycht, Walter Reed Army Inst for Research. Mem: Amer Soc for Clinical Inves, 1950; Amer Psychosomatic Soc, 1947, past pres; Amer Fed for Clinical Research; f, AAAS; fmr mem: Amer Psycht Assn; Sigma Xi; Bx Co Med Cen; AMA; NY State Med Soc; NY Psychoanalytic Soc; Amer Psychoanalytic Assn; Intl Psycho-Analytical Assn; Assn for Psychol Study of Sleep; Psycht Research Soc; study group, Cen for Advanced Psychoanalytic Studies, Princeton, NJ; comm on research students, bd trustees, NY Psychoanalytic Inst; clinical projects research review comm, Natl Inst of Mh since 1967, past mem, small grants comm; org comm, sect of psychosomatic med, World Psycht Assn since 1967; Amer Psychoanalytic Assn; comm on research, Group for Advancement of Psycht; comm on training for research, Bd of Profsl Standards; cons: WHO expert comm on treatment and prevention of psychosomatic disorders; High Point Hosp, Portchester, NY; hons: Phi Eta Sigma; Pi Kappa Epsilon; A Graeme Mitchell Undergrad Ped Soc; Alpha Omega Alpha. Ed-in-chief, Psychosomatic Med, since 1962; mem ed bd, AMA Archives of Gen Psycht, since 1961; contbr to profsl publs. Recipient: Stella Feis Hoffheimer Memorial Prize, 1943. Office: 111 E 20 St, Bronx, NY.

REISMAN, Harry (Zvi), Eng, business exec; b. London, Eng, Mar 9, 1916; s. Hyman and Mildred (Cohen); m. Anne Barnet;

c: Hugh, Sharon. Dep mgr, Eur off, Hamashbir Hamerkazi Ltd, since 1969; dir designate, Paltrade Ltd; buying dir, Victor Valur & Co, 1933-68. Vice-pres: ZF, Gt Brit & Ir; Poale Zion, Gt Brit; chmn, Chevrat Habonim, Gt Brit, mem first group, 1929; vice-chmn: econ comm, ZF; Chalutz Farms Mgmt Comm; treas, Friends Young Poale Zion; mem: Natl Council WJC, British sect; United Syn Dist Council. Spec interest, youth activities. Home: 7 Bridgewater Court, Wembley, Eng. Office: 62 Oxford St, London W1, Eng.

REISNER, Nathan H, US, rabbi; b. Boston, Mass, May 23, 1924; s. Solomon and Rebecca (Lifshitz); BA, cum laude, Harvard Coll, 1944; BJE, Boston Heb Tchrs Coll, 1944; MHL, JTSA, 1949; m. Connie Edell, June 21, 1949; c: Ethelea, Avram, Malka, Yale. Dir, Phila region, United Syn of Amer, since 1959; rabbi: Cong Knesseth Isr, Pittsfield, Mass, 1949-52; Cong Knesseth Isr, Green Bay, Wis, 1952-59. Home: 5422 Woodcrest Ave, Philadelphia, Pa. Office: 1701 Walnut St, Philadelphia, Pa.

REISS, Anselm Anshel, Isr, organization exec; b. Jaroslav, Galicia, Nov 11, 1886; s. Abraham and Sluwa; in Isr since 1925; m. Bathia Menkes, (decd); c: Ruth Levron, Rafael. Mem: Zionist Actions Comm, since 1929; presidium, since 1951; gen secy, Brit Ihud Poalei Zion, 1929-39; vice-pres, Rescue Comm, Pol J, instituted by Pol Govt in exile, London, 1944-46. Served, Aus-Hung Army, WW I. Delg, WZC; mem, exec comm, Chevrat Haovdim. Contbr to press. Home: 8 Feivel St, Tel Aviv, Isr. Office: Histadrut, 93 Arlosoroff St, Tel Aviv, Isr.

REISS, Frederick, US, dermatologist, educator; b. Edelsthal, Aus, Oct 12, 1891; s. Siegmund and Helena (Knoepfmacher); in US since 1941; att U of Vienna, 1909; MD, Royal Hung U, Budapest, 1914; postgrad and research work at U skin clinics: Basel; Vienna; Budapest; Inst of Path, Geneva; Inst of Hygiene, Basel; postgrad study in mycology: Ross Inst for Tropical Med, London, 1929; Hosp St Louis, Paris, 1931; Inst of Parasitology, Paris, 1933; Columbia U, 1944-45; m. Clara Zimmerman, Aug 30, 1935. Asso prof, clinical dermat and syphilology, NYU Postgrad Med Sch, since 1946; asso att dermat, i/c dermat research lab, Bellevue Hosp, NY, since 1946; chief: dermat service, Montefiore Hosp, since 1944; dermat clinic, Manhattan Eye, Ear and Throat Hosp, since 1950; fmr: dermat, Inst of Anat, U of Budapest, 1910-11; lectr, dermat and syphilology, Dung Dai Med Coll, Shanghai, China, 1923-28; clinical prof, head, dermat dept, Natl Med Coll, Shanghai, 1929-36; cons dermat: Lester Chinese Hosp; St Elizabeth Hosp; ARC Hosp; Shanghai Public Hosp for Children, all 1929-41; hon med adv, Chinese Mission of Lepers; clinical chief, Natl Leprosarium, Shanghai, both 1929-41; prof, dermat: St John's U, Shanghai; Women's Chr Med Coll, Shanghai, both 1936-41; dir, anti-venereal clinic of Chinese Med Assn, 1937-39; instr, dermat, Cornell U; phys, out-patient dept, NY Hosp, both 1942-46. Lt, MC, Aus-Hung Army, 1914-18; cons, Surg Gen, US Army, 1946. F: AMA; NY Acad Med; Amer Coll Allergists; Royal Soc Med, London, mem, sect of dermat; Amer Acad Dermat and Syphilology; hon f, NY Acad Scis, pres, div, mycology; dipl, Amer Bd Dermat and Syphilology; fmr: pres des sceances 9th Intl Dermat Cong, Budapest, 1938, mem, comm on terminology, nomenclature and med educ; vice-chmn, Chinese Dermat Soc; past pres, Shanghai Med Soc; mem: NY Med Soc; NY Soc Tropical Med; Soc Investigative Dermat; NE Dermat Soc; corresp mem: Dermat Soc of Nicaragua; Fr, Hung, Aus, It and Brazilian Socs of Dermat; hon mem: Wiener Arzte Gesellschaft; Purkinje Med Soc; Cen Amer Dermat Soc; charter mem, Amer Acad of Compensation Med; life mem, Chinese Assn; hon mem: Port; Indian; Mexican; Iranian; Venezuelan; Greek Dermat Socs; secy gen, Intl Soc Tropical Dermat; past mem, Chinese Med Soc; mem, Sigma Xi, Columbia U; Shriners; fmr: vice-pres, KH; B'nai B'rith, past pres; JNF, past pres. Ed bd: Intl J of Dermat; Mycologia and Mycopathologica Applicata; Jour of Clinical and Experimental Mycology; chmn, ed bd: Dermatologia Tropica; Excerpta Medica, dermat; contbr to sci jours; sects in med books. Recipient: George Washington award, 1965. Home: 1225 Park Ave, New York, NY. Office: 19 E 80 St, New York, NY.

REISS, Rafael, Isr, surgeon; b. Lvov, Pol, Dec 17, 1927; s. Anselm and Bertha (Menkes); in Isr since 1939; MD, U of Paris, 1955; m. Ruth Perl, 1954; c: Ron, Yael. Dir, dept surg, Meir Hosp, Kfar Saba, since 1965; sr lectr, Tel Aviv U Med Sch, since 1967; fmr: chief res, Mt Sinai Hosp, NY; sr surg, Beilinson Hosp, Isr. Lt, Haganah. Mem exec comm: IMA; Isr Surg Soc. Contbr to profsl publs. Home: 19 Moledet St, Kfar Saba, Isr. Office: Meir Hosp, Kfar Saba, Isr.

REISS, Yacoov, Isr, attorney, govt official; b. Oswiencim, Pol, 1912; s. Yosef and Chaya (Kupfer); in Isr since 1935; LLB, Pal Govt Sch, Jerusalem, 1944; m. Ruth Schiffer, Aug 25, 1945; c: Tchiya, Mira. Dep dist atty, Dept of Justice, Haifa and N dists, since 1969; off i/c dist inves dept, Police, 1936-50, asst supt, 1950-63; legal adv, disciplinary courts, Isr Football Referees Assn. Haganah Info Service, 1935-48. Mem: exec off, Hanoar Hazioni, Intelligence, Youth Movement, 1927-35; comm, Haifa dist, Isr Lawyers Assn; exec comm, Govt Lawyers Assn. Hobbies: painting, sculpture, carving wooden puppets. Home: 49 Shukri Hillel St, Haifa, Isr. Office: 11 Hassane St, Haifa, Isr.

REITER, Freda L, US, artist; b. Phila, Pa, Sept 21, 1919; d. Harry and Lilly (Cohen) Leibovitz; att: Moore Inst; Pa Acad of Fine Arts; Fleischer Memorial; Barnes Found; The San Carlos, Mexico City; m. Frank Reiter, Oct 31, 1942; c: Wayne, Diane, Louise. Feature artist; illus; one man shows: Metrop Mus, NYC; Natl Acad, NYC; Acad of Fine Arts, Phila; Carnegie Mus, Pittsburgh; perm collections; Libr of Cong, Wash DC. Art adv: J Fed; Council of J Women; Hadassah. Mem: Artists Equity; Natl Assn Women Artists; club: Print. Home and studio: 1036 Berlin Rd, Haddonfield, NJ.

REITER, Sol M, US, merchant; b. Aus, Oct 1, 1894; s. Judah and Hannah (Burg); m. Jeanette Levin, May 9, 1917. Asso, Moe Meyer Store, since 1925. Pres: United J Charities, 1936-46; JCC, 1945-50; Comty Chest, 1946-48; Temple Beth Jacob; chmn, finance comm, KH, 1944-45; Comty Relations, 1936-51; vice-pres, NY State council, UAHC; mem, natl council, JDC; exec comm: Amer-J League for Isr; United Isr Appeal; NY State chmn, UJA; bd govs, Bonds for Isr; bd, NY Ont region, CJFWF; mem, C of C. Home: 34 Cedar Lane, Windsor, NY. Office: 87 Water St, Newburgh, NY.

REITMAN, Frank H, US, business exec; b. Aus, Dec 25, 1886; s. Adolph and Rissa (Saperstein); in US since 1896; m. 1st; c: Mrs Ned Weissberg; m. 2nd, Jeanette Barth, Jan 26, 1969. Pres, FHR Invest & Loan Corp since 1969; pres, Distillers Exch, 1938-39; chmn, bd, Reitman Inds, 1955-69. Pvt, US Cavalry, 1905-08; mounted police, Panama Canal, 1909-11. Vice-pres: Heb Acad; Home for the Aged; Home for Chronic Sick; f, Brandeis U; trustee, NJ Hosp Dinner; mem: Emil Zucker Lodge, IOBA; bd, Essex Co Council; guest of hon: Brandeis U; JNF; J Natl Hosp, Denver, Colo, hon trustee; J Educ Cen; fmr: chmn bd, Reitman Inds; bd, J Educ Cen. Recipient: Man-of-the-Year: Spirits Sq Club, 1966; NJ Rabb Coll, 1967. Hobbies: travel, golf. Home: 175 Prospect, East Orange, NJ. Office: 715 Park Ave, East Orange, NJ.

REITMEISTER, Louis A, US, author, lecturer; b. NYC, Feb 2, 1903; s. Nathan and Jennie (Crane); att St Lawrence U; m. Betty Richmond, Jan 1, 1931. Lectr, phil and psych, since 1925. Author: Paradise Found, 1926; Ten Commandments of Friendship, 1927; Philosophic Concepts in Crime Prevention, 1928; Music and Philosophy, 1930; Philosophy of Love, 1930; Ten Commandments of Love, 1930; What Life Means to Great Philosophers, 1931; If Tomorrow Comes, 1934; Gist of Philosophy, 1936; When Tomorrow Comes, 1938; An Appeal to Common Sense, 1938; Nature of Power, 1943; The Gods and My Friends, 1947; Nature and Philosophy of Friendship, 3 vols, 1948; By the Way, 1953; A Philosophy of Time, 1959; A Philosophy of Freedom, 1968; ed, Lewis Copeland Publ Co, 1927-31; asso ed, Esthete Mag, 1928-31; cons to Indian Natl Cong, 1928-31. F, Intl Inst of Arts and Letters; found, Albert Einstein Coll of Med; mem: Natl Geog Soc; Amer Mus of Hist; Assn on Amer Indian Affairs; Archaeol Inst of Amer; Amer Acad of Political and Social Sci; Intl Oceanographic Found; Amer Forestry Assn; Defenders of Wildlife. Contbr to educ jours. Home: 100 Hicks Lane, Great Neck, LI, NY.

REKHESS, Jaakov, Isr, organization exec; b. Warsaw, Pol, June 22, 1906; s. Eliezer and Rachel Rechtman; in Isr since 1937; att Commercial HS; m. Toba Segal; c: Nurith Fridman, Eliezer. Dir, JA, Haifa offs; fmr: secy and dir, General Bank of Tel Aviv, 1933-1937; dir, JA off: Paris; Rome. Served Haganah. Pres: Independent Lib Party, Haifa; bd dirs, ACRA, Isr Devl Co; co-found, Hanoar Hatzioni; past mem, Zionist Cen Comm, Pol. Contbr to periodicals. Home: 2 Hanadir St, Haifa, Isr. Office: 2 Palmer Gate, Haifa, Isr.

RELGIS, Eugen, Uruguay, author, editor; b. Jassy, Rum, Mar 2, 1895; s. David and Sofia (Wachtel) Sigler; in Uruguay since 1947; deg, architecture, letters and phil, U of Bucharest, 1917; m. Ana Taubes, Jan 5, 1922; c: Alexander. Author: in Rum, 1912-47; in Span, 1933-69; major works: El Humanitarismo; Los Principios Humanitaritas; Individualismo, Estetica y Humanitarismo; Historia Sexual de la Humanidad; Las Aberraciones Sexuales en la Alemania Nazi; Freud, Freudismo y las Verdades Sociales; Profetas y Poetas; La Internacional Pacifista; Miron el Sordo; Sudamerica, poemas; trans into Rum, Fr, Eng, It, Heb, Esperanto. Found, First Humanitarian Group, Bucharest, Montevideo, Torino, 1923-68; mem: various humanist and pacifist orgs in Eur, Asia, Amer, 1922-69; War Resisters, London, 1947-52; vice-pres, Mahatma Gandhi Research Inst, India; mem: intl movements for disarmament; study mission to Isr, U of Montevideo, 1962; Intl Inst Social Hist, Amsterdam; Natl Acad Social Sci, Sao Paulo; club: PEN, writers in exile sect, NYC and London. Recipient: prize, New Hist Soc, NY, 1933; Cultural Merit 1st class, Bucharest, 1947; Merite National Français 1st class, 1955; candidate, Nobel Peace Prize, 1956. Home: 903 Gaboto, Montevideo, Uruguay.

REMAK, Henry H H, US, educator; b. Berlin, Ger, July 27, 1916; s. John and Hedwig (Salz); in US since 1936; U Bordeaux, 1934; Licencié-es-Lettres, U Montpelier, 1936; MA, Ind U, 1937; PhD, U of Chgo, 1947; m. Inge Grunfeld, Aug 3, 1946; c: Roy, Steven, Renee, Ronald. Prof: Ger, Ind U, since 1960, comparative lit, since 1963, on fac since 1939; staff mem, US Off of Censorship, Chgo, Puerto Rico, 1943-44; visiting lectr, Middlebury Coll, Vt, 1958-1960, dir Ger summer sch, 1967; visiting prof, comparative lit, U Lille, Fr, 1962-63; U Hamburg, Ger, 1967; chmn, W Eur Studies, Ind, 1966. Off, US Merchant Marine, 1944-46. F, Guggenheim Found, 1967-68; mem: MLA; AAUP, mem, council, 1958-61; Sigma Alpha Mu; corresp mem, Academie des Arts, Sci et Belles Lettres of Marseilles. Author: Goethe on Stendhal, 1950; German Reception of French Realism, 1954; co-author: Comparative Literature, 1961; co-ed: Oeuvres de CM Campion, 1945; contbr to lit and scholarly jours. Home: 1212 Maxwell Lane, Bloomington, Ind. Office: Indiana U, Bloomington, Ind.

REMEN, Lazar Eliezer, Isr, obstetrician; b. Bialistok, Russ, Oct 9, 1907; s. Arje and Nehama (Margolis); in Isr since 1933; MD, Med Sch, Jena U, 1930; m. Frieda Feuerstein, July 29, 1928; c: Yona Laor, Uri, Dani. Pvt practice since 1934; mgr, Maternity Hosp, Petah Tikva, 1934-42. Capt, RAMC, Brit Army, 1942-46. Prin contribs: invented Prostigorin, Glycocoll therapy and compound of Glychepar for treatment of Myasthenia Gravis. Chmn, Magen David Adom, Petah Tikva; vice-pres, secy, IMA, Petah Tikva; fmr repr, Histadrut Harefuit Haisraelit, to World Med Assn. Contbr to intl profsl jours. Hobby: chess. Home and office: 102 Rothschild St, Petah Tikva, Isr.

REMEZ, Aharon, Isr, government official, ret army officer; b. Tel Aviv, Isr, May 8, 1919; att Us: Princeton; Harvard, both 1951-53; m. Rita Levy, 1952; five c. Head of Isr Port Authority, since 1971; fmr kibbutz youth instructor, 1937-39; emissary to Zionist youth movement in the USA, 1939-41; head, Min of Defense Purchasing Mission in the USA, 1951-53; aviation adv, Min of Defense, 1953-54; mem, bd dirs, Solel Boneh Ltd; executive dir, Koor Inds Ltd; both 1954-59; adm dir, Weizmann Inst, 1959-60, dir, intl coop div, Min for Fgn Affairs, Jerusalem, 1960-64, adv, intl coop for fgn affairs, 1964-65; Amb to Eng, Court of St James, 1965-71. Haganah; chief of staff, IAF, War of Independence, commander-in-chief, 1948-51. MK, Mapai, 1956-57; chairman, Natl Council for Civil Aviation, since 1960; mem, Kibbutz Kfar Blum, 1947. Hobbies: handicrafts, sculpture. Home: Shikun haKotegim 11, Rehov San Martin, Jerusalem, Isr. Office: Isr Port Auth, Tel Aviv, Isr.

RENOV, Jeremiah, Isr, pilot, business exec; b. Shreveport, La, US, Dec 19, 1922; s. Elias and Lena (Gold); in Isr since 1946; att: Centenary Coll, 1940-42; LSU, 1942-43; m. Beatrice Sirota, June 18, 1945; c: David, Dorit, Amiel, Aviva. Mgn dir, chief pilot: Wings of Isr Air Service Ltd; Exec Airlines Ltd; fmr: chief check pilot, Isr Min of Defense. Aviation cadet, USAF; served IDF. Prin contrib, introduced agric spraying by helicopter in Isr. Home and office: 39 Matzbiim St, Zahala, Isr.

RESEK, J Verne, US, business exec; b. Bklyn, NY, July 10, 1896; s. Morris and Ida (Moses); BS, Case Inst, 1917, ME,

1924; m. Johanna Danziger, June 24, 1929; c: Roger, Diane. Pres, Ind Combustion Inc, since 1957; licensed profsl engr, Wis, since 1936; fmr: devl engr: Perfection Stove Co, 1919-30; Fulton Sylphon Co, 1931-32; chief engr, asst to pres, Cleaver Brooks Co, 1934-57. Served, chem warfare service, US Army, 1918. Dir, AJComm, Milw, since 1958; trustee, Cong Sinai; vice chmn, Milw Co Air Pollution Adv Bd, since 1961; life mem, Natl Oil Fuel Inst; mem: US Natl Produc Auth; Zeta Beta Tau; fmr: trustee, Temple Emmanuel B'nei Jeshurun; pres, Natl Oil Heat Inst of Amer; secy, Amer Soc Mech Engrs, Milw. Contbr to profsl jours. Holder of 9 US patents. Home: 5431 N Mohawk Ave, Milwaukee, Wis. Office: 4465 N Oakland Ave, Milwaukee, Wis.

RESHEF, Eliezer, Isr, organization exec; b. Bucharest, Rum, Feb 16, 1907; in Isr since 1944; s. Heinrich and Amalia (Eckstein); m. Sabina Weber, Oct, 1934; c: Ouriel. Mem exec, Keren Kayemeth LeIsr, since 1961, mgr org dept, head off, Jerusalem, since 1961, fmr: JNF missions to It, Greece, Turkey, dir: Fr; N Afr. Served IDF. Home: 8 Haportsim St, Jerusalem, Isr. Office: Keren Kayemeth Le Israel, Jerusalem, Isr.

RESHEF, Yaakov, Isr, zoologist; b. Petach Tikvah, Isr, June 24, 1937; s. David and Bela (Gelbard) Granek; dipl tchr, Sem Hakibbutzim, Tel Aviv, 1957; m. Nurit Treugoda, Mar 30, 1959; c: Rimon, Hadas. Co-dir gen, Neot Kedumim, Gardens of Isr; fmr, asst dir, Field Educ Cen, Beit Hankin-Kfar Yehoshua. Sgt, IDF, 1957-60. Co-produc, color filmstrips: The Four Species; The Seven Varieties; Tu B'Shvat; traveling exhbs: Tu B'Shvat; Shavuot; Pessach. Spec interests: animals and plants in J heritage; photography. Home: 6 Hashikma St, Kiron, Isr. Office: POB 299, Kiriat Ono, Isr.

RESNICK, Louis B, US, attorney; b. Jeffersonville, NY, Nov 5, 1921; s. Solomon and Ida (Kantrowitz); att: Bklyn Coll, 1938-42; Fordham Law Sch, 1942-43; JD, Columbia Law Sch, 1948; m. Ruth; c: Helene, Jane, Deborah. Partner, Paskus, Gordon & Hyman, since 1958, atty, 1948-57. Cpl, USAAF, It, US Army, IS, 1943-46. Co-chmn: Roslyn Friends, JTSA; FJP, Roslyn div, past chmn, new leadership div, UJA, Roslyn div, past chmn, youth div; trustee: Temple Beth Sholom, Roslyn, NY, past pres; Village of Flower Hill, Manhasset, NY; Heb Arts Sch for Music & Dance, NYC; fmr, mem, bd ed, Yeshiva of Crown Hgts; mem: NY State Bar Assn; Assn of Bar, NYC; NY Co Lawyers Assn; club: Muttontown Golf & Country, past dir. Author: Taxation Problems and Liquidation Sales, 1968. Home: 193 Crabapple Rd, Manhasset, NY. Office: 733 Third Ave, New York, NY.

RESNICK, Nathan, US, educator; b. Bklyn, NY, June 13, 1910; s. Abraham and Fannie (Weinberg); BS, LIU, NY, 1933; BS, Columbia U, 1937; MA, NYU, 1945; studied painting, 1933-45; m. Ernestine Cederholm, May 4, 1943. Dir, librs, LIU, since 1948, librr staff mem since 1933; prof, art, LIU, since 1950, chmn dept art since 1961, fac mem since 1938; dir, pubs and exhbs, LIU, since 1952; dir, LIU press, since 1948; dir of planning, 1965-68; coord, LIU-Bklyn Mus Art Sch. Trustee, Walt Whitman Birthplace Assn, pres since 1963; mem: White House Conf on Educ, 1955; natl secy, Leaves of Grass Centennial, 1955; mem: AAAS; Amer Studies Assn; Amer Acad Political and Social Scis; AAUP; Amer Libr Assn; NY Folklore Soc; Natl Educ Assn; Natl Audubon Soc; Mus of Modern Art; Art Assn, Woodstock, NY. Author: Walt Whitman and the Authorship of the Good Gray Poet, 1948; co-author: The Third Eye, 1962; ed: Life, Land and Water in Ancient Peru, 1962; designed, ed, Songbirds of Amer, 1954. Hobbies: bird watching, space writing, nature study. Home: 72 Barrow St, New York, NY. Office: Long Island U, Brooklyn, NY.

RESNICK, William, Isr, educator, chemical engr; b. Chgo, Ill, 1922; s. Philip and Sarah (Elins); in Isr since 1960; BSc, Purdue U, 1943; MSc, U of Mich, 1945, PhD, 1947; m. Marcia Weiss, Oct 22, 1944; c: Shlomo, David, Sara. Prof and dean, fac of chem engr, Technion, since 1960; asst prof, Ill Inst of Tech, 1947-50; sr lectr, Technion, 1951-56; sr project eng, Standard Oil of Ind, 1956-60. Pres, Isr Inst of Chem Engr; mem: Amer Inst of Chem Engrs; Amer Chem Soc; Amer Soc Elec Engrs. Contbr to profsl jours. Home: 20 Yaarot St, Haifa, Isr. Office: Technion, Haifa, Isr.

RESNIK, Regina, US, opera singer; b. NYC, 1924; d. Samuel and Ruth (Seidler); BA, Hunter Coll; m. Harry Davis, July 18, 1946; c: Michael. Mezzo-soprano: Metrop Opera since 1944; Vienna State Opera; Royal Opera; Covent Garden,

London; Deutsche Oper, Berlin; Grand Opera, Paris; Staats-oper, Stuttgart; Staatsoper, Hamburg; Bayreuth Festival; recording star, London and Columbia Records; Salzburg Festival, 1960; Teatro Colon, Buenos Aires, 1962; appeared for State of Isr Bonds, JNF. Sponsor, Amer-Isr Cultural Soc; hon mem, Hadassah. Office: c/o William L Stein, 113 W 57 St, New York, NY.

RESNIKOV, Philip S, US, insurance cons; b. Chernigov, Russ, May 10, 1903; s. Alter and Bessie (Agronsky); in US since 1904; dipl, Gratz Coll, 1921; BA, U of Pa, 1924, LLB, 1927; m. Rose Rosen, Aug 24, 1928; c: Susan Schultz, Martha Reisman. Life ins cons since 1955; asst mgr, Metrop Life Ins Co, 1947-54; chartered life underwriter, 1946. Pres, Phila Zionist Org, 1950-51; mem, natl exec council, ZOA, since 1947; chmn, bd of dirs, United Heb Schs and Yeshivot, Phila; mem, bd of dirs, Akiba Heb Acad. Mem: Cong Mikveh Isr; Doreshe Daath Soc. Hobby: bridge. Home: 6344 N 8 St, Philadelphia, Pa. Office: 8003 Old York Rd, Philadelphia, Pa.

RESS, Joseph W, US, business exec, attorney; b. Providence, RI, July 30, 1904; s. Morris and Bessie (Flint); PhB, Brown U, 1926, hon LLD, 1966; LLB, Harvard Law Sch, 1929; m. Anne Gordon, June 23, 1932; c: Elizabeth, Joan Reeves. Pres, EA Adams & Son, Inc, since 1949; fmr pres, Miriam Hosp, chmn med matters comm. Past pres, Gen J Comm of Providence; dir, Citizens Trust Bank; trustee em and fmr mem, adv & exec comm, mem, investment comm, all Brown U; trustee, RI Sch Design; mem, pres council, Providence Coll; past campaign chmn and past pres, United Fund, Inc; co-trustee, RI Chari-ties; mem, bd trustees, Temple Emanu-El; fmr dir: YMCA; CJFWF; mem: Phi Beta Kappa; RI Bar Assn; clubs: Turks Head; University. Home: 486 Cole Ave, Providence, RI.

REUBEN, David E, India, jurist; b. Hassan, Mysore State, Sep 3, 1893; s. Ezra and Sarah (Nagavkar); BA, Bombay U, 1913; BA, St Johns Coll, Cambridge, Eng, 1918; Barrister-at-law, Inner Temple, London, 1933; m. Sophie Israel, May 29, 1932; c: Rachel, Elizabeth, Ira. Ret, fmr: mem, exec br, Indian Civil Service, 1918-27; dist judge, High Court, 1928-43; judge, 1943-52; chief justice, High Court of Judicature, Patna, 1952-53. Mem, Bombay Natural Hist Soc. Home: 65 Pali Hill, Bandra, Bombay 50-AS, India.

REUBENI, Aharon, Isr, poet, author, journalist; b. Poltava, Russ, Aug, 1886; s. Zvi and Atara (Kopelevitz) Shimshi; in Isr since 1910; m. Sarah Yermans, 1916. Fmr: ed staff: Ahdut, Doar Hayom, Bustenai, Haboker, Haolam; co-ed: Haolam, Jerusalem, 1940-50. Author: poetry: Leilot Yerush-alaim; Al Yarden Yeriho; Milhemet Yerushalaim; Hamisha veShloshim; hist works: Shem, Ham veYaphet; Kadmut haIvrim; David haMelech; novels; stories; critical essays. Escaped from exile in Siberia, reached Jerusalem in 1910; mem, J delg to London, 1920. Home: 1 Binyamin St, Bet Hakerem, Jerusalem, Isr.

REUBENSTEIN, A Daniel, US, physician, educator; b. Lynn, Mass, Nov 9, 1907; s. Max and Dora (Mamber); BA, cum laude, Harvard Coll, 1928; MD, cum laude, Boston U Sch of Med, 1933; MPH, Harvard Sch of Public Health, 1940; m. Delilah Riemer, Dec 26, 1937; c: Joel, David, Susan. Visiting prof, MIT, since 1967; dir: div of hosps, Mass Dept of Public Health, since 1950, dep commn since 1954; cons: preventive med: Beth Isr Hosp, since 1950; J Memorial Hosp, since 1957; lectr: public health practice, Boston Coll, since 1950; Tufts U Med Sch, since 1958; pres, NE Sinai Hosp; fmr: epidemiolo-gist, div of communicable diseases, dist health off, both Mass Dept Public Health; coord, hosp, Mass Civil Defense Agcy; lectr, Simmons Coll; asso prof, epidemiology, Harvard Sch of Public Health; house off, Boston City Hosp; co-found, Metrop Health Offs Conf. Mem: bd trustees, CJP, Boston since 1962 Mass Med Soc; AMA; Mass Public Health Assn; Amer Public Health Assn; Amer Hosp Assn; NE Hosp Assembly; Gtr Boston Med Soc; council on hosp planning and plant opr, Mass Hosp Assn; Amer Assn of Public Health Officials; Amer Assn of Hosp Planning; Delta Omega; Phi Delta Epsilon; fmr: pres: Mass Cen Health Council; Assn of Hosp Planning Agcys; mem: adv bd, Mass chap, Phys The-rapists Assn; bd dirs, JDC. Contbr to profsl jours. Recipient: citation: Mass Fed of Nursing Homes, 1952; Sr Citizens Assn of Mass, 1954; Award of Merit, Mass Hosp Assn, 1963. Home: 16 Ward St, Newton Center, Mass. Office: 41 Mt Vernon St, Boston, Mass.

REUVEN, Shlomo Mordechai, Isr, business exec; b. Salonica, Greece, Aug 8, 1908; s. Mercado and Oro (Mordoh); in Isr

since 1935; att HS of Commerce, Salonica, 1920-25; m. Shoshana Pessah, Mar 25, 1940; c: Ora Lemkin, Ilana. Gen dir, Ordal Ltd, since 1962. Chief ed, Sion Au Combat, Fr organ of Irgun Tsvai Leumi, Tel Aviv, 1945-48; first sgt, auxiliary med unit, Elisha, 1948-49. Vice-pres, Hitachdut Olei Yevan; pres, Isr-Greece Friendship League; mem: comm: Cen de Recherches Sur le Judaisme de Salonique; Beit Avoth Leon Recanati; B'nai B'rith, Yehuda Halevy lodge; Mitbach Zol Lanitzrachim; fmr: mem: Netziv Betar, Greece; secretariat, Zionist Revisionist Org, Greece; cen comm, Tnuath Haherut, Isr. Author: Au Carrefour Du Reve, poems, 1925; La Calomnie du Sang à Travers Les Ages, 1930; Sous le Ciel Bleu de L'Orient Enchanteur, novel, 1932; chief ed: La Boz Zionista, Salonica, 1930-34; La Nation, 1928-30; Sion Au Combat, Tel Aviv, 1945-48. Spec interests: journalism, Sephardic cmty's folklore and hist, Fr lit. Home: 54 Shalom Aleichem St, Tel Aviv, Isr. Office: 29 Frishman St, Tel Aviv, Isr.

REZNECK, Samuel, US, educator; b. Pol, Aug 4, 1897; s. Benjamin and Celia (Drazner); in US since 1908; AM, Har-vard U, 1921, PhD, 1926; m. Elizabeth Fishburne, Aug 20, 1933; c: Daniel. Prof, hist, political sci, Rensselaer Poly Inst, since 1925. US Army, 1918. Pres, Troy Public Libr, since 1968; vice-pres, Econ Hist Assn, 1957-59; mem: Amer Hist Assn; NY State Hist Assn; AAUP; Upper Hudson Phi Beta Kappa Assn. Author: Education for a Technological Society, 1968; American Depression in the Nineteenth Cen-tury, 1968; contbr to books and scholarly jours. Home: 27 S Lake Ave, Troy, NY. Office: Rensselaer Poly Inst, Troy, NY.

REZNIK, David, Isr, architect; b. Rio de Janeiro, Brazil, Aug 5, 1923; s. Baruch and Rachel (Melamed); in Isr since 1949; att fac architecture, U Brazil, 1944-48; m. Raquel Burstein, Oct 16, 1948; c: Yehoshua, Leah, Baruch. Architect since 1948; asso prof, Technion, Haifa, since 1966. Mem, Assn of Engrs and Architects in Isr. Works executed: Kennedy Me-morial; Journalists Assn Bldg; Soldier's House; Engr's Inst, all Jerusalem; co-architect: Dr Israel Goldstein Syn; Man-chester Bldg of Math, Heb U; Van Leer Found Bldg, all Jerusalem; Isr Pavillion, Montreal World's Fair; master plan for Heb U on Mt Scopus. Recipient: Progressive Architecture Design Award, 1964; Rechter Prize for Architecture, 1965; co-recipient, first prize, Isr Pavillion, NY World's Fair, 1964; first prize, Kennedy Memorial. Home: 7 Achad Ha'am St, Jerusalem, Isr. Office: 4 Narkiss St, Jerusalem, Isr.

REZNIKOFF, Charles, US, author; b. Bklyn, NY, Aug 31, 1894; s. Nathan and Sarah (Wolvoksky); LLB, NYU, 1915; m. Marie Syrkin, 1930. Author: Five Groups of Verse, 1927; Nine Plays, 1927; By the Waters of Manhattan, 1930; Jeru-salem, the Golden, 1934; In Memoriam, 1933, 1934; Testimony, 1934; Early History of a Sewing-Machine Operator, 1936; Separate Way, 1936; Going To and Fro and Walking Up and Down, 1941; The Lionhearted, 1944; The Jews of Charleston, 1950; Inscriptions: 1944-56,1959; By the Waters of Manhattan: Selected Verse, 1962; Testimony: The United States, 1885-90; 1965; Testimony: The United States, 1891-1900, 1968; By The Well of Living and Seeing and The Fifth Book of the Maccabees, 1969; co-author, Family Chronicle, 1963; ed, Louis Marshall, Champion of Liberty, selected papers and addresses, 1957; contbr to periodicals. Home and office: 180 West End Ave, New York, NY.

REZNIKOFF, Marvin M, US, rabbi; b. New Haven, Conn, Dec 9, 1910; s. Frank and Belle (Cohen); BA, Wesleyan U, Middletown, Conn, 1934; MHL, JIR, NY, 1938; att Heb U, Jerusalem, 1946-48; MA, La State U, 1954; m. Shirley Caul-king, Nov 22, 1950; c: Anne, Tamara. Rabbi, Lib Syn, Baton Rouge, La, since 1957 and 1949-55; voluntary visiting J chaplain: La State Insts, since 1950; La State Prison, since 1950; E La State Hosp, since 1950; USPHS Hosp, Carville, La, since 1950; fmr: rabbi, Mohawk St Temple, Amster-dam, NY, 1938-41; asso dir, Hillel Found, Bklyn Coll, 1941-43; rabbi, Temple Judah, Cedar Rapids, Ia, 1955-57. Chap-lain, US Army, 1943-46. Pres: Guidance Cen, 1954-55; Inter-racial Mins Fellowship, 1958-59; ZOA, 1958-59; Manpower Training Comm, 1969; treas, E Baton Rouge Min Assn, 1959-60, 1961-62; mem, bd: Comty Services Council, since 1960; Family Counseling Service, 1953-55, 1957-60; Mh Assn, 1957-60; Comty Advancement, Inc, since 1965, secy since 1968; Baton Rouge Area Alcoholism Info Cen; pres, Operation Upgrade, since 1968; mem, exec bd, Baton Rouge Council on Human Relations, since 1966; chmn, Baton Rouge Zionist Dist, since 1967; dept chaplain, Amer Vets of La, 1952-53, 1954-55; mem: Planning Council of the Baton Rouge Area

United Givers, since 1967; State Health Planning Council, since 1969; B'nai B'rith; ACLU; CCAR. Home: 1220 Colonial Dr, Baton Rouge, La. Study: Liberal Syn, Baton Rouge, La.

REZNIKOFF, Simon, US, educator, attorney; b. St Louis, Mo, Mar 20, 1916; s. Hyman and Sarah (Cheifetz); AB, U of Mo, Columbia, Mo, 1937; LLB, Columbia U, NYC, 1940; m. Ruth Shear, June 12, 1943; c: Carolyn, June, Laura. Prof, bus law, San Diego State Coll, since 1956, coord, grad studies, sch of bus admin, 1956-63; vice-pres, H Reznikoff and Sons, Inc, St Louis, 1940-65; atty, Kramer and Chused, 1940-50; in pvt law practice, 1940-55. Maj, USMCR, 1941-46, ret 1959. Pres: J Comty Cen, 1963-64; Pacific SW Bus Law Assn, 1962-63; vice-pres, Young Audiences, Inc, 1968; treas, San Diego Sym Orch Assn, since 1965; mem, bd dir, United J Fed, 1962-65; bd dirs, JWB, W region. Recipient: Gentleman of Distinction, Musical Arts, 1968. Home: 4786 62 St, San Diego, Cal. Office: San Diego State Coll, San Diego, Cal.

RHEIMS, Maurice, Fr, auctioneer; b. Versailles, Fr, 1910; grad, Sorbonne, Paris; m. Lili Kramer; c: Bettina, Louis, Nathalie. Appraiser since 1935. Author: La Main; Le Cheval d'Argent; Gauguin; Lautrec. Recipient: Croix de Guerre; Commandeur de la Legion d'Honneur. Home: 12A Matignon, Paris, Fr. Office: 1 Rue de Lille, Paris, Fr.

RIBALOW, Harold U, US, author, public relations exec; b. Kiev, Russ, July 1, 1919; s. Menachem and Rose (Charniak); in US since 1921; BS, NYU, 1942; m. Susan Shuck, Oct 26, 1941; c: Reena, Meir. Publicity dir, Devl Corp for Isr, NYC, since 1958. Author: The Jew in American Sports, 1948, 1954, 1959, 1963, 1966; This Land, These People, 1950; These Your Children, 1952; Books on American Jewish Life, 1953; What's Your Jewish IQ? 1954; The History of Israel's Postage Stamps, 1956; The Chosen, 1959; 120 American Jewish Novels, 1962; Fighter from Whitechapel: The Story of Daniel Mendoza, 1962; Autobiographies of American Jews, 1965; Arnold Weskes, a critical study, 1965; Fighting Heroes of Israel, 1967; My Name Aloud, 1969; ed, Independent J Press Service, 1941-42; mgn ed: Cong Weekly, 1946-49, 1950-51; New Pal, 1949-50; Amer Zionist, 1951-53; co-ed, The Great J Books, 1950; sports columnist, Natl J Post, lit columnist, 1950-52; sports ed, JTA, 1956-63; contbr to Ency Judaica; Jews in the Modern World; periodicals. Home: 115-108 220 St, Cambria Heights, New York. Office: 215 Park Ave S, New York, NY.

RIBICOFF, Abraham A, US, legislator; b. New Britain, Conn, Apr 9, 1910; s. Samuel and Rose (Sable); LLB, cum laude, U Chgo, 1933; hon degs: Amherst Coll, Boston Coll, HUC, Dropsie Coll, Yeshiva U, JTSA, U of Cal; m. Ruth Siegel, June 28, 1931; c: Peter, Jane. US Senator, State of Conn since 1963; mem, Conn Leg, 1938-42; judge, Hartford Police Court, 1941-43, 1945-47; chmn, Conn Assembly of Munic Court Judges, 1941-42; mem, US House of Rep, 1949-53; Gov, State of Conn, 1955-61; Secy, HEW, 1961-62. Vice-pres, Bd of Overseers, JTSA, 1967; ed, U Chgo Law Review, 1932; mem: Order of Coif; Dem Party; Amer, Conn, Hartford Co Bar Assns. Home: 30 Woodland St, Hartford, Conn. Office: Sen Off Bldg, Washington, DC.

RICH, Frank H, US, business exec; b. Wash, DC, Apr 13, 1921; s. Herbert and Rosa (Hart); BS, Lehigh U, 1942; att Harvard Grad Sch of Business Admn, 1943; m. 2nd, Anadel Seidman, Mar 15, 1959; c: Frank, Polly, Elizabeth, Ned, Abby. Pres, Rich's Shoe Stores, since 1956, with firm since 1949; customer service mgr, The Hecht Co, 1946-49; lectr, Amer U, 1957-59. Maj, USAF, 1942-46; lt col, 1951-53. Dir: Chevy Chase Cen Merchants Assn, pres, 1957-60; Downtown Park and Shop since 1965; bd trustees: United Givers Fund, 1955-57; Temple Sinai, 1958-61; Natl Footwear Inst; Wash Area Council on Alcoholism; vice-pres, Natl Shoe Retailers Assn; exec, mem steering comm, Retail Bur, Wash Bd of Trade; treas, Wash DC Leadership Comm Inc; mem: Urban Renewal Council, DC; clubs: Rotary; Natl Press; Woodmont Country. Recipient: Bronze Star. Home: 5501 Hawthorne Pl NW, Washington, DC. Office: 1319-21 F St NW, Washington, DC.

RICH, Jacob Morris, S Afr, organization exec; b. Longton, Staffordshire, Eng, Mar 4, 1897; s. Isaac and Sarah (Jacobs); in S Afr since 1939; MA, Cambridge U, 1923, LLB, 1924; m. Sylvia Linken, Feb 4, 1940; c: Margaret, Susan. Secy, S Afr J Bd of Dep, since 1939; mem: natl exec comm, S Afr J Appeal; exec comm, S Afr J Sociol and Hist Soc; asso secy, Coordinating Bd of J Orgs for Cons with UN Economic and Social Council; fmr secy, London J Bd of Dep and Jt Fgn Comm; secy: J Hist Soc of Eng; Soc for J Jurisprudence, Eng. Ed: The J Chronicle, London, 1931-36. Home: 17 Campbell Rd, Parktown W, Johannesburg, S Afr. Office: POB 1180, Johannesburg, S Afr.

RICH, Jacob S, US, rabbi; b. Timkowich, Russ, May 10, 1911; s. David and Celia (Nankin); ordained rabbi, Yeshiva Etz Chaim, 1928; PhD, Loyola U, Chgo, 1948; postgrad studies, Northwestern U, 1948-50; m. Dorothy Raitzik, Aug 4, 1938; c: Michael, Sheldon, Jordan. Rabbi: Beth Shalom Ahavas Achim, since 1959; Adas B'nai Isr, 1940-43; Southtown Heb Cong, 1943-58, all Chgo. Pres, rabb group, Rel Zionists of Amer, since 1960; vice-pres: Rabb Council of Chgo, 1958; JNF, Chgo, 1957; mem: RabCA; Chgo Bd of Rabbis. Contbr to mags. Home: 5650 N Kimball Ave, Chicago, Ill. Study: 5665 N Jersey Ave, Chicago, Ill.

RICHARDS, Bernard G, US, journalist; b. Keidan, Lith, Mar 9, 1877; s. Alexander and Channa (Sirk); in US since 1886; m. Gertrude Gerzunskie, Feb 8, 1903; c: David, Ruth, Joseph, Judah. Chmn, J Info Bur since 1932; pres, Amer J Inst, since 1933; ed, New Era mag; corresp, J Chronicle, London; feature writer; mem of staff: Natl Emergency Council, Wash, DC; US Immigration and Naturalization Service; secy, J Comty, NYC; Amer J delg to Peace Conf, Paris, 1919; found, exec dir, AJCong, 1915-32; chmn, exec comm, J Council of Gtr NY; mem, exec comm, ZOA; exec asst, Dem Natl Comm. Author: The Discourses of Keidansky, 1903. Home: 310 W 106 St, New York, NY. Office: 250 W 57 St, New York, NY.

RICHE, Aaron, US, communal exec; b. Suwalki, Pol, Apr 10, 1883; s. Isaac and Fannie (Goldberg); in US since 1889; att: U Denver, 1903-05; Columbia U ext, 1905-10. Commnr, LA City Civil Defense and Disaster Bd, since 1958; found, Denver J Outlook, 1900; reporter and ed, Denver, 1902-06; PR dir, NY Cen RR, 1907-08; bus mgr: J Gazette and J Daily News, 1908-10; PR counsellor, NYC, 1911-24. Asso dir, US War Dept news bur; asst for publicity, US Secy of War, both 1917-19. Hon vice-pres, ZOA, 1958, pres, LA dist, 1926-28; fmr: chmn: JNF Council, 1933; off, comms, JWB; hon vice-chmn, S Cal ADL Regional Bd; past grand pres, Dist Grand Lodge, B'nai B'rith, since 1956; dir and secy: Cedars of Leb-Mt Sinai Hosp, since 1931; secy and trustee, UJF Fund, 1933-37; secy: LA J Comty Council, since 1936; trustee: J Publ Soc, 1955-61; Natl J Home for Asthmatic Children; J Vocational Service; mem: exec comm, Citizens Water and Power comm of LA; AJCong; AJComm; Amer J Hist Soc; NCCJ; CJFWF; ACLU; ARC; Masons; Amer Isr Soc; Wilshire Blvd Temple; clubs: Covenant, pres, 1934; Concordia, secy, 1927-28; Commonwealth; LA Press; LA Athletic. Contbr: Aaron Riche Youth Fellowship. Recipient: US Treas Dept medal, 1918; citation, US War Dept, 1919; Hillel Key, LA B'nai B'rith, 1949; Mt Sinai Hosp award, 1950; civic award, S Cal B'nai B'rith council, 1951; citation, ZOA, 1952; Diamond Red Feather, LA Comty Chest, 1952; citation, Isr Bonds, 1952; citation, USO-JWB, 1953; United JWF Key award, 1962; civic awards: mayor, LA; city council, LA; Bd of Sups, LA Co; Cal State Sen. Home: 842 S Sycamore Ave, Los Angeles, Col. Office: 590 N Vermont Ave, Los Angeles, Cal.

RICHMAN, Alexander, US, physician; b. New York, NY, Sep 24, 1910; s. Meyer and Mollie (Seminowitz); BS, CCNY, 1928; MD, NY Med Coll, 1932; m. Charlotte Yudell, June 1933; c: Myra Togut, Beverly Richman, Janice Sufrin, Lesley Winaker. Asso att phys, gastroenterology, Mt Sinai Hosp, chief, liver clinic, both since 1956, on staff since 1950; asso clinical prof of med, Mt Sinai Sch of Med, since 1965; att phys: Fordham Hosp; Mother Cabrini Memorial Hosp, both since 1950. Pres, NY Acad of Gastroenterology, 1969; trustee, Park Ave Syn, since 1968; dipl, Amer Bd of Internal Med, 1943, gastroenterology, 1947; f, NY Acad of Med; dir, ZOA, 1948-58; vice-pres, Temple Isr, 1949-50, trustee, 1948-53; mem: AMA; NY State and Co Med Socs; Amer Gastroenterological Assn; Amer Soc for Gastrointestinal Endoscopy; Amer Assn for Study of Liver Diseases. Contbr to med jours. Home: 47 E 88 St, New York, NY. Office: 1050 Fifth Ave, New York, NY.

RICHMAN, Harry, US, author, singer; b. Cincinnati, O, Aug 10, 1895; s. Henry and Kathrine; att, O Mechanics Inst; m. Yvonne Day. Writer, songs: Walking My Baby Back Home; Muddy Waters; Vagabond Song; Danger in Your Eyes Cherie; Say It Again; Moonlight Saving Time; Zeigfeld Follies songs; pianist with Mae West, Nora Bayes; starred in Zeigfeld

Follies; introduced songs: Birth of the Blues; Sunny Side of the Street; I Can't Give You Anything But Love; Puttin on the Ritz. Seaman 1st class, USN, WW I. Co-found, with Sophie Tucker, Amer Guild Variety Artists; mem: Masons 32 deg; life mem, Elks; Musicians Union; ASCAP; Saints and Sinners; Variety Club; Legue Internationale; clubs: Friars; Guardian. Author: A Hell of a Life, 1964. Hobby: flying; holds worlds altitude record for one-motor Amphibians, made first round-trip flight over Atlantic with Dick Merrill, 1936. Home: 151 Ocean Park Blvd, Santa Monica, Cal.

RICHMAN, Michael, Eng, organization exec; b. London, Eng, Dec 25, 1933; s. George and Maude (Lustigman); m. Ruth Rudolph, Dec 15, 1960; c: Alison, Leigh. Organizing exec, JPA, since 1960; fund raising cons. Office: Rex House, 4/12 Regent St, London SW1, Eng.

RICHMAN, Ruth, US, executive dir; b. Silver City, NM, Aug 3, 1909; d. Eli and Rosa Borenstein; BA, Columbia Coll; m. Louis Richman, June 26, 1935; c: Eli. Exec dir, J Conciliation Bd of Amer Inc, since 1956. Mem: Natl Panel Amer Arbitration Assn; Commn on Syn Relations, FJP; Hadassah; Council of J Women. Hobbies: travel, psych, music, art. Home: 157 E 57 St, New York, NY. Office: 225 Broadway, New York, NY.

RICHMAN, Stanley M, US, business exec; b. St Louis, Mo, July 6, 1911; s. Joseph and Emma (Rabinowitz); att U of Ill; LLB, cum laude, Wash U Sch of Law, 1933; m. Barbara Friedman, May 28, 1938; c: Joan Saidel, Judith. Vice-pres, secy, Gen Amer Life Ins Co, since 1966, with firm since 1934; fmr: spec agt, FBI, 1933-34. Chmn, N Cen Round Table, Life Ins Advts Assn, mem exec comm, chmn PR comm, pres, 1967; mem: bd, exec comm, J Hosp; pres, J Family Service Agcy, 1947-49; dir, Family Service Assn of Amer, 1950-56; mem: bd, exec comm, United Fund; exec bd, St Louis council, Boy Scouts of Amer; council pres, St Louis U; trustee, Natl Health and Wfr Assn, 1960-68; mem: PR Soc of Amer; Zeta Beta Tau; Order of Coif; clubs: Advt of St Louis; Media; Westwood Country. Home: 220 Topton Way, Clayton, Mo. Office: 1501 Locust Street, St Louis, Mo.

RICHMOND, Isidor, US, architect; b. Chelsea, Mass, Dec 2, 1893; s. Hyman and Lena (Tanzer); att Boston Architectural Cen, 1911-14, 1922-23; MIT, 1914-16; Amer Acad, Rome, Rotch traveling scholarship, 1923-25; m. Anne Bovarnick, Nov 30, 1933; c: Jean Finegold. Partner, firm, Isidor Richmond and Carney Goldberg, architects and engrs since 1946; fmr with: Cram and Ferguson; Bellows and Aldrich; Guy Lowell; asso architect, Newtone Court Housing Project, Cambridge, Mass; instr, architecture, MIT. Lt, USN, WW I; cdr, USN, 1941-45. Works designed and executed include: Lamson and Hubbard, Boston; chapel, Isabella Thorburn Coll, India; housing projects, schools, libraries, throughout State of Mass; Temple Tifereth Isr, Malden; Temple Agudas Achim, Leominster; Temple Beth Sholom of Nantasket, Hull; Cong Beth Isr, Worcester; Temple Beth Elchim, Wellesley; Temple Isr, Sharon; Temple Tifereth Isr, New Bedford, all Mass; J Comty Cens of Brookline, Brighton, Newton; Sports Cen Bldg, Brandeis U; dormitories, State Coll at Salem; Housing for Elderly, Roxbury, Mass. F, Amer Inst of Architects, 1955; mem: bd trustees, Boston Arts Festival; Beacon Hill Arch commn; Mass State Assn of Architects; Temple Emeth; Masons; past pres: Boston Soc for Architects; Boston Architectural Cen. Recipient: Harleston Parker Gold medal, Boston Soc for Architects, 1949; Award of Merit, Amer Inst of Architects, 1954. Hobbies: flying small planes; figure skating. Home: 56 Baker Circle, Chestnut Hill, Mass. Office: 30 Newbury St, Boston. Mass.

RICHMOND, Sylvia B, US, librarian, journalist; b. Chelsea, Mass, Sept 3, 1905; d. Louis and Sarah (Kabat); att: Columbia U; Boston U; Harvard U; Simmons Coll. Lit ed, Chelsea Record, since 1940; chief libr, Chelsea Public Libr, 1947-66. Mem: Natl League of Amer Penwomen; NE Women's Press Assn; Amer and N Shore Libr Assns; Visiting Nurses Assn; bd mem: Chelsea Memorial Hosp; Agudos Sholom. Contbr to Boston periodicals. Recipient: US Treas Dept citation, 1946; Woman-of-the-Year award, B'nai B'rith, Chelsea, 1944; citation of merit, Children's Cancer Research Found, 1950; hon life member, YWHA; presentation, Cavalcade of Authors, 1952. Hobbies: fishing, travel. Home: 72 Tudor St, Chelsea, Mass. Office: Chelsea Record, Chelsea, Mass.

RICHTER, Charles, US, banker; b. Aus, Oct 17, 1899; s. Pincus and Rebecca (Rothenstreich); in US since 1900; att NYU Sch of Law; m. Miriam Suslow, May 5, 1931; c: Richard, James. Pres, Fed Data Processing Corp; chmn, bd, Richter & Co Inc, since 1959; mem, adv bd, Chem Bank & Trust Co, since 1951, vice-pres, 1951-56; chmn bd, Natl Safety Bank & Trust Co, 1932-51, vice-pres, 1930-32. Mem: Temple Emanu El; B'nai B'rith; Young Men's Philanthropic League; clubs: Fenway Golf, White Plains; City Athletic, NYC. Home: 650 Park Ave, New York, NY. Office: 280 Madison Ave, New York, NY.

RICHTER, Karl, US, rabbi; b. Stuttgart, Ger, Oct 31, 1910; s. Samuel and Josephine (Pick); in US since 1939; att Friedrich Wilhelm U, Breslau, Ger, 1928-33; ordained rabbi, J Theol Sem, Breslau, 1935; hon DD, HUC, 1960; m. Lina Ruth May, Mar 31, 1935; c: Esther Blumenfeld, David. Rabbi, Sinai Temple, Michigan City, Ind, since 1950; lectr, phil, Purdue U, since 1965; rabbi: Ger, 1935-39; Temple Isr, Springfield, Mo, 1939-42; Mt Zion Temple, Sioux Falls, SD, 1943-50. Chaplain, US Med Cen and O'Reilly Gen Hosp, US Army, 1939-42; civilian chaplain, Sioux Falls Army Air Base. Pres: Marshall Kottler lodge, B'nai B'rith, 1957-58; Comty Services Council, 1952-54; chmn: Mich City Ministerial Assn, 1963-65; commn and vice-chmn, Public Housing Auth, 1963-68; vice-pres: Pottawattomie council, Boy Scouts of Amer, 1956-57; Chgo Assn of Reform Rabbis, 1964-65; treas, La Porte Co Family Service Assn; mem bd: ARC; USO; Civic Music Assn; La Porte Co TB Assn; MH Assn, 1955-56; PTA Council, 1952-54; La Porte Co Therapy Cen for Retarded Children, 1960-64; Mich City Comty Scholarship Fund, Inc, 1960-66; Assn for UN; Housing Research Inc, both Mich City; CCAR, 1952-54; Midwest Council for Isr Bonds; Ind J Comty Relations Council; ADL; bd trustees, Alumni Assn of HUC-JIR; mem: Masons; JWF; Sinai Temple Forum comm; Mayor's Comm on Hum Relations; adv bd, Adult and Child Guidance Clinic; Comm on Marriage, Family, Home; exec comm, Chgo Bd of Rabbis, 1959-61; Ind Bd of Rabbis; UAHC; speakers' bur, Ind Fed of Temple Sisterhoods; J Chautauqua Soc; UJA; delg, World Union for Progressive Judaism cong, Amsterdam, 1957; clubs: Knife and Fork, pres; Rotary, vice-pres, 1968-69; Covenant of Ill. Ed: Shma, Bull of Chgo Bd of Rabbis; contbr to J periodicals. Home: 532 Boyd Circle, Michigan City, Ind. Study: 2800 Franklin St, Michigan City, Ind.

RICHTER, William Ben Zion, US, dentist, author, composer; b. Phila, Pa, May 19, 1901; s. Philip and Hanna (Nagler); DDS, Temple U, Phila, 1925. Dentist, author, composer, violinist, music publisher, all since 1925. Author: The Ghetto Struggle, 1934; Sin's Aftermath, 1937; The Cobbler, 1951; North of Society Hill, 1970; songs: Refugee; Keep the Flag of Zion Waving; Out at the Dell; Israel, I'm Dreaming of You; poems; short stories; contbr to J jours. Mem: ASCAP; Pa Assn Dent Surgs; Amer Guild of Authors and Composers. Recipient, citations from: USNR; US Army; US Treas Dept; Amer Legion; 4 Freedoms Found. Hobbies: swimming, hist of J, gen hist. Home and office: 1601 67 Ave, Philadelphia, Pa.

RICHTIGER, Abraham Israel, Eng, business exec; b. Pol, Mar 24, 1891; s. Joseph and Deborah (Moscovitz); in Eng since 1912; att Yeshiva, Pol; m. Joyce Snowman, Mar 30, 1911; c: Rebecca Kaye, Gita Shaw, Toby Meiri. Chmn: JA Aliyah Comm; Chalutz Comm; hon vice-pres, ZF of Gt Brit and N Ir; vice-chmn, Poale Zion; jt treas, Soc Friends of J Refs; mem, bd of deps, Brit Jews. Home: 2 West End Lane, London, Eng. Office: 40 Dean St, London, Eng.

RICKAYZEN, Gerald, Eng, educator; b. London, Eng, Oct 16, 1929; s. Solomon and Jane (Culank); BSc, Queen Mary Coll, London, 1951; PhD, Christ Coll, Cambridge, 1954; m. Gillian Lewin, Dec 20, 1953; c: Alan, Sonia, Martin, Benjamin. Prof, theoretical physics, U Kent, since 1966, fmr, reader physics; lectr, U Liverpool, 1959-66; visiting prof, Cornell U, 1964. Chmn, Canterbury Assn for Advancement of State Educ; gov, Tech HS, Canterbury; mem: Amer Phys Soc; Inst of Physics, Phys Soc. Author: Theory of Superconductivity, 1964; contbr of research papers on theoretical physics. Recipient, Sir John William Lubbock prize, London U, 1951. Hobbies: cello playing, tennis, cinema. Home: 122 Whitstable Rd, Canterbury, Kent, Eng. Office: U of Kent, Canterbury, Eng.

RICKLES, Nathan K, US, psychiatrist; b. Seattle, Wash, Aug 24, 1904; s. David and Tillie (Golan); BS, Northwestern U,

1927, MD, 1928; m. Lynn Bari, Aug 30, 1955; c: Rena. Pvt practice since 1928; dir: Psycht Cen, since 1938; Behavior Clinic, 1938-42, both Seattle; cons: VA, 1939; Surg Gen's Off, US Army, 1942. F: Amer Psycht Assn; AMA; mem council, AAAS; vice-pres, Med Correctional Assn, 1965-69; fmr pres: Wash Mental Hygiene Assn; Electroshock Research Assn; club: Beverly Hills Tennis, pres. Author: Exhibitionism, 1950; Management of Anxiety for General Practitioner, 1962; mem ed bd, Jour of Social Therapy; contbr to sci jours. Home and office: 605 N Alta Dr, Beverly Hills, Cal.

RICKLES, Norman H, US, dental surgeon, educator; b. Seattle, Wash, May 8, 1920; s. Samuel and Anna (Bernstein); DDS, Wash U, Sch of Dent, 1947; MS, U of Cal Grad Sch, SF, 1951; m. Eva Simons, Dec 17, 1950; c: Tamara, Annette. Prof of dent, head, dept of path, U of Ore Dent Sch, since 1956, on fac since 1947. US Army, 1942-44; capt, chief of oral diagnosis and asst chief of research, US Dent Corps, 1952-54. F, dental, oral path, Armed Forces Inst of Path, Wash, DC, 1954-56; dipl, Amer Bd of Oral Path; pres, Amer Acad of Oral Path, 1962-63; mem: Amer Dent Assn; Ore State Dent Assn; Cal Acad of Periodontology; asso, Intl Acad of Oral Path; Intl Acad of Path; Ore Paths Assn; Pacific NW Soc of Paths; Amer Soc of Clinical Paths; Intl Assn of Dent Research; AAAS; Pi Mu Chi; Phi Theta Kappa; Sigma Xi, secy-treas, Portland chap, 1957-59. Contbr to profsl jours. Home: 1515 SW Westwood Dr, Portland, Ore. Office: U of Oregon Dental Sch, 611 SW Campus Dr, Portland, Ore.

RICKOVER, Hyman George, US, naval officer; b. 1900; s. Abraham and Rose; grad, US Naval Academy, 1922; m. Ruth Masters; c: Robert. Admiral, USN; chief, naval reactors br, AEC; fmr: ensign, USN, 1922; qualified submariner, 1930; cons, atomic submarine project, AEC, Oak Ridge, Tenn, 1946-47; i/c nuclear propulsion div. Author: Education and Freedom, 1958; Swiss Schools and Ours, 1961; American Education—A National Failure. Recipient: Egleston medal, Columbia Alumni Assn, 1955; Enrico Fermi award, 1965. Office: c/o Bur of Ships, US Navy, Washington, DC.

RIEGELMAN, Harold, US, attorney; b. Des Moines, Ia, Aug 19, 1898; s. Isaac and Bertha (Meyer); BA, Cornell U, 1914; MA, LLB, Columbia U, 1916; dipl, command and general staff sch, Ft Leavenworth, 1942; m. Gladys Liebman, Nov 1, 1919; c: Ann Ullman, Lois Steckler. Sr partner, Nordlinger, Riegelman, Benetar and Charney, since 1919; counsel, Emb, Rep of China, since 1938; fmr: counsel: NY State Commn to Revise Tenement Housing Law, 1927-29; Vet Relief Commn, 1922-32; asst state atty gen, 1930-31; cons: Army Dept, 1953-58; US Bur of Budget, 1954-56; spec lectr, taxation and govt: NYU, 1938-39; Columbia U, 1939. Capt, US Army WW I; maj, res, 1925; col, 1942, chem off, US Army, 1942-45. Prin contribs: drafted first NY State housing law, 1926; drafted State multiple dwelling law, 1929; reorganized NY PO, 1953; elected by UN Gen Assembly to Admn Tribunal, 1958; mem, US Mission to UN, 1959; Rep candidate for NYC Mayor, 1953; fmr: natl vice-pres, AJC omm, 1949-53; exec comm since 1951; chmn bd, Natl Council on Alcoholism, 1956-59; trustee, counsel, Citizens Budget comm, since 1932; mem: NY State, NYC Bar Assns; NY Co Lawyers Assn; Amer Bar Assn; Council on Fgn Relations; NY State C of C; Amer Legion; VFW; Masons; Zeta Beta Tau, past pres; clubs: Century; Cornell; Natl Rep; Army and Navy; Capitol Hill, both Wash, DC; Amer, London, Eng. Author: War Notes of a Casual, 1931; There's a Nip in the Air, 1946; Caves of Biak, 1955; contbr to profsl jours. Recipient: Wfr Council medal, 1932; Columbia U medal, 1938; Silver Star, 1945; Bronze Star, 1944, 1945; Conspicuous Service Star, NY State, 1945; Order of the Auspicious Star, Rep of China, 1948; f, Royal Society of Arts, London. Hobbies: farming, fishing, painting, horseback riding. Home: 110 E 57 St, New York, NY; Haight Crossroad, Chappaqua, NY. Office: 420 Lexington Ave, New York, NY.

RIEGLER, Eliezer, Isr, banker; b. Rum, Dec 15, 1908; s. Shlomo and Krendelo; in Isr since 1940; CA, Sch of Bus and Banking; m. Esther Strassner, June 23, 1946; c: Netanel, Shmuel. Dir, Bank Hapoel Hamizrachi, Natanya br; councillor, Natanya Munic Council, chmn, agric comm; mem bd dirs: Moatza Datit, treas, Natanya br; Mishav Ltd; Tifareth Banim Ltd; fmr: mgr, Even Chen Ltd. Served Haganah. Mem: cen comm, Natl Rel Party, org and mem exec, local br, cen comm for The Sabbath; fmr, active Zionist movements, Rum. Recipient: entered in Golden Book of JNF. Home: 32 Moshe Shapira St, Natanya, Isr. Office: Bank Hapoel Hamizrachi, Herzl St, Natanya, Isr.

RIEGNER, Gerhart M, Switz, organization exec; b. Berlin, Ger, Sep 12, 1911; s. Heinrich and Agnes (Arnheim); in Switz since 1934; studied law: U Berlin; U Freiburg; U Heidelberg; Sorbonne; Grad Inst of Intl Studies, Geneva; Acad of Intl Law, The Hague, 1929-36. Secy gen, WJC, since 1965, mem of exec, since 1948, legal secy, Geneva off, 1936-39, dir, 1939-48; WJC rep to: Paris Peace Conf; UN Assembly meetings in Eur; UNESCO; ECOSCO; Red Cross; IRO; and ILO conf of non-govt orgs in consultive relationship with UNESCO, 1955-57; conf of consultive non-govt orgs at the UN, 1953-55; fmr intl chmn, World U Service, 1949-55. Contbr to legal and J jours. Home: 25 Ave Wendt, Geneva, Switz. Office: 1 Rue Varembe, Geneva, Switz.

RIEMER, Harry, US, textile specialist; b. Bklyn, NY, May 4, 1893; s. William and Annie (Friedman); hon: MS, Lowell Tech Inst, 1950; D Textiles, Phila Coll of Textiles and Sci, 1954; m. Helen Schwartz, Apr 1, 1919; c: William, Dan. Fmr, asso exec dir, Natl Assn Men's and Boy's Apparel Clubs; ed: American Stationer, 1915-17; Daily News Record, 1917-58; cons, Henry Bach Advt Agcy, 1959-61. War corresp, WW II. Gen cons, Textile Vets Assn, since 1946; hon mem, Natl Council for Textile Educ, since 1950; secy, Alexander D Goode, Ben Goldman lodge, B'nai B'rith, since 1954; adv: NY council, Boy Scouts Amer; NY Cancer Care; mem, Masons, NY Grand lodge, 1954; fmr: vice-pres, NY chap, Quartermaster Assn; trustee, Brotherhood Syn; club: Textile Sq, past pres. Author: Brief for Salesmen, 1950; The World Is Catching Up, 2 vols, 1956. Home: 70 E 10 St, New York, NY. Office: 347 Fifth Ave, New York, NY.

RIESE, Hertha, US, psychiatrist; b. Berlin, Mar 15, 1892; d. Wilhelm and Mathilde (Scheinberger) Pataky; in US since 1940; BS, U Berlin, 1911; MD, U Frankfurt, 1916; BPP, U Lyon, 1935; m. Walter Riese, Aug 7, 1915; c: Renée, Beatrice. Cons psycht, Richmond Public Schs, since 1968; psycht, Friends' Asso for Children, 1966-68; pvt practice, Frankfurt, 1919-33; dir, Family Counselling Clinic, Frankfurt, 1924-30; research worker, Inst of Comparative Brain Research, U Paris; mem, legal commn for alteration of sex leg, Frankfurt; psycht dir, educ therapy cen, Commonwealth of Va, 1943-63; psycht, St Joseph's Villa, 1963-66. F, Amer Psycht Assn; mem: Amer Group Psychotherapy Assn; Assn for Psycht Treatment of Offenders; Amer Acad of Psychotherapy; Amer Med Women's Assn; Hadassah. Author: Die Sexuelle Not Unserer Zeit, 1927; Geschlechtsleben und Gesundheit, Gesittung und Gesetz, 1932; Heal the Hurt Child, 1962; contbr to sci jours. Home: Route 2, Box 397, Glen Allen, Va.

RIESE, Kurt Yeheskel, Isr, manufacturer; b. Berlin, Ger, Jan 16, 1920; s. Willi and Else Lewin; in Isr since 1936; att commercial and tech courses, Tel Aviv, 1938-48; m. Eva Rosenthal, Mar 6, 1945; c: Edna Goldberg, Gabriel. Mgn dir: Oniyah Carbon Paper Factory, since 1948; mem, bd of dirs, STAPEX, Stationery and Paper Export Co; fmr: Dr W Riese and Son Ltd. Found mem, EFORMA, Eur Union of Continuous Forms Mfrs; clubs: vice-pres, Rotary, Tel Aviv-Yaffo, past hon treas, hon secy. Home: 11 Mordechai St, Ramat Gan, Isr. Office: 10 Derech Hashalom, Tel Aviv, Isr.

RIESE, Walter, US, physician, educator, author; b. Berlin, Ger, June 30, 1890; s. Emil and Anna (Rosenthal); MD, U Koenigsberg, 1914; BS, U Lyon, 1936; m. Hertha Pataky, Aug 7, 1915; c: Renée, Beatrice. Em asso prof, neur, psycht, hist of med, Med Coll of Va, since 1941, Rockefeller f, 1933-36 and 1941-43; lectr: Sch of Clinical and Applied Psychol, Richmond Profsl Inst, Coll of William and Mary, since 1952; med fac, neuro-psycht Clinic, Koenisberg, Ger, 1914-15, asst, clinic, 1917-19, chief, nueroanat lab, 1926-27; asst: Hosp for Brain Injured Soldiers, 1919-20; Neur Inst, 1920-26, all Frankfurt/M, Ger; neuropsycht clinic, U of Lyon, Fr, 1933-37; i/c research, Cen Natl de la Recherche Scientifique, 1937-40; asso: dept phys, Sorbonne, 1937-40; Natl Mus of Natural Hist, 1937-40, all Paris; cons neuropath, dept mental hygiene and hosps, Commonwealth of Va, 1941-60; cons, Natl Inst of HEW, USPHS, 1960-63. Author: Vincent van Gogh in der Krankheit, 1926; Das Sinnesleben eines Dichters: Georg Trakl, 1928; Das Triebverbrechen, Untersuchungen über die unmittelbaren Ursachen des Sexual und Affektdelikts, sowie ihre Bedeutung für die Zurechnungsfähigkeit des Täters, 1933; Système nerveux cérébro-spinal, 1940; La pensée causale en médecine, 1950; Principles of Neurology in the Light of History and their Present Use, 1950; The Conception of Disease, Its History,Its Versions and Its Nature,1953; La pensée morale en médecine, premiers principes d'une éthique médicale, 1955; A History of Neurology, 1959; The Legacy of Philippe

Pinel; An Inquiry into Thought on Mental Alienation, 1969; co-author: Die Unfallneurose und das Reichsgericht, 1930; L'idée de l'homme dans la neurologie contemporaine, 1938; Galen on the Passions and Errors of the Soul, 1963; contbr to sci periodicals. Mem: Amer Assn Neuropaths; Amer Assn Hist of Med; Amer Soc Mammalogists; AMA; Acad of Pcychoan; Med Soc of Va; Amer Geriatric Soc; AAUP; Soc of Hist of Heb Med, Paris; Soc Intl d'Expression Path, Paris; Ontoanalytic Assn, Inc, NY. Recipient, research grants, Richmond Area U Cen, 1950, 1952. Home: POB 397, Glen Allen, Va.

RIESMAN, David, US, social scientist, educator; b. Phila, Pa, 1909; s. David and Eleanor (Fleisher); BA, Harvard, 1931, LLB, Law School, 1934; hon LLD: Marlboro Coll, 1954; Grinnell Coll, 1957; St Ambrose Coll, 1965; Oakland U, 1967; U of Cal, 1967; m. Evelyn Thompson, 1936; four children. Ford prof, social sci, Harvard, since 1958; fmr: law clerk to Justice Louis D Brandeis, 1935-36; pvt law practice, Boston, 1936-37; mem fac, U of Buffalo, 1937-41; research f, Columbia U Law Sch, 1941-42; with Sperry Gyroscope Co, NY, 1943-46; mem fac, U of Chgo, 1954-58; dir research, mass communications, Yale U, 1947-49. Author: The Lonely Crowd: A Study of the Changing American Character, 1950; Faces in the Crowd, 1952; Thorstein Veblen, 1953; Individualism Reconsidered and other Essays, 1954; Constraint and Variety in American Education, 1956; Abundance for What? and other Essays, 1964; co-author: The Academic Revolution, 1968. Home: 49 Linnaean St, Cambridge, Mass. Office: Harvard U, Cambridge, Mass.

RIESNER, Daniel J, US, attorney; b. NYC, Oct 25, 1902; s. Henry and Lillian (Wilson); BA, Columbia Coll, 1925, **LLB,** 1927; m. Ruth Gordon, Dec 24, 1926; c: Gordon, Sara Friedman. Mem, Riesner, Jawitz & Holland, since 1927; pres, dir, Educasting Sys Inc; dir: Laser Line Corp; Bartel Laser Communications; Comfax Corp; Computer Pix Inc; Charger Electronics. Pres, Natl Rep Club, 1954-59, delg to natl convs; trustee, Metrop Syn; chmn, AJComn, 1967-68; bd dirs, Columbia Coll Fund; mem: Amer, NY State Bar Assns; Assn of Bar of City of NY; NY Co Lawyers Assn; Phi Sigma Delta; clubs: Old Oaks Country; Columbia U. Author: Practical Politics, 1950. Hobby, painting. Home: 50 E 79 St, New York, NY. Office: 770 Lexington Ave, New York, NY.

RIETTY, Robert Lucio, Eng, editor, actor, director; b. London, Feb 8, 1923; s. Vittorio and Rose (Nay); att Royal Acad of Dramatic Art, London; m. Albertine Shalom, June 1, 1958; c: Jonathan, Anya, Liana. Ed, Gambit, intl drama quarterly; transl; actor: stage, BBC, and TV; org, dir, fgn film soundtracks into Eng; mem: British Actors' Equity Assn; Screen Writers Guild; Royal Soc Authors; Radio Writers Assn; Assn Cinema Technicians. Hobbies: piano, woodwork. Home: 40 Old Church Lane, London, NW9, Eng.

RIFKIN, Harold, US, physician, educator; b. Bklyn, NY, Sep 10, 1916; s. Jack and Rose (Zuckoff); BA, U of Mo, 1935; MD, Dalhousie U, 1940; m. Beatrice Weiss, Nov 25, 1945; c: Janet, Matthew, Phyllis. Clinical prof, med, Albert Einstein Med Coll, since 1962; asso prof, microbiol, NY Med Coll, since 1945; lectr, med, Columbia U, since 1948; chief, diabetes service, Montefiore Hosp, sr attending phys, both since 1955, co-chief, med clinic, since 1957, on staff since 1942; sr visiting phys, Bx Munic Hosp Center, since 1945; cons, metabolism, nutrition, NYC Dept of Health, since 1958; med, Health Ins Plan of NY, 1957-59. Lt-col, US Army MC, 1943-46. Dipl, Amer Bd of Internal Med, 1948; f: Amer Coll of Phys; NY Acad of Med, pres, 1968-70; Amer, NY, Diabetes Assns; sr f, Amer Fed of Clinical Research. Author: Diabetic Glomerulosclerosis, 1952; co-author: Clinical Diabetes Mellitus, 1962; contbr to med jours. Recipient: research grants, USPHS, 1955-59; Henry L Moses prize, 1949, 1952. Home: 4682 Waldo Ave, New York, NY. Office: 35 E 75 St, New York, NY.

RIFKIN, Irving Joseph, US, chemist; b. Sep 11, 1903; s. Harris and Anna (Levine); att: Columbia U Coll of Pharm, 1921-23; Pratt Inst, sch of sci and tech, 1923-25; m. Florence Meisler, Nov 21, 1926; c: Barbara Gutin, Bruce. Partner, chem, Brilco Labs, since 1939; treas, chem, Zodiac Labs Inc, since 1960; secy, dir, Empire State Chem Products Inc; treas, dir, Marryatt Lane Corp. Pres, Ocean Pkwy J Cen, 1966-68; f, Amer Inst Chem; mem: Amer Chem Soc; Columbia U Coll of Pharm, life; ZOA; AJCong; Ave O Temple. Home: 435 Ocean Parkway, Brooklyn, NY. Office: 1551 63 St, Brooklyn, NY.

RIFKIND, Simon H, US, attorney, jurist; b. Meretz, Russia, June 5, 1901; s. Jacob and Celia (Bluestone); in US since 1910; BS, CCNY, 1922; LLB, Columbia U, 1925; hon: DLitt, JTSA, 1950; LLD, Hofstra Coll, 1962; m. Adele Singer, 1927; c: Richard, Robert. Mem, law firm, Paul, Weiss, Goldberg, Rifkind, Wharton and Garrison, since 1950; secy to US Senator Robert Wagner, 1927-33; mem, law firm, Wagner, Quillinan and Rifkind, 1930-41; US Dist Judge, S dist, NY, 1941-50; mem, law firm, Stevenson, Rifkind and Wirtz, Chgo, 1947-61; spec master, Supr Court of US, 1955-61; chmn, Pres RR Comm, 1961-62. Chmn, allocations comm, UJA, since 1949; fmr chmn, exec bd, AJComm; vice-chmn, bd dirs, JTSA, since 1947; mem: NY State Commn on Govt Oprs of NYC, 1959-61; Bd Higher Educ, NYC, 1954-66; bd dirs, NY Co Lawyers Assn; mem, Assn of Bar of City of NY; club: Harmonie. Recipient: Medal of Freedom, 1946; Townsend Harris Medal, CCNY, 1948; Louis Marshall Memorial award, JTSA, 1962. Home: 125 E 63 St, New York, NY. Office: 575 Madison Ave, New York, NY.

RIFTTIN, Jacob, Isr, legislator, farmer; b. Vulka-Profetzka, Pol, Mar 16, 1907; s. Jehuda and Rebeka (Sandomirski); in Isr since 1929; m. Jenia Jones, Jan 1, 1931; c: Jehuda, Nahum. Mem, Kibbutz Ein Shemer, since 1929; MK, since 1929; pres, interior commn: 1st, 2nd, 3rd Knesset; mem: fgn, security comms: 1st, 2nd Knesset; comm for work problems; fmr: mem: political comm, Mapam; Provincial State Council; cen comm, Hashomer Hatzair; exec: Kibbutz Arzi; Histadrut Haovdim; security comm, Va'ad Leumi; Anti-Brit Resistance. Haganah, 1929-48. Contbr to jours. Spec interest: poetry. Home: Kibbutz Ein Shemer, Isr.

RIKELMAN, Herman, US, social worker; b. NYC, July 25, 1911; s. Max and Jennie (LeShak); BS, Fordham U, 1934; MA, Columbia U, 1936; cert, NY Sch of Social Work, 1940; m. Augusta Komarow, Oct 27, 1934; c: Herbert. Cert psychol, NY, Cal; fmr: dir, comty, personal service divs, J Bd of Guardians, 1944-55; exec dir, Karen Horney Clinic, 1955-64. Mem: hon, Natl Council of J Prison Chaplains, secy, 1945-53; Natl Assn of Social Work; Natl Conf of J Communal Services; Amer Psychol Assn; S Cal Soc of Clinical Hypnosis; Amer Assn of Marriage Counselors. Contbr to profsl jours. Recipient: comty award, Mayor's Comm on Youth, 1954; Judea Hall of Fame, 1956. Hobbies: photography, sports. Home: 757 Ocean Ave, Santa Monica, Cal.

RIKOVER, Moshe, Isr, physician; b. Pol, Oct 2, 1907; s. Meir and Berta (Schlomiuk); in Isr since 1935; MD, U Strasbourg, 1932; m. Judith Zylberbaum, 1951; c: Meir, Anat-Marga, Ygal. Chief, dept obstet and gyn, Govt Hosp, Yaffo, since 1949; mem sr staff, Tel Aviv U Med Sch; fmr: Hadassah Hosp, 1935-39; Beilinson Hosp, 1940-42; Kupat Holim, 1943-47. Lt, IDF, 1948-49. Mem: Isr Soc of Obstet and Gyn; Société Française de Stérilité. Home: 13 Dubnov St, Tel Aviv, Isr. Office: Erlich St, Jaffa, Isr.

RIM, Yeshayahu, Isr, psychologist, educator; b. Czernowitz, Pol, Apr 21, 1922; s. Moshe and Ester (Weiner); in Isr since 1944; att Heb U, Jerusalem, 1944-48; PhD, London U, 1953; m. Shulamit Kleeberg, Jan 3, 1950; c: Carmela, Orna. Asso prof, Technion, Haifa, since 1968. Author: Selection of Workers, 1958; Psychology of Work, 1967. Mem: Isr Psych Assn; Intl Assn of Applied Psych. IDF, 1948-51. Home: 46 Shoshanat Hacarmel St, Haifa, Isr. Office: Technion, Haifa, Isr.

RIMALT, Elimelech S, Isr, legislator, teacher; b. Bochnia, Pol, Nov 1, 1907; s. Samuel and Gilli (Suesskind); in Isr since 1939; PhD, Vienna U, 1931, ordained rabbi, Theol Sem, Vienna, 1932; m. Wilma Gelmann, 1933; c: David, Benjamin. MK, since 1951, chmn, fgn affairs comm, 1959-61, 1965-69; mem, security comm, Provisional Govt, 1948; chmn, Lib Party, since 1968; pol and cen comms since 1961; mem, presidium, Gen Zionist Party, 1952, 1959; chmn, Gen Zionist Workers Fed, 1952-61; Isr delgs to UN, 1956, 1958, 1967; fmr: rabbi, Aus, 1933-38; dir, immigration dept, J Comty Council, Vienna, 1938-39; tchr, Bible, Heb hist, elem and secondary schs, Ramat Gan, 1939-45; dir, educ dept, Ramat Gan Munic, 1947-53, dep mayor, 1955-59. Mem, B'nai B'rith. Author: Wechselbeziehungen zwischen dem Aramaischen und dem Neubabylonischen, 1933; contbr to mags. Home: 19 Haam Hatsarfati Blvd, Ramat Gan, Isr. Office: The Knesset, Jerusalem, Isr.

RINDER, Irwin D, US, educator; b. NYC, Dec 20, 1923; s. Aaron and Anita (Tieger); att CCNY, 1940-42; BA, U of Idaho, 1947; MA, U of Chgo, 1950, PhD, 1953; m. 1st, c: Lenore, Tamara, Rose, Deborah, Elliott; m. 2nd, Marion

Hart, Oct 3, 1969. Prof, sociol, Macalester Coll, since 1968; asst prof, Wis State Coll, Milw, 1956-58, mem fac since 1952; prof, sociol, U of Wis, Milw, 1962-68, chmn, dept sociol, 1961-62, mem fac since 1958. USAAC, 1943-45. Bd mem: Wis region, NCCJ, since 1961; Intl Childbirth Educ Assn, since 1962; vice-pres, local 79, Tchrs Union, 1955-56; pres, U of Wis chap, AAUP, 1956-57; f, Amer Sociol Assn; mem: Midwest and Wis Sociol Soc; Soc for Sci Study of Sex; Soc for Sci Study of Social Problems. Author: Polarities in Jewish Identification in The Jews: An American Social Group, 1958; Strangers in the Land: Social Relations in the Status Gap, 1959; co-author: Varieties of Inauthenticity, Psychologically Viewed, 1954; book rev ed, The Sociological Quarterly, since 1960. Spec interest: race and minority relations. Home: 1539 Portland Ave, St Paul, Minn. Office: Macalester Coll, St Paul, Minn.

RINGEL, Herbert A, US, attorney; b. Georgetown, SC, Dec 6, 1908; s. Max and Minnie (Fertel); LLB, U Ga, 1930; m. 1st, Sara Finkelstein (decd); c: Malcolm, Harry, Eleanor; m. 2nd, Martha Strassburger, Sep 7, 1961; step-children: Patricia Lemer, William Spear. Mem, law firm, Smith, Cohen, Ringel, Kohler, Martin and Lowe, since 1945; fmr: with Ringel and Ringel; atty, Brunswick Housing Auth; Glynn Co prosecuting atty, 1936-42; secy, gen counsel, mem bd, Fidelity Fed Savings and Loan Assn, Atlanta, Ga; appd, Spec US Atty, prosecuting war housing frauds, spec asst, both 1947-52. Lt, USN, staff, Admiral Nimitz. Fmr: pres: Gate City lodge, B'nai B'rith; Social Services Index; vice-chmn, bd, J Childrens Service; pres, AJComm; chmn, Fire Prevention Comm; chmn, Leg Comm of Active Voters; pres, The Temple, 1966-68; mem: adv council on naval affairs, Sixth Naval Dist; Atlanta, Ga, and Amer Bar Assns; Amer Judicature Soc; Intl Assn of Ins Counsel; Phi Epsilon Pi; clubs: Standard; Commerce; Lawyers; Optimist; Kiwanis; Masons; Old War Horse Lawyers. Recipient: Navy Unit Citation. Home: 3707 Randall Mill Rd NW, Atlanta, Ga. Office: First Natl Bank Bldg, Atlanta, Ga.

RINOTT, Chanoch, Isr, educator; b. Tarnow, Pol, Mar 1, 1911; s. Jacob and Anna (Weinfeld) Reinhold; in Isr since 1934; att: U Berlin, 1932; U Vienna, 1933; MA, Heb U, Jerusalem, 1939, PhD, 1950; m. Shulamit Gruen, 1935; c: Miriam, Joseph. Dir, Cen for J Educ in the Diaspora, Heb U, Jerusalem, since 1968; org, tchr, First Youth Aliyah, 1934-36; educ sup, JA, Youth Aliyah for Pal, 1939-50, dir of educ, 1950-60; dir gen, Min of Educ and Culture, 1960-67. Author: Joseph Salvador, Life and Views, 1944; Youth Builds its Home, 1953. Contbr to educ and hist jours. Home: 56 Gaza Rd, Jerusalem, Isr. Office: Heb U, Jerusalem, Isr.

RIPSTEIN, Charles B, US, surgeon, educator; b. Winnipeg, Can, Dec 13, 1913; s. Hyman and Bertha (Benjamin); in US since 1949; BA, U Ariz, 1936; MD, McGill U, 1940, dipl, surg, 1949; m. Barbara Adelman, Dec 26, 1950; c: Ellen, Linda. Dir, surg services: Brookdale Hosp Cen; Beth-El Hosp, Bklyn; cons surg: Bx VA and Leb Hosps; Bx Munic Hosp Cen, all since 1958; Misericordia Hosp since 1954; prof, clinical surg, thoracic, Albert Einstein Coll of Med, Yeshiva U, since 1958, fac mem since 1954; visiting prof of surg, U Tel Aviv, since 1969; prof, SUNY Coll of Med, 1952-55; dir, surg services, dept experimental surg, Maimonides Hosp, 1949-55; lectr, f experimental surg, McGill U, 1949. RCAF, 1942-45. FRCS; FACS; dipl: Amer Bd Surg, 1950; Bd Thoracic Surg, 1952; mem: AMA; AAAS; Can Med Assn; Soc of U Surgs. Contbr to med jours. Home: 15 Birch St, Great Neck, NY. Office: Brookdale Hosp Center, Linden Blvd and Rockaway Park, Brooklyn, NY.

RISEMAN, Joseph E F, US, physician, educator; b. Boston, Mass, Aug 31, 1903; s. Joel and Rose (Berger); BS, Harvard U, 1924, MD, 1929; m. Rose Cooper, Dec 20, 1927; c: Barbara Hamburg, Donna Gould. Pvt practice since 1933; asst clinical prof, Harvard Med Sch, since 1952; visiting phys, Beth Isr Hosp, Boston, since 1946; instr in med, Tufts U, 1938-56. Mem: AMA; Mass Med Soc; Amer Soc for Clinical Investigation; AHA; NE Heart Assn; Law Sci Inst. Author: P-Q-R-S-T, 5th ed, 1968; Electrocardiogram Clinics, 1958; Cardiac Arrhymias, 1963. Contbr to med jours. Hobbies: cabinet making, apparatus designing. Home and office: 16 Hawes St, Brookline, Mass.

RITOV, Israel, Isr, organization exec; b. Ossipovice, Russ, Apr 5, 1895; s. Jaacov and Elca (Solowajchic); in Isr since 1932; att: Lidda Yeshiva and Ekaterinoslav U; m. Genia Lashkevich; c: Yaakov. Chmn, bd dirs: KH, JNF, Isr; mem, bd dirs: World KH; fmr dir, Cen Pal Off, Warsaw, Pol; mem: Cooperative Cen of Isr; council, Histadrut; cen comm, Ha'avoda; Zionist Actions Comm; presidium, World Fed Pol Jewry; delg to WZCs. Author: Orakkim beToldoth Zerre Zion-CS; Co-operazia Yatzranit uSherutit; Herzl Berger; ed: Shitituf, Isr; contbr to Heb and Yiddish press. Home: 62 Reiness St, Tel Aviv, Isr. Office: Cooperative Cen, 24 Haarba'a St, Tel Aviv, Isr.

RITTENBAUM, Max, US, business exec; b. Atlanta, Ga, Mar 4, 1914; s. Julius and Annie Minsk; BBA, Emory U, 1935; m. Miriam Orenstein, Jan 18, 1942; c: Ellen Rosenthal, Jeffrey, Alan. Partner, Rittenbaum Bros, since 1942. Maj, USAF, 1942-45. Vice-pres, Atlanta JWF; mem: exec comm, Emory U Bd of Visitors; bd, J Home; bd overseers, JTSA; bd, Natl CJFWF; Ahavath Achim Syn, past pres; pres, Mayfair Club; fmr: pres, Gate City Lodge, B'nai B'rith; chmn: JWF Drive; Isr Bonds. Recipient: B'nai B'rith Man-of-the-Year, 1962; Ben Massell award, Isr Bond Org, Atlanta, 1962. Home: 1886 River Forest Rd, Atlanta, Ga. Office: 691 Houston St NE, Atlanta, Ga.

RITTENBERG, Benjamin B, US, pediatrican; b. Phila, Pa, Feb 28, 1897; s. Ephraim and Anna (Reines); MD, U of Pa, 1921; m. Beatrice Godet, Feb 4, 1923; c: Naomi Barsky, Frances Fish. Pvt practice since 1922; mem, courtesy staff: Albert Einstein Med Center, since 1930, asso ped, 1922-30; Childrens Hosp of Phila, since 1950; chief ped, St Agnes Hosp, 1930-38. Examining phys, WW II. F: Amer Acad Ped; AMA; vice-pres, Phila chap, Amer Friends Heb U; mem: bd trustees, Phi Lambda Kappa, since 1927, past chmn: student loan fund, bd trustees; Phila Co Med and Ped Soc; Pa State Med Soc; ZOA; B'nai B'rith; B'rith Shalom; AJComm; AJCong; Amer J League for Isr; Amer Isr Soc; Har Zion Temple, mem, bd dirs, since 1954; Natl Fed J Men's Clubs, Inc; Amer J Phys Comm; United Fund; Fed J Charities; JTSA; fmr: pres, mem, exec bd, Amer Phys F; chmn, profsl group, Allied J Appeal, also mem, adv comm. Contbr to profsl jours. Recipient, Selective Service medal, 1945. Home: Trianon Apts, Bala Cynwyd, Pa. Office: 4401 Conshohocken Ave, Philadelphia, Pa.

RITTENBERG, Caspar W, US, business exec; b. NYC, Sep 8, 1898; s. Isaac and Annie (Marks); att Yale U, 1918; m. Helene Eisner; c: Richard, Anne Gumley. Partner, Rittenberg Bros, 1919-54; pres, Stonekirk Worsted Co, 1937-53; treas and dir, S Stein & Co, 1941-53. US Navy, WW I. Asso chmn, bd of trustees, Home for Aged and Infirm Hebs of NY, chmn of bd, 1958-61; chmn, functional comm on aged, FJP, NY, 1960-64, trustee since 1953; chmn, retirement planning comm, mem, bd dirs, Community Council of Greater NY, mem, citizens comm on aged; club: Sunningdale Country, pres since 1968. Home: 417 Park Ave, New York, NY.

RITTER, Joseph A, US, pediatrician, educator; b. Lask, Pol, Sep 20, 1903; s. Charles and Nettie (Klein); in US since 1905; BA, U of Pa, 1925, MD, 1928; m. Grace Coyle, 1938; c: Barbara, Michael. Prof, clinical ped, grad sch, U of Pa, since 1959; Schs of Med, U of Pa, since 1961, fac mem since 1948; chmn, ped div, U of Pa-Phila Gen Hosp, since 1936, on staff since 1932; chief, ped dept: Grad Hosp of Pa, since 1942; Wills Eye Hosp, since 1950; fmr: chief of ped: St Agnes Hosp; St Joseph's Hosp; Belmont Hosp. Dipl, Amer Bd of Ped; f: Amer Acad of Ped; Coll of Phys of Phila. Mem: AAAS, AHA; AMA; Phila Ped Soc; Phila Endocrine Soc; Phi Lambda Kappa; Sigma Xi; Alpha Epsilon Pi; Har Zion Temple. Contbr to med jours. Hobbies: cello, fishing, carpentry. Home: 1034 Bryn Mawr Ave, Penn Valley, Narberth, Pa. Office: Phila Gen Hosp, 34th and Civic Ave, Philadelphia, Pa.

RIVKIN, Donald H, US, attorney; b. Davenport, Ia, May 24, 1924; BA, magna cum laude, Yale U, 1948. LLB, 1952; BA, Jurisprudence, Oxford U, 1950, MA, 1953; m. Lois Herman, Dec 29, 1953; three children. Mem, Busby, Rivkin, Sherman & Levy, since 1959; asso: Cravath, Swaine & Moore, 1952-56; Solinger and Gordon, 1956-59. Dir, counsel, Opr Crossroads Afr, Inc; mem: Natl Council Amer Importers; Amer Soc Intl Law; Yale Law Sch Assn; Reform Ind Dems; interreligious coop comm, ADL; Assn of Bar, NYC; Assn Customs Bar; Commerce and Ind Assn; Fr-Amer C of C; British-Amer C of C; Phi Delta Phi; Barristers' Union; Delta Sigma Rho; Phi Beta Kappa; fmr: US repr, comm of experts, Intl Inst for Unification of Pvt Law, Rome; cons, Fund for the Rep, Study of Political Process; pres, Oxford Amer Assn; clubs: Yale, NYC; Federal, Wash, DC. Contbr to law publs. Recipient: Rhodes Scholarship; Thatcher Prize; Ten Eyck Prize;

De Forest Prize; Order of Coif, all Yale U. Home: 16 W 77 St, New York, NY. Office: 750 Third Ave, New York, NY.

RIVKIN, Ellis, US, educator; b. Baltimore, Md, Sep 7, 1918; s. Moses and Beatrice (Leibowitz); BA, Johns Hopkins U, 1941; PhD, 1946; BHL, Baltimore Heb Coll, 1944; m. Zelda Zafren, June 29, 1941; c: Roslyn, Sharon. Adolph S Ochs prof, J hist, HUC-JIR, since 1965, fac mem since 1949; Cyrus Adler postdoc research f, Dropsie Coll, 1946-49; instr, J hist, Gratz Coll, 1946-49; John Simon Guggenheim f, The Hague, 1962-63; visiting prof, Antioch Coll, 1963. Chmn, comm on hist, CCAR; publ comm, J Publ Soc of Amer; mem: Amer Hist Assn; Medieval Acad of Amer; Econ Hist Assn; AAAS; Amer Acad Political and Social Sci; Renaissance Soc of Amer; Acad of Political Sci; Amer J Hist Soc; Soc Bibl Lit and Exegesis; Phi Beta Kappa. Author: Leon da Modena and the Kol Sakhal, 1952; ed bd: HUC Annual; Studies in J Bibliography and Booklore; J Apocryphal Lit, Dropsie Coll, 1968; contbr to hist and J publs. Recipient: Amer Phil Soc grant, 1965. Hobbies: music, art. Home: 7610 Reading Rd, Cincinnati, O. Office: HUC, Clifton Ave, Cincinnati, O.

RIVLIN, Allen, US, screenwriter, producer, publicist; b. Hayward, Wis, Nov 20, 1903; s. Samuel and Rose (Rosenberg); BA, U of Minn, 1925; m. Laura Hornickel, 1952. Freelance writer-produc, since 1931; TV writer and produc, since 1957; newspaper staffs, Chgo and Minneapolis, 1925-27; advt, publicity, NY, Chgo, Hollywood, 1927-31; story exec, MGM, 1955-56. Head, motion picture off, spec services div, US War Dept, 1942-44. Author: Knock on Wood, 1935; screenplays: Joe Smith, American, 1941; The Farmer's Daughter, 1947; Grounds for Marriage, 1950; Timberjack, 1954; The Eternal Sea, 1954; The Man from Texas, 1955; TV plays: Blue Indigo, 1957; The Invisible Man, 1958; Mean Mountain, 1959; Blueprint for Biography, 1959; The Troubleshooters, 1959; The Nobel Prize series, 1963; wrote, directed and produced radio and film documentaries. Dir: Screen Writers Guild, 1946-52; J Film Adv Comm, since 1962; pres: Motion Picture Ind Council, 1951-52; screen br, W div, Writers Guild of Amer, since 1963; co-found, Intl Writers Guild; natl dir, comm for the arts, Dem Natl Comm, 1948-62; PR dir, entertainment producer, Dem Natl Conv, 1960; cons ed, The Octagonian, Sigma Alpha Mu; ed, Writers Guild of Amer newsletter, since 1965. Recipient: awards: Books and Authors, 1954; Photoplay Mag; Look Mag; Box Office Blue Ribbon, all 1948; Valentine Davis, 1963. Home: 8980 Lloyd Pl, Los Angeles, Cal. Office: Box 1644, Beverly Hills, Cal.

RIVLIN, Asher Eliezer, Isr, educator; b. Jerusalem, Isr, Aug 29, 1921; s. Zalman and Hadassa; tchr dipl, Mizrachi Tchr Training Coll, Jerusalem, 1941; MA, Heb U, Jerusalem, 1952; PhD, Cape Town U, S Afr, 1963; m. Tmima Agranowich, June 26, 1945; c: Shai. Head, dept of pedagogy, Tel Aviv U, since 1968, sr lectr, since 1966; dir, dept educ and culture, Netanya ,since 1953; dir, Cape Bd J Educ, S Afr, 1960-64. Served: sgt, Pal units, Brit Army; capt: J Brig; IDF, 1942-48. Author: Achad Ha'am uMitnagdav baSifrut, 1955; Handbook and Syllabus for Hebrew Teachers, 1962; Yom-Yom, 1963; Pulmos baShira, 1966; Mafte'ach Didakti leHora'at haShir, 1968; Mafte'ach Didakti leHora'at haSipur, 1969. Mem, mgmt comm, Isr Bc Auth. Contbr to profsl jours. Recipient: Klausner award, Heb U, 1953. Hobby: classical and synagogue music. Home: 39 Ussishkin St, Netanya, Isr. Office: Tel Aviv U, Tel Aviv, Isr.

RIVLIN, Benjamin, US, business exec; b. NYC, Sep 20, 1898; s. Samuel and Jennie (Feldman); BS, CCNY, 1919; postgrad studies: Columbia U; New Sch for Social Research; CCNY; m. Lena Levy, Dec 21, 1922; c: Edward, Lewis. Chmn, Arista Inds Inc, pres since 1959; pres, Arista Oil Produc Corp, since 1930; treas, bd mem, Isr Devl Corp, since 1954. Fmr bd mem, Amer Friends Heb U, NYC; Citizens Union; ACLU; Amer Assn for the UN; Drug Chem and Allied Trades. Hobbies: gardening, photography, theater, music. Home: 300 E 57 St, New York, NY. Office: 122 E 42 St, New York, NY.

RIVLIN, David Zvi, Isr, diplomat; b. Jerusalem, Oct 16, 1923; s. Zalman and Hadassa; att Heb U, Jerusalem, 1947-48; BA, London U, 1955; m. Ruth Hourvitz, Aug 23, 1949; c: Avital, Gilad. Dir, press relations, spokesman, Isr Fgn Min, Jerusalem, since 1968; fmr: Isr Consul Gen: to Can; NYC; Phila, all 1958-65; dir progs, Army Radio Sta, 1955-58; Jerusalem corresp, Davar, daily. Served: Haganah; J Brigade, Brit Army, 1942-46; capt, IDF. Fmr: JNF emissary for youth and educ to Gt Brit; secy, Jerusalem Journalists Assn. Contbr to Isr radio and press. Home: 13 Rabinovits St, Jerusalem, Isr. Office: Romema, Jerusalem, Isr.

RIVLIN, Haim Hilel, Isr, organization exec; b. Jerusalem, Isr, Oct 16, 1919; s. Zalman and Hadassa; att: Tchrs Sem, Jerusalem; Heb U; m. Esther Benjamini, Feb 26, 1954; c: Ehud, Yaron. Dir gen, Friends of Heb U Assn; fmr: tchr, lectr, schs, youth comms, 1942-45; dir, Brit-Isr Investment, London, 1950-51; owner, PR office, 1954-67. Mem: B'nai B'rith; Isr Soc of Eds of Periodicals; PR Assn of Isr; political comm, Lib Party; mgmt, Histadrut; fmr: co-found, Ben- A Youth Org; educ adv, Fed of Zionist Youth in Gt Brit; chmn, publicity dept, Lib Party. Author: A History of the First Settlers in Eretz Israel, 1947; contbr to publications. Home: 10 Zicharon Yaacov St, Tel Aviv, Isr. Office: 21 Hess St, Tel Aviv, Isr.

RIVLIN, Harry N, US, educator; b. NYC, Dec 30, 1904; s. Samuel and Jennie (Feldman); BSS, CCNY, 1924; MA, Columbia U, 1926, PhD, 1930; m. Eugenie Graciany, Aug 23, 1928; c: Richard, Paula Glickman. Dean, Sch of Educ, Fordham U, since 1966; tchr, public schs, Bklyn, 1924-30; asst prof, educ, CCNY, 1930-39; asst prof, educ, Queens Coll, 1939-57; dean, tchr, educ, CUNY, 1957-66. Pres: educ, psych div, Amer Psych Assn, 1956-57; educ, psych sect, Natl Soc of Coll Tchrs of Educ, 1952-54, natl commn on tchr educ and profsl standards, 1959-62; chmn, Tchrs Exams Adv Bd, Educ Testing Service, 1968-70. Author: Education for Adjustment, 1936, 2nd ed, 1961; Growth, Teaching and Learning, 1957; co-author: Teaching Adolescents in Secondary Schools, 1948; ed: Ency of Modern Education, 1943; The First Years in College, 1965. Home: 205 West End Ave, New York, NY. Office: 302 Broadway, New York, NY.

RIVLIN, Helen A B, US, educator, author; b. Rochester, NY, Apr 9, 1918; d. William and Sarah (Bernstein) Bloom; BA, hons, U Rochester, 1949; AM, Radcliffe Coll, 1950; DPhil (Oxon), Oxford U, Eng, 1953; m. Ephraim Rivlin (div). Professor of ME, Islamic Hist, SUNY, Binghamton, NY, since 1969; asso prof, ME, Islamic Hist, U Md, 1957-69; visiting asst prof, Harvard Summer Sch, 1962; visiting asso prof, SUNY, 1968-69; research, Cen for ME Studies, Harvard U, 1954-56, research asso, 1956-57. Mem: ME Studies Assn; AAUP; Amer Hist Assn; ME Inst; Amer Oriental Soc; Phi Beta Kappa. Author: The Agricultural Policy of Muhammad Ali in Egypt, 1961; contbr: to profsl and gen jours; Ency of Islam. Recipient: f, Rockefeller Found; Social Sci Research Found f; Alice Mary Longfellow f, Radcliffe Coll; Margaret E Maltby f, Amer Assn of U Women; grants from Amer Council of Learned Socs; Women's Scholarship Assn; Amer Phil Soc; Anthony Eden Fund; Xerox Corp; Gen Research Bd, U of Md. Spec interest: Islamic art. Home: 3141 Cornell Ave, Vestal, NY. Office: SUNY, Binghamton, NY.

RIVLIN, Jonathan, Isr, business exec; b. Bradford, Eng, Nov 19, 1932; s. Joseph and Fanny (Hyman); in Isr since 1961; BSc, Manchester U, 1955; m. Joyce Linstill, Aug 17, 1959; c: Hillel, Asaph, Shlomit. Mgn dir, Shaldag Electronics Ltd, since 1969; fmr: head, microwave lab, Elta Elec Ind, 1962-69. Served Brit Army, 1955-57. Mem, Inst of Elec and Electronics Engrs. Recipient: IDF prize, Min of Defense, 1967. Home: 8 Hanavat Selet, Ramat Hasharon, Isr. Office: POB 76, Ramat Hasharon, Isr.

RIVLIN, Moshe, Isr, organization exec; b. Jerusalem, Jan 16, 1925; s. Yitzhak and Esther; att: Mizrachi Tchrs Coll, Jerusalem; Aluma Inst for J Studies; Sch of Political Sci; m. Ruth Arbati; c: Revital, Sarit. Dir gen, JA, since 1960, with org since 1958; Consul of Isr, NYC, 1952-58. Haganah, 1943-47; maj, IDF, 1948-51. Home: 34 Hapalmach St, Jerusalem, Isr. Office: JA, Jerusalem, Isr.

RIVNAY, Ezekiel, Isr, scientist; b. Zicharon Yaakov, Isr, Apr 18, 1899; s. Benjamin and Lea (Courland) Ribniker; BSc, MSc, Mass Agric Coll, 1923-28; PhD, U of Mass, 1931; m. Doucie Levine, Jan, 1948; c: Benjamin, Gershon. Ret since 1964; fmr: head entomology dept, Volcani Inst of Agric Research, 1960-64; entomologist, Agric Res Sta, Rehovot, 1948-60; jr asso entomologist, JAP Agric Experimental Sta, 1931-48. Author: Field Crop Pests in the Near East, 1962; Biological Control of Pests in Israel, 1968; contbr to profsl jours. Home: 11 Alcali St, Rehovot, Isr.

RIWCHUN, Ann S, US, communal worker; b. Leroy, NY, May 3, 1904; d. Harry and Jennie (Parness) Spiller; att U Rochester, NY; m. Meyer Riwchun, Aug 28, 1928. Pres, bd of dirs, Buffalo Assn for the Blind, since 1961; mem, natl bd, JDC; chmn, Nurses Aide Blood Prog Service; natl bd mem, United J Fund; women's comm, Buffalo Philharmonic Orch, pres, 1951-52; mem, natl bd, women's div, UJA, 1956-62. chmn, Buffalo br, 1955. Recipient: woman-of-the-year award, Buffalo Philharmonic Orch Soc, 1956. Spec interest: transcribing Braille. Home: 33 Gates Circle, Buffalo, NY.

RIWCHUN, Meyer H, US, physician, ophthalmologist, educator; b. Buffalo, NY, June 28, 1903; s. Bernard and Edna (Rosenzweig); MD, U Buffalo, 1927; m. Ann Spiller, Aug 28, 1928. Pvt practice since 1929; clinical prof, ophthal, U Buffalo Med Sch, since 1961; mem fac since 1930; cons, ophthal: Vet Hosp, since 1949; Wellaufer Clinic and Buffalo Eye & Ear Hosp, both since 1950; J Old Folks Home, since 1950; att: Deaconess Hosp, since 1930; Buffalo Gen Hosp, since 1959, head dept, since 1960; Children's Hosp since 1942, head dept since 1961. Lt col, US Army MC, 1942-46. Pres: Maimonides Med Soc, 1936-38; Buffalo Eye and Ear Hosp; Buffalo Ophthal Soc, 1940-44; chmn, speakers bur, Buffalo Sight Conservation Soc, 1936-39. Dipl, Amer Bd of Ophthal; f: Amer Coll of Surgs; Amer Acad of Ophthal and Otolaryngology. Mem: AMA; NY State and Erie Co Med Socs; Buffalo Acad of Med; Temple Beth Zion. Contbr to profsl jours. Hobbies: golf, photography. Home: 33 Gates Circle, Buffalo, NY. Office: 191 North St, Buffalo, NY.

ROBBINS, Ira S, US, attorney, housing consultant, public official; b. NYC, June 12, 1900; s. Benjamin and Rebecca (Salwen); BA, Columbia U, 1920, LLB, 1922; m. 2nd, Janet McCloskey, June 20, 1952; c: by 1st m: James, Alice Steinberg. Mem, NYC Housing Auth, since 1958, vice-chmn, 1959-64, 1967-69; counsel: NY State Bd Housing, 1934-39; United Neighborhood Stores, 1936-58; cons, urbanism comm, Natl Resources Comm, 1935-36; spec asst atty gen, NY State, 1938-42; dep commn, State Commn of Housing, 1944-45; staff mem since 1939; counsel, comm on fair rent leg, Natl Defense Adv Comm, 1941; cons, Natl Housing Agcy, 1945-46; exec vice-pres, Citizens Housing and Planning Council of NY, 1948-58; mem, Mayor's Comm for Better Housing, 1954-55; cons, Gov's Conf on Problems of the Aging, 1955; mem: housing adv comm, State Commn Against Discrimination, 1955-59; Gov's Task Force on Middle Income Housing, 1959. Mem: bd govs, Natl Assn Housing and Redevl Officials, since 1958, past pres; bd, Natl Housing Conf, past pres and chmn; bd dirs: Found for Coop Housing, past vice-chmn; Citizens Comm for Children of NYC, bd of dirs; Natl Comm Against Discrimination in Housing, past treas; adv council, NYU Inst in Real Estate, since 1969; hon life mem, Amer Soc of Planning Officials; fmr: vice-pres, counsel, United Neighborhood Houses of NY; pres, Queensview Housing Coop; mem: wfr adv comm, NY J League; natl bd, ADA; exec bd, NY State Comm Against Discrimination in Housing; exec comm, Citizens' Union; Natl Comm on the Aging. Contbr to profsl jours. Recipient, Public Service Award of Merit, Civil Service Leader. Home: 160 E 89 St, New York, NY. Office: 250 Broadway, New York, NY.

ROBBINS, Jerome, US, choreographer, director; b. NYC, Oct 11, 1918; s. Harry and Lena (Rips) Rabinowitz; att NYU; married. Choreographer and dir: West Side Story, 1957 and 1960, co-dir; Gypsy, 1959; Fiddler on the Roof, 1964; The Exception and the Rule, 1968; choreographer: On the Town, 1944; Billion Dollar Baby, 1945; High Button Shoes, 1947; Miss Liberty, 1949; Call Me Madam, 1950; Two's Company, 1952; Bells Are Ringing, 1956; Oh Dad, Poor Dad, Mama's Hung You in the Closet and I'm Feeling So Sad, 1962; dir, plays: Pajama Game; Peter Pan; producer, Funny Girl; co-producer, Mother Courage and Her Children, 1963; choreographer: for ballet, including own co, Ballet: USA; film, The King and I, 1956; TV produc: Peter Pan, 1956, 1960; Ford 50th Anniversary Show, 1953. Mem, theater adv group, Hopkins Cen, Dartmouth Coll. Recipient: Emmy TV Award, for Peter Pan, 1956; Evening Standard Award, for West Side Story, 1959; Donaldson Award, for: Billion Dollar Baby, 1946; High Button Shoes, 1951; NY Drama Critics Award, for The King and I, 1951. Address: 154 E 74 St, New York, NY.

ROBBINS, Samuel Moses, US, dentist; b. Worcester, Mass, June 12, 1902; s. Louis and Sarah (Davidson) Rabinowitz; DDS, Case W Reserve U, 1924; post-grad: NYU; Tufts U; U of Pa; Boston U; U of Ill; cen for continuation of study, U

of Minn; FAGD, 1963; m. Esther Weinberg, July 13, 1924 (decd); c: Allan, Howard. Pvt practice since 1924; bd cert, endodontics; chief cons, Hillcrest Hosp, Cleveland, since 1965. Mem: bd, Park Syn, Cleveland Hgts; comm, Forum Found, Cleveland; photography comm, Acad of Med of Cleveland; life, Amer Dent Assn; O Dent Assn; Cleveland Dent Soc; Amer Pharm Assn; Acad of Med, Cleveland; Amer Soc Dent for Children, past pres, Cleveland chap; Amer Assn Endodontists; Amer Acad Oral Med, past pres, O State chap; Amer Acad Gen Dent; Cleveland Comm, JTSA, NYC; Amer Technion Soc, found, Cleveland chap, 1st pres; Cleveland comm, Weizmann Inst; comm, Heb U; fund comm, Natl J Hosp, Denver, Colo; bd, J Shelter Home, Cleveland; bd, J Relief Soc; AAAS; Fed Dentaire Intl; O Mh Assn; fund comm, Mt Sinai Hosp; life, Alpha Omega, past treas; oldest mem, JWF raising comm; Jt Distribution Comm; found: Cleveland chap, Amer Pharm Assn; Park Syn, past mem bd; Hadassah Sch of Dent Med, Heb U; Sch of Pharm, Heb U; Esther and Samuel M Robbins Student Loan Fund at Hadassah; Case W Reserve U Dent Alumni Assn; Cleveland Health Mus; fmr: pres, Amer Technion Soc; mem, repr assembly, Cleveland Wfr Fed; clubs: Cleveland Playhouse; City, Cleveland, trustee. Contbr to dent jours. Recipient: plaque for 20 yrs service, 25th anniversary Eternal Light; JWF Award, JTSA, NYC; Plaque, Amer Soc Dent for Children. Spec interests: clinical photography, fund-raising. Home: 3333 Warrensville Cen Rd, Shaker Heights, O. Office: 1024 Rose Bldg, 2060 E 9, Cleveland, O.

ROBBINS, Tamar, Isr, actress; b. Odessa, Russ, Nov 4, 1900; d. Aharon and Yehudit (Heller) Rabinovitch; in Isr since 1928; studied under Stanislawski, Moscow, 1920-26; att Drama Sch, Tel Aviv; m. Menakhem Benjamini (decd). Actress, Habimah Theater, since 1917; major roles: Hadibuk; Twelfth Night; Adon Biberman; Amch; Kashe Lihiyot Yehudi; Mirale Efrat; Tuvia Haholev; Maturity; My Son, the Minister; Hayehudi Suss; The Sacred Flame; Fathers and Sons; Hamlet; Barbara Blumberg; Hedva Veani; Shahor Al Gabei; Lavan; Uncle Vanya; Cherry Orchard; War and Peace; The Living Dead; Mademoiselle; My Fair Lady; Separate Tables. Mem, Milo Club. Recipient: Stage Art award, Tel Aviv Munic, 1960. Home: 24 Dov Hos St, Tel Aviv, Isr. Office: Habimah Theater, Tel Aviv, Isr.

ROBERTS, Nathan L, US, publicist; b. NYC, July 27, 1915; s. Labe and Minnie (Tobman) Levine; att CCNY, 1934-35; m. Lois Maker, May 8, 1948; c: Susan Greenspan. Dir, PR, devl dept, JTSA; ed, The Sentinel, PR staff, JWB, 1941-42; UJA PR staff, 1946-5l, asst PR dir, 1951-56; dir, PR: Combined Campaign for Amer Reform Judaism, 1957-62; devl fund for Amer Judaism, 1959-62; dir, public info, CCAR, 1961-63; publicist, UJA, natl, 1962-64; cons, J Affairs, Mayor of NYC, 1964; PR staff, AJCong, 1964-68; dir devl, Dropsie Coll, 1968-69; dir, PR, Amer Technion Soc, 1969. USAF, 1942-45. Mem, exec comm, Amer J PR Soc, since 1963, pres, 1961-62. Home: 117 E 71 St, New York, NY.

ROBERTS, Samuel J, US, jurist; b. Bklyn, NY, Feb 18, 1907; s. Jacob and Anna (Wexler); BS, U of Pa, 1928, LLB, 1931; m. Helene Blumberg, Dec 14, 1934 (decd); c: Barbara Pollock. Asso justice, Supr Court of Pa, since 1963; fmr: asst dist atty; spec dep to atty gen, Commonwealth of Pa; pres, judge, Orphans Court of Erie Co, 1952-63. Served, USN, WW II. Mem: bd, Hamot Hosp, since 1954; Gannon Coll, since 1956; St Vincent's Hosp, since 1957; United Fund. Home: 4107 State St, Erie, Pa. Office: Supreme Court of Pennsylvania, Erie, Pa.

ROBINSON, Antonia, Can, communal leader; b. Gentilly, Que, Can, May 7, 1895; d. Wolf and Janet (Rosenbaum) Seiden; BA, McGill U, 1917; m. Benjamin Robinson, June 24, 1923; c: David, Jonathan, Elaine Waddington. Pres, Intl Council of J Women, 1957-63; pres, Natl Council of J Women of Can, 1953-55. Mem: Intl Alliance of Hosp Volunteers; bd trustees, YM-YWHA; Dominion council; CJCong; bd dirs, Montreal Art Gallery, 1954; fmr mem, bd dirs: Heb U, 1954; J Comty Services; clubs: Women's Can, vice-pres, 1956-58; Themis; Elmridge Golf and Country. Home: 36 Forden Crescent, Westmount, Que, Can.

ROBINSON, Calvin, US, attorney, educator; b. Lowell, Mass, Sept 18, 1905; s. Julius and Rose (Miller); LLB, Northeastern U Law Sch, 1926; LLM, Boston U Law Sch, 1927; m. Sylvia Berman, Aug 2, 1936; c: Majorie, Richard. Pvt practice since 1927; found, dir, Robinson Bar Review, Boston, since 1929; lectr, practical psych, since 1930. Found, treas, J Comty

Chest, Lowell, 1941. Mem: Amer, Mass, and Lowell Bar Assns; Amer Judicature Soc; Bigelow Assn of Masters of Law; Boston U Law Sch Assn; Acad of Political Sci; B'nai B'rith; ZOA; AJCong. Author: Give Yourself One Day, 1952, 1959. Contbr to mags. Home: 193 Lincoln Pkwy, Lowell, Mass. Office: 174 Central St, Lowell, Mass.

ROBINSON, Benjamin, Can, jurist; b. Kovel, Russ, Nov 26, 1892; BA, BCL, QC; m. Antonia Seiden, June 24, 1923; c: David, Jonathan, Elaine Waddington. Ret, 1967; fmr judge, Superior Court, Dist of Montreal, Que, Can. Home: 36 Forden Crescent, Westmount, Que, Can.

ROBINSON, David, US, radiologist; b. Savannah, Ga, Mar 20, 1915; s. Leon and Leah (Shoelson); BS, U of Ga, 1939, MD, 1942; m. Rebecca Drucker, Dec 26, 1940; c: Roslyn, Brenda, Howard. Pvt practice since 1947; chief of radiology: USPHS Hosp, since 1947; Warren A Candler Hosp, since 1958, chief of staff, 1956-57; cons: US Army Hosp, Ft Stewart, Ga; Telfair Hosp. US Army MC, 1943-46. Pres: Radiological Soc, 1966-67; First Dist Med Soc, 1965; dipl, Amer Bd of Radiology, 1947; f, Amer Coll of Radiology; mem: N Amer and Ga Radiological Soc, secy-treas, 1962-63; Amer Roentgen Ray Soc; AMA; Med Assn of Ga; Amer Med Writers Assn; Ga Med Soc; B'nai B'rith; ZOA; Amer Legion; JWV; Masons; Shriners; Alpha Omega Alpha; Exch Club. Contbr to med jours. Hobbies: golf, fishing, woodwork. Home: 4745 Fairfax Dr, Savannah, Ga. Office: 9 Med Arts Cen, Savannah, Ga.

ROBINSON, Dove Myer, NZ, civil servant; b. Sheffield, Eng, June 15, 1901; s. Moss and Ida (Brown); in NZ since 1914; att HS, Manchester, Eng; Devonport Sch, Auckland; m. June 15, 1959; c: Jennifer. Mayor of Auckland, 1959-1965, re-elected, 1968; chmn, Rapid Transit Comm, Auckland Regional Auth, since 1968; pres, Festival Soc; mem: U Council; Regional Auth, all of Auckland, since 1968; chmn, mgn dir, Childswear Ltd, 1940-60. Past chmn: Regional Auth Establishment comm; Metrop Drainage Bd; past mem: City Council; Educ bd; U coll council, all Auckland. Prin contrib, introduced true mass production of children's clothing to NZ. Author: Passenger Transport in Auckland, 1969; contbr to profsl and munic publications. Mem: Royal Soc of Health; NZ Inst of Mgmt; hon mem, Inst of Sewage Purification; pres, Rugby League. Hobbies: boating, fishing, golf, photography. Home: 12A Aldred Rd, Remuera, Auckland, NZ. Office: Civic Admn Bldg, Auckland, NZ.

ROBINSON, Edward G, US, actor; b. Bucharest, Rumania, Dec 12, 1893; s. Morris and Sarah (Goldenberg); in US since 1903; att: CCNY, 1910-12; Columbia U; Amer Acad Dramatic Arts; m. Gladys Cassell, Jan 21, 1927 (div); c: Edward; m. 2nd, Jane Bodenheimer, Jan 16, 1958. Actor, in motion pictures since 1923; leading roles in films include: Little Caesar, 1930; The Little Giant, 1933; Barbary Coast, 1935; Kid Galahad, 1937; Amazing Dr Clitterhouse, 1938; Dr Ehrlich's Magic Bullet, 1940; A Dispatch from Reuters, 1940; The Sea Wolf, 1941; Key Largo, 1948; Ten Commandments, 1956; My Geisha, 1962; debut in silent film, 1923; first sound film, 1929; radio: orig, starred in Big Town series, CBS, 1937-42; stage: since 1916, Darkness at Noon, 1951-52. USN, WW I; with OWI, WW II, broadcast to Eur underground in nine languages. Mem: Actors Equity Assn; Amer Fed Radio-TV Artists; clubs: Lambs, NYC; Masquers, Hollywood, Cal. Recipient: Townsend Harris medal, Alumni Assn CCNY, 1936; Chevalier Legion d'Honneur, Fr, 1952; Eleanor Roosevelt Humanitarian award, 1963. Hobbies: languages, music, pipes, painting, traveling, collecting art. Home: 910 Rexford Dr, Beverly Hills, Cal. Office: c/o William Morris Agcy, 151 El Camino Dr, Beverly Hills, Cal.

ROBINSON, Joel D, US, educator; b. Bklyn, NY, Aug 23, 1925; s. Samuel and Lenora (Miller); BS, Stevens Inst, Hoboken, 1944; m. Barbara Pollitz; c: George, Marc, Stacey. Exec vice-pres, Manhattan Sch of Printing, since 1955; lectr, Amer Mgmt Assn, since 1963; design eng, IBM, 1948-59. Pres, Bklyn Psycht Cens; vice-pres, NY State Private Vocational Schs Assn; secy, Nassau Co Manpower Utilization Comm, 1964-66; exec dir, Nassau Civic Club; mem: exec bd, Natl Rehab Assn; exec comm, NY State ADA; pres, adv bd, Marist Coll; mem: Graphic Arts Tech Found; Intl Assn of Printing House Craftsmen; NY Litho Club; AAAS; Amer Vocational Assn; Manpower Inst of NY; Temple Sinai, LI; AJComm; Histadrut. US Army, 1944-46. Recipient: awards: Pres's Comm on Employment of Handicapped, 1964; US State Dept, AID, 1966, 1968; Natl Rehab Assn, 1967; Marist Coll Development Off, 1968; NY Gov's Comm on Em-

ployment of Handicapped, 1968; Man-of-the-Year, Nassau Civic Club, 1968. Contbr to encys, profsl jours. Hobbies: target shooting, photography. Home: 219 W Broadway, Woodmere, NY. Office: 88 Haddon Rd, New York, NY.

ROBINSON, Michael Aaron, US, rabbi; b. Asheville, NC, Dec 13, 1924; s. Samuel and Esther (Kroman); att NC State Coll, 1941-43; BA, U of Cincinnati, 1948; ordained rabbi, HUC, 1952; m. Ruth Hertzman, Apr 6, 1953; c: Joel, Judith, Sharon. Rabbi, Temple Isr, since 1960; asso rabbi, Temple DeHirsch, Seattle, 1952-55; rabbi, Temple Beth Isr, Pomona, Cal, 1955-60. USN, 1943-46. Natl chmn, J Peace Fellowship; vice-chmn, Fellowship Reconciliation; found mem, Town of Cortlandt Human Rights Commn; chmn, Westchester Comm for SANE, 1963-67; mem: commn on church and state, CCAR; Westchester Bd Rabbis; NY Assn Reform Rabbis; youth commn and ethics comm, Town of Cortlandt. Contbr to profsl jours. Recipient: Brotherhood award, NCCJ, Peekskill area, 1966. Home and study: Glengary Rd, Croton on Hudson, NY.

ROBINSON, Samuel S, Can, physician; b. Kingston, Ont, Can, Oct 15, 1900; s. Joseph and Leah (Segal); MD, CM, Queens U, Ont, 1933. Lectr, Queens U, since 1938; cons dermat, Ongwanada Hosp, Kingston, since 1945; mem staff, Kingston Gen Hosp, Hotel Dieu Hosp; ret cons, Dept of Natl Defense. Can Militia, 1940-46. Fmr pres: Kingston Acad of Med; Kingston and Frontenac Med Soc; Kingston Zionist Soc; Kingston B'nai B'rith lodge; mem: Ont and Can Med Assns. Contbr to med jours. Home: 302 Barie St Kingston, Ont, Can. Office: 301 Brock St, Kingston, Ont, Can.

ROBISON, Adolf C, US, business exec, educator; b. NYC, Feb 4, 1904; s. Louis and Paula (Cohn); BA, Columbia U, 1924; hon degs: Fairleigh Dickinson U, 1966; Kyung Hee U, Korea, 1968; c: Peter, Michael. Pres, Robison Ind Inc, since 1941; chmn bd: Robison of Can Ltd, since 1955; Dyerite Inc, since 1964; dir, Isr Econ Corp, since 1950; fmr, chmn bd, Materials for Isr. Haganah, 1947-49. Chmn bd fs, Fairleigh Dickinson U, since 1966; vice-pres, Friends of Dept of Hebraic Studies, Rutgers U, since 1963; mem: exec comm, Amer-Isr Cultural Found, past vice-pres; natl bd govs, Isr Bonds; NY State exec comm, Histadrut, since 1948; NJ State exec comm, JNF; bd trustees, Teaneck J Cmty Cen, since 1944, past pres; exec comm, Friends of Kyung Hee U, since 1967; bd govs, Hackensack NJ Hosp, since 1968; fmr: pres, Isr Speaks, publ; mem, Teaneck City Council; pres, Teaneck Cmty Chest; trustee, Englewood NJ Hosp; dir: Bergen Co; NJ YMHA. Hobbies: music, tennis, education. Home: 544 S Forest Dr, Teaneck, NJ. Office: 175 Bergen Blvd, Fairview, NJ.

ROBISON, Ann G, US, business exec, civic worker; b. NYC, Nov 19, 1904; d. Boris and Mary (Sugarman) Green; BA, U Me, 1924; MA, Columbia U, 1935; grad, women's inst, JTSA; m. Adolf Robison, Aug 28, 1927; c: Peter, Michael. Vice-pres, Robison Ind Inc, since 1966; treas, Robison-Anton Textiles Co since 1959; dir, Robison of Can since 1957; vice-pres, Robison Found, since 1956; fmr tchr of Fr, New Rochelle, NY. Chmn, spec comm, scholarships and grants, mem bd, adv comm, Rutgers State U, NJ; vice-pres, N Valley br, Amer Assn of U Women; chmn: natl resolutions comm, natl sub-comm on J affairs, new Isr project, all Natl Council of J Women; mem: natl exec comm, Amer-Isr Public Affairs Comm; bd, exec comm, TB Respiratory Diseases Assn of Bergen Co; Phi Beta Kappa; Phi Kappa Phi; bd mem, YM-YWHA, Bergen Co; bd, co repr on state bd, NJ Fed of Rep Women; governing council, Amer Assn for J Educ; bd dirs, J Educ Comm of NYC; mem cabinet, Amer Histadrut Cultural Exch Inst; bd dirs, Natl Found of J Culture; Teaneck Coll Club; life mem: Hadassah; Brandeis U Women; UN Assn; Intl Prog Assn; UJA; bd, Teaneck women's div, Isr Bonds; natl repr: Conf of Pres' of Maj J Orgs; Natl Comty Relations Adv Council; Comm on Comty Relations Aspects of Intl Devls; Conf of J Orgs for Memorial to Six Million; Natl Conf on Soviet Jewry; numerous radio and TV appearances. Contbr to UN publs; weekly column: On the Go, The J Standard. Recipient: Woman-of-the-Year, UJA, Teaneck; Medal of Merit, Fairleigh Dickinson U; Ann Robison House, Girls Dorm, Fairleigh Dickinson U; F award, Amer Assn of U Women, named Ann Robison Award; JNF citation of honor. Home: 554 South Forest Dr, Teaneck, NJ. Office: 175 Bergen Blvd, Fairview, NJ.

ROBISON, Joseph B, US, attorney; b. Crestwood, NY, Apr 8, 1912; s. Louis and Paula (Cohn); BA, Columbia U, 1932, LLB,

1934; m. Helen Feinsod, June 12, 1948; c: Tobias, Phillip. Dir, commn on law and social action, AJCong, since 1964, staff mem since 1946; pvt practice since 1934; sup, briefing sect, NLRB, 1937-46; gen counsel: Natl Comm Against Discrimination in Housing, 1950-68; Natl Assn of Intergroup Relations Officials, 1964-67. Contbr to political and legal jours. Home: 241 W 97 St, New York, NY. Office: 15 E 84 St, New York, NY.

ROCHLIN, Mordecai, US, attorney; b. NYC, Dec 5, 1912; s. Frank and Bessie (Newman); BA, CCNY, 1932; LLB, Columbia Law Sch, 1935; m. Ruth Kane, Dec 24, 1936. Mem, Paul, Weiss, Goldberg, Rifkind, Wharton & Garrison, since 1951; research asst: NY State Law Revision Commn, 1935-36; NY State Constitutional Conv Comm, 1937-38; law asst to Justice Bernard L Shientag, NY Supr Court, 1936-37. Lt, US Army, 1943-46. F, Amer Coll of Probate Counsel. Mem: Assn of Bar, NYC; NY Co Lawyers Assn; Amer Bar Assn. Home: 120 E 81 St, New York, NY. Office: 345 Park Ave, New York, NY.

RODGERS, Richard, US, composer; b. NYC, June 28, 1902; s. William and Mamie (Levy); att: Columbia U, 1919-21; Inst Music and Art, NYC, 1921-23; hon: LLD, Drury Coll, Springfield, Mo, 1949; DMus, Columbia U, 1954; DHL, U of Mass, 1954; DMus: U of Bridgeport; U of Md, both 1962; m. Dorothy Feiner, Mar 5, 1930; c: Mary, Linda. With lyricist Lorenz Hart, composed scores for musicals: The Garrick Gaities, 1925, 1926; Dearest Enemy, 1925; The Girl Friend, 1926; A Connecticut Yankee, 1927; Present Arms, 1928; Chee-Chee, 1928; Spring Is Here, 1929; America's Sweetheart, 1931; Jumbo, 1935; I'd Rather Be Right, 1937; The Boys From Syracuse, 1938; Too Many Girls, 1939; Pal Joey, 1940; composer, co-author: On Your Toes, 1936; Babes in Arms, 1937; I Married An Angel, 1938; composer, co-author, co-produc, By Jupiter, 1942; composer, produc: A Connecticut Yankee (new produc), 1943; Do I Hear a Waltz? 1965; with Hart, composed music for films: Love me Tonight, 1932; Hallelujah, I'm a Bum, 1933; Mississippi, 1935; composed music for ballet, Ghost Town, 1939; with lyricist Oscar Hammerstein, 2nd, composed scores for musicals: Oklahoma! 1943; Carousel, 1945; Allegro, 1947; composer, co-produc: South Pacific, 1949; The King and I, 1951; Me and Juliet, 1953; Pipe Dream, 1955; Flower Drum Song, 1958; The Sound of Music, 1959; with Hammerstein, music for film, State Fair, 1945, for TV musical, Cinderella, 1957; composed scores for TV, documentaries: Victory at Sea, 1952; Winston Churchill: The Valiant Years, 1960; Androcles and the Lion, NBC, 1967; composer, lyricist, produc, No Strings, 1962; co-producer: I Remember Mama, 1944; Annie Get Your Gun, 1946; Happy Birthday, 1945; John Loves Mary, 1947; The Happy Time, 1950. Mem: bd trustees: Barnard Coll; Actors Fund of Amer; NY Philharmonic; bd dirs: ASCAP; Juilliard Sch of Music; pres: NY Music Theater; Lincoln Cen; mem: Authors League Amer; Dramatists Guild, past pres; Natl Inst Arts and Letters; Natl Assn for Amer Composers and Conductors; clubs: Columbia U; Dutch Treat; Players; Century Assn. Recipient: spec Pulitzer award, Oklahoma! 1944; Pulitzer prize, South Pacific, 1950; Donaldson awards: Carousel, 1945; Allegro, 1948; South Pacific, 1949; Pal Joey, 1952; Antoinette Perry awards: South Pacific, 1950; The King and I, 1952; The Sound of Music, 1960; No Strings, 1962; Motion Picture Acad Award for song, It Might as Well Be Spring, 1945; TV Acad award for: Victory at Sea, 1953; Winston Churchill: The Valiant Years, 1962; medal of excellence, Columbia, 1949; 100-Year Assn gold medal, 1950; Columbia Coll award, 1952; dist public service award, USN, 1953; Alexander Hamilton medal, Columbia U, 1956; Christopher award for The King and I, 1956; hum relations award, NCCJ, 1959; award, Advt Fed Amer, 1960; Tex Music Educs award, 1960; gold medal, Poor Richard Club, 1960; Broadway Assn award, 1961; Mary MacArthur Memorial Fund award, 1963; Handel award, City of NY, 1967.

RODIN, Frank H, US, ophthalmologist, educator; b. Homel, Russ, Oct 1, 1892; s. Eli and Bessie (Elkin); in US since 1923; BA, U of Man, Can, 1916, MD, 1920, dipl, educ, 1929; m. Sophia Margulus, Aug 12, 1923; c: Faegal Friedman. Pvt practice since 1927; chief, eye service, Mt Zion Hosp, 1933-35; lectr em, ophthal surg, Stanford U Hosp. Mem: local and intl med societies; Phi Delta Epsilon; club: Concordia-Argonaut. Contbr to med jours. Recipient: $25,000 grant from Metrop Found for research in ophthal, 1935. Home: 2457 Bay St, San Francisco, Cal. Office: 2233 Post St, San Francisco, Cal.

RODITI, Edouard, US, author; b. Paris, Fr, June 6, 1910; s. Oscar and Violet (Waldheim); att Balliol Coll, Oxford, 1927-28; BA, U of Chgo, 1938. Author: Prison Within Prison, poems, three Heb elegies, 1941; Oscar Wilde, A Critical Appraisal, 1947; Poems, 1928-48, pub, 1949; Dialogues on Art, 1960; De l'homosexualité, 1962; Les plus belles lettres D'Eugène Delacroix, 1962; sect on contemporary J painting in book, Jewish Art, pub in Isr, 1959; contrib ed: Arts, since 1959; Arts in Society; European Jewry, London; contbr to: Commentary; World Jewry; Evidences; L'Arche; Der Monat; Encounter; Preuves. Homes: 8 rue Grégoire de Tours, Paris, Fr; 8 Calle Ribbi Mordejai Bengio, Tangier, Morocco.

RODMAN, Morris, US, business exec; b. Russ, Apr 19, 1903; s. Benjamin and Sarah (Hershman); in US since 1909; att Johns Hopkins U, 1924-26; PhG, U of Md, 1928; m. Gertrude Lewis, Aug 7, 1927; c: Ruth Frieman, Judith Bryant, Elizabeth Dubb. Pres, G & R Corp, since 1936; pres, radio sta WGMS, 1949-56. Pres, UJA, Gtr Wash, DC, past chmn; dir, United Isr Appeal; mem, cabinet, Natl UJA; fmr, dir, council, JWF; club: Woodmount Country. Donor: HS, Kiryat Yam, Isr. Recipient: forest in Isr dedicated in his honor, 1970. Home: 2700 Virginia Ave, NW, Washington, DC. Office: 705 18, NW, Washington, DC.

ROEYTENBERG, Efraim, (Fima), Fr, artist; b. Harbin, China, Dec 24, 1916; s. Alexander and Sofia (Fishman); att Chinese Acad of Traditional and Western Painting. One man shows: five in Isr; Baltimore Mus of Art, 1960; Roland, Browse and Delbanco, London, 1962; Gal Jacques Massol, Paris, 1963, 1969; Bineth Gal of Fine Arts, Jerusalem, 1966; Isr Mus, Jerusalem, 1970; group shows: Russ Painters in China; annual shows of Isr Artists and Sculptors Assn; Delius Gal, NY; Bezalel Natl Mus; Isr Art: Helsinki; Oslo; Copenhagen; Stockholm; Goteborg; Modern Art in Isr, Tel Aviv and Jerusalem; Pitt Intl Exhb of Contemporary Painting and Sculpture; Boston Public Libr; Mus of Buenos Aires, Arg; Salon Intl des Galeries-Pilotes, Switz; Libr La Proue, Brussels; Kaleidoscope Gal, Ghent; Bineth Gal, Jerusalem; Art Isr, touring US and Can; Salon des Réalités Nouvelles, Paris; repr in perm collections: Gal Jacques Massol, Paris; Bineth Gal of Fine Arts, Jerusalem. Mem, Isr Assn of Painters and Sculptors. Studios: 9-11 rue Bargue, Paris, Fr; 5 Hazanowitz St, Jerusalem, Isr.

ROFE, Moshe, Isr, public official; b. Haleb, Syria, 1918; s. Shimon and Yafa; in Isr since 1935; att Sch of Law and Econ, Tel Aviv U; m. Rachel Cohen, Aug 30, 1942. Town clerk, since 1951, dep mayor, since 1948, both Haifa Munic, interpreter, 1945; prosecutor and investigator, Isr Police, 1938-45. Served, IDF, 1950-65. Active mem, Sephardic comty, Haifa. Home: 54 Moriya St, Haifa, Isr. Office: 14 Hassan Shukeiri St, Haifa, Isr.

ROGAL, Alvin, US, business exec; b. Pittsburgh, Pa, Feb 25, 1923; s. Hyman and Martha (Ruttenburg); att Shady Side Acad, Pittsburgh, 1941; BS, Cornell U, 1945; m. Ann Lawrence, July 21, 1946; c: Andrew, James. Pres: Rogal Co, Inc, since 1965; Capital for Tech, Inc, since 1963. Ensign, USN, 1945-46. F, Brandeis U; dir: St Francis Gen Hosp; Montefiore Hosp, both Pittsburgh, Pa; dir: YM-YWHA, Irene Kaufmann Cen, vice-pres; CJFWF, NY; United J Fed; ZOA; mem: Mayor's Comm for Exhb Hall Planning, Pittsburgh; citizens comm, Health and Wfr Assn, Allegheny Co, Pa; Pittsburgh Playhouse Assn, past mem exec bd; Million Dollar Round Table; fmr: campaign chmn, pres, United JF of Pittsburgh; chmn, gen assembly, CJFWF; dir, admn comm, JDC. Clubs: Westmoreland Country, Export, Pa, past dir; Standard; Concordia, dir. Hobby, skiing. Home: 1009 Wilkins Heights Rd, Pittsburgh, Pa. Office: Fidelity Bldg, 341 Fourth Ave, Pittsburgh, Pa.

ROGALINER, Stanley D, US, business exec; b. Monessen, Pa, Mar 8, 1915; s. George and Bessie (Romanoff); BS, U of Pittsburgh, 1937; m. Reva Neaman, Jan 21, 1940; c: Lee, Gary. Regional mgr, vegetable oil div, Cargill, Inc, since 1964, with firm from 1956; secy, dir, vice-pres, Falk & Co, 1944-53. Life trustee, Pittsburgh chap, AJComm since 1960, chap chmn, 1958-59; pres, Bus Admn Alumni Assn, U of Pittsburgh, 1961-63; bd dirs: J Comty Relations Council of Pittsburgh, 1955-63; Civic Light Opera Assn, 1960-63; NCCJ, since 1962; mem: Omicron Delta Kappa; Delta Sigma Rho; Pi Lambda Phi; Masons; clubs: Carnegie Rotary; Exec of Chgo. Home: 1954 Linden Ave, Highland Park, Ill. Office: 899 Skokie Blvd, Northbrook, Ill.

ROGALL, Edward Myron, US, business exec; b. Bklyn, NY, Feb 20, 1911; s. Benjamin and Rose (Elias); att CCNY, 1928-31; m. Pearl Goldstein, Sep 1, 1933; c: Elisabeth Weseley, Stephanie. Chmn, commn, City of St Petersburg Housing Auth, since 1964; pres, Eldorado Hotel Corp, since 1954; vice-pres, JH Lopin and Co Inc, 1931-60; pres: Southern Comfort Homes Inc, 1947-57; Ind Affiliates, Inc, 1956-64. Pres: J Comty Cen; Ceres Union, 1957-59; J Comty Council, 1965-67; chmn, Combined J Campaign, 1962-65; mem: Phi Epsilon Pi Frat; Natl Assn Housing and Redevl Off; Amer Hotel Assn. Home: 2150 Pelham Rd, St Petersburg, Fla. Office: 113-60 Gulf Blvd, St Petersburg, Fla.

ROGEL, Dan, Isr, mechanical engr; b. Tel Aviv, Isr, Sep 3, 1935; s. Alexander and Sonia (Pesis) Rogalsky; BSc, Technion, 1962; m. Devora Nudel, July 21, 1956; c: Yael, Eynat. Head div, research and devl dept, Min of Defense, since 1967, mech eng, 1962-67. Contbr to profsl jours. Recipient: Isr Security award, Isr Govt, 1968. Hobbies: photography, traveling. Home: 34 Hashoffim, Kriyat Mozkin, Isr. Office: POB 1, Kiryat Mozkin, Isr.

ROGEL, Shlomo, Isr, physician; b. Hatvan, Hung, July 8, 1927; s. Naphtali and Sarah (Klein) Rosenberg; in Isr since 1949; att Med Sch, U of Budapest, 1946-49; MD, Heb U Hadassah Med Sch, 1953; m. Hanna Sebastian, Sep 15, 1965; c: Adoram, Le'at. Phys-in-chief, internal med, card, Hadassah Med Cen, since 1964; asso prof med, Heb U, since 1967. Gov, bd govs, Heb U; mem: cen comm, Isr Heart Soc; exec comm, alumni assn, Heb U; Soc of Internal Med; fmr: pres, Alumni, Hadassah Med Sch; mem sen, Heb U. Contbr to sci jours. Recipient: Magnes prize, Heb U, 1959; Leiberg prize, IMA, 1964. Home: 3 Bartenura St, Jerusalem, Isr. Office: Hadassah Med Cen, Jerusalem, Isr.

ROGERS, Lawrence S, US, psychologist; b. NYC, July 6, 1913; s. Morris and Esther (Simon); BS, Bklyn Coll, 1933; MA, Columbia U, 1934, PhD, 1940; m. Tessie Deich, Aug 28, 1938; c: Susan, Michael. Chief clinical psych, mental hygiene clinic, VA Hosp, Denver, Colo, since 1947; visiting lectr, genl psych, U Colo, clinical prof, Sch of Med; USPHS, 1946. Chmn, bd dirs, Colo Psych Assn, 1961-62, pres, 1952; mem, exec comm, div of cons psychs, Amer Psych Assn, 1959-62, pres, div psychs in public service, 1952, 1960, mem, council of reprs, 1953-59, 1962-64, 1969-71; chmn, State Bd of Psych Examiners of Colo, 1961-66; mem, profsl adv comm, Colo Assn for MH; pres, Rocky Mt Psych Assn, 1954; f: Soc of Projective Techniques; Amer Acad of Psychotherapists; Amer Psych Assn. Contbr to profsl jours. Home: 1046 Madison, Denver, Colo. Office: 1055 Clermont, Denver, Colo.

ROGOFF, Harry, US, editor, author; b. Berezino, Russia, Dec 11, 1882; s. Isaac and Sarah (Yachnowitz); in US since 1892; BS, CCNY, 1906; m. Anna Kavaler, Sept 1916; c: Julian, Phoebe. Ret. Ed, J Daily Forward, 1951-64. Author: Nine Yiddish Writers, 1915; How America is Governed, 1918; East Side Epic, 1931; History of the US, 5 vols, 1932; The Spirit of the Forward, 1954. Home: 258 Riverside Dr, New York, NY. Office: J Daily Forward, 175 E Broadway, New York, NY.

ROGOFF, Maurice Gerald, Kenya, pathologist; b. Cape Town, S Afr, July 29, 1927; s. Joseph and Ray (Shapiro); in Kenya since 1954; m. Betty Ellis, Nov 21, 1954. Asst dir, Med Services, lab div, Min of Health, Rep of Kenya, since 1963, police surg, 1954-58, police path, 1958-60, spec cons, Forensic Path, 1960-63. Pres: Heb Aid Soc; Chevra Kadisha; Microbiol Soc; chmn, Kenya Blood Donor Org; fmr, pres, Heb Aid Soc, Nairobi. Home: POB 2697, Nairobi, Kenya. Office: Min of Health, POB 30016, Nairobi, Kenya.

ROGOW, Yitzhak, Isr, economist; b. Johannesburg, S Afr, Oct 9, 1936; s. Morris and Janie (Abrahamson); in Isr since 1960; BA, Cape Town U, S Afr; m. Pearl Choritz, Sep 8, 1961; c: Michal, Noam. Dir, dept of info, KH, since 1962; asst, PR dept, Isr Govt Tourist Corp. Sgt, IAF, 1960-61. Repr, Habonim; chmn, WP Zionist Youth Council. Hobby: filming. Home: 6 Brachyahu St, Jerusalem, Isr. Office: POB 583, Jerusalem, Isr.

ROKACH, Itzhak, Isr, business exec; b. Neve Zedek, Jaffa, Pal, Aug 1, 1894; s. Shimon and Rachel (Shostakovski); dipl, Ecole de Commerce, Lausanne, Switz; m. Hilda Gesundheit; c: Miriam, Na'ava. Dir gen, Pardess Syndicate, since 1939; chmn, Mehadrin Ltd; dir, Consolidated Maritime Agcys; mem: Citrus Marketing Bd of Isr, since 1940; Isr Ports Auth,

since 1961; bd dirs, Farmers Fed; fmr: dir, Pardess Co; found, dir, Syndicate for Jaffa Oranges. Mem bd govs, Heb U, Jerusalem; pres, B'nai B'rith, Tel Aviv lodge; hon Rum consul, Tel Aviv-Jaffa; mem bd dirs, Otzar Mifalei Yam; fmr: mem: C of C, Tel Aviv-Jaffa; Seafaring Assn; Tel Aviv City Council. Fmr co-ed, Hadar, monthly. Recipient: Chevalier de la Légion d'Honneur, Fr. Home: Basel St, Herzlia Pituach, Isr. Office: POB 1290, Tel Aviv, Isr.

ROLAND, Alexander, Isr, attorney; b. Beiltz, Bessarabia, July 14, 1911; s. Samuel and Clara (Flanzbaum); in Isr since 1959; MB, fac law, political sci, U of Czernowitz, 1931, PhD, 1933; m. Rachel Segal; c: Leopold. Lawyer and notary s nce 1934; vice-pres, Isr Devl Promotion Co, since 1964. Mem, adv council, J World Cong since 1966. Author: The Resistance to Oppression of Injust Laws, 1934. Spec interest: child, social wfr activities. Home: 19 Nordau Blvd, Tel Aviv, Isr. Office: 79 Allenby Rd, Tel Aviv, Isr.

ROLETT, Daniel M, US, ophthalmologist; b. Nicolaev, Russ, Sep 13, 1899; s. Lazar and Rebecca (Bardacke); in US since 1923; BS, U Crimea, 1922; MD, U Berne, 1930; m. Mary Warshaw, Feb 10, 1927; c: Ellis, Ronald. Pvt practice since 1935; staff phys, ophthal, NY Eye and Ear Infirmary since 1935; cons ophthal, Grasslands Hosp, Valhalla, NY; cons opthal, Burke Found. Pres: Westchester Acad of Ophthal, 1958-60; ZOA, Westchester Co, 1959-60. Contbr to med jours. Hobby: painting. Home: Century Ridge Rd, Harrison, NY. Office: 171 E Post Rd, White Plains, NY.

ROM, Avner, Isr, business exec; b. Eisleben, Ger, Mar 29, 1916; s. Shlomo and Lotte (Stein) Goldstrom; att Tchrs Coll, Breslau; m. Henny Salzmann; c: Danny, Dina, Ilan. Dep mgn dir, Hassneh Ins Co of Isr. Mem various mgmt bds. Contbr to Heb, Eng press. Home: 3 Simtat Hanassi, Herzlia, Isr. Office: 19 Rothschild Blvd, Tel Aviv, Isr.

ROM, Josef, Isr, engineer, educator; b. Warsaw, Pol, Sep 2, 1932; s. David and Mina (Kovensky) Rabinowitz; in Isr since 1935; MSc, Cal Inst of Tech, 1954; PhD, 1957; m. Yael Finkelstein, Feb 14, 1960; c: Dalit, Abraham, Vered. Head, dept of aeronautical engr, Technion, since 1968, asso prof, since 1964; research f, Cal Inst of Tech, 1957-58. Mem, bd dirs: Comm Cen Neve Shaanan, Haifa; Isr Soc of Aeronautics and Astronautics; mem, Amer Inst of Aeronautics and Astronautics. Home: 9 Malal St, Haifa, Isr. Office: Technion, Haifa, Isr.

ROMAN, Bernard, US, attorney; b. Chicago, Ill, July 28, 1908; s. Morris and Bertha (Wertheimer); att: U Wis, 1926-28; LLB, DePaul U, 1932; m. Ruth Goodstein, Sep 18, 1932; c: Richard, Barbara. Pvt practice since 1932. Trustee, B'nai B'rith Found; mem, exec comm, ADL; intl vice-pres, B'nai B'rith, since 1968; chmn, B'nai B'rith Natl Mem Cabinet, 1953-56; mem: Amer, Ill and Chgo Bar Assns; Decalogue Soc of Lawyers; mem, bd dirs, Isaiah Isr Temple, since 1956. Contbr to real estate, tax jours. Home: 8217 S Crandon Ave, Chicago, Ill. Office: 134 N LaSalle St, Chicago, Ill.

ROMANO, Emanuel, US, artist; b. Rome, It, Sep 23, 1905; s. Enrico and Helen (Hirszenberg) Glicenstein; in US since 1928; att: Coll St Pierre, Geneva; Ecole des Beaux Arts, Geneva. One man shows: Kunstverein, Munich, 1917; NYC gals since 1929. Perm Coll: Mus of Fine Arts, Boston; Fogg Mus, Harvard; Metrop Mus, NY; NY Public Libr; Mus of Tex U; portraits executed: Romain Rolland, Andre Gide, Judith Anderson, William Carlos Williams, Carson McCullers, Dmitri Mitropoulos; murals: Metrop Life Ins Co; NY Worlds Fair, 1940; SF Worlds Fair, 1941. Curator, Glicenstein Mus, Safed, Isr; dir, Artists Equity Assn, since 1950. Home and studio: 163 E 74 St, New York, NY.

ROMANO, Giorgio, Isr, author, foreign corresp; b. Padova, It, Sep 8, 1909; s. Girolamo and Ida (Levi); in Isr since 1939; DJur, U Padova, 1932; m. Bianca Segre, Dec 20, 1936. Fmr: secy, J Comty of Milano; dir, It br, KH. Pvt, IDF, 1948-49. Author: Il Cavallo di Vienna, 1959; Israel, hist book for children, 1960; co-author, Theater in Israel, 1969; Ben Gurion, biography, 1967; co-author: Poets of Israel, 1969; regular contbr to periodicals and newspapers in It and Isr. Counsellor: Isr-It league; It Immigrants Assn; past pres, Convegno Ebraico di Milano. Recipient: Silver medal, It Fgn Off, 1961; Cavaliere Officiale, It Govt, 1966; Merito della Repubblica, 1968; Portico d'Ottavia, lit prize, 1968. Spec interests: It jewelry, J hist. Home and office: 19 Keren Kayemeth Blvd, Tel Aviv, Isr.

ROME, Harold Jacob, US, composer; b. Hartford, Conn, May 27, 1908; s. Louis and Ida (Aronson); att Yale Law Sch, 1928-30; BA, Yale U, 1929; BFA, Yale School of Architecture, 1934; m. Florence Miles, 1939; c: Joshua, Rachel. Lyricist and composer for stage, since 1937; composed music for: Pins and Needles, 1937-39; Sing Out the News, 1940; Lunch Time Follies; Star and Garter; Ziegfield Follies, 1943; Stars and Gripes; Call Me Mister, 1946; pop songs: Franklin D Roosevelt Jones; Sunday in the Park; piano suite, Opus New York, 1950; music and lyrics for: Bless You All, 1950; Wish You Were Here, 1952; Fanny, 1954; Sing Song Man (children's album); Destry Rides Again, 1959; I Can Get It For You Wholesale, 1962; The Zulu and the Zayda, 1965. One-man show, paintings, Marble Arch Gal, 1964. US Army, 1943-45. Mem: Dramatists Guild; ASCAP; Yale Club; Players Club. Home: 1035 Fifth Ave, New York, NY. Office: c/o Chappell and Co, 609 Fifth Ave, New York, NY.

ROMIROWSKY, Jacob H, US, rabbi; b. Bronx, NY, July 1, 1922; s. Joseph and Lillian (Hurvitz); BA, Roosevelt Coll, Chgo; ordained rabbi, MHL, JTSA, 1948; m. Blanche Shoulson, Mar 23, 1948; c: Mitchell, Samuel, Reuben. Rabbi: Oxford Circle Comty Cen, since 1954; fmr: Clifton J Cen, NJ; Chev Zedeck Syn Cen, Pottsville, Pa; chaplain, Hahnemann Hosp and Deborah Sanitorium. Pres: NE Zionist Dist; RA, Phila br; mem, bd, NE dist, JCC; mem: Solomon Schechter Day Sch; youth commn, United Syn; J Family Service; speakers' bur, JWF. Recipient: awards: Abraham Freudenheim, ZOA; State of Isr Bond; Brotherhood, Odd Fellows; Legion of Honor, Chapel of Four Chaplains. Contbr to J periodicals. Spec interests: youth work, family counselling. Home: 1122 Gilham St, Philadelphia, Pa. Office: 1009 Unruh St, Philadelphia, Pa.

ROMM, George M, US, business exec; b. Brockton, Mass, Mar 9, 1918; s. Alexander and Ida (Sharfman); att U of Vt, 1936-38; BS, Columbia U, 1940; m. Pearl Marholin, Feb, 1948; c: Douglas, Lisa, Stuart, Jennifer. Pres, Romm and Co, jewelers, since 1946. Lt, USAF, 1942-46, maj, USAF Res since 1962. Mem: bd dirs: Brockton Orch Soc, since 1958; United Fund, since 1959; Commonwealth Org of Dems, since 1961; AJComm, Boston; exec comm, Mass ADA, since 1953; campaign chmn, Child Guidance Clinic, Plymouth Co, since 1958; chmn, Cen Bus Dist; mem: exec bd, Mass Amer-J Comm; Natl Educ Comm of AJComm; Dem City Comm since 1959; Brockton Sch Bd since 1959; fmr: pres: retail div, C of C; Old Colony Assn for MH; mem: bd dirs, YMHA; Brockton Housing Auth; bd dirs: Temple Isr; Natl Amer Vets Comm; U Club of Brockton. Home: 236 Spring St, Brockton, Mass. Office: 162 Main St, Brockton, Mass.

RON, Amiram, Isr, physicist, educator; b. Afula, Isr, Sep 24, 1930; s. Yehuda and Hana (Hachamovitch); EE, Technion, Haifa, 1956; MSc, 1958; DSc, 1960; m. Arza Kanovitch, May 3, 1953; c: David, Ruth, Dana. Prof, physics, Technion, Haifa, since 1968; research asso, Princeton U, 1961-63; asso prof, Technion, 1964-67; visiting prof, UCLA, 1967-68. IDF, 1948-49. Mem, Isr Phys Soc; Amer Phys Soc. Contbr to sci jours. Home: 65 Pinsker St, Haifa, Isr. Office: Technion, Haifa, Isr.

RON, Eliahu, Isr, engineer; b. Ramat Gan, Isr, Aug 4, 1936; s. Moshe and Pnina (Rogatka); BSc, Technion, Haifa, 1960, dipl ing, 1962; MS, Northeastern U, 1965; att MIT, 1967; m. Eliora Zenziper, Aug 7, 1960; c: Michael, Itiy. Chief structural engr, Public Works Dept, since 1968; fmr, cons engr: Lemessorien Asso; Goldberg Asso. Home: 36 Yehuda Hanassi St, Tel Aviv, Isr. Office: 3 Lincoln St, Tel Aviv, Isr.

RON, Shlomo, Isr, electrical engr; b. Losovaja, Russ, Apr 22, 1900; s. Wolf and Anna (Samchan) Rubinstein; in Isr since 1920; att HS of Commerce; Superior J Inst of Sci; dipl, EE, Institut Electrotechnique de Grenoble, Fr, 1927; m. Fany Harris, May 16, 1968; c: Zeev. Cons EE, elec and illumination, since 1961; mem, govt examining bd for elec licensing; fmr: Haifa Town Elec Network, Isr Elec Corp; Tech Consumers, Isr Elec Corp; on UN missions; mem, commn to draft Isr State Elec Ordinance and Regulations. Vice-chmn, Isr Natl Comm of Intl Commn of Illumination; mem: Isr Natl Comm of World Energy Conf; tech council, Assn of Engrs and Architects in Isr, past chmn: Haifa br; electrotech div; Histadrut Engrs Union. Home: 14 Wedgewood St, Haifa, Isr.

RONALL, Joachim O, US, economist; b. Kassel, Ger, Feb 16, 1912; s. Paul and Ida (Stern) Rosenthal; in US since 1957; DJur, Marburg U, 1934; m. Ruth Deutsch, Apr 4, 1952;

c: Daniella, Michael. Econ, research spec, Fed Res Bank, since 1960; adj asso prof, Fordham U; fmr: econ, research spec, UK Commercial Corp, Teheran, 1942-45; commercial services, JA, Govt of Isr, 1945-50; fgn service, Govt of Isr, 1950-57. Mem: Royal Asiatic Soc; Amer Assn of ME Studies; ME Inst; Inst for Mediterranean Affairs; Amer Econ Assn. Co-author: Industrialization in the Middle East, 1960; contbr ed, Ency Judaica. Home: 333 Central Park W, New York, NY. Office: 33 Liberty St, New York, NY.

RONAT, Elhanan Edward, Isr, physicist; b. Galatz, Rum, Sep 3, 1932; s. Wilhelm and Elena (Bauberger) Rosenstein; in Isr since 1966; BS, MIT, 1956; MA, Harvard U, 1958, PhD, 1962; m. Judith Gorenstein; c: Naomi, Ethan. Sr sci, Weizmann Inst, since 1966; fmr: instr, Harvard U, 1962-64; research f, MIT, 1964-66. Master sgt, IDF. Mem: Amer Phys Soc; Sigma Xi. Contbr to profsl publs. Home: 9 Alcali St, Rehovot, Isr. Office: Weizmann Inst, Rehovot, Isr.

RONEN, Joseph, Isr, economist, CPA; b. Rypin, Pol, Feb 22, 1911; s. Izchak and Cyrl (Schnytzer); in Isr since 1933; MA, Sch of Law and Econ, Tel Aviv, 1939; m. Judith Reich; c: Talma Manor, Siva Goren, Yael. Sr lectr, econ, Histadrut Sch, Tel Aviv; CPA, pvt practice; bd, Econ Quarterly; fmr: PR dir, Min of Finance, Isr, 1948-53; adv, Mapai Party, parl faction, Jerusalem, 1954-55. Author: Inflation and Deflation in Eretz Israel, 1944; The Israel Economy, 1958; Public Labor Enterprise in Israel, 1969. Home: 26 Alexandroni St, Ramat Chen, Isr. Office: 6 Achuzat Bait St, Tel Aviv, Isr.

RON-POLANI, Yehuda, Isr, educator; b. Zlotonusha, Russ, Sep 28, 1891; s. Dov and Risi (Blinkin) Polski; in Isr since 1906; att: U of Leipzig, 1912-13; Tchrs Sem, Faine, Ger, 1913-14; m. Miriam Lavit; c: Zafrira Nivron, Talila Kotler; m. 2nd, Shulamith Haiot; c: Ron. Fmr: tchr: elem sch, Rishon le-Zion; Tel Aviv; Herzliya HS; and found, Amlani Sch, Tel Aviv; Bet Alfa; Ben Shemen; Ramat Yohanan. Served: Haganah; IDF. Mem: natl comm, Tchr's Archives Org; ext comm, Ihud Hakvutziot Vehakibbutzim. Ed, Bechol Levavi, 1962; mem ed bd: Hahinuch Hahadash, 1922; Tzror Igrof Hahinuch Hameshutaf, 1961-64; contbr to educ jours. Recipient: Tchrs Org Award, 1969. Home: Kibbutz Ramat Yohanan, Isr.

ROSAN, Samuel D, US, life insurance consultant, broker; b. Bialystock, Pol, Nov 29, 1900; s. Barnet and Anna (Goldberg); in US since 1902; grad, Life Ins Sales Research Bur, 1940; hon deg, Philathea Coll, 1966; m. Miriam Roseman, Jan 21, 1919; div, 1957; c: Howard, Robert; 2nd m. Juliette Hasson, Nov 22, 1957. Asst vice-pres, Standard Security Life Ins Co of NY, supt of agents; gen agt, Continental Assurance Co, 1945-67, found and chmn bd. Trustee, Natl Bus and Profsl Council, dir; past chmn: Life Underwriters Assn of City of NY; life div: FJP; UJA; fmr pres: Life Supervisors Asso of NYC; Independent Ins Brokers Asso of Bklyn, Inc; mem: Ins Fed NY; ins div, Amer Arbitration Asso; Pythagoras Club, fmr pres; Grand Street Boys Club, dir; ADL; B'nai B'rith, NY lodge #1; Bialystoker Home for Aged; UN Asso of NY; US Comm for Refs; Golden Key Soc; Amer Soc of Chartered Life Underwriters; life mem: Renaissance lodge 476, KP; Ins Soc NY; Million Dollar Round Table; Independent Ins Brokers Assn; clubs: 32nd deg Mason; Shriner; Kiwanis. Hobbies: art, travel. Home: 115 Central Park W, New York, NY. Office: 111 Fifth Ave, New York, NY.

ROSAND, Aaron, US, violinist; b. Hammond, Ind, Mar 15, 1927; s. Alan and Ida (Rubin) Rosen; m. Eileen Flissler, Sep 20, 1950. Concert debut with Chgo Sym Orch, under Dr Frederick Stock, 1937, soloist, 1940, 1944; toured extensively, 1937-44; formed NY debut, 1948; toured: Pacific Theater, under auspices US Army Spec Services, WW II; for US: 1948, 1961, 1963; debut with NY Philharmonic Orch, under Leonard Bernstein, 1960; recording artist for: Vox; Turnabout; CBS. Recipient: Chevalier, pour Mérite Culturel et Artistique, Fr, 1965; Gold Medal, Eugene Ysaye Found, 1967. Hobbies: golf, painting, cooking. Home: 67-40 Yellowstone Blvd, Forest Hills, NY. Office: c/o Robert A Gewald Inc, 1 W 58 St, New York, NY.

ROSCHEWSKI, Heinz, Switz, editor, broadcasting exec; b. Zurich, Nov 3, 1919; s. Lazar and Fanny (Grienbaum); m. Suzi Liatowitsch, Jan 14, 1945; c: Ruth. Head, info dept, Swiss Bc Co; chief ed, Volksstimme St Gallen, 1954-67, mem staff since 1943; judge, Dist Court of St Gallen, 1956-67; MP, Canton of St Gallen, 1957-67. Mem, natl comm, Swiss

Socialdemocratic Party. Hobbies: lit, politics. Home: Ankerstr 23, Bern, Switz. Office: Schwartztorstr 21, Bern, Switz.

ROSCHEWSKI, Kurt, Switz, editor; b. Zurich, Switz, Apr 30, 1922; s. Lazar and Fanny (Grienbaum); att Sch of Applied Arts, Basle, 1939-40; m. Lison Neiditsch, July 19, 1951; c: Michael, Catherine. Ed, Israelitisches Wochenblatt, since 1958; fmr: scenarist: Zurich; Solothurn; Basle; bookseller, Zurich, Basle. Served Swiss Army. Mem: cultural comm, J Cmty of Basle, since 1959; council, B'nai B'rith lodge, Zurich, since 1961; delg to Fed of Swiss J Cmtys; mem: cen comm; comm, Poalei Zion, Switz since 1960, past pres; fmr: J Youth Orgs; comm, Omanut, Switz, vice-pres; Verein der Schweitzer Presse. Author, Israelische Reiseimpressionen, 1959. Recipient: award from Swiss Federal Commn for Applied Arts, 1942, 1943, 1944. Home: Freiestr 120, Zurich 7, Switz. Office: Israelitisches Wochenblatt, Florastr 14, Zurich 8, Switz.

ROSE, Alan Charles, Australia, business exec; b. London, Eng, Aug 23, 1923; s. Stanley and Esther (Israel); in Australia since 1948; m. Esta Kingston, July 14,1954; c: David, Caroline, Susan. Mgn dir, Rose Music, Ltd since 1948. Capt, Brit Army, 1944-46. Pres, Austr Friends Heb U; vice-pres, Victorian KH United Isr Appeal. Home: 3 Bromley Court, Melbourne, Vic, Australia. Office: 14 Ross St, S Melbourne, Vic, Australia.

ROSE, Albert, Can, educator; b. Toronto, Can, Oct 17, 1917; s. Mark and Frances (Speigel); BA, hons, U Toronto, 1939; MA, U Ill, 1940, PhD, 1942; m. Thelma Harris, June 7, 1942; c: Jeffrey, Leslie, Janis. Dir, sch of social work, since 1969, prof since 1956, both U Toronto; vice chmn, Metrop Toronto Housing Auth, since 1956; fmr: asst econ, JD Woods and Gordon Ltd; research dir, Comty Chest and Wfr Council of Toronto. Served intelligence corps, Can Army. Mem bd trustees, Holy Blossom Temple, Toronto, since 1959; vice chmn, jt comty relations comm, CJCong, since 1961, fmr chmn, research comm; life mem, Comty Planning Assn of Can, past vice-pres; fmr, sr f, Cen Mortgage and Housing Corp; mem: Natl, US, Can Assns of Social Workers; Amer Stat Assn; Inst of Public Admn. Author: Regent Park-A Study in Slum Clearance, 1958; A People and Its Faith-Essays on Jews and Reform Judaism in a changing Canada, 1959. Recipient: Gold medal, U Toronto. Hobby, philately of Isr. Home: 225 Cortleigh Blvd, Toronto, Can. Office: 273 Bloor St W, Toronto, Can.

ROSE, David, US, business exec; b. Jerusalem, Pal, Dec 24, 1891; s. Joseph and Anna (Rubenstein); in US since 1898; att CCNY, 1906-07; m. Rebecca Shapiro, Nov 25, 1917 (decd). Pres, Bldg & Real Estate Corp; chmn, bd, Amer Technion Soc, pres, 1955-59; vice-pres, YMHA, Bx, 1938-59; active for: New Sch for Social Research; Surprise Lake Camp; Heb U; found and built village of Gan Hannah Leah Rose, Isr. Contr to trade and gen publs. Homes: 39 Oxford Rd, Scarsdale, NY; 150 Central Park S, New York, NY.

ROSE, Herbert Herman, US, rabbi; b. Bklyn, NY, Nov 13, 1929; s. Morris and Etta (Millens); BA, U of Cincinnati, 1950; MHL, HUC, 1955; DHL; m. Esther Burgin, June 5, 1955; c: Judah, Ben Zion, Eve. Rabbi: Temple Or Elohim, since 1962; The Temple, Cleveland, 1957-59; Temple Emanuel, Livingston, NJ, 1959-62. Chaplain, USAF, 1955-57. Secy, NY Assn of Reform Rabbis; chmn, LI Comm for Soviet J, 1966-68; mem: CCAR; JNF. Author: Life and Thought of AD Gordon, 1964. Recipient: Man of the Year, UJA, 1966. Hobbies: classical music, phil. Home: 491 Fox Lane, Jericho, NY. Study: 18 Tobie Lane, Jericho, NY.

ROSE, J Sanford, US, business exec; b. Cleveland, O, Jan 23, 1907; s. Joseph and Phinnie (Cohn); att Spencerian Coll, Cleveland, 1924-25; m. Bobette Sabath, Dec 21, 1941; c: James, Terri D'Ancona. Chmn bd: Elan Corp; Church Chem Corp; Fleetwood Co; pres: Rhodes Pharm Co, since 1944; Oxford Products, Inc; partner, Vitaman Nutrition Labs; treas, 1540 Lake Shore Dr Corp, since 1959, fmr dir; found, Sanford Products, 1930. Clubs: Standard; Lincoln Tennis; Chgo; Racquet, Palm Springs, Cal. Home: 1540 Lake Shore Dr, Chicago, Ill. Office: 200 E Ontario St, Chicago, Ill.

ROSE, Maurice Abraham, Eng, minister; b. Birmingham, Eng, Sep 7, 1925; s. Samuel and May (Finkelstein); BA, hons, London U, 1955, MA, 1957; ordained rabbi, Jews Coll, 1961; m. Cynthia Corman, Mar 31, 1959; c: Simon, Aron, Joseph. Exec dir, Off of Chief Rabbi, since 1962; acad registrar,

lectr, Jews Coll, since 1969; min: Sutton and Dist Syn, 1952-62; Derby Heb Cong, 1952-69. Cpl, RAC, 1949-67. Secy: Conf of Eur Rabbis; Rabb Commn for Licensing of Shochetim; mem, PEN Intl. Home: 86 Leeside Crescent, London, Eng. Study: Adler House, Tavistock Sq, London, Eng.

ROSE, Seymour M, US, attorney, educator; b. LA, Cal, Feb 12, 1928; s. Carl and Lillian (Goldenberg); BA, U of Cal, Berkeley, 1950, LLB, 1955, JD, 1967; m. Suzanne Sloman, 1961; c: Lewis, Carl, Alison. Pvt practice since 1955; lectr, U of Cal, 1955-68. Maj, US Army Res, 1950-68, active duty, 1953-55. Chmn: J Comty Relations Council, Alameda-Contra Costa Cos, 1963; Almaeda Co campaign chmn: Salinger, US Senator, 1964; Lynch, atty-gen, 1966; Robert Kennedy, US Pres, 1968; Cranston, US Senator, 1968; co-chmn, Oakland, Brown, gov, 1958, 1962; vice-chmn, Oakland Housing Auth, 1962-63; supr recorder, Sigma Alpha Mu, 1962; mem: AJComm; Alameda Bar Assn; AJCong; ACLU; Mil Govt Assn; Masons; Dem Party; clubs: Millionaires; Oakland; Synanon. Home: 45 Hillwood Pl, Oakland, Cal. Office: 2150 Franklin St, Oakland, Cal.

ROSEMAN, Ephraim, US, physician, educator; b. Baltimore, Md, Jan 1, 1913; s. Joseph and Sarah (Levitzky); BA, Johns Hopkins U, 1933; MD, U of Md, 1937. Prof, neur, U of Louisville, Sch of Med, since 1949; dir lab of electroencephalography and neur clinic, Louisville Gen Hosp; att neur: Children's Free Hosp; J Hosp; Kosair Crippled Children's Hosp; att neur and electroencephalographer, Norton Memorial Infirmary, neur cons; cons electroencephalographer and dir, lab, Nichols Gen Hosp, cons phys, VA; expert psycht cons to Surg Gen, Training Cen, 3rd Armored Div, Fort Knox; neur cons: Ky Crippled Children's Hosp, Mental Hygiene Clinic, all in Louisville, Ky; Rockefeller f, neurophysiology and research asst in psycht, U of Ill Neuropsychiatric Inst, 1941-42; asst prof, U of Cal, Med Sch, asst dir and asso att neurol of Med Sch Hosp, 1946-47; hosp staff mem: SF City and County, 1946-47; Laguna Honda Chronic Disease of City, County of SF, 1946-47; VA, Palo Alto, 1946-47; Surg Gens off for Letterman Gen, SF, 1947. Lt-col, US Army MC, 1942-52. Pres, Amer br, Intl League Against Epilepsy, 1950-51; pres, S Electroencephalographic Soc, 1951-52; chmn, med exec comm, Ky Cerebral Palsy Assn; mem: prog comm, Amer Acad of Neur, 1949-50, 1951-52; comm, Assn for Research in Nervous and Mental Disease, 1952. Mem: Bd of Psycht and Neur, 1944; AAAS; Amer Neur, Psycht and Med Assns; Amer Soc of Electroencephalography; E and Cen Assns of Electroencephalography; Ky Psycht Assn; Jefferson Co Med Soc; Natl Epilepsy League; Natl Multiple Sclerosis Assn; Natl Rehab Assn; Assn of Mil Surgs of US; N Cal Soc of Neur and Psycht; Louisville Neur Soc; Alpha Omega Alpha. Contbr to med jours. Home: Route 1, Box 79, Prospect, Ky. Office: U of Louisville, 323 E Chestnut St, Louisville, Ky.

ROSEMAN, Kenneth David, US, educator; b. Wash, DC, May 10, 1939; s. Alvin and Edith (Freund); BA, Oberlin Coll, 1961; BHL, MHL, HUC-JIR, 1966; m. Helen Hoodin, Dec 23, 1962; c: Allison. Acting dean, HUC-JIR, since 1968, asst dean, 1966-68. US Army, 1956-57. Treas, First Cincinnati Rehab Corp; mem: CCAR; Metrop Area Rel Coalition of Cincinnati; Natl Assn Student Personnel Admns; bd dirs, J Comty Rels Comm. Contbr to J publs. Home: 7301 Meadowbrook Dr, Cincinnati, O. Office: 3101 Clifton Ave, Cincinnati, O.

ROSEN, Abe S, US, public official; b. Phila, Pa, Apr 14, 1917; s. Harry and Pauline (Sharf); att Temple U, 1934-35; m. Bernice Mittin, June 14, 1942; c: Ellen, Irene. Pres, Phila Convention and Tourist Bur, since 1968; sports writer, Phila Ledger, 1935-42; copy ed, Phila Record, 1943-47; acct exec, Adelphia Assos, 1948-53, partner, 1955-56; dep city repr, PR, City of Phila, 1956-63; vice-pres, Al Paul Lefton Co, 1963-67, dir of commerce, city repr, 1967-68. US Army, WW II. Bd dirs: Fed J Agcys; YM-YWHAs of Phila; Beth Emeth Syn; Phila PR Assn; JDC, 1967; Phila C of C, 1968. Home: 865 Oakfield Lane, Philadelphia, Pa. Office: 1525 JF Kennndy Plaza, Philadelphia, Pa.

ROSEN, Abraham, Isr, educator; b. Budapest, Hung, May 26, 1930; s. Yitzhak and Cornelia (Farkas) Rosner; in Isr since 1949; MSc, Technion, 1958; PhD, 1961; m. Ilana Wurm, Mar 2, 1954; c: Etan, Gad, Michal. Asso prof, Material Sci Dept, Technion, since 1968; metallurgist, U of Cal, Berkeley, 1963-64; sr metallurgist, Atomic Research Cen, Isr, 1964-65; sr lectr, Technion, 1965-68. IDF, 1949-52. Mem: Intl ASM; Sigma Xi, Berkeley, Cal. Recipient: Arnon award, Engrs,

Architects Assn, Isr. Hobbies: music, photography. Home: 55 Einstein St, Haifa, Isr. Office: Technion, Haifa, Isr.

ROSEN, Baruch, Isr, business exec; b. Pol, Aug 10, 1913; att Fr U, Beirut; m. Esther Trushkin; two c. Gen mgr, Atzmon Bonded Warehouses, Ltd; vice-chmn, Silos and Warehouses Ltd; chmn: Express Service Transp; Express Tours; Express Mit'anim, Ltd; econ adv, Min of Defense, dept of resettlement, 1948-50. Mem bd, Tel Aviv-Jaffa C of C; fmr chmn, Isr-Amer C of C. Contbr articles on legal and econ topics. Home: 8 Modigliani St, Tel Aviv, Isr.

ROSEN, B Walter, US, scientist; b. NYC, Feb 2, 1931; s. David and Alice (Blum); BCE, Cooper Union, NYC, 1952; MS, Va Poly Inst, 1955; CE, Columbia U, 1959; PhD, U of Pa, 1968; m. Marcia Melnick, Apr 11, 1959; c: Lynn, Adam. Cons engr, since 1962; aeronautical research sci, NACA, 1952-56; asst tech dir, Avco Research, advanced devl div, 1956-62; visiting asso prof, Technion, Haifa, 1968-69. Tech dir of early ballistic re-entry vehicle progs. Chmn, Structures, Materials Comm, ASME; asso f, AIAA. Contbr to books, jours. Recipient, Guggenheim f. Home: 528 Cardinal Dr, Dresher, Pa. Office: GE Space Sciences Laboratory, King of Prussia, Pa.

ROSEN, Clifford, US, business exec; b. Port Chester, NY, June 4, 1918; s. Jacob and Rose (Rosenfeld); m. Ruth Knopow, March 17, 1946; c: Robert, Bonnie. Partner, B and C Rosen. Pres, J Comty Council, Port Chester, NY; trustee, Cong Kneses Tifereth Isr, pres, 1960-63; dir, Port Chester J Comty Center; pres, Port Chester Zionist Dist; bd member, past pres, Bd of J Educ. Recipient: Combat Infantry Badge, US Army, 1942-45. Home: 252 N Regent St, Port Chester, NY. Office: 449 N Main St, Port Chester, NY.

ROSEN, Daniel, US, surgeon; b. NYC, Oct 19, 1910; s. Isadore and Anna (Kastner); BS, CCNY, 1931; MD, U of Vienna, 1936; m. Dorothy Fireman, Mar 19, 1939; c: Susan, Arnold. Cons: VA Hosp, Brockton Mass since 1954; chief urol, Brockton Hosp, on staff since 1949; asst clinical prof, Tufts U Med Sch, since 1959. Served US Army MC. F, Amer Coll of Surgs; mem: AMA; Mass, Plymouth Co and Brockton Med Socs; NE sect, Amer Urol Assn; Amer Bd of Urol; Masons. Co-author: Studies in Lobotomy, chap 17, Lobotomy and Urinary Bladder, 1950; contbr to Jour of Urol. Home: 78 Belcher Ave, Brockton, Mass. Office: 304 Pleasant St, Brockton, Mass.

ROSEN, David M, US, physician; b. Bklyn, NY, Nov 27, 1910; s. Samuel and Sadie (Roth); BA, Columbia U, 1932; MD, NYU, 1936. Pvt practice, otolaryngology, since 1940; chief of otolaryngology, Trafalgar Hosp; dir, otolaryngology, Sea View Hosp, since 1951, on staff since 1938; asso otolaryngologist, Grand Central Hosp, 1948-63; visiting otolaryngologist, Sydenham Hosp, since 1948; intern: Bellevue Hosp, 1936-37; Kings Co Hosp, 1937-38. Civilian examiner, US Army, 1942-46. Dipl, Amer Bd of Otolaryngology; f, Amer Acad of Ophthal and Otolaryngology. Mem: AMA; NY State Med Soc; NY County Med Soc. Contbr to med jours. Office: 19 W 55 St, New York, NY.

ROSEN, David Moses, Rum, rabbi; b. Moinesti, Rum, July 23, 1912; s. Avraham and Taube (Laksner) Leib; att U Bucharest; m. Amalia Rukenstein. Chief Rabbi, pres, Fed of J Comty, Rum, since 1948; MP, Rum, since 1957; fmr guest lectr, Yeshiva U, NY. Mem: WJC; Heb U, Jerusalem; Conf of Eur Rabbis. Author of studies on Rum Jewry. Home: 17 Maria Rosett, Bucharest, Rum.

ROSEN, Edward, US, educator; b. NYC, Dec 12, 1906; s. Max and Rose (Steckels); BA, CCNY, 1926; MA, Columbia U, 1929, PhD, 1939; m. Sally Fairchild, June 9, 1959; c: Carla. Prof, hist, CUNY, since 1926; visiting prof: MIT, 1957-58; Ind U, 1963-64. US Army, 1943-45. Mem: Phi Beta Kappa; Phi Alpha Theta; Ancient Civilization Group of NY; Intl Acad for Hist of Sci. Author: Three Copernican Treatises, 1939, 2nd ed, 1959; The Naming of the Telescope, 1947; Kepler's Conversation with Galileo's Sideral Messenger, 1965; Kepler's Sommium, 1967; contbr to profsl jours. Home: 315 Riverside Dr, New York, NY. Office: CUNY, New York, NY.

ROSEN, Esther K, US, psychologist; b. Baltimore, Md, Jan 8, 1896; d. Meier and Sophie (Van Leer) Katz; AB, Goucher Coll, Baltimore, 1916; AM, Columbia U, 1917, PhD, 1925; m. Theodore Rosen, Mar 9, 1924 (decd). Ret, 1966; cons psychol, pvt practice since 1928. Dipl in clinical psych; f: Amer Psych Assn; Pa Psych Assn; Soc for Projective Techniques;

mem: Amer Orthopsychiatric Assn; Amer Assn on Mental Deficiency; Amer and Phila Soc of Clinical Hypnosis; Amer Assn of U Women; Phila Art Alliance; bd mem: Social Service Exch; Crime Prevention Assn; Citizens Comm on Public Educ; Assn for J Children; Phila chap, AJComm. Fmr bd mem: United War Chest; USO women's comm; citizens adv comm, WACs; Phila Co Dept of Public Assistance. Author: Comparison of Neurotic and Normal Children, 1925; Psychological Tests in Cyclopedia of Medicine, 1931. Hobby, fgn travel. Home: 1810 Rittenhouse Sq, Philadelphia, Pa.

ROSEN, Frank L, US, allergist; b. Bklyn, NY, Sep 23, 1909; s. Irving and Eva (Oginz); att Columbia U, 1926-29; MD, LI Coll of Med, 1933; m. Sara Sandberg, June 20, 1937; c: Steven, Janet. Pvt practice since 1939; staff: Beth Isr Hosp; St Barnabas Hosp of Newark. Maj, US Army MC, 1942-46. Chmn, air pollution comm, Amer Coll of Allergists; mem: Amer Acad of Allergy; Essex Co Med Soc; Med Soc of NJ, cons, air pollution comm; NJ Allergy Soc; Amer Psychosomatic Soc; Amer Meteorological Soc; AMA; NY Acad Sci; AAAS. Ed, Bull of Essex Co Med Soc, since 1949; contbr to med jours. Hobbies: tennis, bridge. Home: 32 S Munn Ave, E Orange, NJ .Office: 2130 Millburn Ave, Maplewood, NJ.

ROSEN, George, US, physician, educator, historian; b. NYC, June 23, 1910; s. Morris and Rose (Hendleman); BS, CCNY, 1930; MD, U of Berlin, 1935; PhD, Columbia U, 1944, MPH, 1947; m. Beate Caspari, 1933; c: Paul, Susan. Prof, health educ, public health sch, Columbia U, since 1951, fac mem since 1949; asso med dir, Health Ins Plan of Gtr NY, 1950-57; cons, NIH, 1959-64; pvt practice, NYC, 1937-42; health off, NYC Health Dept, 1947-49, dir, bur of public health educ, 1949-50; Fielding H Garrison lectr, Amer Assn for the Hist of Med, 1961; Benjamin Rush lectr, Amer Psycht Assn, 1967; Hideyo Noguchi lectr, Johns Hopkins U, 1968. US Army, 1943-46. Mem: NY Acad of Med; Amer Public Health Assn; Amer Assn for Hist of Med; Amer Sociol Soc; Hist of Sci Soc. Author: History of Miners Diseases, 1943; The Specialization of Medicine, 1944; Fees and Fee Bills, 1945; 400 Years of A Doctor's Life, 1947; A History of Public Health, 1958; Madness in Society, 1968. Trans, ed: Man in Structure and Function, 1938; Einstein-His Life and Times, 1947. Ed: Ciba Symposia, 1938-44; Jour of the Hist of Med, 1946-52; Amer Jour of Public Health, since 1957. Recipient: Grant Squires award, Columbia, 1945; William H Welch medal, Amer Assn for the Hist of Med, 1961; Elizabeth Severance Prentiss award, Cleveland Health Mus, 1964; Edgar C Hayhow award, Amer Coll Hosp Admnr, 1964; Hafner award, Amer Assn for Hist of Med, 1966. Home: 285 Riverside Dr, New York, NY. Office: 600 W 168 St, New York, NY.

ROSEN, Gladys L, US, organization exec; b. Bklyn, NY, Aug 15, 1924; d. Morris and Mildred (Blickstein) Levine; BA, magna cum laude, Bklyn Coll, 1943; BHL, JTSA, 1945; MA, Columbia U, 1944, PhD, 1948; m. Murray Rosen, June 25, 1944; c: David, Jonathan. Exec asso, Amer J Hist Cen, JTSA, since 1959; asst prof, Heb, Rutgers U, 1945-66; lectr, Heb, JTSA, 1966-67. Co-chmn, J Educ, natl women's div, AJCong since 1960, mem, commn J affairs governing council since 1960; vice-pres, Bonoth Hadassah, 1953-56; mem: Amer J Hist Soc; J Publ Soc. Contbr: Samaritan Arabic Commentary on Genesis 37-45, trans and notes, 1948; book revs to Conservative Judaism; Ency Judaica; J publs. Hobby, painting. Home: 16-03 Mandon Pl, Fair Lawn, NJ. Office: 3080 Broadway, New York, NY.

ROSÉN, Haiim B, Isr, linguist; b. Vienna, Aus, Mar 4, 1922; s. Georg and Olga (Gerstl) Rosenrauch; in Isr since 1938; MA, Heb U, Jerusalem, 1943, PhD, 1948; att Ecole des Hautes Etudes, Paris, 1951-52; m. Hannah Stern, June 29, 1953; c: Addy. Prof: gen and Indo-Eur lings, Heb U, since 1949; classics, Tel Aviv U, since 1962; fmr: visiting prof: U of Chgo; Coll of J Studies, Chgo; Sorbonne. Served Haganah. Mem: Perm Intl Comm of Ling; Ling Soc of Amer; Ling Circle of NY; Soc Ling Eur; Group ling d'etudes chamitosemitiques, Paris; Assn pour l'encouragement des études grecques, Paris. Author: Our Hebrew Language, 1955; Good Hebrew; Studies in Syntax, 1958, 67; Eine Laut und Formenlehre der herodotischen Sprachform, 1962; A Textbook of Israeli Hebrew, 1967; contbr to profsl publs; to Ency Hebraica. Home: 13 Brouria St, Jerusalem, Isr. Office: Heb U, Jerusalem, Isr.

ROSEN, Harry R, US, social worker; b. Newark, NJ, May 30, 1926; s. Samuel and Florence (Cohn); AB, U of Miami,

1949; MSW, U of Pa, 1953; m. Shirlee Salowe; c: Roger, Richard, Jan. Exec dir: J Comty Cen, Toledo, O, since 1965; J Comty Cen, Norfolk, Va, 1960-65; women's div, J Comty Council, Essex Co, NJ, 1958-60; Strawberry Mansion Recreation Assn, Phila, 1957-58; prog and camp dir, J Comty Cen, Nashville, 1955-57; dir, teen and coll activities, J Comty Cen, Essex Co, 1949-51; boy's worker, B'nai B'rith Youth Org of NJ, 1946; cons: FJP, Phila, 1957-58; YMHA of Bergen Co, NJ, 1959-60; Natl JWB, 1968-69; instr: U of Tenn Sch of Social Work, 1955-59; Richmond Sch of Social Work, 1960-65; Old Dominion Coll, Norfolk, 1962-65; U of Toledo, 1966-67; lectr: Scaritt Coll, Nashville, 1956-59; Va State Coll, 1964-66. USAAC, 1943-45. Pres: E Cen Region Natl Assn J Cen Workers, 1966-68; Hampton Rds chap, Natl Assn Social Workers, 1962-64; Tenn Valley chap, Amer Camping Assn, 1955-57; chmn: profsl insts comm, Natl Conf J Communal Service, 1968; charter mem, Acad Cert Social Workers; mem: Midwest region bd, Natl Conf of J Comty Service; B'nai B'rith; Rotary. Hobbies: cabinet making, golf, vegetable gardening. Home: 3658 Lainer Dr, Toledo, O. Office: 2275 Collingwood Blvd, Toledo, O.

ROSEN, Hyman J, US, cartoonist; b. Albany, NY, Feb 10, 1923; s. Myer and Ray (Bellin); att Chgo Inst of Hist and Art, 1940-41; m. Elaine Lippman, Sept 11, 1949; c: Edward, Eve, Benjamin. Editorial cartoonist, Times-Union since 1941, cartoons reprinted in Hearst newspapers; profsl journalism f, SUNY, Albany, 1966-67; Stanford U, 1967. Served US Army, WW II. Bd mem: Albany J Comty Cen; Temple Isr; J Social Service; Clinton Sq Neighborhood Assn; Assn of Amer Editorial Cartoonists; comty relations, J Comty Council. Recipient: Top award, Freedoms Found, 1950-55; awards: Natl Safety Council; US Treasury. Home: 77 Marsdale St, Albany, NY. Office: Times-Union, Albany, NY.

ROSEN, Joseph D, US, psychiatrist; b. Poland, Apr 7, 1911; s. Izak and Sophie (Dym) Rosenblatt; MD, Med Sch, Paris, 1936; in US since 1946; m. Anita Slonim, Aug 9, 1960; c: Marc, Emanuel. Asst dir, Aftercare Clinic, Upper Manhattan; pvt practice; fmr: phys: Dutch Consulate, 1943-45; Amer Relief Orgs and JDC, 1946, both in Madrid, Spain; supervising psycht, Manhattan State Hosp, 1953-62. Served Fr Army, WW II. Mem: AMA; NY Co Med Soc; Amer Psycht Assn; Amer Group Therapy Assn; Amer Assn for the Advancement of Psychotherapy. Contbr to psycht jours. Recipient: Medaille des Engagés Volontaires. Hobbies: travel, music, photography. Home and office: 35 E 85 St, New York, NY.

ROSEN, Julius J, US, attorney; b. NYC, May 13, 1914; s. Lewis and Henrietta (Midonick); BA, Columbia Coll, 1935; LLB, Law Sch, 1937; LLM, NYU Grad Sch of Law, 1935; SJD, 1953; m. Mildred Lewis, June 26, 1938; c: James, Harrie. Gen partner, law firm, Austrian, Lance and Stewart; secy dir: Computer Specialties Corp; Time Control Corp; Micro Quoter Inc; gen counsel, Guild of NY Nursing Homes; fmr: asst admnr, Natl War Lab Bd; partner, Rosen and Rowen; admn trial judge; asso gen counsel: S Klein Dept Stores; Grayson-Robinson Stores, Inc. Cdr, USNR, WW II. Mem: NY State Bar Assn; NY Co Lawyers Assn; Nassau Co Bar Assn; Columbia Alumni Assn; NYU Alumni Assn; Tau Epsilon Phi; exec comm, gov council, AJCong, chmn, natl comm on the radical right; vice-pres, LI Columbia Coll Assn; fmr: trustee, Temple Beth El, N Westchester; chmn, Columbia Coll Fund, class of 1935, 1959-61; clubs: Columbia; Columbia Varsity. Author: Strike or Mutiny, 1953. Recipient: bronze lion, Columbia U, 1960; plaque, comty of E Rockaway, 1962. Hobby: tennis. Home: The Churchill, 300 E 40 St, New York, NY. Office: 280 Park Ave, New York, NY.

ROSEN, Leo, US, attorney; b. Kaunas, Lith, Nov 25, 1906; s. Paul and Lina (Tubin); in US since 1909; BA, Wash U, 1926; att U of Mich Law Sch, 1926-27; LLB, cum laude, Yale U, 1929; m. Lucille Gruliow, June 24, 1931; c: Elizabeth, Michael, Charles. Partner, law firm, Greenbaum, Wolff and Ernst since 1945, with firm since 1936; atty: Root, Clark, Buckner, Howland and Ballantine, 1929-34; Reconstruction Finance Corp, NY Loan Agcy, 1935-36. Pres, Riverdale lodge, B'nai B'rith, 1941-42; bd of dirs: Hudson Guild; Brotherhood-in-Action; mem: NYC Adv Council, NY State Commn for Human Rights; Assn of the Bar of NYC; NY State and Amer Bar Assns; NY Co Lawyers Assn; Sigma Alpha Mu; Phi Beta Kappa; Order of the Coif. Home: 5245 Fieldston Rd, New York, NY. Office: 437 Madison Ave, New York, NY.

ROSEN, Lester A, US, business exec; b. Bklyn, NY, Nov 19,

1912; s. Albert and Lena (Davidsburg); BS, U of Pa, 1933; m. Patricia Jefferson, Jan 9, 1945; c: Jefferson, Patricia, Leslie. Agent, Union Cen Life Ins Co, since 1933. Maj, US Army, 1941-46. Chmn, Memphis Hum Relations Commn; bd of trustees: Natl Assn of Life Underwriters; mem, Million Dollar Round Table, Natl Assn Life Underwriters, since 1935, mem exec comm, 1959-63, chmn, 1962; vice-chmn, Memphis Urban League, 1950; co-chmn, Memphis round table, NCCJ, 1960-62; pres: Amer Soc Chartered Life Underwriters, Memphis chap, 1952; Memphis Life Underwriters Assn, 1950; Tenn Assn of Life Underwriters, 1957; mem: bd of dirs, Memphis JWB, 1953-56; Mil Order of WWs; clubs: Sterick; Ridgeway. Home: 4455 Tall Trees Dr, Memphis, Tenn. Office: 2306 Sterick Bldg, Memphis, Tenn.

ROSEN, Marian S, US, attorney; b. NYC, Mar 18, 1934; d. Henry and Ethel (Dushkin) Sirote; AB, U Miami, 1952; LLB, U of Houston, 1954; m. Fred Rosen, June 14, 1953; c: Karen, Gary. Partner, Woody & Rosen; pvt practice, 1955-59 and since 1962; asst to gen counsel, Housing & Home Finance Agcy, Wash DC, 1960-61; partner, Brownfield, Rosen & Malone, 1961-62. Pres, Natl Council of Women, 1958; chmn, United Fund, 1958; bd dirs: Tex Comty Home, 1957-59; Tex Family Counseling Service, 1957-59; mem: Amer, Tex, Fla, Fed Bar Assns; Phi Sigma Sigma; Kappa Beta Pi; Bus and Profsl Women's Club. Home: 415 Carnarvon, Houston, Tex. Office: 918 Houston First Savings Bldg, Houston, Tex.

ROSEN, Martin M, US, investment banker; b. Cincinnati, O, Aug 7, 1919; s. Samuel and Sarah (Fradkin); AB, high honors, U Cincinnati, 1940; MA, U Minn, 1941; m. Judith Jacobs, Mar 27, 1949; c: Andrea, Henry, Yereth, Irene, Marshall, Jania. Pres, First Washington Securities Corp, since 1969; fmr: dir, Far E oprs, World Bank, 1957-61, with org since 1946; exec vice-pres, Intl Finance Corp, 1961-69. Capt, US Army, 1942-46. Mem: Amer Econ Asso; Royal Econ Soc; club: Intl, Wash, DC. Contbr to econ jours. Recipient: decorations: Japan, Colombia, Mauritania, Senegal. Home: 2115 Paul Spring Rd, Alexandria, Va. Office: 1776 K St NW, Washington, DC.

ROSEN, Milton W, US, attorney; b. Braddock, Pa, June 26, 1916; s. Nathan and Bessie (Weissman); BA, Pa State Coll, 1938; LLB, U of Pa, 1941; m. Jene Tucker, July 11, 1944; c: Bruce, Burt, Neil. Pvt practice since 1946; spec atty, Commonwealth of Pa, 1946-54. Capt, USAAC, 1942-46. Pres: B'nai B'rith lodge; NW Pa Council; cdr, JWV Post; judge advocate, Amer Legion post; bd of dirs: Oil City Hosp since 1963; Franklin Club since 1968; MH Soc of Venango Co; exec bd: United Fund; Venango Co Indl Devl Corp; chmn, UJA, 1949; secy-treas, Venango Co Bar Assn, 1953-54; mem: Pa and Amer Bar Assns; clubs: Elks; Oil City Lawyers; Wanango Country. Home: 8 Pleasant St, Oil City, Pa. Office: 36 Natl Transit Bldg, Oil City, Pa.

ROSEN, Nathan, Isr, physicist, educator; b. Bklyn, NY, Mar 22, 1909; s. Joseph and Fanny (Netupsky); in Isr since 1952; MS, MIT, 1930, DSc, 1932; m. Anna Belkes, June 7, 1932; c: Joseph, David. Prof, physics, Technion, since 1952; natl research f: U of Mich, 1932-33; Princeton U, 1933-34; research worker, Inst for Advanced Study, Princeton, 1934-36; prof, theoretical physics, Kiev U, Russ, 1936-38; research worker, MIT, 1938-40; asst prof, Black Mt Coll, 1940-41; prof, U of NC, 1946-52, fac mem since 1941. F: Amer Phys Soc; AAAS; pres, Isr Phys Soc, 1956-58; mem, Isr Acad of Scis and Hum. Contbr to sci jours. Home: 1 Hatsfira St, Neveh Shaanan, Haifa, Isr. Office: Physics Dept, Technion, Haifa, Isr.

ROSEN, Pinhas, Isr, public official, advocate; b. Berlin, Ger, May 1, 1887; s. Shalom and Fanny (Pulvermacher) Rosenblueth; in Isr since 1931; att Berlin U; U of Freiburg; hon deg, Heb U; m. Annie Lesser (decd); c: Karl, Hans, Dina; m. 2nd, Hadassah Perlman (decd); c: Rivka (decd); m. 3rd, Johanna Ettlinger (decd). Pres: Lib Party, since 1961; Progressive Party, 1948-61; pvt practice, Ger; trustee, Solel Boneh, 1923-25; partner, law firm, Smoira, Rosenbluth, Krongold and Bar-Shira, 1932-48; mem, Tel Aviv City Council, 1935-46; pres, Aliyah Hadassa, 1941-48; Isr Min of Justice, 1948-51, 1953-61; MK, 1949-68; counsel, delg, WZC. Mem: bd of dirs, Kartell Judischer Verbindungen, Ger; Blau-Weiss Org, Ger; chmn, Zionist Org, Ger; dir, Zionist Exec, London, Eng, 1926-31. Home: 10 Rambam St, Jerusalem, Isr.

ROSEN, Sanford E, US, rabbi; b. Cleveland, O, May 13, 1920; s. Sanford and Helen (Frank); BA, W Reserve U,

1941; BHL, HUC, 1943, MHL, ordained rabbi, 1947; m. Melba Mells, Mar 19, 1944; c: Ronald, Louise. Rabbi, Peninsula Temple Beth El, San Mateo, Cal, since 1951; visiting lectr, U of SF, since 1968; fmr: rabbi, Temple Beth El, Bakersfield, Cal, 1947-51; student rabbi: Piqua, O; Bluefield, W Va; Shreveport, La; Kokomo, Ind, 1941-47. Found co-chmn, Conf on Rel, Race and Social Concern, since 1967; mem: exec bd, W Assn of Reform Rabbis, since 1948; fmr: bd govs, United Crusade, 1962-65; mem: bd, J Family Service Agcy of SF, Peninsula and Marin Co, since 1965; state bd, Cal Fed for Civic Unity; CCAR, exec bd, 1968-70; Zeta Beta Tau; pres, Bd of Rabbis of N Cal, 1963-65; co-chmn, N Peninsula div, JWF Campaign, 1963; mem: San Mateo Co Child Guidance Clinic comm; comm on Rehab of Prisoners; exec bd, San Mateo Cmty Council, 1957-60; bd alumni overseers, HUC-JIR, 1961-67, bd govs, 1962-65; exec bd, Bay Wfr Planning Fed, 1963-66. Home: 1119 Vernon Terr, San Francisco, Cal. Study: 1700 Alameda de las Pulgas, San Mateo, Cal.

ROSEN, Shlomo, Isr, legislator, organization exec; b. Moravska-Ostrava, Czech, June 21, 1905; s. Shalom and Chaja (Shlachet) Rosenzweig; in Isr since 1926; m. Tsila Hirsh, June, 1926; c: Efraim, Rafael, Noah. MK, chmn, comm for public services; gen secy, Fed of Kibbutz Movement; mem, Kibbutz Sarid, since 1926; exec comm Agric Cen. Served Haganah. Mem, actions comm, WZO. Contbr to lab press. Spec interest: economics. Home: Kibbutz Sarid, Isr. Office: B'rith haTnua haKibbutzith, POB 210, Tel Aviv, Isr.

ROSEN, Warren L, US, surgeon; b. New Orleans, La, Dec 17, 1901; s. Charles and Irma (Leucht); BS, Tulane U, 1922, MD, 1924; postgrad study, U of Vienna, 1926-27; m. Erma Stich; c: John, William. Asst prof, clinical surg, Tulane Med Sch, since 1942; sr surg, Touro Infirmary; visiting surg: Sara Mayo Hosp; Flint Goodrich Hosp. US Army, 1942-45; lt col, hon res, 1945. Mem, bd dirs, Kingsley House and New Orleans Day Nursery, chmn prog personnel comm; org, chmn, doctor's div, Comty Chest, 1938; pres, New Orleans Orchid Soc, 1960-61; trustee, Amer Orchid Soc, 1962-65. Home: 7030 Birch St, New Orleans, La. Office: 3439 Prytania, New Orleans, La.

ROSENAN, Naftali, Isr, scientist; b. Frankfurt/M, Ger, Sep 14, 1901; s. Felix and Louise (Laubner); in Isr since 1933; m. Gertrud Schlesinger, May 4, 1924; c: Uri. Dep dir, Isr Meteorological Service, since 1961, with org since 1948; fmr: sci dir, Pal Meteorological Service, 1938-48. Chmn, mem various working groups and panels of experts of World Meteorological Org. Mem ed bd, Atlas of Isr. Spec interests: J hist, climatology, geneaology. Home: 11 Herzl St, Ramat Gan, Isr. Office: POB 25, Beit Dagan, Isr.

ROSENBAUM, Arthur J S, US, rabbi; b. Fort Worth, Tex, Oct 14, 1915; s. Samuel and Rachel Gershowitz; BA, NYU, 1935; ordained rabbi, Rabbi Isaac Elchanan Theol Sem, 1937; LLD, Blackstone Coll of Law, Chgo, 1941; m. Miriam Kantor, June 20, 1937; c: Sherry, Marcia, Ira. Rabbi, Cong Beth T'fillah, Phila, since 1954; fmr: rabbi: and exec dir, YM-YWHA, Jamaica, NY, 1936-38; Cong Sons of Isr, Binghamton, NY, 1938-45; found, first dir, interfaith activities div, AJComm, 1945-49; exec dir, Bklyn JCC, 1949-54. Chmn, Comty Relations Comm, Bd of Rabbis of Phila, since 1958; pres, Overbrook Park Comty Leaders Conf, since 1961; pres, Phila Rabb Assn; mem: panel of arbitrators, J Comty Relations Council Conciliation and Arbitration Service; comm on law enforcement, Phila Housing Assn; bd: w area, Phila Health and Wfr Council; Phila chap, AJComm; steering comm, citizens adv comm to Sup of Schs on integration and inter-group relations; fmr: mem ad hoc comm on integration, Phila Sch Sys; moderator, Jews in Amer Life, sta WIP, Phila. Recipient: Victory Medal, State of Isr Bonds, 1965; Official Tribute, City of Phila, 1964. Home: 22 Overbrook Pkwy, Philadelphia, Pa. Study: 7630 Woodbine Ave, Philadelphia, Pa.

ROSENBAUM, Asher, Isr, business exec; b. Wishnice, Pol, 1913; s. David and Eidla (Friedman); in Isr since 1934; att Tel Aviv U; m. Lea Aizeshmidt, May 10, 1936; c: Adina, Daphna. Dep gen mgr, gen merchandising mgr, Shalom Stores, since 1964; fmr: dept gen mgr, Hamashbir Lazarchan, 1952-64; fmr, asst gen mgr, rehab dept, Min Defense. Mem: comm, sport and culture, Tel Aviv Munic; Tel Aviv Worker's Council; Lab Party Dist Council; marketing mgmt mem, Isr Mgmt Cen; mem: secretariat, Hapoel Sport Org; Isr Basket-

ball Assn Mgmt. Home: 3A Struma St, Bat Yam, Isr. Office: 9 Achad Haam St, Tel Aviv, Isr.

ROSENBAUM, Charles, US, jurist, attorney; b. Salem, Mass, Apr 9, 1901; s. Samuel and Ida (Adelstein); LLB, U of Denver, 1921; m. Louise Michael, 1928; c: Stanton, Louann Miller. Pvt practice since 1922; judge, Court of 2nd Jud Dist, Colo, 1951-52; mem, Intergovernmental Commn on Eur Migration, Geneva, Switz, 1957; US delg: to White House Confs on Refs, 1958-60; to UN, 1960-61; mem, adv comm, USAF Acad, since 1963. Chmn, arbitration panel, NLRB, WW II. Pres: JCC, 1946-47; Dist Grand lodge, B'nai B'rith, 1937-38, Denver lodge, 1927; chmn, trust fund comm, Comty Chest, 1948-53; vice-pres: Natl J Hosp, 1965-68; Colo Bar Assn, 1944-45; Denver Bar Assn, 1933; mem: Colo Bd of Standards of Child Care, 1945-49; natl exec comm, ADL, 1963-68; clubs: Green Gables Country; Town. Author: Manual on American Citizenship, 1929, reprint, 1935. Recipient: First J Leader of Denver award, Intermountain J News, 1946; Natl Service award, B'nai B'rith Supr lodge, 1957; included in Denver Post Gal of Fame. Hobby: golf. Home: 3500 E Dartmouth, Denver, Colo. Office: 1518 Denver, US Natl Cen, Denver, Colo.

ROSENBAUM, Edward E, US, physician, educator; b. Omaha, Neb, May 14, 1915; s. Samuel and Bessie (Mittleman); BSc, U Neb, Coll of Med, 1936, MD, 1938; MS, U Minn, 1947; m. Davida Naftalin, Feb 17, 1942; c: Richard, James, Howard, Kenneth. Pvt practice since 1938; prof clinical med, U Ore Med Sch, since 1962; chief, rheumatology clinic, 1952-62 and since 1968; intern, J Hosp, St Louis, 1938-39; f: Michael Reese Hosp, Chgo, 1939-40; Mayo Found, Rochester, Minn, 1940-41, 1946-48; chief of med: Holladay Park Hosp, 1956-59; St Vincent's Hosp, 1959. Maj, US Army MC, WW II. Dipl, Amer Bd of Internal Med, 1952; pres, Arthritis and Rheumatism Found, Ore chap, 1950-52; mem: exec comm, Govs Council on Aging, State of Ore, 1962-65; Amer Rheumatism Assn; Portland Acad of Med; Sigma Xi; Alpha Omega Alpha; bd trustees, Temple Beth Isr, 1964-65; bd mem, B'nai B'rith. Contbr to med jours. Home: 4444 SW Fairhaven Dr, Portland, Ore. Office: 333 NW 23 Ave, Portland, Ore.

ROSENBAUM, Irving Joseph, US, rabbi; b. Omaha, Neb, Dec 20, 1922; s. David and Rose (Lederman); BA, U of Chgo, 1942; ordained rabbi, BHL, Heb Theol Coll, 1945; m. Ruth Groner, Feb 27, 1944; c: Roy, Don, Susan, Allan. Rabbi, Chgo Loop Syn, since 1963; natl dir, dept inter-rel coop, ADL, 1944-58; fmr curator, Lasker f prog, civil liberties and civil rights, Brandeis U, 1959-1960. Exec vice-pres, Chgo Bd Rabbis, since 1960; dir, council of rel leaders, Urban League, since 1961; mem:steering comn, Interral Council on Urban Affairs, since 1961; bd dirs, Chgo Loop Syn; bd dirs: Chgo Council on Race and Rel; J Fed of Metrop Chgo; J Council of Urban Affairs; Ida Crown Acad; J Home for Aged; Rel Adv Council; Natl Safety Council; mem:RabCA; Chgo Rabb Council; dir, Rel Educ Assn. Co-autor: Your Neighbor Celebrates, 1955, produc, dir, motion picture, of book, 1949; author, weekly column, Anglo-J newspapers; contbr to profsl publs. Home: 5743 N Bernard St, Chicago, Ill. Study: 72 E 11 St, Chicago, Ill.

ROSENBAUM, Milton, US, psychiatrist, educator; b. Cincinnati, O, Aug 12, 1910; s. Sol and Mary (Michaelson); BS, U of Cincinnati, 1932, MD, 1934; Rockefeller f, Chgo Inst for Psychan, 1940-43; m. Jean Grossman, June 17, 1934; c: Michael, Mary, Elizabeth. Prof and chmn, psycht dept, Albert Einstein Coll of Med, since 1955; dir of psycht, Bx Munic Hosp Cen, since 1955; Cincinnati Gen Hosp; prof, psycht, U of Cincinnati, 1950-55, on fac since 1939; psycht con: Family Ser Agcy, 1944; med adv comm, O State Vocational Rehab Bur, 1945; Children's Hosp, 1946-48; analyst: training, Chgo Psychan Soc, 1950-55; supervising, Chgo Inst for Psychan, 1950-55; visiting prof: Hadassah Med Sch, Heb U, Jerusalem, 1955; U of Puerto Rico Med Sch, 1957. Surg-gen, US Army, 1948-51. Dipl, Amer Bd of Psycht and Neur; f, Amer Psycht Assn, chmn, commn on med educ, 1951. Pres, Amer Psychosomatic Soc, 1957; Cincinnati Soc of Neur and Psycht 1951-52; vice-pres, Amer chap, Intl League Against Epilepsy, 1941-42; chmn, mental hygiene, council, Public Health Fed, 1942-48; commn on med educ, Group for Advancement of Psycht, 1950-53; mem, bd of dirs, NY State MH Assn, 1961-62; O State Mental Hygiene Assn, 1948. Mem: study section, Natl Inst MH, USPHS, 1956-60; AMA; Chgo Psychoanalytic Soc; Assn for Research in Nervous and Mental Diseases; Sigma Xi; Alpha Omega Alpha; Pi Kappa Epsilon. Contbr to books, med jours. Home:

55 Woodbine Ave, Larchmont, NY. Office: Albert Einstein Coll of Med, New York, NY.

ROSENBAUM, Milton, US, rabbi; b. Bronx, NY, Mar 2, 1914; s. Aaron and Rose (Brickner); BA, U of Cincinnati, 1936; MHL, ordained rabbi, HUC, 1940, DD. 1965; m. Thelma Newhouse, May 31, 1942; c: Jonathan, Aaron, Daniel. Rabbi, Temple Emanu-El, since 1956; asst rabbi, Euclid Ave Temple, Cincinnati, 1940-43; rabbi: Temple Beth Jacob, Pontiac, 1946-49; Beth El Cong, Ft Worth, 1949-56. Chaplain, US Army, 1943-46. Bd dirs: JCC of Metrop Detroit; United Heb Day Schs; Midrasha. Home: 526 Hendrie, Royal Oak, Mich. Study: Temple Emanu-El, 14450 W Ten Mile Rd, Oak Park, Mich.

ROSENBAUM, Nathan, US, business exec, author; b. Russ, Aug 15, 1897; s. Morris and Anna (Shatz); in US since 1903; att Temple U, 1916-18; m. Elizabeth Scher, May 27, 1923; c: Arthur, Paul. Pres, Rosenbaum & Co, commercial bankers, since 1924; mortgage broker, 1924-29; pres, Colonial Trust Co, Wilmington, Del, 1930-31. Author: Songs and Symphonies, 1919; Each in His Time, 1925; My Hand and Seal, 1947; A Man From Parnassus, 1951; Create the World, 1956; Collected Poems 1947-67, publ 1968. Mem: Poetry Soc of Amer; Amer Poetry League; f, Intl Inst of Arts & Letters, Switz. Hobby: collector of first editions. Home: 347 Winding Way, Merion, Pa. Office: 1411 Walnut St, Philadelphia, Pa.

ROSENBAUM, Robert Abraham, US, mathematician, educator; b. New Haven, Conn, Nov 14, 1915; s. Joseph and Goldey (Rostow); att St Johns Coll, Cambridge, Eng, 1937; AB, Yale U, 1936, PhD, 1939; m. Louise Johnson, July 1, 1942; c: Robert, Joseph, David. Chancellor, Wesleyan U, since 1970, dean of sci 1963-65, prof, math, since 1953; prof, Reed Coll, 1940-53. Lt cdr, USN, 1942-54. Trustee, Hartford Coll; mem: Amer Math Soc; Math Assn Amer, ed, 1966-68; Phi Beta Kappa, Sigma Xi; AAUP, chap pres. Author: Intro to Projective Geometry and Modern Algebra, 1963; Modern Coordinated Geometry, 1969; contbr to math jours. Home: 29 Long Lane, Middletown, Conn. Office: Wesleyan U, Middletown, Conn.

ROSENBAUM, Shimon, Isr, pediatrician; b. Konigsberg, Ger, Sep 12, 1890; s. Selmar and Pauline (Ladendorff); in Isr since 1933; att U of Freiburg; MD, U of Konigsberg, 1912; m. Vera London, June 18, 1918; c: Gad Rothem. Pvt practice since 1933; asst, U of Breslau Children's Hosp, 1918-20; first asst, Children's Hosp, Marburg, 1920-22; prof, U of Leipzig; dir, Children's Hosp, both 1922-33. Fmr pres, Isr Assn of Peds, 1962; mem, IMA. Author: Keep Healthy in Palestine, 1940; Play Instinct in Man, 1945; Science in School Curriculum, 1946; Man and Climate in Israel, 1946; ed bd, Harefua; contbr to local and fgn publs. Recipient, Parcelsus medal, Ger Phys Assn, 1961. Home and office: 28 Soutine St, Tel Aviv, Isr.

ROSENBAUM, Stanley, US, educator; b. Denver, Colo, Oct 1, 1910; s. Louis and Anna (Block); BA, Harvard U, 1931; MA, U of Denver, 1932; m. Mildred Bockholtz, Nov 27, 1938; c: David, Jonathan, Alvin, Michael. Fac, Eng dept, Florence State Coll, since 1961; partner, Muscle Shoals Theaters, 1932-60. Pres: Ala Council on Human Relations, Muscle Shoals chap, 1963-64; Muscle Shoals MH Assn, 1967-68; Muscle Shoals Lay Diabetes Assn, 1968; lodge pres, B'nai B'rith, 1941, state pres, 1953-54; treas: Florence-Lauderdale Co Libr Bd; Muscle Shoals Regional Libr Bd; mem, regional bd, ADL, 1950-54; pres, Cong B'nai Isr, 1948, 1961. Home: Riverview Dr, Florence, Ala. Office: Florence State Coll, Florence, Ala.

ROSENBAUM, Tibor-Pinchas, Switz, banker, business exec; b. Kisvarda, Hung, 1923; s. Samuel and Lenke (Birnbaum); DRerPol, U of Graz, Aus, 1959; m. Stephanie Stern, 1948; c: Charles, Eric, Evelyn. Ambass Extraordinary and Plen of Liberia at UNESCO, perm repr since 1964; pres: Intl Credit Bank, Geneva, since 1959; Helvis SA, since 1951; chmn: ATA Textile Works, Kiryat Ata; Lodzia Textile Works, Holon; exec bd, Kupat-Am Bank, Tel Aviv, all Isr; co-chmn, Mesurado Fishing Co, Monrovia; treas, mem, governing council, WJC, since 1966; mem, bd: London & Geneva Ins Co, London, since 1965; Mossad Harav Kook, Jerusalem, since 1961; mem: World Exec, Mizrachi Org, Jerusalem; Variety Club Intl; commercial attaché, Liberian Emb, Rome, 1957-63; dir, JA for Pal, immigration dept, Geneva, 1950-65. Prominent mem, J underground, Hung, WW II; Zionist leader of Hung Jewry, i/c, rel Halutz dept; off, UNRRA,

Ger. Pres, Colel Shomrei Hahomot, Switz; vice-pres, J Orthodox Comty, Geneva; vice-chmn, World Assn of J of Hung Descent; mem, bd govs, Bar-Ilan U, Isr; participant: all ZCs since 1946; Isr Econ Conf, 1968; Conf of J Leaders, 1969, both Jerusalem. Author: International Investments in Under-Developed Countries, 1959; Eleh Divrei Shmuel, Heb, 1961; Towards New International Banking Organisation, 1968; contbr to econ jours. Recipient: Grand Band of Human Order of African Redemption; Great Band of Star of Afr, both Liberia. Home: 9 Bertrand Ave, Geneva, Switz. Office: 9 Conseil Général, Geneva, Switz.

ROSENBERG, Abe Eugene, US, attorney; b. Milw, Wis, May 11, 1898; s. Jacob and Jenny (Levitt); BA, U of Ore, 1921, JD, 1923; m. Jeane Kamusher, Feb 14, 1924; c: Edward, Susan Struck. Mem, Rosenberg & Swire, since 1926; dir: May Dept Stores Co, since 1965; Meier & Frank Co, Inc, 1946-66. Exec secy, Pacific region, Natl Bd Coat and Suit Ind, since 1935; pres, Ore JWF, 1940-45; mem: Amer and Ore Bar Assns; Portland C of C; Rep Club. Home: 1205 SW Cardinell Dr, Portland, Ore. Office: Pittock Block, Portland, Ore.

ROSENBERG, Adolph, US, editor, publisher; b. Albany, Ga, Aug 14, 1911; BA, U of Ga. Publisher, Southern Israelite, since 1951, on staff since 1946; reporter: Albany, Atlanta, Wash, DC, 1932-42. USAAC, 1942-45. Pres, Amer J Press Assn, 1966-68; mem: Phi Phi Phi; Jr C of C; Atlanta Hist Soc; B'nai B'rith; Amer J Comm; Sigma Delta Chi; Masons, Scottish Rite; ZOA; Farband; Atlanta Press Club Treas; World Bur of J Journalists, Isr. Home: 1031 Juniper St NE, Atlanta, Ga. Office: 390 Courtland St NE, Atlanta, Ga.

ROSENBERG, Albert J, US, business exec; b. Baltimore, Md, Nov 25, 1909; s. Henry and Laura (Hollender); BS, aeronautical engr, Carnegie Inst of Tech, 1932; MS, Guggenheim Sch of Aeronautics, NYU, 1933; m. Edith Hammond, Nov 26, 1934; c: William, Lawrence. Vice-pres, McGraw Hill Book Co, since 1962, gen mgr, text-film div, 1945-69; aircraft produc, Glenn Martin Aircraft, Budd Mfg Co, 1933; tchg and admn: Baltimore Bd of Educ; Johns Hopkins U; U of Baltimore, all 1934-40; asst dir, Airline War Training Prog, 1941-43; tech adv, US Off of Educ, 1943-45. Co-chmn, film comm, Mamaroneck Free Libr, since 1961. Mem: NY Film Council; Natl Audio-Visual Assn; NEA. Author, Instruction Tests in Aeronautics, 1945; co-author: Photographic Darkroom Procedures, 1947; How to Develop, Print and Enlarge Your Own Pictures, 1948. Contbr to profsl jours. Home: 1015 Nine Acres Lane, Mamaroneck, NY. Office: 330 W 42 St, New York, NY.

ROSENBERG, Alex, US, mathematician, educator; b. Berlin, Ger, Dec 5, 1926; s. Theodor and Rela (Banet); in US since 1949; BA, U of Toronto, 1948, MA, 1949; PhD, U of Chgo, 1951; m. Beatrice Gershenson, Aug 24, 1952; c: Theodore, David. Asst dean, Herzlia and J Tchrs Sem, NYC; prof math, Cornell U, since 1961, past chmn dept math, 1966-69; fmr: prof math, Northwestern U, 1952-61; mem, Inst for Advanced Study, Princeton, 1955-57; visiting research math, Queen Mary Coll. Mem: Amer Math Soc, past ed; Math Assn of Amer, fmr: mem: comm to monitor problems in communications, comm on undergrad progs in math, both Math Assn of Amer, Inst for Advanced Study, Princeton U. Home: 608 Highland Rd, Ithaca, NY. Office: Cornell U, Ithaca, NY.

ROSENBERG, Alex S, US, rabbi; b. Bazin, Hung; s. Philip and Ernestine (Wilheim); in US since 1921; ordained rabbi, Rabbi Isaac Elchanan Theol Sem, 1926; BA, CCNY, 1930; att Columbia U; m. Dora Heiden, Dec 11, 1927; c: Moses, Jacob, Naomi Baumgarten. Rabbi, Cong Ohab Zedek, since 1925, found dir, Ohab Zedek Acad; chaplain, Yonkers Fire Dept, since 1939; rabb admnr of Kashruth, Union of Orthodox J Congs, since 1950; rel dir, JDC, Ger, 1945-47; liaison repr, Syn Council of Amer to Mil Govt, Ger, 1947. Mem, exec comm: Union Orthodox Rabbis US and Can; RabCA. Ed, publisher, Chidushei Horashbas, novellas on Talmud, 2 vols, 1966. Home: 386 Park Hill Ave, Yonkers, NY. Study: 63 Hamilton Ave, Yonkers, NY.

ROSENBERG, Benjamin B, US, social worker, organization exec; b. Czech, May 27, 1909; s. Philip and Ernestine (Wilheim); in US since 1921; BA, O State U, 1930; MA, Johns Hopkins U, 1932; dipl, NY Sch of Social Work, 1940; m. Esther Michaelson, Sep 1, 1935; c: Robert, Paul. Exec dir, Combined J Philanthropies of Gtr Boston, since 1959; fmr instr, Johns Hopkins U, 1935-38; research asst, Md Youth Comm, 1936-37;

boys worker, Fed Settlement, NY, 1938-40; case worker, Natl Ref Service, NY, 1940-41; asso dir, NJ Fed YM-YWHA, 1941-43; exec dir, JCC, Dayton, O, 1944-47; dir, field service CJEWF, 1947-53; exec dir, Gtr Miami J Fed, 1953-59. Pres, Mass Conf on Social Wfr; vice pres, Natl Conv on J Communal Services; mem: adv bd, Mass Dept of Pub Wfr; Interfaith Cons Group, HEW; bd of overseers: Philip Lown School for Contemporary J Studies; Florence Heller Grad Sch for Adv Studies in Soc Wfr, both Brandeis U; bd member, Amer Assn for J Ed; Natl Assn of Soc Workers; Natl Conf J Communal Service; Natl Conf of Social Work; Phi Beta Kappa. Contbr to profsl jours. Home: 6 Sunhill Lane, Newton, Mass. Office: 72 Franklin St, Boston, Mass.

ROSENBERG, Bernard Wayne, US, attorney; b. Ambridge, Pa, Jan 19, 1908; s. Meyer and Sylvia (Wayne); att U Pa, 1923-24; BA, U Mich, 1927, LLB, 1930; m. Harriett Goldberger, Feb 28, 1935; c: Roslyn, Michael. Pvt practice since 1930; secy, Trumbull Plumbing Supply Co, since 1957. Pres: Trumbull Co Bar Assn, 1951-54; B'nai B'rith lodge, 1934; Beth Isr Temple, 1946-49; dir, Warren J Fed. Mem: Amer and O State Bar Assns; Elks; Masons; Temple Rodeph Sholom; Tau Delta Phi, pres, 1927; clubs: Squaw Creek Country, dir, since 1956; Old Erie. Home: 891 Melwood Dr, NE, Warren, O. Office: Union Savings and Trust Bldg, Warren, O.

ROSENBERG, Emanual, US, attorney; b. Decatur, Ill, Sep 27, 1898; s. William and Anna (Marks); att U of Ill, 1916-17; LLB, Northwestern U, 1920; m. Hannah Gervitz, June 18, 1925; c: Elaine Lisberg, Audrey Goodman. Partner, law firm, Rosenberg and Rosenberg, since 1942. Served, WW I. Pres, Macon Co Mh Clinic; hon pres, Temple B'nai Abraham since 1947; pres, Decatur Comty Concert Assn, since 1932; mem: Citizens Adv Comm; Standard Club of Chgo. Home: 267 S Westdale, Decatur, Ill. Office: 1256 Citizens Bldg, Decatur, Ill.

ROSENBERG, Eugene Samuel, US, biochemist; b. NYC, Oct 16, 1935; s. Max and Rebecca (Eisenberg); BS, UCLA, 1957; PhD, Columbia U, 1961; m. Leah Petlak, Sep 3, 1958; c: Robin, Stephanie, Denise. Asso prof, bact, UCLA, since 1968, on fac since 1962. Mem: Amer Biochem Soc; Amer Microbiological Soc. Author: Cell and Molecular Biology, 1970; contbr to sci jours. Home: 842 Hartzell St, Los Angeles, Cal. Office: UCLA, Los Angeles, Cal.

ROSENBERG, Harold, US, author, educator; b. NYC, Feb 2, 1906; s. Abraham and Fanny (Edelman); LLB, St Lawrence U, Bklyn, 1927; hon DL, Lake Forest Coll, 1968; m. May Tabak, Mar, 1932; c: Patia. Prog dir, Longview Found, since 1957, with org since 1944; art critic, The New Yorker Magazine, since 1967; prof, comm on social thought, U of Chicago, since 1966; dep chief, domestic radio bur, OWI, 1943-44; visiting prof, S Ill U, 1965-66. Author: Trance Above the Streets, 1942; The Tradition of the New, 1959; Arshile Gorky, The Man, The Time, The Idea, 1962; The Anxious Object, 1964; contbr to periodicals. Home: 117 E 10 St, New York, NY.

ROSENBERG, Helen O, US, communal worker; b. Phila, Pa, June 26, 1899; d. Daniel and Bess (Dogulov) Ostrow; att Temple U, 1918; m. Max Rosenberg, Sep 22, 1929; c: Sandell Lachman. Natl pres, Women's Amer ORT, 1962-67; chmn, Natl Promotions comm, 1967; head, Women's Amer ORT delgs: Morocco, Tunisia, It, Isr, Fr, Switz, 1958; Fr, It, Switz, Iran, Isr, 1962; mem: exec comm, Amer ORT Fed; World ORT Union. Home: 42 Whitney Rd, Short Hills, NJ. Office: 222 Park Ave S, New York, NY.

ROSENBERG, J Mitchell, US, attorney, public official; b. Bayonne, NJ, Aug 26, 1906; s. Israel and Sarah (Greenberg); BA, NYU, 1927; LLB, Columbia U, 1930, MA, 1939; PhD, New Sch for Soc Research, 1967; m. Helen Emmanuel, 1956. Asst Dist Atty, Kings Co, since 1940; lectr, political sci, New Sch of Social Research, since 1970; asst prof, political sci, RI U, 1966-67; lectr, Bklyn Coll, 1967-69. Mem, bd dirs, Flatbush Zionist dist, AJCong, pres, David Marcus chap; chmn, Newkirk div, Bklyn Boy Scouts; vice-pres, Talmud Torah of Flatbush; secy-treas, Bklyn Zionist Youth comm; trustee, Kings Co lodge, B'nai B'rith; unofficial referee, Munic Court, NYC; mem: UJA; ZOA; Bklyn Bar Assn; Acad Pol Sci; NY State Dist Attorneys Assn. Author: The Story of Zionism, 1946; Jerome M Frank: Jurist and Philosopher, 1970. Recipient: Samuel Sussman Memorial medal, NYU, 1926; plaques, Bklyn Boy Scouts, 1952, 1953. Home:

901 Ave H, Brooklyn, NY. Office: Municipal Bldg, Brooklyn, NY.

ROSENBERG, Jakob, US, art curator, educator; b. Berlin, Ger, Sep 5, 1893; s. Gabriel and Bertha (Rosenbaum); in US since 1936; PhD, U of Munich, 1922; hon: MA, Harvard U, 1942, DArts, 1960; m. Elizabeth Husserl, Dec 22, 1922; c: Ruth Medalia, Wolfgang. Curator of prints, Fogg Art Mus, Harvard U, since 1939, prof em since 1965, fac mem since 1936; asst, print dept, State Mus, Berlin, 1925-30, keeper, 1930-35. German Army, 1914-17. Hon f, Pierpont Morgan Libr, NY; f, Amer Acad Arts and Sci; club: Harvard Fac. Author: Martin Schongauer, 1922; Jacob van Ruisdal, 1928; Die Niederländischen Meister im Berliner Kupferstichkabinett, 1930; Rembrandt, 1948; Great Draughtsmen from Pisanello to Picasso, 1959; Die Zeichnungen von Lucas Cranach, 1960; On Quality in Art, 1967; co-author: Lucas Cranach, 1932; German Expressionism and Abstract Art, 1957. Home: 19 Bellevue Rd, Arlington, Mass. Office: Fogg Art Mus, Harvard U, Cambridge, Mass.

ROSENBERG, Leonard H, US, business exec; b. Baltimore, Md, Dec, 1, 1912; s. Henry and Laura (Hollander); BS, Carnegie Mellon U, 1934; postgrad studies: Loyola Coll; Johns Hopkins U; U of Md; S Methodist U; m. Edna Mazer, Nov, 1936; c: Theodore, Victor, Laurie, Leonard Jr. Found, first pres, The Chesapeake Life Ins Co, since 1956; vice-pres, Stasco Ins Agency, since 1936; pres, The Chesapeake Fund; fmr: dist mgr, Reliance Life Ins Co, 1939-56; bd mem, Bayshore Inds, 1950-61. USAAC, 1941-46, lt-col, ret. Commr, Md Traffic Safety Commn, 1956-66; mem: Pres Nixon's Fed Financial Aid to Higher Educ comm; Gov's Comm to Revise Md Ins Laws; pres: Natl Assn of Life Cos; dir, mem exec comm, chmn finance comm, Natl City Bank of Baltimore; commnr, Md Educ Bc comm; bd trustee, Laurel Gen Hosp, 1956-61; brotherhood bd, Oheb Shalom Temple, 1954-58; bd comm, J Comty Cen, 1954-56; adv bd, Baltimore Sym, 1957-61; pres, Baltimore Comty Cen, 1955-56; bd trustees, Carnegie Mellon U; mem: Inst of Aeronautical Sci; Inst of Navigation; Res Off Assn; clubs: Safety First; Safety Engr; Chestnut Ridge Country; University; Governors; Center. Contbr to profsl jours. Home: 5007 Forest Park Ave, Baltimore, Md. Office: 527 St Paul St, Baltimore, Md.

ROSENBERG, Lester, US, pediatrician; b. NYC, May 4, 1898; s. Saul and Mary (Quint); BS, CCNY, 1917; MD, Cornell U, 1923; m. Ethel Hyman, Sept 24, 1931; c: Mary Marans, Sidney. Pvt practice since 1926; cons ped, Bklyn Hosp, mem staff since 1928; instr, ped, NYU, 1932-33. F: AMA; Bklyn Acad of Peds; Amer Acad of Peds. Mem: Kings Co Med Soc; Phi Delta Epsilon; Alpha Omega Alpha. Contbr to profsl jours. Hobby: poetry. Home and office: 1156 Eastern Pkwy, Bklyn, NY.

ROSENBERG, Louis, Can, organization exec, sociologist; b. Goniendz, Pol, June 17, 1893; s. Joseph and Ella G (Levin); in Can since 1915; BA, U of Leeds, 1913; BS, U of London, 1931; m. Ettie Farber, Sep 5, 1922. Research dir, Bur of Social and Econ Research, Can J Cong, since 1945, staff mem since 1934; fmr: mgr, W off, J Colonization Assn of Can, 1919-40, all Montreal. Mem: bd dirs, YIVO; Amer Stat Assn; Can Soc of Agric Econs; Can Political Sci Assn; Can Hist Soc; Public Libr Bd, Regina; f: Royal Econ Soc; Royal Stat Soc, both Eng; Amer Sociol Assn; fmr: chmn, Consumer's Council; treas, People's Forum; chmn, Public Sch Bd. Author: Canada's Jews, a Social and Economic Study of the Jews in Canada, 1939; The Jewish Community of Winnipeg, 1946; Canadian Jewish Population Studies, 1957; Can ed: Universal Jewish Ency, 1939-40; The Jewish People, Past and Present, since 1944; ed, Canadian Jewish Archives, 1959. Home: 4930 Blvd Ed Monpetit, Montreal, Can.

ROSENBERG, Milton M, US, surgeon; b. Scranton, Pa, Oct 5, 1894; s. Louis and Deborah (Aronson); MD, U of Pa, 1919; postgrad study: U Vienna, 1925-26; U Budapest, 1926; NY Eye and Ear Infirmary, 1927; NY Polyclinic Hosp, 1950; m. Marguerite Gallagher, July 4, 1947. Visiting chief, eye, ear, nose and throat dept: Scranton State Hosp; Mercy Hosp; Comty Cen E; West Side Hosp; St Mary's Hosp, all since 1926. US Army, WW I and II. F: Amer Coll of Surgs; Intl Coll of Surgs; Amer Acad of Plastic Surg; pres, Lackawanna Med Soc, 1933-34, dir, 1934-40. Mem: Amer, Pa, and Lackawanna Med Socs; Pa Acad of Eye, Ear, Nose and Throat; Pa Allergy Assn; JWV; Amer Legion, 1940-48; ZOA; B'nai B'rith; J Comty Cen, past pres; Temple Isr; Masons, 32 deg; Odd

Fellows; Elks; club: Rotary. Home: 216 Conroy Ave, Scranton, Pa. Office: 327 N Washington Ave, Scranton, Pa.

ROSENBERG, Nathan, US, organization exec; b. NYC, Dec 19, 1910; s. Alter and Lena (Rosenberg); BA, CCNY, 1931; MS, Columbia U, 1934, MS, 1943; m. Ruth Friedman, Sept 10, 1936; c: Joseph, Judith Stern, Sarah. Exec vice-pres, Allied JCC, Denver, since 1948; dir: USO, Hawaii, 1939-43; Amer JDC, Chgo, 1943-48. Mem: Mayor's Budget Comm; Metrop Council for Comty Service, both Denver; CJFWF; Amer Assn of Social Work; J Comty Centers, Denver; Mt States Hillel Council; Masons. Home: 234 S Jersey St, Denver, Colo. Office: 400 Kittredge Bldg, Denver, Colo.

ROSENBERG, Norman, US, surgeon; b. NYC, Apr 25, 1916; s. Leo and Rose (Kamerman); BA, U of Pa, 1934; MD, NYU, 1938; m. Ruth Feller, Nov 30, 1940; c: Lois, Ralph. Chief of staff, Middlesex Gen Hosp, since 1967, staff since 1956; cons in surg: Johnson & Johnson Research Found, since 1956; Raritan Valley Hosp; in vascular surg: John F Kennedy Hosp, Edison, NJ; Somerset Hosp, 1960; Roosevelt Hosp, 1961; att surg, St Peters Gen Hosp, since 1946. Off, 39th Portable Surg Hosp, WW II. Dipl, Amer Bd Surg; f, Amer Coll Surg; mem: Intl Cardiovascular Soc; co med coord, Middlesex Co Civil Defense and Disaster Control, 1955-58. Contbr to: Modern Concepts of Hospital Administration, 1962; Fundamentals of Vascular Grafting, 1963; Biophysical Mechanisms in Vascular Homeostasis and Intravascular Thrombosis, 1965. Home: 48 North Dr, East Brunswick, NJ. Office: 10 Lincoln Ave, Highland Park, NJ.

ROSENBERG, Paul, US, physicist; b. NYC, Mar 31, 1910; s. Samuel and Evelyn (Abbey); BA, Columbia, 1930, MA, 1933, PhD, 1940; m. Marjorie Hillson, June 12, 1943; c: Gale. Pres, Paul Rosenberg Asso, cons physicists, since 1945; fmr: chem, Hawthorne Paint and Varnish Corp, NJ; grad asst, lectr, Columbia U; instr, Hunter Coll; research asso, MIT; mem staff: Radiation Lab, NDRC; war comm on radio, Amer Standards Assn. F: AAAS; Inst of Radio Engrs; asso f, Inst of Aerospace Sci; mem: Amer Phys Soc; Sigma Xi; Epsilon Chi; NY Acad of Sci; Amer Assn of Physics Tchrs; Amer Chem Soc; Acoustical Soc of Amer; Armed Forces Communications Assn; RESA, hon ind research soc; Amer Soc of Photogrammetry; Zeta Beta Tau; J Comty Cen, White Plains, NY; clubs: Point Beach; Columbia U; fmr: co-chmn, Natl Tech Comm for Upper Atmosphere and Interplanetary Navigation; gen chmn, Joint Conf on Radio Tech Commn for Aeronautics, Radio Tech Commn for Marine Services and Inst of Navigation; pres, Inst of Navigation; vice pres, AAAS, 1966-68. Contbr to sci and tech jours. Recipient: Talbert Abrams award, Amer Soc of Photogrammetry, 1955. Home: 53 Fernwood Rd, Larchmont, NY. Office: 330 Fifth Ave, Pelham, NY.

ROSENBERG, Paul, US, business exec; b. Chgo, Ill, May 29, 1920; s. Isaac and Sarah (Waintroob); att Armour Inst of Tech; m. Doris Raskin, June 18, 1944; c: Mark, Ira, Sharon. Pres, Lichtenwald Iron Works Co, since 1946. Pres: Asso Talmud Torahs; NW Side J Free Burial Soc; hon pres, Cong Ezras Isr; chmn: bldg comm: Ida Crown J Acad; Heb Theol Coll; Hillel Torah N Suburban Day Sch; syn div, Bonds for Isr; co-chmn, syn div, CJA; bd dirs: Arie Crown Heb Day Sch; J Comty Cen of Chgo; dir, JWF of Metrop Chgo; past pres: Cent lodge, B'nai B'rith; Council of Traditional Syns of Gtr Chgo. Home: 2546 W Jarvis St, Chicago, Ill. Office: 5092 N Kimberly Ave, Chicago, Ill.

ROSENBERG, Ralph P, US, educator, researcher; b. NYC, Apr 15, 1905; s. Barnet and Rose (Weislander); BS, CCNY, 1927; MA, U of Wis, 1928, PhD, 1933; m. Leah Davidson, June 26, 1930; c: Rochelle. Prof, German, Yeshiva U, NYC, since 1952, mem fac since 1934; fac, U of Wis, 1927-34. Mem: MLA; AAUP; Amer Assn of Tchrs of Ger; Intl Comparative Lit Assn. Contbr to scholarly jours. Recipient: U of Wis f, 1927-28; Ford Found Fac, 1951; Grants-in-Aid-of-Research, Amer Council Learned Socs, 1943-45; tour, guest, Ger govt, 1959. Home: 791 Cedar Lane, Teaneck, NJ. Office: Yeshiva U, Amsterdam Ave and 186 St, New York, NY.

ROSENBERG, Richard David, US, business exec; b. Chgo, Ill, Apr 13, 1921; s. Abraham and Minnie (Stashower); BSc, U of Pa, 1942; m. Susan Stern, Sep 28, 1943; c: Carol Troen, Betsy, Daniel, Michael, Jon. Exec vice-pres, Josam Mfg Co, since 1962; dir, First Merchants Natl Bank, since 1968; controller, Alliance Tire & Rubber Co, 1951-56;

vice-pres, i/c, intl oprs, Dayco Corp, 1956-62. Lt, USNR, 1942-46; cdr, Isr Navy, 1949-51. Pres, Mich City United Fund; 1st vice-pres, Dunes Art Found; treas, Memorial Hosp, Mich City; mem: exec bd, Boy Scouts Amer; natl council: JDC; Boy Scouts Amer; natl comm, J Scouting; Natl Small Cities Comm, Council of JWFs; adv bd, Warden of Ind State Prison; fmr: pres: Mich City United JWF; Council Boy Scouts Amer, Pottawattomie; chmn, Bur J Educ, Dayton, O; mem: Rotary Intl; B'nai B'rith, both Mich City. Recipient: Pres' Leadership Award, JCC, Dayton, 1961; Outstanding Citizen of Mich City, Jr C of C, 1967. Hobbies: music, golf; spec interests: J hist, J educ. Home: 8 Shore Dr, Dune Acres, Chesterton, Ind. Office: Josam Mfg Co, Corymbo Rd, Michigan City, Ind.

ROSENBERG, Roy Armand, US, rabbi; b. Baltimore, Md, Dec 22, 1930; s. Harry and Sylvia (Caplan); BA, U of Pa, 1951; MA, ordained rabbi, HUC, 1955, DHL, 1964; m. Ruth Herzberger, Aug 26, 1956; c: Raoul, Risa, Rani, Rianne. Rabbi: Temple Sinai, since 1966; Temple Emanu-El, Rochester, 1953-56; Temple Emanu-El, Honolulu, 1958-66. Chaplain, US Army, 1956-58. Pres, Volunteer Service Bur, 1964-66; chmn: Mayor Comm on Ethics in Govt, Honolulu, 1961-64; Inter-Faith Sem, 1964-66; mem: Hum Relations Comm, New Orleans; Bd J Family and Childrens Service; Bd Alumni Overseers, HUC; club, Rotary. Home: 506 Short St, New Orleans, La. Study: 6227 St Charles Ave, New Orleans, La.

ROSENBERG, Samuel, US, artist, educator; b. Phila, Pa, June 28, 1896; s. Solomon and Anna (Dickstein); BA, Carnegie-Mellon U, 1926; m. Libbie Levin, Dec 24, 1922; c: Murray. Prof, drawing and painting, Carnegie-Mellon U, since 1926; dir, art dept, YMHA, Pittsburgh, since 1926; head, art dept, Chatham Coll, 1937-45; one-man shows: Assoc Amer Artists, 1944, 1947; Bucknell U, 1948; U Tenn, 1948; Arts and Crafts Cen, Pittsburgh; Butler Art Inst; Cheltenham Art Cen; Boston Mus Sch; Pittsburgh Playhouse, all 1950; J Comty Cen, Cleveland, 1951; Carnegie Inst, 1922-37, 1956, 1958, 1965; perm collections: Butler Art Inst; Carnegie Inst; Ency Britannica; Pa State U; Slippery Rock State Tchrs Coll. Mem: Art comm; Asso Artists; Abstract Group, all Pittsburgh; AAUP. Recipient: awards: Pittsburgh Soc of Art, 1928, 1929; Assoc Artists of Pittsburgh, 1917, 1920, 1921, 1930, 1936, 1946, 1948; Butler Art Inst, 1939, 1943, 1947; Martin Lesser, 1941; Carnegie Inst, 1945, 1954; Ind State Tchrs Coll, 1946; Pepsi Cola, 1947, 1948; Jacques Blum, 1947, 1948; Grensfelder, 1953. Home: 2721 Mt Royal Rd, Pittsburgh, Pa. Office: Coll of Fine Arts, Carnegie-Mellon U, Pittsburgh, Pa.

ROSENBERG, Samuel, US, organization exec, teacher; b. Zhagory, Russ, Oct 3, 1907; s. Leib and Yetta (Levitas); in US since 1928; BS, Columbia U, 1931; att: Dropsie Coll; NYU; JTSA; m. Frieda Gershofsky, May 30, 1941; c: Ethan, Rena. Fmr: exec dir, Bur of J Educ, Savannah, Ga, 1954-1969; prin, Heb Public Schs Radviliskis, Lith; tchr, Talmud Torah, Bklyn, NY, 1929-45; acting prin, Temple Isr Rel Sch, Wilkes-Barre, Pa; prin, Savannah Heb Sch, 1946-54. Pres, org, Chug Ivri, Savannah, since 1961; mem exec, Savannah dist, ZOA, since 1947, past financial secy; mem: Natl Council for J Educ; Savannah J Council; J Educ Alliance; fmr: pres, Savannah Zionist Dist; mem comm on public housing, Citizen's Housing Council, NYC. Contbr to periodicals. Home: 340 Oxford Dr, Savannah, Ga. Office: 5111 Abercorn St, Savannah, Ga.

ROSENBERG, Samuel Bernard, Eng, communal exec; b. Nowy Dwor, Pol, Apr 25, 1893; s. Barnett and Rifka (Yarzombeck); in Eng since 1897; m. Sarah Bach, Oct 31, 1915. Pres, Southend and Westcliff Heb Cong, treas since 1944; fmr, mgn dir, S B Rosenberg Ltd. Chmn: Heb Educ Bd; Herzlia Day Sch; bd of govs; Heb classes, bldg comm; pres: New Youth Cen; J Friendly Soc, Southend br; Past Grand Standard, Supr Grand Chap of Eng, Masons, mem, off of numerous lodges. Hobby: collecting objects of art, antiques. Home: Snowdonia, Chalkwell Espl, Westcliff-on-Sea, Essex, Eng. Office: 169-171 High St, Southend-on-Sea, Essex, Eng.

ROSENBERG, Shlomo (Solomon), US, journalist, author; b. Laskarzew, Pol, Apr 23, 1896; s. Henoch and Nehama (Rosenberg); in US since 1941; m. Regina Prashker, Feb 28, 1936; c: Marc, Harold, Rene Frayman. Mem staff, The Jewish Day Journal, since 1942; mem, Chalutz, Pal, 1919-22; actor, Heb stage, 1921; secy to Sholem Asch, 1930-38; mem staff: Hajnt, Yiddish daily newspaper, Warsaw, 1931-38; Pariser Wochenblatt, Di Woch, Illustrierter Wochenblatt, all Paris, 1932-40; publicity staff, UJA, 1943-46. Author: Eli Hacohen's

Toit (poem), 1918; Tswishen Feier un Shwert, 1942; Der Yiddisher Monach, 1943; Yiddishe Heldn, 1943; Rabbi Akiba, 1944; Shlomo Hamelech, 1944; In Kamf far a Neijer Welt, 1945; Der Yiddisher Printz, 1947; Bar Kochba, 1948; Rabbi Meier and Beruriah, 1950; Moshiach's Tsayten, 1950; Der Yiddisher Kenig bei der Volga, 1954; Sholem Asch Fun Der Noent, 1958; Di Kuzrim, 1960; Shabbethai Zevi, 1965. Mem: Yiddish PEN Club; Yiddish Writers Union; LZOA-Poale Zion; Farband Lab Zionist Order. Home: 2950 Bronx Park E, Bronx, NY. Office: 183 E Broadway, New York, NY.

ROSENBERG, Stuart E, Can, rabbi, author; b. NYC, July 5, 1922; s. Hyman and Kate (Weissman); grad, Herzlia Tchrs Sem, 1942; BA, Bklyn Coll, 1942; ordained rabbi, JTSA, 1945, MHL, 1949; MA, Columbia U, 1948, PhD, 1953; m. Hadassah Agassi; c: Rochelle, Ronni, Elissa. Rabbi: Beth Tzedec Cong, Toronto, since 1956; fmr: Temple Beth El, Rochester, NY, 1946-56; lectr, rel, U of Rochester, 1952-56; guest preacher, Church of the Air, CBS. Author: Role and Function of the Rabbi, 1948; The Jewish Community in Rochester, 1843-1925, pub 1954; Man is Free, 1957; The Road to Confidence, 1959; A Time to Speak, 1960; Bridge to Brotherhood, 1961; The Bible is for You, 1961; More Loves Than One: The Bible Confronts Psychiatry, 1963; America is Different: The Making of the American Jew, 1963-64; ed, A Humane Society, 1962; Judaism, 1966; What Do We Believe, 1968; dept ed, Ency Judaica; contbr: weekly syndicated newspaper column, Lines on Life, in US and Can. Vice-pres, Natl Found for J Culture; mem: exec council, RA, chmn, cen Can region, since 1961; rabb cabinet, JTSA; exec, Red Cross; bd trustees, United Comty Fund, both Toronto; Bd of J Orgs in Can; Masons; hon mem, Amer Newspaper Guild; clubs: Variety; Rotary; natl pres, Can J Cultural Found; chmn, UJA, Toronto; chmn, Toronto Rabb f; pres, Rochester dist, ZOA; mem exec, chaplaincy comms, NY Bd of Rabbis. Recipient: award, J Book Council Amer, 1954; Dr Stuart E Rosenberg Chair in J Hist named in his honor, JTSA; Citation for Leadership, Can MH Assn, 1963. Home: 14 Dewbourne Ave, Toronto, Can. Office: 1700 Bathurst St, Toronto, Can.

ROSENBERG, William B, US, attorney; b. Harrisburg, Pa, Aug 19, 1914; s. Robert and Mary (Katzman); BA, Dickinson Coll, 1935; LLB, Columbia U, 1938; m. Yvette Rayben, Mar 13, 1943; c: Joan, David. Partner, law firm, Blumberg & Rosenberg, since 1947; judge, Manville Munic Court, 1949-55. US Army, 1943-46. Pres: Somerset dist, ZOA, 1947-48; Bound Brook J Cen, 1948-51; Somerset Co Bar Assn, 1959; mem: Amer, NJ, Bar Assns; JWV; Amer Legion; Somerset Co Vocational Tech Bd of Educ; Phi Beta Kappa. Home: 121 Agnes Place, Bound Brook, NJ. Office: 35 N Bridge St, Somerville, NJ.

ROSENBLATT, Louise M, US, educator, author; b. Atlantic City, NJ, Aug 23, 1904; d. Samuel and Jennie (Berman); BA, Barnard Coll, 1925; cert d'études, U of Grenoble, Fr, 1926; PhD, Sorbonne, 1931; m. Sidney Ratner, June 16, 1932. Prof, Eng educ, NYU, since 1948; instr, Eng, Barnard Coll, 1927-28, 1929-38; asst prof, Eng, Bklyn Coll, 1938-48; visiting prof, Northwestern U, 1938, 1939; asso chief, W Eur sect, Bur of Overseas Intelligence, Off of War Info, 1943-44, chief Cen Reports sect, 1944-45. Author: L'idée de l'Art pour l'Art, 1931; Literature as Exploration, rev ed, 1968; co-author: Reading in an Age of Mass Communication, 1954; mem, ed bd, College English, 1948-51; contbr to scholarly and profsl jours. Mem: commn on lit, Natl Council Tchrs of Eng, since 1965, fmr mem, bd trustees, research found; MLA; Amer Educ Research Assn; Amer Soc Esthetics; Comparative Lit Assn; NEA; AAUP; fmr: mem: Natl Comm on Eng; comm on Eng, Coll Entrance Examination Bd. Recipient: Guggenheim f, 1942-43; dist lectr for 1970, Natl Council Tchrs of Eng. Hobbies: theater, gardening. Home: 11 Cleveland Lane, Princeton, NJ. Office: NYU, New York, NY.

ROSENBLATT, Richard D, US, business exec; b. NYC, June 18, 1926; s. William and Therese (Steinhardt); att Staunton Mil Acad; Cornell U, 1943-44; grad, W Point Mil Acad, 1949; m. Lois Strauch; c: Amy, Michael, Julie, James, Emily. Pres, Atwood Richards Inc, subsidiary of Chemway Corp, since 1955, dir, Chemway Corp since 1968; pres, Telescreen, Inc, 1959-70. Pilot; interpreter, OSI; liaison off, 1944-54. Clubs: Wings, aviation pioneers; City Athletic, NYC; West Point Soc, NY; Friar's; Presidents, Dem Party. Hobbies: horseback riding, boating, anthropology, flying. Home: 4941 Arlington Ave, Riverdale, NY. Office: 666 Fifth Ave, New York, NY.

ROSENBLATT, Samuel, US, rabbi; b. Bratislava, Czech, May 5, 1902; s. Josef and Taube (Kaufman); in US since 1912; BA, magna cum laude, CCNY, 1921; ordained rabbi, JTSA, 1925; ordained rabbi, Universal Yeshiva of Jerusalem, 1926; PhD, Columbia U, 1927; DD, JTSA, 1965; m. Claire Woloch, Oct 3, 1926; c: David, Judah, Josef. Rabbi: Beth Tfiloh Cong, Baltimore, since 1927; Adath Isr Cong, Trenton, NJ, 1926-27; asso prof, oriental languages, Johns Hopkins U, since 1947, lectr, J lit, 1930-47; Hazard f, Amer Sch Oriental Research, Jerusalem, 1925-26; lectr, Semitic langs, Columbia U, 1926-28; delg, 19th and 23rd ZC, 1935, 1951. Mem: RA; B'nai B'rith; Amer Oriental Soc; Soc of Bib Lit and Exegesis; J Acad of Arts and Scis; AAUP; Conf of J Relations; Rel Zionists of Amer; Amer Acad for J Research; NCCJ. Author: The Highways to Perfection of Abraham Maimonides, 2 vols, 1927, 1938; The Interpretation of the Bible in the Mishnah, 1935; Our Heritage, 1940; This is the Land, 1940; The People and the Book, 1943; The Book of Beliefs and Opinions of Saadia Gaon, 1948; The History of the Mizrachi Movement, 1951; Yossele Rosenblatt, 1954; Hear Oh Israel, 1958; This Night is Different (Passover Seder recording), 1961. Clubs: Mercantile; Woodholme Country. Hobby, travel. Home: 3310 Old Forest Rd, Baltimore, Md. Office: Johns Hopkins U, Dept of Oriental Langs, Baltimore, Md. Study: Cong Beth Tfiloh, Baltimore, Md.

ROSENBLOOM, Charles J, US, investment exec; b. Steubenville, O, Apr 13, 1898; s. Sol and Celia (Neumark); BA, Yale U, 1920; m. Lucile Johnson, Dec 18, 1944. Pres, Rosenbloom Finance Corp. Vice-pres, Pittsburgh Sym Soc; trustee: Carnegie-Mellon U; Pittsburgh Housing Auth, bd mem; hon mem, bd of govs, Heb U, Jerusalem; dir, JTSA; clubs: Harvard, Yale, Princeton, Concordia. Hobbies: collecting art and rare books. Home: 1036 Beechwood Blvd, Pittsburgh, Pa. Office: 521 Union Trust Bldg, Pittsburgh, Pa.

ROSENBLOOM, Fred L, US, attorney; b. Phila, Pa, Apr 9, 1900; s. Herman and Sarah (Labowitz); att U Pa, 1918-21; LLB, Temple U Law Sch, 1932; DLitt, Del Valley Coll of Sci and Agric, 1967; m. Pauline Basen, Feb 6, 1924; c: David, Sanford. Partner, law firm, Schander, Harrison, Segal and Lewis, since 1936; mem fac, Del Valley Coll, since 1948; fmr, field agt, instr, income tax law, US Internal Revenue Bur, 1922-36. Mem: natl exec, past chmn, Phila chap, AJComm; exec, trustee, Del Valley Coll; Temple U Law Alumni Assn; Fed, Amer, Pa, Bar Assns; Masons; clubs: Natl Rep (NYC); Natl Lawyers; Lawyers; Midday; Locust, Phila; lectr, fed taxation, before bar assns; dir, Phila J Comty Relations Council; trustee: Home for J Aged, Phila; Phila Psycht Cen; Fed of J Agcys of Phila; CPA. Contbr to legal periodicals. Home: 1830 Rittenhouse Sq, Philadelphia, Pa. Office: Packard Bldg, Philadelphia, Pa.

ROSENBLOOM, Joseph R, US, rabbi; b. Rochester, NY, Dec 5, 1928; s. Morris and Pearl (Vinik); BA, U Cincinnati, 1950; BHL, HUC, 1952, MHL, 1954, DHL, 1957; m. Cordelia Sherman, June 17, 1952; c: Deborah, Eve, Dena. Rabbi, Temple Emanuel, since 1961; Shaare Emeth, St Louis, 1954-56; Adath Isr, Lexington, Ky, 1956-61; instr, Wash U, since 1961; lectr, U Ky, 1956-61; chaplain, Fed Narcotics Hosp, 1956-61. Mem, bd of delgs, AJComm, since 1958; pres: United Cerebral Palsy of Ky, 1959-61; Lexington Min Assn, 1960; chmn, Ky Commn on Aging, 1958-61. Author: A Biographical Dictionary of Early American Jewry, 1960; A Literary Analysis of the Dead Sea Isaiah Scroll, 1969. Contbr to mags. Home: 541 Purdue, St Louis, Mo. Study: 12166 Conway, St Louis, Mo.

ROSENBLOOM, Morris Victor, publisher, public relations exec; b. Pittsburgh, Pa, Oct 25, 1915; s. Alfred and Corinne (Lorch); BA, U of Pittsburgh, 1936; m. Ronda Robins, May 16, 1953. Pres: Amer Ind Surveys, since 1955, dir, 1947-54; dir, PR Publ Corp, since 1962; found, dir, Amer Ind Surveys, NYC, 1939-41; sr econ, Off Price Mgmt, 1941-42; specialist, War Produc Bd, 1942-43; vice-pres i/c of sales, Diamond Products, Inc, 1946-47; cons to pres, sales mgr, Publicker Ind, Phila, 1947-50; found, exec dir, Inst on Econs Defense Mobilization, 1951-52; asso, Coates & McCormick Inc, NY and Wash, DC, 1954. USN, 1943-46; lt cdr, USNR. Dir, oprs, Natl Citizens Comm for Hoover Report; mem: bd of regents, U of Pittsburgh; natl council, natl PR comm, exec bd and chmn, Boy Scouts Amer; adv to chmn, Fed Maritime Commn; chmn, 1969 world trade award luncheon, Metrop Wash Bd of Trade; mem: Acad Political and Social Scis; Amer Legion; Naval Hist Found; Defense Orientation Conf Assn, vice-pres, 1956-57; PR Soc Amer, dir, Wash chap, since 1962, regional

ROSENBLOOM, repr, natl eligibility comm, counselors sect, since 1963; Amer Political Sci Assn; JWV; Res Offs Assn; US Naval Inst; VFW, mem natl publicity, PR comm, 1953-55; natl panel arbitrators, Amer Arbitration Assn; Intl Platform Assn; Pi Lambda Phi; clubs: Army and Navy; Pitt. Author: The Liquor Industry, 1935, rev ed, 1937; Peace Through Strength: Bernard Baruch and a Blueprint for Security, 1953; co-author: Bottling for Profit, 1940; ed adv bd, PR Quarterly; contbr to profsl jours; lectr. Recipient: Warner award, 1953; Silver Beaver award, Boy Scouts Amer, 1963. Homes: 114 River Dr, Bay Ridge, Annapolis, Md; 2500 Q St, NW, Washington, DC. Office: Headquarters Bldg, 2000 P St, NW, Washington, DC.

ROSENBLOOM, Noah H, US, rabbi, educator; b. Radom, Pol, Sep 29, 1915; s. Michael and Sarah (Weingelb); in US since 1938; tchr's dipl, Yeshiva U, 1939, ordained rabbi, 1942, B Rel Educ, 1945, DHL, 1948; MA, Columbia U, 1945; PhD, NYU, 1958; m. Pearl Cohen, June, 1946; c: Leah, Michaelle. Prof, Stern Coll, Yeshiva U, fac mem since 1954; rabbi: B'nai Isr J Cen, Bklyn, since 1949; Montefiore Heb Cong, Bronx, 1943-46; Tikvath Isr, Phila, 1946-48; instr, Hunter Coll, NY, 1949-54. Mem: RabCA. Author: Luzzatto's Ethico-Psychological Interpretation of Judaism, 1965; contbr to rel and sociol jours. Recipient: Horeb Award, Yeshiva U. Home: 357 Remsen Ave, Brooklyn, NY. Office: Stern Coll, Yeshiva U, New York, NY.

ROSENBLUETH, Cessy W, Isr, social worker; b. Berlin, Ger, Jan 31, 1898; d. Isidor and Alma (Wygodzinesky) Dialoszyinski; in Isr since 1924; att: U Berlin; U Breslau; tchr cert, Breslau Rabb Sch; cert, Sch of Social Work, Jerusalem, 1938; m. Felix Rosenblueth (decd), Jan 6, 1924; c: Tuvia Naooth, Gabriel. Rehab counsellor, Natl Council of Kibbutz Movement, since 1964; social worker, Munic of Haifa, 1943-50; training dir, social workers, Min Wfr, 1951-56; youth employment counsellor, Min Lab, 1956-60. Mem, Women's Council Lab Org; Social Workers Assn; Histadrut; fmr: chmn, WIZO, Jerusalem; secy, Ger Settler's Org. Recipient: UN Observation f, 1950-51. Home: 13 Tomkin St, Tel Aviv, Isr.

ROSENBLUM, Frank, US, labor union exec; b. NYC, May 15, 1887; s. Louis and Annie (Karna); m. Ida Beispiel, Sep 19, 1924; c: Beaty Harris, Leigh, Howard. Gen secy-treas, Amalgamated Clothing Workers of Amer (AFL-CIO), since 1946, found, 1914; vice-pres, ind union dept, AFL-CIO, since 1955; vice-pres, CIO, 1940-55, dir, middlewest textile workers org comm, 1937-39; dir: Amalgamated Trust & Savings Bank, Chgo; Amalgamated Bank of NY; Amalgamated Life Ins Co, Inc; chmn, bd of dirs, Amalgamated Laundry Workers Health Cen, NY; secy and trustee, Amalgamated Ins Fund; secy, Sidney Hillman Found; mem, bd of trustees, Amalgamated Laundry Workers Ins Fund; Amalgamated Cotton Garment and Allied Inds Fund; Amalgamated Neckwear Workers Ins and Retirement Funds; cen states joint bd, Amalgamated Clothing Workers of Amer, Ins Fund; Sidney Hillman Health Cen; Amalgamated Social Benefits Assn; vice-pres, mem of exec bur, World Fed of Trade Unions, 1948-49. Served US Army, WW I. Home: 5701 Sheridan Rd, Chicago, Ill.

ROSENBLUM, Marvin Allan, US, business exec; b. Perth Amboy, NJ, Nov 10, 1930; s. Irving and Anne (Goldstein); BEcon, Rutgers U, 1952; m. Esti Laufer, June 7, 1953; c: Jan, Joshua, Jody. Pres, Precision Polymers Inc, since 1966; vice-pres, Foros Hardware Co, Foros, NJ, 1954-66. Cpl, US Army, 1952. Mem: perm bd, Temple Emanuel, Edison, NJ, past pres; adv bd, Raritan Valley Natl Bank; B'nai B'rith; Soc of Plastic Engrs; YMHA; Metuchen-Edison Racial Relations Council; Plastic Pipe Inst; Natl Swimming Pool Inst; fmr, chaplain, Masons. Home: 2 Renee Ct, Edison, NJ. Office: POB 237, Greenpond Rd, Rockaway, NJ.

ROSENBLUTH, Arthur G, US, organization exec, attorney; b. NYC, Apr 10, 1907; s. Morris and Kate (Gordon); BS, CCNY, 1927, MS, 1943; LLB, cum laude, Fordham U Law Sch, 1930; m. Ina Walit, Oct 15, 1933; c: Alan, Karen. Exec secy, metrop council, B'nai B'rith, since 1944, vice-pres, 1943-44; bus mgr, Metrop Star publ, since 1945; mem, metrop adv bd: ADL, Vocational Service; fmr: tchr, Bd of Educ, NYC, 1927-44; in law practice, Rosenbluth & Rosenbluth, 1930-44; Dir, Queens Coll Hillel Found Bldg Corp; mem, bd of dirs, CCNY Alumni Assn, 1930-36; pres, Franklin D Roosevelt lodge, B'nai B'rith, 1942-43. Mem, Temple Isr, Lawrence, LI. Home: 15 Sutton Lane, Hewlett, LI, NY. Office: 315 Lexington Ave, New York, NY.

ROSENBLUTH, Gideon, Can, educator; b. Berlin, Ger, Jan 23, 1921; s. Martin and Marie (Zellermayer); in Can since 1941; att, LSE; BA, U Toronto, 1943; PhD, Columbia U, 1953; m. Annemarie Fischl, 1944; c: Vera, David. Prof, econ, U of BC, since 1962; fmr: stat, Can Govt; lectr, Princeton U; research asso, Natl Bur of Econ Research, NY; asso prof: Stanford U, 1952-54; Queens U, Kingston, Can, 1954-62. Mem: Can Econ Assn; Amer Econ Assn; Royal Econ Assn. Author: Concentration in Canadian Manufacturing Industries, 1957; The Canadian Economy and Disarmament, 1967; co-author: Canadian Anti-Combines Administration, 1963; contbr to books and academic jours. Office: U of British Columbia, Vancouver, Can.

ROSENBLUTH, Ina Walit, US, communal leader; b. Springfield, Mass, May 30, 1911; d. Alexander and Rose (Labowitz) Walit; BS, Rider Coll, Trenton, NJ, 1930; postgrad, Columbia, 1930-33; m. Arthur Rosenbluth, Oct 15, 1933; c: Alan, Karen. First vice-pres, Natl B'nai B'rith Women, since 1963, natl exec bd, since 1957; past pres, Intl B'nai B'rith Women, 1965-68; mem: intl council, B'nai B'rith, since 1965; natl comm, ADL, since 1957, past natl chmn, NY exec since 1957; natl rel adv comm, Girl Scouts of Amer, since 1957; LI bd, women's div, Fed of J Charities; LI regional bd, B'nai B'rith Youth Org; exec comm: Sisterhood, Forest Hills J Cen; Natl Council of J Women; Temple Isr, LI; Hadassah; found, vice-pres, Conf of Forest Hills, LI Women's Orgs; fmr: natl pres, Phi Eta Sigma; off, Forest Hills chap, Amer Women's Volunteer Service; vice-pres, Queens Coll Hillel Bldg Corp; trustee: Leo N Levi Memorial Hosp, Ark; Natl J Hosp, Denver, Colo; PR chmn, Womens Natl Conf on Hum Relations, Wash, DC; co-chmn, admn comm, Metrop Star; mem: exec comm, Amer-Isr Public Affairs comm; Pres Comm on Employment of the Handicapped. Recipient: awards: B'nai B'rith Women; ADL; Hillel Found; Amer Women's Volunteer Service. Home: 15 Sutton Lane, Hewlett, NY.

ROSENBLUTH, Leo, Swed, cantor, singer, composer; b. Furth, Ger, Jan 11, 1904; s. Simon and Eva (Ephrosi); in Swed since 1931; att U and Konservatorium, Frankfurt/Main, 1922-26; m. Rosa Benkow, May 27, 1934; c: Jeanne-Esti Rosenthal. Chief cantor, choir leader, J Cong, Stockholm, since 1931; leader: J Music Soc, 1941-45; Swed Bromma Choir, 1942-44; concert soloist in Eur, Isr; composer: Folkopera Schulamit; Cantata Hebraica; Trejst; music for The Tenth Man; Tewje and His Daughters; Paddy Chayefski's Holiday Song; commissioned by: Royal Theatre, Stockholm; Swed Bc Co; recordings: Decca, HMV, and Svirsky-Found. Recipient: first prize, Cong for J Culture, NYC, 1949. Home: Kungsholms Strand 155 VIII, Stockholm, Swed. Office: Mosaiska Församlingen, Wahrendorffsgatan 3, Stockholm, Swed.

ROSENBLUTH, Pinchas Erich, Isr, educator; b. Berlin, Ger, July 23, 1906; s. David and Erwine (Barkany); in Isr since 1934; att, Yeshiva Breuer, Frankfurt/M, 1926; PhD, U of Berlin, 1933; tchr dipl, Rabb Sem, Berlin, 1938; m. Matilde Rottenberg, 1934; c: Chava Rachman, David, Moshe. Headmaster, Mikve Isr Sch, since 1945; tchr, J High Sch, Ger, 1932-34; head, Rel Youth Aliyah, 1934-45. Author: Aliyat Hanoar, 1958; Martin Buber, Sein Denken und Winken, 1968. Mem: Cen, Political, Cultural, comms: Natl Rel Party; Hapoel Hamizrahi; Hakibbutz Hadati; J Hist Soc. Contbr to profsl publs. Hobby: collecting hist papers, jours. Home: Shikun Ovdim, Mikve Israel, Holon, Isr. Office: Mikve Israel Sch, Holon, Isr.

ROSENDORFF, Simcha, Isr, physicist; b. Berlin, Ger, Dec 4, 1925; s. Hermann and Hedwig (Zondek); in Isr since 1939; MSc, Heb U, Jerusalem, 1953, PhD, 1957; m. Erika Schrager, Apr 17, 1951; c: Irith, Oriela. Asso prof, Technion, Haifa since 1964, fmr head dept physics. Pvt, IDF, 1948-49. Mem, Amer, Isr Phys Socs. Contbr to sci jours. Home: 82 Horeb St, Haifa, Isr. Office: Technion, Haifa, Isr.

ROSENFELD, Aaron, Isr, business exec; b. Zichron Yaakov, Pal, June 30, 1899; m. Olga Bardash, 1926; c: Zwi, Arie, Israel. Belgian Consul Gen since 1929; consul for Liberia; fmr: staff, ICA, Haifa; Ships Agent and Mfrs Rep. Recipient: Grand Cdr, Order of the Star of Afr; Officier de l'Ordre de la Couronne de Belgique; Chevalier de l'Ordre de Leopold; Crois Civique, 35 yrs of consular service; Chevalier de l'Ordre Grand-Ducal de la Couronne de Chêne, Lux, Verdientst Kreuz Klasse 1, Bundesrepublik Deutschland. Office: 104 Haatzmauth Rd, Haifa, Isr.

ROSENFELD, Abraham I J, Eng, rabbi, author; b. Jerusalem, Isr, Mar 26, 1914; s. Notte and Chaye (Blank); ordained rabbi, Yeshivat Eitz Hayim, 1930; att: Rabbi Kook's Universal Yeshiva, both Jerusalem; Jews Coll, London, 1933-34; m. Miriam Bowman, June 8, 1941; c: Lionel, Susan. Min, Reader, Finchley Syn, London, since 1941; chaplain, U Coll Hosp, London, since 1950; fmr: min, Walford Rd Syn, London, 1934-41; chaplain, Westminster Hosp, 1942-50; hon supr, Finchley Heb Sch, 1945-48; pres, chmn, JNF Commn; hon pres, JPA Comm, both Finchley; vice-pres, JNF for Gt Brit and Ir, since 1952; pres: Friends of British Settler's Assn; The Anglo J Chr Soc; hon pres: Min Assn of Gt Brit and Ir; vice-pres, Finchley Combined Aid; treas, Gt Universal Yeshiva, Jerusalem; hon secy, J Publ Comm; secy: Agudat Achvat-Moses Montefiore lodge, Masons; exec, wfr comm, United Syn; Gen Council JNF, London; chaplain: Waverley Manor; Royal Ear Hosp; mem, house comm, Maurice and Samuel Lyon Home; fmr: found, chmn, Friends of Histadrut Olei Britania; vice-chmn, Regional Comm for Further J Educ; hon secy, Publ of New Heb Grammar; vice-pres, chmn, Finchley Zionist Soc; mem: Masons, King David lodge, Star of David lodge, both London. Author: The Authorised Selichot for the Whole Year, 1956; The Authorized Kinot for the Ninth of Av, 1965; contbr to mags, periodicals. Recipient: Freeman, City of London, 1959. Hobbies: reading; music; travel. Home: 46 Fitzalan Rd, London, Eng.

ROSENFELD, Eva, US, research sociol; b. Warsaw, Pol, Aug 5, 1915; d. Pinhas and Hannah (Handlarz); in US since 1938; LLM, U of Warsaw, 1938; MA, Columbia U, 1946, PhD, 1952. Research sociol since 1968; research asso, bur of applied social research, Columbia U, 1943-45; instr, sociol, Bard Coll, 1946-47; research f, Social Sci Research Council, field work in Isr, 1947-49; jt instr, Isr collectives, Columbia U, 1950-51; asst research prof, research cen for hum relations, NYU, 1952-57; asso dir of research, cen research unit, J Bd of Guardians, 1957-68. Mem, Amer Sociol Soc. Co-author: The Road to H, 1963; contbr to profsl jours. Home: 7 Washington Sq Pl, New York, NY.

ROSENFELD, Hirsh, Can, physician; b. Naumistis, Lith, Dec 10, 1907; s. Joseph and Anna (Levine); in Can since 1924; BA, McGill U, 1928; MD, U Strasbourg, Fr, 1936; m. Dora Kofsky, Feb 18, 1940. Pvt practice since 1937; pres, Drs Hosp, Inc; mem, Montreal Med Clinic. F, Amer Geriatric Soc; natl vice-pres, Amer Phys's F Inc, IMA; vice-pres, Que Pvt Hosps Assn; bd govs, YMHA; mem and patron, Jerusalem Acad of Med; corresp mem, IMA; mem: Can Med Assn; Coll of Phys and Surg; Assn des Médecins de Langue Française du Canada; J People's Sch; J Peretz Sch; club, Montefiore. Home: 31 Maplewood Ave, Outremont, Que, Can. Office: 4575 Park Ave, Montreal, Can.

ROSENFELD, Joseph, Eng, rabbi, educ; b. Jerusalem, Isr, Aug 27, 1909; s. Notte and Chaya (Blank); att Eitz Chaim Sch and Coll, Jerusalem, 1928; U Tutorial Coll, London; Hampstead Inst, London; m. Hilda Cohen; c: Neil, Clive, Gail. Rabbi, Sinai Syn, since 1948; hon supt, Heb classes; min, NW London Syn, 1931-47. Gov, The Gen Bikur Cholim Hosp, Jerusalem, hon secy Brit Aid comm; chmn: The Friend of Incurables, Beth Cholim Mitnavnim, Jerusalem; hon pres, J Vegetarian Soc; mem, Masonic Leadenhall lodge. Contbr to J periodicals. Spec interests: langs, phil. Home: 22 Wessex Gardens, Middlesex, Eng.

ROSENFELD, Joseph B, Isr, physician; b. Sofia, Bulgaria, Mar 19, 1926; s. Bernard and Liza (Carmin); in Isr since 1948; BA, Fr Coll, Sofia, 1944; MD, Hadassah Heb U, 1952; m. Lilli Tadjer, 1957; c: Talia, Randolph, Bernard. Chief, 3rd dept med, Beilinson Hosp, Isr, since 1967; head: renal unit; renal and hypertension clinic, both Beilinson Med Cen, since 1964; fmr: res, internal med, Beilinson Hosp, 1955-58; f, hypertension unit, Hahnemann Med Coll, Phil, 1958-59; research f, renal sect, Tufts U Med Sch, 1959-61; instr, staff mem, hypertension renal unit, Hahnemann Med Coll and Hospital, 1961-63; sr lectr, Tel Aviv U Med Sch, 1967. Pres, Isr Soc of Nephrology; mem: sci council, IMA; council for safety, import of drugs; teaching comm, postgrad med sch, Tel Aviv U; Isr Soc of Card; Amer Fed of Clinical Research; Phila Phys Soc; NY Acad of Sci; f, Amer Coll of Card. Ed, Physical Therapy. Home: 29 Remez St, Tel Aviv, Isr. Office: Beilinson Hospital, Petach Tikva, Isr.

ROSENFELD, Louis Judah, US, urologist, surgeon; b. NYC, Mar 27, 1912; s. Israel and Sarah (Fliegelman); att: Rabbi Jacob Joseph Sch, NYC; Talmudical Acad, NYC; BSc, NYU,

1932; MD, U of Vienna Med Sch, Aus, 1937; m. Elizabeth Silverberg; c: Myrna Fruchtman, William. Asst clinical prof, urol, Albert Einstein Sch of Med; asso att, urol, Beth Isr Med Cen. F, Amer Coll Surgs; mem: bd trustees, Rabbi Jacob Joseph Sch; Young Isr, Fifth Ave; Amer Geriatric Soc, NYC; Amer Urol Assn; AMA. Author: Carcinoma in Diverticula of the Female Urethra, 1964; Aneurysm of the Spermatic Artery, 1964. Spec interests: Heb and Arabic lit and lang. Home and office: 55 E 9 St, New York, NY.

ROSENFELD, Maurice, US, business exec; b. NYC, Feb 21, 1891; s. Jacob and Rose (Eisenberg); m. Allie Leventhal, Jan 1, 1913; c: Ricka Krissel, Irma Canno. Chmn bd, Equitable Paper Bag Co, since 1969, pres, 1922-69. Commn, Saratoga Springs comm, since 1953; trustee, Natl Council on Crime and Delinquency, since 1959; hon life trustee, FJP, NYC; hon trustee: Union Temple, Bklyn; Yeshiva of Crown Hgts, Bklyn; Westchester J Cen, Mamaroneck; Temple Emanu-El; trustee: LI Coll of Med; hon pres, Bklyn Heb Orphan Asylum; a found, Albert Einstein Coll, Yeshiva U. Sponsor, annual boxing tournaments, NYC Parks Dept, 1951-61. Recipient: awards: Mayor Robert Wagner, NYC; Mayor John Lindsay, NYC; UJA, 1968. Home 870 Fifth Ave, New York, NY. Office: 45-50 Van Dam St, LI City, NY.

ROSENFELD, Pinhas Paul, Isr, dairy expert; b. Berlin, Ger, Sep 9, 1912; s. Jakob and Dora (Hutschneker); in Isr since 1934; att: U Berlin; U Brussels; m. Dvorah Ettinger, July 15, 1936; c: Noa Tal, Dina Golan. Adv, expert, bd mem: Tenne-Noga Dairies, since 1969, gen mgr, 1957-67; mgr, dir, United Dairies, 1967-69. Expert: FAO Milk Div; cons panel, Govt Dairy Fed; mem: Food Tech Soc; fmr: secy, Tel Ganim Syn; perm comm of warm countries, Govt Dairy Fed; club: Rotary, Sharon. Author: Sterilized Milk in Warm Countries, 1965; Dairy Products Under Arid Conditions, 1968. Home: 120 Uziel St, Ramat Gan, Isr. Office: Tenne-Noga Dairies, Kfar Shmeriayhu, Isr.

ROSENFELD, Samuel S, US, physician; b. Yedinitz, Russ, Nov 16, 1893; s. David and Pessa (Honigman); in US since 1897; MD, NYU, 1915; m. Vilma Weiward, Oct 14, 1917. Cons, obstet and gyn: J Memorial Hosp, since 1937; Leb Hosp, since 1943. US Army MC, 1917-19. Chmn, Bx Phys div: J Fed of Charities of NY, 1940-41; HIAS, since 1945; UJA, 1946-47; pres: Leb Hosp Alumni Soc, 1936; Bx Obstet and Gyn Soc; f: Amer Coll of Surgs; NY Acad of Med; Amer Acad of Obstets and Gyn; dipl, Amer Bd of Obstets and Gyn. Mem: AAAS; Bx Co Med Soc; Amer Legion; Heb Free Burial Soc. Author: Gynecology and Urology for Nurses, 1931. Contbr to med jours. Home: 1705 Popham Ave, New York, NY. Office: 1882 Grand Concourse, New York, NY.

ROSENFELD, Shalom, Isr, journalist; b. Targowice, Pol, Dec 15, 1914; s. Nathan and Batya; in Isr since 1934; m. Ilana Eckstein, Sep 1, 1959; c: Yoram, Tamar. Dep ed-in-chief, Maariv, since 1959; corresp, J Forward, NY, since 1954; news ed: Hayarden; Hamashkif; Heruth; mem ed bd, Yediot Ahronot daily. Author: Criminal File 124; Strictly Private; trans from Eng: From Cairo to Damascus; The Theory of Modern Capitalism. Home: 23 Chen Blvd, Tel Aviv. Isr. Office: Maariv, 2 Carlebach St, Tel Aviv, Isr.

ROSENFIELD, Harry N, US, attorney; b. NYC, Aug 17, 1911; s. Max and Anna (Kutchai); BA, CCNY, 1931; LLB, Columbia U, 1934; JSD, NYU, 1942; m. Leonora Cohen, June 25, 1936; c: Marianne. Pvt practice since 1953; fmr: secy to chmn, tchrs' retirement bd, Bd of Educ, NYC 1935-42; lectr, NYU Sch of Educ, 1938-42; counsel, US Off of Educ, 1942-44; asst to Fed Security Admnr, 1944-48; US delg, UN Econ and Social Council, Geneva, 1948; commn, DP commn, 1948-52; exec dir, Pres's Commn on Immigration, 1952-53. Chmn, comm on immigration and nationality, Amer Bar Assn, since 1961; mem, exec comm: J Comty Council, Wash, DC, since 1957, 1st vice-pres, 1960-66; Gtr Wash Educ TV Assn, since 1956; bd dirs, Conf on J Relations, since 1936, secy, 1936-42; bd dirs, Amer ORT; mem: Comm on Eur J Cultural Reconstruction; Phi Beta Kappa; Fed Bar Assn. Author: Liability for School Accidents, 1940; Education for Safe Living, 1942; co-author: Immigration Law and Procedure, 1959. Recipient: Founders award, Assn of Immigration and Nationality Lawyers, 1950; Scroll of Merit, HIAS, 1952. Hobby: mountain climbing. Home: 3749 Chesapeake St, NW, Washington, DC. Office: 1735 DeSales St, NW, Washington, DC.

ROSENFIELD, Leonora C, US, educator; b. NYC, Feb 14, 1909; d. Morris and Mary (Ryshpan) Cohen; Certificat d'études Françaises, U of Grenoble, 1928; Diplome superieur d'études de Civilisation Française, Sorbonne, 1929; BA, Smith Coll, 1930; MA, Columbia U, 1931, PhD, 1940; m. Harry Rosenfield, June 25, 1936; c: Marianne. Prof, Fr, U of Md, since 1947; instr: Smith Coll, 1934-35; Bklyn Coll, 1936-46; reader, Bollingen Series (Mellon Found), 1946-47; fac study f, Amer Council of Learned Socs, 1951-52. Mem: MLA; Amer Phil Assn; Amer Assn Tchrs of Fr; AAUP; Hist of Sci Soc; Conf on J Social Studies; Sigma Delta Tau; Phi Beta Kappa. Author: From Beast-Machine to Man-Machine, 1941; Discovering Plato, 1945, paperback, 1960, 1968; Portrait of a Philosopher: Morris Cohen in Life and Letters, 1962. Contbr to scholarly jours. Hobbies: swimming, gardening. Home: 3749 Chesapeake St, NW, Washington, DC. Office: U of Md, College Park, Md.

ROSENLICHT, Maxwell A, US, educator; b. Bklyn, NY, Apr 15, 1924; s. Martin and Julia (Dalinski), AB, Columbia U, 1947; PhD, Harvard U, 1950; m. Carla Zingarelli, 1953; c: Nicholas, Alan, Joanna. Prof, math, U of Cal, Berkeley, since 1959; prof, math, Northwestern U, 1952-59, visiting prof, 1968-69. Pvt, US Army, 1943-46. Mem: Amer Math Soc; Sigma Xi; chmn, bd govs, Pacific Jour of Math, 1963-68. Author: Introduction to Analysis, 1968; contbr to profsl jours. Recipient: Purple Heart; co-recipient, Cole prize, Amer Math Soc, 1960. Home: 263 Forest Lane, Berkeley, Cal. Office: U of California, Berkeley, Cal.

ROSENMAN, Dorothy R, US, civic, worker; b. NYC, Jan 17, 1900; d. Solomon and Serena (Sickles) Reuben; att Montessori Training Sch, 1918; Columbia U, 1921; m. Samuel Rosenman, Sep, 15, 1924; c: James, Robert. Mem, exec comm, Legal Defense and Educ Fund, NAACP; chmn, housing comm, bd mem, United Neighborhood Houses, 1933-38; mem, bd of dirs Citizens Housing Council, 1939, chmn, inves housing comm, 1939-41; mem bd, Henry St Settlement, 1938-42; chmn and org, Natl Comm on Housing, 1941-47; chmn, housing comm, Natl Urban League, 1952-56. Mem, bd of women's div, FJP. Author: A Million Homes a Year, 1945. Contbr to mags. Home: 885 Park Ave, New York, NY.

ROSENMAN, Samuel Irving, US, attorney, jurist; b. San Antonio, Tex, Feb 13, 1896; s. Sol and Ethel (Paler); AB, Columbia U, 1915, LLB, 1920; m. Dorothy Reuben, Sep 15, 1924; c: James, Robert. Partner, law firm, Rosenman, Colin, Kaye, Petschek, Freud and Emil, since 1946; mem, NY State Leg, 1922-26; bill drafting commn, NY State, 1926-28; counsel to Gov Franklin D Roosevelt, 1929-32; justice, NY Supr Court, 1932-43; spec counsel to Pres FD Roosevelt, 1933-45; spec counsel to Pres Truman, 1945-46; mem, Steel Ind Fact Finding Bd, 1949. Mem: NYC, NY State, Amer Bar Assns; Phi Beta Kappa,; Delta Sigma Rho; Phi Epsilon Pi; pres, Assn of Bar of NYC, 1964-66. Author: Working With Roosevelt, 1952; ed, Public Papers and Addresses of Franklin D Roosevelt, 13 vols, 1928-45. Recipient: Medal for Merit, Pres of US, 1946; Legion of Honor, Govt of Fr, 1946. Home: 885 Park Ave, New York, NY Office: 575 Madison Ave, New York NY.

ROSENNE, Shabtai, Isr, attorney, diplomat; b. London, Eng, Nov 24, 1917; s. Harry and Vera (Davis) Rowson; in Isr since 1947; LLB, U of London, 1938; PhD, Heb U, Jerusalem, 1958; m. Esther Schultz, 1940; c: Jonathan, Daniel. Dep perm repr to Isr to UN and legal adv to Min for Fgn Affairs, since 1967; atty, political dept, JA for Pal, 1946-58; mem: Isr delgs to UN Gen Assemblies, 1948, 1957-62, 1964-68, vice chmn, legal comm, Gen Assembly, 1960; Isr delg to Armistice Negotiations, 1949; repr, Isr Govt, intl proceedings and conferences; chmn, Isr delg, UN Conf on Law of Treaties, 1968; mem, Intl Law Comm, since 1962; asso, Inst of Intl Law, since 1963; rapporteur on question of Termination and Modification of Treaties, 1965. Author: Israel's Armistice Agreements with the Arab States, 1951; The International Court of Justice, 1957; The Time Factor in the Jurisdiction of the International Court of Justice, 1960; The World Court: What It Is and How It Works, 1961; The Law and Practice of International Court, 2 vols, 1965; contbr: articles in Heb, Eng, Fr, Span, to profsl publs; to law reviews; Ency Hebraica. Recipient: Isr prize Social Sci and Law, 1960; cert of merit, Amer Soc of Intl Law, 1968. Home: 90 Herzl St, Jerusalem, Isr. Office: 15 E 70 St, New York, NY.

ROSENSAFT, Josef, US, business exec; b. Bendin, Pol, Jan 15, 1911; s. Mendel and Deborah (Shpiro); in US since 1952; att, Yeshiva, Bendin; m. Hadassah Bimko, Aug 18, 1946; c: Menachem. Fmr, scrap iron dealer. Pres, World Fed Bergen Belsen Assns; mem, bd govs, Weizmann Inst Sci, Isr; fmr, chmn: Belsen Comm; Cen Comm for DPs in Brit Zone, Ger. Author: Holocaust and Rebirth, 1965. Hobbies: Fr impressionist art, old Judaica silver. Home and office: 30 E 71 St, New York, NY.

ROSENSTEIN, Arthur, US, architect; b. Boston, Mass, Apr 15, 1890; s. Jacob and Theresa (Epstein); BS, Harvard U, 1912; m. Miriam Gordon, Jan 14, 1946. Pvt practice since 1919. Mem, architectural sect, US Naval Dept, 1917-20. Pres, W End YMHA, 1942-46; vice-pres, Amer Technion Soc,1953; dir, Natl Agric Coll of Pa; treas, NE br, JWB; mem: Bd of Examiners, Brookline; State Bd of Standards, Mass; Harvard Grad Sch of Design; Amer Inst of Architects; Harvard Engr Soc; club: Pinebrook Country. Home: 333 Sunset Ave, Palm Beach, Fla. Office: 16 Lincoln St, Boston, Mass.

ROSENSTEIN, Samuel M, US, attorney; b. Frankfort, Ky, June 7, 1909; s. Robert and Yetta (Urdang); att U of Ky, 1926-29; LLB, U of Cincinnati, 1931; m. Helen Levitan, Aug 22, 1960; c: Elaine Sherman, Lawrence Levitan. Asso justice, US Customs Court, NY, since 1968; partner, Miliken, Handmaker and Rosenstein, Louisville, Ky, since 1931; Smith, Reed and Leary, 1931-46; city prosecutor, Frankfort, Ky, 1933-41; spec asst att gen, State of Ky, 1933-41; spec asst atty gen, State of Ky, 1943-45. USAAC, 1942-43. Hon life mem, Ky State Bar Assn, secy, 1933-50; house of delg, Amer Bar Assn, 1947-49; Louisville Bar Assn; bd of dirs: Amer Cancer Soc, Ky div; J Hosp; J Comty Cen; Conf of J Orgs; NCCJ, 1956-61; pres, J Vocation Service, Louisville; mem, pres adv council, Brandeis U; clubs: Standard Country; Natl Lawyers, Wash, DC. Contbr to legal jours. Home: 400 E 56 St, New York, NY. Office: 45 Customs Court, One Federal Plaza, New York, NY.

ROSENSTOCK, Joseph, US, conductor, composer; b. Cracow, Pol, Jan 27, 1895; s. Bernard and Sabine (Gelberger); att Acad of Music, U of Vienna, 1912-20; in US since 1946; m. Marilou Harrington, 1958; Conductor, Metrop Opera, NYC, since 1960; asst conductor, Vienna Philharmonic Choir,1918; prof, Acad of Music, Berlin, 1920; asst conductor, Stuttgart Opera House, 1921; conductor and music dir: Darmstadt Opera House, 1922-27; Wiesbaden Opera House, Wiesbaden, 1927-29; Metrop Opera House, NYC, 1929; Mannheim Opera House, 1930-33; J Cultural Assn of Berlin, 1933-36; Nippon Philharmonic, Tokyo, 1936-41, 1945-46; conductor,NYC Opera Co, 1948-52, gen dir, 1952-56; music dir: Aspen,Colo Festivals, 1949-53; Opera of Cologne, 1958-60. Compositions include: piano sonata, concerto for piano, songs, choral works, overture for orch, variations for orch. Mem, Amer Fed of Musicians; hon music dir, Japanese Bc Corp. Recipient: Third Order of the Sacred Treasure, Japan. Home: 315 E 72 St, New York, NY. Office: Metropolitan Opera House, New York, NY.

ROSENSTOCK, Werner, Eng, communal leader; b. Berlin, Ger, Apr,10, 1908; s. Joseph and Erna (Lewin); LLD, U of Freiburg; m. Susanne Philipp, Mar 8, 1934; c: Michael. Gen secy, Assn J Ref in Gt Brit, since 1941; secy, Council of Jews from Ger, since 1946; youth secy, legal adv, J Cen Verein, 1926-38; secy, Cen Rep, Reichsvertretung, emigration dept, 1938-39. Comm mem, Hampstead br, Council Chr and Jews; mem, NW London Reform Syn. Ed, ASA Info, since 1946; contbr, Exodus, 1933-39; A Survey of Jewish Emigration from Germany, Leo Baeck Inst Yearbook, 1956. Home: 77 D Compayne Gardens, London, Eng. Office: 8 Fairfax Mansions, London, Eng.

ROSENSWEIG, William, US, dermatologist; b. NYC, Apr 2, 1910; s. Charles and Celia (Scheck); BA, Pa State Coll, 1932; MD, Temple Med Sch, 1936; m.Lois Levy, Dec 28, 1941; c: Richard, Donn, Lawrence, Nancy. Chief, dermat: Nesbitt Memorial Hosp, since 1950; Wyoming Valley Hosp, since 1956; Mercy Hosp, since 1956; cons, VA Hosp. Maj, US Army MC, 1942-46. Vice-pres: J Comty Cen; ZOA, Wilkes-Barre, 1958-60; mem, bd of dirs: Wyoming Valley J Comm, pres, 1958-62; Temple Isr, 1950-54; United Fund, 1957-60; Luzerne Co Med Soc, 1958-62; chmn, UJA, 1957; ed, Luzerne Co Med Bull, 1954-62. Mem: Phila Dermat Soc; Acad of Dermat; AMA; Masons; Shriners. Contbr to med jours. Clubs: Kiwanis, mem bd of dirs; Irem Temple Country. Home: 156 Butler St, Kingston, Pa. Office: 79 W Northampton St, Wilkes-Barre, Pa.

ROSENTHAL, Albert, J, US, educator, atty; b. NYC, Mar 5, 1919; s. Edward and Edith (Rosenberg); BA, U of Pa, 1938; LLB, magna cum laude, Harvard U, 1941; m. Barbara Snowden, June 30, 1953; c: Edward, Thomas, William. Prof, law, Columbia U, since 1964; law clerk: Judge Magruder, US Court of Appeals, 1941-42; Justice Frankfurter, US Supr Court, 1947-48; asst loan off, Intl Bank for Reconstruction and Devl, 1948-50; atty, Dept of Justice, 1950-51; gen counsel, Small Defense Plants Admn, 1952-53; mem, law firm, Golden, Wienshienk, Rosenthal & Mandel, 1953-64. Capt, USAAC, 1942-46. Mem: Tau Epsilon Phi. Ed-in-chief, Harvard Law Review, 1940-41. Home: 15 Oakway, Scarsdale, NY. Office: 435 W 116 St, New York, NY.

ROSENTHAL, Alex, Can, educator; b. Calgary, Can, Oct 16, 1914; s. William and Minnie (Levy); tchrs cert, Camrose Normal Sch, 1934; BS, U Alberta, 1943, BE, 1947, MS, 1949; PhD, O State U, 1952; m. Bessie Sidorsky, Aug, 1947; c: Arthur, Paul, Eve, Valerie. Prof, chem, U of BC, since 1953; fmr: prin, Stirling HS; instr, chem, Vets Vocational Sch; visiting sci, Cambridge U. Served Can Army, 1943-44. F, Chem Inst of Can, past mem exec, Vancouver sect, past ed, Catalyzer; mem: bd dirs, Hillel Found, U of BC; Amer Chem Soc; U Council of Sch of Nursing and Sch of Home Econ, U BC; Sigma Xi; Phi Lambda Upsilon. Contbr to sci jours and monographs. Hobby: photography. Home: 744 W 53 Ave, Vancouver, Can. Office: U of British Columbia, Vancouver, Can.

ROSENTHAL, Anna, US, communal leader; b. NYC, May 17, 1904; d. Isadore and Fannie (Blume) Wallach; BA, Hunter Coll, NYC, 1924; grad studies: Columbia U; CCNY; Fordham U; JTSA; m. Irving Rosenthal, Apr 12, 1927; c: Mitzi Knishkowy, Gilbert. Pres, Fed J Women's Orgs, since 1968; vice-pres: Bx chap, Hadassah; Lower NY State Region, Hadassah, J educ chmn, NY chap; membership and prog, Wash Hgts div, Yeshiva U Women's Org; E coast region, Yeshiva U Women's Org, prog and educ chmn; mem: speaker's bur, leadership training comm, both Natl Hadassah; speakers bur, comm on rel for NYC, NCCJ; leg comm, Ret Tchrs Assn; Hunter Coll Alumni; fmr, pres: prog and educ chmn, Temple Sisterhood; Nation Sorority; Lady Menorah Soc; Henrietta Szold Group, Hadassah, Bx chap; Isr Group, Hadassah, NY chap; Sisterhood, Young Isr of Concourse; Women's Inst, JTSA. Author: plays and poems for children; contbr articles on adult J educ. Home: 975 Walton Ave, Bronx, NY.

ROSENTHAL, Barbara Silver, US, business exec; b. NYC, Aug 14, 1935; d. Maurice and Lily (Jason); BA, Wellesley Coll, 1957; m. Gerald Rosenthal, Feb 19, 1961; c: Matthew Silver, Eric, Jennifer Brooke. Vice-pres, Gerry Sales Co, since 1968; fmr: bus mgr; Amer Wind Sym; Amer Theatre Soc. Pres, Cleveland region, Women's Amer ORT; vice chmn, women's div, JWF; mem: Wellesley Club; Council of J Women; past pres, Jr Auxiliary, Pittsburgh Opera Assn. Spec interests: theatre; bullfights; horseback riding; reading; music. Home and office: 22276 Douglas Rd, Cleveland, O.

ROSENTHAL, Benjamin S, US, attorney, legislator; b. NYC, June 8, 1923; s. Joseph and Ceil (Fisher); att: LIU; CCNY; LLB, Bklyn Coll, 1949; LLM, NYU, 1952; m. Lila Moskowitz, Dec 23, 1951; c: Debra, Edward. Pvt practice since 1949; mem, law firm, Peirez Karmiol & Rosenthal, NYC; mem, US House of Reprs, since 1962. US Army, 1943-46. Mem, exec comm, ADL; vice-chmn, Queens comm on slum clearance and urban devl; mem, Amer Assn for the UN; fmr: pres, J Cen of Jackson Hgts Men's Club; chmn, Jackson Hgts-Elmhurst div, FJP; clubs: Woodside Kiwanis, vice-pres; Queens Lawyers' fmr vice-pres. Home: 88-12 Elmhurst Ave, Elmhurst, LI, NY. Offices: 60-10 Roosevelt Ave, Woodside, LI, NY. US House of Reprs, Washington, DC.

ROSENTHAL, Erich, US, sociologist, educator; b. Wetzlar, Ger, Sep 6, 1912; s. Theodor and Herta (Landau); in US since 1938; att: U of Giessen; U of Bonn, 1931-33; MA, U of Chgo, 1942, PhD, 1948; m. Lillian Mandell, Dec 13, 1947; c: Barbara, Theodore. Prof, sociol, Queens Coll, CUNY, since 1951, dept supr, Sch of Gen Studies, since 1959, fmr grad adv, sociol grad prog; mem grad sociol fac, CUNY, since 1965; fmr: dir research, Chgo bur of war records, JWB; research cons, Group Work Agcys, Chgo; research asso, U of Chgo; asst prof, U of Ia. Mem: Amer Sociol Assn; E Sociol Soc Population Assn of Amer. Author: Jewish Intermarriage in the United States, 1963; Jewish Intermarriage in Indiana, 1967; American Jewish Yearbook; Acculturation without Assimilation? contbr to profsl jours. Recipient: f, Social Sci Research Council, 1942-43; f: Fund for Advancement of Educ, 1955-56; Conf of J Material Claims Against Ger, 1956, 58; field-work grant, Amer Phil Soc, 1959; research f, Natl Found for J Culture, 1962-63. Home: 15 Longview Pl, Gt Neck, NY. Office: Queens's Coll, Flushing, NY.

ROSENTHAL, Franz, US, educator; b. Berlin, Ger, Aug 31, 1914; s. Kurt and Elsa (Kirschstein); in US since 1940; PhD, Berlin U, 1935. Sterling prof of Near E Langs, Yale U, since 1967, Louis M Rabinowitz prof, Semitic Langs 1956-67; instr, Semitic Langs, Lehranstalt fur die Wissenschaft des Judentums, Berlin, Ger, 1937-38; asso prof, Semitic langs, HUC, 1940-48; prof, Arabic, U of Pa, 1948-56. Office of Strategic Services, US Army, 1943-46. F, Amer Acad of J Research; mem: Amer Phil Soc. Author: Die aramaistische Forschung, 1939; A History of Muslim Historiography, 1952; Humar in Early Islam, 1956; Ibn Khaldun: Muqaddimah, 1958; The Muslim Concept of Freedom, 1960; A Grammar of Biblical Aramaic, 1961; Das Fortleben der Antike im Islam, 1965. Recipient: Lidzbarski gold medal, 1938. Home: 80 Heloise St, Hamden, Conn. Office: Yale U, New Haven, Conn.

ROSENTHAL, Harold, US, journalist; b. NYC, Mar 11, 1914; s. Jonas and Charlotte (Morris); m. Alice Stein, Dec 25, 1941; c: Jonas, Jane. Publicist, Natl Football League. Served, USAAF, 1942-45. Author: Baseball Is Their Business, 1952; Baseball's Best Managers, 1961; The Big Game, 1963; co-author (with Jonny Unitas), Playing Pro Football to Win, 1968; contbr to natl mags. Home: 786 Beech Pl, New Milford, NJ. Office: 410 Park Ave, New York, NY.

ROSENTHAL, Henry M, US, educator; b. Louisville, Ky, Jan 9, 1906; s. Louis and Sarah (Abrams); BA, Columbia U, 1925; PhD, 1940; ordained rabbi, JTSA, 1929; m. Rachel Tchernowitz, Sep 15, 1927; c: Lucy, Abigail. Prof, phil, Hunter Coll, CUNY, since 1964, fac mem since 1948; visiting prof, Columbia U, 1962; dir: rel activities, YMHA, 1930-42; Adult Sch of J Studies, 1939-42; lectr: systematic theol, JTSA, 1942-44; Cooper Union, 1945-47; Guggenheim f, 1947-48. Mem: Amer Phil Assn; Phi Beta Kappa. Author: On the Function of Religion in Culture, 1940; co-author: Foundations of Western Thought, 1962; contributing ed, Menorah Journal; contbr: The Philosophy of George Santayana, 1940; educ and lit jours. Home: 65 E 96 St, New York, NY. Office: Hunter Coll, 695 Park Ave, New York, NY.

ROSENTHAL, Irving, US, educator; b. NYC, July 31, 1912; s. Max and Rose (Lifschutz); BSS, CCNY, 1933, MS, 1934; m. Ruth Moss, May 22, 1943; c: David, Robert, Risa. Asso prof, Eng, CCNY, on staff since 1933, asst to pres, 1933-43. Lt, US Army, 1943-45. Chmn, publs comm, CCNY Alumni Assn, since 1953; mem, adv comm on info, Gt Neck Bd of Educ, since 1960; secy, Heb Sch of Williamsburg, Bklyn, 1935-43. Mem AAAU; Coll Eng Assn; Assn for Educ in Journalism; Phi Delta Kappa; Beta Gamma Sigma. Co-author: The Art of Writing Made Simple, 1953; Modern Journalism, 1962; co-ed: Business Letter Writing Made Simple, 1955; A Contemporary Reader: Essays for Today and Tomorrow, 1961; contbr to Ency Judaica, 1968. Recipient: Alumni Service award, CCNY; Army Commendation award. Home: 62 Hampshire Rd, Great Neck, NY. Office: CCNY, New York, NY.

ROSENTHAL, James Yaakov, Isr, journalist; b. Berlin, Ger, Sep 29, 1905; s. Max and Hanna (Salomon); in Isr since 1933; att U of Freiburg, 1925; LLB, LLM, U of Berlin; m. Margard Levinsky, July 7, 1941. Parliamentary, legal corresp, Haaretz, Heb daily, since 1949. Haganah; Army res, 1948-54. Mem: Grand lodge, Theodor Herzl lodge, B'nai B'rith; Ihud Shivat Zion; Tnua L'Yahadut Shel Tora; fmr hon judge, Journalists Org. Ed, Tamzit Itoneynu, 1936-40; co-ed: Press-Echo, Tel Aviv; Yedioth Chadishot, Tel Aviv, 1943-49; contbr to periodicals. Recipient: Aleh; Ot Hahagana. Homes: 71 Maze St, Tel Aviv; 8 Amatzia St, Jerusalem. Office: 56 Maze St, Tel Aviv, Isr.

ROSENTHAL, Jerome Martin, US, business exec; b. NYC, Apr 29, 1907; s. Salomon and Sadie (Newman); LLB, Chgo Law Sch, 1929; m. Birdie Gingiss, Dec 8, 1935. Vice-pres, Natl Airlines Inc, since 1948; pvt practice, law, 1930-41; dir, Ind Relations, Kingsbury Ordinance Plant, 1942-46; staff mem, Airlines Negotiating Conf, 1946-48. F, Royal Soc of Arts; mem: Gtr Miami Aviation Assn; Sigma Alpha Mu;

Lab Law Soc, U of Miami; clubs: Bay Shore Service; Aviation Execs. Home: Miami Beach, Fla. Office: POB Natl Airport Facility, Miami, Fla.

ROSENTHAL, Judah M, US, educator, author; b. Makov, Pol, Jan 21, 1904; s. Mayer and Fayga (Friedman); in US since 1939; J Tchrs Sem, Warsaw, 1926; att Friedrich Wilhelm U, 1928-32; U Leipzig, 1935-37; ordained rabbi, Hochschule für die Wissenschaft des Judentums, Berlin, 1938; PhD, Dropsie Coll, 1942. Prof, Biblical Exegesis, Coll J Studies, since 1944; libr, 1944-65; asso, Cen for J-Chr Studies, Chgo Theol Sem. F, Amer Acad for J Research; mem, ed bd, Ency Judaica. Author: Sheelot Atiqot baTanach, 1948; Hiwi Al-Balkhi, 1949; The Yiddish Translation of the Bible by Yehoash, 1951; Studies and Texts in Jewish History; Literature and Reilgion, 2 vols, 1967; ed: Herev Piphiyot, 1958; Milhamot Adonai, 1963; Meyer Waxman Jubilee Vol, 1967; Prospectives in Jewish Learning, Vol III, 1967; contbr to encys, J periodicals. Recipient: Moses B Newman award, Heb Acad of Amer, 1958. Home: 30 Alfasi, Jerusalem, Isr.

ROSENTHAL, Leighton A, US, business exec; b. Buffalo, NY, Jan 27, 1915; s. Samuel and Sadie (Dosberg); BS, Wharton Sch Finance, U of Pa, 1936; m. Honey Rousuck, June 30, 1940; c: Cynthia, Cole, Jane Rosenthal. Pres, Work Wear Corp, since 1957. USAAC, WW II. Natl vice-pres, Amer Assn for J Educ; vice-pres, Bur of J Educ; trustee: Mt Sinai Hosp; Cleveland J Comty Fed; treas, Cleveland Health Mus; bd overseers, JTSA; clubs: Hillcrest Country; Oakwood Country; Breakers Golf; Clevelander; Commerce. Home: 19001 S Park Blvd, Shaker Hts, O. Office: 1768 E 25th St, Cleveland, O.

ROSENTHAL, Louis A, US, engineer, educator; b. NYC, Aug 16, 1922; s. Meyer and Sadie (Gersh); BEE, CCNY, 1943; MEE, Bklyn Poly Inst, 1947; m. Esther Horodner, May 19, 1946; c: Joel, Bruce, Amy. Prof, EE, Rutgers U, since 1960, fac mem since 1944; staff cons: US Naval Ordnance Labs, since 1950; Union Carbide Plastics Co, since 1954. Sr mem, Inst of Elec and Electronic Engrs; mem: B'nai B'rith; Sigma Xi; Eta Kappa Nu; Tau Beta Pi; Highland Park Conservative Temple. Contbr to profsl jours. Home: 427 Harrison Ave, Highland Park, NJ. Office: Rutgers U, New Brunswick, NJ.

ROSENTHAL, Macha Louis, US, educator, author; b. Wash, DC, Mar 14, 1917; s. Jacob and Ethel (Brown); BA, U of Chgo, 1937, MA, 1938; PhD, NYU, 1949; m. Victoria Himmelstein, Jan 7, 1939; c: David, Alan, Laura. Prof, Eng, NYU, since 1961, mem fac since 1945; instr, Eng, Mich State U, 1939-45. Author: The Modern Poets: A Critical Introduction, 1960; A Primer of Ezra Pound, 1960; Blue Boy on Skates: Poems, 1964; The New Poets: American and British Poetry since WW II, 1967; Beyond Power: New Poems, 1969; co-author: Exploring Poetry, 1955; ed: Selected Poems and Two Plays of William Butler Yeats, 1962; The William Carlos Williams Reader, 1966; The New Modern Poetry: British and American Poetry Since WW II, 1962, 1969; One Hundred Post-War Poems, British and American, 1968; co-ed, Chief Modern Poets of England and America, 1962; poetry ed, The Nation, 1956-61; contbr to: Poetry; Quarterly Review of Literature; Times Literary Supplement; NY Times Book Review; The Spectator, London. F, Amer Council Learned Soc's, 1942, 1956-57; mem: MLA; AAUP; PEN; judge: Natl Book awards, 1960, fmr, mem adv comm. Recipient: F: Amer Council Learned Socs, 1942, 1956-57; Guggenheim, 1960-61, 1964-65; Bullinger Poetry award, 1969-72. Home: 17 Bayard Lane, Suffern, NY. Office: NYU New York, NY.

ROSENTHAL, Mortimer, US, business exec; b. NYC, Feb 9, 1916; s. Jacob and Martha (Weisfeld); BS, CCNY, 1936; MA, Columbia U, 1937; m. Laura Myers, Feb 9, 1941; c: Judy. Vice-pres, sales, Sidney J Kreiss Inc, since 1960, with firm since 1943; mgr, Hess-Taylor Kreiss Inc, 1937-42; chief psych, sta hosp, Ft McClellan, Ala, 1942-43. Treas, Cong Shaaray Tefila; vice-pres, Lawrence Greene Civic Assn; delg, Rockaway Peninsula Civic Assn; mem: Amer Mgmt Assn; Amer Inst of Mgmt; CCNY Alumni Assn; Alumni Assn, Columbia U. Hobbies: stamp collecting, tennis. Home: 720 Virginia St, Far Rockaway, NY. Office: 350 Fifth Ave, New York, NY.

ROSENTHAL, Richard, US, rabbi; b. Usingen, Ger, Apr 14, 1929; s. Carl and Alice (Baum); in US since 1939; BA, Centenary Coll, La, 1949; BHL, MHL, ordained rabbi, HUC, 1954; m. Barbara Miller, Oct 2, 1955; c: David, Deborah,

Robert. Rabbi, Temple Beth El, since 1956; lectr, dept, of rel, U Puget Sound. Chaplain, US Army, 1954-56. Pres, Tacoma-Pierce Co Mh Assn, 1962; chmn, Comty Planning Council, 1965-67; vice-chmn, interfaith adv commn, Dept of Instns, Wash State, since 1962; mem: CCAR; Rotary. Home: 3102 Viewmont, Tacoma, Wash. Study: 5975 S 12, Tacoma, Wash.

ROSENTHAL, Robert, US, pediatrician, educator; b. Odrau, Aus, May 28, 1896; s. Joseph and Fanny (Fadenhecht); MD, U of Vienna, 1922; in US since 1923; m. Juliet Eisenberg, June 27, 1928; pvt practice since 1924; asst clinical prof em, U of Minn, since 1945. Aus Army, 1915-18. Past pres, NW Ped Soc. Mem: Amer Acad of Peds; AMA; Minn State Med Soc; Amer Assn of the Hist of Med; Minn Acad of Med; Ramsey County Med Soc. Contbr to med jours. Home: 2000 Lower St, Dennis Rd, St Paul, Minn. Office: 437 Lowry Med Arts Bldg, St Paul, Minn.

ROSENTHAL, Roy G, US, business exec; b. Seattle, Wash, May 1, 1896; s. Isaac and Milly (Cohn); MA, U Wash, 1919; m. Sadie Kane, Dec 29, 1920; c: Mrs Milton Levitan, Roy, Howard. Pres, U Printing Co, since 1959, vice-pres, 1927-59; fmr: publisher, ed, Montesano Vidette, 1922-27. US Army, WWI. Mem: Sigma Delta Chi; Amer Legion; Masons; Glendale Golf and Country Club, past pres; U Kiwanis, past pres; fmr: pres, ed, Pi Tau Pi Frat; Group Harbor lodge, B'nai B'rith; Temple De Hirsch; mayor, Montesano, Wash, 1926-27; dir publicity, U Wash, 1932-37; presiding chmn, NW region NCCJ. Home: 7231 SE 27, Mercer Island, Wash. Office: 4133 University Way, NE, Seattle, Wash.

ROSENTHAL, Sarah G, US, attorney, communal worker; b. NYC; d. Robert and Rose (Kossoff); BA, Barnard Coll, 1926; LLB, Yale U Law Sch, 1928. Pres, Rose St Devl Corp, since 1955; pvt practice, 1930-39; dir, Cen Sch of Adult Educ, NY, 1940-42; wage and hours insp, US Dept of Lab, 1943-44; atty, War Labor Bd, 1944-47. Chmn, Comm on Civil Rights, 1966-68, mem since 1959; pres: Family Service of New Haven, since 1968; New Haven Co Fed of Dem Women's Clubs; mem: bd dirs, regional ADL; C of C; Munic Fin Offs Assn; exec bd, New Haven Hum Relations Councils; clubs: Brandeis U, Barnard Coll. Home: Kirkham St, Branford, Conn.

ROSENTHAL, Simha Sylvan, Isr, attorney; b. Mariampol, Lith, Mar 13, 1907; s. Abba-Isaac and Lea (Geffen); MSc, U of Nancy, 1927, Ingenieur IAN, 1927; LLM, U of Paris, 1920; m. Rina Scheiner, Aug 3, 1950; c: Abba-Isaac, Esther. Legal adv to Min of Health, since 1963; fmr: pvt law practice, Fr, 1932-40; first asst to Atty Gen of Isr, 1950-63. Contbr to legal periodicals. Hobby: chess. Home: 4 Beth Hakerem St, Jerusalem, Isr. Office: 20 David Hamelech St, Jerusalem, Isr.

ROSENTHAL, Sol Roy, US, biologist, educator; b. Tiktin, Russ, Sep 6, 1903; s. Harry and Sarah (Kahn); in US since 1908; BS, U of Ill, 1925, MD, 1927, MS, 1930, PhD, 1934; m. Dorothy Bobinsky, May 26, 1950; c: Anthony, Wendy. Dir, Inst for TB Research, U of Ill, since 1948, prof, Coll of Med since 1965, on staff since 1940; med dir, Research Found, Ill, since 1948; f: U Freiburg, 1932-33; Pasteur Inst, Paris, 1933-34; dir, Tice labs, Munic TB Sanitarium, Chgo, 1934-48. Maj, US Army, 1944-47. Mem: Amer Assn of Paths and Bacts; Soc of Experimental Biol and Med; Amer Phys Soc; Amer Trudeau Soc; Sociedad de Tisiologia de Cordoba, Arg; Alpha Omega Alpha; Sigma Xi; clubs: Chgo Lit; Oakbrook Hounds. Contbr to med and sci jours. Home: 230 E Delaware Pl, Chicago, Ill. Office: 1853 West Polk St, Chicago, Ill.

ROSENTHALIS, Moshe, Isr, artist; b. Lith, Nov 18, 1922; s. Jacob and Batia (Cohen) Rosenthal; in Isr since 1958; MA, art, U Vilnius, 1950; m. Sarah Engelchin, 1951; c: Raphael, Avner. Tchr: WIZO HS of Art, since 1959; Midrash Lemorim Coll, since 1964; study groups, Bar Ilan U, since 1968. Lith unit, Russ Army, 1942-45. Mem: Isr Painters and Sculptors Assn; Soc of HS Tchrs. Perm coll: govt mus, Russia; Helena Rubinstein Mus, Tel Aviv. Recipient: Red Star; Victory Medal; Letter of Merit, Govt of Russ; Histadrut prize, 1966. Hobby: sports. Home: 15 Fichman St, Ramat Aviv, Isr. Studio: 40/2, Jaffa, Tel Aviv, Isr.

ROSENTHALL, Edward M, Can, educator; b. Montreal, Can, June 3, 1916; s. Samuel and Eva (Cronenberg); BSc, McGill U, Montreal, 1937; MSc, 1938; PhD, Cal Inst of Tech, 1944; m. Sara Segal, Aug 30, 1942; c: Richard, Rosalie, Gilda.

Prof, math, McGill U, since 1954; chmn, dept of math, since 1960, on fac since 1940. Mem: Inst for Advanced Study, Princeton, 1947-48; Amer Math Soc; Can Math Cong; Amer Math Assn; Sigma Xi. Contbr to profsl jours. Home: 3237 Appleton, Montreal, Can. Office: McGill U, Montreal, Can.

ROSENWALD, Edith G, US, communal worker; b. St Paul, Minn, Aug 9, 1893; d. Benjamin and Adelaide (Rau) Goodkind; att: Villa Hessling, Dresden, 1909-11; Pension Canivet, Paris, 1911-12; m. Lessing Rosenwald, Nov 6, 1913; five c. Bd mem: Child guidance Clinic, since 1927; Assn for J Children, since 1943, vice-pres, 1942-50; Phila Mus Coll of Art, since 1958; Fed of J Agencies since 1936; Child Wfr League of Amer, 1935; ARC, Phila chap, 1956-60; pres, Juvenile Aid Soc, Phila, 1935-42; adv bd to dean of women, U of Pa, 1959; club: Cosmopolitan. Home: 1146 Fox Chase Rd, Jenkintown, Pa.

ROSENWALD, Lessing J, US, business exec; b. Chgo, Ill, Feb 10, 1891; s. Julius and Augusta (Nusbaum); att: Cornell U, 1909-11; U of Pa, 1947; Lincoln U, 1954; Jefferson Med Coll, 1954; LaSalle Coll, 1965; Colby Coll, 1966; Beaver Coll, 1966, Phila Coll of Art, 1968; Williams Coll, 1969; m. Edith Goodkind, 1913; c: Julius, Helen Snellenburg, Robert, Joan Scott, Janet Becker. Ret, 1939; fmr chmn, bd dirs, Sears, Roebuck and Co, 1932-39. Fmr chmn bd, Amer Council for Judaism, first pres, 1943-45; hon mem: Phila Mus of Art; Free Lib of Phila; Phila Orch Assn; The Blake Trust, London, Eng; Print Council of Amer; Cong Kneseth Isr; Friends of the U of Pa Libraries; pres, Fed J Charities of Phila, 1930-34; trustee: Lessing J and Edith Rosenwald Found; pres: Rosenbach Found; Natl Gal of Art, Wash, DC; Inst for Advanced Study, Princeton; mem: Amer Council of Learned Socs; Amer Phil Soc; clubs: Philobiblon, past pres; Midday; Franklin Inn. Donor: Rosenwald collection of graphic art and rare books to: Natl Gal of Art; Libr of Cong; both Wash, DC, 1943. Recipient: Royal Order of Vasa, knight 1st-class, Swed. Hobbies: rare books, graphic arts. Home: 1146 Fox Chase Rd, Jenkintown, Pa.

ROSENWALD, William, US, investment exec, communal leader; b. Chgo, Ill, Aug 19, 1903; s. Julius and Augusta (Nusbaum); BS, MIT, 1924; postgrad studies, Harvard U, 1924-25; LSE, 1925-27; hon DHL, HUC, 1944; hon LLD, Tuskegee Inst, 1964; m. Mary Kurtz, June 12, 1938; c: Nina, Elizabeth Williams, Alice. Chmn, bd dirs, Amer Securities Corp, since 1946; dir, Sears, Roebuck & Co, 1934-38; found, William Rosenwald Enterprises, 1936. Natl chmn, UJA, 1942-63 chmn, Isr Emergency Fund; mem: adv bd, Isr Educ Fund; bd govs, AJComm; vice-chmn, JDC, since 1941; trustee-at-large, Fed of J Philanthropies, 1936-61; pres, Natl Ref Service Inc, 1939-44; mem: NY State Commn on DPs; Council on Fgn Relations; dir, Philharmonic Sym Soc of NY; vice-pres, CJFWF, 1937-38; mem, bd trustees, Tuskegee Inst; clubs: Century Country; Sunningdale Country; Harmonie; Sky; Wall St; Tavern. Home: 895 Park Ave, New York, NY. Office: 122 E 42 St, New York, NY.

ROSENZWEIG, Alfred, MM, Belgium, business exec; b. Berlin, Ger, July 20, 1904; s. Curt and Dora (Beermann); LLD, U of Berlin, 1927; m. Anne Kaiser-Bluth, Dec 28, 1932. Mgr, Albatros, petroleum refinery, since 1935; judge, Berlin, Ger, 1931-33. Dir: Fonds de Prêts d'Etudes, Brussels; J Youth Center; co-found and bd mem: Belgian Friends of Heb U, Jerusalem; J Cen Comm, Brussels; bd dirs, Centrale d'Oeuvres Socials Juives, Brussels; bd mem: campaign, UJA; Belgian Friends of Youth Aliyah; mem: J comty, Brussels; Gen Zionist Org; fmr mem: comm for Help to J Ref, Antwerp; comm for re-education for J Ref; J Orphan Asylum. Contbr to legal jours. Home: 91A Ave Jupiter, Brussels/Forest, Belgium. Office: Scheldelaan, Postbus 1, Antwerp, Belgium.

ROZENSWEIG, Kurt Asher, Isr, educator; b. Cologne, Ger, May 15, 1909; s. Siegmund and Martha (Philippi); in Isr since 1933; DMD, Sch of Dent, Bonn, 1933; MPH, Sch of Public Health, Ann Arbor, 1956; m. Ziporah Levin, 1937; c: Sara Meged, Ruth Peled. Chmn, dept preventive dent, Heb U Sch of Dent Med, Jerusalem, since 1959; head dent, public health sect, Tel Aviv U; fmr: staff dent, Hadassah Med Org; dent dir, AJDC Cyprus Camp; dent adv, Min of Health. F, APHA; mem: Alpha Omega; Royal Soc of Health. Eng; fmr: chmn, hon secy, cen comm, Isr Dent Org. Ed, Isr Dent Org Jour, 1961-63; contbr to profsl jours. Recipient: Grabow Dent Research award, Isr Dent Assn, 1962. Spec interest, chamber music. Home: 4 Hehalutz St, Jerusalem, Isr. Office: POB 499, Jerusalem, Isr.

ROSENZWEIG, Leonard, US, physician, psychiatrist; b. Manchester, Eng, Nov 2, 1903; s. Joseph and Rose (Abrahamson); in US since 1905; BA, U Mich, 1926, MD, 1929; m. Dora Coopersmith, May 25, 1934; c: Monica Armour, Herschel, Harry, Suzanne, Joseph. Pvt practice, psycht, phys, since 1948; staff cons, hospitals, since 1946; dir, post-grad training, Mich Soc Psycht and Neur; fmr: cons psycht, Erie Child Study Dept, Erie, Pa, 1933-45; asst supt, Warren State Hosp, Pa, 1940-45; dir, Grand Valley Child Guidance Clinic, Grand Rapids, Mich, 1946-48. F: Mich Neuropsycht Soc; W Mich Soc Psycht and Neur; life f, Amer Psycht Assn; mem: Amer Phys Fellowship, Inc, for IMA; Soc for Sci Study of Sex; AMA; Mich and Kent Co Med Socs; B'nai B'rith; Temple Emanuel, fmr mem, bd trustees. Contbr to profsl jours. Home: 2638 Reeds Lake Blvd, Grand Rapids, Mich. Office: 515 Lakeside Dr SE, Grand Rapids, Mich.

ROSENZWEIG, Saul S, US, educator, psychologist; b. Boston, Mass, Feb 7, 1907; s. David and Etta (Tuttle); BA, summa cum laude, Harvard U, 1929, MA, 1930, PhD, 1932; m. Louise Ritterskamp, 1941; c: Julie, Ann. Prof, psych and med psych, Wash U, St Louis, since 1951, fac mem since 1959; research f, Harvard Psych Clinic, 1929-34; research asso, Worcester State Hosp, Mass, 1934-43; affiliate prof, Clark U, 1938-43; chief psych: W State Psycht Inst and Clinic, Pittsburgh, 1943-48; Community Child Guidance Clinic, Wash U, 1949-59; lectr, U Pittsburgh, 1943-48. F: Amer Psych Assn; Amer Orthopsycht Assn; council repr, Amer Psych Assn, mem, educ and training bd, 1951-53; mem, council, Amer Assn Psycht Clinics for children, 1953-55. Mem: Phi Beta Kappa; Sigma Xi. Asso ed: Journ of Abnormal and Social Path, 1950-56; Zeit f, Psychodiagnostische Psychologie and Persönlichkeitsforschung, 1953-58; Diagnostica, since 1959; adv ed: Jour of Consulting Psych, 1959-64; Jour of Abnormal Psych, 1965-67. Author: Rosenzweig Picture-Frustration Study, psych test, 1948; co-author: Psychodiagnosis, 1949; contbr to psych jours; Ency Britannica. Home: 8029 Washington St, St Louis, Mo. Office: Washington U, St Louis, Mo.

ROSETTENSTEIN, Julius E, S Afr, attorney; b. Johannesburg, S Afr, July 23, 1914; s. George and Clara (Masur); dipl law, 1933; m. Leah Melman, 1960; c: David. Partner, law firm, Reeders, Teager, Rosettenstein, Kotzen, since 1935. Vice-treas, exec, S Afr J Bd of Deps, since 1960; mem governing body, Parktown Boys HS, chmn Parent's Assn; chmn comm, Saxonwold Sch, 1951-54; clubs: Killarney; Balfour Park, 1956-60, hon life mem. Hobbies: tennis, bowls, theater, music. Home: 20 Restanwold Dr, Saxonwold, Johannesburg, S Afr. Office: Palace Bldgs, corner Pritchard, Rissik Sts, Johnnesburg, S Afr.

ROSETTI, Moshe M, Isr, government official; b. London, Eng, Feb 28, 1903; s. Benjamin and Helena (Cohen); in Isr since 1948; att: U London; U Wales; m. Sara Hartstein; c: Helena Galai. Staff ed, Ency Judaica, since 1968; fmr: chief costs clerk, Munic of London, 1927-37; secy, JNF, Gt Brit, 1937; head info dept and pParl agt, JA, London, 1942-48; secy-gen, Knesset, 1948-68. Pres, Assn of Secys Gen of Parl; fmr: mem: J Bd of Deps, Eng; exec, Trade Union; vice chmn, Anglo-Pal Club, Eng. Contbr to local and Brit press. Home: 56 Ussishkin St, Tel Aviv, Isr.

ROSIN, Harry, US, sculptor; b. Phila, Pa, Dec 21, 1897; s. Aaron and Bertha (Baker); att: Phila Mus Sch, 1917-20; Pa Acad Fine Arts, 1923-26; m. Vilna Spitz, 1936; c: Victoria. Instr, sculpture and drawing, Pa Acad Fine Arts, since 1939. Prin works: Connie Mack bronze, 1957; heroic statue, Jack Kelly, Olympic champion, 1965; both in Phila. Exhbs: Chgo Art Inst; Whitney Mus; Metrop Mus; World Fair, Chgo, 1934; SF World Fair, NY World Fair, 1939; Modern Amer Art; Salon de L'Oeuvre Unique; both Paris, 1932. Recipient: Cresson European scholarship, Pa Acad Fine Arts, 1926; Widener, gold medal, 1939; grant, Amer Acad Arts and Letters, 1946; Bouregy prize, Audubon Artists, 1956; Dist Pa Artist, Phila, 1964. Home and studio: New Hope, Pa.

ROSIN, Isodore Rowland, Rhodesia, surgeon; b. Wolverhampton, Eng, May 6, 1903; s. Joseph and Lily (Rudick); in Rhodesia since 1929; BA, MB, BCh, BAO, Trinity Coll, U of Dublin, 1924, MA, MD, 1936; m. Muriel Wolff, Sep 29, 1932; c: Henry, Jean Gilchrist, Richard. Pvt practice, surg, specialist surg, since 1928; hon surg: Rhodesia Children's Home; Salvation Army; visiting surg: St Anne's & Greenwood Park Hosp, Salisbury; cons surg, Mil Forces, Rhodesia. Pres,

Sephardi Heb Cong of Rhodesia, Salisbury; vice-pres: Cancer Assn; Red Cross Soc, both Rhodesia; FRCS; f, Intl Coll of Surgs, 1936; found f, S Afr Coll of Surgs; fmr, active, various communal bodies; past grand lodge off, Eng Freemasonry; past master, Rhodesia Lodge & chap clubs: Salisbury; New. Contbr to British profsl jours. Recipient: OBE, 1958. Home: 30 Mount Pleasant Dr, PO Avondale, Salisbury, Rhodesia. Office: POB 95, Salisbury, Rhodesia.

ROSKIES, Ralph Zvi, US, educator; b. Montreal, Can, Nov 24, 1940; s. Enoch and Malvina (Balaban); in US since 1961; BSc, McGill U, Montreal, 1961; MA, PhD, Princeton U, 1961-65; m. Dolores Dines, June 4, 1963; c: Adina, Julie. Asst prof, physics, Yale U, since 1968, mem fac, since 1965; f, Weizmann Inst, Isr, 1967-68. Mem, Amer Physical Soc; past pres, McGill Hillel Found. Contbr to sci jours. Recipient: U scholar, McGill U, 1957-61; Sidney J Hodgson f, McGill U, 1957-58; Harold Helm f, Princeton U, 1961-62; Moyse Travelling f, McGill U 1962-63; Henrietta and Meier Segals f, Weizmann Inst, 1967-68. Home: 470 Alling Farm Rd, Orange, Conn. Office: Yale U, New Haven, Conn.

ROSLOW, Jerome Morris, US, government official; b. Chgo, Ill, Dec 2, 1919; s. Morris and Mary (Cornick); att Wright Jr Coll, Chgo, 1938-40; BA, cum laude, U of Chgo, 1942; m. Rosalyn Levin, Sep 28, 1941; c: Michael, Joel. Asst Secy of Lab for Policy, Evaluation & Research, US Lab Dept, since 1969; position classification analyst, Army Dept, 1942-43; dir, compensation, War Assets Admn, 1946-48; org and methods examiner, asst mgr, wage and salary div, Off of Secy of Army, 1948-51; dir, policy, salary stabilization bd, Econ Stabilization Agcy, 1952-53; exec, employee relations dept, Creole Petroleum Corp, Caracas, Venezuela, 1953-55; mgr, employee realtions dept, ESSO Eur, Inc, London, Eng, 1966-69. Chief warrant off, US Army, 1943-46. Chmn, compensation council, Natl Ind Cong Bd; asso, Columbia Sem on Lab, Columbia U; mem: bd trustees, Natl Comm on Employment of Youth; Wash, DC; Urban League, Inc; Ind Relations Research Assn; Amer Mgmt Assn; clubs: Fed City; Army-Navy Country. Ed, American Men in Government, 1949; contbr to profsl jours. Home: 4201 Cathedral Ave, NW, Washington, DC. Office: US Dept Labor, 14 and Constitution Ave, Washington DC.

ROSNER, Baruch, Isr, physicist; b. Vienna, Aus, Dec 17, 1931; s. Solomon and Shifra (Stahl); in Isr since 1935; MSc, Heb U, 1958, PhD, 1962; m. Ofra Goitein, July 23, 1956; c: Orly, Shahar, Ayelet. Asso prof, phys, Technion, since 1968; fmr: asso prof, U of Pa; research asso, U of Pittsburg. IDF, 1950-51. Mem: Amer, Isr Phys Socs. Contbr to profsl jours. Home: 67 Pinsker St, Haifa, Isr. Office: Technion, Haifa, Isr.

ROSNER, Fred, US, physician; b. Berlin, Ger, Oct 3, 1935; s. Sidney and Sara (Feingold); in US since 1949; BA, Yeshiva Coll, NY, 1955; MD, Albert Einstein Coll of Med, 1959; m. Saranne Eskolsky, Feb 24, 1959; c: Mitchel, Miriam, Aviva. Asst dir, hematology, Maimonides Med Cen, Bklyn, since 1967, mem staff since 1965; asso visiting phys, Coney Island Hosp, since 1967, asst chief div hematology, since 1965; instr, med, SUNY, Downstate Med Cen, since 1968; asst visiting phys, Kings Co Hosp Cen, Bklyn, since 1968; cons, chronic diseases, USPHS, 1965-67; research asso, neur, Children's Hosp of DC, 1968-69. Epidemiologist, USPHS, 1963-65. Dipl, Natl Bd Med Examiners; f: NY Acad Med; Intl Soc Hematology; asso, Bklyn Soc Internal Med; mem: AMA; Kings Co, NY Med Socs; Amer Soc Hematology; NY Soc for Study of Blood; Amer Assn for Hist of Med; Acute Leukemia Group B; Amer Fed for Clinical Research; Amer Phys' f for IMA; Bklyn adv bd, Leukemia Soc of Amer. Contbr to profsl publs. Recipient: Mosby Co Scholarship Book award, 1957; Mamonides Hosp Research Soc award, 1965, 1967; Michael Reese Hosp and Coll of J Studies Maimonides award, 1969. Home: 750 Elvira Ave, Far Rockaway, NY. Office: 4802 Tenth Ave, Brooklyn, NY.

ROSNER, Jonathan Levi, US, attorney; b. Far Rockaway, NY, Sep 4, 1932; s. Oscar and Miriam (Reinhardt); BA, Wesleyan U, Middletown, 1954; LLB, JD, NYU Law Sch, 1959; m. Lydia Sokol, Dec 23, 1956; c: Beth, Marianne, Joshua. Partner, Rosner & Rosner, since 1963; law clerk, US Dist Judge Bicks, 1959-60; asst atty, US Justice Dept, 1960-63. Cpl, US Army, 1954-56. Dir: Westchester J Comty Services; NYU Law Review Alumni Assn; Hartsdale Lawns Civic Assn; Data Point Corp; Automated Marketing, Inc; trustee, NYU Law Alumni Assn; mem: Order of the Coif; Assn of Bar of NYC; Amer Bar Assn; NY Co Lawyers Assn;

fmr, Dem candidate for Dist Atty, Westchester Co, 1968. Home: 18 Carlyle, Hartsdale, NY. Office: 9 E 41 St, New York, NY.

ROSNER, Oscar Selig, US, attorney; b. NYC, Mar 12, 1897; s. Abraham and Jeanette (Leiner); BS, CCNY, 1917; LLB, NYU Law Sch, 1918; m. Miriam Reinhardt, Jan 25, 1923 (decd); c: Seth, Jonathan; 2nd m. Rosalind Rosenberg, July 8, 1963. Partner, Rosner & Rosner, since 1960; partner, Baker, Obermeier & Rosner, 1925-52; pvt practice, 1952-56; partner, Rosner, Altus & Rosner, 1956-60. Vice-pres: FJP, NY, trustee; Hosp for Jt Diseases and Med Cen, past chmn bd, past pres; mem: NY Co Lawyer's Assn; Bar of NYC; Masons, Beethoven Lodge 661. Hobbies: music, reading, philanthropy. Home: 200 57 E St, New York NY. Office: 9 E 41 St, New York, NY.

ROSNER, Samuel, US, neurosurgeon; b. NYC, May 23, 1912; s. Joseph and Sarah (Findling); att: LIU, 1930-33; Dalhousie U, Halifax, NS, 1933-34; MD, Royal Coll of Phys and Surgs, Edinburgh, 1940; m. Esther Kitay (decd), Oct 21, 1941; c: Evan, Gertrude, Ruth, Saran. Pvt practice since 1945; att neurosurg: It Hosp, since 1962; Gouverneur State Hosp; cons neurosurg, VA Hosp, Lyons, NJ; lectr, neurol sci, Rutgers U Sch of Med; fmr: sr demonstrator, silver medalist in anat, Royal Coll of Phys and Surgs, res surg; res surg, brain injuries unit, Bangour Emergency Hosp, Scotland; chief of neur, neurosurg, cancer research and experimental neur, Stuyvesant Polyclinic, NY, 1950-59; att neurosurg and neurol, Manhattan Gen Hosp, 1951-59. Lt, US Army, MC, 1944-45. Licentiate, Royal Fac of Phys and Surgs, Glasgow; LRCP and S Edinburgh; f: Intl Coll of Surgs, dipl in neurosurg; Amer Coll of Angiology; mem: AMA; Friends of Heb U; IMA; Masons; Young Isr Syn, ritual comm. Hobby, Judaica. Home: 109 Mildred Pkwy, New Rochelle, NY. Office: 1882 Grand Concourse, Bronx, NY.

ROSNER, Seth, US, attorney; b. NYC, June 1, 1931; s. Oscar and Miriam (Reinhardt); AB, Wesleyan U, 1952; JD, Columbia Law Sch, 1955; LLM, NYU Sch of Law, 1960; att Université de Paris, Fr, 1960-61; m. Sara Sheldon. Partner, Rosner & Rosner since 1955; adj asso prof, law, NYU Sch of Law since 1961. Lt, USNR, 1956-59. Trustee, The J Home and Hosp for Aged; mem; exec comm, Wesleyan U Alumni Council; NY Co Lawyers Assn; Amer Bar Assn; NY State Bar Assn; Assn of Bar of NYC; Intl Law Assn; Amer br, World Peace Through Law Cen; fmr, delg, Amer Bar Assn, House of Delgs. Home: 100 Bleecker St, New York, NY. Office: 9 E 41 St, New York, NY.

ROSOFF, Leonard, US, surgeon; b. Grand Forks, ND, May 5, 1912; s. Albert and Sophie (Koblin); AB, U of S Cal, 1931; MD, Sch of Med, U of Tex, 1935; m. Marie Aronsfeld, June 1, 1935; c: Leonard Jr. Prof, surg, U of S Cal Sch of Med; dir of surg, LA Co; sr att surg, Cedars of Leb Hosp, LA; cons staff, Huntington Memorial Hosp, Pasadena. Dipl, Amr Bd of Surgs; f, Amer Coll of Surgs; mem: Pacific Coast Surg Assn; W Surg Assn; Soc for Surg of the Alimentary Tract; AMA; Soc of Grad Surgs; LA Surg Soc; LA Acad of Med; Zeta Beta Tau; Phi Delta Epsilon. Home: 2052 Redcliff St, Los Angeles, Cal. Office: 1200 N State St, Los Angeles, Cal.

ROSOLIO, Shaul, Isr, police officer; b. Tel Aviv, Isr, Aug 12, 1923; s. David and Dora (Arlosoroff); grad, Herzlia Coll; m. Shoshana Massis, Aug 15, 1946; c: Gideon, Michael, Shulamit, Dorit. Chief, Jerusalem and S Isr Sector, police, since 1961, with org since 1949. Off, Haganah, 1941-46; IDF, 1947-49. Hobby: music. Home: 42 King Hezekia St, Jerusalem, Isr. Office: Police Hqrs, Jericho Rd, Jerusalem, Isr.

ROSOVSKY-KAMINER, China, Isr, actress; att, Theatre Inst, Leningrad; Gnessin's Studio, Tel Aviv; m; one c. Actress, found Dorot Theatre; performed in theatres: Habimah; Matate; Ohel. Toured with Dorot Theatre, Eur. Home: 22 Mapu St, Tel Aviv, Isr.

ROSOW, Norman, US, business exec. communal leader; b. NYC, Feb 24, 1904; s. Isaac and Rachel (Bernstein); m. Ethel Lamberg, Oct 21, 1930; c: Patricia, Lazarus, Richard. Pres, NY Brass and Copper Co, since 1957, with firm since 1934. Pres, J Child Care Assn of NY; hon pres, Convalescent Home of NY; trustee, FJP; mem: exec comm, J Hosp and Med Cen of Bklyn; bd dirs, Copper Club; Bus and Defense Service Admn, US Defense Dept; Unity Club of Bklyn; ADL; 52 Assn; active in UJA; fmr: pres, Bklyn J Home for Convalescents; trustee: J Child Care Assn of NY; J Youth Services of

Bklyn; J Cmty Cen of Bklyn; pres: Natl Copper Assn; Copper and Brassware Assn of Amer. Hobbies: sculpture; painting. Home: 1 Fifth Ave, New York, NY. Office: 257 Park Ave S, New York, NY.

ROSS, Beatrice Lifshutz, US, communal leader; b. Denver, Colo, Aug 24, 1905; d. Simon and Mollie Eller (Lifshutz); m. Marion Ross, Aug 30, 1927; c: Barbara Wynn, Harvey, Bruce. Chmn: Reform J Appeal; Natl Fed of Temple Sisterhoods; Cherry Red Heart Ball, 1968; budget chmn, NFTS, SE region; mem bd: S Pinellas MH Assn; Temple Beth El Sisterhood; Bay Front Med Cen; mem: Council of J Women; B'nai Brith Auxiliary Hadassah; Mound Pk Hosp Auxiliary; Symphony Guild; Fla Opera Guild; All Children's Hosp; Pinellas Assn for Retarded Children; Mus of Fine Arts; Stuart Soc of Mus; Natl Home for Asthmatic Children, Denver; fmr: pres, J Cmty Council; chmn, women's div, UJA pres, St Petersburg Opera Guild; vice-pres, Easter Seal Guild. Home: 4936 61st Ave, S, St Petersburg, Fla.

ROSS, I Arnold, US, attorney, accountant; b. Warsaw, Pol, Feb 14, 1897; s. Hyman and Yetta (Bernstein) Rosenzweig; BS, CCNY, 1919, MBA, 1922; JD, NYU, 1927; CPA, NY State, 1927; m. Gertrude Rubin, June 29, 1924; div; c: June Carol Marks, Kenneth; m. 2nd, Sayra Lebenthal, Sep 30, 1955. Pvt practice since 1928; CPA since 1927; adj asso prof, CCNY, since 1967, instr, 1940-42; tchr, NYC HSs, 1927-28; mem, NY State Assembly, 1934; govt appeal agt, Selective Service, NYC, 1942-44; negotiator, price adjustment bd, RFC, 1943-45. US Army, WW I. Active in Rep party, at city, co, state levels; chmn: state affairs comm, Natl Rep Club, 1935-36; mem: Rep Co comm, NY Co, 1932-52 and since 1962; Rep and Lib Party candidate for judge of NY Civil Court, 1963 mem, bd dirs: Baruch Sch of Bus and Public Admn, CUNY, since 1948, pres, 1955; pres, NY lodge, B'nai B'rith, 1955; mem, gen comm, AJComm, 1952-55; fmr: Riverside dist chmn, Boys Scouts of Amer, 1953-59, mem, exec bd, Manhattan council, since 1953, mem, natl council, since 1954; mem: Masons, Elks, Cong Shaaray Tefila, NYC, trustee; J Chautauqua Soc; NY State Soc CPAs; Amer Inst CPAs; Fed, NY, NJ, Conn Bar Assns; Bar Assn of NYC; NY Co Lawyers Assn; Amer Soc Intl Law; Amer Fgn Law Assn, dir since 1966; Inst for Judicial Admn; It-US Cen for Judicial Studies; patron, Intl Bar Assn. Contbr to legal jours. Recipient: CCNY Alumni medal, 1944. Home: 815 Park Ave, New York, NY. Office: 150 Broadway, New York, NY.

ROSS, Daniel G, US, attorney; b. NYC, July 12, 1904; s. Albert and Lena (Goldberg); BA Yale Coll, 1924; LLB, Columbia U, 1927; hon LLB, Heb U, 1961; m. Grace Jarcho, Jan 19, 1934; c: Ann, Loeb, James, Lynn Rosenfeld. Partner, Becker, Ross and Stone. Mem: bd govs, Heb U; Tel Aviv U; fmr pres and chmn bd, Amer Friends Heb U, 1955-62; chmn bd, Amer Friends Tel Aviv U; chmn, Heb U-Technion Jt Maintenance Appeal; mem, bd dirs, JTSA, since 1952; co-chmn, natl council, United HIAS Service, since 1954; vice-pres, Reconstructionist Found; chmn bd trustees, Soc for Advancement of Judaism, 1945-49. Recipient: Scopus award, Heb U. Home: 993 Fifth Ave, New York, NY. Office: 41 E 42 St, New York, NY.

ROSS, Jacob Joshua, Isr, educational admnr; b. Bulawayo, S Rhodesia, Nov 16, 1929; s. Harry and Annie (Wahl); in Isr since 1968; att U of Witwatersrand; MA, U of Capetown, 1950; PhD, U of Cambridge, Eng, 1956; att Yeshiva, Bnei Brak, 1951-2, 1956-8; m. Tamar Wohlgelernter, Mar 28, 1960; c: Elchanan, Dvora, Avraham, Ariel. Gen insp of schs, since 1968; sr lectr, dept phil, Tel Aviv U, since 1968; lectr, chmn, dept phil, Bar Ilan U, 1958-63; visiting prof, Brown U, 1963; dep prin, Jew's Coll, London, 1964-68. Author: The Appeal to the Given, 1969; contbr to phil jours. Home: 30 Metudela St, Jerusalem, Isr. Office: Min of Educ and Culture, Jerusalem, Isr.

ROSS, James, US, business exec; b. Odessa, Russ, Jan 1, 1902; s. Myron and Rebecca; in US, since 1925; LLD, Inst of Intl Law, Moscow, 1922; m. Edith; c: Sally Bach. Pres, Ross Radio Co, since 1930; chmn, bd dirs, Astatic Corp, since 1950. Vice pres, Amer Friends of Heb U; mem, bd dirs: Heb U, Jerusalem; Youngstown J Fed; hon vice-pres, JNF, 1961. Recipient: Hon f, Heb U, Jerusalem, 1969. Home: 4110 Oak Knoll Dr, Youngstown, O. Office: 325 W Federal St, Youngstown, O.

ROSS, Marion B, US, auto dealer; b. Centerville, Ia, Nov 17, 1903; s. Levi and Sadie (Rosen); m. Beatrice Lifshutz, Aug 30, 1927; c: Barbara, Bruce, Harvey. Pres, Ross Chevrolet Inc, since 1951; gen mgr, Luby Chevrolet, Miami, 1939-51. Mem.

bd: Union Trust Natl Bank; St Petersburg C of C; J Comty C; Temple Beth-El; Gulf Coast TB and Respiratory Disease Assn; MH Assn of Fla; Fla Automobile Dealers Assn; fmr pres, UAHC, southeast reg; adv bd, Sci Cen; Boy Scouts, Pinellas area; pres, Goodwill Ind, Suncoast; clubs: Commerce, bd dir; Cosmopolitan, vice-pres; Sunshine City Kiwanis, pres. Home: 4938 61 Ave, St Petersburg, Fla. Office: 2901 34 St, St Petersburg, Fla.

ROSS, Nathaniel, US, psychiatrist, educator; b. NYC, June 11, 1904; s. Harris and Sarah (Lazarus); BA, Columbia Coll, 1924, MD, 1929; cert of grad, NY Psychan Inst, 1941; m. 1st, Barbara Munder, 1929; c: Judith Schooning, John; m. 2nd, Edith Handler, 1963. Pvt practice, psychoanalysis, since 1931; training analyst, Amer Psychoanalytic Assn, since 1948; prof, psycht, SUNY, Downstate Med Cen, since 1963, fac mem, since 1955; psycht prof, Bellevue Psychiatric Hosp, since 1931, staff mem since 1929; research asso, Comm for Study of Suicide, 1937-40; asso neuropsycht, Beth Isr Hosp, 1942-45; cons, Armed Forces Induction Cen, 1942-44; psycht, ARC Cen, 1942-43; att psycht, Hillside Hosp, 1946-48; asso att psychan, Columbia U Psychan Clinic, 1948-52. F: Amer Psycht Assn, since 1966; NY Acad of Med; dipl, Amer Bd Psycht and Neur; vice-pres, Psychoanalytic Assn of NY, 1962; mem: AMA; Intl Psychoanalytic Assn; NY Co and State Med Socs; NY Psychoanalytic Soc and Inst; NY Acad of Med; NY Soc of Clinical Psycht; Phi Beta Kappa; Alpha Omega Alpha. Co-ed: Annual Survey of Psychoanalysis, since 1952; asso ed, Jour of the Amer Psychoanalytic Assn, since 1955. Contbr to profsl jours and books. Hobby: collecting paintings and sculpture. Home: 830 Park Ave, New York, NY. Office: 123 E 75 St, New York, NY.

ROSS, Theodore S, US, rabbi; b. Boston, Mass, Feb 14, 1911; s. Louis and Rebecca (Greenberg); BS, Boston U, 1931; BJEd, Heb Tchrs Coll, Boston, 1931; ordained rabbi, HUC, 1935, DHL, 1941, hon DD, 1960; m. Belle Steinberg, Feb 14, 1949; c: Ira. Rabbi: Temple Sinai, Forest Hills, NY, since 1956; Cong Shaari Zedek, Bklyn, 1936-49; S Shore Temple, Chgo, 1949-51; Temple Isaiah, Forest Hills, 1952-56. Mem, exec bd: CCAR; NY bd of Rabbis, 1947-49; delg, Syn Council of Amer, 1946-49; grand chaplain, Masons, NY, 1948-49; mem, comm, Child Lab, Ind Commn, NY State, 1946-49. Mem, Assn of Reform Rabbis of NYC; CCAR; NY Bd of Rabbis. Home: 110-45 71 Rd, Forest Hills, NY. Study: 71-11 112 St, Forest Hills, NY.

ROSSBACH, J Howard, US, jurist; b. NYC, Dec 19, 1913; s. Max and Mabel (Limburg); BA, Yale U, 1935, LLB, 1938; m. Eleanor Adler Frank, Dec 29, 1947; c: Anne, Sarah, Howard. Judge, Criminal Court of NYC, since 1962; atty: Cook, Nathan, Lehman & Greenman, 1938-40; Guggenheim & Untermeyer, 1946-50; commn, SEC, 1952-53; atty-in-chief, Legal Aid Soc, 1950-55; judge, Court of Spec Sessions, NYC, 1955-62. Lt-col, US Army, 1941-46. Mem: NYC, NY State and Amer Bar Assns; NY Co, Bx and Westchester Lawyers Assns; clubs: Yale of NYC; Cent Country; Riverdale Yacht; City of NY, pres. Contbr to legal jours. Home: 5040 Arlington Ave, New York, NY. Office: 100 Centre St, New York, NY.

ROSSMAN, Joseph, US, attorney; b. Phila, Pa, Oct 5, 1899; s. Louis and Rebecca (Freeman); ChemE, U of Pa, 1922; LLB, George Wash U, 1927, MA, 1927; Master of Patent Law, Wash Coll of Law, 1927; PhD, Amer U, 1930; m. Mildred Katzmann, July 1, 1927; c: Ronald. Pvt practice, patent atty, since 1935; patent examiner, US Patent Office, 1923-35. Mem: Amer Chem Soc; Amer Inst of Chems; Amer Patent Law Assn; Phila Patent Law Assn; Phila, DC, Bar Assns. Author: Psychology of the Inventor, 1931; Patent Law for Chemists, 1932, revised 1935; Protection by Patents and Scientific Discoveries, 1934; co-ed: Patents, Research and Management, 1961; The Law of Chemical, Metallurgical and Pharmaceutical Patents, 1967. Contbr to legal and tech jours. Home: 1714 Rittenhouse Sq, Phila, Pa. Office: Land Title Bldg, Phila, Pa.

ROSTAL, Max, Switz, violinist, composer, educator; b. Teschen, Aus, Aug 7, 1905; s. Joseph and Amalie (Schleuderer); in Switz since 1958; att: State Acad, Berlin, Ger; m. Karoline von Hohenblum, Feb 4, 1945; c: Sybil Eysenck, Angela. Prof: State Acadamy of Cologne, since 1957; Conservatoire, Berne, since 1958; fmr: State Acad, Berlin, 1928-33; Guildhall Sch of Music, London, 1954-58; Recording artist for: Decca Record Co; Argo Record Co; His Master's Voice, all London; Deutsche Grammophone. F, Guildhall Sch of Music; mem, Soc of Musicians, London. Recipient: Mendelssohn Prize,

Berlin, 1925; Bundesverdienstkreuz 1st-class, W Ger, 1968; silver medal, State Acad of Music, Cologne, 1956. Hobbies: motoring, photography. Home: Weststr 12, Berne-Kirchenfeld, Switz.

ROSTEN, Leo C, (Leonard C Ross), US, author, social scientist; b. Lodz, Pol, Apr 11, 1908; s. Samuel and Ida (Freundlich); in US since 1911; PhB, 1930, PhD, 1937; att LSE 1934; m. Priscilla Mead (decd); c: Philip, Madeline, Margaret. m. 2nd, Gertrude Zimmerman, 1960. Spec ed adv, Look Mag, since 1949; fac asso, Columbia U, since 1954; Ford visiting prof of political sci, U of Cal, Berkeley, 1960-61. Dep dir, OWI, 1941-44; spec cons, War Dept, USAAF, 1945-47. Author: The Education of Hyman Kaplan, 1937; The Washington Correspondents, 1937; The Strangest Places, 1939; Hollywood, The Movie Colony, 1941; The Dark Corner, 1948; A Guide to the Religions of America, 1956; The Return of Hyman Kaplan, 1959; Captain Newman, MD, 1961; The Story Behind the Painting, 1962; The Many Worlds of Leo Rosten, 1964; A Most Private Intrigue, 1966; The Joys of Yiddish, 1968. Mem: Amer Political Sci Assn; AAAS; Amer Acad of Political and Social Sci; Phi Beta Kappa; clubs: Cosmos, Wash DC; Chaos, NYC; Authors, London. Recipient: George Polk memorial award, 1954; Freedom Found award, 1955. Office: 488 Madison Ave, New York, NY.

ROSTENBERG, Adolph, US, physician, educator; b. NYC, Sep 27, 1905; s. Adolph and Louisa (Dreyfus); BA, Columbia Coll, 1926; MD, McGill U, 1931; m. Marie Peters, July 30, 1936; c: Susan. Prof of dermat, head of dept, U of Ill, since 1959, asso and prof, dermat, Coll of Med, 1945-49; dermat, FDA, 1939-45; cons, Natl BBB. Mem: AMA; Amer Dermat Assn; Amer Acad of Dermat and Syphilology, chmn: symposium on dermat allergy, 1946-53, on cutaneous testing, 1954-56; Soc of Investigative Dermat; Chgo Dermat Soc, pres, 1957-58; Chgo Allergy Soc; Amer Coll of Allergists; Amer Acad of Allergy; Cosmetic Chems Soc; AAUP; Sigma Xi. Contbr to med jours. Hobby, music. Home: 544 West Wellington, Chicago, Ill. Office: U of Ill, 840 S Wood St, Chicago, Ill.

ROSTENBERG, Leona, US, rare book dealer; b. NYC, Dec 28, 1908; d. Adolph and Louisa (Dreyfus); BA, NYU, 1930; MA, Columbia U, 1933. Partner, Leona Rostenberg Rare Books, since 1944. Mem: Antiquarian Booksellers Assns, Amer and Eng; Amer Hist Soc; Bibliographical Soc Amer; Renaissance Soc Amer; Women's Natl Book Assn. Author: English Stationers in the Graphic Arts, 1599-1700, 1963; Publishing, Printing and Bookselling in England, 1551-1700, 2 vols, 1965; The Subversive Press Under Elizabeth I and James I; contbr to bibliographic and hist jours. Home and office: 152 E 179 St, New York, NY.

ROSTON, Murray, Isr, educator; b. London, Dec 10, 1928; s. Hyman and Matilda (Jacobs); in Isr, since 1956; MA, Cambridge U, 1952; MA, PhD, London U, 1952-61; m. Faith Lehrman, Apr 8, 1956; c: Yardenna, Nina, Yonit. Asso prof, chmn, Eng Dept, Bar Ilan U, since 1956; visiting asso prof, Stanford U, 1966-67. Author: Prophet and Poet, 1965; Biblical Drama in England, 1968; ed, The World of Shakespeare (Heb), 1965. Home: 51 Katzenelson St, Kiryat Ono, Isr. Office: Bar Ilan U, Ramat Gan, Isr.

ROSTOW, Eugene V, US, attorney, economist, educator; b. Bklyn, NY, Aug 25, 1913; s. Victor and Lillian (Helman); BA, Yale Coll, 1933, LLB, 1937; att Kings Coll, Cambridge, Eng, 1933-34; LLD, Cambridge U, Eng, 1962; m. Edna Greenberg, 1933; c: Victor, Jessica, Nicholas. Under-secy of State for Political Affairs, US State Dept, 1966-69; Sterling Prof of Law and Pub Affairs, Yale U, 1965; Dean, Yale Law Sch, 1955-65, fac mem, since 1938, mem, Grad Fac of Econ, since 1944; asso with Cravath, de Gersdorff, Swaine and Wood, NY, 1937-38; visiting asst prof, U of Chgo, 1941; asso, State Dept and Lend Lease Admn, 1942-44; asst to exec secy, UN Econ Commn for Eur, 1949-50; Guggenheim F, 1959-60; f, Kings Coll and Pitt Prof, Amer Hist and Instns, Cambridge U, 1959-60. Chmn: Mayor's Adv Comm on Educ, 1945-49; Emergency Citizen's Comm for DP's, 1947-49—both of New Haven, Conn; mem: Cent Assn of NY; Amer Acad of Arts and Sci; Council of Amer Law Inst; Order of the Coif; Phi Beta Kappa; Alpha Delta Phi. Author: The Recession of 1937-38, Materials for Study of the Control of Industrial Fluctuations, 1941; The Control of the National Economy, 1947; Corporate Recapitalization and Reorganization, 1947; A National Policy for the Oil Industry, 1948; L'Economie Dirigèe aux Etats-Unis, 1950; Planning for Freedom, 1959;

The Sovereign Prerogative, 1962; Law, Power and the Pursuit of Peace, 1968; co-author of J D Poteat of Sturges' Cases and other Materials on the Law of Debtors' Estates, 1940, 49; contbr to profsl and scholarly jours. Clubs: Elizabethan; Graduates (New Haven); Yale of NY. Home: 208 St Ronan St, New Haven, Conn. Office: Yale U, New Haven, Conn.

ROTEM, Lipa, Isr, engr; b. Korosten, Russ, May 13, 1911; s. Benzion and Pesia (Vilensky) Roitman; in Isr since 1923; dipl Ingr, U of Grenoble, 1934; m. Ahava Hajutman, 1935; c: Jair, Jehudit Kotik, Temira Galpas. Dir, cen workshops, Isr Elec Corp, since 1952; erection engr, Reading Sta, 1937-47; maintenance engr, Naharaim Sta, 1947-48; construction engr, Haifa Sta, 1949-52; tchr, Evening Tech Trade Sch, Haifa, Technion, 1952-60, dir, 1960-62. Haganah, 1927-48; IDF, 1948-49. Pres, Mech Assn, Haifa Engr and Architect Org; dir bd, Jr Tech Coll, Technion; host, Mt Carmel Intl Training Cen for Comty Service; org of vocational courses in Histadrut Hanoar Haoved, 1924-29; mem, Engr Club. Contbr to tech, educ jours. Hobbies: music, handicraft. Home: 30A Shoshanat Hacarmel, Haifa, Isr. Office: Isr Electric Corp, Haifa, Isr.

ROTEM, Shmuel, Isr, engineer; b. Haifa, Isr, Nov 22, 1926; s. Moshe and Yehudit (Yosofovitz) Rotwarf; ME, Technion, Haifa, 1951; m. Alisa Stork, June 24, 1953; c: Shai, Eran, Yehudit. Plant mgr, Amer Isr Paper Mills Ltd, Hadera, since 1962; mech engr, Hayama Ship Bldg Co, 1952-53; chief maintenance engr, Dead Sea Potash Works, 1953-57; div head, Isr AEC, 1957-62. IDF, 1944-49. Mem: Assn of Engrs, Architects, Isr; Isr Mgmt Cen; Pulp and Paper Ind. Home: Hofit, Kfar Vitkin, Isr. Office: Amer-Isr Paper Mills Ltd, Hadera, Isr.

ROTEM, Yaacov, Israel pediatrician, author; b. Pol, Nov 25, 1912; s. Israel and Henena (Wilder) Deutsch; in Isr since 1938; m. Frieda Rotenstreich, 1938; c. Yael, Anat. Head, children's dept, Tel Hashomer Hosp, since 1952; phys: Hadassah Hosp, Jerusalem, 1938-39; Kibbutz Negba, 1939; Ein Shemer and dist, 1940-41; children's dept, Cen Hosp, Emek Jezreel, 1941-46; ped, Natanya region Kupat Holim, 1946-52; sr clinical lectr, Heb U, Med Sch; prof, Tel Aviv U Med Sch. Served Haganah. Author: Gidul Banim, 1952; co-author: Sefer Haem, 1952; Heb Med Dict, haDerech leChaim, 1963; Correct Diet for your Child, 1961. Secy, Isr Ped Soc; mem: NY Acad of Scis. Home: 19 Bartenura St, Tel Aviv, Isr. Office: Tel Hashomer Gov Hosp, Ramat Gan, Isr.

ROTENSTREICH, Amalia, Isr, organization exec; b. Lwow, Pol, Nov 23, 1912; d. Moshe and Rosa (Messer) Frostig; in Isr since 1933; att: Heb Coll, U of Lwow; m. Joshua Rotenstreich, Mar 19, 1933; c: Ruth Ahiezer, Mikhal Holzmann, Irith. Chmn, immigration and absorption comm, Pol Immigrants Assn; mem: comm, Hassidei Umot Haolam; club: Rotary. Recipient: award, Pres of Isr. Home: 39 Hashoftim St, Tel Aviv, Isr.

ROTENSTREICH, Joshua, Isr, attorney; b. Kolomyja, Pol, Dec 27, 1910; s. Ephraim and Mirjam (Eifermann); in Isr, since 1933; att, Coll of Journalism, Warsaw, 1929-32; LLD, U Lwow, Pol, 1932; m. Amalia Frostig, Mar 19, 1933; c: Ruth Ahiezer, Michal, Irith. Pvt practice, since 1939; pres, Isr Bar, since 1962; fmr: ME corresp, J Press, 1933-39. Served IDF; chmn, censorship bd, IDF, since 1949. Mem presidium, Isr Bar Assn, since 1938; mem: cen comm, Friends of Heb U; Rotary. Author: History of the Arab National Movement, 1938; mem ed bd: Hapraklit; Psakim; contbr to local and fgn press. Home: 39 Hashoftim St, Tel Aviv, Isr. Office: 2 Har Sinai St, Tel Aviv, Isr.

ROTENSTREICH, Nathan, Isr, educator; b. Sambor, Pol, Mar 31, 1914; s. Ephraim and Mirjam (Eifermann); in Isr since 1932; MA, Heb U, Jerusalem, 1936; PhD, 1938; m. Binah Metzger, Mar 3, 1936; c: Ephrat, Noa. Prof, phil, Heb U, since 1955, dean, Hum, 1957-61, rector, 1965-69; prin, Youth Aliyah Tchrs Coll, Jerusalem, 1944-51. Mem: Isr Acad of Sci and Hum; Intl Inst of Phil. Author: Between Past and Present, 1958; Spirit and Man, 1963; The Recurring Pattern, 1963; Humanism in the Contemporary Era, 1963; Experience and Its Systematization, 1965; Basic Problems of Marx's Philosophy, 1965; On the Human Subject, 1966; From Mendelssohn to Rosensweig, Jewish Philosophy in Modern Times, 1968; contbr to phil mags. Recipient: Ahad Ha'am prize, Heb U, 1936; Tscernichowski prize, Tel Aviv Munic, 1955; Isr Prize for Hum, 1963. Home: 7 Marcus St, Jerusalem, Isr. Office: Heb U, Jerusalem, Isr.

ROTH, Alvin Sydney, US, rabbi; b. Charleroi, Pa, Aug 6, 1917; s. John and Ethel (Handelsman); BA, U of Cincinnati, 1940; ordained rabbi, HUC, 1953; PhD, Northwestern U, 1957; m. Nancy Caplan, Aug 2, 1958; c: Samuel, Emily, Katherine. Rabbi, Cong Beth Emeth, since 1956; asst rabbi, Chgo Sinai Cong, 1953-55. Cpl, USAAC, 1942-45. Chmn, CCAR Comm on Soviet Jewry; past pres, Albany Min Assn; exec comm, Albany Comty Chest; bd govs, HUC-JIR; mem: Phi Delta Kappa. Contbr weekly column to Albany Times-Union. Home: 81 S Manning Blvd, Albany, NY. Study: 100 Academy Rd, Albany, NY.

ROTH, Arthur A, US, surgeon; b. Cleveland, O, Oct 21, 1904; s. Henry and Rose (Bolitzer) att: W Reserve U, 1924-25; O State U, 1927-28; BS, St Louis U, 1930, MD, 1932; m. Lenore Schwartz, Oct 20, 1937; c: Loren. Pvt practice, genito-urinary surg, since 1942; chief, urol Suburban Comty Hosp, since 1957; sr visiting urol, Mt Sinai Hosp, since 1945; cons: Polyclinic, since 1944; Women's Hosp, since 1954; pres, Pfsl Investors, since 1958. Vice-chmn, JWF annual campaign, since 1956; mem: AMA; O State Med Assn; Acad of Med; Amer Urol Assn; Amer Assn for Study of Sterility; Cleveland Urol Soc; Intl Fertility Assn; Endocrine Soc; clubs: Masons; The Temple; Lake Forest Country; Temple Mens. Contbr to med jours. Recipient: award, Amer Urol Assn, 1946. Hobbies: photography, golf. Home: 16100 Van Akin, Shaker Heights, O. Office: 10605 Chester Ave, Cleveland, O.

ROTH, Burnett, US, attorney; b. Newark, NJ, June 13, 1912; s. Hyman and Celia; BS, U of Fla, 1933, LLB, 1934; postgrad study, intl finance, NYU, 1934-35; m. Rosebelle Scher, Sep 6, 1935; c: Paula, Carla, Samuel, Wayne. Pvt practice since 1935. US Army, 1942-45. Natl vice-chmn, ADL, 1960-66, active since 1957; pres: AZC, 1961-65; United Cerebral Palsy, 1959-60; councilman, Miami Beach, 1948-54; mem, Fla and Dade Co Bar Assns. Home: 14 Star Island, Miami Beach, Fla. Office: 420 Lincoln Rd, Miami Beach, Fla.

ROTH, Fred H, US, business exec, civic worker; b. Cincinnati, O, Sep 7, 1899; s. Leopold and Amy (Netter); BA, Williams Coll, 1921; m. Louise Lange, Dec 5, 1928 (decd); c: Patricia Loeb, Marry Benioff; m. 2d, Louise Johnson, Feb 7, 1957. Ret since 1952; fmr vice-pres: Clopay Corp, 1940-52; Roth Shoe Mfg Co, 1928-35. Treas, Antioch Coll, bd govs; chmn, City Charter Comm, 1958-62; exec comm mem, AJComm; pres: J Family Service Bur, 1948-52; United J Social Agencies, 1952-56; Sheltering Oaks Hosp, 1954-57; vice-pres: Urban League, Planned Parenthood Assn. Home: 4804 Cornell Rd, Cincinnati, O.

ROTH, Leor Arie, Isr, painter; b. Tysmenice, Pol, May 17, 1914; s. David and Rivka (Sobel); in Isr since 1933; att, Beaux Arts Sch, Paris, 1950; m. Manja Fogelman; c: David, Salman. Mem, Kibbutz Afikim; painter: Collection of Drawings, 1950; Color Reproductions of Paintings and Drawings, 1963; Mural Painting, 1969; one-man shows, Isr ad abroad; instr, art sch for young Kibbutz artists. IDF, 1948-64. Mem, Isr Artists Org. Hobbies: music, lit. Home: Kibbutz Afikim, Isr.

ROTH, Lester Wm, US, jurist, attorney; b. NYC, Apr 5, 1895; s. Herman and Hannah (Kornfield); LLB, U of S Cal, 1916; m. Gertrude Freedman. July 7, 1926; c: Harlan, Eleanor. Presiding justice, div two, Dist Court of Appeal, Cal, since 1964; pvt practice since 1952; mem, law firm, Lissner, Roth and Gunter, 1920-31; judge, Superior Court of Cal, 1931-36; mem, law firm: Mitchell, Silberberg, Roth & Knupp, 1936-42; Roth & Brannen, 1942-47; dir: Standard Cabinet Works, LA, since 1929; City Natl Bank of Beverly Hills, since 1953; Guaranty Union Life Ins Co, 1940-55; vice-pres, Columbia Pictures Corp, 1947-52. Chmn: Draft Appeal Bd, LA, Cal, 1942-45; Lt, USMC, 1918-19. Natl vice-pres, AJComm, 1951-52; co-chmn, NCCJ, 1957-59; dir: Legal Aid Found, LA; Brandeis Inst; mem: Conf of Cal Judges; Amer Coll of Trial Lawyers; LA Bar Assn; Acad of Motion Picture Arts and Scis; clubs: Hillcrest Country, LA, dir since 1948, pres, 1949-53; Tamarisk Country, dir. Home: 1201 Loma Vista Dr, Beverly Hills, Cal. Office: State Bldg, Los Angeles, Calif.

ROTH, Sol, US, rabbi, educator; b. Pol. Mar 8, 1927; s. Joseph and Miriam (Lamm) in US since 1934; BA, Yeshiva Coll, 1948; ordained rabbi, Isaac Elchanan Theol Sem, 1950; MA, Columbia U, 1953, PhD, 1966; m. Debra Stitskin, Nov 27, 1957; c: Steven. Rabbi, J Cen of Atlantic Beach, since 1956; visiting lectr, dept of phil, Yeshiva Coll. since 1967; rabbi, Temple Ashkenaz, Cambridge, Mass, 1951-52; asst rabbi, Cong Kehilath Jeshurun, NYC, 1954-56. Lt, US Army,

1951-54. Vice-pres, NY Bd of Rabbis; mem: RabCA; Amer Phil Assn. Author: Science and Religion, 1967. Recipient: Commendation Ribbon, US Army, 1952-54. Home: 133 Erie Av, Atlantic Beach, NY. Study: Nassau Ave, Atlantic Beach, NY.

ROTHBARD-SCHWARTZ, Dvorah, US, organization exec; b. Wishegrod, Pol, July 16, 1899; d. Morris and Reila (Klempner); in US since 1914; grad. J Tchrs Sem, 1923 BA, U of Cal, 1933; m. Ignatz Schwartz, Sep 28, 1928. Natl dir, Isr Bonds Issue for Pioneer Women, since 1951; chmn adv bd, Pioneer Women, since 1948, past chmn; vice-pres, J Tchrs Sem; mem: directorate: YIVO, CYCO; natl bd dirs: JNF; KH; AJCong; WJC; Ichud Olami Poalei Zion, Isr; cen comm, Poalei Zion; Farband; Phi Beta Kappa; fmr co-chmn, Natl Comm for Lab Isr. Ed, Pioneer Women; contbr to J publs. Home: 161 W 16th St, New York, NY. Office: 45 E 17th St, New York, NY.

ROTHBERG, Joseph, US, business exec; b. Boston, Mass, May 20, 1909; s. Morris and Annie (Rosenberg); att MIT, 1927-29; m. Dorothy Cohen, Dec 22, 1931; c: Marvin, Ira, Howard. Motion picture producer, since 1944; pres, treas, Dekko Films, since 1944; treas, United Bc Corp, since 1960; research asst, Harvard U, 1930-31; audio visual cons, E Radio Corp, 1933-38; newsreel cameraman, Paramount News; fac mem, Boston U, 1945-53. War corrsp, RAF, W II. Mem: bd of mgrs, Soc of Motion Picture & TV Engrs, since 1960; Audio Engr Soc; Intl Allian·e Theatrical State Employees; Illuminating Engr Soc; Delta Kappa Alpha. Home: 29 Harold St, Sharon, Mass. Office: 126 Dartmouth St, Boston, Mass.

ROTHBERG, Samuel, US, business exec, communal leader; b. Russ, Dec 15, 1910; s. Morris and Bertha; BS, Bact, Phila Coll Pharm and Sci, 1931; hon PhD, Heb U, 1966; m. Jean Culver; c: Michael, Patrick, Kathy, Heidi. Dir, Amer Distilling Co; pres: Isr Inves Corp; Capital for Isr. Founding mem, natl campaign chmn, Isr Bond Org; chmn of bd, Amer Friends of Heb U; natl campaign cabinet, fmr natl chmn for initial gifts, UJA; chmn, bd govs, Heb U; vice-pres, Amer Comm for Weizmann Inst of Sci; bd govs, Amer Assn for J Educ; fmr pres, Peoria J Comty Council. Recipient: Scopus Award, Heb U, 1962. Home: 4739 Grand View Dr, Peoria, Ill. Office: Amer Distilling Co, South Front St and Distillery Rd, Pekin, Ill.

ROTHBORT, Samuel, US, artist; b. Wolkovisk, Russ, Nov 25, 1882; s. Hirsh and Ida (Beckenstein); att Wolkovisk Yeshiva, 1894-96; in US since 1904; m. Rose Kravitz, Aug 28, 1909; c: Henry, Ida, Lawrence, Ruth. Painter since 1905; sculptor since 1925; with Barzansky Gallery, NYC, since 1940; founder of Direct Art movement, 1905. Autobiographical film, The Ghetto Pillow, about Shtetl memories. One man show, Herzl Inst, 1962. Author: Out of Wood and Stone, 1952. Recipient: award, Natl Council of Audio Visual Materials. Hobby: horticulture. Home and studio, 823 Ave S, Brooklyn, NY. Office: c/o Albert Barry & Assos, 485 Rugby Rd, Brooklyn, NY.

ROTHCHILD, Sylvia, US, author, communal worker; b. NYC, Jan 4, 1923; d. Samuel and Bertha (Neuberger) Rosner; att Bklyn Coll, 1939-46; m. Seymour Rothchild, July 8, 1944; c: Alice, Judith, Joseph. Writer, lectr, since 1951; book review columnist, Jewish Advocate, Boston, since 1951; leader, Hadassah study group, Sharon, Mass, since 1953; dir, adult activities, YM-YWHA, 1946-49; org, leader, Golden Age Club, Council of J Women and Hecht House, Boston. Mem: Temple Isr, Sharon; Hadassan; Sharon Civic Orch. Author: Keys to a Magic Door, 1960; Sunshine and Salt, 1964; short stories, articles, reviews in Commentary since 1951; contbr to periodicals. Recipient: JBCA juvenile award, 1960. Hobbies: cello, amateur art. Home and office: 19 Hilltop Rd, Chestnut Hill, Mass.

ROTHENBERG, Beno, Ist, archeologist, author; b. Frankfurt/M, Ger, Oct 23, 1924; s. Chaim and Fanny (Kresch); in Isr since 1933; MA, Heb U; PhD, Goethe U, Frankfurt/M; m. Ruth Buchman; c: Mihal, Daniel, Liora. Research asso, Tel Aviv U, since 1968; archeol surveys, Arabia and Sinai, 1959-69; field dir, HUC, Negev Expedition, 1952-56; dir, Sinai Expedition, 1956-57; ed, Lewin-Epstein publishers, 1964-66; mem, Smithsonian Inst Expedition to Iran, 1968. Brit Army; Haganah. Author: God's Wilderness, 1962, The Hidden Negev, 1967; Archeological Survey of the Elat Area, 1968. Recipient: Negev Lit prize, Elat munic, 1969. Home: 8 Berliner St, Ramat Aviv, Isr. Office: Tel Aviv U, Ramat Aviv, Isr.

ROTHENBERG, Harvey, US, business exec, public official; b. NYC, Feb 6, 1925; s. Philip and Belle (Kirshenbluth); att, U of Pa; BS, NYU, 1949; m. Elaine Feldman, Apr 3, 1951; c: Stephen, Philip. Pres, Philip Rothenberg & Co, since 1955. Lt, USN, 1944-46. Admn asst to Mayor of NY; vice-chmn, NY UJA; found mem, Einstein Coll of Med; campaign mgr, Congressman Ogden Reid, 1962-64. Recipient: 2 Battle Stars, Liberation of Philippines. Home: 232 Oxford Rd, New Rochelle, NY. Office: 350 Fifth Ave, New York, NY.

ROTHENBERG, Nathaniel S, US, attorney, communal worker; b. NYC, Oct 7, 1912; s. Morris and Anna (Shomer); BA, Lehigh U, 1933; att, NYU Law Sch, 1933-34; LLB, St Lawrence U Law Sch, 1936; m. Marjorie Zunser 1946; c: Jonas, Peter. Pvt practice, since 1956; asst to state sup, Home Owners Loan Corp, NY Agcy, 1934-38; mem, law firm, Telsey, Lowenthal, Rothenberg and Mason, 1950-56. Capt, US Army, 1942-46. Chmn, natl admn comm, Amer ZC, 1964-67; dep mem, WZO, since 1965; mem, admn comm, WJC, Amer sec; natl pres, B'nai Zion, 1956-59; vice-pres, ZOA, 1956-60; mem, bd dirs: JNF of Amer; Amer ORT Fed; mem: NY Co Lawyers Assn; Res Offs Assn; Pi Lambda Phi; Cong B'nai Jeshurun; club: Amsterdam Dem. Ed, B'nai Zion Voice, 1959-62. Recipient: Soldier's Medal for Valor, 1943. Home: 225 W 86 St, New York, NY. Office: 55 Liberty St, New York, NY.

ROTHENBERG, Robert E, US, surgeon, educator, author; b. NYC, Sep 27, 1908; s. Simon and Caroline (Baer); BA, Cornell U, 1929; MS, 1932; postgrad study, surg, Royal Infirmary of Edinburgh, Scot, 1934-35; m. Lillian Lustig, 1933; c: Robert, Lynn. Att surg: J Hosp, NY, since 1955; Fr Hosp, NY, 1945-65; mem, bd dirs, Health Ins Plan of Gtr NY, chmn, med group council, 1945-65; clinical asst prof, SUNY U Med Coll, 1952-60. Lt col, US Army MC, 1942-46. Dipl, Amer Bd of Surg; f: Amer Coll Surgs; AMA; mem: Bklyn Surg and NY Co County Med Socs; Amer Public Health Assn; Pi Lambda Phi, Alpha Omega Alpha. Author: Group Medicine and Health Insurance in Action, 1949; Understanding Surgery, 1955; The New Illustrated Medical Ency, 4 vols, 1959; New American Medical Dictionary and Health Manual, 1962; Health and Medical Care After 60, 1963; Reoperative Surgery, 1964; Child Care Ency, 1966; Doctors' Premarital Medical Advisor, 1969. Contbr to med jours. Hobbies: art collecting, travel. Home: 35 Sutton Pl, New York, NY. Office: 870 Fifth Ave, New York, NY.

ROTHENSTEIN, Wolfgang, Isr, educator; b. Amsterdam, June 2, 1923; s. Leo and Johanna (Hollander); in Isr since 1960; BSc, U London, 1948, MSc, 1950, PhD, 1956; m. Mirjam Kaufmann; c: Edna, Arnon, Daniel. Asso prof, nuclear sci, Technion, Haifa, since 1964, fac mem since 1960; fmr: sr lectr, Battersea Polytech, London, 1948-51; research asso, Brookhaven Natl Lab, 1958-60. Sgt, British Army, 1943-46. Mem, Amer Nuclear Soc. Contbr to profsl jours. Home: 8 David Pinsky St, Haifa, Isr. Office: Technion, Haifa, Isr.

ROTHMAN, Marcus, US, organization exec; b. Stryl, Aus, Dec 10, 1912; s. Morris and Esther (Youngman); in US since 1914; BS, CCNY, 1935; m. Sylvia Diamond, Oct 4, 1942; c: Ira, Esther. Admn asst, Nemet Auto Intl Ltd, since 1968; chief, x-ray, physiotherapy, photographic depts, NY State dept of mental hygiene, 1938-45; dist exec, Boy Scouts of Amer, 1945-52; dir, USO, 1956-62, staff mem since 1952; area dir, NY-NJ Natl JWB, 1962-64, asst sales mgr, CUTCO, 1965-68. Mem: Amer Adult Educ Assn; Gulf Coast Comty Service Council; Amer Soc of X-ray Technicians; Amer Registry of X-ray Technicians; contbr to tech jours. Home: 1625 N Thompson Dr, Bay Shore, NY. Office: 153-03 Hillside Ave, Jamaica, NY.

ROTHMAN, Murray Israel, US, rabbi; b. NYC, Mar 16, 1921; s. Hyman and Eva (Esrig); BA, Yeshiva U, 1944; ordained rabbi, MHL, HUC, 1949; m. Charlotte Hamburg, May 28, 1950; c: Jo, Lily. Rabbi, Temple Shalom of Newton, since 1954; asst rabbi, Rodef Shalom Temple, Pittsburgh, 1949-51. Chaplain, USN, 1951-53. Pres, Mass Bd of Rabbis; bd of govs, HUC; bd of dirs, Amer Friends of the Heb U; Newton Comty Council; fmr pres, CCAR, NE region; mem: Newton Fair Housing Comm; natl chaplain, JWV, 1956-57. Chief ed, HUC monthly, 1946-48. Recipient: Naval Commendation Medal, USMC, 1953. Contbr to periodicals. Hobby: photography. Home: 35 Kingston Rd, Newton, Mass. Study: 175 Temple St, Newton, Mass.

ROTHMAN, Robert Aaron, US, rabbi; b. NYC, Mar 31, 1931;

s. Hyman and Eva (Esrig); BA, Yeshiva U, 1953; BHL, HUC, 1955, MHL, hons, 1957. DHL, 1966; m. Sherran Simson, June 7, 1961; c: Dee, Kay. Rabbi Comty Syn, since 1966; visiting prof, Iona Coll, since 1968; instr, HUC Sch of Educ, since 1967; asso rabbi, Temple Isr, Columbus, O, 1959-61; rabbi, Temple Adath Isr, Lexington, Ky; 1961-64. Cdr, USNR. Pres, Rye Interfaith Council; chmn, Interfaith Marriage Comm, FJP; bd dirs: Westchester Co chap, AJ-Comm; Carver Cen of Port Chester; Rotary; mem: CCAR; Alumni Assn HUC-JIR; B'nai B'rith. Contbr to profsl jours. Hobby: photography. Home: 214 Forest Ave, Rye, NY. Study: 200 Forest Ave, Rye, NY.

ROTHMAN, S Lawrence, US, advertising exec; b. Pittsburgh Pa, Dec 4, 1918; s. Saul and Gussie (Litman); att U of Pittsburg, 1937-39; BJour, U of Ga; hon LHD, Indiana Northern U, 1968; m. Constance Friedman, Aug 1, 1943; c: Craig, Stephen, Jane. Pres, Rothman Advt Agcy, since 1958; advt instr, dept of marketing, U of Pittsburgh, 1954-59; sports corresp, United Press Assn, 1940; prog dir, WALB, MBS, 1941-42; partner, Rothman and Gibbons, advt and PR agcy, 1947-57. Lt, US Army, 1942-46. Chmn of Bd, Monongahela Valley Masquers; mem: McKeesport C of C; Pa State Vets Employment Comm; B'nai B'rith; Druids; Pi Lambda Phi; Di Gamma Kappa; McKeesport Little Theater, pres, 1967-68; clubs: Pittsburgh Advt, mem, bd of dirs, 1955-57; Pittsburgh Radio and TV; Cap and Gown, Contbr to mags. Home: 2937. Myer Blvd, McKeesport, Pa. Office: Peoples Union Bank Bldg, McKeesport, Pa.

ROTHMAN, Stuart, US, attorney; b. St Paul, Minn, Apr 14, 1914; s. Harry and Yetta (Rudawsky); BS, LLB, U of Minn; LLM, Harvard Law Sch, 1938; m. Barbara Cohen, Mar 5, 1944; c: Elizabeth, Lucy. Partner, Royall, Koegel, Rogers & Wells; fmr: gen counsel, NLRB, since 1959; solicitor of lab, US Dept of Lab, 1953-59. Chmn, govt div, UJA, since 1958; mem: Amer, Fed Bar Assns; clubs: University, St Paul; Press Club, Wash, DC. Home: 4474 Salem Lane, NW, Washington, DC. Office: 1730 K St NW, Washington, DC.

ROTHMULLER, Marko A, US, educator, composer, singer; b. Trnjani, Yugo, Dec 31, 1908; s. Josip and Ana (Hahn); in US since 1948; att, Acad of Music, Zagreb Yugo, studied privately: composition, Alban Berg, Vienna; voice, Franz Steiner, Vienna; m. Ela Reiss, July 14, 1935; c: Ilan, Daniel. Prof, music, Ind U Sch of Music, since 1962, on staff since 1955; opera appearances include: Covent Garden, London, 1948-54; State Opera, Vienna, 1946-57; Metrop Opera, NYC, 1958-61; performances throughout Eur, S Amer, and US. Compositions: Divertimento for Trombone, Solo Timpani, and String Orch; trios; quartets; songs; ballet music. Recorders: HMV, Bartok, London, Decca. Author: The Music of The Jews, 1954, paperback, 1960, revised and enlarged, 1967. Home: 701 S Park Ave, Bloomington, Ind. Office: Sch of Music, Indiana U, Bloomington Ind.

ROTHSCHILD, Baroness Alix de, Fr, civic worker; b. Frankfurt/Main, Ger, June 30, 1911; d. Baron Philippe, and Lili (Goldschmidt-Rothschild) Schey de Koromla; c: Mrs Maurice Rheims, David. Mayor of Reux, Calvados, since 1953; world patron, Youth Aliyah, chmn Fr sect; chmn, Soc Friends of Musée de l'Homme; vice-chmn, UJA, Fr; mem: Intl bd, Isr Mus, Jerusalem; bd dirs: Rothschild Found; Soc Friends of Musée National d'Art Moderne, both in Paris. Recipient: Chevalier du Mérite Social, 1949; Chevalier de l'Ordre des Palmes Académiques, 1961; Chevalier de l'Ordre des Arts et Lettres, 1964. Homes: 24 avenue Raphael, Paris 16e, Fr; Haras de Reux, Calvados, Fr.

ROTHSCHILD, Bethsabee Beatrice de, Isr, organization exec; b. London, Eng, Sep 23, 1914; s. Edouard and Germaine (Halphen); in Isr since 1962; licenciée es scis, Sorbonne, 1935; m. Donald Bloomingdale, Produc, Bat-Dor Dance Co, since 1968; fmr: biol researcher: Columbia U, 1952-54; NYU; found, Batsheva Crafts Corp Ltd, Tel Aviv. Soldier, Free Fr Women's Auxiliary, 1944-45. Chmn: Batsheva Found for Learning; Batsheva-Bat-Dor Dance Soc; Baron de Rothschild Fund for Sci and Tech, Isr; Baron de Rothschild Found for Advancement of Sci in Isr; fmr: ANTA Dance Panel; pres: Natl Council for Art and Culture in Isr; Isr Dance Panel; Panel mem, Isr Mus, Bezalel br. Author: La Danse Artistique Aux Etats-Unis, 1949. Home: 24 Shamir St, Tel Aviv, Isr. Office: 9 Frug St, Tel Aviv, Isr.

ROTHSCHILD, Carl E, US, physician; b. NYC, May 28, 1917; s. Mervin and Sadie (Miller); BS, U of Med, 1936,

MD, Med Sch, 1940; m. Naomi Bloom, Dec 1, 1946; c: Michael. Pvt practice since 1948. Capt, USAF, 1943-46. Mem: NJ State Med Soc; Bergen Co Med Soc; AMA; f: Amer Acad of Orthopedic Surgs; Amer Coll of Surgs; Dipl, Amer Bd of Orthopedic Surgs. Mem, bd of trustees, Art Cen of Northern NJ. Hobby: sculpture. Home: 1 Brownes Terr, Englewood, NJ. Office: 440 West End Ave, New York, NY.

ROTHSCHILD, Baron Elie Robert de, Fr, banker; b. Paris, Fr, May 29, 1917; s. Robert and Nelly (Beer); licencie en droit, Faculte de Droit; dipl, Institut des Sciences Politiques, Paris; m. Lilliane Fould-Springer, Oct 7, 1941; c: Michael Nathaniel, Nelly Sabine, Gustava. Partner, Rothschild Bros, bankers. Pres: Caisee Israelite de Demarrage Economique; campaign comm, Fonds Social Juif Unife, Recipient: Croix de Guerre; Chevalier de la Legion d'Honneur. Home: 11 rue Masseran, Paris 7, Fr. Office: 21 rue Laffitte, Paris, 9, Fr.

ROTHSCHILD, Friedrich S, Isr, psychiatrist; b. Giessen, Ger, Dec 16, 1899; s. Hesekiel and Bertha (Stein); in Isr since 1936; MD, U of Giessen, 1923; postgrad study, psycht and neur, Us of Heidelberg and Frankfurt, 1924-30; m. Margot Hellmuth, April 5, 1936; Chief psycht, Hadassah U Hosp, Jerusalem, since 1954; clinical asso prof, Heb U Med Sch, 1954-66. Mem, Isr Psychan Soc; corresp mem, Amer Psycht Assn. Author: Symbolik des Hirnbaus, 1935; Das Ich und die Regulationen des Erlebnisvorganges, 1950; Das Zentralnervensystem als Symbol des Erlebens, 1958; contbr to profsl jours. Home: 3 Radak St, Jerusalem, Isr. Office: Hadassah U Hosp, Jerusalem, Isr.

ROTHSCHILD, Fritz A, US, educator; b. Homburg, Ger, Oct 4, 1919; s. Richard and Bella (Strauss); in US since 1948; BRE, JTSA, 1951, ordained rabbi, MHL, 1955. DHL, 1968; m. Lotte Katzenstein, Dec 23, 1950; c: Jonathan. Asso prof, phil of rel, JTSA, since 1960; instr, Pa State U, 1959-60. Mem, RA. Author: Between God and Man: An Interpretation of Judaism from the Writings of Abraham J Heschel, 1959, paperback, 1965; The Concept of God in Jewish Education, 1965; Teaching the Torah: An Essay on Interpretation, 1966; co-author: Theologians: Christians and Jews, 1967; contbr to J publs. Home: 12 Dongan Pl, New York, NY. Office: JTSA, 3080 Broadway, New York, NY.

ROTHSCHILD, Baron Guy de, Fr, banker; b. Paris, Fr, May 21, 1909; s. Baron Edouard and Germaine (Halphen); licencié en droit, Faculté de Droit, Paris; m. Alix Schey de Koromla, Dec 30, 1937; c: David; m. 2nd, Baronne Marie-Hélène de Zuylen de Nyevelt de Haar, Feb 17, 1957; c: Edouard. Pres: Banque Rothschild; Sté Minière & Métallurgique de Penarroya; Five Arrows Securities; second continuation partner: NM Rothschild & Sons; admnr: Francarep; Franco-Britannique de Participations; Sté Le Nickel; Cie du Nord; SAGA National Provincial & Rothschild (Intl) Ltd; New Court; Securities Corp; European Property, London; Femmes d'Aujourd'hui Bruxelles; Rio Tinto Zinc, London. Pres,, Fonds Social Juif Unifie; clubs: Nouveau Cercle, Automobile; Cercle Interallié. Recipient: Officier, Légion d'Honneur; Croix de Guerre, 1939-45; Chevalier du Mérite Agricole. Home: 10 rue de Courcelles, Paris, Fr. Office: 21 rue Laffitte, Paris, Fr.

ROTHSCHILD, Baron James de, Fr, financier; b. Paris, March 19, 1896; s. Baron Henri and Mathilde (Weissweiller); m. Claude Dupont (decd); c: Nicole, Monique de Rothschild; m. 2nd, Yvette Choquet, Oct 21, 1966. Admn, Chemins de Fer de l'Est; mayor, Compiegne, 1935-40, 1945-47. Fr Air Force, 1914-18, 1939-45. Club: Aéro-Club de Fr. Recipient: Croix de Guerre, 1918; Officier de la Légion d'Honneur, 1949. Home: 92-14 rue Saint-Paul, Neuilly sur Seine, Fr.

ROTHSCHILD, Karl, US, psychiatrist; b. Kirchberg, Ger, Nov 29, 1897; s. Julius and Albertina (Salomon); att U's of Frankfurt and Cologne; MD, U of Heidelberg, 1921; in US since 1924; m. Emilie Zemo, Apr 28, 1956. Pvt practice, neuropsycht since 1926; fmr chief, dept of nervous diseases, Middlesex Gen Hosp, New Brunswick, NJ; cons, neuropsycht: St Peters Gen Hosp, New Brunswick, NJ; Roosevelt Hosp, Menlo Park, NJ. F: Amer Coll of Phys (life); Amer Psychiatric Assn (life); Amer Geriatric Soc; Gerontological Soc; AAAS; mem: AMA Union Co and NJ Med Socs; past dep cdr, Sons of Union Vets of the Civil War; club: Rutgers U pres, med sect, 1952. Home: and office 747 W 7 St, Plainfield, NJ.

ROTHSCHILD, Lothar Simon, Switz, rabbi, author; b. Karls-

ruhe, Ger, Dec 7, 1909; s. Ferdinand and Paula (Bloch); PhD, U of Basel, 1932; ordained rabbi, J Theol Sem, Breslau, 1933; DD, HUC-JIR, 1968; m. Thea Katz, 1943. Rabbi em, J Cong, St Gall, rabbi, 1943-68; fmr: lectr, hist of rel, J hist, Handelshochschule, St Gall; chief rabbi, Saar Dist, 1934-38; dir, Ref Aid Movement in Basel, 1938-43; lectr, J hist, U of Basel, 1940-43. Vice-pres, Vereinigung für religiösliberales Judentum in der Schweitz. Author: JC Ulrich und seine Sammlung juedischer Geschichten in der Schweiz, 1933; Schawuoth, 1948; Gesinnung und Tat, 1948; Elias Botschaft, 1950; ed, Tradition und Erneuerung, publ of Lib Judaism Union of Switz, since 1957; contbr to profsl periodicals. Home: Wassergasse 44, St Gall, Switz.

ROTHSCHILD, Louis S, US, business exec; b. Leavenworth, Kan, Mar 29, 1900; s. Louis and Nora (Westheimer); PhB, Sheffield Sci Sch, Yale U, 1920; m. Emily Bettman, 1929. Pres: Standard Real Estate Imp Co, since 1965; Intermediate Credit Corp, 1960-65; Rothschild and Sons, Inc, 1942-46, dir since 1923; dir, Mech Enterprises Inc, since 1965; chmn Fed Maritime Bd, 1953-55; under-secy, US Dept of Commerce, 1955-58; US delg, NATO planning bd for ocean shipping, 1953; chmn, air coordinating comm, 1955-58; mem, govt security commn, 1955-58. USN, WW I. Chmn: City Planning Commn, Kansas City, Mo, 1946-53; Menorah Found for Med Research; dir: Comty Studies Inc; clubs: Oakwood Co; Saddle and Sirloin; Rotary, Kansas City; Capitol Hill; City Tavern Assn, both Wash, DC; Harbor View; Yale, NY. Contbr to trans jours. Hobbies: travel, shooting, riding, Home: 4000 Massachusetts Ave, NW Washington, DC. Office: 1629 K St, NW, Washington, DC.

ROTHSCHILD, Richard C, US, author, organization exec; b. Chicago, Ill, Mar 24, 1895; s. Charles and Justine (Sonnenberg); BA, Yale U, 1916; m. Bessie Newburger ,May 17, 1920; c: Barbara Fogel, Richard. Fmr, advt exec, The Rothschild Co, 1924-35; dir, Parents Mag, 1928-46; lectr, phil New Sch for Social Research, NYC, 1935-38; dir, public educ and info AJComm, 1940-50. Ensign, USN Aviation, 1918. Mem: Manhattan council, NY State Comm Against Discrimination, 1953-64; clubs: Yale, NYC; Sunningdale County. Author: Paradoxy, The Destiny of Modern Thought, 1931; Reality and Illusion, 1934; Three Gods Give an Evening to Politics, 1936. Home and office: 1165 Park Ave, New York, NY.

ROTHSCHILD, Yaacov, Isr, educator, librarian; b. Frankfurt/M, Dec 23, 1909; s. Hugo and Betty (Mayer); in Isr since 1938; PhD, Goethe U, Frankfurt/M; prof deg, U of Heidelberg; libr deg, Heb U, Jerusalem; m. Hadassah Cycowicz, Apr 14, 1940; Dir, grad libr sch, Heb U, since 1969; fmr: sr libr, head dept, J Natl and U Libr, Jerusalem, 1969, on staff since 1959; educ supr, Youth Aliyah Dept, JA, 1951-57; prin, elem schs; dep dir educ, J DP camps, Amer Occupation Zone, Ger; tchr, J secondary schs, Ger. Chmn, comm on cultural activities, Isr Libr Assn; mem bd, Cen for Public Librs; adv, Min of Educ, dept of librs. Contbr to profsl and scholarly jours. Home: 28 Alfasi St, Jerusalem, Isr. Office: Heb U, Jerusalem, Isr.

ROTHSTEIN, Ben, US, art director, artist; b. NYC, Oct 29, 1915; s. Abraham and Gussie (Goldberg); att: Leonardo da Vinci Art Sch, 1934; NY Sch of Ind Art, 1935-39; Pratt Inst, 1940-42; New Sch of Social Research, 1947-50; Fontainebleau Sch of Fine Arts, Fr, 1951; m. Fanny Levine, Sep 28, 1941;. c: Linda. Staff art dir, Sun NY Times, mem staff since 1935, Staff sgt, US Army, 1942-46. One man exhibitions: Anniston Ala, 1945; NYC, 1946; Bridgeport, Conn, 1947. Mem: Amer Newspaper Guild; Fontainebleau Alumni Assn. Recipient: Fashion Group Fine Arts Project, 1955. Home: 614 Antrim Rd, River Vale, NJ. Office: NY Times, 229 W 43 St, New York, NY.

ROTHSTEIN, Irma, US, artist, sculptor; b. Rostov, Russ; d. Emil and Josephine; in US since 1938; att: Women's Acad of Fine Arts, 1927-30; Vienna Art Sch, 1930-36; Sch for Woodcarving, 1931-32. Pvt art classes since 1952; instr City Coll Sch for Gen Studies, 1946-52. Recipient: prizes: Mint Mus of Fine Arts, 1946; Amer Artists Profsl League, 1948; Painters and Sculptors Soc of NJ, 1948; Springfield Art League, 1951, 1958; The Village Art Cen, 1954; Amelia Peabody prize, Natl Assn of Women Artists, 1954. Home: 27 W 15 St, New York, NY.

ROTHSTEIN, Joseph, US, rabbi; b. Yonkers, NY, Nov 1ll, 1916; s. Jacob and Lena (Friedman); BA, Yeshiva Co8,

1939; MA, NYU, 1950; m. Miriam Herman, Dec 29, 1943; c: Deborah, Aaron, Chaim, Judah. Sr Chaplain and admnr, J Cmty Chaplaincy Service of Gtr Phila, since 1955; fmr: rabbi, Mt Kisco, NY; Sundbury, Ont, Can; N Adams, Mass; Cong Sons of Isr, Newburgh, NY; B'rith Sholom Cong, Charleston. Natl pres, Amer Correctional Chaplains Assn; exec bd, RabCA, pres, Phila reg; vice-pres, Talmudical Yeshiva of Phila; mem: exec comm, Interfaith Comm on Chaplaincy, Pa; Phila Bd of Rabbis; Rel Zionist of Amer; Amer Assn of J Prison Chaplains; Amer MH Assn. Author: Sense and Essence, 1954; contbr to Rabbinical Council Sermon Manual. Home: 1616 W Godfrey Ave, Phila, Pa. Study: 1601 Walnut St, Phila, Pa.

ROTHSTEIN, Samuel, Can, educator; b. Moscow, Russ, Jan 12, 1921; s. Louis and Rose (Checov); in Can since 1922; BA U of BC, 1939; MA, 1940; BLS, U of Cal, Berkeley, 1947 PhD, U of Ill, 1954; m. Miriam Teitelbaum, Aug 26, 1951; c: Linda, Sharon. Prof, dir, sch of librarianship, U of BC since 1961, staff member since 1947; fmr: cons, Study of Sci and Tech Info in Can, 1967-69. Served Can Army. Mem: Pacific NW Libr Assn, pres, 1963; bd dirs, Vancouver J Cmty Cen; Assn of Amer Libr Schs, pres, 1968; exec, Pacific div, Can J Cong; BC Libr Assn, fmr pres; Can Libr Assn, fmr mem council; Bibliographical Soc of Can; Can Assn of U Tchrs; mem council, Amer Libr Assn, 1962-68. Author: The Development of Reference Services in American Research Libraries, 1955; co-author: Training Professional Librarians for Western Canada, 1957; contbr to libr jours. Recipient: Carnegie f, 1951-54. Home: 1416 W 40 Ave, Vancouver, BC, Can. Office: U of Brit Columbia, Vancouver, BC, Can.

ROTTENBERG, Jacob Bear, US, accountant; b. Providence, RI, Sep 8, 1918; s. Isaac and Sadie (Rubin); att, Providence Coll, Wash, 1936-39; BA, George Wash U, Wash, DC, 1942, MA, 1947; m. Vera Margolies, Oct 12, 1947; c: Ruth, Marcia, Judith. Office mgr, Northern NE dist ILGWU, since 1951, with org since 1947. Lt, US Army, 1942-46. Pres, Brookline IL Peretz Sch of Workmen's Circle, Inc; financial secy, Golden Ring Camp Inc; mem: exec bd, Workmen's Circle; JCC, Boston. Home: 117 Homer St, Newton, Mass. Office: 33 Harrison Ave, Boston, Mass.

ROTTENBERG, Reuven Robert, Isr, mathematician; b. Cairo, Egypt, Aug 5, 1922; s. Simon and Adela (Marcovitch); in Isr since 1950; BSc, MSc, DSc, technion, 1954-57; m. Noemi Marosi, Aug 22, 1965; c: Shimon, Ora. Sr lectr, math, Technion, since 1967, staff mem since 1957. Electronic engr, Isr Navy, 1952-54. Mem: Isr Math Union; Amer Math Soc. Author: Correspondances entre surface, 1966; Surfaces planaires, 1967. Home: 116 Hagalil St, Haifa, Isr. Office: Technion, Haifa, Isr.

ROTWEIN, Abraham, US, attorney, educator; b. Phila, Pa, Apr 7, 1906; s. David and Fannie (Ostroff); LLB Bklyn Law Sch, 1927; LLM, 1928; m. Joan Green, July 10, 1952; c: Jay, David. Pvt practice since 1929; prof, Bklyn Law Sch, 1928-62. Mem: NYC and NY Bar Assns. Author: Textbook on the Law of Agency, 1936, 2nd ed, 1949; Textbook on Labor Law, 1939; Textbook on New York Pleading and Practice, 1950; 2nd ed, 1956. Contbr to profsl jours. Home: 241 Central Park W, New York, NY. Office: 19 W 44 St, New York, NY.

ROUBACH, Marcelle, Fr, industrialist; b. Metz, Fr, June 14, 1896; d. Gabriel and Palmyre (Michel), Bloch; dipl, Lycee de Metz; m. Louis Roubach, July 29, 1920; c: Jean, Robert. Pres-dir, Le Profil, automobile ind, since 1945; counsellor fgn commerce of Fr, since 1963. Pres women comm, ORT, Fr, since 1938. Recipient: Officier de la Légion d'Honneur. Home: 86 Foch Ave, Paris 16, Fr. Office: 135 rue de la Pompe, Paris 16, Fr.

ROUTTENBERG, Max Jonah, US, rabbi; b. Montreal, Can. Mar 22, 1909; s. Harry and Dora (Garmaise); in US since 1927; att McGill U, 1925-27; BS, NYU, 1930; ordained rabbi, JTSA, 1932, MHL, 1932, DHL, 1949; m. Lilly Soloway, 1931; c: Ruth, Naomi, Aryeh. Rabbi: Temple B'nai Shalom, Rockville Centre, NY, since 1954; Kesher Zion Syn, Reading Pa, 1932-48; visiting prof, JTSA. Sr chaplain, US Army, 1942-45. Pres: RA, 1964-66; vice-pres, JTSA, 1951-54; dir, Cantors Inst and Sem Coll of J Music, 1951-54; lectr on educ and syn admn, Tchrs Inst, 1950-52; mem: ZOA; jt placement comm, Conservative Movement; comm on syn standards, United Syn; commn on chaplaincy, JWB; Amer J,

Hist Soc. Author: Seedtime and Harvest, 1969; contbr to J periodicals. Home: 61 Maine Ave, Rockville Centre, NY. Study: 100 Hempstead Ave, Rockville, Centre, NY.

ROZEN, Chanan, Isr, sales manager; b. Czech, Sep 24, 1918; s. Samuel and Helen (Schlachet) Rosenzweig; in Isr since 1938; m. Lily Rosenbaum, 1941; c: Giora. Sales mgr, Mutzarei Techen, since 1959; fmr: secy, Rasco-United Dairy; mgr, Meonot Poalim; dir, Atlas, war produc, WW II. Pvt, IDF, 1948-67. fmr: secy gen, employees, Isr War Ind; mem: political dept for fgn relations, Mapam; bd dirs: Zavta Club; Revivim, educ inst, Isr Cultural Cen; secy gen, Isr-Czech Friendship League. Corresp, Al Hamishmar daily; radio commentator. Recipient: Gold medal, Czech Soc for Intl Relations, 1965. Home: 120 Uziel St, Ramat Gan, Isr. Office 12 Haarba St, Tel Aviv, Isr.

ROZEN, Irving, US, attorney; b. New Haven, Conn, July 15, 1902; s. Louis and Rose (Surasky); BS, Sheffield Sci Sch, Yale U, 1924; LLB, Yale Law Sch, 1927; m. Celia Slater, Nov 11, 1923; c: Arthur, Stephen. Atty, mem, Weisman Celler, Allan, Spett, and Sheinberg, since 1952; chief regional atty, US Dept of Lab, 1939-47. Chmn, FJP charity drives, 1959; trustee, Temple Gates of Prayer, since 1950; mem: UJA; Fed Bar Assn of Conn and NJ; Fed Bar Assn; Queens Co Bar Assn; clubs: Jefferson Dem, chmn, 1956; Yale, Queens, org and trustee. Ed: Yale Law Jour. Home: 37-42 166 St, Flushing, NY. Office: 1501 Broadway, New York, NY.

ROZIN, Albert, US, teacher, composer; b. Minsk, Russ, June 15, 1906; s. Nathan and Rifka (Granat); in US since 1920; m. Rosanne Lamden; c: Paul. Organist, choir dir, Beth Sholom Peoples Temple, Bklyn, since 1953; tchr, piano, organ. Composer: Hebrew Festival Melodies; Traditional Hebrew Songs, both for piano and organ; liturgical music. Judge, Annual Natl Student Composition Test, Natl Guild Piano Tchrs, Austin, Tex; vice-pres, Asso Music Tchrs League, 1964-68; ed dir, Bklyn Music Tchrs Guild, 1960-69; mem: Piano Tchrs Cong, NY; ASCAP; Bohemians. Contbr to music jours. Home and studio: 1160 Ocean Ave, Brooklyn, NY.

RUBEL, Charles M, US, rabbi; b. NYC, Mar 17, 1905; s. Berl and Anna (Shimelman); BA, CCNY, 1928; MHL, JTSA, 1929; Rabbi, 1931; m. Lillian Yedin, July 6, 1929; c: Sheila Schertzer, Devorah Feldman. Rabbi: Cong Bnai Raphael, since 1967; Northside Heb Cong, 1929-31; Beth El J Cen, Bklyn, 1931-36; Beth Judah Temple, Wildwood, NJ, 1937-39; Kingsway J Comty Cen, Bklyn, 1940-45; Cong Sherah Isr, Macon, Ga, 1947-58: Cong Agudas Achim, Newark, 1958-62; Temple Beth Sholom, Providence, RI, 1962-67. Chaplain: Jackson Memorial Hosp and Sunland Training Cen; JWV; exec bd, RA, 1954-57; mem: Gtr, Miami RA; NY Bd of Rabbis; ZOA; B'nai B'rith; clubs: KP; Kiwanis. Contbr to J jours. Hobbies: J liturgical music, piano, Home: 1320 NW 183 St, Miami, Fla. Study: 1401 NW 183 St, Miami, Fla.

RUBELL, Irwin, US, pediatrician; b. Pinsk, Russ, Jan 27; 1895; s. Meyer and Anna (Ginsberg); in US since 1912; BS, U of Ill, 1919, MD, 1921; m. Julia Brandwein, July 10, 1922; s: Earl. Pvt practice since 1922; cons, Temple Hosp, LA, since 1947; ped em: Cedars of Leb Hosp; Mt Sinai Hosp; asso att phys, Michael Reese Hosp, Chgo, 1925-46; asso ped, Northwestern U Med Sch, Chgo, 1926-46. Mem: AMA; LA Co Med Ass'n; LA Ped Soc; Amer Acad of Ped; Amer Bd of Ped. Contbr to med jours. Home: 10644 Wellworth Ave, Los Angeles, Cal.

RUBEN, Edward Abraham, Kenya, business exec; b. Poltava, Russ, July 13, 1898; s. Hanna Beiness; in Kenya since 1912; HS, Prince of Wales, Nairobi, 1914; m. Helen Biemer, Jan 20, 1924; c: Montague, Jacob. Found, exec chmn, Express Transport Co, Ltd, Nairobi, since 1918; Maj, RASC, WW I; Army Res off, Pres: Kenya Bd of J; Nairobi Heb Cong and every J Org in Nairobi; C of C, Nairobi; Brit Legion; E Afr Pioneer Soc; E Afr Road Fed; E Afr Travel Agts Assn; fmr: chmn, Supply and Transp during Kenya Emergency; mem, Pensions Tribunal; mem: Inst Shipping Agts; Inst of Dirs; Inst Travel Agts. Spec interests: social work, trade union: activities, golf, bridge, chess. Home: POB 458, Nairobi, Kenya. Office: POB 433, Nairobi, Kenya.

RUBENS, Frances, Eng, communal leader; b. London, Eng, Mar 6, 1910; d Frederic and Constance (de Pinna) Weil; m. Alfred Rubens, May 5, 1931; d. Joanna Millan. Chmn, Assn J Women's Orgs in UK; hon vice-pres, Intl Council J Women; vice-chmn, Union of J Women, 1966-67; bd, Bd Deps of Brit

Jews, since 1966; mem: Council of Anglo-J Assn, external Affairs comm; vice-chmn, Lingfield House. Recipient: award, B'nai B'rith 1967. Home: 16 Grosvenor Pl, London, Eng.

RUBENSTEIN, A Daniel, US, physician, educator; b. Lynn, Mass, Nov 19, 1907; s. Max and Dora (Mamber); BA, cum laude, Harvard Coll, 1928; MD, cum laude, Boston U, Sch of Med, 1933; MPH, Harvard Sch of Public Health, 1940; m. Delilah Riemer, Dec 26, 1937; c: Joel, David, Susan. Dir: div of hosps, Mass Dept of Public Health, since 1950; staff mem since 1948; cons preventive med: Beth Isr Hosp, since 1950; J Memorial Hosp, since 1957; coordinator, Mass hosps, Civil Defense Agcy, 1951-62; lectr: Boston Coll, since 1950; Tufts U Sch of Med, since 1958; asso prof. epidemiology, Harvard Sch of Public Health, 1954-60; fac mem from 1945; visiting asso prof, MIT, 1962-67. Pres: NE Sinai Hosp, since 1955; Mass Central Health Council, 1953-54; Assn of Hosp Planning Agencies, 1962-63; med adv bd, Mass chap, Phys Ther Assn, 1957-60; bd trustees, Combined J Philanthropies, Boston, since 1962; bd dirs: JDC, 1962-65; mem: Mass Med Soc; AMA; Amer and Mass Public Health Assn; NE and Mass Hosp Assns; Amer Assn of Public Health Phys; Amer Assn of Hosp Planning; Delta Omega; Phi Delta Epsilon. Contbr to profsl jours. Recipient: citations: Mass Fed of Nursing Homes, 1952; Sr Citizens Assn of Mass, 1954; Mass Hosp Assn, 1963. Home: 164 Ward St, Newton Center, Mass. Office: 41 Mt Vernon St, Boston, Mass.

RUBENSTEIN, Albert H, US, educator; b. Phila, Pa, Nov 11, 1923; s. Leo and Jean (Kaplan); BS, magna cum laude, Lehigh U, 1949; MS, Columbia U, 1950, PhD, 1954; m. Hildette Grossman, Sep 11, 1949; c: Michael, Lisa. Prof of ind engr, Northwestern U, since 1959; asst prof, 1954-59, MIT; Fulbright research scholar, 1955. Mem: Inst of Radio Engrs; Inst of Mgmt Scis; Soc for Applied Anthropology; Oprs Research Soc of Amer. US Army, WW II. Recipient. Purple Heart; Dist Unit Citation. Co-author: Team Research, 1953; ed: Coordination, Control and Financing of Industrial Research, 1955; co-ed: Some Theories of Organization, 1960; contbr to profsl jours. Home: 617 Haven St, Evanston, Ill. Office: Northwestern U, Evanston, Ill.

RUBENSTEIN, Albert Marvin, US, physicist, engineer; b. NYC, May 9, 1918; s. Henry and Esther (Strobel); BA. Bklyn Coll, 1939; MS, U Md, 1949; att, Oak Ridge Sch of Reactor Tech, 1950-51; m. Eleanor Tessler, Jan 6, 1944; c: Shira, Mitchell. Asst to dir of advanced sensors, US Dept of Defense, since 1968; lectr, US Dept of Agric Grad Sch; research staff group leader, Inst for Defense Analyses, 1964-68; adv, Research Projects Agcy, US Dept of Defense, asst dir for ballistic missile defense engr, 1960-64; with Off of Naval Research, 1956-59. Bd dirs, Montgomery Co J Comty, past pres; mem: Amer Inst of Physics; Profsl Engrs, DC; Sigma Pi Sigma; Phi Kappa Phi; fmr: chmn, Bur of Ships Comm on Educ and Training; chmn, rel services, J educ comm, Montgomery Co J Comty. Holder of US Patent (Radar) 1963; US Patent (Space power) 1968. Recipient, USN Civilian Meritorious award, 1954; outstanding performance in missile defense, Off Naval Research, 1959; citation, JTSA, 1964. Spec interests: J rel and hist studies, gen sci, bridge. Home: 2709 Navarre Dr, Chevy Chase, Md. Office: The Pentagon, Washington, DC.

RUBENSTEIN, Benjamin, US, attorney; b. Staraja Siniava, Ukraine, May 5, 1906; s. Jacob and Bessie (Krupnick); in US since 1921; att Manhattan Prep Sch, 1922-24; LLB, St John's U, Sch of Law, 1931; m. Alice Richman, Dec 20. 1969; c Jerome. Atty, United Automobile Workers Union, since 1963; pvt practice, 1933-57; sr partner, Rubenstein & Rubenstein, 1957-63. Pres, Nassau Tenant's Assn, chmn, Tenant's Adv Comm, Nassau Co, NY; commn, Hum Rights Commn, Nassau Co; gen counsel, Nassau Civic Assn; mem: Workmen's Circle, past mem, exec comm; Bar Assn of NYC; panel, Amer Arbitration Assn; panel, NY State Public Employment Relations Bd; US Public Employment Commn; Nassau Co Bar Assn, past mem, exec bd; Nassau Co Lawyers Conf; NY Co Bar Assn; Intl Law Assn; Ind Research Assn; UN Comm; Histadrut; fmr: candidate: for Supr Court Justice, 1958; NY State Assembly, 1968; Mayor, Village of Hempstead, 1969. Recipient: Service award, Amer Arbitration Assn, 1963, 1964. Hobbies: politics, writing, golf, woodworking. Home: 1279 E 17 St, Brooklyn, NY. Office: 60 E 42 St, New York, NY.

RUBENSTEIN, Frank J, US, life insurance counsellor; b. Phila, Pa, Dec 25, 1890; s. Morris and Gitel (Goudiss); tchrs cert, Gratz Coll, Phila, 1912; att U of Baltimore, 1924-26; m. Mary Weinberg, Aug 4, 1918; c: Bernard, Esther Levin.

Asso agcy mgr, Equitable Life Assurance Soc, since 1941. Chmn bd, Baltimore Life Underwriters Assn, 1960; mem: Natl Assn of Life Underwriters; Million Dollar Round Table Baltimore Estate Planning Council; trustee, J Publ Soc of Amer; pres, Menorah lodge, B'nai B'rith. 1939-41 mem: Chizuk Amuno Cong; ZOA Amer-Isr Soc Masons. Contbr to J and ins publs. Recipient: hon citizen of New Orleans, 1956; Equitable's Hall of Fame, 1961, gold medal, 1963. Hobbies: travelling, reading, Home: 100 W Cold Spring Lane, Baltimore, Md. Office: 10 Light St, Baltimore, Md.

RUBENSTEIN, Hyman S, US, psychiatrist; b. Leeds, Eng, Mar 16, 1904; s. Meyer and Rose (Schnéederman); in US since 1904; PhG, U of Md, 1924; MD, 1928; BS, 1932, PhD, 1934; postgrad studies: U of Md Grad Sch, 1930-34; Johns Hopkins Hosp, 1932-35; George Wash U, 1934-35; Baltimore Psychan Inst, 1947-51; Wash, DC, Sch of Psycht, 1946-47, 1948-52; dipl, William Alanson White Inst Psycht, Psychan and Psych, 1958, cert in psychan; m. Ellen Steinhorn, July 21, 1929; c: Madelyn Shapiro, Roberta Herts, Pvt practice, since 1952; visiting phys, psycht, Sinai Hosp, since 1938, on staff since 1935; att phys, sup psycht, Seton Psycht Inst, Baltimore, since 1955; chief, neur, U of Md Sch of Med, 1933-35, on staff since 1929; att phys, neur and psycht, US Army Hosp. Aberdeen, 1951-54; fac mem, Wash Sch of Psycht, 1952-56. Natl pres, Med Student's Aid Soc, 1959-63, mem, natl bd govs, 1958-62, and since 1966; mem: bd dirs, United HIAS Service, Baltimore, since 1962, pres since 1969; natl bd trustees, Amer Phys Fellowship, IMA, since 1958, mem, natl exec comm; asso examiner, Amer Bd Psycht and Neur, 1938-48; f: AMA;AAAS; Amer Psycht Assn Acad of Psychan; mem: Baltimore City Med Soc; William Alanson White Psychan Soc; Sigma Xi; Phi Sigma Delta; Phi Lambda Kappa, natl bd trustees, since 1959, natl pres, 1967; ACLU; United World Federalists; UN Assn; Baltimore Heb Cong. Author: Stereoscopic Atlas of Neuroanatomy, 1947; The Study of the Brain, 1953; cons ed, Psychiatry, Current Medical Digest; contbr to books, encys, and med jours. Recipient: Weaver f, U of Md Sch of Med, 1931-35; Ciba f, Sinai Hosp, 1938-42; Big-Brother-of-the-Year for Md, 1964; corresp mem, honoris causa, IMA, 1964. Home and office: 390 N Charles St, Baltimore Md.

RUBENSTEIN, Laurence H, US, surgeon, educator; b. Chicago, Ill, Feb 7, 1917; s. Abraham and Bessie (Dropin); AA, U of Chgo, 1937; BS, U of Ill, MD, 1941; m. Carol Beck, Dec 16. 1945; c: Nancy, Sally, Laurie, Jonathan. Pvt practice, thoracic surg, since 1948; asso prof, surg, Chgo Med School, fac mem since 1950; att thoracic surg: Michael Reese Hosp; Mt Sinai Hosp. Mem: Soc of Thoracic Surg; Amer Coll of Surg; Amer Coll of Chest Phys; Amer Assn for Thoracic and Cardiac Surg; AMA; B'nai B'rith, Isr mission, 1961. Contbr to med jours. Home: 571 Woodlawn Ave, Glencoe. Ill. Office: 104 S Michigan Ave, Chicago, Ill.

RUBENSTEIN, Richard B, US, business exec; b. Kan City, Mo, Nov 2, 1924; s. Leo and Frances (Hoffman) BSc, US Naval Acad, Annapolis, Md, 1948; m. Jean Lewis, Sep 15, 1949; c: Jane, John, Ann, James. Pres, Blue Ridge Finance Co, since 1962. Cdr, USN, 1942-46. Mem: rel educ comm, Temple B'nai Jehudah; financial comm, bd councilors, Menorah Med Cen; bd and chmn, educ council, J Fed of KC; bd, YMCA; fmr: Cmty Drive; clubs: USNR Offs; Colo Mt Hiking. Hobbies: tennis, mountaineering. Home: 824 W 53 St, Kansas City, Mo. Office: 12009 E 43 St, Kansas City, Mo.

RUBENSTEIN, Richard L, US, rabbi; b. NYC, Jan 8, 1924; s. Jesse and Sara (Fine); att HUC, 1942-45; AB, U of Cincinnati, 1946; MHL, ordained rabbi, JTSA, 1952; MST, Harvard U, 1955, PhD, 1960; m. c: Aaron, Hannah, Jeremy, Nathaniel (decd); m. 2nd, Betty Alschuler, Aug 21, 1966. Dir, B'nai B'rith Hillel Found, chaplain, U of Pittsburgh, Carnegie-Mellon U, all since 1958; lectr, hum, U of Pittsburgh; contbr ed: Reconstructionist Mag, since 1959; rabbi: Temple Beth Emunah, Brockton, Mass, 1952-54; Temple Isr, Natick, Mass, 1954-56; dir: B'nai B'rith Hillel Found, Harvard U, 1956-58. Clubs: Harvard; Yale; Princeton. Contbr to rel jours. Home: 5035 Castleman St, Pittsburgh, Pa. Office: 315 S Bellefield Ave, Pittsburgh, Pa.

RUBEY, Myron Ross, US, merchant; b. Hattiesburg, Miss, Nov 30, 1910; s. Louis and Ida (Block) Rubenstein; m. Mary Rocklin, March 8, 1942; c: Stephen, Robert. Pres, Ross Jewellers Inc, since 1946. Capt, US Army, 1942-46. Regional chmn, AJComm, pres, Mobile div, member, natl exec bd; pres, JWF, Mobile div since 1951; chmn: UJA, 1951-52; Bonds for Isr; pres, Govt St Temple; vice-chmn, United Fund of Mobile; natl cabinet, Amer Isr Public Affairs comm; bd, Ala Hall of Fame, since 1952; mem: Ala State Bd of Educ, since 1953; ZOA; Bnai B'rith; Masons; Shriners. Recipient: Scroll of merit, City of Mobile, 1951; pres citation, 3 bronze stars; Chai award, State of Isr. Home: 301 Bromley Pl, Mobile, Ala. Office: 251 Dauphin St, Mobile, Ala.

RUBIN, Alvin B, US, jurist, educator; b. Alexandria, Ala, March 13,1920;s. Simon and Frances(Prussack);BS, La State U, 1941, LLB, 1942;m.Janice Ginsberg, Feb 17,1946;c:Michael, David. Fed dist judge, since 1966; visiting prof, La State U, since 1946; partner, Sanders, Miller, Downing, Rubin, Kean, 1946-66. Capt, US Army, 1942-46. Vice-pres, Temple B'nai Isr, 1962-64; chmn: La ADL, 1956-58; dir: Legal Aid Clinic, 1950-62; Girl Scouts of Amer, 1952-55; Comty Services Council, 1959; secy, United Givers Fund; arbitrator, Fed Mediation Conciliation Services; bd dirs: C of C; Comty Chest; adv comm, Salvation Army, 1956-59; natl leg comm, Amvets; exec comm, Sym Soc; natl council, JDC; mem: Guidance Cen, Baton Rouge; JWF, New Orleans; Inst Jud Admn; Amer Acad Political and Social Sci; Amer Arbitration Soc; Amer Legion; B'nai B'rith; Phi Delta Phi; Masons; Order of the Coif; La and Amer Bar Assns. Contbr to legal jours. Recipient: Baton Rouge Golden Deeds award, 1962; Brotherhood award, 1968, both NCCJ. Home: 225 Walnut St, New Orleans, La. Office: 400 Royal St, New Orleans, La.

RUBIN, Ephraim Leo, US, educator; b. Bklyn, NY, July 31, 1929; s. David and Libbie (Rabinowitz); BS, CCNY, 1950 MS, 1954, PhD, chem, 1955. Asso prof, aerospace eng and applied mech, Poly Inst of Bklyn, since 1966, fac mem since 1964; visiting lectr, Stevens Inst Tech, 1958-60; research sci: Yeshiva Coll, 1959-60; NYU, 1961-64. Mem: Amer Phys Soc; Amer Chem Soc; Sigma Xi. Contbr to sci jours. Home: 24 W 96 St, New York, NY. Office: Poly Inst of Bklyn, Route 110, Farmingdale, NY.

RUBIN, Ernest, US, government official, educator; b. NYC, May 14, 1915; s. Gershon and Louise (Weinstein). BSS, CCNY, 1937; MA, Columbia U, 1938; PhD, 1947; m. Mary Villon, Oct 15, 1934; c: George, Michael, Eleanor. Dir, Sino-Soviet div, US Dept of Commerce, since 1961, indl econ since 1948; adj prof stat, Amer U, since 1948; fmr: stat-bookkeeper, J Natl Workers Alliance, 1939-41; research analyst, immigrant insp, US Dept of Justice, 1941-48; research econ, Natl Bur of Econ Research, 1948-54. Mem, exec council, Amer Stat Assn; vice-pres, Wash State Soc; mem: AAUP; Math Assn of Amer; Inst of Math Stat; Order of Artus. Author: Unemployment of Aliens in the US in 1940, publ, 1949; co-author: Immigration and Foreign Born, 1954; ed: The American Statistician, 1954, and 1968; contbr to profsl jours. Recipient: UNESCO award, 1955; Rockefeller Travel grant, 1960. Home: 540 S Carlyn Spring Rd, Arlington, Va. Offices: US Dept of Commerce, Washington, DC; American U, 1901 F St, NW, Washington, DC.

RUBIN, Gary Stanley, US, business exec; b. Des Moines, Ia, July 18, 1935; s. Sidney and Ruth (Grund); att, U of Ia, 1953-55; BS, Mich State U, 1957; m. Judith Eirinberg, June 25, 1961; c: Jami, Mark. Dir, marketing, Hockenberg Rubin Co, since 1957. Campaign chmn, JWF, Des Moines; pres, J Comty Cen; regional chmn, UJA Young Leadership Cabinet; mem: B'nai B'rith; JDC; exec comm, Des Moines Wfr Fed; past pres, Tifereth Isr Men's Club. Home: 5131 Robertson Dr, Des Moines, Ia. Office: 1707 High St, Des Moines, Ia.

RUBIN, Hyman, US, business exec, legislator; b. Charleston, SC, Jan 21, 1913; s. Joseph and Bessie (Peskin); att U of NC, 1932-33; AB, magna cum laude, U of SC, 1935; m. Rose Rudnick, May 29, 1940; c: Hyman jr, Jane. Sr partner, J Rubin & Son Co, since 1938; SC State Senator, since 1966; asst mayor, Columbia City Council, 1956-66, mem since 1952. Pres: SC Assn, B'nai B'rith Lodges, 1938; dist grand lodge, B'nai B'rith, 1944-45; state chmn, UJA, 1940-45; pres, bd, Comm Cen for Mentally Retarded Children; past pres and bd mem, Columbia Travelers Aid Soc; trustee, Historic Columbia Found; mem bd: United Comm Services; mem: House of Peace Syn; Elks; Masons; Scottish Rite; Shrine; Columbia C of C; club: Columbia Civitan, past pres. Home: 2428 Wheat St, Columbia, SC. Office: 1742 Blanding St, Columbia, SC.

RUBIN, Martin I, US, chemist, educator; b. NYC, Nov 2, 1915; s. Hyman and Gussie (Buchbinder); BS, CCNY, 1936;

PhD, Columbia U, 1942; m. Edith Feldbau, May 30, 1942; c: Joanne, Richard, Naomi, Deborah. Prof, biochem, Grad Sch, Georgetown U, since 1966, exec head, chem dept since 1955, fac mem since 1948; f: Mt Sinai Hosp, NY, 1939-40; Johns Hopkins U, 1940-41; chem: Wallace & Tiernan Products 1941-46; Schering Corp, 1946-48. Pres, Intl Fed of Clinical Chems; US titular mem, Intl Union Pure and Applied Chem; mem: Amer Rheumatism Soc; Amer Chem Soc; Soc for Experimental Biol and Med; Assn for Clinical Chem: NY Acad of Sci; AAAS; bd dirs, Montgomery Co J Cen. Contbr to profsl jours. Home: 3218 Pauline Dr, Chevy Chase, Md. Office: Georgetown U, Washington, DC.

RUBIN, Max J, US, attorney; b. NYC, Feb 2, 1906; s. Benedict and Ray (Berman); LLB, NYU, 1927; hon deg, HUC, 1962; m. Belle Hirsh, Aug 8, 1929; c: Steven, Matthew. Sr mem, Rubin, Wachtel, Baum & Levin, since 1953; asso partner, Karelsen, Karelsen, Rubin & Rosenberg, 1927-53. Mem, Bd of Regents, NY State, since 1965; pres: Bd of Educ, NYC, 1961-63; NY State Citizens Comm for the Public Schools, 1958-60; Bd of Educ, Great Neck, NY, 1948-52; mem, NY State Delg to White House Conf on Educ, 1955; chmn, lawyers div, Jt Defense Appeal, 1958; mem: NYC, NY State Bar Assn; NY Co Lawyers Assn; N Shore Country Club. Recipient: spec citation, NY Sch Bds Assn, 1952; medal of honor Bklyn Coll, 1964; Alfred E Smith award, NY State Tchrs Assn, 1965. Home: 101 W 55 St, New York, NY. Office: 598 Madison Ave, New York, NY.

RUBIN, Meyer, US, researcher; b. Chgo, Ill, Feb 17, 1924; s. Abe and Esther (Fleischer); BS, U of Chgo, 1947; MS, 1949; PhD, 1956; m. Mary Tucker, June 13, 1944; c: John, Robert, Mark. Geologist, head of radiocarbon dating lab, US Geological Survey, since 1953; mil br, 1950-53. Lt, USAF, weather forecaster, 1943-46. Mem: Geological Soc of Amer; Geological Soc of Wash; Wash Acad of Sci; AAAS. Established glacial chronol by C14 dating. Contbr to profsl jours. Hobbies: archeol, canoeing, tennis. Home: 8215 Cottage St, Vienna, Va. Office: US Geological Survey, Washington, DC.

RUBIN, Milton R, US, ophthalmologist; b. Canton, O, Oct 10, 1910; s. Gabriel and Gertrude (Schwartz); MD, Temple U, 1934; m. Barbara Blatt, June 5, 1934; c: Michal Walke, Amelia Best. Pvt practice since 1938. Maj, US Army MC, 1940-45. Dipl, Amer Bd of Ophthal; f: Amer Coll of Surgs; mem: AAAS; Amer Assn Research in Ophthal; Amer Acad of Ophthal and Otology; Pan-Amer Assn of Ophthal; Pacific Coast Oto-Ophth Soc; Amer, Cal, and Fresno Co Med Assns; B'nai B'rith; Mercury Class Yacht Racing Assn; clubs: Temple Beth Isr Men's; Fresno Yacht; Sierra. Hobbies: sailing, bowling, chess. Home: 4634 Safford St, Fresno, Cal. Office: 1331 Wishon, Fresno, Cal.

RUBIN, Mitchell I, US, pediatrician, educator; b. Charleston SC, Apr 1, 1902; s. Abraham and Eva (Feintuch); att Coll of Charleston, 1919-21; MD, SC Med Coll, 1925; m. Maizie Cohen, Sep 1, 1934; c: Henry, Eve. Prof, ped, U of Buffalo, dept head, 1945-67; att ped, Buffalo Children's Hosp since 1945, ped-in-chief, 1945-67; cons, ped, Erie Co Dept of Health, since 1948; ped, Johns Hopkins U Sch of Med, 1931-45; asso prof, ped, U of Pa Sch of Med, 1931-45. Vice-pres, Soc for Experimental Biol; bd dirs, Buffalo Philharmonic Orch Soc; mem: Med Adv Council; NY State Assn for Crippled Children; Amer Ped Soc; Soc Experimental Biol and Med; AMA; Alpha Omega Alpha; Sigma Xi. Contbr author: Nelson's Textbook of Pediatrics; Handbook of Biological Data; The Child in Health and Disease; contbr to sci and biol jours. Home: 703 West Ferry St, Buffalo, NY. Office: 219 Bryant St, Buffalo, NY.

RUBIN, Mordecai B, Isr, educator; b. Boston, Mass, Aug 8, 1926; s. Samuel and Betty (Altman); in Isr since 1966; BSc, U of Pa, 1947; MA, PhD, Columbia U, 1954; m. Ruth Charney, June 9, 1953; c: Betty, David, Samuel. Asso prof chem, Technion, since 1966; asst prof, Carnegie Inst of Tech, 1958-66; f,Weizmann Inst,1964-65. Served US Army, 1944-46. Mem: Amer Chem Soc; Chem Soc, London. Contbr to sci publs. Home 28 Einstein St, Haifa, Isr. Office: Technion, Haifa, Isr.

RUBIN, Moses J, US, rabbi; author; b. Campolung, Rum, Aug 5, 1892; s. Mendel and Beile (Horowitz); ordained rabbi, Yeshiva Sereth, Rum, 1911; grad, U Cluj, Rum, 1922; m. Sara Farkas, July 5, 1916; c: Samuel, Jacob. Head, rabb court, Borough Park, Bklyn, NY; fmr: rabbi: Rum, 1922-44; Shomre Hadaath Cong, Long Beach, NY, 1950-61. Pres, World Cen of Eur Rabbis, since 1949; chmn presidium, World Cong of Eur Rabbis, Jerusalem, since 1962; pres, Union of Orthodox Rabbis, Rum, 1939-44. Author: Yad Yosef, 1922; Eitz Yosef, 1924; Dorash Moishe, 1929; Die Ideewelt von Samson Rafael Hirsch, 1944. Recipient: Officier of Rum Crown, 1930; citation, CARE, 1959; Home: 1230 43 St, Brooklyn, NY.

RUBIN, Nathan, Eng, communal exec; b. London, Eng, Apr 10, 1921; s. Mark and Annie (Zimmerman); f, Chartered Inst Secys, St Georges; m. Evelyn Goldberg, June 1, 1947; c: David, Gillian. Secy, United Syn, London, since 1968; exec off, London Co Council, 1928-50; secy, London Bd J Rel Educ, 1950-68. Sgt, RAF, 1941-46. Found, gov, hon corresp, J Comprehensive Sch; hon secy: Kosher Sch Meals Service; Conjoint Passover Flour Comm; London J Educ Found; mem, B'nai B'rith, fmr pres, N London lodge. Home: 62 Highfield Ave, Golders Green, London NW 11, Eng. Office: Woburn House, Upper Woburn Pl, London WC1, London, Eng.

RUBIN, Reuven, Isr, artist; b. Galatz, Rum, Nov 13, 1893; s. Joel and Zippora (Rabinowitz); in Isr since 1912; att: Bezalel Art Sch, Jerusalem, 1912; Acad des Beaux Arts, Paris, 1914-15; hon DHL, JIR, NYC, 1945; m. Esther Davis, 1930; c: David, Ariella. Painter, theatrical designer. Envoy, min plen, to Rum, 1948-50. Exhbts: Intl, Venice Biennale, 1948, 1950, 1952; perm collections of museums: Tel Aviv; Ein Harod; Museé d'Art Moderne, Paris; Manchester, Eng; J, NYC; Mus of Modern Art, NYC; Bklyn; Newark, NJ; San Antonio, Tex; Tucson, Ariz; Santa Barbara, Cal; Sarasota, Fla. Author: Godseekers, 1967; My Life-My Art, 1969. Pres, Isr Artists Assn, 1926-28; found, Assn of Painters and Sculptors of Pal, 1923; club: Rotary, Tel Aviv. Recipient: prizes: Lord Plumer, 1927; City of Tel Aviv, 1964. Home and Studio: 14 Bialik St, Tel Aviv, Isr.

RUBIN, Samuel N, US, business exec; b. NYC, Mar 30, 1912; s. Joseph and Anna (Kross); att: Peace Coll, 1928-32; Columbia U, 1934; NYU, 1935; m. Charlotte Ostrow, Apr 14, 1943. Exec vice-pres, Proteus Foods and Inds, Inc; treas: Pacific Bc Corp; Span Bc Sys; partner, Barrios, Hilliard, Sain, CPA 1946-61; US Army, 1942-46. Mem: NY State CPA Soc; Amer Inst of CPA's; Masons. Home: Kent Hollow Rd, New Milford Conn. Office: 477 Madison Ave, New York, NY.

RUBIN, Seymour J, US, attorney, public official; b. Chgo,Ill Apr 6, 1914; s. Sol and Sadie (Bloom); BA, U of Mich, 1935; LLB, Harvard Law Sch, 1938, LLM, 1939; m. Janet Beck, Mar 26, 1943. Partner, law firm, Luney, Karasik, Greene and Hill, since 1948; fgn affairs counsel, AJComm, since 1948; f, Harvard Law Sch, 1938-39; law secy to Judge Augustus N Hand, 1939-40; atty, SEC, 1940-41; chief counsel, OPA, 1941-43; asst legal adv, US Dept of State, 1943-48; legal adv to US delgs abroad, 1945-48; chief, US delg on negotiations with Swed, Spain, Port and Ger external asset matters, 1950-51; cons, Brookings Instn, 1952; chief with rank of US Min, US delg on NATO tax matters, 1953; mem, negotiating delgs for conf on J material claims against Ger, 1952-53; dep admnr, Mutual Defense Assistance Control Act, 1953; cons delg of comm for J claims on Aus, 1953; cons, Dept of State, 1961; gen counsel, Agcy for Intl Devl, 1961-62; personal repr of Pres of US to Bolivia, 1962; US repr to Devl Assistance Comm, with rank of Min, 1962. Mem: Harvard Law Sch Assn; Amer Soc Intl Law; Amer Political Sci Assn; AJComm; Cosmos club. Contbr to profsl jours. Home: 1675 35 St, NW, Washington, DC. Office: 1156 15 St NW, Washington, DC.

RUBIN, Simon S, US, allergist; b. Phila, Pa, Sep 3, 1908; s. Harry and Ida (Reif); BS, Northwestern U, 1930, MD, 1933; m. Anna Chesney, May 24, 1934; c: Herbert, Elliot, Edward Pvt practice since 1938; asso prof, med, Northwestern U since 1938; sr att phys: Methodist Hosp; Mercy Hosp; both since 1945; cons, Sahuaro Sch for Asthmatic Children; Maj, US Army, 1941-45. F: Chgo Allergy Soc; Amer Acad of Allergy; Intl Acad of Med; Intl Soc of Allergology; AMA; mem: NY Acad of Sci; Ind Med Soc; Amer Fellowship Comm for IMA; Lake Co Med Soc; bd dirs, Temple Isr; hon dir, Gary Players. Contbr to med jours. Hobbies: numismatics, philately. Home: 2131 W Fifth Ave, Gary, Ind. Office: 504 Broadway Gary, Ind.

RUBINGER, Naphtali J, US, rabbi; b. Dorna Vatra, Rum, Sep 14, 1924; s. Israel and Honora (Lieberman); in US since 1930; BS, St Johns U, 1944; BHL, JTSA, 1945; ordained Rabbi, Yavone Heb Theol Sem, 1946; MA, John Carroll U, 1956; DHL, Yeshiva U, 1969; m. Charlotte Farkas, June 20, 1943; c: Frederick, Shoshana, Aaron. Rabbi: Cong Habonim, since 1970; fmr Temple B'nai Jacob, 1968-70; Cong Ohav Shalom, Albany, NY, 1956-68; Cong B'nai Avraham, Elyria, O, 1952-56; Jacob Schiff Cong, 1949-52; lectr, J hist, Yavone Heb J Sem, 1949-52. Acting chaplain, US Army, 1944-46. Mem: J Hist Soc; B'nai B'rith; JWV; fmr: pres, Capitol Dist Bd of Rabbis; vice-pres, RabCA; secy, Rabb Council of Springfield, Mass; exec comm: JCC of Albany; J Comty Cen of Albany; pres, Somerset Dist, ZOA. Author:, Abraham Lincoln and the Jews; contbr to J periodicals. Home: 7000 South Shore Dr, Chicago, Ill. Study: 7440 S Phillips Ave, Chicago, Ill.

RUBINOFF, Morris, US, engineer, educator; b. Toronto, Can, Aug 20, 1917; s. Israel and Emma (Nathanson); in US since 1946; BA, U of Toronto, 1941, MA, 1942, PhD, 1946; m. Dorothy Weinberg, Oct 26, 1941; c: Elayne, David, Robert. Prof, elec engr, U of Pa, since 1964; fac mem since 1950; chmn, pres, Pa Research Assos Inc, since 1960; chmn, Energy and Catalytic Corp of Amer, since 1968; dir: Radonics Inc; Caber Corp; both since 1968; fmr: research asst, U of Toronto, 1941-46; research f, instr, Harvard U, 1946-48; research engr, Inst for Advanced Study, 1948-50; chief engr for computers, Philco Corp, 1957-59. Vice-chmn, sci and electronics div, Amer Inst of EEs, since 1962, past chmn, natl joint computer comm; chmn, Phila sect, Assn of Engrs and Architects in Isr; mem: Inst of Radio Engrs, past f, 1962; Amer Phys Soc; Farband; Sigma Xi; fmr vice-pres, chmn, tech comm, Phila chap, Amer Technion Soc. Recipient: Inst of Radio Engrs-Profsl Group on Electronic Computers award, 1955. Home: 517 Anthwyn Rd, Merion, Pa. Office: U of Pa, Phila, Pa.

RUBINOW, Jay E, US, jurist; b. Hartford, Conn, Feb 27, 1912; s. William and Mary (Brodsky); AB, magna cum laude, Harvard Coll, 1933, LLB, 1937; m. Eleanor Schwolsky, Nov 12, 1939; c: Judith, Laurence, David. Judge, Superior Court, Probate Court Admnr, both since 1967; chief judge, Conn Circuit Court, 1960-67; mem, asso bd, Manchester br, Conn Bank and Trust Co, since 1958; in pvt law practice, 1938-60. Pres, Temple Beth Sholom, 1956-59; mem: Conn Safety Comm, since 1961; Capitol Region Planning Auth, 1958-61; Masons; Phi Beta Kappa. Home: 49 Pitkin St, Manchester, Conn. Office: 67 Lafayette St, Hartford, Conn.

RUBINOW, Sol I, US, scientist, educator; b. NYC, Nov 6, 1923; s. Rubin and Sophie (Helfand); BS, CCNY, 1944; MS, Brown U, 1947; PhD, U of Pa, 1951. Prof, Biomath, Grad School of Med Sci, Cornell U Med Coll, since 1964; mem, Sloan-Kettering Inst for Cancer Research, since 1964; physicist, Natl Adv Comm for Aeronautics, 1944-46; research asso, MIT, 1951-54; research f, Harvard U, 1954-56; prof phys, Stevens Inst of Tech, fac mem, 1956-64; sr research sci, Courant Inst of Math, NYU, 1956-64. Mem: Amer Physical Soc; Biophys Soc; Sigma Xi. Contbr to profsl jours. Hobbies: chess, bridge. Home: 2 Washington Sq Village, New York, NY. Office: Cornell U Med Coll, New York, NY.

RUBINSTEIN, Alvin Z, US, educator; b. Bklyn, NY, Apr 23, 1927; s. Max and Sylvia (Stone); BBA, CCNY, 1949; MA, U of Pa, 1950, PhD, 1954; m. Frankie Kimmelman, Nov 12, 1960. Prof, political sci, chmn, grad prog in intl relations, U of Pa, since 1966, mem fac since 1957; visiting prof, U of Cal Santa Barbara; asso, Harvard Russ Research Cen; visiting, lectr: CCNY; Queen's Coll, NY. USN, 1954-56; lt, USNR. Mem: Amer Political Sci Assn; Assn of Asian Studies; Amer Assn of Slavic Studies. Author: The Soviets in International Organizations: Changing Policy Toward Developing Countries, 1953-63, 64; The Foreign Policy of the Soviet Union, 1960; Communist Political Systems, 1966; Yugoslavia and the Non-aligned World, 1969; co-author: Soviet Writings on Southeast Asia, 1968; The Challenge of Politics, 1961; contbr of articles to profsl jours. Recipient: Ford Found f in Intl Relations, 1956-57; Inter U Comm on Travel Grants award, 1957; Amer Phil Soc grants, 1958, 1959, 1968; Rockefeller Found grant, 1961-62; Guggenheim f, 1965-66. Home: Garden Ct Apts, H-405, 47 and Pine Sts, Philadelphia, Pa. Office: U of Pa, Philadelphia, Pa.

RUBINSTEIN, Amnon, Isr, educator; b. Tel Aviv, Isr, Sep 5, 1931; s. Aaron and Rachel (Vilozny); BSc, Heb U, Jerusalem, 1956; PhD, LSE, London, 1961; m. Ronny Havazelet, Jan 7, 1957; c: Tal, Nir. Dean, law fac, Tel Aviv U, since 1969; asso ed, Haaretz, 1964-69. Author: Jurisdiction and Illegality 1965; Constitutional Law of Israel, 1967. Capt, IDF, 1950-52. Mem, Isr Bar Assn. Contbr to profsl jours. Hobbies:

theater, gardening. Home: 30 Alumim St, Tel Aviv, Isr. Office: Tel Aviv U, Ramat Aviv, Isr.

RUBINSTEIN, David, Can, educator; b. Montreal, Can, Mar 4, 1929; s. Louis and Annie (Kooperstock); BSc, McGill U, Montreal, 1949, PhD, 1953, MD, 1957; m. Blanche Rubenstein, June 29, 1952; c: Larry, Bruce, Rhonda. Asso prof biochem and experimental med, McGill U, since 1959; fmr: visiting prof: Heb U, Jerusalem; Weizmann Inst of Sci; research f, Michael Reese Hosp, Chgo. Mem: Amer Soc of Biol Chems; Amer Fed for Clinical Research; Can Soc for Clinical Inves; Can Physiological Soc; Que Coll of Phys and Surgs. Contbr to profsl jours. Home: 1821 Romiti St, Chomedy, Que, Can. Office: McGill U, Montreal, Can.

RUBINSTEIN, Michael, Can, lawyer; b. Lodz, Pol, Mar 2, 1904; BA, McGill U, 1928; LLM, U of Montreal, 1931; att: Columbia U; NYU. Pvt practice since 1931; QC since 1960. Pres, J Lab Comm, Can, since 1937; co-treas, Jt advisory comm on lab relations, Can J Cong, J Lab Comm, since 1947; co-found: J Socialist Verband of Can, 1932, natl pres, 1932-34; Cooperative Commonwealth Fed, Que, 1933, mem, natl council, 1937; chmn, Workmen's Circle, Montreal 1932-38; vice-pres: E region, United J Ref Comm, 1940; Can J Cong, 1940; mem, Montreal City Council, 1940-42. Home 3055 Linton Ave, Montreal, Can. Office: 159 Craig St, W, Montreal, Can.

RUBINSTEIN, Michael A, US, physician, educator; b. Wilno, Pol, Nov 28, 1915; s. Isaac and Esther (Flensberg); att: U of Vilno, U of Paris, MD, PhD; in US since 1940; m. Vera Freudman, 1948; c: Alan, Jonathan, Daniel. Prof of med, Loma Linda U, since 1957; asst prof, U of Vilno, 1939; prof, Yeshiva U, 1941; hematologist and att phys, Montefiore Hosp, 1943-54; fac mem, Columbia U, 1947-54; prof, NY Med Coll, 1950-54; Guest Prof, Sch Med, Tel Aviv U, 1969. Dipl: Natl Bd of Med Examiners, 1942; Amer Bd of Internal Med, 1950; med adv, Consulate Gen of Isr in NY, 1948-53; pres, Amer Heb Med Soc, 1951-53; f: Amer Coll of Phys; NY Acad of Sci; Intl Soc of Hematology; AAAS; AMA; NY Acad of Med. Author: Hormonal Control of Metabolism, 1938; Hemorrhagic Diseases, 1943; Leukemia, 1948; contbr to profsl jours. Home: 803 N Bedford Dr, Beverly Hills, Cal. Office: 414 N Camden Dr, Beverly Hills, Cal.

RUCHAMES, Louis, US, rabbi, educator; b. NYC, May 25, 1917; s. Sam and Yetta (Schaefer); BSS, CCNY, 1937; MA Columbia U, 1940, PhD, 1951; ordained rabbi, JIR, 1943; m. Miriam Lantz, Aug 22, 1943; c: Robert, Barbara. Prof, hist, U of Mass, since 1966, chmn of dept since 1967; dir, B'nai B'rith Hillel Founds: U of Ala; Smith Coll; Amherst Coll, U of Mass, 1943-66. Mem: ACLU; B'nai B'rith; CCAR; Amer J Hist Soc; Amer Hist Assn. Author: Race, Jobs and Politics: The Story of FEPC, 1953; A John Brown Reader, 1959; The Abolitionists: A Collection of Their Writings, 1963; Racial Thought in America, From The Puritans to Abraham Lincoln, 1969; contbr to periodicals. Home: 68 Pierrepont Rd, Newton Lower Falls, Mass. Office: Dept of History, U of Mass, Boston, Mass.

RUCKENSTEIN-CYNOWICZ, Rivka, Isr, advocate, legal adv; b. Czernowitz, Bukovina, 1909; in Isr since 1944; grad: Acad of Commerce, of U Czernowitz. Legal adv, Min of Soc Wfr, org legal dept. Found: Keren Kayemeth le-Israel dept for rescue of Nazi victims' property; pres, B'nai B'rith Women's lodge, Tel Aviv; B'nai B'rith guardians comm for minors and the mentally ill; fmr: vice-pres, Intl Fed of Women Jurists, Paris; pres, found, Union of Women Jurists in Isr. Home: 48a Ben Yehuda St, Tel Aviv, Isr.

RUDD, Jacob L, US, physician; b. Boston, Mass, May 5, 1902; s. Simon and Fanny (Baron) Rudofsky; BA, Harvard Coll, 1924; MD, Harvard Med Sch, 1928; m. Dorothy Wiseman, Sep 3, 1936; c: Edward, Elaine. Cons, dept of rehab, Northeastern U, Mass, since 1966; chief, phys med and rehab: VA Hosp, Boston, since 1960; Brockton VA Hosp, 1953-59; Boston City Hosp, 1947-60; cons: Chelsea Naval Hosp, 1957-60; Neuro Surg Found, Inc, Boston, 1956-60; fmr: surg, US Army, Watertown Arsenal, 1932-42, med mem, US Civil Service Commn, 1932-42. Lt, US Army MC, 1929-30; chief, dept phys med and rehab: Phila Naval Hosp; Pearl Harbor Naval Hosp; both 1942-45; capt, USNR, MC, 1958; ret 1962. Fmr, dipl, Natl Bd Med Examiners; mem: Amer Bd of Phys Med and Rehab; AMA; Mass Med Soc; Amer Acad of Phys Med and Rehab; NE Soc Phys Med and Rehab, past pres; Assn Phys and Mental Rehab; N Amer Acad Manipu-

lation Med, past pres; mem, Mass State Bd of Vocational Educ; chmn, state rehab comm, Mass Dept of Educ; B'nai B'rith; Temple Isr, J Vocational Services; Amer Phys Fellowship, IMA; ZOA; Friends of Harvard Hillel; Phi Delta Epsilon; AMVETS; Disabled Amer Vets, past state rehab off; Amer Legion; Masons 32 deg; clubs: Harvard Varsity; Boston Rotary. Co-ed: Maintenance Theory for the Geriatric Patient, 1968; Selected Readings in Rehabilitation, 5 vols, 1969; Psychological and Sociological Aspects of Physical Fitness; asso ed, Rehab Review since 1954; med adv, ed bd, Amer Archives of Rehab Therapy, since 1958; contbr to med jours. Recipient: Congressional Medal of Merit, 1942; Paul Dudley White award, YMCA Fitness Council, 1968. Home: 50 Massapoag Ave, Sharon, Mass. Office: 17 Court St, Boston, Mass.

RUDEL, Julius, US, musical conductor; b. Vienna, Aus, Mar 6, 1921; s. Jakob and Josephine (Sonnenblum); in US since 1938; conducting dipl, Mannes Coll of Music, NYC, 1942; hon, DMus, U of Vt; m. Rita Gitlis, June 24, 1942; c: Joan, Madeleine, Anthony. Gen dir, NY City Opera Co, since 1957; conductor, since 1943; conductor, opera and orchs in US and abroad, since 1947; musical adv, JFK Cen for Performing Arts, Wash, DC; conductor: "Kiss Me Kate", Vienna Opera, 1956; "Susannah", Brussels World's Fair, 1958; opening performance, Festival of Two Worlds, Spoleto, 1962; cons, Ford Found, commissioning new Amer works. Recipient: gold medal, Natl Arts Club, 1958; Page One award, Newspaper Guild, 1959; Alice M Ditson award, Columbia U, 1959; citation, Amer Assn for Composers and Conductors, 1958; hon insignia, arts and sci's, Aus, 1961; Händel medal, City of NY; citation, Natl Asso Negro Musicians, 1965; hon lt, IDF. Home: 451 West End Ave, New York, NY. Office: New York City Opera Co, Lincoln Center Plaza, New York, NY.

RUDER, William, US, public relations exec; b. NYC, Oct 17, 1921; s. Jacob and Rose (Rosenberg); BSS, CCNY, 1942; m. Helen Finn, Sep 21, 1945; c: Robin, Abby, Brian, Michal, Eric. Pres, Ruder and Finn Inc, since 1962, chmn bd, 1948-62; publicist, Sam Goldwyn Produc, 1946-48; Asst Secy of Commerce, US Govt, 1960-62. USAAF, 1941-46. Trustee: J Bd of Guardians, since 1961; Harrison J Cmty Cen, since 1959; Harrison Bd Educ, since 1958; mem: bd overseers, JTSA, since 1957; bd dirs: Gerber Life Ins Co; NY Med Coll; Flower and Fifth Ave Hosps; mem: bus comm for arts, Westchester Arts Council; NY State Adv Council, innovation in educ; bus leadership adv council, OEO; past vice-chmn, US Comm for UN; mem: Young Pres Org; PR Soc of Amer; US Inter-Amer Council; B'nai B'rith; Fifth Ave Club. Co-author: The Businessman's Guide to Washington. Recipient: Tobe Lecture award, Harvard Grad Sch of Bus Admn, 1961. Home: Beverly Rd, Rye, NY. Office: 130 E 59 St, New York, NY.

RUDIN, Jacob Philip, US, rabbi; b. Malden, Mass Sep 5, 1902;, s. Louis and Dora (Vendrofsky); BA, Harvard Coll, 1924; ordained rabbi, MHL, JIR, 1928, hon DD, 1948; m. Elsie Katz, June 29, 1926 (decd); c: Priscilla Stern, Stephen. Rabbi, Temple Beth El, since 1930; asst rabbi, Stephen S Wise Free Syn, 1928-30. Chaplain, lt cdr, USN, 1942-46. Pres, Syn Council of Amer; chmn, Commn on J Educ: UAHC; HUC-JIR; past pres: Assn Reform Rabbis of NYC; CCAR; fmr: bd govs, HUC-JIR; exec bd, NY Bd of Rabbis. Author: A Haggadah For Children, 1939; So You Like Puzzles, 1940. Home: 20 Chapel Pl, Great Neck, NY. Study: 5 Old Hill Rd, Great Neck, NY.

RUDMAN, Reuben M, US, chemist, educator; b. NYC, Jan 18, 1937; s. Jacob and Deborah (Hurwitz); BA, Yeshiva U, 1957, MHL, 1961; MA, Columbia U, 1959; PhD, Poly Inst of Bklyn, 1966; m. Idelle Menkes, June 26, 1958; c: Zave, Rachel, Benjamin. Asst prof, Adelphi U, since 1967; research collaborator, Brookhaven Natl Lab, since 1967, on staff since 1966. Exec bd, Assn Orthodox J Scis; bd dirs, Yeshiva Tifereth Torah, chmn, 1965-67; mem: Amer Crystallographic Assn; Amer Chem Soc; Intl Union of Crystallography; USA Standards Inst; AAAS; Phi Lambda Upsilon. Contbr to profsl jours. Office: Adelphi U, Garden City, NY.

RUDNIKOFF, Isadore, US, internist; b. Montreal, Can, Feb 19, 1909; s. Max and Sophie (Izenson); in US since 1924; BS, CCNY, 1929; MD, NYU, 1933; m. Sarah Robowsky, 1933; c: Carol Senal, Barbara, Robert. Pvt practice since 1936; pres of med bd, dir of med, Yonkers Gen Hosp, since 1953, on staff since 1939; att phys, Yonkers Profsl Hosp, since 1941. Dipl, Amer Bd Internal Med; f: Westchester Acad of Med; NY Acad of Med; Amer Coll of Phys; Amer Geriatric Soc; Intl Soc of Internal Med; Amer Soc of Internal Med; Yonkers Acad of Med, fmr pres; Westchester Co Med Soc, bd mem: mem: NY State and West Co Med Assns; World Med Assn; AMA; Temple Emanu-El; B'nai B'rith; ZOA; Phi Beta Kappa. Contbr to med jours. Recipient: Pres Medal for Selective Service System work, 1945-46. Hobbies: music, golf, photography. Home: 1200 Midland Ave, Bronxville, NY. Office: 125 Radford St, Yonkers, NY.

RUDOLPH, Bernard G, US, merchant; b. Kovno, Lith, Dec 23, 1885; s. David and Jeanette (Wolfe); m. Lee Levitt, Mar 30, 1913; c: Jay, Mrs D. Ball, Mrs R. Blocher. Pres: ZOA, NY State region, mem natl exec; JWF; Natl Retail Jewelers Assn; pres, bd dirs, St Joseph's Hosp; fmr delg, WZC, Jerusalem; found, lectr series on Judaic studies, Syracuse U. Author: Tell Me More, autobiography, 1965; From a Minyan to a Community—A History of the Jews of Syracuse, New York, 1969. Home: 205 Janet Dr, Syracuse, NY. Office: 541 S Clifton St, Syracuse, NY.

RUDY Zvi, Isr, educator, author; b. Bialystok, Russ June 27, 1900; s. Boris and Sara (Slapak); in Isr since 1934; att Us, Prague, Berlin; Paris; PhD, U of Leipzig, 1926; m. Dora, Horenstein, Mar, 1952. Guest prof, sociol, Free U, Berlin-Dahlem, since 1962; fmr: sci researcher, Acad of J Sci, Berlin, 1928-33; prof, sociol, phil, sch of law and econ, Tel Aviv U, 1935-59. Pres, Phil Soc, Tel Aviv, since 1944. Author: in Heb Gregor Johann Mendel, His Life and Heredity Doctrine, 1935, 2nd ed, 1954; Philosophical Lexicon, 1939; Elements of Sociology, 1944, 3rd ed, 1955; Our Age and Its Outlook, 1950; The Sociology of the Jewish People, 1957; Interpretation of Dreams According to Rabbi Shlomo Almoli, 1960; in Ger: Naturphilosophie im 20 Jahrhundert, 1927; Die biologische Feldtheorie, 1931; Der Staat Israel, 1961; Ethnosoziologie sowjetischer Völker, 1962; Nationalitätenproblem und Nationalitätenpolitik in der USSR, 1962; Die Juden in Der Sowjetunion Europa Verlag Wien, 1966; Die Piktographie Anthropos, 1966; ed, Universal Ency; contbr to Heb, Fr, Ger, jours. Recipient: Bialik prize, 1939; prize, Isr Soc Hist Med and Sci, 1960. Home: 45 Jabotinsky St, Tel Aviv, Isr.

RUFFMAN, Hyman H, US, organization exec; b. Bklyn, NY, Dec 24, 1907; s. Simon and Bella (Kaplan); att, Tchrs Inst JTSA, 1925-29; BS, MA, NYU Sch of Educ; m. Ethel Gerstman; c: Joel, Sharon, Deborah. Exec dir, J Fed, Southern Ill, since 1951, with org since 1947; prin: Temple Beth El, Buffalo, NY, 1935-38; Forest Hills J Cen, 1938-40; educ dir: Heights Temple, Cleveland, O, 1940-43; Pride of Judea Children's Home, 1943-47. Mem: Natl Council of J Educ; Natl Conf of J Communal Service; Ill Wfr Assn. Office: 435 Missouri Ave, E St Louis, Ill.

RUFFMAN, Louis L, US, educator; b. Selz, Pol, Jan 19, 1904; s. Simon and Bella (Kaplan); in US since 1907; dipl, Tchrs Inst, JTSA, 1922; BA, CCNY, 1925; MS, Columbia U, 1933; m. Ruth Meirick, 1931; c: David, Judith. Ret; fmr: asso dir, J Educ Comm, NY, with org since 1940; visiting lectr, Dropsie Coll, 1957-62; ed, J Educ, 1957-61. Pres, Natl Council for J Educ, 1952-54; mem: LZOA; ACLU; ADA; Cong Beth El, S Orange, NJ. Author: The School Assembly Manual, 1940; Curriculum Outline for the Congregational School, 1949; Guide to the Teaching of Torah, 1967; ed, Survey of Jewish Education in New York City; contbr to educ jours. Home: 145 S Kingman Rd, S Orange, NJ.

RUJA, Harry, US, educator; b. Paterson, NJ, Feb 26, 1912; s. Abram and Sarah (Skroopka); BA, UCLA, 1933; MA, U of Chgo, 1934; PhD, Princeton U, 1936; MA, San Diego State Coll, 1953; m. Rose Rosenberg, Dec 22, 1940; c: Michele Rothstein, Ellen Tamarelle, Nancy Scott. Prof, phil, San Diego State Coll, since 1958, mem staff since 1947; instr, phil, UCLA, 1938; tchr, W Jewish Inst, LA, 1936-39; instr, phil, psych, Compton Jr Coll, Cal, 1939-47; visiting asso prof, phil, UCLA, 1946-47; lectr, comparative rel, J hist and phil, Inst Adult J Studies, San Diego, 1948-52; tchr, Beth Isr Cong, San Diego, 1953-64, 1965-68; Hillel counsellor, San Diego State Coll, 1954-64. Mem: Amer Fed Tchrs; Amer Phil Assn; Assn Cal State Coll Profs; Cal State Employees Assn; Temple Isr; fmr: pres, Yiddish Lit and Musical Circle, vice-pres, AAUP, San Diego State Coll chap; chmn, UJA, La Mesa-El Cajon area; pres, ACLU, San Diego chap, mem bd dirs, S Cal; vice-pres: J Social Service Agcy; J Comty Cen; San Diego State Fed Tchrs; pres, Fox lodge, B'nai B'rith. Author: Psychology for Life, 1955; Lebensfuhrüng durch Psychologie,

1958; contbr to scholarly jours. Home: 4664 Troy Lane, La Mesa, Cal, Office: San Diego State Coll, San Diego, Cal.

RUKEYSER, Merryle Stanley, US, author, journalist; b. Chgo, Ill, Jan 3, 1897; s. Isaac and Pauline (Solomon); BLitt, Columbia U, 1917, MA, 1925; m. Berenice Simon, June 25, 1930 (decd); c: Merryle, Louise, William, Robert; m. 2nd Marjorie, Leffler, Aug 1, 1965. Writer, syndicated column, since 1923; pres, Natl Outlook Corp, since 1963; ed writer, Hearst Newspapers, 1931-52; staff, Columbia U, 1918-35. Author: The Common Sense of Money and Investments, 1924; Financial Advice to a Young Man, 1927; Investment and Speculation, 1930; The Doctor and His Investments, 1931; The Diary of a Prudent Investor, 1937; Financial Security in a Changing World, 1940; Life Insurance Property; The Hallmark of Personal Progress, 1958; The Attack on Our Free Choice, 1963; The Collective Bargaining; The Power to Destroy, 1969. Mem: Temple Isr; clubs: Columbia; Beachpoint. Home and office: 21 Glenbrook Dr, New Rochelle, NY.

RULF, Benjamin, Isr, educator; b. Jerusalem, Isr, Nov 6, 1934 s. Shlomo and Ruth (Unna); BSc, Technion, 1958; MSc, 1961; PhD, Poly Inst, Bklyn, 1965; m. Sharon Bard; c: Daphne. Sr lectr, applied math, Tel Aviv U, since 1967; fmr: asst prof, NYU, 1965-67, asso research sci, 1966-67. Isr Navy, 1952-54. Contbr profsl jours. Home: 31 Maale Hatzofim St, Ramat Gan, Isr, Office: Tel Aviv U, Ramat Aviv, Isr.

RULF, Shlomo Frederic, Isr, rabbi; b. Braunschweig, Ger, May 13, 1896; s. Gutmann and Hedwig (Rahmer); in Isr since 1935; PhD, U of Erlangen, 1920; ordained rabbi, Theol Sem, Breslau, 1923; m. Ruth Unna, Oct 3, 1933; c: Itzhak, Benjamin, Jedida Kaouly. Ret; rabbi, congs: Temple, 1922-26; Bamberg, 1926-29; Saarbrücken, 1929-35; tchr: agric sch, Mikve Isr, 1935-37; headmaster, Weizmann elem sch, Nahariya, 1937-58. Author: Weg Der Geretteten, 1963; Derech Geulim, 1965; Ströme im Dürren Land, 1964; bMidbar Maim, 1969. Mem: B'nai B'rith, Gt lodge, Isr; Leo Baeck lodge, Nahariya. Hobby: philanthropic activities. Home: 4 Kaplan St, Nahariya, Isr.

RUNES, Dagobert D, US, editor, publisher, author; b. Zastavna, Aus, Jan 6, 1902; s. Isidore and Adele (Sussman); PhD, U of Vienna, 1924; in US since 1926; m. Mary Talisman, 1931; c: Regeen, Richard. Chief ed and dir, Phil Libr, since 1946; writer, ed, since 1931; dir, Inst for Advanced Educ, 1933-36 ed: The Modern Thinkers, 1923-36; The Current Digest, 1936-40; Who's Who in Philosophy (Tech ed), 1942; The Diary and The Sundry Observations of Thomas A Edison, 1942; co-editor, Ency of the Arts, 1944. Mem: AAAS; Soc of Aesthetics. Author: Der Wahre Jesus, 1927; Goethe, 1934; Dict of Philosophy, 1941; Twentieth Century Philosophy, 1943; The American Way, 1944; A Bible for the Liberal, 1946; Ency of the Arts, 1946; The Selected Writings of Benjamin Rush, 1947; Jordan Lieder, 1948; The Hebrew Impact on Western Civilization, 1949; Letters to My Son, 1950; Spinoza Dict, 1951; Of God, the Devil, and the Jews, 1952; The Soviet Impact on Society, 1952; Pictorial History of Philosophy, 1957; Letters to My God, 1958; Concise Dict of Judaism, 1959; Dict of Thought, 1960, 2nd ed, 1965; Treasury of Philosophy, 1961; Classics in Logic, 1962; The Jew and the Cross, 1965; The War against the Jews, 1968. Contbr to periodicals. Home: 44 W 77 St, New York, NY. Office: 15 E 40 St, New York, NY.

RUPPIN, Gad, Isr, accountant; b. Magdeburg, Ger, Dec 8, 1913; s. Siegfried and Gertrud (Doernberg); in Isr since 1933; att Commercial HS, Hanover, 1931-32; m. Adela Fuchs, Sep 4, 1934; c: Rafael, Doron. Sr partner, Gad Ruppin & Co, CPA's, since 1951; mgr, CPA firms, 1935-47; chief auditor, Isr Min of Defense, 1948-49; dept head, claims against Brit Govt, Isr Min of Fin, 1949-50; spec adv, Off of State Comptroller, 1950-51; mem, bd dirs, Shvilim Ltd, 1949-51; lectr, Isr Mgmt Cen. Maj, IDF. Hon judge and mem, profsl comm, Assn of CPA's in Isr; mem bd, Automobile and Touring Club of Isr; mem: Assn of Cert and Corporate Accntnts, London. Contbr to profsl jours. Hobbies: geography, bridge, tabletennis, twice champion, Hanover and Magdeburg. Home: 20 Shilo St, Ramat Gan, Isr. Office: 7 Levontin St, Tel Aviv, Isr.

RUPPIN, Kurt, Isr, economist, govt official; b. Magdeburg, Ger, Mar 25, 1894; s. Albert and Cecile; in Isr since 1933; dipl, Friedrich Wilhelm, U, 1933; m. Dorothea Jacobsohn, Dec 18, 1921; c: Shulamith Grill, Miriam Tamir. Mem, bd dirs, Isr Land Devl Co, Haifa-Jerusalem, since 1933; fmr: mgr, Haifa Bay Devl Co Ltd, 1933-46; Shikun Ovdim Co,

1947-50; dir, Kishon Port, 1951-54; dir, N dist devl auth, 1955-63. Mem bd, Immigrants of Cen Eur Org; fmr chmn, Ger Jews Immigration Org, 1933-40. Home: 19 Ruth St, Haifa, Isr. Office: 8 Hassan Shukri, Haifa, Isr.

RUPPIN, Rafael, Isr, government official; b. Berlin, Ger, Feb 13, 1919; s. Arthur and Hanna Kahan; in Isr since 1919; studied fishing, Holl; att: Heb U, Jerusalem, 1936-37; LSE, 1937-39; m. Esther Kravtsov, Jan 31, 1948; c: Arthur, Yaron, Eytan. Dir, div maritime educ, Min of Educ and Culture, since 1963; fmr: secy, co-founder, dir, Michmoret fishermen's settlement, 1947-50; dir, Mevoot Yam Nautical Sch, 1950-61; missions on behalf of FAO, Govt of Isr, to India, Eur, Afr; first Isr Ambass to Tanganyika, 1961-63. Served J Brig, Brit Army, 1940-46. Home: Michmoret, Isr. Office: Min of Educ and Culture, Jerusalem, Isr.

RUSKIN, Hans S, Australia, physician; b. Posen, Ger, Mar 7, 1911; s. Gustav and Erna (Konig) Ruschin; in Australia since 1948; MD, U of Berlin, 1934; MSF, SMAE, London, 1945; m. Rozi Weil, Aug 23, 1942; c: Hester Faye. Pvt practice, orthopedist. Lt col, Brit Army MC, WW II. Chmn: standing comm on educ, Exec Council of Austr Jewry, educ comm, Zionist Fed of Austr and NZ, since 1956; educ and cultural comms, Vic J Bd of Deps, since 1956; Mizrachi-Hapoel Hamizrachi, Austr, since 1959; gov, Mt Scopus Coll, since 1954; found gov, Hillel Found of Vic, since 1960; mem: Vic State Council for Educ, since 1956; Austr Lab Party; fmr secy, Kashrut Comm of Vic. Contbr to profsl jours. Home: 40 Otira Rd, N Caulfield, Melbourne, Australia.

RUSLANDER, Selwyn D, US, rabbi; b. Stowe Township, Pa, Jan 7, 1911; s. Fred and Tressa (Fleischman); BA, U of Cincinnati, 1932; ordained rabbi, HUC, 1935; hon degs: Cen State Coll, 1958; HUC-JIR, 1960; U of Dayton, 1968; m. Marguerite Benson, July 25, 1935; c: Gail Levin, Tressa Miller, Judith. Rabbi, Temple Isr, since 1947; fmr: caseworker, supr, Fed Transient Service, 1933-35; rabbi, Port Arthur, Tex, 1935-38; asso dir, Hillel Found, U of Ill, 1938-39; dir youth educ, UAHC, 1939-46; asso rabbi, S Shore Temple, Chgo, 1946-47. Chaplain, USN 1942-46; capt, chaplain corps, USNR. Fmr: pres: Cmty Wfr Council of Dayton and Montgomery Co's; Dayton Urban League; chmn: comm on chaplaincy, CCAR, mem exec bd; O Comm on Delinquency and Crime; vice-chmn, comm on J chaplaincy, JWB. Contbr to profsl jours. Recipient: Testimonial of Service, USAF, 1959. Home: 1957 Burbank Dr, Dayton, O. Study: 1821 Emerson Ave, Dayton, O.

RUSOFF, Louis L, US, biochemist, educator; b. Newark, NJ, Dec 23, 1910; s. Max and Rachel (Rodin); BS, Rutgers U, 1931; MS, Pa State Coll, 1932; PhD, U of Minn, 1940; att Oak Ridge Inst of Nuclear Studies, 1957; m. Sylvia Levin, May 15, 1945; c: Gail, Marsha. Dairy nutritionist, La Agricultural Experimental Station, La State U, since 1950, on staff since 1942; prof, dairy nutrition La State U, since 1950, on staff since 1948; asst, nutrition lab, Fla Agric Experimental station, 1932-37; instr, animal nutrition, U of Fla, 1935-37. Co-counsel, Hillel Found, La State U; f: AAAS; La State U; mem: Amer Chem Soc; La Acad of Sci; Amer Dairy Sci Assn; Amer Inst Nutrition; Amer Soc Animal Production; Sigma Xi; Gamma Sigma Delta; Phi Kappa Phi; B'nai B'rith. Contbr to profsl jours. Recipient: Borden award, 1965. Home: 1704 Myrtledale Ave, Baton Rouge, La. Office: Dept of Dairy Sci, La State U, Baton Rouge, La.

RUTTENBERG, Stanley H, US, economist, b. St, Paul, Minn, Mar 19, 1917; s. Charles and Fannie (Weinstein); BS, U of Pittsburgh, 1937; m. Gertrude Bernstein, 1940; c: Joel, Ruth, Charles. Pres, Stanley H Ruttenberg & Assos, Inc; fmr: asst secy and manpower admnr, US Dept of Lab, 1966-69, staff mem, since 1963; CIO org and field repr in Ohio Valley, 1937-38; asst to dir, Hull House, 1938-39; dir, dept of educ and research, CIO, 1948-55, on staff since 1939; dir, dept of research, AFL-CIO, 1955-62, dir, econ policy comm, 1956-62. Lt, US Army, 1943-46. Vice-chmn, US Natl Comm for UNESCO, 1952; mem, bd dirs: Resources for the Future, Inc, since 1952; Natl Bur of Econ Research, 1940-41, 1948-62; mem: lab comm, Natl Planning Assn, since 1949; Lab-Mgmt Manpower Policy Comm, 1951-62, exec comm, US Natl Comm for UNESCO, 1948-53; Fgn Selective Service Bd, 1950; exec bd, Ind Relations Research Assn; delgs: Intl UNESCO Confs, 1949, 1950; 35th ILO, UN Conv, 1952 Home: 6310 Maiden Lane, Bethesda, Md. Office: Stanley H Ruttenberg and Assos, Inc, 1211 Connecticut Ave, NW, Washington, DC.

RUTTER, Irvin C, US, attorney, educator; b. Bklyn, NY, Nov 8, 1909; s. Simon and Minne (Cowal); BA, Columbia U, 1929, JD, 1931; m. Sylvia Weber, 1938 (decd); c: Elisabeth, Peter. Prof, law, U of Cincinnati, since 1956; dist prof, law, Cincinnati U, 1966; visiting prof, Columbia U, 1964; pvt law practice, NYC, 1931-56; law secy to US Dist Judge, 1931-33 asst US Atty, NYC, 1934-40; spec asst to US Atty Gen, US Dept of Justice, 1940-42; chief enforcement atty, OPA, 1942-44, chief hearing commn, 1944-46; lectr, Columbia U and Practising Law Inst, 1946-51; arbitrator, Amer Arbitration Assn; hearing examiner O Civil Rights Comm. Chmn, Curriculum Comm, Assn of Amer Law Schs; trustee, New Lincoln Sch, NYC, 1950-56; pres, Order of the Coif, Cincinnati chap; mem: NYC Bar Assn; J Comty Relations Comm of Cincinnati. Author: Introduction to Appellate Advocacy, 1958; Legal Drafting, 1959; The Facts Process, 1962; ed: Columbia Law Review, 1929-31; bd eds, Journal of Legal Education. Contbr to legal jours. Recipient: Charles Bathgate Beck Scholar, 1929; James Kent Scholar; Columbia U, 1930. Home: 2930 Scioto St, Cincinnati, O. Office: U of Cincinnati, Cincinnati, O.

RUWITCH, Joseph F, business exec; b. Chgo, Ill, Oct 3, 1911; s. Simon and Selma (Froehlich); AB, U of Mich, 1932, JD, 1934; m. Elizabeth Renard, May 1, 1937; c: Wallace, Joseph jr, Jane. Pres, dir, Renard Linoleum and Rug Co, since 1958; bd dirs: Alvey Conveyor Mfg Co; Bank of St Louis; pvt law practice, 1934-40. USN, 1943-46. Pres: J Fed of St Louis, 1959-60; J Hosp of St Louis, 1963-68; vice-pres, United Fund of Gtr St Louis, 1959; bd mem: Gtr St Louis Comty Chest; Social Planning Council; St Louis Sym Soc; J Family Service Agency; J Child Wfr Assn; J Comty Relations Council; Cong Temple Isr; John Burroughs Sch; bd trustee, St Louis U; mem, Zeta Beta Tau; clubs: Westwood Country, St Charles; Media. Home: 927 Tirrill Farns Rd, St Louis, Mo. Office: 130 Washington Ave, St Louis, Mo.

RYBACK, Martin B, US, rabbi; b. NYC; s. Benjamin and Anne (Shore); BA, NYU; ordained rabbi, MHL, HUC, 1949; m. Betty Behr; 3 c: Rabbi: Temple Ner Tamid, since 1962; fmr: rabbi: Temple Isr, Westport, Conn, 1949-53; Wash Ave Temple, Evansville, Ind, 1953-62; instr, phil and Bible, Evansville Coll; lectr at coll campuses on behalf of J Chautauqua Soc. Past mem, exec bd: MH Assn; Child Guidance Clinic; Sr Citzens Council; past mem: Mayor's Commn on Hum Relations; Ministerial Assn of Evansville; past pres, Ind Bd Rabbis; mem: Adult Educ Commn of Reform Judaism; Rabbi's Comm on Aging and Aged; NCCJ; AJComm; dean, UAHC Youth Camp, Indianapolis; Home: 10335 Downey Ave, Downey, Cal. Study: 10629 Lakewood Blvd, Downey, Cal.

RYCUS, Jacob Louis, Isr, academic secy; b. Montreal, Can, Aug 11, 1913; s. Goodman and Mary (Schwartz); in Isr since 1949; BA, U of Mich, 1933; m. Violet Chulock; c: Abigail, Dena. Acad secy, Weizmann Inst, Rehovot, since 1954; org, Habonim Lab Zionist Youth, US, 1936-40; ed: Isr Speaks; Haganah Speaks, both 1947-49; night ed, Jerusalem Post, 1949-52; dir, Isr off, State of Isr Bonds, 1952-54. M/Sgt, US Army, 1943-46. Home: Neve Weizmann 8, Rehovot, Isr. Office: Weizmann Inst, Rehovot, Isr.

RYPINS, Stanley, US, educator, author; b. Evansville, Ind, Feb 1, 1891; s. Isaac and Esther (Franklin); BA, U of Minn, 1912; MA, 1913; Rhodes Scholar, Oxford U, 1914-17; PhD, Harvard U, 1918; m. Evelyn Pessin, Sep 2, 1941. Prof em, Eng lit, Bklyn Coll, since 1962, fac mem since 1931; instr, U of Minn, 1918-20; prof, chmn, Eng dept, dean, academic studies, SF State Coll, 1921-30. Mem: MLA; AAUP; Soc for Old Testament Study: club; Andiron. Author: Revolutions, Mexican and Russian in Renascent Mexico, 1935; The Ferrara Bible at Press: A Bibliographical Study, The Library, 1956; contbr to profsl jours. Spec interest: Bibl paleography, cryptography. Home: 8 W 13 St, New York, NY.

RYSKIND, Morrie, US, playwright; b. NYC, Oct 20, 1895; s. Abraham and Ida (Etelson); BL, Columbia U, 1917; m. Mary House, Dec 19, 1929; c: Ruth, Allan. Playwright: Louisiana Purchase, 1940; co-author, with George S Kaufman: Animal Crackers, 1927; Strike Up the Band, 1929; Of Thee I Sing, 1932; screen writer: The Coconuts, 1930; Animal Crackers, 1931; Night at the Opera, 1936; My Man Godfrey, 1937; Penny Serenade, 1940; Claudia, 1943; poet: Unaccustomed As I Am, 1921; columnist: Wash Star Syndicate. Dir: Beverly Hills Rep Club, since 1950; Amer J League Against Communism, since 1948. Recipient: Pulitzer Prize, 1932. Home and office: 605 N Hillcrest Rd, Beverly Hills, Cal.

S

SAAL, Joseph, US, surgeon; b. NYC, Sept 11, 1909; s. Nathan and Feni (Bittner); BS, CCNY, 1929; MD, BCh, U St Andrews, 1933; m. Sylvia Schwartz, June 21, 1941; c: Harry, Michael, Andrew, Frederick. Att orthopedic surg: Bkln J Hosp, since 1958; J Chronic Diseases Hosp, since 1958; Adelphi Hosp, since 1953; orthopedic res, Hosp for Jt Diseases, 1943-46. Amer Coll Surgs, 1954; Amer Acad Orthopedic Surgs; NY Acad Med; dipl, Amer Bd Orthopedic Surgs; mem: AMA; Kings Co and NY State Socs. Home: 786 E 19 St, Brooklyn, NY. Office: 622 Ocean Ave, Brooklyn, NY.

SAAR, Tuvia, Isr, TV broadcaster; b. Jerusalem, Apr 4, 1935; s. David and Lisa (Jelenetz) Nesher; att: Nautical Sch, Haifa; Heb U, Jerusalem; m. Medy Jacob, Jan 28, 1965; c: Gal, Ran. Head, Tel Aviv newsroom, Isr TV, since 1968; chief ed, Army Radio, 1958-59; mil corresp, Kol Isr, 1959-65, radio spokesman, prog ed, 1965-68. Lt, Isr Navy, 1953-58; capt IDF, 1958-59. Mem: Union Israeli Journalists. Recipient: Sinai Campaign, Six-Day War decorations. Home: 79 Hauniversita St, Tel Aviv, Isr. Office: Isr TV, Hakirya, Tel Aviv, Isr.

SABAGH, Victor, Guat, electrical engr; b. Guatemala City, Guat, Apr 19, 1924; s. Ezra and Sarina (Kaire); BS, U Mich, 1947; m. Sara Palatchi, Feb 5, 1950; c: Ezra, Clara. Power plant chief, ee, Instituto Nacional De Electrificacion, since 1967; ee, Empresa Electrica de Guatemala SA, 1947-51; mgr, Almacen Lazaro 1953-68. Pres, Jorge Garcia Granados Lodge, B'nai B'rith; off, Bet El Reform Cong; adv, Instituto Einstein Heb Day Sch, fmr pres; Macabi; off Zionist; mem, Colegio De Ingenieros. Spec interests: J hist, music. Home O Av A 1-84, Guatemala City, Guat. Office: POB 1102, Guatemala City, Guat.

SABAH, Nahon, Isr, business exec; b. Tangier, Dec 14, 1917; s. Yomtob and Sol (Nahon); in Isr since 1958; Diplomé d'Etudes Commerciales; m. Gladys Lasry, June 17, 1940; c: Yomtob, Sol Toaff, Samuel, Yehuda. Chmn, Unico Mortgage & Invest Bank, since 1961; bd dirs: Isr Gen Bank; United Mizrachi Bank; Zim; Clal; dir, Assurances Sabah, Morocco, till 1936. Mem, fmr mem various communal orgs. Home: 77 Emek, Hefer St, Netanya, Isr. Office: 25A Lilienblum St, Tel Aviv, Isr.

SABAS, Marcos, Greece, chemist, educator; b. Athens, June 14, 1928; s. Ninos and Fortuni; grad, chem, U Athens, 1953; m. Artemis Yacoej, March 29, 1953; c: Albert, Nadia. Chem, dir, tcch sch, Min of Lab. Secy gen, Athens J Comty; vice-pres, Organisme de Secours et de Rehabilitation des Juifs de Grece, 1964-65; secy gen, cen bd, J Comtys of Greece, 1966-67. Home: 112, 3 September St, Athens, Greece.

SABEL, Harry, Isr economist, administrator; b. London, Eng, Jan 1, 1909; s. Avraham-Abba and Leah (Swidler); in Isr since 1948; att: Oxford U; BA, E Ham Tech Coll, London; m. Gladys Shapiro, Aug 30, 1931; c: Pamela Loval, Robert. Sr exec, dept dir, JNF Head Off, Jerusalem, since 1952, fmr, dir: Brit; S Afr; fmr owner London cos; chmn, mgr dir, Lloyd Manhatten Group of Cos, 1948; pres off, Isr Govt, 1948-49; fmr dir, budget div, JA. Capt: Brit Army, 1939-45; IDF, 1948-49. Chmn: JNFW, London, 1945-48; Hitachdut Olei Britania, Jerusalem, 1951-56; mem bd dirs, Jerusalem YW-YMHA, since 1965; mem: Haganah Lodge, B'nai B'rith; club, Rotary, Jerusalem. Contbr numerous articles and brochures. Hobbies: photography; carpenting, engr, motoring. Home: 3/5 Neve Granott, Jerusalem, Isr. Office: JNF Head Office, Jerusalem, Isr.

SABIN, Albert B, Isr, medical researcher, educator; b. Bialystok Russ, Aug 26 1906; s. Jacob and Tillie (Krugman); in Isr since 1969; BS, NYU, 1928, MD, 1931, hon DS, 1959; hon: DHL, HUC-JIR, Cincinnati, 1960; LHD, Coll Conservatory of Music, Cincinnati, 1960; DS: Temple U, Phila, 1961; O State U, 1961; D HC, U Brazil; DS: Bowling Green State U, O, 1961; Miami U, Oxford, O, 1963; DHC, Heb U, 1964, PhD, 1964; DS, U Newcastle upon Tyne, Eng, 1965; DS, Albert Einstein Coll of Med, NY, 1966; DHC: Universi-taria Gama Filho of Rio De Janeiro, Brazil, 1967; Universidad Nacional de la Plata, Arg, 1967; Universidade de Sao Paulo, Brazil, 1967; U Messina, 1969; m. Sylvia Tregillus, Sep 12, 1935 (decd); c: Deborah, Amy. Pres, Weizmann Inst, Re-, hovot, since 1969; research asso, bact, NYU Coll of Med, 1926-31; house phys, M Bellevue Hosp, NY, 1932-33; f, NRC, Lister Inst, London, Eng, 1934; mem, sci staff, Rockefeller Inst Med Research, NY, 1935-39; asso prof, pediatrics, U Cincinnati Coll of Med and The Children's Hosp Research Found, 1939-43, prof, ped, 1946-60, dist service prof, 1960-69; cons, US Army, serving with Commission on Virus and Rickettsial Diseases, Armed Forces Epidemiological Bd; special missions to Panama, Japan, Korea, China and Ger, 1941-62; cons, USPHS, since 1947; cons, Select Comm on Govt Research; House of Reprs, since 1963; O State Regents Prof, 1968-69. Lt col, US Army, serving with Bd for Inves Epidemic Diseases, Off of Surg Gen; spec missions to ME, Afr, Sicily, Okinawa Phillipines, 1946-46. Prin contribs: discovery B virus; devl oral polio vaccine; first isolation of protozoan parasite, toxoplasma. Pres, Infectious Diseases Soc of Amer, 1968-69; trustee NYU, since 1966; mem, bd govs: Heb U, Jerusalem, since 1965; Weizmann Inst of Sci, Rehovot, Isr, since 1965; mem: Armed Forces Epidemiological Bd, since 1963; natl adv council, Natl Inst Allergy and Infectious Diseases, since 1965; Natl Acad Sci; Assn Amer Phys; Amer Assn Immunologists;-AAAS; Amer Epidemiological Soc; Amer Pediatric Soc; Amer Soc for Microbiol; Amer Soc Tropical Med and Hygiene; Soc for Clinical Inves; Soc for Experimental Biol and Med; Soc for Ped Research; Harvey Soc; Alpha Omega Alpha; Sigma Xi; corresp mem, Royal Acad of Med, Belgium; hon mem: Soc of Microbiols, Epidemiologists, and Infections. Diseases, Russ; Brazilian Ped Soc; Med Soc of Santiago, Chile; Academia Nacional de Medicina, Brazil; Hung Acad of Scis; Serbian Acad Sci and Arts; It Soc Experimental Biol; British Ped Assn; It Soc of Peds; f: Amer Acad Arts and Scis; Assn Amer Phys; Natl Acad Sci; Amer Acad Tropical Med; hon f: Royal Soc Health, London, Eng; club, NYU. Contbr to profsl jours. Recipient: Theobald Smith award, med scis, AAAS, 1939; Mead Johnson award, Amer Acad Peds, 1941; Legion of Merit, US Army, 1945; Gold Medal award, Phi Lambda Kappa, 1957; H T Ricketts Award, U Chgo, 1959; med alumni award, NYU, 1960; Sachs award, Cincinnati Inst Fine Arts, 1960; William Cooper Procter award, Children's Hosp Research Found, Cincinnati, 1960; alumni achievement award, Wash Sq Coll, NYU, 1961; James D Bruce Memorial award, Amer Coll Phys, 1961; dignity of man award, Kessler Inst, 1961; Chapain award, City of Providence and RI Med Soc, 1962; Mordecai Ben David award, Yeshiva U, 1962; Robert Koch medal, Robert Koch Found, W Ger, 1963; Wm G Anderson Award, Amer Assn for Health, Phys Educ and Recreation, 1963; Oscar B Hunter Award, Amer Therapeutic Soc, 1963; Henrietta Szold award, Hadassah, 1963; Albert Gallatin award, NYU, 1963; Order of Merit,Bavaria, 1964; Intl Antonio Feltrinelli prize, Accademia Nazionale dei Lincei, Rome, Italy, 1964; Liceaga gold medal, Govt Mex, 1964; 1964 Gov's Award, State of O. 1965; gold medal, It Govt, 1965; Intl Dag Hammarskjoeld Award, Intl Assn of Dipl Corresp, 1965; Albert Lasker Clinical Med Research award, 1965; Scoups Award, Amer Friends Heb U, 1965; Gran Oficial Orden Hipólito Unánue, Govt of Peru, 1966; Order of Yugoslav Flag with Ribbon, 1966; Murray-Green Award, AFL-CIO, 1967; gold medal, City of Naples, It, 1967; Addingham medal, Eng, 1967; Matricola d'Onore, U Pavia, It, 1967; Ordem de Merito Medico, Govt Brazil, 1967; Servidor Emerito Honorario do Estado de Sao Paulo, Brazil, 1967; Orden de Mayo al Merito, Govt Arg, Mangia d'Oro Medal, City of Sienna, It 1968; decoration, Aztec Eagle-Sash, Mex, 1969; gold Medal, Royal Soc Health, 1969. Home and office: Weizmann Institute, Rehovot, Isr.

SACHAR, Abram L, US, historian, educator; b. NYC, Feb 15, 1899; s. Samuel and Sara (Abramovitz); MA, Wahington U, St Louis, 1920; PhD, Cambridge U, Eng, 1923; hon: DLitt, Educ, 1950; LHD, Boston U, 1952; LLD: U of RI, 1953; Wash U 1953; Jufta U, Mass, 1955; U Mass, 1957; Northeastern U, Boston, 1959; Calvin Coolidge Coll, 1963; Notre

Dame U, 1964; Bowdouin Coll, 1964; DLitt. U of Ill, 1964; Providence Coll, 1965; LHD, Boston Coll, 1966; LLD: Lafayette Coll, 1968; Brandeis U, 1968; DSc, Norwich U, 1968; DHL, U Santa Clara, 1968; m. Thelma Horowitz, June 6, 1926; c: Howard, Edward, David. Chancellor, Brandeis U, since 1968, pres, 1948-68; instr, hist U Ill, 1923-29; dir, B'nai B'rith, Hillel Found, 1928-33; natl dir, 1933-48; news analyst, WNBC radio, 1944, cons on educ, Mass, 1950; trustee, Aspen Inst of Humanistic Studies 1950; F, Amer Acad Arts, and Scis, since 1952; trustee: Amer ORT Fed; Amer J, Hist Soc; mem: Comm on Future Pvt and Independent Higher Educ in NY; US Adv Comm on Intl Educ and Cultural Affairs; Commn to Study Non-Public Higher Educ in State of Ill; Mass Comm for Fulbright Awards; bd govs: Heb U, Jerusalem; Natl Hillel Found, hon chmn; bd trustees: Kennedy Memorial Libr; Pal Endowment Funds, Inc; mem: Eleanor Roosevelt Memorial Fund; Phi Beta Kappa; Phi Epsilon Pi; B'nai B'rith; clubs: Harvard; Hasmonic; Belmont Country; Pinebrook Country. Author: Factors in Jewish History, 1927; A History of the Jews, 1929, 23rd ed, 1967; Sufferance is the Badge, 1939; contbr to jours of opinions. Home: 66 Beaumont Ave, Newtonville, Mass. Office: Brandeis: U, Walthan, Mass.

SACHAR, Howard Morley, US, historian, author; b. St. Louis, Mo, Feb 10, 1928; s. Abram and Thelma (Horwitz); BA, Swarthmore Coll, Pa, 1947; MA, Harvard U, 1950, PhD, 1953; m. Eliana Steimatsky, July 23, 1964; W, c: Sharon, Michele. Prof hist, George Wash U, Wash DC, since 1965; instr, U Mass, 1953-54; dir: Hillel Found, UCLA, Stanford U, 1954-61; Hiatt Inst, Brandeis U, 1961-65. Author: The Course of Modern Jewish History 1958; Aliyah: The Peoples of Israel, 1960; From the Ends of the Earth, 1964; The Emergence of the Middle East, 1914-1924, pub 1969. Mem: publ comm. J Publ Soc, trustee, 1965-67; Amer Hist Assn; Amer J Hist Soc. Home: 9807 Hill ridge Dr, Kensington, Md. Office: George Washington U, Washington, DC.

SACHAROV, Aharon, Isr, business exec; b. Jerusalem, Aug 20, 1916; s. Itzhak and Rivka (Ben Tovim); att Sch of Commerce, Tel Aviv; LSE; m. Phyllis Kahn, Apr 6, 1941; c: Alexander, Ruth, Yael. Chmn, mgr dir: Sahar Ins Co, Ltd; Mivtah Ltd, ins agcy; Sahar Inves Corp, dep chmn, Isr Reinsurance Ltd. Served, Haganah, maj, IDF. Home: Herzliya Pituah, Isr. Office: Sahar House, 23 Ben Yehuda St, Tel Aviv, Isr.

SACHAROV, Israel, Isr, business exec; b. Jerusalem, May 1, 1912; s. Itzhak and Rivka (Ben Tovim); att HS of Commerce, Tel Aviv; m. Lea Lifshitz, Aug 20, 1940; c: Tamar, Shulamit. Mgn dir, IM Sacharov and Sons, Ltd, Tel Aviv, since 1950; mem bd dirs; TAAL Mfrs of Plywood Ltd; Sahar Ins Co Ltd; Merkaz Shivuk Levidel Isr Ltd; chmn bd, co-owner, Hayom, Heb daily; fmr: mem bd dirs, Frachtwanger Bank Ltd; Kupat Am Bank Ltd; Jordania Gen Ins Co of Isr Ltd; Haboker, Heb daily; Mutual Emergency Inst Fund; mem, ins council, Min of Finance. Served, Haganah; off, Brit Army, World War II. Mem: exec cen comm, council, Lib Party of Isr; C of C, Tel Aviv-Jaffa; council, Sch of Law and Econ, Tel Aviv; Mem cen comm, Maccabi Sports Org; hon treas. Home: 30 King David Blvd, Tel Aviv, Isr. Office: 61 Rothschild Blvd, Tel Aviv, Isr.

SACHER, Michael Moses, Eng, business exec; b. Manchester, Eng, Oct 17, 1917; s. Harry and Miriam (Marks); related to: 1st and 2nd Lord Marks of Broughton; Lord Sieff of Brimpton, life peer; MA, New Coll, Oxford, 1968; m. Audrey Glucksman, Sep 29, 1938; c: Simon, Elizabeth, Susan, Jeremy, Michael. Asst mgn dir, Marks and Spencer Ltd, i/c food group, with firm since 1938. Maj, RASC, 1939-45. Chmn, JPA, fmr treas; vice-pres, JNF, Gt Brit and Ir, fmr pres, treas; hon vice-pres, ZF, London; gov: Weizmann Inst, Rechovot; Heb U, Jerusalem; Reali Sch, Haifa, all Isr; f, Royal Philatelic Soc; club, asso mem, Royal Yacht. Spec interests, hobbies: communal work for Isr and Zionist Orgs; stamp collecting, particularly: Pal Forerunners, Mandate, ME. Home: 15 Upper Phillimore Gdns, London W8, Eng. Office: 47 Baker St, London, Eng.

SACHS, Arieh, Isr, educator; b. Tel Aviv, Isr, Mar 24, 1932; s. Mendes and Celia (Zelitan); BA, Johns Hopkins U, Baltimore, 1954, MA, 1955; att Sorbonne U, Paris, 1956; PhD, Cambridge U, London, 1960; m. Gaby Aldor. Asso prof, Eng dept, Heb U, Jerusalem, since 1969; dir, Heb U Theater, since 1969; dir, adapter, The Deluge, 1966; Alice in Wonderland, 1967; Aristophanes' Peace, 1968; Everyman, 1969. Pvt, Palmach, 1948; Lt, IDF, since 1951. Author: Passionate Intelligence, 1967; The English Grotesque, 1969; ed, Studies in

the Drama, 1967. Recipient: Phi Beta Kappa; Woodrow Wilson F; Ot Ha'Atzmaut. Home: 20/128 Ein Roggel, Jerusalem. Isr. Office: Heb U, Jerusalem, Isr.

SACHS, Arieh Erich, Isr, musician; b. Katowice, Ger, Feb 22, 1908; s. Joseph and Johanna (Ittmann); BA, State U, Berlin, 1931; MA, U Erlangen, 1933; att Pal Conservatoire, Jerusalem, 1934-35; m. Esther Gruenewald, Sept 27, 1935; c: Neomi, Daliot, Yair. Produc, musical progs, Isr Bc Authority, since 1968, i/c instrumental, contemporary, Israeli music, since 1948; staff pianist, Pal Bc Service, 1936-42, sr produc, music section, 1942-48; regular piano, harpsichord appearance in Isr towns and settlements; ret magistrate by decree of W Ger Min of Justice, since 1951; music critic: Massa, Lamerhav, 1952-53. Found, Collegium Musicum, Jerusalem, 1953; mem: musical examination br: artists section, Isr Labor Fed since 1948; Min of Educ and Culture; Amer-Isr Cultural Fund; mem: Isr Journalist's Assn; AFA comm for org of cultural activities for res of besieged Jerusalem, 1948; Soc Friends Isr Mus; Isr SPCA. Composer: piano arrangements, cantoral and J music; contbr to Isr music jours. Hobbies: antiquities, nature and landscape of Isr. Home: 10 Saadia Gaon St, Jerusalem, Isr. Office : Helene Hamalka St, Jerusalem, Isr.

SACHS, Howard F, US, attorney; b. Kan City, Mo, Sep 13, 1925; s. Alexander and Rose (Lyon); BA, Williams Coll, 1947; JD, Harvard, 1950; m. Susanne Wilson, May 31, 1960; c: Alex, Adam. Partner, Spencer, Fane, Britt & Browne, since 1962; law clerk, Albert A Ridge, US Dist Judge, 1950-51. US NAVY, 1944-46. Prin contribs: assisted drafting and defending legality of first civil rights leg in Mo; assisted in drafting subsequent civil rights ordinances for Kan City. Chmn, J Comty Relations Bur, Kan City, since 1968; mem, exec bd, Natl J Comty Relations Adv Council, since 1968; trustee, Cong B'nai Jehudah; Kan City Commn on Hum Relations; fmr pres: Jackson Co Young Dem, 1959-60; Urban League, Kan City, 1957-58; co-chmn, NCCJ, Kan City, 1958-60; chmn, AJComm, Kan City, 1963-65, hon chmn since 1965; mem: Amer, Kan City Bar Assns; Lawyers Assn of Kan City; Phi Beta Kappa. Contbr to legal and historical jours. Home: 816 W 68 Terr, Kansas City, Mo. Office: 1000 Power & Light Bldg, Kansas City, Mo.

SACHS, Leo, Isr, biologist; b. Leipzig, Ger, Oct 14, 1924; s. Eliyahu and Louise (Lichtblau); in Isr since 1952; BS, U Wales, 1948; PhD, U Cambridge, 1951; m. Rachel Eliash, Dec 12, 1950; c: Shlomith, Judith, Mordechai, Naomi. Prof, head, dept virology and genet, Weizmann Inst of Sci since 1960. Home: Neve Weizmann, Rehovot, Isr. Office: Weizmann Inst of Science, Rehovot, Isr.

SACHS, Leonie F, US, educator; b. Berlin, Mar 5, 1908; d. Hermann and Elizabet (Leuchtag) Feiler; in US since 1937; PhD, U Berlin, 1931; m. George Sachs, 1932 (decd); c: Daniel, Benjamin. Asso prof, Span, Hunter Coll, since 1968, asst prof, 1961-68; research asst, ling, Centro de Estudios Históricos, Madrid, 1933-36; HS tchr, modern langs, Walden Sch, NYC, 1947-55; prof, Ger, Sarah Lawrence Coll, 1955-61; visiting prof, Span, U of Cal, Berkeley, 1962; lectr, J org, NYC, local Hillel Founds, since 1944; dean, women, annual natl summer insts, B'nai B'rith Hillel Founds, 1952-64. Mem: MLA; Amer Assn Tchrs Span and Port; AAUP; Lincoln Sq Syn, since 1966. Mem: ed bd, Cong Bull, Beth Hillel of Wash Heights, 1959-66; contbr to lang jours. Spec interests: J phil and mysticism. Home: 160 West End Ave, New York, NY. Office: 695 Park Ave, New York, NY.

SACHS, Mendes H, Isr, citrus grower, business exec; b. Baltimore, Md, US, Nov 17, 1907; s. Philip and Mary (Brodie); in Isr since 1931; att: U of Md, 1924-26; Harvard U, 1927; BS, U of Cal, Berkeley, 1929; m. Celia Zelitan, Feb 14, 1930; c: Arieh, Tsvi. Mgn dir, Mehadrin Ltd, citrus growers; mgr, Pardess-Gan Chaim Coop Soc; dir: Citrus Marketing Bd, Isr; Citrus Control Bd, Isr; Bank Leumi Ltd; Bank Leumi Trust Co Ltd; Union Bank of Isr; Ihud Ins Co. Trustee, Natl and U Inst of Agric; bd govs, Heb U, Jerusalem. Contbr articles to jours. Home: Gan Chaim, Isr. Office: 18 Mohilever St, Tel Aviv, Isr.

SACK, Bessie K, attorney; b. Pittsburgh, Pa, Jan 9, 1908; d. Abraham and Lillian (Silverman) Kann; BA, U Pittsburgh, 1927, LLB, 1930; m. Frank Sack, Dec 17, 1931; c: Gerry, Marilyn, Jeanabbey Lynn. Dep dir, Pittsburgh field off, Fed Housing Admn, since 1965; pvt practice since 1930; spec counsel to closed bank div, 1936-40; price atty, OPA, 1944-46; auditor, atty, inheritance tax div, Commonwealth of

Pa, 1956-57; tchr, 1954-56; spec asst, Atty Gen Dept of Justice, Commonwealth of Pal, 1957-65. Bd dirs: Girl Scouts; mem: state and co bds, Amer Assn U Women; W Pa Penal Affairs Comm; Hadassah; Council J Women; Allegheny Co Bar Assn; Women Lawyers; Rodef Sahlom Sisterhood; clubs: Lawyers Coll. Home: 2D Chatham Center, Pittsburgh, Pa. Office: Fed Housing Admn, Pittsburgh, Pa.

SACKLER, Harry, US, organization exec; playwright; b. Bohorodczany, Aus-Hung, Aug 22, 1883; s. Shalom and Sarah (Schmerler); in US since 1902; att NYU Law Sch, 1906-08; hon D es Lettres, JTSA, 1967; m. Leah Breger, July 12, 1905. Ret; mem, ed staff: Dos Yiddishe Folk, 1909-11; Hadror, 1911-12; J Morning Jour, 1913-14; secy J Comty of NY, 1917-18; org dept, ZOA, 1918-23; admn secy, J Educ Assn, 1923-26, all NYC; free-lance writer, 1927-40; exec-secy, JCC, Bklyn, NY, 1940-44; dir, Yiddish publicity, JDC, 1944-45. Author: 4 vols of Yiddish plays, 1925-28; Festival at Meron, 1935; Sefer Hamachzoth, plays, 1948; Hakesheth Be'anan, 1948; U'sfor Hakohavim, 1961; Hylva B'Meron, 1963; Beyn Eretz V'Shamayim, 1964; Masach U'Masechoth, 1964; Sof Posuk, 1966; Oleloth, 1966; plays produced: Yiskor, 1923; Jose of Yokrath, 1923; The Tsaddik's Journey, 1926; Major Noah, 1928, all NYC; Rahab, Habimah, Pal, 1933; filmed, Yiskor, Vienna, Aus, 1924. Recipient: 1st prize for Yiddish Lit in Amer, 1929; Louis LaMed Prize, 1944, 1948. Home: 323 W 38 St, New York, NY.

SACKMAN, Robert, US, business exec; b. NYC, May 3, 1918; s. David and Therese (Berkowitz); BS, George Wash U; m. Sylvia Koonin, Apr 20, 1941; c: Barbara Coigny, Ellen. Pres. TIME/DATA Corp, Palo Alto, Cal since 1966; dir, cons, Vidar Corp, Mt View, Cal since 1966; chief, research and devl, exec agcy, Defense Dept, 1946-53; exec vice-pres Ampex Corp, 1953-64; bd dirs, ORRADIO, 1959-60; chmn, bd, VSC Corp, 1964-66; bd dirs, ORTEC, 1965-66. USN, 1943-46. Mem, Sigma Tau; fmr: dir, Cong Beth Am, LA, Cal; co-chmn, JWF, tech sect. Contbr to mgmt and tech jours. Home: 70 Stern Lane, Atherton, Cal. Office: 490 San Antonio Rd, Palo Alto, Cal.

SACKS, Albert M, US, educator; b. NYC, Aug 15, 1920; s. Harry and Minnie (Miretsky); BBA, magna cum laude, CCNY, 1940; LLB, magna cum laude, Harvard U, 1948; m. Sadelle Rader, Nov 22, 1945; c: Margery, Janet. Asso dean, Harvard U, Law Sch since 1968, on fac since 1952; law clerk: colon Judge Augustus N Hand, 1948-49; Justice Felix Frankfurter, 1949-50. Dir, Mass Admn Procedure Study Project, 1953-54; chmn, Atty Gen Comm on Civil Rights and Civil Liberties, Mass since 1967; reporter, Adv Comm on Fed Rules of Civil Procedure, Judicial Cong of US; mem, Mass and DC Bar Assns. Contbr to profsl jours. Home: 64 Lincoln St, Belmont, Mass. Office: Harvard U Law Sch, Cambridge, Mass.

SACKS, Muriel Elsie, Eng, gynecologist; b. London, Eng, Jan 21, 1895; d. Marcus and Caroline (Kohn) Landau; MD, BS, London Sch of Med; MRCS; FRCS, Royal Free Hosp, London; m. Samuel Sacks, June 22, 1922; c: Marcus, David, Michael, Oliver. Cons surg since 1960; gyn surg: E G Anderson Hosp, 1922-60; Marie Curie Hosp, 1923-60; J Hosp, London, 1928-60. Fmr: pres: Med Women's Fed; J Hosp Med Soc, both London; chmn, JPA, Drs and Dents comm. Author: Women of Forty, 1956; Change of Life, 1958. Home: 37 Mapesbury Rd, London N W2, Eng.

SACKS, Norman P, US, educator; b. Phila, Pa, Feb 11, 1914; s. Louis and Pauline (Brody); BS, Temple U, Phila, 1935; MA, U of Pa, 1937, PhD, 1940; m. Miriam Bronstein, Sep 15, 1943; c: Laurie, Julie, Robert. Prof, Span and Port, dir, Latin-Amer Cen, U Wis, since 1961; tchr, Latin, Phila Schs, 1936-39; asst instr, romance lang, U of Pa, 1938-40; instr, Span, Temple U, 1945-46; prof, Span, Oberlin Coll, 1946-61; visiting prof: U of Cal, 1942-43, 1949; W Reserve U, 1957-58; U of S Cal, 1959; U of NM, 1959-60; U Wis, 1960; Harvard U, 1964; guest lectr, Fgn Service Inst. Mem: MLA; Amer Assn Tchrs Span and Port, fmr pres; Ling Soc of Amer; AAUP; Amer Council on Teaching Fgn Langs; Latin Amer Studies Assn. Author: The Latinity of Dated Documents in the Portuguese Territory, 1941, 3rd ed, 1966; Spanish for Beginners, 1951, 2nd ed, 1957; Cuentos de hoy y de ayer, 1956, rev ed, 1965; Modern Spanish, 1960; cons, lang devl prog US Off of Educ; ed, Comparative Romance Linguistics Newsletter; contbr to profsl jours. Recipient: Dist Alumnus Award, Temple U, 1964. Hobbies: travel, photography. Home: 918 Swarthmore Ct, Madison, Wis. Office: U of Wis, Madison, Wis.

SACKS, Samuel I, US, attorney, civil engr; b. Wilmington, Del, July 8, 1892; s. Jacob and Bessie (Berman); BS, U Pa, 1913, CE, 1916; att: Gratz Coll, Phila, 1914-18; Neff Coll, 1918; LLB, Temple U Law Sch, 1925; m. Cecilia Linker, Oct 12, 1915; c: Marjorie Abrams, Lee. Pvt practice, atty and cons engr, since 1925; CE: Dept of City Transit, 1913-19; Wm Linker Co, 1919-25; legal adv, Draft Bd, all Phila, Pa. USN, WW I. Cons, Major's Adv Comm for Revision Phila Bldg Code; f: AAAS; Soc of CE; mem: Phila Bar Assn; Natl Soc Profsl Engrs, fmr vice-pres; hon mem, Société des Ingénieurs Professionnels, Fr; United Syn of Amer; fmr: hon pres, Temple Beth-Zion Beth-Isr; commn, Old Guard, Phila; pres, Strawberry Mansion Recreation Assn; co commn, Amer Legion. Co-author: The Business of Home Building, 1950; contbr on engr and law to profsl jours. Home: 1208 The Windsor, Philadelphia, Pa. Office: 719 Land Title Bldg, Philadelphia, Pa.

SACKTON, Alexander H, US, educator; b. Galveston, Tex, Jan 30, 1911; s. Tobias and Matilda (Littman) Sakowitz; BS, U of Pa, 1931; BA, Cambridge U, 1934; MA, Harvard U, 1936, PhD, 1941; m. Ivria Adlerblum, May 11, 1944; c: John, David, Margaret, Elizabeth. Asso prof, Eng, U Tex, since 1950, asst prof, 1946-50; instr, Eng, A & M Coll, Tex, 1936-38; asst prof, Eng, U Del, 1945-46. USAAF, 1942-45. Mem: MLA; AAUP; Modern Humanities Research Assn; chmn, allocations comm, JCC, Austin, 1958-60. Author: Rhetoric as a Dramatic Language in Ben Jonson, 1948; contbr to Tex Studies in Eng; Modern Lang Quarterly. Hobbies: collecting original prints; photography. Home: 2525 Spring Lane, Austin, Tex. Office: U of Tex, Austin, Tex.

SADE, Jacob, Isr, physician; b. Berlin, Ger, June 3, 1925; s. Nahum and Ronja (Feinberg); MD, med sch, Geneva, 1951; m. Ruth Gariny; c: Joau, Ayelet, Nadav. Chief, dept otolaryngology, Weizmann Inst of Sci since 1962; phys: Tel Hashomer Hosp, 1952-62; Mass Ear and Eye Hosp, 1955-58; Wash U, 1958-59. Mem: Amer Coll Surgs; Isr Surg Assn; Isr Otolaryngological Assn; Acad Ophthal and Otolaryngology. Contbr articles to med jours. Office: Weizmann Inst of Sci, Rehovot, Isr.

SADEH, Dror, Isr, physicist; b. Tel Aviv, Isr, Feb 25, 1932; s. Shmuel and Devorah; MSc, Hcb U, Jerusalem, 1955; Doctorat d'Etat, Sobonne, Paris, 1960; att: UCLA, 1965-66; Naval Research Labs, Wash, DC, 1966-68; m. Haya Rubinstein, Nov 6, 1955; c: Shmuel, Michal, Yonatan. Asso prof, astrophysics, Tel Aviv U, since 1968; mem, Isr AEC, 1955-68; prof, U Cal, 1965-68. Sci br, IDF, 1955-57. Mem: Amer Astronomical Soc; Amer Phys Soc. Recipient: gravitational award, Gravitational Soc, 1967. Contbr to profsl jours. Home: 20 Neve Reim, Ramat Hasharon, Isr. Office: Physics Dept, Tel Aviv U, Tel Aviv, Isr.

SADEH, Pinhas, Isr, poet, novelist; b. Lvov, Pol, July 17, 1929; s. Itzchak and Haya (Krochmal) Feldman; in Isr since 1934; div. Author: Massah Duma, poems, 1951; haChaim keMashal, autobiographical novel, Eng trans, Life as a Parable, 1966, adapted for stage and produced 1968; Al Matzavo Shel ha-Adam, novel, 1967; Mot Abimelech veAliyato haShamiyma beZro'ot Imo, a story, 1969; Sefer haShirim, poems, 1947-70; haEssev haAdom Boer leAt, haNahar haYarok Zorem la'Ad, a story, 1970; haNessia, diary of a journey, 1971; also children's books; poems trans into Arabic, Eng, Fr, Ger, Hung, Span, Latin. Home: 3 Ychonathan St, Ramat Gan, Isr.

SADEH-SADOWSKY, Nachum, Isr, physician; b. Kovno, Lith, Jan 13, 1900; in Isr since 1930; MD, U Berlin, 1925. Pvt practice, specialist, ear, nose, throat; co-found, ear surg, Assuta Hosp, Tel Aviv, since 1935; adv, throat diseases, Isr Anti-TB League. Prin contribs: introduced fenestration oprs into Isr; prin investigator, research and demonstration, pilot project on rehab of deaf persons in Isr with Helen Keller House, Tel Aviv. Found, fmr pres, League for Better Hearing, Tel Aviv; initiator, Intl Course of Audiology, Stockholm; fmr, pres, Archaeol Soc Tel Aviv. Ed, Acta Oto-Laryngologica Orientalia, periodical; contbr to profsl publs. Home: 47 Rothschild Blvd, Tel Aviv, Isr.

SADOFF, Benjamin, US, investor; b. Odessa, Russ, Nov 6, 1900; s. Abraham and Rebecca; in US since 1903; m. Dina Cohen; c: Howard (decd). Pres, 20th Cent Inves Co; partner, Empire Bldg, since 1968; bd dir, First Wis Bank; fmr: dir, Natl Exch Bank; pres: Amer Motors Products; Wells Mfg Co; vice-pres, Sadoff Iron and Metal Co. Pres, Templ Beth Isr; chmn: Rienzi Cemetery Assn; YMCA; Oshkosh U Found;

UJA; JNF; NCCJ, Wis; mem, Elks; bd dirs: Ripon Coll; Marian Coll, Fond du Lac; ARC; fmr: pres: Assn of Commerce; Badger Council, Boy Scouts; B'nai B'rith; hon chmn, Mh Dir; clubs: Rotary, fmr dir; Exch, fmr pres; S Hills, fmr pres. Hobbies: golf; breeding and showing saddlebred horses. Home: Lakewood Beach, Fond du Lac, Wis. Office: 20 Forest Ave, Fond du Lac, Wis.

SAENGER, Gerhart H, US, psychologist, educator; b. Berlin, Ger, Mar 18, 1910; s. Isidor and Olly (Hirsch); in US since 1937; PhD, U Basel, Switz, 1937; att: U Berlin, Ger, 1931-33; Columbia U, NYC, 1937-38; m. Mya Ceha, June 6, 1959. Chief psych, Mh research unit, dept mental hygiene, State of NY, since 1961; prof, psycht, Upstate Med Sch, Syracuse, NY, since 1961; research dir, IS, OWI, 1941-43; dir, sociol research labs, CCNY, 1943-46; prof, grad dept psych, NYU, 1950-61, prog dir, cen for applied sociol research, 1956-61; research cons, AJComm, 1950-55; lectr, Syracuse U, 1961-65; guest prof, U Groningen, Holland, 1966-67. Mem: Amer Psych Assn; Psych Study Sociol Issues Soc; Amer Sociol Soc. Author: Das Realitatsproblem, Erlebnis und Erkeunbarkeit der Realitat, 1936; Today's Refugees, Tomorrow's Citizens, 1941; The Social Psychology of Prejudice, 1953; The Adjust-Adjustment of Severely Retarded Adults in the Community 1957; Factors Determining the Institutionalization of the Retarded, 1960; Medical, Psychological and Social Adjustment of Former Patients of a Children's Orthopedic Hospital and Rehabilitation Center, 1962; co-author, Outpatient Treatment of Alcoholism, 1966; contbr to profsl jours. Hobbies: skiing, photography. Home: 6 Sycamore Terr, Syracuse, NY.

SAFADI, Florence, US, artist, educator; b. NYC, July 18, 1925; d. Louis and Mollie (Mazer) Kurland; att Bklyn Col, 1939-41; BFA, Cooper Union Art Sch, 1946; studied painting with; George Grosz, Art Students League, NYC, 1955-57; Louis Bouche, Natl Acad of Design, NYC, 1954-57; m. 2nd, Harvey Einbinder; c: Jonathan. Found, inst, glass workshop, YM-YWHA, NYC, since 1967; instr: art dept, Yeshiva Moses Soloveichik, NYC, since 1968; art dept, Rodeph Sholom Rel Sch, since 1956; art dept, Hell's Kitchen, since 1950; etching, Young Judea Youth Group, NYC, 1954-55; fmr instr: art dept, Park E, NY, Bklyn J Comty Cen. One-man shows: Red and White Gal, NY, 1967; Interfaith Cen, NY; Natl Design Cen, NY; Chem Corn Bank, NY; group show, ACA Gal, NY. Prog dir, charter found, Glass Craft Soc; secy, Poalei Zion; mem: Artist-Craftsman, NYC; Cooper Union Alumni Soc. Recipient: Hallgarden Traveling award for Painting, Natl Acad of Design, 1957; Dr Weler Drawing award, Natl Acad of Design; Isidor Hallgarten award, Natl Acad of Design. Home: 308 W 97 St, New York, NY. Office: YM-YWHA, Lexington Ave and 92 St, New York, NY.

SAFIR, Jesse, US, attorney; b. NYC, Nov 4, 1901; s. Harry and Gussie (Ragovin); BCS, NYU, 1921, LLB, 1924; m. Harriet Picker, Mar 25, 1928 (decd); c: Joan Wiener, Alan; 2nd m. Ellen Bailey, 1954. Partner, law firm, Safir and Kahn, since 1928; mayor, Village of Hewlett Neck, LI, since 1958. Trustee, Mt Vernon Hosp, 1948-50; pres, Free Syn of Westchester, 1941-46; mem: natl council, JDC; AJComm; B'nai B'rith; Alpha Epsilon Pi; clubs: Metrop Country; Woodmere Country, pres, 1965-67. Home: 155 Dolphin Dr, Woodmere, NY. Office: 633 Third Ave, New York, NY.

SAFRAI, Schmuel, Isr, educator, author; b. Warsaw, Pol, June 16, 1919; s. Moses and Rivkah (Gefen); in Isr since 1922; ordained Rabbi, Yeshiva Merkaz HaRav, Jerusalem; MA, PhD, Heb U, Jerusalem; m. Chaya Fahn, 1944; c: Chana, Zeev. Sr lectr, Heb U, since 1956; mil rabbinate, 1933-67. Author: The Temple in the Life of Jewish People, 1963; The Jewish People in the Time of Second Temple, 1964; Pilgrimage at the Time of Second Temple, 1965; Atlas Carta of the Time of Second Temple, 1967; History of the Jewish People, 1969; contbr articles on J hist talmudical period. Recipient: Ot Hagana, Ot Komemiut, Ot Sinai. Home: 21 Bethar St, Jerusalem, Isr. Office: Heb U Jerusalem, Isr.

SAFRAN, Alexandre, Switz, rabbi; b. Bacau, Rum, Sep 12, 1910; s. Bezale and Finkel; PhD, U Vienna, 1933; m. Sarah Reinharz, 1936; c: Esther, Avinoam. Chief rabbi, Geneva, since 1948; lectr on J thought, U Geneva, since 1948; rabbi, Bacau, 1933-39; chief rabbi, Rum, Bucharest, 1939-48; mem, Rum Sen, 1940; found, J U, Bucharest, 1941; head: Tarbuth, 1942; Inst for High Rabb Studies in Rum, 1943; Yabneh, 1944. Dir, J Underground Activities, Rum, WW II; saved J population Rum from deportation through personal intervention with Papal clergy and govt officials. Pres: ORT, OSE, Rum;

Mizrachi Fed, Rum; cen comm, Rum Zionist Org; repr, Agudath Isr World Org to: UN Eur Off; intl comm, Red Cross; High Commn for Refs, Geneva, all since 1948; participant in confs: Intl Conf J and Chr, Seelisberg, 1947, Fribourg, 1948; Rencontres Internationales de Genève, since 1949; hon pres, B'nai B'rith, Geneva; fmr: guest lectr of UJA to J theol instns, US; delg, WZC; Conf Intl J Orgs, Paris; co-found, United J Educ and Cultural Found of Eur. Author: La Cabale, 1960. Home: 11 rue Marignac, Geneva, Switz. Study: 10 rue St Léger, Geneva, Switz.

SAFRAN, Hyman, US, business exec; b. Detroit, Mich, Feb 9, 1913; s. Elias and Freda (Mendelson); att Wayne U, 1929-32; m. Leah Yoffee, July 25, 1937; c: Sharon, Fred, Kenneth, James. Pres, Safran Printing Co, since 1932; vice-pres, Rotary Manifold Forms Corp since 1952. Pres: web offset sect, Printing Ind of Amer, 1955-56; JWF, since 1964; vice-pres, Council of J Fed and Wfr funds, since 1968; bd trustees, Cong Shaarey Zedek, since 1948, pres, 1957-58; exec comm, JCC, since 1950; bd mem, Sinai Hosp, since 1960; mem: JWV. Recipient: Louis Marshall Award, 1960; Web Offset Award, Printing Ind of Amer, 1961. Hobbies: travel, photography. Home: 19350, Parkside Ave, Detroit, Mich. Office: 3939 Bellevue Ave, Detroit, Michigan.

SAFRAN, Nadav, US, educator; b. Cairo, Egypt, Aug 25, 1925; s. Joseph and Jeanne (Abadi); in US since 1950; BA, Brandeis U, 1954; MA, Harvard U, 1956, PhD, 1958; m. Anna Balicka, June 9, 1955; c: Janina, Abigail, Elizabeth. Prof, govt, Harvard U, since 1968, mem fac since 1958. Mem: Amer Political Sci Assn; Amer Fgn Service Assn; Phi Beta Kappa. Author: Egypt in Search of Political Community, 1961; The US and Israel, 1963; From War to War, 1969. Recipient: Guggenheim F; Ford F. Home: 3 Wyman St, Cambridge, Mass. Office: Harvard U, Cambridge, Mass.

SAFRO, Paul, US, certified public acctnt; b. Warsaw, Pol, May 29, 1912; s. Meyer and Fannie (Zelznick); in US since 1932; att CCNY; m. Miriam Scheck, June 12, 1938; c: Julia Edelman, Marti Kopp, Naomie Kolbrenner, Adele. Sr partner, Safro, Gould and Rudolph, CPA's and predecessor firms, since 1961; bd mem, Flushing Natl Bank; owner, Paul Safro, CPA, 1939-61. Vice-pres: natl ZOA, fmr finance chmn; LI Zionist Found; LI council, JNF; mem, bd trustees: Temple Beth El, Cedarhurst, LI; Emet Rabbi Herzog World Acad; bd dirs, United Isr Appeal; found, Eleanor Roosevelt Inst for Cancer Research; mem: NY State Soc of CPA's; Amer Inst CPA's; NY Stat Soc CPA's; fmr: pres, Five Towns Zionist Dist; chmn, S Shore and acctnts div, Isr Bonds. Author: Pay as You Go Tax Explained, 1943; Your Tax Guide, 1948; contbr to profsl jours. Home: 11 Cooper Beech Lane, Lawrence, LI, NY. Office: 225 Broadway, New York, NY.

SAGALOWITZ, Benjamin, Switz, publicist; b. Witebsk, Russ, June 3, 1901; s. Zwi and Henrietta (Burland); in Switz since 1914; DJur, U Switz. Perm contbr to J press in Switz, Swiss press; ed, Das Jüdische Heim, Zionist monthly; corresp, J periodicals abroad; head publicity, press dept, Schweizerischer Israelitischer Gemeindebund, 1938-64; corresp, trials, Protocols of Elders of Zion, Berne, 1933-37; David Frankfurter trial, Chur, 1936; War Crimes Trial, Nuremberg, 1948-49; Eichmann trial, Jerusalem, 1961-62; Auschwitz trial, Frankfurt/M, 1963-65; numerous war crimes trials in Ger; researcher on Nazi war crimes. Mem: cen comm, Swiss Zionist Org; Social Dem Party, Zurich; delg: WZC, Jerusalem, 1960-61, 1968; Poalei Zion Hitachduth to conf Ichud Olami. Home: 52 Reisbachstr, Zurich, Switz.

SAGALOWITZ (Sagal), Wladimir, Switz, artist; b. Witebsk, Russ, May 18, 1898; s. Zwi and Henrietta (Burland); studied med, U Zurich, 1917-21; m. Lucie Ausderau, May 27, 1944; c: Nina, Gabriella. Artist, painter, and newspaper cartoonist, since 1929; columnist, text and drawings, Swiss dailies; art critic, Omanut, 1945-58; works include drawings of prominent Zionist personalities. Volunteer, Fr Army, 1940. Recipient: hon mention, Süddeutschen Rundfunks, 1957; gold medal, Biennale, Ancona, It, 1966, hon dipl with gold medal, 1967, Medaglia della Rivista Internationale, 1968. Hobby: collecting autographs. Home: Zollikerstr 211, Zurich, Switz.

SAGHER, Felix, Isr, physician, educator; b. Innsbruck, Aus, June 12, 1908; s. Josef and Ida (Zeisel); in Isr since 1938; m. Ruth Dostrovsky, 1942; c: Uri, Tamar. Head, dept dermat and venereology Hadassah U Hosp, Jerusalem, since 1956; prof, dermat and venereology, Heb U-Hadassah Med Sch, since 1958; dir, Hosp for Hansen's Diseases, Isr Min of Health, since 1949; fmr, visiting prof, UCLA. Secy, Dermat Soc of Isr; secy gen, treas, Intl League Dermat Socs; hon mem: dermat socs: Austr; Brit; Greece; Cuba; India; Iran; Pol; S Afr; Spain; Den; Yugo; Pacific Dermat Assn; corresp mem: Amer Dermat Assn; Dermat Assn: Arg; Brazil; Finland; Fr; Mexico; Venezuela. Author: chap, Mastocytosis (Urticaria Pigmentosa) in book Cutaneous Manifestations of the Reticulo-endothelial Granulomas, 1960; Mastocytosis and the Mast Cell, 1967; contbr to med jours. Hobby: bridge. Home: 19 Alharizi St, Jerusalem, Isr. Office: Hadassah U Hosp, Jerusalem, Isr.

SAGNER, Alan L, US, business exec; b. Baltimore, Md, Sep 13, 1920; s. Samuel and Mary (Rappaport); BA, U of Md, 1942; m. Ruth Levin, Oct 25, 1945; c: John, Deborah, Amy. Builder-devl, Levin-Sagner Homes, since 1948; sales mgr, Sagner Inc, clothing mfr, 1943-47. Pres, Newark Beth Isr Med Cen, since 1967; gen chmn, UJA, Essex Co 1962-63, chmn, natl young leadership council, 1962-64; club, Livingston Rotary, pres, 1956. Hobbies: tennis, politics. Home: 2 Crest Circle, S Orange, NJ. Office: 200 E Mt Pleasant Ave, Livingston, NJ.

SAHAR, Yeheskel, Isr, business exec; b. Jerusalem, Jan 10, 1907; s. Itzhak and Rivka (Ben Tovim) Sacharov; att LSE, 1936-39; m. Dina Ginsburg, 1945; c: Elhanan, Gideon, Michael. Dir, Sahar Ins Co Ltd, since 1962; pvt secy to Chaim Weizmann, 1936-40; insp gen, Isr Police Force, 1948-58; Isr ambass, Aus, 1958-60. Maj, Brit Army, 1940-46. Hobby: art collecting. Home: Kfar Shmaryahu, Isr.

SAIFER, Abraham, US, researcher; b. Phila, Pa, Nov 13, 1911; s. Michael and Eva (Stern); BS, CCNY, 1934; MS, Poly Inst, Bklyn, 1952, PhD, 1961; m. Shirley Schoenfeld, June 20, 1948; c: Madlyn, Michael, Steffen. Chief, dept biochem, Isaac Albert Research Inst, Kingsbrook J Med Cen, since 1950; biochem: Queens Gen Hosp, 1935-42; Manhattan Beach VA Hosp, 1946-50. Capt, US Army MC, 1942-46. Chmn, NY Metrop sect, Amer Assn Clinical Chems, 1963; mem: Phi Lambda Epsilon; Amer Chem Soc; NY Acad of Sci. Contbr to profsl jours. Recipient: cert, Amer Bd Clinical Chem, 1952; Vansl-yke Award, 1966. Office: 86 E 49 St, Brooklyn, NY.

SAINT-LOU, Maurice, US, artist; b. Paris, Fr, Oct 24, 1897; s. Zeida and Louise (Silberman) Wolff; in US since 1950; att HS, Paris; D, honoris causa, Commonwealth U, Cal; hon prof, Institut Humaniste, Paris; m. Jeanne Beroy, Dec 27, 1945; One man shows: Fr, US, Mexico; represented: in mus: Honfleur, Fr; Phila Independence Hall; City Hall, Phila; Beaumont, Texas; in embs: Mexican, Wash, DC; Fr, Mexico; Isr, Paris; Fr Gen Consulate, Houston. Violinist, Paris Conservatory, 1915; movie dir, producer, 1926-46. Fr Army, 1940. Hon adv, Columbus Assn; hon mem, Intl Mexican Acad; life mem, Amer Intl Inst; mem: Société des Beaux Arts, Nice, Fr; Fine Arts and Educ Council, Intl Amer Inst, Wash, DC. Recipient: Chevalier of the Sovereign Greek Order of St Dennis of Zante and Cross of Grand-Officier; cdr, Cross of Nichan-Iftikar of Tunis; silver medal, Japanese Red Cross; gold medal, arts, sciences et lettres, Paris; Merite de France et des Colonies; cross of acad hon, Acad Council Amer Inst. Home: 1315 Bath St, Santa Barbara, Cal.

SAKLAD, Bernard, US, attorney; b. Boston, Mass, July 18, 1930; s. Saul and Lillian (Cohen); JD, Suffolk U Law Sch, Mass, 1956; BA, first class hons, Brandeis U; att, Harvard-Radcliffe Archival Inst; m. Ann Kotchen, June 8, 1958; c: Martin, David, Sharon. Pvt practice since 1960; head scholarly and reference dept, Libr Bookseller, 1957-60. Mem: Wig and Robe Soc; Brandeis U Alumni Assn; Suffolk U Law Sch Alumni Assn; Amer J Hist Assn; B'nai B'rith, fmr pres, Fall River Lodge; Amer, Mass, Bristol, Fall River Bar Assns; Friends of SMTI; bd dirs, Adas Isr Syn; lawyers div, United Fund; UJA; Cancer Fund, fmr spec gifts chmn; pres, Fall River JCC; club, Somerset–Swansea Kiwanis. Home: 230 Regan Rd, Somerset, Mass. Office: 56 N Main St, Fall River, Mass.

SALAMON, Benjamin, Isr, business exec; b. Kaunas, Lith, May 7, 1929; s. Meir and Jeta (Shapiro); in Isr since 1936; MA, Heb U, Jerusalem, 1952; PhD, LSE, 1956; m. Pearl Nahum, July 3, 1955; c: Londa, Orlitte, Talya. Mgn dir, Yeda Research and Devl Co, since 1962, secy gen, 1958-62; dir: Miles-Yeda, since 1967; Cidco, since 1968; Ingram Glass Isr, since 1969; dep dir, inves cen, Min of Commerce and Ind, 1957-58, chief econ asst, devl areas, 1957. Sgt, border police, IDF, 1948-49. Mem, exec, Independent Lib Party; fmr: vice-pres, World Fed Lib Youth; chmn, youth, Independent

Lib Party; mem exec, Isr Student Assn, UK. Recipient: UN Intl Essay award, 1953. Hobby: painting. Home: 12 Mapu St, Tel Aviv, Isr. Office: Yeda Research and Devl Ltd, Weizmann Inst of Sci, Rehovot, Isr.

SALAMON, Chaim Ande, Isr, business exec; b. Timisoara, Rum; s. Moshe and Emilia (Grosz); in Isr since 1938; MJur, Heb U, Jerusalem, 1956; MBA, Chgo U, 1967; m. Miriam Heller, July 13, 1949; c: Dan, Ilana, Yael. Pres, Isr Ind Services Inc, NY, since 1969; gen mgr, Scherr-Tumico (Isr) Ltd, 1963-64; Isr consul, Chgo, Ill, 1964-67; admn mgr, Leyland-Ashdod Motor Corp Ltd, 1961-63; mgr budget dept, asst secy, Amer Isr Paper Mills Ltd, 1959-61; mgr, issue dept, chief security off, Bank of Isr, 1954-59; mem: Kibbutz Maagan, 1944-50; Kvutzat Nitzanim, 1940-44; gen mgr, Zenith, Isr, 1968-69; co-mgn dir, Beth Shean Nazareth Textile Works, 1967-68. Org illegal immigration, E Eur, 1947-50; sgt, J Brig, Brit Army, 1939-45; sgt: Haganah, J Settlement Police, IDF, 1938-50. Recipient: Afr, It Stars; defense medal, Brit Army, IDF decorations. Homes: 36 Yehuda Hanassi St, Neve Avivim, Isr; 430 E 64 St, New York, NY. Office: 500 Fifth Ave, New York, NY.

SALAND, Gamliel, US, physician; b. Pal, Jan 1, 1898; s. Sundel and Rachel (Margolis); in US since 1906; BA, Columbia Col, 1920, MD, Coll Phys and Surgs, 1922; m. Mollie Mandler, June 28, 1921; c: Eugene. Pvt practice since 1922; cons phys, Heb Home and Hosp for Chronic Sick, since 1935, pres, mem bd, since 1950; chief med off, NYC Fire Dept, since 1956; cons phys, Bx Hosp, since 1958. US Army, 1918. F, AMA; FACS; dipl, Amer Bd Internal Med; mem: Bx Co, NY State Med Socs; Presbyterian Hosp Alumnus Soc. Contbr to med jours. Home: 920 E 199 St, N Miami Beach, Fla.

SALCZER-ELIAZ, Joseph Zwi, Isr, business exec; b. Ma'd, Hung, Aug 13, 1903; s. Pinchas and Jozefin (Teitelbaum) Salczer; in Isr since 1948; att tech sch, wines; m. Miriam Goldstein, Jan ,1948; c: Kate Paldi, Moshe. Found, dir, Eliaz wine cellar, Benyamina, Isr. Mem: natl, commercial comms, Rel Party. Home: 13 Ahad Ha'am St, Haifa, Isr.

SALERT, Irving W, US, government official; b. NYC, July 4, 1914; s. Sigmund and Dena (Halpern); grad, Rand Sch of Social Sci, 1932; att: NYU, 1930-32; New Sch for Social Research, 1931-33; m. Estelle Sheld, Feb 21, 1937; c: Susan, Barbara. Fgn service off, Off Intelligence and Research, State Dept, since 1968; org, Amalgamated Clothing Workers, 1937-41; dir, NY State, CIO Comty Services Commn, 1941-43; natl field dir, J Lab Comm, 1944-51; lab attache, US Emb, Brazil, 1952-57, 1st secy, Buenos Aires, 1957-62; chief, lab sect, Mexico, 1962-68. Mem: Fgn Service Assn; Amer Political Sci Assn; Amer Lab Educ Services. Office: Dept of State, Washington, DC.

SALINGER, Hans, Isr, radiologist; b. Berlin, Ger, July 10, 1897; s. George and Marianne (Cohn); in Isr since 1933; att Us: Berlin, Heidelberg, Ger; m. Nora Ehrlich, Oct 26, 1930; d. Miriam Lior. Pvt practice since 1938; prof em, radiology, U Tel Aviv, since 1969, clinical prof, 1966-69; asso prof radiology, Heb U, Jerusalem, since 1956; cons, radiology, Beilinson Hosp, Petah Tikvah, since 1967, dir, X-ray dept, 1936-67. Contbr publs on radiological subjects, Eng, Heb, Ger. Hon dipl, Isr Radiological Soc; mem: IMA; Isr Radiological Soc. Home: 26 Joseph Zion St, Ramat Gan, Isr. Office: 3 Bialik St, Tel Aviv, Isr.

SALITERNIK, Zvi, Isr, malariologist, government official; b. Proskurov, Russ, May 16, 1897; s. Haim and Rachel (Dibnis); in Isr since 1920; MSc, Heb U, Jerusalem, 1937, PhD, 1945; m. Susanne Lissauer, Dec 24, 1930; c: Shulamith, Ruth. Adv for malaria and schistosomiasis, Isr Min Health since 1962; chief insp: Malaria Research Inst, Pal Govt, 1922-29; Nesher Factory, Ltd, Portland Cement Works, 1929-36; exec off, malaria comm, adv: Va'ad Leumi; Hadassah Med Org, insp; Workers Sick Fund, 1936-47; chief insp, Workers Sick Fund, 1929-44; WHO fs in: Gt Brit; Greece; USA; Turkey, 1953; Thailand; India; It; Port; Switz, 1957; Yugo; Rum, 1961; mem, med mission Mali, 1961. Prin contrib: devl methods for control mosquitos and snails; control and eradication of malaria and schistosomiasis. Mem: IMA; Isr Microbiol Assn; Isr Assn for Advancement Sci; Amer Mosquito Control Assn; corresp mem, Experta Medica, Amsterdam; fmr: Min Health delg to: intl congs: Athens; Turkey; WHO Intl Assembly, Geneva. Author: Malaria in Israel, 1930; Survey of Water Sources for Antimalaria Treatment, 1954; Malaria and Its Eradication, 1965; contbr to profsl jours. Recipient, Isr Prize,

1962. Home: 16 Arlosoroff St, Jerusalem, Isr. Office: Min of Health, Jerusalem, Isr.

SALK, Jonas Edward, US, research scientist; b. NYC, Oct 28, 1914; a. Daniel and Dora (Press); BS, CCNY, 1934; MD, NYU, 1939; hon: Des Lettres, JTSA; PhD, Heb U; DHL, Yeshiva U; m. Donna Lindsay, June 8, 1939; c: Peter, Darrell, Jonathan. F, dir, Salk Inst for Biol Studies, San Diego, Cal, since 1962; mem expert adv panel on virus diseases, WHO; f, chem, NYU Coll of Med, 1935-36, Christian A Herter f, chem, 1936-37, experimental surg, 1937-38, f, bact, 1939-40; asso prof, dept epidemiology, Sch of Pubilc Health, U Mich, 1946-47, f, med sci, NRC, 1942-43, research f, epidemiology, 1943-44; Commonwealth prof experimental med, Sch of Med, U Pittsburgh, 1957-62, Commonwealth prof preventive med, 1955-57, on fac since 1947, dir Virus Research Lab, 1947-62; mem, cons staff, Music Hosp for Contagious Diseases, Pittsburgh, 1948-56; mem, commn on influenza, Army Epidemiological Bd, 1944-54; cons epidemic diseases: Secy of War, 1944-47; Secy of Army, 1947-54. Prin contrib: discoverer of the Salk polio vaccine, 1954. F: AAAS, Amer Public Health Assn; hon f, Weizmann Inst of Sci; mem: Assn Amer Phys; Amer Soc for Clinical Inves; Amer Epidemiological Soc; Amer Assn Immunologists; Amer Coll Preventive Med; AMA; Soc for Experimental Biol and Med; Soc of Amer Bacts; Phi Beta Kappa; Alpha Omega Alpha; Sigma Xi; Delta Omega. Contbr to sci jours. Recipient: Criss award, AMA, 1955; Chevalier, Legion of Honor, 1955; Cong Medal for Civilian Achievement, 1956. Home and office: 2444 Ellentown Rd, La Jolla, Cal.

SALKIN, David, US, physician, educator; b. Ukraine, Russ, Aug 8, 1906; s. Samuel and Eva (Sturman); in US since 1929; MD, U Toronto, 1929; m. Bess Adelman, Sep 12, 1934; c: Barbara, Robert. Dir, VA Hosp San Fernando, Cal, since 1967, chief of staff since 1948; clinical prof: thoracic diseases, Loma Linda U, since 1961; med, U of Cal; supt, med dir, Hopemont Sanitarium, W Va, 1934-48; asso clinical prof, UCLA, 1951-61. Pres: Cal Thoracic Soc, 1962; LA Trudeau Soc, 1957; mem, bd dirs, TB and Health Assn, Cal, since 1960; mem: LA, Cal Med Assns; Amer Coll Phys; Amer Thoracic Soc; Amer Coll Chest Phys; Amer Therapeutic Soc; Sigma Xi; Comty Concert Assn; TB and Health Assn of LA. Contbr to profsl jours. Recipient: VA Commendation; hons, Amer Acad TB Phys. Home and office: VA Hosp, San Fernando, Cal.

SALL, George L, US, business exec; b. Phila, Pa, June 25, 1903; s. Jacob and Goldie (Axelrod); att Lehigh U, 1922-24; m. Mary Cohen, 1926; c: Betty Malmud, Marianne Perilstien, Roberta Moss. Vice-pres, Einstien Med Cen, since 1957; chmn, Golden Slipper Found; bd mem: Gratz Coll; Fed J Agcys; Har Zion Temple; Amer Cancer Soc; bd overseers, JTSA; mem: Masons; Sigma Alpha Mu; clubs: Golden Slipper Sq; Green Valley Country; Locust, pres. Recipient, awards: JTSA; Allied J Appeal; JWV; LA Sanatorium, JWB. Home: 220 W Rittenhouse, Philadelphia, Pa. Offic: 2255 E Butler St, Philadelphia, Pa,

SALMAN, Jaacov, Isr, civil servant; b. Bialystok, Russ, Sep 9, 1926; s. Eliahu and Rachel (Rog); in Isr since 1939; att IDF Coll; m. Atara Lashciver, Sep 13, 1949; c: Dita, Uzi, Amir. Dir, govt cos, since 1968; dep commn income tax, 1954-60; dir, property tax, 1960-66; dep dir gen, Min of Finance, 1966-68. Lt col, IDF, 1948-54. Home: 5 Schiller St, Jerusalem, Isr. Office: Min of Finance, Jerusalem, Isr.

SALMON, Karel, Isr, conductor, composer; b. Heidelberg, Ger, Nov 13, 1897; s. Hermann and Julie (Marx); in Isr since 1933; att: Heidelberg U, Berlin U, 1915-20; Acad of Art, Berlin; m. Esther Müller, Sep 25, 1933; Ret; dir transcriptions, Kol Isr, 1958-62; music dir: 1948-57, music dir, Pal Bc Service, 1936-48; conductor Baden-Baden, Hamburg, since 1920; music tchr, choral conductor Heb U Conservatory, 1933-36; radio, 1948-62. Composer: David and Goliath, opera 1930; Der Ton, oratorio, 1932; Ali Beer, fantasy based on popular song, 1937; haSevivon, 1941; Suite on Greek Themes, 1943; Shir haMavet, 1944; Am Isr Hai, 1948; Concerto for Piano & Orch, 1947; Jerusalem, 1948; Adon Olam, 1949; Nights in Canaan, sym, 1950; Youth Sym, 1951; Daliah, dance rhapsody, 1953; Nedarim, opera, 1955; cantatas: Ingathering of the Exiles, 1956; For the Sake of Jerusalem, 1958; Divertimento for Wind Instruments, 1958; Concerto for 2 pianos, 1959-60; Concertino for Oboe, 1960; Concertino for Xylophone, 1961; Sephardic Suite 1, 1961; Sym for Amateurs, 1961; Sephardic Suite II, for orch, 1963; Tour Times Methusalem, opera, 1965; The

Life of Man, Cantata, 1967. Home: Beit Zayit, Jerusalem, Isr.

SALOMON, Harald, Den, sculptor, engraver; b. Oslo, Nor, May 8, 1900; s. Simon and Johanna (Einstein); att Royal Danish Acad, 1921-27; m. Else Magnussen, Mar 21, 1925; c: Lilian. Sculptor in marble, bronze stoneware, china; worked Rorstrans Porcelain Mfg, Swed, 1943-45; medal designer: King Christian X; King Frederik IX; King Gustav Adolph V; royal mint engraver: coins for Danish mint and official medals; works in: Alborg Mus; Tonder Mus; Natl Mus, Copenhagen; Fyns, Stift Mus; HC Andersen Mus; Frederiksborg; Bergen; Stockholm; Oslo; Upsala; Paris Mint Cabinet; portrait reliefs: King Christian X; Queen Alexandrine; King Frederik X and Queen Ingrid at Frederiksberg Town Hall; medal of Dag Hammarskjold; other portraits. Recipient: bronze medal, Intl Medal Exhb, Madrid; 1st Grade Knight of Dannebrog; 1st Grade Knight of St Olav Order of Norway; Danish Red Cross. Home and studio: Skovtoftebakken, Virum, Copenhagen, Den.

SALOMON, Irving, US, diplomat, educator, columnist, rancher; b. Chgo, Ill, Aug 23, 1897; s. Abraham and Ella (Polachek); att Northwestern U, 1915-18; hon LHD, Western U, Cal, 1959; m. Cecile Leibowitz, Sep 25, 1937; c: Abbe Wolfsheimer. Pres: Gold Coast Pictures; Mt Palomar Ranchos; chmn bd, Royal Metal Mfg Co, Chgo, since 1942; prof political sci: San Diego State Coll; U of Cal, San Diego, both since 1965; cons: US War Dept, 1947; Munitions Bd, 1949; Ford Found and its repr to UNESCO conf, Paris 1951; Fund for Adult Educ, 1952, 1953; chmn, US delg, UNESCO conf, Paris; Geneva, 1953; vice-chmn, US delg, ECOSOC; exec cons, Fund for Advancement of Educ, 1954-55; US delg, UN Gen Assembly, 1958; undersecy for UN, State Dept, 1962-63. Mem: exec bd, Gov Cal, Bd Educ TV, 1953-54; Natl Citizens Comm for educ TV, 1952-54, treas, 1953-54; chmn, JDC, 1946-48, 1962; bd chmn: Ballet of San Diego; Pala Catholic Mission; mem, natl finance council, JWB; mem bd: Brandeis U; AJComm; Inst Intl Educ; UNICEF; US Comm for the UN; UN Assn of US; fmr chmn: World Fed UN; Fgn Policy Assn; Atlanta U; Georgetown U; Cal Western U; Clairmont U of Theel, Methodist; San Diego Sym Assn; Old Globe Theater; YMCA; Child's Guidance Clinic; Scripps Research Inst; clubs: Guyamaca; Harmony; Standard; San Diego; Kona Kai. Author: Retire and Be Happy, 1951; College and University Management, 1953; contbr to weekly press. Home: Rancho Lilac, Escondido, Cal; 3200 Sixth Ave, San Diego, Cal.

SALOMON Isidore L, US, poet, translator; b. Hartford, Conn, Dec 10, 1899; s. Joseph and Elizabeta (Segall); BA, CCNY, 1923, MS, 1924; m. Frances Slobodin, June 28, 1925; c: Joanne Helfer. Conducted poetry workshop, Bd of Educ, NYC, 1948; chmn, Evenings of Poetry, NY Public Libr, 1949. Students Army Training Corps, 1918. Author: Unit and Universe, poems, 1959; Dino Campana; trans: Carlo Betocchi, 1963; Orphic Song, 1968; reviewer, Saturday Review; Poetry, Chgo; contbr to Poetry Northwest, Minn Review. Mem: Acad Amer Poets; PEN; Authors Guild; James Joyce Soc; MacDowell Assn. Recipient: annual award, Poetry Soc of Amer, 1948, 1957; EA Robinson in poetry, MacDowell Colony, 1949; $10,000 award, Natl Council on Arts, 1966; gold metal, Marraki Stuly, birthplace of Campana, 1968. Hobbies: music, fishing. Home: 12 Stuyvesant Oval, New York, NY.

SALOMON, Mordoqueo (Mordecai) I, US, physician, educator; b. Minsk-Mazowiecki, Pol, Jan 26, 1906; s. Joseph and Ida (Perkal); D Natural Scis, U Brussels, Belgium, 1929; MD, U Geneva, Switz, 1933; m. Sophie Lewin, 1930; c: Ruth King, Hillel. Pvt practice in US since 1943; att phys, Knickerbocker Metrop, BS Coler; Flower Hosps, all since 1954; clinical prof, NY Med Coll; prof: biol and phys, U Cochabamba, Bolivia Sch Med, 1935-37, biol, U Oruro, Bolivia, 1938; phys, mining companies, Oruro, Bolivia, 1935-38; pvt practice, phys, La Paz, Bolivia, 1938-42. Mil phys, Bolivian Army, 1933, chief sanitary control, 1934-35. F: NY Acad Med; Amer Coll Card; Amer Coll Chest Phys; asso, f, NY Acad Gastroenterology; bd mem: United Isr World Union; B'nai Zion. Contbr to sci and med jours. Hobbies: big game camera hunting. Home: 501 E 79 St, New York, NY. Office: 1350 Madison Ave, New York, NY.

SALOMON, Milton, US, soil chemist, educator; b. Passaic, NJ, June 19, 1914; s. Joseph and Florence (Stein); BS, RI State Coll, 1937; MSc, Va Poly Inst, Blacksburg, Va, 1938; PhD, NC State Coll, Raleigh, NC, 1952; m. Betty Mayer,

June 9, 1946; c: David, Deborah, Judith. Prof, agric chem, U of RI, since 1958, mem fac since 1939; soil cons, Natl Wild Life Fed; research f, Va Agric Experimental Sta, 1937-38. US Army, 1941-46. F, AAAS; mem: Amer Soc Agronomy; Soil Sci Soc of Amer; Intl Soil Sci Soc; Sigma Xi; Phi Kappa Phi; Alpha Zeta. Contbr to profsl jours. Recipient: Silver Star; Brit Mil Cross; Purple Heart. Home: 51 Cherry Rd, Kingston, RI. Office: U of RI, Kingston, RI.

SALOMON, Wolfgang Zeev, Isr, commission, shipping agt; ins broker; b. Berlin, Ger, Mar 27, 1907; s. Gabriel and Alice (Wolff); in Isr since 1935; att HS, Berlin; m. Margot Berliner, Feb 17, 1935; c: Ruth, Reuben. Dir: Salomon Bros Co Ltd; Lucy Borchard Shipping Ltd; Keren Ins Broker Ltd; Turon Ltd; Philippine consul, Haifa, since 1954, fmr with Corn Exch, Berlin, Ger. Mem: C of C; Chamber of Shipping; Assn Commn Agts; Consular Corps, Haifa; Masons, Haifa; club: Skal, Mt Carmel. Home: 5 Maabarot St, Haifa-Carmel, Isr. Office: 5 Habankim St, Haifa, Isr.

SALOMONOWITZ, Adolf Konrad, Isr, obstetrician; b. Morav-ska-Ostrava, Czech, July 15, 1915; s. Nathan and Gusti (Wnuczek); in Isr since 1949; MD, U Prague, 1945; m. Berta De Vanoni, Apr 27, 1945; c: Peter, Franz. Dir, Health Cen, Kiryat Shemona, since 1955; first asst, MD, Women's dept; Karlsbad, 1945-48; Hadera, 1949-51, Tiberias, 1951-55. Lt, MC, Czech Army, IDF, 1945-64. Author: Anemias of Preg-nancy, 1961; Anemias of Pregnancy and Treatment, 1963. Pres, Magen David Adom, Kiryat Shemona; fmr pres: Cancer Org, Kiryat Shemona; Crippled Children Org; Anti TB League. Recipient: work prize, Histadrut; D Ziman prize, Min of Health, 1967; hon citizen of Kiryat Shemona. Hobby: photography. Home: 16 Hagalil St, Kiryat Shemona, Isr. Office: Health Cent, Kiryat Shemona, Isr.

SALPETER, Edwin Ernest, US, educator; b. Vienna, Aus, Dec 3, 1924; s. Jakob and Friedericke (Horn); in US since 1949; MS, U Sydney, Austr, 1945; PhD, U Birmingham, Eng, 1948; hon DSc, U Chgo, 1969; m. Miriam Mask, Apr 1, 1950; c: Judy, Shelley. Prof, physics and astrophysics, Cornell U. F, Amer Acad Arts and Sci; mem: Natl Acad Sci; Intl Astronomical Union; Amer Phys Soc. Author: Quantum Mechanics, 1957. Home: 116 Westbourne, Ithaca, NY. Office: Cornell U, Ithaca, NY.

SALPETER, Eliahu Arnost, Isr, journalist; b. Slatina, Czech, Jan 11, 1927; s. Nahman and Cornelia (Horowitz); att: Sch of Journalism, Prague U, 1947-49; Heb U, 1949-51; m. Ruth Freiman, 1960; c: Ron, Noam. Ed writer, mem ed bd, Ha'-aretz, since 1968; dipl corresp, 1957-61, Wash corresp, 1953-56, 1961-65, mgn ed, 1965-68; columnist, JTA, since 1965, bur chief, Jerusalem, 1956-61; on staff: AP, Prague, 1948-49; Jerusalem Post, 1950-53. Mem: Isr Journalists Assn; Isr Fgn Policy Assn; club, Natl Press, Wash, DC. Home: 28 Rem-brandt St, Tel Aviv, Isr. Office: 56 Mazeh St, Tel Aviv, Isr.

SALPETER, Julius G, Isr, business exec; b. Kishkar, Hun, Mar 10, 1902; s. Simha and Tova (Hauser); in Isr since 1921; grad, Tech Coll, Budapest, 1920; m. Rachel Golden-berg, 1930; c: Simha, Oded. Mgn dir, Shikun Esrachi Ltd, since 1961; fmr, mem, Tel Aviv City Council. Mem, exec comm, Lib Party, chmn, munic comm; pres: Isr-Ceylon Fri-endship Soc; Isr-Ceylon C of C; Hung Immigrants Assn; mem, Masons, Hermon lodge. Recipient: first prize for immi-grants housing plan, Dept of Public Works, Govt of Isr, 1950. Home: 19 Dov Hos St, Tel Aviv, Isr.

SALTEN, David G, US, educator; b. NYC, Aug 23, 1913; s. Max and Gertrude (Brauer); BS, NYU, 1933; PhD, 1944; AM, Columbia U, 1939; m. Frances Brown, Sep 12, 1936; c: Phoebe, Cynthia, Melissa. Exec vice-pres, FJP, since 1966; lectr, grad educ prog, Hunter Coll, since 1947; supt schs, Long Beach, NY, 1950-62; lectr, educ admn, NYU, 1958-60; supt schs, New Rochelle, NY, 1962-65; witness: Little Rock Sch integration case, Fed Court, 1958; US Cong hearing on spec educ, 1960; US resourcer, World Mh Cong, Paris, 1961. F, AAAS; NY State Mental Hygiene Council, since 1968; White House Conf on Educ, 1955, 1960; Amer Assn Sch Admns; Amer Educ Research Assn; Amer Psych Assn. Au-thor: Basic Mathematics, 1957; Education of the Gifted,1961; contbr to profsl jours. Home: 10 The Esplanade, New Ro-chelle, NY. Office: 41 Park Ave, New York, NY.

SALTMAN, Abraham, US, business exec; b. Liverpool, Eng, July 26, 1905; s. Joseph and Fanny (Herman); in US since 1908; grad, Natl Security Sem, Ind Coll, Armed Forces, 1965-

66; m. Syd Schultz, Jan 26, 1930; c: Richard, Stuart. Pres: Package Store, since 1933; Realty Devl Corp, since 1946; chmn bd, J Saltman and Co, since 1923, co-owner, 1923-40; dir: Holyoke and Westfield RR Co, since 1936, pres, 1958; mem, bd trustees, Comty Savings Bank; pres, R & S Devl, 1953-68; dir, Regional Business Devl, 1953-68; vice-pres, Highland Mfg, 1960-67. Chmn, City of Holyoke Gas and Ele-ctric Comm, since 1963; PR comm, Amer Public Power Assn, since 1964; chmn bd, Public Works, City of Holyoke, 1958-63; mem: Mayor's Ind Devl Adv Comm; Natl Liquor Stores Leg Comm; Amer Public Works Assn; Govs Adv Comm, Ind Devl; dir: Pioneer Valley Assn, 1957; CJA; NCCJ; chmn: Holyoke ZC, since 1948, vice-pres, NE Zionist Re-gion, 1948; UJA, 1957; delg, AJComm, since 1955; mem: ADL regional bd; ZOA, life; pres: YMHA, 1927; Cong Sons of Zion, 1948; dir: J Comty Center, 1942; Red Feather Agcys, 1946; Jr Achievement Found, 1955; Holyoke Hosp, 1946; mem, bd trustees, Robert Newcomb Fund; fmr chmn C of C Conv Bur; pres em, Holyoke Masonic Assn, since 1968; mem: Masons, 33 deg; Shriner; Holyoke C of C; clubs: Wyckoff Golf and Country; Pioneer Valley Shrine, Holyoke Boys', dir, 1956. Home: 208 Walnut St, Holyoke, Mass. Office: 444 High St, Holyoke, Mass.

SALTMAN, Avrom, Isr, historian, educator; b. Whitely Bay, Eng, Nov 17, 1925; c. Isaac and Miriam (Rosenberg); in Isr since 1957; BA, Cambridge U, 1945, MA, 1949; PhD, London U, 1951; m. Ilse Rabinowicz, 1953. Head, dept Hist, Bar Ilan, since 1957, prof hist, since 1961, mem sen, since 1960, rector, 1964-65; lectr Hist, London U, 1948-57. F, Royal Hist Soc, London; mem, Isr Council for Higher Educ. Au-thor: History of Hendon Synagogue, 1953; Life of Theobald, Archbishop of Canterbury, 1956; The Cartulary of Tutbury. Priory, 1961; The Cartulary of Dale Abbey, 1967. Contbr to Hist jours. Home: 5 San Martin St, Ramat Gan, Isr. Office: Bar Ilan U, Ramat Gan, Isr.

SALTZ, Nathan Jacob, Isr, educator, surgeon; b. NYC, Nov 1, 1912; s. Morris and Jenny (Feierstein); in Isr since 1952; BS, U Fla, 1934; MS, Emory U, Atlanta, Ga, 1935, MD, 1939; m. Armen Bagdasaroff, Apr 14, 1950; c: Jenny, David. Prof, surg, Hadassah-Heb U, Med Sch, Jerusalem, since 1963; chmn depts of surg, Rothschild-Hadassah U Hosp, since 1962. Capt US Army, MC, 1941-45. F, Amer Coll Surg; dipl, Amer Bd Surg; spec affiliate, AMA; mem of council, Isr Surg Soc; mem: Société Internationale de Chirurgie; James IV Assn; Surg; Phi Delta Epsilon. Contbr to profsl jours. Recipient. Bronze Star. Home: 10 Alkalay St, Jerusalem, Isr. Office: Hadassah U Hosp, Jerusalem, Isr.

SALTZMAN, Maurice, US, physician; b. Lith, Apr 15, 1894; s. David and Drazne (Edeiken); in US since 1912; MD, Jeff-erson Med Coll, 1922; m. Sophie Aaron, Sep 16, 1924; c: Marguerite, Edward, Herbert. Cons, Albert Einstein Med Cen; asst prof, otorhinology, Temple U Med Sch. Prin contrib: inaugurated teaching and audiology, 1942. Mem: AMA; Phila Co Med Soc; Coll of Phys, Phila; Amer Acad Ophthal and Otolaryngology; Pa Acad Ophthal and Otolaryngology; Phila Laryngological Soc; Temple U Educ Fund; Jefferson U Alumni Fund; Histadrut; Friends Heb U; Allied J Appeal; United Fund. Author: Clinical Audiology, 1949; contbr to med jours. Home and office: 2037 Spruce St, Philadelphia, Pa.

SALTZMAN, Samuel L, US, surgeon, educator; b. Hinsdale, NH, Feb 19, 1898; s. Louis and Augusta (Persky); PhB, cum laude, Yale U, 1920; MD, NY Med Coll, 1926; Oculi et auris Chirurgus,NY Ophthal Hosp, 1931.Dir, ophthal and oph-thal surg, Sea View Hosp; visiting eye surg, Metrop Hosp; asst visiting eye surg, Flower and Fifth Ave Hospitals; asst clinical prof, ophthal, lectr, phys, NY Med Coll; dir ophthal, chief med staff, Heb Home for the Aged, Riverdale, NY; visiting ophthal,Bird S Coler Hosp; cons, ophthal, Natl Council to Combat Blindness, mem sci adv comm, resident eye surg, Mt Sinai Hosp, 1932-33; asst prof, NY Ophthal Hosp, 1931-35, 1935-38, all NYC. Dipl, Amer Bd Ophthal, f: Amer Acad of Ophthal and Otolaryngology Amer Coll of Surgs; AMA; Amer Geriatric Soc; mem: AAAS; Oxford Ophthal Cong;Assn for Research in Ophthal; corresponding secy, Alumni Assn of NY Med Coll, 1945. Contbr to med jours. Home and office: 334 W 86 St, New York, NY.

SALTZSTEIN, Harry G, US, surgeon; b. Wash, DC, Nov 11, 1890; s. Abraham and Fannie (Cohen); PhB, Yale U, 1914; MD, Johns Hopkins U, 1918. Pvt practice since 1923; prof em, Wayne State U, fac mem since 1952; cons surg: Harper Hosp; Sinai Hosp, since 1952. Dipl, Amer Bd Surg; f,

Amer Coll Surgs; mem: Detroit Acad of Surg; Amer Gastroenterology Soc; Amer Soc Clinical Oncology; Soc Head and Neck Surgs; Temple Beth El; club, GreatLakes. Contbr; to profsl jours. Home: 850 Whitmore Rd, Detroit, Mich. Office: 850 Whitmore Rd, Detroit, Michigan.

SALZMAN, Leon, US, psychiatrist, educator; b. NYC, July 10, 1915; s. Morris and Sarah (Wolf); BS, CCNY, 1936; MD, Royal Coll Phys and Surgs, Edinburgh, Scotland, 1940; Dipl, Wash Sch Psycht, 1945; m. Ann Bailin, 1950; c: Susy, Terry, Carol, Sarah. Pvt practice since 1945; clinical prof, psycht, Georgetown U, on fac since 1948; visiting prof, psycht, Catholic U Sch Psychol, since 1953; cons: ARC, since 1947; Glendale Santitarium, since 1948; St Elizabeth's Hosp, since 1955. F, Amer Psycht Assn; dipl, Amer Bd of Neur and Psycht; mem: local, state, natl med soc's; Wash Psychoanalytic Soc; St Elizabeth Med Soc; Amer Psychoanalytic Soc; fmr pres, Amer Acad of Psychan. Author: Developments in Psychoanalysis, 1962; Obsessive Personality, 1968; contbr to med jours. Home: 7402 Barra Pl, Bethesda, Md. Office: 1610 New Hampshire Ave NW, Washington, DC.

SALZMAN, William Simcha, US, business exec; b. Toefipoll, Russ, June 29, 1883; s. Samuel and Yetta (Feder); in US since 1908; att Yeshiva in Russ; m. Minnie Reich, May 31, 1905; c: Alexander, Sarah, Herbert. Ret; pres, Standard Bag Co, 1923-1966, mem firm since 1913; asso with Salzmann Ltd, Isr, since 1936. Acad Heb Lang bldg, Jerusalem, erected and named for William and Minnie Salzman. Bd trustees,Soc for Advancement Judaism, since 1932; dir, Heb Tchrs Inst, since 1928, pres, 1943-47, hon pres, since 1947; hon mem, Acad Heb Lang, Jerusalem; dir J Educ Comm, 1949; mem, B'nai B'rith; vice-pres, Hadoar. Home: 1120 Park Ave, New Yotk, NY,

SALZMANN, Harold Irving, US, rabbi; b. Cleveland, O, Aug 6, 1922; s. Bernard and Rae (Busch); att U Cincinnati, 1943-45; BA, Ohio U, 1945; BHL HUC-JIR, 1944, ordained rabbi, MHL, 1950; m. Audrey Pastor, Oct 8, 1950; c: Ariel, Joshua. Rabbi: Temple Anshe Amunim, Pittsfield, Mass, since 1954; Temple Judah-Beth Jacob, Cedar Rapids, Ia, 1950-52. Chaplain, US Army, 1952-54. Mem: CCAR, treas, NE area, since 1961; Mil Chaplains Assn of Amer;Assn J Chaplains Armed Forces; Mass Bd Rabbis;Berkshire Co Rabb Assn; Alumni Assn, HUC-JIR; Phi Beta Kappa; B'nai B'rith; Soc Isr Philatelists; pres,Pittsfield Area Min Assn,1958-59; gen chmn, J Wfr Campaign, Pittsfield, 1957; J Chaplain, Berkshire Co Boy Scouts of Amer, 1954-63; pres, Cen Berkshire Clergy Assn, 1966-67; club, Rotary, dir, since 1960. Spec interest: philatelic hist, Holy Land. Home: 48 Revere Pkwy, Pittsfield, Mass. Study: 26 Broad St, Pittsfield, Mass.

SALZMANN, Jacob Amos, US, orthodontist; b. Phila, Pa, Oct 1, 1901; s. Abram and Sarah (Ammerman); DDS, U of Pa Coll Dent, 1923; m. Leah Wishoff, Feb 24, 1924; c: Jerome, Rhoda. Pvt practice since 1923. Att orthodontist em, Mt Sinai Hosp, NYC, since 1966, att orthodontist, 1944-46. dir, cleft palate cen, 1950-66. F: Amer Coll Dents; Amer Pub Health Assn; fmr pres, Amer Assn Orthodontists; dir, Amer Bd Orthodontics; mem: White House Conf for Children, 1950-60; NE Soc Orthodontists; Intl Assn for Dent Research; hon mem, Isr, Ger, Mexican and S Orthodontics Assns. Author: Practice of Orthodontics, 1966; ed em, NY Jour of Dent; review ed, Amer Jour of Orthodontics, since 1939; contbr articles on growth and development. Recipient: Ketcham award, Amer Assn Orthodontists, 1966; dist service award, Orthodontic Found for Research and Educ, 1966; award of merit, U, of Pa Dent Alumni, 1966. Home: 135 Continental Ave, Forest Hills, NY. Offices: 654 Madison Ave, New York, NY; 1 E 100 St, New York, NY.

SAMBURSKY, Daniel, Isr, composer; b. Königsberg, Ger, Apr 4, 1909; s. Menachem and Selma (Kabak); in Isr since 1933; att music conservatory, Danzig, 1928-30; U Berlin, 1930-33; m. Chermona Schaoni, July 15, 1935; c: Ophra. Music tchr, Tchrs Sem, since 1948; composer, since 1933; music tchr, secondary schs, 1933-48. Composed: three books of songs for school and people, 1945-1969; numerous songs, camera music, choirs, etc. Mem: ACUM. Hobbies: astronomy, photography. Home: 13 Baron Hirsch St, Tel Aviv, Isr.

SAMBURSKY, Shmuel, Isr, educator; b. Königsberg, Ger, Oct 30, 1900; s. Menahem and Selma (Kabak); in Isr since 1924; att U Berlin; PhD, U Königsberg, 1923; m. Miriam Grünstein, 1938; c: Shlomith Cheyette. Prof, hist and phil of sci, Heb U, Jerusalem, since 1960, dept chmn since 1959; mem fac, physics dept, since 1928, dean, fac sci, 1957-59; visiting f:

St Catherine's Coll, Oxford, 1965, All Souls Coll, 1967; visiting prof, U Heidelberg, 1968. Vice-chmn, Isr natl comm: for UNESCO, since 1959; mem, Isr Acad Sci; fmr dir, vice-chmn, Research Council of Isr. Author: The Physical World of the Greeks, 1956; Physics of the Stoics, 1959; The Physical World of Late Antiquity, 1962; contbr to local, fgn sci jours; encys. Recipient: Rothschild prize in hum, 1967; Isr Prize in hum, 1968. Home: 3 Kikar Magnes, Jerusalem, Isr. Office: Heb U, Jerusalem, Isr.

SAMET, Seymour, US, organization exec, educator, comty relations cons; b. Newark, NJ, Dec 3, 1919; s. Isadore and Sylvia (Birn); BA, Montclair State Tchrs Coll, 1941; MEd, Sch of Educ, U Miami; grad studies: New Sch for Social Research, 1946; Columbia U, 1947-52; Group Dynamics Lab, Bethel, Me; m. Elaine Rosenberg, Oct 3, 1943; c: Anita, Robert. Natl dir, intergroup relations and social actions, AJComm, NYC, since 1968, SE area dir, 1952-64; tchr, hist and econ, Barringer HS, Newark, 1941; prog service dir, Essex Co Intergroup Council; asst exec secy, comty relations comm, JCC, Essex Co, 1949-52; mem fac, workshop in hum relations, Rutgers U, 1951-52; exec dir, Dade Co Comty Relations Bd, Fla, 1963-64; dir, prog evaluation and devl, comty relations service, US Justice, Dept, 1964-68. US Army Signal Corps, 1942-46. Mem: Phi Alpha Theta; Kappa Delta Pi; Natl Comm Against Discrimination in Housing; Natl Assn Intergroup Relations Officials; Assn J Comty Relations Workers. Recipient: Seymour Samet Hum Relations Libr, established in Dade Co, Fla Bd Public Instrn. Home: 150 West End Ave, New York, NY. Office: 165 E 56 St, New York, NY.

SAMISH, Rudolf Moshe, Isr, horticulturist, educator; b. Carlsbad, Czech, Mar 20, 1904; s. Wilhelm and Ida (Altschul); in Isr since 1935; att U Prague, 1922-24; BS, U Cal, Berkeley, 1929, PhD, 1934; m. Zdenka Kohn, June 26, 1927; c: Jochai, Michael. Head, dept horticulture, Agric Research Sta, Rehovot, since 1960, horticulturist, 1935-45, head, div pomology and viticulture, since 1945; asso prof, horticulture, Heb U since 1959, on fac since 1946. Mem: Isr Botanical Soc; Amer Soc Plant Physiologists; Amer Soc Horticultural Sci; Sigma Xi; club, Rotary. Contbr to sci publs. Home: 16 Ruppin St, Rehovot, Isr. Office: Volcani Inst Agric Research, Beit Dagon, POB 6, Rehovot, Isr; Fac of Agr, Heb U, Rehovot, Isr.

SAMISH, Zdenka, Isr, food technologist, educator; b. Prague, Czech, Mar 13, 1904; p. Otto and Wilma (Wurm) Cohen; in Isr since 1934; MS, U of Cal, Berkeley, 1933; m. Rudolf Samish, June 26, 1927; c: Jochai, Michael. Head, dept food tech, Agric Research Sta, Rehovot, since 1940; sr lectr, fac of agric, Heb U. Pres, Inst Food and Nutrition Scis, since 1958; mem: bd dirs, Consumers Assn of Isr; Standards Inst; Inst Food Technologists; Phi Tau Sigma; Sigma Xi, all US; Soroptimists Intl; Intl Org U Women. Contbr to profsl and sci publs. Home: 16 Ruppin St, Rehovot, Isr. Offices: Volcani Inst of Agric Research, Rehovot, Isr; Fac of Agric, Heb U, Rehovot, Isr.

SAMITZ, M H, US, physician, educator; b. Phila, Pa, Dec 18, 1909; s. Philip and Rachel (Rabinowitz); MD, Temble U Sch of Med, 1933; MSc, U of Pa Grad Sch of Med, 1945; m. Doris Rubin, 1945; c: Phyllis, Joel. Prof, dermat, U Pa Sch of Med; prof, dir dermat, Grad Div of Med, U Pa; visiting prof dermat: Hahnemann Med Coll; and cons in dermat, Pa Coll of Pod Med; chief, dept dermat, Grad Hosp, U Pa; med dir, Skin and Cancer Hosp, Phila, 1953-54. Capt, MC, US Army, 1942-44. F: Coll Phys, Phila; Amer Acad Dermat; Soc of Investigative Dermat; Amer Coll Allergists; FACP; AAAS; mem: Amer Inst Biol Sci; AAUP; Amer Soc Microbiol; Amer Inst Biol Sci; AAUP; Amer Soc Microbiol; Amer Ind Hygiene Assn; Bockus Alumni Intl Soc Gastroenterology; Intl Soc Tropical Dermat; Pan Amer Med Assn; Pa Allergy Soc; Phila Dermat Soc; corresp mem: Arg Dermat Assn; Uruguay Dermat Assn; Phila Acad Natural Sci; Franklin Inst. Author: chaps in med textbooks; contbr to med jours. Home: 1715 Pine St, Phildelphia, Pa. Office: Dunring Labs, U of Pa, Philadelphia, Pa.

SAMPLINER, Paul H, US, publisher; b. Cleveland, O, May 16, 1898; s. Philip and Gizella (Falter); att U of Pa, 1920; m. Jan 3, 1922; c: Philip, Joan Ben-Avi. Pres, Independent News Co, since 1932; treas, Natl Comics Publs Inc, since 1953, secy, 1946-53; bus mgr, Screenland Publishing Co, 1923; pres, E Distributing Corp, 1924-32. Maj, USAAF, 1942-44. Chmn, natl exec comm, ADL, since 1960, chmn, natl campaign cabinet, ADL Appeal; club, Harmonie. Home: 150 Central

Park S, New York, NY. Office: 909 Third Ave, New York, NY.

SAMPSON, Joseph S, India, communal worker; b. Bombey, India, Aug 28, 1899; s. Solomon and Rebecca (Hayeem); desc of Hayeem S Kehimkar, found Israelite HS; att: New Poona Coll, Poona, 1917-19; Elphinstone Coll, Bombay, 1920-21; m. Mary Payne, Dec 28, 1930; c: Regina, Sylvia, Juliet. Pres: Sir Elly Kadoorie Sch, 1954-56 and since 1960; J Coop Banking Soc, since 1959, fmr secy; vice-chmn, ORT, India, since 1960; treas, Bombay Zionist Assn, since 1958, fmr vice-pres; mem: Aliyah Comm, since 1958; comm, Cen J Bd, since 1947, fmr treas; fmr pres, Titareth Isr Syn. Capt, Indian Army, WW II. Recipient: 1939-45 medal, gen service medal; Burma Star; Victory Medal; AFI Efficiency Medal with Bar. Home: Khurshed Bldg, Wylie Rd, Bombay, India.

SAMSON, John Murray, Eng, solicitor; b. London, Apr 30, 1946; s. Sidney and Bessie (Zane); LLB, hons, King's Coll, London, 1967. Solicitor. Chmn, Fed Zionist Youth; London vice-pres, ZF, Gt Brit and Ir; hon vice-pres, Cen Young Zionist Soc, chmn, 1965-67; chmn, NW Hafinjan Young Zionists, 1962-64. Home: 96 Camlet Way, Hadley Wood, Hertfordshire, Eng.

SAMSON, Julius L, US, attorney; b. Detroit, Mich, Apr 22, 1911; s. Louis and Tillie (Klempner); att UCLA, 1928-31; BA, U of S Cal, 1933; JD, Southwestern U, Cal, 1936; m. Sylvia Crystal, July 3, 1941; c: Sharri Drori, Lee, Herschel, Rachel. Pvt practice since 1939; sr partner: Samson, Sternfeld, Goldwasser & Sisskind, 1958-62; Samson & Goldwasser, 1962-65. Pres: Beth Jacob Cong, Beverly Hills, Cal; Rel Zionists of Amer, LA Region; natl vice-pres, Union Orthodox Congs of Amer, fmr pres, Pacific Coast Region; bd dirs: Hillel Heb Acad; B'nai B'rith, Dist Grnad Lodge 4; mem: B'nai B'rith, fmr pres Boris D Bogen Lodge, fmr pres, S Cal Council; Amer Bar Assn; LA Co Bar Assn; fmr: pres, Camp Moshava; bd dirs, Rambam Torah Inst; regional dir, B'nai B'rith Youth Org; Dist Grand Aleph Godol, Aleph Zadik Aleph, B'nai B'rith; natl commn, B'nai B'rith Adult J Educ Commn. Recipient: man of year, Hillel Heb Acad, 1965. Home: 1441 Glenville, Los Angeles, Cal. Office: 7461 Beverly, Los Angeles, Cal.

SAMTER, Max, US, physician, educator; b. Berlin, Ger, March 3, 1908; s. Paul and Clair (Rawicz); in US since 1937; att: U Freiburg, Ger; U Innsbruck, Aus; MD, U Berlin, 1933; m. Virginia Svarz, Oct 17, 1947; c: Virginia. Prof, med, U of Ill Coll of Med, since 1961, mem fac since 1946; pvt med practice, Berlin, 1933-37; asst dispensary phys and research in hematology, Johns Hopkins Hosp, Baltimore, Md, 1937-38; guest f, anat, U of Pa, 1938-43. Capt, US Army MC, 1943-46. Dipl, Amer Bd Internal Med, fmr chmn, subspecialty bd allergy; pres, Intl Assn Allergology; fmr pres, Amer Acad Allergy; mem: AMA; Amer Coll Phys; Sigma Xi; Alpha Omega Alpha. Co-ed: Regional Allergy, 1954; Immunological Diseases, 1965. Home: 645 Sheridan Rd, Evanston, Ill. Office: U of Ill, Coll of Med, 840 S Wood St, PO Box 6998, Chicago, Ill.

SAMUEL, Coral Cynthia, Eng, civic worker; b. London, Eng, Aug 10, 1927; d. Albert and Frances (Singer) Julius; att Wokingham Co Girls Sch, Berks, 1940-46; m. Louis Fineman, Feb 3, 1948 (decd); c: Lynne, Peter. m. 2nd, Basil Samuel, Feb 20, 1962. Pres, Union of J Women; hon secy, Alice Model Nursery, Stepney; vice-pres, City of Westminster Soc for Mentally Handicapped Children; chmn, Frances House Nursery, 1964-67; treas, Guardee Comm, 1965-67. Hobbies: children, opera, music. Home: 49 Melbury Rd, London, W 14, Eng.

SAMUEL, David Herbert, Isr, chemist; b. Jerusalem, July 8, 1922; s. Edwin and Hadassah (Goor); grandson of Herbert Samuel, Ist Brit high commn, Pal; MA, Oxford, 1948; PhD, Heb U, 1953; m. Rinna Grossman, Dec 12, 1960; c: Judith, Naomi. Sherman Prof Phys Chem, Weizmann Inst of Sci, since 1967; research f: Harvard, 1957-58; U of Cal, 1965-66. Capt, Brit Army, 1942-46; IDF, 1948-49. Bd dirs: Isr Sci Tch Cen; Weizmann Sci Press; mem: Faraday Soc; Isr Chem Soc. Contbr articles on isotope chem, phosphorus and brain biochem. Home: Shikun Neve Weizmann, Rehovot, Isr. Office: Weizmann Inst of Sci, Rehovot, Isr.

SAMUEL, Edwin Herbert, 2nd Viscount of Mt Carmel and of Texteth, Liverpool, UK, lecturer, author; b. London, Eng, Sep 11, 1898; s. Herbert and Beatrice (Franklin); in Isr, with intermittence since 1917; BA, Balliol Coll, Oxford U, 1920; att Columbia U, NY, 1932-33; m. Hadassah Goor, Dec 6, 1920; c: David, Dan. Sr prin, Isr Inst of Public Admn, since 1945; dist off, Brit Mandatory Govt in Pal: Jerusalem, 1920-25; Ramallah, 1925-26; Jaffa, 1926-27; asst secy to High Commn, Pal, 1927-30; asst dist commn, Galilee, 1933-34; dep commn, immigration, 1934-39; postal and telegraph censor 1939-42, chief censor, 1942-45, press consor,1944-45; dir of Bc, 1945-48; lecr: Witwatersrand U, Johannesburg, 1953; Heb U, Jerusalem, 1953-69; visiting prof: ME govt, Dropsie Coll, Phila, Pa, 1948-49; political sci, SUNY, Albany, 1963; U Pittsburg, Pa, 1970; Eur dir, Conquest of the Desert exhb, Jerusalem, 1950-53. Lt, Royal Field Artillery, 1917-19; on Gen Staff intelligence, Pal, attached to Zionist Commn, 40th J Battalion, Royal Fusiliers. Pres, PATWA Assn, Gt Brit; mem: Lab Party, House of Lords, Gt Brit; council Anglo-Isr Assn, London; Friends Heb U, Gt Brit; Isr PM's Comm Soc Nomination Dir Ger; adv, PR and Publicity, Magen David Adom. Author: A Primer on Palestine, 1933; A Handbook of the Jewish Communal Villages, 1938, 2nd ed, 1945; The Theory of Administration, 1947, trans in Heb; Problems of Government in the State of Israel, 1956, in Span, 1957; British Traditions in the Administration of Israel, 1957; Structure of Society in Israel, 1969; Anglo-Israel Contacts 1948-68, pub 1969; collected short stories: A Cottage in Galilee, 1957; A Coat of Many Colours, 1960; My Friend Musa, 1963; The Cucumber King, 1965; His Celestial Highness, 1968; illustrated children story, Captain Noah and Hist Ark, 1965; ed: HaMinhal, Heb quarterly for public admnrs, 1950-60; Public Admn in Israel and Abroad, annual since 1960; mem: ed bd, Netivey Irgun ve-Minha, Heb bimonthly for admnrs; dir, London J Chronicle; contbr articles to J and non-J jours, in Isr, Gt Brit, S Afr, US. Recipient: Companion, Order of St Michael and St George. Home: 15 Rashba St, Jerusalem, Isr.

SAMUEL, Ester, Isr, educator; b. Oslo, Nor, May 16, 1933; d. Jitzhak and Henriette (Pollak); father was chief rabbi, Nor; in Isr since 1946; BA, Heb U, Jerusalem, 1958; MA, PhD Columbia U. Asso prof, stat, Heb U, since 1969, on fac since 1962. Mem: Inst Math Stat. Contbr to intl stat jours. Home: 3A Givat Beit Hakerem, Jerusalem, Isr. Office: Hebrew U, Jerusalem, Isr.

SAMUEL, Eva, Isr, ceramist, painter; b. Essen, Ger, Nov 26, 1904; d. Salomon and Anna (Friedlander); in Isr since 1932; att: Schs of Handicarfts, fine arts: Essen, Stuttgart; artists village, Woryswede; studied with sculptor, Will Lommert. Ceramist, pvt workshop, Rishon le Zion; Margaretenhohe, Essen, 1926-30; Hayotzer, Jerusalem, 1932; found, Kad vaSefel, Rishon le Zion, 1934. World exhbs: NY, Paris, Brussels, Milan; exhbs of paintings: Bezalel, Jerusalem, Tel Aviv Mus; represented in mus: Munich, Florence, Paris, Ein Harod, Haifa. Mem: Isr Painters, Sculptors, Isr Ceramic Artists Assns. Recipient: several prizes. Home: 17 Menashe Habilui St, Rishon le Zion, Isr. Studio: 9 Yudelevitz St, Rishon le Zion, Isr.

SAMUEL, Hadassah, viscountess, Isr, communal worker; b. Jaffa, June 6, 1896; d. Yehudah and Rachel (Neiman) Goor; grad, Women's Tchrs' Sem, Tel Aviv; att, U Geneva; m. Edwin Samuel, Dec 6, 1920; c: David, Dan. Chmn, WIZO, Isr, 1932-51; bd mem: Fr-Isr Assn; Mikveh Isr Agric Sch; Bezalel Mus; Brit Ivrit Olamit. Home: 15 Rashba St, Jerusalem, Isr.

SAMUEL, Howard D, US, union official; b. NYC, Nov 16, 1924; s. Ralph and Florence (Weingarten); BA, Dartmouth Coll, 1946; att Columbia U, 1948; m. Ruth Zamkin, Apr 15, 1948; c: Robert, Donald, William. Dir, Sidney Hillman Found, since 1951; vice-pres, Amalgamated Clothing Workers of Amer since 1966; fac mem, New Sch for Social Research. US Army, 1943-46. Vice-chmn, Westchester Co Dem Comm, chmn, White Plains Comm; bd dirs: ACLU; NY Urban Coalition; bd govs, Ethical Culture Schs; mem, Phi Beta Kappa. Co-author: Congress at Work. 1952; Government in America, 1957; ed, Toward a Better America, 1968. Home: 7 Sherman Ave, White Plains, NY. Office: 15 Union Sq, New York, NY.

SAMUEL, Jochanan, Isr, army officer, organization exec; b. Berlin, Ger, Feb 28, 1914; in Isr since 1938; att, U and Tchr's Inst, Berlin; IDF, Command and Staff Coll; m. Irma Seligmann; two c. Gen secy, Amer-Isr Cultural Found, since 1963; lt col, on staff and command posts, IDF, 1948-62. Co-found and mem, Ein Hod. Home: 3 Simtat Mazal Schor St, Tel Aviv, Isr.

SAMUEL, Maurice, US, author; b. Macin, Rum, Feb 8, 1895; s. Isaac and Fanny (Acker); in US since 1914; att Vic U, Manchester, Eng, 1911-14; m; c: Gershon, Eva. Author: You Gentiles, 1924; I, the Jew, 1926; What Happened in Palestine, 1929; On the Rim of the Wilderness, 1930; Jews on Approval, 1932; Beyond Woman, 1934; The Great Hatred, 1940; The World of Sholom Aleichem, 1943; Harvest in the Desert, 1944; Prince of the Ghetto, 1948; Web of Lucifer, 1949; The Gentlemen and the Jew, 1951; Level Sunlight, 1953; Certain People of the Book, 1955; The Professor and the Fossil, 1956; The Second Crucifixion, 1960; Little Did I Know; recollections and reflections, 1963; Blood Accusation, 1966; Light on Israel, 1968; transl works of Bialik, Sholem Asch, Shmarya Levin. Recipient: annual prize, Saturday Review, for the World of Sholom Aleichem, 1944; Stephen Wise award, 1956. Home: 515 West End Ave, New York, NY.

SAMUEL, Shellim, India, attorney, author; b. Bombay, India, Oct 8, 1922; s. Rahamim and Shegula (Samson); BA, hons, St Xavier's Coll, Bombay, 1942; LLB, Govt Law Coll, Bombay, 1944; MA, Sch of Econ and Sociol, Bombay, 1945. Advocate: in High Court, Bombay, since 1948; Supr Court of India, since 1955; prof, econ: Khalsa Coll, 1945-46; St, Xavier's Coll, 1946-55. Pres: Bombay Zionist Assn, since 1960, mem exec comm, since 1945; B'nai B'rith Lodge 2626; mem: exec comm, J Relief Assn, since 1955; PEN Guild of India; fmr pres, Sir Elly Kadoorie Sch. Author: Civics for the General Reader, 9th ed; Intermediate Economics; co-author, Principles of Economics; ed, Indo-Israel Review, since 1958. Spec interest: hist of Bene Isr of India. Home: Colaba Court, Flat 18, Colaba Rd, Bombay, India. Office: Bombay Mutual Chambers, 19/21 Hamam St, Fort, Bombay, India.

SAMUELS, Ernest, US, educator, biographer; b. Chgo, Ill, May 19, 1903; s. Albert and Mary (Kaplan); PhB, U Chgo, 1923, JD, Law Sch, 1926, MA Grad Sch, 1931, PhD, 1942; m. Jayne Porter Newcomer, Aug 24, 1938; c: Susanna, Jonathan, Elizabeth. Prof, Eng, Northwestern U, since 1954, chmn, Eng dept, 1964-66; atty, Samuels & Samuels, Chgo, 1933-37; instr, Eng, State Coll of Wash, 1937-39; Leo S Bing visiting prof, U of S Cal, 1966-67. Pres: Northwestern U Chap, AAUP, 1954-55; N Ill, Wis, chap, Amer Studies Assn, 1960-61; mem: Ill Comm of Scholars, State of Ill Bd of Higher Educ; MLA; ACLU, Amer Studies Assn, adv comm, Comm on Intl Exch of Persons, Wash DC, 1961-65; corresp mem, Mass Hist Soc. Author: The Young Henry Adams, 1948; Henry Adams: The Middle Years, 1958; Henry Adams, The Major Phase, 1964; mem, adv comm, publ; contbr lit publs; contrib ed, Major Writers of Amer. 1962; bd eds, Amer Lit Mag. Recipient: Guggenheim F, 1955-56; Fullbright Lectureship to Belgium, 1958-59; Bancroft prize, Columbia U; Francis Parkman prize, Soc of Amer Hist, 1959; Pulitzer prize, biography, 1965. Home: 3116 Park Pl, Evanston, Ill. Office: Northwestern U, Evanston, Ill.

SAMUELS, Gertrude, US, journalist, author, photographer; b. Manchester, Eng; d. Sam and Sarah (Benjamin); in US since 1922; att George Wash U, 1934-37; c: Paul. Staff writer, Sunday dept, NY Times, since 1943; staff writer-photographer, Sunday Mag, since 1947; ed staff: NY Post, 1937-41; Newsweek Mag, 1941-42; Time Mag, 1942-34; spec cons, UN Intl Children's Emergency Fund, 1948; war corresp: Korea, 1951: Six-Day War, 1967. Author: B-G, Fighter of Goliaths: The Story of David Ben Gurion, 1961; The People vs Baby, novel, 1967; The Corrupters, play, 1969; The Secret of Gonen, 1969. Mem: Amer Newspaper Guild; Authors League; Amer Soc Mag Photographers; UN Corresp Assn. Recipient: George Polk award, educ reporting, LIU; 2 Page One awards, Newspaper Guild, natl reporting; citation, Overseas Press Club. Office: 229 W 43 St, New York, NY.

SAMUELS, John Arnold, US, dentist; b. Toledo, O, July 6, 1912; s. Max and Libby (Rosenthal); DDS, Case W Reserve U, 1937; m. Miriam Wolf, Sep 22, 1938; c: Margaret Silver, Marshall, Alan. Instr, oral biol and med, Case W Reserve U, Cleveland, O, since 1965. Capt, US Army, Dent Corps, 1944-46. Pres, Cleveland Dent Soc; treas, Alumni Assn Sch of Dent, Case W Reserve U; mem: O Dent Assn; Alpha Omega, fmr natl pres; cofound, fmr chmn, policy bd, Heb U Sch of Dent. Hobbies: old cars, photography, gardening. Home: 23425 Bryden Rd, Shaker Heights, O. Office: 12429 Cedar Rd, Cleveland Heights, O.

SAMUELS, Martin, US, business exec; b. Bklyn, NY, July 2, 1924; s. Louis and Anna (Schneider); BBA, Pace Coll, NY, 1949; LLB, U Miami, 1954; n. Irene Stern; c: Richard, Law-

rence, Robert, David. Exec vice-pres, treas, Food Fair Stores, since 1967, admn asst to chmn bd, 1956-67; staff acctnt, Abbess, Morgan & Altemus, 1949-55; vice-pres, Norward Corp and Norgas Corp, 1955-56. Sgt, US Army, 1943-45. Mem: Amer Inst CPAs; Fla Inst CPAs. Recipient :Purple Heart. Home: 7721 SW 134 Terr, Miami, Fla. Office: 8101 Biscayne Blvd, Miami, Fla.

SAMUELS, Samuel, US, educator; b. Boston, Mass, Aug 16, 1908; s. Nathan and Sophia (Mannos); AB, Harvard U, 1929; MEd, Boston U, 1951; m. Jennie Samuels, Dec 27, 1936; c: James. Dir, guidance, schs, Revere ,Mass, since 1954, tchr, 1936-54. Cdr, USNR, 1944-66. Mem, exec bd, Revere Tchrs Assn, since 1965; bd dirs, Cong Tifereth Isr, 1962-65; pres, Adult Educ Assn, 1963-65; fmr natl cdr, natl exec committeeman, JWV, led JWV Convocation to Isr, 1968; mem: VFW; Amvets; Brotherhood Syns. Hobbies: working with youth groups. Home: 14 Wilson St, Revere, Mass. Office: 153 Beach St, Revere, Mass.

SANDBERG, Hannah, US, artist; b. Safad, Pal; studied with Benjamin Yair, Joseph Zaritzky; m. Mordecai Sandberg; c: Abraham, Judith, Joseph, Michael. One-man shows: Lynne Kottler Gals, NY, 1956; NY Public Libr, 1957; Educ Alliance, 1961; group show, John J Meyers Gal, 1963; exhb, 18 paintings from Book of Psalms, JTSA, 1967. Home: 865 Columbus Ave, New York, NY.

SANDBERG, Moshe, Isr, business exec; b. Kecskemet, Hung, Mar 29, 1926; s. Shlomo and Miriam; in Isr since 1948; MA, Heb U; m. Bracha Rabinovitch, Nov 1, 1951; c: Shlomit, Nava. Vice-chmn, Ind Devl Bank of Isr; chmn: IDBI Inves Corp; Deco Inves Corp; dep chmn, Isr Corp, all since 1968; bd dirs: El Al Airlines, since 1966; Inst for Planning and Devl, since 1966; dep dir, Internal Revenue, Govt of Isr, 1958-63, dir, budgets, 1964-68; econ adv, Min of Finance, 1963-68. Chmn, Found for Gifted Sportsmen; council mem, Yad Vashem; exec bd, Technion; dep exec, Inst of Applied Social Research, 1951-58; mem, Econ Research for Social Sci. Author: My Longest Year, 1968. Home: 11 Tiapust St, Tel Aviv, Isr. Office: 9 Ahad Haait St, Tel Aviv, Isr.

SANDERS, Albert Zu Kalna, US, engineer, industrialist; b. NYC, May 25, 1920; s. Benjamin and Frances (Adelson) Zu Kalna; BS, Columbia Sch Engr, 1941; m. Edith Steinberg, 1951; c: James, Avis. Pres, Allen-Stevens Corp, since 1946. Lt, USAAC, 1944. Prin contrib: devl of efficient die casting machinery. Contbr to tech sours. Home: 501 E 87 St, New York, NY. Office: 33-53 62 St, Woodside, NY.

SANDERS, Ira E, US, rabbi; b. Rich Hill, Mo, May 6, 1894; s. Daniel and Pauline (Ackerman); BA, U Cincinnati, 1918; ordained rabbi, HUC, 1919, hon DD, 1954; MA, Columbia U, 1928; LHD, U Ark, 1951; m. Selma Loeb, 1922; c: Fora. Ret; rabbi: Cong B'nai Isr, Little Rock, Ark, 1926-63; Cong Knesseth Isr, Allentwon, Pa, 1919-24; Temple Isr, NY, 1924-26; instr, sociol, U Ark, 1927-43. Pres: Little Rock Public Libr, 1947, mem, bd trustees, since 1930; Ark Lighthouse for the Blind, since 1941; and org, Planned Parenthood Assn of Ark; Human Betterment League, since 1941; Council of Social Agcys, Little Rock, 1927-29; and found, Little Rock Sch of Social Work, 1927-33; and found, Ark J Assembly, 1931; and org, JWF; Urban League, 1939, both of Little Rock; SW Assembly Rel Sch Tchrs, 1937; FJP, 1932; chmn and org, Pulaski Co Public Wfr Commn, 1933; Gov's Commn for DP's 1946; co-found, Assn J Rel Sch Tchrs of E Pa; treas, Ark TB Assn, since 1927; secy, HUC Alumni Assn, 1926-41; mem: exec bd, UAHC, 1949-53; mem, Natl TB Assn; CCAR; club, Rotary. Recipient: testimonial during Brotherhood Week, Rotary Club, 1951. Home: 4623 Crestwood Dr, Little Rock, Ark.

SANDGROUND, Jack H, US, educator, researcher; b. Johannesburg, S Afr, Feb 2, 1899; s. Charles and Sarah (Freeder); in US since 1922; MS, U of S Afr, 1920; DS, Johns Hopkins U, 1925; m. Rose Plotler, Nov 2, 1929; c: Mark. Ret; research asso, Haskins Labs 1957-70; Webb scholar, U of S Afr, 1922-25; curator, Mus Comparative Zool, Harvard U. 1927-37; asso prof, microbiol, Harvard Med Sch, 1925-38; f, Guggenheim Found, 1938-39; chief, tropical research lab, Eli Lilly & Co, 1939-47; parasitologist, cons, Bellevue Hosp, NYC, 1947-53; visiting prof, zool, Dartmouth Coll, 1952-53; asso prof, microbiol, NY Med Coll, 1954-57. Mem: Amer Soc Tropical Med; Amer Soc Protozoologists; Soc for Experimental Biol and Med. Contbr to profsl jours. Home: 2030 Sgate St, Santa Barbara, Cal.

SANDGROUND, Mark B, US, attorney; b. Brookline, Mass, June 6, 1932; s. Jack and Rose (Plotler); BA, U Mich, 1952; LLB, U Va, 1955; m. Marcia Gurevich, June 20, 1959. Spec counsel, US Sen Antitrust Comm, since 1952; gen counsel, Warrant Off Assn, USCG; law clerk, State Dept, NY, 1954; spec asst to Atty Gen, Justice Dept, 1955-56; lectr: law, Amer U Sch of Law, 1959, E Psychoanalytic Assn. Dir: Friends Corcoran Art Gal, pres, 1968-69; Canterbury Sch; secy, comm on Ethics and Grievance, DC Bar Assn; pres, Wash chap, U Mich Alumni Assn, mem bd of dirs; fmr pres, John Bassett Moore Soc on Intl Law; clubs: Natl Press; Capitol Hill. Contbr to law reviews. Home: 3508 Sterling Ave, Alexandria, Va. Office: 944 Washington Bldg, Washington, DC.

SANDMEL, Samuel, US, educator, author; b. Dayton, O, Sep 23, 1911; s. Morris and Rebecca (Lenderman); BA, Mo U, 1932; ordained rabbi, HUC, 1937; PhD, Yale U, 1949; m. Frances Fox, June 23, 1940; c: Charles, Benjamin, David. Prof, Bible and Hellenistic lit, HUC, since 1952, provost, 1957-66; rabbi, Heb Benevolent Cong, Atlanta, 1937-39; prof, J lit and thought, Vanderbilt U, 1949-52. Chaplain, USN, 1942-46. Author: Philo's Place in Judaism, 1956; A Jewish Understanding of the New Testament, 1957; The Genius of Paul, 1958; The Hebrew Scriptures, 1963, 1968; We Jews and Jesus, 1965; Herod: Profile of a Tyrant, 1967; We Jews and You Christians: An Inquiry into Attitudes, 1967; ed: Old Testament Issues, 1968; First Christian Century in Judaism and Christianity, 1969; contbr to rel jours. Mem: Soc Bibl Lit; Amer Schs Oriental Research; Amer Oriental Soc; club, Shamus. Recipient: Pres f, Brown U, 1951. Hobbies: music, theater. Home: 3875 Clifton Ave, Cincinnati, O. Office: 3101 Clifton Ave, Cincinnati, O.

SANDROW, Edward T, US, rabbi; b. Phila, Pa, Dec 23, 1906; s. Nahum and Molly (Cohen); BA, U of Pa, 1929; ordained rabbi, JTSA, 1933, DHL, 1952, DD, 1962; MA, Colombia U, 1940; m. Miriam Slavin, 1933; c: Nahma. Rabbi, Temple Beth El, Cedarhurst, LI, since 1937; visiting prof, pastoral psycht, JTSA, since 1964, homiletics, 1954-56, 1962-63, adj prof, Tchrs Inst, f, Lehman Inst of Ethics; rabbi, Neveh Shalom, Portland, Ore, 1933-37; teaching f, NYU, 1948-52; lectr, radio series, The Living Word, 1953. Chaplain, US Army, 1942-46; fmr, maj, US Army Res. Chmn, bd govs, NY Bd Rabbis, since 1968, pres, 1966-68; fmr pres: RA; Intl Org Conservative Rabbis; found, fmr pres, JCC, Five Towns and Rockaway; chmn: Chaplaincy Comm, JWB, since 1968; Bd of Educ, Brandeis J Day Sch; fmr vice-pres, J Chaplains Assn; mem, bd govs, Amer Assn J Educ; mem, bd overseers, JTSA; mem, bd dirs: JTA; Amer Friends Heb U; Five Towns Comty Chest; Natl JWF; Five Towns United Fund; natl council, JDC; Histadrut Cultural Exch Comm; mem, exec comm, Five Towns Comty Council, found, fmr pres, group relations comm; mem: NY State Comm, 1960 White House Conf on Children and Youth; Natl Council for J Educ; NY Conf of Social Work; functional comm, FJP, Gtr NY; exec comm, natl exec council, ZOA; rabbis' natl adv council, UJA, since 1960; exec bd, J Comty Services of LI; planning and coord bd, Assn for Aid of Crippled Children; spec comm on housing, NY State Commn Against Discrimination; exec comm, Nassau Co Mh Assn; Amer Acad J Research; AAAS; Amer Assn for Pol and Social Sci; Phi Delta Kappa; Acad of Rel and Mh; exec comm, Nassau Heart Assn; club, Woodmere Country. Co-author: Young Faith, 1956; Judaism and Psychiatry, 1956; chmn, bd dirs, Hadoar; contbr to jours. Recipient: first annual Cumming award, FJP, Gtr NY, 1961; natl service award, JTSA, 1965. Home:Broadway and Woodlane, Woodmere, NY. Study: Temple Beth El, Cedarhurst, NY.

SANES, Samuel, US, physician, educator; b. Rochester, NY, June 26, 1906; s. Joseph and Esther (Gottlieb); BA, U Buffalo, 1928, MD, 1930. Prof, path, U Buffalo Med Sch, prof, legal med, 1954-66, on fac since 1968; moderator, Med Round Table Broadcasts, WBEN Radio and TV, since 1952; res, path, Buffalo Gen Hosp, 1931-34, asst path, 1934-41, asso path, 1935-52; path and dir, labs, Niagara Falls Memorial Hosp, 1939-40; asso path, Buffalo Children's Hosp, 1935-42; path, Buffalo Emergency Hosp, 1941-42; asso path and exec dir, E J Meyer Memorial Hosp, 1942-46, dir, path, 1946-61; dir, path, Erie Co Lab, 1946-54; Erie Co path and deputy med examiner, 1946-61; lab cons, Buffalo Police Dept, since 1946; cons path: Millard Fillmore Hosp, since 1946; De-Graff Memorial Hosp, N Tonawanda, NY, 1942; Brooks Memorial Hosp, Dunkirk, NY, 1950; US Vets Hosp, Batavia, NY, 1946-50, Buffalo, since 1959; coord, U Buffalo modern

med series broadcasts, WBEN-TV, 1953-56. Dipl, Amer Bd Path; pres: NY State div, Amer Cancer Soc, 1966-67, Erie Co chap, 1948-50, 1960-62; W NY sect, NY Soc Paths, 1959, 1964; NY State sect, JWB, since 1958; Med Union, 1954-55; Erie Co Medico-Legal Forum, 1953-56; Erie Co Med Soc, 1952-53; NY State Assn Public Health Labs, 1954; Buffalo J Cen 1956-58; chmn, sect path, NY State Med Soc, 1953-54, legal med, 1956-57; mem, bd govs, United J Fed, Buffalo, 1955-58; mem, bd dirs: Erie Co Visiting Nurses Assn, 1952-53; ZOA, Buffalo, 1955-61; mem: Coll Amer Paths; Western NY Soc Paths; subcomm, phys-comty relationships, Natl Commn of Chronic Illness, 1953-54; AMA, AAAS; Amer Assn Paths and Bacts; Amer Acad of Forensic Scis; Amer Soc Clinical Paths; Amer Soc Parasitologists; Intl Acad Path; Buffalo Acad Med; Maimonides Med Soc; bd regional advs, ADL, 1955-56; Sigma Xi; Alpha Omega Alpha. Contbr to prof jours. Recipient: outstanding citizen award, Buffalo Evening News, 1953; deans award for contrib to teaching, U Buffalo Med Sch, 1963, sr students' awards for teaching, 1963, 1967. Home: 246 Brantwood Rd, Eggertsville, NY. Office: Millard Fillmore Hosp, Buffalo, NY.

SANGER, Eleanor N, US, radio exec; b. NYC, Sept 20, 1900; d. Edward and Lotta (Tachau) Naumburg; att Ethical Culture Tchr Training Sch, 1916-19; m. Elliott Sanger, Feb 8, 1921; c: Elliott, Kenneth. Ret; program cons, radio sta, since 1961, gen asst, 1936-42, program dir, 1942-61; tchr, Ethical Culture Sch, 1920-21. Mem, bd dirs: Naumburg Orchestral Concerts; club, Womens City, treas, 1958-60. Recipient: one of 30 women honored for exceptional contribs to life of NYC, 1946. Hobbies: art, painting, music. Home: 75 Central Park W, New York, NY.

SANGER, Elliott M, US, radio exec; b. NYC, Mar 2, 1897; s. Isaac and Frances (Meyers); B Litt, Sch of Journalism, Columbia U, 1917; m. Eleanor Naumburg, Feb 8, 1921; c: Elliott, Kenneth. Mem, bd dirs, Interstate Bc Co, subsidiary of the NY Times, Sta WQXR, since 1944, co-founder, WQXR, 1936; in field publicity and advt, 1918-36. Contbr to jours. Recipient: award, outstanding achievement in journalism, Alumni Assn Sch of Journalism, Columbia U, 1952. Home: 75 Central Park W, New York, NY.

SANGER, Morton H, US, business exec; b. Dallas, Tex, Oct 17, 1904; s. Asher and Stella (Hochstadter); BS, U of Pa, 1925; m. Hortense Landauer, Oct 15, 1934; c: Anne, Mary, John. Vice-pres, EM Kahn & Co, since 1926. Pres, JWF, 1952-54; dir: Comty Chest, 1951; Salvation Army, 1953; pres, J Family Service, 1968-69. clubs: Columbian, pres, 1941; Downtown; Salesmanship. Home: 5923 Averill Way, Dallas, Tex. Office: EM Kahn & Co, Dallas, Tex.

SANHEDRAI, Tova, Isr, legislator; b. Tarnopol, Pol, Sep 23, 1906; d. Salamon and Esther (Gluckman) Diamand; in Isr since 1934; att Heb Tchrs Coll, Tarnopol, 1924-28; m. Israel Sanhedrai, 1938; c: Uri. MK since 1959, vice chmn: Knesset, since 1963; United Natl Rel Org, since 1960; mem exec comm, Hapoel Hamizrachi,since 1950; mem, Natl Assembly, 1944-49. Co-found, chmn, Women's Workers Org, 1934-50; found, Fed of Hapoel Hamizrachi Women, US, Can; delg: 19th; 24th ZCs; chmn, Isr Social Wfr Assn; mem, Zionist Exec; head, Isr delg, Intl Conf of Social Services, Rome, 1961. Contbr to jours; lectr, Kol Isr radio. Home: 43 Louis Marshall St, Tel Aviv, Isr. Office: The Knesset, Jerusalem, Isr.

SAPEIKA, Norman, S Afr, pharmacologist, educator; b. Oudtshoorn, Cape Province, Jan 17, 1909; s. Raphael and Leah (Klass); BA, 1928; MB, ChB, hons, 1932; PhD, 1935; MD, 1950; m. Simone Silverberg, 1943; c: Raphael, Karin, David. Prof, pharm, U Cape Town, since 1965, asso prof, 1956-65; external examiner to Pretoria U, since 1946. Treas, mem council, Royal Soc of S Afr, since 1951, f, since 1944; mem: regional council, S Afr Red Cross Soc; Bd J Deps; Friends Heb U; IMA. Author: Actions and Uses of Drugs, 8th ed; Food Pharmacology, monograph; co-author, Xenopus Laevis: a Bibliography; contbr to local, fgn publs. Hobbies: carpentry, mt rambling. Home: 21 Oakhurst Ave, Rondebosch, S Afr. Office: U Cape Town, Med Sch, Cape Town, S Afr.

SAPERSTEIN, Harold I, US, rabbi; b. Troy, NY, Dec 9, 1910; s. David and Rose (Lasker): BA Cornell U, 1931; MHL, DD, HUC-JIR, 1935; att Columbia U, NYU; m. Marcia Rosenblum, Dec 22, 1940; c: Marc, David. Rabbi, Temple Emanuel, Lynbrook, NY, since 1933. Vice-pres: NY Bd Rabbis; Amer Bd World Union for Progressive Judaism, mem governing body; mem: Syn Council of Amer; rabb adv comm, ORT;

inter-rel comm, ADL; fmr pres, Assn Reform Rabbis NY; chmn, Comm on Isr Projects, CCAR; bd govs, HUC-JIR. Home: 170 Hempstead Ave, Malverne, NY. Study: Ross Plaza, Lynbrook, NY.

SAPERSTEIN, Nathan, US, attorney; b. NYC; att NYU; LLB, Bklyn Law Sch; m. Mary; c: Louis, Diana Wolf, Sandy. Pvt practice since 1930; bd dirs: E Coast Ins Co; Eagle Ins Co. Pres, Natl Council Young Isr; vice-pres, syn commn, FJP; bd dirs: Yeshiva of Cen Queens; Lake Peekskill Temple Isr; found, Young Isr of Kew Garden Hills; mem: Mizrachi-Hapoel Hamizrachi; KP. Office: 3 W 16 St, New York, NY.

SAPERSTON, Alfred M, US, attorney; b. Buffalo, NY, Apr 7, 1898; s. Willard and Julia (Wolfson); LLB, Cornell U, 1919; m. Josephine Lee, Nov 24, 1924, c: Frances Klingenstein, Lee. Partner, law firm, Saperston, Wiltse, Duke, Day and Wilson, fmr Saperston, McNaughton & Saperston, since 1921; dir, Mfrs and Traders Trust Co, Buffalo. Flier, USMC, WW I. Natl chmn, Cornell Fund, mem admn bd, Cornell U Council; vice-pres, dir: City of Buffalo Planning Assn; Children's Aid Soc for Prevention of Cruelty to Children; dir: Arthritis and Rheumatism Found; Cornell U Bar Co chap; Cornell Alumni Assn, fmr pres; Western NY Educ TV Corp; and fmr pres, Children's Aid Soc, Erie Co; United Fund, Buffalo and Erie Co; NCCJ; trustee, mem exec comm, Cornell U Bd Trustees; mem: Cornell U Law Sch Council; exec, C of C, fmr dir; mem exec: Erie Co Adoption Bur; Niagara Frontier chap, AJComm; natl council: Jt Defense Appeal; JDC; mem: Amer, NY, Erie Co Bar Assns; Marine Corps League; Amer Legion; Amer Law Inst; Temple Beth Zion, fmr pres, Men's Club; fmr: chmn, first UJA dr, Buffalo; natl judge advocate; dir: Cancer Soc, Buffalo chap; Munic Research Bur; Epilepsy League; pres: United J Fed, Buffalo; Comty Wfr Council, Erie Co; Cornell U Law Assn; Fed Cornell U Men's Clubs of US; clubs: Buffalo; Mid-Day; Marshall; fmr pres: Cornell, Buffalo, NY; Gtr Buffalo Ad; Westwood Country; Lawyers of Buffalo. Home: 85 Nottingham Terr, Buffalo, NY. Office: 815 Liberty Bank Bldg, Buffalo, NY.

SAPERSTON, Howard T, US, attorney; b. Buffalo, NY, Oct 30, 1899; s. Willard and Julia (Wilson); att: Cornell U, 1917-18; LLB, Syracuse U,1921; m. Nan Basch, Oct 6, 1937; c: Howard, Willard. Partner, law firm, Saperston, Wiltse, Duke, Day and Wilson, and predecessor firms, since 1922; mem, bd dirs, Bank of Buffalo, since 1951; mem, adv bd, Transcontinent TV Corp, 1958-64. Pres: Temple Beth Zion, 1953-55; Comty Volunteer Service Bur, 1942-44; United Fund, Buffalo and Erie Co, 1956-57, dir, trustee; United J Fed, Buffalo, 1952-54; vice-pres: Federated Health Fund, Buffalo and Erie Co, 1951; CJFWF for NY and Ont, 1952-54; United Health Found, Western NY; Buffalo area council, Boy Scouts, mem bd dirs: Buffalo Gen Hosp; chmn: council, U Buffalo, 1958-65; West NY region, JDA, 1950-54; United Negro Coll Fund, 1950; Comty Chest-Red Cross Appeal, 1955; annual dinner, 1959; vice-chmn, civic comm, 125th anniversary, Buffalo, 1958; asso chmn, special gifts, U Buffalo campaign, 1958, 1959; mem, bd regents, Canisius Coll; mem, bd: Western NY, ADL; Buffalo Urban League; ARC; Buffalo J Cen, 1940-44; mem, bd visitors, Syracuse U Coll of Law; mem: Grosvenor Soc; Albright-Knox Art Gal; Buffalo Soc Natural Scis; NY State, Erie Co Bar Assns; Amer Judicature Soc; adv bd, Cerebral Palsy Assn, Western NY; adv bd, Camp Lakeland; Western NY regional bd, ADL; natl council, Joint Defense Appeal; natl council, United HIAS Service; JDC; Amer Legion; Buffalo C of C; Buffalo Hist Soc; Buffalo Pub Libr; Buffalo Fine Arts Acad; Masons; Shriners; clubs: Buffalo; Buffalo Athletic; Westwood Country; Automobile; Palm Beach Natl Golf and Country; Cornell Buffalo; Buffalo Lawyers; Marshall; Buffalo, Advt, fmr secy, bd mem. Recipient: outstanding citizen award, Buffalo Evening News, 1955; Brotherhood award, NCCJ, 1956; Pres Med, Canisius College, 1963; Silver Beaver Award, Boy Scouts of Amer, 1954; natl award, NCCJ, 1966; Dist Citizens Achievement Award, 1968. Hobbies: golf, tennis, travel. Home: 226 Depew Ave, Buffalo, NY. Office: 815 Liberty Bank Bldg, Buffalo, NY.

SAPINSLEY, John, US, business exec, educator; b. Providence, RI, Apr 10, 1922; s. Milton and Elsa (Schwed); BA, magna cum laude, Brown U, 1942; m. Lila Manfield, Dec 23, 1942; c: Jill, Carol, Joan, Patricia. Dir, Providence Mutual Fire Ins Co, since 1958; bd incorporators, Citizens Trust Co, since 1962; teaching asst, econ, Brown U, since 1968; pres, Carol Wire & Cable Corp, 1952-64. Lt ,USN, 1942-45. Dir: Pawtucket Comty Fund, since 1952; Miriam Hosp, since 1950;

Temple Beth-El, since 1951; J Comty Cen, 1950-53; Brotherhood Temple Beth-El, since 1947; AJComm, Providence, since 1951; Pawtucket YMCA since 1952; Narragansett Council Boy Scouts, since 1953; Big Brother Movement, since 1953; Jr Achievement, since 1953; commn, RI Commn Higher Educ, since 1964; prog dir, RI Council Econ Educ, 1968; natl council, Jt Defense Appeal, since 1952; mem, Phi Beta Kappa; club, Ledgemont Country. Home: 25 Cooke St, Providence, RI.

SAPIR, Boris, Holland, historian; b. Lodz, Pol, Feb 24, 1902; s. Moses and Anna (Gozhanski); JUD, U Heidelberg, Ger, 1932; m. Berti MacDonald, July 9, 1948; c: Leo, Anna. Mem, Inter-U Project on Hist of Menshevik Movement, since 1959; sr f, Intl Research Inst of Social Hist, since 1967; dir, research dept, JDC, 1948-66; dir: Russ dept, Intl Inst of Social Hist, Amsterdam, Holland, 1936-40; project on hist J Comty in Cuba, 1941-44. Mem: Atcan Found, NY; Amer Hist Assn; fmr mem exec comm, Intl, Socialist Youth, Belgium; secy, gov body, Russ Social Dem Party, 1944-52. Author: Dostojewsky und Tolstoi über Probleme des Rechts, 1932; Marx gegen Hitler, 1934; Liberman et le Socialisme Russe, 1938; The Jewish Community of Cuba, 1948; Vpered. 1873-1877—Founding Activities-Liquidation, 1969; co-ed, Against the Current, 1952-54; contbr to intl publs. Home: Rondom Zon, Noolseweg 65, Blaricum, Holland. Office: Keizersgracht 264, Amsterdam, Holland.

SAPIR, Pinchas, Isr, politician; b. Suvalki, Pol, 1909; s. Mordechai and Tova Koslowski; in Isr since 1929; m. Shoshana Gibvanski, 1931; c: Rina Tal, Amos, Tzfira Holtzman. Min finance, since 1969; asst dir, dir Mekorot, 1937-47; dir gen, Min of Defense, dir gen, Treasury, 1947-55; min commerce and ind, 1955-63, min finance, commerce and ind, 1963-65; min finance, 1965-68. Secy gen, Isr Lab Party, 1968-69. Home: 9 Arlozorov, Kfar Saba, Isr. Office: Min of Finance, Hakirya, Jerusalem, Isr.

SAPIRSTEIN, Milton R, US, psychiatrist; b. NYC, Nov 30, 1914; s. Isidore and Fanny (Berkowitz); BS, CCNY, 1934; MD, NYU Coll of Med, 1938; cert, Psychoanalytic Clinic for Training and Research, Columbia U, 1948; m. Lillian Brizel, Dec 27, 1937; c: Frederic, Victor. Head, div org psycht, Mt Sinai Hosp, since 1958, head, div comty psycht, since 1966; prof, clinical psycht, Mt Sinai Med Sch, since 1966, fac mem since 1942; asso att psycht, Psychoanalytic Clinic for Training and Research, Columbia U, since 1948; f, neurophys, Yale U, 1939; res psycht, Hillside Hosp, 1941-42; instr, pharm, NYU Coll of Med, 1942-43; sr cons, psycht, Bx Vets Hosp, 1952-56. Chmn, comm on devl, Amer J Phys Comm, since 1960; mem: Amer Psychoanalytic Assn; Amer Psychoanalytic Soc; Amer Acad Neur; NY Co Med Soc; NY Neur Soc; Assn for Psychoanalytic Med; club, N Shore Country. Author: Problems of Emotional Security, 1949; Paradoxes of Everyday Life, 1955; contbr to profsl jours. Home: 983 Park Ave, New York, NY. Office: 110 E 87 St, New York, NY.

SAPOWITCH, Joseph, A, US, merchant; b. Buffalo, NY, Jan 1, 1893; s. Harris and Masha (Friedland). m. Jeanette Strauss, May 29, 1922 (decd); c: Leonore Glauber, Miriam Schiff. Pres: S Side Furniture Co; Seneca Cazenovia Parking Corp. Pres: Kadimah Day Sch; Cong Beth Abraham; hon pres, Bur for J Educ; vice-pres, Amer Assn for J Educ; mem: bd trustees, Temple Beth Zion; bd govs, Fed J Social Service; bd trustees, org, Perseverance Lodge 946, Masons, fmr master, Buffalo; UJA; fmr: pres, S Buffalo Bus Men's Assn; org, first secy Zionist Dist; clubs: S Buffalo Lions, dir; Montefiore. Recipient: citation for 20 years service, Amer Assn J Educ. Hobbies: music, golf. Home: 110 Chatham Ave, Buffalo, NY. Office: 2196 Seneca St, Buffalo, NY.

SARACHAN, Goodman A, US, attorney; b. Russ, Sep 30, 1898; s. Harry and Sara (Gordon); in US since 1904; BA, U Rochester, 1918; LLB, Harvard Law Sch, 1921; m. Evelyn Simon, Mar 9, 1930; c: Donna Lawrence, Niki Singer, Richard. NY State Commn Investigation, since 1958, acting chmn; arbitrator, NY State Bd Mediation, since 1956; exec asst, Congressman Meyer Jacobstein, 1923-29; counsel and research dir, Monroe Co Govt Revision Commn, 1934-35; first asst, US atty, W Dist NY, 1935-45; Judge, Supr Court, NY State, 1955. USNR, 1918-22. Mem, natl bd, Amer Friends Heb U, since 1950; chmn, scholarship comm, Iota chap, Phi Beta Kappa, since 1953, fmr, mem exec bd, pres; mem: bd trustees, Bur J Educ, Rochester, since 1945, fmr pres; finance comm, Phi Epsilon Pi, fmr natl vice-pres; Amer, NY State,

Monroe Co Bar Assns; Rochester Civic Music Assn; Rochester Mus of Arts and Scis; Memorial Art Gal of Rochester; fmr mem: bd mgrs and exec comm, U Rochester Alumni Assn; bd trustees: Temple Beth El; Temple Brith Kodesh, Rochester, NY; bd dirs, J Young Men's and Women's Assn, Rochester; club, Harvard, Rochester. Contbr to legal jours. Home: 87 Maybrooke Rd, Rochester, NY. Office: Executive Bldg, 36 Main St, W Rochester, NY.

SARACHAN, Herman A, US, organization exec; b. Vilna, Russ, Sep 14, 1894; s. Aaron and Sara (Gordon); in US since 1903; BS, U Rochester; MS, Cornell U, 1923; m. Emma Alderman, 1921; c: Morton. Ret; asst dir, YMHA, Rochester, NY, 1945-65, dir, men's dormitories, 1936-45; instr, mech engr: Cornell U, 1919-21; U Rochester, 1921-23; off mgr, Hickey-Freeman Clothing Co, 1923-26, purchasing agt, 1926-35. Mem: Natl Assn J Cen Workers; Amer Assn Group Workers; Acad Certified Social Workers; J Home for Aged; Rochester Consistory; Shriners; comm on libr and mus, asst grand lectr, i/c sch of ritual, Masons, fmr dist dep grand master, fmr mem grand lodge comm on relief and unemployment, fmr pres, Masonic Service Bur; fmr: pres, JNF Council; secy, ZOA; dept scout commn; clubs: City; Group Workers. Author: Campaigning For Members, 1949; History of Masonry in Monroe County, 1959; ed, Damascus News-Monthly Shrine News Mag; contbr to Masonic jours. Recipient: Dist Masonic Service award, 1958; hon 33rd deg Mason, 1961. Hobbies: violin, choral music. Home: 46 Gorham St, Rochester, NY. Office: Masonic Temple, 875 Main St E, Rochester, NY.

SARASOHN, Israel J, US, rabbi; b. Vilna, Lith, Dec 15, 1891; s. Raphael and Bessie (Silver); in US since 1893; BA, cum laude, Clark U, Worcester, Mass, 1912; MA, U Cincinnati, 1914; ordained Rabbi, HUC, 1916. Chaplain, NC Home for J Aged, Winston-Salem, NC; rabbi Leavenworth, Kan, chaplain, Fed Insts, 1925-42; JWB repr, 1925-42; chaplain, Amer Legion Post, 1938-42; rabbi: Temple Moses Montefiore, Marshall, Tex, 1946-52; Temple Beth El, Corsicana, Tex, 1952-56; Temple Oheb Shalom, Goldsboro, 1956-61, Em, 1961; lectr, NCCJ, Tex; J Chautauqua lectr, 1962; fmr, rabbi, Temple Beth-El, Rocky Mount, NC. Chaplain, US Army, 1918-19. Dir: Rocky Mount Mh Assn; Mid-Atlantic Assn Reform Rabbis; NC Assn Rabbis; mem: Assn J Chaplains; CCAR; Amer Legion; C of C, Rocky Mount; Alumni Assn, HUC-JIR; B'nai B'rith, fmr lodge pres; AJComm; Mil Chaplains Assn, fmr: pres, Min's Assn; dir, Harrison Co Red Cross Chap, Marshall Tex; Corsicana secy, J Fed; pres, Kallah of Tex Rabbis; chaplain, Amer Legion Higgins Post, Corsicana; club, Rotary. Recipient: award as chmn profsl div, United Fund Campaign, 1959; citation, JWB, 1962. Home and study: NC Home for J Aged, Winston Salem, NC.

SAREL, Shalom, Isr, chemist, educator; b. Jerusalem, Oct 25, 1918; s. Moshe and Miriam (Ashvili); MSc, Heb U, Jerusalem, 1942, PhD, 1946; m. Meira Imber, Sep 9, 1947; c: Miriam, Dan, Tal. Head, dept pharmaceutical chem, Heb U, Jerusalem, since 1956, prof since 1964, on fac since 1955; research asso, O State U, 1952-54; guest research prof, Mich State U, 1965-66; guest lectr: intl symposium, Belgium, Switz, Isr, Eng, Ir; Eur and Amer Us. Group leader, sci sect, IDF, 1947-49. Prin contribs: alfa-lactam chem; synthesis of cardenolides and bufadienolides; vinyl-cyllopropane chem; cyclic carbonates and sulfites. Author: Identification and Characterization of Organic Compounds, 1947; mem, ed bd, Isr Jour of Chem; contbr to profsl jours. Fmr pres, Isr Chem Soc; mem: Amer Chem Soc; Chem Soc, London; Soc Chem de Fr; Swiss Chem Soc; Isr Chem Soc; AAAS. Home: 36 Jabotinsky St, Jerusalem, Isr. Office: Heb U, Jerusalem, Isr.

SARFATIS, David, Greece, physician; b. Athens, Greece, Nov 30, 1920; s. Mark and Eugene (De Kalo); MD, U Athens, 1942; deg, hygienist, Athens Sch of Hygiene, 1951; m. Gina Asseo, July, 1945; c: Eugene. Dir, Min Social Services, since 1950, dir, various divs of min throughout Greece, 1950-60. Res off, Mil Sanitary Service, 1946-50. Gen secy, Cen Isr Consulate, Greece. Recipient: Laureate, twice, Greek Govt; War Cross. Home: 13 M Voda St, Athens, Greece. Office: 17 Aristotelus St, Athens, Greece.

SARFATTI, Gad, Isr, educator; b. Pisa, It, Nov 5, 1916; s. Gualtiero and Eilosa (Levi); in Isr since 1939; DMath, U Florence, It, 1937; PhD, Heb U, Jerusalem, 1955; m. Rachel Levi, Apr 8, 1946; c: Biniamin, Eliav, Miriam. Asso prof, Heb lang, Bar Ilan U, Ramat Gan, since 1969, on fac since 1962; mem, Kibbutz Tirat Zvi, 1940-47. Lt, IDF, 1948-50.

Author: Mathematical Terminology in Hebrew; Scientific Literature of the Middle Ages, 1968. Contbr to profsl publs. Home: 5 Hamelech George St, Jerusalem, Isr. Office: Bar Ilan U, Ramat Gan, Isr.

SARGON, Joseph Isaac, US, business exec; b. Bombay, India, May 19, 1906; s. Isaac and Dinah (Ezra); in US since 1941; m. Dorothy Cohen, Feb 11, 1942; c: Rosalind, Marilyn Brier, Dinah, Joyce, Edward. Pres, NE Modernizing Co, since 1943. Pres: Home Improvement Contractors Assn, since 1965; Natl Home Improvement Contractors Assn, 1958-60; NE region, ZOA; vice-pres: NE region, JNF; NE region, United Syn of Amer; fmr pres, Temple Beth Zion, fmr pres, Brotherhood; mem: Masons; B'nai B'rith. Found, ed, Beth Zion Mag, 1952-64; ed, J Tribune, Bombay, 1927-40. Recipient: Solomon Schechter award for publs, United Syn of Amer, 1961. Home: 59 Corey Rd, Brookline, Mass. Office: 319 Allston St, Brookline, Mass.

SARIG, Arie, Isr, government official; b. Kedainiai, Lith, Feb 15, 1913; s. Shraga and Olga (Gigus) Sirkin; in Isr since 1936; BS, law, State U, Lith, 1935; m. Yocheved Gigus, Sep 20, 1938; c: Gideon. Asst dir gen, Min of Defense, since 1966, secy gen, 1948-50, dir, org and admn, 1953-66; secy gen, Hapoel Sports Org, 1936-41; mgr, workers provident fund, Tel Aviv Munic, 1941-43; head, purchasing mission, Legation of Isr, London, 1950-52. Arrested twice by Brit Govt, brought before mil court, Sirkin-Rachlin Arms Trial, for alleged arms transp for Haganah. Pres, Isr Football Assn; mem: cen commn, Hapoel Sports Org; exec, Isr Olympic Comm; delg, Histadrut and Hapoel, US, 1947. Hobbies: music, sports. Home: 40 Yehuda Hamaccabi St, Tel Aviv, Isr. Office: Hakiryah, Tel Aviv, Isr.

SARIG, Shmuel, Isr, scientist, editor; b. Shavli, Lith, May 3, 1909; s. Zvi and Rivkah (Rubenstein); in Isr since 1924; att Heb U, Jerusalem, 1947-48; m. Shoshana Shurer, 1947; c: Nirah Cohen, Roni Gofer, Dorith. Dir: Lab for Research for fish Diseases, since 1947; Min of Agric. Prin contrib: research in identification and control of fish diseases; teaching, adv, fish farmers in control of diseases. Secretariat, council, chmn of expert comm, Fish Breeders Assn in Isr; mem, Wildlife Disease Assn, US; various posts in Kibbutz Haartzi movement. Ed, Bamidgeh, bull on fish culture in Isr, since 1948; fisheries div; contbr numerous papers on fish culture to jours. Hobby: philately. Home: Kibbutz Nir David, Isr. Office: Lab for Research of Fish Diseases, Nir David, Isr.

SARLOUIS, Abraham, Isr, diplomat; b. Amsterdam, Holland, Feb 9, 1916; s. Lodewyk and Lea (Asscher) Hartog; in Isr since 1951; att U Amsterdam, 1935-41; PhD, U Leiden, 1950; m. Clara Weiss, Mar 22, 1953; c: Ilana, Ayala. Isr Ambass to Dominican Rep and Jamaica, since 1967; with research dept, Min for Fgn Affaisr, 1951-57; secy, Emb, Montevideo, 1957-61; dep dir, Latin Amer sect, Min for Fgn Affairs, 1961-64; chargé d'affairs, ambass, Quito, Ecuador, 1964-67; tchr, Greek, Latin J Gymnasium Leauwerden, 1941-42. Concentration Camps, Westerbork, Holland, Bergen-Belsen, Ger, 1943-45. Mem: B'nai B'rith, Montevideo, since 1958. Spec interests: ancient hist; archaeol; ling; Bible study. Home: 32 Hapalmach St, Jerusalem, Isr. Office: 38 Sarasota Ave, Santo Domingo, Republica Dominicana.

SARNA, Nahum M, US, educator; b. London, Eng, Mar 27, 1923; s. Jacob and Milly (Horonzick); in US since 1951; BA, U London, 1944, MA, 1946; dipl, J Coll, 1955; PhD, Dropsie Coll, 1955; m. Helen Horowitz, Mar 23, 1947; c: David, Jonathan. Dora Golding Prof Bibl Studies, Brandeis U, since 1965; libr, asst prof Bible, Tchrs Inst, JTSA, since 1957; asst lectr, Heb, U Coll, London, Eng, 1946-49; educ worker, JA, Isr, 1949-50; lectr, Gratz Coll, Phila, 1951-57; visiting prof: Bibl studies, Andover-Newton Theol Sch, 1966-67; Bible, Dropsie Coll, Pa, 1967-68; visiting asso prof, rel dept, Columbia U, 1964-65. Mem: Soc for Bibl Lit and Exegesis; Amer Oriental Soc; Isr Exploration Soc; Archons of of Colophon; Amer Acad for J Research; B'nai B'rith Adv Bd on Adult J Educ; trustee, Boston Tchrs Coll; cons, Melton Research Cen; fmr asso trustee, Amer Schs for Oriental Research. Author: Understanding Genesis, 1966; ed, trans, Bible trans comm, J Publ Soc; contbr to scholarly publs, encys. Recipient: award, JBCA, 1967. Home: 22 Russell St, Brookline, Mass. Office: Brandeis U, Waltham, Mass.

SARNAT, Bernard G, US, plastic surgeon, educator; b. Chgo, Ill, Sep 1, 1912; s. Isadore and Fanny (Sidran); BS, U Chgo, 1933, MD, 1936; MS, U of Ill, 1940, DDS, 1940; m. Rhoda

Gerard, Dec 25, 1941; c: Gerard, Joan. Pvt practice since1956; asst, histology, U of Ill Coll of Dent, 1937-40; res, oral, plastic surg; Cook Co Hosp, 1940-41; instr, histology path, Loyola U, 1941-42; dept surg, Wash U Med Sch, 1942-46; prof, dir, dept oral plastic surg, St Louis U Coll Dent, 1945-46; prof, head, dept oral, maxillofacial surg, U of Ill Coll Dent, 1946-56, clinical asst prof, plasric surg, Coll of Med, 1949-56; Cons: oral surg, Hines VA Hosp, 1951-56; gen plastic and maxillo-facial surg, V.A regional office, Ill, 1950-56. Found, Amer Soc Plastic and Reconstructive Surgs; mem: Phi Epsilon Pi; Phi Delta Epsilon; Alpha Omega; Sigma Xi; Amer Coll Surgs; AAAS; Plastic Surg Research Council; Amer Assn Plastic Surgs; Amer Bd of Plastic Surgs; Amer Assn Physical Anthro-pologists. Author: Oral and Facial Cancer, 2nd ed, 1957; Sur-gery of the Temporomandibular Joint, 1962; chaps: Tumors of the Neck, in Textbook of Pediatrics, 1950; Tongue in Health and Disease, in Diseases of Digestive System, 1953; Facial Plas-tic Surgery, in Skin Surgery, 1962; Developmental Facial Ab-normalities, in Pain and Mandibular Function; Facial Ab-normalities, in Current Pediatric Therapy; ed, contbr The Tem-poromandibular Joint, 1951, 1964; contbr to profsl jours. Home: 616 N Maple Dr, Beverly Hills, Cal. Office: 435 N Roxbury Dr, Beverly Hills, Cal.

SARNAT, Marshall Jordan, Isr, educator; b. Chgo, Ill, Aug 1, 1929; s. Maurice and Dena (Lew) Sarnatzky; in Isr since 1950; BA, Heb U, Jerusalem, 1955; MA, Northwestern U, 1957, PhD, 1959; m. Carmela Shenker, Jan 11, 1956; c: Don, Iddo. Head, dept bus admn, Heb U, since 1969, sr lectr, since 1967, on fac since 1959. Pvt, IDF, Res. Author: The Development of the Securities Market, in Israel, 1966; Saving and Invest-ment Through Retirement Funds, 1966. Mem: Beta Gamma Sigma, Northwestern U, 1957. Home: 34 Nayot St, Jerusalem, Isr. Office: Heb U, Jerusalem, Isr.

SARNOFF, David, US, business exec; b. Minsk, Russ, Feb 27, 1891; s. Abraham and Lena (Privin); in US since 1900; att spec courses, elec engr, Pratt Inst, Bklyn, NY; hon: DSc: St Lawrence U, 1927; Marietta Coll, 1935; Suffolk U, 1939; Pa Mil Coll, 1952; U Notre Dame, 1955; Temple U, 1958; DLitt, Norwich U, 1935; LLD: JTSA, 1946; Bethany Coll, 1946; John Carroll U, 1950; U of Pa, 1952; Fair-leigh Dickinson Coll, 1953; Pratt Inst, 1954; U of S Cal, 1954; Fordham U, 1955; Dropsie Coll, 1957; U of RI, 1957; Okla City U, 1962; LHD, U Louisville, 1950; DEng, Drexel Inst of Tech, 1953; DCS, Oglethorpe U, 1958; Bos-ton U, 1948; m. Lizette Hermant, July 4, 1917; c: Robert, Ed-ward, Thomas. Chmn, bd RCA, since 1947, gen mgr 1921, vice-pres, gen mgr, 1922-29, exec vice-pres, 1929-30, pres, 1930-47; dir, chmn bd, RCA Communications, Inc, NBC; messenger, Commercial Cable Co, 1906, wireless operator, 1907-12, chief radio insp, later commercial mgr, until RCA-Commercial Cable merger, 1919. Signal Corps Res, US, Army, 1931, brig gen, 1944. Pres, Armed Forces Communications. and Elec Assn, 1946-48; f: J Acad Arts and Sci; JTSA; chmn, Inst Elec and Electronics Engrs; Royal Soc Arts, London; mem, bd trustees: Educ Alliance; Pratt Inst; Thomas A Edison Found; NYU; mem: Radio Free Eur Corp; Mil Order World Wars; World Rehab Fund; Intl Radio and TV Soc; Naval Order of US; Council on Fgn Relations; Grand St Boys Assn; Vet Wireless Operations Asso, life mem and hon pres; Beta Delta Sigma; Radio Pioneers; Amer Legion; Tau Delta Phi; hon mem, Brit Inst Radio Engrs; clubs: Me-trop, Wash, DC; Army and Navy, Wash, DC; Econ, NY, India House; Poor Richard; Cent Country; Engrs, Phila. Re-cipient: Legion of Merit, US War Dept, 1944; medal of merit, US, 1946; Cross of Chevalier, Legion of Honor, Fr Govt, 1935, off, 1940, cdr, 1947; first hon f, Weizmann Inst of Sci, Isr, 1952; Hall of Fame, Educ Alliance, 1954; US Sen tribute, 1961; medal, RA, 1962. Office: 30 Rockefeller Plaza, New York, NY.

SARNOFF, Dorothy, US, singer; b. NYC, May 25, 1919; d. Jacob and Belle (Roosin); BA, Cornell U; m. Milton Ray-mond. Appeared in theater producs: Rosalinda, 1942-44; Magdalena, 1948; The King and I, 1951-53; My Darlin' Aida, 1953; appeared with NYC Opera Co; NYC; Phila; St Louis Munic; LA Civic Light; New Orleans; La Scala; numerous solo appearances in US and Can; guest appearances: radio and TV; NBC; CBS;ABC; supper clubs throughout US; lectr, Art of Conversation. Found, Dorothy Sarnoff's Speech Cosmetics and Speech Dynamics Inc, 1966. Mem: Amer Guild of Variety Artists; Amer Fed TV and Radio Artists; Amer Guild of Musical Artists; Actor's Equity. Author: How to Sound as Good as You Look, 1969. Recipient: wo-

man of achievement award, Albert Einstein Med Coll, 1964. Home and office: 40 Central Park S, New York, NY.

SARTANI, Arie, Isr, artist; b. Kutno, Pol, Sept 9, 1920; s. Zvi and Hana Rak; in Isr since 1936; att: Beaux Arts, 1949-51; Grand Chaumiers, 1949-51, both, Paris; m. Amira Feuer-stein, 1955; c: Gil, Revital, Jasmine. Exhb: Independent Artists, Paris, 1949; Katya Gronov Gal, Paris, 1967; repre-sented in various perm and pvt collections. Secy, Org of Kib-butz Ha'artzi Painters, 1964-66. Recipient: Struck Prize, Haifa, Munic, 1962; 2nd intl prize, Monaco Exhb, 1967. Home and studio: Kibbutz Merhavia, Isr.

SARWER-FONER, Gerard J, Can, psychiatrist; b. Volkovisk, Pol, Dec 6, 1924; s. Michael and Ronia (Cablan); in Can since 1932; BA, U Montreal, 1945, MD, 1951; D Psycht, McGill U, 1955; m. Ethel Scheinfeld, May 28, 1950; c: Micha-el, Gladys, Janice, Henry. Asso prof, psycht, McGill U, Sch of Med, since 1966, on fac since 1955; visiting prof, psycht, Laval U, Que, since 1964; dir, dept psycht, Queen Elizabeth Hosp of Montreal, since 1966; asso psycht, dir research, J Gen Hosp, 1955-66; cons, dir dept research, Queen Mary Vets Hosp, 1955-60. Lt col, Royal Can MC. Dir, Can Psycht Assn; treas, Que Psycht Assn; mem: adv panel in psycht, Defense Research Bd, Can; comm on spec psycht, Royal Coll Phys and Surgs, Can; f: Amer Psycht Assn, fmr pres, Que dist; Amer Geriatric Soc; charter, Amer Coll of Neuropsy-chopharm; mem: Can Psychoanalytic Soc; Intl Psychoana-lytic Assn; Amer Soc Biol Psycht; Can Med Assn; Mon-treal Clinical Soc; Amer Orthopsycht Assn; Can Friends Heb U; fmr, f psycht, Montreal Medico-Chirurgical Soc. Author: The Dynamics of Drug Therapy, 1960; Research Conference on The Depressive Group of Illnesses, 1966; contbr to psycht jours. Recipient: Can Forces Decoration. Home: 613 Cote St Antoine Rd, Montreal, Can. Office: McGill U Sch of Med, Montreal, Can.

SAS, Louis F, US, educator, author; b. Chelsea, Mass, Jan 12, 1908; s. Samuel and Bessie (Furman); BA, CCNY, 1928; MA, Columbia U, 1930, PhD, 1937; m. Anne Greenstein, Aug 1, 1931; c: Bernard. Prof, dept romance langs, CCNY, since 1958, chmn, grad comm, romance langs, since 1967, on fac since 1929; visiting prof: Yehiva U, since 1945; Man-hattan Sch of Music, since 1956. Mem: Amer Assn Tchrs Span; AAUP; Phi Beta Kappa, fmr pres, Gamma chap; fac chap, AJCong, pres since 1961; fmr: secy, Amer Assn Tchrs Fr, pres, metrop chap, mem natl chap. Author: Noun Declen-sion System in Merovingian Latin, 1937; Les Grands Savants Français, 1939; Quienes son los arios?, 1941; staff cons for Random House Dict of the Eng Lang, prepared romance etymologies; contbr to: Enc Hebraica, Isr; philological publs; ed, Fac Facts; ed bd, Gen Educ News. Recipient: Guggenheim f to S Amer, 1940-41; f, Amer Council Learned Soc, 1950-51; Ford Study Comm grant, CCNY, 1954. Hob-bies: travel, philately. Home: 475 W 186 St New York, NY. Office: CCNY, New York, NY.

SASSO, Moses de Castro, US, rabbi; b. St Thomas, VI, Feb 2, 1894; s. David and Emmeline (de Castro); m. Esther Robles, Apr 5, 1936; c: Emmeline Brenner. Rabbi, Heb Cong of St Thomas, VI, since 1914; mem, Selective Service Bd of US. Mem, chaplain, Harmonic Lodge, Masons. Recipient: cita-tions of appreciation for work in Selective Service. Hobbies: philately, numismatics. Home and study: 2 A C Commandant Gade, St Thomas, Virgin Islands.

SASSON Eliahu, Isr, cabinet min; b. Damascus, Syria, Feb 2, 1902; s; David and Sarah; U deg, St Joseph Coll, Beirut; in Isr since 1927. Ret; Isr Min of Police, 1967-69; Min of Posts, 1961-67; corresp, Arabic and Heb newspapers, 1919-31; ed, Arabic newspaper, El-Hayat, Damascus, 1920; jour-nalist, Jerusalem, 1927-33; head, Arabic dept, JA for Pal, 1933-48; dir, dept for ME, Min for Fgn Affairs, 1948-50; mem delg: to UN, 1947-49, 1961; to Armistice Agreement with Egypt, 1949; for peace talks with the Arab Countries, Recon-ciliation Comm of UN, Lausanne, Switz, 1949; Isr min: Turkey, 1950-52; It, 1953-57, Ambass, 1957-60; head, Isr delg to coronation of Pope John the 23rd, Rome, 1958; ambass, Switz, 1961. Recipient: Chevallier de la Grande Croix de Saint Silvestre, Vatican, 1959; Cavaliere Granda Ufficiale dell' Ordine di Sant'Agata, State of San Marino, 1961; Cavaliere di Gran Croce al Merito della Repubblica Italiana, Govt of It, 1961. Home: 24 Lincoln St, Jerusalem, Isr.

SASSON, Moshe, Isr, diplomat; b. Damascus, Syria, 1925; s. Eliahou and Jael (Zghoul); in Isr since 1927; att Heb U, Jerusalem; m. Tova Sockolov, 1949; c: Orna, Reuven. Repr of PM, admn areas, since 1967; attache, Isr delg to Lausanne, 1949; in ME dept, Min for Fgn Affairs, 1950; vice-consul, 2nd secy, Isr emb, Athens, 1952-55; dep, Isr delg, Eur off, UN, Geneva, 1955-57; acting dir, ME dept, Min Fgn Afiffairs, Jerusalem, 1957-60; min, Isr legation, Ankara, 1960-66; dir, dept armistice affairs, Fgn Off, Jerusalem, 1966-67. Office: Off of PM, Hakirya, Jerusalem, Isr.

SATIN, Estelle H, US, communal leader; b. NYC, Dec 8, 1898; d. Mark and Ida (Lamport) Hurewitz; att Barnard Coll, NY, 1915-19; m. Morris Satin, Maz 7, 1943; c: Morton, Samuel, Naomi. Chmn, Woman's Div, FJP; natl pres, Yeshiva U Women's Org; fmr pres, Sist J Cen; mem: Hadassah; NY chap, Brandeis U. Spec interest: music. Home: 80 Central Park W, New York, NY.

SATOVSKY, Abraham, US, attorney; b. Detroit, Mich, Oct 15, 1907; s. Samuel and Stella (Benenson); BA, U Mich, 1928, LLB, 1930; m. Toby Nayer, Sep 4, 1938; c: Sheldon, James. Pvt practice since 1930. Life bd mem, Cong Shaarey Zedek, Detroit, fmr pres, life hon pres, Men's Club, fmr pres, Young Peoples Soc; life hon pres, Great Lakes region, Natl Fed J Men's Clubs, found and fmr pres; chmn, friend court and family law comm, Detroit Bar Assn, mem, consitutional comm; mem, Mich Bar Assn; bldg chmn, lawyers comm, United Fund and Torch Dr; bd mem, Detroit Service Group, chmn, profsl div; mem: adv council, United Syn of Amer, fmr mem, exec comm; adv, profsl div, Allied J Campaign; mem: exec comm, JTSA; United Heb Schs; ZOA; B'nai B'rith, fmr vice-pres, Gtr Detroit Council, pres, Detroit lodge; AJCong, fmr bd mem; Brandeis U; Pi Lambda Phi Alumnus Club; Yeshivah Beth Yehuda; fmr: co-chmn, interfraternal div, Detroit Round Table of Catholics, Prots and Js; bd mem, JWF; public panel mem, Detroit War Lab Bd; pres, Phi Beta Delta; bd mem: JWB; Detroit JCC; fmr worker, US War Bond Drs. Contbr to Torch mag. Recipient, awards: JTSA; United Found; Allied J Campaign. Home: 18480 Muirland, Detroit, Mich. Office: 16536 Wyoming, Detroit, Mich.

SATZ, David M Jr, US, attorney; b. NYC, Jan 14, 1926; s. David and Maria (Lowenberg); BA, Harvard Coll, 1948; LLB, U of Pa, 1951; m. Susan Steiner, May 14, 1954; c: Constance, David. US atty, dist of NJ, since 1961; with Lum, Fairlie & Foster, 1952-54; dep atty gen, State of NJ, 1954-58, 1st asst, 1958-61. USAF, 1944-45. Bd trustee: AJ Comm, NJ, since 1958; Hosp Cen, Orange, NJ since 1963; United Comty Fund; asso mem, Zeta Beta Tau; mem: Essex Co, NJ State, Amer, Bar Assns; fmr pres, NJ chap, Fed Bar Assn. Home: 283 West End Rd, S Orange, NJ. Office: Fed Bldg, Newark, NJ.

SAVEL, Lewis Eugene, US, obstetrician, gynecologist; b. NYC, Nov 9, 1911; s. Morris and Rose (Siegel); BS, NYU, 1932, MD, 1936; m. Harriet Rubin, Jan 21, 1940; c: Susan. Pvt practice since 1938; chief, obstet-gyn, Beth Isr Hosp, Newark, since 1958, pres, med staff, since 1968; ed, Jour Beth Israel, since 1962. Chmn, med adv comm, Essex Co Comm on Planned Parenthood; med comm, Visiting Nurses Assn co-chmn, phys comm, UJA, Esscx Co; f: Amer and Intl Coll Surgs; Amer Coll Obstet and Gyn; dipl, Amer Bd Obstet and Gyn; mem: NJ Obstet and Gyn Soc; Phi Delta Epsilon. Contbr to profsl jours. Home: 370 Beech Spring Rd, S Orange, NJ. Office: 468 Irvington Ave, S Orange, NJ.

SAVIN, Robert Shevryn, US, business exec; b. Bridgeport, Conn, Mar 17, 1925; s. Harry and Agnes (Jacobs); att U Bridgeport, 1951-52; m. Barbara Low, July 15, 1951; c: Deborah, Scott. Pres, IPCO Hosp Supply Corp, since 1965, with firm since 1955. PFC, Eur Theatre of Oprs, 1943-46. Trustee, Truman Peace Cen; dir, Health Inds Assn; mem, Young Pres' Org; fmr, chmn, med and surg dir, UJA, NY. Hobbies: golf, philanthropy. Home: 1045 Nautilus Lane, Mamaroneck, NY. Office: 161 Sixth Ave, New York, NY.

SAVIR, Yehuda, Isr, attorney; b. Warsaw, Pol, Jan 7, 1925; s. Israel and Paula (Lipshitz) Svislotzky; in Isr since 1929; LLM, S Methodist U, Dallas, Tex, 1958; admitted to Lincoln's Inn, London, 1951; MJur, Heb U; m. Edna Rosen, Sept 3, 1965. Pvt practice since 1959; instr, Heb U, 1957-58, lectr, S Methodist U, 1963-64. Hon secy: Isr Assn for UN, Maccabiah Village, 1960-63; exec comm, Independent Lib Party, Tel Aviv; Masons; Isr Bar Assn; fmr chmn: Movement for Changing Election System, Tel Aviv; Circle Friends Zora Theater. Contbr to law jours. Office: 31 Rothschild Blvd, Tel Aviv, Isr. Home: 24 Michal St, Tel Aviv, Isr.

SAWYER, David A, US, social worker; b. Boston, Mass, Sep 15, 1917; s. Edward and Annie (Stone); BS, U Mass, 1940; MS, Springfield Coll, Mass, 1941; m. Sylvia Rubinow, Sep 17, 1941; c: Ronnie, Warren. Asso dir, employment policy prog, US Treasury Dept, since 1968; dir, youth, J Comty Cen, Springfield, Mass, 1940-42; asst dir, YM-YWHA, Baltimore, Md, 1946-48; dir: J Comty Cen, Winthrop, Mass, 1948; NE div, AJCong, 1948-50; Mass Comm Fair Educ Practices, 1949-50; Ind J Comty Relations Council, Ind Comty Relations Council; Citizens Comm for Separation of Church and State, all 1950-54; Cen States area, AJComm, 1954-59; exec dir, Commn Council on Hum Relations, Wash, DC, 1959-62; spec asst, inter-group relations, Commanding Gen, US Army Material Command, 1962-66; dir, comty relations, chief, Ind Fair Employment, Dept of Defense, 1966-68. Mem: Natl Assn Social Workers; Natl Assn Intergroup Relations Officials; Assn Comty Relations Workers; Was h Urban League; NAACP; Acad Cert Social Workers; Alpha Epsilon Pi; Masons; Torch Intl Club. Recipient: Omega Psi Phi Prat, hum relations award, 1960; cert of merit, Bd of Commns, 1962. Home: 2228 Richland St, Silver Spring, Md. Office: US Dept of Treasury, Wash, DC.

SAX, Julius M, US, business exec; b. Amsterdam, Holland, May 9, 1915; s. Frederik and Isabella (van Gelder); in US since 1940; dipl, Sch of Commerce, Amsterdam, 1929-33; m. Rose Frisch, Nov 19, 1944; c: Frederic, Helen. Vice-pres: Lubell & Sax Inc, since 1948; Leo Frisch & Co Inc, since 1955; partner, Fred Sax Co, Amsterdam, 1937-40; mgr, sales promotion, Remington Rand, Inc, 1940-41. Sgt maj, US Army, 1942-46. Pres, Frederik & Isabella van Gelder Sax Found Inc; dir, Diamond Mfrs and Importers Assn Amer; secy, exec comm, Keren Yaldenu, Inc; mem: Parents Council, Barnard Coll, NYC; JWV, Jerome Schary Post 264; ZOA, dist 7; fmr: pres, Young Zionist Org, Holland; natl treas, Masada, Young Zionist Org Amer; treas, Parents Sch, Rama, Sch. Spec interests: philately, peace for Isr and neighbors. Home: 120 E 81 St, New York, NY. Office: 580 Fifth Ave, New York, NY.

SAX, Leonard B, US, lawyer, business exec; b. Cincinnati, O, June 4, 1917; s. Ben and Goldie (Quitman); JD, Northwestern U, 1942, BSC, 1949; att: Loyola U, 1939; U Chgo, 1955; Harvard U, 1957-58; Stanford U, 1958; m. Dolly Cedar, Sept 15, 1942; c: Wyn, Donald, Linda, Kurt. Pres, Amer Buff Intl, since 1957, secy-treas, 1946-47; treas, Ajax Hardware Mfg Co, LA, since 1958. Mem: Amer Bar Assn; Ill State C of C; Young Pres Org; W Cen Assn; Chief Exec's Forum. Contbr to legal jours. Hobby: collecting antique watches. Home: 48 Meadoview Dr, Northfield, Ill. Office: 624 W Adams St, Chicago, Ill.

SAYPOL, George M, US, surgeon, educator; b. NYC, Sep 4, 1911; s. Louis and Minnie (Michakin); BS, NYU, 1931, MD, 1935; m. Grace Levenson, June 8, 1947; c: Marjorie, David. Dir, surg: Manhattan State Hosp, since 1955; LI J Hosp att Surg; Queens Hosp Cent; att surg: U Hosp; Bellevue Hosp, since 1958; cons surg: United Hosp, Portchester, NY since 1962; NY Infirmary; White Plains Hosp; asso prof, clinical surg, NYU Post-Grad Med Sch, since 1954. Lt col, US Army, MC, 1942-46. Dipl, Amer Bd Surg; f, Amer Coll Surgs; mem: NY Surg Soc; NY Acad Med; AMA; Alpha Omega Alpha; Sigma Xi. Contbr numerous articles to med jours. Home: 297 Daisy Farms Dr, Scarsdale, NY. Office: 82-68 164 St, Jamaica, NY.

SCHAAR, Bernard E, US, chemical engr; b. Cincinnati, O, Apr 1, 1884; s. Edward and Bella (Rosenthal); Chem Engr, U Cincinnati, 1908; m. Sarah Blumenthal, 1918. Ret; pres, Schaar and Co, mfg sci apparatus, 1909-55. F, AAAS; pres: Chgo sect, Amer Chem Soc, 1932-33, mgn ed, Chem Bull, 1921-33; Chgo br, Amer Assn Sci Workers, 1941; councillor, Amer Inst Chems, since 1954, hon mem since 1958; mem, bd dirs: Save the Dunes Council, since 1959; Near W Side Planning Bd, 1947-56; J Vocational Service, since 1956; mem, bd trustees, Hull House, since 1951; mem: Fed Amer Scis; Tau Beta Pi; Mayor's Comm for Sr Citizens Hall of Fame, 1962; Ill delg, White House Conf on Aging, 1961; clubs: City, Chgo; Chgo Chem. Contbr to sci publs. Recipient: honor scroll, Chgo Chap, Amer Inst Chems, 1952; citation, goodind race relations, Chgo Urban League, 1954; citation, org sci clubs, Chgo Boys Clubs, 1955; citation with Sarah Schaar, J Sr Citizen Couple, 1960. Home: 1360 Lake Shore Dr, Chicago, Ill.

SCHACH, Leonard L, S Afr, theater dir; b. Cape Town, S Afr,

Sep 10, 1918; s. Solomon and Edith (Lazarus); BA, U Cape Town, 1938, MA, 1939, LLB, 1941. Dir-mgr, Leonard Schach Producs, since 1949, fmr, Leonard Schach Cockpit Players; dir, Playhouse Theatre, Johannesburg, since 1960; among perm dirs, Cameri Theater, Tel Aviv, since 1964; directs annually, Belgium, Eng; directed plays for: U Cape Town, drama dept, 1949-51; Natl Theatre of S Afr, 1952-55, 1962; lectr, arts, drama, U Cape Town, controller, U Little Theatre; theater surveys to Eur, US, 1947-48, 61; S Afr repr to: Conf of Intl Theatre Inst, UNESCO, Prague, 1948; Intl Theatre Conf on Children's Theater, Paris, 1951-52; guest dir: Manchester, Eng; US; among plays directed: Diary of Anne Frank; Look Back in Anger; Twelfth Night; The Miracle Worker; Arms and the Man; Back to Methusala; The Firstborn; Long Day's Journey into Night; The Corn is Green; View From the Bridge; The Heiress; The Tenth Man; Antigone; The Lady's Not for Burning; Inherit the Wind; The Glass Menagerie; The Crucible; Cat on a Hot Tin Roof. Mem: Artistic Council, U Cape Town; comm, Comty Chest; Cape Town regional bd, Natl Theatre Org; chmn, S Afr Assn Theatre Mgmt. Author: The Zulu War, 1879, pub, 1939. Recipient: coronation medal, for services to theater; spec scholarship to US; David's Harp, for producs: After the Fall; Case of Robert Oppenheimer and Hedda Gabler; Brussels Drama Critics Circle Award, for Fr producs of Arthur Miller and Shakespeare. Hobbies: music, antiques, travel. Homes: POB 593, Cape Town, S Afr; 18 Netiv Hamazalot, Jaffa, Tel Aviv, Isr.

SCHACHAT, Walter S, US, ophthalmologist; b. NYC, July 30, 1916; s. Abraham and Lillian (Borut); BS, NYU, 1936, MD, Sch of Med, 1940; m. Francine Bonat, Jan, 1941; c: Andrew. Att ophthal surg, Manhattan Eye and Ear Hosp, since 1959; sr cons, ophthal NYC Dept of Health, since 1955; instr, ophthal: Tulane U Coll Med, 1943-46; NYU Coll Med, 1946-50; NY Med Coll. USPHS, 1943-46. Dipl, Amer Bd Ophthal; f: Amer Public Health Assn; Royal Soc Health; Amer Coll Surgs; NY Acad Med. Contbr to profsl jours. Home: 975 Park Ave, New York, NY. Office: 799 Park Ave, New York, NY.

SCHACHNER, Bruno, US, attorney, educator; b. Aus, Aug 1, 1911; LLB, Columbia U, 1933. Pvt practice since 1933; asst US atty, 1939-51; asso prof, NY Law Sch, 1947-50; spec counsel, cong comm on internal revenue adm, 1951-52; counsel, Secy Gen, UN, 1952-54; guest lectr at Us. Mem: Assn Bar, NYC; Amer Bar Assn; Amer Soc Intl Law; club, Chaos. Ed: Columbia Law Review, 1931-33; Fed Bar Journal, 1946-49. Home: 400 E 57 St, New York, NY. Office: 655 Madison Ave, New York, NY.

SCHACHT, Lawrence, US, business exec; b. NYC, Oct 17, 1905; s. Barnet and Eva (Biarski); ME, Stevens Inst of Tech, Hoboken, NJ, 1927; m. Aleen Ginsberg, June 29, 1934; c: Michael, Barbara Marshall. Pres: Schacht Steel Construction, Inc, since 1933; Schacht Found, Inc, since 1951; chmn bd, Standard Dredging Corp, since 1968; dir: Royal Natl Bank, since 1952; Amer Tech Soc, since 1958; Natl Bx Bank, 1949-58; Isr Investors Corp, 1959-65. Natl chmn, UJA, since 1967, mem, natl exec comm, since 1962, vice-pres, NY, since 1966, gen chmn, 1963-65; bd govs: Daughters of Isr, since 1956; Pleasant Valley Home, since 1956, chmn bldg comm, 1960-62; chmn, mem natl bd govs, State of Isr Bonds, NYC, 1954, hon chmn, Essex Co, 1958, chmn, 1956-58; bd trustees: Amer Friends Tel Aviv U, since 1966; Hillside Ind Found, 1953-60; J Comty Council, Essex Co, NJ; mem exec comm, Amer Isr Public Affairs Comm; mem: Soc Founders Albert Einstein Med Coll; Vascular Research Found; Amer Isr C of C; Soc Amer Mil Engrs; Pi Lambda Phi; clubs: Green Brook Country, Caldwell, NJ; Boca Rio Golf, Boca Raton, Fla. Hobby: golf. Homes: 216 Crestwood Dr, South Orange, NJ; 200 E 57 St, New York, NY; 1200 S Ocean Blvd, Boca Raton, Fla. Offices: 200 E 42 St, New York, NY; 465 Hillside Ave, Hillside, NJ.

SCHACHTEL, Hyman Judah, US, rabbi; b. London, Eng, May 24, 1907; s. Bernard and Janie (Spector); in US since 1915; BA, U Cincinnati, 1928; BHL, HUC, 1928, ordained rabbi, 1931; EdD, U Houston, 1948; DHL, Southwestern U, 1955; DD, HUC-JIR, 1958; m. Barbara Levin, Oct 15, 1941; c: Bernard, Ann. Chief rabbi, Cong Beth Isr, Houston, Tex, since 1943; civilian chaplain, Ellington Field, Tex, 1943-45; rabbi, W End Syn, NYC, 1931-43. Pres: SW region, CCAR; Houston Rabb Assn, 1963; Kallah Tex Rabbis, 1963; vice-pres, NY Bd J Mins; dir: Harris Co Red Cross; San Jacinto Girl Scout Council; mem: Slum Clearance Comm;

Liturgy Comm of Crime Commn, both Houston; Gov's Comm on Marriage and Family, NY; HUC Alumni Assn; AJComm, NCCJ; fmr co-chmn, Civil Defense Comm, NY; clubs: Westwood Country; Fac; Petroleum; Houston Kiwanis, dir. Author: Life of Mendelson, 1929; Maimonides Rabbi, 1931; Eternal People Drama, 1936; Friday Night Service, 1952; Enjoyment of Living, 1954; The Life You Want to Live, 1956; The Shadowed Valley, 1962; fmr columnist, Bell Syndicate; delivered invocation at Johnson Inaugural, Wash, DC, 1965. Home: 2527 Glenhaven, Houston, Tex. Study: 3517 Austin, Houston, Tex.

SCHACHTEL, Irving I, US, attorney, business exec; b. London, Eng, Mar 2, 1909; s. Bernard and Janie (Spector); in US since 1914; BA, U Buffalo, 1928; LLB, Columbia Law Sch, 1931; hon LLD, Hartwick Coll, 1948; m. Elinor Weiler, Apr 30, 1944; c: Ellen, Mary, Roger. Pres, Sonotone Corp, 1946-68, vice-pres, 1942-46; partner, law firm, Franchot & Schachtel, 1935-42. Pres: Natl Hosp for Speech Disorders, 1959-64; Profsl Children's Sch, 1958-63; Amer Hearing Aid Assn, 1947-52; fmr trustee, Westchester Co Council Social Agcys; exec comm, Heb HS, NYC, 1950-54; adv bd, Selective Service, 1941-45; mem, Mayor's Reception Comm, 1954-62; mem: NYC Bar Assn; ASCAP; club, Columbia U. Author: Patent Pools and the Anti-Trust Laws, 1932; Planning for Tax Economy, 1938; Conserving Our Children's Hearing, 1948. Recipient: pres citation, 1946. Home: 885 Park Ave, New York, NY.

SCHACHTER, Haim, Isr, business exec; b. Falticeni, Rum, Aug 19, 1902; s. Schneur and Riva; in Isr since 1939; att Carl U, Prague; m. Boehm; c: Ada Taiber, Ruth Abramovicz. Gen mgr, Tamis Ltd, since 1951; fmr mgn: leather factory, Rum; Palmach Ltd, Isr. Owner of many patents in US, Eng, Ger, Fr, It and Isr. Home: 15 Eilath St, Givatayim, Isr. Office: 7 Timnah St, Holon, Isr.

SCHACHTER, Melech, US, rabbi, educator, lecturer; b. Bucovina, Rum, Apr 10, 1913; s. Moses and Miriam (Fuchs); in US since 1929; BA, Yeshiva Coll, 1937; PhD, Dropsie Coll, 1946; m. Claire Tunis, Nov 21, 1937; c: Sara, Hershel. Prof, J law, rabb dept, Yeshiva U, since 1951; prof, Talmud, Stern Coll for Women, since 1958; f, Dropsie Coll, 1944-46; rabbi: Cong Sons of Halberstam, Phila, Pa, 1946-51; Cong Adath Jeshurun, Bx, 1952-63. Mem: RabCA, fmr, coord, Beth Din; NY Bd Rabbis; Dropsie Coll Alumni; Rabb Alumni, Yeshiva U; fmr, pres, Phila Council Rabbis. Author: The Babylonian and Jerusalem Mishna, 1959; contbr to profsl jours and periodicals; lectr at various instns. Home: 1684 Morris Ave, Bronx, NY.

SCHACHTER, Oscar, US, attorney; b. NYC, June 19, 1915; s. Max and Fannie (Javits); BS, CCNY, 1936; LLB, Columbia U, 1939; m. Mollie Miller, 1936; c: Judith, Ellen. Dep exec-dir, dir research, UN Inst for Training Research, since 1966, dir, gen legal div, UN, 1952-66, dep dir, 1946-52, sr legal counselor, 1946-48; asst gen counsel, UNRRA, 1944-46; visiting lectr, intl law, Yale U, since 1955; sr atty, FCC, 1941-42; prin divisional asst, US State Dept, 1942-44. F: World Acad Art and Sci; Intl Acad Astronautics; pres, Amer Soc Intl Law, since 1968; mem, governing council, Inst Intl Org, Sussex, Eng, since 1965; asso, Institut de Droit International, since 1965; mem: Council on Fgn Relations, NY; adv council, dept politics, Princeton U; Pres council, NYU Cen on Intl Studies; Intl Law Assn; Phi Beta Kappa; hon mem, Fundación Internacional Eloy Alfaro. Co-author: Across the Space Frontier, 1952; mem, bd eds, Amer Jour of Intl Law; ed in chief, Columbia Law Review, 1938-39; contbr to legal publs. Recipient: Kent Scholar; Ordronaux Prize, both Columbia U. Home: 36 Sutton Pl S, New York, NY. Office: UN, New York, NY.

SCHACHTER, Yehoshua O, Isr, chemist, educator; b. Horodenka, Russ, Jan 26, 1911; s. Shmuel and Adela (Spitz); in Isr since 1940; grad ChemE, Tech U, Vienna, 1935; PhD, Heb U, Jerusalem, 1947; m. Elsa Campos, Mar 17, 1942; c: Rivka Hashimshoni, Shmuel. Prof, chem, Bar Ilan U, Ramat Gan, since 1960; prin res off, Natl Res Council, 1949-52; research dir, Isr Mining Ind, 1952-60. Capt, IDF, 1948-49. Patents in field applied and phys chem. Contbr papers on applied and phys chem. Mem: Amer Chem Found; Isr Chem Found; Isr Inst of Chem Engrs. Home: 92 Bialik St, Ramat Gan, Isr. Office: Bar Ilan U, Ramat Gan, Isr.

SCHACK, William, US, author, editor, chemist; b. Bklyn, NY, Aug 3, 1898; s. Abraham and Hannah (Weinstock); BA,

Cornell U, 1918; m. Sarah Pitkowsky, 1922. Free-lance author since 1927; research chem, Natl Bur Standards, Wash, DC, 1919; ed: Paper, 1920; The Ind Digest, 1921; Fairchild Publs, 1924-26; Social Service, Dept of Wfr, NYC, 1932-35; ed, sup, Index of Amer Design, 1936-38; all NYC; Plastics mag, NYC, Chgo, Ill, 1944-48; publicity service, NYC,1948-55. Pvt, US Army, 1917; ed, automotive publs, ordnance dept, US War Dept, 1941-44. Author: And He Sat Among the Ashes, 1939; A Manual of Plastics and Resins, in ency form, 1950; Art and Argyrol, 1960, rev ed, 1963; co-author, Extrusion of Plastics, Rubber and Metals, 1952; contbr to profsl and gen publs. Home: RR3, W Redding, Conn.

SCHACTER, Herschel, US, rabbi; b. Bklyn, NY, Oct 10, 1917; s. Pincus and Miriam (Shimelman); BA, Yeshiva U, 1938;' ordained rabbi, Rabbi Isaac Elchanan Theol Sem, 1941; m. Pnina Gewitz, 1948; c: Jacob, Miriam. Rabbi: Mosholu J Cen, since 1946; Cong Agudat Shalom, Stanford, Conn, 1941-42; mem, homiletics fac, Yeshiva U, 1954. Chaplain, US Army, 1942-45. Mem: Exec comm, RabCA, fmr chmn, Isr comm; comm on J chaplaincy, JWB; fmr: chmn, Conf Pres Maj J Orgs; vice-pres, pres, Rel Zionists of Amer; pres, Yeshiva U Rabb Alumni; official guest of Isr Govt, 1955; mem, 1st rabb delg to survey J life in USSR, Pol, Rum, Czech, studied J life Rum, Hung; Defense Dept mission to J mil personnel in Eur, Japan; first J chaplain to work in Buchenwald Concentration Camp; led UNRRA Transp of J Children from Buchenwald to Switz; escorted transp of Hung ref from Aus to US. Author: Critique of Reconstructionism, 1956. Home: 3330 Rochambeau Ave, Bronx, NY. Study: 3044 Hull Ave, Bronx, NY.

SCHAECHTER, Joseph, Isr, educator, author; b. Kudrynce, Galicia, Sep 16, 1901; s. Shoel and Sarah (Distenfield); in Isr since 1938; ordained rabbi, 1926; PhD, U Vienna, 1931; m. Netti Dlugacz, 1943; c: Shoel. Tchr: Bible and Aggadah, A D Gordon Tchrs Sem, since 1959, prin, 1953-59; Talmud, Bible, Hebräisches Pädagogium, Vienna, 1922-29, 1935-38; Rambam Inst, Vienna, 1935-38; Shalva HS, Tel Aviv, 1938-40; Reali HS, Haifa, 1940-50; Reali Tchrs Sem, 1948-50; sup, Isr HS's, 1951-52. Author: Prolegomena zu Einer Kritischen Grammatik, 1935; Mavo Kazar leLogistika, 1937; Mikhilta deRabbi Ishmael, 1944; Commentary on Mishne Torah laRambam, 1945; Mavo leAggadah, 1949; meMadah leEmunah, 1953; Mavo laTalmud, 1957; Pirkei Talmud, textbooks, 1957; Sefer haAggadah leVatei haSefer, 1957; Pirkei Hadrakha beTanakh, 1960; Otzar haTalmud, Lexicon, 1963; Shvilim beHinuch haDor, 1963; Yahadut veHinuch baZman Hazeh, 1956; Mavo laTanach, 1959; contbr on phil, Talmud and Judaica to learned publs in Eur and Isr. Mem: Vienna Circle of Moritz Schlick. Recipient: Ruppin award, Haifa munic, 1968. Home: 7 Tel Hai St, Haifa, Isr. Office: A D Gordon Tchrs Sem, Haifa, Isr.

SCHAEFFER, Morris, US, physician virologist, educator; b. Berdichev, Russ, Dec 31, 1907; s. Samuel and Celia (Sellman); in US since 1913; BA, U Ala, 1930, MA, 1930; PhD, NYU, 1935, MD, 1944; m. Josephine Wintzer, Nov 5, 1943; c: Debora, Colin, David, Jessica. Gen dir, Bur Labs, NYC Dept Health, since 1959; mem, Public Health Research Inst, since 1959; natl cons, Surg Gen, USAF, 1959-64; mem, Surg Gen's adv comm of influenza, USPHS, 1959-64; adj prof med, NYC Sch Med, since 1960; mem, WHO panel of experts on virus diseases, since 1960; cons: USPHS, NIH, since 1961, mem, bd viruses and cancer, chmn, panel on cancer virology, 1961-63; USPHS cons: Natl Communicable Disease Cen since 1961; VA Hosp, NY, since 1969; bact, NYC Dept Health, 1932-42; lectr, public health, Hunter Coll, NYC, 1942-44; house off, Boston City Hosp, 1944-45; res ped, Cleveland City Hosp, and Childrens Hosp, 1945-48; asst prof, ped, W Reserve U, Cleveland, 1945-48; dir, virus lab, USPHS, Montgomery, Ala, 1949-59; cons, VA Hosp, Montgomery, Ala, 1950-59; asso prof, bact and immunology, Emory U Ga, 1951-59; visiting lectr, Tulane U Med Sch, New Orleans, La, 1952-59. F: AAAS; NY Acad Sci; NY Acad Med; Amer Public Health Assn; found mem, Amer Bd Preventive Med and Public Health; mem: Soc Experimental Biol and Med; Amer Coll of Preventive Med, charter mem; Amer Soc Microbiol; Amer Acad Microbiol; Amer Bd Microbiol; Research Soc of Amer; Sigma Xi; Delta Omega; Alpha Omega Alpha. Author: Experimental Poliomyelitis, 1940; contbr to med jours and books. Hobbies: photography, travel. Home: 65 Edgars Lane, Hastings-on-Hudson, NY. Office: 455 First Ave, New York, NY.

SCHAFFER, Bernardo, Isr, physician; b. Kicinief, Rum, May

21, 1904; s. Samuel and Matilde (Zaidemberg); in Isr since 1964; MD, Med Sch, Buenos Aires, 1927; m. Aida Sevlever. Chief, obstet and gyn dept, Sharei Zedek Hosp, Jerusalem, since 1964; prof, med sch, Rosario, Arg, chief obstet dept, Saenz Pena Hosp, Rosario, both 1956-64. Mem, Obstet and Gyn Soc, Isr; att intl confs, congs. Contbr numerous reports to med jours, Buenos Aires. Home: 5 Balfour St, Jerusalem, Isr. Office: Sharei Zedek Hosp, Jerusalem, Isr.

SCHAFFER, Walter, S Afr, educator; b. Cologne, Ger, Oct 5, 1906; s. Hermann and Clara (Anschel); in S Afr since 1910; MSc, Rhodes U, Grahamstown, PhD, 1940; att Cambridge U, Eng, 1953-60; m. Gladys Levinsohn, Sep 25, 1932; c: Dona Strauss, Herman, Benjamin. Asst prin, U Cape Town, since 1969, prof, physics, since 1954. Capt, S Afr Air Force, 1940-46; chmn: WP Priorities Bd; Jt Matriculation Bd; mem: WP ZC; Cape comm, J Bd Deps; various U bodies; mem: S Afr Inst Physics; Royal Met Soc. Contbr papers on dynamics of atmosphere, crystallography, to various sci jours. Spec interests: J, ancient hist, sci. Home: 6 Norfolk Close, Highstead Rd, Rondebosch, Cape, S Afr. Office: U Cape Town, Rondebosch, Cape, S Afr.

SCHAFLER, Leo, Eng, organization exec; b. Czernowitz, Aus, Aug 25, 1890; s. Abraham and Jety (Welzer); in Eng since 1938; LLD, U Vienna, U Czernowitz, 1913; DL; m. Regina Katz, Nov 2, 1920; c: Paul. Dep gen secy, ZF, since 1960, secy, 1942-60; mgn ed, The Jewish Observer and Middle East Review, since 1964; advocate, pvt practice, Vienna, Aus, 1920-38. Aus Army WW I. Home: 37 Sandringham Court, London W 9, Eng. Office: ZF, 4/12 Regent St, London SEW 1, Eng.

SCHAFLER, Samuel M, US, rabbi; b. NYC, Feb 20, 1929; s. Benjamin and Ethel (Schnapp); BSS, CCNY, 1950; MHL, ordained rabbi, JTSA, 1952; m. Sara Edell; six c. Rabbi: Temple Gates of Prayer, since 1961; Knesseth Isr Syn, Gloversville, NY, 1952-55; asst dir, United Syn Commn on J Educ, 1955-61. Bd mem: Syn Council; comm on J law, RA; pres: RA, Queens, NY, 1965-66; Metrop NY, 1966-68; mem: AJCong; Educ Assembly; Natl Council for J Educ. Ed: The Synagogue School, 1955-61; Our Age, 1957-61. Hobbies: Mil hist, architecture. Home: 144-63 37 Ave, Flushing, NY. Study: 38-20 Parsons Blvd, Flushing, NY.

SCHAGRIN, Elihu, US, rabbi; b. Wilmington, Del, June 20, 1918; s. Charles and Frances (Schwartz); BA, U of Pa, 1940; MHL, ordained rabbi, JIR, 1946; m. Dorothy Wallach, June 17, 1945; c: Gail, Charles, Judith. Rabbi: Temple Concord, since 1953; Beth Isr Cong, Coatesville, Pa, 1945-53; instr, Sem, Lincoln U, 1950 chaplain, VA Hosp, 1945-53. Pres, found, Chester Co (Pa) Mh Comm, 1949-53; pres: Gtr Coatesville Interracial comm, 1949-53; Family and Children's Service Soc, 1961-63; Binghamton Minnisterial Assn, 1958-59; gen chmn, United J Fund campaign, J Fed, Broome Co, 1969; chmn, profsl dir, United Fund, Broome Co, 1966; bd dirs: Broome Co chap, ARC, 1955-68; min bd, Planned Parenthood Assn, Broome Co; Broome Co council, NY State Div Hum Relations; Mayor's Adv Comm on Urban Renewal; Citizen's Adv Comm on Social Wfr; mem: bd, Alumni Assn, HUC-JIR, 1965-68; exec bd, CCAR; Metro Interfaith Services; U of Alumni Assn; Masons; club, Rotary, fmr pres. Author, chap, History of Jews of State of Delaware, 1946. Recipient: award, Broome Co Med Soc, 1967. Home: 5 Chapin St, Binghamton, NY. Study: 9 Riverside Dr, Binghamton, NY.

SCHALLINGER, Gideon, Isr, architect, town planner; b. Brno, Czech, Feb 1, 1909; s. Adolf and Gisela (Raucher); in Isr since 1930; dipl, architect, Tech HS, Brno, 1929; m. Lore Hopf, July 3, 1947; c: Ilana, Eldad. Pvt practice, Haifa, since 1933; planned: settlements: Kiryat Bialik; Shavey Zion; Regba; res quarters: Haifa; Tel Aviv; Kiryat Bialik; Dolphin House Hotel, Shavey Zion; Bank Leumi le Isr, Tiberias; public bldgs: schs; cinemas; civic cen's; syns throughout Isr; asst to Richard Kauffmann, architect, Jerusalem, 1930-33. Served, Haganah; IDF. Mem: Assn Engrs and Architects in Isr, chmn, Haifa Br, since 1968; panel, Haifa Outline Scheme; Dist Town Planning Commn, N Isr; fmr chmn, Inst Architects in Haifa; club, Rotary, Kishon-Haifa Bay, fmr pres. Hobbies: arts; philately; photography. Home: 15 Yefeh Nof St, Haifa, Isr. Office: 6 Bialik St, Haifa, Isr.

SCHANIN, Norman, Isr, educational exec; b. Bklyn, NY, Nov 26, 1922; s. Charles and Jeane (Fishman); BA, NYU, 1943, MA, 1948, EdD, 1959; BRE, Tchrs Inst, JTSA, 1948; m. Roslyn Fleischer, Dec 22, 1946; c: David, Jonathan, Hillel.

Prin, David Yellin Heb Tchrs Coll, Jerusalem, since 1968; tchr, youth leader, E Midwood J Cen, 1939-43; dir, Bklyn Zionist Youth Commn, 1944; asst prin, youth dir, Park Ave Syn, NYC, 1946-47; natl dir, Young Judea, 1947-52; educ dir, Forest Hills J Cen, 1952-68. US Army, 1944-46. Fmr pres, Educs Assembly; mem: Natl Council for J Educ; Metrop Prin's Council, United Syn, fmr pres; Assn for Supervision and Curriculum Devl; dept elem sch prin's, NEA; prin's council, Assn of United Syn Sch's in Queens, NY. Author: Young Judea-A Survey of A Jewish Youth Movement in 1951-52, pub 1958; Israel in the United Synagogue Youth Program, 1957; T'filla V'Hag Latamid, 1960; contbr to J press. Home: 7 Tchernichovsky St, Jerusalem, Isr. Office: David Yellin Heb Tchrs Coll, Jerusalem, Isr.

SCHANKER, Louis, US, artist, educator; b. NYC, July 20, 1903; s. Samuel and Fanny (Rosner); att: Cooper Union Art Sch; Art Student League; studied in Fr, Spain, It. Asso prof, fine arts, Bard Coll, since 1949; murals: Neponsit Beach Hosp, 1937; radio sta WNYC, 1939; numerous one-man shows including painting, sculpture, wood cuts, prints; one-man shows of oils: Walker Art Cen, Minneapolis, Minn, 1959; Lucien Gal, NY, 1960; exhbs: Mus Modern Art; Philips Memorial Mus; Metrop Mus; Bklyn Mus; Whitney Mus; Toledo Mus. Mem: Sculptors Guild Inc; Coll Art Assn; Fed Modern Painters and Sculptors; club, artist. Author: Line Form Color, 1949. Recipient: Purchase Prize 1947, 1949. Home: Sag Harbor, NY. Studio: Stamford, Conn.

SCHANZER, Albert D, US, attorney, jurist; b. Arva Komidat, Hung, Aug 18, 1890; s. Isidore and Rosa (Stiller); in US since 1898; LLB, cum laude, NYU, 1912; m. Minnie Cohen, July 2, 1922; c: Jane, Herbert. Pvt practice; mem, NY State Leg, 1930-37; councilman, NYC, 1938-39; borough secy, Bklyn, 1940; appeals commn, NY Unemployment Ins Div, 1941-46; city magistrate, NY, 1950-58; fmr, judge, Court of Spec Sessions, NYC. US Army, 1919. Hon chmn, JNF of Amer; Bklyn comapign chmn, Isr Bonds; mem: Masons; KP; Moose; B'rith Abraham; United Friends Mutual Aid Assn; fmr: pres, J Big Brother and Big Sister Assn; found, Bklyn Region, ZOA; co-chmn, Bklyn div, UJA; club, Arrowbrook. Recipient: forest of 25,000 trees planted in his name in Isr. Home: 38 School St, E Williston, NY. Office: 66 Court St, Brooklyn, NY.

SCHAPIRO, Aronhold C, US, attorney; b. Portsmouth, O, Feb 25, 1893; s. Abraham and Cecelia (Schloss); LLB, O State U, 1914; m. Regina Half, Sep 28, 1920; c: Felice Klein. Partner, Kimble, Schapiro, Stevens, Harsha and Harsha, since 1943; dir, O Bar Title Ins Co, since 1957; atty in pvt practice, 1914-43; mem, Civil Service Commn, 1916-17; asst city solicitor, 1930-35, all Portsmouth, O. US Army, 1918-19. Pres, Cong Beneh Abram, since 1960, secy 1947-60; f, O Bar Assn Found, fmr mem, bd trustees, fmr pres, O Bar Assn; Amer Bar Assn Found; mem: B'nai B'rith; Zeta Beta Tau; Elks; Masons; Family Service of Scioto Co, fmr mem bd dirs; fmr: mem, Commn of Grievances and Discipline, Supr Court of O; bd dirs: Portsmouth J Wfr Assn; Portsmouth Bar and Libr Assn; Scioto Planning Comm; Jud Council of O; chmn, YMCA Town Hall Comm; club, Exch. Home: 2319 Micklethwait Rd, Portsmouth, O. Office: 600 Natl Bank Bldg, Portsmouth, O.

SCHAPIRO, Barry Jay, US, research social worker; b. NYC, Dec 18, 1942; s. Harris and Gwen (Heimowitz); BS, CCNY, 1965; MSW, Hunter Coll, NYC, 1967; m. Frances Federman, June 17, 1967. Research social worker, since 1969; social worker, J Comty Cens Assn, 1967-68. Pres, found, Mitzvah Credit Union; vice-pres: W Cen chap, Natl Assn J Social Workers, fmr secy; JCAA Employees Union; mem: Natl Assn J Cen Workers; Mo Consumers Assn. Spec interests: mental retardation, consumer affairs, econ, photography. Home: 1035 Llewellyn Lane, Olivette, Mo. Office: 11001 Schuetz Rd, St Louis, Mo.

SCHAPIRO, Meyer, US, educator; b. Shavly, Lith, Sep 23, 1904; s. Nathan and Fanny (Adelman); in US since 1907; AB, Columbia U, 1924, PhD, 1931; m. Lillian Milgram, 1928; c: Miriam, Ernest. U prof, Columbia U, since 1966, prof, fine arts, 1954-66, on fac since 1928; instr, fine arts: NYU, 1932-36; New Sch for Social Research, 1938-52; Warburg Inst, London U, 1947, 1957; Heb U, Jerusalem, 1961; Charles Eliot Norton Prof, Harvard U, 1966-67; Slade prof, Oxford U, 1968. F, Amer Acad Arts and Scis. Bd eds, Jour of Hist of Ideas; contbr articles on modern and medieval

art. Recipient: Guggenheim f, 1939, 1942. Home: 279 W 4 St, New York, NY. Office: Columbia U, New York, NY.

SCHAPPES, Morris U, US, editor, historian; b. Kamenets-Podolsk, Ukraine, May 3, 1907; s. Haim and Ida (Urman) Shapiro; in US since 1914; BA, CCNY, 1928; MA, Columbia U, 1930; m. Sonya Laffer, Apr 6, 1930. Ed, J Currents, since 1958; instr: Eng, CCNY, 1928-41; div J studies, Jefferson Sch of Social Scis, 1948-57; Sch J Knowledge, NY, 1958-69. Mem: presidium, Yiddisher Kultur Farband; Amer Hist Assn; Amer J Hist Soc; Conf on J Social Studies; Assn for Study of Negro Life and Hist; YIVO; fmr mem, bd dirs, Sch of J Studies. Author: Letters from the Tombs, 1943; Prose and Poetry of Emma Lazarus, 1944; Letters of Emma Lazarus, 1949, 3rd rev ed, 1967; A Documentary History of the Jews in the US, 1654-1954, rev ed, 1965; fmr mem, ed bd, J Life; contbr to scholarly jours. Home: 700 Columbus Ave, New York, NY. Office: 22 E 17 St, New York, NY.

SCHARF, Mendel Ovadia, Isr, advocate, notary; b. Bohorodczany, Aus-Hung, July 13, 1913; s. Lipa and Berta (Karliner); in Isr since 1933; dipl, Hebrew U, Jerusalem, 1935; LLB, London U, 1945; m. Malvine Rosen, June 9, 1949; c: Zivya, Daphne, Zeev. Pvt practice, since 1938; Vaad Leumi, Natl Council Pal Js 1938-48; legal adv, cons, JNF, 1933-63. Capt, IDF, 1948-49. Mem: Bar Assn, Jerusalem. Contbr to profsl jours. Prin interest: Gamarah study. Home: 21 Balfour St, Jerusalem, Isr. Office: 33 Jaffa Rd, Jerusalem, Isr.

SCHARF, Robert, US, economist; b. Vienna, Aus, Sep 22, 1899; s. Arnold and Mathilde (Saphier); in US since 1938; att Berlin U, 1919-21; PhD, Kiel U, 1922; postgrad studies, State U of Commerce, Berlin, 1923. Prof em, Georgia Inst Tech, since 1967, prof, social scis, chair of phil, 1949-67; lectr, Atlanta Bur J Educ; cartel econ: Osram Gesellschaft, Berlin, Dresden, 1922-36, Tungsram, Vienna, 1937-38; educ dir, Saxony Assn, Retail Merchants and Dept Stores, 1927-33. Dir, J Youth Org, Dresden Saxony, 1933-36; mem: Amer Econ Assn; Amer Phil Assn; AAUP; Amer Soc Eng Educ; S Econ Assn; Amer Acad Pol and Social Sci; Elks; Phi Eta Sigma; fac adv, Alpha Epsilon Pi; Maimonides Lodge, B'nai B'rith, Dresden, Saxony; clubs: Atlanta Bicker, pres; Aus, pres; Atlanta Press; New World, Atlanta. Author: Stimmungstraining, 1927; The Three-Legged Ostrich, 1956; Investment Dilemmas?, 1961; contbr to profsl publs. Hobby: art collector. Home: 2179 Willow Ave NE, Atlanta, Ga. Office: Ga Inst of Techn, Atlanta, Ga.

SCHARF, Salo (Shlomo), Isr, business exec; b. Chemnitz, Ger, May 21, 1915; s. Abraham and Adela (Lazar); in Isr since 1934; m. Sara Finkler, Sep 1937; c: Noemi, Jaron. Mgn dir: Travex Ltd, since 1946; Travex Ltd Sightseeing and Tours; Lucky Drive Ltd, Hertz; adv, mem comms, Govt Tourist Corp. IDF, 1947-48. Clubs: Skal of Isr, pres since 1962, chmn, natl council Skal Clubs; Jerusalem Sports, bd mem; Jerusalem Rotary, fmr hon-secy. Hobbies: bridge, tennis. Home: 21 Redak St, Jerusalem, Isr. Office: 8 Shamai St, Jerusalem, Isr.

SCHARFSTEIN, Zevi H, US, educator, author; b. Dunayevtzy, Russ, Mar 15, 1884; s. Dov and Hannah (Bocser); in US since 1914; hon, DHL: JTSA, 1919; Coll of J Studies, Chgo, 1954; m. Rose Goldfarb, 1914; c: Ben Ami, Sulamith Chernoff. Prof em, JTSA, since 1957, prof, J Educ and Heb lit, 1917-57; prin: Safa Berura, Brzezany, 1906; Tarnow, 1909, both in Pol; secy, bur J educ, Heb Tchr Assn, Aus, to 1914; head, textbook dept, Bur J Educ, NYC, 1914-21. Author: Jewish Education in Palestine, 1930; Lexicon on Hebrew Synonyms, 1939; Methods of Teaching Hebrew, 1942; Methods of Teaching Bible, 1942; The Jewish Primary School, 1943; History of Jewish Education in Modern Times, 5 vols, 1945-65; Hebrew Writers for Children, 1947; Springtime, autobiography, 1953; Forty Years in America, autobiography, 1957; A Teachers Way of Life, 1959; Talks to Teachers, 1962; Lexicon of Ideas and Epigrams, 3 vols, 1966; Great Jewish Educators, 1961; textbooks for teaching Heb; ed, Heb tchrs quarterly, Shevile Hachinuch, since 1938. Hon pres: Heb Tchrs Fed, since 1954; chmn, bd license, J Educ Comm, 1938; club: Heb PEN, pres, 1950-57. Recipient: Louis LaMed lit prize; Kessel prize, Mex; Educ Prize, Munic of Tel Aviv, Isr. Home: 310 W 105 St, New York, NY.

SCHARLACK, Louis J, US, business exec; b. Chgo, Ill, Mar 2, 1899; s. Meyer and Mary (Arbetter); m. Mamie Kray, May 27, 1928; c: Miriam, Meyer. Partner, Southern Jewelry Co; secy-treas, Southern Music Co, 1947; pres: Losoyo Plaza Corp, 1954; 212 Losoyo Corp, 1954. Chmn, armed forces commn,

JWB, 1944-58. Fmr pres: Talmud Torah; Temple Beth El; fmr vice-pres, bd dirs, C of C; bd dirs, J Social Service Fed, since 1924; life mem, Scottish Rite, Masons; mem: B'nai B'rith; ZOA; YMCA; Masons; Shriners; fmr natl esquire table tennis champion, fmr Tex, La state champion, men's div; club, San Antonio Optimist, life mem. Home: 455 E Rosewood, San Antonio, Tex. Office: 325 Alamo Plaza, San Antonio, Tex.

SCHARY, Dore, US, playwright, director, producer, motion picture exec; b. Newark, NJ, Aug 31, 1905; s. Herman and Belle (Drachler); hon: DHumL, Coll of Pacific, Cal, 1951; DFA, Lincoln Coll, Ill, 1960; m. Miriam Svet, Mar 5, 1932; c: Jill Robinson, Joy Stashower, Jeb. Theatrical playwright, dir and produc, since 1957; dir, little theater shows; actor-playwright, on and off Broadway; publicity and newspaper work, all 1926-32; writer, motion picture studios, 1932-40; exec produc: MGM Studios, 1940-43; vice-pres i/c produc, 1948-56; Selznick Intl, 1943-46; exec vice-pres, RKO Studios, 1947-48. Author, screen plays: Edison the Man; Young Tom Edison; Boys' Town; produc, films: I'll be Seeing You; Till the End of Time; The Spiral Staircase; The Farmer's Daughter; The Bachelor and the Bobby-Soxer; Battleground; Go For Broke; Bad Day at Black Rock; The Swan; Designing Woman; The Hucksters; Battle of Gettysburg; Sunrise at Campobello; Sup: Joe Smith, American; Journey for Margaret; Lassie Come Home; Lost Angel; Bataan; Mr. Blandings Builds His Dream House; The Window; The Set-up; Crossfire; co-produc, The Theater Guild: Sunrise at Campobello, author; A Majority of One, dir; The Highest Tree, author and dir; The Prosecutor, dir; The Unsinkable Mollie Brown, dir; The Devil's Advocate, author and dir; Something about a Soldier, dir; author: Hannukah Home Service, 1950; Case History of a Movie, 1950; For Special Occasions, 1962; co-author, Storm in the West, 1963; contrb to natl publs. Off, gov, League of NY Theatres; mem, bd dirs: Amer Theater Wing; JTSA; Walter Reade Org, Inc; Interracial Council for Bus Opportunities; chmn, natl commn, B'nai B'rith-ADL; pres, Dramatist Guild Fund; mem: United World Federalists; Screenwritres Guild; Screen Producers Guild; UN Assn; NJ State Council on Arts; Natl Citizens Comm for Bc. Recipient: Academy award, for original screenplay, Boys' Town, 1938; Tony award, for Sunrise at Campobello, 1958. Home: 10 E 70 St, New York, NY. Office: 850 Seventh Ave, New York, NY.

SCHATZ, Arthur H, US, attorney; b. Hartford, Conn, Dec 31, 1918; s. Nathan and Dora (Goldberg); AB, Cornell U, 1940, LLB, Law Sch, 1942; m. Cecil Ruskay, Feb 11, 1945; c: Ellen, Robert, Daniel. Sr partner, Schatz and Schatz, since 1951; cons, med jurisprudence, since 1955; lectr, co-moderator, First Amer Cong on Legal Med and Law Sci Problems, Chgo, 1957; delg, 2nd intl meeting, Forensic Path and Med, NYC, 1960, 3rd intl meeting, London, 1963; visiting lectr: U Conn, 1959-62; Cornell U Law Sch, 1959-63; lectr, NE Law Inst, 1960. Donor with wife, Celia Pessin Scholarship, Technion, Haifa, Isr, 1962. Lt, USCG Res, 1942-45. Found mem: Law Sci Acad of Amer, Austin, Tex; Law Sci Found of Amer, Austin; chmn, ed comm, mem policy comm, mem exec council, Amer Acad Forensic Sci; mem: prog comm, Soc Med Jurisprudence, NY, since 1958; adv council, NE Law Inst, since 1956, exec comm since 1957; comm on insts, Hartford Co Bar Assn, fmr mem exec comm; Natl Assn Claimants Compensation Attys; Amer Bar Assn; Amer Judicature Soc; Beth El Temple, Conn; ZOA; AJCong; Amer Friends Heb U; Amer Technion Soc. Author: Medical Terms for Lawyers Relating to Head and Back, 1958; Check-List for Plaintiffs Personal Injury Attorneys, 1958; Soft Tissue Injuries and Remote Effects of Injuries-Medical Preparation and Proof, 1960; contrb to profsl publs. Home: 77 Norwood Rd, W Hartford, Conn. Office: 750 Main St, Hartford, Conn.

SCHATZ, Julius, US, organization exec; b. NYC, Aug 3, 1915; s. Max and Freda (Czerwinski); BA, NYU, 1934, MA, 1936; m. Sophie Sipser, July 3, 1945; c: William, Eric. Dir, Commn on J Affairs, AJCong, dir, Comty Services, since 1948. Co-chmn, Natl Council on Adult J Educ; vice-chmn: Natl J Music Council; Natl Comm for the 6,000,000; secy: Natl Comm on Yiddish and E Eur Culture; Natl Council on Art in J Life; fmr chmn: Natl Council on J Audio-Visual Materials; Natl Conf Prog Dirs; fmr mem, exec comm, Film Council of Amer; mem: exec comm: Assn J Comty Relations Workers; JBCA; publs comm, Natl Conf cf J Communal Service; Comm on Syn Relations, FJP, NYC. Home: 92-31 57 Ave, Elmhurst, Queens, NY. Office: 15 E 84 St, New York, NY.

SCHATZKI, Erich, US, engineer; b. Ger, Jan 23, 1898; s. Ferdinand and Beate (Stern); in US since 1941; dipl engr, Inst of Tech, Darmstadt, Ger, 1923; DEng, Inst of Tech, Berlin Charlottenberg, Ger, 1929; m. Ruth Koller, Sep 13, 1925; c: Thomas, Karin, Arlin. Devl engr since 1966; instr, Bklyn Poly Inst, 1948-49; aeronautical engr, Junkers Aircraft Corp, Ger, 1924-25; chief engr, airline pilot, Deutsche Lufthansa, Ger, 1926-33; tech repr in US, Swissair, 1933-34; chief engr: Fokker Aircraft Corp, Holland, 1934-38; Koolhoven Aircraft Corp, Holland, 1938-40; tech mgr, El Al Airlines, Isr, 1949; tech adv, Govt of Isr, chief engr, IAF, 1949-50; project, devl engr, Republic Aviation Corp, 1943-49, 1950-53; pres, Schatzki Engr Corp, 1953-56, 1957-58; vice-pres, engr, Penn Tex Corp, 1956-57; dir engr, Isr Aircraft Ind, 1958-62. Home: 123-60 83 Ave, Kew Gardens, NY. Office: Bilnor Corp, 300 Morgan Ave, Brooklyn, NY.

SCHAUDINISCHKY, Leo Herzl, Isr, acoustician; b. Eydtkuhnen, Prussia, Ger, June 4, 1905; s. Aharon and Rebecca (Fellmann); dipl Ing: Hein Hertz Inst; F Schwingungs-Forschung; m. Eva Wolff, 1932; c: Ruth Haeftrathi, Dan. Head, dept applied acoustics, Technion, since 1960, sr research asso; prin contribs: new diagnostic methods; new hearing instruments; hearing aid restoring binaural hearing to one-side deaf people; shape conforming electrode. Isr Repr, Association Internationale Contre le Bruit; mem: Org for Econ Coop and Devl; Isr Comma for Konowitz Law; Intl Inst for Med Elec and Biol Engr. Author: Law and Noise; contbr to publs. Spec interests: music reproduction. Home: 31 Hatichon St, Haifa, Isr. Office: Technion, Haifa, Isr.

SCHAUMANN, David, It, rabbi; b. Aug 6, 1910; s. Emanuel and Regina (Scherzer); deg classical studies, U Turin, 1942; m. Anita Wolkowicz, Dec 28, 1950; c: Donia, Danni. Chief rabbi, Milan, since 1969, asso rabbi, 1943-45; dir: J Sch, Milan, since 1947; dir, Found for Higher Studies in Judaism, since 1951; chief rabbi, Genoa, 1945-58. Vice-pres, JNF, It, since 1945; delg, WZC, 1951, 1959, 1963, 1968; mem, rel and cultural dept, Zionist org, It; fmr pres, ZF, It. Home: Via Morosini 14, Milan, It. Office: Via Eupili 5-8, Milan, It.

SCHAVER, Emma, US, concert singer; b. Kaminskoe, Russ; d. Jacob and Anna (Velinsky) Lazaroff; att: Detroit Conservatory of Music; Juilliard Sch of Music; studied with: Boghetti, Devries, McClellan, Sebastien; hon deg, JTSA; m. Morris Schaver; c: Isaac. Debut: sang "Cavalleria Rusticana" at inaugural performance of Detroit Civic Opera Co; performed with: San Carlo Opera Co; Cincinnati Opera Co; Mex City Opera Co; guest soloist with: Detroit Sym Orch; Isr Sym Orch; Kol Zion L'Gola Sym Orch; Haifa Sym Orch; toured: US; Can; Brazil; Chile; Uruguay; Arg; Eur and Isr, 1932, 1935, 1948, 1951, 1953; mem, first culture mission sponsored by WJC and UNRRA to visit DP camps, Ger, 1946; recorded albums: Ghetto Songs, I Believe, 1947; Heb and J Songs, From the Heart of a People, Jerusalem, 1953; Concert tour in Pol, 1961. Author: Mir Zeinen Do, 1947. Pres: Cen Overall Supply Co; Morris and Emma Schaver Found; chmn: women's div, Isr Bonds, Detroit; Morris and Emma Schaver Publs Fund for J Studies, Wayne U, Detroit; mem, bd dirs: Amer-Isr Cultural Found; AMPAL; Isr Devl Corp of Amer; Amer Friends Heb U; Pioneer Women Org of Amer; LZOA; Natl Lab Comm for Isr; mem, gov council, Amer Assn for J Educ; found, Harry S Truman Cen for Advancement of Peace, Jerusalem. Recipient: Eleanor Roosevelt Humanities Award, 1967. Home: 25259 Ingleside Dr, Southfield, Mich.

SCHECHNER, Sheridan, US, business exec; b. Newark, NJ, Jan 4, 1905; s. Samuel and Fannie (Sheps); BCS, NYU, 1925; m. Selma Schwartz, Nov 15, 1927; c: David, Arthur, Richard, William. Pres, Barton Savings & Loan Assn, since 1962. Fmr pres, North NJ Region, United Syn of Amer; bd mem, overseers, JTSA, since 1959; pres, Oheb Shalom Syn, 1951-55; mem, Amer Inst of Real Estate Appraisers. Home: 4 Walnut Court, S Orange, NJ. Office: 1166 Raymond Blvd, Newark, NJ.

SCHECHTMAN, Charles T, US, surgeon; b. Pol, Aug 15, 1901; s. Joseph and Rebecca (Gorbach); BS, U of Vt, 1923, MD, 1926; m. Sylvia Shakin, Oct 25, 1932; c: Sheila Weinberg, Rebecca, Jonathan. Sr surg: New Brit Gen Hosp, since 1940; New Brit Memorial Hosp, since 1948; cons, eye, ear, nose and throat, VA Hosp, Newington, Conn, since 1938. Pres: Hartford Co Med Assn, 1948; New Brit Med Soc, 1942; New Brit J Fed, 1952-53; Temple B'nai Isr, 1945-47; B'nai B'rith, New Brit, Conn, 1938; Med Alumni Assn, U Vt; 1st vice-pres, Conn State Med Soc, 1954-55; mem: Eye Care Comm, Conn;

Commn Geriatric Study, Conn; bd dirs, New Brit Memorial Hosp; trustee, U of Vt; mem: Amer Acad Ophthal and Otolaryngology; Pan-Amer Soc Ophthal; NE Acad Ophthal; NY Soc Clinical Ophthal; AMA; club, Indian Hill Country. Home: 62 Dover Rd, New Britain, Conn. Office: Cedar Lake Med Center, New Britain, Conn.

SCHECHTMAN, Joseph B, US, author, communal worker; b. Odessa, Russ, Sep 6, 1891; s. Boris and Sarah (Faier); in US since 1941; LLD, U Berlin, 1914, Novorossisk U, 1915; m. Rachel Davidson, May 23, 1936; c: Lea, Alexander, Miriam. Mem: actions comm, WZO; exec, WJC; chmn, World Party Council, Brit-Herut-Hatzohar, all since 1946; research f, Inst J Affairs, 1941-43, dir, Research Bur on Population Movements, 1943-44; cons, US Off Strategic Services, 1944-45; dep mem exec, JA for Isr, 1948-51, mem exec, 1965-68; mem: All Russ J Cong, Petrograd, 1917; Ukranian Natl Assembly, Kiev, 1917; J Natl Secretariat, Kiev, 1918. Author: in Russ: The Jews and the Ukranians, 1917; Jews and National Movements in Free Russia, 1917; Under the Sign of Palestine, 1918; The Pogroms of the Volunteer Army, 1932; in Fr: Les Pogromes en Ukraine sous le Gouvernements Ukrainiens, 1927; in Ger: Die Jüdische Irredenta, 1929; Transjordanien im Bereiche des Palästina-mandates, 1937; in Eng: European Population Transfers, 1946; Population Transfers in Asia, 1949; The Value of Galut Yemen, 1950; The Arab Refugee Problem, 1951; The Vladimir Jabotinsky Story: vol 1, Rebel and Statesman, 1956, vol 2, Fighter and Prophet, 1959; On Wings of Eagles; Plight, Exodus, and Homecoming of Oriental Jewry, 1961; Star in Eclipse: Soviet Jewry Revisited, 1961; Postwar Population Transfers in Europe, 1944-55, pub, 1962; The United States and the Jewish State Movement, 1966; Zionism and Zionists in Sòviet Russia, 1966; Jordan-A State That Never Was, 1968; co-ed: Unser Weg, Paris, 1930-31; Rasswiet, Berlin, 1922-24, Paris, 1926-34. Home: 85-43 168 Pl, Jamaica, NY.

SCHEER, Eva, Nor, journalist, author; b. Oslo, Nor, Mar 13, 1915; d. Salomon and Hanna (Scheer) Kaldosin. Corresp: Arbeiderbladet, Nor Govt newspaper, since 1947; Jewish Chronicle, London, since 1949; on lectr tours about Isr; columnist for 5 mags and newspapers; lectr: Dept Educ; Dept Defense; adv to theater, TV. Author: We Are Building in the Sand, 1948; We Meet in Jerusalem, 1951; Teddy Bear at Wavelength, 1954; A Textbook About Israel, 1966; Israel-Land of the Double Promise, 1967; contbr to: anthols; encys; textbooks; trans: The Children of the Umbrella-Maker by Jascha Galuwanjuk, 1947; The Only Performance by Willy Corsari, 1952; Children's Book Serial, 1956. Co-found, Norway-Isr Soc. Home: Bogstadv 3, Oslo, Nor.

SCHEFFLER, Israel, US, philosopher, educator; b. NYC, Nov 25, 1923; s. Leon and Ethel (Grunberg); BA, Bklyn Coll, 1945, MA, 1948; MHL, JTSA, 1949; PhD, U of Pa, 1952; hon AM, Harvard U, 1960; m. Rosalind Zuckerbrod, June 26, 1949; c: Samuel, Laurie. Victor S Thomas prof, educ, phil, Harvard U, since 1964, prof, educ, 1961-64, on fac since 1952; Guggenheim f, 1958-59. Author: The Language of Education, 1960; The Anatomy of Inquiry, 1963; Conditions of Knowledge, 1965; Science and Subjectivity, 1967; ed, Philosophy and Education, 1958; contbr to educ and phil jours. Mem: Amer Phil Assn; Assn for Symbolic Logic; Phil of Educ Soc; AAUP; John Dewey Soc; Aristotlian Soc; charter mem, Natl Acad Educ. Home: 3 Woodside Rd, Newton, Mass. Office: Harvard U, Cambridge, Mass.

SCHEIBER, Alexander, Hung, educator, rabbi; b. Budapest, Hung, July 9, 1913; s. Lajos and Mária (Adler); deg, U Budapest, 1937; ordained rabbi, Rabb Sem of Hung, 1938; D, HC, HUC, 1960; m. Livia Bernáth, 1942; c: Mária. Prin, Natl Rabb Sem of Hung, since 1950; chief rabbi, town of Dunaföldvár, Hung, 1940-44; prof, U Szeged, 1949. Corresp mem, J Hist Soc of Eng. Author: Mikszáth Kálmán és a keleti folklor, 1949; The Kaufmann Haggadah, Eng, pub Budapest, 1957; Corpus Inscriptionum Hungariae Judaicarum, 1960; Hebräische Kodexüberrestse in ungarländischen Einbandstafeln, 1969; ed: Heller Jubilee Volume, 1941; Semitic Studies in Memory of Immanuel Löw, 1947; co-ed: Ginzeh Kaufmann, 1949; Ignace Goldziher Memorial Volume, 1958; Monumenta Hungariae Judaica, vols V-XI, 1958-68; Löw: Fauna und Mineralien der Juden, 1969. Home: Kun utca 12, Budapest, Hung. Office: József körút 27, Budapest, Hung.

SCHEIN, Clarence J, US, surgeon; b. NYC, Jan 15, 1918; s. Benjamin and Fannie (Feldman); BS, cum laude, NYU, 1938, MD, 1942; m. Ada Frenkel, Sep 1, 1960. Pvt practice since 1948; asso prof, surg, Albert Einstein Coll of Med, since 1956; asso surg, Montefiore Hosp, since 1948. Mem: Amer Coll Surgs; NY Soc for Thoracic Surg; Acad of Med; Soc Acad Surgs; AAAS; Amer Bd Thoracic Surg; Amer Bd Gen Surg; Amer Coll Gastroenology; Phi Beta Kappa. Contbr to profsl jours and films. Home: 5400 Fieldston Rd, Riverdale, NY. Office: 111 E 210 St, New York, NY.

SCHEINBERG, Peritz, US, physician, educator; b. Miami, Fla, Dec 21, 1920; s. Mendel and Esther (Asch); AB, Emory U, 1941, MD, 1944; m. Dollye Selby, Sep 19, 1942; c: Philip, Richard. Chmn, dept neur, prof, U Miami Sch of Med, since 1958, fac mem since 1952; instr, Duke U Med Sch, 1949-50; research asso, U of Miami med research unit, 1950-52. USNR, 1944-45, 1953-55. Vice-pres, Miami chap, AJComm, 1959-61; med adv bd, Natl Multiple Sclerosis Soc; dipl: Amer Bd Intl Med; Amer Bd Psycht and Neur; FACP; f, Amer Acad Neur; mem: Assn Research in Nervous and Mental Disorders; Amer Fed for Clinical Research; S Soc for Clinical Research; Phi Beta Kappa; Omicron Delta Kappa; Alpha Omega Alpha; Sigma Xi. Contbr numerous articles to med jours. Home: 66 Bay Hgts Dr, Miami, Fla. Office: U of Miami Sch of Med, Miami, Fla.

SCHEINER, Samuel Leo, US, organization exec; b.Minneapolis, Minn, Sep 22, 1908; DJ, U Minn, 1930; m. Sally Levenson, Oct 1, 1933; c: Susan Druskin, James. Exec dir, J Comty Relations Council, Minn, since 1939; atty, pvt practice, 1931-39; instr, hum relations: Minneapolis, St Paul schs; Us; Minn Bur Criminal Apprehension; Suburban Police Chief's Sch on Police-Comty Relations. Sgt, US Army, 1944-46. Vice-pres, Assn J Comty Relations Workers; natl leg off, JWV; mem, exec comm, Amer Rehab Inst and Found; bd dirs: UN Assn; United World Federalists; chmn, subversive activities comm, 5th dist, Amer Legion; tmr pres, Arthur Brin lodge, B'nai B'rith; mem: Gov's Hum Rights Commn; civil rights comm, Minn Bar Assn; Gov's Crime Prevention Commn; AJComm; AJCong; J Lab Comm. Recipient: state cert, State of Minn, 1951; humanitarian award, St Paul Mt Zion, 1951; hum relations awards: WCCO Radio; Minneapolis Fair Employment Practices Commn; Twin City Council of Clubs; 4-H Movement, Minn; dist service award, mayor of Minn; award: Freedom Found; NCCJ; Minn UN; Minneapolis Cen Lab; Columbus Heights HS, Minn; Minneapolis Ramsey Jr HS PTA. Spec interest: piano, golf, bridge. Home: 3023 Lynn Ave S, St Louis Park, Minn. Office: 211 Produce Bank Bldg, Minneapolis, Minn.

SCHEINERT, David, Belgium, author; b. Pol, May 29, 1916; s. Jacob and Fela (Józefowicz); in Belgium since 1924; m Suzanne Servais 1941. Author: L'Apprentissage Inutile, 1948; Le Coup d'Etat, 1950; Le Flamand aux Longues Oreilles, 1960; Le Mal du Docteur Laureys, 1962; La Contre-Saison, 1966; Un Silence Provisoire, 1968; play, L'Homme qui allait à Götterwald, 1970; 7 collections of poems; one collection of short stories; adaptation, Cantique des Cantiques (Song of Songs). Recipient: Prix Rossel, for Le Flamand aux Longues Oreilles, 1961. Home: Parklaan 200, Overijse, Belgium.

SCHEINFELD, Amram, US, social scientist, author; b. Lewisville, Ky, June 1, 1897; s. Solomon and Sanna (Sachs); att: U Wis; NYU; New Sch for Social Research; art sch: Milw; NY; Paris; m. Dorothy Suratt, 1951. Mag writer since 1930; newspaper reporter, ed, cartoonist: newspapers in Milw, Baltimore, NY, 1916-26; King Features, McNaught Syndicates, 1924-34. Author: You and Heredity, 1939; Women and Men, 1944; Postscript to Wendy, novel, 1948; The New You and Heredity, 1950; The Human Heredity Handbook, 1956; Why You are You 1959; The Basic Facts of Human Heredity, 1961; Your Heredity and Environment, 1965; Twins and Supertwins, 1967; contbr to natl mags and profsl jours. F: Amer Sociol Soc; NY Acad Sci; AAAS; Eugenics Soc; Eng; asso: Columbia U Seminar on Human Genetics; Inst Psychol Research; Tchrs Coll; bd mem, Comty Guidance Service, NYC; mem: Amer Psychol Assn; Amer Soc Hum Genetics; Genetics Soc of Amer; Amer Genetics Assn; Natl Council Family Relations; Natl Assn Sci Writers; Soc Mag Writers. Recipient: Saturday Review Anisfield-Wolf award, 1966. Home and office: 37 W 12 St, New York, NY.

SCHEINGARTEN, Milton L, US, architect; b. NYC, Mar 3, 1911; s. Morris and Clara (Kleinman); att: Columbia U, 1928-34; George Wash U, 1937-38; m. Shirley Solomon, Nov 3, 1934; c: Rena Safer, Sheva. Pvt practice since 1958;

asst architect to Eric Mendelsohn, 1934-37; architect, USN Dept, 1938-44; partner, Levy & Scheingarten, 1944-58. Found, trustee, dir, NJ Soc of Architects, since 1968; fmr: pres, Suburban J Cen, Linden; vice-pres: NJ Zionist Region; NJ council, JNF; city chmn, Isr Bonds; mem: Amer Inst Architects; Isr Assn Architects and Engrs; Columbia U Alumni. Contbr to profsl jours. Recipient: Cert of merit, NJ Soc of Architects, 1950-51. Home; 59 Edgewood Rd, Linden, NJ. Office: 1 Broad St, Elizabeth, NJ.

SCHELITZER, Walter Z, Isr, real estate broker; b. Posen, Ger, Apr 3, 1906; s. Wilhelm and Julie (Peiser) Chrzelitzer; in Isr since 1936; m. Gertrud Boehm, Sep 8, 1931; c: Ofra Jacoby. Owner, Schelitzer Gen Brokers and Trustees, Tel Aviv, since 1944; asst mgr: Freiherr von Richthofen, AG, 1925-27; Quabis Bread Factory, 1927-30; both in Breslau; mgr, Halpaus Bread Factory, Gleiwitz, 1930-33; gen mgr, O H Feinbaeckerei, Frankfort/M, 1933-36. Found, first pres, Maldan, Isr Real Estate Brokers Assn, hon pres, since 1959; chmn, council, Isr Philharmonic Orch Assn, since 1961; fmr grand pres, B'nai B'rith Grand Lodge No 14; fmr vice-pres, Supr Lodge; fmr pres, Bialik Lodge; mem, Tel Aviv comm, Cen Eur Immigrants Assn; council mem: Intl Real Estate Fed; Mus Assn; Tel Aviv Assn for Contemporary Music. Home: 118 Hayarkon St, Tel Aviv, Isr. Office: 24 Yavneh St, Tel Aviv, Isr.

SCHENFELD, Rina, Isr, dancer; b. Tel Aviv, Isr, Dec 16, 1938; s. Israel and Deborah (Zekel); att: Martha Graham's Sch for Contemporary Dance; Juilliard Dance Sch; Conn Coll, all US; m. Uri Feigenblat, 1961; c: Tamar. Soloist, asst to artistic dir, Batsheva Sch of Dance, Tel Aviv; fmr: found, dance group; mem, Lyric Theatre of Anna Sokolow; created Fado, a solo dance; choreographed: Figures; Jephta's Daughter, Blindman's Buff; outstanding roles: Errand into the Maze; Cave of the Heart; The Mythical Hunters; Side Show; Voices of Fire. Home: 14 Harav Friedman, Tel Aviv, Isr.

SCHENK, Faye Libby, US, communal leader; b. Des Moines, Ia, Sep 17, 1909; d. Naphtali Zeichik; BA, Drake U, Des Moines, 1926, MA, 1932; m. Max Schenk, Sep 3, 1933; c: Mina Hechtman, Alice Raphael. Natl pres, Hadassah, since 1968. fmr natl vice-pres, secy, treas, found and 1st pres, Wash Hgts group, NY chap, fmr pres, Bklyn Pkwy chap; mem: Actions Comm, World Zionists Org; Pres' Conf Natl J Org; bd govs, Heb U, Jerusalem; delg, WZCs. Home: 115 Central Park W, New York, NY. Office: 65 E 52 St, New York, NY.

SCHENK, Max, US, rabbi; b. Berne, Switz, Jan 9, 1905; s. Sigmund and Minna (Schneider); in US since 1907; BA, CCNY, 1925; MHL, ordained rabbi, HUC-JIR, 1928, hon DD, 1954; m. Faye Zeichik, Sep 3, 1933; c: Mina Hechtman, Raphael. Rabbi: Cong Shaari Zedek, Bklyn, NY, since 1949; Temple Judah, Cedar Rapids, Ia, 1928-32; YM-YWHA Syn, NY, 1933-39; Temple Emmanuel, Sydney, Austr, 1939-49; fmr lectr: ext div, Sydney U, Austr Army Educ Dept. Vice-pres, Bklyn div, AJCong; dir: TB and Health Assn, Bklyn; J Educ Comm of NY, since 1960; mem: natl rabb advi council, UJA; CCAR; speaker's bur, JWB, UJA; fmr: pres, Bklyn Bd of Rabbis; chmn exec comm, pres, co-chmn, chaplaincy comm, vice-pres, NY Bd Rabbis; pres, Bklyn Assn Reform Rabbis; mem exec comm: NY Assn of Reform Rabbis; JCC, Bklyn; pres, Alumni Assn, HUC-JIR, mem bd govs; rel adv, Girl Scouts of Amer; mem: admn council, ZOA; Jt Leg Comm on Child Wfr; in Austr: pres, ZF, Austr and NZ; hon pres, Youth Aliyah, Austr and NZ; patron, Friends Heb U; dir, JWB for SW Pacific; delg: Austr, NZ WZC's, London; United Pal Appeal, Eng. Co-ed, Australian J Review, 1940-49, contbr to periodicals. Home: 115 Central Park W, New York, NY.

SCHENKER, Avraham, Isr, US, organization exec; b. Bklyn, NY, Oct 15, 1918; s. Joseph and Esther (Eisenberg); att CCNY, 1937; m. Sima Altman, 1940; c: Hillel, Naomi. Mem, exec, JA, Jerusalem, since 1968, dep mem, Amer sect, 1956-68; natl vice-chmn, AZC, since 1961; hon chmn, JNF of Amer, since 1960; mem, exec: World Union of Mapam, since 1955; WJC, since 1968. US Army, 1944-46. Mem: Assn for Help of Retarded Childern; Monthly Rev Assos; New Outlook Assos; Farband Lab Zionist Order; fmr: secy: Hashomer Hatzair Zionist Youth: Hechalutz of Amer; dir, Camp Shomria, NY; admn secy, Natl Comm for Lab Isr; Progressive Zionist League; natl chmn, Amers for Progressive Isr; mem bd dirs, UJA; vice-chmn, WJC, Amer sect. Author: The Bi-national Position of Hashomer Hatzair, 1944; chmn, ed bd, Israel Horizons, 1952-68; contbr to periodicals. Hobby:

philately. Home: 1151 E 12 St, Bklyn, NY. Office: POB 92, Jerusalem, Isr.

SCHENKER, Benjamin N, US, surgeon; b. Buffalo, NY, June 27, 1901; s. Nathan and Risa (Rothenberg); BS, Fordham U, 1923; MD, Cincinnati Electric Med Sch, 1928; m. Jeanette Adelberg, Feb 21, 1942; c: Arlene, Sheila. Pvt practice since 1930; att phys, St Francis Hosp, Jersey City; att surg: Greenville Hosp; Margaret Hague Hosp; Courtesy Med Cen, all Jersey City, since 1930, sci f, instr, chem, Fordham U, 1922-23. Capt, US Army MC, 1942-45. Pres, Cong Tifereth Isr; Mem: AMA; Hudson Co Med Soc; Eclectic Med Soc, fmr pres; UJA Isr Bonds; Yeshiva of Hudson Co; Mizrachi; ZOA; B'nai B'rith; JWV; Amer Legion; KP; Masons; Shriners. Contbr to med jours. Hobby: photography. Home: 38 Kensington Ave, Jersey City, NJ. Office: 249 Eighth St, Jersey City, NJ.

SCHENKER, Léon-Max, Fr, naval engr, educator; b. Warsaw, Pol, June 24, 1903; s. Elimelech and Ida (Fajncyn); in Fr since 1928; att Poly Inst, Warsaw, 1921-24; Off Sch, Grudziadz, Pol, 1924-25; grad, Poly Inst, Nantes, Fr, 1930; licencié des sciences mathématiques, Faculté des Sciences, Rennes, 1931; m. Cecile Budovniczy, April 30, 1930; c: Claude. Prof, atomic energy and electrodynamics, Faculté de Nantes; head, research lab, Navy Yard, Nantes, since 1930; collaborator, Sci Research Bur of Fr. Pol Army, 1921-26, off, 1924-26. Co-found, pres: Assn J Engrs and Technicians in Fr; Friends of Isr, both since 1949; Zionist Org, 1946; pres, WJC, 1948; found; J Schs, in W Fr; Ligue Internationale d'Amis d'Action Sioniste; mem, ZF of Fr. Author: Sur pluies dans les déserts, 1953; Ouvrage Sociologique et économopolitique sur le Judaisme. Recipient: Virtuti militaris, Pol, 1921. Spec interests: meteorology, atomic weapons. Home and office: 16 av des Primevères, Nantes, Fr.

SCHEPS, Abraham, Arg, economist, public official; b. Entre Rios, Arg, May 9, 1912; s. Luis and Ana (Kaler); DSc, Econ and Natl CA, U Buenos Aires; m. Paulina Heller, Feb 21, 1942; c: Margarita, Violeta. Econ adv, Arg C of C; Arg adv, Inter-Amer Council of Commerce and Prod, delg exec comm, NY, 1956, Buenos Aires, 1957, Sao Paulo, 1958, Guayaquil-Quito, 1959, Montevideo, 1961; adv to pvt enterprises; expert, Arg commn, Latin-Amer Free Trade Zone Assn; fmr: exec mem, Coll of Grads of Econ Scis, Fed Capital; found and first pres, Jr C of C, Arg; asst, Inst of Public Admn, Fac of Econ Scis; invited by US State Dept to carry out research on custom unions, Org of Amer States, 1943-44; mem, Arg mission to ILO, Geneva, 1956; delg, Conf of Econ Min of Amer Countries, Buenos Aires, 1957; delg, Comm of 21, Buenos Aires, 1959; repr, Profsl Council of Econ Scis, natl conv, Buenos Aires, 1959; delg, Inter-Governmental Conf on Free Trade Zone, Montevideo, 1959, 1960; delg, 1st Arg Cong of Jt Stock Cos, Buenos Aires, 1960; delg, Cong of Intl C of C, Copenhagen, 1961; delg, conf of Punta del Este, Uruguay, 1961; adv, official Arg delg, negotiations of Montevideo Pact, 1961, invited to lecture by US State Dept. Home: 2781 Malabia, Buenos Aires, Arg.

SCHERAGA, Harold Abraham, US, educator; b. Bklyn, NY, Oct 18, 1921; s. Samuel and Etta (Goldberg); BS, CCNY, 1941; AM, Duke U, Durham, NC, 1942, PhD, 1946, hon ScD, 1961; m. Miriam Kurnow, June 20, 1943; c: Judith, Deborah, Daniel. Todd Prof Chem, Cornell U, since 1965, prof, chem, since 1958, chmn, dept chem, 1960-67, mem fac since 1947; mem, adv panel in molecular biol, NSF, 1960-62; Harvey lectr, NYC, 1968; Gallagher lectr, CCNY, 1968-69. Chmn, Cornell sect, Amer Chem Soc, 1955-56, fmr councillor; mem: exec comm, div biol chem, Amer Chem Soc, 1966-69; council, Biophys Soc, 1967-70; research career award comm, Natl Insts Gen Med Sci, NIH, 1967-71; biochem training comm, 1963-65; exec comm, Amer Profs for Peace in ME; Ithaca Bd Educ, 1958-59; Amer Soc Biol Chem; Biophys Soc; Faraday Soc; AAAS; Natl Acad Sci; Amer Acad Sci; Amer Inst Chem; Phi Beta Kappa; Sigma Xi; Phi Lambda Upsilon. Author: Protein Structure, 1961; Theory of Helix-Coil Transitions in Biopolymers, 1969; co-ed, Molecular Biol, Acad Press, since 1961; mem: adv bd, Biopolymers, since 1963; ed adv bd, Biochemistry, since 1969; ed bd, Physiol Chem & Physics, since 1969; contbr to sci jours. Recipient: Eli Lilly Award in biochem, 1957; Guggenheim f, Fulbright research scholar: Carlsberg Lab, Copenhagen, Den, 1956-57; Weizmann Inst, Isr, 1963; NIH spec f, Weizmann Inst, Isr, 1970. Hobbies: golf, skiing. Home: 212 Homestead Terr Ithaca, NY. Office: Dept of Chem, Cornell U, Ithaca, NY.

SCHERAGO, Morris, US, microbiologist, educator; b. Rum, Dec 25, 1895; s. Israel and Bessie (Jacobs); in US since 1899; BS, Cornell U, 1917; DVM, 1919; hon DSc, Honoris Causa, U Ky, 1966; m. Jane Stone, Sep 5, 1920; c: Earl, Emily Rubin. Ret; prof, bact, renamed microbiol, U Ky, 1924-66, chmn dept, 1923-66, on fac since 1919; lab asst, USPHS, NY, 1918; asst, comparative path and bact, Cornell U, 1918-19; bact, Life Ext Inst, NYC, 1919; asst bact, NY State Dept Health, Albany, 1920; visiting prof, bact, Wash U School of Med, St Louis, assigned to tech and econ mission, US Mutual Security Admn, med schs in Bangkok, Thailand, 1951-52; cons: hematology, Jockey Club; bact, USPHS Hosp, Lexington, Ky; Institut de Salubridad y Enfermedades Tropicales, Mex. Dipl, Amer Bd Microbiol; f: Amer Acad Microbiol; Amer Coll Allergists; Amer Public Health Assn; asso f, Amer Soc Clinical Paths; mem: AAAS; AAUP; Amer Assn Immunologist; Soc Amer Bacts, fmr councillor; Conf State and Provincial Public Health Lab; Amer Soc Profsl Biol, exec secy, since 1961; S Assn Sci and Ind, exec comm, 1941-43; Valley Allergy Soc; Ky-Tenn Soc Microbiol, pres, 1940-41; Ky Acad Sci, pres, 1948-49; Ky Public Health Assn; Royal Soc Health, London, Eng; Sigma Xi; B'nai B'rith, pres, 1928; bd dirs, Comty Chest, 1923-34; Boy Scout Council, 1923-26; clubs: U Ky Research, fmr pres; Lions, fmr pres. Co-author: Reading Assignments for Lectures on Bacteriology for Medical Students; Laboratory Exercises in General Bacteriology; collaborator, 4th ed, Diagnostic Procedures and Reagents; ed: Biological Abstracts, allergy sect; asst ed, Quarterly Review of Allergy and Applied Immunology; mem, ed bd, Annals of Allergy; contbr to sci and med jours. Recipient: dist prof of year, U Ky, 1950-51; U Ky Alumni award, 1955; King award, Ky Acad Sci, 1941; research grants: Amer Coll Allergists, 1947-49; O Valley Allergy Soc, 1953; Ky Heart Assn, 1958-62; NIH, 1956-64. Home: 255 Shady Lane, Lexington, Ky.

SCHERBERG, Max G, US, aeronautical engr; b. Russ, Mar 7, 1902; s. Jacob and Bessie (Keiner); in US since 1904; BS, Wash U, St Louis, Mo, 1925; att U Chgo, 1927-28; PhD, U Minn, 1931; m. Goldie Steinberg, Jan, 1930; c: Lee, Neal. Research sci, Aeronautical Research Labs, Wright Patterson Air Force Base, chief, applied math br, 1949-54; asst tech dir, 1954-60; mem, dept math, Coll of Engr and Grad Sch, 1928-40; aerodynamicist, Chance Vought Aircraft, 1940-45; engr specialist and aerodynamicist, McDonnell Aircraft, 1945-49. Prin contribs: directed aerodynamic design of fighter aircraft XP88; designed and patented spec valve for pulse-jet engine; designed and experimentally checked polynomial analog computer. Mem: council, Dayton-Cincinnati br, Inst Aeronautical Scis, 1960-61; treas, Minn sect, Amer Fed of Tchrs, 1937-38; AAAS; bd dirs, Temple Isr, Dayton, O, 1956-59. Contbr to profsl jours. Hobby: music. Home: 1506 Cory Dr, Dayton, O. Office: Wright Patterson Air Force Base, Dayton, O.

SCHERF, David, US, physician, educator; b. Aus, Oct 18, 1899; s. Isaac and Regina (Kreindler); in US since 1938; MD, U Vienna, 1922; m. Gertrude Goetz, Apr 11, 1930. Prof, clinical med, NY Med Coll, since 1953, asso prof, 1938-53; privatdozent, U Vienna, 1935-38. F: Amer Coll Chest Phys; Amer Coll Card, vice-pres; hon f: Swiss, Arg, Fr, Brazil Heart Assns; mem: AHA; AAAS; corresp hon mem, Vienna Med Soc. Author: Cardiovascular Diseases; Clinical Electrocardiography; co-author, Extrasystoles and Allied Arrhythmias; contbr to med jours. Hobby: photography. Home: 10 E 85 St, New York, NY. Office: 1 E 105 St, New York, NY.

SCHERMAN, Harry, US, publisher, author; b. Montreal, Can, Feb 1, 1887; s. Jacob and Katharine (Harris); in US since 1889; att Wharton Sch of Finance and Sch of Law, U of Pa, 1905-07; m. Bernardine Kielty, June 3, 1914; c: Katharine, Thomas. Chmn bd, Book-of-the-Month Club Inc, since 1950, pres, 1931-50, co-found, 1926; free-lance writer, NYC, 1907-12; advt: Rutherauff & Ryan; J Walter Thompson, 1912-16; co-org, The Little Leather Library Corp, 1916, pres; partner, advt agcy with Maxwell Sackheim, 1920-26. Author: The Promises Men Live By, 1937; Will We Have Inflation, 1941; The Last Best Hope of Earth, 1941; contbr on econ and monetary subjects. Dir, Natl Bur Econ Research, since 1937, pres, 1950-51, 1954, chmn bd, 1952-53, 1955-56, hon trustee, 1967; trustee, Comm for Econ Devl, since 1967; clubs: Cent; Players; Lotos. Home: 322 E 57 St, New York, NY. Office: 280 Park Ave, New York, NY.

SCHERMER, Robert, US, dentist; b. Czech, June 6, 1920; s. Harry and Anna (Rosenwater); in US since 1921; DDS, O State U, 1943; m. Gertrude Chertoff, Dec 8, 1947; c: Bruce,

Carol. Pvt practice since 1943. Capt, US Army, Dent Corps, 1943-46. Chmn: dent div, JWF, Cleveland, O; Cash Day, UJA, Cleveland, fmr chmn, dent div; mem: campaign team, Metzenbaum for US Sen; Alpha Omega; Amer Dent Assn, both Cleveland, O; fmr: pres, Cleveland Acad for Dent Studies; bd mem, B'nai B'rith U Lodge; club, Beechmont Country, Cleveland. Contbr to dent jours. Hobbies: art collector, sculpturing, golf, photography, travel. Home: 19950 Shaker Blvd, Shaker Heights, O. Office: 510 Euclid Ave, Cleveland, O.

SCHIBY, Baruch, Greece, journalist, author; b. Thessaloniki, Greece, May 15, 1906; s. Jacob and Reyna (Beracha); att Amer Mission Sch, Thessaloniki; m. Rachel Chaim, Mar 27, 1945; c: Jacob, David, Malka. Mgr, J Comty, Thessaloniki, since 1948; journalist, ed-in-chief: Independent; El Pueblo; La Prensa, 1925-48; ed, mgr, Delfiká Tetradia, periodical, 1964. Greek resistance, WW II, aided escape of chief rabbi Elia Barzilay. Pres, Circle Arts and Letters, N Greece; mgn mem, Delphic Org; mem: J cultural org; Thessaloniki Frat; fmr: participant in various phil congs; Greek repr, Zionist Lab Party; active in establishment: Salonica U; Salonica Intl Fair. Author: The Burning Bush, 1968; Haggadah shel Pessah, with comments, hist, colored pictures, 1969, both in Greek; History of the Jewish People; contbr numerous articles and confs on J subjects in Greek and Fr. Spec interests: phil, archaeol, theol. Home: 39 Vas Heracliou, Thessaloniki, Greece. Office: 24 Vas Heracliou, Thessaloniki, Greece.

SCHIEBER, David, Isr, engineer; b. Rum, May 30, 1938; s. Shalom and Gisella (Fuhrmann); in Isr since 1951; MSc, Technion, Haifa, 1962, DSc, 1965; m. Nira Leimann; c: Tamar, Yoav. Sr lectr, Technion, Haifa, since 1966. Lt, IDF, 1960-62. Numerous patents in field of elec engr. Contbr to intl profsl jours. Home: 7 Simtat Ehud, Haifa, Isr. Office: Technion, Haifa, Isr.

SCHIEBER, Eric, Fr, organization exec; b. Wizenka, Aus-Hung, June 9, 1915; s. Léon and Jenta (Udelsmann); in Fr since 1938; att 1st Viennese Handelsakademie, Vienna; dipl, U Vienna, Law, 1938; m. Gita Sochaczewska, 1951; c: Judith, Emmanuel. Admn dir, ORT, Fr, since 1957; ed: ORT a ses Amis; Nouvelles de l'ORT, both since 1964. Secy gen: J Art Mus, Paris; Repr Council Traditional Judaism of Fr; mem: B'nai B'rith. Home: 31 rue du Fbg Poissonnière, Paris, Fr. Office: 10 Villa d'Eylau, Paris, Fr.

SCHIEBER, Jakob, Isr, business exec; b. Russ, July 9, 1905; s. Meshulam and Bluma (Zloczower); in Isr since 1941; dipl, atty, U Czernowitz; m. Manea Godelman; c: Jehudith Blachman. Mgr: Univers Ltd, travel off, since 1954; Romis, import-export, since 1967, both Tel Aviv. Sgt, Rum Army, 1930-31. Mem, Masons, Tel Aviv; found, 1st cdr, Betar, Rum; fmr: mem: Ketzin Shilton Betar Olamit; Ketzin Galil, Haifa; i/c illegal immigration from Rum. Author: Haivri, Heb textbook; contbr to Yiddish and Rum press. Home: 118 Arlosoroff St, Tel Aviv, Isr. Office: 17 Rambam St, Tel Aviv, Isr.

SCHIEBER, Michael Misho, Isr, physicist, educator; b. Vatra-Dornei, Rum, Nov 4, 1928; s. Menahem and Pnina (Margalit); in Isr since 1952; grad, Inst Poly, Bucharest, 1951; PhD, Heb U, Jerusalem, 1961; m. Bella Friedman, May 24, 1953; c: Pnina, Dorit. Asso prof, experimental physics, Heb U, since 1968, on fac since 1966; research asso, Weizmann Inst, Rehovot, 1957-62; research f: Imperial Coll, London, 1962-63; Harvard U, Boston, 1963-64; Natl Magnet Lab, MIT, 1964-66. Secy gen, Intl Comm on Crystal Growth; mem: Sigma Xi, Harvard U; Amer Phys Soc; Amer Ceramic Soc. Author: Experimental Magnetochemistry, 1967; prin ed, Jour of Crystal Growth, N Holland, since 1967; contbr to sci jours. Home: 4 Brenner St, Jerusalem, Isr. Office: Heb U, Jerusalem, Isr.

SCHIFF, Alvin Irwin, US, educator; b. Boston, Mass, Aug 8, 1926; s. Jacob and Miriam (Schriebman); BA, Yeshiva U, 1947, tchrs dipl, 1948, PhD, 1959; MA, Columbia U, 1950; m. Miriam Fleschner, Aug 31, 1952; c: Debra, Linda. Prof, chmn, dept J educ, Ferkauf Grad Sch of Humanities and Social Scis, Yeshiva U, since 1965; visiting prof, social sci research, CCNY, since 1968; asst prin, Heb Inst of LI, 1952-55; instr to asso prof and sup, student teaching, Yeshiva U, 1948-65; educ cons, J Educ Comm of NY, 1956-65. Prin contrib: research in contemporary J educ. Pres, JCC, Oceanside; vice-pres, Natl Council for J Educ; chmn, comm for certification of prins, Natl Bd License; mem: educ planning comm, CJFWF; natl adv comm, dept educ and culture and dept of Torah and culture, JA; commn on J educ, COJO; governing bd, Amer

Assn for J Educ; Natl Conf J Communal Service; AAUP; Natl Council Young Isr; fmr, chmn, Oceanside J Forum. Author: The Jewish Day School in America, 1966; Haggadah Latalmid, 1969; nine tchrs manuals; ed, Teachers Guide to World Over mag, 1959-65; asso ed, Jewish Education, since 1967; contbr to educ publs. Recipient: cert of award, Yeshiva U, 1964; Natl Bible Contest Citation, Dept Educ and Culture, JA, 1966; Bernard Revel Memorial Award, Yeshiva Coll Alumni Assn, 1968. Hobbies: Isr society, comparative J educ, tennis. Home: 33 Jordan St, Oceanside, NY. Office: 55 Fifth Ave, New York, NY.

SCHIFF, Dorothy, US, publisher; b. NYC, Mar 11, 1903; d. Mortimer and Adele (Neustadt); att Bryn Mawr Coll, 1920-21; m; c: Mortimer Hall, Adele Hall, Sarah-Ann Backer; m. 4th, Rudolf Sonneborn, Aug 18, 1953. Owner, publisher, NY Post, since 1943, dir, vice-pres, treas, 1939-42, pres, publisher, 1942. Dir: Mt Sinai Hosp, 1934-38; Women's Trade Union League of NY, to 1939; NYC Bd Child Wfr, 1937-39; mem: NY Dem State Comm, 1952-54; Ellis I Investigating Comm, 1934. Office: 75 West St, New York, NY.

SCHIFF, Harold, Can, educator; b. Kitchener, Ont, June 24, 1923; s. Jacob and Lena (Bierstock); BA, U Toronto, 1945, MA, 1946, PhD, 1948; m. Daphne Line, Nov 30, 1948; c: Jack, Sherry. Prof, chem, dean, Fac of Sci, York U, Toronto, since 1965; cons: Ballistic Research Lab, US Army; Can Armament and Research Establishment; Environmental Sci Service Admn, Boulder, Colo; postdoc f, Natl Research Council, Ottowa, 1948-50; Nuffield f, Cambridge U, Eng, 1959-60; asso prof, chem, McGill U, Montreal, 1956-65; fmr cons, Geophysics Corp of Amer. F, Chem Inst, Can, vice-chmn, chem educ div, chmn, Montreal sect, 1953-54; mem: asso comm on space research, NRC; comm on research, McGill U; Sigma Xi; Can Assn U Tchrs. Co-author: Chemistry of Lower and Upper Atmosphere, 1961; contbr to profsl jours. Home: 60 Denwoods Dr, Toronto, Ont, Can. Office: York U, Toronto, Ont, Can.

SCHIFF, Herbert H, US, business exec; b. Columbus O, Oct 6, 1916; s. Robert and Rebecca (Lurie); BBS, U of Pa, 1938; m. Betty Topkis, June 19, 1938; c: Suzanne Gallant, Patricia Hershorin, Jane Fleckner. Chmn bd, SCOA Inds, Inc, since 1968, pres, since 1965, with firm since 1938. Chmn, consumer relations comm, Amer Retail Fed; active hon dir, Volume Footwear Retailers Amer; dir, O Retail Merchants; trustee, United Isr Appeal; mem: finance comm, Comm for Econ Devl; bd trustees: Natl Shoe Inst; United J Fund and Council, mem, exec bd, fmr pres; bd dirs: Columbus Baseball Club; J Cen; Heritage House; Hillel Found, O State U; natl council, JDC; CJFWF; United HIAS; adv council newspaper eds, Pres' Assn; adv bd, Youth Civic Bd; cabinet, UJA; natl exec comm, AJComm; fmr dir, Natl Footwear Mfr Assn; mem: Emergency Econ Stabilization Adv Comm; Rensselaer Mgmt Devl Council; Pres' Club, O State U; natl council, Fgn Policy Assn; Newcomen Soc N Amer; Amer Econ Preparatory Comm; B'nai B'rith; clubs: Athletic, Columbus; Standard, Chgo; Winding Hollow Country, Columbus. Home: 1620 E Broad St, Columbus, O. Office: 35 N 4 St, Columbus, O.

SCHIFF, John M, US, banker; b. Roslyn, NY, Aug 26, 1904; s. Mortimer and Adele (Neustadt); BA, Yale U, 1925; BA, MA, New Coll, Oxford U, 1927; m. Edith Baker, May 3, 1934; c: David, Peter. Partner, Kuhn, Loeb & Co, since 1931, with firm since 1929; dir: Getty Oil Co; Uniroyal, Inc; Kennecott Copper Corp; Madison Fund, Inc; LA and Salt Lake RR; Westinghouse Elec Corp; CIT Financial Corp; Gt Atlantic and Pacific Tea Co; trustee, Provident Loan Soc; fmr, asso with: Bankers Trust Co, NY; Mo Pacific RR, St Louis, Mo, 1927-29. Cdr, USNR, 1945. Trustee, dir: Nassau co council, Boy Scouts Amer; NY Zool Soc; JWB; NYU; NY Public Libr; Visiting Nurse Service, NY; clubs: Grolier; River; Creek; Piping Rock; Turf and Field; Meadow Brook; Natl Golf; Metrop, Wash, DC. Home: Berry Hill Rd, Oyster Bay, NY. Office: 40 Wall St, New York, NY.

SCHIFF, Leon, US, physician, educator; b. Riga, Latvia, May 1, 1901; s. Mordecai and Esther (Liebschutz); in US since 1905; BS, U Cincinnati, 1922, MD, 1924, MS, 1927, PhD, 1929; m. Augusta Miller, June 9, 1925; c: Herbert (decd), Gilbert, Eugene. Prof, med, U Cincinnati, since 1958, mem fac since 1930; dir, gastric research labs, Cincinnati Gen Hosp; att phys: J Hosp; Gen Hosp. F: AAAS; Amer Med Authors; FACP; mem: Amer Soc for Clinical Inves; Cen Soc for Clinical Research; Amer Gastroenterological Assn; Amer Assn for Study Liver Diseases, fmr pres; Intl Assn for Study

Liver; AMA; Subspecialty Bd Gastroenterology, 1953-57; affiliate, Royal Soc Med, Gt Brit. Author: Differential Diagnosis of Jaundice, 1946; Clinical Approach to Jaundice, 1952; ed, Diseases of the Liver, 1956, 1963, 1969; contbr to texts and med jours. Hobby: photography. Home: 5300 Hamilton Ave, Cincinnati, O. Office: Holmes Hosp, Cincinnati, O.

SCHIFF, Leonard J, US, physician; b. Plattsburgh, NY, Sep 28, 1910; s. Leo and Fanny (Schiff); BA, Cornell U, 1931; MD, Albany Med Coll, 1935; m. Laura Taylor, 1938; c: Gordon, Joseph. Dep commn, Clinton Co Dept of Health, since 1954; dir, health service, State U Coll, since 1957; att phys: Phys Hosp; Champlain Valley Hosp, both since 1940; health off, Plattsburgh, 1953-54. Fmr: pres: Clinton Co Health Council; Clinton Co Med Soc; Beth Isr Cong; secy, treas, Northeastern NY Diabetes Assn, secy, 4th dist, NY State Med Soc; dir: Plattsburgh C of C; Comty Chest; Clinton Co Council Comty Services; mem: Elks; B'nai B'rith. Contbr to med jours. Home: 19 Grace Ave, Plattsburgh, NY. Office: State U Coll, Plattsburgh, NY.

SCHIFF, Saul, US, business exec; b. Lith, Apr 15, 1897; s. Efraim and Sarah (Touff); in US since 1905; BA, U Cincinnati, 1921; m. Mollie Shapiro, Nov 6, 1927; c: Barbara Passloff, Carole Straus, Simone Englander. Cons, A S Beck Shoe Corp, since 1962, vice-pres, dir, 1947-62; dir: Musler-Price Co; First Isr Bank and Trust Co of NY. Co-found, Albert Einstein ' oll of Med; chmn: shoe ind campaigns, UJA, 1950-53; retail div, UJY Fund, 1958; shoe ind div, Golden Anniversary Boy Scout Capital Camp Campaign, 1960; shoe div, Natl Fund for Med Educ, 1961-62; sponsor, Herbert H Lehman Inst of Ethics; bd trustees, Home for Aged and Infirm Heb, NY; clubs: Econ; Fenway Golf; Lotos; Winding Hollow. Recipient: Louis Marshall award, JTSA, 1960. Home: 60 Park Rd, Scarsdale, NY.

SCHIFFER, Irvine, Can, psychoanalyst, educator; b. Toronto, Can, Feb 8, 1917; s. Abraham and Anna (Cohen); MD, U Toronto, 1941; psychan, Boston Psychoanalytic Inst, 1957; m. Ellen Norgan, Apr 21, 1949; c: Marc, David, Susan, Laura. Asst prof, psycht, U Toronto, since 1960, research prof, political econ, since 1968; teaching analyst: Can Psychoanalytic Soc, 1958; Can Inst of Psychan, 1958. Capt, RAMC. Mem: med and psychoanalytic socs; Sigma Alpha Mu. Contbr to profsl jours. Recipient: Afr and It Stars, 1943. Hobby: music. Home: 91 Gordon Rd, Willowdale, Ont, Can. Office: 300 St Clair Ave W, Toronto, Can.

SCHIFFMANN, Mina, Isr, scientist; b. Lwow, Pol, Dec 11, 1909; d. Samuel and Anna (Rikower) Nadel; in Isr since 1933; dipl eng agronom, U Nancy, Fr, 1930; dipl, in path, Inst Natl Agronomy, Paris, 1932; MSc, U Paris, 1933, DSc, 1938; m; c: Joram, Edna, Raphael. Sr lectr, plant path, Heb U, Rehovot, since 1952; head dept, research on storage of fruits and vegetables, Volcani Inst of Agric Research, since 1962; lectr, mycology, Tel Aviv U, 1952-60. Head, Haganah Women's Group, Rehovot, 1938-41. Prin contrib: research in biol of fungi and bact causing diseases of fruits and vegetables; control of plant diseases. Fmr i/c, local group, Magen David Adom, Rehovot; mem, Hashomer Hatzair, Pol. Contbr to Isr and intl jours. Spec interest: immigration to Isr. Home: 31 Rupin St, Rehovot, Isr. Offices: Volcani Inst of Agric Research; Fac of Agric, Heb U, Rehovot, Isr.

SCHIFMAN, Ben B, US, editor; b. Kan City, Mo, Apr 20, 1913; s. Aron and Celia (Sambursky); att Amer Inst Banking; m. Mary Lapin, 1937; c: Stanley, William, Elinor. Treas: Kan City Star Co, since 1966, bd dirs, since 1967, financial ed, since 1955; Cadillac Printing and Lithography, since 1966; bd dirs, Flambeau Paper Co, since 1967; reporter, UP, 1930-34. Chmn, finance comm, Kehilath Isr Syn, since 1959, trustee, since 1952; area dir, Boy Scouts of Amer, since 1950; pres, Soc Amer Bus Writers, 1966-67; vice-pres, Jr Achievement, since 1960; mem: Sigma Delta Chi; Kan City Soc Financial Analysts; clubs: Kan City; Intl Fgn Trade; Kan City Press. Home: 2108 W 70 St, Mission Hills, Kan. Office: 1729 Grand Ave, Kansas City, Mo.

SCHIFRIN, Sol S, US, physician; b. NYC, Aug 5, 1906; s. Samuel and Anna (Grunin); AB, Columbia Coll, 1926, MD, Coll Phys and Surgs, 1930; m. Fannie Galuten, Aug 19, 1934; c: Barry, Alvin, Rhoda. Att obstet, gyn, J Memorial Hosp, since 1962, fmr pres, med bd; visiting obstet gyn, Fordham Hosp, since 1950. Mem: Bx Gyn and Obstet Soc, fmr pres; Bx phys comm, UJA; f: Amer Coll Surgs; Amer Coll Obstets and Gyn; NY Acad Med; mem, Masons, fmr master. Hobbies: music, photography. Home: 194 Elk Ave, New Rochelle, NY.

SCHIMEL, Adolph, US, attorney, business exec; b. Vienna, Aus, 1899; s. Herman and Betty (Scharf); in US since 1904; BA, CCNY, 1920; LLB, Harvard, 1923; m. Muriel Lobar; c: Jane, Judy. Pvt practice since 1924; vice-pres, gen counsel, Universal Pictures. Dir, chmn, law commn, Motion Picture Assn; bd dirs, Will Rogers Memorial Fund; asso trustee, Cong Kehilath Jeshurun; trustee, J Child Care Assn; mem: Amer Bar Assn; Bar Assn, NYC; CCNY Alumni Assn; Harvard Law Sch Alumni Assn; club, City Athletic. Home: 176 E 71 St, New York, NY. Office: 445 Park Ave, New York, NY.

SCHIMELMAN, Joseph, US, rabbi; b. NYC, May 14, 1918; s. Meyer and Rose (Wieder); BA, cum laude, Yeshiva U, 1939; MA, Columbia U, 1942; PhD, Burton Coll, 1963; cert, public HS tchr; m. Gertrude Budin, Sep 6, 1941; c: David, Seymour, Mark, Frances. Rabbi: Cong Tifereth Isr, Glen Cove, NY, 1955-64; West Haven, Conn, 1942-44; Watertown, NY, 1944-47; Portsmouth, NH, 1947-51; Cumberland, Md, 1951-55; civilian chaplain: US Army, Pine Camp, NY, 1944-47; Portsmouth Naval Prison and Hosp, 1947-51; fmr: chief of clergy, NH, Civil Defense, Allegany Co, Md; tchr: phil, SUNY, Suffolk; J phil, J hist, Central HS; siocal studies, Harborfields CSD 6. Mem: Mayor's Comm on Race Relations; Citizens Adv Comm on Urban Renewal, Juvenile Delinquency; Public Sch Liaison Comm; Family Service Agcy; LI Assn of Rabbis, pres, 1960-61; N Shore Min Assn, pres, 1961-62; Nassau-Suffolk Assn Rabbis, vice-pres, 1961-64; NY Bd Rabbis; Mizrachi; B'nai B'rith; LI Prin Assn; club, Rotary. Home: 2 Pine Place, Glen Cove, NY.

SCHINDEL, Jehuda, Isr, physician; b. Tarnow, Pol, Mar 15, 1915; s. Asher and Rosa (Dresner); in Isr since 1950; MD, Med Sch, 1938; ear, nose, throat specialist, U Clinic, Erlangen, 1950; m. Dina Dresner, 1948; c: Asher, Doron, Karen. Head, ear, nose, throat dept, Beilinson Hosp, Petah Tikva, since 1966; sr lectr, Tel Aviv U Med Sch, since 1967. Mem: Intl Coll Surgs; Isr Ear, Nose, Throat Assn; Isr Surg Assn. Contbr to med jours. Home: 34 Bloch St, Tel Aviv, Isr. Office: Beilinson Hosp, Petah Tikva, Isr.

SCHINDLER, Alexander Monroe, US, rabbi; b. Munich, Ger, Oct 4, 1925; s. Eliezer and Sali (Hojda); in US since 1938; BSS, CCNY, 1949; BHL, MHL, ordained rabbi, HUC-JIR, Cincinnati, O, 1949-53; m. Rhea Rosenblum, Sep 29, 1956; c: Elisa, Debra, Joshua, Jonathan, Judith. Vice-pres, UAHC, since 1967; dir, NE council, 1959-63, natl dir, educ, 1963-67; asso rabbi, Temple Emanuel, Worcester, Mass, 1953-59. Cpl, ski troops, US Army, 1944-46. Mem: presidium, World Council J Educ; exec comm, CCAR; governing council, World Union for Progressive Judaism; bd trustees, HUC; fmr: dir, Jt Commn on J Educ, UAHC and CCAR; regional dir, NE area, Fed Reform Temples. Author: From Discrimination to Extermination, 1950; fmr, lit ed, CCAR Jour; found ed, Dimensions; head, UAHC Publs Prog; contbr to scholarly and profsl jours. Recipient: Bronze Star; Purple Heart; 3 combat ribbons. Home: 6 River Lane, Westport, Conn. Study: 838 Fifth Ave, New York, NY.

SCHINDLER, Pesach, US, educator; b. Munich, Ger, Apr 11, 1931; s. Alexander and Esther (Zwickler); in US since 1940; BA, Bklyn Coll, 1954; MS, Yeshiva U, 1964; m. Shulamith Feldman, June 30, 1954; c: Chaya, Gitah, Meyer, Nehama, Avraham. Asst natl dir, dept educ, United Syn Amer, since 1965; educ dir, Adath Isr Cong, Toronto, Can, 1959-65; natl exec dir, B'nai Akiva of N Amer, 1953-54. Natl chmn, Assn Amers and Cans for Aliyah; chmn, Shaarei Tefillah Cong Youth Commn; found, pres, Isr Inves Assn of Toronto, 1962-63; mem: Educs Assembly; Bklyn Coll Alumni; Natl Council for J Educ. Author: A Hebrew High School in Your Community, 1967; A Manual for the Solomon Schechter Day School, 1969; ed, Igeret, publ for Solomon Schechter day schs; contbr to profsl jours. Hobby: classical music. Home: 431 Beach 25 St, Far Rockaway, NY. Office: 218 E 70 St, New York, NY.

SCHINDLER, Richard D, US, physician; b. Strassburg, Ger, June 27, 1891; s. Wolf and Caecile (Joseph); in US since 1935; att: Freiburg U; Munich U; Koenigsberg U; MD, U Berlin, 1917; m. Bella Seckback. Radiologist, pvt practice; fmr: asst, Westend Krankenhaus; Virchow Krankenhaus; Charité, all Berlin, Ger. Mem: AMA; Rudolf Virchow Med Soc; B'nai B'rith; Amer J KC Frat. Author: Principles of a

New Therapy with High Speed Electrons, 1940; contbr to med jours. Hobby, collecting medieval art. Home and office: 360 Central Park W, New York, NY.

SCHIRN, Otto, US, organization exec; b. Vienna, Aus, Aug 23, 1908; s. Joseph and Taube (Kriss); in US since 1941; DEcon and Bus dept, Vienna U, 1932; att Inst of Journalism, Brussels, Belgium; m. Yvonne Kurz, Dec 27, 1939; c: Robert, Vivian, Daniel. Chmn, United LA Memorial Comm, since 1966; ed writer, fgn corresp, L'Independence Belge, Brussels, 1932-38; asst dir, org dept, WJC, NY, 1942-45; found, first chmn, Young Zionist Actions Comm, NY, 1943-44; w coast dir, United Isr Appeal; vice-chmn, Amer Zionist Council of LA, 1945-56; w coast coord, JA econ dept, 1951-53; dir, LA JCC, 1953-56; dir, w coast region, AJCong, 1957-61; mem, exec comm, World Union of J Youth, 1939-41. Contbr to J mags. Home: 1706 Garth Ave, Los Angeles, Cal.

SCHISCHA, Adolph, Eng, business exec; b. Vienna, Aus, Mar 21, 1915; s. Simon and Julia (Stern); in Eng since 1939; att Yeshiva, Galanta, 1930-36; m. Amelia Winegarten, Sep 1, 1943; c: Leah, Joseph, Shulamit. Bus interests, dir, property cos, since 1943. Council mem: J Hist Soc, Eng; J Mus, London; Anglo-J Archives; mem, B'nai B'rith, First Lodge of Eng. Ed, Derasha le'Rosh Hashana, 1955; Toldoth Rabbanay Verpelet, 1959; Ma'or Hachayim, 1960; contbr to hist and bibliographical jours, Eng, Heb, Ger. Hobbies: bibliophile, autographs, hist research. Home: The Coppice, Pasture Rd, Letchworth, Hertfordshire, Eng.

SCHLANG, David, Aus, educator, lawyer, translator; b. Krakow, Pol, July 8, 1906; s. Aron and Chana (Jeruth); in Aus since 1950; DJur: U Jagiel, Krakow, U Vienna; dipl trans, Inst for Trans, U Vienna; m. Tola Weinberg, 1933, (died in concentration camp, Auschwitz); m. 2nd, Dora Rath, 1947; c: Norbert. Asst prof, U Vienna, since 1964, trans for Heb and Pol, since 1965; trans, Court of Vienna; pvt practice, law, Krakow, Pol, 1934-39. Concentration camps: Plashow, Gross-Rosen, Brunnlitz, 1939-45. Gen leader, Vienna br, Intl Comm for Intellectuals, Geneva, since 1956; gen secy, ZF, Aus, since 1960; gen secy, Zionist Lab Movement, Vienna; fmr, pres, Poale Zion, Pol; Aus delg to WZC, Jerusalem, 1965; mem: clubs: Soz Akad, Vienna; U Lectrs, U Vienna. Ed mem, Renaissance monthly, since 1962. Home and office: 2/7 Steindl St, Vienna, Aus.

SCHLANG, Joseph, business exec; b. NYC, Feb 24, 1911; s. Alexander and Blanche (Cohen); BCS, NYU, 1930; m. Bernice Breitbart, June 8, 1944; c: Stuart. Org, partner, Schlang Bros & Co, real estate, NYC, since 1934; mgr: 80, 89, 67 and 41 Broad St; 100 Gold St; 132 Nassau St; 30 Pine St; 67 Wall St; 15 Moore St; 27 William St and others; ltd partner: Majidot Realty Corp, since 1958; 67 Wall St, since 1957; 80 Broad St Mortgage, since 1956; 1036 Park Ave Assos, since 1960; NY Stock Exch firm, Kalb, Boorhis & Co, since 1958; pres, Schlang Manuscript Co, Inc, since 1965; owner, Candee, Smith & Howland Co, 1944-55; dir, part owner, Fork Lift Truck Rental Corp, Bond Indsl Maintenance Corp, 1956-57; owner, 271 Central Park W, 1958-59; ltd partner: 975 Park Ave, 1957-60; 1165 Park Ave, 1957; asso publisher: Graphic History of J Heritage, 1963; The Bible and Modern Medicine, 1963; adv, Libr of Presidential Papers, since 1966. Asst treas, Downtown Hosp, 1945-57; natl council, NY Met Opera, since 1960, 1st patron since 1962; sponsor, NYC Opera since 1962; secy, dir, Kehillah, NYC; mem exec comm, dir, Synagogue Council of Amer, since 1947; pres: Schlang Found, Inc; Broad St Found; Barclay Found; treas: Elias Cohen Found; Found for a Graphic History J Lit; dir, bd review and concilliation in J Schools, Milah Bd, NY; dir, Cong Kehilath Jeshurun, NY, since 1957; co-found, Albert Einstein Coll Med; Technion, Isr; mem: US and NY Power Squadron; NY Real Estate Bd; Natl Assn Real Estate Bds; Manuscript Soc of Amer; Natl Assn Owners, Mgrs and Builders; mem exec comm, dir, Union Orthodox J Cong Amer; clubs: Town; P and C Inves, fmr pres; 100 Club VP; Lancers'; Colonial Yacht. Author: Survey of the Financial District of NYC, booklet, 1940; Financial District of NYC, booklet, 1956; contbr to newspapers and mags. Recipient: award: Amer J Lit Found, 1960; statesman award, Synagogue Council Amer, 1964. Home: 35 E 84 St, New York, NY. Office: 75 Maiden Lane, New York, NY.

SCHLEIN, Irving, US, composer; b. NYC, Aug 18, 1905; s. Morris and Gussie (Friedman); grad pharm, Coll of Pharm, Bklyn, 1927; cert, piano: NY Coll of Music, 1928; Juilliard Sch of Music, 1930; BA, CCNY, 1936; m. Ann Seigal, Feb

28, 1932; c: Peter, Stephen, Leland, Paul. Conductor: Broadway produc; Shubert, 1932-45; Feuer & Martin, 1945-50; tchr, lectr. Composer: Dance Overture, 1940; Slave Songs of the US, 1967; Let God's Children Come Home, 1969. Mem: ASCAP; Natl Assn Composers and Conductors; Amer Fed Musicians; United Fed Tchrs. Recipient: awards: for Dance Overture, 1940; for Festive Cantata, B'nai B'rith, 1945. Home: 650 Ocean Ave, Brooklyn, NY. Office: 2500 Nostrand Ave, Brooklyn, NY.

SCHLESINGER, Benjamin, Can, educator, social worker; b. Berlin, Ger, July 20, 1928; s. Abraham and Esther (Trisker); BA, Sir George Williams U, 1951; MSW, U Toronto, 1953; PhD Cornell U, 1961; m. Rachel Aber, Mar 29, 1959; c: Peter, Leo, Esther, Michael. Prof, Sch of Social Work, U of Toronto, on fac since 1960; social worker: J Immigrant Aid Soc, Montreal, 1947-51; Children's Aid Soc, Toronto, 1953-56; fac mem, Aloka, World Assembly of Youth, Mysore, India, 1959-60. Mem: Vanier Inst of Family; Council on Social Work Educ; Soc for Study Psychol Issues; Natl Council Family Relations; Can Assn Social Workers; Phi Delta Kappa. Author: The Multi-Problem Family, 1963; Poverty in Canada and the United States, 1966; The One Parent Family, 1969; contbr numerous articles to profsl jours. Home: 415 Roselawn Ave, Toronto, Can. Office: U of Toronto, Sch of Social Work, Toronto, Can.

SCHLESINGER, Hugo, Brazil, author, journalist, economist; b. Biala, Pol, May 5, 1920; s. Simon and Jetty; dipl, econ and admn, Cracov, Pol; U Florence, It; m. Janina Landau, Apr 14, 1946; c: Ricardo, Claudio. Dir-supt, Soc Brasileira De Comedia, since 1964; dir, Newsreel Mundo Em Noticias, since 1965. Author: Bomba, Il Paese di Silvio Spaventa, 1943; Quid est Varitas?, 1943; L'Arte Polacca, 1944; English Proverbs and Sayings, 1944, 2nd ed, 1945; Guerra e Pace (Dal Diario di un Soldato), 1945; Paderewski e L'Italia, 1945; Zyd Polski, 1945; "Pononica" Brasileira, 1947; Glossario Cinematografico, 1951; Brasil Nâo Pode Parar, 1954; Enciclopedia Da Industria Brasileira, 1953, 2nd ed, 1954, 3rd ed 1959; Aspectos Psicologios DE Venda, 1955, 2nd ed, 1964; Brasil Em Cifras, 1956; Pequeno Dicionario Do Comercio Exterior, 1956; Geografia Industrial Do Brasil, 1956, 2nd ed, 1959; Metodos Basicos De Venda, 1964; Pesquisâs E Analise Do Mercado, 1964; Preparação Profissional Do Vendedor, 1964; Publicidade E Promoçâo De Vendas, 1964; Quem Matou Cristo?, 1965; Simplismente Gente, 1966; Crianças No Mundo Sem Deus, 1967; Enciclopedia Brasileira De Administração E Negocios, 8 vol, 1968; A Musica E O Amor Na Via De Chopin, 1968. Dir, Casa de Cultura de Isr; pres, Editora B'nai B'rith; co-pres, Conselho Fraternidade Cristao-Judaica; mem, B'nai B'rith, loja Osvaldo Aranha, Sao Paulo. Home: 421, rua Ubatuba, Sao Paulo, Brazil. Office: 89/7, rua St Ifigenia, Sao Paulo, Brazil.

SCHLESINGER, Mordechai Jafe, Isr, rabbinical judge; b. Zlatemorauce, Czech, Jan 5, 1909; s. Samuel and Berta (Friedman); att Rabbi HS, Bratislava, Czech; m. Irene Klein; c: Samuel. Chmn, Rabb Court Tel Aviv; fmr chief rabbi, Eisenstadt, Aus. Author: Ud Majzal Meesh; S'fat Hameil; Mishberei Jam. Home: 5 Zvi Brook St, Tel Aviv, Isr. Office: Rabb Dist Court, Tel Aviv, Isr.

SCHLESSEL, Stanley Wolf, US, educator; b. Bklyn, NY, Feb 7, 1927; s. Samuel and Bertha (Goldberg); BS, LIU, 1949; MA, Columbia U, 1950; m. Gloria Landau; c: Ronnie, Rosalyn. Dir, youth dept, Intercoll Council, Armed Forces Div, Natl Council Young Isr, since 1951; tchr, borough coord student activities, supt, student activities, Sch Dist 29, NYC, coord, comty relations, Bd of Educ, since 1951. US Army, 1945-46. Charter mem: Natl Assn Social Workers, since 1955; Acad Social Workers, since 1960; mem, Phi Delta Kappa. Recipient: natl service award, Natl Intercollegiate Council Young Isr, 1966. Home: 466 Buckingham Rd, Lawrence, NY. Office: 3 W 16 St, New York, NY.

SCHLICHTER, Jakub G, US, physician, educator; b. Bochnia, Pol, Aug 10, 1912; s. Samuel and Dora (Fluhr); in US since 1943; att: U Vienna, 1932-38; BM, U Lausanne, 1938, MD, 1940; m. Nelly Chabloz, Oct 15, 1941; m. 2nd, Lois Newman, Oct 3, 1965. Pvt practice since 1947; asst prof, med, Northwestern U, since 1952; att phys, Michael Reese Hosp, Chgo, since 1959, research asso, cardiovascular dept, since 1947, f, 1944-47; asso att phys, card, Children's Memorial Hosp, Chgo, since 1950; asst med: U Hosp, Lausanne, 1938-40; Gibraltar Camp Hosp, Jamaica, BWI, 1942-43; asst path, Mt Sinai Hosp, NYC, 1943-44. Maj, US Army, 1953-55.

Dipl: Bd Internal Med; Bd Cardiovascular Diseases; f: Amer Coll Chest Phys; Council Clinical Card; FACP; mem: AMA; AHA; Intl Heart Assn; Soc for Study Arteriosclerosis; NYAcad Sci; AAAS; Soc Biol and Med; Ill and Chgo Med Socs. Contbr to sci and med jours. Hobby: photography. Home: 2130 N Lincoln Park W, Chicago, Ill. Office: 55 E Washington St, Chicago, Ill.

SCHLOSS, Leo, educator, accountant; b. NYC, Dec 9, 1914; s. Joseph and Rose (Schrier); BBA, St John's U, 1938; m. Ruth Hochman, July 3, 1940; c: Raela, Joan. CPA since 1942; prof, dept acctnt, Coll Bus Admn, LIU, since 1942, dept chmn, 1944-58, asso dean, 1954-58, fac mem since 1943. Chmn, ed comm, Acctnt Tchrs' Guide, Amer Acctnt Assn, 1953; mem: Amer Inst CPAs; AAUP; Fac Assn, Acctnt Soc, LIU; Amer Acctnt Assn; Amer Inst Acctnts; NY State Soc CPAs; Amer Friends Heb U; Alpha Epsilon Pi; Odd Fellows; Madison J Cen; Alpha Phi Omega; Optimates, LIU. Recipient: Chancellor's medal, outstanding educ, LIU, 1968. Contbr to profsl jours. Home: 1845 E 28 St, Brooklyn, NY. Office: 225 Broadway, New York, NY.

SCHLOSS, Ruth, Isr, painter; b. Nürnberg, Ger, Nov 22, 1922; d. Ludwig and Dina (Elsas); att Bezalel Art Sch, Jerusalem; m. Benjamin Cohen; c: Raya, Nurit. Illus: Mor Hehamor; Nissim vehaGdi; painter: Album of Drawings, 1964; Album of Paintings and Drawings, 1968. Mem: Isr Assn Painters and Sculptors. Home: 12 Hazore'ah St, Kfar Shmaryahu, Isr.

SCHLOSS, William L, US, industrial banker; b. Monmouth, Ill, Feb 3, 1909; s. Eli and Clare (Rose); AB, U Mich, 1930; m. Jane Mathews, Dec 3, 1935; c: Ellen Flamm, Judith Klaon, Robert, Thomas. Pres, Indianapolis Morris Plan, since 1936; chmn bd, Econ Finance Corp, since 1947; partner, Schloss Bros. Dir, mem, exec comm: Bd for Fundamental Educ; Cen Ind Boy Scout Council; pres: JWF; Indianapolis Heb Cong, 1942; bd dirs: ARC, 1953-59; Natl United Fund, Gtr Indianapolis; AJComm; mem: Comty Chest; Amer Ind Bankers Assn; Ind Consumer Finance Assn; Consumer Bankers Assn; B'nai B'rith. Home: 2 W 64 St, Indianapolis, Ind. Office: 110 E Washington St, Indianapolis, Ind.

SCHMERLING, Louis, US, chemist; b. Milw, Wis, Apr 20, 1912; s. Max and Bertha (Frumin); BS, U Wis, 1932; PhD, Northwestern U, 1935; m. Annette Frazin, July 25, 1937; c: Judith Kaas, Michael. Research chemist, Universal Oil Products Co, since 1935; lectr, organic chem, Northwestern U, 1941-42. Holder: numerous US patents. Mem: nomenclature comm, NRC; Amer Chem Soc; Amer Inst of Chems; Phi Beta Kappa; Sigma Xi; Phi Lambda Upsilon. Contbr to chem publs. Recipient: Ipatieff prize, catalytic chem, 1947; Precision Sci Co award, petroleum chem, 1951. Home: 183 Lawton Rd, Riverside, Ill. Office: Universal Oil Products Co, Des Plaines, Ill.

SCHMIDT, William M, US, pediatrician, educator; b. Cincinnati, O, Oct 20, 1907; s. Joseph and Esther (Newman); BS, U Cincinnati, 1928, MD, 1931; hon AM, Harvard, 1960; m. Lena Fullerton, Dec 24, 1937; c: Mark, Hannah, Sarah, James. Prof, maternal and child health, Harvard Sch Public Health, since 1960; cons, child health, Children's Hosp, Boston; instr, ped, Cornell U Med Coll, 1935-41; instr, preventive med, 1937-41; dir, HS health study, NY Dept Health and Progressive Educ Assn, 1937-38; admn dir, coop study nutrition, USPHS, NYC Dept Health, Cornell U of Med Coll, Milbank Memorial Fund, 1938-41; with US Children's Bur, 1941-44; med adv, JDC, 1945-49, 1953-57; alternate mem, sub-comm on med projects, UNICEF, 1948-49. F: Amer Acad Ped; Amer Public Health Assn; dipl: Amer Bd Ped; Amer Bd Preventative Med; mem: med adv, bd, JDC; expert comm on maternity care, WHO, 1952, panel maternity care, 1952-57; participant, White House Conf Children and Youth, 1959, 1960; Amer Ped Soc; Soc Ped Research; Soc for Research in Child Devl; Royal Soc of Health; exec bd, Mass Comm on Children and Youth. Author: Health for High School Pupils, 1939; Report on Maternal and Child Health in US Zone of Germany, 1950; co-author: chap, Problems of Childhood, in Preventive Medicine in Modern Practice, 1942; preliminary report, Midcentury White House Conf, Sch Health Services, 1950; contbr to med jours. Home: 49 Monmouth St, Brookline, Mass. Office: 55 Shattuck St, Boston, Mass.

SCHNEERSOHN, Baruch Simon, Isr, educator, author; b. Cracow, Pol, Aug 28, 1913; s. Joseph and Nehama (Frankel);

in Isr since 1947; ordained rabbi, Yeshivat Hachmei, Lublin, 1935; m. Rosa Weidenfeld, June, 1945; c: Joseph, Nahum. Dean, Kohav Miyaacov Rabb Coll, Jeruaslem, since 1950; fmr, dean, Rabb Coll, Lod, Isr, 1952-56. Author: eight books and numerous Talmudic and Halakah commentaries; fmr, mem ed comm, HASHAS HaIsraeli Hashalem. Dir, Hafetz Hessed Soc. Home: 9 Elkana St, Jerusalem, Isr. Office: 12 Chana St, Jerusalem, Isr.

SCHNEEWEISS, Joachim, Austr; b. Hanover, Ger, June 3, 1927; s. Jakob and Brucha (Brand); in Austr since 1939; MB, BS, Sydney U, 1950; m. Sybil Jackson, 1960; c: Gerald, David, Daniel. Hon asst phys, Prince Henry Hosp; cons chest phys, Parramatta Dist Hosp, NSW; hon asst phys, Rachel Forster Hosp, Sydney; hon tchr, clinical med, U of NSW; acting govt med off, Norfolk I, 1952; med registrar, Royal Postgrad Med Sch, London, 1948-61. Mem: Austr Med Assn; Austr Lab Party; exec: ZF, Austr and NZ; State ZC, NSW; presently: chmn, Isr comm, Exec Council Austr Jewry; vice-pres, NSW J Bd Deps; mem: comm, Austr J Hist Soc; fmr pres: Zionist Youth League; Sydney U J Students Union; chmn, Austr Zionist Youth Council; hon secy, F of J Drs of NSW; club, U. Chmn, Australian J Quarterly; found, co-ed, The Bridge. Hobby: photography. Home: 44 Park Parade, Bondi, NSW, Austr. Office: 185 Macquarie St, Sydney, NSW, Austr.

SCHNEIDER, Alan, US, theatrical dir; BA, U Wis; MA, Cornell U; m; two c. Asso dir: Wash Arena Stage, 1961-63; Tyrone Guthrie Theater, 1964; artistic dir, Ithaca Festival Theater, 1965-69; lectr: Yale U; Johns Hopkins U; Columbia U; Circle-in-the-Sq; Hofstra Coll; U Wis; Stanford U; Catholic U. Dir: Broadway produc: A Delicate Balance; Slapstick Tragedy; Malcolm; Entertaining Mr Sloane; Tiny Alice; Ballad of the Sad Cafe; Who's Afraid of Virginia Woolf?; Kataki; Miss Lonelyhearts; The Glass Menagerie; The Skin of Our Teeth; Anastasia; All Summer Long; The Remarkable Mr Pennypacker; The Gingham Dog; I Never Sang for my Father; The Birthday Party; You Know I Cant' Hear You When the Water's Running; Off Broadway produc: The Zoo Story; Do Not Pass Go; The Dumbwaiter; The Collection; Happy Days; The American Dream; Measure for Measure; Krapp's Last Tape; The Summer of the Seventeenth Doll; Endgame; A Long Way From Home; Amer premieres: Herakles; Caucasian Chalk Circle; The Dumbwaiter; Clandestine on the Morning Line; Twelve Angry Men; The Circus of Dr Lao; Waiting for Godot; Jim Dandy; Lute Song; Burning of the Lepers; TV and film: Eh, Joe?; Act Without Words; Waiting for Godot; The Secret of Freedom; The Life of Samuel Johnson; The Years Between; Oedipus the King; dir, plays: abroad; regional theaters: Wash; Chgo; Boston; SF; Houston. Mem: Phi Beta Kappa. Contbr to books, periodicals. Recipient: grant, Ford Found, 1958-61; Guggenheim f, 1956. Home: 30 Scenic Dr, Hastings-on-Hudson, NY.

SCHNEIDER, Alfred R, US, broadcasting exec; b. Bklyn, NY, Apr 25, 1926; s. Sol and Lena (Schneider); att Hamilton Coll, 1949; LLB, Harvard Law School, 1952; m. Jane Harris, July 26, 1953; c: Leland, Jeffrey, Elizabeth. Vice-pres, asst to exec vice-pres, ABC, since 1960, atty, asst dir bus affairs, 1952-54; asst dir bus affairs, exec asst to pres, CBS, 1955-60. Mem: Phi Beta Kappa. Home: 65 Shore Dr, Larchmont, NY. Office: 1330 Ave of the Americas, New York, NY.

SCHNEIDER, Anna W, US, labor mediator; b. Boston, Mass, Mar 21, 1896; d. Joseph and Rebecka (Seidel) Winestock; m. Jesse Schneider, Oct 15, 1929. Commn, Fed Mediation and Conciliation Service, since 1922, first woman ever to be appd to this position, has served longer than any other govt mediator; bus agt, Neckwear Workers Union, 1917-20. Prin contribs: formulated new techniques for lab mediation. Org: Mass Suffrage Assn; Boston League Women Voters; mem: Council J Women; Lab Relations Research Assn; Sisterhood, Temple Emanuel; volunteer service auxiliary, Westbourgh State Hosp, trustee; Brandeis U Women's Auxiliary; fmr: pres, leg repr, Women's Trade Union League; dir, lab div, Natl Rep Campaign, 1932. Recipient: award from US Govt, 1957. Spec interest, hobbies: care of mentally ill; cooking, bridge. Home: Westboro, Mass. Office: 340 Main St, Worcester, Mass.

SCHNEIDER, Benjamin, US, business exec; b. NYC, Sep 10, 1907; s. Albert and Rebecca (Barr); Pharm G, Bklyn Coll of Pharm, LIU, 1928; m. Nettie Roth, June 25, 1933; c: Herbert. Pres, Intercontinental Mgmt Services, Inc, since 1964; gen

sales mgr, Harrower Lab, 1946-53; pres: Purdue Frederick Co, 1953-61; M R Thompson, 1961-64. Mem, bd trustees, Bklyn Coll of Pharm, since 1960, pres, Alumni Assn, 1957-59; chmn, drug div, NY Heart Assn, since 1959; chmn bd, J Pharmaceutical Soc Amer, 1962; pres, Charles Polimer Lodge, Brith Abraham, 1940-43; mem: Amer and NY State Pharmaceutical Assns; Masons; clubs: Drug and Chem Sq, chmn, PR dept, since 1960; Pharmaceutical Advt; Sales Execs. Recipient: visual presentation award, Sales Exec Club, 1955; alumni award, Bklyn Coll of Pharm, 1960; heart of gold citation, AHA, 1962. Home: 520 E 89 St, New York, NY. Office: 120 Broadway, New York, NY.

SCHNEIDER, Benjamin, US, physician; b. Phila, Pa, Nov 18, 1908; s. Max and Elizabeth (Forman); BA, U of Pa, 1929, MD, 1933; m. Anne Lipkin, May 14, 1933; c: Joyce Zeluck, Robert. Pvt practice since 1934; med dir, Montour Co, since 1957; Fed Aviation med examiner, since 1947; clinician, Child Health Cen, Danville, since 1958; Selective Service med examiner, since 1941; electrocard: Bloomsbury Hosp; Sunbury Pa Hosp, both since 1949; dir, Shamokin State Hosp, Pa, 1937-40; chief, med practice dept, Bloomsbury Hosp, 1951-57, chief, med dept, 1957-58; dep med dir, Civil Defense Montour Co. Pres: bd dirs, Danville State Hosp, Pa, since 1955; sect on gen practice, Pan Amer Med Assn; vice-pres, 3rd World Cong on Gen Practice, New Delhi, India; chmn, Pa Steering Comm for Continuing Post-Grad Educ in Psycht; secy-treas, Susquehanna unit, Pa AJCong; dir: Montour Co Cancer Soc; Pa TB and Health Assn; Montour Co TB and Health Assn, fmr pres; Danville chap, ARC, since 1949; f: AMA; Amer Coll Chest Phys; Acad Psychosomatic Med; asso F, Aero-Space Med Assn; regional mem, Co Bd Mh; mem: Amer Acad Gen Practice, regional mem, Mh Comm; comm on Mh, Pa Acad Gen Practice, fmr pres; comm Mh, Pa Med Soc; World Med Assn; coord comm for med educ, cen Pa; Regional Med Prog; adv council, Pa, Del, Md, AJComm; exec comm, Pa Med Comm for Political Activity; at-large and delg, Pa adv council, AJComm; Amer Geriatric Soc; Amer Trudeau Soc; U of Pa Susquehanna Valley Alumni Soc, fmr pres; Civil Aviation Med Examiners Assn; Phi Lambda Kappa; B'nai B'rith; Elks; Montour Co Dem Club; fmr: pres, Northumberland Co Med Soc; Montour Co Med Soc; dir, Temple B'nai Zion, Danville; Temple Beth El, Sunbury; chmn: blood prog, NE, Pa; UJA Fund. Mem, ed comm, Manual of Cancer for the General Practitioner. Recipient: Selective Service Medal. Hobby: swimming. Home and office: 123 E Market St, Danville, Pa.

SCHNEIDER, Morris H, US, attorney; b. NYC, Sep 10, 1910; s. Philip and Bessie (Haas), BS, St John's U, NY, 1932, JD, 1935; m. Estelle Simon, Feb 7, 1937; c: Alan, Betsy Seitler. Co atty, Nassau Co, since 1965, chief dep co atty, 1964-65, sr dep co atty, 1962-64; partner, law firm, Schneider and Edelstein, 1936-62. Pres, Cen Syn of Nassau Co, fmr pres, Men's Club; vice-pres, lawyers div, Nassau Co FJP; counsel, Nassau Comty Coll; chmn, Nassau Co Traffic Safety Comm; secy, Nassau Co Ethics Bd; mem: Health Wfr Council; Youth Bd; Off Econ Opportunity Council; Scenic Easement Comm; Crime Council, all Nassau Co; Citizen's Adv Comm, Sch Dist 21, Rockville Cen, NY; Natl Inst Munic Law Offs; Comm on Law Off Procedure and Salary; Comm on Munic Lab Relations; grievance comm, lab law comm, Nassau Co Bar Assn; Bklyn, NY State Bar Assns; bd dirs, Nassau Co Legal Services Comm Inc, chmn, personnel comm; mem: KP; Masons; fmr: mem bd trustees, Metrop Conf, Fed Natl Temple Brotherhoods; Rockville Cen JCC; dir, hon chmn, United Fund drive, Rockville Cen; trustee, Mid-Village Civic Assn; chmn, sub-comm, Exec Mgmt Info Comm, Nassau Co; mem: bd dirs, South Shore YM-YWHA; Nassau Co Task Force for Aging; Sheriff's Adv Comm; Educ's Leg Comm. Fmr ed, The Nassau Lawyer. Recipient: man of year, Men's Club, Cen Syn, 1968; award, Rockville Cen UJA, 1969. Hobby: flowers, shell collecting. Home: 386 Raymond St, Rockville Center, NY. Office: Exec Bldg, West St, Mineola, NY.

SCHNEIDER, Tobias, S Afr, physician; b. London, Eng, May 1, 1905; s. Aaron and Annie (Comaroff); in S Afr since 1912; MB, BCh, U Witwatersrand, 1927; MD, FRCP, Edinburgh, 1958; m. Hilda Lavin, Dec 4, 1956; c: Caron, Alan. Hon cons phys, Johannesburg Hosp, and phys i/c, Diabetic Clinic. Capt, S Afr MC, 1942-46. Natl pres, Assn Phys of S Afr, since 1961; mem, Fed Council, Med Assn, S Afr, since 1946, chmn, ethical comm, since 1958, pres, Transvaal br, 1952-53; chmn, Metabolic, Endocrine and Diabetic Soc, since 1961; pres: Med Grad Assn, U Witwatersrand; United Heb Cong of Johannesburg, 1958, 1966-70; chmn, exec council, S Afr J Bd Deps, 1960-65; mem, med exec, S Afr ZF; fmr vice-chmn, Magen David Adom, S Afr. Author: Observations in Diabetes Mellitus, 1958; contbr to med jours. Recipient: bronze medal for meritorious services, Med Assn of S Afr. Home: 11 Fifth Ave, Lower Houghton, Johannesburg, S Afr. Office: 43 Harvard Bldg, Joubert & Pritchard Sts, Johannesburg, S Afr.

SCHNEIDERMAN, Clarence, Can, surgeon; b. Montreal, Can, Apr 1, 1918; s. Morris and Edith; BSc, McGill U, 1937, MD, 1941; m. Ronnie Schneiderman, Dec 5, 1949; c: Edwina, Martin, Ian, Jane. Urol-in-chief, J Gen Hosp; cons urol: Queen Elizabeth Hosp; Queen Mary Hosp, all since 1956. MC, Royal Can Army, 1942-45. Exec off, Can Urol Assn; pres, Que Assn Urols; exec, northeast sect, Amer Urol Assn; f, Amer Coll Surgs; fmr pres, Montreal Clinical Soc; clubs: Elmridge Country; Montreal Urol, fmr pres. Hobbies: golf, fishing. Home: 115 Stratford Rd, Hampstead, Que, Can. Office: 5845 Côte des Neiges, Montreal, Can.

SCHNEIDERMAN, Harry, US, editor, organization exec; b. Savine, Pol, Jan 23, 1885; s. Samuel and Deborah (Rothman); in US since 1890; BS, CCNY, 1908; m. Tillie Saymon, Jan 18, 1917; c: Herbert, Florence Dobrer, Lois King. Ret; ed, Who's Who in World Jewry, 1955, 1965; on staff, AJComm, NY, 1909-49; asst secy, 1914-45; ed, Amer J Year Book, 1920-48; contbr ed, J writer, J Tribune, NY, 1923-28; lectr on J in US, Sch of Educ, NYU, 1936-37; ed, Contemporary J Record, 1938-45. Co-found, JBCA, 1940, vice-pres, since 1947; secy, Emergency Comm for J Refs, 1924-28; mem: publ comm, J Publ Soc of Amer, Phila; Amer J Hist Soc; Conf on J Relations; Maimonides Benevolent Soc. Author: The Jew in American History (Jewish Tribune), 1922-23; The Jews of Nazi Germany: A Handbook of Facts Regarding their Present Situation, 1935; trans: Der Golem by Chayim Bloch, 1925; The Wells of Girar by Ruben Rotgeisser, 1953; ed: Eng trans of Josef S Bloch's Israel und die Voelker, 1927; Two Generations in Perspective: Notable Events and Trends, 1846-1956; co-chmn, Amer adv bd, Standard Jewish Ency, 1959; contbr: chap to, Our Racial and National Minorities, 1937, rev ed, One America, 1945; articles: Universal J Ency; Amer J Year Book; Amer Year Book. Home: 514 W 114 St, New York, NY.

SCHNEIERSON, S Stanley, US, microbiologist; b. NYC, May 15, 1906; s. Isaac and Anna (Levine); BA, Cornell U, 1928; MD, LI Coll of Med, 1932; m. Marianne Katz, July 21, 1950; c: Martine. Prof, microbiol, Mt Sinai Sch Med; dir, microbiol, Mt Sinai Hosp, since 1960, on staff since 1934; research asst, Pasteur Inst, Paris, 1939. Cdr, USN, 1941-46. F: Amer Coll Phys; NY Acad Med; Amer Acad Microbiol; NY Acad Scis; AAAS; dipl: Amer Bd Path; Amer Bd Microbiol; mem: Soc Experimental Biol and Med; Amer Soc for Microbiol; Amer Assn Paths and Bacts. Contbr to med jours. Home: 64 E 86 St, New York, NY. Office: 1 E 100 St, New York, NY.

SCHNEK, Georges Arthur, Belgium, educator; b. Warsaw, Pol, Aug 22, 1924; s. Michel and Malvina (Fokschanska); in Belgium since 1925; att Engr Sch Chem, Brussels, 1945-47; docteur ès sciences, U of Paris, 1951; m. Sarah Deutsch, Oct 15, 1955; c: Ariane. Asst prof, U of Brussels Fac Med, since 1969; chief: Toraude Labs, 1952-58; Coles Labs, 1959-69; chef travaux, U Libre, Brussels, 1964-68. Found, pres, Fonds du Prêt d'Etudes; found, admnr, Youth Cen; admnr, Centrale des Oeuvres Sociales Juives, past pres, all Brussels; found, Union J Students, Belgium, fmr secy gen; found, Fed J Youth, Belgium. Lt, Fr Resistance, 1943-44. Mem: Société Belge: Biochimie; Chimie. Contbr publs on lysozyne and hemoglobin, protein structure. Recipient: Fr Resistance Medal. Hobbies: violin, tennis. Home: 75 A Huysmans St, Brussels, Belgium. Office: 50 Roosevelt St, Brussels, Belgium.

SCHNEOUR, Elie Alexis, US, research scientist; b. Neuilly-sur-Seine, Fr, Dec 11, 1925; s. Zalmon and Salomea (Landau); father, J writer and novelist; desc of Hassidic Rabbi Schneour Zalman; BA, Columbia, 1947; MA, U Cal, Berkeley, 1955; PhD, UCLA, 1958; hon DSc, Bard Coll, Columbia, 1947; m. Joan Brewster, Jan 22, 1955; c. Mark, Alan. Research neurochem, City of Hope Natl Med Cen, since 1969; chem, research and devl, JAE Co, NY, 1948-51; f, Natl Cancer Inst and teaching, research asst, U Cal, 1951-58; sr research f, AHA, 1958-62; research asso, genet dept, Stanford U Med Cen, 1962-65; asso prof, biol dept, U Utah, 1965-69; fmr: exec secy mem, steering comm, Natl Acad Scis Space Sci Bd Study

Group on Biol, and Exploration of Mars; chmn, W Research Council, on Basic Bioscis for Manned Orbiting Missions, NASA and Amer Inst Biol Scis; cons: ind, tech, mgmt to various maj corps; ed, to maj coll publisher; instr, Biol Sci Curriculum Study Prog on Tchrs Training, Natl Sci Found. Mem: biomed research bd, Research Found for Multiple Sclerosis; AAAS; Amer Chem Soc; Amer Inst Biol Scis; Amer Soc for Neurochem; Inst of Elec and Electronics Engrs; NY Acad Scis; Soc for Experimental Biol and Med; Sigma Xi; Phi Sigma Soc. Co-author: Life Beyond the Earth, 1965; The Search for Extraterrestial Life, 1968; contbr to sci publs. Recipient: William Lockwood Prize, Columbia U; John Bard Scholar in Sci and Math, Columbia U. Home: 1000 S Ninth St, Arcadia, Cal. Office: City of Hope Natl Med Cen, Durate, Cal.

SCHNIER, Jacques, US, sculptor; b. Constanza, Rum, Dec 25, 1898; s. Benjamin and Matilda (Leibo); in US since 1901; BA, Stanford U, 1920; MA, U of Cal, 1939; m. Dorothy Lilienthal, Jan 29, 1949; c: Claude, Rebecca. Prof em, U of Cal, since 1966; prof, sculpture, 1936-66; civil engr, HI, Cal, 1919-24; designed: US half-dollar commemorating SF-Oakland Bay Bridge, 1936; nine monumental sculptures for SF World's Fair, 1939; represented in perm collections: Hist Soc of SF; Palace of Legion Honor Mus; Chase Natl Bank Numismatic Collection; SF Mus Art; Santa Barbara Mus Art; Mills Coll Art Gal; Heb U, Jerusalem; Stanford U Mus; Oakland Art Mus; Honolulu Acad Art; Smithsonian Inst; one-man shows: Stanford U Art Mus, 1962; Santa Barbara Mus Art, 1963; Crocker Art Mus, 1963; U of Cal, Ryder Art Gal, 1965. Mem: Phi Gamma Delta. Author: Sculpture in Modern America, 1948; contbr: Yearbook for Psychoanalysis; art and psychoanalytical jours. Recipient: first sculpture award, Seattle Art Inst, 1928, 1929; SF Art Assn, 1928; gold medal and Adele Hyde Morrison award, Oakland Art Gal, 1936, 1948; third sculpture award, Intl Exhb, Phila, 1949; third biennial, Santa Barbara Mus of Art, 1959; grant, Inst Creative Arts, U of Cal.

SCHNITMAN, Joseph Irving, US, dentist; b. New Haven, Conn, July 29, 1911; s. Siah and Diana (Zimmerman); BS, DDS, U of Pittsburgh, 1934; cert mouth rehab, NYU, 1957; m. Jane Asheim; c: Paul, Deenabeth, Susan, Harriett. Pvt practice since 1934; lectr, State and City Dent Socs. Lt col, US Army, Dent Corps, 1953-56. Chancellor cdr, KP; mem: Amer Dent Assn; Conn State Dent Assn; New Haven Dent Assn; club, Woodbridge Country, Conn. Hobbies: tennis, golf. Home: 18 Vernon Ct, Woodbridge, Conn. Office: 291 Whitney Ave, New Haven, Conn.

SCHNITZER, Edward, US, engineer; b. Newark, NJ, Aug 12, 1915; s. Harry and Jennie (Lassar); att Inst of Construction and Design, 1950-51; BCE, Poly Inst, Bklyn, 1952; m. Lillian Alcosser, Oct 23, 1937; c: Harriet Storch, Arthur. Found, chief exec, firm of cons engrs, since 1952; chief engr, Nassau Co, NY, since 1967, sup bldgs, 1962-67; chief engr, Dreier Structural Steel Co, 1949-52; cons, Bd of Educ, Valley Stream Union Free Sch, 1953-55; designer: Levitt Houses, Whitestone, NY, 1955; 1st prestressed concrete bridge, LI, 1956; expert in nuclear shielding; cons, NY State Div of Housing, 1959. USNR, 1945-46. Mem: Soc Amer Mil Engrs; NY State Soc Profsl Engrs; Natl Soc Profsl Engrs; KP; JWV; Disabled Amer Vets; mem, Nassau Co Dem Comm, 1954-69; found, pres, Franklin Terr Civic Assn; regular Dem candidate for off of Supr of Highways, 1961; field commn, Sr Scouting, Boy Scouts Amer, 1942; skipper, natl flagship, Sea Scouts Amer, 1944; club, Toroh. Contbr to profsl publs. Recipient: Victory Medal, 1946; bronze plaque, Queens C of C, 1957, 1960; medal, Soc Amer Mil Engrs, 1962. Home: 1088 Park Lane N, Franklin Square, NY. Office: Nassau Co Exec Bldg, Mineola, NY.

SCHNITZER, Jeshaia, US, rabbi; b. Phila, Pa, Jan 25, 1918; s. Phillip and Jennie (Galler); BA, U Del, 1940; ordained rabbi, HUC-JIR, 1944; MSW, NY Sch of Soc Work, Columbia U, 1949; EdD, Tchrs Coll, 1954; m. Hilde Maier, 1947; c: Jonathan, Lisa. Rabbi: Temple Shomrei Emunah, specializing in family and marriage counseling, since 1951; Free Syn Soc Service Dept, NYC, 1947-49; and rel dir, YM-YWHA, NYC, 1949-51. Chaplain, US Army, 1945-47. Pres: bd rabbis, Essex Co, 1959-61; Northern NJ Region, RA, since 1962; Northern NJ div, Amer Assn Marriage Counselors, 1962; mem: soc planning comm, Soc Service Agcys, 1952-54; bd, ARC, 1953-54, both in Montclair, NJ; Amer Assn for UN; Assn J Chaplains; Alumni Assns: U Del; HUC; Columbia U. Author: A Study of the People's Synagogue, Its History,

Organization and Function in the Educational Alliance, 1949; A Human Relation Center in the Synagogue, 1954; New Horizons for the Synagogue, 1956; Rabbis and Counseling: Report on a Project; The Ideals of Jewish Marriage–Perspectives of the Man-Woman Relationship; contbr to Conservative movement publs. Recipient: B'nai B'rith Americanism Award. Hobby: covered bridges. Home: 144 Midland Ave, Montclair, NJ. Study: 67 Park St, Montclair, NJ.

SCHNITZER, Shmuel, Isr, journalist; b. The Hague, Netherlands, July 25, 1918; s. Moshe and Gusta (Weindling); in Isr since 1939; att Yesodé Hatora, Yeshiva and bus sch, Antwerp; m. Malka Ajchenblat, Sep 1941; c: Moshe, Arieh. Political writer, chief news ed, Maariv daily; head, Kol Isr panel of theater critics, 1963-66; lectr, Technion, Haifa, 1966; mil corresp, IDF, 1953-56. Author: African Adventures; Aliyah Picturebook; trans numerous books into Heb from Eng, Fr, Dutch, Ger, including: Anne Frank's Diary, Herzl's Altneuland, Balzac's Père Goriot. Mem: Assn Isr Journalists. Spec interests: J hist, archaeol. Home: 7 Hirschenberg St, Tel Aviv, Isr. Office: Maariv, Tel Aviv, Isr.

SCHNURER, Harold T, US, attorney; b. NYC, Oct 8, 1904; s. Bert and Louisa (Teller); BS, CCNY, 1924; LLB, Columbia U, 1927; m. Bernice Lunin, Oct 6, 1957; c: Anthony, Eric, Danielle. Regional dir, Ariz, US Small Bus Admn, since 1963; asso counsel, NY Co Ambulance Chasing Inves, 1928-30; pres: Carolyn Schnurer Inc; Beachwear Corp of Amer, both 1945-55; dep commn, NY State Dept of Commerce, 1955-59. Maj, NY State Guard, 1947-54. Exec dir, Maricopa Co Dem Cen Comm; exec bd, Ariz Dem Council; pres: Phoenix chap, AJ Comm, 1966-68; Twelfth Regiment Vet Off Assn, 1961; bd dirs: J Comty Cen, Phoenix; bd govs, Jt Defense Appeal, 1953-62; mem: B'nai B'rith; Masons; Alpha Epsilon Pi. Home: 5750 E Indian Bend Rd, Scottsdale, Ariz.

SCHOCKEN, Gershom G, Isr, publisher; b. Zwickau, Ger, Sep 29, 1912; s. Salman and Lilli (Ehrmann); in Isr since 1933; att: Heidelberg U, 1932-33; LSE, 1935-36; c: Racheli, Amos, Hillel. Ed, publisher, Ha'aretz, Heb daily, since 1939; dir, Schocken Pub Co, Ltd, since 1939; MK, Progressive Party, 1955-59; chmn, Itim, Isr News Agcy, 1950-55, 1960-62. Home: 19 Vitkin St, Tel Aviv, Isr. Office: 56 Maze St, Tel Aviv, Isr.

SCHOCKEN, Theodore, US, publisher; b. Zwickau, Ger, Oct 8, 1914; s. Salman and Lilli (Ehrmann); in US since 1937; MBA, Harvard Bus Sch, 1940; m. Dora Landauer, Apr 11, 1941; c: Miriam Michael, Naomi, Eva. Pres, Schocken Books Inc, since 1945; dir, Schocken AG, dept stores, 1933-37; partner, Schocken Verlag, pubs, 1935-38, both Ger. Lt, US Army, 1942-45. Dir, Schocken Inst for J Research, Jerusalem; mem, bd overseers, JTSA; club, Harvard, NY. Hobbies and spec interests: J books; sports; shell collecting. Home: 117 Old Army Rd, Scarsdale, NY. Office: 67 Park Ave, New York, NY.

SCHOCKEN, Uli, Isr, opera singer; b. Berlin; d. Leo and Josepha (Weissbart), mother well-known Eur, Isr singer; in Isr since 1939; studied under Lottie Leonard; att Royal Coll of Music, London; granted personal scholarship by Prof Ben-Zion Dinur, Isr Min of Educ and Culture; m. Yehuda Efroni, Aug 25, 1953; c: Leor, Josefa. Appeared: Habimah Theater: Midsummer Night's Dream; Cry My Beloved Country; leading parts, Isr Natl Opera: Faust; Fledermaus; title role, Shulamith, Ohel Theater; Operetta Theater, leading part in Silva and Byaderra by Kalman; star, local productions: Pajama Game; My Fair Lady; West Side Story; under direction of Musical Ensemble sponsored by Baroness De Rothschild; toured as multi-lingual folksinger. IDF, 1952-53. Home and office: 9 Frishman St, Tel Aviv, Isr.

SCHOEM, Gerald N, US, organization exec; b. Passaic, NJ, Mar 22, 1922; s. Herman and Mae (Minkoff); att NYU, 1938-40, 1943-45; m. Sara Richman, June 7, 1942; c: Mark, David. Exec dir: Har Zion Temple, since 1952; BMH Cong Denver, Colo, 1949-52; partner, Harold Nixon Inc, ind realtors, Hackensack, NJ, 1945-49. Pres: Temple Beth Isr, Maywood, NJ, 1946-49; Natl Assn Syn Admnrs, 1958-60; vice-pres, NJ region, United Syn of Amer, 1948-49. Home: 5211 Lebanon Ave, Philadelphia, Pa. Office: Har Zion Temple, 54 and Wynnefield Ave, Philadelphia, Pa.

SCHOEN, Alfred, US, business exec; b. Ger, Apr 22, 1916; s. Kaufmann and Theresa (Heiman); in US since 1936; att Yeshiva, Frankfurt; m. Carla Gans, Oct 4, 1941; c: David, Michael. Pres: Gen Foam Div, Tenneco Chem Inc, since 1953. US Army, 1943-46. Pres: Riverdale J Cen; UJA Bonds;

Maimonides Inst for Mentally Handicapped, Yeshiva U. Hobbies: art, traveling. Home: 617 W 227, New York, NY. Office: 640 W 134, New York, NY.

SCHOEN, Myron Erwin, US, organization exec; b. Bx, NY, Jan 9, 1920; s. Murray and Anna (Stern); BBA, CCNY, 1948; m. Charlotte Klepper, Jan 10, 1944; c: Deborah, Marc. Dir, J Commn on Syn Admn, UAHC-CCAR, since 1962, secy, bd Cert for Temple Admns, UAHC-CCAR-NATA, since 1963; dir, off syn admn, UAHC, 1957-62; asst to natl dir, B'nai B'rith Hillel Found, 1950-53; exec dir, Stephen Wise Free Syn Found, 1954-57. S/sgt, US Army, 1943-45. Secy, Inter-Faith Research Cen for Rel Architecture, Inc, 1965; exec bd, Natl Assn for Temple Admns; hon mem, Guild for Rel Architecture, 1966; mem: Natl Assn Church Bus Mgrs; Amer Cemetery Assn. Author: Successful Synagogue Administration, 1963; columnist, Natl Jewish Post and Opinion, since 1960. Home: 45 Fairview Ave, NY. Office: 838 Fifth Ave, New York, NY.

SCHOENBERG, Irving B, military officer; b. St Joseph, Mo, Nov 5, 1925; s. Morris and Mary (Hochman); att U Kan, 1943; Cornell, 1944; BA, US Mil Acad, West Point, 1948; MA, U of Md, 1959; grad, Ind Coll of the Armed Forces, Wash, DC, 1967; MS, Bus Admn, George Wash U, 1969; m. Ann Hoffman, June 24, 1956; c: David, Jeffrey. Col, cdr, Air Force Contract Maintenance Cen, USAF, since 1969; admn off, 301st Bomber Wing, 1948-51; asst wing insp, 307th, Bomb Wing, 1951-52; asst prof, air sci, Air Force ROTC, U Md, 1952-55; White House aide, 1954-56; prog and analysis off and exec off, off of leg liaison, Off Secy of Air Force, 1955-59; maj, missile flight cdr and group exec off, USAF, Eur, 1959-62; missile oprs staff off, Off Dir of Oprs, USAF Hqr, Wash, DC, 1962-69; chief, spec projects br, Off Secy of Air Force, 1964-65; dep exec asst to the Under Secy of the AF, 1965-66, exec asst, 1967-69. Served: US Army, WW II, USAF, Korea. Mem: Natl Soc Scabbard and Blade; Assn Grads US Mil Acad; Phi Kappa Phi; Pi Sigma Alpha; Pi Tau Pi; Royal Order WWs; Soc of Logistics Engrs; Masons. Hobbies: amateur theatricals; squash rackets; handball; tennis; travel. Home: 1053 Saratoga Dr, Fairborn, O. Office: Air Force Maintenance Cen, Wright-Patterson Air Force Base, O.

SCHOENBERGER, Guido L, US, art hist, educator; b. Frankfurt/M, Ger, Feb 26, 1891; s. Jacob and Pauline (Mayer); in US since 1939; PhD, U Freiburg, 1917; att U Berlin, 1911-12; privatdozent für Kunstgeschichte, U Frankfurt, 1924; m. Martha Kaufmann, Apr 11, 1923; c: Eva Heimer, Lisa Cohen. Research f, em, J Mus, JTSA, since 1961, research f, 1947-61; adj prof and lectr, hist art, NYU; asst, Inst Fine Arts, Frankfurt U, Ger, 1919-24; privatdozent, 1924-35; curator, Hist Mus, Frankfurt, 1928-35. Mem: Natl Geog Soc; Blue Card; Coll Art Assn of Amer. Author: Beiträge zur Baugeschichte des Frankfurter Doms, 1927; Der Frankfurter Dom, Das Bauwerk, 1929; The Drawings of Mathis Gothart Nithart, called Gruenwald, 1948; co-author, J Ceremonial Art, 1959; contbr to art periodicals. Home: 115-25 84 Ave, Richmond Hill, NY.

SCHOENEWALD, Jacob, Isr, adjustor, surveyor; b. Dortmund, Ger, Sep 17, 1908; in Isr since 1935; att U's Bonn; Munich; DJur; DRerPol; m; one c. Adjustor for leading ins co's including Lloyds of London. Mem, exec bd, Ilan, Isr Soc for Crippled Children; club, Rotary, Tel Aviv-Yaffa, fmr pres, mem bd, dist I99. Home: 42 Oranim St, Kfar Shmaryahu, Isr. Office: 22 Maze St, Tel Aviv, Isr.

SCHOLEM, Gershom G, Isr, educator, author; b. Berlin, Ger, Dec 5, 1897; in Isr since 1923; PhD, Munich U, 1922; hon DHL, HUC-JIR, NY; m. Fania Freud. Prof em, Heb U, Jerusalem, since 1966, prof, Kabbala, 1933-66; lectr, 1925-33; head, dept Hebraica, Judaica, U Libr, 1923-27; visiting Strock lectr, JIR, US, 1938, 1949; visiting prof, Brown U, Providence, RI, 1956-57. Pres, Isr Acad Sci and Hum, since 1968. Author: Das Buch Bahir, 1923; Bibliographia Kabbalistica, 1927; Catalogus Codd Kabbalisticorum, 1930; P'rakim leToldot Sifrut haKabbala, 1933; Raayon haGeula baKabbala; Die Geheimnisse der Schöpfung, 1935; Major Trends in Jewish Mysticism, 1941; Halomotov shel haShabatai Rabbi Mordechai, 1944, Eng ed, 1965; belkvot Mashiah, 1947; Reshith haKabbala, 1948; Seder haMisko'ot beMada'ei haYahadut, 1950; Shabtai Zvi vehaTenua haShabtaith, 2 vols, 1957; Jewish Gnosticism and Talmudic Tradition, 1960; Zur Kabbala und ihrer Symbolik, 1960, Eng ed, 1965; Ursprung und Anfänge der Kabbala, 1962, Fr ed, 1966; Von der mystischen Gestalt der Gottheit, 1962. Home: 28 Abarbanel Rd, Jerusalem, Isr. Office: Heb U, Jerusalem, Isr.

SCHONFELD, Hyman Kolman, US, dentist, researcher, educator; b. NYC, Aug 5, 1919; s. Adolph and Bessie (Mintzer); BA, Bklyn Coll, 1940; DDS, NYU, Coll of Dent, 1943; MPH, U of NC, Sch of Public Health, 1960, PhD, 1962; m. Muriel Kleiman, Jan 30, 1944; c: Warren, Judith. Asso prof, public health, Yale Y Sch of Med, since 1969, sr research asso, since 1964; pvt practice, 1946-56; dent, Cen State Hosp, 1957-59; clinical research asso, biometrician, Warner-Lambert Research Inst, 1962-64. Capt, US Army, Dent Corps, 1944-46. Mem: Amer Public Health Assn; Amer Stat Assn; Amer Dent Assn; Conn State Dent Assn; New Haven Dent Assn. Contbr to dent and public health jours. Home: 343 Augusta Dr, Orange, Conn. Office: 60 College St, New Haven, Conn.

SCHONFELD, Lazar, US, rabbi, broadcaster; b. Backo, Petro-vośelo, Yugo, July 17, 1880; s. Moritz and Leontina (Paskesz); in US since 1925; att Coll of Szeged, Hung; U Budapest; U Vienna; Yeshiva, Bonyhad and N Surany, Hung; Rabb Coll, Pressburg, Czech, all 1894-1907; m. Sarah Furth, Jan 5, 1908; c: Nelly, Magda Mescheloff, Frank, Gabriel. Fmr rabbi, Cong Beth David Agudath Achim, Bx, NY; chief rabbi: Pakrac, Vinkovci, Yugo, 1907-13; Nagykaroly, Hung, now Carei, Rum, until 1925. Prin contrib: discoverer of J archive in Pressburg. Hon vice-pres, Union Orthodox Rabbis of Amer and Can; hon pres: Rabb Bd, Bx, Rabb Bd, Boro Park, Bklyn; Soc Satmar and Vicinity; exec mem, Mizrachi Org of Amer; delg, WZC, Basel, 1946, Jerusalem, 1951. Rel lectr, Hung progs, VOA, since 1952; weekly radio broadcasts, WPCH, NYC, 1927-33; contbr articles to rabb and sci jours. Recipient: decoration by Emperor Karl of Aus-Hung, 1917, for services in WW I; street in Nagykaroly, Carei, Rum, named for him; medal from US Govt for vol service of finances for WW II. Home: 934 46 St, Brooklyn, NY.

SCHONFELD, Moses, US, radio correspondent, lecturer,writer; b. London, Eng, Nov 19, 1910; s. Victor and Rachel (Stern-berg); in US since 1938; att U London, 1933; Columbia U, 1944; m. Ruth Bitensky, 1939; c: Debbie, Jo-Ann,Victor. UN corresp, radio commentator; pres: Jo-Deb Enterprises, Inc, since 1945; Schonfeld Trading, Inc, since 1946; Sun-Fast Textiles, Inc, 1940-61; staff mem, Derby and Co, London, 1927-33; prop, Schonfeld and Co, 1933-39; pres: Victor Ship Corp, 1962; Ace Devl Corp, 1953. Pal Police, 1936; aide to Col Lord Josiah C Wedgwood, 1937-38; pres: Manhattan chap, Amer Friends Heb U, 1954; Amer sect, Commn on Status J War Orphans in Eur, 1949; chmn bd, Youth Ref Comm, UK, 1932-33; found: Tel Aviv Forum, 1934; Givat Miller settlement for employees of Tel Aviv Munic, 1935; hon secy, Amer Chap, Rel Emergency Council, 1941-48; secy, Dominion League for Pal, 1936-38; spec off, UN repr for ZOA, 1956-62; spec cons, Ambass Henry Cabot Lodge, 1960; delg, White House Conf on Small Bus; mem: Amer sect, WJC; Amer Zionist Council; Seafood Producers Assn; hon secy, Westchester Rel Inst and Westchester Day Sch; hon fire chief, NYC Fire Dept; club, UN. Author: Pales-tine as a British Dominion, 1938; The Mark of the Swastika, 1941; Nutrition Problems in Relief and Rehabilitation, 1944; Blueprint for Post-War Reconstruction, 1945; lit and drama ed, The Light Magazine, NY. Contbr to periodicals. Hobby: art. Home: Greacen Point, Mamaroneck, NY. Of-fice: UN, Room 371, New York, NY.

SCHONFELD, Solomon, Eng, presiding rabbi; b. London, Eng, Feb 21, 1912; s. Victor and Rachel (Sternberg); att Us: London, Vienna; PhD, Königsberg U, 1933; ordained rabbi, Yeshivot: Slabodka, Kovno; Tirnau, Slovakia, both 1933; m. Judith Hertz; c: Victor, Jonathan, Jeremy. Presiding rabbi, Union Orthodox Heb Congs, since 1933; chmn, prin, J Secondary Schs Movement; rabbi, Adath Isr Syn, 1933-60. Pres, Council J Day Schs in Gt Brit; chmn, Comty Cens for Isr Org; dir, Chief Rabbis Council, 1938-50; chmn, Bd Orthodox J Educ, 1945-60. Author: Jewish Religious Educa-tion, 1943; Universal Bible, 1953; Message to Jewry, 1958; Why Judaism, 1963; Sayings of the Fathers, 1969. Home: 73 Shepherds Hill, London N6, Eng. Study: 86 Amhurst Park, London N16, Eng.

SCHONTHAL-BERTRAN, Aviva Haia, Isr, educator; b. Lvov, Pol, Jan 31, 1928; d. Bruno and Meta (Lau); in Isr since 1963; BA, Hunter Coll, 1949; MA, 1951; dipl d'etudes, Sorbonne, Paris, 1955; PhD, Columbia U, NYC, 1957; m. Shabetai Bertran; c: Hanna, Lea. Asst prof, Fr lit, Bar Ilan U, Ramat Gan, since 1963; tchr: Fisher Sch of Langs, NY, 1947-49;

Rabbi S R Hirsch HS, NY, 1950; Berlitz Sch of Langs, Paris, Fr, 1954-55; Theodore Roosevelt HS, NY, 1956-58; lectr, Columbia U, 1955-58; instr: Universidad do Brasil, 1959-60; and visiting lectr, Alliance Francaise, Brazil, 1959-61; Inst Brasil-Estados Unidos, 1959-61; Queen's Coll, Flushing, NY, 1961-62; Alliance Française, NY, 1962; i/c ed research in fgn langs, NH Wilson Co, NYC, 1950-53; chmn dept Fr, Beth Jacob Tchrs Sem, NYC, 1955-56; teaching Fr ins-tructorships: CCNY; Alliance Française, NY; Yeshiva U Cen HS; Mannes Coll of Music, NY, 1962-63. Contbr to jours. Recipient: f, Bryn Mawr Coll, 1951; Fr Govt Research f; Fr Govt Patronship. Home: 5 Kedushat Yomtov St, Yismach Moshe, Kiryat Ono, Isr. Office: Bar Ilan U, Ramat Gan, Isr.

SCHOOLER, Lee, US, public relations exec; b. Chgo, Ill, June 15, 1923; s. David and Mary (Lippert); BS, Roosevelt Coll, Chgo, 1945; m. Rachelle Margulas, Nov 15, 1959. Chmn: PR Bd, Chgo, found, 1948; Financial Relations Bd Inc; PR Bd of Can; dir, US comm, Care of Eur Children, 1946; produc, moderator, Press Conf, TV prog; writer, produc, radio sta KWTO, WBAB, Atlantic City, NJ, 1946; lectr, Eng, Roosevelt Coll, 1946-47. US Army, 1943-45. Dir, ACLU; chmn, bd trustees, Mundelein Coll; natl exec, ADL, B'nai Brith; mem: AJComm; PR Soc of Amer; adv bd, Ill Youth Commn; bd, Traveler's Aid Soc; Intl Coll Surgs, Hall of Fame; All Chgo Citizens Comm; Chgo Assn Commerce and Ind; Ill Assn Commerce; Amer Legion; Amer Vets Comm; Ill, Chgo Hist Socs; Mus Modern Art; Chgo Art Inst; Amer Fed of Arts; clubs: Exec's; Publicity; Standard; Art Collectors, all Chgo; Lincoln Park Tennis, dir. Recipient: Billionaire Anniversary medal, City of Paris, Fr; Loyola U of Citizens Key; cert, extraordinary service, State Dept, 1951; award for meritorious service, Freedom Found. Hobbies: horses; riding; tennis; photography; travel; art; Amer hist. Home: 43 E Elm St, Chicago, Ill. Office: 75 E Wacker Dr, Chicago, Ill.

SCHOOLMAN, Bertha S, US, communal worker; b. NYC, Dec 9, 1897; d. Wolf and Frimet (Bardowitz) Singer; BA, Hunter Coll, 1919; postgrad study, Tchrs Coll, Columbia U, 1921-23; grad, tchrs inst, JTSA, 1921, postgrad study, 1922-23, 1946; m. Albert Schoolman, June 25, 1922; c: Judith Taller, Frima Kain. Mem, natl bd, Hadassah, since 1935, natl secy, 1940-41, natl vice-pres, 1941-43, natl chmn, Pal Comm, 1941-47, Youth Aliyah, 1956-60; co-chmn, Youth Aliyah Mgmt Comm, JA for Isr, 1947-53, mem since 1960; dep mem, Zionist Gen Council, WZO; mem: gov bd, J Recon-structionist Found, since 1945; bd govs, Amer Assn for J Educ, since 1945; Amer Assn for UN; Freedom House, Alumni Assn, Tchr's Inst, JTSA, Hunter Coll; delg, 5 WZCs, 1946-64; mem exec, AZC, 1939-61, alternate mem since 1961; chmn, exec comm, World J Child's Day, Jerusalem, 1949-53; tchr, Cen J Inst, Soc for Advancement Judaism, 1919-23; dir, children's summer camping, 1922-46; White House Conf, 1960. Recipient: Alumni award, Tchr's Inst, JTSA, 1947. Hobby: camping. Home: 415 Central Park W, New York, NY.

SCHOOLNIC, Jacob W, US, physician; b. NYC, June 8, 1906; s. Harry and Ester (Polock); BA, U of W Va, 1926; BS, Med Sch, 1928; MD, Rush Med Coll, 1931. Pvt practice since 1931; instr of med to nurses, E Liverpool City Hosp, since 1932, mem, med staff, since 1932, chief, med, since 1953. F: Amer Coll Phys; Amer Coll Allergists; dipl, Amer Bd Internal Med; mem: Amer, O Socs Internal Med; pres: E Liverpool J Fed, 1935-51, 1960-61; B'nai B'rith lodge, 1935-40; Columbiana Co Med Soc, 1940; dir, J Home for Aged, Pittsburgh, Pa; mem: Amer Acad Allergy; AHA; AMA; O State Med Assn; Amer Diabetes Assn; Pittsburgh Allergy Soc; Intl Corresp Club Allergy; J Chautauqua Soc; C of C; AJComm; Phi Sigma Delta; Temple B'nai Isr; clubs: Rotary; E Liverpool Country. Hobbies: golf, chess. Home: 2545 Parkway, E Liverpool, O. Office: 130 W 5 St, E Liverpool, O.

SCHORR, Daniel, US, journalist, news commentator; b. NYC, Aug 31, 1916; s. Louis and Tillie (Godiner); BSS, CCNY, 1939. Chief, CBS News Bur for Ger and E Eur in Bonn, 1960-66; CBS, Wash corresp, CBS News, since 1966, spec assignments in Latin Amer and Eur, reopened CBS Moscow Bur, 1955, chief, news bur for Ger and E Eur, Bonn, 1960-66; asst ed, JTA, 1934-41; news ed, Aneta, Dutch News Agcy, 1941-46; corresp in Low Countries for: CBS; Chr Sci Monitor; NY Times; London Daily Mail, 1948-53. US Army, 1943-45. Mem: Overseas Writers Assn; Radio TV Analysts; clubs: Overseas Press; Natl Press. Recipient: citations for excellence in radio-TV reporting from USSR, Overseas Press Club; Off of Orange Nassau, 1955. Office: 2020 M St, NW, Washington, DC.

SCHORR, Norman A, US, business exec; b. Bklyn, NY, Jan 1, 1920; s. Morris and Anna (Fessler); AB, U Mich, 1940; m. Thelma Mermelstein, Mar 5, 1955; c: Susan, Marjorie, Elizabeth. Pres, Norman A Schorr & Co, PR firm, since 1952; newsman, UPI, 1940-41; PR repr, Westinghouse Elec Corp, 1941-43, 1946-52. Lt, US Army Signal Corps, 1943-46. Mem: natl exec bd, Amnesty Intl of US; exec bd, NY chap, AJComm; bd trustees, Soc for Advancement Judaism; exec council, NY profsl chap, Sigma Delta Chi; public service comm, PR Soc of Amer; Ind Publicity Assn; fmr: chmn, PR comm, Amer Vets Comm; PR counsel, Amer-Isr C of C and Ind Inc; clubs: Lenox Hill, mem, exec comm; Overseas Press of Amer. Author: chap in Handbook on Public Relations, 1960. Recipient: Asiatic-Pacific Theater Decoration; Amer Campaign Medal; WW II Victory Medal; Silver Anvil, PR Soc of Amer, 1965. Home: 470 West End Ave, New York, NY. Office: 5 E 42 St, New York, NY.

SCHORR, Samuel, Isr, educator; b. Kutov, Pol, June 22, 1915; s. Alexander and Esther (Lwow); in Isr since 1926; att Heb U, Jerusalem, 1933-35; MD, R U, Bologna, It, 1939; m. Head, dept diagnostic radiology, Munic and Govt Med Cen, Tel Aviv-Jaffa; dean, fac continuing med educ, Tel Aviv U, prof, diagnostic radiology, since 1967; clinical asso prof, Heb U, Jerusalem, since 1959; chief phys, x-ray dept, Hadassah Hosp, 1947-57. F, sci council, Intl Coll Angiology; hon f, Amer Coll of Radiology. Contbr to radiological lit. Home: 40 Chen Blvd, Tel Aviv, Isr. Office: Weizmann Ave, Tel Aviv, Isr.

SCHORSCH, Emil, US, rabbi; b. Huengheim, Ger, Jan 12, 1899; s. Isaak and Karoline (Hirschheimer); in US since 1940; ordained rabbi, J Theol Sem, Breslau, Ger, 1928; PhD, U Tuebingen, 1925; m. Fanny Rothschild, Dec 28, 1926; c: Hanna Hahn, Ismar. Rabbi em, Mercy and Truth Syn, Pottstown, Pa; fmr: chaplain: Pennhurst State Sch; Valley Forge Army Hosp; rabbi, J Comty, Hannover, Ger. Mem: B'nai B'rith, fmr pres, Hannover lodge; RA; Bd of Rabbis, Phila; club, Optimist. Author: Die Lehrbarkeit der Religion, 1929; contbr articles on phil and psych of Judaism. Home: 37 Victory Ave, Vineland, NJ.

SCHOSSBERGER, Janos, Isr, physician; b. Budapest, Hung, Oct 4, 1914; s. Alexander and Rachel (Reichardt); att Vienna Med Sch; m. Stella Kalmar, Apr 5, 1936; c: Michael, Evi, Eli, Ruthi. Dir: psycht, Kfar Shaul Work Village; Child Psycht Unit, Merkaz Lemaan Hayeled; visiting prof: W Psycht Inst, Pittsburgh, 1967-68; Johns Hopkins Hosp, Baltimore, 1968-69. Maj, IDF MC. Prin contribs: psychoanalytic communication theory, aggression theory, systems theory (social psycht). Mem: IMA; Isr Psychan Assn; Intl Psychan. Contbr papers, articles to sci jours. Hobbies: sci fiction, music, photography, life's deployment. Home: 27 Harakevet St, Jerusalem, Isr. Office: Kfar Shaul Work Village, Jerusalem, Isr.

SCHOTT, Stuart, US, research exec; b. Newport, Ky, Apr 28, 1913; s. Morris and Jennie (Spector); BS, U Ky, 1933; MA, U Cincinnati, 1934, PhD, 1936; m. Laurene Davis, June 18, 1939; c: Susan, Nancy. Vice-pres, research, US Ind Chem Co, since 1957, on staff since 1950. Maj, US Army, 1942-46. Bd trustee, Rockdale Ave Temple; mem: Amer Chem Soc; Soc Chem Industry; Soc for Hist Tech; club, Chem. Home: 5300 Hamilton Ave, Cincinnati, O. Office: 1275 Section Rd, Cincinnati, O.

SCHOTTLAND, Charles I, US, social worker, educator, administrator; b. Chgo, Ill, Oct 29, 1906; s. Harry and Milly (Lustberg); AB, UCLA, 1927; Social Work Cert, NY Sch Social Work, 1929; att U of S Cal Law Sch, 1929-33; hon deg, Boston U, 1969; m. Edna Greenberg, June 7, 1931; c: Richard. Dean, Florence Heller Grad Sch for Advanced Studies in Social Wfr, Brandeis U, since 1959, dean U fac, 1961-63; admnr, Cal Relief Admn, 1933-36; exec dir, Fed JWO, 1936-41; asst to chief, Children's Bur, US Dept of Lab, 1941-42; asst dir, UNRRA for Ger, 1945; dir, Cal Dept of Social Wfr, 1950-54; commn, social security, HEW, 1954-58. Lt col, WW II. Chmn: US comm, Intl Conf Social Work, 1961-62; deans adv comm, Fed Social Wfr Agcys, Council on Social Work Educ, 1969-70; mem: exec bd, Amer Public Wfr Assn; exec comm, Natl Conf on Social Wfr, pres, 1959-60; Natl Assn Social Workers Inc, pres, 1967-69; Intl Council on So-

cial Wfr, pres, 1968-72; Natl Social Wfr Assembly; Save the Children Fed; J Big Brothers Assn; comm social security experts, Intl Lab Off; prin adv, US deleg, UN Social Commn, 1955-57; group of experts, Econ and Social Council, 1959; chmn, Income Maintenance Comm, White House Conf on Aging, 1959-60; mem: AJComm; Amer Legion; JWV; Zeta Beta Tau; club: Cosmos, Wash. Author: Federal Social Security: A Guide to Law and Procedure, 1959; The Social Security Program in the United States, 1963; ed, The Welfare State, 1967. Recipient: J Koshland award for outstanding exec in social work in Cal, 1954; alumnus of year, U of Cal, 1960. Home: 61 Fairgreen Place, Chestnut Hill, Mass. Office: Brandeis U, Waltham, Mass.

SCHRAG, Allen Israel, US, business cons, attorney, business exec; b. NYC, July 19, 1925; s. Carl and Sadie (Bernhard); AB, Columbia Coll, 1944; LLB, Yale Sch of Law, 1947; m. Bella Fink, Oct 15, 1950; c: Howard, Jonah, Carl. Financial cons since 1968; econ and legal cons, Triangle-Pacific Forest Products Corp, since 1968, trouble-shooter, secy, treas, house counsel, Precisionware, Inc, 1950-68, financial control, and credit and collection mgmt, of Triangle-Pacific Forest Products Corp subsidiaries, analyzing mergers. Pres, Yeshivah of Flatbush, NY, fmr trustee, dir, mem bd educ, chmn comms; trustee, E Midwood J Cen; life mem: John Jay Assn, Columbia U; ZOA; Bklyn JCC, dir; Phi Beta Kappa; NY Bar Assn. Co-author: Comparative Compilation of Federal Transportation Statutes, 1949; contbr to law jours. Recipient: Dist Communal Service, Bklyn JCC, 1968. Home: 3379 Bedford Ave, Brooklyn, NY.

SCHRAG, Otto, Ger, merchant, author, translator; b. Karlsruhe, Ger, Oct 11, 1902; s. Hugo and Bella (Sulzberger); att Us: Freiburg; Munich; PhD, U Heidelberg, 1934; m. Alice Vittali, July 30, 1953; c: Peter. Pres: Schrag Malz AG; Malzfabrik Gengenbach AG; Malterie Lix, Ebers Münster, Fr. Ref in Eur, 1940-41; concentration camp, St Cyprien, 1941. Author: The Locusts, 1943; Sons of the Morning, 1945; Bedrock, 1947; Die Antwort, 1952; trans: From Here to Eternity; Rock Wagram; other works. Home: Quettigstr 17a, Baden-Baden, Ger.

SCHRAGE, Samuel Awner, US, communal leader; b. Belo Horizonte, Brazil, Dec 12, 1935; s. Feiuisch and Scheindla (Lieberman); desc of Reb Elimelech Meligensk; in US since 1949; ordained rabbi, United Lubavitchen Yeshivoth, 1960; MS, LIU, 1968; dipl, public admn, NYU, 1967; m. Rose Levine, Feb 25, 1962; c: Abraham, Aryeh. Prin, hum resources spec, NYC, since 1968; admn asst, United Lubavitchen Yeshivot, 1962-64; asst to mayor, NYC, 1965-68. Formed Maccabees, citizens group, 1964; cons, law enforcement agencies. Home: 724 Montgomery St, Brooklyn, NY. Office: 38 Park Row, New York, NY.

SCHRAGER-OSTRYNSKI, Fajwel, Fr, organization exec; b. Krynki, Pol, May 2, 1907; s. Zalmand and Jenta (Efront); in Fr since 1927; att: U Grenoble, 1927-28; U Nancy, 1928-29; m. Fejga Stupnik, Dec, 1936; c: Solange. Dir, ORT Union and ORT, Fr, since 1950; secy gen, Arbeter Ring, Paris and repr, J Lab Comm, NY, in Paris, 1945-50; mem, bd dirs: Fonds Social Juif Unifié, Paris; Union des Anciens Combattants Juifs; Arbeter Ring. Served Fr Army. Contbr to Yiddish publs. Home: 18 bis Ave de Versailles, Paris 16, Fr. Office: 10 Villa d'Eylau, 44 av Victor Hugo, Paris 16, Fr.

SCHRAMEK, Alfred, Isr, surgeon; b. Cieszyn, Pol, July 10, 1917; s. Wilhelm and Cecilia (Schajowicz); in Isr since 1950; att Med Sch, Prague, 1938; MD, Med Sch, Vienna, 1950; m. Mona Lipanski, Aug 12, 1945; c: Nomi. Head, dept vascular surg, Rambam Hosp, since 1965. MC, IDF. Mem: Surg Soc; Société Européenne de Chirurgie Cardiovasculaire. Contbr to med jours. Home: 2 Leon Blum St, Haifa, Isr.

SCHRAYER, Max Robert, US, business exec; b. Chgo, Ill, Nov 17, 1902; s. Robert and Jennie (Weber); BS, U Mich, 1923; m. Mildred Mayer, Oct 25, 1924; c: Helaine Freeman, Jean Adler, Robert. Pres, Associated Agcys, Inc, since 1966. Pres, Better Govt Assn; vice-chmn, Roosevelt U; dir, JWF, Metrop Chgo; mem, Chgo chap, Chartered Property and Casualty Underwriters; fmr: pres, gen chmn, CJA; pres: KAM Cong; Beth Am Cong; Chgo fed, UAHC; dir, UAHC; club, U of Mich, Chgo, fmr pres. Home: 4950 Chicago Beach Dr, Chicago, Ill. Office: 175 W Jackson Blvd, Chicago, Ill.

SCHREIBER, Bruno B, It, educator; b. Trieste, It, Feb 19, 1905; s. Alberto and Alice (Cerf); deg, natural sci, U Padua,

1927; m. Ada Fano, May 23, 1943; c: Fabio. Prof, zool, U Parma, since 1952; asst prof, U Milan, 1930-52. Lt, It Army. Corresp mem, Instituto Lombardo di Science e Lettere; club, Rotary. Contbr to sci jours. Home: Via Goito 16, Parma, It. Office: U of Parma, Parma, It.

SCHREIBER, Flora Rheta, US, educator, writer, broadcaster; b. NYC, Apr 24, 1918; d. William and Esther (Aaronson); cert, Cen Sch of Speech Training and Dramatic Art, with U London, 1937; BS, New Coll, Columbia U, 1938, MA, 1939; att: Mus Modern Art Motion Picture Sch; NYU Radio Workshop. Asst prof, Eng and speech, dir, PR, John Jay Coll of Criminal Justice, CUNY; dir, radio, TV and film writing workshop, New Sch for Soc Research, since 1953; psycht ed, Sci Digest, since 1964; corresp-columnist, Bell McClure Syndicate; cons: NBC press dept; BBD & O, advt agcy; fmr mem, speech dept: Bklyn Coll, Adelphi Coll; former instr, Exeter Coll, Eng; produc, Bklyn Coll Radio Forum, WNYC, 1944-46; dir, radio and TV workshop, Adelphi Coll, 1948-51. Mem: Authors League of Amer; Soc Mag Writers; Speech Assn of Amer; Eng Inst, Columbia U; AAUP; Intl Platform Assn; Amer Assn U Women; Natl Council on Crime and Delinquency; fmr: mem, dept of audio-visual instrn, NEA; Theater Lib Assn. Author: Biography of William Schuman, 1954; Your Child's Speech: A Practical Guide for Parents for the First Five Years, 1956. Contbr to mags, radio, TV. Home: 32 Gramercy Park S, New York, NY. Office: CUNY, New York, NY.

SCHREIBER, Georges, US, artist, author; b. Brussels, Belgium, Apr 25, 1904; s. Herman and Pauline (Lenneberg); in US since 1928; att Acad of Fine Arts: Berlin, Ger, 1922; Duesseldorf, Ger, 1923; m. Lillian Yamin, Sep 28, 1941; c: Joan Hoberg-Petersen. Mem, art fac, New Sch for Social Research, NY, since 1958. Paintings in perm collections: Metrop Mus; Bklyn Mus; Whitney Mus; Syracuse Mus; Mus Davenport, La; Mus Terre Haute, Ind; HUC, Mus, Cinn, O; Cinn Mus; Newark Mus; Toledo Mus; LA Mus; Tel Aviv Mus; Libr of Cong; Bibliotheque Nationale, Paris; MIT; Rutgers U; Smith Coll. Author and illus: Portraits and Self-Portraits, 1936; Bambino The Clown, 1947; Professor Bull's Umbrella, 1954; Bambino Goes Home, 1959; illustrated book, Ride on the Wind, by Lindbergh and Dalgliesh, 1957; contbr to mags. Artist corresp, War and Navy Dept, Wash, DC, 1943-44, Arctic Documentary assignment, 1943, US Submarine at War documentary, 1944; creator of official War Loan posters for US Treasury, 1942-44. Dir, NY chap, Artists Equity, 1948-49, natl dir, 1949-52. Recipient: Tuthill prize, Art Inst, Chgo, Ill, 1932; gold medal, NY Art Dirs Club, 1943; first prize, Mus Modern Art Competition, NYC, 1943; silver medal, US Treasury for dist services, 1944; Purchase Prize, first annual print exhb, Bklyn Mus, NY, 1948. Home and studio: 8 W 13 St, New York, NY.

SCHREIBER, Samuel S, US, engineer, business exec; b. Butler, Pa, May 23, 1908; s. Barry and Doris (Miller); BS, Case Inst of Tech, 1929; m. Phyllis Levy, 1937; c: Dale, James. Chmn, bd, pres, dir, Triple Cities Corp, Binghampton, NY; chmn, bd, Emerald Isle Hotel, Dublin, Ir; pres and dir: Yonkers Transit Corp; Crompond Construction Corp, Yonkers, NY; pres, Standard Operating Service Rent-a-Car Lic, Binghampton; treas, dir: Crompond Realty Corp, Yonkers; NY City Bus Conf; asst treas, Springhill Corp, Chgo, Ill; dir: First Westchester Corp, New Rochelle, NY, all since 1952; construction engr, Sam W Emerson Co, Cleveland, O, 1929-30; engr, W R Rhoton Co, 1930-31; utility engr, Forest Hills Devl Project, Cleveland, O, 1932-33; mem, Berger, Schreiber and Asso, cons engrs, and vice-pres, Sam S Schreiber Co, Cleveland, 1933-36; chief engr, exec asst, City State RR Commn, Cleveland, 1936-41; staff engr, exec asst, Transit Bd, City of Cleveland, 1942-43; cons engr, W C Gilman Co, NYC, 1943-50; gen mgr for trustee: Yonkers RR Co, 1950-52, pres, dir, 1952-60; Third Ave Transit Corp; Surface Transp Corp; Westchester St Transp Co, Inc; Westchester Elec RR Co; Warontas Press, Inc, all NY, 1950-52; vice-pres and dir, Surface Transp Advt, Inc, NY, 1950-52; chmn, bd, pres, dir, BEJ Corp, Binghampton; pres, dir, Cross County Coach Corp, Yonkers; exec vice-pres, Ghana (Afr) Econ Devl Corp, NYC; vice-pres, dir, Cross County Inves, Inc, Yonkers; treas, dir: Dana Schreiber Mortgage Co; Dana Schreiber Co, Inc; Beckman Investing Corp, NYC; Lee Communications, Inc, NYC; Windward Corp, Chgo, Ill; dir, Hudson and Manhattan RR Co and subsidiaries, NYC, all 1952-60. Dir: Yonkers C of C; United Givers of Yonkers, Inc; Civic and Commerce Assn, New Rochelle, NY, 1952-60; mem: bus adv comm, Yonkers Visiting Nurses Assn; Mayor's

Traffic Adv Comm, Yonkers; pres council, Amer Inst of Mgmt, NY; coord comm, Bd of Educ, New Rochelle; planning bd, City of New Rochelle, all 1952-60; Amer Transit Assn; Bx Bd of Trade, Inc; Sigma Alpha Mu; club, Yonkers. Home: Spring Hill Farm, Box 151, Purchase, NY. Office: 152 Downing St, Yonkers, NY.

SCHROTTER, Bruno, Eng, dental surg; b. Bielitz, Pol, 1899; MD, Vienna, Aus, 1924; LDS, RCS, Eng. Pvt practice: Vienna, 1927-39; London. Aus Army, WW I. Found, Fed for Sch of Dent, Heb U, Jerusalem, 1952; mem, Igul; activities with: Isr Dent Sch; Friends Heb U, Eng; fmr: pres, J Med Students Assn, Vienna; mem: exec, Jüdischer Hochschulausschuss; J Acad Frat, Emunah, Vienna; Haschahar, Zionist Org; delg to 15th ZC, Basle, 1927. Home: 388 Upper Richmond Rd, London SW15, Eng. Office: 92 Harley St, London W1, Eng.

SCHUHL, Pierre-Maxime, Fr, educator, author; b. Paris, June 28, 1902; s. Lucien and Lucie (Schuhl); licencié es sciences, 1923; agrégé de philosophie, Ecole Normale Supérieure, 1925; docteur es Lettres, Paris, 1934. Chmn, dept phil, Sorbonne, Paris, since 1962, on fac since 1938; dir: Revue Philosophique; Libr of Contemporary Phil, both since 1952; lectr, U Montpellier, 1936; prof, U Toulouse, 1938. Fr Army, WW I. Pres: Soc Moreaude, Tours, 1968-69; Soc J Studies, 1949-52; Soc Hellenic Studies, Paris, 1964-65; mem, Natl Council Sci Research. Author: Platon et l'Art de son Temps, 1933; Machinisme et Philosophie, 1938; Etudes sur la Fabulation Platonicienne, 1947; La Pensée de Lord Bacon, 1949; Trois Essais de Montaigne, 1951; Le Merveilleux, la Pensée et l'Action, 1952; L'Oeuvre de Platon, 1954; Etudes Platoniciennes, 1960; Le Dominateur et les Possibles, 1960; Imaginer et Réaliser, 1963; Le Merveilleux et l'Imagination, 1969. Recipient: Chevalier de la Légion d'Honneur, 1950; Officier de l'Instruction Publique, 1947; Croix des Services Militaires Volontaires, 1947; Commandeur des Palmes Académiques, 1967. Office: Sorbonne, Université de Paris, Paris, Fr.

SCHÜLLER, Hans, Ger, merchant; b. Hildesheim, Jan 5, 1915; s. Adalbert and Ellen (Cassler); m. Josephine Braulitsch, Aug 8, 1948; c: Eva, Ruth, Michael. Owner, Schüller & Co, leather wholesalers, since 1945, found, Hamburg br, 1948. Ref in Eur, 1938-45; liaison off, Brit 8th Army, 1945. Chmn: Fed J Businessmen, State of Hesse; W Ger Assn of J Businessmen and Ind; mem: finance commn, J Comty of Frankfurt/M. Office: Kaiserstrasse 16, Frankfurt/Main, Ger.

SCHULMAN, Elias, US, author, librarian, editor; b. Slutzk, Russ, Sep 28, 1907; s. Falk and Bessie (Barhon); in US since 1921; att: CCNY, 1931-35; Yiddish Sci Inst, Vilna, Pol, 1935-36; Dropsie Coll, 1958-62, f, 1961-62, PhD, 1965. Libr, J Educ Comm, NYC. Author: A Critique of the Yiddish Encyclopedia, 1942; A History of Yiddish Literature in the USA, 1943; Young Vilna, 1946; Problems in the Interpretation of Yiddish Literature, in Heb, 1969; ed, Der Wecker; co-ed: Getzelten, NY, 1943-46; Biographical Dict of Yiddish Literature, vol 7; contbr: to Ency Judaica; of studies, essays, reviews to: Unzer Tseit; Yivo Bletter; Literarische Bletter; Oifn Shvell; Insich; Yearbook of Yiddish Sci Inst; Amer J Yearbook; Judaism, Cong bi-weekly. Mem: World Cong for Yiddish Culture; Comm for Yiddish Academic Dict; club: Yiddish PEN. Home: 2720 Broadway, New York, NY. Office: 426 W 58 St, New York, NY.

SCHULSOHN, Samuel J, US, rabbi; b. Aus, May 16, 1902; s. Wolf and Czarne (Raucher); in US since 1948; ordained rabbi, Hildesheimer Rabbiner Sem, Berlin, 1925; PhD, U Berlin, 1927; licentiate in law, U Czernowitz, 1932; m. Netty Beutel, Apr 16, 1940. Chaplain, Kings Co Hosp, NY, since 1956; rabbi: J Comtys of Sereth and Bukowina, 1928-34, and Caransebesch, 1934-35; Syn Mare, Bucharest, 1936; J Comty of Czernowitz, 1936-46; Fargarasch, 1947; and spiritual leader, concentration camps, Cariera de Piatra on Bug and Tulczyn, Pololia-Transistria, where deported, 1942-44; Cong Beth Isr, NYC, 1948-50; Brighton Beach J Cen, Bklyn, 1955-57; practicing atty, 1932-42; chaplain, Kingston Ave Hosp, 1951-56; lectr in US and Eur. Chmn, mem bd dirs, identification comm, World Org of Rabbi Nazi Victims, fmr, delg before Ger Bundestag, Parl, Restitution Comm and before various chancellors and mins, to identify E Eur Rabbi Nazi victims; found, pres, Bukowiner Friends, NYC; co-found, vice-pres, B'nai B'rith, Rum lodge; co-found, mem bd dirs, Rum Fed of Amer, chmn, comm for Ger restitution to J of Rum and Bukowina; mem: NY Bd Rabbis; Bklyn Bd

Rabbis; Union Ref Rabbis from Eur; exec comm, Assn to Perpetuate Memory of Ukrainian Js; J Hist Circle, NYC; fmr: guest of Ger govt; speaker on behalf UJA, Isr Bonds. Author: History of the Jews in Bukowina, 1744-1948; co-ed, contbr, Memorial Book for Jews in Bukowina, Tel Aviv, 1958; contbr to: Ency Judaica; Juedisches Lexikon, both Berlin; Ger, Yiddish and Eng periodicals in US and abroad. Home: 2915 W 5 St, Brooklyn, NY.

SCHULSON, Hyman A, US, attorney; b. Jerusalem, Dec 25, 1912; s. Solomon and Minnie (Schnitzer); in US since 1917; BA, Brown U, 1933; LLB, Yale U, 1936; m. Ruth Hendricks, Aug 8, 1950; c: David, Henry, Anne. Pvt practice since 1951; atty, NLRB, 1937-38; trial atty, Chgo, 1938-39; counsel, ZOA, 1940-42. US Army, 1942-46. Wash repr counsel, AZC, 1946-50; repr, JA for Pal before UN, 1947-50; exec dir, counsel, ORT, 1950-51; mem: Bar Assns, NYC; Wis and DC Bar Assns; ZOA; Cong Shearith Isr; AJCong; AJComm; Amer J Hist Soc; Amer J Tercentenary Comm; J Publs Soc of Amer; ORT; Reconstructionist Found; Amer J Soc for Service; Amer Comm for Weizmann Inst of Sci; Amer Friends Heb U; Fund for Israel Insts; Amer Technion Soc; JNF; United Isr Appeal; Phi Beta Kappa. Home: 25 W 81 St, New York, NY. Office: 55 Liberty St, New York, NY.

SCHULTZ, Henry Edward, US, attorney, communal leader; b. NYC, June 18, 1906; s. Julius and Esther (Block); LLB, NY Law Sch, 1929; hon DH, W Va State Coll, 1961; m. Rose Yellin, 1930; c: Roger, Michael, Jane. Vice-pres, gen counsel, The J B Williams Co, Inc. Hon natl chmn, ADL, since 1963, natl chmn, 1952-62; mem: bd trustees, Queens Speech and Hearing Cen; bd dirs, Sarah Delano Roosevelt House; off and dir, Eleanor Roosevelt Cancer Fund; mem, Bd Higher Educ, NYC, since 1941. Home: 565 Park Ave, New York, NY. Office: 767 Fifth Ave, New York, NY.

SCHUMACHER, Vincent James, US, dentist; b. Pittsburgh, Pa, Apr 14, 1928; s. James and Vera (Kertavich); BS, Loyola U, Chgo, 1949, DDS, 1955; m. Patricia O'Donovan, Dec 17, 1955; c: Suzette, Vincent, Dawn, Anthony, James, Kimberley.Pvt practice since 1955; asst prof, endodontics, Loyola U Dent Sch, since 1969; asso att, Michael Reese Hosp, Chgo, since 1966. Capt, US Army, 1956-60. Vice-pres, Dent Clinic, Michael Reese Hosp; secy, Odontographic Soc Chgo; mem: Intl Coll Dent; Delta Sigma Delta; Pierre Fauchard Acad; Coll Endodontic Study Club; Amer Dent Assn; Ill State Dent Soc; AMA; Chgo Dent Soc; Amer Assn Endodontists; N Suburban Dent Assn; Histopath Study Club. Home: 1381 Lincoln Ave, Highland Park, Ill. Office: 55 E Washington, Chgo, Ill.

SCHUR, Ira A, US, accountant; b. Boston, Mass, Apr 11, 1901; s. John and Rachel (Aronson); att NYU; m. Ethel Goldstein, 1932; c: Jane Brown, Susan, Edith. Mgn partner, S D Leidesdorf and Co; vice-pres, treas and dir, Baker, Evans and Co, Inc; treas, dir: Murray Hill Operating Co, Inc; Pershing Sq Bldg Corp; secy, dir, 1185 Tenants Corp. Chmn: natl retirement comm, Amer Inst CPAs, 1957-66; comm on investing soc's funds, NY State Soc CPAs, 1961-64; comm on fiscal and service acctnt, Comm on Standards and Accreditation Services for Blind, 1964-65; bequests and founds comm, ARC, 1968; finance comm, Inst for Advanced Study, Princeton, NJ, since 1964; vice-chmn, BBB of NYC, 1955-58; vice-pres, Cong Emanu-El, NYC, since 1961; treas: Mt Sinai Hosp, since 1955; Mt Sinai Sch of Med, CUNY; Acctnts Found, since 1952; Psychoanalytic Research and Devl Fund; Natl Accreditation Council for Agcys Serving Blind and Visually Handicapped, since 1966; secy bd, NY State Bd CPA Examiners, 1950-53; trustee, FJP, 1942-55; dir, Natl Info Bur, since 1966; mem: CPA Grievances Comm, NY State, 1944-48; steering comm, Project Adv Comm for Natl Health Council-Natl Social Wfr Assembly Uniform Acctnt Project, 1962-64; Natl Assembly for Social Policy and Devl, since 1967; Intl Lay Council, Intl Card Found, since 1964; State of NY-Dept Social Wfr Adv Council on Charities Registration, since 1966; NY Stock Exch Panels of Arbitrators, since 1965; council, Columbia U Sch Gen Studies, 1952-64; Royal Photographic Soc of Gt Brit; clubs: Acctnts of Amer; Harmonie, NY, pres, 1956-58; City Athletic, NY, gov, 1942-52; Grand Argentier, Commanderie de Bordeaux, Inc; Grand Officier, Confrerie des Chevalier du Tastevin; Argentier, Confrerie de la Chaine des Rotisseurs; Camera, NY; Boston Camera; Pinnacle, NY; 60 East, NY. Home: 1185 Park Ave, New York, NY. Office: 125 Park Ave, New York, NY.

SCHUR, Robert J, US, rabbi; b. Cincinnati, O, Sep 15, 1921; s. Louis and Maxine (White); BA, U Cincinnati, 1945; MHL, HUC, 1949; m. Rolly Friedman, Mar 25, 1945; c: Sally Selman, William. Rabbi, Cong Beth-El, Fort Worth, Tex, since 1956; asst rabbi, Beth Isr, Houston, Tex, 1949-52; rabbi, Gemiluth Chassodim, Alexandria, La, 1952-56; dir, SW Council, UAHC, 1954-59. Chmn, J Soc Service Agcy; fmr chmn: Comm on Youth, CCAR; Fed Agcys Serving Handicapped; health and hosp sect, Tarrant Co Comty Council; health and hosp comm, Ft Worth C of C; Child Wfr Adv Bd; mem, bd: Big Brothers Assn; Comty Action Agcy; Child Study Cen, fmr vice-pres; Ft Worth Sym Assn; J Fed, Ft Worth; fmr bd mem, Gen Mins Assn; mem: Metrop Ft Worth Urban Policy Conf; Ft Worth C of C Educ Comm; Tex br, ACLU; Kallah Tex Rabbis; UAHC Comm on Youth; Gov's Comm, White House Conf on Children and Youth, Wash, DC, 1960; active in Natl Fed of Temple Youth Leadership Training Insts; speaker on coll campuses; AJComm; B'nai B'rith; Natl Fed Temple Youth. Recipient: annual award, Health and Hosp Sect, Comty Council, 1961; J man of year, B'nai B'rith, Ft Worth, 1962; annual brotherhood award, Ft Worth Chap, NCCJ, 1966. Home: 2825 Harlanwood Dr, Fort Worth, Tex. Study: Cong Beth-El, PO Box 2232, Fort Worth, Tex.

SCHURR, Arie, Isr, police officer; b. Jerusalem, Nov 11, 1912; s. Solomon and Bertha (Rivlin); att Technion, Haifa, 1929-30; m. Esther Glasner, Aug 27, 1937; c: Avital, Yoram, Gideon. Cdr, chief, CID, Isr Police Hqr, Tel Aviv, since 1963, dep dist cdr, Haifa, 1949-52, head, identification dept, Police Hqr, 1951-63. Maj, IDF, 1947-49. Home: 22 Yosef Hagalili St, Ramat Gan, Isr. Office: 14 Harakevet St, Tel Aviv, Isr.

SCHUSTER, Aron, Netherlands, rabbi; b. Amsterdam, Aug 8, 1907; s. Izak and Rosa (Pakter); licencié ès lettres, 1936; ordained Rabbi, Hatarath Horaä, 1941; m. Eva Packter, 1936; three c. Pres, Chief Rabbinate for Netherlands, since 1968; prin, Rabbis and Tchrs Sem, since 1951; chief rabbi: Amsterdam, since 1955; provinces Noord Brabant, Limburg, 1951-55; province Overijsel, 1954-55. Home and study: Joh Verhulststr 29, Amsterdam, Netherlands.

SCHUSTER, Max Lincoln, US, editor, publisher; b. Kalusz, Aus, Mar 2, 1897; s. Barnet and Esther (Steiglitz); in US since 1897; B Litt, Columbia Sch of Journalism, 1917; m. Ray Haskell. Co-found, pres, chief exec off, and ed in chief, Simon and Schuster, Inc, book pubs, NYC, 1924-66; pres, ed in chief, chmn, ed bd, The Inner-Sanctum Library of Living Literature; asso with People's Book Club; co-found, co-dir, Ray and M Lincoln Schuster Ed Research Assos, NY; fmr: mem, bd dirs, Ency Britannica, Inc; asso with Pocket Books, Inc; dir, Business Reports, Inc; copy boy, NY Evening World, 1913; corresp: Boston Evening Transcript; United Press Assns, NY, mem, Wash Staff; United Press Assn; chief, publ info sect, bur war risk ins, US Treasury Dept; dir, publ, USN, 4th, 5th, Victory Loan Campaigns; asso in journalism, Grad Sch of Journalism, Columbia U; mem: org comm, NY World Fair, 1964. F, Amer Geographic Soc; chmn, journalism fund, Pulitzer Sch of Journ Alumni Assn; found, Soc for Prevention Cruelty to Newspaper Readers; mem, bd trustees, Montefiore Hosp; mem: Friends Scripta Mathematica; Bibliographical Soc of Amer; Shakespeare F; clubs: Three Hours for Lunch; Wednesday Culture Club That Meets on Fridays; Downing St Young Men's Marching; Dutch Treat; Rockefeller Center Luncheon; The Book Table; High Fidelity Friends of WQXR; Sea Cliff Garden. Author: Eyes on the World: A Photographic Record of History in the Making, 1935; ed: A Treasury of the World's Great Letters, 1940; Book Series on the Wisdom of the (S) Ages; contbr to periodicals. Homes: 11 E 73 St, New York, NY; Cow Neck Farm, Sands Point, LI, NY.

SCHUTZMAN, Noah Norman, US, business exec; b. Wilmington, Del, July 23, 1920; s. Isador and Ida (Goldman); BS, U Del, 1941; m. Helen Tomases, Apr 1, 1951; c: David, Daniel, Sara. Pres, Snelling & Snelling, since 1957; sales mgr, S & S Wholesale Co, 1949-56. Lt: Isr Army, 1948-49; US Army, 1941-45. Pres, J Comty Cen; vice-pres, J Fed, Del; Middle-Atlantic region, JWB. Home: 705 Coverly Rd, Wilmington, Del. Office: 917 Washington, Wilmington, Del.

SCHWAB, Bernard S, US, rabbi; b. St Paul, Minn, Feb 28, 1932; s. William and Mollie (Kamil); ordained rabbi, 1955; BS, Wis State U, 1961; BHL, Heb Theol Coll, Chgo; MTh, Coll of Bible-Lexington Theol Sem, 1962; m. Edith Minovitz,

Aug 7, 1955; c: Charles, Mollie, Michael. Rabbi, Cong Ohavey Zion, Lexington, Ky, since 1962; rabbi: Cong Beth Isr, Stevens Point, Wis, 1957-61; Cong Beth El, Ft Dodge, Ia, 1961-62. Mem: Alpha Gamma; B'nai B'rith; fmr: mem, Gov's Commn for Higher Educ; Isr Bond Chmn for Gtr Lexington. Home: 212 Conn Terr, Lexington, Ky. Study: 120 W Maxwell St, Lexington, Ky.

SCHWAB, Joseph J, US, biologist, educator; b. Columbus, Miss, Feb 2, 1909; s. Samuel and Hortense (Jackson); PhB, U Chgo, 1930, MS, 1936, PhD, 1938; m. Rosamond McGill, Sep 13, 1932; c: Jill. William Rainey Harper prof, natural scis, prof, educ, U Chgo, since 1949; cons, visiting prof, U Puerto Rico, 1948-57; f, Cen for Advanced Study in Behavioral Scis, 1958-59; Inglis lectr, Harvard U, 1961. Mem: Genetics Soc of Amer; Sigma Xi. Author: The University of Chicago Science Program, in Science in General Education, 1947; The Natural Sciences, in Idea and Practice of General Education, 1950; Eros and Education, 1958; The Teaching of Science as Enquiry, 1962; BSCS Biology Teachers' Handbook, 1963; Structure of the Disciplines: Problems, Topics, Issues, 1964; College Curriculum and Student Protest, 1969; contbr to profsl jours. Recipient: Quantrell Award for Teaching, 1945, 1965. Hobbies: electronics, music. Home: 5501 S Kenwood Ave, Chicago, Ill. Office: U of Chgo, 5835 S Kimbark Ave, Chicago, Ill.

SCHWAB, Robert Sidney, US, psychiatrist, neurologist; b. St Louis, Mo, Oct 3, 1903; s. Sidney and Helen (Stix); BA, Harvard U, 1926, MD, 1931: MA, St Johns Coll, Cambridge, 1929; m. Dorothy Miller, Aug 26, 1932. Dir, Brain Wave Lab, asso neur, Mass Gen Hosp, Boston; asst clinical prof, neur, Harvard Med Sch; cons neur: Mass Eye and Ear Infirmary, Boston; Metrop State Hosp, Waltham, Mass; US Naval Hosp, Chelsea, Mass; res neur, Mass Gen Hosp, 1935; res psycht, Boston Psychopathic Hosp, 1936. Cdr, USN, 1941-46. F, Amer Acad Neur; dipl, Amer Bd Neur and Psycht; mem: Amer Electroencephalographers Assn, pres, 1951; E Assn Electroencephalographers, pres, 1946; Amer Psychiatric Assn; Amer Neur Assn; Assn for Research in Nervous and Mental Disease; Boston Soc for Neur and Psycht; Gt Brit, Fr, It Encephalographic Assns; vice-pres, Intl Assn of Electroencephalographics Socs; clubs: Cambridge Cruising, Eng; Harvard, Boston. Author: Electroencephalography in General Practice, 1951; asso ed, Jour of EEG; contbr to med jours. Home: 81 Border St, Cohasset, Mass. Office: Mass Gen Hosp, Fruit St, Boston, Mass.

SCHWAB, Rose L, US, educator; b. Bklyn, NY; d. Samuel and Molly (Sbinowitz) Levine; BA, MA, Cornell U; grad studies, Columbia U Tchrs Coll; m. Joseph Schwab, Aug 25, 1942. Dist supt, Dist 27, Bd of Educ, NYC, since 1965, staff supt, 1962-65. Bd govs: J Tchrs Comty Chest; NY Acad Public Educ; pres, Natl Council Admn Women in Educ, 1959-61, pres, NY br, 1954-56; mem: Amer Assn Sch Admn of NY; J Tchrs Assn; club, Cornell, NY. Home: 8579 88 St, Woodhaven, NY. Office: 8505 102 St, Richmond Hill, NY.

SCHWAB, Simon, US, rabbi, author, educator; b. Frankfurt/M, Ger, Dec 30, 1908; s. Leopold and Hannah (Erlanger); in US since 1936; att: Torah Inst, Yeshiva, Frankfurt, 1924-26; Telshe Rabb Coll, Lith, 1926-29; ordained rabbi, Mirrer Rabb Coll, Pol, 1931; m. Recha Froehlich, Oct 22, 1933; c: Moses, Judith, Joseph, Myer, Jacob. Rabbi, Cong K'hal Adath Jeshurun, since 1958; dean: Rabb Sem of Beth Midrash Jeshurun; Samson Raphael Hirsch Mesivta HS, all NYC; asst rabbi, Darmstadt, Ger, 1931-33; dist rabbi, Ichenhausen, Ger, 1933-36; rabbi, Cong Shearith Isr, Baltimore, Md, 1937-58; fmr prof, homiletics and practical rabbinics, Ner Isr Rabb Coll; hon rabbi, Chevra Ahavas Chessed, both Baltimore. Fmr pres: bd educ, Beth Jacob Sch for Girls; Agudath Isr, 1940-45; praesidium, Council Orthodox Rabbis, 1950-52; mem, bur kosher meat and food control, Union Orthodox Rabbis, all Baltimore. Author: Heimkehr ins Judentum, 1934; Beth Hashoevah, 1942; Shemesh Marpe, 1951; These and Those, 1965. Home: 736 W 186 St, New York, NY. Study: 4343 Broadway, New York, NY.

SCHWAB, William, US, educator; b. Bad Kreuznach, Ger, Nov 8, 1923; s. Samuel and Maly (Israel); in US since 1938; BA, Bethany Coll, 1945; MA, U Wis, 1947, PhD, 1951; postgrad studies: U London, 1949; U Mich, 1952, 1955-56. Prof, Eng, Oakland U, since 1965, on fac since 1953; asst prof, Eng, Eng Lang Inst, summers, 1953-55, 1956; instr, Eng, Purdue U, 1950-53; Fulbright prof of Eng, U Philippines, 1954-55; Fulbright lectr: ling, methods teaching Eng, U Philippines, Ateneo

de Manila U, 1963-64; 5th Amer Studies Sem, Manila, 1968; mem: Philippine long-range planning team, Fulbright-Hays Prog, 1967. Mem: MLA; Amer Ling Socs. Author: Guide to Modern Grammar and Exposition, 1967; contbr to profsl jours. Recipient: grant, Amer Council Learned Socs, 1952. Home: 729 Wallace, Birmingham, Mich. Office: Oakland U, Rochester, Mich.

SCHWALBERG, Alfred W, US, business exec; b. NYC, Aug 8, 1898; s. Morris and Rachel (Balender); BCS, NYU, 1917; m. Carmel Myers, Oct 30, 1951; c: Martin, Elizabeth, Ralph, Susan, Mary. Fmr pres, Paramount Film Distributing Corp; auditor, Vitagraph Co, 1926-42, vice-pres, 1942-48; gen sales mgr, Intl Picture Corp, 1944; vice-pres, Eagle Lion Pictures Corp, 1946. Mem: Masons; B'nai B'rith; club, Variety Intl. Home: 171 57 St, New York, NY.

SCHWARCZ, Moshe, Isr, educator; b. Hung, Oct 3, 1925; s. Kalman and Helen; MA, Heb U, Jerusalem, 1951, PhD, 1958; m. Mirjam Klein, Dec 12, 1950; c: Eliezer, Chava, Joseph, Ronit. Asso prof, Bar Ilan U, since 1968, sr lectr, 1963-68, chmn, dept phil. Author: Language, Myth, Art, 1966. Recipient: Warburg Prize, Heb U, 1958-60; Ramat Gan Prize for J Studies, 1968. Home: 3 Simtat Hamaalot, Ramat Gan, Isr. Office: Bar Ilan U, Ramat Gan, Isr.

SCHWARTZ, Aaron R, US, legislator, attorney; b. Galveston, Tex, July 17, 1926; s. Joe and Clara (Bulbe); att Tex A and M; LLB, U Tex Law Sch, 1951; m. Marilyn Cohn, July 14, 1951; c: Robert, Richard, John, Thomas. State senator, Tex, since 1959; in pvt law practice since 1951; asst co atty, 1951-53; mem, Tex House of Reprs, 1954-58. USN, 1944-46; USAF Res, 1950-55. Mem, natl commn, ADL, fmr chmn, SW region; fmr chmn: Isr Bond Drive; JNF campaigns, Galveston Co. Home: 10 South Shore Dr, Galveston, Tex. Offices: 307 Cotton Exch Bldg, Galveston, Tex; 2034 Houston Natural Gas Bldg, Houston, Tex; Senate Chamber, State Capitol, Austin, Tex.

SCHWARTZ, Abraham J, US, business exec; b. Galicia, Aus, Aug 18, 1894; s. Max and Clara (Rosenstock); in US since 1905; m. Celia Lavender (decd); c: Gladys Frant, Phobe Atterman, Stanford; m. 2nd, Beatrice Gold, May 1961. Ret: pres, AJ Schwartz & Co, clothing mfr, 1918-50; partner: Widener Bldg, Phila; 1 Park Ave, NYC; 2 Park Ave; Manhattan Hotel; Astor Hotel. Chmn, Richmond Hill chap, Bonds for Isr; mem, bd dirs, Merchants Bank of NY; Cong Beth Isr, Richmond Hill, pres, 1937-43; J Comty Service, LI, 1937-50; a found, UJA, NY, 1938; vice-pres, Queens Fed J Charities, 1937-50; mem: B'nai B'rith; AJCong; ZOA; United HIAS Services; FJP; Queens Co Grand Jurors Assn; Masons. Home: 85-30 Somerset St, Jamaica, NY.

SCHWARTZ, Adolph K, US, attorney; b. St Louis, Mo, May 8, 1915; s. Jacob and Bess (Kurtz); BA, Wash U, 1936, LLB, 1939, JD, 1968; m. Beatrice Kantor, Sep 2, 1945; c: John, Nancy, Lucylle. Pvt practice. USN, USCG, 1942-45. Vice-pres, J Comty Relations Council, since 1965; mem: Amer and St Louis Bar Assns; Nu Beta Epsilon; fmr: chmn, St Louis Council on Hum Relations; pres: J Child Wfr Assn; Clayton Public Libr; bd dirs, J Family Service Agcy; bd govs, children's div, Gtr St Louis Comty Chest; mem: Social Planning Council; bd, J Feds; pres, St Louis Co C of C. Ed in chief, Mo Bar Jour, 1940-42; contbr to legal jours. Home: 28 Aberdeen Pl, Clayton, Mo. Office: 1015 Locust St, St Louis, Mo.

SCHWARTZ, Alan Earl, US, attorney; b. Detroit, Mich, Dec 21, 1925; s. Maurice and Sophia (Welkowitz); BA, with distinction, U Mich, 1947; LLB, magna cum laude, Harvard Law Sch, 1950; m. Marianne Shapiro, 1950; c: Marc, Kurt, Ruthanne. Sr partner, law firm, Honigman, Miller, Schwartz and Cohn; chmn, bd: Cunningham Drug Stores Inc, since 1968; Cyphernetics Corp; Arlan's Dept Stores Inc, 1963-64; Federal's Inc, 1966-68; dir: SOS Consolidated Inc; Macoid Inds Inc; Allied Supermarkets Inc; Kaiser-Frazer, Inc and Willys Motors, Inc, 1954; spec asst counsel, NY Crime Commn, 1951. Ensign, USN, 1943-46. Pres, Wayne State U Press; vice-pres: Detroit Sym Orch; JWF, Detroit; chmn, Mayor's Rehab Comm for City of Detroit, since 1957; trustee: Detroit Grand Opera Assn; Cranbrook Sch; Harper Hosp; dir: J Home for Aged; March of Dimes; United Found; ways and means comm, Gov's State Council for Arts; clubs: Standard City, Detroit; Franklin Hills Country. Home: 17651 Hamilton Rd, Detroit, Mich. Office: 2290 First National Bldg, Detroit, Mich.

SCHWARTZ, Albert M, US, surgeon; b. NYC, Nov 11, 1907; s. Herman and Rachelle (Rohrlich); BS, NYU, 1928, MD, 1931; m. Estell Franck, May 2, 1959. Att surg for vascular surg, Beth Isr Med Cen; cons surg, Morrisiana City Hosp. Lt col, MC, US Army, 1941-46. Chmn, bd dir, Home of Old Isr; treas, Amer Bd Surgs; f: Amer Coll Surgs; NY Acad Med; AMA; Amer Geriatric Soc; NY Heart Assn; pres, NY Co Med Soc; asst treas, NY State Med Soc; mem, Phi Delta Epsilon; club, City Athletic. Contbr to med jours. Hobbies: photography, collecting Don Quixotiana. Home: 410 E 57 St, New York, NY. Office: 1148 Fifth Ave, New York, NY,

SCHWARTZ, Arnold Manuel, US, attorney; b. Bklyn, NY, June 5, 1901; s. Marcus and Pauline (Moscowitz); att CCNY; LLB, Bklyn Law Sch, 1927; m. Rita Holtzmann, Dec 24, 1926; c: Phoebe, Lisa Kramer. Pvt practice; fmr US govt appeal agt. Dir: Fed J Charities; regional group, Commercial Law League; gov, Bklyn J Cen; trustee: Bklyn Bar Assn; Trafalgar Hosp; mem: B'nai B'rith; Amer Judicature Soc; ZOA; NY State Bar Assn; Amer Bar Assn; fmr pres, PTA; club, Bklyn Lawyers. Spec interests: J culture, legal aid. Recipient: Cong Medal of Merit. Home: 163 Eastern Parkway, Brooklyn, NY. Office: 105 Court St, Brooklyn, NY.

SCHWARTZ, Arthur H, US, attorney; b. NYC, Nov 18, 1903; s. Louis and Ida (Rothstein); BA, Columbia U, 1923, LLB, 1926; m. Dorothy Blaine, Aug 5, 1928 (decd); c: Anne, Lois; m. 2nd, Betty Spare, Feb 14, 1958. Partner, Schwartz and Frohlich, since 1936; counsel: Jt Leg Comm on Leg Practices and Expenditures, 1945-46; NY State Comm to Study Need for State U; NY State Comm on Coord State Activities, 1948-59; spec counsel, The Jockey Club, 1949; justice, Supr Court, NY State, 1952. Mem: commn on character and fitness, First Judicial Dept, since 1949; NY State Law Revision Commn, since 1960; counsel, Rep State comm, 1945-52; mgr, NY State for Gov Thomas E Dewey pres campaign, 1944; counsel, Citizens Comm for Javitz, 1956; pres, NY Bar Assn, 1958-59; trustee, Fed Bar Assn, 1955-58; vice-pres, NYC Bar Assn, 1949; mem, bd dirs, NY Co Lawyers Assn, 1949-55; mem: Amer Bar Assn; Amer Coll Trial Lawyers; NY Dist Attys Assn; Legal Aid Soc, dir; NCCJ; bd visitors, Columbia Law Sch; NY chap, AJComm; lawyers and motion picture divs, J Defense Appeal and UJA; FJP; Cinema Lodge, B'nai B'rith, trustee, since 1953; Soc Amer Magicians; Munic Art Soc; Metrop Mus of Art; Phi Beta Kappa; clubs: Manhattan; Natl Rep. Recipient: Cong Medal for services rendered as appeal agent, 1950. Home: 3 E 69 St, New York, NY. Office: 19 E 70 St, New York, NY.

SCHWARTZ, Barry Dov, US, rabbi; b. Boston, Mass, July 22, 1940; s. Melvin and Frances (Polonsky); att Heb U, Jerusalem, 1959-60; B J Ed, Heb Tchrs Coll, 1959; AB, Boston U, 1961; ordained rabbi, JTSA, 1965. Rabbi, Cong Beth Mordecai, since 1967; fmr rabbi, Cong Kehillath Isr, Brookline, Mass. Chaplain, capt, USAF, 1965-67. Prin contrib: discovered ancient syn and four remaining Js in Azores, Port. Fmr vice-pres, Student Org, JTSA; mem, RA. Contbr to rel jours. Recipient: SAC Educ Award, USAF, 1966. Hobbies: writing, criminology. Home: 23 Smith St, Perth Amboy, NJ. Study: 224 High St, Perth Amboy, NJ.

SCHWARTZ, Buky, Isr, sculptor; b. Jerusalem, 1932; att: Avni Inst of Fine Arts, Tel Aviv; St Martin's Sch of Art, London. One-man shows: Dugith Gal, Tel Aviv, 1963; Rina Gal, Jerusalem, 1963; Massada Gal, Tel Aviv, 1965; Isr Pavilion, Venice Biennale, 1966; Hamilton Gal, London, 1967; Tel Aviv Mus, 1969; group exhbs: Tel Aviv; Jerusalem; Berlin; London; Leeds; Vienna; Intl Symposium of Sculpture in Ger and Aus; commns: brass sculpture, Hilton Hotel, Tel Aviv; bronze sculpture, Knesset, Jerusalem; Pillar of Heroism, Yad Vashem, Jerusalem; Fronts, Fac of Educ, Bar Ilan U; stainless steel, El Al, Johannesburg, S Afr; sculpture and gates, Yad Vashem, Jerusalem; sculpture garden, Weizmann Inst; fountain, seashore, Eilat; chess set, Intl Chess Olympiad. Recipient: Sainsbury award for sculpture, 1961, 1962; Dizengoff prize, 1965. Home: 14 Zvilson St, Tel Aviv, Isr.

SCHWARTZ, Chaya, Isr, artist; b. Pol, 1916; d. Abraham and Michal; in Isr since 1930; att: Bezalel Art Sch, Jerusalem, 1933; Scandinavian Acad, Paris, 1934-36. One-man shows: US; London; S Afr; Paris, Isr, Rome, 1962; participated in Venice Biennale, 1958. Recipient, Dizengoff Prize, 1942; 1948, 1960. Homes: 10 Mazal Dagim St, Old Jaffa, Isr; Artists Colony, Safed, Isr.

SCHWARTZ, David L, US, rabbi; b. NYC, Oct 14, 1922; s. Jacob and Minnie (Joskowitz); BA, Bklyn Coll, 1944; ordained rabbi, MHL, JIR, 1947; tchr cert, NYU, 1952; m. Sandra Friedman, Nov 26, 1949; c: Debra, Philip. Rabbi, Temple Beth Ha-Sholom, since 1957; chaplain, US Fed Penitentiary, Lewisburg, since 1965; rabbi: Temple Beth-Ha-Sholom, Niagara Falls, NY, 1951-52; Temple B'nai Abraham, Hagerstown, Md, 1952-57; chaplain, Newton D Baker Vet Hosp, 1953-57. Mem: CCAR; f, World Heb Fed. Home: 145 Union Ave, Williamsport, Pa. Study: 425 Center St, Williamsport, Pa.

SCHWARTZ, Edgar L, US, business exec; b. NYC, Mar 30, 1896; s. Sigmund and Fanny (Berg); BS, Cornell U, 1917; m. Eleanor Frank, Apr 29, 1924; c: Frank, Marion Class. Pres, Nathan Frank's Sons, Inc, dept store, since 1950, mgr, 1926-50; advt and sales mgr: Schwartz & Langbein, 1922-26; A Sherwin & Bros, 1919-22, both NYC. Lt, US Air Service, WW I; maj, NY Guard, 1940-48. Mem: Natl Retail Merchants Assn; NY State Council Retail Merchants Assn; Masons; Elks; Amer Legion; Boys State Comm; Pi Lambda Phi; fmr: pres: Ogdensburg C of C; St Lawrence Council, Boy Scouts Amer; 6th Regiment Infantry Assn; cdr, Amer Legion Post; clubs: Ogdensburg Country; Rotary. Recipient: Silver Beaver Award, Boy Scouts, Amer, 1949. Hobby: travel. Home: 412 Jay St, Ogdensburg, NY. Office: 224 Ford St, Ogdensburg, NY.

SCHWARTZ, Edward, US, ophthalmologist; b. Portland, Me, May 26, 1909; s. Louis and Ethel (Shelling); BS, Bowdoin Coll, 1930; MD, Jefferson Med Coll, 1934; att Grad Sch of Med, U of Pa, 1938-39; m. Sylvia Winn, Aug 18, 1935; c: Rochelle, Louis. Ophthal: pvt practice, since 1935; Chester Hosp, Pa, asso, 1935-37; Sacred Heart Hosp, 1958-60; clinical asst, ophthal, Mt Sinai Hosp, 1935-37; asst chief of surg, ophthal, Phila Gen Hosp, 1937-52; chief, eye sect, Bruns Gen Hosp, 1942-45. Capt, US Army, MC, 1942-45. F: Amer Acad Ophthal and Otolaryngology, 1948; Amer Med Soc; dipl, Amer Bd Ophthal; mem: Del Co Med Soc; Pa Med Soc; Phi Beta Kappa; Phi Lambda Kappa; Amer Legion; JWV; Masons. Contbr to med jours. Hobby: tennis. Home: 103 Harvey Rd, Chester, Pa. Office: 112 E Ninth St, Chester, Pa.

SCHWARTZ, Edward P, US, business exec; b. Minneapolis, Minn, Oct 15, 1903; s. Mayer and Daisy (Gruenberg); att U Minn, 1922-23; m. Mae Frydenlund, May 28, 1927; c: Betty Smith. Vice-pres, Ad Art Advt Co, Minneapolis, since 1944; reporter, Minneapolis Daily News, 1923; with circulation dept, Minneapolis Tribune, 1925-27; with advt dept, Phila Public Ledger, 1927-28; asst mgr, Pioneer Printers, Minneapolis, 1934-37; with ind relations dept, Hanford Engr Works, Pasco, Wash, 1943; ed, Portland Daily Journal of Commerce, 1944; with ed dept, Minneapolis Tribune, 1944. Chief barker (pres), Variety Club of NW, Tent 12; pres, Henry Miller Lit Soc, since 1957; mem: B'nai B'rith; ZOA; Temple Isr; Elks; C of C; NW Ind Eds; Printing Ind of Twin Cities; Intl Geneva Soc; Minn Hotel Assn; fmr: pres, B'nai B'rith Lodge; secy, Minneapolis Housing and Redevelopment Auth; clubs: Minneapolis Advt; Minn Press; Minn Valley Country. Recipient: award, Newspaper Guild of Twin Cities, 1953. Home: 15 S First St, Minneapolis, Minn. Office: 1521 Hennepin Ave, Minneapolis, Minn.

SCHWARTZ, Elliot S, US, educational dir; b. Bklyn, NY, Oct 30, 1921; s. Israel and Clara (Schwartz); BA, Bklyn Coll, 1942; MA, Columbia U, 1943; Heb Tchrs Dipl, Herzliah Tchrs Acad, 1941; m. Florence Greisman, Sep 3, 1943; c: Charles, Paul, Sidney. Educ dir, Cong Beth Shalom, since 1967; prin, J Cen of Jackson Hts, 1946-50; educ dir: Cong Shaarey Zedek, Detroit, 1950-55; Temple B'nai Sholom, Rockville Cen, 1955-67. US Army, Signal Corps, 1944-46. Pres, prin council, LI Assn Cong Schs, 1962-64; bd dirs, Educs Assembly of United Syn Amer; mem: Natl Council for J Educ; Heb Prins Assn. Contbr to profsl jours. Recipient: award, outstanding prin, United PTA, 1961-62; Solomon Schechter award, 1952, 1965. Home: 63 E 106 Terr, Kansas City, Mo. Office: 620 W 95 St, Kansas City, Mo.

SCHWARTZ, Emanuel King, US, psychologist; b. NYC, June 11, 1912; s. Harry and Sarah (Fried); PhD, NYU, 1937; DSc, New Sch for Social Research, 1948; cert, psychotherapy and psychan, Post Grad Cen for Mh, NY, 1950; m. Reta Shacknove, Feb 3, 1943. Dean, dir training, Post Grad Cen for Mh, NY, since 1947; adj prof, psych, Grad Sch, NYU, since 1964; clinical prof, Post-Doctoral Inst, Adelphi U, since

1964. Lt, US Army, 1943-46. Mem: Phi Beta Kappa. Co-author: Psychoanalysis in Groups, 1962. Recipient: 2 vol Festschrift in his honor, entitled New Directions in Mental Health, 1969. Hobbies: theater, travel. Home: 12 E 87 St, New York, NY. Office: 124 E 28 St, New York, NY.

SCHWARTZ, Ferdinand F, US, physician, educator; b. Cleveland, O, Mar 15, 1902; s. Ellis and Rose (Weiss); BS, U of W Va, 1927; MD, Rush Med Coll, Chgo, 1929; postgrad work, Polyclinic of NY, 1946; Allgemeines Krankenhaus, Vienna, Aus, 1959; m. Jessie Gerk, 1957; c: Stephen, Rose. Asso prof, phys med, Med Coll of Ala, since 1954, fac mem since 1950; owner, med dir, Birmingham Inst Phys Med and Rehab, since 1946; cons: Hilcrest Hosp; Partlow Sch and Hosp, Tuscalosa, Ala; Charlanne Sch for Motor and Speech Defects, since 1948; VA Hosp, Birmingham, Ala, since 1952; VA Hosp, Tuscalosa, since 1948; Spastic Aid of Ala, since 1948; Multiple Sclerosis Soc of Ala, since 1951; chief, phys med: Northington Gen Hosp, 1943-45; Walter Reed Hosp, 1946; staff mem: Highland Baptist Hosp; Jefferson-Hillman Hosp; S Highland Infirmary; Austin Lewis Hosp. Maj, MC, 1942-46. Dipl, Amer Bd Phys Med and Rehab; f, Intl Coll Angiology; fmr pres, B'nai B'rith, Birmingham; mem: bldg fund comm, Jerusalem Acad Med; bd, Ala Arthritic Soc; Amer Rheumatic Soc; Pres, and Gov Comms on Hiring Handicapped; NY Acad Scis; Ala Acad Sci; AMA; Ala Med Assn; S Med Assn; Mil Surgs Assn; Acad Phys Med and Rehab; Royal Soc Health, Eng; Cong of Phys Med; Corrective Therapy Assn; Geriatric Assn; Ultrasonics Acad; Hosp Assn; Amer Med Writers Assn; AAAS; World Med Assn, Ala State chmn; Amer Med Soc, Vienna, Aus, life, gold key mem; phys f, IMA, Jerusalem Acad Med; exec bd, Birmingham Mus; Knesseth Isr Temple, fmr pres, men's club; Elks; YMCA; hon mem: It Phys Med Soc; Dominican Med Assn; Natl Fed of Med, S Amer; Mexican Soc for Phys Med and Rehab; Atlantic-Pacific Med Soc, Barranquilla, Colombia; Latin Amer Cong Phys Med; Rehab Soc of W Ger; club, Lions. Mem, ed staff, Ger and Span Archives of Phys Med; contbr to med jours. Hobbies: travel, music, art. Home: 5305 11 Ave S, Birmingham, Ala. Office: 916 S 20 St, Birmingham, Ala.

SCHWARTZ, Harold, US, orthodontist; b. Phila, Pa, Nov 22, 1902; s. Louis and Clara (Oser); MS, Northwestern U, 1941; BS, U Chgo, 1937; DDS, Loyola Dent Sch, Chgo, 1924; m. Ruth Smith, Dec 6, 1934; c: Sandra Bartky, Jeffrey. Pvt practice since 1924; research asso, Northwestern U Dent Sch, 1960-65. Pres, Midwest Component, Edw H Angle Soc Orthodontists; Alpha Omega; Amer Dent Assn; Amer Orthodontic Assn. Contbr to dent jours. Home: 676 DeTamble Ave, Highland Park, Ill. Office: 1811 St Johns, Highland Park, Ill.

SCHWARTZ, Harry, US, journalist, educator; b. NYC, Sept 10, 1919; s. Sam and Rose (Schnell); BA, Columbia U, 1940, MA, 1941, PhD, 1944; m. Ruth Blumner, June 8, 1941; c: William, John, Robert. Specialist, Soviet affairs, NY Times, since 1948; U prof, econ, SUNY, New Paltz, since 1967; mem fac: Columbia U, 1940, 1941, 1943, 1947 and since 1961; Bklyn Coll, 1941-42; Syracuse U, 1946-54; served with US govt: War Produc Bd; Dept of Agric; Off Strategic Services; State Dept, 1942-46. Mem: Amer Econ Assn; Amer Stat Assn; Council on Fgn Relations; Phi Beta Kappa. Author: Russia's Soviet Economy, 1950; The Red Phoenix, 1961; Russia Enters the 1960's, pub, 1962; Tsars, Mandarins and Commissars, 1964; The Soviet Economy Since Stalin, 1965; An Introduction to Soviet Economy, 1968; Prague's 200 Days, 1969. Office: 229 W 43 St, New York, NY.

SCHWARTZ, Harry E, US, rabbi; b. Kishinev, Russ, July 10, 1899; s. Mordecai and Rachel (Malias); in US since 1908; BA, U of Pa, 1921; ordained rabbi, MHL, JTSA, 1925, DD, 1965; m. Helen Climo, 1945; c: Joel, Shalom, Beryl. Rabbi em, Cong Beth Isr, since 1967, rabbi, 1963-67; rabbi: Cong Beth El, Waterbury, Conn, 1925-32; Patchogue J Cen, NY, 1932-33. Treas, RA, 1944; chmn, educ and youth, LI Zionist Region, 1938; exec council: NY Bd Rabbis, 1953; Syn Council Amer; admn bd, Comty Chest; mem: B'nai B'rith; Cancer Soc; Multiple Sclerosis Assn; C of C. Author: Passover–It's Significance, Observance, and Practices; The Jewish Trinity; The Essence of Jewish Life. Spec interest: J liturgical music. Home: 1495 NE 167 St, N Miami Beach, Fla.

SCHWARTZ, Herbert Ellis, US, attorney, educator; b. LA, Cal, Dec 17, 1936; s. Milton and Mildred (Solomen); BS, UCLA, 1958, LLB, 1961; m. Harriet Jacobs, June 15, 1958;

c: Steven, Gregory, Daniel. Prof, law, UCLA Sch of Law, since 1962; lawyer, since 1964; teaching f, research asst, Harvard Law Sch, 1961-62. Secy-treas, trustee, LA Phi Sigma Delta Found; mem: Amer Bar Assn; Beverly Hills Bar Assn; U Policies Commn, UCLA. Recipient: Elijah Watt Sells Gold Medal, Amer Inst CPAs, 1958. Office: UCLA Sch of Law, Los Angeles, Cal.

SCHWARTZ, Hy H, US, publisher; b. Chgo, Ill, June 27, 1921; s. Aaron and Helen (Levinsky); BBA, Northwestern U, 1943; m. Elsie Kalmikoff, Dec 28, 1947; c: Carol, Larry. Vice-pres, United Bus Publs, since 1959; asst, publisher, Amer Trade Mags, 1945-59. Vice-pres, Chgo Sch for Retarded Children, since 1962, found pres, Mitzvah chap, 1959-62; mem, bd dirs, Niles Township J Comty Cen, since 1962, pres, Cen Civic Improvement Assn, 1959-61; pres, Skokie Home Owners Council, 1961; mem, bd dirs, Skokie Valley Traditional Syn. Contbr monthly column to: Drycleaning World; Institutional Laundry; Marketing News. Home: 2528 Harrison, Glenview, Ill. Office: 100 E Ohio St, Chicago, Ill.

SCHWARTZ, Jeanna Moscovici, Isr, physician; b. Bucharest, Rum, Jan 23, 1921; d. Abraham and Melania (Kopolovici); in Isr since 1959; MD, J Med Sch, Rum, 1947; m. Otto Moscovici, Jan 4, 1954; c: Ariel. Sr lectr: dept med microbiol, Tel Aviv U, since 1965, on fac since 1959, fac continuing med educ, since 1969; phys, Cantaculino Hosp, Bucharest, 1948-49; instr, Med Sch, Bucharest, 1948-50; instr, lectr, Post-Grad Sch for Phys and Pharms, Bucharest, 1952-58; sr researcher, 1951-56, chief of lab, 1956-58. Prin contribs: research immunology; virology; bact. Mem: Isr Immunology Soc; Isr Microbiol Soc; Isr Allergology; Soc Clinical Path; Soc Gen Microbiol, London; Asso des Medecins Etrangers de L'Inst G Roussy, Fr. Contbr to profsl publs. Hobby: clay modeling. Home: Gannot, Isr. Offices: Tel Aviv U, Ramat Aviv, Isr; 155 Herzl St, Tel Aviv, Isr.

SCHWARTZ, Joseph Joshua, US, communal leader; b. Russ, Mar 23, 1899; s. Abraham and Goldie (Preil); in US since 1907; ordained rabbi, Rabbi Isaac Elchanan Theol Sem, 1923; PhD, Yale U, 1927; Sterling Research F, 1928-29; hon DHL: Yeshiva U, 1950; Brandeis U, 1960; Dropsie Coll, 1963; hon PhD, Heb U, Jerusalem, 1968; m. Dora Rashback, Mar 6, 1923; c: Nathan. Vice-pres, Isr Bonds Org, since 1955; instr: Amer U, Cairo, to 1928; LIU, Bklyn, NY, 1930-33; dir, public info, Fed J Charities, Bklyn, NY, 1929-31, exec dir, 1931-38; secy, JDC, 1939-40, chmn, Eur exec council, 1940-49, dir gen, 1950-51; exec vice-chmn, UJA, 1951-55. Mem, 1st, 2nd Jerusalem Econ Conf, invitation Govt of Isr; asst, report to Pres Truman by Earl G Harrison; mem, Intergovernmental Comm on Refs, on conditions of DPs in Amer Zone, Ger; vice-pres, Capital for Isr, Inc; pres, Ency Judaica Research Found; mem: American Oriental Soc; bd govs, Dropsie Coll; J Acad of Arts and Sci; fmr pres, Natl Conf on J Social Wfr; vice-pres, NY State Conf on Social Work. Contbr: papers, on Semitics, Semitic lit, J affairs; fmr ed, Scripta Mathematica. Recipient: Mordechai Ben David award of Yeshiva U for public service to J Comty, 1946; Chevalier, Fr Legion of Honor, 1947; Stephen Wise award, 1950; Scopus award, Heb U, Jerusalem, 1964. Home: 164 Central Park W, New York, NY. Office: 215 Park Ave S, New York, NY.

SCHWARTZ, Larry, US, publisher; b. NYC, Mar 25, 1922; s. Samuel and Esther (Levy); BA, Union Coll, 1941; att: Columbia U Sch of Bus, 1941-42; Yale U, 1943-44; U Mich, 1944-45; Columbia U Inst for Intl Affairs, 1946-47; m. Shelia Frackman, June 30, 1949; c: Nancy, Jonathan, Elizabeth. Pres, Pub Ind Devl Corp, since 1962; sr vice-pres, Lester Harrison Advt Inc, since 1966; asso with: R H Macy & Co; Gen Elec Co; ABC; partner, Wexton Advt Agcy, 1947-53, pres, 1953-62; lectr: Mgmt Inst, NYU, 1957-59; City Coll of Bus, 1950-57. Lt, Mil IS, US Army, 1943-46. Vice-pres, League of Advt Agcys; mem: Young Pres's Org; Phi Beta Kappa; Kappa Nu, natl vice-pres, 1948-49, natl secy, 1949-51; club, Sales Exec. Recipient: Pres Unit Citation, WW II. Home: 1 Dogwood Dr, Kings Point, NY. Office: 210 E 50 St, New York, NY.

SCHWARTZ, Lawrence W, US, rabbi; b. NYC, Dec 13, 1902; s. Eugene and Rose (Schwab); BA, Columbia Coll, 1924; MA, Tchrs Coll, Columbia U, 1926; ordained rabbi, MHL, JIR, 1928; att: U Berlin, 1928; Heb U, Jerusalem, 1928-29; DE, Columbia U, 1941; hon DD, HUC, NY, 1954; m. Vera Bendheim, 1931; c: Lawrence, June. Rabbi, Jewish Comty Cen, White Plains, NY, since 1930; asst rabbi, Temple Isr,

Boston, Mass, 1929-30; instr: JIR, NY, 1936-46; HUC Sch for Tchrs, NY, 1938-42. Pres: Westchester Council Rabbis, 1938-40; White Plains JCC, 1941-43; White Plains Council Comty Services, 1944-48; Westchester council, NY State Comm Against Discrimination, 1948-58; Ministerial Assn, White Plains, 1957-58; mem: CCAR; Zeta Beta Tau; Kappa Delta Pi; chaplain, Civil Air Patrol, White Plains Squadron, since 1953. Author: Curriculum Development in a Jewish School, 1941. Recipient: White Plains Hum Relations Award, 1958. Home: 15 Blackthorn Lane, White Plains, NY. Study: 252 Soundview Ave, White Plains, NY.

SCHWARTZ, Louis B, US, attorney, educator; b. Phila, Pa, Feb 22, 1913; s. Samuel and Rose (Brown); BS, Wharton Sch of Finance and Commerce, 1932; LLB, U of Pa Law Sch, 1935; m. 1st, Berta Woslon, 1937 (div); c: Johanna, Victoria; m. 2nd, Miriam Robbins, 1964. Benjamin Franklin Prof, Law, U of Pa, since 1946; prof, law: U of Cal, 1950; Columbia U, 1947; Salzburg Seminar in Amer Studies, 1960; visiting prof: Harvard Law Sch, 1963; Cambridge U, 1965; atty, SEC, 1935-39; chief, sect: criminal div, US Dept of Justice, 1939-43, anti-trust div, 1945-46; reporter, model penal code, Amer Law Inst, 1952-61. Communications off, USNR, 1944-45. Mem: natl bd, ADA; exec comm, Phila Defender Assn, since 1950; Atty Gen's Comm to Study Anti-Trust Laws, 1955-56; ACLU; adv council, Natl Defender Project, since 1966; Comm on Minimum Standards for Criminal Justice, Amer Bar Assn, since 1966; adv comm, Pre-Arraignment Code, Amer Law Inst, since 1966; dir, Natl Commn on Reform of Fed Criminal Laws, since 1967. Author: Free Enterprise and Economic Organization, 1959, 3rd ed, 1966; Model Penal Code of American Law Institute, 1963; Police Guidance Manuals, 1968; contbr to legal jours. Home: 510 Woodland, Philadelphia, Pa. Office: 3400 Chestnut St, Philadelphia, Pa.

SCHWARTZ, Marvin, US, physician, educator; b. Detroit, Mich, Apr 28, 1914; s. Morris and Dora (Raskin); AB, Wayne U, Detroit, 1935, MD, Coll of Med, 1939, MS, 1945; m. Selma Gates, June 18, 1939; c: Lee, Arbey, Julie. Pvt med practice, specializing in cardiovascular diseases, since 1949; asst clinical prof, med, card, U Ore Med Sch, since 1945; teaching f, card, Wayne State U Med Sch, Detroit Receiving Hosp, 1943-45. F: Amer Coll Chest Phys; Amer Coll Card; Council Clinical Card, AHA; mem: AMA; Amer Bd of Internal Med; Portland Acad Med; AHA; Amer Fed for Clinical Research; Sigma Xi; club, Tualatin Country, pres, 1961. Contbr to med jours. Hobbies: golf, photography. Home: 3021 NW Greenbriar Terr, Portland, Ore. Office: 2256 NW Lovejoy St, Portland, Ore.

SCHWARTZ, Maurice L, US, rabbi; b. Newark, NJ, Oct 18, 1928; s. Abraham and Pauline (Scher); BA, Yeshiva Coll, 1953; ordained rabbi, Rabbi Isaac Elchanan Theol Sem, 1954, 1959; m. Rachel Bilitzky, Nov 15, 1953; c: Avrom, Etiel, Hayim, Rivka. Rabbi: Young Isr, Parkchester, NY, since 1958; Carmel Syn, Bx, NY, 1954-58. Pres, co-found, Kolel Rabbi Moshe Shatzkes Inc, Kfar Chasidim, Isr, since 1959; bd mem, Yeshiva Torah V'Emunah, Bx; mem: RabCA; Union Orthodox Rabbis; B'nai B'rith; Metrop Bd Orthodox Rabbis; exec comm, United Yeshiva Fund, Bx; Council of Young Isr Rabbis; exec comm, Rabb Alumni, Yeshiva U. Home: 1470 Parkchester Rd, Bronx, NY. Study: 1375 Virginia Ave, Bronx, NY.

SCHWARTZ, Melvin, US, physicist, educator; b. NYC, Nov 2, 1932; s. Harry and Hannah (Shulman); PhD, Columbia U, NY, 1958; m. Marilyn Fenster, Nov 25, 1953; c: David, Diane, Betty. Prof, physics: Stanford U, Calif, since 1966; Columbia U, 1963-66, on fac since 1958. Prin contrib: co-discoverer of Muon Neutrino; various experiments in high energy physics. F, Amer Phys Soc. Contbr numerous sci articles. Recipient: Hughes prize, Amer Phys Soc; Guggenheim f. Home: 770 Funston Ave, San Francisco, Cal. Office: Stanford U, Stanford, Cal.

SCHWARTZ, Morton K, US, biochemist; b. Wilkes-Barre, Pa, Oct 22, 1925; s. Norman and Dorothy (Kanter); BA, Lehigh U, 1948; MA, Boston U, 1949, PhD, 1952; m. Delia Corr, Oct 28, 1966; c: Gary, Ronald. Att biochem, chmn, biochem dept, Memorial Hosp for Cancer and Allied Diseases, since 1967; asso mem, Sloan Kettering Inst Cancer Research, since 1960; asso prof, biochem, Sloan Kettering div, Cornell U, since 1962; biochem, LI J Hosp, 1956-57. Elec tech, USN, 1944-46. Mem: NY Acad Sci; Harvey Soc; Amer Assn for Cancer Research; Amer Soc Biol Chems; Amer Assn Clinical

Chems; Amer Chem Soc; AAAS; Sigma Xi; Tau Delta Phi. Contbr to profsl publs. Recipient: predoc f, Natl Cancer Inst, USPHS, 1950-52. Home: 21 Chatham Pl, White Plains, NY. Office: 444 E 68 St, New York, NY.

SCHWARTZ, Murray L, US, attorney, educator; b. Phila, Pa, Oct 26, 1920; s. Harry and Isabelle (Friedman); BS, Pa State Coll, 1942; LLB, U of Pa, 1949; m. Audrey James, Feb 12, 1950; c: Deborah, Jonathan, Daniel. Prof, law, UCLA, since 1958; law clerk, Supr Court Judge Fred M Vinson, 1949-51; spec asst to US Atty Gen, 1952-54; first dep city solicitor, Phila, 1955-56. Lt, USNR, 1944-46. Author: Professional Responsibility and the Administration of Criminal Justice, 1961; co-author, Federal Censorship: Obscenity in the Mail, 1961; contbr to legal periodicals. Home: 1339 Marinette Rd, Pacific Palisades, Cal. Office: UCLA, Los Angeles, Cal.

SCHWARTZ, Myer, US, business exec; b. Phila, Pa, Jan 1, 1919; s. Morris and Rebecca (Moscowitz); att: U of Pa, 1940; Temple U, 1944; m. Helen Kaufman, Jan 3, 1947. Vice-pres, E Area mgr, Stone Container Corp, since 1969, gen mgr since 1962, with corp since 1942. Dir, Amer-Isr C of C; trustee, FJA; mem, bd govs, Isr Bond Org. Recipient: Jacob Mayer Award, Amer-Isr C of C, 1959; Chai Award, Isr Bond Org, 1966. Home: 250 S 17, Philadelphia, Pa. Office: Tulip & Decatur Sts, Philadelphia, Pa.

SCHWARTZ, Nathan H, US, attorney; b. Chgo, Ill, July 24, 1906; s. Abraham and Ethel (Shapiro); LLB, De Paul U, Chgo, 1928; m. Harriet Bernstein, Aug 22, 1929; c: Lois Husman, Ronald. Ret; pvt practice since 1928; fmr govt appeal agt, Selective Service Sys. Pres: Found for Emotionally Disturbed Children, 1960; De Paul U Alumni Assn, 1953; Nathan & Harriet Found, 1950-62; De Paul U Sym Assn; dir: Bur on J Employment Problems; fmr mem, bd dir, St Joseph Hosp; John Howard Assn; fmr dir: Chgo Urban League; Decalogue Soc of Lawyers; Bd J Educ; fmr chmn: Chgo Isr Bond Drive; Citizens Comm Catholic Interracial Council; Chgo comm, Truman Libr Comm; trustee, Coll J Studies; mem: lay bd trustees, De Paul U; Ill Comm for Equal Job Opportunities; gov council and life mem, AJCong; bd trustees, Chgo Soc Weizmann Inst; bd dirs: Amer Friends Heb U, fmr pres, Chgo chap; Amer-Isr C of C and Ind; ACLU; fmr dir, J Comty and Family Service; fmr vice-pres, a found, Multiple Sclerosis Found, Chgo; fmr vice-pres, Temple Sholom; fmr vice-chmn, Council Against Discrimination; mem: Chgo, Amer, and Ill Bar Assns; life mem: Art Inst of Chgo; AJCong; Chgo Hist Soc; NAACP; clubs: City, Chgo bd dirs; Bryn Mawr Country; Standard; Covenant, Ill, fmr dir, vice-pres; Execs; Brandeis U, Chgo, mem bd and secy. Home: 3750 Lake Shore Dr, Chicago, Ill. Office: 111 N Wabash Ave, Chicago, Ill.

SCHWARTZ, Robert M, US, engineer; b. NYC, Jan 20, 1920; s. Joseph and Bessie (Spinner); BMech Engr, CCNY, 1941; MS, Newark Coll Engr, 1950; att Stevens Inst of Tech, 1951; m. Lillian Moskowitz, Oct 14, 1941; c: Nancy, Susan, Deborah. Chief engr, US Army Munitions Command; visiting lectr, Stevens Inst of Tech. Lt cdr, USNR. Mem: Amer Soc Mech Engrs; Tau Beta Pi. Contbr articles on ordnance engr, applied mech, missile engr. Home: 42 Erskine Dr, Morristown, NJ. Office: Dover, NJ.

SCHWARTZ, S Alvin, US, rabbi, organizational exec; b. Baltimore, Md, May 8, 1928; s. Norton and Kate (Spector); BA, Yeshiva Coll, 1950; ordained rabbi, Yeshiva U, 1952, MA, 1955; m. Ivy Ebenstein, June 14, 1953; c: Hanita, Shimshon, Jonathan. Exec dir, Amer off, Boys Town, Jerusalem, since 1967; exec dir: Heb Theol Coll, Skokie, Ill, 1962-67, dir comty relations, 1953-62; Council Traditional Syns, 1953-61; Pa region, AJCong, 1961-62. Mem: RabCA; Rel ZOA. Home: Teaneck, NJ. Office: 165 W 46 St, New York, NY.

SCHWARTZ, Samuel, US, rabbi; b. Velki Sevlyvs, Hung, Dec 25, 1880; s. Jacob and Miriam (Gelb); in US since 1904; grad, Rabb Sem, Budapest, 1904; ordained rabbi, HUC, 1909, hon DD, 1947; BA, U Chgo, 1914; m. Charlotte Ulmer, 1917; c: Ruth, James. Rabbi em, Oak Park Temple, since 1947, rabbi, 1920-47; fmr, rabbi: B'nai Jeshurun, Cleveland, O; Ahavath Chesed, Jacksonville, Fla; Emanu-El, Montreal, Can. Mem: B'nai B'rith; Free Sons; ZOA; hon life mem, CCAR; fmr, pres: Chgo Rabb Assn; W Side Mins Assn; clubs: Standard; Covenant. Author: Tell Thy Children, autobiography, 1959. Home: 308 N Taylor Ave, Oak Park, Ill.

SCHWARTZ, Sidney H, US, book dealer, educator; b. Tykocin, Pol, Dec 15, 1905; s. Jacob and Sarah (Olstein); in US since 1923; att: Coll J Studies; Lewis Inst; m. Penina Parmet, June 22, 1929; c: Maxima Wax, David. Owner, Goodman Bros Hebrew Book Store, since 1956; Chgo corresp, The Day, 1930-33; tchr: Talmud Torah-Heb Sch, St Joseph, Mo, 1927-30; Capitol City Heb Sch, St Paul, Minn, 1935-40; prin: Cong Beth Isr Schs, Flint, Mich, 1940-43; Englewood Heb Sch, Chgo, Ill, 1943-47; educ dir: Duluth Heb Inst, Duluth, Minn, 1947-50; Albany Pk Heb Cong Schs, Chgo, 1950-53; B'nai Jacob Cong Schs, Chgo, 1953-56. Pres: A D Gordon br, LZOA, since 1965; hon pres, Bialik-Bogdansky Farband, since 1964, mem, coord comm, LZOA, pr, United Lab Zionist Org, Chgo, and Farband-LZOA; secy, Histadrut Ivrith, since 1943; fmr pres, Chgo Heb Tchrs Union; natl vice-pres, Fed Heb Tchrs and Prins Amer, 1950-53; fmr secy, Midwest Fed Heb Tchrs; found: Heb Prins Assn, Chgo; secy, NW br, Zeire Zion and Poalei Zion, Chgo, 1923-27, 1931-33; AJCong, pres, 1937-40, St Paul; Chgo Bd J Educ; Amer Assn J Educ; Natl Council J Educ; Albany Pk Heb Cong; B'nai Jacob Cong; B'nai B'rith; mem: Chgo Zionist Council; JNF council. Home: 2610 W Rosemont Ave, Chicago, Ill. Office: 2611 W Devon Ave, Chicago, Ill.

SCHWARTZ, Sidney L, US, investment banker; b. San Francisco, Jan 3, 1886; s. William and Henrietta (Gump); att U Cal, 1904-06; hon LLD, U Santa Clara; m. Alice Wolff, June 22, 1913; c: Marie Barnston, Elizabeth Cosgriff. Ltd partner, Sutro & Co, since 1959, sr partner, 1930-59, with firm since 1906; dir: Radium Oil Co; New Comstock Mines; pres, SF Stock Exch, 1923-30, 1942-44; mem, bd govs, NY Stock Exch, 1944-51. Fmr pres, bd trustees, SF Rotary Found; dir: Heb Home for Aged Disabled, 1954-62; hon dir, Big Bros, SF; mem, Inves Bankers Assn; treas, mem, bd trustees, Fogel Loan Fund, 1937-50; hon dir, Pacific Coast Stock Exch; pres, Old Time Athletics Assn, 1951-52; mem: adv bd, U Santa Clara Sch of Bus; Lowell Alumni Assn; Masons; hon mem, Beta Gamma Sigma; fmr mem, bd dirs, Mt Zion Hosp; clubs: Stock Exch; Rotary; Commonwealth; Merced Golf and Country. Home: 1750 Taylor St, San Francisco, Cal. Office: 460 Montgomery St, San Francisco, Cal.

SCHWARTZ, Steven O, US, physician, educator; b. Hung, July 6, 1911; s. Otto and Henrietta (Lemburger); in US since 1923; BS, Northwestern U, 1932, MS, 1935, MD, 1936; m. Ruth Deimel, Apr 24, 1942; c: Kay, Ann, James. Pvt practice, hematology, since 1938; att hematologist: Ill Masonic Hosp, since 1941; Columbus Hosp, since 1950; Mother Cabrini Hosp, since 1951; cons hematologist, Hines VA Hosp, since 1956; sr att phys, Chgo Wesley Memorial Hosp, since 1955; prof med, Northwestern U, since 1959; cons, Highland Park Hosp, since 1950; hematologist, Hektoen Inst for Med Research, Cook Co Hosp, Chgo, 1945-68; dir, hematology lab, att hematologist, 1939-68; prof: internal med, Cook Co Grad Sch, 1939-68; hematology, Chgo Med Sch, 1947-55; asso hematology, Michael Reese Hosp, chief, Mandel Clinic, 1938-50; asst prof, U of Ill, 1942-47. F: Chgo Soc Internal Med; Intl Acad Med; mem: Amer Fed for Clinical Research; Amer Coll Phys; AAAS; Intl Soc Hematology; Human Genetics Soc of Amer; Eur Soc Hematology; Amer Assn for Cancer Research; Amer Hematology Soc; Inst of Med, Chgo; Masons; Phi Delta Epsilon; Sigma Xi. Author: Hematology in Practice, 1960; asst ed, Blood, Journal of Hematology, 1946-50; contr to med jours. Home: 2185 Linden Ave, Highland Park, Ill. Office: 720 N Michigan Ave, Chicago, Ill.

SCHWARTZ, Theodore Morris, US, judge; b. NYC, Aug 3, 1909; s. Louis and Ida (Rothstein); att CCNY, 1928; LLB, Bklyn Sch, 1931; m. Helen Flanagan, July 28, 1934. Chmn, Employees Compensation Appeals Bd, Lab Dept, Wash, DC, since 1955; procurement engr, War Dept, 1942-45; asst Atty Gen, NY State, 1945-51; gen counsel, NY State Workmens Compensation Bd, 1951-55. Recipient: meritorious award, Lab Dept, 1961. Hobbies: music, electronics, photography. Home: 5225 Connecticut Ave, Washington, DC. Office: Lab Dept, 14 & Constitution Ave, Washington, DC.

SCHWARTZ, William B Jr, US, business exec; b. Atlanta, Ga, Nov 14, 1921; s. William and Ruth (Kuhn); BS, U of NC, 1942; m. Sonia Weinberg, Dec 3, 1942; c: William, Arthur, Robert. Ret; vice-pres, Natl Service Inds, 1945-68; presently engaged in real estate and inves, USN, 1942-45; lt, USNR. Vice-pres, Big Brothers Assn; mem bd: Heb Benevolent Cong, fmr pres; J Comty Cen; J Children's Service; Natl Comty Relations Adv Comm; Florence Crittenton Services; Emory U Bd

Visitors; pres council, Ogelthorpe U; fmr pres, Atlanta Bur J Educ; club, Kiwanis, secy, bd mem. Hobbies: golf, boating. Home: 35 Valley Rd NW, Atlanta, Ga. Office: 1422 W Peachtree St NE, Atlanta, Ga.

SCHWARTZ, William Samuel, US, artist; b. Smorgon, Russ, Feb 23, 1896; s. Samuel and Taube (Reznikoff); in US since 1912; att: Vilna Art Sch, 1908-12; Art Inst of Chgo, 1915-17; studied singing: under Karl Stein, Auditorium Conservatory of Music, Chgo, 1915-18; under Francesco Daddi, 1918-19; m. Mona Turner, Aug 15, 1939. Represented in perm collections: Art Inst of Chgo; Detroit Inst Arts; Libr of Cong; US Dept Lab; Art Alliance, Phila; Acad Fine Arts; Madison Art Assn, Wis; Little Gal, Cedar Rapids, Ia; Us: Ill, Neb, Mo, Wyo, Minn, Chgo; Ill State Normal Sch; Bradley U; Ill State Tchrs Coll; Chgo Normal Coll; Standard Oil Co, NJ; Amer People's Ency; Tel Aviv Mus, Isr; Ein Harod Mus, Isr; Dallas Mus; Oshkosh Mus, Wis; Montclair Mus, NJ; SF Mus; Joslyn Mus, Omaha; Santa Barbara Mus, Cal; Denver Mus; U Wash Mus, Seattle; Davenport Libr, Ia; Glenco and Chgo Librs, Ill; Cincinnati Libr; Musée d'Art Juif, Paris, Fr; Des Moines Art Cen, Ia; Union League Club, Chgo; murals: Cent of Progress Exposition, 1933; Cook Co Nurses Home, Chgo, 1935; Fairfield PO, 1936; Eldorado PO, 1937; Pittsfield PO, 1938; represented in pvt and public collections in Fr, Ger, Russ, Swed, Czech; appeared as tenor in operas, including: The Bartered Bride; Rigoletto; La Traviata; Il Travatore; Aida; Cavaleria Rusticana; also operatic roles in concerts, vaudeville. Recipient: 1st Albert Kahn prize, Detroit, 1925; 1st prize, Temple Beth El Sisterhood, Detroit, 1926; Marshall Fuller Holmes prize, Chgo Inst Art, 1927; MV Kohnstamm prize, 1930; Clyde M Carr prize, 1930; Mr and Mrs Jules F Brower prize, 1945, 1963; Munic Art League prize, 1952; prize, Covenant Club, 1936, 1941; 1st purchase prize, Monticello Coll, Godfrey, Ill, 1939; 1st prize, watercolors, Union League Club, Chgo, 1959. Home and studio: 880 N Lake Shore Dr, Chicago, Ill.

SCHWARTZBERG, Ralph M, US, attorney; b. Negaunee, Mich, June 16, 1906; s. Harris and Sophia (Feldman); LLB, U Mich, 1928; m. Celia Kaplan, Aug 17, 1930; c: Hugh, Joel, Burton. Sr partner, Schwartzberg & Barnett, since 1939; pres, Ambass Hotel Corp, Jacksonville, Fla; Buffalo Merchandise Warehouses Inc, Buffalo, NY; The Flying Carpet Motor Inn, Inc, Des Plaines, Ill; Buffalo Chgo Corp, Buffalo, NY. Mem, bd dirs, Bd J Educ; trustee, Coll J Studies; dir, Ner Tamid Cong, North Town; mem: Amer, Chgo, and Ill Bar Assns; hon supr chancellor, Tau Epsilon Rho; pres, Tau Epsilon Rho Scholarship Found; clubs: U Mich; Covenant, Ill; Twin Orchard Country. Home: 5600 N Francisco Ave, Chicago, Ill. Office: 11 S La Salle St, Chicago, Ill.

SCHWARTZMAN, Daniel, US, architect; b. Baltimore, Md, Dec 9, 1908; s. Abraham and Ethel (Benjamin); BArch, U of Pa, 1931; postgrad studies, Ecole Nationale Supérieure des Beaux-Arts, Paris, 1933-34; m. Dorothy Kemmler, Feb 24, 1933; c: John, Ellen. Architect, NYC, since 1936; fac mem, Sch of Architecture, Pratt Inst. Chmn, architects adv panel, UAHC; natl vice-pres, Amer Inst Architects, 1968-69; trustee: J Bd Guardians; Natl Inst Architectural Educ; exec mem, Intl Union Architects; mem, Architects League of NY, fmr pres; club, Grolier. Contbr to profsl jours. Recipient: Edward C Kemper Award, 1964; House Beautiful Mag Award; NY State Architects Assn Award; Baltimore C of C Award; Peale Mus Award. Home: 110 Prospect Ave, Sea Cliff, NY. Office: 90 Park Ave, New York, NY.

SCHWARTZMAN, Louis, US, organization exec, educator; b. Baltimore, Md, Jan 25, 1909; s. Samuel and Rebecca (Sherman); BA, LLB, U Md, 1931; att: Johns Hopkins U, 1931-34; U Baltimore, 1935; BHL, Baltimore Heb Coll, 1942, EdD; att Dropsie Coll, 1947-52; m. Bernice Shpritz, July 21, 1941; c: Susan Chasan, Linda Marvan, Barnett. Exec dir, Bur J Educ, Gtr Miami, since 1949; book review ed, J Educ Mag; educ cons, S Fla J Comtys; instr, Living Heb, first Heb TV program; prin, and asst exec dir, Bd J Educ, Baltimore, 1926-44; dir, Asso Heb Schs, Wilmington, Del, 1954-55; exec dir, Atlanta Bur J Educ, 1946-49; educ dir, YM-YWHA, Wilmington, 1954-55; Hillel councilor, Ga Tech, Emory U, 1946-49; instr, Heb, Heb civilization, U Miami, 1950-54. Pres, Children's Service Bur, Miami, 1959-60; vice-pres: Natl Council for J Educ, 1961-63; natl Young Judea, 1939; fmr youth dir, Seaboard Region, ZOA; mem, Natl Assn Heb Coll Profs. Co-author: Hebrew Thru Values; contbr to publs; author, plays and cantatas for children. Home: 1917 SW 19 Ave, Miami, Fla. Office: 940 Lincoln Rd, Miami Beach, Fla.

SCHWARTZMAN, Sylvan D, US, educator, author, rabbi; b. Baltimore, Md, Dec 8, 1913; s. Jacob and Rose (Padve); BA, U Cincinnati, 1936; MHL, ordained rabbi, HUC, Cincinnati, 1941; PhD, Vanderbilt U, Nashville, Tenn, 1952; m. Sylvia Cohen, Sep 22, 1940; c: Judith Apple, Joel. Prof, J rel educ, HUC-JIR, Cincinnati, since 1950; dir, rel educ, Temple Isr, Boston, Mass, 1939-40; rabbi: Cong Children of Isr, Augusta, Ga, 1941-47; Vine St Temple, Nashville, 1948-50; dir, field activities, UAHC, NY, 1947-48. Author: The Story of Reform Judaism, 1947; Reform Judaism in the Making, 1951; Religious School Administration, 1951; Religious School Teaching, 1952; Rocket to Mars, 1953, Sephardic ed, 1969; Once Upon a Lifetime, 1958; Into the Underground Kingdom, 1960; An Orientation to God, Prayer and Ethics, 1961; An Orientation to the Religious Home, Temple and Jewish Home, 1961; The Commitments of Confirmation, 1961; co-author: Meeting Your Life Problems, 1959; Our Religion and Our Neighbors, 1959; The Living Bible, 1962; The Non-Text Sermon, 1965; Reform Judaism—Then and Now, 1970; contbr to educ and rabb jours. Mem: CCAR; Vanderbilt Alumni Assn; Rel Educ Assn; HUC-JIR Alumni Assn; Comm on J Educ; exec comm, Natl Assn Temple Educs. Home: 2561 Erie Ave, Cincinnati, O. Study: HUC, Clifton Ave, Cincinnati, O.

SCHWARZ, Binyamin, Isr, educator; b. Vienna, Aus, Dec 7, 1919; s. Arthur and Alice (Pappenheim) Zacharias; in Isr since 1938; MSc, Heb U, Jerusalem, 1942; PhD, Wash U, St Louis; m. Ruhama Agai, Apr 17, 1962. Prof, math, Technion, Haifa, since 1967, on fac since 1955; with Research and Devl Dept, Min Defense, Isr, 1949-55. Royal Artillery, J Brig, 1942-46; capt, IDF, 1948-55. Mem: Isr Math Union; Amer Math Soc. Author: papers on pure math. Home: 4 Havradim Rd, Haifa, Isr. Office: Dept of Math, Technion, Haifa, Isr.

SCHWARZ, Boris, US, musician, educator; b. St Petersburg, Russ, Mar 13, 1906; s. Joseph and Rose (Kaplan); in US since 1936; att: Sorbonne, Paris, 1925-26; U Berlin, 1930-36; PhD, Columbia U, 1950; m. Patricia Yodido, June, 15, 1941; c: Joseph, K Robert. Prof, music,Queens Coll, since 1941, chmn, dept music, 1949-52, 1953-56, leader, Queens Coll String Quartet, since 1949; conductor: Queens Coll Orch Soc, since 1946; YMHA Sym, NYC, 1939-41; debut, violinist, Hannover, Ger, 1921; concert tours, Eur, 1921-25, 1927-36; concertmaster, Indianapolis Sym, 1937-38; first violinist, NBC-Toscanini Sym, 1938-39; mem fac, Natl Music Camp, Interlochen, Mich, summers, 1938-41. Mem: Société française de musicologie, Paris; Amer Musicological Soc; Intl Musicological Soc, Basel, Switz; Gesellschaft für Musikforschung, Kassel, Ger. Author: Music in Soviet Russia, 1970; contbr to encys and music jours. Recipient: Ford Found Award, 1952; Guggenheim f, 1960; selected for cultural exch prog between US and USSR, Amer Council Learned Socs, 1962. Hobby: photography. Home: 50-16 Robinson St, Flushing, NY. Office: Queens Coll, Flushing, NY.

SCHWARZ, Chaja, Isr, artist; b. Pol, 1916; in Isr since 1930; att Bezalel Sch of Arts and Crafts, Jerusalem; studied under Paldi; Zaritzky, Tel Aviv. One-man shows: Paris, 1950, 1964; London, 1953, 1964; Rome, 1962; Tel Aviv Mus, 1949, 1961; Mus Modern Art, Haifa, 1961; Jerusalem, 1961; Petah Tikva Mus, 1965; Negev Mus, Beersheva, 1966; group exhbs: Venice Biennale, 1958; Exhb J Painters of Paris Sch, Paris, 1959; Marseille, 1964; Migdal David Exhb, Jerusalem, 1961; Mus Modern Art, Haifa, 1969. Recipient: Dizengoff Prize, Tel Aviv Munic, 1944, 1949, 1960. Home: 10 Simtat Mazal Dagim St, Jaffa, Isr; Summers: Kiryat Hatzarayim, Safad, Isr.

SCHWARZ, Charles D, US, surgeon; b. Fiume, It, Sep 22, 1903; s. Desider and Olga (Herzfeld); in US since 1946; MD, U Zagreb, Yugo, 1926; m. Eva Rubinstein, Sep 22, 1941. Sr surg asst, Beth Isr Hosp, NY, since 1949; surg: Zakladna Hosp, Zagreb, 1926-29; Universitaetsklinik, Leipzig, Ger, 1929-33; att surg, Mercur Hosp, surg, Compensation Bd, 1933-41, both Zagreb. Mem: AMA; NY Co, NY State Med Socs; NY Acad Scis. Contbr to fgn med and sci jours. Recipient: Sveti Sava Reward, King Alexander, Yugo, 1926. Home and office: 88 Central Park W, New York, NY.

SCHWARZ, Joseph, US, rabbi; b. Korschenbroich, Ger, Feb 17, 1906; s. Hermann and Rosalie (Klein); in US since 1949; att: U Cologne, 1928; U Breslau, 1925-27, 1928-30; ordained rabbi, J Theol Sem, Breslau, 1932; hon DD, HUC-JIR, Cincinnati, 1962; m. Anneliese Levy, Nov 17, 1936; c: Michael, David. Rabbi, Temple Beth El, since 1949; rabbi: Liegnitz,

Ger, 1932-36; Hildesheim, Ger, 1936-38; Manila, Philippines, 1938-49. Pres: Min Assn, 1956-57, Interfaith Conf on Rel and Race, 1964-65; bd dirs, Assn for Retarded Children, 1953-58; mem: CCAR; B'nai B'rith; ZOA; club, Rotary. Contbr articles on hist of J in the Philippines. Home: 432 Cayoga Rd, Benton Harbor, Mich. Study: 214 Britain Ave, Benton Harbor, Mich.

SCHWARZ, Peter, Yugo, physician; b. Hung, Apr, 1890; s. Samuel and Rose (Schwarz); in Yugo since 1920; MD, Budapest U, 1917; m. Kornelia Stark, Dec 16, 1920. Sci adv, Inst for Preventive Med; chief, liquor lab, Clinic of Neur; chief, bacteriological dept, Hygiene Inst, 1920-32, pvt lab, 1932-41; dir, Inst for Med Research, 1949-61, all Novi Sad. Fmr: pres: J Comty, Novi Sad; Sports Club Juda Maccabi; vice-pres: Zionists Revisionists of Yugo; Assn Phys, Novi Sad. Author: monograph, Serial Examinations in Laboratory Practice; contbr to profsl jours. Recipient: Order for Service to People, III deg, 1948. Hobby: sabre fencing. Home: U1 J N A 47, Novi Sad, Yugo. Office: Inst for Preventive Medicine, Novi Sad, Yugo.

SCHWARZ, Stefan, W Ger, journalist, engineer; b. Chrzanow, Pol, Oct 12, 1910; s. Aron and Gusta (Grajower); att U Prague; dipl engr, Deutsche Technische Hochschule, 1933; m. Dora Dunkelblum, Dec 6, 1949. Free lance journalist since 1945; corresp, J and Pol press in Prague and Cracow, 1926-39; mgn engr, chem factory, Pol, 1939; ed, found, J jour, The Moment, 1946; liaison off between Mil Govt in Straubing, Regensburg, UNRRA, and persecuted persons. In Ger concentration camp, 1942-1945. Chmn, J Comty, Straubing, since 1945; co-found, Friends for Heb U, Cracow, 1928; J Cong of Straubing (rebuilding Syn), 1945; Regional Comm for liberated J in US Zone, Regensburg and Munich; mem: exec bd, Regional Comm, Regensburg and Council of Cen Comm, Munich; J Writers Union, Munich; Zionist Org, Ger; Moazah des Ichud Olami in Isr; mem bd, Akademie für Politische Bildung, Tutzing Bayern; head off and union of J Engrs; Landesverband der Israelitischen Kultusgemeinden in Bayern. Author: T G Masaryk und seine Einstellung zum Judentum, 1949; Die Juden in Bayern im Wandel der Zeiten, 1963; Aus der Geschichte der Juden in Straubing, 1968; contbr papers and articles to various jours. Home: 16 Gabelsbergerstr, Straubing, W Ger.

SCHWARZBAUM, Haim, Isr, author, archivist; b. Warsaw, Pol, Sep 24, 1911; s. Jacob and Esther (Shpiro); in Isr since 1937; att: Tchr Sem,Warsaw; U Warsaw; Heb U, Jerusalem; m. Judith Avritzer, Mar 7, 1941; c: Devora Rav-Aha, Moshe. Archivist, Govt of Isr, since 1950; libr, Cen Bur of Stat, 1940-50. Pvt, IDF, 1948-50. Prin contrib: research, J folklore contrib to world folklore. Vice-pres, Isr Folklore Soc, since 19.5; mem, Intl Soc Folklore Research. Author: Studies in Jewish and World Folklore, 1968; contbr numerous studies, essays, articles on folklore. Home: 5 Habitachon St, Kiron, Isr. Office: 50 Jabotinski St, Givatayim, Isr.

SCHWARZ-GARDOS, Alice, Isr, author, journalist; b. Vienna, Aus; d. Emanuel and Margarethe (Freistadt) Schwarz; desc of Heinrich Heine, Karl Marx; in Isr since 1940; att Coll, Bratislava, 1936-38; m. Eliahu Gardos, Oct 12, 1964. Mem, ed staff: Yedioth Chadashot since 1962; Yedioth Hayom, 1949-62; secy, Royal Navy Stores Off, Haifa, 1942-47. Mem: control, disciplinary court, Haifa Jour Assn; club, Isr PEN. Author: Schiff Ohne Anker, 1960; Die Abrechnung, 1962; Versuchung in Nazareth, 1963; Yoel und Yael, 1963; Entscheidung im Jordantal, 1965; contbr to: press, periodicals, anthols. Recipient, Youth Prize: for Lit, Neue Freie Presse, 1935; Pan-Eur, Vienna, 1935. Hobbies: gardening; Oriental arts and crafts. Home: 3 Arava St, Hadera, Isr. Office: 19/21 Jaffa St, Haifa, Isr.

SCHWEBER, Silvan Samuel, US, physicist, educator; b. Strasbourg, Fr, Apr 10, 1928; s. David and Dora (Edelman); in US since 1942; BS, CCNY, 1947; MS, U of Pa, 1949; PhD, Princeton U, 1951; m. Miriam Fields, June 14, 1945; c: Simone. Prof, physics, Brandeis U, since 1955; instr, Princeton U, 1951-52; postdoc f, Cornell U, 1952-54; sr postdoc f, Carnegie Tech, 1954-55. Author: Relativistic Quantum Field Theory, 1961; Quantum Electrodynamics, 1963. Spec interest: Isr. Home: 22 Turnine Mill Rd, Lexington, Mass. Office: Brandeis U, Waltham, Mass.

SCHWEID, Eliezer, Isr, author, educator; b. Jerusalem, Sep 7, 1929; s. Zevi and Osnat (Rosin); PhD, Heb U, 1960; m. Sabina Fuchs, Oct 14, 1953; c: Michal, Jacob, Rachel. Sr lectr, J phil, Heb U, Jerusalem, since 1965. Palmach, 1947-48. Mem: Heb Writers Assn; Société Internationale pour L'etude de la Philosophie Medievale; Zionist Conf in Isr. Author: Shalosh Ashmuroth, 1964; Iyunim Bishmona P'rakim, 1965; Haerga Limlot Hahaviah, 1968; Ad Mashber, 1969; mem ed bd, Petahim, mag; contbr to periodicals. Recipient: Valenrod Award. Home: 11 Yishay St, Jerusalem, Isr.

SCHWEIG, Joel, US, physician; b. Tarnopol, Aus, Apr 6, 1893; s. William and Amalia (Wischnowitzer); in US since 1924; MD, U Vienna, Aus, 1918; m. Sidonia Gelles, 1926; c: Noel. Pvt practice since 1924; chief of clinic, skin dept, Mt Sinai Hosp, since 1942; att dermat: Union Health Cen, since 1940; Hillside Hosp, since 1952; asso dermat, Beth Isr Hosp, since 1944; cons, Lexington Sch for Deaf, since 1930, all NYC. Aus Army, 1914-18. Hon pres, Amer-Pol Med Soc, since 1956; mem: NY State Med Soc; AMA; ZOA; AJCong; fmr pres, Bklyn Dermat Soc. Contbr to med jours. Hobbies: bridge, chess. Home: 170-40 Highland Ave, Jamaica, NY. Office: 133 E 58 St, New York, NY.

SCHWEITZER, Avram, Isr, journalist; b. Budapest, Hung, Jan 15, 1923; s. Yoshua and Shoshana (Berger); in Isr since 1946; att: U Budapest, 1942-46; King's Coll, Cambridge, 1952-53; m. Ora Zuckerman, July 30, 1950; c: Yitzhak, Yoram. Econ ed, Haaretz, since 1955; econ, Treasury Dept, 1949-55. Mem, cen comm, Isr Lab Party. Home: 8 Yoash St, Tel Aviv, Isr. Office: 56 Mazeh St, Tel Aviv, Isr.

SCHWEITZER, Jerome W, US, educator; b. Tuscaloosa, Ala, Dec 28, 1908; s. Abe and Mary (Spiro); BA, U Ala, 1930, MA, 1932; PhD, Johns Hopkins U, 1940; att U Mex, 1946; m. Anne Stoler, Oct 1, 1931. Prof, romance langs, U Ala, since 1951, fac mem since 1930, dir, publicity, 1931-37; reporter, Tuscaloosa News, 1926-28; instr, Span, Johns Hopkins U, 1935-39; chief ed, Fort Benning Bayonet, 1942-46. Lt col, US Army, 1942-57, US Army Res. Pres, Ala Alpha, 1959-60; mem: MLA; Amer Assn Tchrs Span and Port; S Atlantic, MLA; Phi Sigma Delta; Phi Beta Kappa; Sigma Delta Pi; Los Comediantes; Ala Educ Assn; club, U. Author: Georges de Scudery's "Almahide", 1939; The Scuderys Revisited, 1968; co-author: The Parisian Stage, Vol III, 1961; Le Theatre de Tristan L'Hermite, edition critique, 1969; contbr to: Cabeen's Critical Bibliography of 17th Century French Lit Section, The Contemporaries of Pierre Corneille, 1961. Home: 14 Arcadia Dr, Tuscaloosa, Ala. Office: Box 1043, U Ala, Tuscaloosa, Ala.

SCHWEITZER, Mitchell David, US, jurist; b. Bridgeport, Conn, Mar 14, 1905; s. David and Dora (Schachman); AB, Columbia Coll, 1926; LLB, Columbia Law Sch, 1928; m. Sylvia Brandt, Aug 11, 1938; c: Daniel, Richard, Leonard. Justice, Supr Court of NY since 1962; judge: NYC Munic Court, 1946-54; NY Co Court of Gen Sessions, 1955-62. Pres: Children's Free Dent and Optometric Clinics; trustee, Brookdale Hosp Cen; mem: B'nai B'rith; Young Men's Philanthropic League; Masons; Grand St Boys Assn. Home: 785 Fifth Ave, New York, NY. Office: 100 Center St, New York, NY.

SCHWENGER, Lloyd S, US, attorney; b. Cleveland, O, Apr 21, 1906; s. Sigmund and Belle (Rickersberg); BA, Princeton U, 1927; LLB, Harvard Law Sch, 1930; m. Helen Rosenthal Mervis, July 9, 1959; c: Francis Mervis. Partner, Daus, Schwenger and Kottler, since 1934. Pres, J Comty Fed, Cleveland; trustee: Mt Sinai Hosp, Cleveland; ADL; mem: Amer, Ohio, and Cleveland Bar Assns; fmr: vice-chmn, B'nai B'rith Youth Org; secy, Council Educ Alliance, Cleveland. Home: 13800 Fairhill Rd, Shaker Heights, O. Office: 1290 Union Commerce Bldg, Cleveland, O.

SCHWENK, Erwin, US, researcher; b. Prague, Bohemia, Oct 19, 1887; s. Adolf and Johanna (Reiss); in US since 1933; BChE, Technische Hochschule, Vienna, 1909, D Natural Scis, 1910; m. Rascha Schapiro, Aug 4, 1914; c: Lilli Hornig. Ret; research asso, Worcester Found for Experimental Biol, 1949-61; asst: U Erlangen, Ger, 1912-14; Kaiser Wilhelm Inst, Ger, 1914-16; dir, research, Verein f Chem Metall Produktion, 1916-28; asst dir, Schering AG, Berlin, 1928-33; dir, research and vice-pres, Schering Corp, Bloomfield, NJ, 1933-48. Mem: Natl Acad Arts and Scis; NY Acad Scis; London Chem Soc; Amer Chem Soc; Amer Soc Eur Chems; Amer Inst CEs. Author: Grundlagen und derzeitiger Stand der Chemotherapie, 1913; contbr to profsl jours. Home: 207 Loetscher Pl, Princeton, NJ.

SCHWIMMER, H Victor, US, attorney; b. Bklyn, NY, Apr 6, 1904; s. Samuel and Anna (Perlin); BS, Lehigh U, 1926; JD, St John's U, 1931. Pvt practice, NYC, 1931-35 and since 1945; ed staff, Intl Travel Register and Living Age Mag, 1928-29; asst counsel, Relief Admn Inves, NYC, 1936; atty, NY off, SEC, 1936-43; asso, law firm, Chadbourne, Wallace, Parke and Whiteside, 1943-44. Chmn, registrants advisory bd, Selective Service, 1940-43; mem: NY State, Amer Bar Assns; Assn Bar, NYC; US and E Lawn Tennis Assns; Pi Lambda Phi; clubs: Lehigh U, NYC, pres; Bankers of Amer; Metrop Country. Recipient: spec cong award, 1946. Home: 345 E 57 St, New York, NY. Office: 120 Broadway, New York, NY.

SCHWISBERG, Cyril E, Can, attorney; b. Montreal, Jan 21, 1908; s. Samuel and Malca (Edgar); BA, McGill U, 1927, BCL, 1931; m. Louise Beausejour, Dec 28, 1955; c: Samuel. Pvt practice since 1962; partner, Schwisberg and Schwisberg, 1933-54. Natl pres, Zionist Men's Assn, 1958-64; mem, natl off comm, exec comm, chmn, ZOC, 1959-64; mem, comm for Young Judaea, since 1962; hon dir, Chevra-Kadishah, B'nai Jacob Syn, since 1961, hon counsel, 1959-64; mem, exec comm, JNF, 1959-64; pres, Sons of Zion, 1928; mem: Loge L'Alliance-Fr Lodge, B'nai B'rith; Les Amis de L'Art; exec, hon off, Regiment de Maisonneure; YMHA; Pi Lambda Phi. Home: 250 Clarke Ave, Westmount, Can. Office: 1010 St Catherine St, W, Montreal, Can.

SCIAKY, Ino, Isr, dentist; b. Salonica, Greece, June 29, 1912; s. Daniel and Mathilde (Cazes); in Isr since 1937; DMD, Institut Dentaire, Geneva, 1936; m. Maggy Haddad, June 25, 1965; c: Nira, Daniel, Yael. Dean, Sch of Dent Med, Heb U, since 1965. Haganah, 1938-48; capt, IDF, 1948-50. Mem: FICD; FACD; IDA; AD; ADA; IADR. Hobby: photography. Home: 37 Rambam, Jerusalem, Isr. Office: Sch of Dent Med, Heb U, Jerusalem, Isr.

SCIAKY, Joseph Moses, Greece, attorney; b. Athens, Greece, Apr 1, 1918; s. Moses and Rachel (Saporta); law deg, U Athens, 1942; m. Despina Vaki, Jan 17, 1955; c: Marice. Atty since 1942; legal adv, Evangelismos Hosp, since 1951. Sgt, Greek Army, 1943-46. Mem: Masons; off council, Masonic lodge of Athens, orator; B'nai B'rith, fmr vice-pres, Philon lodge; secy-gen, Union ME Ex-Servicemen; treas, Union Greek Zionists; pres, Relief and Rehab Org of Greek Jews; clubs: Touring of Greece, mem council; J of Athens, fmr council mem. Author: Bitter Truths, 1952; trans, The Teaching of Contempt, 1966; lectr, on J subjects. Recipient: Dist Service Medal; 3rd class Mil Cross. Spec interest: hist of Greek Jewry. Home: 5 Gelonos St, Athens, Greece. Office: 76 Academia St, Athens, Greece.

SCIAMA, Dennis William, Eng, scientist; b. Manchester, Eng, Nov 18, 1926; s. Abraham and Nelly (Ades); MA, PhD, Cambridge U; m. Lidia Dina, Nov 26, 1959; c: Susan, Sonia. F: All Souls Coll, Oxford, since 1970; Trinity Coll, Cambridge, 1952-56, Peterhouse, 1963-70; lectr, math, Cambridge, 1961-70. Pvt, Brit Army, 1947-49. Author: The Unity of the Universe, 1959; The Physical Foundations of General Relativity, 1969. Mem: Royal Astronomical Soc. Hobbies: music, food, wine, theater, cinema, lit. Home: All Souls Coll, Oxford, Eng. Office: Dept of Astrophysics, S Parks Rd, Oxford, Eng.

SCLAR, Isaac, Scotland, business exec; b. Glasgow, Scotland, Mar 13, 1899; s. Philip and Fanny (Elkin) Clare; EE, 1st class hons, City and Guilds, Beath Tech Engr Coll, Fife, 1918; m. Doris Shulman, June 10, 1931; c: Fiona Cohen. Chmn, mgn dir, James Scott Ltd, elec holdings, since 1947, with firm since 1918. Prin contrib: initiated: Isaac Sclar Scholarship, for Post Grad Award, U Strathclyde; Isaac Sclar Prize, for best Elec Apprentice Student in Scotland; created, Isaac Sclar Charities Fund, donating to various charities, particularly educ. Vice-pres, Anglo-Isr C of C; hon pres, JPA, Glasgow, fmr, jt chmn, comm mem; gov, Calderwood, Lodge Sch, Glasgow; comm, Elec and Electronics Inds Benevolent Assn; mem: Glasgow J Bd of Educ; Glasgow J Reprs Council; fmr pres, Elec Contractors Assn, Scotland; chartered engr, f, Inst of EEs; f, Inst of Dirs; club, Rotary, Dumferline, hon mem, fmr pres. Home: 6 Egidia Ave, Giffnock, Glasgow, Scotland. Office: 80/110 Finnieston, Glasgow, Scotland.

SCRINOPSKIE, E Leslie, US, business exec; b. Topeka, Kan, Apr 17, 1922; s. Myer and Donna (Seff); m. Harriette Spector, Apr 17, 1948; c: Nancy, Ronald. Engaged in pvt business. Cpl, USAF, 1942-45. Pres, Kan State B'nai B'rith Assn; Capt of Guard, Arab Shrine Temple AAONMS; mem:

High Twelve; Elks; Amer Legion; VFW; Masons, Topeka Consistory Masonic Order; fmr: pres, B'nai B'rith, Topeka Lodge; treas, Temple Beth Sholom; mem bd, Off Econ Opportunity. Home: 3150 Westover Rd, Topeka, Kan. Office: 909 Kansas Ave, Topeka, Kan.

SEAGER, Esther, Eng, municipal official; b. Cardiff, S Wales, Eng, March 5, 1905; d. Harris and Miriam Harris; att: Dudley Bus Coll; m. Maurice Seager, June 18, 1930; c: Harry, David. JP, Smethwick, since 1950, councillor, 1945-62, dep mayor, 1950-54, mayor, 1955-56. Prin contrib: initiated road safety device, accident prevention measure, used near elem schs and on RR crossings; org young children club in 1942, to promote understanding between peoples of different rels and natls. Chmn, Poale Zion, 1952-54. Contbr to J jours. Home and office: 77 Waterloo Rd, Smethwick, Warley, Worcs, Eng.

SEASONGOOD, Murray, US, attorney; b. Cincinnati, O, Oct 27, 1878; s. Alfred and Emily (Fechheimer); BA, Harvard U, 1900, MA, 1901, LLB, 1903; hon LLD: Marietta Coll, Marietta, O, 1950; NYU, 1951; Wilmington Coll, 1963; Miami U, 1963; U Cincinnati, 1964; hon DHL, HUC-JIR, 1962; m. Agnes Senior, Nov 28, 1912; c: Janet Hoffheimer Jr. Mem, Paxton & Seasongood, since 1927; asso lawyer, Paxton & Warrington, 1903-09; mem, Paxton, Warrington & Season-good, 1909-27; part-time prof, Coll of Law, U Cincinnati, 1925-59, prof em since 1959; mayor, Cincinnati, 1926-30. Chmn, Cincinnati Planning Commn, 1926-30; mem, loyalty review bd, US Civil Service Commn, 1947-53; pres: Natl Assn Legal Aid Orgs, 1945-48; Natl Munic League, 1931-34, hon vice-pres, 1934-39, mem council, since 1939; hon vice-pres, Natl Legal Aid and Defender Assn, since 1953, dir, 1949-53; mem: hon life, bd trustees, Home for J Aged, Cincinnati; adv bd, JDC, since 1945; natl council, Amer Friends Heb U, since 1958, mem, adv bd, since 1962; adv comm, J Publ Soc Amer, since 1962; bd govs, HUC, 1913-42; exec comm, AJComm, 1938-47; Cincinnati, O State and Amer Bar Assns; Amer Law Inst; Rockdale Ave Temple; trustee: Julius Rosenwald Fund, 1930-34; Clovernook Home and Sch for Blind, since 1958, vice-pres, since 1962; clubs: Queen City; Lit, fmr pres; Harvard Fac, Cambridge; Harvard, NY. Author: Local Government in the United States, A Challenge and an Opportunity, 1933; Cases on Municipal Corporations, 1934, 2nd ed, 1941, co-author, 3rd ed, 1953; chap on Municipal Corporations in Ballantine's Problems in Law, 2nd ed, 1937, 3rd ed, 1949. Recipient: Good Citizen award, Natl Munic League, 1951; Good Neighbor award, Plum St Temple, 1959; citation, NCCJ, 1961. Home: 2850 Grandin Hollow Lane, Cincinnati, O. Office: 1616 Union Central Bldg, Cincinnati, O.

SEBBA, Felix, S Afr, educator; b. Cape Town, S Afr, Nov 21, 1912; s. Isidor and Ernestine (Carmel); MSc, U Cape Town, PhD, 1936; DIC, Imperial Coll, London, 1939; postgrad studies: U Cambridge, Eng, 1939-40; Princeton U, 1952; m. Margot Ellison, Jan 17, 1954; c: Mark. Prof phys chem, U Witwatersrand, since 1957, head, dept chem and biochem, since 1965; sr tech off, Royal Aircraft Establishment, Farn-borough, Eng, 1943-46; lectr, sr lectr, U Cape Town, 1946-57. S Afr Air Force, 1940-43. Prin contribs: invented ion flotation, 1959. F: Royal Inst Chem; Chem Soc; mem: Faraday Soc; Soc Chem Ind; Sigma Xi; fmr pres, Cape Chem Soc. Author: Ion Flotation, 1962. Hobbies: music, travel, garde-ning. Home: 177 Retha Rd, Northcliff, Ext 2, Johannesburg, S Afr. Office: U of Witwatersrand, Johannesburg, S Afr.

SEBBA, Shalom, Isr, artist, stage designer; b. Tilsit, Jan 14, 1897; s. Jakob and Marie (Meisel); in Isr since 1936; grad, Art Acad, Koenigsberg, 1919. One-man shows, Tel Aviv Mus, 1945, 1955, 1961; executed scenic and stage designs for theaters in: Berlin; Stockholm; Munich; Darmstadt; Tel Aviv; in collaboration with: Leopold Jessner; Tyrone Guthrie; Gustav Hartung; murals: The Happy Haul, Sharon Hotel, Herzliya; Resurrection, Yad leBanim, Givatayim; Samson, Civic Cen, Ashkelon; The Guardian, 2 fresco paintings, Technion, Haifa; Brotherhood, Hamlin House, Tel Aviv; Tech Symbols, ORT Sch; participated in: intl exhb, Dresden, 1920; Intl Lab Off Art Exhb, 1957. Recipient: Dizengoff prize, Tel Aviv Munic. Home and studio: 28 Hapisgah St, Giva-tayim, Isr.

SEBBAG, Gabriel, Isr, public official; b. Mekness, Morocco, May 15, 1933; s. Moses and Rebecca (Toledano); in Isr since 1952; att: Ind Tech Sch, Beersheva; Beit Berl U, Tel Aviv; m. Simha Zafrani, June 26, 1954; c: Doron, Dorith, Avital. Mayor, Dimona, Isr, since 1966; lab mgr, Kibbutz Ginosar,

1952-57; chmn, workmen's comm, Dead Sea Potash Works, 1958-62, produc mgr, 1962-66. Regimental sgt, MC, IDF. Hon chmn, Foyer Culturel Français; mem, Rotary of Dimo-na; fmr: mem local exec, Isr Lab Party; natl exec, Histadrut. Ed in chief, Niv Yam Hamelah; contbr to Isr press. Recipient: Silver Medal, City of Paris; Gold Medal, City of Belfort; Bronze Medal, City of Marseilles; City of Saint-Amande-Les-Eaux, all Fr. Hobbies: theater, music, camping, gardening. Home and office: Dimona, Isr.

SECUNDA, Sholom, US, composer, conductor; b. Alexandria, Russ, Aug 23, 1894; s. Abraham and Anna (Nedobeika); in US since 1908; att: Juilliard Sch of Music, 1914-20; Columbia U, 1913-14; Cooper Union Coll, NY, 1912-13; m. Betty Almer, Oct 25, 1927; c: Sheldon, Eugene. Composer: Sympho-nic Sketches; Yemenite Dance; Song of the East; Danse des Odalisques; Tango de la Luna; String Quartet in C Minor; opera, Sulamith, 1925; popular song, Bei Mir Bist Du Shein; 60 operettas, including: Mein Yiddish Meidel; Katja's Wed-ding; Mashka; Israel and America; Die Freiliche Mishpoche; liturgical compositions; popular and classic songs in Yiddish and Heb; scores: Tevye the Dairyman; Kol Nidre; Sholom Aleichem's Motye Peishe dem Chazins; complete musical setting: High Holy Day; Festival and two Sabbath Services; Kabbalat Shabbat; Shabbat Hamalkah; Lichvod Shabbat; all complete services recorded, Columbia Records, under di-rection of composer. Musical dir, Concord Hotel, since 1946; prof, J music, JTSA, since 1965; conductor, Concord Sym Orch, Kiamesha, NY, 1947; chorus boy, Comedy Theater, NYC, 1916-17; tchr, music, 1915-23; conductor: concert orchs, all major radio networks; at: Madison Sq Garden, NYC, 1948; Civic Opera Theater, Chgo, 1953; Waldorf-Astoria; Commodore Hotel; Astor Hotel, all NYC; lectr: NYU, 1939-41; Hunter Coll, 1939. USNR, 1918. Pres: Soc of J Composers, since 1934; mem: ASCAP; Asso Musicians of Gtr NY; In-dependent Alexandria Benevolent Assn; Workmen's Circle; Farband-LZOA; clubs: Amer-Isr; Yiddish Theatrical Al-liance; Heb Actors. Author: Sholom Secunda's Memoirs, 1969; fmr music critic, J Daily Forward. Home: 590 Fort Washington Ave, New York, NY.

SEDLER, Robert Allen, US, educator, lawyer; b. Pittsburgh, Pa, Sep 11, 1935; s. Jerome and Esther (Rosenberg); BA, U Pitts-burgh, 1956, JD, 1959; m. Rozanne Friedlander, Jan 24, 1960; c: Eric. Prof, law, U Ky, since 1968; fac mem since 1966; asst, asso prof, St Louis U, 1961-65; asst dean, asso prof, Haile Selassie I U, Ethiopia, 1963-66. Prin contribs: participant in civil rights litigation; sch segregation, discri-mination in housing, freedom of expression against sedition charges. Treas, Phi Beta Kappa; bd dirs: Ky Civil Liberties Union; St Louis AJCong, 1961-63; mem: Order of Coif; Amer and Ky Bar Assns; Amer Judicature Soc. Author: The Con-flict of Laws in Ethiopia, 1965; Ethiopian Civil Procedure, 1968; contbr to legal jours. Home: 3461 Keithshire, Lexing-ton, Ky. Office: U of Ky, Lexington, Ky.

SEEBACHER, J Ira, US, journalist; b. Phila, Pa, Jan 29, 1911; s. Ira and Ferdinanda (Morris); grandfather, Jacob Seebacher, 1st J elected to NY State Sen; att CCNY, 1929-31; m. Sophie Smoliar, Mar 23, 1946; c: Jay. Sports ed, columnist, Morning Telegraph, since 1939; vice-pres, Photo Ind News, Inc, since 1956. NY Natl Guard, 1927-30. Club: Collectors, NY. Hobby: philately. Home: 48 Knollwood Rd, S Roslyn, LI, NY. Office: 525 52 St, New York, NY.

SEECOF, David P, US, pathologist, educator; b. NYC, Dec 25, 1895; s. Morris and Jennie (Berlowitz); MD, U and Bellevue Hosp Med Coll, 1918; m. Anna Robertson, June, 1948. Cons, path, Vet Hosp, Castle Point, NY, 1957; path, Montefiore Hosp, 1921-27; asso with Dr I Levin, 1919-21; asso prof, path, U Colo, 1927-29; dir lab, City Hosp, Cleveland, and asst prof, path, W Reserve U, 1929-33; dir, labs, J Gen Hosp, Montreal, Can, 1934-37; asst prof, path, Einstein Med Coll, Yeshiva U, 1956-57; asst visiting path, Bx Munic Hosp Cen, 1956-57. US Army, 1917-18. Dipl, Amer Bd Paths; mem: NY Acad Med; NY Path Soc; AAAS; Amer Assn Paths and Bacts; Amer Assn for Cancer Research; Soc for Experimental Biol and Med; Intl Acad Path; NY State Path Soc; NY Acad Scis; Endocrine Soc; Can Phys Soc; Sigma Xi; Phi Delta Epsilon; Assn Amer Orthodox J Scis; Mizrachi. Contbr to med jours. Home and office: 1970 Daly Ave, Bronx, NY.

SEEGAL, David, US, research dir, educator; b. Chelsea, Mass, June 23, 1899; s. Morris and Rose (Beerman); MD, Harvard Med Sch, 1928; m. Emily Carrier, July 8, 1925. Dir, research service, 1st div, Goldwater Memorial Hosp, Columbia U

Coll Phys and Surgs, 1942-47 and since 1951, prof med, Columbia U, since 1951; dir research, div chronic diseases, Wfr I, 1936-42; prof med: LI Med Coll, 1947-48; State U Med Cen, Bklyn, 1950-51; att phys, Presbyterian Hosp, 1956, asso att phys, 1945-47, 1952-56; cons, epidemic diseases, US Secy of War, 1942-45; research cons, Public Health Research Inst, NYC. Mem: adv comm, Unitarian Service Comm; med adv council, Masonic Found for Med Research and Hum Wfr; med and sci comms, Arthritis and Rheumatism Found; comm on med educ, NY Acad Med; NY Comm on Study Hosp Internships and Residencies; Assn Amer Phys; Assn Amer Med Colls; Amer Soc Clinical Inves; Amer Assn Immunologists; Soc for Experimental Biol and Med; Amer Rheumatism Assn; Harvey Soc; AAAS; Alpha Omega Alpha; Omega Club; f, AMA; fmr, vice-pres, Assn for Research in Nervous and Mental Diseases; delg, Natl Conf on Chronic Diseases, Chgo, 1951. Mem: ed bd, The Pharos of Alpha Omega Alpha; adv bd, Familiar Medical Quotations, 1968; contbr: chaps to med surveys, books and proceedings; to med jours; co-ed, Jour of Chronic Diseases, 1955. Recipient: Army and Navy cert of appreciation,1948. Home:39 Claremont Ave, New York, NY. Office: Welfare Island, New York, NY.

SEGAL, Bernard, US, rabbi, organization exec; b. Lipno, Pol, Nov 15, 1907; s. Eli and Gittel (Zucker); in US since 1922; BS, Columbia U, 1931; MHL, ordained rabbi, JTSA, 1933, DHL, 1950, hon DD, 1964; m. Hattie Clark, Nov 25, 1934; c: Gita, David. Exec dir, United Syn of Amer, since 1953; rabbi, Queens J Cen, 1934-40. Chaplain, US Army, 1940-45. Exec, vice-pres: RA, 1945-49; JTSA, 1949-53; dir, Natl Ramah Commn, 1950-54; mem, Mayor's Comm on Housing, NYC, 1954-58; bd dirs, Comm on Rel in Amer Life, 1954-56; Assn for Middle Income Housing, NYC, since 1960; pres, Assn J Chaplains, US Army and Navy, 1945-47. Home: 110-21 73 Rd, Forest Hills, LI, NY. Office: United Syn Amer, Broadway and 122 St, New York, NY.

SEGAL, Bernard G, US, attorney; b. NYC, June 11, 1907; s. Samuel and Rose (Cantor); BA, U of Pa, 1928, LLB, 1931, Gowen f, 1931-32; hon LLD: Franklin and Marshall Coll, 1953; Temple U, 1954; Dropsie Coll, 1966; m. Geraldine Rosenbaum, Oct 22, 1933; c: Loretta Cohen, Richard. Sr partner, Schnader, Harrison, Segal and Lewis, since 1936; instr: political sci, Wharton Sch, U of Pa, 1928-32, public finance, Grad Sch, 1934-35, lectr, Law Sch, 1931-35, 1945-47; bus, govt, Amer Inst of Banking, 1935-37; North lectr, law, Franklin and Marshall Coll, 1936-37; legal asst, Amer Law Inst, 1932-33; Amer reporter on contracts, Intl Cong Law, The Hague, 1932; dep atty gen, Commonwealth of Pa, 1932-35, drafted banking and bldg law codes, 1933, Milk Control Law, 1934. Pres, Amer Bar Assn, 1969, mem, house delgs, 1952-54, 1957-61, mem, council, sect on judicial admn, since 1963; hon pres, Allied J App, fmr pres, chmn bd; chmn: comm on intl communications, World Peace Through Law Cen, since 1963; Commn on Judicial and Cong Salaries, 1953-55; co-chmn, Lawyers Comm for Civil Rights Under Law, 1963-65; spec master, RR Reorg, US Court Appeals, Third Circuit, since 1945; bd dirs: Amer Judicature Soc, 1958-61; Brandeis Lawyers Soc; PA Judicial Nominating Commn, 1964-65; vice-pres: bd govs, Dropsie Coll; Amer Law Inst; life f, Amer Bar Found, mem, bd dirs; mem, bd Fs, Inst Judicial Admn, since 1968; f, Amer Coll Trial Lawyers, mem bd regents, fmr pres; bd trustees: U of Pa, life mem; Albert Einstein Med Cen; J Publ Soc of Amer, fmr vice-pres; Ency Judaica Research Found; trustee, Chapel of Four Chaplains; lay bd trustees, Villanova U; bd dirs: Fed JAs, life mem; Gtr Phila Movement, charter mem; found, Fed Bar Assn; Amer Arbitration Assn; Medico Inc; Legal Aid Soc, Phila, 1935-68; United Fund, Gtr Phila; J League for Isr; hon dir, J Family Service; chancellor, Phila Bar Assn, 1952, 1953; mem: Council Legal Opportunities, since 1968; Jt Comm for Effective Admn Justice; Natl Conf Bar Pres; Inter-Amer Bar Assn; Intl Bar Assn; Assn Bar, NYC; Fed Bar Assn; Fed Communication Bar Assn; Assn Interstate Commerce Practioners; standing comm on rules of practice and procedure, Judicial Conf of US, since 1959; Atty Gen's Natl Comm to Study Anti-Trust Laws, 1953-55; exec comm, Atty Gen's Natl Conf on Court Congestion and Delay in Litigation, 1958-61; Natl Citizens Comm for Comty Relations, since 1964; State Dept Adv Panel on Intl Law, since 1967; adv comm, United States Mission, UN, 1967-68; Fed Judicial Conf, Third Circuit, since 1945; Bd Law Examiners, Phila, 1940-46; City of Phila Adv Comm on Commitment, Detention, and Discharge of Prisoners, 1953-55; spec comm on anti-poverty prog, Phila, OEO, since 1967; Admn Conf of US, since 1968; adv comm, Natl Legal Service

Prog, OEO, since 1968; Pa Judicial Council, since 1968; bd law, U of Pa Sch; jt bd, Annenberg Sch of Communications; house delgs, Pa Bar Assn, fmr mem, exec comm; Order of Coif; Delta Sigma Rho; Tau Epsilon Rho; clubs: Natl Lawyers, charter mem, bd govs, since 1959; Locust; Union League; Socialegal; Midday; Lawyers; Pen and Pencil; Intl Variety; Pa Soc; Adm; Ambass; Fed City, Wash, DC. Chmn, intl hon bd, Ency Judaica; contbr to legal and gen publs. Recipient: award, Pa Bar Assn, 1962; Dedication Day Award, Fed Bar Assn, 1968. Home: 155 Rose Lane, Haverford, Pa. Office: 1719 Packard Bldg, Philadelphia, Pa.

SEGAL, Erich, US, educator, author; b. Bklyn, NY, June 16, 1937; s. Samuel and Cynthia (Shapiro); AB, Harvard U, 1958, AM, 1959, PhD, 1965. Asso prof, classics and comparative lit, Yale U, since 1968, asst prof, classics, 1964-68; teaching f, hum, Harvard U, 1959-64. Author: Roman Laughter: The Comedy of Plautus, 1968; Euripides: A Collection of Critical Essays, 1968; Love Story,1970; screenplays:Yellow Submarine; The Games; Love Story; RPM; Cyrano; Railroad Bill; trans, Plautus: Three Comedies, 1969; contbr to reviews and profsl jours. Recipient: Guggenheim f, 1968. Hobby:long-distance running. Home: 3092 Yale Station, New Haven, Conn. Office: Yale U, New Haven, Conn.

SEGAL, Maurice S, US, physician, educator; b. Ponadel, Lith, July 31, 1907; s. Louis and Liba (Horwitz); in US since 1909; BS, Tufts U, 1928, MD, cum laude, 1932; m. Sylvia Wyman, Apr 17, 1937; c: Peter. Prof med, Tufts U, since 1950, mem fac since 1932; dir, dept inhalation therapy and Lung Station (Tufts), Boston City Hosp, since 1946, mem staff since 1933; med cons, social security admn, council of appeals, HEW, since 1959; asso in med, Beth Isr Hosp, Boston, 1950; cons, chest diseases: Faulkner Hosp, Jamaica Plain, Mass, 1952; Mt Auburn Hosp, Cambridge, 1952; J Memorial Hosp, Boston, 1952; mem, cons staff, Winthrop Comty Hosp, 1950; admnr, USPHS Res, 1952. Dipl: Natl Bd Med Examiners; Amer Bd Internal Med; FACP; f: Amer Coll Chest Phys, fmr pres, NE states chap; Amer Coll Allergists; Amer Acad Allergy; mem: AMA, fmr cons on pharm and chem; Amer Trudeau Soc; Amer Therapeutic Soc; Mass Med Soc; Sigma Xi; Alpha Omega Alpha; chmn, class of 1936, 25th year reunion, Tufts U Med Sch. Author: The Management of the Patient with Severe Bronchial Asthma, 1950; co-author: Chronic Pulmonary Emphysema, Physiotherapy and Treatment, 1953; Effective Inhalation Therapy,1953; mem, ed staff, Annals of Allergy, since 1950; contbr: chaps to med books, numerous papers to med jours; guest lectr on chest diseases, to med schs and socs: US; Can; Mexico; Guat; Fr; It; Aus; Eng; Switz; etc. Recipient: grant-in-aids from: USPHS; Found for Research in Bronchial Asthma and Related Diseases; Tobacco Ind Research Comm; Pharmaceutical houses, for research and studies on cardio-pulmonary function in health and disease. Home: 1010 Memorial Drive, Cambridge, Mass. Office: Lung Station (Tufts), Boston City Hosp, 818 Harrison Ave, Boston, Mass.

SEGAL, Mendel, Can, accountant; b. Montreal, Jan 2, 1902; s. Moses and Sarah (Budyk); BComm, McGill U, Montreal, 1923; m. Bessie Mains, 1935; c: Charles. Office mgr, J Gen Hosp, Montreal, since 1936. Secy, men's assn, Shaar Hashomayim, Montreal; mem: council, Montreal Friends Heb U; Amer Assn Hosp Acctnts; Hosp Financial Mgmt Assn; fmr: pres, Masonic Club, McGill U; chancellor, Omicron chap, Tau Epsilon Phi. Home: 3864 Wilson Ave, Montreal, Can. Office: 3755 Côte St Catherine Rd, Montreal, Can.

SEGAL, Mendel, US, business exec; b. Chattanooga, Tenn, June 8, 1914; s. Samuel and Rebecca (Lewis); att Emory U, 1931-33; m. Mynette Kahn, Jan 22, 1939; c: Joe. Mgn partner, Stein Printing Co, since 1943, with firm since 1935; pres: Oak Realty Co; Segal Services Inc. Pres: Gate City lodge, B'nai B'rith; Metrop Atlanta Mh Assn; exec bd, NCCJ, Atlanta; bd men, BBB, Atlanta; mem: Fulton Co Mh Comm; cen bd, Atlanta J Home for Aged; Natl Defense Exec Res; clubs: Atlanta Advt; Standard Town and Country, Progressive. Author: How to Sell Printing Creatively, 1955; How to Develop Your Personal Selling Power, 1966; Sales Management for Small and Medium-Sized Businesses, 1969. Recipient: Man of year award, Atlanta Club of Printing House Craftsman, 1959; Printers Ink-AFA silver award, Atlanta Advt Club, 1961. Home: 475 Hillside Dr NW, Atlanta, Ga. Office: 2161 Monroe Dr, NE, Atlanta, Ga.

SEGAL, Meyer, US, dentist; b. Bklyn, NY, May 19, 1892; s. Samuel and Fanny (Gamse); DDS, Georgetown U Sch of

Dent, 1917; m. Sara Winograd, Aug 9, 1925; c: Beverly Leonard. Pvt practice since 1926; various govt positions, 1920-26. Life mem, Amer Dent Assn; Chgo Dent Soc; mem: B'nai B'rith, Jackson Park Lodge 1408; Masons, fmr master, Wash Emblem Lodge 965; organizer, Adult J Educ Study Group, Ben Z Nudelman Lodge, B'nai B'rith, 1961; fmr: chmn, B'nai B'rith Summer Inst of Judaism, Chgo, Ill; recording secy, S Side Heb Cong, Chgo, Ill. Contbr to dent jours. Recipient: plaque, B'nai B'rith Adult Educ Prog, Gtr Chgo B'nai B'rith Council, 1959; Samuel J Graff Memorial Award, Jackson Park Lodge 1408, B'nai B'rith, 1961. Hobbies: music, golf, gardening, langs, adult J Educ. Home: 7439 S Chappel, Chicago, Ill. Office: 757 W 79, Chicago, Ill.

SEGAL, Mordechai, Isr, educator; b. Orynin Podolia, Ukraine, Dec 25, 1903; s. Aaron and Rachel (Lieberson); in Isr since 1925; att: CCNY, 1920-24; Biol Pedg Inst, Tel Aviv, 1931-32; m. Yetta Caller (decd); c: Rachel Rabinowitz; m. 2nd, Lina Rosenzweig; c: Michal, Ruth, Naomi, Aaron (decd, 1962, lt, IAF). Head, found, Sem Hakibbutzim, Tchrs Coll, since 1939; mem, Cen Educ Bd, Hakibbutz Hameuchad, since 1933; headmaster, kibbutz sch, Kfar Guiladie, 1933-38; found, first Halutz Farm in US, Flagtown, NJ, 1924. Mem: Natl Bd Educ Council for Higher Educ, Interkibbutzim Educ Comm; fmr: secy, J Studies Org, NY; mem: exec comm, Natl Tchrs Union of Isr; Parl Comm for Educ Reform. Author: Essays on Education, 1956; Bible Values as Human Values, 1959. Home: Kibbutz Givat Hayim Meuchad, Isr. Office: Seminar Hakibbutzim, Bnei Ephraim St, Tel Aviv, Isr.

SEGAL, Nachman Nathan, Isr, author; b. Dorohoi, Rum, Feb 10, 1900; s. Bernard and Sara (Popliker); BS, U Rum, 1924; m. Anna Paskal, 1933; c: Oktombriwa Groper. Herborist, Consort Intl, Bucharest, 1944-49; writer, Cenaclu Menora Jour, 1949-69. Author: Flora Spontana, 1966. Hobbies: botany, chem, herboristics. Home: 9 Hamelech David St, Kahane David, Haifa, Isr.

SEGAL, Robert E, US, organization exec; b. Chillicothe, O, Dec 11, 1903; s. Max and Betty (Bloom); BA, O State U, 1925; m. Jane Sickles, June 22, 1932; c: Ellen Landau, William. Exec dir, JCC, Metrop Boston, since 1944; reporter, promotion mgr, Cincinnati Post, 1925-35; asst publisher, Chillicothe Scioto Gazette, 1935-40; secy, JCC, Cincinnati, 1940-44. Mem, exec bds: World Affairs Council, Mass sect, UNICEF; NCCJ; Natl Comty Relations Adv Council; chmn, Boston-Suburban Comm, Mass Commn Against Discrimination; vice-chmn, Mass Adv Comm, US Commn on Civil Rights; pres: Temple Shalom, Newton, Mass, 1950-53; Boston Intergroup Relations Council, 1951-53; mem: Phi Beta Kappa; Sigma Delta Chi; Zeta Beta Tau; Pi Delta Epsilon; Amer Soc of Newspaper Eds, 1937-40; club, Cincinnati Civic, pres, 1930-31. Home: 50 Verudale Rd, Newton Highlands, Mass. Office: 72 Franklin St, Boston, Mass.

SEGAL, Robert Mandal, US, attorney; b. Worchester, Mass, Mar 21, 1915; s. Abe and Bella (Perry); AB, Amherst Coll, 1936; LLB, Harvard U, 1942; att U Chgo; f, Brookings Inst, Wash, DC, 1938-39; m. Sharlee Mysel, June 17, 1941; c: Terry, Ellen. Sr partner, Segal and Flam, since 1950; counsel, Mass State Lab Council, AFL-CIO, since 1955; NE counsel, Amer Fed TV and Radio Artists, since 1948; lectr, Harvard Bus Sch, since 1960; econ, War Produc Bd, 1942-43. US Army, 1943-45. Pres, JCC, Metrop Boston; NE chmn, J Lab Comm; mem, Educ Compact Council of Mass; co-chmn, Lab Relations Comm, Boston Bar Assn; adv comm, ACLU, Mass; chmn, Bar-Press Comm of Mass; mem: Amer Bar Assn; ADA; Phi Beta Kappa; Delta Sigma Rho; fmr: trustee, Temple Shalom, W Newton; dir, W Newton Coop Bank; mem, house delgs, Amer Bar Assn; mem: exec council, Boston Bar Assn; Mayor's Minority Comm; Harvard Law Sch Alumni Assn; natl vice chmn, Harvard Law Sch Fund. Contbr to legal publs. Recipient: 5 Battle Stars, World War II. Home: 74 Sylvan Ave, W Newton, Mass. Office: 11 Beacon St, Boston, Mass.

SEGAL, Samuel, Lord Segal of Wytham, Eng, communal leader, physician; b. London, Eng, Apr 2, 1902; s. Moshe and Leah (Frumkin); MA, Jesus Coll, Oxford, 1923; MRCS, LRCP, Westminster Hosp, London, 1927; m. Molly Rolo, Mar 18, 1934; c: Maureen Hadfield, Valerie Pelham. Mem, House of Lords; MP for Preston Lancs, House of Commons, 1945-50; house phys, casualty off, Westminster Hosp, London, 1928-30; sr clinical asst, Gt Ormond St Children's Hosp, London, 1930-31; regional med off, Min of Health, 1951-63. RAF, med br, 1939-46. Chmn: Anglo-Isr Assn; Natl Soc for Mentally Handicapped Children; vice-chmn, Lab Friends of Isr; numerous other; fmr: treas, Oxford J Cong; dep for Oxford, Bd of Deps; hon F, Jesus Coll, Oxford; council, Oxford Soc; clubs: RAF; United U; Oxford; Cambridge; others. Home: Wytham Abbey, Oxford, Eng. Office: 27 Chester, London SW1, Eng.

SEGAL, Shmuel, Isr, actor; b. Pol, Dec 14, 1924; in Isr since 1934; att: Habima Dramatic Sch; London Acad of Music and Arts; m. Nediva Tidhar; c: Guri, Ami. Actor with Habima Theater; maj roles: Comedy of Errors; Taming of the Shrew; Merchant of Venice; Twelve Angry Men; The Caine Mutiny; The Enemies; Snutit beHof Matumba; Shmo Holech le Fanav; Shalom Aleichem Trio, Die Kleine Mentschelach; toured with Habima: NY; London; Paris; Vienna; one-man shows on stage, radio; numerous records. Home: 16 Blum Blvd, Tel Aviv, Isr. Office: Habima Theater, Tel Aviv, Isr.

SEGAL, Simon, US, attorney, organization exec; b. Radziechow, Pol, Mar 21, 1909; s. Schmarje and Rose (Pfeffer); licencié en droit, U Paris, 1929; D en droit, 1932; dipl, Ecole Libre des Sciences Politiques, Paris, 1930; postgrad, Columbia U; m. Sonia Sorokine, Dec 24, 1940. Dir, fgn affairs dept, AJComm, since 1940; mem: Carnegie Endowment for Intl Peace, 1935-36; Fgn Policy Assn, 1937-39. Author: L'individu en droit international positif, 1932; Le domaine reśervé, 1934; New Poland and the Jews, 1938; New Order in Poland, 1940; Problems of Minorities Regarding an International Bill of Right, 1943. Home: 130 Judson Ave, Dobbs Ferry, NY. Office: 165 E 56 St, New York, NY.

SEGAL, Stanley Solomon, Eng, educator; b. London, Eng, Oct 11, 1919; s. Fredil and Chavid (Gershcovitz); tchr cert, Goldsmith Coll Educ, U London, 1950; dipl, educ of handicapped children, Inst of Educ, London, 1955; MEd, Inst of Educ, Leicester, 1970; m. Tamar Shuster, Apr 29, 1945; c: Valerie Sinason, Alan. Prin, Ravenswood Village Settlement, since 1970; juvenile magistrate, since 1961; headmaster: Spec Sch for Educationally Subnormal Pupils, 1959-66; Spec Sch for Handicapped Pupils, 1966-69, both Inner London Auth. Cpl, Royal Signals, 1940-46. Hon prin, Coll of Spec Educ; educ cons, Advisory Cen for Educ, Cambridge; fmr: gen secy, chmn, Guild Tchrs Backward Children; mem, adv comm, Spec Educ; initiated, org: natl conf, Backward Child, 1957, 1958, 1959; intl conf, Backward Child, County Hall, London, 1960; led delg, Brit Council to Study Spec Educ in USSR; lectr, broadcaster, on handicapped children, 1951-69; mem: Natl Union Tchrs; Working Party on Needs of Handicapped, Natl Bur for Coop in Child Care. Author: 11 + Rejects?, 1961; The Space Age series, 1964; Teaching Backward Pupils, 1966; No Child is Ineducable, 1968; ed: Forward Trends in the Treatment of the Backward Child, Backward Children in USSR; The Working World series, 1966; contbr numerous articles to profsl jours. Recipient: Life Pres, Guild Tchrs of Backward Children, 1969. Home: 11 Ravensdale Ave, Finchley, London N12, Eng. Office: Ravenswood Village, Crowthorne, Berkshire, Eng.

SEGAL, Zeev, Isr, engineer; b. Minsk, Russ, Nov 17, 1913; s. Nahum and Esther (Berman); desc of Rabbi Shmuel Mohilever, found Mizrachi Movement; BSc, 1st class hons, Vic U, Manchester, 1936, MSc, 1937; AFRACS, RAF Service Coll, 1942; m. Claire Rosenberg, Jan 3, 1943; c: Michelle Hipshman, Jonathan. Cons engr, produc efficiency methods, since 1964; cons to Isr Aviation Ind; sr erection engr, Dimona Atomic Reactor, 1962-64; sr erection and maintenance engr, Isr Elec Corp, 1951-62. Squadron leader, RAF, 1941-47; 1t col, IDF, 1948-51. Prin contribs: devl and intro into use time and lab saving method, for maintenance and overhaul of aircraft engines and parts. Found, Isr Inst of Aeronautical Sci; mem: Inst MEs, Eng; Isr Soc for Bibl Research; asso f, Royal Aeronautical Soc; fmr: chmn, Tel Aviv br, ME's Assn; vice chmn, Manchester Youth ZC; treas, Manchester Tarbut Soc; Tel Aviv Country Club. Author: The Jet Propulsion Engine, 1959; contbr tech articles and brochures on efficient use of manpower, rationalization of ind, ind safety, aviation, productivity. Recipient: Kaplan Productivity Prize, Isr Inst of Productivity, 1958. Hobbies: long-distance swimming; Bible Quizzes. Home and office: 11 Kish St, Ramat Gan, Isr.

SEGAL, Zev, Isr, social psychologist; b. Nahalal, Isr, May 28, 1925; s. Rafael and Rivka; BS, George Williams Coll, Chgo, Ill, 1955, MS, 1956; PhD, NYU, 1962; m. Ruth Dubi, Sep 7, 1948; c: Rafi, Adi. Dir, div comm work, Haifa Munic, since 1964; fmr: instr in cmty org, Paul Baerwald Sch of Social

Work, Heb U, Jerusalem. Lt, IDF, 1947-51. Mem: Natl Council on Family Relations, US. Author: The Stork's Secret — How We Are Born and Grow, 1966; The Secret of Youth, a guide to adolescents, 1968; The Secret of Marriage, 1968. Hobbies: photography, sculpture. Home: 18A Maneh Hill, Haifa, Isr. Office: Munic of Haifa, Isr.

SEGAL, Zvi, Isr, advocate, notary; b. Leningrad, Russ, Nov 9, 1908; s. Zeev and Klara; MJ, Latvian U, Riga; m. Lea Tschetchik; c. Zeev. Pvt practice since 1947; secy gen, Natl Sick Fund, 1936-44. Lt, IDF, 1948-49. Chmn, Isr-Finland Assn; acting chmn, cen court, Lib Party; bd mem: legal adv, Latvian and Estonian Immigrants Assn; Isr Philharmonic Orch Assn; mem, B'nai B'rith, Isr. Home: 25 Zamenhoff St, Tel Aviv, Isr. Office: 88 Rothschild Blvd, Tel Aviv, Isr.

SEGALL, Harold N, Can, physician, educator; b. Jassy, Rum, Oct 18, 1897; s. Fischel and Creina (Solomon); in Can since 1899; MD, MC, McGill U, 1920; f: research, Path Dept, Royal Vic Hosp, 1921-22; Henry D Walcott, Harvard U, 1922-23; research, Dalton Scholar, card dept, Mass Gen Hosp, 1923-24; att U Coll, London, Eng, 1924-26; m. Dorothy Caplin, Mar 6, 1934; c. Carol, Jack. Asso prof med, McGill U, since 1949; cons phys, dept card, J Gen Hosp, since 1960, sr phys, chief card dept, 1934-60; hon att phys, Montreal Gen Hosp, since 1960, asso phys, 1945-60. Chmn educ comm, Que Heart Found, since 1958, fmr pres; mem: Phys Soc of Gt Brit; AHA; Montreal Clinical Soc; Can Phys Soc; Sigma Xi; Zeta Beta Tau; FACP; fmr: pres, Can Heart Assn; vice-pres, Natl Heart Found of Can; chmn, Louis Gross Memorial Lectr Comm. Contbr to med jours. Home: 4100 Cote des Neiges Rd, Montreal, Can. Office: 5845 Cote des Neiges, Montreal, Can.

SEGALMAN, Ralph, US, social worker; b. NYC, July 15, 1916; s. Samuel and Celia (Lasky); BA, U Mich, 1937, MSW, 1944; PhD, Cen for Hum Relations and Comty Studies, NYU, 1966; m. Anita Cohen, 1940; c. Robert, Ruth, Daniel. Asso prof, social work, U Tex, Austin, since 1967; field work: Consultation Bur of Detroit; Bur Old Age Assistance, Ann Arbor, both 1937-39; J case worker, Child and Family Service, Peoria, Ill, 1939-42; state dir, JWB-USO, Ariz, 1942-43; exec dir, J Fed, Springfield, Ill, 1943-45; dir, Vienna area, JDC, attached to US forces in Aus, 1945-46; intake sup, cons on ref settlement, J Soc Service Bur, Chgo, Ill, 1947; exec dir, J Fed and Cen, Sioux City, Ia, 1947-51; lectr, social work, Morningside Coll, Sioux City, 1948-52; exec dir, J Fed, Waterbury, Conn, 1953-61; exec dir, JCC and Cen, El Paso, Tex, 1961-65; asso prof sociol, U Tex, El Paso, 1965-67. Dir, Isr Bond Campaign, 1955-58; vice-pres, United Cerebral Palsy, 1957, chmn, prog services, 1953-58; conducted Crippled Childrens' Study for State of Isr, 1958; chmn: bd, mem inst, Comty Council, 1959, profsl workers inst, 1958; Conn Chap, comm on intl social work, Natl Assn Social Workers; mem: Amer Sociol Assn; Amer Psych Assn; Amer Assn for Psych Study Social Issues; Amer Assn Social Workers; Amer Assn Group Workers; Assn for Study Comty Org; Natl Conf J Communal Service; Natl Assn J Cen Workers; J Natl Workers Alliance; Conn State Comty Relations Council, 1953-58; Acad Cert Social Workers; bd, Waterbury Heb Free Loan Assn; Waterbury Comm to Employ Physically Handicapped, 1958; B'nai B'rith, 1954-58; regional exec, ADL bd, 1957-58; Alpha Kappa Delta. Contbr to profsl and Anglo-J jours. Recipient: State of Isr Medal, 15th Anniversary, 1963. Home: 1906 Rio Grande, Austin, Tex. Office: Sch of Social Work, U of Tex, Austin, Tex.

SEGALOFF, Walter Sherman, US, merchant; b. NYC, July 1, 1931; s. Charles and Bess (Moscowitz); BA, U Mich, 1954; m. Jacki Drucker, Sep 19, 1956; c. David, Peter. Pres, Va Speciality Stores, since 1958. Vice-pres, Newport News JCC; pres, Newport News J Comty Cen; mem: natl bd, young leadership bd, UJA; Sigma Alpha Mu; frat U of Mich; several comty orgs. Recipient: retailer of year, 1960; outstanding man of year, City of Newport News Jr C of C. Home: 30 Mac Irvin Dr, Newport News, Va. Office: 32 and Washington Ave, Newport News, Va.

SEGEL, Jacob Yonny, US, artist, teacher; b. NYC, Feb 14, 1912; s. Solomon and Rose (Greenblatt); BSS, CCNY, 1933, MS, 1946; m. Truda Rosenblat, June 6, 1934; c. Shari. Asst prof, mech drawing, art appreciation, Bx Comty Coll, NY; art instr: New Sch for Social Research; Pratt Inst; ind designer: Donald Deskey Assos, 1946-47; Weldwax Corp, 1947; Kastar, 1952-53; DuPont, 1953-58. USAF, tech instr, convalescent training program, 1943-45. Works exhibited: Metrop Mus Art;

Amer Mus Natural Hist; Brussels World's Fair. Mem: Coll Art Assn; Artist-Craftmen of NY. Author: Drafting Made Simple, 1962; contbr to art jours. Home: 9 Stuyvesant Oval, New York,NY. Office: Bx Comty Coll,120 E 184 St, Bronx, NY.

SEGEL, Louis J, US, rabbi, organization exec; b. Leeds, Eng, Sep 14, 1896; s. Isaac and Amelia (Friedman); in US since 1906; BA, Mount Union Coll, 1918; BH, HUC, 1927, ordained rabbi, 1929; m. Isabelle Sands, Oct 15, 1930; c. Celia. Ret; exec dir, J Comty Relations Council, Alameda and Contra Costa Cos, Cal, 1944-62; rabbi: Anderson, Muncie and Marion Congs, Ind, 1929-30; Joplin, Mo, 1930-32; Panama, Rep of Panama, 1940-44. US Army, 1918. Mem: AJComm; B'nai B'rith; First Heb Cong, Oakland. Contbr to SF Chronicle and J mags. Home: 1818 Gouldin Rd, Oakland, Cal.

SEGOE, Ladislas, US, consulting engr, city planner; b. Debreczen, Hung, Aug 17, 1894; s. Adolph and Leona (Kohn); in US since 1921; dipl engr, Tech U, Budapest, 1919; m. Vilma Czittler, Mar 24, 1926. Head, Ladislas Segoe and Assos, Cincinnati, O, since 1928; cons on city or regional plans for: Cincinnati; Detroit; Pittsburgh; Seattle; SF; Buffalo; Rochester; state planning commns; fed agcys; engr, town planning projects, Yugo Govt, 1920-21; res city planner, Tech Adv Corp, NY, 1921-24; jr mem co, 1924-26; exec secy, planning engr, Cincinnati City Planning Commn, 1926-28; lectr: postgrad sch, public admn, U Cincinnati, 1930-42; Sch of City Planning, Harvard U; Carnegie Inst Tech; visiting prof, grad sch, div city planning, U Cincinnati, 1966-67; US delg, Inter-Amer Cong Munics, Santiago, Chile, 1941. Pres, Albert Bettman Found Comty Planning; mem: bd, Better Housing League, Gtr Cincinnati Inc; Amer Soc Planning Officials; Amer Inst Cons Engrs; Amer Soc CEs; Amer Inst Planners; Inst Traffic Engrs; fmr: dir, urbanism comm, Natl Resources Comm; mem, jury of awards, Carson, Piere, Scott and Co, centenniel competition for redevl downtown Chgo. Co-author: Our Cities, Their Role in the National Economy, 1937; Urban Planning and Land Politics, 1939; Urban Government, 1939; prin author, Local Planning Administration, 1941; contbr profsl articles. Recipient: Dist Service award, Amer Inst Planners, 1957, 50th Anniversary award, 1967. Home: 1767 E McMillan St, Cincinnati, O. Office: 811 Gwynne Bldg, Cincinnati, O.

SEGRE, Attilio Isidore, It, pharmacist; b. Finale Ligure, It, May 8, 1904; s. Emanuele and Olimpia (Treves); DCh, U Torino, 1924; Pharm, U Ferrara, 1926; m. Sara Colombo, Sep 6, 1936; c. Renata, Ariel, Claudio. Pharm, Perrucchetti Pharm, since 1963; export mgr, Farmitalia (Montedison), 1948-63. Vice-pres, KH, It. Home: Via San Maurilio 23, Milan, It. Office: Farmacia Perrucchetti, Piazzale Perrucchetti 4, Milan, It.

SEGRE, Augusto Moshe, It, educational dir; b. Casale Nonferrato, It, Apr 1, 1915; s. Ezechiele and Sornaga (Bendetta); ordained rabbi, Rabb Coll, Rome; PhD, law, U Rome; m. Iris Steinmann, May 31, 1949; c. Maurizio, Tamar. Educ dir, Union J Comtys, It, since 1959; adv to J Comty, Asti. Partisan forces WW II. Fmr: mem: DELASEM, aid to J refs; Aliyat Hanoar; secy gen, ZF, It. Author: series of books on J holy days; prefaces to many books on Bibl hist; about 200 articles to periodicals. Hobbies: books, hist, phil. Recipient: cert granted by Marshal Alexander. Home: 55 Via del Conservatorio, Rome, It.

SEGRE, Beniamino, It, mathematician, educator; b. Turin, It, Feb 16, 1903; s. Samuele and Leonilda (Segre); DMath, U Turin, 1923; D honoris causa, U Bologna; m. Fernanda Coen, Mar 20, 1932; c. Sergio, Silvana Cicala. Prof, higher geometry and dir, Inst of Math, U Rome, since 1950; prof: U Bologna, 1931-39; U Manchester, Eng, 1942-46. Found, Unione Matematica Italiana; pres, Accademia dei Lincei; mem: Société Mathématique de France; Amer Math Soc; Tensor Soc; Accademia Nazionale dei XL, Accademia delle Scienze, Turin; Société Royale, Liège, Belgium; Accademia delle Scienze dell'Instituto di Bologna; Natl Acad of Sci, Buenos Aires; Instituto Lombardo di Scienze e Lettere; Royal Acad of Belgium; Accademia Petrarca di Arti e Scienze; hon mem: London Math Soc; Palatinum Lions Club. Contbr: numerous publs in math. Recipient: Gold Medal: for Culture and Sci of It Rep; from Acad Natl de XL; Gold Pen, It Rep. Hobbies: chess, swimming, hiking. Home: Viale Ippocrate 79, Rome, It. Office: U of Rome, It.

SEGRE, Bruno (pseudonym **Sicor**), It, attorney, journalist; b. Turin, Sep 14, 1918; s. Dario and Ottavia (Avondo); LLD,

U Turin, 1940. Pvt practice since 1948; a leading defender of conscientious objectors before It mil courts. Political prisoner, 1942; mem, Justice and Liberty underground movement, Piedmont, established comm to help wounded and imprisoned J, 1944-45. Pres, It Fed Cremation; Piedmont delg, Citizens of World; mem: leader comm, It Socialist party; cen comm, Associazione Nazionale Libero Pensiero, Giordana Bruno, Rome; admn political candidate, Turin and Piedmont, 1951-53; delg to intl cong: Fribourg, 1948; London, 1950; Geneva, 1951; E Berlin, 1952; Bern, 1953; Warsaw; Stockholm; Moscow; Helsinki; Chgo. Found, ed, L'Incontro, monthly mag, since 1949; contbr to political jours. Home: Via Gaidano 8, Turin, It. Office: Via della Consolata 11, Turin, It.

SEGRE, Emilio G, US, nuclear physicist, educator; b. Tivoli, It, Feb 1, 1905; s. Giuseppe and Amelia (Treves); in US since 1938; PhD, U Rome, 1928; m. Elfriede Spiro, Feb 2, 1936; c: Claudio, Amelia, Fausta. Prof, physics, U Cal, Berkeley, since 1946; asst prof, physics, U Rome, It, 1930-32; asso prof, 1932-35; prof, physics, and dir, lab, U Palermo, It, 1935-38; research asso, radiation lab, U of Cal, 1938-43; physicist, group leader, Los Alamos Lab, 1943-46; visiting prof, U of Ill, 1951-52; Rockefeller f, 1931-32; Fulbright f, 1951; Guggenheim f, 1958. Prin contrib: co-discoverer: Slow neutrons; elements: Technetium, Astatine, Plutonium, Antiprotons. F, Amer Physical Soc; mem, bd govs, Tel Aviv U; trustee, U Research Assn, Wash, DC; mem: Natl Acad Sci; Accademia Nazionale Lincei, Roma; Uruguayan Soc of Sci; Heidelberg Akademie der Wissenschaften. Ed: Experimental Nuclear Physics, 1951-55; contbr to profsl publs. Recipient: title, hon prof, S Marcos U, Lima, Peru, 1954; Hoffmann Medal, Deutsche Chemische Gesellschaft; Donegani Lecturer, Accademia dei Lincei, Italy, 1951; Cannizzaro Medal, Accademia Lincei; Nobel Prize in Physics, 1959; Grande Ufficiale Merito della Repubblica, It. Office: U of Cal, Berkeley, Cal.

SEGRE, Marco C, It, industrialist, author; b. Tivoli, It, Sep 28, 1893; s. Giuseppe and Amelia (Treves); DEngr, U Rome, 1919; m. Rosa Guastalla, Feb 11, 1926; c: Renata Trucchi, Giuseppe, Claudio. Mgn dir, Società Cartiere Tiburtine, Rome, since 1929; pres, Società Cartiere Sibilla, since 1923; fmr: asst prof, mech ,U Rome, 1919-23. Off, It Air Force. Vice pres: Gen Confd of It Ind, Rome, since 1945; It PR Assn, since 1956; Soc Cartiere Tiburtine e Industrie Affini, since 1959; Società Carte ed Affini, Rome, since 1959; pres: Industrialists Union of Lazio, since 1944; Comitato Nazionale per l'organizzazione Scientifica, since 1959; mem mgmt comm, Geneva; mem: Consiglio Superiore di Statistica, since 1957; Commissione Ministeriale per la Instruzione Professionale, Min for Public Educ, since 1961; Comitato Internazionale dei Prezzi, since 1946; Intl Acad of Mgmt, Geneva; councillor, Soc for Financial Initiative, since 1957; Instituto Nazionale Previdenza Dirigenti Aziende Industriali; club, Rotary. Author: Corso di Esercitazioni Collaudo dei Motori, 1918; Un Nuovo Freno Dinamometrico, 1920; I Tormenti Vibratori dei Motori Aeronautici, 1921; Sulla Misura a Distanza del Livello di un Liquido Contenuto in un Serbatoio, 1921; Industria e Confindustria, 1949; Iniziativa Pubblica ed Iniziativa Privata di Fronte alla Disoccupazione dei Paesi Sovrapopolati, 1953; L'Organizzazione Scientifica ed il suo Divenire, 1963; L'Economia Italiana nel Dopoguerra ed i suoi Sorluppi Futuri, 1963. Recipient: Cavaliere di Gran Croce al Merito della Repubblica Italiana, 1952; Gavaliere al Merito del Lavoro, 1953; Gold Medal, for services to profsl instrn, Min of Public Educ, 1960. Home: Via Taramelli 15, Rome, It. Office: CNOS, Foro Traiano 1A, Rome, It.

SEGY, Ladislas, US, art collector and dealer, author; b. Budapest, Hung, Feb 10, 1904; s. Bela and Malvine (Sohr); in US since 1936; hon DLitt, Cen State Coll, Wilberforce, O, 1953; m. 2nd, Helena Muniz de Souza, 1957. Dir, Segy Gal, NYC, specializing in Afr art, since 1960; lectr, Afr sculpture ·in Amer Colls and Us, and in S Amer. Collections exhibited in colls and mus in US and Can. F, Royal Anthropological Inst, London; mem: Intl Afr Inst; Royal Afr Soc, both in London; Intl Soc for Gen Semantics; Amer Soc for Esthetics; NY Acad of Sci; Société des Africanistes, Paris. Author: African Sculpture Speaks, 1952, 3rd ed, 1961; African Art Studies, 1958; African Sculpture, 1959; co-produc, film, Buma-African Sculpture Speaks; contbr numerous papers pertaining to Afr art. Home: 35 W 90 St, New York, NY. Office: 708 Lexington Ave, New York, NY.

SEID, Ruth (pen name, **Jo Sinclair**), US, author; b. Bklyn,

NY, July 1, 1913; d. Nathan and Ida (Kravetzky). Author: Wasteland, 1946; Sing at My Wake, 1951; The Changelings, 1955; Anna Teller, 1960; included in anthols: A Treasury of American Jewish Stories;Cross Section; Social Insight Through Short Stories; This Way to Unity; America in Literature; Of the People; Theme and Variation in the Short Story; The American Judaism Reader; Tales of Our People, Great Stories of the Jew in America; contbr to natl mags, J mags. Producer: The Long Moment, play, 1950; radio plays, Cleveland radio sta, for ARC, 1941, 1943, 1947; The Jane Wyman Show, TV, 1957; asst dir, PR, ARC, 1942-46. Mem: Authors Guild Amer. Recipient: Harper Prize Novel Award, for Wasteland, 1946; 2nd Prize, Fund for Rep, natl TV competition in civil liberties, for 1-hour play, We Can't Be the First, 1955; Ohioana Libr Book Award, 1956; Harry and Ethel Daroff Memorial Fiction Award, J Book Council Amer, 1956; Cert of Recognition, Brotherhood Week, NCCJ, all three awards for novel The Changelings; Ohioana Libr Book Award, for novel Anna Teller, 1961; lit award, Cleveland Arts Prize, 1961; Wolpaw Playwriting Grant, J Comty Cen, Cleveland, O. Home and office: 8351 Fairmount Rd, Novelty, O.

SEIDEL, Hilel, Isr, journalist, labor exec; b. Krakow, Pol; s. Eliezer and Debora (Ausübel) Langerman; m. Golda Syrkin; c: Dorith, Dita. Mem, exec bur, Histadrut; head, pensions dept, and chmn, Ind Lib Workers Movement, all since 196i. Ghetto fighter during WW II; after war, head of: Z Youth Movement Akiva; Aliya B, in Pol. Mem: council, Yad Veshem Libr; exec bur, Lib Party. Hobby: philately. Home: 31 Brandeis St, Tel Aviv, Isr. Office:93 Arlozorov St, Tel Aviv, Isr.

SEIDEL, Joseph, Isr, business exec; b. Zamosc, Pol, June 4, 1920; s. Moshe and Esther (Eisenberg); in Isr since 1950; dipl econ, Econ HS, Pol. Chmn, exec, Inst for Petroleum Research and Geophys, since 1966; mgn dir, Transp Co Ltd, Tel Aviv since 1969; bd dirs: Timna Copper Mines, mem exec; Inst for Petroleum Research and Geophys Assn; Isr Mining Inds Inst for Research and Devl; Negev Ceramic Materials Ltd; dir gen, Min of Devl, 1966-68; mgn dir, Hachofer Ltd, 1964-66; mgr, Rassco Ltd, 1952-64; bd dirs, Isr Ports Auth, 1966-68; fmr chmn of various govt commns; mem, comm for absorption of 20,000 families, JA, 1968. Author: Project Evaluation, Organization Systems. Spec interests: classical, folk music; swimming; tennis; chess. Home: 3 Golani St, Ramat Chen, Isr. Office: 3 Achuzat Beit, Tel Aviv, Isr.

SEIDELMAN, Morris Bernard, US, social worker; b. Libau, Latvia, Feb 13, 1902; s. Michael and Sarah (Fleischman); in US since 1905; LLB, St John's U, 1930; BA, CCNY, 1940; MSW, Columbia U, 1943; PhD studies; m. Sara Farber, Apr 3, 1932. Exec dir, Family Services, since 1963; instr, Utica Coll since 1959. Fmr pres, Natl Assn Social Workers; state treas, Exec Forum, Family Service, since 1966; mem: prog comm, NY State Wfr Council, 1967-70; Mohawk chap, Natl Assn Social Workers; mem: Cen Homemaking Service; Utica Comty Chest and Planning Council. Author: The ORT Story, 1953. Spec interests: oil painting, sociol, dramatics. Home: 46 Emerson Ave, Utica, NY. Office: 209 Elizabeth St, Utica, NY.

SEIDEMANN, Hans, US,obstetrician and gynecologist; b. Fraustadt, Ger; s. Simon and Bianca (Goldstaub); in US since 1933; att Us: Breslau, 1920-22; Munich, 1922-23; Berlin, 1923-24; MD, Breslau U, 1926; m. Ilse Cohn, Feb 26, 1933; c: Robert. Sr visiting phys, obstet and gyn, Mt Sinai Hosp, since 1953; on staff since 1935. Maj, US Army, 1924-46. Dipl, Amer Bd Ostet and Gyn; F, Amer Coll Surgs; mem: AMA; Cleveland Obstet and Gyn Soc; Amer Coll Obstet and Gyn. Contbr to med jours. Home: 19425 Van Aken Blvd, Shaker Heights, O. Office: 14077 Cedar Rd, Cleveland, O.

SEIDEN, Norman Jack, US, business exec; b. Worcester, Mass, Feb 24, 1925; s. Samuel and Anna (Schweitzer); BS, Purdue U, 1945; m. Barbara Cohen, Mar 3, 1946; c: Stephen, Pearl, Mark. Pres: Melnor Inds Div, Beatrice Foods Co; Melnor Mfg; Everain Inds; Carol Ind Park Inc; Bridge Ind; bd dirs: Jaclyn; Lexington Research Inves. Pres, United J Fund, Englewood; vice-pres: Young Pres Org, E area; Englewood J Comty Cen; J Wfr Council; natl bd, Isr Bonds; co-chmn, ADL; asst treas, Amer Technion Soc; exec comm, Stonehurst Home Owners Assn; adv bd, War Peace Report; mem: Amer Soc ME; Pi Tau Sigma Engr Soc. Home: 54 Oxford Dr, Tenafly, NJ. Office: 1 Carol Pl, Moonachie, NJ.

SEIDENFELD, Morton A, US, psychologist, educator; b. Spokane, Wash, Sep 21, 1906; s. Samuel and Fanny (Gross);

BS, U Wash, 1927; MS, U of Pa, 1933, PhD, 1937; m. Miriam Clair, 1932; c: Carol, Sue-Ellen. Dep asst admnr, off research, demonstration and training, Social and Rehab Service, HEW, since 1960; co-dir, psych clinic, St Christopher's Hosp for Children, Phila, 1934-38; dir: psych services and rehab, Natl J Hosp, Denver, Colo, 1938-40; rehab, TB Inst of Chgo and Cook Co, Ill, 1940; psych services and public educ, Natl Found for Infantile Paralysis, NYC, 1945-60; prof, clinical psych, Yeshiva U, NY, 1949-56, asso dir, psych clinic, 1950-56. Col, US Army, first clinical psych, Off Surg Gen, 1940-45. Dipl, clinical psych, Amer Bd Examiners in Profsl Psych; f: Amer Psych Assn; Amer Orthopsycht Assn; AAAS; Amer Public Health Assn; NY Acad Scis; Acad Psychosomatic Med; Soc for Projective Techniques and Rorschach Inst; Soc of Public Health Educs; Royal Soc of Health, Eng; fmr chmn: perm resolutions comm, Conf of World Orgs Interested in the Handicapped; adv guidance bd, Fifty-Two Assn; comm on cert, NY State Psych Assn; vice-chmn, Natl Conf for Coop in Health Educ; cons, delg, Pres White House Conf on Children and Youth, 1950; mem: commn on J educ, UAHC; NY adv bd, ADL; comm on chaplaincy, JWB, 1944; Amer Psychosomatic Soc; E Psych Assn; Natl Acad of Rel and Mh; Intl Soc for Wfr of Cripples; Intl Union for Health Educ of Public; Va Acad Sci; Cen Syn, Nassau Co, NY, fmr pres; Res Offs Assn; Phi Delta Kappa; Psi Chi; asso, Amer Coll of Card; delg, Amer Natl Council for Health Educ of Public, 1958; club, Cosmos. Mem, ed bd, Quarterly Rev of Neur and Psycht; contbr to psych and educ publs. Recipient: B'nai B'rith Service award; 52 Assn award; Commendation Ribbon, US Army; Superior Service award, HEW. Hobby: photography. Home: 5410 Connecticut Ave, Washington, DC. Office: HEW, Washington, DC.

SEIDENMAN, Ludwik, US, attorney; b. Warsaw, Pol, Dec 28, 1906; s. Szymon and Helen (Erlich); in US since 1943; LLM, U Warsaw, 1928; LLB, cum laude, NY Law Sch, 1957; m. Ida Heller, July 26, 1931. Atty, NYC; mem, Pol emb staff, USSR, 1941, legal counselor, 1942-43; corresp, JA, WJC, J Lab Comm, USSR, 1941-43; vice-consul, Pol Consulate Gen, Jerusalem, 1943; Pol consul, NYC, 1945. Hon counsel, Pol Inst of Arts and Sci in Amer; dir, Pol Assistance Inc; vice-pres, Club of Pol J, NYC; trustee, Wanda Roehr Found; mem: NY Bar; NY Co Lawyers Assn. Home: 1200 Fifth Ave, New York, NY. Office: 50 E 42 St, New York, NY.

SEIDLIN, Joseph, US, mathematician, educator, author; b. Pavlograd, Russ, May 23, 1892; s. Moses and Gittel (Schmigelsky); in US since 1906; BS, Columbia U, 1915, MA, 1916, PhD, 1930; hon ScD, Alfred U, 1965; m. Ada Becker, Dec 22, 1917; c: John. Fac cons, Agric and Tech Coll, SUNY, since 1965; dean, Grad Sch, Alfred U, 1947-62; prof, 1924-32, head dept, math, 1933-37, head dept educ, acting dean, Coll Lib Arts, 1959-60, on fac since 1920. Prin contrib: instrumental in establishing Cen Inst of Math, U of Concepcion, Chile. Author: Elementary College Mathematics, 1926; A Critical Study of the Teaching of Elementary College Mathematics, 1931; co-author, Spherical Trigonometry, 1943; ed, tchrs dept, Natl Math Mag; contbr articles on teaching math. F: Amer Math Soc; AAAS; mem: Math Assn of Amer; AAUP; Natl Educ Assn; Assn of School Admnrs; Sigma Xi; Phi Delta Kappa. Home: 37 Main St, Alfred, NY. Office: Agric and Tech Coll, SUNY, Alfred, NY.

SEIDMAN, Jacob Stewart, US, certified public acctnt; b. NYC, Sep 8, 1901; s. Louis and Fanny (Goldfarb); BCS, magna cum laude, NYU, 1921, BS, cum laude, 1928; JD, cum laude, Fordham U, 1924; LLM, cum laude, St Lawrence U, 1925; m. Jan Sherman, Dec 29, 1950. Partner, Seidman and Seidman, CPAs, NYC, since 1921. Capt, USNR, WW II. Delg, Natl Tax Assn Convs, 1926-29; acctnt cons, appropriations comm, US House of Reprs, 1948, 1950; mem, exec, budget and finance comms, NY Bd Trade, since 1957; adv comm, Comptroller's Off, NY State, 1956-59; acad council, advanced training cen, Internal Revenue Service, 1952-54; acctnt task force, Hoover Commn, 1953; head, US exch mission on acctnt to Soviet Union; pres: Amer Inst CPAs, 1959-60, chmn, tax comm, mem, exec council and exec comm; NY State Soc CPAs; NYU Commerce Alumni Fed; comm on econ, bd standards and planning, Living Theater; vice-chmn, disaster relief comm, NY chap, ARC, since 1948; trustee, Hosp for Jt Diseases, NYC; treas, bd trustees, Amer Acad Dramatic Arts; mem, bd dirs, Natl Parkinson Found; hon f, acctnt, LIU, 1956; cons, taxation adv bd, Pace Coll; Soc Bus Adv Professions; Amer Acctnt Assn; Natl Assn Cost Acctnts; Natl Security Ind Assn; Navy League; Council on Accountancy for State NY; natl policy adv comm, United Shareowners

of Amer, Inc; Alpha Epsilon Pi; Beta Gamma Sigma; Alpha Beta Psi; Delta Mu Delta; acctnts adv comm, law comm, FJP; clubs: NYU Men in Finance, fmr pres; Sphinx; Arch and Sq; Econ; Acctnts. Author: Seidman's Legislative History; Federal Income and Excess Profits Tax Laws, 4 vols; tax contbr, NY Times, since 1959; tax columnist, NY Herald Tribune, 1936-57; contbr to newspapers, profsl jours and theatrical mags. Recipient: John T Madden Memorial award, NYU, 1955; award for outstanding service, Jt Defense Appeal, 1956; named acctnt of year, NY State Soc of CPAs, 1956; NYU Alumni Meritorious Service award, NYU, 1962. Home: 2 E 67 St, New York, NY. Office: 80 Broad St, New York, NY.

SEIDMAN, Jeannette S, US, business exec, civic worker; b. Russ, June 15, 1887; d. Solomon and Sophia Kaplan; m. Nathan Seidman (decd); c: Lloyd, Bert, Benedict. Chmn bd, Inter-Racial Press of Amer Inc, since 1955, pres, 1948-55. Cons, Savings Bond div, US Treasury Dept; Natl Assn Women Shareholders in Amer Bus; found and prin, Kaplan Sch, Bklyn, NY, 1904-15; found and head, Bklyn Women's Forum, 1912; co-found, Comty Service League, now Child Guidance Org, 1914; leader, 23rd assembly dist, Woman Suffrage Party; charter men, League Women Voters; life mem, Brandeis U; mem, inter-commn comm, NCCJ; NY League Bus and Profsl Women, observer at intl conv, Swed, 1954; Advt Women of NY; Amer Assn for UN; Natl Council J Women; Hadassah; AJComm; clubs: NYC; Women's. Recipient: dist service medal, US Treasury, 1961. Home: 320 E 42 St, New York, NY. Office: 305 Madison Ave, New York, NY.

SEIDMAN, Lloyd G, US, business exec; b. Bklyn, NY, Sep 27, 1913; s. Nathan and Jeannette (Kaplan); BA, Columbia Coll, 1932; m Judith Kaplan, Sep 4, 1936; c: Elinor Berlin, David. Asst sup, Jack Tuikert & Partners, Inc, since 1962; vice-pres, West Weir and Bartel, and predecessor co, Donahue and Co, 1936-61; pres, educ sci div, US Inds, 1961-63; affiliated with: Montgomery Ward, 1932-34; Lord and Thomas, 1934-36. Fmr pres: Davenport Neck Assn; Columbia chap, Delta Sigma Rho; chmn: publ, New Rochelle Volunteers for Stevenson, 1956; advt, bond dr, war activities comm, Motion Picture Ind; secy, New Rochelle Dem City Comm, 1959-62; mem: exec bd, Citizens for a Better New Rochelle, 1960-62; Amer Acad Political and Soc Sci; B'nai B'rith; Delta Sigma Rho; co committeeman, Westchester Co Dem Comm, 1958-62; clubs: Columbia Players; New Rochelle Dem. Recipient: citation, Natl Soc for Programmed Instrn; citation, for outstanding service, War Agcys of US Govt. Hobby: oil painting. Home: 180 West End Ave, New York, NY. Office: 1414 Ave of the Americas, New York, NY.

SEIDMAN, Phillip K, US, certified public acctnt; b. Bklyn, NY, June 8, 1907; s. Louis and Fanny (Goldfarb); att Columbia U, 1925-27; LLB, Memphis Law Sch, 1936; m. Leone White, Oct 7, 1944. Partner, Seidman and Seidman, CPA, since 1928; lectr: Southwestern Coll, 1940; S Law Sch, 1940-41; U Tenn, 1941-42; Amer Inst of Banking, Memphis, 1942; Ill U Tax Inst, 1969. Lt cdr, USN, 1942-45. Endowed, M L Seidman Memorial Town Hall lectrs, Memphis State U. Aide de Camp, col, staff, Tenn Gov, since 1963; pres: Memphis Coll Accountancy, since 1946; Memphis State U, 1957-60; Goodwill Inds, 1965-67, mem, bd dirs, 1940-60; Family Services; bd dirs: St Joseph Hosp, since 1969; Memphis Ballet Soc; Sr Citizens; Comty Chest, Shelby Co, 1956-59; Opera Theater, 1959 and since 1967; mem, adv comm, Salvation Army; mem: Tenn State Bd Accountancy, 1950-53; Tenn Soc CPAs; Amer and Tenn Bar Assns; Assn CPA Examiners, pres, 1960; Amer Acctnt Assn; Amer Legion; VFW; Mil Order WWs; S Econ Assn; Amer Acad Political Sci; Amer Natl Theater Acad; clubs: City, Baton Rouge; Summit; Rivermont; Army and Navy, pres, 1959 and since 1968, all in Memphis. Co-author: Seidman's Legislative History, Federal Income and Excess Profits Taxes, IV vols. Home: 807 Kimbrough Towers, Memphis, Tenn. Office: 63 S Main Building, Memphis, Tenn.

SEIDMAN, Saul, US, jurist; b. Hartford, Conn, June 24, 1904; s. Nathan and Ella (Meiselman); BA, Yale, 1925, LLB, 1927; m. Lillian Hertz, Nov 26, 1925; c: Richard. US Referee, Bankruptcy Court, since 1960; mem, Bd Aldermen, City of Hartford, 1935-37; judge, Hartford Police and Juvenile Court, 1937-39. Pres, Hartford Zionist Dist, 1944-45; vice-pres: HIAS, since 1956; Hartford J Fed, since 1960; Hartford J Comty Cen, since 1950; Hartford Council Social Agcys, 1939-40; CJFWF, 1958-61; bd dirs, Hartford J Social Service, since

1940; mem, exec comm, Gtr Hartford Comty Chest, 1950-53; pres, Hospital Council Gtr Hartford, 1968-70; mem: local and natl barr assns; club, Rotary. Home: 87 Ferncliff Dr, West Hartford, Conn. Office: US Dist Court, Hartford, Conn.

SEIFTER, David, Belgium, merchant; b. Trzebinia, Pol, Dec 6, 1897; s. Abraham and Chaja (Goldberg); in Belgium since 1920; att Yeshiva Chrzanow, Pol, 1916; ordained rabbi, Hochschule für Jüdisches Wissen, Berlin, Ger, 1920; m. Rachel Mandelbaum, Jan 15, 1924; c: Edith Katz, Noemi Katz. Diamond merchant since 1925; vice-pres, J Coop Bank, since 1947. Pres, KH, since 1964; hon secy, Tachkemoni Sch, since 1945; hon dir, Magbit, since 1950; mem: comm, J Cen Found Romi Goldmuntz; Council of Comty (Shomre Hadass), since 1958; B'nai B'rith; Bourse Diamantaire; club, Diamond. Spec interests: J hist, Bible. Home: 57 Ave de France, Antwerp, Belgium. Office: 74 rue des Fortifications, Antwerp, Belgium.

SEIGLEMAN, Merton, Eng, anaesthetist; b. Salford, Eng, June 19, 1923; s. David and Bertha (Beckerman); MRCS, LRCP, U Manchester, Med Sch, 1953. Cons anaesthetist, Blackburn Group of Hosps, since 1961; spec f, Cleveland Clinic, 1960-61; mem, Manchester City Council, 1962-65. Sgt, Queens Royal Regiment, 1942-44. Mem: Assn Anaesthetists, Gt Brit and Ir; Brit Soc Med Hypnosis; Manchester Med Soc; World Volunteer Movement, Volunteer's Union, Isr; Natl Geog Soc. Hobbies: photography, amateur radio. Home: 47 Meade Hill Rd, Higher Crumpsall, Manchester, Eng. Office: Royal Infirmary, Blackburn, Eng.

SEIGLER, Max, Can, insurance broker; b. Rum, Jan 24, 1897; s. Lazarus and Dora; in Can since 1898; att Mt Royal Bus Coll; m. Anna Monblatt, May 3, 1923; c: Esther Schubert, Sheila Diamond. Pres: Max Seigler Co, ins and mortgage brokers; Granite Mortgage Corp; alderman, Montreal City Council, 1930-62, served intermittently as acting mayo, repr, city, Coronation of King George VI, 1937. Fmr chmn, Montreal Water Bd; fmr commn, Health and City Planning Bds; hon gov: Children's Memorial Hosp; J Gen Hosp; YM-YWHA; vice-pres: United Talmud Torahs, Montreal; J Hosp of Hope; dir, Can Friends Technion U; mem: Can J Cong; Zionist Men's Org; KP; Mount Royal Lodge, B'nai B'rith; 1st Natl Can leadership mission to Isr, 1960; club, Montefiore. Recipient: citation, services rendered to comty, Civic Leaders, 1950; Seigler Clinic, erected by Montreal City Council, 1931. Home: 4555 Bonavista Ave, Montreal, Can. Office: 4521 Park Ave, Montreal, Can.

SEILER, Jacob M, US, business exec; b. NYC, Dec 17, 1908; s. Louis and Rebecca (Kraut); BS, NYU, 1929, LLB, 1930; m. Muriel Pulvermacher, Sep 20, 1959; c: Elaine, Lewis, John Heffer, Jane Heffer. Chmn bd, AJ Armstrong Co, since 1962, exec since 1956; law practice, 1931-41; org partner, Newmont Factors, 1935-46. Pres, Natl Commercial Finance Conf, 1960-62, chmn, 1962-64; chmn, finance and factors group, UJA; trustee, Muscular Dystrophy Assn; mem: FJP, Jt Defense Appeal; clubs: Fairview Country, Greenwich, Conn; City Athletic, NYC. Contbr to trade jours. Hobbies: golf, skiing, swimming. Home: 1020 Seahaven Dr, Mamaroneck, NY. Office: 850 Third Ave, New York, NY.

SEITZ, Peter, US, arbitrator; b. NYC, May 17, 1905; s. Samuel and Clara (Kopelson) Seitzick; BS, NYU, 1926, JD, Law Sch, 1928; m. Myra Tolins, Dec 23, 1931; c: Michael, Johanna. Full time arbitrator since 1956; impartial chmn, Hotel Ind, NYC; govt official, 1934-51; vice-pres, Liebmann's Breweries, Inc, 1951-56. Mem: bd of govs, Natl Acad of Arbitrators; Ind Relations Research Assn, fmr mem, natl exec bd; Assn Bar, NYC; Columbia U Sem on Lab. Home and office: 285 Central Park W, New York, NY.

SELA, Matityahu Edmund, Isr, business exec; b. Aus, Mar 1, 1911; s. Siegfried and Jeanette (Weitzmann) Silberstein; in Isr since 1936; D Jur, U Innsbruck, 1934; m. Yehudith Back; c: Arnon, Ehud. Head, gen control dept, Zim Lines, since 1969, head personnel, 1966-68; police constable, Pal Police, 1937-45; lawyer, Tel Aviv, 1945-48; chief, Police, Tiberias div, 1948-49, dep chief, Tel Aviv Dist, 1950-51, head, econ dept, 1951-53, head, Haifa Dist, 1953, head, CID, police hqr, 1958-63; adv to Insp Gen, Police, Afr, 1959-60. Mem: Maccabi Cen Comm; Maccabi, Haifa; Intl Police Org. Hobbies: sport, hunting. Home: 19A Ehud St, Haifa, Isr. Office: Atzmaut St, Haifa, Isr.

SELA, Michael, Isr, scientist, educator; b. Tomaszow, Pol, Mar 6, 1924; s. Jakob and Rivka (Aleskowski) Salomonwicz; in Isr since 1941; MSc, Heb U, Jerusalem, 1946, PhD, 1954; m. Margalit Liebmann, June 20, 1948; c: Irit, Orlee. Prof, immunology, head, dept chem immunology, Weizmann Inst of Sci, mem fac since 1950. Prin contribs in fields of: structure and functions of proteins; synthetic protein models; chem basis of antigenicity. Chmn, Isr Immunological Soc; found mem, Isr Biochem Soc, fmr pres; mem: NY Acad Sci; Isr Chem Soc; Amer Chem Soc; AAAS; hon mem, Amer Soc Biol Chems; fgn mem, Max Planck Soc; mem: Eur Molecular Biol Org; Intl Cell Research Org; WHO Expert Adv Panel on Immunology; Brit Biochem Soc; Brit Soc for Immunology. Ed, New Perspectives in Biology, 1964; mem, ed bd: Weizmann Sci Press of Isr; Biochimica et Biophysica Acta; Archives of Biochem and Biophysics; Eur Jour of Biochem; Immunochemistry; Excerpta Medica; Current Topics in Microbiol and Immunology; contbr to profsl jours. Recipient: Isr Prize in Natural Scis, 1959; Rothschild Prize in Chem, 1968; Otto Warburg Medal, Ger Biochem Soc, 1968. Home and office: Weizmann Inst of Sci, Rehovot, Isr.

SE-LAVAN, Yoseph, Isr, literary critic; b. Shpola, Russ, Dec 15, 1906; s. Yaacov and Feige (Omansky) Salauan; in Isr since 1923; att Tchrs Sem, Jerusalem; MA, Heb U, Jerusalem, 1933; m. Batia Stravinsky; c: Jonathan, Amos; m 2nd, Shoshana Broitman; c: Shay, Adi. Fmr tchr, sup, lit and grammar, various Heb HS, 1940-69. Author: Roman Roland, 1942; Yosef Haim Brenner, 1947; Shmuel Yosef Agnon; The Poetry of S Shalom, 1952; Yosef Haim Brenner for the Young; World Literature, 2 vols, 1958-64. Mem: cultural org, Histadrut; Isr Writers Union; fmr: Hecalutz Org; educ org, Histadrut; Tchrs Org. Home: 91 Jabotinsky St, Tel Aviv, Isr. Office: 1 May St, Holon, Isr.

SELA WEINER, Yehudith, Isr, music teacher; b. Novy-Bohumin, Czech, Oct 27, 1923; d. Peretz and Elisheva (Tobias) Haas; in Isr since 1938; att Agric Sch Ben Shemen; kindergarten tchr cert, Tchrs Sem, Tel Aviv, 1944; music tchrs cert, Tchrs Music Sch, Tel Aviv, 1956; m 2nd, Anat Sela; one c. Composer, music and rhythm tchr, since 1956. Mem: ACUM; Isr Org of Rhythmic Tchrs. Composer: Children's Plays for Elem Sch; Pictures in Music on the Market, radio sketch, 1967; Let's Get Together, children's opera, 1958. Recipient: Cultural Award, Munic Council, Emek Hayarden. Hobbies: wood working, children's lit. Home: Kibbutz Degania B, Isr.

SELBY, Woolf, Eng, business exec; b. London, Eng, Apr 27, 1893; s. Abraham and Agie (Levy-Segal) Schwalbe; att Whitechapel Found Sch, London; m. 2nd, Kate Kloot, July 11, 1954. Hon gen and finance secy, JPA, S dist, since 1961; warden, Southend and Westcliff Heb Cong, since 1963; dir: Mortimer Box Co Ltd, since 1939; Selby Securities Ltd, since 1954. Treas, Southend and Dist Aid Soc; mem, St Leonard Lodge, Masons, Essex. Spec interests: communal activities. Home: 79 Chalkwell Ave, Westcliff-On-Sea, Essex, Eng. Office: 132 Great Portland St, London, W1, Eng.

SELDIN, Harry M, US, oral surgeon; b. Russ, Feb 4, 1895; s. Mendel and Bertha (Arsh); in US since 1905; DDS, NYU, 1918; att Rhodes Acad, NYC; PhD, Heb U, Jerusalem, 1964; m. Tena Ritter, Apr 17, 1921; c: Evelyn Rakower, Lila Kramer, Marlene Cohen. Practicing oral surg, cons oral surg: Harlem Hosp, since 1934; Peekskill Hosp, since 1942; NY Infirmary, since 1956; instr, oral surg, NYU Coll of Dent, 1919-26; chief, dept gen anesthesia, 1926-31; asst visiting oral surg, Bellevue Hosp, 1925-28; asst dir, div dent, Dept Hosp, NYC, 1928-30, dir, 1930-34. Prin contrib: designer, 18 surg instruments for removal of roots and teeth. Pres: Amer Soc Oral Surgs, 1956; Metrop NY Soc Oral Surgs, 1951-53; hon prof: maj and minor surg, Natl U, Mex; oral surg, Sch of Dent, U Montreal, Can; oral surg, Sch of Dent, U San Domingo; hon pres, Assn de Cirujanos de Cuba; "padrino", Acad Mexicana de Ciruglo Oral; hon mem: Amer Soc of Anesthetists; Federacion Odontological Latinamericana; Assn Odontological del Peru; Acad de Estomatologia del Peru; Yokosuka Dent Assn; Amer Stomatological Soc of Japan; Soc Dent de El Salvador; Omicron Kappa Upsilon; Alpha Omega; mem, bd govs: Tel Aviv U; Heb U; f: Intl Coll Dents; Intl Coll Anesthetists; Amer Coll Dents; mem: Amer Dent Assn; Dent Soc of NY; bd dirs, Amer Friends Heb U; dipl: Amer Bd Oral Surg; NY State Bd of Oral Surg. Author: Practical Anesthesia for Dental and Oral Surgery, 1934; contbr to med publs. Recipient: prize, Anesthesia Research Soc, 1934; meritorious service award, NYU, 1948; cert service, Meharry Med Coll, 1950;

decorated with Symbol of Isr, 1952; service award, Alpha Omega Frat, 1954. Home: Mill St, Putnam Valley, NY. Office: 57 W 57 St, New York, NY.

SELDOWITZ, Morton, US, physician; b. NYC, Aug 5, 1895; s. Max and Celia (Lipshitz); BS, Columbia U, 1917, MD, 1919; m. Esther Weinstein, June 20, 1926; c: Marjorie Sontag, Joan Silver. Pvt practice since 1921; dir, ped ambulatory services, cons ped, J Hosp and Med Cen of Bklyn; ped, J Hosp, Bklyn, 1927-62. Pres, ped sect, Kings Co Med Soc, 1953-54; licentiate, Amer Bd of Ped. Contbr to ped jours. Home and office: 601 E 15 St, Brooklyn, NY.

SELIG, Martha, US, social worker; b. NYC, Dec 25, 1912; d. Jacob and Sadie (Hammer) Keiser; BA, Hunter Coll, NYC, 1932; MS, CCNY, 1933; att Columbia U Tchrs Coll, 1933-38; dipl, NY Sch Social Work, 1939; m. Kalman Selig; c: Judith Rubenstein, Elaine Gould. Exec dir, Comty Services, FJP, NY, since 1968, cons, family and children's services, 1946-67; caseworker, sup, J Child Care Assns, 1938-44; exec dir, J Comty Services, LI, 1944-46. Pres, Natl Conf J Communal Service; vice-chmn, NYC Commn for Foster Care of Children; bd dirs, Council of J Feds and Wfr Funds; mem: Natl Assn Social Workers; Natl Conf Social Wfr; fmr mem: NY State Jt Leg Comm on Child Care Needs; NY State Wfr Conf. Contbr to sociol jours. Recipient: Naomi Lehman Memorial Awards, 1960. Home: 22 E 88 St, New York, NY. Office: 130 E 59 St, New York, NY.

SELIG, Rudolf L, US, attorney, business exec; b. Weinheim, Ger, Aug 24, 1889; s. Sigmund and Zerline (Rapp); in US since 1938; LLD, U Heidelberg, 1912; att: U Freiburg; U Berlin; m. Berta Siegel, Apr 5, 1925; c: Dorit Paul. Atty, pvt practice, 1917-33; adv, cons, fgn exch laws, Mannheim, Ger, 1933-37; pres: Superior Mfg Inc, 1941-54; Superior Smelting, 1945-47; Matchless Metals, 1947-54. Mem: AJCong; UJA; ZOA; Odd Fellows; B'nai B'rith; club, Amer Continental, hon pres. Contbr to mags. Hobby: translating. Home: 440 West End Ave, New York, NY.

SELIGER, Martin Menahem, Isr, educator; b. Eisenach, Ger, Sep 5, 1914; s. Max and Paula (Frank); in Isr since 1936; MA, Heb U, Jerusalem, 1940, PhD, 1955; m. Eva Hollander, Aug 18, 1937; c: Daniela Gordon, Yael Gordon. Asso prof, political sci, Heb U, Jerusalem, since 1967, chmn, dept political sci, 1963-67, on fac since 1956; tchr, headmaster, HS, Ramat Gan, Kfar Saba, 1941-54; prin, Tchr Training Coll, 1954-56. Author: European Policy in Near East, 1941; The Liberal Politics of John Locke, 1968; contbr to periodicals. Fmr council, secretariat mem, Kfar Saba br, Mapai; mem: Isr, Intl, Amer Political Sci Assns. Hobby: tennis. Home: 14 Hatibonim St, Jerusalem, Isr. Office: Heb U, Jerusalem, Isr.

SELIGMAN, Adrian, US, attorney; b. NYC, Nov 27, 1906; s. Sigmund and Mathilda (Beringer); BA, CCNY, 1927; att: Columbia U Law Sch, 1927-29; NYU Sch of Educ, 1931; JD, NYU Law Sch, 1931; m. Irene Brown, Aug 6, 1933; c: Elissa Brezner, Martin. Ret; first dep state reporter, Court of Appeals, 1953-68, dep state reporter, 1938-53; legal research, city sch law, State Comptroller's Off, 1950-51, all Albany, NY; civil service examiner, NYC, 1933-34; spec counsel, Town of Eastchester, Westchester Co, 1932-35. Fmr: pres, Tifereth Isr Inst Syn; dir, B'nai B'rith Lodge; counsel: Temple Isr; JCC; trustee, J Social Service; gifts div, ARC; co-chmn, State dir, JWF, all Albany, NY; mem: Albany Co Bar Assn; J Comty Cen. Contbr to legal jours. Homes: 15 S Main Ave, Albany, NY; Lake Luzerne, NY.

SELIGMAN, Arnold Max, US, surgeon; b. St Johnsbury, Vt, Mar 30, 1912; s. Maurice and Sylvia (Crestin); BA, Harvard Coll, 1934, MD, Harvard Med Sch, 1939; m. Blume Appel, Mar 3, 1940; c: Myron, Dale, Garry, Stanley. Surg in chief, Sinai Hosp, Baltimore, since 1954; prof, surg, Johns Hopkins U Sch of Med, since 1968, asso prof, 1954-68; asso dir, surg, research, surg, res, Beth Isr Hosp, 1949-54. Pres, Histochem Soc, 1954; mem: bd dirs, Amer Assn for Cancer Research, 1958-61, 1967-70; AMA; AAAS; Amer Acad Arts and Scis; Amer Bd Surgs; Amer Coll Surgs; Amer Surg Assn; Phi Beta Kappa; Alpha Omega Alpha; Sigma Xi; club, Surg Biol. Contbr to profsl jours. Home: Rt I, Box 208, Park Hts Ave, Owings Mills, Md. Office: Sinai Hosp, Belvedere and Greenspring Aves, Baltimore, Md.

SELIGMAN, Ben B, US, economist; b. Newark, NY, Nov 20, 1912; s. Reuben and Toby (Katz); AB, Bklyn Coll, 1934; MS, Columbia U, 1936; m. Libby Contract, Oct 1, 1938; c: Robert, Ruth. Prof, economics, dir, Lab Cen, U Mass, since 1965; wage analyst, NY State Dept of Lab, 1941-42; commodity analyst, OPA, 1942-45; mgn ed, Labor & Nation mag, 1945-46; econ, Council J Feds, 1946-53; dir, Off for J Population Research, 1949-50; lectr, econ, Bklyn Coll, 1947-49; dir, comty services, J Lab Comm, 1953-55; dir, Wash off, AJComm, 1955-56; intl affairs specialist, United Auto Workers, 1956-57; dir, dept educ and research, Retail Clerks Intl Assn (AFL-CIO), 1957-65. Mem: Amer Econ Assn; Ind Relations Research Assn, exec comm; Assn for Evolutionary Econs, pres, 1970. Author: Main Currents in Modern Economics, 1962; Most Notorious Victory: Man in An Age of Automation, 1966; Permanent Poverty: An American Syndrome, 1968; Economics of Dissent, 1968; ed: Poverty As A Public Issue, 1965; Aspects of Poverty, 1968; contbr articles on econs to mags and jours. Spec interest: social econs. Recipient: Guggenheim f, 1967; dist alumnus award of hon, Bklyn Coll, 1968. Home: 53 Wildwood Lane, Amherst, Mass. Office: 125 Draper Hall, U of Mass, Boston, Mass.

SELIGMAN, Bernard, US, physician; b. NYC, Aug 25, 1898; s. Jacob and Esther (Levy); BS, NYU, 1916; MD, NYU and Bellevue Med Coll, 1920; att U Vienna, 1928; m. Edith Duberstein, June 28, 1928; c: Stephen, Joan. Cons phys, J Hosp, Bklyn, fmr, att phys in med and endocrinology, mem staff, since 1929; phys i/c, adult health services, Cancer Detection Clinic, fmr, chief; cons phys: Kings Co Hosp, since 1966, mem staff, since 1929; Dept of Health, NYC, since 1950; mem, staff, J Chronic Diseases Hosp, 1940-50, lectr, 1947-52; att phys, Heb Convalescent Home, 1939-47; instr: LI Med Coll, 1935-39; State U Med Coll, Bklyn, 1948-69. Dipl, Amer Bd Internal Med; FACP; em mem, Amer Assn for Study Internal Secretions; hon chmn, J hosp phys, FJP; mem: Royal Soc Health; AMA; Kings Co Med Soc; NY Acad Sci; NY Diabetic Soc; Intl Soc Internal Med; NY Endocrinological Soc, fmr mem exec comm; ZOA; med adv comm, Visiting Nurses' Assn, Bklyn; bd dirs, Alumni Assn, NYU Med Cen; comm, Isr Bonds; Flatbush Bd of Review; Boy Scouts Amer; fmr: chmn, Bklyn phys, UJA; vice-pres, Prospect Park J Cen; chmn, Parents Assn, NYU Med Coll, class of 1956; club, Drs' Bklyn, fmr pres. Contbr to med jours. Hobbies: golf, painting. Home and office: 163 Ocean Ave, Brooklyn, NY.

SELIGMAN, Hans, Switz, banker; b. Frankfurt/M, Apr 11, 1899; s. Milton and Maria (Sans); in Switz since 1935; att: U Frankfurt, 1918-19; U Munich, 1921-22; m. Inge Schürch, Feb 22, 1933; c: Peter, Petra, Thomas. Pvt banker, Basle, since 1935; mem staff, banking firms: Dreyfus, Berlin, 1919-23; Mauricio Hochschild, S Amer, 1924-25; Seligman Bros, London, 1927-28; Hugo Oppenheimer & Sohn, Berlin, 1928-31. Ger Army, WW I. Mem: Pvt Bankers Assn; Swiss Bankers Assn; clubs: Rennverein; Casino Tennis; Kunstverein; Montreux Golf. Contbr yearly reports to Natl Zeitung, Bazle. Hobbies: sports, agric. Home: Kappellenstr, Basle, Switz. Office: 12 Rittergasse, Basle, Switz.

SELIGMAN, Max, Isr, attorney; b. Swansea, Wales, Oct 12, 1902; s. Haim and Becky (Jackson); in Isr since 1921; grad: Cardiff Tech Coll; Jerusalem Law Sch; m. Malka Kert, 1925; c: Aura, Sheila. Pvt practice, Tel Aviv, since 1930; agric worker, Pal, 1921-22; secy: Judea Ins Co, 1922-30; Pal Potash Ltd, 1923-29; Pal Mining Syndicate, 1923-30; leading defense atty for Resistance Movements before Brit courts in Pal.Chmn, Isr-Brit Commonwealth Assn; mem, Royal Geog Soc, London; fmr Grand Master, Masons, Isr, Isr repr grand lodges in Eng, India; co-found, Yeshurun Syn, Jerusalem; clubs: Menorah, Jerusalem, co-found; Tel Aviv Commercial and Ind, mem bd. Home: 87 Rothschild Blvd, Tel Aviv, Isr. Office: 24 Rambam St, Tel Aviv, Isr.

SELIGMAN, Raphael David, Bahamas, attorney; b. Dublin, Ir, Nov 29, 1919; s. Ephraim and Esther (Wigoder); in Bahamas since 1957; BA, Trinity Coll, Dublin, Ir, 1939, MA, LLB; m. Lorna Duke, Aug 12, 1939; c: Arthur, Helene, Edgar. Partner: Henderson & Seligman, since 1967; Elyan, Seligman & Co, solicitors, Dublin, 1942-57; acting stipendiary magistrate, circuit justice, Bahamas, 1962-67. Council mem, Nassau Heb Cong; fmr: hon legal adv: Dublin Bd Shechita; Beth Hamidrash Hagadol, Dublin; fmr pres, Dublin J Dramatic Soc; mem: Bahamas Bar Assn; Inc Law Soc of Ir; B'nai B'rith, Nassau; clubs: Kiwanis, Nassau; Royal Aero, London; Royal Nassau Sailing; Bahamas Contract Bridge, dir. Hobbies: theater, bridge, lit. Home: L'Aiglon, The Grove, Nassau, Bahamas. Office: 326 Bay St, Nassau, Bahamas.

SELIGMAN, Selig J, US, television produc; b. NYC, Jan 24, 1918; s. Jacob and Bella (Nemenoff); BA, NYU, 1937; LLB, Harvard U, 1940; LLM, Harvard U, 1941; m. Muriel Bienstock, Mar 28, 1948; c: Joel, Brad, Dale, Lucy, Adam. Pres, Selmur Producs, since 1960; exec produc, TV series: Combat; Day in Court, since 1960; Gen Hosp, since 1963; Shindig; Young Marrieds; Mickey Show; Garrison's Gorillas; exec produc, theatrical motion pictures, Smashing Time; Charly Candy; Hell in Pacific; asst to vice-pres, United Paramount Theaters, 1948-50; vice-pres, Northio Theaters Corp, 1951-53; sta mgr, KABC-TV, LA, 1953-60; vice-pres, ABC, 1958-60. Mem: Phi Beta Kappa. Author: Honey on the Hill, 1953. Home: 2606 Nottingham Ave, Los Angeles, Cal. Office: 4151 Prospect Ave, Hollywood, Cal.

SELIGSOHN, Ernst Chaim, Isr, attorney, patent atty; b. Berlin, Ger, July 4, 1903; s. Martin and Berta (Simon); in Isr since 1934; LLD, U Freiberg, 1927; assessor, U Berlin, 1928; m. Lili Katz, Dec 25, 1927; c: Ruth Tuteur, Emanuel, Uri. Patent atty since 1934; atty since 1940; mem, law firm, Berlin, 1929-33. Mem, appeal tribunal, Isr Bar; fmr pres, Supr Tribunal, Isr Bar Assn. Author: Outlines of the Law of Copyright, Trade Marks and Designs in Israel, 1963. Home: 7 Ruppin St, Tel Aviv, Isr. Office: 60 Rothschild Blvd, Tel Aviv, Isr.

SELIGSOHN, Uri, Isr, physician; b. Isr, Feb 6, 1937; s. Ernst and Lili (Katz); MD, Heb U Sch of Med, Jerusalem, 1963; m. Hana Gavrieli, Oct 8, 1958; c: Yael, Gavriel. Specialist, hematology, Tel Hashomer Hosp, since 1969; 1st asst, med, since 1968. Lt, IDF, 1954-57. Home: 3 Havazelet St, Ramat Hasharon, Isr. Office: Tel Hashomer Hosp, Tel Hashomer, Isr.

SELIGSON, David J, US, rabbi; b. NYC, June 10, 1907; s. Abraham and Bella (Silberblatt); BPd, Tchrs Inst, Yeshiva Coll, 1925; BS, Columbia U, 1929; BHL, HUC, 1933, DHL, 1954, DD, 1958; m. Minnie Cohen, July 12, 1938; c: Michelle, Jill. Rabbi: Cen Syn, NYC, since 1945; Cong Beth Judah, Ventnor City, NJ, 1933-35; Lib J Syn, Birmingham, Eng, 1935-40; Port Chester Heb Cong, Port Chester, NY, 1940-42; chaplain, NY dept Amer Legion; lectr: J hist and lit, Selly Oaks Coll, Birmingham, Eng, 1937-38; Anglo-J Lectr Bur, Eng, 1938-39. Chaplain, US Army, 1943-45. Pres: NY Bd Rabbis, 1954-55; Assn Reform Rabbis, 1952-54; chmn, Westchester br, JNF, 1941; mem: bd govs, HUC; ZOA. Home: 165 E 72 St, New York, NY. Study: 123 E 55 St, New York, NY.

SELIGSTEIN, Milton B, US, physician; b. Memphis, Tenn, June 14, 1893; s. Barney and Bertha (Schwab); MD, U Tenn, 1916; m. Mary Cook, Aug 10, 1948; c: Bernice Salomon. Semiret; phys, eye, ear, nose and throat, since 1923; staff doctor, B'nai B'rith; phys, gen practice, 1917-18. Lt, US Army, MC, 1918-19. Mem: Memphis, Shelby Co, S Tenn Med Assns; AMA; Acad Eye, Ear, Nose and Throat; Masons; Shriners. Home: 868 East Dr, Memphis, Tenn. Office: 67 Madison Ave, Memphis, Tenn.

SELIKOFF, Irving J, US, physician; b. Bklyn, NY, Jan 15, 1915; s. Abraham and Tilli (Katz); BS, Columbia U, 1935; MD, Royal Colls, Scotland, 1941; m. Celia Schiffrin, Feb 4, 1946. Att phys, Mt Sinai Hosp; prof, comty bd, dir, environmental sci lab, both Mt Sinai Sch of Med; att phys, Seaview Hosp, since 1947; training staff appointments: Mt Sinai Hosp, NY; Newark Beth Isr Hosp, NJ; Seaview Hosp, 1941-47. Prin contribs: introduced isoniazid for treatment of TB, 1952. F: Amer Coll Chest Phys, pres, NJ chap; Amer Public Health Assn; pres, NY Acad Sci, 1969; mem: Amer Trudeau Soc; AMA; fmr: chmn, sect on med, NJ Acad of Med. Author: Management of Tuberculosis, 1956; ed in chief, Environmental Research; contbr to med jours. Recipient: Lasker Award in Med. Home: 505 Upper Blvd, Ridgewood, NJ. Office: 750 Broadway, Paterson, NJ.

SELIKSON, Eleazar, Isr, jurist; b. Riga, Russ, 1906; s. Samuel and Rose; in Isr since 1936; att U Jena; DJ, U Riga; m. Sofija, 1933. Chief magistrate, Tel Aviv, since 1962; fmr atty, pvt practice. Club: Rotary, Tel Aviv-Jaffa, fmr vice-pres. Author: Euthanasia; Civil Procedure in Palestine; contbr to legal jours. Spec interests: admn law, writing, stamps. Home: 1 Gluskin St, Tel Aviv, Isr. Office: 1 Weizmann St, Tel Aviv, Isr.

SELINGER, Michael Benhaim, Isr, auditor; b. Chrzanow, Pol, Feb, 1911; s. Haim and Gusty (Michnik); in Isr since 1930; att HS, Pol; m. Esther Wahl, 1934; c: Bathsheva Zacharia, Marganit. Dir, dept control monies and acct, Histadrut, since 1959; dir of control, JA, 1954-59. Cen control bd: United Workers Party; Histadrut; found, muhtar: Kvutzat Usha; Nir Zvi settlement; dir, Youth Aliyah, Ger, Aus, 1945-48; mem, world exec, Gen Zionist Org and Youth Movement. Spec interest: agric. Home: Nir Zvi, Isr. Office: 93 Arlosoroff St, Tel Aviv, Isr.

SELLA, Eliahu, Isr, civil servant; b. Isr, Jan 31, 1937; s. Yossef and Henya Boukstein; dipl, Levinsky Tchrs Sem, 1958; LLB, Hebrew U, Jerusalem, 1964; m. Gilah Friedman, Oct 15, 1959; c: Iris, Cigalit. Adv to Pinchas Sapir, Min of Finance, dir, bur, since 1968; asst to civil service commn, govt of Isr, 1960-63; exec asst, budgeting dept, Min of Finance, 1963-66, econ asst, dir bur, 1966-68. IDF, 1955-58. Hobby: coins and medals collecting. Home: 39 Harav Berlin St, Jerusalem, Isr. Office: Min of Finance, Jerusalem, Isr.

SELLA, Itzhak, Isr, author, educator; b. Skierniewice, Pol, 1902; s. Jacob and Feiga (Rack); att: yeshiva, grad tchr, 1935; m. Chava Katariwa. Writer and lectr; fmr: dir, tchr, schs in Ger and Isr; ed, Prozdor, Isr Min of Educ publ. Author: tales for children, novels, plays; two plays performed in Heb, Ohel and Matate theaters; play trans into Yiddish, performed in US, Austr, Arg. Chmn, Org for Prozelytes and Propagation of Judaism. Recipient: Pinski Prize, Haifa, 1969, for play Hasaneigor Hagadol. Hobby: violin playing. Home: 6 Smuts Blvd, Tel Aviv, Isr.

SELLERS, Rose Zakarin, US, librarian; b. Bklyn, NY, Jan 25, 1910; d. Kalman and Ida (Voronoff) Zakarin; BA, Hunter Coll, 1930; BS, Columbia U, 1933; MA, NYU, 1950; m. Jesse Sellers, 1947. Asso libr, asso prof, Bklyn Coll, since 1947, on staff since 1934. Pres: Libr Assn, CCNY, 1963-64; Fac-Hillel Assos, Bklyn Coll, since 1968; mus div, Spec Librs Assn, 1966-67, fmr chmn, geog and map group, New York chap; adv: Metrop Bd, Phi Sigma Sigma, 1954-60; Beta Nu Chap, Phi Sigma Sigma, 1964-65; mem: Amer Mus Natural Hist; Citizens for Clean Air; Defenders of Wildlife; Friends Prospect Park; Friends South St Seaport Mus; John Burroughs Memorial Assn; Natl Audubon Soc; Natl Parks Assn; NY Zool Soc; Wilderness Soc; Amer Friends Heb U; Amer Profs for Peace in ME; Bklyn Mus; Columbia U Sch Libr Service Alumni Assn; Country Dance Soc; Folk Festival Council; Victorian Soc in Amer; Hadassah; Pioneer Women; Libr Assn, NYC; clubs: Sierra; NY Libr, fmr pres. Contbr to profsl and educ periodicals. Recipient: John Cotton Dana publicity award, 1948, 1951, 1958; Libr Relations Council award, 1958; Natl Libr Week Award, Spec Libr Assn, 1964; guest lectr, dedication ceremony, Grad Libr Sch Bldg, Heb U, 1964; Pyramid award, Phi Sigma Sigma, 1965; H W Wilson Libr Recruitment award, 1968. Hobbies: folk and square dancing, travel, home-made movies. Home: 4640 Bay Pkwy, Brooklyn, NY. Office: Bklyn Coll Libr, Brooklyn, NY.

SELLY, Meier, Isr, advocate, translator, editor; b. Russ, 1893; s. Pessach and Miriam (Beker) Bogdanovsky; in Isr since 1912; grad, Heb Tchrs Coll, Jerusalem, 1915; att U Vienna; licensed, Pal Govt Law Courses; m. Batia Goldberg, 1925; c: Mia Segal. Chief draftsman, ed, official publ, Min of Justice, since 1948; secy, Lab Party, Jerusalem, 1919-21; secy, Hechalutz World Org, 1924-26; mgn ed: Davar, daily; Am Oved, pub house, 1927-48. Lt, Turkish Army. Co-found, Histadrut; mem: Heb Lang Acad; Lab Party; Histadrut; fmr: mem exec bd, J Comty in Jerusalem; delg of Jerusalem, 1st Asefat Hanifcarim. Home: 24 Eben Ezra St, Jerusalem, Isr. Office: Min of Justice, Jerusalem, Isr.

SELTZER, Albert Pincus, US, physician; b. Rum, Aug 12, 1903; s. Pincus and Ida (Sunshine); in US since 1905; MD, Temple U Med Sch, 1928; MSc, U Pa Grad Sch of Med, 1943, DSc, med, 1944; postgrad studies: U Bordeaux, Fr; Columbia U; NYU; hon LLD, Shaw U, 1953; m. Sylvia Superstein, Nov 5, 1944; c: Benjamin, Marjorie. Asso prof, otolaryngology, U Pa Grad Sch of Med, since 1958; chief, otolaryngology: Phila Gen Hosp, since 1954; Mercy-Douglass Hosp, since 1942; Albert Einstein Med Cen, since 1941; chief, plastic and reconstructive surg: St Lukes Hosp, since 1940; Comty Hosp; att plastic surg, St Josephs Hosp; lectr, Amer Acad of Otolaryngology, since 1952; acting surg, USPHS, 1931-32. Prin contrib: inventor, 25 surgical instruments. Hon f, Portman's Found, Fr; pres, Profsl Circle and Med League; mem: AAAS; AMA; Pa State, Phila Co Med Socs; Phila Laryngological Soc; Amer, Pa

Acads Ophthal and Laryngology; Intl Coll Surgs; Amer Coll
Surgs; Amer Soc Facial Plastic Surg; Amer Otorhinologic
Soc for Plastic Surg; hon mem, Reading Ear, Eye, Nose and
Throat Soc; dipl, Amer Bd Otolaryngology; fmr pres, Phila
chap, Amer J Phys F of IMA. Author: The Plastic Surgery
of the Nose, 1949; Diseases of the Ear, Nose and Throat,
1950; Your Nasal Sinuses and Their Disorders, 1951; contributing ed: World Book Ency; to cons, Smith, Kline and
French; Family Medical Guide; contbr to med jours. Recipient: man of year, VFW, 1959; Honor Key, Amer Acad
of Otolaryngology. Home and office: 2104 Spruce St, Philadelphia, Pa.

SELTZER, Dov, Isr, composer; b. Yassi, Rum, Jan 26, 1932;
s. Joseph and Fanny (Unger) Zeltzer; in Isr since 1948; att
Haifa Conservatory; dipl, Mannes Coll of Music, NYC,
1957, BS, 1960; m. Graziella Fontana, May 14, 1948; c: Mas-
simo. Asst prof, Mannes Coll, 1957-59. Staff sgt, IDF, 1950-53.
Composer for theater, motion pictures, syms, records; for:
Megillah of Itzik Manger, 1966; Kazablan, 1967; I Like Mike,
1968; theater: Don Juan, Broken Pitcher; films: Boat of
Dreams, Isr; Fortune, Isr, Fr; 8 Following 1, Isr; Truck to
Cairo, Isr, Ger; Three Days and a Child; Tevia and His
Daughters, all Isr; My Love in Jerusalem, Isr, It; musicals:
The Revisor; Utz li Gutz li, both Isr; sym, Prophecy and
Poetry of the Bible. Mem: Amer Fed Musicians; Amer Guild
Authors and Composers; ACUM; club, Variety, Isr. Recipi-
ent: Harp of David award, composer of year, Yediot Acharo-
not, 1966, 1968. Home: 19 Hamevo'ot St, Savyon, Isr.

SELTZER, Herbert Abraham, US, hospital exec; b. Boston,
Mass, Feb 28, 1907; s. Solomon and Edith (Abramson); BA,
Harvard U, 1928, MA, 1929; ordained rabbi, JTSA, 1933,
MA, 1949; m. Judith Thurman, Mar 3, 1968. Exec dir, Home
and Hosp, Daughters of Jacob, since 1940; asst exec dir,
Brooklyn Heb Home and Hosp, 1936-40. Chmn, Admnr
Conf, 1944-46, 1968-69; treas, Natl Assn J Homes for Aging,
1967; dir, Amer Assn Homes for Aging, 1962; mem, Amer
Coll Hosp Admnrs. Home: 1155 Park Ave, New York, NY.
Office: 321 E 167, New York, NY.

SELTZER, Joseph G, US, physician; b. Toronto, Can, Oct 13,
1907; s. Hyman and Mary (Needle); in US since 1933; MD,
U Toronto, 1933; m. Margaret Harris, Dec 14, 1934; c: Carol
Rose, Georganne Greenstein. Pvt practice, phys, internist,
since 1937; mem, staff: Orange Memorial Hosp; Fla Sani-
tarium and Hosp, both since 1937; dir, Fla Natl Bank, Orlando.
Mem: Amer, Fla and S Med Assns; Orange Co Med Soc;
Intl Coll Angiology; Amer Coll Geriatrics; World Med Assn;
AHA; Amer Diabetic Assn; Cen Fla Devl Comm; Orlando
Sr C of C; Temple Lib Judaism, fmr pres; club, Dubsdread
Country. Contbr to med jours. Hobbies: swimming, golf.
Home: 711 Park Lake Circle, Orlando, Fla. Office: 725 Mag-
nolia Ave, Orlando, Fla.

SENED, Alexander, Isr, author; b. Wloclawek, Pol, July 21,
1921; s. Chaim and Jafa (Drachman) Sendrovitz; in Isr since
1934; att U Tel Aviv, 1964-67; m. Jonat Sack, June 1, 1948;
c: Joav, Itai. Chmn, Hakibbutz Hameuhad Pub House, since
1964; secy, Kibbutz Revivim. Palmach, 1941-48. Co-author:
Adama leLo Zel, 1952; Bein Hametim uVein Hahaim, 1964;
Hanisaion Hanosaf, 1968. Recipient: awards: Ussishkin, Jerusalem, 1951; Kugel, Holon, 1956; Brenner, 1965. Home:
Kibbutz Revivim, Isr. Office: 27 Soutin St, Tel Aviv, Isr.

SENED, Yonat, Isr, author; b. Czestochowa, Pol, Aug 11, 1926;
d. Joseph and Helena (Dawidowicz) Sack; in Isr since 1948;
att Underground HS, Warsaw, 1940-43; U Geneva, Switz,
1946-48; m. Alexander Sened, June 1, 1948; c: Joav, Itai.
IDF, 1948. Co-author: Adama leLo Zel, 1952; Bein Hametim
uVein Hahaim, 1964; Hanisaion Hanosaf, 1968. Awards:
Ussishkin, Jerusalem, 1951; Kugel, Holon, 1956; Brenner,
1965. Home and office: Kibbutz Revivim, Isr.

SEPPILLI, Alessandro, It, physician, educator; b. Trieste, It,
May 7, 1902; s. Giacomo and Emma (D'Ancona); MD,
U Florence, 1926; m. Anita Schwarzkopf, Sep 9, 1923; c:
Tullio. Dir, Inst of Hygiene, U Perugia; first asst, Inst of
Hygiene, U Padua, 1928-38; prof, hygiene, U Modena, 1938;
ref in Brazil, 1938-48. Mem: It Assn Hygiene and Public
Health; Società Internazionale Microbiologia; Federazione
Italiana contro TB; Società Italiana Malaie Infette e Paras-
sitarie; Associazione Italiana Idroclimatologia e Terapia Fisica;
Società Italiana Gerontologia; Società Italiana Genetica ed
Eugenica. Contbr to publs in hygiene and microbiol. Home:
Via degli Olivi 24, Perugia, It. Office: POB 324, Perugia, It.

SER, Isaac, Isr, physician; b. Lodz, Pol, Oct 16, 1908; s. Mena-
hem and Ita (Kopelman); MD, U Strasbourg, Fr, 1932;
m. Sophie Kurower, Aug 17, 1939; c: Hedva. Cons phys,
internal diseases and diabetes, Cen Clinic, Kupat Holim,
Tel Aviv, since 1949; head, Inst for Postgrad Studies, IMA,
Tel Aviv, since 1964; mem staff, J Hosp, Lodz, Pol, 1932-39;
visiting phys: Hôpital de la Pitié, Paris, 1935; Hôpital Hôtel-
Dieu, Paris, 1938; J Hosp, Getto, 1940-44; Steno Memorial
Hosp, Gentofte, Copenhagen; Hosp Beaujon, Paris; Kings
Coll Hosp, London; Hammersmith Hosp, London, all 1954-55.
Pres, Isr Diabetic Assn; mem: sci council, IMA; Med Council
Sick Fund; Isr Assn for Internal Med; Isr Endocrinology
Soc; Eur Assn for Study Diabetes; Isr repr, Intl Diabetes
Assn. Contbr to profsl publs. Home and office: 22 Mapu St,
Tel Aviv, Isr.

SERBEN, Reuben, US, dentist; b. Jan 19, 1902; s. Joseph and
Betty (Schiffman) Serebrenik; att CCNY, 1920-21; DDS,
NYU, 1925; m. Sylvia Hyman, Apr 15, 1944; c: Barry, Ro-
berta. Ret; pvt practice, 1925-65; dent surg, US Civil Service,
1955-60. Capt, US Army, Dent Corps, 1942-46. Pres, Allied
Ret Med Group, Gtr Miami, found, organizer; cdr, JWV,
Post 415; chancellor cdr, KP, U Lodge; mem: Amer Dent
Assn; 1st Dist Dent Soc; NY State Dent Soc. Contbr to
dent jours. Recipient: achievement cert, Allied Retired Med
Group, Miami, 1970; Key to Dade Co, City of Miami, 1970.
Spec interests: public speaking, group organizing, lectures,
painting. Home: 6061 Collins Ave, Miami Beach, Fla.

SERETAN, Edward L, US, physician; b. NYC, Apr 23, 1916;
s. Charles and Molly (Abrams); BS, NYU, 1936; MD, St
Louis Sch of Med, 1940; m. Enid Stollerman, Aug 31, 1947;
c: Douglas, Clifford. Asso att ophthal, Queens Gen Hosp,
since 1969; ophthal: Booth Hosp; LI J Hosp; Hillside Hosp;
pvt practice since 1950; asst att ophthal: Manhattan Eye
and Throat Hosp; Queens Gen Hosp, both 1950-56. Lt col,
US Army MC. F: Isr Acad Med; Amer Acad Ophthal and
Otolaryngology; Amer Coll Surgs; mem: AMA; Amer Bd
Ophthal; NY Acad Med; AAAS; Pan Amer Assn Ophthal;
NY State, Queens Co, Nassau Co Med Socs; Nassau Acad
Med; World Med Assn; Isr Med Soc; Barraquer Inst Ophthal;
Phi Delta Epsilon; Alpha Omega Alpha; Masons; NY Zool
Soc; Mus Natural Hist; US Power Squadron; Gt Neck
Power Squadron. Contbr to med jours. Hobbies: swimming,
boating, fishing. Home: 413 Congress Ave, E Williston, LI,
NY. Office: 111-32 76 Ave, Forest Hills, NY.

SERLIN, Yosef, Isr, attorney, legislator; b. Bialystok, Pol,
Feb 24, 1906; s. Jacob and Rosa (Leszczynski); in Israel
since 1932; MJ, U Warsaw, 1929; m. Dina Basevich, 1932;
c: Omri, Itamar. MK, fmr Lib Party, chmn, Gahal, since
1968, dep speaker, 1951-52, and since 1961; Min of Health,
1952-55; pvt law practice since 1933. Mem, world exec,
World Confd of Gen Zionists; delg to WZCs. Contbr to
newspapers. Office: 6 Ahuzat Bayit St, Tel Aviv, Isr.

SERR, David Michael, Isr, physician; b. Leeds, Eng, Aug 4,
1925; s. Harry and Jeanne (Harris), in Isr since 1951; MD,
U Leeds Med Sch, 1948; m. Meirah Zussman, 1951; c: Ronnie,
Jonathan, Yaakov. Dir, dept obstet and gyn, Tel Hashomer
Govt Hosp, since 1968, dep dir, 1964-68; asso prof, Tel Aviv U,
since 1969; house phys, dept internal med, St James Hosp,
Leeds, 1948; house surg, dep obstet, St Marys Hosp, Leeds,
1950; asst, obstet, gyn, Sharei Zedek Hosp, Jerusalem, 1951;
chief phys, dept obstet, gyn, Rothschild-Hadassah U Hosp,
Jerusalem, 1964, on staff since 1951; sr research f, U Glasgow,
1957; f, population council, Rockefeller Inst, NY, 1958; lectr,
NYU, 1958; sr lectr, Heb U, 1965-68, on fac since 1958.
RAMC venereologist, Mil Hosp, Glasgow, 1948-50. Mem:
natl comm, natl treas, Isr Soc Obstet and Gyn; Intl Fertility
Assn; Isr Soc Study Fertility; secy, Isr Soc for Biol and Med
Engr. Contbr to profsl publs. Recipient: f, Goodenday Trust,
Friends Heb U, 1957; research f, Rockefeller Inst, 1958, re-
search grant, 1960; fac prize, for research on sex chromatin
and chromosomes; research grant, Natl Council for Research
and Devl, 1966. Home: 23 Maale Habonim St, Ramat Gan,
Isr. Office: 28 Bloch St, Tel Aviv, Isr.

SETER, Mordecai, Isr, composer, educator; b. Novorossysk,
Russ, Feb 26, 1916; s. Izhak and Bracha (Kapustin) Staro-
minsky; in Isr since 1926; dipl in: composition; counterpoint;
harmony; piano, École Normale de Musique, Paris, 1937;
studied with Paul Dukas and Nadia Boulenger; m. Dina
Persner, Aug 31, 1939; c: Boaz, Aia. Prof, composition, Isr
Acad of Music, Tel Aviv, since 1950. Prin compositions:
Sabbath Cantata, 1940, performed in Isr, NYC; Festivals, for

chorus, 1947; Motets, for chorus, 1951, performed in Fr, Isr, It; Sonata, for two violins, 1952; Ricercar, for strings, 1956; Divertimento, for orch, 1958; Sinfonietta, for orch, 1958; Tikkun Hatzot, Midnight Vigil, for orch, 1959, performed in: Isr, Milan, Geneva, NYC; variations, for orch, 1959, performed in: Isr, Swed, Switz, Australia; Tikkun Hatzot, oratorio for choir, voice and orch, 1961; The Legend of Judith, ballet commissioned by Martha Graham and performed in: Isr, Yugo, Pol, Swed, Holland by Martha Graham Dance Co, 1962; Yemenite Suite, for orch and voice, 1963, performed in: Isr, Eur; Part Real Part Dream, 1964, ballet performed by Martha Graham Dance Co in US; The Daughter of Jephtah, 1965, a ballet commissioned by Bat-Sheva Dance Co, performed in Isr and abroad; Jerusalem, a sym for choir and orch, 1966, commissioned by the Isr Festival of Music; Hallet, for choir, 1967; Rounds, for orch, 1968, performed in Isr. Recipient: Tel Aviv Munic Prize, for Sabbath Cantata, 1945, for Sonata, 1954; ACUM Composers Prize, 1958 and UNESCO Prize, Paris, 1961, both of Ricercar; Italia Prize for Tikkun Hatzot, 1962; Isr State Prize for Music, 1965. Home: 1 Karny St, Ramat Aviv, Isr. Office: 7 Lilienblum St, Tel Aviv, Isr.

SETTEL, Arthur, US, government official, author; b. Bklyn, NY, Nov 26, 1911; s. Joseph and Dora (Rosenberg); BLitt, Columbia U, 1932; m. Helen Rhein, Mar, 1942; c: Mrs David Humphers, Marshal, Jonathan. Spec asst for public info, Off of Commn Customs, Treasury Dept, Wash, DC, since 1962; Near E corresp, United Press; mgn ed, Egyptian Mail; feature writer, Pal Post, all 1934-38; dep chief, public info div, US Mil Govt, Ger, 1946-49; dir, PR div, Off US High Commn, Ger, 1949-52; chief, promotion, VOA, 1952-53; audience-bldg and publicity, CBS, 1953-55; dir, PR, KLM Royal Dutch Airlines, 1955-58; cons to: US Dept of State, on Brussels World Fair; Depts of Commerce and Agric; AEC, on US exhb at New Delhi World Agric Fair, 1958-59; dir, publs, Bur Fgn Commerce, 1959-62. USAF, 1942-45. Mem: Sigma Delta Chi; clubs: Natl Press, Wash, DC; Overseas Press of Amer. Author: Year of Potsdam, 1948; This Is Germany, 1950; Calvalcade of Europe, 1960; contbr to mags and newspapers in US and Eng. Home: 3313 Ross Pl, NW, Washington, DC. Office: Bur of Customs Treasury Dept, Washington, DC.

SEVER, Mordechai Moshe, Isr, author, editor; b. Bessarabia, Russ, Jan 1, 1906; s. Moshe and Rachel (Morgenstern); in Isr since 1923; att Yeshiva; Heb Gymnasium, Bessarabia; m. Rivka Berlin; c: Amatzia, Mira. Ed, exec comm, Histadrut, since 1951; ed, Harashut Hakomit, 1954-59; lab, train sta, Haifa, 1923-24; employee, Hadassah Med Org, Haifa, 1925-43; writer, Davar newspaper, 1925-43; secy, educ insts, Kiryat Haim, 1943-46. Served IDF. I/c, info, Blood Bank, Magen David Adom. Author: Bishlihut Ha'oved haIvri, 1963; haIsh uFoalo, 1969; contbr, trans poetry; critic. Home: 13 29th of November St, Tel Aviv, Isr. Office: 93 Arlosoroff St, Tel Aviv, Isr.

SEVERE, Alis, Isr, physician; b. Berne, Switz, July 16, 1912; s. Raphael and Rebecca (Swerdlov); MD, U Lyon, Fr; m. Zina; c: Amiram. Head, med unit for civil service employees, Govt Isr, Min Health. Home: 23 Tchernichovsky St, Jerusalem, Isr. Office: Min of Health, Jerusalem, Isr.

SEVER-SVERDLIK, Isaac, Isr, author, journalist; b. Yalta, Russ, Dec 18, 1914; s. Abraham and Ziporah (Krasniansky); father, found, Bnei Yerushalaim, first Zionist org in Russ; in Isr since 1923; grad, Inst Local Govt, HS Law and Econ, 1952; BA, Bar Ilan U, 1968; m.; c: Betty Frenkel, Giora, Mordehai, Roman; m. 2nd, Lusia Ronis, 1969. Author, journalist, trans, since 1936; fmr: PR off, Petah Tikva Munic. Haganah, 1936-48; IDF, 1948-49. Mem: Natl Comm for Accident Prevention; Rotary, Petah Tikva, ed, local bull; hon mem, cen comm, Herut; fmr: secy, Profsl Civic Employee Org; active: Betar, youth movement; Herut Party. Author: Lectures in Local Government, 1951; Face of the Orient, 1946; Days Under British Military Supression, 1947; History of Petah Tikva for Students; trans of classic prose and poetry; trans into Heb: Queen of Atlantis; Pier Benuit; Of Human Bondage; Nomads of the North; Prince of Egypt; East of Eden; Captain Blood; Well of Loneliness; contbr numerous original publs in prose and poetry. Spec interests: Egyptology; ancient cultures, lit, poetry, art. Home: 42 Montefiore St, Petah Tikva, Isr.

SEYMOUR, Milton A, US, attorney; b. NYC, Dec 15, 1909; s. Abraham and Pauline (Walerstein) Sadolsky; att U Coll,

NYU, 1927-28; LLB, Bklyn Law Sch, 1931; m. Mary Denker, June 16, 1938. Mem, law firm, Katz, Robinson, Brog and Seymour, since 1968; fmr mem, Multer, Nova and Seymour, 1948-68; US Govt Agt, WW II; chief area rent atty, Bx OPA, 1943-46. Counsel, dir, Shield of David Inst for Retarded Children, since 1948; vice-chmn, Bx div, JTSA, since 1952; trustee, asst secy, chmn, law comm, Bx Leb Hosp Cen; vice-chmn, exec comm, NY bd, ADL; vice-chmn, Bx div, Fed for Support J Philanthropies, since 1960; mem: grievance comm, Assn Bar, NYC; Bx Co Bar Assn, fmr pres; NY State, Fed Bar Assns; clubs: Hampshire Country; Lawyers of of NY; fmr: asst chmn, Bx campaign, Jt Defense Appeal; chmn, Bx lawyer's div, UJA. Home: 200 E 66 St, New York, NY. Office: 10 E 40 St, New York, NY.

SHAANAN, Avraham, Isr, editor; b. Weldirz, Pol, Nov 3, 1919; s. Joseph and Sarah (Muhlrad) Friedfertig; in Isr since 1935; MA, Heb U, Jerusalem, 1943, PhD, 1945; att Sorbonne and l'École des Hautes Études Sociales, Paris, 1946-47; m. Mina Langsam, 1941 (decd); c: Joseph, Shlomo. Lit ed, Davar, daily, since 1957; asso prof, Heb and comparative lit, Bar-Ilan U, since 1967; tchr, Reali HS, Haifa, 1945-46; lectr, comparative lit, Tel Aviv U, 1957-61; cultural counselor, Isr emb, 1963-66. Maj, IAF, War of Independence. Author: Olam Hamahar, 1952; Iyunim beSifrut haHaskalah, 1952; Hilel Korin, 1955; Dictionary of Modern Literature, 1958; Trends in Modern Hebrew Literature, 4 vols, 1962-63. Recipient: Klauzner award, Tel Aviv munic, 1945; Milo Lit award, 1967. Home: 16 Zichron Yaakov St, Tel Aviv, Isr. Office: 45 Shenkin St, Tel Aviv, Isr.

SHAARI, Yehuda, Isr, attorney, legislator; b. Siret, Rum, Feb 8, 1920; s. Jacob and Lea (Klein) Scheuermann; in Isr since 1941; att U Czernowitz, 1938-39; grad, law sch, Tel Aviv U, 1955; m. Paula Breitner, Nov, 1946; c: Ariela. MK since 1961; mem, exec bur, Histadrut, head, legal, pension depts, mem, trade union dept; dep Min of Devl; chmn, bd dirs, Elec Corp of Isr; mem, Kibbutz Alonei Aba, 1941-49. Served, IDF. Mem, secretariat, Hevrat Ovdim; chmn exec comm, Lib Lab Movement; fmr: mem exec, Hanoar Hazioni, Rum; delg, Intl Fed of Trade Unions. Author: Israeli Society at the Crossroads, 1958; The Liberal Challenge of Israel, 1961; contbr to the press. Home: 5 Pinhas St, Tel Aviv, Isr. Office: 48 King George St, Tel Aviv, Isr.

SHABAN, Abel, S Afr, business exec, journalist; b. Krakinovo, Lith, June 15, 1914; s. Chaim and Rikle (Dembo); in S Afr since 1927; m. Sarah Liberman, Feb 25, 1933; c: Martin. Found, chmn, mgn dir, Alpha group of co's, S Afr, 1944, among them: Alpha Free State Holdings Ltd; Alpha Ind Devl Corp; Alpha Steamship Co; Alpha Union and Overseas Finance Corp; co-found, Union Stock Exch in S Afr; dir: Jesma Inves Ltd; Safe Inves Trust; Beta Secys Ltd; ed: Afr J Newspaper, 1930-34; J Opinion, 1937; Fgn Affairs, 1940-43; World Opinion, 1940-43. Hon pres: World Union OSE, since 1952; S Afr ORT-OSE, 1952-66; vice-pres, World Union ORT, 1955-65; S Afr HIAS, since 1951; mem: exec, WJC, since 1953; gen council, S Afr J Appeal, since 1952; hon con, S Afr Journalists Assn, since 1946; fmr: mem exec, J Bd Deps; natl chmn, United Communal Fund; club, J Guild. Home: 57 St Patrick's Rd, Johannesburg, S Afr. Office: POB 8659, Johannesburg, S Afr.

SHACHAL, Moshe, Isr, legislator; b. Jerusalem, May 20, 1935; s. David and Aviva (Rabla); deg, econ and political sci, Haifa Div, Heb U, 1966; att Tel Aviv U, 1967; m. Sarah Sher; c: Ofer, Idit. Mem, council, Haifa Munic, since 1965; secy, Haifa Lab Council, since 1966; mem exec: Shikun Ovdim Ltd; Carmel Bank Haifa; Lab Party Cen. Home: 57A Einstein St, Haifa, Isr. Office: 43 Hechalutz St, Haifa, Isr.

SHACHNAI, Eliahu, Isr, organization exec; b. Russ, Apr 2, 1898; s. Isaak and Ester (Sachnowitz); in Isr since 1921; m. Mirjam Gershenowitz; c: Yael Fromer, Herzl, (another son killed in action, Isr War of Independence). Mem, mgmt, Magen David Adom, 1938-65; lab worker, Heb U, Jerusalem, 1925-30; dir, Kofer Hayishuv, 1938-41; insp, food dept, found, Inst of Commerce and Ind, 1948-51. Haganah, 1921-42; IDF, War of Independence, Sinai War. Mem: Histadrut Haovdim Haklali; Isr-Amer Friendship Assn, 1949-69. Home: 23 Lotos Rd, Haifa, Isr.

SHACHNAI, Herzel, Isr, master mariner; b. Jerusalem, Dec 1, 1923; s. Eliahu and Miriam; att Nautical Sch, Haifa, 1938-41; m. Aviva Tivon, July 24, 1959; c: Asaf. Sr pilot, Haifa Port, since 1959; master mariner since 1953; fmr: with Atid Navigation Co; sailed on first Isr passenger ship, Kedma. Brit Navy, 1943-45; Merchant Navy, 1945-47. Home: 18 Hasport St, Haifa, Isr.

SHACHOR, Binyamin, Isr, communal leader; b. Jerusalem, Isr, 1916; s. Moshe and Sara (Yemini); att Etz Haim Yeshiva, 1921-35; m. Sara Cohen, Aug 15, 1940; c: Ephraim, David, Zeev. MK since 1961; dep Min, Rel Affairs, Jerusalem, since 1966. Mem, exec: Rel Zionists of Isr; HaPoel haMizrahi; Sharei Zedek Hosp, Jerusalem; Bnai Akiva Yeshiva. Home: 12 Smuts Blvd, Tel Aviv, Isr. Office: Min of Rel Affairs, Jerusalem, Isr.

SHACHTER, Haim, Isr, editor, author; b. Rum, Apr 13, 1911; s. Jacob and Henna (Breneg); in Isr since 1936; BA, hons, Us Belfast; London; m. Avigail Cohen, Mar, 1937; c: Uri (killed in action, Apr, 1960), Eldad. Ed: JA Press Service, JA Publs, since 1948, fmr ed, JA Digest of Press and Events; examiner, Isr Min of Educ, since 1939; sr master, Heb HS, Jerusalem, 1942-48; lectr, Sch Higher Studies, Jerusalem, 1945-48. Author: The New Universal Hebrew Dictionary, 2 vols, 1969; Four-Volume Encyclopedia Dictionary, English-Hebrew; A History of English Literature, Heb, 1945; The Concise English-Hebrew Dictionary, 1966; numerous Eng lang textbooks for Isr HSs; trans into Eng works of: Aaron Barth; Eliezer Steinman; contbr to Anglo-J press, J periodicals in Fr, Ger, Span, Yiddish. Hobbies: music, book collecting. Home: 5 Marcus St, Jerusalem, Isr.

SHADMI, Nachum, Isr, military off; b. Kishinev, Bessarabia, Russ, 1898; s. Meir and Batsheba (Utchitel) Kramer; att mil off sch, Odessa, Russ, 1917; m. Shoshana Goldberg, 1921; c: Issaschar. Ret; chmn, controller's bur, Lab Party, 1958-68, mem secretariat; cdr, Galil line, Haganah, 1937-40; cdr, Jerusalem line, 1941-45; cdr, J Defense, Eur, N Afr, 1948-58; staff, gen adj, 1948; pres, Mil Court of Appeal, 1948-58. Mem: Lab Party; active in pensioners assn, IDF. Home: 13 Hatam-Soffer St, Tel Aviv, Isr.

SHADMON, Asher Sinai, Isr, mining cons; b. Amsterdam, Holland, July 29, 1922; s. Schulem and Hava (Klugman-Sinai) Braunfeld; in Isr since 1950; BSc, hons, King's Coll, London, 1948; postgrad, Royal Sch of Mines, 1948-49; MSc, Technion, Haifa, 1964; m. Miriam Figler, Dec 20, 1953; c: Joshua, Batsheba, Pia, Rama. Marble devl cons, UN Devl Prog, Philippines, since 1969; coord, Earth Scis Council, Min of Devl, Jerusalem, since 1968; drilling sup, water div, Min of Agric, 1950; geologist, Isr Mining Ind, Timna, 1951; head, Quarries Sect, tech adv to controller of mines, Min of Devl, 1954-56, sr mining engr, 1956-68. Served, IDF; active, Aliyah B, War of Independence. Prin contrib: specialist, geo-environmental scis; cons practice in construction materials. Fmr: exec mem: Zionist Youth Fed; U ZC; ZF, Gt Brit; pres, King's Coll, J Soc; found mem, Misrad Aliyah, repr, ZF Admn Comm; hon secy, auditor, Isr Geological Soc; hon secy, Isr Assn for Advancement of Sci; chmn, IUGS Commn, Engr Geology; pres, Intl Assn Engr Geology. Contbr articles to profsl publs. Recipient: Tully Medal, London, 1946; Six-Day War Ribbon. Home: 56 Nayot St, Jerusalem, Isr.

SHAETER, Jacob, Isr, rabbi; b. Frumusica, Rum, Dec 31, 1896; m. Adina; four c. Ret; rabbi: Galatz, Rum, 1913-20; Manchester, Eng, 1920-26; N Ir, 1926-54. Vice-pres: JNF; Mizrachi Org; fmr, dean of res, J Students, Queens U, Belfast; hon instr, Belfast Talmudical Soc; vice-pres: Belfast ZC; Belfast J Student Union. Author: The Student's Guide Through the Talmud; Machaze Avraham veLeecutey Yaacov; Dovev Siftei Yeshenim veCheker haLacha; She'erit Yaakov; Meshelcha b' divrei "Hazal". Home: 12 Narkis St, Jerusalem, Isr.

SHAFAT, Avraham Joseph, Isr, attorney; b. Budapest, Hung, Apr 10, 1930; s. Shmuel and Margit (Leb) Schwartz; in Isr since 1949; MJ, Heb U, Jerusalem; m. Batia Rosenberg, Jan 20, 1958; c: Milka, Michal, Chagit, Lea, Shmuel. Legal adv, Min of Interior, since 1968. Staff sgt, IDF, 1950-52. Mem: World Council Mishmeret Tzeirah; Miflagah Datit Leumit, fmr mem hon court. Contbr: articles on elections and election sys. Home: 16 Ben Zion St, Jerusalem, Isr. Office: Hakirya, Jerusalem, Isr.

SHAFFER, Jerome A, US, educator; b. Bklyn, NY, Apr 2, 1929; s. Joseph and Beatrice (Leibowitz); BA, Cornell U, 1950; PhD, Princeton U, 1952; m. Olivia Connery, Sep 3, 1960. Prof, U Conn, since 1967; asst prof, Swarthmore Coll, 1955-58, asso prof, 1958-67. Secy, Swarthmore chap, AAUP,

1960-62; exec secy, Council for Phil Studies, since 1965; pres, Swarthmore chap, Phi Beta Kappa, 1958-61; mem, Amer Phil Assn. Author: The Philosophy of Mind, 1968. Recipient: Korean Service decoration; Study F, Amer Council Learned Soc, 1963-64. Office: Dept of Phil, U of Conn, Stons, Conn.

SHAFRAN, David, Isr, rabbi, educator; b. Rum, Jan 8, 1915; s. Hanoch and Zivia (Rubinovich); in Isr since 1958; BA, U Bucharest, 1938, PhD, 1940; rabb dipls: Chief Rabbis of Rum: Dr Jacob Itzhak Nemirower of Transylvania; Itzhak Klein; Haim Rabinowitz; m. Zipora Landman, Mar 15, 1945; c: Zivia Silvia. Tchr since 1960; rabbi, Ahdut Kodesh Syn, Rum; tchr, Fukshenyano Kultura, both 1940-48; in jail as objector to Communism, 1954-56; insp, Rel Sem for Tchrs, Jerusalem, 1959-60; ed, Menora, 1959-65; Rum broadcasts, Kol Isr, 1954-60; fgn corresp, Rum broadcasts, Radio Free Eur, 1960-65. Author: Personality of the Professor, 1939; From the Moral of the Centuries, 1940; Pakuda, 1941; Saadia Gaon, 1942; Missions Humanities, 1944; The Moral Pedagogy by F W Foester, 1945; Judaism-Conception and Mission, 1946; The Active Bible, 1947; Writers from the Rumanian Aliyah, 1959; Fragments from His Creations, in memory of Rabbi Hanoch Shafran, 1960; Jacob Groper, 1962; Synagogue of My Youth, 1964; Maimonides, 1965; Satan, 1965; Germany of Yesterday-Germany of Today, 1965; Zishe Portugal, 1966; Where in Israel, 1967; Chronicle of the Nazi Disaster, 1967; My Country in the War of Six Days, 1968; Questions and Answers for My Generation, 1969. Fmr mem: Masons, Rum; Cen Comm of Rum Zionists. Hobby: music. Home: 2 Gordon St, Jerusalem, Isr.

SHAFRAN, Menahem Beir, Isr, rabbi; b. Bacau, Rum, July 20, 1913; s. Bezalel and Reinhartz (Finkel); in Isr since 1956; ordained rabbi, J Theol Fac, Vienna, 1937; PhD, Vienna U, Basel U, 1939; m. Malca Bourshtein, Dec 12, 1939; c: Meshulam, Bezalel, Amikam. Rabbi, Comty of Ramat Aviv, since 1956; headmaster, Rel Munic HS; chief rabbi, Ploiesti, Rum, 1940-56. Mem, B'nai B'rith; fmr, chmn: Zionist Org; Mizrachi; WJC, all Rum. Author: Die Inneren and Kulturellen Verhaeltinisse in der Bukovina, 1939; co-author, Chibat Zion in Roumania, 1958; contbr to periodicals in Rum, Isr. Spec interests: educ, hist, public work, rel activities. Home: 15 Fichman St, Ramat Aviv, Isr. Study: Eben Ezra St, Herzilya, Isr.

SHAFRIR, Eleazar, Isr, educator; b. Cracow, Pol, Sep 19, 1924; s. Marcus and Rose (Lempel) Spiegel; in Isr since 1944; MS, Heb U, Jerusalem, 1952, PhD, 1955; m. Aviva Rutenburg, June 8, 1950; c: Ehud, Eviathar, Ora. Asso prof, biochem, Heb U-Hadassah Med Sch, since 1965; dir, lab clinical biochem, Hadassah Hosp, since 1964; visiting sci, Natl Heart Inst, Bethesda, Md, 1957-58; visiting prof, Harvard Med Sch, 1967-68. Prin contribs: fat transp metabolism research; study of biochem and phys of edipose tissue; diabetes, obesity diseases of fat metabolism. Mem: several intl profsl and learned socs. Asso ed, Isr Jour of Med Sci; contbr to Isr and fgn profsl jours; co-author, various books. Home: 57 Hechalutz St, Jerusalem, Isr. Office: Hadassah U Hosp, Jerusalem, Isr.

SHAFRIR, Herman Naftali, Isr, educator; b. Berlin, Ger, Dec 25, 1919; s. Jacob and Miriam (Grünberg) Steiger; in Isr since 1936; BSc, Technion, Haifa, 1944, DSc, 1956; m. Hanna Bauman; c: Anat, Avraham. Head: dept nuclear sci, Technion, since 1968, radiation safety unit, 1963-68. Capt, IDF, 1947-49. Contbr to intl jours. Mem: Amer Nuclear Soc; Intl Radiation Protection Soc; Isr Chem Soc. Home: 21 Smolenskin St, Haifa, Isr. Office: Dept Nuclear Sci, Technion, Haifa, Isr.

SHAGASS, Charles, US, psychiatrist, educator; b. Montreal, Can, May 19, 1920; s. Morris and Pauline (Segal); in US since 1958; BA, McGill U, 1940; MD, CM, 1949, dipl, psycht, 1953; MS, U Rochester, 1941; m. Clara Wallerstein, Nov 1, 1942; c: Carla, Kathryn, Thomas. Prof, Temple U Med Coll, since 1966; dir, electro-phys lab, Royal Vic Hosp, Montreal, 1952-58; lectr, asst prof, McGill U, 1952-56; prof, State U Ia, Coll of Med, 1960-66. Flying off, RCAF, 1941-45. Asst secy, Soc for Biol Psycht, since 1967; f, Amer Psychiatric Assn; mem: AMA; Amer Coll Neuropsychopharm; Amer Electroencephalohraphic Soc; Amer Psychosomatic Soc; Amer Psychopath Assn; Group for Advancement of Psycht; E Assn Electroencephalographers; Collegium Intl Neuropsychopharmacologicum. Contbr to med jours and texts. Home: 1301 Spruce Lane, Wyncote, Pa. Office: 3300 Henry Ave, Philadelphia, Pa.

SHAHAM, David, Isr, author; b. Warsaw, Pol, Jan 27, 1923; s. Eliezer and Varda Steinman; in Isr since 1924; att New Sch for Social Research, NY, 1949-50; LLB, Tel Aviv U, 1956; m. Rina Gologorsky, Nov 20, 1948; c: Mylatte, Dalitte. Co-owner, Shaham Lewensohn Aylon Agcy; mem Kibbutz, 1945-51; on educ mission to USA, 1948-51; ed youth mag, 1941-45; chmn bd, Adv Agcy Radio Corp, 1962-66; mem bd, Radio Corp, 1962-66. Capt, IDF, 1951-53. Author: novels, Harpatkaot Ahitam; Lo Ba Beheshbon; Shalom Lefetah; short stories: Yom Ehad Shehu Harbeh; Hamidron Haaroh; Sheela Shel Zman; plays: Haerev Haaharon; The Boss; contbr articles to mags. Mem: Comm Checking Isr Info Services; initiating comm, Citizens for Eshkol, 1965. Hobby: violin playing. Home: 14 De Haas St, Tel Aviv, Isr. Office: 16 Helsinki St, Tel Aviv, Isr.

SHAHAM, Nathan, Isr, author; b. Tel Aviv, Jan 29, 1925; s. Eliezer and Varda (Briskman) Steinman; m. Ktina Panitch, 1951; c: Boaz, Orit, Yavin. Ed, Sifriat Poalim, since 1961; vice-chmn, Isr Bc Auth, since 1968; ed, Hotam, weekly, 1964-66; secy, Kibbutz Bet Alpha, 1952-54, 1967-68. Mem: ACUM; Intl Theater Inst. Author: Dagan Veoferet, 1948; Haelim Atzelim, 1949; Hem Yagiu Machar, 1951; Yohanan Bar Hama, 1953; Tamid Anachnu, 1954; Even Al PihaBe'er, 1956; Kvar Mutar leGalot, 1958; Shikun Vatikim, 1958; Pgishot beMoskva, 1958; Masa leEretz Kush, 1961; Zebiglal, 1961; Chochmat haMisken, 1962; Kav LiDmit, 1962; Reach Hadarim, 1964; Masa beEretz Israel, 1967; Masa beEretz Nodaat, 1968; Guf Rishon Rabim, 1968; plays: Hem Yagiu Machar, 1951; Kra li Siomka, 1952; Cheshbon Chadash, 1954; Arba Enaim veEporon, 1959; Mechir haKeren, 1960; Zug Ofanayim, 1969; Chufsha baKfar, 1959; Mi Makir Mi Yodea, 1960. Recipient: Habima award, 1953; 40 years award, Histadrut, 1961; Shlonsky award, 1958; award for children's books, Min Culture and Educ, 1959; Isr Bc Sys drama award, 1960. Office: Isr Bc Auth, Jerusalem, Isr. Home: Kibbutz Bet Alpha, Isr.

SHAHAR, David, Isr, author; b. Jerusalem, Dec 12, 1926; s. Meir and Sarah (Hurwitz); att Hebrew U, Jerusalem; m. Shulamith Weinstock, 1956; c: Meir, Dina. Author: Al Hachalomot, 1955; Yerah Hadvash veHazahav, 1959; Caesar; Maggid haAtidot; Heichal haKelim haShvurim; works have been trans into: Eng, Fr, Danish, Nor, It, Span, Arabic. Lt, IDF. Mem: Heb Writers Assn; ACUM. Recipient: PM prize for lit creation, 1969. Hobby: painting. Home: 17 Hovevey Zion St, Jerusalem, Isr.

SHAI, Joshua N, Isr, diplomat, atty; b. Jerusalem, Oct 10, 1905; s. Samuel and Hannah (Danon) Behar; grad, Jerusalem Law Sch, 1930; law deg, 1957; m. Rivka Simha, July 2, 1935; c: Samuel, Aron. Adv, Min for Fgn Affairs, since 1968; Isr ambass to: Costa Rica; El Salvador; Guat; Honduras; Nicaragua; Panama, 1959-64; Isr diplomatic repr to Greece, 1964-68; secy, dept immigration, JA, 1924-38, dep dir, 1938-48, on missions to org immigration to Pal, in Greece, 1935, Aden, 1937-38, 1942, Eur, 1946-47; dir, immigration, naturalization services, Isr Govt, 1948-57; established Isr Tourist Offs, NYC, Paris, 1949; mem, Isr delg, Intl Comm for Eur Migration, Geneva, 1955; consul gen, Istanbul, Turkey, 1957-59. Fmr: bd dirs: Amidar; Anti-TB League; Rotary, Istambul; Maccabi Org; legal comm, Va'ad Leumi. Contbr to local publs. Hobby: hiking. Office: Min for Fgn Affairs, Jerusalem, Isr.

SHAIN, Rose W, US, voice tchr; b. Lith; d. Isaac and Hannah (Yaffe) Wies; MA, Staley Coll, 1937, D Art of Oratory, 1940; att Harvard U; MEd, Mass State Coll, 1960; m. Mark Shain (decd); c: Esther Osborne, Thelma Wisefield, Gloria Regney, Myron. Voice tchr and coach; conductor, Temple Emeth choral group; fmr dean, Staley Coll, vocal dept; lectr, Boston U; conducted courses for Mass Div U Ext; appeared in concerts, opera, theater and radio. Mem: Natl Assn Tchrs Singing; NE Music Forum; Hadassah; B'nai B'rith; Sisterhood Kehillath Isr; Women's Scholarship Town Meeting, mem, Brookline; clubs: Recital; Profsl Womens; Mass Fed of Music. Fmr music ed, Brookline Mag. Recipient: named NE queen of air, NBC. Home: 4 Stedman St, Brookline, Mass.

SHAIN, Samson A, US, rabbi; b. Boston, Mass, May 1, 1906; s. Jacob and Sarah (Levine); BA, Harvard Coll, 1929; MHL, ordained rabbi, JIR, 1933; DD, HUC-JIR, 1961; m. Lillian, Litoff, Feb 13, 1944; c: Paula Strassman, Joyce Bronstein, Judy Teitelbaum. Rabbi, Shaarai Shomayim, since 1956; org, first rabbi, The Cape Cod Synagogue, 1933-35; rabbi: Sunnyside Cen, LI, NY, 1935-48; Nassau Comty Temple, LI, 1948-51; Cong House of Isr, Hot Springs, Ariz, 1951-56. Chaplain, US Army, 1942-46, lt col, USAF Res, since 1946. Delg, 7th World Jamboree, Aus, 1951; fmr pres, Lancaster br, NCCJ; bd trustee, JIR, 1940-43; exec comm, CCAR, 1955-57; mem, Masons; club, Lancaster Torch, fmr pres. Contbr to Brandeis Avukah Annual, Place Name Mags. Address: 508 N Duke St, Lancaster, Pa.

SHAINMARK, Eliezer L, US, editor, business exec; b. Warsaw, Pol, Sep 13, 1900; s. David and Libby (Kahn); BS, NYO, 1921; m. Edythe Witt, Jan 31, 1925; c: Norman. Pres, ed, Gilmark Features Syndicate, since 1958; PR adv, NYC Econ Devl Admn, since 1962; reporter, Norfolk, Virginian Pilot, Richmond Times Dispatch, 1923-25; night ed, feature ed, NY Graphic, 1925-29; night ed, NY Jour-Amer, 1929-35; asst mgn ed, Chgo-Amer, 1936-41, mgn ed, 1941-45; mgn ed: Hearst Wash Bur, 1947; Chgo Herald Amer, 1948-50; ed asst to pub, Esquire, Coronet mags, 1950-51; asst to admnr, FSA, 1952-53; vice-pres, Guild Films, NYC, 1953-58. Prin contribs: 1st Amer journalist to expose Hitler's atrocities in Amer press; initiated important psychol warfare prog against Facists and Nazis, WW II; proposed to B'nai B'rith world wide PR drive for direct peace negotiations between Isr and Arab States, 1968. Mem: Soc Amer Eds; Sigma Delta Chi; clubs: Silurians; Natl Pres, PR Offs Soc, fmr pres. Publisher ed, Unsolved Murders, 1954. Recipient: citation for war aid, US Treasury and Army. Home: 2686 Bailey Ave, New York, NY. Office: 225 Broadway New York, NY.

SHAINSKY, Israel Sam, US, farmer; b. Kiev, Russ, May 10, 1896; s. Avrum and Esther (Adamsky); in US since 1914; m. Fanny Steinman, July 11, 1922; c: Muriel Robbins, Cecelia Cohen, Allen. Ret; poultry dealer, farmer, 1922-64; mem adv bd, Bank of Amer. Bd mem, Sonoma Valley C of C; pres, treas, Sonoma Valley Hosp Dist; mem: Cong Beth Shalom; Temple Beth Ami; B'nai B'rith; fmr: pres, Sonoma Valley Hist Soc; exec bd, Sonoma Valley Vintage Festival; clubs: Kiwanis, treasurer; Sonoma Valley Garden, fmr vice-pres. Hobbies: gardening, comty service. Home: 21498 Shainsky Rd, Sonoma, Cal.

SHAIR, Hilliard Milton, US, physician, surgeon; b. Bklyn, NY, Mar 31, 1909; s. Nathan and Jennie (Goldstein); BA, MA, Columbia U, MD, Med Sch, att Postgrad Med Sch, 1946-48; m. Jane Martin, May 19, 1943; c: Robert, Joseph, Harry, David. Dermat, Phys and Surgs Clinic, Quincy, Ill, since 1948. Maj, US Army MC, 1941-46. Lectr: on Isr in Western Ill; Southeastern Ia; Northeast, Iowa, since 1963; talks on: Bibl trans; Bibl criticism; Judaism; fmr: pres: Comty Chest; ARC Drives; Quincy Sym Orch; Adams Co Med Soc; chmn, UJA, Quincy, Ill area; club, Rotary, fmr pres. Spec interests: study Heb and Bible, theater acting roles. Home: 166 N 18, Quincy, Ill. Office: 1101 Maine, Quincy, Ill.

SHAKOW, David, US, psychologist, educator; b. NYC, Jan 2, 1901; s. Abraham and Eva (Leventhal); BS, Harvard U, 1924, MS, 1927, PhD, 1942; m. Sophie Harap, June 1, 1926; c: Alice Piller, Naomi, Alexander. Sr research psychol, Natl Inst Mh, Bethesda, Md, since 1967, chief, psych lab, 1954-66, cons, 1946-54; cons, USPHS, since 1947; asst in psychopath, McLean Hosp, Waverly, Mass, 1923-24; asst psychol, Worcester State Hosp, 1924-25, chief psychol, dir, psych research, 1928-46; cons psychol, Worcester Child Guidance Clinic, 1928-46, acting dir, 1945-46; br cons, chief clinical psychol, VA, 1946-48; chief psychol, Ill Neuropsycht Inst, 1946-54; prof, psych: U Chgo, 1948-54; U of Ill Coll of Med, 1946-54, professorial lectr, 1954-61; cons: clinical psych, Group for Advancement Psycht, 1947-55. Surg Gen, US Army, 1948-54. F: Amer Psych Assn, fmr mem: council, policy and planning bd, fmr pres, div clinical psych, chmn, comm on training in clinical psych; Amer Orthopsychiatric Assn; Soc for Psych Study Social Issues; mem: Sigma Xi; E Psych Assn; Midwestern Psych Assn; Amer Psychosomatic Soc, fmr, mem council; Amer Psychopath Assn, fmr mem council; fmr: mem: natl adv subcomm on clinical psych, VA; hon mem, Wash Psychoanalytic Soc; Amer Bd Examiners in Profsl Psych; div anthropology and psych, Natl Research Council, mem, comm on psycht, div med scis; career investigator selection comm, Natl Inst Mh, panel cons, hist of med, screening comm, psych; Fulbright Comm; bd dirs, Found Fund for Research in Psycht; psycht and neur adv comm, VA; adv group, Ford Found Prog for Support of Research in Mh; asso mem, Chgo Analytic Soc; club, Cosmos. Author: Clinical Psychology as Science and Profession: A Forty-Year Odyssey, 1969; co-author, The Influence of Freud on American Psychology, 1963; cons ed and contbr to profsl jours. Recipient: Saltonstall and Bassett Scholarships; James Walker f; Detur Prize, all Harvard U;

dist contrib award, div clinical psych, Amer Psych Assn, 1959; Collier Lectr, U Rochester, 1960; Stanley R Dean Research award, U Mich, 1962; Helen Sargent Memorial award, Menninger Found, 1965. Home: 4001 Dresden St, Kensington, Md. Office: Natl Inst of Mh, Bethesda, Md.

SHAKOW, Zara, US, theater dir; b. NYC; d. Abraham and Eva (Leventhal); training: The Actor's Studio; Neighborhood Playhouse; Vakhantangov Theater; Inst for Advanced Studies in Theater Arts; Amer Theater Wing; Lessac Inst for Voice and Speech; Amer Acad Dramatic Arts; theater courses: New Sch; Hunter Coll; CCNY; div. Dir: Province of Ontario Council of Arts; Dominion Theatre, Winnipeg; Chamber Theater, Tel Aviv; Equity Theater, NY; Shaw Soc of Amer; Amer Children's Theater, LA; Hollywood Theater Alliance Children's Theater; comty theaters: NY; NJ; Cal; stock: Conn; Clinton Playhouse; Mass: Barn Theater; Priscilla Beach Theater; Yarmouth Playhouse; produc sup, Haifa Munic Theater; cons dir, adjudicator: Min of Culture and Educ; Cultural Div, Lab Fed, both Isr; acting instr, coach: Acting Training Cen; Theater Workshop; Haifa Munic Theater Studio and Repertory Co; Manitoba Theater Cen and Drama Sch; Chamber Theater Drama Sch; Columbia Pictures; lectr: 92nd St Y; United Coll, Winnipeg; participated as mem panel, guest on TV progs. Author: The Theater in Israel, 1964; Curtain Time, for J youth, 1968; contbr to Ency of World Drama; Emcy on Isr; profsl jours. Mem: Soc of Stage Dirs and Choreographers; Actors Equity Assn; Amer Educ Theater Assn; ZOA; Hadassah; Assn Intl du Theatre pour l'enfance et la jeunesse. Home: 910 West End Ave, New York, NY. Office: 160 W 73 St, New York, NY.

SHALEV, Mordechai, Isr, diplomat; b. Brno, Czech, July 24, 1915; s. Menahem and Mariska (Benet) Friedmann; in Isr since 1939; att Masaryk U, Brno, 1934-38; MA, Amer U, Wash, DC, 1954; m. Shoshana Sachs, Apr 4, 1941; c: Michael, Chava, Menahem. Dir, consular div, Isr Min for Fgn Affairs, since 1967; ed, Radio Week, Jerusalem, 1946-47; 2nd secy, Isr, Emb, Wash, DC, 1951-56, 1st secy, 1956-57; info div, Isr Min for Fgn Affairs, 1958-59, press off, spokesman, 1959-60, head, dir gen off, 1960-61; Isr consulate gen, LA, 1961-65; ambass, Ghana, 1965-67. Lt, Brit Army, 1942-46; capt, IDF, 1948-49. Home: Neve Granott 1, Jerusalem, Isr. Office: Min for Fgn Affairs, Jerusalem, Isr.

SHALEV, Zalman, Isr, business exec, government official; b. Haifa, 1923; m; two c. Mgn dir, AEL Isr, Ltd, since 1966; fmr col, chief signal and elec off, IDF, with IDF since 1948. Dep chmn, Isr Govt Comm and Elections Council. Home: 36 Yehuda Hanassi St, Neve Avivim, Tel Aviv, Isr.

SHALEV-TOREN, Puah, Isr, author; b. Tel Aviv, Mar 29, 1930; d. Haim and Sarah (Aisenberg); MA, Heb U, Jerusalem, 1952; m. Haim Toren, Nov 4, 1952; c: Ron. Author: Haruzim Mibein Kiflei Hamenifa, 1956; Libi Er, 1964; monograph on AB Gottlober; trans of seven books by Tagore. Mem: Heb Writers Assn in Isr. Recipient: Miss Jerusalem, 1954; Zipora Klausner prize. Hobbies: music, painting. Home: 19 Shmaryahu Lewin St, Jerusalem, Isr.

SHALHEVET, Joseph, Isr, scientist; b. Jerusalem, Apr 29, 1931; s. David and Bella (Zeldin) Brandeis; BS, U Cal, Berkeley, 1954; MS, Cornell U, 1955, PhD, 1958; m. Jacqueline Braun, Sep 21, 1957; c: Sarit, Ron. Head: dept soil and water, Volcani Inst for Agric Research, since 1969, div soil salinity and mgmt, since 1967, on staff since 1962. Pvt, IDF, 1948-50. Mem: Sigma Xi, Cornell U; Amer Soc Soil Sci; fmr secy, Isr Soc Soil Sci. Contbr to sci jours. Home: 14 Einstein St, Rehovot, Isr.

SHALIT, Leon, Isr, business cons; b. Riga, Russ, Jan 18, 1905; s. Morduch and Frieda (Frumkin); in Isr since 1963; att: Boersen Kommerzschule, Riga, 1911-15; Count Tenischeff, Petrograd, 1915-18; St Edwards, Oxford, Eng, 1919-23; MA, St Catherine's Coll, Cambridge, Eng, 1927; m. Lilly Shalit, Apr 17, 1952. Cons since 1963; mgr, London N Trading Co, 1927-33; sr exec, Marks and Spencer, London, 1935-63. Maj, J Brig, 1940-45; lt col, Quartermaster's Br, IDF, 1948-49. Adv, JA, Isr Purchasing Commn, 1951-52; repr, Isr Treasury Dept, Paris, for Fr credit purchases; vice-chmn, Anglo-Isr Archaeol Soc, 1952-63; mem, exec: ORT, London, 1958-63; Anglo-Isr C of C. Recipient: campaign medals, Haganah; cert, for over $1,000,000 in export, Isr Min of Trade and Commerce. Hobbies: archaeol, gardening, riding. Home and office: 12 Hanof St, Savyon, Isr.

SHALIT, Lilly, Isr, organizational worker; b. Brasow, Rum, Mar 22, 1912; d. Lazar and Elena (Gross); in Isr since 1933; tchrs cert, Nancy U, 1930; m. Leon Shalit, Apr 17, 1952. Secy, Mischar veTaasia Co Ltd, org of trade exhbs abroad, 1933-39, 1944-48; org fairs: Paris; Bulgaria; trade info off, US World Fair, 1939; org, itinerary propaganda exhb on behalf of UJA, JA Rio de Janeiro, Sao Paulo, Montevideo; sup printing, Pal Govt Trade Catalogues; secy, Pal Airways Ltd, 1937-39; co-mgr, Intrameccan Ltd, 1948-52; head, dept fgn stamp issues, Isr Govt, 1963-66. Observer, exec, World WIZO; fmr: mem: bd, Zionist Org, Bucharest; exec: Youth Aliyah, London; Brit Women's ORT. Home: 12 Hanof St, Savyon, Isr.

SHALOM, Shin, Isr, author, poet; b. Parczew, Pol, Dec 28, 1904; s. Avraham and Ester (Golda) Shapira; in Isr since 1922; att: Mizrachi Tchrs Sem, 1922-25; U Erlangen, 1930-31; m. Ora Fried, 1931. Tchr: Rosh Pina, 1927; Jerusalem, Hadera, 1927-30; Nuremberg, Ger, 1930-31. Chmn, Isr Writers Assn. Author: beLev haOlam, 1927; Mi? 1930; Yoman baGalil, 1932; Mittokh haLehavot, 1936; Shirim, 1939; Sefer haShirim VehaSonnetot, 1940; Panim el Panim, 1941; haYad haShnia, 1942; Shabbat haOlam, 1944-45; Ilan Bakhut, 1946; Shirim, 1949; Adama uShmei Shamayim, 1949; haNer lo Kava, 1952, 1961; libretto for opera Dan HaShomer; Adama, play; Shirei Kommiouth Israel, 1958; baMetakh haGavoah, selected stories, 1956; Bein Tcheleth Lelavan, 1958; Sefer Hai Roi, 1962; Collected Works, 8 vols, 1968. Recipient: Key, City of Newark, NJ, 1961; citizen, Haifa, 1961; Bialik prize, 1941; Brenner prize, 1949; Tchernichovsky prize, 1950; Joseph Kassel prize, 1956; Ruppin prize, 1957; Ramat Gan prize, 1963. Home: POB 6095, Haifa.

SHALON, Rahel, Isr, scientist, educator; b. Sieradz, Pol, Apr 15, 1904; d. Hanoch and Gitel (Lifszyc) Znamirowski; in Isr since 1925; att Inst Tech, Warsaw, Pol, 1923-25; BSc, Technion, Haifa, 1930, CE, 1931; m. Uriel Shalon, 1929. Prof, CE, Technion, since 1952, head, bldg research sta, since 1953, sr vice-pres, academic affairs, 1965-66, vice-pres i/c research, 1963-65, dean, sch grad studies, 1959-62, mem fac since 1931. Haganah, 1925-48; maj, IDF, 1948-49. Chmn, intl research groups on concrete, reinforced concrete, windows and indoor climate in hot countries; fmr pres, perm comm, Reunion Internationale des Laboratories d'Essais et de Recherches sur les Materiaux et les Construction; fmr chmn: Haifa br, Assn Engrs and Architects in Isr; perm comm, concrete products, Amer Concrete Inst; exec bd, Intl Council for Bldg Research; mem: Intl Research Group On Corrosion On Reinforcement; Council for Higher Educ, since 1958; fmr: mem: Sci Research and Devl Council; Council Engr and Architecture, fmr mem, cen comm; 1st, 2nd Govt Educ Bd; Isr natl commn, UNESCO. Author: Cement and Concrete, 1939; Cementitious Materials, 1964; ed, In the Field of Bldg, since 1952; contbr to local, fgn profsl jours. Office: Technion, Haifa, Isr.

SHALON, Uriel, Isr, engineer, business exec; b. Moscow, Russ, May 21, 1899; s. Savely and Clara (Roniger) Friedland; in Isr since 1925; dipl engr, Petrograd Poly, 1920; m. Rahel Znamirowski, 1929. Chmn bd, Shemen, Isr Oil Co Ltd, Haifa, since 1967, mgn dir, 1940-67, with firm since 1928; mem, bd dirs, Timna Copper Mines; engr, oil fields, Baku, 1920-22; mgr, machinery dept, Solel Boneh, Tel Aviv, 1926-28; mem, Haifa Munic Council, 1951-57. Chmn exec, Isr Standards Inst; vice-pres, bd govs, Technion, Haifa; mem, Munic Council, Tel Aviv; chmn, Isr-Amer Soc; fmr: pres, Assn Engrs and Architects in Isr; found, bd mem, Isr Inst Productivity; chmn: Tzerie Zion, Caucasus; Haifa emergency council; head, Hechalutz Training Dept, Constantinople; gen secy, world exec, Hitachdut Zionist Lab; mem: World Hechalutz comm, Berlin; cen comm, Hapoel Hatzair, Tel Aviv; JCC, Haifa; chmn, Hadar Hacarmel Local Council; munic counselor, Haifa; club, Rotary, fmr pres. Fmr mem, ed bd, Arbetsvolk, Histadrut monthly, Berlin. Hobby: photography. Home: 30 Vitkin St, Ahuza, Haifa, Isr. Office: Shemen Oil Industry, Haifa, Isr.

SHALOWITZ, Morton, US, rabbi; Chgo, Ill, Dec 27, 1923; s. Milton and Mary (Halpert); BA, Cen YMCA Coll, Chgo, 1945; att U Chgo, 1945-46; BHL, ordained rabbi, Heb Theol Coll, 1949. Rabbi, Temple Beth Isr, since 1963; asso rabbi, Kehiloth Isr Syn, Kan City, 1954-57; rabbi: Heska Amuna Cong, Knoxville, 1957-62; Cong Yehudah Moshe, N Miami, 1962-63. US Army, 1952-54, found, 1st syn in Korea Beth Yehee Shalom, 1954, chaplain, maj, US Army Res. Mem: RabCA; ZOA; Rel Zionists of Amer; B'nai B'rith. Home:

6 Woods Pl, Fund du Lac, Wis. Study: 149 E Division St, Fund du Lac, Wis.

SHALTIEL, Shmuel, Isr, scientist; b. Thessaloniki, Greece; s. Shabetay and Renee (Bourla); in Isr since 1944; MSc, Heb U, Jerusalem, 1960; PhD, Weizmann Inst, Rehovot, 1964; m. Sarah Mass, May 10, 1956; c: Orna, Ruth. Sci, dept chem inmunology, Weizmann Inst of Sci, since 1964, lectr since 1967; research asso, U Wash, Seattle, 1964-66. Prin contribs: studies on: structure and function of enzymes and antibodies; vitamin B6 and its biol functions. Mem: Amer Chem Soc; Isr Biochem Soc; Isr Immunological Soc. Co-ed, sci column, Ha'aretz daily, since 1963; contbr of numerous publs to sci jours. Home: Shikun Ovdei Mahon Weizmann 9, Rehovot, Isr. Office: Weizmann Inst of Sci, Rehovot, Isr.

SHAMES, Irving Herman, US, educator; b. Boston, Mass, Oct 31, 1923; s. Louis and Dinah (Crystal); BS, Northeastern, U, Boston, 1948; MS, Harvard U, 1949; PhD, U Md, 1953; m. Sheila Shapiro, 1954; c: Lisa, Bruce. Fac prof, SUNY, Buffalo, since 1969, prof, chmn, div interdisciplinary studies, 1962-69; prof, chmn, dept engr sci, Pratt Inst, 1957-62, acting chmn, physics dept, 1960-61. Staff sgt, US Army, 1943-46. Mem: AAUP; ASEE; AIAA. Author: Engineering Mechanics, 1959; Mechanics of Fluids, 1962; Mechanics of Deformable Solids, 1964. Home: 805 N Forest St, Williamsville, NY. Office: 3435 Main St, Buffalo, NY.

SHAMGAR, Meir, Isr, advocate; b. Danzig, Pol, Aug 13, 1925; s. Eliezer and Dina (Bonfeld); in Isr since 1939; att: Heb U, Jerusalem; U London, Ext; Govt Law Classes, Jerusalem; m. Geula Nave; c: Anat, Ram, Dan. Atty gen, State of Isr, since 1968; mil advocate gen, 1961-68; legal adv, Min of Defense, 1968. Col, IDF, 1948-68; mem, Irgun Zevai Leumi, 1939-1948; interned by Brit, exiled to Afr, 1944-48. Contbr to profsl jours. Home: 12 Shakhar St, Jerusalem, Isr. Office: Jaffa Rd, Jerusalem, Isr.

SHAMIR, Meir, Isr, diplomat; b. Arad, Rum, Dec 5, 1920; s. Shlomo and Aurelia (Zahler); dipl, Ecole des Hautes Etudes Internationales, Paris, 1950; BA, Heb U, Jerusalem, 1963; m. Marli Roeder, Sep 24, 1954. Chargé d'affaires, Isr Emb, Bumako, Mali, since 1967, ambass-designate, since 1969. with Min for Fgn Affairs, since 1949, served in embs: Paris, Rome, London, Wash, counselor, Isr Emb, Ivory Coast, 1966-67. Office: POB 205, Bamako, Mali.

SHAMIR, Moshe, Isr, novelist, playwright; b. Safed, Sep 15, 1921; s. Arie and Ella (Ahronsohn); m. Zvia Frumkin, June 6, 1946; c: Ennula, Yael, Elyahu. Dir, immigration dept, JA, London; fmr mem, Kibbutz Mishmar HaEmek; found, ed, Bamaheneh, IDF weekly, 1948-50; co-ed: BaShaar; Omer; Massa. Served Palmach; capt, IDF. Author: Hu Halach baSadot; Tachat haShemesh; Bemo Yadav; Ad Eilat; Yedidav haGdolim shel Gadi; 1:0 leTovatenu; Nashim Mechakot baChutz; Melech Bassar vaDam; haHut haMeshulash; beKulmus Mahir; haGalgal haChamishi, haGvool; Ness LoKara Lanu; haChaim im Ishmael; plays: Kilometer 56; Beth Hillel; Leil Sufa; Soph haOlam; Milchemet Bnei Or; Agadot Lod; Bait beMazav Tov; haLaila leIsh; haYoresh; Shyv'a leOrlan; beChazara leYehudith. Chmn, cen comm, Land of Isr Movement. Recipient: Ussishkin prize, 1949; Brenner prize, 1953; Bialik prize, 1955. Home: 3 Rosanis St, Tel Aviv, Isr.

SHAMIR, Nachum, Isr, business exec; b. Cracov, Pol. Mar 30, 1917; s. Abraham and Hedva (Seiden) Wachsmann; in Isr since 1934; att: Hebrew U, Jerusalem, 1938-41; Columbia Bus Admn for Grads, NY, 1953-54; m. Malka Fass; c: Michael, Hedva, Uriel. Gen mgr: The Isr Corp Ltd, since 1968; Shilumim Corp, 1955-63; Hassneh Ins Co, 1962-64; econ min to US, Isr Govt, 1964-67; head, Aliyah off, It, JA, 1948-50, treas, Aliyah, Eur, 1951-52; head defense mission to US, Min of Defense, 1952-55. IDF, 1948. Dir: Friends Cameri Theater; Jt Comm Theaters in Isr; fmr: chmn, Isr Shipyard, Haifa; mem exec, treas, Mapai Party. Home: 41 Haoranim St, Kfar Shmaryahu, Isr. Office: 32 Ben Yehuda St, Tel Aviv, Isr.

SHAMOSH, Tuvia, Isr, journalist; b. Aleppo, Syria, 1914; s. Moshe and Rina; in Isr since 1934; att: U Beirut; Tel Aviv U Law Sch; m. Ada Turkieh, Mar 15, 1938; c: Rina Plesser. Ed: Sada A'Tarbiah, since 1952; Arabic quarterly of Histadrut, since 1969; Alyom, daily 1966-68, subed, 1948-66; subed, Haquiqat Al Amr, weekly, 1937-60. Mem: Histadrut, fmr mem exec; Org of Journalists; Org for Fgn Policy.

Home: 13 Ben Ezra Rd, Tel Aviv, Isr. Office: 17 Hagra St, Tel Aviv, Isr.

SHAN, Nava, Isr, actress; b. Prague, Czech, Sep 1, 1920; d. Salomon and Magda (Eckstein) Schonn; in Isr since 1948; att: U Prague, 1938-39; U Munchen, 1967-69; c: Orah. Actress: Munic Theatre, Haifa, since 1961; Munic Theatre, Prague, 1938-40; Munic Theatre, Brno, Czech, 1945-48; Habima, Isr, 1950-56; fmr mem: Kibbutz Neot Mordechai; Kibbutz Givat Brenner; appeared in one-woman show in all kibbutzim, Contbr to press in Isr, Czech. Home: 26 Margalit St, Haifa, Isr. Office: Munic Theatre, Haifa, Isr.

SHANE, Bernard, Can, labor org; b. Russ, June 3, 1890; s. Evadie and Leba; m. 2nd, Emma Baskin, May 25, 1934; c: Evelyn Raphael, Hugo. Mgr, ILGWU locals, Montreal, since 1934, vice-pres since 1950, org, Toronto, 1929-31; org: dressmakers, Chgo, 1931-34; Montreal cloakmakers, Montreal, 1934, dressmakers and embroidery workers, 1937. Chmn, Jt Comm to Combat Racial Intolerance, Montreal, since 1946, natl chmn for Can since 1950; Can treas, J Lab Comm; mem, Workmen's Circle frat delg, Trades and Lab Cong to AFL Conv, SF, 1951; gen vice-pres, Can Lab Cong, delg, Conv of Intl Confd Free Trade Unions, Vienna, Aus, 1955. Home: 6300 Lennox Ave, Montreal, Can. Office: 405 Concord St, Montreal, Can.

SHANEDLING, Philip D, US, ophthalmologist; b. Eveleth, Minn, Aug 4, 1912; s. Isadore and Felicia (Rodgers); BS, U Chgo, 1933, MD, 1936; m. Dorothy Winkler, Aug 15, 1948; c: Arlene. Pvt practice since 1940; instr, U Chgo, 1939-40; sr attending ophthal, chmn, eye dept, Mt Sinai Hosp, since 1958. US Army, 1943-47. Chmn: LA Co Ophthal Soc, 1960; co-chmn, phys div, United JWF, 1960; treas, Natl Soc Ophthal; f: Amer Coll Surgs; Amer Bd Ophthal; mem: Public Health League; LA Co Art Mus; Natl Soc for Prevention Blindness; Natl Med Found for Eye Care; LA Phys Art Soc; Pan Amer Assn Ophthal; Amer Acad Ophthal; AMA; LA Co Med Soc; Phi Beta Kappa; Phi Sigma Delta; Phi Delta Epsilon; B'nai B'rith. Contbr to med jours. Hobby: painting. Home: 1011 Maybrook Dr, Beverly Hills, Cal. Office: 6333 Wilshire Blvd, Los Angeles, Cal.

SHANI, Alexander, Isr, electrical engr; b. Satu-Mare, Rum, Mar 4, 1923; s. Yehuda and Margaret (Hertz) Fuchs; in Isr since 1949; Dipl, Engr, Inst of Tech, Munich, 1948; MSc, Isr Inst Tech, 1956, DSc, 1958; m. Ceslawa Hirschfeld, 1951; c: Aliza, Rachel. Found, mgr, ALEF Research and Devl, since 1969; adj asso prof, fac elec engr, agric engr, Isr Inst Tech, since 1967, fac mem since 1960; engr, Isr Bc Sta, 1948-51; research engr, sci dept, Isr Min Defense, 1951-53, sr project engr, 1953-58; research asso, SEA Paris, 1958-60; head, computer group, sci dept, Isr Min Defense, 1960-65, head elec div, 1961-65; co-found, 1st tech dir, ELBIT Computers Ltd, 1965-69. Mem bd dirs, chmn of comm for research, Isr Inst for Info Processing; chmn, Isr sect, Inst Elec and Electronic Engrs, 1964-65; co-found, 1st chmn, Isr Natl Assn for Automatic Control, 1965-67; mem, Assn Engrs, Isr. Mem, ed bd, Jour of Assn of Engrs, Isr; contbr to profsl jours. Recipient: award, exact sci, Histadrut Haovdim, 1958; Isr Defense award, PM of Isr, 1965. Home: 118A, Jaffe Nof, Haifa, Isr. Office: 6 Shulamith St, Haifa, Isr.

SHANKER, Albert, US, union leader; b. NYC, Sep 14, 1928; s. Morris and Mamie (Burko); att Columbia U, 1949-52; BA, hons, U of Ill; m. Edith Gerber, Mar 18, 1961; c: Adam, Jennie, Michael. Pres, United Fed Tchrs, AFL-CIO, since 1964, secy, asst to pres, 1962-64; vice-pres: Amer Fed Tchrs, field repr, 1959; NYC Cen Lab Council; NY State AFL-CIO. Vice-pres, J Lab Comm; exec comm, Workers Defense League; asso, U Sem Lab, Columbia U; bd dirs: United Housing Found; NYC Council Econ Educ; League for Ind Dem; bd trustees, Cen for Urban Educ; bldg and devl fund, Wiltwyck Sch for Boys. Ed, United Teacher; contbr to profsl jours. Hobbies: photography, classical records, electronic gadgets. Home: RFD 1, Putnam Valley, NY. Office: 260 Park Ave S, New York, NY.

SHANKMAN, Jacob K, US, rabbi; b. Chelsea, Mass, Oct 22, 1904; s. Isaac and Dina (Kestin); BA, Harvard U, 1923, MA, 1925; BHL, HUC, 1926, ordained rabbi, 1930; hon DD, 1955; m. Miriam Frankenstein, June 12, 1930; c: Judith Kosak, Diane Panish, Michael. Rabbi: Temple Isr, New Rochelle, NY, since 1937; Temple B'rith Sholem, Troy, NY, 1930-37. Chaplain, lt cdr, USNR, 1943-46. Pres, World Union for Progressive Judaism, since 1964, Amer dir since 1957, chmn exec since 1959; bd govs, HUC; pres: Assn Reform Rabbis, NY, 1957; Westchester Council Rabbis, 1962; Alumni Assn, HUC-JIR, 1958-59; Council Social Agcys, Troy, 1936-37, New Rochelle, NY, 1942-43; mem, exec bd, CCAR, 1940-42, chmn, comm on church and state, 1951-55; club, Harvard, Westchester. Contbr to J periodicals. Home: 2 Glenwood Ave, New Rochelle, NY. Study: 456 Webster Ave, New Rochelle, NY.

SHANOK, Louis Morrison, US, communal leader; b. Russ, Feb 15, 1905; s. Moshe and Yehudis (Narotsky); in US since 1908; PhB, Yale U, 1926, att Yale Law Sch, 1925-27; dipl, Grad Sch for J Social Work, NY Sch for Social Work, 1928; D Jur, Creighton Law Sch, 1930; m. Sylvia Ellovich, June 10, 1934; c: Michael, Mrs Abraham Tsafarty. Exec dir: New Haven J Comty Cen, since 1944; Port Chester J Cen, NY, 1934-44; J Comty Cen, Fall River, Mass, 1932-34; asst exec dir: Irene Kaufmann Settlement, Pittsburgh, Pa, 1930-32; FJP, Omaha, Neb, 1928-30. Mem: Natl Assn Social Workers; Acad Cert Social Workers; Natl Assn J Cen Workers; dir, USN League. Contbr: articles to profsl jours; book revs. Recipient: Grad Study f, Grad Sch Social Work, 1927. Hobbies: reading, writing. Home: 589 Fountain St, New Haven, Conn. Office: 1156 Chapel St, New Haven, Conn.

SHAPERO, Harold S, US, composer, educator; b. Lynn, Mass, Apr 29, 1920; s. Hyman and Jessie (Gorbatch); AB, Harvard U; m. Esther Geller, Sep 20, 1945; c: Hannah. Asso prof, music, Brandeis U, since 1951; lectr, Salzburg Sem in Amer Studies, 1950. Composer: Four Hand Piano Sonata; Sonata for Piano and Violin; Serenade in D for String Orch; On Green Mountain; Sym for Classical Orch, commissioned by Koussevitsky Found; The Travelers, overture, commissioned by Houston Sym Orch; Credo, commissioned by Louisville Orch; Until Night and Day Shall Cease, cantata, commissioned by Amer J Tercentenary. Mem: Phi Beta Kappa. Recipient: Knight prize, Harvard, 1941; Prix de Rome, Amer Acad, 1941, 1950; Fulbright award, Rome, It, 1949-50. Home: 9 Russell Circle, Natick, Mass. Office: Brandeis U, Waltham, Mass.

SHAPERO, Nate S, US, business exec, civic worker; b. Detroit, Mich, Sep 27, 1892; s. Samuel and Augusta (Metzger); Pharm G, Ferris Inst, Mich, 1912, PhB, 1921, hon LLD, 1942; hon LLD, U Detroit, 1955; m. Ruth Bernstein, Jan 27, 1924; c: Ray, Marianne Schwartz. Chmn bd: Cunningham Drug Stores, Inc, Detroit; Marshall Drug Co, Cleveland, O; dir: Natl Bank of Detroit; Warner-Lambert Pharmaceutical Co, NYC. USN, WW I. Natl chmn, multiple-stores sect for War Bonds, WW II; dollar-a-year man, US Treasury Dept, WW II; pres: Sinai Hosp; United Found; Gtr Detroit Hosp Fund, all Detroit; mem, bd trustees: Detroit Inst of Tech; U Detroit, Mich; Detroit Comty Fund; Metrop Polio Found, Detroit; Weizmann Inst of Sci, Rehovot, Isr; f, Brandeis U; fmr pres: Natl Assn Chain Drug Stores, NYC; Bd Fire Commns, Detroit; Mich State Wfr Commn; Temple Beth El, Detroit; fmr mem, bd: Ferris Inst; Amer Cancer Soc; Natl Found for Infantile Paralysis; Detroit Bd Commerce; War Chest of Metrop Detroit, WW II; fmr mem: Mich Crippled Childrens' Commn; clubs: Harmonie, NY; Advt, NY; Standard, Detroit; Gt Lakes; Hundred, Detroit; Boys of Mich, mem bd. Home: 18151 Hamilton Rd, Detroit, Mich. Office: 1927 12 St, Detroit, Mich.

SHAPERO, Sanford M, US, rabbi; b. Cincinnati, O, Mar 4, 1929; s. David and Leah (Adler); BA, U Dayton, 1950; BHL, HUC-JIR, 1952, MHL, 1954, ordained rabbi, 1955, DHL, 1959; m. Harriet Plotkin; c: Andrea, Seth, Jonathan, Adam. Exec vice-pres, Alliance Diversified Services Inc; lectr: Elmira Coll for Women; Briarcliff U; Columbia U; rabbi: B'nai Isr, Elmira, NY, 1956-59; Park Ave Temple, Bridgeport, Conn, 1959-64; Temple Emanuel, Beverly Hills, 1964-68. Chaplain, USN, 1955-56. Research cons on geriatrics and dementia: City of Hope Med Cen, LA; med staff, SF Hosp, 1968; co-found, Bridgeport br, Acad Rel and Mh; pres, Bridgeport Pastors Assn, 1963; vice-pres, NE Region, CCAR, 1960; cons on youth problems and drug addiction, Govs Comm, NY State, 1958, Conn Police Depts; bd overseers, HUC-JIR; bd dirs, USO; YMCA; club, Rotary. Specinterests: aviation, archaeol. Home: 2140 Burr St, Fairfield, Conn. Office: 608 Ferry Blvd, Stratford, Conn.

SHAPEY, Ralph, US, composer, conductor; b. Phila, Pa, Mar 12, 1921; s. Max and Lillian (Paul); studied: violin, with Emanuel Zetlin, 1938-42; composition, with Stefan Wolpe, 1945-48; m. Vera Klement; c: Max. Prof, music, dir, Con-

temporary Chamber Players, U Chgo, since 1964; instr, U of Pa, 1963-64; asst conductor, Natl Youth Admn Sym Orch, Phila, 1939-42; guest conductor, Phila Sym Orch at Robin Hood Dell, 1942; mem, Adolf Busch Chamber Players, 1946-47; tchr, Bklyn Free Musical Soc, Sch of Music, 1946-48; mem, bd dirs, tchr, Contemporary Music Sch, NY, 1949-50; tchr, 3rd St Settlement Sch of Music, 1951-53; US Army, 1942-45. Various concerts of new music, NYC, 1950-64; guest conductor of sym orchs: Buffalo; Chgo; London. Compositions: String quartets I, II, III, IV, V, VI; Sonatas: no 1 for piano; violin and piano; cello and piano; Variations for piano; 3 Essays on Thomas Wolfe for piano; quintet for 4 strings and piano; 7 little pieces for piano; Suite for piano; Quartet for oboe and 3 strings; Cantata for narrator, 3 solo voices, chamber orch and percussions; Fantasy for sym orch; Symphony no 1; Concerto for clarinet and chamber group; Trio for 2 strings and piano; Mutations for piano; Duo for viola and piano; Rhapsody for oboe and piano; Songs of Eternity, for female voice, piano and orch; Preludium and Fantasia for organ; Walking Upright-8 songs for female voice and violin; Ontogeny, for sym orch; Concerto for violin and orch; Evocation, for violin, piano and percussion; Form, for piano; Soliloquy for narrator, string quartet and percussion Rituals for sym orch; Movements for woodwind quartet; This Day, for female voice and piano; De Profundis for solo contra bass and instruments; Dimensions for soprano and instruments; In cantations for soprano and instruments; Discources for four instruments; Piece for violin and instrument. Convocation for chamber group; Chamber Sym for 10 solo players; Birthday Piece for Stefan Wolpe for piano; Seven, for piano 4 hands; Brass Quintet; Sonance, for Carillon; Configurations, for flute and piano; String Trio; Partita, for solo violin and for violin and 13 players; Poeme, for viola and piano; For Solo Trumpet; Partita-Fantasy, for cello and 16 players; Deux, for 2 pianos; Songs of Ecstasy, for soprano with piano, percussion and tape; Reyem or Musical Offering, for flute, violin, piano; all recordings; works commissioned by: Joseph Marx, 1951; Alma Morgenthau, 1953; Dimitri Mitropoulos, 1955; Fromm Found, 1960, 1967; Richard Waller, 1960; Bert Turetzky, 1960; Lewis Kaplin, 1962; Max Pollikoff, 1962, 1965; Milton and Peggy Salkind, 1963; Daniel Robins, 1964; Kindler Found, 1965; Sue Ann Kahn, 1965; Francis Burnett, 1966; Rhoda Lee Rhea, 1966; U Chgo, 1966; Ronald Anderson, 1967; Koussevitzky for Libr of Cong, 1967; Philip Lorenz and Ena Bernstein, 1967. Mem: Composers Catalogue, Inc; Intl Soc for Contemporary Music; Amer Composers Alliance; Amer Music Cen. Recipient: George Gershwin award, hon mention for Fantasy for Sym Orch, 1951; Frank Huntington Beebe Award, 1953; MacDowell Colony f, 1956-58; Clarinet Concerto, one of two works chosen to represent the US at Festival of Intl Soc for Contemporary Music, Strasbourg, Fr; It Govt grant, 1956-60; Brandeis creative arts award, 1962; Edgar Stern Family Fund award, 1962; William and Noma Copley Found award, 1962; Arts and Letters award, 1966; Nüremberg Recording award, 1966. Home: 150 W 92 St, New York NY. Office: U of Chgo, Dept of Music, Chicago, Ill.

SHAPIRA, Itzhak, Isr, farmer, organization exec; b. Pol, Aug 2, 1905; s. Menahem and Esther (Rosen); desc, 9th generation of Baal Shem Tov, Ture Zahav; in Isr since 1926; m. Lotte Friedler, 1928; c: Ruth, Joram, Hadassa. Secy gen, Agric Workers Org of Isr, since 1956; secy, moshavot dept, 1948-55; mem, Moshav Zofit; org, J workers in Petah Tikva, 1926-36; co-org, Hitashvut Haelef, 1930-34; secy, workers council: Raanana, 1940-44; Kfar Saba, 1944-47. Mem: Zionist Actions Comm; exec, Histadrut; secretariat, Mapai Party; co-org, Gordonia, Hitahdut, Hechalutz and Heb schs abroad. Home: Moshav Zofit, Isr. Office: 126 Allenby Rd, Tel Aviv, Isr.

SHAPIRA, Izhak, Isr, educator; b. Drohobycz, Pol, Oct, 1907; s. Abraham and Esther (Rabinovitch); in Isr since 1922; BA, hons, Queen Mary's Coll, London, 1933, MA, 1935; m. Betty Rosenberg, 1935; c: Sheila Schoenberg. Prin: Reali HS, Haifa, since 1955, vice prin, 1944-54; secondary sch, Kiryat Motzkin, 1939-44. Author: History of Modern Times, 4 vols, 1955-58; contbr essays and articles to daily press. Home: 10 Ehud St, Ahuza, Haifa, Isr. Office: POB 4920, Haifa, Isr.

SHAPIRA, Raphael, Isr, rabbi, educational dir; b. Lapitz, Russ, June 16, 1920; s. Israel and Taybe (Mankewitz); att Yeshivot: Etz Haim; Petah Tikva; Hebron; m. Zahawa Robman; c: Arieh, Simha, Hadassah, Shoshana, Haim Yakov. Pres, yeshivot: Tifereth Isr; Tifereth Hacarmel, both Haifa; found, head, coll for postgrads: Tifereth Hacarmel; Yarhei Kala. Mem: Comm for Observation Shabbat; Comm for Purification Family; Comm for Maintenance Mikvot. Home: 37 Pewsner St, Haifa, Isr. Study: 1 Geulah St, Haifa, Isr.

SHAPIRA, Rina, Isr, educator; b. Tel Aviv, Jan 28, 1932; d. Shraga and Devorah Netzer; BA, MA, Heb U, Jerusalem; PhD, Columbia U, NY, 1965; m. Uri Shapira, Dec 25, 1951; c: Irit, Opher, Michal. Chmn, dept sociol, Tel Aviv U. Prin contribs: studies on students in Isr; youth movements in Afr. Mem: Amer Sociol Assn; Isr Sociol Assn. Contbr articles on sociol and sociol of educ. Home: 9 Levi Itshak St, Tel Aviv, Isr. Office: Tel Aviv U, Ramat Aviv, Isr.

SHAPIRA, Yechiel, Isr, naval officer, business exec; b. Warsaw, Pol, Oct 8, 1921; s. Shmuel and Leah (Lichter); in Isr since 1935; att: Off's Gunnery Sch, 1951; Staff Off's Sch, 1957-58; m. Edna Kabak; c: Sara, Uri. Gen mgr, Beit Shean Textile Mills, since 1968; instr, Staff, and Command Coll, IDF, 1958-60; head, Naval IS, 1960-64; Naval attaché to W Eur, 1964-67, in Navy since 1948; ret with rank cdr, 1968. Haganah, 1938-40; J Brig, Brit Army, 1940-46; Aliyah Bet, Eur, 1946-48; Home: 32 Nordau St, Ramat Hasharon, Isr. Office: Beit Shean, Isr.

SHAPIRO, Alvin P, US, physician, educator; b. Nashville, Tenn. Dec 28, 1920; s. Samuel and Mollie (Levine); AB, Cornell U, 1941; MD, LI Coll of Med, 1944; m. Ruth Thomson, Aug, 1951; c: Debra, David. Prof, med, U Pittsburgh, since 1967, fac mem since 1956; att phys: VA Hosp, since 1960; Presbyterian U Hosp, since 1957; med teaching f, internal med, Commonwealth Fund Psychosomatic Prog, att phys, Cincinnati Gen Hosp, 1949-51; instr, internal med, U Cincinnati, 1949-51; asst prof, U Tex, 1951-56; att phys: Parkland Hosp; VA Hosp, both Dallas, 1951-56. Capt, US Army MC, 1946-47. Adv bd, council on high blood pressure research, AHA; mem: Amer Fed Clinical Research; Amer Soc Clinical Inves; Amer Coll Phys; Assn Amer Med Colls; NY Acad Sci; AMA; AAAS. Co-author: Clinical Evaluation of New Drugs, 1959; ed bd, Psychosomatic Medicine, since 1962; contbr to profsl jours. Home: 6212 Hampton St, Pittsburgh, Pa. Office: U of Pittsburgh, Sch of Med, Pittsburgh, Pa.

SHAPIRO, Arthur N, US, manufacturer, business exec; b. Haverhill, Mass, Aug 26, 1910; s. Harry and Fanny (Roffman); m. Sara Swartz, Nov 25, 1934; c: Ellen, Jane, Harriet, Lawrence. Pres: Shapiro Bros Shoe Co Inc, Auburn, Me, since 1937; Losarge Footware Inc, since 1956, with firm since 1927. Pres: Auburn Shoe Mfrs Assn, 1959-60; B'nai B'rith, 1943-44; J Comty Cen, 1955-56; Beth Jacob Syn, 1958-59; NE bd, ADL, 1953; treas, Auburn Taxpayers Assn, 1944; mem: bd dirs, Comty Chest, since 1940, exec comm, 1951; Zoning Bd, Auburn, 1947, personnel comm, 1952; Auburn PTA, 1950; ARC; Auburn C of C, 1953-54; adv comm, publicity bur, State of Me; Lewiston-Auburn J Fed; fund-raising comm, UJA, since 1937; USO, 1941-43; Cen Me Hosp, 1946; St Mary's Gen Hosp, 1948; US Bond Dr, since 1941; mem: Auburn Sports Assn; Masons; Shriners; Elks; Kiwanis; clubs: Martindale Country; Beth Jacob Men's, fmr pres. Home: 94 Shepley St, Auburn, Me. Office: Shapiro Bros Shoe Co, Auburn, Me.

SHAPIRO, Ascher H, US, consulting engr, educator; b. Bklyn, NY, May 20, 1916; s. Bernard and Jennie (Kaplan); SB, MIT, 1938, ScD, 1946; m. 2nd, Regina Lee, June 4, 1961; c: Beverly, Peter, Martha, Mary, Mathew. Ford prof engr, MIT, since 1962, mem fac since 1938, head dept mech engr, since 1965; cons ME since 1938; mem, tech sub-comms, Natl Adv Comm for Aeronautics; dir, Project Dynamo for AEC, 1952-53; visiting prof, applied thermodynamics, U Cambridge, 1955-56. Princ contribs: holder of patents on fluid metering apparatus, combustion chambers, propulsion system and aerothermopressor. Found, chmn, Natl Comm for Fluid Mech Films, since 1960; f: Amer Acad of Arts and Sci; Soc of MEs, mem exec comm, hydraulics divs; f, Inst Aeronautical Sci; mem: Natl Acad Sci; council, Atlantic Union Comm; Amer Soc for Engr Educ; AAAS; Sigma Xi; Tau Beta Pi; Pi Tau Sigma. Author: The Dynamics and Thermodynamics of Compressible Fluid Flow, vol I, 1953, vol II, 1954; Shape and Flow, The Fluid Dynamics of Drag, 1961; writer and prin in educ pictures in fluid dynamics; mem ed bd, Journal of Applied Mechanics, 1955; contbr to tech jours; delivered Akroyd Stuart Memorial Lectures, U Nottingham, Eng, 1956. Recipient: Naval Ordinance Devl award, 1945; Army-Navy Cert of Merit, 1947; Richards Memorial award, Amer Soc MEs, 1960, Worcester Reed Warner medal, 1965. Hobbies: sailing, gardening, sports.

Home: 6 Chapman St, Arlington, Mass. Office: MIT, Cambridge, Mass.

SHAPIRO, Betty K, US, communal worker; b. Wash, DC, Sep 26, 1907; d. Nathan and Mollie (Begorad) Kronman; m. Michael Shapiro, July 5, 1936. Intl pres, B'nai B'rith Women, since 1968, natl exec comm since 1959, natl chmn: mem comm, 1961-65, citizenship and civic affairs, 1957-61, public affairs, 1965-68, pres, dist No 5, 1955-56; pres, Argo chap, 1951-52, repr, Eur Crusade for Freedom trip, 1958, mem, ADL comm, since 1962, secy, Md-DC regional adv bd, 1955-57; mem: exec, JCC, Gtr Wash, since 1955, fmr secy; volunteer adv bd, DC Gen Hosp, since 1950; ARC; United Giver's Fund; League of Women Voters, Wash area; Amer Assn for UN; auxiliary, Heb Home for Aged Ladies; DC chap, Brandeis Women; NCCJ; Hadassah; fmr: pres, Natl Council J Jrs; exec comm, chmn gen solicitation, women's div, UJA; area chmn, Cancer Crusade; bd trustees, J Comty Cen; secy, off mgr, HIAS, all Wash, DC. Home: 6943 33 St, NW, Washington, DC.

SHAPIRO, Carl Frederick, US, journalist; b. Jersey City, NJ, Feb 28, 1938; s. Dorothy (Sharrow); att Montclair State Coll, NJ, 1956-58. Mgn ed, Independent Publ, since 1968; free lance writer; dir, Soc of Baroque Music, 1962-68; journalist: Paterson News; Westchester Historian, both 1968-69. Mem: ASCAP. Composer popular and choral music. Hobbies: music, lit. Home: 327 E 32 St, Paterson, NJ. Office: POB 162, Park Station, Paterson, NJ.

SHAPIRO, Charles Samuel, US, journalist; b. Phila, Pa, Feb 26, 1920; s. Harry and Elizabeth (Rantz); BS, U of Pa, 1941; LLB, U of Pa Law Sch, 1948; m. Charlotte Broder, Mar 8, 1953; c: Charles, Elizabeth, Susan. Ed, J Exponent, since 1963; atty, Phila, 1948-49; reporter, Bethlehem Globe-Times, Pa 1950-51; sports writer, Atlantic City Press, 1951-53; entertainment ed, Wilmington, Sunday Star, 1953-54; regional ed, TV Guide, 1954-63. Lt, USN 1942-46. Mem bd, Gtr Phila br, ACLU; fmr: chmn, Abington Dem Comm; mem bd: Phila YM-YWHA; SE Pa ADA. Recipient: cited for advancing cause of equal justice under law, Phila Bar Assn, 1969. Hobbies: golf, swimming. Home: 1155 Lindsay Lane, Rydal, Pa. Office: 1513 Walnut St, Philadelphia, Pa.

SHAPIRO, David, Isr, educator, chemist; b. Veshinty, Lith, Aug 10, 1903; s. Joseph and Bathsheva (Kagan); in Isr since 1933; att U Berlin 1922-24; PhD, U Kiel, 1927; m. Karola Reis, 1934; c: Yael. Prof, organic chem, Weizmann Inst of Sci, since 1954, sr chem, 1939-54. Prin contrib: synthesis of brain constituents, 1952-68. Mem: Isr, Amer, Brit Chem Socs; World Fed Neur; Multiple Sclerosis Research Comm. Contbr to profsl jours. Recipient: Weizmann Prize, 1955. Home: Neve Weizmann, Meonot Wolfson B, Rehovot, Isr. Office: Weizmann Inst of Sci, Rehovot, Isr.

SHAPIRO, David, US, rabbi; b. Jerusalem, Dec 12, 1907; s. Nathan and Nechama (Avner); in US since 1920; LLB, Bklyn Law Sch, 1933; ordained rabbi, Yavne Theol Sem, 1939; m. Leila Sinaiko, Aug, 1933; c: Herman, Judith. Rabbi: Temple Sinai, Hollywood, Fla, since 1952; J Comty, Green Bay, Wis, 1939-44; exec dir, AJCong, Chgo, 1944-49. Pres: Gtr Miami Rabb Assn; Midwest Zionist Org, 1949-52; chmn, UJA, Wis, 1949-52; mem: B'nai B'rith; ZOA; Comm of 100, Hollywood, Fla; club, Rotary. Home: 1150 S North Lake Dr, Hollywood, Fla. Study: Johnson and 12 Ave, Hollywood, Fla.

SHAPIRO, David, US, artist, educator; b. Aug 28, 1916; s. Jacob and Ida (Katz); att: Educ Alliance Art Sch, NY, 1934-36; Amer Artists Sch, NY, 1936-38; m. Cecile Peyser, June 18, 1944; c: Deborah, Anne. Asst prof, fine arts, Hofstra U, since 1961; tchr: Smith Coll, Mass, 1946-47; GWV Smith Mus of Art, Springfield, Mass, 1946-47; Bklyn Coll, summer, 1947; U of BC, Can, 1947-49; Comty Cen, Temple Rodeph Sholom, NY, 1949-51, 1953-55. One-man shows: U Art Gal, U of BC, 1948; Vancouver Art Mus, Can, 1949; Ganso Gal, NY, 1951; Ann Ross Gal, White Plains, NY, 1955; Milch Gal, NY, 1958, 1961, 1963; exhbs: Harry Salpeter Gal, NY, 1951; John Heller Gal, NY, 1952; Il Camino Gal, Rome, It, 1952, 1953; Ganso Gal, NY, 1953, 1954, 1955; Milch Gal, 1956-62; The Contemporaries, NY, 1957; natl and traveling exhibs: Pa Acad Annual; Whitney Annual; Chgo Art Inst; Bradley U; Cincinnati Art Mus; Audubon Annual; Bklyn Mus; Munson-Williams-Proctor Inst; Brandeis U; Seattle Art Mus; SF Mus of Art; Terry Art Inst; Carnegie Inst; Riverside Mus; U of Ga; Bordighera Mus, It; Alliance of Altoona; City Art Mus, St Louis; Houston Mus of Fine Arts; Art Inst, Zanesville; Little Gal, Phila; NW Printmakers Annuals; Natl Acad of Design; U of S Cal; Rochester Mus Fine Arts; New London Mus; Gal ENIT, Rome, It; US Info Agcy Traveling Graphics Exhibs; Fulbright Painters Exhb; represented in perm collections: Bklyn Mus Fine Arts, Springfield; Libr of Cong, Wash, DC; U of BC, Vancouver; Fine Arts Div, US Treasury, Wash, DC; Metrop Mus, NYC; Phila Mus, Pa; Slater Memorial Mus, Norwich, Conn; works reproduced in: Life; Time; Art News; Pictures on Exhibit; NY Times; Newsday; LI Daily Press; official observer, UNESCO Intl Conf of Artists, 1952. Pres, Soc Amer Graphic Artists; mem: Artists Equity Assn; Coll Art Assn; Comm on Art Educ; fmr: chmn, visual arts comm, U of BC, dir, art U gal. Author: Visual Design-Canadian Architecture, 1949. Recipient: purchase award, US Treasury Dept, 1942; 1st prize, Springfield Art League Annual, 1947; purchase prize, Bklyn Mus Print Annual, 1947; citation, Art for Dem Living Exhib, 1950; purchase prize, Libr of Cong Print Annual, 1950; Fulbright f, It, 1951-53; purchase prize: E States Art Exhb, Springfield Mus Fine Arts, 1957; 49th Annual, Soc Amer Graphic Artists. Home: 124 Susquehanna Ave, Great Neck, NY. Office: Hofstra U, Hempstead, NY.

SHAPIRO, David Solomon, US, rabbi; b. Phila, Pa, Dec 7, 1909; s. Solomon and Dinah (Epstein); BS, Lewis Inst, Chgo, 1936; ordained rabbi, Heb Theol Coll, Chgo, 1934, DHL, 1955; m. Etta Feinberg, June 21, 1937; c: Iolet, Dena. Rabbi, Cong Anshe Sfard, Milw, since 1948; lectr, dept Heb studies, U Wis, since 1963; rabbi: B'nai B'rith Jacob, Savannah, Ga, 1936-38; Brith Shalom, Erie, Pa, 1938-41; Knesses Isr, Indianapolis, Ind, 1941-48. Found, Hillel Acad, day sch, Milw; mem, RabCA. Author: Yeshode HaDat HaUniversalit, 1936; Midrash David, 1954; Torath Moshe VeHanevim, 1961; asso ed, Hadarom; mem, ed bd, Tradition; contbr ed, Judaism; contbr to J jours. Hobby: music. Home: 4903 W Townsend, Milwaukee, Wis. Study: 3447 N 51 St, Milwaukee, Wis.

SHAPIRO, Eli, US, educator; b. NYC, Jan 13, 1916; s. Samuel, and Pauline (Kushell); AB, hons, Bklyn Coll, 1936; AM, Columbia U, 1937, PhD, 1945; m. Beatrice Ferbend, Jan 18, 1946; c: Stewart, Laura. Prof, finance, Harvard Bus Sch, since 1962; staff mem, Bur Econ Research, since 1955; instr, asst prof Bklyn Coll, 1936-46; research asso, Natl Bur Econ Research 1938-40; econ analyst, US Treasury, 1941; head, consumer spending sect, div research, OPA, 1942; prof, finance, Sch of Bus, U Chgo, 1946-52; asso dean, Sch of Ind Mgmt, MIT, 1954-57, prof, finance, 1952-61; dep dir, research, Commn on Money and Credit, 1958-61; cons: Intl Cooperation Admn; Off, Eur Econ Coop; Eur Productivity Agcy; Inst for Defense Analyses; Jt Chiefs of Staff; US Treasury Dept; Council Econ Adv; Arthur D Little, Inc; mem, research adv bd, Comm for Econ Devl, since 1961. USN, 1942-46. Mem, adv bd: Bus Horizons; Intl Mgmt; F, Amer Acad Sci; mem: Amer Finance Assn; Amer Econ Assn; Mgmt Sci Assn. Author: Development of Wisconsin Credit Unions, 1946; co-author: Personal Finance in the United States, 1942; Money and Banking, 1941, 1948, 1953, 1958; contbr to bus jours. Hobbies: woodworking, gardening. Home: 514 Parker St, Newton Centre, Mass. Office: 209 Morgan Hall, Harvard Bus Sch, Boston, Mass.

SHAPIRO, Ezra Z, US, attorney, communal leader; b. Volozhin, Pol, May 7, 1903; s. Osias and Esther (Brudno); in US since 1906; LLB, O Northern U, 1925; m. Sylvia Lamport, Nov 27, 1932; c: Rena Blumberg, Daniel. Pvt practice, Cleveland, O, since 1925; dir of law, City of Cleveland, 1933-35. Chmn, KH, since 1971; hon pres, Amer J League for Isr, since 1960, pres, 1957-60; vice-chmn, Cleveland Comty Relations Bd; mem: natl bd govs, Amer Comm for Weizmann Inst of Sci, since 1950; natl bd trustees, Amer Friends of Heb U, since 1955; bd trustees, Cleveland J Comty Fed, since 1934; gen council, WZO, since 1951; vice-chmn, World Confd of Gen Zionists, repr, exec, JA; Amer, O, Cleveland Bar Assns; Park Syn; fmr: pres: Cleveland JCC; Cleveland Bd J Educ; natl vice-pres: UJA; Amer Assn for J Educ; natl bd govs, State of Isr Bond Org; delg, WZCs; club, City, Cleveland. Home: 13900 Shaker Blvd, Cleveland, O. Office: KH, Jerusalem, Isr.

SHAPIRO, George M, US, attorney; b. NYC, Dec 7, 1919; s. Samuel and Sarah (Milstein); BS, cum laude, LIU, 1939; LLB, Kent Scholar, Columbia Law Sch, 1942; m. Rita Lubin, Mar 29, 1942; c: Karen Raban, Stanford. Partner, Proskauer, Rose, Goetz and Mendelsohn, since 1955; off of counsel to

Gov NY State, 1945-54, counsel to Gov Thomas E Dewey, 1951-54; counsel, majority leader, pres pro tem, NY State Sen, 1955-59; chief counsel, NY State constitutional revision comm, 1960-61. Chmn, council, State U Colls of Med, since 1954; fmr: mem: bd trustees, LIU; bd of visitors, Columbia Law Sch; comm on policy and prog, Rep Natl Comm; exec bd, AJComm; chmn, comm on civil rights and liberties; clubs: Harmonie; Brae Burn, NY. Recipient: alumnus of year award, LIU, 1954; citation, Amer Isr C of C, 1961. Home: 1160 Park Ave, New York, NY. Office: 300 Park Ave, New York, NY.

SHAPIRO, Harold, US, attorney, public official; b. Pereyaslov, Russ, May 1, 1906; s. Max and Fannie (Bernstein); DJur, Marquette U, 1927; m. Sylvia Chinio, June 14, 1953; c: Remma. Atty: Miami Beach, Fla, since 1946; Milw, Wis, 1927-43; for Ind Theater Owners Assn, 1941-43; gen counsel, Motion Picture Ind of Wis, 1941-43; mem, Milw Motion Picture Commn, 1941-43; councilman, Miami Beach, Fla, 1955-59, mayor, 1953-55. Lt, USN, 1943-45. Mem bd dirs: J Home for Aged; J Fed, both Gtr Miami; Bur J Educ; Miami Beach Music and Arts League; mem: Civic League; C of C; Elks; Amer Legion; JWV; Masons; Miami Consistory; Mahi Shrine; radio round table, NCCJ; fmr: pres, Miami Beach Zionist Djst; chmn, JNF Council, Gtr Miami; cdr, JWV. Author: Trial Manual for Deck Court and Summary Court Martial Cases, 1944; commentator, local radio sta, 1949-53. Home: 2383 N Bay Rd, Miami, Fla. Office: 927 Lincoln Rd, Miami Beach, Fla.

SHAPIRO, Harold Roland, US, attorney; b. Bklyn, NY, Jan 4, 1904; s. Hayman and Celia (Merowitz); BS, NYU, 1924; DJur, NYU Law Sch, 1926; MA, Columbia U, 1938; m. Pauline Wolinsky, Oct 3, 1933; c: Jonathan, Salem. Asst Dist Atty, NY Co, since 1943; fmr: lectr, summers, Bklyn Coll, 1932-33; code auth counsel, Natl Recovery Act, 1933-35; prof, NYU Law Sch, 1934-41; asso, Harper and Matthews, 1941-43. Mem: bd, NY Soc for Deaf, FJP, since 1954, fmr pres, lay spiritual leader to J deaf; fmr, exec bd, Manhattan Council, Boy Scouts of Amer, chmn J comm, mem Natl J Comm on Scouting, fmr secy; comm on criminal courts, NY Co Lawyers Assn, chmn comm on state leg since 1967; Assn Bar, City NY; Masons; Grand St Boys Assn; fmr: mem: B'nai B'rith, dep to Inwood Lodge, pres, Wash Hgts Lodge, chmn, Manhattan ADL comm. Author: What Every Young Man Should Know About War, 1937; Six Million Speak, 1957; co-author: The National Industry Recovery Act: An Analysis, 1933; Trade Associations in Law and Business, 1938; contbr to periodicals. Home: 790 Riverside Dr, New York, NY. Office 155 Leonard St, New York, NY.

SHAPIRO, Harry, US, rabbi, teacher; b. Jerusalem, July 10, 1904; s. Mordecai and Ita (Gottlieb); in US since 1924; rabbi, Chgo Heb Theol Coll, 1927; att: U Wis, 1929-31; U Tex, 1931-32; BA, Baylor U, 1934; m. Sadye Fair, July 29, 1945; c: David, Judith, Martin. Tchr, Chgo J Acad, since 1962; J chaplain, Chgo State Hosp, since 1961; rabbi: Agudas Achim Cong, Corsicana, Tex, 1933-44; B'nai Zedek Cong, Kenosha, Wis, 1945-52; Beth Hillel Cong, Chgo, Ill, 1952-59. Mem: RabCA; Chgo Rabb Council; Mizrachi-Hapoel Hamizrachi; Chgo Bd Rabbis; secy, B'nai B'rith, Bismarck, ND, 1927; treas, Yeshiva Alumni, 1929; pres, Min Assn, Corsicana, Tex, 1937. Recipient: award, UJA, 1956-57. Hobby: music. Home: 5722 N Christiana Ave, Chicago, Ill. Study: State Hosp, 6500 W Irving Park, Chicago, Ill.

SHAPIRO, Harry L, US, anthropologist; b. Boston, Mass, Mar 19, 1902, s. Jacob and Rose (Clemens); AB, Harvard, 1923; MA, 1925, PhD, 1926; m. Janice Sandler, June 26, 1938 (decd); c: Thomas, Harriet, James. Prof, anthropology, Columbia U, since 1943; curator, Amer Mus Natl Hist, chmn, dept anthropology, 1942-69; with mus since 1926; research prof, Hawaii, 1930-35; asso, Bishop Mus, Honolulu. Dir: Louise Wise Services; Field Found; f: Natl Acad Arts and Sci; Amer Acad Arts and Sci; hon f, Die Anthropologische Gesellschaft, Wien; mem: Amer Ethnological Soc; Amer Assn Phys Anthropologists; Amer Anthropological Assn; AAAS; Natl Research Council; Amer Eugenics Soc; Social Sci Research Council. Author: Heritage of the Bounty, 1936; Migration and Environment, 1939; Aspects of Culture, 1956; The Jewish People, 1960; ed, Man, Culture and Soc, 1956; contbr to sci jours. Recipient: Theodore Roosevelt Dist Service Medal, 1964. Home: 26 E 91 St, New York, NY.

SHAPIRO, Henry, US, journalist; b. Rum, Apr 19, 1906; s. Simon and Buca (David); in US since 1920; BA, CCNY,

1929; LLB, Harvard U, 1932; m. Ludmilla Nikitina, June 11, 1937; c: Irina. Moscow bur mgr, UPI, since 1937; pvt law practice, NY, 1932-33; fgn corresp, Reuters, 1934-37; corresp, ABC, 1957-61; US War corresp, 1944-45; visiting lectr, U Cal, 1962-63; guest prof, U Tel Aviv, 1964. Pres, Anglo-Amer Press Assn, Moscow, 1942-43; mem: Alumni Assn, CCNY, Harvard U. Author: L'URSS Apres Staline, 1954. Recipient: natl headliner award, 1944, 1963; Nieman f, Harvard, 1954; dist achievements award, U of S Cal, 1960; Ford Found grant, 1962; Sigma Delta Phi Profsl Journalistic award,1965. Home and office: 220 E 42 St, New York, NY.

SHAPIRO, Herbert, US, physiologist; b. NYC, Nov 21, 1907; s. Morris and Sarah (Goldberg); BS, Columbia U, 1929, MA, 1930; PhD, Princeton U, 1934; m. Jeanette Halper, Sept 1, 1946; c: William, Marcia. Asso mem, research lab, Albert Einstein Med Cen, Phila, since 1961; Francis Hinton Maule f, Princeton U, 1932-33; f, NRC, U Chgo, 1930-35; Guggenheim f, biophysics, U Coll, London, 1937-38; asst prof, phys, CCNY, 1937; instr, phys: Vassar Coll, 1939-41; Hahnemann Med Coll and Hosp, 1941-43; staff mem, radiation lab, MIT, 1943-45; chief, biophysics sect, Edgewood Arsenal, Med Research Div, 1946; spec research f, NIH, 1947; research asso, U of Pa, 1948, asst prof, phys med, 1950-53; head, phys div, research dept, Wills Hosp, Phila, Pa, 1954-56; research asso, Women's Med Coll, Phila, Pa, 1958-61. F, AAAS; mem: Amer Phys Soc; Soc for Experimental Biol and Med; Amer Soc of Zool; Histochem Soc; Walter Reed Soc; Marine Biol Lab Corp; Sigma Xi; Intl Soc for Cell Biol; corresp mem, Soc Italiana della Zootecnica. Contbr to sci Jours. Home: 6025 N 13 St, Philadelphia, Pa. Office: Research Lab, Albert Einstein Med Center, Philadelphia, Pa.

SHAPIRO, Isaac, US, neuropsychiatrist, educator; b. London, Eng, Nov 3, 1899; s. David and Dora (Schulberg); in US since 1903; att Union Coll, 1918-20; MD, Albany Med Coll, 1924; m. Helen Goldsmith, Oct 1, 1925; c: Arthur, Elinor Brownstein. Pvt practice since 1926; asso prof, neur, Albany Med Coll, since 1937; neuropsycht: Ellis Hosp, since 1940, with hosp since 1924; E NY Orthopedic Hosp; att neuropsycht, City Hosp; cons neuropsycht, St Claire's Hosp; all Schenectady, NY; asst att neur, Albany Hosp; postgrad neur and psycht, Neuro-Psychiatric, Inst, Columbia U, 1931; cons, care and treatment polio patients, Schenectady Co, 1931; asso prof, neur, Russel Sage Coll, 1937; chmn, neuropsycht, Med Adv Bd 44, WW II, US Army, 1917. Dipl, Amer Bd of Neur and Psycht; f: Amer Coll Phys; Amer Acad Neur; Amer Psychiatric Assn; dir; Schenectady Co, Child Guidance Clinic, Mental Retarded Assn; vice-pres, Northeastern Sight Conservation Assn; chmn, Muscular Dystrophy Assn; J Home for Aged; chmn, sect neur and psycht; NY State Med Soc; fmr pres, Schenectady Co Med Soc; mem: Schenectady Bd Educ, 1952-59; wfr Bd, Schenectady Co; sub-comm on health, TB amd Heart Assn; Epileptic Soc; AMA; Natl Neuro-Psychiatric Assn; Natl Assn Epilepsia; Mohawk Valley Neuro-Psychiatric Soc; Kiwanis; Masons; J Comty Cen, Schenectady; Phi Sigma Delta; club, Kiwanis. Contbr to med jours. Recipient: Cong citation medal and cert, 1946. Home: 1764 Eastern Pkwy, Schenectady, NY, Office: 1603 Union St, Schenectady, NY.

SHAPIRO, J Irwin, US, jurist; b. NYC, Oct 13, 1904; s. Joseph and Dora (Buntzer); BS, NYU, 1925, LLB, 1926; m. Kate Gleitsman, May 30, 1926; c: Dianne Gasworth. Judge, Supr Court, Queens Co, NY, since 1962; chief, asst dist atty, Queens Co, 1948-51; city magistrate, LI City, 1951-54; justice, Domestic Relations Court, NYC, 1954; commn investigation, NY State, 1955-57; judge: City Court, NYC, 1957-60; Co Court, Queens Co, 1960-62. Pres C of C, Rockaways, 1950-52; bd dirs, Wyckoff Hgts Hosp; member: NY State and Queens Co Bar Assn. Home: 165 Noye Lane, Woodmere, NY. Office: 88-11 Sutphin Blvd, Jamaica, NY.

SHAPIRO, Jacob, US, attorney; b. NYC, Apr 30, 1887; s. Morris and Rachel (Gabarsky); BS, CCNY, 1906; JD, NYU, 1908; m. Gertrude Seligman, Mar 2, 1919; c: Marcia Segerman, Irwin. Ed in chief, Real Estate News, since 1961, law ed since 1942; treas, Gtr NY Mutual Ins Co, since 1964, dir, 1942-64; mem, Shapiro & Frieder, 1925-41. Chmn, Bkln Heb Home and Hosp for Aged; pres, Gtr NY Taxpayers Assn, 1953-54; mem: Selective Service Draft Bd; Bklyn J Cen: CCNY Alumni; NYU Alumni; NY Co Lawyers Assn. Author: Interesting Realty Decisions, 1941. Home: 135 Eastern Pkwy, Brooklyn, NY. Office: 225 Broadway, New York, NY.

SHAPIRO, Jacob Shimshon, Isr, government official; b. Elisavet-

grad, Russ, 1902; in Isr since 1924; att U Cracow, Pol; LLB, Law Sch, Jerusalem; m. Aya Hecht; c: Gamliel, Rahel Kleinman, David. Min of justice, since 1966; found mem, Kibbutz Givat Hashlosha, 1925; 1st atty gen, Govt of Isr, 1948-50; mem, 2nd and 3rd Knessets. Mem, Isr Lab Party. Office: Min of Justice, Jerusalem, Isr.

SHAPIRO, Joseph G, US, attorney; b. NYC, Jan 18, 1886; s. Barnet and Esther (Spitz); LLB, cum laude, Yale U, 1907; m. Helen Rosenstein, June 19, 1917; c: Howard, Carol Shepard, Elaine Silver. Pvt practice since 1907; chmn, Comm on Admission to Bar, since 1954; prosecutor, Shelton, Conn, 1913-20. Corp counsel, 1917-22, judge, City Court 1920-31; acting judge, Court Common Pleas, 1928; mem, Judicial Council of Conn, 1927-31; chmn, City Court Judges, 1930. Pres: Bridgeport Comty Forum, 1926-39; Bridgeport Bar Assn, 1948; mem: life, exec bd, UAHC, fmr pres NE council; bd govs, World Union for progressive Judaism; exec comm, Syn Council of Amer; trustee: Palmer Memorial Inst; Park Ave Temple, fmr pres; chmn, trial commn, Masonic Grand Lodge, Conn; mem, comm on rules and grievances, US Dist Court for Conn, secy, 1938; mem: Amer, NY, and Conn Bar Assns; NYC and Co Lawyers Assns; Amer Judicature Soc; Intl Assn Ins Counsel; Chi Tau Kappa; hon life mem, Masonic Grand Lodge, Isr; life mem, Amer Law Inst. Asso ed, Dimension. Hobbies: travel, lecturing. Home: 25 Cartright St, Bridgeport, Conn. Office: 855 Main St, Bridgeport, Conn.

SHAPIRO, Judah J, US, educator; b. NYC, June 12, 1912; s. Solomon and Bella (Silverman); Tchrs Dipl, Tchrs Inst, Yeshiva U, 1930; BA, CCNY, 1934; att Columbia U, 1934-36; EdD Harvard U, 1948; m. Florence Snyder, 1934; c: Jeremy, Daniel. Secy, Natl Found for J Culture, since 1959; lectr, hist, sociol, HUC-JIR Sch of J Communal Service; prof, sociol J Tchrs Sem and Peoples U; feature writer, New Middle East, London; lectr, J Orientation Training Sems; educ cons; instr, Heb, Sholem Aleichem Mitlshul, 1930-34; tutor, sociol, CCNY, 1934-36; club dir, 92nd St YMCA, NYC, 1934-36; asst exec dir, Bx YM-YWHA, 1936-39; exec dir, United J Comty, Harrisburg, Pa, 1939-42; dir, Hillel Found: Cornell U, 1942-43; Harvard U; MIT; Simons Coll; Boston U; Tufts Coll, all 1943-46, asso natl dir, 1946-48, natl dir, 1957-60; civilian chaplain, Harvard U, 1943-45; dir, cultural and educ reconstruction; JDC, 1948-54; Conf J Material Claims Against Ger, 1954-57. Mem: bd dirs, YIVO; natl council, JDC, cultural chmn; Natl Conf J Communal Service, fmr pres; natl comm, JBCA; Natl Council for J Educ; Farband; fmr: chmn, Hadassah Youth Reference Bd; secy, Natl Assn J Cen Workers; club: Harvard, NYC. mem, ed bd, Jewish Heritage; contbr to periodicals. Home: 302 W 86 St, New York, NY.

SHAPIRO, Karl Jay, US, poet, editor; b. Baltimore, Md, Nov 10, 1913; s. Joseph and Sarah (Omanski); att Johns Hopkins U, 1937-39; hon DHL, Wayne State U, 1961; m. Evalyn Katz, Mar 25, 1945 (div); c: Katherine, John, Jacob, Elizabeth; m. 2nd, Teri Kovach, July 31, 1967. Prof, Eng, U Cal, Davis, since 1968; poetry cons, Libr of Cong, 1946-47; asso prof, writing, Johns Hopkins U, 1947-1950; fmr prof, Eng: U Neb; U of Ill, Chgo Circle Campus, 1967-68. US Army, 1941-45. Author: Poems, 1935; Person, Place and Thing, 1942; The Place of Love, 1942; V-Letter and Other Poems, 1944; Essay on Rime, 1945; Trial of a Poet, 1947; Bibliography of a Modern Prosody, 1948; Poems, 1940-53; Beyond Criticism, 1953; Poems of a Jew, 1958; In Defense of Ignorance, 1960; Selected Poems, 1968; White-Haired Lovers, poems, 1968; To Abolish Children, 1968; ed: Poetry — A Magazine of Verse, 1950-56; Newberry Libr Bull; Prairie Schooner; contbr poetry to lit mags. F, Amer Letters, Libr of Cong, 1953-54; mem: Soc Midland Authors; Phi Beta Kappa; Amer Arts and Scis. Recipient: Jeanette S Davis prize, 1942; Guggenheim f, 1945-46; Levinson prize, 1943; Contemporary Poetry prize, 1943; Amer Acad Arts and Letters grant, 1944; Pulitzer prize, poetry, 1945; Shelley Memorial prize, 1945; co-recipient, Bollingen prize, poetry, 1968. Home: 1119 Bucknell Dr, Davis, Cal.

SHAPIRO, Leon, US, organization exec, writer; b. Korsun, Russ, July 14, 1905; s. Mark and Frida (Sheinblum); in US since 1941; Dipl, Social Sci, Kiev U, 1923; Licencie en Droit, U Toulouse, 1928; m. Luba Shapiro, 1946. Asst exec dir: Memorial Found for J Culture, since 1964; Conf on J Material Claims Against Ger, since 1955; writer, Russ, E Eur, Amer Jewish Year Book, since 1946; lectr, Russ-Jewish hist, Rutgers U, since 1969. Contbr: articles on Russ Jewry to profsl jours. Home: 171 W 71 St, New York, NY. Office: 215 Park Ave, S, New York, NY.

SHAPIRO, Manheim Simeon, US, social worker; b. Bklyn, NY, Sep 5, 1913; s. Solomon and Bella (Yanowitz); att: Bklyn Coll, 1930-34; U Mich, 1943-45; New Sch for Social Research, 1950-56; m. Esther Binder, Mar 21, 1935, (decd); c: Ezra. Sociol cons, lectr, since 1969; dir: prog and publs, B'nai B'rith Youth Orgs, 1946-49; J communal affairs, AJComm, 1949-66; cons, numerous J orgs, 1966-68; exec dir, Bur for Careers in J Service, 1968-69. F, Amer Sociol Assn; mem: Acad Cert Social Workers; Natl Assn Social Workers; Natl Assn Intergroup Relations Officials; Adult Educ Assn; Natl Assn J Cen Workers; Assn J Comty Relations Workers; Council on Adult Educ, Amer Assn for J Educ; Natl Conf J Communal Service; Soc for Sci Study Rel. Contrib ed, Nat J Digest, since 1967; mem, ed bd, Reconstructionist; contbr to profsl jours. Home: 5 Ridgeview Ave, West Orange, NJ.

SHAPIRO, Maurice Ansel, US, educator, engineer b. Denver, Colo, June 4, 1917; s. Joseph and Henrietta (Peiser); BA, Johns Hopkins U, 1941; MEngr, U Cal, 1949; m. Anne Klakovich, Aug 14, 1945; c: Karla, Mark, Deborah, Joel, Lisa. Prof, environmental health engr, Grad Sch of Public Health, U Pittsburgh, fac mem since 1951; asst sanitarian, res corps, USPHS, 1941-47; engr research asso, Amer Public Health Assn, 1949-51; visiting prof, Technion, Haifa, 1965-66. F, Amer Public Health Assn; member: Amer Soc CEs; Amer Technion Soc; Amer Water Works Assn; Water Pollution Control Fed; Sigma Xi. Home: 5557 Forbes Ave, Pittsburgh, Pa. Office: U of Pittsburgh, Grad Sch of Public Health, Pittsburgh, Pa.

SHAPIRO, Maurice M, US, physicist; b. Jerusalem, Nov 13, 1915; s. Asher and Miriam (Greenbaum); in US since 1921; BS, U Chgo, 1936, MS, 1940, PhD, 1942; m. Inez Weinfeld, Feb 8, 1942 (decd); c: Karla, Ellen, Raquel; m. 2nd, Marion Gordon, Aug 20, 1968. Chief sci, Lab for Cosmic-Ray Physics, USN Research Lab, Wash, DC, since 1965, chair, cosmic-ray physics, since 1966, head, cosmic-ray br, 1949-65, sup, nucleonics div, 1953-65; lectr, physics, U of Md, since 1949; cons, Capitol Radio Elec Inst, since 1958; instr: math and physics, Chgo City Coll, 1937-41; math, Gary (Ind) Coll, 1942; experimental physicist, USN Dept, 1942-44; lectr, George Wash U, 1934-44; group leader, mem, coord council, Los Alamos Lab, U Cal, 1944-46; sr physicist and lectr, nucleonics, Oak Ridge Natl Lab, Tenn, 1946-48; cons; Fairchild Engine and Aircraft Corp, 1948-49; Argonne Natl Lab, U Chgo, 1949; asso prof, physics, U of Md, 1950-51; cons, nuclear products div, ACF Inds, 1956-58; lectr, Enrico Fermi Intl Sch Physics, Varenna, It, 1962; Guggenheim f, visiting prof, physics, Weizmann Inst of Sci, Isr, 1962-63. Mem, visiting comm, Bartol Found, Franklin Inst, Phila, since 1966; delg: Int Conf Nuclear Physics, Oxford-Harwell, Eng, 1950; Intl Union Pure and Applied Physics, Fr, 1953, Guanajuato, Mex, 1955, Varenna, It, 1957, Geneva, 1958, Moscow, 1959, and 1960, Kyoto, Jap, 1961, CLARC, Mex, 1961, Bolivia, 1962, cosmic ray conf, Jaipur, India, 1963, London, 1965, Calgary, 1967, Budapest, 1969; Chmn: US Intl Geophysical Year Commn on Interdisciplinary Research, Natl Acad Scis, 1958-60; exec comm, Assn Los Alamos Scis, 1946; Assn Oak Ridge Engrs and Scis, 1947-48; pres, Phil Soc, Wash, DC; cons, panel on cosmic radiation, US Natl Comm for Intl Geophys Year; mem: bd, Technion Soc of Wash; Amer Astronomic Soc; It Phys Soc; panel on emulsion experiments, Natl Acad Scis; Space Sci Bd; Fed Amer Scis; Sigma Xi; Phi Beta Kappa; US steering comm, Intl Coop Emulsion Flights; f: Amer Phys Soc; AAAS; Wash Acad Sci. Mem, ed bd, Astrophysics and Space Sci, since 1967. Recipient: dist civilian service award, USN Dept, 1967. Home; 6511 Elgin Lane, Bethesda, Md. Office: Naval Research Lab, Washington, DC.

SHAPIRO, Max, S Afr, business exec, b. Libau, Russ, Feb 7, 1896; s. Solomon and Freda (Lewinson); in S Afr since 1907; m. Hilda Whitaker, Sep 11, 1946; Dir, chmn: Park Cinemas 1952 Ltd; Odeon Cinemas Ltd; chmn, Hildemax Properties Ltd; mgn dir, chmn, Bank Properties Ltd; appd Commn of Oaths, 1928. Mem, exec comm, Assn C of C in S Afr, since 1946; found, pres, Commercial Exch, since 1956; found, pres, Vereeniging and Dist Heb Benevolent Soc, since 1958; mem exec, Publicity Assn; hon life pres, Vereeniging C of C; hon life vice pres, Vereeniging United Heb Inst; fmr: mem: adv council, vice pres, pres, C of C; Town Council; bd, Commercial and Tech HS; pres, Heb Inst, vice-chmn of council. Home: 8 Brandmuller Dr, Three Rivers, Vereeniging, S Afr. Office: POB 227, Vereeniging, S Afr.

SHAPIRO, Max A, US, rabbi; b. Worcester, Mass, Jan 23, 1917; s. Samuel and Clara (Wolfgang); BA, Clark U, 1939; MEd, Boston Tchrs Coll, 1940; BHL, HUC, 1952, ordained rabbi, 1955; EdD, U Cincinnati, 1960; m. Bernice Clein, 1944; c: Susan, Steven. Rabbi, Temple Isr, Minneapolis, Minn, since 1963; mem fac, Hamline U, St Paul, since 1958; USAAF, 1941-46. Pres: Minn Rabb Assn, 1962-64; and founder, Minn Council on Rel and Race, 1967; vice-pres: Minneapolis Urban Coalition, 1968; Amer Friends Heb U, since 1960; dir: J Fed; JDC, mem, natl council; AJComm; ADL; delg, White House Conf on Children and Youth, 1960, mem: Minn State Commn on Hum Rights, since 1967; Amer Acad of Rel; bd, Alumni Overseers, HUC-JIR, since 1966; Hennepin Co Hosp Adv Comm; J Commn of J Educ, CCAR; exec comm, Gov's Comm on Youth; CCAR; B'nai B'rith; Acad Rel and Mh; AJ Cong. Author: A Passover Story, 1959; In Time of Grief; Living as a Reform Jew; contbr to rel jours. Home: 2830 Inglewood Ave, Minneapolis, Minn. Study: 2324 Emerson Ave, Minneapolis, Minn.

SHAPIRO, Michael Ronald, US, business exec; b. LA, Cal, Feb 26, 1940; s. Issadore and Rebecca (Friesh); cert spec course, Northwestern U, Chgo, Ill, 1956; JD, U of S Cal, 1964; BA, UCLA, 1969; c: David, Brian. Pres: Prophesy Records; Gulf Pacific Inds, since 1968; pvt practice since 1965; law clerk, Hon Walter Ely, US Dist Court of Appeals, 9 Circuit, 1964-65; asso: Kadison & Quinn, LA, 1965-66; Irmas & Rutter, Beverly Hills, Cal, 1966-68. Mem: Phi Delta Phi; State Bar of Cal; Amer Bar Assn; LA Co Bar Assn, exec council; Amer Judicature Soc; World Affairs Council; Town Hall; UCLA Alumni Assn; U of S Cal Alumni Assn; Citizens for Cal Higher Educ, interim chmn. Co-author: How to Make a Hit on a First Date, 1965; contract songwriter, Beechwood Music Corp; producer of: musical version HAIR; various albums for: Atlantic Records; Uni Records; Hour Glass Records. Recipient: Silver Key award, Amer Law Student Assn, 1964. Home: 11926 Goshen, Los Angeles, Cal. Office: 8961 Sunset Blvd, Los Angeles, Cal.

SHAPIRO, Morris A, US, physician; b. Glens Falls, NY, Aug 13, 1909; s. David and Dora (Schulberg); AB, Union Coll, Schenectady, NY, 1932; MD, Albany Med Coll, 1936; m. Hester Blatt, Dec 21, 1941; c: Susan, William. Pvt practice, card, since 1946; chief of staff, Ellis Hosp, since 1962, att med since 1950, att card since 1958; att med, St Claire's Hosp, since 1954, att card since 1957; cons card: Northeastern NY Orthopedic Hosp, since 1951; Comty Hosp, since 1957; J Home for the Aged, Troy, NY since 1959; asso med, Albany Med Coll, since 1948. Maj, US Army. F: Amer Coll Card; Amer Coll Chest Phys; FACP; cert, Amer Bd Internal Med; mem: bd, Schenectady Mus, since 1961; Schenectady Recreational Adv Comm, since 1961; AMA; Schenectady Co Med Soc, fmr vice-pres; NY State Med Soc; AHA; Schenectady Health Assn; fmr: chmn, AHA Fund Drive, Schenectady; Gov for Upstate NY, Amer Coll Card. Contbr to med jours. Recipient: Silver Star; Oak Leaf Cluster; Purple Heart; Pres Unit Citation; 6 Battle Stars. Hobbies: astronomy, photography, golf. Home: 2009 Lexington Pkwy, Schenectady, NY. Office: 1603 Union St, Schenectady, NY.

SHAPIRO, Morris J, US, surgeon; b. Rochester, NY, Oct 21, 1913; s. Simon and Rose (Goldstein); BA, hons, U Rochester, 1933, MS, 1934; MD, Jefferson Med Coll, 1938; m. Miriam Fischer, Mar 27, 1946; c: Barbara, Donna. Pvt practice since 1942; clinical asst prof, surg, U Rochester Med Sch, on fac since 1952. Maj, US Army, 1942-46. Pres, United JWF, Rochester; Genesee Valley Med Found; vice-pres, JCC of Rochester; bd dirs: Comty Chest of Rochester; Council Social Agcys, Rochester; J Family Service; J Young Men's and Women's Assn, 1956-59; J Home and Infirmary; dipl, Amer Bd of Surg; f, Amer Coll of Surgs; mem: Phi Beta Kappa; Alpha Omega Alpha; AMA; Phi Lambda Kappa; Phi Epsilon Pi. Recipient: 4 battle stars. Home: 3750 Elmwood Ave, Rochester, NY. Office: 720 East Ave, Rochester, NY.

SHAPIRO, Naftoli, Scotland, rabbi; b. Mir Minsk, Pol, May 5, 1906; s. Sender and Rivka (Arrol); in Eng since 1933; ordained rabbi, Rabb colls: Mir, Radun, Lomza; MA Glasgow U, 1939; m. Rose Slotki, Sep 26, 1952. Rabbi, Gt Cen Syn, since 1956; prin, Glasgow Rabb Coll since 1933. Pres, Tifereth Bachurim; hon pres, Glasgow Sabbath Observance Org; fmr pres, Glasgow Ritual Council. Hobbies: chess, reading, walking. Home: 12 Leslie, Glasgow, Scotland. Study: Gt Cen Syn, Glasgow, Scotland.

SHAPIRO, Philip, US, labor exec; b. Vilna, Russ, May 20, 1896; s. Benjamin and Rebecka (Shapiro) Kaslov; in US since 1908; m. Beatrice Chaikes, 1919; c: Lawrence, Sylvia Lindsey,

Connie Roth. Chmn, United Heb Trades of State NY, since 1969; fmr pres, Delicatessen Union Local 60, AFL-CIO. Vice-chmn, United HIAS Council of Orgs; vice-pres, Union Label and Service Dept, State of NY; mem exec bd, Natl Lab Comm for Lab Isr. Home: 190 Shakespeare Ave, Bronx, NY. Office: 175 E Broadway, New York, NY.

SHAPIRO, Raymond N, US, plastic surgeon; b. Bklyn, NY, June 29, 1915; s. Simon and Ida (Shakefsky); BS, NYU, 1935, MD, 1938; DDS, 1940; m. Beryl Petchesky, Jan 24, 1942; c: Peter, Donald. Pvt practice since 1948; cons: St John's Episcopal Hosp; Carson C Pecks Memorial Hosp; att plastic surg, LI J Hosp; asso plastic surg, Kings Co Hosp; clinical asst prof, plastic surg, State U Downstate Med Cen, 1957. US Army MC, 1942-45. F: Amer Coll Surgs; Amer Coll Dent; mem: bd zoning appeals, Village of Hewlett Harbor; NY Acad Med; Nassau Acad of Med; AMA; Amer Dent Assn; Nassau Co Med Soc; 2nd Dist Dent Soc; Amer Soc of Maxillo-Facial Surgs; Amer Soc for Cleft Palate Rehab; NY Acad of Sci; AAAS, clubs: US Power Squadron; Woodmere Bay Yacht; Virgin I Yacht. Contbr to plastic surg jours. Home: 1110 Seawane Dr, Hewlett Harbor, NY. Office: 230 Hilton, Hempstead, NY.

SHAPIRO, Sam O, US, business exec; b. Chgo, Ill, Dec 28, 1902; s. Pincus and Sarah (Greenwald); AB, U of Ill, 1923; div; c: Alan, Richard; m. 2nd, Toni Dale, Apr 14, 1965. Vice-pres, dir, Cowles Mag and Bc Inc, since 1952; staff, circulation dept, Chgo Tribune and Liberty Mag, 1924-31; circulation mgr, Macfadden Publ 1931-38, vice-pres, 1941-48. Natl commn, NY exec comm, ADL; chmn, publ ind div: UJA; Fed Heb Charities of NY; f, Brandeis U. Home: 300 E 57 St, New York, NY. Office: 488 Madison Ave, New York, NY.

SHAPIRO, Samuel, US, educator; b. Ellenville, NY, Aug 23, 1927; s. Abraham and Ethel (Victor); BS, CCNY, 1948; MA, PhD, Columbia U, 1948-56; m. Gloria Kaufman, June 19, 1959; c: Iabel, David. Asso prof, U Notre Dame, since 1963. Cpl, USAF, 1945-47. Author: Richard Henry Dana, 1961; Invisible Latin America, 1963. Hobbies: chess, gastronomy, oenology, camping. Home: 305 Wakewa St, South Bend, Ind. Office: U of Notre Dame, Notre Dame, Ind.

SHAPIRO, Sarya, Isr, journalist; b. Grodek, Pol, Jan 12, 1910; s. Mordechai and Miriam (Weissenberg); in Isr since 1926; att Herzliya Sch, Tel Aviv; m. Yochewed Mozenerg, Oct 8, 1938; c: Thaira, Ariella. Sr reporter, head Tel Aviv office, Jerusalem Post, since 1948; columnist, Haboker, Heb daily, 1935-48; mil corresp, IDF, 1948-60. Mem, Journalists Assn, Tel Aviv. Ed: The Loyal Rebel Papers, 1964; trans stories into Heb. Home: 6 Hakerem St, Tel Aviv, Isr.

SHAPIRO, Solomon B, US, rabbi; b. Rum, Mar 29, 1922; s. Mordecai and Molly (Rabinowitz); desc Baal Shem Tov; in US since 1922; ordained rabbi, Mesifta Talmudical Sem, 1943; BA, Bklyn Coll, 1943; DD, Phila Coll, 1962; m. Mildred Sodden, 1946; c: Mordekai, Brocha, Miriam, Mala. Rabbi: Cong B'nai Abraham, E Flatbush, since 1947; Cong Degal Mordecai, since 1947; chaplain: Kingsbrook J Med Cen; Kings Co Hosp Cen: lectr, comparative rel, Kings Co Sch of Nursing; prin, Beth Rivkah Sch for Girls, 1943-45; rabbi, Cong Anshei Ozaritz, Bklyn, 1945-47. exec-dir, Mesifta Rabbi Chaim Berlin, 1946-48. Pres, Rabb Alumni Mesifta Torah Vodaath Talmudical Sem; vice-pres: Rabb Alliance of Amer, 1957-59; Rabb Bd, E Flatbush, since 1959; mem, bd trustees: Union Orthodox Rabbis, US and Can, since 1960; Rabb Alliance of Amer, since 1959; mem, bd dirs, Bklyn Assn for MH; mem: exec, RABCA, since 1961; Rabb Bd Gtr NY; Amer Sociol Assn; Amer Correctional Assn; Free Sons of Isr; Mizrachi Org of Amer. Contbr to Rabb Jours. Recipient; awards: State of Isr 1957, 1958, 1959; J Chronic Disease Hosp, 1958; Educ Inst of Amer, 1962; Yeshiva and Meshivta, Eastern Pkwy, 1969. Hobby: photography. Home: 831 Linden Blvd, Brooklyn, NY. Study: 407 E 53 St, New York, NY.

SHAPIRO, Solomon, K, US, rabbi; b. Jerusalem, Apr 23, 1920; s. Jacob and Gittle (Kehane); in US since 1929; BA, Bklyn Coll, 1942; ordained rabbi, Yavne Heb Theol Sem, 1942; att NYU, 1944-46; m. Rebecca Mandel, Dec 28, 1946; c: Eli, Vivian, Harold, Stanley, Abraham, Maharshal. Rabbi, Cong Yeshiva Yavne, exec dir, Yavne J Theol Sem, since 1950; prin, Heb Inst S Bklyn, 1938-43; rabbi: Cong Beth Isr, Stevens Point, Wis, 1946-47; Temple Beth Isr, Salisbury, Md, 1947-50. Pres. Beth Tziporah Heb Inst; trustee, Machon Maharshal Sem, Jerusalem, Isr; mem: bd dirs, RaCA; NYC

Dept Social Services. Home: 718 E 7 St, Brooklyn, NY. Study: 510 Dahill Rd, Brooklyn, NY.

SHAPIRO, Sylvia L, US, communal worker; b. NYC, Mar 10, 1910; d. Solomon and Anne (Lamport) Lamport; BA, Hunter Coll, 1931; m. Ezra Shapiro, 1932; c: Rena, Daniel. Chmn: natl service comm, natl bd, Hadassah, since 1967, women's div, Bonds for Isr, Cleveland, 1960-61; pres, Cen States Region, 1948-50, natl vice-pres, 1950-53; mem, bd trustees, Bur J Educ, Cleveland, since 1953; mem, bd govs, Coll J Studies, Cleveland, since 1958; mem, natl bd, women's div, State of Isr Bonds, since 1962; chmn Cleveland br, 1960-61; mem, bd Gtr Cleveland Women's Comm for Civil Rights; mem: Cleveland chap, women's comm, Brandeis U; Public Wfr Comm, J Comty Fed; exec, women's cabinet, UJA, 1960-64; Women's City Club of Cleveland; Alpha Epsilon Phi; Park Syn, club, Women's City, Cleveland. Home: 13900 Shaker Blvd, Cleveland, O.

SHAPRAY, William, Can, chartered acctnt; b. Montreal, Oct, 24, 1901; s. Harris and Minnie (Joseph); BComm, McGill u, 1920; m. Lillian Schuander, Mar 17, 1929; c: Donald, Howard. Owner, Wm Shaprey and Co, chartered acctnts, since 1924. Pres, Montreal chap, Can Friends Heb U, 1956-58, treas, 1937-53; mem, Inst Chartered Acctnts, Que. Home: 17 Forden Ave, Westmount, Que, Can. Office: 210-11 Drummond Bldg, 1117 St Catherine St, W Montreal, Can.

SHARE, Nathaniel S, US, rabbi; b. Montreal, Can, May 12, 1908; s. Moses and Dora (Levey); in US since 1917; BHL, HUC, Cinn, 1929; BA, U Cincinnati, 1931; ordained rabbi, HUC, 1932, hon DD, 1958; MSW, Tulane U, Sch of Social Work, 1959; m. Isabelle Burr, Aug 4, 1935; c: Susan (decd); Jonathan. Rabbi, Cong Gates of Prayer, New Orleans, since 1934. Mem: CCAR, exec bd mem, 1951-53; B'nai B'rith; Acad Rel and Mh; fmr pres, La Assn for Retarded Children, 1954-57. Home: 4918 S Galvez St, New Orleans, La. Study: 1139 Napoleon, Ave, New Orleans, La.

SHAREF, Zeev, Isr, cabinet minister, legislator, b. Izvor-Szeletin, Rum, Apr 21, 1906; s. Meir and Rachel (Pomeranz); in Isr since 1925; m. Henya Udin, 1940; c: Klonymus, Yair, Zippor, Zvi. Min of Housing, since 1969, Min of Commerce and Ind, 1966-69, Min of Finance, 1968-69; MK since 1965; dir, Fgn Trade Bank Ltd, since 1963; mem, Kibbutz Givat Brenner, since 1935; official, Pal Workers Fund, 1925-28; mem, Kibbutz Shfayim, 1929-31; on Zionist missions to Pol, Latvia, Aus, Fin, 1931-35; secy: Hapoel, 1935-40; Haganah, 1940-44; political dept, JA, 1944-47; i/c preparation admn blueprint for J State, laid organizational and manpower found for future govt mins, 1947-48; secy, Govt of Isr, dir gen, Off of PM, 1948-57; civil service commn, 1951-54; dir, state revenue, Min of Finance, 1954-61; spec adv to PM Levi Eshkol, 1964-65; chmn, Ports Auth, 1962-66. Author: Three Days (May 12-15, 1948), pub in: Heb; Eng; Fr; ed: Das Buch von Arbeit, (Yiddish), 1933; Hahoger, 1938; Chaim Arlosoroff Yoman Yerushalaim, 1948; contbr to local and fgn press. Office: Min of Housing, Jerusalem, Isr.

SHARENSON, Bessie Neveloff, US, dentist; b. Yomul, Russ, Jan 15, 1894; d. Bernard and Mollie (Wessler) Neveloff; in US since 1897; att Columbia U, 1916-19; m. Reuben Sharenson, Apr 21, 1921; c: Naomi Copeland, Isabel Davidoff. Pvt practice since 1916; dent: Jt Bd of Sanitary Control, Ladies Garment Union, 1916; home off, Metrop Life Ins Co, NY, 1918-21; Forsyth Dent Clinic, Boston, 1921-23. Hon pres: NE Region, Hadassah, Boston; League J Women's Orgs, Boston; fmr: pres: Heb Tchrs Coll, Brookline, Mass; Pal Heb U Scholarship Assn; Boston City Fed of Org; secy, Pal Agric Assn, Boston; life mem: Pal Agric Assn; Hadassah; Beth Isr Hosp, Boston; Childrens Home; Heb Tchrs Coll, Brookline; Brandeis U; J Memorial Hosp, Boston; ZOA; Kehillath Isr Sisterhood, Brookline; Mizrachi Rel Zionists Amer; mem: J Womens Health Assn; J Rehab Cen, Rosindale, Mass; Sisterhood, Adath Sharon, Mass; Friends of Boston Sym. Home and Office: 1812 Beacon St, Brookline, Mass.

SHARFMAN, Isaiah Leo, US, economist, educator; b. Polonnoe, Russ, Feb 19, 1886; s. Nathan and Rhoda (Shikes); in US since 1894; AB, Harvard Coll, 1907; LLB, Harvard Law Sch, 1910; hon LLD, Brandeis U, 1964; m. Minnie Shikes, July 7, 1910; c: Nelson, Warren, Marcia Gilmartin. Prof em, U Mich, since 1955, prof, econ, 1914-55, Henry Carter Adams U prof, 1947-55, chmn, dept econ, 1927-54, fac mem since 1912; prof, law and pol sci, Imperial Pei-Yang U, 1910-11; visiting prof, Stanford U, summer, 1939. Chmn: Pres emergency bds in RR lab disputes, since 1937, arbitration boards under RR Lab Act, intermittently since 1941, referee, Natl RR Adjustment Bd, since 1936; pres, Amer Econ Assn, 1945; trustee, Brandeis U, since 1955; chief investigator, Commn Regulation of Pub Utilities, Natl Civic Fed, 1912-13; dir: inves anti-trust policy, Natl Ind Conf Bd, 1923-24; research on admn law and procedure for Commonwealth Fund, 1925-37; mem: adv comm on RR employment to Fed Coord of Transp, 1933-36; adv comm on economists and social scis, Pres Comm on Civil Service Improvement, 1939; NLRB, 1942-43; Natl RR Lab Panel, 1943-46; AAUP; Amer Stat Assn; Amer Political Sci Assn; Acad Political Sci; Mich Acad Sci, Arts and Letters, fmr pres; Amer Friends Heb U; Conf on J Natl Studies; Amer Econ Assn, fmr pres; AJComm; J Acad of Arts and Scis; f: Int Inst of Arts and Letters; Ind Relations Research Assn; Natl Acad Arbitrators; Amer J Hist Soc. Author: Railway Regulation, 1915; The American Railroad Problem, 1921; The Interstate Commerce Commission, 5 vols, 1931-37; co-found: Harvard Menorah Soc, 1907; Menorah Jour, 1915; ed asso, Amer Econ Rev; contbr: Ency of the Social Scis; profsl jours. Recipient: James Bar Ames prize, legal writing, Harvard Law Sch, 1939; Dist f, Amer Econ Assn, 1965. Home and office: Cosmos Club, 2121 Massachusetts Ave, NW, Washington, DC.

SHARGEL, Yaacov Zvi, Isr, author; b. Chelem, Pol, Dec 8, 1905; s. Yitzhak and Bela; in Isr since 1926; att: High Tech Inst, 1930-36; m. Fira Zavels, Oct 3, 1934; c: Daniel, Sarah Wolfson. Cultural admn mgr, Munic Petah Tikva, since 1961; fmr ed lit sect: Israel Shtime; Katif, munic almanac. Haganah, 1929-49. Author Yiddish poems: In Bloen Licht, 1938; Fun Vei un Gloiben; 1958; Sunike Shvelen, 1968. Hobby: philately. Home: Shikun Mapam, 1 Yitzhaki St, Petah Tikva, Isr. Office: 2 Aliya St, Petah Tikva, Isr.

SHARI, Reuben, Isr, government official, attorney; b. Kishinev, Bessarabia, Apr 21, 1903; s. Moshe and Zipora (Gutterman) Schreibman; in Isr since 1925; att Jassy U, 1920-24; m. Anita Zuckerman, 1924; c: Binyamina Dmiel, Yael Levin, Chava Sekeles. Ret; Civil Service Commn, 1962-67; fmr mem, cen comm, Mapai; secy, Lab Council: Rehovot, 1934-43; Jerusalem, 1943-48; dep mayor, Jerusalem, 1949-51; MK, Mapai, 1949; fmr dep Min of Transport and Communications. Mem: Haganah Command; Jerusalem Emergency Council internal security and recruiting dept during siege. Co-found, Zeirei Zion, Bessarabia; Mapai; Histadrut delg, Zionist, Lab and Agric Cong. Home: 11 Rashba St, Jerusalem, Isr.

SHARLITT, Herbert Victor, US, business exec; b. NYC, July 12, 1912; s. Michael and Matilda (Goldstone); BA, U Mich, 1933; MBA, Grad Sch of Bus, 1935. Pres, Transco Plastics Corp, since 1940. Lt, USAF, 1942-46. Pres: land lodge 16, B'nai B'rith; J Vocational Service Agcy, Cleveland; mem: Phi Beta Kappa, Phi Epsilon Pi. Recipient: Army commendation medal, WW II. Home: 3715 Warrensville Cen Rd, Cleveland, O. Office: 3828 E 91 St, Cleveland, O.

SHARMAN, Brian, Eng, business exec, communal leader; b. Chelm, Pol, May 2, 1908; s. Chaim and Chaja; in Eng since 1932; deg, State Heb Sem, Warsaw, Pol, 1928; dipl, City Lit Inst, U London, 1944; m. Jessica Mestel, Mar 19, 1944; c: Vivian Laurence, Helen, Julian. Dir, B J Sharman Investments, Ltd, since 1959; headmaster, Heb Schs, Tarbuth, Pol, 1928-32; sub-ed, Jewish Post, London, 1933-35; corresp, Warshaw Newspapers, London, 1933-39; dir, World J Press, Photonews, 1935-37; sub-ed, London produc, Yavneh, geog atlas and globe, Heb for Isr, 1945-50. Pres, Hertford dist Zionist Socs; fmr: repre: bd mgmt, dist council, Syn; United Syn, both Hertford. Hobby: lectr on J topics to various J and Zionist socs. Home: 15 Beechwood Gardens, Ilford, Essex, Eng. Office: Ilford Lane Chambers, Ilford, Essex, Eng.

SHARNOVA, Sonia, US, voice tchr, singer; b. Chgo, Ill, May 2, 1896; d. Joseph and Leah (Levi) Shapiro; studied and sang in Eur, 1924-28; m. L J Luechauer, 1924 (div); 2nd m. I T Feingold, 1936 (decd). Tchr, singing, since 1937; instr, chmn, voice dept, Chgo Conservatory; soloist, contralto; German Opera Co, 1929-30; Chgo Civic Opera Co, 1939-40; Cincinnati Opera, 1932-33; St Louis Opera, 1936-39. Mem: Natl Assn Tchrs Singing, fmr pres, Chgo chap; Soc Amer Musicians, pres, 1964-65; Sigma Alpha Iota, hon mem; Hadassah. Contbr to profsl jours. Home: 1360 Lake Shore Dr, Chicago, Ill. Office: Chgo Conservatory, 64 E Van Buren St, Chicago, Ill.

SHARON, Arieh, Isr, architect; b. Yaruslav, Pol, May 28, 1900; in Isr since 1920; grad, Bauhaus, Dessau, 1929; m. Haya

Sankowsky, 1932; c: Eldar, Uri, Yael. Partner, Arieh and Eldar Sharon, architects, town planners, since 1964; mem, Kibbutz Gan Shmuel, 1920-26; i/c architectural off, Hannes Meyer and Fed Sch for Trade Unions, Berlin, Ger, 1929-31; pvt, practice, Tel Aviv, 1931-39; town planner, 1940-48; dir, natl planning dept, PM's off, 1948-53; UN expert, regional planning, India, Burma, 1954; partner with B Idelson, 1955-64. Works executed: exhb bldg for Histadrut: co-op housing schemes; old Beilinson Hosp; housing estates; kibbutzim; sch comtys; kibbutz dining halls; Beilinson Hosp Cen; Regional Hosp, Beersheva; Ichilov Munic Hosp, Tel Aviv; Ezrat Nashim Mental Hosp; Eilat Regional Hosp; Rehovot Health Cinic; Isr Pavilion, Intl Exhb, Brussels; fac chem, students dorms, Heb U, Jerusalem; cen libr, Churchill Auditorium, Sen Technion, Haifa; sci labs, San Martin Guest House, Weizmann Inst Sci; Workers Bank of Isr, head off, Tel Aviv; Wingate Inst for Phys Educ; JA Bldg; Solel Boneh Bldg; other bldgs, hosps, mus in Isr and abroad in partnership with son Eldar; urban design, reconstruction scheme for Old Jerusalem and surrounding areas. Pres, Assn Engrs and Architects in Isr, since 1965; hon mem: Royal Inst for Brit Architects, since 1962; Akademie der Kuenste, Berlin, since 1965; Bund Deutscher Architekten, since 1965; chmn: Standards Inst of Isr; natl council, Natl Parks and Nature Res; fmr mem exec, Intl Union of Architects. Author: Physical Planning in Israel; Collective Settlements in Israel; Hospitals in Israel and the Developing Countries; contbr to profsl jours. Recipient: Isr prize, architecture, 1962; Gold Medal, Mex Inst for Architecture, 1963; 1st prize, architecture competition for: Ezrat Nashim Mental Hosp; Wingate Inst for Phys Educ. Home: 244 Hayarkon St, Tel Aviv, Isr. Office: 70 Hayarkon St, Tel Aviv, Isr.

SHARON, Haya, Isr, actress; b. Russ, d. Aharon and Bela Sankovsky; in Isr since 1925; m. Arieh Sharon; c: Eldar, Uri. Mem, Ohel Theatre; leading roles: Naama in Salomon The King; Hermione in Winter's Tale; Mrs Ford in Merry Wives of Windsor; Nicole in Bourgeois Gentilhomme; Toinette in Malade Imaginaire; Malkale in Joshe Kalb; Belka in Fishke Hahiger; Shifra in Haktuva; Bessi Burgess in The Plough and The Stars. Mem, Art Council. Home: 244 Hayarkon, St, Tel Aviv, Isr.

SHARON, Henry Hanan, Isr, economist, business exec; b. Tel Aviv, Oct 20, 1929; s. Julius and Anna (Goldman) Steinberg; BA, MA, PhD, U of Cal, Berkeley, 1948-54; att U London, 1963-65; m. Hadassah Greengrass, Dec, 24, 1958; c: Eiran, Gil. Dep dir, JA Cos Bur, since 1966; dir: Isr Land Devl Co; Rassco; Maskit; Sharon and Galei Kinereth Hotels, since 1966; cons on corp mgmt: Isr Govt; Solel Boneh; Eur cos, 1959-66; JA Repr, London, 1963-66; external relations dir, JA, 1956-59; exec, intl finance, Richfield Oil, 1950-54. IDF, 1948, 1954-56. Prin contrib: pioneer, mgmt research, Isr, developing countries. Chmn, finance sect, Isr Mgmt Cen, Tel Aviv; mem dir comm, org of Isr Academicians, fmr: mem, natl comm: Isr Political Assn; Isr Assn for UN; mem, Amer Soc Intl Law. Contbr numerous research papers to Isr and intl jours. Hobbies: music, theater, golf, horseback riding. Home: 4 Gur Arie St, Tel Aviv, Isr. Office: 17 Kaplan St, Tel Aviv, Isr.

SHARON, Nahum, Isr, educator b. Lutzk, Ukraine, Dec 20, 1912; s. Joseph and Esther (Boyko) Shtrachman; in Isr since 1949; c: Ruth, Joseph. Dir, research dept, Educ Cen, Histadrut, since 1962, mem, exec, culture cen, since 1968, mem, comty council, since 1960; mem, cen comm, and political commn, Mapam, since 1968; repr, JA mission to Cuba, 1960-62. Pol Army, 1937-38; Russ Army, 1941-42. Mem, Yiddish Writers and Journalists Assn; fmr: mem, bd dirs, KKL, Pol; ed, Hamishmar newspaper; secy, Hashomer Hatsair Party, Pol. Author: Israel, Problems and Political Parties, 1958; ed, Sefer Lotzk, 1960; mem, ed bd: Basha'ar; Isr Shtime; Mosti, newspaper, Pol, 1946-49. Home: 15 Fichman, Tel Aviv, Isr. Office: 93 Arlosoroff, Tel Aviv, Isr.

SHARON, Nathan, Isr, scientist; b. Brisk, Pol, Nov 4, 1925; s. Abraham and Esther (Kozlouski) Shtrikman; in Isr since 1934; MSc, Heb U, Jerusalem, 1950, PhD, 1953; m. Rachel Itzikson, Jan 13, 1948; c: Esther, Osnath. Prof, molecular biol, Weizmann Inst, Rehovot, Isr, since 1968, on fac since 1954; visiting asso prof, Albert Einstein Coll of Med, NY, 1963; research asso, dept biol chem, Harvard Med Sch, 1962-63; asst biochem, biol dept, Brookhaven Natl Lab, NY, 1958-59; research f, dept med, Harvard Med Sch, 1957-58; research f, biochem research lab, Mass Gen Hosp, 1956-57; research asst, Dairy Research Lab, Agric Research Sta,

Rehovot, 1949-53. Palmach, Haganah, 1943-45; lt, IDF, 1947-49. Mem: adv comm, Natl Council for Research and Devl, Isr; Biochem Soc of Isr; Isr Chem Soc; Amer Chem Soc; Intl Sci Writers Assn; fmr, Assn for Advancement in Isr. Co-ed: What is New in Science, Heb, vol I, 1961, vol II, 1965; sci ed, Mada, Heb monthly; fmr, sci ed, Kol Isr radio; contbr to sci jours. Home: 19 Zimchey Hayehudim St, Ramat Aviv, Isr. Office: Weizmann Inst of Sci, Rehovot, Isr.

SHATIL, Joseph Ernest, Isr, economist; b. Berlin, Ger, Dec 19, 1909; s. Armin and Antonia (Pollack); in Isr since 1943; m. Ruth Prager; c: Jonatan, Ezra, Giora. Econ ed, Al Hamishmar daily, since 1968; agric worker; econ adv, Kibbutz Artzi; econ, inter-kibbutz fed. Prin contribs: econ adv and research in kibbutz econ. Mem: sci comms for various research insts; econ dept, Kibbutz Arzi Fed; fmr: secy, Cen Comm J Youth Movements, Ger; secy, Youth Aliyah, Ger; delg, Eur off, Youth Aliyah. Author: Economic Planning After the War, 1944; Kibbutz Economy in Israel, 1955; L'Economie Collective du Kibbutz Israelien. Home: Hazorea, Isr.

SHATKAY, Adam, Isr, scientist; b. Lodz, Pol, Sep 2, 1921; s. Joseph and Sydonie (Tartakower); in Isr since 1933; MSc, Heb U, Jerusalem, 1951; PhD, Weizmann Inst, Rehovot, 1964; m. Sara Huber, 1952; c: Michal, Hagit. Research Asso, phys chem, Weizmann Inst, since 1965; co-found, commanding off, Mil Flying Sch, Ghana, 1959-61. Pilot, RAF, 1940-45; lt col, IAF, 1948-63. Chmn, Sci Workers Org, Weizmann Inst; mem: Aeronautical Engrs, Isr; Amateur Astronomers; chief pilot, Isr Flying Club, 1951. Author: Toldot Ne'ureha shel Tayeset A, 1950; contbr to profsl jours. Recipient: stars: Afr; It; medals: Defense; Independence; Sinai; 6 Days War. Hobbies: flying, fencing. Home: 42 Be'eri St, Rehovot, Isr. Office: Weizmann Inst of Sci, Rehovot, Isr.

SHAVIT, Avraham Buma, Isr, business exec; b. Tel Aviv, Sep 14, 1927; s. Peretz and Sima (Vinshelbaum); att Sch of Art, Cambridge, London, 1946-47; m. Yaffa Boltianski, Aug 17, 1948; c: Oren, Sima. Dir: Shavit and Sons, Elec, Gas, Metal Works, since 1952; Kenes-Org Congs, Spec Events, since 1967. Maj, IAF. Mem: exec, Mfr Assn Isr; pres, Jr Chamber of Isr; vice-pres, Jr Chamber Intl. Home: 26 Alumim, Afeka, Isr. Office: 39 Allenby St, Tel Aviv, Isr.

SHAVIT, Moshe A, Isr, business exec; b. Pol, Sep 10, 1916; s. Yehuda and Fani (Katriel) Varshavsky; in Isr since 1936; att Technion, Haifa, 1936-38; m. Ora Goldberg, Nov, 1945; c: Zipora, Yehuda. Gen mgr, Agrexco Agric Export, Co since 1964; secy, Kibbutz Neve, mgr, Nahshon, both 1940-44; dir, Dept Fisheries, Min Agric, 1953-64; treas, JA, Ger, 1948-51. Mem: council, Ports Auth. Author: articles in brochure for fishermen. Home: 20 Seren Dov St, Ramat Chen, Isr. Office: 119 Hachashmonaim St, Tel Aviv, Isr.

SHAVIV, Giora, Isr, astrophysicist; b. Haifa, Aug 16, 1937; s. Moses and Yatska (Alembik); BSc, Technion, Haifa, 1959, MSc, 1960, PhD, 1965; m. Edna Levite, June 15, 1965; c: Guy-Erez. Head, astrophysics group, Tel Aviv, U, since 1969. Pvt, sci corps, IDF, 1960-65. Spec interest: architecture. Office: Tel Aviv U, Ramat Aviv, Isr.

SHAW, Abraham D, US, rabbi; b. Kansas City, Kan, Nov 5, 1909; s. Morris and Essie (Bloomgarten); BA, U Cincinnati, 1932; BH, HUC, 1932, ordained rabbi, 1936, hon DD, 1961; grad study, Johns Hopkins U, 1941, 1942; m. Maxine Friedson, Sep 18, 1940 (decd); c: David, Helaine. Rabbi, Temple Oheb Shalom, Baltimore, since 1940, life tenure since 1956, affiliated since 1936. Pres, Menorah Lodge, Baltimore, 1940-48; chmn: clergymen's adv comm, Planned Parenthood, Baltimore; 1st vice-pres: Middle Atlantic Region, CCAR; Clergy Brotherhood of Baltimore; fmr mem, bd: Baltimore chap, ARC; Baltimore Bd J Educ; Baltimore J Council; NCCJ; United World Federalists; AJComm; mem: Md State Scholarship Bd; Citizens Planning and Housing Comm; Masons; B'nai B'rith; Baltimore repr, AJCong, 1943; bd, World Union for Progressive Judaism; Natl Rabb Pension Bd; clubs: Rotary; Golden Eagle; Suburban; Woodholme. Author: Life of Jacob Emden, 1936; contbr to centennial hist Oheb Shalom Cong, 1953. Home: 7121 Park Heights Ave, Baltimore, Md. Study: 7310 Park Heights Ave, Baltimore, Md.

SHAY, Arnold Leo, US, tailor, lecturer; b. Bendsburg, Pol, Feb 16, 1922; s. Alexander and Sara (Druch); in US since 1949; m. Bella Saionz, Aug 12, 1947; c: William, Shirley. Custom tailor, since 1945; head fitter, Al Berman, 1957-61.

Inmate, concentration camps: Aushwitz; Oranienburg, Sachsenhausen, Dachau. Chmn: Assn J New Amers; pres: Soc Isr Philatelists, trustee, JNF League Men's Orgs; mem: Bayse Newcomb Lodge, Masons; Amer, Ger, Polonus, Judaica Historical Philatelic Socs; Postal Hist Soc; Soc Isr Philatelists; clubs: Masonic Stamp, Phila, found; War Cover; 906 Stamp; Universal Autograph Collectors. Author, lectr on WW II, philately, specializing in ghetto and concentration camp aspects. Recipient: awards at intl stamp exhbts for concentration camps and Judaica material. Home: 205 Haverford Rd, Wynnewood, Pa. Office: 2228 Bryn Mawr Ave, Philadelphia, Pa.

SHAZAR, Shneur Zalman, Isr, President of Israel; b. Mir, Russ, Oct 6, 1889; s. Yehuda and Sarah (Ginsburg) Rubaskov; in Isr since 1924; grad, Acad of J Studies, St Petersburgh, 1911; research work under Prof Simon Dubnow; att: U Freiburg; U Strasbourg, 1912-14; U Berlin, 1917-20; m. Rachel Katznelson, 1920; c: Roda. Third Pres, State of Isr, since 1963; exec comm, Histadrut, 1925-49; co-found, Davar, lab daily, 1925, mem, ed bd, 1925-48, acting ed, 1931-33, ed, 1938-48; Histadrut missions to: US, 1927, 1932, 1934-36; Eur, 1929, 1934-36; JA missions to US, 1954; delg to WZCs from 1921; Histadrut delg: ITUC, Stockholm, 1930; Intl Socialist Confs: Vienna, Hamburg, Berlin; mem: presidium, World Zionist Actions Comm, 1923-51; Yishuv Electoral Assembly, 1948; Isr Constituent Assembly, 1949; mem, JA delg to UN Gen Assembly, 1947; MK, 1st, 2nd, 3rd, Knesset; 1st Isr Min of Educ and Culture, 1949-50, introduced compulsory elem educ; mem, exec, JA, Jerusalem, 1951-63. Pres' visits: Nepal; Uruguay; Chile; Brazil; all 1966; Can, 1967; Wash, DC, 1966. Author: Toldot Bikoret haMikra, 1925; Lasalle ha-Yehudi haGermani, 1926; Masber haUma beMashber ha-Olam, 1941; Shem leAbba, memoirs, 1941; Kokhve Boker, 1950; Or Ishim, 1956; trans, poems by Rachel from Heb to Yiddish; Sefunot, vols III, IV; fmr ed: Ahdut Ha-avoda, 1930-32; Davar Year Book, 1936-43; political and lit periodicals, Histadrut and Mapai Party; contbr of Heb, Yiddish essays to jours. Recipient: Ussischkin Prize, for Kokhve Boker; Bialik Prize, for Or Ishim, Tel Aviv Munic. Home and office: The President's House, Jerusalem, Isr.

SHAZAR-KATZNELSON, Rachel, Isr, editor; b. Bobruisk, Russ, 1888; d. Nissan and Selde (Rosowski) Katznelson; in Isr since 1912; grad, Women's U Petersburg; att Acad J Studies; m. Zalman Shazar, 1920; c: Roda. First Lady of Isr since 1963; found, ed, Dvar-Hapoelet, since 1934; fmr: agric worker; mem Kibbutz Kineret; Tel Adashim; Women's Workers Group, Jerusalem. Hon presidium, Zionist Actions Comm; delg to ZCs; mem: Women's Workers Council, 1930-63; cen cultural comm, Histadrut, 1924-27; exec comm, Mapai; mem Lab Party. Author: Masot veRishimot, 1946; Al Admat haIvrit, 1967; ed: Im Paamei haDor, anthol of 25 years of Dvar Hapoelet, 1964. Recipient: Brenner prize, 1947; Isr prize, 1958; Chaim Greenberg prize, Pioneer Women in US. Home: The President's House, Jerusalem, Isr.

SHEAR, Murray Jacob, US, biomedical scientist; b. Bklyn, NY, Nov 7, 1899; s. Victor and Henrietta (Robinson); BS, CCNY, 1920; MA, Columbia U, 1922, PhD, 1925; m. Rose Roseman, 1935; c: David, Jonathan, Victor. Spec adv, lab chem pharm, Natl Cancer Inst, since 1963, chief, 1946-63; cancer researcher, USPHS, 1931-39; asst chem, Columbia U, 1923-25; research chem, admn off, ped research lab, J Hosp, Bklyn, 1925-31; research f, Harvard U, 1931-39. US Army, 1918. Prin contribs: research in mechanism deposition of bone salts, genesis tumor with chems, chemotherapy and immunology of cancer. Chmn: bd, Civil Service Examiners, NIH, 1947-51; chemotherapy comm, Intl Union Against Cancer, 1954-62; pres: Bethesda Chevy Chase J Comty Group, 1942; Amer Assn for Cancer Research, 1960-61; mem: Soc for Experimental Bio and Med; Amer Soc Biol Chems; Amer Chem Soc; Wash Acad Med; Wash Acad Scis; Royal Soc Med, London; Societa Italiana di Cancerologia; ZOA; AJComm; Amer Soc Pharm and Experimental Therapeutics; clubs: Harvard, Boston; Cosmos, Wash. Home: 5203 Battery Lane, Bethesda, Md. Office: National Cancer Inst, Bethesda, Md.

SHEARER, Zoe S, Rhodesia, business exec; b. London, Eng, May 1, 1916; d. William and Bertha (Leventhal) Friedland; m. Harold Shearer (decd). Head, Mfrs Exhb Cen, Salisbury, since 1968; dir: Shearer Ltd; Va Export Ltd; Enterprise Holdings Ltd; inves adv, Dalrymple Turner, Stock and Share Brokers, Johannesburg, S Afr, 1935-50; gen mgr, Cen Afr Trade Fair and Bulawayo Agric Soc, 1962-67. Asst provincial commandant, S Afr Women's Auxiliary Services, WW II. Found, natl life pres, Women's Voluntary Services, Cen Afr since 1953; Fmr pres, Ex-Service Women's League, Salisbury. Author, produc, musicals; ed, cook books. Recipient: OBE; Asso Rhodesian Advt award, 1966; Rhodesian of year, Lions Clubs, Rhodesia, 1967. Home: Peter House, Monmouth Rd, Avoodale, Salisbury, Rhodesia.

SHECHTER, Moshe, Isr, physician; b. Lubashovka, Ukraine, Apr 10, 1896; s. Samuel and Etja (Glusberg); in Isr since 1933; ordained rabbi, Rabb Sem, Kishinev, 1914; MD, U Kharkov, 1923; MD, U Berlin, 1931; m. Riva Itelson, 1924; c: Chanoch, Aja. Pvt practice, specializing in internal med and metabolism, since 1933; chief med adv to Isr Min of Finance on people disabled during Nazi regime, since 1957; lectr, endocrinology to postgrad students; asst, Charité Med Clinic, U Berlin, 1923-33; research worker, biol dept, Kaiser Wilhelm Inst, Dahlem, Berlin, 1931-33. Mem: cen comm, sci council, IMA; nutrition comm, Health Council, State of Isr; B'nai B'rith; Scottish Rite; Masons. Co-ed: Ha-Talmud veChachmath Harefua; The Medical and Health Thesaurus; contbr to local and fgn med jours. Home: 10 Modigliani St, Tel Aviv, Isr. Office: 105 Rothschild Blvd, Tel Aviv, Isr.

SHECTER, Pearl S, US, artist, teacher; b. NYC, Dec 17, 1913; d. Daniel and Anna (Mantel) Schechter; MFA, Columbia U Sch of Fine Arts, 1938; att: Hans Hofmann Sch of Painting, 1947-51; New Bauhaus Sch of Art, 1941; Harvard U Grad Sch, 1962-63. Art dir, Little Red Schoolhouse, since 1945; art lectr: NYU, since 1945; Queen's Coll, 1940-41; Wm and Mary Coll, 1941-45; U Va, 1941-45; res art tchr, Newton Harvard Creative Art Cen. One-man shows: Amer House Gal, 1953; Mus Natural His, 1949-1951; Contemporaries Gal, 1955; IFA Gal, 1957, 1958, 1959; group exhbs: Walker Mus; Va Mus Fine Arts; Huntington Gal; Cleveland Mus; Inst Contemporary Art; Camino Gal; Contemporary Mus Art; Schaeffer Gal; James Gal; Tweed Gal, Minn; Contemporary Liturgical Art, Phila, Pa; exhbs: Alice Nosh Gal, NY; Lehigh U, Lichtfield Gal; Bridgeport Art Cen; Carnegie Endowment Cen; City Art Mus, Mo; repr in: Betty Parsons collection; traveling group exhbs; mus, gals in US; in pvt collections: Miami U Mus; Mus Natural Hist; NYU; Prof Guilio Mazzon,It; Mme Henriette Noyer, Fr; John F Kennedy Libr; Spaeth Found Coll; paintings reprinted in books: Modern Art; Art in America. Mem: Experiments in Art Tech; Artists Equity Assn. Home and studio: 60 E 9 St, New York, NY.

SHECHTERMAN, Abraham, Isr, civil engr; b. Odessa, Russ, Dec 3, 1910; s. Zvi and Miriam (Friedman); in Isr since 1924; CE, Royal U, Ghent, Belgium, 1935; m. Sara Doubovsky (decd); c: Yizhak, Elinoar Mazor, Tamar; m. 2nd, Judith Sieff, May 21, 1962. Cons engr, since 1946; mgn dir, Netivot Devl Co Ltd, Tel Aviv; mem, bd dirs cos; MK since 1969; mem, Munic Council, Tel Aviv, 1955-69, dep mayor, 1957-59, chmn, appeal comm for Tel Aviv-Jaffa town planning, since 1959; chmn, floods comm, since 1956, head, health dept, 1957-59; head, Jaffa Munic Admn, 1957-59, chmn, tendering comm, 1955-57; chmn, city devl comm, Tel Aviv-Jaffa, 1955-59; mgr, Sdom Dead Sea Works of Pal, 1943-46; work mgr, Pal, Potash Co, Dead Sea, 1943-46; cons engr, Kaiser-Frazer of Isr, Haifa, 1950-55. Chmn, Irgun Zvei Leumi, 1936-48. Chmn Found for Advancement of Med, Tel Aviv; mem presidium, Zionist Org; chmn, Friends of Theater in Isr; pres, Isr Council, Herut Party, since 1961, fmr mem exec; mem: Betar since 1927, gen staff, aviation cdr; bd dirs, KH; B'nai B'rith; clubs: Rotary; Pilots, Tel Aviv, fmr pres. Contbr to profsl jours, daily press. Spec interest: aviation, co-found of aviation in Pal. Home: 20 Dubnov St, Tel Aviv, Isr. Office: 14 Hagdud Haivri, Tel Aviv, Isr.

SHECHTERMAN, Judith Hannah, Isr, communal leader; b. Manchester, Eng, Sep 26, 1921; d. Israel and Rebecca (Marks) Sieff; in Isr since 1959; m. Avraham Shechterman; c: Sara Minster, Michaela, Marcus. PR head, World Wizo, Tel Aviv; fmr: ind and retail mgmt, Marks and Spencer, 1937-44; org, Balfour Services Club for J Servicemen, London, 1942-46; Min Info, overseas Bc, London, 1944-45. Fmr mem: council, Fed of Women Zionists, Eng; council, JNF, Eng; vice chmn, Friends Isr Philharmonic Orch; mem: B'nai B'rith, Rebecca Sieff Lodge, Tel Aviv; Weizmann Inst. Home: 20 Dubnov St, Tel Aviv, Isr. Office: Wizo, 38 David Hamelech St, Tel Aviv, Isr.

SHECHTMAN, Harry, US, attorney; b. Paris, Fr, Aug 19, 1912; s. Solomon and Rose (Pollack); in US since 1915; BS, LIU, 1933; LLB, Columbia Law Sch; m. Betty Goodman, Nov 20,

1940. Pvt practice. Vice-chmn, natl mem cabinet, B'nai B'rith; pres, LIU Alumni Assn, 1965-67; chmn, Elmhurst Salvation Army appeal, 1959-61; bd govs, Jt Defense Appeal; mem: NY Co Lawyers Assn; J Cen, Jackson Hts. Home: 8015 41 Ave, Elmhurst, NY. Office: 21 E 40 St, New York, NY.

SHEDLOVSKY, Theodore, US, chemist, educator; b. Leningrad, Russ, Oct 29, 1898; s. Alexander and Bertha (Weinstein); in US since 1908; BS, MIT, 1918, PhD, 1925; m. Beatrice Paul, May 16, 1929; c: Richard, Julian, Alexandra. Prof, Rockefeller Inst, since 1957, on staff since 1927; civilian cons, Navy Dept, 1944. Vice-pres, NY Acad Scis, 1942, 1960; mem: Natl Acad Scis, Amer Chem Soc; Electrochem Soc; Biophys Soc; bd mem: Consumers Union of US, 1950-60; Med Letter-Drug and Therapeutic Info Inc. Author: Electrochemistry in Biology and Medicine, 1955; asso ed, NY Acad Scis Jour, 1938-42; contbr to profsl jours. Hobbies: music, chess. Home: 419 W 118 St, New York, NY. Office: Rockefeller Inst, New York, NY.

SHEFFERMAN, Abe, US, attorney; b. Baltimore, Md; s. Adler and Freda (Scolnick); LLB, Georgetown U, 1917; m. Belle Blattberg, Nov 19, 1922; c: Sholom, Ivan, Eleanor Anderson. Ret: exec dir, Adas Isr Cong, Wash, DC, 1937-61; att, 1919-37. Pvt, US Army, 1917-19. Found, fmr pres, Natl Assn Syn Admnrs; pres, B'nai B'rith lodge; leader: Masonic Lodge; music, Adas Isr Cong; with JWB, Fr, 1919; mem: ZOA; Isr Bonds; Big Bros; social action comm, United Syn. Home: 2800 Quebec, Washington, DC.

SHEFTEL, Arie, Isr, civil servant; b. Vilna, Lith, Feb 3, 1905; s. Itzhak and Esther (Kolbovsky) in Isr since 1947; att: HS Political Sci, Vilna; Tchrs Sem, Vilna; m. Pola Rabinovitz, 1946; c: Esther, Hana. Mayor, Rishon le Zion, 1952-54, and since 1965; dir; cen of info, State of Isr, since 1954; mem, First Knesset, 1949-52; fmr: tchr, Vilna; researcher, Inst J Hist, Pol. Dir, Brit Ivrit Olamit, Isr; mem: Yad Vashem; Partisans' Org WW II; Cen Mapai; Cen Dept of Coop; B'nai B'rith. Office: Munic, Rishon le Zion, Isr.

SHEINKMAN, Jacob, US, attorney; b. NYC, Dec 6, 1926; s. Shaia and Bertha (Rosenkrantz); BS, Cornell U, NY, 1949, LLB, 1952; cert, econ, Oxford U, Eng, 1949; m. Betty Johnson, 1954; c: Michael, Joshua, Mark. Vice-pres, Amalgamated Clothing Workers of Amer, since 1968, gen counsel, since 1958, staff mem since 1953; practising law inst, Cornell U, since 1965; mem, Minimum Wage Bd, US Dept of Lab, for Puerto Rico, 1959, 1962; legal asst, NLRB, 1952-53. USN, 1944-46. Secy-trustee, Amalgamated Cotton Garment and Allied Inds Fund, since 1965; chmn, attys comm, Natl Found Health and Wfr and Pension Plans, Inc, since 1968; co-chmn, comm wfr, pension and other related plans, Amer Bar Assn, since 1965; dir: Comty Services, Inc, since 1965; Riverboy Corp (Coop City), since 1967; United Housing Found, 1959-65; Intl Rescue Comm, since 1966; J Lab Comm, since 1965; Mus Graphic Arts, since 1967; Assn Pvt Pension Plans, Inc; mem: adv comm, NYU Civil Liberties Cen, since 1965; planning comm, NYU Conf on Lab, since 1965; panel arbitrators, Amer Arbitration Assn, since 1959; NYC Council on Poverty, 1965-66; Larchmont Temple; Workmen's Circle; Phi Kappa Phi; Amer Vet Comm. Contbr to legal publs. Home: 23 Mayhew Ave, Larchmont, NY. Office: 15 Union Sq, New York, NY.

SHEINMAN, Kannon, US, oral surg; b. Pinsk, Russ, Mar 23, 1889; s. Frederick and Sara (Kurchin); in US since 1891; att CCNY, Coll Dent and Oral Surg, 1904-07; DDS, Columbia U, 1910; MD, honoris causa, Oriental U, Wash, DC, 1920; postgrad, U Vienna, U Berlin, Med Schs, 1922-23; m. Anne Garfinkel, Feb 10, 1938. Ret; pvt practice, oral surg, 1918-1950; chief, dept oral surg, Leb Hosp, 1919-24; instr, oral surg, Post-Grad Dept, Allied Dent Council for number years. Lt, US Army, MC, 1918. F, NY Inst Clinical Path; life mem: 1st Dist Dent Soc of NY, NY State Dent Soc, Amer Dent Assn; mem: UN Assn; Dent Alumni Columbia U; Alumni Columbia U; fmr; pres, found, N Dent Soc; mem: Local Bd 84, NY Selective Service; Intl Anesthesia Research Soc. Contbr to dent jours; presented a symposium on newer concepts of dent educ, in form of a tri-cornered debate before Jt Sci Session of Allied Dent Council; fmr, ed: Bull of N Dist Dent Soc; Dent Outlook. Recipient: Clarkson Cowl Gold medal, Coll Dent and Oral Surg, Columbia U Spec interests: pragmatic phil, lectr on econs, political and sociol conditions. Home: 800 West Ave, Miami Beach, Fla.

SHEK, Y Zeev, Isr, diplomat; b. May 13, 1920; s. Pessakh and Rachel (Weitzen); in Isr since 1946; att: U Prague, 1939; Heb U, Jerusalem, 1946-47; m. Alisa Ehrman, 1947; c. Ruth, Daniel, Rachel. Isr ambass, Aus, since 1968; dir, youth dept, J Comty, Prague, 1941; dir, off for collection of documents on J persecutions, 1945; mem, staff, Eur div, Isr Min for Fgn Affairs, 1948-50; 2nd secy, Isr emb, Prague, 1950-52, charge d'affaires, 1952-53; political secy, Min for Fgn Affairs, Jerusalem, 1953-56; counselor, emb London, 1956-60; min plenipotentiary, Paris, 1960-63; dir, W Eur Dept, Min Fgn Affairs, 1963-67. Chmn, research comm on Theresienstadt Ghetto. Contbr of articles on Nazi persecutions of Js. Home: Hechalutz St, Beit Hakerem, Jerusalem, Isr. Office: Isr Min for Fgn Affairs, Jerusalem, Isr.

SHELEF, Samuel, Isr, lawyer; b. Poltava, Russ, Dec 15, 1905; s. Michael and Ester (Zerikovsky) Fichelef; in Isr since 1926; att Us: Harkov, Odessa, Russ, Social, Econ Scis; licencie, Docteur en Droit, Toulouse, Fr; m. Bela Komar, July 1934; c. Ora, Michael. Pvt practice since 1939; Isr ambass, Philippines, 1963-65. Chmn, Isr Inst of Intl Relations, Tel Aviv; mem: Council Assn Friendship with Asian Countries, Jerusalem; exec bd, L'Association Isr-Fr; Comm for Fgn Relations, Lab Party, Isr. Author: Le Statut International de la Palestine Orientale, 1932; chief ed, Intl Outlook. Home: 12 Ruth St, Tel Aviv, Isr. Office: 20 Achad Haam St, Tel Aviv, Isr.

SHELEF, Zvi, Isr, engineer; b. Tel Aviv, Dec 17, 1929; s. Zeev and Jaffa (Eliashevitz) Shteinshleifer; MSc, Imperial Coll, London, 1958; m. Joan Ratcliff, 1960; c: Naomi, Dalia, Ofra, Tamar, Roneet. Mgr, Tamam Precision Instruments Ind. Isr, since 1963; mgr devl engr Ellicot Bros, UK, 1959-61; sr sup engr CEC, US, 1961-63. Sgt, IAF, 1948-51. Home: 5 Hazivoni, Ganei Yehuda, Isr. Office: Lod Airport, Lod, Isr.

SHELESNYAK, Moses C, US, endocrinologist, physiologist, educator; b. Chgo, Ill, June 6, 1909; s. Jonas and Faye (Levitt); in Isr since 1950; BA, U Wis, 1930; PhD, Columbia U, 1933; att Columbia Coll Phys and Surgs, 1933-35; NY Sch of Social Work, 1938-39; m. Rosyln Benjamin, Jan 1942; c: Henry, Betty Sonheimer. Dir, Interdisciplinary Communications Prog, Smithsonian Instn, since 1969; instr, phys, pharm, Chgo Med Sch, Ill, 1935-36; lectr, hum growth, New Coll, NY, 1936-37; research asso: Mt Sinai Hosp, 1936-40; Beth Isr Hosp, 1940-42; dean, Boys Heb Orphan Asylum, 1938-40; head, environmental phys and ecology br, US Off Naval Research, 1946-49; initiated establishment of Pt Barrow Lab for Arctic Research, 1946-47; visiting lectr, geog, McGill Summer Sch, Montreal, Can, 1948; lectr, ecology, Johns Hopkins U, 1949-50; dir, Baltimore-Wash Off, Arctic Inst of N Amer, 1949-50; visiting prof, Coll de Fr, 1960; prof, endocrine and reproduction phys, head, biodynamics dept, Weizmann Inst of Sci, Rehovot, Isr, 1958-69. Lt cdr, USN, 1942-46. F: AAAS; Amer Soc Study of Sterility, corresp mem; Arctic Inst of N Amer; Eugenics Soc, London; Soc for Research in Child Devl; Soc Royale Belge, gyn and obstets, hon fgn corresp mem; mem: hon comm panel, hum ecology, arid zones, UNESCO; panel, on neuroendocrinology, Interdisciplinary Brain Research Org; research comm, Intl Planned Parenthood Fed; expert adv bd, biol hum reproduction, WHO; Isr Comm for Naples Zool Sta; natl council, Isr Soc for Protection of Nature; founding mem; Intl Soc Research in Biol Reproduction; council on public health, adv to exec comm, Histadrut; adv comm, Intl Training Prog in Phys of Reproduction, Worcester, US; Isr Soc for Experimental Biol and Med, pres, since 1962; council, exec comm, Assn for Advancement Sci of Isr, 1954-56; Aero Med Assn; AAUP; Amer Chem Soc; Amer Polar Soc; Arctic Circle, Ottawa Can; Biochem Soc of Isr; British Glaciological Soc; Endocrine Soc Amer; Hakluyt Soc; Hist of Sci Soc; Inst of Aeronautical Scis; Isr Chem Soc; NY Acad Scis; Soc for Experimental Biol and Med; Soc Research in Child Devl; Soc for Study of Fertility; Can Arctic Expedition, Muskox, 1945-46; clubs: Cosmos, Wash, DC; Explorers, NYC. Ed: Ovum Implantation; Proceedings for Population Conf, Growth of Population-Consequences and Control; corresp ed, Jour of Reproduction and Fertility, London since 1960; contbr to sci publs, Recipient: Oliver Bird prize, for research in reproductive phys, 1958; f: med, Columbia U, 1932-33, child study, Gen Educ Bd, 1936-38; Friedsam Research, Beth Israel Hosp, NY, 1940-42; Sir Simon Marks, Eng, 1957-58. Home: 1353-28 St, NW Washington, DC. Office: 1025-15 St, NW, Washington, DC.

SHEMANO, Jacob, US, business exec; b. Russ, Feb 15, 1913; s. Samuel and Jennie (Milkin); in US since 1917; att: SF State Coll, 1931; Amer Inst Banking, 1932-35; m. Rhoda Borsuk, May 19, 1940; c: Richard, Gary. Chmn bd; Liberty Natl Bank, since 1968; Gary Financial Corp, since 1968; pres: Natl Consumers Credit Plan, since 1952; Natl Finance Corp, 1945-52; found, pres, Golden Gate Natl Bank, 1961-67. Chmn, Housing Auth, SF city and Co; dir, Cong Beth Sholom; co-chmn, finance comm, JWF Campaign; bd dirs: NCCJ; St Anthony's Dining Room; pres: J Educ Soc, SF, 1953-56; dist 4, B'nai B'rith, 1957; W co-chmn, UJA, 1956; mem: Amer, Cal, Independent Bankers Assns; Masons; Shriners; clubs: Hunter's Point Boys; Concordia-Argonaut; Lake Merced Golf and Country. Home: 2190 Washington, San Francisco, Cal. Office: 130 Montgomery St, San Francisco, Cal.

SHEMEN, Nachman, Can, rabbi, author, organization exec; b. Chodel, Pol, Mar 15, 1912; s. Solomon and Gitl (Eichenthal) Boimoil; in Can since 1930; ordained rabbi, Warsaw, 1929; m. Toby Rosenberg, May 10, 1936; c: Aviva, Honey, Orah, Larry. Dir: orthodox div, Can J Cong, cen region, Toronto, since 1954; secy, Can Fed for Aid to Pol J in Isr, since 1940; cons, Cen Fund for Traditional Insts of United JWF of Toronto mem: Torah V'Avoda movement, Cong Torah V'Avoda. Author: Facism in Eurose, 1933; between War and Peace, 1939; Rabbi Judah Yudl Rosenberg, 1943; Rabbi Judah Leib Graubart, 1943; Jewish Attitude Towards the Non-Jew, 1945; Biography of a Warsaw Rabbi, 1949; Lublin, 1951; Religious Socialism, 1953; Dos Gezang Fun Chasiduth, 2 vols, 1959; Jewish Attitudes Toward Labor,1963; Jewish Attitude Towards the Woman, 2 vols, 1968-69; ed: Yiddish Neies, bull, United JWF and cen region, Can J Cong, since 1956; Sefer Hayovel, Talmud Torah Etz Chaim, 1943; The Voice of Religious Labor; contbr to local and fgn press. Home: 197 Lonsmount Dr, Toronto, Can. Office: 150 Beverley St, Toronto, Can.

SHEMER, Gideon, Isr, actor; b. Tel Aviv, May 24, 1928; s. Yechiel and Rachael (Rudoy); m. Livnat Shalem, Oct 1, 1968; c: Haleli. Actor since 1958; roles in the theater; My Fair Lady; After the Fall: The Oppenheimer Affair; The Simple Man: the Rattle of a Simple Man; Hedda Gabler; The Price; Love and All That Jazz; parts in Isr films Lt, IDF, 1948-50. Home: 8 Cremieux St, Tel Aviv, Isr. Office: Cameri Theater, 101 Dizengoff St, Tel Aviv, Isr.

SHEMER, Naomi, Isr, song writer; b. Kibbutz Kinneret; d. Meir and Rivka (Shafriri) Sapir; att Isr Acad, Tel Aviv; dipl, Jerusalem Music Acad; m. Mordechai Horowitz; c: Haleli. Writer: popular songs for theaters, soloists, groups, films; composed lyrics and music, Jerusalem of Gold; author, All My Songs, 1968. IDF, 1953-54. Mem: ACUM. Recipient: 1st prize, Intl Contest, Pesaro, It; Kinor David award, 1967; Home: 12 Biltmore St, Tel Aviv, Isr. Office: POB 3342, Tel Aviv, Isr.

SHEMTOV, Victor, Isr, government official; b. Sofia, Bulgaria, 1915; in Isr since 1939; m. Gretti Eliezer; c: Iris, Shmuel. Min of Health since 1969; mem, cen comm, Mapam Party; MK, 5th and 6th Knesset; fmr mem, Knesset finance comm; mem, Vaad haPoel, Histadrut, since 1961; mem: Parl delg to Belgium, 1968; Isr delg, Inter-Parliamentary Assn, Senegal. Contbr to mags and press. Home: 5 Mohilver, Jerusalem, Isr.

SHENHABI, Mordechai, Isr, communal leader; b. Russ, Sep 13, 1900; s. David and Chana (Eisenberg) Elfenbein; in Isr since 1919. Found, dir: Lemaan Yerushalayim, since 1958; Ot Hamutzar Hayerushalmi; Yad Vashem Memorial Auth, 1942-55; fmr: 1st econ secy, Mishmar Haemek, co-found, educ inst; dir, Heb lang courses, Hashomer Hatzair, org first pioneer group, repr to Pol and Ger, head Tel Chai Group. Served, Haganah. Prin contribs: planned and directed entry ind produc into agric kibbutzim. Co-found: Hashomer Hatzair, Vienna; Beit Hatanach Haolami; co-dir, World Hashomer Hatzair; mem: Kibbutz Arzi; Mapam; Histadrut; fmr: delg: WZCs; found conv, Histadrut; repr to Pol, JNF; helped to salvage J property in Nazi Ger, Czech, Yugo. Contbr to Heb jours. Home: Kibbutz Mishmar Haemek, Isr. Office: 17 Hebron Rd, Jerusalem, Isr.

SHENKEN, Leon I, NZ, psychiatrist; b. Auckland, NZ, Mar 6, 1927; s. Louis and Rachel (Lazarus); MB, ChB, U Otago, 1949; dipl, psychol med, Royal Coll Phys and Surgs, Dublin, Eire, 1953; m. Brenda Mendoza, Dec 14, 1955; c: Hilary, Mark, Jonathan. Pvt practice since 1954; visiting psycht specialist, Auckland Hosp; sr house off, U Glasgow, 1952-53. Mem: NZ Psychol Soc; Med Assn of NZ; Austr and NZ Coll Psychts; SWn Comm; chmn, Auckland J Day Sch Comm

Contbr to med jours. Home: 12 Rockwood Pl, Epsom. Auckland SE, NZ. Office: 72 Remuera Rd, Auckland, NZ.

SHENKIN, Brian Kevin, NZ, barrister, solicitor; b. NZ, Oct 10, 1940; s. Israel and Phyllis (Ross); LLB, Auckland U, 1962; m. Vivien Shieff, Dec 16, 1963; c: Paul, David. Pvt practice, barrister, solicitor. Vice-pres, Auckland Zionist Soc; secy: ZC, NZ; Friends Heb U, 1962-68. Spec interest: Judaica. Home: 215 Riddell St, Auckland, NZ. Office: 159 Queen St, Auckland, NZ.

SHENKIN, Henry Arnold, US, surgeon, educator; b. Phila, Pa, June 25, 1915; s. Julius and Rose (Rosenbaum); BA, U of Pa, 1935; MD, Jefferson Med Coll, 1939; m. Renee Frieden-berg, Jan 11, 1940; c: Budd, Robert, Katherine, Emily. Clinical prof, neurosurg, Temple U Sch of Med; dir, neurosurg, Episcopal Hosp. F, Amer Coll Surgs; mem: AMA; Assn for Research in Nervous and Mental Diseases; Harvey Cushing Soc. Home: 265 St Joseph's Way, Philadelphia, Pa. Office: Episcopal Hosp, Philadelphia, Pa.

SHER, Zeev, Isr, lawyer; b. St Polten, Aus, May 1, 1930; s. Azriel and Helena (Steiner) Schachter; in Isr since 1936; MJur, Heb U, 1936; LLM, Harvard U, 1957; m. Rivka Grayevsky, Sep 4, 1956; c: Uzi, Dina, Neta. Dep atty gen, since 1968, asst atty gen, 1953-68; legal adv to Bank of Isr, since 1963; registrar, patents, designs and trademarks, since 1959. Home: 1 Shahar St, Jerusalem, Isr. Office: 19 Jaffa St, Jerusalem, Isr.

SHERBER, Daniel A, US, physician; b. NYC, Feb 21, 1914; s. Sol and Sarah (Engelberg); AB, Columbia Coll, 1934; MD, Columbia U Coll Phys and Surgs, 1938; m. Florence Klein-berg, Aug 13, 1955; c: Harvey, Kenneth. Internist, pvt prac-tice, since 1938; dir, metabolic research lab, Fordham Hosp, since 1950; dir, med, United Home for Aged Hebrews, New Rochelle, since 1949; cons phys, New Rochelle Hosp; re-search f, endocrinology, Bklyn J Hosp, 1945-48, adj med, 1949-51; sex endocrinologist, City Hosp, NYC, 1950. Lt col, US Army MC, 1941-45. Dipl, Amer Bd Internal Med; f: Amer Coll Phys; Council on Arteriosclerosis; mem: AHA; Amer Therapeutic Soc; Soc Nuclear Med; AMA; Endocrine Soc; Clinical Soc Diabetes Assn; AAAS; NY Acad Sci; Westchester Co Med Soc; Intl Soc Internal Med; B'nai B'rith; Temple Isr Brotherhood. Contbr to med jours. Home: 333 Oxford Rd, New Rochelle,NY. Office:140 Lockwood Ave, New Rochelle, NY.

SHERE, Eugenia Shereshevski, Isr, psychologist; b. Kowno, Lith; d. Moses and Judith (Gersten) Levitan; PhD, Jena U, Ger. Asso prof, clinical psych, Bar Ilan U, since 1964; fmr: re-search asso, Clark U, Worcester Mass; chief clinical psych, The Memorial Hosp, Worcester. Author: Mother-Child Interaction in Cerebral Palsy, monographs, 1966; New Thou-ghts on Old Age, 1964. F, Amer Psych Ass. Home: 4 Hevra Hadasha St, Tel Aviv, Isr. Office: Bar Ilan U, Ramat Gan, Isr.

SHERER, Moshe, US, rabbi, communal leader; b. Bklyn, NY, June 18, 1921; s. Chaim and Basya; ordained rabbi: Mesifta Torah Vodaath Rabb Sem, Bklyn; Ner Isr Rabb Coll, Balti-more; m. Deborah Fortman, Nov, 1943; c: Rochelle Langer, Elkie, Shimshon. Exec pres, Agudath Isr of Amer, since 1967; prof, homiletics, Mesifta Torah Vodaath, since 1948; chmn ed bd, Dov Yiddishe Vort; asso ed, The Jewish Observer. Mem exec: and found, Natl J Commn on Law and Public Affairs; Citizens for Educ Freedom; J Restitution Successor Org. Recipient: dist service award: for Passage of Federal Educ Aid Bill, by Pres Lyndon Johnson, 1965; for NY State Textbook Bill, by Citizens for Educ Freedom, 1966. Home: 1626 52 St, Bklyn, NY. Office: Suite 910, 5 Beekman St, New York, NY.

SHERESHEFSKY, Judah Leon, US, educator; b. Pinsk, Russ, Oct 15, 1892; s. Jacob and Menia (Fidelman); in US since 1912; att Carnegie Inst Tech, Pittsburgh, Pa, 1918-21; BCh, U Pittsburgh, 1923; PhD, Johns Hopkins U, 1926; att Camb-ridge U, 1937-38; m. Pauline Miller, Nov 15, 1928; c: Ruth Reynolds. Prof em, Howard U, Wash, DC since 1958, head, chem dept, 1930-58; ind research f, Mellon Inst, U Pitts-burgh, 1928-30; research sci, Manhattan Project, Columbia U, 1943-44; prof, phys chem, Technion, Haifa, Isr, 1950-52, 1st dean of fac, 1951-52, organized fac and curriculum of pure sci. Prin contribs: discovered anomallous water and other liquids in capillaries; theory of surface tension of solutions; two-dimensional Condensation of liquids. Mem: Acad Adv

Council, J Tchrs Sem; Amer Chem Soc; AAUP; AAAS; Amer Technion Soc. Contbr to sci jours. Recipient:post doc f, Johns Hopkins U, 1928; merit award, Amer Chem Soc, Div of Colloid and Surface Chem, 1968. Hobbies: music, gar-dening. Home: 9023 Jones Mill, Chevy Chase, Md.

SHERIFF, Batsheva, Isr, poet, educator; b. Tel Aviv, June 28, 1937; d. Meir and Tova; BA, Heb U, Jerusalem, 1960; div; c: Yosef, Zeev. HS tchr since 1960. Author: Poems, 1961; Not All the Rivers, 1968. Home: 28 Ha'Avoda St, Tel Aviv, Isr.

SHERIFF, Noam, Isr, composer; b. Ramat Gan, Jan 7, 1935; s. Meir and Tova (Katz); att: Heb U, Jerusalem, 1955-59; Hochschule für Musik, Berlin, Ger, 1960-62; studied: compo-sition with Paul Ben-Haim and Boris Blacher; conducting with Igor Markevitch; m. Zafrira Shapira, Aug 25, 1959; c: Eran. Prof: orchestration, Acad of Music, Jerusalem 1965-67; orch and conducting, Natl Acad Music, Tel Aviv, 1967-68; leading arranger, folk and light music, Isr Bc. Sgt maj, IDF, Mil Sym Orch, 1952-54. Composer: Festival Pre-lude, for orch, 1957; Song of Degree, for orch, 1959; Ashrei, for alto, flute, 2 harps or harp and piano, 1961; Music, for woodwinds, trombone, piano and double bass, 1961; Destina-tion 5, for brass and percussion instruments, 1962; Sonata for piano, 1962; Heptaprisms, ballet music, 1965; Metamorph-osis on a Galliard, for orch, 1965; Chaconne, for orch, 1968; two Epigrams, for chamber orch, 1968; Pieces for Choir A Cappella. Recipient: 1st prize: Isr Philharmonic orch, for Festival Prelude, 1957, for Song of Degrees, Isr Philhar-monic World Tour, 1959. Hobbies: painting, phil, electro-nics. Home: 22 Moaz Aviv St, Tel Aviv, Isr.

SHERMAN, Arthur, US, educator, sculptor, writer; b. NYC, May 12, 1920; s. Herman and Fay; BMus, Juilliard Sch of Music, 1949; MMus, Manhattan Sch of Music, 1951; hon, PhD, CUNY, 1969; all NYC; m. Claire Fuchs, Jan 8, 1951; c: Claudia. Prof, dir, performing arts, NYC Comty Coll, since 1964; stage dir, W Mich Opera Assn, Bklyn Lyric Opera Co, since 1969; dir, Clearview Theater Workshop, since 1965; fmr: dir-produc, Adirondack Arts Festival; dir: Schroon Crest Playhouse; Pleasantville Children's Theater; hour show, Jane Morgan, Kennebunkport, Me, also wrote original material; dir-produc, numerous plays, musicals, operas; produc, Not While I'm Eating, also sketches and lyrics; performed as: singer, actor, variety; writer: A Minute! A Minute; So What; Lenore And the Wonder-House; In the Grass Of Jungle, ballet, performed in Isr, 1968; Jericho cantata; sculptor, one-man shows:NYC Gals; Bar Harbor, Me; Grand Rapids, Mich. USN, 1943-46. Pres: NYCC chap, United Fed Coll Tchrs; bd dirs, Bklyn Lyric Opera Co; contbr, Comty Service Cen, LI; mem: ASCAP; Amer Educ Theater Assn; NY State Music Assn; Two Year Colls. Recipient, Asian-Pacific Ribbon. Home: 144-45, 35 Ave, Flushing, Queens, NY. Office: NYC Coll, 285 Jay St, Brooklyn, NY.

SHERMAN, Charles Bezalel, US, author, editor, organization exec; b. Kiev, Russ, Jan 14, 1896; s. Phillip and Bella (Sher-man); in US since 1911; m. Dora Rich, June 1, 1918, (decd); c: Anita Glassman, Selma Stone; m. 2nd Minna Markowitz, May 29, 1966. Prof sociol, J Tchrs Sem; lectr sociol, Stern Coll, Yeshiva U; gen secy, mem world bur, Amer Left Poalei Zion Party, 1923-38; field dir, J Lab Comm, 1938-44; lab dir, ADL, 1944-47; dir, natl affiliates, AJCong, 1951-53; cultural dir, Lab Zionist Org, NYC, 1955-61; ed, Left Poalei Zion Publs, 1923-50. Bd dirs, YIVO, since 1952; fmr: cen comm, LZOA; Amer Sociol Assn. Author: The Communists in Palestine, 1939; Jews and Other Ethnic Groups in the US, 1948; Jewish Communal Organizations in the US, 1949; Israel and the American Jewish Community, 1951; Three Cen-turies of Growth, 1955; Labor Zionism in America, 1957; The Jew Within American Society—A Study in Ethnic In-dividuality, 1961; ed bd, Zionist Ency; contbr to: J Frontier; J Social Studies; Reconstructionist; Judaism; Congress Bi-Weekly; Kemfer; Zukunft; Yiddish Ency; J People, Past and Present. Recipient, awards: LaMed; JBCA. Home: 1 Tennis Court, Brooklyn, NY.

SHERMAN, David, S Afr, rabbi; b. Boston, Mass, US, Sept 13, 1909; s. Abram and Shifra (Lubovsky) Shershevsky; in S Afr since 1946; BS, Boston U, 1930; ordained rabbi, HUC, 1934, DD, 1959; m. Bertha Cohen, Jan 7, 1947; c: Saralee, Gail, Jessica, Rena. Rabbi, Cape Town J Reform Cong, since 1946; dir, J Comty Cen, Binghamton, NY, 1937-39; rabbi, Adas Emuno, Hoboken, NJ, 1939-45; dir, comty relations, Amer J Conf, 1945-46, secy, rescue comm, 1945-46. Pres, S Afr

Council for Progressive J Educ, 1950-52; mem, CCAR. Home: Savannah, Alster Ave, Cape Town S Afr. Study: Temple Isr, Upper Portswood Rd, Cape Town, S Afr.

SHERMAN, E David, Can, physician; b. Sydney, Can, Mar 15, 1908; s. Frederick and Sara (Epstein); MD, MC, McGill U, 1932; m. Janet Brodsky, 1938 (div); c: Neil; m. 2nd, Anne Donner, 1955. Pvt practice, internal med and gerontology, Montreal, since 1956; res: Women's Gen Hosp, Montreal, 1931-33; Mt Sinai Hosp, NYC, 1933-35; att phys: City of Sydney Hosp; St Rita Hosp, both 1935-46; Marine Hosp; Vets Hosp, both 1942-46, all Sydney, NS; practiced, NYC, 1947-55; mem staff: NY Hosp; Bellevue Hosp, NY; instr med, Cornell U Med Coll, all 1950-55; co-phys in chief, Maimonides Hosp and Home for Aged, 1956; mem, geriatric clinic and med staff, J Gen Hosp, Montreal, 1956; lectr, geriatrics, Sch of Rehab, U Montreal, 1958, vice pres, inst gerontology, 1962; dir research, Rehab Inst, Montreal, 1962. Royal Can Army MC, 1943-44. Dipl, internal med, Royal Coll of Phys; FACP; f: Amer Geriatrics Royal Soc of Arts, mem, bd dirs; Gerontological Soc; Royal Soc Med; Intl Coll Angiology Soc, fmr pres; NY Acad Sci; chmn, comm on aging, mem bd dirs, Quebec Med Assn; cons comm on aging, Can Wfr Council; med dir, sheltered workshop, J Vocational Service; mem: hon life, St John Ambulance Assn; Shaare Zion Syn; Temple Emanuel; St James Lit Soc; Masons; Phi Lambda Pi; fmr: chmn, comm on aging, mem gen council, Can Med Soc; mem council, Intl Assn of Gerontology; pres: Sydney Acad Alumni Assn; YMHA; Sydney br, Can J Cong; B'nai B'rith, Cape Breton; vice pres, Sydney Red Cross Soc. Abstract ed, Nova Scotia Med Bull, 1942-46; contbr to Amer and Can jours. Recipient: Malford W Thewlis award, Amer Geriatrics Soc, 1965. Home and office: 4330 Hampton Ave, Montreal, Can.

SHERMAN, Irving H, US, banker; b. NYC, Dec 25, 1900; s. Frank and Sophie (Kaufman); BA, Cornell U, 1922; m. Marie Vandeputte, Nov 20, 1941. Vice chmn, AG Becker & Co Inc, since 1961, with firm since 1925; dir, Deltown Foods Inc, since 1960. Treas, JDC since 1960, admn comm mem; mem: Beta Sigma Rho; club, Cornell, NY. Home: 812 Park Ave, New York, NY. Office: 60 Broad St, New York, NY.

SHERMAN, Jerome Nathaniel, US, rabbi; b. Everett, Mass, Nov 13, 1936; s. Abraham and Anna (Grunberg); BA, Harvard U, 1958; BHL, MHL, ordained rabbi, HUC, 1963; MA, Boston U; PhD, U Houston, 1968; m. Ruth Goldberger, Sep 29, 1962; c: Marc, Scott, Rhonda. Rabbi, Temple Isaiah, Lafayette, Cal, since 1966; instr, lang lab, HUC, 1960-62; rabbi, Cong Beth Isr, Houston,1963-68; Fmr lectr: U Houston; Acad Chr and Culture; San Jacinto Jr Coll, Sch of Nursing; J Chatauqua Soc. Chmn, radio-TV dept, N Cal Bd Rabbis; mem: bd, Contra Costo Co MH Assn; bd dirs, J Family Services, Alameda and Contra Costa Cos; Lafayette Rotary; J Comty Relations Council, Alameda and Contra Costa Cos; Min Assn; NW Council, UAHC; Pacific Assn Reform Rabbis; CCAR; E Bay Bd Rabbis; Amer Psychol Assn; fmr: cons, Houston Commn on J Educ; pres, Houston Rabb Assn; rabb adv, Tex-Okla Fed, Temple Youth; mem: bd trustees, Model Sch, Houston; U Area Rotary Club of Houston; Houston Jr C of C; clergy adv comm, Planned Parenthood Assn of Houston; bd dirs, JCC. Author: series for Sunday newspapers on fact-finding mission to ME. Home: 37 Sarah Lane, Moraga, Cal. Study: 3800 Mt Diablo Blvd, Lafayette, Cal.

SHERMAN, Mandel, US, psychiatrist, psychologist; b. Chgo, Ill, June 7, 1896; s. Joseph and Marian (Seidl); BS, U Chgo, 1917; MD, Rush Med Coll, 1921; PhD, U Chgo, 1927; m. Marjorie Lipman; c: Marion. Pvt practice, psycht and psych, Beverly Hills, Cal; psycht, Ill Inst for Juvenile Research, 1922-24; asso, Northwestern U Med Sch, 1923-26; dir, Wash Child Research Cen, Wash, DC, 1927-31; adj prof, child devl, U Md, 1928-31; profsl lectr, George Wash U, 1928-31; prof, educ psych, U Chgo, 1931-50; dir, Reiss-Davis Clinic, 1950-53. Mem: AMA; Cal Med Assn; Amer Psychiatric Soc; Amer Psych Soc; pres, Emotional Health Assn since 1958. Author: The Process of Human Behavior, 1929; Hollow Folk, 1933; The Development of Attitudes, 1933; Mental Hygiene and Education, 1935; Infant Behavior, monograph, 1936; Basic Problems of Behavior, 1941; Intelligence and its Deviations, 1945; Psychology for Nurses, 1947. Home: 9255 Doheny Rd, Los Angeles, Cal. Office: 9201 Sunset Blvd, Los Angeles, Cal.

SHERMAN, Martin A, US, educator, musician; b. NYC, June 19, 1918; s. David and Bella (Handelsman); Dipl, piano, Juilliard Sch of Music, 1937; MA, NYU, 1948; m. Marsha Tofilowsky, Feb 27, 1942; c: Nina. Prof, music, Rutgers U,

since 1969, asso prof, 1958-69, on fac since 1952, dir, band, 1951-58; choir dir, Highland Park Conservative Temple, NJ, 1952-55. US Army, 1942-46. Mem: Amer Musicological Soc; Coll Music Soc; AAUP. Contbr to encys and periodicals. Home: RD 4, Freehold, NJ. Office: Rutgers U, New Brunswick, NJ.

SHERMAN, Samuel, US, physician; b. Carnegie, Pa, July 15, 1910; s. Markus and Josephine (Schermer); BS, U Pittsburgh, 1932; MD, St Louis U, 1936. m. Constance Sameth; c: Jeffrey, Patricia. Pvt practice, phys med and rehab, Pittsburgh since 1946; chief, phys med and rehab depts, Montefiore and Passavant Hosps, Pittsburgh; cons, phys med and rehab: Oakland VA Hosp; Penn Cen RR; Pittsburgh Centerville Med Clinic; J Home for Aged; Jones & Laughlin Steel Corp; Homestead Hosp; Pittsburgh VA Regional Off; Leech Farm VA Hosp; Butler VA Hosp. Maj, US Army MC, 1942-46. Mem: Alpha Omega Alpha. Contbr to med jours. Home: 6582 Beacon St, Pittsburgh, Pa. Office: 3500 Fifth Ave, Pittsburgh, Pa.

SHERR, Abraham I, US, business exec; b. NYC, July 4, 1910; s.Ivens and Ethel (Kurlan); MBA, Harvard Sch of Bus Admn, 1932; m. Jean Frank, Apr 23, 1944; c: Barbara, Rita, Alan. Pres, dir, Fownes Bros & Co Inc. USCG, 1942-45. Club: Beachpoint Country. Home: 120 East End Ave, New York, NY. Office: 411 Fifth Ave, New York, NY.

SHERR, Rosalie, Eng, organization secy; b. London, Nov 8, 1912; d. Nathan and Sarah (Stiller) Gassman; m. Leonard Sherr, June 17, 1950; c: Sarah. Gen secy, Fed Women Zionists, Gt Brit and Ir, since 1940; chmn, World WIZO Youth Cen, 1936-40. Co-chmn, cultural comm, J Free Sch, Parent/ Tchrs Assn. Author: The Story of F.W.Z., 1968; contbr to J and Zionist publs, articles of interest to women. Recipient: British Empire Medal, King George VI, Blitz Sep 1940. Spec interests: civil defense, music, gardening, writing. Home: 25 Oman Ave, London NW2, Eng. Office: 107 Gloucester Pl, London W1, Eng.

SHERRICK, Lester S, US, business exec; b. Norfolk, Va, Sept 23, 1903; s. Samuel and Alexina (Jacobs); BS, U Va, 1924; m. Mildred Loewner, 1935; c: Lona Gruber, Charles, Carol Warschauer. Asso gen agent, John Hancock Mutual Life Ins Co, since 1960, affiliated since 1928; salesman, Sherrick Selling Agcy, 1925-28. Pres: Ohef Sholom Temple, 1957-60; Norfolk JCC, 1948-49; Norfolk Life Underwriters Assn, 1936; B'nai B'rith, 1942; S Region, CJFWF, 1955; vice-pres, Beth Sholom Home of Va, 1954; dir, Norfolk Chap, AJComm, since 1958; mem, exec bd: Tidewater Council, Boy Scouts of Amer, 1941-68, adv council since 1968; Norfolk J Comty Cen, since 1951; Ohef Temple Shalom, since 1950; natl council, JDC; mem: Pi Tau Pi; Natl Assn Chartered Life Underwriters; club, Lafayette Yacht. Recipient: Silver Beaver, Boy Scouts of Amer, 1937; dist service award, B'nai B'rith, 1952; first citizen award, Norfolk J Comty Cen, 1958. Home: 1363 Brunswick Ave, Norfolk, Va, Office: 4101 Granby St, Norfolk, Va.

SHERRY, Sol, US, physician, educator; b. NYC, Dec 8, 1916; s. Hyman and Ada (Greenman); BA, NYU, 1935, MD, 1939; m. Dorothy Sitzman, Aug 7, 1946; c: Judith, Richard. Prof, chmn med dept,Temple U, since 1968; asst prof, NYU,1948-51; dir: May Inst for Med Research, Cincinnati, 1951-54; med dept, J Hosp of St Louis, 1954-58; prof, Wash U Sch of Med, 1958-67. Flight surg, USAAF, 1942-46. Chmn: comm on thrombosis, NIH; selections comm for clinical inves, US VA; cons: council on drugs, AMA; Research and Devel Command, US Army; mem: Inst Soc of Haemostasis and Thrombosis; Assn Amer Phys; Amer Soc Clinical Inves; Cen Soc for Clinical Research; Amer Phys Soc; Phi Beta Kappa; Alpha Omega Alpha; Sigma Xi; club, Interurban. Ed bd: Circulation, Med, Thrombosis et Diathesis Hemorrbogrea; Jour of Chronic Diseases; contbr to sci jours. Recipient; US Typhus Comm medal, control typhus in Bavaria. Home: 408 Sprague Rd, Narberth, Pa. Office: 3400 N Broad St, Philadelphia, Pa.

SHERWIN, Richard Elliott, Isr, lecturer, poet; b. Malden, Mass, Aug 21, 1933; s. Morris and Edith (Broidy); in Isr since 1964; BA, UCLA, 1959; PhD, Yale U, 1963; m. Rachel Domke, Aug 17, 1958; c: Elisabeth, Yael, Reuben. Sr lectr, Eng, Bar Ilan U, since 1966; visiting lectr, Eng, Tel Aviv U, since 1965; asst prof, Carleton Coll, 1962-64; visiting prof, UCLA, 1968. Sgt, USAF, 1951-55. Reviews in Carleton Miscellany, 19th Century Fiction; poems in Reconstructionist, Image; essay in The Shakespearean World, 1968. Secy, Org Isr U

Tchrs of Eng, since 1966. Hobbies: ancient hist, theol, social psych. Home: 6 Tor Hazahav St, Herzliya, Isr. Office: Bar Ilan U, Ramat Gan, Isr.

SHERWOOD, Richard E, US, attorney; b. LA, Cal, July 24, 1928; s. Benjamin and Jennie (Goldeen); BA, Yale U, 1949; LLB, magna cum laude, Harvard U, 1952; m. Dorothy Romonek, July 25, 1953; c: Elizabeth, Benjamin. Partner, O'Melveny & Myers; pvt practice since 1955; Sheldon traveling f, Harvard U, 1953-54; law clerk, Justice Felix Frankfurter, US Supr Court, 1954-55. Lt USAF, 1952-53. Pres, Planned Parenthood/World Population, LA; finance chmn, Dem State Cen Comm, 1966-68; bd trustees, LA Co Mus of Art; bd delgs, AJComm since 1958; comty relations comm, LA JWF Council; mem: Commn on Cal State Govt Org and Econ, 1962-67; Amer, Cal, LA Co Bar Assns; Aurelian Honor Soc; club, Hillcrest Country. Home: 9606 Heather Rd, Beverly Hills, Cal. Office: 611 W 6 St, Los Angeles, Cal.

SHESHINSKI, Eytan, Isr, economist, educator; b. Haifa, Isr, June 29, 1937; s. Baruch and Alice (Praschker); BA, Heb U, Jerusalem, 1961, MA, 1963; PhD, MIT, Boston, 1966; m. Ruth Abramovizc, Aug 16, 1960; c: Yael, Hadar, Michal. Sr lectr, dept econ, Heb U, Jerusalem, since 1967; asst prof, Harvard U, 1966-67. Sgt, IDF, 1955-58. Contbr: articles to profsl jours. Home: 38 Ramban St, Jerusalem, Isr. Office: Heb U, Jerusalem, Isr.

SHESTACK, Jerome J, US, attorney; b. Atlantic City, NJ, Feb 11, 1923; s. Isadore and Olga (Shankman); AB, U of Pa, 1943; LLB, Harvard Law Sch, 1949; m. Marciarose Schleifer, Jan 28, 1951; c: Jonathan, Jennifer. Partner, Schnader, Harrison, Segal & Lewis, since 1956; spec asst to legal counsel for Gov Adlai Stevenson, Ill; teaching f, Northwestern Law Sch, both 1949-50; asst prof, La State U Law Sch, 1950-52; first dep city solicitor, City of Phila, 1953-55; lectr: U of Pa Law Sch, Rutgers Law Sch, 1953-61. Lt, USN, 1943-46. Pres, Phila chap, Amer J League for Isr, since 1957; vice-pres, J Publ Soc, since 1965; bd dirs: Fed JAs, Gtr Phila; Amer Friends Heb U, Phila since 1959; bd govs: JTSA; Heb U; bd overseers, Gratz Coll, since 1959; bd trustees, World Affairs Council, 1954-57; chmn, individual rights and responsibilities sect, Amer Bar Assn; natl adv comm, OEO; mem: Phila Bar Assn, chmn, comm on local govt, 1961; Pa Bar Assn; Order of Coif; Pi Gamma Mu; club, Harvard. Contbr to legal jours. Home: 2201 Parkway, Philadelphia, Pa. Office: Packard Bldg, Philadelphia, Pa.

SHEVAT, Levy, Isr, business exec; b. Kovel, Russ, Aug 3, 1909; s. Yaakov and Mindel (Burstein); in Isr since 1936; att HS, Kovel, Russ; m. Leah Lesman, Mar 4, 1947; c: Yaakov, Anat. Dir, co-found, Zim Isr Navigation Co, since 1949, head finance div. Active illegal immigration to Pal; IS, Haganah. Contbr: essays on illegal immigration, JA. Home: 3 Maabarot Rd, Haifa, Isr. Office: 7/9 Ha'atzmaut Rd, Haifa, Isr.

SHIBOLETH, Dov Menachem, Isr, business exec; b. Kedainiai, Lith, Nov 10, 1908; s. Getzel and Alte (Tubin) Sang; in Isr since 1925; att Sch of Law and Econ, Tel Aviv. m. Sara Bonstein. c: Amnon, Tamar. Gen mgr: Mortgage & Inves Bank Ltd, Haifa, since 1957; Carmel Mortgage & Inves Bank, since 1962; chmn, bd, Bat Galim Sea Shore Enterprise, 1943-68; gen mgr: Shibolet & Co, 1944-57; Natl Ins Off, 1946-57. Pal Police Force, 1929-44. Mem: exec bd, Union of Banks, Isr; Moshe Sharet Inst of Oncology; bd, Friends of Technion; Va'ad Lema'an Hachayal; cen comm, Maccabi; Masons. Hobby: golf. Home: 30 Hayarkon St, Haifa, Isr. Office: 22 Haneviim St, Haifa, Isr.

SHIBOLETH, Mordechai, Isr, advocate; b. Siret, Rum, Sep 20, 1924; s. Menachem and Haya (Wasserman) Vevic; in Isr since 1948; LLB, Sch of Law and Econs, Tel Aviv U, 1957; BA, Tel Aviv U, 1959; LLM, Heb U, Jerusalem, 1960; postgrad studies, U London, 1969; m. Deborah Goldenzweig, July 10, 1951; c: Rina. Dep dist atty, Tel Aviv, head, fiscal dept, since 1969, dep dist atty, Cen Dist, 1965-69; prosecutor, Tel Aviv, 1960-65. IDF, 1948-49. Author: High Court Control of Administrative Action, 1960. Spec interests: archeol, politics, Judaism. Home: 21 Yehezkiel St, Tel Aviv, Isr. Office: 1 Weizmann St, Tel Aviv, Isr.

SHIDLOVSKY, Alisa, Isr, organization exec; b. Romani, Russ, Mar 9, 1895; d. Yaakov and Zipora (Kropitzki) Tchitliyonk; in Isr since 1913; att Agric Sch, 1913-16; m. Aharon Shidlovsky; c: Hadassah Din, Rivka Shalev. Chmn,

Mash'en, Histadrut mutual fund; mem: secretariat, Women Workers Council, 1946-69; insp comm, Kupat Holim, 1953-69; secretariat, Lab Party, 1963-69. Fmr: on missions to: Eng; Pol; Swed; US; delg, World Cong, 1963. Contbr to the press. Home: Kvutzat Kinereth, Isr. Office: 97 Bloch St, Tel Aviv, Isr.

SHIENTAG, Florence Perlow, US, attorney; b. NYC, Sep 12, 1912; d. David and Esther (German) Perlow; LLB, NYU, 1931, BS, 1940; att Columbia U; m. Bernard Shientag, June 8, 1938 (decd); m. 2nd Monte Sideman, Sep 30, 1959. Pvt practice, NYC, since 1952; law aide, Thomas E Dewey, spec dep dist atty, NY, 1937-38; law secy, Mayor Fiorello H LaGuardia, NYC, 1940-43; judge, Domestic Relations Court, 1941-43; asst US Atty, S Dist, NY, 1944-52. Pres,Women's Bar Assn, 1940; chmn, domestic relations court comm, NY County Lawyers Assn; mem: NY Co Lawyers Assn; Fed Bar Assn; Bar Assn, NYC; dir, YM-YWHA; It-Amer Assn for Sicily; Intl Cultural Cen for Youth, found, trustee; Lincoln Sq Neighborhood Cen; Family Location Service. Contbr to legal jours. Home: 737 Park Ave, New York, NY. Office: 665 Fifth Ave, New York, NY.

SHIFF, Chaim, Isr, business exec; b. Pol, Feb 8, 1924; in Isr since 1937. Prop, mgr: President Hotel; Orgil Hotel; Judea Gardens Hotel; Dolphin House; Chen Orgil cinemas; Sirtei Chen Films. Brit Army, 1940-45; Irgun Zvei Leumi, interned at Acre and Latrun. Office: President Hotel, Jerusalem, Isr.

SHIFTAN, Zeev L, Isr, geologist; b. Goerlitz, Ger, June 22, 1920; s. Max and Dina (Meyer) Schueftan; in Isr since 1939; MSc, Heb U, Jerusalem, 1944; m. Judith Eschwege, 1944; c: Dina, Anath, Yoram. Chief hydrogeologist, Tahal Cons Engrs, since 1967; dep dir, head hydrogeology div, Geological Survey, Min of Devl, 1963-66; fmr: tech adv, Resources and Transp Div, UN, NY; groundwater devl work: Spain; Iran; Afr; Latin Amer. Prin contribs: devl groundwater resources in Isr, spec achievements in Eilat, Jerusalem, Sodom. Mem: Isr Geological Soc, fmr pres. Contbr to profsl jours. Hobby: photography. Home: 6 Katznelson Rd, Jerusalem, Isr. Office: 54 Ibn Gvirol St, Tel Aviv, Isr.

SHILLO, Yitzchak, Isr, actor; b. Bendzin, Pol, Aug 23, 1920; s. Yosef and Zivia (Piekarsky) Shulman; in Isr since 1935; att, Habima Dramatic Sch; Paris, London, New York drama schs; m. Aviva Gor; c: Tamar. Actor, theaters: Habima, 1939-48; Cameri, 1948-58; NY; LA; maj roles: The Trial; As You Like It; Tartuffe; on stages and TV, NY. Recipient: Intl Theater Inst. Home and office: 8 Kikar Malchei Israel St, Tel Aviv, Isr.

SHILO, Efraim, Isr, agricultural admnr; b. Pol, Mar 5, 1916; s. Symcha and Chaja (Naiman) Szulc; in Isr since 1936; att U. Frankfurt; m. Jedida Ert; c: Nurith, Ada, Erella, Chaia Dir, Cen for Planning and Devl in Agric Settlements, since 1966; agric mgr, Tirat Zvi, 1951-53, 1961-63; agric planner Beisan Valley, 1958-61; dep dir, JA Agric Settlement Dept, 1964-66; head agric planning, Tahal, Casvin Iran Project, 1962-63. I/c illegal immigration: Fr; N Afr, 1946, 1947-51; Balkans, 1946-48. Mem, bd dirs: Mekorot Water Co; Intl Soc for Rural Coop; Cen for Agric Econ Research; fmr vice-chmn regional bd, Beth Shean. Author: Agricultural Planning; Economic Structure of the Kibbutz. Spec interests: lit, hist. Home: Kibbutz Tirat Zvi, Isr. Office: Hakiryah, Tel Aviv, Isr.

SHILO, Moshe, Isr, civil servant; b. Riga, Latvia, July 6, 1902; s. Itzhak and Malka (Wilenzyk) Brachman; grad, HS for Admn and Commerce, Ger; m. Stefania Ehrlich-Neufeld, 1926; c: Uri. Adv to dir-gen, Min of Defense, since 1967; secy-gen, Cen Comm for Knesset Elections, since 1948; secy, Hechalutz Cen, Ger, 1926-30; mem, Kibbutz Givat Brenner, 1930-33; secy, munic div, exec, Histadrut, 1937-42, asst to dir, immigration div, 1946-47; asst secy to dir gen, PM's off, 1948-50; secy gen, Min of Defense, 1950-53; dir, IDF Archives, 1953-67; dir, Assistance from Isr, to DP's, Cyprus, 1947-48. Sgt, Royal Engrs, Brit Army, 1942-46. Chmn Arbitration Bd for Civil Employees in IDF; bd, Naval Off Sch, Acre; vice-chmn, Archive Assn of Isr; mem: Supr Archives Council; Histadrut; Org of Sr Civil Servants; active secretariat, Vets Assn in Isr. Contbr to daily and profsl press. Recipient: Kaplan prize, efficiency in admn; cert, outstanding citizen, by late Pres Ben Zvi. Hobbies: lit music; gardening. Home: 17 Soutine St, Tel Aviv, Isr. Office: Hakiryah, Tel Aviv, Isr.

SHILOAH, Amnon, Isr, musicologist; b. Lanus, Arg, Sep 28, 1928; s. Joseph and Ora (Cohen); in Isr since 1941; MA, Heb U, Jerusalem, 1952; dipl: Isr Acad of Music, 1953; Conservatoire Natl, Paris; PhD, Sorbonne, Paris, 1963; m. Analia Haimovici, Mar 1, 1957; c: Eldad, Noga. Research f, sr lectr, dept musicology, Heb U, since 1965; sr producer, J traditional music, Isr radio, since 1965; with Kol Isr Orch, 1953; music critic, Isr press, 1954-58; music producer, broadcaster, Isr radio, 1958-60; lectr, oriental music: Musicology Inst; Musée Guimet; Fr radio, all 1964; i/c folklore sect, Isr radio, 1965; lectr, musicology, U Ill, 1968. Mem: exec comm, Isr Musicological Soc. Recipient: scholarships: Fr Govt, 1960; Cen Natl de la Recherche Sci, 1962-65. Home: 1 Shmuel Klein St, Jerusalem, Isr. Office: Heb U, Jerusalem, Isr.

SHILOH, Isaac Samson, Isr, jurist; b. Gliniany, Pol, Aug 21, 1913; s. Israel and Chaya (Ehrlich) Schimmel; in Isr since 1926; LLB, hons, U London, Eng, 1936; cert, classical Arabic, Sch of Oriental Studies, 1937; Barrister, Inns of Court, Middle Temple, London, 1938; m. Rachel Schurr, Mar 31, 1944; c: Ilan, Joseph. Judge, Dist Court, Tel Aviv, since 1965; magistrate, Magistrate's Court, 1945-52; lectr, Heb U, Jerusalem, since 1952. Sgt, RAF, 1942-45. Contbr to profsl jours. Home: 17 Nezach Israel St, Tel Aviv, Isr. Office: Dist Court, 1 Weizmann St, Tel Aviv, Isr.

SHILON, Matthew, Isr, architect; b. Lwow, Pol, Aug 17, 1920; s. Herman and Anna (Bund) Schleyen; in Isr since 1938; BSc, engr architect, Technion, Haifa, 1947; m. Liliana Szajn, Sep 27, 1949. Pvt practice since 1953; asst, Technion, Haifa, 1946-48; chief planner, Upper Galilee Region, Govt Planning Bur, 1949-53; cons, Min of Educ, 1958-60. Bd dirs, Wingate Inst for Phys Educ, 1960-68; chmn, Inst of Architects, Tel-Aviv, 1965-69; mem, Engrs and Architects Assn, Isr. Recipient: awards in architectural competitions. Home: 46 Be'eri St, Tel Aviv, Isr. Office: 8 Hagilboa St, Tel Aviv, Isr.

SHIMKIN, Leon, US, publisher; b. Bklyn, NY, Apr 7, 1907; s. Max and Fannie (Nickelsberg); BS, NYU, 1926; m. Rebecca Rabinowitz, Aug 17, 1930; c: Emily Gindin, Michael. Chm bd, Simon and Schuster, Inc, since 1957, began career as acctnt, then, bus mgr and treas; co-found, Pocket Books, Inc, 1939, pres, since 1950; dir, Golden Press, Inc, since 1958. course, book NYU; Comm for Econ Devl; fmr, org, dir, Trustee: NYU; Comm for Econ Devl; fmr, org, dir, course, book publishing, NYU. Recipient: Madden Memorial Award, for outstanding bus achievement, NYU, 1960. Home: 8 East Dr, Larchmont, NY. Office: 630 Fifth Ave, New York, NY.

SHIMONI, Emanuel, Isr, diplomat; b. Johannesburg, S Afr, Mar 30, 1931; s. Mordehai and Rachel (Katz); BA, Witwatersrand U, Johannesburg, 1951; m. Rayla Samuels, Aug 15, 1954; c: Michal, Ophir. Councilor, Isr emb, Ottawa, Can, since 1969; head: educ min's bur, 1962-64; dep prime min's bur, 1964-66; fgn min's bur, 1966-69. Gen secy: Zionist Socialist Youth, S Afr, 1948-50; Zionist Socialist Party, S Afr, 1950-53. Home: 51 Harav Uziel St, Jerusalem, Isr. Office: Fgn Office, Jerusalem, Isr.

SHIMONI, Shimon, (pen name, **L Haim Shimoni)**; Isr, surveyor, political leader, author; b. Suvalki, Pol, July 26, 1900; s. Ahron and Fruma (Zviling) Vorobeiczyk; tchrs dipl, tchrs Sem, Lith, 1922; licensed surveyors cert, Survey Dept, Isr Govt, 1954; m. Sara Taub, 1961 (decd); c: Guta. Ret; surveyor, Survey Dept, Isr Govt, 1948-67. Mem: cen comms: Poalei Zion, Lith, 1920-24, Isr, 1924-44; Achdut Ha'avodah Poalei Zion, Isr, 1946-48; workers' council, exec comm, Haifa, since 1967; Mem: Lab Party, since 1968; exec comm, Rothschild Hosp, Histadrut delg, N and S Amer, 1949-50. Author: Barrg Aroif, 1951; Tag Aus, 1954; Untervegs, 1956; Nechin, 1959; Gang, 1962; Bazalt, 1966; co-author Israel Per Dentro, 1957; contbr in Heb and Yiddish to local, fgn press. Home: Maimon 15, Neve Shaanan, Haifa, Isr.

SHIMONI, Yaacov, Isr, diplomat, author; b. Berlin, Ger, Apr 9, 1915; s. Fritz and Lotte (Saling) Simon; in Isr since 1936; att tchrs Sem, Jerusalem, 1938-40; m. Miriam Schoenbrunn, 1938; c: Yair, Yakhin, Michal. Mem, Kibbutz Givat Hayim, 1936-41; staff mem, Arab sect, political dept, JA, 1941-48, dir, research sect, 1946-48; dep dir, Near E dept, Isr Fgn Off, 1948-49, dir, Asian dept, 1949-52; counselor, Isr Emb, Wash, DC, 1952-55; Min to Burma, 1955-57, concurrently accredited to Philippines, Ceylon and Laos; dir: E Eur dept, Min for Fgn Affairs, 1957-60, Asian dept, 1960-64; govt lectr, Heb U, Jerusalem, 1957-64; ambass to Swed, 1964-68. Author: The Arabs of Palestine, 1947; The Arab Minority

in the State of Israel, 1950; The Arab States, 1952, 1959; The Countries of South Asia-Their National Movement and their Independence, 1960; Contemporary Asia—a political history, 1961; The Arab States—Their Contemporary History and Politics, 1965; trans: the German Republic, by Rosenberg, 1942; Fifty Years of Socialism, by Baer, 1943: ed, Ha-Mizrah heHadash, 1949-52; contbr to Ency Hebraica. Home: 17 Redak St, Jerusalem, Isr.

SHIMSHONI, Daniel, Isr, educator; b. Pittsburgh, Pa, Sep 20, 1919; s. Isaac and Sarah (Raisin) Levin; in Isr since 1948; BS, Princeton U, 1941; MSc, Cal Inst of Tech, 1942; PhD, Harvard U, 1958; m. Rose Freeman, 1946; c: Jonathan, Michael, Abigail, Isaac. Prof, political sci, Tel Aviv U, since 1965; aerodynamicist, Convair, US, 1941-48; dir gen, Natl Council for Research and Devl, Off of PM, Jerusalem, 1959-65. IAF, 1948-56. Chmn, Isr Found Trustees. Contbr to sci publs. Home: Hanassi St, Herzliya Pituah, Isr. Office: Tel Aviv U, Ramat Aviv, Isr.

SHIMSHONI, Michael, Isr, scientist; b. Berlin, Ger, Mar 22, 1927; s. Samson and Charlotte (Struck), Buttenwieser; in Isr since 1935; BSc, EE Technion, Haifa, 1951; MSc, U Wales, 1958; PhD, Wiezmann Inst, Rehovot, 1962; m. Miriam Stern, July 5, 1955; c: Ilan-Moshe, Oded, Ehud. Sr sci, dept applied math, Weizmann Inst of Sci, since 1962; sr visiting lectr, U Cambridge, 1962; research asso, Cal Inst of Tech, 1962-64. Served Haganah; lt, IAF, 1952-55. F, Royal Astronomical Soc; mem, Seismological Soc of Amer. Home: 11 Hazayit St, Rehovot, Isr. Office: Weizmann Inst of Sci, Rehovot, Isr.

SHINBANE, Abraham Mark, Can, attorney; b. Winnipeg, Man, Aug 29, 1891; s. Jacob and Leah (Perilmuter); BA, U Man, 1912; LLB, 1915; postgrad, Chgo U Law Sch; m. Ancy Hertz, Sep 17, 1957, Sr mem, Shinbane, Dorfman, Kanee, Aenteleff & Cohan: QC since 1931; atty with: Hugh Phillips, 1912-15; Crown Counsel, Min Justice, 1928-57. Natl vice-pres, Friends Heb U, since 1949; chmn, Man comm, policy and platform, Lib Party; fmr: chmn, JDC, Man, 1925-28; pres, ZOC, 1930-38; hon vice-pres, Can J Cong, 1930-33; dir: Hillel Found, 1937-41; Alumni Assn, U Man, 1929; hon treas: Cen Council Social Agcys, Gtr Winnipeg, 1935-40; Man Fed Lib Progressive Assn, 1930-35; Winnipeg Sym Orch, 1931-36; bd mem, Family Bur, Winnipeg, 1935-48; clubs: Can of Winnipeg; Winnipeg Press; Can; Glendale Country. Home: 1191 Wellington Crescent, Winnipeg, Can. Office: 703 Paris Bldg, 259 Portage Ave, Winnipeg, Can.

SHINEDLING, Abraham I, US, rabbi, teacher, editor; b. Menominee, Mich, Sep 8, 1897; s. Moses and Dora (Morris); BA, Cincinnati U, 1919; ordained rabbi, HUC, 1920; MA; Columbia U, 1928; hon DD, HUC-JIR, 1959; m. Helen Lowenstein, 1929; c: Sidney. Tchr, Heb: College Albert, Albuquerque, since 1957; prin, rel sch, Santa Fe J Temple and Comty Cen, since 1962; part-time rabbi: Santa Fe, since 1963; Carlsbad J Cong, Carlsbad, NM, 1964-68; mem, staff, Amer J Archives, Cincinnati, since 1950; rabbi: Congs in Ga, Mo, Tex, NC, 1920-26; chaplain, Westchester Co Penitentiary and Jail, E View NY; tchr, social worker, Westchester Co for Natl Council J Women, both 1932-43; chaplain, Fed House of Detention, NYC, 1942-43; rabbi: Congs in La, Ala, 1943-47; Cong Ahavath Shalom, Bluefield, W Va, 1947-50; Cong Beth El, Beckley, W Va, 1950-56; chaplain: Beckley W Va Hosp, 1951-56; Fed Reformatory for Women, Alderson, W Va, 1951-54; lectr, coll and Us for J Chautauqua Soc, 1946-58; tchr, Heb, B'nai Isr Cong, Albuquerque, 1956-57; part time rabbi and tchr, Los Alamos J Cen, NM, 1956-57; lectr before church groups, service clubs, and other NM orgs on subjects of J and rel interest. Secy-treas, Beckley Min Assn; secy, B'nai B'rith, Beckley, both 1953-56; charter mem, Natl Council for J Chaplains in Penal Insts, 1937-43; mem: Temple Albert Men's Club; Albuquerque; U Cincinnati Alumni Assn; HUC-JIR Alumni Assn; CCAR. Author: History of the Los Alamos Jewish Center, 1958; West Virginia Jewry: Origins and History, 1850-1958, 3 vols 1963; co-author: History of the Beckley Jewish Community; History of Congregation Beth El, (The Beckley Hebrew Assn), 1955; trans, History of the Jews after the Fall of the Jewish State, by Ismar Elbogen, 1926; asst ed, trans, Universal J Ency; contbr of numerous articles to: Universal J Ency; Natl Ency and Ency of J Knowledge and Year Book. Home: 615 Aliso Dr, Albuquerque, NM.

SHINITSKY, Moshe I, Isr, business exec; b. Vielun, Pol, Sep 9, 1909; s. Mordechai and Rachel (Krimolovsky); in Isr since 1922; att Yeshiva; m. Dvora Shklonovsky, 1933; c: Zeev, Meira, Amos. Owner, Shinitsky and Co, mfr agric machinery; dep chmn, Kupat Am Bank Ltd, since 1958; dir, ins and finance co, since 1957; mem, control comm, Halvaah Vehissahon Bank Ltd. Maj, IDF. Chmn: Marmorek St Syn; Friends of Midrashia, Pardess Hannah; mem bd: Isr Syns; B'nai B'rith; Isr-Brit Commonwealth Assn; clubs: Isr Ins; Ind and Commercial. Spec interest: J studies. Home: 13 Berdischevsky St, Tel Aviv, Office: 75 Nahlat Binyamin St, Tel Aviv, Isr.

SHINNAR, Felix Elieser, Isr, economist; b. Stuttgart, Ger, Apr 17, 1905; s. Chaim and Jenny (Schiffmann) Schneebalg; in Isr since 1934; att: Us: Tubingen, Frankfurt; DJur, U Heidelberg, 1927; m. Alisa Oppenheimer, 1941; c: Michael. Chmn, Delek, Isr Fuel Corp, since 1951; bd mem, Isr Chemicals, Ltd; fmr: mgr, Gen Trust Co, 1934; official receiver, Amtsgericht, Berlin-MiHe, 1934; mgn dir, Haaretz daily, Tel Aviv, 1937-48; controller, fuel, Isr Min of Finance, 1952; econ adv, Isr Discount Bank, Ltd; econ counselor: Isr Legation, London; Isr Fgn Min; jt head, Isr delg, Ger reparations negotiations, Vassenaar, Ger; head, Isr mission to Fed of Ger in personal rank of ambass plen, 1953-66. Home: Beth Shinnar, Tel Ganim, Ramat Gan, Isr.

SHINNAR, Reuel, US, educator; b. Vienna, Aus, Aug 15, 1923; s. Emil and Rosa (Storch) Bardfeld; in US since 1962; BSc, Technion, Haifa, 1945, MSc, 1952; DSc, Columbia U, 1957; m. Miryam Halpern, June 22, 1948; c: Shlomo, Meir. Prof, chem engr, CCNY, since 1964; tech mgmt, Isr Mil Inds; asst prof, Technion, 1958-62; visiting research f, Princeton U, 1962-64. Pvt, IDF, 1948-49. Mem: Great Neck Syn; profsl socs. Contbr to profsl publs. Home: 110 Ash Dr, Great Neck, NY. Office: CCNY, New York, NY.

SHIPTON, Sidney Lawrence, Eng, solicitor; b. London, July 25, 1929; s. Harold and Rose (Horowitz); LLB, London U, 1951. Pvt practice since 1955.Vice-pres, London, Zionist Fed, of Gt Brit and Ir; jt hon secy, Brit sect, WJC, chmn, constitution comm; vice-chmn, Gen Zionist Admn Comm; hon vice-pres: ZF Educ Trust; Fed Zionist Youth; vice-chmn, Aliyah Jt Liaison Comm; co-chmn, bd govs, Clapton J Day Sch; dir, Zionist Review Ltd; vice-pres, Hendon Una and Charter Soc; mem: fgn affairs comm, J Bd Deps; London bd, JTA; dep mem: Zionist Actions Comm; Jt Comm for Youth Affairs; mem: Medico-Legal Soc; J Hist Soc; Law Soc, fmr, hon secy, young mem's group; Brit Acad Forensic Sci; U London Convocation; fmr: chmn, Fed Zionist Youth; hon secy, hon treas, ZF; mem, WZO Reorg Comm; delg, World ZCs. Author: The Arab Refugee Problem, 1966; Towards a Practical Zionism, 2nd ed, 1969; mem, ed bd, Zionist Year Book; fmr, ed, The Young Zionist. Recipient: hon vice-pres and JNF Golden Book Cert, Fed Zionist Youth. Spec interests: ME and intl politics, law and criminology, book collecting. Home: 46 Brent St, London NW 4, Eng. Office: 70 New Cavendish St, London W1, Eng.

SHISTER, Joseph, US, educator, lab arbitrator; b. Russ, Nov 27, 1917; s. Eli and Pearl (Millman); BS, U Montreal, Can, 1939; MA, Harvard U, 1940, PhD, 1941; in US since 1939; m. Edna Tuch, 1941; c: Neil, Jayne, Gail, Diane. Prof, chmn, dept ind relations, SUNY, since 1950; instr, econ, Cornell U, 1942-43; cons econ, NLRB, 1944; research asso, Rockefeller Found for Study Trade Unionism, 1944-45; asst prof, econ: Syracuse U, NY, 1945-46; Yale U, 1946-49; visiting prof: Tufts U; Wesleyan U; U Montreal; spec adv lab leg, Gov of Conn, 1948-50; public mem: Natl Wage Stabilization Bd, 1951-52; NY State Minimum Wage Bd, 1957-59; NY State Mediation Bd, 1965-68; mem, Buffalo Public Employment Relations Bd, since 1967; moderator, Buffalo Round Table of the Air, since 1952; chmn, Emergency Dispute Bd, 1961, 1962, 1964; mem, White House Conf on Natl Econ Issues, 1962; referee, Natl RR Adjustment Bd, since1960; impartial umpire for lab disputes between cos and unions; spec repr, Mayor, Buffalo, for settling emergency lab disputes. Chmn, acad div, United Negro Coll Fund; mem, exec bd: Ind Relations Research Assn; Temple Beth Am; mem: Natl Acad Arbitrators; Amer Econ Assn; AAUP; Fed Mediation and Conciliation Service; Amer Arbitration Assn; Phi Beta Kappa; Beta Gamma Sigma; club, Harvard. Author: Insights into Labor Issues, 1948; Job Horizons, 1949; Conflict and Stability in Labor Relations, 1952; Economics of the Labor Market, 1956; Essays in Labor Economics and Industrial Relations, 1956; Public Policy and Collective Bargaining, 1962; contbr articles to profsl mags. Recipient: named one of Buffalo's Ten Outstanding Citizens, 1954. Hobbies: music; art; travel. Home: 200 Brantwood Rd, Snyder, NY. Office: SUNY, Buffalo, NY.

SHIZGAL, David T, Can, dentist; b. Maciejow, Pol, May 15, 1913; s. Todres and Esther (Hendler); in Can since 1926; DDS, McGill U, 1939; m. Rita Dash, Oct 19, 1941; c: Elaine, Peter. Pvt practice, dent surg, Montreal, since 1946; lectr, dept dent anat, McGill U, since 1946. Capt, Army Dent Corps, 1941-45. Mem: Can Technion Soc; Can Dent Assn; Que Coll Dent Surgs; Montreal Endodontia Soc, fmr pres; McGill Grads Soc; Friends Heb U; Shaar Zion Syn, mem, Mens Club; fmr pres, Mt Royal Dent Soc. Recipient: Star of It, Fr and Ger campaigns; Defense of Eng and Can Medals; Can Voluntary Service Medal and Clasp. Home: 4465 Harvard Ave, Montreal, Can. Office: 1396 St Catherine St W, Montreal, Can.

SHIZGAL, Sender, US, rabbi; b. Montreal, Can, Mar 28, 1939; s. Abraham and Esther (Liechtstein); in US since 1959; BA, Yeshiva Coll, 1960; ordained rabbi, Isaac Elchanan Theol Sem, NY, 1962; MHL, Bernard Revel Grad Sch, NY, 1962; m. Chava Salit, Sep 13, 1959; c: Esther, Shlomo, Ben-Zion. Rabbi, Cong Rodphey Shalom, since 1962. Fmr: chmn, UJA, Roosevelt, NJ; secy, RabCA, Phila. Recipient: Paul Orentlicher French prize, Yeshiva Coll, 1960; Premier Prix-Journalisme, Cercle Français, NY, 1960. Home: 10 Keefe Ave, Holyoke, Mass. Study: 1800 Northampton St, Holyoke, Mass.

SHKLARSKY, Elisha, Isr, educator; b. Pal, 1912; s. Bezalel and Yehudit; BSc, Technion, Haifa, 1935; CE, 1936; m. Chawa Rieber, 1938; c: Dan, Ruth, Gad. Prof, hwy and airport engr, Technion, since 1965; vice pres, academic affairs, since 1966; dean, fac architecture, town planning, since 1967, dean, civil engr fac, 1961-66, on fac since 1967; cons engr, road, airfield engr to public insts in Isr, since 1945; head, hwy and soil engr lab, 1959-61, head dept, 1957-59. Mem: Assn Engrs and Architects, Isr; Intl Soc of Soil Mechs. Contbr articles to profsl jours. Office: Technion, Haifa, Isr.

SHLOMM, Gregory, US, business exec; b. Simferopol, Russ, Jan 30, 1904; s. Boris and Sophie (Salnaja); in US since 1941; att Ecole Superieure de Commerce, Lausanne; m. Raissa Markowski, Nov 24, 1932; c: Boris. Pres: Amicale Ind Inc; Amicale Yarns; Amicale Trading Co; Atlantic Wool Combing; Woonsocket Spinning Co; Amicale Fabrics Inc; in wool waste and specialty fiber bus, Fr until 1941. Trustee, mem finance comm, Cong Rodeph Sholem; bd dirs, Long Beach Hosp, 1962; mem: B'nai B'rith; NY, Boston Wool Trade Assns. Home: 88 Central Park W, New York, NY. Office 1040 Ave of Americas, New York, NY.

SHLONSKY, Vardina, Isr, pianist, composer; b. Kremenchug, Russ, 1913; d. Tuvia and Zipora (Braverman); student of: Egon Petri, Arthur Schneider; studied composition in Paris under: Nadia Boulanger; Max Deutch; Edgar Varese. Acad prof of music, since 1929; music tchr: Berlin, 1927; Paris, 1927-31; composer, Habimah, Ohel theaters, 1931-33. Mem: Assn of Composers, Tel Aviv; ACUM, Tel Aviv. Compositions: Poem Hebraique; String Quartet; Hodaya; Images Palestinien, 1931; Let's Sing, children's songs, 1959; Eleven Postcards, 1954; Opus for Singer, Cello, Piano; Esprit on Spirit; Symfonfie, Heb songs; Sonata for Violin and Piano, 1, 2; Compositions, 1969; Eupony, for Chamber Orch; Five songs for Voice and Orchestra; Reflexion Orchestral, five movements for orch; Imagination; Fantasy, both for cello and piano. Recipient: 1st prize, Paris, for Poem Hebraique; Bela Bartok prize. Hobbies: drawing, journalism. Home: 10 Hofien St, Ramat Aviv, Isr.

SHMUELI, Eliezer, Isr, plant physiologist; b. Pol, 1919; s. Josef and Taube (Bekenstein) Szmulewicz; in Isr since 1937; PhD, Heb U, Jerusalem, 1952; m. Nehama Schmusch; c: Dan, Yosef, Hannah. Head, div irrigation, Volcani Inst, Bet Dagan, since 1960; tchr, Ein Harod Agric HS, 1943-45; sr sci, research comm, Jordan Valley Settlements, 1945-57; lectr, Tel Aviv U, 1956-64. Fmr chmn, Comm for Prevention Frost Damage in Agric; fmr mem, Min Comm for Efficient Use Water in Agric; mem: Isr, Intl, Soil Sci Socs; Isr Botanical Soc. Author: Studies on the Banana, 1952; contbr to sci publs. Recipient, awards: J Students Assn, Manchester U; Natural Sci Assn, Tel Aviv, both for MSc thesis. Hobbies: philately, floriculture. Home: 53 Yahalom St, Ramat Gan, Isr. Office: Volcani Inst, Bet Dagan, Isr.

SHMUELI, Ephraim, Isr, author, teacher; b. Lodz, Pol, Nov 28, 1908; s. Mordekhai and Frieda (Strykowski) Szmulewicz; in Isr since 1933; grad, J Theol Sem, Breslau, 1933; PhD, U Breslau, 1933; m. Kath Perle, Oct 12, 1933; c: Mikhal Jacoby,

Gila. Prof, phil, Cleveland State U, since 1967; tchr, Govt Tchrs Coll, Haifa, 1954-67; dir, dean, Tchrs Training Coll, Haifa, 1949-53. Author: Tradition and Revolution, 1942; History of the Jewish People in Modern Times, 7 vols, 1940-57; Cervantes, 1953; Giordano Bruno, 1953; Man of the Renaissance, 2 vols 1954; Faith and Heresy, 1961; Problems of Jewish People in Our Times, 1960; Don Isaac Abravanel and the Expulsion from Spain, 1963; Identity, Assimilation and the Impact of Israel, 1966; trans into Heb: Utopia by Thomas More; Political Writings of Machiavelli; Politics as vocation by Max Weber; The Letters of Spinoza. Recipient: Tchernichowsky prize, 1947. Homes: 16 Boaz St, Mt Carmel, Haifa, Isr; 14015 Superior, Cleveland, O.

SHMULEWITZ, Icek, US, journalist; b. Kielce, Pol, Mar 14, 1911; s. Chaim and Blima (Tchorz); in US since 1954; att Kielce HS; m. Miriam Krakowski, Oct 2, 1946; c: Esther, Aaron. Staff writer, J Daily Forward, 1954-69. Mem: Workmen's Circle; Farband; I L Peretz Writers Union; YIVO Cultural Cong; fmr, mem bd, Workmen's Circle, Paris. Hobby: reading. Home: 500A Grand St, New York, NY. Office: 175 E Broadway, New York, NY.

SHNEERSON, Mordekhai, Isr, government official; b. Kiev, Russ, Jan 5, 1913; s. Aharon and Chaya (Tversky); in Isr since 1924; licence es droit, Sorbonne U, Paris, 1938, jist dipl; m. Miriam Tchertok, June 6, 1946; c: Yael, David. Dir, Eur 2 Div, Min for Fgn Affairs, since 1969; counselor: Legation, Buenos Aires, 1949-52; Legation, Rio de Janeiro, 1952-55; min, Isr Emb, Paris, 1957-60; Isr Ambass: Mexico, 1960-63; Japan, 1963-66. Haganah, 1936-42; RAF, 1942-46. Recipient: Commandeur Legion d'Honneur. Hobbies: music, art. Home: 2 Ibn Ezra St, Jerusalem, Isr. Office: Hakiryah, Jerusalem.

SHNEERSON, Pinchas, Isr, farmer; b. Russ, 1893; s. Arie and Yacheved (Hamerman); in Isr since 1908; m. Esther Halperin, 1922. Ret; co-found, Kibbutz Kfar Gileadi, 1916-33; mem, Hashomer; dir, Kfar Etzion, 1933-38; with planning dept, Tel Aviv Munic, 1940-59. Hashomer, 1909-20; Haganah, 1920-48. Active cen comm, Mapam; mem, council, Histadrut. Contbr to press. Home: 15 Zamenoff St, Tel Aviv, Isr.

SHNEIDERMAN, Samuel L, US, journalist, author, lecturer; b. Kazimierz, Pol, June 15, 1906; s. Abraham and Chana (Mandelbaum); att Warsaw U, 1927; in US since; 1940; m. Eileen Shimin, Mar 15, 1933; c: Helen, Benjamin. UN corresp, Amer, Isr and Eur newspapers, since 1945; feature writer, The Day, J jour; ed, Trybuna Akademicka, Warsaw, 1927-31; staff mem, Paris corresp for Nasz Przeglad; Chwila; Nowy Dziennik; Hajnt, all Pol, until 1939. Author: Gilderne Feigl, 1927; Feiern in Shtodt, 1932; Zvishn Naievkes un Eifel Turem, 1935; Krieg in Shpanien, 2 vols, 1939; Between Fear and Hope, 1947; The Warsaw Heresy, 1959; Ilya Ehrenburg, 1968; ed, Anthol of Yiddish and Heb Prose and Poetry, Pol trans, 1934; co-ed, One Thousand Years Pinsk, 1943; ed: The Warsaw Ghetto, diary of Mary Berg, 1944; Neurim B'zel Ha-Mavet, ghetto memoirs by Miriam Biederman, 1960; My Story, by Gemma LaGuardia Cluck, 1962; translated works of Pol and Fr poets into Eng; wrote script and directed documentary film in Pol, The Last Chapter, 1967; contbr to publs. Home: 280 Ninth Ave, New York, NY.

SHNITKA, Theodor K, Can, physician; educator; b. Calgary, Can, Nov 21, 1927; s. Abraham and Pearl (Freifeld); BS, U Alberta, Edmonton, 1948, MS, 1952, MD, 1953; postdoc research f, Johns Hopkins U Sch of Med, Baltimore, 1959-61. Prof, path, Fac of Med, U Alberta, since 1967, on fac since 1954; on active att staff, U Alberta Hosp, since 1961. Can Naval Res, 1945-59. Prin contrib: established electron microscopy unit, Fac of Med, U Alberta, 1961-63. Mem: Alberta and Can Med Assns; Alberta Soc Path; Can Assn Path; NY Acad Sci; Electron Microscope Soc of Amer; Histochem Soc of Amer; AAAS; Amer Soc for Experimental Path; Amer Soc for Cell Biol; Can Soc for Cell Biol; Intl Acad Path: Alpha Omega Alpha; cert spec in path, CRCP of Can, 1958. Ed: Gastric Secretion; Mechanisms and Control, 1967; contbr to profsl jours. Recipient: John S McEachern Memorial f, Can Cancer Soc, 1959-60. Hobbies: photography, music. Home: 9823-106 St, Edmonton, Can. Office: U Alberta, Edmonton, Can.

SHOCHET, Azriel, Isr, educator; b. Motol, Pol, Mar 18, 1906; s. Aharon and Sarah (Brinberg); in Isr since 1926; att Heb Tchrs Coll, Jerusalem, 1927-30; MA, Heb U, 1938, PhD, 1956; m. Ahuvah Wachtel, 1938; c: Janir. Sr lectr, U Coll,

Haifa, since 1963, head, dept J hist, since 1967; tchr, Heb Tchrs Coll, Jerusalem, 1946-64, vice-prin, 1960-64. Author: Im Hilufai Tekufot, 1960; co-ed Vol 4, Educational Ency; pub, Sefer Yehufat of Shlomo Ilin Verga. Contbr: Heb Ency; to Heb educ and hist jours; J hist textbooks. Home: 18 Eder St, Haifa, Isr. Office: Coll of Haifa, Haifa, Isr.

SHOCHET, Fred K, US, editor, publisher; b. Baltimore, Md, Aug 24, 1915; s. Louis and Ethel (Silverman). Ed, publisher, The J Floridian, since 1939. Pres, Amer Assn Eng-J Newspapers, 1953; dir: Fla Press Assn, 1943; J Comty Cen, 1948; ZOA, 1949; J Home for Aged, 1951, all Miami, Fla; dir, Gtr Miami J Fed; trustee, B'nai B'rith; AJComm; fmr pres, Natl Assn Eng-J Newspapers; mem: J Cens Assn; Sigma Delta Chi; Alpha Epsilon Pi; club: Elks; Lions, fmr pres. Hobbies: boating, fishing. Home: 651 NE 30 Terr, Miami, Fla. Office: 120 NE 6 St, Miami, Fla.

SHOENBERG, David, Eng, physicist; b. St Petersburg, Russ, 1911; s. Isaac and Esther (Eisenstein); in Eng since 1914; BA, PhD, Trinity Coll, Cambridge U; m. Catherine Fischmann, Mar 14, 1940; c: Ann La Roque, Peter, Jane. Reader in physics, Cambridge U, since 1952; head, Mond Lab, since 1947. Author: Magnetism, 1949; Superconductivity, 1938, 1952. F, Royal Soc of London, 1953. Recipient: Fritz London award, Intl Award Soc, 1964. Home: 2 Long Rd, Cambridge, Eng. Office: Royal Soc, Mond Laboratory, Free School Lane, Cambridge, Eng.

SHOFMAN, Joseph, Isr, legislator; b. Warsaw, Pol, June 12, 1903; s. Shalom and Tamara (Kirslowin); in Isr since 1940; LLM, U Warsaw, 1927; m. Hannie Salberg-Lassger, July 12, 1967; c: Hanna Itzhaki. MK since 1955. Mem, cen comm, Herut Part, chmn, exec, 1962-65; Jabotinsky Order; chmn, Zionist Revisionist Party in Pol, until 1939; Pal, 1945-46; Contbr: articles to daily press. Hobby: classical music. Home: 8 Dizengoff St, Tel Aviv, Isr.

SHOHAM, Avigdor, Isr, government official; b. Koenigsberg, Ger, Aug 8, 1915; s. Herman and Rosa (Glaser) Silberstein; in Isr since 1939; Gymnasium, Koenigsberg, 1933; m. Edith Neugeboren, Jan 25, 1939; c: Rajah, David. Dir, dept for official guests, Min for Fgn Affairs, since 1968; kibbutz mem, 1939-42; staff, JA, Jerusalem, 1945; secy, dept for resettlement ex-soldiers, 1945-46, staff, political dept, 1947-48; dir, dept Finance, Min for Fgn Affairs, 1948-52; consul, i/c consulate gen, Zurich, Switz, 1952-55; 1st secy, chargé d'affairs, Isr Legation, Finland, 1955-58; dep dir, Dept for Intl Coop, 1960-63; min, Isr Emb, Rio de Janeiro, 1963-65; ambass, Columbia, Guyana, 1965-68. Brit Army, 1942-45. Mem, Zionist org, Ger, 1933-39; cen exec, Zionist Pioneer Movement, Ger, 1937-39. Recipient: Afr Star, Brit Army; Haganah, Volunteer, State Fighters Medals, Isr. Hobbies: classical music, tennis, golf. Home: 60A Shmarjahu Levin, Jerusalem, Isr. Office: Min Fgn Affairs, Jerusalem, Isr.

SHOHAM, David J, Isr banker; b. Tel Aviv, June 9, 1923; s. Zeev and Zilla; MA, Heb U, Jerusalem, 1951; m. Dina Rezky, 1949; c: Avshalom, Dorit. Mgn dir, Isr Gen Bank Ltd since 1965; dep controller, fgn exch, Min of Finance, 1952-56; econ counselor, Isr Emb, London, 1957-59; mgn dir, Fgn Trade Bank Ltd, 1959-65. J Brig, WW II; battalion cdr, Isr War of Independence. Home: 62 29th of November St, Tel Aviv, Isr. Office: Isr Gen Bank Ltd, Tel Aviv, Isr.

SHOHAM, Zilla, Isr, agriculturist; b. Jaffa, Nov 27, 1895; d. Israel and Fanny (Belkind) Feinberg; father was co-found Rishon leZion, Gedera and Hadera; mother was one of the four Bilu women; att: U Berlin, 1914-19; U London, 1920-21; U Vienna, 1921; m. Zeev Shoham, 1919. Mem: control commn, Pardess Syndicate Coop Soc Ltd, mem coop, since 1941; control comm, Citrus Marketing Bd of Isr, since 1960. Chmn, agric educ dept, World WIZO; mem: status women comm, legal advisory bur, WIZO, women's equal rights comm; Farmers Assn of Isr; U Women's Assn; Intl Alliance of Women. Home: 16 Ben Yehuda St, Haifa, Isr.

SHOHAT, Joseph, Isr, educator; b. Rovno, Pol, May 21, 1908; s. Avram and Krejna (Rejseles); in Isr since 1936; MA, State U, Warsaw, 1932; MJ Studies, Inst J Studies, 1932; m. Elisheva Skurkovicz, 1936; c: Avshalom, Doron. Dep dir gen, Min of Educ and Culture, since 1960, dist insp, 1957-60; head, pedg council, secondary educ; tchr, Reali HS, Haifa, 1936-47; acting prin, Tchrs Training Coll, Haifa, 1947-51. Exec bd: Yad Vashem; John Dewey Sch of Educ; Heb U; Council of Art and Culture, Min of Educ; natl comm vice-chmn,

UNESCO, Isr, 1960-69. Author: hist texts for secondary schs. Home: 22 Hattibonim, Jerusalem, Isr. Office: 22 Shivtei Yisrael, Jerusalem, Isr.

SHOHET, Abraham Edward, Isr, editor; b. Baghdad, Iraq, Dec 12, 1913; s. Ezekiel and Roza (Ramond); in Isr since 1953; BA, hons, St Xaviers Coll, U Bombay, 1935; m. Daphne Nagler, Sep 18, 1938; c: Uri, Ruth, Aviva. Ed, Technion Mag and other publs, since 1962; gen sales mgr, Hindustani Lever Ltd, Bombay, 1940-53; marketing dir, Pal Edible Products, Isr, 1953-56; sales mgr, Amer Isr Paper Mills, 1959-62. Vicechmn, Haifa br, Isr Brit Commonwealth Assn; initiator, J Cen Bd, Bombay; fmr: official repr in India, JA for Pal; pres, Zionist Org of Bombay; hon ed, The J Advocate, Bombay; club, Rotary, Carmel. Hobbies: camping, swimming. Home: 21 Kidron St, Haifa, Isr. Office: Technion City, Neve Sha'anan, Haifa, Isr.

SHOHET, Harmon, US, dentist; b. Roxbury, Mass, Feb 28, 1897; s. Jacob and Fannie (Kaplan); att Tufts Coll, 1914-15; DMD, cum laude, Harvard U Dent Sch, 1918; m. Grace Cohen, June 5, 1928; c: Marcia, Stephen; m. 2nd, Evelyn Collins, Oct 14, 1955. Pvt practice since 1918; instr, chem, Harvard U Dent Sch, 1917-18, crown and bridge prosthesis, 1919-26, spec lectr, postgrad dept, 1956-57; instr, Forsyth Dent Infirmary, 1922; spec lectr, Tufts U Dent Sch, postgrad dept, 1958-62; lectr, US, Can, Mex, Isr and Eur, on facial pains related to temporomandibular jt problems, mouth rehab and restorative dent; lectr, Japan, China, Thailand, Singapore. US Army, WW I. Prin contrib: originator, single casting technique for removable bridge work, the Shohet semi-veneer, the Shohet semi-clasp and the Shohet bridge pontic. F: Amer Acad Dent Sci; Amer Equilibration Soc; Gtr NY Acad of Proshodontics; Harriet N Lowell Research Soc; mem: exam comm, Harvard Sch Dent Med; Amer Dent Assn; Mass Dent Soc; Gtr Boston Dent Soc; Harvard Odontological Soc; Royal Soc of Health, Eng; Phi Sigma Tau; Omicron Kappa Upsilon; Alpha Omega; clubs: Oakly Country; Harvard, Boston; New Cent Commonwealth Country. Contbr to dent jours. Home: 10 Emerson Pl, Boston, Mass. Office: 20 Commonwealth Ave, Boston, Mass.

SHOMRON, Gideon, Isr, civil servant; b. Lodz, Pol, Mar 30, 1921; s. Leon and Miryam (Garfunkel) Silberstrom; in Isr since 1934; Dipl, Public Service Coll, 1948; m. Helen Wiseman, 1950; c: Ari, Avidan. Dir, Off, Pres of Isr, since 1965; attache, Isr Mission to UN, NY, 1948-49; vice-consul, Isr Consulate Gen, NY, 1949-51; prin asst, Isr Fgn Min, Jerusalem, 1951-55; 1st secy: Isr Emb, Stockholm, 1955-58; Moscow, 1958-60; counselor, Isr Consul Gen, London, 1960-63; head, dir gen off, Isr Fgn Min, 1963-65. Home: 28 Nayot, Jerusalem, Isr. Office: 17 Alharizi St, Jerusalem, Isr.

SHOR, David D, US, rabbi; b. New Orleans, La, Apr 2, 1913; s. Joseph and Janette (Waldstein); BA, U Cincinnati, 1934; att S Methodist U, 1933; BHL, HUC, 1934; ordained rabbi, 1937; hon DD, HUC, LA, Cal, 1962; m. Bettye Rothschild, Oct 4, 1942 (decd); c: Judith, Frances. Rabbi, Temple Albert, since 1948; JWB chaplain: Sandia Base; Manzano Base; Kirtland Air Force Base; VA Hosp, Albuquerque, NM, all since 1948; B'nai B'rith Hillel counselor, U of NM, since 1949; rabbi: Lib J Syn, London, Eng, 1937-38; Cong Moses Montefiore, Marshall, Tex, 1938-40; Temple Beth Ell, Helena, Ark, 1940-42; Cong B'nai Isr, Hattiesburg, Miss, 1946-48. Chaplain, maj, US Army, 1942-46. Mem: adv commn, NM Fair Employment Practices Commn, 1961; W States, Commn on Higher Educ, 1955; Commn on MH, 1955; pres, Albuquerque Min Alliance, 1957-58; 1st vice-pres, Pacific Assn Reform Rabbis, 1969-70; mem, bd: Albuquerque JWF, since 1948; Albuquerque Home for J Aged, since 1961; Albuquerque Boys' Club, 1948-52; Visiting Nurses Assn, 1954-55; MH Soc, 1950-56; Council Social Agcys, 1956-60; United Fund, 1957-61; Goodwill Inds, 1948-50; YMCA, 1959-60; mem: CCAR; W Assn Reform Rabbis; Assn of J Chaplains; Interrel Council, U of NM. Contbr to local, J jours. Home: 3309 Hastings Ave, NE, Albuquerque, NM. Study: 1006 Lead Ave, SE, Albuquerque, NM.

SHOR, Zvi, Isr, artist; b. Russ, Dec 27, 1898; s. Pinhas and Ruth (Schwartzbart); in Isr since 1921; att: Yeshiva Kaminitz; Acad Gran Chumiere; Acad Colorossy, both Paris; m. Rivka Levin, 1942; c: Ruth Habas, Avinoam. Prin, art sch, Petah Tikva, since 1949; one-man shows: Mus: Tel Aviv; Jerusalem; Bat Yam; Holon; Haifa; Petah Tikva; Ramat Gan, all Isr; Ariz; Gal de Niveau, Paris; maj works exhb: Isr; Eur; US; S Afr. Mem: found, Painters and Sculptors Assn of Isr. Recipi-

ent: Dizengoff award, Tel Aviv Munic, 1939, 1949. Home: 4 Geser St, Tel Aviv, Isr.

SHORE, Herbert Harold, US, social service admnr; b. NYC, Oct 23, 1925; s. Isadore and Mollie (Algus); BS, CCNY, 1948; MS, Columbia U, 1952; att N Tex State U; m. Selma Epstein, Aug 29, 1948; c: Debra, Wendy, Andrew. Exec dir, Dallas Home and Hosp for J Aged, since 1953; instr: SW Med Sch, U Tex, Sch Social Work; N Tex State U; Worden Sch Social Work, Tex; Inst Gerontology, U Mich; group worker, comty cens, NY, 1943-49; asst dir, Drexel Home, Chgo, 1950-53. Fmr pres: Amer Assn Homes for Aging; Natl Assn J Homes for Aged; Tex Gerontological Soc; fmr chmn, div on aging, Dallas Council Social Agcys; exec vice-pres, Tex Soc on Aging, fmr pres; f, Gerontological Soc; mem: Natl Adv Comm Housing Elderly, US Dept Housing and Urban Devl; bd dirs, Dallas Co Comty Action Comm; Natl Assn Social Workers; Adul Educ Assn; Natl Council on Aging; Tex, Dallas Social Wfr Assns; Tex, Dallas Mh Socs; Pres Task Force on Nursing Home and Related Facilities Caring for Elderly; Natl Conf J Communal Service; Natl Conf Social Work; Amer Hosp Assn; Amer Coll Hosp Admrs; Tex Assn Homes for Aged. Co-ed, Geriatric Institutional Management, 1964; ed, Newsletter, Tex Soc on Aging; fmr mem, ed bd, Jour of J Communal Service; contbr: chaps in books; to profsl publs. Recipient: hon award, Amer Assn Homes for Aging. Home: 5839 Meaddowcrest Dr, Dallas, Tex. Office: 2525 Centerville Rd, Dallas, Tex.

SHORESH, Shmuel, Isr, legislator; b. Rovno, Russ, Jan 11, 1913; s. Jacob and Fania (Buslik) Shternberg; in Isr since 1924; m. Hana Ben-David, 1935; c: Jakov, Israela Levy, Yehudith. Found, mem Moshav Bet Sharim, since 1936, secy, chmn, 1936-41; MK, 1955-69; secy, local lab council, Magdiel, 1934-36; chmn, local council, Nahalal, 1945-49. Info off, Haganah. Mem: exec comm, settlement and agric movement, Tel Aviv. Contbr: articles on problems of agric econ and coop farming. Home: Bet Sharim, Isr. Office: Knesset, Jerusalem, Isr.

SHOR-SAVENEANU, Moshe Maur, Isr, author, editor; b. Saveni, Rum, Jan 5, 1910; s. Solomon and Henia (Baratz); in Isr since 1951; att Journalism Sch, Paris; m. Malvina Rudberg. Chief ed, Facla, Rum daily since 1963. Author: numerous works 1928-1948, in Rum; Israel râde, 1952; Legea Trupului Roman, 1953; Strul din RPR, 1954; Geografia Israelului, 1960; Istoria Israelului, 1961; Numai Dumnezeu nu Face Umbrà, 1968; Bàrbatii Vàd prin Ochii Femeilor, 1969; Fiecare Iubire cu soarte ei, 1969; O Femeie a Fost Siluità, 1969; all Tel Aviv; trans into Rum, The Life of Moshe Dayan, 1967; Bible commentator. Mem, Igud Haitonayim; fmr master, Masons, fmr Gt Architect, Grand Lodge. Hobby: philately. Home: 145 Haalouf David St, Ramat Gan, Isr. Office: 52 Harakevet St, Tel Aviv, Isr.

SHOSHANI, Yitzhak, Isr, journalist; b. Bialystok, Pol, May 1, 1914; s. Fishel and Hannah (Shlafmitz) Rosenthal; in Isr since 1938; att Gymnasia Ivrit, Bialystok, 1928-32; m. Lea Jalovski, 1943; c: Hannah Sherman, Avraham. Mgr, sup, Laborers Council, since 1963; mem secretariat, Histadrut Cultural Cen, since 1960; mem, Kibbutz Kfar Menahem, 1938-45; mgr, sup, Lab Exch Cen, 1949-58; org mgr, MAPAM Cen, 1958-60. Mem: Yiddish Writers and Journalists Org, Isr; bd, Org Immigrants from Pol; exec comm, Histadrut; cen secretariat, MAPAM; fmr mem: Kfar Saba Town Council; head off, World Fed Pol J. Contbr to Heb, Yiddish jours. Hobbies: acting; stage mgn. Home: 18 Weisel St, Tel Aviv, Isr. Office: 126 Allenby St, Tel Aviv, Isr.

SHOSHANY, Mordechai, Isr, architect; b. Plock, Pol, July, 1914; s. Naftali and Chaia (Treitel); in Isr since 1922; BA, Technion, Haifa, 1940; m. Rifka Cohen; c: Ruth Pagirsky, Benjamin. Chief architect, public works, Isr Govt, since 1965. Maj, engr corps, IDF, 1948-67; chief first naval engr, Civil Defense. Mem: Assn Engrs and Architects in Isr; Histadrut, engr chap. Lectr; contbr to profsl jours. Home: 18 Yellin, St. Tel Aviv, Isr. Office: 3 Lincoln St, Tel Aviv, Isr.

SHOSTECK, Robert, US, organization executive. b. Newark, NJ, Apr 25, 1910; s. Saul and Bessie (Rubin); AB, George Wash U, 1937, AM, 1953; cert, Radcliffe-Harvard Summer Prog, 1957; m. Dora Rabinovitz, May 9, 1936; c: Herschel, Sara. Curator, B'nai B'rith Exhibition Hall, Wash, DC; asst chief, placement, Natl Roster Sci and Specialized Personnel, 1940-45; dir, research, B'nai B'rith Vocational Service, 1945-59. Mem: Amer J Hist Soc; Amer Assn Mus; Amer Assn for

State and Local Hist; Amer Personnel and Guidance Assn; Manuscript Soc; Soc J Bibliophiles; form pres, J Hist Soc, Gtr Wash, 1960-62. Author: Careers in Retail Business Ownership, 1946; Small Town Jewry Tell Their Story, 1953; College Finder, 1959; College Guide for Jewish Youth, 1959; Potomac Trail Book, 1968; Weekender's Guide, 1969; numerous career guidance pamphlets. Home: 10002 Gardiner Ave, Silver Spring, Md. Office: 1640 Rhode Island Ave, NW, Washington, DC.

SHOULBERG, Harry, US, artist; b. Phila, Pa, Oct 25, 1903; s. Max and Tessie (Derfler); att: CCNY, 1931-35; Amer Artists Sch, 1936-38; m. Sylvia Hendler, June 1, 1931; c: Ted. Art dir, Studio Art Gal, since 1938; repr in perm collections: Metrop Mus Art; Norfolk Mus Art; NJ State Tchrs Coll; Denver Mus; Baltimore Mus; SF Mus; George Walter Vincent Smith Mus, Springfield, Mass; Tel Aviv Mus; Ein Harod Mus, Isr; Brooks Memorial Gal; Milw Art Inst; Carnegie Inst; US State Dept; NY State Tchrs Coll; one-man exhbs: Harbor Gal; Modern Age Gal; Frances Webb Gal; Salpeter Gal; Natl Serigraph Soc; Denver U; Hudson Guild. Mem: Silvermine Guild of Artists; Audubon Soc of Artists; Soc Painters in Casein; Natl Serigraph Soc; Amer Print Club; NJ Soc Painters and Sculptors; Bklyn Soc of Artists. Recipient: Emily Lowe award; Albert Kapp award; Tanner prize; Jane Peterson prize; first prize: Guild Hall; Bx House; second prize, Parrish Mus; purchase prize, Milw Art Inst; Grumbacher Award; Peterson Medal of Honor. Home and studio: 567 Ave of the Americas, New York, NY.

SHRAGA, Alexander, Isr, attorney; b. Bucharest, Rum, Mar 12, 1923; s. Lascar and Lucy (Rosner); in Isr since 1947; LLM, U Bucharest, 1947, BSc, econ, 1947; PhD, U Milan, 1948; m. Rachael Kirstein; c: Yael, Michal. Mem, council, atty, Givatayim Munic. Capt, IDF. Mem: B'nai B'rith, Rambam Lodge. Contbr to profsl jours, newspapers. Home: 21 Gordon St, Givatayim, Isr. Office: 5 Weizmann St, Givatayim, Isr.

SHRAGAI, Eliyahu, Isr, public relations dir; b. Jerusalem, Jan 8, 1929; s. Shlomo and Miriam; tchrs dipl, Tchrs Training Coll, Jerusalem, econ politice deg, Geneva U, Switz; m. Miriam Armon; c: Yinon, Enat. Dir, press, PR, Zim Isr Shipping Co, since 1954; tchr, Kfar Saba, until 1945; journalist, parl reporter, Knesset, 1950-51. Home: 6 Gilboa St, Haifa, Isr. Office: 7 Ha'atzmauth Rd, Haifa, Isr.

SHRAGAI, Shlomo Zalman, Isr, journalist; b. Gorszkovitz, Pol, Dec 31, 1899; s. Moshe and Frumet (Weingarten) Faiwlowicz; in Isr since 1924; m. Miriam Shpilberg, 1924; c: Yehuda, Eliyahu, Ovadya, Efrat. Ret; mem, JA exec, 1954-68; first J mayor, Jerusalem Munic, 1950-52. Author: Thumim; Hazon veHagshama; Tahlichei haGeula vehaTmura; Sha'a vaNetzah; Pa'amei Geula; Gerangel Far Yidishkait; Shabato Shel Israel; Vohin Yidishe Shmoesn; Zmanim; contbr numerous articles to newspapers. Found, rel settlements: Kiruat Sandz; Yismah Moshe; Matisdorf; co-found, Hapoel Hamizrachi; mem, Zionist Gen Council; fmr: mem: exec, Vaad Leumi; Zim Council; Hapoel Hamizrachi Bank; directorate, KH; delg, ZCs. Home: 8 Keren Kayemet St, Jerusalem, Isr. Office: POB 7109, Jerusalem, Isr.

SHRAGOWITZ, Moses Joshua, US, rabbi; b. Timkowitz, Russ, Jan 12, 1895; s. Mordecai and Rashe (Turetzky); in US since 1923; ordained rabbi; Seminarjum Duchowne of Kletsk, Pol, 1923; m. Hinde Shragowitz, June 9, 1922; c: Jacob, Bessie Kra, Sarah Lander. Rabbi: Kneses Tifereth Isr, since 1937; Kneses Tifereth Isr, Mt Kisco, NY, 1923-25; Heb Cong, Linden, NJ, since 1937; Agudath Achim and Cong Anshe Chesed, Somerville, NJ, 1926-37. Life mem, Rel Zionists of Amer, Mizrachi; mem: Anshei Zedeck; Timkowitz. Hobbies: music, chess, swimming. Home and study: 105 Haseco Ave, Port Chester, NY.

SHTERN, Israel H, (Ish Yair), Can, poet, writer, educator; b. Pol, June 25, 1914; s. Abraham and Gittel (Zimmerman); in Can since 1937; BS, Sir George Williams U, Montreal, 1944; MA, NYU, 1953; MS, McGill U, 1957, PhD, 1961; m. Amalia Udovitch, Aug 4, 1944; c: Adele, Avrom, Yona. Lectr, math, physics, Sir George Williams U, 1944-46; asst prof, math, McGill U, 1961-66, mem fac since 1956; asso prof, math, Loyola Coll, Montreal, 1966-69. Author: Fables, 1967; Out of the Burning Bush, 1968; pub poems, short stories, essays, in Eng and Yiddish mags and anthols in Eng, Switz, Greece, India, Philippines, Brazil, Can, US. Mem: Can Math Cong; Can Assn U Tchrs; Farband Lab Zionist Order; J Peretz Schs; J Public Libr; YIVO; United Poets Laureate Intl;

World Poetry Soc Intercontinental; Centro Studi E Scambi Internazionali; Can Poetry Soc; J I Segal Fund for J Culture in Can; intl corresp, Poesie Vivante; fmr pres, Fed J Tchrs, Montreal. Recipient: 2 gold medals, laurel wreath, Intl Rizal, Poet Laureate Intl, 1967-68; dist service citation and dipl, World Poetry Soc Intercontinental, 1968; Centro Studi Dipl of Merit and Medal of Hon, Centro Studi E Scambi Internazionali, 1969. Home: 6741 Baily Rd, Montreal, Can.

SHTRIKMAN, Shmuel, Isr, engineer; b. Brisk, Pol, Oct 21, 1930; s. Avraham and Esther (Kozlovsky); in Isr since 1934; BSc, Technion, Haifa, 1953; Engr, 1954; DSc, 1958; m. Rachel Chdorovsky, Sep 27, 1955; c: Hadas, Ilan, Yoram. Prof, Weizmann Inst, Isr, since 1966; visiting sci, Imperial Coll, London, 1960; sr staff physicist, Franklin Inst, 1960-62; visiting prof, U of Pa, 1964-65. IDF, 1958-50. Recipient: Weizmann award, Tel Aviv City, 1968. Home: 1 Hasharon St, Rehovot, Isr. Office: Weizmann Inst of Sci, Rehovot, Isr.

SHTULL, Jacob, US, rabbi; b. Montreal, Can, Nov 18, 1925; 1925; s. Yekuthiel and Blima (Schwartz); BS, Sir George Williams Coll, Montreal, 1946; ordained rabbi, MHL, JTSA, 1953; m. Rita Estrin, Dec 25, 1951; c: Kiva, Simcha, Dina, Ora. Rabbi, Mayfield Temple, since 1957; lectr, Inst J Studies; rabbi: B'nai Isr Cong, London, Can, 1953-56; Cong Beth Am, 1956-57. mem: RA, secy, Northern O region. Home: 3532 Blanche Ave, Cleveland Heights, O. Study: 3040 Mayfield Rd Cleveland Heights, O.

SHUBART, Stanley C, US, engineer; b. Denver, Colo, June 17, 1906; s. Benedict and Daisy (Newhouse); BS, U Colo, 1927; m. Rita Sanders, Sep 19, 1929; c: Sally Schein, Stana Cooper. Partner, Schloss and Shubart, since 1935; sales engr, Link-Belt Co, 1925-35. US Army, 1941-46. Fmr pres: Rocky Mt Coal Miners Inst; Natl J Hosp Denver; mem: Amer Ordnance Assn; Res Offs Assn of US; Mil Order of WWs; Amer Inst Mining Engrs; Amer Council for Judaism; B'nai B'rith; Amer Legion. Recipient: Army Commendation Ribbon. Home: 550 E 12 Ave, Denver, Colo. Office: 1626 Wazee St, Denver, Colo.

SHUBOW, Joseph Shalom, US, rabbi, writer lecturer; b. Olita, Lith, Sep 26, 1899; s. Morris and Esther (Lasker); in US since 1907; AB, Harvard, 1920, AM, 1921, PhD, 1959; MHL, ordained rabbi, JIR, 1933; hon DArt of Oratory, Staley Coll, 1950; m. Beatrice Citron, 1928; c: Judith Habibah, Jehiel. Rabbi, Cong B'nai Moshe, Brighton, Mass, since 1933; chaplain: Vet's Hosp, W Roxbury, Mass, since 1946; New Boston Vets Hosp, since 1952; lit ed, Boston J Advocate, 1923-35; corresp, feature writer, JTA, 1924-31; field secy, Amer Econ Comm for Pal, 1931-32. US Army, 1943-46. Pres: Gtr Boston Rabb Assn, since 1950; NE div, AJCong, 1941-43; hon pres since 1943; Harvard Zionist Soc, 1920-21; vice-pres: admn, ZOA, since 1961; and co-found, Avukah, Amer Student Zionist Org, 1925; dir, Watch and Ward Soc, since 1949; mem: interim comm, AJConf, 1943; price panel, War Price and Rationing Bd, Brighton, 1941-43; men's council, Boston Aid to the Blind; Amer Acad for J Research; Amer Soc for Pol Sci; RA, life, CCAR; Amer Legion JWV; Amvets; Mil Chaplains Assn of US; Amer J Hist Soc; NAACP; delg, WZCs; clubs: Harvard, Boston; Sidney Hill Country. Author: Peretz B Moshe Smolenskin; Zionism, Jewish Nationalism and European Nationalism; Great Men and Great Ideas; ed, Brandeis Avukah, 1936; co-ed, Opinion, since 1949; contbr to Boston and Anglo-J Press. Recipient: Bronze Star Medal, 1945; Jacob Schiff prize, Harvard Coll, 1920; Dante prize, Cambridge Dante Soc, Harvard U, 1921; Bowdoin prize, Harvard U; Boston J Comty prize, 1920; Charles W Eliot prize, JIR, 1932; Louis Marshall prize, Heb U, 1933; prize, ZOA, 1951; plaque, Amer J Lit Found, 1956. Home: 125 Holland Ave, Brookline, Mass. Study: 1845 Commonwealth Ave, Brighton, Mass.

SHUBOW, Leo, US, rabbi, lecturer; b. Olita, Lith, July 22, 1903; s. Morris and Esther (Lasker); in US since 1906; BA, Harvard Coll, 1924; BS, NYU, 1927; MHL, ordained rabbi, JIR, 1932; m. Pauline Kniznik, 1938; c: Dorothy, Morris, Charles. Rabbi, Temple B'nai B'rith, Somerville, Mass, since 1946; chaplain: State Prison Colony, Norfolk, Mass, since 1947; Youth Service Bd of Mass, since 1951; rabbi: Temple of Isr, Amsterdam, NY, 1932-35; Temple Emanuel, Newton, Mass, 1935-38; Genesis Heb Cen, Tuckahoe, NY, 1938-46; lectr, service clubs; church and temple orgs; comty forums; illus with own movies of Isr; led tour of Isr as guest of El Al Airlines, and corresp of Boston Herald Traveler, 1968; delivered essay, Beginnings of Brandeis Zionism, Herzl Inst,

NY. Yeoman, secy, Intl Ice Patrol, USCG, 1924-25. Pres: Somerville Min Alliance, 1968; Constitution Lodge, B'nai B'rith, 1959-60; Zionist dists, Yonkers, NY, 1940-42; Middlesex, NY, 1949-51; chaplain; Eastchester, NY Fire Dept, 1938-46; Henry Price Masonic Lodge, Oakley Chap, USCG; vice-pres: Zionist Regions: Westchester, NY, 1944-46; NE, 1956, 1963, mem, exec bd, since 1947; Mass Bd of Rabbis, 1952-55; mem, exec bd: AJCong; Somerville Comty Council; ARC; mem: natl exec comm, ZOA, since 1958; CCAR; NY Bd Rabbis; Amer J Hist Soc; fmr mem, standing and adv comm, Boston Latin Sch Alumni; clubs: New Cent, Boston Camera. Author: Israel Lives Again, 1952; Iceberg Dead Ahead, 1959; contbr: articles on Jacob de Haas for Herzl Year Book, vol 5, for Boston J Advocate; to newspapers and mags; Isr corresp, Boston Traveler, 1937, 1949. Recipient: Salomon Schechter Award, 1952; Boston J Advocate Carnation award, 1957; citation, Boston Latin Sch Alumni. Home: 172 Central St, Somerville, Mass. Study: 201 Central St, Somerville, Mass.

SHUER, David Stanley, US, social welfare admr; b. Holyoke, Mass, Jan 16, 1914; s. Max and Sarah (Jacobson); BSS, Springfield Coll, Mass, 1941; MSW, Columbia U Sch Social Work, 1949; m. Grace Bruder, Dec 22, 1946; c: Herbert, Martin. Exec dir: Elmira J Cen; JWF and Comty Council, all since 1968; Toledo J Cen, 1956-64; J Cen and Comty Council, Bangor, Me, 1964-68; lectr, sociol, hum relations, U Toledo, 1958-64; social work, Elmira Coll, 1968-69; spec cons, OEO, State of Me, 1964. Pvt, US Army, 1942-45. Mem: Natl Assn Social Workers; Natl J Cen Workers; B'nai B'rith; fmr pres, Me Adult Educ Assn. Author: Adult Programs in Jewish Centers, 1967; program guides, JWB. Recipient: PR award, Toledo Comty Chest, 1960; comty service award, Toledo J Cen, 1960. Hobby: writing, speaking, music, golf. Home: 821 W Church St, Elmira, NY. Office: 115 E Church St, Elmira, NY.

SHUGAR, Joseph L, Can, surgeon; b. Montreal, Apr 8, 1919; s. Harry and Dora (Hochmitz); BSc, McGill U, 1941, MDCM, 1943; m. Anne Sirota, June 27, 1943; c: Richard, Donna, William. Orthopedic surg, chief orthopedic service, J Gen Hosp, since 1962, mem att staff since 1952; att staff: Montreal Childrens Hosp; Reddy Memorial Hosp, both since 1952; mem fac, McGill U, since 1956. MC, Royal Can Army, 1943-46. FRCS; FACS; dipl, Amer Bd Orthopedic Surg; mem: Assn of Orthopedic Surgs, Que; Amer Acad Orthopedic Surgs; Que Soc of Orthopedics and Traumatology; Can Med Assn; Alpha Omega Alpha. Recipient: Can Voluntary Service Medal and Clasp; 1939-45 Star. Home: 4530 Madison Ave, Montreal, Can. Office: 6000 Côte des Neiges, Montreal, Can.

SHUGER, Leroy W, US, chemist, business exec; b. Baltimore, Md, Jan 11, 1910; s. Morres and Sophie (Navanvorich); BS, Johns Hopkins U, 1930, PhD, 1934; m. Joyce Tramer, Dec 25, 1935; c: Jill, Maura. Vice-pres, Baltimore Paint & Chemical Corp. Prin contrib: inventor, numerous patents, principally in the field of reflectorized traffic paint. Chmn, Md Chap, Amer Inst of Chems; bd dirs, Natl Paint Varnish & Lacquer Assn; mem: Amer Chem Soc; Amer Soc for Testing Materials; Hwy Research Bd; AAAS; Phi Sigma Delta; Har Sinai Cong; club, Woodholme Country. Recipient: George B Heckel award, for making greatest contrib to paint ind mgmt, 1968. Home: Shuger Hill Rd, Pikesville, Md. Office: 2325 Hollis Ferry Rd, Baltimore, Md.

SHULEMSON, Sydney Simon, Can, printing exec; b. Montreal, Oct 22, 1915; s. Saul and Rebecca (Rosenberg); att McGill U, 1933. Div mgr, Apex Press, Ltd, Montreal. RCAF, 1941-45; squadron commanding off, Royal Can Air Cadets, 1946-51. Fmr pres, B'nai B'rith; fmr master, Masons. Recipient: dist service order, Gt Brit; Dist Flying Cross, Gt Brit. Home: 3600 Ridgewood Ave, Montreal, can.

SHULIMSON, I Adrian, US, chemical engr; b. Kiev, Russ, Mar 11, 1902; s. Aharon and Faygeh (Kliegman); in US since 1902; BA, Columbia U, 1923, CE, Engr Sch, 1925; m. Edith Kliegman, Mar 11, 1928; c: Victor, Miriam Becker. Purchasing off, Kliegman Bros Inc, since 1927; cons engr since 1925; research engr: Amer Borch Engr Corp, 1925-26; Forest Elec Co, 1926-27. Prin contribs: research, US patent on electrolytic rectification, 1929; donated research lab in bio-chem to Hadassah-Heb U Med Sch, Jerusalem. Chmn, spec gifts, UJA since 1950; mem bd, Jamaica J Cen since 1945; found; Amer Soc for Technion, past bd mem; mem: charter, Ussishkin Club, JNF; Amer Chem Soc; Amer-Isr Cultural Found; fmr pres, Jamaica Zionist Dist. Hobbies: photography; work for

State of Isr. Home: 170-38 82 Ave, Jamaica, NY. Office: 76-01 77 Ave, Glendale, NY.

SHULMAN, Albert M, US, rabbi; b. Russ, March 21, 1902; s. Morris and Rachel (Nemirov); in US since 1904; BA, U of S Cal, 1926, MA, 1927; MHL, ordained rabbi, JIR, 1932, hon DD, HUC-JIR, 1960; m. Rose Rosenberg, June 15, 1924; c: Jeremy, Naomi. Rabbi, Temple Beth-El, S Bend, Ind, since 1934; lectr, Ind U Cen. Chaplain, lt cdr, USN, 1943-46. Chmn, S Bend Housing Auth; fmr pres: St Joseph Co Min Assn; Intl Relations Council; B'nai B'rith; S Bend ZionistDist; St Joseph Co United Found; O, Mich, Ind Rel Educs; Natl Assn for Prevention Blindness; vice-chmn, Amer Council, Amer Legion, fmr Ind State, natl chaplain; mem adv bd, Beatty Memorial Hosp; bd mem: S Bend UN Org; ARC; YMCA; NCCJ; mem, gov's adv, Comm on Mh, since 1958; State Comm on the Aged and Aging; mem: Elks; Masons; Alpha Kappa Delta; club, Rotary. Recipient: brotherhood award, NCCJ, 1958. Home: 1411 Northside Blvd, South Bend, Ind. Study: 305 W Madison St, South Bend, Ind.

SHULMAN, Cynthia B, US, communal worker; b. Boston, Mass, Aug 6, 1931; d. Frank and Sarah (Goldfarb) Brezniak; AB, Smith Coll, 1952; m. Leon Shulman, June 22, 1952; c: Steven, Kenneth, William. Pres, women's div, Heb Rehab Cen for Aged, since 1967; vice-pres: NE br, Natl Women's League, since 1968; League of J Women's Orgs, since 1968; pres, Sisterhood Temple Emanuel, 1965-67; fmr vice-pres: Newton Hadassah; Brookline Hosp; J Vocational Aid Soc; Natl Council J Women; bd mem, Mass Kidney Found; mem: Brandeis U Womens Comm; Heb Tchrs Coll; Recuperative Cen; Beth Isr Hosp; League Women Voters; Family and Children's Service; Dana Hall and Smith Coll Alumni Assns. Hobbies: theater, skiing. Home: 11 Gralynn Rd, Newton Center, Mass.

SHULMAN, Harold, US, educator; b. Newark, NJ, Feb 12, 1925; s. Elias and Rose (Schneiberg); BA, George Wash U, 1948; ordained rabbi, Ner Isr Rabb Coll, 1951; MA, Johns Hopkins U, 1952; PhD, NYU, 1958; c: Batya, Jacob, Tzipporah. Asst prof, math, Herbert H Lehman Coll, since 1964; research asso, NYU, 1958-60. Treas, Assn Orthodox J Sci. Home: 144-43 Jewel Ave, Flushing, NY. Office: Herbert H Lehman Coll, Bronx, NY.

SHULMAN, Harry Manuel, US, educator, author; b. Chicago, Ill, Oct 16, 1899; s. Isaac and Millie (Monaschewitz); PhB, U Chgo, 1921; att Columbia U, 1923-31; m. Daga Stalstjerna, 1927. Prof em, CUNY, since 1967, prof, sociol, 1956-67, fac mem since 1938; mem, comm on grad studies, 1961-67; dir, Hawthorne-Cedar Knolls Sch, 1934-36; 1st dep commn, NY City Dept of Correction, 1954-56; cons, US Bur Budget, 1964; exec secy, NJ State Crime Commn, 1967-68. Served, WW I. Author: Slums of New York, 1938; Juvenile Delinquency in American Society, 1961; contbr, reports to NY State Crime Commn. Home: 50 Park Terr E, New York, NY.

SHULMAN, Irving, US, author; b. Bklyn, NY, May 21, 1913; s. Max and Sarah (Ress); AB, Ohio U, 1937; AM, Columbia U, 1938; m. Julia Grager, July 9, 1938; c: Joan Alexander, Leslie Eddy. Asst prof, Eng, Cal State Coll, LA, 1964-65; teaching asst, UCLA, 1962-64. Author: The Amboy Dukes, 1947; Cry Tough, 1949; The Big Brokers, 1951; The Square Trap, 1953; Children of the Dark, 1955; Good Deeds Must be Punished, 1955; Calibre, 1956; The Velvet Knife, 1959; The Short End of the Stick, 1959; The Roots of Fury, 1961; Harlow, 1964; Valentine, 1967; other titles under pseudonyms; screenplays; short stories. Pres, Phi Epsilon Pi Alumni Assn of S Cal, since 1959; bd dirs, Ohio U Alumni Assn for S Cal, 1958-62; mem: Eng Grad Assn, NYU; Eng Grad Assn, UCLA; Writers Guild of Amer, W; AAUP; Acad Motion Picture Arts and Sci. Recipient: dist service key, Phi Epsilon Pi, 1961, achievement citation, 1963. Spec interests: chess, philately. Office: Reece Halsey Agcy, 8733 Sunset Blvd, Los Angeles, Cal.

SHULMAN, Nisson Elchanan, US, rabbi; b. Bklyn, NY, Dec 12, 1931; s. Moses and Rose (Port); BA, magna cum laude, Yeshiva U, 1952, ordained rabbi, 1955, MA, 1960; m. Rywka Kossowsky, Nov 27, 1958; c: Eliahu, Nehama. Rabbi, Cong Sons of Isr, Yonkers, NY, since 1962; chaplain, USNR Training Cen, Whitestone, NY, since 1962; mem fac, Yeshiva U Torah Leadership Sem, since 1959; rabbi, educ dir, Gt Neck Syn, 1955-56; rabbi, N End Syn, Bridgeport, Conn, 1958-62. Lt cdr, USNR, since 1956. Chmn, Yonkers Bd Rabbis; mem: exec comm, RabCA since 1959, fmr chmn, rel observance comm; Rabb Alumni, Yeshiva U, since 1960; Mil Chaplains Assn; B'nai Zion; fmr: pres, Rabb Council, Conn; mem, exec comm, Rel Zionists of Amer. Recipient: Gottesman scholarship for advanced Talmudic research, 1952; Minna Belkin Memorial award, 1952; alumnus of year, annual banquet, Yeshiva Etz Hayim, Boro Park. Home: 112 Belvedere Dr, Yonkers, NY. Study: 155 Elliott Ave, Yonkers, NY.

SHULMAN, Oscar, US, business exec; b. Vilna, Russ, Apr 10, 1911; s. Isaac and Anna (Mintz); in US since 1917; m. Anne Fidelman, Nov 14, 1937 (decd); c: Dori; m. 2nd, Ethel Shapiro, Apr 13, 1969. Pres, maj stockholder, I Shulman and Son Co, since 1948. Pres, Cong Shombay Hadath; mem: bd dirs: J Home for Aged, Syracuse, NY; J Comty Cen; Elmira JWF, NY, fmr campaign chmn; mem: Jessie L Cooley Lodge 966, Masons; Elks; Elmira Shrine; Corning Consistory, NY; fmr, pres, dir, West NY chap, Inst Scrap Iron and Steel; club, Kiwanis. Hobbies: bowling; golf; billiards; music. Home: 82 Greenridge Dr W, Elmira, NY. Office: 197 E Washington Ave, Elmira, NY.

SHULMAN, Stephen, N, US, attorney, b. New Haven, Conn, Apr 6, 1933; s. Harry and Rea (Karrel); BA, Harvard Coll, 1954; LLB, Yale Law Sch, 1958; m. Sandra Still, Aug 14, 1954; c: Harry, Dean, John. Res counsel, Cadwalader, Wickersham & Taft, mem, Kane, Shulman & Schlei, since 1967; ind relations, Bendix Aviation Corp, 1954-55; law clerk, Supr Court Justice Harlan, 1958-59; visiting asst prof law, U Mich Law Sch, 1959; asso law firm, Covington & Burling, 1959-60; asst, US Atty, Wash, DC, 1960-61; exec asst to Secy Labor, 1961-62; dep asst, Secy Defense, 1962-65; gen counsel, USAF, 1965-66; chmn, Equal Employment Opportunity Comm, 1966-67. Mem: Order of Coif; Cum Laude Soc; Phi Alpha Delta; Book and Gavel; Conn, Wash, DC, and Supr Court Bars. Ed in chief, Yale Law Jour, vol 67. Home: 3732 N Oakland St, Arlington, Va. Office: 1000 Connecticut Ave, NW, Washington, DC.

SHULOV, Aharon, Isr, zoologist, educator; b. Jelisavetgrad, Russ, Nov 5, 1907; s. Shlomo and Chava (Doskovsky); in Isr since 1926; att: Heb U, Jerusalem, 1926-32; U Padua, It, 1933; DSc, U Naples; m. Jocheved Pressman, 1930; c: Michael, Shlomith. Asso of zool, Heb U, Jerusalem, since 1959, head dept, entomology and venomous animals, asst in zool, since 1939, lectr since 1951; found, Jerusalem Biblical Zoo, dir, since 1950. Mem: Isr Zool Soc; corresp mem, Zool Soc, London; Intl Acad Zool; exec comm, Agra, India; Ecology Soc of Amer; Inst Paris Execs; Isr Entomology Soc. Contbr to profsl jours. Recipient: research grants: Brit Colonial Off; US Dept Agric; Hadassah Med Org; Isr PM Off; NIH, US; Isr Acad Sci and Hum. Home: Meonoth Ovdim b/25, Rehavia, Jerusalem, Isr. Office: Hebrew U, Jerusalem, Isr.

SHULVASS, Moses Avigdor, US, educator, author; b. Plonsk, Pol, July 29, 1909; s. Meyer and Rebecca (Michelson); in US since 1948; ordained rabbi, Tachkemoni Rabb Coll, Warsaw, Pol, 1930; MA, PhD, U Eerlin, 1934; m. Celia Cemach, Apr 4, 1935; c: Phyllis, Ruth. Dist Service Prof J Hist, chmn,dept grad, studies, Coll J Studies, Chgo, Ill, since 1951; instr, rel, Rabbiner Sem, Berlin, 1934; author, lectr, ed, in Pal, 1935-47; prof, rabb lit and hist, Baltimore Heb Coll, 1948-51; visiting lectr, hist, Yeshiva U, summer 1949; lectr, Heb, Ner Isr Rabb Coll,Baltimore,1949-51.Author: Die Juden inWurzburg, 1934; Bibliographical Guide to Jewish Studies, 1935; Rome and Jerusalem, 1944; The Jews in Spain from 1391 to 1492, pub 1948; Jewish Life in Renaissance Italy, 1955; In the Grip of Centuries, 1960; Between the Rhine and the Bosporus, 1964; compiler, trans, Pirkei Hayim, autobiographical fragments, by Shmuel David Luzzato, 1950; ed: Jewish Historical Texts Series, 1948-52; Italy, J quarterly; contbr to jours in Eng, Heb, Yiddish. Vice-chmn, Heb Culture Council, Chgo; research secy, comm on hist of Hassidim, YIVO, 1948-49; mem, bd, Hist Soc of Isr, 1946-48; mem: natl council, Histad ruth Ivrith of Amer; Natl Council for J Educ; Natl Bd Licence, for teaching personnel in Heb Schs in Amer, since 1957; JBCA; Conf on J Relations; clubs: Heb PEN; Yiddish PEN. Recipient: LaMed Lit prize, 1956. Home: 6537 N Ashland Ave, Chicago, Ill. Office: Coll of J Studies, 72 E 11 St, Chicago, Ill.

SHUMAN, Hyman Boris, US, business exec; b. Buffalo, NY, Oct 6, 1926; s. Philip and Ida (Aliotz); att Millard Fillmore Coll, 1947-48; m. Yvonne Velleman, June 21, 1963; c: Miriam, Aviva. Pres: Philip Shuman & Sons, Inc, since 1961, partner, 1947-60; Shuman Plastics, since 1961; Shuman Plastics Intl,

Ltd, since 1962; Peckham-Adam Corp, since 1962; Shuman Plastics of Can, since 1968. Pvt, US Army, 1945-46. Participant, N Amer sect, Council Econ and Ind Devl for Isr, since 1968; mem, profsl comm, plastics, since 1968; mem: bd dirs,Buffalo Heb Benevolent Loan Assn; UJF, Buffalo, allocations comm, spec gifts event; Kadimah Sch; chmn, Buffalo Council, JNF; profsl services comm, J Family Service, Erie Co, NY; bd govs, Isr Bonds; bd, Capital for Isr; Soc Plastic Engrs; participant, Econ Conf of the PM of Isr, 1968, 1969. Hobbies: philately, numismatics, study of hist and antiquities. Home: 723 Parkside, Buffalo, NY. Office: 35 Neoga St, Depew, NY.

SHUMER, Herbert M, US, business exec; b. Bklyn, NY, July 16, 1914; s. Samuel and Kate (Harris); grad, Cooper, Union, 1936; m. Minna Schipper, June 21, 1936; c: Neil, Lenore. Plant mgr, Bacig Mfg Co, since 1942; owner, Lordent Co, 1936-42. Mem: sch bd, Temple Hillel, Valley Stream, NY, found and pres, 1955-57; Free Sons of Isr; Hapoel Hamizrachi; Young Isr. Home: 1046 Rosedale Rd, Valley Stream, NY. Office: 132 W 21 St, New York, NY.

SHUMIATCHER, Abraham Isaac, Can, lawyer; b. Gomel, Russ, Apr 16, 1890; s. Judah and Chassia (Rasin); in Can since 1911; att U Alberta; m. Hessia-Luba Lubinsky, Sep 21, 1913; c: Minuetta Kessler, Morris. Barrister-at-law, Shumiatcher & Shumiatcher, since 1930; QC since 1940. Hon life mem, IL Peretz Sch; fmr pres: Farband, LZOA; B'nai B'rith; House of Jacob Cong; 1st vice-pres, Calgary br, Can J Cong; mem: bd educ, Calgary Heb Sch; exec, Calgary br, ZOC; Bar Assn; Law Soc, Alberta; Can Bar Assn; Commercial Law League of Amer; clubs: Can; Calgary Musical. Home: 918 Ridge Rd, Calgary, Can. Office: 603 Grain Exch Bldg, Calgary, Can.

SHUNAMI, Shlomo, Isr, librarian, bibliographer; b. Hung, 1894; s. Shalom and Borbala (Fuchs); dipl, Ecole de Bibliothécaires, Paris, 1921; m. Alma Levy; c: Gideon, Nurith. Tchr J bibliography, Grad Librr Sch, Heb U, since 1956; counselor, Inst for Heb Bibliography, Jerusalem, since 1964; chief bibliographer, Ency Judaica, Jerusalem, since 1968; libr: HUC Libr, 1929-30; Harvard U libr, Cambridge, Mass, 1960-61; J Natl and U Librr, Jerusalem, 1921-61. Prin contribs: salvaging cultural property looted by Nazis, 1949-62. Mem: bd, Isr Librr Assn;librr terminology commn, Heb Lang Acad. Ed: Yad la Kore,Isr Librr Assn,1946-62;Bibliography of J Bibliographies, 1936, 2nd ed, 1965; contbr: to Heb, Eng jours; to Heb Ency. Recipient: Dr I Shapiro award, Heb U, 1965. Home: 25 Alfasi St, Jerusalem, Isr. Office: Heb U Libr, Jerusalem, Isr.

SHUR, Barnett Israel, US, attorney; b. Antileptos, Lith, July 15, 1905; s. Joseph and Ethel (Brickman); in US since 1908; BS, Harvard U, 1926; LLB, Boston U, 1930; m. Clarice Geller, July 10, 1938, c: George, Janet. Sr partner, Bernstein, Shur, Sawyer & Nelson; corp counsel, City of Portland, since 1946; corporator: Me Med Cen; Me Savings Bank. Dir, Natl JWB; pres; Portland Boys Club Assn; United Fund, Gtr Portland, 1962-63; Cumberland Co Bar Assn, 1964-65; Natl Inst Munic Law Offs, 1956-57; chmn, State of Me Land Damage Bd; mem, Portland Comm on Fgn Relations; club, Portland Rotary. Home: 24 Wadsworth St, Portland, Me. Office: 443 Congress St, Portland, Me.

SHUR, Yaakov, Isr, civil engr; b. Wolkowisk, Russ, 1907; s. Nahum and Tzyrl; in Isr since 1934; dipl civil engr, Polytechnion, Warsaw, 1934; m. Esther Tofilovski, Jan 2, 1934; c: Avihu, Sarah Dar. Dir, chief engr, Solel Boneh Overseas, since 1959, mgn dir, since 1964, engr, 1940-44, chief engr, 1944-59; cons engr, Architect Wittman, 1934-40. Sgt, Pol Army, 1932-34; Haganah, 1937-48. Mem: Assn Architects and Engrs. Home: 31 Hanassi Ave, Haifa, Isr. Office: Solel Boneh, Solel Boneh Sq, Haifa, Isr.

SHUREM, Abraham M, Can, organization exec; b. Rovno, Pol, June 16, 1901; s. Ovshea and Miriam (Appel); att Moscow U, 1919-20; in Can since 1921; m. Rachel Appel, Sep 14, 1924; c: Shulamith. Ret; natl exec dir, Can Assn for Lab Isr, 1942-68; natl vice-chmn, actions comm, Lab Zionist Movement of Can, since 1943, exec dir, 1939-42; br chmn, Farband LZOA, since 1953; mem, ed bd, Dos Vort, 1943; secy-treas, Amalgamated Clothing Workers Union of Amer, Montreal, 1936-39. Hon natl secy, Can Histadrut Campaign; vice-chmn, Montreal Histadrut Campaign; mem: dominion council, Can J Cong; exec comm, United Zionists of Can; bd dirs, Can Pal Trading Co; co-org, Hechalutz, Ukraine and Pol, 1918-19; secy, party br,

Poale Zion, Montreal, 1928-36. Home: 4845 Bourret Ave, Montreal, Can. Office: 5780 Decelles Ave, Montreal, Can.

SHURIN, Zvi H, US, rabbi; b. Lith, Nov 22, 1922; s. Moses and Ruth (Davidowitz); in US since 1940; ordained rabbi, Hebron Yeshiva, Jerusalem, 1940; att Columbia U, 1943-49; m. Dorothy Trivosh, Feb 15, 1949; c: Sorele, Yafalee, Ahuva, Shulamith, Kalman. Rabbi, Cong Sons of Isr, Jersey City, NJ, since 1948; chaplain, med cen, Jersey City, since 1953; educ cons, supt, Joseph Shapiro Tchr Training Inst of Torah Umesorah, Natl Soc of Heb Day Schs in US and Can; adv, Natl Yeshiva Tchrs Bd of License, Post Grad In-Service Sems of Torah Umesorah; Heb lectr: Torah Umesorah Inst for Higher J Studies, Spring Valley, NY, 1945; Young Isr Inst for Adults, NY, 1945-46; rabbi, Beekman Ave J Cen, Bx, NY, 1945-48. Prin contrib: instrumental in establishing kosher meal prog in Med Cen, Jersey City. Mem: admn, exec bds, Union of Orthodox Rabbis in US and Can; found, chmn, Savy-Seidman Memorial Fund; found, hon chmn, United Chevrah Kadishah; mem: exec bd, UJA, Jersey City; asso bd dirs, J Comty Cen; Heb Free Loan Assn; bd educ, Yeshiva of Hudson Co, Union City, NJ; HebronYeshiva Alumni. Recipient: plaque of honor, Council of Kashruth and Traditional Judaism, 1956; Torah Scroll of Honor, Cong Sons of Isr, 1957. Home: 23 Wayne St, Jersey City, NJ. Study: 294 Grove St, Jersey City, NJ.

SHURMAN, Michael M, US, educator; b. St Louis, Mo, Aug 4, 1921; s. Michael and Dorothy (Mendelsohn); BA, U Wis, 1943, MA, 1946, PhD, 1951. Prof, physics, U Wis, since 1961, asso dean, sci, 1962-65, on fac since 1955; staff mem, physicist, Los Alamos Sci Lab, 1952-55. Served, US Army. Mem: Amer Phys Soc; Amer Assn Physics Tchrs. Home: 1732 N Prospect Ave, Milwaukee, Wis. Office: Physics Dept, U of Wis, Milwaukee, Wis.

SHUSTER, Zachariah, US, organization exec; b. Lomza, Russ; in US since 1927. Dir, Eur off, AJComm, Paris, since 1949, PR since 1939, ed, Comm Reporter, 1945-47; fmr staff writer, The Day, NY; contbr to: Zukunft, Hadoar, The Nation, Commentary, Menorah Jour, Contemporary J Record. Office: 30 rue La Boetie, Paris, Fr.

SHUTZBERG, Jaacow, Isr, farmer; b. Drohbycz, Pol, Jan 29, 1906; s. Asher and Rachel (Finkelstein); in Isr since 1926; att Technicum, Neustadt, Ger, 1923-25; m. Adina Fenster, 1929; c: Tamar, Ilana, Schmuel.Mem, Kibbutz Merhavia, since 1926; fmr mem: cen comm, Agric Cen, Labor Movement; council, Natl Ins; council for water resources and irrigation; budget comm, JA; cen exec, Tnuva; govt council of the coop of Isr. Haganah, 1927-48. Repr, kibbutz movement, exec of agric cen, Histadrut; mem: council, Mapam; Supr Court, Histadrut; fmr: delg to WZCs; mem exec comm, Hakibbutz Haartzi. Contbr to jours. Home: Kibbutz Merhavia, Isr.

SHUVAL, Hillel I, Isr, engineer; b. Wash, DC, July 16, 1926; s. Louis and Rose (Suskind) Schwefel; in Isr since 1948; BS, U of Mo, 1948; MPH, U Mich, 1951; m. Judith Tannenbaum, 1952; c: Yael, Rama, Tamar. Asso prof, environmental health, Heb U-Hadassah Med Sch, since 1965; sanitary engr adv, Min of Health, since 1965, chief sanitary engr, 1958-65; visiting asso prof: Technion, Haifa, since 1965; sch public health, U Mich, 1961-62, 1967. US Army, 1944-46; IDF, 1948-49. Vice-pres, Intl Assn for Water Pollution Research; mem, WHO: Expert Adv Panel on Environmental Health; Expert Comm on Water Pollution Control in Developing Countries; f, Amer Public Health Assn; mem: Amer Soc CEs; Isr Assn Engrs and Architects; fmr: mem exec comm, Intercollegiate ZF of Amer. Contbr to profsl jours. Hobby: archaeol. Home: 38 Bethlehem Rd, Jerusalem, Isr. Office: Heb U Med Sch, Jerusalem, Isr.

SHUVALSKY, Morris Moshe, US, rabbi; b. Baltimore, Md, June 28, 1925; s. Hillel and Sarah (Kucher); att Johns Hopkins U, 1944-47; ordained rabbi, Ner Isr Rabb Coll, 1949; MEd, Duquesne U, 1959; m. Esther Lafferman, Apr 22, 1955; c: Tzipora, Tsivia, Jacob. Rabbi: Beth Jacob Amunath Isr Cong, since 1963; United Orthodox Syns, Vaad Hakashrus, Woodbine, NJ, 1948-50; Ahavath Sholom Cong, Baltimore, 1950-56; Cong Ohave Isr, Brownsville Pa, 1957-60; Ahavath Isr Cong,Trenton, NJ, 1962-63; Hillel dir, U of W Va, 1958-59; chaplain, Apple Creek State Hosp, O, 1961-62. Vice-pres, Atlantic City Mizrachi, since 1963; hon vice-pres: JNF, Atlantic City; ZOA; exec secy, chmn, Rabb Comm, Mikveh Soc; mem: Beth Din J Orthodox Council; RabCA; Ner

Isr Rabb Coll Alumni; Duquesne U Alumni. Contbr to Heb, Yiddish and Eng jours. Home: 117 Oriental Ave, Atlantic City, NJ. Study: Congress and Pacific Aves, Atlantic City,NJ.

SHVA, Shlomo Yosef, Isr, journalist, author; b. Galicia, 1929; s. Mordechai and Haya (Rosenvaser) Schwartz; in Isr since 1936; m. Zaharira Harifai; c: Aya-Chaya. Journalist: Al Hamishmar; Lamerhav, all Heb dailies. IDF, 1948-50. Author: Anashim Hadashim beHarim HaGvohim, 1953; Makom Sheein Lo Shem, 1957; haTzayad, 1967; Shevet haNoazim, 1969; Yamim shel Zahav, play; co-author, Nodedei Laila, 1965; contbr to press. Home: 14 Zecharya St, Tel Aviv, Isr.

SHVO (Shvom), Yitzhak, Isr, advocate; b. Warsaw, Pol, Dec 18, 1899; s. Abraham and Khaya (Feinstein); in Isr since 1925; dipl, advocate, Warsaw U; att Sorbonne U, Paris; m. Yehudit, 1930; c: Youval, Ilana. Pvt practice since 1937; legal adv, Histadrut Housing Co, since 1937; dir gen, Min of Interior, 1957-60. Mem: ZC Court; Histadrut High Court; Histadrut Council; Lab Party Council; Govt Coop Council; Govt Munic Council; Natl Council, Habimah Theatre; pres, Isr Football Assn High Court; vice-pres, Discipline Appeal Comty, Isr Bar Assn. Home: 37 Hen Blvd, Tel Aviv, Isr. Office: 6 Warburg St, Tel Aviv, Isr.

SHWADRAN, Benjamin, US, educator, editor; b. Jerusalem, Sep 12, 1907; s. Mendel and Anna Susman (Deleon); in US since 1928; att Heb U, Jerusalem, 1926-28; BA, Clark U, 1938, MA, 1939, PhD, 1946; m. Dorothy Derman, Mar 20, 1935; c: Aiton, Avivah. Ed: ME Affairs, since 1950; Council for ME Affairs Press, since 1957; secy, Council for ME Affairs, since 1950; Pal Affairs, 1947-50; ME ed, Hadoar, 1942-60; prof, ME studies, Yeshiva U, since 1960; dir, research dept, AZC, 1943-50; lectr, ME studies, New Sch for Social Research, 1945-49; prof, ME studies and dir, ME Inst, Dropsie Coll, 1957-59; guest lectr, Us:Harvard; Columbia; Colo; Chgo; NYU; Clark; Pittsburgh; Notre Dame; Butler; Lehign; Rutgers; lectr, Fgn Policy Assn; research prof, Tel Aviv U, 1968-69; has appeared on TV, radio. Mem: Political Sci Assn; f delg, Jersey City, NJ, Amer J Conf, 1943-48. Author: The Middle East, Oil and the Great Powers, 1955, 1959; Jordan a State of Tension, 1960; The Power Struggle in Iraq, 1960; General Index Middle Eastern Affairs, 1968; collaborating author, Palestine, A Study of Jewish, Arab and British Policies, 1947; contbr to scholarly jours. Home: 2061 Belmont Ave, Elmont, NY. Office: 432 Fourth Ave, New York, NY.

SHWARTZ, Pinhas, Isr, organization exec; b. Pol, 1909; in Isr since 1927; att: Amer U, Beirut; HS of Law and Econ, Tel Aviv; m. Miriam; c: Aldea, Gedalyahu, Shoshana. Gen secy: Union Artisans and Small Mfrs, since 1949, Tel Aviv br, since 1937; initiator, co-found: Bank Lemelacha Ltd, 1954; Lab Rehabilitation Co, Ltd, 1961; Co for Devl of Lab Ltd, 1963; several export cos. Mem: Yerid Hamizrach Corp; Tel Aviv Master Plan Adv Council. Home: 18 Zeitlin St, Tel Aviv, Isr.

SHWARZ, Zvi, Isr, attorney; b. Bessarabia, Jan 2, 1896; att: LSE J Coll, London; Heb U, Jerusalem; m; c: Ruth Dayan, Reumah Weizmann. Mem, Isr Legal Council, since 1948; tchr, Merhavia, Isr, 1915-18; lectr, Workers Sem, Jerusalem; secy, KH, London, 1921-28, Jerusalem, 1928-34; chmn, Rehavia Council, Jerusalem, 1940-48. Mem: exec, Isr Bar Assn; Jerusalem Bar Assn, fmr vice-chmn; bd govs, exec, Heb U; Histadrut Supr Court; JA Disciplinary Court; exec: Isr UNO Assn; Amer-Isr Soc; bd dirs, Beth Hanoar Haivri, Jerusalem; vice-chmn, Jerusalem Haganah Assn; club, Rotary, Jerusalem. Contbr: essays to lab jours. Homes: 38 Hapalmach St, Jerusalem; 114 Eshel St, Herzliya, both Isr. Offices: 33 Jaffa Rd, Jerusalem; 24 Montefiore St, Tel Aviv, both Isr.

SHWAYDER, King David, US, business exec; b. Denver, Colo, Aug 12, 1910; s. Jessie and Nellie (Weitz); att: U Colo; U of Pa; m. Rose Friedland, Dec 30, 1934; c: Keith, Jessie Harsham. Pres, Samsonite Luggage Co, fmr, Shwayder Bros Inc, since 1961, exec vice pres, Denver off, 1960-61, with firm since 1930; bd dirs: Denver US Natl Bank; Public Service Co of Colo. Regional vice-pres, Luggage and Leather Goods Mfrs Assn; regional co-chmn, pres, mem exec comm, Colo Assn Commerce and Ind; bd dirs: Mile High United Fund; Regis Coll; Allied JCC; mem: Denver exec bd, natl council, Boy Scouts of Amer; C of C, city, natl levels; Gov's Supr Court Nominating Commn; Gov's Comm on Higher Educ; Gov's Econ Devl Council; adv panel, Denver Research Inst, U Denver; pres council, Brandeis U; B'nai B'rith ADL; bd trustees, J Comty Cens of Denver; Temple Emanuel; Denver, Art Mus; Den Sym Soc; Phi Sigma Delta; Colo Photographic Arts Cen; Photographic Soc of Amer; clubs: Rotary, Denver; Green Gables Country, bd dirs: Town; Brown Palace. Spec interests: golf, photography. Home: 9 Cherry Hills Dr, Engelwood, Colo; summer, 6010 W Jewell Ave, Denver, Colo. Office: 1050 S Broadway, Denver, Colo.

SICHERMAN, Esther, US, attorney; b. Buffalo, NY, Oct 29, 1900; d. Harry and Lena (Block) Lieberman; LLB, U Buffalo Law Sch, 1922; m. Jacob Sicherman, Sep 14, 1923; c: Barbara. Tax cons, Niagara Mohawk Power Corp, since 1965; tax atty: W div, Niagara Mohawk Power Corp, 1926-65; Niagara Lockport & Ontario Power Co, predecessor co, 1923-26. Mem, tax comm: Buffalo C of C; Bar Assn of Erie Co; mem: NY State Assessors Assn; Natl Tax Assn; Intl Assn of Assessing Officers; club, Counselers. Home: 135 Jewitt Pkwy, Buffalo, NY. Office: 535 Washington St, Buffalo, NY.

SICRON, Moshe S, Isr, statistician, educator; b. Jerusalem, Dec 21, 1928; s. Isaac and Hadassa (Shaltiel); BA, Heb U, Jerusalem, 1952, MA, 1956; PhD, U of Pa, Phila, 1968; m. Sara Kutner, June 30, 1961; c: Noam, Ayala. Dep dir, Cen Bur of Stat, since 1962; sr lectr, Tel Aviv U, since 1965. Mem: Intl Union, Population Study; Amer Stat Assn; Population Assn of Amer. Author: Immigration to Israel, 1948-53, pub, 1967; contbr to profsl publs. Home: 26 Tchernichovsky St, Jerusalem, Isr. Office: Cen Bur of Stat, Jerusalem, Isr.

SIDEMAN, Samuel, Isr, engineer, educator; Haifa, Feb 6, 1929; s. Gad and Ester (Richter); MChemE, Bklyn Poly Inst, NY, 1955; DSc, ChemE, Technion, Haifa, 1960; m. Naomi Rubin, Dec 16, 1956; c: Anat, Gil. Prof, ChemE, Technion, Haifa, since 1966, dean, students, since 1969, lectr, sr lectr, 1957-64; plant mngr, Garan Chemicals, LA, Cal, 1955-57; prof, Okla State U, 1964-65. Capt, IDF, 1947-49. Co-found, Isr Inst ChemEs, 1963, pres, 1965-66; fmr chmn, Assn Technion Profs, Lectrs; mem: Amer Inst ChemEs; Inst Engr Educ; Sigma Xi; Author: Direct Contact Heat Transfer in Advances in Chemical Engineering, 1966; contbr: to tech, sci, intl jours; books; reports to Isr Natl Council for research and devl. Recipient: citation, Amer Inst ChemEs, 1965; Arnan award, Isr Assn Engrs and Architects, 1968. Spec interest: Civic Comm for Advancement of Drug Educ. Home: 14 Palmach St, Haifa, Isr. Office: Technion, Haifa, Isr.

SIDEMAN, Sydney, US, surgeon, educator; b. Chgo, Ill, May 1, 1904; s. Moses and Ida (Behr); BS, U of Ill, 1925, MD, 1927; m. Fay Adelman, July 5, 1931; c: Susan, Michael. Orthopedic surg since 1929; att orthopedic surg, Michael Reese Hosp, since 1930, fmr pres med staff, chmn, dept orthopedic surg; chmn, dept orthopedics, Weiss Memorial Hosp, since 1957, fmr pres med staff; att orthopedic surg, Cook Co Hosp, since 1947, on staff since 1932; prof, orthopedic surg, Cook Co Sch of Med, since 1947; asso prof, orthopedic surg, Northwestern U Med Sch, since 1953, on fac since 1930; cons, US Naval Hosp, San Diego, since 1967; Scripps Memorial Hosp, since 1967; U Hosp, San Diego, since 1967; Children's Hosp, San Diego, since 1968; jr att surg, St Luke's Hosp, 1929-30. Lt, US Army Res; capt, USNR, ret since 1964. F: Amer Coll Surgs; Intl Coll Surgs; cert, Amer Bd Orthopedic Surgs; mem: AMA; Amer Acad Orthopedic Surgs; Clinical Orthopedic Soc; Chgo Orthopedic Soc, fmr pres; W Orthopedic Assn; Ill Med Assn; Chgo Med Soc; Assn Mil Surgs; Insts Med, Chgo, San Diego; Amer Fracture Assn; Phi Delta Epsilon; Sigma Alpha Mu. Contbr to med jours. Home: 1219 Coast Blvd, La Jolla, Cal.

SIDORSKY, David, US, educator; b. Calgary, Can, July 7, 1927; s. Myer and Ella (Blumenthal); in US since 1944; BA, NYU, 1948, MA, 1953; BHL, JTSA, 1950; PhD, Columbia U, 1962; m. Rhoda Goldstein, Feb 4, 1952; c: Robert, Gina, Emily. Asso prof, phil, Columbia U, since 1966, on fac since 1959. Home: 448 Riverside Dr, New York, NY. Office: Columbia U, New York, NY.

SIEFF, Israel Moses, Baron of Brimpton, Eng, business exec; b. Manchester, Eng, May 4, 1899; s. Ephraim and Sarah; BS, BCom, U Manchester; m. Rebecca Doro, 1910 (decd); c: Michael, Marcus, Daniel (decd) Judith Shechterman. Pres, Marks and Spencer Ltd, with firm since 1915; farmer. Vicepres, WJC, chmn, Eur exec; hon pres, ZF of Gt Brit and Ir; pres, Anglo-Isr C of C, fmr chmn; hon pres, Jt Pal Appeal; pres: Political and Econ Planning, fmr chmn; Inst J Affairs; chmn, bd govs, Carmel Coll; established Daniel Sieff Research Inst, Rehovot, Isr, 1934; hon f and mem bd govs, Weizmann

Inst of Sci, Rehovot; f: Royal Anthropological Inst; Royal Geog Soc; Brit Inst Mgmt; mem: Court of Patrons, Royal Coll Surgs, Eng; exec, JA; fmr: vice-pres, Multiple Shops Fed; secy, Zionist Commn. Office: Michael House, Baker St, London W1, Eng.

SIEGAN, Harold Aaron, US, attorney; b. Chgo, Ill, Oct 3, 1914; s. Joseph and Bertha (Paster); LLB, De Paul U, 1938; m. Bernice Rubinoff, June 19, 1938; c: Elayne Feder, Kenneth, Jerold. Master in chancery, Circuit Court, since 1955; partner, Siegan & Rubinoff, since 1940. Pres: Council Traditional Syns, Gtr Chgo, 1964-66; Cong KINS, W Rogers Park, 1958-60; co-chmn, Syn Div, CJA, Chgo, 1960-61; bd govs, Isr Bonds; bd dirs, Bernard Horwich Cen of J Comty Cens, Chgo. Home: 2825 W Jarvis, Chicago, Ill. Office: 33 N Dearborn, Chicago, Ill.

SIEGEL, Arthur, US, composer, pianist; b. Lakewood, NJ, Dec 31, 1923; s. Nathan and Fanny (Kahn); att: Amer Acad of Dramatic Arts; Juilliard Sch of Music. Composer: show and popular music; for Broadway shows: New Faces of 1952, 1956, 1962, 1968; songs include: Monotonous: Love is a Simple Thing; Penny Candy; He Takes Me Off His Income Tax; piano arranger for Eddie Cantor's one man show at Carnegie Hall and on tour, 1950; wrote children's record albums for RCA, Columbia; recorded, Peanuts album, with Kaye Ballard for Columbia Records; wrote spec material songs for: Hermione Gingold; Imogene Coca; Gypsy Rose Lee; Mitzi Green; Kaye Ballard; Eddie Cantor; Eartha Kitt. Hobbies: collecting old books, records, theater progs, sheet music. Home and office: 29 W 65 St, New York, NY.

SIEGEL, Barry D, US, organization exec; b. Newark, NJ, Feb 17, 1931; s. Herman and Sue (Nutes); BA, Bowling Green State U, 1952; att Rutgers U, 1952-53; m. Nancy Dreskin, Aug 4, 1955; c: Abby, John. Exec secy, Zeta Beta Tau natl frat, since 1961; asst exec dir, Tobacco Merchants Assn of US, 1955-60. US Signal Corps, 1953-55. Mem: Zeta Beta Tau; Pi Sigma Alpha; Rho Sigma Mu; bd dirs, Brotherhood, Temple B'nai Jeshurun, Short Hills, NJ; club, Bowling Green Alumni, Metrop, NY, pres since 1959. Home: 5 Darby Terr,Livingstone, NJ. Office: Statler Hilton House, New York, NY.

SIEGEL, Barry N, US, educator; b. Chgo, Ill, June 4, 1929; s. Mandel and Marry (Schulman); AB, U Cal, 1951, PhD, 1957; m. Jetta Rackow, Jan 20, 1952; c: Ronald, Daniel, Naomi. Asso dean, Lib Arts, prof, econ, U Ore since 1961; asst prof, econ, U Utah, 1957-61; Smith-Mundt lectr, Mex 1960; Fulbright lectr, Yugo, 1967-68. US Army, 1946-47. Mem: Amer Econ Assn; Amer Finance Assn; Royal Econ Soc. Author: Inflation and Economic Development: The Mexican Experience, in Span, 1960; Aggregate Economics and Public Policy, 1960, 3rd ed, 1970. Home: 325 Sunset Dr, Eugene, Ore. Office: U Oregon, Eugene, Ore.

SIEGEL, Benjamin V, US, pathologist, educator; b. NYC, Dec 14, 1913; s. Nathan and Anna (Krieger); BS, U Ga, 1934; MA, Columbia U, 1937; PhD, Stanford U, Cal, 1950; m. Jane Morton, June 30, 1961; c: Marilyn, Benjamin, Andrew. Prof, path, U Ore Med Sch, since 1961; instr, research f, Stanford U, 1950-53; research asso, lectr, U Cal, Berkeley and SF, 1954-61. USAAC,WW II. F: Amer Acad Microbiol; AAAS; NY Acad Sci; Intl Acad Path; mem: Phi Beta Kappa; Phi Kappa Phi; Sigma Xi; Phi Sigma. Contbr to sci jours. Recipient: Pres Unit Citation. Hobbies: tennis, hiking; photography. Home: 3900 SW Pendleton St, Portland, Ore. Office: U of Ore Med Sch, Portland, Ore.

SIEGEL, David, US, attorney; b. Bklyn, NY, Jan 18, 1909; s. Eser and Rebecca (Swirsky); att NYU, 1925-27; LLB, Bklyn Law Sch, 1930; m. Sophie Zablinsky, Feb 21, 1942 (decd); c: Arlene, Inez. Attaché, Supr Court, Kings Co, Bklyn, NY, since 1949, presently in incompetents div; pvt law practice, 1932-49; law and personal asst, Judge J Vincent Keogh, 1952-62. USAAF, 1942-46, capt, Res, until 1953. Charter mem, Mt Alvernia Interfaith Movement; mem, trustee, Park Slope J Cen, fmr pres; mem: Bklyn ORT Soc; Bikur Cholim Visiting Sick Soc; Bklyn, Inc; Assn J Court Attachés Inc; Amer Legion; Supr and Surrogate's Court Attachés Assn; St Vincent's Hosp Assn; B'nai B'rith. Recipient: Amer Campaign Medal; Asiatic Pacific Campaign Medal; Victory Medal. Hobbies: violin, music, writing. Home: 1948 76 St, Brooklyn, NY. Office: Supr Court Bldg, Brooklyn, NY.

SIEGEL, Edward, US, physician; b. NYC, Sep 22, 1912; s. Jack and Ida (LeVine); BA, Cornell U, 1933; MA, U of Pa,

SIEGEL, 1934; MD, U Md, 1938; m. Gretchen Broody, Sep 25, 1945; c: Jane, Andrea. Pvt practice since 1941; chief of staff, CV/PH Med Cen, since 1948; med examiner, FAA; cons to: NY State Dept Health; VA; USAF; NY State Compensation Bd; ophthal surg, NY Ear and Eye Infirmary, 1945-48. Lt col, US Army, 1941-45; col, Res MC. Delg, AMA; vice-pres, Plattsburgh Bd Educ; mem council, NY State Med Soc; f, Intl Coll Surgs; mem: Pan Amer Assn Ophthal; WHO; Amer Soc Ophthal; Aerospace Med Soc; Assn for Research in Ophthal; AMA; NY State Med Soc; Clinton Co Med Soc, fmr pres; Elks; VFW; Amer Legion; fmr: pres: Temple Beth Isr; YMCA; B'nai B'rith; Youth Commn; mem: bd dirs, C of C; Cancer Soc; Comty Services; YMCA; club, Rotary. Co-author: Ency of Ophthalmology, 1950. Recipient: Pres Citation for Comty Services; Citizen of Year, 1964. Home: 41 Broad St, Plattsburg, NY. Office: 61 Brinkerhoff St, Plattsburg, NY.

SIEGEL, Eli, US, author; b. Dvinsk, Latvia, Aug 16, 1902; s. Mendel and Sarah (Einhorn); in US since 1905; m. Martha Baird, 1944. Found, and tchr, Aesthetic Realism, since 1940; writer: Johns Hopkins Horizons, 1922; Modern Quarterly, 1923; Baltimore American, 1925; book reviewer: Lit Review of NY Evening Post, 1926; Scribner's, 1931-35. Author: The Aesthetic Method in Self-Conflict, 1946; Psychiatry, Economics, Aesthetics, 1946; The Meaning of the Hebrew Kaddish, 1954; Is Beauty the Making One of Opposites?, 1955; Hot Afternoons Have Been in Montana: Poems, 1957; Art as Life, 1957; Shakespeare's Hamlet: Revisited, 1963; James and the Children: A Consideration of Henry James's The Turn of the Screw, 1968; Hail, American Development, 1968; The Williams-Siegel Documentary, 1970; contbr poems, articles and reviews in periodicals. Recipient: Poetry prize, Nation mag, 1925. Home and office: 67 Jane St, New York, NY.

SIEGEL, Erich, US, pediatrician; b. Brieg, Ger, Dec 10, 1885; s. Herman and Paula (Juliusberger); in US since 1940; att U Berlin, 1904-08; grad, U Heidelberg, 1909; MD, U Leipzig, 1911; m. Susi Frankfurter Apr 15, 1920; c: Ruth Sachs, Ellen, Anne Moradpour. Pvt practice; mem, outpatient div, ped dept, Mt Sinai Hosp, NY; ped, Berlin, Ger, 1913-38; head, Ped Wfr Clinic, Berlin J Comty, 1920-38. Ger Army, WW I. Mem: AMA; NY State Med Soc; NY Co Med Soc; Amer Assn for Mental Deficiency; NY Acad of Scis; Rudolf Virchow Med Soc, NY, bd mem, 1951-61; Park Ave Syn, NYC. Home and office: 151 W 86 St, New York, NY.

SIEGEL, Henry, US, physician; b. NYC, Oct 16, 1910; s. William and Pauline (Berkowitz); BS, cum laude, CCNY, 1933; MD, NYU, 1937; m. Julia Vinograd, Sep, 1934 (decd); c: Edward, Marian; m. 2nd, Lillian Niefeld, Aug, 1968. Exec dep chief med examiner, NYC, since 1961; asso prof, forensic med, NYU, since 1961; hon research prof, Rutgers U, since 1958; chief path, Kings Co Hosp, 1950-55; asso prof, path, State U, Coll of Med, 1950-55; asso prof, Albert Einstein Coll of Med, 1955-58; att path, Bx Munic Hosp Cen, 1955-58. US Army MC, 1944-46. Chmn, legal med, NY State Med Soc; secy, NY Path Soc, 1956-58; mem: AMA; Coll Amer Path; Amer Acad Forensic Sci; Amer Assn Path and Bact; Amer Soc Clinical Path; NY Acad Med; Phi Beta Kappa. Contbr to sci jours. Home: 343 E 30 St, New York, NY. Office: 520 First Ave, New York, NY.

SIEGEL, Herbert J, US, business exec; b. Phila, Pa, May 7, 1928; s. Jacob and Fritzi (Stern); BA, Lehigh U, 1950; m. Anna Levy, June 29, 1950; c: John, William. Bd chmn, pres, Chris-Craft Inds, Inc, since 1968, dir, since 1967; dir, Piper Aircraft Corp, since 1971; vice-pres, dir: Bev-Rich Producs, 1955-56; Westley Inds, 1955-58; Phila Ice Hockey Club, 1955-60; bd chmn: Fort Pitt Inds, 1956-58; Seeburg Corp, 1958-60; Centlivre Brewing Corp, 1959-61; Gen Artists Corp, 1960-63, pres, 1960-65; Baldwin-Montrose Chem Co, Inc, 1960-68, merged into Chris-Craft; dir: Paramount Pictures Corp, 1965-66; Hemisphere Hotel Corp, 1969-70. Club: Friars. Home: Tower East, 190 E 72 St, New York, NY. Office: 600 Madison Ave, New York, NY.

SIEGEL, Irving, US, physician, educator; b. Lomza, Pol, May 1, 1907; s. Samuel and Rebecca (Rockowitz); in US since 1911; BA, Crane Jr Coll, 1926; BS, U of Ill Coll of Med, 1928, MD, 1930; m. Joyce Rozner, Aug 13, 1942; c: Pamela, Michael, Sheila. Asso prof, obstet, Chgo Med Sch, since 1947; instr, Mt Sinai Hosp, Chgo, Ill, since 1947, with hosp since 1933; att obstet Cook Co Hosp, since 1959; dir, med educ, Edgewater Hosp, Chgo; pvt practice obstet and gyn, Chgo, 1933-41. Lt, US Army MC, 1941; lt col, chief of service,

obstet and gyn, Fort Benning, Ga, 1946-47, res off since 1941. Dipl, Amer Bd Obstet and Gyn, 1943; f: Amer Coll Surgs; Intl Coll Surgs; mem: AMA; Amer Fed Clinical Research; Chgo Med Soc; Ill State Med Soc; Chgo Gyn Soc; Ill Soc for Clinical Research; Amer Med Writers Assn; AAUP; Phi Lambda Kappa, pres, Chgo Alumni chap, 1950-51, 1968-70; Alpha Omega Alpha. Contbr to med jours. Home: 5054 N St Louis Ave, Chicago, Ill. Office: Mt Sinai Hosp, 2750 W 15, St, Chicago, Ill.

SIEGEL, Keeve Milton, US, educator, business exec; b. NYC, Jan 9, 1923; s. David and Rose (Jelin); BS, Rensselaer Poly Inst, 1948, MS,1950; m. Ruth Boerker, June 22, 1951; c: Leigh, David. Chmn bd, KMS' Ind Inc, since 1967; dir, Mech Tech, Data Sci Ventures; prof, dept engr, U Mich, 1957-67, head radiation lab, 1957-61, mem fac since 1948; chmn bd, pres, Conductron Corp, 1960-67; mem, adv group radio experts in space, NASA, 1960-64; visiting prof, Oakland U, 1967-68; sci adv bd, USAF, 1958-66; cons, US Army, 1958-61. US Army, 1942-45. F: Inst Elec and Electronics Engrs; AAAS; mem: Amer Math Soc; Amer Phys Soc; Phi Sigma Delta; asso mem, Amer Inst Aeronautics and Astronautics; mem at large, natl comm, URSI, fmr vice-chmn, Intl Commn VI; fmr mem bd, Beth Isr Comty Cen. Co-author: Methods of Radar Cross-Sect Analysis; asso ed, Transactions Profsl Group of Antennas and Propagation, Inst of Radio Engrs, 1960-65; mem, ed bd: Jour of Research Bur of Standards; Jour of Math Physics; contbr to profsl jours. Recipient: award for meritorious civilian service, Dept Air Force, 1966. Home: 276 Indian River Pl, Ann Arbor, Mich. Office: 220 E Huron St, Ann Arbor, Mich.

SIEGEL, Lawrence J, US, certified public acctnt; b. St Louis, Mo, Sep 18, 1937; s. Ben and Ann (Gornstein); BS, BA, Wash U, St Louis, 1959; m. Judith Schechter, July 19, 1959; c: Nancee, Stephen. Partner, Gordon, Siegel & Co, CPAs, since 1968; staff acctnt, Lopata, Lopata & Dubinsky, CPAs, 1961-64; pvt practice, 1964-68. Lt, US Army, 1959-61. Info secy, St Louis B'nai B'rith Council; delg, Mo State Assn, B'nai B'rith; mem: J Fed, St Louis; Amer Inst CPAs; Mo Soc CPAs; Pi Lambda Phi; fmr pres, Archway Lodge, B'nai B'rith. Home: 12188 Lake Meade Dr, St Louis, Mo. Office: 225 S Meramec Ave, St Louis, Mo.

SIEGEL, Martin, US, rabbi; b. Bklyn, NY, May 27, 1933; s. Samuel and Helen (Berger); BS, Cornell U, 1955; MHL, BHL, HUC, 1960; m. Judith Tobias, Nov 19, 1963; c: Sally. Rabbi, Temple Sinai of LI, since 1967; prof, J Studies, Wheeling Coll, since 1966. Lt, USN. Pres, Five Towns Coalition; secy, Rel Council of the Five Towns; co-dir, Natl Comm on J-Chr Insts. Home: 946 Allen Lane, Woodmere, NY. Study: 131 Washington Ave, Lawrence, NY.

SIEGEL, Milton P, US, international exec; b. Des Moines, Ia, July 23, 1911; s. Barney and Silvey (Levenson); att Drake U, Des Moines; m. Rosalie Rosenberg, May 25, 1934; c: Betsy. Asst dir-gen, WHO, since 1947; dir finance and stat, Ia Emergency Relief Admn, 1933-35; regional off positions, chief fiscal off, Farm Security Admn, Dept of Agric, 1935-44; dir, office for Far E, UNRRA, 1944-45; asst dir produc and marketing, Dept of Agric, 1945-47; visiting prof, U Mich, 1967. Mem: Amer Public Health Asso; perm commn on contribs, League of Red Cross Soc. Recipient: Sam Beber award, 1960. Hobbies: philately, photography, music. Home: 1 rue Viollier, Geneva, Switz. Office: WHO, Geneva, Switz.

SIEGEL, Morris, US, epidemiologist, educator; b. NYC, Mar 2, 1904; s. Henry and Martha (Heller); BA, CCNY, 1924; MD, NYU, 1928; MPH, Johns Hopkins Sch of Public Health, 1939; m. Miriam Amdur, Sep 16, 1933; c: Robert, Nancy. Prof, environmental med, comty health, SUNY Downstate Med Cen, since 1959, on staff since 1952; visiting lectr, epidemiology, Harvard Sch of Public Health; phys, research labs, NYC Health Dept, 1935-40; asso, Research Inst, NYC, 1941-47. Dipl, Amer Bd Preventive Med and Public Health; mem: NY Acad Med; Harvey Soc; Amer Public Health Assn; Amer Coll Preventive Med; Amer Epidemiological Soc; Med Soc Co, NY; Sigma Xi; Phi Beta Kappa; Alpha Omega Alpha. Contbr to med jours. Home: 345 E 69 St, New York, NY. Office: 450 Clarkson Ave, Brooklyn, NY.

SIEGEL, Morton, US, educator; b. NYC, Dec 5, 1924; s. Samuel and Esther (Sackin); deg, Tchrs Inst, Yeshiva U, 1943; BA, summa cum laude, Yeshiva Coll, 1945; MA, Columbia U, 1946, PhD, 1952; m. Pearl Fox, June 28, 1949; c: Deborah, Daniel, Dinah. Dir: educ, United Syn of Amer, Comm on

J Educ, both since 1964, educ placement service, 1949-53, dept youth activities, 1952-64; Camp Ramah, 1954; United Syn Youth for Isr Pilgrimage, 1958-62; educ, Laurelton J Cen, 1946-53. Mem: Natl Council J Educ; Educ Assembly. Home: 133-08 228 St, Laurelton, NY. Office: 218 E 70 St, New York, NY.

SIEGEL, Norman, US, rabbi; b. Safed, May 5, 1914; s. Herman and Esther (Barsel); in US since 1920; BA, Yeshiva Coll, 1934; ordained rabbi, Rabbi Isaac Elchanan Theol Sem, 1938; MHL, JTSA, 1960; grad, US Army Command and Gen Staff Coll, 1960; m. Vivienne Horowitz, June 16, 1946; c: Aaron, Judith. Rabbi, J Cen of Kings Hwy, since 1957. Chaplain, US Army, 1941-46; col ,US Army Res, since 1967; instr: US Army Chaplain Sch; Command and Gen Staff Coll. Mem: RA; Natl Beth Din; J Service Chaplains Assn; NY Bd Rabbis. Recipient: Bronze Star, 1945. Home: 1839 Ocean Pkwy, Brooklyn, NY. Study: 1202 Ave P, Brooklyn, NY.

SIEGEL, Reuven, US, rabbi; b. Baltimore, Md, May 18, 1922; s. Herman and Esther (Barsel); BA, Yeshiva U, 1942; ordained rabbi, MHL, JTSA, 1945; m. Pearl Solomon, July 30, 1961; c: Arnon, Judith. Rabbi: E 55 St Conservative Syn, since 1967; Cong Tifereth Isr, Duluth, Minn, 1945-49; asso rabbi, Temple B'nai Abraham, Newark, NJ, 1949-51; rabbi: Temple Beth Sholom, Providence, RI, 1953-55; Temple Adath Isr, Bx, 1955-67. Chaplain, USN, USMC, Korea, 1951-53; cdr, USNR. Pres, Gtr NY chap, Mil Chaplains Assn, since 1967; bd mem: Bx Planned Parenthood Org; Bx chap, NCCJ; J Music Forum; mem, J Chaplains Assn. Recipient: Pres Unit Citation; 2 battle stars. Home: 751 Walton Ave, Bronx, NY. Study: 308 E 55 St, New York, NY.

SIEGEL, Saul R, US, business exec; b. NYC, Nov 24, 1909; s. Morris and Jennie (Baliof); LLB, St Johns U, 1934; m. Irma Bernstein, June 27, 1936; c: Ronald, Nancy. Pres: Elliot, Green & Co Inc, since 1951; Elgrebead Corp; Yarn Merchants Assn; vice-pres, Albeck Realty Corp. Pres, US Stone and Bead Importers Assn, since 1952; bd dirs, United HIAS Service; mem: Sigma Tau; clubs: Natl Dem; Lone Star Boat. Home: 2670 Rockaway Ave, Oceanside, NY. Office: 37 W 37 St, New York, NY.

SIEGEL, Seymour, US, rabbi, educator; b. Chgo, Ill, Sep 12, 1927; s. David and Jeanette (Morris); BA, U Chgo, 1951; ordained rabbi, MHL, DHL, JTSA, 1955. Prof, JTSA, since 1955; asst dean, HH Lehman Inst of Ethics, since 1960. Secy, RA; bd govs, J Mus; bd eds, J Publ Soc; mem: B'nai B'rith; Amer Acad J Res. Author: Judaism: A Guide, 1969; co-author, Jewish Dietary Laws, 1962; contbr to jours. Home: 380 Riverside Dr, New York, NY. Office: 3080 Broadway, New York, NY.

SIEGEL, Seymour N, US, radio exec; b. NYC, July 29, 1908; s. Isaac and Anne (Natelson); BS, U of Pa, 1929; MA, Columbia U, 1932; m. Nancy Davids, 1943 (div); c: Constance, Cynthia; m. 2nd, Frances Ladd Hanen, 1959; step-c: Sarah, Deborah, John. Dir, radio communications for NYC, since 1947; dir, WUHF, TV channel 31; coord, Civil Defense, since 1950; chief stat, Morris and Smity, 1929-34; prog dir, radio sta, WNYC, 1934-37. Cdr, USN, 1941-45; capt, Supply Corps, USNR. Pres, Natl Assn Educ Broadcasters, 1950-52; mem: Jt Comm on Educ TV, 1951-53; Radio Advisory Comm to Pres of US, 1951; clubs: Natl Rep; U Pa; Overseas Press. Contbr to profsl jours. Recepient: Off, Order of Orange-Nassau, Netherlands, 1952; Legion of Honor, 1953. Home: 417 E 57 St, New York, NY. Office: 2500 Munic Bldg, New York, NY.

SIEGEL, Shirley Adelson, US, attorney; b. NYC, July 3, 1918; d. Henry and Rose (Zagor) Adelson; BA, hons, Barnard Coll, 1937; f, LSE, 1937-38; LLB, Yale Law Sch, 1941; m. Elwood Siegel, Sep 22, 1946; c: Eric, Ann. Gen counsel, Housing and Devl Admn, NYC, since 1966; asso, law firms: Proskauer, Rose, Goetz and Mendelsohn, 1941-45, 1951-52; Pacht, Tannenbaum, 1948-50; Rosenman, Goldmark, Colin & Kaye, 1953-59; exec dir: Citizen's Housing Council, NY, 1945-46; Citizen's Housing Council, LA, Cal, 1946-48; cons, housing and city planning sect, UN, 1953; asso counsel, Temporary Comm on Courts, NY State, 1953; legal cons, Park, Rercreation and Open Space Project, NJ, NY, Conn Metrop region, 1958-59; lectr, MIT, 1962-63; asst atty gen, NY State, i/c Civil Rights Bur, 1959-66. Mem: exec comm, AJComm, NY; adv bd to counselor of J students, Columbia U, since 1962; ACLU; comm on housing and urban devl, Assn Bar, NYC; NY Co Lawyers Assn; Hadassah; League Women Voters; Regional Plan Assn; NY, Cal, US Supr Court Bars; Phi Beta Kappa;

fmr: mem: housing adv council, Manhattan Council, NY State Comm Against Discrimination; bd dirs, housing chmn, Cal Fed Civic Unity; asso counsel, comm on law and social action, AJCong; club; Women's City, NY. Author: Better Housing for Everyone, 1954; The Law of Open Space, 1960; co-author, Toward City Conservation, 1959; contbr to legal reviews. Recipient: woman of year, Mademoiselle Mag, 1948; Home: 317 W 89 St, New York, NY. Office: 100 Gold St, New York, NY.

SIEGEL, Sidney, US, physicist; b. NYC, Jan 10, 1912; s. Lester and Eva (Sokoloff); BA, Columbia U, 1932, PhD, 1936; m. Lilyan Ferges, Aug 22, 1937; c: Maria Watt, Anne Podney, Laura, Gail. Vice-pres, Atomics Intl div, Amer Rockwell Corp, since 1950; research asst, Columbia U, 1933-37; research sci: to dir, physics dept, Westinghouse Co, Pittsburgh, 1937-50; Oak Ridge Natl Lab, Tenn, 1946-48; research asso, Cal Tech, Pasadena, 1951-52. Pres, Amer Nuclear Soc, 1966-67; f, Amer Phys Soc; mem, Sigma Xi. Contbr to profsl jours. Home: 612 El Cerco Pl, Pacific Palisades, Cal. Office: POB 309, Canoga Park, Cal.

SIEGEL, Stanley E, US, educator; b. Long Branch, NJ, May 7, 1928; s. Charles and Ida (Frankel); BA, Wash and Jefferson Coll, 1949; MA, U Md, 1950; PhD, Rice U, 1953; m. Norma Stein, Aug 23, 1953; c: Charles, David, Martin. Prof, hist, U Houston, since 1963, fac mem since 1957; B'nai B'rith Hillel counselor since 1953. Vice-chmn, professions div, Houston UJA, since 1956; bd dirs, Cong Beth Yeshurun, 1958-59; mem: S Hist Assn; B'nai B'rith; ZOA. Author: A Political History of the Texas Republic, 1836-45, pub, 1956. Home: 4107 Leeshire, Houston Tex, Office: Cullen Blvd, Houston, Tex.

SIEGMEISTER, Elie, US, composer; b. NYC, Jan 15, 1909; s. William and Bessie (Gitler); BA, Columbia Coll, 1927; dipl: École Normale de Musique, Paris, 1931; Julliard Grad Sch, NYC, 1938; m. Hannah Mersel, Jan 15, 1930; c: Miriam, Nancy. Prof, music, composer in residence, Hofstra U, since 1966, on fac since 1949; composer, conductor, ed of music, since 1927; tchr, music: Bklyn Coll, 1934; New Sch for Social Research, 1937-38; U Minn, 1948; org, dir, Amer Ballad Singers, concerts at Town Hall and throughout US, 1940-46; compositions performed by: Arturo Toscanini; Leopold Stokowski; Dimitri Mitropoulous; Phila Orch; NY Philharmonic Sym; Eur, Austr, Isr, orchs. Composed: three syms, 1947, 1950, 1957; Ozark Set, 1943; Prairie Legend, 1943; Western Suite, 1945; Wilderness Road, 1945; Sunday in Brooklyn, 1946; Funnybone Alley, 1946; Lonesome Hollow, 1946; Summer Night, 1947; From My Window, 1949; Divertimento, 1953; concerto for clarinet and orch, 1956; concerto for flute and orch, 1960; Theater Set, 1960; Dick Whittington and his Cat, 1966; Five Fantasies of the Theater, 1967; The Face of War, 1968; two string quartets; sextet for brass and percussion; two piano sonatas; three violin piano sonatas; maj theater scores include: Doodle Dandy of the USA, 1942; Sing Out Sweet Land, 1944; Darling Corie, 1952; Miranda and the Dark Young Man, 1955; The Mermaid in Lock No 7, 1958; The Plough and the Stairs, 1960-69; fim score, They Came to Cordura, 1959; over 100 songs; music for piano, voice and piano, band. Vice-chmn, Amer Music Cen; mem: ASCAP; Natl Assn Amer Composers; Amer Fed Musicians; AAUP; Amer Guild Authors and Composers; Screen Composers Guild; Composers and Lyricists Guild of Amer, 1st vice-pres; Phi Beta Kappa. Author: The Music Lovers' Handbook, 1943; Work and Sing, 1944; Songs of Early America, 1945; American Folk Song Choral Series, 1954; Invitation to Music, 1961; Harmony and Melody, 2 vols, 1965-66; The New Music Lovers' Handbook, 1969; co-author, A Treasury of American Song, 1940. Home: 56 Fairview Ave, Great Neck, NY.

SIERRA, Sergio, J, It, rabbi; b. Rome, Dec 21, 1923; s. Giorgio and Grazia (Perugla); DLitt, U Rome, 1948; ordained rabbi, Rabb Coll of Rome, 1949; m. Ornella Pajalich, Jan 30, 1949; c: Tamar, Ora, Jonathan. Head, Rabb Sch, Margulies-Disegni; chief rabbi: J Comty, Turin, since 1959; J Comty, Bologna, 1949-59; lectr, Heb U, Bologna, 1950-59. Councilor, Union It J Comtys; mem, It Rabb Council, since 1951; Contbr to J and gen press. Home: Via Pietrio Giuria, 26, Turin, It.

SIEVER, Raymond, US, geologist, educator; b. Chgo, Ill, Sep 14, 1923; s. Leo and Lillian (Katz); BS, U Chgo, 1943, MS, 1947, PhD, 1950; m. Doris Fisher, Mar 31, 1945. Prof, geology, Harvard U, since 1965, on fac since 1956; asso, geology, Woods Hole Oceanographic Inst, since 1957; geologist, Ill Geological Survey, on staff since 1943. F, Amer Acad Arts and Sci; mem: Geological Soc of Amer; Amer Assn Petroleum

Geologists; AAAS; Geochem Soc; Sigma Xi. Contbr to geological jours. Recepient: Assn pres award, sci paper, Amer Assn Petroleum Geologists, 1952; paper award, Jour of Sedimentary Petrology, Soc Econ Paleontologists and Mineralogists, 1959. Hobbies: fencing, piano, photography. Home: 4 Madison St, Belmont, Mass. Office: Hoffman Lab, Harvard U, Cambridge, Mass.

SIGAD, Eliahu, Isr, artist; b. Ponievez, Lith, 1901; s. Joseph and Golda (Fuhr); in Isr since 1925; att: U Riga; Acad Callarossi, Paris; m. Rina Spielman, 1935; c: Ran. Art tchr since 1934. One-man shows: Tel Aviv: 1933, 1943, 1950, 1955, 1960; Jerusalem: 1952, 1955; works exhibited at: NYC, 1939, 1947, 1954, 1958; Can, 1956; Biennale, Sao Paulo, 1956; S Afr, 1957; Scandinavia, 1958; Greece, 1958; Chile, 1960. Mem: Intl Assn Plastic Arts; Milo; fmr: head delg, Intl Cong Plastic Arts, Yugo; gen secy, mem council, Isr Painters and Sculptors Assn. Recepient: Dizengoff prize, 1946; first prize, Tiberias Landscape, 1955; second prize, Isr 10th Anniversary Exhb, Ramat Gan, 1958. Home and studio: 35 Sirkin St, Tel Aviv, Isr.

SIGAL, Benjamin C, US, attorney, educator; b. Phila, Pa, Mar 27, 1906; s. Abraham and Pauline (Cohen); BA, U Pittsburg, 1927; LLB, Harvard Law Sch, 1930; m. Esther Lencher, Sep 25, 1936. Gen counsel for trade unions; dir, lab-mgmt educ prog, U Hawaii, since 1965; exec asst to lab mems, War Lab Bd, Wash, DC, 1942-46; mem, Natl Wage Stabilization Bd, 1952-53. Bd trustee, Temple Emanu-El, since 1967; mem: atomic energy comm, Fed Bar Assn, 1962-63; comm on intl control, atomic energy, Amer Bar Assn, 1962-63; Dem Cen Comm, 1948-52; pres, Wash chap, ADA, 1948-50. Home: 4999 Kahala Ave, Honolulu, Hawaii. Office: 333 Queen St, Honolulu, Hawaii.

SIGMON, Jackson M, US, attorney; b. Bethlehem, Pa, Apr 15, 1917; s. William and Jeanette (Marcus); BA, U Pittsburgh, 1938; MA, Fletcher Sch Intl Law and Diplomacy, 1939; LLB, Duke U, 1942; grad studies, Balliol Coll, Oxford U, Eng, 1945; m. Ruth Friedman, Aug 22, 1948; c: Mark, Hillary, Jill, Jan, William, Erica. Dep atty gen, Commonwealth of Pa, since 1962; partner, law firm, Sigmon, Briody and Littner; Rep state committeeman, 18th leg dist, Commonwealth of Pa, since 1958; asst city solicitor, trial counsel, Bethlehem, 1962. Lt, US Army, 1942-46. Mem: Amer Bar Assn; Pa Bar Assn, fmr mem, house of delgs; fmr pres, Northampton Co Bar Assn; mem: Brith Shalom Comty Cen; ZOA; B'nai B'rith; Disabled Amer Vets; Amer Legion; Pi Lambda Phi; Hon First Defenders; Masons; clubs: Optimists; Locust Valley Country; Moselem Springs Country. Recipient: Croix de Guerre, 1945; Bronze Star, 1945. Home: 3464 Mountainview Circle, Bethlehem, Pa. Office: 146 E Broad St, Bethlehem, Pa.

SILBAR, Sidney J, US, urologist, educator; b. Milw, Wis, Oct 20, 1895; s. Jacob and Matilda (Toch); BS, U Wis, 1916; MD, Marquette U, 1921; MS, U Pa, 1924; m. Anita Feld, Aug 5, 1923; c: John, Matilda. Pvt practice; asso prof, Marquette U Sch of Med, since 1926; mem, exec bd, Mt Sinai Hosp, Milw, chief, urol, 1946, chief, surg, 1948. Lt col, US Army MC, 1942-45. Dipl, Amer Bd Urol; mem, exec bd: N Cen sect, Amer Urol Soc; Milw J Comty Cen; mem: Wis, Chgo, and Milw Urol Socs; Milw Med Soc; Profsl Men's Orch; Shrine Band, both Milw; club, Brynwood Country. Contbr to med jours. Hobbies: gardening; tropical fish. Home: 7511 N Lake Dr, Milwaukee, Wis. Office: 2040 W Wisconsin Ave, Milwaukee, Wis.

SILBER, Max I, US, business exec, civic worker; b. Manchester, NH, Feb 15, 1911; s. Oscar and Anna (Slovack); m. Edith Kamenske, June 20, 1934; c: Natalie Weil, Allan. Pres, treas, N Kamenske & Co, Inc, since 1949, supt, 1933-40, vice-pres, 1940-49. Found: Nathan E and Harry S Kamenske scholarship, Brandeis U, 1951; Max Silber trophy, best woman athlete, Brandeis U, annually, 1955; Colo Sch of Mines, scholastic achievement awards annually, 1962; presented fully equipped campsite to Camp Carpenter, Daniel Webster Council, Boy Scouts of Amer, 1955. Mem, bd dirs: YMCA, Nashua, NH, since 1959; Nashua Comty Chest, since 1959, pres, 1961; Temple Beth Abraham, mem, sch bd, since 1953, pres since 1951; mem: natl council, Boy Scouts of Amer, since 1946, natl J Comm on scouting, since 1958, exec bd, region I, since 1954, vice-chmn, 1962; exec bd, Daniel Webster council, since 1943, pres, 1953-56, fmr council commn; chmn, NE jamboree comm, 1957-60; mem, bd govs mfrs council, C of C, Nashua, 1962; vice-chmn, disaster comm, ARC, since 1952; chmn, Nashua CJA, 1951-55; Council of Ingot Brass and Bronze

Ind; ZOA; United Syn of Amer; Masons; Shriners; Brotherhood, Temple Beth Abraham; clubs: Nashua Rotary, fmr pres; Nashua Country; Brandeis U, life mem. Recipient: Eagle Scout, bronze, gold, silver palms; scouters' key, scoutmaster's key, arrow head award, silver beaver, silver antelope, vigil hon award, all Boy Scouts of Amer; golden deeds award, Nashua Exch Club, 1953; service award, Nashua J Comty, 1957; tribute of hon award, Temple Beth Abraham, 1961; citizen of year, Nashua C of C, 1960; J Advocate Carnation award, 1961. Hobbies: photography, sports. Home: 34 Wood St, Nashua, NH. Office: 5 Otterson Ct, Nashua, NH.

SILBERBERG, Alexander, Isr, scientist; b. Vienna, Aus, Feb 24, 1923; s. Joseph and Josephine (Konstantinowsky); in Isr since 1953; BSc, U Witwatersrand, Johannesburg, S Afr, 1943; PhD, U Basel, Switz, 1952; m. Leah Abrahams, Mar 30, 1948; c: Josephine, Yeshayahu. Prof, phys chem, Weizmann Inst, since 1963. Cpl, S Afr Army, 1944-46. Council mem: Intl Org Med Physics; Intl Soc of Hemorheology; mem Amer: Phys Soc; Chem Soc; AAAS; Isr Microcirculation Soc; Biophys Soc. Contbr to sci jours. Home: 3 Rupin St, Rehovot, Isr. Office: Weizmann Inst, Rehovot, Isr.

SILBERBERG, Ruth, US, physician, educator; b. Kassel, Ger, Mar 20, 1906; d. Ludwig and Kaethe (Plaut) Katzenstein; in US since 1937; MD, U Breslau, 1931; m. Martin Silberberg, Dec 27, 1933. Prof, path, Wash U Med Sch, since 1968, on fac since 1944, research path, 1937-40; asst path, Barnes and Allied Hosp, since 1960; U Breslau, 1930-33; path, J Hosp, Breslau, 1933; research path, Dalhousie U, Halifax, 1934-36; asst path, NYU, 1941-43; acting path, J Hosp, St Louis, Mo, 1945-46; path, Barnard Skin and Cancer Hosp, St Louis, 1947; asso path, St Louis City and Mo Pacific Hosp, 1947-59. Pres, St Louis Path Soc, 1949; mem: Soc for Experimental Path; Soc for Experimental Biol and Med; Amer Assn Path and Bact; Soc for Growth and Devl; AAAS; Amer Soc for Cancer Research. Ed bd: Growth, 1960; Pathologia and Microbiologia, 1960; contbr to med jours and books. Home: 18 S Kings Hwy, St Louis, Mo. Office: Wash U Med Sch, St Louis, Mo.

SILBERBERG-CHOLEWA, Israel, US, educator, journalist, author; b. Szydlow, Pol, Mar 30, 1898; s. Mordechai and Sarah (Cholewa); in US since 1922; att U Copenhagen, 1918-22; m. Esther Machebansky, June 2, 1923; c: Ruth Flapan. Danish corresp, The Day, NYC, 1919-22; ed, Yugntshtime, Copenhagen, 1921-22; co-ed, Kinder Jour, 1940-50; dir: Sholem Aleichem Mitlshul, 1950-52; Sholem Aleichem Cen and Day Sch, Bensonhurst, Bklyn, 1952-57. Author: Denmark, 1967; Mentsh Un Folk, 1967; arranged, Leivick-Essays and Speeches, 1963; co-author, Anthology in Yiddish-Literature, 1969; ed: Passi dem Chasens, sch ed, 1946, 3rd ed, 1961; Tevye der Milchiker, sch ed, 1963; trans Scandinavian lit into Yiddish; contbr essays on J and Scandinavian lit and educ to J Press. Club: PEN. Recipient: Zukunft prize for essay on Henry Nathansen, 1946. Home: 7601-21 Ave, Brooklyn, NY.

SILBERBLATT, Beryl, US, physician, educator; b. NYC, Mar 15, 1906; s. Solomon and Dora (Cohen); MD, Columbia U, 1929; m. Mildred Rubin, Oct 27, 1935; c: Katherine, Steven. Clinical prof, obstets and gyn, NY Med Coll, since 1955; visiting obstets and gyn: Flower Fifth Ave Hosp; Metrop Hosp; Bird S Coler Hosp; chief gyn, malignancy service, Metrop, Bird S Coler Hosps; guest prof: Ankara U, Turkey, 1959; Tohoku U, Sendai, Japan, 1962. Contbr to med jours. Hobbies: music, theater. Home: 1133 Park Ave, New York, NY. Office: 1001 Park Ave, New York, NY.

SILBERG, Moshe, Isr, jurist; b. Skaudvile, Lith, 1900; s. Hillel and Asna (Jaffe); in Isr since 1929; att U Marburg, 1921-23; DJur, U Frankfurt, 1926; m. 2nd, Prina Bartfeld, 1945; c: Etan, Osnat. Justice, Isr Supr Court, since 1950, acting justice, 1949-50, dep pres, since 1965; visiting prof, law personal status, Heb U, since 1954; lectr, Talmudic law, since 1959; tchr, Tahkemoni Rel Sch, Tel Aviv, 1929-31; pvt law practice, Tel Aviv, 1934-48; judge, dist court, Tel Aviv, 1948-49. Author: Hiring and Contracting in Talmudic Law, 1927; Personal Status in Israel, 1957; Principia Talmudica, 1961; contbr to local press. Recipient: Bialik prize, 1958; Isr prize, 1964. Home: 45A King George St, Jerusalem, Isr. Office: Supr Court, Jerusalem, Isr.

SILBERG, Sidney, Eng, rabbi; b. Leeds, Eng, June 27, 1934; s. Max and Millie (Taylor); BA, MA, ordained rabbi, J Coll, 1962; m. Isabelle Riff, July 11, 1957; c: Deborah, Dov, Allon.

Rabbi: Jesmond Heb Cong, since 1967; Ealing Dist Syn, London, 1962-67; asst min, Hampstead Garden Suburb Syn, 1957-62. Mem: B'nai B'rith. Contbr to El Am Talmud, Isr. Spec interests: J day sch movement, art, philately. Home: 16 N Jesmond Ave, Newcastle-upon-Tyne, Eng.

SILBERG, Yoel, Isr, stage and film director; b. Tel Aviv, Mar 30, 1927; s. Ben-Zion and Tova (Geisiner); att Old Vic Drama Sch, London, 1952-53; m; three c. Dir: plays: Kazablan; I Like Mike; film, The Simchon Family; first asst dir: films: Exodus; Judith; The Best of Enemies; plays: Habimah Theater; Ohel Theater, both Isr, US theater group. IDF, 1947-50. Hobby: sports. Home: 10 Zacharya St, Tel Aviv, Isr.

SILBERLING, Edwyn, US, attorney; b. Jersey City, NJ, Aug 4, 1924; s. Louis and Rose (Router); BA, Harvard Coll, 1947, LLB, Harvard Law Sch, 1949; m. Margaret Pargellis, 1949; c: Stephen, Amy, Elizabeth, Peter, Louise. Partner, law firm, Mulligan, Silberling and Jacobson; and predecessor firms, since 1950; asst dist atty, NY Co, 1951-57; spec asst to atty gen, NY State, i/c of: inves into political corruption, Suffolk Co, 1957-61; spec asst to US Atty Gen, chief, sect on organized crime and racketeering, Dept of Justice, 1961-63; Suffolk Co Commn of Hum Relations, 1963-69; lectr, trial practice, Practising Law Inst. USAC, 1943-46. Co-chmn, Nassau Co Bar Assn, Comm on Post-Admission Legal Educ, 1967-68; mem: law reform comm, Assn Bar, NYC, 1951-54; comm on courts of superior jurisdiction, 1959-60, grievance comm, since 1969; NY regional adv bd, ADL, mem, exec comm, Wash, DC. Home: 72 Ketewemoke Dr, Huntington, NY. Office: 36 44 St, New York, NY.

SILBERMAN, Charles E, US, journalist, editor, economist; b. Des Moines, Ia, Jan 31, 1925; s. Seppy and Cel (Levy); AB, Columbia Coll, 1946; postgrad studies, Columbia U, 1946-49; m. Arlene Propper, Sep 12, 1948; c: David, Richard, Jeffrey, Steven. Mem bd eds, Fortune Mag, since 1961, asso ed, 1953-60; dir, Carnegie Corp Study, Educ of Educators, 1966-69; tutor, econ, CCNY, 1947-48; lectr, econ, Columbia U, 1955-66, mem fac, since 1949. Author: The Myths of Automation, 1966; Crisis in Black and White, 1964; Crisis in Classroom, 1971; contrib author: Markets of the Sixties; The Negro Challenge to the Business Community; The Free World and the New Nations; contbr to: Fortune; Harpers; Commentary; other mags. USNR, 1943-46. Chmn, comm on rel and race, mem exec comm, Syn Council of Amer; f, Natl Assn Bus Econs; mem: natl progs comm, ADL; bd overseers, Lown Grad Cen for Contemporary J Studies, Brandeis U; natl domestic affairs comm, AJComm; bd dirs, Amer Histadrut Cultural Exch Inst; bd dirs, Citizens Advocate Cen; visiting comm, Haverford Coll; bd trustees, Free Syn, Westchester; Amer Econ Assn. Recipient: B'nai B'rith Four Freedoms Lit award, 1965; NCCJ Superior Merit award, 1965, 1967; Loeb award, for dist bus and financial writing, 1966; Schoolbell award, NEA, 1967. Home: 110 Stuyvesant Plaza, Mt Vernon, NY. Office: Time and Life Bldg, Rockefeller Center, New York, NY.

SILBERMAN, Curt C, US, attorney; b. Wuerzburg, Ger, May 23, 1908; s. Adolf and Ida (Rosenbusch); in US since 1938; DJur, summa cum laude, U Wuerzburg, 1931; LLB, Rutgers U, Newark, NJ, 1947; m. Else Kleeman, 1935. Pvt practice since 1948. Pres, Amer Fed J from Cen Eur, since 1962; trustee, Leo Baeck Inst, NY, since 1962; bd dirs, J Restitution Successor Org, since 1962; hon trustee, J Counseling and Service Agcy of Essex Co, Newark, NJ; trustee: J Philanthropic Fund of 1933 Inc, NY; NY Found of Nursing Homes Inc; mem presidium, Council of J from Ger, since 1962; chmn, Comm on Comparative Jurisprudence, NJ State Bar Assn; fmr: pres, J Family Service Assn; vice pres, NY State AJCong; chmn, frat and syn div, UJA, Essex Co; pres, J Unity Club, Newark, NJ. Lectr, contbr articles on: intl, pvt law; ref problem; contemporary J scene; problem of political educ. Home: 11 Aspen Rd, West Orange, NJ. Office: 589 Central Ave, East Orange, NJ.

SILBERMAN, Lou Hackett, US, educator; b. San Francisco, June 23, 1914; s. Lou and Myrtle (Mueller); AB, U Cal, Berkeley, 1934; BHL, HUC, 1939, MHL, 1941, DHL, 1943; ordained rabbi, 1942; m. Helen Epstein, June 14, 1942; c: Syril, Deborah Cohn. Chmn, dept rel studies, Vanderbilt U, since 1970, Hillel prof J Lit and Thought, since 1952; f, instr, HUC, 1941-43; asst rabbi, Temple Emanuel, Dallas, Tex, 1943-45; rabbi, Temple Isr, Omaha, Neb, 1945-52; visiting prof, Judaiste Inst, U Vienna, Aus, 1965-66. Chmn, Comty

Relations Comm, J Fed, Nashville, Tenn; fmr: vice chmn, Natl J Comty Relations Adv Council; mem: Amer Acad Rel; Soc Bibl Lit; Amer Soc for Study Rel; Amer Theol Soc; Assn for J Studies; Studiorum Novi Testamenti Societas; B'nai B'rith; CCAR. Home: 600 Hillwood Dr, Nashville, Tenn. Office: Divinity Sch, Vanderbilt U, Nashville, Tenn.

SILBERMAN, Richard, T, US, business exec, b. LA, Cal, Apr 22, 1929; s. Isadore and Sophie (Mechanic); BS, San Diego State Coll, 1950; m. Roberta Rosenfeld, July 1, 1951; c: Jeffrey, Karen, Craig. Vice-chmn, treas, dir, Foodmaker Inc, since 1965; mem, bd dirs, exec comm, S Cal First Natl Bank, since 1968; pres: Electronics Intl Mgmt Ltd, 1960-65; Electronics Corp Advs, 1960-65; exec vice pres: Electronics Intl Capital 1960-65; Electronics Capital Corp, 1959-65; vice-pres: Electronics Inves Mgmt Corp, 1959-65; Electronics Inves Corp, 1954-65; asso prof, physics, San Diego State Coll, 1949-50; partner, Video Service, 1950-57; vice pres: Brown Corp, 1951-52; Video Antenna Sys, 1953-57; pres, Kin Tel div, Cohu Electronics, 1952-59. Mem: Sigma Phi Sigma; Inst Radio Engrs. Recipient: outstanding alumni award, San Diego State Coll, 1959. Home: 4021 Miller St, San Diego, Cal. Office: POB 783, San Diego.

SILBERMAN, Samuel Joshua, US, business exec; b. NYC, Apr 17, 1915; s. Alfred and Dorothy (Lichtenstein); att Harvard U, 1932-34; hon LLB, Fairleigh Dickinson U, Rutherford, NJ, 1968; m. Lois Voltter, July 2, 1960; c: Douglas, Rita, Alfred, Allen, Jane, Peter. Ret since 1969; chmn, bd, chief exec off, Consolidated Cigar Corp, until 1968, held various positions in corp, 1934-68. Lt cdr, USCG, 1941-45. Pres, Gulf and Western Found; chmn, Coast Guard Acad Found; dir: Gtr NY Fund; Council JWF; trustee: Fairleigh Dickinson U; FJP, fmr pres, NY; mem: Temporary NY State Commn to Revise Social Services Law; Natl Comm for Social Work Educ, Council on Social Work Educ; bd govs, ASPIRA; Gov Comm on Social Problems; Temple Emanu-El; fmr: delg, US to 14th Intl Conf on Social Wfr, Helsinki, Finland, 1968; trustee, NCCJ; mem: Gov Comm on Public Wfr; Adv Bd NY Jt Leg Comm to Revise Social Wfr Law; clubs: Harvard, NYC; St Croix, St Croix, VI. Co-author: A New Yardstick for Profit Analysis, 1955. Recipient: 12th Biennial Citation, Who's Who in Amer, 1962; Pres' Medal, Hunter Coll, CUNY, 1966, with wife. Home: 885 Park Ave, New York, NY. Office: 113 E 79 St, New York, NY.

SILBERMANN, Alphons, Ger, sociologist, author; b. Cologne, Ger, Aug 11, 1909; s. Salomon and Bella (Eichtersheimer); DJur, U Freiburg; Laureat de l'Inst de Fr. Prof: U Cologne; U Lausanne; fmr lectr, St Conservatory of Music, Sydney, Austr. Author: Of Musical Things, 1949; La musique, la radio et l'auditeur, 1954; Introduction à une sociologie de la musique, 1955; Wovon lebt die Musik-Die Prinzipen der Musiksoziologie, 1957; Musik, Rundfunk und Horer, 1959; Das Imaginare Tagebuch des Herrn Jacques Offenbach, 1960; Vom Wohnen der Deutschen, 1963; Ketzereien eines Soziologen, 1965; Bilschirm und Wirklichkeit, 1966; Vorteile und Nachteile des Kommerziellen Fernnsehens, 1968; contbr to sociol publs and music jours. Home: 142 Philipstr, Cologne, Ger. Office: U of Cologne, Ger.

SILBERNER, Edmund, Isr, economist, historian; b. Boryslaw, Pol, Apr 20, 1910; s. Manes and Rachel (Pomeranz); MA, Hochschule Fur Welthandel, Vienna, 1932; PhD, U Geneva 1935; Dipl, Grad Sch for Intl Studies, Geneva, 1939; m. Regina Rothenberg, Sep 19, 1938; c: Naomi, Nora. Prof, Heb U, Jerusalem, since 1967, asso prof, 1956-67, on fac since 1951; f: Grad Sch for Intl Studies, Geneva, 1936-38; Geneva Research Cen, 1939-41; asst to dir, Intl Conf on Capital Movement, 1939; editor in chief, Annuaire des Banques d' Emission, 1939; privat-docent, U Geneva, 1939-41; mem, Inst for Advanced Study, Princeton, NJ, 1942-43; visiting lectr; Princeton U; US Army Specialized Training Prog, 1943-44; econ: Fr Supply Council, 1944-45; Fr emb, 1945-46, both Wash, DC, lectr, asst prof, Princeton U, 1946-50; f, Intl Inst Social Hist, Amsterdam. 1964-65. Mem: Amer Econ Assn; Amer Hist Assn. Author: L'Oeuvre Economique d'Antoine-Elisee Cherbuliez, 1935; La Guerre dans la Pensée économique du 16e au 18e siècles, 1939; The Problem of War in Nineteenth Century Economic Thought, 1946; Moses Hess, An Annotated Bibliography, 1951; Socialism and the Jewish Problem 1800-1917; Heb 1954; La Guerre et la Paix dans l'histoire des doctrines economiques, 1957; The Works of Moses Hess, an Inventory of his Signed and Anonymous Publications, Manuscripts and Correspondence, 1958; Socialisten zur Judenfrage, 1962; Un Manuscrit inedit de David Ricardo sur le probleme monetaire, 1940; Moses Hess Briefwechsel, 1959; Heinrich Graetz Briefe an Moses Hess, 1961; Moses Hess, Die Geschichte Seines Lebens, 1966; Johann Jacoby Korrespondent 1816-49. Recipient: Award Laureat l'Acadamie des sciences morales et politiques, Paris, 1940; Laureat de l'Universite de Geneve, 1940; Home: 5 Hapalmach St, Jerusalem, Isr. Office: Heb U, Jerusalem, Isr.

SILBERSCHEIN, Fanny, Switz, social worker; b. Moscow, Russ, Feb 16, 1901; d. Arieh and Eva (Syrkin) Danzig; in Switz since 1938; att, Ecole Sociale, Geneva; m. Abraham Silberschein, June 8, 1944, (decd). Gen secy, Amis du Village d'Enfants Suisses en Isr, Kiriat Yearim, Fr Switz, since 1955; social worker, J comty, Dresden, Ger, 1936-38; dir, Intl Comm for Help to Intellectuals, Geneva, Switz, 1938-61. Home: 10 Ave Miremont, Geneva, Switz.

SILBERSCHLAG, Eisig, US, educator, author; b. Stryj, Aus, Jan 8, 1903; s. David and Bertha (Pomerantz); in US since 1920; PhD, U Vienna, 1926; m. Milka Antler, 1938. Pres, Heb Coll, since 1968, dean since 1947, prof, Heb lit, since 1944, fac mem since 1932; instr, J hist, Tchrs Inst, JTSA, 1930-31; Bibl hist, Sch for Tchrs, HUC, 1931-32. Author: Tehiyah-u-Tehiyah be-Shirah, 1938; Kimron Yamai, 1959; Saul Tschernichowsky: Poet of Revolt, 1968; trans; contbr poems, essays to jours. Pres, Assn Pres and Deans Heb Colls; dir, Goslava and Abraham Joseph Stybel Found for Heb Lit; vice-pres, Natl Council for J Educ; fmr pres, NE Assn for Hebraic Culture; fmr trustee, Touroff Fund; mem: JBCA; Amer Acad for J Research. Recipient: prize, ZOA, 1938; La Med prize, 1943; Tschernichowsky prize, Munic of Tel Aviv, 1950. Home: 50 The Fenway, Boston, Mass. Office: 43 Hawes, Brookline, Mass.

SILBERSTANG, Edwin, US, author; b. Bklyn, NY, Jan 11, 1930; s. Louis and Fay (Berkowitz); BA, U Mich, 1950; LLB, Bklyn Law Sch, 1957; m. Lynn Sandage, Mar 16, 1969; c: Julian, Joyce, Allan. Author since 1964; atty, Silberstang & Silberstang, 1958-64. Spec agt, Counter-intelligence Corps, US Army, 1951-53. Author: Rapt in Glory, 1964, 1969; Nightmare of the Dark, 1967, 1968, 1969. Recipient: Edwin Silberstang Collection, Mugar Libr, Boston U, 1969. Home: POB 569, Woodstock, NY.

SILBERSTEIN, Aron, Switz, rabbi, author; b. Kunszentmarton, Hung, Nov 20, 1905; s. Alexander and Terezia (Klain); in Switz since 1945; PhD, U Budapest,1930; m. Minia Belchatowska; c: Juli, Noemi. Rabbi: J Cong, Bienne, since 1949; Siklos and Hodmezovasarhely, Hung, 1930-44; concentration camp, Bergen-Belsen,1944. Author: Farissol Abraham, 1930; History of the Jews at Siklos,1932; History of the Jews of Hodmezovasarhely, 1934; Holidays of Israel, 1957; Heilige Bruderschaft, History of the Chevra of Bienne, 1966.Contbr to J press. Home and study: 12 Gartenstr, Bienne, Switz.

SILBERSTEIN, Werner, Isr, physician, goverment official; b. Berlin, Ger, Nov 24, 1899; s. Walther and Lea (Levy); in Isr since 1933; MD, U Berlin, 1924; m. Ronya Kolodny, 1924. Ret; dir: Govt Cen Labs; div public health labs, Min of Health, Jerusalem, both 1948-65; asst, Robert Koch Inst for Infectious Diseases, Berlin, 1926-33, later reinstated and appd sci adv; bacteriologist, Hadassah Hosp, Jerusalem, 1933-38; research work, Microbiol Inst, Istanbul U, Turkey, 1938-42; bacteriologist, Pal Govt, Jerusalem, 1943-48. Pres, Isr Inst for Sacred Music, Jerusalem; mem: cen comm, Isr Phys Org; comm, Isr Soc Clinical Path. Contbr to Isr fgn press. Spec interests: hist of med, music. Home: 5 Brenner St, Jerusalem, Isr.

SILBERT, Doris, US, educator, musicologist; b. Buffalo, NY, Nov 12, 1901; d. Herman and Helena (Slonim); BA, Barnard Coll, 1923; MA, Smith Coll, 1925. Prof em, Smith Coll, since 1967, prof, 1947-67, dean, 1960-65, on fac since 1925; tchr, Hunter Coll, 1927, summer sessions, 1927-29. Mem: Musicological Soc; Phi Beta Kappa. Ed: Smith Coll Musical Archives: Vol VII, Balletto, 1945; Vol XII, T A Vitali Sonatas, Op 4, 1954; contbr to musical publ; Collier's Ency. Home: 61 Crescent St, Northampton, Mass.

SILK, Dennis Peter, Isr, author; b. London, Eng, July 10, 1928; s. Jack and Deborah; in Isr since 1955; att Clark's Coll; London Coll. Author: A Face of Stone, 1964; Billy Doll, 1966; Retrievements: A Jerusalem Anthol, 1968; contbr lit mags. Hobby: storytelling. Home: 19/73 Abu Tor, Jerusalem, Isr.

SILK, Donald, Eng, lawyer; b. London, Eng, Sep 6, 1928; s. Robert and Polly; att Magdalen Coll, Oxford, 1940-47, MA, New Coll, Oxford, 1951; Cert d'Assiduite, Acad of Intl Law, The Hague, 1952; m. Angela Buxton, Feb 9, 1959; c: Benjamin, Joseph, Rebecca. Sr partner, Silk, Miller and Co, solicitors, since 1968; dep chmn, Silk's Estates Ltd, since 1968; sole partner, Donald Silk and Co; dir, Zionist Review Ltd. Chmn: ZF of Gt Brit and N Ir, vice-pres, secy, treas, 1958-67; Gen Zionist Admn Comm, Herzlia Sch; found, life pres, Marylebone J Soc; gov, Robert Montefiore Sch; vice-chmn, WJC, dep mem, world exec, hon secy, 1962-68; vice-pres, Fed Zionist Youth, chmn, 1953-55; trustee, council mem, Chichester Festival Theatre; mem, actions comm, World Zionist Org; mem, Eur Shnat Sherut Exec; exec mem: Bd Dep Brit J; World Confd of Gen Zionists; mem: Law Soc; Brit Law Assn; B'nai B'rith; Commn on Law of Contempt of Court, sponsored by Justice Intl Commn of Jurists. Ed, bd mem, Jewish Observer and Middle East Review; contbr to gen and educ jours. Hobbies: numismatics, model engr, kibbutz devl, activating youth and students. Home: 16 Winnington Rd, London, N2, Eng. Office: 130 Seymour Pl, London,W1, Eng.

SILMAN, Gerald John, Eng, business exec; b. Leeds, Eng, May 28, 1918; s. Morris and Ellen (Cohen); MA, U Cambridge, 1939; m. Christine Feldman, 1940; s. Lionel. Mgn dir, dir, several cos. Capt, Brit Army, 1939-45. Vice-chmn: ZC, Leeds; bd govs, Leeds J Day Sch; W Riding Hillel Found; fmr chmn: Educ Comm Talmud Torah, Leeds; Cambridge U Zionist Soc; mem, B'nai B'rith, Leeds. Home: 4 Crescent Gardens, Leeds, Eng. Office: Hope Mfg Co, Sheepscar St, Leeds, Eng.

SILTON, Maurice Z, US, physician; b. Boston, Mass, May 6, 1906; s. Meyer and Fannie (Lurinsky); BS, Harvard U, 1928; MD, Rush Med Coll, U Chgo, 1932; m. Hilda Strimling, 1938; c: Naomi, Myrna, Robert. Pvt practice, obstet and gyn, since 1935; asso clinical prof, dept obstet and gyn, U of S Cal, since 1935; sr att and chmn, dept obstet and gyn, Cedars of Leb Hosp and Clinics, since 1938; asst, dept bact, U Chgo, 1929-30; att gyn, LA TB Sanatorium, 1938; Mt Sinai Hosp and Clinics, 1939; sr att staff obstet and gyn, Queen of Angels Hosp, 1938-47. Lt cmdr, USNR MC, 1943-46. F: Amer Coll Surgs; Intl Coll Surgs; Amer Coll Obstet and Gyn; Amer Soc Abdominal Surgs; Amer Geriatrics Soc; mem: bd dirs, Sinai Cong, 1952-53; Amer J Phys F Comm for IMA, 1951; Amer Soc for Study Sterility; LA Obstet and Gyn Soc; AMA; Cal, World, and LA Co Med Assns; Intl Fertility Assn; Phi Delta Epsilon; Tau Epsilon Phi; J Big Brothers Assn; ZOA; clubs: Harvard, S Cal; LA Profsl Men's; U of S Cal Med Fac; Brentwood Country. Contbr to profsl and med mags. Hobbies: golf, photography. Home: 116 S Las Palmas Ave, Los Angeles, Cal. Office:6360 Wilshire Blvd, Los Angeles, Cal.

SILVER, Brian Lionel, Isr, scientist, educator; b. London, Eng, Feb 6, 1930; s. Barnett and Rebecca (Greenstein); in Isr since 1958; BSc, PhD, U Coll, London, m. Esther Asher, May 28, 1961; c: Sharon. Asso prof, chem, Technion, since 1969; research asst, Weizmann Inst, 1960-63; research f: U Cambridge, 1963-64; U Coll, London, 1966-67. Sgt, Royal Armored Corps, Brit Army, 1948-50. Contbr numerous sci papers and revs. Home: 12 Hahursha St, Haifa, Isr. Office: Technion, Haifa, Isr.

SILVER, Charles H, US, industrialist b. Dec 5, 1888; s. Simon and Anna (Herschkowitz); hon: LLD, Fordham U; LHD, Yeshiva U; DSc, St Johns U; m. Hannah Bernstein, Jan 4, 1912; c: Evelyn Bernstein, Natalie Moscow, Robert. Pres: Beth Isr Med Cen; Amun-Isr Housing Corp; Joseph and Helen Yeamans Levy Found; cons to mayor, NYC; fmr: exec asst to Mayor Wagner for educ and ind devl; vice-pres, dir, Amer Woolen Co; public interest dir, bd, Fed Home Loan Bank of NY; mem bd dirs, NY World's Fair Corp; adv, US delg to UN Commn on Human Rights. Pres: Cong Bnei Jeshurun, NYC; Grand St Boys Found, vice-pres, Grand St Boys Assn; Intl Syn, Kennedy Intl Airport; trustee, Urban League; vice-pres, Albert E Smith Memorial Found; co-found, Albert Einstein Coll of Med; mem: Regional Export Expansion Council; bd trustees, Yeshiva U; bd dirs, NY Council on Econ Educ; Gov's Council on Rehab; natl exec bd, AJComm; fmr, Pres Truman's Intl Security Commn; bd overseers, JTSA; exec comm, FJP; econ adv comm, Fordham U. Recipient: citation, Yeshiva U; Star of It Solidarity; Medallion of NYC; Papal Knighthood of St Sylvester; annual brotherhood award, JWV, NYC Council, 1968; NY Co Med Assn Citizens award, 1968; Victory Medal, State of Isr. Home: 101 Central Park W, New York, NY. Office: 10 Nathan D Perlman Pl, New York, NY.

SILVER, Daniel Jeremy, US, rabbi; b. Cleveland, O, Mar 26, 1928; s. Abba and Virginia (Horkheimer); AB, Harvard U, 1948; MHL, ordained rabbi, HUC, 1952; PhD, U Chgo, 1960:; m. Adele Zeidman, July 19, 1956; c: Jonathan, Michael, Sarah. Rabbi, The Temple, since 1956; adj prof, rel, Case-W Reserve U, since 1968; rabbi, Beth Torah Cong, Chgo, 1954-56. Lt, chaplain, USN, 1952-54. Pres: Natl Found for J Culture; Cleveland ZC; chmn, public wfr comm, Cleveland J Fed; mem, CCAR; fmr: mem, exec bd: UA; Cleveland J Fed; CCAR; Amer-Isr Public Affairs Comm; Cleveland Council Econ Opportunities; Cleveland Urban Coalition. Author: From the Rabbi's Desk, 1962; In the Time of Harvest, 1963; Maimonidean Criticism and the Maimonidean Controversy (1180-1240), 1966; Judaism and Ethics, 1969; ed, CCAR Journal, since 1964. Home: 2841 Waybridge Rd, Cleveland, O. Study: U Circle and Silver Park, Cleveland, O.

SILVER, Edward S, US, attorney, government official, jurist; b. NYC, Nov 17, 1898; s. David and Sarah (Einstein); BSS, CCNY, 1920; LLB, Harvard Law Sch, 1924; hon LLD, Yeshiva U, 1967; m, Regina Bublick, Nov 18, 1924; c: David, Jonathan, Sarah Bunim. Commn, NY State Inves Commn, since 1969; asst US atty, 1925-29; spec asst US atty, 1929-31; Commn, Alien Enemy Hearing Bd, E Dist, NY, 1942-45; judge, Surrogates Court, 1945-69; dist atty, Kings Co Bklyn, 1954-64, chief asst dist atty, 1946-54. USN, WW I. Chmn: NYC Bonds for Isr, 1964-68; tech adv comm, Detached Workers Project, Juvenile Delinquency, since 1950; Bklyn Bonds for Isr, since 1952; J adv comm and vice-pres, Natl J Comm, Boy Scouts of Amer; subcomm on prosecution problem, and mem, comm on scope and prog, Amer Bar Assn; hon pres, Natl Council of Young Isr; pres, Civil Cen Clinic, since 1955; mem, governing council and commn on law and social action, AJCong; mem, bd dirs: exec comm, Bklyn JCC; Hillel Found; Rabb Sem of Amer; UJA; Bklyn Region, NCCJ; exec comm, Bklyn div, FJP, NY; lawyers div, Amer Friends Heb U; JWB; mem, bd trustees, Bar Ilan U, Isr; mem: chaplaincy adv bd, NY Bd Rabbis; ed bd, Natl Probation and Parole Assn Jour; natl exec bd, Vaad Hapoel, Rel Zionists of Amer; Amer comm, Natl Sick Fund of Isr, Inc; adv bd, Natl Assn for Prevention Addiction to Narcotics; Amer Legion; JWV; NY State, and Fed Bar Assns; Assn Bar, NYC; NY Co Lawyers Assn; NY State and Natl Dist Attys Assns; NAACP; Urban League; Youth Council Bur; Grand St Boys Assn; B'nai B'rith; Men's League of Bklyn; hon mem: Detective Endowment Assn; (life) commn on syn relations, FJP; Affiliated Young Dems of NY State; club, City Coll. Recipient: award of honor, State of Isr, 1954; medal from Isr PM Sharett, devotion to Isr and for promotion of bonds, 1954; man of year award, Kings Co JWV, 1957; award of merit, Dist Attys Assn of State of NY, 1958; award of honor, Parents Assn for Children with Retarded Mental Devl, Inc, 1961; Furtherance of Justice award, Natl Dist Attys Assn; Townsend Harris medal, Alumni Assn, CCNY; Edward S Silver Chair on Criminal Law and Criminality, established at Heb U, Jerusalem; other awards from profsl and philanthropic orgs. Home: 222 E 17 St, Brooklyn, NY. Office: 295 Madison Ave, New York, NY.

SILVER, Emanuel, Eng, physician; b. Newcastle-on-Tyne, Eng, Dec 9, 1922; s. Rose (Kraut); MBBS, Durham U, 1944; DA, Royal Coll Surgs, 1964; m. Stella Cohen, Aug 22, 1946; c: Michele, Alan. Phys since 1948; clinical asst, anaesthetics, Sunderland Group Hosp, since 1964. Lt, RAFVR, 1946-48. Vice-chmn, Newscastle-on-Tyne Bd Schechita; council mem: Jesmond Heb Cong; Newscastle-on-Tyne Repr Council; mem, Fac of Anaesthetists. Home: 11 Glastonbury and Rove, Newcastle-on-Tyne, Eng. Office: 37A Heaton Rd, Newcastle-on-Tyne, Eng.

SILVER, Harold, Isr, social worker; b. Kliusi, Russ, May 18, 1900; s. Anchel and Rebecca (Raginsky); PhB, U Chgo, 1922; MSS, Grad Sch for J Social Work, 1934; m. Fannie Kravchik, Dec 31, 1922; c: Reuben, Rena Schwartzberg. Sr tchr, Paul Baerwald Sch of Social Work, Heb U, since 1965; cons on family services, Min of Social Wfr, Jerusalem, 1963-65; dir, J Family and Children's Service, 1933-65; lectr, social work, Wayne State U, 1934-53, both Detroit, Mich. Mem: Natl Conf on J Communal Service, Farband-LZOA; Isr Assn Academic Social Workers; fmr: pres, mem exec comm, Natl Conf on J Communal Service; chmn, comm on personal standards and practices, natl bd, exec comm, Natl Assn Social Workers; mem adv comm on children's services: Mich State Social Wfr Commn; Mich State Leg Comm on Child Care. Recipient: citation, natl Conf J Communal Service, 1949; merit award, Detroit chap, Natl Assn Social Workers, 1954.

Home: Kibbutz Urim, Negev, Isr. Office: Heb U, Jerusalem, Isr.

SILVER, Isidore, US, educator; b. NYC, Aug 13, 1906; s. David and Dora (Weinstein); BA, CCNY, 1929; att Harvard U, 1929-30; PhD, Columbia U, 1938; m. Edith Schuman, Feb 21, 1943. Rosa May Dist U Prof in Hum, Wash U, St Louis, Mo, since 1967, prof, romance langs, 1957-67; tchr, NYC HSs, 1937-43; research analyst, US Army, Wash, DC, 1943-45; asst prof, Fr, Brown U, 1945-48; prof Fr, U Conn, 1949-57. Chmn: Fr II Group, MLA, 1953; comparative lit sect, Amer Assn Tchrs Fr, 1963; mem: Renaissance Soc of Amer; Assn Guillaume Budé; Assn Intl des Etudes Françaises; Intl Comparative Lit Assn. Author: The Pindaric Odes of Ronsard, 1937; ed, Les Oeuvres de Pierre de Ronsard, Texte de 1587, vols I-VI, 1966-68; co-ed: Pierre de Ronsard: Oeuvres complétes, tome XV, 1-2 parties, 1953-57; tome XVII, 1-2-3 parties; tome XVIII, 1-2 parties, 1961; edition critique par Paul Laumonier, 1959-60; Ronsard and the Hellenic Renaissance in France, Vol I: Ronsard and the Greek Epic, 1961; contbr to profsl jours. Recipient: Guggenheim f, 1948-49; Amer Phil Soc Grants, 1950, 1951, 1961; Fulbright award, 1955-56; grant, Amer Council Learned Soc, 1960-61, Home: 7259 Cornell Ave, St Louis, Mo. Office: Washington U, St Louis, Mo.

SILVER, Maurice Lee, US, neurosurgeon; b. New Brit, Conn, Apr 23, 1918; s. Adolph and Rebecca (Caplan); BS, CCNY, 1938; PhD, U Chgo, 1941; MD, Loyola U, 1945; m. Edna Haun; c: Phebe, Alan, William, Ben, Mitchell, Miriam. Chief, neur surg dept: Miriam Hosp, Providence, RI, 1952-60; St Joseph's Hosp, 1957-60; Kaiser Found Hosp, Honolulu, Hawaii, 1960-63; instr, anat: U of Chgo, 1940-41; Loyola U, 1943-44; lectr, neuro-anat, Johns Hopkins U, 1949-50. Dipl, Amer Bd Neur Surg; f, Intl Coll Surgs; mem: AMA; Amer Assn Anats; Amer Assn Neur Surgs; Soc for Experimental Biol and Med; Amer Assn Neuropath; Acad Cerebral Palsy; Cong Neur Surgs; Sigma Xi. Contbr to profsl jours. Home: 204 Wailupe Circle, Honolulu, Hawaii. Office: Suite 617, Ala Moana Bldg, Honolulu, Hawaii.

SILVER, Melvin J, US, attorney; b. St Paul, Minn, Nov 12, 1904; s. Alexander and Edith (Silberstein); BA, U Minn, 1924; LLB, St Paul Coll of Law, 1927; m. Eleanor Kaufman, 1930; c: Sandra Alch. Pvt practice since 1927; sr mem, law firm, Silver and Ryan, and predecessor firms, since 1946; gen counsel: US Arlington, Inc; Twin city Textile Mills, Inc. Chmn: bd dirs, Sacred Design Assos, Inc; Nathan and Gertrude Shapira Scholarship Found; dist grand lodge, Americanization comm, B'nai B'rith; initial gifts comm, Comty Chest, St Paul, 1937-42; U Minn Scholarship Found, 1954; Edward Hoffman and William Ginsberg Memorial Funds, 1954; Isr Bond Comm; pres, Minn Lodge, B'nai B'rith, 1933-34; fmr chief justice, Alpha Tau Mu; mem: Bd of Educ; Masons, 32 deg; Shriners; capt, ARC drive; clubs: Standard; Hillcrest Country. Recipient: award, B'nai B'rith, 1951; scroll of honor, St Paul Bd of Educ, 1952. Home: 2029 Upper St Dennis Rd, St Paul, Minn. Office: Minnesota Bldg, St Paul, Minn.

SILVER, Samuel, US, govt official, attorney; b. Wilmington, Del, Nov 10, 1914; s. Abraham and Sophia (Levine); att U Del, 1931-33; AB, Amer U, Wash, DC, 1935; LLB, U of Pa Law Sch, 1939; m. Edith Newman, July 2, 1944; c: Ira. Ind relations adv, US Dept of Defense, since 1958, dep dir, off ind relations, 1953-58. Mem: bd of dirs, govt div, UJA. Home: 8808 Spring Valley Rd, Chevy Chase, Md. Office: Dept of Defense, Washington, DC.

SILVER, Samuel, US, physicist, educator; b. Phila, Pa, Feb 25, 1915; s. Boris and Molly (Agrin); MA, Temple U, 1937; PhD, MIT, 1940; hon DSc, Temple U, 1963; m. Marjorie Euster, Dec 28, 1938; c: Daniel, Deborah. Dir, space sci lab, U Cal, Berkeley, since 1960, prof, engr sci since 1953, on staff since 1947; instr, asst prof, Okla U, 1941-43; staff, radiation lab, MIT, 1943-46; Guggenheim f, 1953-54, 1960-61. Pres, Intl Union Radio Sci, 1966-69, chmn, intl comm on radio waves and circuits, 1954-60; f: Amer Phys Soc; Inst Elec and Electronic Engrs; Amer Geophys Union; mem: US Natl Acad Engrs: AAAS; NY Acad Sci; Sigma Xi; clubs: Commonwealth of Cal; Cosmos. Hobby: photography. Office: U of Cal, Berkeley, Cal.

SILVER, Samuel Manuel, US, rabbi; b. Wilmington, Del, June 7, 1912; s. Adolph and Adela (Hacker); BA, U Del, 1933; ordained rabbi, MHL, HUC, 1940; m. Elaine Shapiro, Feb

8, 1953; c: Leon, Joshua, Barry, Noah, Daniel. Rabbi, Temple Sinai since 1959; dir, Hillel Found, U Md, 1940-42; asst rabbi, Anshe Chesed Cong, Cleveland, 1946-52; ed, Amer Judaism, UAHC, 1952-59. Chaplain, US Army, 1942-46. Chmn, social action comm, Stamford-Darien Council of Churches; fmr pres: Assn J Chaplains; Min League, Stamford and Darien; natl chaplain, JWV, since 1965; mem: CCAR; NY Board of Rabbis; natl exec bd, ZOA. Author: Portrait of a Rabbi: Biography of Rabbi Barnett Brickner, 1957; How To Enjoy This Moment, 1968; ed, The Quotable American Rabbis, 1968. Home: 53 Nutmeg Lane, Stamford, Conn. Study: Lakeside Dr, Stamford, Conn.

SILVER, Solomon, US, physician; b. NYC, Jan 23, 1903; s. Adolph and Rachel (Halpern); att Columbia U, 1921-23; MD, Bellevue Med Sch, 1927; m. Mildred Shapiro, Apr 11, 1937. Clinical prof, med, Mt Sinai Sch of Med, since 1967; cons phys, Mt Sinai Hosp, since 1966, att phys since 1946; asst clinical prof, med, Columbia U Coll Phys and Surgs, since 1946. Mem: Amer Thyroid Assn; AMA; Amer Coll Phys; NY Acad Med; Endocrine Soc; Amer Fed Clinical Research. Author: Radioactive Isotopes in Clinical Practice, 1958; Radioactive Isotopes in Medicine and Biology, 1962; Radioactive Nuclides in Clinical Medicine, 3rd ed, 1968; contbr to med publs. Home: 1088 Park Ave, New York, NY. Office: 35 E 85 St, New York, NY.

SILVERBERG, Michael Joel, US, attorney; b. Rochester, NY, Aug 12, 1932; s. Goodman and Minnie (Krovetz); BA, U Rochester, 1954; LLB, Columbia Law Sch, att U Strasbourg, Fr, 1958-59; m. Charlotte Goldman, June 19, 1955; c: Mark, Daniel. Partner, Phillips, Nizer, Benjamin, Krim & Ballon since 1967; asso atty, 1960-67; instr, Columbia Law Sch, 1957-58. Mem: exec bd, NY chap, AJComm; NYC, NY State, Amer Bar Assns. Recipient: Fulbright Scholar, U Strasbourg, 1958-59. Home: 205 West End Ave, New York, NY. Office: 477 Madison Ave, New York, NY.

SILVERMAN, Abner D, US, government official; b. NYC, Jan 8, 1909; s. Abraham and Kate (Goodman); LLM, NYU, 1934; m. Eleanor Frankel, June 8, 1934; c: Kate. Gen dep, Housing Assistance Admn, Dept Housing and Urban Devl, since 1967, on staff since 1948; asst comm: mgmt, Public Housing Admn, since 1956; pvt practice, real estate brokerage and property mgmt, NYC, 1928-38; dir, div local auth mgmt, US Housing Auth, 1938-44; dep asst commn project mgmt, Fed Public Housing Auth, 1944-48; dir mgmt, Amer Comty Builders, 1948. US Army Engrs, 1943-44. Mem: Lambda Alpha, Hon Intl Land Econ Frat, 1968; Natl Assn Housing and Redevl Officials; Fed Bar Assn; NY State Bar. Author: Selected Aspects of Administration of Publicly Owned Housing, 1961; contbr to real estate publs. Recipient: dist service award, Home Finance Agcy, 1958; Rockefeller public service award, 1959. Hobby: photography. Home: 9908 Parkwood Dr, Bethesda, Md. Office: 7 and D St, SW, Washington, DC.

SILVERMAN, Albert A, US, attorney, business exec; b. Copenhagen, Den, Oct 14, 1908; s. Louis and Anna (Mendelsohn); in US since 1909; LLB, Loyola U, 1940; m. Gertrude Adelman, 1929 (div); c: Violet Blumenthal; m. 2nd, Florence Cohen, 1939 (decd). Pres, Vilter Mfg Corp, since 1949, dir since 1945; secy-treas, Cen Ill Co, 1932-42; secy, Rep Drill and Tool Co, 1942-44; asst to treas, Hansen Glove Corps, 1944-45. Pres, Vilter Found, Inc; trustee, Cong Emanu-El B'nai Jeshurun, Milw; mem: gov bd, and lay adv bd, St Joseph's Hosp, Milw; Wis Devl Auth; Cen Ind Devl Comm, Milw Mayor's Econ Growth Council, 1963-66; dir, Milw J Comty Cen; mem: Amer, Chgo, Milw and Wis Bar Assns; Amer Soc Heating, Refrigeration and Air-conditioning Engrs; Amer Foundrymen Soc; Master Brewers Assn of Amer; Milw Assn of Commerce; natl prog comm, ADL, and regional bd, Wis; Wis Soc for J Learning; B'nai B'rith; Zool Soc of Milw Co; Masons, 32 deg; Shriners; Loyola U Alumni Assn; YMCA; clubs: Wis; Emanuel Temple Men's; Milw Athletic; Milw Press. Recipient: citation of merit, Radio Sta WEMP, Milw, 1967; man of year, 1967 award, UNICO Natl, Milw chap, 1967. Home: 1626 N Prospect Ave, Milwaukee, Wis. Office: 2217 First St, Milwaukee, Wis.

SILVERMAN, Alter, US, rabbi; b. Landwarow, Pol, Dec 10, 1909; s. Mordecai and Ida (Wolf); in US since 1926; ordained rabbi, Slobodka Yeshiva, Lith, 1926; BS, NYU, 1931; LLB, Bklyn Law Sch, 1934; m. Edith Breuer, Oct 14, 1945; c: Diane, Ralph, Rubin, Ricka, Marc. Prin, Downtown Talmud Torah, since 1955; rabbi, Cong Anshei Tov, Sunnyside, since 1951; lectr: Young Isr Inst for J Studies, since 1948; Heb Tchrs

Training Sch for Girls, 1945-53; rabbi: Cong Anshei Tov, Bklyn, 1938-41; Heb Educ Alliance of Greenpoint, Bklyn, 1941-51. Exec mem, Union Orthodox Rabbis of US and Can; mem: RabCA; Rabb Bd Gtr NY; Heb Prins' Assn. Home: 47-36 41 St, Sunnyside, NY. Study: 45-16 48 Ave, Woodside, NY.

SILVERMAN, Alvin M, US, journalist, author, public relations cons; b. Louisville, Ky, Jan 16, 1912; s. Alvin and May (Michaels); att W Reserve U, 1930-33; m. Phyllis Israel, Nov 22, 1936; c: Sue, Lorrie, Jane. Pres, Pearl-Silverman Agcy, PR cons, since 1965; Cleveland Plain Dealer, 1957-65, ed columnist, 1941-65, on staff since 1930; mem: bd dirs, Tiffin Amusement Co; Ellet Co; Bklyn Devl Corp. Mem: White House Corresp Assn; Sigma Delta Chi; Zeta Beta Tau; fmr mem: Cleveland Mayor's Fair Employment Practice Comm adv bd; O Gov's Racial Relations Bd; Mayors Comm on Comty Relations; comm, City Council Cancer Fund; clubs: Gridiron; Natl Press; City of Cleveland; Woodmont Country. Author: The American Newspaper, 1965. Recipient: headliner award, best news story, 1941, best feature, 1952, best column, 1953, best weekly column, 1959, 1961, Cleveland Newspaper Guild; man of year award, Lambda chap, Zeta Beta Tau, 1962. Hobbies: golf, dancing. Home: 4740 Connecticut Ave, NW, Washington, DC. Office: 1125 17 St, NW, Washington, DC.

SILVERMAN, Benjamin, US, attorney; b. Savannah, Ga, Jan 23, 1911; s. Harry and Dora (Grushewesky); att Gilbert Johnson Law Sch; m. Edith Berman, Mar 30, 1941; c: Victor, Donna, David. Pvt practice since 1935; atty, Savannah Ind and Domestic Water Supply Commn, 1946-48; mem, Bd of Public Educ, Chatham Co and City of Savannah, 1959-60. Mem: Amer, Savannah, Ga Bar Assns; bd govs, Savannah J Council, since 1957; life, bd dirs, J Educ Alliance, since 1952, fmr pres; Shriners Ritualistic Potentate Alee Temple, fmr pres; Ritualistic Divan; knight cdr of honor, Masons; venerable master of consistory, Scottish Rite, 1968; fmr pres: Savannah Aerie, Eagles; Savannah Lodge, B'nai B'rith; Savannah Dist, ZOA; Hebrah Gemulith Hesed. Home: 4661 Cumberland Dr, Savannah, Ga. Office: 301-304 Two Whitaker Bldg, Bay and Whitaker Sts, Savannah, Ga.

SILVERMAN, Charlotte, US, epidemiologist; b. NYC, May 21, 1913; d. Harry and Gussie (Goldman); BA, Bklyn Coll, 1933; MD, Woman's Med Coll of Pa, 1938; MPH, Johns Hopkins Sch of Hygiene and Public Health, DPH, 1948. Chief, population studies prog, Natl Cen for Radiological Health, since 1968; asst prof, epidemiology, Johns Hopkins Sch of Hygiene and Public Health, since 1956; with USPHS, 1944-45; asst dir, dir, bur TB, Baltimore City Health Dept, 1946-56; chief, div epidemiology and communicable disease control, Md State Dept Health, 1956-59, chief, off planning and research, 1959-62; cons, research utilization br, Natl Inst Mh, 1962-67. F: Amer Coll Preventive Med; Amer Public Health Assn. Author: The Epidemiology of Depression, 1968; contbr to med jours. Recipient: F, Amer Assn U Women, 1941-42. Home: 4977 Battery Lane, Bethesda, Md. Office: Natl Cen for Regiological Health, Rockville, Md.

SILVERMAN, Daniel, US, physician; b. Phila, Pa, May 8, 1910; s. Charles and Fannye (Silberstein); BA, U Wis, 1932; MD, Jefferson Med Coll, 1937; qualified, psychan, Inst Phila Assn for Psychan, 1951; m. Adeline Rubin, June 13, 1936; c: Robert, Peter, Paula. Asso prof, neur, psycht, U of Pa, since 1959, mem fac since 1946; electroencephalographer: Grad Hosp, U of Pa, since 1946; Albert Einstein Med Cen; Cooper Hosp; Bryn Mawr Hosp, all since 1959; psychan, pvt practice, since 1951; asst surg, USPHS Med Cen for Fed Prisoners, 1940-43; training and supervising psychan, Inst of Phila Assn for Psychan, 1963. US Army, 1943-46. Mem: Phila Co Med Soc; AMA; Phila Psycht Soc; Amer Psychoanalytic Assn; Amer Electroencephalographic Soc, pres, 1969; Amer Psycht Assn; Assn for Research in Nervous amd Mental Diseases; AAAS; Kenesset Isr; fmr: chmn, Amer Bd of Qualification in Electroencephalography; pres: Phila Assn for Psychan; mem bd dirs, ed, Bulletin; E Assn for Electroencephalographers, councilor; Phila Neur Soc; club, Rydel Country. Author: chaps in Handbook of Correctional Psychology, 1946; Psychosomatic Medicine, 1962; contbr to profsl jours. Recipient: meritorious service unit plaque, 1945; 2 Bronze Stars, 1945; Clinical Essay prize, Inst of Psychan, London, 1953. Hobbies: music, lit, golf, photography. Home and office: 408 Waring Rd, Elkins Park, Pa.

SILVERMAN, Godfrey Edmond, Isr, editor; b. Liverpool, Eng, Aug 30, 1934; s. J Alex and Enid (Vernick); in Isr since

1967; att Sorbonne, Paris, 1956; BA, Oxford, 1958, MA, 1962; dipl, J studies, J Coll, London, 1961. Asst ed, world lit dept, Ency Judaica, since 1967; dir, Eur off, Bar Ilan U, 1961-66. Russ interpreter, RAF, 1953-55. Hon vice-pres, Ilford and Dis Mizrachi Soc, Eng; ex-officio, Histadrut Olei Britannia, Jerusalem; life mem: Oxford U Union; Oriel Soc, Oxford; fmr: chmn: Oxford U Isr Group; Us Zionist Council; chmn, vice-chmn, Inter-U J Fed; mem, natl exec, Brit Mizrachi Fed; Hitachdut Olei Britannia; mem: Council of Hillel Fed, London; J Hist Soc of Eng. Fmr mem ed bd, Jewish Review; contbr of Articles to Anglo-J press. Hobbies: cantorial music, photography, travel. Home: 9 Habanai St, Bet Hakerem, Jerusalem, Isr. Office: POB 986, Jerusalem, Isr.

SILVERMAN, Ira, US, business exec; b. Bklyn, NY, Mar 10, 1912; s. Irving and Gertrude (Lazarus); att: O State U, 1930-32; NYU, 1932-33; m. Lillian Rappaport, June 24, 1934; c: Stephen. Pres, Elton Leather Corp, since 1954. US Army, 1943-46. Pres, J Comty Cen, Fulton Co, since 1961; Gloversville lodge, B'nai B'rith, 1952-54, pres, Upstate NY Council, 1958-59, mem, bd govs, dist 1, 1958-61, justice, dist court, 1961. Recipient: 3 battle stars. Hobby: fruit farming. Home: Phelps St, Gloversville, NY. Office: 47-49 Spring St, Gloversville, NY.

SILVERMAN, Joseph, US, scientist, educator; b. NYC, Nov 5, 1922; s. Jakob and Mary (Chechick); BA, Bklyn Coll, 1944; AM, Columbia U, 1948, PhD, 1951; m. Joan Jacks, Jan 14, 1951; c: Joshua, David. Prof, nuclear engr, U Md, since 1961; cons, US Dept of Defense, in applied radiation chem to Den, since 1966, with dept since 1962; dir research, Walter Kidde Nuclear Labs, 1952-55; sr sci, bd dirs, Radiation Applications Research Corp, 1959-65. US Army, 1944-46. Prin contrib: atomic battery, 1956; process for removal of strontium 90 from milk, 1959. Secy, isotopes and radiation div, Amer Nuclear Soc; f, Amer Inst Chem; delg to confs: Intl Atomic Energy Agcy, Warsaw, 1959; Salzburg, 1963; Seventh Japan Conf on Radioisotopes, 1966; mem: Amer Chem Soc; Amer Phys Soc; Chem Soc of Wash; Wash Nuclear Soc; Sigma Xi. Contbr to profsl jours. Home: 320 Sisson St, Silver Spring, Md. Office: U of Md, College Park, Md.

SILVERMAN, Leon, US, attorney; b. NYC, June 9, 1921; s. Joseph and Sadie (Zitrin); BA, Bklyn Coll, 1942; LLB, Yale Law School, 1948; att LSE, 1948-49; m. Rita Schwartz, Aug 14, 1949; c: Susan, Jane. Partner, Strasser, Spiegelberg, Fried & Frank, since 1960; asso, Riegelman, Strasser, Schwartz & Spiegelberg, 1949-53; asst US Atty, dist, NY, 1953-56; asst dep, Atty Gen, US Dept of Justice, 1958-60; counsel, Gov Comm on Human Rights, 1967-68. US Army, 1942-45. Counsel, Beth Din of Amer Inc; bd dirs, Legal Aid Soc; f, Amer Coll Trial Lawyers; mem: Amer, NYC, NY State, Fed Bar Assns; Fed Bar Assn of NY, NJ, Conn. Home: 16 Oak Dr, Great Neck, NY. Office: 120 Broadway, New York, NY.

SILVERMAN, Maurice Martin, US, physician; b. Toronto, Can, Mar 28, 1907; s. Louis and Fannie (Cohen); BS, U Mich, 1928; BM, Wayne Med Sch, 1930, MD, 1931; m. Helen Whitman, June 23, 1929; c: Agnes Schussler, Anita Zalesin. Surg: St Marys Hosp since 1931; Mt Carmel Mercy Hosp, since 1939; instr, Mercy Coll; med adv, US Army, Selective Service. Pres, B'nai B'rith; vice-pres, Cong B'nai David; dipl, f, Inter-Coll Surgs; mem: Amer Med Soc; Wayne Co and Mich State Med Socs. Contbr to sci publs. Recipient: Pres Citations, Selective Service Adv, since 1941. Home: 17589 Westhampton Rd, Southfield, Mich. Office: 17301 28 Mile, Detroit, Mich.

SILVERMAN, Morris, US, rabbi, author; b. Newburgh, NY, Nov 19, 1894; s. Simon and Lena (Friedland); AB, Phi Beta Kappa, O State U, 1916; MA, Columbia U, 1917; ordained rabbi, JTSA, 1922, MHL, 1947, DHL, 1952, hon DD, 1956; hon DHumL, O State U, 1965; m. Althea Osber, June 29, 1919; c: Hillel, Arthur. Rabbi em, Emanuel Syn, Hartford, since 1961, rabbi, 1923-61; rabbi: Mt Sinai Temple, Bklyn, NY, 1917-20; Temple Isr, Wash Hgts, NYC, 1920-23. Cofound, dir, Mt Sinai Hosp, since 1923; dir: United J Charities; J Fed; Heb Home for Aged; J Comty Cen, all Hartford, since 1923; mem, chmn, Human Rights and Opportunities Commn, Conn, since 1943; hon pres, Conn Valley United Syn, Amer, since 1963; mem: Amer Acad J Research; Amer J Hist Soc; B'nai B'rith; AJCong; AJComm; NCCJ; ZOA; Hartford Citizens Comm for Civic Progress; fmr: pres: Assn Mins and Rabbis, Hartford; Conn br, United Syn Amer; chmn: Rabb Comm on Sem Affairs, Conn; rabb assembly, Amer, World

J Comm; co-chmn, Clergy Mgmt Conf; mem: Defense Council; ARC Adv Council, both Hartford; exec comm, RA; bd, Overseers JTSA; clubs: hon mem: Tumble Brook Country; Knights of Pythias. Author: Heaven on Your Head, 1964; History of Hartford Jews 1659-1969, pub 1970; ed: Junior Prayer Book: For Sabbath and Festivals, 1933, for High Holidays, 1936; High Holiday Prayer Book, 1939, Isr ed, 1963; Official Prayer Book, Sabbaths, Festivals, 1945; Weekday Prayer Book, 1956; Passover Haggadah, 1959, Span ed, 1962; co-ed: Prayer Book for Summer Camps, 1954; Sidderenu. Recipient: Gtr Hartford Citizen award, 1950; Freedom Found medal and prize, 1951, 1952; citation, Conn State Leg, 1961. Home: 195 Ridgefield St, Hartford, Conn.

SILVERMAN, Morris, US, educator; b. Bx, NY, Mar 20 1924; s. Samuel and Lena (Fridson); BA, Yeshiva U, 1945, BRelE, 1953, MS, 1961; MA, Bklyn Coll, 1949; m. Gilda Semmel, 1948; c: Samuel, Elliot, Gail. Registrar, Yeshiva U, since 1960, coll registrar, 1949-60, U coord admissions, 1955-58, prof, hist, since 1966, on fac since 1953; asst libr, Yeshivah of Flatbush, Bklyn, 1945-48. Mem: Amer Schs of Oriental Research; AAUP; NEA; Amer Assn for Higher Educ; Soc for Advancement Educ; Amer, ME Assns of Coll Registrars; Citizens Union, NYC; B'nai Zions; Rel Zionists of Amer; Amer Friends of Isr; Exploration Soc. Home: 1271 E 9 St, Brooklyn, NY. Office: 500 W 185 St, New York, NY.

SILVERMAN, Oscar A, US, educator; b. Uniontown, Pa, Feb 13, 1903; s. George and Leah (Cohen); BA, Yale U, 1925, PhD, 1941; MA, U Wis, 1926; m. Margaret de Morini, 1932 (div); c: Clare, Ann. Prof, Eng SUNY, Buffalo, since 1943, dir em librs, since 1968, dir, librs 1960-68, on fac since 1926; asst, Eng, U Wis, 1926-28; f, Grad Sch, Yale U, 1928-30; instr, Biarritz-Amer U, Biarritz, Fr, 1945-46; visiting f, gen educ, Harvard U, 1953-54. Clubs: Grolier, NY, Thursday, Buffalo. Ed: The Management of Universities, 1955; James Joyce's Epiphanies, 1956; book reviewer on radio sta in Buffalo, 1940-47. Home: 786 W Ferry St, Buffalo, NY. Office: SUNY, Buffalo, NY.

SILVERMAN, S Richard, US, audiologist, educator; b. NYC, Oct 2, 1911; s. David and Sarah (Sheiken); BA, Cornell U, 1933; MS, Wash U, 1938, PhD, 1942; DL, Gallaudet, 1961; DHL, HUC, 1962; LLD, Emerson U, 1966; m. Sara Hill, Sep 3, 1938; c: Rebecca. Chmn, Natl Adv Comm on Educ for Deaf, HEW, since 1966; dir, Cen Inst for Deaf, St Louis, Mo, since 1947, Rockefeller f, 1933-35, instr, 1935-41, admn exec, 1941-47; prof, audiology, Wash U, St Louis, since 1949, mem staff since 1946, lectr, otolaryngology, Med Sch, 1946-49; dir, hearing and deafness project, US Off Sci Research and Devl at Cen Inst for Deaf, 1944-46; audiological cons to: US Secy of War, 1944-46; USAF, 1951; guest lectr: U Tex; State U of Ia; Northwestern U; Pa State Coll; U Tenn; Ind State Tchrs Coll; U London, Eng; U Utrecht, Netherlands. F: Royal Soc Med, Eng; Amer Speech and Hearing Soc, fmr pres; hon F, Amer Coll Dents; pres, Alexandre Graham Bell Assn for Deaf, since 1957; mem bd: Amer Hearing Soc, since 1956; Social Planning Council, since 1957; mem, adv councils on: Handicapped Children, S Regional Educ Bd, since 1956; speech and hearing, HEW, since 1957; mem: bd mgrs, St Louis League for Hard Hearing; comm on hearing in children, Amer Acad of Ophthal and Otolaryngology, since 1957; Acoustical Soc Amer; Volta Speech Assn for Deaf; Conf of Execs, Amer Schs for Deaf; Natl Forum on Deafness and Speech Path; Natl Adv Council on Vocational Rehab; AAAS; Sigma Xi; Sigma Alpha Mu; Kappa Delta Pi; Phi Delta Kappa; St Louis Ear, Nose and Throat Soc; Kan City Otolaryngological Soc; Cleveland Otolaryngological Soc; La Federacion Argentina de Sociedades de Otorinolaringologia; Sociedad de Oto-Rino-Laringologia de Rio de Janeiro; Sociedad Chilena de Oto-Rino-Laringologia; club, Cosmos, Wash, DC. Asso ed: The Laryngoscope; Jour of Speech and Hearing Disorders; Jour of Exceptional Children, 1948-53; contbr to US, fgn profsl publs. Recipient: cert of appreciation, US War Dept, 1946; hons, Amer Speech and Hearing Assn, 1954; dist alumni assn, Wash U Second Cent Convocation, 1955; Edward Allen Fay award, Conf of Execs, Amer Schs for Deaf, 1965. Home: 7574 Cornell Ave, University City, Mo. Office: 818 S Kings Hwy, St Louis, Mo.

SILVERMAN, Samuel J, US, jurist, attorney; b. Odessa, Russ, Sep 25, 1908; s. Benjamin and Ida (Karlitsky); in US since 1913; BA, Columbia U, 1928, LLB, U Law Sch, 1930; m. Claire Gfroerer, Aug 21, 1941. Surrogate, NY Co, since 1967; sr atty, US RR Retirement Bd, 1936-37; asst corp counsel, NYC, 1938-40; asst to trustee, Asso Gas and Elec Co, in reorg, 1940-44; head atty, Fgn Econ Admn, 1944; lectr, Practising Law Inst, Harvard, Yale, Columbia Law Schs, 1955-60; mem, law firm, Paul, Weiss, Rifkind, Wharton and Garrison, 1946-62; justice, NY State Supr Court, 1963-66. F, Amer Coll Trial Lawyers; chmn, civil rights comm, NY Co Lawyers Assn, 1950-57; dir, U Settlement, since 1961; spec counsel, NY State Dem Comm, 1962; mem: Assn Bar, NYC; Phi Beta Kappa. Home: 210 E 68 St, New York, NY. Office: 31 Chambers St, New York, NY.

SILVERMAN, Saul, US, organization exec; New Orleans La, June 27, 1924; s. Samuel and Fannie (Aronson); BS, Loyola U, 1949; MA, MS, NYU, 1951; grad work: Columbia U, 1949-50; U Mich, 1953-55; m. Rita Geiges, Dec 18, 1949; c: Barry, Michael. Exec-dir: Phoenix J Fed, since 1966; Phoenix JCC, 1966-68; Salt Lake City United J Comty Cen and Wfr Fund, 1963-66; fmr exec-dir, Holyoke CJA and J Cen, Mass; fac mem, Ariz State U Grad Sch; fmr fac mem: U Utah; U Conn; U Omaha. US Army, 1943-46. Chmn: Migrant Opportunity Prog, since 1967, mem bd mgrs, 1967-68; Mayor's Comm "Phoenix Forward," natl bd mem, JDC; charter mem: Natl Assn Social Workers; Natl Assn J Communal Service; mem, steering comm, W Region leadership conf, UJA; mem: Midrasha-Phoenix J Educ Prog, 1966-68; Temple Beth Isr; J Family and Children Service; Phoenix Bikkur Cholim; Hillel Council, Gtr Phoenix; Gtr Phoenix Council, ADL; Amer Friends Heb U; ZOA; Amer Camping Assn; J Publ Soc; Utah Gov Conf on Aging, 1965-66; fmr pres: B'nai B'rith lodge, Neb sect, Amer Camping Assn; Neb group work sect, Natl Assn Social Workers; Omaha council, Adult Educ Council. Recipient: citation, B'nai B'rith lodge, Omaha, 1959; adm, Neb Navy, 1959; medal, State of Isr, 1963. Hobbies: travel, music, photography, sports. Home: 1241 E Gardenia Dr, Phoenix, Ariz. Office: 1718 W Maryland Ave, Phoenix, Ariz.

SILVERMAN, Sol, US, attorney; b. San Francisco, June 25, 1900; s. Jacob and Anna (Cohn); AB, U Cal, Berkeley, 1923, JD, 1926; m. Frances Bernstein; c: Jack, Sol; m. 2nd, Carolyn Stern, Dec 22, 1946. Pvt practice since 1926; publisher, ed, Emanu-El and J Jour, 1930-45. Pres: JNF; ZOA, SF dist; chmn, Histadrut; mem: SF Bar Assn, bd dirs, chmn, SF Bar Jour; Cal State Bur, delg, mem, leg comm, chmn, Cal State Bar Jour; Amer Judicature Soc; Amer Bar Assn; Natl Conf Commns Uniform State Laws; Cal Commn on Uniform State Laws; delg, Natl Leg Conf; Interstate Coop Commn; commn, Constitutional Rev Commn, Cal; chmn, Cal Comm for Boxing Safeguards; life mem: U Cal Alumni; clubs: Press; Commonwealth. Spec interests: Isr, law. Home: 1200 California St, San Francisco, Cal. Office: 1901 Mills Tower, 220 Bush St, San Francisco, Cal.

SILVERMAN, William B, US, rabbi; b. Altoona, Pa, June 4, 1913; s. Simon and Rae (Friedland); BA, W Reserve U, O, 1935, BHL, 1937; MHL, ordained rabbi, HUC, 1941, DHL, 1966; hon DD, Northland Coll, 1950; m. Pearl Biales, June 23, 1940; c: Joel, Eldon. Rabbi: B'nai Jehudah, Kan City, Mo, since 1960; Temple Beth-El, Battle Creek, Mich, 1941-43; Temple Emanuel, Gastonia, NC, 1943-46; Temple Emanuel Duluth, Minn, 1946-50; Cong Ohabai Sholom, Nashville, Tenn, 1950-60; civilian chaplain, Fort Custer, Mich, 1941-43. Organized adv comm, Juvenile Court, Gastonia, 1944; chmn, Minn Gov's Commn on Parents and Family, 1949; mem: Boy Scouts; speakers bur, NCCJ; comm on psycht, CCAR; Mo Health and Wfr Div; Juvenile Delinquency Comm; natl prog comm, B'nai B'rith; Zionists; Radio and TV Council; club, Rotary. Author: The High Cost of Jewish Living, 1948; Judaism and Christianity Compare Notes, 1949; The Still Small Voice, 1953; Strength of Faith, 1954; The Still Small Voice Today, 1957; Rabbinic Stories for Christian Ministers and Teachers, 1958; God Help Me, 1961; Religion for Skeptics, 1967; Judaism and Christianity-What We Believe, 1968; Basic Reform Judaism, 1969; conductor, radio and TV progs. Home: 8401 Briar Lane, Prairie Village, Kansas City, Mo. Study: 712 E 69 St, Kansas City, Mo.

SILVERMAN, William M, US, attorney; b. Boston, Mass, Oct 21, 1896; s. Isadore and Rebecca (Kudisch); AB, Harvard U, 1918, LLB, 1920; m. Edith Bronstein, June 28, 1928; c: Richard, Donald. Head, law firm, Silverman, Kudisch & O'Neil, since 1942; pvt practice since 1920; mem, Mass Leg, 1927-28. Ensign, USNR, WW I. Mem, bd trustees, Temple Isr, Boston, Mass, since 1956; vice-pres, NE region, UAHC, since 1952; mem: bd, Coat and Suit Natl Recovery Bd; Brookline Rep Town Commn; commn, Interstate Compact Minimum Wage, 1939-44; pres, Commercial Law League of Amer, 1945-46;

mem: Boston, Norfolk Co, Mass Amer Bar Assns; Amer Law Inst; Sigma Alpha Mu; Masons; Shriners; AJComm. Home: 60 Longwood Ave, Brookline, Mass. Office: 100 State St, Boston, Mass.

SILVERS, Seymour H, US, dermatologist; b. Lodz, Pol, May 21, 1901; s. Nathan and Dina (Reingold); in US since 1920; BA, U of ND, 1925, MS, 1926; MD, Columbia U, 1928; m. Sarah Rashal, June 28, 1931; c: Anita, David. Cons, dermat div, Kings Co Hosp Cen, since 1967; clinical asso prof, SUNY Sch of Med, since 1956; att dermat: Wyckoff Hgts Hosp; Bethany Deaconess Hosp; Menorah Home and Hosp, all Bklyn, NY; cons, Selective Service bds, WW II. Dipl, Amer Bd Dermat and Syphilology; f: Amer Coll Phys; NY Acad Med; Amer Acad of Dermat and Syphilology; Amer Geriatrics Soc; fmr pres, secy, ed of Bklyn Dermat Soc; mem: AMA; NY State and Kings Co Med Soc; Amer Med Writers Assn; AAAS; ACLU; club, Roslyn Country. Contbr to profsl jours. Recipient: Selective Service Medal, US Cong, 1945; cert of appreciation, US Pres, 1945. Home: 17 Horseshoe Lane, Roslyn Heights, NY. Office: 928 Bushwick Ave, Brooklyn, NY.

SILVERSTEIN, Abe, US, engineer; b. Terre Haute, Ind, Sep 15, 1908; s. Joseph and Eva (Levine); BS, Rose Poly Inst, Terre Haute, 1929, ME, 1934; hon DSc, 1959; hon DEngr, Case Inst Tech, Cleveland, O, 1958; hon DHL, Yeshiva U, NY, 1960; hon, D Applied Sci, Fenn Coll, Cleveland, 1964; hon DSc, John Caroll U, Cleveland, 1967; m. Marion Crotser, Dec 5, 1950; c: Judith, Joseph, David. Dir, Lewis Research Cen, NASA, Cleveland since 1961, chief, engine installation research div, 1943-45, chief, wind tunnel and flight research div, 1945-49, chief, research, 1949-52; asso dir, 1952-58, dir, off of space flight progs, Wash, DC, 1958-61; aerodynamic research engr, Natl Adv Comm for Aeronautics, Langley Field, Va, 1929-40, head, full scale wind tunnel, 1940-43. F: Amer Inst Aeronautics and Astronautics; Amer Astronautical Soc; Royal Aeronautical Soc; mem: adv council, Baldwin-Wallace Coll; Intl Acad Astronautics; Natl Acad Engr; Tau Beta Pi; Carnegie-Mellon U Mech Engr Visiting Comm; trustee, Cleveland State U; Case W Reserve U; repr US: Jt meeting, Inst of Aeronautical Scis and Royal Aeronautical Soc, London, 1947; lectr: Inst of Aerospace Scis, 1948; 49th Wilbur Wright Memorial Lecture, London, 1961; presented paper to 5th Cong Intl Council of Aeronautical Scis, London, 1966; Biennial Theodore von Karman Memorial Lecture, 10th Isr Annual Conf on Aviation Astronautics, Tel Aviv, Isr, 1968. Contbr to tech and sci jours. Recipient: exceptional civilian service award, USAF, 1960; medal, NASA, 1961; career service award, Natl Civil Service League, 1962; Sylvanus Albert Reed award, Amer Inst Aeronautics and Astronautics, 1964; Louis W Hiel Space Transport award, 1967; NASA dist service medal; Rockefeller Public Service award, 1968. Home: 21160 Seabury Ave, Fairview Park, O. Office: 21000 Brookpark Rd, Cleveland, O.

SILVERSTEIN, Reuben, B, US, physician; b. Bklyn, NY, Aug 17, 1905; s. Hyman and Yetta (Brodsky); att NYU, 1922-25; MD, NY Med Coll, 1929; m. Mollie Silver, Nov 24, 1929; c: Lois Werner, Seth. Pvt practice since 1930; adj gyn and obstet, Bklyn Women's Hosp, 1930-33, adj roentgenologist, 1933-53; asso att roentgenologist, E NY Dispensary, Bklyn, 1933-35; examining phys, Selective Service, Queens, 1941-45; med instr, ARC, Jamaica, 1942-45. F: NY Card Soc; Amer Coll Angiology; Amer Geriatric Soc; mem: Amer Acad of Gen Practice; NY Med Coll Alumni Assn; Kings Co Med Soc; Laurelton J Cen; Phi Lambda Kappa; B'nai B'rith. Recipient: Selective Service Medal, US Cong, 1945; Cert Appreciation, Pres US, 1945. Home: 226-14-137 Ave, Laurelton, NY. Office: 122-17 134 St, S Ozone Park, NY.

SILVERSTEIN, Saul, US, accountant; b. NYC, Aug 29, 1916; s. Morris and Hannah (Schneider); BBA, CCNY, 1936, CPA, 1940; m. Helen Garlen, Aug 11, 1940; c: Deborah, Daniel. Pvt practice since 1945; regional inves staff, OPA, 1942-44; civilian technician, US Army, 1944-45. Pres: Kiwanis, 1964; Temple Beth El, 1958-60, 1963-65, 1968; Zionist dist, 1947-48; Cerebral Palsy Assn, 1951-52; vice-pres, C of C, 1953-54; secy-treas, Glen Falls Hosp, since 1957; treas, Isr Emergency Fund, 1967; chmn, Glen Falls UJA, 1968-69; bd dirs: Glen Falls Forum, 1952-55; Comty Service Council, 1953-54; mem: NY State Soc CPAs; Amer Inst CPAs. Home: 15 Lincoln Ave, Glen Falls, NY. Office: 50 Everts Ave, Glen Falls, NY.

SILVERSTEIN, Saul M, US, business exec; b. Boston, Mass, Aug 25, 1900; s. Jacob and Rebecca (Rajunsky); BS, MIT,

1921, MS, 1922; m. Rebecca Berger, 1928; c: Lee, Phyllis Rubinovitz, Barbara Gersin. Chmn, Rogers Corp in Rogers, Manchester, Woodstock, Conn, and Chandler, Ariz, since 1966, pres, 1946-66, on staff since 1930; instr, ChemE, Grad Sch, MIT, 1922-23; research engr, Guggenheim Bros, NYC, 1923-24; dir, ind research div, Bigelow, Kent, Willard and Co, Boston, 1924-30; vice-pres and org, First Natl Bank, Manchester, 1950-58; lectr, conductor sems abroad, sponsored by US State Dept, in ind and lab, since 1952; conductor, mgmt sems abroad. Hon life pres, Temple Beth Sholom, since 1949, pres, 1938-49; vice-pres, Council for Intl Progress in Mgmt, since 1959; trustee, States Exposition; mem, bd dirs, Newington Hosp for Crippled Children; mem: B'nai B'rith; AJCong; ZOA; Haifa Technion Soc; Masons; adv comm, CIPM's Intl Enterprise F Prog; Conn State Commn, Child Lab Laws; Manchester Hum Relations Commn; hon mem, Beta Gamma Sigma; club, Stein. Recipient: citations: JTSA, 1949; VFW, 1957; Jr C of C, Manchester. 1958; Govt of Turkey; McAuliffe Medal, Diocesan Lab Inst, Hartford, 1959; hum relations award, Soc for Advancement of Mgmt,1961. Home: 28 Stephen St, Manchester, Conn. Office: Rogers Corp, Rogers, Conn.

SILVERSTONE, Alex Eli, Eng, rabbi, author; b. Manchester, Eng, Mar 9, 1897; s. Simon and Matilda (Levenson); ordained rabbi, Yeshiva, Manchester, 1918; MA, PhD, U Manchester, 1924; m. Helen Amias (decd); c: Sheila Nadel, Valerie Bach, Naomi Chachik; m. 2nd, Jessie Weitzman, Sep 5, 1946. Rabbi em, Southport Heb Cong, since 1967, rabbi, 1927-67; rabbi, Sunderland Heb Cong, 1924-27. Officiating chaplain, Brit Army, 1940-45. Author: Aquila and Onkelos, 1931; The Great Beyond, 1932; Marganita Tava, Heb Responsa, 1956; ed, What I Believe, by fourteen modern thinkers; trans, Tractate Shebuoth (Soncino Talmud); contbr lit articles to: Jewish Chronicle, Jewish Review, both London; S Afr Jewish Observer, Johannesburg; other publs. Pres: Friends Heb U; mem, Convocation, Manchester U, both Southport br; fmr: pres: Mizrachi Soc; Zionist Soc, both Southport; chaplain, to two successive mayors, Southport. Home: 37 Alexandra Rd, Southport, Lancs, Eng.

SILVERSTONE, Max, Isr, banker, accountant; b. Eng, Mar 3, 1909; s. Solomon and Sophia (Katz); in Isr since 1933; BSc, physics, U Liverpool, Eng, 1929, BSc, 1st class hon, math, 1930, dipl, educ, 1931; m. Jeanette Cohen, Aug 13, 1933; c: Raphael, Esther Daniels. Asst gen mgr, chief insp, Bank Leumi le-Isr, Tel Aviv, Isr; research on tides, U Liverpool, 1932-33; math, sci master, Corinth Coll, Cheltenham, Eng, 1931-32; math, sports master, King Edward VI Sch, Bury St Edmunds, Eng, 1933; AACCA, London 1938; CPA, Isr, 1954. Mem: Adv Council, Brit Immigrants' Assn, Isr; Amer Intl Acad; Masonic bodies: US; grand royal arch chap, Isr, 1st grand prin; asso: Assn CPAs and Corp Acctnts, London; Inst of Taxation, London; Inst of Bankers, London; Inst of Internal Auditors: NY; Isr. Office: Bank Leumi le-Isr, Head Office, POB 2, Tel Aviv, Isr.

SILVERZWEIG, David F, US, attorney; b. Pol, Feb 22, 1907; s. Samuel and Fannie (Fromer); in US since 1914; LLB, U Chgo, 1933. Pvt practice. Mem, bd dirs, Amer Friends Heb U; bd mgrs, Decalogue Soc of Lawyers, since 1940, pres, 1943-44, ed, Jour, 1939-47; pres, Chgo, council, AJCong, 1952-55; mem, bd dirs, Bur on J Employment Problems, 1953-55; mem: Chgo, Ill, and Amer Bar Assns; Amer J Hist Soc; United HIAS Service; ACLU; Chgo Loop Syn; club, Covenant. Home: 6433 N Newgard Ave, Chicago, Ill. Office: 100 N LaSalle St, Chicago, Ill.

SIMA, Miron, Isr, artist; b. Proskurov, Russ, Jan 22, 1902; s. Benjamin and Bela (Sobol); in Isr since 1933; studied: State Sch of Art, Odessa, 1920-22; State Acad of Fine Arts, Dresden, 1924-30. Found, dir, Jerusalem Sch for Painting and Sculpture, 1939-44. One-man shows: Tel Aviv Mus, 1936, 1940; Petrides-Bosc Gal, Paris, 1947; Natl Bezalel Mus, Jerusalem, 1950, 1959; John Heller Gal, NY, 1958; Doll and Richards Gal, Boston, 1953; Albert H Wiggin Gal, Boston Public Libr, 1953; Mus Modern Art, Haifa, 1956; exhbs drawings from Eichmann Trial, Jerusalem, Tel Aviv, Haifa, 1961; Nassauischer Kunstverein Mus, Wiesbaden, 1967; Kunstverein Salzgitter, 1967; Mus Göttingen, 1967; group shows: 100 Years of Painting in Saxonia, Ger; Ger Graphic, Prague; Sachsischer Kunstverein, Dresden; Art in Homes, Dresden; Dresdner Kunstgenossenschaft Exhb, Dresden; Intl Exhb, ILO, Geneva; Intl Exhb of Black and White, Lugano; Biennale, Venice; Intl Biennale Exhb of Prints, Tokyo; Exhb of Isr Art, Mus d'Art Moderne, Paris; Intl Exhb of Gravure, Ljubliana; Intl Prints, Cincinnati; Exch Exhb of Graphic

Art, Belgrade, Tokyo, Warsaw; Mostra Intl della Grafica, It; Triennale of Color Woodcuts, Capri, It; represented in mus and public collections: Natl Bezalel Mus, Jerusalem; Mus Tel Aviv; Mus Modern Art, Haifa; Mishkan le'omanut, Ein Harod, Isr; Metrop Mus; Mus Modern Art, both NY; Mus Fine Arts, Boston; Wiggin Collection, Boston Public Libr; Mus Fine Arts, Phila; Fogg Mus Art, Mass; Mus Arts, Baltimore; Truman Mus, Mo; SF Mus Art; Cal Palace of Legion of Honor, SF; Co Mus, LA; UAHC; Dropsie Coll, Phila; Brandeis U, Mass; J Mus, SF; J Mus, Boston; Graphic Collection, Eidgenossenschaftliche Technische Hochschule, Zurich; Pol Natl Mus, Warsaw. Publs: Reminiscences of Pogroms, 1924; Journey into the Orient, 1926; Hannah Rovina on Stage and in Life, 1937; Jerusalem, 1952; Facing the Sad Symbol, 1969. Recipient: prize, City of Dresden, 1932; Dizengoff prize, Tel Aviv, 1936, 1938; prize, City of Jerusalem, 1957; medal, City of Jerusalem, 1969. Home and studio: 6 Ben Sira St, Jerusalem, Isr.

SIMIAN, Maurice Ludwig, Isr, animal trainer; b. Plotsk, Lith, Oct 4, 1917; s. Alfonses and Fruma (Cohen); in Isr since 1935; grad, biol, Heb U, Jerusalem, 1941; m. Zippora Skepitsky, Apr 14, 1936; c: Moshe, Shlomo, Ruth. Chief dog controller, Tel Aviv Munic, since 1954; adv on animal breeding, Weitzmann Inst, since 1952; chief dog trainer, IDF, 1948-51. Maj, IDF. Prin contrib: invention of Simian Dog Muzzle; Simian method of detecting dog meat in meat products. Pres: Intl Fed for Advancement Space Flight; Heb Friends of Plotsk; asso mem: Intl Soc of Dog Breeders. Author: Dogs-My Life, 1953; Breeding of Animals in Hot Climates, 1958. Recipient: Golden Bone award, Isr Dog Soc, 1963. Hobbies: chess, Mah Jongg. Home: 37 Hazait St, Ramat Gan, Isr. Office: 84 Mikveh Israel St, Tel Aviv, Isr.

SIMKE, Ernest E, Phillippines, bus exec; b. Berlin, Ger, June 10, 1908; s. Leopold and Berta (Koschminski); in Philippines since 1932; m. Rita Broniatowski, May 29, 1941 (decd); c: Susan, Jack. Hon Isr Consul-Gen, since 1950; asst gen mgr, vice-pres, Levy Hermanos Inc, since 1948; pres, Estraco Inc, since 1949; expert, hides and skins: Arnhold & Co, Ltd, Shanghai, 1928-30; Olivier-Chine, Hankow, 1930-32. Treas, J Comty, Philippines, since 1950, pres, 1947-50; mem: Amer C of C; Philippine C of C; Makati Mfrs Assn; Masons; Guatama Consistory; clubs: Valley Golf; Manila Polo; Span Casino; Army and Navy; Bagulo Country. Spec interests: Intl politics, hist. Home: 24 Cambridge Circle, N Forbes Pk, Makati, Rizal, Philippines. Office: POB 3150, Manila, Philippines.

SIMKIN, Benjamin, US, physician; b. Phila, Pa, Apr 17, 1921; s. Aaron and Rebecca (Schor); AB, magna cum laude, U of S Cal, 1941, MD, Sch of Med, 1944; m. Muriel Shapiro, 1947; c: Barbara, Jonathan. Att phys in med, and chief, endocrinology, Cedars-Sinai Med Cen, LA, since 1960, research f, med, 1946-47; pvt med practice since 1950; asst clinical prof, med, U of S Cal Sch of Med, since 1950; f, metabolic and endocrine research, Michael Reese Hosp, Chgo, 1947-48; research f, diabetes, May Inst for Med Research, J Hosp, Cincinnati, 1948-49. Mem: Endocrine Soc; Soc for Experimental Biol and Med; W Soc for Clinical Research; Amer Fed for Clinical Research; AMA; Amer Diabetes Assn; Phi Beta Kappa; Sigma Xi; Phi Kappa Phi; concert master, LA Doctors' Symphony Orch. Contbr to med jours. Hobbies: music, violin. Home: 701 Amalfi Dr, Pacific Palisades, Cal. Office: 6423 Wilshire Blvd, Los Angeles, Cal.

SIMMENAUER, Felix, Eng, author-architect; b. Berlin, Ger, Oct 9, 1903; s. Heinrich and Selma (Ottenstein); in Eng since 1961; att: Kunstgewerbe und Handwerker Schule, 1921-22; Humboldt Schule, 1923-25, both Berlin; Ill Inst of Tech, Chgo, 1947; m. Charlotte Schwarzmann, June 15, 1937. Ret; asso, Prof Bruno Paul, architect, 1927-31; own firm, 1931-61; tchr, art and interior design, YMCA, Chgo, Ill; lectr, J Art, Theodor Herzl Soc, London. Vice-chmn, Northeast Hyde Park Council, Chgo, Ill, 1956-58; mem: Amer Inst Interior Designers, Ill; Cartell J Student Frat, Gt Brit. Contbr articles and poems to J publs; produc, dir: films: Maccabim, 1931; The First Maccabiah, Tel Aviv 1932; author, dir, Theodor Herzl Night, play, Berlin 1931. Recipient: gold and bronze medals, athletics, I Maccabiah, Tel Aviv 1932; spec commendation, Amer Inst Interior Designers; Good Citizen award, Hyde Park Kenwood Comty Conf, both 1956. Hobbies: painting, writing. Home: 25 Princess Court, Queensway, London W2, Eng.

SIMON, Abraham, US, rabbi; b. NYC, Sep 30, 1909; s. Harry and Sarah (Horowitz); BA, CCNY, 1928; Dipl, Tchrs Inst,

JTSA, 1927, MHL, ordained rabbi, 1932, DD, 1966; m. Fannie Friedenberg, Oct 30, 1932; c: Ruth Ritterband, Israel, Judith. Rabbi; Cong Beth Abraham, since 1965; Middleton Heb Assn, NY, 1934-48; chaplain, NYC Reformatory, 1934-48. Maj, USAAF, 1943-46. Co-chmn, NCCJ, Bridgeton; exec: Bridgeton Ministerial Assn; Commn on J Chaplaincy, JWB; chaplain, Bridgeton Rotary; mem, RA; club, Rotary. Home: 5 Russell Sage Ave, Bridgeton, NJ. Study: Fayette St and Belmont Ave, Bridgeton, NJ.

SIMON, Arthur Sigmund, US, merchant; b. Chgo, Ill, Oct 22, 1891; s. Charles and Leah (Rosenthal); m. Besse Simon; c: Charlotte Hurwick. Pres, Simon Bros, Inc, wholesale grocers, since 1924. Pres, JWF, 1946-47; Comty Chest, 1944; B'nai B'rith, 1933; Temple Beth El, 1932-41; chmn, UJA, 1948; all South Bend, Ind; trustee, Bellefaire J Children's Home, Cleveland, O; mem: Izaak Walton League; Culver Mil Acad; Fathers' Assn; Masons, 32 deg; Shriners; clubs: Rotary; Ind; City. Home: 307 S Coquillard Dr, South Bend, Ind. Office: 402-20 South Joseph St, South Bend, Ind.

SIMON, Benjamin, US, psychiatrist, neurologist; b. Ponievej, Russ, May 31, 1903; s. Max and Eva (Yudelevit); in US since 1905; att Johns Hopkins U, 1921-23; BA, Stanford U, 1925; MA, 1927; MD, Wash U, 1931; att Boston Psychoanalytic Inst, 1950-55; m. Sarah Scrimshaw, 1935; c: Robert, John, Richard. Pvt practice, psycht and neur, since 1949; pres, Bay State Med Assos; dir, psycht, Westborough State Hosp, Mass, since 1960; cons: psycht and neur, Symmes Hosp, Arlington, Mass, since 1949; psycht, VA Hosp, Bedford, Mass, since 1950; lectr, postgrad sems, psycht and neur: Conn, since 1947; Mass, since 1950; lectr: Harvard U, since 1956; Boston U, since 1950; Wesleyan U, Trinity Coll, both Conn, 1947-49; asst, phys, Stanford U, 1926-27; res in neur, Boston City Hosp, 1933-34; sr psycht, Worcester State Hosp, Mass, 1936-41, on staff from 1934; Rockefeller f, neur, Natl Hosp, London, 1937-38, med registrar 1938; clinical dir, Conn State Hosp, Middletown, 1941-49; asst clinical prof, psycht and Mh, Yale U Sch of Med, 1947-50; att psycht, VA Hosp, Newington, Conn, 1947-50; dir, Ring Sanatorium, Arlington Hgts, Mass, 1949-59; asst clinical prof, psycht, Tufts U Sch of Med, Boston, Mass; cons: HEW, USPHS. Lt col, US Army MC, 1942-46, chief, neuropsycht service, Mason Gen Hosp, 1943-46, cons, Fac of Command and Gen Staff Coll, Ft Leavenworth, 1948. Dipl: Natl Bd Med Examiners; Amer Bd Psycht and Neur; Bd Mental Hosp Admnr; f: AMA; Mass Med Soc; Amer Psycht Assn; Amer Assn on Mental Deficiency; Amer Group Psychotherapy Assn; AAAS; Amer Acad Psychan; Amer Coll Psychts; chmn: adv comm on occupational therapy educ, Council on Med Educ and Hosps, 1957-63, comm on therapeutic care, 1957-68; prog comm, Mass Psycht Assn, since 1953; Mass Med Soc, 1957-58; pres: Mass Soc for Research in Psycht, 1952-53; NE dist br, Amer Psycht Assn, 1956-57; Natl Assn Pvt Psycht Hosps, 1958-59; Middlesex chap, Res Offs Assn of US, 1947-48; vice-pres: Amer br, Intl League Against Epilepsy, 1951-52; Mass Psycht Soc, 1954-55; mem: Commn on Vets, since 1961; Smith, Kline and French awards Comm, since 1961; med adv council, Amer Occupational Therapy Assn, since 1954, mem, adv comm, field cons in psycht, since 1961; profs adv bd, Amer Registry Phys Therapists, since 1958; bd dirs, Assn Gen Hosp Psychts, since 1963; Assn Mil Surgs of US; Group for Advancement of Psycht; Assn for Research in Nervous and Mental Diseases; NE Soc of Psycht; NE Soc for Group Psychotherapy; Conn State Med Soc; Conn Soc for Neur and Psycht; Conn Coop Labotomy Comm; Boston Soc for Neur and Psycht; Natl, Conn and Mass Assns for Mh; Conn Soc for Mental Hygiene; Mystic Valley and Arlington Mh Assns; Johns Hopkins, Stanford and Wash U Alumni Assns; Alpha Omega Alpha; Sigma Xi; Amer Legion; Task Force to Study Gtr Participation Psychts in State and Local Med Socs, since 1968; Task Force Redistricting Areas, since 1968; hon mem, Que dist br, Amer Psycht Assn, since 1968; clubs: Arlington-Lexington Drs; Boston. Author: Toward Therapeutic Care, 1961; Crisis in Psychiatric Hospitalization, 1969; co-atuhor: Rehabilitation of the Mentally Ill: Social and Economic Aspects, 1957; The Interrupted Journey, 1966; produc psycht film, Let There Be Light, with Johns Huston, 1946; mem, ed comm, Intl Jour of Group Psychotherapy, since 1953; contbr to profsl publs. Recipient: Army commendation medal, 1946; Legion of Merit, 1946; Meritorious Service Unit Plaque, 1946. Hobbies: photography, fencing. Home: 141 Hillside Ave, Arlington Heights, Mass. Office: 10 Hawthorne Pl, Charles River Park, Boston, Mass.

SIMON, Bernard, US, journalist, organization exec; b. W New York, NJ, May 7, 1920; s. Max and Mary (Kell); BSc, NYU, 1941; m. Dorothy Ligeti, May 24, 1942; c: Gary, Linda, David. Dir, PR, B'nai B'rith, since 1956; newspaper reporter, 1936-46; asst dir, PR, ADL, 1947-58. Mem: Amer PR Assn; Amer J PR, Soc; club, Natl Press. Contbr to natl publs. Home: 2405 Colston Dr, Silver Spring, Md. Office: 1640 Rhode Island Ave, Washington, DC.

SIMON, Caroline K, US, jurist, public official; b. NYC, Nov 12, 1900; d. David and Julia (Feist) Klein; LLB, NYU, Law Sch, 1925; m. Leopold Simon; c: Cathy Silver, Lee; m. 2nd, Irving Halper, June 30, 1953. Judge, NY Court of Claims, since 1963; mem, State Wfr Council, Comm on Discrimination in Employment, 1943-45; commn: State Workmen's Compensation Bd, 1944-45; State Youth Commn, 1956-59; legal adv, US Delg, UN Hum Rights Commn, 1958; Secy of State, NY State, 1959-63; dir, group activities, Off Civilian Defense and mobilization adv, 2nd Corps Area, WW II. Rep Party candidate, for Pres, City Council, NY, 1957. Mem: exec comm, bd trustees, Natl Council on Crime and Delinquency; judicial, Inst of Judicial Admn; bd dirs, Freedom House; hon mem bd trustees J Bd of Guardians; life mem, admn comms, AJ Comm, fmr, vice-pres; bd trustees, Fed and Employment Guidance Service, mem, comm on job placement, comm on rehab, research and demonstrations, common law, mem, women's exec and personnel comms, JWB; comty relations comm, NY Fed Reform Syns; Temple Emanu-El; mem: Comm on Project Hire, Fed and Employment Guidance Service; NY Co L vyers Assn; NY State Bar Assn; Assn Bar, NYC; Amer Bar Assn, mem, sect judicial admn, mem, adv comm to spec comm on crime and prevention control, Fed Mediation and Conciliation Service; adv bd, Bur Safety and Accident Prevention, Div of Safety; Inter-Amer Bar Assn; World Peace Through Law Cen; patron, Intl Bar Assn; sponsor, Commn for Intl Due Process of the Law; mem, Interracial Colloquy; delg, White House Conf on Children, 1950, 1960; hon, bd mem, Manhattan chap, Brandeis U Natl Women's Comm. Contbr to legal jours. Recipient: award, woman of achievement, Women's Intl Exposition, 1957; woman of month, Amer Womens' Assn, 1959; citation and testimonial dinner, Mass Comm of Catholics, Prot and J, 1960; woman of year, Beth Isr Hosp Sch of Nursing, 1960; Bond Between Us award, outstanding service to Isr, 1960; citation and testimonial dinner, Assn for Help of Retarded Children, 1960; woman of achievement, Fed J Women's Orgs, 1961; citation and testimonial dinner, Temple Ohabei Shalom, Boston, 1961; annual brotherhood award, Temple Emmanu-El, NYC, 1961; outstanding citizenship award, Amer Heritage Found, 1961; Salute to Woman award, for dist achievement, 1962; pres citation, NYU, 1962. Home: 227 E 57 St, New York, NY. Office: 270 Broadway, New York, NY.

SIMON, David H, Isr, researcher; b. Jerusalem, Oct 12, 1928; MA, Heb U, Jerusalem, 1951; postgrad studies in agric econ, LSE, 1952-53; m. Edna Salamon; c: Avner, Amos, Yoav. Dep dir, applied research, Auth for Research and Devl, Heb U, since 1968; gen mgr, Yissum Research Devl Co, Heb U, since 1966; mem, bd dirs, Ames-Yissum Ltd; dir; tech assistance dept, PM, off, 1960-62, dep dir gen, admn, 1961, dir, and follow-up org unit, 1963-64; tourism promotion dept, tourist services dept, Min of Tourism, 1962-66; mem, bd dirs: and mgn dir, Isr Prog for Sci Trans Ltd, 1961; and exec comm, Ancient Jaffa Devl Corp Ltd, 1962-66; secy gen, Govt Tourist Corp, 1964-65; secy and coord, comm for planning the devl of tourism, 1965-70. Mem: Isr Mgmt Assn. Home: 74 Tchernchovsky, Jerusalem, Isr.

SIMON, Emanuel Ernst, Isr, physician; b. Berlin, Ger, July 23, 1898; s. Jehuda and Emilie (Hirschhorn); in Isr since 1924; att U: Berlin, Munich, Wuerzburg, 1918-23; MD, U Wuerzburg, 1923; HS Phys Educ, 1923-24; postgrad studies: Swed, Den; m. Zeruja Auerbach, 1930; c: Joab, Gad, Rachel. Vice-pres, Research Council Sport and Phys Educ, UNESCO, since 1964, sci secy, research comm, 1960-64; phys, tchr: Reali HS, Haifa, 1924-27; dept phys hygiene, Nathan Strauss Health Cen, 1929-36; dir, dept phys educ: Vaad Leumi, 1939-48; Min of Educ and Culture, 1949-53, spec adv, 1953-59. IDF, 1948-49. Hon pres, Isr Sports Med Assn, since 1960, chmn, 1956-60; mem: IMA; Isr Phys Educ Tchrs Assn; Intl Sport-Med Fed; Fédération Internationale d'Education Physique; Maccabi Org; Intl Soc Sports Psych; hon mem, Span Assn of Sports-Psych; fmr mem, exec comm, Maccabi World Union. Author: Keep Fit, 1931; Posture Gymnastics, 1935; Track and Field Athletics, 1935, 1927; Natural Exercises, 1939; The Child and Sport, 1943, 1961; Rehabilitation, 1948; co-author, Theory of Physical Education, 1940; co-ed:

The Feet, 1942; International Research of Sport and Physical Education, 1964; contr to sci jours. Recipient: Ruhemann award, Ger Soc of Sports Med, 1959; plaque, Min of Educ, Fr, 1961; DOV HOS, Munic Tel Aviv-Jaffa, 1968. Hobbies: photography, long-distance running. Home: 40 Ruppin St, Tel Aviv, Isr.

SIMON, Ernest E, Isr, biochemist; b. Berlin, Ger, July 11, 1902; s. Hans and Elisabeth (Mirauer); in Isr since 1935; PhD, U Berlin, 1925; m. Edith Kahan, 1946; c: Elieser. Prof em, dept biodynamics, Weizmann Inst of Sci, mem staff since 1935; research asst, Kaiser Wilhelm Inst, Berlin-Dahlem, 1925-33; sci guest: Biol Sta, Arcachon, Fr, 1933; Institut de Biologie Physico-Chimique, Paris (Edmond de Rothschild Found), 1934; visiting sci: Mass Gen Hosp, Boston, 1953; NIH, Bethesda, Md, 1960. Prin contrib: worked with Dr Weizmann on problems of the mechanism of the acetonebutanol fermentation; devl ind method for the dehulling of carob seeds in order to obtain a gum used as thickening agt in textile ind; established action of seven carbon sugar mannoheftulose as a reversible block of insulin secretion and as acceleration of gluconeogenesis. Contr: papers in biochem, endocrine phys. Home: Meonot Wolfson D, Neve Weizmann, Rehovot, Isr. Office: Weizmann Inst of Sci, Rehovot, Isr.

SIMON, Ernst A, Isr, educator, author; b. Berlin, Ger, Mar 15, 1899; s. Gotthold and Caecilie (Leppmann); in Isr since 1928; PhD, Heidelberg U, 1923; att Us: Berlin, Frankfurt; m. Tatiana Rappoport, Mar 16, 1925; c: Uriel, Hanna. Prof em, educ, Heb U, Jerusalem, since 1967, prof, 1955-67, dir sch of educ, since 1966, dir, info and org dept, 1935, chmn, dept educ, 1944-46; co-ed, Der Jude, 1923-28; sch tchr: Ger, 1926-28; Pal, 1928-33; co-dir, with Martin Buber, J adult educ and tchrs training prog, Ger, 1934-35; dir, Heb Tchrs Training Coll and its model sch, Jerusalem, 1939-40; visiting prof educ: JTSA, 1946-47, 1962; Judaism, LA, Cal, 1956-57. Mem, bd dirs, Ihud League for J-Arab Coop; fmr, hon secy, Brith Shalom. Author: Ranke und Hegel, 1928; Die Psychologie des Jüdischen Witzes, 1929; Das Werturteil im Geschichtsunterricht, 1931; Bialik, 1935; Henrietta Szold, 1945; The Crisis in Zionism in Education, 1947; The Educational Meaning of Socratic Irony, 1948; Pestalozzi ve-Korczak, 1949; Goethe and Religious Humanism, 1950; Are We Still Jews?, 1951; Revelation and Religious Experience, 1953; The Philanthropists and Jewish Education, 1953; Pestalozzi's Teachings, 1953, 2nd ed, 1962; Reconstruction Within Destruction, Jewish Adult Education in Nazi Germany as Spiritual Resistance, 1959; The Ends of Secondary Education in Israel, 1961; Bridges, Collective Essays, 1965; Leo Baeck, Last Representative of German Jewry, 1968; co-author: Modern Hebrew Linguaphone Course, 3 vols, 1935; Franz Rosenzweig Briefe, 1935; co-ed: Towards Union in Palestine, 1947; Educational Encyclopedia, 1959; hon ed, Ba'ayoth, 1945-47. Recipient: prize, City of Jerusalem, 1955; Isr Educ Prize, 1967. Home: 35 Ben Maimon St, Jerusalem, Isr. Office: Heb U, Jerusalem, Isr.

SIMON, Ezekiel Helmut, Isr, educator, administrator; b. Katowitz, Ger, May 6, 1912; s. Bernard and Alma (Glogovsky); in Isr since 1936; PhD, Humboldt U, Berlin, 1934; m. Pnina Feuer, Feb 7, 1937; c: Ehud, Ido. Headmaster, Dvir HS, Ramat Gan, since 1954; asst headmaster, tchr Eng lang and lit, Munic HS, 1941-53. Author: Guide to English Composition; Guide to English and American Poetry; Guide to Macbeth; Guide to Choice Pages; Grammar in Action. Home: 66 Rashi St, Tel Aviv, Isr. Office: 38 Sharet St, Ramat Gan, Isr.

SIMON, Isidore, Fr, physician; b. Bala, Rum, Nov 5, 1906; s. Henri and Regine (Abraham); MD, Fac Med, Paris, 1933; m. Fride Madeleine; c: Laurette, Jean. Pvt practice, neuropsycht; asst, phys, Med Fac, Paris; prof, hist of Heb med, Centre Universitaire d'Etudes Juives, Paris, since 1967; asst, neuropsycht to prof Laignel Lavastine, 1932-36; asst, endocrinology, to Dr Welti, 1936-39. Capt, Fr Army, WW II, chief mil hosp, Aix-les-Bains and Coubert. Found, Soc d'Hist de la Med Heb; found and ed, Revue d'Histoire de la Médecine Hébraique, since 1948; lauréat, Acad Natl de Med, Paris, 1967; pres: Société Medicale de l'Opera, since 1961; Brith Ivrith Olamit, Fr, since 1960; corresp mem, Intl Acad of Hist of Med; fmr: secy gen: Magen David Adom; Friends Heb U, Fr; pres, Fed of Fr Maccabi. Contr to: med-hist press; profsl jours; Ency Judaica. Recipient: Star and Cross, Amer Intl Acad, US, 1952; Légion d'Honneur, 1962. Home and office: 177 Blvd Malesherbes, Paris, Fr.

SIMON, Jarrett Bernard, US, optometrist; b. Ft Worth, Tex, Nov 16, 1915; s. Arthur and Ida; att: U Tex; Spartan Sch of Aeronautics; Natl Sch of Banking; OD, S Sch Optometry; m. Lillian Unell, June 15, 1960; c: Theodore, Leslie. Optometrist since 1940; fmr: with: mgn transit dept, Citizen's Bank; credit dept, Goldstein-Magel Co. Pvt, USAC. Pres, B'nai B'rith, fmr state secy; mem: Masons; Shriners; active in Boy Scouts of Amer for 40 yrs; club, Tri-State Financial, pres. Recipient: Scouters Key; Scouters award; Pres Star award; Shofer award; Golden Sun award; Order of Arrow. Home: 1221 Roland St, Joplin, Mo. Office: Miners Bank Bldg, Joplin, Mo.

SIMON, Joachim N, US, business exec; b. Ger, 1912; s. Julius and Johanna (Friedberg); in US since 1921; att LSE, 1934-36; m. Henrietta Hirsch, 1938; c: Joanne, Ellen. Asst mgr, Isr Discount Bank, NYC, since 1963, with bank since 1962; vice-pres: Isr Corp of Amer, 1949-62; Pal Econ Corp of NY, 1954-62; secy, initiator, Ency Judaica Inc, 1959-62; dir, Inca Corp, 1956-60. Mem: Amer Arbitration Assn. Hobby: farming. Home: 49 Brush Lane, Greenslawn, NY. Office: 511 Fifth Ave, New York, NY.

SIMON, John, Eng, business exec; b. Bamberg, Ger, April 19, 1914; s. Sidney and Bertha (Steinberger); in Eng since 1935; med: U Lausanne, 1933; U Grenoble, 1934-35; m. Diana Hassan, Sep 29, 1941; c: Barbara, Richard. Mgn dir, HS Simon Ltd, since 1935. Chmn, Morris Feinmann House for Old Refs; vice-pres, B'nai B'rith Dist, chmn, N Region, 1965-67, pres, Menorah Lodge, 1957-58; treas, Fed Jewish Youth Soc, 1946-49; mem, Inst of Dirs. Hobbies: Wfr of old people, Isr, golf. Home: 11 Elmroad, Didsbury, Manchester, Eng. Office: Phoenix Mills, Piercy St, Manchester, Eng.

SIMON, Manfred, Fr, jurist; b. Nuremberg, Mar 4, 1898; s. Leo and Helene (Falck); Docteur en droit: U Bologne, It, 1923; U Paris, 1927; m. Marguerite Godard, Mar 21, 1934. Ret; presiding judge, Court of Appeals, Paris, 1963-65, judge, 1958-65; head juridical adv service, Free Fr, 1941-44; chief, mission, UNRRA, 1944-46; counselor, Council of State, 1947-55; legal adv, UN, 1948-49, 1951-58; dep dir, public prosecutions, Courts of Appeal, Riom and Amiens, 1955-58. Mem: Union Fédérale des Magistrats; Assn des Magistrats Résistants; Société de Législation Comparée; Assn des Juristes Eur; cen comm, Alliance Isr Universelle; Combattants Volontaires de la Résistance; Jean Moulin Club. Contr to legal publs. Recipient: Chevalier de la Légion d'Honneur; Croix du Combattant; Croix du Combattant Volontaire de la Résistance; Médaille de la France Libre. Home: Chemin des Bluets 2, Lausanne, Switz.

SIMON, Max M, US, architect; b. NYC, Jan 3, 1909; s. Louis and Sara (Blechowsky); BA, NYU, 1934; m. Rose Sobin, June 23, 1940; c: David, Lois. Pvt practice since 1946; works' executed: Linwood Apts, Ft Lee, NJ; Exec House, St Louis, Mo; Teaneck J Comty Cen, NJ; Temple Beth El, Laurelton, LI; Collonades, Lynbrook, LI; architect: Dept of Wfr, NYC, 1934-40; Manhattan Project, NY, 1942-45; chief architect, Naval Installations, Newport, RI, 1940-42; guest lectr: Columbia U; Architects Council; spec cons, Bklyn Poly Inst, drafting NYC bldg code, 1966-68; cons, City Council, NYC on housing maintenance code, 1967. Chmn, city planning and zoning comm, since 1949; trustee, Comty Chest, Harrison; fmr: pres: Bx chap, Amer Inst Architects; B'nai B'rith, Harrison Lodge; chmn: educ comm, NY State Assn Architects, fmr secy; Planning Bd, Town of Harrison; vice-pres: Architects Council, NYC; J Comty Cen, Harrison; mem bd dirs, NY Soc of Architects. Author: So You Want to Build; asso ed, NY Architect. Hobbies: photography, choral singing. Home: Genesee Trail, Harrison, NY. Office: 1841 Broadway, New York, NY.

SIMON, Max Michael, US, surgeon; b. Poughkeepsie, NY, Sep 15, 1899; s. Isaac and Goldie (Katz); BS, Union Coll, Schenectady, 1921; MD, Cornell U Med Sch, 1925; m. Zerline Lehman, Nov 18, 1928 (decd); c: Georgene Dreishpoon, Babette Stall, Fredrica Goodman; m. 2nd, Dusty Taylor, Sep, 1968. Sr att surg, St Francis Hosp, Poughkeepsie, since 1939, mem, med surg bd, since 1940, fmr, chief of staff; cons surg: Highland Hosp, since 1951; Matteawan State Hosp, since 1956, both Beacon, NY; Harlem Valley State Hosp, Wingdale, NY, since 1957; mem staff, NY Hosp for Jt Diseases, 1925-26; house surg, NY Leb Hosp, 1926-28. US Army, 1917-18; 1st lt, Med Offs Res Corps, 1925. Prin contribs: originator, Simon triangle for localization and protection of laryngeal nerve in thyroid surg, 1942. Dipl, Intl Bd Surg, mem adv bd, since 1957, bd govs since 1958; FACS; hon f: Madrid Coll Surgs, Spain, 1952; Roman Coll Surgs, It;

Miss Valley Med Soc, Quincy, Ill, 1956; pres, Hudson Valley Guild, Intl Coll Surgs, since 1941, fmr gen chmn, NE Surg Cong; dir, Amer J Phys Comm, since 1950; mem: AMA; NY State and Duchess Co Med Socs; Kappa Nu; Phi Delta Epsilon; Vassar Temple, fmr pres; Schomre Hadath; Amer Legion; Elks; fmr, gen chmn, Intl Cong of Surgs, NYC; Masons; club, Vassar Temple Mens. Contbr to med publs. Home and office: 96 Hooker Ave, Poughkeepsie, NY; summer home: Fox Run Farm, Pleasant Valley, NY.

SIMON, Morris, US, attorney; b. Rowne, Pol, Sep 2, 1901; s. Nathan and Etta (Bokser); att NYU, 1919-21; LLB, Albany Law Sch, 1924; m. Estelle Greenspan, July 1, 1928; c: Wilma Machover, Alberta Hauser, Ruth. Sr partner, law firm, Murphy, Aldrich, Guy, Broderick and Simon. Pres, J Comty Cen, 1946-47; trustee: J Home for Aged; Temple Beth El; J Council, all Troy, NY; mem: Masons; hon mem, Justinian Law Soc. Hobby: violin. Home: 1 Mc'Leod Rd, Troy, NY. Office: 297 River St, Troy, NY.

SIMON, Ralph, US, rabbi; b. Newark, NJ, Oct 19, 1906; s. Isaac and Yetta (Biddleman); BA, CCNY, 1927; ordained rabbi, MHL, JTSA, 1931; MA, Columbia U, 1943; grad study, Oriental Inst, U Chgo, 1944-47; m. Kelsey Hoffer, 1931; c: Matthew, Tamar Hoffs, Jonathan. Rabbi: Cong Rodfei Zedek, Chgo, Ill, since 1943; Cong Rodef Sholom, Johnstown, Pa, 1931-36; J Cen, Jackson Hgts, NY, 1937-43; Pres: Chgo Bd Rabbis, 1952-54; RA, 1968-69, vice-pres, Chgo Council, since 1943, mem, exec comm, since 1952; vice-chmn, Ill Bd Mh Commn, since 1957; mem, bd dirs: J Fed, Chgo, 1949-61; found, Camp Ramah, Wis, 1947; mem: Citizens, Gtr Chgo, 1953-59; Chgo Commn on Youth Wfr, since 1958; Council Hyde Park and Kenwood Churches and Syn; Bur for Careers in J Service; clubs: Covenant, Ill; Standard, Ill; Idlewild Country. Recipient: Ralph Simon Chair in J Ethics and Mysticism, JTSA, 1958. Home: 5000 East End Ave, Chicago, Ill. Study: 5200 Hyde Park Blvd, Chicago, Ill.

SIMON, Roy D, US, insurance agent; b. Chgo, Ill, Dec 11, 1910; s. Albert and Irene (Levy); att U of Ill, 1928-29; Chartered Life Underwriter, Amer Coll of Life Underwriters, 1936; m. Fannie Bowman, Oct 10, 1945; c: Ann, Roy. Life ins agent, Penn Mutual Life Ins Co, since 1933; asst to pres, Famous Clothiers, 1929-33. USNR, 1942-45. Mem: exec comm, Chgo chap, AJComm; sponsoring comm, Chgo HS Intergroup Relations Conf; fmr pres: Highland Park Comty Chest; Chgo Assn of Life Underwriters; Natl Assn of Life Underwriters; natl committeeman, Ill Life Underwriters Assn, 1960-62; mem, Amer Soc Chartered Life Underwriters; club, Downtown. Hobbies: tennis; bridge. Home: 1540 Sheridan Rd, Highland Park, Ill. Office: 221 N LaSalle St, Chicago, Ill.

SIMON, S William, US, physician; b. Cincinnati, O, Aug 12, 1905; s. Moses and Belle (Trost); BS, U Chgo, 1924, MS, 1926; MD, Rush Med Coll, 1929; m. Florence Elisburg, Aug 8, 1937. Pvt practice; staff, Michael Reese Hosp, 1932-40; chief, allergy clinic, Brown Gen Hosp, VA Cen, 1947-68. Lt col, US Army MC, 1940-47; col, flight surg, O Air Natl Guard, 1948-60. F: Intl Allergology; Amer Acad Allergy; Amer Coll Allergists; Amer Geriatric Assn; pres, O Valley Allergy Soc, 1952; mem: AMA; Chgo Allergy Soc; Amer Assn Hist of Med; Assn Mil Surgs; Intl Corresp Soc Allergy; Air Force Assn; Disabled Amer Vet. Recipient: Bronze star, 1945. Contbr to profsl jours. Spec interest, hist of med. Home: 505 N Lake Shore Dr, Chicago, Ill. Office: 185 N Wabash Ave, Chicago, Ill.

SIMON, Seymour, F US, attorney, government official; b. Chgo Ill, Aug 10, 1915; s. Ben and Gertrude (Rusky); BS, Northwestern U, 1935, JD, 1938; m. Rosalyn Schultz, May 26, 1954. Pvt law practice, since 1946; mem, bd dirs, Natl Gen Corp; alderman, 40th Ward, Chgo, 1955-61, and since 1967; Dem committeeman, since 1959; pres: Bd of Commn, Cook Co, Ill, 1962-66; Forest Preserve Dist, Cook Co, 1962-66. USN, 1942-45. Dir: Schwab Rehab Hosp; Cong Shaare Tikvah; trustee, Temple Beth Isr; mem: Chgo, Ill State Bar Assns; B'nai B'rith; Amer Legion; VFW; JWV; Phi Beta Kappa; club, Standard. Recipient: Order of Coif, 1938; Legion of Merit medal. Home: 5900 N Christiana, Chicago, Ill. Office: 39 S LaSalle St, Chicago, Ill.

SIMON, Sidney, US, artist, educator; b. Pittsburgh, Pa, May 21, 1917; s. James and Minnie (Lipman); BA, Pa Acad Fine Arts, 1941; BFA, U Pa, 1941; div; c: Mark, Teru, Rachel, Nora, Juno; m, 2nd, Renee Simon. Artist in residence, Amer Acad, Rome, It, 1969-70; tchr: Cooper Union, 1946-48; Bklyn

Mus Art Sch, 1949-52; dir, Skowhegan Sch of Painting and Sculpture, 1942-58; tchr: New Sch for Social Research, 1965-69; Parsons Sch of Design, NY, 1962-63; works in public and private collections. Capt, US Army, 1941-45, official war artist, 1942-45. Vice-pres, Artists Equity Assn, 1958, dir, treas, 1947-58; f, Pa Acad Fine Arts; mem: Cent Assn, NYC. Recipient: Emien Cresson f, 1940; Edwin Austin Abbey f, 1941; Bronze Star, 2 Pres Unit Citations, 5 Battle Stars, WW II. Home and office: 95 Bedford St, New York, NY.

SIMON, Solomon, US, dentist, author; b. Kolikovichi, Russ, July 4, 1895; s. Eurichim and Mere (Lifschitz); in US since 1913; DDS, NYU, 1924; m. Lena Fischer, Mar 27, 1920; c: David, Judith, Miriam. Asso prof, Bibl lit, J Tchrs Sem, since 1964; ret dent, in practice since 1924. US Army, 1918. Mem: Kings Co Dent Soc, fmr chmn mem comm; YIVO; PEN club; J Ethical Culture Soc, fmr vice-pres; Soc Bible Lit; fmr mem exec, Allied Dent Council. Author: Levik's Golem, 1927; Schmerl Nar, 1931; Dos Kluge Schniderl, 1933; Kinder Yoren—Yiddische Schreiber, vol I, 1936, vol II, 1945; Robert's Ventures, 1938; Levik's Kinder Yoren, 1938; Helden fun Helm, 1942; The Wandering Beggar, 1942; The Wise Men of Chelm and Their Merry Tales, 1945; In Die Teg fun die Nviim, 1947; Yidn Zvishn Felker, 1949; Medinat Israel un Eretz Israel, 1950; Amoleke Yidn, 1952; Yehoshua un Shoftim, 1952; Tuch-Yidishkeit, 1954; My Jewish Roots, 1956; In der Teg Fun Der Ershte Niviim, 1959; Chachomim un Akshonim, 1963; More Wise Men of Chelm, 1965; sr author: The Rabbis and Bible Teacher's Resource Book on the Pentateuch, 1966; The Early Prophets, 1969; co-author: Maises Fun Agadata, 1936; Chumesh far Kinder, 1940; ed: Schulblatt, 1940; Kinder Journal, 1947-50, asso ed, 1940-47; staff mem, NY Morning Jour since 1951; Di Presse of Arg since 1949; contbr to Yiddish periodicals. Recipient: Mordecai Stolier lit award, 1956; Kessel libr award, Mex. Home: 215 E 43 St, Brooklyn, NY.

SIMON, Walter M, US, attorney; b. Denver, Colo. June 3, 1909; s. Saling and Lara (Lowenstein); AB, cum laude, U Colo, 1930; LLB, Harvard, 1933; m. Anne Menkofsky, Dec 2, 1940; c: Laurence, Peter. Pvt practice since 1934. Trustee, Natl J Hosp, Denver, pres, 1960-62; mem, exec comm, ADL, Denver, chmn, 1955-59, mem, exec comm, Mt States region, chmn, 1954-57; mem, B'nai B'rith; clubs: charter mem: Town; 26, both Denver. Home: 518 Bellaire St, Denver, Colo. Office: 1640 First Natl Bank, Denver, Colo.

SIMON, Yohanan, Isr, artist; b. Berlin, Ger, Nov 3, 1905; s. Moritz and Henriette (Sichel); in Isr since 1936; att: U Berlin; Ecole des Beaux Arts, Paris; studied with: Max Beckman; Peter Rasmussen; m. Sarah Katz (div); m. 2nd, Finy Leitersdorf; c: Nizana Kadmon, Ayah. Mem, Kibbutz Gan Shmuel, 1936-53. One-man shows: Gal Jeanne Castel, 1935; Tel Aviv Mus 1943, 1947, 1954, 1958; Haifa Pevsner Hall, 1947; Beitenu, Haifa, 1950; Ben Uri Gal, London, 1951; O'Hara Gal, London, 1954, 1959; Mus di Arte Moderna, Sao Paulo, 1954; Hebraica, Buenos Aires, 1955; Galeria de Lima, 1956; Mikra Studio, Tel Aviv, 1956; Jerusalem Artists House, 1958; Gal Plaats, The Hague, 1959; Boisserée Gal, Ger, 1959; Art Cen, Lima, Peru, 1961; Gal Cruz Azul, Guat, 1962; San Salvador Galeria Forma, 1962; Gal Feingarten Gal, 1962; Miami Mus Modern Art, 1962; Walcheturm Gal, 1964; Berlin 1965; intl collective shows, Biennale: Venice, 1948, 1958; Sao Paulo, 1953; repr shows of Isr Art in: Eur; US; Can; S Amer; S Afr; India; Japan; Austr; public collections; Tel Aviv Mus; Bezalel Natl Mus; Munic Mus, Haifa; Mus Ein Harod; Munic Mus Art, Herzliya; Natl Mus Jeu de Paume, Paris; Mus Chalons S Marne; Mus Marseille; Mus Manchester; Ben Uri Collection, London; Mus de Arte Moderna, Sao Paulo; Hebraica Collection, Buenos Aires; Fine Arts Mus, Montreal; Miami Mus Modern Art. Fmr: served Fr Army, 1934; Haganah, IDF, 1948-49. Fmr head, cen comm, Isr Painters and Sculptors Assn; club, Rotary, Sharon. Recipient: Dizengoff Prize, 1946, 1953, 1961; prize: Cong for J Culture, 1951; Zichron Yaacov, local council, 1952; Isr Olympic Comm; Jubille prize, Ramat Gan Munic, 1958; Histadrut prize, 1960. Home and Studio: 2 Derech Ha-Be'er, Kfar Shmaryahu, Isr.

SIMONS, Edward L, US, chemist; b. NYC, May 9, 1921; s. Maurice and Julia (Schlossberg); BS, CCNY, 1941; MS, NYU, 1943, PhD, 1945; m. Elaine Lief, June 6, 1943; c: David, Richard. Mgr, fuel cells prog, Gen Elec Research and Devl Cen, since 1967, with Cen since 1951; asst prof, chem, Rutgers U, 1946-51. Dir, Natl Assn Corrosion Engrs, 1959-62; chmn: Boy Scout Troup Comm, J Comty Cen, 1962-66; educ comm,

Temple Gates of Heaven, 1953-54; mem: Amer Chem Soc; Alumni Assn; Chem Alumni, both of CCNY; NYU Chem Alumni; Phi Beta Kappa; Sigma Xi; Phi Lambda Upsilon. Co-author: Dushman's rev, Scientific Foundations of Vacuum Technique, 1962; contbr to sci jours. Recipient: Young Author Award, Natl Assn Corrosion Engrs, 1956. Hobbies: bicycling, magic. Home: 10-C-2 Randi Rd Schenectady, NY. Office: Gen Elec Research and Devl Cen, Schenectady, NY.

SIMONS, Leonard N, US, advertising exec; b. Youngstown, O, July 24, 1904; s. Jack and Mina (Williams); hon: LLD, Wayne State U, 1957; DHL, HUC-JIR, 1964; m. Harriette Lieberman, Jan 21, 1930; c: Mary Zieve, Susan Nagler. Partner, Simons-Michelson Co, advt agcy, since 1929; mem, bd dirs, City Natl Bank, Detroit; visiting lectr, NYU Sch Bus Admn; advt dir, Mich war finance comm, US Treasury, World War II. Pres: Detroit Historical Commn; Temple Beth El, Detroit; chmn: United Negro Coll Fun, Mich; Allied J Campaign, Detroit; SE Mich div, Amer Cancer Soc; vice-pres, Detroit Grand Opera Assn; mem, bd dirs: Marygrove Coll, Detroit; Sinai Hosp; J Home for Aged, fmr chmn, exec bd; U Mich Hillel Found; Wayne State U Hillel Found; NCCJ; Detroit Round Table of Catholics, J and Prots; ADL, Mich; JWF, Detroit, fmr vice-pres; Detroit Service Group; SE Mich div, Natl Found for Infantile Paralysis; J Hist Soc, Mich; Wayne State Fund; UAHC; United Comty Service, Detroit; AJComm; Midrasha Coll J Studies, Detroit; f, Brandeis U; mem: adv bd, Wayne State U Press; natl council, JDC; Amer J Hist Soc; Soc J Bibliophiles; Mackenzie Hon Soc, Wayne State U; hon mem, JWV; hon asso mem, Zeta Beta Tau; fmr mem, bd dirs: Amer Friends Heb U; J Publ Soc of Amer; clubs: Hundred, Detroit; Franklin Hills Country, fmr pres; Standard City; Adcraft, Detroit; Bankers. Recipient: leadership award, Urban League, Detroit, 1966; testimonial resolution, City of Detroit, 1951; Americanism award, Amer Legion, 1956; outstanding citizen, Probus Club, 1962; citation, St Cyprian's Prot Episcopal Church, 1958; Fred Butzel award, JWF, Detroit, 1963; man of year, Detroit lodge, B'nai B'rith, 1956-57; Democratic Living award, ADL, Mich, 1957; award, Hist Soc Mich; citation, Detroit Bd Educ, 1958; gold medal: US Army; US Treasury; World War II citations: ARC; USAC; USN; USCG; USMC; War Shipping Admn; Nurses Corps. Spec interests: hist, traveling, book collecting. Home: 19005 Parkside, Detroit, Mich. Office: Lafayette Bldg, Detroit, Mich.

SIMONSOHN, Berthold, Ger, sociologist; b. Bernburg, Ger, Apr 24, 1912; s. Alfred and Sidonie (Fried); att Halle Saale and Leipzig Us for Law and State Sci, DJur, 1934; att Zurich U, 1947-50; Prof, social pedg and youth rights, Frankfurt U, since 1961; J social work, Stettin, Hamburg, 1938-42; concentration camps, Theresienstadt, Auschwitz, Dachau, 1942-45; mgr, J Com Social Sci, Hamburg, Frankfurt, 1951-61; tchr delg, Pedagogics Inst, Hessen, 1959-61. Contbr to profsl jours. Office: 42 Feldbergstrasse, Frankfurt am Main, 6, Ger.

SIMONSOHN, Shlomo, Isr, educator; b. Breslau, Ger, Oct 30, 1923; s. Isaac and Dora (Wertheim); in Isr since 1933; MA, Heb U, 1946; PhD, London U, 1952; m. Gabriela Manfield, May 19, 1957; c: Raphael, Daniela. Prof, J hist, chmn dept, Tel Aviv U, chmn, Diaspora research inst. Lt, IDF, since 1946. Mem: Isr Hist Soc; World Union J Studies; Amer Acad for J Research. Author: Leon Da Modena, 1953; Responsa Ziqnei Yehuda, 1957; Clipeus Et Gladius, 1960; History of the Jews in the Duchy of Mantua, 1962-64; contbr to profsl jours, encys. Recipient: Ben-Zvi prize, 1964. Home: 71 Kaplan St, Herzliya, Isr. Office: Tel Aviv U, Tel Aviv, Isr.

SIMONSON, Ernst, US, physiologist, educator; b. Tiegenhof, Ger, June 26, 1898; s. Max and Kathe (Paechter); in US since 1939; MD, U Greifswald, Ger, 1924; m. Sophie Schemel, 1931; c: Walter. Prof em, U Minn, prof, phys hygiene, since 1944; dir, Medico-elec Research, Mt Sinai Hosp, since 1966; cons, hosp, since 1952; cons, VA Hosp, Minneapolis, since 1952; privatdozent, ind psych, U Frankfurt, 1928-34; prof em; sci dir, Inst of Lab, Kharkov, 1935-37; research asso, Mt Sinai Hosp, Milw, Wis, 1939-44. F, Gerontological Soc; corresp mem, Ger Phys Soc; mem: NY Acad Sci; Amer Phys Soc; Soc for Experimental Biol and Med; AAUP; comm, NRC, 1946-51; hon mem: Sociedad Peruana de Cardiologia; Brasil Soc de Geriatria. Mem, ed bd: Jour of Applied Physiology, 1948-55; Amer Heart Jour; Jour of Electrocardiography; contbr to profsl jours. Recipient: Cert of merit, Amer Coll Sports Med. Home: 5104-26 Ave S, Minneapolis, Minn. Office: Lab of Physiological Hygiene, U of Minn, Minneapolis, Minn.

SIMRI, Uriel, Isr, scientific director; b. Vienna, Aus, May 22, 1925; s. Mendel and Toni (Broczyner) Singer; in Isr since 1934; BSc, CCNY, 1952; MSc, W Va U, 1965, EdD, 1966; m. Ita Schwarzman, Apr 16, 1959; c: Dror, Ronnie, Merav. Sci dir, Wingate Inst for Phys Educ, since 1969; dir, athletics, Haile Selasse U, Addis Ababa, Ethiopia, 1962-64; lectr, Phys Educ Tchrs Coll, Isr, 1957-69; adv to Govt Singapore, 1969. IDF, 1948-49. Mem, bd, Isr Phys Educ Tchrs Assn; corresp mem: Intl Comm for Standardization Phys Fitness Tests; Intl Research Comm on Hist Sports and Phys Educ. Author: 20 books; 5 trans; 5 research projects; contbr numerous articles. Hobbies: bridge, chess, philately. Home and office: Wingate Inst for Phys Educ and sport, Wingate PO, Isr.

SIMS, Matilda K, US, communal worker; b. Phila, Pa, Feb 8, 1908; d. Abraham and Ida (Lesnick) Klugman; att: Penn State; Detroit City Coll; Wharton Sch; m. Leonard Sims, June 8, 1930; c: Bennett. Natl chmn, leadership training, B'nai B'rith Women, since 1961, intl pres, 1963-65, chmn, intl afiairs, 1965-68; natl commn, ADL, 1965-71; exec bd, comty relations comm, JCC; bd trustees, Natl J Hosp, Denver, since 1961; vice-pres, JWB, 1956. Recipient: service awards: ARC, 1950; B'nai B'rith, 1948, 1959; Woman of Valor award. Home: 24280 Berkley, Oak Park, Mich.

SINAI, Isaac Robert, US, educator, author; b. Lith, Oct 10, 1924; s. Boris and Ella (Zotnick) Skikne; in US since 1963; educ: in S Afr; m. Anne Witten, Aug 18, 1946; c: Joshua. Asso prof, political sci, LIU Bklyn, since 1966; free lance journalist, Johannesburg, London, Paris, 1946-51; ed, Work, jour, Isr Fed Lab, 1952-55; off, intl relations dept, 1957-60; repr, Isr Lab Party on Secretariat Asian Socialist Conf, Rangoon, Burma, 1955-57 info off, Isr Fgn Off, 1962. IDF, Army, 1952-53. F, Rockefeller Found, 1965-66; mem: Amer Political Sci Assn; Amer Hist Assn; Amer Acad Political and Social Scis. Author: The Challenge of Modernization, 1964; In Search of the Modern World, 1967; contbr: US, Isr, Eur, Asian publs. Home: 677 West End Ave, New York, NY. Office: LIU, Brooklyn, NY.

SINCLAIR, Solomon, Can, educator; b. Rocanville, Can, Jan 14, 1905; s. Isaac and Freda (Dubin); BSA, U Sask, 1932, MS, 1937; PhD, U Minn, 1953; m. Elsie Osten, Feb 5, 1933; c: Carole, Grant, Fern. Dir, Natural Resources Inst, U Man, since 1968, prof, head, dept agric econ, 1953-66, mem fac since 1945; dist agriculturist, 1929-31; farm mgr, 1932-39; asst dir, Prairie Farm Assistance Admn, 1939-45; Ford Found Prog Specialist, Kenya Min of Agric, Nairobi, 1966-68; chmn, adv comm, Freshwater Fish Marketing Corp, 1969. F, Agric Inst, Can; charter mem, Man Inst Agrologists; vice-chmn, mem, bd govs: Maimonides Coll; Hillel Found, U Man; mem: ZOC; Amer Farm Econ Assn; Amer Econ Assn; Fisheries Research Bd, Can; fmr pres: Sask Young Lib Assn; Agric Inst, Can; Regional B'nai B'rith; clubs: Kiwanis; Breezy Bend Country. Contbr to sci and farm jours. Home: 804-155 Wellington Crescent, Winnipeg, Can. Office: U of Man, Winnipeg, Can.

SINCOFF, Ethel Raymonde, US, communal leader; b. NYC, Dec 10, 1897; d. Harry and Anne (Levin) Krulewitch; att Tchrs Coll, NYC; m. Jacob Sincoff, Dec 24, 1914; c: Jeane Theodore, Marjorie Kogan. Trustee, J Mus, NYC; mem: Natl bd, women's div, Technion, Haifa; Amer Assn Mus; overall bd, women's div, J Fed; Advanced Gifts Comm; Manhattan Bd Fed; fmr vice-chmn: NY chap, Hadassah; Women's Div, AJComm; fmr co-chmn, fund raising, Women's Div, UJA; fmr pres, women's div, Cong Bnai Jeshurun; club, Harmonie. Prin contrib: established Jacob and Ethel Sincoff Gal, J Mus, NYC. Recipient: Elbert Weinberg Bronze Plaque, JTSA. Home: 880 Fifth Ave, New York, NY.

SINGER, David, Austr, solicitor; b. Sydney, Jan 19, 1936; s. Simon and Tonia (Zucker); BA, U Sydney, 1955; BLL, 1st class hons, 1958; m. Carole Goodman, Aug 7, 1960; c: Deborah, Simon, Shuli. Asso partner, Legal Firm, David Landa Stewart & Co, since 1963; partner, Barkell & Peacock, solicitors, 1960-63. Hon secy: Masada Coll, Lindfield; Youth Educ Sem; bd mem, North Shore Syn; fmr council mem, NSW bd of J Educ; mem: Einstein lodge, B'nai B'rith; club, Monash Country. Gen ed, Austr, The Australian Lawyer, legal monthly publ. Home: 29 Sugarloaf, Castlecrag, NSW, Austr. Office: 187 Maquarie, Sydney, NSW, Austr.

SINGER, Jacob, US, business exec; b. NYC, July 8, 1902; s. Louis and Tillie (Wollen); att NYU Law Sch, 1920-24; m. Julia Epstein, Dec 18, 1923; c: Rene Ivler, Barbara Sigman,

Myron. Pres, Mt Leb Cemetery, since 1937; secy: Mt Carmel Cemetery, since 1937; Cedar Grove Cemetery Assn, since 1937. Pres: Home of Old Isr; Isr Sr Citizens Housing Corp, Seagirt Village, Far Rockaway, NY; Isr Golden Age Fund, Inc, since 1969; mem: bd dirs, J Conciliation Bd Amer; Pi Alpha Lambda. Hobby, fishing. Home: 430 Shore Rd, Long Beach, NY. Office: 7800 Myrtle Ave, Brooklyn, NY.

SINGER, Josef, Isr, engineer, educator; b. Vienna, Aus, Aug 24, 1923; s. Zvi and Etel (Isler); in Isr since 1933; BSc, Imperial Coll, U London, 1948; dipl, Imperial Coll, 1949; M Aeronautical Engr, 1957; m. Shoshana Praeger, June 29, 1954; c: Gideon, Tamar, Uri. Prof, aeronautical engr, Technion, since 1965, asso prof, 1961-65, mem fac since 1955, head, dept, 1958-60, 1965-67. Tech, RAF, 1943-46; engr off, maj, head, test and devl sect, engr dept, IDF, 1949-55. Fmr, chmn, Isr Soc Aeronautics and Astronautics; asso f, Inst of Aerospace Scis, US; f: Inst Mech Engrs, Eng; Royal Aeronautical Soc, Eng; corresp mem, Intl Acad of Astronautics. Contbr to sci jours. Home: 9 Malal St, Haifa, Isr. Office: Technion, Haifa, Isr.

SINGER, Jules B, US, business exec; b. NYC, Sep 19, 1899; s. William and Estelle (Manes). BA, Columbia Coll, 1920; m. Anne Cassler, Apr 29, 1923. Marketing cons since 1960; vice-pres, Fed Advt Agcy, 1938-52, with firm since 1920; vice-pres, dir, Grey Advt Agcy, 1952-60. Fmr chmn, N Amer Mensa; bd dir, Sales Exec, NY, 1958-69; mem: Free Syn; club, Harmonie. Author: Your Future in Advertising, 1960. Home: 151 E 80 St, New York, NY. Office: 370 Lexington Ave, New York, NY.

SINGER, Lav, Yugo, jurist, attorney; b. Zagreb, Yugo, Sep 13, 1901; s. Miha and Sharlote (Wild); LLB, Fac of Law, Zagreb, LLD; m. Vally Reiss. Asst public prosecutor, People's Repl of Croatia, pres, court of discipline, since 1947; court official till 1929; atty till 1941. Interned, concentration camp, Lopud and Hvar, 1942. Mem, Natl Commn for War Crimes of Croatia, 1945-47; pres, J Comty, Zagreb, 1952; vice-pres, Fed J Comtys in Yugo; secy, Assn Jurists, since 1950. Home and office: Zagreb, Yugo.

SINGER, Marcus, US, anatomist, educator; b. Pittsburgh, Pa, Aug 28, 1914; s. Benjamin and Rachel (Gershenson); BS, U Pittsburgh, 1938; MA, Harvard U, 1940, PhD, 1942; m. Leah Horelick, June 8, 1938; c: Robert, Jon. Henry Wilson Payne Prof Anat, dir dept, Sch of Med, W Reserve U, co-dir, developmental biol cen, since 1961; asst prof, anat, Harvard Med Sch, 1942-51; prof, zool, Cornell U, 1951-61; asso ed, Jour of Morphology. F: Amer Acad Arts and Scis; AAAS; mem: Amer Assn of Anat; Growth Soc; Amer Soc Zool; AAUP; Soc for Study of Growth and Devl, treas; Sigma Xi. Author: The Brain of the Dog in Section, 1962; co-author, The Human Brain in Sagittal Section, 1954; contbr to studies on regeneration; anat and phys of nervous sys; to biol jours. Home: 2905 Berkshire Rd, Cleveland Heights, O. Office: W Reserve U, Cleveland, O.

SINGER, Morris Milton, US, attorney; b. NYC, Oct 30, 1905; s. Eisig and Leah (Kessler); JD, Dickinson Law Sch, Pa, 1926; m. Sara Waldman, July 12, 1950; c: Betty Davidson, Wayne. Atty since 1928. Pres, Fed J Agcys, Atlantic County; dir: Atlantic City Cmty Concerts; NJ br, ACLU; mem, NJ State, Bar Assn; fmr: exec secy, Atlantic Co Bar Assn; dir: Atlantic Co Heart Fund; Atlantic City J Cmty Cen. Hobbies: fishing; bridge. Home: 10 S Bartram Ave, Atlantic City, NJ. Office: 1537 Atlantic Ave, Atlantic City, NJ.

SINGER, Paul, Isr, physicist; b. Roman, Rum, July 22, 1934; s. Daniel and Carolina (Pinsler); in Isr since 1951; BSc, cum laude, Technion, 1956, MSc, 1958, DSc, 1961; m. Yocheved Gastfreund, July 28, 1958; c: Iddo, Orna. Head, dept physics, Technion, since 1969, asso prof since 1964; research asso, Northwestern U, 1961-63, visiting prof, 1967-68; research sci, Columbia U, 1963-64. Mem: Isr Phys Soc, mem council, 1966-67; Amer Phys Soc. Contbr to intl jours. Home: 6A Yaarot St, Haifa, Isr. Office: Technion, Physics Dept, Haifa, Isr.

SINGER, S Fred, US, physicist, educator; b. Vienna, Aus, Sep 27, 1924; s. Joseph and Anne (Kelman); in US since 1940; BEE, O State U, 1943; AM, Princeton U, 1944, PhD, 1948. Dep Asst Secy for Sci Progs, Dept of Interior, Wash, DC, since 1967; instr, physics dept, Princeton U, 1943-44; physicist, Johns Hopkins U, Applied Physics Lab, Silver Spring, Md, 1946-50; sci liaison off, Off Naval Attaché, US Emb, London,

Eng, 1950-53; prof, physics dept, U Md, 1959-64, on fac since 1953, dir, cen for atmospheric and space physics, 1959-64; visiting researcher, Jet Propulsion Lab, Cal Inst Tech, Pasadena, Cal, 1961-62; dir, Natl Weather Satellite Cen, US Weather Bur, Suitland, Md, 1962-64; prof, atmospheric sci, dean, Sch of Environmental and Planetary Scis, U Miami, 1964-67. USN, 1944-46; capt, USAF Res, 1950-55. F: Amer Physical Soc; Amer Inst Aeronautics and Astronautics; Amer Geophys Union; Amer Astronautical Soc; AAAS; Brit Interplanetary Soc; Royal Astronomical Soc; head: sci evaluation group and sci cons, select comm on astronautics and space explorations, US House of Reprs, 1958; tech panel on rockets and tech panel on cosmic rays, US Natl Comm for Intl Geophys Year, 1957-58; chmn: subcomm on basic research, comm on sci and tech, US C of C, 1960-62; comm on Sci and oceanography, comm of 21, Miami-Dade Co C of C, 1965-66; comm on publs, Amer Geophys Union, since 1968; sci comm, Amer Astronautical Soc, since 1967; cons, Pres Commn on Marine Sci, Engr and Resources, since 1967; off, Pan-Amer Med Assn, Space Med Sect, since 1959; dir, Amer Astronautical Soc, 1960-66; gov, Natl Space Club, Wash, DC, 1960-64, and since 1968; mem: Intl Acad Astronautics, since 1961; Intl Sci Radio Union; Amer Meteorological Soc; environmental pollution adv bd, US C of C, 1966-67; spacecraft oceanography adv group, USN Oceanographic Off, 1966-67; adv bd, Missiles, Space and Range Pioneers, since 1967; Lunar Intl Lab Comm, Intl Acad Astronautics, since 1964; repr, Dept of Interior: Comm on Environmental Quality of Fed Council of Sci and Technology; Comm on Ocean Exploration and Environmental Scis; Comm on Multiple Use of Coastal Zone, Natl council on Marine Resources and Eng Devl, since 1967; participant and lectr in numerous intl congs in US, It, Arg, Spain, Aus, Isr, Greece, Pol. Asso ed, ICARUS, Intl Jour of Solar Sys; org of numerous spec courses and confs, 1964-68; mem, ed bd, Planetary and Space Sci; contbr: many research papers on astronomy, astronautics to publs. Recipient: official commendation from Pres Eisenhower for outstanding achievement in devl satellites for sci purposes, 1958; dist alumnus award, O State U, 1958; one of ten outstanding young men of 1959, US Jr C of C; First Astronautics Medal for Sci, Brit Interplanetary Soc, 1962; US Dept of Commerce gold medal, 1965. Home: 2302 Kalorama Rd, NW, Washington, DC. Office: Dept of the Interior, Washington, DC.

SINGER, Shmuel, Isr, advocate; b. Bucharest, Rum, June 7, 1900; in Isr since 1940; att: U Bucharest; U Rome; m. Etella; c: Lya, Moshe. Advocate and notary; fmr co-found, pres, ed, publisher, Hashmonea; co-found, Poale Zion group, Renashterea, Rum, 1926; leader, J Party and its repr, Rum Parliament, 1930-31; delg: ZCs; 1st WJC; negotiated with Rum and Ger on Rum J fate. Home: 5 Hashmonaim St, Haifa. Office: 35 Hameginim Ave, Haifa.

SINKIN, William R, US, business exec; b. San Antonio, Tex, May 19, 1913; s. Nathan and Bella (Rashall); BBA, U Tex, 1934; m. Fay Bloom, 1942; c: Nathan, Lanny. Pres: N Sinkin, Inc, since 1943; N Sinkin Dept Stores, since 1950; Goodwill Inds, 1945-48; San Antonio Fair, Inc, 1962-63; Hemistan, since 1968; and chmn, bd, Tex State Bank, since 1969. Chmn: planning, San Antonio Urban Coalition, 1969; AJComm, 1944-48; UJA, 1944-46; Public Housing Auth, 1949-52; co-chmn, NCCJ, 1947-53; vice-chmn, commns comm, Natl Assn Housing Officials, 1954; mem, bd dirs: Tex Safety Assn, Inc, 1952-53; Bexar Co Hosp, since 1967; mem: J Soc Service Fed, 1947-49; C of C. Recipient: award, Natl Assn Housing Officials, 1953; Master Publicist award, 1964; Outstanding Citizen award, 1966; Brotherhood award, NCCJ, 1966; Intl Relations award, St Mary's U, 1967. Home: 215 Crescent, San Antonio, Tex. Office: 718 N Cherry, San Antonio, Tex.

SINYKIN, Melvin B, US, gynecologist, obstetrician; b. Sioux City, Ia, Jan 1, 1912; s. Solomon and Fanny (Sachs); MB, U Minn, 1935, MD, 1936; m. Julianne Harris, Apr 29, 1951; c: Carol, Stuart, Richard. Pvt practice since 1940; chief med staff, Mt Sinai Hosp, 1958, on staff since 1951; clinical instr, obstet, U Minn since 1942. Maj, US Army, 1942-46, Fmr pres, Minn State Soc Obstet and Gyn; f, Amer Coll Surgs; mem: Amer Bd Obstet and Gyn; AMA; Amer Coll Obstet and Gyn; Minneapolis Acad Med. Ed staff, Modern Medicine, since 1950; contbr to med jours. Hobbies: photography, lapidary. Home: 2525 Thomas Ave S, Minneapolis, Minn. Office: 127 S 10 St, Minneapolis, Minn.

SIPORIN, Mitchell, US, artist, educator; b. NYC, May 5, 1910; s. Hyman and Jennie (Dressler); att Art Inst, Chgo, 1928-32; m. Miriam Tane, Nov 11, 1945; c: Judith, Rachel. Prof, found, dept fine arts, Brandeis U, since 1951, Charles Bloom Prof arts of design; executed frescos for St Louis PO, 1939-42; artist-in-res, Amer Acad, Rome, 1966-67; sr Fulbright research f, It, 1966-67; paintings in perm collections: Metrop Mus, NY; Mus Modern Art, NY; Whitney Mus, NY; Fogg Art Mus, Cambridge, Mass; Art Inst, Chgo; U of Ia; U Ill; U of NM; U Ariz; U Ga; U Neb; Smith Coll; Cranbrook Acad; Wichita Mus; Newark Mus; Johnson Collection, Natl Art Collection, Smithsonian Inst. Artist, hist sect, US Army, 1942-45. F: Amer Acad, Rome; Guggenheim Memorial Found, 1945-47; trustee, Boston Art Festival; mem, Artists Equity Assn. Recipient: Prix-de-Rome, 1949-50; grant, Inst of Arts and Letters, 1956. Home: 300 Franklin St, Newton, Mass. Office: Brandeis U, Waltham, Mass.

SIRAT, Colette, Fr, educator; b. Paris, Fr, Nov 2, 1934; d. Abraham and Laura (Arner) Salamon; BA, Fac of Phil, Toulouse, 1955, MA, 1956; dipl, Ecole Pratique des Hautes Etudes, Sorbonne, 1962, PhD, 1963; m. René Sirat, 1951; c: Hélène, Gabriel, Annie. Dir, studies, Ecole Pratique des Hautes Etudes, sect IV, Sorbonne, since 1969; engr, Natl Cen Sci Research, Paris, 1956-63. Found, Comm of Heb Paleography, Fr-Isr org, dir, Fr team. Author: Les Théories des Visions Surnaturelles dans la Pensée Juive du Moyen-Age, 1969. Home: 9 rue Berthollet, Paris 5, Fr.

SIRAT, René Samuel, Fr, educator; b. Bône, Algeria, Nov 13, 1930; s. Ichoua and Oureida (Attlan); in Fr since 1948; ordained rabbi, Séminaire Israelite de Fr, Paris, 1952; dipl, Ecole Natl Langues Orientales Vivantes, Paris, 1957; MLitt, Strasbourg, PhD, 1965; m. Colette Salamon, Dec 18, 1951; c: Hélène, Gabriel, Annie. Prof, modern Heb, U Cen of Oriental Langs, since 1966; i/c course, Sorbonne, dir, U Cen of J Studies, both Paris, since 1969; rabbi, Toulouse, ACIT, 1952-55; dir, studies: ACIP, 1955-63; CUEJ, since 1965. Fr Army, 1954-55. Hon pres, Union J Students of Fr; pres, Naguilah, group of blind, handicapped J; mem natl council, FSJU. Home: 9 rue Berthollet, Paris 5, Fr. Office: 2 Rue de Litte, Paris, Fr.

SIRIS, Elaine Kappel, US, communal leader; b. NYC, Mar 26, 1923; d. Samuel and Minnie (Senowitz) Kappel; att Conn Coll, 1940-41; Columbia U, 1941-42; m. Burt Siris, Aug 15, 1941; c: Peter, Margot Helphand, Penny Kappel. Gen chmn, NY UJA, since 1968, chmn, women's div, 1958-62, chmn, bd, women's div, 1962-65; secy, Amer Zionist Youth Found; trustee, Council of JWF Funds; mem: admn comm, JDC; bd Isr Educ Fund. Home: 103 Greenhaven Rd, Rye, NY.

SIRLUCK, Ernest, Can, educator; b. Winkler, Man, Apr 25, 1918; s. Isaac and Rose (Nitikman); BA, U Man, 1940; MA, U Toronto, 1941, PhD, 1948; LLD, Queen's U, 1968; m. Lesley McNaught, 1942; c: Robert, Katherine. Vice-pres, U Toronto, since 1969, dean, Sch Grad Studies, since 1964, prof, Eng, since 1962, lectr, U Coll, 1946-47; prof, U Chgo, 1958-62, on fac since 1947; overseas f, Churchill Coll, Cambridge U, 1966; Guggenheim f, 1953-54. Pres, Midwest (now, Newberry Libr) Renaissance Conf, 1951-52; found pres, Renaissance Eng Text Soc, 1959-65; chmn, various sect, MLA, since 1957; Ont Comm Grad Deans, since 1962; vice-chmn, Adv Jt Council, Ont Grad Deans and Librs, 1967-68; mem, bd dirs: Cen for Continuing Educ, Chgo, 1960-62; Midwest Inter-Libr Cen, Chgo, 1963-65; mem, bd govs, Ont Inst for Studies in Educ, since 1965; mem: final rev comm, Canada Council, 1963-65; Woodrow Wilson Dissertation F Selection Comm, 1964-68; Can Comm for Commonwealth Scholarships and Fs, 1964-67; Comm on Intl Educ, Amer Assn of Grad Schs, 1964-66; policy comm, Amer Assn Grad Schs, since 1966; U Comm on St Lawrence Cen for the Arts, since 1966; sci council, Canada Council Study of Research in Can Us, 1967-69; Ont Grad Appraisals Comm, 1967-69; Royal Soc of Can; Assn Can U Tchrs of Eng; Can Assn U Tchrs; AAUP; Can Civil Liberties Assn; Renaissance Eng Text Soc; f: corp, Massey Coll, since 1963; Royal Soc of Can, since 1967. Author: Complete Prose Works of John Milton, Vol II, 1959; Paradise Lost: A Deliberate Epic, 1967; contbr and ed numerous articles to educ jours. Home: 185 Balmoral Ave, Toronto, Canada. Office: University Coll, U of Toronto, Toronto, Canada.

SISKIN, Edgar Elias, US, rabbi; b. Edinburgh, Scotland; s. Hyman and Dora (Berkowitz); in US since 1921; BA, U Cincinnati, 1928; ordained rabbi, HUC, 1929; PhD, Yale U, 1941; m. Lillian Margolin, July 6, 1946; c: Jonathan, Joshua, Sharon. Rabbi: N Shore Cong, since 1948; Cong Mishkan Isr, New Haven, 1930-38; visiting f, anthropology, Yale U, 1941-43, asst prof, 1946-48. Chaplain, USNR, 1943-46. Pres:

Chgo Bd Rabbis; fmr pres: Chgo Assn Reform Rabbis; N Shore F Rabbis; Alumni Assn, HUC-JIR; bd dirs, Rel Educ Assn of Amer; bd council, Rel and Intl Affairs; f, Amer Anthropological Assn; mem, CCAR. Author: The Impact of the Peyote Cult Upon Shamanism Among the Washo Indians, 1941; The Impact of American Culture Upon the Jew, 1952. Home: 928 Oak Dr, Glencoe, Ill. Study: 840 Vernon Ave, Glencoe, Ill.

SISSELMAN, Mina, Isr, artist, art critic; b. Tel Aviv; d. Pinchas and Bella (Cohen); BA, NY Sch of Art, 1950. Artist and painter since 1930; art critic since 1950. Mem: Isr Assn Painters and Sculptors. Recipient: Dizengoff prize, 1958; Histadrut prize, 1964. Home: 3 Mendele St, Tel Aviv, Isr.

SITCHIN, Zecharia, US, economist; b. Baku, Russ, Jan 11, 1920; s. Itzhak and Yaffa (Barsky); BCom, hons, U London, Eng, 1942; m. Rina Regenbaum, Sep 16, 1941; c: Edna, Ella. Pres, Intercontinental Trailsea Corp, since 1967; asst town clerk, Tel Aviv Munic, 1944-49; secy, dir, econ dept, Tel Aviv-Jaffa C of C, 1949-52; found, exec dir, Amer Isr C of C, NY, 1953-65; Brit Army, 1940-44. Mem: panel arbitrations, Amer Arbitration Assn. Ed, Economic Horizons, since 1959; fmr, mem ed staff, Haboker daily, Tel Aviv; ed, Hamishmar, commerce jour; contbr to mags. Home: 310 W 86 St, New York, NY. Office: 11 Broadway, New York, NY.

SITTON, David, Isr, editor; b. Jerusalem, Jan 8, 1909; s. Nisim and Esther; m. Bilha Horowitz; c: Dov, Dikla Ben Shaul, Avinoam. Ed, Bama'araha, Sephardic comty newspaper, Isr, since 1961; chmn exec comm, Sephardic Comty, since 1957; fmr: mem, ed bd: Hayarden; Haolam; Haboker, Heb dailies; Hon secy, found, World Sephardic Cong; fmr: on missions to J comtys abroad; mem, Revisionist Movement; delg, WJC. Author: Studies on Ethnic Problems in Israel; contbr to mags and press. Office: 12A Hahavatselet, Jerusalem, Isr.

SIVAN, Reuben, Isr, educator, lexicographer; b. Jerusalem, June 28, 1912; s. Kaddish and Esther (Cohen) Silman; MA, Heb U, 1946, PhD, 1965; m. Doreen Micznik, Mar 3, 1967; c: Esther; lectr, tchrs colls, since 1962; info off, Heb Lang Acad, since 1968, dir, radio program on Heb usage, Isr Bc; tchr, Min of Educ, 1933-48, press off, 1949-52, ed, publs, 1956-62; lectr, Heb, Leeds U, 1953-55. Cpl, Brit Army, 1942-45; lt, IDF, 1948-49. Mem: World Union J Studies; Brit Soc for Old Testament Studies. Author: Better Hebrew Usage, 1969; co-author, The Megiddo Modern English-Hebrew, Hebrew-English Dictionary, 1966; trans: sci, scholarly books; contbr to jours. Home: 10 Bet Hakerem St, Jerusalem, Isr. Office: Heb Lang Acad, Jerusalem, Isr.

SKEER, David, US, attorney; b. Kan City, Mo, Aug 27, 1916; s. William and Florence (Alisky); BA, U Mo, 1937; JD, U Chgo, 1939; m. Janet Reinhardt, June 25, 1942 (decd); c: John, Berkley; m. 2nd, Tillie Feingold, Sep 2, 1966. Partner, Sheffrey, Ryder & Skeer, since 1961, legal adv, Harzfelds Inc, 1939-43; pvt practice, 1946-51; partner, Barnett & Skeer, 1951-61. Lt cdr, USN, 1943-46. Chmn, Mh Commn, State of Mo, since 1966; pres: Mo Assn for Mh, 1960-63; Lawyers Assn, Kan City, 1961-62; Kan City Res Theater, 1947-50; councilor, Menorah Med Cen and Hosp; bd mem: J Home for Aged; Natl Assn for Mh; bd govs, Mo Bar Assn. Author: Condemnation Appraisal Practice, 1961. Hobbies: composing music, theater. Home: 1207 W 66 St, Kansas City, Mo. Office: 1011 Commerce Bldg, Kansas City, Mo.

SKIRBALL, Jack H, US, motion picture producer, business exec; b. Homestead, Pa, June 23, 1896; s. Abram and Sarah (Davis); BHL, ordained rabbi, HUC-JIR, 1921; BA, W Reserve U, 1923; hon DHL, HUC-JIR, 1955; m. Audrey Marx, April 7, 1949; c: Sally, Agnes. Pres: Skirball Produc, since 1949; Bowlero Corps, since 1955; Vacation Village, Inc, since 1961; rabbi, Euclid Temple, Cleveland, 1921, Evansville, Ind, 1921-23; gen mgr in charge produc, Educ Films of Amer,1933-39; lectr, J Chautauqua Soc. Films produc: Birth of a Baby, 1937; Shadow of A Doubt, 1945; Saboteur, 1946; Magnificent Doll, 1948; Guest Wife, 1945; Payment on Demand, 1951; produc stage play, Jacobowsky and the Colonel, 1947. Chmn, exec bd, HUC-JIR, LA, since 1958; pres, S Cal dist, UAHC, 1953-54; fmr: pres, S Ind Red Cross Soc; chmn, Anti-TB Soc; mem, Comty Chest Comm; mem: B'nai B'rith; Masons. Home: 722 N Elm Dr, Beverly Hills, Cal. Office: 9033 Wilshire Blvd, Beverly Hills, Cal.

SKLAR, George, US, novelist, playwright, screenwriter; b. Meriden, Conn, June 1, 1908; s. Ezak and Bertha (Marshak);

BA, Yale U, 1929, att Dept of Drama, 1929-31; m. Miriam Blecher, Aug 21, 1935; c: Judith, Daniel, Zachary. Author: novels: The Two Worlds of Johnny Truro, 1947; The Promising Young Men, 1951; The House-warming, 1953; The Identity of Dr Frazier, 1961; plays, co-author: Merry-Go-Around, 1932; Peace on Earth, 1933; Stevedore, 1934; Parade, 1935; Laura, 1946; And People All Around; author, Life and Death of an American, 1939. Mem: Authors' League of Amer; Phi Beta Kappa; Dramatists' Guild, exec council, 1938-42. Recipient: John Golden writing award, NYC, 1938. Home: 530 N Fuller Ave, Los Angeles, Cal.

SKLAR, Samuel B, US, consulting chemist, physicist; b. Russ, May 14, 1897; s. Chaim and Anna (Rose); in US since 1911; att U Minn, 1918-21; DSc, U Leipzig, Ger, 1926; hon PhD: U Vienna, 1926; U Istanbul, 1928. Research chem and physicist; visiting prof: U Tenn, 1926-27; U Minn, 1927; pres, Sklar & Co, Inc, mfr own inventions, 1926-29; dir, research, Standard Research Labs, Pittsburgh, 1930-41; part-time tchr and student guidance counselor, Braille Tech Sch, Columbia U, 1946-50. Capt, WW I. Prin contribs: inventions including: invalid bed and fracture table; accoustic elements; variable time alarm devices; with Dr J Weiner, expansion compensation device for valve actuation; improvement for process in making vinly resin composition; process for making dent porcelain; electrodepositing indium; red rubber composition. F: Amer Acad Psychosomatic Med; hon, Intl Inst Arts and Letters; asso, Fr Acad Sci; mem: AAUP; AMA; Fed Amer Scis; Amer Assn Physics Tchrs; AAAS; Soc Med Jurisprudence; Natl Tchrs Assn; Assn Française pour L'Avancement des Sciences, Paris; Chartered Inst Amer Inventors; Kaiser Wilhelm Soc for Promotion Sci; J Grad Soc, Columbia U; hon, Orthodox J Scis; Soc for Steel Treating; Ceramic Soc; Boy Scouts Amer; Police Athletic League; Amer Legion; B'nai B'rith; Hillel Soc; Span Port Syn; Masons; Odd Fellows; Beta Sigma Rho; Sigma Alpha Mu; Phi Sigma Delta; Sigma Beta Phi; clubs: Chemist, London; Stratoliner; 100,000 Mile United Airline. Author: The Happy Man and Other Essays, 1923; Glorious Dream of Youth, 1931; A Pamphlet on Industrial Research, 1931; Closeness to Marriage, 1948. Recipient: S Cotton Assn award, for devl chem process for extermination boll weevil, 1925; medals: from Pope Pious XII, 1955; from Pope John, 1959; Rosicrucian Order award as humanist, 1958; hon commns from Govs of: Neb; NM; Okla; Ga; Ky; Tex; complimentary letters and autographed photographs from Presidents: Truman; Eisenhower; Johnson; Nixon. Office: 400 W 119 St, New York, NY.

SKLARE, Marshall, US, sociologist, educator; b. Chgo, Ill, Oct 21, 1921; s. Irving and Bee (Lippman); MA, U Chgo, 1948; PhD, Columbia U, 1953; m. Rose Bernards, June 8, 1947; c: Daniel, Judith, Joshua. Prof, sociol, Yeshiva U, since 1966; dir, div sci research, AJComm, 1956-65, study dir, 1953-55; Fulbright lectr, Heb U, 1965-66; visiting prof, Amer Studies, Brandeis U, 1969-70. F: Amer Sociol Assn; Conf on Social Studies; Rel Research Assn; Rel Educ Assn. Author: Conservative Judaism, An American Religious Movement, 1955; ed, The Jews: Social Patterns of an American Group, 1958; co-author, Jewish Identity on the Suburban Frontier, 1967. Home: 1001. E 21 St, Brooklyn, NY. Office: 55 Fifth Ave, New York, NY.

SKLORMAN, Gene, US, business exec, b. Canton, O, Oct 27, 1909; s. Lewis and Sarah (Levine); div; c: Sheryl. Dist mgr, Mutual of Omaha Ins Co, since 1954; real estate broker, LA, Cal, 1945-49; owner, clothing and shoe store, Canton, O, 1936-42. Cpl, US Army, 1943-45. Second vice-pres, Wooster C of C; chmn, spec gifts, Wayne Co Cancer Soc; mem: bd trustees, Wooster United Fund; Wayne Co Life Underwriters; Amer Legion; B'nai B'rith, fmr pres; Wooster Moose; chmn, UJA; pres, Hillel org, Kent State U; fmr: mem finance comm, chmn, spec invitation, Wayne Co Reps; club, Lions, fmr mem, bd. Recipient: recognition dinner, Wooster J Comm, 1967; Retention of Mem award, Dist Grand Lodge 2, B'nai B'rith. Home: 1715 Harold St, Wooster, O. Office: 141½ E Liberty St, Wooster, O.

SKOLSKY, Sidney, US, journalist; b. NYC, May 2, 1905; s. Louis and Mildred (Arbeit); att NYU; m. Estelle Lorenz, August 27, 1928; c: Nina Marsh, Steffi Grant. Hollywood columnist, NY Post, since 1939; publicist, 1925-29; Broadway columnist, NY Daily News, 1929-33, Hollywood columnist, 1933-39; producer: Jolson Story, 1946; Cantor Story, 1956. Author: Times Square Tintypes, 1930; Hollywood and the Movies, TV documentary; Hollywood: The Golden Era,

TV spec. Home: 160 S Orange Dr, Los Angeles, Cal. Office: c/o NY Post, 75 West St, New York, NY.

SKULSKY, Shlomo Yehuda (pen name, **Ben Israel Hadoni, Shas**), Isr, author, teacher; b. Volhynia, 1912; s. Israel and Etti(Grinbaum); in Isr since 1941; att Tchrs Sem, Vilna, Pol: MA, Heb U, Jerusalem, 1963; m. Felicia Grabshrift, July 2, 1947; c: Edia. Lit ed: Herut, 1948-65; Yediot Aharonot, 1946-48, both Heb dailies. Active, Irgun Zvei Leumi, taken prisoner, Latrun. Author: poetry: Bein haBt'arim, 1942; Ashira Lach, Tel Aviv, 1948; poems and stories for children; some trans into Eng, It; trans: Konrad Wollenrod, Grazyna; poems by Adam Michewicz; stories by Jules Verne, others; ed, several anthols; contbr to newspapers and periodicals.Mem: Sem Tchrs Org; fmr: leader, Betar; mem, Vaad Hapicuach. Home: 5 Armonmi St, Ramat Gan, Isr.

SKORNIK, Robert Gady, Isr, physiotherapist; b. Paris, Fr, Oct 19, 1940; s. Victor and Feiga (Fingelbaum); in Isr since 1957; att schs: Kibbutz; IDF; m. Simona Dayan, Oct 12, 1961; c: Ady, Guy. Isr Judo champion, since 1965. Mem: Kodokan, Tokyo, Japan. Hobbies: swimming, shooting. Home: 2 Ariel St, Tel Aviv, Isr. Office: 9 Hess St, Tel Aviv, Isr.

SKURNIK, Sender, Finland, manager; b. Helsinki, Sep 12, 1906; s. Moses and Sara (Skurnik); engr deg, Nordic Corresp Inst, Stockholm, 1946; m. Sassie Knaster, Mar 18, 1928; c: Harry, Dorothea Aviva. Mgr, Oy Textil Ab, Helsinki, since 1949. Econ, J Cong, Helsinki, 1945-49, treas, 1949-60; clubs: J Bridge, Helsinki; Hamilton, London. Recipient: Medal of Liberty 11 class, 1942, 1 class, 1944. Home: Sörnäs Strandväg 3 B 30, Helsinki, Finland. Office: Sörnäs Strandväg 3, Helsinki, Finland.

SKY, Harry Zvi, US, rabbi; b. Newark, NJ, Apr 17, 1924; s. Louis and Ida (Lozea-Furman); BA, Yeshiva U, 1949; MHL ordained rabbi, JTSA, 1951; m. Ruth Levinson, Dec 24, 1950; c: Rina, Uri, Ari. Rabbi, Temple Beth El, since 1961; lectr, U Me, since 1965; rabbi: Brith Sholom, 1956-59; Temple Beth El Zedeck, Indianapolis, Ind, 1959-61. Mem: Reconstructionist Found, NAACP; AJCong; Isr Affairs Comm; RA; Amer J Hist Soc; Portland Model Cities Health Prog; fmr chmn, Human Relations Council, Portland; pres, Interfaith Council of Clergy, Portland; club, Rotary, Portland. Author: Inspirational Anthology, 1968; contbr to rel and gen jours. Recipient: humanitarian, Salvation Army Centennial award, 1955; humanitarian, City of Scarboro, Me, 1965; citation, UJA, 1967. Home: 24 Catherine, Portland, Me. Study: 400 Deering Ave, Portland, Me.

SLADOWSKY, Yitzchak, Alfred, US, rabbi, educ; b. Hamburg, Ger, Jan 1, 1932; s. Jacob and Greta (Kanarek); in US since 1936; BA, Yeshiva Coll, 1954; MA, Columbia U, 1955; ordained rabbi, Isaac Elchanan Theol Sem, 1956; m. Frayda Gelman, Feb 27, 1955; c: Esther, Rayla, Saul, Chava, Deborah, Rachel. Rabbi, Forest Park J Cen, since 1958; instr, Yeshiva U, HS, since 1962; rabbi, Edison J Cen, 1956-58; fmr lectr: Adult Educ Inst; E NY YM and YWHA. Chmn, prins council, Talmud Torah Council, Queens; mem, bd educ, Yeshiva of Cen Queens; bd dirs, Heb HS of Queens; fmr mem, exec bd, Rabb Alumni, Yeshiva U; mem: RabCA; Rel Zionists of Amer. Home: 90-50 Union Turnpike, Glendale, NY. Study: 90-45 Myrtle, Glendale, NY.

SLAVIN, Marese, US, dietitian; b. Paterson, NJ, June 28, 1914; d. Charles and Matilda (Levine) Cohen: BS, W Reserve U, 1937; m. Emanuel Slavin, 1947; c: Charlene. Cons dietitian since 1963; admn dietitian, City Hosp, 1940-45. Pres, Cleveland chap, Hadassah; mem, Amer Dietetic Assn. Home: 3813 Claridge Oval, Cleveland, O.

SLAVITT, Jacob, US, attorney; b. Ger, Apr 20, 1907; s. Frank and Rachel (Huneau); in US since 1907; att Newark Inst of Arts and Scis, 1921-23; BCS, NYU, 1927; LLB, Rutgers Law Sch, 1930; m. Sylvia Berman, Jan 17, 1942; c: Richard, Alan. Pvt practice since 1930; mem, bd, Bank of Bloomfield; chmn, Ind Devl Commn, Newark; tax commn, Newark, 1945-49, pres, Tax Bd, 1949-54. Pres: Heb Free Loan Assn; YMHA, 1940-45; Ezekiel Lodge, B'nai B'rith; chmn: bd, Heb Acad; Econ Devl Commn to Isr; UJA; hon, Isr Bond Campaign; mem: Gov's Educ Auth Commn; Gov's Commn on Local Property Taxation; bd, Home for Chronic Sick; pres council, Brandeis U; Amer and Essex Co Bar Assns; Newark Area Redevl Corp. Recipient: Arthur Szyk award, State of Isr, 1952; Big Wheel Isr Bond award, 1953; Americanism award, B'nai B'rith, 1953; Levi Eshkol award of honor, 1954; Brotherhood award, NCCJ, 1966. Home: 725 Elizabeth Ave, Newark, NJ. Office: 17 Academy St, Newark, NJ.

SLAVSON, Samuel R, US, psychotherapist, author; b. Poltava, Russ, Dec 25, 1891; s. Schlomo and Fanny (Tarsy); in US since 1904; BS, Cooper Union, 1913; att: CCNY, 1914-15; Tchrs Coll, 1921-22; m. Cornelia Goldsmith; c: Robert, Hertha Klugman, Gerda Cooke. Cons, group psychotherapy: Children's Village, since 1957; Northside Youth Consulatation Service, Manhasset, NY, since 1958; J Bd of Guardians, NY, 1934-56; Bridgeport, Conn Mental Hygiene Soc, 1945-48; Comty Service Soc, 1946-51; J Child Guidance Clinic, Newark, NJ, 1947-51; Hudson Guild, 1949-57; Youth Consultation Service, 1950-58; cons, staff devl, Bklyn State Hosp, NY, 1964-68; dir, group therapy evaluation project, Children's Village, Dobbs Ferry, NY, 1957-64; research psych, Malting House Sch, Cambridge, Eng, 1927-29; fac mem: NYU, 1935-41; Springfield Coll, 1939-40; Yeshiva U, 1950-53. Chmn, commn on group therapy, WHO, 1948; found, first pres, Amer Group Psychotherapy Assn, 1942-44; mem: AAAS: NY Acad of Scis; Amer Orthopsycht Assn; Amer Acad Political and Social Scis; Soc Applied Anthropology; Inst Soc Psycht, Eng. Author: Science in the New Education, 1934; Creative Group Education, 1937; Character Education in a Democracy, 1939; Introduction to Group Therapy, 1943; Recreation and Total Personality, 1946; The Practice of Group Therapy, 1947; Analytic Group Psychotherapy, 1950; Child Psychotherapy, 1952; Re-Educating the Delinquent, 1954; The Fields of Group Psychotherapy, 1956; Child-Centered Group Guidance of Parents, 1958; A Textbook of Analytic Group Psychotherapy, 1964; Reclaiming the Delinquent, 1965; Because I Live Here: Vita-Erg Therapy With Repressed Psychotic Women, 1969; ed, Intl Jour of Group Psychotherapy, since 1951. Recipient: Dr Adolf Meyer award, service to Mh, 1956. Home: 321 E 18 St, New York, NY.

SLEPIAN, Joseph, US, engineer; b. Boston, Mass, Feb 11, 1891; s. Barnet and Annie (Bantick); BA Harvard U, 1911, MA, 1912, PhD, 1913; postgrad study: Göttingen, Ger, 1914; Sorbonne, 1914; hon, DEng, Case Inst, 1949; m. Rose Myerson Nov 10, 1918; c: Robert, David. Ret; Asso dir, research, Westinghouse Elec Corp, 1938-58, research engr, 1916-38; mem, fac, Cornell U, 1914-15. Prin contrib: holder, prin patents on lightning arresters, circuit breakers and rectifiers. Mem: Amer Math Soc; Amer Phys Soc; Amer Inst EEs; Inst Research Engrs; Amer Assn Physics Tchrs; Natl Acad Scis; Phi Beta Kappa. Contbr to sci pubs. Recipient: John Scott medal, City of Phila, 1932; Westinghouse Order of Merit, 1935; Lamme medal, Amer Inst EEs, 1942, Edison medal, 1948. Home: 115 Lancaster St, Pittsburgh, Pa. Office: Westinghouse Research Lab, E Pittsburgh, Pa.

SLESENGER, David Serge, Eng, business exec; b. Newcastle-upon-Tyne, Eng, Dec 21, 1937; s. Joseph and Mabel (Levy); m. Jacqueline Greene, Aug 20, 1960; c: Joseph, Deborah. Mgn dir, Slesenger & Sons Ltd. Lt, RASC, 1956-58. Hon treas: Newcastle J Nursery Sch; Newcastle J Day Sch; hon secy, Jesmond Heb Cong. Spec interests: J educ, photography. Home: 2 Westfield Park, Gosforth, Newcastle-upon-Tyne Eng. Office: 15/19 Westmorland Rd, Newcastle-upon-Tyne, Eng.

SLESINGER, Zalmen, US, educator; b. Jerusalem, Pal, May 14, 1906; s. Abraham and Sheindel (Schlessinger); in US since 1923; BS, NYU, 1929; f, Dropsie Coll, 1930; PhD, Tchrs' Coll, Columbia U, 1936; m. Ella Schapira, 1946. Dir, dept pedg and curricular materials, Amer Assn for J Educ, since 1948; exec-secy: Natl Council on Adult J Educ, since 1965; Natl Council on J Audio-Visual Materials, since 1949, mem, bd of rev, 1949; prin, Shaarei Tefilah Heb Sch, Far Rockaway, NY, 1941-48; head, Heb dept, J Cen Sch, Far Rockaway, NY, 1941-48. Mem: exec comm, Natl Council for J Educ; Natl J Music Council, since 1952; ed bd, J Education, since 1950. Author: Education and the Class Struggle, 1937; Survey of Jewish Education in Southern Illinois, 1943; Survey of Jewish Education in Rural Maine, 1944; Audio-Visual Program Aids for the Jewish Festivals, 1957; Teaching Bible Through Audio-Visual Aids, 1961; co-author: Outline of a Curriculum on Israel, 1950; The Jewish School—Your Child and You; The Jew in America, 1954; ed: The Pedg Reporter, since 1949; The J Audio-Visual Rev, since 1949. Home: 920 E 17 St, Brooklyn, NY. Office: 101 Fifth Ave, New York, NY.

SLESS, Herzl, Eng, physician; b. Cork, Ir, Feb 9, 1922; s. Joseph and Julia (Fox); in Eng since 1946; MB, BCh, BAO,

LM, DObst, MRCGP, U Coll, Cork; m. Ruth Levy, Jan 31, 1922; c: Marion, Josepha, John, Sara. Phys with Garland, Sless & Curtis. Chmn, Brighton Hillel House; hon life vice-pres, J Soc, Sussex U; grand vice-pres, B'nai B'rith Dist Grand Lodge, Gt Brit and Ir; dep, Bd Deps of Brit J; mem: Coll Gen Practitioners; Sussex Unity Masonic Lodge. Hobby: caravaning. Home: 294 Dyke Rd, Brighton, Sussex, Eng.

SLESSNER, Charles, US, scientist; b. Lafayette, Ind, Nov 10, 1915; s. Carl and Esther (Krushen); BS, Purdue U, 1937, MSE, 1940, PhD, 1944; m. Ruth Shapiro, Aug 20, 1940; c: Carolyn, Robert, Sharon, Dianne, Daniel. Sci adv, tech exch br, dir of intl affairs, AEC, since 1966, with commn since 1946; adj prof, math, Montgomery Coll, Rockville, Md, since 1966; research chem Purdue U, 1937-44; research asst, Columbia U, 1944-45; research sci, Carbide amd Carbon Chemicals Corp, NYC 1945-46. Mem: Amer Chem Soc; Atomic Ind Forum; Phi Lambda Upsilon; Sigma Xi. Contbr to profsl jours. Home: 12921 Moray Rd, Silver Spring, Md, Office: AEC, Washington, DC.

SLIFKIN, Lawrence Myer, US, physicist; b. Bluefield, W Va, Sep 29, 1925; s. Isaac and Eva (Baden); BA, NYU, 1947; MA, PhD, Princeton U, 1950; m. Miriam Kresses, July 4, 1948; c: Anne, Rebecca, Merle, Naomi. Prof, U of NC, since 1963; fac mem since 1955; research asst prof, U Ill, 1950-54; asst prof, U Minn, 1954-55. US Army, 1944-46. Bd trustees, Beth El Cong, 1961-62; f, Amer Phys Soc; mem, Soc Photographic Sci and Engrs. Contbr to sci jours; cons to govt off and labs. Home: 313 Burlage Circle, Chapel Hill, NC. Office: Dept of Physics, U of NC, Chapel Hill, NC.

SLOAN, Henry Siegmund, US, writer, editor; b. Berlin, Ger, Mar 27, 1926; s. Siegmund and Else (Berndt) Ehrlich; in US since 1937; AB, SF State Coll, 1950; MA, NYU, 1952; att, U of Cal, Berkeley, 1953-55; PhD, NYU, 1962. Asso ed, Current Biography, since 1961; contbr: Ency Americana; Americana Annual, both since 1965; Midcentury Authors; Current Biography; social case worker, LA Co Bur of Public Assistance, 1955-58; free-lance writer, ed, Lewis Hist Publishing Co and other firms, 1958-60. Cpl, US Army, 1944-46. Mem: Amer Hist Assn; Amer Acad Political and Social Sci; Phi Alpha Theta; Mensa; Leo Baeck Inst. Hobbies: hiking, swimming, travel, folk music. Home: 210 W 70 St, New York, NY. Office: c/o H W Wilson Co, 950 University Ave, Bronx, NY.

SLOANE, Paul, US, psychiatrist; b. Phila, Pa, Jan 15, 1902; s. Solomon and Anna (Israelit) Slonimsky; BA, U of Pa, 1921; MD, Jefferson Med Coll, 1925; m. Vera Taplinger, Feb 11, 1940; c: Richard, Barbara. Em sr att psycht, Albert Einstein Med Cen, since 1967, chmn, psycht dept, 1953-67; asso prof, U of Pa, since 1964; fac mem, Phila Psychiatric Assn for Psychan, since 1949; lectr, neur, Temple U Med Sch, 1931-42; neur, St Joseph's Hosp, 1931-36; sr att neur, Mt Sinai Hosp, 1935-53; lectr, psycht, Phila Psychiatric Hosp, 1946-53; clinical prof, neuro-psycht, Hahnemann Med Coll, 1948-58; dir, res training, educ, Phila Psychiatric Cen, 1953-57; lectr, Moore Coll of Art, 1965. Secy, trustee, J Publ Soc; mem: bd dirs: J Y's and Cens, Phila; Germantown J Cen; Amer Psychiatric Assn; Phila Psychiatric Assn; Pa Psychiatric Soc; Phila Co Med Soc; Phila Assn for Psychan; Intl Psychoanalytic Assn; fmr: chmn, admn bd, Phila Assn for Psychan, repr councilor, Amer Psychoanalytic Assn, 1951-53. Ed, jour, Phila Psychiatric Hosp, 1956-68; contbr to sci jours. Home: 1025 W Cliveden St, Philadelphia, Pa. Office: D-108 Presidential Apts, Philadelphia, Pa.

SLOBODKIN, Louis, US, sculptor, illustrator, author; b. Albany, NY, Feb 19, 1903; s. Nathan and Dora (Lubin); att, Beaux Arts Inst of Design, NY, 1918-23; m. Florence Gersh, 1927; c: Lawrence, Michael. Works include: Lincoln, Interior Bldg, Wash, DC, 1939; figure, Postmaster Gen Reception Room, Wash, DC, 1935; three sandstone panels, N Adams, Mass, 1942; granite eagles, Johnstown, Pa, 1937; Bethsheba, bronze, Tel Aviv Mus, Isr, 1940; Shulamith, 1933; God's head, 1945; Fo'castle Waltz, 1940; bronze, Tami, Toni, 1952; illus: The Moffats, 1941; The Middle Moffat, 1942; Sun and Wind and Mr Todd, 1943; Rufus, 1943; The Hundred Dresses, 1944; all by Eleanor Estes; Peter the Great, by Nina Brown Baker, 1943; Many Moons, by James Thurber, 1944; Tom Sawyer, by Mark Twain, 1946; Jonathan and the Rainbow, by Jacob Blank, 1950; Gertie The Horse, by Margaret Glendenning, 1951; Alhambra, by Washington Irving, 1953; The Magic Fishbone, by Charles Dickens, 1953; exhb: Metrop Mus; Bklyn Mus; Mus Natural Hist, all NY; Corcoran Gal, Wash, DC; Phila Art Mus; Chgo Art Inst; Simmons Coll, Boston; Rochester Art Mus. Author: Magic Michael, 1944; Friendly Animals, 1944; Clear the Track, 1945; Fo'castle Waltz, 1945; Adventures of Arab, 1946; Seaweed Hat, 1947; Hustle and Bustle, 1948; Bixxy, 1949; Sculpture Principles and Practice, 1949; Mr. Mushroom, 1950; Dinny and Danny, 1951; Our Friendly Friends, 1951; Space Ship Under Apple Tree, 1952; Circus April 1, 1953; Mr Petersand's Cats, 1954; The Late Cuckoo, 1962; Three-seated Space Ship, 1962; Moon Blossom and the Golden Penny, 1963; Yasu and the Strangers, 1963; The Polka-dot Goat, 1969; Round-trip Space Ship, 1969; author and illus: One is Good, 1956; The Little Mermaid, 1956; Thank You-You're Welcome, 1957; Melvin the Moose Child, 1957; The First Book of Drawing, 1958; The Wide Awake Owl, 1958; The Space Ship Returns, 1958; Trick or Treat, 1959; Excuse Me-Certainly, 1959; co-author, Too Many Mittens, 1958. Mem: bd dirs, Artists' Equity; Sculptors' Guild; Authors' Guild. Recipient: 22 medals, Beaux Arts Inst of Design, 1918-22; Louis Tiffany Found F, 1923; hon mention, Chgo War Memorial, 1932; commn for Fed Bldg, 1934; Fed Bldg, NY World's Fair, 1938; Caldecott Medal, Amer Libr Assn, 1943. Homes: 209 W 86 St, New York, NY; Ocean Beach, NY.

SLOCHOWER, Harry, US, psychoanalyst, author, educator; b. Bukovina, Aus-Hung, Sep 1, 1900; s. Mayer and Frieda (Schnapp); in US since 1913; BSS, CCNY, 1923; MA, Columbia U, 1924, PhD, 1928; grad studies: U Munich, 1925; U Berlin, 1926; U Heidelberg, 1926; Natl Psych Assn for Psychan, NYC, 1953-58; div; c: Joyce. Practising psychan, since 1948; mem, fac, New Sch for Soc Research, NYC, since 1947; visiting prof, Drew U; mem; fac, Bklyn Coll, 1930-56; Theodor Reik Clinic, 1956-58; f: Guggenheim, 1929-30; Bollingen Found, 1950-55; lectr, Wm A White Inst for Psycht, 1948-50. Author: Richard Dehmel, Der Mensch und der Denker, 1928; Three Ways of Modern Man, 1937; Thomas Mann's Story, 1938; No Voice is Wholly Lost, Writers and Thinkers in War and Peace, 1945; Mythopoesis: Myth Patterns in the Literary Classics: From the Book of Job to the Existentialists, 1969; chaps in books; Reichl's Philosophischer Almanach, 1927; Goethe-a Symposium, 1932; The Philosophy of Ernst Cassirer, 1949; Spiritual Problems in Contemporary Literature, 1952; Foundations of World Organization, 1952; ed, Guide to Psycht and Psych Lit, 1955-57; contbr to: Ency of the Social Scis; Collier's Ency; American People's Ency; lit and educ jours. Mem: Council Psychan Psychotherapists; Assn for Applied Psychan; Amer Group Psychotherapy Assn; NY Soc of Clinical Psych; Inter-Amer Soc of Psych. Hobbies: chess, tennis. Home: 221 E 18 St, Brooklyn, NY. Office: 46 E 73 St, New York, NY.

SLONE, Henry O, US, engineer; b. Philipsburg, Pa, May 25, 1925; s. Ruben and Goldie (Slone); BS, MS, Carnegie-Mellon Inst, 1949; m. Maxine Green, Oct 18, 1953; c: Minda, Sheila, Reuben. Project mgr, asst div chief, NASA Space Power Systems since 1949. US Army, 1944-46. Pres, Beth Isr-W Temple; treas, Cleveland Council on Soviet Anti-Semitism; mem, B'nai B'rith. Contbr to tech publs. Home: 15375 Sandalhaven Dr, Cleveland, O.

SLONIM, Emanuel, Isr, judge; b. Jerusalem, Apr 18, 1915; s. Shlomo and Esther; LLB, LSE, 1938; barrister-at-law, Middle Temple, London, 1939; m. Julia Levinson, Mar 14, 1948; c: Alina, Osnat, Reuel. Judge, Dist Court, Haifa, since 1949; advocate, 1941-48. Maj, Mil Court, IDF. Chmn: Isr-Brit Commonwealth Assn; Haifa-Portsmouth and Haifa-Hackney twinning comms; mem comm, Wfr of Soldiers Commn; dist supt, Haifa, Isr Grand Lodge; master, Mt Carmel Masons, Haifa, 1957-58; mem comm, Haifa Sym Orch; 1st prin, Mt Carmel Royal Arch, chap 804, Haifa. Hobbies: bridge, golf. Home: 27 Horeb St, Haifa, Isr. Office: Dist Court, Haifa, Isr.

SLONIM, Moses J, US, educator, real estate cons; b. Hartford, Conn, Mar 5, 1894; s. Nathan and Anna (Berman); att: NYU; Sorbonne U, Paris; LLB, U of Pa, 1916; m. Sophia Golland, Feb 15, 1922. Dir, dept land econ and real estate, and lectr, Wash U, since 1931; real estate cons, St Louis, since 1925; in law practice, Hartford, Conn, 1917. US Army, WW I. Hon pres, St Louis Council, AJCong, since 1955, fmr pres, natl exec comm; mem: natl exec comm, ZOA; Amer Real Estate Urban Econ Soc; natl comm on educ, Natl Assn Real Estate Bds, since 1952; Amer Inst Real Estate Appraisers; Acad Sci; Histadrut Ivrit, Amer; fmr: pres: St Louis div, AZC; ZOA, St Louis; delg, Amer J Conf, field secy, Pal Found Fund; Fac, Wash U. Contbr articles on land

econ and related subjects, also subjects of J interest to publs. Home: 7545 York Dr, St Louis, Mo. Office: Wash U, St Louis, Mo.

SLONIM, Sima, Isr, artist; b. Jaffa, Nov 7, 1910; d. Schneur and Hanna (Slonim); att: Acad Grand Chaunier, Collorosy Acad, both Paris; Westminster Tech Inst of Art, London; m. Reuven Wartenberg; c: Ariela Madder, Asnat. Art tchr, Oranim, Kibbutz Tchrs Sem; one-man shows: Beit-Pevsner, 1945; Mikra Studio, Tel Aviv, 1955; Artists House, Jerusalem, 1955; 220 Gal, Tel Aviv, 1962; Mus Modern Art, Haifa, 1964; Chemerinsky Gal, Tel Aviv, 1966; exhbs in Eng, Netherlands, Switz; represented in pvt collections. Recipient: Dizengoff prize, Tel Aviv Munic, 1942, 1962; Herman Struck prize, Haifa Munic, 1950, 1955; Malach prize, Ein Hod, 1959. Home: 67 Sea Rd, Haifa, Isr. Studio: Ein Hod Artists Village, Isr.

SLONIMSKY, Henry, US, educator; b. Minsk, Russ, Oct 9, 1884; s. Moses and Sarah (Epstein); in US since 1890; att: Harvard Coll, 1901-02; U of Pa, 1902-03; U Berlin, Ger, 1905-07; PhD, U Marburg, Ger, 1912; m. Minnie Tennenbaum, Sep 1927. Prof em, HUC-JIR, NY, since 1952, mem fac: HUC, since 1922, JIR, since 1924; lectr, Columbia U, 1914-15; instr, asso, Johns Hopkins U, 1915-21. Home: 375 West End Ave, New York, NY.

SHLONIMSKY, Nicolas, US, author, musicologist, composer, conductor; b. St Petersburg, Russ, Apr 27, 1894; s. Leonid and Faina (Vengerova); in US since 1923; att St Petersburg Conservatory, 1910-18; m. Dorothy Adlow, July 30, 1931; c: Electra Yourke. Tours as pianist: Eur, 1921-22; US since 1923; S Amer, 1941-42; instr, Eastman Sch of Music, 1923-25; conductor, Pierian Sodality, Harvard, 1928-30; visiting prof, Colo Coll, 1940, 1948-49; instr, Russ, Harvard U, 1946-47; lectr, music: Simmons Coll, 1948-49; UCLA, 1946-47; conductor, Apollo Club Chorus, 1947-49; guest conductor: Paris; Berlin; Budapest; Havana; SF; LA; Hollywood; S Amer; hon prof, Brazilian Conservatory of Music, 1941; traveled as Amer specialist under auspices of State Dept to: Russ; Pol; Yugo; Greece; Isr; Rum; Bulgaria, 1962-63; mem adv panel, Off of Cultural Exch, State Dept. Compositions: music for ballet, orch, piano, voice; author: Music since 1900, pub, 1937; Music of Latin America, 1945; Thesaurus of Scales and Melodic Patterns, 1947; The Road to Music, 1947; A Thing or Two About Music, 1948; Lexicon of Musical Invective, 1953; ed: 4th-8th eds, International Cyclopedia of Music and Musicians, 1946, 1949, 1952, 1956, 1958; 5th ed, Baker's Biographical Dictionary of Musicians, 1958; mem, ed bd, Ency Britannica, since 1958, compiler, annual music surveys, Ency Britannica Year Book, since 1951; prog annotator for LA Philharmonic Orch, 1966-69. Home and office: 151 W 88 St, New York, NY.

SLOTKI, Judah Jacob, Eng, educator; b. Jerusalem, Pal, Mar 10, 1903; s. Israel and Sarah (Lowenstein); in Eng since 1912; BA, hons, Manchester U, 1923, MA, 1925, dipl, educ, 1924, PhD, 1939; m. Phyllis Gittelson, June 29, 1948; c: Ian, Angela. Dir, Heb educ, Manchester area, since 1955; gov, Manchester Coll of Educ; vice-prin, Manchester Talmud Torah, 1927-42; supt, J Educ Bd, 1942-46; dir, Leeds Educ Bd, 1946-55. Prin contrib: established Steinart Day Training Coll for Heb Tchrs. Chmn: JNF Educ Comm; Manchester J Study Circles, 1924-46; Manchester Mizrachi; vice-pres, Brit Mizrachi Org; exec, Manchester Zionist Cen Council; hon secy, U Sem for Hebraic Studies, 1923-39; mem, B'nai B'rith. Author: Midrash Rabba, commentary and trans; Commentary on Ruth, Daniel, Ezra, Nehemiah; New Children's Festival Book, 1962; Bible Textbooks for schs; contbr, articles on Hebraic studies to profsl jours. Home: 11 Castelton Rd, Salford, Eng. Office: Emanuel Raffles House, Upper Park Rd, Salford, Eng.

SLOTKIN, Edgar A US, surgeon; b. Buffalo, NY, Jan 8, 1909; s. Nathan and Carolyn (Beck); BS, Hobart Coll, 1930; MD, U Buffalo, 1934; m. Alma Rosenquist, Feb 1, 1942; c: Edgar, Ellen. Asst clinical prof, urol, SUNY, since 1963; urol, Buffalo Gen Hosp, since 1963; att urol, Children's Hosp, since 1946. Maj, NY State Guard, 1941-45. Mem: AJComm; Buffalo Acad of Med; Erie Co and NY State Med Socs; AMA; Amer Urol Assn; Amer Coll Surg; Amer Acad Ped; Soc for Ped Urol; Maimonides Med Soc; U Buffalo Alumni; club, Westwood Country. Contbr to med jours. Home: 33 Burbank Terr, Buffalo, NY. Office: 50 High St, Buffalo, NY.

SLOTKIN, Hugo, US, business exec; b. Bklyn, NY, June 12, 1912; s. Samuel and Fanny (Rivkin); att LIU; m. Babette

Walsey, Sep 22, 1935; c: A Donald, Mitchell, Curtis, Todd. Pres, Hygrade Food Products Corp, meat packers, since 1949, chmn bd, since 1968, with co since 1931. Vice-chmn, dir, exec bd, Amer Meat Inst; pres, E Meat Packers Assn, 1945-46; dir: Detroit service group, Allied J Campaign; Sinai Hosp Detroit; mem, bd of dirs, United Found, Detroit; mem: Chgo Bd Trade; Inedible Animal Fat Advisory Comm; clubs: Bankers of Amer; Lawyers; Standard; Franklin Hills Golf; Harmonie, NY. Hobbies: golf, farming. Home: 19201 Strathcona Dr, Detroit, Mich. Office: 11801 Mack Ave, Detroit, Mich.

SLUTSKY, Yehuda, (pen name, **Sallou**), Isr, author; b. Shchorsk, Russ, Nov 10, 1915; s. Avraham and Musia (Zimerinov); in Isr since 1925; PhD, Heb U, Jerusalem; m. Lea Blezowski, 1937; c: Nehora Gabbay, Ofra Dayagi, Hanna Tamari. Lectr, Tel Aviv U. Author, co-ed, The History of the Haganah; contbr chaps: Lexicon Hasifrut Haivrit; Ency Lehalutzei Haishuv Uvonav. Home: 74 Arlosoroff St, Ramat Gan, Isr.

SLUTZKI, Arie, Isr, judge; b. Turetz, Russ, Jan 1, 1904; s. Gad and Zelda (Bitenski); in Isr since 1944; Magister Juris; Vienna U, 1929; m. Jaffa Grinberg, 1946. Judge, Dist Court, Haifa, since 1961; atty, 1933-54; magistrate, 1954-61. Author: Factory Law, 1962. Home: 27a Hayim Rd, Haifa, Isr.

SLYOMOVICS,Vera, Can, communal leader; b. Bustino, Czech, Mar 19, 1926; in Can since 1948; BA, Charlles U, Prague, Czech; m. Josef Slyomovics; c: Peter, Susan. Vice-pres, Can dist, B'nai B'rith; mem bd: Can JIAS; B'nai B'rith Hillel Youth Org; mem: UN Org; Free Eur Org; active: aid of Czech J; preservation of J monuments in E Eur; fmr: secy, Czech U Student Council; participated in Haganah transp, 1945-48. Home: 711 Bertrand Circle, Montreal, Can.

SMILG-BENARIO, Michael, Arg, journalist, author; b. St Petersburg, Russ, Mar 16, 1895; s. Josef and Jeanette (Benario) Smilg; in Arg since 1937; att St Anne Sch, Russ; m. Hanna Levy, June 27, 1922; c: Josef, Chief cd, Semanario Israelita, since 1969; currently, researcher on J problems; journalist: Münchener Neueste Nachrichten 1919-20; Prager Presse, 1920-24; Nieuwe Rotterdamsche Courant, 1921-25; Die Weltbühne, 1928-33; Pariser Tageblatt, 1935-37; dir, Deutsche Freiheit, 1934-35. Author: Von der Demokratie zur Diktatur, 1920; Der Zusammenbruch der Zarenmonarchie, 1929; Von Kerensky zu Lenin, 1930; La Conspiracion Mundial del Nacismo, 1939; Death and Resurrection of Democracy in Europe, Span, 1943; Die Ritualmordlegende im Zaristischen Russland, Span, 1968. Spec interest, hist studies. Home: 1995 Conde St, Buenos Aires, Arg.

SMITH, Alfred E, US, real estate broker; b. Chgo, Ill, Dec 28, 1905; s. Morris and Bella (Simons); m. Ida Cohen, Apr 8, 1930; c: Linda, Myrna. Pres, Heb Cemetery, 1954; dir: Merchants Assn, 1930; BBB, 1954; Temple Isr, 1933-53; ARC, 1948-51; Travelers Aid, 1946; Oasis Temple, Shriners, 1932; dir, Royal Order of Jesters, 1953; chmn: Civil Service Commn, 1954; co-found, Fed J Charities, 1938 all Charlotte; mem, Masons; club, Lions, pres, 1932. Home: 2216 Pembroke Ave, Charlotte, NC. Office: 218 Latta Arcade, Charlotte, NC.

SMITH, Gadiel M, US, physician, educator; b. NYC, Oct 9, 1912; s. William and Rebecca (Silverman); BS, CCNY, 1932; MD, U Geneva, 1936; m. Anita Cooper, Aug 17, 1940; c: Deborah, Bettina. Staff phys, VA Hosp, since 1951; asst prof, clinical med, NY Coll of Med. Chmn: fgn affairs comm, AJComm; lecture comm, YM-YWHA's, Essex Co; prof comm, Temple Emanuel, 1st vice-pres, 1959-61; f: Amer Coll of Phys, dipl, Amer Bd of Internal Med; FACP. Contbr articles on internal med. Home: 19 Mounthaven Dr, Livingston, NJ. Office: VA Hospital, E Orange, NJ.

SMITH, Herbert Allen, Isr, statistician; b. Pittsburgh, Pa, Feb 2, 1923; s. Nathan and Esther (Lifshitz); in Isr since 1950; BSc, U Pittsburgh, 1943; MA, PhD, Columbia U; m. Emma Newburger, 1950; c: Yoav, Raphael, Esther. Dir, Manpower Planning Auth, Min of Lab since 1962; dep dir, Cen Bur of Stat, 1955-62; stat adv, Econ Adv Staff, Govt of Isr, 1955; kibbutz mem, 1950-55. Sgt, USAF, 1943-46. Author: Manpower Strategy for Developing Countries, 1967; Israelis Vote, 1969. Spec interests: election analysis, writing plays. Home: 10 Berechiyahu St, Jerusalem, Isr. Office: Min of Lab, Jerusalem, Isr.

SMITH, Joseph, US, rabbi; b. Bklyn, NY, May 17, 1920; s. Emanuel and Edna (Falk); BS, CCNY, 1942; BHL, Sem Coll

J Studies, 1941; MHL, ordained rabbi, JTSA, 1946; m. Henrietta Lichtman, Apr 2, 1944; c: Penina, David. Rabbi, Beth Shalom, Whittier, Cal, since 1964; mem fac, dept rel,Whittier Coll; rabbi; B'nai Isr, Burlington, NJ, 1946-48; B'nai Isr, Steubenville, O, 1948-52; Beth El Syn, Waterbury, Conn, 1952-64. Pres, San Gabriel Valley Rabb Assn; chmn, comm on Soviet Jewry, Bd Rabbis S Cal; mem exec, Dial Help; secy, Acad of Rel and Mh, Whittier; J Chaplain, Nelles Sch for Boys; mem, Alumni Assn, Tchrs Inst. Home: 201 S Norma St, La Habra, Cal. Study: 14564 E Hawes St, Whittier, Cal.

SMITH, Nora, US, psychiatrist; b. Fulda, Ger; d. Max and Bella (Nussbaum); Tchrs Dipl, Heb Tchrs Training Sch for Girls, 1955; BS, Bklyn, Coll, 1956; MD, SUNY, 1960. Dir, Infant Evaluation Service, Staten I Mh Cen, since 1969, staff psycht, since 1967, f, child and comty psycht, 1964-67. Prin contrib: research in child devl. Secy, mem, bd govs, Assn Orthodox J Sci; mem: Amer Psychiatric Assn; NY Council on Child Psycht; Med Soc Kings Co. Offices: 380 E 18 St, Brooklyn, NY; 657 Castleton Ave, Staten Island, NY.

SMOLAR, Boris (Ber), US, editor; b. Rovno, Russ, May 27, 1897; s. Leizer-Leivia and Mariam, (Shearer); in US since 1919; att Northwestern U, 1921-24; m. Genia Lewin, Feb 26, 1934. Ed in chief em, JTA, since 1967; ed in chief 1924-67, fmr chief Eur corresp in London, Paris, Berlin,Moscow, Jerusalem; regular weekly column, Between You and Me, in Eng-J press, also appearing in Span, Ger; Port; Yiddish; Heb; ed staff mem, J Daily Forward, 1920; roving corresp, NY World, 1928-30. bd dirs, natl commn, JDC; Amer Acad Political and Social Sci; UN Corresp Assn; bd dirs, YIVO; club, J Writers. Author: Yiddish and Heb: Drei Prinzn; The Witch; Die Lebendige Aritmetik; Kinderwelt; The Kiddies Corner, NY. Recipient: citation for promoting Chr-J amity in US, NCCJ; Isr Govt Silver Medal, bronze peace medal, 10th Anniversary Medal, other awards from Isr Govt; Alumna Pax Amoris Medal, Pope Paul VI, 1965. Home: 147 W 79 St, New York, NY. Office: 760 First Ave, New York, NY.

SMOLI, Eliezer, Isr, author; educator; b. Ukraine, Aug 15, 1901; s. Avraham and Gitle; in Isr since 1920; att: Tchrs Sem, Jerusalem; m. Shoshana Levin, 1929; c: Shulamit Vitkon, Tamar Ben Josef, Ret; fmr tchr: Degania, Kfar Gileadi, Kfar Mahal, Tel Aviv; sch insp, Sharon region, 1948-66; sent to Berlin to prepare young people for immigration to Isr, 1934-36. Author of 15 books for youngsters, including: Anshei Bereshit; Bnei Hayore; Laila baMishalt; Tziporim Be Israel; El haMabua; Bein Hermon veGilboa; contbr to press. Recipient: Bialik award, 1935; Isr, award 1956. Home: Ramatayim, Isr.

SMOTRICZ, Israel, Isr, educator; b. Wiznitz, Russ, Apr 26, 1908; s. David and Rachel (Sternhell); in Isr since 1935; PhD, U Vienna, 1932; m. Sidonia Reif, Sep 22, 1935. Tchr, hist, geog, Herzlia Gymnasium. Author: Mahapechat, 1848 beAustria, 1957; Historya Hadasha 1789-1830, pub 1958; Sefer Limud beHistoria Hadasha 1492-1753, pub 1961; Kitzur Toldot Germanya, 1871-1965, pub 1967. Mem: Theodore Herzl Lodge, B'nai B'rith; cultural activity, Isr Lab Org. Home: 13 Maccabi St, Tel Aviv, Isr. Office: 106 Jabotinsky St, Tel Aviv, Isr.

SMULEVITZ, Henry S, US, attorney; b. Radom, Pol, May 14, 1909; s. Berryl and Gertrude (Milman); in US since 1920; att: NYU Law Sch,1929; Chgo Law Sch, 1930-31; LLB, 1932; m. Frances Givel, Apr 27, 1941; c: Alan, Gloria. Pvt practice since 1934; acting judge, juvenile court, 1951-55; atty, City of Hammond: Dept of Redevl, Urban Renewal; Bd of Bldg Contractors. Pres: B'nai B'rith, Ind State, 1954-55, E Chgo lodge, 1939-40, mem natl commn vocational service, since 1956, secy, 1959-62; co-found, E Chgo Forum; mem: exec comm, ADL, Midwest, 1952-64; Amer Bar Assn, comm antitrust law; Ind Bar Assn, comm criminal jurisprudence, 1953; E Chgo Bar Assn; Amer Judicature Soc; Decalogue Soc Lawyers, Chgo; Beth Sholom Cong; Beth El Temple. Home: 7246 Knickerbocker Pkwy, Hammond, Ind. Offices: 4520 Indianapolis Blvd, E Chicago, Ill; 5305 Hohman Ave, Hammond, Ind.

SNAPIR, Nachum, Isr, scientist, educator; b. Tel Aviv, Isr, Oct 3, 1934; s. Yehiel and Sara; BSc, Heb U, Jerusalem, 1959, MSc, 1962, PhD, 1966; m. Yael Avneri, June 5, 1956; c: Orit, Galia, Arnon. Lectr, Heb U, since 1967. IDF, 1952-55. Prin contrib: improving artifical insemination and fertility in poultry. Mem; World Poultry Sci Assn. Contbr to sci publs.

Home: 6 Hagra St, Rehovot, Isr. Office: Fac of Agric, Heb U Rehovot, Isr.

SNAPIRI, Nachum, Isr, auditor; b. Wilno, Pol, July 9, 1911; s. Aharon and Esther (Golomb) Wirszup; in Isr since 1930; att: Heb U, Jerusalem, 1930-34; m. Sarah Diskin, Mar 8, 1942; c: Abraham, Yehuda, Yair. Treas, Internal Auditors in Isr, since 1968; sportwriter, novel trans, 1932-40; internal auditor: Natl Lab Org; Natl Sick Fund in Isr, both 1940-69. Irgun Zvei Leumi, 1931-42; IDF. Coord, Fgn Friendship Assns; hon secy, Isr-Amer Assn; mem comm, Acctnts Assn; secy, mem supr control comm, Natl Lab Org; El Al Students Corp; mem Va'ad Kehila; fmr: world comm, J from Wilna; cen comm, Brit Rishonim. Hobby: chess. Home: 57 Rambam St, Jerusalem, Isr. Office: 2 Ben Yehuda St, Jerusalem, Isr.

SNEIDER, Leopold J, US, business exec; b. Burlington, Vt, May 19, 1896; s. Charles and Fannie (Silverman); BA, NYU, 1918; LLB, Columbia U, 1921; att New Sch for Social Research, 1925-30; m. Frances Magid, Sep 22, 1921; c: Richard. Ret; partner; Magid Handbags, 1936-63; A I Magid Co, 1922-36. Mem: NYC Sch Bd, 1940-46; Ind Comm 41, US Dept of Labr, 1941; mfr adv bd, OPA, 1943-45; bd dirs: J Reconstructionist Found, since 1940; Soc for Advancement of Judaism, since 1936; Amer Econ Comm for Pal, 1944-48; vice-pres, Pal Gals, 1945-48; mem: Natl Council J Cultural Agcys. B'nai B'rith; Pi Lambda Phi; Tau Kappa Alpha; Intercoll Soc. Author: What is the American Way, 1936; Where Business Fails the Businessman, 1965; ed bd, The Reconstructionist, since 1962. Home: 19 E 88 St, New York, NY.

SNIDER, Jack Engler, US, dentist; b. Jacksonville, Fla, Mar 19, 1923; s. David and Annie (Engler); DDS, Emory U, 1946; postgrad: U of NC, 1955; NYU, 1965; m. Shirley Wexler, Nov 24, 1946; c: Harold, Carolyn, Marlene. Pvt practice, since 1946; vice-pres, Reliance Mutual Fund, 1961-68. Lt, USN, 1946-48. Pres: J Family and Children's Services; Temple Ahavath Chesed Brotherhood, 1956-57, mem, bd trustees, 1956-66; fmr: vice-chmn, Fla Sch for Deaf and Blind; vice-pres, B'nai B'rith lodge, campaign chmn, Comty Chest; exec bd, Jacksonville JCC; bd dirs: River Garden Home for Aged; bd trustees: Hope Haven Children's Hosp; mem: Alpha Omega; Tau Epsilon Phi; clubs: Lions; Beauclers Country. Hobbies: coin collecting, fishing. Home: 3741 Montclair, Jacksonville, Fla. Office: 3645 Hendricks, Jacksonville, Fla.

SNITOW, Virginia L, US, communal leader; b. NYC; d. Louis and Tania (Rosenberg) Levitt; BA, Hunter Coll, 1931; m. Charles Snitow, Nov 2, 1935; c: Ann, Alan. Natl vice-pres, AJCong since 1964, pres womens div, since 1964; secy-treas, Leadership Conf of J Women's Orgs; delg, Dem Party Conv, 1968; mem: League of Women Voters; Pan-Pacific and SE Asia Women's Assn; Women's Intl League for Peace and Freedom; hs tchr, Eng, NYC, 1932-47. Home: 81 Walworth Ave, Scarsdale, NY. Office: 331 Madison Ave, New York, NY.

SNYDER, Herman E, US, rabbi; b. New Bedford, Mass, July 7, 1901; s. Moses and Dora (Genensky); BA, U Cincinnati, 1926; BHL, HUC, 1926, ordained rabbi, 1928, DD, 1956; att: U Chgo; U Ill; m. Adele Biederman, Feb 11, 1934; c: Julia Shlaferman, Jane. Rabbi, Sinai Temple, Springfield, Mass, since 1947; counselor, Hillel Found, since 1947; rabbi, Brith Sholom Temple, Ill, 1928-47. Chaplain, USN, USMC, 1942-45. Pres: Juvenile Delinquency Commn; ARC chap; Fgn Policy Assn; New Eng region; CCAR, fmr financial secy; Comty Council Social Agcys; E New Eng Conf Lib Rabbis; secy, HUc-JIR, Alumni Assn, fmr pres; corporator, Five Cents Savings Bank; mem: exec bd, Mass Bd Rabbis; bd, United Fund, since 1949; exec bd, Mass Commn on Children and Youth; fmr: pres: J Social Service Bur; B'nai B'rith; secy, Springfield J Fed; chmn, USO; cdr, JWV Post; club, Rotary. Author: The History of Brith Sholom Temple and the Jewish Community of Springfield, Ill, 1937; contbr to Universal J Ency. Recipient: citation, outstanding clergyman, Jr C of C, Springfield, 1954. Home: 50 Colony Rd, Longmeadow, Mass. Study: 1100 Dickinson St, Springfield, Mass.

SNYDER, Jerry Norton, US, attorney; b. Cheyenne, Wyo, Jan 18, 1932; s. Benjamin and Esther (Stark); att: U Neb; U Colo; BS, LLB, U Denver; m. Marilyn Epstein, Feb 27, 1957; c: Brent, Leslie, Tabie. Atty since 1956. USAF, 1951-52. Pres, Lodge 171, B'nai B'rith; trustee: BMH Cong; mem: Zeta Beta Tau Frat; Phi Delta Phi. Home: 5950 E Cedar Ave, Denver, Colo. Office: 718 17 St, Denver, Colo.

SNYDER, Mitchell, Isr, statistician; b. Phila, Pa, Nov 4, 1938; s. Frank and Dorothy (Miller); in Isr since 1968; BA, BHL, Yeshiva U, NY, 1960; MS, NYU, 1962; PhD, U Chgo, 1965; m. Rebecca Brill, Sep 13, 1963; c: Isaiah, Yaffa. Head, dept sci applications, Computer Cen, Bar Ilan U, since 1969, lectr, dept math, since 1968; mem, tech staff, Bell Telephone Labs, 1965-68. Mem: Inst Math Stat; Amer Stat Soc; Math Assn Amer; Assn Computer Machinery; AACI; fmr pres: NJ chap, Assn Orthodox J Scis; U Chgo chap, Yavneh. Author: Comparison of Multivariate Test Statistics, 1964; Winsorizing with a Covariate, 1967. Spec interest, Torah. Home: 14 Kedushat Yom Tov St, Yismach Moshe, Isr. Office: Bar Ilan U, Ramat Gan, Isr.

SOBEL, Eli, US, educator; b. NYC, Jan 17, 1915; s. Martin and Lena (Filenbaum); BA, U Ala, 1937; MA, 1938; PhD, U Cal, Berkeley, 1946; m. Margaret Forster, Dec 2, 1944; c: Jeffrey. Prof, Germanic Lang and Lit, UCLA, since 1946, asso dean, Coll Letters and Sci, 1957-64; chmn, dept Germanic langs, 1964-69; cons, Council of Grad Schs in US, since 1966; mem: sr accrediting commn, W Assns Schs and Colls, since 1965. Lt cdr, USN, 1942-45. Vice-pres, Philol Assn, Pacific Coast, 1952-54; mem: rel educ comm, Temple Isaiah, LA; ed bd, Amer Assn Tchrs Ger; MLA; Renaissance Soc Amer, found; Phi Sigma Delta; Zeta Beta Tau; Hillel Guild. Author: Sebastian Brant and Ovid, 1952; Alte Newe Zeitung; A Sixteenth Century Collection of Fables, 1958; The Tristan Romance in the Meisterlieder of Hans Sachs, 1963; Liebesspiele, 1970; contbr: numerous articles, revs. Recipient: silver star, Pres unit citation, 9 combat stars, citation from Philippines Pres, World War II; Guggenheim f, 1959; DAAD F, W Ger govt, 1966. Spec interest: Renaissance and Reformation books and manuscripts. Home: 2207 Kelton Ave, Los Angeles, Cal. Office: Dept of Germanic Langs, UCLA, Los Angeles, Cal.

SOBEL, I Jerome, US, physician; b. Strimba, Hung, July 16, 1899; s. Shimon and Sura (Wieder); in US since 1905; BS, Loyola U, MD, Strich Coll of Med, 1927; att: Columbia U; U Mich; Fordham U; Wayne U; m. Dorothy Martinique, June 25, 1932 (decd); c: Marcia, Beth; m. 2nd, Anne Nakonechna, Dec 1963; c: Tamara, Michael. Pvt practice since 1928; mem, courtesy med staff: Beth Isr Hosp, since 1928; Passaic Gen Hosp, since 1928; St Mary's Hosp, since 1936, fmr asso i/c phys therapy, all Passaic. Lt, SATC, 1918; lt, USNG, 1928-33. Chmn, comm for chronically ill and indigent, Passaic Co Med Soc, since 1957; bd mem: YM-YWHA, since 1936; Hillel Acad, since 1950; B'nai Isr Old Age Home, since 1955; chmn, mem comm, Amer Phys F for IMA, fmr natl pres; mem: Amer Assn for Automotive Med; AMA; Amer Geriatric Soc; Passaic Co Med Soc; B'nai B'rith; Amer Legion; JWV; YMCA; fmr: natl pres: Phi Lambda Kappa; Med Student Aid Soc; counselor in E for Loyola U; clubs: Lions; Passaic Practitioners, fmr pres; Boosters, fmr chmn. Ed, Phi Lambda Kappa Quarterly, since 1946; contbr to med jours. Recipient: dist award, man of year award, both Amer Phys F for IMA, 1969. Home: Jefferson Lakes, Stanhope, NJ. Office: 136 Broadway, Passaic, NJ.

SOBEL, Samuel, US, chaplain, rabbi; b. Greensboro, NC, July 14, 1916; s. Isaiah and Mary (Witten); BA, Yeshiva U, 1941; MA, Columbia U, 1944; ordained rabbi, HUC-JIR, 1945; att, Union Theol Sem, NY, 1953; EdD, Jackson Coll, Honolulu, Hawaii, 1956; m. Shirley Monat, Aug 18, 1946 (decd); c: Arleen, Barbara, Karen. Capt, dist chaplain, Naval Dist of Wash, since 1968; staff chaplain, Mil Sea Transp Service, Atlantic Area, 1963-65, exec dir, Armed Forces Chaplain Bd, Dept of Defense, Wash, DC, 1965-68, USN chaplain since 1945, first J chaplain appt to regular USN rank capt; rabbi, B'er Hayim Cong, Cumberland, Md, 1944; mem, fac, Jackson Coll, 1954-56. Treas, Mil Chaplains Assn of US; mem: CCAR; NY Bd Rabbis; fmr pres, Hampton Roads Rabb Assn. Author: I Love the House, 1962; ed, A Treasury of Jewish Sea Stories, 1965. Recipient: Four Chaplains awards: Res Off's Assn of US, 1955, B'nai B'rith, 1964; Bronze Star with Combat V; Purple Heart; Legion of Merit. Home: 4305 Federal St, Rockville, Md. Office: District Chaplain, Headquarters, Naval District of Wash, Washington, DC.

SOBELOFF, Irene E, US, communal worker; b. Rakonitz, Aus-Hung; d. David and Sophie (Popper) Ehrlich; att: Tchrs Training Sch, Baltimore; Columbia U; grad, Md Inst of Art and Design, 1909-16; m. Simon Sobeloff, May 19, 1918; c: Eva Goldstrom, Ruth Mayer. Recording secy, Natl Council J Women, 1946-53, pres, mid-Atlantic conf, 1936-40; recording secy, asso treas, United for New Amers, 1948-50, bd mem to

1953; chmn, public wfr citizenship, public affairs, Americanization, Md Fed of Women's Clubs, since 1935; pres, Fed J Women's Orgs of Md, 1943-46; chmn, Nationality Council of Md, since 1940; mem: League Women Voters; Women's Civic League; B'nai B'rith Women; Hadassah; Women's Intl League for Peace and Freedom; NCCJ. Home: 2404 W Rogers Ave, Baltimore, Md.

SOBELOFF, Isidore, US, organization exec; b. Baltimore, Md, Aug 30, 1899; s. Jacob and Mary (Kaplan); m. Edith Mozorosky, July 30, 1932; c: Jonathan. Lectr, W Coast Sch for Communal Service, HUC, since 1969; city ed, Cumberland, Md, Daily News, 1920-22; dir: J Comty Cen, Jersey City, NJ, 1922-25; PR, FJP, NY, 1925-30; mgn ed, J Social Service Quarterly, 1932-36; dir, public educ, Wfr Council, NYC, 1934-37, ed, Better Times, social work publ, 1934-37; cons, fund-raising and publicity Travelers Aid Soc, 1930-34; exec vice-pres, JWF, Detroit, 1937-64; exec dir, J Fed-Council, Gtr LA, 1964-68; fmr lectr, Training Bur for J Social Work. Pres, Natl Conf J Social Welfare, 1945; bd mem: CJFWF, 1940; JWB; JDC; Natl Found J Culture; JTA; Mich Wfr League; United Comty Services of Detroit; Health and Wfr Council, LA; org, Natl War Fund; mem: UJA missions to Eur and Isr from 1949. Home: 9221 Charleville Blvd, Beverly Hills, Cal.

SOBELOFF, Simon E, US, jurist, government official; b. Baltimore, Md, Dec 3, 1894; s. Jacob and Mary (Kaplan); LLB, U Md, 1915, hon LLD, 1954; hon: LHD, HUC, 1956; DLitt, New Sch for Social Research, 1956; LLD: Morgan State Coll, 1955; Dropsie Coll, 1959; m. Irene Ehrlich, May 19, 1918; c: Ruth Mayer, Evva Goldstrom. Chief judge, US Court of Appeals for Fourth Circuit, since 1956; US atty, Dist of Md, 1931-34; arbitrator, men's clothing ind, Md, 1934-36; city solicitor, Baltimore, 1943-47; chmn, commn on admn org, State of Md, 1951-52; chief judge, Court of Appeals, Md, 1952-54; solicitor gen of US, 1954-56. Fmr natl vice-pres, AJCong, co-found, Baltimore br, 1932, fmr pres; vice-pres, Prisoners Aid Assn, mem, bd dirs; pres, B'nai B'rith lodge, 1925; fmr pres: Bd J Educ; J Council; mem, bd dirs, Asso J Charities since 1925, all in Baltimore; trustee, Brandeis U; club, Phoenix. Home: 2404 W Rogers Ave, Baltimore, Md. Office: 630 US Court House, Baltimore, Md.

SOCOLOW, A Walter, US, attorney; b. NYC, Feb 4, 1907; s. Harry and May (Stein); BS, CCNY, 1927; LLB, Harvard U, 1930; m. Edith Gutman, May 28, 1933; c: Robert, Daniel, Joan. Pvt practice since 1930. Pres, J Educ Comm, NY, 1968; chmn, Manhattan div, United Syn of Amer, 1958-61; trustee, FJP; adv council, Soc for Advancement of Judaism, since 1952, chmn, bd trustees, 1949-52; natl planning comm, JTSA, 1953-60; bd dirs, J Reconstructionist Found Inc, since 1945; mem, JDC, since 1950; master, Marshall lodge, Masons, 1938. Author: The Law of Radio Broadcasting, 2 vols, 1939. Home: 45 E 82 St, New York, NY. Office: 580 Fifth Ave, New York, NY.

SOETENDORP, Jacob, Netherlands, rabbi, author; b. Amsterdam, July 5, 1914; s. Abraham and Jansje (van der Glas); ordained rabbi, Rabb Sem, Amsterdam; Dr HC: U Amsterdam; Heb U, Jerusalem; Leo Baeck Coll; Leiden U; m. Miriam Blits, Jan 11, 1940; c: Abraham, David, Bentsion, Leah. Rabbi, Lib J Cong, Amsterdam, since 1955. Author: Een Staat Herrijst, 1948; De Huidige Toestand van het Joodse Volk, 1952; Schepping en Ondergang in het oude Oosten, 1955; Symboliek der Joodse Religie, 1958; Phoenix Bijbel Pockets, 1962; Ontmoetingen in Ballingschap, 1964, 1966, 2 vols; De Wereld van het Optimisme, 1969. Mem: Nederlandse Zionistenbond; Genootschap v d Joodse Wetenschap; Rotary Intl; Ancient Order of Foresters; B'nai B'rith. Hobbies: art, music. Home: A J Ernststraat 21, Amsterdam, Netherlands. Study: Graafschapstraat 8, Amsterdam, Netherlands.

SOETENDORP, Sjalom Awraham, Netherlands, rabbi; b. Amsterdam, Netherlands, Feb 16, 1943; s. Jacob and Miriam (Blits); ordained rabbi, Leo Baeck Coll, London, 1967; f, HUC-JIR, 1967-68; m. Sipora Vanyssel, Aug 15, 1965; c: Aviva. Rabbi, Lib J Cong, The Hague, Netherlands, since 1968; fmr rabbi: Manchester; NY State. Mem: Pres Youth Sect for Progressive Judaism; World Council of Faith. Home: 856 Laan van Meerdervoort, The Hague, Netherlands, Study: 12 Stad Houdelaaw, The Hague, Netherlands.

SOFFER, Alfred, US, physician; b. S Bend, Ind, May 5, 1922; s. Simon and Bessie (Rokach); MD, U Wis, 1945; m. Isabel Weintraub, July 22, 1956; c: Jonathan, Hillel, Joshua. Med admnr, AMA, since 1962; ed in chief, Diseases of the Chest, since 1968; exec dir, Amer Coll Chest Phys, since 1969; prof, med, Chgo Med Sch, U Health Sci, since 1968; chief, cardiopulmonary labs, Rochester Gen Hosp 1958-62. Capt, US Army MC, 1946-48. F: Amer Coll Phys; Amer Fed for Clinical Research, asso f, Amer Coll Card; fmr mem, bd dirs: Temple Beth El; J Social Service Bur; pres, Rochester Reconstructionist F, 1961; natl speakers bur; Hadassah; United Syn of Amer; ZOA. Author: Clinical Aspects of Chelation, 1963; contbr to profsl jours. Home: 325 Alexis Court, Glenview, Ill. Office: 112 E Chestnut St, Chicago, Ill.

SOFFER, Harry N, US, attorney; b. Russ, Dec 29, 1902; s. Louis and Kate (Kramer); in US since 1910; LLB, Wash U, Mo, 1924; m. Ruth Coopersmith, June 26, 1960. Pvt practice since 1924. Vice-pres, B'nai Amoona Cong; fmr pres: Achad-Haam Heb Sch; B'nai B'rith lodge; provisional judge, Munic Courts; bd dirs: YM-YHWA; Children's Home of St Louis; election bd, St Louis Co, 1961-69; mem: St Louis and Mo Bar Assns; Lawyers Assn of St Louis. Home: 8701 Delmar, University City, Mo. Office: 722 Chestnut St, St Louis, Mo.

SOFFER, Milton David, US, educator, chemist; b. NYC, Dec 11, 1914; s. Henry and Hannah (Kleinman); BS, U Ark, 1937; MA, Harvard U, 1939, PhD, 1942; m. Rosanne Smith, Feb 16, 1957; c: Katherine Barns, Roderick, Frederic. Sophia Smith Prof, chem, Smith Coll, since 1970, mem, grad fac since 1960, mem fac since 1942, prof, chem, 1956-70; f, Natl Defense Research Comm, Purdue U, 1941-42; visiting prof, U Mass, 1962; visiting sci-in-res, Hollins Coll, 1963; cons to ind; research grantee: Research Corp, 1946-52; NSF, 1952-68; Guggenheim f, Oxford U, 1950-51; NSF sr postdoc f, Harvard U, 1958-59. Mem: AAAS; AAUP; Amer Chem Soc; Soc Harvard Chem; Sigma Xi; club: Harvard, Pocumtuck Valley, Mass. Contbr to profsl jours. Home: Poplar Hill Rd, RFD, Haydenville, Mass. Office: Sabin-Reed Hall, Smith Coll, Northampton, Mass.

SOHLBERG, David, Isr, educator; b. Basel, Switz, July 9, 1924; s. Marcus and Margaretha (Hausdorff); in Isr since 1955; PhD, U Basel, 1955; m. Chava Kahn, Oct 15, 1958; c: Jael, Michal, Shay. Sr lectr, head, dept classical studies, Bar Ilan U, Ramat Gan; guest sr lectr, Tel-Aviv U. Home: 21 Bnei Moshe St, Tel Aviv, Isr. Office: Bar Ilan U, Ramat Gan, Isr.

SOIHETMAN, Meir, Isr, government official; b. Russ, Aug 7, 1917; s. Mordhai and Hana (Meiler); in Isr since 1936; CED, Fac de Droit, Paris; ordained rabbi, Paris; PhD, U Mo; m. Miriam Kaniel; c: Eliav, Hana-Ora. Dep dir gen, Min of the Interior, since 1960, insp gen of natl elections. Home: 7 Narkis St, Jerusalem, Isr. Office: Min of Interior, Jerusalem, Isr.

SOKAL, Robert R, US, educator; b. Vienna, Aus, Jan 13, 1926; s. Siegfried and Klara (Rathner); in US since 1947; BS, St Johns U, Shanghai, China, 1947; PhD, U Chgo, 1952; m. Julie Yang, Aug 12, 1948; c: David, Hannah. Prof, biol sci, SUNY, Stony Brook, since 1969; prof stat biol, U Kan, 1961-69, on fac since 1951; Hillel counselor, 1955-61; biol instr, Shanghai Amer Sch, 1946-47; asst, zool, U Chgo, 1950-51; NSF sr post doc f, U Coll, London, 1959-60; Fulbright prof, Tel Aviv U, Heb U, both Isr, 1963-64. Mem: Biometric Soc; Soc of Naturalists; Amer Soc of Zool; Genet Soc of Amer; Soc for Study of Evolution, fmr vice-pres; Entomological Soc of Amer; Sigma Xi; B'nai B'rith, fmr lodge pres; fmr: f, Chgo Natural Hist Mus; mem bd, Kan Sch of Rel. Author: The Principles of Numerical Taxonomy, 1963; Biometry, 1969; Statistical Tables, 1969; contbr to profsl jours. Home: 35 Gernet Pl, Elmont, NY. Office: SUNY, Stony Brook, NY.

SOKOBIN, Alan Mayor, US, rabbi; b. Newark, NJ, Mar 8, 1926; s. Max and Pauline (Ferster); BA, Syracuse U, 1950; MAHL, HUC, 1955; ThD, Burton Coll, Colo, 1962; m. Miriam Levy, May 19, 1957; c: Sharon, Jonathan. Rabbi, Temple Bnai Isr, since 1960. Mem: Commn on Justice and Peace; CCAR; Commn on Social Action; UAHC. Home: 35 Garnet Pl, Elmont, NY. Study: Temple Bnai Isr, Elmont, NY.

SOKOLOF, Herbert, US, business exec; b. Bklyn, NY, Jan 18, 1928; s. Alfred and Adelaide (Crystal); BBA, Pace Coll, 1950; MBA, CCNY, 1957; m. Gladys Epstein, Mar 31, 1958; c: Ellen, Steven, Allison. Vice-pres: Color Card Corp, since 1963; and treas, Channel Marine Service, since 1959; comptroller, Durelle Fabrics Corp, 1961-63; treas, vice-pres, Auralfone Corp, 1958-61; sr partner, accnt firm, Sokolof Kane, 1958. Warrant off, US Army, 1952-54. Pres, Woodhaven J Cen; vice-pres: Woodhaven-Cypress Hills Cmty Assn; Pace Alumni Assn, Queens; fmr: vice-pres, E Meadow J Cen; treas, JWV; chmn, Forest Pkwy Tenants Comm; club, Rep. Recipient: Korea Medal; Spec Defense Dept Medal; cert of award, Yeshiva U, 1966; testimonial dinner, Woodhaven J Cen, 1967; citation and breakfast, UJA, 1968; plaque and breakfast, State of Isr Bonds, 1968; award citation, Rabbi Isaac Elchanan Theol Sem, 1968; citation, FJP, 1967. Hobbies: sports, collecting antique shaving mugs. Home: 80-50 Forest Pkwy, Woodhaven, NY. Office: 34-42 41 St, Long Island City, NY.

SOKOLOFF, Leon, US, pathologist; b. Bklyn, NY, May 9, 1919; s. Barnet and Ray (Cohen); BA, NYU, 1938; MD, 1944; m. Barbara Snow, June 2, 1950 (decd); c: Michael, Naomi. Chief, sect on rheumatic diseases, lab of experimental path, Natl Inst Athritis and Metabolic Diseases, NIH, Bethesda, Md, since 1952; instr, path, NYU, 1947-50, asst prof, 1950-52. Mem: Amer Assn Paths and Bacteriol; Sigma Xi; Harvey Soc. Contbr to med jours. Home: 6804 Laverock Court, Bethesda, Md. Office: Natl Inst of Arthritis and Metabolic Diseases, NIH, Bethesda, Md.

SOKOLOVSKY, Mordechai, Isr, chemist; b. Tel Aviv, Dec 27, 1936; s. Yehuda and Sonia (Fishlin); MSc, Heb U, Jerusalem, 1960; PhD, summa cum laude, Weizmann Inst, Rehovot, 1964; m. Ruth Gerti, Nov 14, 1964. Asso prof, U Tel Aviv, dept biochem; research f, Harvard U, 1964-66; asso f, 1966-67; research f, Peter Bent Brigham Hosp, Boston, 1964-67. IDF, 1954-56. Mem: Chem Socs, Isr, London, Amer. Contbr to jours. Recipient: Bloch award, Weizmann Inst, 1963. Home: 136 Achad Haam St, Tel Aviv, Isr. Office: U of Tel Aviv, Ramat Aviv, Isr.

SOKOLOWSKI, Jerzy Ftanislaw, Isr, scientist; b. Cracow, Pol, Mar 29, 1928; s. Zygmunt and Stefania (Moszkowska) Horowitz; in Isr since 1956; MSc, Wroclaw Tech U, Pol, 1952; m. Rina Glimovsky, Aug 31, 1966; c: Eldad. Sr sci, Weizmann Inst of Sci, since 1957; research asst, Inst for Nuclear Research, Pol, 1955-57; i/c devl lab, Factory of Elec Components, Pol, 1954-55; research asst, Acad of Med, Pol, 1953-54. Contb: to publs in field nuclear instrumentation and experimental nuclear physics. Home: 12 Neve Weizmann, Rehovot, Isr. Office: POB 26, Rehovot, Isr.

SOKOLY, Laszlo, US, dentist; b. Vac, Hun, May 1, 1926; s. Aladar and Terezia (Heksh); in US since 1957; att Dent Sch of Budapest; DDS, Geogetown U, 1963; m. Annamaria Orban, July 3, 1952; c: Kathy, Thomas. Asst prof, dent, Georgetown U Dent Sch, since 1963; pvt practice since 1963. Mem: Royal Soc Health, Eng; Amer Dent Assn; Amer Dent Sch Assn; DC Dent Soc; Maimonides Dent Soc; Alpha Omega; club, Georgetown U Alumni. Contbr chaps in: Dentist Laboratory Technical Relation, 1964; Dental Health Team, 1970. Recipient: restorative dent award, Georgetown U Alumni Club, 1963; John Burke Memorial award, Opr Dent Assn, 1963. Hobby: soccer. Home: 6626 Hillmead, Bethesda, Md. Office: 1722 Eye St, Washington, DC.

SOLAR, Hervey L, US, business exec; b. Lynn, Mass, Aug 31, 1908; s. Harry and Lena (Newburgh); BS, Harvard U, 1929, LLB, 1933; m. Mildred Beckerman, May, 1938; c: Richard, Barry, Robert, Alan. Vice-pres, Walcott Corp, since 1942; trustee, Amesbury Properties Trust; partner, Todd Asso; corporator, Grove Hall Savings Bank, since 1960; treas, Window Shop, Cambridge, Mass. Overseer, Sch Contemporary Studies, Brandeis U; mem: bd govs, Hum Relations Cen, Boston U; trustee: CJA, fmr chmn women's apparel div; Temple Isr since 1962; fmr: chmn, Boston campaign, Friends Heb U; bd dirs, J Family and Children's Service; pres, J Vocational Service. Home: 75 Shaw Rd, Chestnut Hill, Mass. Office: 1050 Commonwealth Ave, Boston, Mass.

SOLE, Moshe Zeev, Isr, rabbi; b. Munkacs, Hung, Sep 12, 1908; s. Shlomo and Rivka (Frenkel); in Isr since 1939; PhD, U Prague, 1933; Rabb Sem, Berlin, 1931-33; Theol Sem, Bresalu, 1929-31; m. Betty Wislicki, Dec 8, 1936; c: Shoshana Lichtman, Rivka. Secy, rabb court, Jerusalem, since 1945; rabbi, Czech, 1933-39; secy, J Comty, Jerusalem, 1939-45; Mem: Heb Writers Assn; Brit Ivrit Olamit; Jerusalem Phil Soc; B'nai B'rith. Author: books and articles on rel, phil. Home: 3 Alfasi St, Jerusalem, Isr. Office: 40 Jaffa Rd, Jerusalem, Isr.

SOLENDER, Sanford Lewis, US, social worker; b. Pleasantville, NY, Aug 23, 1914; s. Samuel and Catherine (Goldsmith); BS, NYU, 1935; MA, Columbia U, 1937; m. Ethel Klonick, June 19, 1935; c. Stephen, Peter, Ellen, Susan. Exec vice-pres, JWB, since 1960; dir: J Cen div, 1948-60; boys work, Neighborhood House, Bklyn, 1935-36; activities, assr dir, Bx House, NYC, 1936-39; head worker, Madison House, NYC, 1939-42; exec dir, Council Educ Alliance, Cleveland, O, 1942-48. Chmn, planning comm, Intl Conf J Communal Service; first vice-pres, Natl Council J Communal Service; mem: Natl Conf Lawyers and Social Workers; Health and Wfr Task Force, Natl Adv Council on Status Women; bd dirs: Natl Assembly for Social Policy and Devl; USO; Bur Careers in J Service; Natl Educ Adv Comm of Hadassah; bd overseers, Florence Heller Grad Sch for Advanced Studies, in Social Wfr, Brandeis U; US Comm, Intl Conf Social Work; visiting comm, U Coll of Arts and Sci, NYU; bd trustees, Council of Intl Progs for Youth Leaders and Social Workers; Cong Emanu El, Mt Vernon, NY; NY state Citizens Comm for Public Schs; fmr: mem, Natl Adv Council on Public Wfr HEW, Commn on Social Policy and Action. Pres, Natl Assn J Cen Workers; mem, Bd Educ, City of Mt Vernon; pres, Natl Conf Social Wfr. Mem ed, bd J Social Service Quarterly, since 1946; contbr to social service jours. Home: 121 Country Ridge Dr, Port Chester, NY. Office: 15 E 26 St, New York, NY.

SOLOFF, Louis A, US, cardiologist, educator; b. Paris, Fr, Oct 2, 1904; s. Abraham and Rebecca (Wagenfeld); in US since 1905; BA, U of Pa, 1926; MD, U Chgo, 1930; m. Mathilde Robin, Dec, 25, 1934; c: JoAnn. Prof, med, chief, div card, Temple U Health Sci Cen, since 1956, on fac since 1941; chief, med, card Episcopal Hosp; dir, lab, St Joseph's Hosp and Eagleville Sanatorium, 1938-47. F: Amer Coll of Phys; Phila Coll of Phys; dipl, Bd, of Card; mem: Phila Co, Pa State Med Socs; AMA; AHA; Amer Fed for Clinical Research; Assn U Card; Sigma Xi. Contbr to med jours. Home: 1901 Walnut St, Philadelphia, Pa. Office: 3401 N Broad St, Philadelphia, Pa.

SOLOFF, Mordecai Isaac, US, rabbi, educator, author; b. Igumen, Russ, July 2, 1901; s. Lippman and Rivko (Goldberg); in US since 1910; BS, CCNY, 1923; MA, Tchrs Coll, Columbia U, 1927; ordained rabbi, MHL, HUC, 1940, DD, 1965; m. Eve Miller, Nov 1924; c: Rav, Tamar Brower. Rabbi: Temple Jeremiah, fmr, Temple Isr, Westchester, LA, since 1952; Cen Syn, Nassau Co, NY, 1942-44; fmr prin, sup: Cong Chizuk Amuno, Baltimore; Beth-El, Providence; Shaare Zedek, Detroit; Temple Emmanuel B'nai Jeshurun, Milw; tchr, Heb, Sunday Schs, Bklyn, Bx, NY, 1919-23; staff mem: Bur J Educ, NY, 1924-27; Bd J Educ, Chgo, 1927-29; Baltimore, 1946-52; rabbi, Bnai Sholom, Essex, Md, 1948-52. Mem: CCAR. Author: When the Jewish People Was Young, 1934; How the Jewish People Grew Up, 1936; How the Jewish People Lives Today, 1940; Jewish Life and Work Book, 1950; Our Prayerbook, 1950; contbr to Universal J Ency and J educ mags. Home: 8045 Emerson Ave, Los Angeles, Cal. Study: 78333 Airport Blvd, Los Angeles, Cal.

SOLOFF, Rav Asher, US, rabbi; b. Bklyn, NY, Jan 4, 1927; s. Mordecai and Eve (Miller); BA, U Cincinnati, 1947; MHL, ordained rabbi, HUC-JIR, 1951; PhD, Drew U, Madison, NJ, 1967; m. Harriet Leibowitz, Jan 27, 1952; c: Rebecca, Sharon, Michael. Rabbi, E End Temple, since 1959; instr, HUC-JIR Sch of Educ since 1967; rabbi, Temple Isr, Lafayette, Ind, 1951-52; asst rabbi, Temple B'nai Jeshurun, Newark, NJ, 1954-59. Chaplain, lt, US Army, 1952-54. Pres, Essex Co Bd Rabbis; treas, Assn Reform Rabbis, NY; chmn, UJA, 1966-68; mem: exec comm, CCAR; LZOA; ACLU; UN Assn. Home: 60 Gramercy Park, New York, NY. Study: 398 Second Ave, New York, NY.

SOLOFF, Solomon, US, optometrist; b. Bridgeport, Conn, Nov 8, 1913; s. Meyer and Esther (Gimborg); att: NYU, 1932-37; OD, cum laude, N Ill Coll Optometry, 1940; m. Yetta Zagorin, Oct 11, 1942; c: Judith, David. Pvt practice since 1940. Vice-pres, North NJ Region, United Syn of Amer, 1961-65; bd trustee, treas, Ocean Co Coll; bd dirs: Co council, Boy Scouts of Amer; Cong B'nai Isr, since 1951; hist, Shalom lodge, Masons since 1955; bd trustee, Comty Memorial Hosp, 1963-66; co-chmn, Toms River UJA, 1952, 1961; mem: Toms River Bd Educ; Ocean-Monmouth Optometric Assn; Amer Optometric Assn; NJ Optometric Soc; Eye Research Found; B'nai B'rith; Farband; AJCong; C of C; club, Kiwanis. Home: 306 Washington St, Toms River, NJ. Office: 28 Robbins St, Toms River, NJ.

SOLOMON, Alan David, Isr, mathematician; b. NYC, Apr 6, 1940; s. Charles and Ella (Lowenschutz); in Isr since 1967; BS, CCNY, 1959; MS, NYU, 1960, PhD, 1963; m. Faiza Nabi, Sep 12, 1968. Sr lectr, math, Tel Aviv U, since 1967; asst prof, research sci, NYU, 1963-67. Mem: Amer Math Soc; Solar Energy Soc; Soc for Ind and Applied Math. Contbr: research papers in applied math. Home: 29 Sokolov St, Tel Aviv, Isr. Office: Tel Aviv U, Ramat Aviv, Isr.

SOLOMON, Bertha, S Afr, legislator; b. Russ, Jan 1, 1892; BA, LLB; widow. Advocate, Supr Court, Johannesburg; mem, Provincial Council of Transvaal, 1933-38; MP for Jeppe, 1938-58. Life vice-pres, Natl Council Women S Afr. Author: Time Remembered, autobiography. Home: 4 Riviera Mansions, Killarney, Johannesburg, S Afr.

SOLOMON, Gus J, US, jurist; b. Portland, Ore, Aug 29, 1906; s. Jacob and Rose (Rosencrantz); PhB, U Chgo, 1926; LLB, Stanford U, 1929; m. Elisabeth Willer, Mar 18, 1939; c: Gerald, Phillip, Richard. Chief judge, US Dist Court, Ore, since 1958, judge since 1948. Vice-pres, AJCong, since 1959; mem, natl civil rights comm, ADL, since 1956, mem bd and exec comm, regional bd, since 1956, pres, 1960-61; bd regents, U Portland; mem, bd visitors, U Oregon Law Sch; exec bd, AJComm. Home: 2323 SW Park Pl, Portland, Ore. Office: 615 US Court House, Portland, Ore.

SOLOMON, Izler, US, conductor, educator; b. St Paul, Minn, Jan 11, 1910; s. Harry and Eva (Levin); att Mich State Coll, 1928-31; hon DMus: Pacific U; Butler U; Anderson Coll; Franklin Coll; hon LLD, Ind Cen; m. Sorelle Melamed, Nov 26, 1931 (decd): c: Joseph (decd); m. 2nd, Elizabeth Westfeldt, Feb 26, 1961. Conductor, musical dir, Indianapolis Sym Orch, since 1956; music dir, Aspen Festival, Aspen, Colo, since 1956; instr violin, Mich State Coll, 1931-36; conductor, musical dir, Columbus Philharmonic Orch, O, 1941-56; prof music, O State U, 1947-56; conductor: Ill Sym Orch, Chgo, 1956; Women's Sym Orch, Chgo, 1940-41; New Orleans Summer Pops Sym, 1943-44; guest conductor: Buffalo Philharmonic Orch, 1936; Detroit Civic Orch, 1936; Les Concerts Symphoniques de Montreal, 1939-42; NBC Sym Orch, 1939-42, 1947; Phila Orch, 1940; Detroit Sym Orch, 1945; Vancouver Sym Orch, 1945; Chgo Grand Park Sym, 1945-47; Hollywood Bowl Sym Orch, 1946-47; Isr Philharmonic Orch, 1948; BBC Orch, London, 1962; NY Philharmonic Orch, Carnegie Hall, spec series for HS students—Lincoln Cen Educ Prog, 1962. Home: 4553 Broadway, Indianapolis, Ind. Office: Murat Theater, Indianapolis, Ind.

SOLOMON, Joseph C, US, psychiatrist, educator; b. Pretoria, S Afr, Jan 12, 1904; s. Jacob and Nellie (Gartenlaub); in US since 1906; BA, Syracuse U, 1924, MD, 1927; postgrad study: Paris; Vienna; m. Ruth Freeman, Mar 21, 1930; c: George, Daniel. Pvt practice, psychan, since 1946; asso clinical prof, psycht, U Cal Med Sch, since 1946; cons: Mt Zion Hosp, SF, since 1948, asso chief, dept psycht, 1939-48; f, Natl Comm for Mental Hygiene, Baltimore, 1936-39; asso prof, psycht, U Md, 1937-39. Maj, US Army, 1942-46, surg, 1946-53. Dipl, Amer Bd Neur and Psycht; f: Amer Acad Psychan; Amer Psycht Assn; Amer Orthopsychiatric Assn; charter mem, Amer Acad child Psycht; mem: SF Psychoanalytic Soc; Alpha Omega Alpha. Author: Soliders and Psychiatry in War, 1944; A Synthesis of Human Behavior, 1954; chap in Therapeutic Use of Play in Projective Techniques, by Anderson & Anderson; Ego Defenses in Childhood in Case Studies, by Burton; contbr to sci and med jours. Home: 34-25 Ave, San Francisco, Cal. Office: 2211 Post St, San Francisco, Cal.

SOLOMON, Kenneth Ira, US, certified public acctnt, attorney; b. Chgo, Ill, Feb 1, 1942; s. Morris and Freida (Krupka); BS, U of Ill, 1963, MS, 1964; JD, U Chgo Law Sch, 1967; m. Ellen Lewis; c: David, Michael. Partner, Laventhol, Krekstein, Horwath & Horwath, since 1970, asso dir, educ, 1968-70; asso prof, acctnt bus law, Chgo City Coll, 1964-67; asst prof, law, Case W Reserve U, Cleveland, O, 1967-68; spec lectr, panel mem at SEC and acctnts liability confs: Amer Mgmt Assn; SUNY Law Sch; Ill Soc of CPAs; Amer Accounting Assn; Georgetown U Law Sch. Chmn, comm: Decalogue Soc of Lawyers; Ill Soc CPAs; mem: Phi Kappa Phi; Beta Gamma Sigma; Beta Alpha Psi. Author: Partnerships-Tax and Accounting Treatment, 1964; Lawyer's Guide to Accounting Theory and Practice, 1970; contbr to tax and legal jours. Home: 7840 W Church St, Morton Grove, Ill. Office: 111 E Wacker Dr, Chicago, Ill.

SOLOMON, Maurice D, US, rabbi; b. I humen, Russ, Sep 25, 1911; s. Abraham and Anna (Nisnevich); in US since 1920, BS, Ill Inst of Tech, 1932; ordained rabbi, Heb Theol Coll, Chgo, 1934; hon DHL, Jewish U of Amer, 1960; m. Betty Mallin, Apr 15, 1934; c: Gloria Parelman, Ronald, Leon, Sheila. Rabbi: Kehilath Isr Syn, since 1934; Cong Tifereth Sforad, 1934-35; dir, dietary dept, Menorah Hosp, 1936; chaplain, Amer War Dads, 1942-45; dir, Sch of J Studies, 1947, all Kan City, Mo; visiting lectr: W Eur; Scandinavia; Mediterranean countries; Russ, 1964. Pres, Rabb Assn Kan City, since 1962; mem: RabCA; Mizrachi-Rel Zionists of Amer, Alumni Assn Heb Theol Coll; Union Orthodox Congs in Amer; rabb adv council, UJA; B'nai B'rith, hon; Alpha Epsilon Phi; fmr delg: Council Feds and Wfr Funds, Atlanta, Ga; World Conf Ashkenazi and Sephardic Syns, Jerusalem; overseas delg, UJA. Author: Homiletical Digest, 1952; Story of Purim, 1945; Survey of Orthodox Community of Kansas City, 1945; ed, bull, Rabb Assn of Heb Theol Coll, 1935-40; contrib ed, Kansas City J Chronicle, since 1934. Spec interest: sociol. Home: 437 E 64 Terr, Kansas City, Mo. Study: 800 E Meyer Blvd, Kansas City, Mo.

SOLOMON, Norman, Eng, rabbi; b. Cardiff, Wales, May 31, 1933; s. Phillip and Esther (Lewis); MA, Cambridge U, 1954; PhD, Manchester U; BMus, London U; ordained rabbi, J Coll, London, 1961; m. Doris Strauss, Aug, 1955; c: Jacob, Miriam, David, Baruch. Sr min, Greenbank Dr Heb Cong, since 1966; dir, rel studies, King David HS; min, Whitefield Heb Cong, Manchester, 1961-66. Home: 24 Sinclair Dr, Liverpool, Eng. Study: Greenbank Dr Heb Cong, Liverpool, Eng.

SOLOMON, Ram, Isr, attorney; b. Sofia, Bulgaria, Oct 11, 1917; s. Nissim and Buka (Farhi); in Isr since 1941; LLM, Sofia U, 1950; m. Bellina Kokashvilli, Dec 20, 1945; c: Rina. Pvt practice since 1950; legal adv, Isr Min of Police, 1948-52, dir, 1949-52; Commn of Prisons, Govt Prison Service, 1948-52. Haganah, 1947-48. Prin contrib: org sys of penal instns in Isr. Judge, Disciplinary, Appeals Court, Isr Bar; chmn, Isr-Japan Friendship Assn; mem: Criminology Soc; fgn relations comm, Isr Bar; fmr: gen secy: and found, League of Socs for Rehab of Offenders; Zionist Youth Cen, Sofia; Maccabi Sport Movement, Bulgaria. Author: Treatment of Offenders, 1951. Recipient: Inscribed in JNF Golden Book. Hobbies: stamps; coins. Home: 8 Um Blvd, Tel Aviv, Isr. Office: 37 Jaffa Rd, Tel Aviv, Isr.

SOLOMON, Reuben A, US, physician, educator; b. Indianapolis, Ind, Aug 17, 1893; s. Hyman and Rose (Center); BS, Ind U, 1915, MD, 1917, cum laude, 1918; grad study, Harvard U, 1927; m. Caroline Bamberger, Dec 12, 1927; c: Rose, Richard. Pvt practice since 1919; clinical prof, Ind Sch Med and Dent, since 1941; staff: Ind U Hosps; Indianapolis Gen Hosp; Methodist Hosp; St Vincent's Hosp, all since 1919. Capt, Amer Expeditionary Force, WW I; chief med examiner, Marion Co Draft Bd, WW II. Dipl, Amer Bd Internal Med; FACP; mem: AMA, Ind State Med Assn; Indianapolis Med Soc; Amer Legion; B'nai B'rith; Shriners; Indianapolis Heb Cong; Alpha Omega Alpha; Phi Beta Pi. Contbr to med jours. Home: 5330 N Penn St, Indianapolis, Ind. Office: 414 Hume Mansur Bldg, 23 E Ohio St, Indianapolis, Ind.

SOLOMON, Robert D, US, pathologist, educator; b. Delavan, Wis, Aug 28, 1917; s. Lewis and Sara (Ludgin); BS, U Chgo, 1938; MD, Johns Hopkins U, 1942, postgrad studies, 1957-60; m. Helen Fisher, Apr, 1943; c: Susan, Wendy, James, William. Dir, labs, Doctor's Hosp, since 1967; asso clinical prof, U S Cal, since 1960; path, Ill State Hosp, 1949-50; asso dir, Terre Haute Lab, 1950-56; asso path, Sinai Hosp, Baltimore, 1954-60; cons path, Baltimore Vet Hosp, 1954-60; asst prof, U Md, 1958-60; asso path, dir path research, City of Hope Med Cen, Cal, 1960-67. US Army MC, 1943-46. Prin contribs: demonstration of reversibility of artherosclerosis in animals. Mem: AMA, Coll Amer Paths; Amer Soc Clinical Path; Amer Chem Soc; Intl Acad Path; Amer Coll Phys; Phi Beta Kappa; Sigma Xi; club: Rotary. Contbr to med jours. Hobbies: astronomy, philately, electronics. Home: 1625 Calle Arroyo, Diablo, Cal. Office: Doctor's Hosp, San Leandro, Cal.

SOLOMON, Samuel, Can, research dir; b. Pol, Dec 25, 1925; s. Nathan and Rachel (Greenberg); in Can since 1936; BS, McGill U, 1947, MS, 1951, PhD, 1953; m. Sheila Horn, 1953; c: David, Peter, Jonathan. Prof, depts biochem and experimental med, McGill U, since 1960; dir, endrocrine lab, Royal Vic Hosp, since 1960; asst prof, Columbia U, 1959-60;

on fac since 1953. Mem: Amer Chem Soc; Endocrine Soc; AAAS; Can Biochem Soc; Harvey Soc; Montreal Physiological Soc; Amer Soc Biol Chems; Chem Inst of Can; Sigma Xi. Co-ed, Chemical and Biological Aspects of Steriod Conjugation; asso ed, Can Jour of Biochem, since 1966; mem, ed bd, Endocrinology, 1962-63; contbr to profsl jours. Home: 260 Kenaston Ave, Montreal, Can. Office: Royal Vic Hosp, Montreal, Can.

SOLOMON, Saul, US, physician, educator; b. Montreal, Can, Oct 26, 1905; s. Charles and Toba (Smilovitz); BA, McGill U, 1926, MD, 1930; in US since 1930. Visiting phys, Bellevue Hosp; asso visiting phys, U Hosp; att phys, Polyclinic Hosp, asso prof, clinical med, NYU, since 1955; pneumonia research, 1933-34. Col, US Army MC, chief of med service, 1940-45. F: Amer Coll phys; Amer Coll Chest Phys; Amer Coll Card; Amer Rheumatism Assn; mem: AMA; NY Co Med Soc; Amer Thoracic Soc. Author: Tuberculosis, 1952; contbr to med jours. Hobbies: swimming, tennis. Home: 33 East End Ave, New York, NY. Office: 755 Park Ave, New York, NY.

SOLOMON, Syd, US, artist, educator; b. Uniontown, Pa, July 12, 1917; s. Jack and Edith (Bennett); att: Ecole des Beaux Arts, Paris; Chgo Art Inst; m. Ann Cohen, Dec 29, 1941; c: Michele, Michael. Mem, dir fac, Famous Artists Sch Inc, since 1952; prof art, New Coll, Sarasota, Fla; tchr, Pittsburgh Art Inst, 1947-49; dir, Sarasota Sch of Art, 1950-59; dir, art teaching, Ringling Mus of Art, 1952-58. US Army, WW II. One-man exhbs: Fla Gulf Coast Art Cen; Tampa Art Cen; Tampa Art Assn; Sarasota Art Assn; Stetson U; Lowe Gal; Ringlin Mus of Art; Barry Coll, Miami; Jerusalem, Haifa, Tel Aviv, all Isr; Amer Fed of Art; Saidenberg Gal; McClung Mus; U Tenn; represented in: Baltimore Mus of Art; Delgado Mus of Art; Butler Mus of Amer; DeWhitte Mus of Art; Clearwater Art Mus; Walter P Chrysler Mus; Wadsworth Anthenum; Whitney Mus of Amer Art; Ringling Mus of Art; Guggenheim Mus, NYC; Cincinnati Mus of Art; Phila Mus; Lower Gal Mus; Rose Mus, Brandeis U; Adelphi Coll Mus. Mem: Artists Equity; Amer Watercolor Assn. Contbr to Art publs. Recipient: five Bronze Stars; gold medal of honor, Audubon Artists, 1957; Fla intl purchase award, 1952; watercolor purchase award, Bulter Mus of Art, 1957; 1st prize, Riverside Mus, 1957; 1st purchase natl oil award, Sarasota Art Assn, 1958; painting of year, 1958, 1962; 1st award, Lower Gal, U Miami, 1952; watercolor purchase award, Birmingham Mus, 1956; Hare award, 1956-57; Clark award, Soc of Four Arts, 1961. Home and studio: 2428 Portland St, Sarasota, Fla; summer, E Hampton, NY.

SOLOMON, Victor Martin, US, rabbi, educator; b. Bklyn, NY, Dec 13, 1928; s. Abraham and Tilla (Kirstein); ordained rabbi, Rabbi Isaac Elchanan Theol Sem, NY, 1955; BA, Yeshiva U, 1950; MA, Hunter Coll, 1954; STD, Temple U, 1960; STM, NY Theol Sem, 1967; m. Marcia Cohen, May 24, 1953; c: Samuel, Shimon Yitzchak. J chaplain, USAF, since 1967; prof, chmn, psych dept, Sophia U, Tokyo, Japan, since 1969; rabbi: Cong Ezrath Isr, Phila, Pa, 1955-63; Cong Ahavath Achim, Fairfield, Conn, 1965-67; instr: U Bridgeport, Conn, 1964-67; Sacred Heart U, 1965-67; Fairfield U, Conn, 1965-67. Capt, USAF since 1967. Mem: RabCA, fmr mem, exec comm; Metrop Assn for Applied Psych; Amer Sociol Assn; fmr, vice-pres: Yeshiva U Rabb Alumni; Rabb Council of Conn. Author: A Handbook on Conversions to the Religions of the World, 1965; ed, Rabbinical Council of America Sermon Manual, 1967. Recipient: Phil Award, Yeshiva U, 1950; Intl Brotherhood Award, Delta Tau Kappa, 1966; Brotherhood Award, Gtr Bridgeport Council of Churches, 1968. Hobbies: writing, basketball, swimming. Home and study: 6100th Support Wing, APO San Francisco 96323.

SOLOMONS, Michael, Isr, gynecologist; b. Dublin, Ir, May 3, 1919; s. Bethel and Gertrude (Levy); MB, U Dublin, 1941, FRCPI, 1959, FRCOG, 1965; m. Joan Maitland; four c. Gyn, Drumcondra Hosp; asst gyn, Mercer's Hosp; visiting obstet, Rotunda Hosp. Lt, RAFVR, 1945-47. Examiner, Royal Coll Surgs; f comm, Royal Coll Phys; council mem, Dublin J Progressive Cong; mem, Dublin Obstet Visiting, Soc; clubs: U; Kilburny Golf; Carrickmines Tennis. Author: Life Cycle, 1963; contbr to med jours. Hobbies: racing, tennis, skiing. Home and office: 42 Fitzwilliam Sq, Dublin, Ir.

SOLOMONS, Samuel Isaac, Eng, rabbi; b. London, Eng, Oct 6, 1903; s. Jacob and Freda; att J Coll, London, BA, hons, U Coll, London. Rabbi, Bournemouth New Reform Syn, since 1953. Mem, exec, Council Reform and Lib Rabbis. Recipient: Hollier Heb Scholarship, U Coll, London, 1925; Hester Roths-

child Scholarship, U Coll London, 1926. Hobby, music. Home: 44 Ave Court, The Avenue, Bournemouth, Eng. Study: 53 Christchurch Road, Bournemouth, Eng.

SOLOTAROFF, Theodore H, US, editor; b. Elizabeth, NJ, Oct 9, 1928; s. Ben and Rose (Weiss); BA, U Mich, 1952; MA, U Chgo, 1956; m. Lynne Friedman, Sep 4, 1950; c: Paul, Ivan; m. 2nd, Shirley Fingerhood, 1965; c: Jason. Ed: New Amer Review, since 1967; Asso ed, Commentary, 1960-66; ed, NY Herald Tribune, Bookweek, 1966; ed: An Age of Enormity, 1962; writers and Issues, 1969; contbr to lit jours. USN, 1946-48. Mem: Phi Beta Kappa. Home: 310 W 79 St, New York, NY. Office: 1301 Sixth Ave, New York, NY.

SOLOV, Zachary, US, choreographer, dancer. Chief choreographer, ballet master, Metrop Opera, since 1951; fmr choreographer: Lambertsville, NJ Music Circus; Yale U Dramatic Assn; Pittsburgh Playhouse; shows for China-Burma-India theater, US Army Spec Services; SF Opera, 1965-67; Dallas Opera, 1968; Kan City Performing Arts Festivals, 1967-69; fmr danced with: Littlefield Ballet; Amer Ballet Co; Dance Players; Ballet Theater; Broadway produc; TV shows. Home: 300 W 54 St, New York, NY. Office: Metrop Opera Assn, New York, NY.

SOLOW, Anatole Abraham, US, educator; b. Davos, Switz, Aug 10, 1913; s. Natan and Dora (Trilling); in US since 1939; BArch, Ecole Spéciale d' Architecture, Paris, 1935; MA, urban planning, Sch of Planning for Natl Devl, London, 1939; m. Ruth Scheiner, Feb 2, 1937; c: Jonathan, Daniel. Prof, urban and regional planning, U Pittsburgh, since 1964; research asst, MIT, 1939-40; research asso, Amer Public Health Assn, 1941-47; chief, div housing and planning, Org Amer States, 1947-59; physical regional planning adv, US Agcy for Intl Devl, 1959-64; cons on urban planning and housing: US Natl Housing Agcy, 1947; Isr Min of Lab and Reconstruction, 1948; Guat, 1949, Ecuador, 1951, Panama, 1955, Costa Rica, 1956; Min of Public Works, El Salvador, 1967-69; visiting prof, U of Pa, 1952-58. Cpl, engr corps, US Army, 1942-45, Mem: Amer Inst Planners; asso, Brit Town Planning Inst. Author: The Role of Industrial Estates, Areas and Zones in Urban and Regional Development, 1966; Housing Conditions of Urban Low Income Families in Latin America, 1966; Plans, Tools and Techniques for Implementation of Urban Planning, 1967. Hobbies: photography, tennis. Home: 5458 Covode St, Pittsburgh, Pa. Office: U of Pittsburgh Grad Sch of Public and Intl Affairs, Pittsburgh, Pa.

SOLOW, Robert Merton, US, economist; b. Bklyn, NY, Aug 23, 1924; s. Milton and Hannah (Sarney); BA, Harvard, 1947, MA, 1949, PhD, 1951; hon LLD, U Chgo, 1967; m. Barbara Lewis, Aug 19, 1945; c: John, Andrew, Katherine. Prof, econ, MIT, since 1958, on fac since 1950; sr econ, Council Econ Advs, 1961-62; Marshall lectr, U Cambridge, 1963; Devries lectr, Rotterdam, 1963; Wicksell lectr, Stockholm, 1964; Eastman visiting lectr, Oxford U, 1968-69; Radcliff lectr, Warwick U, 1968-69. Tech sgt, US Army Signal Corps, 1942-45. Pres, Econometric Soc, 1964-65; vice-pres: Amer Econ Assn, 1968-69; AAAS, 1970-71. Author: Capital Theory and the Rate of Return, 1963; The Sources of Unemployment in the US, 1964; Price Expectations and the Behavior of the Price Level, 1970; Growth Theory, 1970; co-author, Linear Programming and Economic Analysis, 1958; contbr to jours. Recipient: David A Wells prize, Harvard, 1951; John Bates Clark Medal, Amer Econ Assn, 1961. Spec interest: sailing, skiing. Home: 95 Martha's Point Rd, Concord, Mass. Office: MIT, Cambridge, Mass.

SOLTES, Avraham, US, rabbi; b. NYC, Mar 3, 1917; s. Mordecai and Ida (Levy); BSS, CCNY, 1937; MA, Tchrs Coll, Columbia U, 1938; ordained rabbi, MHL, JIR, 1942; hon DD, Philathea Coll, London, Ont, 1961; Titular Cruz Eloy Alfaro, 1962; DHL, HUC, 1967; m. Sara Rudavsky, June 19, 1938; c: Marnin, Michal, Z Ori, Dafna, Eyton. Vice-pres, comty relations, Glen Alden Corp, since 1969; J Chaplain, US Mil Acad, West Point, since 1963; chaplain, dir rel educ, Pleasantville Cottage Sch, 1941-53; dir, Hillel Found: Cornell U, 1943-45; McGill U, Montreal, 1945-46; asso rabbi, Cong Rodeph Shalom, NY, 1946-49; rabbi: Temple Sharay Tfilo, E Orange, NJ, 1949-64; Temple Emanuel, Gt Neck, NY, 1964-69. Chmn, Natl J Music Council, since 1963; mem: exec bd, Amer-Isr Cultural Found, since 1963; JBCA, since 1965; gov bd, J Liturgical Music Soc, since 1965; bd dirs: JWB, since 1964; Talbot-Perkins Child Adoption Agcy; Assn J Chaplains; pres, Gt Neck Assn of Mins, Priests and Rabbis, 1968-69. Author: Palestine in Poetry and Song of the Jewish Diaspora, 1942; Invocation—A Sheaf of Prayers, 1959; Off the Willows, 1969; Cantatas: The Vision of Moses, 1953; Israel Reborn, 1958; Maccabean Miracle Reborn, 1967; Jerusalem of Light, 1968; co-author: Oratorios: Golden Gates of Joy, 1966; Song of Esther, 1968; Prayer Books for Children and Youth, 1941-69. Office: 711 Fifth Ave, New York, NY.

SOLVEY, Joseph, Austr, engineer; b. Tomsk, Russ, Apr 16, 1910; s. Leo and Emma (Fliat) Soloveicik; in Austr since 1940; dipl physics, math, Lith U, Kaunas, 1930; CE, Ecole Natl Supérieure de L'Aeronautique, Paris, 1932; MME, U Melbourne, 1947; m. Lily Bruml, Mar 12, 1946. Prin research sci, Aeronautical Research Labs, since 1947; technician, Air Force, 1933-37; f sch insp, ORT Tech Sch, 1937-38; design engr, Commonwealth Aircraft Corp, 1940-47; mem: exec council, Austr Jewry; exec, ZF, Austr and NZ, since 1962, fmr pres, chmn; Vic J Bd Deps; asso f, Royal Aeronautical Soc, London; Inst of Aero-Space Sci, NY; fmr pres: Vic Zionist Org; State Council, Vic. Contbr to profsl jours. Home: 2/29A Hamden Rd, Victoria, 3143, Austr. Office: Fisherman's Bend, Melbourne, Austr.

SOMEKH, Fred S, Isr, accountant; b. Basra, Iraq, July 17, 1911; s. Sasson and Simcha (Somekh); in Isr since 1934; att Regent Poly, London; m. Rifka Malaton, May14, 1937; c: Dan, Gad. Sr partner, Somekh, Chaikin, Citron and Co, CPA's, since 1949; sr acctnt, Russell & Co, 1935-49. F: Assn CPA's in Isr, pres; Assn Cert and Corp Acctnts, London; Inst Costs and Works Acctnts, London; mem: auditors council, Min of Justice, since 1961; club, Rotary, fmr pres. Spec interests: comty service; psych; music. Home: 129 Rothschild Blvd, Tel Aviv, Isr. Office: 5 Achuzat Bait St, Tel Aviv, Isr.

SOMEN, Israel, Kenya, business exec; b. London, Jan 25, 1903; s. Louis and Sophie (Lurie); m. Sophie Biemer, May 17, 1931; Chmn, mgn dir, Hutchings Biemer Ltd, furniture and bedding mfr, since 1926; alderman, Nairobi City Council, since 1952, mem, Council, 1947-52, dep mayor, 1954-55, mayor, 1955-57. Lt Col RASC. U Coll, Nairobi; fmr pres, Bd Kenya Jewry; life vice-pres, Nairobi Heb Cong; hon consul for Isr, 1950-63. Recipient: MBE, 1943. Home: PO Box 1334, Nairobi, Kenya.

SOMMERBURG, Miriam, US, sculptor; b. Hamburg, Ger; d. David and Nanny (Munk) Cahn; in US since 1946; studied abroad: sculpture with Richard Luksch; design, Friedrich Adler; m. Rudolf Sommerburg, Feb 10, 1927 (decd); c: Sascha, Dmitri, Sonia Rabin, Peter, Gioconda. One-man shows: UAHC, NYC; YMHA, NYC, 1963; exhbs: Atlantic City Art Cen; Silvermine Guild of Artists, Conn; New Sch for Social Research, NY; The Contemporaries, NY; Grand Cen Art Gals, NY; J Tercentenary Traveling Exhbs; Fla S Coll Intl Exhb; Allied Artists of Amer; Soc of Young Amer Artists; Cal Soc of Etchers; Creative Arts Assos; Bklyn Soc Artists; Soc Amer Graphic Artists; Natl Assn Women Artists; Audubon Artists; Boston Art Mus; Isaac Delgado Mus, New Orleans, La; Whitney Mus, NY; Bklyn Mus; Syracuse Mus; Pa Acad, Phila; Berlin Acad Fine Arts, Berlin, Ger; Brussels, Antwerp, Ghent, Ostend, all Belgium; with USIS: Burlington Gals, London; Stedeljik Mus, Amsterdam, Holland; Edinburgh, Scot; San Remo, Italy; Museo des Belles Artes, Buenos Aires, Arg; Mus Modern Art, Rio de Janeiro; Acad Arts and Letters; NY Bd of Trade, 1968; New Delhi, Bombay, Calcutta, Madras, Hyderabad, Baroda, all India, 1965-66; Alpes Maritimes, La Napoule, Musée de Cognac, Cannes, all Fr, 1965-66; Vera Cruz, Mexico City, Monterey, all Mex, 1964-65; represented in perm collections: Metrop Mus, NY; Springfield Art Mus, Mo; Fla S Coll; Norfolk Mus; pvt collections in US and abroad. Mem: Audubon Artists; Natl Assn Women Artists; Soc Contemporary Artists; Amer Soc Contemporary Artists; Creative Arts Assos; Artists Equity Assn; Print Council of Amer. Recipient: awards: Village Art Cen, 1947-51, 1949-51, 1960; Creative Gal, 1951; Fla S Coll, 1952; Knickerbocker Artists, 1954; Painters and Sculptors of NJ, 1955; Amer Soc of Contemporary Artists, 1958, 1962, 1964; Silvermine Guild Artists, 1959; design in hardwoods, 2 awards, Chgo, 1959; Natl Assn Women Artists, 1961; Audubon Artists Medal for Creative Sculpture, 1966. Home and studio: 1825 First Ave, New York, NY.

SOMMERS, Allen, US, public relations exec, journalist; b, Oct 26, 1918; s. Robert and Clara (Ressler); att Temple U, 1936-38; m. Ruth Lehrer, Mar 16, 1941; c: Erica, Carl. Pres, Allen Sommers Asso Co, PR agcy, since 1946; reporter, feature writer, Phila Evening Ledger, 1936-42; ed, Atlantic City World, 1942; corresp: NY Herald Tribune; Phila In-

quirer; Chr Sci Monitor, 1946-47; vice-pres, co-owner, Gtr Phila Mag, 1952-57; weekly bus column, NY Herald Tribune, 1952-58. USMC, 1942-46. Pres, Asso Bus Writers of Amer, 1953-55; mem: Phila Press Assn; PR Soc of Amer; Phila PR Assn; Marine PR Assn; Amer Vets; Masons; B'nai B'rith; clubs: Pen and Pencil; Poor Richard. Co-author: Iwo-Hell's Half Acre, 1946. Home: 115 David Rd, Bala-Cynwyd, Pa. Office: Lewis Tower Bldg, Philadelphia, Pa.

SOMPOLINSKY, David, Isr, bacteriologist, educator; b. Copenhagen, Den, Aug 6, 1921; s. Simson and Chana (Kucinsky); DVM, Vetr and Agric HS, Copenhagen, 1946; PhD, Heb U, Jerusalem, 1962; m. Illona Malik, 1946; c: Leah, Sara, Izchak, Rifka, Mordehai, Rachel, Eliyahu, Jacob, Abraham, Nehama. Prof, bact, Bar Ilan U, since 1968; on fac since 1960; dir, bact lab, Asaf Harofe, Govt Hosp, since 1951, staphylococcus reference lab, since 1959; research asst, State Vetr Hosp, Copenhagen, 1946-51. Contbr to profsl jours. Home: 18 Dror St, Rishon le Zion, Isr. Office: Bar Ilan U, Ramat Gan, Isr.

SONNABEND, Roger P, US, business exec; b. Boston, Mass, Sep 17, 1925; s. Abraham and Esther (Lewitt); BS, MIT, 1946; MBA, Harvard Bus Sch, 1949; m. Elsa Golub, July 17, 1949; c: Andrea, Stephanie, Jacqueline, Alan. Pres, exec vice-pres, dir, Hotel Corp of Amer, since 1956; gen mgr: Nautilus, Hotel & Beach Club, Atlantic Beach, NY, 1947-50; Whitehall Hotel, Palm Beach, Fla; Samoset Hotel, Rockland Me, both 1950-54; pres, gen mgr, Brewster Wholesale Corp, Boston, 1949-51; vice-pres, gen mgr, Somerset Hotel, Boston, 1951-53; exec, vice-pres, gen mgr, Sonnabend-Operated Hotels, 1954-56. Lt, USNR, 1943-46, inactive duty supply corps, 1946-56. Mem, exec comm, regional chmn, Natl Alliance Businessmen; intl pres, Young Pres Org, 1961-63, conv chmn, 1960; mem: bd dirs, exec comm, NCCJ, 1959-62, vice-chmn, Northeast div, 1961-68, co-chmn NE area since 1960; dir, Newton Taxpayers Assn,1960-66; finance chmn, hotel sect, US comm for UN, 1958-63; vice-chmn, NE, Natl J Hosp, Denver, Colo, 1958-62; bd govs, Boston U Hum Relations Cen, since 1960; div chmn, Boston Red Feather Campaign, 1955; corp, Peter Bent Brigham Hosp, since 1959; bd dirs, Natl Training Labs, 1961-66; AJComm; adv comm, Harvard-Radcliffe Prog on Bus Admn; adv bd, Harvard Students Agcys, 1960-67; chmn: trades and and professions div, businessmen's council mem, exec comm, CJP, 1962-66; co-chmn, Boston Arts Festival, 1962-64; treas, dir, US Squash Racquets Assn, 1959-61; pres, dir, Mass Squash Racquets Assn, 1960-61; mem: Amer Soc Travel Agts; natl export expansion comm, US Dept of Commerce; Amer, NE and Mass Hotel Assns; clubs: Harvard, Boston. Hobby: sailing, boating, sports. Home: 129 Wentworth Rd, Rye, NH. Office: 390 Commonwealth Ave, Boston, Mass.

SONNEBORN, Tracy M, US, educator, research; b. Baltimore, Md, Oct 19, 1905; s. Lee and Daisy (Bamberger); BA, Johns Hopkins U, 1925, PhD, 1928, hon DSc, 1957; m. Ruth Meyers, June 6, 1929; c: Lee, David. Dist prof, zool, Indiana U, since 1953; f, NRC, 1928-30; research asst, asso, asso in zool, Johns Hopkins U, 1930-39; Natl Sigma Xi lectr, 1947. Mem: Amer Soc Zools, fmr pres; Amer Soc Naturalists, fmr pres; Genetics Soc of Amer, fmr pres; Soc for Study Evolution, fmr vice-pres; Intl Soc Cell Biol; Natl Acad of Sci; Amer Phil Soc; Amer Acad Arts and Scis; Harvey Soc; Amer Soc Protozool; Soc for Growth and Devl; Amer Eugenics Soc; Ind Acad Sci, fmr chmn, zool sect; Human Genetics Soc; Marine Biol Lab; AAUP; Phi Beta Kappa; Sigma Xi; Beta Beta Beta; f, AAAS; fgn mem, Royal Soc, London 1964; hon mem: Faculdad de Biolgia y Ciencias Medicas, U de Santiago de Chile; Soc de Biol de Santiago de Chile; Soc Medica de Concepcion, Chile; Soc de Biol de Concepcion, Chile. Author: The Control of Human Heredity and Evolution, 1965; mem ed bd: Genetics, 1947-62; Journal of Experimental Zoology, 1948-60; Physiological Zoology, 1948-60; Cytologia, fgn collaborator; Annual Review of Microbiology, 1954-58; Jour of Morphology, 1946-49; adv bd, Experimental Cell Research; contbr to sci pubs. Recipient: Kimber Gentics award, Natl Acad of Sci, 1959; Mendel medal, Czech Acad of Sci, 1965; co-recipient, prize, AAAS, 1946. Home: 1305 Maxwell Lane, Bloomington, Ind. Office: Ind U, Bloomington, Ind.

SONNENBERG, Benjamin, US, public relations cons; b. Brest-Litovsk, Pol, July 12, 1901; s. Harry and Ida (Bedder); m. Hilda Caplan, 1924; c: Helen, Benjamin. Pres, Publicity Consultants, Inc, since 1937; in PR since 1928. Club: Lotos. Recipient: Chevalier de la Legion d'Honneur. Home: 19 Gramercy Park, New York, NY. Office: 20 Gramercy Park, NY.

SONNENFELD, Fritz, Isr, business exec; b. Brno, Czech, Nov 29, 1904; s. Alexander and Sophie (Singer); att Prague U, Czech; m. Shoshana Carmel, 1942. Owner, Cinema Shderoth, Tel Aviv, since 1939; mgr, Sunfilm, Tel Aviv, since 1939; fmr mgr, Continental Steel Trading Co of Prague, Tel Aviv. Mem: B'nai B'rith; Masons; Union Film Distributors in Isr; Cinema Owners Assn of Isr; club, Variety, Isr. Hobby: bridge. Home: 15 Haneviim St, Tel Aviv, Isr. Office: Sunfilm, 24 Allenby St; Cinema Shderoth, 80 Rothschild Blvd, both Tel Aviv, Isr.

SOPHER, Aaron, US, artist; b. Baltimore, Md, Dec 16, 1905; s. Samuel and Jennie (Saperstein); att Md Inst Fine Arts, m. Antoinette Weidenhamer, 1935; c: Erika, Christine. Freelance artist since 1927. Works in permanent collections: Cone Collection, Walters Art Gal; Addison Gal Amer Art; Baltimore Mus Art; Munic Mus, Baltimore, Md; Dumbarton Oaks Collection; Bklyn Mus; Phillips Memorial Gal; C Law Watkins Memorial Collection; Edward Bruce Memorial Collection, all three, Wash, DC; Nelson Gutman Collection, Baltimore; Norfolk Mus; in pvt collections; illus, books: Rivers of Eastern Shore, 1944; Portfolio of Maryland Institutions, 1949; Princess Mary of Maryland, 1956; People, People, poems, 1956; The Bull on the Bench, 1967; The Hospitalized Child and His Family, 1967; contbr, illus to: New Yorkers; Harpers Mag; Baltimore Sun; Wall Street Jour; Johns Hopkins Mag; Washington Post. Mem: Artists Equity Assn; Baltimore Mus Art; Corcoran Gal Art. Recipient: 1st prize, Baltimore Evening Sun Contest, 1936, 1943, 1946, 1953, 1956; Life in Baltimore Show, Munic Mus, 1951, 1952, 1953, purchase awards, 1941, 1944, 1st drawing award, 1956; purchase prize, Drawing Annual, Norfolk Mus, 1956; award for drawing, Corcoran Gal of Art, regional exhb, 1953; hon mention, Wash Water Color Club, US Natl Mus, 1956; water color prize, Munic Mus of Baltimore, 1960. Hobby: chess. Home and studio: 500 W University Pkwy, Baltimore, Md.

SORANI, Settimio, It, engineer, social worker; b. Rome, Dec 9, 1899; s. Giustino and Elisa (Sorani); att Engr U, Rome, 1919-22; m. Lina Sorani, Apr 22, 1925. Ret; secy, J Comty, Florence, 1955-65; employee, Unione Italiana di Assicurazione, 1922-38; mgr: Delagazione Assistenza Emigranti Ebrei, 1939-47; Pal Off for It, Rome, 1945-48; immigration off, Isr legation, Rome, 1948-51; mgr, KH, It, 1952-55. Capt, It Army, 1917-22. Hon pres, B'nai B'rith, Florence; collaborator: KH; Keren Kayemet; mem, Comitato Assistenza Ebrei, Rome, 1935-39; vice-pres, It ZF, 1946-49; pres, three homes for children recovered from monastery after WW II, Padri Degli Orfani, 1944-48. Recipient: Croce di Guerra; Cavaliere di Vittorio Veneto; inscription, golden book, Keren Kayemet. Home: 13 Via Capo di Mondo, Florence, It.

SORKIN, Cylvia Aaron, US, educator, business exec; b. St Louis, Mo, Nov 29, 1914; d. Leo and Laura (Messenberg); BBA, Wash U, St Louis, 1935, MBA, 1936, PhD, 1941; m. Harry Sorkin (decd); c: Harlan, Lianne; m.2nd, Harry Shatzman, June 20, 1963. Bus cons, lectr, St Louis, since 1944; appears regularly, KTVI-TV, St Louis; asst prof, commerce and finance, Sch of Bus, Wash U, 1943-49, chmn, grad sch, div on counseling and personnel, 1947-49, on fac since 1936; lectr, Amer Inst Banking, St Louis, 1950-54: mem, US Defense Dept, Defense Adv Comm on Women in Services, Wash, DC, 1953-57; own TV prog, Dr Cylvia Sorkin Show, KSD-TV, St Louis, 1958-60; daily radio prog, Think It Over, KMOX, St Louis, 1961-62. Mem: Amer Assn U Women; Amer Acad Political and Social Sci; Amer Legion Auxiliary; Natl Off Mgmt Assn; Amer Econ Assn; Amer Stat Assn; Chgo Area Bus Tchrs Assn; Natl Assn Bus and Profsl Women's Clubs; clubs: St Louis Zonta; Fac. Contbr to mags. Recipient: US Army Cert of Merit, May, 1958. Home: 2 Jaccard Lane, St Louis, Mo.

SORKIN, Nathaniel, US, jurist; b. NYC, Jan 10, 1912; s. Abraham and Ida (Panish); LLB, cum laude, St John's U, 1935. Judge, Civil Court, NYC, since 1962; pvt law practice, 1936-41, 1951-55; law secy, Justice Charles Marks, Munic Court, 1941-46; law asst, Commn of Inves, NYC, 1946-47; dep commn, NYC Dept of Inves, 1947-51; commn, Temp City Housing Rent Commn, NYC, 1948-50; munic court justice, 1955-62. Pres: Cong Ahavath Isr, 1953-54; Wash Hgts, B'nai B'rith, 1952-54; chmn, Upper Manhattan dist, Boy Scouts of Amer, 1964-66; vice-chmn, Wash Hgts div, UJA, 1952-55; bd, NY ADL, since 1965; co-dir, Dist War Finance Comm, WW II; mem: Mayor's Adv Comm on Handicapped, since 1968; Amer, NY State, NYC Bar Assns; NY Co Lawyers Assn; Amer Judicature Soc, Elks, Masons; club, Lawyers Square. Recipient: Philonomic Council Key;

US Treasury Dept award. Home: 800 Riverside Dr, New York, NY. Office: 111 Centre St, New York, NY.

SOROF, Sam, US, researcher; b. NYC, Jan 24, 1922; s. Morris and Bella (Blank); BS, CCNY, 1944; PhD, U Wis, 1950; m. Phyllis; one c. Sr mem, div biochem, Inst for Cancer Research, since 1961, oncologist since 1952; f, Natl Cancer Inst, 1950-51; visiting sci, biochem inst, Uppsala U, Sweden, 1956. USNR, 1944-46. Mem: Amer Assn for Cancer Research; Amer Soc Biol Chem; AAAS; Amer Chem Soc; NY Acad, of Sci. Contbr to profsl jours. Home: 310 S Easton Rd, Glenside, Pa. Office: 7701 Burholme Ave, Philadelphia, Pa.

SORREL, Jerome M, US, orthodontist; b. NYC, June 27, 1922; s. Simon and Lee (Lesenger); BA, cum laude, U Tenn, 1943; DMD, U Louisville, 1946; postgrad cert, orthodontics, Columbia U, 1956; m. Norma Ruby, Dec 21, 1957; c: Lawrence, Gail. Pvt practice; mem, orthodontic staff: J Memorial Hosp, 1947-49; Leb Hosp, 1956-58; mem, orthodontic panel, NY Dept of Health; dent cons, Boys Club of NY, 1948; cons orthodontist, Comty Service Soc, NY, 1956-57; clinical staff, orthodontics, Columbia U Sch of Dent and Oral Surg, 1956-60; staff researcher, orthodontic div, Columbia U, 1956-60; adj att orthodontist, Grand Cen Hosp, 1961-63; clinician Northeastern Soc Orthodontists; lectr, Heb U Sch of Dent, Jerusalem, 1960. Chmn: Oral Hygiene Comm, Gtr NY, 1963; Gtr NY Children's Dent Health Week, 1962; Gtr NY Isr Bond Drive, 1961, treas, 1960; cultural comm, dent div, UJA, 1952, mem exec comm, 1954; oral hygiene comm, E Dental Soc, since 1955; intl chmn, research and clinicians comm, Alpha Omega, since 1970; delg, Intl Dent Cong, London, 1952; pres: Empire State lodge, B'nai B'rith, 1949-50; Columbia U Orthodontic Group, 1954-56; Alpha Omega, 1960-61, natl regent, dist 3, 1963; vice-pres: Quaker Ridge Scarsdale Homeowners Assn; Columbia U Orthodontic Alumni Soc, 1962; f: NY Acad Dent; mem: Northeastern Soc of Orthodontists; Eur Orthodontic Soc; Amer Assn Orthodontists; adv comm, continuing dent educ, NYU Coll of Dent; AAUP; Amer Assn Dent Eds; Amer Ac d Dent Med; NY State Soc Dent for Children; AAAS; Fed Dentair Intl; NY State Dent Soc; Amer Dent Assn; JWV; Amer Legion. Author: Emotional Factors Influencing Oral Malocclusions in Identical Twins, 1955; A Study on Facial Growth and Development, 1955; ed, Alpha Omega Bull, 1957-59; asso ed, E Dent Soc Bull, since 1960; contbr to profsl jours. Recipient: cert of award, orthodontics, Seton Hall Coll of Dentistry, 1957; meritorious award, E Dent Soc, NY, 1971. Home: 4 Windward Lane, Scarsdale, NY. Office: 263 West End Ave, New York, NY.

SORREL, William E, US, neuropsychiatrist, educator; b. NYC, May 27, 1913; s. Simon and Lee (Lesenger); BS, NYU, 1932; MA, Columbia U, 1934, MD, 1939; postgrad studies: Postgrad Cen for Psychotherapy, 1944-46; Inst for Psychan, 1946-48; cert psycht and examiner, NY State Dept of Mental Hygiene, 1946; PhD, NYU, 1963; m. Rita Marcus, July 1, 1950; c: Ellyn, Joy, Beth. Pvt practice, psycht, NYC; asso att neuropsycht and chief, clinical child psycht, Lebanon Hosp, since 1947; asso psycht: Morrisania Hosp, since 1959; Trafalgar Hosp, since 1962, chief, psycht, 1966-69; att psycht, Gracie Sq Hosp, since 1959; off, instruction, St Louis U Med Sch, 1940-41; asso psycht: Tenn State Hosp Sys, 1941-44; Seton City Hosp, 1955; asso att neuropsycht and chief, clinical psycht, J Memorial Hosp, NY, 1946-59; asst prof to prof, Yeshiva U, 1952-61, psycht-in-chief, asso dir, Yeshiva U Psychol Cen, 1955-61; psycht cons, LIU Grad Cen, 1955-60; visiting prof, psycht, Heb U, Jerusalem, 1960; mem, Amer Psycht Commn to Russ, Pol, Czech, 1963; visiting prof: psycht, U of Tokyo Med Sch, 1964; NYU Inst of Tech, 1968; visiting lectr, NYU, 1970. F: Amer Assn Psychoanalytic Phys, fmr treas; Amer Psycht Assn, fmr pres, dist br; Amer Acad Psychotherapy; Amer Assn for Advancement of Psychotherapy; pres, Amer Soc Psychoanalytic Phys, 1971-72; mem: AMA; NY State and Co Med Socs; Amer Med Writers Assn; Bx Soc Neur and Psycht, fmr pres; NY Soc Clinical Psycht; E Psycht Research Assn; AAUP; Assn for Research in Nervous and Mental Diseases; Amer J Phys Comm; B'nai B'rith; fmr: vice-pres, Golden Years Found for Sr Citizens; cons, Daytop Village; Amer delg to Intl Cong on Mh, London, Eng. Author: Neurosis in a Child, 1949; A Psychiatric Viewpoint on Child Adoption, 1954; Shock Therapy in Psychiatric Practice, 1957; An Experimental Approach to the Prediction of Success with Electroshock Therapy, 1962; The Schizophrenic Process, 1963; Psychodynamic Effects of Abortion, 1967; contbr to med jours; lectr, 1st World Cong on Fertility and Sterility, 1955. Recipient: Sir William Osler Intl Hon Med Soc

Gold Key, 1939; 3rd prize, for oil paintings, NY State Med Art Exhibit, 1954; Founders Day Award, NYU, 1963; Silver medal, Amer Psychiatric Assn, 1970. Home: 23 Meadow Rd, Scarsdale, NY. Office: 263 West End Ave, New York, NY.

SORRIN, Sidney, US, dentist; b. NYC, Jan 15, 1900; s. Alexander and Dina; DDS, Coll of Dent, NYU, 1921; postgrad studies, periodontia, oral diagnosis, Coll Oral and Dent Surg, Columbia U, 1923-24; m. Ruth Kandell, 1926; c: Edward. Prof, chmn, dept periodontia and oral med, Coll of Dent, NYU, since 1959, fac mem since 1925; periodontist, Montefiore Hosp, since 1931; cons, periodontia, oral med, VA Hosp, NYC, since 1958; fmr chief, periodontia clinics: Mt Sinai Hosp; Sydenham Hosp; Midtown Hosp. Chmn: pathodontia sect, First Dist Dent Soc, 1937; dent div, FJP, 1955; pres: Amer Acad Oral Med, 1947, co-found, 1946; Omicron chap, Omicron Kappa Upsilon, 1940; Alpha Omega, 1940; found mem, Isr Sch of Dent Med; life mem, bd govs, Henry Oldtimers, Henry St Settlement; f: Amer Coll Dents; AAAS; Amer Acad Oral Med; mem: Amer Soc Periodontists; Amer Acad Periodontology; Amer Dent Assn; AAUP; Intl Assn for Dent Research; Fed Dentaire Intl; Sci Research Soc of Amer; Dent Alumni Assn; NYU Coll of Dent; Albert Gallatin Assos, NYU; Northeastern Soc Periodontists; dent adv comm, Dept of Health, NYC, 1950-53; med emergency div, Off of Civil Defense, NYC; Asociacion de Cirujanos Orales de Cuba, hon; Metrop Opera Guild, NYC; Temple Isr of NY; sponsor, NYU Dent Cen; fmr mem: NY Inst of Clinical and Oral Path; NY Health and TB Assn; clubs: Alpine Country; Century; NYU; One Hundred. Author: Practice of Periodontia, 1960; co-author: Practice of Periodontia, 1928; Textbook of Periodontia, 1938, publs comm, Jour of Dent Med; contbr to textbooks, dental, med and lay jours. Recipient: dist service award, Acad of Dent Med, 1948; service citation, NYU, 1955; service medallion, NYU Alumni Assn, 1960; man of year award, Alpha Omega frat, 1969; Samuel Chas Miller award, Amer Acad Oral Med, 1969. Hobbies: collecting antique miniatures; painting; singing; golf. Home: 130 E 75 St, New York, NY. Office: 745 Fifth Ave, New York, NY.

SOSKIS, Philip, US, social worker; b. Russ, July 4, 1910; s. Harry and Ida (Soskis); in US since 1920; BA, Bklyn Coll, 1933; MSW, Columbia U Sch Social Work, 1944; m. Anne Katchka, June 25, 1939; c: David. Exec dir, NY Assn for New Amers, Inc, since 1952, asst dir, 1949-52; case sup, case cons, admnr, NYC Dept of Wfr, 1934-37, dir, training, 1945-47; admnr, United Service for New Amers, 1947-49. Pres: Natl Conf J Communal Services, 1962-63; hon, Natl Assn J Family, Children's and Health Services, since 1968, found and co-chmn, 1966-68; chmn: alumni fund, mem, exec comm, Alumni Assn, Sch of Social Work, Columbia U, 1962-66; prog comm, annual workshop, Amer Immigration and Citizenship Conf, 1960-61; FJP, NY, 1964-66; prog comm for insts, NY State Conf Social Wfr, 1946; asso chmn, social service div, UJA, Gtr NY, since 1961, 2nd vice-chmn, NY chap, Natl Assn Social Workers, 1961-63; bd mem, since 1968; mem: adv bd, social service exch, Comty Council, Gtr NY, since 1958; Natl Conf Social Wfr. Contbr to profsl jours. mem Home: 915 E 7 St, Brooklyn, NY. Office: 15 Park Row, New York, NY.

SOURKES, Theodore L, Can, educator; b. Montreal, Can, Feb 21, 1919; s. Irving and Fannie (Golt); BS, McGill U, Montreal, 1939, MS, 1946; att Queens U, Kingston, Ont, 1941-42; PhD, Cornell U, NY, 1948; m. Shena Rosenblatt, 1943; c: Barbara, Myra. Prof, biochem, dept psycht, McGill U, since 1965, asso prof, psycht, 1959-65; sr research biochem, Allan Memorial Inst of Psycht, since 1953, hon lectr, dept biochem, since 1959; teaching asst, biochem, Cornell U, 1946-48; asst prof, pharm, Georgetown U Med Sch, Wash, DC, 1948-50; research asso, Merck Inst for Therapeutic Research, Rahway, NJ, 1950-53. Can Res Army, 1943-44. Pres, Montreal Phys Soc, since 1962; fmr pres, Sir Arthur Currie Home and Sch Assn; mem: Can Phys Soc; Can Biochem Soc; Amer Soc Biol Chems; Amer Chem Soc; NY Acad Scis; Sigma Xi; Can Soc for Study Hist and Phil of Sci; Sons of Isr Benevolent Soc, Montreal. Author: Biochemistry of Mental Disease, 1962; mem, ed bd, Can Jour of Biochem; contbr to profsl jours; ed bd, Canadian Jour of Biochem. Home: 4645 Montclair Ave, Montreal, Can. Office: 1025 Pine Ave, W Montreal, Can.

SOUZA, Ernest Henriques de, Jamaica, photographer; b. Kingston, Jamaica, Sep 28, 1933; s. Ernest and Nora (Henriques). Profsl photographer since 1954; salesman, collector, Brandon & Co, 1950; cost acctnt, Stanley Motta, 1950-53; clerk, acctnt

dept, Lascelles de Mercado, 1953-54. Dir, lay reader, rel sch tchr, asst to rabbi, United Cong of Israelites, Jamaica, fmr pres; treas, chaplain, B'nai B'rith Jamaica Lodge 2593, found mem, fmr pres; treas, Council and Exec, Girl Guides Assn; mem: I Council and Exec, Boy Scouts Assn; hon mgr, Jamaica Scout Shop; fmr dir, Jamaica Children's Service Soc; mem, bd mgmt, Jamaica Youth Corps; various offs held in Masonic lodges and chaps; has acted as spiritual leader of J Comty; represented J Faith in prayers prior to Jamaica's Independence; mem: Royal Photographic Soc; life mem: Cancer Soc; Wolmer's Old Boy's Assn; Wolmer's Lodge, 1506; found mem: Profsl Photographers Assn, Jamaica; St Michaels Lodge 1634; Jamaica Camera Club; others. Recipient: Gevaert Gold medal and Blue Ribbon award, for photo contest to commemorate Jamaica's Tercentenary of Brit Rule, 1955; Thanks Badge, Girl Guides Assn, 1962; cert of merit, for services, Jaycees chap, Jamaica, 1963, 1965, 1967; Torch award, Girl Guides Assn, Jamaica, 1967; Life Senator, Jr Chamber Intl, Kingston Jr Chamber, 1969. Hobbies: movies, scouting and social work, collecting coins, stamps, fishing amateur radio, preserving hist records. Home and office: 2 Somerton Ave, Kingston 6, Jamaica, W Indies.

SOWDEN, Dora Leah Levitt, Isr, journalist; b. Krakenovo, Russ, Mar 29, 1917; in Isr since 1967; d. Marcus and Reisa (Levitt); BA, U Witwatersrand, 1936, MA, 1938; m. Lewis Sowden. Isr corresp for S Afr newspapers, and Dance Magazine, NY; free-lancer; music critic, Sun Times, Johannesburg, 1952-67; music and film critic, Rand Daily Mail, 1954-67; freelance jour, 1936-51; org, S Afr Book Exhb, London, 1947; tutor, J Coll, London, 1949; research secy, S Afr J Hist Soc, 1951-54; ed, Federation Chronicle, 1954-55. Hon secy, S Afr PEN Club, 1953-59, S Afr delg, PEN Congs. Contbr to: The Story of Fifty Years, 1953; The Jews in South Africa, 1955. Home: 9/49 Zangwill St, Jerusalem, Isr.

SOWDEN, Lewis S, Isr, author, editor; b. Manchester, Eng, Mar 25, 1905; s. Isaac and Henda (Mofson); MA, U Witwatersrand, 1927; m. Dora Levitt. Asst ed, Rand Daily Mail, 1951-66; corresp, UN, 1949. Author: plays: The Fugitive, 1934; The Man in the Checks, 1935; Red Rand, 1937; The Gold Earth, 1944; Ramses the Rich, BBC, 1956; The Kimberley Train, 1958; poems: The Charmed Fabric, 1943; Reverie, illus by Alva, London, Eng, 1954; Poems with Flute, 1955; Poems From the Bible, 1960; survey, The S Afr Union, pub, NY, 1943; London, 1945; novels: The Man Who Was Emperor, 1947; Star of Doom, 1948; Lady of Coventry, 1949; The King of High Street, 1950; Tomorrow's Comet, 1951; Family Cromer, 1952; The Crooked Bluegum, 1955; Kop of Gold, 1956; anthol, The Land of Afternoon, 1968. Fmr chmn, PEN club. Home: 9/49 Zangwill St, Jerusalem, Isr. Office: Ency Judaica, Jerusalem, Isr.

SOYER, Raphael, US, artist; b. Russ, Dec 25, 1899; s. Abraham and Bella (Schneyer); in US since 1914; att Natl Acad Design and Art Students League, NY, 1919-22; m. Rebecca Letz, Feb 8, 1931; c: Mary. First one-man exhb, Daniel Gal, NY, 1929; exhbs: Valentine Gals; Rehn; Macbeth; Asso Amer Artists Gals, NY, 1953; retrospective exhb, Whitney Mus Amer Art, 1967; perm exhbs: Reclining Figure, Metrop Mus; Girl in Brown, Portrait of Artist's Parents, Office Girls, Whitney Mus, NY; Pensive Girl, Carnegie Mus, Pittsburgh; Bus Passengers, H Shulman Coll, Conn; Passengers in RR Sta, Corcoran Gal, Wash; fmr instr: Amer Art Sch; Art Students League. Mem: Amer Inst of Arts and Letters. Author: A Painter's Pilgrimage, 1962; Homage to Thomas Eakens Etc, 1966. Recipient: Kunstamm prize, Chgo Art Inst, 1933; Temple Gold Medal, Pa Mus, 1946; Isr prize, Corcoran Mus, 1952; $100 Prize, USA, 1959. Studio: 54 Second Ave, New York, NY.

SOYPHER, Maurice J, US, attorney, legislator; b. Baltimore, Md, Feb 17, 1911; s. Benjamin and Sophie (Hoffman); LLB, U Baltimore, 1935; m. Marion Mazaroff, Aug 25, 1940; c: Richard. Pvt practice since 1936; mem: Md House of Delgs, since 1951; Baltimore City Council, since 1951; spec liason, Gen Assembly of Md on city leg, from Baltimore Mayor; asst counsel, Reconstruction Finance Corp, Wash, DC, 1937-39. US Army, 1943-46. Pres, Brotherhood of Agudas Achim Cong, 1952-54; sr vice-cmdr, JWV, Md, 1950-51; headmaster, Upsilon Lambda Phi, 1931-32; mem: ZOA; B'nai B'rith; KP; Lawyers Civic Assn; Natl Assns Claimants' Compensation Attys; Baltimore, Md Bar Assns. Home: 5814 Berkeley Ave, Baltimore, Md. Office: 906 Munsey Bldg, Baltimore, Md.

SPAER, Arnold, Isr, lawyer; b. Danzig, Mar 28, 1918; s. Mark and Ada (Lifshutz); in Isr since 1934; dipl, Govt Law Sch, Jerusalem, 1942; m. Maud Rosenbaum, Jan 10, 1954; c: Michael, Daniel, Uriel. Atty, notary public, since 1944; sr partner, Spaer, Toussia and Cohen, since 1960; jr partner, Bernard Joseph and Co, 1938-49; partner: Shuarz, Caspi, Spaer and Co, 1949-54; Schuarz, Spaer and Toussia Cohen, 1954-60. Capt, legal and gen staff, IDF, 1948-68; legal adv to mil gov, Jerusalem, 1948-49. Law council, Min Justice, 1956-62; Bar Council, Isr Advocates Chamber, 1962-64. Spec interests: numismatics, hist, archaeol. Home: 3 Hovevei Zion St, Jerusalem, Isr.

SPARER, Malcolm M, US, rabbi; b. Bx, NY, Aug 12, 1926; s. Samuel and Anna (Distler); AB, CCNY, 1943; MA, U Wis, 1947; ordained rabbi, 1953; DD, Cen Sch of Rel, Ind, 1968; m. Erna Reichel, Aug 11, 1945; c: Ruth, Arthur, Jennifer, Shoshana. Rabbi, Beth El Syn, since 1966; rabbi, NYC, 1952-59; asso rabbi, B'nai David Cong, LA, 1960-66; exec dir, Rabb Council of Cal, LA, 1959-66. Chaplain, JWV, Ia-Neb; vice-pres, Des Moines br, ZOA; coord, Union Orthodox J Cong, first social action conf; fmr chmn, J Comm on Scouting, San Fernando Valley Council; pres, Co Ministerium, 1956-58; juvenile affairs coord, Co Superior Court; mem: Gov's Comm for Educ and Integration; Natl Family Relations Council; Chgo Rabb Council; bd dirs, Rambam Torah Inst; bd, Yeshiva U Syn Council; Rabb Council, UJA; Natl Rabb ORT Comm. Author: Curriculum for Religious School, 1966; Profiles of Clergy, 1958; lectr to regional conf various service orgs; dir, produc, moderator, 1st W coast TV prog on Day Sch Educ; moderator, B'nai B'rith radio prog, Lest We Believe; ed, Rel News Desk, Rel News Service; TV, radio coord for Rabb Council of Cal; contbr to publs. Recipient: Beaver Award, Boy Scouts, 1960; Pres Citation, 1946. Home: 102 Cummins Pkwy, Des Moines, Ia. Study: 954 Cummins Pkwy, Des Moines, Ia.

SPECTER, Jack Edward, US, business exec; b. Phila, Pa, Feb 6, 1898; s. Bernard and Rose (Goldsmith); m. Ann Duberstein, June 30, 1940; c: Goiffon, Meiselman, Garfield, Ret; motion pictures, 1920-25; own bus, 1925-55; personal repr, Fr Line, 1955-65. Cpl, US Army, 1918-19. Prin contrib: promoting Fr-Amer relations, specifically regarding Judaism. Hon cdr, JWV, Fr, Gt Brit, dep fgn affairs off, US; life mem: Hon Legion, NY Police Dept; Masons; mem: Fed Fr War Vets, NY; Fr Forever; Verdun War Vets; Free Fr War Vets; Belgian War Vets Amer; Dunkirk War Vets, Gt Brit; fmr mem, Gold Star Mothers, US Emb, Paris, Fr. Recipient: dipl and citations, NYC; Soc of Fr Legion of Honor Med WW II; Assn Natl Fr Croix de Guerre Medal WW I; Assn Natl Medaille de la France Liberée Medal WW II; hon: Ky col; gen, Fr Army, WW II; Silver Medal, Citizen City of Paris. Hobbies: sculpturing; photography, fishing. Home: 210 W 89 St, New York, NY.

SPECTER, Melvin H, US, attorney; b. E Chgo, Ind, July 12, 1903; s. Moses and Sadie (Rossuck); BA, U Mich, 1925; JD, U Chgo Law Sch, 1928; m. Nellie Rubinstein, Feb 1, 1927; c: Lois Kanz, Michael. Pvt practice since 1928; atty, Bd of Park Commns, 1930-39. Secy, E Chgo Bar Assn, fmr pres; dir, Comty Chest Assn, since 1940; pres, E Chgo Public Librs, since 1958, mem bd trustees, since 1956; hon dir, ARC, since 1950, dir, 1937-50; dir: Salvation Army Adv Bd, since 1929, fmr pres; Visiting Nurses Assn, since 1941, fmr pres; Anselm Forum, since 1955; Twin City Recreation Cen, since 1956, fmr vice-pres; E Chgo Boys Club of Amer, since 1957; mem: Phi Beta Kappa; Ind State Bar Assn, fmr mem, House of Delgs; Delta Sigma Rho; Wig and Robe; B'nai B'rith; Beth Sholem Cong, E Chgo; Temple Beth El, Hammond, Ind; Elks; KP; Amer Bar Assn; Amer Judicature Soc; Amer Acad of Political Sci; Commercial Law League of Amer; fmr: chmn, brotherhood week, NCCJ; dir, Comty Concert Assn; club, Kiwanis, fmr pres. Recipient: citation, for dist public service, U Chgo Alumni Assn, 1958. Home: 4213 Baring Ave, E Chgo, Ind. Office: 823 W Chicago Ave, E Chicago, Ind.

SPECTOR, Dorothy B, US, communal worker; b. Boston, Mass, Dec 1, 1906; d. Max and Sophia (Lipshires) Baer; m. Carl Spector, Jan 14, 1936; c: Arthur, Edzia Weisberg. Natl vice-chmn, women's div, UJA, since 1957; found mem, mem natl bd, Brandeis Women's Comm, since 1948; chmn: comm on J educ, Combined J Philanthropies, since 1959; Isr comm, JCC, since 1960; fmr chmn, CJA; first chmn, Isr Bonds, 1954; mem: Natl Comm for Overseas Needs, CJFWF; bd govs, Amer Assn J Educ, since 1961; fmr: natl vice-pres, Hadassah, pres, Boston, NE Region; mem, bd govs, Comm to Audit State Needs. Home: 154 Sewall Ave, Brookline, Mass.

SPECTOR, Dov, Isr, engineer; b. Petah Tikva, Aug, 1913; s. Gershon and Lana (Dropkin); deg, elec and mech engr, Manchester Coll of Tech, 1937; m. Ziva Feller, Dec 9, 1939; c: Tamar, Yechiel, David, Avner. Pres: Spector Cathodic Protection, Spectronix Ltd, D Spector Cons Engrs, since 1951; civil engr, Royal Engrs Hqr, 1937-40; asst controller, heavy ind, Pal govt, 1940-44; head, tech div, Min of Defense, 1947-48. Prin contribs: to devl Corrosion Engr, Cathodic Protection; several inventions patented; promotor application of wind power, corrosion engr, automation, in Isr. Chmn: Isr Corrosion Group; Corrosion Comm of Isr Petroleum Inst; educ comm, Intl Cong on Metallic Corrosion, mem, perm council; sr mem, Inst Elec and Electronic Engrs, US; mem, intl comm, Intl Water Supply Assn. Author: Corrosion and its Prevention, Heb, 1961; instructional pamphlets on corrosion prevention; contbr to tech mags. Hobbies: gardening, photography, do-it-yourself projects. Home: 36 Har Dafna St, Savyon, Isr. Office: 22 Harakevet St, Tel Aviv, Isr.

SPECTOR, Irwin, US, educator; b. Garwood, NJ, Jan 11, 1916; s. George and Tillie (Weinberg); BS, NJ State Coll, 1936; MA, Columbia U, 1940; PhD, NYU, 1952; dipl, conducting, Conservatory of Music, U Paris, 1954; m. Jane Hoffman, Jan 22, 1944; c: Jerome, Alan, George. Prof, music, Ill State U, since 1957, composer in res, since 1959; visiting prof, music hist, U Kan; sup of music, Morris Township public schs, 1936-42; instr, music: Union Co Band and Orch Sch, 1934-37; NJ State Coll, 1938-41; Monmouth Coll, 1947-48. US Army, 1942-46. Mem: Intl Musicological Soc; Gesellschaft fur Musikforschung; Natl Assn for Amer Composers and Conductors; Renaissance Soc; AAUP; fmr, secy, Midwest chap, Amer Musicological Soc. Contbr to music jours. Recipient: Bronze Star. Home: 903 Sudduth Rd, Normal, Ill. Office: Ill State U, Normal, Ill.

SPECTOR, Sidney, US, government official; b. Cleveland, O, Sep 16, 1915; s. Abraham and Eva (Kristol); AB, Miami U, 1939; AM, U Chgo, 1948; m. Zelda Garber, 1943; c: Richard, Abby. Exec asst to Mayor Carl B Stokes, Cleveland, since 1968; dir, research, Council of State Govts and Govs' Conf, 1949-59; secy, Cong of Chief Justices, 1950-59; dir, Interstate Clearing House on Mh, 1954-59; staff dir, Sen Comm on Aging, 1959-61; asst admnr, Off of Housing for Sr Citizens, US Housing and Home Finance Agcy, 1961-66; asst to Secy, Dept of Housing and Urban Devl, 1966-68. USN, 1943-46. Vice-chmn, legislative comm, Natl Assn for Mh; secy, Fed-State Conf on Aging; cons, mental hosp inst, Amer Psycht Assn; mem, bd: Chgo Soc for Mh; S Suburban Syn; mem: social wfr research comm, Amer Gerontological Assn; Amer Soc Public Admnrs; Natl Assn Housing and Redevl Officials; Amer Political Sci Assn; AAAS; Md Assn for Mh. Co-author: Reorganizing State Government, 1950; The 48 State Court Systems, 1951; Occupational Licensing in the States, 1952; Training and Research in State Mental Programs, 1953; Public Authorities, in the States, 1954; The States and Their Older Citizens, 1955; The Aging and the Aged in the US: A National Problem, 1960. Recipient: South Pacific ribbons. Hobbies: tennis, music. Office: Mayor's Office, Cleveland, O.

SPEIZMAN, Morris, US, business exec; b. Lodz, Pol, Aug 31, 1905; s. David and Elka (Bornstein); in US since 1905; dipl, Phila Textile Inst, 1927; m. Sylvia Valenstein, Mar 4, 1934; c: Lawrence, Robert. Pres: Morris Speizman Co, Inc, since 1937; S Mill Equipment Corp, since 1946; Carolina Knitting Machine Corp, since 1954; chmn bd, Speizman Inds, Inc, since 1967; dir, Bank of Charlotte, since 1957. Chmn, NC region, UJA, 1949, 1952, 1959, 1960; pres: World Council Syns, 1968-70; Charlotte Fed of J Charities, 1948-50; hon life pres, Temple Isr, Charlotte, pres, 1952-54; chmn: bd dirs, Mercy Hosp, Charlotte; NC region, UJA, 1949, 1952, 1959, 1960; mem: natl council, JDC; J Defense Appeal; United Services for New Amer, 1948-52; S regional council, ADL, 1952-53; exec comm, natl planning and campaign comm, JTSA, 1952-53; natl vice-pres, United Syn of Amer, 1955-57; 1961-63, 1967-69; co-chmn, NC Bonds for Isr Campaign, 1951-52; dir, Charlotte C of C, 1963; Salvation Army, Charlotte; machinery dealers, War Produc Bd, 1942-45; mem: Masons; civitan; clubs: Amity Country; Carolina Golf; Harmonie, NYC. Contbr to knitting trade publs, 1941-62. Home: 435 Colville Rd, Charlotte, NC. Office: 508 W 5 St, Charlotte, NC.

SPELLBERG, Mitchell A, US, gastroenterologist, educator; b. Russ, Apr 27, 1908; s. William and Molly (Milman); in US since 1921; AA, Crane Jr Coll, 1929; BS, Loyola U, 1932; MD, U of Ill, 1933, MS, 1939; m. Anna Rosen, June 18, 1933;

c: Victor, Robert. Clinical prof, med, U of Ill, since 1966, fac mem since 1950; acting chmn, gastroenterology div, Michael Reese Hosp, since 1967, staff mem since 1953; cons, gastroenterology, Vet Hosp. Lt col, US Army MC, 1941-46. F, Amer Coll of Phys; mem: Amer Gastroenterological Soc; AAAS; AMA: NY Acad of Sci; Chgo Med Soc; Chgo Soc of Internal Med; Chgo Heart Assn; Chgo Diabetes Assn; Sigma Xi. Author: Diseases of the Liver, 1954; contbr to med jours. Home: 7408 S Clyde Ave, Chicago, Ill. Office: 111 N Wabash Ave, Chicago, Ill.

SPELLER, Cyril Alfred, Eng, estate agent; b. London, Sep 4, 1919; s. Isaac and Annice (Rabinovitch). JP for Bournemouth, since 1959; Bournebouth corresp, J Chronicle, until 1961. Vice-pres; treas, Council of Chr & J, both Bournemouth; secy: Fabian Soc, 1945-55; JPA comm, 1955-65; vice-pres, agt, Lab Party, 1959-64, all Bournemouth; mem, B'nai B'rith, Bournemouth. Hobbies: psych, watching TV. Home: 5 Earls Court, 9 Gervis Rd, Bournemouth, Eng.

SPERBER, Daniel, Isr, educator; b. Ruthin, Wales, Nov 4, 1940; s. Samuel and Miriam (Schorr); in Isr since 1968; att: Yeshiva Kol Torah, Jerusalem, 1958-59; Yeshiva Hebron, 1959-62; BA, Courtauld Inst of Art, U London, 1965; PhD, U Coll, London, 1968. Lectr, Talmud, J Hist, Bar Ilan U, since 1968. F, Royal Numismatic Soc; comm mem, Anglo-Isr Archaeol Assn. Contbr to profsl jours. Home: POB 7366, Jerusalem, Isr. Office: Bar Ilan U, Ramat Gan, Isr.

SPERBER, David Sol, US, attorney; b. NYC, July 28, 1939; s. Meyer and Pauline (Lerner); BA, UCLA, 1961, LLB, Sch of Law, 1964; m. Jeanine Dias, Jan 23, 1967; c: Toby. Pvt practice since 1968; dep Atty Gen, State of Cal, 1964-68. Mem: Co Cen Comm, LA Co Cen Comm, 59 Assembly Dist; LA Co Bar Assn and sects: Trial Lawyers, Criminal Law and Procedure, Real Property; LA Lawyers Speakers Bur; fmr, chmn, Student Judicial Bd, UCLA; clubs: Lawyers, LA. Hobbies: photography, water and snow skiing. Home: 3666 Keyston, Los Angeles, Cal. Office: 2501 W 3, Los Angeles, Cal.

SPERKA, Joshua S, US, rabbi; b. Wloclawek, Pol, Nov 15, 1905; s. Shlomo and Libe (Friedman); in US since 1921; ordained rabbi, Heb Theol Coll, Chgo, 1930; BS, Lewis Inst of Chgo, 1931; MA, U Mich, 1933; m. Yetta Peiman, May 31, 1931; c: Shlomo, Judith, Joel, Chava. Rabbi, Cong Young Isr, Greenfield-Oak Park, Mich, since 1961; chaplain, Mich State Prisons, since 1941; rabbi: Beth Tfilah Moses, Mt Clemens, Mich, 1931; Beth Isr, Ann Arbor, Mich, 1932; Cong Bnai David, Detroit, Mich, 1933-53. Pres: JNF Council, 1936-38; AJCong, 1940-42; League for Rel Lab in Isr, since 1947, all Detroit; vice-pres: Mizrachi Org, Detroit, midwest region, Amer Prison Chaplains Assn, since 1952; secy, Mich Syn Conf, 1939-41; mem, bd: Yeshiva Beth Yehudah, since 1943; govs, JWF, since 1950; J Comty Cen, since 1950; JCC, 1945-48, all Detroit; hon pres, Fed of Pol Js; hon chaplain, JWV, Mich. Author: Eternal Life, 1939; Proverbs To Live By, 1967. Home: 14281 Wales Ave, Oak Park, Mich. Study: 15150 W Ten Mile Rd, Oak Park, Mich.

SPERLING, Melitta, US, psychiatrist; b. Aus, Oct 15, 1899; d. Hersch and Rachel (Bierman) Wojnilower; in US since 1938; MD, U Vienna, 1924; m. Otto Sperling, Mar 28, 1929; c: George, Eva Cockcroft. Clinical prof, psycht, SUNY, since 1949, training analyst, sup, Psychoanalytic Inst, Downstate Med Cen, since 1949; head, dept child psycht, J Hosp, Bklyn, 1940-53. Prin contrib: Originator, simultaneous treatment mother and child in child psycht. Mem: Natl Council J Women; Amer, Intl Psychoanalytic Assns; Psychoanalytic Assn, NY; NY Psychoanalytic Soc; Amer Psychiatric Assn; Amer Orthopsychiatric Assn; Amer Acad Child Psycht; Amer Psychosomatic Assn. Contbr to sci jours. Recipient: Intl Essay prize, psychan, 1947. Home and office: 960 Park Ave, New York, NY.

SPERLING, Milton M, US, motion picture producer; b. NYC, July 6, 1912; s. Charles and Bessie (Diamond); att CCNY, 1929-32; m. Betty Warner, July 12, 1939; c: Susan, Karen, Debora, Matthew. Pres, Milton Sperling Producs, since 1962; scenario writer, 20th Century-Fox, 1934-38, produc, 1938-41; exec produc, pres, US Pictures, 1945-62. Capt, USMC, WW II. Chmn, UJA Motion Pictures Div, 1966; vice-pres: Amer-Isr Cultural Found; Brandeis Camp Inst; bd overseers, U of Judaism, chmn, 1955-60; treas, UCLA Theater Group; mem: W Coast Council, JWV since 1962; Screen Produc Guild, treas, 1959-60; Screen Writers Guild,

bd dirs, 1937-39. Home: 1116 La Collina Dr, Beverly Hills, Cal. Office: 9255 Sunset Blvd, Los Angeles, Cal.

SPERLING, Otto E, US, psychiatrist, educator; b. Vienna, Aus, Dec 14, 1899; s. Simon and Rose (Pfeffer); in US since 1938; MD, U Vienna Med Sch, 1924; grad, Vienna Psychoanalytic Inst, 1929; m. Melitta Wojnilower, Mar 28, 1929; c: George, Eva. Psychan in pvt practice since 1939; clinical prof, psychoanalytic med, SUNY Med Cen, since 1948; cons psycht: Hillside Hosp; Bklyn J Hosp. F: Amer Psychiatric Assn; Amer Acad Child Psycht; mem: NY Psychoanalytic Assn; Amer Psychoanalytic Assn; Amer Psychosomatic Soc; B'nai B'rith; Masons. Contbr to profsl jours. Home: and office: 960 Park Ave, New York, NY.

SPERO, Carl M, US, insurance broker; b. NYC, June 2, 1902; s. Frank and Stella (Levy); m. Mildred Wolfe, Jan 22, 1930; c: Michael. Pres, Spero Whitelaw Co Inc, since 1934, found, 1928. Pres: Assos of Dalton Sch, 1953; Stuyvesant Neighborhood House, 1938-48; Amer Soc Chartered Life Underwriters, 1951-52; pres, NY chap, 1941-42; mem, bd trustees: FJP, 1938-48; Educ Alliance, since 1952; Emanu-El Stuyvesant J Comty Cen, since 1960; treas, Wiltwyck Sch for Boys, since 1960; mem, Fed Grand Jury Asso. Home: 139 E 95 St, New York, NY. Office: 386 Park Ave, New York, NY.

SPETNER, Lee Mordecai, US, physicist; b. St Louis, Mo, Jan 17, 1927; s. Abraham and Rose (Raskas); BS, Wash U, 1945; PhD, MIT, 1950; m. Julia Borvick, Oct 22, 1950; c: Abba, Solomon, Daniel, Sharon. Physicist, Applied Physics Lab, Johns Hopkins U, since 1951; lectr, applied mech, Wash U, 1946-47; research asso, MIT, 1950-51. USN, 1945-46. First pres,Yeshiva HS, Gtr Wash; former pres, Cong Shomrai Emunah; bd dirs: Heb Acad of Wash; pres, Assn Orthodox J Scis; mem: Amer Phys Soc; Inst Radio Engrs; AAAS; Commn II, Intl Sci Radio Union. Contbr to profsl jours. Recipient: Shofar award, Natl Council Young Isr. Home: 7801 13 St NW, Washington, DC. Office: 8621 Georgia Ave, Silver Spring, Md.

SPICEHANDLER, Ezra, Isr, educator; b. Bklyn, NY, Apr 6, 1921; s. Abraham and Esther (Orkin); BA, U Cincinnati, 1942; ordained rabbi, MHL, HUC, 1945, PhD, 1951; m. Shirley Horn, Aug 20, 1944; c: Reena, Judith. Dir, J studies, HUC Bibl and Archaeol Sch, Jerusalem, fmr prof, modern Heb lit, Cincinnati Sch, HUC-JIR, asso prof, 1956-60, instr, NY Sch, 1951-54, asst prof, 1955-56. Pres, Cincinnati ZC, 1956-64; dep mem, actions comm, World Zionist Org, since 1961; natl vice-pres, LZOA, 1960-62; art and lit comm, CCAR, 1958-61; mem: Amer Oriental Soc; MLA; Assn Profs of Heb. Author: The Modern Hebrew Poem Itself, 1965; co-author, Perakim Biyahadut, 1962. Recipient: Natl Defense fgn lang f, 1960-61; Fulbright research grant study in Iran, 1962-63. Home and office: 13 King David St, Jerusalem.

SPIEGEL, Albert Alexander, US, lawyer; b. McKeesport, Pa, Mar 9, 1916; s. Joseph and Grace (Breyer); BA, U Pittsburgh, 1937; LLB, Harvard Law Sch, 1940; m. Bernice Lerner, Jan 16, 1944; c: Carolyn Tisherman, Mark, Paul, David. Pvt practice since 1941. Capt, US Army, 1942-44. Vice-chmn, comm on fed planning for J educ, CJFWF; vice-pres, mem bd, J Fed Council Gtr LA, secy, J Comty Found; chmn: Bur J Educ, LA; bd govs, U of Judaism; trustee: J Publ Soc Amer; and mem: natl campaign cabinet, UJA; bd, Amer JDC; bd overseers, JTSA; natl governing council, Amer Assn for J Educ; bd: Sinai Temple, LA; AJComm, LA; State Bar, LA Co Bar, Santa Monica Area Bar Assns, bd trustees, Santa Monica Hosp; fmr: gen chmn, United JWF; fmr pres: Beth Sholom Temple, Santa Monica, Cal; JCC, Bay Cities; Santa Monica Bay Zionist Dist; J Comty Cen, Bay Cities; B'nai B'rith Lodge. Home: 807 N Elm Dr, Beverly Hills, Cal. Office: 641 N Sepulveda Blvd, Los Angeles, Cal.

SPIEGEL, Arie, Isr, manufacturer; b. Lodz, Pol, July 12, 1907; s. Hanoch and Malka (Pilicer); in Isr since since 1925; m. Chana Lange; c: Amos, Gideon. Mgn dir, Hanoch Spiegel Ltd, since 1939; fmr: found mgn dir, chmn bd, Bet-Sha'an-Nazareth Textile Works, 1959-68; found, dir Sharon Textile Works, 1945-69. Fmr: mem, presidium, Mfg Assn of Isr, chmn, textile div. Home: 55 Frishman St, Tel Aviv, Isr. Office: 24 Abulafia St, Tel Aviv, Isr.

SPIEGEL, Ernest A, US, neurologist, educator; b. Vienna, Aus, July 24, 1895; s. Ignaz and Elise (Fuchs); desc of Rudolph Fuchs, trans Bible into Ger; in US, since 1930; MD, U Vienna,

1918; hon MD, Zurich, 1965; m. Anna Adolf, Aug 1, 1925. Prof em, Temple U Sch of Med, since 1937, prof, head dept experimental neur, 1930-37; docent, U Vienna Med Sch, 1924-30. Prin contribs: devl, with H T Wycis, method to produce cicumscribed lesions in the brain with guided electrodes. F: Coll of Phys, Phila; AMA; AAAS; hon f, Amer Electroencephal Soc; pres, Intl Soc for Research in Stereoencephalotomy; hon mem, Ger Neur Soc; mem: Amer Neur Assn; Amer Phys Soc; Soc Experimental Biol; Amer Therapeutic Soc; Phila Neur Soc, fmr pres; Phila Phys Soc; Assn Nervous and Mental Diseases; fmr councilor, Electroshock Research Assn. Author: Tonus of Skeletal Muscles, 1923; Centers of Autonomic Nervous Systems, 1925; Experimental Neurology, 1928; co-author: Stereoencephalotomy, vol I, 1952, vol II, 1962; Neurology of the Eye and Ear, Ger ed, 1930, Span ed, 1936, Eng ed, 1945; Confinia Neurologica, since 1938; Process in Neurology and Psychiatry, since 1946. Recipient: Otto Foerster Medal, 1965. Home: 6807 Lawnton Ave, Philadelphia, Pa. Office: Research Dir, Natl Parkinson Found, 880 NE 69 St, Miami, Fla.

SPIEGEL, Guido, It; PhD, U Padua. HS tchr, appd prof. Hon repr, JA; mem cen comm, JNF, fmr mem exec, ZF, It. Home: 20 Carli St, Trieste, It.

SPIEGEL, Henry W, US, educator, author; b. Berlin, Ger, Oct 13, 1911; s. Isaac and Auguste (Fuld); in US since 1936; JUD, U Berlin, 1933; PhD, U Wis, 1939; m. Cecile Wasserman, May 2, 1947; c: Robert, Richard. Prof, econ, Catholic U, since 1950, on fac since 1943; asst prof, econ, Duquesne U, 1939-42; lectr: Mich State Coll, 1942; U Wis, 1947; Johns Hopkins U, 1949-50; Howard U, 1954-63; Dumbarton Coll, 1955-59; Trinity Coll, 1956-62; Ind Coll of Armed Forces 1957, 1959, 1961; U Idaho, 1958; U Md, 1959, 1962-63; U Wash, 1961; U Cal, Santa Barbara and Berkeley, 1962; U Va, 1965; econ, US State Dept, 1945; cons: Pres Materials Policy Commn, 1951; Public Adv Bd for Mutual Security, 1952; Comm Public Works, House of Reprs, 1962; adv: Villanova U, Havana, 1954; natl panel, Amer Arbitration Assn, since 1959. Master sgt, US Army, 1942-45. Author: Land Tenure Policies at Home and Abroad, 1941; The Economics of Total War, 1942; The Brazilian Economy, 1949; Current Economic Problems, 1949, 1955, 1961; Introduction to Economics, 1951; Development of Economic Thought, 1952; Du Pont on Economic Curves, 1955; Rise of American Economic Thought, 1960; mem bd eds: Social Science, since 1953; Handbook of Latin American Studies, 1946-60; contbr to profsl periodicals. Mem: Royal Econ Soc; Amer Econ Assn; AAUP; Catholic Econ Assn; Amer Farm Econ Assn; Amer Political Assn; Assn for Latin Amer Studies; mgmt comm, Inst of Ibero Amer Studies; Amer Acad Political Sci; Phi Beta Kappa; Gamma Mu, fmr chancellor, Atlantic region; Artus; Academic Council for Heb U. Recipient: Guggenheim f, for research in Latin Amer. Hobbies: book, autograph collecting; walking; music. Home: 6848 Nashville Rd, Lanham, Md. Office: Catholic U, Washington, DC.

SPIEGEL, Irving Joshua, US, surgeon, educator: b. Fort William, Ont, Can, Aug 16, 1915; s. Jeremiah and Dora (Sloved); in US since 1937; MD, U Toronto Sch of Med, 1937; m. Rosalynde Green, 1942; c: Virginia, Jonathan, Petra. Asso prof, neur surg, Chgo Med Sch, since 1955; chief, neurosurg, Michael Reese Hosp; cons neurosurg: Edgewater Hosp; W Side VA Hosp; Provident Hosp; Belmont Hosp; Amer Hosp; S Chgo Comty Hosp; S Shore Hosp; Cen Comty Hosp; Louis A Weiss Memorial Hosp; Martha Washington Hosp; asst res: neuropsycht, State Hosp, Howard, RI, 1938-39; neur surg, Boston City Hosp, 1939-40; sr res, neur surg, St Luke's Hosp, Chgo, Ill, 1940-41; chief res: neur surg, Cook Co Hosp, Chgo, 1941-42; neur and neur surg, Neuropsychiatric Inst, Chgo, 1942; asso prof, neur surg, U of Ill, 1946-55. Maj, US Army MC, 1942-46. Pres, Neur Soc of Amer, 1956; chmn, specialty div, Intl Coll Surgs; mem: Royal Soc Med; Amer Bd Neur Surg; Neur So of Amer; Harvey Cushing Soc; AMA; Ill State Med Soc; Cook Co Med Soc; Chgo Med Soc; Assn Mil Surgs of US; Cong Neur Surgs; Chgo Neur Soc; Intl Bd Surg; Interurban Neurosurgical Soc; Cen Neurosurgical Soc; Phi Delta Epsilon; Sinai Temple; clubs: Standard; Adventurer's, Chgo; Shikar-Safari. Contbr to med jours and publs. Hobbies: archeol; hunting, fishing. Home: 6801 S Bennett Ave, Chicago, Ill. Office: 53 E Washington, Chicago, Ill.

SPIEGEL, John P, US, psychiatrist, educator; b. Chgo, Ill, Mar 17, 1911; s. Modie and Lena (Strauss); BA, Dartmouth Coll, 1934; MD, Northwestern U Sch of Med, 1939; m.

Babette Schiller, Aug 1, 1935; c: Heli, Adam, Mary, Pauline. Prof, social psycht, Florence Heller Sch for Advanced Studies in Social Wfr, Brandeis U, since 1966, dir, Lemberg Cen for Study of Violence, since 1966; asso att phys, Cook Co Psychopathic Hosp, 1947-49; lectr: Sch of Social Service Admn, U Chgo, 1949-51; child care course, Chgo Inst of Psychan, 1950-52; asso dir, Inst for Psychosomatic and Psycht Research and Training, Michael Reese Hosp, 1951-53, mem staff, since 1938; asso, Lab of Social Relations, Harvard U, 1954-66, asso clinical prof, psycht, Med Sch, 1957-66. Psycht cons, US 12th Air Force, 1942-44; chief, profsl services, USAF Hosp, St Petersburg, Fla, 1944-46. F: AMA; Amer Psycht Assn; chmn, comm on family, Group for Advancement of Psycht, since 1950; mem: Amer Bd Psycht and Neur; Assn Psycht Facilities, Chgo, Inc; Amer Psychosomatic Soc; Chgo Psychoanalytic Soc; Natl Council on Family Relations; fmr: vice-pres, Ill Soc Mh; mem: comms on psycht disaster studies, stress, both, NRC; Conf on Group Processes, Josiah Macy Jr Found; comm to frame unified theory of behavior, Chgo. Co-author: Men under Stress, 1945; War Neuroses, 1946; contbr to med jours. Home: 10 Channing Pl, Cambridge, Mass. Office: Lemberg Cen for the Study of Violence, Waltham, Mass.

SPIEGEL, Moshe, US, translator; b. Ostropol, Russ, Feb 16, 1899; s. Solomon and Fanny (Kaminker); in US since 1913; att Drexel Inst. Trans: The Last Revolt by J Opatoshu, 1952; The Travels and Adventures of Benjamin III, 1949, The Nag, 1954, by Mendele Mocher Sephorim; Hamlet and Don Quixote by Turgeniev; After the Fair, by Sholem Aleichem; In This World and the Next, by I L Peretz, 1958; In The Thicket by Solomon Simon, 1962; The Restless Spirit, Zalman Shneour, 1962; World History of the Jews by Dubnov, 1968. Author: play, Count Leo Tolstoy; contbr: Treasury of Russian Literature, 1945; Treasury of Yiddish Stories, 1954; Sholem Aleichem Panorama; lit jours. Home: POB 1003, Philadelphia, Pa.

SPIEGEL, Sam, US, film producer; b. Aus, 1904; s. Simon and Regina (Schwitz); in US since 1939. Pres, Horizon Pictures Inc, since 1948; among pictures produc: Tales of Manhattan; African Queen; On The Waterfront; The Bridge on the River Kwai; The Chase; Suddenly Last Summer; Lawrence of Arabia; Nicholas and Alexandra; The Dilke Story; One of our Brains is Draining. Recipient: Irving Thalberg Memorial award, 1965. Office: 711 Fifth Ave, New York, NY.

SPIEGEL, Samuel A, US, jurist, attorney; b. NYC, April 26, 1914; s. Max and Gussie (Zeller); LLB, St John's U Law Sch, 1936; m. Charlotte Neuman, 1942; c: Jill, Maura. Justice, NY State Supr Court, since 1966; law practice, Spiegel and Davis, 1937-62; Civil Court Judge, 1962-66; law instr, USN, 1943-46; guest lectr, housing, govt, legislation, CCNY; Pace Coll, LIU, 1956-62. Prin contribs: sponsored, housing, civil rights, aid to educ and other social legislation. US Army, 1942; USN, 1943-46. Fmr pres, Stuyvesant Polyclinic Hosp; pres, found, Samuel Dickstein Lodge, B'nai B'rith, 1953; Seward Park HS Alumni, since 1931; Clark House Alumni Assn, 1936; chmn, Local Sch Bd 3, NYC, 1960-62; chancellor-commn, Lenton Lodge 680, KP, 1951; mem, bd dirs: Grand St Settlement, since 1948; Young Men's Philanthropic League; E Side Torah Cen, since 1959; mem: Dowtown Talmud Torah, since 1955; HIAS, since 1956; Amer Bar Assn; NY Co Lawyers Assn; Plaintiff Trial Lawyers Assn; Inter-Faith Movement, Inc; E Side C of C; Amer Legion; JWV, Grand St Boys Assn; Workmen's Circle. Author: The Forgotten Man in Housing, 1959. Recipient: commendation, outstanding legal work, USN, 1945; service awards: Grand Lodge, Dist l, 1956, Dickstein Lodge, 1957, B'nai B'rith; Clark House Alumni Assn, 1957; Health Found, 1958; UJA, 1959; Downtown Torah, 1959; leadership award, NJJC, 1959; E Side Post, JWV, 1960; Morros Dickstein Post, VFW 1958, legislative service award, 1961; alumnus of year, Seward Park High Sch, 1960, first mem, Seward Hall of Fame, 1961; Corlears Comty award, 1961. Home: 577 Grand St, New York, NY. Office: 60 Centre St, New York, NY.

SPIEGEL, Yeshajahu, Isr, author; b. Lodz, Pol, Jan 14, 1906; s. Moshe and Sarah (Brown); in Isr since 1951; m. Charlotte Titel. Tchr, Yiddish lit and lang, 1929-38, 1946-48; govt official, Min of Finance, 1951-64. Author: poetry: Mitn Ponym Tsu Der Zun, 1930; Un Geworn Iz Licht, 1949; short stories: Malchus Geto, 1947; Intern Ibern Geto, 1948; Mentshn In Thehom, 1949; Licht Funem Opgrunt, 1952; Vint un Vortslen, 1955; Di Brik, 1963; Malchut Geto, 1952; novel: Flamen Fun Der Erd, 1966; Shtign Tsum Himl, 1966;

stories, poetry, appear in Eng, Dutch, Fr, Ger anthols. Fmr secy, Union Yiddish Writers, Warsaw; mem: Org J Writers, Tel Aviv; ACUM; clubs: Heb PEN; Yiddish PEN. Recipient: Max Kessel prize, 1952; Fr-Yiddish Culture Cong award, Paris, Yiddish PEN Club Cen prize, 1968: Fishl Bimko prize. Home: Borohov St, Givatayim, Isr.

SPIEGEL-ADOLF, Mona, US, chemist, educator; b. Vienna, Aus, Feb 23, 1893; d. Jacob and Hedwig (Spitzer) Adolf; in US since 1931; BS, U of Vienna, 1918; m. Ernest Spiegel, Aug 1, 1925. Prof em, Temple U Sch of Med, since 1966, prof, head dept, colloid chem, 1931-66; demonstrator, path histology and bact, U Vienna, 1915-18, asst, med colloid chem, 1919-30, docent, med chem, 1931; cons, Fed Inst of Serumtherapy, Vienna, 1927-29. F, AAAS; mem: Amer Soc Biol Chem; Amer Chem Soc; Biochem Soc, Eng; Amer Crystological Soc; Amer Optical Soc; Amer Assn U Women; Sigma Chi. Author: The Globulins, 1930; The Steinkopff, 1930; co-author, X-Ray Diffraction in Biology and Medicine, 1947; contbr to profsl jours. Home: 6807 Lawnton Ave, Philadelphia, Pa.

SPIEGELMAN, Anna R, US, physician, educator; b. Bklyn, NY, Sep 22, 1903; d. Morris and Fannie (Derjawitz); BA, Adelphi Coll, 1923; MD, LI Coll Hosp, Med Sch, 1927. Pvt practice since 1930; asst prof, clinical med, NYU Postgrad Med Sch, since 1952; att phys: Sea View Hosp; Sydenham Hosp; asso phys: Bellevue Hosp; U Hosp. F: Clinical Soc; NY Diabetes Assn, 1944; mem: AMA; AHA; Amer Diabetes Assn; Geriatrics Assn; NY Acad Scis; NY State and Co Med Soc; NY Diabetes Assn; NY Heart Assn; Amer Public Health Assn. Contbr to profsl jours. Hobby: music. Home: 90 Riverside Dr, New York, NY. Office: 121 E 60 St, New York, NY.

SPIEGELMAN, Sol, US, educator; b. NYC, Dec 14, 1914; s. Max and Eva (Kramer); BS, CCNY, 1937; att Columbia U, 1939-41; PhD, Wash U, 1944; hon DS: Rensselaer Poly Inst, 1966; Northeastern U, 1966; St Louis U, 1968; m. Helen Wahala, 1939; c: Willard, George, Marjorie. Prof, microbiol, U of Ill, since 1949; lectr, physics and applied math, Wash U, 1942-44, instr, bact, Sch of Med, 1945, asst prof, 1946; spec postdoc f, USPHS, U Minn, 1948. F, Amer Acad Arts and Scis; mem: Amer Soc Microbiol; Soc Gen Microbiol, Brit; Soc Gen Physiologists; Soc Amer Naturalists; Natl Acad of Scis; Phi Kappa Phi. Contbr numerous sci papers. Recipient: Pasteur award, Ill Soc for Microbiol; Jesup lectr, Columbia U, 1963; Ciba lectr, 1964; Alumni Citation award, Wash U, 1966; Gehrmann lectr, Philips lectr, Bertner Found award in Cancer Research; Dyer lectr, NIH; Harvey lectr, NY Acad Med, 1968. Home: 610 W Green St, Champaign, Ill. Office: U of Ill, Urbana, Ill.

SPIEGLER, Samuel, US, organization exec; b. Wilmington, Del, Oct 24, 1906; s. Harry and Yetta (Aaron); m. Anne Berdit, June 8, 1930. Dir, info, Natl J Comty Relations Advisory Council, NY, since 1946; ed: Journal of Intergroup Relations, 1959-64; Occupational Index, 1934-38; asst dir, dir research, J Occupational Council, 1938-46. US Army, 1943-45. Pres, Assn J Comty Relations Workers, 1961-63; mem: Amer J PR Soc; Natl Conf J Communal Service; Natl Assn Intergroup Relations Officials: JWV. Author: Your Life's Work, 1944; pamphlets on occupations for use in counseling, 1936-40. Home: 5 Peter Cooper Rd, New York, NY. Office: 55 W 42 St, New York, NY.

SPIELBERGER, Joseph, Isr, business exec; b. Kosice, Czech, Oct 28, 1904; s. Hermann and Karolina (Monig); in Isr since 1935; EE, Poly, 1927; m. Fanny Sparer; c: Tirzah, Edrah. Dir, tech adv, mem bd, Elco, since 1949, tech dir, 1935-49; engr, K Engel, Budapest, 1927-35. Prin contrib: Found first Isr electro-mech ind; specialist in bldg elec transformers. Mem: Isr Assn Engrs and Architects; B'nai B'rith; fmr: mem exec, Zionist Org, Hung; pres, Mizrachi, Hung. Contbr: articles in field of elecs. Spec interest: Judaica. Home: 1 Lean St, Ramat Gan, Isr. Office: 23 Jabotinsky St, Ramat Gan, Isr.

SPIELMAN, Herbert, US, govt official; b. Bayonne, NJ, Oct 13, 1920; s. John and Leah (Tobias); BS, CCNY, 1946; PhD, U Chgo, 1949; m. Sally Sweet, Mar 26, 1947; c: Terry, Elena. US State Dept Fac Adv to Defense Intelligence Sch, since 1968; political off, Amer Emb, Bangkok, 1966-68, NATO affairs, State Dept, 1962-64; Bur W Eur affairs, 1964-66; hist tchr: Thornton Jr Coll, 1948, Amer U, Wash, 1952; spec asst to chmn, US Natl commn for UNESCO, 1949-50; intel-

ligence research spec, 1950-51; hist, hist div, State Dept, 1951-57; political off, US delg to NATO, Paris, 1957-62. US Army, 1943-46. Mem: Amer Fgn Service Assn. Hobbies: golf, swimming. Home: 381 N St, SW, Wash, DC. Office: Dept of State, Washington, DC.

SPIES, Gerty, Ger, author; b. Trier, Ger, Jan 13, 1897; d. Sigmund and Charlotte (Kahn) Gumprich; att HS, Ger; div. Started to write after being freed from three years imprisonment in Nazi camp Theresienstadt; author: numerous poems, essays, stories, novels, pub in Ger publs and on TV, Bayern; Theresienstadt, poems, 1947. Mem comm, Gesellschaft für christlich-jüdische Zusammenarbeit, Bayern; mem: Germania-Judaica, Köln; Deutsch-Englische Gesellschaft; Verband Deutscher Schriftsteller. Hobbies: playing violin, nature, hiking. Home: Schleissheimerstrasse 452/VII, Munich, Ger.

SPIESMAN, Manuel G, US, physician, educator; b. Chgo, Ill, Oct 30, 1900; s. Gabriel and Louisa (Weinstein); BS, Chgo Med Sch, 1925, MD, 1926; hon LLD, Natl Coll of Can, 1946; m; c: Renee Jans, James, Anthony; m.2nd, Christine Baker, 1961. Practicing proctologist since 1926; proctologist, att staff, Edgewater Hosp, 1934-63; head, GI rectal clinic, Cook Co Hosp, 1929-33; asst in surg to Dr Max Thorek, 1934-37; adj, surg, Mt Sinai Hosp, 1936-49; asso prof, proctology, Chgo Med Sch, 1930-63, all Chgo. Served USN. F: Intl Acad Proctology, pres, 1955-56; AMA; Amer Coll Gastroentero-logy; mem: Cook Co Med Soc; Ill Med Soc; Masons; club, Corinthian Yacht, Chgo. Author: An Outline of Proctology, 1939; Essentials of Clinical Proctology, 1946, rev ed, 1957; contbr to profsl jours; held 14 sci exhbs; proctologic movies shown at med socs meetings. Hobbies: painting, sailing. Home: 7445 S W 78 Ct, S Miami, Fla.

SPILLER, Andrées Hecht, Uruguay, industrial exec; b. Abony, Hung, Sep 12, 1913; s. Aladar and Elizabeth (Hecht); in Uruguay since 1930; att HS, Cluj, Rum; m. Elizabeth Kwek-silber, June 13, 1940; c: Carlos, Pablo. Ind exec since 1934; owner, 1st factory with pressured foundry; did 1st exportation of faucets and fittings, both Uruguay; jeweller: Albano, 1930-31; Jourdan & Co, 1931-34. Hon pres, ORT, since 1967, pres, 1954-66, treas, 1952-54, vocal, 1950-52; mem: B'nai B'rith, Oriental Lodge; Unified Campaign. Hobbies: music, chess. Home: T Narvaja 880, Montevideo, Uruguay. Office: J Paullier 1875, Montevideo, Uruguay.

SPIRA, Ralph, Isr, physician; b. Cracow, Pol, Aug 1, 1913; s. Benjamin and Salomea (Spira) Naftali; in Isr since 1952; MD, med sch, U Paris; Med Coll, Edinburgh; m. Miriam Walk, Mar 30, 1947; c: Judith, Daniella. Dir, phys med dept, Assaf Harofe Hosp, since 1956; rehab cons, Min of Defense, since 1952. Maj, IDF, 1952-54. Hon med adv, Ilan-Isr Found for Handicapped Children. Author: Influence of Sport Ac-tivities on Rehabilitation of Paralytic Subjects, 1967. Home: 12 Nehardea St, Tel Aviv, Isr. Office: Asaf Harofe Hosp, Zrifin, Isr.

SPIRA, Yeshayahu, Isr, broadcasting exec, editor; b. Krakow, Pol, Dec 20, 1903; s. Zev and Rosa (Hof); in Isr since 1940; att Poly Inst, Lwow, Pol, 1920-21; PhD, Jagellonian U, Krakow, 1926; att Conservatory of Music, Lwow, Krakow, 1926; m. Hadassah Moldavsky; c: Zev, Gony. Dir, radio, Isr Bc Auth, since 1969, fmr dir gen, planning, dir progs, with auth since 1948; controller, Heb prog, Voice of Jerusalem, radio, 1946-48; dir, Childrens Immigrant Camps, Jerusalem, 1943; org, musical activities in kibbutzim. Composer: songs and J folklore. Chmn: music sect, mem bd, Isr Council for Culture and Arts; scholarship comm, mem, Isr Bd, Isr-Amer Cultural Found; co-found, Gordonia Youth Movement, Pol; mem, bd: Isr Commn for UNESCO; Merkaz Hachinuch; mem, bur radio programming commn, Eur Bc Union, Geneva, Switz. Home: 90 Hashalom Rd, Tel Aviv, Isr. Office: Beit Hashidur, Hamalka Melisanda, Jerusalem, Isr.

SPIREA, Andrei, Isr, composer; b. Bucharest, Rum, Jan 21, 1932; s. Aurel and Adriana (Lupescu); in Isr since 1959; MA, Acad of Music, U Bucharest, 1953; m. Batsheva Dat, Oct 1, 1963; c: Avinoram; Smadar. Lectr, Tel Aviv U Acad of Music, since 1968; fmr: tchr, instr of chamber music, regional studios, sponsored by kibbutzim. Composer: Diverti-mento for Orchestra, 1961; Music for Brass, 1964; Sinfonia da Camera for Viola and 17 Instruments, 1964; Concerto for Piano and Orchestra, 1964-65; Concerto for Violin and Or-chestra, 1964-66; Quintet for Clarinet and Strings, 1965; Wood-wind Quintet, 1968-69; Partita for Piano, 1967-68; Allegro for Orchestra, performed in public concert under

Sergiv Commisiona, Rum. Mem: League of Composers in Isr. Home: 29 Brandeis St, Tel Aviv, Isr.

SPIRN, Charles Arnold, US, rabbi; b. Pol; s. Juda and Rose (Kleiner); in US since 1943; BA, cum laude, Yeshiva U, 1947; ordained rabbi, Rabbi Isaac Elchanan Theol Sem, 1951; m. Regina Volfovsky; c: Beth, Neil. Rabbi, Cong Anshe Zedek, Yonkers, NY, since 1951; lectr, Fr dept, Yeshiva U, 1963-65; established first Greystone Rel Sch, Yonkers, 1955. Vice-pres, Rel Zionist Youth, Bklyn, 1943-45; co-chmn, convention, Rabb Alumni, Yeshiva U, 1959; secy, ed comm, RabCA; found, Yonkers Coll J Studies, 1959; Gtr Yonkers Bd Rabbis, Yonkers Bd of Educ; Mayor's appointee as J Repr to Yonkers Comty Action Comm, 1965-66; org: first Isr Bond Dr in Yonkers, 1957, and subsequent dr; first Anti-Poverty Dr in Yonkers; City-Wide Rally for Soviet Jewry, 1966; mem, exec bd; Brandeis dist, ZOA; J Fed; mem, bd dirs, Heb Acad, Yonkers; mem: B'nai B'rith; B'nai Zion; Isr Commn, RabCA; fmr: active in Zionist movement, J Student Org, and Boy Scout movement, all in Fr. Contbr: Le Flambeau, The Torch, Fr lit publ of Yeshiva U, ed-in-chief, 1945-47; to J periodicals. Home: 270 N Broadway, Yonkers, NY. Study: 6 Ingram St, Yonkers, NY.

SPIRO, Saul S, US, educational dir; b. Jerusalem, Oct 21, 1906; s. Moshe and Rachel (Slonim); in US since 1928; att Etz Hayim Yeshiva; grad, Mizrachi Tchrs Coll, 1926; at Heb U, 1927; ordained rabbi, 1928; att U Vt, 1930; m. Dorothy Mazel, Apr 27, 1930; c: Saul, Herzl, Rena. Dir, Bur of J Educ, Dayton, O; fmr dir, educ, Fairmount Temple, Cleveland, O; prin, Solomon Kluger Yeshiva, NY, 1930; supt, SW dist, Pa J Rel Schs, dean, Tchrs Training Coll, lectr, Coll of J Studies, Pittsburgh, 1936-40; natl field dir, secy, exec dir, ZOA, 1940-46; educ dir, Burlington, Vt, 1958; lectr, U Vt, 1959. Mem: Natl Council J Educ; Educs Assembly; Natl Assn Temple Educs; fmr: pres, Heb Tchrs Assn, Pittsburgh; ZOA, Pittsburgh dist, tri-state Zionist region; Vt J Council; Histadrut Ivrit. Author: Joy of Jewish Living; Fundamentals of Judaism; Biographical Study of Ludwig Lewisohn, 1938; Hebrew Grammar, 1938; Teacher's Manual for Religious Schools, 1962; lit ed, Amer J Outlook; Pittsburgh ed, Vt J Voice; contbr to Anglo-J press. Recipient: awards from Natl Assn of Temple Educs, HUC, for educ progs. Home: 5516 Joyceann Dr, Dayton, O. Office: 184 Salem Ave, Dayton, O.

SPITZ, Berthold Uri, Isr, business exec; b. Nuremburg, Ger, Nov 10, 1922; s. Julius and Helena (Wolff); in Isr since 1954; att: Rosenberg Inst; Brighton Tech Coll; m. Regine Alcalay; c: Naomi, Robert. Dir: Modehaus Sallinger, since 1955; Rimon Moden, since 1969; chief of communications, El Al, 1951-53. Royal Engrs, 1942-46; capt, IDF, 1948-50. Pres, Textile and Fashion Comm, Ger; mem: presidium, Ger-Isr C of C; club, Lions. Hobbies: golf, fishing, hunting, flying. Home: 52 Chen Blvd, Tel Aviv, Isr. Office: 38/29 Straubing St, W Ger.

SPITZ, Hans, Austr, business exec; b. Vienna, Aus, Nov 19, 1911; s. Leopold and Ida (Porges); in Austr since 1939; BCom, U Vienna, 1933; DEcon, DCom, U Florence, It, 1935; Acctnt deg, U Vienna, 1937; m. Toni Schoenberg, Nov 25, 1934; c: Eva Lustig. Dir of cos since 1948. Austr Army, 1942-46. Asso Australasian Inst Cost Acctnts; Soc of Acctnts; Intl vice-pres, mem, bd govs, B'nai B'rith, fmr pres, dist 21, fmr pres, Menorah lodge, Melbourne lodge; dir, Austr J Wfr Soc. Home: 29 Longview Rd, Melbourne, Austr. Office: 323 Montague St, Melbourne, Austr.

SPITZ, Henry, US, attorney, b. NYC, Oct 21, 1903; s. Herman and Dora (Dinenberg); BSS, CCNY, 1925; LLB, Columbia U, 1928; m. Rose Schrier, Feb 16, 1936; c: Harlan, Arnold. Gen counsel, NY State Div Hum Rights, since 1945; asso with: Kaye, McDavitt and Scholer, 1928-30; Hartman, Sheridan, Tekulsky, Pegora & Banton, 1930-33; Greenbaum, Wolff & Ernst, 1933-34; attorney, rehab and liquidation div, NY State Dept of Ins, 1934-36; pvt law practice, 1936-45. Mem: Assn Bar, NYC; Columbia U Alumni Assn; CCNY Alumni Assn; Phi Beta Kappa; Hillcrest J Cen. Home: 80-64 Surrey Pl, Jamaica, NY. Office: 270 Broadway, New York, NY.

SPITZER, Jack J, US, banker; b. NYC, Sep 11, 1917; s. Ira and Jennie (Brody); BEcon, UCLA, 1938; m. Charlotte Braunstein, Dec 21, 1941; c: Jill, Robert. Pres, chmn bd: Sterling Savings and Loan Assn, since 1966; Brentwood Savings, 1959-66. Lt, US Army, 1943-46. Chmn, B'nai B'rith Youth Commn; pres, Riverside United J Fund; vice-pres, Student Inter-rel Cen, U Cal, Riverside; fmr: pres: B'nai B'rith Lodge; Amer Friends Afr; intl pres, AZA of B'nai B'rith. Recipient: Army Commendation Ribbon. Home: 1105 Via Vallarta, Riverside, Cal. Office: 3855 Market St, Riverside, Cal.

SPITZER, Max David, US, attorney; b. Aus, Aug 2, 1906; s. Benjamin and Tillie (Schechter); in US since 1913; BCS, NYU, 1927, LLB, 1930, JD; m. Lucille Peters, Feb 2, 1947; c: Robert. Sr partner, law firm, Kahr & Spitzer & Howard, NYC; mem: bd, Royal Natl Bank, NY; adv comm, Title, Guarantee, Co; fmr, mem bd, Diana Stores Corp. Staff sgt, US Army, 1943-45. Co-found, Albert Einstein Med Sch; mem: exec comm, Kings Co chap, Amer Legion; Park Ave Syn; Assn Bar, NYC; NY Co Lawyers Assn; fmr: chancelor, KP Lodge; cdr, Amer Legion Post; pres, AJCong; active: Young Isr; UJA; found, Soc of J Thought and Culture; club, Town, NYC, 1st vice-pres. Home: 1025 Fifth Ave, New York, NY. Office: 405 Park Ave, New York, NY.

SPITZER, Moshe Maurice, Isr, publisher; b. Boskovice, Aus, July 8, 1900; s. Maximilian and Eveline (Karpelis); in Isr since 1939; att U Vienna; PhD, U Kiel, Ger, 1926; m. Pepa Hammerman, 1940; c: Daniel, Immanuel, Ester. Prop, mgr, Tarshish Books, since 1941; research asst, Prussian Acad Sci and Hum, Berlin, 1927-28; dir, Schule der Judischen Ingeun, Berlin, 1929-32; asst to Prof Martin Buber, 1932-34; ed, dir, Shodejn Verlag, Berlin, 1932-39; dir, pub dept, JA, Jerusalem, 1945-60; co-found, dir, Jerusalem Typefoundry, Jerusalem, 1951-63. Prin contrib: introduction of new standard in Heb typography in Pal; creation of new Heb type faces. Chmn, panel, visual arts, Isr Arts Council; mem, adv council on coins and notes, Bank of Isr; adv publs, Isr Acad Sci and Hums, since 1965. Pub: papers on: Old Indian phil, lit, hist; Heb letters; trans Sanskrit and Ger into Heb. Hobby: art collecting. Home and office: 14 Hakeshet St, Jerusalem, Isr.

SPIVACK, Robert Gerald, US, journalist; b. Dayton, O, Apr 28, 1915; s. Mose and Leah (Tahl); BA, U Cincinnati, 1936; m. Adrienne Rauchwerger, Apr 18, 1940; c: Lorna, Miranda. Wash columnist, NY Herald Tribune Syndicate, Inter Publishers Newspaper Syndicate, since 1961; ed and pres, Reporters' New Syndicate, since 1968; political writer and reporter, NY Post, 1944-53; Wash corresp, 1953-61. Mem: Overseas Writers; Omicron Delta Kappa; Sigma Tau Phi; Amer Newspaper Guild; Albany Soc; Legislative Corresp Assn; Inner Circle, NY; clubs: Natl Press; Wash Athletic. Co-ed, Candidates, 1960, contbr to: Our Sovereign State; The American Century; natl mags. Home: 2113 Paul Spring Rd, Alexandria, Va. Office: Natl Press Bldg, Washington, DC.

SPIVAK, Lawrence Edmund, US, tv-radio producer; b. NYC; s. William and Sonya (Bershad); AB, Harvard; hon: LLD, Wilberforce U; DLitt, Suffolk U; LHD, Tampa U; m. Charlotte Beir Ring; c: Judith Frost (decd); Jonathan. Produc, found, Meet the Press, radio since 1945, tv since 1947; bus mgr, Antiques Mag, 1921-30; asst to publisher, Hunting and Fishing, Natl Sportsman mags, 1930-33; bus mgr, Amer Mercury, 1934-39, publisher, 1944-50; found, publisher, Ellery Queen's Mystery Mags, Mag of Fantasy and Sci Fiction, Mercury Mystery Books, Bestseller Mysteries, Jonathan Press Books, all until 1954. Mem: Radio and TV Corresp Assn; clubs: Fed City; Natl Press; Harvard. Recipient: best public service award, O State, 1950; Sylvania award, 1951; Peabody award for tv news, twice. Home: Sheraton Park Hotel, Washington, DC. Office: 2660 Woodley Rd, NW, Washington, DC.

SPIVAK, Sydney Joel, Can, attorney; b. Winnipeg, Can, May 23, 1928; s. Malek and Rose (Portigal); LLB, U Man, 1951; LLB, Harvard U; m. Mira Steele, May 29, 1955; c: Lori, Harold, Diane. Min, Dept Commerce and Ind, Province Man, since 1966; fmr, barrister, Spivak and Spivak. Mem: bd govs Maimonides Coll; B'nai B'rith; fmr: pres, Rainbow Stage; mem: bd, Man Theater Cen; Man Hist Soc; JWF Bd; exec, Can Friends Heb U; club, Harvard, Man. Hobby: tennis. Home: 1516 Mathers Bay W, Winnipeg, Can. Office: 302 Leg Bldg, Winnipeg, Can.

SPIVAKOVSKY, Jascha, Austr, concert pianist, educator; b. Smela, Russ, Aug 18, 1896; s. David and Rahel (Placson); in Austr since 1938; att Klindworth-Scharwenka Conservatoire, Berlin, Ger, 1907-10; studied with Mayer Mahr, 1912; m. Leonore Krantz, 1926; c: Rahel, David, Michael. Tchr, master class in piano, U Melbourne Conservatorium, 1934-62; first concert tour in Eur, 1910; toured Eur and US annually since 1910, playing under: Nikisch, Furtwängler, Richard

Strauss, Sir Malcolm Sargent; toured Isr, 1952; formed Spivakovsky-Kurtz Trio, with brother Tossy as violinist, Edmund Kurtz as cellist, 1933. Pres, Vic Friends of Isr Philharmonic Orch, since 1937. Home: 76 St Georges Rd, Toorak, Victoria, Austr.

SPIVAKOVSKY, Tossy, US, violinist; b. Odessa, Russ, Feb, s. David and Rahel (Placson); in US since 1939; att Berliner Hocheschule fur Musik; studied with: Arrigo Serato; Willy Hess; m. Erika Lipsker, Nov 21, 1934; c: Ruth. Concert debut, Berlin, 1918; toured Eur as soloist with leading orchs, 1918-33; concert-master, Berlin Philharmonic, 1926; toured Austr and NZ, 1933-39; instr violin, Melbourne Conservatorum, Austr, 1934-39; Amer debut with Cleveland Orch under Artur Rodzinski, 1942; first Carnegie Hall recital, NYC, 1942; introduced Bartok Violin Concerto to Amer with Cleveland Orch, 1943. Composer: three cadenzas to Beethoven's Violin Concerto; cadenzas to Mozart concertos. Recordings: Columbia Masterworks; Concert Hall Soc; ARC-Victor; Everest; Epic; Vanguard. Mem: Amer Fed Musicians. Hobby: chess. Home: 70 Weston Rd, Westport, Conn. Office: c/o Columbia Artists Mgmt, 165 W 57 St, New York, NY.

SPIVEK, Ephraim, US, social worker; b. Chgo, Ill, Feb 1, 1917; s. Herman and Gertrude (Peters); BA, U Chgo, 1939; att Sch of Social Service Admn, U Chgo, 1939-41, MA, 1946; m. Ilse Pincuss, Apr 14, 1946; c: Beverly, Roberta. Exec dir, United J Fed: case worker, J Family Service, Kan City, Mo, 1941-42, Chgo, 1946; subscription secy, J Fed Chgo, 1949-49; fmr exec dir, JCC, Norfolk, US Army, 1942-46. Mem: B'nai B'rith; Cong Ohef Sholem; JWV; B'rith Sholem Lodge; AJComm; club, Torch. Recipient: Purple Heart. Home: 209 N Blake Rd, Norfolk, Va. Office: 7330 Newport Ave, Norfolk, Va.

SPLAVER, Sarah, US, counseling psychologist, author; b. NYC; d. Morris and Rose (Farber); PhD, NYU Sch of Educ, 1953. Practicing psychol and guidance cons since 1950; cons, HEW, since 1962; personnel sup, US War Dept, 1943-45; dir, guidance, Rhodes Sch, NY, 1946-50. Author: Opportunities in Vocational Guidance, 1949; High School Students and Occupational Books, 1953; Opportunities in Guidance, 1961; Careers in Personnel Administration, 1962; Your Career—If You're Not Going to College, 1963; Your Personality and You, 1965; Your Handicap-Don't Let It Handicap You, 1967; Your College Education-How to Pay for It, 1968; Some Day I'll Be a Doctor, 1967; Some Day I'll Be an Aerospace Engineer, 1967; Some Day I'll Be a Librarian, 1967; ed in chief, Guidance Exch; organizer, Socio-guidrama series, playlets for teenagers; contbr to profsl and popular jours; over 50 occupational abstracts; handiguides for secondary schs; lectr on educ, guidance, and psychol subjects. F, Intl Council Psychols, fmr co-chmn, comm on problems of children; mem: profsl; Natl Vocational Guidance Assn; life, Amer Personnel and Guidance Assn; Metrop Assn Applied Psychol; AAAS; NY Personnel and Guidance Assn, fmr mem, bd trustees; educ chap, B'nai B'rith; Authors Guild. Recipient: cert, commendation, from Mayor LaGuardia, for service as sup of interviews, Civil Defense Volunteer Off, WW II. Hobbies: photography; golf. Home and office: 3310 Rochambeau Ave, Bronx, NY.

SPORN, Philip, US, engineer, business exec; b. Galicia, Aus, Nov 25, 1896; s. Isak and Rachel (Kolker); in US since 1907; EE, Columbia U Sch of Engr, 1917, postgrad study, 1917-18; hon DEngr: Stevens Inst Tech, 1948; Ill Inst Tech, 1953; Bklyn Poly Inst, 1955; Tri-State Coll, 1959; Rensselaer Poly Inst, 1968; D honoris causa, U Grenoble, Fr, 1950; hon LLD: Hanover Coll, 1953; Columbia U, 1966; hon DHL, Marshall Coll, 1956; hon DS: O State U, 1957; Ind Inst Tech, 1958; hon D Tech Scis, Technion, Haifa, 1959; m. Sadie Posner, Sep 10, 1923; c: Deborah Gilbert, Arthur, Michael. Cons, Amer Elec Power Co, since 1961, vice-pres i/c all engr activities, 1934, exec vice-pres, 1945, mem staff since 1920, pres, Amer Elec Power Service Corp and subsidiary cos, 1947-61; chmn, Sea Water Conversion Comm, Govt of Isr, since 1959; cons: US War Produc Bd, 1942-45; Oak Ridge Nuclear Project, Monsanto Chem Co, 1947; lectr, Ind Coll of Armed Forces, 1948; visiting prof, engr, Cornell U, 1962; pres, dir: Ind-Ky Elec Corp; O Valley Elec Corp, all 1952-67; pres, Nuclear Power Group, 1955, vice-pres, 1956, dir, 1957-61; chmn, research and devl comm, E Cen Nuclear Group, 1958-67, chmn, working comm, 1957; mem: elec utility defense adv council, Defense Elec Power Admn, 1950-52; elec power comm, Natl Security Resources Bd, 1947-53; visiting comm for nuclear engr and reactor depts, Brookhaven

Natl Labs, 1953-57; AEC, US and ad hoc adv comm on reactor policies and progs, 1959; State Dept ad hoc adv comm on US Policy Toward Intl Atomic Energy Agcy, 1962; chmn: ad hoc adv comm on coop between Elec Power Ind and AEC, 1949-51; gen adv comm, Fed Power Natl Commn Power Survey 1962-64; mem: bd dirs, Ky Spindletop Research Cen, 1960-68; policy comm on power capacity and pooling, Edison Elec Inst 1960-67, mem, natl defense comm, 1961-67, mem, tech appraisal task force on nuclear power, 1958-61; exec comm, Assn Edison Illuminating Cos; chmn, US natl comm, Conf Intl des Grandes Réseaux Electriques; US delg, Geneva Conf on Peaceful Uses of Atomic Energy, 1955, accredited observer, 2nd Conf, 1958; mem, gen tech adv comm to Off of Coal Research, Interior Dept, since 1960; dir, Atomic Ind Forum, 1959-67, vice-pres, 1961; mem, natl research council comm on dispersal and disposal of radioactive wastes, Natl Acad Scis, chmn, comm on power supply for the Zeus Multi-Function Array Radar installations, since 1962; comm on commercial uses of atomic energy, US C of C, 1955-60, comm on new frontiers of tech, 1961-63; nuclear energy comm, Natl Assn of Mfrs, 1958-61; trustee, Comm for Econ Devl, since 1957, mem, comm on research and policy since 1960; dir, trustee, Natl Fund for Med Educ, 1958-63. F: hon mem, Amer Inst MEs; AAAS; mem: adv comm, bus and ind, AJ-Comm, since 1949; fmr: chmn, bd dirs, Amer Technion Soc, 1940-42; vice-chmn, exec comm, dir, Natl Coal Policy Conf, 1959-67; natl chmn, spec gifts campaign, NCCJ, 1958-59; dir, Advt Council, 1958-61; gov, Weizmann Inst of Sci, since 1958, dir, Amer Comm, since 1958; mem: visiting comm, dept elec engr, MIT, since 1958; adv council, Sch Engr, Columbia U, since 1955; engr coll council, Cornell U, since 1958; fmr, adv council, elec engr dept, Sch of Engr and Applied Sci, Princeton U, 1958-63; mem: Amer Soc CEs; Natl Acad Scis; Natl Acad Engr; Eta Kappa Nu; Sigma Xi; Tau Beta Pi; Columbia U Assos; Franklin Inst; hon mem, Fr Soc Electricians; clubs: Econ; Engrs; City Midday, all NYC. Author: The Integrated Power System, 1950; Energy: Its Production, Conversion and Use in the Service of Man, 1963; Foundations of Engineering, 1964; Research in Electrical Power, 1965; Fresh Water from Saline Waters, 1966; Vistas in Electrical Power, 1969; Technology, Engineering and Economics, 1969; co-author, Heat Pumps, 1957; contbr to tech jours. Recipient: natl 1st prize, Amer Inst Elec Engrs, 1928, Edison Medal, 1945; Egleston Medal, Columbia U Sch Engr Alumni Assn, 1956; medal for excellence, Columbia U, 1948; John Fritz Medal, Amer Soc CE, Amer Inst Mining and Metallurgical Engrs, Amer Soc Mech Engrs, Amer Inst EE, 1955; Chevalier, Fr Legion of Hon, 1956; Conservation Service award, Interior Dept, 1960; medal, Amer Soc Mech Engrsl 1962; dist engr in ind award, NY chap, NY State Soc of Profs, Engrs, 1962; Faraday Medal, Inst of Elec Engrs, 1969. Home: 320 E 72 St, New York, NY. Office: 140 Broadway, New York, NY.

SPORN, Rose Evelyn, US, teacher, communal leader; b. Kan City, Mo, Nov 2, 1919; d. Max and Lena (Friedman) Kurs; BS, Tchrs Coll, Kan City, 1940; grad work, U Mo, 1965; m. David Sporn, Dec 31, 1941; c: Wendy, Debby. Tchr, sup: primary dept, Beth Shalom, since 1938; music, J Cmty Cen, since 1964; free lance writer; tchr, Kan City Public Schs, 1940-43; personnel worker, US Govt, 1943-45. Prin contrib: creating materials, methods for elem, pre-sch levels. Chmn, Natl Adult J Educ, B'nai B'rith Women, fmr, pres, Dist II; mem: Beth Shalom Sisterhood; Brandeis Women; Council J Women; AHA; fmr PR chmn, Girl Scout Council. Author: A Religious School Primary Grades Curriculum, 1969; Mornings with Music, 1969; The Power of Positive Programming; scripts for TV, radio. Recipient: Pres Tribute Dinner, B'nai B'rith, 1960; This is Your Life, B'nai B'rith Women, 1956; tribute, 25th teaching anniversary, Beth Shalom. Spec interest: children. Home: 710 E 73 St, Kansas City, Mo. Office: 620 W 95 St, Kansas City, Mo.

SPOTTS, Leon Herbert, US, educator; b. Phila, Pa, Nov 6, 1933; s. Joseph and Sylvia (Sher); BA, hons, U Pa, 1955; BHL, Gratz Coll, 1955; PhD, Dropsie Coll, 1959; m. Sara Taub, July 7, 1962; c: Joanne. Cons, secondary educ; prin, Heb HS, since 1964; dir, tests, measurements, Gratz Coll 1957-59; dir, rel educ, Park Syn, 1959-64. Recording secy, Natl Council for J Educ; mem, Natl Conf J Communal Ser-, vice. Author: Voice of Wisdom, 1965; Wisdom Literature of the Bible, 1967; Budgeting and Financing of Central Agencies for Jewish Education, 1968; Teachers Guide to the Jewish Catastrophe in Europe, 1968; contbr to profsl jours. Home: 265 W Mt Pleasant Ave, Philadelphia, Pa. Office: 10 St and Tabor Rd, Philadelphia, Pa.

SPRAFKIN, Benjamin R, US, social work exec; b. Chgo, Ill, Jan 14, 1910; s. William and Rebecca; BA, CCNY, 1931; grad dipl, Columbia U Sch of Social Work, 1933; MA, Columbia U, 1934, dipl, psych, 1935; m. Dora Berman, Dec 24, 1935; c: Reva Wurtzburger, Robert. Exec dir, J Family Service of Phila, since 1942; case worker, J Family Service of NY, 1932-36, sup, 1936-41. Pres, Pa Council Family Service Agcys; vice-pres, Phila-Camden Social Service; asso trustee, U Pa; bd dirs: Family Service Assn Amer, 1949-67; mem: Natl Assn Social Workers; Assn J Agcy Execs. Contbr to profsl jours. Home: 1901 Walnut St, Philadelphia, Pa. Office: 1610 Spruce St, Philadelphia, Pa.

SPRING, Leonard, H, US, advertising exec; b. Detroit, Mich, June 14, 1922; s. Harry and Selma (Baeder); BS, NYU, 1946; m. Helene Lowenfeld, Mar 8, 1946; c: Lesley, Meryl. Vice-pres: Hardman Sklar Fluerbach Becker Inc, since 1968; The Zlowe Co, 1954-66; Ted Gravenson Inc, 1966-67; Don Kemper Co, 1967-68. Pres: E End Temple; Natl Fed Temple Youth, 1948-50; secy, NY Fed Reform Syn. Home: 390 First Ave, New York, NY. Office: 4 W 58 St, New York, NY.

SPRITZER, David Joseph, Peru, rabbi; b. Mt. Vernon, NY, Oct 16, 1940; s. Abraham and Helen (Seidner); in Peru since 1967; BA, Stanford U, 1962; MHL, ordained rabbi, JTSA, 1967; att Heb U, 1960-61; m. Judith Friedman, Oct 16, 1960; c: Alisa, Doniel, Ahavya. Rabbi, Sociedad de Beneficencia Israelita de 1870, since 1967; prof, J hist, Semenario Santa Toribio, since 1967; rel tchr, Colegio Leon Pinelo, Franco Peruno San Silvestre and Britannica Peruano, since 1967. Active: revitilization J rel life in Lima, Peru; youth work; org first Catholic-J dialogue; mem, B'nai B'rith. Contbr to J jours. Home: Manco Capac 179, Miraflores, Lima, Peru. Study: Libertad 675, Miraflores, Lima, Peru.

SPRITZER, Ralph S, US, attorney, educator; b. NYC, Apr 27, 1917; s. Harry and Stella (Theuman); BS, Columbia U, 1937, LLB, 1940; m. Lorraine Nelson, 1950; c: Ronald, Pamela. Prof, law, U Pa, since 1968; gen counsel, Fed Power Commn, 1961-62; first asst to Solicitor Gen, US Dept of Justice, 1962-68, staff mem since 1946. Served, Judge Advocate Gen Dept, US Army,1941-46. Mem: NY, Supr Court Bars; Fed Bar Assn. Recipient: Superior service award, US Dept of Justice, 1960; Tom C Clark award, Fed Bar Assn, 1968. Home: 2117 Pine St, Philadelphia, Pa. Office: 3400 Chestnut St, Philadelphia, Pa.

SPRUCH-PEWZNER, Abraham A, Isr, physician; b. Brody, Pol, June 17, 1893; s. Moshe and Chane (Spruch) Pewzner; att Us: Lwow; Pisa; Siena; MD, U Rome, 1929; m. Toybe Szteynberg, May 25, 1921; found, chmn, Birth Fund in Isr; fmr, phys, Florence, It. Contbr: articles on problems of J demography and the necessity to increase the J population; first to warn of the dangerous demographical situation of J after WW II. Home: 36 Montefiore St, Tel Aviv, Isr. Office: POB 1038, Tel Aviv, Isr.

SQUADRON, Howard Maurice, US, attorney; b. NYC, Sept 5, 1926; s. Jack and Sara (Sherry); BA, CCNY, 1946; LLB, Columbia Law Sch, 1947; m. Lorraine Vlosky (decd); c: William, Richard, Diane. Partner, law firm, Squadron, Alter and Wein rib, since 1954; atty: Phillips, Nizer, Benjamin and Krim, 1951-53; Stroock, Stroock and Lavan, 1950. Capt, Judge Advocate, US Army Res, since 1953. Chmn: exec comm, Found for Amer Dance; NY chap, UN Assn; co-chmn, coordinating council, AJCong; dir, Interracial Council for Bus Opportunity; mem: NY State Bar Assn; Amer Bar Assn. Hobby: tennis. Home: 25 W 81 St, New York, NY. Office: 292 Madison Ave, New York, NY.

SREBNIK, Saly, Eng, business exec; b. Plauen, Ger, June 5, 1912; s. Jacob and Rachel; in Eng since 1938; m. Irma Steinberg, Sep 21, 1940; c: Ralph. Mgn dir since 1965; dir, United Textiles, Tudex Ltd, 1938-47; mgn dir, Silkinese Ltd, 1949-59. Staff Sgt, RASC, 1943-47. Chmn, Geulah Zionist Soc; secy, Geulah, Mizrachi JPA; chmn, Vocational Service, Paddington Rotary Club, 1962-65; club, Ealing Golf. Recipient: 1939-45 Star; Defense Medal. Hobbies: music, golf, skiing. Home: 7 Allandale Ave, Finchley, London, Eng. Office: Windsor Rd, Bedford, Eng.

SROLE. Leo, US, educator, sociologist; b. Chgo, Ill, Oct 8, 1908; s. William and Rebecca (Epstein); BS, Harvard Coll, 1933; PhD, U Chgo, 1940; m. Esther Alpiner, Dec 27, 1941; c: Ira, Rebecca. Prof, social scis, dept psycht, Columbia U Coll Phys and Surgs, since 1965; chief, psycht research, social

scis, NY State Psycht, since 1965; cons, WHO; prof, chmn, dept sociol, Hobart Coll, 1941-42; dir, UNRRA, Landsberg, Ger, J DP camp, 1945-46; div dir,Bur Applied Social Research, Columbia U, 1947-48; research dir, ADL, 1948-52; prof, sociol, Cornell Med Coll, 1952-59; research prof, Albert Einstein Med Coll, 1959-61; prof, sociol, SUNY Downstate Med Cen, Bklyn, 1961-65. Psychol, USAAF, 1943-45. Mem: Soc for Study of Social Issues; Soc for Applied Anthropology; Amer Sociol Soc. Author: Social Systems of American Ethnic Groups, 1945; Mental Health in the Metropolis: The Midtown Manhattan Study, 1962; contbr to mags. Home: 151-39 25 Ave, Whitestone, NY. Office: 722 W 168 St, New York. NY.

STABINS, Samuel J, US, surgeon; b. Watertown, NY, Mar 14, 1901; s. Jacob and Dora (Cohen); MD, Emory U, 1925; m. Paula Gates, Mar 7, 1930; c: Ann Sewell, Paula Davis. Prof em, clinical surg, U Rochester, since 1966, on staff from 1948; surg in chief em, Genesee Hosp, since 1956, surg in chief, 1946-56; bd dirs: Bausch & Lomb Inc, since 1968; Comty Savings Bank, since 1967; cons surg, Vet Hosp, Canadaigua, 1947-60. USN, 1942-45. Chmn: Monroe Comty Coll; local chap, AJComm, 1956; found, 1st pres, Soc U Surgs, 1939; vice-chmn, Rochester-Monroe Co ARC; bd govs, Amer Coll of Surgs, 1961; hon bd; Baden St Settlement, 1961; Monroe Co Cancer Assn; mem: Amer Surg Assn; clubs: Irondequoit Country; U of Rochester, mem, bd trustees; Genesee Valley; Automobile, Rochester; Contbr to profsl jours. Home: 1600 E Ave, Rochester, NY. Office: 267 Alexander St, Rochester, NY.

STABINSKY, Raymond Ralph, US, business exec; b. NYC, Jan 11, 1925; s. Louis and Fannie (Podeswa); m. Helene Yanell, Nov 24, 1946; c: Steven, Jeff, Brad. Pres: The Textile Stores Inc, since 1949; Louis Stabinsky & Sons, since 1964. Cpl, US Army, 1943-46. Chmn: UJA, Norwalk; Isr Bond Dr, Norwalk; Norwalk J Cen, 1964-66, pres, 1960-64; bd dirs, Temple Shalom; mem: Pres Club, JWB; B'nai B'rith, JWV. Spec interest: Bibl studies. Home: 15 Muriel, Norwalk, Conn. Office: 234 Atlantic, Stamford, Conn.

STACK, Norman A, US, organization exec; b. NYC, July 70, 1919; s. Solomon and Sadie (Heiken); BSS, CCNY, 1940; MS, 1943; m. Ida Hankin, Oct 22, 1944; c: Gerald, Richard. Exec dir, J Comty Relations Council, St Louis, since 1963; instr, Human Relations Workshop, St Louis U, since 1963; dir, guidance dept, Wash Hgts YM-YWHA's, 1944; asso dir, J Vocational Service, Boston, 1944-46, exec dir, Toronto, Can, 1946-48; asst dir, United JWV, Toronto, 1948-50; dir, W Cen area, AJComm, 1951-63. Mem: Amer Psych Assn; Amer Sociol Assn; Assn J Communal Workers. Contbr to profsl jour. Home: 6915 Dartmouth St, University City, Mo.

STAFFORD, Julius, NZ, business exec; b. Hlohovec, Czech, Nov 30, 1912; s. Albert and Blanche (Einzig) Schnitzer; in NZ since 1930; LLD, D political sci, Comenius U, Bratislava, Czech, 1938; m. Carmel Goldstone, Jan 20, 1944; c: Carole Emanuel, Albert. Mgn dir: Import & Merchants, since 1947; Stemco Ltd, 1947-69. NZ Expeditionary Forces, WW II. Pres: Youth Aliyah; Zionist Soc; B'nai B'rith Lodge 2293; bd mem, Wellington Heb Cong; mem exec, dist Grand Lodge 21, B'nai B'rith, NZ; mem: ZC, Olympic Council, NZ; fmr NZ Sabre Champion and NZ Empire Games Team Mem, fencing; fmr vice-pres, NZ Fencing Fed; intl pres, FIE jury; NZ Panel Natl Pres, FIE; mem, Masonic Blue. Home: 38 Ngatoto, Khandallah, Wellington 4, NZ. Office: 2, Pretoria St, Lower Hutt, NZ.

STAGMAN, Joseph, US, surgeon; b. Chgo, Ill, Mar 11, 1909; s. Samuel and Rose (Snitovsky); BS, U of Ill, 1930; MS, MD, Coll of Med, 1932; m. Dolyne Rosin, May 21, 1935; c: Robert, Terry. Pvt practice, ear, nose, throat, and plastic surg, since 1935; cons, otolaryngology, Forkosh Memorial Hosp; att, otolaryngology, Michael Resse Hosp; asso att, otolaryngology, 1956-60, adj, att, 1935-56; instr, otolayngology, U of Ill, 1935-40; adj att, Ill Eye and Ear Infirmary, 1943-50. Dipl, Bd of Otolaryngology; f: AMA; IMA; mem: Amer Acad Ophthal and Otolaryngology; Ill and Chgo Med Socs; Natl J Hosp, Denver; bd govs, Med Student Aid Soc, fmr vice-pres; bd dirs, Phi Lambda Kappa, since 1956, fmr natl vice-pres; ZOA, Chgo; J Chautauqua Soc; J Fed, Chgo; Art Inst, Chgo; Alpha Omega Alpha; Chgo Mus Natural Hist; AJCong; AJComm; club, Entertainers and Actors. Contbr to med jours. Recipient: Jeweled Key, Phi Lambda Kappa, 1950. Homes: 5733 N Sheridan Rd, Chicago, Ill; Lakefront Dr, Beverly Shores, Ind. Offices: 55 E Washington St, Chicago, Ill; 622 Diversey Pkwy, Chicago, Ill.

STAJNER, M Aleksandar, Yugo, economist; b. Apr 30, 1913; s. Makso and Eva (Spicer); in Yugo since 1929; grad, Acad of Trade, 1929; pre-grad, High Econ and Commercial Sch, 1947; m. Alice; c: Tamora. Councilor for social ind inves; collaborator, Five Year Plan for Econ Devl of Yugo, 1947-51; secy, econ councilor, Yugo Govt, 1946-48; mem, exec, Chamber of Fgn Trade, 1951-53. Mem, exec Fed of J Cmtys of Yugo, since 1945; fmr: working comm, Fed J Youth Soc Yugo; admn comm, Assn Econs, Serbia; State Inst for Phys Culture; pres: Yugo-Amer Soc; Yugo-E Afr Soc; J Cmty, Belgrade. Contbr to profsl jours. Home: Alekse Nenadoviéa 25, Belgrade, Yugo. Office: Interexport Kolaréeva 8-10, Belgrade, Yugo.

STALSON, Benjamin, S Afr, organization exec; b. Transvaal, S Afr; s. Alexander and Molly (Bukantz), BA, U Witwatersrand. Exec dir, United Progressive J Cong, since 1941. Hon life pres: Transvaal Inter-Club Goodwill Assn; Temple Guild; hon life mem: Boksburg N Soccer Assn; United Progressive J Cong; found, Camp Caplan; hon life mem, co-found, hon life vice-pres, Alan Isaacs Camp; club, Montagu Country, found, hon life pres. Home: 30 Grace Rd, Mountain View, Johannesburg, S Afr. Office: Temple Isr, Paul Nel and Claim Sts, Johannesburg, S Afr.

STAMLER, David Marcus, Eng, educator; b. London, Eng, Nov 4, 1928; s. Herman and Bronia (Rosshandler); BA, Oxford U, 1954; att Brandeis U, 1954-55; m. Micheline Lindenbaum, Sep 8, 1957; c: Jonathan, Rebecca, Daniel, Tamar. Headmaster, Carmel Coll, since 1962. Mem: B'nai B'rith. Author: Backdoor to Tragedy. 1957. Recipient: Fulbright f, 1955. Spec interests: early Persian pottery, modern art. Home and office: Carmel Coll, Wallingford, Berks, Eng.

STAMMELMAN, Mortimer J, US, chemist, business exec; b. NYC, Dec 27, 1897; s. Joseph and Rose (Rattner); BA, Columbia U, 1920, MA, 1921, PhD, 1924; m. Florence Siff, Nov 1935; c: Joseph. Pres, The Atmos Products Co, since 1925; chem, Intl Arms & Fuse Co, 1917; chief chem, Dusenberg Motors Co, 1918; tchr lab courses, chem, Columbia U, 1919-23. Pres, NY Tobacco Table, 1958, 1959, asst teas, 1947-57; Tobacco Salesman Assn of Amer, 1949-53, vice-pres, since 1953; chmn, Columbia Coll Fund, class of 1919, 1960; f: Amer Inst Chem; AAAS; mem: Amer Chem Soc; UJA; Fed J Charities; NCCJ; JWB; B'nai B'rith; ADL; Phi Lambda Upsilon; Sigma Xi. Recipient: man of year award, 1960, service award, 1968, NY Tobacco Table; Deans award, Columbia Coll, 1960, 1969; hon guest, UJA, 1968. Contbr to trade papers. Home: 10 E End Ave, New York, NY. Office: 13 E 17 St, New York, NY.

STAMPFER, Joshua, US, rabbi; b. Jerusalem, Pal, Dec 28, 1921; s. Elijah and Nehamah (Frank); in US since 1923; BS, U Chgo, 1942; MS, U Akron, 1944; O State U, 1945; MHL, JTSA, 1949; att: Heb U; U Neb, 1951; m. Goldie Goncher, Feb 13, 1944; c: Shaul, Meir, Noam, Nehama, Elana. Rabbi, Cong Neveh Shalom, Portland Ore, since 1953; lectr, Portland State Coll; educ dir, Young People's League, 1948; head counselor, Brandeis Camp Inst, 1949, 1950, 1952; Hillel dir, U Neb, 1949-53; rabbi, Cong Tifereth Isr, Lincoln, Neb, 1949-53; a found, Camp Solomon Schechter. Dir, World Sem for J Service, 1967; mem: RA; B'nai B'rith. Home: 2800 SW Peaceful Lane, Portland, Ore. Study: 2900 SW Peaceful Lane, Portland, Ore.

STANETZKY, Jan, (Pawel Granitzky), Isr, physician; b. Lwow, Russ, Oct 22, 1901; s. Noe and Rebeka, (Tieger) Steinwurzel; in Isr since 1957; PhD, U Lwow; DMD, Stomat Acad, U Poznan; MD, U Wroclaw; m. Danuta Rosenblatt, Mar 5, 1932. Head, microbiol dept, Govt Hosp, Jaffa, since 1961; prof, HS, Pol, 1927-39; head, microbiol dept, Inst of Public Health, 1953-57. Author: Pol: The Prager of Grass, 1926; The Book of Songs, 1928. Mem: IMA; Isr Microbiol Assn. Contbr numerous articles to profsl publs. Recipient: grants, sci studies: Min of Health, 1967; WHO, 1969. Hobby: music. Home: 11 Bnei Moshe St, Tel Aviv, Isr. Office: Govt Hosp, Jaffa, Isr.

STANFORD, Myron S, US, attorney; b. Bendzin, Pol, Mar 22, 1907; s. Joseph and Dora (Rettman); in US since 1920; BA, W Reserve U, 1929, LLB, 1931; m. Florence Shapero, 1934; c: Donald, Richard, Barbara. Pvt practice since 1931; counsel for planning survey, O State Hwy Dept, 1936-37; city prosecutor, Cleveland, O, 1941-45. Pres: United J Rel Schs, 1962; B'nai B'rith Mid-day Lodge, 1962; Cleveland Masada Youth, 1931-38; Migdal Zion, 1938-47; chmn, cultural comm, Natl

Masada, 1933-35, co-org, 1933; trustee: Bur of J Educ; J Cmty Cen; chmn, cultural arts adv comm; delg: assembly, mem, J Comty Fed, 1947-52; ZOA conventions secy, Cleveland ZOA Dist, 1935; mem: adv comm, J Drama Cen; Cleveland, Cuyahoga, Amer and Inter-Amer Bar Assns; Amer Arbitration Assn; Phi Beta Kappa; Order of Coif; Masons; club: Fairmont Temple Men's, pres, 1954-55. Hobbies: photography, travel, amateur acting. Home: 2646 Endicott Rd, Shaker Heights, O. Office: 250 Leader Bldg, Cleveland, O.

STANG, Arnold, US, actor; m. Joanne Taggart; c: David, Deborah. Appeared: TV: Bonanza; Ed Sullivan; Dean Martin; Hallmark Playhouse; I've Got a Secret; What's My Line; To Tell the Truth; Bob Hope; Frank Sinatra Specs; Jackie Gleason; US Steel Hour; Alcoa Presents; Playhouse 90; December Bride; Milton Berle; Jack Benny; Red Skelton; McHale's Navy; Wagon Train; Top Cat; Broadside; Jerry Louis; Bewitched; Johnny Carson; Batman; Merv Griffin; You Don't Say; Mike Douglas; on Broadway: Front Page; A Funny Thing Happened on the Way to the Forum; Wedding Breakfast; Wallflower; Sailor Beware; All in Favor; Same Time Next Week; stock: Why I Went Crazy; Don't Drink the Water: Death Knocks; Luv; Tobacco Road; Odd Couple; Rattle of a Simple Man; Charlie's Aunt; Annie Get Your Gun; Finian's Rainbow; Seven Year Itch; Three Men on a Horse; Will Success Spoil Rock Hunter?; Say Darling; The Gazebo; Blood, Sweat and Stanley Poole; The Poor Nut; Wish You Were Here; The First Year; No Time for Sergeants; films: The Man With the Golden Arm; Pinnochio in Outer Space; My Sister Eileen; They Got Me Covered; So This is New York; staring roles: It's a Mad Mad Mad Mad World; The Wonderful World of the Brothers Grimm; Skidoo; The Aristocrats; Hello Down There; Dondi; Alakazam the Great; Second Fiddler; Seven Days Leave; Let's Go Steady; Hepcats: Double for Della; Arnold the Benedict; Honorable Myrtle; The Expectant Father. Starred in 32 short subjects; humorous recordings. Address: ASCAP, 575 Madison Ave, NY.

STANHILL, Gerald, Isr, scientist; b. London, Eng, Apr 28, 1929; s. David and Minnie (Paril) Stanhill; in Isr since 1958; att Heitcordshire Inst of Agric, St Albans, Eng; BSc, Reading U, Eng, 1953, PhD, 1956; m. Rachel Bechler; c: David, Michal. Head, dept agric meteorology, asso prof, Volcani Inst of Agric Research, since 1965; sr research worker, 1958-65; sci off, Agric Research Council, Gt Brit, 1954-58. Prin contrib: research in crop water requirements in agric. Mem: Royal Meteorological Soc; Soc for Experimental Biol, both Eng; Isr Soil Sci Soc; Meteorological Soc; found, J Soc, Reading U. Contbr to various jours. Spec interest: J mysticism. Home: 7 Hanasi Harishon St, Rehovot, Isr. Office: Volcani Inst of Agric Research, Rehovot, Isr.

STANTON, Stuart Moss, Isr, insurance; b. London, Eng, Mar 13, 1938; s. Harvey and Leah (Moss); in Isr since 1962; Asso Chartered Ins Inst, Holborn Coll, 1962; m. Nitza Kollman, Sep 9, 1962; c: David, Harel. Served, RAF, IDF. Hon secy Brit Settlers Assn; mem: Chartered Inst Ins, Eng. Hobbies: photography, philately. Home: 6 Herut St, Ramat Gan, Isr.

STARK, Arthur, US, arbitrator; b. NYC, Mar 7, 1919; s. Louis and Jennie (House); BA, U Chgo, 1939, MA, 1941; m. Dorothy Copeland, July 9, 1955; c: Jeffery, Margo, Laura Steele. Fulltime arbitrator since 1957; contract, arbitrator, impartial chmn, umpire: Gen Motors, IUE; United Airlines, ALPA; Xerox Corp, ACWA; others; mem panel: Amer Arbitration Assn; Fed Mediation and Conciliation Service; NY, NJ, State Mediation Services; others; prin field examiner, acting regional dir, NLRB, 1942-47; asst exec dir, NY State Bd of Mediation, 1947-51, exec dir, 1951-57; lectr, econ Columbia U Sch of Gen Studies, 1952-66; visiting prof, Cornell U Sch of Ind and Lab Relations, 1957; mem: Pres Emergency Bds in airlines and RR inds, 1955, 1959, 1960, 1961; Pres Bds of Inquiry, 1956, 1962; chmn or mem: NY State Minimum Wage Bds, 1961, 1962; US Minimum Wage Bds, Puerto Rico, 1963, 1964, 1969. Mem: Natl Acad Arbitrators; Ind Relations Research Assn; Amer Arbitration Assn; Intl Assn on Social and Lab Leg. Contbr to Profsl jours. Hobbies: music, photography, painting. Home: 203 W 86 St, New York, NY. Office: 165 W 46 St, New York, NY.

STARK, Victor, Isr, business exec; b. Yugo, Feb 2, 1904; s. Joseph and Anna (Guttman); in Isr since 1935; m. Camilla Braun, Sep 14, 1929; c: Thea Bloch. Hon Consul Yugo, Haifa, since 1957; mgn dir: Volta Factory of Elec Materials, Ltd;

Yugoslav Trade and Shipping Agcys, both Haifa, since 1935; gen mgr, Agricola, Agric Machine Distributors, Yugo, 1928-35. Mem: Mfrs Assn; Chamber of Shipping; club, Caesarea Golf and Country. Home: 37 Givat Downes, Ahuzat-Carmel, Haifa, Isr. Office: 2 Haneemanim St, Haifa. Isr.

STARK, William, US, business exec; b. NYC, Sep 25, 1917; s. Sidney and Sadie (Braham); BA, U Pittsburgh, 1938; att Harvard U Law Sch, 1939; m. Olga Bernstein, July 26, 1940; c: Sally Lee, Hilary. Pres: Penn Overall Supply Co, since 1950, with firm since 1939; AAA Uniform Service Co, since 1950; US Ind Glove Co, since 1950. Pres, Hill City Youth Munic, 1961-62; vice-pres: United J Fed, since 1962; bd dirs, YM-YWHA since 1962; fmr pres, Inst Ind Launderers, mem, research and devl comm; mem: Amer Soc Safety Engrs; J Chautauqua Soc; Masons; U Pittsburgh Alumni Assn; clubs: Lions, Rotary. Hobbies: music, amateur pianist and bass viola player, golf. Home: 5847 Aylesboro Ave, Pittsburgh, Pa. Office: 2236 La Place St, Pittsburgh, Pa.

STARKMAN, Moshe, US, journalist, author; b. Mosty Weilke, Galicia. Sep 25, 1906; s. Israel and Sophie (Seligman-Steger); in US since 1921; att: Yiddish Tchrs' Sem, 1926; CCNY, 1932-33; m. Rachel Ravitch, 1936; c: Monica, Reeva. Staff mem, J Day-Journal, NYC, since 1932, city ed, The Day, 1939-43. Mem: Yiddish Writers Union; YIVO; Histadrut Ivrith; JBCA; ZOA; club, Yiddish PEN, vice-pres. Ed: Hemshekh, Yiddish poetry anthology, 1945; Yiddish Sect, J Book Annual, vols 2-4, 8, 12; Heb-Yiddish 70th Anniversary Vol in honor of Shlomo Bichel, 1968; 80th Anniversary Vol in honor of Abraham Golomb, 1969; co-ed, Heb-Yiddish Berish Weinstein Anniversary Vol, 1967; asso ed, Leksikon Fun der Nayer Yiddisher Literatur, since 1956; contbr to lit mags, in Yiddish, Heb and Eng. Home: 4700 Broadway, New York, NY. Office: 183 E Braadway, New York, NY.

STAROBINSKI, Jean, Switz, educator; b. Geneva, Nov 17, 1920; s. Aron and Szajndla (Frydman); licence es lettres, Geneva U, 1942, doctorat es lettres, 1958, MD, 1960; m. Jaqueline Sirman, Aug 15, 1954; c: Michel, Peirre, Georges. Prof, hist of ideas, Geneva U, since 1958, Fr lit since 1962; asst prof, Johns Hopkins U, Baltimore, 1954-56; prof, U Basel, 1959-61. Served Swiss Army. Pres: Rencontres Internationales de Genève; Societe Jean-Jacques Rousseau,Geneva; Societe Suisse de philosophie; mem: jury, prix des Critiques, Paris. Author: Montesquieu, 1953; JJ Rousseau: La Transparence et l'Obstacle,1958; L'Oeil Vivant, 1961; Histoire de Traitment de la Mélancolie, 1961; L'invention de la liberté, 1964. Recipient: Prix Femina Vacaresco. Hobby: music. Home: 12 rue de Candolle,Geneva, Switz. Office: U de Genève, Geneva, Switz.

STARR, Arnold, US, surgeon, educator; b. Boston, Mass, Oct 20, 1903; s. Benjamin and Sarah (Bornstein); MD, Tufts Coll Med Sch, Boston, 1928; m. Frances Tolman, Oct 2, 1933 (decd); c: Betty, David, Jonathan; m. 2nd Thelma Reingold, July 1959. Clinical prof em, Tufts U Med Sch, prof, since 1943; clinical asso, surg, Harvard U Med Sch, instr, 1948; visiting surg, Beth Isr Hosp, Boston, since 1951. Mem: Boston Surg Soc; Amer Bd Surg; club, Harvard. Contbr to profsl jours. Home: 120 Sewall Ave, Brookline, Mass. Office: 416 Marlborough St, Boston, Mass.

STAUB, Milton, US, business exec; b. Kaschau, Hung, Apr 15, 1904; s. Samuel and Charlotte (Gross); in US since 1914; att: U Akron, 1920-21; O State U, 1921-22, 1927-29; m. Martha Goldsmith, Apr 20, 1928. Pres: Gustav Hirsch Org,Columbus, O, since 1959, with firm since 1939; Gustav Hirsch Org of Alaska, Inc, Anchorage, Alaska; Eastmoor Elec Co, Columbus; Incore Elec Co, Cincinnati, O; Sky Way Bc Corp, Columbus; Second Securities Corp, Columbus; Inter City Auto Service, Columbus; Waverly House Motel, Columbus; dir: Elyria Lorain Bc Corp, Elyria, O; First Natl Bank, Nelsonville, O; United Utilities of O, Inc, Mansfield, O; acctnt: Goodyear Tire and Rubber Co, 1922-24; various firms, 1924-26; auditor and acting treas, United Woolen Co, 1926-29. Found f, Acad Electrical Contracting; pres: Temple Isr; Cen O Chap, NECA; vice-pres and trustee: O Soc for Prevention Blindness; Heritage House; chmn, Natl Jt Apprenticeship Training comm; co-chmn, Natl Manpower Comm; trustee: Franklin Co Polio Soc; Natl Elec Contractors Assn; gov, Cen O Chap, NECA, 1954-67; treas, Variety Clubs of Amer, Tent No 2; mem: Council on Ind Relations, Supr Court, Elec Ind; Midwestern Airborne Video Educ Comm; O State Safety Comm; US Independent Telephone Assn; O

Independent Telephone Assn; Independent Telephone Pioneers of Amer; O Soc of NY; Columbus C of C; clubs: Columbus Athletic; Winding Hollow Country; O State U Pres. Home: 17 Meadow Park Ave, Columbus, O. Office: 1347 W Fifth Ave, Columbus, O.

STAUB, Peter, Rhodesia, business exec, legislator; b. Breslau, Ger, May 14, 1911; s. Hugo and Kate (Schüfftan); in Rhodesia since 1950; att: Columbia U, NY; U Copenhagen, Den; m. Cynthia Daniels, June 4, 1947; c: Petronella, John, Hugh. Mining, financial ed, Rand Daily Mail and Sunday Times, Johannesburg, 1936-44; MK, Fed of Rhodesia and Nyasaland; S Afr Army, WW II. Chmn, Natl Assn Youth Clubs, since 1959; vice-pres, Rhodesian Econ Soc; mem, Masons. Author, Industrial Development in Rhodesia, 1954; contbr of articles to econ jours. Hobby; fishing. Home 1 Wavell Rd, Highlands, Salisbury, Rhodesia. Office: POB 3643, Salisbury, Rhodesia.

STEADMAN, Harvey S, US, business exec; b. Jacksonville, Ill, Nov 4, 1907; s. Louis and Lena (Blair); BA, U Wis, 1927; m. Catherine Bell, Jan 31, 1928; c: Louis, Marie, Sandra. Pres, Liquid Glaze Inc, since 1957; owner, Steadman's Furniture, since 1923; pres: Steadman's Inc, 1938-45; Better Housekeeping, 1945-54. Mem, govtecon comm, Natl Mfrs Assn; co-chmn govt leg comm, C of C; maj, United Fund of Lansing; hon pres,Mich B'nai B'rith Council, Jacob H Schiff Lodge, Lansing; chmn, health wfr comm, dist 6; fmr: org and secy treas, JWF; secy-treas, Temple Beth El; secy-treas, Cong Schaarey Zedek, all Lansing; mem: Alpha Epsilon Pi; Elks. Home: 441 Glenmoor Rd, E Lansing, Mich. Office: 735 May St, Lansing, Mich.

STEARNS, Anna, Can, educator; b. Skala, Aus-Hung, Sep 3, 1904; d. Abraham and Rosa (Weiser) Seidner; in Can since 1938; tchrs cert, Tchrs Sem, Vienna, 1924; att U Vienna; MA, U Ottawa and Montreal, 1950, PhD, 1954; m. Eugene Stearns, Sep 18,1927; c: Ada Weinthal, Eva Libman. Asst prof, ethnology, U Montreal, since 1957; mem, Research Inst of Mid and E Eur, since 1954, contrib ed, Etudes Slaves, pub by dept of Slavic studies,since 1952. Mem: Inter-U Comm on Can Slava; Can Assn of Slavists; MLA; fmr: Can Council of Chr and J; lectured, Catholic Info Cens; lectr, sch for adults, Temple Emanu El, since 1954. Author: L'Ajustement psychologique de L'immigrant Européen au Canada,1952; The European Intellectual and His Problem of Integration, 1954; L'arc Trompeur, 1958; Bible as Literature; The Jewish Contribution to Civilization; Israel and the Jewish Image in Different Countries in the World; Newcomers to Canada: A Problem in Creative Reorientation, 1960; contbr to scholarly jours. Home: 4000 Beaconsfield Ave, Montreal, Can. Office: U of Montreal, Montreal, Can.

STECKEL, Leonard, Ger, stage dir, actor; b. Knihinin, Hung, Jan 8,1901; s. Markus and Eva (Bazar); m. Jo Mihaly; c: Anja; m. 2nd. Stage dir, actor, radio and TV performances: Berlin; Munich; Hamburg; Köln; Vienna, since 1953; staged over 100 plays, many first- performances, some at Cameri Theatre, Tel Aviv; latest roles (first performance, world premiere: Meteor, by Dürrenmatt; Prize, by Miller; Staircase, by Dyer; fmr, actor, stage dir, Schauspielhaus, Zurich, Switz. Home: Bartningallee 16, Berlin, Ger.

STECKERL, Alfredo, Colombia, industrialist; b. Vienna, Aus, Apr 24, 1903; s: Josef and Berta (Bauer); m. Rosa Fuchs, Sep 18, 1924; c: Griselda Sasson; Susana Schmulson. In pvt bus since 1941; secy, Mercur Bank, Vienna, 1921-25; mgr, I Steckerl & Co, Vienna, 1925-38. Hon pres, Colegio Hebreo Union; pres, Centro Israelita Filantropico; repr, HIAS; cofound and mem: B'nai B'rith; mem bd dirs, Banco de la Costa and Exec Club; hon mem, Sociedad Mejoras Publicas; mem bd dirs, C of C and Fenalco; club, Rotary, chap Barranquilla. Home: Carrera, 54 70-15, Barranquilla, Colombia. Office: Calle 37 46-104, Barranquilla, Colombia.

STEEFEL, Robert David, US, attorney; b. Rochester, NY, May 5, 1901; s. Joseph and Sadie (Lang); BA, Harvard U, 1922, LLB, 1924; m. Margaret Lane, Dec 18, 1929; c: Caren Haldenstein, Edward. Mem, Stroock & Stroock & Lavan, since 1937, asso 1924-36; dir, gen counsel, Big Apple Supermarkets, Inc; gen counsel: Hotel Pierre; Sherry-Netherland Hotel; Durst Org; Charles F Noyes Co; bd adv, The Title Guarantee Co. Trustee: FJP; Montefiore Hosp,since 1930; Hosp Council of NY; exec comm, AJComm, 1944-54; mem: Task Force on Child Abuse, NYC; Assn Bar, NYC; NY Co Lawyers Assn; clubs: Harmonie, Cent Country. Home: 1125 Park Ave, New York, NY. Office: 61 Broadway, New York, NY.

STEIGER, Aaron Armin, US, business exec; b. Aus, Sep 19, 1909; s. Louis and Sarah (Braun); in US since 1919; BA, W Reserve U, 1930, LLB, Law Sch, 1932; m. Donna Jarboe, Dec 12, 1949; c: Cheryl. Pres: Tel A-Sign Inc, since 1950; Gatch Wire Goods Co, since 1961; dir, Elec Neon Mfg Co, since 1961; vice-pres, Natl Metal Products Co, 1940-45; pres, Elec Devices, 1946-50. Chmn: CJA; Jt Defense Appeal; J Fed; NCCJ; pres, Cleveland Lodge, B'nai B'rith, 1941; mem: Masons; Sigma Alpha Mu; Sigma Delta Chi; Tau Kappa Alpha; Phi Delta Gamma; Phi Beta Kappa; clubs: Standard; Ravisloe Country, chmn. Contbr to trade jours. Home: 900 Lake Shore Dr, Chicago, Ill. Office: 3401 W 47 St, Chicago, Ill.

STEIGRAD, Joseph, Austr, surgeon; b. Jaffa, Pal, Jan 28, 1902; s. Samuel and Pearl (Greenstein); in Austr since 1904; MB, ChM, U Sydney, 1926, FRACS, 1933; hon deg, Postgrad Commonwealth Med Education Univ, NSW; m. Heather Wilson, May 19, 1938; c: Stephen, Peter. Hon cons, surg: Royal Alexandria Hosp for Children; Royal S Sydney Hosp; hon cons, Ped surg, Prince Henry Hosp and Prince of Wales Hosp; cons, dept preventative dent, United Dent Hosp, Sydney; lectr, surgical diseases of children, U Sydney 1953-61; hon surg to Gov Gen of Austr, 1946-50. Austr Army MC, since 1926, served WW II, hon brig, ret Royal Austr Army MC, hon col. Mem: bd mgmt, Royal Alexandria Hosp for Children, since 1962; Austr Med Assn; Far West Children's Med Scheme, since 1962; Austr J Wfr Soc, since 1962; Sydney Legacy; dep hon dir, Children's Med Research Found, Sydney, since 1962; chmn, bd govs, rehab fund, J Ex-Serviceman's Assn, NSW; pres: Austr Ped Assn, 1960-61; Fellowship J Doctors, NSW, 1956-61; YMHA; fmr: mem bd mgmt, Temple Emanuel, Sydney; mem, United Services Inst; club, Imperial Service. Contbr to med pubs. Recipient: CBE; mention in dispatches, efficiency decoration. Home: 18 Balfour Rd, Rose Bay, Sydney, NSW, Austr. Office: High St, Randwick, NSW, Austr; Box 1, PO Kensington, NSW, Austr.

STEIMAN, Sidney, US, rabbi; b. Boston, Mass, June 22, 1922; s. Benjamin and Anna (Greez); BA, cum laude, Yeshiva U, 1944; MHL, ordained rabbi, JTSA, 1949; MA, Boston U, 1950; PhD, Brandies U, 1959; m. Shirley Green, June 3, 1946; c: Ben, Aron, Debra. Rabbi, Cong Beth-El Zedeck, since 1961; affiliate prof, Chr Theol Sem, since 1968; visiting prof, Marian Coll; rabbi, Temple Beth Hillel, Mattapan, Mass, 1949-61. Pres, Ind Council Rabbis; bd dirs: Ind Sch Rel; Ind J Comty Relations Council, pres, 1963-66; Marion Co Mh Assn; JWF, Indianapolis; pres, RA, NE region, 1961; fmr chancelor, State Lodge, KP, Boston; fmr chaplain of day, House of Repr, US Cong; fmr mem, Rabb Cabinet, JTSA; mem: Moument lodge, Masons, Indianapolis; Natl Hon Frat Social Scis; Chgo Bd Rabbis; Ind Acad Social Sci; AAUP; Amer Acad Political and Social Sci; World Union J Studies; club, Kiwanis. Author: Custom and Survival, 1963. Hobbies: golf, photography, bridge. Home: 437 E 84 St, Indianapolis, Ind. Study: 600 W 70 St, Indianapolis, Ind.

STEIMATZKY, Yeheskel, Isr, publisher; b. Russ, Jan 16, 1900; s. Mordechai and Mussia (Talan); in Isr since 1925; att: Commercial Inst, econ deg, Moscow; law deg, Humbold U, Berlin; m. Berta Fish, Dec 29, 1935; c: Eliana Sachar, Eri, Eliora, Elisheva. Gen mgr, Steimatzky's Agcy Ltd, pubs, book retailers, distributors. Fmr: cen comm, Hechalutz, Russ; delg, 13th ZC; cen comm, Revisionist Party, Pal. Publisher: Pal guides; Heb globes; Heb atlases; art books; children's books; text books in Heb; Isr albums in Eng. Home: 9 Shmaryahu Levin St, Tel Aviv, Isr. Office: Steimatzky's Agency, Citrus House, Tel Aviv, Isr.

STEIN, Alexander T, US, attorney; b. Lancaster, Pa, Oct 10, 1905; s. Herman and Dora (Wilson); BA, magna cum laude, Franklin and Marshall Coll, 1927; m. Blanche Lurio, Mar 28, 1933; c: Donald. Sr partner, law firm, Stein, Storb and Mann, since 1958; pvt practice, since 1931. Co-chmn, UJA, 1960-61; mem: bd of dirs and advs, J Comty Cen, since 1950; bd of trustees, Free Public Libr, since 1945; bd of dirs, Osteo Hosp, since 1951, past pres, all Lancaster; vice-pres, Lancaster Bar Assn, since 1961; legal adv, League of Women Voters; mem, exec bd, Lancaster Co council, Boy Scouts, 1940-55; trustee, Temple Shaarai Shomayim; treas, USO, Lancaster; mem: comm for revision of constitution of Pa; Pa Bar Assn; Amer Bar Assn; Elks; B'nai B'rith; Phi Beta Kappa; clubs: Lions, pres, 1954-55; Boys, dir and mem of bd, both Lancaster; Big Brothers, vice-pres, Lancaster Co. Home: 11 Orchard Rd, Lancaster, Pa. Office: 53 N Duke St, Lancaster, Pa.

STEIN, Arnold, US, educator, author; b. Brockton, Mass, Apr 27, 1915; s. Benjamin and Dora (Markovitz); BA, Yale U, 1936; MA, Harvard U, 1938, PhD, 1942; m. Bess Dworsky, June 20, 1942; c: Jonathan Deborah. Prof, Eng, U Wash, Seattle, since 1953, asso prof, 1948-53; instr, U Minn, 1940-46; asst prof, O State U, 1946-48. US Army, WW II. Mem, Pacific NW advisory bd, ADL, since 1962; chap pres, AAUP, 1956-57. Author: Perilous Balance, poems, 1945; Answerable Style, 1953; Heroic Knowledge, 1957; John Donne's Lyrics, 1962; George Herbert's Lyrics, 1968; ed, Theodore Roethke: Essays on the Poetry, 1965; contbr to lit jours. Recipient: Ford f, 1953; Guggenheim f, 1959. Home: 265 149 NE, Bellevue, Wash. Office: U Wash, Seattle, Wash.

STEIN, Calvert, US, neuropsychiatrist; b. Newcastle-on-Tyne, Eng, Apr 6, 1903; s. Harry and Lily (Phillips); in US since 1912; premed cert, Tufts U, 1924, MD, 1928; LLB, Northeastern U, 1938; att: Columbia U; Yale U; Harvard U, all 1933-53; m. Lucille Weinstein, Nov 26, 1929; c: Elinor Leavitt, Mildred Sobel. Pvt practice, neur and psycht, since 1938; cons, Westover Air Force Base, since 1958; lectr, neur and psycht, Springfield Coll grad sch, 1948-66, visiting asso prof, clinical psycht, since 1966; neuropsycht, Springfield Hosp, since 1938; official examiner: US Civil Service; USRR, retirement bd; VA, US Army Induction Bd, all since 1946; guest lectr, Columbia U Med Sch, since 1964; courses, lectrs and demonstrations: hypnosis and psychodrama; psychotherapy, Can, Eng, Isr and Fr; gen practice, Oakland-Berkeley, 1929-31; sr phys, psycht and neur, Monson State Hosp, Palmer, Mass, 1931-38; neuropsycht, child guidance clinic and outpatient neur dept: Springfield Hosp; NE Med Cen; Boston Psychopathic Hosp; all 1931-38; spec lectr, analytic psych and social psych, Amer Intl Coll, 1949-51. Capt, USN MC, 1941-46, res, 1946-62. Dipl: Natl Bd Med Exams, 1929; Amer Bd Psycht, 1936; Neur, 1937; f: Amer Psychiatric Assn, 1940, life f, since 1961; Amer Soc of Group Psychotherapy; Amer Soc Group Psychotherapy and Psychodrama, pres, 1964-66; Amer Soc of Clinical Hypnosis, vice-pres, and training fac; pres, Sinai Temple, 1947-49, mem exec bd of Brotherhood; mem: Amer Acad Neur; E Assn Electroencephalographers; Maimonides Med Assn; AMA; Mass Med Assn. Author: Nothing to Sneeze At: Introduction to Psychosomatic Medicine, 1949; Hidden Springs of Human Action, 1952; Practical Psychotherapeutic Techniques, 1968; Practical Psychotherapy in Nonpsychiatric Specialties, 1969; Practical Family and Marriage Counseling; Practical Pastoral Counseling; contbr ed, Amer Jour of Group Psychotherapy; contbr articles to med jours. Recipient: First Prize, NE Psychiatric Assn, 1936. Hobbies: handicrafts, choral singing, fishing, gardening. Home: 71 Meadowbrook Rd, Longmeadow, Mass. Office: 146 Chestnut St, Springfield, Mass.

STEIN, Charles Jay, US, business exec; b. Pittsburgh, Pa, May 23, 1910; s. Louis and Ida (Rosenbloom); att: U Pittsburgh, 1930; Pa State U, 1931; LLB, Cumberland Law Sch, 1933; m. Janis Harrison, June 4, 1938; c: Charlotte Sigman, Robert, Louis, David. Pres and chmn, bd dirs, Roberts Enterprises, Inc; Roberts Lumber Co; Louis Wholesale Co; Stein Devl Corp; Sigman Realty Corp; David Acceptance Corp; owner, lumber yards, since 1938; atty, Corpus Christi, 1933-34; legal dept, US Govt, Wash, DC, 1934-35. USN, 1944-46. Pres: Wheeling Comty Council, 1959-60; Woodsdale Temple, 1952-53, bd mem, 1950-56; club, Elks. Home: 13 Woodlawn Court, Wheeling, W Va. Office: 2146 Market St, Wheeling, W Va.

STEIN, Emanuel, US, economist, educator; b. NYC, Oct 9, 1908; s. Jacob and Yetta (Liebreich); BS, NYU, 1928, MA, 1930, PhD, 1933; m. Florence Gordon, Dec 23, 1934; c: Barbara, Kenneth. Prof, econ, dept head, NYU, 1946-67, mem fac, since 1930, chmn: dept of econ, Wash Sq Coll, 1952, soc sci group, Grad Sch of Arts and Sci, 1946-60; exec-dir, Inst Lab Relations and Soc Security, 1948-62; public mem: Natl War Lab Bd, 1943-45; Wage Stabilization Bd, 1950-52. Mem: arbitration panel, Fed Mediation and Conciliation Service; NY Bd of Mediation; NJ Bd of Mediation; Amer Abitration Assn; Amer Econ Assn; NY Public Employment Relations Bd; NYC Off of Collective Bargaining; Natl Acad Arbitrators; NJ Statutory Bds of Arbitration; Phi Beta Kappa. Author: Labor Problems in America, 1940; Government and the Investor, 1941; Labor Cases and Materials, 1941. Ed, Proceedings of Annual NYU Confs on Labor, vols 1-15. Home: 234 E Penn St, Long Beach, NY. Office: NYU, New York, NY.

STEIN, Gabriel, Isr, educator; b. Budapest, Hung, May 24, 1920; s. Arthur and Zelma (Weiss); in Isr since 1938; MSc,

Heb U, Jerusalem, 1946; PhD, Kings Coll, U Durham, Eng, 1950; m. Pauline Epstein, Aug 2, 1950; c: Tamar, Asher. Prof phys chem, Heb U, since 1960; head dept since 1953, mem fac, since 1951; demonstrator, research f, U Durham, 1948-51. Brit Army 1940-44. Contbr to sci jours. Recipient: Weizmann Prize, 1960. Home: 15 Shmuel Hanagid St, Jerusalem, Isr. Office: Heb U, Jerusalem, Isr.

STEIN, Hannah R, US, organization exec; b. Berlin, Ger; d. Arthur and Salome (Blumstein); in US since 1949; att: Ravensfield Coll, London, Eng; Ecole Benedict, Neuchatel, Switz; Pittman's Coll, London; hon DHum, Philathea Coll, London, Ont, Can. Exec dir, Natl Council J Women, since 1959, repr, Council of Pres of Maj J Orgs; pres, Fed of Zionist Youth of Gt Brit and Ir, 1944-46, mem exec comm, 1946-48; bd dirs, Amer Immigration Citizenship Conf; conf of execs, Natl Social Wfr Assembly; house of delgs, Council on Social Work Educ; exec comm, women's div, JWB; planning comm, Natl Conf on Social Wfr, 1963; secretariat, World Confd of Gen Zionists, 1946; found, Herev Leet village in Isr; delg: White House Conf on Children and Youth; White House Conf on the Aging, 1961; mem: Women in Comty Services; Intl Platform Assn; PR Soc of Amer; Amer J PR Soc; Fgn Press Assn, London; Bnai Zion; J Reconstructionist Found; life, ZOA; Hadassah; Eye Bank for Sight Restoration; Pres Comm on Employment of Handicapped; Bnai Jeshurun Temple; asst to exec dir, dir, ZOA, 1953-59, mem, natl exec council, 1960-62. Lectr, W Eur, Can, US; corresp, intl, Eur confs. Recipient: UJA award for philanthropic leadership. Office: 1 W 47 St, New York, NY.

STEIN, Harry, Can, educator; b. London, Eng, Dec 29, 1902; s. Jacob and Kate (Stoller); in Can since 1912; BA, Man U, 1922, MA, 1935; PhD, Minn U, 1942; m. Lorice Badner, Mar 30, 1929; c: Leonard, Carole Doane, Keith. Dir, grad studies, and prof, educ psych, U of BC, since 1956; prin: sch, Sifton, Man, 1925-28; Benito HS, Man, 1928-34; counselor, Winnipeg schs, 1934-46; prof, educ, U Man, 1946-56; visiting prof, U of S Cal, 1951, 1953, 1956, 1959, 1961, 1963. Lt, Cadet Services, Can, 1942-50. Pres: Pacific region, Can J Cong, mem, natl exec, both since 1960; Bur J Educ, Winnipeg, 1935-38; vice-pres, J Home for Aged, Vancouver, since 1963; mem, bd: Beth Isr Syn, since 1958; UJA, Vancouver, since 1960; mem: Can Assn Profs of Educ; Phi Delta Kappa; Masons; club, J Musical, Winnipeg, pres, 1935-40. Contbr to educ publs. Recipient: Boyd Traveling F, U of Man, 1938. Home: 204-2191 W 39 Ave, Vancouver, BC, Can. Office: Coll of Educ, U of BC, Vancouver, BC, Can.

STEIN, Hava, Isr, geneticist, researcher; b. Berlin, Ger, Aug 3, 1924; d. Bruno and Luba (Lurje); in Isr since 1933; MSc, Heb U, Jerusalem, 1947, agric deg, Rehovot, 1950; PhD, U Wis, Madison, 1957. Research asso, plant, genet sect, Weizmann Inst, since 1963, research asst, 1958-63. Pvt, IDF, 1948-49. Chmn, Isr Botanical Soc, 1966-69; secy, Genet Soc Isr, 1965-68; adv, comm on recommendation of agric varieties. Spec interests: biology, language, philology. Home: 131 Ben Yehuda St, Tel Aviv, Isr. Office: Weizmann Inst, Rehovot, Isr.

STEIN, Irvin, US, surgeon, educator; b. Fayetteville, NC, Oct 17, 1906; s. Kalman and Fannie (Berman); BA, U of NC, 1926; MD, Jefferson Med Coll, 1930; m. Dorothy Bluthenthal, 1934; c: Jane, Margery, Katherine. Chief orthopedic surg, Phila Gen Hosp, since 1941; asso prof, chmn, of dept, orthopedic surg, Albert Einstein Med Cen, S div, since 1950; cons, orthopedic surg, Eagleville Sanatorium, since 1936; mem, att staff, U of Pa Hosp, since 1934; asso prof, orthopedic surg, U of Pa, fac mem, since 1934; in surg pathology, Johns Hopkins U and Hosp, 1931-32; chief res, Phila Orthopedic Hosp, 1932-33; asst res and asst instr, Johns Hopkins, Hosp, 1933-34; chief res, Children's Hosp Sch, 1934; lectr dept of radiology, grad sch, U of Pa, 1938-46; asst chief: Orthopedic Hosp, 1934-41; Methodist Hosp, 1938-41; visiting orthopedic surg, Children's Seashore Home, Atlantic City, NJ, 1939-58. Dipl, Amer Bd Orthopedic Surgs, since 1938; f: Amer Coll Surgs; Intl Coll Surgs; Amer Acad Orthopedic Surgs; Coll of Phys, Phila; Amer Rheumatism Assn; Amer Geriatics Soc; Amer Gerontological Assn; Amer Assn Med Writers; mem: AMA; Pa State Med Assn; Phila Co Med Soc; Orthopedic Research Soc; Assn for Study of Neoplastic Diseases; Johns Hopkins Med and Surg Assn. Author: Living Bone in Health and Disease, 1955; contbr to med jours. Recipient: Cert of Award, for sci exhbts, Amer Acad Orthopedic Surgs. Home: 3251 Huntington Valley, Pa. Office: 1936 Spruce St, Philadelphia Pa.

STEIN, Israel Chaim, US, rabbi; b. Hartford, Conn, Oct 3, 1937; s. Jacob and Rose (Abrahamson); BA, Trinity Coll, Conn, 1959; MHL, ordained rabbi, JTSA, 1964; m. Roslyn Berkowitz, Mar 29, 1959; c: Jeremy, Jay, Eli, Seth. J Cen, Bayside Hills, since 1968; asso rabbi, Temple Beth El, Rochester, NY, 1966-68. Chaplain US, Army, 1964-66. Secy, vice-pres, Rochester Bd Rabbis; bd govs, JWF, Rochester; bd dirs, Heb Acad, N Queens; mem: Assn J Chaplains; NY Bd Rabbis; RA; Comm on Syn Relations; Phi Beta Kappa. Home: 48-50 Oceania St, Bayside, NY. Study: 212 St and 48 Ave, Bayside, NY.

STEIN, Joseph Bernard, US, business exec; b. Stanford, NC, Aug 16, 1910; s. Kalman and Fannie (Berman); att, U NC, 1926-31; m. Herlyn Yalovitz, June 18, 1935; c: Marica, Janet. Pres: Capitol Dept Store, Inc, since 1946; K's Exclusive Shoes since 1951; Populaire, Inc, since 1952; Cape Fear Inds, Inc, since 1958; Comty Devl Corp, since 1959; observation worker, J B Ivey Co, 1930; mem, 3rd Army Adv Comm, 1952, 1954. Dir: C of C, pres, 1949-53, 1958-59, vice-pres, Jr C of C, 1935; Red Cross, 1952; Methodist Coll Campaign, 1969; pres: B'nai B'rith, 1949; Cumberland Co Alumni Assn, 1949; state chmn, UJA, 1951-52; chmn: steering comm, Bicentennial Celebration; bldg, comm, Beth Isr Comty Cen, 1947, pres, 1950; co-org, USO, 1941, org in Cumberland Co; mem: bd gov Beth Isr Syn, 1947-54; Cumberland Blind Assn; Federate Charities, all Fayetteville, NC; club, Lions, past pres. Recipient: Man of Year; B'nai B'rith, 1958; Faytetteville Kiwanis Club, 1969; C of C, realtors group, 1969; Brand Name award, for Dept Stores, 1952. Home: 105 Dobbin Ave, Faytteville, NC. Office: 126 Hay St, Fayetteville, NC.

STEIN, Leon, US, composer, conductor, educator, author; b. Chgo, Ill, Sep 18, 1910; s. Harry and Rebecca (Lazar); BMus, DePaul U, 1931, MMus, 1935, DMus, 1949; m. Anne Helman, Oct 30, 1937; c: Robert, Kenneth. Dean, DePaul U Sch of Music, since 1966, dir grad div, since 1950, chmn, dept of theory and composition, since 1948, mem fac, since 1931; dir, City Sym Orch, Chgo, since 1963; conductor, Comty Sym Orch, since 1946; guest conductor: Ill Sym, 1935; Chgo Civic Orch, 1940; DePaul U Orch, 1942, 1943; Kenosha Sym, 1944; f, conducting, Chgo Sym Orch, 1937-40; conductor, USN Concert Band and Orch, Ill, 1944-45; chmn, Coll of J Studies Inst of Music, 1952-57. Composer: orchestral works, syms, chamber music, concertos, songs, opera. Chmn, Intl Soc for Contemporary Music, Chgo, 1954-55; mem: Amer Musicological Soc; Phi Gamma Mu; Sinfonia Frat; AAUP. Author: Hassidic Music, 1943; The Identity of Jewish Music, 1943; An Analytical Study of Brahms' Variations on a Theme by Haydn, 1944; Jewish Music Today, 1945; The Problems of Ernest Bloch, 1946; The Anti-Semitism of Richard Wagner, 1949; The Racial Thinking of Richard Wagner, 1950; Structure and Style, 1962; Anthology of Musical Forms, 1962; contbr to: sect on great orch works, U of Knowledge Ency, 1938; profsl jours. Recipient: performance awards, Ill Sym, 1935; Amer Composers Commn award, 1950; performance awards: U Composers Exch, 1952; 1953; 1954; SW Composers Symposium, 1954; co-winner, Midland Found Natl Contest, 1955. Home: 4050 Greenwood St, Skokie, Ill. Office: DePaul U, Chicago, Ill.

STEIN, Leon, US, editor; b. Baltimore, Md, Jan 18, 1912; s. Jacob and Freda (Barcun); BA, CCNY, 1934; m. Feb 2, 1936. Ed, Justice, ILGWU, since 1952. Pres, Intl Lab Press Assn, 1964-65; mem: Ind Relations Research Assn; AJCong; Cutters Local 10, ILGWU. Author: The Triangle Fire, 1962; trans, Education of Abraham Cahan, 1969; ed, American Labor, 60 vols, 1970. Home: 1142 E 4 St, Brooklyn, NY. Office: 1710 Broadway, New York, NY.

STEIN, Louis, US, organization exec; b. NYC, May 7, 1917; s. Samuel and Sonia (Burstein); BS, CCNY, 1942; m. Edith; c: Kit. Dir, PR, Beth Isr Hosp, since 1960; reporter, NY Times, 1940-42; dir, PR: CCNY, 1946-48; Council of J Fed of Wfr Funds, 1948-60. Sgt maj, USAAC, 1942-45. Chmn: PR sect, Mass Hosp Assn, 1961; comm on ethics and standards, Amer PR Soc, 1958-60; pres, Mid-Nassau Comty Guidance Cen, 1954-56; vice-pres, NE Hosp PR Assn; mem, PR Soc Amer. Ed: Building the Successful Campaign, 1957; Year Round Interpretation, 1960. Home: 19 Garrison Rd, Brookline, Mass. Office: 330 Brookline Ave, Boston, Mass.

STEIN, Louis Ronald, US, musician, business exec; b. St Louis, Mo, Apr 12, 1930; s. Harry and Celia (Zarfas); BA, Wash U, St Louis, Mo, 1951; att: Yale U, 1951-52; U of S Cal, 1959-63; m. Harlene Hiken, Dec 23, 1951; c: Harise, Hollie, Jaciyn,

Victor. Theatrical film composer, since 1955; admnr, US Educ Films, since 1966; owner, music publ, recording, produc cos, since 1958; asst to music dir: Munic Opera, St Louis, 1950-51, 1954; Greek Theatre, LA, 1955; music dir, Amer Intl Pictures, Hollywood, Cal, 1958-60; asst prof, music, San Fernando Valley State Coll, 1960-62; asso music dir, Phoenix Star Theater, Arizona, 1964. Composer: Road Without End, from The Littlest Hobo, 1958; Of Love and Desire, Katherine's Love Theme, theme from Dime With a Halo, all 1963; music from: Getting Straight; The Rain People, both 1969; 75 theatrical film scores; serious compositions for concert and sym; guest appearances as conductor and solo pianist; produc, educ film, National Parks—A Road for the Future, 1968; film and music critic for mags and jours. Cpl, US Army Spec Services, 1952-54. Civil defense instr, Northridge, Cal; chmn, film festival comm, Audio-Visual Educ Assn, Cal; mem bd: and adult educ comm, Temple Ramat-Zion, Northridge, Cal, secy, Brotherhood, 1965-66; Composers and Lyricists Guild Amer, Hollywood, Cal; mem: fgn lang film sect, Acad Motion Picture Arts and Scis; Screen Composers Assn; ASCAP; charter, Songwriters Hall of Fame; Screen Actors Guild; dept audio-visual instrn, NEA; charter, LA Libr Assn; Amer Fed Musicians, local 47; life: Alpha Epsilon Pi; US Chess Fed; club, Northridge Chess, found, pres, 1966-67. Recipient: Keys; Omicron Delta Kappa; Natl Collegiate Players; Thyrsus and Quad Show Service; Pres Unit Citation; hon life mem, Asso Students, San Fernando Valley State Coll, 1961; 2-year Service Button, J Big Brothers, LA, Cal, 1968. Spec interests: chess, teaching civil defense and med self-help, short wave radio. Home: 17414 Devonshire St, Northridge, Cal.

STEIN, Martin H, US, surgeon; b. Lith, Dec 8, 1890; s. Hillel and Goldie (Blatt); in US since 1904; MD, Medico-Chirurgical Coll, Phila, Pa, 1914. Att surg em, St Elizabeth Hosp, Elizabeth, NJ, since 1954. Lt, US Army, WW I. Amer Coll Surg, 1937; mem, AMA. Hobbies: travel, music, golf, bridge. Home: 60 Elmora Ave, Elizabeth, NJ.

STEIN, Mimi, US, author, broadcaster, storyteller; b. Port Elizabeth, S Afr; d. Benjamin and Bluma (Sendzul); in US since 1939; att, NYU, 1954. Conducts programs: radio, TV, since 1955; J Home Show, since 1962; storytelling to children: public schs; Educ Alliance; radio; TV; ed asst, Americana Ency, 1944; radio show, S Afr, Mimi Speaking, 1967. Volunteer, storytelling: FJP; Hosp for Jt Diseases; Park Ave Syn; NY Hosp; Children's Zoo; mem, ASCAP. Author: My Little World, record, 1956, song book, 1956; God and Me, 1960; Two Oxen for Lobola, 1964; Mort the Mascot Mouse, 1968; Majola, a Zulu Boy, 1969; Puleng of Lesotho, 1969; contbr to press, mags, Ency Americana. Hobby: making hats and necklaces. Office: 329 E 83 St, New York, NY.

STEIN, Morris J, US, attorney; b. Russ, Mar 16, 1905; s. Israel and Bessie (Beiser); in US since 1907; LLB, Bklyn Law Sch, St Lawrence U, 1926; m. Ella Katz, July 2, 1930; c: Susan, Janet. Judge of Civil Court, NYC, since 1968; pvt practice, Bklyn, NY, since 1927; asso atty, jt leg comm, Housing and Multiple Dwellings, 1946-48; mem, City Council, NY, 1949-68; chmn, Comm of Gen Wfr, 1962-68. Pres: Brighton and Manhattan Beach C of C and Civic Assn, 1945-46; Manhattan Beach Comty Group, Inc, 1947-48; and co-found, Oceanfront, Youthtown Comty Cen, Inc, NY, 1945; co-found, chmn, exec comm, Manhattan Beach Recreation Cen, Inc, 1947; Mem, bd dirs: Asso YM-YWHA's, Gtr NY; Temple Beth El, Manhattan Beach; hon mem, counsel, Coney Island Research Inst; mem: comty adv bd, Coney I Hosp; Bklyn Bar Assn; club, Bklyn Lawyers. Home: 257 Coleridge St, Brooklyn, NY. Office: 120 Schermerhorn St, Brooklyn, NY.

STEIN, Nathaniel Edward, US, stockbroker; b. NYC, Aug 4, 1904; s. Samuel and Anna (Blyweiss); att U Maine, 1920-22; m. Helen Hecht, Oct 3, 1927; c: Nancy Zeldes, Michael. Br mgr, Newburger Loeb and Co, since 1949. Treas, mem bd, Amer J Hist Soc; mem: bd, Vocational Camp for Blind; Whitney Mus; fmr pres, Manuscript Soc; clubs: Grolier, City Athletic. Contbr to Manuscript Soc Jour. Hobby: collecting Amer hist manuscripts. Home: 15 E 91 St, New York, NY. Office: 931 Madison Ave, New York, NY.

STEIN, Richard, Isr, educator; b. Czech, May 11, 1898; s. Leopold and Karolina; in Isr since 1949; att U Prague; m. Batia Lampel, 1928; c: Ruth Zif. Prof ophthal, U Tel Aviv, since 1964; head eye dept, Tel Hashomer Hosp, since 1949; sr lectr, U Prague, 1932-38. Head, Isr Ophthal Soc. Home and office: 20 Hess St, Tel Aviv, Isr.

STEIN, Walter, US, artist; b. Bklyn, NY, Nov 30, 1924; s. Louis and Fannie (Maidenberg) Grushka; att: Cooper Union Art Sch, 1941-42; New Sch for Social Research, 1946-49; NY U, 1949-50, all NYC; Academia di Belle Arte, It, 1950-51; m. Sally Coogan, June 28, 1946. Tchr: pvt, 1954-55, 1962-63; Cooper Union, 1968-69; One man shows: gals: Graham, NYC, 1964; Durlacher Bros, NYC, 1951, 1953, 1955, 1957, 1959, 1961, 1962; Swetzoff, Mass, 1951, 1957; Mayo Hill, Mass, 1953; Hilson, Mass, 1957; Mus of Art, RI Sch of Design, Providence, 1958; Vassar Coll, NY, 1959; repr in collections: Boston Mus of Fine Arts; Chgo Art Inst; Fogg Art Mus; Mus of Modern Art; Phillips Collection; Yale U Art Gal; Walter P Chrysler Collection. Sgt, USAAF, 1942-45. Publs: Elegy by Chidiock Tichborne, drawings, 1967; A Common Botany, woodcuts and engravings, 1956; Natural History by Jules Renard, lithographs, drawings, 1960; All That Sunshine, watercolors, 1967; Toulouse Lautrec, Bonnard, Stein, 1967. Home and studio: 11 Cooper Sq, New York, NY.

STEIN, William H, US, biochemist; b. NYC, June 25, 1911; s. Fred and Beatrice (Borg); BS, Harvard Coll, 1933; PhD, Columbia U, 1938; m. Phoebe Hockstader, June 22, 1936; c: William, David, Robert. Mem and prof biochem, Rockefeller Inst, since 1952, on staff since 1938; cons, Chem-Biol Coord Cen, 1951-56; f, lectr, Amer Swiss Found, 1956; Harvey lectr, 1957; Philips lectr, 1962; visiting prof, U Chgo, 1960; Harvard U, 1964. Natl chmn, US Natl Comm for Biochem, 1964-68; mem: bd trustees, Montefiore Hosp; med adv bd, Heb U-Hadassah Med Sch; finance comm, Amer Soc of Biol Chems; sci counselor, Natl Inst for Neur Diseases and Blindness; Natl Acad of Scis; Amer Acad of Arts and Scis; Biochem Soc, Eng; Amer Chem Soc; AAAS; Harvey Soc; Sigma Xi. Ed, Jour of Biol Chem, since 1968, asso ed, 1964-68, ed comm, 1955-58, chmn 1958-61; contbr to sci jours. Hobbies: music, tennis. Home: 168 E 74 St, New York, NY. Office: Rockefeller Inst, 66 St, and York Ave, New York, NY.

STEIN, Yechezkiel, Isr, professor; b. Cracow, Pol, May 15, 1926; s. Joshua and Mina (Blum); in Isr since 1942; att med sch, Switz, 1946-49; MD, med sch, Jerusalem, 1952; m. Olga Weindling, Oct 1947. Prof of med, head Lipid Research Lab, head dept med B, Hadassah U Hosp. IDF, 1948. Author: numerous sci publs. Home: 5 Shalom Aleichem St, Jerusalem, Isr. Office: Heb U-Hadassah Med Sch, Jerusalem, Isr.

STEINBACH, Alexander Alan, US, rabbi, author; b. Baltimore, Md, Feb 2, 1894; s. Abraham and Sarah (Wolfe); BA, Johns Hopkins U, 1917; MA, Atlantic U, 1930; ordained rabbi, HUC, 1930, hon DD, 1956; m. Sadye Silberstein, June 8, 1919; c: Ruthanne Greenspan. Rabbi em, Temple Ahavath Sholom, Bklyn, NY, rabbi, since 1934; rabbi: Cong Ahavath Sholom, Bluefield, W Va, 1921-22; Temple Beth El, Norfolk, Va, 1922-34. Capt, US Army, 1943-46. Hon pres, JBCA; fmr pres: NY Bd Rabbis; hon chmn, Natl Poetry Day, 1958, 1959; mem, bd dirs: Natl Home for Asthmatic Children, Denver, since 1935; Bklyn Juvenile Guidance Cen, since 1936; Bklyn Assn for Mh, since 1938; Bklyn JCC, since 1939; J Educ Comm, NY, since 1940; hon mem: Mark Twain Soc, since 1935; Eugene Field Soc, since 1937; mem: ceremonies comm, CCAR, since 1959, liturgical comm, since 1960; educ, culture comm, JA of Isr, since 1960; Syn Council Amer. Author: Treatise Baba Mezia, 1929; Sabbath Queen, 1936; When Dreamers Build, poetry, 1937; What is Judaism? 1937; Musings and Meditations, 1941; In Search of the Permanent, 1946; Bitter-Sweet, 1955; Faith and Love, 1959; Through Storms We Grow; ed: Jewish Book Annual, since 1954; In Jewish Bookland, since 1960; NY Bd Rabbis Bull, 1950-60; Recipient: first prize: Bookfellow Poetry Annual, 1940; Amer Poetry League Contest, 1949. Hobby: music. Home: 2310 Ave R, Brooklyn, NY. Study: 1609 Ave R, Brooklyn, NY.

STEINBERG, Aaron Zacharovich (pen name, M Avrelin), Eng, author; b. Dvinsk, Russ, June 12, 1891; s. Zorach and Chiena (Elyashev); desc, Rashi, in Eng since 1934; att fac of Phil, 1908-14; DJ, Law Fac, 1913, both Heidelberg, Ger; m. Sophie Rosenblatt, Apr 4, 1935, (decd). Hon mem, governing council, WJC, since 1968, mem, exec bd, and dir cultural dept, 1948-68, repr in UNESCO, 1945-67; mem, mgmt bd, Inst of J Affairs, London, since 1967; prof, phil, secy phil assn, St Petersberg, 1918-23. Author: The Two Chambers System in Russia, 1913; Dostoievsky's Philosophy of Freedom, 1924; Dostoievsky in London, 1932; Dostoievsky, 1966; co-author, The History of the Jewish People, 3 vols, 1936-38; ed, Dubnow Centenary vol, 1963; trans: from Russ into Ger, Dubnow's World History of the Jewish People, vols I-X, 1925-29; from

Heb into Ger, Dubnow's History of Chasidism, 1931, 1969; co-ed, co-author: Ency Handbook: The Jewish People—Past and Present; Gen Ency, Yiddish, 1946-52; mem, adv bd, The Jewish Journal of Sociology, since 1964; contbr to Russ, Ger, Eng, Fr, Heb, Yiddish, publs. Hon pres: Brit sect, J Research Inst, YIVO, since 1952; Assn J Journalists in Gt Brit, since 1962; hon vice-pres, Brit sect, WJC, chmn research comm, 1942-47; co-found, mem bd: Inst of Higher J Studies, St Petersburg, 1918-23; J People's Coll, London, 1935-38; co-found, YIVO, Berlin, 1924; mem bd, Inst of J Learning, London, 1940-45. Hobbies: chess, fine arts. Home: 81 Eton Pl, Eton Coll Rd, London NW3, Eng. Office: 55 New Cavendish St, London, Eng.

STEINBERG, Abraam, US, ophthalmologist; b. Pittsburgh, Pa, May 12, 1910; s. Jacob and Pearl (Caplan); BA, U Mich, 1932, MD, 1935; m. Dorothy Israel, Jan 31, 1932; c: Susan, Mark. Asso in ophthal, Montefiore Hosp, since 1958, sr att phys, since 1961; chmn, out-patient dept, phys comm, since 1963, ophthal i/c, eye clinic, since 1955. Capt, US Army 1942-46. F: Amer Bd Ophthal; Amer Bd Surg; mem: Pittsburgh Ophthal Soc; AMA; Assn for Research in Ophthal. Hobbies: music, sculpture. Home: 5139 Penton Rd, Pittsburgh Pa. Office: 3401 Fifth Ave, Pittsburgh, Pa.

STEINBERG, Abraham, (pen name, Abe Steinberg), US, composer, train conductor; b. NYC, Mar 21, 1897; s. Morris and Fannie (Scheps); m. Gussie Eisenberg, June 28, 1924. IRT conductor, NYC Transp Dept, 1916-66; with ASCAP, since 1963. USNR WW I. Life mem, Disabled Amer Vets, chap 23, Bx, since 1963, post hist; mem, Dorshei Tov Anshei Tov cong; mem: Mt Sinai Anshei Emet cong; Sinai J Cen cong; Master Mason, Amity Lodge, 323, 1948-69. Composer, author, including: America I'm For You, 1917; Israel I'm For You, 1967; appears on TV and radio as guest star; contbr: poems, jingles, to jours and mags. Recipient: Career Civil Service award, City Hall, 1960. Home: 195 Bennet Ave, New York, NY. Office: 370 Jay St New York, NY.

STEINBERG, Arnold David, US, dentist; b. Warsaw, Pol, Oct 25, 1930; s. Morris and Leila (Baum); in US since 1938; att U of Ill, Chgo, 1948-50, MS, 1964; DDS, Northwestern U Dent Sch, 1954; m. June Bender, June 14, 1953; c: Steven, Barbara, Ruth, Mark. Pvt practice, since 1956; asst prof, periodontics, U of Ill Sch of Dent, since 1967, research asso, biochem dept, Med Sch, 1964-67; asso att, Michael Reese Hosp, Chgo, since 1968, tchr, dent for handicapped; dir, Lincoln Dent Caries Study, Ill State Dent Soc, 1963-67. Capt, USAF, 1954-56. F: Intl Coll Dents; Acad for Gen Dent; Amer, Coll of Dents; vice-pres, Acad Dent of Handicapped; co-found, med chmn, Chgo chap, Natl Tay-Sachs Assn, mem, natl adv group, 1959-60; bd dirs: Akiba J Day Sch, 1967; Cong Rodfe Sholom, 1968; mem: Soc Dent for Children; Intl Assn Dent Research; Amer Dent Assn; Ill State Dent Soc; AAAS; Amer Assn Mental Deficient; Alpha Omega. Author: Dentist's Handbook of Office and Hospital Procedures, 1963; contbr: chap on Dentistry For Handicapped; to dent jours. Recipient: Man of Year, Chgo Natl Tay-Sachs Assn, 1961. Hobbies: bri c[..] handball. Home: 1710 E 91 Pl, Chicago, Ill. Office: 982 !S Crawford, Evergreen Park, Ill.

STEINBERG, Arthur Irwin, US, dentist, educator; b. Pittsburgh, Pa, Sep 16, 1935; s. Ben and Sylvia (Jacobs); BS, U Pittsburgh, 1957, gradwork, 1957-59, DMD, cum laude, 1963; dipl, periodontology, Harvard U, 1966; m. Barbara Ehrenkranz, May 23, 1959; c: Sharon, Mindy, Michael. Asso prof, period-ontology, Temple U Sch of Dent, since 1967; pvt practice, periodontics, since 1967; asst prof, dept of periodontology, SUNY, Buffalo, 1966-67; asso periodontics, Phoenixville Hosp, Pa, 1968-70, att periodontist, since 1970, infections, control comm, since 1969. Mem: Amer Dent Assn; AMA; Amer Acad Periodontology; Harvard Odontological Soc; Harvard Dent Alumni Assn; Masons, 32 degree; Beta Beta Beta, B'nai B'rith; Zeta Beta Tau; Shriners, Lulu Temple, Phila; Alpha Epsilon Delta; Omicron Kappa Upsilon; Sigma Xi; fmr mem: Health Physics Soc; Amer Public Health Assn; Gtr Boston Dent Soc; AAUP ins comm; Pa Soc Periodontists, Blue Cross comm, Pa Co Dent Soc. Contbr to sci jours. Recipient: awards: Alfred I Wise, 1963; Gold Foil, Amer Acad of Gold Foil Operators, 1963; W Pa chap, Amer Soc Dent for Children, 1963; first prize, sr student Amer Dent Assn clinics, 1963; Fulbright-Hays award, 1970-71. Hobby: music. Home: 1681 Pheasant Ln, Norristown, Pa. Office: Temple U, 3223 N Broad, Philadelphia, Pa.

STEINBERG, Bernhard, US, physician; b. NYC, June 18,

1897; s. Murry and Sara (Sprinborg); att, Fordham U, 1918; MD, Boston U, 1922; m. Roberta Riman, Feb 13, 1932; c: Bernard, Michael. Asso clinical prof, research path, Loma Linda U Sch of Med, Cal, since 1964; f, Natl Research Council, 1924-26; Crile Research f, W Reserve U, 1927-28; dir, inst of med research, Toledo Hosp, 1942-64, path and dir of labs, 1927-64; lectr, forensic med, U Toledo and police dept, 1938-64; cons, O State Ind Commn, 1943; sr surg, USPHS, 1949. Hon mem, Phi Kappa Phi; mem: AMA; Amer Assn Paths and Bacts; Amer Bd Path; Amer Assn Immunologists; Fed of Amer Socs of Experimental Biol; Amer Soc Hematology; Intl Soc Hematology; Amer Fed Clinical Research; Tri-State Post-Grad Med Assn, fmr pres; clubs: Rotary; Torch of Toledo, fmr pres. Author: Infections of the Peritoneum, 1944; I Had An Idea, 1952; contbr to med jours. Recipient: Silver Medal, Amer Soc Clinical Paths, 1937; First Cincinnati Proctologic award, 1951. Home: PO Box 633, Claremont, Cal.

STEINBERG, Charles LeRoy, US, physician; b. Louisville, Ky, Dec 24, 1903; s. Joseph and Mary (Rosenbleib); BS, U Louisville, 1927, MD, 1929; m. Audrey Davidson, Mar 22, 1933; c: Kermit, Wendy. Pvt practice, since 1933; sr clinical instr med, U Rochester, mem staff, Strong Memorial Hosp; cons, internal med Wayne Co Comty Hosp, since 1957; sr visiting phys, Rochester Gen Hosp, since 1949, dir, arthritis clinic, since 1933, asso chief med, 1947-48. Lt cdr, USNR, WW II. FACP; trustee, Rochester Acad Med; chmn, Med Conf of Rochester Regional Hosp Council; mem, bd dirs: Health Assn, Rochester Monroe Co, mem, exec comm, since 1956; Visiting Nurse Assn, since 1955; mem: planning commn Council Social Agcys; AAAS; AMA; AHA; Amer Rheumatic Assn; Comty Chest; club, Midvale Country, mem bd dirs, since 1957. Author: Arthritis, Rheumatism and Allied Disorders, 1954; contbr to: Rheumatic Diseases, by W B Saunders, 1950; Progress in Arthritis, 1959; contbr to med jours. Recipient: First Honor, clinical research, NY State Med Soc, 1947; Citation Award of Merit, for teaching, Rochester Acad of Med, 1952. Hobbies: golf, swimming, fishing. Home: 228 Danbury Circle N, Rochester, NY. Office: 176 S Goodman St, Med Center, Rochester, NY.

STEINBERG, Charles S, US, communications exec; b. NYC, Oct 23, 1913; s. Herman and Henrietta (Side); BA, NYU, 1937, MA, 1939, PhD, 1954; m. Hortense Rosenson, Dec 1952; c: Harriet. Vice-pres, public info, CBS TV network, since 1959, dir, info services, 1957-59; dir of educ, Book-of-the Month Club, 1942-43; E dir, PR, Warner Bros Pictures, 1943-56; lectr, New Sch for Social Research and NYU, 1944-60. Mem: Radio and TV Execs Soc; Natl Soc for Study of communication; Phi Beta Kappa; club, City. Author: The Mass Communicators; Public Relations, Public Opinion and Mass Media, 1958; contbr to profsl publs. Home: 515 Beach 131 St, Belle Harbor, LI, NY. Office: 485 Madison Ave, New York, NY.

STEINBERG, Eliot, US, business exec; b. NYC, June 5, 1923; s. Joseph and Rose (Graff); BS, Poly Inst Bklyn, 1943, MS, 1947; m. Judith Silverstein, Aug 3, 1947; c: Robert, Julian, Andrew. Dir, research admn, Warner-Lambert Pharmaceutical Co, Morris Plains, NJ, since 1958, chemist, 1947-52, mgr, research admn, 1952-58. US Army, 1944-46. Pres, Morris Township Bd of Educ, 1965-68; mem: bd dirs, NJ Council for Research and Devl; Morristown Comty Concerts; Temple B'nai Or, Morristown, NJ, pres, 1964-65; mem: Amer Chem Soc; NY Acad Scis; Amer Inst Chems; Urban League; ACLU; B'nai B'rith; AAAS. Hobby: music. Home: 29 Raynor Rd, Morristown, NJ. Office: Warner-Lambert Pharmaceutical Co, Morris Plains, NJ.

STEINBERG, Ellis P, US, researcher; b. Chicago, Ill, Mar 26, 1920; s. Solomon and Sarah (Saphir); BS, U Chgo, 1941, PhD, 1947; m. Esther Abraham, Dec 16, 1944; c: Sheryl, David, Deborah. Sr sci, Argonne Natl Lab, since 1943; jr chem, US, War Dept, 1941-43; US delg to 1st UN conf on peaceful users of Atomic Energy, Geneva, 1955; chmn, Gordon Conf on Nuclear Chem, 1961. Mem: Bd of J Educ, Park Forest, since 1951, pres, 1955; bd, Park Forest B'nai B'rith Lodge; Amer Phys Soc; Amer Chem Soc; Research Soc Amer; Park Forest Sym Orch; Park Forest Art Cen. Contbr to sci publs. Recipient: Guggenheim f, 1957-58. Hobbies: music, athletics, painting, Home: 194 Westwood Dr, Park Forest, Ill. Office: 9700 S Cass Ave, Argonne, Ill.

STEINBERG, Erwin R, US, educator; b. New Rochelle, NY, Nov 15, 1920; s. Samuel and Lea (Neumann); BS, NY State

Tchrs Coll, 1941, MS, 1942; PhD, NYU, 1956; m. Beverley Mendelson, Aug 15, 1954; c: Marc, Alan. Dean, Margaret Norrison Carnegie Coll, since 1960, and Coll of Hum and Soc Scis, since 1965, both Carnegie-Mellon U, prof, Eng, since 1960, fac mem, since 1946. USAAF, 1943-46. Chmn, Conf on Coll Composition and Communication, 1960; mem, bd dirs, Natl and Pa Councils of Tchrs of Eng, 1960; mem: MLA; Kappa Delta Phi; Phi Delta Kappa. Author: The Stream of Consciousness Technique in James Joyce's Ulysses, 1958; Communications in Business and Industry, 1960; co-author, Suggestions for Evaluating Junior High School Writing, 1958; ed: The Rule of Force, 1962; Insight Series, 1968-69; co-ed, Personal Integrity, 1961; contbr to scholarly jours. Recipient, Carnegie Teaching award, 1956. Hobby: tennis. Home: 1376 N Sheridan Ave, Pittsburgh, Pa. Office: Carnegie-Mellon U, Schenley Park, Pittsburgh, Pa.

STEINBERG, Jack, US, attorney; b. Seattle, Wash, Jan 6, 1915; s. Solomon and Mary (Rashall); BA, U Wash, 1936, DJ, 1938; m. Frieda Rashbam, May 6, 1939; c: Roosevelt, Mary, Quentin. Pvt practice, law, since 1938; ed, The Washington Examiner, 1960-63; judge pro tem, Seattle Munic Court, 1952-54. Pvt, Wash Natl Guard. Pres: Emanuel Cong, 1968; Seattle ZOA, 1962-63; Seattle Heb Sch, 1950; mem: Wash State Gov's Commn on Status of Women, 1964-65; Wash State Bar Assn; Amer Judicature Soc; B'nai B'rith. Home: 6826 43 Ave NE, Seattle, Wash. Office: 1311 Joseph Vance Bldg, Seattle, Wash.

STEINBERG, Leo, US, art historian, writer; b. Moscow, Russ, July 7, 1920; s. Isaac and Nehama (Esselson); Fine Arts Dipl, Slade Sch, U London, 1940; PhD, Inst of Fine Arts, NYU, 1960. Prof, Hunter Coll, NYC. Home: 211 Central Park W, New York, NY.

STEINBERG, Martin R, US, physician, educator; b. Russ, June 5, 1904; s. Harry and Rose (Remez); BA, U of Pa, 1923; MD, Temple U, 1927; MMS, U of Pa, 1930; m. Cecily Kaplan, June 30, 1931; c: Deborah, Howard. Practice, otolaryngology, since 1929; dir, Mt Sinai Hosp, NY, since 1948; chmn dept, prof, admn med, Mt Sinai Sch of Med; asst prof, otolaryngology, Grad Sch of Med, U of Pa, 1935. Lt col, US Army MC, 1942-45. F: NY Acad of Med; Amer Acad of Orl; Amer Coll of Hosp Admnrs; pres: Hosp Assn NY State; Gtr NY Hosp Assn, 1954-55; chmn, med adv comm, Sidney Hillman Health Cen; bd trustees, Amer Hosp Assn; mem, NY State Hosp Review and Planning Council. Contbr to med jours. Home: 45 Arleigh Rd, Great Neck, NY. Office: 11 E 100 St, New York, NY.

STEINBERG, Marvin D, US, podiatrist; b. Syracuse, NY, May 2, 1909; s. Leon and Mae (Blaustein); att LIU, 1928-31; PodD, Coll of Podiatry, 1945; m. Ruth Wollner, Aug 19, 1939; c: Lloyd, Elise. Dir, dept podiatry, J Memorial Hosp, on staff since 1953; cons, Bx Munic Hosp, since 1958. Prin contribs: inventor: surg Trephine, keramin solution for warts; new instrument and operation for ingrown nails. F, AAAS; chmn, bd govs, St Luke Hosp Coll of Podiatry, Phila, since 1961; scope of practice comm, NY State Podiatry Soc, 1958-63; dir, NY State Research Podiatry Soc, 1952-62; mem: specialists panel, Workmen's Compensation, NY State Bd; NY Acad Sci; Amer Podiatry Assn; hon mem, NJ Podiatry Soc. Contbr to profsl jours. Home: 12 Lawrence Park Ct, Bronxville, NY. Office: 630 Ft Washington Ave, New York, NY.

STEINBERG, Moses Wolfe, Can, educator; b. Ottawa, Can, Feb 16, 1918; s. Louis and Leah (Sanders); BA, hons, Queens U, Kingston, 1943, MA, 1944; PhD, U Toronto, 1952; m. Esther Cohen, July 29, 1945; c: Daniel, David, Ruth, Jerome, Eliot. Prof, dept Eng, U of BC, since 1946; with Can Civil Service, 1935-40. Dominion councilor, CJCong, since 1955; chmn: Vancouver Poetry Cen, 1958-62; J Centennial Comm of BC, 1958; interim dir, Hillel Found, U of BC, 1961-62; pres, Hum Assn of BC, 1955-56; secy-treas, Assn Can U Tchrs Eng, 1961-62. Author: Aspects of Modern Drama, 1960; ed: Papers of the Shaw Festival, 1956; A M Klein, The Second Scroll, 1961; Thomas Hardy, Tess of the D'Urbervilles; dir, Prism Poetry Mag; contbr to lit jours. Recipient: Can Council Research award, 1962, 1969. Home: 4361 Cambie St, Vancouver, BC, Can. Office: U of BC, Vancouver, BC, Can.

STEINBERG, Nathaniel P, US, artist; b. Jerusalem, Feb 15, 1893; s. Sol and Sarah (Saphir); in US since 1901; att Art Inst, Chgo, Ill, 1912-15; m. Isabel Schuham, Oct 15, 1939. Ret; ed artist, Chgo Amer, daily, from 1938, advt artist, 1919-39. Exhbs: Art Inst, Chgo; Libr of Cong; Natl MusWash,

DC; Mus: Denver; LA; Palm Beach; Detroit; Wichita; Seattle; Indianapolis; NY and Paris; perm collections: Isr Mus; Libr of Congress; Smithsonian Inst. Mem: Palette and Chisel Acad of Fine Arts, vice-pres, 1959, pres, 1960-61; Painters and Sculptors Soc; Chgo Soc of Etchers, bd dirs, since 1952. Recipient: award of merit, Chgo Soc of Etchers, 1935, 1949, hon mention, 1953; gold medal, Palette and Chisel Acad, 1954, 2nd water color prize, 1958, Gold Star award, 1966; prize, Indiana Soc of Etchers, 1946; Pennell award, Amer Soc of Etchers, 1950; Artists Guild award, 1955; Bruce Parsons award, 1957. Home and studio: 82 Ellis St, Douglas, Mich.

STEINBERG, Paul M, US, educator; b. NYC, Jan 29, 1926; s. Abraham and Lena (Schimelman); BSS, CCNY, 1946, MS 1948; ordained rabbi, MHL, HUC-JIR, 1949; EdD, Columbia U, 1961; m. Trudy Strudler, June 15, 1947; c: Alana, Alan. Dean, prof, human relations and educ, HUC-JIR, NY, since 1958; guest lectr, Sch of Social Work, Jerusalem, Isr, 1949-50; dir, B'nai B'rith Hillel Found, Berkeley, Cal, 1950-52; chaplain, FDR Vets Hosp, Montrose, NY, 1952-57; rabbi, Temple Israel, N Westchester, 1952-58. F, AAAS; mem: bd dirs, Mh Assn, Westchester Co, 1952-57; exec bd dirs, Council Higher Educ Instns NYC, since 1962; CCAR; Amer Psych Assn; Amer Personnel and Guidance Assn; Phi Delta Kappa; AAUP. Recipient: Guggenheim f, 1949; NY State Dept of Educ, Intl Research Grant, 1967. Home: 54 Rutledge Rd, Scarsdale, NY. Office: 40 W 68 St, New York, NY.

STEINBERG, Uziel, Isr, certified public acctnt; b. Muktchevo, Czech, Aug 15, 1924; s. Israel and Chaya; in Isr since 1949; Engr, Tech U, Prague, 1949; m .Irene. Klein, May, 1955; c: Ruth, Michael, Benjamin. CPA; govt off, since 1950; dep commn, Income Tax, 1960-62, commn, 1962-65; controller, Fgn Exch, dir, Inves Auth, 1966-67. Mem exec comm: ORT, Isr, World ORT Union; mem, Assn Public Acctnts in Isr; club, Variety, treas. Home: 22 Yair St, Ramat Hen, Isr. Office: 9 Ahad Haam, Tel Aviv, Isr.

STEINBERG, Zeev Wolfgang, Isr, musician, composer; b. Dus seldorf, Ger, Nov 27, 1918; s. Paul and Margarete (Hirschland); in Isr since 1934; att HS, Trier Mosel, Ger, 1927-34; m. Chava Weil, Feb 17, 1938; c: Naomi Barzely, Amnon. Mem, Isr Philharmonic Orch, since 1942, leader viola sect, since 1968; mem, The New Isr String Quartet; agric laborer: Kibbutz Ein Harod, 1934-36; Moshav Beer Tuvia, 1936-37; taxidriver,Tel Aviv, 1937-42. Composer: Seven 2-part pieces for harpsichord, 1949; Sonata for 2 violas, 1955; Canonic Pieces for string-quartet or orch, 1959; 6 Miniatures for violoncello and piano, 1962; Concerto da camera for viola and strings, 1962; Concerto da camera No 2 for violin and 8 instruments, 1964; Praeambulum, Fughetta and Tocatta for organ, 1967-68; The Story of Rahab and the Spies, for 3 speakers, contralto, 2 recorder-flutes, violoncello, harpsichord, 1968-69. Home: 13 Golomb St, Kiryat Ono, Isr.

STEINBERGER, Itzhak Tibor, Isr, physicist, b. Miskolc, Hung, Mar 13, 1928; s. Moshe and Frida (Guttmann); in Isr since 1946; MSc, Heb U, Jerusalem, 1952, PhD, 1957; m. Eva György, Dec 18, 1951; c: Jonathan, Meshulam. Asso prof, Heb U, dept physics, since 1968, mem fac, since 1953; visiting asso prof, U of S Cal, 1966-68. IDF, 1948-49. Mem: Isr, Amer, Eur, Phys Socs; Isr Crystallographic Soc. Contbr to sci jours. Home: 351 Neve Granot, Jerusalem, Isr. Office: Heb U, Physics Dept, Jerusalem, Isr.

STEINBRINK, Stuart H, US, attorney; b. Bklyn, NY, Feb 5, 1908; s. Meier and Sadie (Bloch); BA, Princeton U,1927; LLB, Columbia U, 1930; m. Carolyn Strauss, June 18, 1933 (decd); c: Richard, Barbara Levine; m. 2nd, Therese Obermeier Kamins, June 24, 1962. Vice-pres and gen counsel, Universal Amer Corp; asso, Mudge, Stern, Williams & Tucker, 1930-43; mem, law firm: Levien & Singer, 1951-59; Levien, Steinbrink & Beaudet, 1960-61; asst secy, Kings Co Lighting Co, 1953-57; fmr asso govt appeal agent, Selective Service Sys; mem, Alien Enemy Hearing Bd, WW II. Dir, Comty Council of Gtr NY, chmn, Contbrs Info Bur fmr dir: Bklyn Child Guidance Cen; and secy, Bklyn Bur; of Comty Service; fmr chmn: personnel practices, Bklyn Heb Orphan Asylum; Soc Service Exch Comm, Wfr Council of NY; fmr vice-chmn, borough, FJP, NY; fmr vice-pres, J Youth Services, Bklyn; trustee, Cong Beth Elohim, fmr chmn, rel sch comm; mem: Bklyn, NY State and Fed Bar Assns; NY Co Lawyers Assn; Phi Beta Kappa; Cum Laude Soc; club, Princeton, NY. Home: 77 Park Ave, New York, NY. Office: 200 Park Ave, New York NY.

STEINBROCKER, Otto, US, physician, educator; b. Aus, July 17, 1898; s. Harry and Eva (Warburg); in US since 1899; BS, NYU, 1925, MD, 1927; m. Elizabeth Braverman, May 17, 1929; c: Ann, Dan. Cons phys, Hosp for Jt Diseases, since 1963; att phys, chief, arthritis clinic, Lenox Hill Hosp, since 1951. F, Intl Coll Anesthesia; pres; Amer Rheumatism Assn, 1950-51; NY Rheumatism Assn, 1946-47; mem: local, state, natl med socs; Acad Med; AAAS; Arthritis and Rheumatism Found; Alpha Omega Alpha; hon, Rheumatism Assns of Arg & India; Ligue Internationale Contre le Rheumatisme. Author: Arthritis in Modern Practice, 1941; contbr to med jours. Home: 208 E 72 St, New York, NY. Office: 121 E 60 St, New York, NY.

STEINCROHN, Peter J, US, physician, author; b. Hartford, Conn, Nov 28, 1899; s. Myer and Pearl (Brownstein); att, NYU, 1917-19; MD, U of Md, 1923; m. Patti Chapin, Feb 8, 1936; c: Barbara Davis. Med syndicated columnist: McNaught Syndicate, NYC; fmr, Bell Syndicate, from 1955; moderator, med TV prog, WTHS TV, Miami, Fla; cons, internal med: Mt Sinai Hosp, Hartford, Conn, att phys, 1927-52, chief of staff, 1940; McCook Memorial Hosp, att phys, 1928-52. US Army, WW I. F: Amer Coll Phys; AMA; vice-pres: Conn State Med Soc, 1940; Hartford Heart Assn, 1950; co-chmn: med adv bd, Co Rehab Soc, Hartford; publicity comm, Gtr Miami Heart Assn, 1959; mem, bd dirs: Hartford Co Med Soc, 1941; Hartford Cancer Soc, 1945; mem: adv bd, Visiting Nurses Assn, since 1951; hon comm, Muscular Dystrophy Assn, 1953; Temple Beth Isr; club, Phys Masonic. Author: More Years for the Asking, 1940; You Don't Have to Exercise, 1941; Heart Disease is Curable, 1942; Forget Your Age, 1943; What to do for Angina Pectoris and Coronary Occlusion, 1945; What to do for High Blood Pressure, 1946; You and Your Fears, 1947; Heart Worry and its Cure, 1948; How to Stop Killing Yourself, 1949, rev, 1962; The Doctor Looks at Life, 1952; You Can Increase Your Heart Power, 1958; Mr. Executive: Keep Well—Live Longer, 1960; Your Life to Enjoy, 1963; Common Sense Coronary Care and Prevention, 1964; You Live as You Breathe, 1965; How to Get a Good Night's Sleep, 1966; How to Be Lazy, Healthy and Fit, 1968; contbr to periodicals and med jours. Hobbies: music, sports. Home and office: 1430 Ancona Ave, Coral Gables, Fla.

STEINDLER, Adolfo, It, educator; b. Camenari, Dalmatia, May 28, 1918; s. Umberto and Laura (Mopurgo); DMath, U Rome, 1940; m. Giuliana Megrelli, Oct 27, 1962. Schoolmaster, secondary sch, since 1965, tchr, since 1945; prof of math, U Trieste, 1950-53. Lt, It Army. Pres, Trieste br, mem natl council, Natl Union Secondary Schs; fmr, pres, Associazioni tra Laureati dell'Università di Trieste. Contbr to sci jours. Home: Via E De Amicis 31, Trieste, It.

STEINER, Alfred, US, physician, educator; b. Richmond, Va, July 1, 1910; s. Samuel and Estelle (Jacobs); BS, U Richmond, 1930; MD, Med Coll, Va, 1933; DMS, Columbia U, 1938; m. Margaret Allen, July, 1944; c: Joseph, Julie, Betsy. Pvt practice, card and internal med, since 1938; asso prof, clinical med, Coll of Phys and Surgs, Columbia U, NY, since 1958; att phys med, Columbia research service, Goldwater Memorial Hosp, NYC, since 1939; Mem: AMA; Med Soc Co NY; council on arteriosclerosis, AHA; Amer Fed for Clinical Research. Contbr to med jours. Recipient: Dist Alumnus award, Phi Alpha frat; A Walter Suiter Memorial Lectureship, NY State Med Soc. Home: 544 E 86 St, New York, NY. Office: 630 Park Ave, New York, NY.

STEINER, Harry, US, attorney; b. Newark, NJ, Nov 28, 1897; s. Joseph and Lena (Melnick); BA, Columbia U, 1918, LLB, 1920; att Harvard U, 1919; m. Helen Garlin, Oct 27, 1926; c: Susan Satz, James. Pvt practice, since 1920; mem, Schapira, Steiner & Walder, since 1965; asst gen counsel, War Produc Bd, 1945; Civilian Produc Admn, 1945-47. USN, WW I. Natl exec comm, AJComm, since 1955, chmn, Essex Co, 1952-54; chmn: UJA, 1942, 1952; Hum Relations Council, 1950, both Orange, NJ; pres, Zeta Beta Tau Found, 1952-62; vice-pres, NJ Mh Assn, 1957-62; vice-chmn, Essex Co Intergroup Council, 1952-54; publs comm, Commentary, since 1959; comty relations comm, JCC, Essex Co, since 1951, trustee 1955-60; adv bd, NJ commn for law and social action, AJCong, since 1951; mem, NJ Planning Bd, since 1965; club, E Orange Golf. Home: 241 Heywood Ave, Orange, NJ. Office: 17 Academy St, Newark, NJ.

STEINER, Joe Paul, US, business exec; b. Chgo, Ill, June 14, 1916; s. Lewis and Mabel (Quitman); m. Sylvia Siegel, June 13, 1940; c: Judith, Maureen, Raymond. Gen agt, Guaranty Income Life Ins Co; repr, furniture and rug mfrs, 1938-40; US Govt service, 1944-46. Pres, La state, B'nai B'rith, 1950, 1954, pres, bd dirs, 1950-51; chmn, civic affairs, C of C; treas, mem bd, Temple B'nai Isr; mem, bd of finance, Comty Chest, 1953-54; mem, bd dirs: Gen Agents and Mgmt Conf, Sales Mgmt and Execs, Baton Rouge; N Baton Rouge Merchants Assn, 1950; mem: Baton Rouge Life Underwriters Assn; Million Dollar Round Table, 1969, 1970; clubs: pres: Young Men's Bus, 1951, La State, 1960; Temple B'nai Isr Men's, 1959; mem, Kiwanis. Recipient: B'nai B'rith Service award, 20 years, 1938-58; Outstanding B'nai B'rith for La award, 1961; Outstanding Citizen award, N Baton Rouge Merchants Assn; Outstanding Mem, La Young Men's Bus Club, 1958, 1960. Home: 4900 Claycut Rd, Baton Rouge, La. Office: 1986 Dallas Dr, Baton Rouge, La.

STEINER, Lee R, US, psychologist, lecturer; b. Superior, Wis, Nov 18, 1901; d. Harry and Sarah (Skolnick) Rabinowitz; BA, U Minn, 1924; MS, Smith Coll, 1929; training: clinical psych, with Andew Brown, 1932-34; psychan, with Alfred Adler and Douglas Campbell, 1932-34; m. Alfred Steiner, 1935 (decd); m. 2nd, Samuel Melitzer, Apr 22, 1949; Psychol, pvt practice, since 1932; lectr, since 1932; with radio sta WEVD since 1948; psychiatric social worker: inst for child guidance, Commonwealth Fund Teaching Cen, 1928-29; Inst for Juvenile Research, 1929-31; lectr: radio sta, WGN, Chgo, 1934; Ill Soc for Mental Hygiene, 1934-35; radi sta WINS, NY, 1938; CBS networks, 1953; instr: U Chgo, 1931-32; Fordham U, NY, 19ᵗˢ-36; Rand Sch of Social Sci, 1939-40; Rutgers U, 1940-44, Hunter Coll, 1944-48; Atlanta U, 1944; William and Mary Coll, 1945; Queens Coll, 1948-49. Pres, and found, Acad of Psychols in Marital Counseling; mem: Amer, Inter-Amer, E and NY State Psych Assns; AAUP; Natl Conf on Family Relations. Author: Where Do People Take Their Troubles, 1945; A Practical Guide for Troubled People, 1952; Make the Most of Yourself, 1954; Understanding Juvenile Delinquency, 1960; Romantic Marriage—The Twentieth Century Illusion, 1963; scripts for radio and TV; contbr to profsl jours. Office: 45 W 81 St, New York, NY.

STEINER, Melvin D, US, physician, eduator; b. Columbus, Tex, Mar 15, 1911; s. Abe and Ruth (Wampold); BS, Tulane, U, 1934; MD, 1936; m. Jane Blumenthal, Apr 16, 1940; c: Carol, Sidney, Jerome. Pvt practice, since 1939; asst clinical prof, obstet, gyn, Tulane Med Sch, since 1947; sr visiting surg, New Orleans Charity Hosp, since 1955; chief, obstet, gyn, Flint-Goodrich Hosp, since 1967; courtesy staff, Saro Mayo Hosp, since 1955; chief, gyn, Touro Infirmary, 1960-65, sr gyn, since 1952. Dipl, Amer Bd of Obstet and Gyn; f: Amer Coll Obstet and Gyn; Amer Coll Surgs; mem: AMA; La State Med Soc; Orleans Parish Med Soc; New Orleans Obstet and Gyn Soc, vice-pres, 1958-60; Temple Sinai; Zeta Beta Tau; Phi Delta Epsilon. Home: 1 Dunlieth Ct, New Orleans, La. Office: 209 Med Arts Bldg, 3439 Prytania St, New Orleans, La.

STEINER, Philip G, US, business exec; b. Baltimore, Md, Apr 20, 1901; s. Sigmund and Emma (Lowenbach); BA, U Mich, 1923; m. Desiree Harris, Jan 20, 1934; c: Philip, Richard. Pres, Tom Collins Jr Co, since 1927; vice-pres: Par Beverage Corp, since 1938; Kenner Products Co, since 1948; all Cincinnati. Mem, exec comm, Jt Defense Appeal, since 1956; AJComm, since 1957, chmn, Cincinnati chap, 1957-59, treas, 1950-52; mem, bd: JDC; HIAS; Natl Syn Council, since 1956; J Comty Relations Comm; J Comty Cen; J Vocational Service; Mayor's Friendly Relations Comm; NCCJ, since 1953; JWF, pres, 1955, 1960-62, chmn bd, 1956; Sheltering Oaks Hosp, pres since 1959; trustee, J Hosp, since 1955; chmn: Residential Comty Chest Campaign, 1956; Thrift Shop, 1952; Libson F Cancer Research, 1953, all Cincinnati; hon life mem, Amer Contract Bridge League, vice-pres, chmn exec comm 1934-35, winner, natl championships, 1935, 1938; mem: B'nai B'rith; Wise Temple; club, Losantiville Country, pres, 1954-56. Recipient: Herbert H Lehman award, State of Isr Bonds, 1967; Guardian of Menorah award, B'nai B'rith, 1968. Hobby: Contract bridge. Home: 4044 Rose Hill Ave, Cincinnati, O. Office: 912 Sycamore St, Cincinnati, O.

STEINFELD, Samuel S, US, legislator; b. Louisville, Ky, Feb 15, 1906; s. Emile and Florence (Simons); LLB, U Louisville, 1928; m. Flora Loebenberg, July 24, 1929; c: Helane Grossman, James. Justice, Court of Appeals of Ky, since 1967; atty, 1928-66, partner, Steinfeld & Steinfeld, 1934-66; dir: Llewellyn Laundries Inc and subsidiaries, since 1940; Jos T Griffin Co, since 1955; and secy, Modern Loan Co and subsidiaries, since 1947; and pres, Lorenza Realty Co, since 1950; Louisville Taxicab Co, since 1966; co atty, Jefferson Co, Ky, 1946-49; dir and secy: S Cab Corp, 1962-67; S Tank Lines, 1966-67. Dir: J Comty Cen, since 1953, pres, 1958-60; Fire Prevention Bur of Louisville, since 1956; chmn: Ky Judicial Conf, since 1968; election comm, Jefferson Co, 1954-65; Rep Co exec comm, 1939-66, alternate delg, Rep Natl Convs, 1940, 1956; mayor's citizen's adv comm, 1962-66; leg adv comm, 1949-60; mem: bd govs, midwest sect, JWB, 1959-60; bd trustees, Adath Isr Cong; Amer Bar Assn; Amer Judicature Soc; Louisville Bar Assn; Ky State Bar Assn; Commercial Law League of Amer; Ky Hist Soc; clubs: Young Men'sRep, Ky, fmr pres; Lincoln of Ky; L, U of Louisville. Chmn, prin draftsman, Rules of Practice of Jefferson Circuit Courts, pub, 1953. Recipient: Dist Law Alumni award, U Louisville, 1966. Spec interests: politics, civic activities. Home: 3512 St Germaine Ct, Louisville, Ky. Office: State Capitol Bldg, Frankfort, Ky.

STEINHORN, Elihu Jacob, US, rabbi; b. NYC, July 29, 1937; s. Louis and Leah (Freeman); BA, BRE, MHL, MS, Yeshiva U; m. Deborah Birnbaum, Jan 27, 1958; c: Tova, Darona, Nechama, Aleeza. Rabbi, BMH Cong, Denver, Colo, since 1967; asso prof, U of Cal, 1962-63; headmaster, N Shore Heb Acad, 1964-66; exec dir, Yavneh, Rel Students Assn, 1966. Chaplain, USAF. Dean, Denver Adult Inst J Studies; mem: RabCA; NEA. Author: In the Campus Climate, 1967. Home: 765 York St, Denver Colo. Study: 560 Monaco Pkwy, Denver, Colo.

STEINITZ, Franz S, US, physician; b. Beuthen, Ger, June 22, 1910; s. Hugo and Gertrud (Friedländer); in US since 1937; MD, U Munich, 1934; m. Jeanne Sonnenschein, Dec 15, 1946; c: Gail, Hugo, Paul. Att phys, Edgewater Hosp, Chgo, since 1939, chmn, dept gen practice, 1962; pres med staff, 1966; mem, med staff, Michael Reese Hosp, Chgo, since 1939, research f, cardio-vascular diseases, 1939-42. Capt, US Army MC, 1943-45. Pres: Edgewater Regional Chap, Ill Acad of Gen Practice, 1968-69, chmn, comm on ins, 1954; Temple Ezra, 1949-50, 1961-63; chmn: Commn on Intl Affairs, Amer Acad of Gen Practice, 1969; Chgo group, Amer J KC Frat, since 1950; United HIAS Service, Chgo, since 1950; mem: AMA; AHA; Isr Med Assn. Contbr to sci publs. Recipient: Citation for Bravery, WW II, 1944; Bronze Star medal, 1945. Home: 730 Sheridan Rd, Evanston, Ill. Offices: 30 N Michigan Ave, Chicago, Ill; 3653 W Lawrence Ave, Chgo, Ill.

STEINITZ, Hans J, US, editor; b. Berlin, Ger, Mar 9, 1912; s. Ludwig and Erna (Rothenberg); in US since 1947; att Us: Berlin; Heidelberg; Basel, D Political Sci and Law, m. Lore Oppenheimer, May 15, 1948; c: Lucy. Ed, Aufbau, newspaper, since 1966; asso ed, 1964-65; US corresp for Swiss and Ger press, 1947-64. Fr Army, 1939-40; pres, Fgn Press Assn, 1959-62, life mem; mem: PEN Intl; Intl Assn of Ger Writers Abroad; club, Rotary, NY. Author: Regierungs und Verfassungsformen des Auslandes, 1948; Der Siebte Kontinent; Ringen um die antarktische Eiswelt, 1958; Mississippi, Geschichte eines Stromes, 1967; contbr to press; public lectrs: radio and TV. Hobby, mountain climbing. Home: 65 Park Terrace W, New York, NY. Office: 2121 Broadway, New York, NY.

STEINITZ, Herman, Isr, physician; b. Ger, Oct 17, 1900; s. Hans and Gertrud (Appel); in Isr since 1933; att Us: Berlin; Freiburg; Breslau; MD, 1923; c: Hannah Rosen. Pvt practice, since 1933; cons in gastroenterology, Gen Workers' Sick Fund, Tel Aviv, since 1936; asst J Hosp, Berlin, 1925-28; third asst, Munic Hosp, Hufeland, Berlin, 1928-33. Contbr to med jours. Hobby: music. Home and office: 26 Ben Zion Blvd, Tel Aviv, Isr.

STEINKOPF, Maitland B, Can, attorney, legislator; b. Winnipeg Can, Sep 10, 1912; s. Max and Hedwig (Mayer); LLB, U Man, 1936; m. Helen Katz, Apr 4, 1947; c: Marilyn, Justine, Alison, Max, Jocelyn, Winifred. Min of Public Utilities and Provincial Secy, Man; QC, since 1961; pres: J Leckie Co, Ltd; R S Robinson's Sons; L H Packard & Co; Dayton Shoe Mfg Co; Can W Shoe Mfg Co; Polo Park Centre; dir: Monarch Life Assurance Co; Isr Hotels Intl; Czech Consul, W Can, 1937-48. Queen's Own Cameron Highlanders, 1940; lt col, Royal Can Ordance Corps, 1945. Chmn, Man March of Dimes campaign, 1962; gen chmn State of Isr Bonds, 1961-62; pres, Man Travel and Convention Assn, 1959-60; mem, bd trustees: Winnipeg Gen Hosp; U of Man Found; mem: Man and Can Bar Assns; Sigma Alpha Mu; Masons; C of C, Winnipeg; Gen Monash Legion; clubs: Glendale, Elmhurst; Rotary; Motor Country. Recipient: MBE, 1944. Hobby: golf. Home: 203 Oxford St, Winnipeg, Can. Office: 806 Somerset Bldg, 294 Portage Ave, Winnipeg, Can.

STEMATSKY, Avigdor, Isr, artist; b. Odessa, Russ, 1908; s. Zvi and Sara (Hoffman) Steimatsky; in Isr since 1920; att: Bezalel Art Sch, Jerusalem; acads, Paris, 1930-32; Tchr: Avni Inst of Art, Tel Aviv; pvt. Exhb, biennales: Venice, 1948, 1956; Menton, 1951; Sao Paulo, 1955; group exhbs: Mus of Modern Art, Paris, 1960; Gal Charpentier, 1963; NY Mus of Modern Art, 1964; Eng; Can; S Amer; Japan; Rum; and others; one man shows: Isr Mus; gals: Paris, Holland, Swed. Served IDF. Co-found, New Horizons Group. Recipient: Dizengoff Prize, Tel Aviv Munic, 1941, 1956; Milo Prize, Tel Aviv Artists, 1966; 1st prize, selected Isr artists exhb, Jerusalem, 1967. Home: 22 Bnei Dan St, Tel Aviv, Isr.

STEMATSKY, Tamar, Isr, virologist; b. Isr, d. Yaacov and Miriam (Simma) Gottlieb; MSc, Heb U, Jerusalem, 1946, PhD, 1953; m. Avigdor Stematsky; c: Noa. Sr lectr, virology, Tel Aviv U, since 1963; dep i/c, Virus Epidemiological Lab, Tel Aviv-Jaffa Min of Health, since 1968; guest sci: Children's Hosp, U of Phila, 1951; Public Health Research Inst, NYC, 1952-55; Cancer Research Inst, Paris, 1960; Natl Inst Med Research, London, 1966. Lt, IDF, War of Independence. Contbr to med and virological jours. Recipient: Surasky Prize, Heb U Med Sch, 1957; Home: 22 Bnei Dan St, Tel Aviv, Isr. Offices: Tel Aviv, U, Ramat Aviv, Isr; Virus Epidemiological Laboratories, Tel Aviv-Jaffa, Isr.

STEN, Ephraim Frederic, Isr, stage, radio dir; b. Zloczow, Pol, Feb 20, 1928; s. Adolf and Anna (Mann) Sternschuss; in Isr since 1957; att Politechnion, Gliwice, Pol, 1946-48; Art of Theater, Warsaw, 1948-53; m. Tamar Kaplan, Dec 19, 1962; c: Hagith, Oded. Chief drama produc, Isr Bc Auth, since 1963; stage dir, Modern Theater, Zabne, 1948-53; ed, dir, Pol Radio, Katowice, 1951-53; artistic mgr, dir, Estrada Theater, Gdansk, 1953-57. Served IDF. Mem, ACUM. Contbr: satire, Szpilki, weekly, 1950-57; short stories, Isr press, 1957-60. Hobby: documentary radio programs, writing. Home: 39 Beeri St, Tel Aviv, Isr. Office: Isr Bc Auth, Hakirya, Tel Aviv, Isr.

STENGEL, Erwin, Eng, physician; b. Vienna, Aus, Mar 25, 1902; s. Abraham and Franziska (Popper); MD, U Vienna, 1926; LRCP, MRCS, Us: Bristol, Edinburgh, 1942; m. Anna Kohl, 1935. Em prof, psycht, U Sheffield, Eng, since 1967, prof, 1956-67; fmr dozent, neur, psycht, U Vienna, Aus; reader, psycht U London, 1950-56. Pres: Intl Assn for Suicide Prevention; Royal Medico-Psych Assn, 1966-67; hon mem: Brit Psych Soc; Deutsche Gesellschaft für Psychiatrie und Nervenheilkunde. Author: Suicide and Attempted Suicide, 1964, 1969; co-author, Attempted Suicide, 1958. Home: 7 Montrose Ct, Hull Turrets Close, Sheffield, Eng.

STERLING, Julian A, US, surgeon, educator; b. Phila, Pa, Jan 30, 1913; s. Alexander and Elsie (Walkowitz); BA, U of Pa, 1932, MD, 1936, MS, 1937, DSc, 1951; m. Madeline Shaffer, 1942; c: Elsie, Ralph. Sr att surg, Albert Einstein Med Cen, since 1956; asst prof, Temple U Sch of Med, since 1958; instr em, U of Pa Sch of Med, since 1955, asst prof surg, Grad Sch Med, since 1956. US Army, 1941-46. F: AAAS; Amer Coll Surgs; Intl Coll Surgs; Amer Coll Gastroenterology; Amer Med Writers Assn; AMA; Phila Coll Phys; Phila Acad Surg; mem: Amer, Pa, Phila Med Assn. Author: Biliary Tract, 1955; Guide to Surgical Management, 1959; Experience with Biliary Atresia, 1959; The Acute Abdomen, 1967; contbr: chap in Traumatic Med and Surg for the Atty, 1962; to med jours; ed in chief, Jour, Albert Einstein Med Cen, since 1958; asso ed em, Amer Jour Gastroenterology. Home: 610 Wyncote House, Wyncote, Pa. Office: 1351 W Tabor Rd, Philadelphia, Pa.

STERLING, Theodor David, US, educator, author; b. Vienna, Aus, July 3, 1923; s. William and Sarah (Schwarzman); in US since 1940; BA, MA, U Chgo; PhD, Tulane U, New Orleans; m. Nora Moskalik, June 20, 1948; c: Elia, David, Elsie. Prof, dept computer sci, Washington U, St Louis, Mo; pres, MEDCOMP Research Corp; prof, dir, computing cen, Coll of Med, U Cincinnati, 1958-66. US Army, 1942-46. Author: Computers and the Life Sciences, 1965; Introduction to Statistical Data Processing, 1968; A Guide to PL/I, 1969; Computing and Computer Science, 1970; ed: Computation in Radiology, 1971; Proc, 2nd Conf on Visual Prosthesis, 1971. Home: 7220 Greenway, St Louis, Mo. Office: Dept of Applied Math and Computer Sci, Wash U, St Louis, Mo.

STERMAN, Max M, US, physician, educator; b. Lith, Feb 6, 1896; s. Moses and Hannah (Much); in US since 1906; MD, Coll Phys and Surgs, Columbia U, 1919; att Sch of Public

Health and Admn Med, 1947; f: Parasitology and Tropical Med, Cen Amer, 1956; Leprosy Sem, USPHS Hosp, Carville, La, 1965; m. Lillian Sage, May 17, 1931; c: Miriam, Sara Shapira. Public health phys, epidemology, phys i/c tropical disease, diagnostic service, Wash Hgts Health Cen, NYC, Dept of Health, 1947-67; diagnostician, 1943-47, health referral service, 1967, asso phys, tropical med, parasitology, Knickerbocker and Elmhurst Gen Hosps, since 1955; asst clinical prof, Flower and Fifth Ave Hosps, NY Med Coll, since 1944; instr, tropical diseases, Coll Phys and Surgs, Columbia U, since 1951; asst att phys: City Hosp, Wfr I since 1942; Mt Sinai Hosp, 1922-26; Beth David Hosp, 1927-30; Vanderbilt Clinic, 1927-29; Beth Isr Hosp, 1930-40. US Army Res, 1919. Trustee, Cong Ohab Zedek, since 1953; mem: NY Co, State Med Socs; AMA; Amer Public Health Assn; Amer Soc Tropical Med and Hygiene; NY Soc Tropical Med; KP. Co-author: Animal Parasites in Man, 1961; contbr to med jours. Spec interests: Heb bibliography and abbreviations, chess. Home: 220 W 93 St, New York, NY. Office: 272 W 90 St, New York, NY.

STERN, Abraham A, US, educator, social worker; b. NYC, Dec 27, 1927; tchr dipl, Yeshiva U, 1947, BA, 1948, MS, 1950; PhD, NYU, 1964; att: NY Sch of Social Work; Columbia U; m. Marjorie Harris, Dec 24, 1954; c: Rebecca, Deborah, Judith, Sharon, Faith. Dir, found, youth bur, Yeshiva U, since 1954, instr, Tchr's Inst, since 1951; asst dir, youth dept, Natl Council Young Isr, 1949-51; cons, youth: Union of Orthodox J Cong, 1951-53, Cong Shearith Isr, 1961; dir Mizrachi Youth of Amer, 1952-54; staff, YMHA, Bx, Williamsburg, 1960. Chmn, educ comm, Monsey Comty Syn, 1960-61; mem: mayor's comm, rel leaders, NYC Youth Bd; Mizrachi Youth Commn, 1952-54; Natl Assn J Cen Workers; Social Work Alumni, Yeshiva U. Author: You and Your Group, 1957; Youth Ideas, 1958; Supervisory Concepts and Practices, in Public and Voluntary Social GroupWork Organizations; ed youth sect, P'rakim, 1950-53; contbr to J Jours. Recipient: service cert, Yeshiva U, 1961; Founders Day award, NYU, 1965. Office: Yeshiva U, Amsterdam Ave and 186 St, New York, NY.

STERN, Adolph, US, attorney; b. NYC, July 28, 1882; s. Max and Rae (Glick); LLB, NYU, 1903; m. Blanche Moshkovitz, Aug 11, 1915; Pvt practice, since 1903; mem, NY State Assembly, 1907-14; asst corp counsel, NYC, 1914-20; city magistrate, 1927-37. Grand secy, B'rith Abraham, since 1950, grand master, 1924-26; chmn, bd of dirs, Eighth St Day Nursery; mem, bd of dirs: United HIAS Service; J Convalescent Home; admn comm, AJCong; adv comm, JWB; mem: Masons; KP; Odd Fellows; Sanders Assn; Boy Scouts. Home: 446 E 20 St, New York, NY.

STERN, Alexander W, US, physicist, engineer; b. NYC, Nov 30, 1898; s. William and Kate (Lewin); CE, Cooper Union, 1921; att CCNY, 1921-22; participated, symposia on theoretical physics, U Mich, 1931-33; m. Bertha Gendel, June 29, 1924; c: Kathryn Braunstein. Ret; CE, Bur of Highway Design, Bklyn, NY, 1924-62; guest lectr, U Ia, 1953; mem, Inst Theoretical Phys, U Copenhagen, Den, 1955-56, 1963-64. F, AAAS; mem: Sigma Xi; Amer Phys Soc; NY Acad of Scis. Author: The Role of Mathematics in Physical Theory, 1928; Cosmic Radiation, 1932; Trend of Modern Physics, 1933; Nuclear Showers, 1946; A Trend in Contemporary Physics, 1949; Space, Field and Ether, 1952; Concepts of Modern Physics, 1953; Physics of Atomic Energy, 1955; The Idea of Complementarity in Psychology, 1956; Quantum Physics and Biological Systems, 1964; The Third Revolution in 20th Century Physics, 1964; contbr to sci jours. Home: 101 California Ave, Santa Monica, Cal.

STERN, Alfred, US, educator, author; b. Baden, Aus, July 18, 1899; s. Julius and Rose (Kohn); in US since 1944; PhD with distinction, U Vienna, 1923; m. Gloria Pagán y Ferrer, Nov 15, 1946. Prof phil, Universidad de Puerto Rico, Mayagüez, since 1968; prof em, Cal Inst of Tech, Pasadena, since 1968, prof, 1947-68; Inst de Hautes Etudes de Belgique, Brussels, 1936-40; Ecole Libre des Hautes Etudes, NY, 1945-46; lectr: Sorbonne, Paris, 1934-39; U of S Cal, LA, 1946-60; visiting prof: Universidad Nacional de Mexico, 1942; Universidad de Buenos Aires, 1959. Lt, Aus Army, WW I; volunteer, Fr Army, WW II. Mem: Amer Phil Assn, pres, 1964-65; Alliance Française; Société Européenne de Culture, Venice, It. Author: Die Philosophischen Grundlagen von Wahrheit, Wirklichkeit, Wert, 1932; Philosophie des Valeurs, 1936; Filosofia de la Politica, 1943; Philosophie du Rire et des Pleurs, 1949; Sartre—His Philosophy and Psychoanalysis, 1951, 1967; Philosophy of

History and the Problem of Values, 1962; books publ in Eur, Latin Amer, US, Japan; contbr to: Ency Americana, scholarly jours. Recipient: Academic Palms, Officier d'Academie, Fr, 1950; Knight of Legion of Honor, Fr, 1954. Home: Luna 270, San Juan, Puerto Rico. Office: Departamento de Humanidades, Universidad de Puerto Rico, Mayagüez, Puerto Rico.

STERN, Arthur, Isr, physician; b. Pol, June 20, 1879; s. Joseph and Hulda (Boehm); att Us Freiburg, Berlin, Munich, 1898-1903, MD, 1903; m. Else Wertheim, 1919; c: Hanna, Liesel. Pvt practice; neur cons, Bikur Holim Hosp, Jerusalem; dir, Givat Shaul Asylum. Staff dr, Ger Army, 1914-18. Author: In Bewegten Zeit, 1968; Die Genetische Tragödie der Familie Theodor Herzl, 1965; contbr to jours. Recipient: Gold Medal, U Freiburg, Ger. Spec interest: genet. Home: 8 Bezalel St, Jerusalem, Isr.

STERN, Arthur C, US, engineer; b. Petersburg, Va, Mar 14, 1909; s. Harry and Marie (Rosenstock); ME, Stevens Inst of Tech, NJ, 1930, MS, 1933; m. Dorothy Anspacher, Jan 16, 1938; c: Richard, Elizabeth, Robert. Prof, air hygiene, Sch Public Health, U of NC, since 1968; dir, NYC air pollution survey, 1935-38; chief, engr unit, div ind hygiene, NY State Dept of Lab, 1942-54; chief, lab, engr and phys scis, div air pollution, USPHS, Robert A Taft Sanitary Engr Cen, Cincinnati, 1955-62; dir, Natl Cen for Air Pollution Control, 1962-68. Dipl: Amer Sanitary Engrs; Amer Bd of Ind Hygiene; chmn, sectional comm on ind ventilation, US Standards Inst; mem: comm on air pollution controls, Amer Soc Mech Engrs; air pollution comm, Amer Ind Hygiene Assn; ed, internal relations comm, Air Pollution Control Assn; Pi Lambda Phi; cons, profsl examination service, Amer Public Health Assn. Ed: Air Pollution, 3 vols, 1968. Home: Castillian Villa E7, Chapel Hill, NC. Office: POBox 630, Chapel Hill, NC.

STERN, Bernard H, US, educator; b. NYC, Dec 17, 1911; s. Samuel and Anna (Cone); BA, Bklyn Coll, 1932; MA, Columbia U, 1934; PhD, NYU, 1940; cert, Japanese studies, U Colo, 1943; m. Lisbeth Sachs. Prof, Eng, asso dir, Sch of Gen Studies, Bklyn Coll since 1958, dean of summer session and spec baccalaureate degree prog for adults, since 1968, on fac since 1933. USN, 1942-47. Mem: AAUP; MLA; Union Temple, Bklyn; Bklyn Coll Alumni Assn, vice-pres, 1950-58; Alpha Sigma Lambda, pres, 1945-58; Phi Beta Kappa; club, Andiron, NY. Author: Rise of Romantic Hellenism in English Literature, 1940; Reading for Pleasure, 1948; How Much Does Adult Experience Count? 1955; Adults Grow in Brooklyn, 1955; Adult Experience and College Degrees, 1960; Never Too Late for College, 1962; contbr to profsl jours. Recipient: USN unit commendation medal, 1945; grant, Ford Found, 1954-56. Home: 39 Plaza St, Brooklyn, NY. Office: Bklyn College, Brooklyn, NY.

STERN, Bernice F, US, communal worker; b. Seattle, Wash, July 25, 1916; d. Abe and Josephine (Gumbert) Friedman; att U Wash, 1933-35; m. Edward Stern, May 7, 1935; c: Edward, David. Hon natl vice-pres, Natl Council J Women, since 1965, vice-pres, 1952-65, chmn, W region, 1946-48; vice-chmn, Seattle chap, AJComm, since 1962; chmn, natl comm, Can-Amer Relations, 1949-53, pres, Seattle sect, 1942-45, mem since 1936; mem, bd dirs: Seattle Federated J Fund, 1944-53; Temple deHirsh Sisterhood, 1949-52; Amer Assn for UN, since 1959; Planned Parenthood, 1955-60; vice-pres: Mayor's Civil Unity Comm, since 1960; Seattle and Kings Co Health and Wfr Council, 1951-53; Braille transcriber, Seattle Social Cen for Blind, since 1936; instr, Braille to sighted women; mem: Kings Co Council, 1969; ARC; clubs: Grendale Golf; Wash Athletic. Home: 2709 W Galer, Seattle, Wash.

STERN, Bessie C, US, statistician; b. Hornell, NY, Feb 14, 1888; d. Leopold and Julia (Mehlinger); BA, Cornell U, 1909; MEd, Harvard U, 1921; att: Columbia U; Chgo U; Johns Hopkins U; Goucher Coll. Ret; stat, dir of finance, stat, educ measurements, Md State Dept Educ, 1921-48; tchr, Fr, Ger, Silver Creek HS, NY; examiner, comm on sch inquiry, NYC Bd of Estimates and Apportionment, 1911-1914, comm on educ, 1914-18; stat, div of planning and stat, US Shipping Bd; off mgr, Price & Price, Paterson, NJ; instr, stat, educ admn, Johns Hopkins U, 1928. Leader, bus, profsl unit, Baltimore League of Women Voters, 1949-64; treas, Leg Clearing House of Md, 1961-67; mem bd, Cen Scholarship Bur, since 1952, financial secy, 1955-60, life mem; hon mem, Md Libr Assn, mem, leg and planning comm, since 1950; mem: Amer Assn Sch Admnrs; NEA; Md State Tchrs Assn; Amer Educ Research Assn; Amer Stat Assn; Phi Beta Kappa.

Author: annual reports of Md State Dept Educ, 1921-47. Recipient: citation, Hood Coll, 1951. Hobbies: piano playing, cooking, identifying birds. Home: 4307 Springdale Ave, Baltimore, Md.

STERN, Charles, US, broker; b. Newark, NJ, Apr 25, 1910; s. Joseph and Fannie (Tenzer); BS, U of Pa, 1931; m. Irene Rush, Feb 16, 1937; Vicki Abrams, Judith. Partner, Stern Bros, since 1957; secy, Confection Cabinet Corp, 1947-57. Pres: J Comty Found; JCC, 1964-66, both Essex Co, NJ; vice-pres: United HIAS; J Counseling Service Agcy, 1963-64. Home: 627 Mountain Dr, S Orange, NJ. Office: 111 Broadway, New York, NY.

STERN, Edward A, US, educator; b. Detroit, Mich, Sep 19, 1930; s. Jack and Rose (Kravitz); BS, Cal Inst of Tech, 1951, PhD, 1955; m. Sylvia Sidell, Oct 30, 1955; c: Hilary, Sharon, Miriam. Prof, physics, U Wash, since 1966; research f, Cal Inst of Tech, 1955-57; asst prof, U of Md, 1957-60, asso prof, 1960-65, prof, 1965-66. F, Amer Phys Soc; co-found, Cong Bet Shalom, 1968; treas, Gtr Wash State Solid Physics Colloquia, 1959-63; chmn, J Comty Cen of Prince Georges Co, 1959-61; mem, Sigma Xi. Contbr to books and profsl jours. Recipient: NSF grad fs, 1952-55; Guggenheim Found award, 1963-64. Home: 9536 42 NE, Seattle, Wash. Office: U Wash, Seattle, Wash.

STERN, Edward F, US, business exec; attorney; b. Seattle, Wash, Aug 6, 1905; s. Leopold and Louise (Friend); LLB, U Mich, Ann Arbor, 1928; m. Bernice Friedman, May 7, 1935; c: Edward, David. Vice-pres, Amer Discount Corp, since 1937; law asso: Leopold M Stern, 1928-30; Eggeiman & Rosling, 1930-32; law partner, Stern & Stern, 1932-37. Mem: natl exec bd, AJComm, since 1959, chmn, Seattle chap, 1957-59; bd dirs, Fed J Fund of Seattle, since 1950; pres, Cong Temple DeHirsch, 1947-48; mem: Amer, Seattle, Wash State Bar Assns, treas, Seattle, 1934; Pi Tau Pi, natl pres, 1939-40; Kappa Nu; clubs: Wash Athletic; Glendale Golf and Country. Home: 2709 W Galer St, Seattle, Wash. Office: 222 Queen Anne Ave N, Seattle, Wash.

STERN, Ernest, US, government official; b. Frankfurt, Ger, Aug 25, 1933; s. Henry and Henny Stern; in US since 1947; BA, Queens Coll, 1955; MA, Flectcher Sch of Law and Dipl, Boston, Mass, 1957, PhD, 1964; m. Zina Gold, June 23, 1957. Asst admnr, prog and policy coord, Agcy for Intl Devl, since 1969, asst dir, India, 1965-67, dep dir, Pakistan, 1967-68; dep dir, Pearson Commn, World Bank, 1968-69. Mem: council, exec comm, Soc Intl Devl; Amer Econ Assn. Recipient: Hon award, Agcy Intl Devl, 1964; Meritorious award, W A Jump Memorial Found, 1964, 1967. Home: 3001 Veazey Terr, NW, Washington, DC. Office: Agcy for Intl Devl, State Dept, Washington, DC.

STERN, Friedel, Isr, artist; tchr, b. Leipzig, Ger; d. Feivel and Louise (Rosenfeld); in Isr since 1938; att Bezalel Art Sch, Jerusalem. Art tchr, Bezalel Sch, since 1964. Haganah; Brit Army, 1942-46. Mem, Assn of Graphic Deisigners. Author: In Short, Israel, 1958; illus several books; contbr to jours. Recipient: mentioned in dispatches; 2nd, 5th Prize, Intl Cartoon Exhb, Montreal, Can. Hobbies: travelling; radio and TV Panels. Home: 8 Yehoash St, Tel Aviv, Isr.

STERN, Gardner H, US, business exec; b. Chgo, Ill, Aug 3, 1904; s. Harry and Cora (Weinberg); BA, Yale U, 1926; m. Hanchen Strauss, Feb 12, 1927; c: Gardner, Harry, John, Jeffrey. Chmn, finance comm, Hillman's Inc, with firm, since 1926; dir: Chgo Title & Trust Co; Hillison & Etten Co. Cdr, USNR, 1942-45. Dir: AJComm, 1946; Jt Defense Appeal, 1947; Comty Fund, 1950, all Chgo; trustee: U Chgo; Chgo Educ TV Assn; mem: Chgo comm, United Negro Coll Fund; clubs: Standard; Lake Shore Country; Chgo; Commercial, Chgo; Mid-Day; Yale, Chgo; Tavern. Home: 1440 Lake Shore Dr, Chicago, Ill. Office: 28 W Washington St, Chicago, Ill.

STERN, Hans Chanan, Isr, engineer; b. Zwickau, Ger, Oct 22, 1924; s. Karl and Bertha (Gerson); in Isr since 1939; att Technion, Haifa, 1939-40; BSc, U London, 1944; m. Gila Baar, Oct 6, 1949; c: Dan, Dorit. Mgn dir: Isafos Engr Co Ltd, since 1961; Pernix Enthone, Isr, since 1968; owner, elec workshop, 1945-47; dir, Metal Finishing sect, Min of Ind and Commerce, 1949-59; ind cons, 1959-60. Sgt, Brit Army, 1942-44; maj, IDF, 1947-48; mem: exec, B'rith Hakoah 1909; transp comm, munic Ramat Gan; Inst of Metal Finishing, London; clubs, Lions Intl, Ramat Gan, pres,

1968-69; mem, control comm, Isr Automobile. Recipient: Brit: 1939-45 Star; Afr Star; Defense Medal; War Medal, 1939-45; 8th Army Clasp; Oak Leaf; Isr: Ot Haganah; Ot Komemiut; Ot Hitnadvut; Oy Sinai; Itur Lochamei haMedina. Hobbies: music, sports, photography, stamps. Home: 25 Hamaagal St, Ramat Gan, Isr. Office: 17 Hazanhanim St, Givataim, Isr.

STERN, Harry Joshua, Can, rabbi, author; b. Lith, Apr 24, 1897; s. Morris and Hinda (Markson); BHL, HUC, 1919, ordained rabbi, 1922; BA, U Cincinnati, 1920; att U Chgo, 1926; hon LLD, McGill U, 1938; hon DD, HUC, 1947; m. Sylvia Goldstein, July 4, 1937; c: Stephanie Glaymon, Justine Bloomfield. Rabbi: Temple Emanu-El, Montreal Can, since 1927; Temple Isr, Uniontown, Pa, 1922-27. Overseer, HUC-JIR; secy, first WJC, Genera, Switz, 1936; mem: Can Penal Assn; CCAR; UAHC; Bible Soc Can; ZOC; Royal Empire Soc; Amer Acad Political and Social Sci; B'nai B'rith; Masons; Pi Lambda Phi; clubs: Kiwanis; Canadian. Author: Jew and Christian, 1927; Judaism and the War of Ideas, 1934; The Jewish Spirit Triumphant, 1943; Martyrdom and Miracle, 1950; My Pilgrimage to Israel, 1951; Entrusted With Spiritual Leadership, 1962. Recipient: Coronation medal, King George VI, Gt Brit, 1937; B'nai B'rith Hum award, 1967. Home: 3238 The Boulevard, Westmount, Que, Can. Study: 4100 Sherbrooke St W, Westmount, Que, Can.

STERN, Henry B, US, social worker; b. New Haven, Conn, Dec 6, 1926; s. Emanuel and Sophie (Brown); BS, CCNY; MSW, Wash U, St Louis; cert, social wfr, Brandeis U; m. Lila Simon, Feb 22, 1953; c: Jonathan, Dena, Adam. Exec dir, Social Work Vocational Bur, since 1968; profsl positions, JCC, 1949-62; exec dir, J Comty Cen and Council, Lawrence, Mass, 1959-62; social work cons, Mass Rehab Commn, 1963-64; personnel cons, JWB, 1964-68. Sch comm, Bethpage J Comty Cen, 1965-67; sch bd, JCC, Lawrence, Mass, 1959-63; mem: Natl Conf J Communal Service; Natl Assn J Cen Workers; Natl Assn Social Workers; Council on Social Work Educs; Judaica Hist Philatelic Soc. Contbr to J publs. Home: 6 Jane Dr, Old Bethpage, NY. Office: 386 Park Ave S, New York, NY.

STERN, Isaac, US, violinst; b. Kreminiesz, Russ, July 21, 1920; s. Solomon and Clara (Jaffe); in US since 1921; studied with Naoum Blinder; att SF Conservatory of Music, Cal, 1930-37; m. Vera Lindenblit, Aug 17, 1951; c: Shira, Michael, David. Concert violinist; mem, Stern-Istomin-Rose Trio; NY debut 1937; Carnegie Hall, NY debut, 1943; appeared in concerts throughout the world; soloist with world's leading orchs; appeared at maj Amer festivals, including: Lewisohn Stadium, NY; Robin Hood Dell, Phila; Ravina Park, Chgo; fgn festivals: with Pablo Casals, at Prades and Perignan; Edinburgh; Venice; Isr; invited to inaugurate Mann Auditorium, Tel Aviv, 1957; US repr on US natl day, at Brussels World Fair, 1958; played role of Eugene Ysaye, in Tonight We Sing, 1952. Pres: Carnegie Hall; Amer-Isr Cultural Found; mem, Natl Council on Arts, since 1965; unofficial US musical ambass. Recording artist for Columbia Masterworks; recordings include: Tchaikovsky, Brahms and Wieniawski concerts; pressings of Prades, Perpignan Festivals; double concerti, with David Oistrakh. Office: Hurok Attractions, Inc, 730 Fifth Ave, New York, NY.

STERN, J David, US, publisher; b. Phila, Pa, Apr 1, 1886; s. David and Sophie (Muhr); BA, U of Pa, 1906; LLB, 1909; m. Juliet Lit, Nov 22, 1908; c: David, Jill, Meredith, Jonathan. Ret; owner and publisher: Camden Evening Courier, NJ, 1919-47; Camden Morning Post, NJ, 1926-47; Phila Record, Pa, 1928-47; New Brunswick Times, NJ, 1912-14; Springfield News, Ill, 1914-19; Springfield Record, Ill, 1915-19; gen mgr, Providence RI News, 1911; publisher, NY Post, 1933-39. Author: Eidolon, 1932; Memoirs of a Maverick Publisher, 1962. Homes: 944 Fifth Ave, New York, NY; 160 Wells Rd, Palm Beach, Fla.

STERN, Jacob, Isr, psychologist; b. Berlin, Ger, Aug 30, 1913; s. David and Rachel (Davidson); in Isr since 1945; ordained rabbi, tchr cert, Rabbiner Sem, Berlin, Ger, 1939; PhD, U Zurich, Switz, 1945; m. Jeannette Erlanger, Aug 29, 1939; c: Rachel Asher, Shalom, Eli, Ishak. I/c wfr offs auth, Min of Social Wfr, since 1969, youth rehab dept, 1948-69; dir: Home for J Children, Basel, Switz, 1939-45; children's home, Jerusalem, 1945-48. Haganah, IDF, 1946-55. Contbr articles on educ, psych to jours. Home: 8 Pouah St, Jerusalem, Isr. Office: 8 King David St, Jerusalem, Isr.

STERN, Joseph S, Jr, Isr, business exec; b. Cincinnati, O, Mar 31, 1918; s. Joseph and Miriam (Haas); BA, Harvard U, 1940; MBA, 1943; m. Mary Stern, June 14, 1942; c: Peter, William, Peggy. Pres, J S Stern Jr & Co; dir: US Shoe Corp, since 1956, vice-pres, 1955, pres, 1965-68; Cen Trust Co; Lamb Communications Inc, Toledo, O; adj prof, bus policy, U Cincnnati, USNR, 1943-46. Pres: Friends of Public Libr, 1959-61; Cincinnati Comm for Refs, 1950-55; I M Wise Temple, 1959-61; secy, bd trustees, Cincinnati Public Libr; mem, visiting comms, libr, resources, Harvard bd of overseers; vice-pres, Cincinnati Country Day Sch, since 1958; club, Harvard, Cincinnati, pres, 1966, treas, 1954-56. Home: 3 Grandin Pl, Cincinnati, O. Office: US Shoe Corp, Cincinnati, O.

STERN, Jossi, Isr, artist; b. Hung, Sep 26, 1923; s. David and Katherine (Wiess); in Isr since 1939; BA, Bezalel Art Sch, Jerusalem; one-man shows: Yonas Gal; Rinah Gal; Jerusalem Artists House; Bet HaAam, all Jerusalem; Mikra Studio Gal; Chamerinski Gal, both Tel Aviv; exhbs in US; Can; London; instr, graphic arts, Bezalel Sch. War illus, Haganah, IDF. Pub works: woodcuts for The Golden Camp by Asher Barash; beGius Maleh, 1948; beOhalei Gadna, 1949; Jerusalem, album; Yossi Stern—sketches and drawings; Daf Kravi, war sketches; contbr to Heb dailies. Recipient: Struck prize; travelling grant, Isr Min of Educ, 1949; UNESCO study grant to US, 1966; Asher Safari prize. Home: 23 Nachlat Zadock, Jerusalem, Isr.

STERN, Leah G, US, communal worker; b. Nov 28, 1909; d. Isaac and Bessie (Rogosin) Gordon; att Bklyn Coll; m. Mordecai Stern, Feb 8, 1928; c: Ariel, Pnina Grinberg. Exec vice-pres, women's branch, Union Orthodox J Congs of Amer, since 1962, natl chmn, speakers bur, 1943-54, natl pres, 1954-56; natl pres, Histadruth Harabonioth. Transliterated, Grace After Meals, for transcription into Braille. Home: 210 E 15 St, New York, NY. Office: 84 Fifth Ave, New York, NY.

STERN, Leo, US, stockbroker; b. Bklyn, NY, Dec 21, 1895; s. Fred and Emma (Simon); BS, Columbia U, 1915, MA, 1916; m. Marjorie Phillips, March 11, 1926; c: Robert, Walter, Richard. Partner, Newburger Loeb & Co, since 1935, head of research, 1930-35; dir emeritus, Alloys Unlimited, dir, 1960-68. US Army, 1916-17. Home: 10 Beechwood Dr, Larchmont, NY. Office: 5 Hanover Sq, New York, NY.

STERN, Louis, US, stockbroker; b. Newark, NJ, Feb 29, 1904; s. Joseph and Fannie (Tenzer); BS, U of Pa, 1924; m. Frances Baum, 1929; c: Robert. Partner, Stern Bros, since 1937. Pres: JWB, since 1965; Council J Feds and Wfr Funds, 1963-65; fmr pres: J Comty Council; YM-YWHA, both Essex Co, NJ; co-chmn, Interreligious Comm on Poverty; mem bd, United Isr Appeal. Home: 521 Henderson Dr, South Orange, NJ. Office: 50 Broadway, New York, NY.

STERN, Madeleine B, US, author, rare book dealer; b. NYC, July 1, 1912; d. Moses and Lillie (Mack); BA, Barnard Coll, 1932; MA, Columbia U, 1933; Guggenheim f, 1943-45. Partner, Leona Rostenberg, rare books, since 1945. Author: The Life of Margaret Fuller, 1942; Louisa May Alcott, 1950; Purple Passage: The Life of Mrs Frank Leslie, 1953; Imprints on History; Book Publishers and American Frontiers, 1956; We the Women: Career Firsts of Nineteenth-Century America, 1963; So Much in a Lifetime: The Story of Dr Isabel Barrows, 1964; Queen of Publishers' Row: Mrs Frank Leslie, 1965; The Pantarch: A Biography of Stephen Pearl Andrews, 1968; Heads and Headlines: The Phrenologizing Fowlers, 1970; contbr to scholarly jours. Mem: MLA; Antiquarian Booksellers Assn of Amer; Phi Beta Kappa. Home: 40 E 88 St, New York, NY. Office: POBox 188, Gracie Sta, New York, NY.

STERN, Malcolm Henry, US, rabbi; b. Phila, Pa, Jan 29, 1915; s. Arthur and Henrietta (Berkowitz); BA, U of Pa, 1935; ordained rabbi, MHL, HUC, 1941, DHL, 1957, hon DD, 1966; m. Louise Bergman, May 25, 1941. Dir, rabb placement, CCAR, since 1964; asst rabbi, Cong Keneseth Isr, Phila, 1941-47; rabbi, Cong Ohef Shalom, Norfolk, Va, 1947-64. Chaplain, USAAC, 1943-46. F, treas, Amer Soc Genealogists; pres: Mid-Atlantic RA, 1962-63, Hampton Rds RA; hon chmn, UJA campaign, Norfolk, 1963-64; mem: exec council, Amer J Hist Soc; Interracial Min F; club, Rotary, Norfolk, 1948-64. Author: Americans of Jewish Descent, 1960; ed, Union Songster, 1960; contbr to J publs. Spec interests: Genealogy, Amer J hist, classical and J music. Home: 300 E 71 St, New York, NY. Office: 790 Madison Ave, New York, NY.

STERN, Marks, Isr, civil engineer; b. Tomashov, Pol, Oct 10, 1899; s. Simon and Malka (Jacobovich); in Isr since 1921; ACGI, BSc, London U, 1920. Sr partner, M Stern and Partners, cons engrs, since 1949; dist engr, PWD, Pal, 1921-48; dir, public works, Isr Govt, 1948-49; cons engr: new port of Eilat; Natl Stadium, Ramat Gan. Sapper, Royal Engs, Brit Army, 1917-19; F, Inst of Civil Engrs; pres, Assn of Engrs and Architects of Isr. Home and office: 10 Binyamin St, Ramat Gan, Isr.

STERN, Michael, It, journalist, author; b. NYC, Aug 3, 1910; s. Barnett and Anna (Agulansky); BS, U Syracuse, 1932; m. Estelle Goldstein, Nov 11, 1934; c: Michael, Margaret Dorsen. Fgn corresp, Fawcett Publs, since 1942; reporter: Syracuse Jour, 1929-33; NY Jour, 1931-32; Middletown Times Herald, 1932-33; staff writer, McFadden Publs, 1935-42; adv, John Harlen Amen inves into alliance between crime and politics, NY, 1939-42; host, TV prog, The City, CBS; exec vice-pres, Itam Films, Inc; war corresp with Allied Forces, WW II. Mem, clubs: Overseas Press of Amer; Aquasanta Golf; Olgiata Golf. Author: The White Ticket, 1936; movie, The Memphis Belle, 1943; Into the Jaws of Death, 1944; No Innocence Abroad, 1954; An American in Rome, autobiography, 1963; Faruk: A Biography, 1966; Via Veneto, 1970; co-author, Flight From Terror, 1941; contbr to Amer mags, widely reprinted in It. Recipient: citation for war front coverage, US, 1941-45. Hobby: painting. Home: Via Proceno 5, Rome, It.

STERN, Mordechai C, Isr, politician, economist, business exec; b. Vienna, Aus, Oct 16, 1914; s. Netanel and Rose (Pinkas); in Isr since 1934; att: U Vienna, 1933-34; Sch of Acctnt and Bus Admn, Jerusalem, 1942-45; m. Yehudit Kronheim, May 19, 1946; c: Azgad, Jacob. Mem exec, Near E Trade Fair Co; mgr, Haavara, 1934-39; dept secy, Bank Leumi leIsr, Ltd, 1939-42; insp, Income Tax Dept, 1942-45; mgn dir, Rassco, Ltd, 1945-66; MK, 1965-69. Mem, natl exec, Lib Party; chmn: Isr Soc for Rehab of Disabled; Forum for J Thought; bd, trustees, Bar Ilan U; mem exec, Isr Found for Handicapped Children; mem bd: Sharei Zedek Hosp, Jerusalem; Heichal Shlomo; Cen Eur Immigrants Assn; Soc for Isr Philharmonic Orch; Isr Opera; John Kennedy Memorial Fund; mem, B'nai B'rith; fmr mem: Tel Aviv Munic Council; natl exec, Progressive Party. Author of books and articles. Home: 38 Brandeis St, Tel Aviv, Isr.

STERN, Neuton S, US, physician, educator; b. Memphis, Tenn, April 9, 1890; s. Maurice and Hattie (Mauss); BA, Harvard U, 1912, MD, 1915; m. Beatrice Wolf, Nov 24, 1924; c: Thomas, Robert. Clinical prof med em, U Tenn Med Coll, asst prof, phys, 1919-22, asso prof, since 1930; teaching f, phys, Harvard U Med School, 1916. Lt, US Army MC, 1917-19. F: Amer Coll Phys; mem: AHA; AMA; S Med Assn; Tenn State, Memphis, Shelby Co Med Socs. Author: Clinical Diagnosis, 1933; The Bases of Treatment, 1957; fmr ed, Memphis Med Jour. Recipient: Medal of Honor, Fr Rep; Establishment of Neuton S Stern visiting lectureship, U of Tenn Med Coll. Home: 684 Center Dr, Memphis, Tenn. Office: 899 Madison Ave, Memphis, Tenn.

STERN, Pavao, Yugo, physician, educator; b. Yugo, Mar 17, 1913; s. Josip; MD, Med Fac, 1936; m. Bosiljka Srkoc, Nov 19, 1945; c: Milan. Prof, pharm, med fac, Pharm Inst, Sarajevo, since 1948; pharm, Kastel & Co, 1937-45; asst prof, Med Fac, Zagreb, 1945-48. Contbr to profsl jours. Home: Obala 6, Sarajevo, Yugo. Office: Pharm Inst, Sarajevo, Yugo.

STERN, Percival, US, civic worker; b. Amite, La, Jan 31, 1880; s. David and Bertha (Leopold); BEE, cum laude, Tulane U, 1899; m. Lillian Burkson, Apr 20, 1903 (decd); c: Lois Brown; m. 2nd, Elsie Kahn Levin, Nov 2, 1938. Ret; pres, Interstate Elec Co, 1912-52, gen mgr, 1903-12; org Autolee Stores, 1928, sold 1952. Found mem: Natl Automotive Wholesale Assn, 1932; Intl House; Intl Trade Mart; Co-org, New Orleans C of C, 1913; chmn bd: City Trust, since 1953; hon Jr Achievement since 1953; mem, bd trustees, Gtr New Orleans Educ TV Found, since 1958; hon mem, Intl Grad Achievements, Inc, since 1961. Club, Research. Donor to: Tulane U for nuclear lab; Newman Sch; J Comty Cen; Touro Infirmary; Jr Achievement. Recipient: Times Picaynne award, 1963. Hobbies: hunting, fishing. Home: 4040 Tulane Ave, New Orleans, La. Office: 801 Hibernia Bank Bldg, New Orleans, La.

STERN, Richard G, US, educator, author; b. NYC, Feb 25, 1928; s. Henry and Marion (Veit); BA, U of NC, 1947; MA,

Harvard U, 1949; PhD, U of Ia, 1954; m. Gay Clark, Mar 14, 1950; c: Christopher, Kate, Andrew, Nicholas. Prof, Eng, gen studies in hum, U Chgo, since 1965, fac mem since 1955; lectr U Heidelberg, 1950-51; educ adv, Dept of Army, 1950-52; instr, Eng: Coe Coll, 1952-53; U of Ia, 1953-54; Conn Coll, 1954-55; visiting prof: U Venice, 1962-63; U of Cal, Santa Barbara, summers, 1964-68; SUNY, Buffalo, 1966; Harvard U, 1969. Mem: Phi Beta Kappa; Philol Soc. Author: Golk, 1960; Europe, or Up and Down With Baggish and Schreiber, 1961; In Any Case, 1962; Teeth, Dying and Other Matters, 1964; Stitch, 1965; Honey and Wax, 1966. Recipient: Longwood award; Natl Inst of Arts and Letters award; Natl Found in Arts and Hum F Rockefeller award; Friends of Lit award. Office: U Chgo, Chicago, Ill.

STERN, Richard M, US, investment counselor; b. NYC, Nov 12, 1890; s. Jacob and Eva (Posnanski); AB, CCNY, 1911; MA, Columbia U, 1922; m. Elizabeth Loeb, July 13, 1928. Econ and inves cons, since 1938; rabbi: Temple Isr, New Rochelle, NY, 1912-23; Vine St Temple, Nashville, Tenn, 1923-26; broker and stat: Colvin & Co; Wertheim & Co, both NYC, 1927-33; stat, Sterling Natl Bank, NY, 1935-38. Mem: bd trustees, exec bd, UAHC, mem, new congs comm, since 1957; exec comm, CCAR, 1925-26; Rabb Pension Bd, since 1959; hon vice-pres, NY Fed Reform Syns, since 1968; chmn, jt capital pension fund, UAHC and CCAR. Contbr to banking jours. Home and office: 1435 Lexington Ave, New York, NY.

STERN, Sol Victor, US, dentist; b. London, Eng, June 8, 1906; s. Simon and Mildred (Tannenbaum); in US since 1910; DDS, Marquette U, Milw, Wis, 1930; m. Margaret Leviant, June 18, 1933; c: Marsha Belfer, Caren Rouske, Renee. Dent, since 1930. Pres, Beth El Ner Tamid Syn; mem bd: Milw J Cmty Cen; United Syn Amer; Natl Conf of J Men's Clubs; mem: B'nai B'rith, Wash Park; Zionist Org, Milwaukee; Natl Wfr Bd; Masons, Harmony Lodge; Amer Dent Assn; Wis Dent Assn; Gtr Milw Dent Soc; Alpha Omega Dent Frat; Alpha Omega Alumni Assn, fmr pres; Marquette Alumni Assn; Marquette Dent Alumni Assn; Mitchell St Advancement Assn; Royal Arch Masons; Consistory; fmr chmn, Milw Co NCCJ; clubs: Lions, pres, 1945-46; Beth El Ner Tamid Men's, 1957-59. Contbr to profsl jours. Recipient: Man of Year, Beth El Ner Tamid Syn, 1960; Covet award, Milw J Comty Cen, 1963. Hobbies: art, woodcarving. Home: 2608 Lefeber Ave, Wauwatosa, Wis. Office: 1206 W Mitchell St, Milwaukee, Wis.

STERN, William, US, organization exec; b. Yaroslav, Aus-Hung, July 7, 1910; s. Jacob and Jennie (Lieberman); in US since 1911; BA, LIU, 1931; MA, NYU, 1932; m. Lucille Moskowitz, 1937. Admn dir, Workmen's Circle, since 1963, natl dir, youth and Eng-speaking div, 1946-63, NYC, dir, 1938-46. Pvt, US Army, 1943-45. Mem bd: Workers Defense League, chmn, natl action comm, 1948-57; Lower E Side Neighborhood Assn, co-chmn, 1962-64; and vice-chmn, J Lab Comm, since 1947; Radio Sta WEVD, NY, 1961-65; League for Ind Democracy; AJConf on Soviet Jewry; NY Fraternal Cong, pres, 1967-68; Inst for J Affairs; United Housing Found, since 1960; Rochdale Housing Coop, since 1960; Comm for Yiddish in NY High Schs, since 1958; ORT; and vice-chmn Jewish Daily Forward Assn, Workers Defense League, chmn 1948-57; mem: natl council, JWB, since 1951; natl exec comm, J Socialist Verband, since 1956; exec comm, Cong for J Culture, 1948; Rand Sch for Social Scis, 1954-57; Amer Vets Comm; Dem Social Fed; Lib Party. Columnist, Workmen's Circle Call, since 1938, ed, since 1946. Home: 573 Grand St, New York, NY. Office: 175 E Broadway, New York, NY.

STERN, Zahava Odes, Isr, sculptress; b. Plungian ,Lith, Sep 29, 1916; d. Shalom and Gita (Sacks); in Isr since 1936; att U Kowna, 1934-36; m. Gabriel Stern, June 22, 1940; c: Miriam, Deganit. Sculptress, since 1938; perm exhbs, Artist's Colony, Safed; tchr, phys educ and dance. Mem, Isr Painters and Sculpturers Assn, since 1960. Author: Album, 1967. Home: 250 Borodezky St, Tel Aviv, Isr. Studio: Artist's Colony, Safed, Isr.

STERNAU, Herbert, US, insurance underwriter; b. NYC, Dec 24, 1899; s. Albert and Aimee (Rosenthal); c: Virginia Moore, Thomas. Spec agt, Northwestern Mutual Life Ins Co, since 1924. Mem: exec comm and bd, Amer Social Health Assn; bd: Park W Neighborhood Assn; W Side Schs Comty Cen; Puerto Rican Cultural Cen; YMCA; Park to Hudson Urban Renewal Citizens Comm; W Side Housing Comm; Bloomingdale-Parkwest Health Comm; Mayor's Comm on Puerto Rican Affairs; Riverside Public Health Comm; exec comm, NY chap,

AJComm; City-Wide Slum Prevention Comm. Recipient: dist service award, Victory Loan Dr, 1945, Manhattan comty sales div, War Finance Comm; award, El Consejo de Organizaciones Hispano Americanas de Nueva York, 1952. Home: 5 Riverside Dr, New York, NY. Office: 1775 Broadway, New York, NY.

STERNBERG, Erich Walter, Isr, composer; b. Berlin, Ger, May 31, 1891; s. Phillipp and Anna (Buki); in Isr since 1932; att Askanisches Gymnasiam, Berlin, 1907-10; m. Ella Thal, Tel Aviv; c: Miriam Davidson, Ruwen, Tamar Aljagor, Michel, Judith. Composer: The 12 Tribes of Israel; The Story of Joseph; The Raven; My People; Dialogues with the Wind; The Distant Flute; Praise Ye; Paysant Songs; Sonate für Klavier; Der Wegbruder; String Quartet With Alto Solo; Toccata for Piano; Capriccio; Allegro; Horah for 7 Voices; Overture to Comedy, for orch; Harken, Israel, for orch; Dr Dolittle, children's opera; Amcha Suite, for orch; Quodlibet, for orch; The Ressurection of Israel, oratorio; Study, for orch; Noah's Ark, for orch. Recipient, Engel Prize, Tel Aviv Munic, twice. Home: 20 Ruppin St, Tel Aviv, Isr.

STERNBERG, Harry, US, artist; b. NYC, July 19, 1904; s. Simon and Rose (Brand); att: Art Students League, NYC; m. Mary Gosney, Nov 9, 1946; c. Leslie. Tchr, Art Students League, NYC; head, art dept, summer campus, U of S Cal, Idyllwild, Cal; graphics, San Diego State Coll, 1967-68. Exhibited paintings and graphics since 1932; ACA Gal, NYC, more than 15 years; retrospective exhb, Garelick Gal, Detroit, 1958; U Minn, 1959; one-man shows, Heritage Gal, 1963, 1964; ACA Gal, 1968; works represented in perm collections: Art Students League, NY; Whitney Mus; Mus of Modern Art; Metrop Mus; H de Young Memorial Mus; Syracuse U Mus; Fogg Mus; Bklyn Mus Art; Addison Gal Amer Art; Cleveland Mus Art; Libr Cong; NY Public Libr; U Minn; Amer Archives, Wash, DC; Victoria and Albert Mus, London; Biblioteque Nationale, Paris; Natl Mus, Tel Aviv, NZ Mus Art. Hon mem, Art Students League. Produc; dir, Many Worlds of Art, film, 1960; author: Silk Screen Color Printing, 1942; Modern Methods and Materials of Etching, 1949; Composition and Abstract Drawing, 1954; Woodcut, 1962. Recipient: Guggenheim f, 1936; purchase prize, natl competition, Asso Amer Artists, 1946, 1947, 1953; Dir's prize, Audubon Artists, 1955; awards: 100 Fine Prints of Year, 1937-39; Print Club, Phila, 1941-42. Hobby: inventing and designing. Home: 1606 Conway Dr, Escondido, Cal. Studio: 1718 Valley Pkwy, Escondido, Cal.

STERNBERG, Paul, US, surgeon, educator; b. Chgo, Ill, Dec 18, 1918; s. David and Sarah (Kopeka); BS, Northwestern U, 1938, MD, 1940; m. Doris Betty Feitler, Dec 24, 1949. Asso prof, Ophthal, Chgo Med Sch, since 1947; att ophthal: Michael Reese Hosp; Cook Co Hosp; res ophthal, U of Ill, Eye and Ear Infirmary, 1942-43, att ophthal, 1948-52; f, ophthal, Cornell Med Sch and Wilmer Inst, 1943-44. F: AMA; Amer Coll of Surgs; mem: Chgo Ophthal Soc; Amer Acad of Ophthal and Otolaryngology; Assn for Research in Ophthal; Pan-Amer Cong of Ophthal. Contbr to med jours. Home: 359 Surfside Pl, Glencoe, Ill. Office: 111 N Wabash Ave, Chicago, Ill.

STERNEFELD, Daniel, Belgium, conductor; b. Antwerp, Nov 25, 1905; s. Alexander and Dina (Frank); att: Conservatoire, Antwerp; Mozarteum, Salzburg. First conductor, Radio-Tel, Belgium, since 1948; fmr prof, Conservatoire d'Anvers, Antwerp. Served Belgium Army. Recipient: Chevalier de l'Ordre de la Couronne; Officier de l'Ordre de Léopold II; It decoration. Hobbies: fishing, gardening. Home: 83 ave R Gobert, Brussels, Belgium. Office: RTB, Place Eugen Flagey, Brussels, Belgium.

STERNFELD, David (pen name, **David Rakia**), Isr, artist; b. Vienna, Aus, Dec 16, 1928; s. Ernst and Ester (Malz); in Isr since 1938; att Ecole Nationale Superieure des Beaux Arts, Paris, 1955-60; m. Laurence van der Ark, Mar 11, 1960; c: Mark, Karin. One-man shows: Paris, 1958; Jerusalem, 1958, 1960, 1962, 1964, 1966, 1968; Zurich, 1959; The Hague, 1960; London 1961; Tel Aviv, 1961, 1967; Amsterdam, 1967; Arnhem, 1967, 1969; Eilat, 1969; art illustrations for: Emily Dickinson, 1965; Miriam Jalan Stekelis, 1966; Martin Buber, 1969. IDF, 1947-48. Prin contribs: works donated to: IDF; Jerusalem Munic; Keren Kayemet leIsr. Mem: Isr Assn of Painters and Sculptors; Jerusalem Artists; Paris Artists; comm, J Painters, Paris. Recipient, Prix Etranger, Mus of Modern Art, Paris, 1958. Hobbies: ballet, architecture. Studio: 29 Keren Kayemet St, Jerusalem, Isr.

STERNFELD, Leon, US, physician, public health official; b. Bklyn, NY, June 15, 1913; s. Solomon and Goldie (Levine); BS, U Chgo, 1932, MD, 1936, PhD, 1937; MPH, Columbia U, 1943; m. Ruth Schwartz, Aug 25, 1934; c: Kay, Barbara. Dep commn health, Commonwealth of Mass, since 1961; asso prof, maternal and child health, Harvard U; lectr, public health, Simmons Coll; asso phys, Children's Med Cen, Boston, since 1957; jr epidemiologist, asst dist state health off and dir, bur of med rehab, NY State Dept of Health, 1941-50; asst dir, TB div, Mass Dept of Public Health, 1950-52; asso dir, field training unit, Harvard Sch of Public Health, 1952-53; public health commn, Cambridge, Mass, 1955-61. Maj, US Army MC, 1953-55; col, US Army Res. Dipl: Amer Bd of Peds, 1944; Amer Bd Preventative Med, 1952; f: Amer Public Health Assn; Mass Public Health Assn, pres, 1959-60; Mass Med Soc; Phi Beta Kappa; Sigma Xi. Contbr to med jours. Recipient: Commendation, Rep of Korea. Hobbies: music, philately. Home: 360 Ward St, Newton Centre, Mass. Office: Dept of Public Health, State House, Boston, Mass.

STERNLICHT, Sanford, US, educator, author; b. NYC, Sep 20, 1931; s. Irving and Sylvia (Hilsenroth); BS, State U Coll, Oswego, NY, 1953; MA, Colgate U, 1955; PhD, Syracuse U, 1962; m. Dorothy Hilkert, June 4, 1956; c: David, Daniel. Prof, Eng, State U Coll, Oswego, NY, since 1959, research f, 1965, 1969; Leverhulme visiting f, U York, Eng, 1965-66; Lt cdr, USNR. Mem: AAUP; MLA; USN Inst; NY State Eng Council; Navy League; Fac Assn, SUNY; counselor, B'nai B'rith Hillel Found, Oswego, NY. Author: Uriah Phillips Levy, The Blue Star Commodore, 1961; Gulls Way, 1961; Love in Pompeii, 1967; co-author: Yankee Racehorse with Sails, 1970; The Black Devil of the Bayous, 1970; contbr to: Saturday Evening Post; NY Times; NY Herald Tribune; Chr Sci Monitor; Can Poetry; Can Forum; Writer's Digest. Recipient: SUNY Research Found Fs, 1963, 1965, 1969; annual new poets' award, Writer mag, 1963; NY State U Research Found f, 1963; Amer Council of Learned Socs, travel grant, 1969. Home: 87 Sheldon Ave, Oswego NY. Office: State U Coll, Oswego, NY.

STERNS, Fred James, US, merchant; b. Bangor, Me, May 4, 1908; s. Harry and Bessi (Schiro); BS, Colby Coll, 1929; m. Sarah Hoos, May 24, 1932; c: Richard, Harvey. Owner and mgr, Sterns, Inc, since 1929. Pres: C of C, Skowhegan, Me, 1952; bd, Fairview Hosp, 1952; chmn, Pittsfield dist, UJA, 1953; mem: ZOA; B'nai B'rith; AJComm; Masons; Odd Fellows; Tau Delta Phi; Phi Gamma Mu; club, Lions. Home: 12 Dyer St, Skowhegan, Me. Office: 1 Madison Ave, Skowhegan, Me.

STERNSTEIN, Joseph P, US, rabbi; b. Bklyn, NY, Aug 20, 1924; s. Charles and Bertha (Milman); LLB, St Johns U, 1943; BA, Bklyn Coll, 1944; ordained rabbi, MHL, JTSA, 1948, DHL, 1961; JD, St Johns U Sch of Law; m. Geraldine Cohen, Dec 21,1947; c: Judith, Rachel, Gerson, Hillel. Rabbi: Temple Anshe Chesed, NYC, since 1964; Cong Tifereth Isr, Glen Cove, LI, 1948-50; Beth Abraham Syn Cen, Dayton, O, 1950-61; exec dir, US head off, JNF, 1961-64. F, Herbert A Lehman Inst of Talmudic Ethics, JTSA; natl chmn, commn on educ prog, and speakers bur, ZOA, since 1954; chmn: UN Comm of Syn Council; Inst of Intermarriage, NY Fed; Metrop Council, Klal Isr comm, both RA; Natl Young Zionists Actions Comm, 1945-48; Chalutziuth commn, ZOA, 1948-50; speakers bur, New-Dayton Comm, 1957; vice-chmn, natl rabb cabinet, JTSA; natl pres, Massada Young Zionists of Amer, 1945-47, pres, Mh Assn, Dayton, Montgomery Co, 1953-55; exec mem, Natl Zionists Youth Comm, 1945-47; asst to exec dir, Amer Zionist Emergency Council, 1946-49; mem: Pal bur, JA, 1947-49; ZOA delg to Eur, Isr, 1958; mem, state bd dirs, O Mh Assn, 1953-57; New-Dayton Comm, 1957; gen comm, ACLU, O. Author: American Zionism: Diagnosis and Prognosis, 1954; Theology of Gerer Rebbe, Heb, 1961; contbr to Zionist publs. Home: 845 W End Ave, New York, NY. Study: 251 W 100 St, New York, NY.

STIASSNY, Franz Dov, Isr, farmer, bus exec; b. Czech, Oct 13, 1902; s. Siegmund and Marie (Schostal); in Isr since 1933; att Us: Munich; Frankfurt; PhD, 1925; m. Kaete Weiss, Sep 17, 1927; c: Gad, Shimon, Esra, Rahel. Chmn, bd dirs: Zeraim Ltd, Gedera; Cotton Gin; mem bd dirs: Wine Growers Coop, Rishon leZion, Zichron Yaacov; Isr Elec Corp, Haifa; other cos. Haganah, 1934-48. Chmn: fgn relations comm, Isr Farmers Fed; control comm, govt vegetable bd; local council, Gedera, 1947-48, councilor, 1935-47; bd mem: Isr Farmers Fed; govt bds: cotton, wine, seed produc. Recipient: medals:

Haganah; Civil Defense. Home: 28 Kerem Hazeitim, Savyon, Isr. Office: 10 Zukerman St, Gedera, Isr.

STILLERMAN, Maxwell, US, educator, physician; b. Bklyn, NY, Jan 25, 1909; s. David and Rose; att Columbia U, 1926-28; MD, LI Coll Med, 1932; m. Carolyn Rachlin, 1945; c: Rosalind, Roberta, Diane. Asso prof, clinical peds, Cornell U Med Coll, NYC, since 1962; att ped: LI J Hosp, since 1955; N Shore Hosp, since 1954; asso att ped, NY Hosp, since 1967, asst att ped, 1956-67; investigator: Natl Found for Infantile Paralysis, 1939; streptococcal studies, Natl Inst of Health and NY Heart Assn, 1956-57, 1961-63; clinical investigator: Eli Lilly & Co, 1956-70; Squibb Inst for Med Research, 1961-63; Bristol Lab, 1966; Wyeth Labs, 1969-70. F, Measles Convalescent Serum Lab, 1938-41; mem: Amer Acad Peds; NY Acad Scis; NY Ped Soc. Contbr: Poliomyelitis Studies, 1939-41; Measles Studies, 1939-44; Mild Neonatal Toxoplasmosis, 1957; Streptococcal Studies, 1956-70. Home and office: 20 Polo Rd, Great Neck, NY.

STIM, Menahem, US, attorney; b. Stanislau, Aus-Hung, Jan 15, 1895; s. Isaac and Sophie (Friedman); in US since 1913; BSc, NYU, 1922, LLB, 1927; m. Annie Spunt, Dec 24, 1918; c: Allen, Joseph, Edward. Mem, law firm: Curran, Mahoney, Felix & Stim, since 1959; Blake, Stim & Curran, 1932-43; Curran & Stim, 1943-56; Curran, Mahoney, Cohn & Stim, 1956-59. US Army, 1917-18. Vice-commn and judge advocate, Amer Legion, NY Co, 1945-50; mem: Amer Bar Assn; NY Co Lawyers Assn; AJCong; ZOA; lawyers div, UJA; Grand St Boys Assn; club, Lawyers. Contbr to legal jours. Recipient: Purple Heart; Silver Cross. Home: 25 Neptune Blvd, Long Beach, LI, NY.

STITSKIN, Leon D, US, educator, rabbi; b. Cracow, Pol, July 2, 1910; s. Samuel and Anna (Zisner); in US since 1919; ordained rabbi, rabbi Isaac Elchanan Theol Sem, 1932; BA, Hiram Coll, 1932; PhD, Yeshiva U Sch of Educ, 1956; m. Dorothy Gerston, July 2,1933; c: Rochelle Dicker,Debbi Roth, Miriam Krater. Dir, comty relations and spec publs, prof, J phil, Yeshiva U, since 1953; rabbi: Beth Isr, Warren O, 1932-42; Beth Joseph, Rochester, NY, 1942-50; Comty Cen, Phila, Pa, 1950-53; found, acting dir, W Coast Inst of J Studies, Yeshiva U, 1962. Prin contrib: found and Exponent of phil of J personalism. Secy, RabCA, 1958, treas, 1949; mem: Acad of Research; Alumni Assn Yeshiva U; ZOA; AJCong; Mizrachi; B'nai B'rith; NY State Bd of Rabbis; NY State Bd for Equality in Educ. Author: Judaism as a Religion, 1937; Judaism as a Philosophy, 1960; Anthology of Studies in Torah Judaism, 1968; Personalism—A definition of Jewish Philosophy, 1969; ed: Sermon Manual, 1948, 1956; Studies in Torah Judaism, since 1960; Studies in Judaica; co-ed, Tradition, since 1959; contbr to religious jours. Recipient, annual award, JWV. Home: 1569 49 St, Brooklyn, NY. Office: Yeshiva U, Amsterdam Ave and 186 St, New York, NY.

STIVELMAN, Barnet P, US physician; b. Podol, Russ, Jan 27, 1892; s. Koppel and Ethel (Packer); in US since 1906; MD, NY State U Coll Med, 1914; m. Maria de Zwaan, 1941; c: Robert. Ret; pvt practice; med dir, Montefiore Hosp Sanatorium, 1917-25; chief examining phys in NY, City of Hope, Cal, 1927-47; fmr cons phys: Amer Med Cen, Denver, Colo; Harlem Hosp. Lt comdr, USNR, 1936-41. F: Amer Coll Phys; NY Acad Med; NY Thoracic Surgs; f em, Amer Coll Chest Phys; mem, AMA. Contbr to med jours. Hobbies: travel, photography. Home: 25 Central Park W, New York, NY.

STIX, Regine K, US, physician; b. Cincinnati, O, Nov 22, 1895; d. Joseph and Ella (Maertz) Kronacher; BA, Wellesley Coll, 1916; MA, U Cincinnati, 1922, MD, 1922; m. Thomas Stix, Sept 1, 1921; c: Thomas, Barbara Lipke. Ret; research cons, Dept Health, NYC, chief, secondary sch health service, 1945-50, coord, children's cardiac service, 1952-54, research asso, 1954-68; research asso, Milbank Memorial Fund, 1932-41. F: Amer Public Health Assn; NY Acad of Med; mem: Population Assn of Amer; Soc for Research in Child Devl. Co-author: Controlled Fertility, 1940. Home: 55 E 9th St, New York, NY.

STOCK, Ernest, Isr, journalist; b. Frankfurt, Ger, Aug 6, 1924; s. Leo and Jule (Marx); in Isr since 1961; BA, Princeton U, 1948; MS, Columbia U, 1949, MA, 1957, PhD, 1963; m. Bracha Heiblum, Feb 11, 1951. Dir, Jacob Hiatt Inst of Brandeis U, Jerusalem, since 1966; fgn news ed, Jerusalem Post, 1949-50; Jerusalem corresp, UP, 1949-50; asst to natl dir, B'nai B'rith Hillel Founds, 1950-52, research f, Ford

Found Grant to Study Amer-Isr relations, 1953-54; cons on overseas studies CJFWF, 1954-61; repr in Isr, JA for Isr, 1961-65. Mem: Phi Beta Kappa; club, Princeton. Author: Israel on the Road to Sinai, 1967; From Conflict to Understanding: Jews and Arabs in Israel, 1968; contbr to periodicals. Home: Nayot 6, Jerusalem, Isr.

STOCK, Mario, It, business exec; b. Spalato, July 31, 1906; s. Emilio and Irma (Hirschel); BA, hons, Trinity Hall, Cambridge, Eng, 1927, MA, 1933; m. Beata Oblath, 1936; five c. Pres Saec Cement Co, since 1952. Pres, J Comty, Trieste, 1948-68; mem, Cen Council It J, 1946-51, 1956-61. Home: Vio Torino 34, Trieste, It.

STOCK, Sigmund, Austr, manufacturer; b. Deutschkreutz, Aus, 1897; s. Alexander and Karoline (Lederer) Feigelstock; in Austr since 1939; m. Helene Koppel, 1923; c: Eric, Garry, Ilse Lamm. Mfr, since 1920. Life pres, Revisionist Party, Austr, since 1942; treas: United Isr Appeal of Vic, since 1948; treas, mem exec, ZF; KH, both Australia and NZ; mem: world exec, Herut-Hatzohar, since 1960; Bd Deps, Vic, since 1954, fmr treas; exec, Mt Scopus Coll; past dep mem, Actions Comm, WZO. Home: 112 Summerhill Rd, Glen Iris, Austr.

STOJKOVITCH-FREUND, Marija Rosalia Bella (stage name, **Rahela Ferari**), Yugo, dramatic actress; b. Belgrade, Yugo, Aug 27, 1911; d. Bella and Emilia (Leiner) Freund; theatrical study, Budapest, Hung, 1936-39; m. Aleksandar Stojkovic, 1941; c: Darko, Sasa. Stage actress, Yugo; appears in films, on TV and radio. Recipient: October award, State of Yugo, 1962; Steria award, Steria Pozorje, 1964. Home: 87 Revolucije, Belgrade, Yugo. Office: 54 M Tito St, Belgrade, Yugo.

STOLLERMAN, Gene H, US, physician, educator; b. NYC, Dec 6, 1920; s. Maurice and Sarah (Mezz); BA, Dartmouth Coll, 1941; MD, Columbia U, 1944; m. Corynee Miller, Jan 21, 1945; c: Lee, Anne, John. Prof, chmn med dept, U of Tenn Coll of Med, since 1965; phys in chief, City of Memphis Hosps, since 1965; med dir, Irvington House for Cardiac Children, 1951-55; instr, NYU Coll of Med, 1951-55; asst prof, Northwestern U Med Sch, 1962-64, on fac since 1955; dir, Samuel J Sackett Found, 1955-64. Capt, US Army MC, 1946-48. Chmn: Research Career Devl Award Comm; NIAMD, NIH; Expert Adv Panel on Cardiovascular Diseases, WHO; mem: bd dirs, Cen Soc Clinical Research; Amer Bd Internal Med; Assn Amer Phys; Amer Soc for Clinical Inves; Amer Assn Immunologists; Infectious Diseases Soc of Amer; Amer Fed Clinical Inves; Amer Coll Phys; Arthritis Found; Amer Rheumatism Assn; AMA; Streptococcus Commn; Armed Forces Epidemiological Bd; Phi Beta Kappa; Alpha Omega Alpha; Sigma Xi. Ed: Advances in Internal Medicine; contbr to sci jours. Home: 5892 Shady Grove Rd, Memphis, Tenn. Office: 951 Court Ave, Memphis, Tenn.

STOLLMAN, Samuel S, Can, rabbi, educator; b. Ozaritch, Russ, Sep 4, 1922; s. Isaac and Shifra (Shapiro); BS, Columbia U, 1946; ordained rabbi, Yeshiva U, NY, 1947; MA, Wayne State U, 1959, PhD, 1964; m. Deborah Levin, Nov 16, 1948; c: Shifra, Yacov, Aryeh, Nehemya. Rabbi, Shaar Hashomayim Cong, Windsor, Ont, since 1949; asst prof, Eng dept, U Windsor, since 1967; found, prin, Heb Orthodox Cen Day Day Sch, Scranton, Pa, 1948-49; found, Windsor Heb Day Sch, 1969. Pres, Windsor Council, JNF; mem: RabCA; B'nai B'rith; Mizrachi Org; Mayor's Rel Comm of Windsor. Home: 1365 Victoria Ave, Windsor, Can. Study: 115 Giles Blvd, E Windsor, Can.

STOLPER, Israel, US, educator, attorney; b. Guadavpils, Latvia, Aug 12, 1893; s. Zalmon and Rose (Margolis); in US since 1900; LLB, Northeastern U Sch of Law, 1915; AB Harvard U, 1945, AM, PhD, 1962; AM, Boston U, 1947; m. Ann Crystal, Feb 22, 1922; c: Albert, Saul. Prof, chmn dept, govt and econ, Suffolk U, since 1947; pvt law practice, 1917-38; mem, planning div, Gen Elec Co, 1940-46. US Army, WW I. Mem: AAUP; Amer Political Sci Assn; Acad of Political Sci. Home: 295 Spiers Rd, Newton Centre, Mass. Office: Suffolk U, 20 Derne St, Boston, Mass.

STOLPER, Pinchas Aryeh, US, rabbi, editor, author; b. Bklyn, NY, Oct 22, 1931; s. David and Nettie (Rosch); att Tchrs Inst, Yeshiva U, 1947-49; BRE, JTSA, 1951, att grad sch, 1951-52; BA, Bklyn Coll, 1952; ordained rabbi, Mesivta Rabbi Chaim Berlin and Gur Aryeh Inst for Advanced J Research, 1956; att New Sch for Social Research, since 1952;

m. Elaine Liebman, Nov 22, 1955; c: Akiva, Michal, Malka. Natl dir, Natl Conf Syn Youth, since 1959; asst to prin, Beth Isr Talmud Torah, E Flatbush, 1950-53; tchr: Bnai Sholom Rel Sch, Rockville Cen, LI, 1951-52; Cong Agudath Sholom, Bklyn, 1953-54; Hillcrest J Cen Rel Sch, 1954-55; asst rabbi: Cong Beth Isr, E Flatbush, 1954-56; Young Isr, Bedford Bay, 1955-56; dir, LI Zionist Youth Commn, 1956-57; dir Pr, admn dean, adv to English speaking students, Ponevez Yeshiva, Bnei Brak, Isr, 1957-59. Natl Pres, Brith Trumpeldor, Amer, 1950-53; delg, World Conf, Brith Trumpeldor World Org, Jerusalem, 1951; mem, natl exec bd: Rabb Alliance, Amer, 1965-67; Amer Zionist Youth Council, 1949-53; mem, exec comm, United Zionists-Revisionists, Amer, 1956; cons: World J Youth Conf, Jerusalem, 1964; N Amer J Youth Conf; trustee, Gur Aryeh Inst for Advanced J Scholarship, 1965-68; repr, Union Orthodox J Congs at White House Conf on Children and Youth, 1961; bd dirs: Chaim Berlin Torah Schs-Mesivta Rabbi Chaim Berlin Rabb Acad; Natl J Music Council; Natl Assn Dirs, Natl J Youth Orgs; mem, comms, Union Orthodox J Congs. Author: Day of Delight, 1961; Tested Teen Age Activities, 1961, 1964; Sabbath Day of Delight, 1962; Tefilah, 1963; What Happened on Sinai, 1966; Prayer, The Proven Path, 1967; The Road to Responsible Jewish Adulthood, 1967; asso ed, Igereth Haigud; ed, found, Jewish Youth Monthly; ed: Hadar, 1953; mem, ed bd, Jewish World; 1953-54; contbr to J and Heb publs. Recipient: Alumni Amudim award, Mesivta Rabbi Chaim Berlin-Gur Aryeh Inst, 1967. Home: 703 Rockaway Pkwy, Bklyn, NY. Office: 84 Fifth Avenue New York, NY.

STOLPER, Saul James, US, production engr, business exec; b. Revere, Mass, Feb 25, 1926; s. Israel and Ann (Crystal); BS, Boston U, 1948; m. Frances Liberman, May 11, 1950; c: David, Edward, Michael, Elizabeth. Treas, mem, bd dirs: Gen Devices Co, Inc, since 1950; Coll-Ind Bronze, Inc. US Army, WW II. Prin contribs: pioneer in use of numerical controlled equipment used in produc of parts in Mercury, Saturn, Gemini, Apollo space progs. Worshipful Master, Garden City lodge, Masons. Recipient: Award of Achievement, Asso Inds of Mass, for significant contrib to moon landing, 1969. Home: 111 Exeter St, Newton, Mass. Office: 589 Granite St, Braintree, Mass.

STONE, Dewey D, US, business exec, communal leader; b. Brockton, Mass, Aug 31, 1900; s. Morris and Idletta (Stone); BBA, Boston U, 1920, hon DHumL, 1950; LLD, Stonehill Coll, 1958; hon f, Weizmann Inst of Sci, Isr, 1960; m. Anne Abrams, June 28, 1923. Pres, Harodite Finishing Co; mem bd dirs: Converse Rubber Co; Crosby Valve & Gage Co; Ashton Valve Co; T Noonan Sons Co, all Mass; Costal Footwear Corp, Puerto Rico Trusteed Funds, Inc. US Army, WW I. Prin contrib: The Dewey D and Harry K Stone Sci Bldg, Boston U, 1947. Hon chmn UJA; chmn: bd govs, Weizmann Inst of Sci, Isr; JA for Isr, Inc, since 1960; Amer Comm for Weizmann Inst; bd, Brandeis Youth Found; natl chmn, United Isr Appeal; trustee: and incorporator, Cardinal Cushing Gen Hosp; Stone Charitable Found; vice-pres, Amer J League for Isr; mem: bd dirs: CJFWF; Friends of Heb U; Zionist House; Camp Young Judea; Isr Bond Corp; Amer-Isr Cultural Found; Isr Econ Corp; Isr Fgn Trade Credits Corp; bd trustees: and asso found, Boston U; Heb Tchrs Coll; fmr vice-pres, ZOA; mem: JWV; Amer Legion; B'nai B'rith; YMHA; Masons, 32nd deg; Cong Agudas Achim, Brockton; Temple Isr, Brockton; Zeta Beta Tau. Recipient: Man of Year, Zeta Beta Tau, 1947; cert of merit, JWV, 1952. Home: 53 Arlington St, Brockton, Mass. Office: Harodite Finishing Co, Dighton, Mass.

STONE, Earl S, US, rabbi; b. Childs, Pa, July 2, 1914; s. Ben and Bertye (Breakstone); BA, Syracuse U, NY, 1935; ordained rabbi, MHL, HUC-JIR, 1939; m. Judith Wilensky, June 4, 1942; c: Theodore, Jeremy. Rabbi, Temple Emanuel, Denver, Colo, since 1956; student counselor, Syracuse U, 1945-48; asso rabbi, The Temple, Cleveland, O, 1948-56. Chaplain, US Army, 1941-45. Mem: bd of govs, HUC-JIR; exec bd, CCAR, 1952-54; ZOA; Res Offs Assn, natl chaplain; Cleveland Mh Assn; ARC; Zeta Beta Tau; club, Rotary Intl. Recipient: Bronze Star, 1946. Home: 3400 E Dartmouth Ave, Denver, Colo. Study: Temple Emanuel, 51 Grape St, Denver, Colo.

STONE, Irving, US, author; b. SF, Cal, July 14, 1903; s. Charles and Pauline (Rosenberg) Tennenbaum; BA, U of Cal, Berkeley, 1923; MA, U of S Cal, 1924, Des Lettres, 1965; hon DLitt, Coe Coll, Ia, 1967; hon LLD, U of Cal, Berkeley,

1968; m. Jean Factor, Feb 11, 1934; c: Paula, Kenneth. Biographer, novelist, since 1956; teaching f: econ: U of S Cal, 1923-24; U of Cal, Berkeley, 1924-26; mem fac: U of Ind, 1948; U Wash, 1961; U of S Cal, 1966; art critic, LA Mirror-News, 1959-60; lectr, Cal State Colls, 1966. Author: Pageant of Youth, 1933; Lust for Life, 1934; Dear Theo, 1937; Sailor on Horseback, 1938; False Witness, 1940; Clarence Darrow for the Defense, 1941; They Also Ran, 1943; Immortal Wife, 1944; Adversary in the House, 1947; Earl Warren, 1948; The Passionate Journey, 1949; We Speak for Ourselves, 1950; The President's Lady, 1951; Love is Eternal, 1954; Men to Match my Mountains, 1956; The Biographical Novel, 1957; The Agony and the Ecstasy, 1961; I, Michelangelo, Sculptor, 1962; The Irving Stone Reader, 1963; The Story of Michelangelo's Pieta, 1964; The Great Adventure of Michelangelo, 1965; Those Who Love, 1965; There Was Light: Autobiography of a University, Berkeley, 1868-1968, pub, 1970; co-ed, Lincoln: A Contemporary Portrait, 1962; books trans into many langs; Magnificent Doll, screen play; contbr to books and mags. Prin contrib: found, Irving and Jean Stone lit prizes. Pres: LA Dante Alighiere Soc; and found, Fs for Schweitzer, S Cal, since 1955; Cal Writers Guild, 1960-61; Beverly Hills Improvement Assn, 1964-65; found: Acad of Amer Poets, 1962-66; Cal State Coll Comm for the Arts, 1967; vice-pres, Eugene V Debs Found, Terre Haute, Ind, since 1963; trustee, Douglass House Found, Watts, Cal, 1967-68; mem: Authors League of Amer; PEN; Soc of Amer Hists; Acad of Motion Picture Arts and Scis; W Writers of Amer; Acad of Political Sci; Hist Soc of S Cal; Renaissance Soc of Amer; Cal Civil War Centennial Commn, 1961-65; Eleanor Roosevelt Memorial Found, 1963; Amer Assembly, Columbia U, 1963-67; adv bd, U Cal Inst for Creative Arts; Cal Citizens Comm for Higher Educ, 1964; Cal State Comm on Public Educ, 1966-67; contributing mem, Amer Sch for Cisssical Studies, Athens, Greece; specialist on Culture Exch, US State Dept, to: Soviet Union, Pol, Yugo, Eur, 1962; participant, Arden House Conf on US and E Eur, 1967. Recipient: Christopher award; Silver Spur, W Writers Amer; Golden Lily, Florence, It; Rupert Hughes award; Commendatore, Rep It; gold medal: Council Amer Artists Socs; Commonwealth Club, Cal; Amer Revolution Round Table award, 1966; Lit Father of Year, 1966; gold trophy, Amer Women in Radio, TV, 1968. Office: c/o Doubleday and Co, Garden City, NY.

STONE, Irving I, US, business exec; b. Cleveland, O, Apr 5, 1909; s. Jacob and Jennie (Canter) Sapirstein; m. Beatrice Wieder, Aug 6, 1931; c: Hensha Millstein, Neil, Myrna Tater, Judy Weiss. Pres, Amer Greetings Corp, since 1960, with co, since 1923. Pres, Heb Acad, Cleveland; vice-pres: J Comty Fed, Cleveland; Telshe Yeshiva; Bur of J Educ; team capt, graphic arts div, and bd mem, UA, Gtr Cleveland; mem, bd: Young Isr, Cleveland; Cleveland Art Inst. Home: 20011 N Park Blvd, Shaker Heights, O. Office: 1300 W 78 St, Cleveland, O.

STONE, J Jacques, US, attorney; b. NYC, Aug 10, 1907; s. Benjamin and Betsy (Goldman); BA, CCNY, 1928; LLB, Harvard U, 1931; m. Janet Stone, Sep 20, 1940; c: Toni, Carol. Pvt practice, since 1932; Pres: Cen Syn, 1969; J Educ Comm, NY, 1965-68; Natl Fed Temple Brotherhoods, chancelor J Chautauqua Soc, 1963-65; NY Lodge 1, B'nai B'rith, 1958-60; mem, bd trustees: UAHC; FJP, NY; mem: Natl Civil Rights Commn, ADL; Natl Hillel Commn; AJ Comm; NY Co Lawyers Assn; Harvard Law Sch Assn. Home: 1165 Park Ave, New York, NY. Office: 22 E 40 St, New York, NY.

STONE, Jerome H, US, business exec; b. Chgo, Ill, Mar 18, 1913; s. Joseph and Mary (Hefter); att: Northwestern U; DePaul U Law Sch; m. Evelyn Teitelbaum, Aug 19, 1936; c: James, Ellen, Cynthia. Exec vice-pres, chief off off, Stone Container, since 1968, with firm since 1946; vice-pres, SC Inds, since 1962; mem mgmt adv bd, Paperboard, Packaging; partner, J H Stone & Sons, 1938-46. Chmn: bd, Roosevelt U; rel activities comm, Chgo and Gt Lakes UAHC Fed; public info comm, Fibre Box Assn, fmr pres; dir: Evanston Hosp; Ill Children's Home and Aid Soc; pres: Intl Corrugated Case Assn, Paris 1961-63; J Vocational Service, 1953-55; N Shore Cong Isr, 1961-65; vice-pres, J Fed, Metrop Chgo, 1967-68; clubs: Standard, Chgo; Northmoor Country, dir; Arts, Chgo; Mid-America, Chgo. Hobbies: golf, art, music. Home: 212 Maple Hill Rd, Glencoe, Ill. Office: 360 N Michigan Ave, Chicago, Ill.

STONE, Julius, Austr, educator, author, jurist; b. Leeds, Eng;

July 7, 1907; s. Israel and Ellen (Cohen); BA, Oxford U, 1928, BCL, 1929, DCL, 1935; LLM, U Leeds, 1930; Rockefeller f in social scis, 1930; DJS, Harvard U, 1932; m. Reca Lieberman, Aug 1934; c: Michael, Jonathan, Eleanor. Challis prof, intl law and jurisprudence, U Sydney, since 1942, acting dean, fac law, 1954-55, 1958-59; academic dir, Harry S Truman Cen for Advancement of Peace, Jerusalem, Isr; asst lectr, U Coll, Hull, 1930; prof, intl law and diplomacy, Fletcher Sch Law and Diplomacy, 1933-36, visiting prof, 1949; instr, asst prof law, Harvard Law Sch, 1932-36; prof, dean fac, Law sch, Auckland U Coll, NZ, 1938-42; visiting prof: NYU; Columbia U; Harvard U; Hague Acad of Intl Law; Charles Inglis Thompson guest prof, U of Colo; Rosco Pound lectr, U Nebraska, all 1956, 1957; John Field Sims Memorial Lectr, U New Mexico, 1959; visiting prof, Indian Sch of Intl Studies, Delhi, 1960. Asso, Inst Intl Law; councilor, Austr sect, Intl Comm, Jurists, acting pres, 1962; found, exec mem, Austr Social Sci Research Council; first pres, Austr br, Intl Law Assn, 1959, official observer, Eichmann Trial; chmn, NSW research group, Austr Inst Intl Affairs, 1942-45; vice-chmn, PM'S Comm on Natl Morale and with Directorate of Research, LHQ, lt col; Austr delg, 6th UNESCO Gen Conf, Paris, 1951; chmn, Austr UNESCO Comm for Social Scis, 1950-60, mem, Austr repr, 2nd Corning conf on the individual in the modern world; mem comm, Friends of Heb U; hon mem, Amer Soc Intl Law. Author: International Guarantees of Minority Rights, 1932; Regional Guarantees of Minority Rights, 1933; Law in the Modern State, 1939; The Atlantic Charter-New Worlds for Old; Stand Up and Be Counted, 1944; Colonial Trusteeship in Transition, 1945; The Province and the Function of Law, 1946, 1961; Legal System and Lawyer's Reasonings, 1964; Human Law and Human Justice, 1965; Social Dimensions of Law and Justice, 1966; The Middle East Under Cease-Fire, 1967; No Peace, No War in the Middle East, 1969; co-autor: Law and Society, 3 vols, 1949; Legal Controls of International Conflict, 1954, 1958; Sociological Inquiries Concerning International Law, 1956; Aggression and World Order, 1958; Legal Education and Public Responsibility, 1959; Quest for Survival, 1961; The Eichmann Trial and the Rule of Law, 1961; The International Court and World Crisis, 1962; gen ed, Sydney Law Review, 1953-60, mem ed comm; radio and TV commentator on intl affairs, Austr Bc Commn, since 1945; contbr to Anglo-Amer legal publs. Recipient: award, Amer Soc Intl Law, 1956; prize, Legatum Visserianum, Leyden U, Holland, 1956. Home: 1 Holland Rd, Double Bay, NSW, Austr. Office: 167 Phillip St, Sydney, Austr.

STONE, L Joseph, US, educator; b. Wash, DC, May 20, 1912; s. Nahum and Esther (Levinson); BA, Cornell U, 1933; MA, Columbia U, 1934, PhD, 1937; m. Beatrice Berlin, 1933 (decd); c: Deborah Nelson, Miriam Leavitt, Susannah Eldridge. Prof, psych, Vassar Coll, since 1949, chmn, dept of child study, 1955-61, fac mem, since 1939, dir, Vassar Film Series, since 1940; instr psych: Columbia U, 1935-37; Bklyn Coll, 1938-39; CCNY, 1940-42; research asso, Sarah Lawrence Coll, 1937-39; lectr, New Sch for Soc Research, 1945-56; mem staff, Dutchess Co Mh Clinic, 1950-65; Fulbright research grant, U of Oslo, Nor, 1957-58. Lt cmdr, USPHS, 1944-46. Dipl, Amer Bd Examiners Prof Psych; f: Amer Psych Assn; Amer Orthopsychiatric Assn; Soc Projective Techniques; Soc Research Child Devl; NY State Psych Assn, pres, 1952; World Fed of Mh; E Psych Assn; mem: adv council, psych, Bd Regents, SUNY, 1958-66; Sigma Xi; fmr dir, Catherine St Comty Cen, Poughkeepsie, NY. Co-author: Childhood and Adolescence; A Psychology of the Growing Person, 1957, 1968; contbr to profsl jours. Office: Vassar Coll, Poughkeepsie, NY.

STONE, Martin L, US, physician, educator; b. NYC, June 11, 1920; s. Isaac and Margaret (Usoskin) Goldstein; BS, Columbia U, 1941; MD, NY Med Coll, 1944, MMS, 1949; m. Dorothy Freedman, Mar 21, 1943; c: Robert. Prof and chmn, dept of obstet and gyn, NY Med Coll, since 1956, on staff since 1953; att, obstet and gyn, Metrop Hosp, since 1956, asso visiting phys, 1953-56; att obstet and gyn, Flower and 5th Ave Hosps, since 1956, asst att obstet and gyn, 1953-56; att gyn, Bird S Coler Hosp and Home, since 1956; cons: Mitchell Air Force Base, since 1957; Bx Vets Hosp, since 1957; chief, obstet and gyn, Tilton Gen Hosp, 1946-47; asso visiting gyn, Otisville Munic Sanatorium, 1953; cons: Fitkin Memorial Hosp, Neptune, NJ; Perth Amboy Hosp, NJ; Southampton Hosp, NY; City of Hope, LA. F: NY Acad Sci; NY, Amer Gyn Socs; NY Obstet Soc; hon, f: NJ Obstet and Gyn Soc; Brazilian Soc of Obstet and Gyn; treas, Alumni Assn, secy Alumni Fund, both NY Med Coll; chmn, tissue comm, chmn, out-patient dept comm, both Metrop Hosp; obstet cons, maternity and newborn div, Dept Health, NYC; secy-treas, and prog chmn, Dist II, Amer Coll of Obstet and Gyn, 1959; secy, sect obstet and gyn, Acad of Med, 1961; co-investigator, collaborative research prog, Natl Inst Neur Diseases and NIH; mem: med adv bd, Planned Parenthood NY; sci adv, council, Menen Baby Found; Amer Coll Surgs; Amer Bd Obstet and Gyn; Amer Coll Obstet and Gyn; Amer Soc for Study of Sterility; NY Fertility Soc; AAAS; Intl Fertility Assn; Amer Comm on Maternal Wfr; Assn of Amer Med Coll; Med Soc of NY Co; Med Soc NY State; AMA; Intl Coll Surgs; Amer Acad Cerebral Palsy; asso, mem, Amer Acad of Neur. Contbr to med jours. Recipient: Alumni of Year award, NY Med Coll, 1960. Home: 110 E End Ave, New York, NY. Office: 1249 Fifth Ave, New York, NY.

STONE, Marvin L, US, journalist; b. Burlington, Vt, Feb 26, 1924; s. Samuel and Anita (Abrams); AB, Marshall U, 1947, hon Des Lettres, 1968; MSJ, Columbia U, 1949; m. Sydell Magelaner, Nov 20, 1949; c: Jamie, Stacey, Torren. Asso exec ed, US News & World Report, since 1960; assignment, Huntington Herald Dispatch, W Va, 1941-43; Eur corresp, Intl News Service, 1949-52, Far E dir, 1952-58; Sloan f in service, Columbia U, 1958-59; cons to chief of Army Research and Devl, 1959-60. Lt, USN, 1943-46. Pres, Fgn Corresps Club, Japan, 1956-57; vice-pres, Columbia Journalism Alumni, 1960-62; sponsor, The Atlantic Council; mem, Amer Acad Political and Social Soc; clubs: White House Corresps Assn; Natl Press; Overseas Writers, all Wash, DC; Overseas Press, NY. Author: Man in Space 1960. Recipient: Pulitzer Travelling f, Columbia U, 1950; Holmes Award for Fgn Corresp, Intl News Service, 1954; Hon award, Columbia U 50th Anniversary, 1963. Home: 6368 Waterway Dr, Falls Church, Va. Office: 2300 N St NW, Washington, DC.

STONE, Melvin Lewis, US, business exec; b. Portland, Me, May 1, 1921; s. David and Gertrude (Cohen) Epstein; att Portland Jr Coll, 1939-41; BS, Boston U, 1943; m. Frances Lempert; c: Charles, David. Pres: Stone Enterprises Inc, since 1965; Downeast TV, since 1963; and treas, gen mgr, Rumford Bc Co, since 1952; Rumford Publ; vice-pres, gen mgr, Casco Broadcasters Corp, 1957-65. Capt, Army Corps of Engrs, 1943-47. Pres: and org, NE Press Assn; J Fed of Portland; fmr pres: Me Press Assn; Me Radio-TV Broadcasters Assn; chmn, CJA, 1964; vice-pres: J Home for Aged, 1965-68; Temple Beth El, 1963-65; mem: B'nai B'rith; AJ Comm; ACLU; clubs: Lions; Sales Marketing Execs; Portland Advt. Recipient: Bronze Star. Home: 6 Highland, Portland, Me. Office: 440 Forest Ave, Portland, Me.

STONE, Michael Edward, Isr, educator; b. Leeds, Eng, Oct 22, 1938; s. Julius and Reca; in Isr since 1966; BA, U Melbourne, Austr, 1959; att Heb U, Jerusalem, 1960-61; PhD, Harvard U, 1965; m. Nira Weintraub, 1961; c: Aurit. Research f, J Hellenism, Heb U, Jerusalem, since 1966; asst prof, U of Cal, Santa Barbara, 1965-66. Secy, Isr Soc Hist of Rels; mem: Soc Rel in Higher Educ; Soc Bibl Lit. Author: The Testament of Levi, 1969; The Manuscript Library of Armenian Patriarchate of Jerusalem, 1969; dept ed, Apocrypha and Pseudepigrapha, Ency Judaica. Contbr articles to scholarly jours. Home: 10b Hatomer St, Jerusalem, Isr. Office: Heb U, Jerusalem, Isr.

STONE, Morris, US, dentist; b. Beverly, Mass, Apr 14, 1923; s. Benjamin and Mary (Goldberg); BS, Tufts U, Mass, 1944, DMD, Sch of Dent, 1947; m. Gail Rogers, May 2, 1948; c: Beverly, David. Pvt practice, since 1947; instr, clinical dent, Tufts U Dent Sch, Boston, Mass, 1950-59. Pvt, US Army, 1943-44; capt, 1952-54. Pres: Roxbury Dent Soc, 1960; Dudley Assn, 1962; mem: Temple Emeth, S Brookline, Mass; Royal Soc Health, Eng; Metrop Dist Dent Soc; Mass Dent Soc; Amer Dent Assn; KP; Masons. Hobby: stamp and coin collection. Home: 480 Dudley Rd, Newton, Mass. Offices: 1352 Bedcon St, Brookline, Mass; 1085 Blue Hill Ave, Dorchester, Mass.

STORCH, Harold Jacob, US, supermarket exec; b. Pol, June 9, 1910; s. Jacob and Esther; in US since 1923; m. Ruth, June 24, 1934; c: Elaine Retting, Gerald. Owner, secy, mem, bd dirs, Key Food Stores, since 1936. Chmn, food ind, State of Isr Bonds; vice-pres, Harvest Lodge, B'nai B'rith, 1967-70; mem: UJA; ADL; Cong Sons of Isr; club: Food Ind Sq, fmr pres. Hobbies: bridge, golf. Home: 967 Midwood Rd, Woodmere, NY. Office: 6928 Fifth Ave, Brooklyn, NY.

STRASFOGEL, Ignace, US, conductor; b. Warsaw, Pol, July 17, 1909; s. Ludwik and Salomea (Goldberg); in US since 1933; att Hochschule für Musik, Berlin, 1923-27; m. Alma Lubin, July 23, 1934; c: Ian, Andrew. Asso conductor, Metrop Opera Co, since 1960; musical dir, Kathryn Long Opera Sch, on musical staff, since 1950; asst conductor, Berlin State Opera, 1930; composer, conductor, Max Reinhardt Producs, Berlin, 1929-32; official pianist, NY Philharmonic Sym Soc, 1935-45; guest conductor: Ballet Russe, Naumberg Concerts, both NYC; NYC Sym, Latin Amer tour, 1938-42; Grand Theater Opera House, Geneva, Switz, 1968; conducted: NY Philharmonic, Lewisohn Stadium, 1944, Cen Park Mall; Carnegie Hall; Cincinnati Summer Opera, 1958-65; summer concerts, New Orleans; Grant Park Series, Chgo; Phila Orch, Acad of Music; Buffalo Philharmonic; Natl Sym Orch, Wash, DC; Dr's Orch Soc, 1947-50; New Friends of Music Series, Town Hall, NYC, 1948-50; Metrop Opera Auditions of Air, 1954-57; Metrop Opera Spring Tour, 1957; Metrop Opera, NYC. Recipient: Mendelssohn State Prize, composition, Berlin, 1926; Medal of Liberation, King Christian X, Denmark, 1945. Home: 161 W 54 St, New York, NY. Office: Metrop Opera, Lincoln Center Plaza, New York, NY.

STRASSBURGER, Eugene B, US, attorney; b. Pittsburgh, Pa, Sep 23, 1886; s. Samuel and Julia (Morganstern); BA, Harvard U, 1908, LLB, 1910; hon LLD, Duquesne U Law Sch; m. Constance Block, May 10, 1915; c: Eugene, Joan Obernauer, Martha Ringel. Mem, law firm, Strassburger & McKenna, since 1919; vice-pres, atty, Grant Bldg Inc, since 1927; secy, dir, atty: The Emerson Press, Inc; Keystone Box Co, both since 1946; dir, atty: Pittsburgh Outdoor Advt Co; York Furniture Inc, both since 1935; atty: Gearing Lumber Co, since 1910; Royal of Pittsburgh, Inc, since 1945; instr, negotiable instruments and suretyship, Duquesne U Law Sch, 1920-42. US Army, WW I. Vice-pres and trustee, Rodef Shalom Cong, since 1949, pres, 1941-49; trustee: UAHC, since 1936, vice-pres, 1948-56; Natl J Hosp, Denver; and secy, Maurice and Laura Falk Found; chmn, Law Libr Comm, Allegheny Co; mem: exec comm, council, Amer Law Inst; Amer, Pa, and Allegheny Co Bar Assns; Amer Judicature Soc; Orphans Court Rules Comm; Harvard Law Sch Assn, W Pa, pres, 1951-52; council, Harvard Law Sch Alumni Assn; visiting comm, bd overseers, Harvard Coll on ME studies, 1954-55, 1955-56; clubs: Concordia; Harvard-Yale-Princeton; Hundred, Pittsburgh; Westmoreland Country; Civic, Allegheny Co; Pa Soc; Bungalow Island Fishing, chmn of bd. Hobbies: bridge, fishing. Home: 6515 Beacon St, Pittsburgh, Pa. Office: 2602 Grant Bldg, Pittsburgh, Pa.

STRASSBURGER, Eugene B, Jr, US, attorney; b. Pittsburgh, Pa, Mar 27, 1917; s. Eugene and Constance (Block); BA, Williams Coll, 1938; LLB, Harvard U, 1941; m. Jane Schanfarber, Aug 19, 1941; c: Eugene, Edwin, Elaine. Practicing atty, since 1942. USN, 1942-45. Natl bd mem, NCCJ, since 1967, co-chmn W Pa and W Va, 1956-62; trustee, Pittsburgh chap, AJComm; mem: Allegheny, Pa and Amer Bar Assns; Amer Law Inst. Recipient: Asiatic Pacific Area Service decoration with 8 battle stars; Philippine Liberation Ribbon, one star. Hobbies: golf, bridge, philately. Home: 1530 Beechwood Blvd, Pittsburgh, Pa. Office: 2602 Grant Blvd, Pittsburgh, Pa.

STRAUCH, Morris L, US, attorney; b. NYC, Feb 7, 1909; s. Isadore and Sophie (Plesofsky); BA, U Tenn, 1930; att Harvard Law Sch, 1930-32; m. Nettie Brooks, Sep 1, 1946; c: Ilsa. Pvt practice, since 1933; partner, Goodman, Glazer, Strauch & Schneider. Capt, US Army, 1942-46. Pres: dist grand lodge, 7, B'nai B'rith, 1955-56, Tenn state assn, 1950; Fed J Wfr Agcys, Memphis, 1954-56, vice-pres, 1952-54; Shelby Co chap, U Tenn Alumni Assn, 1949-62; natl commn, ADL, 1956-62; chmn, AJComm, Memphise, 1952-53; treas, J Comty Cen, 1958-60, vice-pres, 1960-62; bd trustees: B'nai B'rith Home and Hosp for Aged, Inc; Leo N Levi Memorial Hosp; mem: Amer, Tenn, Memphis, Shelby Co Bar Assns; Masons; Phi Kappa Phi. Home: 1142 Fair Meadow Rd, Memphis, Tenn. Office: 1400 Commerce Title Bldg, Memphis, Tenn.

STRAUS, David III, US, advertising exec; b. Newark, NJ, Nov 5, 1916; s. David and Pauline (Schwartz); BS, Ind U, 1939; m. Lizbeth Spero, Nov 26, 1947; c: Robin, Martha. Sr vice-pres, Zlowe Co, Inc, since 1961; advt mgr, Ronson Corp, 1940-42; acct exec, Lewin, Williams & Saylor, 1945-52; vice-pres, secy, Ovesey & Straus, Inc, 1952-61. Lt, USAF. Mem, bd trustees: Temple B'nai Jeshurun, Newark, NJ; mass media comm, AJComm; mem bd, J Counseling and Service Agcy. Home: 63 Collinwood Rd, Maplewood, NJ. Office: 770 Lexington Ave, New York, NY.

STRAUS, Donald Blum, US, business exec; b. Middletown, NJ, June 28, 1916; s. Percy and Edith (Abraham); AB, Harvard U, 1938, MBA, 1940; m. Elizabeth Allen, Sep 7, 1940; c: David, Robert, Sara. Pres, Amer Arbitration Assn, since 1963; research asst, Harvard Grad Sch of Bus Admn, 1941-42; chief of personnel, CAB, 1942-43; vice-pres, Mgmt Employee Relation, Inc, 1946-53; exec dir, Atomic Energy Lab Relations Panel, 1948-53; instr, NYU, 1950-51; vice-chmn, review and appeals comm, Wage Stabilization Bd, Wash, DC, 1952; vice-pres, Health Ins, Gfr NY, 1953-61; mem, NY State Mediation Bd, 1956-59; cons and arbitrator, 1961-63; lab bds: econ cons, NYC Transit Fact Finding bd, 1950; secy, Pres Emergency Bd, Amer Airlines Dispute, 1951; mem, Lab Secy's Foreign Flag Review Bd; exec secy, Pres Bd Inquiry, Maritime Dispute, both 1961; mem, Pres Emergency Bd 142, 1962. Air combat intelligence off, USN, 1943-45. F Amer Public Health Assn; chmn, exec comm, Panned Parenthood of Amer, since 1965, chmn bd, 1962-65; trustee, Milton Acad, Mass; mem: review comm, Asso Hosp Service of NY; Council on Fgn Relations; comm on Second Regional Plan; Cent Assn; bd: NY Fund for children; Educ Alliance, fmr pres; Amer Found on Automation and Employment; State Charities Aid Assn; UN Assn, 1964-65; fmr: mem, overseers comms to visit Harvard U; chmn, sem Jt Conf Group Health Fed of Amer, Amer Lab Health Assn; mem: Markle Scholarship Bd Comm; bd: Group Health Assn; Public Educ Assn; United Neighborhood Houses. Contbr to profsl publs. Recipient: Stanley Isaacs award, for dist public and comty service, 1965. Home: 44 E 73 St, New York, NY. Office: 140 W 51 St, New York, NY.

STRAUS, Ernst G, US, mathematician, educator; b. Munich, Ger, Feb 25, 1922; s. Elias and Rahel (Goitein); in US since 1941; att Heb U, Jerusalem, 1938-41; MA, Columbia U, 1942, PhD, 1948; m. Louise Miller, Nov 23, 1944; c: Daniel, Paul. Prof math, UCLA, since 1948; asst to Albert Einstein, Inst for Advanced Study, Princeton, NJ, 1944-48. Mem, Amer Math Soc. Mgn ed, Pacific jour of Math, 1956-59; contbr to sci jours. Home: 526 Bienveneda, Pacific Palisades, Cal. Office: U Cal, Los Angeles, Cal.

STRAUS, Jack Isidor, US, business exec; b. NYC, Jan 13, 1900; s. Jesse and Irma (Nathan); BA, Harvard U, 1921; hon: LLD, Adelphi Coll, 1955; DCS, NYU, 1958; m, Margaret Hollister, Apr 29, 1924; c: Patricia Toohey, Pamela McLean, Kenneth. Chmn, exec comm, R H Macy and Co Inc, since 1968, chmn bd, 1956-68, pres, 1940-56, on mgn staff since 1922; dir: Continental Can Co since 1964; FidelityUnion Trust Co, Newark, since 1967; NYC Public Devl Corp, since 1966, and vice-chmn, since 1968; Econ Devl Corp NYC, since 1965; trustee, Greenwich Savings Bank; dir: and vice-pres, Macy's Bank, 1941-67; Safeway Stores, Inc, 1956-59; LI RR, 1954-56. Lt, US Army, 1919. Hon f, Amer Coll of Hosp Admnrs; chmn: retail stores div, NY United Service Org; bd trustees, Roosevelt Hosp, since 1965; Mayor's Comm for Pedestrian Safety, 1957-58; dir: Gtr NY Fund, 1942-64, hon dir, since 1964; Police Athletic League, since 1961, vice-pres, since 1964; Amer Arbitration Assn, since 1955; public gov, NY Stock Exch, 1964-68; fmr secy, J Bd Guardians; mem: traffic adv comm, NYC, since 1954; Amer Soc Fr Legion of Honor; life, Acad of Political Sci; visiting comm: Harvard U Sch of Bus Admn, 1938-65; U Resources, 1964-67; bd overseers, Harvard Coll, 1950-54; mem at large, Empire State Found, since 1952; clubs: Harvard, NYC; Piping Rock; The Creek. Recipient: Cross of Off, Order of Leopold II, Belgium, 1951; Chevalier de la Legion d'Honneur, Fr, 1951; Stella della Solidarieta Italiana di seconda classe, 1952. Home: 19 E 72 St, New York, NY. Office: 151 W 34 St, New York, NY.

STRAUS, Oscar S II, US, business exec; b. NYC, Nov 6, 1914; s. Roger and Gladys (Guggenheim); AB, Princeton, 1936; m. Marion Miller, 1941; c: Oscar. Pres and dir, Straus Exploration Inc, since 1968; partner, Guggenheim Brothers Ltd, since 1959; limited partner, Salomon Bros; dir: Anglo-Lautaro Nitrate Corp; Tehidy Minerals Ltd; Camborne Mines, Ltd; pvt secy, Intl Lab Off, Geneva, Switz, 1937-38; US Fgn Service Off, 1940-42; divisional asst, State Dept, 1942-43, 1944-45; chmn, finance comm, Amer Smelting and Refining Co, 1946-59; pres, Guggenheim Exploration Co, 1963-68. Lt, USCG, Res, 1943-44. Chmn, natl comm, Inst on Man and Sci; co-chmn, NCCJ; pres, Theodore Roosevelt Assn, 1948-58; dir: Daniel and Florence Guggenheim Found; and pres, Fred L Lavan-

burg Found; Clear Pool Camp, 1948-68; trustee: U Andes, 1959-63; and secy, treas, Roger William Straus Found; mem: adv council, econ dept, Princeton U; US Trade Mission to Peru, Ecuador, 1959; clubs: Princeton U; River; Bankers of Amer, NYC; Mining; Megantic Fish and Game; Royal Nova Scotia Yacht Squadron; Chester Yacht, Nova Scotia; The Bd Room. Spec interests: yachting, skiing, tennis. Home: 228 E 62 St, New York, NY. Office: 120 Broadway, New York, NY.

STRAUS, William L Jr, US, anatomist, anthropologist, educator; b. Baltimore, Md, Oct 29, 1900; s. William and Pauline (Gutman); BA, Johns Hopkins U, 1920, PhD, 1926; f; Natl Research Council, W Reserve U, 1926-27; Guggenheim Memorial Found, U Coll, London, 1937-38; m. Henrietta Hecht, Sep 19, 1926 (decd); m. 2nd, Bertha Nusbaum, June 15, 1955; c: Pauline Rauh. Prof, anat and phys anthropology, Johns Hopkins U, since 1957, fac mem, since 1927; hon research asst, U Coll, London, Eng, 1937-38; visiting prof, anat, Wayne State U, 1950. F, AAAS, vice-pres and chmn, sect anthropology, 1956, acting chmn, ed bd, 1953; pres: Amer Assn of Phys Anthropologists, 1953-55; Johns Hopkins Chap, Sigma Xi, 1957-58; mem: Anat Bd, State of Md, 1947-52; Amer Assn of Anats; adv bd, Patuxent Inst Md, 1955-60; Natl Acad Scis; Amer Soc Mammalogists; Amer Soc Zools; Marine Biol Lab, Woods Hole, Mass; Amer Inst of Human Paleontology; hon, Phi Beta Kappa; Soc of Vertebrate Paleontology; Baltimore Zool Soc; Amer Anthropological Assn; corresp mem, Zool Soc, London. Mem, ed bd: Human Biology, since 1953; Folia Primatologica, since 1962; co-ed: Yearbook of Physical Anthropology, 1951; The Anatomy of the Rhesus Monkey, 1953; Forerunners of Darwin, 1745-1859; acting chmn, ed bd, Science and Scientific Monthly, 1953; asso editor, Amer Jour Anat, 1946-58; contbr to jours and books. Recipient: medal and award in phys anthropology, Viking Fund, 1952; achievement citation, Phi Epsilon Pi, 1957. Hobbies: painting, art. Home: 7111 Park Heights Ave, Baltimore, Md. Office: Johns Hopkins U Sch of Med, Baltimore, Md.

STRAUSS, Amelia C, US, attorney; b. Knoxville, Tenn, Sep 25, 1908; d. Gerson and Mattie(Rabinowitz) Corkland; LLB, U Tenn, 1930; m. Harry Strauss, June 18, 1933; c. Jo Anne George; Madelyne Bailey. Partner, Strauss & Strauss, since 1934; mem, Campbell & Corkland, 1931-34. Pres: bd Childrens and Family Bur, Knoxville, 1948-50; Knox Area Mh Assn, 1969; women's sect, Tenn Bar, 1947-48; vice-pres: Natl Assn of Women Lawyers, Tenn, 1948-50; natl B'nai B'rith Women, 1961-62; Florence Crittenton Home Bd, 1969; vice-chmn, ADL Natl Commn, 1969, mem since 1959; regional dir, Bus and Profsl Women's Group, 1945; mem: Tenn Mh Assn Bd, since 1965; Knox Co Juvenile Court Adv Bd, 1968; Regional Libr Bd, E Tenn, 1949; budget comm, United Fund, 1951; Knoxville Bar Assn; Phi Kappa Phi; Order of Coif. Contbr to legal journals. Home: 925 Southgate Rd, Knoxville, Tenn. Office: 800 Burwell Bldg, Knoxville, Tenn.

STRAUSS, Bernard V, US, psychiatrist, educator; b. Bklyn, NY, Dec 21, 1910; s. Max and Clara (Falk); BS, Columbia U, 1931; MD, LI Coll Med, 1935; m. Seena Mandell, 1935; c: Saul. Pvt practice, since 1940; clinical asso prof, psycht, SUNY Med Sch, since 1947; sr psychiatric cons, i/c psychiatrice res training prog, VA Hosp, Bklyn, since 1950; psychiatric cons: Mental Hygiene Clinic, NY regional off VA, since 1961; Danbury Hosp, Conn; dir: child guidance clinic, Maimonides Hosp, 1937-45; mental hygiene clinic, Kings Co Hosp, 1941-45. Dipl, Amer Bd Psycht and Neur, 1942; f: Amer Psychiatric Assn; Amer Orthopsychiatric Assn; mem: Bklyn Psychiatric Soc; Fairfield Co, Conn State Med Socs. Contbr to med jours. Home and office: Arrowhead Point, Brookfield, Conn.

STRAUSS, Clifford M, US, business exec; b. Memphis, Tenn, May 17, 1904; s. Fred and Carrie (Schuster); m. Roselyn Lieber, Aug 5, 1926; c: Carolyn (decd), Peggy Greenbaum, Jean Mintz. Pres: F Strauss & Son, Inc, Monroe, La and Affiliates, chmn, bd: New Orleans, Tallulah; Gulf Island Corp; chmn bd: Strauss Liquor Corp, Monroe, Shreveport; Strauss Distributors Inc; devl, operator: Eastgate Shopping Cen; Southside Shopping Cen; Northgate Shopping Cen; K-Mart Plaza Shopping Cen. Chmn, Carolyn Rose Strauss Rehab Cen; fmr pres: United Givers Fund; C of C; Cong B'nai Isr; Wine and Spirits Whoesalers, Amer; Public Affairs Research Council, La. Home: 3706 Deborah Dr, Monroe, La. Office: 2930 Commerce St, Monroe, La.

STRAUSS, Elias, US, physician, educator; b. Roosevelt, NY, Feb 13, 1913; s. Henry and Ray (Friedman); BS, NYU, 1933; MD, Columbia U Med Sch, 1937; m. Sophie Simmons, Aug 21, 1941; c: Henry, James, Robert. Pvt practice, since 1948; clinical prof preventive med, chmn dept, Southwestern Med Sch, U Tex, since 1954. Major, US Army MC, WW II. Mem: Amer Coll Phys; Amer Soc for Clinical Research; Amer Fed for Clinical Research; AMA; S Soc for Clinical Inves; AHA. Contbr to profsl jours. Home: 6307 Glendora, Dallas, Tex. Office: 3707 Gaston Ave, Dallas, Tex.

STRAUSS, Gideon, US, banker; b. Berlin, Ger Apr 16, 1915; s. Max and Ida (Rosenfeld); m. Ruth Kanterowicz, 1939 (div); c: Yair, Noa; m. 2nd, Renate Calé, 1954; c: Sharon, Eran, Adin. Vice-pres, intl dept, Rosenthal & Rosenthal, Inc, since 1966, sr vice-pres, Rosenthal Intl Ltd, Nassau; fmr: US repr, Bank Leumi leIsr, exec vice-pres, mgr, NY br, Bank Leumi; pres, Leumi Financial Corp, NY; mem, head of staff, Anglo-Pal Bank Ltd, Tel Aviv, 1936-48; consul, econ dept, Consulate Gen of Isr, NY, 1948-50; Isr delg, econ and social comm, UN Gen Assembly, 1949-50. Contbr to jours. Home: 205 W End Ave, New York, NY. Office: 1451 Broadway, New York, NY.

STRAUSS, Herbert Arthur, US, educator, communal leader; b. Würzburg, Ger, June 1, 1918; s. Benno and Magdala (Hinterneder); in US since 1946; PhD, U Bern, Switz, 1946; att: Columbia U, 1949; New Sch for Social Research, 1949-51; m. Lotte Schloss, 1944; c: Jane. Asso prof, hist, CCNY, since 1960, on fac 1948-54; exec-dir, Amer Fed of Jews from Cen Eur, since 1964; chmn, B'rith Yehudim Zeirim, Ger, 1936-38; f: Commn on Eur J Cultural Reconstruction, 1946-48; New Sch for Social Research, 1949-51; asst to asso prof, acad dept, Juilliard Sch, NY, 1954-60. F: Leo Baeck Inst, 1963; Amer Council Learned Socs, 1963; Social Sci Research Council, 1963; Memorial Found for J Culture, 1956, 1960, 1966; mem, bd dirs: Self Help of Emigrés from Cen Eur, NY; NY Nursing Home Found; J Philanthropic Fund of 1933, since 1968; Kew Gardens Nursing Home Co, since 1968; mem, scholarship comm, Robinson Scholarship Fund, NY. since 1965. Author: Staat, Buerger, Mensch, 1948; other books; contbr to Ency Judaica; J publs. Recipient: numerous awards, including: NAACP, Phi Alpha Theta, Alpha Sigma Lambda. Home: 90 Lasalle St, New York, NY. Office: CCNY, 139 St at Convent Ave, New York, NY.

STRAUSS, Israel, Isr, certified public acctnt; b. Haifa, Apr 7 1930; s. David and Rivka (Kaplan); att Tel Aviv Sch of Law and Econ, 1950-54; m. Amalia Ben-Ya'acov, Feb 10, 1953; c: Ehud, Opher. Free-lance CPA, since 1962; chief insp, Income Tax, 1954-57; head, inves dept, Migdal Ins Co, 1957-62; lectr on income tax. Capt, IDF. Mem, presidium, profsl council, numerous other comms, Inst of CPAs, Isr. Author: Key to Income Tax Cases, 1965; brochures and articles on income and estate taxes. Home: 10 Frankel St, Tel Aviv, Isr. Office: 3 Ahuzat Bayit St, Tel Aviv, Isr.

STRAUSS, Joseph M, US, rabbi; b. Detroit, Mich, Jan 7, 1917; s. Isadore and Fannie (Hostein); BA, teaching cert, Wayne State U, 1937; ordained rabbi, MHL, HUC, 1943; att: Northwestern U; U Chgo, both 1945; DD, HUC-JIR, 1968; m. Elizabeth Shapiro, June 24, 1945; c: Sharon, Herschel. Rabbi: and found, Temple Menorah, since 1946; Temple Beth El, Helena, Ark, 1943-44; Beth El Cong, Chgo, 1944-46. Pres: Interfaith F, W Rogers Park; Chgo Assn of Reform Rabbis, 1967-69; mem: CCAR; ZOA; B'nai B'rith; Chgo Bd of Rabbis; club, Covenant. Hobbies: swimming, golf. Home: 2948 W Greenleaf, Chgo, Ill. Study: 2800 W Sherwin Ave, Chicago, Ill.

STRAUSS, Julius, US, business exec; b. Stuttgart, Ger, July 21, 1899; s. Salomon and Frieda (Neter); in US since 1936; att U Munich; m. Eva Korps, Nov 24, 1927; c: Rosemary, Peter. Chmn bd, Gen Cigar Co, NY, since 1963, pres, 1949-62, with firm since 1936. Lt, Ger Army, 1916-19. Finance chmn, Boy Scouts, Manhattan; fmr ind chmn: FJP; UJA; club, Golden Age, Gt Neck, trustee. Hobbies: music, golf, gradening. Home: 1 Brentwood Lane, Great Neck, NY. Office: 605 Third Ave, New York, NY.

STRAUSS, Karl M, US, business exec; b. Minden, Ger, Oct, 5, 1912; s. Albrecht and Mathilde (Lilienfeld); in US since 1939; BS, Munich Inst Tech, 1933; m. Irene Vollweiler, Jan 1939. Vice-pres, produc, Pabst Brewing Co, since 1959, with co since 1939. Fmr pres, Master Brewers Assn Amer, pres, S Cal dist, 1950; dir: Malting Barley Improvement Assn, since 1959; Brewing Ind Research Inst, since 1961; mem: B'nai B'rith; Amer Soc Brewing Chems; Milw Grain Exch; Minneapolis Grain Exch; club, New Home, vice-pres, 1946. Home: 8515 N Manor Lane, Milwaukee, Wis. Office: 917 W Juneau Ave, Milwaukee, Wis.

STRAUSS, Leo, US, educator; b. Kirchhain, Ger, Sep 20, 1899; s. Hugo and Jennie (David); in US since 1938; PhD, U Hamburg, 1921; m. Miriam Bernson, June 20, 1933; c: Jennie. Prof, political sci, Claremont Men's Coll; Hutchins Dist Service prof, political sci, U Chgo, since 1949; research asst, Acad for J Research, Berlin, 1925-32; prof, fac mem, New Sch for Social Research, 1938-49. Mem, Amer Acad of J Research. Author: Religions-Kritik Spinoza's Berlin, 1930; Philosophie und Gesetz, 1935; The Political Philosophy of Hobbes, 1936; On Tyranny, 1948; Persecution and the Art of Writing, 1952; Natural Right and History, 1953; Thoughts on Machiavelli, 1958; What is Political Philosophy? 1959. Home: 145 E 11 St, Claremont, Cal. Office: Claremont Men's Coll, Claremont, Cal.

STRAUSS, Leonard Harold, US, business exec; b. Kan City, Kan, Nov 12, 1917; s. Harry and Anna (Cohn); BS, Carnegie Mellon U, Pittsburgh, Pa, 1939; m. Marilyn Ross, Nov 27, 1968; c: Leslie, Susan Feld. Pres: Inland Cold Storage Co, since 1946; Cousins Realty Co, since 1948; dir: Parkview Gem Inc, since 1960; Commercial Natl Bank, since 1962; Brown-Strauss Corp, since 1969. Capt, USAF, 1942-46. Pres, dir, Menorah Med Cen; vice-pres, dir, Kan City J Comty Cen; gov, Kan City J Fed. Home: 8449 Somerset Dr, Shawnee Mission, Kan. Office: 6500 Inland Dr, Kansas City, Kan.

STRAUSS, Walter, Israel, physician; b. Berlin, Ger, Jan 11, 1895; s. Moritz and Elizabeth (Ferber); in Isr since 1934; m. Anni Freudenthal, Oct 28, 1926; c: Uziel. Prof em, preventive med, Heb U Med Sch, Jerusalem, prof since 1950; lectr, asso prof, Berlin U, 1921-33; dir, Hadassah Health Cen, Jerusalem, 1939-49. Contbr to profsl publs. Home: 8 Shlomo Molcho St, Jerusalem, Isr.

STRAUSS, Walter, US, insurance broker; b. Stuttgart, Ger, July 25, 1905; s. Heinrich and Frieda (Neumond); PhD, U Heidelberg, 1926; law referendar, U Tübingen, 1928; CLU, Amer Coll Life Underwriters, 1950; m. Inge Wassermann, Dec 21, 1940; c: Brigitte, Frank, Marion. Ins broker since 1937; atty, Ger, 1932-36. Pres, Blue Card Inc; chmn, Org J from Württenberg; Friends of Fritz Busch Soc; leader, J Youth, Stuttgart, Ger, 1933-36; mem: Life Underwriters, Amer Soc of CLUs, NY. Music reporter, newspapers: Ger, Switz. Home: 621 W 227 St, Riverdale, NY. Office: 41 E 42 St, New York, NY.

STRAX, Selig, US, surgeon; b. NYC, June 23, 1913; s. Jacob and Molly (Pelchovicz); BS, NYU, 1931, MD, 1935; m. Blanche Isaacson, Aug 14, 1937; c: Thomas, Susan, Lisa. Sr clinical asst surg, Mt Sinai Hosp, since 1950; asso visiting surg, Harlem Hosp, since 1948; sr surg, USPHS, since 1957, on staff since 1943. Dipl, Amer Bd Surg; f, Amer and Intl Colls Surgs; Amer Soc Abdominal Surgs; NY Acad Med. Home: 10-53 Totten St, Beechhurst, NY. Office: 1056 Fifth Ave, New York, NY.

STREAN, George Joshua, Can, surgeon, educator; b. Montreal, Can, 1898; s. Max and Rachel (Pearson); BA, McGill U, 1918; MD, 1921; m. Hilda Blumer, 1928; c: Joan Solomon, Maxine Sigman. Pvt practice, obstet and gyn, since 1926; hon cons, Dept of Obstet and Gyn, J Gen Hosp, fmr, dir; fmr: asst prof, Obstet and Gyn, McGill U; mem, courtesy staff, Dept of Obstet and Gyn, St Mary's Hosp; demonstrator in chem, McGill U, 1922-23; att obstet, Herbert Reddy Memorial Hosp, 1926-35; gyn, Herzl Inst, 1926-40; mem, courtesy staff, Royal Vic Hosp. Capt, res, RCAMC. F: Royal Coll Surgs; Royal Coll Obstet and Gyn, chmn, Can Council, Amer Coll Surgs; Intl Coll Surgs, fmr pres, Can chap, Amer Coll Obstet and Gyn; pres, Que sect, JNF; fmr pres: Montreal Medico-Chirurgical Soc; Montreal Obstet and Gyn Soc; Montreal Clinical Soc; NE Soc Nuclear Med; chmn, adult educ, Shaar Hashomayim, Montreal; fmr chmn: Montreal Campaign for Albert Einstein Coll Med, 1954; Can Cancer Soc Campaign, Montreal, 1955; Red Cross Soc Campaign, Montreal, 1954; CJA, 1951-52; fmr vice-chmn, Campaign for Sir George Williams U; hon treas, Second World Cong, Intl Fed of Obstet and Gyn, 1958; mem, bd trustees, Fed J Comty Services; mem, bd govs: Hillel Found, McGill U; YM-YWHA; fmr mem, bd dirs: Marriage Counseling Cen, Wfr Fed Montreal; QMA, 1961-64; mem: Natl Council, JDC; Soc of Obstets and Gyns of Can; NY Acad of Sci; Can Med Assn; comm, IMA; Coll of Phys and Surgs of Provence of Que; Amer Comm on Maternal Wfr; Med Alumni Assn, Chgo U; Montreal Phys Soc; McGill U Tchrs Assn; Surgs of Provence of Que; Phi Delta Epsilon; Pi Lambda Phi; Sigma Xi; fmr mem: mem adv bds: Can Cancer Soc; Cancer Research Soc; Cancer Aid League; Maternal Wfr Comm, Mt Royal Lodge, B'nai B'rith; Corinthian Lodge; Masons; clubs: Canadian, Montreal; Montefiore; Elmridge Gold and Country; Greystone Curling; Westmount Munic; Old Boys, Montreal HS. Contbr to textbooks, med jours; ed, proceedings of IFGO, 2 vols, 1958. Recipient: f: Rockefeller, 1925; Guggenheim, 1927. Home: 656 Landsdowne Ave, Westmount, Que, Can. Office: 1538 Sherbrooke St W, Montreal, Que, Can.

STREIFLER, Edward Isaac, Isr, engineer; b. Vienna, Aus, July 1, 1921; s. Jonas and Lotte (Heller); in Isr since 1939; CE, Technion, Haifa; m. Cipora Aysenfeld, July 13, 1945; c: Joseph, Raphael. Dir, planning and devl, Koor Inds Ltd, since 1963; coord, Jt US-Isr sea water desalinization project, since 1964; dir, construction and installations, Min of Defense 1957-60; pres, Solcoor Inc, NY, 1960-63. Lt col, engr corps, IDF, 1947-57. Prin contrib: spec mil installation, first research reactor. Mem, bd govs, Technion, Haifa, since 1968; mem, bd dirs: Tech Communication Cen, since 1967; Assn of Architects and Engrs in Isr, since 1969; mem: US Mil Engrs; Amer Assn Civil Engrs. Contbr to jours. Home: 24 Lipsky St, Tel Aviv, Isr. Office: 99 Ben Yehuda St, Tel Aviv, Isr.

STREIFLER, Max B, Isr, neuropsychiatrist; b. Jazlovice, Aus, May 2, 1915; s. Jonas and Lotti (Heller); in Isr since 1938; att med fac, Vienna, MD U Beirut; MSC, Heb U, Jerusalem; med study Hadassah U Hosp, Jerusalem; US; m. Blanka Redner; c: Nurit, Jonathan. Clinical lectr, neur, Heb U Med Sch; sr clinical lectr, neur, Tel Aviv U Med Fac; head, dept neur, Ichilov-Hadassah Hosps, Tel Aviv; mem: sci socs. Contbr to profsl jours. Home: 53 David Hamelech Blvd, Tel Aviv, Isr. Office: Hadassah-Ichilov Hosp, Tel Aviv, Isr.

STRICKER, Stefan, Isr, engineer, educator; b. Baden, Aus, Aug 8, 1903; s. Moritz and Margaret (Bloch); in Isr since 1934; dipl, engr, Technische Hochschule, Vienna, 1927; m. Anna Silberberg, 1931. Asso prof, Technion, since 1959, dean fac, 1963-65, mem fac, since 1952; EE, Elin AG, Vienna, 1928-31; self employed, 1932-34; engr, Isr Elec Corp, 1934-52; guest lectr, UCLA, 1959-60; guest worker, Natl Bur of Standards, Wash, DC, 1965-66, guest research project, guest researcher, 1967-68; visiting prof, U Minn, 1966. Mem: Inst EEs, Eng; sr, Inst Elec and Electronics Engrs, US, various comms: Standards Inst, Isr; Min Devl; Min Labor. Contbr to profsl and sci jours. Hobby: chamber music. Home: 13 Adam Hacohen St, Haifa, Isr. Office: Engr Technion Fac, Haifa, Isr.}

STRIKS, Haim, Isr, attorney, business exec; b. Berlin, Ger, Aug 20, 1927; s. Michael and Leonie (Eitinger); in Isr since 1933; grad, Sch of Law and Econ, Tel Aviv, 1951; m. Aliza Gevirtz, June 27, 1950; c: Shelly, Michal. Partner, law off, Haim Zadok, Barzel, Deouell & Co, since 1968; gen counsel, secy, Rural and Suburban Settlement Co, 1953-68. IDF, 1948-49. Mem: Isr Bar Assn; Masons. Home: 10a Ruppin St, Tel Aviv, Isr, Office: 33 Lillienblum St, Tel Aviv, Isr.

STRIMLING, David B, Swed, attorney, organization exec; b. Växjö, Swed, Oct 27, 1907; s. Chaim and Sara (Nachemsohn); LLB, U Lund, 1932; m. Signe Schwartzberg, Aug 21, 1938; c: Siv, Lena, Jan. Comty secy, since 1944; law practice, 1938-44. Mem, B'nai B'rith. Hobbies: theater, fishing, bridge. Home: Roskildevägen 9b, Malmö, Swed. Office: Kamrergatan, 11, Malmö, Swed.

STRIP, Asriel C, US, attorney; b. Antwerp. Belgium, Apr 13, 1936; s. Menachem and Regina (Gunzig); BA, O State U, JD, 1960; m. Dorothy Danziger, Aug 24, 1958; c: Wendy, Michael. Partner, Harris, Lias & Strip, attys. Off, Natl Guard. Mem: comm on legal aid and indigent defenders, Amer Bar Assn, repr evaluating legal aid progs on Indian reservations, and progs; spec comms: on law and poverty, on civil disorder, social workers and lawyers, Columbus Bar Assn; O St Bar Assn; Franklin Co Trial Lawyers Assn; O Acad Trial Lawyers; Amer Trial Lawyers Assn; planning comm, Orphan's Day, O St Fair; vice-pres: E Sertoma Club, Columbus; pres, State Assn of B'nai B'rith Lodges; fmr: mem, City of

Columbus Traffic Commn; pres, Legal Aid and Defenders Soc, Columbus. Home: 1692 Gaynor Rd, Columbus, O. Office: 16 E Broad St, Columbus, O.

STROOCK, Alan Maxwell, US, atty; b. NYC, Nov 12, 1907; s. Solomon and Hilda (Weil); AB, magna cum laude, Harvard U, 1929; LLB, cum laude, Yale U, 1934; LLD, JTSA, 1961; m. Katherine Wyler, June 12, 1931; c: Robert, Mariana Leighton, Daniel. Partner, Stroock & Stroock & Lavan, since 1942; law clerk, Justice Benjamin N Cordozo, US Supr Court, 1934-36; asso, Stroock & Stroock, NYC, 1936-37, partner, 1939-42; asst corp counsel, NYC, 1938. Bd trustees, NYU, since 1955; pres, corp, JTSA, since 1963, chmn bd, 1947-63; vice-pres, AJComm, 1948-51, 1955-58, chmn admn comm, 1958; trustee: at large, FJP, NY, since 1960; Horace Mann Sch for Boys, 1946-59; mem: visiting comm: Harvard dept hist, dept phil, 1956-62; US Natl Commn, UNESCO, since 1965; NY Co Lawyers Assn; NY Law Inst; Amer Bar Assn; Assn Bar, NYC, grievance comm, 1951-54, 1960-63; Phi Beta Kappa; Order of Coif; clubs: Lawyers; Harmonie, NYC. Homes: 875 Fifth Ave, New York, NY; 60 Kerry Lane, Chappaqua, NY. Office: 61 Broadway, New York, NY.

STROUSE, Beatrice E, US, communal worker; b. Baltimore, Md, Sep 20, 1906; d. Jacob and Mary (Oppenheimer) Engel; att Goucher Coll, 1924-27; m. Samuel Strouse, Feb 27, 1936; c: Joan Sandler. Mem 'bd, Natl Council J Women, 1949-53, and since 1955, chmn, service to fgn born, 1949-53; coord, Meals on Wheels Service for Aging, since 1960; mem, commn on problems of aged, Baltimore City, since 1961; secy, mem, exec comm, United Service for New Amers, 1949-53. Hobby: photography. Home: 1959 Greenberry Rd, Baltimore, Md.

STROUSE, Samuel Salabes, US, business exec; b. Baltimore, Md, July 8, 1905; s. Jay and Sarah (Salabes); att Johns Hopkins U, 1922-30; m. Beatrice Engel, Feb 27, 1936. Ret; partner: Cahn, Miller & Strouse Inc, 1958-67; Kaufman, Strouse 1950-58. Pres: Bd J Educ, Baltimore; Temple Oheb Shalom, Baltimore, 1956-58; mem J Hist Soc, Md. Author: Ten Jewish Leaders in America, 1968. Home: 2216 Ken Oak Rd, Baltimore, Md.

STUBENHAUS, Harold, US, attorney; b. NYC, Nov 1, 1917; s. Jacob and Rose (Umansky); AB, LIU, 1938; LLD, Fordham U, 1941; m. Violet Nauke, Sep 17, 1943; c: Selena, Michael, Joanne. Atty: since 1941; with Paul Kellner, 1941-42. Sgt, US Army, 1943-46. Dir, United Syn Amer, exec comm, NY metrop region pres, Westbury Heb Cong, 1956-58; mem: recreation commn, Village of Westbury, NY; Alpha Mu Sigma. Hobbies: fishing, travel, recreation. Home: 591 Oxford St, Westbury, NY. Office: 245 Post Ave, Westbury, NY.

STULBERG, Julius, US, musician, educator; b. Kisielin, Pol, June 2, 1913; s. Max and Rebecca (Pudick); in US since 1920; BS, Mich State U, 1935, MA, 1938; studied violin and chamber music with: Michael Press, 1931-38; Hans Letz, 1939-40; Bronislaw Huberman, 1942; Louis Persinger, Julliard Sch, 1947; m. Esther Leiberman, Sep 7, 1941; c: David, Joseph, Bernard, Mira. Prof music, W Mich U, Kalamazoo, since 1945, acting head, dept music, 1965-66; sym conductor, since 1945; fac adv, Hillel Chap; conductor, Kalamazoo Jr Sym Orch, since 1943; guest conductor; clinician; tchr, master classes; recitals; soloist, all mid-W; tchr, violin, viola, Mich State U, Lansing, 1934-35; concertmaster, Lansing Sym Orch, 1941-45; civilian instr, math, US Air Corps, 1943-44. Vice-pres, Cong of Moses, 1963; mem: Kalamazoo Arts Council; Sinfonia; Amer String Tchrs Assn; Natl Fed of Music Clubs; Mich Educ Assn; Mich Music Tchrs Assn; Jr Sym Bd; W Mich U Rel Council; B'nai B'rith; Masons; hon mem, Mich State Band and Orch Assn. Author: A Violin Method for Adult Beginners, 1938. Recipient, Sertoma award for service to mankind, 1965. Home: 443 Pinehurst Blvd, Kalamazoo, Mich. Office: W Mich U, Kalamazoo, Mich.

STULBERG, Louis, US, labor union exec; b. Pol. Apr 14, 1901; s. Benjamin and Jenny; in US since 1919; att, U Chgo. 1921; m. Bebe Friedman, 1929; c: Judith. Pres: ILGWU, since 1966, vice-pres, 1947-66, gen org, Midwest, 1924, co-dir, gen org dept, 1941, mem, since 1919; vice-pres, ind union dept, AFL-CIO; fmr: mgr, local 62, Undergarment and Negligee Workers Union, ILGWU; bus agt, asst gen mgr, Cutters Union, local 10. F, Brandeis U; mem bd trustees: Mutual Redevl Houses Inc; E River Housing Corp; bd dirs, HIAS; natl debt comm, Twentieth Cent Fund; exec comm: City of Hope; Deborah Sanitarium and Comty Services Inc; Pres Comm on Consumer Interests; trade union comm: Histadrut;

Amer ORT; treas, Negro Lab Comm, 1947; mem, Public Devl Corp of NY. Home: 25 Central Park W, New York, NY. Office: 1710 Broadway, New York, NY.

STULBERG, Morris, US, business exec; b. Battle Creek, Mich, May 5, 1922; s. Max and Rebecca (Pudick); att Mich State U, 1940-43; BBA, U Mich, 1947; m. Charlotte Kaufman, June 22, 1947; c: Alan, Irving, Daniel, Michael. Pres: Marshall Iron & Metal Co, since 1964, vice-pres, 1949-64, on staff since 1947; Morris Inves Co Inc, since 1963. US Army, WW II. Mem: Cong of Moses, Kalamazoo, Mich; fmr mem bd: C of C; Family Counciling Service; Marshall Civic Theater; Marshall Music Assn; regional council, Boy Scouts Amer; regional adv bd, ADL; Calhoun Co Comty Services; Marshall Bd of Educ; club, Rotary. Recipient: outstanding achievement award, Jr C of C, Mich, 1959; Bronze Star. Spec interests: comty theater, lecturing to non-J groups on J topics, horses. Home: 311 N Grand St, Marshall, Mich. Office: 420 W Spruce St, Marshall, Mich.

STULMAN, Julius, US, business exec, author, publisher; b. NYC, Apr 11, 1906; s. Joseph and Ida (Goldstein); att NYU; m. Paula Lesser, (div); c: Stephen, Joan; m. 2nd, Janis Carter, Dec 26, 1956. Pres, Lumber Inds; chmn, Lumber Exch Terminal; dir: Meadtex Corp; Found, Life Ins Co of Amer; publisher, Main Currents in Modern Thought. Author-publisher: Fields Within Fields---Within Fields, Man, Mankind, The Universe, 1968; Economic Fluctuations, 1968; Climbing to Mankind Solutions, 1968. Author: The World Institute, 1949; Western Aid to Asia's Sub-Continent, 1951; Worldwide Trends and Insights, 1956-57; More Needed Than Money, 1956; World Economic Development, 1961; Evolving Mankind's Future, 1967. Pres: World Inst Inc; World Inst Council Inc; found, Stulman Found; dir, vice-pres, Found for Integrative Educ. Home: 870 UN Plaza, New York, NY. Office: 777 UN Plaza, New York, NY.

STULMAN, Stephen Lloyd, US, investment banker; b. NYC, May 2, 1931; s. Julius and Paula (Lesser); BA, Yale U, 1952; att Columbia U Grad Sch of Bus, 1952-53; m. Elga Kron, Nov 15, 1953; c: Andrea, Jessica, James, Laura. Vice-pres, dir, Lumber Inds, Inc, since 1969; pres, Amer-Isr Marketing Corp, since 1966; exec vice-pres, dir, Lumber Exch Terminal, Inc, 1957-66; vice-pres, Isr Ind Services, 1967-68; dir: Isr Research and Devl Corp; Amer Friends Heb U; Amer Friends Tel Aviv U; Pal Endowment Funds; PEC, Isr Econ Corp, 1968-69; Childville, Inc; World Inst Council; and vice-pres, Amer-Isr C of C; chmn: NY Leadership Council, 1966-67; Volunteers for Isr Products, 1966-68; pres, Isr Cancer Found; off, Amer Assn J Educ; mem: steering comm, PM's Council for Isr Econ Devl; exec comm: JTA; UJA, Gtr NY; Natl Young Leadership Cabinet, UJA; bd govs, Weizmann Inst Sci; clubs: Yale, NY; NY Tennis. Home: 1088 Park Ave, New York, NY.

STURM, Ephraim H, US, organization exec; b. NYC, May 5, 1924; s. Sam and Bertha (Liebowitz); BA, Bklyn Coll, 1944; MA, Columbia U, 1946; m. Marion Schneck, Sep 5, 1948; c: Ava, Ira, Jay, Joel. Exec vice-pres, Natl Council of Young Isr, since 1958, fmr natl dir, dir staff, since 1952, registrar, Young Isr Inst for Adult J Studies, 1948-50; ed, Young Isr Viewpoint, 1950-52; lectr, phil, Yeshiva U, since 1962, Ferkauf Grad Sch, since 1967; guest lectr, NYU, since 1957; asst prin, Yeshiva, Brighton Beach, 1947-48. Mem, bd dirs: Natl Assn Heb Day Schs PTA, since 1955; Rabb Alliance, since 1954; secy, Council of Young Isr Rabbis, since 1950; mem: bd of license, J Educ Comm, since 1956; exec bd, Mesivta Talmudical Acad, since 1955; RabCA; Phi Delta Kappa; Rabb Alumni, Yeshiva U. Contbr author: The Sanctity of the Synagogue, 1959. Recipient: cert of merit, Natl Assn of Heb Day Schools PTA, 1956; award of merit, intercollegiate council, Natl Council of Young Isr, 1957; hon award, State of Isr Bonds, 1958; plaque, Pace Coll. 1959; comty service award, FJP, 1962; man of year award, Young Isr of Far Rockaway, 1967; alumni award, Talmudical Acad, 1968. Home: 744 Empire Ave, Far Rockaway, NY. Office: 3 W 16 St, New York, NY.

STUTSCHEWSKY, Joachim J, Isr, composer, teacher, author; b. Romny, Ukraine, Feb 7, 1891; s. Kalman and Liuba; in Isr since 1938; grad, hons, Leipzig Conservatoire, 1911; m. Julia Bliudz, Jan, 1945. Composer: works include: The Songs of Radiant Sadness; Concertino for clarinet and string orch; Terzetto for wind instruments; Sextet for wind instruments; Fantasia for oboe, harp and strings; Concertante Music for flute and strings; Safed sym poem, for orch; Isr, sym suite, 1964; Soliloquia, for viola solo, 1964; Music for Strings,

1965; Calling Voice, for horn solo, 1965; Three for Three violoncellos, 1967; Four Movements, for wind quartet, 1967; Brass Quintet, 1967; Quatre Inattendus for piano, 1967; fmr: mem, Jena String Quartet, 1911-14; appeared in concerts; soloist and teacher, Switz, 1914-24, and Vienna, 1924-38; toured Cen Eur; co-found, J natl music movement, Eur; musical insp, cultural dept, Vaad Leumi, Pal, 1938-48. Mem: Isr League of Composers; Music Tchrs Assn; club, Milo Artists. Author: The Art of Cello Playing, 6 vols, 1924; Studies for a New Technic of Playing the Violoncello; Mein Weg Zur Jüdischen Musik, 1935; Jewish Music, 1946; Folk Songs of Eastern European Jewry, 1946; 120 Hassidic Melodies, 1950; The Cello and its Masters, History of Cello Playing, 1950; Kelzmorim-Jewish Folk Musicians, 1959; Hassidic Tunes; Shabbat, both 1967; collection of articles and lectures, 1969; Der Wilner Balebessl, 1968; Memoirs, 3 vols, Ger. Recipient: Engel prize, City of Tel Aviv, 1951, 1959, prize of honor, 1967; prize, Milo Club, 1959; Piatigorsky prize, Violoncello Soc of NY, 1963. Home: 37 Bodenheimer St, Tel Aviv, Isr.

SUBOTNIK, Louis, US, certified public acctnt; b. Bialystok, Pol, Jan 11, 1911; s. Berl and Feiga (Wasilkowski); in US since 1941; DCS, U Liege; Master's deg, Columbia U, 1944; m. Emma Bouskela, 1939; c: Daniel, Rena. Pvt practice, CPA, since 1947; repr, JNF, 1933-41; acctnt, various orgs, 1941-47. Chmn, Farband Br 430; bd mem, Natl Comm Lab Isr; mem: NY State CPAs; Amer Inst CPAs. Contbr to econ jours. Home: 276 Riverside Drive, New York, NY. Office: 500 Fifth Ave, New York, NY.

SUCHARD, Sigmund Samuel, S Afr, rabbi; b. Johannesburg, July 4, 1939; s. Edward and Minnie; att Telshe Yeshiva, 1957-68; m. Rachel Spivak; c: Mordechai, Ziporah, Chayan, Shneir. Dean, Menorah HS, since 1969; lectr: Yeshiva Coll, since 1968; Telshe Yeshiva, 1966-68. Home: 70 Ridge St, Johannesburg, S Afr. Office: Ridge at Long Ave, Johannesburg, S Afr.

SUD, Ira, US, rabbi; b. Samgorodok, Russ, June 26, 1910; s. Shaya and Pessie (Piliper); in US since 1939; ordained rabbi, Jüdisches Theologisches Sem, Breslau, 1937; BA, Siena Coll, NY, 1945; m. Vera Herrmann, Apr 11, 1937; c: Joan, Riah. Rabbi, Temple Ezra, Chgo, Ill, since 1961; rabbi: Cheb-Eber, 1935-38; Maisel Syn, Prague, Czech, 1938-39; co-adjutor to Chief Rabbi of Prague, 1939; rabbi: Tifereth Isr Inst, Albany, NY, 1940-45; J Cen, Arlington, Va, 1945-50; Ohev Sholom Syn, Chester, Pa, 1950-61. Chaplain: civilian defense, Del Co, Pa; Pa Mil Coll, both 1950-61; mem: exec bd, Chgo Bd of Rabbis; B'nai B'rith, chmn, AJE, Dist 6; ZOA; RA; Leo Baeck Inst; Amer J Hist Soc. Home: 6230 Kenmore Ave, Chicago, Ill. Study: Ezra Cong, 2620 W Touhy Ave, Chicago, Ill.

SUDAKOFF, Harry, US, financier, builder; b. NYC, June 10, 1903; s. Max and Dora; m. Ruth Erdie, Oct 15, 1927; c: Michael. Own firm since 1925; Price Control Bd, WW II. Chmn: bd, Assn of Builders of Gtr NY, 1948-54; UJA, since 1953; FJP, since 1955; mem, bd govs, Jt Defense Appeal, since 1958; trustee, J Comty Services, LI; mem: exec, LI div, CARE; Masons; club, Glen Head Country, mem, bd of govs and acting pres. Recipient: awards from: Pres Truman; FJP; Jt Defense Appeal; USA. Home: 12 Lighthouse Rd, Kings Point, Great Neck, NY. Office: 116-55 Queens Blvd, Queens, NY.

SUDARSKY, Jerry M, Isr, business exec; b. Nizhni Novgorod, Russ, June 12, 1918; s. Selig and Sara (Ars); in Isr since 1967; BA, U of Ia, 1939; BS, Poly Inst Bklyn, 1942; m. Mildred Axelrod, Aug 31, 1947; c: Deborah, Donna. Found, chmn, Isr Chems Ltd, since 1968; pres, JMS Inc, since 1966; found, exec vice-pres, Bioferm Corp, 1946-61; gen mgr, Intl Mineral & Chem Corp, 1961-66. USN, 1943-46. Prin contrib: numerous patents in field fine chem and insecticides. Bd govs, treas, Heb U; bd govs, Technion; fmr pres, Kern Co J Wfr, 1965-67; mem: Amer Chem Soc; AAAS. Home: 7 Havakuk St, Tel Aviv, Isr. Office: 19 Keren Hayesod St, Jerusalem, Isr.

SUGARMAN, Norman A, US, attorney; b. Cleveland, O, Sep 12, 1916; s. Simon and Esther (Goldstein); AB, W Reserve U, 1938, LLB, 1940; m. Joan Green, Oct, 20, 1940; c: Joel, Janet, Elaine, Nancy, Lawrence. Partner, law firm, Baker, Hostetler, and Patterson, since 1954; spec asst to chief counsel, US Internal Revenue Service, 1940-51, asst commn, 1952-54; lectr, George Wash U Law Sch, 1950-52. US Army, 1943-45. Pres, Tax Club of Cleveland, 1966-67; mem, bd of trustees: Temple Tiffereth Isr, since 1960; J Family Service, 1955-61; Bellefaire, 1957-61; mem: endowment comm, J Comty Fed, Cleveland, since 1955; exec comm, Cleveland Bar Assn, 1960-63; council ,tax sect, Amer Bar Assn, 1962-65; Cuyahoga, O State and Fed Bar Assns; Tax Inst, Inc; Amer Law Inst; club, Tax, Cleveland, pres, 1966-67. Contbr to legal jours. Home: 2677 Green Rd, Shaker Heights, O. Office: 1956 Union Commerce Bldg, Cleveland, O.

SUGARMAN, Robert R, US, attorney, educator; b. NYC, June 17, 1898; s. Samuel and Dorothy (Kahn); BA, CCNY, 1920; LLB, cum laude, Bklyn Law Sch, 1926, JD, summa cum laude, 1927; m. Clara Barb, June 29, 1957. Prof, law, Bklyn Law Sch, since 1927; arbitrator, small claims court, Civil Court of NYC, since 1933; mem, comm on character and fitness, Apellate div, Supr Court, since 1958; mgr, unlisted securities dept, NY Commercial ,1920-21; asst mgr, law dept, Title Guarantee & Trust Co, NY, 1923-27. US Army, 1918. Chancellor, philonomic council, Hon Soc, Bklyn Law Sch, since 1935; fmr vice-pres, Bklyn Council, Boy Scouts of Amer; vice-chmn, lay bd, Cumberland Hosp, Bklyn, NY, since 1951; fmr cdr, Kings Co, Amer Legion; fmr chief, Mish-E-Na-Mo, Amer Indian Soc, NY; mem: NY State Bar Assn; Bklyn Bar Assn; Amer Bar Assn; Fed Bar Assns of NY, NJ and Conn; Lock and Key; Kappa; Phi Iota Theta; hon mem: Iota Theta; Soc of Old Brooklynites. Author: Law of Partnership, 1937, 1966; Cases on Law of Agency and Partnership, 1949, supplement, 1966; contbr to legal jours. Recipient: Good Citizenship award, Retreads, USA; Soc Old Brooklynites; Americanism award, Amer Legion. Home: 441 Ocean Ave, Brooklyn, NY. Office: 110 E 42 St, New York, NY.

SUGERMAN, Bernard, Austr, jurist; b. Sydney, NSW, July 5, 1904;s.Solomon and Florence (Green); LLB, U Sydney, 1925; m. Sara Rosenblum, Jan 4, 1928; c: David, Alan. QC, since 1943; judge: Supr Court, NSW, since 1947; Court of Appeal, since 1966; Land and Valuation Court, NSW, 1947-61; lectr, contracts, torts, mercantile law, U Sydney, 1925-43; judge, Commonwealth Court of Conciliation and Arbitration, 1946-47. Pres, Friends of Isr Philharmonic Orch; vice-pres, Friends of Heb U; dir, Benevolent Soc, NSW; club, University. Ed: Australian Law Jour, 1927-46; Commonwealth Law Reports, 1942-46; Australian Digest, 1934-39. Home: 9 Yamba Rd, Bellevue Hill, Sydney, Austr. Office: Supr Court, Sydney, Australia.

SUHL, Yuri, US, author; b. Pol, July 30, 1908; s. Isaiah and Miriam (Fiksel); in US since 1923; att: Bklyn City Coll, 1929-30; NYU, 1930-31; clinic for profsl writers, NYU, 1949-53; m. Isabelle Shugars, June 24, 1950. Author: One Foot in America, 1950; Cowboy on a Wooden Horse, 1953; Ernestine Rose and the Battle for Human Rights, 1959; 4 vols of poetry in Yiddish; ed and trans, They Fought Back: The Story of Jewish Resistance in Nazi Europe, 1967; writer, research worker, Universal J Ency, 1937-38. Morale dept, US Army, 1942-44. Mem, Authors Guild, Amer. Home: 274 E 10 St, New York, NY.

SULMAN, Felix Gad, Isr, pharmacologist, educator; b. Berlin, Ger, Mar 30, 1907; s. Bernhard and Hedwig (Witkowsky); in Isr since 1933; DVM, Vetr Fac, Berlin, 1930; MD, Med Fac, 1933; m. Edith Grzebinasch; c: Nurith, Irith, Prof, head applied pharm dept, Heb U, Jerusalem, since 1956, on fac since 1940; asst, Hadassah U Hosp, 1934-40.Cdr, youth org, Haganah. Hon f, Arg Pharm Soc; vice chmn, Isr Philharmonic Orch Comm, Jerusalem; found, Abu Gosh Musical Festival, Isr; mem: NY Acad of Scis; Endocrinology Soc; Soc Experimental Biol and Med, US; Royal Soc Med, Eng, Soc Endocrinology, Eng. Author: Hormones, 1962; Hypothalmic Control of Lactation, 1969; co-author: The Antigonadotropic Factor with Consideration of the Antihormone Problem, 1942; Psyche und Hormon, 1960; ed, Refuah Veterinarit; ed bd, Eur Jour pharm; contbr numerous articles to profsl jours. Home: 2 Abarbanel St, Jerusalem, Isr. Office: Heb U, Jerusalem, Isr.

SULTANIK, Kalman, US, organization exec; b. Miechow, Pol, Apr 12, 1916; s. Samuel and Gitla (Wechadlowski); att: Sch of Econ, Tel Aviv, 1949-51; Columbia U, 1954-57; m. Bronia Burganski, 1947; c: Aaron, Samuel. Exec vice-chmn, World Conf Gen Zionists, since 1953, secy gen, Isr off, 1950-53, mem, Zionist Gen Council since 1960; co-found, Ichud movement, postwar Pol and Ger, 1946-48; mem, Cen Comm Liberated J, Munich, Ger, 1947; secy, Constructive Enterprises Fund of Gen Zionists, Isr, 1948; mem, exec bd, haOved haZioni, Isr, 1949; delg ZC, 1946. Contbr on Zionism and Isr. Hobbies: art collecting, philately. Home: 10 W 66 St, New York, NY. Office: 30 E 42 St, New York, NY.

SULZBERGER, Frank Leopold, US, business exec; b. Chgo, Ill, Dec 3, 1887; s. Solomon and Clara (Frank); att U Chgo; m. Helen Becker, 1911; c: Kate Levi, Ann Wolff, Jean Meltzer. Chmn bd, Enterprise Paint Mfg Co, since 1951, with firm since 1905, vice-pres, 1909-31, pres 1931-51. Mem, bd of trustees, U Chgo, vice-chmn, 1954-56, life trustee since 1957; trustee: Comm for Econ Devl, since 1955; Chgo Comty Trust, 1948-53; dir: AJComm; J Charities, 1930, pres, 1935-38; Mercantile Natl Bank, 1940-57; Comty Fund Chgo, 1936-57; fmr, JDC; Natl Paint Varnish and Lacquer Assn, 1958-60; fmr, SE Chgo Commn; bd mem, J Fed, Chgo; vice-chmn, Ill Public Aid Commn, 1942-54; pres: Amer Paint and Varnish Assn, 1927; Chgo Paint Varnish and Lacquer Assn, 1921-22; life mem: U Chgo Alumni Assn; Chgo Natural Hist Mus; governing life mem, Art Inst of Chgo; clubs: Quadrangle, U Chgo; Standard; Lake Shore Country; Tavern; Commercial; Cen Mfg Dist. Recipient: citizens award, Ill Wfr Assn, 1954; Julius Rosenwald award, J Fed, 1962. Home: 5454 S Shore Dr, Chicago, Ill. Office: 2841 S Ashland Ave, Chicago, Ill.

SUMMERS, Allan, US, rabbi; b. Ukraine, Jan 25, 1913; s. Issie and Faige (Katz) Sudnovsky; in US since 1925; tchr cert, Yeshiva U, 1933; UCLA, 1937; MA, U of S Cal, 1939; ordained rabbi, Heb Theol Coll of Amer 1943; m. Ethel Fischer, Aug 28, 1946; c: Rebecca, Felice, Elliot; Rabbi, Anshe Emet Syn, LA, since 1949; tchr: Beth Jacob, 1930-40; Samuel Gompers Jr HS, 1943-44; LA, Cal, 1943-49. Vice-pres, Rabb Council, Cal, 1953-54; corresp secy, 1955; mem: Hapoel Hamizrachi. Author: Basic Jewish Law, 1949; A Jewish Boy, pamphlet, 1951. Home: 8838 Key St, Los Angeles, Cal. Study: 1490 S Robertson Blvd, Los Angeles, Cal.

SUMNER, Michael, Can business exec; b. NYC, Dec 13, 1904; c. Samuel and Sarah (Benstein); BA, NYU, 1928; m. Eva Woolovich, June 21, 1935; c: Samuel, Benjamin. Pres, Sumner Printing and Pub Co, Ltd, since 1929. Dir, Shaar Hashomayim Syn, since 1934; chmn bd, Windsor Chesed Shel Emes; pres: Windsor JCC, 1950; Inst Phys Med and Rehab, Inc, Essex Co, 1956-66; vice-pres, Council on Group Relations; mem: exec bd: Can Council Chr and J, Ontario; Comty Council, since 1940; Can J Cong, since 1950; cen region ZOC; bd dirs, Riverview Hosp; bd, Rel Sch, since 1935; bd, St Leonard's House; Sr Citizens Cen; sen, Assumption 1951-64. Office: 680 E C Row St, Windsor, Can.

SUPER, Arthur Saul, S Afr, rabbi; b. Gt Yarmouth, Eng, July 1, 1908; s. Isaac and Lena (Bull); in S Afr since 1960; BA, MA, Emmanuel Coll, Cambridge, 1929; dipl OS, Sch of Oriental Studies, London, 1932; ordained min, J Coll, London, 1933; ordained refo 1 m rabbi, 1964; DLitt et Phil, U of S Afr, 1968; m. Tilla Hyams; c: Bernard, Stacia. Chief min, United Progressive J Cong, Johannesburg, chmn, ecclesiastical adv comm, since 1965; fmr: educ dir, Cong Shaar Hashomayyim, Can; lectr, J Higher Educ Cen, London; sr min, United Heb Congs of Leeds, registrar Beth Din; min, Bayswater Syn, London; pres, Anglo-J Preacher's Union. Chaplain, Brit Army, 1940-45. Author: Children's Haggadah, 1932; Israel-State and Religion, 1946; Alonei Yitzhak, 1956; Theodor Herzl Story, 1960; The Reform Haggadah, 1967; fmr ed: Zionist Record & S Afr J Chronicle; Zionist Rev; asst ed, chief writer, dipl corresp, Jerusalem Post; Eng news ed, Isr Radio; trans novels by Shalom Aleichem; publ lectrs, Five Generations of Life, 1820-1968. Hobbies: writing, conversation. Home: 141 Jan Smuts Ave, Johannesburg, S Afr. Office: Paul Nel St, Hillbrow, Johannesburg, S Afr.

SUPINO, Giulio, It, hydraulic engr, educator; b. Florence, It, Oct 8, 1898; s. I Benvenuto and Valentina (Finzi); DEngr, U Bologna, DMath; DHC, Technische Hochschule, Munich, Ger, 1955; m. Camilla Benaim, Dec 26, 1934; c: Valentina Viterbo. Prof and dir, dept hydraulics, U Bologna, since 1934, except 1938-45. It Army, 1917-19. Mem: Consiglio Superiore Lavori Pubblici; Istituto Superiore di Sanita; Accademia Nationale dei Lincei, Rome; Academie des Sciences, Inscriptions et Belles Lettres, Toulouse, Fr; fmr vice-pres, Intl Assn Hydraulic Research. Author: Le Reti Idrauliche, 1938, 1965; Idraulica, 1956; contbr to sci jours. Recipient: 2 Croce di Guerra. Home: Via S Domenico 7, Bologna, It. Office: U Bologna, Via Risorgimento, Bologna, It.

SUPINO, Paolo, It, army officer, author; b. Pisa, It, Nov 25, 1893; s. Raffaele and Elena (Gallico); DEngr, U Rome, 1924; staff off, State War Coll, 1930; m. Emma Esdra, Sep 15, 1929; c: Laura, Giulio, Silvia. Ret; fmr gen, It Army, since 1961, secy-gen to Min of War, 1946-47, cdr: Sch of Applied Arms, 1949-51, War Coll, 1951-52, Armoured Div, Centauro, 1952-53, active service, since 1914. Author: Considerazioni sulla Battaglia Moderna, 1951; Aspetti della Guerra Moderna, 1952; Problemi dell'Esercito, 1954; Saggi sulla Ricerca Operativa e l'Automazione, 1958; Contributo alle impostazione di una concesione operativa moderna, 1961; Della Strategia classica alle nuove strategie, 1963; Strategia globale, 1965; contbr of articles to natl and fgn revs. Recipient: Grande Ufficiale al Merito della Repubblica Italiana; Ordine Mauriziano. Home: Via Olono 3, Rome, It.

SURKIS, Mordecai, Isr, public official; b. Stanislawow, Pol, Jan 21, 1908; s. Moshe and Rivka; in Isr since 1933; m. Lola Regenbogen; c: Shlomo. MK, chmn of Internal Affairs Comm; fmr mayor, Kfar Saba; chmn, Local Council, 1951-62; chmn, Union of Local Authorities in Isr, since 1959; org, illegal immigration from It and E Eur, 1945-47; dir, immigration dept, Histadrut, 1947-51. J Brig, WW II. Mem, cen comm, Mapai; dep mem, exec Histadrut; mem, Zionist Gen Council; delg to: mayors' congs, Rome, 1955, The Hague, 1957; exec comm, Intl Union Local Auths, Vienna, 1961, Osterbeck, 1962. Home: Brenner St, Kfar Saba, Isr.

SURKS, Sylvan N, US, physician; b. NYC, Feb 25, 1916; s. Jacob and Rose (Hollander); BS, NYU, 1937; MD, Chgo Med School, 1943; m. Harriet Schwartz, July 29, 1955; c: Denaa, Laura. Dir, dept of anesthesiology, LI J Med Cen, since 1954; anesthesiologist in chief, LI J Med Cen, Queens Hosp Cen Affiliation, since 1964; clinical asso prof, dept anesthesiology, SUNY Coll of Med, NYC, since 1956, on staff since 1952; asso visiting anesthesiologist, King's Co Hosp, since 1952; gen practice, 1946-48; chief, anesthesiology sect, VA Hosp, Bklyn 1950-52. Capt, US Army MC, 1944-46. Dipl, Amer Bd Anesthesiology; f, Amer Coll Anesthesiologists, 1953; mem: AMA; Amer Soc Anesthesiologists; NY State Soc Anesthesiologists; Intl Anesthesia Research Soc; Kings Co Med Soc; NY Acad Scis. Contbr to med jours. Hobby: photography. Home: 15 Merrivale Rd, Great Neck, NY. Office: 270-05 76 Ave, New Hyde Park, NY.

SUSAYEFF, Zalman, Isr, business exec, manufacturer; b. Riga, Feb 14, 1911; s. Eliahu and Miriam; in Isr since 1935; att U of Riga; m. Rulija Felduhn, 1935; c: Eliora, Mikhal, Gur. Main shareholder, dir, Plaro Produc Corrugated Cardborad, Ltd; MK, Gen Zionists, 1951-59; dep min of Commerce and Ind, 1953-55. Pres: Importers and Wholesalers Assn in Isr, 1949-50; C of C, Tel Aviv-Jaffa, 1950-52; Mfrs Assn of Isr. Office: 19 Shamir St, Tel Aviv, Isr.

SUSLAK, Howard R, US, business exec; b. NYC, Apr 24, 1920; s. Sigmund and Estelle (Robinson); grad, Juilliard Sch of Music, 1942; BA, NYU, 1942; MBA, U Pa, 1943; m. Adele Barnett, June 19, 1949; c: Brian, Neil, Valerie, Pamela. Pres, MacDonald & Co, Inc, since 1962, with firm since 1945; chmn, mgn dir, Ind Mgmt Cons Ltd, London, Eng, since 1949; dir: George Hopkinson Ltd, 1949-52; Roberts Pharm Labs Ltd, 1949-54; and chmn, exec comm, Stablond Labs Ltd, 1950-54. US Engr Corps, WW II. Dir: Purchase Comty House; Purchase Assn; vice pres, life mem, Phi Beta Kappa Alumni Assn, NY; trustee, Eddie Cantor Camp Comm, Surprise Lake Camp; org, corporate gifts comm, Metrop Opera Assn; adv, Anglo-Amer pruduc teams in London assisting postwar recovery, 1949-52; mem: pres council, Amer Inst of Mgmt; scholarship award comm, Phi Beta Kappa, fmr chmn; exec comm, Newcomen Soc of N Amer; Amer Mgmt Assn; Comm of Econ Devl; clubs: Harmonie, NY; Royal Automobile, Lodnon; Royal Automobile Country, Eng; Econ, NY. Contbr to jours. Home: Convent Lane, Rye, NY. Office: 532 Madson Ave, New York, NY.

SUSMAN, Abraham B, US, pediatrician; b. Kingston, Ont, Can, Aug 14, 1903; s. Max and Annie (Chananie); in US since 1928; BA, MD, CM, Queens U, Can, 1921-28; m. Rose Elson, Feb 19, 1933; c: David, Gerson. Pvt practice, since 1933; dir, peds, prof, peds and att ped, NY Polyclinic Med Sch and Hosp, since 1957, on staff since 1935; on staff, Grand Cen Hosp, NY, 1935-63, att ped, 1955-63. Licentiate, Amer Bd of Peds; mem: AMA; NY State Med Soc. Hobby: gardening. Home: 114 W 70 St, New York, NY. Office: 115 Central Park W, New York, NY.

SUSMAN, Samuel Isaac, Eng, minister of religion; b. Liverpool, Eng, June 18, 1911; s. Felix and Annie; min dipl, Talmudical Coll, Telz, Lith, 1932; m. Sarah Swift, Dec 17, 1933; c: Doreer, Roy. Sr min, Leicester Heb Cong, since 1952; asst

min, Bristol Heb Cong, 1934-44; sr min, Plymouth Heb Cong, 1944-52. Chaplain, Brit Army, 1946. Pres, JPA, Leicester; vice-pres, Maccabi Assn, Leicester; mem, B'nai B'rith. Spec interests: youth and social activities. Home: 12 Stanley Rd, Leicester, Eng. Study: Syn, Highfield St, Leicester, Eng.

SUSMAN, Milton K, US, attorney, advertising exec, univer-city admnr; b. Pittsburgh, Pa, Dec 15, 1906; s. David and Rebecca (Brockstein); AB, Harvard U, 1929; LLB, U Pittsburgh, 1932; m. Minnie Spero, Oct 18, 1936; c: Brooks. Columnist, J Chronicle, Pittsburgh, since 1963; pvt practice, atty, 1932-42; ed, J Criterion, 1933-63; pres, Milton K Susman Asso, Pittsburgh, 1946-64. US Army, 1942-46. Bd dirs: Heb Inst, Pittsburgh; YM-YWHA; Craig House-Technoma; Heb Free Loan Assn; Home for Crippled Children; NCCJ; mem: speakers bur, UJA; ACTION-housing; AJ Comm; NAACP; Rodef Shalom Cong; Phi Beta Kappa; Delta Sigma Rho; Sigma Delta Chi; Phi Epsilon Pi. Home: 5819 Ferree St, Pittsburgh, Pa. Office: 104 Rockwell Hall, Duquesne U, Pittsburgh, Pa.

SUSSER, Bernard, Eng, rabbi; b. London, Eng, Sep 29, 1930; s. Mendel and Sophia (Cohen); BA, U London; asso f, J Coll, London; m. Sylvia Rosenblatt; c: Helen, Jacob. Min, Sunderland Heb Cong, since 1965. Chaplain, Royal Navy, 1961-65. Chmn, Sunderland Mizrahi Soc. Ed: Sunderland J Review; contbr to jours. Spec interests: Anglo J hist. Home: 2 Wadsley Sq, Sunderland, Eng.

SUSSKIND, David, US, rabbi; b. NYC, July 7, 1923; s. Joseph and Rose (Last); BA, Yeshiva Coll, 1944, cert, Tchrs Inst, 1946; MHL, odrained rabbi, JIR, 1949; m. Bernice Meppen, Sep 1, 1947; c: Sandra, Brian, Jonathon. Rabbi: Temple Beth-El, since 1957; Cong Shearith Isr, Wharton, Tex, 1949-51; Euclid J Cen, Cleveland, 1951-53; Temple Lib Judaism, Orlando, Fla, 1953-57; civilian chap, 1953-56. Pres, S Pinellas Mh Assn, 1962-64; vice-pres: SE Assn, CCAR, 1967-69; Council on Human Relations; bd dirs: Adult Mh Clinic; JCC, St Petersburg; clergy chmn, United Fund of Pinellas Co, 1967; mem: CCAR. Home: 100 79 St, Petersburg, Fla. Study: 400 Pasadena Ave, St Petersburg, Fla.

SÜSSKIND, Nathan, US, educator; b. Stropkov, Czech, Sep 6, 1906; s. Pinchas and Ida (Weinberger); in US since 1921; BA, CCNY, 1929, MEd, 1930; PhD, NYU, 1942; m. Matilda Blaufuchs; c: Fay, Edwin. Asso prof, Ger, CCNY, since 1932, dir Inst for Yiddish Lexicology, since 1966; guest prof, J Tchrs Sem, since 1961; tchr, prin: E Concourse J Cen; Mt Eden J Cen, both 1926-29, 1936-37; civilian instr, trans of secret documents, training prog, US Army, 1941-43; guest prof, Yiddish, Yeshiva U, 1955-61; chmn, bd educ: E Concourse J Cen, 1932-40; New Brighton J Cen, 1945-50; treas, Coll Yiddish Assn, since 1961; mem: academic council, J Tchrs Sem, since 1961; ling circle, sci council, YIVO, found comm, libr and archives, 1935; found comm, tech cons vice-chmn, 1969; Gtr Yiddish Dict, 1954-56; Phi Beta Kappa; AJCong; United Fed of Tchrs; Friends of Heb U; Ling Soc Amer; Ling Circle NY; Amer Assn Tchrs of Ger; Verein deutscher Lehrer. Contbr to: Universal J Ency; scholarly publs. Hobbies: lay preaching, hiking. Home: 1927 University Ave, Bronx, NY. Office: CCNY, Convent Ave and 130 St, New York, NY.

SUSSMAN, Ettel, Isr, author, singer; b. Pol; d. Abraham and Deborah (Liebmann); att Conservatoire Nationale Fr. Recital tours, concerts, operas: Fr; US; Can; Gt Brit; Belgium; Holland; Den; Swed; Nor; Switz; It; Isr; N Afr. Composer: Chinese Poets on Animal Life; Chansons pour petits brigands; Le Cantique des Cantiques; Recordings: From Lully to Rameau, French Operatic Airs; Schumann-Mozart; Debussy-Fauré-Ravel; Moussorgski; Enfantines; Chants et Danses de la Mort; Sans Soleil; Lully. Recipient: Grands Prix de Chant et d'Art Lyrique, Fr; Lauréate au Concours International d'Exécution Musicale de Genève. Home: 17 Hamitnadew, Tel Aviv, Isr.

SUSSMAN, Helen P, US, communal worker; b. Charlestown, Mass, Nov 24, 1905; d. Harry and Jennie (Friedman) Perlmutter; att Pace Inst, Boston, 1927-29; m. Louis Sussman, 1935; c: Ruth, Michael. Life mem and natl exec comm mem, Natl Women's League of United Syn of Amer, natl pres, 1954-58; training: educ chmn, Belleville-Nutley chap, Hadassah; council mem, Torah Fund-Residence Hall, JTSA; chmn, adult educ, Sisterhood, Cong Ahavath Achim, 1968-69, mem, bd Cong Ahavath Achim, 1968-69; natl planning comm, JTSA, 1954-59; exec comm: J Braille Inst of Amer, 1956-58;

exec, JWB, 1956-58. Home: 66 Van Reyper Pl, Belleville, NJ. Office: 3080 Broadway, New York, NY.

SUSSMAN, Jerry, US, hotel exec; b. NYC, Mar 20, 1922; s. Louis and Bessie (Levinson); BBA, CCNY, 1942; m. Esther Waloman, Mar 20, 1922; c: Kenneth, Marc, Lester, David. Exec dir, Carillion Hotel, Miami Beach, Fla, since 1959; co-owner, Sans Souci Hotel and Howard Johnson Motor Lodge, since 1966; mgr dir, Sorrento Hotel, 1949-52; co-owner, Johnina Hotel, 1952-57; Crown Hotel, 1957-59. Lt, US Army, Engrs Corps, 1942-46. Pres, Miami Beach C of C; vice-pres: United Syn of Amer, pres, SE region, 1960-62; S Fla Hotel and Motel Assn; Hospitality Lodge, B'nai B'rith, 1966-69; Temple Menorah, 1950-53; mem: CCNY Alumni, S Fla chap; Beta Gamma Sigma. Recipient: Comty Service award, Civic League, Miami Beach, 1960; Hall of Fame; Insts Mag, 1968. Hobbies: swimming, horseback riding, walking, travel. Home: 1576 Daytona, Miami Beach, Fla. Office: 6801 Collins Ave, Miami Beach, Fla.

SUSSMAN, Leonard R, US, organization exec; b. NYC, Nov 26, 1920; s. Jacob and Caroline (Marks); AB, NYU, 1940; MS, Columbia U, 1941; m. Marianne Gutmann, May 28, 1958; c: Lynne, David, Mark. Exec dir, Freedom House, since 1967, ed, publs, org of academic confs in Public Affairs Inst; Caribbean corresp, UP and Bus Week, 1942; press secy, Gov Puerto Rico, 1943; found, dir, Puerto Rico info off in US, 1946-48; PR counsel to ins and ind cos, 1952-55; exec dir, Amer Council for Judaism, 1955-66, found quarterly issues, created textbook series in rel educ; dir, rel educ, 1949-55. US Army, 1943-46. J repr, curriculum comm, Council of Lib Churches, 1956-59; accredited observer, UN, 1961-66; club, Overseas Press. Author: Puerto Rico Handbook, 1948; contbr to newspapers and mags. Recipient: Legion of Merit, WW II; Black Cat award, Press and Union Club of SF, 1962. Hobby: photography. Home: 210 E 73 St, New York, NY. Office: 20 W 40 St, New York, NY.

SUSSMAN, Louis, US, atty, accountant; b. Jersey City, NJ, Aug 2, 1908; s. Samuel and Bertha; BCS, NYU, 1928; LLB, John Marshall Law Coll, 1935; m. Helen Perlmutter, Sep 15, 1935; c: Ruth, Michael. Prin, Louis Sussman & Co, CPAs, NY and NJ, since 1930. Pres: Cong Ahavath Achim, Belleville, NJ, 1958-60, trustee, legal chmn, 1942-62; ZOA, Belleville-Nutley Dist; chmn, Belleville, UJA; mem: JCC, Essex Co; NY State Soc CPAs. Home: 66 Van Reyper Pl, Belleville, NJ. Office: 26 Journal Sq, Jersey City, NJ.

SUSSMANN, Yoel, Isr, jurist; b. Krakow, Pol, Oct 24, 1910; s. Meyer and Nicha (Bauminger); in Isr since 1934; DJ, U Heidelberg, 1933; att U Cambridge, Eng, 1937; LLB, London U, 1946; m. Eva Salomon; c: Daphne Barlev; m. 2nd, Rina Klebanov, 1954; c: Amnon, Amir. Judge, Isr Supr Court, since 1953; atty, pvt practice, 1938-49; Deputy Judge Advocate Gen, 1948-49; judge, Dist court, Tel Aviv, 1949-53; lectr, Heb U Law Sch. Capt, IDF. Chmn, Cen Electoral Comm, 4th Knesset, 1959. Author: Das Wechselrecht Palästinas, 1937; Bills of Exchange, 1945; Dinei Shtaroth, 1951, 1967; Arbitration, 1953, 1962; Civil Procedure, 1959, 1967. Home: 13 Balfour St, Jerusalem, Isr. Office: Supr Court, Jerusalem, Isr.

SUSZ, Hanan, Isr, business exec; b. Vienna, Aus, Mar 20, 1920; s. Franz and Amalia (Breisach); in Isr since 1949; m. Elisheva Schmidt, Aug 10, 1950; c: Ruth, Michael. Owner, mgn dir, Kidron Trading Co, Ltd, since 1961; jt gen mgr, Casa Kavlin, La Paz, Bolivia, 1938-39; mgr, life ins dept, Migdal Ins Co Ltd, 1949-54; mgn dir, Israel Corp Amer, Isr Ltd, vice-pres, NY. Hon repr, JA for Pal and Govt of Isr, Bolivia, 1945-49; club, Rotary of Sharon, 1957. Home: Kaplan St, Herzliya, Isr. Office: 10 Carlebach St, Tel Aviv, Isr.

SUTZKEVER, Abaram, Isr, editor, poet; b. Smorgon, Lith, July 15, 1913; s. Herz and Reine (Fainberg); in Isr since 1947. Ed, Yiddish quarterly, Die Goldene Keit, since 1948. Fought in Vilna ghetto, WWII, mem, org partisan fighters; 1943, flown to Moscow; 1944, returned to Vilna with Red Army, participated in rescue of J books, writings; witness Nurnberg Trial, 1946. Author: poetry: Lieder, 1937; Valdiks, 1940; Die Festung, 1946; Lieder fun Ghetto, 1946; Yiddishe Gass 1948; Gehaimshtot, 1948; In Feier Woggn, 1952; Sibir, trans into: Heb, Eng, 1952; Fun Drei Veltn, 1953; Ode zu der Toib, 1955; In Midbar Sinai, 1957; Oazis, 1960; Geistike Erd, 1961; Kol Nidre, 1961, trans into Fr, 1950; Poetishe Verk, 1963; Firkantike Oises Umoifsim, 1968; Lider fun jam Hamoves, 1968. Fmr pres, Writers Assn in Isr. Recipient:

first prize, Assn J Writers in Vilna Ghetto, 1942; two prizes, WJC, 1950, 1956; prize, Le Parisien, Fr daily, 1950; UNESCO choice for publ, 1961, Siberia, trans into Eng by Jacob Zontag, illus, Marc Chagall. Home: 20 28th of November St, Tel Aviv, Isr. Office: 16 Be'eri St, Tel Aviv, Isr.

SVIRSKY, Leon, US, journalist, author; b. Ekaterinoslav, Russ, May 11, 1904; s. Solomon and Maria (Rosow); in US since 1904; BA, Yale Coll, 1927; m. Helen Spencer, Feb 8, 1930; c: Marcia Dexter, Peter; m. 2nd, Ruth Hotaling, Sep 4, 1954. Mayor, Royal Palm Beach, Fla; writer, ed cons: ed, Real Estate Daily News, 1927-29; reporter: NY World, 1929-31; NY World-Telegram, 1931-37; writer, asso ed, Time Mag, 1937-47; Nieman f, Harvard U, 1945-46; co-found, mgn ed, Sci Amer, 1948-58; ed, vice-pres, Basic Books, Inc, 1958-63; co-author: ed, Your Newspaper, 1947; Twentieth Century Unlimited, 1950; Scientific American Reader, 1953; contbr to mags. Co-found, Amer Newspaper Guild, 1934; mem: Natl Assn Sci Writers; club, Royal Palm Beach Country. Home and office: 764 Camellia Dr, Royal Palm Beach, Fla.

SWACK, Elmer, US, business exec; b. W Salem, O, Oct 14, 1915; s. Myer and Bella (Gryhnam); BA, O State U, 1939, MSc, 1942; dipl, Coll J Studies, Chgo, 1950; m. Anne Goldschlager, Aug 30, 1952. First vice-pres, M Swack Iron and Steel Co, since 1954; housing admnr, Fed Public Housing Auth, 1942-45; public housing mgr, Chgo Housing Auth, 1945-50; with JA, 1950-52. Chmn, Zanesville Planning Commn; pres: Beth Abraham Cong, Zanesville, 1955-58; B'nai B'rith lodge, 1958-60; chmn, Isr Bonds comm, 1960, 1962; mem: Amer Political Sci Assn; ZOA; Histadrut Ivrith; Natl Assn Housing and Planning Officials. Home: 880 W Taylor St, Zanesville, O. Office: 167 Kensington Ave S, Zanesville, O.

SWARSENSKY, Manfred Eric, US, rabbi; b. Mareinfliess, Ger, Oct 22, 1906; s. Jacob and Louise (Lewinsky); in US since 1939; PhD, U Würzburg, 1929; ordained rabbi, Hochschule für die Wissenschaft des Judentums, Berlin, 1932; m. Ida Weiner, Oct 24, 1952; c: Sharon, Gerald. Rabbi: Temple Beth El, since 1940; J Comty, Berlin, 1932-39; asst rabbi, Temple Sholom, Chgo, 1939-40. Bd dirs: ARC; Dane Co Mh Assn; Inter-faith Dialogue Comm of Madison Area Clergymen; ADL; Madison Gen Hosp; Dane Co Child Guidance Clinic; United Givers Fund; J Wfr Council; mem, natl bd: JWB; JDC; HIAS; mem: Equal Rights Council, Dept Ind, Lab, Hum Relations; Family Life Educ Adv Comm, Madison Sch Bd; Leo Baeck Inst; CCAR; Wis Soc for J Learning; B'nai B'rith; clubs: Rotary; Madison Lit. Author: The Liturgy of the Samaritans, 1929; The Jewish Year, 1935; From Generation to Generation, 1955. Recipient: org award, Isr Bonds, 1959; citizen award, NCCJ, 1967. Home: 3995 Plymouth Circle, Madison, Wis. Study: 2702 Arbor Dr, Madison, Wis.

SWARTZ, David, Can, surgeon; b. Osviecim, Pol, May 1, 1904; s. Aba and Pessie (Junger); in Can since 1904; MD, U Man, 1928. Hon cons, urol: Deer Lodge Hosp, on staff since 1945; Misericordia Hosp; Gen Hosp, all Winnipeg. Maj, RAMC, 1942-45. F, Royal Coll of Surgs, Edinburgh, 1935, Can, 1947; pres: Winnipeg Med Soc, 1953-54; Can Urol Assn, 1959-60; hon mem, Brit Assn Urol Socs; mem: Man and Can Med Assns; Can Urol Assn; N Cen sect, Amer Urol Assn; Brit Assn Genito-Urinary Surgs. Contbr to med publs. Home: 235 Park Blvd, Winnipeg, Can. Office: 332 Med Arts Bldg, Winnipeg, Can.

SWARTZ, Harry, US, physician, author; b. Detroit, Mich, June 21, 1911; s. Isaac and Anne (Srere); BA, U Mich, 1930, MD, 1933; postgrad study, allergy, NYU Med Coll and Clinics, 1936-38; m. Eve Sutton, Oct 3, 1942; c: Mark. Mem, outpatient staff, allergy dept, Roosevelt Hosp, since 1946; chief, allergy dept, adj prof, med, NY Polyclinic Med Sch and Hosp, since 1957; att phys, Bx State Hosp; gen practice, Detroit, 1935-36; pvt practice, allergy, NYC, 1937-42. Maj, US Army, chief, allergy dept, Tilton Gen Hosp, Fort Dix, NJ, 1942-46. F: Amer Acad Allergy; Coll of Allergists; AMA; Geriatrics Soc; Intl Acad Applied Nutrition; NY Allergy Soc; NY State and Co Med Socs; NY Acad Sci; AAAS; Phi Beta Kappa; Phi Kappa Phi; Alpha Omega Alpha; dipl, Bd Clinical Immunology and Allergy; pres, Health Field Validation Corp. Author: Allergy, What It Is and What To Do About It, 1949, Brit ed, 1950; Fr, It eds, 1951; rev ed, 1960, 1966; Brit and Brazilian eds, 1962; Your Hay Fever and What To Do About It, 1951, rev ed, 1962; The Allergic Child, 1954, rev ed, 1962; The Intelligent Layman's Medical Dictionary,

1955, paperback, 1960; How To Master Your Allergy, 1961; The Story of Your Body, 1962; The Allergy Guide Book, 1966; ed, Med Opinion and Review; author of short stories, essays in mags under pseudonym since 1940; contbr to med jours, periodicals, chaps on allergy for med textbooks. Home: 6 W 77 St, New York, NY. Office: 105 E 73 St, New York, NY.

SWARTZ, Jacob H, US, physician; b. Brestowitz, Russ, May 10, 1896; s. Asher and Rachel (Rosofsky); in US since 1906; MD, Harvard Med Sch, 1960; postgrad studies: Harvard U; Mass Gen Hosp; m. Janet Heller, Nov 21, 1922; c: Morton. Ret from clinical practice; researcher, tchr, Mass Gen Hosp, hon phys since 1966; first chief, dept dermat, Beth Isr Hosp, Boston, Mass, 1929-39; fmr: mem bd consultation, Mass Gen Hosp; cons dermat: Mass Eye and Ear Infirmary; Brooks Hosp; Addison Gilbert Hosp; Exeter Hosp, NH; J Memorial Hosp; lectr, mycology, Harvard Med Sch. Prin contrib: actively engaged in investigative work in dermat and med mycology; described a new contrast stain and a new rapid stain for fungi in skin, nails, hairs and a new anti-fungal antibiotic-mycoticin. Mem: AMA; Amer Dermat Assn; Mycological Soc Amer; Amer Acad Dermat; Soc for Investigative Dermat; NY Acad Sci; hon, NE Dermat Assn, fmr pres; Mass Med Soc, fmr chmn, dermat sect; hon, Boston Dermat Club, fmr pres; Temple Isr, Boston; hon, Eugene Field Soc. Author: Elements of Medical Mycology, 1943, 2nd ed, 1949; Dermatology in General Practice, 1953; co-author, Diagnosis and Treatment of Skin Diseases, 1935; contbr to med textbooks. Home: 101 Monmouth St, Brookline, Mass. Office: 483 Beacon St, Boston, Mass.

SWERDLOFF, Simcha Mendel, Isr, engineer; b. Polozk, Russ, July 13, 1896; s. Mendel and Frida; Dipl, engr, Tech U, Charkov, 1921; m. Nechama Swerdloff, Aug 27, 1918; c: Sara Alroy. Engr, Histadrut, fmr mgr, ind educ; fmr: engr, JA; cen bd, Solel Boneh; mgr, ind dept, Hamiashis Homen. Cen Councillor, Assn Engrs and Architects in Isr. Contbr to profsl jours. Home: 5 Arnon St, Givatayim, Isr. Office: Histadrut, Tel Aviv, Isr.

SWERSKY, Barry Raymond, Isr, advocate; b. Witbank, S Afr, Feb 20, 1939; s. Joel and Sonia (Behrman); in Isr since 1965; BA, LLB, U Johannesburg, 1958-61; m. Anne Kirson, Dec 15, 1963; c: Nava, Guy, Micha. Pvt practice, Tel Aviv, since 1967; with Swersky, Fernbach and Fine, since 1969; partner, Swersky and Ciuin, Johannesburg, 1963-65. Exec comm mem, Bat Dor dance co and studios; mem, Isr Bar Assn. Home: 93 Zahal St, Kiron, Isr. Office: 68 Ibn Gevirol St, Tel Aviv, Isr,

SWICHKOW, Louis J, US, rabbi, author; b. Chgo, Ill, July 13, 1912; s. Joseph and Dora (Shafrin); BS, DePaul U, Chgo, 1934; ordained rabbi, Heb Theol Coll, 1935; MA, Marquette U, Milw, 1943; DHL, JTSA, 1956; m. Gertrude Astrachan, Feb 11, 1936; c: Rosalie, Morton, Daniel, Deborah. Rabbi, Beth El Ner Tamid Syn, since 1937. Pres: Milw chap, AJCong, 1939-42; Milw ZC, 1940-59; Wis Council Rabbis, 1961-63, 1966-68; fmr mem, bd dirs: Milw JWF; Milw J Council; Family Law Comm, Wis legislative Council, 1957-59; mem: Gov's Family Code Review Comm, 1960; Milw Commn on Comty Relations, 1961-65; Milw Family Court Adv Comm, 1963-68; Milw Juvenile Court Comm, since 1967; RA. Author: Invocations, 1943, 1951, 1964; A History of B'nai B'rith in Milwaukee, 1962; The History of the Jews in Milwaukee, 1963. Recipient: Milw Co Hist Soc award, 1959. Home: 3323 N Sherman Blvd, Milwaukee, Wis. Study: 3725 N Sherman Blvd, Milwaukee, Wis.

SWIDLER, Joseph Charles, US, lawyer; b. Chgo, Ill, Jan 28, 1907; s. Abraham and Dora (Cromer); att: U of Ill; U Fla; PhB, U Chgo, 1929, JD, 1930; m. Gertrude Tyrna, 1944; c: Ann, Mark. Mem, law firm, Swidler & Belnap, Wash, DC, since 1965; pvt law practice, Chgo, 1930-33; asst solicitor, US Dept of Interior, 1933; mem, legal dept, TVA, 1933-57, gen counsel, secy, chmn bd, TVA Retirement Sys, 1945-57; counsel, Alien Property Bur, 1941, power div, War Produc Bd, 1942; pvt practice, cons, utility mgmt: Knoxville, 1957-58; Nashville, 1958-61; chmn, Fed Power Commn, 1961-65; mem, Water Resources Council, 1964-65; US Repr, Water for Peace Conf, 1967. USNR, 1943-45. Club, Fed City, Wash. Home: 9504 Michaels Ct, Bethesda, Md. Office: 1750 Pennsylvania Ave, NW, Washington, DC.

SWIG, Benjamin Harris, hotel owner and operator; b. Taunton, Mass, Nov 17, 1893; s. Simon and Fanny (Levy); grad, Taunton HS; hon degs: U Santa Clara, 1962; HUC-JIR, 1964; Brandeis U, 1966; m. Mae Aronowitz, Dec 24, 1916 (decd);

c: Melvin, Betty Dinner, Richard. Chmn bd: Fairmount Hotel Co, SF, since 1945; W Dairy Products Inc, since 1946; and public interest dir, Fed Home Loan Bank, SF; bd dirs: Cartier Inc; Lilli Ann Corp; pres: Fairmount-Roosevelt Hotel Co; Fairmount-Dallas Hotel Co; fmr, real estate operator, Boston, NYC, 1925-45. Chmn, site comm, mem, exec comm, Citizens Comm for SF Worlds Fair, 1970-71; mem: natl bd, NCCJ, natl exec comm, natl spec gifts comm, SF adv bd; mem: natl bd trustees, Children's Asthma Research Inst and Hosp; bd govs, Eleanor Roosevelt Cancer Found; natl council, Eleanor Roosevelt Memorial Found; chmn, exec comm of state adv bd, Salvation Army; natl adv bd dirs, Assn of US Army, pres, SF chap; found, chmn, bd dirs, Careers Unlimited for Women; mem, natl council: JDC; Amer Soc for Technion; Albert Einstein Coll of Med, W coast chmn, SF chap, soc of founders; Jt Defense Appeal, natl trade and ind cabinet, chmn, mem comm; JWB; Syn Council Amer; mem: bd, ZOA; natl bd delgs, AJComm; bd trustees, Brandeis U; reg chmn, Brandeis U Assos; natl bd dirs, JNF, pres, Gtr W reg; natl bd govs, State of Isr Bonds-Devl Corp of Isr, natl and SF exec comms, W reg chmn, bd trustees; exec comm, UJA, natl chmn, Isr Educ Fund, co-chmn, comty activities comm, reg co-chmn; natl cash comm, W coast; bd govs, W Coast U of Judaism, vice-chmn, bd of overseers; bd dirs: JTA; JTSA, bd overseers, exec comm of natl planning comm, natl chmn, Herbert H Lehman Inst of Ethics; PEC-Isr Econ Corp; UAHC, natl vice-chmn, combined campaign, chmn, Youth Inst Comm, W coast chmn, devl fund for Amer J; Isr Investors Corp; Amer Friends Tel Aviv U; chmn, N Cal reg, Amer-Isr Cultural Found; asso chmn, natl adv comm, Dropsie Coll; chmn, adv group, SF and reg; co-chmn, natl life mem comm, J Chautauqua Soc; vice-pres, bd mem, J Heritage Found; bd mem, Modern Heb Day Sch; admn bd, HUC-JIR, Cal; exec bd, Heb Free Loan Assn of SF; finance, inv comm, Amer J Hist Soc; legacy devl comm, ADL; natl bd, Brandeis Clubs; trustee, Ency J Research Found; soc of hon fs, City of Hope; natl adv comm, JWV; honorary: vice-chmn, W coast div, Yeshiva U; chmn, J Rel Educ for Retarded Children; dir, J Wfr Fed, SF, Marin Co, and Peninsula; gov and f, Hed U, Jerusalem; vice-pres, Amer Friends of Heb U; co-chmn, finance comm, SF World Trade Cen Auth, chmn, adv comm; bd trustees, U Santa Clara, pres, The Heritage Found; mem: Cal and SF C of C; SF Real Estate Bd; United Bay Area Crusade; United World Federalists; bd dirs, Dominican Convent, Motherhood, and Novitiate, Mission San Jose; mem, temples and syns: Emanu-El, Beth Isr, Sherith Isr, Beth Sholom, Ner Tamid, all SF; Beth Am, Palo Alto; Beth El, San Mateo; Judea, Daly City; clubs: Commonwealth; Concordia-Argonaut; Press; Union League, all SF. Recipient: awards: China Relief Legion, 1941; Combined J Appeal, Gtr Boston, 1951; PM of Korea, 1954; UJA, Gtr NYC, 1958; ZOA, 1961; Boys Clubs of Amer, 1961, 1963; Boys Town of Italy, 1962; UJA, 1962, 1963; Louis Marshall medal, JTSA, 1962; Medal of Valor, State of Isr, 1963; Papal Knighthood, 1966; AJComm, 1966; leadership medallion, Amer Friends Heb U, 1966; J Fed and Council, Gtr Seattle, 1967; knight cdr, court of honor, SF Scottish rite, Masons, 1967; f, Isr Educ Fund, State of Isr, 1968; Archbishops Youth award medal, Catholic Youth Org, 1968. Home and office: Fairmount Hotel, San Francisco, Cal.

SYKES, Melvin Julius, US, attorney; b. Baltimore, Md, Jan 9, 1924; s. Philip and Sara (Kline); AB, hons, John Hopkins U, 1943; LLB, magna cum laude, Harvard Law Sch, 1948; m. Judith Konowitz, Sep 24, 1950; c: David, Rachel, Daniel, Israel. Pvt practice since 1949. Staff sgt, USAAF, WW II. Trustee, Baltimore Heb Coll; mem: comm on state relation to church schs; standing comm on rules, practice, procedure, Md Court of Appeals; Phi Beta Kappa; Menorah lodge, B'nai B'rith; Baltimore J Council; Asso J Charities; gov council, Amer Assn for J Educ; fmr: reporter, State comms: to study judiciary; to revise public utility laws; pres, Baltimore City Bar Libr; mem: Baltimore City Charter Revision comm; Md Constitutional Conv comm. Author: Maryland Law Encyclopedia Procedure Forms, 1964; Sykes Probate Forms, 1966. Home: 3811 Fords Lane, Baltimore, Md. Office: 906 Munsey Bldg, Baltimore, Md.

SYLK, Harry, S, US, business exec; b. Philadelphia, Pa, Apr 6, 1903; s. Benjamin and Lena (Hunn); m. Gertrude Bardy, Jan 5, 1930; c: Robert, Leonard, Norma. Chmn, bd, Consolidated Sun Ray Inc, since 1959, pres, Sun Ray Drug Co, 1946-59; pres, radio stas: WPEN, Phila, since 1949; WSAI, Cincinnati, since 1959; WALT, Tampa, since 1959; treas, Phila Eagles Inc; dir, Diners Club Inc, since 1955. Chmn, Allied J Appeal, 1954-56; gen chmn, Phila Isr Bonds, 1958-59;

mem, bd of dirs: Albert Einstein Med Cen; Phila Coll of Osteopathy; Har Zion Syn; Amer Friends of Heb U; mem: natl campaign cabinet, UJA; adv bd, City of Hope; Masons; clubs: Golden Slipper Sq, pres, 1951; Green Valley Country; Locust; Equity. Home: 350 Highland Ave, Merion, Pa. Office: 2212 Walnut St, Philadelphia, Pa.

SYLK, William H, US, business exec; b. Philadelphia, Pa, July 7, 1907; s. Benjamin and Lena (Hunn); BSc, Temple U, JD, Law Sch; m. (decd); c: Richard, Kenneth, Thomas. Pres: Penrose Inds Corp; Sun Ray Drug Co, both since 1948; pres, William Penn Bc Co, 1951-69. Pres, Isr Histadrut Found; trustee, Temple U; bd mem, Ind Valley Bank; Har Zim Temple; natl vice-pres, ZOA; chmn, United Israel Appeal; vice-chmn, Ampal; club: Locust. Home: 400 Bryn Mawr Ave, Bryn Mawr, Pa. Office: 1321 Arch, Philadelphia, Pa.

SYME, Monte Robert, US, rabbi; b. Winnipeg, Can, July 1, 1930; s. Max and Anne (Meitin); in US since 1941; BA, U Man, 1941; MA, U Pittsburgh, 1960; m. Sonia Hendin; c: Daniel, David, Michael. Rabbi: Temple Isr of Detroit, since 1953; Cong B'nai Abraham, 1947-53. Fmr pres, Family Service Soc, metrop Detroit; cabinet, ADL; bd dirs: internal relations comm, JCC; Dearborn Rel Cen, U Mich; Mich Council for Study of Abortion; Credit Counseling Cens, Inc; trustee, Mich Inter-Profsl Assn on Marriage, Divorce, and The Family. Home: 3490 Parkland Dr, Birmingham, Mich. Study: 17400 Manderson Rd, Detroit, Mich.

SYMON, Eva, Austr, editor; b. Budapest, Hung, May 18, 1928; d. Adolph and Antonia (Weiss) Simon; in Austr since 1959; BA, U Budapest, 1956; m. Joseph Symon, Feb 23, 1947; c: John, Juliane. Ed, Austr J Times, since 1965; fmr: journalist, Hung. Mem, Austr J Appeal. Author: children's stories, radio plays. Hobby: painting. Home: 64 Millwood Ave, Chatwood, NSW, Austr. Office: 140 Darlinghurst Rd, Sydney, Austr.

SYRKIN, Marie, US, educator, author, editor; b. Switz, March 22, 1899; d. Nachman and Basya (Osnos); in US since 1907; BA, Cornell U, 1920, MA, 1922; m. Charles Reznikoff, May 27, 1930; c: David. Prof em, Eng, Brandeis U, since 1966, asso prof, 1950-66. Ed, J Frontier, since 1948. Author: Your School, Your Children, 1944; Blessed is the Match, 1947; Way of Valor, 1955; Nachman Syrkin, 1961; Golda Meir: Woman With A Cause, 1964; contbr to lit jours. Exec mem, JA, 1965-68; mem, LZOA. Home: 180 West End Ave, New York, NY.

SYRKIN, Simon, Isr, engineer; b. Kiev, Russ, Apr 20, 1906; s. Nachman and Cecylja (Temkin); in Isr since 1925; ing dipl, Poly, Hannover, Ger, 1925; m. Batami Kolodny, 1931; c: Nachman. Cons engr since 1932; dir, S Sirkin, Cons Engrs Ltd, since 1962; fmr: sup engr, Pica, 1926-29; dist engr, KRL, 1929-32. Col, Brit Army, 1940-45; Haganah, since 1926; lt col, IDF, 1948-55. Mem, exec comm, Assn of Engrs and Architects in Isr; co-found, Hapoel Sports Org; past chmn, Assn of Water Engrs; mem: NY Acad of Sci; Amer Assn of CEs. Recipient: Off de la Legion d'Honneur. Home: 19 Hatamar St, Tel Aviv, Isr. Office: 8 Shalag St, Tel Aviv, Isr.

SZABAD, George M, US, attorney, business exec; b. Nizhni Novgorod, Russ, Feb 21, 1917; s. Michael and Nita (Szereszewski); in US since 1934; BS, Columbia U, 1937, LLB, Law Sch, 1939; m. Shirley Meyers, Nov 8, 1938; c: Peter, Ellen. Mem, Blum, Haimoff, Gersen, Lipson and Szabad, since 1949, with firm since 1947; vice-pres, counsel, secy, Burndy Corp, Norwalk, Conn, since 1956, mem, bd dirs, since 1954; mem, bd dirs: BICC-Burndy Ltd, Eng, since 1959; York Research Corp, since 1960; Burndy, Mexico, since 1961; asso counsel to trustee, Asso Gas and Elec Co, 1940-42; chief, appellate sect, US Dept of Lab, 1942-47; chief, manpower sect, USSR div, US Dept of State, 1945-46; pres, spec counsel, secy, dir, Tel Autograph Corp, 1953-58; secy, dir, Nuclear Corp of Amer, 1955-56. USCG Res, 1943; OSS, US Army, 1945. Pres, dist 2, Scarsdale bd of educ, 1960-62; bd dirs, Family Counseling Service; mem, bd govs, chmn, natl educ comm, AJComm, fmr pres, Westchester chap; treas, Consular Law Soc, 1951-55; mem: NYC, Amer, and Fed Bar Assns; Amer Inst Mgmt; E Scarsdale Assn; clubs: Garth Rd Dem, pres, 1948-50; Scarsdale Dem; Scarsdale Town, bd govs, pres, 1966-67; Mamaroneck Beach and Yacht. Contbr to legal jours. Hobbies: photography, philately, sports. Home: 16 Continental Rd, Scarsdale, NY. Office: 270 Madison Ave, New York, NY.

SZABOLCSI, Bence, Hung, educator, musicologist; b. Budapest, Hung, Aug 1899; s. Miksa and Malvina (Boskovitz);

att: U Budapest; Budapest Acad of Music; Leipzig Conservatory of Music; deg, U Leipzig, 1923; m. Klára Gyözö, 1928; c: Eva, Gábor (decd). Prof, Budapest Acad of Music, since 1945, academician since 1948; dir, Bartók archives, Musicological Inst, Hung Acad of Higher Learning, since 1969. Forced lab service, WW II. Mem: Intl Soc Musicologists; Aus, Finnish, It, socs of musicians; past pres, Hung League Musicians, 1951-62. Author: A zene története (The History of Music), 1940, 3rd ed, 1968; A melódia története (The History of Melody), 1950, Eng ed, 1965; Beethoven, 1947; Daybreak in Europe, 1948; Bartók, 1956; Centuries of Hungarian Music, 1959-61; Crossroad, 1963; trans into Hung, The History of the Jews, Dubnov, 1935; contbr to mags and profsl jours. Recipient: Kossuth prizes: 1951, 1965; Order of Red Flag, 1954. Home: Pozsonyi ut 40, Budapest, Hung.

SZAPIRO, Shlomo, Isr, chemist; b. Siedlce, Pol, Apr 19, 1927; s. Nathan and Nehama (Morgensztern); in Isr since 1957; MS, phys chem, MPh, math, U Lodz, Pol, 1952; PhD, phys chem, Feinberg Grad Sch, Weizmann Inst, 1966; m. c: Tsila. Research asso, Soreq Nuclear Research Cen, since 1967; fmr: research asst, Inst of Tech, Lodz, 1951-57; research jr and asso, Weizmann Inst, 1957-67. Mem, Isr Chem Soc. Contbr to profsl jours. Recipient: prize, Pol Chem Soc, 1956. Spec interest: classical music. Home: 123 Shalma Rd, Tel Aviv, Isr. Office: Soreq Nuclear Research Cen, Yavneh, Isr.

SZEFTEL, Marc, M, US, educator; b. Starokonstantinov, Russ, Feb 10, 1902; s. Uriel and Anna (Kovner); in US since 1942; LLM, U Warsaw, 1925; D en droit, U Brussels, 1934, lic, Slavic philology and hist, 1939; att Columbia U, 1943-45; m. Catherine Grouse, 1949; c: Tatiana, M Watson. Prof, Russ hist, U Wash, since 1961; fmr: lectr, U Brussels, 1936-40; prof, Ecole Libre des Hautes Etudes, 1942-45; visiting asso prof, Columbia U, 1950-54; prof, Cornell U, 1945-61. Pres, Conf of Slavic Hists, 1963-64; mem: AAUP; Amer Hist Assn; Société Jean Bodin pour l'étude de l'histoire des institutions; Intl Commn for Hist Repr Parl Insts; Société d'Histoire de Droit; Book and Bowl Lit Soc; Phi Beta Kappa. Author: Documents de Droit Relatifs à la Russie Mediévale, 1963; Russia Before 1917; pub 1966; co-author: La Geste du Prince Igor, 1948; contbr to: Fr, Belgian, and Amer hist periodicals; Encyclopedia Britannica. Recipient: fs: Belgian-Amer Educ Found, 1943-45; Russ Inst, Columbia U, 1949-50, 1952-53; Guggenheim, 1959-60; Amer Council of Learned Socs, 1964-65; All Souls Coll, Oxford U, 1968-69. Home: 926 Harvard Ave E, Seattle, Wash. Office: U of Wash, Seattle, Wash.

SZEINBERG, Arieh, Isr, biochemist; b. Pol, Nov 8, 1918; s. Zalman and Leah (Shapiro); in Isr since 1937; MS, Heb U, 1942, PhD, 1950; m. Bilha Becker, Nov 6, 1945; c: Amir, Leora. Prof, head dept, chem path, Tel Aviv U Med Sch, and Sch of Continuing Med, both since 1963; head, Inst of Chem Path, Tel Hashomer Govt Hosp, since 1953; fmr: lab dir, Hayarkon Hosp, Tel Aviv, 1944-53; visiting sci, Columbia U, 1959-60. Lt, IDF, 1948-67. Prin contribs: research: biochem genet of J nation; inborn errors of metabolism; biochem of mental retardation; pharmaco-genets. Mem: Intl Soc of Hematology; Eur Soc of Human Genets; Fed of Eur Biochem Socs. Recipient: Henrietta Szold award, Tel Aviv Munic, 1959; Meier award, Workers Sick Fund, 1961. Home: 17 Nathan Hechacham St, Tel Aviv, Isr. Office: Tel Hashomer Govt Hosp, Tel Aviv, Isr.

SZEMERE, Samu, Hung, author, educator; s. Sándor and Anna (Bader) Stern; DPhil; U prof; m. Renée Horvát (decd); c: Tamás (decd). Prof, Natl Rabb Sem of Hung, since 1945; prin, Natl J Tchrs Sem, 1927-42. Author: Az Esztétikai Játékelmélet (The Esthetic Theory of Play), 1940; I Dialoghi Bruniani de la Causa, Principio ed Uno, pub in It, 1917; Giordano Bruno, 1917; Main Currents of Modern Philosophy, 1923; Spengler's Philosophy, 1924; Pedagogy and Philosophy, 1929; Art as an Interpretation of Reality, 1936; Studies in Philosophy, 1941, all in Hung; Art and Humanity, A Study of Thomas Mann's Esthetic Opinions, 1967, 2nd ed, 1968; contbr to: Heller Jubilee volume, 1941; Semitic Studies in Memory of Immanuel Löw, 1947; trans into Hung: all phil works of Spinoza, 4 vols. Pres, J Hung Lit Soc; corresp mem, Acad of Higher Learning. Recipient: Order of Merit for Outstanding Work. Home and office: József Körút 27, Budapest, Hung.

SZENES, Michael, Mordechai, US, rabbi; b. Budapest, Hung, Sep Sep 5, 1916; s. Moric and Ilona (Grünfeld); in US since 1947; PhD, U Budapest, 1940; ordained rabbi, Rabb Sem of

Hung, 1942; m. Mignon Spira, June 6, 1941; c: Harold, Miriam, Myron, Hanna. Rabbi, Cong Gates of Heaven, since 1959; Hillel counselor, Union Coll; fmr: asst rabbi, instr in rel, Lib Cong, Budapest, 1941-47; rabbi, Temple Myer David, Claremont, NH, 1948-51; adv to J students, Dartmouth Coll, 1948-51; Sinai Temple, Sioux Falls, SD, 1951-53; Temple Beth Jacob, Concord, NH, 1953-59; adv to J Students, U of NH, 1953-59. Chmn, educ comm, Hum Rights Commn; vice-chmn, Hum Rights Commn, Schenectady Co; pres, Capitol dist, Bd of Rabbis, 1964-66; chmn NH comm, 1960 White House Conf, 1958-59; mem: CCAR; exec comm, Clergy Profsl Assn, Schenectady. Home: 125 Elmer Ave, Schenectady, NY. Study: 852 Ashmore Ave, Schenectady, NY.

SZILARD, Claire, Isr, artist; b. Budapest, Hung; studied: Free Acad, Budapest, 1940-44; Ecole des Beaux Arts, Switz, 1945; Accademia di Bella Arti, It, 1955. Perm exhb, own studio, Old Jaffo, since 1967; one-man shows: Salle Beauregard-Mutuelle Artistique, Geneva, 1948; Gal Kirchgasse, Zurich, 1950; Chemerinsky Art Gal, Tel Aviv, 1954, 1956, 1960; Bet Zvi, Ramat Gan, 1961; Gal LaFontanella, Rome, 1962; exhbs: Gal Motte, Geneva; Isr House, London; Gal Motte, Paris; 5 Artists, Zurich; Beit Yad LeBanim, Petah Tikva; group shows in Isr and abroad. Prin works: fresco buono wall paintings, public bldgs, Zurich; ARTA lithograph; stained glass windows for public bldgs, syns, pvt houses. Mem, Isr Artists Assn. Home and studio: 11 Mazal Dagim St, Yaffo, Isr.

SZNAJDER, Jaime, Uruguay, administrator, physician; b. Pol, Oct 8, 1927; s. Gidali and Sprintze (Zak); in Uruguay since 1931; BS, Sch of Med, Paysandu, 1948; MD, Montevideo, 1957; MPH, U Mich, 1966; m. Sylvia Donner; c: Joyce, Lita. Asst gen admnr of med care, Sindicator Médico del Uruguay Plan, since 1967; chief res, govt hosp Maciel, Min Health, 1958-64; dir, govt hosp, Pereira Rossell, 1966-68; under-secy of health, cabinet mem, 1968-69. First J cabinet min in Uruguay. Pres, found mem, Uruguayan Public Health Specialists Assn; mem of bd, Pan Amer Med Confd, 1964-70; pres, J Profsl Assn; vice-pres, B'nai B'rith (Artigas); mem bd dirs: J Old Age Home; Youth for Understanding; gen secy, Fed of Students, 1949-50; secy, intl relations, Med Soc, Uruguay, 1958-62; club: Rotary, Pocitos, co-found, bd mem, 1966-69. Author: Cost of Health in Uruguay, 1966; contbr to profsl jours. Spec interests: J hist, politics. Home: 2574 Brasil Ave, Montevideo, Uruguay. Office: 1938 Colonia St, Montevideo, Uruguay.

SZOLD, Zip F, US, communal worker; b. Savannah, Ga, Apr 19, 1888; d. David and Cissie (Solomons) Falk; AB, Bryn Mawr Coll, 1918; m. Robert Szold, Sept 4, 1917; c: Miriam Seligman, Ruth Ginzburg, Betty Krainis, Joan Zheutlin. Mem, natl bd, Hadassah, since 1921, natl pres, 1929-31. Home: 334 Pelhamdale Ave, Pelham, NY.

SZONDI, Leopold, Switz, psychologist, psychiatrist, author, educator; b. Neutra, Hung, Mar 11, 1893; s. Abraham and Therese (Kohn) Sonnenschein; in Switz since 1944; MD, U Budapest, 1919; m. Lili Radvanyi, 1926; c: Veronika, Peter. Pvt practice, psych, since 1944; head, sem for experimental drive-psych and psych of fate, Inst for Applied Psych, Zurich, since 1952; pres, comm for Szondi-drive diagnostics and fate psych, since 1951; fmr: dept head, Graf Albert Apponyi Poliklinik, Budapest, 1923-26; found, dir, State Labs for Research in Psycho-Path, Coll for Med Pedg, Budapest, 1927-41. Mem:

Swiss Soc for Psych. Author: Schwachsinn und innere Sekretion, 1923; Schwachsinn, 1925; Wachstumsstörungen und innere Sekretion, 1926; Zur Psychometrie der Tests, 1929; Revision der Neurastheniefrage, 1929; Über Art und Wert der Konstitutionsanalyse bei Schwachsinnigen, 1930; Studien zur Theorie und Klinik der Endokrinen Korrelationen, 1931; Konstitutionsanalytische Beiträge zur Revision der Neurastheniefrage, 1931; Konstitutionsanalyse von 100 Stotteren, 1932; Konstitutionsanalyse Psychisch abnormer Kinder, 1933; Methodik der Familien und Zwillingsforschung, 1935; Die Rolle der Vererbungslehre in der Praxis, 1936; Die Neurotiker im Lichte der Psychoanalytischen, Neuroendokrinen und Erbpathologischen Forschungen, 1936; Analysis of Marriages, 1937; Heilpaedagogik in der Prophylaxe der Nerven und Geisteskrankheiten, 1939; Treib und Erziehung, 1939; Schicksalsanalyse, 1944, 1948; Triebpathologie vol I, 1951, Ich Analyse, vol II, 1956; Heilwege der Tiefenpsychologie, 1956; Experimentelle Triebdiagnostik, 3 vols, 2nd ed, 1960; Schicksalsanalytische Therapie, Lehrbuch der passiven und aktiven Psychoanalyse, 1963; Freiheit und Zwang in Schicksal des Einzelnen, 1968; Kain, Gestalten des Bösen, 1969; Thanatos and Cain, American Imago, 1964. Home and office: 3 Dunantstr, Zurich, Switz.

SZTOKFISZ, David, Isr, author; b. Lublin, Pol, Nov 2, 1912; s. Shalom and Hendel (Morgenstern); m. Rivka Rosenbush, Jan 29, 1937; c: Jerucham, Shalom. Ed, Folk und Zion, since 1970; fmr: corresp, Arbeiterzeitung, Warsaw, 1930-38, gen secy, Poale Zion Left, Warsaw, 1940-48. Head, org in Pol for J DPs. Author: Mordechai Oren, The Story of a Political Prisoner in Prague, 1959; Margaret Larkin, The Six Days of Yad Mordechai, 1967; Dialogue of Combat, 1969. Ed, Memorial Books: The Heroism and the Destruction of Markushow, 1955; Frampoler, 1966; Wyshkow, 1964; Falenica, 1967; Kutno and Surroundings, 1968; Chorostkow, 1968; Rubiezewiche and Surroundings, 1968; Demblin-Modrzyc, 1969; Drohicin, 1969; Kazimiers, 1970; Gniewassow, 1970; co-editor: The Book of Lublin, 1952; Tarnow, 1954; Lublin volume, Ency of the J Diaspora, 1957; Rohatin: The History of a Jewish Community, 1962; ed: Israel Stimme; Kol Nechei Milchama monthly; Heid haIrgun. Pres: The Lubliners, Isr; Genia Levi-Garfinkel Lit Funds comm; mem: Cen Comm of Mapam; exec, World Union of Mapam Parties in Isr; Mandelsberg-Shildkraut Funds comm, Heb U scholarships; Dr Abraham Kershman Memorial scholarships comm. Home: 14 Hazanchanim St, Ramat Gan, Isr. Office: Hamishmar, Hamasger St, Tel Aviv, Isr.

SZWARC, Michael, US, chemist, educator; b. Bedzin, Pol, June 9, 1909; s. Meyer and Regina (Pregier); chem engr, Warsaw Poly, 1932; PhD, organic chem, Heb U, 1942; PhD, phys chem, Manchester U, 1947, DS, 1949; m. Marja Frenkel, Aug 6, 1933; c: Raphael, Meira. Dir, Polymer Research Cen, SUNY, Coll of Forestry, Syracuse; prof, phys and polymer chem, SUNY Coll of Forestry, Syracuse U, since 1952, research prof since 1956; fmr: lectr, phys chem, U Manchester, 1949-1952; Royal Soc visiting prof, U Liverpool, 1963-64; Nobel guest prof, Uppsala U, Swed, 1969-70. F, Royal Soc, London, 1966; mem: Amer Chem Soc; Chem Soc, London; Faraday Soc. Contbr to profsl jours. Recipient: f, U Manchester, 1949; Sigma Xi award, Syracuse chap, 1955; dist prof of chem, SUNY, 1964; Amer Chem Soc awards: Syracuse sect, 1966, 1969. Home: 406 Hillsboro Pkwy, Syracuse, NY. Office: SUNY, Syracuse, NY.

T

TABACHNICK, Avrohom B, US, journalist, author; b. Russ, Aug 22, 1902; s. Jacob and Feige (Dorfman); in US since 1921; att J Tchrs Sem, 1924-26; m. Freda Janovsky, Oct 20, 1926; c: Ann. Night ed JTA, since 1941. Mem: Yiddish Writers Union. Author: In Sheid, poetry, 1936; Der Man fun Lied, essay, 1941; Dichter und Dichtung, poetry, 1949; Abba Stolzenberg, essay, 1951; Metsh in Cholem, essay, 1962, Collection of Essays, Dichter und Dichtung, 1965, Der Yunger Manger, essay, 1967; Itzig Manger Und De Yiddische Balade, essay, 1968; ed, Vogshall, Yiddish literary quarterly, since 1958; contbr to Yiddish periodicals. Club, Yiddish PEN. Recipient: N Chanin Cultural Found prize, 1966. Home: 266 E Broadway, New York, NY. Office: 660 First Ave, New York, NY.

TABACHNIK, Joseph, US, rabbi; b. Kaunas, Lith, June 1, 1922; s. Moses and Sara (Perlman); in US since 1930; BA, Yeshiva U, 1943; MHL, ordained rabbi, JTSA, 1946; grad studies, Columbia U; m. Miriam Fertig; c: Emanuel, Rena, Naomi. Rabbi: W Suburban Temple Har-Zion, since 1964; Tifereth Isr, Albany, NY, 1946-52; Temple Beth El, S Orange, NJ, 1949-52; Cong B'nai Jacob, New Haven, Conn, 1952-62. Treas, RA, past exec bd mem; past pres, Essex Co Bd of Rabbis; past chmn, Comty Relations Council; mem: B'nai B'rith; Chgo Bd of Rabbis; clubs: Standard; Brookwood Country, Covenant. Contbr to J jours. Home: 1500 Bonnie Brae, River Forest, Ill. Study: 1040 N Harlem, River Forest, Ill.

TABACZNIK, David, Isr, communal leader; b. Warsaw, Pol, Aug 12, 1908; s. Joseph and Taube-Etta (Zukerman); in Isr since 1929; att Tech Sch, Pol; m. Riva Pfeffer; one c. Vicemayor, Petah Tikva, since 1950. Served Haganah, sent on fgn missions. Secy, Hevrat Haovdim; mem: exec council, Zionist Org; Arab div, KH. Contbr to periodicals. Home: 86 Herzl St, Petah Tikva, Isr. Office: 2 Aliyah St, Petach Tikva, Isr.

TABB, J Yanai, Isr, educator; b. Russ, 1907; s. Azriel; in Isr since 1954; BS, LIU, 1932; MA, U Chgo, 1944, PhD, 1952; m. Jean Goldberg, 1934. Prof, ind relations and soc sci, Technion, dir, ext div, 1954-56, chmn, dept of gen studies, 1957-61; adv, manpower devl, Govt of Ceylon, 1961-62. Pres, Isr Ind Rel Research Assn; mem, bd dirs, Isr Elec Corp; mem: Intl Council Ind Relations; Isr Council Mgmt Cen. Author: Labor Relations in Israel; Human Factor in Production; Personnel Management in a Developing Enterprise; Workers Participation in Management; Israel's Socio-Economic Planning; contbr to profsl jours. Home: 5 Eshkolot St, Haifa, Isr. Office: Technion, Haifa, Isr.

TABIB, Mordechai, Isr, author; b. Isr, 1910; s. Tabib and Shoshana; m. Hana Kantorowitz, 1934; c: Lea, Gal. Author: keEssev Hassadeh, 1948; Derech shel Afar, 1953; keArar baArava, 1957; Kinoro shel Yossi, 1960; Shlomo haMelech vehaDevora, 1960; Tikun Hatzoth; Masah laAretz haGdola, 1968. Recipient: prizes: Ruppin, 1950; two Ussishkin, 1954; Aharonowitz, 1956; Italia. Home: 8 Shivat Zion St, Rishon leZion, Isr.

TABOR, Harry Zvi, Isr, physicist; b. London, Eng, Mar 7, 1917; s. Charles and Rebecca (Weinstein); in Isr since 1949; BSc, hons, Heb U, 1937, PhD, 1956; m. Vivienne Landau; c: Sharona, Dalia. Dir, Natl Phys Lab of Isr, Natl Council for Research and Devl, Off of PM, since 1950; fmr: dep dir reasearch, Electroflo Co, 1948-49, research physicist, 1938-48; adv, govt and UN agcys. Chmn, Sci Research Found, Isr; mem, adv council, Brit ZF, Isr; f, Inst of Physicists, London; fmr: chmn, found, Jerusalem Citizens Org; leader, Brit Habonim Movement. Contbr to profsl jours. Home: 13 Hameyasdim St, Jerusalem, Isr. Office: Dan Danciger Bldg, Heb U, Jerusalem, Isr.

TABOR, Maurice S, US, insurance exec; b. Buffalo, NY, Dec 10, 1894; s. Leo and Rose (Fleishman); m. Miriam Geismar, Feb 25, 1926; c: John. Gen agt, Travelers Ins Co, since 1919. Maj, US Army, 1917-1919. Press: Buffalo Life Underwriters,

1948; J Fed for Social Services, 1945-46; NY Stage reg, CJFWF, 1949-50; Council of Social Agcys, 1953-54; Temple Beth Zion, 1955-56, 1965-67; Comty Chest of Buffalo & Erie Co, 1960; clubs: Montefiore; Westwood Country. Home: 142 Rumsey Rd, Buffalo, NY. Office: 800 Wallbridge Bldg, Buffalo, NY.

TACKEFF, Bertram C, US, business exec; b. Boston, Mass, Dec 1, 1923; s. Michael and Lena (Goldstein); BS, Boston U, 1945; MBA, U Chgo, 1946; m. Sterra Stone, Aug 8, 1946; c: Jo Ann, Matthew, Roger. Pres: Pies Cold Storage Co, Inc; New Boston Freezer Co; Food and Fibre Inc. Served, USAAC, 1943. Dir, Amer Meat Inst, since 1952; exec comm, Combined J Philanthropies, Boston; vice-chmn, fellows, Brandeis U; trustee, Beth Isr Hosp. Home: 49 Princeton Rd, Brookline, Mass. Office: 960 Massachusetts Ave, Boston, Mass.

TADMOR, Dov, Isr, business exec; b. Pol, Aug 28, 1929; s. Nachum and Hinda (Lichter) Racimor; in Isr since 1948; LLB, sch of law and econ, Tel Aviv U; m. Sara Wackerman, Mar 16, 1954; c: Lihi, Eran. Mgr, Property and Bldg Co Ltd, since 1961; legal adv, Tel Aviv Munic, 1954-56; secy, legal adv, Delek of Isr, 1956-61. Sgt, IDF, 1948-50. Mem: chmn, Young Businessmen Assn, Isr; treas, Friends of Tel Aviv U; Isr Bar Assn. Contbr to profsl jours. Home: 18 Pumbedita St, Tel Aviv, Isr. Office: 16 Simtat Bet Hashoeva St, Tel Aviv, Isr.

TADMOR, Hayim, Isr, educator; b. Harbin, China, Nov 18, 1923; s. David and Frieda (Kaznitz) Frumstein; in Isr since 1935; MA, Heb U, 1949, PhD, 1954; postgrad study: London U, 1951-52; U Chgo, 1955-57; m. Miriam Skura, Mar 25, 1953; c: Naomi, David. Asso prof, Heb U, since 1966, fac mem since 1958; visiting lectr, Coll J Studies, U Chgo, 1955-57. IDF, 1947-48. Contbr: History of the Jewish People, Vol I; The Ancient Times, 1969; co-ed, Ency Mikrait; contbr to scholarly jours. Home: 19 Balfour St, Jerusalem, Isr. Office: Dept of Assyriology, Heb U, Jerusalem, Isr.

TADMOR, Jacob Trocker, Isr, nuclear scientist; b. Cetatea, Rum, Nov 4, 1924; s. Nissan and Frieda (Schachter) Trocker; in Isr since 1949; att Poly, Bucharest, 1944-47; CE, Technion, 1950, MSc, 1956; nuclear engr deg, Saclay, Fr, 1957; PhD, Heb U, 1964; m. Sara Grungross, June 24, 1958; c: Noga, Carmel. Dir, nuclear safety, Isr AEC, since 1966; head, nuclear safety group, Soreq Nuclear Research Cen, since 1962, staff mem since 1955; fmr: research chem, Chem and Fertilizers, Haifa, 1953-55; visiting sci, Oak Ridge Natl Lab, US, 1966-67. Sci br, IDF, 1953-55. Mem: Isr and Amer Chem Socs; Health Physics Soc; Assn des Ings en Genie Atomique, Fr. Contbr to sci jours. Home: 37 Weizmann St, Rehovot, Isr.

TADMOR, Zehev, Isr, educator; b. Ocna Mures, Rum, Feb 6, 1937; s. Izchak and Sarah (Farkas); in Isr since 1950; BS, Technion, 1959, MS, 1963; DSc, Stevens Inst of Tech, 1966; m. Ciporah Spitzer, Apr 2, 1960; c: Ellad. Asst prof, chem engr, Technion, since 1968; vice-pres, dir research, Sci Process and Research, Inc, Highland Park NJ, since 1969; fmr: Isr research engr, Western Elec Co, 1964-68; research engr, Isr Min of Defense, 1960-63. Cpl, IDF, 1959-62. Mem: Soc of Rheology; Soc of Plastics Engrs; Isr Chem Engr Soc. Author: Principles of Plasticating Extrusion, 1969. Recipient: Herman Mark f, Plastics Inst of Amer, 1964. Home: 70 Shoshanat Hacarmel St, Haifa, Isr. Office: POB 4910, Haifa, Isr.

TADZER, Isak, Yugo, physician, educator; b. Dec 24, 1916; s. Salis and Ida (Rodriguez); MD, 1941; in Yugo since 1944; m. Milena Rueh, Nov 11, 1946; c: Salis, Slavjanka. Lectr and prof extraordinary, med fac, U Skopje, since 1951; asst prof, Regius prof, pathophys, 1947-51; head, Inst for Pathophys, Med Fac and Isotope Lab. Fmr: secy, Macedonian Assn Phys; ed, Macedonian Med Rev. Contbr to Yugo and fgn profsl jours. Recipient: Order of Labour, III deg; award for org and application of isotopes. Macedonia. Hobby, modern music. Home: Ul, 11 Oktomvri 62, Skopje, Yugo. Office: Medical Faculty, Skopje, Yugo.

TAFT, Eric Hyman, Austr, dermatologist; b. Melbourne, Austr, Feb 12, 1923; s. Boris and Ettel (Zeigermacher); BM, BS, U Melbourne, 1945; DM, U Sydney, 1956; m. Evelyn Sibel, Mar 23, 1948; c: Jonathan, Judith, Deborah, Natalie. Hon dermat, Prince Henry's Hosp, since 1957; censor-in-chief, Austr Coll of Dermat since 1966. Vice-pres, Cong Temple Beth Isr, Melbourne; chmn: Vic State fac, Coll of Dermat; med lit comm, Prince Henry's Hosp; fmr: pres: Austr Fellowship; IMA; hon secy, Dermat Assn of Austr; clubs: Collingwood Football; Social; Eastern Golf. Contbr articles to profsl jours. Hobbies: reading, photography, golf. Home: 21 Stoke Ave, Kew, Vic, Australia. Office: 33 Collins St, Melbourne, Australia.

TAFT, Pincus, Austr, physician; b. Melbourne, Austr, June 24, 1920; s. Morris and Rose (Wittner); m. Tamara Heselev; c: Lisa, Jennifer. Phys i/c, Downie Metabolic Research Unit, Alfred Hosp, since 1963; cons endocrinologist, Royal Women's Hosp, since 1954; hon endocrinologist, Royal Melbourne Hosp, 1950-63. Capt, Austr Army, MC, 1942-46. Pres: Endocrine Soc of Austr; Profsl Adv Comm, J Wfr Soc; mem: Amer Diabetes Assn; Amer Endocrine Soc. Contbr articles to med jours. Office: 37 Spruzen Ave, N Kew, Vic, Austr.

TAFT, Ronald, Austr, psychologist, educator; b. Melbourne, Austr, June 3, 1920; s. Hirsh and Olga (Mushatsky); BA, Melbourne U, 1939; MA, Columbia U, 1941; PhD, U Cal, Berkeley, 1951; m. Ellen Braumann, Apr 1, 1943; c: Barbara Mushin, David. Prof, social psych, Monash U, since 1968; fmr: ind psychol: Dept Aircraft Produc, 1942-44; Austr Inst of Mgmt, 1942-47; reader in psychol: Melbourne U; U of W Austr, 1951-66. F, Austr Psychol Soc, past chmn; mem: Social Sci Research Council Austr; gov body, Intl Union Psych Sci; Temple Beth Isr; Hillel Found of Vic; Friends of Heb U; found pres: Temple David Cong, Perth; Melbourne J Youth Council, 1942-44. Author: From Stranger to Citizen; co-author: Clinical Inference and Cognitive Theory; contbr to profsl jours. Spec interest: research on J Comty of Melbourne. Home: 5 Charles St, Kew, Vic, Austr. Office: Monash U, Clayton, Vic, Austr.

TAGLIACOZZO, Carlo, It, consulting engr, educator; b. Rome, It, Jan 21, 1904; s. Giacomo and Annina (Ascoli); D Engr, U Rome, 1927, DMaths, 1931; m. Lida Aelion, May 23, 1945. Prof, libero docente, U Rome, since 1946; fmr: prof, U Rome, 1929-38; prof, U of Sao Paulo, Brazil, 1941-46. Chmn, Roman comm, KH, since 1950. Author: Sulla Stabilita' Dell' Equilibrio Elastico-Riassunto Di Un Corso Di Lezioni Dettate L'Anno Accademico, 1934-35; Nel R. Instituto Superiore D'Ingegneria, 1935; Concreto Armado-Preleções Sobre Calculos de Resistencia, 1942; contbr to profsl jours. Home and office: 7 Lungotevere Mellini, Rome, It.

TAISHOFF, Sol J, US, editor, publisher; b. Minsk, Russ, Oct 8, 1904; s. Joseph and Rose (Order); in US since 1906; m. Betty Tash, March 6, 1927, c: Joanne Cowan, Lawrence. Ed, publisher: Broadcasting Magazine, since 1931; Television Magazine, 1960-68; fmr: staff mem, AP, Wash DC, 1920-26; reporter, radio columnist, US Daily, 1926-31. Sr mem, Inst of Radio Engrs; mem: Bc Pioneers, pres, 1960; Sigma Delta Chi, natl pres, 1957-58; White House Intl Corresp Assn; clubs: Overseas Writers; Natl Press; Broadcasters; Woodmont Country. Recipient: award U, of Mo, 1953; Wells Memorial Key, Sigma Delta Chi, 1960; award, Natl Assn of Broadcasters, 1966; Paul W White award, 1967. Home: 4201 Cathedral Ave NW, Washington, DC. Office: 1735 De Sales St NW, Washington. DC.

TAKSERMAN-KROZER, Rachel, Isr, physicist; b. Ukraine, Russ, July 31, 1921; d. Gdaliahu and Luba (Sokolowska) Takserman; in Isr since 1968; MSc, U Taschkent, Russ, 1947; DSc, Inst of Gen Chem, Warsaw, 1961; docent, Tech U, Lodz, 1966; m. Simon Krozer; c: Anatol, George, Viktor. Sr lectr, Technion, since 1969; fmr: asst, sr asst, Tech U, Tashkent, 1947-48; sr asst, lectr, U Leningrad, 1948-49; sr research f, Inst of Gen Chem, Warsaw; asso prof, Inst of Fundamental Problems, Warsaw; visiting prof: Sci Inst of High Molecules, Sci Inst of Petrochem Ind, both Russ, 1962; Sci Inst of High Molecules, Prague, 1965. Mem: Pol Chem Sci Soc; Pol Phys Sci Soc, both 1959-68. Author, chap in Structure of Macromolecules in Solutions, 1968; contbr to profsl publs. Recipient: sci award: Pol Chem Soc, 1963; directorate, Inst of Gen Chem, Pol, 1964. Home: 116a UNO Ave, Haifa, Isr. Office: Technion, Haifa, Isr.

TAL, Alexander, Isr, musician; b. Timisoara, Rum, Oct 21, 1932; s. Ferdinand and Rosalia (Ida) Deutel; in Isr since 1951; att Acad of Music: Tel Aviv; Bucharest; div; c: Michal. Leader: Isr Chamber Ensemble, since 1966; New Isr String Quartet, since 1957; fmr: leading violinist, soloist, Isr Philharmonic Orch, 1954-66; Recipient: Prize, Isr 10th Anniversary comm. Spec interests: theater, hist. Home: 13 Onkelos St, Tel Aviv, Isr. Office: 103 Ibn Gvirol St, Tel Aviv, Isr.

TAL, Israel, Isr, army officer; b. Safed, Isr, Sep 13, 1924; s. Ben-Zion and Penina (Pilpel); BA, Heb U; m. Hagith Kipnis, Mar 15, 1949; c: Penina, Yair. Maj gen, cdr, armored corps, IDF, since 1964, with IDF since 1948; fmr: Haganah, J Brigade, Brit Army, 1942-46. Recipient: Isr Defense award, 1961. Office: Israel Defense Forces, Isr.

TAL, Josef, Isr, musicologist, composer; b. Poznan, Pol, Sep 18, 1910; s. Julius and Ottilie (Bloch) Gruenthal; in Isr since 1934; m. Pola; c: Eithan. Head, musicology dept, Heb U, since 1965; dir, Rubin Acad of Music, Jerusalem, 1948-52. Recipient: UNESCO f, Engel prize, Tel Aviv; composers prize, ISCM, labor union, Tel Aviv. Home: 2 Devora Hanevia St, Jerusalem, Isr. Office: Heb U, Jerusalem, Isr.

TAL, Miriam, Isr, critic, writer, b. Smolensk, Russ, June 29, 1910; d. Abraham and Anna (Karpilov) Rosental; in Isr since 1930; att Heb U, Jerusalem, 1932; div. Art critic: Gazith, since 1958; Ariel; beTerem; Jerusalem Almanach; Orot; Renaissance; Revivim; Youth Horizon; Haboker daily, 1949-65; La Vie Culturelle en Israel, Brussels, 1957-64; Hayom, daily, 1966-69. Author: Hebrew novel, 1937; Kav leKav, 1964; numerous prefaces, bibliographies to art books, one-man shows, portfolios. Cpl, British Army, 1943-44. Mem: Intl Assn Art Critics; adv council, Div of Plastic Arts, Min of Educ. Home and office: 5 Hazanowitz St, Jerusalem, Isr.

TAL, Uriel, Isr, historian; b. Vienna, Aus, Dec 23, 1929; s. Israel and Sarah (Sommer) Taubes; in Isr since 1940; BA, Heb U, Jerusalem, 1955, MA, 1959, PhD, 1963; m. Miriam Shoshani, 1949; c: Yizhr, Judith. Acting chmn, dept hist J thought, Heb U, since 1969, fac mem, dept J Hist; visiting prof, modern J Hist, HUC-JIR, Cincinnati, O, 1970-72; Capt, Haganah, 1946-48; IDF since 1948. Mem: steering comm, Isr Interfaith Comm, Jerusalem; comm on contemporary Judaism, Isr Hist Soc, Jerusalem. Author: Jews and Christians in the Second Reich, 1870-1914, A Study in the Rise of German Totalitarianism, 1969; Patterns in the Contemporary Jewish-Christian Dialogue, 1969; contbr to scholarly publs. Home: 5 Shmuel Klein Str, Jerusalem Isr. Offices: Heb U, Jerusalem, Isr; HUC-JIR, Clinton Ave, Cincinnati, O.

TALIANOFF, George Joseph, US, attorney; b. NYC, Nov 14, 1910; s. Morris and Fannie (Goldstein); BA, Cornell U, 1931; JD, Bklyn Law Sch, 1935; att, New Sch for Social Work, 1936; m. Lucille Sable, Jan 26, 1936; c: Susan Rubin, Marsha. Pvt practice since 1948; spec asst atty-gen, State of Fla, 1953-55, 1959. Chmn, natl comty service comm, ADL; Fla chmn, Soc of Fellows, ADL; vice-pres, Temple Emanuel, since 1949; mem: Fla, Dade Co, Miami Beach, Amer Bar Assns; past pres, B'nai B'rith: Miami lodge; State lodge. Hobbies: golf, chess. Home and office: 420 Lincoln Rd, Miami Beach, Fla.

TALKAR, Raymond Samuel, Isr, community leader, b. Bombay, India, Aug 11, 1913; s. Samuel and Mazel Tov (Moses) Enoch; in Isr since 1957; m. Sophie Solomon, Oct 8, 1939; c: Mazal-Nathan, Samuel, Esther Benshabat. Staff mem, Negev Inst for Arid Zone Research, since 1959; fmr: off asst: E D Sasson and Co Ltd, Bombay, 1937-44; Off of Textile Commnr, 1944-56. Air raid warden, IDF, 1957-61. Mem: B'rith Rishonim, Assn of Vet Zionists in Isr; fmr: secy, Isr Brotherhood, Bombay; delg, B'nai Isr Conf, 1937-43; mem, J Wfr Assn, New Delhi; found, Temple of Man, Beersheva, 1957; secy, B'nai Isr Youth Day, Bombay, 1937-44; mem, Zionist Assn Bombay, 1938-56; att: 25th, 26th, 27th Zionist Congs; Herzl Centenary, Jerusalem. Spec interests: visiting hosps, aged persons homes, orphanages. Home: 25 Giora Joseftal St, Beersheva, Isr. Office: Negev Inst for Arid Zone Research, Beersheva, Isr.

TALL, Baruch, Isr, government official; b. Przansyz, Pol, 1907; s. Zvi and Sara (Glowinski); m. Repr of Defense Min, cen comm of V'ad Leman leHayal, since 1960; fmr: kibbutz mem, 1930-1939; emissary to Hechalutz, Eng, 1939-1946; dir mobilization, Defense Min, 1947-51; secy, org dept, Mapai, 1951-57; dir, popular export dept, Min of Trade, 1957-60. Mem, cen comm, Isr Amer Soc; fmr mem, secretariat, cen comm, Mapai. Author, Sefer, Kalin 1965. Hobbies: photography, rare books on Pal, Isr. Home: 26 Amsterdam St, Tel Aviv, Isr. Office: 8 Arbaah St, Tel Aviv, Isr.

TALMI, Emma, Isr, legislator, educator; b. Warsaw, Pol, Apr 1905; in Isr since 1924; m; three c. MK, dep speaker, Knesset, mem educ, finance comms; mem: Kibbutz Mishmar HaEmek; Mapam Party Secretariat, political cen council; fmr: kindegarten tchr; agric tchr; agric worker; bldg worker. Mem secretariat, Women's Workers Council; delg, Zionist Congs. Author: Purim be'Elul; leEt Ohalim; Tail Al Hadneister; Bein Gvulot; Mishmar HaEmek Bama'aracha; fmr ed, Hedim, of Kibbutz Arzi. Home: Kibbutz Mishmar HaEmek, Isr.

TALMI, Ephraim, Isr, editor, journalist, poet; b. Szerpc, Pol, Sep 9, 1905; s. Abraham and Mindel (Borstein) in Isr since 1925; m; c: Menahem, Doron. Ed, Davar leYeladim, since 1956. mem, ed staff, Davar since 1944. Author: Broshim baLeil, 1941; Ephraim Ish Hulda, 1943, 1945; beEmda Kidmit, 1949; baMatzor ubaKrav, Et veShelach, beKav haEsh, Israel baMaaracha,1949; Sadot Yerukim, 1953; co-author: haNegev, haGalil, Yerushalaim, 1954; miDan veAd Eilat, 1954; leArtzi, 1955; Gluiot min haMoledet, 1959; Shloshim Shnot Haganah; Nofei Moledet, 1961; Madrich Hadash leTiyul Shel Kaiitz, 1962; Israel, 1961; New Israel Guide, 1962; a geographical dict, 1962; Albom Kinneret, 1964; Albom Emek Israel, 1965; Ma veMi beMilchemet haAtzmaut, 1965; Albom haYarden, 1966; Pinot baMoledet, 1966; Yerushalaim veHagada haMaaravit, 1967; Magen vaShelach, 1968; ed; anthology, Sippurei Yam, 1952. Haganah, 1925-48, ed staff, Bamachaneh, 1937-48; Tel Aviv Civil Guard, 1940-44; mil corrrespt, 1948-50. Mem: Heb Writers Assn; Isr Journalists Assn. Recipient: Sokolov award, Tel Aviv Munic, 1954. Home: 33 Bezalel St, Tel Aviv, Isr. Office: 45 Shenkin St, Tel Aviv, Isr.

TALMI, Igal, Isr, physicist, educator; b. Kiev, Ukraine, Jan 31, 1925; s. Moshe and Lea (Weinstein); in Isr since 1925; MSc, Heb U, 1947; D, Natural Sci, ETH, Swiss Fed Inst of Tech, Zurich, 1952; m. Chana Kivelewitz, Aug 8, 1949; c: Yoav, Tamar. Prof, physics, Weizmann Inst of Sci, since 1958, fac mem since 1954; visiting: f, Princeton U, 1952-54, asso, prof, 1956-57; prof, 1961-62, 1966-67. Palmach, 1941-43; IDF, 1947-49. Mem: Amer Phys Soc; Isr Phys Soc; Isr Academy of Scis and Humanities. Co-author: Nuclear Shell Theory, 1963; contbr to sci jours. Home: Neve Weizmann, Rehovot, Isr. Office: Weizmann Inst of Sci, Rehovot, Isr.

TALMI, Menachem, Isr, author; b. Ramat Gan, Isr, Sep 19, 1926; s. Ephraim and Tova. Staff mem, Maariv; fmr mem: Kibbutz Mitzpe Yam; Kibbutz Izrael. Served Givati Unit, 1948. Author: Lichiot, Lichiot, 1949; Yechi haOmetz, 1951; haBachurim Lo Hichzivu, 1952; Kach Lacham Israel, 1953; Kach Hitgonen Israel, 1954; Sefer Hanegev, 1954; Sefer Hagalil, 1955; Sefer Yerushalaim, 1956; Hamatos Himrih Bachatzot, 1955; haTzalahat haMeofefet, 1955; Hanazir beEe haAlmogim, 1956 beOz Rucham, 1956; haKnufiya Shel Haiimo, 1957; Shayarot beEsh, 1957; Kach Lachamnu BeSinai, 1957; Yishuvim beEsh, 1958; Yalkut Derachim, 1958; Michnasei Or haYaguar, 1960; Israel, Madrich Hadash, 1960; Kol haAretz Lexicon, 1962; Yam Kinneret, 1965; Yam haMelech, 1966; Tzochek Mi sheTzoochek Acharon, 1969; Yerushalaim veHagada haMa'aravit, 1967; pub 15 children's books about the War of Independence; 2 books on Isr geog; co-ed; 3 anthols; contbr to press. Recipient: Lamdan award, Ramat Gan Munic, 1956. Home: 10 Gordon St, Tel Aviv, Isr. Office: Maariv, 2 Carlebach St, Tel Aviv, Isr.

TALMI, Yoav, US, composer, conductor; b. Merhavia, Isr, Apr 28, 1943; s. Avraham and Sara; dipl, Rubin Music Acad, Tel Aviv, 1964; postgrad dipl, Juilliard Sch of Music, 1968; m. Erella Gottesmann; c: Gil. Asso conductor, Louisville Orch, since 1968; music dir, Ky Chamber Orch, since 1969; mem fac: U Louisville, since 1968; Juilliard Sch of Music, 1967-68. Served IDF orch, 1961-63, composed IDF official march. Recorded: CBS; Louisville Records. Recipient: full scholarship, Amer-Isr Cultural Found, 1968; Koussevitsky, Memorial Conduction prize, Boston Sym Orch, 1969. Hobby: painting. Home: 3 Hawthorne Hill, Louisville, Ky. Office: 211 Brown Bldg, Louisville, Ky.

TALMON, Jacob L, Isr, educator; b. Rypin, Pol, June 14, 1916; s. Abraham and Zipora (Lichtenstein); MA, Heb U, 1939; att Sorbonne, 1939; PhD, LSE, 1943; m. Irena Bugajer, Nov 23, 1961. Prof modern hist, Heb U; visiting f: St Catherine's Coll, Oxford; Inst for Advanced Study, Princeton,

1967-68; visiting prof, MIT, 1968-69; secy, Pal comm, asst secy, fgn affairs comm, Bd of Dep of Brit Jews, 1944-47. Mem, The Isr Academy of Scis and Humanities. Author: The Origins of Totalitarian Democracy, 1952; The Nature of Jewish History-Its Universal Significance, 1957; Political Messianism — The Romantic Phase, 1960; The Unique and The Universal, 1965; Romanticism and Revolt, 1967; Israel among the Nations, 1968. Recipient: Israel prize; grant, Rockefeller Found. Home: 41 Ramban St, Jerusalem, Isr. Office: Heb U, Jerusalem, Isr.

TALMON, Michael, Isr, government official; b. Jerusalem, Isr, June 26, 1922; s. Eliahu and Lea (Waltz) Cohen; m. Rachel Katz, Mar 31, 1943; c: Eliahu, Bathsheva, Shay. Div dir, Isr Land Admn, since 1969; dir, Negev region, Min of Housing, since 1963; fmr dir: Negev region, Agric Settlement Dept, 1949-60; WRD, 1960-63. Home: 46 Gershon St, Beersheva, Isr. Office: 6 Shamai St, Jerusalem, Isr.

TALMON, Shemaryahu, Isr, educator; b. Skierniwice, Pol, May 28, 1920; s. Litman and Hella (Ell) Zelmanowicz; in Isr since 1939; MA, Heb U, 1945; PhD, 1956; c: Efrath, Tamar, Nogah, Tammy; m. 2nd, Peninah Genio, Mar 18, 1969. Asso prof, Heb U, since 1966; prin, Haifa U Coll, since 1968; fmr: lectr, Leeds U, 1949-51; prof, Brandeis U, 1961-63; visiting lectr, Harvard U, 1961-62. Capt, IDF. Mem: Soc of Oriental Studies, Eng; Amer Oriental Soc; Isr Exploration Soc. Author: Biblica; Vetus Testamentum; Tarbiz; Textus; Beth Miqra; contbr to profsl jours. Home: 4 Beth Ha'Arabah, Jerusalem, Isr. Office: Heb U, Jerusalem, Isr.

TALMON (Monsohn), Zvi, Isr, educator, composer, conductor; b. Jerusalem, Isr, Dec, 1922; s. David and Sarah (Rabinovitz) Monsohn. BA, Isr Acad of Music, Jerusalem; m. Rivka Rohald; c: Rachel Gayer, Baruch, Orna. Choir, orch conductor, Gen Orphanage for Girls; choir master: Hechal Shlomo Syn; Tiferet Zvi Syn. Mem: ACUM; League of Composers in Isr. Composer: lithurgical music based upon tradition but constructed as Western music; Rinat haHechal; Ron Lan, choir songs; Paatey Mizrach, piano sonata for young people; laMenatseach Mizmor, Biblical songs; Tsliley Dror uMoledet, for solo and group singing; Tav Ron, for choir; Et haZamir, for choir; Pirkey Shira unGinah laYom haZikaron laShoah velaGvurah. Spec interest: methodical aids in teaching Talmud. Home 22 Ben Maimon St, Jerusalem, Isr. Office: General Orphanage for Girls, Kiriat Moshe, Jerusalem, Isr.

TAMARI, Amiram, Isr, tchr, artist; b. Hadera, Isr, Mar 22, 1913; s. Michael and Zipora (Kipper) Teitelman; in Isr since 1913; att: Julien Acad, 1935; De la Grande Chaumiere, 1936-37, both Paris. Artist, painter, since 1937; tchr, hist of art, since 1946. Royal Engrs, British Army, 1941-46; IAF, 1948. Mem: Isr Painters and Sculptors Assn; Isr Tchrs Union. Recipient: Dizengoff awards, Tel Aviv Munic, 1943, 1944; African Star. Home: 8 Tzidon St, Tel Aviv, Isr. Office: 193 Ben Yehuda St, Tel Aviv, Isr.

TAMIR, Alexander, Isr, musician, educator; b. Vilna, Pol, Apr 2, 1931; s. Noah and Fenia (Kowarski) Wolkowyski; in Isr since 1945; honor grad, Acad of Music, Jerusalem, 1952; studied with pvt tchr, Tel Aviv. Mem, Eden and Tamir, intl known duo pianists, Hurok Concerts, Inc; prof, Rubin Acad of Music, Jerusalem, since 1958; dir, Targ Music Cen, since 1969. Pvt, IDF, 1948-50. Composed: Shtiler, Shtiler; recorded: London, Decca. Recipient: Silver medal, Vercelli Intl Competition, It, 1956. Home: Ein-Kerem, Jerusalem, Isr. Office: POB 410, Jerusalem, Isr.

TAMIR, Joseph, Isr, public official, journalist; b. Berdichev, Russ, Mar 5, 1915; s. Naphtali and Aliza (Toshpe) Kwentzel; in Isr since 1925; att sch of law and econ, Tel Aviv, U, 1935; m. Naomi Manevich, 1939; c: Diza, Naphtali. MK, Gahal, since 1965; secy-gen, Lib Party, since 1951, mem natl exec comm, chmn, info bur; mem, bd staff, Haboker daily, since 1940, US corresp; mem, Tel Aviv Munic Council, adr.in bd, since 1959; ed staff: Haaretz, 1933-40; Maariv, 1948-56; Kol Israel weekly. Mil corresp, IDF, 1948. Chmn, Subur.n Journalists Assn; vice-chmn, Isr-Amer Friendship League; pres, Maccabi Sports Org,Petach Tikva, 1930-45; delg, Maccabi World Cong, Prague, 1933; found, Natl Council for Beautification of Isr. Author: The Campaign on Israel's Eastern Borders, 1949. Home: 53 King David Blvd, Tel Aviv, Isr. Office: 66 Ibn Gvirol St, Tel Aviv, Isr.

TAMIR, Max Mordecai, US, city planner; b. Haifa, Isr, May 17, 1912; s. Matatyahu and Hanna (Horowitz); in US since 1943; PhD, Sorbonne, 1938; m. Vicki Levy, July 6, 1956; c: Edith, AaDean. Dir, planning, research and devl, transp admn, City of NY, since 1967; pres, chmn bd, Directomat Inc, 1957-66; dir, dept of traffic, City of NY, 1952-57. Served Fr underground, Maquis, WW II. Prin contrib: invented Directomat machine, built Pal Pavilion, Intl Fair, Paris, 1937. Mem: Amer Inst of Planners; Inst of Traffic Engrs; Soc of Munic Engrs; Assn of Engrs and Architects in Isr. Author: La Mer Morte et une ville à son bord, 1937; Les expositions internationales à travers les âges, 1938. Recipient: Lauréat de l'Académie des Beaux Arts, Paris, 1939. Home: 785 West End Ave, New York, NY.

TAMIR, Noah, Isr, author, educator; b. Bessarabia, Russ, 1890; s. Israel and Zipora (Zevin); in Isr since 1910; att, Tchr Sem, Jerusalem, 1911-14; m. Bella Dvosis, 1924; c: Uzi. Ret, since 1954; author: Shalviya, 1939; El meEver laMoledeth, 1944; haRabi miBelz uKfilo, 1961; Seminaristim beMa'avak Am, 1963; Asher Siparti leIladim, 1957; Chagim Mesaprim, 1959; Agadat Motho Shel Yeshu veUvdath haGenocide, 1960; velIrushalaim, Ircha, 1967; ed: Beit Sifreinu, 1957; Sefer Kalarash, 1966. Home: 94 Weizmann St, Tel Avvi, Isr.

TAMIR (Katznelson), Shmuel M, Isr, public official, attorney; b. Jerusalem, Isr, March 10, 1923; s. Reuven and Batsheva (Nagel) Katznelson; att, Heb U, law degree, Jerusalem Law Sch, 1948; m. Ruth Gurevitch, 1947; c: David, fell in action, Liora, Noga, Josef. MK; chmn, exec comm, Free Center Party; pvt law practice since 1948. Mem: Isr comm, Intl Commn of Jurists; natl supr court, Isr Bar Assn; acting cdr, IZL, Jerusalem dist, 1946-47; co-found, Herut movement, 1948. Contbr to press, profsl jours. Home: 189 Haeshel St, Herzliya Pituach, Isr. Office: 15 Rothschild Blvd, Tel Aviv, Isr. Isr.

TAMIS, Abraham B, US, physician, educator; b. NYC, Oct 26, 1899; s. Louis and Anna (Frantzman); BS, NYU, 1920; MD, Bellevue Med Coll, 1922; m. Lillian Rosenthal, Oct 18, 1925; c: Florence, Robert. Pvt practice, obstetrics and gyn, since 1930; asst clinical prof, Albert Einstein Coll of Med; cons gyn; Montefiore Hosp and Med Cen; Bx-Leb Hosp Cen; NY Polyclinic Hosp and Med School; NY Infirmary; J Memorial Hosp; gyn, Kingsbridge House. Chmn, phys div, Bx chap, UJA, 1952; trustee, Fed J Philanthropies; dipl, Amer Bd of Obstets and Gyn; f: Amer Coll of Surg; Amer Coll of Obs and Gyn; mem: NY Acad of Med; AMA; Bx Co Med Soc, pres, 1950; Bx Obstets and Gyn Soc; Bx Bd of Trade; Bx Wfr and Health Council; Phi Delta Epsilon; Alpha Omega Alpha; NY Gyn Soc; Masons. Contbr to med jours. Home: 169 E 69 St, New York, NY. Office: 2 E 85 St, New York, NY

TAMMUZ, Benjamin, Isr, editor, author, sculptor; b. Russ, July 11, 1919; s. Joseph and Sofia (Segal) Kammerstein; in Isr since 1924; att Sorbonne, 1951; m. Miryam Solberg, Nov 11, 1946; c: On, Jonathan. Lit ed, weekly lit supplement, Haaretz daily, since 1965; ed, Yom Yom daily, 1948-59; art critic, Haaretz daily, 1948-58. Author: Sands of Gold; Closed Garden; A Boat Sails to Sea; A Night on the Western Bank; trilogy: The Life of Elyakum; Castle in Spain; The Book of Hallucinations; ed: Art in Isr, 1964; sculptor: Monument to Fallen Aviators, Independence Garden, Tel Aviv. Mem: Isr Writers Assn; Painters and Sculptors Assn. Home: 13 Levi Itzhak St, Tel Aviv, Isr. Office: Haaretz, Maze St, Tel Aviv, Isr.

TANENBAUM, Marc H, US, rabbi, org exec; b. Baltimore, Md, Oct 13, 1925; s. Abraham and Sadie (Siger); BS, Yeshiva U, 1945; MHL, ordained rabbi, JTSA, 1950; m. Helga Weiss, Feb 6, 1939; c: Adena, Michael. Natl dir, dept of interreligious affairs, AJComm, since 1961; TV panelist, ABC, CBS; PR counsel, Eternal Light radio prog, NYC, 1946-50; lit ed, PR dir, Henry Schuman Inc, publishers, 1950-52; rabbi: Northeast Heb Cong, Wash DC, 1952; J Cen, Lake Mahopac, 1953; fmr: exec dir, Syn Council, Amer; pres, Marc H Tanenbaum Assos, PR. Cons: childrens bur, HEW; Pius XII Rel Educ Resource Cen, Monroe, Mich; prog chmn, Natl Conf on Race and Rel; mem, conv prog comm, Rel Educ Assn; mem, rel adv comm, US Comm for UN; mem, bd dirs, Inter-Amer Literacy Found; fmr: vice-chmn, exec comm, White House Conf on Children and Youth; mem, natl adv council, White House Conf on Aging; natl vice-chmn, ARC; vice-pres, Rel in Amer Life; mem: Natl Commn for UNESCO; natl rel policy comm, Girl Scouts Amer and Camp Fire Girls Amer; bd of dirs, Clergymen's Econ Inst; Council of trustees,

United Seamen's Service. Author: A Guide to Jewish Traditions and Holy Days; Our Moral and Spiritual Resources for International Cooperation; co-author: Jewish-Chiristian Dialogue; contbr to: Vatican II: An Interfaith Appraisal; Torah and Gospel; The Star and the Cross; and scholarly, rel, popular jours. Spec interest: advancement of Catholic-J understanding. Recipient: Coronet award, St Edwards U. Home: 83-06 Victor Ave, Elmhurst NY. Office: 1 65 E 56 St, New York, NY

TANNE, David, Isr, government official; b. Ger, June 3, 1909; s. Israel and Pearl (Acker); in Isr since 1933; att, U Berlin; m. Helga Jacob; c: Hagit, Hovav, Michael Kushnir, Ariel. Dir gen, Min of Housing since 1953; bd mem, banking and building cos; leading org and dir, Isr housing enterprises, mortgage banks; Ger sect, JA, Haifa, 1933-48; dir Absorption dept, JA, Tel Aviv, 1949-53. Contbr to profsl publs. Home: 32 Giv'ati St, Ramat Gan, Isr. Office: Min of Housing, Hakirya, Tel Aviv, Isr.

TANNENBAUM, Samuel W, US, attorney; b. NYC, March 3, 1890; s. Max and Lena (Falk); BA, Columbia U, 1910, MA, 1912, LLB, 1912; m. Frieda Stone, June 4, 1922; c: Claire Ollstein, Ellen Shadick. Partner, Johnson and Tannenbaum, law firm since 1945; copyright counsel and cons: MGM; Warner Bros; Paramount; Universal-Intl; Walt Disney, all since 1945; United Artists since 1953; NBC, CBS; 20th Century Fox; ABC; Desilu; lectr on copyright and unfair competition: Practicing Law Inst; NYU Law Sch; NY Law Sch; Columbia U; Yale U, 1954; arbiter, Motion Picture Fed Consent Degree, 1943-45. Ensign, USN, WW I. Found, pres, Copyright Soc of USA, 1953-54, trustee since 1961; mem: panel of experts on copyright, UNESCO, 1950-54; Amer Bar Assn, chmn, copyright div, 1961-62; Assn of Bar, City of NY; NY Co Lawyers Assn, 1942-61; NY Patent Law Assn; Fed Bar Assn; JCCen, White Plains; pres, Men's club; Masons, past master. Author: Copyright Problems, 1952; Fatal Errors in Copyright, 1949; Uses of Titles for Copyrighted and Public Domain Works, 1958; The US Copyright Statute; Uses of Characters in Literature; contbr to legal jours. Recipient: awards: Fed Bar Assn, 1959; Practicing Law Inst, 1960; Columbia Coll Dean, 1965. Hobbies: piano, painting. Home: 430 E 86 St, New York, NY. Office: 250 W 57 St, New York, NY.

TANNENBAUM, Robert, US, educator; b. Cripple Creek, Colo, June 29, 1915; s. Henry and Nettie (Porges); AA, Santa Anna Jr Coll, 1935; AB, U of Chgo, 1937, MBA, hons, 1938, PhD, 1949; m. Edith Lazaroff, Feb 4, 1945; c: Judith, Deborah. Prof, Grad Sch of Bus Admn, UCLA, since 1957, fac mem since 1948; instr, acctnt, Okla A & M Coll, 1937-39; research asst, teaching f, U of Chgo, 1939-42. Lt, USN, 1942-46. F, Natl Training Labs; mem: Amer Econ Assn; Amer Psych Assn; Amer Sociol Assn; Ind Relations Reserach Assn; LA Co Psych Assn; Phi Beta Kappa; Beta Gamma Sigma; Soc for Psych Study of Social Issues. Co-author: Leadership and Organization: A Behavioral Science Approach, 1961. Home: 12800 Kling St, North Hollywood, Cal. Office: Brad Sch Bus Admn, UCLA, Los Angeles, Cal.

TANNENWALD, Theodore, US, jurist; b. Valatie, NY, July 28, 1916; s. Theodore and Myra (Barnet); AB, summa cum laude, Brown U, 1936; LLB, magna cum laude, Fay dipl, Harvard Law Sch, 1939; m. Selma Peterfreund, Aug 3, 1940; c: Peter, Robert. Judge, US Tax Court, since 1965; professorial lectr, George Wash U Law Sch, since 1968; partner, Weil, Gotshal & Magnes, NYC, 1939-65; spec asst, US Secy of State, 1961; mem, Pres' Task Force on Fgn Assistance, 1961. Chmn, comm on Isr, AJComm; vice-chmn, bd govs, HUC-JIR; mem: Council on Fgn Relations; Phi Beta Kappa; Sigma Xi; fmr, mem, bd trustees, SUNY. Home: 2916 Albemarle St, NW, Washington, DC. Office: 1111 Constitution Ave, NW, Washington, DC.

TANNHAUSER, David S, Isr, educator; b. Ludwigshafen, Ger, Dec 13, 1927; s. Siegfried and Kaete (Riess); in Isr since 1934; dipl, phys, ETH, Zurich, 1954; PhD, U Chgo, 1957; m. Pia Miglioretto, 1954; c: Nomi, Daniel, Jonathan. Asso prof, Technion, since 1968. IDF, 1947. Mem, Amer Phys Soc. Contbr to profsl jours. Hobby: flying airplanes. Home: 66 Horeb St, Haifa, Isr. Office: Technion, Haifa, Isr.

TANNY, Shlomo, Isr, journalist, author; b. Pol, Nov 27, 1919; s. Joseph and Esther (Bochner) Koszycki; in Isr since 1929; m. Tirzah Brandstatter, Aug 12, 1946; c: Michal, Joseph. Head, info dept, Histadrut, since 1967, Hasbarah dept, since 1967;

Mem, ed bd, Haaretz daily 1944-50, 1959-66; chief ed, Davar le Yeladim weekly, 1954-56. War corresp, 1948-49; chief ed, Bamahaneh, maj, IDF, 1950-54; mem: cen comm, Heb Writers Assn, 1956-68; Journalists Assn; Soc for Protection of Nature; world comm, Isr Tenth Anniversary, 1958-59. Author: Shlosha Chizim VaEth, reportage, 1950, 1956; poetry: Pgishat haOhavim, 1947; Erettz haChaim, 1954; Kokchvei Derech, 1956; Lifnei Yamim Chadashim, 1961; The Moment Came, 1967; children's books: Yonim baChalom, 1958; Chaverim, 1961; Agadath haBayit haTzochek, 1962; contbr to local and fgn jours. Home: 9 Derech Haifa, Tel Aviv, Isr. Office: Histadrut, 93 Arlozorov, St Tel Aviv, Isr.

TAN-PAI, Yehoshua, Isr, journalist, poet; b. Kishinev, Russ, July 2, 1914; s. Shaul and Manea (Brill) Boudesky; in Isr since 1934; m. Aliza Mautner; c: Shaul (killed in action), Gittit, Miriam. Dir, Jerusalem off, Haaretz daily, since 1951. Ed bd mem since 1942; found, Sifriyat haShaot Pub House; ed, Hed Yerushalayim, 1944-45. Chmn, Jerusalem Journalists Assn; mem, arts and culture comm, Min of Educ and Culture; mem: Authors Assn; B'nai B'rith. Author: meAlef ad Tav, 1937; Variatziot al haAviv, 1942; Adam beKfar, 1942; Shirei ha Choshech veHareut, 1944; Kol haAdam, 1951; French-Heb Dict, 1966; transl: Maupassant, Balzac, Baudelaire, Rimbaud, Shakespeare, Ezra Pound, Chekhov, Tolstoy; anthol of Eng and Amer poetry, 1968. Home: Ramat Hagolan St., Jerusalem, Isr. Office: Haaretz, Jerusalem, Isr.

TANSMAN, Alexandre, Fr, composer; b. Lodz, Pol, June 18, 1897; s. Moses and Anna (Gourvitch); law deg, U Warsaw, 1919; m. Colette Cras, Dec 7, 1937 (decd); c: Mireille Zanuttini, Countess Marianne Martinozzi. Composer: operas: Le Serment, Sabbatai Levi, Il Usignolo de Bobdie; choral works for choir and orch: Isaiah the Prophet, Psalms; ballets; syms; orchestral, chamber works; concert tours throughout Eur, US, Far East, Isr. Hon mem, intl music socs. Recipient: Juji-Thimpo medal, Japan, 1933; Coolidge medal, Libr of Cong, 1941. Home: 3 rue Florence Blumenthal, Paris, Fr.

TANZER, Abraham Herman, S Afr, rabbi; b. Brooklyn, NY, Oct 13, 1935; s. Jacob and Vita (Pollak); in S Afr since 1963; att Telshe Yeshiva, Cleveland, 1950-59, postgrad inst, 1959-63; Kaufman Pedg Inst, Cleveland, 1957-63; m. Marcia Charrick, Nov 2, 1959; c: Chaya, Nechoma, Boruch, Dov, Goldi. Head, Yeshiva, Coll Yeshiva Bet Yitzhak, since 1963; rabbi, Glenhazel Heb Cong, since 1965; fac mem, Heb Acad of Cleveland, 1961-63. Chmn of mgmt, Menorah Primary Sch; council: Rabb Assn of S Afr; United Mizrachi of S Afr; hon mem, Heb Order of David lodge, Jerusalem. Home: 66 Nicholson Ave, Glenray, Johannesburg, S Afr.

TANZMAN, Joseph, Can, physician; b. Warsaw, Pol, March 9, 1903; s. Jacob and Helen Belle (Shocken); MD, CM, McGill U, 1927; m. Celia Soltz, Feb 16, 1936; c: Isabel, Sandra. Pvt practice, obstet and gyn, since 1946, gen practice, 1929-39; fmr chief, dept of obstet and gyn: St John Gen Hosp; St Joseph Hosp. Can Army, 1939-45. Chmn bd School Trustees, St John, 1953-61; fmr pres: St John lodge, B'nai B'rith, 1959-61; dir, Can and Maritime Auto Assn; pres, St John Med Soc, 1935; bd commns, St John Gen Hosp; mem: Cong Shaarei Zedek, pres, 1932-39; mem: Can Med Assn; New Brunswick and St John Med Socs; Masons. Recipient: OBE. Hobbies: music, gardening. Home: 617 Sand Cove Rd, St John, NB. Office: 112 Hazen St, St John, NB, Can.

TARAGIN, Nathan, US, rabbi; b. Preili, Latvia, Aug 25, 1913; s. Mendel and Fradel (Wolfe); in US since 1929; BA, Yeshiva Coll, 1936, ordained rabbi, 1938; MA, Brown U, 1942; m. Beatrice Schunfenthal, Mar 21, 1947; c: Francine, Marvin. Chaplain: Morrisania City Hosp; Leb Hosp, both since 1953; Beth Isr Med Cen, since 1968; rabbi: J Cen of Highbridge, Bx, since 1953; Cong Sons of Abraham, Providence, 1938-43; Cong Ahavath Isr, Phila, 1944; Young Isr of Claremont Pkwy, 1944-52. Mem: RabCA; NY Bd Rabbis; Bx Council Rabbis; Rabb Alumni Assn, Yeshiva U. Author: The Anthropology of the Talmud and Midrash, 1942. Home: 1340 Merriam Ave, Bronx, NY. Office: 1178 Nelson Ave, Bronx, NY.

TARG, Max, US, business exec; b. Zawiercie, Pol, Sep 10, 1895; s. Mandel and Scheindel Targownik; in US since 1913; LLB, Chgo Law Sch, 1922; m. Fannie Wexler, May 6, 1920; c: Bernice Weissbourd. Fmr: cen mgr, Targ and Dinner Inc, since 1920. US Army, 1917-19. Pres, Amers for a Music Libr in Isr, since 1950; mem: Poale Zion; B'nai B'rith; JWV; AJCong; Amer Friends Heb U; Amer Technion Soc; Friends of Music Inst; Isr Bonds; Amer J Hist Soc; J Publ Soc Amer;

Masons; fmr: pres: Natl Assn Music Merchandise Wholesalers; pres and found, Music War Council Amer club, Covenant. Contbr to trade mags. Recipient: citations and honors for contribs to advancement of music in US and Isr. Home: 2400 Lakeview, Chicago, Ill. Office: 2451 N Sacramento St, Chicago Ill.

TARG, William, US, editor; b. Chgo, Ill, Mar 4, 1907; s. Max and Esther (Solomon) Torgownik; m. Anne Jesselson, May 1, 1933 (decd); c: Russell; m. 2nd, Roslyn Siegel, July 30, 1965. Ed in chief, vice-pres: GP Putnam's Sons, since 1965; World Publ Co, 1942-64. Clubs: Grolier, NYC; Rowfant, Cleveland; Caxton, Chgo. Author: 10,000 Fare Books and Their Prices, 1936; Rare American Books, 1941; The American West, 1946; Carousel for Bibliophiles, 1947; Bouillabaisse for Bibliophiles, 1955; Bibliophile in the Nursery, 1957. Home: 101 W 12 St, New York, NY. Office: 200 Madison Ave, New York, NY.

TARGOW, Abram M, US, physician, educator; b. Rochester, NY, June 19, 1907; s. Morris and Rose (Portyansky) Torgovetsky; AB, U Mich, 1927; PhD, U Chgo, 1934, MD, 1935; m. Jeanette Goldfield, Jan 11, 1935; c: Patricia, Richard. Pvt practice, specializing in allergy, since 1937; clinical prof em, U of S Cal, since 1964, fac mem since 1959; asst in pharm, U Chgo School of Med, 1930-34. Pres, LA Allergy Soc, 1956; vice-pres, Amer Coll Allergists, 1955-56; mem: AMA; AAAS. Contbr to med jours. Home: 1835 N Doheny Dr, Los Angeles, Cal. Office: 9400 Brighton Way, Beverly Hills, Cal.

TARLOV, Malcolm A, US, business exec; b. Norwalk, Conn, Aug 6, 1921; s. Harry and Rose (Marcus); att Clark U, 1938-40; m. Harriett Barbakoff, March 11, 1946; c: Mark, Jill. Owner, Tarlov Ins Agency. Staff sgt, US Army, 1942-45. Pres, Norwalk J Comty Cen; exec comm, natl comm, Rotary Assn, Conn; found, secy, Norwalk Little League, 1952; chmn, Norwalk UJA, 1960; natl cdr, JWV, 1966-67; exec dir, Natl Vets for Humphrey, 1968. Recipient: Eur Theater ribbon, five battle stars. Home: 15 Winding Lane, Norwalk, Conn. Office: 31 West Ave, Norwalk, Conn.

TARNOWSKI, Bernard, Belgium, business exec; b. Hanover, Ger, July 31, 1910; s. Josef and Genia; att, Talmud Torah Sch, Hamburg, Ger. Chmn, Tarnowski & Co, since 1951. Natl pres, ORT, Belgium; pres: Mémorial aux Matyrs Juifs de Belgique; Comité de Direction de la Centrale d'Oeuvres Sociales Juives; Commn de Construction de l'École Israélite; Comité d'Aide aux Réfugiés d'Afrique du Nord; fmr: vice-pres, B'nai B'rith; mem of exec, KH; mem found, Solidarity Funds for Isr. Home: 163 Orban Ave, Brussels, Belgium. Office: 4 rue de la Chancellerie, Brussels, Belgium.

TARSCHYS, Bernard, Swed, educator, broadcasting exec; b. Stockholm, Swed, Aug 6, 1905; s. Salomon and Rebecka (Kartow); MPh, U Stockholm, 1929, PhD, 1949, hon docent, 1949; ordinary U lectr, 1955; m. Karin Alexanderson, Mar 11, 1933; c: Rut Lindmark, Eva, Hedvig Block, Nils. Lectr and reader, Sem for Tchrs Training, U Stockholm, since 1949; tchr since 1933; mem, perm staff, Dagens Nyheter, since 1947; lectr, head, cultural dept, Swed radio and TV; adv to Min of Educ, 1950, 1951, 1954. Vice-chmn, Union of Tchrs in Training Colls, since 1950; mem: Primary Sch Bd; Libr Comm; Natl Salaries Comm; Zionist Fed; Swiss-Isr Soc; Soc of Authors; fmr: vice-chmn, Pedg Soc; chmn, sch and libr bds, J Parish Council, 1949-69; mem bd, Natl Assn Civil Servants; press repr, Swed Assn of Tchrs; club, Idun. Contbr to periodicals. Home: 3 Hjortstigen, Lidingö, Swed.

TARSHIS, Sam W, US, business exec; b. Braelov, Russ, Feb 15, 1902; s. Welvel and Pearl (Perkel); in US since 1913; m. Emma Solomon, Feb 23, 1930; c: Laurence, Anne. Owner, S W Tarshis Co, since 1928; pres, NW Furniture Mart Inc, 1964-66. Pres, J Comty Cen, since 1954; natl vice-chmn, Jt Defense Appeal, since 1953; vice-chmn, Wash State Adv comm, US Commn on Civil Rights, since 1958; natl bd, United Service New Amer; commn, natl ADL, since 1953; mem: ZOA, hon life; B'nai B'rith, pres, 1952; jt interim comm on facilities and oprs, Wash State Leg, 1966-67. Recipient: awards: ZOA, 1948; UJA, 1950; Jt Defense Appeal, 1953, 1961; ADL, 1953; Man of Year, B'nai B'rith, 1963. Home: 4416 51 St NE, Seattle, Wash. Office: 121 Boren Ave N, Seattle, Wash.

TARSHISH, Abraham, Isr, editor; b. Bobruisk, Russ, Oct, 1900; s. Yoel and Gita (Osowsky); in Isr since 1920; m. Jocheved Malkiman; one c. Ed: haKibbutz haMeuchad Publishing, since

1950; laMerhav daily; mem, ed bd, Al haMishmar daily; fmr, gen secy, Kibbutz haMeuchad. Mem: political and cen comms. Histadrut; cen comm, Lab Party; cen secretariat, Lab Zionist Movement; Journalists Union, Isr. Home: Kibbutz Ein Harod, Isr. Office: Kibbutz haMeuchad Publishing, 22 Sutin St, Tel Aviv, Isr.

TARSHISH, Allan, US, rabbi; b. Baltimore, Md, Oct 12, 1907; s. Robret and Mina (Jacobson); BA, U of Cincinnati, 1929; ordained rabbi, HUC, 1932, DHL, 1939, hon DD, 1958; m. Miriam Grad, Jan 7, 1934; c: Bennett, Deborah. Rabbi: Temple Jeremiah, since 1960; Temple Beth Isr, Hazelton, Pa, 1936-47; Cong Kahal Kadosh Beth Elohim, Charleston, SC, 1947-60. Mem, Masons; fmr: pres: N Shore Interfaith Clergy, 1967-69; Hillel counselor, The Citadel, 1950-60; chmn, comm on contemporary hist, CCAR, 1958-61, mem, exec comm, 1955-57; bd govs, HUC, 1963-67. Author: Not by Power: The Story of the Growth of Judaism, 1952; The Economic Life of American Jewry in Mid-19th Century, 1958; contbr articles to Anglo-J publs, J Ency. Home: 256 Lincoln Dr, Glencoe, Ill. Study: 860 Oak St, Winnetka, Ill.

TARSKI, Alexander, Isr, composer, conductor; b. Lodz, Pol, Nov 10, 1921; s. Eliahu and Berta (Kupfer) Tabaksblat; in Isr since 1957; MA, Acad of Music, 1948; m. Irene Shuk, 1948; c: Dana. Conductor: Isr Natl Opera, since 1957; Hed Arzi Recording Co; Radio Lodz, 1946-51; Warsaw Opera, 1951-57; Tashkent Opera; Stockholm Opera. Mem: ACUM, Isr Composers League. Recipient: prizes, Pol Competition for Young Pianists, 1936-38. Office: Isr Natl Opera, Allenby St, Tel Aviv, Isr.

TARTAKOWER, Arieh, Isr, scholar, author; b. Brody, Pol, Sep 24, 1897; s. Nathan and Sophie (Fichman); in Isr since 1946; LLD, U Vienna, 1920, DPolSc, 1923. Co-chmn, exec comm, WJC, since 1948; chmn, Isr sect, WJC, since 1948; found, Hitachdut Zionist Lab Org, Pol, 1922-39; exec comm, World Heb Confed, Brit Ivrit Olamit, since 1959; found, pres, Isr Assn for the UN, 1949-52; fmr lectr: Inst J Sci, Warsaw; Heb U; dep-dir, Inst J Affairs, NY, 1940-46. Author: Toldoth Tnuat haAvoda haYehudit, 3 vols, 1928-30; Zarys Socjologji Zydostwa, 1938; Yiddishe Emigrazie un Yiddishe Emigrazie Politik, 1939; Nedudei haYehudim baOlam, 1947; haAdam haNoded, 1954; haChevra haYehudit, 1957; ha-Chevra haIsraelit, 1959; Megilat haHityashvut, 1958; In Search of Home and Freedom, 1958; haHityashvut haYehudit baGola, 1959; haLeumiut haYehudit, 1962; Shivtei Israel, 3 vols, 1966-69; contbr to publs. Home: 45a King George Blvd, Jerusalem, Isr. Office: WJZ, 1 Ben Yehuda St, Jerusalem, Isr.

TAS, Jacques, Isr, physician; b. Amsterdam, Holland, Mar 14, 1910; s. Elias and Deborah (de Wilde); in Isr since 1939; MD, U Amsterdam, 1934; m. Ina Andreson, Feb 26, 1944; c: Vza, Ido. Head allergy unit, Hadassah Hosp, since 1964; asso clinical prof, dermat and venerology, Heb U, since 1963. Pres, Isr Soc of Allergy, 1960-65; mem bd, Bezalel Natl Mus, 1949-59; mem, Collegius Intl Allergologium. Contbr: chapters in textbooks; profsl jours. Home: 8 Ben Labrat St, Jerusalem, Isr. Office: Hadassah Hosp, Jerusalem, Isr.

TATZ, Gershon, Isr, public official; b. Lith, Sep 10, 1914; s. Mordechai and Tova; in Isr since 1935; att Rabb Sem, Kovno; m. Ida Friedmann, 1938; c: Yair, Jochevet. Mayor of Nahariya, since 1947, dep mayor, 1941-47; pres, Nahariya Devl Co, since 1948. Mem: cen comm, Mapai; secretariat, Histadrut. Contbr to local press. Office: Town Hall, Nahariya, Isr.

TAUB, Abraham H, US, mathematician, educator; b. Chgo, Ill, Feb 1, 1911; s. Joseph and Mary (Sherman); BS, U Chgo, 1931; PhD, Princeton U, 1935; m. Cecilia Vaslow, 1933; c: Mara, Nadine, Haskell. Prof, math: U of Cal, Berkeley, since 1964; Inst Advanced Study, Princeton, 1935-36, 1940-41; Wash U, Seattle, 1946-48, mem fac since 1936; Haskell Research prof, applied math, Digital Computer Lab, U of Ill, 1948-64. Physicist, Natl Defense Research Comm, Princeton U, 1942-45. F, Amer Phys Soc; mem: Amer Math Soc; AAAS; mem, adv council, applied math, Natl Bur Standards, 1949-54; chmn, comm on research and training in applied math, NRC, 1952-54. Contbr to profls jours. Home: 242 Yale Ave, Berkeley, Cal. Office: Math Dept, U of Cal, Berkeley, Cal.

TAUB, Samuel J, US, allergist, educator; b. Chgo, Ill, Nov 18, 1894; s. Louis and Rose (Goodman); MD, U of Ill, 1916; postgrad, Cornell Med Sch, 1918; m. Thelma Golde, Dec 23, 1917; c: Bernadine, Elias, Robert. Prof em, Chgo Med Sch, since 1961, fac mem since 1939; regional cons, Natl Home for Asthmatic Children, Denver; att staff: Michael Reese Hosp, 1920-40; Cook Co Hosp, 1926-60; Mt Sinai Hosp, 1948-50; Columbus Hosp since 1950; Louis A Weiss Hosp since 1953. Lt, US Army MC, 1917-18. F: AMA; Amer Acad Allergy: Amer Coll Phys; hon, Port, Span and Fr Allergy Socs; mem: Chgo Allergy Soc; Sigma Xi; club, Standard. Author: Essentials of Clinical Allergy, 1945; Clinical Allergy, 2nd ed, 1951; contbr to med jours. Home: 3180 N Lake Shore Dr, Chicago, Ill. Office: 6 N Michigan Ave, Chicago, Ill.

TAUB, William, Isr, educator; b. Elberfeld, Ger, Aug 25, 1914; s. Ludwig and Edith (Freymann); in Isr since 1939; CE, U Geneva, 1933, PhD, chem, 1939; m. Marguerite Hemmerdinger, Oct 9, 1947; c: Edith, Jonathan. Asso prof, chem, head, med chem group, Weizmann Inst, since 1960; sci dir, Yeda research and devl co, Weizmann Inst since 1963; fmr: research chem: D Sieff Research Inst, 1939-41; tech dir, Pal Pharm Produc Ltd, 1941-46; sr sci, Weizmann Inst. Pvt, sci corps, IDF, 1948-50. Mem: exec, NRC of Isr; adv comm, Admission of New Drugs, Min of Health; Isr, Fr Chem Soc's; fmr: chmn, Pharm comm, Isr NRC; mem exec, Isr Chem Assn. Home: 55 Hanasi Harishon Ave, Rehovot, Isr. Office: POB 26, Rehovot, Isr.

TAUB, Yitzchak Julius, Isr, economist; b. Bratislava, Czech, Jan 16, 1927; s. Yecheskel and Berta (Landau); in Isr since, 1939; BA, econ, MJur, Heb U; m. Marit Lifshitz, Feb 1, 1957; c: Gad, Hagar. Secy gen, Bank of Isr, since 1966, asst to gov since 1961; fmr: journalist; econ, research dept, Bank of Isr. Served, Palmach. Chmn, bd dirs, Khan Theatre Jerusalem; mem: Isr Journalists Assn; Academic Workers in Isr. Home: 7 Neve Sha'anan St, Jerusalem, Isr. Office: Bank of Isr, Jerusalem, Isr.

TAUBE, Herman, US, organization exec, columnist; b. Lutzow, Pol, Feb 2, 1918; s. Aaron and Miriam (Mandel); in US since 1947; att Heb Gymnasium, Lodz, Pol, 1933-36; Mesifta Coll for J Studies, Machazikei Hada'ath, Lodz, 1936-39; m: 5 children. Columnist, Jewish Week, Wash, DC, since 1968; regional dir, Histadrut Council: Md, Va, Del, Wash, DC, since 1968, exec dir, Histadrut campaign, Wash, DC, 1965-67; writer, corresp: J Hist Commn, Hessen, Ger, 1945-47; J Daily Forward, Baltimore ed, 1947-50; asst dir, org dept, Histadrut, NY, 1950-51; pres, owner, Taube Markets, Inc, Baltimore, 1951-65. Medic, war prison camp and hosps: Pol, Ger, WW II. Mem: bd, HIAS of Baltimore, Inc; Woodmoor Heb Cong; bd dirs, Farband, Wash, DC; Baltimore Isr Histadrut Assn, co-found, 1st exec dir; Ind B'rith Sholom, Baltimore, past mem, exec assembly; club: Sholom, co-found, past bd mem. Author: The Unforgotten, 1948; Remember, 1952; The Last Train, 1967; Empty Pews; contbr to J periodicals. Home: 12618 Eastbourne Dr, Silver Spring, Md.

TAUBENHAUS, Leon Jair, US, physician; b. Newark, Del, Dec 29, 1912; s. Jacob and Esther (Hirshensohn); BA, Rice U, 1933; MD, Tulane U, 1937; MPH, Harvard U, 1955; hon DHumL, Mass Coll Optometry, 1967; div; c: Jair Pruitt, Marsha. Dir, Cmty Health Services, Beekman-Downtown Hosp, since 1968; fmr: pvt practice, 1945-57; public health phys, Mass Dept Public Health, 1955-57; dir, public health, Brookline Health Dept, 1957-64; dep-supt, ambulatory services, Boston City Hosp, 1964-66; dep commn, comty health services, Boston Dept Health and Hosps, 1966-68; hosp appointments: asso, preventive med, Beth Isr Hosp, 1959-68; med staff, Peter Bent Brigham Hosp, 1962-68; teaching appointments: lectr, public health, Harvard Sch Public Health, 1955-64; asst clinical prof, public health, Tufts Sch Dent Med, 1960-62; lectr, public health admn, Florence Heller Grad Sch Advanced Studies in Social Wfr, Brandeis U, 1961-68; lectr, preventive med: Tufts Sch Med, 1964-68; Harvard Med Sch, 1964-68; clinical prof, Boston Sch Med, 1964-68. Lt cdr, US Navy med corps, 1941-45. Dipl, Amer Bd Preventive Med; f: Amer Public Health Assn; Amer Coll Preventive Med; Amer Coll Emergency Phys; mem: Royal Soc Health, London; AMA; Asso Mgmt Public Health; Amer Geriatrics Soc; AAAS; Hosp Mgmt Sys Soc Gtr NY; Amer Asso Public Health Phys; Ind Med Assn; Med Assns, State and Co, NY; Assn Tchrs Preventive Med; fmr bd dirs: Norfolk Co Tuberculosis and Health Assn; Mass Tuberculosis and Health League; Mass Health Council; Mass Heart Assn; mem: adv comm, cons, USPHS neur and sensory disease service prog; fmr comm mem: White House Conf on Aging; APHA; Natl Found Kidney Diseases; Mass Dept Public Health; Mass Task Force on Mh; Mass Hosp Assn; mem:

Mass Leg Study Commns on Dent Health of Children and Multiphasic Screening; hon life mem, Mass Health Off Assn, since 1964; hon mem, Brookline Dent Soc, since 1963; Author: Pre-school Vision Screening, 1969; contbr to profsl jours. Recipient: pres unit citation, with 1st div, USMC, Guadalcanal, 1942. Home: 55 W 14 St New York, NY. Office: Beekman-Downtown Hosp, New York, NY.

TAUBER, Abraham, US, educator; b. NYC, Nov 8, 1912; s. Aaron and Fanny (Landau); BSS, CCNY, 1931; MA, Columbia U, 1932, PhD, 1958; m. Rhea Sapodin, May 26, 1936; c: Lucy, June, Peter. Ret, 1966; dean, fac, Bronx Community Coll, CUNY, 1958-66; sr prof, speech, Yeshiva U, 1938-66; tchr, Bx HS of Sci, 1939-58; adj prof, speech, CCNY, 1932-58; dir, speech cen, YMHA, 1939-49. ARC, overseas, WW II. Pres, Amer Soc of Geolinguists; trustee: Grand St Boys Found; fmr, Temple Emanuel, Parkchester; mem: exec comm, ADL, NY region; Phi Beta Kappa; Kappa Delta Pi; Phi Delta Kappa; B'nai B'rith; FJP. Author: Spelling Reform in the United States, 1958; Gorge Bernard Shawon Language, 1963. Home: 441-16 N Broadway, Yonkers, NY. Office: Yeshiva Coll, New York, NY.

TAUBER, Gerald E, Isr, educator; b. Vienna, Aus, Oct 31, 1922; s. Friedrich and Helene (Kreidl); in Isr since 1965; BA, hons, U Toronto, 1946; MA, U Minn, 1947, PhD, 1951; m. Lydia Rudoler, Oct 21, 1956; c: Peter, Robert, Chanan. Prof, physics, Tel Aviv U, since 1968, visiting prof, 1965-68; fmr: instr: math, ORT Sch, Que, 1941-42; physics, Bishop Strachan Sch, Toronto, 1944-45; teaching asst, U Minn, 1946-50; sessional lectr, McMaster U, 1950-52; postdoc f, NRC, 1952-54; prof, physics, W Reserve U, 1961-65, fac mem since 1954. Can Offs Training Corps, 1955-57. Mem: Amer Phys Soc; Cleveland Phys Soc; AAUP; Can Assn of Physicists; Sigma Xi; fmr: adv bd, B'nai Akiba, Cleveland; dir, B'nai Akiba, Minn; bd mem, Hillel Found, W Reserve U; vice-pres, Bar Ilan chap, Rel ZOA; chmn, Zionist Youth Council, Toronto, 1945. Author: The Scientific Endeavor of Israel, 1961; contbr to: Grolier's Book of Knowledge; profsl jours. Home: 30 Ofakim, Afeka, Isr. Office: Tel Aviv U, Ramat Aviv, Isr.

TAUBER, Stephen J, US, chemist; b. Vienna, Austria, Jan 8, 1932; s. Joseph and Alice (Frankfurther); in US since 1941; BA, Cornell U, 1952; AM, Harvard U, 1953, PhD, 1958; m. Erika Graf, Jan 1, 1961; c: Andrew. Chief, info sci sect, supervisory oprs research analyst, Natl Bur Standards, since 1968, chem, data processing systems, 1962-68; asst prof, chem, Smith Coll, 1959-62. Mem: Amer Chem Soc; prog, long-range planning comm, Div Chem Lit; Assn Harvard Chems; Assn for Computing Machinery; AAAS; Phi Beta Kappa; Sigma Xi. Adv bd, Jour of Chem Documentation; contbr to Computing Reviews; profsl jours. Hobby: philately. Recipient: postdoc research f, NRC of Can, 1958-59; Princeton f, public affairs, 1967-68. Home: 3816 Williams Lane, Chevy Chase, Md. Office: Natl Bur of Standards, Washington, DC.

TAUBMAN, Arthur, US, business exec; b. Astoria, NY, July 15, 1901; s. Maurice and Sophie (Tupper); m. Grace Weber, 1929; c: Stephanie Low, Nicholas. Pres: Advance Stores Co, Roanoke, Va, since 1932; Alliance Tire & Rubber Co, Hadera, Isr, since 1952; Cordovan Associates Inc, Dayton, O, since 1957; chmn, Automotive Assn Inc, NYC, since 1960; dir: First Natl Bank, since 1951; Dominion Bankshares Corp; both Roanoke. USN, 1917-18. Dir: Memorial Hosp; Salvation Army; trustee: Gill Found; Burrell Memorial Hosp; Northcross Sch; bd mem, Roanoke C of C; mem: Temple Emanuel, fmr pres; AJComm; NCCJ; US C of C; Masons; Amer Legion; Kiwanis; club: Quarter Century, pres, 1954, dir since 1954. Home: 2802 Stephenson Ave, Roanoke, Va. Office: First and Main Sts, Roanoke, Va.

TAUCHNER, Maximilian, Ger, lawyer, journalist; b. Vienna, Aus, May 7, 1917; s. Salo and Sala (Schmer); in Ger since 1950; MA, Us of Cracow and Lwow, both Pol, 1940; DJur, Us of Graz and Munich, 1957; m. Henriette Salamon, 1941; c: Paul. Law off for Ger restitutions since 1952; journalist, corresp, J jours in Munich, since 1950; lawyer; ed, J rev, Opinia, corresp intl jours, Pol, both 1945-50. Pres, KKL, Munich, exec mem, Ger; vice-pres, J Comty, Munich; exec mem J Comty, Bavaria; Eur exec mem, Independent Lib Zionist Party, Paris off; fmr: mem, ZC, E and W Galizia; mem, cen council, Hanoar Hazioni; past chmn: Ichud, Pol; council of Pol Jews; KKL and KH, Pol; mem delg, Pol J, Pol-Isr negotiations, 1949-50. Home and office: 6/11 Possartstr, Munich, Ger.

TAVOR, Moshe, Isr, journalist, author; b. Czech, June 29, 1903; s. Otto and Gisela (Kaufmann) Tauber; in Isr since 1939; DJur, Prague U; m. Nora Heller. Corresp, Frankfurter Allemeine Zeitung, Isr, since 1960; fmr: head bur, parl corresp, Davar daily, 1950-57, 1960-63; press attaché, Isr-Mission, Ist Emb, Cologne, 1957-60, 1963-66. Mem: Assn of Isr Journalists; Fgn Press Assn in Isr; fmr mem, cen comm, Zionist Org, Czech. Author: Jerusalem, pictorial book, 1969, Ger ed, Wir und die Nachbarn, trans by Ben Gurion. Home: 32 Gaza Rd, Jerusalem, Isr.

TAX, Sol, US, anthropologist, educator; b. Chgo, Ill, Oct 30, 1907; s. Morris and Kate (Hanowitz); PhB, U Wis, 1931; PhD, U Chgo, 1935; m. Gertrude Katz, July 4, 1933; c: Susan, Marianna. Prof, anthropology, U Chgo, since 1948, dept chmn, 1955-58, head, Coll of Social Sciences, 1962-63, dir, U extension, 1963-68, fac mem since 1940; acting dir, Cen for Study of Man, Smithsonian Inst, since 1968, spec adv to inst secy since 1965; dir, Mesquakie Indian project, U Chgo-State U of Ia, since 1948; anthropological field work: Algeria, 1930; Apache Indians, NM, 1931; Cen Algonquin and Fox Indians, 1932-34; Mayan Indians, Guat and Mex, 1934-35; ethnologist, Carnegie Inst of Wash, 1934-48; f, Cen for Advanced Study in Behaviorial Scis, 1969-70. F: Amer Anthropological Assn; Amer Ethnological Assn; Amer Folklore Soc; Soc for Amer Archaeol; Sociedad Mexicana de Antropologia; Sociedad de Geografia e Historia de Guatemala; hon f: Royal Anthropological Inst, Gt Brit; Children Anthropological Soc; Slovakian Anthropological Soc; chmn: comm on educ, training, and research in race relations, 1952-56; self-study on behavioral scis, since 1953; both U Chgo; delg: NRC, 1947; UNESCO conf, Paris, 1952; coord, Amer Indian Chgo conf, 1961; mem: US Natl Commn for UNESCO, 1960-66; bd of advs, Ill State Mus, since 1954; Sigma Xi. Author: Civilizations of Ancient America, 1951; Acculturation in the Americas, 1951; Heritage of a Conquest, 1952; Indian Tribes of Aboriginal America, 1952; Appraisal of Anthropology Today, 1953; Penny Capitalism, A Guatemalan Indian Economy, 1953; The Draft: A Handbook of Facts and Alternatives, 1968; The People vs The System, 1968; ed: Current Anthropology, since 1958; Viking Fund publications in anthropology, 1960-68; sect, Middle Amer Ethnology, Handbook of Latin Amer Studies, 1943-53; microfilm collections, Middle Amer Cultural Anthropology manuscripts, since 1945; Evolution after Darwin, 3 vols, 1960; Amer Anthropologist, 1953-56, asso ed, 1947-52. Recipient: Viking Fund medal, 1962-65. Home: 5537 S Woodlawn Ave, Chicago, Ill. Office: U Chicago, Chicago, Ill.

TAXMAN, Philip W, US, business exec; b. Rock I, Ill, Mar 3, 1905; BA, U of Ia, 1928. Ret since 1950; stockbroker, Chgo, 1928-35; retail bus, New Orleans, 1935-50. Mem: natl bd: HUC-JIR; State of Isr Bonds; bd dir: Beth Isr Temple; JCC; Maricopa Comty Cancer Soc; Beth El Syn; fmr gen chmn: JWF, UJA, 3 years, emergency chmn, 1967; club: found, Cent Country; Kiwanis. Recipient: Man of Year award: City of Hope, 1964; Bonds for Isr, 1969. Home: 6529 N Central, Phoenix, Ariz.

TAXON, Jordan I, US, rabbi; b. Columbia, O, May 12, 1917; s. Morris and Edyth (Schottenstein); BA, O State U, 1938, BSc, 1938; MA, Northwestern U, 1940; LLB, Southern Law U, 1942; MHL, ordained rabbi, JIR, 1947; m. Gloria Seidel, July 3, 1949; c: Janet, Morse, Naomi. Rabbi, Syn Emanu-El, since 1964; chaplain, VA Hosp, Charleston, since 1965; Hillel adv, The Citadel, since 1967; rabbi: Temple Beth El, Cranford, NJ, 1946-52; Tri City J Cen, Rock I, Ill, 1954-64. Chaplain, US Army, 1952-54. Mem: RA; NY Bd of Rabbis; ZOA; B'nai B'rith; JWV; Chgo Bd of Rabbis; Assn J Chaplains; Mil Chaplains Assn; Assn Mh Chaplains; clubs: Masons; Shriners; Sojourners; Exch. Co-author: Anthology of Prayers; Sermons for Special Occasions. Recipient: Tanenbaum Scholarship, JIR, 1947. Home: 42 Sixth Ave, Charleston, SC. Study: 78 Gordon St, Charleston, SC.

TAYAR, Abraham R, Isr, legislator; b. Tunisia, Jan 29, 1924; s. Daniel and Zizete; att Fr Tchrs Sem; m. Hilda Kriser, May, 1947; c: Pnina, Daniel, Nitza. MK; pres of exec, Free Cen Party; mem, exec, Histadrut haKlalit, Vaad Hapoel, 1965-69; secy gen, Betar, Tunisia, 1945-47. Ed in chief, LeAn Chadash, monthly. Hobby: painting. Home: Hanita St, Neve Shaanan, Haifa, Isr. Office: The Knesset, Jerusalem, Isr.

TAYLOR, Henry K, US, roentgenologist, educator; b. NYC, May 9, 1894; s. Hyman and Rebecca (Keller) Schneider; MD, NYU, Col of Med, 1915; m. Eva Kane, June 23, 1930; c:

Sara Rabbino. Pvt practice since 1924; cons roentgenologist: Mary Manning Walsh Home, since 1951; Goldwater Memorial Hosp, since 1967, staff mem since 1939; NYU-Bellevue Med Cen, since 1959, staff mem since 1950; roentgenologist, Inst of Phys Med and Rehab, since 1959; impartial specialist, Workmen's Compensation Bd, since 1940; fmr roentgenologist: Vets Bur; Beth David Hosp; Harlem Hosp, all NYC; Sea View Hosp, Staten I, 1931-39; asso dir, dept of radiology, Beth Isr Hosp, 1936-39; asso prof, dept of radiology, NYU Coll of Med, 1946-50, fac mem, 1934-36, 1941, 1942-45; instr, radiology, Columbia U, 1937-39; clinical prof, radiology, NY Post Grad Med Sch, 1950-52. US Army MC, WW I. F: Amer Coll Radiology; Amer Coll Chest Phys; Amer Acad Compensation Med; AMA; Amer Coll Phys; dipl, Amer Bd Radiology; mem: NY State and Co Med Socs; Amer and NY Roentgen Socs; Radiological Soc of N Amer; NYU and Beth Isr Hosp Alumni Assns; Alpha Omega Alpha. Contbr to med jours. Home: 480 Park Ave, New York, NY. Office: 63 E 66 St, New York, NY.

TAYLOR, Milton S, US, pharmacist, bus exec; b. NYC, Mar 3, 1908; s. Simmon and Fannie (Schlamn); PharmG, Columbia U, 1928; m. Zelda Funk, Feb 18, 1951; c: Adam, Joshua. Pres, Caswell-Massey Co, Ltd, pharmaceutical supplies, since 1937. F, Coll of Apothecaries; mem: Amer Pharmaceutical Assn; NY State Pharmaceutical Assn; Amer Inst of Hist of Pharm; Columbia U Alumni Assn; natl exec comm, ZOA, 1950-54, natl vice-pres, 1932-36; chmn, Amer Zionist Youth Comm, 1952-55. Asso ed, Masada Jour, 1932-36; ed, Zionist Observer, 1951. Home: 601 Bleeker Ave, Mamaroneck, NY. Office: 518 Lexington Ave, New York, NY.

TCHETCHIK, Alexander, Isr, educator; b. Pinsk, Russ, Aug, 21, 1895; s. Abraham and Esther (Stoupak); in Isr since 1920; att U Lausanne, 1915-19; m. Tamara Goldenberg, Aug 11, 1925; c: Esther Steinfeld, Israel. Prof, Technion-Isr Inst Tech, since 1950; fmr mgr, Isr Elec Co, 1920-57. Vice-pres, Intl Commn on Illumination; f: IEE; Eng Illumination Soc, both London; fmr: pres, Assn of Engrs and Architects in Isr; chmn, natl commn, WEC. Author: Fundamentals of Engineering, 1969. Home: 5 Yitzhak, Ave, Haifa, Isr. Office: Technion, Haifa, Isr.

TEAR, Morris William, US, optometrist; b. NYC, Mar 20, 1914; s. Sam and Lillie (Wolf); BS, Columbia U, 1934, MS, 1953; OD, Mass Coll Optometry, 1962; m. Edna Edelson, Oct 20, 1935; c: Sheila Stransky, Howard. Pvt practice since 1935. F: Amer Acad Optometry; NY Acad Optometry; mem, NY State Optometric Assn. Mem: steering comm, natl youth commn, United Syn of Amer; chmn, youth commn, NY region; co-found, fmr chmn, Westbury Heb Cong; chmn, UJA, Westbury 1939-46; adv bd, adult educ, Westbury Sch System; club: Kiwanis, past pres; Sunrise lodge Masons. Home: 544 Rockland St, Westbury, NY. Office: 287 Post Ave, Westbury, NY.

TEDESCHI, Gad (Guido), Isr, educator; b. Rovigo, It, May 17, 1907; s. Attilio and Paolina (Del Vecchio); in Isr since 1939; DJur; m. Elda Finzi, July 9, 1933; c: Silvia Gutman. Prof, civil law, Heb U, since 1949. Chmn, adv comm, law of contracts, Min of Law. Author: Studies in Israel Law, 1952, 2nd ed, 1960; Studies in Israel Private Law, 1958, 2nd ed, 1966. Recipient: Isr prize, 1954; Rothschild prize, 1965. Home: 6 Disraeli St, Jerusalem, Isr. Office: Heb U, Jerusalem, Isr.

TEDESCHI, Vittorio, It, educator, attorney; b. Genoa, It, July 13, 1910; s. Ettore and Delia (Sacerdote); PhD, Law Sch, U Genoa, 1930; m. Bianca Luzzati, Jan 28, 1940; c: Delia, Noemi. Asso prof, comparative pvt law, U Genoa, since 1935; lectr, civil law, U Rome, 1935; It pvt law, U Geneva, 1945; adv, It-J Communities Union, 1940-43, 1965-69. Mem: It Inst of Leg Studies; Societe de Legislation Comparee. Author: Il Domicilio nel Diritto Internazionale Privato, 1933; Del Domicilio, 1936; Il Diritto Privato Comparato, 1936; Il Trasferimento della Proprieta nella vendita Mobiliare, 1937; Prescrizone Estintiva e Decadenza, 1948; L'Anticrest, 1932; Vendita di Cose Mobili nel Diritto Anglo-Americano, 1952; profilo dell'Agency nel Diritto Nordamericano, 1961. Home: Via Maragliano 2, Genoa, It.

TEICH, Arthur, US, attorney; b. Trenton, NJ, Jan 30, 1915; s. Benjamin and Anna (Cohen); BS, U of Pa, 1935; LLB, Harvard Law Sch 1938; m. Sylvia Agress, Aug 6, 1944; c: Nancy, Jonathan. Pvt practice since 1939; pres, Natl Beer Distributors, since 1954; sr mem, Teich, Groh & Robinson, law firm. since 1961; pres, Mercer Mortgage Co, 1946-61;

secy treas, The Blatt Co, 1956-66. US Army, 1941-46. Bd dirs, Stacy Savings and Loan Assn, since 1955; natl fiscal control bd, Alpha Epsilon Pi, 1953-61, and since 1967, natl pres, 1950-52, natl supr bd govs, 1939-53; pres, J Fed of Trenton, 1955-57, bd dirs, chmn exec comm, 1959-60; state dir, Beverage Distribution Assn, 1957-59; bd dirs: J Conty Cen, 1953-62; chmn, UJA campaign, 1952-53, big gifts chmn, 1958, mem campaign cabinet, 1954-59; delg, Trenton region, UJA Conf, 1952-57; bd trustees: Del Valley United Fund, 1954-58, chmn, profsl div, 1960 and 1961; Trenton J Cen Assn, 1953-62; Gtr Trenton Council, 1957-58; Legal Aid Soc of Mercer Co, 1950-55; mem: Mercer Co Bar Assn; NJ Bar Assn; Amer Bar Assn; club: Greenacres Country, life mem, pres, 1959-60, bd dirs, since 1952. Recipient: UJA cert, 1952-53; UJA award, 1957; Order of the Lion award, Alpha Epsilon Pi, 1955; Gitelson award, Alpha Epsilon Pi, 1958. Home: 20 Glenwood Ave, Trenton, NJ. Office: 143 E State St, Trenton, NJ.

TEICHER, Morton Irving, US, social worker, educator; b. NYC, Oct 3, 1920; s. Sam and Celia (Roth); BSS, CCNY, 1940; MSW, U of Pa, 1942; PhD, U of Toronto, 1956; m. Mildred Adler, Apr 10, 1941; c: Phyllis, Oren. Dean, Wurzweiler Sch of Social Work, Yeshiva U, since 1956; cons, Sch of Social Work, Bar Ilan U, since 1965, mem, acad adv council; fmr: chief social worker, VA, 1946-48; asst prof, chief psycht social worker, U of Toronto, 1948-56. Lt, US Army, 1942-46. Prin contribs: found, schs of social work: Yeshiva U; Bar Ilan U; U Zambia. Exec-secy, Natl Conf of J Communal Service; f: Soc for Applied Anthropology; Amer Anthropological Assn; mem: Natl Assn of Social Workers, Weschester chap, pres; Amer Ethnological Assn; Natl Assn of J Cen Workers; Amer Assn of Higher Educ; Council of Social Work Educ; Intl Council of Social Wfr; bd mem, Beth El Syn, 1957-61. Author: Windigo Psychosis, 1960; book rev ed, Jour of J Communal Service, 1960-68; mem, ed bd, Human Organization, Soc for Applied Anthropology, 1963-66; contbr to psycht, social work, and anthropological jours. Home: 50 Gateway Rd, Yonkers, NY. Office: 55 Fifth Ave, New York, NY.

TEICHMAN, Jacob, Switz, rabbi; b. Tallya, Hung, Jan 15, 1915; s. Eugen and Rosa (Schwarz); in Switz since 1959; ordained rabbi, J Theol Sem, Budapest, 1942; D Phil, Royal U of Scis, Budapest, 1940; dipl, sci libr, Heb U, 1959; m. Agnes Porjes, Feb 27, 1944; c: George-Jehuda, Daniel. Rabbi, Israelitische Kultusgemeinde, since 1959; fmr: rabbi, tchr Judaica, J Comty, Budapest, 1940-56; sci collaborator, PR officier, Yad vaShem, Jerusalem, 1957-58; chief libr, Bar Ilan U, 1959. Vice-pres, Swiss br, J World Bible Org; mem: Union of Rabbis of Switz; Conf of Eur Rabbis; B'nai B'rith; Hillel House comm, Zurich; Mizrachi Org; Chr-J Coop Org. Author: The Spirit of Judaism, 1939; The Colors of the Bible, 1940, both Hung; contbr to periodicals in Hung, Isr, Switz. Home: Gerechtigkeitsgasse 14, Zurich, Switz. Study: J Comty Cen, Lavaterstr 33, Zurich, Switz.

TEICHMAN, Sabina, US, artist; b. NYC; d. Maurice and Esther (Goldberg) Goldman; BA, Columbia U, 1941, MA, 1943; m. David Teichman, Dec 25, 1923; c: Wendy. One-man shows: Harry Salpeter Gal, NYC, 1947, 1949, 1952, 1955; ACA Gal, 1956, 1960, 1963; Rome ACA, 1965; exhbts: 1956, 1958; U of Puerto Rico, 1962; Fairleigh Dickinson Coll, 1954; ACA, 1955-69; N Truro Art Cen; Amer Acad of Arts and Letters; perm collections: Bezalel Natl Mus; Tel Aviv Mus; Whitney Mus; Butler Mus; U of Puerto Rico Mus; Brandeis U; Living Arts Found Collection; Bklyn Mus; Vatican Mus; James Michener Found Collection; Chrysler Art Mus; Finch Mus; Smithsonian Inst, Wash, DC. Mem: Natl Assn Women Artists Equity Assn; Provincetown Art Assn. Home: 11 E 93 St, New York, NY. Studio: 27 E 22 St, New York, NY.

TEICHOLZ, Bruce B, US, business exec; b. Rzeszow, Pol, Feb 20, 1914; s. Isaac and Helen (Glucker); in US since 1952; att: Acad of Econs and Bus, Pol, 1932-35; U of Vienna, 1947-49; U of Frienze, 1950-51; CCNY, 1959-61; m. Eva Saar, July 30, 1952; c: Thomas, Debbie. Real estate exec since 1954; partner, Woodhole Mgmt Co, since 1954; dir, Polski Lloyd AG, Pol, 1937-39; pres, Exclusive Knitting Mills, NJ, 1952-54. Rescue and underground work, WW II. Pres, Beekman Sutton lodge, B'nai B'rith, since 1968; chmn of admn comm, Natl ORT League, since 1963; pres exec comm mem, Amer ORT Fed, since 1963; mem: Ins Brokers Assn; Real Estate Brokers Assn; adv comm, New Dem Club, since 1964; fmr: pres: ORT, Vienna, 1945-48; Intl Comm for Refugees and Inmates from Concentration Camps, Eur, 1945-51;

Zionist Org, 1948-50; vice-pres, Pol Help and Rescue Comm, Hung, 1943-45. Contbr to J press. Recipient: Letters and citations for rescue and underground work, WW II: Pol Cen Comm, Budapest, 1946; Hqrs, Eur Command, 1948; JDC, 1950; Rep of Aus, 1950; Intl Comm J Ref and Inmates from Concentration Camps, 1951; Comm of Illegal Immigration, Govt of Isr, 1964; cdr, BRICHA, Eur, 1967; HaMossad LeAlia, Govt of Isr, 1964; Golden Book award, JNF, 1946, 1951; citation award, B'nai B'rith, 1965, 1966; Man of the Year, ORT, 1967; Medal of Haganah, Govt of Isr, 1968. Hobbies: tennis, skiing, reading, music, travel. Home: 410 E 57 St, New York, NY. Office: 347 E 53 St, New York, NY.

TEITELBAUM, David, US, attorney; b. NYC, Nov 20, 1906; s. Raphael and Tessie (Schlanger); BS, NYU, 1926; LLB, Harvard Law Sch, 1929; m. Sylvia Lowenthal, Nov 11, 1937; c: Richard, Ray. Partner, law firm, Donovan, Leisure, Newton, and Irvine, since 1937; fmr, spec asst to US Atty Gen, Wash, DC, 1930-31; asso, law firms, 1931-37. Mem: Amer, NY Co, and NYC Bar Assns; clubs: Harvard; Broad St. Homes: 44 W 77 St, New York, NY; Cross Highway, Westport, Conn. Office: 2 Wall St, New York, NY.

TEITELBAUM, Harry A, US, psychiatrist, neurologist; b. Bklyn, NY, Oct 7, 1907; s. Louis and Gertrude (Levine); BS, U of Md, 1929, MD, 1935, PhD, 1936; m. Marjorie Shively, Oct 30, 1947; c: Paul, Joan. Pvt practice since 1946; asst prof psycht, Johns Hopkins Med Sch, since 1962, researcher, Pavlovian lab, since 1946; head, div, neuropsych, U of Md Med Sch, since 1952. Maj, US Army, 1942-45. Dipl, Amer Bd of Psycht and Neur; f: Amer Psycht Assn; AAAS; mem: Amer Psychopath Assn; Amer Psychosomatic Assn; NY Acad of Sci. Author: Psychosomatic Neurology, 1964; asst ed, Conditional Reflex; contbr to profsl jours. Recipient: Fredenwald f, 1931-32; Hitchcock f, 1933; Weaver f, 1935-36. Home: 5605 Greenspring Ave, Baltimore, Md. Office: 200 W Cold Spring Lane, Baltimore, Md.

TEITELBAUM, Herbert D, US, rabbi; b. SF, Cal, May 14, 1926; s. Jacob and Shirley (Bergstein); BA, NYU, 1947; MA, Tchrs Coll, Columbia U, 1950; ordained rabbi, MHL, JTSA, 1951; m. Robin Wagenfeld, March 24, 1957; c: Joshua, Adam. Rabbi: Temple Beth Jacob, since 1957; Temple Beth Israel, SF, 1953-55; Sinai Temple, LA, 1955-57. Chaplain, US Army, 1951-53. Vice-pres: Western Regional RA; Bd of Rabbis of N Cal; mem: RA of N Amer. Recipient: Bronze Star; Freedom award, State of Isr. Home: 94 15 Ave, Atherton, Cal. Study: 1550 Alameda de Las Pulgas, Redwood City, Cal.

TEITELBAUM, Irving, US, counselor, psychotherapist; b. NYC, May 5, 1923; s. Chiel and Sadie (Reinhard); BA, Bklyn Coll, 1947; MS, Yeshiva U, 1951; PhD, Dropsie U, 1964; att Inst for Practising Psychotherapists, 1966; m. Phyllis Abrams; c: Shifra, Ozer. Asst prof, counseling, Coll Discovery, since 1968; staff psychol, Bklyn Comty Counseling Cen, since 1968; Heb tchr, Beth El J Cen, Bklyn, 1948-52; owner Empire Lion Sales Co, 1952-57; Heb tchr, Union Temple, Bklyn, 1957-63; registered repr, Zim Unified Services, 1968. Mem: bd dirs, Queens Co Mh Soc, Hollis, NY; AAUP; Amer, NY State, and Bklyn Psychol Assns; Bklyn Mh Assn; Amer and NY Personnel and Guidance Assns; Assn for Applied Psychan. Contbr to profsl jours. Recipient: Mark Dreyfus scholarship. Hobby: piano, clarinet, trumpet. Home: 1504 48 St, Brooklyn, NY. Office: Queensborough Comty Coll, Bayside, NY.

TEITELBAUM, Maurice Joel, US, dentist; b. Newark, NJ, June 19, 1919; s. Max and Rebecca (Berner); att Bucknell U, Lewisburg, Pa, 1936-39; DDS, Temple U, Phila, Pa, 1943; m. Dorothea Epstein, Nov 22, 1942; c: Ronni Lipman, Barbara, Kenneth. Pvt practice since 1943. Capt, US Army, Dent Corps, 1951-53. Treas, NJ Libr Trustee Assn; secy, Newark Public Libr Trustee Bd, past pres; mem: bd dirs, Young Isr, Newark, NJ; Essex Co Dent Soc; Amer Dent Soc; ASCAP, NY; fmr: co-chmn, 1st Isr Fair in Amer; mem, bd dirs, Newark YMHA. Author: book and lyrics, musical, Hooray Its A Glorious Day....And All That, 1966; ed, TIC Mag, since 1969; contbr to mags; fmr, ed, Newark Dent Club Jour. Recipient: awards: Natl Dent Lab, 1962; State of Isr, 1963. Hobbies: philately, chess. Home and office: 174 E Mt Pleasant Ave, Livingston, NJ.

TEITELBAUM, N Simcha, US, educational admn; b. Jerusalem, Isr; s. Aron and Chaje (Mandelbaum); att Yeshivot: Tifereth Zvi; Hebron; both Jerusalem; ordained rabbi, Rabbi Isaac Elchanan Theol Sem, NY, 1953; BA, U Buffalo, 1957;

MA, U Pitt, 1963; m. Elly Mayer; c: Aron, Naomi. Dean, Yeshiva HS, Queens, since 1954; prin: Ahavath Achim Heb Sch, Buffalo, 1954-57; Hillel Acad of Pittsburgh 1957-63; Yeshiva of Cen Queens, 1963-67. Prin contrib: founded Hillel Acad HS, Pittsburgh; Yeshiva HS, Queens. Pres, Natl Conf of Yeshiva Prins; fmr chmn, bd dirs; mem: RabCA; Natl Assn of Secondary Sch Prins; bd: Samuel A Fryer Educ Research Found; Ozar haTorah; Natl Assn of Heb Day Sch PTA's; Rel ZOA; fmr cultural chmn, NY Council, Hapoel Hamizrachi. Home: 70-33 173 St, Flushing, NY. Office: 148-15 Archer Ave, Jamaica, NY.

TEITELMAN, S Lloyd, US, surgeon; b. Cleveland, O, Nov 30, 1911; s. Ben and Esther (Fink); BA, U Mich, 1932; MD, Northwestern U, 1937; m. Bobette Wilson, Aug 31, 1940; c: Peter, Mari, Andrew. Pvt practice, surgery, since 1946; att surg, Michael Reese Hosp, since 1946; clinical asst prof, surg, Chgo Med School. US Army MC, 1942-46. Mem: Alpha Omega Alpha; Pi Lambda Phi; Phi Delta Epsilon. Contbr to profsl jours. Hobbies: piano, golf. Home: 5502 Hyde Pk Blvd, Chgo, Ill. Office: 55 E Washington St, Chicago, Ill.

TEITLER, Otto Chaim, US, business exec; b. Vienna, Aus, Sep 17, 1925; s. Bernhard and Klara (Wald); in US since 1949; att Heb U, 1946-48; intern, UN Secretariat, NYC, 1950; BEcon, Columbia U, 1952; MBA, Harvard U Grad Sch of Bus, 1954. Exec vice-pres, Inst For Devl of Metal Working Inds, Machine Tools Intl, since 1964; gen mgr, Primary Inds Corp, Primary Intl, 1958-63. Lt, Brit Navy; Isr Navy, Palmach, 1942-49. Prin contrib: ind devl in Asia, Afr. Mem: adv bd, Inst for Intl Study and Research, NYC; bd trustees, Tibet Council; council, Asia Soc; Heb Sch for Arts and Dance; ed bd, Jour of East-West Trade; Soc for Intl Devl; Harvard Bus Sch Assn; Amer Can Metal Working Comm for Isr. Home: 33 East End Ave, New York, NY. Office: 420 Lexington Ave, New York, NY.

TEKOAH, Yosef, Isr, diplomat; b. Mar 4, 1925; s. Shaul and Dvora; grad, law, U L'Aurore, China; MA, Harvard U; m. Ruth, April 15, 1951; c: Michal, Gilead, Yoram. Perm repr, UN, since 1968; instr, intl relations, Harvard U, 1947-48; delg, UN Gen Assembly, 1948; dep legal adv, head treaties sect, Min for Fgn Affairs; liaison off, IDF-Fgn Min, 1949-53; dir, armistice affairs, officio head, Isr delg, mixed armistice commns, Egypt, Syria, Leb, Jordan, 1954-58; mem, Isr delgs: UN Security Council, 1953-56; UN Gen Assembly, 1956; participant, negotiations with UN Secy Gen, 1955-57; Isr repr: armistice talks with Egypt, Gaza frontier, 1955; negotiations with UN, Mt Scopus access, 1957-58; dep perm repr, UN, 1958; acting perm repr, 1959-60; ambass: Brazil, 1960-62; Russ, 1962-65; asst dir gen, Min for Fgn Affairs, 1966-68. Office: Min for Fgn Affairs, Jerusalem, Isr.

TELLER, Edward, US, physicist, educator; b. Budapest, Hung, Jan 15, 1908; s. Max and Ilona (Deutch); in US since 1935; att: Tech Inst, Karlsruhe, 1926-28; U Munich, 1928-29; PhD, U Leipzig, 1930; hon degs: Yale U, 1954; U Alaska, 1959; Fordham U, George Wash U; U of S Cal; St Louis U; all 1960; Rochester Inst of Tech, 1962; LLD: Boston Coll, 1961; Seattle U, 1962; U Cincinnati, 1962; U Pittsburgh, 1963; m. Augusta Harkanyi, Feb 26, 1934; c: Paul, Susan. Prof-at-large, U of Cal, since 1960, prof since 1953; cons, Livermore br, U of Cal Radiation Lab, 1952-53; asso dir, Lawrence Radiation Lab, Livermore, since 1954, dir, 1958-60; research asso: Leipzig U, 1929-31; Göttingen U, 1931-33; Rockefeller f, study with Niels Bohr, Copenhagen, 1934; lectr, U London, 1934-35; prof: George Wash U, Wash, DC, 1935-41; Columbia U, 1941-42; physicist, Manhattan Engr dist, 1942-46; prof, U Chgo, 1946-52; asst dir, Los Alamos Sci Lab, 1949-52; dir, hydrogen bomb prog 1950. Prin contribs: to chem, molecular, and nuclear physics, and quantum theory; development of thermonuclear weapons, and applications for their peaceful uses. F: Amer Nuclear Soc; Amer Phys Soc; mem, bd govs, Tel Aviv U; mem: adv bd, USAF; Natl Acad of Sci; Amer Acad of Arts and Sci; Amer Ordnance Assn; fmr gen adv comm, AEC. Co-author: The Structure of Matter, 1949; Our Nuclear Future, 1958; The Legacy of Hiroshima, 1962; The Constructive Uses of Nuclear Explosives. Recipient: Joseph Priestly Memorial award, Dickinson Coll, 1957; Alber Einstein award, 1959; Gen Donovan Memorial award, 1959 Midwest Research Inst award, 1960; Living History award Research Inst of Amer, 1960; Thomas E White award, 1962 Enrico Fermi award, 1962; Golden Plate award, 1961 Robins award, 1963. Home: 1573 Hawthorne Terr, Berkeley

Cal. Office: U of Cal, Lawrence Radiation Lab, Berkeley, Cal.

TELLER, Judd L, US, communal leader, author; b. Tarnopol, Pol, May 5, 1915; s. Sholem and Elke (Landau); in US since 1921; tchrs cert, Tchrs Coll, Yeshiva U, 1932; BA, CCNY, 1935; MA, Columbia U, 1940, PhD, 1948; m. Frances Beck, Mar, 1932. Coord, intl progs for B'nai B'rith, since 1969; fmr: found, chmn, Amer Histadrut Cultural Exchange, 1963-68; political secy, WZO, 1956-58; first secy, Pres Conf of Major J Orgs; public affairs dir, JA for Pal, 1952-56. Author: Lieder Vun Der Tzeit, poems, 1934; Scapegoat of Revolution, 1954; The Kremlin, The Jews and the Middle East, 1954; The Jews: Biography of a People, 1966; Strangers and Native: Evolution of the American Jew, 1968; ed, Independent J Press Service; fmr ed, Palcor News Agcy, 1941-48; contbr to periodicals; lectr: panelist on TV public affairs progs.Home: 1316 New Hampshire Ave NW, Washington, DC. Office: 1640 Rhode Island Ave NW, Washington, DC.

TELLER, Sidney A, US, lecturer; b. Chgo, Ill, Apr 4, 1883; s. George and Josephine (Zuckerman); att: Inst of Tech, 1904; U Chgo, 1909; m. Julia Pines, July 27, 1916 (decd). Lectr since 1910, intl tours, radio since 1922, TV since 1947; chem engr, 1903-07; supt, Deborah Boys Home, 1907-08; dir: Stanford Park, Chgo, 1910-16; Irene Kaufman Settlement, Emma Farm Assn, Pittsburgh, 1916-42. Established: Julia P Teller Scholarship Fund, at Allegheny Co Scholarship Assn; Sidney and Julia Memorial Fund, at Irene Kaufmann Settlement; Sidney and Julia Teller Cancer Research Funds, at Michael Reese Hosp, and at Montefiore Hosp, Pittsburgh; Sidney and Julia Teller Fund, at U Chgo, U of Ill, U of Pittsburgh. Mem: ACLU; adv council, Urban League; NCCJ; AJComm; Natl Recreation Assn; Boys Clubs of Amer. Recipient: medal, Boys Club of Amer, 1941; spec dipl, Mexico, 1952; honored in Pittsburgh for 50 years of distinguished services by: U of Pittsburgh, The J Centers, Heb Free Loan Assn, Allegheny Co Scholarship Assn, Sr Citizens Club, 1968. Home: 5528 Hyde Park Blvd, Chicago, Ill.

TEL-NIR, Nathan, Isr, organization exec; b. Brno, Czech, July 9, 1917; s. Usiel and Stephanie (Lubinger) Landesberg; in Isr since 1934; m. Hayah Vishnitzky, July 4, 1944; c: Dan, Usiel, Ram. Exec dir, Isr Natl Council for Prevention of Accidents, since 1959. Lt col, IDF, Tel Aviv br; 1936-59. Pres, Lions Club, Tel Aviv; hon treas, Isr PR Assn; mem, exec comm, Isr Fundraisers Assn; hon secy, Zeveth. Contbr to local press. Special interests: astronomy; archaeol; physics; chess. Home: 11/3 Moaz Aviv, Tel Aviv, Isr. Office: 29 Yehud -Hayamit, Tel Aviv, Isr.

TELPAZ, Gideon, Isr, author; b. Petah Tikva, Isr, Aug 26, 1936; MA, Heb U, 1961. Placement off for immigrant tchrs, Min of Educ, since 1968. Author: Shechunt Chapp, 1966; Massahay Ish haChooshchash, 1969; Fear Has No Color, 1969, all short story collections. Mem: ACUM; Heb Writers Assn in Isr. Recipient: Anna Frank prize, Amer-Isr Cultural Fund, 1961; ACUM prize, 1961; Valenrod prize, Heb Writers Assn in Isr, 1969; award, Bd of Culture and Art, 1966. Home: 68 Ein Karem, Jerusalem, Isr.

TELSNER, David, Isr, organization exec; b. Lith, Sep 1, 1908; s. Hirsh and Sylvia (Cohen); in Isr since 1969; att Yeshiva, Riga, Latvia, 1925-29; ordained rabbi, Yavne, NY, 1943; att grad sch, Yeshiva U, NY; m. Edith Roth, 1945. c: Debbi, Zvi, Sylvia. Dir, rel dept, Min of Absorption, since 1969; rabbi, Cong Tiferet Eliezer, NY, 1946-68; exec dir, Hapoel Hamizrach, US, 1950-53; asst dir, Torah educ dept, JA, NY, 1954-64, dir, rel dept, aliyah dept, 1964-68. Chmn, org comm, Irgun Havatikim. Ed, Misrach Weg, NY, 1962-68. Recipient: Rabbi Herzog award, Mizrachi Org of US, 1968. Hobbies: bicycling, music. Home: 7 Narkis St, Jerusalem, Isr. Office: Min of Absorption, Hakirya, Jerusalem, Isr.

TELZER, Ralph, Eng, organization exec; b. Blackpool, Eng, May 5, 1933; s. Cecil and Rose (Fisher); att Manchester Grammar Sch, 1945-50; m. Edna Birzansky, Sep 7, 1958; c: Sholam, Yitzchok. Admn secy, J Day Schs, since 1966; secy, Broughton Syn, since 1959; org secy, Mizrachi-Hapoel Hamizrachi, 1958-60; admn secy, Manchester-J Blind Soc, 1960-66. Hon secy, Manchester Friends of Bar Ilan U; jt hon secy, Manchester and Dist Sabbath Observance League; council mem, Holy Law Cong; comm mem, Manchester Kollel; treas, Manchester Torah Va'Avodah, 1956-57; asso: Soc of Commercial Acctnts; Brit Inst of Commerce; Inst Off

Mgmt; Brit Inst Mgmt. Hobbies: cricket, reading. Home: 69 Catherine Rd, Manchester, Eng. Office: J Day Schs, Beth David, Bury New Rd, Prestwich, Eng.

TEMERSON, Jake Harry, US, business exec; b. Birmingham, Ala, Mar 29, 1900; s. Charles and Gertrude (Berlin); BS, U Ala, 1923, LLB, 1929. Mem, Charles Temerson & Sons; dealer and broker of scrap iron, fabricator and distributor of new steel; dir, City Natl Bank, Tuscalosa. Pres: southeastern chap, Inst of Scrap Iron and Steel; Tuscaloosa Personnel Assn; Fed J Charities, 1948; mem, B'nai B'rith; club, Kiwanis. Home: 16 Audubon, Tuscaloosa, Ala. Office: 2120 Fourth St, Tuscaloosa, Ala.

TEMIANKA, Henri, US, conductor, concert violinist; b. Greenock, Scotland, Nov 19, 1906; s. Israel and Fanny (Hildebrand); in US since 1939; att: Berlin Hochschule; Paris Conservatoire Natl; grad, Curtis Inst, Pa; m. Emmy Cowden, Jan 28, 1943; c: Daniel, David. Found, conductor, Cal Chamber Sym, since 1958; concert appearances include: Edinburgh Festival, 1953; Beethoven Cycle, London, 1953; Osaka Festival, 1960; guest conductor: Buenos Aires Philharmonic, 1959; LA Philharmonic Orch, 1959-61; visiting prof: UCLA; Royal Conservatory, Toronto; Brigham Young U; Utah; Aspen Inst, Colo; Amer String Tchrs Conf; Natl Music Camp, Interlochen, Mich; Acad of the West, Santa Barbara, Cal; LA Conservatory; Boise Jr Coll; recorded for: RCA; Delta; Kappa. Contbr to Amer, Eur periodicals. Home: 2195 Patricia Ave, Los Angeles, Cal. Office: Chamber Sym Society of Cal, 6715 Hollywood Blvd, Hollywood, Cal.

TEMKIN, Alex, US, business exec; b. Madison, Wis, Feb 6, 1916; s. Jake and Celia (Kress); LLD, U Wis, 1939; m. Pauline Brody, Aug 29, 1942 (div); c: Frances, Joan, Ruth. Exec pres: Mohawk Bldg Corp; Midwest Steel Co; pres: Mohawk Homes; Mayfair Homes; owner, Temco Steel; pvt practice, law, 1939-41. US Army, 1941. Mem, bd: Madison J Welfare Council, pres, 1957-59; Beth Isr Cen, pres, 1959-61; mem, B'nai B'rith. Hobbies: swimming, golf. Home: 4817 Sheboygan Ave, Madison, Wis. Office: 4400 Sycamore Ave, Madison, Wis.

TENDLER, Moses D, US, rabbi; b. NYC, Aug 7, 1926; s. Isaac and Bella (Baumrind); BA, NYU, 1947, MA, 1951; ordained rabbi, Yeshiva U, 1948; PhD, Columbia U, 1958; m. Sifra Feinstein, Dec, 1948; c: Rivka, Yacov, Mordechi, Aaron, Hillel, Sara, Rus BasSheva, Eliyahu. Rabbi, Monsey Kehilla, since 1967; prof, biol, Yeshiva Coll, since 1963, asst prof, Talmud, since 1967, asst dean, 1956, lectr, Talmud, 1949. Mem: RabCA; Union Orthodox Rabbis of USA and Can; AAAS; Soc Amer Microbiols; Torrey Botanical Club; Comprehensive Med Soc; Amer Soc Clinical Pharm & Chemotherapy. Contbr to sci and educ jours. Home: 4 Cloverdale Lane, Monsey, NY. Office: Yeshiva U, New York, NY.

TENE, Benjamin, Isr, author, poet; b. Warsaw, Pol, Dec 10, 1914; s. Shmuel and Frymet (Licht) Tenenbaum; in Isr since 1937; m. Sara Chapnik, June 1, 1937; c: Yael Bahat, Abraham. Ed, Mishmar leYeladim, since 1948. Author: poems: Mechora, 1939; Masa baGalil, 1941; beHeret haDvai, 1945; Tmolim Al haSaf, 1947; Ktzir hapele, 1957; Sha'alul Tha'alul, 1962; Shirim uPeomot, 1967; trans: Ehad meIr uShnaim miMishpacha; Shirim uBaldot, by Itzik Manger, and others. Fmr mem, Kibbutz Eilon, 1937-48; mem: Heb Writers Assn in Isr; club: PEN. Home: 8 Karni St, Tel Aviv, Isr. Office: Al Hamishmar, Hamsasger St, Tel Aviv, Isr.

TENENBAUM, Shea, US, author; b. Lublin, Pol, Apr 14, 1908; s. Abraham and Rachel (Grossman); in US since 1934. Author: A Visitor to the World, 1937; The Sphinx, 1938; Children of the Sun, 1942; Gold and Rust, 1943; The Writing on the Horizon, 1947; Harvest, 1949; In the Image of God, 1951; A Hand is Writing, 1953; Poets and Generations, 1955; The Earth Remains Forever, 1957; Anna Frank, 1958; The Truth Shall Be Your Star, 1960; The Angel of Life, 1963; Isaac Ashmedai, 1965; Job of Lemberg, 1967; Personalities By My Desk, 1969; contbr to J periodicals. Mem: J Natl Workers Alliance; club: Yiddish PEN. Recipient: award, Amer Comm for Emigre Scholars, Writers and Artists, 1946; Zvi Kessel prize, Mex, 1951; Karl Rotman Stipendium, Cong for J Culture and NY sect, J PEN Club, 1967. Home: 45-35 44 St, Long Island City, NY.

TENENBLATT, Mordecai Anczel, Isr, journalist, author; b. Jezierjany, Galicia, Aus, Mar 27, 1888; s. Avraham and

Zivia (Ginsberg); in Isr since 1935; m. Chaya Beer, May 18, 1918; c: Ada Moran, Ranana Meridor. Dir, Isr News Agcy, since 1958, with firm since 1935; Eur corresp-in-chief: NY Forward, 1919-1920; J Corresp Bur, Vienna, 1920-34; ed in chief, JTA, London,1934-35. Author: Prakim Chadashim leToldot Eretz Israel uBavli, 1970; co-author: Leshoneinu. Aus Army, WW I. Fmr mem: Jerusalem Journalists Comm; cen comm, Galicia Zionist Org, Vienna, 1930. Contbr to periodicals. Hobby: Chess. Home: 17 Sd Ben Maimon, Jerusalem, Isr. Offffice: 59 Sheinkin St, Tel Aviv, Isr.

TENZER, Herbert, US, attorney; b. NYC Nov 1 1905; s. Michael and Rose (Bernstein); LLB, NYU, 1927; m. Florence Novor, June 29, 1930; c: Barry, Diane Sidel. Sr mem, law firm, Tenzer, Greenblatt, Fallon & Kaplan, since 1937; dir, Amer Trust Co; chmn, bd of dirs, Barton's Candy Corp, 1940-60, ret; mem, US Cong, 1964-68. Dir: NYU Law Alumni Assn; NY Co Lawyers Assn; trustee: Candy & Confectionery Worker, local 452, pension fund, wfr fund; dir, Confectioners Ind Relations Bd; co-found, UJA of Gtr NY, chmn: gen campaign, 1970, campaign cabinet, 1971; chmn, confectionery div: NYC Cancer Comm; UJA; org and past chmn, confectionery div, FJP; pres, Natl Council to Combat Blindness, Inc; dir, Chronic Disease Hosp, Bklyn, NY; chmn: Maimonides Inst for New Devl; south shore div, Albert Einstein Coll of Med, mem, pres' council; trustee, Yeshiva U; hon pres, Cong Beth Shalom, Lawrence, LI, pres, 1952-57; hon pres, Yeshiva of Crown Heights, Bklyn, pres, 1932-49; chmn, bd overseers, Hillel Sch, Lawrence; mem: Grand St Boys Assn; B'nai B'rith; KP; club: Woodmere. Recipient: Statesman award, Synagogue Council Amer, 1962; man of the year, LI chap, NCCJ, 1967. Home: 15 Waverly Pl, Cedarhurst, NY. Office: 235 E 42 St, New York, NY.

TEPER, Lazare, US, economist; b. Russia, Jan 16, 1908; s. Gedeon and Esther (Bogatirsky); in US since 1927; AM, Johns Hopkins U, 1930, PhD, 1931. Dir of research, ILGWU,since 1937; research asst, Johns Hopkins U, 1931-34; instr, econ, Brookwood, 1934-36; dir of research, stat bd, Dressmakers Union, 1935-37. US Army, 1943-45. F: AAAS; Amer Stat Assn; mem: bd of dirs: Natl Bur Econ Research; Fed Employment and Guidance Service; adv comm, Amer Stat Assn, to US Bur of the Census, 1956-68; lab adv council, US Bur of Lab Statistics; mgmt-lab textile comm; repr, ICFTU, on UN Stat Commn; Amer and Metrop Econ Assn; Ind Relations Research Assn; Amer Marketing Assn: Econometric Soc; Acad of Political Sci. Author: Hours of Labor, 1931; Women's Garment Industry, 1937. Recipient: Bronze Star; Conspicuous Service Cross, NY State, 1947. Home: 650 West End Ave, New York, NY. Office: 1710 Broadway, New York, NY,

TEPFER, Sanford S, US, educator; b. Bklyn, NY, March 24, 1918; s. Albert and Rose (Ulman); BS, CCNY, 1938; MS, Cornell U, 1939; PhD, U of Cal, Berkeley, 1950; m. Bertha Fliess, May 6, 1942; c: David, Mark, Gary, Fred. Co-chmn, dept of biol, U of Ore, since 1968, prof since 1967, fac mem since 1955; instr: botany, U of Ariz, 1950-54; biol, Ore Coll of Educ, 1954-55. US Army, 1942-46. Member: Sigma Xi; Botanical Soc of Amer; Intl Soc of Plant Morphologists; Cal Botanical Soc. Hobbies: hiking, camping, scouting, skiing. Home: 2011 Elk Dr, Eugene, Ore. Office: U of Oregon, Eugene, Ore.

TEPLITZ, Saul I, US, rabbi; b. Vienna, Aus, Aug 1, 1921; s. Mendel and Esther (Landau); in US since 1922; BA, U Pittsburgh, 1941; ordained rabbi, MHL, JTSA, 1945, DHL, 1956; m. Miriam Artz, June 11, 1944; c: Howard, Daniel, Michael. Rabbi: Cong Sons of Isr, since 1963; Laurelton J Cen, 1944-60; J Comty Cen, Harrison, NY, 1960-63. Natl chmn: United Syn Youth comn; Coll Atid, org of the Conservative Movement; Heb High Sch comm of the United Syn; natl vice-chmn, Amer J Conf on Soviet Jewry; chmn, comm of rabbi and social worker, vice-chmn, comm syn relations, both FJP: mem: exec comm, RA, fmr pres, metrop br; exec comm, Syn Council Amer; panel of judges, J Conciliation Bd of Amer; cabinet, JTSA. Author: Best Jewish Sermons, 9 vols, biennially since 1952; contbr to Anglo-J periodicals. Home: 20 Neptune Ave, Woodmere, NY. Study: Cong Sons of Isr, 111 Irving Place, Woodmere, NY.

TEPPER, Morris, US, meteorologist; b. Jerusalem, Mar 1, 1916; s. Benjamin and Anna (Goldman); in US since 1922; BA, Bklyn Coll, 1936, MA, 1938; PhD, Johns Hopkins U, 1952; m. Sandra Levin; c: Andrew, Bradford. Dep dir, off of space applications progs, NASA, since 1966, dir of meterology since 1961, chief, meteorological satellite program, 1959-61;

chief, severe local storms research unit, US Weather Bur, 1946-59. Weather off, USAAC, 1943-46. Chmn, working group 6, mem, working group 2, Comm on Space Research; mem: global atmospheric research prog, Intl Council of Sci Unions; intl relations comm, Natl Acad of Sci; US Natl Comm for Intl Hydrological Decade; exec comm, Experimental Inter-Amer Meteorological Rocket Network; Interagency Comm for World Weather Progs; Amer Meteorological Soc; Amer Inst Aeronautics and Astronautics; Wash Acad Scis. Recipient: Meissinger award, Amer Meteorological Soc,1950; Dist Alumni award, Bklyn Coll, 1961; Exceptional Service medal, NASA, 1966. Home: 107 Bluff Terrace, Silver Spring, Md. Office: NASA, Washington, DC.

TEPPER, Sid, US, composer; NYC, June, 25, 1918, s. Abraham and Annie (Leamseader); att, NY Sch of Dentistry; m. Lillian Monkarsh, Feb 7, 1948; c Susan, Michelle, Brian, Warren, Jacqueline. Composer; fmr spec material writer for: Elvis Presley, Hildegarde, Misha Auer, Bobby Breen; staff writer, Mills Music Inc, 1944-48. US Army, spec services, 1941-45. Mem: ASCAP; KP; Midway J Center; JWV; LI Civic Assn; Amer Fed of TV Artists. Composer: The Woodchuck Song; Bagel and Lox; Red Roses for a Blue Lady; New Orleans; Naughty Lady of Shady Lane; Stop! and Think It Over; special material, Elvis Presley films: Blue Hawaii, King Creole, Loving You, Jailhouse Rock. Home and office: 29 Deerpath Lane, Syosset, NY.

TERR, Mischa Richard, US, composer, conductor; b. Odessa, Russ, April, 1,1909; s. Bernard and Mina (Rabinovich); in US since 1922; att Odessa Imperial Conservatory; m. Stella Eskin, Oct 11, 1962; Pres: West Bay Distributors; R Michael Terr Prod; MRT Publishing Co; fmr: cellist: Imperial Sym Orch, Seattle, LA; films: sound recorder, composer, producer. Music dir, sup, USO units, Santa Ana AF Base, 1943-44. Sup, music dir, Independent Motion Pictures Assn; mem: ASCAP; Musicians Union, local 47, LA. Hobbies: cooking, collecting paintings and liquors. Home and office: 2473 Crestview Dr, Los Angeles, Cal.

TERRACINI, Umberto, It, attorney, legislator; b. Genoa, It, July 27, 1895; s. Jair and Adele (Segre); DJur, U of Turin, 1 1920; m. Marialaura Gayno, 1948; c: Massimo. Senator, It Sen, since 1948; found, mem exec, It Communist Party, since 1921; mem, It Socialist Party, 1911-21; political prisoner, condemned for anti-fascism, 1928-43; mem: Consulta Nazionale, 1945; It Constituent Assembly, 1946-48, pres, 1947-48. It Army, 1918-20; partisans, WW II. Pres: It Assn Dem Lawyers; Soc for Assistance to Politically Persecuted: It-Bulgarian Cultural Relations Assn; Assn for Persecuted Anti-fascists. Home: Via Mangili 3, Rome, It. Office: Senato della Repubblica, Rome, It.

TETON, Joseph B, US, physician, educator; b. Sochochin, Pol., Dec 14, 1909; s. Isaac and Fanny (Sarna); in US since 1922; BS, U of Ill Coll of Med, 1931; MD, 1934; m. Shirley Newberger, Nov. 21, 1940; c: John, Andrew, Nancy. Asst prof, obstet and gyn, U of Ill Coll of Med, since 1950; att obstet and gyn, Lutheran Gen Hosp, since 1962; cons gyn: Elgin State Hosp, 1940-49; health service, U of Ill, 1947-57; Kankakee State Hosp, 1949-61; asso att gyn, Cook Co Hosp, 1949-53; sr att obstet and gyn, Henrotin Hosp, 1947-58. Dipl, Amer Bd Obstet and Gyn, 1945; FACS, 1946; f, Chgo Gyn Soc, 1950; found f, Amer Coll Obstet and Gyn, 1950; mem, Amer Comm on Maternal Wfr. Contbr to jours. Home: 1133 Michigan Ave, Wilmette, Ill. Office: 64 Old Orchard, Skokie, Ill.

TEVETH, Shabtai Amotz, Isr, journalist; b. Tel Aviv, Isr; s. Dov and Shifra; att: Heb U, Jerusalem; Temple U, Phila, Pa; m. Ora Leibovitz; c: Yael, Shaul, Yoav. Mem, ed staff, H'aretz daily. Lt, infantry, IDF, 1948-67. Mem: munic comm for beautification of Tel Aviv; club: Variety. Author: Affluence and Anxiety, 1962; Tanks of Tamuz, 1969. Recipient: Prix Italia, 1967; award, Isr Press Assn, 1967. Hobby: collecting dicts. Home: 28 Soutine St, Tel Aviv, Isr. Office: 56 Maze St, Tel Aviv, Isr.

TEXON, Meyer, US, physician; b. NYC, Apr 23, 1909; s. Morris and Eva (Kaizer); AB, cum ladde, Harvard U, 1930; MD, NYU, 1934; m. Ami Gold, Oct 26, 1941; c: Stephen, Sylvia. Asst prof, forensic med, NYU Sch of Med, since 1957; asst med examiner, NYC, since 1957; staff phys, Mt Sinai Hosp; asso att phys: Fr Hosp; NY Infirmary. Capt, US Army, 1941. Chmn, comm on public health, NY Co Med Soc; FACP; f: NY Acad of Med; Amer Coll of Card; council of clinical card, AHA; council on arteriosclerosis, AHA; dipl: Amer Bd of Internal Med; Amer Bd of Cardiovascular Disease. Author: Heart Disease and Industry, 1954; chaps in: Atherosclerotic Vascular Disease, 1957; Atherosclerosis and Its Origin, 1953; contbr of numerous papers on heart disease and atherosclerosis. Recipient: Hektoen Silver medal, AMA, 1958. Home: 365 West End Ave, New York, NY. Office: 3 E 68 St, New York, NY.

TEZMAN, Yusuf, Turkey, postal expert; b. Ankara, Turkey, Sep 23, 1911; s. Hayim and Simha (Alaton) Levi; m. Refika Albukrek-Ender, Apr 11, 1929; c: Semiha Bali, Meral Habib, Feride Elyazar. Dir of co-ordination, pvt trade co, since 1966; fmr, dir intl postal sect, PTT Gen Directorate, on staff since 1930. Mem, Masons. Home: Atac Sokak 46/4, Yenisehir-Ankara, Turkey.

THALHEIMER, Ross J, US, psychoanalyst, educator; b. Baltimore, Md, Nov 21, 1905; s. Samuel and Merla (Friedenwald); AB, Johns Hopkins U, 1925, PhD, 1929; att Cambridge U, Eng, 1925-26, postdoc work: 1932-33; NY Psychoanalytic Inst, 1947-48; m. Helen Kehlman, 1951. Found, exec dir, Comty Guidance Service Inc, NY, since 1953; pvt practice, psychan, since 1946; dir: Intl Council on Psych Dangers to World Peace, since 1960; Inst for Practicing Psychotherapists, since 1960; fmr: instr: Johns Hopkins U, 1927-28; U Wash, Seattle, 1928-29; prof, U Baltimore, 1935-38; educ dir, Amer Fed of Tchrs, 1938-39; dir, Madison House Psycht Clinic, NYC, 1951-52. Clinical psychol, US Army, 1940-45. F, Amer Psychol Assn; mem: bd dirs, Assn for Psycht Treatment of Offenders Inc, 1950-54; Assn for Advancement of Psychotherapy; NY State Psychol Assn; Amer Phil Assn; Natl Psychol Assn for Psychan; pres, Thalheimer Found Inc. Donor: annual Thalheimer awards to NAACP; Natl Urban League. Contbr to profsl jours. Home and office: 161 W 54 St, New York, NY.

THALHIMER, Morton G, US, business exec; b. Richmond, Va, Oct 17, 1889; s. Gustavus and Pauline (Lohnstader); att U of Pa; m. Ruth Wallerstein, Oct 11, 1920; c: Morton jr, Peggy Lewis. Chmn bd, Morton G Thalhimer Inc, since 1967, pres since 1913; chmn, bd dirs, Neighborhood Theater, Inc; dir, Broad-Grace Arcade Corp; dir em: Richmond TV Corp, vice-pres; State-Planters Bank of Commerce and Trusts; Spotless Co. Capt, US Army, WW II. Fmr pres, Va Real Estate Fed; chmn, bd and exec comm, Richmond Memorial Hosp; mem, bd govs, Amer Soc Real Estate Counsellors; mem, bd dirs and/or trustees: Firemens Mutual Aid Assn; adv bd, YMCA; adv bd: VA Home for Incurables; Will Rogers Memorial Hosp; Sheltering Arms Hosp; VA Mus of Fine Arts; Robert E Lee Boy Scout Trust; Historic Richmond Found; Temple Beth Ahabah; mem: Amer Soc Real Estate Counsellors; Amer Inst Real Estate Appraisers; Natl Assn Real Estate Bds; Intl Real Estate Fed; Mortgage Bankers Assn; Real Estate Mgmt Inst; Columbia Assos; Collector's Circle; Va Comm on the Arts and Humanities; Masons; clubs: Bull and Bear; Executives; Jefferson-Lakeside; Forum; Variety; 2300. Home: 4 Paxton Rd, Richmond, Va. Office: 1013 E Main St, Richmond, Va.

THAU, Avshalom, Isr, architect; b. Kosice, Czech, June 18, 1916; s. Ozjas and Cecylja (Altheim); in Isr since 1934; BArch, Technion, 1938, dipl ing, arch, 1941; m. Lea Baum, July 27, 1939; c: Shulamith Spitz. Sr lectr, architecture, town planning, Technion, since 1967; pvt practice since 1967; fmr: engr, tech dept, Solel Boneh, 1941-48. Planning off, engr corps, IDF, 1948-67. Prin contribs: research on structural surfaces stressed to curvature. Mem: Assn of Engrs and Architects in Isr. Author: Architectural Integration of Installations for: Drying Domestic Laundry, 1964; Waste Disposal, 1966; Solar Water Heaters, 1968; contbr to sci and profsl publs. Recipient: Aleh. Home: 114 Hanasi Ave, Haifa, Isr. Office: Technion, Haifa, Isr.

THEILHEIMER, Feodor, US, mathematician; b. Gunzenhausen, Ger, June 18, 1909; s. Gustav and Rosa (Waldmann); in US since 1937; PhD, U of Berlin, 1936; m. Henriette Rubel, Dec 19, 1948; c: Rachel. Math, Naval Ship Research and Devl Cen, since 1953; asst prof, math, Trinity Coll, 1942-48; math, Naval Ordnance Lab, 1948-53. Pres, Chavruta, Heb speaking org, 1962-64. Home: 2608 Spencer Rd, Chevy Chase, Md. Office: Naval Ship Research and Devl Cen, Washington, DC.

THEMANLYS, Pascal, Isr, administrator, author, journalist; b. Paris, Fr, Sep 27, 1909; s. Louis and Claire; in Isr since

1949; att Ecole Pratique des Hautes Etudes, Sorbonne; m. Raymonde Litkin, Sep 18, 1947. Dir, Fr sect, JA. Author: Le Monocle d'Emeraude, poems, 1924; Le Souffleur, 1927; Figures Passionées, 1930; Les Merveilles du Becht, Vie du Baal Shem Tov, 1934; Grands d'Israel, 1938; Cocktails de Fruits, 1938; Influences, 1949; Max Theon et la Philosophie Cosmique, 1954; Un Itineraire de Paris à Jerusalem, 1963; ed: Idéal et Réalité, Paris, 1928-32; Renaissance, Jerusalem, 1954-56; La Semaine Israelienne, Jerusalem, 1952-62. Contbr to Fr periodicals; Fr & Isr radio. Secy-gen, Amitiés Israel-Fr, Jerusalem. Recipient: Palmes academiques francaises. Home: 3 Maadereth St, Jerusalem, Isr. Office: JA, Jerusalem, Isr.

THEODOR, Oskar, Isr, entomologist; b. Königsberg, Ger, Oct 3, 1898; s. Emil and Lina (Rudberg); in Isr since 1919; att U of Königsberg, PhD, 1928; m. Margarete Aron, Mar 17, 1921; c: Daniel, Emanuel. Prof em, parasitology, Heb U, since 1967, mem fac since 1925. Brit Army, 1942-45. F, Royal Entomological Soc, London; fmr chmn, Assn of Academic Workers in Isr. Author: books, chaps in textbooks; contbr to jours. Home: Beth Hakerem, Jerusalem, Isr. Office: Heb U, Jerusalem, Isr.

THEODORE, Frederick H, US, physician; ophthalmologist; b. NYC, Apr 4, 1908; s. Benno and Luba (Biscow); AB, Columbia Coll, 1927; MD, Columbia U Coll of Phys and Surg, 1931; m. Jeanne Sincoff, Feb 6, 1940; c: Andrea, William. Pvt practice; att ophthal: Mt Sinai Hosp, since 1960; Manhattan Eye, Ear and Throat Hosp, since 1956. Maj, US Army MC, 1942-45. Pres: Manhattan Ophthal Soc, 1962-63; NY Soc for Clinical Ophthal, 1954-55; chmn, sect on ophthal, NY Acad of Med, 1968-69; clubs: Harmonie, NY; Beachpoint, Mamaroneck. Prin contbrs: org and classified ocular allergies, 1958; pointed out role of saprophytic fungi in postoperative eye infections; first described disease of Superior Limbic Reratoconjunctivitis, 1963. Author: Ocular Allergy, 1958; ed, Complications after Cataract Surg, 1965; mem, ed bd, Jour of Ped Ophthal; asso ed: AMA Archives of Ophthal; Eye, Ear, Nose and Throat Monthly; contbr to med books and profsl jours; spec lectureships. Recipient: dist service medal, Acad of Ophthal and Otolaryngology, 1960. Home: 1120 Park Ave, New York, NY. Office: 625 Park Ave, New York, NY.

THOMAS, Lawrence Jay, US, physician, educator; b. Bklyn, NY, Dec 23, 1913; s. Samuel and Dina (Topilsky); BS, NYU, 1934; MD, George Wash U, 1938; m. Beatrice Pfursich, May 21, 1939; c: Stephen, Judith. Asst clinical prof, med, George Wash U, since 1959, mem fac since 1942; res phys, DC Gen Hosp, 1939-40; f, George Wash Hosp, 1940-42. Pres: Phi Lambda Kappa, 1962, treas, 1955-61; Med Students Aid Soc, 1963-66; FACP, 1948; f, Amer Bd of Intl Med, 1945; mem: AMA; Amer Diabetes Assn; AHA; Amer Fed Clinical Research. Contbr to profsl jours. Home: 1422 Jonquil St NW, Washington, DC. Office: 1712 Eye St NW, Washington, DC.

THON-HOLLANDER, Nella, Uruguay, organization leader; b. Cracow, Pol, Apr 11, 1908; d. Osias and Maria (Bach) Thon; grad, law and phil, U Pol, 1932; m. Repr, WJC, in Uruguay; fmr: tchr, Heb Coll, Cracow; ed, Vär Röst, Stockholm; dir, WJC, Stockholm. Contbr to periodicals. Home: 1570 Cebollati, Montevideo, Uruguay. Office: WJC, 1119 Rio Branco, Montevideo, Uruguay.

THROPE, Norman Harold, US, business exec; b. NYC, Sep 15, 1915; s. Julius and Bessie (Cohen); BS, NYU, 1936; AM, Harvard U, 1937; m. Shirley Porton, Nov 30, 1941; c: Aileen Grossberg, Martin, David. Pres, Form Fit Plastics, since 1968; vice-pres, Middlesex Paper Tube Co Inc, since 1953. Pres, Lowell Heb Comty Cen and Temple Beth El; dir: UJA; Beth-El Cemetery Corp; mem: B'nai Br'ith; Masons; Amer Packaging and Handling Engrs; Harry S Truman Libr Found. Home: 831 Westford, Lowell, Mass. Office: 345 Chelmsford St, Lowell, Mass.

THURMAN, Harold, US, professional mgmt cons; b. Boston, Mass, May 9, 1904; s. Jacob and Bella (Rabinowitz); BA, Harvard Coll, 1925, cert, Harvard Bus Sch, 1941; m. Melanie Thurman, Aug 14, 1935; c: Jane, Deborah. Financial cons since 1959; pres: Thurman Co, 1936-50; Miami Natl Bank, 1957-59. Dir, J Family Service, since 1967; bd mem: Cedars of Leb Hosp, since 1959; United Fund, since 1958; vice-chmn, Large City Budgeting Conf, since 1959; secy, Assn Mgmt Cons, since 1967; vice-pres: Friends of Heb U, since 1960; Brandeis U, Miami, since 1959; Hillel Found, U Miami,

1956-58; Gtr Miami J Fed, 1959-67; fmr chmn: Combined J Appeal, 1960; Sr Citizens of Dade Co Wfr, 1956-57; mem: Temple Isr, chmn, rel sch 1953-59, pres, 1963-65; Masons; club: Harvard, Miami, mem, exec comm, since 1958. Recipient: hon pres, J Big Brother Assn, since 1948; hon vice-pres, Bur J Educ, since 1958. Home: 700 Biltmore Way, Coral Cables, Fla. Office: 1610 Congress Bldg, Miami, Fla.

TICKTIN, Max David, US, rabbi; b. Phila, Pa, June 30, 1922; s. Israel and Sarah (Pincus);BA, U Pa, 1942; ordained rabbi, MHL, JTSA, 1947; m. Esther Kelman, Nov 25, 1945; c: Hannah, Deborah, Ruth. Dir, natl leadership training dept, B'nai B'rith Hillel Founds, since 1964; dir, Hillel Found, U Chgo, since 1964; dir, B'nai B'rith Hillel Found, U Wis, 1948-64 Home: 5528 Kenwood, Chicago, Ill. Office: 5715 S Woodlawn Ave, Chicago, Ill.

TIDHAR, David, Isr, author editor, publisher; b. Jaffa, Isr, June 7, 1897; s. Moshe and Esther (Nirenberg) Todresowitz; m. Rivka Kapiluto: c: Esther, Moshe. Ed and publisher, Ency leChalutzei haYishuv uBonav, since 1947. Off, J Legion, Pal, 1918; mem, Neveh Shalom, defense group, 1921; insp, New City Police, Jerusalem, 1921-26; found, dir, pvt inquiry and inves off, 1931-47. Co-found: Maccabi, Isr; Haganah, Tel Aviv Mus, 1931; Jabotinsky Inst, 1940; mem: B'nai B'rith; Masons. Author: Chotim veChataim, 1924; Bein haPatish, vehaSaddan, 1932; beMadim uBelo Madim, 1938; beSherouth haMoledeth: 1912-60, 1961; co-ed: haBalash. Home: 62 Shenkin St, Tel Aviv, Isr.

TIEMANN, Arthur Edmund, US, statistician; b. Boston, Mass June 5, 1918; s. Harry and Sarah (Sisson); AB, Harvard U, 1939; att Amer U, Wash, DC, 1940-41, 1947-49; m. Riboline Youngwitz, Apr 19, 1944; c: Robert, David, Zachary. Chief, stat services div, World Bank, since 1967, on staff since 1966; asst prof, stat, George Wash U; fmr: asso dir, progress reports and stat div, USN, 1950-62; chief, planning methods br, airports service, FAA, 1964-66, staff planning officer, 1962-64. Capt, US Army, 1941-46. Pres, Montgomery Co J Comty, Chevy Chase; chmn, adult educ: Bd J Educ, Wash, DC; B'nai B'rith, Wash area; exec bd, JCC of Gtr Wash; mem: Amer Stat Assn; Amer Econ Assn; Oprs Research Soc Amer; ZOA; AJCong; J Publ Soc of Amer. Contbr to profsl jours. Recipient: Bronze Star. Home: 9314 Harvey Rd, Silver Spring, Md. Office: 1818 H St NW, Washington, DC.

TIFTY, Meir, Isr, organization exec; b. Habil, Iraq, 1933; s. Zion and Sarah; in Isr since 1951; m. Frieda Kiriah, 1954; c: Sarah, Ziviah, Yehudit, Ilan. Mem, secretariat, Natl Org Agric Workers, since 1968; fmr secy: profsl org; lab council, both Tavneh. IDF, 1952-54. Mem: local council; Histadrut council; Mgmt Cen Ins Fund, Agric Workers. Home: 914 Chissachon, Yavne, Isr. Office: 126 Allenby Rd, Tel Aviv, Isr.

TIKOFSKY, Ronald Sherwood, US, educator; b. Bklyn, NY, May 21, 1930; s. Abraham and Gussie (Garcon); BA, Bklyn Coll, 1952; MA, 1953; PhD, U of Utah, 1957; m. Rita, May 30, 1958; c: Melissa, Andrew. Prof, psych, speech, U Mich, since 1968, chmn, psycholings prog, since 1966, fac mem since 1958; instr, U Pittsburgh, 1957-58. Prin contrib: Found, Acad of Aphasia. Pres: Temple Beth Emeth, dir, rel sch; Metrop Detroit Fed of Reform Syns; fac adv comm, U Mich Hillel Found; chmn: Ann Arbor UJA, 1960-62; Ann Arbor Isr Bonds Comm, 1969-70; mem, Acoustical Soc Amer; f, Amer Speech and Hearing Assn; mem: Amer Psych Assn; AAAS. Contbr: Speech, 1960; Language Problems in Adults, 1966. Hobbies: music, art, tennis. Home: 379 Brookside, Ann Arbor, Mich. Office: U Mich, 182 Frieze Bldg, Ann Arbor, Mich.

TILLIS, Herman H, US, physician; b. Newark, NJ, Dec 11, 1907; s. Morris and Pauline (Block); BS, NYU, 1928; MD, U Louisville Med Coll, 1931; m. Evelyn Goldstein, Aug 30, 1936; c: Blanche, Alan. Chief, arthritis: Beth Isr Hosp, since 1942; Presbyterian Hosp, since 1942; mem, Health Dept, since 1937; all Newark; fmr, clinical asst, arthritis, Bellevue Med Coll, 1942. Co-chmn, Phys Bonds for Isr, since 1951; keyman, UJA, since 1940; mem: bd trustees, NJ Arthritis and Rheumatism Found; Phys Cmty Chest; AMA; NJ and Essex Co Med Socs; B'nai B'rith; AJComm, NY Rheumatism Soc; Amer Rheumatism Soc; Heb Orphanage and Sheltering Home; Temple B'nai Jeshurun; YMHA; NJ Rheumatism Soc, pres, 1952. Home: 243 S Harrison St, East Orange, NJ. Office: 109 S Munn Ave, East Orange, NJ.

TIMBERG, Sigmund, US, attorney; b. Antwerp, Belgium, Mar

5, 1911; s. Arnold and Rose (Mahler); in US since 1916; BA, Columbia U, 1930, MA, 1930, LLB, 1933; m. Eleanor Ernst, Sep 22, 1940; c: Thomas, Bernard, Rosamund, Richard. Pvt practice since 1954; lectr: Parker Sch Fgn and Comparative Law, Columbia U, since 1967; Practicing Law Inst, NYC, since 1949; sr atty, Solicitor's Off, US Dept of Agric, 1933-35, chief, soil conservation sect, 1935-38; sr atty, SEC, 1938-42; staff mem, Temp Natl Econ comm, 1938-39; chief, property relations and ind org div, reoccupation br, Bd Econ Warfare and Fgn Econ Admn, 1942-44; delg, Anglo-Amer Telecommunications Conf, Bermuda, 1945; spec asst to Atty-Gen, anti-trust div, Dept of Justice, 1944-46, chief, judgment and enforcement sect, 1946-52; delg, Geneva Copyright Conf, 1952; secy, UN Comm on Restructive Bus Practices, 1952-53; prof, law, Georgetown U Law Sch, 1952-54. Mem: Amer, Intl, Fed, and NYC Bar Assns; Amer Soc Intl Law; Amer Econ Assn; Amer Fgn Law Assn; Amer Law Inst; Amer Patent Law Assn; Conf on Sci, Phil and Religion; Columbia Law Alumni of Wash; John F Kennedy lodge, B'nai B'rith; clubs: Cosmos, Natl Lawyers; Natl Capitol Dem: Torch; Columbia U. Contbr to legal publs. Home: 3519 Porter St NW, Washington, DC. Office: 815 15 St NW, Washington DC.

TIMEN, Jacob, Isr, actor; b. Nikolaev, Russ, Feb 28, 1903; s. Shlomo and Rosalia (Sklovsky); in Isr since 1925; att Odessa U, 1919-20; grad, Odessa Dramatic Sch, 1922; m. Rivka Rabinovitch, Feb 21, 1932; c: Gabriella, Shlomo. Actor since 1922; one-night shows, Isr, since 1959; radio and TV; staff mem: Dramatic and Satirical Theater, Nikolaev, 1922-25; Heb and Natl Theaters, Pal, 1925-27; co-found, mgmt, performer, satirical theaters: Hakumkum, 1927-28, Hamatateh, 1928-55; org, actor, Hevraya theater group, 1955; dir, puppet theater, visiting new settlements, 1958-59. Served Haganah; enertainer: J troops, Brit Army, WW II; IDF, Isr War of Independence. Club: Milo Theatre. Recipient: decoration, Haganah. Home: 29 Gordon St, Tel Aviv, Isr.

TIMNAT, Yaakov, Isr, scientist; b. Trieste, It, June 22, 1923; s. Haim and Paola (Levi) Manheimer; in Isr since 1940; MSc, Heb U, 1947, PhD, 1959; m. Shushana Segal, July 29, 1947; c. Hanna Reich, Gil. Asso prof, head propulsion and combustion lab, dept aeronautical engr, Technion, since 1965; fmr: sr research off, sci dept, Isr Min of Defense, 1951-65; research asso, Cornell U, 1960-61; sr research f, Cal Inst of Tech 1961-62. Haganah; Palmach, 1942-48; IDF, 1948-49. Prin contribs: research in field of combustion, propulsion, detonation and high temperature gases. Mem: AIAA, US; Isr Aeronautical and Astronomical Soc, past chmn; Isr Phys Soc; Isr Astronautical Soc, past chmn. Contbr to sci jours. Home: 95 Hagalil St, Haifa, Isr. Office: Technion, Haifa, Isr.

TINSLEY, Milton, US, surgeon, educator; b. Chgo, Ill, June 6, 1910; s. Abraham and Sarah (Klingman); att U of Chgo, 1929-31; BS, U of Ill, 1933, MD, 1937, MS, 1939; m. Phyllis Silverman, Feb 27, 1947; c: Abigail, Stephen, Peter, Elisa. Prof, dept head, neurosurg, Chgo Med Sch, since 1950; att surg, dept head, neurosurg, Michael Reese Hosp, since 1947; att neurosurg: VA, since 1948; Mt Sinai Hosp, since 1940; cons: Oak Park Hosp, since 1948; St Elizabeth Hosp, since 1948; Alexian Bros Hosp; VA Hosp, since 1948; asst prof, neurosurg, U of Ill, 1937-46; att neurosurg, Cook Co Hosp, 1940-50. Lt col, US Army MC, 1941-46. Mem, Anshe Emet Cong; club: Covenant, Chgo. Contbr to med jours. Recipient: Purple Heart, 1943; Bronze Star, 1945. Home: 442 Wellington St, Chicago, Ill. Office: 55 E Washington St, Chicago, Ill.

TISCHLER, Morris, US, business exec, scientist; b. Newark, NJ, Mar 28, 1922; s. David and Sadie (Bach); att Johns Hopkins U, 1946-50; BS, U of Md, 1950, MA, 1952; att Morgan State Coll, 1954; m. Ruth Shafer, June 16, 1946; c: Joel, Alan, Bruce, Mark, Joanne. Vice-pres, Electronic Aids Inc, since 1964, fmr pres, with firm since 1958; cons, intl tech educ; US State Dept; fmr: tchr, electronics, Forest Park HS, 1946-58; dir, med electronics, U of Md, 1950-62; prof, dept head, Baltimore Comty Coll, 1958-62. Staff sgt, US Army, 1943-46. Prin contribs: patented first transistor pacemaker, device for heart stimulation, provided unit to Pres Eisenhower, 1959; developed electronic training aids for technical and vocational educ; established vocational training progs in over 25 countries; holder of 5 patents in med and educ equipment, 1957-64. Mem: IEE; NEA; ZOA. Author: 22 manuals for teaching electronics, 1959-68; contbr to med and educ jours. Home: 3100 Shelbourne Rd, Baltimore, Md. Office: 6101 Falls Rd, Baltimore, Md.

TISHLER, Max, US, chemist; b. Boston, Mass, Oct 30, 1906; s. Samuel and Anna (Gray); BS, Tufts U, 1928; MS, Harvard U, 1933, PhD, 1934; hon: DS, Tufts U, 1956; DS, Bucknell U, 1962; DSc, Phila Coll of Pharm and Sci, 1966; D Engr, Stevens Inst of Tech, 1966; m. Elizabeth Verveer, June 17, 1937; c: Peter, Carl. Sr vice-pres, research and devl, Merck and Co, since 1969, pres, research labs, Merck, Sharpe and Dohme div, 1956-69, staff mem since 1937; research asso, chem, Harvard U, 1934-36, instr, 1936-37. Mem: bd trustees, Tufts U, chmn, visiting comm, chem dept; asso trustee, Science U, Pa; visiting comms: sch of public health and dept chem, Harvard U; trustee, Union Coll; bd govs, Weizmann Inst; natl adv council, Hampshire Coll; bd of visitors, fac health scis, SUNY, Buffalo; Amer Chems Soc, chmn, organic chem div, 1952, councilor, 1951; councilor: Amer Inst Chems, 1959-61; Soc Chem Ind, 1957; f: NY Acad of Sci; Amer Acad Arts and Sci; mem: Swiss Chem Soc; Chem Soc of London; Natl Acad of Sci; ed in chief, Organic Syntheses, 1959. Contbr to profsl jours. Recipient: bd dirs award, (established annual Max Tishler visiting lectureship at Harvard U, and annual Max Tishler scholarship at Tufts U), Merck and Co, Inc, 1951; Amer Inst of Chems scroll, 1960; medal, Ind Research Inst, 1961; medal, Soc Chem Ind, 1963; Rennebohm lectr, sch of pharm, U Wis, 1963; chem lectr award, Royal Swed Acad of Engr Scis, 1964; Kauffman Memorial lectr, O State U, 1967; chem pioneer award, Amer Inst of Chems, 1968. Hobby: gardening. Home: 857 Knollwood Terr, Westfield, NJ. Office: Merck and Co, Inc, Rahway, NJ.

TISHMAN, David, US, business exec; b. NYC, Apr 22, 1889; s. Julius and Hilda (Karmel); LLM, NYU Sch of Law, 1910; hon LLD, NYU, 1960; m. Ann Valentine, Jan 8, 1914; c: Robert, Alan, Virginia Rand. Chmn, bd dirs, Tishman Realty and Construction Co, since 1948, pres, 1928-48; vice-pres, Julius Tishman and Sons, Inc, 1912-28. Dir, Citizens Housing and Planning Council of NY, Inc; mem, bd of trustees: Citizens Budget Commn; NYU Med Cen; NYU Law Cen Found; NYU; bd of dirs, ARC, NY chap; Masons; clubs: Sunningdale Country, Scarsdale; NYU, dir. Recipient: meritorious service award, NYU, 1955. Home: 930 Fifth Ave, New York, NY. Office: 666 Fifth Ave, New York, NY.

TITIEV, Mischa, US, educator, anthropologist; b. Krementchug, Russ, Sep 11, 1901; s. Jacob and Rose (Ornstein); MA, Harvard U, 1924, PhD, 1935; m. Estelle Berman, Aug 12, 1935; c: Robert, Jay. Prof, anthropology, U Mich, since 1951, on fac since 1936; field dir, cen for Japanese studies, Okayama, Japan, 1951; field work, anthropology: Hopi Indians, Ariz, 1932-34; Araucanian Indians of Chile, 1948; asst mus curator, jr archeol, Natl Park Service, 1935; chief, New Delhi Research and Analysis Off, India. Historian, China-Burma-India Theater, OSS, 1944-45. Mem: Amer Anthropological Assn; AAAS; Far E Assn; Amer Ethnological Assn; Assn for Asian Studies; Phi Kappa Phi; Sigma Xi. Author: Old Oraibi, A Study of the Hopi Indians of the Third Mesa, Ariz, 1944; Araucanian Culture in Transition, 1951; The Japanese Colony in Peru, 1951; The Science of Man, 1954, revised ed, 1963; Introduction to Cultural Anthropology, 1959; contbr to profsl jours. Home: 910 Heather Way, Ann Arbor, Mich. Office: U of Mich, Ann Arbor, Mich.

TOBIAS, Abraham Joel, US, artist; b. Rochester, NY, Nov 21, 1913; s. Israel and Jennie (Warnick); att: Cooper Union Art Sch, 1930-31; Art Students League, 1931-33; Federal Arts Projects, 1938-40, all NYC; m Carolyn Patt, Oct 29, 1949; c: Maya. Artist-in-res, Adelphi Coll, since 1947, instr, painting and drawing, lectr on art, executing series of murals on campus; visiting lectr, art program, Assn of Amer Colls; lectr, mural paintings, Howard U, Wash, DC, 1954. US Army, 1942-43; art dir, intelligence div, USAAF, 1943-44; graphic designer, OSS, Wash, DC, 1945. Murals: Sect of Fine Arts, Wash DC; PO, Clarendon, Ark, 1942; Midwood HS, Bklyn, 1943; Founders Libr, Howard U, 1946; James Madison HS, Bklyn, 1952; Adelphi Coll, 1948-54; Charles H Silver Clinic, Beth Isr Hosp, NYC, 1954; Domestic Relations Court, Bklyn, 1956; Bklyn Poly Inst, 1957-58, 1963; perm collection: Bklyn Mus; NY Public Libr; Rochester Public Libr; LA Mus; Howard U; one-man shows: Delphic Studios, 1935, 1937, 1939, New Sch for Social Research, 1937; Howard U, 1938; Everhart Mus, 1939; exhb: Mus of Modern Art; Bklyn Mus; Adelphi Coll; Architectural League of NY; NYC Munic Art Comm; SF Mus. Mem: Architectural League of NY; Natl Soc of Mural Painters; Arists Equity Assn. Recipient, awards: Natl Fine Arts commn; Natl Mural Competition; Post Office commn, Clarendon, Ark, 1940; Architectural League, 1952. Home: 98-51 65 Ave, Rego Park, Queens, NY.

TOBIAS, Charles H, Jr, US, attorney; b. Cincinnati, O, Apr 16, 1921; s.Charles and Charlotte (Westheimer); BA,Harvard Coll, 1943, LLB, 1949; m. Mary Kaufman, June 15, 1946; c: Jean, Thomas, Robert. Partner, Steer, Strauss, White & Tobias. Lt, USNR, 1943-46. Bd mem: City Charter Comm; Valley Temple; Asso J Agencies; Comty Relations Comm; The J Hosp; Cincinnati J Fed; mem: J Vocational Service of Cincinnati, pres, 1962-64; Cincinnati chap, AJComm, chmn, 1964-67; div co-chmn: UJA, 1956; JWF, 1962; club: Losantville Country. Home: 88 Mt Pleasant Ave, Cincinnati, O. Office: 2215 Central Trust Tower, Cincinnati, O.

TOBIAS, Norman, US, dermatologist; b. Elmira, NY, June 26, 1898; s. Sol and Jennie (Cohen); MD, NYU, 1921; m. Agnes Blumberg, June 26, 1939; c: Sally, Susan. Pvt practice since 1923; asso prof, dermat, St Louis U, 1930-56. Mem: AMA; S Med Assn; Soc for Inves of Dermat; Amer Acad of Dermat; curator, mus, Shaare Emeth Temple; clubs: Rotary. Author: Essentials of Dermatology, 5th ed, 1956; contbr to med jours. Hobbies: travel, photography. Home: 700 S Meramec Ave, Clayton, O. Office: 634 N Grand Ave, St Louis Mo.

TOBIAS, Phillip V, S Afr, anatomist, educator; b. Durban, S Afr, Oct 14, 1925; s. Joseph and Fanny (Rosendorff); BSc, U Witwatersrand, 1945, BSc, hons, 1946, MB, 1950, PhD, 1952, DSc, 1967; postgrad studies, Cambridge U, 1955-56. Prof, anat, U Witwatersrand Med Sch, since 1959, mem fac since 1951. F, Royal Soc of S Afr; chmn, Kalahari Research comm; found, pres, Inst for Study of Man in Afr; pres, Anat Soc S Afr, 1968-70; first chmn, S Afr Soc for Quaternary Research, 1969; mem: council, S Afr Assn for Advancement of Sci, vice-pres, 1968-69; mem: S Afr Archaeol Soc, fmr pres; Anat Soc of Gt Brit and Ir; Royal Anthropological Inst, London; Geog Soc, Lisbon; Anthropological Soc, Paris; Amer Soc for Hum Genet; Amer Assn Phys Anthropologists; Inst for Study Hum Biol; S Afr J Sociol and Hist Soc; Assn Sci Writers of S Afr, pres, 1963-64; fmr: mem: exec, Educ League of S Afr; exec, Jan Hofmeyr Memorial Found; internal mgmt comm, Gt Syn, Johannesburg; educ comm, S Afr J Bd Deps; bd govs, King David Schs, Johannesburg. Author: The African in the Universities, 1951; Chromosomes, Sex-cells, and Evolution, 1956; Man's Anatomy, 1963-64, 2nd ed, 1967; Man's Brain, 1963; Olduvai Gorge, vol II, 1967; Man's Past and Future, 1969; contbr to books and sci jours. Recipient: Abe Bailey traveling f, 1952-53; British Assn medal, 1953; Nuffield f, 1955; Rockefeller traveling f, 1956; S L Sive traveling f, 1956; Simon Biesheuvel medal, 1966; S Afr medal, 1967. Hobbies: archaeol, philately, Africana, music. Home: 602 Marble Arch, Goldreich St, Johannesburg, S Afr. Office: U of Wirwatersrand, Johannesburg, S Afr.

TOBIN, Irwin Morris, US, diplomat; Boston, Mass, July 8, 1913; s. Hyman and Goldie (Learner); BS, Tufts U, 1933; MA, Clark U, 1934; MA, Fletcher Sch Law and Diplomacy, 1935; PhD, Brown U, 1941; m. Rosalyn Ricklin, Apr 4, 1936; c: Ruth, Joseph, Deborah, David. Dir, off research and analysis, USSR and E Eur, US State Dept, since 1970; dir, World Affairs Council, RI, 1935-42; asst prof, RI State Coll, 1942-44; field repr, OWI, London, 1944; inteligence off, OSS, 1944-45; Eur lab adv, dep spec cons to Sec, US State Dept, Wash, DC, 1945-52; fgn service off, 1st secy, lab attache: Vienna, Aus, 1952-56, Bonn, Ger, 1956-58; staff, Natl War Coll, 1958-59; off i/c NATO Political Affairs, US State Dept, 1959-61, dep dir, off Eur regional affairs, 1960-62; adv, intl affairs, off sci and tech, White House, 1963-65; counselor, Amer Emb, Belgrade, Yugo, 1965-69. Mem: Amer Political Sci Assn; Amer Assn Slavic Studies. Hobbies: music, philately, outdoors. Home: 7110 Wilson Lane, Bethesda, Md. Office: Dept of State, Washington, DC.

TOBOLOWSKY, Hermine D, US, attorney; b. San Antonio, Tex, Jan 13, 1921; d. Maurice and Nora (Brown) Dalkowitz; att Incarnate Wood Coll, 1938-39; Trinity U, San Antonio, 1939-40; LLB, U of Tex Sch of Law, 1940-43; m. Hyman Tobolowsky, Aug 19, 1951. Pvt practice since 1943. Mem, Natl Adv Health Council, to Surg Gen of US; leg chmn, legal adv, Tex Fed of Bus and Profsl Women's Clubs, fmr pres; mem, bd dirs: Dallas Citizens Traffic Assn; Dallas Equality Assn; mem: Tex Bar Assn; Dallas Fed of Womens Clubs; Kappa Beta Pi; Alpha Lambda Delta; Temple Emanu-El; hon mem, Delta Kappa Gamma. Contbr to periodicals. Hobbies: drama, music. Home and office: 647 Desco Dr, Dallas, Tex.

TOBRINER, Mathew O, US, jurist; b. SF, Cal, Apr 2, 1904; s. Oscar and Maud (Lezinsky); AB, magna cum laude, Stanford U, 1924, MA, 1925, LLB, Harvard Law Sch, 1927; SJD, Sch of Law, U of Cal, 1932; m. Rosabelle Rose, May 19, 1939; c: Michael, Stephen. Asso justice, Supr Court of Cal, since 1962; partner, law firm, Torbriner, Lazarus, Brundage & Neyhart. 1936-59; asso justice, Dist Court of Appeal, div 1, 1959-62, USCG, 1943-45. Chmn, J Comty Relations Council, SF, 1962-64; pres, Legal Aid Soc of SF, 1961-63; mem: Amer, Cal, and SF Bar Assns; Phi Beta Kappa; Delta Sigma Rho; clubs: Barristers, co-founder, second pres, 1930; Commonwealth, quarterly chmn, 1960. Co-author: Principles and Practices of Cooperating Marketing, 1926; contbr to law jours. Hobby: water-color painting. Home: 3494 Jackson St, San Francisco, Cal. Office: State Bldg, 350 McAllister St, San Francisco, Cal.

TOBY, Jackson, US, sociologist, educator; b. NYC, Sep 10, 1925; s. Phineas and Anna (Weissman); BA, Bklyn Coll, 1946; MA, econ, Harvard U, 1947, MA, sociol, 1949, PhD, 1950; m. Marcia Lifshitz, Aug 1, 1952; c: Alan, Gail. Prof, sociol, chmn of dept, Rutgers U; cons, youth devl prog, Ford Found, 1959-63. USN, WW II. Mem: Amer Sociol Soc; E Sociol Soc; ACLU; ADA; AAUP. Author: Sociological Studies in Scale Analysis, 1954; Social Problems in America: Costs and Casualties in an Acquisitive Society, 1960; Contemporary Society, 1964; contbr to sociol and criminological jours. Home: 17 Harrison Ave, Highland Park, NJ. Office: Rutgers U, New Brunswick, NJ.

TOLEDANO, J R, Morocco, industrialist; b. Tangier, Morocco, July 5, 1906; s. Raphael and Rachel; desc, Rabbi Daniel Toledano, chief rabbi, Spain, 1492; m. Rosette Benacerraf, Jan 12, 1949; c: Raphael, Rachel. Pres: Conserveries de la Gironde, Agadir, since 1934; Cooperative Marocaine de la Conserve, Casablanca, since 1954; vice-pres, Morocco Fed of Canners. Pres, Moroccan br, WJC, 1946-60; fmr mem, bd, J Comty of Casablanca; active mem, J philantropic orgs, Casablanca, since 1929. Home: Villa Rosette, Allee des Buttes, Casablanca, Morocco. Office: 37 rue Ait Ba-Amrane, Casablanca, Morocco.

TOLEDANO, Meyer, Morocco, attorney; b. Casablanca, Morocco, July 13, 1918; s. Isaac; Licence en droit, Fac of Law, U Bordeaux, Fr; dipl, law and admn studies, Morocco. Pvt practice, law, Casablanca, since 1943; dir, cabinet, Min of Natl Econ, Morocco, 1956-57; head, govt missions: to London, 1957; to Havana, 1959; temp dep gov, Fonds Monetaire Intl, New Delhi, 1958; econ counselor, Embs of Morocco, Paris and Wash, DC, 1957-59; vice-pres, munic council, Casablanca, 1960; counselor, Min for Fgn Affairs, 1959-61. Vice-pres, ORT, Morocco, 1959; active in J youth orgs, 1949-55; pres: Alliance-Sports; treas, La Goutte de Lait, 1961. Office: Passage Tazi, Casablanca, Morocco.

TOLKOWSKY, Dan, Isr, business exec, military off; b. Tel Aviv, Jan 17, 1921; s. Samuel and Anne (Goldberg); BSc, ACGI, London, 1941; m. Miriam Beitner, Nov 18, 1948; c: Ronnie, Gideon, David. Mgn dir, Discount Bank Inves Corp, since 1965, exec mgr and dir, 1961-65; fmr: mech engr, research dept, Inst of Automobile Engrs, London; produc engr, research dept, Inst of Automobile Engrs, London; produc engr, Structural and Mech Devl Engrs Ltd, Slough, Eng; exec mgr, Isr Inves and Finance Corp, Tel Aviv, 1959-61. Flight-lt, RAF, WW II; chief-of-staff, IAF, 1951-53, commanding off, brig-gen, 1953-58, maj-gen, res. Asso mem, Brit Inst of Mgmt. Home: 22 Asael St, Zahala, Tel Aviv, Isr. Office: Discount Bank Inves Corp, POB 1688, Tel Aviv, Isr.

TOLMAS, Hyman C, US, pediatrician; b. New Orleans, La, Feb 1, 1922, s. Charles and Cecile (Bressler); BS, Tulane U, 1943, MD, Sch of Med, 1945; m. Constance Cohen, June, 1950; c: Jean, Alan. Pvt practice since 1946; chief, ped sect, Mercy Hosp, since 1957; coord, ped sect, Hotel Dieu Hosp, since 1958, chief sect, 1957-58; sr ped, Touro Infirmary, since 1958; sr visiting ped, Charity Hosp, since 1950, mem staff since 1951; clinical asst prof, ped, Tulane U Sch of Med, all New Orleans. Lt, USNR, Med Corps, 1946-48. Dipl, Amer Bd Ped; f, Amer Phys F Comm of IMA; found, past pres, New Orleans Ped Soc; mem: New Orleans Grad Med Assembly; Orleans Parish Med Soc; La State Ped Soc, past secy; La State Med Soc; AMA; Amer Acad Ped. Contbr to med jours. Hobby: golf. Home: 466 Crystal St, New Orleans, La. Office: 2049 Metairie Rd, New Orleans, La.

TOMARIN, Adelle, Can, communal leader; b. Toronto, Can, Jan 21, 1919, d. Morris and Sarah (Saliter) Slepkov; m. Harry Tomarin, Nov 23, 1939; c: Larry, Seymour. Mem, bd dirs: Toronto Wfr Council; B'nai B'rith Women, fmr pres, dist 22; chmn, Ontario comty services, Can J Cong. Hobby: painting. Home: 18 De Cou Rd, St Catharines, Can.

TOMER, Ben Zion, Isr, poet, govt official; b. Pol, 1928; s. Arie and Sara (Weissmann) Teitelbaum; in Isr since 1943; att Heb U, 1955; m. Ruth Rinzler; c: Ran. Councilor, Off of Dep PM, since 1969; lectr, various kibbutzim sems; ed, Masa, Lamerhav newspaper, 1954-55; cultural councilor, Isr Emb, Brazil, 1966-68. Served IDF. Author: Nahar Chozer, 1957; Derech haMelech; Al Kav haMashve, 1969; Yaldei haTzel, play, performed by Habimah Theatre. Recipient, awards: Baratz, 1963; ACUM, 1968. Home: 182 Ibn Gvirol St, Tel Aviv, Isr.

TOPIOL, Meilich, Fr, manufacturer; b. Stosov, Pol, July 18, 1910; s. Moise and Rose (Segal); c: Simon, Louise. Pres, Topiol Frères et Cie. Pres: Independent Zionist Org; exec, UJA, Fr; JA, Fr. Mem, clandestine comm, J Defense, during occupation, WW II. Home: 139 rue de Longchamps, Paris 16, Fr. Office: 24 rue de la Voie des Bancs, Argenteuil, Val d' Oise, Fr.

TORCZYNER, Harry, US, attorney; b. Antwerp, Belgium, Nov 8, 1910; s. Numa and Rosa (Weisslitz); LLD, Brussels U, 1933; LLB, Columbia U, 1943; m. Marcelle Siva, June 6, 1939; c: Evelyne, Denise. Pvt practice since 1946; gen counsel: Amer-Isr C of C and Ind; Diamond Trade Assn of Amér; Govt of Ivory Coast; Govt of Sierra Leone; fmr: cons, OWI, 1944, mem, rev bd, 1942-45; spec counsel, JA for Pal, at UN Spec Assembly, 1947. Chmn, comm on comparative law, Fed Bar Assn, NY, NJ, Conn, since 1953; mem, natl exec, ZOA, since 1949; exec mem, AZC, since 1949; Amer-Isr Comm, since 1954; vice-chmn, NY State Joint Leg Comm on Narcotic Study, 1957-59. Author: Miettes, 1952; Forgery in Art and the Law, 1956; Coin De Désert, 1958; contbr to law jours. Office: 521 Fifth Ave, New York, NY.

TORCZYNER, Jacques, US, business exec; b. Antwerp, Belgium, July 8, 1914; s. Numa and Rachel (Weisslitz); in US since 1940; Ing Commercial, Brussels U, Solvay Institute, 1935; m. Berthe Pintel, Sep 15, 1938; c: Ernest, Robert. Gen mgr, Rassco Isr Corp, since 1967, dir of devl, 1961-67; in diamond trade, 1940-59. Pres, ZOA, since 1965, chmn, natl exec council, 1962-65; found, vice-pres, World Union of Gen Zionists, since 1957; mem, presidium, World Zionist Actions Comm, since 1956; found, mem bd, Amer-Isr C of C, since 1952; delg, WZCs, 1946, 1951, 1956, 1960, 1964, 1968. Home: 124 W 79 St, New York, NY. Office: 535 Madison Ave, New York, NY.

TORCZYNER, Joshua, US, merchant; b. Vienna, Aus, Sep 29, 1910; s. Eisig and Sarah (Wolfgang); in US since 1941; m. Juana Spitzer, Jan 9, 1940; c: Jerome, Judith. Owner, Pacific Diamond Co, since 1948; wholesale jewelry salesman, newspaper writer, Vienna, 1929-38. Underground leader, J youth work, Belgium, 1940-41. Chmn: Bay Area Zionist Council, since 1967; Maccabi, Aus region, 1938-39, dir, World Maccabi Aid Comm, Switz, 1939-40; pres: SF HaKoah, 1964, found, 1945, hon pres since 1951; SF dist, ZOA, Nordau dist, 1950-51; Chess Friends of N Cal; N Cal Soccer Football Assn; Louis D Brandeis House, 1956; vice-pres: AZC; US Maccabi Assn, NY 1942-43; SF chap, JNF, 1954-55; co-found, J Refugee Org, Havana, Cuba 1941; repr, Vienna J Comty to Zionist Cong. Pub and ed, Pacific Diamond Lore mag. Home: 3003 Hillside Dr, Burlingame, Cal. Office: 760 Market St, San Francisco, Cal.

TORCZYNER, Moses, US, business exec; b. Vienna, Aus, May 25, 1905; s. Eisig and Sarah (Markin); in US since 1941; desc of Moses Cordovero, Kabbalist of the 16th cent; m. Martha Bergmann, Feb 28, 1937; c:Even, Jimmy. Pres, M Torczyner & Co, Inc, since 1956. Vice-pres, ZOA, pres, Manhattan reg, natl chmn: educ, Heb programming; bd mem, UJA; Amer Assn for J Educ; JNF; mem: Histadrut Ivrit; Hadoar; Friends of Heb U; Amer-Isr C of C. Home: 15 W 47 St, New York, NY. Office: 576 Fifth Ave, New York, NY.

TOREN, Eli, Isr, rabbi; b. Cologne, Ger, 1920; in Isr since 1951; att Heide Yeshiva, Belgium; ordained rabbi, Ostrova Yeshiva, Czech, 1939; att Us: Ger; Fr; Switz; Queens Coll, NY; m. Kitty Frank, May 12, 1950; c: Tanya-Tehila; Eitan Avraham. Dir, spec assignments, Min Rel Affairs, 1952-63, and since 1965; dir-gen, Keren Yaldenu Org, since 1955; fmr: head, Bnei Akiva, Switz, 1945; org, youth wfr dept in ref camps; tchr, youth orgs, Switz, 1948-49; dir, immigration, JA, Cen Amer, 1963-65; repr, reconstruction J quarter, old city Jerusalem, 1967; Mem, Fr underground forces, WW II, smuggled J children from concentration camps to Switz. Mem, PM comm for Black Panther problems. Home: 1 Balfour St, Jerusalem, Isr. Office: Min of Rel, Jerusalem. Isr.

TOREN, Haim, Isr, author, publishing exec; b. Dumbraveni, Bessarabia, Aug 18, 1913; s. Aaron and Rachel (Weisser); in Isr since 1933; MA, Heb U, 1937; m. Puah Shalev, Nov 4, 1952; c: Ron. Dir, The Magnes Press, Heb U, since 1949; broadcaster on lit topics. Mem: Govt Film Censorship Bd; comm for approval of visiting artists from abroad; exec bd: Heb Writers Assn; Heb PEN Cen in Isr, ed, bulletin. Author: Sifrutenu haYafa meBialik ad Yamenou, 3 vols, 1944-54; Shirei Ahava beIsrael, 1948; Beth Aba, 1955; beZel Ganim, 1960; monographs: MM Dolitzky; AK Shapiro; JK Kantor; MZ Mane; Prof J Klausner; ed: Iturim, 1948; Sifrei Mophet, 1951; Yerushalayim biYtzirat haDorot, 1951. Hobby: music. Home: 19 Shmaryahu Levin St, Jerusalem, Isr. Office: The Magnes Press, Heb U, Jerusalem, Isr.

TOREN-FRANK, Kitty, Isr, flower painter; b. Amsterdam, Holland, Nov 6, 1922; d. Isaac and Sara (Deleeuwe); in Isr since 1951; att Ind Sch, Zurich; BA, MA, Bezalel Sch of Art, Jerusalem; att St Carols Academia, Mex; m. Eli Toren; c: Tanya, Etan. Flower painter, Heb U, Jerusalem; painter: Old City, Jerusalem; murals for youth cens. Dutch underground, helped save children from Gestapo, 1940-45. Fmr dir, Haachshara for Isr Pioneers, Holland. Author: Flora Palestina, 1966; textbooks. Home: 10 Balfour St, Jerusalem, Isr.

TORRES, Henry, Fr, attorney, legislator; b. Les Andelys, Fr, Oct 17, 1891; s. Fernard and Berthe (Levaillant); licencié en droit, U of Paris, 1911; div; c: Jean, George (decd). Pvt practice, law, since 1948; visiting prof, law fac, Université Francaise, NYC, since 1945; fmr: dep, Alpes-Maritimes, 1932-36; vice-pres, fgn affairs comm, Chambre des Députés, 1933; prof, law fac: U of Rio de Janeiro; U of São Paulo; both 1940-41; dir, France-Amérique, 1942-46; vice-pres, Haute Cour de Justice, 1954; pres, sup council, Radio-TV Francaise, 1958-59; pres, Soc Intl de Diffusion de l'Audio-Vision; senator for the Seine, 1948-58. War Service, 1914-18. Author: Le Procès des Pogroms, 1928; France, Terre de Liberté, 1939; Pierre Laval, 1941; La Machine Infernale, 1943, Accusés Hors Série; de Clemenceau â de Gaulle. Recipient: Croix de Guerre, Mil medal, both 1918; Médaille de la France libre, 1945. Home: 35 Ave Hoche, Paris 8, Fr.

TORY, Avraham, Isr, advocate; b. Lith, Dec 10, 1909; s. Zoruch and Sara (Prusak) Golub; in Isr since 1947; BJ Kaunas U, Lith; m. Pnina Ushpitz, Aug 8, 1945; c: Shulmit Karby, Alina, Zila. Pvt practice, advocate since 1952, notary since 1962. Co-found, mem exec, MAKOZ, Zionist underground, Ghetto Kovno, secy, J comm of Ghetto, 1941-44; mem delg: Anglo-Amer Inquiry comm, It; to PM of It; to Chief of Allied Command, It, all 1946; secy-gen, Merkaz Lagola, illegal immigration cen; segen, IDF, chief, mil atty unit, 1955-64. Vice-chmn, cen elections comm, Knesset; chmn, fgn relations comm, Independent Lib Party; mem: presidium, Zionist World Action comm; council, Israeli Bar, vice-chmn, pension fund, 1958-67; OTZMA council, Bank Leumi leIsr; comm, Intl Maccabi Games; Maccabi Village; council, Isr-It Friendship League; pres, Herzl lodge, B'nai B'rith; fmr: WZCs; org comm, 1st World Cong of J Lawyers and Jurists, Isr, 1969; exec mem, Fgn Advocates Org in Isr; mem, World Zionist Court of Honor, 1955-64; co-found, Holocaust Memorial, Kibbutz Tel-Ytz; vice-chmn, Hanoar Hazioni, Lith, 1929-41. Author: The Escape from the Ninth Fort, 1958; Maccabi the World Over, 1958-60; Rosh Galuta, in Eichal Sheshaka, 1963; ed, Al Hupim, monthly ref publ, 1946-47; contbr to mags in Isr, Lith, It. Special interests: sports, J and Zionist affairs. Home: 17 Nerdaa St, Tel Aviv, Isr. Office: 61 Yehuda Halevi St, Tel Aviv, Isr.

TOSK, Morris Max, US, rabbi; b. Paterson, NJ, June 26, 1924; s. Solomon and Eva (Damsky); BBA, Pace Coll, 1949; BHL, MHL, ordained rabbi, HUC-JIR, 1958; m. Anita Finkelstein, Jan 25, 1948; c: Stephen, Nadine, Shari. Rabbi, Temple Beth Am, since 1954; Heb tchr: Paterson, NJ, 1946-49; and youth dir, Pottsville, Pa, 1949-53; dep reg dir, B'nai B'rith, 1952-53. Cpl, US Army, 1943-46. Mem: CCAR; NY Bd of Rabbis;

NY Fed of Reform Rabbis; Essex Co Bd of Rabbis; NJ Assn of Reform Rabbis; NAACP; Comty Chest; Cmty Day Nursery; Kiwanis; fmr: chmn, Mayor's Commn on Civil Rights, 1963-64; treas, Combined Clergy of Bayonne, 1958-61. Recipient: dist service citation, B'nai B'rith, 1960; cert of recognition, NCCJ, Bayonne, 1966; comty relations award, AJCong, Bayonne, 1966. Home: 120 W 43 St, Bayonne, NJ. Study: 111 Ave B, Bayonne, NJ.

TOUREL, Jennie, US, mezzo-soprano, concert and opera; b. June 18, 1910; in US since 1941; educated in Fr and Switz. Fac mem, vocal dept, Juilliard Sch of Music, since 1963; tours throughout US and Can, since 1942; opera debut as Carmen, Opera Comique, Paris, 1933; concert debut with Toscanini, NY Philharmonic, 1942; joined Metrop Opera, 1944; soloist with all maj US and Can sym orchs; debut, Teatro Munic, Rio de Janeiro, 1944; toured S Amer; debut, London, 1947; debut, Isr, 1949; toured S Afr, 1954; Aspen Festival, 1957; toured Japan, 1961; appeared on Mt Scopus, first concert after liberation, conductor, Leonard Bernstein, 1967; recorded for: Columbia, Odyssey. Lang repertory: Fr, It, Russ, Ger, Eng, Port, Pol, Heb. Recipient: Chevalier, Order of Arts and Letters, Fr, 1967. Office: c/o, Sheldon Soffer Mgmt, 130 W 56 St, New York, NY.

TOURKOW, Frederick Reinhold, US, attorney; b. Smyrna, Turkey, Sep 6, 1918; s. Samuel and Sophia (Margolis-Kalvariski); in US since 1920; att U Dayton, 1936; LLB, Georgetown U, 1939, LLM, 1940; m. Leah Schwartz, Jan 17, 1943; c: Deborah, Joshua, Samuel. Mem, law firm: Tourkow, Danehy and Crell, since 1964; Tourkow, Dennis and Danehy, 1955-64; Tourkow and Dennis, 1951-55; chmn bd, secy, Gerberhaus Motor Hotel Inc, and Gerber-haus Restaurant Inc, since 1958; found, bd mem: Gt Northern Life Ins Co, Ft Wayne, since 1953; pres, Northern Imperial Corp, since 1958; pres, New Haven Wire and Cable Co, since 1958; Heinold Elevator Co, Inc, since 1958; secy. William A Braun; Ft Wayne Wilbert Vault Works, Inc, since 1948; fmr: asso, Miller and Meyring, 1940-46; mem, Frankenstein and Tourkow, 1946; pvt practice, 1947-51. Maj, USAAF, 1944-45. Bd mem, Ft Wayne J Fed, since 1960, pres, 1966-68; secy, natl exec comm, JWV, since 1968; chmn natl ins comm, 1958-59; dir, Natl Shrine to the J War Dead, since 1966; delg: All-Amer Conf to Combat Communism, 1958; Natl Comty Relations Adv Council, 1962; mem: Cong B'nai Jacob, pres, 1950-52; Masons, 32 deg, Scottish Rite; B'nai B'rith; ZOA; Georgetown U Alumni Assn; Fraternal Order of the Police; VFW; Amer Legion; Amer Judicature Soc; Amer, O State, Ind State and Allen Co Bar Assns; Izaak Walton League; Law-Sci Acad of Amer; Commercial Law League; Travelers' Protective Assn; Ft Wayne C of C; VA Volunteer Service Comm; Natl Armed Services comm; Amer-J Tercentenary Comm, 1954; clubs: Ft Wayne Press; Optimist. Recipient: 3 battle stars; Bronze Star; Meritorious Service award. Home: 5616 Old Mill Road, Fort Wayne, Ind. Office: 814 Anthony Wayne Bank Bldg, Fort Wayne, Ind.

TOUROVER, Denise, US, communal worker; b. New Iberia, La, May 16, 1903; d. Leopold and Blanche (Coguenhem) Levy; LLB, George Wash U, Law Sch, 1924; m. Raphael Tourover, Nov 14, 1926; c: Blanche Medelle Berenson. Repr, natl bd, Hadassah, Wash, DC, liaison off for negotiations with US govt agcys, since 1940, mem, natl bd, since 1939, natl vice-pres, 1946-50, life mem, natl hon council, since 1959, pres: Wash chap, 1936-39, Seaboard reg, 1939-41; mem, actions comm, WZO, since 1956; delg, WZC, 1939, and since 1946; mem, exec comm, JCC, Gtr Wash, since 1940; natl exec, women's div, UJA, 1958; mem: Amer and DC Bar Assns; B'nai B'rith; League of Women Voters; Amer Assn for the UN; NCCJ; sisterhood, Adas Israel Cong; Natl Civil Liberties Clearing House; Phi Sigma Sigma, natl pres, 1953-58; Delta Sigma Rho. Hobby: coin collecting. Recipient: cert for service, Amer Food for Peace Council, The White House, 1965; award, Natl Council Women, 1968. Home: 1884 Columbia Rd, NW, Washington, DC. Offices: Munsey Bldg, NW, Washington, DC; Hadassah, 65 E 52 St, New York, NY.

TOURY, Jacob, Isr, educator; b. Beuthen, Ger. Jan 5, 1915; s. Max and Meta (Freund) Koenigsberger; MA, Heb U, 1940, PhD, summa cum laude, 1960; m. Eva Aron, Aug 10, 1941; c: Gideon, Irith, Erman. Sr lectr, modern J hist, Tel Aviv U, since 1962; tchr, asst prin, Haifa Tech HS, Technion, 1938-61; lectr: Haifa U Coll, 1954-61; Technion, 1958-61; didactics, Heb U, 1961-64. Lt, IDF, 1948-49. Author: Die Politischen Orientierungen der Juden in Deutschland, 1966; Turmoil Confusion in the Revolution of 1848, pub 1968; contbr to textbooks, scholarly jours. Home: Herzliya, Isr. Office: Tel Aviv U, Tel Aviv, Isr.

TOUSSIA-COHEN, Leah, Isr, attorney; b. Saarbrucken, Ger, Apr 4, 1932; d. Arthur and Esther (Mecklemburg) Löwenherz; MJ, Heb U, 1955; widow; c: Tamar, Asnath. Chief asst, Haifa dist atty, since 1964. Sgt, IDF, 1950-52. Fmr, hon secy, La Societe Israeliene de Criminology, 1964-66, Home: 14 Kabirim St, Haifa, Isr. Office: Hassan Shukeri St, Haifa, Isr.

TOUSTER, Ben, US, communal leader; b. NYC, Apr 8, 1893; s. Oscar and Betty (Ehrlich); m. Bertha Landau, Feb 22, 1920; c: Irwin, Saul. Ret; fmr business exec, pres, Cinderella Hat Co, NYC, since 1919. US Army WW I. Chmn bd, CARE, since 1967, vice-pres, 1953-57, treas, 1957-67; hon vice-chmn, UJA, Gtr NY, since 1954, found, 1939; dir: Touro Syn Natl Historic Shrine; Alliance Israelite Universelle, Amer br, since 1953; exec bd, AJComm, since 1950; mem, bd govs, adv council, NY Bd of Rabbis; asso chmn bd, United Hias Service, since 1960, exec comm, since 1954, fmr pres; trustee: Maimonides Med Cen, Bklyn, vice-pres since 1958; FJP, NY, since 1945; J Home and Hosp Aged, NY, since 1952; mem: natl council, JDC; natl council, JTSA; hon pres, YM and YMHA, Boro Park, since 1955, pres, 1949-55; hon trustee, Temple Emanu-el, Boro Park, Bklyn; JWB pres club; HIAS, pres, 1952-54; CJFWF, dir, exec comm, 1953-59; Natl Conf J Communal Service; Amer Asso J Educ; lay mem, Brith Milah Bd, NY; clubs: Overseas Press; Advertising; Grand St Boys; mem: publ comm, Commentary, since 1950. Home: 41 Park Ave, New York, NY.

TOVIYAHU, David, Isr, communal leader; b. Zolkiev, Galicia, Nov 20, 1898; s. Joseph and Miriam (Landau) Taube; in Isr since 1920; att: Yeshiva, Zolkiew; Lwow U, Vienna, 1917-20; m. Lea Rotbart, Aug, 1926; c: Rina Dotan, Dan. Chmn of exec, U of Negev, since 1965; bd dirs, Chevrat Chashmal; fmr: farmer, Kibbutz Geva, 1922-27; mem, exec, Solel Boneh, 1950-63, building worker, 1930-49; mayor, co-found, devl, City of Beersheva. Club: Rotary. Haganah, 1921-48. Spec interests: archaeol, J hist, reading. Home: 2 Assaf Simhoni St, Beersheva, Isr. Office: U of Negev, Beersheva, Isr.

TOW, Abraham, US, pediatrician, educator; b. NYC, May 12, 1899; s. Harris and Anna (Gold); att: CCNY, 1915-17; Columbia U, 1917-19; MD, Tulane U, 1921; m. Elsa Robison, Dec 27, 1925; c: William. Chief of peds, Guyan Valley Hosp, since 1960; clinical prof, peds, NY Polyclinic Med Sch, 1937-57; asso ped, NY Polyclinic Hosp, 1937-58. Pvt, US Army, WW I, lt col, WW II. Mem: W Va Ped Soc; AMA; NY Acad of Med; Amer Acad of Peds; Amer Med Workers Assn; Amer Vets Comm; Soc of Amer Wars. Author: Diseases of Newborn, 1937; contbr to med jours. Office: Guyan Valley Hosp, Logan, W Va.

TRAGER, Bernard H, US, lawyer, govt official; b. New Haven, Conn, July 18, 1906; s. Harry and Ida (Ruttenberg); LLB, NYU, 1928; m. Mina Rubenstein, Aug 25, 1929; c: Roberta Cohen, Philip. Mem, Trager, Kleban and Trager; in pvt practice since 1929. Chmn, Conn Bd of Pardons, since 1959; trustee, Peoples Saving Bank, since 1964; dir, Bridgeport Hosp, since 1970; mem, gov's comm on criminal admn, since 1967; dir, Title Guarantee Fund; mem: financial adv comm, City of Bridgeport; bd dir: Conn State Prison; Conn Bd of Parole; pres: Bridgeport Bar Assn, 1959-61; Conn Bar Assn, 1964-65; mem, house of delgs, Amer Bar Assn, 1965-66; pres, Conn Conf of Social Work, 1948-49; mem: Bridgeport JCC, 1944-46; NE region, CJFWF, 1952-54; mem, natl bd dirs, CJFWF, 1954-61; chmn, Natl Comty Relations Adv Council, 1953-57; mem, bd dirs, NYU Law Alumni Assn, 1958-62; vice-pres, AJCong, 1958-60; chmn, Mayor's Comm Human Rights, Bridgeport, 1958-62; asso chmn, Amer J Tercentenary Comm, 1953-54; trustee: Natl Health and Retirement Assn, 1955-68; Cong Rodelph Sholom, 1953-57; mem, natl exec council, United Syn of Amer, 1957-59; bd dirs, United HIAS Service, 1956-58; pres, bd asso, U Bridgeport, 1964-66; gov's comm on DP's, Conn, 1947-50; clubs: Algonquin; Birchwood Country; NYU; Natl Lawyers. Home: 25 Cartright St, Bridgeport, Conn. Office: 955 Main St, Bridgeport, Conn.

TRAGER, Frank N, US, educator; b. NYC, Oct 9, 1905; s. Benjamin and Eda (Schapiro); BS, NYU, 1927, MA, 1928, PhD, 1951; m. Helen Gilbson, Oct 9, 1936. Prof, intl relations, NYU, since 1953; instr, phil, John Hopkins U, 1928-34; research asst, Amer Coll of Learned Socs, 1931-34; field surveys, resettlement admn, and lab relations, US Govt, 1934-38;

exec, AJComm, 1938-43; asst to pres, NCCJ, 1945-46; prog dir, ADL, 1946-51; dir, Tech Coop Admn, Point Four prog, Burma, 1951-53; Carnegie Research f, Council on Fgn Relations, 1957-58; visiting prof: Yale U, 1960-61; Natl War Coll, 1961-63. USAAC, 1934-45. Secy, Baltimore J Unity Comm, 1933-34; fmr bd mem: Inst of Intl Lab Research; Assn for Asian Studies; Inst of Pacific Relations; mem: Amer Political Sci Assn; Council on Fgn Relations; Asia Soc; club, NYU Fac. Author: Building a Welfare State in Burma, 1954, 2nd ed, 1958; Why Viet Nam?, 1966; Burma, From Kingdom to Republic, 1966; co-author: Burma, 1956; Burma's Role in the UN, (1948-55), 1956; Marxism and Southeast Asia, 1959; Why Federations Fail, 1968. Recipient: Butler f, phil, 1927-28. Office: Wash Sq Coll, NYU, New York, NY.

TRAGER, Gerry Amelia, US, business exec, communal leader; b. Hartsville, SC, May 22, 1920; d. Joseph and Frances (Morninstar) Levkoff; m. Leo Trager, Mar 31, 1946; c: Helen, Janet. Secy-treas, Custom Hall, since 1958; fmr profsl singer, 1938-46. Pres: Key Women; Fairfield Co chap, womens div, Amer Soc for Technion; mem: bd dirs, J Family Service; womens auxiliary, Park City Hosp; B'nai B'rith; Hadassah; fmr: vice-pres, United J Council, 1965-67; chmn, United J Campaign, 1951-69; pres: J Women's Service League, 1953-54; J Fed Women's Clubs of Gtr Bridgeport, 1962-65; bd govs, J Cmty Cen; regional chmn: ADL; Americanism and Civic Affairs, B'nai B'rith; bd: Cmty Chest and Council of Gtr Bridgeport; chmn , Mother's March of Dimes; mem, mayor's comm, housing for underprivileged. Hobbies: music, art, golf. Home: 188 Skytop Dr, Fairfield, Conn. Office: 105 Meadow St, Fairfield, Conn.

TRAGER, Jesse, US, dentist; b. Baltimore, Md, May 24, 1911; s. Harry and Minnie (Sussman); DDS, U of Md Dent Sch, 1934; m. Rose Hecht, June 13, 1937; c: Alan, Mark, Frances. Ret from pvt practice; fmr: dir, outpatient dept, Sinai Hosp and Mt Pleasant Hosp; owner and dir, Camp Woodbine. Dist chief, youth mobilization prog, civil defense, WW II. Fmr pres: Menorah lodge and Dist Grand lodge 5, B'nai B'rith; Md-DC Assn of B'nai B'rith Lodges; Md sect, Amer Camping Assn; mem: Baltimore J Council; Baltimore, Md State, and Amer Dent Assns; Amer Acad of Dent Med; Amer Soc for Children's Dent; Amer Assn of Endodontists; Amer Acad of Dent Hist; Royal Soc of Health, Eng; Pierre Fauchard Acad; Alumni Assn, Baltimore Coll of Dent Surg; Alpha Omega, fmr intl pres; Alumni Assn, Sch of Dent, U Md, fmr natl treas; Masons. Recipient: meritorious service award Alpha Omega, 1948; legion of honor, Natl B'nai B'rith Youth Comm, 1950. Home: RD 1, Woodbine, Md.

TRAGER, Seymour, US, certified public acctnt, attorney; b. Bklyn, NY, Jan 19, 1924; s. Max and Mary (Goldstein); BBA, CCNY, 1946; JD, St John's U, 1949; m. Joan Schwartz, Mar 27, 1948; c: Marlene, Barbara, Michael. Partner, Ferber & Trager, attys and CPAs, since 1949. Staff sgt, USAAC, 1942-45. Chmn, fund-raising, Temple Torah, secy, pres, men's club; ADL repr, B'nai B'rith, Queens Co; mem: Masons, Brandeis lodge; Amer Inst CPAs; NY State Soc CPAs; Amer Inst of Attys-CPAs; Tax Study Group of NYU. Recipient: unit citation, 6 battle stars, WW II; outstanding service, Temple Torah, 1966; man of the year, Isr Bond Drive, Little Neck-Douglaston Comty, 1970. Home: 57-16 263 St, Little Neck, NY. Office: 511 Fifth Ave, New York, NY.

TRAMER, Hasn, Isr, organization exec, editor; b. Silesia, Ger; s. Wilhelm and Irma (Altmann); in Isr since 1933; PhD, U Breslau; ordained rabbi, J Theol Sem, Breslau; m. Antonie Schattner. Gen secy, ed, "MB", Wochenzeitung des Irgun Olei Merkaz Europa; ed: Bull of Leo Baeck Inst; Robert Weltsch anthol, 1961; In Zwei Welten, Sigfried Moses anthol, 1962; Kurt Blumenfeld Memoirs, 1962; contbr to publs adv bd, United Restitution Org; bd, Isr sect, Leo Baeck Inst. Home: 23 Pinsker St, Tel Aviv, Isr. Office: 15 Rambam St, Tel Aviv, Isr.

TRANIN, Earl J, US, business exec; b. Russia, July 15, 1897; s. Bennett and Rebecca (Esrig); in US since 1903; m. Leona Kessler, May 26, 1918; c: Shirley Morantz, Marian Shultz, Donald. Pres, Paper Supply Co, since 1918. Fmr: pres, Heart of Amer Paper Trade Assn, 1956-58; mem, bd dir, Natl Paper Trade Assn, 1951-59; regional chmn, paper ind, NRA, 1934; dollar-a-year man, Surplus Commodities Corp, 1945-46; chmn, cen budget comm, J Fed and Council of Gtr Kans City, chmn, campaign cabinet, pres, 1947-49; gen campaign chmn, 1949, 1954; mem: natl campaign cabinet, UJA; bd,

CJWF; Kehilath Isr Syn, pres, 1944-48; bldg trustee and bd mem, J Comty Cen; chmn bd, Menorah Med Cen; bldg trustee and bd mem, J Family and Children Service; mem, bd of trustees, Rockhurst Coll; all Kan City; mem: B'nai B'rith; Masons, past master. Home: 6400 Ward Pkwy, Kansas City, Mo. Office: 2915 Southwest Blvd, Kansas City, Mo.

TRAUB, Fredrick B, US, microbiologist; b. Czech, Sep 5, 1911; s. Arthur and Bertha (Levitus); in US since 1943; MD, Charles U, Prague, 1936, DPH, 1938; m. Ella Baumgartl, Mar 29, 1939. Dir, blood bank and chief, div of microbiol, J Hosp of Bklyn, since 1950, with hosp since 1943; research f, Cambridge U, Eng, 1940-43; asst clinical path, Addenbrooke's Hosp, Cambridge, 1942-43. Czech Army, 1936-39. Pres, Sagamore Lake Civic Assn; f, Coll of Amer Paths; mem: AMA; NY Co Med Soc; Amer Assn of Immunologists; Soc of Amer Microbiols; Soc for Gen Microbiol. Home: RFD 2, Carmel, NY. Offices: J Hosp of Bklyn, 555 Prospect Pl, Brooklyn, NY; 405 E 72 St, New York, NY.

TRAUM, Eliahu Eduard, US, educator; b. Vienna, Aus, July 1, 1924; s. Eisig and Cypre (Kuttenplan); in US since 1965; BSc, dipl Ing, Technion, Haifa, 1948, MSc, 1950, DSc, MIT, 1957; m. Shoshanna Goldfinger, Nov 11, 1947; c: Rivka, Dorit, Ruth. Prof, construction, Harvard U, since 1968, dir, tech prog, Grad Sch of Design, since 1968; sr lectr, Technion, 1958-65; prin, E Traum & Asso, 1958-65. Mem, Intl Assn Shell Structures; fmr mem: bd govs, Technion; planning bd, Haifa Munic. Contbr to profsl jours. Recipient: 4th prize, intl competition, Lincoln Inst, 1967. Home: 227 Mason Terr, Brookline, Mass. Office: Harvard U, Cambridge, Mass.

TRAURIG, Max R, US, attorney; b. Newark, NJ, May 3, 1898; s. William and Nettie (Raydner); BA, Yale U, 1920, LLB, 1923. Pvt practice since 1923; dir, Waterbury Natl Bank, since 1949. Col, US Army, 1941-45. Mem, bd trustees, Conn State comty, Reg Comty Colls, since 1965; pres, The Waterbury Found, since 1968, dir since 1959; vice-pres: NE reg AJComm, since 1960, chmn, Waterbury unit, since 1960, mem, natl exec bd, since 1961; J Home for Children, since 1952; Comty Workshop, since 1955; Child Guidance Clinic; Gaylord Farm Hosp and Sanitarium, pres, 1956-60; Comty Council, 1954-60; Comty Chest, 1948-51; J Fed Appeal, 1947-54; Beth El Syn, 1925-41; ARC, 1948-52; AHA, 1954-57; Legal Aid Bur, 1956-57; corporate mem: The Waterbury Hosp, charter mem; Citizens for Gtr Waterbury, Inc; mem: Amer, Conn, and Waterbury Bar Assns; Friends of Yale Hillel; B'nai B'rith; Masons; Reserve Off Assn, fmr pres, Woodbury chap, fmr vice-pres, State of Conn; clubs: Yale, NY; Army and Navy, Wash, DC; Waterbury; Rotary, pres, 1952. Recipient: Bronze Star; Croix de Guerre with palm. Home: 174 Euclid Ave, Waterbury, Conn. Office: 111 W Main St, Waterbury, Conn.

TREIGER, Leah F, US, organization exec; b. Woodbine, NJ, June 14, 1907; d. Solomon and Golda (Yellin) Farber; BA, magna cum laude, U of Wash, Seattle, 1927; att: Grad Sch J Social Work, JTSA; NY Sch Social Work, Columbia U; Sch of J Studies, JTSA, 1955-57; m. 1st, Baruch Treiger (decd); m. 2nd, Samuel Schimmel, 1961. Exec dir, Natl Women's League, United Syn of Amer, since 1962, mem, natl bd, natl field dir, 1955-62; dir, womens-c dept, Neighborhood House, Portland, Ore, 1927-29; sr caseworker, J Family Service, NYC, 1930-33; exec dir: J Big Sisters, Toronto, 1934-36; Council Soc Agcys, Travelers Aid, Tacoma, 1939-42. Fmr: pres, Hadassah, Portland, Ore, educ chmn, Toronto; mem: B'nai B'rith Women; Pioneer Women; League of Women Voters; Council of Social Agcys; Council of J Women; Mayor's Comm for Youth; Councils of Syn and Church Women, Ore; Wash; Nev; NJ; Pa; Phi Beta Kappa. Hobbies: J arts and crafts; travel. Home: 90 La Salle St, New York, NY. Office: 3080 Broadway, New York, NY.

TREIMAN, Israel, US, attorney; b. Odessa, Russ, June 2, 1900; s. Marcus and Dora (Neidenburg); in US since 1906; MA, Wash U, 1922, LLB, 1924; PhD, Oxford U, 1927; m. Jeanne Fredlob, Dec 20, 1935; c: Ruth, Ellen. Pvt practice since 1944; prof, law, Wash U, 1930-40; chief atty, OPA, US govt, 1940-42, hearing commnr, 1942-44. Chmn, drafting comm, constitutional amendment on judical selection, St Louis Bar, 1940; pres, Lib Forum of St Louis, 1956-57. Mem: Order of the Coif; Phi Beta Kappa; club: Columbian, pres, 1947. Contbr to legal jours. Recipient: Rhodes Scholarship, Oxford U, 1927. Home: 11 Crestwood Dr, Clayton, Mo. Office: 611 Olive St, St Louis, Mo.

TREIMAN, Sam Bard, US, physicist, educator; b. Chicago, Ill, May 27, 1925; s. Abraham and Sarah (Bard); att Northwestern U, 1942-44; SB, SM, PhD, U Chgo, 1946-52; m. Joan Little, Dec 26, 1952; c: Rebecca, Katherine, Thomas. Prof, physics, Princeton U, since 1963, on fac since 1952. USN, 1944-46. Mem, Amer Phys Soc. Contbr to profsl jours. Home: McCosh Circle, Princeton, NJ. Office: Princeton U, Princeton, NJ.

TREISTER, Leizer, US, teacher, author; b. Opatov, Pol, Apr 15, 1905; s. Samuel and Chanah (Alter); in US since 1937; m. Fannie Stitsky, July 2, 1932; c: Rochelle. Tchr, Yiddish lit and hist, Sholem Aleichem Inst, NYC, since 1937; co-ed, Hemschech, NYC, 1939. Author: in di Shtile Teg, 1933; Ariber di Bregen, 1942; play, Der Pastech Kenig, 1955; contbr of short stories and essays in Yiddish to periodicals; trans, The Philosophy of Purpose, by Dr S Belkin, 1959. Recipient: 1st prize, for King Saul, 1949; prize, for Opshtam, Cong for J Culture, 1954. Mem, Farband; club: PEN. Home: 1466 49 St, Brooklyn, NY.

TRENCHER, Bernard, US, attorney; b. NYC, May 2, 1896; s. Pincus and Lena (Greenspan); LLB, NYU Law Sch, 1917; m. Bessie Gelula, July 4, 1922; c: Lenore Appelson, Phyllis Kraft. Pvt practice; spec referee, Supr Court, State of NY; examiner, bar admission, First Judicial dept. Govt appeal agt, Selective Service System, 1940-45. Fmr: chmn on judiciary, Bx Co Bar Assn; pres, YM-YWHA, Bx, dir; chmn, Bx Co Fed for Support of J Philanthropies Campaign, 1948, 1949; mem: NY State, Amer and NYC Bar Assns; Amer Judicature Soc; club: Briar Hall Golf and Country. Recipient: selective service medal, US Cong; citations: US Treas; ARC; Gtr NY Fund; NY War Fund; Civilian Defense Volunteer Off, all WW II; Felix M Warburg Memorial award, 50 years service, FJP. Home: 175 E 74 St, New York, NY. Office: 535 Fifth Ave, New York, NY.

TREPP, Leo, US, rabbi, educator; b. Mainz, Ger, Mar 4, 1913; s. Maier and Selma (Hirschberger); in US since 1940; PhD, U of Würzburg, 1935; ordained rabbi, Rabb Sem, Berlin, 1932-36; m. Miriam de Haas, Apr 26, 1938; c: Susan. Prof, phil and hum, Napa Coll, since 1951, dir, study travel, 1956-67; rabbi: Cong Beth Sholom, Napa, since 1962; Oldenburg, Ger, 1936-38; Greenfield, Mass, 1940-44; Somerville, Mass, 1944-46; Tacoma, Wash, 1946-48; Berkeley, Cal, 1948-51; J Comty Cen, Santa Rosa, Cal, 1951-61. Mem: Napa City Planning Commn, since 1964; senate adv, Napa Coll Adult Forums, since 1967; natl adv bd, Relations in Educ Found, 1956-66; Amer Phil Assn; RA; B'nai B'rith. Author: Taine, Montaigne, Richcome, 1935; Eternal Faith, Eternal People, A Journey Into Judaism, 1962; Die Landesgemeinde der Juden in Oldenburg, 1965 Judaism, Development, and Life, 1966; Das Judentum, Entwicklung und Lebensformen, 1969; contbr to J, phil, rel, and profsl jours. Hobbies: travel, music. Home: 295 Montecito Blvd, Napa, Cal. Office: Napa Coll, Napa, Cal.

TREPP, Walter, US, business exec; b. Witzenhausen, Ger, Sep 30, 1919; s. Isaac and Else (Wahlhaus); in US since 1938; m. Emily Nussbaum, Dec 26, 1948; c: Elaine, Sharon, Howard. Pres, Statolet Corp, since 1950. US Army, 1942-46. Pres, Cong Ahavath Thora; bd dirs: Moriah Sch; J Comty Cen; United J Fund; J Wfr Council, all Englewood. Home: 416 Gloucester, Englewood, NJ. Office: 63 71 St, Guttenberg, NJ.

TRETTER, Maxwell H, US, attorney, housing cons; b. NYC, Dec 3, 1905; s. Leon and Esther (Dicker); BA, Cornell U, 1927; LLB, Cornell Law Sch, 1929; m. Beatrice Dicker, Dec 24, 1929; c: Franklin, Flora. Pvt practice, 1930-34 and since 1947; chief counsel, Fed Public Works Admn, NY and all NE, 1934-38; asst corp counsel, NYC, 1938-40; exec dir, NYC Housing Auth, 1944-47, with auth since 1940; gen counsel, Natl Assn of Housing and Redevl Officials; lectr, housing, Columbia U, 1955-58; club: Cornell, NY. Recipient: scholarships: Leopold Schepp found, 1928; Boardman, 1929. Home: 62 Malvern Rd, Scarsdale, NY. Office: 485 Lexington Ave, New York, NY.

TREUHAFT, William C, US, business exec; b. Oct 21, 1892; att: Adelbert Coll; W Reserve U; MIT, 1910-14; hon degs: W Reserve U, 1958, Case Inst Tech, 1967; m. Elizabeth Marting, 1934. Chmn of bd: Armalux Glass Inds Ltd; bd dirs: Jamestown Finishes; Stonhard-Tremco Ltd; fmr: pres, Sterling Products Co, 1916-28; found, pres, Tremco Mfg Co, 1928-66. Lt, USNR aviation, WW I. Chmn: Case-W Reserve

U; natl comm, Council on Social Work Educ; endowment fund, J Comty Fed; visiting comm, Sch of Applied Social Sci; vice-chmn, Amer Mgmt Assn; pres, UA of Gtr Cleveland, 1966-67; bd trustees: Amer Fund for Dental Educ; Sunny Acres Hosp; Ursuline Coll for Women; steering comm, Cuyahoga Co Chronic Illness Cen; adv council, Cleveland Mus of Art; planning commn, Mt Sinai Hosp; mem: Cleveland Little Hoover Commn; The Temple; clubs: Oakwood Country; Mentor Harbor Yachting. Recipient: Charles Eisenman award, 1950; dist service award, Comty Chest, 1954; medal for public service, Cleveland C of C, 1958; pres achievement award, Case Inst of Tech, 1965; meritorious service award, United Comty Funds and Councils of Amer, 1967; outstanding service award, Cleveland Wfr Fed, 1967. Home: 19200 Shaker Blvd, Cleveland, O.

TREUMANN, Otto Heinrich, Netherlands, graphic designer, commercial artist; b. Fürth, Ger, Mar 28, 1919; s. Max and Babette (Besela); in Netherlands since 1935; att: Realgymnasium, Nuremberg, 1932-35; Amsterdam Graphic Sch, 1935-36; New Art Sch, Amsterdam, 1936-40; m. Jettie Van de Velde-Olivier, 1945; c: Rene Babette. Free-lance graphic designer, since 1945; adv, tchr, Bezalel Sch, Jerusalem, 1969. Mem, resistance movement, during Ger occupation, WW II. Bd dirs: JNF; Hachsharah and Aliyah, munic adv comm, graphic design, Amsterdam; pres, Graphische Vormgevers Nederland, 1955-61; mem: munic council of art, Amsterdam, 1964-67; Alliance Graphique Internationale. Recipient: five poster awards, City of Vienna, 1948; prizes, City of Amsterdam, 1948, 1956; prize, Calcutta, 1959; DA Thieme award, Netherlands Printers Fed, 1960; Typomundus cert of merit, for El Al emblem, 1967. Home: 144, Vondelstraat, Amsterdam, Netherlands.

TREVES, David, Isr, scientist; b. Milan, It, June 28, 1930; s. Mordehai and Irma (Rosenberg); in Isr since 1939; BSc, magna cum laude, Technion, 1953, Ingenieur, EE, 1954, MSc, 1956, DSc, 1958; m. Nehama Kanchuk, Aug 10, 1954; c: Yoram, Daniel, Ron. Prof, Weizmann Inst, since 1968. IDF, 1948-1950. Mem: Amer Phys Soc; Isr Phys Soc. Contbr to sci jours. Home: 13 Ussishkin St, Rehovot, Isr. Office: Weizmann Inst of Sci, Rehovot, Isr.

TRICHTER, Benjamin, US, ophthalmologist; b. Bklyn, NY, June 30, 1917; s. Abraham and Molly (Haller); BS, CCNY, 1938; MD, Georgetown U Sch of Med, 1942; att NYU Grad Sch of Med, 1947-48; m. Alice Waks, May 17, 1942; c: Robert, Marjorie. Pvt practice since 1950. USNR, 1943-46. Mem: Amer Coll of Surgs; Amer Bd of Ophthal; Amer Acad of Ophthal and Otolaryngology; Bklyn Ophthal Soc. Home: 821 Central Ave, Woodmere, NY. Office: 515 Ocean Ave, Brooklyn, NY.

TRIFON, Raphael, Isr, economist; b. Oct 17, 1929; s. Joseph and Gina (Mandel); BA, Heb U, 1953; PhD, LSE, 1957; m. Tseira Kashtan, June, 1952; c: Yoav, Tamar. Asso prof, econ, Technion, since 1966, fac mem since 1961; sr econ adv, Isr Civil Service, 1957-58; asso prof, research asso, U of Man, Can, 1958-61. Served, IDF Res. Mem: Amer Econ Assn; Inst of Mgmt Scis. Contbr to profsl jours. Hobbies: photography, astronomy. Home: 26 Hantke St, Haifa, Isr. Office: Technion, Haifa, Isr.

TRILLING, Diana, US, literary critic, author; b. NYC, July 21, 1905; d. Joseph and Sadie (Forbert) Rubin; BA, Radcliffe Coll, 1925; m. Lionel Trilling, June 12, 1929; c: James. Contbr, lit criticism, essays on social and political subjects: Partisan Rev; Commentary; Encounter; The Amer Scholar; New Leader; NY Times; Look; Harper's Bazaar; The Reporter; ed, with critical introduction: The Viking Portable D H Lawrence, 1947; Selected Letters of D H Lawrence, 1958; author: Claremont Essays, 1964. Chmn, Amer Comm for Cultural Freedom, 1955-57. Recipient: Guggenheim f, 1950-51. Home: 35 Claremont Ave, New York, NY.

TRILLING, Lionel, US, educator, author; b. NYC, July 4, 1905; s. David and Fannie (Cohen); BA, Columbia U, 1925, MA, 1926, PhD, 1938; hon DLitt: Trinity Coll, 1955; Harvard U, 1962; Northwestern U, 1964; Case-W Reserve U, 1968; m. Diana Rubin, June 12, 1929; c: James. Prof, lit, Columbia U, since 1948, fac mem since 1931; Eng instr: U of Wis, 1926-27; Hunter Coll, 1927-30; sr f, sch of letters, Ind U, 1950. Mem: Natl Inst Arts and Letters; Amer Acad Arts and Sci; Cent Assn; club: Athenaeum, London. Author: Matthew Arnold, 1939; E M Forster, 1943; The Middle of the Journey, 1947; The Liberal Imagination, 1950; The Opposing Self,

1955; Freud and the Crisis of Our Culture, 1957; A Gathering of Fugitives, 1958; Boy and Culture, 1966; The Experience of Literature, 1967; ed: The Portable Matthew Arnold, 1949; The Letters of John Keats, 1950. Home: 35 Claremont Ave, New York, NY. Office: Columbia U, New York, NY.

TROPE, Harry, S Afr, communal worker; b. Posvityn, Lith, June 1, 1892; s. Aizik and Bessie (Trusfus); in S Afr since 1911; m. Sylvia Lipman, Apr 16, 1913 (decd); c: Samuel, Robert, Percy, Alice; m. 2nd, Florrie Jacobs, May 29, 1943. Ret; fmr: trading and farming, Orange Free State; wholesaler of liquor, fancy goods; mfr, wholesaler of perfumes. Hon vice-pres, S Afr ZF, mem, exec comm, since 1937; natl chmn, Isr United Appeal, since 1952; mem exec, Poalei Zion of S Afr, since 1937; mem: World Zionist Gen Council since 1960; dir, JNF; clubs: Automobile and Bowling. Home: 10 Gleneagles, Killarney, Johannesburg, S Afr.

TROSK, George, US, attorney; b. NYC, Sep 22, 1890; s. Samuel and Bertha (Friedman); LLB, NY Law Sch, 1911; m. Gertrude Sigmund, Dec 24, 1919; c. Marian Zimmer. Pvt practice since 1911; mem, Upstate Mediation Bd, panel of arbitrators; fmr: counsel: inves of magistrates courts, 1931; dist attys off, NY Co, 1931; chief asso, Seabury inves, NYC, 1932; spec-dep, NY State Atty-Gen, Albany Co election fraud inves, 1944; inves of wfr dept, NY, 1947; mem, counsel, commn to inves NY State pari-mutuel harness racing, 1953-54; spec asst, NY State Atty-Gen, inves of employer-employee wfr funds, 1953; impartial arbitrator, Bldg Service Employees-Midtown Realty Owners Assn. Lt, US Army, 1918-19; mem, NYC panel, War Labor Bd, 1946. Mem: Amer and NY Co. Bar Assns; AJComm; Masons. Home and office: 860 Fifth Ave, New York, NY.

TROSTLER, Rudolf Reuven, Isr, architect; b. Vienna, Aus, Mar 21, 1908; s. Herman and Regina (Hirsch); architect, Acad for Applied Arts, Vienna, 1929; m. Corina Kleiner, Nov 2, 1938; c: Jacob, Naomi. Pvt practice since 1929; Hamehandes Co, 1946-56; R Trostler Ltd, 1956-69. Lt, Engr Corps, IDF, 1948-56. Mem: Lions Intl; Masonic Orders, Isr. Home: 5 Shlomo Molcho St, Jerusalem, Isr. Office: 5 Heleni Hamalka St, Jerusalem, Isr.

TROTZKY, Daniel, US, educational exec; b. New Bedford, Mass, Dec 25, 1903; s. Hyman and Ida; BCS, NYU, 1924; LLB, St Lawrence U, 1930; m. Rhoda Cohen, 1938; c: Howard, Arthur. Found, fmr pres: Roosevelt Sch; Young Israel; vice-pres, Heb High Schs-J Educ comm; chmn: Food Train for State of Isr, 1948-49; Machinery and Materials for Isr, 1948-49; Salute to Isr, Madison Sq Garden Events, 1949-50; arrangements comm, Mayor's Comm on Scholastic Achievement, NYC; dir: B'nai B'rith; and found, Idlewild Syn JF Kennedy Intl Airport, NY; mem: bd govs, ADL; panel, Amer Arbitration Assn; NY Co Grand Jurors Assn; ZOA, life; AJCong; AJComm; Grand St Boys Assn; Amer Assn Sch Admnrs. Home: 27 W 86 St, New York, NY.

TROY, Abraham, Australia, engineer; b. Riga, Latvia, Sept 19, 1904; s. Ben-Zion and Zissa (Friedman); in Austr since 1927; EE, Poly Inst of Arnstadt, 1927; BA, U of W Austr, 1968; m. Leah Leventhal, Aug 21, 1928; c: Deborah, Fay. Fmr: mgr, Neon Elec Co, from 1929. Pres: State ZC, since 1955; JNF of Perth, 1941-59; Perth Heb Cong, 1952-53; treas, 1955-60; mem, Bd of Deps, 1958-61. Home: 50 Carnarvon Crescent, Mt Lawley, W Australia.

TRUNK, Isaiah Elezer, US, historian; b. Kutno, Pol, July 21, 1905; s. Itzhak and Frymet (Bornstein); father, found, Mizrachi Movement in Pol; in US since 1954; PhD, U Warsaw, 1929; DHL, JTSA, 1969; m. Celia Baar, Sep, 1948; c: Gabriel. Mem, commn of research, YIVO, since 1959; ed staff: J Hist Inst, Warsaw, 1947-50; Beth Lohamei Hagetaot, Isr, 1951-53. Mem: Workmen's Circle, NY; Hist Soc of Isr. Author: History of the Jews in Kutno, 1934; History of the Jews in Plotzk, 1237-1656, pub 1939; Geshtalten un Gesheeiushn, 1962; Studies in Yiddishe Geshichte in Pol, 1963; numerous hist studies; contbr to hist publs. Recipient: awards: Diana Blumenfeld Found, 1965; JBCA, 1967. Home: 144-39 37 Ave, Flushing, NY. Office: 1048 Fifth Ave, New York, NY.

TRUSTMAN, Alan R, US, attorney, screenwriter; b. Boston, Mass, Dec 16, 1930; s. Benjamin and Julia (Myerson); AB, Harvard U, 1952; LLB, 1955; m. Renee Rapaporte, June 26, 1955; c: John, Laurie, Steven. Partner, Nutter, McClennen & Fish, since 1963, with firm since 1955. Mem: bd trustees,

Combined J Philanthropies Gtr Boston Inc; social planning, budget comms, Asso J Philanthropies; chmn, Brookline United Fund Area, 1957-58; fmr dir: United Cerebral Palsy Assn Gtr Boston; Harvard Hillel Houses; J Family and Children's Services; vice-chmn, Brookline Redevelopment Auth, 1958-64; mem, Amer Cancer Soc. Screenwriter: The Thomas Crown Affair, 1968; Bullitt, 1968. Home: 70 Lyman Rd, Brookline, Mass. Office: 75 Federal St, Boston, Mass.

TSAMRIYON, Tsemah Moshe, Isr, educational admnr; b. Raseiniai, Lith, Nov 19, 1919; s. Gedalia and Henia (Kaplan) Halperin; in Isr since 1938; PhD, U Munich, 1951; m. Penina Kagan, Nov 27, 1947; c: Gania, Daliya. Dir: State Tchrs Coll, Haifa, since 1963; Galilee HS, Tiberias, since 1953, tchr, 1951-60; Haifa Munic HS "A", 1960-63. British Army and J Brigade, 1941-46; Haganah; IDF, until 1968. Chmn, jury comm for Rupin Prize, Haifa Munic; mem, Tchrs Org, Isr Off of Educ and Culture; fmr, mem: youth movement, J State Party, Haifa; comm, Vaad Brigada; cen comm, United Revisionists in Ger and Eur. Author: Wegweiser, in Yiddish, 1949; booklets on Old Testament and hist; co-author, Torat Hachibur, 1964; ed, Unser Welt, Yiddish weekly, 1948-51; contbr on educ, Bible, hist, natl problems, in Isr and abroad. Hobby: collector of papers and mags. Home: 14 Nahalal St, Haifa, Isr. Office: State Tchrs Coll, Tschernichovsky St, Haifa, Isr.

TSANIN, Yeshayahu M, Isr, author; b. Sokolow, Pol, Apr 1, 1906; s. David and Tova; in Isr since 1940; m. Debora Alter; c: Zeev. Chief ed: Lezte Nyes, since 1949; Illustrirte Weltwoch, since 1956. Mem: exec, Intl J Journalists Assn; Comm of Daily Eds; Press Council; B'nai B'rith; club: PEN. Author: Vivat Lebn, 1933; Oyf Zumpiker Erd, 1936; Shabesdike Shmuessn, 1957; The Complete Heb Yiddish Dict, 1960; Tvishn Felker un Geter, 1964; Oyf di Vegn Fun Yiddishn Goyrl, 1966; Artapanos Kumt Aheim, 1966; Decdents Fun a Moshiah, 1967; Darquey Hagoral Hayehudi, 1967; Fremde Himlen, 1968. Pres, Assn of Yiddish Writers in Isr. Home: 29 Stricker St, Tel Aviv, Isr. Office: 52 Herskeveth St, Tel Aviv, Isr.

TSCHACBASOV, Nahum, US, artist; b. Baku, Russ, Aug 31, 1899; s. Stephen and Sonia (Tibel); in US since 1906; att: Lewis Inst, 1915; Armour Inst of Tech, 1916-17; Art Inst, all Chgo; Columbia U; art insts, Paris, 1932-34; m. 1st, Esther Sorokin, Apr 26, 1929; c: Sondra Bellow; m. 2nd, Irene Zevon, 1966. Art tchr since 1937; one-man shows: Salon des Tuilleries, Paris, 1933; Secession Gal, 1935; ACA Gal, 1936, 1938, 1940, 1942; Perls Gal, 1944, 1946, 1947, 1948, all of NYC; Arts and Crafts Club, New Orleans, 1945; SF Mus of Art; Colo Springs Fine Arts Cen; U of Tex; James Vigeveno Gal, LA, all 1946; William Rockhill Nelson Gal, 1950; Walker Art Gal, 1951; John Heller Gal, NYC, 1951, 1953; Kan State Coll; Richmond Profsl Inst; O State U; Indiana State Tchrs Coll, Pa; Us of Neb; Colo; Fla State; Mo; NC; Pa Coll for Women; Allegheny Coll, all 1953; J Mus, NYC, 1955-56; Arlington State Coll; Huntington Coll; Mercer Coll; Ohio U; Union Coll; repr in natl exhbs: Whitney Mus of Amer Art; Metrop Mus of Art; Mus of Modern Art, all NYC; Pa Acad of Fine Arts; Corcoran Gal; Carnegie Inst; Cincinnati Art Mus; City Art Mus, St Louis; Va Mus of Fine Arts; Art Inst of Chgo; Walker Art Cen, Minneapolis; Springfield Mus of Fine Arts, Mass; perm collections: Whitney Mus of Amer Art; Bklyn Mus; J Mus, all of NYC; Newark Mus Assn, NJ; Phila Mus of Art; Butler Art Inst; Us of Ill; Me; Neb; Cornell; Ga; Ala; Brandeis U; Smith Coll; US State Dept, Wash, DC; Dallas Mus of Fine Arts; Pa Acad; Mus of Tel Aviv; Lycoming Coll; Glassboro State Coll; Ore State Coll; Bethune Cookman Coll; Menninger Clinic, Topeka, Kan; Topeka Pub Libr; Pensacola Art Cen; Edison Jr Coll; La Jolla Art Mus; Devereux Found, Scottsdale, Ariz; Watkins Inst; Miss State Coll for Women; Sacramento State Coll; Baldwin Wallace Coll; Columbia Mus of Arts and Crafts, Ga. Contbr to art jours. Recipient: Pepsi-Cola Art award, 1947. Home: 222 W 23 St, New York, NY.

TSEVAT, Matitiahu, US, Hebraist, educator; b. Kattowitz, Ger, July 15, 1913; s. Adolf and Lotte Kober (Pinczower); in US since 1949; tchr cert, Theol Sem, Breslau, 1936; MA, Heb U, 1948; PhD, HUC, 1953; m. Miriam Krieg, Nov 12, 1949; c: Daniel, Joel, David. Prof of Bible, HUC, since 1966, asst prof, 1957-61, asso prof, 1961-66; spec libr, Semitic collection, 1954-63; dir, J studies, HUC Bibl and Archaeol Sch, Jerusalem, 1964-66. Council mem, World Union J

Studies, Jerusalem; mem: Soc Bible Lit; Amer Oriental Soc Author: A Study of the Language of the Biblical Psalms, 1955; ed, HUC Annual; contbr to profsl jours. Hobbies: music, hiking. Home: 764 Red Bud Ave, Cincinnati, O. Office: HUC, Clifton Ave, Cincinnati, O.

TSOUR, Seev, Isr, legislator; b. Kvynki, Pol, Aug, 1911; s. Shneur-Zalman and Ziporah (Efroimson) Stein; in Isr since 1931; att Technikum, Wilno, 1926-29; m. Lea Hahamovitz, 1937; c: Tzafrira, Ivria. MK since 1965; mem: bd dirs, Isr Elec Corp; council, Land Auth; fmr: secretariat: haKibbutz haMeuchad, 1941-43, and 1952-55, Merkaz Halai, 1945-49; dep Min of Agric, 1955-59; political secy, Achdut Avoda, 1962-65. Mem, ed bd, laMerchav, contbr to press. Home: Sdeh Nahum, Isr. Office: The Knesset, Jerusalem, Isr.

TSUR, Bomba Joseph, Isr, stage and screen actor; b. Haifa, Isr, Dec 26, 1928; s. Shlomo and Esther (Kliger) Waltser; studied, Reali, Haifa, 1935-47; Brit Drama League, 1958-60; m. Minna Baal-Teshuva, May 8, 1958; c: Amnon, Tal, Shlomo. Actor since 1950; produc since 1960; haMatateh Satirical Theater, 1950-53; Cameri Theater, 1953-58; Isr motion pictures: Hem Hayu Asara; Chavura sheKazot; Fortuna; Chor baLevana; Dalia vahaMalahim; Tealat Blaumilch; prin stage roles: My Fair Lady, (Doolittle), 1963-64; Fiddler on the Roof, (Tevye), 1964-66; The Brave Soldier Shweik (Shweik), 1966-67; The Odd Couple, 1967-68. Entertainment troupe, IDF, 1947-1950. Recipient: Kinor David award, Yediot Achronot, 1967. Home and office: 36 Sderot Nave Oved, Herzliya Pituach, Isr.

TSUR, Hilel, Isr, educator, teacher; b. Riga, Latvia, Dec 12, 1909; s. Yakov and Rahel (Hait) Stein; in Isr since 1928; att: Agric HS, Mikveh Isr; tchrs courses, Rubin Coll, 1956-58; m. Shulamith Sluzky, Jan, 1934; c: Yakov, Yigal, Athara Kochava, Ephrath Paz. Vice-mgr, Messiloth Public Sch, since 1968; mem, Natanya Munic, since 1935, fmr dep mayor. Sgt-maj, IZL underground movement, prisoner-of-war, Eritrea, Sudan. Mem: cen comm, Herut; Order of Name of Zeev Jabotinsky; found mem, Betar movement. Home: 14 Tiomkin St, Natanya, Isr.

TSUR, Jacob, Isr, diplomat, public official; b. Vilno, Lith, Oct 18, 1906; s. Shmuel and Bella (Felmann) Tchernowitz; in Isr since 1921; att U Florence, 1924-25; Sorbonne, 1925-29; m. Vera Gotlib, Apr 21, 1928; c: Dalia Dovrat, Shmuel. Chmn, bd dirs, JNF, Keren Kayemeth leIsrael, since 1960, PR off, Jerusalem, 1929-48; spec missions to Belgium, Greece and Bulgaria, 1934-35; repr, JA, in Cairo; liaison off with GHQ, Brit Forces in Egypt, both 1943-45; first Isr emissary to liberated Greece, 1945; chmn, recruiting comm for besieged Jerusalem, 1946-47; first Isr min: Arg; Uruguay; Paraguay; Chile, all 1949-53; ambass to Fr, 1953-59; acting dir-gen, Isr Min for Fgn Affairs, 1959; chmn, bd dirs, Zionist Gen Council, 1960-68. Pres, Cen Inst for Cultural Relations with Iber-O-Amer; found, Isr Cultural Inst in Buenos Aires; mem: Histadrut; Mapai; B'nai B'rith. Author: Sunrise in Zion, 1965; Prelude for Suez, 1967; An Ambassador's Diary in Paris, 1967; contbr to Heb, Span and Fr periodicals. Recipient: Grand Officier, Legion d'Honneur, Fr, 1959. Home: 8 Mevo Yoram, Jerusalem, Isr. Office: JNF, POB 283, Jerusalem, Isr.

TUBIN, Yehuda, Isr, author; b. Kovno, Lith, Aug 5, 1908; s. Bendet and Hana (Viener); in Isr since 1931; att agric sch, Nancy, Fr, 1927-29; m. Shulamit Vulkan, Jan 10, 1936; c: Ilana Avin, Haran, Benjamin. Author: Avot haMarxism uShe'elat haYehudim, 1954; liShe'lat haYehudim beYameinu, 1968; contbr to newspapers. Served, J Brig, Brit Army, 1942-46. Mem, Kibbutz Bet Zera. Home: Kibbutz Bet Zera, Isr.

TUCAZINSKY, Nisan Aaron, Isr, rabbi, educator; b. Jerusalem, Isr, 1922; s. Yechiel and Toibe; ordained rabbi, Etz Hayim, Jerusalem; m. Zelda Zeibald. Rabbi, dean, dir, Etz Hayim, Jerusalem, Isr. Spec interest: astronomy. Home: 3 Ishtori Haparchi, Jerusalem, Isr. Study: 115 Jaffo, Jerusalem, Isr.

TUCHMAN, Barbara W, US, author, historian; b. NYC, Jan 30, 1912; d. Maurice and Alma (Morgenthau) Wertheim; BA, Radcliffe Coll, 1933; hon DLitt: Yale U; Columbia U; HUC; New Sch for Social Research; U Mass; Bates; m. Lester Tuchman, June 18, 1940; Lucy, Jessica, Alma. Fmr: research asst, Inst Pacific Relations, NYC, 1934; Tokyo, 1935; ed asst, The Nation, NYC, 1936, Spain, 1937; staff writer, The War in Spain, London, 1937-38; Amer corresp, New Statesman and Nation, London, 1939; ed, OWI, NY, 1943-45. Trustee, Radcliffe Coll, since 1960; council mem: Authors League; Authors Guild. Author: The Lost British Policy, 1938; Bible and Sword, 1956; The Zimmermann Telegram, 1958; The Guns of August; The Proud Tower, 1966. Recipient: Pulitzer Prize for gen non-fiction, 1963. Home: 875 Park Ave, New York, NY.

TUCHMAN, Maurice Simon, US, librarian; b. Bklyn, NY, Sep 14, 1936; s. William and Rose (Luria); mother, Rose Halpern, Hadassah pres; BA, Bklyn Coll, 1958; MLS, Sch of Libr Sci, Columbia U, 1959; BHL, JTSA, 1964; m. Helene Bodner, Aug 30, 1959; c: Joel, Miriam. Libr, Heb Coll, Mass, since 1966; cataloguer: Buffalo and Erie Co Public Libr, 1959-60; NY State Maritime Coll, 1962-64; cataloging cons, Mid-Hudson Librs, 1964-66. US Army, 1960-62. Mem: Assn J Librs; Theol Libr Assn. Contbr to J Advocate. Hobbies: sport, reading, philately, J bibliography. Home: 1909 Commonwealth St, Auburndale, Mass. Office: Heb Coll, 43 Hawes St, Brookline, Mass.

TUCKER, Harold, Eng, real estate devl; b. London, Eng, Feb 4, 1930; s. Alec and Esther (Perper); m. Shirley Silver, July 2, 1952; c: Barry, Steven, David. Real estate devl, Harold Tucker & Son, since 1952; exec off, Bd of Trade, 1950-52. RAF, 1948-50. Conservative candidate, opposed PM Harold Wilson at Huyton gen election, 1964. Pres, S Manchester Heb Cong; councillor, Manchester City Council; vice-chmn, S Manchester J Youth Council; gov: John Dalton Coll Tech; Mather Tchr Training Coll; Manchester Evening Cens; chmn: Bldg Sub-Comm for Manchester Educ; Royal Natl Life Bd Inst, 1964-67; council mem, Salford U; dep chmn, Manchester Art Gals comm, 1965-66; mem: Freemasonry; Rotary. Hobbies: reading, golf, bridge. Home: 69 Gouldon Rd, Didsbury, Manchester, Eng. Office: 4 Church Rd, Northenden, Manchester, Eng.

TUCKER, Richard, US, opera and concert tenor, cantor; b. Bklyn, NY, Aug 28, 1915; s. Samuel and Fannie (Chiplewutzer) Ticker; hon DFA: Notre Dame U; Adelphi Coll; St Johns U; m. Sara Perelmuth, Feb 11, 1936; c: Barry, David, Henry. Leading tenor: Metrop Opera House, since 1945; La Scala, Milan, and Rome Opera Houses, since 1969; radio and TV; cantor, annually, J High Holy Days, Passover; toured Amer, S Amer, Eur, Asia, Isr; officiated, Sabbath services, Gt Syn, Isr, 1963; toured Vietnam, 1967; entertained Isr troops, 1967; fmr cantor, Bklyn J Cen. Sponsor: Alyn Crippled Hosp, Jerusalem; scholarships, coll and U's, Isr. Recorded: Columbia, RCA-Victor, Angel. Recipient: commendatore, Order of Merit, It; Artistic and Cultural award, Isr; Handel medallion, NYC; First Annual B'nai B'rith award; Justice Louis B Brandeis medal; Natl Interfaith Council award; gold plaque,State of Isr; gold medal, City of Vienna. Hobbies: golf, poker, trading stocks,bonds, real estate. Office: c/o Columbia Artists Mgmt, 165 W 57 St, New York, NY.

TUFT, Louis, US, allergist, educator; b. Phila, Pa, Sep 14, 1898; s. Harry and Edith (Kofsky); BS, U of Pa, 1916; MD, 1920; postgrad study, NY Hosp and Cornell Med Sch, 1927; m. Carlyn Manasses, July 1, 1930; c: Janet Garvin, Betsy, Harry. Pvt practice since 1923; fmr chief, allergy clinic, Temple U Sch of Med, staff mem since 1931; clinical prof em, med, fac mem since 1955; allergy cons: Vets Hosp, Coatesville, Pa, since 1949; Vets Outpatient Clinic, since 1950; Vets Hosp, since 1953, both Phila; asst, Mt Sinai Hosp, 1923-28; asst instr, U of Pa, 1924-31, instr, grad sch, 1928-33; dir, Pa State Health Labs, 1937-39. F: AAAS; Amer Acad of Allergy, pres, 1940; Amer Coll of Phys; mem: AMA; Phila Co Med Soc; Phila Path Soc; Amer Assn of Immunologists; Phila Allergy Soc; Phila Coll of Phys; Amer Assn for the Study of Allergy; Phi Lambda Kappa; clubs: Phila Alumni; Philmont Country. Author: Clinical Allergy, 1937, 2nd ed, 1949; Clinical Immunology, Biotherapy and Chemotherapy, 1941; contbr to med jours. Hobbies: music, golf. Home: 4613 Larchwood Ave, Philadelphia, Pa. Office: 1530 Locust St, Philadelphia, Pa.

TULIN, Abraham, US, attorney; b. Besdjez, Russia, Mar 26, 1882; s. Shaia and Bassia (Shulman); in US since 1890; BA, Yale U, 1903; LLB, Harvard U, 1906; DS, hon causa, Technion, 1957; m. Anna von Lepel, Oct 9, 1936. Pvt practice since 1919; fmr, asso with law firms, 1906-19; secy to Justice Edward B Whitney, 1910-11; asst to chief, Herbert Hoover: Amer Relief Admn; Supr Econ Council of Versailles Peace Conf, both 1919; chief, Amer Mission to S Russ and Armenia, 1919. Capt, US Army, WW I. Chmn bd, Amer Soc for Technion, 1956-61, hon chmn since 1961; Amer delg to Intl Zionist Confs and Congs: London, 1919-20; Basle, 1927, 1931; Prague, 1933; dep mem, Zionist Actions comm, 1931-33; mem, exec comm: ZOA, 1919-20, 1929-33, mem, admn in charge of publs, 1929-33; Amer Zionist Emergency Council, 1940-47; chief counsel for JA and all Amer Zionist orgs, before Anglo-Amer Commn of Inquiry on the Pal Question, 1945; and before UN Gen Assembly, 1947; mem, Assn of Bar of NY; club: Yale. Co-author: The Basic Equities of the Palestine Problem, 1947; compiler, annotator: Book of Documents, submitted to Gen Assembly of UN for JA of Pal, 1947. Recipient: named in his honor: forest on Mt Carmel, Haifa, 1959; chair of humanities, Technion, 1961. Home: 330 W 72 St, New York, NY. Office: 1000 Fifth Ave, New York, NY.

TULIN, Anna Johanna von Lepel, US, communal worker; b. Berlin, Ger, Dec 15, 1903; in US since 1932; m. Abraham Tulin, Oct 9, 1936. Vice-pres, Lepel High Frequency Labs, 1932-36. Natl vice-pres, Hadassah, 1953-57; mem, bd govs, Heb U, 1953-57; repr, Council of Voluntary Agencies under UNRRA, 1946-50; fmr, Hadassah: chmn, purchasing and shipping, 1941-46; natl treas, 1946-50; natl chmn, Youth Aliyah, 1950-53; chmn: med org, 1953-57; natl med cen comm, 1957-62; finance and budget, 1963-66; wills and bequests, 1966-69. Home: 330 W 72 St, New York, NY. Office: 65 E 52 St, New York, NY.

TULIPMAN, Boaz Joseph, Isr, scientist, executive; b. Jerusalem, Mar 6, 1926; s. David and Shifra (Singer); att Technion, 1945-50; Harvard Bus Sch, 1965; m. Ahuva Twerdin, Mar 30, 1950; c: Yael, David, Nily, Tamar. Dir: Nuclear Research Cen, Negev, since 1966; bd mem, Isr AEC, since 1966; fmr: project mgr, Isr AEC, 1951-60; head, engr dept, Negev Phosphates, 1961-63; dep dir-gen, Min of Devl, 1963-65. Maj, infantry, IDF, 1947-49. Home: 12 Sokolov St, Beersheva, Isr. Office: POB 107, Beersheva, Isr.

TUMARKIN, Isaia, Isr, attorney; b. Witebsk, Feb 1, 1893; in Isr since 1957; att: Vilna Pedg Inst; Leningrad Pedg Inst; law fac, Yassi, Rum; m. Esther. Pvt practice, Isr, since 1957; fmr: found, dir, tchr, Heb Tarbut Schs, Yassi, 1944; legal cons, J Natl Party, Rum, 1944-49; legal adv, Isr Legation, Bucharest, 1949-51. Fmr: found, Maccabi, Kishnev; exec mem, JWC, Rum, 1944-49; active Zionist and fund-raiser; Rum delg, WJC, 1948. Home: 16 Tzimhei Hayehudim, Ramat Aviv, Isr.

TUMARKIN, Ygael, Isr, artist; b. Dresden, Ger, 1933; in Isr since 1935; studied sculpture under: Rudolf Lehmann, 1954; Berthold Brecht, 1955-57. One-man shows: Bezalel Mus, Jerusalem; Galerie Lohr, Frankfurt; Tel Aviv Mus; Isr Mus; Paris; Ger; NY; group exhbs: Carnegie Inst; Mus of Modern Art, NY; Biennale, Venice; maj monuments: The Arad Panorama, 1963; Andarta Lashoa, Nazareth, 1964; Peace Monument, 1965; Seamen Monument, 1969; War and Peace, 1969; designed theater sets in Ger, Netherlands, Isr; around-the-world tour with exhibitions, 1957-62. Recipient: 1st prize, for Hulikat Fighters, 1965; Sandberg award, 1968; 1st award, for Seamen Monument, 1968. Home: 2 Sokolov St, Tel Aviv, Isr.

TUMIN, Melvin Marvin, US, sociologist; b. Newark, NJ, Feb 10, 1919; s. Robert and Rose (Yawitz); att: U Newark, 1934-38; BA, U Wis, 1939; MA, 1940; PhD, Northwestern U, 1944; m. Sylvia Yarost, June 18, 1948; c: Jonathan, Zachary. Prof, sociol and anthropology, Princeton U, since 1947; asso prof, sociol and anthropology, Wayne State U, 1944-47; fmr visiting prof, Tchrs Coll, Columbia; visiting research sociol, Educ Testing Service, 1969-70. Cons: curriculum devl dept, since 1964, regional lab adv panel, since 1965, both HEW; research and devl sect, Agcy for Intl Devl, 1964-68; coroner, Mercer Co, NJ, 1961-66; bd govs, Lenberg cen for study of violence, Brandeis U, since 1966; dir, task force on individual violence, Natl Commn on Causes, Prevention of Violence, 1968-69; mem: steering comm, longitudinal evaluation of headstart progs, Educ Testing Service, since 1968; comm on health care for the urban poor, Amer Hosp Assn, since 1968; exec council, Amer Sociol Assn, 1960-63; fmr pres: Amer Anthropological Assn; E Sociol Assn, 1967-68; Society for Study of Social Problems, 1966-67; mem: Phi Beta Kappa, Sigma Xi; Sociol Research Assn; ed bd: Public Opinion Quarterly; Social Education; Amer Educ Research Jour; Amer Sociol; Social Problems. Author:

Caste in a Peasant Society, 1952; Segregation and Desegregation: A Summary of Research 1951-56, supplements, 1957-59; Desegregation: Resistance and Readiness, 1958; An Inventory and Evaluation of Research and Theory in Anti-Semitism, 1960; Social Class and Social Change in Puerto Rico, 1961; Education, Social Class and Intergroup Attitudes in England, France, and Germany, 1964; Quality and Equality in American Education, 1966; Social Stratification, 1967; Research Annual on Intergroup Relations, 1966, 1967, 1968; Education and National Goals: A Model for the Measurement of the Effectiveness of Educational Systems, 1969; Reader in Social Stratification, 1969; Comparative Perspective on Race Relations, 1969; Crimes of Violence: Causes and Preventions, 1969; co-author: Social Life: Structure and Function, 1948; ed, Race and Intelligence, 1963. Recipient: sr f, Council of the Hums, Princeton U, 1957-58, 1965-66; Fulbright sr research scholar, Oslo, Nor, 1960-61, It, 1967; Guggenheim Found f, 1969-70. Home: 119 Fitzrandolph, Princeton, NJ. Office: Sociol Dept, Princeton, NJ.

TUNICK, Stanley B, US, accountant, attorney, educator; b. NYC, Mar 6, 1900; s. Abraham and Mary (Bloch); BA, CCNY, 1919, MBA, 1923; JD, St Lawrence U, 1928; PhD, NYU, 1938; m. Mildred Superior, June 26, 1942; c: Andrew, Richard. Partner, Tunick and Platkin, CPA's, since 1928, atty since 1929; prof em, acctnt dept, CCNY, since 1962, chmn dept, 1956-62, mem fac since 1931; dir, secy, Dorex Inc, since 1967; dir, treas, Thirty Third Equities Inc, since 1948; trustee, treas, Wallace Whittaker Found, since 1959; vice-pres, Kamber Mgmt Inc, since 1957. Lt Col, US Army engr corps, 1942-46, org res since 1946. Mem, NY State Bd CPA Examiners, past chmn; hon dir, Asso Alumni, CCNY; mem: natl panel, Amer Arbitration Assn; Amer Inst CPA's, mem, natl council, since 1967; Amer Accounting Assn; NY State CPAs, bd dirs, 1948-51; Phi Delta Kappa; Iota Theta; Beta Gamma Sigma; Phi Beta Kappa; Beta Alpha Psi; Delta Phi Epsilon; chmn, acctnts div: UJA, 1963; Bonds for Isr, 1957; clubs: Acctnts; Town, NYC. Author: Outlines in Accounting, 1961; co-author: Fundamental Accounting Theory and Practice, 1950, 3rd ed, 1963; co-ed, NY Tax Course, annually, 1939-62; cons ed, Fed Tax Course, 1957-66. Recipient: Alumni Service medal, Asso Alumni, CCNY, 1940; commendation medal, US Army, 1946; Townsend Harris medal, CCNY, 1966; Bernard M Baruch medallion, Bernard M Baruch Sch Alumni, 1968; guest of honor, Fed J Charities, 1968. Hobbies: prestidigitation, philately, numismatics. Home: 252 DeMott Ave, Rockville Cen, NY. Office: 2 Park Ave, New York, NY.

TURAK, Nartan, US, salesman; b. Brest-Litovsk, Russ-Pol, Aug 9, 1899; s. Chaim and Leah (Wargaftig); in US since 1906; m. Sadie Baris, Sep, 1943; c: Lucille (decd), Alice. Field repr, Great Yiddish Dict, mem, exec bd; fmr: sales mgr, Becker Bros Engraving Co; found, treas, United Engraving Works Inc, 1918-54. Mem, Employing Brass Engravers Assn; Workmen's Circle; co-found, vice-pres, Freeland League for J Territorial Colonization; secy, Alveltlicher Yiddisher Cong, 1935-38; rep: Freie Shriften, Warsaw, 1926-31; Dos Freie Vort, London, 1935-36; chmn, comm for publ, Dr I N Steinberg Memorial Book, 1960; exec bd, Sviva, lit mag, since 1962. Hobby: cabinet making. Home: 76-12 35 Ave, Jackson Heights, NY. Office: 1048 Fifth Ave, New York, NY.

TURECK, Rosalyn, US, concert pianist, conductor; b. Chgo, Ill, Dec 14, 1914; d. Samuel and Monya (Lipson); grad, cum laude, Juilliard Sch, 1935; hon degs: Colby Coll, 1964; Roosevelt U, 1968; Wilson Coll, 1968. Debut, age 9, Chgo, 1923; NY debut, Carnegie Hall, Phila Orch, 1936; soloist with leading sym orchs, US and Europe; annual US tours, since 1935; Eur tours, since 1947; toured S Afr, 1959, S Amer, 1963; soloist: Isr Philharmonic; Kol Isr Orch; Isr Festival, all 1965. First woman to conduct the NY Philharmonic in its regular concert series. Instr: Phila Conservatory of Music, 1935-42; Mannes Coll of Music, 1940-44; Juilliard Sch of Music, 1945-55; Columbia U, 1953-55; visiting prof of music, Wash U, St Louis, 1964-65; regents lectr, U of Cal, San Diego, 1966, prof of music, 1966. Found: Composers of Today, Contemporary Music Soc, NY, 1949; Tureck Bach Players, London, 1959; Intl Bach Soc Inc, dir, 1966; Inst for Bach Studies, dir, 1968. Mem: Amer Musicological Soc; Incorporated Soc of Musicians, London; Royal Musical Assn, London. Records: Decca, HMV, Capitol. Author: Introduction to the Performance of Bach, 3 vols, 1959-60; contbr to periodicals. Recipient: 1st prize, Gtr Chgo Piano Playing Tournament, 1928; f, Juilliard Grad Sch; Schubert

Memorial award, 1935; First Town Hall Endowment award, 1937. Offices: c/o Columbia Artists Mgmt Inc, 165 W 57 St, New York, NY; Ibbs and Tillett, 124 Wigmore St, London, Eng.

TURETSKY, Morris, UK, rabbi; b. Manchester, Eng, Jan 22, 1926; s. Ben and Freda (Friedman); MA, U Manchester, 1952; PhD, U Leeds, 1963; m. Rachel Yodaiken, Sep 2, 1952; c: Sorrel, Jonathan, Geoffrey, Daniel, Michael. Rabbi: Dayan Leeds Beth Din, since 1948; New Cen Vilna Syn; min, Sunderland Heb Cong, 1951-54. Chmn, educ, Selig Brodetsky Sch; vice-pres, Leeds Mizrachi; exec, Leeds J Repr Council. Home: 31 Kings Mount, Leeds, Eng.

TURKEL, Henry, US, physician, researcher; b. Podwoloczyska, Aus, June 29, 1903; s. Hillel and Frieda (Segal); in US since 1922; BA, O State U, 1931; MA, U Mich, 1932, MD, 1936; hon DSc, Lane Coll, 1961; m. Jeanne Marcus; c: Margot Chapman, Ellen Kallick, Hope van Riper, Robert. Phys, research in mental retardation; lectr, med schs and hosps, Amer, Eur, Cuba, 1959-63; visiting prof: U Haiti, Lane Coll. Cons, US surg gen's off, US Army, 1945-54. Prin contribs: invented Turkel instruments for bone marrow infusion and tissue biopsies; devl treatment for genetic anomalies. Mem: AMA; Amer Acad Gen Practice; Amer Geriatric Soc; Amer Acad Forensic Sci; Amer Public Health Assn; Amer Inst Chems; Amer Chem Soc; Inst Clinical Chems; AAAS; Amer Pharm Assn; Amer Assn Mental Deficiency; Amer Med Writers Assn; Assn Mil Surgs of US, life mem; Assn Biol and Tropical Med, Cuba; Amer Med Soc, Vienna; Eur Soc Hematology; Intl Soc Comprehensive Med; Intl Soc Hematology; IMA; Jerusalem Acad Med; Mich Acad Art and Scis; Michigan State Med Soc; Mich Soc Hematology; DC Med Soc; NY and NJ Acads Sci; NY Microscopical Soc; NC Acad Sci; Natl Assn Drs US; Phi Lambda Kappa; Psychosomatic Med; Public Health Assn, Cuba; Royal Soc Med; Royal Soc Health; Royal Soc Tropical Med and Hygiene, all London; Research Soc Amer; Sociedad Medica Dominicana; S Soc Cancer Cytology; Wayne Co Med Soc; Phil Soc of Eng. Author: textbook, Trephine Technique of Bone Marrow Infusion and Tissue Biopsies, 11th ed, 1964; contbr to profsl jours. Recipient: Natl Order de la Santa Publique, Haiti, 1961; Order of Merit, Saint Hubertus, It, 1953; Order of Merit, Intl Red Cross, Cuba, 1958; award: Clara Maas Found, 1962; Found Internacional Eloy Alfaro, Panama, 1965. Hobbies: chess, travel. Home and office: 8000 W Seven Mile Rd, Detroit, Mich,

TURKOW, Jonas, theatrical director, author; b. Warsaw, Pol, Feb 15, 1898; s. Naftal and Gita (Gotowizna); in Isr since 1967; m. Diana Blumenfeld, May 15, 1925 (decd); c: Margarita; m. 2nd, Sonya Margolis, 1967. Archivist, theater dept, YIVO, 1958-67; found, dir, J Comty Theaters: Cracow, 1926-37; Warsaw, 1930; Vilna, 1932; J Chamber Theater, Pol, 1936; prin, tchr, Heb J Theater Sch, Vilna, 1933; dir, Kulturbund Theater, Danzig, 1938; head: J Soc Wfr, 1939-41; cen off, theater and entertainment, Warsaw Ghetto, 1939-42. Active mem, resistance movement, Pol, WW II; personal appearance tours of DP Camps for UNRRA, 1945, for Farband, 1947. Found, WAGRO, Warsaw Ghetto Resistance Org, NYC; pres, Writers and Actors Union of Jews in Pol, 1944-45; mem exec, Cen Comm of Polish Jews, 1944-45. Author: Wegwaizer far Dramatishe Kraisen, 1924; Azoi Is Es Geven, 1948; In Kamf Far'n Leben, 1949; Farloshene Shtern, 2 vols, 1953; Joe Paull, 1959; Noch Der Bafrayung, 1959; Hay'd Heita Warsha Jehudit, 1969; Ala Golom, 1969; Mordecai Anielevich El Levantamento Del Ghetto De Varsovia, 1968; The Warsaw Ghetto Uprising, 1968; co-ed, Yiddisher Theater in Europe Zvishn Beide Weltmilchomes, 1969. Mem: Farband; Heb Actors Union of Amer; clubs: Amer-Isr; J Writers and Artists. Recipient: Zwi Kessel lit prize, Mex, 1954; Ot haLochem baNazim and Ot haLochem HaMedina, both Govt of Isr. Home: 5 Harav Uziel St, Bat Yam, Isr.

TURKOW, Marc, Arg, organization exec, journalist, author; b. Warsaw, Pol, May 11, 1904; s. Naftal and Gita (Gotowizna); in Arg since 1939; m. Beatrice Braunstein. Secy, S Amer br, WJC, since 1959, mem, exec, since 1961, repr for Arg since 1954; dir, HIAS, S Amer, 1946-54; found and dir, ed comm: Dos Poilishe Identum; co-ed, Moment, daily, Warsaw, parl corresp before L of N, Geneva, Switz; gen secy, Anti-Hitlerist Comm, Pol, and delg, Anti-Hitlerist comm, Amsterdam, Geneva, London, 1933-34. Pres, S Amer Fed of Polish J; vice-pres, World Fed of Pol J. Author: Polacy, Zydzi i Mechesi, 1930; Gdansk Na Wulkanie, 1932; Rewolucja Amerykanska, 1937; Brif fun E R Kaminska, 1927; Roosevelt's Amerike, 1937; Oif Idishe Felder, 1938; Malka Owsianij Dertzailt, 1946; Di Letzte fun a Groisn Dor, 1954. Home: Aguero 1775, Buenos Aires, Arg. Office: Corrientes 1979, Buenos Aires, Arg.

TURNER, Herbert D, US, engineer, government official; b. NYC, Feb 24, 1923; s. Leo and Mollie (Dobrikin); BS, Case Inst of Tech, 1950; att: St Catherine's Soc; U Oxford, Eng, 1950-51; m. Edna Gluck, Sep 11, 1948; c: Mark, Steven, Perry. Chief, tech assistance policy div, AID, Agcy for Intl Devl, US State Dept, since 1967, staff mem since 1960; fmr: tool and die maker, design craftsman, mech engr: Perfection Steel Body Co; Monsanto Chem Co; Intl Gen Elec Corp, all 1940-51; produc assistance spec, Fgn Oprs Admn, US Mission, Copenhagen, 1951-56; dep dir, tech coop, div Intl Coop Admn, US Mission, NATO, Paris, 1956-60. USAAC, WW II. Mem: Amer Soc Mech Engrs; Amer Soc Tool Engrs; Research Inst Mgmt Sci. Hobbies: music, art, gardening. Home: 3419 Cummings Lane, Chevy Chase, Md. Office: AID, US Dept of State, Washington, DC.

TURNER, Justin G, US, business exec, lectr; b. Chgo, Ill, Nov 5, 1898; s. Oscar and Bessie (Taxey); att U Chgo, 1916-18; LLB, DePaul U, 1920; hon degs: Lincoln Coll, 1955; U Judaism, 1960; m. Gertrude Levin, July 27, 1932; c: Paul, Barbara. Partner: Turner Inves, realtors, since 1950; Town Inves, Chgo and LA, 1932-50; Pickwick Realty and Inves Co; Turner and Turner, law firm, 1921-43. Served, US Army, 1918. Pres: S Cal J Hist Soc, 1952-62, hon pres since 1963; Natl Civil War Council, since 1958; Hist Soc of S Cal, 1962-63; Friends of UCLA Libr, 1957-60; Manuscript Soc, 1951-53; Civil War Round Table of S Cal, 1955-56; Chgo B'nai B'rith Council, 1933-35; chmn: bd govs, U Judaism, LA, 1951-62; libr bldg comm, JCC, LA; J Book Month comm, LA; Amer Tercentenary comm, S Cal; Civil War Centennial; Jewish Hist commn; Lincoln Sesquicentennial Assn of Cal; co-chmn, B'nai B'rith Archives; trustee, Natl Found for J Culture; f, Pierpont Morgan Libr, NYC; mem: Amer Hist Assn, life; MLA; Assn for State and Local Hist; Amer Studies Assn; Book Club of Cal; Ill Hist Soc; Keats-Shelley Soc; Miss Valley Hist Assn; Pacific Coast Hist Assn; Renaissance Soc of Amer; Soc of Amer Archivists; Confederate Research club, London; Mus Assn of LA; Southwest Mus; J Hist Soc of Eng; Friends of Bancroft Libr, Berkeley; Clements Libr, Ann Arbor; Honnold Libr, Claremont; Henry Huntington Libr, San Marino; Lincoln Memorial U Libr, Harrogate, Tenn; Occidental Libr, LA; Yale Libr Assn; John Carter Brown Libr; hon mem, Alpha Epsilon Pi; Shriner; Masons; clubs: Hillcrest Country, LA; Tamarisk Country, Palm Springs; Grolier, NY; Covenant, Chgo. Author: Mary Lincoln and Her Letters, 1969; mem, ed bd: Civil War History; Manuscripts; publs of S Cal Hist Soc; contbr to hist jours. Recipient, citations: U Judaism; JWV; Amer J Tercentenary comm; Manuscript Soc, 1953; Civil War Round Table, 1955; diploma of honor, Lincoln Memorial U, 1962. Spec interests: Lincolniana, Amer manuscripts, Judaica, golf. Home: 423 S Rexford Ave, Beverly Hills, Cal. Offices: 2389 Westwood Blvd, Los Angeles, Cal; 33 N La Salle St, Chicago, Ill.

TURNER, Reuben, UK, communal leader; b. Karlsruhe, Ger, Jan 8, 1924; s. Morris and Bluma (Kosiner); in Eng since 1933; att Yeshivah Eitz Chaim, London; m. Anne Straus, Feb 5, 1947; c: Marion Posen, Norman, Leila. Dir, ZF Syn Council, since 1967; ed, Gates of Zion, since 1967; min of rel, United Syn, 1948-67. Chmn, J Music Council; hon org, Brit Olim Parents Assn; pres, Assn of Mins, 1962-67; hon

prin, Brixton J Kindergarten, 1950-67; cultural dir, Maccabi Union of Gt Brit, 1960-65. Author: The Jewish Quiz Book, 1961; Judaism, A Way of Life, 1965. Hobbies: youth work, educ, music. Home: 30 Eastside Rd, London, NW11, Eng. Office: Rex House, 4/12 Regent St, London, SWI, Eng.

TUSSMAN, Malka Heifetz, US, author; b. Russ, May 16, 1896; d. Bozukh and Gitle (Shadkrem) Heifetz; in US since 1937; m. Solomon Tussman, Feb 12, 1914; c: Joseph, Hugh. Fmr, Yiddish tchr, U of Judaism, LA. Author: Lieder, 1949; Mild Mine Wild, 1958; Shadows of Remembering, 1965. Mem, PEN NY. Home: 605 San Vincent St, Santa Monica, Cal.

TUVIN, Sarah Z, US, communal worker; b. Baltimore, Md, Sep 15, 1908; d. Abraham and Katie (Kleinman) Zarwitz; m. Alfred Tuvin, Nov 8, 1931; c: James, Carl. Fmr, dept store exec, Stewart & Co, 1922-32. Pres, seaboard reg, Hadassah, since 1958, mem, natl bd, since 1952, pres, Baltimore chap, 1953-55; co-chmn, womens div, Asso J Charities and Wfr Fund; mem, bd, JWF, Baltimore. Home: 3900 N Charles St, Baltimore, Md.

TWERSKY, Eshia H, US, rabbi; b. Chicago, Ill, July 21, 1930; s. Henach and Hava (Jerusilimsky); att Telshe Yeshiva, Cleveland; W Reserve U; ordained rabbi, BHL, Heb Theol Coll, 1955; m. Toby Halberstam, 1953; c: Boruch, Joseph, Ruchama, Deborah. Rabbi, Cong Lev Someach, since 1954. Dir, Assn of Orthodox Syn of Chgo; bd dirs: Telshe Yeshiva Arie Crown School-Boys Youkov Sch; mem: RabCA; Chgo Rabb Council; Union of Orthodox Rabbis of Amer. Home: 3253 W Hollywood Ave, Chicago, Ill. Study: 5555 N Bernard St, Chicago, Ill.

TWORKOV, Jack, US, artist, educator; b. Biala, Pol, Aug 15, 1900; s. Hyman and Esther (Singer); in US since 1913; att: Columbia U, 1920-23; Natl Acad, 1923-25; Art Students League, 1925-26; m. Rachel Wolodarsky, 1935; c: Hermine, Helen. Prof em, art, Sch of Art and Architecture, Yale U, since 1969, Leffingwell prof of art, chmn, art dept, 1963-69. One-man shows: Stable Gal, 1957, 1959; Egan Gal, 1947, 1949, 1952, 1954; Baltimore Mus of Art, 1948; Walker Art Cen, Minneapolis, 1957; 10-year retrospective exhb: Holland Goldowsky Gal, Chgo, 1960; Castelli Gal, 1961; Whitney Mus, 1963-69; group shows: Mus of Modern Art, 1958; Osaka Intl Festival, Japan, 1958; Carnegie Intl, 1952, 1958; Whitney Mus annuals, since 1952; Chgo Art Inst; Pa Acad; Corcoran; Documenta 11, Kassel, Ger, 1959; Amer Vanguard, Aus and Yugo, USIA exhbt, 1961-62; perm collections: Watkins Gal; Amer U; Baltimore Mus of Fine Arts; New Paltz State Tchrs Coll; Walker Art Cen, Minn; Santa Barbara Mus; Hartford Athenenum; Whitney Mus; Mus of Modern Art; Metrop Mus of Art; Albright; Cleveland Mus; James Michener Found. Contbr to periodicals. Home and studio: 161 W 22 St, New York, NY.

TZUR, Michael, Isr, government official; b. Berlin, Ger, May 1, 1923; s. Chaim and Helena (Feiner) Leibermann; in Isr since 1934; att fac of law, Tel Aviv U; m. Ruth Beinhacker, June 4, 1948; c: Yael, Danny. Chmn, bd dirs: ZIM Isr Navigation Co; Haifa Refineries; Isr Petrochem Enterprises; bd dirs: ATA Textiles; Beged-Or; fmr, dir gen, Isr Min of Commerce and Ind, 1958-66, with min since 1952. Lt, IDF, 1948-49. Author: Israel's Industrial Future, 1960-65, pub 1959; contbr to local press. Recipient: decoration, War of Independence; commander, Order of Merit, Rep of Cen Afr; commandeur, L'Ordre National, Ivory Coast. Home: 6 Tel Hai St, Katamon, Jerusalem, Isr. Office: Zim House, 42 Haatzmaut St, Haifa, Isr.

U

UCHILL, David R, US, business exec; b. Bessarabia, Rum, Mar 24, 1909; s. Morris and Rose (Sidikman); m. Rose, Mar 22, 1931; c: Sherman, Patsy, Lawrence. Vice-pres, Horsman Dolls, Inc, since 1949; owner, Peoples Furniture Co, Denver, Colo, since 1940. Bd govs, Amer Financial and Devl Corp for Isr, since 1951; natl cabinet, UJA. Home: 6 Tideway, Great Neck, NY. Office: 200 Fifth Ave, New York, NY.

UCKER, Paul, US, economist; b. Zurich, Switz, July 24, 1904; s. Solomon and Ida (Pick); in US since 1939; PhD, U Zurich, 1935; m. Bertha Weinhouse, Feb 12, 1947; c: David. Inves securities broker, Reynolds & Co, SF, since 1952; econ research analyst, Swiss bus firms, 1935-39; journalist, Swiss newspapers, in Swiss, NY, SF, 1939-41; econ cons, free-lance writer, econ periodicals, 1941-46; research analyst, Nuremberg War Crimes Trials, 1946. Mem: ZOA, SF, since 1941; AJ Cong; B'nai B'rith, SF lodge 21; secy, Hechaver, Zionist student org, Zurich, 1928-34. Author: Die Italienische Agrarpolitik seit 1925 unter besonderer Berücksichtigung des Kampfes um das Getreide, 1935; Die Bierbesteuerung im Ausland und in der Schweitz, 1936. Home: 2035 28 Ave, San Francisco, Cal. Office: 425 Montgomery St, San Francisco, Cal.

UCKO, Sinai, Isr, educator; b. Gleiwitz, Nov 7, 1905; s. Nathan and Else (Weissenberg); in Isr since 1935; att: U Vienna; U Breslau; Theol Sem, Breslau; PhD, U Königsberg, 1929; ordained rabbi, Hochschule für die Wissenschaft des Judentums, 1930; m. Ruth Loew, 1931; c: Elisheva, Dina. Prof, head educ dept, Tel Aviv U, since 1956; tchr, Youth Aliyah, until 1946; prin, Tchrs Training Coll, until 1954; supr tchrs educ, Isr Min Educ and Culture, until 1958. Served Haganah. Author: Gottesbegriff in der Philosophie Herman Cohens; Al haOsher vehaTov; co-ed, Iyyun, phil quarterly; contbr ed, Judaism; contbr to profsl jours. Recipient: Henrietta Szold Prize, Jerusalem, 1968. Home: Nof Yam, Herzliya, Isr. Office: Tel Aviv U, Tel Aviv, Isr.

UDELL, Jerome I, US, business exec; b. NYC, Jan 24, 1898; s. Max and Jane (Walcoff); BA, cum laude, CCNY, 1918; m. Sophie Spector; c: Edith Fierst, Helen Lowenstein. Specialist: mergers, acquisitions, since 1964; bd dirs: Bank of N Amer, since 1946, Standard Prudential United Corp, since 1964; chief: clothing br, research and devl bur, Quartermasters Corps, US Army, 1943; Textile, Clothing, Leathergoods Div, Off Fgn Relief, Rehab, WW II; chmn, Max Udell Sons & Co, 1946-64; adv to Korean Min Commerce and Ind, Agcy Intl Devl, 1965, 1966. Dir: Beth Isr Med Cen, NYC, since 1931; United Service for New Amers; JDC; Clothing Mfrs Assn US, 1933-64; pres: Philanthropic Fifty, 1957, 1958; Cith College Fund, 1962-63, treas, 1958-62; vice-pres, trustee, UJA, since 1958, city chmn, NY, 1948-54; trustee, FJP, chmn, clothing ind dr; vice-pres, Clothing Mfrs Exch, 1933-64; treas: Natl Citizens Political Action Comm, 1944-45; Herbert H Lehman's Senatorial Campaign, 1949; mem, Phi Beta Kappa. Recipient: medals: Gold Pell; Alumni Service, CCNY Alumni Asso, 1947, Centennial, 1964; awards: Townsend Harris, CCNY, 1954; Phi Epsilon Pi Alumni, 1958. Home: 300 Central Park W, New York, NY.

UDWIN, Saul, Rhodesia, engineer, legislator; b. Königsberg, Russ, June 22, 1922; s. Mailach and Bluma (Rome); in Rhodesia since 1948; BSc, U Witwatersrand, S Afr, 1947; m. Flora Bernstein, Dec 3, 1952; c: Leon, Robert, Dennis, Jennifer. Sr partner, Udwin & Vrettos, cons engrs, since 1950; MP, Fed Assembly, since 1958; main cons engr, Beira oil pipe line; engr: Sir Alfred Macalpine Ltd; Ashkelon, Isr. S Afr Army, 1939-44. F, Amer Assn Civil Engr; hon treas, Fed Party; mem: J Bd Deps; S Afr and Rhodesian Inst Civil Engr. Home: 22 Lawson Ave, Milton Pk, Salisbury, Rhodesia. Office: POB 3093, Salisbury, Rhodesia.

UKHMANI, Azriel, Isr, editor; b. Sanok, Pol, Mar 17, 1907; s. Haim and Gela (Fenig) Schwarz; in Isr since 1932; m. Rivka Gurfein, 1932; c: Rachel Hillel. Ed, Sifriat Poalim, publishers, since 1953; mem, Kibbutz Ein Shemer, since 1932, secy Karkur Lab Council, 1936-38; org, settlement dept, Hakibbutz Haarzi, Hashomer Hatzair, 1940-43; secy, A Hamishmar daily, 1943-47; counsellor, Isr legation, Warsaw, 1948-50. Mem, cen comm Heb Writers Assn. Author: leAiver haAdam, 1953; Tchanim veZurot, 1957; Kolot Adam, 1963; Aval Layla Layla Ani, 1968; Achshav KsheKvar Shachah haRuah, 1969; contbr to anthols, periodicals. Hobbies: gardening, philately. Home: Kibbutz Ein Shemer, Isr. Office: Sifriat Poalim, POB 526, Tel Aviv, Isr.

ULAM, Stanislaw Marcin, US, mathematician, educator; b. Lwow, Pol, Apr 13, 1909; s. Jozef and Anna (Auerbach); in US since 1936; DMath Scis, Poly Inst, Lwow, 1932; m. Françoise Aron, Aug, 1941; c: Claire. Prof, chmn, math dept, U Colo, since 1967; cons, Pres Sci Adv Comm, since 1960; prof, visiting prof, math: Princeton Inst for Advanced Study, 1936; Harvard U, 1936-40, 1951; U Wis, 1941-43; U of S Cal, 1946; MIT, 1956-57; U Colo, 1961; research adv, Los Alamos Sci Lab, 1956-67, staff mem, 1943-56. Mem: Amer Acad Arts and Scis; Natl Acad Scis; Amer Phil Soc; Amer Math Soc; Amer Phys Soc; Math Council. Author: A Collection of Mathematical Problems, 1960; Mathematics and Logic, 1968; contbr to profsl jours. Hobbies: chess, tennis. Home: 775 Pleasant St, Boulder, Colo. Office: Math Dept, U Colo, Boulder, Colo.

ULIN, Alex W, US, surgeon, educator; b. Phila, Pa, Apr 13, 1913; s. Wolf and Rebecca (Werbner); AB, U Pa, 1933, MD, 1937; postgrad studies, U Cincinnati Med Sch, 1939-42; m. Ruth Brody, Jan 3, 1943 (decd); c: S Reid, Robert; m. 2nd, Harriet Wolf, Sep 4, 1966. Dir med research, Ethicon Inc, since 1968; dir, surg research, Hahnemann Med Coll and Hosp, since 1951, sr att surg since 1951, clinical prof, since 1960, on staff since 1946; chief surg, Phila Gen Hosp, since 1956, staff mem since 1953; sr cons surg, mem research comm, VA Hosp, since 1955, staff mem since 1953; res, asst surg, Cincinnati Gen Hosp, 1939-42; cons surg, Sidney Hillman Med Cen, 1951; chmn, dept surg, Albert Einstein Med Cen, 1955-67. Maj, US Army, 1942-46. Dipl, Amer Bd Surg, 1948, 1948; f: AMA; Amer Coll Surgs; Phila Coll Phys; Phila Acad Surg; chmn, hosp div, Allied J App, 1954; mem: Phila Co and Pa State Med Socs; Phila Phys Soc; AAAS; Mont Reid Surg Soc; NY Acad Scis; Phi Beta Kappa; Alpha Omega Alpha; Sigma Xi. Contbr to med jours. Home: Cedarbrook Hill Apts, Wyncote, Pa. Office: 1500 Vine St, Philadelphia, Pa.

ULLMANN, Jacob Walter, US, business exec; b. NYC, Aug 12, 1927; s. Siegfried and Irma (Lichtenstadter); att MIT, 1943-44, 1954-55; BChE, NYU, 1948; MSE, U Mich, 1949; m. Regina Figatner, Sep 15, 1968. Tech asst to vice-pres, Union Carbide Corp, since 1966; sr engr, Oak Ridge Natl Lab, 1950-66. Vice-pres, Amer Technion Soc; mem, bd govs: Technion, Haifa; Weizmann Inst, Rehovoth, both Isr. Home: 1175 York Ave, New York, NY. Office: 270 Park Ave, New York, NY.

ULLMANN, John E, US, educator; b. Vienna, Aus, Dec 25, 1923; s. Ernest and Anna (Hönigsfeld); in US since 1948; BSc, U London, 1948; MS, Columbia U, 1951, PhD, 1959; profsl engr, NY State; m. Eva Gruenwald, Aug 30, 1953; c: James, Catherine. Prof, mgmt, chmn, dept mgmt, marketing, bus stat, Hofstra U, NY, since 1961; cons: urban problems, transp, ind marketing; plant engr: Natl Gas & Oil Engine Co Ltd, 1941-48; Worthington Corp, 1948-50; planning engr, Bechtel Corp, 1948-50; planning engr, Bulova Research and Devl Labs, 1954-57; lectr, Columbia U, 1957-58; asst prof, econ of engr, Stevens Inst Tech, 1958-61. Co-author: Manufacturing Management: An Overview, 1969; ed, Conversion Prospects of the Defense Electronics Industry, 2nd ed, 1969; contbr to profsl jours. Home: 2518 Norwood Ave, North Bellmore, NY. Office: Hofstra U, Hempstead, NY.

ULLMANN, Theodor D, Isr, physician, educator; b. Würzburg, Ger, Apr 28, 1908; s. Simon and Pepi (Saenger); in Isr since

1934; MD, Julius-Maximilian U, Würzburg, 1933; m. Lisa Findler, 1945; c: Edna, Simon. Head phys, internal diseases dept, Hadassah Rothschild U Hosp, since 1940, head, clinical research lab, since 1957; asso prof, med, Heb U Sch Med, Jerusalem, since 1960; acting head, med dept, A, Hadassah U Hosp, since 1968. Pres, Isr Soc Nephrology, since 1965. Contbr to profsl jours. Home: 28 Abarbanel St, Jerusalem, Isr. Office: Hadassah Rotschild U Hosp, Jerusalem, Isr.

UMANSKY, David, US, business exec; b. Bklyn, NY, May 1, 1913; s. Joseph and Rose (Katz); att U Richmond, Va, 1933-36; BS, CCNY, 1938; m. Pearl Kaplan, June 17, 1939; c: Barbara Lustig, Linda. Pres, Reliable Remover & Lacquer Corp, exec secy, since 1951; estimator, Joseph Umansky Plumbing and Heating, 1938-40; with construction batallion, munition plants, 1941-44. Pres, Men's Assn, Cong Rodeph Sholom, NYC, since 1961; exec bd mem, Natl Fed of Temple Brotherhoods, since 1963; vice-pres, Thomas Jefferson Alumni Assn, fmr pres; Jefferson Athletic Alumni Assn; mem: Masons; B'nai B'rith; Phi Sigma Delta; fmr: lay judge, J Conciliation Bd Amer; instl repr, Boy Scout Troop 583; fmr active in coll and profsl football. Author: Passing, Punting and Place Kicking, 1938. Recipient: Medal of Honor, for saving life of drowning man, Mayor James J Walker, 1929. Home: 322 W 72 St, New York, NY. Office: 42-56 Crescent St, Long Island City, NY.

UNGAR, Alexander Lawrence, US, orthodontist; b. NYC, Nov 15, 1906; s. John and Victoria (Von Falkenheim); att NYU, 1924-26; DDS, U of Pa, 1932; cert, orthodontics: NYU, 1934; Columbia U, 1937; m. Helene Rosenson, Feb 22, 1942; c: Judith Leibowits, John, Vicki. Pvt practice, since 1934; chief, orthodontics, head dent clinics: J Memorial Hosp; Sydenham Hosp; child research div, NYU Dent Sch; dent, 1932-34. Lt col, Dent Corps, US Army, 1940-46. F: Intl Coll Dent, 1958; Amer Coll Dent, 1962; NY Acad Dent; pres, bd dirs, Heb HS of Five Towns; trustee Temple Beth El, Cedarhurst; treas, SED frat, fmr pres; fmr: delg, Amer Dent; Assn; chancellor cdr, KP; mem: bd govs, NY State Dent Soc; 1st Dist and E Dent Socs, fmr pres; AAAS; Amer Assn Orthodontists; Federation Dentaire Internationale; Amer Dent Assn; Northeastern Soc Orthodontists. Recipient: Army Commendation Medal. Author: Incidence and Effect of Premature Loss of Deciduous Teeth, 1937. Hobbies: painting, sculpture, bridge. Home: 829 Cent Ave, Woodmere, LI, NY. Office: 211 Central Park W, New York, NY.

UNGAR, André, US, rabbi, educator; b. Budapest, Hung, July 21, 1929; s. Bela and Frederika (Rujder); in US since 1959; BA, hons U London, 1951, PhD, 1954; m. Judy Bell; c: Michelle, Ethan, Eli. Rabbi, Temple Emanuel, Westwood, NJ, since 1961; lectr, Rutgers U, since 1963; fmr: rabbi, Eng, S Afr, Can. Expelled by S Afr govt for opposing racism; participant: civil rights movement Ala, Miss, Wash DC, NJ, since 1959; peace movement; alternate delg, Dem Natl Conv, 1968; mem: RA; AAUP. Author: Living Judaism, 1958; Resistance Against Tyranny, 1966; contbr to rel and political jours. Home: 41 St Nicholas Ave, Westwood, NJ. Study: 111 Washington Ave, Westwood, NJ.

UNGAR, Benjamin, Isr, cantor; b. Jaslo, Aus, Sep 24, 1907; s. Moses and Reisel (Feuer); in Isr since 1938; att: Yeshiva, Vienna, Trnava; Conservatory, Vienna, Magdeburg; m. Henni Haendler, Dec 3, 1933; c: Miriam Tauber, Varda. Chief cantor, Gt Syn, Tel Aviv, since 1959; participant: Kol Isr; Kol Zion la Gola; Galei Zahal radio stas; fmr: cantor: Tel Aviv, 1939-59; high holidays, Stockholm, 1953, 1954. Haganah, 1938-47; IDF, 1947-63. Pres, Cantors Assn Isr; mem: B'nai B'rith; Masons. Recordings: Liturgical Recitatives and Nigune Chassidim, 1961; Liturgical Recitatives, 1969. Home: 14 Natan Hehacham St, (Lessing), Tel Aviv, Isr. Office: Great Synagogue 110 Allenby St, Tel Aviv, Isr.

UNGAR, Eric Edward, US, engineer; b. Vienna, Aus, Nov 12, 1926; s. Irwin and Sabina (Schlesinger); in US since 1939; BS, Wash U, St Louis, 1951; MS, U of NM, 1954; DEng, NYU, 1957; m. Goldie Becker, July 1, 1951; c: Judith, Susan, Ellen, Sharon. Mgr, applied physics dept, Bolt Beranek and Newman Inc, since 1967, sr engr sci, 1958-67; aero-ordinance engr, Saudia Corp, 1951-53; asst prof, research sci, NYU, 1956-57, instr, 1953-56. Lt, US Army, 1944-48. F, Acoustical Soc Amer, since 1968; F, bd mem, Temple Emanuel, Newton, Mass, chmn, adult educ comm; mem: Amer Soc Mech Engrs; Amer Inst Aeronautics and Astronautics; Tau Beta Pi; Sigma Xi; Pi Mu Epsilon; Pi Tau Sigma; Phi Kappa Phi. Contbr to books: Structural Damping, 1959; Mechanical Design and Systems

Handbook, 1964; Dynamics of Structured Solids, 1968; contbr to engr and sci jours. Home: 15 Considine Rd, Newton Centre, Mass. Office: 50 Moulton St, Cambridge, Mass.

UNGAR, Henry, Isr, pathologist, educator; b. Berlin, Ger, Jan, 1906; s. Bernhard and Gisella (Haimovici); in Isr since 1935; MD, U Berlin, 1930; m. Ruth Bestermann, July 1933; c: Deborah Tal, Ayalah. Chief, dept path, Heb U-Hadassah Med Sch, since 1950, prof path, Hadassah U Hosp, since 1954; asst path, U Berlin, 1931-33; res, lab div, Montefiore Hosp, NY, 1934-35; visiting prof, path, Sch Med, U Cal, 1952-53. Pres: IMA sci council, 1959-61; Intl Soc Geog Path, 1966-69; mem: Isr Assn Paths; Intl Assn Clinical Path; Intl Acad Path; Soc of Experimental Biol and Med Contbr to profsl jours. Spec interest: viola player. Home: 38 Metudela St, Jerusalem, Isr. Office: Heb U-Hadassah Hosp, Jerusalem, Isr.

UNGAR, Paul, Austr, communal worker; b. Vienna, June 9, 1895. Honorary life mem JNF, Austr and NZ, fmr pres, mem, JNF Council; exec mem, Zionist Fed of Austr and NZ; vice-pres, United Israel Appeal, NSW; Honary Dir, J Bd of Deputies of NSW. Home: 71 Mona Vale Rd, Pymble, Sydney, Australia.

UNGER, Abraham Alfred, Isr, industrialist; b. Cracow, Aus, June 20, 1906; s. Chaim and Rachel (Wachsmann); in Isr since 1934; deg, metallurgy, U Vienna; m. Gisela Attermann, Oct 8, 1946; c: Raphael, Evelyne. Owner, pres, Dental-Sahav-Unger, since 1935. Found, pres, Dent Gold Mfrs and Importers Assn; co-found, exec mem, Hitahdut Olei Aus; mem: Masons; B'nai B'rith; fmr dir, Pal Off, Vienna; mem, Zionist Org, Aus; contbr to Zionist publs. Home: 21 Hen Blvd, Tel Aviv, Isr. Office: 8 Herzl St, Tel Aviv, Isr.

UNGER, Allen Norman, US, business exec; b. Newport News, Va, Dec 1, 1912; s. William and Rose (Berger); BS, U Va, 1934; m. Helen Goldstein; c: Jane, William. Ret; fmr vice-pres, finance, Noland Co, Inc, Newport News, 1959-69. Pres, Jr C of C, Hampton Rds, Va, 1948; co-chmn, Allied J Appeal, Newport News, 1952. Home: 52 Manteo Ave, Hampton, Va.

UNGER, Jerome, US, rabbi; b. NY, Oct 1, 1906; AB, NYU, 1928; AM, U Cincinnati, 1929; ordained rabbi, MHL, HUC-JIR, 1935; m. Anne Kaplan, 1935; c: Judith Thalberg, David. Dir public affairs, ZOA, since 1964; comm, Unity for Palestine, 1946-48, asso exec dir, 1948-49; rabbi, Vassar Temple, Poughkeepsie, NY, 1935-46; chaplain, US Mil Acad, West Point, 1943-46; mil police guard, Hyde Park Estate, 1943-46; dir, AZC, 1949-64. Repr J people, dedication, Hyde Park Roosevelt Shrine, 1946. Study: 145 E 32 St, New York, NY.

UNGER, Lester J, US, physician; b. NYC, Aug 1, 1888; s. Hermann and Sophia (Jarecky); BA, CCNY, 1909; MA, Columbia U, 1910, MD, Coll of Phys and Surgs, 1913; m. Beatrice Raphael, Sep 14, 1922; c: Roger, Harlow. Dir: blood and plasma bank, NYU Med Cen, U Hosp, since 1948; blood bank, St Luke's Hosp, Women's Hosp Div, since 1940; att transfusionist, St Clare's Hosp, since 1940; att hematologist, Lutheran Hosp, since 1917; cons hematologist: St Joseph's Hosp, Far Rockaway, since 1930; NY Infirmary for Women and Children, since 1950; Fr Hosp, since 1948; att transfusionist, Hosp for Jt Diseases, 1920-51; asst surg, Post-Grad Hosp, 1922-48; dir, blood and plasma bank, 1940-48; cons hematologist, Englewood Hosp, NJ, 1935; att phys, U Hosp, Bellevue Hosp, both 1950-54; pres, bd dirs, Blood and Plasma Exch Bank, 1941. F, Intl Soc of Hematologists; mem: Med adv comm, AMA; NY State Med Soc; NY Co Med Soc; NY Acad Med; State Path Soc; Amer Assn Clinical Path; AAAS; Soc for Experimental Biol and Med; Amer Assn Blood Banks; Amer Acad Forensic Scis; Amer Soc Hum Genetics; NY Acad Scis; Soc for Study of Blood; Civil Defense Comm; Alpha Omega Alpha. Contbr of numerous articles to med jours. Recipient: Work in blood transfusion and hematology, selected for time capsule buried at site of last World's Fair in NY, to be excavated in 5000years. Home: 1192 Park Ave, New York, NY. Office: 135 E 74 St, New York, NY.

UNGER, Menashe, US, journalist, author; b. Zabno, Aus-Hung, Nov 12, 1899; s. Sholem and Blume (Horowitz); ordained rabbi, Broder Yeshiva, Vienna, 1917; att Heb U, Jerusalem, 1925-30; m. Ruth Brilliant, Nov 25, 1936; c: Jehudith Menucha. Staff mem, The Day Morning Jour, NYC, since 1934, columnist since 1950. Author: Chasidus un Lebn, 1946; Pszysche un Kock, 1949; Gut Yom Tov Kinder, 1950; Moadim Le-Simcha, 1953; Die Chassidishe Welt, 1954; Chassidus un

Yom-Tov, 1957; Reb Yisroel Baal Shem Tov, 1963; Sefer Kedashim, 1967; Religiezer Widershtand, 1968. Mem: Yiddish Writers Union; club, PEN. Home: 150 W 96 St, New York, NY. Office: 183 E Broadway, New York, NY.

UNGER, Sidney E, US, rabbi; b. NYC, May 7, 1896; s. Adolph and Julia (Klein); BA, U Cincinnati, 1925; ordained rabbi, HUC, 1928, hon DD, 1958; MEd, Temple U, 1938; STD, 1938; m. Evelyn Winsberg, May 25, 1941; c: Edwin, Carol Adelstein. Rabbi Em, Cong Beth Ha-Tephila, Asheville, NC, rabbi since 1946; asst rabbi: Rodeph Shalom, 1928-33; Temple Judea, 1933-40, both Phila, Pa; Beth Elohim, Charleston, SC, 1945-46. Lt, US Army, WW I; chaplain, maj, WW II. Mem: bd dirs, Civic Music Assn; exec bd, CCAR, 1947-49; bd dirs, Asheville Biltmore Coll, 1948-57; B'nai B'rith; Masons; Pi Lambda Phi; Phi Delta Epsilon; club, Lions. Ed: weekly radio prog, Hear, Oh Israel, WWNC, Asheville; contbr to J publs. Home: 1 Lynmar Ave, Asheville, NC.

UNNA, Moshe, Isr, legislator; b. Mannheim, Ger, Nov 22, 1902; s. Itzhak and Gittel (Goitein); in Isr since 1927; dipl, agronomist, Agric Coll, Berlin, 1922; att Hildesheimer Rabb Coll, 1920-22; m; c: Ruth, Yedida, Matanya-Zvi; m. 2nd, Sabina Gutman; c: Shlomit, Gabriella, Hillel-Josef, Tirza. Isr Religious Party leader; farmer, mem, Kvutzat Sde Elyahu; exec comm, haPoel haMizrachi, since 1942, dir: youth immigration dept, 1939-40; MK, 1949-69, chmn: comms: constitution and leg, law; fgn policy and defense; econ; council, rel educ in govt schs, 1955-56, 1968-69; dep min, Isr Min Educ and Culture, 1956-58. Bd dirs, Mikveh Isr Agric Sch; co-found: Kfar Avraham, 1932; Kfar Hanoar Hadati, 1938, head, bd dirs, 1956-66; fmr mem, secretariat; haKibutz haDati; Kvutzot Rodges and Tirat Zvi; delg, WZCS; mission abroad, 1933-34. Author, Beshvilei haMahshava ve haMaase; Shutafut shel Emet; contbr to local rel press. Home: Kvutzat Sde Elyahu, Isr.

UNSDORFER, Julius, Eng, rabbi; b. Bratislava, Czech, May 10, 1919; s. Solomon and Jenny (Stern); in Eng since 1939; ordained rabbi, Yeshiva Coll, Bratislava, 1939; MA, U Manchester, 1953; PhD, U Leeds, 1962; m. Ada Jaffe, Sep 15, 1940; c: Paula Goldblum, Malka, Golda Solomon, Sr rabbi, Holy Law Cong, Manchester, since 1950; rabbi: Bratislava, 1938-39; Kahal Chassidim, Manchester, 1940-50. Hon rel dir, gov, King David Schs; vice-pres, Mizrachi Fed, Gt Brit, chmn, Manchester Mizrachi, 1955-60; hon chaplain: Lord Mayor, 1964-65; J Lads Brig; mem, exec comm, NCCJ. Author, Jewish Bride's Book, 1956. Home: 124 Albert Ave, Prestwich, Manchester, Eng.

UNTERBERG, Sigmund, Can, attorney, organization exec; b. Aus, Dec 17, 1896; s. Isaac and Regina (Tenenbaum); in US since 1940; D, law and political econ, U Vienna, 1921; dipl, Acad of Commerce, 1922; m. Hedwig Kempler, June 14, 1931; c: Paul Mary. Exec treas, off, mem natl exec, Can J Cong, since 1965, controller to 1943; exec dir, United J Relief Agcy, since 1968; mgr, Can-Isr Corp, since 1953; dir: United J Tchrs Sem, since 1952; J Immigrant Aid Soc, since 1963; trustee, Cong Charities Comm; dir, CJCong Mus and Archives, since 1968. Dir, Jt Adv Lab Comm; mem: jt comm on lab relations; Jt Comm, Can J Cong and B'nai B'rith; Cong Shaar Hashomayim; Temple Emanu-El; delg, Assembly of J Feds and Wfr Funds; club, Can. Recipient: Can Centennial Medal, Govt of Can. Home: 4439 Harvard Ave, Montreal, Can. Office: 493 Sherbrooke St W, Montreal, Can.

UNTERMAN, Issar Y, Isr, chief rabbi; b. Brisk, Lith, 1886; s. Eliahu and Sheine (Fisher); in Isr since 1947; att Yeshivas: Brisk, Mir, Maltch; ordained rabbi, Rabbi Volozin Yeshiva; m. Rachel Yellin (decd); c: Avraham, Yaakov, Mordechai, Baruch, Elhannan, Zvi, Esther. Chief rabbi, Ashkenazi, of Isr, since 1964; chief rabbi, Tel Aviv-Jaffa and Dist, and pres, Rabb Courts, Tel Aviv, 1947-64. Mem: World Mizrachi; cen comm, Mizrachi; delg, WZCs since the 12th; fmr pres: JNF; KH, Liverpool, Eng, vice-pres, Gt Brit. Author: Shevet Meyehuda, 1955; contbr to rabb jours. Home: 21 Keren Hayesod, Jerusalem, Isr. Office: Chief Rabbinate, Jerusalem, Isr.

UNTERMAN, Mordecai Maurice, Eng, rabbi; b. Porozow, Pol, Mar 18, 1917; s. Iser; in Eng since 1924; ordained rabbi, Mir Theol Coll, Pol; m. Ruth Harris; c: Rochelle, Reva. Rabbi: Marble Arch Syn, London, since 1961; Cardiff Syn, 1937-46; pres, Hove Syn, 1950-52; dir, Bar-Ilan U, Isr, 1960-61. Vice-chmn, trustee, Ravenswood Found Mh; hon

dir, Chief Rabbi's Cabinet. Home: 32 Gt Cumberland Pl, London, W1, Eng. Study: Marble Arch, Syn, London, W1, Eng.

UNTERMEYER, Jean Starr, US, author, lecturer; b. Zanesville, O, May 13, 1886; d. Abraham and Joanna (Schoenfeld) Starr; att Columbia U, 1905; m. Louis Untermeyer, Jan 23, 1907 (div); c: Richard (decd). Tchr, lectr: New Sch for Soc Research, 1948-56; Olivet Coll, 1936-37; tchr, Writers Sch, League of Amer Writers, 1938-39. Author: poetry: Growing Pains, 1918; Dreams out of Darkness, 1922; Steep Ascent, 1927; Winged Child, 1936; Love and Need, 1940; Private Collection, a memoir, 1965; Job's Daughter, 1967; trans, from Ger: Schubert, The Man, 1928; The Death of Virgil, by Hermann Broch, 1945; contbr, critical revs to: NY Times; Saturday Rev of Lit; Chgo Herald-Tribune; Voices. Hon mem, bd, Amer-Isr Cultural Found; mem: Authors League of Amer; Poetry Soc of Amer; club, PEN. Recipient: Ford Madox Ford Chair of Creative Lit, Olivet Coll, Mich, 1940. Hobbies: music, cooking. Home: 235 E 73 St, New York, NY.

UNTERMEYER, Louis M, US, author, editor; b. NYC, Oct 1, 1885; s. Emanuel and Julia (Michael); hon DHL, Union Coll; hon DLitt, New England U; m. Jean Starr, Jan 23, 1907; (div); m. 2nd ,Virginia Moore, 1926; m. 3rd, Esther Antin, 1933; m. 4th, Bryna Ivens, 1948; c: Richard Starr (decd), John, Lawrence, Joseph. Author: Modern American Poetry, 1921, 1962; Modern British Poetry, 1920, 1962; This Singing World, 1923; Moses, novel 1928; The Book of Living Verse, 1932; From Another World, autobiography, 1939; A Treasury of the World's Great Poems, 1942; Doorways to Poetry, 1951; The Magic Circle, 1953; Makers of the Modern World, 1955; Lives of the Poets, 1959; Britannica Library of Great American Writing, 2 vols, 1960; Long Feud: Selected Poems, 1962; The World's Great Stories, 1964; Labyrinth of Love, 1965; Bygones: An Autobiography, 1965; The Firebringer and Other Great Stories, 1968. Vicepres, mgr, jewelry bus, 1923; poetry ed, The Amer Mercury, 1934-37; poet in residence: Knox Coll; Amherst Coll, both 1937; U Mich, 1939-40; U Kan City, 1939; Ia State Coll, 1940; sr ed publs, OWI, 1942; ed: Armed Services Eds, 1943-44; Decca Records, 1944-57; appd, cons in poetry, Libr of Cong, 1961; contbr of prefaces, critical revs to: New Republic; Yale Rev; Saturday Rev of Lit; anthols; ed, various mags. Mem: Natl Inst Arts and Letters. Recipient: Gold Medal, Poetry Soc of Amer; hon Phi Beta Kappa: Harvard U, Tufts U. Home: Great Hill Rd, Newton, Conn.

URBACH, Ephraim E, Isr, Talmudist, educator; b. Wloclawek, Pol, May 26, 1912; s. Israel and Esther (Spiegel); in Isr since 1938; ordained rabbi, J Theol Sem, Breslau, 1933; att U Breslau, 1930-33; DLitt, U Rome, 1935; m. Hannah Pinczower, 1943; c: Abraham, Joseph, Meir, Esther, Rachel, Naomi. Prof, Talmud and Midrash, Heb U, Jerusalem, since 1953; lectr, J Theol Sem, Breslau, 1935-38; tchr, Gimnasia Ivrit, Jerusalem, 1939-41; prin, Maale Secondary Sch, 1945-50; sup, Secondary Schs, Min Educ, 1950-51; dir, Dept Higher Educ, Min of Educ, 1952-53. Chaplain, Brit Army, 1942-45; IDF. Mem: Heb Lang Acad; Isr Acad Scis, Humanities; bd, Hist Soc of Isr; hon secy, Mekize Nirdamin Soc. Author: Etudes sur la Littérature Polémique au Moyen Age, 1935; Arugat haBossem, Vol I-IV, 1939-63; Religious and Social Tendencies in the Talmudical Teachings of Charity, 1951; Baale haTossafot, 1955; The Rabbinical Laws of Idolatry in 2nd and 3rd Centuries, in the Light of Archeological and Historical Facts, 1959; The Laws Regarding Slavery as a Source for Social Hist of the Period of the Second Temple, The Mishna and Talmud, 1963; Class Status and Leadership in the World of the Palestinian Sages, 1966; contbr to learned jours. Recipient: Isr Prize for J studies, 1955. Home: 22 Hatibbonim St, Jerusalem, Isr. Office: Heb U, Jerusalem, Isr.

URBACH, Symcha Bunim, Isr, rabbi, educator; b. Warsaw, Pol, Dec 31, 1913; s. Boruch and Sarah (Naparstek); in Isr since 1941; ordained rabbi, Yeshiva, Pol; att: U Bordeaux, Fr, 1935; Heb U, Jerusalem; m. (decd). Sr lectr, phil, Bar Ilan U, since 1956; rabbi: Tivon, 1949-67; Sdeh Jacob, 1946-49. Author: Toldot Neshama Ahat, 1953; Amudei haMahshava haYisraelit, 3 vols, 1951. Mem, B'nai B'rith; haPoel haMizrachi. Recipient: awards: Harav Kuk; Hantziv; Harav Harlap; Rel Explanation, Heichal Shlomo, chief rabbinate, Tel Aviv; Jerusalem. Home: 15 Klee St, Tel Aviv, Isr. Study: U Bar Ilan, Rmat Gan, Isr.

URBONT, Carl, US, organization exec; b. NYC, Dec 25, 1915; s. Albert and Pauline; AB, NYU, 1941; MS, Columbia U,

1948; ED, Tchrs Coll, Columbia U, 1966; m. Genia Ukrainsky, 1948; c: Aviva, Albert. Exec dir, 92nd St YM & YWHA, since 1956, asst exec dir, 1951-56; actor, with Eva LeGallienne, George S Kaufman and the Theatre Guild, until 1941; tchr, sociol, Wash Sq Coll, 1946, 1948; exec dir, Emanuel Brotherhood, 1947-49; dir, cultural and educ rehab, JDC, Paris, 1949-51. Vice-pres, Natl Assn J Cen Workers, since 1960, secy, 1958-60; mem, bd of dirs, Yorkville Civic Council since 1960; pres, Metrop Assn of J Cen Workers, 1954-56. Recipient: Israel Cummings award, FJP, 1960. Home: 82 North Chatsworth Ave, Larchmont, NY. Office: 1395 Lexington Ave, New York, NY.

URIEL, Gila, Isr, administrator; b. Cracov, Pol, Jan 23, 1913; s. Eliezer znd Sophia (Billig) Stamm; in Isr since 1924; cert: HS Law and Econ, 1938; LSE, 1939; Oriel Coll, Oxford U, 1953. Dir, org and training div, Tel Aviv Munic, since 1954; dir of studies, Public Admn Inst, co-ed, Haminhal Quarterly, 1946-56. F, UNPA, UN, since 1953; RIPA, London, since 1939; IIAS, Brussels, since 1950; mem, Poetry Soc, London. Author: Human Relationship in Public Administration, 1953; Office Administration, Heb, 1959; Efficiency and Training, 1963; ed bd: Public Admn in Isr and Abroad, Annual; Org and Admn, Jerusalem, since 1960. Spec interests: translating, reciting, broadcasting, lectr on world poetry. Home: 9 Prague St, Tel Aviv, Isr. Office: Tel Aviv Munic, Tel Aviv, Isr.

URY, Josef Franz, Isr, educator; b. Karlsruhe, Ger, Feb 12, 1909; s. Jakob and Deborah (Schloss); in Isr since 1934; Dipl, Tech Hochschule, Dresden, Ger, 1932; MSc, Technion, 1963; m. Sara Oppar, Sep 8, 1935; c: Jacob, Dan. Asso prof, mech engr, Technion, since 1959, fac mem since 1952, dean, fac mech engr, 1964-65; produc and maintenance: Assis Ltd, Ramat Gan, 1934-38; Pal Frutarom Ltd, Haifa, 1938-49; maintenance, sup, design, Tnuva, Haifa, 1950-52. Mem: Assn Engrs and Architects, Isr; Inst of ME; AAAS. Contbr to engr sci jours. Home: 86 Hatichon St, Neve Shaanan, Haifa, Isr. Office: Technion, Haifa, Isr.

URY, Zalman F, US, rabbi, educational cons, educator; b. Stolpce, Pol, Dec 17, 1924; s. Abraham and Cypa (Borishansky) Fajwusowitz; in US since 1947; ordained rabbi, Beth Medrash Govoha, Lakewood, NJ, 1948; BS, Wash U, St Louis, Mo, 1955; MA, Loyola U, LA, 1962; DEduc, UCLA, 1966; m. Eva Perl, Aug 30, 1945; c: Celia Rabinowitz, Natali Amster, Ramma, Israel. Head cons, Bur of J Educ, LA, since 1959, i/c, orthodox schs; lectr, educ, Yeshiva U, since 1963; rabbi, Young Isr Beverly Hills, since 1967; prin: Epstein Acad, St Louis, Mo, 1952-57; Hillel Acad, Beverly Hills, 1957-59. Mem: Natl Council J Educ; Torah Umesorah. Author: The Mussar Movement, 1969; contbr numerous articles and curricula guides in Eng and Heb. Spec interest: research in ethics and character educ. Home: 465 S Wetherly Dr, Beverly Hills, Cal. Office: 590 N Vermont Ave, Los Angeles, Cal.

USSISHKIN, David, Isr, archaeologist, educator; b. Jerusalem, Isr, Oct 21, 1935; s. Samuel and Elsa (Schönberg); grandson, Menahem Ussishkin; MA, Heb U, Jerusalem, 1961, PhD, 1966; m. Ann Herzfeld, Dec 27, 1964; c: Iddo. Lectr, Tel Aviv U, since 1967; participant in various archaeol excavations and projects. IDF, 1953-55. Contbr of articles to sci jours. Home: 3 Neve Granot, Jerusalem, Isr.

USSISHKIN, Samuel, Isr, attorney; b. Ekaterinoslav, Russ, May 19, 1899; s. Menahem Mendel and Esther (Paley); in Isr since 1922; LLB, U Cambridge, Eng, 1922; m. Elsa Schoenberg, 1926; c: Jacob. Pvt practice since 1924; lectr, Sch of Law and Econ, Tel Aviv, 1936-46. Mem, bd dirs, Keren Kayemet leIsr; dep chmn, Zionist Org Tribunal; delg, ZCs. Author: Prakim baHok haBriti, 1927; Maarav baMizrah, 1931; Shitot haShilton baKeisarut haBritit, 1937; Mishtar haMedini beBritania, 1944. Home: 7 Ussishkin St, Jerusalem, Isr.

USSOSKIN, Moshe, Isr, civic worker; b. Moghilew Podolsk, Russ, Mar 8, 1899; s. Elijahu and Dvora (Kassjansky); in Isr since 1941; m. Mirjam Griner, Mar 29, 1934; c: Elischewa Barak. Vice-chmn, Tel Aviv Devl Co; mem, bd dirs, Isr Land Devl; Jerusalem Econ; Binyanei Haooma; dir, Cen Bank for J Coop, Credit Societies in Rum, 1928-41. Dir, JDC and Amer Jt Reconstruction Found for the Balkan countries, Hung, Turkey, 1928-41; dir gen, and treas, United Isr Appeal, 1949-68; mem, presidium, World Fed of Bessarabian J; mem, bd of govs, Heb U; rep, United Isr Appeal, delg, ZC; exec, comm, Friends of Jerusalem Artists House. Author: Social Welfare Among Jews in Saloniki; The Cooperative Movement Among Jews in Old Rumania; numerous articles in Isr and fgn periodicals. Home: 16 Arlosoroff St, Jerusalem, Isr.

UVEELER, Mark, US, organization exec; b. Warsaw, Pol, Dec 7, 1904; s. Wolf and Sarah (Brandes) Juwiler; in US since 1941; att U Warsaw, 1926; m. Luba Syman, June 8, 1949. Dir, dept cultural and educ reconstruction, Conf on J material claims against Ger, since 1956, secy since 1962; exec dir, Memorial Found J Culture; tchr, Yiddish sch sys, Warsaw, 1922-23; gen secy: Intl Union Leathergoods Workers, Pol; J Printers Union, Pol, 1924-26; exec dir: J Actors Union, Pol, 1926-32, 1936-39; YIVO, NYC, 1944-56. Mem: exec bd, Soc Friends of YIVO, Warsaw, 1932-39; cen bd, YIVO, Vilna, Pol, 1939-40. Home: 5 W 86 St, New York, NY. Office: 215 Park Ave S, New York, NY.

UZAN, Aron, Isr, government official; b. Tunisia, Nov 1, 1924; s. Shlomo and Aliza Garbi; in Isr since 1949; att Yeshiva Sasa, 1938-42; m. Jenie Amano, 1949; c: Shlomo (fell in action 1970), Rina, Eiran, Amos, Joav. Dep Min of Agric, since 1965; chmn, Crop Ins Fund, Ltd, since 1967; secy, Moshav Gilat, 1954-57; dir, Negev Purchasing Org, 1957-65. Cpl, IDF, 1950. Mem, secretariat: Lab Party; Moshav Movement; mem, reg bd Merchavim, 1952-65; chmn: Negev Purchasing Org; Devl Co, Negev Moshav, 1958-65; Devl Co Lachish Moshav, 1963-65; club, Econ for Negev Devl. Home: Moshav Gilat, Isr. Office: 10 Hakirya D, Tel Aviv, Isr.

UZIEL, Baruch, Isr, attorney, legislator; b. Thessaloniki, Greece, Aug, 1901; s. Moshe and Rachel (Attias); in Isr since 1914; grad: Tchrs Sem, 1919; Govt Law Courses, 1932, both Jerusalem; m. Mandy Semo, Oct 30, 1936; c: Moshe, Rachel Farhi. Pvt practice, since 1934; MK, since 1961, chmn, Educ Comm; tchr: Rehovot, Petah Tikva, 1920-31. Mem: World Zionist Exec Comm, since 1956; secretariat, haOved haZioni, since 1936; exec, Lib Party, mem, political comm, chmn, sect; Sephardic and Oriental comtys; fmr chmn, Inst for Study of Saloniki Jewry; past dep Grand Master, Yehudah Halevi lodge, B'nai B'rith; mem: bd, Recanati Parents' Home; Isr Bar Assn; fmr mem: Zionist exec bd educ; ZC Court of Honor, presidium, Maccabi. Author: Travels in Palestine, 1927; stories on life of the Jews in Thessaloniki; contbr articles on Sephardic folklore, to Isr and Judeo-Sephardic press; ed: Thessaloniki Archives, 1962; Saloniki Ir vaEm beIsrael. Home: 15 George Eliot St, Tel Aviv, Isr. Office: 34 Jaffa Rd, Tel Aviv, Isr.

V

VADNAI, Georges-Joseph, Switz, rabbi; b. Gödöllö, Hung, July 23, 1915; s. Abraham and Giselle (Lang); ordained rabbi, Ecole Rabbinique, Paris, 1942; PhD, Sorbonne, Paris, 1951; m. Anne-Laure Braunschweig, 1944; c: Gabriel, Raphael. Rabbi of Lausanne, since 1948. Secy-gen, World Union of J Students, 1946-48; mem, exec, Zionist Youth of Fr, 1945-46. Author: Histoire des Juifs en Croatie-Slavonie aux 18e et 19e Siècles, 1950; contbr to J and Chr publs. Home and study: 2 Chemin de Lucinge, Lausanne, Switz.

VAGINSKY, Samuel, Isr, artist; b. Haifa, Isr, Oct 24, 1937; s. Avigdor and Shulamit; att Midrasha Leziur, Tel Aviv; m. Malka, Oct 11, 1962; c: Efrath, Idoh. Art tchr. One-man shows: gals: Katz, 1960; Chemarinsky, 1961, 1966; Shulamith, 1964; Dugit, 1969, all Tel Aviv; Yad Lebanim, Petah Tikva, 1967; participated, exhbs sponsored by Isr Painters and Sculptors Assn. Mem, Isr Painters and Sculptors Assn. Home: 6 Hess St, Petah Tikva, Isr.

VAGO, Bela Adalbert, Isr, historian; b. Sighet, Rum, June 6, 1922; s. Avraham and Frieda (Fuchs); MA, fac of phil, U Cluj, Rum, 1947, PhD, 1949; m. Lidia Rosenfeld, 1945; c: Raphael, Ariel. Sr lectr: hist dept, Heb U, Jerusalem; and head hist dept, Haifa U, both since 1964; lectr: Bolyai U, Cluj, 1949-57; Parhon U, Bucharest, 1957-58. Author: The Szekler Society in the XVIIIth Century, 1957; contbr of studies on: intl relations in Southeast Eur; natl problems; anti-semitism; Hung and Rum Jewry; fascism. Home: 4 Morad Hazamir, Haifa, Isr. Office: Haifa U, Haifa, Isr; Hebrew U, Jerusalem, Isr.

VAGO, Tibor, Isr, physician; b. Uzhorod, Czech, June 19, 1914; s. Emmanuel and Sidonia (Lichtig); in Isr since 1949; MD, Charles U, Prague, 1947; visiting research f, obstets and gyn, Harvard Med Sch, Boston, 1965; m. Stephania Hendel, Sep 9, 1949. Head, dept obstets and gyn, Govt Hosp, Ashkelon, since 1961; sr res, Schweitzer Hosp, Tiberias, 1949-53; asst head, dept of obstets and gyn, Assaf Harofe Hosp, 1953-61. Mem: Intl Coll of Surgs; IMA; Isr Assn for Research in Fertility; Isr Soc for Obstets and Gyn; Intl Soc for Clinical and Experimental Hypnosis. Author: Gynecology; contbr to profsl jours. Hobbies: pipe collecting, hunting, painting. Home: 13 S Africa Blvd, Afridar, Ashkelon. Office: Govt Hosp, Ashkelon, Isr.

VAINSHENKER, Itshak (pen name, **S Masin**), Uruguay, teacher, author, community clerk; b. Terebna, Bessarabia, Rum, Apr 18, 1914; s. Nahum and Ghelman (Masi); in Uruguay since 1944; att Idishn Shul Farain Sem, Tchernovitz; m. Iocheved Roizman, Dec 28, 1938; c: Judith Lifschitz, Ury. Yiddish-Heb PR, Comité Central Israelita Del Uruguay, since 1949; tchr: Shalom Aleichem HS, since 1957; Ahad Haam Tchrs Sem, since 1965; practical trans of Yiddish, Heb; exec secy, ORT-OSE, Uruguay, 1944-49; consulate official, Isr Emb, 1949-53. Prin contrib: initiator of J schs, study of contemporary Jewry. Pvt, Rum Air Force, 1936-37. Co-found, Confraternidad Christiana, Uruguay; secy, pedg commn, Scholem Aleikhem HS; bd mem, Shifra Staroshevsky Cultural Fund; secy, cultural commn, J Comty, 1966; mem: B'nai B'rith; Circulo de la Prensa, Uruguay; Poalei Zion; Mapai; bd dirs, IWO, Uruguay. Author: Far Alt Naie Hiskhaivusn, 1948; Poshet Mitokh Libshaft, 1955; Boiers un Mitboiers fun Idishn Ishuv in Uruguay, 1957; Urugvortzlen, 1969; trans ino Yiddish: Transnistrie by M Karp, 1950; from Heb, Babi Yar, The Song and the Songster by Shlomo Eyen-Shoshan, 1962, contbr to: Enciclopedia Judaica Castellana, Mexico, 1948; Gt Dict of Yiddish Lang, NY; world J press. Home: 18 de Julio 2135/102, Montevideo, Uruguay.

VAINSTEIN, Rose, US, librarian; b. Edmonton, Alberta, Can, Jan 7, 1920; d. Nathan and Jane (Simenstein); AB, Miami U, Oxford, O, 1941; BLS, W Reserve U, 1942; MS, U of Ill, 1952; research scholar, Fulbright f, Eng, 1952-53. Prof, libr sci, U Mich, since 1968; jr libr, Cayahoga Co libr, Cleveland, O, 1942-43; young people's libr, Bklyn Public Libr, 1943-44; br libr, Contr Costa Co Libr, Martinez, Cal, 1948-51; libr

cons, Cal State Libr, Sacramento, 1953-55; head, ext dept, Gary Public Libr, Ind, 1955-57; spec, public librs, Off Educ, Wash, DC, 1957-61; asso prof, Sch Librarianship U of BC, Can, 1961-64; dir: public librs research study, BC, U of BC, 1963-64; Bloomfield Township Public Libr, Mich, 1964-68. Armed forces, libr, US, Japan, 1944-48. Bd dirs: public libr assn comm, ALA, 1958-61, adult services div, 1961-64, libr educ div, 1968-71; chmn, ASD/RSD interdivisional comm, orientation of adult readers to use of libr, 1968-69; mem, research comm, assn hosp and instn librs, 1969-71; chmn, good teaching award comm, Beta Phi Mu, 1961-62, mem, exec council, 1960-63; co-chmn, intellectual freedom comm, Cal Libr Assn, 1955-56; pres, Dist III, Mich Libr Assn, 1968-69; spec cons, librs for hosps comm, BC Libr Assn, 1961-63; life mem, Can Libr Assn, since 1963; mem: Inst Profsl Librs, Can, since 1961; Libr Assn, Eng, since 1952; Mich Adult Educ Assn, since 1965; Pacific NW Libr Assn, since 1961; Spec Librs Assn, since 1961; clubs: Hadassah, Ann Arbor, since 1968; Altrusa Intl, since 1966; Women's Research, since 1968. Contbr to profsl jours. Hobbies: travel, music, ballet. Home: 201 Medford Rd, Ann Arbor, Mich. Office: Sch Libr Sci, U Mich, Ann Arbor, Mich.

VAJDA, Edward R, US, organization exec; b. NYC, Nov 18, 1912; s. Adolph and Theresa (Rippner); LLB, Atlanta Law Sch, 1934; m. Laura; c: Teresa, Debra. Exec vice-pres, Amer Technion Soc, since 1967; exec dir, Chgo Young Judea, 1938-40; field repr, Natl Ref Service, 1940; mem, comty service dept, JDC, 1941-43, 1946-47; natl field dir, UJA, 1962-67, dir, Cen States region, 1948-55; dir allocations, 1955-61. US Army, 1943-46. Home: 65 Central Park W, New York, NY. Office: 1000 Fifth Ave, New York, NY.

VALERO, Aaron, Isr, physician; b. Jerusalem, Feb 19, 1913; s. Nissim and Esther (Kokia); att Amer U, Beirut, 1930-32; MB, ChB, Med U, Birmingham, Eng, 1938; postgrad: SUNY; U of S Cal, 1953-55; m. Miriam Shaposhnik, Feb 16, 1941; c: Ron, Amira. Head, med dept, cardio-respiratory lab, Rambam Govt Hosp, Haifa, since 1957, sr clinical lectr, since 1965; head, med dept, dir of hosp, Poriah Hosp, Tiberias, 1955-56. Capt, RAMC, 1941-46; IDF, 1946-48. Mem: Intl Heart Assn; Intl Chest Phys Assn; Intl Internal Assn. Contbr of over 50 articles to med jours. Hobbies: painting, golf. Home: 3 Yair Katz St, Mt Carmel, Haifa, Isr. Office: Rambam Hosp, Haifa, Isr.

VALERO, Aron H, Isr, attorney; b. Jerusalem, Aug 3, 1914; s. Joseph and Lea (Sheikewitz); BA, St John's Coll, Cambridge U, 1935, LLB, 1936, MA, 1937; Barrister at Law, Middle Temple Bar, London, 1937; m. Atara Golombek, Sep 10, 1939; c: Simha Cohen, Moses, Leora. Pvt practice, atty and notary, since 1939; chmn, Govt Civil Service Comm, 1968-69. Mem: hqrs, Haganah, Jerusalem, 1948; Mil Gov's Council, Jerusalem, 1948-49. Chmn, Jerusalem Landlords Assn, since 1956; dep chmn, treas, and mem, exec comm, Isr Sephardic Union, 1948-52; pres, Haganah Lodge, B'nai B'rith, 1958-59; mem: Govt Commns on Rents, 1957-60, 1965; presidium, Isr Bar Assn, since 1959; Isr Bar Council, since 1960; council, exec comm, Isr Chamber of Advocates, since 1962; exec, Isr-Amer Soc, since 1957; adv bd, Isr Law Reports, since 1961; delg, World Sephardic Cong, Paris, 1951; co-found, Binyanai Haooma; club: Jerusalem Lions, pres, 1961-62, dist gov, Lion Intl, 1964-65. Hobbies: music, photography. Home: 10 Ussishkin St, Jerusalem, Isr. Office: 10 Ben Yehuda St, Jerusalem, Isr.

VALEVICI, Rita, Uruguay, communal leader; b. Vienna, Aus, Oct 5, 1926; d. David and Malcia (Gottesmann) Kirmayer; in Uruguay since 1953; att HS, Vienna, Aus; m. Abraham Valevici, Apr 10, 1948; c: Harry, Melly. Pres, Youth Org, B'nai B'rith, vice-pres, treas, B'nai B'rith Women Hatikvah; mem: WIZO; U of Jerusalem, vice-pres, 1956-58. Home: Bulevar España, 2780/8, Montevideo, Uruguay.

VALOBRA, Lelio Vittorio, It, attorney; b. Genoa, It, Mar 2, 1900; s. Aronne and Ester (De Benedetti); DJur, U Genoa,

1920; m. Angela Imelio, Aug 8, 1938; one c. Pvt practice since 1923; hon consul gen of Isr, Genoa, since 1950. Lt, It Army, 1915-18. Pres: Volunteer Org of First Aid, Genoa; Delegazione Assistenza Emigranti Ebrei, 1939-49; mem: exec, Union J Comties, since 1935; B'nai B'rith; J comty, Genoa, 1933-35; delg, WJC, Switz, 1948. Home: Piazza Vittoria 4-9, Genoa, It.

VAN AMERONGEN, Eduard, Isr, journalist; b. Amsterdam, Netherlands, Mar 24, 1912; s. Simon and Henriette (Kulker); in Isr since 1951; m. Rachel Frankfoorder; c: Jitschak, Mirjam. Journalist since 1945; chess tchr; chess ed, Lamerhav, since 1965; dir: Nieuw Israelietisch Weekblad; Joachimsthal's Boekhandel, both 1938-50. Author: 133 Traps in the Openings, 1958; 222 Combinations, 1963. Hobbies: chess, classical music, lit. Home: 9 Bar Ilan Blvd, Bat Yam, Isr.

Van CREVELD, Simon, Netherlands, pediatrician; b. Amsterdam, Aug 21, 1894; s. Abraham and Henriette (Bos); BA, U Amsterdam, 1918; MD, U Groningen, 1922; m. Elizabeth Van Dam, Sep 17, 1924. Dir, hemophilia clinic, Huizen, since 1964; prof, head dept ped, U Amsterdam, 1938-64. Prin contribs: original work on glycogen disease, hemophilia and allied disorders. Hon mem, fgn sci socs. Contbr publs on biochem and ped. Recipient: Royal Distinction, 1955. Home: Johannes Vermeer St 87, Amsterdam, Netherlands. Office: Hemophilia Clinic, Huizen, Netherlands.

VAN DAM, Hendrik George, Ger, attorney; b. Berlin, Nov 8, 1906; s. Jacques and Meta Cohen; m. Wilma Wreden. Secy gen, Cen Council of J in Ger, since 1950; legal adv: Cen Wfr Orgs of J in Ger; Assn of J Comtys in N Ger; J Relief Unit, 1946-50; journalist, Netherlands and Switz, 1933-41. Allied Forces: Eng, Netherlands, Ger, 1941-46. Club: Anglo-Ger, Hamburg. Contbr to legal publs. Recipient: Grand Service Cross, W Ger, Fed Rep. Home: 5 Golzheimer Platz, Düsseldorf, Ger. Office: 49 Fischerstr, Düsseldorf, W Ger.

Van EMDE BOAS, Conrad, Netherlands, psychoanalyst; b. Rotterdam, June 17, 1904; s. Simon and Mietje (Katan) Boas; MD, Leiden U, 1930; specialized as psycht and psychan, 1927-32; m. Magda Starkenstein, July 26, 1941; c: Menno, Carel, Walter, Peter. Psycht-sexologist and psychan since 1932; cons sexologist, since 1954; fmr: asst dir, med dir, Dr Aletta Jacobshuis birth control clinic. Pres, Dutch Assn for Med Sexology; Netherlands repr, intl vice pres, Intl Planned Parenthood Fed, since 1953; hon pres, found, sexological clinics in Netherlands, past pres, med bd; mem: Dutch Med Socs; Deutsche Gesellschaft für Sexualforschung; hon, Amer Assn for Group Psychotherapy; Eugenic Soc of Gt Brit; Assn Intl des Critiques d'Art; Soc Européenne de Culture; club, PEN. Author: The Periodical Infertility in Women, 9th ed, 1957; Shakespeare's Sonnets and their Connection with the "travesti-double" plays, 1951; Abortus Provocatus, 1952; Encyclopedia of Sex Science, Dutch version, 1952; Introduction to the Study of Pornography, 1967; Obscenity and Pornography Anno 1966, 1967; co-author: Mems en gemeenschap, 1950; Sex, Society and the Individual, 1953; Geistige Hygiene, Forschung und Praxis, 1955; Das Psychoanalytische Volksbuch, 5th ed, 1957; Encyclopedia of Sexual Behavor, 1960; mem ed bd, sect on sexology: Netherlands Med Jour; Excerpta Medica; contbr to Dutch and fgn jours. Hobby: art. Home and office: 80 Stadionweg, Amsterdam, Netherlands.

VAN PRAAG, Siegfried Emanuel, Belgium, author, educator; b. Amsterdam, Netherlands, Aug 8, 1899; s. Henri and Grietje (de Jongh); grad, U Amsterdam, 1923; m. Hilda Sanders, Apr 16, 1924; c: Herman, Ganna. Prof Fr, Nutsacademie, Rotterdam, since 1957; commentator, ed, Belgian Natl Radio, London, 1942-44. Author: novels: De Weegschaal, 1925; Sam Levita's Levensdans, 1925; La Judith, 1930; Cabaret der Plaatsvervangers, 1932; Julie de Lespinasse, 1934; Madame de Pompadour, 1936; Jezus en Menachem, 1951; Marianne's Lyfwacht, 1951; Seizoenen, 1957; Marceline, 1959; Jerusalem van het Westen, 1961; Dokter de Sola, 1968; De Jakobsladder, 1969; stories: Een man van aanzien, 1931; Son Anglaise, 1944; Daughter of France, 1945; The Road of Nostalgia, 1947; Saul, 1947; Op enkel Spoor, 1949; De Grote Hypnose, 1952; essays: The Western Jews and their Literature since 1860; publ, 1926; In Eigen en Vreemden Spiegel, 1928; Het Ghetto, 1930; Wereldburgers, 1933; Essai d'une Typologie Juive, 1938; The Passions of the Soul, 1939. Mem: comm, Assn of Dutch Authors; Dutch Soc for J Sci; club, Intl PEN, Dutch sect. Recipient: Officier d'Academie, Fr, 1940; prize, Assn of Amsterdam Booksellers, for novel about

destruction of Amsterdam J Comty. Home: 27 ave Antoine Depage, Brussels, Belgium.

Van ZWANENBERG, Saal, Netherlands, industrialist; b. Oss, Netherlands, Apr 21, 1899; s. Arnold and Catharina (Levisson); hon MD, U Utrecht, 1955; m. Nettie van Gelder (decd); c: Kittie Schudel; Irene Hannivoort. Pres, NV Koninklijke Zwanenberg-Organon, since 1910. Hon f, Royal Soc of Arts and Inds, London; mem: De Witte Soc, The Hague; Joods Wetenschappelijk Genootschap, Amsterdam, club, Dutch, London, Recipient: Ridder, Order Nederlandsche Leeuw; Cdr, Order Oranje-Nassau; Ridder, Order Pius IX, 1954; Freeman, City of Oss. Hobbies: sci, music. Home: Amersfoortseweg 17, Apeldoorn, Netherlands. Office: Koninklijke Zout-Orfanon, Arnhem, Netherlands.

VAROD, Shimshon, Isr, veterinary surg; b. Liverpool, Eng, June 22, 1926; Charles and Rebecca (Miller) Pink; in Isr since 1950; BVSc, vetr fac, Liverpool U, 1943, MRCVS, 1949; m. Edith Ayhan; c: Shmuel, Yonathan, Michal. Area vetr surg, hachklait, Tel Mond, since 1950; JA repr, Young Poalei Zion, Volunteer Union, London. Lt, IDF, MC, 1953-55. Chmn, Western Settlers Assn, Netanya; mem: natl exec: Brit Settlers Soc; Isr Vetr Assn, 1960-63; Brit Vetr Assn; leader, Habonim, Gt Brit, 1943-48. Spec interests: current events, hist. Home and office: 14 Yoel Salomon St, Netanya, Isr.

VARON, Benjamin (Benno Weiser); Isr, diplomat, author; b. Cernowitz, Aus-Hung, Oct 4, 1913; s. Leon and Gusti (Weinreb) Weiser; att Med Sch, Vienna, 1932-38; m. Miriam Laserson; c: Leonard, Daniela. Isr Ambass to Paraguay, since 1968; dir: Latin Amer dept, JA, NY, 1948-60; Cen Inst for Cultural Relations Isr-Ibero Amer, Jerusalem, 1960-64; ambass to: Dominican Rep and Jamaica, 1946-67. Author: Yo Era Europeo; El Mirador del Mundo; Visitenkarte, poems. Home: 3750 Mariscal Lopez, Asuncion Paraguay. Office: 221 Alberdi, Asuncion, Paraguay.

VASHITZ, Joseph, Isr, educator; b. Hamburg, Ger, Dec 29, 1910; s. Joshua and Anna (Buber); in Isr since 1936; att: U Berlin, 1929-34; Heb U, Jerusalem, 1967-69; m. one c. Dir, lectr, Cen for Arab Studies, Givat Haviva, Isr, since 1963 journalist, Al Hamishnar, 1945-52; ed, Al Mirsad, 1952-63; Sgt, IDF Res. Bd mem, Isr Orientalist Soc. Author: The Arabs in Palestine, 1947; contbr to jours. Home: Kibbutz Lehavot Habashan, Isr. Office: Givat Haviva, Isr.

VEIS, Arthur, US, biochemist; b. Pittsburgh, Pa, Dec 23, 1925; s. Fred and Sarah (Landis); BS U Okla, 1947; PhD, Northwestern U, Ill, 1950; m. Eve Zenner, June 24, 1951; c: Judith, Sharon, Deborah. Prof, biochem, asso dean, grad and med schs, Northwestern U, since 1965, asso prof, 1960-65; instr, U Okla, 1950-52; research chem, Armour & Co, 1952-60. Lt, USNR, 1943-46. Councilor, Amer Chem Soc; mem: NY Acad Sci; Amer Soc of Biol Chems; Biophys Soc. Author: Macromolecular Chemistry of Gelatin, 1964; Biological Polyelectrolytes, 1970. Recipient: f, Guggenheim Found, 1967. Home: 7633 Lowell, Skokie, Ill. Office: 303 E Chicago Ave, Chicago, Ill.

VENEZKY, Julian B, US, communal leader; b. Bridgeton, NJ, May 16, 1909; s. David and Gussie (Barr); att: U Md George; Wash Law Sch; m. Madelynn Venezky, Nov 9, 1942; c: Gail, Linda. Natl chmn for regions, State of Isr Bonds, chmn, natl exec comm, treas, 1951-55; mem, UJA natl campaign comm, 1963, natl chmn for regions, 1947-48, chmn, natl campaign cabinet, 1948-50; natl chmn, Amer Isr Public Affairs Comm; mem, bd dirs, Weizmann Inst of Sci; clubs: Creve Coeur; Standard, Peoria. Home: High Point Rd, Peoria, Ill. Office: State at Water St, Peoria, Ill.

VENEZKY, Richard Lawrence, US, educator; b. Pittsburgh, Pa, Apr 16, 1938; s. Bernard and Isabel (Zeisel); BEE, Cornell U, 1961, MA, 1962; PhD, Stanford U, 1965; m. Karen Gauz, Aug 2, 1964. Asso prof, computer sci, U Wis, since 1965. Chmn, Midwest region, Amer Profs for Peace in ME; bd dirs, Madison J Wfr Council; mem: AAAS; Ling Soc Amer; Intl Reading Assn; Assn for Computing Machinery. Author: The Structure of English Orthography, 1970; contbr to educ jours. Home: 2228 Hollister, Madison, Wis. Office: U Wis, Madison, Wis.

VENOUZIOU, Victor Solomon, Greece, engineer; b. Larissa, Greece, Sep 15, 1929; s. Solomon and Esther (Kapeta); att Poly, Greece, 1948-52; m. Sultana Albagli, Apr 4, 1965. Engr contractor since 1955. Greek Army, 1952-54. Secy, Salonica

J Comty bd; pres, J Comties of Greece Congr, 1964, 1966, 1967; vice-pres, J Comty, Karditsa, 1952-62. Home: 25 Sarandaporou St, Salonica, Greece. Office: 24 Dimitriou Gounari St, Salonica, Grece.

VENTURA, Moshe, Isr, educator, author; b. Izmir, Turkey, Dec 6, 1893; s. Jacob and Rosha Ventura; ordained rabbi, Rabb Sem, Istanbul, 1914; Diplôme de Pédagogie, Inst de Psychol, Paris, 1923; licence es lettres, Sorbonne, Paris, 1925, Docteur d'etat, 1935; m. Miriam Uziel, Jan 21, 1923; c: Ruth Dotan, Jacob, Violette Maidemberg, Abraham. Lectr, J phil, Bar Ilan U, Isr; chief rabbi, Alexandria, Egypt, 1938-48; lectr, J phil, Yeshiva U, NY, 1950-52; head: tchrs sem, Ramsgate, Eng, 1953-54; Histadrut Rel Tchrs Sem, Jerusalem, Kfar Sava, 1961-67. Author: Le Livre du Kuzari, 1934; La Philosophie de Saadia Gaon, 1935; Le Kalam et le Péripatétisme d'Après le Kuzari, 1935; Introduction to Jewish Philosophy, 1959; Psychology for Teachers, 1966; Kitsur Mishne Tora Leharambam, 1967; The Terminology of Logic by Maimonides, 1969. Home: 39 Reading St, Tel Aviv, Isr.

VERDIGER, Avraham, Isr, legislator; b. Lodz, Pol, May 6, 1921; s. Jacob and Jenetta (Woidislavsky); in Isr since 1947; m. Chaja Kiss, July, 1947; c: Mordchai, Nechama, Allice, Hanoch. MK since 1968; gen secy, Poalei Agudat Isr, since 1961, gen secy, Eur, 1946-48, mgr, immigration dept, 1948-56; mgr, Shearim daily. Home: 16 Mazada St, Tel Aviv, Isr. Office: 114 Allenby St, Tel Aviv, Isr.

VERLINSKY, Nahum, Isr, business exec; b. Adjamka, Russ, Oct 13, 1895; s. Jonathan and Hassia (Szereszewsky); in Isr since 1925; att: Psychoneur Inst, Petersburg; law fac, Odessa U; fac econ, Poly Inst, Odessa; m. Dina Radomiselsky; c: Michael (decd). Dir gen, Tnuva Ltd, since 1916, gen mgr, 1937-58; chmn, Post Bank; mem, bd dirs; Bank Leumi le-Israel; Citrus Marketing Bd; Citrus Control Bd; Gen Mortgage Bank; Bank Igud; Bank Leumi Investment Co; Tnuva Export; Ind Devl Bank Isr; Isr Agric, Devl Exhbs; mem: secretariat, Hevrat Ovdim; cen comm, Intl Coop Alliance; Govt Agric Council; Govt Coop Council; Milk Marketing Bd. Mem: united KH-Keren Kayemet leIsr natl comm; delg: WZCs; Histadrut, to Intl Congs of Coop Alliance: Copenhagen, Den, 1951; Lausanne, Switz, 1960; Eng, 1963; Aus, 1966; to Intl Dairy Congs: Swed, 1949; Netherlands, 1953; It, 1956; Eng, 1959; Den, 1962. Author: The Marketing of Agricultural Product; Impressions from a Visit to US and England; Dairy Marketing in England; Problems of Agricultural Supply and Marketing; Changes in Agricultural Supply and Demand; contbr to local press. Home: 53 David Hamelech Blvd, Tel Aviv, Isr. Office: 17 Yehuda Halevy St, Tel Aviv, Isr.

VERNON, Raymond, US, economist; b. NYC, Sep 1, 1913; s. Hyman and Lillian (Sonnenberg) Wisotsky; BA, CCNY, 1933; PhD, Columbia U, 1941; hon MA, Harvard, 1959; m. Josephine Stone, Aug 9, 1935; c: Heidi Wortzel, Susan Leinwand. Prof, intl trade, inves, Harvard Bus Sch, since 1959; research asst, Natl Bur Econ Research, 1934-35; lectr, Amer U, 1941-49; asst dir, trading and exch div, SEC, 1943-46, with comm, 1935-46; vice-chmn, US delg, Gen Agreement on Tariffs and Trade, Geneva, 1952-53; mem, US delg, intl trade confs, 1948-54; acting dir, Off of Econ Defense and Trade Policy, State Dept, 1953-54, with dept, 1946-54; dir: planning and control, Hawley and Hoops, Inc, Newark, 1954-56; Metrop Region study, 1956-59; Harvard Devl Adv Service, 1962-65; acting dir, Harvard Cen for Intl Affairs, 1966-68. Mem: Amer Econ Assn; Council on Fgn Relations; Phi Beta Kappa. Author: Regulation of Stock Exchange Members, 1941; Organizing for World Trade, 1955; Anatomy of a Metropolis, 1959; Metropolis: 1985, pub 1960; Myth and Reality of Our Urban Problems, 1965; Manager in the International Economy, 1968. Recipient: Meritorious Service award, State Dept, 1952. Home: 1 Dunstable Rd, Cambridge, Mass. Office: Harvard Bus Sch, Boston, Mass.

VERSHBOW, Herman, US, manufacturer; b. Lomza, Pol, Nov 20, 1893; s. Herschel and Rebecca (Finkelstein); in US since 1912; att Wentworth Inst, Boston, 1916-19; m. Jennie Polansky, March 20, 1920 (decd); c: Arthur, Daniel; m. 2nd, Peggy Abrams, Dec 15, 1968. Co-found, treas, Modern Die & Machine Co, since 1926; co-found, pres, Eastern Steel Rack Co, since 1928; dir, Serv-O-Lift Corp, since 1957. Hon pres, life trustee, Temple Ohabei Shalom, pres 1964-67; trustee: Heb Tchrs Coll; Bur J Educ; mem: AJComm; Masons; Shriners; life mem, J Chautauqua; club, Gtr Boston,

Brandeis, hon life dir. Home: 340 Kent St, Brookline, Mass. Office: 166 Pleasant St, Boston Mass.

VERTÉS-LEBOURG, Paul, It, author, translator; b. Merzokovesd, Aug 10,1883; s. Adam and Fanny (Lebourg); grad, Sorbonne; m. Ánna Misdarys, 1939. Tchr of Fr, until 1939. Author: Echos français de la lyre italienne, 1920; Poètes de Hongrie, 1921; Echos lyriques de Trianon, 1922; Prêtres Poètes de Hongrie, 1924; Les Consciences se réveillent 1926; Poétesses de Hongrie, 1929; Poétesses de Pologne, 1929; Poétesses Allemandes, 1931; Poétesses du XXe siècle, 1948; Poétesses d'Italie, 1953; Poétesses du Peuple de la Bible et du Décalogue, 1954; Disapora Poetica-Anthologia; Résistance Bimillénaire du Peuple Biblique; contbr to: Information Juive, Paris; Revue Centrale, Brussels. Active in underground against fascists, WW II. Mem: Assn de la Presse Française; Société Lafontaine; Académie Ronsard; Académie Petofi; Alliance Israëlite Universelle. Home: 13 Via S Agostino, Udine, It

VEXLER, Esther, US, communal leader; b. San Antonio, Tex, Jan 1, 1918; d. Meyer and Mary (Arbetter) Scharlack; att: Mills Coll; UCLA, both Cal; BA, U Cal, Berkeley, 1940; m. Harold Vexler; c: Jack, Stuart, M Jill. Chmn: Mh, Bexar Co Bd of Commns for Mh and Mental Retardation; comty services, Tex Assn for Mh; pres: San Antonio sect, Natl Council of J Women, 1959-60, pres, SW region, 1961-65, mem natl bd, 1961-65; J Social Service Fed, 1966-68; bd mem, New Orleans J Home Service; San Antonio bd dirs: League of Women Voters; Econ Opportunity Devl Corp; Women in Comty Service; exec dir, pres, Bexar Co Mh Assn; vice-pres, Tex Assn Mh; mem: Natl Women's Comm for Civil Rights, 1963; gov's comm on Mh needs, 1963-65; leg secy, Tex Assn for Social Wfr, 1964-65. Recipient: Headliner award, Theta Sigma Phi, 1964; Outstanding Volunteer, San Antonio Express-News, 1966; NCCJ Brotherhood award, 1967; Hannah award, San Antonio sect, Natl Council of J Women, 1967. Spec interests: arts and crafts, family needs. Home: 330 Park Hill Dr, San Antonio, Tex.

VIDGOFF, I Jack, US, surgeon, educator; b. Bogopol, Russ, Dec 24, 1901; s. Jacob and Anna (Nemirofsky); in US since 1905; BS, U Wash, 1923; MD, U Ore, 1927; m. Elaine Rabinowitz, Jan 3, 1932; c: Joel, Joan. Pvt practice since 1931; att, staff surg: Cedars of Leb Hosp; Mt Sinai Hosp; asso sr att surg: Co Gen Hosp; Temp e Hosp, all LA; asso clinical prof surg, Coll of Med Evangelists, LA; instr, surg, U of S Cal, 1931-38. Maj, US Army MC, 1942-46. F, Amer Coll Surgs; mem: LA Surg Soc; AMA; Cal Med Assn; LA Co Med Assn; Phi Delta Epsilon; Zeta Beta Tau; clubs: Profsl; Men's, Wilshire Blvd Temple. Contbr to med publs. Home: 451 Comstock Ave, W Los Angeles, Cal. Office: 633 Wilshire Blvd, Los Angeles, Cal.

VIENER, Jacob M, US, business exec; b. Charles Town, W Va, Aug 31, 1912; s. Hyman and Rebecca (Mozenter); BS, U of Pa, 1934. Partner, Hyman Viener & Sons. Lt cdr, USNR, 1942-46. Pres: Richmond JCC; Secondary Metal Inst; vice-pres: Richmond chap, ARC; United Givers Fund, Richmond; mem: natl bd govs, USO; bd, Natl JWB; J Cen; Beth Sholom Home for Aged, bldg fund chmn; Boys Club; natl bd, Navy League of US; Temple Beth El; 1965 crusade chmn, Richmond Cancer Soc; clubs: Rotary, bd men; Boys. Recipient: Bronze Star Medal, WW II. Home and office: Richmond, Va.

VIGÉE, Claude A, Isr, educator, author; b. Bischwiller, Fr, Jan 3, 1921; s. Robert and Germaine (Meyer), PhB, U Strasbourg, 1939; PCB, U Caen, 1940; att U Toulouse, 1940-42; MA, O State U, 1945, PhD, 1947; m. Evelyn Meyer, Nov 29, 1947; c: Claudine, Daniel. Prof, modern Fr lit, Heb U, Jerusalem, acting chmn, dept of Romance studies, 1963-67; asst prof, Romance langs, O State U, 1947-49; visiting lectr, modern Fr lit, Wellesley Coll, 1949-50; asso prof, Fr lit, Brandeis U, 1952-58, prof, 1958-61, chmn, dept, Eur langs and lits, 1956-59, chmn, Sch of Hum, 1958-59. Mem: MLA; AAUP; Assn Intl des Etudes Françaises; Union des Écrivains pour la Vérité, Author: La Lutte avec L'Ange, 1950; Avent, 1951; Aurore Souterraine, 1952; Cinquante Poemes de R M Rilke, 1952; La Corne du Grand Pardon, 1955; L'Eté Indien, 1958; Les Artistes de la Faim, essais, 1960; Révolte et Louanges, essais; Le Poème du Retour Canaan d'Exil, 1962; Mission de Canaan, 1967; La Lune d'Hiver, 1969; contbr to Fr lit publs. Recipient: Palmes Académiques, 1960; Ordre National du Mérite, 1965. Home: 27 Ben Maimon Ave, Jerusalem, Isr. Office: Heb U, Jerusalem, Isr.

VILENSKA, Esther, Isr, legislator; b. Vilna, Pol, June 8, 1918; d. Mordecai and Sonia (Trakeniski); in Isr since 1938; MA, Heb U, Jerusalem, 1942; m. Zvi Breitstein, Nov 14, 1943; c: Sarah, Joseph. Mem: political comm, Communist Party of Isr, since 1944, cen comm, 1944; exec comm, Histadrut, since 1949; sch tchr, 1940-43; mem, Electoral Assembly; chief ed, Kol Haam, communist party newspaper, both 1944-51; MK, 1951-65; Author: Outlines of Israel Path to Socialism, 1968. Home: 6 Dik, St, Kiryat Shalom, Tel Aviv, Isr. Office: POB 1843, Tel Aviv, Isr.

VILENTCHUK, Isaac J, Isr, engineer, business exec; b. Briansk, Russ, Dec 7, 1894; s. Jacob and Rebecca (Sirkin); in Isr since 1926; Engr, St Petersburg Poly Inst, Russ, 1920; m. Lydia Nurok, Nov 5, 1946; c: Bar-Atid, Nathan. Exec vice-chmn, Govt Sea Water Conversion Commn, since 1958; mech engr, hydroelectric power plant, Pal Elec Corp, 1927-30; chief engr, gen mgr, Pal Water Co, 1930-49; adv, Isr Govt, on power devl, 1948-53; dir, mgr, Mekorot Water Co, 1949-55; mem, Tel Aviv Munic Council, 1951-55; chmn, bd dirs and exec comm, Isr Minning Inds, 1955-63. Mem, exec comm, Haganah, Jerusalem, 1932-40; chmn, War Produc Bd, War of Independence, 1947-49. Mem, bd govs and council, Haifa Technion, since 1948; pres, Isr Assn Engrs and Architects, 1947-55, vice-pres, 1944-47; chmn, cen comm, Hitahdut Zionist Labor Party, Russ, 1922-26. Contbr to profsl publs. Hobby: gardening. Home: 19 Hazait St, Tel Aviv, Isr. Office: POB 7050, Hakirya, Tel Aviv, Isr.

VILENTCHUK, Lydia, Isr, engineer, scientist; b. Moscow, Apr 7, 1907; d. Julius and Miriam (Jacobson) Nurock; in Isr since 1933; dipl ing, Tech U, Berlin, 1930; att London U Coll, 1952-53; m. Isaac Vilentchuk, Nov 5, 1946; c: Alexander Wolberg. Head, dept of documentation, Cen of Sci and Tech Info, since 1960; lectr, documentation: Libr Sch, Heb U, since 1956; Technion, extension courses, since 1958; civil engr, 1930-40; dir, tech libr, info off, Assn Engrs and Architects, Isr, 1946-68. Lt, ATS, Brit Army, 1941-46. Chmn: Isr Soc of Spec Libr and Info Cens; examination comm, Isr Libr Assn, mem exec comm; mem: Assn Engrs and Architects in Isr; Inst of Info Scis. Contbr of papers and articles on documentation topics. Recipient: Afr Star, Brit Defense Min; Defense medal; War medal, all 1939-45; Volunteers Decoration, 1965; Fighters for the State Decoration, 1968. Home: 19 Hazayit St, Tel Aviv, Isr. Office: 84 Hahashmonaim St, Tel Aviv, Isr.

VILNAY, Zev, Isr, author, lecturer; b. Haifa, June 12, 1900; s. Avraham and Haya (Freiman); grad: Heb Tchrs Sem, Jerusalem; Sch of Oriental Studies, London U; PhD, Dropsie Coll, US; m. Esther Margoliash, 1939; c: Oren, Matan. Author: The Village of the Hashmonaim, 1925; The Ancient History of the Valley of Jezreel, 1926; Legends of the Land of Israel, 1929, 6th ed, 1962; Legends of Palestine, 1932; Haifa, Present and Past, 1936; Madrich Eretz-Israel, 4 vols, 1941, 3rd ed, 1955; Palestine Guide, 1935, in Heb, Eng, Ger, Pol; The History of the Hebrew Map of the Holy Land, 1944; Israel's War of Liberation, 1949, 4th ed, 1955; Sacred Shrines in the Holy Land, 1950, 2nd ed, 1963; The Coasts of Israel and Her Neighbors, 1953; 2nd ed, 1962; The Land and the Bible, 1954; Place-names in Israel, 1955; Israel Encyclopedia, 3 vols, 1956; Minorities in Israel, 1959; Monuments of the War of Liberation, 1959; Lachish Region, 1960; Ramla, Past and Present, 1961; The Holy Land in Old Prints and Maps, 1961, Eng ed, 1962; Jerusalem—the Capital of Israel, vol I, The New City, 1960, vol II, The Old City, 1962; Ashkelon—New and Old, 1963; The Guide to Israel, 12th enlarged ed, in Eng, 1969; The New Israel Atlas, 1968, Eng ed, 1968; Yehudah veShomron, 1968; Sinai—Past and Present, 1969. Served, Haganah. Mem: Govt Place-names Comm; council, Isr Exploration Soc; visiting lectr in: Eng, US, and Isr. Contbr to local and sci press. Home: 15 Radak St, Jerusalem, Isr.

VINAVER, Chemjo, Isr, musician; b. Warsaw, Pol, July 10, 1900; s. David and Rachel (Rosenfeld); in Isr since 1959; studied with Hugo Ruedel and Siegfried Ochs, Berlin, Ger, 1920-26; m. Mascha Kaléko, 1935; c: Steven. Dir: Vinaver Chorus; Vinaver Symphonic Voices; Eur concert debut, State Acad of Music, Berlin, 1926; choral concerts, Eur, Pal, 1926-38; choirmaster, liturgical music, J Comty, Berlin, 1928-38; choir dir, Radio Berlin, 1925; music dir, Habimah Theater, Pal, 1928; dir, Hanigun , male choir, 1933-35; ed, music column, Jüdische Rundschau, 1935-38; recorded for Odeon Co, Berlin; Amer concert debut, Canegie Hall and Town Hall, NY, 1939; concerts, Town Hall, 1940-46; first

series, concerts with Vinaver Chorus, Times Hall, 1947-48, second series, Town Hall, 1948-50. Prin works: stage music for: Ger stage, 1928; Theater Guild, NY, 1939; The Seventh Day, a Sabbath-eve service, 1946; dir, world premiere, Haggadah, oratorio by Paul Dessau, performed, Jerusalem, 1962; Anthology of Jewish Music, 1954; Chassidic Cantata, 1970; contbr to profsl publs. Home: 33 King George Ave, Jerusalem, Isr.

VINCZE, Ilona, Isr, musician; b. Budapest, Hung, Dec 14, 1902; d. Edward and Caroline (Lefkovics) Kraus; in Isr since 1936; tchr's dipl, performer's dipl, RAM, Budapest, 1924; m. Laszlo Vincze, Aug 12, 1930; c: Adam. Sr lectr, Isr Acad Music, Tel Aviv U, since 1966; soloist, major orchs, including Isr Philharmonic Orch; tchr piano, Pal Conservatory of Music, Jerusalem, 1936-47; tchr, methodics: Isr Conservatory; Acad Music, Tel Aviv, both 1945-66. Prin contrib: introduced teaching of piano methodics in Isr. Author of articles on music. Recipient: Liszt Prize, 1923; Senn Prize, 1924, both Royal Acad, Budapest. Spec interest: research in music educ. Home: Hakidma 5, Herzliya, Isr.

VINCZE, Laszlo, Isr, musician; b. Budapest, Hung, May 23, 1904; s. Moric and Regina (Mellinger); in Isr since 1935; grad, RAM, Budapest, 1924; DL, U Budapest, 1927; m. Ilona Kraus, Aug 12, 1930; c: Adam. Sr lectr, Isr Acad Music, Tel Aviv U, since 1966; mem, law off, Budapest; corresp, La Revue Musicale, Paris, both 1933-35; intl concerts: mem: Hung Trio, 1925-35; Pal (Isr) String Quartet, 1939-51; found mem, cellist, Isr Philharmonic Orch, 1936-68; dir, Isr Conservatoire and Acad Music, 1945-52. Hobbies: gardening, poetry. Home: Hakidma 5, Herzliya, Isr.

VINEBERG, Philip Fischel, Can, attorney, educator; b. Mattawa, Can, July 21, 1914; s. Malcolm and Rebecca (Phillips); BA, McGill U, 1935, MA, 1936, BCL, 1939; att Ecole Libre des Sciences Politiques, Fr; hon f, Bar Ilan U; fmr f, Brandeis U; m. Miriam Schachter, Dec 19, 1939; c: Robert, Michael. QC; atty, Phillips, Vineberg, Goodman, Phillips & Rothman, since 1939; Batonnier, Bar of Montreal, 1969-70; lectr, econ, Sir George Williams U, 1936-39; teaching positions: educ, econ, political sci, commercial and corp law, McGill U, 1939-68; econ cons, Can Wartime Prices and Trade Bd, 1942-45; mem, Fed Govt Conciliation Bds, dealing with RR wages and working conditions, 1958, 1960. Fmr chmn, bd govs, Can Tax Found; gov, YMHA; bd dirs, United Talmud Torahs; dir, Can Friends of Technion; vice-pres: Can Friends Alliance Israelite Universelle; Bar, Province Quebec, 1969-70; trustee, J Gen Hosp; natl council, Can Bar Assn; clubs: Reform; Elmridge; Montefiore; U; Cercle Universitaire. Author: The French Franc and the Gold Standard, 1936, rev ed, 1948; contbr to econ and legal jours. Home: 32 Summit Crescent, Montreal, Can. Office: 1 Place Ville Marie, Montreal, Can.

VIRSHUBSKI, Mordechai, Isr, attorney; b. Leipzig, Ger, May 10, 1930; s. Menahem and Sabina (Hauskind); in Isr since 1939; MJ, Heb U, Jerusalem, 1953; m. Viola Israel, Nov 3, 1955; c: Gabriel, Rafael. City atty, Tel Aviv, since 1966; legal adv, Isr Water Commn, 1955-66; adv on water leg and admn: Peru, Chile, Columbia, Iran, Ethiopia. Chmn, music comm, Isr-Amer Cultural Found; mem bd, mem theater comm; mem: Isr Bar Assn; UN list of experts on water leg and admn. Contbr of various publs on water leg and admn. Hobbies: music, lit. Home: 8 Eduard Bernstein St, Tel Aviv, Isr. Office: Munic Tel Aviv, Kikar Malchei Isr, Tel Aviv, Isr.

VITAL, David, Isr, educator; b. London, Eng, Apr 10, 1927; s. Meir and Barbara (DePorte) Grossman; in Isr since 1934; BA, hons, New Coll, Oxford U, 1951, DPhil, St Antony's Coll, 1966; m. Alisa Waxman, May 1, 1957; c: Tamar, Adam, Ruth. Asso prof, political studies, head dept, political studies, Winston S Churchill Prof, Intl Relations, all Bar Ilan U, Isr, since 1968; civil servant, PM's Office, Fgn Min, 1954-66; lectr, Intl Relations, U Sussex, Eng, 1966-68. Lt, IDF, since 1956. Mem: Inst for Strategic Studies; Political Studies Assn. Author: The Inequality of States, 1967; The Making of British Foreign Policy, 1968. Recipient: De Osma Studentship, Oxford U, 1951. Home: 75 Hazorea St, Kfar Shmaryahu, Isr. Office: Dept Political Studies, Bar Ilan U, Ramat Gan, Isr.

VITAL, Iochanas, Greece, business exec; b. Patras, Greece, Feb 28, 1916; s. Zacharias and Rebecca (Iochanan); grad, Panal Ash Coll, Yorkshire, 1935; m. Rosetta Levy, Dec 12,

1948; c: Philip, Paul. Mgn dir, textile firms, since 1940. Pvt, Greek Army, 1937-39. Vice-pres, Athens J Comty; dir, Athens Comm Youth Program, 1945-48; mem bd, Cen Bd J Comty, Greece; mem, B'nai B'rith, Athens; club, Rotary, Athens. Home: 5 Ipsilantou St, Athens, Greece. Office: 11 Metropolis Sq, Athens, Greece.

VITALE, Carlo, It, artist, educator; b. Milan, It, Nov 20, 1902; s. Pio and Alessandrina (Segre); grad, U Pavia, 1922; att: Acad Fine Arts of Brera, Milan, 1918-20; Acad Fine Arts, Florence, 1926; m. Irma Schulz, 1945; c: Adriana, Elio. Prof, Acad Fine Arts of Brera, since 1961; painter, since 1926; exhbs: Venice; Rome; Milan; Naples; Lausanne; Buenos Aires; Bern; Munich; Salons des independants, 1939; Salons des Tuileries, 1939, both Paris, perm exhbs, It and abroad; works appear in: Artisti Italiani Contemporanei; Dizionario dei Pittori Italiani Contemporanei; Collana Disegnatori ed Incisori del 1900; Istituto Europeo Storia d'Arte. Lt, It Artillery. Mem: Soc Artisti and Patriotica; Soc per le Belle Arti ed Esposizione Permanente. Recipient: gold and silver medals for artistic merits. Spec interest: ancient illus books. Home: Via Ajaccio 1, Milan, It. Office: Via Carnaghi 2, Milan, It.

VITERBO, Carlo Alberto, It, editor; b. Florence, It, Jan 23, 1889; s. Umberto and Matilde (Levi); DL, U Pisa; m. Nella Uzielli, June 24, 1918; c: Giuseppe. Ed, Israel, It weekly, since 1944; fmr, atty. Capt, It Army, WW I. Hon pres: It ZF, since 1961, fmr pres; KH, It, fmr pres; mem, B'nai B'rith; fmr vice-pres, Isr Comty, Florence. Author: Una via verso l'ebraico, 1968; Elef Milim, It ed, 1957. Spec interests: Falashas, hist, lit. Home: 1 Largo Don G Mozosini, Rome, It.

VITTA, Edoardo, It, attorney, educator; b. Florence, It, Feb 27, 1913; s. Cino and Emma (Melli); DJur, U Florence, 1935; postgrad studies: Holland; Switz; Fr; US; m. Ilda Segre, 1940; c: Johanan, Nathanel. Dean fac econ, U Cagliari, since 1968, prof public law, since 1959; fmr: lectr: Sch Law and Econ, Tel Aviv; intl law, Govt Law Sch, Jerusalem; U Madrid; U Valladolid; Mogadishu U; Strasbourg; Hague Acad Intl Law, 1969; secy, legal council, JA, Jerusalem, 1948; legal adv, Dept Legal Planning, Isr Min Justice, 1949-52. Prin contrib: helped prepare first laws relating to constitutional org of new state of Isr. Author: La Validite des traités internationaux, 1940; The Conflict of Laws of Personal Status in Palestine, 1947; Organization of the State, 1949; Prospettive del diritto internazionale, 1968; contr books; numerous articles on: intl treaties, conflicts of laws, responsibility of states. Home: Corso Moncalieri 56, Turin, It. Office: U Cagliari, Sardinia, It.

VODICKA, Ruth, US, sculptor; b. NYC, Nov 23, 1921; d. Julius and Rachel (Weiner) Kessler; att: CCNY, 1938-40; Music Sch Settlement, 1943-44; studied with O'Connor Barrett, 1946-49; att: Sculpture Cen, 1948-52; Art Students League, 1956-57; New Sch, 1962; m. Otokar Vodicka, May 15, 1945; c: Phyllis. Tchr: Emanu-El Midtown Y, since 1966; Queens Youth Cen, Bayside, LI, 1953-56. One-man shows: Assn Amer Artists, 1956; Sunken Meadows, LI, 1957; Krasner Gal, 1959; Roosevelt Field Art Gal, Garden City, 1960; New Gal, Provincetown, Mass, 1961; Angeleski Gal, 1962; Mari Gal, Larchmont, NY, 1962, Larchmont, NY, 1967; in perm collections: Norfolk Mus, Va; Montclaire State Coll, NJ; Grayson Co State Bank, Tex; pvt collections; participated exhbs: Tex Traveling; Amer J Tercentenary 1954-55; Amer Fed of Arts, 1957-58; S Amer Traveling, 1963-64; Art Inst, Chgo; SF Mus; Art Alliance, Phila; Dallas Mus; Corcoran Gal, Wash, DC; Cleveland Mus; Whitney Mus; Pa Acad; Detroit Inst Arts; Riverside Mus, NYC; Sculptors Guild, since 1955; Audubon Artists, since 1954; New Burlington Gal, London; Gal Claude Bernard, Paris; Museo des Bellas Artes, Buenos Aires; commn, Eternal Light, Temple of J Comty Cen, Harrison, NY, 1965; demonstrated steel welding, art film, SF Mus; appeared, Voice of Amer newsreel; Prin contrib: pioneered in adapting bronze and brass welding to sculpture. Mem: Sculptors Guild, Audubon Artists; Natl Assn Women Artists; Amer Soc Contemporary Artists. Recipient: prizes: Natl Assn Women Artists, 1954, 1957, 1963; Natl Acad Design, 1955; Audubon Artists, 1957; awards: Silvermine Guild, New Canaan, Conn, 1957, 1958; Bklyn Soc of Artists, 1959, 1st prize, 1962; medal of hon, Painters and Sculptors Soc of NJ, 1962, award 1963. Home: 33 E 22 St, New York, NY. Studio: 97 Wooster St, New York, NY.

VODOVOTZ, Marcos, Isr, physician; b. Buenos Aires, Arg, Sep 1, 1910; s. José and Teresa (Wolcowicz); in Isr since 1966;

MD, Med Fac, U Buenos Aires, 1934; m. Judith Heller, Mar 10, 1938; c: Daniel, Horacio. Med dir, Cen Emek Hosp, Afula, Isr, since 1966; hon asst phys, med, clinic, Hosp Ramos Mejia, 1934-44, asst phys, 1945-51; head, clinic, Hosp Israelita Ezrah, 1940-41, asst phys, 1941-53, dep dir, 1955, head, med services, 1958-59, organizer, i/c night cons clinic; pyhs, Instituto Nacional de Gastronenterologia, 1954-56; med ir, J Hosp Ezrah, Buenos Aires, 1962-65, asso prof dozent, Fac of Med, 1955-65, lectr, dept gen path and med. Pres: Confed of Gen Zionists, S Amer; Lib Zionist Org, Arg, since 1959, vice-pres, 1953-59; vice-pres, Maccabi, 1947-49; secy, Med Assn of Cen Emek Hosp; mem: Zionist Actions Commn, WZO; Asociacion Medica Arg; Sociedad Arg de Gerontologia y Geriatria; Soc Arg de Gastroenterologia; B'nai B'rith; exec comm, Federacion Sionista Arg, 1934-53; Vaad Hakehilot, 1956-59; delg, WZCs, 1956, 1960. Home: Cen Emek Hosp, Afula, Isr.

VOET, Andries, US, research chemist; b. Amsterdam, Netherlands, Nov 21, 1907; s. Herman and Maria (Boom); in US since 1939; MS, U Amsterdam, 1931, PhD, 1935; m. Henriette Mogendorff, Jan, 5,1933 (decd); c: Louise Blumberg, Marion, Donald, Martin; m. 2nd, Rebecca Cohen, 1964. Research chem, since 1935; dir, ink research, JM Huber Corp, since 1943; mem, staff, US Govt Tech Intl Intelligence Agy, 1945-46. Holder of numerous patents, US and other countries. F, NY Acad of Scis; pres: Temple B'nai Israel, Amarillo, Tex, 1945-56, vice-pres, 1953, mem bd, since 1952; mem: Amer Chem Soc; Amer Phys Soc; clubs: Borger Country; Borger Chess, pres, 1962. Author: Ink and Paper in the Printing Process, 1952, Russ, 1954, Japanese, 1958. Contbr to sci publs. Home: 901 Country Club Rd, Borger, Tex. Office: JM Huber Corp, Borger, Tex.

VOGEL, Dan, US, educator; b. Bklyn, NY, Feb 12, 1927; s. Samuel and Esther (Braff); BA, Bklyn Coll, 1948; MA, Rutgers U, 1949; PhD, NYU, 1956; m. Sybil Ehrenfeld, Mar 25, 1950; c: Simeon, Mindel, Jeremy. Prof, Eng, Yeshiva U, since 1962; instr, 1949-55; lectr, CCNY, 1957-58. Natl delg, Natl Council of Young Isr, 1954-55; mem, MLA. Contbr to scholarly jours; mem, ed bd, Tradition mag. Home: 1160 E 12 St, Brooklyn, NY. Office: Stern Coll for Women, Yeshiva U, 253 Lexington Ave, New York, NY.

VOGEL, Ruth D, US, jurist; b. Buffalo, NY, Feb 25, 1917; d. Nate and Clara (Goodman) Dozoretz; LLB, cum laude, U Buffalo Law Sch, 1938, postgrad studies, 1956; m. Irving Vogel, Dec 24, 1939; c: Barbara, Donna. Fmr, city judge, Tonawanda, NY, since 1957, acting city judge, 1956-57; in private law practice since 1954; atty, Dept Social Wfr, Erie County, 1939-41; mem, law firm, Falk, Phillips, Twelvetrees & Falk, 1945-49. Mem: W NY regional adv bd, ADL; Amer Bar Assn; NY State Bar Assn; Erie Co Bar Assn; Natl Council on Crime and Delinquency; Natl Assn Munic Judges; Hadassah; B'nai B'rith; Temple Beth Zion; Order of Eastern Star; Order of Amaranth; Pioneer Women of Amer. Home: 439 Delaware St, Tonawanda, NY.

VOGELMANN, Mordechai, Isr, rabbi; b. Pol, Sep 19, 1898; s: Nachum and Sophie (Pfeffer); in Isr since 1940; att: U Bern, Switz, 1918-20; U Zurich, 1920-22; DLetters, U Florence, 1924; m. Bella Lau, 1927; c: Lea Goldfeld. Chief rabbi of Kiryat Motzkin, since 1940; prof, It Rabb Coll, Florence, 1923-26; chief rabbi, J comty, Katowice, Pol, 1927-40. Chmn, Rel Council of Kiryat Motzkin. Author: Beth Mordechai, responsa and halacic research, 1969; contbr to periodicals. Home and study: 40 Ussishkin St, Kiryat Motzkin, Isr.

VOGHERA, Giorgio, It, author; b. Trieste, It, Aug 19, 1908; s. Guido and Paola (Fano); deg classics, Dante Alighieri, Trieste, 1925. Writer, trans, journalist, since 1962; employee, Ins Co, Trieste, 1926-38, 1946-62; mem, Kibbutz Givat Brenner, 1939-46. Author: Quaderno D'Israele, 1967; contbr of articles to It press. Recipient: Portico D'Ottavia, J Comty, Rome, 1968. Home: 2 Via Tor San Piero, Trieste, It.

VOLCANI, Raanan, Isr, educator; b. Jaffa, Nov 11, 1910; s. Meir and Sara (Rubin); BS, U Cal, Davis, 1934; PhD, Heb U, Jerusalem, 1952; m. Drora Beker, June 10, 1935; c: Yael, Zvi, Meir. Prof, animal husbandry, dept agric, Heb U, since 1960; research worker, Volcani Inst Agric Research, since 1934, head div animal husbandry since 1958, head dept of dairy husbandry, 1938-48. Served Haganah. Contbr over 120 papers to sci jours. Home: 13 Hankin St, Rehovot, Isr. Offices: Heb U, Fac of Agric, Rehovot, Isr; Volcani Inst Agric Research, Rehovot, Isr.

VOLINI, Clara, Gruïa, Isr, dancer, choreographer; b. Lugosh Rum, Nov 16, 1922; d. Arpad and Ilona (Teichner) Wolf; in Isr since 1966; att Ballet Sch, Bucharest, 1930-42; m. Abraham Gruïa, Apr 5, 1945. Ballerina, Isr Natl Opera, since 1966; visiting tchr, Rubin Acad of Music, Jerusalem; fmr: with: J Theater Barasheum; Savoy show theater; Opera and Ballet Theater, tchr, ballet, character dance, 1948-66, all Bucharest; dancer, choreographer, Rum TV; prin solo parts at Opera, Bucharest: Span dances, Carmen; ethiopian slave dance, Aida; Hung dances, Coppelia and Swan Lake; Nutcracker Suite; theater dance, The Fountain; guest performances: Russ; Armenia; Bulgaria; Ger; Isr Opera, Tel Aviv: solo in: Coppelia; Fledermauss; Peer Gynt. Author: poems, in Universul Copiilor; contbr to Revista Mea, Isr. Hobby: decorative painting. Home: 47/3 Hatayasim Rd, Tel Aviv, Isr.

VOLK, Bruno W, US, physician, researcher; b. Vienna, Aus, Sep 25, 1909; s. Emil and Stefanie (Ganz); in US since 1938; MD, U Vienna, 1934; m. Ida Ehrlich, Sep 14, 1939; c: Judy. Dir, Isaac Albert Research Inst, Kingsbrook J Med Cen, since 1955, dir of labs, since 1946; clinical prof, path, Downstate Med Cen, SUNY, since 1960; asst path, Cook Co Hosp, Chgo, 1946-48; visiting asso prof, Albert Einstein Coll Med, Yeshiva U, Bx, 1956-60. US Army, 1944-46. Past pres, NY Pathol Soc; mem: adv bd, Natl Tay-Sachs Assn; Amer Assn Paths and Bacts; Amer Diabetes Assn; Amer Soc Clinical Path; NY Acad Med; NY Acad Scis; Endocrine Soc; Amer Soc Experimental Path. Co-author: chapters, med books, contbr of over 250 articles to profsl jours. Home: 95-07 70 Ave, Forest Hills, NY. Office: 86 E 49 St, Brooklyn, NY.

VOLLI, Gemma E, It, teacher, communal worker; b. Trieste, It, May 24, 1900; d. Ignazio and Elvira (Pincherle); DPhil, U Bologna, 1922. Ret; tchr, classic schs, 1922-38, 1945-58. Found, WIZO, Trieste, 1930, pres, Bologna sect, 1947-58; trustee, Karen Kayemet leIsrael, Bologna, since 1946. Contbr of articles and short storis. Spec interests: hist research, hist of Diaspora social problems, contbr of J to cultural and political life in It. Home: Via Bambaglioli 6-2, Bologna, It.

VOLTERRA, Edoardo, It, attorney, educator; b. Rome, Jan 7, 1904; s. Vito and Virginia (Almagia); DJur, U Rome, 1926; D hon causa: U Brussels; U Louvain; U Prague; U Paris; U Cracow; m. Nella Mortera, Sep 15, 1929; c: Laura, Virginia. Prof, Roman law: Rome U, since 1951; U Cagliari, 1926-29; U Parma, 1929-31; U Pisa, 1931-32; U Bologna, 1932-38, 1945-51, rector, U Bologna, 1945-47; dep, Province of Rome,

1944-45; mem, Consultore Nazionale, 1945-46. With It partisans, WW II. Author: Collatio Legum Mosaicarum et Romanarum, 1930; Diritto Romano e Diritti Orientali, 1937; Instituzioni di Diritto Privato Romano, 1960; contbr of over 300 articles to profsl jours. Recipient: Medaglia d'argento al valore, militare; Croce di guerra; Medaglia Garibaldina; Medaglia d'oro Ben Scuola; cavaliere di Gran Croce Merito, Repubblica Italiana. Home: Via Porta Pinciana 6, Rome, It.

VORSPAN, Albert, US, organization exec; b. St Paul, Minn, Feb 12, 1924; s. Ben and Fanny; BA, NYU, 1946; m. Shirley Nitchun, June 16, 1946; c: Charles, Roberta, Kenneth, Deborah. Dir, commn on social action, UAHC, since 1953; asst natl coord, Natl Comty Relations Adv Council, 1948-52. USN, 1943-46. Author: Giants of Justice, 1960; Jewish Values and Social Crisis, 1968; My Rabbi Doesn't Make House Calls, 1969; co-author: Justice and Judaism, 1956; A Tale of Ten Cities, 1962; contbr to mags. Home: 134 Harris Ave, Hewlett, NY. Office: 838 Fifth Ave, New York, NY.

VREDENBURG, Max D, Netherlands, composer; b. Brussels, Belgium, Jan 16, 1904; s. Isaac and Eva (Sanson); in Netherlands since 1946; studied under Paul Dukas, Paris, 1926-27; m Cornelia Sluizer, Jan 5, 1937. Dir, Dutch sect, Jeunesses Musicales, Youth and Music, since 1953; found, Natl Youth Orch, 1946. Interned by Japanese, Java, 1942-45. Compositions: orch; choral works; songs; film music; stage music for: Rachel Kämpft mit Gott, by Stefan Zweig; Herodes, by Abel Herzberg; Die einzige Lösung; wrote chapters on film and ballet music; co-author, Musikale Ommegang. Mem: Amsterdam Art Council; bd, Dutch Music Copyright Bur; Fgn Press Assn, Netherlands; Société Européenne de Culture; Assn of Dutch Composers. Home: Stadionweg 212, Amsterdam, Netherlands. Office: 51 Jacob Obrechtstraat, Amsterdam, Netherlands.

VURE, Ellis, Isr, physician; b. Leeds, Eng, Mar 17, 1916; s. Julius and Fanny (Bilson); att med sch, Leeds; m. Betty Goletka, Oct 3, 1945; c: Yossef, Shoshana. Head, chidren's dept B, Assaf Harofe Hosp, since 1951. Batallion med off, London Yeomanry, 1942-45; maj, IDF: brig dr, Givati, 1948-49; commanding off, field hosp, Sinai Campaign, 1956; phys i/c receiving room, Assaf Harofe Hosp, Six-Day War, 1967. Mem: BMA, Isr Ped Assn; IMA; Isr Astronomical Assn; Masons; chmn, Leeds Zionist Org, 1946-48; mem comm, Isr Polio Found, Ilan, Givatayim, 1962-66; Isr Bridge Fed; club, Rotary. Recipient: mentioned in dispatches, 1945. Hobbies: fishing, bridge. Home: 40 Sireni St, Givatayim, Isr. Office Assaf Harofe Govt Hosp, Sarafand, Isr.

W

WACHENHAUSER, Arie, Isr, artist; b. Warsaw, Pol, June 12, 1917; s. Mose and Sara (Cancevik); in Isr since 1939; att: Practical Arts Sch, Warsaw, 1931-34; Avni Studio, Tel Aviv, 1939-51; Art Tchr's Sch, 1951-52; m. Liza Bogomilska, 1941; c: Zameret. One-man shows, gals: Katz, Tel Aviv, 1945, 1954; Tzemerinsky, Tel Aviv, 1962, 1963; Senta Tafts Art Cen, Sydney, 1964; Rina, Jerusalem, 1965; Murray Greenfield, NY, 1965; Chagall House, Haifa, 1968. Cpl, IDF Med Corps, 1947-49. Mem: Painters and Sculptors Assn of Isr; club, Milo. Home and studio: 45 Reines St, Tel Aviv, Isr.

WACHOLDER, Ben Zion, US, educator; b. Ozarow, Pol, Sep 21,1924; in US since 1947; s. Pinhas and Feiga (Lederman); att Yeshiva, Baranowicze, 1937-39; BA, ordained rabbi, Yeshiva U, 1951; PhD, UCLA, 1960; m. Touby Kamil, July 9, 1952; c: Fay, Sholom, David, Hannah. Prof, Talmud and rabbinics, HUC, since 1967; tchr: Fort Worth, 1952-55; Rambam Jr HS, LA, 1955-56; libr, HUC, LA, 1956-63. Mem: World Cong J Studies; Amer Soc Bibl Exegesis; Amer Oriental Soc; CCAR. Author: Nicolaus of Damascus, 1962; contbr to J and scholarly jours. Home: 7648 Greenland Pl, Cincinnati, O. Office: HUC, Cincinnati, O.

WACHTEL, Helena, Den, communal worker; b. Czech; d. Moritz and Klara (Herschan) Hajek; PhD, U of Vienna, 1935; m. Frederik Wachtel, Apr 15, 1952; c: Frank Fisher. Chmn, ZF of Den, since 1965, mem bd since 1961; asso: emigration dept, J comty, Stockholm; HIAS; JDC; all 1945-52; pres, WIZO, Den, 1958-63. Home: Maltevangen 14, Gentofte, Copenhagen, Den.

WACHTEL, Jacques L, US, chemist; b. Donora, Pa, Nov 20, 1918; s. Max and Blanche (Katten); BA, Oberlin Coll, 1939; PhD, Yale U, 1942; m. Rose Edlin, Sep 30, 1945; c: Alan, Janet, Ruth. Mgr, quality control, Amer Chicle div, Warner-Lambert Pharm Co, since 1959; asso, N region research lab, US Dept of Agric, 1941-45; head, dept of chem, asst to dir, Schenley Labs Inc, 1945-50; head, chem devl lab, E R Squibb & Sons, 1950-59. Mem: Amer Chem Soc; Sigma Xi. Contbr to profsl jours. Recipient: award, Lasker Found, 1946; dist service award, US Dept Agric, 1947. Home: 1037 Ironbound Ave, Plainfield, NJ. Office: Warner-Lambert Pharm Co, Long Island City, NY.

WACHTELL, Hanns H, Australia, business exec; b. Vienna, Aus, Mar 29, 1908; s. Isidor and Adelaide (Bondi); in Austr since 1939; LLD, U Vienna, 1931; m. Ilse Pollak, May 21, 1935; c: Jeanette Kitchener. Asst gen mgr, Protector Safety Inds Ltd, since 1967; mem, law firm, Rumpler, Goldberger, Wachtell, Vienna, 1937; JP; dir, Blok van Rooyen & Co Jewry; Ltd, 1941-67. Mem: mgmt comm, Exec Council of Austr exec; NSW J Bd Deps; grand treas, Dist Grand lodge 21, B'nai B'rith of Australia and NZ, 1962-64; pres: Sir John Monash lodge, B'nai B'rith, 1957-58; Kingsford-Maroubra Heb Cong, Sydney, 1951-59; Jüdischer Judenbund, Vienna, 1937. Home: 40 Nagle Ave, Maroubra, Australia. Office: 1/17 Buckingham St, Sydney, Australia.

WAGNER, Charles A, US, poet, journalist, educator; b. NYC, Mar 10, 1901; s. Morris and Fanny (Haut); BA, Columbia U, 1923, MA, 1924; Nieman f, Harvard U, 1945; m. Ruth Warters, 1924; m. 2nd, Celia Bernstein, July 9, 1930; c: Carl, Carol. Book reviewer, Cosmopolitan Book Corp, 1922-23; tchr, Eng, NYC HSs, 1924-26; feature writer, NY World, 1924-25; drama critic, NY Morning Telegram, 1926; book rev ed, Bklyn-Times Union, 1928-31; ed, Bobbs Merrill Publishers, 1932; book reviewer, INS, 1933-35; instr, journalism: NYU, 1950-52; CCNY, 1951-52; ed in chief, NY Sun, Mirror Mag, 1957-63, staff mem since 1935. Author: Poems of the Soil and Sea, 1923; Nearer the Bone, 1930; contbr of poetry Saturday Rev; NY Times; The Measure; ed: Prize Poems, 1932; Titans of American Journalism, 1933; Harvard: Four Centuries and Freedoms, 1950; New Poems, 1954. Exec secy, Poetry Soc Amer; mem: Amer Acad Political Sci; Amer Phil Soc; NY Newspaper Guild; Nieman Soc of Fs; clubs: Overseas Press; Columbia U; Harvard; Natl Arts, NYC. Recipient:

Repr Poet of US for UNESCO, Intl Biennale Poetry, Belgium, 1968. Hobby: painting. Home: 106 Morningside Dr, New York, NY. Office: 142 E 35 St, New York, NY.

WAGNER, David H, US, surgeon, educator; b. Dorchester, Wis, Sep 30, 1905; s. Abraham and Sarah (Rockstein); BA, U of Wis, 1927; MD, U of Ill, 1930; m. Vivian Wolfson, Sep 12, 1929. Prof, surg, Chgo Med Sch, since 1966, fac mem since 1948; att surg: Michael Reese Hosp, since 1957, pres, med staff, since 1970, on staff since 1951; Cook Co Hosp, since 1957; asso clinical prof, surg, Chgo Med Sch, since 1959, fac mem since 1948; fmr, instr, surg anat, U of Ill Med Sch, 1937-49, staff mem since 1937. Asst chief surg, Army Evacuation Hosp, 1941-45. Mem: AJCong; Amer Coll Surgs; Amer Bd Surg; AMA; Chgo Surg Soc; Chgo Med Soc; AAAS. Contbr to med jours. Recipient: Arquin Memorial Prize for Research, U of Ill, 1934; Bronze Star, 1945. Home: 5000 East End Ave, Chicago, Ill. Office: 25 E Washington St, Chicago, Ill.

WAGNER, Isaac, US, certified public acctnt; b. Aus, Mar 2, 1893; s. Alter and Chaya (Lecker); in US since 1901; dipl, Northwestern U Sch of Commerce, 1919, CPA, 1919; m. Birdie Goldenstein, Dec 29, 1938; c: Joan Satoloe, William. Sr partner, Katz, Wagner, and Co, since 1922. Mem, bd trustees, B'nai B'rith Found of US; pres, Chgo B'nai B'rith Council, 1929; exec comm, Natl Hillel Commn, since 1955; bd mem: Amer Med Center, Chgo comm, since 1937; Leo N Levi Memorial Hosp, since 1950; B'nai B'rith Henry Monsky Found; Chgo Loop Syn; Amer Friends of Hebrew U, Chgo comm; Natl J Hosp at Denver, midwest region comm, both since 1949; mem, bd of govs, Supreme lodge, B'nai B'rith, 1958-65; bd: J Fed Metrop Chgo, 1952-64; Cong B'nai Zion, 1952-57; pres, Chgo B'nai B'rith Council, 1929; mem: Amer and Ill Socs of CPA's; Ill and Chgo Assns of Commerce; Delta Mu Delta; clubs: Bryn Mawr Country; Brandeis U; Gtr Chgo, mem bd trustees; Covenant, fmr pres. Home: 1038 W Albion, Chicago, Ill. Office: 105 W Adams St, Chicago, Ill.

WAGNER, Jerry, US, attorney; b. New Haven, Conn, Aug 2, 1926; s. Nathan and Clara (Themper); BS, Yale U, 1947; LLB, Harvard U, 1949; m. Sarah Hurvitz, May 30, 1950; c: Jonathan, Paula, Michael. Atty since 1949; state repr, State of Conn, 1959-60; counsel, sen majority, Conn Leg, 1967-68; spec asst, J affairs, Natl Citizens for Humphrey, 1968. USAAF, 1945. Chmn, Hartford J Comty Relations comm; natl dir, United Syn of Amer; pres: Conn div, AJCong; Midrasha Heb HS; Beth Hillel Syn, 1957-59; Conn J Comty Relations Council, 1960-63; mem: Conn Bar Assn, leg comm; Hartford Co Bar Assn, exec comm; NAACP; JWV; Urban League. Home: 4 Craigemore Rd, Bloomfield, Conn. Office: 860 Park Ave, Bloomfield, Conn.

WAGNER, Maurice, Rhodesia, organization exec; b. Pol, June 24, 1908; s. Oizer and Esther; in Rhodesia since 1951; att Jews Coll, London; MA, U Coll, London, 1931, tchrs dipl, 1932; m. Channa Fisher, Dec 1, 1932; c: Stella, Deborah. Gen secy, Cen Afr J bd of deps, since 1951; secy-gen, United J Educ and Cultural Org, 1947-48; headmaster, Avigdor HS, London, 1948-51. Chaplain, Brit Army, 1944-46. Home: 51 Athlone Ave, Bulawayo, Rhodesia. Office: POB 1456, Bulawayo, Rhodesia.

WAGNER, Philip, US, attorney; b. NYC, Jan 15, 1904; s. Frederick and Pauline (Kline); LLB, St Johns Coll of Law, 1928; m. Edith Horowitz, June 6, 1940; c: Paula, Marsha. Gen trial atty, since 1959; asst dist atty, NY Co, 1931-37; sr atty, SEC, 1938-56; lst dep supt of banks, NY State, 1956-59. Head, war bond drives, Yorkville, 1942-43; appeal agent, local selective service bd 12, mem, bd 8, since 1945. Pres: Soc for the City of NY, 1957-58; Manhattan lodge, Free Sons of Isr, 1936; mem: Fed Bar Assn; NY Co Lawyers Assn; Cen Syn; B'nai B'rith; Elks; club, Kehilath Jeshurun Men's. Recipient: Selective Service medal, 1946. Home: 425 E 86 St, New York, NY. Office: 305 Broadway, New York, NY.

WAGNER, Stanley M, US, rabbi, educator; b. NYC, Apr 1, 1932; s. Albert and Stella (Ludmer); tchrs dipl, Yeshiva U, 1952, BRE, BA, 1953, ordained rabbi, 1956, MHL, DHL, 1964; m. Simmy Parczewski, June 14, 1956; c: Frady, Chaya. Rabbi: Baldwin J Cen, since 1961; Onaway Zion, Lexington, Ky, 1957-61; instr, ancient languages and literature, U of Ky, 1957-61. Pres, Nassau-Suffolk Assn of Rabbis; hon pres, LI Commn of Orthodox Rabbis; chmn: rabbinic adv comm: Nassau-Suffolk JNF Regional Council; ORT; film comm, Youth Bur of Yeshiva U; mem, natl exec bd: Rel Zionists of Amer; Rabb Alumni of Yeshiva U; ZC; panelist, Amer Arbitration Assn. Contbr to rel and scholarly jours; ed, rabb alumni proceedings, 1961-62, 1965-67. Recipient: Ky Col, 1960. Home: 257 W Seaman Ave, Freeport, NY. Study: 885 E Seaman Ave, Baldwin, NY.

WAGNER, Victor, UK, communal leader; b. London, Eng, Aug 22, 1920; s. Alfred and Rose (Wagner); matriculation, Tottenham Grammar Sch, London, 1936; m. Bette Golker, Mar 11, 1947; c: Gideon, Sheira. Secy, and secy for marriages, Brondesbury Syn, since 1959; secy, A Wagner and Sons, 1946-50; repr, Confed Life Assn, 1950-56; secy, Hendon Syn, 1956-59. RAF, 1941-46. Vice-chmn, Syn Secys Assn; hon secy: London J Male Choir; Golders Green Estate Rate Payees Assn; Zion House, Hampstead, 1963-66; Christs Coll Parents Assn, 1964-65; member, Moorfields 4949 lodge, Freemasons. Hobbies: J Mus, assisting charitable orgs, local politics. Home: 37 Cheviot Gardens, London NW2, Eng. Office: Brondesbury Syn, Chevening Rd, London, NW6, Eng.

WAHRHAFTIG, Hy Liebling, US, business exec; b. Zborow, Aus, Jan 21, 1896; s. Samuel and Rachel (Liebling); in US since 1906; m. Sophie Fishman, Mar 23, 1920; c: Joseph, Stephen, Bernice. Pres, Monarch Oil Co, since 1945. Treas, Heb Day Sch, Sullivan, Ulster and Orange counties, since 1954; dir, Monticello Hosp, 1926-32; co-chmn: JNF, 1938; UJA 1944; army and navy comm, JWB, 1937-52; ZC, Sullivan Co, 1941-48; pres, Monticello Zionist dist, 1934-52; treas: J Gen Aid Assn, 1928-38; J Comty Center, 1938-46; Heb Sch, 1930-49; chmn, soldier's gift comm, Rotary Club-J Comty Cen, 1941-47; mem: Monticello Syn; KP; Odd Fellows; club, Rotary. Home: 8 Lakewood Ave, Monticello, NY. Office: St John St, Monticello, NY.

WAINER, Abraham, Finland, jurist; b. Viborg, Finland, Feb 4, 1905; s. Marcus and Haija (Goldberg); license in law, U Helsinki, 1928; m. Sarah Rosenberg, Jan 29, 1933; c: Deila, Dina. Sr judge, Town Court of Helsinki, since 1967, judge, 1960-67, state atty, 1947-60; asst under secy, Min of Finance, Helsinki, 1945-47. Dep, J Comty Helsinki, 1950-60; mem cen bd, J Comtys in Finland, 1949-60; mem, Assn of Finnish Lawyers. Home: Pihlajatie 20 B, 14, Helsinki 27, Finland.

WAISMAN, Gabriel, (B Mandel), Isr, author; b. Radom, Pol, Aug 17, 1901; s. Samson and Gitla (Silverman); in Isr since 1949; att: music sch, Tarnopol, Pol; sch of painting, Radom, Pol, m. Lea Mandel, 1936; c: Ilana Manes, Shoshana Pekarski. Author and lectr; fmr, dir, Folk's U, Stettin, Pol, 1946-49. Mem: ACUM, Assn of Yiddish Writers and Journalists in Isr. Author: Radomer Folklore; Kinder Maisalach; Dos Telerl Fun Himel; Vegen Mazel. Recipient: awards: Radom J Comty, 1939; Baltimore Lutzk Landsmanshaft, 1957. Home: 2 Nachshon St, Kiryat Borochov, Ramat Gan, Isr.

WAISMAN, Harry A, US, pediatrician, educator; b. Milwaukee, Wis, Apr 25, 1912; s. Morris and Rachel (Schulner); BS, U Wis, 1935, MS, 1937, PhD, 1939, MD, 1947; m. Ethel Katz, Aug 18, 1940; c: Donald, Karen, David. Prof, ped, U Wis, since 1958, fac mem since 1950; research asso, U of Ill, 1949-50. US Army, 1944-45. F: Amer Bd of Nutrition; Amer Bd of Peds; mem: Amer Acad of Peds; Amer Ped Soc; Amer Soc Biol Chems; AAAS, Soc for Experimental Biol and Med; Royal Soc of Med; Amer Assn for Cancer Research; Amer Assn on Mental Deficiency; Cen Soc for Clinical Research; Cen Soc for Ped Research; Soc for Ped Research; Soc for Research in Child Devl; Phi Lambda Upsilon; Gamma Alpha; Sigma Xi; bd mem, Temple Beth El, Madison. Co-author: Vitamin Content of Meat, 1941; contbr to med jours. Recipient: Borden award, 1947. Home: 4625 Gregg Rd, Madison, Wis. Office: 1300 University Ave, Madison, Wis.

WAKSMAN, Byron H, US, educator; b. NYC, Sep 15, 1919; s. Selman and Deborah (Mitnik); father, Nobel Laureate; BS, Swarthmore Coll, 1940; MD, U of Pa, 1943; m. Joyce Robertroy, Aug 11, 1944; c: Nan, Peter. Prof, microbiol, Yale U Sch of Med, since 1963, dept chmn since 1964; fmr asso bact, Mass Gen Hosp; asst prof, bact and immunology, Harvard U Sch of Med, 1954-63; f, Mayo Found, 1946-48; NIH postdoc f, Columbia U, 1948-49. US Army, 1946-48. Mem: Amer Assn of Immunologists, councilor since 1965, pres, 1970-71; Amer Soc of Microbiol, councilor since 1967; Soc of Experimental Biol and Med; Brit Soc for Immunology; Soc Fr d'Immunologie; Reticuloendotheliol Soc; Transplantation Soc; Amer Public Health Assn. Contbr to profsl jours. Hobbies: chamber music, langs. Home: Rock Hill Rd, Woodbridge, Conn. Office: Yale Sch of Med, New Haven, Conn.

WAKSMAN, Selman A, US, microbiologist, researcher, educator; b. Priluka, Russ, July 22, 1888; s. Jacob and Fradia (London); in US since 1910; BS, Rutgers Coll, 1915, MS, 1916; PhD, U Cal, 1918; hon degs: Rutgers U; Princeton U; RI State Coll; Pa Mil Coll; Phila Coll of Pharm and Sci; Brandeis U; Jacksonville U; hon MD: Us: Liege; Madrid; Athens; Strasbourg; Heb; hon LLD: Yeshiva U, NY; Keio U, Japan; hon DHL, HUC; m. Deborah Mitnik, Aug 5, 1916; c: Byron. Prof em, microbiol, dir em, inst of microbiol, Rutgers U, since 1958, on faculty since 1920; bact: Cutter Labs, 1918; Takamine Labs, 1919-20; org, div of marine bact, Woods Hole Oceanograhic Inst, 1931, marine bact, 1931-42, trustee since 1942; cons: US Dept of Agric; NRC; US Off of Sci Research and Devl; Sloan-Kettering Inst; Charles Mickle f, U Toronto, 1950. Prin contribs: isolated, with assos and students, new antibiotics including: actinomycin, 1940; clavacin, streptothricin, 1942; streptomycin, 1942; grisein, 1946; neomycin, 1948; fradicin; candicidin; candidin. Pres: comm III, Intl Soc of Soil Sci, 1927-35; Soc of Amer Bacts, 1944; vice-pres, Amer Soc of Agronomy, 1930-32; corresp mem, French Acad of Scis, since 1937; mem: Natl Acad of Scis; Amer Acad of Arts and Scis; Alpha Zeta; Phi Beta Kappa; Sigma Xi. Author: Enzymes, 1926; Principles of Soil Microbiology, 1927, 1932; The Soil and the Microbe, 1932; Humus, 1936, 1938; Microbial Antagonisms and Antibiotic Substances, 1945, 1947; The Actinomycetes, 1950; Soil Microbiology, 1952; SN Wingradsky, 1953; Guide to Actinomycetes and their Antibiotics, 1953; My Life with the Microbes 1954; ed: Streptomycin—Nature and Practical Applications, 1949; lit on: streptomycin, 1948, 1952; neomycin, 1952, 1956; the actinomycetes, 3 vols, 1959-62; contbr to sci and profsl publs. Recipient: awards: Nobel prize, physiology and med, 1952; Passano Found, 1947; Carlsberg Labs; and Emil Christian Hansen medal, both Denmark, 1947; Albert and Mary Lasker, Amer Public Health Assn, 1948; Amory, Amer Acad of Arts and Scis, 1948; NJ Agric Soc medal, 1948; John Scott, 1949; Page One, 1949; NJ State Veterans, 1949; Amer Pharm Mfgs, 1949; Leeuwenhoek medal, Netherlands Acad of Scis, 1950; cdr, Legion of Honor, Fr, 1950; Order of Merit of the Rising Sun, Emperor of Japan, 1952; humanitarian awards: B'rith Sholom, 1952; Variety Clubs, 1953; St Vincent award, Acad of Med, Turin, 1954. Home: 16 Logan Lane, Piscataway, NJ.

WALBA, Harold, US, educator; b. Chelsea, Mass, March 10, 1921; s. Joseph and Anna (Kamenetsky); BS, Mass State Coll, 1946; PhD, U Cal, Berkeley, 1949; m. Beatrice Alpert, Oct 12, 1945; c: David, Jeffrey. Prof, chem, San Diego State Coll, since 1958, dept chmn, 1960-63, fac mem since 1949; teaching f, U Cal, 1946-48; DuPont research f, 1948-49; research asso, Scripps Inst of Oceanography, 1951. Lt, USAAC, WW II. Mem: Amer Chem Soc, chmn, San Diego sect, 1958-59; AAAS; Phi Kappa Phi; AAUP; Alpha Epsilon Pi; Sigma Xi. Contbr to chem jours. Recipient: DFC; Air Medal with clusters. Home: 3870 Carancho St, Lemon Grove, Cal. Office: San Diego State Coll, San Diego, Cal.

WALBE, Joel, Isr, teacher, musicologist, composer, b. Shepetovka, Ukraine, 1900; s. Shalom and Chaya-Hinda (Feller); in Isr since 1920; att Vienna Konservatorium, 1933-37; PhD, U Vienna, 1964; m. Adina Kaplan; c: Ayala Yiftah, Israel. Music tchr, Levinsky Tchrs Coll, since 1937; tchr, lectr, Cantors Sem, Sela, Tel Aviv. Mem: Isr Assn Composers; ACUM; Milo, Tel Aviv. Compositions: Cantata leShabat; Cantata leChag haBikurim; Quintet for oboe and strings; variations on theme, Shir Geshem; music for plays: haChoma; Adloyada; Concertino; Ballad for orch, 1945; Symphony in B, 1956; Cantata Ilioth, 1959; The Yordan, cantata, 1967; Ginossar, string quartet, 1968. Contbr to music jours. Recipient: Yoel Engel prize, Tel Aviv Munic, 1954. Home 29 Zamenhoff St, Tel Aviv, Isr. Office: Levinsky Tchrs Coll, Tel Aviv, Isr.

WALBORSKY, Harry M, US, educator; b. Lodz, Pol, Dec 25, 1923; s. Israel and Sara (Miedowicz); BS, CCNY, 1945; PhD, O State U, 1949; m. Jan 8, 1953; c: Edwin, Eric, Lisa, Irene. Prof, chem, Fla State U, since 1950; cons, Dow Chem Co; research asso: Cal Inst of Tech, 1948-49; UCLA, 1949-50. Mem: Amer Chem Soc; London Chem Soc; Sigma Xi; Phi Lambda Upsilon. Contbr to profsl jours. Home: 2223 Ruagdh Ride, Tallahassee, Fla. Office: Fla Stat U, Tallahassee, Fla.

WALD, Fanny Judith, US, communal leader; b. NYC, Mar 1, 1901; d. Abba and Mindel (Potasher) Reiser; att: Columbia U; NY Sch Social Work; Fordham Sch Social Work; m. Henry Minsky; c: Marvin Minsky; m. 2nd, Albert Wald, May 24, 1955; c: Charlotte Porson, Ruth Amster. Delg to UN, from women's br, Union Orthodox J Congs of Amer; delg to Isr mission, liason to Isr consulate, from NY chap, Hadassah; repr, from Natl J women's orgs, to Natl JWB; chmn, Riverdale chap, League Women Voters, 1950-52; pres, Educ Council and Isr Gorup, Hadassah, 1956-60; mem, adv bd, FJP, 1961-65; vice-pres, conf comm, Natl J Women's Orgs, 1966-68. Home: 993 Park Ave, New York, NY.

WALD, George, US, educator; b. NYC, Nov 18, 1906; s. Isaac and Ernestine (Rosenmann); BS, NYU, 1927; MA, Columbia U, 1928, PhD, 1932; hon MA, Harvard U, 1944; hon MD, U Bern, 1957; hon DSc: Yale U, 1958; Wesleyen U, 1962; NYU, 1965; McGill U, 1966; Clark U, 1968; Amherst Coll, 1968; m. Frances Kingsley, May 14, 1931; c: Michael, David; m. 2nd, Ruth Hoffmann Hubbard, June 11, 1958; c: Elijah, Deborah. Higgins prof, biol, Harvard U, since 1968, fac mem since 1934; asst instr, biol, NYU, 1927-28; asst, biophysics, Columbia U, 1928-32; NRC f, biol: Kaiser Wilhelm Inst, Berlin; Dahlem, Heidelberg; Us of Zurich and Chgo, 1932-34. F: Natl Acad of Scis; Amer Acad of Arts and Scis; Amer Phil Soc; lectr, Natl Sigma Xi, 1952; mem: Amer Phys Soc; Optical Soc of Amer; Soc of Biol Chems; Soc of Gen Phys. Co-author: General Education in a Free Society; Twenty-six Afternoons of Biology, 1962; contbr to profsl jours. Recipient: Nobel Prize, physiology and med, 1967; Eli Lilly award, Amer Chem Soc, 1939; Lasker award, Amer Public Health Assn, 1953; Rumford medal, Amer Acad of Arts and Scis, 1959; Ives medal, Optical Soc of Amer, 1966; Karrer award, U of Zurich, 1967; T Duckett Jones award, Whitney Found, 1967; Bradford Washburn award, Boston Mus of Sci, 1968. Home: 21 Lakeview Ave, Cambridge, Mass. Office: Biol Labs, Harvard U, Cambridge, Mass.

WALD, Lewis, US, business exec; b. Boston, Mass, May 23, 1894; s. Simon and Leah (Hanenbarg); AB, Harvard Coll, 1916; m; c: Harriet, Robert, Lois. Pres, Ind Experience Inc, placement agcy for ret people, since 1960; fmr, pres and chmn bd, Vellumoid Co, Worcester, Mass, with firm since 1916. Co-chmn, NCCJ; treas, AHA; trustee, Mechanics Savings Bank; mem: Temple Emanuel, fmr pres; Mass State commn to study employement of older people; fmr pres: Employers Assn of Worcester Co; Mh Assn of Worcester Co; club, Harvard. Home: 4 Otsego Rd, Worcester, Mass.

WALD, Samuel S, US, oral roentgenologist, educator; b. NYC, Feb 5, 1906; s. Benzion and Lena (Wahler); DDS, NYU, 1928; m. Shirley Blau, June 12, 1932; c: Grover, Naomi. Clinical prof, radiology, diagnosis, and oral cancer, NYU Coll of Med, Bellevue Med Cen and Postgrad Med Sch, since 1930; asso prof, roentgenology, NYU Coll of Dent, since 1928; spec lectr, roentgenology and oral diagnosis, USN Dent Sch, Bethesda, since 1947; cons: Comty Service Soc of NY, since 1930; USN Hosp, St Albans, NY, since 1948; VA, Bklyn, since 1951; Dent Info Bur, since 1950; insp, east coast, Naval Dent Activities, since 1951; fmr, head, dept of roentgenology, Guggenheim Dent Clinic and Sch for Dent Hygienists, NYC, 1930-42. USN, 1942-45, rear adm, USNR. Dipl, NY State Bd of Oral Surg, 1947; f: NY Acad of Scis; NY Acad of Dent; Amer Coll of Dents; Amer Acad of Oral Roentgenology; cons to commn, chmn of adv comm on radiology, NY State Dept of Health; mem: NYU chap, Omicron Kappa Upsilon; Amer Dent Assn; NY State Dent Assn; Sci Research Soc of Amer; panel on tumors of oral cavity, Natl Cancer Inst, Amer Cancer Soc; Natl Cancer Conf; AAUP; Pan-Amer Med Assn, secy, sect of dent and oral surg; Mil Order of World Wars; Assn of Mil Surgs of US; USNR Med and Dent Offs Assn, pres, 1940-46. Author: Manual of Dental Roentgenology, 1936; Clinical Dental Roentgenology—Technic and Interpretation, 1940, 4th ed, 1957, Span ed, 1947, Ger ed, 1954; contbr to med and dent

jours. Recipient: awards: Public Health Assn of NYC, 1955; NYU, 1965; med and surg bur, USN, 1968. Home: 420 E 72 St, New York, NY.

WALDINGER, Ernst, US, educator, author; b. Vienna, Aus, Oct 16, 1896; s. Solomon and Anna (Spinath); in US since 1938; PhD, U of Vienna, 1921; m. Beatrice Winternitz, Feb 4, 1923; c: Hermann, Ruth. Prof em, Ger, Skidmore Coll, since 1965, fac mem since 1947; free-lance writer, lectr, since 1921; ed, trade mag, Allegemeiner Tarif Anzeiger, Vienna, 1922-38. Lt, Aus Army, WW I; mem, US War Dept, WW II. F, Intl Inst of Arts And Letters, Lindau, Ger; mem: AAUP; MLA; Amer Assn of Tchrs of Ger; NY State Fed of Fgn Lang Tchrs; Intl Germanistenverein, Copenhagen; PEN Center, Ger writers in fgn countries, London. Author: poems: Die Kuppel, 1934; Der Gemmenschneider, 1937; Die Kühlen Bauernstuben, 1941; Musik für diese Zeit, 1946; Glück und Geduld, 1952; Zwischen Hudson und Donau, 1958; Gesang vor dem Abgrund, 1960; Ich kann mit meinem Bruder sprechen, 1965; contbr to periodicals, and to radio progs in US, Aus, Ger, Swed. Recipient: Julius Reich Dichterstiftung für Lyrik, 1934; Theodor Körner Found award, 1958; award, City of Vienna, 1960, golden medal of honor, 1966. Home: 372 Central Pk W, New York, NY.

WALDMAN, Lester J, US, organization exec; b. NYC, Mar 5, 1907; s. Henry and Ruth (Rindskopf); BS, LIU, 1931; LLB, St. Lawrence U, 1931; m. Blanche Weinstein, July 29, 1947; c: Michael. Natl dir, org and planning, ADL, since 1959, with org since 1949; spec dep to atty gen, NY, 1936; lectr, hum relations, grad sch of educ, LIU, 1951-54. Mil psychol, adj gen dept, US Army, 1942-46. Dir, Soc for Deaf, since 1950; trustee, FJP; vice-pres, men's club, Cong Emanu-El; mem: NY and Fed Bars; Amer Psych Assn; Adult Educ Assn; Natl Assn of Intergroup Relations Officials; Phi Epsilon Pi; Masons; dir, Bur of Intercultural Educ, 1952-54; pres: NY lodge 1, B'nai B'rith, 1940-42; LIU Alumni Assn, 1932-42. Home: 340 E 64 St, New York, NY. Office: 315 Lexington Ave, New York, NY.

WALDOR, Milton A, US, attorney, legislator; b. Newark, NJ, Sep 28, 1924; s. Jack and Rose (Lowe); JD, Rutgers U Law Sch; m. Mona McClosky, June 11, 1950; c: Mitchell, Cathy. NJ state senator, since 1968; atty, Waldor and Hochberg, since 1951. Lt, USAAC, WW II. Leg chmn, JWV, natl cdr, 1965-66, natl judge-advocate, 1964-66; mem: Essex Co Bar Assn; Amer Trial Lawyers Assn; Sigma Alpha Mu. Author: Peddlers of Fear, 1966. Recipient: DFC; Chinese Star of Honor; Air medal with oak leaf cluster; Papal award, Pope Paul VI, 1966; citation of the year, B'nai B'rith, 1967. Home: W Orange, NJ. Office: 1180 Raymond Blvd, Newark, NJ.

WALERSTEIN, Isidor, US, physicist, educator; b. Lubartow, Pol, Mar 1, 1905; s. Abraham and Taube (Tenenbaum); in US since 1929; BA, U Toronto, 1926; PhD, U Chgo, 1929. Prof, physics, Purdue U, since 1948, fac mem since 1929. Mem: Amer Phys Soc; Amer Assn Physics Tchrs; pres, Lafayette J Charities, 1950-57. Contbr to sci jours. Home: 1334 Sunset Lane, W Lafayette, Ind. Office: Purdue U, W Lafayette, Ind.

WALIN, Moshe, Isr, impresario; b. Vilna, Pol, May 7, 1906; s. Zvi and Sarah (Vilkomirsky); in Isr since 1920; att: Tech HS, Vilna, 1924-25; theater arts, Hatai Sch, Isr, 1926-28; m. Shoshana Ukrainitz, 1936; c: Daniel. Impresario since 1930; co-found, Kibbutz Hakovesh, 1926; actor: Hatai theater, 1926-28; Kumkum, satirical theater, 1928-29; org, weekly Artists Evenings, 1929-45; found, dir, Li-La-Lo, satirical musical theater; concert tours in Eur, USA, Afr. Discovered: Braha Zefira, Sarah Osnath, Shoshana Damari, Hanna Aharoni. IDF, 1948-50. Author: From an Impresario's Diary, 1942. Recipient: named in Isr Golden Book, 1946. Hobby: art. Home: 7 Hataz St, Tel Aviv, Isr. Office: 1 Hess St, Tel Aviv, Isr.

WALKIN, Samuel D, US, rabbi; b. Gruzd, Lith, 1904; s. Aron and Rachel (Sorotzkin); in US since 1946; ordained rabbi, att yeshivas: Slobodka; Mir; and Radum; m. Cilia Sacharow, 1932; c: Chaya Small, Esther Poupko, Moishe, Chaim, Rachel. Rabbi: Beth Aron Cong, Bklyn; found, Yeshiva Beth Aron, Kew Gardens; fmr, rabbi, Lokatsh, Pol. Vice-pres, Union of Orthodox Rabbis; mem, presidium, Poale Agudath Isr. Home and study: 119-16 83 Ave, Kew Gardens, NY.

WALL, Max B, US, rabbi; b. Pol, July 23, 1915; s. Louis and Gertrude (Heller); AB, Yeshiva U, 1938; ordained rabbi, MHL,

JTSA, 1942; hon DHum, U of Vt, 1969; m. Miriam Peyser, Oct 18, 1942; c: Mindy, Naomi, Shira. Rabbi, Ohavi Zedek Syn, since 1946; fac mem: Champlain Coll; St Michael's Coll; chaplain for all state instns; rabbi, Cong Beth El, Woodbury, NJ, 1942-43. Chaplain, US Army, 1943-46. Bd trustees: Champlain Coll; Med Cen Hosp of Vt; member: NY Bd of Rabbis; RA; ZOA; Vt Council of Social Wfr; club, Intl Rotary. Home: 472 North St, Burlington, Vt. Study: 188 N Prospect St, Burlington, Vt.

WALLACE, Mike, US, journalist; TV interviewer and commentator; b. Boston, Mass, May 9, 1918; s. Frank and Zina (Sharfman); AB, U Mich, 1939; m. Lorraine Perigord, Aug 21, 1955; c: Christopher. Correspondent, CBS News, since 1963; asso: radio, since 1939; TV, since 1946; reporter, air edition, Chgo Sun-Times, 1941-48; free-lance journalist, radio and TV, 1953-63. USNR, 1943-46. Chmn: US State Dept cultural exch delg, Radio-TV to USSR, 1958; exec vice-pres, Acad of TV Arts and Scis, 1960-61; mem, Sigma Delta Chi; clubs: Overseas Press, The Players, Town Tennis. Author: Mike Wallace Asks, 1958; contbr to periodicals. Recipient, awards: Robert E Sherwood, 1957; Emmy, 1957-58; George Foster Peabody, 1963. Home: 133 E 74 St, New York, NY. Office: 524 W 51 St, New York, NY.

WALLACH, David Abraham, US, attorney; b. NYC, Sep 2, 1895; s. Elias and Clara (Wallach); att NYU, 1915; LLB, Bklyn Law Sch, 1917; att Columbia U, 1925-26; m. Madeleine Spiro, Oct 6, 1926; c: Barbara Juster, Edward. Pvt practice since 1917; pres, Empire State Mutual Ins Co, 1923-29. Mem, cabinet: FJP, NYC; UJA; trustee, Union Temple, Bklyn; mem, Bklyn Bar Assn; fmr, delg, Natl Dem Conv, 1948; club, Lawyers of Fed. Hobby: music. Home: 135 Eastern Parkway, Brooklyn, NY. Office: 32 Court, New York, NY.

WALLACH, Eli, US, actor of stage, screen, TV; b. Bklyn, NY, Dec 7, 1915; s. Abraham and Bertha (Schorr); BA, U Texas, 1936; MA, educ, CCNY, 1938; m. Anne Jackson, 1948; c: Peter, Roberta, Katherine. Actor in Broadway plays: Mr Roberts; The Rose Tattoo; Camino Real; The Teahouse of the August Moon (NY and London); Major Barbara; Rhinoceros; The Tiger; The Typists; Luv; The Staircase; TV actor: The Lark; The Battler; movies: The Brain (Fr); Baby Doll; The Misfits; The Victors; Lord Jim; The Magnificent Seven. Recipient: awards: Donaldson; Perry; Theatre World Critics; all for The Rose Tattoo; Brit Acad, for Baby Doll; dist medal, AJCong. Home: 90 Riverside Drive, New York, NY.

WALLACH, Ira, US, author; b. NYC, Jan 22, 1913; s. Morris and Rose (Sims); att Cornell U, 1930-31; m. Devera Sievers, Jan 25, 1941; c: Leah Sievers. Author: The Horn and the Roses, 1947; How to be Deliriously Happy, 1950; Hopalong-Freud, 1951; Hopalong-Freud Rides Again, 1952; Gutenberg's Folly, 1954; How to Pick a Wedlock, 1956; Muscle Beach, 1959; The Absence of a Cello, 1960; for stage: Phoenix, '55, 1955; The Absence of a Cello, 1964, co-author: Drink to Me Only, 1959; Smiling the Boy Fell Dead, 1961; for screen: Boys Night Out, 1962; Don't Make Waves, 1967, co-author: The Wheeler-Dealers, 1963; Hot Millions, 1968. Mem: Writers Guild of Amer; Dramatists Guild of Amer; PEN; Airplane Owners and Pilots Assn. Home and office: 345 W 58 St, New York, NY.

WALLACH, Luitpold, US, educator, author; b. Munich, Ger, Feb 6, 1910; s. Karl and Rosa (Schneeweis); in US since 1939; PhD, U Tuebingen, 1932; PhD, Cornell U, 1947. Prof, classics, U of Ill, since 1967; asso mem, Cen for Advanced Study, U of Ill, 1969-70; fmr lectr: Hamilton Coll; Cornell U; U of Okla; Harpur Coll; prof, classics, Marquette U, 1962-67. Mem: Amer Philol Assn; Amer Hist Assn; Medieval Acad of Amer; Phi Beta Kappa; Phi Kappa Phi; Eta Sigma Phi; Sigma Tau Delta. Author: Berthold of Zwiefalten's Chronicle, 1958; Alcuin and Charlemagne, 1959, 2nd, ed, 1968; Liberty and Letters: The Thoughts of Leopold Zunz, 1959; The Classical Tradition, 1966; contbr to hist and philol jours. Recipient: fs: Fund for Advancement of Educ, 1952; Amer Council of Learned Socs, 1960; Marquette U Fac, 1967; Leo Baeck Inst, 1967. Hobbies: rowing, hiking. Office: U of Ill, 361 Lincoln Hall, Urbana, Ill.

WALLACH, Michael, UK, journalist; b. Frankfurt/M, Ger, Feb, 1918; s. Ber and Maria (Roth); in Eng since 1936; BS, U Coll, London; m. Maisie Marks, Mar, 1941; c: Sharon. Ed writer, J Chronicle, London, since 1965, ed: supplements, color mag; ed, J Year Book, since 1969; asso with BBC, 1946-49;

secy, Off of Chief Rabbi, United Heb Congs, Brit Commonwealth, 1951-62. Brit Army, 1940-46; Brit mil govt, Ger, 1944-46. Pres, Slig Brodetski lodge, B'nai B'rith, 1962-63, fmr, vice-pres, Ben Yehuda Heb-speaking lodge; secy, Conf Eur Rabbis, 1957-62; mem: natl exec, Mizrachi Org, 1952-59; exec, Council of Chr and J, chmn, publ comm. Fmr ed, News from Zion; chmn, Rel Weekly Press Group, 1969-70; contbr to Heb and Anglo-J press. Home: 47 Delamere Rd, London W5, Eng. Office: 25 Furnival St, London EC4, Eng.

WALLACH, Sidney, US, public affairs cons, journalist; b. Horochow, Pol, July 4, 1905; s. Don and Bertha (Steinberg); in US since 1912; BA, CCNY, 1925; att Columbia U, 1925-26; m. Idalee Burrows, Aug 17, 1929 (decd); c: Rosanne Stein, Don; m. 2nd, Pauline Rudnick, Feb 5, 1967. Pres, Sidney Wallach Assos, since 1942; exec vice-pres, Amer Inst for Tropics, since 1952; Eur corresp, Seven Arts Feature Syndicate, 1928-29; exec dir: AJComm, 1933-42; counsel: JWB, 1942-43; NCCJ, 1942-44; Amer Council for Judaism, 1943-50. Exec dir: Theodore Roosevelt Centennial commn, 1955-59; Amer Chess Found; trustee, Oliver Wendell Holmes Assn; mem: West End Syn; Amer Arbitration Assn. Author: Hitler, Menace to Mankind, 1933; The Theodore Roosevelt Roundup, 1959; ed: Perry's Expedition to the China Seas, 1953; City College Alumnus, 1948-51; Modern Mexico, 1945-50; mgn ed: J Tribune, 1931; Young Judean, 1932; co-found, Contemporary J Record (now Commentary), 1939; contbr to periodicals. Recipient: alumni medal, CCNY, 1947. Home: 12 Beekman Pl, New York, NY.

WALLACH, Yehuda Lothar, Isr, educator, ret army off; b. Haigerloch, Ger, Mar 12, 1921; s. Louis and Minna (Rotheimer); in Isr since 1936; BA, Heb U, 1962; PhD, Oxford U, 1965; m. Chava Turetzky, Sep 2, 1940; c: Roni, Eliezer, Uri. Sr lectr, mil hist, Tel Aviv U, since 1965. Haganah; IDF, armor, gen staff, 1944-65; cdr: infantry battalion, Givati Brig, 1948; Battalion and Brig Cdr's Sch; cen task force, mechanized brig, Sinai Campaign; mem, army spokesman's dept, Six-Day War. Mem, Isr Fgn Policy Assn. Author: Das Dogma der Vernichtungsschlacht, 1967; Die Lehren von Clausewitz und Schlieffen und ihre Wirkungen in zwei Weltkriegen, 1967; Die Kriegslehre von Friedrich Engels, 1968; The War of the Maccabees. Hobbies: travelling, camping. Recipient: ALA medal. Home: 27 Ben Zvi Ave, Ramat Gan, Isr. Office: Tel Aviv U, Ramat Aviv, Isr.

WALLENSTEIN, Meir, UK, educator; b. Jerusalem, May 3, 1903; s. Shimon and Sarah; att Tchrs Training Coll, Jerusalem; MA, Manchester U, 1935, PhD, 1946; m. Sara Rabi, 1946. Reader, modern and medieval Heb, U Manchester. Chmn, Tarbut Soc, Manchester; jt hon secy, Friends of Heb Lang Acad, Eng; adv mem, Heb Lang Acad, Jerusalem; mem: FRAS; PEN, Jerusalem. Author: Some Unpublished Hymns from the Cairo Archives, 1956; The Nezer, Hymn from the Dead Sea Scrolls, 1957; ed, Melilah; contbr to scholarly jours. Spec interest: Genizah fragments. Home: 11 Heathland Rd, Salford, Eng. Office: U Manchester, Manchester, Eng.

WALLER, Herbert S, US, rabbi; b. Memphis, Tenn, Oct 23, 1914; s. Jacob and Helen (Schlesinger); BA, U Cincinnati, 1935; MA, 1937; BH, MHL, cum laude, ordained rabbi, HUC-JIR, 1939; ThD, S Baptist Theol Sem, Louisville, 1949; DD, HUC, 1964; m. Sylvia Steinberg, Sep 14, 1938; c: David. Rabbi, Cong Adath Isr, since 1947; moderator, weekly Interfaith panel, WLKY-TV; lectr, Bellarmine Coll; rabbi, Temple B'nai Isr, Columbus, Ga, 1939-47. Ky state chmn, natl RabCA combined campaign for HUC-JIR and UAHC; mem, bd of alumni overseers, HUC-JIR; bd mem: Blue Cross Hosp Plan Inc; Lincoln Found; Assn Moral and Spiritual Values; Comty Concert Assn; bd mem, pres, Louisville Bd of Educ, 1960-66; mem: natl recruitment comm, HUC-JIR; AJ-Comm; B'nai B'rith; Phi Beta Kappa; Amer bd of World Union for Progressive Judaism; Ky Council on Hum Relations; comm on church and state, CCAR; mem, lectr speakers bur: NCCJ; J Chautauqua Soc; ARC; Louisville Comty Chest; clubs: Conversation; Kiwanis. Author: Heinrich Heine—His Relationship with Jews and Judaism, 1937; Three Systems of Hebrew Vocalization Historically Considered, 1937; The Evolution of the Practice of not Pronouncing the Divine Name in Biblical Literature, 1938; Leopold Zunz—The Creative Years, 1939; The Unity of the Book of Amos, 1949; Home: 612 Cressbrook Dr, Louisville, Ky. Study: 834 S 3 St, Louisville, Ky.

WALLER, Peter Louis, Australia, educator; b. Siedlce, Pol, Feb 10, 1935; s. Jacob and Hilda (Sklarsz); in Austr since 1938;

LLB, hons, U Melbourne, 1955; BCL, Oxford U, 1958; m. Wendy Poyser, Jan 11, 1959; c: Anthony, Ian, Eleanor. Sir Leo Cussen Prof of Law, Monash U, since 1965, dean, fac of law, since 1969; sr lectr, U of Melbourne, 1949-65; bicentennial f in criminal law, U of Pa, US, 1964-65. Capt, Austr Army Res since 1966. Exec mem, Austr Us Law Schs Assn, 1966-67, 1968-69; mem: B'nai B'rith, Harmony lodge, past pres; Freemasons, Melbourne U, past master. Co-author: Cases and Materials in Criminal Law, 1962, 2nd ed 1965; An Introduction to Law, 1966; Cases and Materials on the Legal Process, 1966. Hobbies: reading, films, theater. Home: 2 Hartley Ave, Caulfield, Australia. Office: Law Sch, Monash U, Clayton, Australia.

WALLERSTEIN, Morton L, US, attorney; b. Richmond, Va, Dec 7, 1890; s. Joseph and Clare (Ullmann); BA, U of Va, 1911; LLB, Harvard U Law Sch, 1914; m. Ruth Cohn, Sep 1, 1919; c: Elizabeth Bingham, Catherine White, Morton Jr. Mem, Wallerstein, Goode, Adamson, Dobbins, and Shuford, since 1921; asst to Atty Gen of Va, 1914-16; asst counsel, Va State Tax Bd, 1916-17; counsel, Public Works Admn, 1933-36. USN, WW I. Pres: Amer Munic Assn, 1927; Amer Soc of Planning Officials, 1934; Richmond JCC, 1947-48; exec secy, League of Va Munic, 1921-41, counsel since 1941; chmn: region 2, Natl Resources Planning Bd, 1935-43; Va Planning Bd, 1933-38; mem: Amer Bar Assn; Amer Law Inst; Delta Sigma Rho; Masons. Contbr to legal jours. Recipient: dist citizens award, Richmond JCC, 1956; dist public service award, Va Citizens Planning Assn, 1959. Home: 1601 Pope Ave, Richmond, Va. Office: Travelers Bldg, Richmond, Va.

WALLERSTEIN, Robert Solomon, US, psychiatrist, psychoanalyst; b. Berlin, Ger, Jan 28, 1921; s. Lazar and Sally (Guensberg); in US since 1923; BA, Columbia Coll, 1941; MD, Columbia U Coll Phys and Surgs, 1944; cert, Topeko Inst Psychan, Kan, 1958; m. Judith Saretsky, Jan 26, 1947; c: Michael, Nina, Amy. Chief, dept psycht, Mt Zion Hosp, since 1966; training and supervising analyst, SF Psychoanalytic Inst, SF, since 1966; clinical prof, psycht: Langley Porter Neuropsychiatric Inst; U of Cal Sch Med; both since 1967; chief psychosomatic sect, staff psycht, Winter VA Hosp, Topeka, Kan, 1951-53, cons, psychosomatic sect, 1954-66, on staff since 1949; dir, dept research, sr psycht, Menninger Found, Kan, 1965-66, on staff since 1954; cons: psychiatric staff, Topeka State Hospital, 1957-66; lectr: Menninger Sch Psycht, 1951-66; Topeka Inst Psychan, 1959-66, training and supervising analyst, 1966-66. Capt, US Army MC, 1946-48. Pres, Topeka J Fed, 1958; f: Amer Psychiatric Assn; Amer Coll Phys; Amer Orthopsychiatric Assn; mem: Mh research career award comm, Natl Inst Mh, chmn, 1968-70; Amer Psychoanalytic Assn, exec council, 1968-72; Intl Psychoanalytic Assn; SF Psychoanalytic Soc; Cen for Advanced Psychoanalytic Studies, Princeton; Group for Advancement Psycht, chmn, research comm, 1958-66; AMA; Cal Med Assn; SF Med Soc; AAAS; Amer Bd Psycht and Neur, cert in psycht, 1953; fmr mem, Amer Psych Assn. Co-author: Hospital Treatment of Alcoholism: A Comparative, Experimental Study, 1957; The Teaching and Learning of Psychotherapy, 1958; Prediction in Psychotherapy Research: A Method for the Transformation of Clinical Judgments into Testable Hypotheses, 1968; ed bd: US ed, Intl Jour of Psychoanalysis; Psych Issues; Archives of Gen Psycht; Jour Nervous and Mental Diseases; Jour Psychiatric Research, 1963-64; Jour Amer Psychoanalytic Assn, 1965-67, 1969-71; contbr to profsl jours, publs. Recipient: f: Phi Beta Kappa, Columbia, 1940; Alpha Omega Alpha, Columbia, 1944; Cen Advanced Study Behavioral Scis, Stanford U, 1964-65. Hobbies: tennis, hiking. Home: 290 Beach Road, Belvedere, Cal. Office: Mt Zion Hosp, 1600 Divisadero St, San Francisco, Cal.

WALTZER, Herbert, US, educator; b. Bklyn, NY, May 29, 1930; s. Samuel and Pearl (Bernstein); AB, NYU, 1951, MA, 1954, PhD, 1959; m. Marilyn Fischvogt, June 11, 1962; c: Adam, Sarah, Samuel. Prof, political sci, Miami U, since 1966, fac mem since 1957; instr, govt, NYU, 1954-55. USAF, 1955-57; capt, ret, res. Author: American Government: Principles, Institutions, and Processes, 1962; co-author: Ideas in Action: Modern Political Ideologies, 1969; contbr to The Politics of Reapportionment, 1962. Mem: Amer, Midwest, and S Political Sci Assns; O Conf of Political Sci and Econ; Pi Sigma Alpha. Recipient: Penfield f, NYU. Home: 609 Melinda Dr, Oxford, O. Office: Miami U, Oxford, O.

WARACH, Bernard, US, social work exec; b. NYC, Feb 10, 1921; s. Joseph and Frances (Farber); BSS, CCNY, 1940; MS, Sch Social Work, U Pittsburg, 1942; m. Shirley Wagner,

May 10, 1950; c: Joshua, Jonathan, Beth. Exec dir, J Assn for Services for Aged, since 1968; field repr: agric marketing admn, US Dept Agric, W Va, Vt, 1942-44; chief supply div, displaced persons prog, wfr off, UN Relief and Rehab Admn, 1944-47; asst exec dir, Irene Kaufmann Settlement House, Pittsburgh, 1948-52; exec dir, Mosholu Neighborhood Cen, NY, 1952-54; lectr: schls social work: Adelphi Coll, 1954-57; Hunter Coll, 1957-59; NYU, 1959-60; acting exec dir, J Assn Neighborhood Cens, 1956-57; gen dir, Asso YM-YWHAs, Gtr NY, 1966-68, asso gen dir since 1957. Chmn, profsl educ comm, Natl Assn J Cen Workers, 1960-66; mem: Natl Assn Social Workers, Nassau Co, Acad Social Work; Phi Beta Kappa. Author: Program Planning for Bus Trips, 1954; Group Leaders Handbook, 1960; contbr to profsl jours. Home: 10 Hampshire Rd, Great Neck, NY. Office: 33 W 60 St, New York, NY.

WARBURG, Edward M M, US, communal leader; b. White Plains, NY, June 5, 1908; s. Felix and Frieda (Schiff); BS, Harvard Coll, 1930; hon DHL: Brandeis U, 1955; HUC-JIR, 1955; m. Mary Prue, Dec 6, 1939; c: Stephen Currier, stepson (decd), David, Daphne. Hon chmn, JDC, chmn, 1941-65, co-chmn, 1939-41; instr, art, Bryn Mawr, 1931-33; mem, archaeol expedition, Iran, 1933; staff mem, Mus Modern Art, 1934-35. Maj, US Army, 1942-45, served in civil affairs sect, and displaced persons div, 1st Army. Pres, UJA, Gtr NY, 25 years; mem: bd govs, Heb U; bd trustees, Amer-Isr Cultural Found; chmn, Amer Patrons Isr Mus, found, fmr mem, exec comm; hon trustee: NY Mus Modern Art; Inst Intl Educ, fmr mem, bd dirs, exec comm; adv comm, Voluntary Fgn Aid; spec asst, cultural affairs, Gov, State of NY; mem, NY State Bd Regents. Recipient: Bronze Star, Officier de l'ordre de la Couronne, Belgium; Herbert Lehman award, UJA, Gtr NY; cdr, Order of Merit; cdr, Order of Solidarity, both Rep of It. Home: 730 Park Ave, New York, NY. Office: 277 Park Ave, New York, NY.

WARBURG, Erik, Den, cardiologist, educator; b. Copenhagen, Feb 3, 1892; s. Alexander and Agnes (Levy); m. Vigga Valentiner, Apr 28, 1925; c: Niels, Mette. Prof, internal med, U Copenhagen, since 1931, rector, 1956-58. Chmn: Danish Sci Card Soc; Danish Gen Card Soc. Recipient: cdr: Order of the Dannebrog; Icelandic Falcon; Legion of Honor. Home: H C Andersens Blvd 48, Copenhagen, Den. Office: Rigshospitalet, Copenhagen, Den.

WARBURG, Frederick M, US, banker, business exec; b. NYC, Oct 14, 1897; s. Felix and Frieda (Schiff); BA, Harvard U, 1919; m. Wilma Shannon, Mar 4, 1946. Partner, Kuhn, Loeb & Co, since 1931, with firm since 1922; trustee, Amer Optical Co, since 1951; partner, Amer Intl Corp, 1919-24; asso: M M Warburg & Co. Hamburg, Ger, 1921-22; Lehman Bros, 1927-30. Lt, US Army WW I, res, 1919-37, col, spec services div, WW II. Trustee: Smith Coll; Middlesex Sch, Mass; NY Found; FJP; dir: Gtr NY Council, Boy Scouts of Amer; Natl Recreation Assn; USO; Natl Travelers Aid Assn; clubs: River; Harvard, NY and Boston; Wall St, NY; Tavern, Boston. Recipient: army commendation ribbon, WW II. Home: 6 Riverview Terr, New York, NY. Office: 30 Wall St, New York, NY.

WARBURG, James Paul, US, author, business exec; b. Hamburg, Ger, Aug 18, 1896; s. Paul and Nina (Loeb); BA, Harvard U, 1917; m; c: April, Andrea, Kay; m. 2nd, Joan Melber, 1948; c: James, Jennifer, Philip, Sarah. Dir, Polaroid Corp; pres: Fontenay Corp; Bydale Co; fmr: banker; RR dir. Lt, USN aviation, WW I; dep dir, propaganda policy, OWI, WW II. Trustee, Inst for Policy Studies, Wash, DC; mem, Council on Fgn Relations. Author: Wool and Wool Manufacture, 1920; Cotton and Cotton Manufacture, 1921; Hides and Leather Manufacture, 1921; Acceptance Financing, 1922; Three Textile Raw Materials, 1923; The Money Muddle, 1934; It's Up To Us, 1934; Hell Bent for Election, 1935; Still Hell Bent, 1936; Peace in our Time? 1940; Our War and Our Peace, 1941; Foreign Policy Begins at Home, 1944; Unwritten Treaty, 1945; Germany, Bridge or Battleground? 1947; Put Yourself in Marshall's Place, 1948; Last Call for Common Sense, 1949; Faith, Purpose and Power, 1950; Victory Without War, 1951; How to Co-exist, 1952; Germany: Key to Peace, 1953; The United States in a Changing World, 1954; Turning Point Toward Peace, 1955; Agenda for Action, 1957; The West in Crisis, 1959; Reveille for Rebels, 1960; Disarmament: The Challenge of the Nineteen Sixties, 1961; The Long Road Home, autobiography, 1962; Time for Statesmanship, 1964; The United States in The Postwar World, 1965; Vietnam: Proposal for Policy Modification, 1965;

Western Intruders, 1966; Crosscurrents in the Middle East, 1968; Wanted: A New American Approach to Peace, 1968; verse: And Then What? 1931; Shoes, Ships and Sealing Wax, 1932; Man's Enemy and Man, 1942; Home: Greenwich, Conn. Office: 60 E 42 St, New York, NY.

WARBURG, Miriam, Switz, communal worker; b. Marburg, Ger, Oct 19, 1895; d. Karl and Gertrud (Cohn) Goldberg; m. Gustav Warburg, Apr 23, 1943. Mem exec, Youth Aliyah, Geneva, since 1960; life mem, bd mgmt, Youth Aliyah, Isr; repr, Intl Council J Women at UN, Geneva; fmr, gen secy, Youth Aliyah, Gt Brit. Author: graphology textbooks; fmr corresp, Berliner Tageblatt. Recipient: Henrietta Szold award, Eng, 1965. Home: 8B Ave de Miremont, Geneva, Switz.

WARBURG, Siegmund George, Eng, banker, business exec; b. Tuebingen, Ger, Sep 30, 1902; s. Georges and Lucie (Kaulla); in Eng since 1933; att, Hum Sem, Urach; m. Eva Philipson, Nov 8, 1926; c: George, Ann Biegun. Dir, S G Warburg, London, since 1946; partner, MM Warburg, Hamburg, 1930-38; dir, New Trading Co, London, 1938-46; partner, Kuhn, Loeb & Co, NY, 1946-64. Gov, Weizmann Inst, Rehovot. Recipient: knighthood, Queen of Eng, 1966. Home: 95 95 Eaton Sq, London SWI, Eng. Office: 30 Gresham St, London EC2, Eng.

WARDI, Chaim, Isr, educator, editor; b. Pol, Apr 19, 1901; s. Dov and Rosa (Elwing) Rosenfeld; in Isr since 1919; att Us: Rome, Florence, Turin; PhD, U Pisa, 1926; m. Hannah Bing, June, 1966 (decd); c: Yorai, Eynel. Sr lectr, church hist, Tel Aviv U, since 1952; ed, Chr News from Isr, since 1949; visiting f, Inst of Arts and Hum Studies, Penn State; fmr: instr, It hist and culture, Heb U, 1932-40; lecture tours: Eur, 1936, Asia, 1939; dir, Chr Comtys dept, Isr Min for Rel Affairs, counsellor, Chr Affairs, 1948-68; tchr, Amer Inst of Holy Land Studies. Prin contribs: advised Isr govt in relations with Chr churches in Isr and abroad, repr Isr at Chr church assemblies in Amer, Eur, and Asia. Brit Army, 1941-46. Mem, B'nai B'rith. Fmr ed, Ency Hebraica; contbr to periodicals, and scholarly jours; trans, It to Heb, Home: 1 Brenner St, Jerusalem, Isr.

WARHAFT, Sidney, Can, educator; b. Winnipeg, Can, Dec 8, 1921; s. Benjamin and Bertha (Glassman); BA, hons, U Man, 1949; att, U Paris, 1949-50; MA, Northwestern U, 1952, PhD, 1954; m. Marion Glassman, 1953; c: Mark. Prof, head, Eng dept, U Man, since 1958; fac mem since 1954; asst prof: U Mich, 1955-57; U of S Cal, 1957-58; RCAF, 1942-45. Mem: Can Assn U Tchrs; Assn Can U Tchrs of Eng; Renaissance Soc of Amer; MLA. Co-ed, English Poems, 1250-1660, pub 1961; ed, Francis Bacon: A Selection of his Works, 1965; contbr to profsl jours. Home: 312 Waverley St, Winnipeg, Man, Can. Office: U Man, Winnipeg, Man, Can.

WARHAFTIG, Zerah, Isr, government official; b. Warsaw, Pol, Feb 2, 1906; s. Yerucham and Malka (Feinstein); in Isr since 1947; LLM, U Warsaw, 1939; LLD, Heb U, 1967; m. Naomi Klein, 1939; c: Emanuel, Nili, Itamar, Yacov, David. MK since 1949; Isr Min of Rel Affairs since 1961, dep min, 1951-59; mem, exec, Natl Rel Party; fmr: pvt law practice, Warsaw, 1936-39; vice-chmn, Cen Pal Off, Warsaw, 1936-39; dep dir, Inst of J Affairs, NY, 1943-47; dir, law dept, Vaad Leumi, NY, 1947; lectr: J Law Research Inst, Isr Min of Justice; law fac, Heb U. Mem: World Zionist Action Comm; cen comm: KH; World Mizrachi; Amer Soc for Intl Law; exec council: WJC; Hechal Shlomo; fmr: vice-pres: Mizrachi; Hecalutz Hamizrachi, Pol; Hapoel Isr-Amer C of C and Ind; Jerusalem Phil Soc; Hist Soc, Isr; Hamizrachi, US; delg to WJCs. Author: Starvation over Europe, 1943; Relief and Rehabilitation, 1944; Where Should They Go?, 1946; Uprooted, 1946; HaChazaka baMishpat Halvrey, 1965; contbr to periodicals. Home: 7 Narkis St, Jerusalem, Isr. Office: Min for Rel Affairs, 30 Jaffa Rd, Jerusalem, Isr.

WARMBRAND, Martin J, US, business exec, communal leader; b. NYC, 1926; att: CCNY; U Buffalo; New Sch for Social Research, NY. Gen contractor; real estate mgr. Instr, US Army rehab unit. Mem, comm on Black Jews, FJP; admnr, Family Counseling Service; fmr: prog dir, Natl Fed Temple Brotherhoods; acting admnr, Amer Pro-Falasha comm; temple admnr, The Brotherhood Syn; mem, Bushwick Comty Action Assn. Prin contbr: research and contact with Black J congs and the Beta Isr Comty, Ethiopia. Author: The Black Jews of

America, 1969; contbr to Amer and fgn press. Home: 182-25 Wexford Terr, Jamaica Estates, NY.

WARMBRUNN, Hans, US, business exec; b. Frankfurt, Ger, May 19, 1911; s. David and Lilly (Guckenheimer); in US since 1941; law deg, Us: Grenoble; Berlin; Frankfurt; grad, Col Sch of Mines, 1943; MA, Columbia U, 1960; m. Olga Lewandowsky, Nov 22, 1933; c: Ruth Bean, Eva Herndon, Arlene Saxonhouse. Vice-pres, treas, H D Sheldon and Co, since 1946; partner; Oliveirax Warmbrunn Ltd, Port, 1935-41; testing engr, Tin Processing Corp, Tex, 1943-44. Pres, J Philanthropy Fund of 1933, Inc; vice-pres, NY Found of Nursing Homes Inc; treas, Self-Help of Emigres from Cen Eur, Inc; mem exec comm, Amer Fed of Jews from Cen Eur; fmr, treas, J cmty, Oporto, Port. Spec interests: modern art, peace orgs. Home: 11050 68 Dr, Forest Hills, NY. Office: 104 Fifth Ave, New York, NY.

WARNER, Jack Milton Jr, US, motion picture produc, importer; b. SF, Cal, Mar 27, 1916; s. Jack L and Irma (Rogell); AB, cum laude, U of S Cal, 1938; m. Barbara Richman, May 30, 1948; c: Elizabeth, Deborah. Pres, Warner Products Inc; fmr asso, Warner Bros Pictures Inc: mem, theatre dept and distributor, 1946-49; produc, London, 1948-49, produc exec, 1951-57; vice-pres, TV commercial and ind films div, 1957-59. Lt-col, US Army, Signal Corps, WW II; col, res. Pres, LA Co Assn for Mh, 1958-59; supr secy, Zeta Beta Tau, 1960; mem, natl adv council, Assn of US Army. Recipient: 5 battle stars, N Afr, Mediterranean, and Eur theatres, Occupation of Ger ribbon. Hobby: photography. Office: 9320 Santa Monica Blvd, Beverly Hills, Cal.

WARSEN, Allen A, US, educator; b. Warsaw, Pol, June 19, 1903; s. Jacob and Anna (Turower) Warshawski; in US since 1932; BA, Wayne State U, 1936, MSW, 1938; m. Sara Cohen, 1930 (decd); c: Annette. Tchr, social sci, Detroit Bd of Educ, since 1938. Found: J Research Cen, Detroit; Dir's Council of J Rel, Metrop Detroit, first pres; J Hist Soc of Mich, hon pres; trustee, Detroit Fed of Tchrs; delg, JCC, Metro-Detroit; mem: B'nai B'rith; Alumni Assn, Wayne State U; club, Metrop Detroit Social Studies. Author: Jewish Communal Institutions in Detroit; co-ed, Michigan J Hist Mag; contbr to jours. Hobbies: photography, travel, book collecting. Home: 21721 Parklawn, Oak Park, Mich. Office: 18445 Cathedral, Detroit, Mich.

WARSHA, Avigdor, Isr, attorney; b. Antopol, Russ, June 11, 1930; s. Yehoshua and Sarah (Berg); in Isr since 1939; MJ, Sch of Law and Econs, Tel Aviv U, 1954; m. Aviva Kiev, Oct 28, 1962; c: Mira, Gad. Mayor, local council, Kiryat Ono, since 1969; Intl B'nai B'rith Legal Counsel in Isr. Sgt-maj, IDF. Exec comm, B'nai B'rith Bldg, Tel Aviv; secy, judge, Disciplinary Court, Tel Aviv dist, Isr Bar Assn; fmr exec comm: Isr Sports Assn; Isr Football Assn; chmn, Herut Youth Movement, Tel Aviv; mem: B'nai B'rith; Isr Bar Assn; Isr-Amer C of C Isr and Ind; Jerusalem Phil Soc; Hist Soc, Isr; Exploration Soc; club: Commercial and Ind, Tel Aviv. Recipient: Itur Lochamei Hamedinah; decorations: War of Independence; Mivzah Kadesh; 6 Day War. Home: 13 Rothschild St, Kiryat Ono, Isr. Office: 123 Rothschild Blvd, Tel Aviv, Isr.

WARZAGUER, Jaime (Szroitman, Ben Shalom), Uruguay, educator, journalist, author; b. Dubienka, Pol, Apr 20, 1911; s. Abraham and Sara (Landsberg); in Uruguay since 1934; tchr dipl, Lehrer Sem, Vilna; m. Esther Szroit, 1933; c: Raquel Barszcz. Headmaster, Shalom Aleichem Sch, Montevideo, since 1950; counselor, Kehila, 1946-58. Delg: WZCs; Movimiento Zionista Mundial; secy, mem, Zionist Lab Movement and its action comm, Jerusalem. Author: Sixty Days in Medinat Israel, 1965; contbr to jours in Uruguay, Isr. Home: Martin C Martinez 2548/3, Montevideo, Uruguay. Office: Constitucion 2484, Montevideo, Uruguay.

WASSERMAN, Helen Bernstein, US, communal leader; b. Portland, Me, July 4, 1929; d. Israel and Rebecca (Thurman) Bernstein; BA, magna cum laude, Radcliffe Coll, 1951; MS, and tchrs cert, U Bridgeport, 1965; m. Edward Wasserman, Aug 19, 1951; c: David, Daniel. Co-chmn, ed comm, mem, steering comm, Urban Coalition Gtr Bridgeport; vice-chmn, commn on cmty relations, United J Council, Gtr Bridgeport; adv, past chmn, Sch Volunteer Assn; mem bd: Conf of Women's Orgs; Hall Neighborhood House; Child Guidance Clinic of Bridgeport; Fed of J Women; Conn Sym Orch; fmr: pres, Gtr Bridgeport sect, Natl Council of J Women, 1965-67; mem: Bridgeport Hosp Auxiliary; Fairfield Co Med

Assn Auxiliary; sisterhood, Cong, Rodeph Shalom; Hadassah; Brandeis Women, life; Technion, life; League of Women Voters; Phi Beta Kappa; Radcliffe Club; Amer Assn of U Women; NCJW, life; Amer Assn UN. Home: 25 Harwick Rd, Fairfield, Conn.

WASSERMAN, Jack, US, art historian, educator; b. NYC, Apr 27, 1921; s. William and Pearl (Bajcz); BA, NYU, 1949, MA, 1953, PhD, 1961; m. Ambretta Amati, July 6, 1952; c: Shara, Talya. Prof, chmn, dept art hist, U Wis, since 1962; curator, Art Hist Gal, since 1964; instr, NYU, 1953-54; U Conn, 1954-60; asst prof, Ind U, 1960-62. Cpl, USAAC, 1942-45. F, Royal Soc Arts, London; mem: Phi Beta Kappa; Coll Art Assn; Soc Architectural Hists; hon mem, Amici di Brera, Milan. Author: Ottaviano Mascarino, 1966; contbr to profsl jours. Recipient: Fulbright award; Fels Fund award. Home: 2715 N Lake Dr, Milwaukee, Wis. Office: U Wis, Milwaukee, Wis.

WASSERMAN, Louis R, US, physician, researcher, educator; b. Bklyn, NY, July 11, 1910; s. Jacob and Ethel (Ballin); AB, Harvard Coll, 1931; MD, Rush Med Coll, U Chgo, 1935; m. Julia Weisskoff, 1957. Dir, hematology dept, Mt Sinai Hosp, since 1957; research collaborator, Brookhaven Natl Lab, since 1960; chmn, dept clinical sci, Mt Sinai Sch of Med, since 1968, prof, med, since 1966; asso clinical prof, Coll of Phys and Surgs, Columbia U since 1960; research f, Donner Lab of Med Physics, U of Cal, 1946-50, cons, radiation lab, 1948-52. US Army, 1942-46. Councillor, Intl Soc Hematology, since 1968; pres, Amer Soc Hematology, 1966-69; f; NY Acad of Sci; Amer Coll of Phys; dipl, Amer Bd Internal Med; mem: Harvey Soc; Amer Assn Cancer Research; Amer Soc Clinical Oncology; Soc for Experimental Med and Biol; Amer Fed Clinical Research; NY Acad of Med; Alpha Omega Alpha; Sigma Xi. Contbr to profsl jours. Home: 1200 Fifth Ave, New York, NY. Office: Mt Sinai Hosp, New York, NY.

WASSERMAN, Max J, US, economist, educator; b. St Louis, Mo, June 6, 1895; s. Bennett and Rose (Meyer); BA, Cornell U, 1918; AM, U of Ill, 1921; att, U Chgo, 1921-22; PhD, U Lyon, Fr, 1925; m. Rose Brosseau, Aug 4, 1925; c: Bennett, Lawrence, Max Jr. Visiting lectr, econ, Ky State Coll, since 1965, sr staff econ, Spindletop Research Inc, since 1965; asst prof, econ, U of Ill, 1925-34; econ, US Dept Agric, 1934-35; dir, finance div, Resettlement Admn, 1935-37; chief, stat sect, Social Security bd, 1937-41; intl econ, US Dept Commerce, 1941-59; visiting prof, intl commerce, U of Ky, 1959-65. Lt, pilot, USAAC, 1918-19. F: U Lyons, Fr, 1922-23; Amer Field Service, Fr, 1923-25; Social Sci Research Council, Fr, 1927; mem: Amer Econ Assn; Phi Beta Kappa; Zeta Beta Tau. Author: l'Oeuvre de la Federal Trade Commission, 1925; co-author: Modern International Economics: A Balance of Payments Approach, 1962; International Finance, 1963; The Common Market and American Business, 1964; The Balance of Payments, 1965; contbr to profsl and bus publs; commentator, VOA, 1952-53. Home and office: 1104 Fountaine Rd, Lexington, Ky.

WASSERMANN, Ita, Isr, chemist; b. Bucharest, Rum, May 11, 1922; d. Simha and Malia (Altman) Tutelman; in Isr since 1961; MSc, U Bucharest, 1951; div. Research chem, isotopes, Weizmann Inst, since 1961; fmr research chem: Metallurgical Inst of Research, Bucharest, 1948-58. Author: Analytical Biochemistry, 1964; Chemistry and Industry, 1964; contbr to sci jours. Home: 29 Haganah St, Rehovot, Isr. Office: Weizmann Inst, Rehovot, Isr.

WASSERSTROM, Evelyn, US, communal leader; b. Boston, Mass, Sep 11, 1927; d. Joseph and Tena (Drew) Yaffe; att: Kan City Jr Coll; Kan City Art Inst, both Mo, both 1946-47; m. Dexter Wasserstrom, Dec 25, 1948; c: Tena, Bruce. Project dir, housing survey, Kan City Assn for Retarded Children, since 1969; tchr, pre-sch music dept, J Comty Cen, since 1967; tchr, primary dept, music dir, Cong Beth Sholom, since 1967; fmr, commercial artist, United Films Inc, 1947-48. Intl treas, B'nai B'rith Women, mem, natl bd, since 1965, fmr chmn, comm for Natl Anti-Poverty Prog; natl ADL chmn for B'nai B'rith Women, mem: natl commn of ADL, since 1963, exec comm, Plains States reg adv bd; co-chmn, Metrop Action! (umbrella org of 30 Gtr Kans City orgs working for human relations and civil rights); mem bds: NCCJ; J Comty Relations Bur; J Educ Council; Friends of Metrop Jr Coll; sch bd and sisterhood, Cong Ohev Sholom; moderator, Panel of Amer Women, since 1967; pres: YMCA; PTA, Sch for Exceptional Children. Spec interest: retarded children. Home: 449 W Dartmouth Rd, Kansas City, Mo.

WASSERSUG, Joseph D, US, physician, author; b. Boston, Mass, Oct 19, 1912; s. Jacob and Dora (Blank); BA, cum laude, Harvard Coll, 1933; MD, cum laude, Tufts Coll Med Sch, 1938; m. Leona Alberts, Nov 3, 1940; c: Rona, Richard, Robin. Pvt practice, internal med, since 1945; acting phys, Quincy City Hosp, since 1945; asst: Lakeville State Sanitarium, 1939-41; Norfolk Co Hosp, 1941-45; instr, Tufts Coll, 1945-61; asst phys, Boston City Hosp, 1945-62; visiting phys, Boston State Hosp, 1946-68; cons, Medfield State Hosp, 1951-66. F, Amer Coll Chest Phys: bd dirs: Quincy J Comty Cen; Norfolk Co Health and TB; mem:AMA, Amer Heart Assn; Amer Thoracic Soc; Amer Soc Internal Med; Mass Med Soc; B'nai B'rith; Alpha Omega Alpha; clubs: Harvard; Tufts. Author: Your Rheumatism and Backaches, 1947; Your Coughs, Colds, and Wheezes, 1949; Hospital with a Heart, 1961; Medicated Fables for Mice & Men, 1962; Understanding Your Symptoms, 1964; How to be Healthy and Happy After Sixty, 1966; fmr, syndicated columnist, NY Herald-Tribune, 1962-65; contbr to med jours. Recipient: Humanitarian award, Hay Fever Prevention Soc, 1958. Home: 44 Highfield Rd, Quincy, Mass. Office: 22 Spear St, Quincy, Mass.

WATERMAN, Jerame A, US, business exec; b. Hawkinsville, Ga, Nov 6, 1883; s. Maurice and Henrietta (Maas); BS, Mercer U, 1902; m. Daisy Guggenheimer, Sep 14, 1922 (decd); c: Cecile Essrig, Regena Bragin. Chmn bd, Maas Bros, Inc, since 1958, with firm since 1907. US Army, WW I; USAAC, WW II. Cdr, Mil Order of WW's; bd trustees, U Tampa; mem: Res Offs Assn; J Comty Cen; B'nai B'rith; Natl Aeronautics Assn; Ret Offs Assn; Amer Legion; Elks; Jesters; Wings; Natl Aviation; fmr pres, Comty Chest; vice-pres, Air Force Assn; mem bd, PR, City of Tampa; clubs: Palm Bay; Miami; U, Tampa; Palme Ceia Golf and Country; Tampa Yacht and Country; MacDill Off's; River; Marco Polo, NY. Author: An Inspiration A Day, 1950. Home: 2401 Bayshore Blvd, Tampa, Fla. Office: POB 311, Tampa, Fla.

WATTERS, Gertrude, US, communal worker; b. Buffalo, NY; d. Isaac and Fannie (Stettenheim) Wile; m. 2nd, Leon Watters, 1936; c: Robert Nathan, Mrs Charles Lazarus. Pres: Beth Zion Sisterhood, Buffalo, 1920-25; Lakeland Camp; Natl Fed Temple Sisterhoods, 1935-41, 1st vice-pres, 1930-35; 1st vice-pres, mem exec bd: NY State br, Women's Auxiliary Cong Emanuel, NYC; J Braille Inst of Amer; UAHC; NY sect, Natl Council J Women; womens' div, NY FJP, 1936-49; League of Women Voters, Erie Co. Home: 995 Fifth Ave, New York, NY.

WAX, Bernard, US, historian; b. Phila, Pa, Apr 4, 1930; s. Samuel and Anna (Kaminker); BA, U Chgo, 1950; MA, 1952; att U of Wis, 1955-59; m. Dolores Nemchek, Mar 26, 1953; c: Ann, Steven, Stuart, Dir, Amer Hist Soc, since 1966; field services sup, Ill State Hist Libr, 1961-66, staff mem since 1959. Bd dirs, Springfield J Fed, 1965-66; mem: Cook Co Local Records comm 1961-66; Ill Local Records commn, 1961-66; Amer Hist Assn; Amer Assn State and Local Hist; Org of Amer Hists; Natl Trust for Hist Preservation; Assn of J Librs. Home: 21 Blake Rd, Brookline, Mass. Office: 2 Thornton Rd, Waltham, Mass.

WAXMAN, Nissan, Isr, rabbi; b. Starofin-Slutzk, Russ; s. Reuven and Sheina (Rivin); in Isr since 1964; att: Yeshivas: Pol; Lith; ordained rabbi, Riets, NYC, 1927; att, CCNY; m. Sara Schwartz, Feb 4, 1933; c: Shulamith, Abraham, Chaim, David. Secy-gen, Rabb Courts, Tel Aviv, since 1964; fmr: rabbi, Lakewood, NJ, 1932-44; exec dir, Heb Day Sch, Baltimore, 1944-46; Feder Council, Rel Org, NYC; org Bet Medrash Gavoha Rabb Coll, Lakewood, NJ. Fmr mem: Union of Orthodox Rabbis; RabCa. Co-ed: Shutzk Yizkor Book, 1962; contbr to rabb jours. Home: 15 Trumpeldor St, Petach Tikva, Isr. Study: 33 King David St, Tel Aviv, Isr.

WAYNE, George J, psychiatrist, educator; b. NYC, Sep 13, 1914; s. Irwin and Eva (Bloom); BS, Bklyn Coll, 1934; MD, U of W Ont Med Sch, Can, 1939; certs of grad: med field service sch, US Army, 1941; aviation med sch, USAAC, 1943; FACP, 1958; m. Kyra Petrovskaya, Apr 21, 1962; c: Robin, Ronald. Pvt practice, psycht and psychan, since 1947; med dir, Edgemont Hosp, since 1957; prof, psycht, UCLA, since 1966, fac mem since 1953; sr cons, Brentwood Vets Hosp, since 1955, on staff since 1950; med dir, LA Neur Inst, 1946-57. Maj, USAAC, med corps, 1941-45. F: Amer Psycht Assn; Gerontological Soc; dipl, Amer Bd of Psycht and Neur, mem: Aerospace Psychoanalytical Assn; AMA; Cal and LA Co Med Assns. Ed, Emergency Psychiatry, 1967; contbr: chaps in books; to profsl jours. Hobbies: art, travel. Home: 259 St Pierre Rd, Los Angeles, Cal. Office: 4841 Hollywood Blvd, Los Angeles, Cal.

WAYSMAN, Simon, Isr, scientist, business exec; b. Luck, Pol, Oct 18, 1921; s. Michael and Rachel (Kierzner); in Isr since 1952; ing dipl, Inst de Electrochimie, Grenoble, 1943; BSc, Geneva U, 1945; m. Elaine Natengel, 1953; c: Danny, Karine, Guy. Owner, gen mgr, Shachlavan Chems Ltd, since 1945; co-owner, factories: Fr, Turkey; dir: Blancomme, 1947-50; Par-jons, 1950-52. Capt, Fr Army. Prin contribs: development of protective coatings, road marking materials. Fmr chmn, local council Ganei Yehuda; club, Rotary, Savyon. Home: 38 Havradim St, Ganei Yehuda, Isr. Office: POB 9042, Tel Aviv, Isr.

WEBBER, Carmel Roma, Eng, communal leader; b. London, Eng, Apr, 26, 1912; d. Paul and Romana (Yanczyk) Good-man; att U Coll, London, 1932-33; m. George Webber, July 27, 1933; c: Judith Humphrey, Marilyn Lehrer, Jonathan. Chmn, Fed of J Women Zionists of Gt Brit; grand vice-pres, Dist Grand Lodge, B'nai B'rith; pres, First Women's Lodge, B'nai B'rith. Hobbies: travel, music. Home: 79 Kingsley Way, London, N2, Eng.

WEBER, Joseph, US, organization exec; b. NYC, Jan 18, 1926; s. Hugo and Goldie (Weber); BA, Bklyn Coll, 1950; MA, Columbia U, Tchrs Coll, 1951; m. Barbara Waxman, June 29, 1952; c: Laurie, Jeffrey. Asso dir, Gtr NY Fund, since 1969, dir, agcy relations, since 1961; teaching staff: mgmt sci dept, grad div, Stevens Inst of Tech; grad sch, Fordham Sch of Social Service; sup, NY State Sept of Lab, 1946-48; asst prog sup, YM-YWHA, NYC, 1946-52; asst coord, student activities, Bklyn Coll, 1948-52; teaching f, sociol, U Tex, 1953; dir, multiple comty oprs, USO, Austin, Tex, 1952-53; asst dir of oprs, natl USO, NY, 1955-58; staff asso, personnel dept, United Funds & Council of Amer, 1957-61. USAAC, 1944-46. Mem: Amer Psych Assn; Natl Assn of Social Workers; Acad of Cert Social Workers; Masons; Alpha Kappa Delta, Kappa Delta Phi. Home: 4 Wayne Court, Ardsley, NY. Office: 100 E 42 St, New York, NY.

WEBER, Lazar Joseph, Isr, chemical engineer, economist; b. Bucharest, Rum, July 14, 1903; s. Joseph and Pauline (Davi-dov); in Isr since 1936; att: U Berlin; Technische Hochschule, Berlin-Charlottenburg; m. Daniella Gurian. Researcher, tchr, Berlin Technische Hochschule, 1926-33; tech dir, Sapic Chem Ind, 1934-36; mem: sr staff: Pal Potash, 1936-48; JA, 1949-54; mem, Council of Sci Research, Govt of Pal, 1944-47; cons, tech dept, Shilumim Corp, 1952-53; mem: econ adv staff, PM's Off, 1954-57; ind adv group, Min of Finance, 1954-57; ind adv, Min of Commerce and Ind, 1951-60. Chmn, Jeru-salem br, Pal Chem Org, 1944-47; pres, chmn, mem exec council, Isr Chem Soc, 1949-50. Co-author: econ studies commissioned by Govt of Isr Mins and Bank of Isr; contbr to econ and chem jours, in Isr and Ger. Hobby: music. Home: 9 Schmuel Hanagid St, Jerusalem, Isr.

WEBERMAN, Benjamin, US, journalist; b. Bronx, NY, Mar 27, 1923; s. Sol and Sadie (Wolfe); BS, CCNY, 1943; cert, mech engr, U of Md, 1944; MBA, NYU Grad Sch of Bus, 1955; m. Sylvia Berger, Nov 15, 1947; c: Nancy, Lynn. Financial ed, Amer Banker, since 1964; econ, Intl Stat Bur, 1946-51; financial ed: NY Jour of Commerce, 1951-59; NY Herald-Tribune. Treas, NY Financial Assn, 1954, mem, bd govs; mem: Amer Stat Assn; NY Soc of Security Analysts; clubs: Bankers; Lambs. Home: One Albert Court, Kings Point, NY. Office: 67 Pearl St, New York, NY.

WEBMAN, Arnold I, US, physician, b. Pol, Feb 22, 1906; s. Isaak and Bertha (Stein); in US since 1920; BS, U Chgo, 1930; MD, U Neb Coll of Med, 1934; m. Lucille Polishok, June 21, 1936; c: Vivian, Estelle, Jerry. Asst dir, Neb State Health Dept, since 1965; pvt practice, Superior, Neb, 1940-63; city phys, 1945-63; chief of staff, Brodstone Memorial Hosp, 1949-59. Pres, Nuckolls Co Med Soc, 1952-54, secy, 1954, delg to state med soc, 1946-51; mem, bd dirs, ARC; vice-pres, B'nai B'rith, Cen Neb lodge, since 1950; mem: Neb State Med Soc; AMA; Amer Psycht Assn; Masons; Scottish Rite, 32 deg; Rep Valley Shriner's pres, 1956; club, Superior Kiwanis, pres, 1957-58. Rep Valley. Contbr to med jours. Recipient: plaque, Superior Kiwanis, 1958. Hobby: photo-graphy. Home: 3210 S 28 St, Lincoln, Nev.

WECHSLER, David, US, psychologist, educator; b. Lespedi, Rum, Jan 12, 1896; s. Moses and Leah (Pascal); in US since 1902; BA, CCNY, 1916; MA Columbia U, 1917, PhD, 1925; Amer f, U Paris, 1920-22; m. Ruth Halpern, 1939; c: Adam, Leonard. Area cons, VA Hosps, since 1945; psychol: Bur of Child Guidance, NY, 1922-24; Bklyn Social Service Bur, 1926-30; chief psycht, Bellevue Hosp, 1932-67; adj prof, psychol, NYU Grad Sch, 1945-65; clinical prof, NYU Med Sch, 1945-65; visiting prof, psychol, Heb U, 1967. US Army, 1918-19; cons, US Secy of War, 1941-43. F, AAAS; dipl, Amer Bd of Examiners in Profsl Psychol, 1951; mem: NY Acad of Sci; Sigma Xi; vice-pres, Amer Friends of Heb U, since 1965; bd govs, Heb U, since 1967; pres: Amer Psychopath Assn, 1959; clinical div, Amer Orthopsycht Assn, 1945; clinical div, Amer Psychol Assn, 1945. Author: Mea-surement of Emotional Reaction, 1925; Wechsler-Bellevue Adult Intelligence Scale, 1939; Wechsler Intelligence Test for Children, 1948; Range of Human Capacity, 1955; Measure-ment and Appraisal of Adult Intelligence, 1958; Wechsler Pre-School and Primary Scale of Intelligence, 1967; contbr to sci and educ jours. Home: 145 E 92 St, New York, NY.

WECHSLER, David, Switz, author; b. Zurich, Switz, Dec 28, 1918; s. Lazar and Amalie (Tschudi); PhD, U Zurich, 1945; m. Johanna Caspers, Sep 15, 1945; c: Barbara, Thomas, Peter, David. Mgr, publicity, Dia-Reklame AG, Zurich, since 1946; screenwriter, Praesens-Film AG, Zurich, 1945-54. Author: films: The Search, 1947; The Village, 1954; The Right To Be Born, 1966; novels: The Village, 1952; Spiel ohne Regeln, 1955; Ein Haus zu Wohnen, 1961; Ein Bündel blauer Briefe, 1962; play, Wege zum Rahel, 1961. Mem: Acad of Motion Picture Arts and Scis, LA; Schweizerischer Schrift-stellerverein. Recipient: Oscar, Acad award, for The Search, Acad of Motion Picture Arts and Scis, 1948. Home: Burenweg 4, Zurich, Switz. Office: Kirchgasse 32, 8001 Zurich, Switz.

WECHSLER, Gabriel A, US, organization exec, public re-lations counselor; b. Bklyn, NY, Dec 28, 1908; s. Charles and Bessie (Glassburg); att Marquand Sch of Ins, Columbia U, 1924; m. Miriam Pullan, Dec 29, 1929; c: Charles. Asst ad-mnr, munic service admn, NYC, since 1965; head, PR, Gabriel A Wechsler, since 1948; exec dir, B'nai B'rith council, Gtr Phila, 1959-61; dep commn, dept of purchase, NYC, 1961-65. Gen secy, City Fusion Party, NYC, since 1933; chmn, PR and research, Grand lodge, KP, since 1955; secy, dept sociol, Bklyn Inst Arts and Scis, 1936-38; head, Wash bur, Amer League for Free Pal, 1940; natl secy: Emergency comm to Save J People of Eur, 1942; comm for a J Army of Stateless and Pal Jews, 1939-41; natl dir, Amer comm for Natl Sick Fund of Isr, 1942-44; exec dir, pres, natl Haym Salomon Memorial comm, 1951; campaign dir, City of Hope, 1966-69. Found ed, The Answer, 1943; mem, ed bd, Middle East and the West, since 1954. Home: 215 E 80 St, New York, NY. Office: 156 W 44 St, New York, NY.

WECHSLER, Herbert, US, attorney, educator; b. NYC, Dec 4, 1909; s. Samuel and Anna (Weisberger); BA, CCNY, 1928; LLB, Columbia U Law Sch, 1931; LLD: U Chgo, 1962; Harvard U, 1967; m. Doris Klauber, Apr 13, 1957. Harlan Fiske Stone prof, constitutional law, Columbia U, since 1957, mem, law fac, since 1933; dir and secy, Amer Law Inst, since 1963, chief reporter on model code of penal law, since 1951; mem, NY comm to revise penal law and criminal code, since 1961; counsel to US Senator Robert F Wagner, 1938; spec asst to US Atty Gen, 1940; asst Atty Gen of US, 1944-46; tech adv, Intl Mil Tribunal, Nuremberg, Ger, 1945-46. Mem: Amer Bar Assn; Assn Bar of NYC; Phi Beta Kappa; Cent Assn; NY temp housing commn, 1948-50; adv comm on criminal procedure, US Supr Court, 1940-42; Pres commn on law enforcement and admn of justice, 1965-67. Author: Principles, Politics, and Fundamental Law, 1961; co-author: Criminal Law and Its Administration, 1940, 1956; The Federal Courts and the Federal System, 1953; contbr to legal jours. Home: 179 E 70 St, New York, NY. Office: Columbia U Law Sch, New York, NY.

WECHSLER, James A, US, editor, author; b. NYC, Oct 31, 1915; s. Samuel and Anna (Weisberger); BA, Columbia U, 1935; m. Nancy Fraenkel, Oct 5, 1934; c: Michael, Holly. Editorial page ed and columnist, New York Post, since 1961, mem, Wash Bur, 1947-49, ed, 1949-61; ed: Columbia Spectator, 1934-35; The Student Advocate, 1936-37; asst ed: The Nation, 1938-39; PM, 1940-41, chief, Wash Bur, 1942-44. US Army, 1945. Mem, natl exec comm, ADA, since 1947; natl bd, ACLU, 1953. Author: Revolt on the Campus, 1935; Labor Baron, 1944; The Age of Suspicion, 1953; Reflections of an Angry Middle-Aged Editor, 1959; co-author, War Propaganda and the United States, 1940. Recipient: Wash award, Amer Vets Comm, 1948; Florence Lasker Civil Liberties award, 1968. Home: 420 West End Ave, New York. Office: NY Post, 75 West St, New York, NY.

WECHSLER, Tovia, Isr, historian, author; b. Libau, Latvia, June 12, 1889; in Isr since 1935; att Us: Tuebingen; Hamburg; m. Miriam Munin; c: Abraham, Yacob, Meir, Ester Cohen. Author: poems, From Within and Without; Hidden Elements of Israel's Tradition, 1968; contbr to Eng and Heb jours. Spec interest: ancient Isr hist. Home: 45 Keren Kayemet St, Jerusalem, Isr.

WECHTER, William Julius, US, biochemist; b. Louisville, Ky, Feb 13, 1932; s. Louis and Elsa (Stauss); att Ill Inst of Tech, 1949-50; AB, U of Ill, 1953, MS, 1954; PhD, UCLA, 1957; m. Roselyn Greenman, Aug 24, 1952; c: Laurie, Diane, Julie. Research head, hypersensitivity diseases research, Upjohn Co, since 1968, sr sci, 1957-67; fmr: teaching asst, UCLA, 1954-56; visiting scholar, Stanford U, 1967-68. Pres, Temple B'nai Isr; mem: Amer Chem Soc; AAAS; Sigma Xi; Phi Lambda Upsilon; ACLU; Citizens to Advance Public Educ; delg, Dem Co conv, 1964-66. Contbr to profsl jours; holder of eighteen US patents, 1959-67. Spec interest: film criticism. Home: 2820 Taliesin Dr, Kalamazoo, Mich. Office: Upjohn Co, Kalamazoo, Mich.

WEDECK, Harry E, US, classicist, author; b. Sheffield, Eng, Jan 11, 1894; s. Simon and Anne (Shapiro); in US since 1923; MA, first class hons, medalist, Edinburgh U, 1916; diplomé, Caen U, 1920; att: Sorbonne, 1920; Columbia U, 1924-25; m; c: Edmund, David; m. 2nd, Slata Kominsky, 1937. Lectr, classics: New Sch for Soc Research, since 1968; Bklyn Coll, 1951-68; reviewer: Natl J Monthly, since 1945; Classical Weekly, since 1928; Cong Weekly, 1949-50; Chgo J Forum, 1953-56; Classical Jour, 1953-59; Latomus, Belgium, 1951-60; asso ed, Latin Notes, 1929-36; lit ed, Bombay J Tribune, 1931-34; ed: Latin Texts, 1934-40; Orbis Latinus, 1936-37; gen ed, Pitman Latin Series, 1939; reviewer: Tomorrow, 1945-48; NY Times, 1946-50. Served, WW I. Mem: Medieval Acad of Amer; Amer Classical League; Amer Phil Assn; clubs: NYC Classical; NY Medieval. Author: Narrationes Biblicae, 1928; Humor in Varro, 1929; Living Language, Book II, 1934; Third Year Latin, 1938; Latin Poetry, 1940; Mortal Hunger, 1947; Dictionary of Magic, 1956; Dictionary of Classical Allusions, 1957; Treasury of Witchraft, 1961; Dictionary of Aphrodisiacs, 1961; Erotic Literature, 1962; Medieval Reader, 1964; Dictionary of Middle Ages, 1964; co-author, Renaissance, 1967; trans: Principles of Cartesian Philosophy, 1961; Fountain of Life, 1962; Aristotle Dictionary, 1962; Classics in Logic, 1962; contbr to learned jours, periodicals, in US and abroad. Recipient: prize for study of languages, Urdu and Pushtu, Govt of India, 1917. Spec interests: travel, the Orient. Home: 425 E 79 St, New York, NY. Office: New Sch for Social Research, New York, NY.

WEHLE, Kurt, US, business exec; b. Jablonec, Czech, Apr 29, 1907; s. Siegfried and Marie (Altschul); in US since 1951; DJur, Prague, 1930; MBA, NYU, 1953; m. Hana Loewy, May 19, 1946; c: Eva Friedner, John, Susan. Asso dir, Med Cen, and Hosp for Joint Diseases, since 1967, with hosp since 1958; secy-gen, JCC, Prague, 1945-48; atty, asst dir, JDC, Paris, 1948-51; head, Czech and Aus depts, United Restitution Org, 1951-61. Chmn, bd, Soc for Hist of Czech Jews, pres, 1961-67; chmn, action comm, ZO, Czech, 1946-48; vice-pres, Mapai, Czech, 1946-48; co-found, Soc for Hist of Czech Jews in NY; fmr vice-pres, B'nai B'rith. Contbr to political and legal jours. Home: 82-34 265 St, Floral Park, NY. Office: 1919 Madison Ave, New York, NY.

WEICHMANN, Herbert Kurt, Ger, public official; b. Landsberg, Ger, Feb 23, 1896; s. Wilhelm and Irma (Guttentag); att Us: Breslau; Frankfurt, Heidleberg; NYU, 1940. Pres of Sen, Lord Mayor, City of Hamburg, since 1965; mem, pres, Bundesrat; fmr, personal asst to PM, Prussia; min councilor, Prussian State Min, Berlin, until 1933; econ, author, Paris, 1933-40; pub accnt, NYC, 1941-48; controller gen, Hamburg, 1949-57, senator of finances, 1957-65; dir; Continental Elektroindustrie AG, Düsseldorf; Hamburger Wasserwerke GmbH; Hamburger Gaswerke GmbH; chmn, bd, Hamburgische Landesbank-Girozentrale; dep chmn, Hamburgische Wohnungsbaukasse; fmr: lectr, U Hamburg; prof, U Edmonton, Can. Mem: Amer Soc Intl Inst; Wissenschaftsrat; Inst Intl de Finances Publiques; Inst Intl des Scis Admns, both Brussels; clubs: Overseas; Press, Hamburg. Author: Das Werden eines

neuen Staates; Alltag in USA; Alltag in der Betriebswirtschaft; Handwörterbuch der Sozialwissen schaften; co-author: Neuordnung der öffentlichen Haushalte; Reform der öffentlichen Haushalte; Haushaltssysteme des Auslands; Les depenses de guerre en Allemagne. Address: 36 Gänsemarkt, Hamburg, Fed Rep of Ger.

WEIDENBAUM, Murray, US, government official; b. Bx, NY, Feb 10, 1927; s. David and Rose (Warshaw); BS, CCNY, 1948; MA, Columbia U, 1949; PhD, Princeton, 1954; m. Phyllis Green, June 13, 1954; c: Susan, James, Laurie. Asst secy, econ policy, US Treas Dept, Wash, DC, since 1969; corp econ, Boeing, 1958-63; sr econ, Stanford Research Inst, 1963-64; chmn, dept econs, Washington U, St Louis, Mo, 1964-69. Clubs: Cosmos, Wash, DC; Natl Econs, Wash, DC. Author: Modern Public Sector, 1969. Recipient: Townsend Harris medal, CCNY, 1970. Home: 124 Grafton, Washington, DC. Office: US Treas Dept, 15 & Pennsylvania Ave, NW, Washington, DC.

WEIDER, Ben, Can, publisher, physical fitness expert; b. Montreal, Can, Feb 1, 1923; s. Louis and Anna (Nudelman); m. Huguette Drouin, 1959; c: Louis, Eric, Mark. Publisher and ed, Weider athletic and sports publs, since 1946; pres, Weider Sports Equipment Co, since 1958; pres and dir, Weider Inst of Phys Culture Ltd, since 1960; lectr, demonstrator of new athletic training methods, concentrated foods, in over 70 countries. Can Army, 1941-45. Chmn, Intl Fed of Body-Builders, since 1947; mem: Temple Emanuel; Shaare Zedek Syn; B'nai B'rith; club, Lord Reading Yacht. Author: L'Histoire de Louis Cyr, 1960; Jeune Toute Sa Vie, 1961; Manger Bien et Rester Svelte, 1962; La Culture Physique pour Tous, 1962. Contbr to publs. Hobbies: archaeol, bible hist. Office: Wieder Bldg, 2875 Bates Rd, Montreal, Que, Can.

WEIDMAN, Jerome, US, author, novelist; b. NYC, Apr 4, 1913; s. Joseph and Anne (Falkovitz); att: CCNY, 1930-33; Wash Sq Coll, 1933-34; NYU Law Sch, 1934-37; m. Elizabeth Payne, Jan 18, 1943; c: Jeffrey, John. Author: I Can Get It for You Wholesale, 1937; What's in It for Me, 1938; The Horse That Could Whistle Dixie, 1939; Letter of Credit, 1940; I'll Never Go There Anymore, 1941; The Lights Around The Shore, 1943; Too Early to Tell, 1946; The Captain's Tiger, 1947; The Price is Right, 1949; The Hand of the Hunter, 1951; Give Me Your Love, 1952; The Third Angel, 1953; Traveler's Cheque, 1954; Your Daughter Iris, 1955; A Dime a Throw, 1956; The Enemy Camp, 1958; Before You Go, 1960; My Father Sits in the Dark, 1961; The Sound of Bow Bells, 1962; Word of Mouth, 1964; Other People's Money, 1967; The Center of the Action, 1969; plays: Fiorello, 1959; Tenderloin, 1961; I Can Get It For You Wholesale, 1962; The Mother Lover, 1969; Back Talk, essays, 1963; The Death of Dickie Draper, short stories, 1965. Co-recipient: Pulitzer Prize in Drama, for Fiorello, 1960. Home and studio: 1035 Fifth Ave, New York, NY.

WEIL, Adolfo, Arg, business exec; b. Buenos Aires, Arg, Sep 26, 1911; s. Hermann and Jeanne (Braun); att Haute Ecole de Commerce, Strasbourg, Fr; m. Clara Rosenbaum, Dec 7, 1946. Pres: Adoclar SA, since 1967; Clarel SA, since 1959; Imra SA, 1950-59; Fmr: secy, Chamber of Importers; pres, Beth-El Comty; dir: Latin Amer Rabb Sem; Daia, Arg Fed of J Socs; pres, secy, Cong Israelita, Buenos Aires, 1945-62; pres: B'nai B'rith Youth, 1940-44; Consejo Juvenil Hebreo, 1942-44; mem bd, Charter and Found, World Council of Syns, since 1959. Home: 1703, Virrey-Loreto, Buenos Aires, Arg. Offce: 2580 Olazabal, Buenos Aires. Arg.

WEIL, Alfred J, US, allergist, microbiologist, researcher; b. Mainz, Ger, April 27, 1900; s. Edmund and Elisabeth (Hochheimer); in US since 1936; MD, U Munich, 1923; m. Elisabeth Seligman (decd); m. 2nd, Hilde Heymann, 1952; c: Peter, Eva. Consultant, allergy and microbiol, since 1968; att microbiol, Bx-Leb Hosp Cen, 1948-68; head, immunological research: Lederle Labs; Amer Cyanamid Co, 1937-48. F: Amer Coll of Allergists; Amer Public Health Assn; Coll Amer Pathologists; NY Acad of Scis; NY Acad of Med. Author: Salmonellae and Shigellae, 1953; contbr to profsl jours. Home and office: 143 Forest Ave, Pearl River, NY.

WEIL, Arthur, US, physician; b. Braunschweig, Ger, Oct 3, 1887; s. Abraham and Helene (Coblenzer); in US since 1923; MD, U Berlin, 1914, MD, U Halle, 1919. Ret; cons, US Army VA, 1949-54; asst, U Halle, 1912-19; privatdozent, phys, 1919-21; neuropath, Montefiore Hosp, NYC, 1924-28; asso prof, neuropath, Northwestern U, 1929-44. Surg gen, US

Army Inst of Path, 1945. F: NY Acad of Med; Amer Neur Assn; mem: Amer Assn of Neuropaths, pres, 1934; hon, Acad of Scis, Lima, Peru. Author: Internal Secretion, 1920, 3rd ed, 1923; Textbook of Neuropathology, 1933, 2nd ed, 1945; ed, Jour of Neuropath and Experimental Neur, 1953-66, asso ed, 1942-53. Recipient: plaque, Amer Assn of Neuropaths, 1959; hon pres, 4th Intl Cong of Neuropath, 1961. Hobby: music. Home: 104-40 Queens Blvd, Forest Hills, NY.

WEIL, Erwin A, US, business exec; b. Frankfurt/M, Ger, Aug 1, 1909; s. Theodore and Martha (Hirschhorn); in US since 1935; grad, Muster-Schule, Frankfurt, 1928; LLB, law schs: U Frankfurt, U Berlin, 1931; m. Gisela Meyer, Dec 26, 1963; c: Martha, Vice-pres, Amer Metal Climax Inc, since 1968, secy, since 1957, with firm, 1935-43 and since 1946. Purser, US Merchant Marine. 1943-46. Mem: Amer Soc of Corporate Secys Inc; clubs: Rockefeller Cen Luncheon; Harvard. Home: 40-45 Hampton St, Elmhurst, NY. Office: 1270 Ave of Americas, New York, NY.

WEIL, Gérard Emmanuel, Fr, educator; b. Strasbourg, Fr, Nov 5, 1926; s. Henri and Suzanne (Haguenauer); ordained rabbi, Rabb Sch, Paris, 1954; D semitique, fac des lettres, U Strasbourg, 1961; Des lettres, Sorbonne, 1969; m. Ninette Bauer, May 29, 1952; c: Eve, Dan, Batyah, Noémie, Marc-Elie, Yaël, Gad, Nagdimon. Prof, fac of letters, U Nancy, dir, Inst of Comparative Semitic Langs, both since 1965; head, Bible sect, research of Semitic linguistics dept, Inst of Research and Hist of Texts, Massorétique; ed, Massorah collection, rabbi, Saverne, Fr, 1954-56; i/c of research, Natl Cen of Sci Research, 1956-65. Served, Fr Maquis. 1943-47; IDF, War of Independence; prin mil chaplain, 1956-61. Author: Elie Lévita, humaniste et massorète, 1469-1549, pub 1963; Initiation à la Massorah, 1964; Massorah Parva, 1968-70; contbr to scholarly jours. Recipient: Prix Delalande-Guérineau, Académie des Inscriptions et Belles Lettres, Paris, 1965; Croix du Combattant; Croix du Combattant Volontaire; Croix des Bléssés; Croix de la Résistance; 1943-47. Office: faculté des lettres, Inst de Langues Sémitiques Comparées, 23 Blvd Albert 1, Nancy, Fr.

WEIL, Herman, US, psychologist, university admnr, educator; b. Alsace-Lorraine, Dec 15, 1905; s. Leopold and Selma (Israel); in US since 1938; PhD, U Marburg, 1929; educ deg, Pedg Inst, Kassel, 1933; postdoc f, U of Ia, 1939; m. Bertha Weiler, 1931; c: Gunther. Asso dean, coll of letters and sci, U Wis, since 1967, chmn, honors prog for superior students, since 1960, prof and chmn, dept of psych, 1944-61; prof: Neb Cen Coll, 1939-40; Milw Sch of Engr, 1940-43; head, dept of educ and psych, Wis State Coll, 1944-57, dir, workshops in hum relations, 1952-56; cons to US State Dept and Off of Educ, sch project, Ger, 1954; adv, sch of nursing, Mt Sinai Hosp, Milw, 1954-56. Pres: Wis Soc for J Learning, 1957-59; AAUP, U Wis-Milw chap, 1959-60; Wis Psych Assn, 1962-63; Milw Co Psych Assn, 1961-62; chmn: J Adult Educ Prog, 1962-63; mem: Amer Psych Assn; intergroup relations comm, Gtr Metrop Milw, 1958-61; natl educ commn, NCCJ, 1955-60, co-chmn, Wis region since 1952, natl co-chmn, schs and colls, brotherhood week, 1957; region adv comm, Wis ADL, 1958-65; midwest comm on discrimination in higher educ, Amer Council on Educ, 1950-53; Wis Gov's commn on hum rights, 1953-56, dir, rel educ, Temple Emanu-El B'nai Jeshuran, 1945-56; counselor, Milw B'nai B'rith Hillel Counselorship, 1950-60, Author: Milwaukee Makes Instructional Changes, 1950; co-author: Psychology of Human Types, 1930; contbr to profsl jours. Recipient: Human Relations award, B'nai B'rith, Milw, 1952; Brotherhood award, Wis NCCJ, 1959; citation, Intl Inst, Milw Co, 1960. Hobby: philately. Home: 2027 E Lake Bluff Blvd, Milwaukee, Wis. Office: U Wisconsin, Milwaukee, Wis.

WEIL, Joseph, US, engineer, educator, university admnr; b. Baltimore, Md. July 19, 1897; s. Isaiah and Bertha (Adler); BSE, Johns Hopkins U, 1918; MS, U Pittsburgh, 1926; hon DSc, Jacksonville U, 1960; m; c: Marvin; m. 2nd, Cyrille Buchman, 1964. Provost, NY Inst of Tech, since 1966; dean, Coll Engr, U of Fla, 1938-66, prof, elec engr, since 1931, coord, CAA pilot traning courses, fac mem since 1921. Region adv, engr sci, and mgmt war training, Off of Educ, 1942-45; educ coord, Adjutant Gen's dept, US War Dept, 1942-46; S region repr, War Manpower commn, engr sci and mgmt training, 1943-45; tech cons, Eglin AF base, 1952-58. F: Amer Inst EEs, chmn, Fla sect, 1935, secy-treas, 1926-35, life mem since 1959; Fla Engr Soc, pres, 1940, dir, 1934-38; Inst Radio Engrs; pres: Fla State Bd Engr Examiners, 1946-47, secy-treas

since 1939, mem natl council; Gainesville lodge, B'nai B'rith, 1939; vice-pres, Fla Fed, 1941; dir: Amer Soc for Engr Educ, 1942-46, chmn, 1946-47; Natl Soc Profsl Engrs, 1946-47; nuclear div, Instrument Soc Amer, 1956-57; mem, tech adv group, Air Research and Devl Command; nuclear dir, Amer Inst Chem Engrs; engr comm, Interstate Oil Compact commn; ind adv comm, Fla Devl Commn; Commn de la CAE; Comm de métérologie radio-électrique; mem: Amer Nuclear Soc; AAUP; Newcomen Soc Amer; Amer Technion Soc; Sigma Tau; Tau Beta Phi; Phi Kappa Phi; Phi Beta Delta; Pi Lambda Phi; club, Rotary. Contbr to profsl jours. Recipient: pres medal, Fla Engr Soc, 1945; Naval Ordnance Devl award, 1946; Big Pi medallion, Pi Lambda Phi, 1951; dist service cert, Natl Council State Bds Engr Examiners, 1955; man of the year, U Fla, 1956; award, Fla Engr Soc, 1956; citation, Tampa lodge, B'nai B'rith, 1956; scroll, engr fac, Fla U Coll, 1957; awards: Jacksonville U, 1958; Fla State C of C, 1961; Miami-Isr, 1962. Hobbies: gardening, photography. Home: 195 S Middleneck Rd, Great Neck, NY. Office: NY Inst of Technology, Old Westbury, LI, NY.

WEIL, Rolf Alfred, US, educator; b. Ger, Oct 29, 1921; s. Henry and Lina (Landauer); in US since 1936; BA, U Chgo, 1942, MA, 1945, PhD, 1950; m. Leni Metzger, Nov 3, 1945; c: Ronald, Susan. Pres, Roosevelt U, since 1966, dean, Coll of Bus Admn, 1957-65, fac mem since 1946; research analyst: Cowles commn for research in econ, 1942-44; Ill Dept of Revenue, 1944-46; lectr, adult educ div, Ind U, 1945-55. Mem, bd trustees, Roosevelt U, since 1961; off, bd mem, Selfhelp Home for Aged Inc, Chgo; mem: Amer Econ Assn; Amer Finance Assn; AAUP; commn on fed revenues and expenditures, Chgo Assn of Commerce and Ind; Inves Analysts Soc of Chgo; club, Rotary. Contbr to profsl jours. Home: 3015 Simpson St, Evanston, Ill. Office: Roosevelt U, Chicago, Ill.

WEIL, Roman L, US, attorney; b. Montgomery, Ala, Oct 5, 1912; s. Lee and Esther (Roman); BA, U of Ala, 1932, LLB, 1935; att Harvard U, 1932-33; m. Charlotte Alexander, June 28, 1938; c: Roman Jr, Judith, Carol, Kenneth. Partner, law firms: Rushton, Stakely and Johnston, since 1942; Weil, and Stakely, 1935-42. USMCR, 1942-45. Chmn: City of Montgomery planning commn; Kahl Montgomery, pres, 1959-61; Amer Bar Assn; Zeta Beta Tau; Standard, pres, 1947-48; Rotary. Contbr to profsl jours. Home: 3552 Thomas Ave, Montgomery, Ala. Office: 1201 Bell Bldg, Montgomery, Ala.

WEIL, Shraga, Isr, painter, graphic artist; b. Nitra, Czech, Sep 24, 1918; s. Izhak and Leah I (Tausig); in Isr since 1947; att: Umprum Art Sch, Prague; Acad Beaux Arts, Paris; m. Sarah Taub, July 4, 1941; c: Ran, Efrat. Prin works: entrance doors, with brass reliefs, Knesset bldg; cooper relief doors: Tel Aviv Hilton Hotel; Wolfson House, Weizmann Inst; entrance doors, Pres Residence, Jerusalem; murals for Isr Pavillon at World's Fair, 1967 and Bar-Ilan U; one-man shows: Tel Aviv Mus: Hazorea and Elat Mus; Ben-Uri Gal, London; graphic works: The Love of Samson; Tracks in the Desert; The Song of Songs; Ecclesiastes; The Dead Sea Scrolls; author: Song of Songs, 1958; Kohelet, 1965. Mem: Isr Painters and Sculptors Assn; Kibbutz Artists Org. Recipient: Dizengoff Art Prize, Tel Aviv, 1959. Home: DN Lev Hasharon, Kibbutz Haogen, Isr.

WEIL, Simon, US, business executive; b. Nashville, Tenn, July 6, 1897; s. Harry and Marien (Jacobs); m. Carrie Foley, Oct 30, 1923; c: Marien Garner, Elsye Heyman. Chmn of bd: Kuhn Bros Co Inc; Kuhn's 5c-10c-25c and $1.00 Stores; pres, Big K Discount Stores, since 1948. US Army, 1918-19. Vice-chmn, exec comm, natl commn, ADL; pres: The Temple, 1959-60, mem, bd dirs; B'nai B'rith Nashville lodge, 1941-43; vice-pres, ZOA, Nashville dist, 1940-52; bd dirs: Natl Variety Assn; Sr Citizens Inc; C of C; Boys Club; Comty Relations comm; bd govs, JCC, treas, secy, vice-pres, 1940-52; mem: Masons; Elks; Shriners; Club, Woodmont. Recipient: cert of merit, Natl ARC. Home: 3405 West End Ave, Nashville, Tenn. Office: 3040 Sidcot Dr, Nashville, Tenn.

WEILAND, Fred, US, attorney, business exec; b. Cincinnati, O, Jan 27, 1896; s. Samuel and Regina (Grossman); LLB, U Cincinnati, 1917; m. Ruth Friedman 1950; c: Janet Solinger, Marilyn Klein, Richard, Lois. Pvt practice since 1917; dir, secy: Frederick Iron & Steel Co; Ludowici Celadon Co. USN, WW I. Mem: bd, Orthodox J Home for Aged, since 1920; exec comm and council, United J Social Agcys, 1925-45.

Home: 2444 Madison Rd, Cincinnati, O. Office: 1401 Enquirer Bldg, Cincinnati, O.

WEILE, Eric Ignatz, US, business exec, legislator; b. Gera, Thuringia, Ger, Sep 29, 1907; s. Louis and Hedwig (Michaelis); in US since 1938; m. Helen Grevinsky, Sep 28, 1940; c: Spencer, Lisa. Mem, Md House of Delgs, since 1966, chmn, tourism and recreation comm. Pres: Optimist Intl, Wash, DC; Langley Pk C of C; B'nai B'rith 5; treas, JWB, Wash, DC; mem: bd,Temple Isr, Silver Spring, Md; bd dirs, JCC, Wash, DC; Restaurant Assn of Gtr Wash. Recipient: awards: C of C; B'nai B'rith. Hobbies: books, photography. Home: 921 Ray Rd, Hyattsville, Md. Office: 1325 University Blvd, Langley Pk, Md.

WEILER, Jack D, US, realtor, communal leader; hon DHL, Yeshiva U. Found, pres, Realty Found, NY; mem bd dirs, PEC Isr Econ Corp; chmn bd: Amer; United; Atlantic; Intercontinental Assos; built over 12,000 housing units in Isr; Natl chmn, UJA, 15 yrs, mem: exec comm, natl campaign cabinet, chmn, trustees, UJA NY, chmn, UJA Gtr NY, 9 yrs, hon chmn, real estate div; natl secy-treas, State of Isr Bond org; mem: natl exec comm, bd dirs, chmn bd overseers, Albert Einstein Coll Med, mem soc founds, JDC, chmn, natl council, vice-chmn, mem: exec comm, admn comm; mem, adv bd, Isr Educ Fund; chmn bd, lay adv council, NY Bd Rabbis; natl treas, mem bd, United Isr Appeal; mem bd dirs, Amer comm, Weizmann Inst Sci; mem adv bd, Amer Friends Heb U; fmr: vice-pres, chmn bldg comm, FJP; pres, chmn bd dirs, Lebanon Hospital, Bx, hon pres; mem bd: trustees, dirs, JTSA; J Cen Manhattan; mem: spec comm on racial and rel prejudice, Mayor John Lindsay, NYC, 1968; Fifth Ave Syn; Cong Kehilath Jeshurun; Moshulu J Cen; Beth El Syn-Cen, New Rochelle; Temple Isr, White Plains; NY Real Estate Bd; Commerce & Ind Assn, NY; Ave of Amers Assn; Third Ave Assn; Grand St Boys' Assn; Natl Realty Club. Recipient: Universal Brotherhood f, JTSA; Herbert H Lehman Ethics award; hon alumnus, Brandeis U, 1948; Realty Man of Year: Real Estate Sq Club, 1956; Realty Found, NY, 1962. Home: 936 Fifth Ave, New York, NY. Office: 437 Madison Ave, New York, NY.

WEILER, Julius Vilayi, Isr, engineer, business exec; b. Lemberg, Aus, June 8, 1908; s. Elias and Cecilia (Fendrich); in Isr since 1936; dipl ing, Tech U, Lemberg, 1934; sr exec sch course, MIT, 1958; m. Pela Hoelzel, Jan 30, 1938; c: Ellan, Zev. Mgn dir, Isr Electro-Optical Ind Ltd, since 1942; sr lectr, Technion, Haifa, 1952-62; vice-pres, i/c of engr, Isr Mil Ind, Min of Defense, 1960-68. Haganah: IDF, hqr, arms design, 1948-51. Prin contrib: engineered Uzi submachine gun, delivered to IDF, and for export. Pres, Mech Engr sect, Isr Assn of Engrs and Architects; fmr, leader, Zionist Academic Movement, Lemberg; delg, ZC, Lucerne, 1933; mem: Inst Mech Enrs; Inst Produc Engrs, both London. Contbr to jours of Engrs Assn. Recipient: Kaplan Productivity award, 1956; decorations: War of Independence, Haganah, and Sinai Campaign decorations. Hobbies: photography, music. Home: 7 Elisha St, Tel Aviv, Isr. Office: POB 2700, Tel Aviv, Isr.

WEILER, Moses Cyrus, Isr, rabbi, organizational exec; b. Riga, Latvia, Mar 23, 1907; s. Zalman and Hannah (Halevi-Hurwitz); in Isr since 1958; BA, U Del, 1929; BHL, HUC, 1931, ordained rabbi, 1933, hon DD, 1944; grad studies, Heb U, 1958-60; m. Una Gelman, Mar 1, 1942; c: Daniel, Adam, Arnona, Gideon, Joseph, Benjamin. Personal adv to chmn, bd dirs, JNF, Jerusalem, on intl J orgs and Amer Jewry, since 1962; mem exec: WJC, since 1960; World Heb Org, since 1958; Maritime League, since 1958; vice-pres, World Union for Progressive Judaism, 1949-58; established MC Weiler Sch for Afr Children, 1945; mem world exec: ORT, 1946-60; Oeuvre de Secours aux Enfants, 1946-58; natl vice-pres, United Isr Appeal; mem exec: S Afr J Bd of Deps; ZF; delg, WZCs; pres, Isr Maritime League; vice-chmn: non-party Assn of S Afr Zionists, JNF; J Sociol Hist Soc; found: S Afr Progressive J Movement; Soc J and Chr, fmr vice-pres; chief min, United Progressive J Cong, Johannesburg, 1946-58; lectr tours and fund-raising missions: Afr, Eur, USA, S Amer, Austr, NZ. Recipient: awards and scholarships in his name: Weiler Scholarship to Heb U, S Afr Union of Temple Sisterhoods; Weiler Park, Eilas, S Afr Friends Isr Maritime League; bursary, Technion, Haifa; Rabbi Weiler Heb Sch, Johannesburg; Leo Baeck Sch, Haifa. Home: 4 Nachshon St, Jerusalem, Office: POB 283, Jerusalem, Isr.

WEILERSTEIN, Sadie R, US, author; b. Rochester, NY, July 28, 1894; d. Bernard and Tillie (Berger) Rose; BA, U Rochester, 1917; m. Reuben Weilerstein, July 29, 1920; c: Hershel, Judith, Deborah, Ruth. Tchr, Rochester Sch for the Deaf, 1917-20. Author: What Danny Did, 1928, 1944; The Adventures of K'tonton, 1935; What the Moon Brought, 1942; Little New Angel, 1947; The Singing Way, poems, 1946; Mollie and the Sabbath Queen, 1949; Our Baby, 1950; Dick, The Horse that Kept the Sabbath, 1955; Jewish Heroes, vol I, 1953, vol II, 1956; Ten and a Kid, 1962; K'tonton in Israel, 1964. Mem: Hadassah; Mizrachi Women; B'nai B'rith Women; JNF Council, Atlantic City; Technion, women's div; Assn of U Women; bd, Natl Women's League, United Syn of Amer, 1930-50; NJ Audubon Soc; Alumnae Assn, U Rochester; JBCA. Recipient: J Juvenile award, JBCA, 1956; Yovel award, Natl Women's League, United Syn of Amer, 1967; Jerusalem award, Isr Bonds, 1969. Hobbies: gardening, birdwatching. Home: 129 Virginia Ave, Atlantic City, NJ.

WEILL, Denise, Fr, psychologist; b. Paris, Oct 6, 1926; d. Emmanuel and Raisa (Epstein) Lefschetz; dipl psych, Inst of Psych, U Paris, 1947; m. Jacques Weill, July 8, 1948; c: Barbara, Caroline, Fabrice, Nicolas. Dir: Centre de Réadaptation, since 1957; Hôpital de Jour et Centre Medico Psychopedagogique; psychol: Service Social des Jeunes, 1945-50; Hôpital Bretonneau, 1950-52; Hôpital des Enfants Assistés, 1955-57. Titulaire, Intl Assn Applied Psych; mem: Alliance Israélite; Soc de Psych. Author: Pour l'Equilibre de Votre Enfant; contbr to sci publs. Home: 6 bis rue Bachaumont, Paris, Fr. Office: CEREP, 50 rue du Fg Poissonniere, Paris, Fr.

WEILL, Eugène, Fr, communal worker, attorney; b. Strasbourg, Oct 18, 1906; s. Rene and Suzanne (Bloch); att U Strasbourg; m. Margo Meyer, Jan 10, 1932, c: Gilberte Gougenheim. Atty, fmr judge, Tribunal de Seine. Secy-gen, and mem, cen comm, Alliance Israelite Universelle; delg, Conseil Consultatif d'Organisations Juives, to UN Gen Assembly, and to UNESCO conf; mem: Conseil Représentatif des Juifs de France; exec comm, United J Social Fund; admn council, Soc J Studies. Recipient: officier, Legion d'Honneur. Home: 21 rue Viete, Paris 17, Fr. Office: 45 rue La Bruyere, Paris 9, Fr.

WEILL, Milton, US, business exec; b. NYC, Oct 21, 1891; s. Charles and Rose (Strauss), BA, Columbia U, 1913; m. Teresa Jackson, Mar, 1922. Chmn bd: Arrow Mfg Co, since 1961, with firm since 1926; Arrow Case Mfg Co, Ltd, Toronto, since 1961; dir: MCI Plastics Corp, since 1962, pres, 1959-62; Mt Palomar Ranchos Inc, since 1956; pres, AMC Realty Corp, since 1959; partner, Weil-Biow-Weil Advt Agcy, 1916-20; vice-pres, A J Donahue Sales Corp, 1920-23. Lt, US Army, WW I. Asso chmn bd, FJP, NY, since 1954, pres, 1951-54; bd mem: UJA, Gtr NY; Natl JWB, since 1942, chmn, armed forces div, 1946-50, vice-pres, 1948-67; JDC, 1948-1965; 92nd St YM-YWHA, 1919-51, vice-pres, 1940-51; mem, exec bd, Asso YM-YWHAs of Gtr NY; mem, bd trustees, bd govs, AJComm, since 1946, hon life mem of exec bd; bd of overseers, Brandeis U Grad Sch of Social Wfr, since 1960, f since 1965; hon trustee, Park Ave Syn, trustee since 1929, vice-chmn, bd, 1938-47; hon dir, Surprise Lake Camp, dir, 1920-51; mem, natl council, USO, dir, and dir of camp shows, both 1951-55; chmn, Gtr NY Fund, 1951-54, bd mem, 1951-57; hon life mem, Paul Revere lodge, Masons; clubs: Twenty-Four Karat; City Athletic; Harmonie; Old Oaks Country. Recipient: Purple Heart. Hobbies: golf, theater. Office: 567 52 St, West New York, NJ.

WEILL, R Adrienne, Fr, engineer; b. Paris, June 28, 1903; d. Léon and Cécile (Kahn) Brunschvicg; licence ès scis, Sorbonne, 1923, postgrad studies, lab of radioactivity, 1923-25; widow; one c. Contractual engr, naval arms and construction, Fr Navy, 1951-68; sci adv, consultative comm, Louvre Mus Lab; sci research, Cavendish Lab, Cambridge, Eng, 1940-45. Vice-pres, Fr Assn U Women; mem: Assn of U Grad Women; Fr Soc Metallurgy; club, Paris Soroptimist. Contbr to profsl jours. Recipient: Médaille Commémorative des Forces Françaises Libres; chevalier de l'Ordre National du Mérite. Home: 56-60 rue de l'Amiral Mouchez, Paris, Fr.

WEIN, Berel, US, rabbi, attorney; b. Chgo, Ill, Mar 25, 1934; s. Zev William and Esther (Rubinstein); grandson, Rabbi Chaim Z Rubenstein, founder Heb Theol Coll, Skokie, Ill; BA, Roosevelt U, 1954; ordained rabbi, BHL, Heb Theol Coll, 1955; JD, DePaul U, 1956; DHL, Heb Theol Coll, 1967; m. Jackabed Levin, June 28, 1955; c: Miriam, Chaim, Dena, Sarah. Rabbi, Beth Isr Cong, since 1964; fac admnr, Mesivta of Gtr Miami, since 1964; atty, Abrams and Linn, 1956-58; pvt practice, 1958-64. Secy, Orthodox Rabb Council of Gtr Miami; vice-pres: Bais Yaakov Sch, Chgo, 1960-64; Telshe Yeshiva, Chgo, 1960-64; mem, RAbCa. Contbr to rel jours. Hobbies: Talmudic research, writing. Home: 3711 Prairie, Miami Beach, Fla. Study: 711 40 St, Miami Beach, Fla.

WEIN, Isadore R, US, business exec; b. Harrison, NJ, June 2, 1914; s. Max and Nettie (Manber); PhC, Rutgers U, 1934; m. Jeanette Abrams, 1940; c: Alan, Robert, Gary. Vice-pres, since 1944: Modern Clothing Co; Home Credit Clothing Co; Modern Furniture Co; Publix, Inc; vice-pres, A and W Inves Co, since 1952; owner, Wein's Pharm, Newark, NJ, 1934-40. USN, 1944-45. Pres: Temple Beth-El, since 1946, chmn bd, 1950-62, served as rabbi; Raleigh Co Cancer Assn, since 1946; B'nai B'rith lodge, 1942-43; Civitan Intl, 1957, lt-gov since 1959; vice-pres: Beckley Bus Bur, 1952-53; chmn: Hum Rights Commn, 1965-69; Mercantile Bd; UJA; Bonds for Isr; mem, bd dirs: C of C, since 1959, treas since 1957; Mountaineer Family Health Plan; Epic Drama, W Va; Raleigh Co United Fund, 1953-54; Pittsburgh Home for the Aged; mem: ZOA; Temple Bene Kedem; Social Wfr Assembly; Amer Legion; Masons; Elks; KP; Moose; Shriners; clubs: Beckley Tennis, vice-pres since 1960; Black Knight Country, mem, bd dirs; 40 & 8. Hobbies: philately, coin collecting. Home: 107 Queen St, Beckley, W Va. Office: 411 Neville St, Beckley, W Va.

WEINBERG, Alvin M, US, nuclear physicist, researcher; b. Chgo, Ill, Apr 20, 1915; s. J L and Emma (Levinson); BA, U Chgo, 1935; MA, 1936, PhD, 1939; m. Margaret Despres, June 14, 1940; c: David, Richard. Dir, Oak Ridge Natl Lab, since 1955, with lab since 1945; research asso: math, biophysics, U Chgo, 1939-41, metallurgical lab, 1941-45. F: Amer Nuclear Soc; Amer Phys Soc; mem: Amer Acad of Arts and Scis; Natl Acad of Scis; Pres Sci Adv comm, since 1960; USAF Sci Adv bd, 1956-59; Amer Nuclear Soc, pres, 1959-60. Recipient: E O Lawrence Memorial award, 1960; Atoms for Peace award, 1960. Home: 111 Moylan Lane, Oak Ridge, Tenn. Office: POB P, Oak Ridge, Tenn.

WEINBERG, Avraham A, Isr, psychiatrist; b. Hamburg, Ger, Aug 22, 1891; s. Isaac and Sara (Elias); in Isr since 1939; m. Georgine Cohen, May 10, 1917; c: Joost, Theodora Lazer. Pvt practice since 1939; research worker, Inst of Phys, Holland, 1910-17; asst, Groningen U Hosp of Neur and Psycht, 1917-19; conservator, sci dir, Psycht Lab, 1919-23; pvt practice, Groningen, 1923-39; mem, exec council, Psycho-Tech Inst Found, 1938-39. Corresp f, Amer Psycht Assn; pres, hon dir, Isr Found for Study of Adjustment Problems, since 1951; bd mem: Isr Mh Assn; YM-YWHA, Jerusalem; pres, Isr Soc for Med Psychotherapy; mem: IMA; Isr Neur and Psycht Assn; B'nai B'rith; Assn for Neur and Psycht of Netherlands. Author: Psychosociology of the Immigrant, 1949; Migration and Belonging, 1961; contbr to profsl jours. Home and office: 21 Ramban Rd, Jerusalem, Isr.

WEINBERG, Bernard, US, educator; b. Chgo, Ill, Aug 23, 1909; s. Willam and Anna (Goldstein); PhB, U Chgo, 1930, PhD, 1936; dipl, U Paris, 1931. Prof, Romance langs, U Chgo, since 1955, visiting prof, 1947, chmn dept, 1958-67; prof, fac mem, Wash U, St Louis, 1937-49; prof, Northwestern U, 1951-55, fac mem since 1949. Capt, USAAC, 1942-45. Mem: AAUP; Amer Assn Tchrs of Fr; MLA; Intl Fed for Modern Langs and Lits; Amer Assn Tchrs of It; Assn Internationale des Etudes Françaises; Newberry Libr Renaissance Conf; Renaissance Soc of Amer; Phi Beta Kappa. Author: French Realism: The Critical Reaction, 1830-1870, pub 1937; Critical Prefaces of the French Renaissance, 1951; French Poetry of the Renaissance, 1954; History of Literary Criticism in the Italian Renaissance, 1960; The Art of Jean Racine, 1964; The Limits of Symbolism, 1967; co-author: The Evolution of Balzac's Comedie Humaine, 1941; Critics and Criticism, Ancient and Modern, 1951; contbr to Amer and Eur scholarly jours. Recipient: f for Fr, Amer Field Service, 1934-35; Guggenheim fs: 1947-48, 1956-57; Fulbright awards: for It, 1951-52, for Fr, 1962-63. Office: U Chgo, Chicago, Ill.

WEINBERG, Dudley, US, rabbi; b. St Louis, Mo, Aug 11, 1915; s. Morris and Mollie (Rothman); BA, Carleton Coll, 1935; BHL, MHL, DD, HUC, Cincinnati, 1941; att: Boston U, 1951-52; Harvard U, 1953-55; m. Marian Myers, June 16, 1940; c: Avrom, Myra, Jonathan. Sr rabbi, Cong Emanuel B'nai Jeshurun, since 1955; asst rabbi, Temple Isr, Memphis, Tenn, 1941-43; sr rabbi, Temple Ohabei Shalom, Brookline, Mass, 1945-55. Chaplain, US Army, 1943-45. Pres: Gtr Milw Conf on Rel and Race; Wis Council of Rabbis; trustee: Milwaukee JWF; UAHC; chmn, commns on wor-

ship, CCAR and UAHC; planning comm, Milw United Comty Services; bd govs, Inst of Pastoral Care; exec bd, CCAR; mem, Phi Beta Kappa. Contbr to rel jours. Hobbies: violin, chamber music. Home: 1100 E Lexington Blvd, Milwaukee, Wis. Office: 2419 E Kenwood Blvd, Milwaukee, Wis.

WEINBERG, Felix Jiri, Eng, physicist; b. Aussig, Czech, Apr 2, 1928; s. Victor and Nelly (Altschul); in Eng since 1945; BSc, DSc, PhD, U London, 1951-61; m. Jill Piggott, July 26, 1954; c: John, Peter, Michael. Prof, combustion physics, Imperial Coll, U London, since 1967, fac mem since 1956. Inmate, concentration camps: Theresienstadt, Auschwitz, Buchenwald, 1942-45. F, Inst of Physics, 1961; mem: Inst of Fuel; Brit sect, Combustion Inst; libr comm, Royal Inst. Author: Optics of Flames, 1963; Electrical Aspects of Combustion, 1969; contbr to profsl jours. Spec interests: comparative rel, skindiving, flying. Home: 59 Vicarage Rd, London SW 14, Eng. Office: Imperial Coll, London SW 7, Eng.

WEINBERG, Gladys D, US, curator, archaeologist; b. NYC, Dec 27, 1909; d. Israel and Carrie (Dreyfuss) Davidson; BA, NYU, 1930; PhD, Johns Hopkins U, 1935; m. Saul Weinberg, Apr 17, 1942; c: Susanna. Curator, Mus of Art and Archaeol, U of Mo, since 1962; f, Amer School of Classical Studies, 1932-33, 1936-38, acting libr, 1947-48; asst curator, Princeton U Art Mus, 1939-43; trans, US State Dept, Istanbul and Athens, 1943-45; ed, archaeol mag, 1952-67; dir for excavations: Greece, 1959; Isr, 1964-67. Hon life mem: Amer Assn U Women; Archaeol Inst. Author: The Antikyhera Wreck Reconsidered, 1966; co-author: Small Objects From the Pnyx: I, 1942; Corinth: The Minor Objects, 1952. Home: 1401 Anthony St, Columbia, Mo. Office: U of Mo, Columbia, Mo.

WEINBERG, Joseph L, US, architect; b. Omaha, Neb, Nov 12, 1890; s. Louis and Mollie (Lazar); BA, Harvard U, 1912; m Edith Lazarus, May 28, 1933; c: Judith Weidenthal, Daniel Lang. Partner, Weinberg, Teare, Fischer, and Herman, since 1949; in pvt practice, 1919-23; partner, Morris & Weinberg, 1923-30; mem, fac: Sch of Architecture, W Reserve U, 1925-41; John Huntington Polytech Inst, 1930-41; partner, Weinberg, Laure, and Teare, 1946-49; planning cons, Cleveland Neighborhood Conservation project, 1945-46. US Army, WW I; chief architect, 5th construction zone, quartermaster corps, 1941-42, chief engr, architect, US Dist Engrs Office, Kingsport, Tenn, 1942-44. F: Amer Inst of Architecture, 1949, pres, Cleveland chap, 1938-39; Intl Inst of Arts and Letters, 1960; pres: Arch Soc of O, 1937-38; Cleveland lodge 16, B'nai B'rith, 1925; Dist Grand lodge, 1925-26; mem: adv comm, US Housing Auth, 1947-59; comm on the elderly, Cleveland Wfr Fed, since 1956; exec, campaign and planning comms, JWF, fmr chmn, builders' div: exec comm, J Cultural Garden; adv comm, Home for Aged Colored People, 1950-59; bd of trustees, Montefiore Home for Aged, 1946-60; Natl Planning Assn; Amer Soc for Aesthetics; AAAS; Amer Acad of Poliiical and Social Scis; Suburban Temple; clubs: Oakwood Country; Commerce; Harvard, Cleveland; Longboat Key Gold, Sarasota. Recipient: awards for design, Cleveland C of C, 1941, 1953, 1957, 1961, 1966, 1967; natl award of merit, Amer Inst of Arch, for O'Neill-Sheffield Reg Center, Lorain, O. 1955. Home: 19101 Van Aken, Shaker Heights, O. Office: 29th fl, Terminal Tower, Cleveland, O.

WEINBERG, Julius R, US, philosopher, educator; b. Zanesville, O, Sep 3, 1908; s. Solomon and Dolores (Chase); BA, O State U, 1931, MA, 1932; PhD, Cornell U, 1935; m. Ilse Heimann, June, 1938; c: Marilyn, Mark. Vilas Prof of Phil, U Wis, since 1964, prof since 1947; instr, Cornell U, 1937-38; Howald Scholar, O State U, 1938-39; fac mem, U Cincinnati, 1941-47. Author: An Examination of Logical Positivism, 1936, 1937; Nicolaus of Autrecourt, 1948; History of Medieval Philosophy, 1964; contbr to profsl jours. Home: 584 Park Lane, Madison, Wis. Office: U of Wis, Madison, Wis.

WEINBERG, Kurt, US, educator; b. Hannover, Ger, Feb 24, 1912; s. Paul and Frieda (Wolff); in US since 1941; MA, Trinity Coll, 1949; PhD, Yale U, 1953; m. Florence Byham, May 8, 1955. Prof, Fr, Ger, comparative lit, U Rochester, since 1962; instr: Yale U, 1950-51, 1952-53; Hunter Coll, 1953-54; visiting prof, Ia State U, 1954-55; visiting lectr, U of BC, 1955-57, asst prof, 1957-62. Fr Army, 1939-40; US Army, 1942-45. Mem: MLA; clubs: Elizabethan; Yale U. Author: Henri Heine, romantique défroqué héraut du symbolisme français, 1954; Kafkas Dichtung die Travestien des Mythos, 1963; co-compiler, C Von Faber Du Faur: German

Baroque Literature, 1959; contbr: Ency of Poetry and Poetics, 1965; Ency of Phil, 1967; Ency of World Lit in the 20th Century, 1967; chap, André Gide, in Der moderne franzosische Roman, 1968; and to scholarly jours. Recipient: Sr Sterling f, Yale U; Guggenheim f, 1960-61. Office: U Rochester, Rochester, NY.

WEINBERG, Sidney R, US, physician; b. Bklyn, NY, Feb 9, 1912; s. Hyman and Minnie (Slotnick); BS, NYU, 1933, MD, 1937; m. Goldie Winkler, Dec 6, 1938; c: Jane, Geltner, Emily Schulman, Winkler. Chief, urol div, J Hosp, Bklyn, since 1963; clinical prof, Downstate Med Cen, Bklyn, since 1963. Lt, US Army, 1938-42. Pres, Bklyn Urol Soc; club, Unity, Bklyn. Author: The Ureter, 1967; contbr to med jours. Home: 212 Beach 139, Belle Harbor, NY. Office: 142 Joralemon, Brooklyn, NY.

WEINBERG, Tobias, US, physician, educator; b. Baltimore, Md, Mar 3, 1910; s. David and Yetta (Goodman); BA, Johns Hopkins U, 1930, MD, 1933; m. Rhoda Perlo, July 14, 1940; c: David. Path-in-chief and dir labs, Sinai Hosp, since 1940; prof, path, U Md Med Sch, since 1968, fac mem since 1955; asso prof, Johns Hopkins Med Sch, since 1961; dir of lab, Happy Hills Hosp for Children, since 1968; cons path: Springfield State Hosp; Mt Pleasant Sanitorium; Kernan's Hosp; Lutheran Hosp; fmr: res, med, Baltimore City Hosp, 1933-36; med asst, Johns Hopkins U, 1934-36; asst and f in path, Mt Sinai Hosp, NY, 1936-40; path: Beth Isr Hosp, Passaic, NJ, 1939-40; St Joseph's Hosp, Baltimore, 1943-45; Levindale Home, Baltimore, 1945; asso prof, path, U Md Dent Sch, 1951-59. F: AMA; Coll of Amer Paths; dipl, Amer Bd Path; mem: Amer Assn of Paths and Bacts; AAAS; Intl Acad of Paths; Amer Assn for Study of Neoplastic Diseases; Med and Chirurgical Fac of Md; Baltimore City Med Soc; Sigma Xi; Har Sinai Cong. Contbr to med jours. Hobbies: fishing, photography. Home: Hooks Lane, Pikesville, Md. Office: Sinai Hosp, Baltimore, Md.

WEINBERG, Vladimir, US, physician; b. Odessa, Russ, Feb 6, 1892; s. Samuel and Dora (Misroch); in US since 1923; MD, Zurich U, 1916; m. Florence Trachenberg, July 10, 1920. Pvt practice, NYC, since 1925. Phys, Russ Army, 1916-19. Pres, Fellows of Odessa, since 1943; mem: Amer phys comm, IMA. Author: How to Preserve Health, 1945; weekly med column, Novoye Russkoye Slovo, NY, since 1925. Home: 124 W 72 St, New York, NY.

WEINBERG, Werner, US, educator; b. Rheda, Ger, May 30, 1915; s. Eli and Paula (Grünewald); in US since 1948; grad, Heb Tchrs Sem, Wurzburg, 1936; MA, U Louisville, 1953; PhD, HUC, 1961; m. Louise Halberstadt, Dec 21, 1938; c: Koni, Barrie. Asso prof, Heb langs and lit, HUC, since 1965. Mem: AAUP; Ling Soc Amer; Soc Bibl Lit; Natl Assn Profs Heb. Author: Die Reste des Jüdischdeutschen; The Problems of the Hebrew Spelling Reforms; contbr to scholarly jours. Home: 735 Red Bud Ave, Cincinnati, O. Office: 3101 Clifton Ave, Cincinnati, O.

WEINBERG, Yeshaya, Isr, theater mgr, business exec; b. Warsaw, Pol, July 14, 1918; s. Samuel and Chana (Zuckerman); in Isr since 1933; m. Chana Lutsky, May 15, 1959; c: Michal, Benjamin. Dir gen, Cameri Theatre, Tel Aviv, since 1961; mem, Kibbutz Elon, 1935-55; asst dir, govt mechanization cen, PMs off, Jerusalem, 1956-61. Sgt, J Brig, Brit Army, 1942-46. Pres, Isr Cen of the Intl Theater Inst; mem: Natl Council on Culture and Art; club: Variety. Home: 134 Jabotinsky St, Tel Aviv, Isr. Office: 101 Dizengoff St, Tel Aviv, Isr.

WEINBERG, Zvi Zevulun, Isr, author, editor; s. Eliezer and Ira-Tairah (Stern); in Isr since 1921; ordained rabbi, Rabbi Ulterman's Yeshiva; tchrs cert, Grudna, 1912; m. Menuha Alperin; c: Dvorah Gretz, Jonah, Tzirah Artzi. Ret since 1950; fmr: tchr, HS, Warsaw, 1913-20; sch dir, Zicharon Yaacov, 1920-21; dir, sch insp: Bat Shlomo, 1920-21; Atlit; Shfeya kindergarten, Zichron Yaacov; tchr, insp, Heb studies, Ascola HS, Warsaw, 1922-34. Fmr: found, chmn, Heb Writers and Journalists Assn, Pol; mem: Cen Comm on Cultural Affairs, Pol; Lit Council of Writers Assn, Pol; club: PEN, vice-chmn. Author: Tziyurim veSipurim, 1913-14; Yaldut, 1920; Bayit uRehov, 1932; biDrahim Avelot, 1942; Mehitzot, 1943; Gami, 1944; Asher Avar, vols, 1954, 1957; Adam beOhalo, vol 4, 1957; Hem Halchu, 1957; Ehad meHem, 1st vol, 1963; Darchei Enosh, 1st vol, 1966; Tzeirim beDoram, 3rd vol, 1968; ed: Kolot, monthly, 1923-24; Resheet, 1933-34. Recipient: hon citizenship, Tel Mond. Home: Tel Mond, Isr.

WEINBERGER, Andrew D, US, attorney; b. Obecha, Hung, Aug 20, 1901; s. Joseph and Josephine (Sonnenschein); in US since 1904; att NYU, 1919-20; LLB, NY Law Sch, 1925; hon LLD, Wilberforce U, 1959; m. Sylvia Budinoff, Aug 17, 1924; c: Eric, Anthony, Michael. Pvt practice, specializing copyright and civil liberties, since 1926; visiting lectr: Grad Sch of Public Admn, NYU, 1953-56; U Mexico, 1959-60; U Tokyo, 1960-61. USCG, res, WW II. Mem: bd dirs, NAACP, 1943-67; Amer and NY State Bar Assns; NY Co Lawyers Assn. Author: Freedom and Protection: The Bill of Rights, 1962; contbr: appendix, Man's Most Dangerous Myth: the Fallacy of Race, 4th ed, 1963; and to legal and social sci jours. Home: 3 Sheridan Sq, New York, NY. Office: 230 Park Ave, New York, NY.

WEINBERGER, Aron, US, organization exec; b. Auschwitz, Pol; DJur, U Cracow, Pol; m; two c. Dir, Found for JNF, NY; bus mgr, Midstream, J quarterly; fmr: practicing atty, Pol; ed asst, Phaidon Press Ltd, Vienna and Holland; sales promotion mgr, W De Haan, book pubs, Holland; mgn dir, Phaidon SA, Switz; gen mgr, Phaidon E and W Libr of NY; rel and fgn ed, sales promotion mgr, Farrar, Straus & Cudahy. Organized "Remember" comm, which recorded testimony from fmr inmates of concentration camps. Inmate, concentration camps: Vught, Westerbork, Bergen-Belsen, Biberach/Riss; co-leader, Zionist underground, Bergen-Belsen; camp capt, Biberach/Riss, Ger, elected by camp inmates after liberation; interpreter, liaison off, mil govt, Fr, occupation zone, Ger, WW II. Fmr: found, Akiba Gen Zionist Movement, Pol; pres, Hashachar, Zionist academic org, Yagello U, Cracow; mem: Zionist exec, ZC, both Pol; ZC, Holland; chmn, intl affairs comm, AJCong, Queens div, mem, govt council. Lectr, and contbr to periodicals. Office: JNF Inc, 42 E 69 St, New York, NY.

WEINBERGER, Bernard, US, rabbi; b. Sanz, Pol, Apr 13, 1929; s. Joshua and Ester (Birnbaum); ordained rabbi, Yeshiva Torah Vodaath Mesivta, 1952; att, Beth Medrash Elyon, 1947-52; BA, Bklyn Coll, 1951; MA, NYU, 1960; PhD, Philathea Coll, 1960; cert social worker, NY State, 1968; m. Anne Fox, Jan 23, 1956; c: Linda, Martin, Marc, Debra. Rabbi, Young Isr of Bklyn, since 1955; rabb cons, YM-YWHA of Williamsburg, since 1968; found sponsor, W Coast Talmudic Sem, LA, 1953-54; admr, Yeshiva Torah Vodaath and Mesivta, Bklyn, 1954-57. Pres, Rabb Alliance of Amer, since 1967; vice-pres, Council of Young Isr Rabbis, since 1961; syn comm, FJP; natl pres, Agudath Isr Youth of Amer, 1949-51; mem, NYC Council Against Poverty. Contbr to Anglo-J periodicals. Home. 225 Division Ave, Brooklyn, NY. Study: 563 Bedford Ave, Brooklyn, NY.

WEINBERGER, Philip M, US, rabbi; b. Sanz, Pol, Sep 8, 1926; s. Joshua and Esther (Birnbaum); ordained rabbi, Mesifta Talmudical Sem, 1950; MA, U of Me, 1958; DD, Philathea Coll, 1963; m. Hannah Slutsker, Apr 17, 1954; c: Judah, Deborah, Samuel. Rabbi; Cong Anshe Sholem, since 1958; Cong B'nai Yessocher, Bx, 1950-54; Beth Abraham, Bangor, 1955-58. Exec bd, Union Orthodox Rabbis of Amer; mem: RabCa, Rabb Alliance of Amer, fmr vice-pres; Rel Zionists of Amer. Radio lectr, "Voice from the Synagogue." Home: 59a Locust Ave, New Rochelle, NY. Study: 50 North Ave, New Rochelle, NY.

WEINBLUM, Mordechai, Isr, engineer; b. Jerusalem, Dec 10, 1931; s. Nechemia and Hadassah; MS, Technion, 1956; m. Tamara, Aug 10, 1954; c: Dafna, Ofra, Dalia. Dir, The Agric Engr Inst, since 1968, fac mem since 1966; head, machinery div, Min of Agric, 1962-65. Contbr to profsl jours. Home: 7 Hashomrim St, Rehovot, Isr. Office: Beth Dagan, Isr.

WEINER, A Herbert, US; b. Boston, Mass, Oct 27, 1919; s. Simon and Celia (Blank); BA, U Mass, 1942; ordained rabbi, HUC, 1946; m. Shirley Jacobs, 1952; c: Jonathan, Carmi, Alisa. Rabbi, Temple Isr, since 1948. Radio off, US Merchant Marine, 1944-45. Author: The Wild Goats of Ein Gedi, 1961; ed, Therefore Choose Life, from works of Rabbi Abba Hillel Silver, 1967; 9½ Mystics: The Kabbalah Today, 1969; contbr to jours. Home: 31 Park Rd, Maplewood, NJ. Study: 432 Scotland Rd, S Orange, NJ.

WEINER, Abe, US, artist, teacher; b. Pittsburgh, Pa, Nov 5, 1917; s. Nathan and Rose (Einbund); cert of painting, Carnegie Inst of Tech, 1941; m. Anne Weisberg, Nov 8, 1947; c: Shari, Kim, Jonathan. Artist; asst dir, tchr, Ivy Sch of Profsl Art, since 1961; lectr, contemporary painting; exhbs: Asso Artists of Pittsburgh, since 1941; Carnegie Intl Exhbs; Chgo

Art Inst; Metrop Mus of Art; Bulter Art Inst; Carnegie Inst, natl shows; Three Rivers Arts Festival, Pittsburgh; West-moreland Art Mus, Pa; commn, mural and mosaic, Alumin-um Co of Amer. Mem: Asso Artists of Pittsburgh; Pittsburgh Council of Arts. Recipient: 1st prize 1941, 2nd prize, 1945, judges prizes 1958, 1959, Asso Artists of Pittsburgh; Bulter Art Inst award; Allegheny Co Fair painting prize; Three Rivers Art Festival purchase award, 1968. Home: 1636 Den-niston St, Pittsburgh, Pa. Office: Ivy Sch of Profsl Art, Pitts-burgh, Pa.

WEINER, Alfred L, US, dermatologist, educator; b. North Vernon, Ind, Apr 13, 1911; s. Samuel and Molly (Moel); BA, U Cincinnati, 1933, MD, 1937; m. Janet Lackner, June 17, 1940; c: Wendy, Stuart, Toben. Pvt practice since 1939; asso prof, dermat, U Cincinnati Coll of Med, since 1959; fac mem since 1949; asst dir, dermat dept, U Cincinnati Med Cen; dir, dermat dept, J Hosp, since 1957, att phys since 1944; chief clinician in dermat, out patient div, Cincinnati Gen Hosp, since 1953. F: AMA; Amer Acad Dermat; dipl, Amer Bd of Dermat and Syphilology; charter pres, Noah Worcester Dermat Soc; mem: Soc for Inves Dermat; Cincinnati Dermat Soc, fmr pres; Acad of Med, Cincinnati; Wise Temple; Sigma Alpha Mu Alumni; club: Losantiville Country. Contbr to med jours. Home: 7340 Aracoma Forest Dr, Cincinnati, O. Office: 2825 Burnet Ave, Cincinnati, O.

WEINER, Erwin, US, public official; b. Chgo, Ill, Dec 5, 1911; s. Sam and Ida (Goldsholl); att Chgo Normal Coll, 1929-33; Northwestern U, 1933-34. m. Claire Gassin, Sep 11, 1938; c: Neil, James. Cons, Chgo Park dist, since 1968, exec with dist since 1948; bd dirs: Main State Bank, Chgo, since 1966; Pro-vident Hospital, since 1964; La Rabida Children's Hosp and Research Cen, since 1965. Bd mem, JNF, since 1960; chmn, Amer comm, Isr Torah Research Inst, since 1966; gen chmn, Gtr Chgo State of Isr Bonds, since 1967; bd govs, Heb U, Jerusalem, since 1969; mem, natl bd dirs: Amer comm, Weiz-mann Inst of Sci, since 1966; J Home for Aged; B'nai B'rith; Amer Friends Heb U; JNF; mem: J Hist Soc; Temple Beth Isr; chmn, Chgo conv, Natl Park Recreation Assn, 1969. Recipient: man of the-year, Amer comm, Weizmann Inst, 1965. Home: 2946 Balmoral St, Chicago, Ill.

WEINER, Eugene Carl, US, administrator, rabbi; b. NYC, Sep 14, 1933; s. Morris and Ann (Lesky); BA, Columbia Coll, 1955; ordained rabbi, MHL, JTSA, 1960; m. Anita Herzog, Dec 28, 1954; c: Daniel, David, Dir, Herbert H Lehman Inst of Ethics, JTSA, since 1965; asso registrar, JTSA, 1960-62; rabbi, Beth Jacob Cong, 1962-65. Bd dirs: Amer Movement for Arab-J Coop; Org of Multi-Racial Jews; United World Federalists; mem: RA; Amer Sociol Assn. Home: 350 Central Park W, New York, NY. Office: 3080 Broadway, New York, NY.

WEINER, Frank J, US, attorney, educator; b. Boston, Mass, Mar 9, 1929; s. Benjamin and Anna (Braverman); BS, Boston U, 1950; MBA, Northeastern U, 1963; LLB, Portia Law Sch, 1965; m. Helen Cabitt, Aug 21, 1955; c: Richard, Michael. Atty since 1965; lectr and instr, Northeastern U, since 1957; fmr: gen traffic mgr, Cargo-Imperial Freight Lines, 1953-58; transp cons, 1958-65. Cpl, US Army, 1951-53. Pres, Temple Beth Abraham, Canton, Mass, vice-pres, 1960-61, 1966-68; dir: Assn of ICC Practitioners, 1st dist; mem: Motor Carriers Lawyers Assn; Mass, Norfolk Co, and Boston Bar Assns; Mass Trial Lawyers Assn; Mayflower lodge, B'nai B'rith; lawyer's comm, Histadrut; Farband; Isr Emergency Fund; Metrop Dist commn, Gtr Boston CJP; fmr chmn; Canton CJP; Tau Epsilon Phil; Brotherhood lodge, AF and AM. Home: 44 Kings Rd, Canton, Mass. Office: 536 Granite Rd, Braintree, Mass.

WEINER, Harry, US, orthopedist; b. Kiev, Russ, Aug 12, 1901; s. Solomon and Sophie (Gendell); in US since 1905; MD, NYU and Bellevue Hosp, 1924; m. Charlotte Rabiner, Feb 6, 1925; c: Norma Heit. Att orthopedist, J Sanitarium and Hosp for Chronic Diseases, since 1949; orthopedic cons, Kings-brook J Med Cen; asso att orthopedist, Kings Co Hosp, since 1946; instr, orthopedics, postgrad div, Bellevue Med Cen, since 1940; att orthopedist em, Maimonides Hosp, on staff since 1942. F, Amer Coll of Surgs, since 1953; pres: med bd, J Chronic Disease Hosp, 1960-62; Ocean Med Soc, 1950; mem: Amer and NY Rheumatism Assns; AMA; Kings Co and NY State Med Assns; Phi Lambda Kappa, pres, Bklyn alumni. Contbr to med jours. Home and office: 1017 Ave R, Brook-lyn, NY.

WEINER, Herbert E, US, foreign service officer, economist; b. NYC, Mar 2, 1921; s. Jacob and Beatrice (Kauftheil) BSS, CCNY, 1941; MA, Columbia U, 1943; PhD, 1957; att US Naval War Coll, Newport, RI, 1965-66; m. Eva Feiman, June 19, 1957. Counselor for econ affairs, US Emb, Lisbon, since 1966; fmr: instr, econ, CCNY, 1946-47; 3rd secy, US Emb, London, 1948-49; vice-consul, lab attaché, US Consulate-Gen, Sydney, 1949-53; chief, Brit Commonwealth affairs, US Dept of Lab, 1953-57, lab adv for Far East, 1957-59; mem, US delg to ILO, 1959-61; 1st secy, counsul, US Emb, Ottawa, 1961-65. Mem: Amer Fgn Service Assn. Author: British Labor and Public Ownership, 1960; contbr to scholarly jours. Recipient: Pres Unit Citation, 11th Airborne Div. Office: US Emb, Lisbon, Port.

WEINER, Herman, US, attorney, organization exec; b. Phila, Pa, July 4, 1906; s. Isaac and Pearl (Gantman); LLB, Temple Law Sch, 1930; m. Bertha Bitman, July 6, 1936; c: Arlene Meth. Atty since 1930. Pvt, US Army, 1943-45; govt appeal agt of Selective Service Sys. Natl vice-pres, ZOA; mem bd, J Cmty Relations Council, Phila; exec bd, Bonds for Isr; cdr, Phila Variety post 713, Amer Legion; fmr: state cdr, JWV, 1957-58, cdr, Haim Parnes post, 1968-69; mem: Ma-sonic Order Shekinah lodge; AJCong; Temple Law Alumni; fmr, pres: Har Sinai lodge, B'nai B'rith; B'nai Yiddish of Phila; panel, Amer Arbitration Assn; clubs: 32 Carat, pres, 1948-49; Odd Fellows, past noble, Grand Menorah lodge. Spec interest: revival of Yiddish, and J culture and hist. Home: 117 WB Green Hills Apts, Philadelphia, Pa. Office: 1412 Fox Bldg, 1612 Market St, Philadelphia, Pa.

WEINER, Jacob, Isr, organization exec; b. Radautz, Aus, Mar 19, 1894; s. Moshe and Rebekka (Mimeles); in Isr since 1939; DJur, U Vienna, 1920; m. Johanna Schmidt. Ret, 1969; fmr: dir, Hillel Remedy Factory Ltd, Haifa, 1945-68; prokurist, Credit-Anstalt Bankverein Vienna Zuckerfabriks, Aus, 1930-38; acting dir, JA for Pal 1940-43; dir, Mfrs Assn, Haifa, 1943-45. Lt, Aus-Hung Army, 1914-1918; inmate concentration camps: Dachau, Buchenwald, 1938-39. Fmr chmn, Comm of Ger colony, Haifa, 1947-53; mem: court of Natl Ins Inst, Isr; Isr-Amer Friendship Soc; fmr, mem, Akademische Verbindung Kadima, Vienna. Recipient: medals: Gold Cross with crown; Bronze Cross; Silver Cross, all Aus-Hung Army, WW I. Home: 6 Beth Lehem St, Haifa, Isr.

WEINER, Josephine S, US, communal worker; b. Detroit, Mich, April 8, 1912; d. Milford and Mollie (Sillman) Stern; BA, U Mich, 1933, MA, 1934; tchrs cert, Wayne State U; m. Leonard Weiner, June 18, 1936. Fmr: tchr, public schs, Detroit. Pres: Natl Council of J Women, since 1967, Detroit sect, 1941-43; women's div, JWF, 1951-53; vice-pres, J Comty Cen, 1947-50; bd mem, United Comty Services of Metrop Detroit, since 1957, chmn: women's comm, 1955-57, 25th anniversary celebration; bd member, natl women's div, UJA, 1953-56; bd govs: Heb U, Jerusalem; bd mem, Natl Found for J Culture; mem, Mayor's Youth Comm, 1944-46. Home: 25564 Wareham Dr, Huntington Woods, Mich.

WEINER, Leonard, US, dentist, periodontist; b. NYC, Aug 4, 1913; s. Harris and Eva (Ossin); BA, Yale U, 1936; DMD, Harvard U, 1940; m. Doris Goldman, Dec 14, 1940; c: Charles, Elizabeth. Pvt practice since 1940; staff mem: St Mary's Hosp; Pima Co Hosp; Tucson Med Cen; visiting lectr, U of S Cal Dent Sch. US Army, 1941-46. F: Amer Coll Densists; Amer Assn Endontists; dipl: Amer Bd Periodonto-logy; Amer Bd Endodontics; pres: W Soc of Periodontology, since 1967; Natl Fed Regional Periodontal Orgs, 1968-69; Amer Friends of Heb U, 1956-57; ZOA, 1947-48; vice-pres, Temple Emanuel, Tucson; chmn, CJA, 1949; mem: Amer and Ariz State Dent Assns; Amer Acad Periodontology; Colo Dent Found; Histo-Path Study Club; Alpha Omega; Sigma Xi. Contbr to profsl jours. Home: 3348 E 4 St, Tucson, Ariz. Office: 12c Med Sq, 1601 N Tucson Blvd, Tucson, Ariz.

WEINER, Otto F, US, attorney; b. Chgo, Ill, Nov 6, 1898; s. Adolph and Paula (Frisch); PhB and JD, U Chgo; m. Norma France, Sep 11, 1927; c: Kenneth, Ann Bandolik. Pvt practice since 1920; fmr: asst corp counsel, City of Chgo, 1931-36; asst atty, Ill Commerce Commn, 1937-38. Served, USN. Pres, 49th Ward Regular Dem Org; mem: natl B'nai B'rith Youth Commn; regional bd, ADL; fmr pres: Gtr Chgo B'nai B'rith Council; Dist Grand lodge, 6 B'nai B'rith; mem: Ill and Chgo Bar Assns; Temple Sholem; Amer Legion, Hobby: bridge. Home: 330 W Diversey Pkwy, Chicago, Ill. Office: 134 N LaSalle St, Chicago, Ill.

WEINER, Robert H, US, administrator, social worker; b. Bridgeport, Conn, Jan 8, 1919; s. Joseph and Sarah (Kaufman); BA, U Buffalo, 1940; MSSA, W Reserve U, 1942; m. Jane Lasner, June 28, 1942; c: Jerome, Marilyn, Exec dir, J Comty Cen of Gtr Wash, DC, since 1958; prof dir, YM-YWHA, Louisville, 1944-46; asst dir, J Comty Cen, Buffalo, 1946-53; exec dir, J Comty Cen, San Antonio; 1953-58; fmr lectr: U Buffalo Sch of Social Work and Med; Howard U Sch of Social Work. Pres: Montgomery Co, Recreation Bd, 1969-70; Wash Comty Music Sch; mem: Montgomery Co Comty Services Coord Commn; Middle Atlantic chap, Natl, Assn of J Cen Workers, chmn, 1963-64; natl bd, 1964-66; Natl Assn of Social Workers; precinct chmn, Dem Party, 1963-67. Contbr to profsl jours. Home: 2631 Colston Dr, Chevy Chase, Md. Office: 6125 Montrose Rd, Rockville, Md.

WEINERMAN, Robert Arthur, US, business exec; b. Hartford, Conn, July 23, 1922; s. David and Anna (Schwartz); BA, Yale U, 1944; MS, MIT, 1948; m. Harriet Chaikind, June 29, 1947; c: Leslie, Lynne, Harry. Pres, Southern NE Contracting Co, since 1958. Lt, USAAC, 1943-46. Chmn, Hartford Bldg Commn; pres: Emanuel Syn, 1960-62; Hartford J Comty Cen, 1966-68; vice-pres, Hartford J Fed, 1956-68; mem: Comty Chest budget comm; The Loomis Council; club: Rotary. Recipient: award, Hartford J Fed. Hobbies: reading, tennis, travel. Home: 76 Westerly Terr, Hartford, Conn. Office: 526 Farmington Ave, Hartford, Conn.

WEINERT, Bernard, Isr, business exec; b. Stanislavov, Aus-Hung, May 20, 1898; s. Michael and Anna (Mahler); in Isr since 1936; PhD, U Zurich, 1921; m. Hella Weinmann, 1924; two c. Swissair repr to Isr, 1947-69; repr, Keren Kayemeth, Eur, 1924-30; journalist in Switz, 1930-36; secy, JA for Pal, non-Zionist dept, Jerusalem, 1936-38; repr: Swiss Natl Tourist Office; Swiss trade commn to Pal, both 1938-47; hon Swiss Council, Tel Aviv, 1947-50. Alternate mem, bd govs, Heb U, Jerusalem; mem bd, Soc of Friends of Heb U; club: SCAL, Isr, pres. Contbr to jours. Home: 22b Dubnov St, Tel Aviv. Office: 41 Ben Yehuda St, Tel Aviv, Isr.

WEINFELD, Abraham C, US, attorney; b. Budzanow, Aus-Hung, Feb 22, 1896; s. Moses and Brane (Schutzman); in US since 1921; DJur, U Vienna, 1920; LLB, Columbia U, 1926; m. 1st; c: David; m. 2nd, Merna Resnikoff, Apr 18, 1948. Ret, 1965; fmr: atty, Kugel and Telsey, NYC, 1927-31; pvt practice, NYC, 1932-35; atty-adv, US Dept Agric, 1937-65. Mem: Fed Bar Assn; Columbia Law Sch Alumni Assn; fmr: chmn: Comm for Isr Scholarships, 1962-64; vice-chmn and exec comm, govt div, UJA, 1962-64; pres, N Va Zionist dist, 1961-63; mem, natl exec council, ZOA, 1961-65. Author: Labor Treaties and Labor Compacts, 1937; Towards a United States of Europe, 1942; Basic Jewish Ethics and Freedom of Will, 1968; contbr to law revs and Zionist press. Hobby: hiking. Home: 7306 Valleycrest Blvd, Annandale, Va.

WEINGART, Irving A, US, rabbi; b. Chgo, Ill, Sep 1, 1907; s. Samuel and Sima (Bakalshok); PhB, U Chgo, 1929; ordained rabbi, Heb Theol Coll, Chgo, 1933; MA, Drake U, 1951; PhD, Cen Sch of Rel, Ind, 1951; m. Hella Graubart, June 19, 1934; c: Samuel. Rabbi: Tifereth Isr Syn, since 1945; chaplain: VA Hosp, Knoxville and Des Moines, since 1950; B'nai Jacob Cong, Fort Wayne, Ind, 1933-45; instr, social sci, Drake U, 1941-42; Divinity Coll, 1968. Civilian chaplain, Baer Field Air Base, Fort Wayne, WW II. Chmn, Des Moines Rabbinate; pres: Ia Bd of Rabbis, since 1961; cen states region, RA; speakers bur, NCCJ; bd: U of Ia Sch of Rel; UN Speakers Bur; adv comm, Des Moines Public Libr; lectr, Chautauqua Soc; bd mem, Des Moines JWF; admn bd, Des Moines chap, ZOA, 1938, mem natl exec bd, 1962, pres, 1961-67; mem, Gov Harold E Hughes crisis comm, 1968. Author: Bible and Talmud, A Source for the Development of Medical and Dental Knowledge, 1951; mem, perm panel, weekly radio prog. Home: 4915 Woodland Rd, Des Moines, Ia. Study: 924 Polk Blvd, Des Moines, Ia.

WEINGARTEN, Hilde Kevess, US, artist; b. Berlin, Ger, d. Morris and Clara (Leitner); in US since 1938; studied art, Berlin, 1937-38; grad, Cooper Union Art Sch, 1947; att Art Students League, NYC, 1941-42; m. Arthur Kevess, Jan 28, 1951; c: Ruth, Robert. One-man shows: Carlebach Gal, NYC, 1949; Hicks St Gal, Bklyn, 1962, 1968; Contemporary Arts Inc, NYC, 1963, 1968; works exhb: Seattle Art Mus; Denver Art Mus; Dallas Mus of Fine Arts; Phila Print Club; Phila Art Alliance; Bklyn Mus; Riverside Mus; AAA Gal; ACA Gal; all NYC; Cleveland Mus of Art; gals: Albright, Corcoran, Rochester Memorial; Fujikawa, Osaka, Japan;

Peter Cooper, NYC; Paul Kessler, Provincetown; Bezalel Mus, Jerusalem; perm collections: Provincetown Art Assn, Donnell Art Libr; Lever House, NYC. Bd dir, Artists Equity, NY, since 1964; mem: Natl Assn of Women Artists; League of Present-Day Artists; Provincetown Art Assn. Recipient: Annual purchase prize, Collectors Amer Art, 1947-65. Home: 140 Cadman Plaza, Brooklyn, NY.

WEINGARTEN, Yerachmiel, Isr, editor, administrator; b. Warsaw, Pol, Dec 23, 1902; s. Wolf and Sarah (Panasky); in US, 1946-68, in Isr since 1968; grad, Pol State Tchrs Sem, 1923; att Warsaw U, 1927; m. Anna Margel, May 28, 1926; c: Jaala, Alexander. Ed in chief, LeMishpacha, publ of Histadrut Ivrit of Amer, since 1963; fmr: ed: Alim leSifruth, 1926-1929; Eeton Katan, 1928-32; co-asso, Janusz Korczak's Children's Home; co-ed, Maly Przeglad, both 1927-31; tchr, lectr, Pol, 1927-39; ed, Central, pub house, 1935-38; lectr, JTSA, NY, 1947; secy-gen, Histadrut Ivrit of Amer, 1953-57. Mem: exec, Farband, 1952-55; exec, Heb World Union, Jerusalem, since 1954; Natl Council for J Educ; fmr: pres, Union J Rel Tchrs Pol Schs, 1928-37; vice-pres, Heb Writers Union, 1935; found: and exec dir, Can Heb Culture Fund, 1942-46; and dir, J Natl Day Schs Kinneret, Bklyn, Bx, and NY, 1946-53. Author: A Velt in Flamen, 1941; Amenu beAvar ubaHove, 6 vols, 1945; Heb lang and hist textbooks, since 1932; co-author: Sefer Chadash, part I, 1953, part II, 1956; contbr to Heb, Yiddish publs. Home and office: 21 Beeri St, Tel Aviv, Isr.

WEINGARTNER, Henry W, US, business exec; b. Flehingen, Ger, Sep 4, 1914; s. Victor and Emma (Pfaelzer); in US since 1937; att Technische Hochschule, Karlsruhe, 1934-36; m. Ilse Sternberg, Jan 6, 1946; c: Marilyn. Pres, Henry Weingartner & Co, Inc, since 1956. Lt, US Army, mil intelligence, 1943-45. Comm mem, UJA, Eastchester; pres: Genesis Heb Cen, Tuckahoe, 1953-61, bd chmn, 1961-63; mem, Hutchinson lodge, B'nai B'rith. Recipient: Bronze Star; spec citation; field commission; all WW II. Home: 45 Interlaken Dr, Eastchester, NY. Office: 217 Broadway, New York, NY.

WEINHOLTZ, Yehuda Salomon, Isr, engineer; b. Warsaw, Pol, Feb 5, 1917; s. Salomon and Eva; deg, tech of metal work, Tech Inst; m. Dafna; c: Revital, Irit. Head, professions definition and classification dept, Isr Fed of Lab, since 1962; tech adv, ORT, Ger, 1945-50; maintenance engr, Voit, Ger, 1946-49. Home: 4 Jecheskel, Ramat Chen, Isr. Office: 93 Arlosoroff, Tel Aviv, Isr.

WEINHOUSE, Sidney, US, administrator, biochemist, researcher; b. Chgo, Ill, May 21, 1909; s. Harry and Dora (Cutler); BS, U Chgo, 1933, PhD, 1936; m. Sylvia Krawitz, Sep 15, 1935 (decd); c: Doris, James, Barbara. Dir, Fels Research Inst, Temple U Med School, since 1963; asso dir since 1961; prof, biochemistry, Temple U, since 1947; fmr: research asso: U Chgo, 1936-43, Office of Sci Research Devl, 1941-44; research chem, Houdry Process Corp, 1944-50; head, dept of metabolic chem, Lankenau Hosp Research Inst, and Inst for Cancer Research, 1950-61. Sci adv comm, Damon Runyon Memorial Fund; fmr: chmn, comm on biochemistry, div of chem and chemical tech, Natl Acad of Sci-NRC; mem, natl adv cancer council, US Dept HEW; chmn, biol div, Amer Chem Soc; mem: Natl Adv Council on Environmental Health; Amer Chem Soc; Amer Asso of Biological Chemists; Amer Diabetes Assn; Soc for Experimental Biol and Med; Temple Judea. Co-ed, Advances in Cancer Research; mem, ed bd, Jour of Biol Chem; contbr to profsl publs. Recipient: Eli Lilly f, 1936-38; Coman f, 1939-41. Home: 6419 Lawnton Ave, Philadelphia, Pa. Office: Fels Research Inst, Temple U, Philadelphia, Pa.

WEININGER, Freed, Isr, poet, artist, psych social worker; b. Czernowitz, Rum, July 29, 1915; s. Chaim and Yetta (Friedman); in Isr since 1968; att U Czernowitz; MSW, Wayne State U, 1962; m. Leah Kessler; c: Yehudi. Psycht social worker, Kfar Tikvah, Kiryat Tivon, since 1969; fmr: tchr, Workmens Circle Sch, Bridgeport, Conn; tchr and prog asst, J Comty Cen, Detroit; sr psycht social worker, Psycht Clinic, Buffalo, 1963-68; field instr, Sch of Social Wfr, Buffalo State U. Author: Narzissen, 1937; Ovnt Baim Prut, 1942; A Pastuch in New York, 1951; Baim Prut, La Plata Un Yarden, 1966. Painting exhbs: Havana, Cuba, 1946; Ward Eggleston Gals, NY, 1948; J Artists Exhb, J Mus, NY, 1948, 1950; Intl Inst, Detroit, 1958; Anna L Werbe Gals, Detroit, 1960; annual exhb: Mich Artists, Detroit Inst of Art, 1960; Har Sinai Temple, Phila, 1960; Sisti Gals, Buffalo, 1965; Annual Western NY Exhbs, Albright Knox Art Gal, Buffalo, 1964-

1966. Mem: Natl Assn of Social Workers; club: Yiddish PEN, secy, 1948-50; Agudat Sofrei beIsrael. Recipient: Bimko poetry prize, Cong for J Culture, NY, 1967. Home: 3a Nuriot Kiryat Tivon, Isr.

WEINREB, Arye, Isr, physicist; b. Vienna, Aus, Aug 26, 1921; s. Jacob and Regine (Hojda); in Isr since 1938; att: Yeshivat B'nei Akiva, Kfar Haroeh, 1940-43; Mikveh Isr Agric Sch, 1938-40; MSc, Heb U, 1951, PhD, 1957; m. Fanny Mayer, Sep 3, 1950; c: Rachel, Ester, Yonina. Asso prof, experimental physics, Heb U, since 1967; research adv, Bar Ilan U; fmr: research asso, Argonne Natl Lab, Ill, 1958-61. Segen Mishne, IDF, since 1948. Chmn, Org of Rel Scis in Isr, 1964-66; adv, Keren Yaldenu; mem: AAAS; Isr Phys Soc. Contbr to profsl jours. Spec interests: rel educ, rel and sci. Home: 8 Shiler St, Jerusalem, Isr. Office: Heb U, Jerusalem, Isr.

WEINRONK, Jack, S Afr, business exec; b. Port Elizabeth, S Afr, July 16, 1915; s. Bernard and Sarah (Fisher); m. Sarah Farber, Aug 2, 1947; c: Brian, Jennifer, Eileen, Stanley. Dir: Weinronk's Furniture House Ltd, since 1945; Bluewater Bay Township Ltd, since 1947; Perfect Holdings Ltd, since 1947; Simax Estates Ltd, since 1948; Brisan Investments Ltd, since 1955; Vilink Investments; Jeback Investments. Capt, S Afr AF, WW II. Perm mem exec, ex-officio, S Afr J Bd of Deps, E province, chmn, 1960-62, exec since 1955; mem exec, Summerstrand Heb Cong, chmn, 1956, 1967, 1968. Recipient: award of merit, Royal Life Savings Soc. Spec interests: motorcycle racing; aviation, holder of civil pilot's, instructor's and gliding licences. Home: 8 Eleventh Ave, Summerstrand, Port Elizabeth, S Afr. Office: 42 Main St, Port Elizabeth, S Afr.

WEINRYB, Bernard, US, economist, educator; b. Turobin, Pol, May 15, 1901; s. Elazar and Toba (Kremer); in US since 1939; grad, J Theol Sem, Breslau, Ger, 1930; PhD, U Breslau, 1933; att, Columbia U, 1941-43; m. Doris Infield, 1942; c: Max, Joan, Ely. Prof, hist, econs, Dropsie Coll, since 1949, chmn, hist dept, since 1967, dir, research project, hist material and rabb lit, since 1959, dir, intergroup research project, 1957-59; fmr: libr, Breslau, 1931-33; ed staff, Ency Judaica, Berlin and Zurich, 1933-34; lectr, asst prof, schs of social work and econs, Pal, 1935-39; research asso, Mossad Bialik, Heb U, 1935-37; lectr, hist, Herzliah Tchrs Sem, 1940-41; dean, J Tchrs Sem, 1941-48, both NYC; lectr, Bklyn Coll, 1948-51; research cons: AJComm, 1949-50; Zionist Emergency Council, 1944-49; area spec, econs, US State Dept, 1951-55; lectr, Columbia U, 1950-56; prof, J hist, Yeshiva U Grad Sch, 1948-64. Fmr mem: commn on intl affairs, AJCong, 1957-62; publ comm, Amer J Hist Soc, 1959-63; mem: Amer Econ Assn; Natl Council for J Educ; ME Inst; AAUP; fmr mem, Vaad haKehilla, Jerusalem, 1937-39. Author: Studien zur Wirtschaftsgeschichte der Juden in Russland und Polen im 18 bis 19 Jahrhundert, 1933; Neueste Wirtschaftsgeschichte der Juden in Russland und Polen, 1934; Der Kampft um die Berufsumschichtung, 1936; Mechkarim beToldot haKalkalah behaChevrah shel Yehuday Polin, 1939; beReshith haSozialism haYedhudi, 1940; Jewish Emancipation Under Attack, 1942; The Yishuv in Palestine, 1947; Jewish Vocational Education, History of Training in Europe, 1948; Text and Studies in the Communal History of Polish Jewry, 1950; haDor haSheni beEretz Yisrael, 1954; The Beginning of East European Jewry, 1962; co-author: The Jews in the Soviet Satellites, 1953; ed: The Jewish Review, 1943-48; Catalogue of the Hebrew Manuscripts, J Theol Sem, Breslau, 1965; The Dropsie College Study of Jewish Textbooks, 1965; Jewish School Textbooks and Intergroup Relations, 1965; contbr to econ, hist, and learned publs. Home: 6036 N 13 St, Philadelphia, Pa. Office: Dropsie Coll, Broad & York Sts, Philadelphia, Pa.

WEINSHAL, Jacob, (Johann Bayer, Benjamin Doeg, I H Eytan, Dr Weill); Isr, physician, author; b. Tiflis, Caucasus, Nov 1, 1891; s. Ben Zion and Carolina (Landau); in Isr since 1922; att U Dorbat, Estonia; MD, U Basle, 1916; m. 1st; c: Arieh; m. 2nd, Amelia Okween, 1951. Pvt practice, med, electrotherapy, surgery. Phys, Russ Army, 1916-21. Head, haZohar Movement, Pal, 1925-28; mem: J Supr Leg Body, 1925-28; natl council; Tel Aviv city council; delg, J Cong, Jerusalem, 1937, 1951. Author: The Illegal, 1938; Hans Herzl, 1941; The Last Jew, 1944; Marko Baruch, 1946; The Legend of Onkelos, 1948; Giants in the Desert, 1952; In the Shadow of Titus' Arch, 1952; Jabo, 1955; The Blood on the Threshold, 1956; The Battle on the Menorah, 1957; Herodus, My Brother, 1960; haRishon beKovshei haHar, Ben-Josef, 1968; Irma, Pirkei Chaim shel Poresh Gadol, 1968; ed: leHasskala Zionit Academait, 1915; haTzafon, 1926-27; haChevrah, 1940-46;

contbr to periodicals, books. Recipient: awards for lit: Jabotinsky; B'nai B'rith; both 1969. Home and office: 106 Allenby Rd, Tel Aviv, Isr.

WEINSHEL, Edward M, US, psychiatrist; b. Milw, Wis, Aug 21, 1919; s. Michael and Ella (Berkowitz); BA, U Wis, 1941; MD, 1943; m. Anta Broseil, Aug 31, 1941; c: Julie, John. Training dir, Mt Zion Hosp, since 1966, chief, psycht, 1961-66; fmr: res, Wis Gen Hosp and Mendota VA Hosp, 1946-48; cons, J Comty for Personal Service, 1953-56. US Army, 1944-46. Ed bd, Jour of Amer Psychoanalytic Assn, 1966-69; mem: AMA; Amer Psychiatric Assn; N Cal Psychiatric Assn; SF Psychoanalytic Soc and Inst; Amer Psychoanalytic Assn; Cal and SF Co Med Socs; Phi Beta Kappa; Alpha Omega Alpha. Contbr to psychiatric jours. Home: 135 Presidio Ave, San Francisco, Cal. Office: 2380 Sutter St, San Francisco, Cal.

WEINSTEIN, Alexander, US, biologist, researcher, science hist; b Astrakhan, Russ, Nov 22, 1893; s. Henry and Helen (Mirski); in US since 1900; BS, Columbia U, 1913, AM, 1914, PhD, 1917; m Eva Wechsler, Nov 26, 1917; c: Alexandra Garcia-Bryce. Researcher, Commonwealth Fund grant, Harvard U, since 1951, research f, biol, 1951-54; fmr: asst zool, Columbia U, 1916-17; Sigma Xi research f, 1921-22, lectr, 1928; research grant, Amer Phil Soc, 1937-42; research asst, genet, Carnegie Inst of Wash, 1917-19; ed and stat work, Sci Press, 1920-21; Johnston scholar, Johns Hopkins U, 1922-23; NRC f, 1923-24, asso, zool hist of sci, 1930-36; Intl Educ Bd f, Cambridge U, 1924-25; asso, zool, U of Ill, 1926-27; prof, genet, U Minn, 1928-29; instr, physics, CCNY, 1942-49. F, AAAS; mem: Amer Soc Naturalists; Amer Soc Zool; Genet Soc of Amer; Amer Phys Soc; Hist of Sci Soc. Contbr: Heredity and Development, to Chemistry in Medicine, 1928; Ency of Social Scis; and to profsl and sci jours. Home: 41 Linnaean St, Cambridge, Mass. Office: Biol Labs, Harvard U, Cambridge, Mass

WEINSTEIN, Baruch Borris, Isr, public official, journalist; b. Balta, Russ, Sep 15, 1898; s. Shmuel and Batya; in Isr since 1924; ML, U of Laws, Odessa, Russ. Mem, presidium, Zionist Actions Comm, since 1946, fmr journalist, Russ, Berlin, and Pal-Isr; mem: cen comm, haChaver, Zion students org; gov body, Tzeirei Zion movement; delg, first all-Russ Zion Conf after Feb Revolution; inmate, Soviet Prison, for Zionist Activities, 1922-24. Mem, Provisional State Council of Isr, until 1949; co-found, Jours Org in Pal; fmr pres, Theodor Herzl lodge, B'nai B'rith; mem: Masons. Contbr to intl Zionist publs, in seven languages. Spec interest reading, writing, lit. Home: 20 Mane St, Tel Aviv, Isr. Office: 68 Ibn Gvirol St, Tel Aviv, Isr.

WEINSTEIN, David, US, linguist, educator; b. Boston, Mass, June 26, 1927; s. Herman and Fanny (Katzoff); BHL, Heb Tchrs Coll, 1950, MHL, 1953; MEd, Harvard U, 1952, DEd, 1956; m. Sandra Bargad, June 29, 1958; c: Noah. Pres, Coll of J Studies, since 1964, prof, lang educ, since 1964; cons, Lang Research Inst, Harvard U, 1954-63, asso in educ, 1961-63; prof, educ, and registrar, Heb Tchrs Coll, 1956-63. Cpl, US Army, 1945-47. Dir, Comty Youth Theater; vice-pres, Chgo chap, Rel Educ Assn, 1965-67; mem: AAUP; MLA; Amer Assn J Educs; Natl Conf J Educs; REA; Phi Delta Kappa. Author: Hebrew Through Pictures, 1954; First Steps in Reading Hebrew, 1955; Heb-Eng/Eng-Heb Pocket Dictionary, 1961; Modern Jewish Educational Thought, 1964; Essential Hebrew By Examples, 1964. Hobby: swimming. Home: 354 Seven Pines Circle, Highland Park, Ill. Office: 72 E 11 St, Chicago, Ill.

WEINSTEIN, Edwin A, US, psychiatrist, educator; b. NYC, Feb 18, 1909; s. Louis and Minnie (Fogel); BA, Dartmouth Coll, 1930; MD, Northwestern U, 1935; m. Lucy Strong, Apr 10, 1947; c: Lucy, Robert. Pvt practice, research, teaching, in neur and psychiatry, since 1942; cons: Walter Reed Army Inst of Research, since 1952; VA, since 1954; sr cons, Peace Corps, since 1966; attending neur, Mt Sinai Hosp, since 1947; prof, neur, Mt Sinai Sch of Med, since 1968; f, William Alanson White Inst of Psycht, since 1947. US Army, 1942-46. Mem: Amer Neur Assn; Amer Psycht Assn. Author: Cultural Aspects of Delusion: A Psychiatric Study of the Virgin Islands, 1961; co-author: Denial of Illness: Symbolic and Physiological Aspects, 1955. Recipient: Bronze Star. Home: 1200 Fifth Ave, New York, NY. Office: 1212 Fifth Ave, New York, NY.

WEINSTEIN, George, US, certified public accountant; b. NYC, Mar 20, 1924; s. Morris and Sara (Broder); BS, U of Ill, 1944; MBA, NYU, 1947; m. Shirley Greenberg, 1945; c: Stanley,

Jerrald, Sara. Partner, Morris J Weinstein, Groothius, & Co, NYC, since 1944; exec-secy, Illini Union Bldg Co, Champaigne, Ill, 1944; acctnt, Homes and Davis, 1944. Chmn bd: People's Inves's Corp; Brookside Mgmt Co; dir: SE Enterprises, Inc; Azalea Meats, Inc; Southland Provision Inc; and pres, Natl Diversified Inds, Inc. Chmn, bd, N Shore Heb Acad, since 1958; active in drives for UJA and HIAS; ambass, Yeshiva U; mem: Amer Inst Acctnts; NY Soc CPAs; Tau Delta Phi, fmr natl treas; clubs: Masons; Westmoreland; Presidents, U of Ill; Admirals; Ambassadors. Home: One Cow Lane, Kings Point, NY. Office: 501 Fifth Ave, New York, NY.

WEINSTEIN, Israel, US, physician, educator; b. NYC, May 26, 1893; s. David and Frieda (Chester); BA, CCNY, 1913; MA, Columbia U, 1915, MD, 1926, PhD, 1930; ScD, NYU, 1917. Ret since 1948; bact, lab of Dr William H Park, 1914; tchr, biol, NYC HSs, 1914-22; instr, phys, Columbia U Coll of Med, 1926-30; asst prof, bact and hygiene, NYU Med Coll, 1930-33, asst prof, preventive med, 1933-37; asst dir, Bur of Health Educ, NYC Health Dept, 1936-46; commnr of health, NYC, 1946-47. US Army, 1918-19, lt col, MC, 1942-46. F: NY Acad of Med; AMA; Amer Public Health Assn; dipl, Natl Bd of Med Examiners; mem: Phi Beta Kappa; Sigma Xi; Alpha Omega Alpha. Fmr, ed, Neighborhood Health, publ of NYC Health Dept, 1936-42; contbr to med jours. Recipient: Purple Heart, 1945; Bronze Star, 1945. Home: 55 Pierrepont St, Brooklyn, NY.

WEINSTEIN, Jack B, US, jurist, educator; b. Wichita, Kan, Aug 10, 1921; s. Harry and Bessie (Brodach); BA, Bklyn Coll, 1943; LLB, Columbia Law Sch, 1948; m. Evelyn Horowitz, Oct 21, 1946; c: Seth, Michael, Howard. US Dist Judge, E dist of NY, since 1967; adj prof, Columbia Law Sch, since 1967, fac mem since 1952, adv comm, Columbia Law Sch project on intl procedure, 1961-64; fmr: law clerk, Judge Stanley Fuld, NY Court of Appeals, 1949-50; pvt practice, 1950-52; spec counsel, NY Jt Leg comm, motor vehicle problems, 1952-54; counsel, State Senator Seymour Halpern, 1952-54; chmn, lay bd, Riverside Hosp for Adolescent Drug Users, 1954-56; reporter, cons, NY State temp comm on courts, 1955-58; reoprter, adv comm, NY State Sen Financial comm, 1957-61; mem, adv narcotics council, NYC, 1960-62; Nassau Co Atty, 1963-65; adv comm on evidence, US Judicial Conf, since 1969. USN, 1943-46, lt, res. Mem: AAUP. Assn Bar of NYC; NY State Bar Assn; Soc Public Tchrs of Law; comm on fed rules, Amer Bar Assn, since 1960; Temple Emanuel, Gt Neck, NY; FJP; ACLU, bd dirs, NY, 1957-63; AJCong. Author: revision, NY Vehicle and Traffic law, 1955; revision, NY Civil Practice, 1962; co-author: Cases and Materials on Evidence, 1947; Cases and Materials on Elements of Civil Litigation, 1962; New York Civil Practice, 9 vols, 1965; A Constitution for New York State, 1967; Manual of New York Practice, 1967. Home: 69 Station Rd, Great Neck, NY. Office US Courthouse, 225 Cadman Plaza E, Brooklyn, NY.

WEINSTEIN, Jacob, US, business exec; b. Phila, Pa, Oct 5, 1898; s. Abraham and Bertha (Daschel); m. Annette Schwartz, June 21, 1936; c: Shirley Koplik, Beatrice. Pres and gen mgr, Web-Jamestown Corp; pres: Web Machinery Co; Weinstein Co, all Jamestown, NY; treas, Vac Air Alloys; fmr: partner, Jamestown Furniture Cen; pres, Surplus and Salvage Co. Mem exec, and trustee, Temple Hesed Abraham; co-chmn, NCCJ; active in UJA; mem: Elks Masons, 32 deg; Shriners; YMCA; clubs: Rotary; Moonbrook Country. Hobbies: golf, fishing. Home: 125 Ellis Ave, Jamestown, NY. Office: 109 N Main St, Jamestown, NY.

WEINSTEIN, Jacob J, US, rabbi; b. Stephin, Russ-Pol, June 6, 1902; s. Benjamin and Shaindel (Weinstein); in US since 1907; BA, Reed Coll, 1923; att: New School for Social Research, 1923-24; rabbi, Heb Union Coll, 1929, DD, 1955; m. Janet Harris, Aug 10, 1931; c: Ruth, Daniel, Judith, Deborah. Rabbi em, KAM Temple, Chgo, since 1967, rabbi, 1939-67; fmr rabbi: Cong Beth Isr, Austin, Texas, 1929-30; Cong Shearith Isr, SF, 1930-32; dir: Sch for J Studies, NYC, 1932-35; Sch for J Studies, SF, 1939-35. Natl chmn, Natl Comm for Isr Lab, since 1959; pres: Hyde Park Council of Churches and Syns, 1948-50; Chgo Bd of Rabbis, 1947-49 mem: Pres Comm on Equal Employment Opportunity, since 1961; business ethics advisory comm, US comm, US Dept of Commerce, since 1961; mem: CCAR, pres, 1965-67; Chgo Bd of Rabbis; Poale Zion; B'nai B'rith; clubs: Standard; Covenant. Author: The Place of Understanding, 1959; contbr to Anglo-J press. Hobbies: nature study, mountain climbing. Recipient: awards: NCCJ; Mayor's Comm on Human Rights; Roosevelt Coll; Immigrant League Service; Histadrut; B'nai B'rith women's

auxiliary; elected to Lincoln Acad, 1967. Home: 1080 Francisco St, San Francisco, Cal.

WEINSTEIN, Laurence A, US, business exec: b. Madison, Wis, Dec 3, 1923; BBS, U Wis, 1945, LLB, 1947; m. Frances Lipton, May 25, 1945; c: Daniel, Miriam. Pres, Gen. Beverage Sales Co, since 1951, secy, 1947-51. Pres Temple Beth El, 1961-63; bd dirs, JWF, since 1951, pres, 1057-59, campaign chmn, 1953-54, co-chmn, gifts comm, 1952-53; co-chmn, State of Isr Bonds, 1952; pres, Wis Wine and Spirit Inst, 1959-61; vice-pres: wholesale comm, C of C; and bd mem, Wine and Spirit Wholesalers of Amer; bd dirs: Madison Family Service, 1959; UAHC; CJFWF; mem, Order of Coif. Home: 1134 Waban Hill, Madison, Wis, Office: Verona and McKee Rds, Madison, Wis.

WEINSTEIN, Lewis H, US, attorney, community leader; b Arany, Lith, Apr 10, 1905; s Jacob and Kuna (Romanow); in US since 1906; BA, magna cum laude, Harvard Coll, 1927, LLB, Harvard Law Sch, 1930; m Selma Yeslawsky, Sep 2, 1932; c: David, Louise. Partner, law firm, Foley, Hoag, and Eliot, since 1946; lectr, law, Harvard Law Sch, since 1960; sr visiting lectr, city planning, MIT, 1961-68; fmr: partner, Rome, Weinstein & Wolbarsht, 1930-45; asst corp counsel, Boston, 1934-45; gen counsel, Boston Housing Auth, 1938-45; cons, US Housing Auth, 1940-42; chmn, Mass State Emergency Housing commn, 1946-47; Housing Bd; Housing Council, both Mass State, 1948-52. Lt col, US Army, 1942-45, civil affairs off, gen staff, 1944; col, Judge Advocate Gens Corps, US Army Res, 1952-65; ret, 1965. Chmn, Amer J Conf on Soviet Jewry, since 1968; admn comm, J Comty Council, since 1947, pres, 1953-55; trustee, Heb Tchrs Coll, since 1947, pres, 1947-53; bd trustees, exec comm, Combined J Philanthropies, since 1950, life mem, pres, 1954-57; mem, exec comm, Gtr Boston Armed Forces adv comm, since 1949; chmn, 1956-58; bd dir: Bureau J Educ, since 1946; Assn US Army, Mass Bay chap; fmr: pres, Council of J Feds and Wfr Funds, 1965-65, life mem; chmn: Conf of Pres of Maj Amer J Orgs, 1963-65; Natl Comty Relations Adv Council, 1960-64, life mem: mem, exec comm, Pres Kennedy's and Pres Johnson's Comm Equal Opportunity in Housing; mem adv comm to Mass Depts Educ, Mh, Commerce and Devl; pres, Mass Mil Govt Assn; trustee: Beth Isr Hosp, Heb Rehab Cen for Aged; Temple Mishkan Tefla; f: Amer Assn J Educ; Amer Bar Found; Amer Coll Trial Lawyers; Brandeis U, and mem, bd overseers; Florence Heller Grad Sch; Lown Cen Contemporary J Studies; visiting comm, Harvard Bd Overseers; natl council, natl JWB and JDC; Comm 300, Amer J Tercentenary; mem, human rights and housing, urban devl comms, World Peace Through Law; mem, adv comm, Mass Dept Comty Affairs; natl bd dirs, NCCJ; exec council, Amer J Hist Soc; trustee, Boston Five Cents Savings Bank; mem: Amer, Mass, and Boston Bar Assns; Phi Beta Kappa; club, Harvard of Boston. Author: liberetto for operetta, So Let 'Em Foreclose; contbr to profsl periodicals. Recipient: Legion of Merit; Bronze Star; chevalier, Fr Legion of Honor; Croix de Guerre; mil medal, Pope Pius XII; natl citation, NCCJ, 1957. Spec interests: writing, music, theater, teaching. Home: 56 Varick Rd, Waban, Mass. Office: 10 Post Office Sq, Boston, Mass.

WEINSTEIN, Louis, US, physician, educator; b Bridgeport, Conn, Feb 26, 1909; s Harry and Minnie (Rubinstein); BS, Yale U, 1928, MS, 1930, PhD, 1931; MD, Boston U, 1943; m. Ethel Raport, Oct 7, 1934; c: Allen, Carol. Prof, med, Tufts U Sch of Med, since 1957; asso phys-in-chief, infectious disease service, NE Cen Hosp, since 1957; lectr, infectious disease, Harvard Med Sch, since 1950; asso phys, Mass Gen Hosp; asst prof, med, fac mem, Boston U, 1943-57. Mem: Mass Med Soc; AMA; Amer Fed for Clinical Research; Amer Soc for Clinical Inves; Assn of Amer Phys; Amer Acad of Arts and Scis; Amer Acad of Microbiol; Soc for Experimental Biol and Med; Amer Coll of Phys; Soc for Investigative Dermat; Sigma Xi; Alpha Phi Delta Epsilon. Author: The Therapeutic Application of Lactobacillus Acidophilus, 1936; The Practice of Infectious Disease, 1958; Streptomycin and Dihydrostreptomycin, in Med Ency, 1958; contbr to med jours. Hobby: music. Home: 26 Graylock Rd, Newtonville, Mass. Office: NE Center Hosp, 171 Harrison Ave, Boston, Mass.

WEINSTEIN, Pal, Hung, physician, educator; b Sátoralja Ujhely, Hung, Sep 5, 1906; s. Tóbiás and Rosalie (Braun); dipl, U Budapest Sch of Med, 1930; DSc, 1960; m. Ilona Kardos. Prof and chief ophthal, Med Postgrad Sch, U Budapest, since 1939; mem staff: eye clinic, U Budapest, 1930-36; sect of ophthal, Budapest Polyclinic, 1936-39. Ordinary mem,

Ophthal Soc, UK, since 1959; delg mem, Fr Ophthal Soc, since 1959; hon mem, Mex Ophthal Soc, since 1966; corresp mem, E Ger Ophthal Soc, since 1969; fmr pres, Hung sect, WJC. Author: Monograph on Glaucoma, in Eng, 1953; four books on ophthal; contbr to profsl jours. Hobby: collecting paintings. Home: Balassi, Bálint utca 9/11, Budapest, Hung,

WEINSTEIN, Roy, US, physicist, educator; b. NYC, Apr 21, 1927; s. Harry and Lillian (Ehrenberg); SB, MIT, 1951, PhD, 1954; m. Janet Spiller, Mar 20, 1954; c: Lee, Sara. Prof, physics, Northeastern U, since 1960; visiting physicist, Stanford U, 1966-67, cons, since 1967; mem, policy adv, Cambridge Electron Accelerator, Harvard U, since 1967; bd dirs, Ikor Inc, since 1965; asst prof: Brandeis U, 1954-56; MIT, 1956-59. USNR, 1945-46. Mem: Amer Phys Soc; Amer Assn Phys Tchrs; Masons; Sigma Xi Author: Nuclear Physics and Applications, 1963; contbr to profsl jours. Recipient: f, NSF, 1959-60, 1969-70. Home: 10 Daniels St, Lexington, Mass. Office: c/o Physics Dept, Stanford U, Stanford, Cal.

WEINSTEIN, Samuel J, US, certified public acctnt; b. Rum, Feb 6, 1908; s. Hyman and Malka (Kupershlac); in US since 1920; BA, U Buffalo, 1934; m. Sophie Schaffer, Mar 17, 1935; c: Erwin, Sandra. CPA since 1941; res partner, Roberts & Leinwander Co, 1935. Chmn, UJA, 1965; vice-pres, bd mem, United J Fed; chmn, Isr Bond Drive, 1955; treas, ZOA, 1953; bd mem: Buffalo ADL Exec Comm; Temple Emanuel, 1948; mem: NY State Soc of CPA's; Amer Inst of CPA's; B'nai B'rith; Masons; Odd Fellows; clubs: Montefiore; Westwood Country. Home: 25 Mardel Way, Buffalo NY.

WEINSTEIN, Sidney Moses, US, business exec; b. Portland, Me, Jan 30, 1917; s. Jacob and Kuna (Romanow); AB, cum laude, Harvard, 1939; MS, NYU, 1943, PhD, 1951; m. Ethel Blanck, Aug 25, 1940; c: David, Daniel, Michael. Vice-pres, Tanatex Chem Corp, since 1957; research chem, Apex Chem Co, 1940-44, research dir, 1944-52; pres, Chem-Plex Co, Inc, 1952-57. F, Amer Inst Chems; pres, JCC, Essex Co, NJ; vice-pres, United Comty Fund, Gtr Newark; trustee, Gtr Newark Urban Coalition; natl bd, ADA; bd overseers, Philip Lowe Inst Contemporary J Studies, Brandeis U; mem: Amer Chem Soc; Amer Assn Textile Chems and Colorists; AAAS; Temple Isr, Oranges and Maplewood; AJComm; Urban League, Sigma Xi, Phi Lambda Upsilon; fmr: pres, NJ "Y" camps; vice-pres, J Voc Service, Essex Co, 1963-66; club, Harvard, NY. Holder of US patent: Dying Synthetic Fibers with Alkyl Naphthalene Composition. Hobbies: tennis, reading. Home: 48 Rock Spring Rd, Orange, NJ. Office: Page and Schuyler Aves, Lyndhurst, NJ.

WEINSTEIN, Sol, US, author; b. Trenton, NJ, July 29, 1928; s. Samuel and Chai (Shmoorok); att NYU, 1946-49; m. Ellie Eisner, May 29, 1955; c: David, Judith. Author: Loxfinger; Matzohball; On the Secret Service of His Majesty, The Queen; You Only Live Until You Die; contbr to Playboy; moderator, radio progs. Home: 54 Rain Lily Rd, Levittown, Pa.

WEINSTEIN, Walter H, US, business exec; b. NYC, Jan 5, 1905; s Max and Bertha (Arbus); BSE, Wharton Sch of Finance and Commerce, 1924; m. Anita Fried, June 17, 1933; c: Suzanne. Treas, dir: Sirwein Realty Corp, 1928-61; Natl Chromium Corp, 1928-61; pres, Russeks Fifth Ave, 1950-57; fmr, vice-pres, dir: Ind Natl Bank and Trust; Continental Bank and Trust Co; spec asst, RFC, 2nd Fed res dist, 1934-37. Chmn, bd govs, Home and Hosp of Daughters of Jacob, since 1957; alternate trustee, FJP; mem: Sigma Alpha Mu; Masons. Home: 19 E 88 St, New York, NY Office: 1008 Fifth Ave, New York, NY.

WEINSTEIN, William Joseph, US, attorney; b. Detroit, Mich, Dec 9, 1917; s. Joseph and Bessie (Abramovitch); LLB, Wayne State U, 1940; m. Evelyn Ross, Apr 5, 1942; c: Patricia, Michael. Sr partner, Gussin, Weinstein, & Kroll, since 1965. Brig gen, USMCR, since 1941. Vice-pres, Cong B'nai David; dir, Detroit Bar Assn; chmn, negligence sect, Mich Bar Assn; natl vice-pres, USN League; f: US Coll Trial Lawyers; Intl Acad Trial Lawyers. Contbr to law jours. Recipient: Man-of-the-year, Isr Bonds, 1967. Home: 1300 Lafayette E, Detroit, Mich. Office: 1935 First Natl Bldg, Detroit, Mich.

WEINTRAUB, Claire C, US, civic worker; b. Miami, Fla, June 1, 1905; d. Isidor and Ida (Hirch) Cohen; AB, U Miami, 1928; hon DHumL, U Miami, 1959; m. Sydney Weintraub, Oct 16, 1928; c: Albert. Natl chmn, Volunteers Natl Easter

Seal Soc; exec comm, Fla Children's commn; bd, Crippled Children's Soc; Temple Isr Sisterhood; J Home for Aged; Goodwill Ind; chmn, Practical Nurse bd; pres: Dade Co Citizens Safety Council; Miami sect, Council of J Women, 1936; Fed of Women's Clubs, 1942; Visiting Nurse Assn, 1944; Health Council, 1945; fmr pres: Mus of Sci and Natural Hist; Fla State Crippled Children and Adults Soc; mem: Delta Phi Epsilon. Recipient: Outstanding Citizen award, B'nai B'rith, 1951; Outstanding Alumni, U Miami, 1955; Silver Medallion award, NCCJ. Home: 3030 Brickell Ave, Miami, Fla.

WEINTRAUB, Joseph, US, attorney, business exec; b. Waynesboro, Ga, Dec 10, 1904; s. Sigmond and Anne (Goodman); att: U of Va, 1922-25; NYU, 1925-26; m. Hortense Katz, Jan 27, 1929; c: Joanne, Michael. Head, law firm, Weintraub, Martin & Schwartz, since 1943; US mgr, Swiss Natl Ins Co, Basel; chmn bd: Pan Amer Bank of Miami; Amer Title Ins Co; Atico Financial Corp; S Atlantic Title Ins Co; Tex Title Guaranty Co; Commercial Mgmt Co; dir: Commercial Aseguradora, SA, Guat City; Columbia Title Ins Co; Real Estate Title Ins Co, both of Wash, DC; Continental Corp; Continental Ins Co; Fidelity & Casualty Co of NY; Niagara Ins Co; Seaboard Fire & Marine Ins Co; pres, Gibson Security Co. USCG, WW II. Fmr pres: Opera Guild, Miami; Miami-Dade C of C; Gtr Miami Traffic Assn; Dade Co Research Assn; dir: United Fund Dade Co; Miami Heart Inst; adv bd, Salvation Army; citizen's bd, U Miami; trustee, Cedar Leb Hosp; fmr trustee, Temple Isr; mem: Amer and Dade Co Bar Assns; Amer Judicature Soc; clubs: Westview Country; Rotary; Wall St; Marco Polo; Masons; Shriners; Elks. Recipient: award, U Miami bd trustees, 1962. Home: 1021 N Greenway Dr, Coral Gables, Fla. Office: POB 3131, 901 NE Second Ave, Miami, Fla.

WEINTRAUB, Lewis A, US, rabbi; b Uscilug, Pol, June 10, 1918; s. Meyer and Annie (Brenner); in US since 1938; BA, Yeshiva Coll, 1941; ordained rabbi, MHL, JTSA, 1944; m. Fannie Goldberg, June 17, 1951; c: Samuel, Fred, Rebeccah. Rabbi, Temple Isr, since 1955; acting rabbi, Temple Beth El, Fall River, 1944; asst rabbi, Beth Hamedrosh Hagodol, Denver, 1946-47; rabbi, Syn Emanu-El, Charleston, SC, 1947-55. Chaplain, Can Army, 1944-46. Pres: Wash region, RA, since 1968; Wash Bd Rabbis, 1962-64; exec council, JCC of Gtr Wash, since 1961; bd dirs: Louis D Brandeis Zionist dist; UJA of Gtr Wash; mem: jt commn on social action, RA-United Syn; J Reconstructionist Found; J Publ Soc Amer; Assn J Chaplains; JWB; Montgomery Co Human Relations commn, 1961-65. Home: 511 E Indian Spring Dr, Silver Spring, Md. Study: 420 University Blvd E, Silver Spring, Md.

WEINTRAUB, Richard, Isr, public official, editor, farmer; b. Krakow, Pol, July 24, 1903; s Yitzhak and Dina (Reisher); in Isr since 1946; m. Dora Alter; c: Ruth Klein. Mem: Histadrut Council; cen and political comms, Mapam, mgn ed, Bashaar, party bimonthly; mem: Histadrut Agric Council, 1933-60; cen salary comm, Histadrut, 1939-41; delg to WZC's, 1920, 1923. Brit Army, 1939-46. Fmr ed: Hashomer Hatzair, 1939-40; Chedim, 1961; Al Hamishmar, Mapam daily 1962-63; contbr to press. Recipient: Brit War medal, WW II. Home: Kibbutz Merhavia, Isr.

WEINTRAUB, Russell J, US, attorney, educator, author; b. NYC, Dec 20, 1929; s. Harry and Alice (Lieberman); BA, NYU, 1950; LLB, Harvard Law Sch, 1953; m. Zelda Kresshover, 1953; c: Sharon, Harry, Steven. Prof, law, U of Tex, since 1965; teaching f, Harvard Law Sch, 1955-57; prof, law, U of Ia, 1957-65. US Army, 1953-55. Bd dirs, Agudas Achim Syn, 1959-65; trustee, Sch of Rel, U of Ia, 1958-65; mem: commn on conflict of laws, Amer Assn of Law Schs; NY, Ia Bar Assns; AAUP; Phi Beta Kappa; Psi Chi; B'nai B'rith. Author: The Iowa Law of Workmen's Compensation, 1960; Contemporary Values and the Responsibility of the College, 1962; Cases and Materials on the Conflict of Laws, 1967; contbr to: Annual Supplements, Moore's Federal Practice, 1960, 1961; legal jours. Home: 7204 Sungate Dr, Austin, Tex. Office: U Tex Sch of Law, Austin, Tex.

WEINTRAUB, Ruth G, US, educational admnr, educator; b. NYC, Feb 15, 1909; d. Morris and Pessa (Noah) Goldstein; BA, Hunter Coll, 1929; JD, NYU, 1931; MA, Columbia U, 1932, PhD, 1939; m. Solomon Weintraub, Aug 26, 1930; c: Jonathan. Dean of social scis, Hunter Coll, since 1968, dir, grad studies in arts and scis, 1956-68, chmn, dept of political sci, 1956-60, fac mem since 1929; visiting prof, grad sch, NYU, 1948-49. Vice-pres: Academic Freedom comm, NYU, 1952;

metrop JWB, since 1960, chmn, personnel and training comm, natl JWB, 1958-62; dir, Citizenship Clearing House for Southern NY, 1957-62; mem, bd dirs, YM-YWHA, Bx, chmn, personnel comm; mem: ACLU; natl council, Amer Political Sci Assn, 1956-58, natl prog comm, 1959-60; exec comm, Coll-Fed Agcy Council, NY Civil Service region; leg comm, Citizens Union, 1942-60. Author: Government Corporation and State Law, 1939; How Secure These Rights, 1949; Administrative Questions and Political Answers, 1966; co-author: Goals for Political Science, 1951; contbr to political sci and educ jours. Home: 55 Central Park W, New York, NY. Office: Hunter Coll, 695 Park Ave, New York, NY.

WEINTRAUB, Sidney, US, economist, educator; b. NYC, Apr 28, 1914; s. Aaron and Martha (Fisch); BCS, NYU, 1935, PhD, 1941; att LSE, 1938-39, PhD, math 1968; m. Sheila Tarlow, Aug 25, 1940; c: Eliot, Arthur. Prof econ: U of Pa, since 1950; St John's U, 1946-50; econ: Inst Intl Finance, 1935-37; US Treas, 1941-42; Fed Res Bank of NY, 1942-43; cons: US Forest Service, 1957-58; Natl Council Applied Econ Research, India, 1964; Fed Power Commn, 1965-67; FCC, 1966-68; Amer specialist, US State Dept, 1968. US Army, 1943-46. Mem: Amer Econ Assn; Royal Econ Soc; Econometric Soc; AAUP; hon mem: Mark Twain Soc; Beta Gamma Sigma. Author: Price Theory, 1949; Income and Employment Analysis, 1951; Theory of Income Distribution, 1958; Forest Service Price and Appraisal Policies, 1958; A General Theory of the Price Level, 1959; Classical Keynesianism, Monetary Theory, and the Price Level, 1961; Wage Theory and Policy, 1963; Intermediate Price Theory, 1964; Employment Growth and Income Distribution, 1966; contbr to profsl jours. Recipient: Ford Found Research f, 1956-57. Home: 926 Morgan Ave, Drexel Hill, Pa. Office: U of Pa, Philadelphia, Pa.

WEINTRAUB, Sidney, US, diplomat; b. NYC, May 18, 1922; s. Reuben and Sarah (Litwin); BBA, CCNY, 1943; MA, BJ, U of Mo, 1948; MA, Yale U, 1958; PhD, Amer U, 1966; m. Gladys Katz, Aug 11, 1946; c: Jeffrey, Marcia, Deborah. Dep asst secy, intl finance and devl, US State Dept, Wash, DC, since 1969; with State Dept: Madagascar; Mexico City; Tokyo; Bangkok; Wash, DC, since 1949; city ed, Post-Herald, Beckley, W Va, 1948; econ counselor, dir, AID mission, Santiago, Chile, 1966-69. Staff sgt, US Army, 1943-46. Mem: Amer Econ Assn; Amer Fgn Service Assn; Beta Gamma Sigma; Sigma Delta Chi. Author: Trade Preferences to Less Developed Countries, 1966; mystery novels; contbr to econ and fgn affairs jours. Recipient: superior service award, US State Dept, 1964. Home: 5152 Linnean Terr, NW, Washington, DC. Office: US Dept of State, 2201 C St, NW, Washington, DC.

WEINTRAUB, Sydney E, US, surgeon; b. Taylor, Pa, May 16, 1908; s. Joseph and Rebecca (Karp); BS, U Pittsburgh, 1928; MD, Jefferson Med Coll, 1932; m. Hilda Branker, Dec 18, 1934; c: Linda, Neil. Asso surg in charge of vascular surg, proctology, Easton Hosp, since 1948, asst to chief surg, 1933-37, asst surg, 1938-48. Lt, US Army, MC, 1942-43. Found and f, Intl Acad of Proctology, 1948; pres: E Pa region, mem, exec council, United Syn of Amer, since 1946; J Comty Cen, 1940-42; Children of Abraham Cong, 1940-47; vice-pres, ZOA lodge, 1945; treas, UJA, 1938; bd mem, Comty Chest, 1941, all of Easton; chmn, social service, E Pa dist, B'nai B'rith, 1939-42, pres, Easton lodge, 1937-39. Mem: NY Acad of Scis. Ed, Amer Jour of Proctology, since 1948; contbr to profsl jours. Home: 3641 Timberlane Dr, Easton, Pa. Office: 1834 Washington Blvd, Easton, Pa.

WINTRAUB, Wiktor, US, educator, author; b. Zawiercie, Pol, Apr 10, 1908; s. Maurycy and Rebeka (Dobrzynski); in US since 1950; MA, U Cracow, 1929, PhD, 1930; hon, MA, Harvard U, 1954; m. Anna Tennenbaum, June 29, 1934 (decd). Prof, Slavic langs and lit, Harvard U, since 1959, fac mem since 1950; lit critic, Warsaw, 1934-37; Fr govt scholarship, Paris, 1937-39; press off, Pol Emb, Moscow, Kuibishev, 1941-42; ed, W Drodze, Jerusalem, 1943-45; staff mem, Pol, Min of Info, London, 1945; free-lance writer, London, 1945-50. Author: The Style of Jan Kochanowski, 1932; The Poetry of Adam Mickiewicz, 1954; Literature as Prophecy, 1959; asso ed, Harvard Slavic Studies, since 1953; co-ed, Orbis Scriptus, 1966. Mem: Pol Inst Arts and Scis in Amer; Pol Soc of Arts and Scis Abroad, London; MLA; Amer Assn of Teachers of Slavic and Eastern Eur Langs. Recipient: Guggenheim f, 1953. Home: 383 Broadway, Cambridge, Mass. Office: 171 Widener, Harvard U, Cambridge, Mass.

WEINTROUB, Benjamin, (pen name, Binim); US, editor, publisher, attorney; b. Odessa, Russ, Sep 4, 1891; s. David and Chai (Zukerman); in US since 1906; att Kan City Sch of Law, 1910-12; LLB, Chgo Kent Sch of Law, 1916; PhB, U Chgo, 1931; m. Ruth Malik, Aug 22, 1926; c: Dolly Anste, Laura Hollander. Ed and publisher, The Chgo J Forum, since 1942; gen mgr, The Chgo J Chronicle, 1922-41; fmr ed, The Decalogue Jour. Vice-pres, HIAS Chgo chap; exec secy, Amer J Hist Soc, Chgo chap; fmr pres and treas, The Decalogue Soc of Lawyers; clubs: City, bd govs; Covenant, bd dirs since 1952. Home: 1309 Ritchie Court, Chicago, Ill. Office: 179 W Washington St, Chicago, Ill.

WEINZWEIG, John J, Can, composer, educator; b. Toronto, Can, Mar 11, 1913; s. Joseph and Rose (Burshtyn); BMus, U Toronto, 1937; MMus, Eastman Sch of Music, U Rochester, 1938; hon DMus, U Ottawa, 1969; m. Helen Tenenbaum, July 19, 1940; c: Paul, Daniel. Prof, music, U Toronto, since 1952; tchr, music and composition, Royal Conservatory of Music, Toronto, 1939-60. RCAF, 1943-45. Found and pres, Can League of Composers, since 1951; mem, bd dirs: Composers, Authors, and Publishers Assn of Can; Can Music Cen; cultural comm, Can J Cong. Composer: Israel, cello sonata, 1949; Dance of Massadah, for baritone, 1951; Am Yisroel Chai, for mixed chorus, 1952; violin concerto, 1954; Wine of Peace, for soprano and orch, 1957; Red Ear of Corn, ballet; concerto for harp and chamber orch, 1967; Dummiya, for orch, 1969; string quartet; composed for: radio, films, Natl Film Bd of Can. Records: Columbia, Can Broadcasting Corp. Recipient: Olympic Silver medal, London, 1948; award, Can Council Sr Arts, 1968. Home: 107 Manor Rd, Toronto, Can. Office: Edward Johnson Bldg, U Toronto, Toronto, Can.

WEIS, Paul, Switz, international lawyer; b. Vienna, Aus, Mar 19, 1907; DJ, U Vienna, 1930; PhD, U London, 1954. Spec adv, UN High Commn for Refs, Geneva, since 1967, dir, legal div, 1961-67; fmr: ind, Vienna; mem: Vienna Lab Court; Arbitration Tribunal for Social Ins, 1930-38; legal secy, research dept, WJC, London, 1944-47; legal adv, Intl Ref Org, Geneva, 1951-61. Author: The Undermining of the Nationality Concept in German Law, 1943; Statelessness as a Legal-Political Problem, 1944; Protection Against Group Defamation, 1944; Nationality and Statelessness in International Law, 1956. Home: One rue du Vidollet, Geneva, Switz.

WEISBERG, Joseph Gotland, US, editor, publisher, attorney; b. Boston, Mass, June 10, 1911; s. Abraham and Sarah (Brin); AB, Harvard Coll, 1933, LLB, 1936; m. Marjorie Elbinger, May 7, 1939; c: Lawrence, Helaine. Co-publ, exec ed, J Advocate, since 1948; asso ed, 1941-52; law partner, Brin & Weisberg, 1936-41. Vice-pres; Temple Isr, Boston; Pres Council of Brandeis U; mem: natl council, JDC; exec council, Amer J Hist Soc; exec comm, Asso Syns of Gtr Boston; trustee, Combined J Philanthropies, Gtr Boston; mem: Mass Bd of Educ; Gov's Comm on Youth Fitness; Mass Educ Communications Commn; Boston and Fed Bar Assns; Amer-J Press Assn, fmr pres; NE Press Assn; Natl Assn State Bds Educ; Alpha Mu Sigma; clubs: Overseas Press; Harvard; Belmont Country, Gtr Boston Brandeis, vice-pres. Contbr to publs. Hobby: golf. Home: 39 Chatham St, Brookline, Mass. Office: 251 Causeway St, Boston, Mass.

WEISBERGER, Isarel, US, educator; b. Poughkeepsie, NY, Jan 27, 1909; s. Benjamin and Pearl (Singer); dipl, U Paris, Fr, 1932; BA, MEd, CCNY, 1935; DEd, Grad Sch of Educ, Yeshiva U, 1961; m. Tobi Schnur, June 2, 1936; c: Avram, Penny Sclair. Dist cons, J Educ Comm of NY, since 1947; cons: Conservative Syn Schs, Queenn, NY; Akiba Heb Acad, Bx; fmr chmn, J Educ Comm Staff Org, repr, to NY Co-ord Comm of Jews, Protestants, and Roman Catholics for Released Time; dir, USO-JWB, Natl Wfr Bd, 1942-45, admn asst, Natl J Wfr Bd, 1945-47. Civilian chaplain, J Wfr Bd, WW II. Mem: bd, J Tchrs Retirement Assn; exec comm, Educators Council, JNF; Natl Council of J Educ; bd, Yeshiva R M Soloveichik; bd, Cong Mt Sinai Anshe Emes. Author: Siddur Katon, 1948; contbr to J educ jours. Home: 95 Cabrini Blvd, New York, NY. Office: 246 W 58 St, New York, NY.

WEISEL, Alfred, US, educational exec; b. Rum, July 27, 1920; s. Nathan and Gussie (Moldovan); BA, Yeshiva Coll, 1942; tchrs dipl, Heb Tchrs Inst, 1943; MA, NYU, 1948; att Dropsie Coll, 1949-52, 1957-58; m. Helen Hersh, Jan 1, 1949; c: Aviva, David, Ilana, Hillel. Educ dir, Emanuel Syn, since 1952; field dir and leader, Young Judea; tchr, Mt Eden Cen, 1942-46, both Bx; prin, Temple Emanuel, Paterson, NJ, 1946-52. Mem: natl exec council, Educators Assembly, chmn, nominations comm, pres, 1959-61, pres, Conn region, 1955-57; steering comm, Natl Youth Commn of United Syns, chmn, publ comm; Natl Council for J Educ; elementary sch princ dept, Natl Educators Assembly; Gtr Hartford Conservative Syn, pres, educ council, 1956-58; Zionist Youth Commn, Hartford, chmn, 1953-57; Conn Youth Commn, chmn, 1963-65; ZOA. Contbr to jours and press. Hobbies: painting, drawing. Home: 18 Tecumseh Rd, W Hartford, Conn. Office: 160 Mohegan Dr, W Hartford, Conn.

WEISENFELD, Shirley, US, physician; b. NYC, Oct 31, 1923; d. Benjamin and Amelia (Stempel); BA, summa cum laude, NYU, 1943; MD, Coll of Med, 1946; m. Stanley Slater, May 23, 1951; c: Leonard, Michael. Att phys and research asso, dept of med, J Hosp and Med Cen of Bklyn, since 1968; asso dir, 1964-68, staff mem, since 1961; att phys, State U Hosp, dept of med, since 1967; asst prof, med, SUNY Downstate Med Cen, Bklyn, since 1962; fac mem since 1957; asso phys, chief of isotope unit, J Chronic Disease Hosp, Bklyn, since 1957, on staff since 1954. Mem, bd dirs, Blue Feather auxiliary, Asso for Help of Retarded Children, since 1964; mem: AAAS; Worcester Found for Experimental Biol; Intl Platform Assn; Research Soc of SUNY; NY State and Kings Co Med Socs; AMA; NY Diabetes Assn; Endocrine Soc; Amer Diabetes Assn; Amer Fed for Clinical Research; Mamonides Hosp, Bklyn, 1950-51; Sloan-Kettering Inst, NY, 1951-52. Phi Sigma Sigma; Phi Beta Kappa. Contbr: chap in book, Clinical Diabetes Mellitus, 1962; to med jours. Recipient: research fs, endocrinology, Hobby: travel. Home: 945 E 10 St, Brooklyn, NY. Office: 555 Prospect Pl, Brooklyn, NY.

WEISER, Louis Leon, US, business exec; b. NYC, Mar 22, 1918; s. Joseph and Elizabeth (Geltner); BA, Bklyn Coll, 1939; m. Anita Kovarsky, June 5, 1943; c: Ronnie, Roberta. Exec vice-pres, Knickerbocker Travel, since 1965; pres, Council Vacation Service, since 1967; exec vice-pres, Natl Conf of Shomrim Socs, pres, 1963-64; Lt of detectives, NYC Police dept, 1961-65, asst commn of inves, 1964-65. Secy, Shomrim Soc, NYC Police dept, pres, 1954-55; 1st vice-pres, Council of J Orgs in Civil Service; pres, Munic lodge, B'nai B'rith 1964-65. Home: 119-14 231 St, Cambria Hgts, NY. Office: 1212 Sixth Ave, New York, NY.

WEISFOGEL, Israel, US, rabbi; b. London, Eng, Aug 18, 1917; s. Barnett and Rose (Singer); in US since 1940; ordained rabbi, Mir Yeshiva, Pol, 1940; MA, Trinity Coll, Comm, 1957; m. Bella Kranzler, Nov 31, 1943; c: Gerald, Rhoda, Deborah. Rabbi, Cong Kodimoh, since 1959; chaplains: State Sch for Retarded, since 1964; Amer Intl Coll; Springfield Coll, both since 1968; exec dir, Mirrer Yeshiva, NY, 1940-51; rabbi, Cong Beth Isr, Wallingford, Conn, 1951-59. USAAC, 1942-43. Vice-pres: RabCA; Vaad Harabonum of Mass; chaplian, first reg, JWV; mem: personnel adv bd, City of Springfield; RabCA Delg to Russ, 1965; delg, Eur Conf of Rabbis, London, 1965; fmr pres, Rabb Council of Conn, 1957-59. Ed: RabCA Manial of Holiday Sermons, 1967. Home: 23 Spruceland Ave, Springfield, Mass. Study: 124 Sumner Ave, Springfield, Mass.

WEISGAL, Meyer W, Isr, communal leader; b. Kilol, Pol, Nov 10, 1894; s. Solomon and Lea (Friedman); in US since 1905; in Isr since 1949; att Columbia U ext courses: m. Shirley Hirshfeld, June 10, 1923; c: Emanuel, Helen, David. Chancellor, Weizmann Inst of Sci, since 1970, pres, 1966-69, chmn, exec council, 1949-66; was closely affiliated with first pres of Isr, Dr Chaim Weizmann, was his personal political repr in US; org, Amer comm for Weizmann Inst, exec vice-chmn since 1947; chmn bd, Yad Chaim Weizmann natl memorial, since 1952; natl secy, ZOA, US, 1921-30; org, secy gen, Amer sect, JA for Pal, 1943-46; vice-pres, Amer Financial and Devl Corp for Isr, 1951; chmn, World comm for Isr 10th anniversary celebrations, 1958-59. Ed: The Maccabean, 1918-21; The New Palestine, 1921-30; Bialik's Poems, 1926; Herzl Memorial Book, 1929; The J Standard, Toronto, 1930-32; Chaim Weizmann: Statesman, Scientist, Builder of the Jewish Commonwealth, 1944; Chaim Weizmann, A Biography by Many Hands, 1962. Theatrical producer: Romance of a People, 1933; The Eternal Road, 1936; dir gen, Pal Pavilion, NY Worlds Fair, 1939-40. Home: Neve Weizmann, Rehovot, Isr. Office: Weizmann Inst of Sci, Rehovot, Isr.

WEISGALL, Hugo David, US, composer, conductor; educator; b. Ivancice, Aus-Hung, Oct 13, 1912; s. Adolph and Aranka (Stricker); in US since 1920; att: Peabody Conservatory, 1927-30; Curtis Inst, 1936-39; studied composition with Roger Sessions, 1934-41; PhD, Johns Hopkins U, 1940; m. Nathalie

Shulman, Dec 28, 1942; c: Deborah, Jonathan. Chmn, fac, Cantors Inst, JTSA, NYC, since 1952; fac mem, Juilliard Sch of Music, since 1957; prof, Queens Coll, since 1960; fmr conductor: Har Sinai Temple Choir, 1931-42; "Y" Alliance Orch, 1935-42; String Sym, Baltimore, 1936-38; natl Youth Admn Orch, Baltimore, 1940-41; guest conductor; London Sym Orch, 1943-45; London Philharmonic Orch, 1944; BBC Sym Orch, 1944; Orchestre de la Chapelle Musicale de la Reine Elisabeth, 1945, 1946, Radio Natl Belge, both in Belgium; instr, composition, Cumington Sch of Arts, Mass, 1948-50; dir: Inst of Musical Arts, Baltimore, 1949; Hilltop Musical Co, Baltimore, 1951-56; lectr, music, Johns Hopkins U, 1952-56; conductor, Chizuk Amuno Choir and Chorus, Baltimore, 1958-59; dist visiting prof, music, Pa State, U, 1959-60; composer in res, Amer Acad, Rome, 1966-67. US Army, 1942-46; asst mil attaché, govts-in-exile, 1945-46; cultural attaché, Amer Emb, Prague, 1946-47. Pres, Amer Music Cen, since 1963; asst, Lincoln Cen Fund, since 1965; mem: ASCAP, Phi Beta Kappa. Composer: operas: The Tenor, 1951; The Stronger, 1952; Six Characters in Search of an Author, 1957; Purgatory, 1958; Athaliah, 1962; Nine Rivers from Jordan, 1968; ballets: Quest, 1937; One Thing is Certain, 1939; Outpost, 1947; Hymn for chorus and orch, 1941; Overture, Amer Comedy, 1942; Soldier Songs, 1944-45; A Garden Eastward, cantata After Moses Ibn Ezra, 1952. Recipient: Bearns prize, Columbia U, 1931; travelling f, Curtis Inst, 1938; Ditson f, Columbia U, 1944; award, Amer Inst Arts and Letters, 1954; Guggenheim fs, 1956, 1961, 1966; Ford commn; Koussevitzky commn; decoration, Order of White Lion. Home: 81 Maple Dr, Great Neck, NY. Office: 3080 Broadway, New York, NY.

WEISL, Wolfgang Zeev von, Isr, physician, author; b. Vienna, Aus, Mar 27, 1896; s. Ernst and Charlotte (Popper-Michlup); in Isr since 1922; MD, med fac, U Vienna, 1921; att Law Sch, U Vienna, 1922-23; m. Noemi Zuckermann, June 8, 1927; c: Dan, Elda Karassikoff, Eliana Rubin, Amarel. Owner, Parksanatorium, Gedera, since 1940; corresp, Wiener Zeitung, since 1967; corresp, Vossische Zeitung, Neue Freie Presse, 1924-32; chief phys: Sanatorium Wilhelmshöhe, Kassel, 1929-31; dietetic dept, Sanatorium Purkersdorf, Aus, 1933-37. Artillery off, IDF; historian for Isr artillery. Co-found, Revisionist Party, 1924, pres, 1930-31, 1943-44; mem, presidium, New Zionist World Org, 1937-40; vice-grand master, B'nai B'rith, Isr, 1948-59; dir, Eur bur, Gen Zionist World Confd, Paris, 1957-58; mem: Va'ad Leumi, 1925-31; WJC, 1955-59. Author: Kampf ums Heillige Land, 1925; Zwischen Teufel und Rotem Meer, 1927; 92 Days Prison and Hunger Strike, 1946; Allah and Albion, 1947; co-author: Allah ist Gross, 1934; Gerson's Diet-Therapie der Lungentuberkulose. Contbr to med, mil, J jours. Home and office: Parksanatorium, Gedera, Isr.

WEISMAN, Abner Irving, US, physician, educator; b. NYC, Jan 4, 1909; s. Samuel and Celia (Siegel); BA, NYU, 1928; MD, NY Med Coll, 1932; m. Martha Behrman, Aug 26, 1950; c: Martha, Henry, Raymond, Bonita, Celia. Clinical prof, obstet and gyn, NY Med Coll, since 1959; pvt practice, obstet and gyn, since 1933; att obstet, gyn; Flower-Fifth Ave Hosp, since 1956; J Memorial Hosp, since 1949; fmr asst surg, US-PHS, 1944-46. Pres, Weisman Mus Ancient Med of the Amers; mem: AMA; Amer Coll Surgs; NY Acad Med; Amer Coll Obstet and Gyn; NY Co Med Soc. Author: You Can Have a Baby, 1942; Spermatozoa and Sterility, 1942; contbr to profsl jours. Spec interests: archaeol, philately, Americana, Lincolniana. Home: 162 E 95 St, New York, NY. Office: 133 E 73 St, New York, NY.

WEISMAN, Gertrude, US, civic worker; b. St Louis, Mo, Mar 24, 1897; d. Louis and Sadie (Saks) Birenbaum; att Epstein Music Conservatory, St. Louis; m. Hyman Weisman, Dec 24, 1916; c: Alan. Active in volunteer wfr work since 1917; natl pres, B'nai B'rith Women's Supr Council, 1949-51, pres: dist Grand Lodge, 1944-45, Mo State Assn, 1939-40, Mo chap, 1934-37, secy, 1934-47; pres, J Child Wfr Agcy, 1951-52, mem bd, 1943-50, 1953; J Children's Home, Inc, 1953-55, hon life exec secy since 1918, secy since 1920; J Child Wfr Assn, 1956-57; dir, St Louis J Fed, repr to natl bd, Natl Found for Infantile Paralysis; non-govt liaison off to UN, 1949-51; mem: bd trustees, Natl J Hosp, Denver, Colo since 1949; exec bd, hon vice-pres, Leo N Levi Hosp, Hot Springs, Ark, since 1949; natl adv comm, VA; Atty Gen's Citizenship Comm, both 1949-51; Mo State Adv comm, Natl Found for Infantile Paralysis; mem, speakers bur; Civil Defense Appeal; ARC; War Chest; Comty Chest; mem: Mo Wfr Agcy; United Heb Temple; United Order of True Sisters; Order of Eastern

Star, matron, St Louis chap, 1932, grand repr, 1942-45; Amer Legion; regional chmn, In-camp and Hosp Work, WW II; organized scholarship fund for students. Recipient: Amer Legion State Dept highest award for child wfr work, 1939; citations from govt and pvt agcys for war work. Home: 7539 Cromwell Dr, Clayton, Mo.

WEISMAN, Jacob I, US, physician; b. Chelsea, Mass, Mar 4, 1907; s. Joseph and Minnie (Bortman); BA, cum laude, Harvard U, 1928; MD, cum laude, Boston U Sch of Med, 1932; m. Doris Feeney, Sep 1, 1933; c: Sandra, Marilyn. Phys in chief, Springfield Hosp, since 1957, internist, 1943-51, card, 1953-57, dir, cardio-vascular sect, dept of med, 1957-68; att phys and card, Munic Hosp, 1951; sr phys, Essex Co TB Sanatorium, 1932-34; pvt practice, 1936-41. Capt, US Army, MC, 1941-43. F, Amer Coll of Card; asso f, Amer Coll of Phys; pres, co-found, W chap, Mass Heart Assn; mem: Amer Trudeau Soc; Amer Diabetic Soc; AHA; Masons; Shriners; B'nai B'rith; Amer Vets Comm; clubs: Maimonides Med; Pavlo Med. Contbr to profsl jours. Home: 147 Wheelmeadow Dr, Longmeadow, Mass. Office: 151 Maple St, Springfield, Mass.

WEISMAN, Joseph, US, artist, teacher; b. Schenectady, NY, Feb 17, 1907; s. Solomon and Lena (Goldberg); att: Chouinard Sch of Art, 1927-31; LA Art Cen Sch, 1932-33; m. Eva Bober, Dec 24, 1930 (div, 1965); c: David, Daniel. Art instr, LA City Bd of Educ, since 1954; art ed, Pan Mag, Pasadena, 1940-41; tech illus, Douglas Aircraft Co, 1942-44; matte shot artist, MGM studios, 1944-46; scenic artist: 1946-51; 20th Cent Fox, 1951-52. Exhbs: LA Co Mus, Pasadena Mus, Santa Barbara Mus, San Diego Mus, Oakland Art Gal, SF World's Fair, Art Inst of Dayton, Pa Fine Arts Acad. Mem: Artists Equity Assn. Recipient: Civitan medal, for art editing, 1927; 1st prize, for portrait painting, Cal State Fair, 1940; 2nd prize, for prints, Westwood Village Art Assn, 1952. Hobbies: hiking, philately. Home and studio: 3229 Larissa Dr, Los Angeles, Cal.

WEISMAN, Milton C, US, attorney; b. NYC, Art 11, 1895; s. Karl and Rebecca (Hornstein); att; Syracuse U; LLB, Fordham Law Sch; m. Helen Gray, June 29, 1920; c: Margaret Rice, Patricia Taylor. Partner, law firm, Weisman, Celler, Allan, Spett, & Sheinberg; dir: Fedders Corp; Trans-Lux Corp; Kinney Natl Service Corp; NY, Susquehanna & Western RR. Trustee, FJP, NY; chmn, exec comm, Home and Hosp of Daughters of Jacob; mem: Amer Bar Assn; NY Co Assn; clubs: Cavendish; Private Lanes. Home: 575 Park Ave New York, NY. Office: 1501 Broadway, New York, NY.

WEISMAN, Seymour S, US, organization exec; b. NYC, Apr 27, 1919; s. Alex and Rose (Silbermintz); BSS, CCNY, 1939; MSW, NY Sch of Social Work, Columbia U, 1946; PhD, NYU, 1958; m. Betty Scott, Sep 4, 1952; c: Julie, Scott. Exec secy, CCNY Alumni Assn, since 1956, program cons, JWV, since 1956, asst natl exec dir, 1950-56. US Army, 1942-46. F, Amer Sociol Assn; mem: bd dirs, JWB; Amer Public Admn Soc; Amer J Comty Relations Workers. Author: Case Study of a Flood Stricken City, 1958. Recipient: Bronze Star; Purple Heart; award, Amer Heritage Found, 1952. Home: 3 Shadow Lane, Norwalk, Conn. Office: Alumni Assn of CCNY, Finley Study Cen, New York, NY.

WEISMANN, Walter W, US, business exec; b. NYC, Aug 11, 1891; s. Abraham and Minnie (Kirschner); grad: Cooper Union, 1915; NYU, 1919; m. Dorothy Altermann, 1920; c: Marjorie Zeidman, Florence Weinberg, Helen Weinberg. Chmn, bd dirs: Aetna Ind Corp, NYC, since 1942; Trimont Mfg Co, Mass, since 1940; Oscar Heineman Corp, Chgo, since 1945; Champlain Spinners Inc, Whitehall, NY, since 1951; Modern Globe Inc, Mich, since 1952; Kaynee Co, O, since 1952; DeLuxe for Boys Inc, NYC, since 1954; Graton and Knight, Mass, since 1956; Eisendrath Glove Co, Wis, since 1957; W F Dougherty & Sons, Phila, since 1959; F H Hill Co, Cleveland, since 1959; dir, L H Shingle Co, Camden, since 1956; pres, William Bayley Co, since 1964; dir, Trans-Lux Corp, since 1967. Natl vice-pres, UAHC, since 1968; hon chmn, Cong Rodeph Shalom, since 1967, pres, 1949-67, bd trustees since 1949; bd dirs, Beth Isr Hosp, since 1944; bd trustees, United Home for Aged Hebrews, New Rochelle, since 1958; chmn, Gtr NY combined campaign, UAHC-HUCR-JIR, 1952; vice-pres, NY Fed of Reform Syns; asso treas, UAHC, 1961-62; clubs: Bayshore Yacht; Harmonie, NYC; Standard, Atlanta; Grand St Boys. Recipient: man-of-the-year, Amer Reform Judaism, 1955. Home:

880 Fifth Ave, New York, NY. Office: 565 Fifth Ave, New York, NY.

WEISS, Aaron, US, attorney, librarian; b. Bklyn, NY, Dec 29, 1906; s. Benjamin and Anna (Kessler); att, NYU, 1926-27; Bklyn Law School, 1928-31; m. Evelyn Meyers, July 26, 1940. Chief law asst, Civil Court of NYC, since 1968, prin law libr, 1961-68; pvt law practice, 1932-46; prin law libr, City Court, NYC, 1946-61. Sgt, US Army, 1943-45. Judge advocate, Bklyn council, Kings Co, VFW, 1946-47, chmn, resolutions comm, 1946-59, mem, Flatbush Memorial Post; mem: NY Co Lawyers Assn; Law Libr Assn of Gtr NY. Home: 50 Lenox Rd, Brooklyn, NY. Office: Civil Court of the City of NY, 111 Centre St, New Yorkk, NY.

WEISS, Abraham, Isr, educator, rabbi; b. Podhajce, Galicia, Mar 23, 1895; s. Berl and Sarah (Geller); in Isr since 1964; ordained rabbi, Rabb Sem Vienna, 1921; PhD, U Vienna, 1921; hon DHL, Yeshiva U, NY, 1967; m. Perl Kramer, Sep 3, 1933; c: Moshe, Cypora, Benjamin. Prof, Talmud and Rabbinics, Bar Ilan U, since 1928; rector, Inst for Sci J Studies, Warsaw, 1936-38. Vice-pres: Polish Mizrachi; KH, both 1933-39; mem: World Zionist Action comm of JA, 1935-46; First Judenraat,Warsaw,1939-40; Acad of J Research; club: PEN. Author: On The History of the Development of the Babylonian Talmud, 1929; Literary Development of the Babylonian Talmud, Vols, I, II, 1937-39; The Development of the Talmud as a Literary Unit, 1943; The Talmud in its Development, 1954; Court Procedure, 1956; Studies in the Literature of the Amoraim, 1962; Studies in the Law of the Talmud on Damages, 1966; entbr to Heb and scholarly publs. Home: 29 Ben Maimon St, Jerusalem, Isr. Office: Bar Ilan U, Ramat Gan, Isr.

WEISS, Alfred, Isr, radiologist, physician; b. Bolechow, Pol, Mar 27, 1914; s. Shmuel and Jeanette; in Isr since 1948; att med sch, U Zurich, 1931-34; MD, med sch, U Milan, 1937; m. Eugenia Rabinowicz; c: Shalom, Sarah. Sr lectr, Tel Aviv U Med Sch, since 1968; head, x-ray dept, Beilinson Hosp, since 1969, asst dir, 1948-60; head x-ray dept, haSharon Hosp, 1960-68. Mem, sci comm, Isr Radiological Soc. Contbr to profsl jours. Spec interest: mammography. Hobby: music, piano. Home: 19 Hagalili St, Ramat Gan, Isr. Office: Beilinson Hosp, Petach Tikva, Isr.

WEISS, Alvin L, US, attorney; b. Pottstown, Pa, July 19, 1926; s. Thomas and Jennie (Klein); AB, Ursinus Coll, 1949; LLB, Columbia U Law Sch, 1952. Partner, law firm, O'Donnell, Weiss, Mattei, Scuhoza & Henry, since 1955; asso, Rutter, O'Donnell Mauger, 1952-55. US Army, 1944-46. Pres, E Pa region, United Syns, since 1968, vice-pres, 1962-68; bd dirs: Pottstown Public Libr, since 1958; Mongomery Bar Assn, since 1958; Cong of Mercy and Truth, since 1952, pres, 1958-62; Pottstown J Fed, since 1958, chmn, 1956-58; mem: Pa Bar Assn. Home: 259 Chestnut St, Pottstown, Pa. Office: 41 High St, Pottstown, Pa.

WEISS, Benjamin, US, business exec; b. Chgo, Ill, Mar 31, 1910; s. Elias and Bertha (Kronenvirth); m. Helen Moskovitz, Aug 1, 1937; c: Calvin, Daniel. Owner Machinery Liquidating Co, since 1946; vice-pres, Ind Rental Service Inc, since 1946; fmr: shop supt, Interstate Machine Co, 1929-34; partner, Herben Machine Co, 1934-37; sales mgr, Harvey Goldman & Co, 1937-39. Mem, bd trustees: Detroit League for the Handicapped, since 1958; Unied Heb Schs of Detroit, since 1954; Blind Service Cen, metrop Detroit, since 1960; exec bd, Detroit chap, Archives of Amer Art; bd mem: Machinery Dealers Natl Assn, since 1947, pres, 1955-56; Cong B'nai Moshe, Oak Park, since 1950, pres, 1956-57; Natl Fed J Men's Clubs, since 1956, pres, Gt Lakes region, 1956-57; chmn, mem, Zionist Org, Detroit, 1947-48; chmn, Unied Heb Schs Transp comm, 1967-69; bd overseers, JTSA, 1968; mem: B'nai B'rith; ZOA; Gt Detroit Bd of Commerce; Detroit Hist Soc; club, men's, Cong B'nai Moshe, pres, 1952-53. Recipient: award, JTSA, 1954. Home: 18660 Pennington Dr, Detroit, Mich. Office: 3920 23 St, Detroit, Mich.

WEISS, Charles, US, bacteriologist, educator; b. Brzesko, Pol, Oct 18, 1894; s. Solomon and Fannie (Seelengut); in US since 1905; BS, CCNY, 1915; MS, NYU, 1916; PhD, U of Pa, 1924, MD, 1924; m. Dorothy Wilkes, Aug 1, 1920; c: Margery, Dottie, Charles Jr. Ret, 1959; cons, since 1959; asso, experimental biochem, Research Inst for Cutaneous Med, Phila, 1919-23; f, mem, NRC, Columbia U, 1925-26; asst prof, bact, sch of tropical med, 1926-28; dir, lab, Presbyterian Hosp, San Juan, Puerto Rico, 1926-28; asso prof, applied bact and immunology, Wash U Med Sch, St Louis, 1928-32; asso prof, research med, Hooper Found, U Cal, 1932-44; dir, clinical and research lab, Mt Zion Hosp, SF, 1932-44; dir, lab, J Hosp, Phila, 1944-50; head, dept of microbiol, N Div, Albert Einstein Med Cen, 1950-59. F: NY Acad of Scis; Amer Soc Clinical Paths; Amer Coll Paths; AAAS; dipl, clinical path, clinical microbiol, Amer Bd Path; pres: SF dist, ZOA; Dorshe Daath, 1952-54; mem: Amer Assn Immunologists; Phila Co Med Soc; Soc Amer Bacts; Soc Experimental Biol and Med; Amer Assn Experimental Path; Sigma Xi. Contbr to med jours; J Social Studies. Recipient: research grants from: AEC; NIH; Commonwealth Fund; Natl TB Assn; AMA; Columbia Found; Sigma Xi; Memorial Found J Culture. Spec interest: sci research on circumcision, funded by grants. Home: 412 W Mt Airy Ave, Philadelphia, Pa.

WEISS, David, Can, social worker; b. NYC, Nov 4, 1914; s. Phillip and Sarah (Cohen); in Can since 1947; BSS, CCNY, 1937; dipl, social work, NY Sch of Social Work, Columbia U, 1940; m. Raye Acker, Sep 18, 1938; c: Harriet, Jay. Exec dir, Baron de Hirsch Inst, J Child Wfr Bur, since 1947; spec lectr, Ottawa Sch of Social Work, St Partick's Coll, since 1960; commentator, moderator, Forum TV prog, Channel 12, since 1961; lectr: Buffalo Sch of Social Work, 1946; McGill U Sch of Social Work, 1952-60; admn asst, YMHA's, NYC, 1936-38, dir, clubs, ext activities, East NY, 1938-40; caseworker, J Family Wfr Soc, NYC, 1939-43; spec adv, Selective Service Bd, 1941-43; dir, men's and boy's work, Rochester J YM-YWHA, 1943-44; casework sup, J Social Service Bur, Rochester, 1944-47; visiting lectr: Sir George Williams U; Saidye Bronfman Cen. Chmn, casework sect, Montreal Council of Soc Agencies, 1950-53, mem, bd govs, 1953-56; mem, bd dirs, Montreal Marriage Counseling Cen, 1955-58; mem, bd trustees, A and H Bronfman Trust Fund for Soc Work Educ and Training, 1955-61; mem: exec comm, Natl Conf Communal Service; Can Assn of Soc Work; Natl Conf of Family Relations; Can and intl congs on soc work; Corp of Profsl Soc Worker, Que, Superior Council of the Family, Min of Family and Social Wfr, Que. Author: Principles of Administration in Social Agencies, 1956; Advice, Not Judgment, 1963. Recipient: Queen Elizabeth II Coronation medal, 1953; Can Centennial medal, 1967. Home: 5000 St Keran, Montreal, Can. Office: 3600 Van Horne Ave, Montreal, Can.

WEISS, David, (pen name, **D Halivni**), US, rabbi, educator; b. Polyana Kobelecky, Czech, Oct 2, 1927; s. Callel and Fanny (Weiss) Weiderman; in US since 1942; ordained rabbi, Yeshiva of Sighetul, Rum, 1944; BA, Bklyn Coll, 1953; MA, NYU, 1956; DHL, JTSA, 1958; m. Ann Hager, Dec 9, 1953; c: Bernard, Ephraim, Isaiah. Adj prof, rel, Columbia U, since 1967, fac mem since 1957; prof, rabbinics, JTSA, since 1968, prof, Talmud, 1967-68; visiting prof, Talmud, Bar Ilan U, 1966-67. Mem, Amer Acad for J Research. Author: Sridim mePeirush haRah al Taanit, 1959; Sources and Traditions, Vol 1, 1968. Home: 435 Riverside Dr, New York, NY. Office: 3080 Broadway, New York, NY.

WEISS, David Walter, Isr, biologist, educator; b. Vienna, Aus, July 6, 1927; s. Hillel and Julia (Kohn); in Isr since 1968; BA, cum laude, Bklyn Coll, 1949; PhD, Rutgers U, 1952; PhD Med, Oxford U, 1957; m. Judith Weintrob Mar 25, 1951; c: Hillel, Joshua, Jeremy. Prof, dept of immunology, Heb U-Hadassah Med Sch, since 1968; annual lectr, Brandeis Camp Inst, Brandeis, Cal, since 1966; prof, U Cal, Berkeley, 1957-68. Cpl, US Army, 1946-48. Chmn: J Fac Group, U Cal, Berkeley, 1960-68; Acad Comm on Soviet Jewry, 1966-68; Modern Day Sch, Oakland, 1958-64; bd mem, exec, Cong Beth Jacob, Oakland, 1957-60. Contbr to profsl jours. Recipient; Ger occupation ribbon; spec performance citation, both WW II; dist alumnus award, Bklyn Coll, 1961. Home: 20a Radak St, Jerusalem, Isr. Office: Heb U-Hadassah Med Sch, Jerusalem, Isr.

WEISS, Emilio, US, microbiologist; b. Pakrac, Yugo, Oct 4, 1918; s. Edoardo and Vanda (Schrenger); in US since 1939; att: U, Rome, It, 1936-38; AB, U Kan, 1941; MS, U Chgo, 1942, PhD, 1948; m. Hilda Damick, June 23, 1943; c: Natalie, Elizabeth. Dir, microbio dept, Naval Med Research Inst, Natl Naval Med Cen, since 1954; fmr: research asso, U Chgo, 1948-50; asst prof, U Ind, 1950-53; br chief, biol labs, Ft Detrick, Md, 1953-54. US Army, 1943-46. Mem: Amer Soc of Microbiol; Soc for Experimental Biol and Med; Amer Assn of Immunologists; Sigma Xi. Contbr to sci jours. Home: 3612 Raymond St, Chevy Chase, Md. Office: Naval Med Research Inst, Bethesda, Md.

WEISS, George Herbert, US, mathematician; b. NY, Feb 19, 1930; s. Morris and Violet (Mayer); att CCNY, 1948-50; AB, Columbia U, 1951; MA, PhD, U Md, 1958; m. Delia Orgel, Dec 20, 1951; c: Miriam, Alan. Chief, phys scis lab, NIH, since 1964; f, Weizmann Inst of Sci, 1958-59; physicist, Naval Ordinance Lab, 1959-61; asst research prof, Inst for Fluid Dynamics and Applied Math, U of Md, 1960-64; visiting prof, Johns Hopkins U, 1967-68; sr Fulbright f, Imperial Coll, London, 1968-69. US Army 1954-56. Mem, Assn of Orthodox J Scis. Author: Lattice Dynamics in the Harmonic Approximation, 1963; bd of eds, Transportation Research; contbr to profsl jours. Recipient: award, Wash Acad of Scis, 1967. Hobby: photography. Home: 1105 N Belgrade Rd, Silver Spring, Md. Office: NIH, Bethesda, Md.

WEISS, Gerald N, US, surgeon; b. New Orleans, La, June 14, 1932; s. Arthur and Amelia (Levy); BA, Tulane U, 1943, MD, 1945; m. Elaine Bresler, Feb 1, 1948; c: Harlan, Gray, Lauren. Pvt practice since 1957; mem: surg staff: Lake Charles Memorial Hosp; St Patricks Hosp; Lake Charles Charity Hosp; mem, teaching fac, Amer Soc Abdominal Surgs; clinical instr, dept surg, Tulane U Sch Med, 1948-49; phys, surg, Goldsmith Clinic, La, 1951-57; gen surg, Belize Gen Hosp, Brit Honduras, 1962; mem, med and surg staff, Guatemalan villages, 1968; instr, dept zool, McNeese State Coll; clinical instr, dept surg, La State U Sch Med, 1961-1964, 1966-1968; spec cons, Govt of Brit Honduras, 1962. Capt, base surg, USAAC med corps, 1946-49; fleet surg, US Power Squadron, Lake Charles chap, 1962-64. Mem: found: Law Sci Inst; Law Sci Acad; Amer Soc Abdominal Surg, exec comm; Alpha Omega Alpha; AMA; SE Surg Cong; Pan Amer, S, La State, 7th dist, Orleans parish, and Calcesieu Parish Med Assns; Amer Coll Surgs; Amer Bd Surg; Amer Geriatrics Soc; Amer Thoracic Soc; Natl Bd Med Examiners; NY Acad Scis; Intl Coll Surgs; Assn Amer Phys and Surgs; bd, Lake Charles Guidance Cen; exec bd, Boy Scouts of Amer, Calcesieu area; La Assn for Mh, SW La chap, past pres. Contbr to profsl publs. Recipient: Hurricane Audrey citation, Calcesieu parish, 1957; Medalist paper, SE Surg Cong, 1960; Al Merito honor, Govt of Guatemala, 1968; Gold medal, Law Sci Acad Amer, 1968. Home: 2001 21 St, Lake Charles, La. Office: 1611 Foster St, Lake Charles, La.

WEISS, Ira Francis, US, banker, b. Providence, RI, Oct 19, 1909; s. Abraham and Minnie (Chernoff); att CCNY, 1926-28; Columbia U, 1931-33; LLB, St Lawrence U Law Sch, 1931; m. Gladys Abbott (div); c: David, Michael, John. Sr vice-pres, Natl Bank of N Amer, since 1970; fmr: asst secy, Credit Utility Co, 1937-42; pvt law practice, 1933-37; sr vice-pres, Trade Bank and Trust Co, 1961-70, exec since 1945, staff mem, 1926-33. Sgt, US Army, 1942-45. Mem: natl exec bd, AJComm, treas, NY chaps; natl panel, Amer Arbitration Assn; Natl and NY Robert Morris Assos; NY Credit and Financial Mgmt Assn; fmr: trustee: Temple Sharey Tefilo, E Orange, NJ, 1963-65; pres, East End Temple, NYC, 1948-49; asst mgr, United Fund, Glen Ridge, NJ, 1959-60; secy, NY Fed of Reform Syns, 1950-52; mem: Civic Conf Comm, Glen Ridge, NJ, 1961-63; J Comm on Scouting, NYC, 1950-53; speakers bur, United Cerebral Palsy Soc of NY, 1950-53; Home: 330 E 46 St, New York, NY. Office: 44 Wall St, New York, NY.

WEISS, Isidore I, US, psychiatrist; b. Kalnik, Hungary, Aug 20, 1906; s. Herman and Hannah (Berkowitz); in US since 1914; BS, CCNY, 1927; MD, U Edinburgh, 1931; m. Florence Elias, 1936; c: Judith, Karen. Asst supt, Stockton State Hosp, since 1940; cons psychiatrist and neur, San Joaquin Gen Hosp; staff mem, corrections dept, Ind Dept of Med Care, 1938-40. US Army MC, 1942-46. F, Amer Psychiatric Assn; dipl, Bd of Psycht and Neur; mem: Amer Acad of Neur; Amer Geriatric Assn; AMA; Cal and San Joaquin Co Med Socs; J Comty Council, pres, 1950-52; Cong Adas Jeshurun, pres, since 1954. Contbr to med journals. Home: 560 E Acacia St, Stockton, Cal.

WEISS, Jerome S, US, attorney; b, Chgo Ill, Feb 7 1909; S. Morris and Fannie (Salamson); PhB, U Chgo, 1928, JD, cum laude, Law Sch, 1930; m. Gertude Levy, June 20, 1947; c: Marlene Plotkin, Stanton Berlin. Sr partner, law firm, Sonnenschein, Levinson, Carlin, Nath & Rosenthal, since 1942, asso, 1930-42. US Court of Mil Appeals, WW II. Chmn and secy, correctional services adv bd, Ill Youth Commn; mem: Citizens Comm of Family Court; vice-chmn, spec comm on defense of indigent persons, Amer Bar Assn, chmn, spec house comm; mem, comm on character and fitness, Ill Supr Court, since 1951, chmn, 1956-57;

chmn, Family Court adv comm, 1955-57; mem: Chgo Bar Assn, pres, 1958-59; Intl, Fed, Seventh circuit, and Ill Bar Assns; Decalogue Soc of Lawyers; Natl Legal Aid Assn; life mem: and f, Amer Bar Assn; Amer Bar Found; U Chgo Law Rev Eds; B'nai B'rith; Alpha Epsilon Pi Alumni Assn; pres: U Chgo Law Sch Alumni Assn; Temple Sholom, bd dirs; Wfr Council of Metrop Chgo; chmn bd, lawyers div, J Fed of Metrop Chgo; gov and secy, Sarah Siddons Soc Inc; dir, Juvenile Protective Assn, since 1954, pres, 1958-61; mem: bd dirs, Alumni Found, U Chgo; visiting comm, U Chgo; adv bd, Edwin Mandel Legal Aid Clinic; clubs: Natl Lawyers, Wash, DC; Law; Standard; City; Downtown; Order of the Coif. Fmr ed, Chicago Bar Record. Recipient: alumni citation, U Chgo, 1962; Hobby: walking. Home: 247 E Chestnut St, Chicago, Ill. Office: 69 W Washington St, Chicago, Ill.

WEISS, Josef, Isr, executive; b. Flamersheim, Ger, Nov 30, 1902; in Isr since 1938; DJur, Us: Bonn, Frankfurt, Heidelberg; m. Ruth Abraham, July 14, 1929; c: Mirjam Kareth, Chanan. Mgn dir, Delek, Isr Fuel Corp Ltd; hon consul of the Philippines, Tel Aviv, since 1959; dir, financial dept, JNF head off, Jerusalem, 1942-52; repr, Bank Leumi leIsrael, for Eur, Zurich, 1953-56; adv, to Min of Finance, on compensation claims against Ger. Mem, bd of govs, Weizmann Inst; mem, exec bd, Isr Technion Soc; hon treas: Friends of Mus haAretz; Isr Cancer Assn; f, Isr Petroleum Inst. Home: 16 Hagiva St, Savyon, Isr. Office: 6 Ahuzat Bait St, Tel Aviv, Isr.

WEISS, Joseph H, US, radiologist; b. Denver, Colo, Nov 26, 1951; s. Harry and Sarah (Fine); BS, U Denver, 1936; MD, U Colo Sch of Med, 1939; m. Ruth Huttner, June 12, 1945; c: Marcy, Jack, Gary, Cindy. Pvt practice, radiology; cons, Long Beach Dept of Public Health; radiologist, Gen Rose Memorial Hosp, 1949-62; clinical instr, U Colo Med Cen, 1948-62; alternate chief, radiology, Denver Gen Hosp, 1949-57, chief, 1948-49. Maj, US Army, 1941-46. Dir, Lakewood C of C; bd dirs: Temple Isr; Long Beach J Comty Cen; mem: NY Acad of Scis: Amer Coll Radiology: Radiological Soc of N Amer; Soc of Nuclear Med; AMA; Rocky Mt Radiological Soc; B'nai B'rith; ADL Council; Temple Emanuel, secy, 1951-52; clubs: Men's, Rotary. Recipient: Hartford Found grant, research on cineradiography, 1958. Hobby: photography. Home 3625 Country Club Lane, Lakewood, Cal. Office: 5220 Clark Ave, Lakewood, Cal.

WEISS, Julius, US, attorney; b. NYC, Mar 1, 1894; s. Moritz and Henriette (Freuder); BA, CCNY, 1915; LLB, Columbia U, 1918; m. Helen Stern, Feb 25, 1923; c: Janet Goodman, Carol Wohl, David. Pvt practice since 1919; law firm, Weiss, Bronston, Rosenthal and Heller, since 1959; dir, gen counsel, PEC-Isr Econ Corp, since 1926; pres, Pal Endowment Funds, since 1965, trustee since 1945; fmr: chmn, bd dirs, Union Bank of Isr, 1958-61; Can Isr Cen Bank Ltd, 1945. US Army, WW I; adv to registrants, Selective Service Bd, New Rochelle. Chmn, law comm, Westchester Co Dem comm; fmr: pres, Bd of Educ, New Rochelle, NY; vice-pres, dir, Ref Econ Corp, 1934-50; trustee, Comty Coll, Westchester Co. Ed bd, Columbia Law Rev, 1917-18. Recipient: Purple Heart. Home: 66 Crawford Terrace, New Rochelle, NY. Office: 295 Madison Ave, New York, NY.

WEISS, Leon Paul, US, physician, educator; b. Bklyn, Oct 4, 1925; s. Isidor and Florence (Reif); att CCNY, 1942-44; MD, LI Coll Med Med Sch, 1948; m. Ellen Tarter-Fishbein, June 19, 1949; c: Stephen, Philip, Alice, Marisa, Nataniel, Eve. Prof, anat, Johns Hopkins U Med Sch, since 1967, fac mem since 1960; fmr: asst prof, anat, Harvard Med Sch, 1958-60. Capt, US, Army, 1953-55. Mem: Amer Assn Anatomists; Amer Soc Cell Biol; Histochem Soc; Amer Assn Immunology. Author: Histology, 1966. Home: 1808 Dixon Rd, Baltimore, Md. Office: 709 N Wolfe St, Baltimore, Md.

WEISS, M David, US, administrator, rabbi; b. Pittsburgh, Pa, July 15, 1927; s. Joshua and Sarah (Deutsch); BA, Franklin and Marshall Coll, 1945; att U Pittsburgh, 1947-49; ordained rabbi, MHL, JTSA, 1953; att: Brandeis U, 1954-56; Harvard U, 1957-59; div; c. Janna, Deborah. Exec dir, Asso Syns of Mass, since 1967; exec vice-pres, Mass Bd of Rabbis, since 1967; chaplain, McLean Hosp, Belmont; acting prin, found mem, Solomon Schechter Day Sch; fmr: asst rabbi, Cong Kehillath Isr, Brookline, Mass, 1953-55; rabbi, Temple Isr, Sharon, Mass, 1955-62; asso rabbi, Temple Emanuel, Newton, Mass, 1962-67. Cpl, USAAC, 1945-46. Chmn: United Rabb Chaplaincy Commn of Mass; social action commn, NE United Syn of Amer, dir, Young People's League; mem: admn comm:

JCC of Gtr Boston; NE Zionist region; bd dirs: Mass Conf of Social Wfr; Packard Manse Ecumenical Cen; Solomon Schechter Day Sch; exec comm: Natl J Wfr Bd; Amer Zionist Youth Comm; delg, Natl J Cmty Relations Adv Council; vice-pres, NE AJCong, 1965-67; mem: NE Rabb Soc; Combined J Philanthropies of Gtr Boston; Acad of Rel and Mh; Assn of Mental Hosp Chaplains; ACLU. Contbr to J jours. Home: 145 Langley Rd, Newton, Mass. Study: 177 Tremont St, Boston, Mass.

WEISS, Martin Joseph, US, chemist; b. NYC, May 4, 1923; s. Meyer and Nadia (Rind); AB, NYU, 1944; PhD, Duke U, 1949; postdoc f, Hickrill Research Found, 1949-50; m. Audrey Wasserberg, Apr 15, 1951; c: Eric, Richard, Laurence. Group leader, pharm research, Lederle Labs, since 1950. Mem: Amer Chem Soc; Chem Soc, London; AAAS; Sigma Xi; Phi Lambda Upsilon; Temple Emanuel,Westwood, NJ, fmr pres. Contbr to chem jours. Home: Oradell, NJ. Office: Lederle Labs, Pearl River, NY.

WEISS, Mika Miksa, US, rabbi; b. Kiskunfelegyhaza, Hung, Oct 19, 1913; s. Ferenc and Terez (Hollander) Weiszman; in US since 1961; PhD, Pazmany Peter U, 1939; ordained rabbi, J Theol Sem, Budapest, 1941; MHL, U Judaism, LA, Cal, 1966; m. Maria Brull, Oct 22, 1946; c: Pter. Rabbi: Temple Beth Hayim, since 1966; Cong of Oroshaza, Hung, 1939-44; chief rabbi: Debrecen, Hung, 1946-57; Finland, 1957-61; rabbi, J Comty Cen, Flemington, NJ, 1962-63; Cong Mishkan Tephilo, Venice, Cal, 1963-66. Inmate, Nazi concentration camps, 1944-45; chaplain, Free Hung Army, 1945-48. Chmn, mem, Zionist Orgs, Hung, 1946-48; chaplain, Camp of Horsching, Aug, 1945; mem: B'nai B'rith Fredslogen, Stockholm, 1959-61; RA; Masons. Contbr to J jours. Home: 14535 Benefit St, Sherman Oaks, Cal. Study: 4302 Van Nuys Blvd, Sherman Oaks, Cal.

WEISS, Miriam Schlein (pen name, **Miriam Schlein**), US, author, juvenile writer; b. NYC, June 6, 1926; d. William and Sophie (Bigleisen) Schlein; BA, Bklyn Coll, 1947; m. Harvey Weiss, June 23, 1954; c: Elizabeth, John. Author, childrens books: The Four Little Foxes; Shapes; Go With the Sun, all in 1952; Fast is Not a Ladybug; When Will the World be Mine, all in 1953; The Sun Looks Down; How Do You Travel; Elephant Hevd; Heavy is a Hippopotamus, all in 1954; Oomi, the New Hunter; Little Red Nose; It's About Time; City Boy, Country Boy; Puppy's House; Big Talk; Lazy Day, all 1955; Deer in the Snow; Henry's Ride, both in 1956; Something for Now,Something for Later; The Big Cheese; Little Rabbit, the High Jumper; Amazing Mr. Pelgrew; A Bunny A Bird, A Funny Cat; Here Comes Night, all in 1957; The Bumblebee's Secret; Home, The Tale of a Mouse; Herman McGregor's World, all in 1958; The Raggle Taggle Fellow; Little Dog Little; The Fisherman's Day; Kittens, Cubs and Babies, all in 1959; My Family; The Sun, The Wind, the Sea and the Rain, all in 1960; Laurie's New Brother; Amuny, Boy of Old Egypt, all in 1961; The Pile of Junk; Snow Time, both in 1962; The Way Mothers Are; The Snake in the Carpool; The Big Green Thing, all in 1963; Billy, the Littlest One, 1966; contbr: adult fiction to mags. Mem: Authors League of Amer. Home and office: 8 Reimer Rd, Westport, Conn.

WEISS, Myron, US, editorial counsel; b. Cleveland, O, July 14, 1894; s. Alex and Rose (Katz); BA, Harvard U, 1914; att: Cleveland Law Sch; schs in Fr; hon D Art Oratory, Staley Coll, Boston, 1937; m. Lucie Wiese, 1928. Ed counsel since 1938; publisher, arts commentator, since 1939; counsel, Metals Info Libr, since 1957; fmr: asso ed, Time Mag, 1925-38; asso, Time-Life-Fortune-Architectural Forum, and March of Time radio, 1925-38. Served US Army, Mex border, 1916-19. Mem: Amer Soc for Metals; Amer Soc for Hist of Metals; Amer Public Health Assn; Amer Geneitc Assn; AAAS; reference bd, Staley Coll; panel, Amer Arbitration Assn; hon, Pan Amer Med Assn; delg: Intl Hygiene Cong, Dresden, 1930; Natl Health Conf, Wash, DC, 1938; Amer Sci Cong, 1940; Natl Health Assembly, 1948; rapporteur, World Metallurgical Cong, 1947; club, Natl Press. Author: Joseph Nashe McDowell, MD; ed: Men, Metals and Modern Magic; Casting Design Process; Bedside Management of Heart Patient; Birtcher Medical World Book; In Defense of Love. Office: 130 W 57 St, New York, NY.

WEISS, Paul, Isr, business exec; b. Landau, Ger, Dec 26, 1899; s. Hermann and Helene (Guggenheim); in Isr since 1933; DRerPol, U Frankfurt/Main, 1923; m. Tilly Guggenheim, 1924; c: Ruth, Edna. Ret, 1968, fmr mgn dir, Zori Pharm &

Chem Ind Co Ltd, 1933-68; staff mem: banks, Frankfurt, Stuttgart, 1919-28; pharm factory, Munich, 1928-33. Chmn, pharm sec, Isr Mfrs Assn. Home: 6 Bialik St, Tel Aviv, Isr.

WEISS, Paul, US, philosopher, educator; b. NYC, May 19, 1901; s. Samuel and Emma (Rothschild); BSS, CCNY, 1927; MA, Harvard U, 1928; PhD, 1929; Sears traveling f, 1929-30; LHD, Grinnell Coll, 1960; resident scholar, SUNY, 1969-70; m. Victoria Brodkin, 1928 (decd); c: Judith, Jonathan. Heffer prof, phil, Catholic U of Amer, since 1969; cons: Great Books Found; Inst for Phil Research; fmr: instr, Harvard Coll, 1930-31; instr, Radcliffe Coll, 1930-31; prof, phil, Bryn Mawr Coll, 1940-46, chmn, phil dept, 1944-46; fac mem since 1931; Jonathan Sterling prof, phil, Yale U, 1963-69, fac mem, since 1945; visiting prof, Heb U, 1951. F, Ezra Stiles Coll; first pres: C S Pierce Soc; and found, Metaphys Soc of Amer, 1951; first chmn, Amer Friends of Heb U, New Haven; treas, found, Phil of Educ Soc, Inc; trustee, Amer Assn ME Studies; mem: found, Conf on Space, Phil and Rel; Amer Phil Assn; Phi Beta Kappa; Judaism; fmr mem, Amer Soc Aesthetics; clubs: Aurelian Soc; Morys; NY Philosophical; Elizabethan. Author: Nature of Systems, 1929; Reality, 1938; Nature and Man, 1947; Man's Freedom, 1950; Modes of Being, 1958; Our Public Life, 1959; The World of Art, 1961; Nine Basic Arts, 1961; History: Written and Lived, 1962; Art and Religion, 1963; The God We Seek, 1964; Philosophy in Process, 1965; The Making of Men, 1968; Sport: A Philosophic Inquiry, 1969; co-author: 7th Intl Cong of Phil, 1930; American Philosophy Today and Tomorrow, 1935; Approaches to World Peace, 1944; Perspectives on a Troubled Decade, 1950; Moral Principles of Action, 1952; Personal Moments of Discovery, 1953; Right and Wrong, 1967; found, ed, Rev of Metaphysics, 1947-63; co-ed: Collected Papers of Charles S Pierce, 6 vols, 1931-35; ed bd, Judaism. Recipient: Guggenheim f, 1938; Rockefeller-Rabinowitz grant for study in Isr and India, 1954; Townsend Harris medal, 1963; lectr: Aspen Inst, 1952; Chancellor's Forum, U Denver, 1952; Powell, Orde Wingate, 1954; U Ind, 1958; Gates, Grinnelll Coll, 1959; Matchette, Purdue, 1959; Wesleyan, 1963; Aquinas, Marquette U, 1963; Phi Beta Kappa, 1968-69; E-W Conf of Phil, 1969. Office: Catholic U of Amer, Washington, DC.

WEISS, Robert Burton, US, town manager; b. Medford, Mass, June 9, 1922; s. William and Esther (Herman); BA, Boston U, 1947; MGA, U of Pa, 1948; m. Gloria Weiner, June 15,1947; c: Peter, Jay, Wendy. Town mgr: Manchester, since 1965; S Berwick, Me, 1949-52; Windsor, Conn, 1952-64. Sgt, US Army, 1942-45. Dir, Gtr Hartford Sym Soc; mem: Phi Beta Kappa; Amer Soc for Public Admn; Intl City Mgrs Assn, fmr vice-pres; Conn Mgr Assn, fmr pres; Masons; Kiwanis. Hobby: tennis. Home: 71 Lakewood Cen, Manchester, Conn. Office: Town Hall, Manchester, Conn.

WEISS, Samson R, US, rabbi; b. Emden, Ger, May 9, 1910; s. Aron and Judith (Schweiger); in US since 1938; att Us: Breslau, 1928; Berlin, 1929; Zurich, 1933; Prague, 1934; ordained rabbi, Yeshiva Mir, 1933; PhD, summa cum laude, U Dorpat, Estonia, 1938; m. Helen Carlebach, 1936. Exec vice-pres, Union of Orthodox J Congs of Amer, since 1956; rabbi: Cen Syn, since 1945; J Tchrs Coll, Würzburg, Ger, 1934-38; prof, codes, Rabb Acad Ner Isr, Baltimore, 1938-40; dean, Talmudical Acad, Yeshivath Beth Yehudath, Detroit, 1941-44; dir, Torah Umesorah, NYC, 1944-45; dir: natl council, Young Isr, NY, 1947-50; found, dir, Inst for J Studies, 1945-56. Bd chmn: Amer Friends of Shaare Zedeck Hosp; Amer Friends of Mirrer Yeshiva, both in Jerusalem; mem: RabCA. Ed bd, contbr: Viewpoint, since 1945; J Life, since 1956; contbr to Ger-J press. Home: 1570 53 St, Brooklyn, NY. Office: 84 Fifth Ave, New York, NY

WEISS, Samuel, US, journalist; b. Pulawy, Pol, Sep 6, 1897; s. Mendel and Machle (Sigman); in US since 1925; att J People's Inst, Chgo, 1926; m. Florence Kornberg, 1942. Ed, repr, J Daily Forward, Pacific coast, since 1968; co-ed: Gerechtigkeit, since 1950; Wecker, since 1942; dir, Yiddish publicity, ILGWU, 1957-68. Mem: J Lab comm; YIVO; Workmens Circle; Yiddish Writers Union; ORT; UJA. Author: The Jewish Labor Movement in America, article in Gen Ency in Yiddish, 1957; contbr to J press. Home: 1275 N Havenhurst Dr, Los Angeles, Cal. Office: 509 N Fairfax Ave, Los Angeles, Cal.

WEISS, Samuel A, US, jurist; b. Krotovocz, Pol, Apr 15, 1902; s. Israel and Sadie (Golden); in US since 1902; BS, Duquesne U, 1925, LLB, 1927, hon LLD, 1959; m. Jeannette Hoffman, 1930; c: Sandra (decd), James, Joy Cohen. Ret, 1968; judge, Court of Common Pleas, Allegheny Co, Pa, 1946-68; fmr:

pvt law practice, 1927-45; le , Pa House of Reprs, 1934-38; congressman, US House of Reprs, 1940-46. Pres, Pa Conf of State Trial Judges, since 1965; natl vice-pres, B'nai B'rith, since 1949, McKeesport lodge, 1935, 1937, Dist lodge, 1946, mem, exec comm, Supr lodge, 1948,1950; pres: Roselia Foundling and Maternity Hosp, since 1953, and mem of bd; chmn, UJA, tri-state area, W Pa-Eastern O-W Va, since 1945; mem, bd dirs: ZOA; United J Fed; Beth Shalom Syn; Montefiore Hosp, both of Pittsburgh; Boys Club of McKeesport; mem, bd trustees: Duquesne U; McKeesport Hosp; pres, E Intercoll Football Officials Assn, 1933; dep commr, referee, Natl Profsl Football League, 1942-50; mem: Amer Acad Pol Sci; Sigma Alpha Mu; Elks; Eagles; Moose; Lions; Odd Fellows; KP. Author: Sammy Blows His Whistle, 1952. Recipient: Outstanding Alumus award, Boys Club, 1950; plague, Isr Fgn Min Moshe Sharett, 1951; awards for service to vets: VFW, 1945; Amer Legion, 1946; Disabled Amer Vets, 1946; AMVETS, 1949; Dapper Dan, 1950; JWV, 1953; Tri-State, Athletic Assn award, 1955; sportsman-of-the-year, Allegheny Co, Pittsburgh, 1958; f, Intl Acad, 1958. Home: 4601 Fifth Ave, Pittsburgh, Pa.

WEISS, Stanford L, US, business exec; b. West Chester, Pa, Jan 28, 1927; s. Morris and Anna (Cantor); att US Merchant Marine Acad; BA, U Mich, 1949; MBA, Harvard U, 1951; m. Geraldine London, Jan 30, 1949; c: Richard, Marilyn. Vice-pres, Triangle Shoe Co, since 1954; fmr: asst to merchandise mgr, John Wannamaker Dept Store, Phila, 1951-52, asst fur buyer, 1952-53. Pres, J Fed, Gtr Wilkes-Barre; vice-pres, Pa-Md-Del region, AJComm, since 1967; pres, Parents Council, Wyoming Sem, Kingston, Pa; treas, Homemakers Service, Luzerne, since 1968; vice-pres, Wyoming Valley United Fund, since 1967; mem: bd trustees, Wyoming Valley J Comty Cen, since 1959, bd dirs since 1966; exec, Wilkes-Barre AJComm; vice-chmm, Kings Coll Pres Council, 1968-69; Masons: Shriners; Rotary; club: Westmoreland Country, Wilkes-Barre. Home: 654 Westmoreland Ave, Kingston, Pa. Office: POB 1391, Kingston, Pa.

WEISS, Theodore R, US, educator, editor, author; b. Reading, Pa, Dec 16, 1916; s. Nathan and Mollie (Weinberg); BA, Mulhenberg Coll, 1938, hon deg, 1968; MA, Columbia U, 1940; m. Renée Karol, June 6, 1941. Prof, writing, hum, Princeton U, since 1968, poet-in-res, 1966-67; reader, poetry bd, Wesleyan U Press, since 1964; ed, Quarterly Rev of Lit, since 1943; prof, Eng, Bard Coll, since 1946; fmr: instr: U Md, 1941; U NC, 1942-44; Yale U, 1944-46; lectr: New Sch for Social Research, 1955-56; Harvard U; Yale U; Boston U; Wellesley Coll; Barnard Coll; Bennington Coll; Wash U; visiting poet, MIT, 1961-62. Mem, Natl Book Award comm for poetry. Author: Selections from the Notebooks of Gerard Manley Hopkins, 1945; The Catch, 1951; Outlanders, 1960; Gunsight, 1962; The Medium, 1965; The Last Day and the First, 1968; contbr to periodicals. Recorded own poems for Yale U, Harvard U, and Libr of Cong. Recipient: Ford Found f, 1953-54; Wallace Stevens poetry award, 1956; grant, Natl Found Arts and Humanities, 1967. Home: 26 Haslet Ave, Princeton, NJ.

WEISSBARG, Julius, Isr, business exec; b. Slavuta, Russ, Aug 5, 1903; s. Aron and Clara (Hendelman); dipl in econ, DRerPol, Albertus U, Königsberg; m. Njuta Abramsky; c: Judith Kalir. Mgr, Citrus Marketing Bd of Isr, since 1946; fmr guest lectr: Us, agric schs. Chmn, shipping comm, Isr Export Inst; fmr vice-pres: Isr-Can C of C; Isr-Belgium C of C. Home: 52 Hovevi Zion St, Tel Aviv, Isr. Office: 69 Haifa Rd, Tel Aviv, Isr.

WEISSBERG, Guenter, US, educator, international atty; b. Kassel, Ger, May 14, 1929; s. Max and Ida (Israel); in US since 1940; AB, magna cum laude, NYU, 1951; JD, Columbia U Sch of Law, 1954; PhD, Columbia U, 1959; cert, Hague Acad of International Law, The Netherlands, 1952. Prof, political sci, Colby Coll, since 1970, asso prof, 1965-70; cons, Amer Law Inst, Phila, 1956-59; lectr, intl law: Columbia U, 1959-60, 1961; Rutgers Sch of Law, 1964; visiting asst prof, gvt, Cornell U, 1960-61; visiting prof, political sci, George Washington U, Wash, Dec, 1 1964; fmr, research asso to Hon Philip C Jessup. Mem: NY Bar; Assn of Bar NYC; Amer Soc Intl Law; Amer Political Sci Assn; Amer br, Intl Law Assn; Phi Beta Kappa; Pi Sigma Alpha. Author: The International Status of the United Nations, 1961; Recent Developments in the Law of the Sea and the Japanese-Korean Fishery Dispute, 1966; contbr to intl law and political sci jours. Home: 72a Elm, Waterville, Me. Office: Colby Coll, Waterville, Me.

WEISSBERG, Victor H, US, rabbi, b. Highland Park, Mich, June 26, 1927; s. Isadore and Ruth (Friedman); PhB, U Chgo, 1948; BHL, HUC, 1950, MHL, 1954, DHL, 1970; att: U Cincinnati, 1950-53; Heb U, 1951-52; m. Tamar Libovsky, Feb 12, 1952; c: Amyra, Ariel, Alona. Rabbi, Temple Beth-El, since 1954; spec lectr, Bible, Heb, Chgo Coll of J Studies, since 1955, dir, preparatory dept, since 1958; fmr: case worker, Hamilton Co Wfr Dept, 1949-50; dir, educ asst, rabbi, Temple Isarah Isr, Chgo, 1953-54; chaplain, Cook Co Jail, 1955-59. USN, 1945-46. Vice-pres, Histadrut Ivrit, since 1961; fmr: vice-pres, Hyde Park Kenwood Council Churches and Syns, 1954-55; secy, Chgo Bd of Rabbis, 1956-58, mem, exec comm, 1961; mem: CCAR; Zionist Youth Commn; Phi Delta Kappa; club: Kiwanis. Contbr to J jours. Recipient: scholarship, Cleveland Zionist Fed, 1951. Home: 4820 W Sherwin Ave, Lincolnville, Ill. Study: 3050 W Touhy Ave, Chicago, Ill.

WEISSBERGER, L Arnold, US, attorney; b. NYC, Jan 16, 1907; s. Harry and Anna (Lenson); AB, cum laude, Harvard U, 1927; LLB, cum laude, Harvard Law Sch, 1930. Head, law firm specializing in theater law, since 1939; fmr: atty: Guggenheim and Untermeyer, 1930-34; Riegelman, Hess and Hirsch, 1935-39. US Army, 1942-43. Dir: Fountain House; Amer Inst of Music; Dance Notations Bur Inc; John Golden Fund Inc; pres, New Dramatics Comm Inc; found, Tel Aviv Mus Patrons Inc; trustee, chmn, Friends of Theater Collection, Mus of NYC; trustee, Harlem Ear and Eye Hosp; mem: Bar Assn of NYC; Amer Natl Theater and Acad; Phi Beta Kappa; fmr: dir, vice-pres, Bx House; trustee, FJP Socs. Contbr to profsl jours. Home: 10 W 86 St, New York, NY. Office: 120 E 56 St, New York, NY.

WEISSBROT, Eleaser, Isr, educator; b. Kiev, Russ, Sep 17, 1917; s. Shlomo and Tema (Nehamkin), in Isr since 1935; att Heb U, 1935-38; BA, U Chgo, 1945; asso mem, corp of cert secys, BICA, London, 1949-52; m. Ruth Zwerling, Feb 16, 1943; c: Nurit Levi, Ethan, Orna. Prin, dir: The Brit Tutorial Insts; The Heb Tutorial Inst, both since 1950, with insts since 1943. Found of first Heb correspondence coll in the world. Served: Haganah; IDF. Monitor, David Yellin lodge, B'nai B'rith; pres, Alumni Soc of Chajes-RG, Vienna; mem: Intl and Eur Councils of Corresp Educ; B'nai B'rith; Rotary; fmr: prin, Higher Comm Coll; chmn, YMCA educ comm; Isr repr, Intl Council Corresp Educ, UNESCO, 1969. Contbr to profsl jours. Hobbies: music, travel, science, sport, Zionism. Home: 9 Balfour St, Jerusalem, Isr. Office: POB 1259, Jerusalem, Isr.

WEISSMAN, George, US, business exec; b. NYC, July 12, 1919; s. Samuel and Rose (Goldberg); BBA, CCNY, 1939; m. Mildred Stregack, June 4, 1944; c: Paul, Ellen, Daniel. Pres, chief operating off, Philip Morris Inc, since 1967, with firm since 1952; mem bd: Miller Brewing Co, since 1969; Benson & Hedges, Can, Ltd, since 1958; publicity adv, Samuel Goldwyn Producs, 1946-48; PR acct exec, Benjamin Sonnenberg, 1948-52. USN, 1942-46. Div chmn, UJA, since 1963, vice-chmn, 1958-63; trustee: Lincoln Cen Fund; Bernard Baruch Coll Fund, CUNY; Asso YM-YWHAs, Gtr NY; dir: Film, Soc, Lincoln Cen; chmn, parents comm, Swarthmore Coll; mem: grad adv bd, Bernard Baruch Coll; Natl Citizens comm, United Comty Campaigns; Beta Gamma Sigma; Council for Higher Educ; fmr: mem, adv council, Lincoln Cen; chmn, FJP dr, NY tobacco div, head, service unit, Gtr NY Fund; natl vice-chmn, Comty Funds and Councils of Amer; div chmn, UJA; dir, CCNY Alumni Assn; clubs: Economic, NY; Natl Press; Chems. Recipient: young-exec-of-the-year, Natl, Assn Tobacco Distributors, 1954; award, tobacco div, FJP, 1963; Townsend Harris medal, CCNY Alumni Assn, 1968; award, Bernard M Baruch Coll Alumni Soc, 1968; knight off, order of merit, It, 1965; cdr, order of merit, It, 1970. Home: 81 Manursing Way, Rye, NY. Office: 100 Park Ave, New York, NY.

WEISSMAN, K B, US, business exec, accountant; b. NYC, May 22, 1906; s. Joseph and Celia (Kittner); att Pace Coll, NY, 1923-26; m. Rosalind Dworsky, Mar 12, 1932; c: Alan. Ret since 1949; fmr pvt practice, acctnt, 1926-33; asso, Wek Sales Co, financing of commodities, 1933-49. Donor: $1.5 million to Coll of Dent, NYU, 1965. Bd mem: Amer-Isr Cultural Found, since 1960; Optometric Cen of NY, since 1959; Lyric Arts Opera Found; pres, K B Weissman Found; co-found: Albert Einstein Coll of Med; Metropolitan Star, publ of B'nai B'rith, NY; active in organized charities. Home: 350 Beechmont Dr, New Rochelle, NY.

WEISS-ROSMARIN, Trude, US, author, editor; b. Frankfurt, Ger; d. Jacob and Celestine (Mulling) Weiss; in US since 1931; PhD, U Wurzburg, 1931; c. Moshe. Ed: The J Spectator, since 1936; Isr abstracts sect, Jour of Ecumenical Studies; lectr, Grad Sch of Educ, NYU. Author: Religion of Reason, 1936; The Hebrew Moses: An Answer to Sigmund Freud, 1939; Judaism and Christianity: The Differences, 1943; Jewish Survival, 1949; Saadia, 1959; contbr to: Ency Judaica; Ency of the Social Scis; and periodicals. Natl co-chmn of educ, ZOA, 1949-51; adv bd: JBCA; Natl J Curriculum Inst; mem: Amer Acad of Rel; Soc for Sci Study of Rel. Office: 250 W 57 St, New York, NY.

WEISTROP, Jerome, US, rabbi; b. Bx, NY, Oct 27, 1929; s. Solomon and Rose (Cooperman); BS, NYU, 1950; BRE, JTSA, 1950; MHL, ordained rabbi, JTSA, 1954; cert, marriage counseling, U of Pa, 1963; m. Francine Slepikoff, June 11, 1950; c: Penina, Aviva, Jonathan, Debra. Rabbi: Temple Shalom, since 1967; Temple Isr, Upper Darby, Pa, 1959-67; chaplain: Elwyn Inst, 1959-67; Haverford State Hosp, 1962-67. Fmr, chmn: funeral standards comm, sabbath promotion comm, RA, Phila br; rel freedom comm, J Comty Relations Council, Phila; bd mem, Milton Housing for the Aged; mem: Acad of Rel and Mh; Amer Assn of Marriage Counselors. Author: Choosing Jewish Careers; chap, Teaching to be Different, in Keys to Understanding; contbr to rel jours. Home: 37 Hills View Rd, Milton, Mass. Study: 180 Blue Hill Ave, Milton, Mass.

WEITZ, Emil, US, business exec, sports org, author; b. Jamnica Pol, May, 18, 1905; s. David and Rachel (Herman); in US since 1948; att: Intl Sch Bus Admn, Vienna, 1926-28; U Cracow, 1932-33; Heb U, 1934-46; Loughborough Coll, Eng, 1938-39; m. (decd); c: Amira Spier. Pres, Isr Coin Distributors Corp, since 1950; fmr: dir: Pal Sport Team, Maccabia, Tel Aviv, 1935; Pal athletic participation, Workers Olympic Games, Antwerp, 1937; ref children's camp, Dovercourt, Eng, 1938; Pal athletic participation, Intl Sports Competition, Cairo, 1940; Amateur Athletic Assn, Pal, 1939-45; JNF Youth Dept, 1941-48; nation and land exhb, Tel Aviv, 1945; org: Admatenu, relay race, Syrian border to Jerusalem, 1944; torch relay race, Jerusalem to NJ, 1968; found: Amer-Isr Sport Comm, 1948; Isr delg to Olympics, Helsinki, 1952; vice-pres, Amer-Worlds Fair Corp; gen mgr, Amer-Isr pavilion, NY Worlds Fair, 1964; mgn dir, Isr 20th anniversary exhb, 1968. Creator, exhbs: 4000 Years of J Hist; A Century of J Hist; exhb in US, Can, Isr. Author: Thoughts and Ideas, 1932; On the Ruins of Stanislavov, 1947; All Are Jews; A Glimpse into Jewish History Through Philately, 1968; contbr to publs in five langs. Hobby: philately. Office: 327 Park Ave S, New York, NY.

WEITZ, Joseph, (pen names: Ben Porat, Yoref Hagalili); Isr, public official; b. Wolhynia, Russ, Jan, 1890; s. Abraham and Raica (Klibaner); in Isr since 1908; att U Odessa, 1905; m. Ruhama Altshuler, 1912; c: Raanan, Sharon. Dir gen, Isr Lands Auth; fmr: agric worker: Rehovot; Hadera; Petah Tikva; Galilee; all 1908-15; chmn, Isr Soil Devl Council; dir, land and soil devl dept, 1932-59; dep chmn, JNF, 1959-67. Chmn, sub-comm for naming agric settlements. Author: ha-Gefen; Pardes veGan; haYaar beEretz Israel; Shivat ha-Minim; Beth Shaan; haSharon; haHar; Eretz haGalil; Emek Hefer; Nof veAdam; Sadeh veGan; Kocha shel Eretz Israel; Hitnahluteinu beTkufat haSaar; Siah Sade; Ginat Veradim; Yomanei veIgrot leBanim, 5 vols, 1935-64; Dapim Rishonim; Bintivi; Kavim leDioknaot; haNadneda haAzuva; contbr to jours. Home: 16 Hechalutz St, Bet Hakerem, Jerusalem, Isr.

WEITZ, Martin M, (pen name, Misli); US, rabbi, author; b. Denver, Colo, Aug 2, 1909; s. Joseph and Rachel (Kaufman); att: Colo State Col of Educ, 1925-27; U Denver, 1931; Harvard Chaplains Sch, 1943; BA, U Cincinnati, 1932; ordained rabbi, HUC, 1934, hon DD, 1959; DHumL, Colo State Coll, 1963; DD, Lincoln U, 1967; m. Margaret Kalach, Aug 5, 1934; c: Myshlee Levinson, Jonathan. Dir, Cen for Interfaith Studies, Lincoln U, mem fac since 1967; rabbi, Adas Shalom Temple, Havre de Grace, Md; fmr: found dir, B'nai B'rith Hillel Found, Northwestern U; dir, educ, Temple Sholom, Chgo, both 1934-37; rabbi: Beth Hillel Cong, Kenosha, Wis, 1937-43; Temple B'nai Jeshurun, Des Moines, Ia, 1946-47; Cong House of Isr, Hot Springs, Ark, 1948-51. Capt, U Army, 1943-46. Chmn, adv council, Comty Coll of S Jersey; co-found, Atlantic Co Bd Rabbis; hist, Alumni Assn of HUC; mem: CCAR; Amer bd, World Union of Progressive Judaism; UJA; J Chautauqua Soc; NCCJ. Author: Jewish Community Studies, 1936; Wind Whispers, 1950; Directory of Reform Rabbinate, 1952, 1955, 1963, 1967; Tercentenary Confirmation Manual, 1954; Year Without Fear, 1955; Life Without

Strife, 1958; Decalogues of Our Days, 1962; Race and Religion Review, 1968; Campus on a Compass, 1969; co-author: Ten Commandments for Modern Living, 1952; ed: The Hour Glass; annual manuals for World Union of Progresive Judaism; The Hour Glass; contbr to J periodicals. Recipient: spec commendation, US Army, 1945. Hobbies: old books, coins, hiking. Home: Oxford, Pa. Office: Lincoln U, Pa.

WEITZMAN, Alan Gordon, US, rabbi; b. Cincinnati, O, Oct 29, 1934; s. Isadore and Ella (Lisner); BA, U Cincinnati, 1955; BHL, MHL, HUC-JIR, 1960. Rabbi: Cong Oheb Sholom, since 1964; Indianapolis Heb Cong, 1960-64. Pres: Berks Co Ministerium; Berks Co Mh Assn; secy, AJComm; bd mem: Fellowship House; Mh and Mental Retardation; Planned Parenthood; Campfire Girls. Hobby: sports. Home: 50 N 4 St, Reading, Pa. Study: 13 and Perkiomen, Reading, Pa.

WEITZMAN, George, US, attorney; b. Bklyn, NY, June 4, 1910; s. Samuel and Celia (Feuer); AB, Lafayette Coll, 1931; JD, NYU Law Sch, 1935; m. Frieda Joseph, June 27, 1942; c: Ellis. Partner, law firm, Goodman & Weitzman, since 1936; fmr: 1st dist atty, Northampton Co; hearing examiner, Dept of Revenue, Pa; spec asst atty gen, Pa. Lt, US Army, 1942-46, Pres: Northampton Co Bar Assn; Lafayette Coll Alumni, Easton area Comty Chest, J Comty Cen; chmn, UJA campaign; trustee, Temple Covenant of Peace; exec comm, United Fund, 1938-68; bd dirs, J Comty Cen, 1946-51. Home: 222 E Pierce St, Easton, Pa. Office: Drake Bldg, Easton, Pa·

WEITZMAN, Leonard, US, organization exec; b. May 4, 1923; s. Joseph and Irene (Fleit); BS, U Pittsburgh, 1943, ML, 1947; m. Harriet Reich, Aug 3, 1947; c: Richard, Mark, Steven, Barbara, Nancy. Exec dir, Vocational Rehab Cen of Allegheny Co, since 1952, with org since 1947; cons: vocational rehab, US Dept HEW; Social Security Admn. US Army, 1943-47. Pres: Natl Assn Sheltered Workshops and Homebound Progs Inc; bd mem, J Comty Relations Council; vice-chmn, Pittsburgh chap, AJComm, since 1958; vice-pres, Allegheny Co Scholarship Assn; dir, Pa Rehab Assn; chmn: Julia Pines Teller Award for Handicapped; Pittsburgh Comm on Employment of Handicapped, 1958-59; metrop div, UJA, 1955-57; mem: Mayor's and Gov's comms for Handicapped; Natl Rehab Assn; Amer Personnel and Guidance Assn; club: Rodef Shalom Men's, vice-pres since 1963. Hobbies: golf, tennis, squash, bowling. Home: 5654 Darlington Rd, Pittsburgh, Pa. Office: 908 Penn Ave, Pittsburgh, Pa.

WEIZMANN, Ezer, Isr, business exec, ret army off; b. Tel Aviv, Isr, 1924; s. Yehiel and Yehudit; nephew of Chaim Weizmann, first pres of Isr; studied aeronautics, Eng, 1946-47; m. Reuma Shamir; two c. Business exec, shipping co, since 1971; maj gen, chief, gen staff br; fmr, Min of Transp, 1970. Haganah, 1939-48; fighter pilot, RAF, 1942-46, active duty in India; cdr, first wing, IAF, 1949; lt col, chief of oprs, 1950-53; cdr, IAF, 1958-66. Chmn, Herut Party, since 1971. Office: Hqrs, IDF, Isr.

WEIZMANN, Herzl G, Isr, agricultural settlement expert; b. Druskenik , Lith, July 25, 1905; s. Moses and Zinaida (Riwlin); nephew of Chaim Weizmann, first pres of Isr; DAgron, Inst for High Agronomic Studies, Naples, It, 1927; att: UCLA, 1932; Fed Training Cen, Wis, 1947; m. Yaffa-Shura Ledermann, May 10, 1931; c: Rafael, Uriel, Edna. Sr cons, OECD (Org Eur Coop and Devl), Paris; visiting prof, ME Tech U, Ankara, Turkey; cons to FAO, UN; chief land settlement off, intergovt comm for Eur migration, Geneva, since 1953; fmr: field mgr, Pal Plantations Ltd, 1928-39; soil conservation spec, Agric Research Sta, Rehovot, 1940-44; exec secy, agric settlement planning bur, JA for Pal, 1945-50; co-mgr, agric and resettlement jt planning cen, Isr Govt and JA for Pal, 1951-52. Served, Haganah. Mem comms: United Isr Appeal, Geneva, since 1959; fmr: Pal Agron Assn, 1940-42; Agric Research Sta Staff Assn, 1943-45. Contbr to Isr, It, and Swiss periodicals. Hobbies: music, photography, motoring. Home: 5 Tsimhei Hayehudim St, Ramat Aviv, Isr.

WELCMAN, Nathan, Isr, educator; b. Kutno, Pol, Apr 20, 1919; s. Jacob and Mata (Klar); in Isr since 1937; BSc, MSc, Technion; PhD, U Cambridge, Eng, 1961; m. Leah Weisberg, Apr 20, 1948; c: Dahlia, Jacob. Sr lectr, chem, Technion, since 1966. J Brigade, Brit Army, 1941-46; segen, sci corps, IDF, 1948-50. Coord, chem tchrs, Reali HS, Haifa; natl coord, Training of Chem Technicians; mem: Amer and Isr Chem Socs; Chem Soc, London. Author: General Chemistry

for Universities, 1967; contbr to sci jours. Home: 22 Sport Rd Haifa, Isr. Office: Technion, Haifa, Isr.

WELFELD, Marvin J, US, attorney; b. Chgo. Ill, Dec 8, 1905; s. Herman and Sarah (Bows); BA, U Mich, 1927; DJ, Northwestern U, 1930; m. Ann Adriance, Dec 2, 1955; c: Lewis, Martin, Geri Lasky, Marvin Jr; m. 2nd, Joyce Wagner, Aug 9, 1969. Partner, law firm, Welfeld, Fleischman & Chaimson, since 1935; fmr: Slottow & Leviton, 1930-31; Schwartz, Welfeld & Perlman, 1931-35. Mem: bd of dirs: JWF of metrop Chgo; Lyric Opera of Chgo; co-chmn, special gifts div, CJA, chmn: lawyers, city and country clubs divs; fmr: vice-pres, Brandeis Asso of Chgo; chmn, Denver Hosp drive; mem: Amer, Ill, and Chgo Bar Assns; Phi Epsilon Pi; clubs: Standard; Ravisloe Country; Execs. Hobbies: photography, farming. Home: 2130 Lincoln Park W, Chicago, Ill. Office: 33, N Dearborn St, Chicago, Ill.

WELS, Richard H, US, attorney; b. NYC, May 3, 1913; s. Isidor and Belle (Hoffman); BA, Cornell U, 1933; LLB, Harvard U 1936; m. Marguerite Samet, Dec 12, 1954; c: Susan, Amy. Partner, law firm, Wels and Marcus, and predecessor firms, since 1946; dir: Cornell Theaters, Inc; Nine Eleven Park Inc; fmr: spec asst dist atty, NY Co, 1936-37; asso, law firm, Handel and Panuch, 1937-38; mem, legal staff, asst to chmn, SEC, 1938-42; spec asst to US Atty and Atty Gen of US, 1940-42; spec counsel, House Naval Affairs comm, 79th Cong; gen counsel, Bowling Props Assn of Amer, 1952-61. Lt, USN, 1942-46. Chmn, bd trustees, Bleuler Psychotherapy Cen, Islands Research Found; mem, bd trustees, William Alanson Inst, Bleuler Psychotherapy Cen; chmn comms: improvement of family law, Assn of Bar of NYC; mil justice, NY Co Lawyers Assn; bowling and allied trades div, UJA, since 1961; vice-chmn: AJComm, mem, natl exec bd; Amer Parents comm; vice-pres, Cornell Alumni Assn of NY, 1953; mem: Amer, Fed, and FCC Bar Assns; Amer Judicature Soc; Inter-profsl comm on marriage, div, and family courts; Amer Legion, vice-cmdr, advt men's post; Pi Lambda Phi; Sunningdale Country; Natl Lawyers, Wash, DC; Harvard, NY; Cornell, NY; Harmonie, mem, bd govs. Contbr to profsl publs and mags. Home: 911 Park Ave, New York, NY. Office: 18 E 48 St, New York, NY.

WELT, Isaac D, US, researcher; b. Montreal, Can, May 13, 1922; s. David and Norma (Younger); in US since 1946; BS, McGill U, 1944, MS, 1945; PhD, Yale U, 1949; m. Rhoda Litwin, Dec 30, 1945; c: Selma, Murray, Bernard. Prof and dep dir, Cen for Tech and Admn, Amer U, Wash, DC, since 1964; fmr: asso dir and chief, Inst for Advancement of Med Communication, Wash off, 1961-64; researcher, Public Health Research Inst, NY, 1949-51; asso dir, radio-isotope unit, VA Hosp, Houston, 1951-53; asst prof, biochem, Baylor U Coll of Med, 1951-53; researcher, Natl Acad of Scis, 1953-61; professorial lectr, chem, Amer U, 1955-61; participant, spec sems, sci and tech info, Isr, 1969. Pres, Amer Documentation Inst, Potomac Valley chap, 1960-61; adult educ volunteer, J Cen, Arlington-Fairfax, since 1955; mem: Amer Chem Soc; AAAS; Med Libr Assn; Sigma Xi; ZOA. Author: Index-Handbook of Cardiovascular Agents, 1960; asso ed: Amer Documentation, since 1961; ed, abstract and index, Methods of Info in Med, since 1961; contbr to profsl jours. Hobbies: astronomy; gardening; woodworking. Home: 117 N Edgewood St, Arlington, Va. Office: Amer U, Washington, DC.

WELTCHEK, Harry, US, attorney; b. Elizabeth, NJ, May 10, 1901; s. Morris and Rebecca (Diamond); BS, U of Pa, 1923; LLB, Columbia U Law Sch, 1926, MA, grad sch, 1931; m. Elma Garber, Oct 19, 1927; c: Roy, Abby. Partner, law firm, Weltchek & Weltchek, since 1927; atty, Township of Clark, 1931-41. Pres: Union Co Assn, 1954; Cong B'nai Isr, Elizabeth, 1945-49; Elizabeth J Council, 1950; mem: YMHA; Intl Brotherhood of Magicians; club: Shackamaxon Country. Author: Rules of Land Warfare, 1931; History of Union Country Bar Association, 1952. Home: 585 Newark Ave, Elizabeth, NJ. Office: 27 Prince St, Elizabeth, NJ.

WELTSCH, Robert, Isr, journalist; b. Prague, Czech, June 20, 1891; s. Theodor and Frieda (Boehm); in Isr since 1938; JD, U Prague, 1914; DHL, with hons, HUC-JIR, 1969; m. Irene Leiser, 1951; c of previous m: Reuben, Shoshana Gumpert, Daniela, Tal. London corresp, Haaretz daily, since 1947, ed staff mem since 1940; fmr: ed, Judische Zeitung; journalist, Wiener Morgenzeitung, both Vienna, 1918-19; ed, Judische Rundschau, Berlin, 1919-38; free-lance writer, Pal, 1938-40. Mem bd, Leo Baeck Inst, since 1955, chmn, London bd. Author: Zionistische Politik, 1928; Ja-sagen Zum

Judentum, 1933; contbr to books: Martin Buber, 1961; Chaim Weizmann, 1962; Entscheidimpihr-1932, pub, 1966; ed: Leo Baeck Inst yearbooks, since 1955; contbr to J press. Hobbies: opera, LP records. Home: 7 Credition Hill, London NW, Eng. Office: Haaretz, 56 Maze St, Tel Aviv, Isr.

WENDER, Herbert, US, educator, author; b. Atlanta, Ga, Feb 8, 1900; s. Joseph and Lonna (Seltzer); BA, Oglethorpe U, 1921; att Columbia U, 1922; PhD, Johns Hopkins U, 1927; m. Sybil Landman, Sep 15, 1931; c: Stephen. Prof, hist, LIU, since 1946; fmr: instr, O State U, 1928-34; head, hist dept, Paterson Coll, 1934-42; prof, Concord Coll, 1942-44. Mem, Amer Hist Assn. Author: Southern Commercial Conventions, 1930; Growth of Modern Thought and Culture, 1959: co-author: The World Since 1914, pub, 1953; Contemporary Social Science, 1954; Development of Historiography, 1954. Home: 605 Grove St, Clifton, NJ. Office: Long Island U, Brooklyn, NY.

WENDEROW, Baruch, Isr, engineer; b. Kiev, Russ, Mar 8, 1921; s. Menachem and Sara; in Isr since 1925; Reali Sch, 1935-40; BS, Technion, 1946; div; c: Adi, Iron. Dir, fgn oprs, Tahal Water Planning for Isr, Ltd, since 1963, with org since 1952; fmr: water engr, Haifa Munic, 1947; dist engr, Min of Agric, 1949-52. Capt, IDF, 1947-49. Mem: Assn of Engrs and Architects of Isr; club: Lions, Haifa. Hobbies: music, history, photography, bridge. Home: 5 Zerubavel St, Haifa, Isr. Office: Tahal, 59 Ibn Gvirol St, Tel Aviv, Isr.

WENKERT, Ernest, US, chemist, educator; b. Vienna, Aus, Oct 16, 1925; s. Moses and Elcie (Seidmann); in US since 1941; BS, U Wash, 1945, MS, 1947; PhD, Harvard U, 1951; m. Ann Davis, June 22, 1948; c: Naomi, David, Daniel, Deborah. Prof, chem, Ind U, since 1961; instr, Lower Columbia Jr Coll, 1947-48; prof, Ia State U, 1959-61, fac mem since 1951; visiting prof, U Cal, Berkeley, 1961; Fulbright lectr, Institut de Chimie des Substances Naturelles, Gif-sur-Yvette, Fr, 1963; acting head, dept organic chem, Weizmann Inst of Sci, 1964-65; visting prof, U of Paris, 1968. Mem: Amer Chem Soc, chmn, 1958; Chem Soc, London; Sigma Xi; Phi Lambda Upsilon. Contbr to profsl jours. Recipient: Guggenheim f, 1965-66. Hobbies: stamp collecting, hiking. Home: 711 S Clifton Ave, Bloomington, Ind. Office: Ind U, Bloomington, Ind.

WERB, Morris R, US, rabbi; b. NYC, Oct 5, 1913; s. Israel and Sarah (Rakito); BA, Yeshiva U, 1936, ordained rabbi, 1937; MA, NYU, 1943, PhD, 1959; m. Helen Beiber, Aug 15, 1938; c: Hillel, Sherry. Rabbi, Cong Agudath Isr, since 1939; chaplain, Essex Co Penitentiary, since 1943; instr, sociol, Fairleigh Dickinson U; fmr, rabbi, Temple B'nai Zion, Bloomfield, NJ, 1938-39. Mem: RA; Bd of Rabbis of NY; Bd of Rabbis, Essex Co, pres, 1955-57; Prins Council of the J Educ Assn, exec; 1953-55; Amer Sociological Soc. Author: A Study of Jewish Suburbia, 1959; contbr to J publs. Home: 10 Florence Pl, Caldwell, NJ. Study: Cong Agudath, Isr. Caldwell, NJ.

WERBACH, Samuel, US, business exec; b. Felshteen, Russ, Jan 22, 1905; s. Menachem and Jocheved (Kanfer); in US since 1925; m. Martha Robbins, Apr 3, 1938; c: Melvyn, Joan. Owner, Werbach's Admiration Jewelry Co, since 1950; partner: Venus Bead & Novelty Co, 1930-37; Universal Jewelry Co, 1937-50. Vice-pres, Westchester Zionist Region since 1958; mem: natl exec comm, ZOA, since 1961; fmr: pres, Genesis Zionist, dist 151; trustee, Genesis Heb Cen, Tuckahoe, NY 1953-60; club: Optimist Intl. Home: 130 Puritan Ave, Yonkers, NY.

WERBALOWSKY, Seymour, US, attorney; b. Kingston, NY, Mar 7, 1926; s. Isadire and Ida (Smith); att: NYU, 1943; Princeton U, 1945; BA, Pa State U, 1947; LLB, Albany Law Sch, 1950; m. Nina Lakretz, Dec 4, 1955; c: Jeffrey, Eric, Kevin Partner, law firm, Richter & Werbalowsky, since 1951; investigator, Atty Gen of NY State, 1950-52. USN, 1944-46. Dir: Gateway Inds for Handicapped; Salvation Army; Ulster Co Bar Assn; vice-pres, Cong Ahavath Isr; fmr pres: Kingston lodge, B'nai B'rith, Hudson Valley Council; J Comty Cen; mem: Amer and NY Bar Assn; comm, Ulster Co bd of elections, since 1954; Pi Lambda Phi; 40 and 8 Soc; Masons. Hobbies: gardening, golf, sports. Home: 86 Sherry Lane, Kingston, NY. Office: 86 John St, Kingston, NY.

WERBEL, Ben, business exec; b. Nov 23, 1898; s. Philip and Anna (Footman); m. Mollie Katz, June 16, 1923; c: Edward, Walter, Morton, Harvey. Asso, display advt bus; secy, bd

of justices, criminal div, Supr Court, Kings Co; NY State assemblyman, 1948-54. Chmn, fund-raising drives: Isr Bond; Food for Isr; Red Mogen David; March of Dimes; UJA; Poale Agudath Isr; FJP, all Bklyn; pres, Yeshiva Torah M'Zion, since 1950; vice-pres, JNF, since 1948; vice-chmn: ZOA, Bklyn, since 1948; Pride of Judea Children's Home; dir: NY Youth and Adult Cen; YMHA; mem: Sign Display and Pictorial Union; Boy Scouts; KP; Apex Soc, Inc. Home: 1132 E 99 St, Brooklyn, NY. Office: 360 Adams St, Brooklyn, NY.

WERBELL, Frederick E, US, investment banker, rabbi; b. Stockholm, Swed, June 19, 1941; s. Joel and Anna (Jacobson); in US since 1963; att: Carmel Coll, Eng, 1953-55; Gymnasium, Sockholm, 1956-60; BA, with hons, Jews Coll, U London, 1963; BA, BHL, Yeshiva U, 1964; MA, oradined rabbi, JTSA, 1968; m. Elaine Pesrow. Inves banker, Bruns, Nordeman & Co, since 1969; lectr, Amer Acad of J Rel, NYC; rabbi: N Shore J Cen, LI, 1964-66; Temple Beth Sholom, Syracuse, 1966-68; vice-pres, Ken J Pesrow Corp, 1966-69. Mem: life, B'nei Akiva, Swed; Harvest lodge, B'nai B'rith; Amer reg comm, Council for Isr Econ Devl. Author: History of the Jews in Sweden. Spec interests: contemporary J hist, sociol. Home: 500 E 83 St, New York, NY. Office: 580 Fifth Ave, New York, NY.

WERBER, Eugen Moshe, Yugo, actor, director; b. Subotiza, Yugo, Jan 25, 1923; att Commercial Acad, Novi Sad. Actor, mem, Ben Zmanenu Theater, Belgrade, since 1960; dir: radio, theater, TV, movies, since 1945. Served, Yugo army. Mem: comm for civilization matters, J Comty in Belgrade, 1960-70; Fed of J Comty of Yugo, 1961-70. Trans: Shalom Aleichem, by Bialik; Tuvia haCholer, by Aloni, 1971; works by Kishon. Home: 11000 Bolgrade, Vele Nigrissove 14, II, Yugo.

WERBIN, Benzion, Isr, physician; b. Omsk, Russ, Jan 21, 1913; s. Yossef and Nehama; in Isr since 1913; MD, U Rome; m. Fania Israel, 1915; c: Dorit, Nahum. Head, childrens dept, Hadassah Hosp, Tel Aviv, since 1950; sr lectr, Tel Aviv U. Mem: ped orgs; Isr Heart Soc. Contbr to profsl jours. Home and office: 89 Rothschild Blvd, Tel Aviv, Isr.

WERMAN, Robert, Isr, educator; b. Bklyn, NY, May 2, 1929; s. Sidney and Rose (Sutton); in Isr since 1967; AB, NYU, 1948, MD, 1952; m. Golda Spiera, Feb 14, 1954; c: Michael, Aaron, Rachel. Prof, neurophysiol, Heb U, since 1969; asst prof, Columbia U, 1960-61; prof, Ind U, 1961-69. Lt, USN, 1954-56. Contbr to sci jours. Home: One Nahalat Tsadok St, Jerusalem, Isr. Office: Heb U, Jerusalem, Isr.

WERNE, Benjamin, US, attorney, educator, rabbi; b. Russ, Apr 15, 1904; s. Isaac and Marie (Lemon); in US since 1904; ordained rabbi, Columbus, O, 1923; BA, S Methodist U, 1926; LLB, St John's U, 1930; JD, NYU, 1932; m. Ruth Weiss, Aug 30, 1935; c: Mary Jane. Pvt law practice since 1943; lectr: lab law and collective bargaining, Practicing Law Inst, since 1952; med jurisprudence, Coll of Phys and Surgs, Columbia U, since 1941; lab counsel: Natl League of Cities; Natl Assn of Cos, both Wash, DC; US Conf of Mayors; NY State Conf of Mayors; rabbi: Temple Tefereth Isr, Columbus, O, 1923-25; Jamaica J Cen, 1925-30; Temple Emanuel, Yonkers, 1930-35; prof, NYU Grad Sch of Bus Admn, 1951-64. Mem: panel, Amer Arbitration Assn; Amer, NY State, NYC Bar Assns; NY Co Lawyers Assn; bd mem: United Med Service; NY Acad of Sci; Natl Adv Bd, Practicing Law Inst; Cen Syn of Nassau Co, fmr chmn, educ comm, bd trustees. Author: Business and the Robinson—Patman Act, 1938; Rogers on Expert Testimony, 1941; Guide for Labor Law, 1950; Law on Labor Relations, 1951; Management's Objectives in Collective Bargaining, 1953; Law and Practice of the Labor Contract, 2 vols, 1957; Industrial Relations Digest, 1958; Administration of the Labor Contract, 3 vols, 1963; Labor Relations Law and Practice, 2 vols, 1966; Collective Bargaining for Public Employees, 1968; Current Labor—Management Problems, 1969; Law for Doctors, 1969. Home: 66 Allen Rd, Rockville Centre, NY. Office: 122 E 42 St, New York, NY.

WERNER, Alfred, US, art critic; b. Vienna, Aus, Mar 30, 1911; s. Ignatz and Friedericka (Silberstein); in US since 1940; PhD, U Vienna, 1934; m. Judith Mayer, 1953. Art critic; contbr ed, Arts Mag, since 1954; ed, Die Stimme und Gerechtigkeit, Vienna, 1935-36; lit dir, Jüdische Kulturstelle, Vienna, 1936-38; ed, Universal J Ency, 1942-44; asso ed, Chgo J Forum, 1943-60; ed: Little Book Art Series, 1948-49; survey reports, Off of J Info, AJCong, 1953; lectr, Sch of Gen Studies, CCNY, 1955-58. Asso, OWI, 1943. Author: Gebet aus der Tiefe, poems, 1935; Der Blick Nach Innen, poems, 1936; Richard Beer-Hoffman, 1936; Alexander Watin und Die Jüdische Volkskunst, 1937; biographies: Utrillo, 1952; Dufy, 1953; Rousseau, 1957; Modigliani, 1962; Pascin, 1962; Barlach, 1966; Chagall, 1968; Degas Pastels, 1969; contbr to art jours. Home: 453 Hudson St, New York, NY. Office: Hotel Bryant, Broadway, and 54 St, New York, NY.

WERNER, Eric, US, musicologist, educator; b. Vienna, Aus, Aug 1, 1901; s. Julius and Helene (Donath) in US since 1938; att Us: Graz; Prague; Vienna; Berlin; Goettingen, 1919-28; PhD, U Strassbourg, 1928; D with hons, HUC, 1967; m. Elisabeth Mendelssohn, 1932, Head, dept of musicology, Tel Aviv, U, 1967-71; referendar, Landschulheim am Solling, 1925-26; asst prof, Saarbruecken Conservatory, 1926-33; study assessor, J Gymnasium, Breslau, 1935-38; prof, liturgical music, HUC-JIR, 1939-67; F, Intl Musicological Soc; mem: CCAR; Amer Musicological Soc; Soc for the Advancement of Judaism; Intl Cong of Catholic Church Music; corresp mem: Hung Acad of Scis; Amer Acad of J Research. Author: In the Choir Loft, 1958; The Sacred Bridge, 1959; Mendelsshohn: A New Image of the Composer and His Age, 1963; From Generation to Generation, 1968; contbr to J and profsl jours. Recipient: Guggenheim f. Spec interests: advanced math, cooking. Home: 900 W 190 St, New York, NY. Office: 40 W 68 St New York, NY.

WERNER, Herbert Levy, US, management cons; b. Berlin, Ger, June 9, 1908; s. Berthold and Alice (Hamburger); in US since 1938; att HS, Berlin, 1917-26; deg, textile engr, Reutlingen Coll, 1930; m. Stella Werner, June 28, 1938; c: Laurel, Beryl, Jeffrey. Chmn bd, Werner Assos, Inc, (subsidiary of Leasco Data Processing Equipment Corp), since 1938, chmn, mgmt cons comm, Leasco, since 1969; dir, mem exec comm, vice-pres, Fulton Inds Inc, 1956-68. Chmn: Isr Bond drive, Westchester Co; bd dirs, PEC; bd trustees, Westchester J Comty Services; FJP; asso chmn, Contbr to profsl publs. Home: 77 Feninmore Rd, Larchmont, NY. Office: 1450 Broadway, New York, NY.

WERNER, Shmuel, Isr, business exec; b. Dortmund, Ger, Feb 18, 1914; s. Menachem and Gitel (Stern); in Isr since 1933; chef, Hotelerie Sch, Strasbourg, 1933; m. Simcha Gross, 1934; c: Amnon, Dan. Mgn dir, Pundakim Catering Ltd, since 1965; dir, Mat'am, kosher frozen foods, Kibbutz Chefez Chaim, since 1969. Found, secy, Kibbutz Ein Gev, 1937. IDF,1934-65. Mem, Chain des Rotisseurs. Home: 24 Habrosh St, Savyon Isr. Office: Lod Airport, Isr.

WERNER, Shoshana, Isr, administrator, social worker, ret army officer; b. Lvov, Pol, 1912; d. David and Sarah (Yarmush); in Isr since 1933; grad, Paul Baerwald Sch of Social Work, Versailles, Fr; BA, Heb U, 1956. Natl secy, Assn of Social Workers in Isr, since 1960; exec secy, dept for higher educ, Vaad Hapoel; agric worker, Rehovot, 1933; i/c, Beit Hachalutzot, immigrants home for girls, Tel Aviv, 1946-48. Haganah, research work in explosives, 1933-39; capt, Brit Army, 1942-46; org, CHEN, women's sect, IDF, 1948, cdr in chief, col, CHEN, 1948-52. Chmn, The Council of Social Agencies, Tel Aviv area; head, women's sect, Mapai Party, 1956-60; mem: Org for Social Workers; Academicians Dept for Social Scis. Hobby: swimming. Home: 61 Pinsker St, Tel Aviv, Isr. Office: 93 Arlosoroff St, Tel Aviv, Isr.

WERNICK, Nissim, US, rabbi; b. Bklyn, NY, Mar 17, 1939; s. William and Edith (Sabon); BS, LIU, 1961; MHL, JTSA, 1963, ordained rabbi, 1966; PhD, Brigham Young U, Sch of Rel, 1968; m. Diane Lewis, Dec 18, 1962; c: Stuart, Bruce. Rabbi, Cong Shearith Isr, since 1968; lectr, Emory U, since 1969; chaplain, Ga State U, since 1968; speech therapist, Eng tchr, Bobover Yeshiva, 1957-62; rabbi, Cong Montefiore, 1966-68; guest prof, Brigham Young U, 1967-68. Natl bd, JDC; bd dirs: JCC of Atlanta; Concerned Clergy of Atlanta, 1968-69; mem: RA; Ecumenical Council, Ga State U; Min Assn, Salt Lake City, 1966-68; Atlanta Natl Council of J Feds; AJComm; Isr Bonds; Sigma Alpha Mu. Author: Mormonism and Jewish Literature, 1969. Spec interests: composer, author, performer of musicals and dramas, lectr on civil rights, Mormonism, Israel. Home: 1205 Spring Valley Lane, NE, Atlanta, Ga. Study: 1180 University Dr, NE, Atlanta, Ga.

WERSHUB, Leonard Paul, US, urologist, educator, author; b. NYC, May 5, 1901; s. Samuel and Rosa (Schwartz); att: Columbia Coll, 1919-22; Yale U, 1922-24; MD, NY Med Coll, 1927; m. Miriam Goldblatt, June, 1923; c: Stuart. Prof

urol, NY Med Coll, since 1939, fac mem since 1932; dir, urol, Heb Home for the Aged, since 1952. Maj, US Army Res Med Corps, 1928-37. Pres, med bd, Flower-Fifth Ave Hosps, 1966-69; hon f, Madrid Acad of Surg; f: Amer Coll of Surgs; Intl Coll of Surgs; dipl, Amer Bd of Urol. Curator, medical memorabilia, 1965-69. Author: Urology and Industry, 1956; Sexual Impotence in the Male, 1959; The Human Testis: A Clinical Treatise, 1962; One Hundred Years of Medical Progress, 1967; Urology from Antiquity to the 20th Century; contbr to profsl jours. Recipient: Legion of Merit, US Cong; alumni medal, NY Med Coll. Home: 1136 Fifth Ave, New York, NY. Office: 115 E 61 St, New York, NY.

WERTHEIMER, Ernst, Isr, physiologist, educator; b. Bühl, Ger, Aug 24, 1893; s. Leo and Hermine ((Wertheimer); in Isr since 1934; MD, U Heidelberg; m. Ruth Lehmann, 1928; c: Ayala, Neomi, Ada. Dorit. Prof, biochem, Heb U, since 1953, dean, med fac, 1953-57, fac mem since 1934; dir, chem lab, Hadassah Hosp, since 1934; asso prof, phys, U Halle, Ger, 1928. Mem, Isr Acad of Sci and Humanities. Contbr to profsl jours. Recipient: Isr prize; Banting medal, Toronto, 1960. Home: 26 Abarbanel St, Jerusalem, Isr. Office: Heb U, Jerusalem, Isr.

WERTHEIMER, Howard M, US, editor, attorney; b. Cleveland, O, April 11, 1893; s. Daniel and Rose (Oppenheimer); BS, Harvard U, 1915; LLB, W Reserve U, 1918. Drama critic, radio sta WERE, Cleveland, since 1967; ed, J Rev and Observer, 1918-64. Perm chmn, class of 1918, W Researve U Law Sch; mem: Amer Fed of Radio and TV Artists; clubs: Press, Cleveland; Harvard. Home: 12701 Shaker Blvd, Cleveland, O. Office: 1220 Huron Ave, Cleveland, O.

WERTHEIMER, Joseph, US, business exec; b. Cleveland, O, Apr 14, 1894; s. David and Bertha (Rosenbloom); BS, Case Inst of Tech, 1916; m. Theresa Schemnitz, June 21, 1921; c: Irwin, Elaine Graham, Milan, William. Pres and chmn of bd, Turner Printing Machery in Inc, since 1922, ret; experimental engr, Natl Tube Co, Lorain, O, 1916-17; chem, produc supt, Amer Borvisk Co, 1919-20; asso prof, metallurgy, U Kan, 1920-21; metallurgist, Cleveland Drop Forge Co, 1921-22. Lt, US Army, 1917-18. Natl vice-pres, Amer Technion Soc; hon pres, Chgo chap; trustee, Isr Inst of Tech, Haifa, Isr; pres, ZOA, NS Shore div, Chgo, 1936-38; mem: Printers Supplymen's Guild; Ill Press Assn; Intl Assn Printing House Craftsmen; Amer Legion; B'nai B'rith; Amer Friends of Heb U; N Shore Temple Isr; clubs: Standard, Chgo; Palm Beach Country. Recipient: meritorious, award, Case Inst of Tech, 1956. Homes: 1111 Pebblewood Lane, Glencoe, Ill; 250 Bradley Pl, Palm Beach, Fla. Office: 732 Sherman St, Chicago, Ill.

WERTHEIMER, Zeev, Isr, business exec; b. Ger, July 16, 1926; s. Eugen and Lina, m. Miriam Wallach; c: Eitan, Ruth, Ptach. Mgr, Iscar Ltd, since 1952; with Defense Min. Palmach, 1944-47. Home: 104 Herzl St, Nahariya, Isr. Office: POB 34, Nahariya, Isr.

WERTMAN, Moshe Efraim, Isr, government official; b. Tomaszow, Pol, Feb 20, 1924; s. Israel and Sara (Wektman); in Isr since 1947; m. Malca, Aug 31, 1949; c: Elisha, Nurit, Ehud. MK since 1966; secy-gen, Isr Lab Party, Haifa, since 1968; mem, exec, Haifa Lab Council, 1959; secy-gen, Lab Party, 1964-68. Sgt, IDF, 1947-49. Home: 28 Bet St, Halfa, Isr. Office: Knesset, Jerusalem, Isr.

WESTBURY, Jack, Eng, public official, valuation surveyor; b. London, Eng, June 24, 1914; s. Isaac and Rachel (Chyte) Wieselberg; att: Pitmans Cen Coll, 1928-30; NW Poly, 1932-34; m. Rachel Lieberman, May 7, 1939; c: Frances, Judith. Alderman, London Borough of Lambeth, since 1968, dep-mayor since 1969, councilor, 1964-68; sr partner, Westburys, since 1959; dir, Curtis Estates London Ltd, since 1939. Pvt, RASC, 1941-44. Warden, Brixton Syn; chmn: standing comm, United Syn Movement; adv comm, Dept Health and Social Security; Highways & Works comm, both Lambeth; Hitherfield, Sunnyhill & Julians group schs; Anglo-J Philanthropic Soc; vice-chmn, Batterson Grammar Sch; gov, JFS Comprehensive Sch, Inner London Educ Auth; mem: J Comm for HM Forces; Southeast London Rent Tribunal, Min Housing; Streatham Citizens Advice Bur comm; London Council Social Service; London Boroughs Assn. Home: 24 Woodbourne Ave, London, Eng. Office: 120 Streatham Hill, London, Eng.

WESTHEIMER, Frank H, US, chemist, educator; b. Arlington, Md, Jan 15, 1912; s. Henry and Carrie (Burgunder); BA, Dartmouth Coll, 1932; hon DSc, 1961; MA, Harvard U, 1933, PhD, 1935; m. Jeanne Friedmann, Aug 31, 1937; c: Ruth, Ellen. Prof, chem, Harvard U, since 1954, chmn, chem dept, 1959-62; prof, U Chgo, fac mem, 1936-54; sup, explosives research lab, Natl Defense Research comm, 1944-45; visiting prof, U Cal, 1955, 1958; Morell lectr, U Cambridge, 1962. Mem: Pres Sci Adv comm, since 1967; Natl Acad of Scis. Ed bd, jour of Amer Chem Soc; contbr to profsl jours. Recipient: Naval Ordnance Devl award, 1946; Army-Navy cert, 1948. Home: 46 Rockmont Rd, Belmont, Mass. Office: Harvard U, Cambridge, Mass.

WESTHEIMER, Robert I, US, stockbroker; b. Cincinnati, O, Oct 25, 1916; s. Irvin and Duffie (Heinsheimer); BA, Cornell U, 1938; m. Ruth Welling, Nov 12, 1945; c: Ann, Sally, Richard. Dir and vice-pres, Hayden, Stone Inc, since 1963; fmr, acct exec, Westheimer & Co, 1938-42, partner, 1945-63; dir: Cincinnati Equitable Ins Co; Access Corp; Cincinnati Financial Corp; IHC Corp; Carousel Fashions Inc. Cons, USAAF, 1942-45. Dir: exec bd, AJComm; Boys Clubs, Cincinnati; trustee: Cincinnati BBB; Comty Chest & Council, vice-chmn, allocations div; fmr: pres: J Family Service Bur; Cincinnatus Assn; dir, Family Service Assn of Amer; chmn, Comty Health and Wfr Council; clubs: Queens City; Bankers; Losantiville Country; Cincinnati Stock and Bond. Recipient: award of merit, USAAF; citations: Air Material Command; Air Transp Command, all WW II. Home: 455 Rawson Woods Lane, Cincinnati, O. Office: 3 E Fourth St, Cincinnati, O.

WETTSTEIN, Hyman, US, educator, rehab specialist; b. Bklyn, NY, Aug 26, s. Philip and Minnie (Diner); BS, NYU, 1937, MA, 1948, dipl, rehab, 1955; m. Rosalie Saks, Nov 5, 1939; c: Howard, Ellen, Joel. Asst prof, health and phys educ, Yeshiva U, since 1951, dir, intramurals, since 1957, fac mem since 1937; chief, corrective therapy, Bx VA Hosp, since 1968, staff mem since 1946, instr, phys educ, and basketball coach, HS, Yeshiva U, 1940-42, and since 1947; dir, metrop J HS Leagues, since 1951; guest lectr, corrective therapy and phys rehab: NYU, since 1948; Clumbia U Tchrs Coll, since 1956; visiting prof, LIU, since 1957; supervising recreation tchr, Bx, 1934-35; playground dir, NYC Parks Dept, 1937-42; prin, Bd of Educ Comty Cen, Bx, 1950. Chief, USN, 1942-45, specialist, phys fitness and rehab prog; guest lectr, USN phys educ, U Richmond, 1943; phys dir, VA Hosp, Perry Pt, Md, 1945-46; chief, corrective phys rehab, VA Hosp, Ft Howard, Md, 1946. Developed aids now used nationally to help disabled automobile drivers. Chmn: bd dirs, Metrop J HS League, since 1964; natl cert bd, Amer Corrective Therapy Assn, 1964-66, natl leg comm, 1968; cert comm, Natl Assn for Phys and Mental Rehab, since 1962, co-found, 1946; pres: E States chap, Amer Assn for Phys and Mental Rehab, 1962, NY chap, 1964; commn, Dr Jacob Byer Memorial post, AMVETS, 1949, 1956; mem, bd dirs, J Comty Cen, Spring Valley, NY, 1960; mem: exec bd, Bx post, DAV, 1947-52; AAUP. Films: co-author, Driver Training for Severely Disabled, 1955; produc, dir, Courage Takes the Wheel, 1966. Recipient: VA awards: aids for disabled, 1956, 1957, 1958; corrective therapy work, 1957; public service, 1967; treatment of disabled, 1967; fac awards: Yeshiva U Athletic Assn, 1955, 1958. Home: One Northbrook Rd, Spring Valley, NY.

WEXLER, Bernard C, US, medical researcher, educator; b. Boston, Mass, Apr 30, 1923; s. William and Dora (Russia); BS, U Ore, 1947; MA, U Cal Coll of Med, 1948; PhD, basic med sci, Stanford U Coll of Med, 1952. Asso prof, experimental path, U Cincinnati Coll of Med, since 1962, fac mem since 1956; dir, May Inst for Med Research, J Hosp, since 1964, with org since 1956; inves, AEC, Stanford Research Inst, 1950-52; dir, endocrine and path labs, Baxter Labs, Morton Grove, Ill, 1952-56. US Army, 1942-46. F, Amer Gerontological Soc; mem: Acad of Med, Cincinnati; AAAS; Amer Assn for Lab Animal Sci; Amer Assn of Paths and Bacts; Amer Diabetes Assn; Amer Psychosomatic Soc; Amer Soc of Experimental Path; Assn of Amer Med Colls; Biol Stain Commn; AHA councils: arteriosclerosis, cerebrovascular disease, high blood pressure research; Diabetes Assn of Cincinnati; Endocrine Soc; honor soc, U Cal; NY Acad of Sci; Sigma Xi; Soc of Experimental Biol and Med; Soc for Study of Reproduction. Contbr to med research jours. Recipient: Merrell scholar in gerontology, 1953-57; advanced research f, AHA, 1960-62; research career award, Natl Heart Inst, Natl Insts of Health, 1962-69. Home: 7640 De Mar Rd, Indian Hill, Cincinnati, O. Office: 421 Ridgeway Ave, Cincinnati, O.

WEXLER, David J, US, surgeon; b. Bklyn, NY, Nov 13, 1906; s. Jacob and Sarah (Wexler); BS, CCNY, 1927; MD, Tufts Med Sch, 1931; m. Ida Schwartz, 1934; c: Charles, Howard, Joan. Sr surg and gyn, Southside Hosp, Bay Shore, since 1934; pres, med bd; sr surg, Good Samaritan Hosp, W Islip, since 1959; dir, surg, Cen Islip State Hosp, since 1965, adv council, nursing sch, staff mem since 1951; att surg, Pilgrim State Hosp, W Brentwood, since 1962; cons, surg, Brookhaven Memorial Hosp, Patchogue, since 1956; dir, Group Health Inc, NY, since 1958; fire surg, Islip Terr Volunteer Fire Dept, 1934; asso att gyn, female sex endocrine clinic, J Hosp, Bklyn, 1957-66, staff mem since 1944. Inventor of surgical and gyn devices. F: Amer Coll of Surgs; Intl Coll of Surgs; pres: Suffolk Co Acad of Med, since 1958; Suffolk Co Med Soc, 1957; fmr, chief med off, civil defense: Town of Islip; Suffolk Co; dir, Happy Landing Fund of Suffolk Co, since 1963; mem: AMA; NY State Med Soc; Intl and Pacific Coast Fertility Assns; Amer Soc for the Study of Sterility; NY Acad of Sci; Amer Phys Fellowship of IMA; Southside Clinical Soc; Suffolk Surg Soc; LI Phys; B'nai B'rith; Temple Sinai, Bay Shore; club, Lions, Islip. Contbr to profsl jours. Hobbies: painting, photography, amateur radio, fishing. Home: 161 W Bayberry Rd, Islip, NY. Office: 111 Carleton Ave, Islip Terrace, NY.

WEXLER, Jack, US, physician; b. Aus, Apr 15, 1913; s. Harry and Sophie (Teiplitzki); in US since 1922; AB, W Va U, 1935; MD, Med Coll of Va, 1939; m. Ruth Gherman, 1946; c: Bruce, Richard, Steven. Phys, Johns Hopkins Hosp, since 1952, instr, med sch, since 1952; cons, card, VA, since 1951; att phys, Sinai Hosp, Baltimore, since 1950; tutor, med, Harvard Med Sch, 1942-43. Maj, US Army MC, WW II. Chmn: Baltimore chap, AJComm, 1962-63; educ evaluation comm, Baltimore Heb Cong, 1964-68, mem, bd of electors, 1960; vice-chmn, Baltimore J Council, 1963-64; mem: adult educ comm, J Comty Cen; Md State and Baltimore City Med Socs; Amer Coll of Phys; AHA; Phi Beta Kappa. Contbr to profsl jours. Recipient: Harvard research f, 1942-43; commendation ribbon, WW II; research grant, NIH. Special interests: golf, semantics. Home: 7 Swanhill Dr, Baltimore, Md. Office: 222 W Cold Spring Lane, Baltimore, Md.

WEXLER, Jakov, Isr, artist; b. Libau, Latvia, Nov 15, 1912; s. Tuvia and Sara (Krupnik); in Isr since 1935; att Acad of Art, Hamburg, Ger; m. Miriam Shternberg, 1950; c: Itamar, Avital. Dir, Avni Inst Fine Arts, Tel Aviv, since 1966. IDF, 1948-50. One-man shows: Gal Jonas, 1945; Artists House, 1953, both Jerusalem; Tel Aviv Mus, 1948, 1955; Artists House, Tel Aviv, 1953; Tokanten Gal, Copenhagen, 1950; Artists House, Haifa, 1955; Haifa Mus, 1959; Gal Lara Vincy, Paris, 1956; exhbs: Biennale of Sao Paulo, 1953-61; Salon d'Automne, Paris, 1955; Exhb of Contemporary Art, Musée d'Art Moderne, Paris, 1956; Biennale of Graphic Art, Tokyo, 1960, 1966; Art Isr, NY Mus of Modern Art, 1964; Gal Charpentier, Paris, 1964; Intl Graphic Art, Vancouver, 1966. Mem, New Horizons Group. Recipient: Dizengoff prize, 1942; Herman Struck prize, 1945; JA prize, 1945. Home and studio: 6 Ovadia St, Ramat Chen, Isr.

WEXLER, Samuel H, US, business exec, manufacturer; b. Fall River, Mass, Feb 25, 1904; s. Lewis and May (Perlitch); BBA, Boston U, Coll of Bus Admn, 1924; m. Etta Goldstein, June 26, 1927; c: Robert, Jerrold. Pres, Selig Mfg Co: Leominster, and Fitchburg, Mass; Siler City, NC; Monroe, La; Elora, Can; Copenhagen, Den, since 1931; dir: Leominster Realty Co; Devonshire Realty Co; Monroe Realty Co; Siler City Realty Co; public acctnt, 1924-26; sales mgr, Freeman Parlor Furniture Co, 1926-31. Dir, Natl Furniture Mfrs Assn; natl furniture chmn, UJA, 1946-48, chmn and pres, Leominster campaign, 1949-50; f, Brandies U, since 1966; mem: pres council and natl ind planning comm; bd of trustees, Temple Agudas Achim; B'nai B'rith; Masons; club, Mt Pleasant Country. Home: 781 W St, Leominster, Mass. Office: 54 Green St, Leominster, Mass.

WEXLER, William A, US, optometrist; b. Toledo, O, July 16, 1913; att U Toledo; grad, S Coll of Optometry, Memphis, 1937; m. Dorothy Levy. July 18, 1937; c: Allan, Edward, Raymond. Pvt practice since 1941. World pres, B'nai B'rith, since 1965; affiliated since 1939; co-chmn, World Conf J Orgs; chmn, Amer Conf J Orgs; pres: JCC, Savannah, 1961-63; J Comty Cen, 1947-48; S region, CJFWF, 1963-65; S sect, JWB, 1951-52; vice-pres: Conf Material Claims Against W Ger; Natl J Hosp, Denver; Leo N Levi Hosp, Hot Springs, Ark; chmn: UJA, Savannah, 1951-56; Isr Bond Comm, 1957-63; vice-chmn: Third Armed Forces Services Region, JWB;

alderman, Munic of Savannah, 1947-48; mem: exec comm, Memorial Found for J Culture; World Council of Educ; ZOA, life; fmr: Savannah Bd J Educ; natl council, JDC, finance comm, USO of Savannah; bd, UM Assn. Recipient: man of the year, JWV, Savannah, 1955. Home: 623 E 49 St, Savannah, Ga. Office: 139 Bull St, Savannah, Ga.

WEYNE, Arthur, US, journalist; b. NYC, June 19, 1908; s. Asher and Chaya (Kushiner); m. Joyce Bobkin, June 15, 1930; c: Bruce, Mark. Ed, The Cleveland J News, since 1964; pub, The J Record, 1957-59; staff mem, PR dept, UJA, 1959; ed, The Amer Examiner, 1959-64. Mem: Amer J Press Assn; Amer J PR Soc. Author: Joshua The Redeemer, 1952; The Less Said, 1964; Getting Out the Paper, journalism guidebook. Recipient: best comty newspaper awards, CJFWF, 1954, 1955, 1956. Home: 13855 Suprior, Dr, E Cleveland, O. Office: 2108 Payne Ave, Cleveland, O.

WHARTMAN, Eliezer Leonard, Isr, radio journalist; b. Phila, Pa, May 16, 1920; s. Isadore and Ethel (Dyner); in Isr since 1958; BE, Temple U, 1942; Heb tchrs cert, Gratz Coll; att Heb U, 1964-66; m. Drora Neeman; c: Moshe, Yisrael, Yifat. Head, ME bur, MBS, since 1960; instr, Eng dept, Heb U, since 1966; dir, publs, AZC, 1962-67; corresp, Westinghouse Bc Co, 1964-67. US Army, info and educ div, 1942-46; Haganah; IDF, 1948-49. Bd mem, Mevakshei Derech Cong, Jerusalem; fmr, chmn, Jerusalem br, AACI. Contbr to Anglo-J publs. Home: 2 Nayot, Jerusalem, Isr. Office: c/o Govt Press Info Off, Jerusalem, Isr.

WHITE, Allen Jordan, US, stockbroker; b. Boston, Mass, Oct 24, 1927; s. Benjamin and Lillian (Stein); BS, Boston U, 1951; m. Janice Myers, June 24, 1951; c: Nancy, David. Pres, A J White, Carlotti and Co, stockbrokers, since 1959; dir: Quaker City Ind, NJ; Hydroski Intl, Fla; Viking Air Lines, RI; World Ind, Cal; Elmwood Sensors, RI. Lt, US Army finance dept, 1945-49. Pres: Temple Sinai, Cranston, RI; Frat Order of Police, E Providence; commn, RI State Comm for Hum Rights; mem: Warwick City Rep comm, since 1967; Tau Delta Phi; Social Financial Analysts, RI; fmr dir: Navy League; Providence Plantation; club, E Providence Rotary, fmr dir. Home: 115 Love Lane, Warwick, RI. Office: 320 Waterman Ave, E Providence, RI.

WHITEMAN, Maxwell, US, librarian, author; b. Phila, Pa, Jan 17, 1914; s. Tobiah and Nechamah (Millman); m. Elizabeth Delano, May 8, 1937; c: Bethel. Archival and hist cons, Union League of Phila, since 1964; antiquarian, bookseller, 1935-53; asst dir, Amer J Archives, 1955-57; libr, Dropsie Coll, 1959-64. Mem: publs comm, J Publ Soc Amer, since 1956; exec council, Amer J Hist Soc, 1956-67. Author: A Century of Fiction by American Negroes, 1955; Mankind and Medicine, 1966; Pieces of Paper: Gateway to the Past, 1967; While Lincoln Lay Dying, 1968; co-author, The History of the Jews of Philadelphia from Colonial Times to the Age of Jackson, 1957; ed, Afro-Amer series. Home: 414 Westview Rd, Elkins Park, Pa. Office: 140 S Broad St, Philadelphia, Pa.

WICE, David H, US, rabbi; b. Petersburg, Va, Feb 1, 1908; s. Henry and Rose (Cooper); BA, Wash and Lee U, 1927, MA, 1928, hon DD, 1948; ordained rabbi, HUC, 1933; hon DHL, 1954; m. Sophie Salzer, Feb 22, 1934; c: Carol, David. Rabbi: Cong Rodeph Shalom, since 1947, life tenure since 1952; Temple Isr, Omaha, Neb, 1933-41; Temple B'nai Jeshurun, Newark, NJ, 1941-47; lectr, Judaism: J Chautauqua Soc; World Union for Progressive Judaism. Mem, natl bd, Family Service Assn, since 1959, natl press, 1961-67; dir, Amer group, World Union for Progressive Judaism, 1944-55; chmn, comm on family, CCAR, 1967, E reg, 1958-61; bd govs, and bd overseers, HUC-JIR, both 1948-52; mem: Marriage Council; Planned Parenthood; New Americans; NCCJ; J Comty Relations Council; Fed of J Agencies; J Comty Chaplaincy Service, found pres; Bd of Rabbis, pres, 1954-56; Phi Beta Kappa; Kappa Phi Kappa. Home: 21 Latham Pkwy, Melrose Park, Pa. Study: 615 N Broad St, Philadelphia, Pa.

WIDELOCK, Daniel, US, microbiologist, researcher; b. NYC, Apr 24, 1911; s. Barnet and Fannie (Cohen); BS, LIU, 1932; MS, NYU, 1933; PhD, 1937. Dep dir, bur of labs, NYC Health Dept, since 1966; serologist, USPHS, 1940-45. Lt col, US Army, 1942-45, col res, ret. F: Amer Acad of Microbiol; NY Acad of Sci; Amer Public Assn Health; dipl, Amer Bd of Microbiol, mem, expert comm on treponematosis, WHO, since 1951. Contbr to sci jours. Home: 2960 Grand Concourse,

New York, NY. Office: Public Health Labs, 455 First Ave, New York, NY.

WIDLITZ, Paul J, US, jurist; b. Newark, NJ, Aug 11, 1914; s. Meyer and Rose (Kaplan); BA, Pa State U, 1936; LLB, NYU Law Sch, 1939; m. Beatrice Landsman, 1944; c: Phyllis Schwartz, Stephen. Justice of Supr Court, State of NY, since 1962; judge: Dist Court of Nassau Co, 1951-56; Co Court of Nassau Co, 1957-61. Lt, USAAF, 1943-46. Chmn, bd dirs, pres, Heb Acad of Nassau Co; trustee, Isr Comty Cen, Levittown; fmr chmn, Boy Scouts drives, Nassau Co; pres, Co Judges Assn, State of NY; delg, NY State Constitutional Conv, 1967; mem: Guiding Light lodge, B'nai B'rith; Masons; Amer Legion; JWV; NY State and Nassau Co Bar Assns. Recipient: Silver Beaver award, Boy Scouts of Amer; gold medal, VFW; medal of merit, JWV; annual award, S Nassau Co Lawyers Assn, 1960; Norman F Lent Memorial award, Criminal Courts Bar Assn, 1966. Home: 36 Raspberry Lane, Levittown, NY. Office: Nassau Co Supr Court Bldg, Supr Court Dr, Mineola, NY.

WIDMAN, Alfred B, S Afr, attorney; b. Capetown, S Afr, June 25, 1921; s. Morris and Rebecca (Abrams); att Natal U; m. Lillian Margolis, Aug 29, 1948; c: Myrisse, Jonathan. Pvt practice since 1948. Capt, S Afr Army, 1940-45. Mem, provincial council, Orange Grove, Transvaal, since 1959; city councilor for Berea, Johannesburg City Council, since 1961, mem, mgmt comm, with portfolio of health and amenities; leader, United Party, in City Council; chmn: Aesthetic Control comm; Rand Stadium comm; Johannesburg Regional Council, mem actions comm; vice-chmn, Natl Kidney Found of S Afr; chmn: Mus of Man; Mus of Sci; exec gov, Johannesburg Civic Theater Assn; mem: exec, Witwatersrand Agric Show; bd, Edenvale Hosp; Parkview Greenside Heb Cong; bd govs, Waverly Girls Sch; charter, The Lions; Highlands N Boys Sch; adv comm, Marriage Guidance Assn; comm, Johannesburg Munic Pension & Provident Fund; exec, Transvaal Munic Assn and Council of Reef Munics; comm, Photographic Mus; club, Huddle Park Gold, pres. Hobbies: golf, boats, fishing. Home: 27 Eighth Ave, Highlands N Ext, Johannesburg, S Afr. Office: 4 Victory House, 34 Harrison St, Johannesburg, S Afr.

WIEN, Lawrence A, US, attorney; b. NYC, May 30, 1905; BA, Columbia Coll, 1925; LLB, Columbia U Law Sch, 1927; hon LLD: LIU, 1962; Brandeis U, 1962; m. Mae Levy, July 21, 1929; c: Enid Morse, Isabel Malkin. Sr mem, law firm, Wien, Lane, Klein and Malkin; pvt law practice since 1928; heads numerous inves groups controlling commercial bldgs, apt houses, shopping cens and hotels, including: Empire State Bldg; Plaza Hotel, NYC; mem, bd dirs: Consolidated Edison Co; Borden Inc; Jonathan Logan Inc; Morse Shoe Inc. Chmn, bd trustees, Brandeis U; asso chmn, bd trustees, FJP, NY, pres, 1960-63; vice-chmn: bd dirs, Lincoln Cen for Performing Arts, Inc; bd trustees, Inst of Intl Educ; trustee: Columbia U; Educ Bc Corp; Citizens Budget Commn; mem, bd dirs: UN Assn of USA; Comty Blood Council, NY; pres, Charles and Rosanna Batchelor Memorial Inc; mem, host country adv comm for UN; fmr: trustee, Norwalk Hosp, Conn; off, City Fusion Party; mem: Amer and NY State Bar Assns; Assn Bar City of NY; natl panel of arbitrators, Amer Arbitration Assn; clubs: Columbia U; Birchwood Country, Westport, Conn; Golf at Aspetuck, Easton, Conn; Palm Beach Country, Fla; Desert Inn Country, Las Vegas; Harmonie. Office: 60 E 42 St, New York, NY.

WIENER, Alexander S, US, physician, serologist, educator; b. NYC, Mar 16, 1907; s. George and Mollie (Zuckerman); AB, Cornell U, 1926, MD, SUNY Downstate Med Sch, 1930; hon deg, honoris causa, Toulouse U, 1969; m. Gertrude Rodman, June 15, 1932; c: Jane Einhorn, Barbara Krevit. Owner, dir, Wiener Labs, since 1935; att immuno-hematologist: J Hosp, Bklyn, since 1952, mem staff since 1932; Adelphi Hosp, Bklyn, since 1952, mem staff since 1940, pres, med staff, since 1960; prof, forensic med, NYU Coll of Med, since 1968, fac mem since 1938; serologist, Off of Chief Med Examiner, NYC, since 1938; cons to hosps; lectr: Practicing Law Inst; Law Inst, both 1938-40. Prin contribs: pioneer co-discoverer: Rh blood factor, 1937; role of Rh in blood transfusion reactions, 1939; introduced Rh typing in selection of blood donors, 1940; discoverer, Rh-Hr types and mechanism of their heredity, 1942; co-discoverer, blood factors, Ca, U, Rh^a, Rh^b, Rh^c, Rh^d, M^e, devised method of treatment of erythroblastosis fetalis by exch transfusion, 1944-46; demonstrated evolution of human blood groups; found blood groups of non-human primates for use in experimentation and transplantation, FACP; f: Amer Coll Clinical Paths; AMA; Coll of Amer Paths; Intl Soc of Hematology and Blood Transfusion; AAAS; NY Acad Med; NY Acad Scis; Amer Acad Forensic Scis; mem: Union Temple, Bklyn; Amer Assn Immunologists; Amer Bd Path; Kings Co Med Soc; Amer Doc Genet; Research Soc Amer; Amer Assn Blood Banks, Soc for Study of Blood, found, first pres; Soc Med Jurisprudence; NY State Soc Med; Amer Assn Phys Anthropologists; NY State Soc Paths; Blood Banks Assn, NY; Royal Soc Med, London; Phi Delta Epsilon; Phi Beta Kappa; Phi Beta Kappa Assos; Alpha Omega Alpha; hon: Mystery Writers Amer; Associatión Mexicana de Transfución y Hematologia. Author: Blood Groups and Transfusions, 3rd ed, 1943; Rh-Hr Syllabus, The Types and Their Application, 2nd ed, 1962; Rh-Hr Blood Types, Applications in Clinical and Legal Medicine and Anthropology, 1954; Advances in Blood Grouping, 1961, vol II, 1965, vol III, 1970; co-author, Heredity of Blood Groups, 1958; mem, ed bds: Nouvelle Revue Française d'Hématologie; Acta Genetica Medica et Gemellologiae, Rome, since 1952; Amer Jour Forensic Scis, co-found, 1956; Jour Forensic Med, S Afr, since 1964; Transfusion, since 1962; Experimental Medicine and Surgery, since 1952; Laboratory Digest, since 1951; contbr to profsl jours. Recipient: Phi Delta Epsilon prize, 1931; Silver medal, Amer Soc Clinical Path, 1943; Alvarenga prize, Coll of Phys, Phila, 1945; Lasker award, Amer Public Health Assn, 1945; Ward Burdick award, Amer Soc Clinical Path, 1946; Army-Navy cert, 1948; Oscar, Youth United, 1951; award, Passano Found, 1951; Modern Med award, 1953; Alumni medal, SUNY, Coll of Med, 1955; Karl Landsteiner award, Amer Assn Blood Banks, 1956; Carlos J Finlay medal, Havana, Cuba, 1958; order of accomplished analytical bio-chems, Amer Bd of Bio-Analysts, 1961; research grants, USPHS, since 1961; Joseph F Kennedy Jr Found award, for research in mental retardation, 1966; award of honor, FJP, NY, 1966; Emily Cooley lectureship, Amer Assn of Blood Banks, 1966. Hobbies: music, piano and composing, theater, math, tennis. Home: 90 Maple St, Brooklyn, NY. Office: 64 Rutland Rd, Brooklyn, NY.

WIENER, Aron, Isr, engineer; b. Pol, Aug, 1912; s. Shimshon and Hencia (Wexler); in Isr since 1935; CE, U Brno, Czech, 1935; m. Shifra Miller, 1945; c: Ruth, Michel. Dir gen, Tahal, cons engineers, Water Planning for Israel, Ltd, since 1956; chief eng, Mekoroth, 1949-60, staff mem since 1942. Prin contrib: designed master plan for devl of irrigation and munic water supplies. Home: 6 Rembrandt St, Tel Aviv, Isr. Office: 54 Ibn Gvirol St, Tel Aviv, Isr.

WIENER, Ernest Edouard, Belgium, army off; b. Brussels, Apr 13, 1882; s. Edouard and Annie (Spielmann); att, Military Sch; dipl, CE, Ecole d'Application de l'Artillerie et du Génie, 1905; EE, Inst Electrotechnique de Montefiore, Liège, 1909. Ret lt-gen, 1946; dir, and second in command, elec services, mil constructions and bldgs, 1919-27; mem, perm comm, Dept of Electricity, 1925-32; dir, studies, Mil Sch, 1929-36. Maj-gen, cdr, forces and transp, 1936-40; prisoner-of-war in Ger, 1940-45. Pres, Comité Electrotech Belge, 1959-61, hon pres since 1961; hon pres, Intl Electrotech comm, since 1959; first vice-pres, Inst Belge de Normalisation; mem, found, gen secy, Assos des Ingénieurs issus de l'Ecole d'Application de l'Artillerie et due Génie, 1922, counsellor since 1933; pres, Consistoire Central Israélite de Belgique, 1938-56. Recipient: Grand Officier de l'Ordre de la Couronne; Grand Officier de l'Ordre de Léopold, JJ; Croix de Guerre WW I avec palmes, 1916; Croix de l'Yser; Military Cross, Eng; Chevalier de la Légion d'Honneur, Fr; Croix de Guerre, Fr: Commandeur de l'Ordre de la Couronne, Yugo; Commandeur de l'Ordre Royal de Georges I, Greece. Home: 42 Marie-Louise Sq, Brussels, Belgium.

WIENER, Marion P, US, communal worker; b. Little Rock, Ark, May 9, 1903; d. Louis and Weetie (Siesel) Pfeifer; att Cinn Conservatory of Music, 1920-21; m. Samuel Wiener, Apr 15, 1926; c: Sam jr, Earl. Mem: Shreveport Recreational Council; exec bd, Shreveport J Fed, org, 1941, exec bd, women's div; bd, Shreveport Comty Council; fmr chmn: Braille comm and nurses aide corps, ARC; fmr pres: Genevieve Children's Home and Service Bur; Natl Council of J Women; org: Golden Age Club, 1949; Sick Loan Closet, 1947; bd mem: Hadassah; B'nai Zion Temple Sisterhood; Caddo-Bossier Council of Social Agencies; Comty Chest; Assn for the Blind; Shreveport Sym Soc; Sym Soc Women's Guild; League of Women Voters, all of Shreveport, La; natl women's div, UJA. Home: 615 Longleaf Rd, Shreveport, La.

WIENER, Marvin S, US, rabbi, educational dir, editor; b. NYC, Mar 16, 1925; s. Max and Rebecca (Dodell); BS, CCNY, 1944, MS, 1945; BHL, JTSA, 1947, MHL, ordained rabbi, 1951; m. Sylvia Bodek, 1952; c: David, Judith. Dir, Natl Acad for Adult J Studies, United Syn of Amer, and ed, The Burning Bush Press, both since 1958; cons, Frontiers of Faith, NBC-TV series, 1951-57; registrar, Rabb Sch, JTSA, 1951-57; dir, Cantors Inst, Coll of J Music, JTSA, 1954-58; fac coord, Sem Sch, and Womens Inst, JTSA, 1958-64. Hon chmn, bd of rev, Natl Council for J Audio-Visual Materials, chmn, 1967-68; co-chmn, J Bible Assn, 1960-63; trustee, Jt Retirement Bd, JTSA, since 1959, secy; mem: Adult Educ Assn of US; Amer Acad for J Research; Council of Natl Orgs for Adult Educ; Natl Council for J Educ; RA; NY Bd of Rabbis. Ed: Adult J Educ, since 1958; Past and Present, selected essays by Israel Friedlander, 1963; J tract series, since 1964. Home: 67-66 108 St, Forest Hills, NY. Office: 218 E 70 St, New York, NY.

WIENER, Meyer, US, attorney; b. Pol, Mar 4, 1915; s. Noah and Anna (Mostofsky); BA, Bklyn Coll, 1936; LLB, Bklyn Law Sch, 1938, JDS, 1940; m. Celia Reiter, Mar 11, 1945; c: Meryl, Donna. Pvt practice, since 1939. Chmn bd, pres, Natl Council of Young Isr; pres, Young Isr, 1954-56; pres, Young Isr Bklyn, 1948-49, exec comm since 1951; mem, bd of educ, Yeshiva Crown Hgts, Bklyn. Home: 925 E 14 St, Brooklyn, NY. Office: 26 Court St, Brooklyn, NY.

WIENER, Philip P, US, educator, author; b. NYC, July 8, 1905; s. Elias and Sophia (Friedman); BS, CCNY, 1925; MA, Columbia U, 1926; PhD, U of S Cal, 1931; att, U Paris, 1931-32; hon DHL, Kenyon Coll; m. Gertrude Schler, Aug 24, 1934; c: Leonard, Marjorie. Prof, phil, Temple U, since 1968; chmn, phil dept, CCNY, 1959-65. Vice-pres, Intl Soc for Hist of Ideas, since 1960; pres, Peirce Soc, 1958-59; mem: Amer Phil Assn; Hist of Sci Soc; Brit Soc for Phil of Sci. Ed, Jour of the Hist of Ideas, since 1940; ed-in-chief; Dict of Ideas, 1967-70; and trans, Duhem's Aim and Structure of Physical Theory, 1954; author: Evolution and the Founders of Pragmatism, 1949; Leibniz, 1951; Readings in Philosophy of Science, 1953; Selected Writings of C C Peirce, 1966; Dict of History of Ideas, 1967-70; co-author, Basic Problems of Philosophy, 1947. Home: Dorchester Apt, Rittenhouse Sq, Philadelphia, Pa. Office: Temple U, Philadelphia, Pa.

WIENER, Robert A, US, certified public acctnt; b. NYC, Jan 9, 1918; s. George and Rose (Fink); BS, NYU, 1938; m. Annabelie Kalbfeld, Jan 1, 1941; c: Marilyn, Mark, Marjorie. Sr partner, Robert A Wiener & Co; in pvt practice, since 1946; asso prof, taxation, Pace Coll; lectr: CCNY; Annual Tax Inst, NYU; fmr, partner, Kohleriter, Spandurf, and Wiener. US Army, 1943-45. Mem: NY State Soc CPAs, fmr, chmn, insolvency and re-org comm; Amer Inst CPAs; Pi Lambda Phi; clubs: Natl Rep; Collectors; NYU; Young Men's Philanthropic League. Recipient, Bronze Star. Home: 132 E 35 St, New York, NY. Office: 10 E 40 St, New York, NY.

WIENER, Samson, US, business exec; b. Shreveport, La, Dec 27, 1907; s. Eli and Selma (Lowenstein); BA, U Mich, 1928; m. Fan Gardner, Mar 12, 1939; c: Thomas, Nancy. Pres and gen mgr, Wiener Lumber Co, since 1954; vice-pres: Krause and Managan, Inc, Lake Charles, La; Crowell Lumber Co, since 1960; dir: Lufkin Foundry and Machinery Co, since 1954; Angelina and Neches River RR Co, since 1957. Dir: Lumbermans Assn, Texas, since 1961, 1st vice-pres; N Dallas C of C; and vice-pres, Natl Lumber and Building Materials Assn; dir: Dallas chap, Amer Council for Judaism, since 1945; Big Bros of Amer, fmr pres; mem: exec comm, bd trustees, Tex Scottish Rite Hosp for Crippled Children; adv council, Dallas Comty Chest Trust Fund; fmr: pres, Brotherhood of Temple Emanu-El, Dallas, 1939-40; dir, Dallas Crime commn, 1962; vice-chmn, delinquency sect, Dallas Council of Social Agcys, 1938-39; mem: Masons, 33 deg, past master of consistory; Shriners; B'nai B'rith; Pi Tau Pi; Sigma Alpha Mu; clubs: Park Cities Rotary, fmr pres; Columbian, fmr secy. Recipient: lumberman-of-the-year, Lumbermens Assn of Tex, 1963; Brotherhood award, NCCJ, 1968. Home: 4408 Lorraine Ave, Dallas, Tex. Office: Wiener Lumber Co, POB 35125, Dallas, Tex.

WIENER, Samuel G, US, architect; b. Monroe, La, Dec 26, 1896; s. Sam and Tillie (Loeb); BS, U Mich, 1920; att, Ecole de Beaux Arts, Paris, 1920-23; studied with Eliel Saarinen, Ann Arbor, Mich, 1923; m. Marion Pfeifer, Apr 15, 1926; c: Samuel jr, Earl. Head, Samuel G Wiener and Assos.

Ensign, USN, WW I. F, Amer Inst of Architects; fmr: first pres, N La chap, Amer Inst of Architects; pres, Shreveport J Fed; mem: La Bd of Architectural Examiners; airport adv bd; building appeals bd, both Shreveport; Tau Sigma Delta; Zeta Beta Tau. Author: Venetian Houses and Details, 1928; contbr to architectural jours. Home: 615 Longleaf Rd, Shreveport, La. Office: Commercial Bank Bldg, Shreveport, La.

WIENER, Theodore, US, librarian, rabbi; b. Stettin, Ger, Sept 28, 1918; s. Max and Toni (Hamburger); in US since 1934; att Syracuse U, 1935-36; BA, U Cincinnati, 1940; MHL, ordained rabbi, HUC, 1943. Sup, Heb lang unit, descriptive cataloging div, Libr of Cong, since 1964; head cataloger, HUC-JIR Libr, 1963-64, on staff since 1950; fmr: rabbi: Sioux City, Ia, 1943-44; Port Arthur, Tex, 1944-47; Corsicana, Tex, 1947-48; chaplain, Home for J Aged, 1958-64. Mem, Min Alliance, 1944-47; secy, J Fed, 1945-47; vice-pres, Day Nursery, 1946-47; secy, B'nai B'rith, 1946-47, all Port Arthur; mem, exec bd, J Fed, Sioux City, 1945-46; secy, Zionist dist, Corsicana, 1947-48; mem: CCAR; Alumni Assn of HUC; comm on aged, J Family Service Bur, Cincinnati, 1959-64; mem council, Assn of J Librs, 1966-68, vice-pres, research and spec librs div, since 1968. Author: bibliographies: The Writings of Leo Baeck, 1954; The Writings of Samuel Cohon, 1956; co-trans: Bernhard Felsenthal's Letters to Osias Schorr, 1958; co-author: The Writings of Solomon B Freehof, 1964; contbr to: Universal J Ency, 1943; Studies in Bibliography and Booklore, 1953-65; J Book annual, 1959-58; Israel Bettan Memorial vol, 1961; The Book of Knowledge annual, 1968. Home: 1701 N Kent St, Arlington, Va.

WIESEL, Elie, US, author, journalist; b. Szighet, Rum, Sep 30, 1928; s. Salomon and Sarah (Feig): in US since 1956; att, Sorbonne, 1948-51; hon Des Lettres, JTSA-HUC. Chief fgn corresp, Yediot Aharonot, Tel Aviv, since 1947; staff mem, J Daily Forward, since 1957. Mem: UN and Fgn Corresps Assns; Authors League, US. Author: Night, 1960; Dawn, 1961; The Accident, 1962; The Town Beyond the Wall, 1964; The Gates of the Forest, 1966; The Jews of Silence, 1966; Legends of Our Times, 1968; A Beggar in Jerusalem, 1970; One Generation After, 1971. Recipient: Prix Rivarol, 1964; J Heritage award, 1965; Rememberance award, 1965; Prix Medicis, 1968. Home: 239 Central Park W, New York, NY.

WIESEL, Uzi, Isr, musician, cellist, educator; b. Tel Aviv, Isr, Jan 8, 1927; s. Mordechai and Miriam (Gelber); att, Heb U, 1945-47; dipl, Isr Acad, Tel Aviv, 1950; BA, CCNY, 1953; MS, Juilliard Sch of Music, 1954; m. Aviva Hess, Nov 8, 1960; c: Arnan. Found, mem, Tel Aviv String Quartet, since 1961; sr lectr, head, cello dept, Tel Aviv U, since 1965; concert artist, soloist with Isr Philharmonic and other orchs, Isr, US, Eur; recordings: Columbia, Concert Hall. Soc. Author: Cello Tutor, 1969; Arrangements for Cello and Piano, 1969. Recipient: Piatigorski award, 1954; highest award, Juilliard Sch of Music, 1957; 2nd awards: Intl Concours, Moscow, 1961; Casals Intl Concours. Home: 14 Motzkin Blvd, Tel Aviv, Isr

WIESNER, Jerome Bert, US educator, communications engr; b. Detroit, Mich, May 30, 1915; s. Joseph and Ida (Friedman); BS, U Mich, 1937, MS, 1940, PhD, 1950; m. Laya Wainger, Sep 2, 1940; c: Stephen, Zachary, Elisabeth, Joshua. Provost, MIT, since 1966, prof, elec engr, since 1950, fac mem since 1946, asso dir, research lab of elec, 1949-52, dean of sci, 1964-66; cons: IBM Co; Celanese Corp, dir; Kerr-McGee Oil Co, all since 1964; dir, Sprague Elec Co; fmr: asso dir, U Mich Bc Service, 1937-40; chief engr, Libr of Cong, 1940-42; staff, MIT Radiation Lab, 1942-45; staff, U Cal Los Alamos Lab, 1945-46; spec asst to the Pres on sci and tech, 1961-64. F: Inst Radio Engrs; Amer Acad of Arts and Scis; chmn, Pres's Sci Adv comm, 1961-64; mem: AAUP; elec adv group, AEC; Army Sci Adv comm, 1956-61; adv bd, TV Fund, Inc; tech adv comm, Amer Found for the Blind; Geophys Union; Amer Soc Engrs; Acoustical Soc of Amer; Natl Acad of Scis; Phi Kappa Phi; Sigma Xi; Eta Kappa Nu; Tau Beta Pi. Author: Where Science and Politics Meet, 1964. Recipient: medal of honor, Electronic Inds Assn, 1961. Home: 61 Shattuck Rd, Watertown, Mass. Office: MIT, Cambridge, Mass.

WIESS, Bernard, US, attorney; b. Union City, NJ, June 20, 1903; s. Frank and Rebecca (Prince); BA, Yale Coll, 1924; LLB, 1926; m. Mildred Simons, June 9, 1929; c: Myron, Diana. Partner, law firm, Wiess & Costa, since 1928; dir em, First Fed Savings & Loan Assn of Port Jervis; mem, adv bd, Monticello br, The County Trust Co, White Plains, NY;

judge and surrogate, Sullivan Co, 1929-33. Dir, NY State Natl War Fund; govt appeal agt, draft bd 311; chmn, finance drive, ARC, all WW II. F, Amer Coll Probate Counsel; secy, chmn, UJA, Monticello, since 1939; mem: Sullivan Co Bar Assn, pres, 1941; Assn of Bar, NYC; NY State Bar Assn, mem, exec comm, 1953-58; Amer Bar Assn; Elks, exalted ruler; Rotary, past pres; KP; Phi Beta Kappa; fmr: vice-pres, Empire State ZOA, secy, Monticello dist; treas, Salvation Army. Fmr, ed, Yale Law Jour. Recipient: Silver Beaver award, Orange-Sullivan council, Boy Scouts Amer. Home: 24 Bedford Ave, Monticello, NY. Office: 230 Broadway, Monticello, NY.

WIGODA, Paul Theodor, US, attorney, municipal official; b. Peoria, Ill, June 18, 1922; s. Hugh and Rebecca (Citron); att: U of Ill, 1940-42; BA, Roosevelt U, 1950; JD, DePaul U, 1950; m. Rose Woloshin; c: William, Gary, Robert. Pvt practice since 1950; alderman, Chgo City Council, 49th ward, since 1959; instr, political sci, Mundelein Coll, Loyola U. USN, 1942-45. Pres: Cong B'nai Zion; Abiba lodge, B'nai B'rith; mem, bd dirs, Chgo Bd of J Educ; trustee: Mundelein Coll; Coll of J Studies, both Chgo, Home: 1535 W North Shore, Chicago, Ill. Office: 111 W Washington St, Chicago, Ill.

WIGODER, Geoffrey Bernard, Isr, editor, journalist; b. Leeds, Eng, Aug 3, 1922; s. Louis and Paula (Lubelski); in Isr since 1949; MA, Trinity Coll, Dublin, 1944; PhD, Oriel Coll, Oxford, London; att: Jews' Coll, London; JTSA, NY; m. Deborah MacDwyer, 1949; c: Shimson, Meir. Dep ed-in-chief, Ency Judaica, since 1967; dir, audio-visual dept, Inst of Contemporary Jewry, Heb U, since 1959; fmr: dir, Eng broadcasts, radio Kol Zion Lagolah, 1950-60; dir, fgn broadcasts, radio Kol Isr, 1960-67. Ed: Abraham bar Hayya's Meditations of the Sad Soul, 1969; exec ed, Standard J Ency, 1959; co-ed: Ency of the J Rel, 1966; J Lexicon, 1969; contbr to: Jerusalem Post; Davar; J press; fmr corresp, BBC. Home: 11 Hameyasedim St, Bet haKerem, Jerusalem, Isr.

WIGODER, Philip Isidore, UK, dentist; b. Lith, Mar 25, 1885; in Eng since 1892; LDS, 1911; LRCP; LRCS, both 1915; m. Rebekah Jacobs, June 2, 1920; c: Basil, Pamela. Hon cons dent surg: Home for Aged, since 1915; Manchester Children's Hosp, 1918-45; demonstrator, Manchester Dent Hosp, 1911-12. Hon life pres, Manchester and Salford Zionist Cen Council, since 1952, past pres: hon life vice-pres, Friends of Heb U, since 1940; Jt Pal Appeal, since 1940; fmr: pres, Friends of Habonim, Manchester; exec treas, Public Dent Service, Gt Brit and Ir; chmn, E Lancashire br, Public Dent Service Assn. clubs: Masons; Rotary; Reform; Country. Author: Oral Bacteriology, 1910; A Trip to Italy and Palestine, 1935; contbr to med jours. Spec interest, Isr. Home: 6 Spath Rd, Machester, Eng. Office: 2 St John St, Manchester, Eng.

WIGODSKY, Herman S, US, physician, business exec; b. Sioux City, Ia, June 12, 1915; s. Harry and Riva (Rozran); BA, Yankton Coll, 1936; BS, U of SD, 1937; MS, Northwestern U, 1938, MB, 1940, PhD, 1940, MD, 1941; m. Joann Pincus, Mar 6, 1946; c: Ann, Dan, John. Secy-treas: The Pincus Co, since 1950; The Olmos Co, since 1960; C Z Realty Co, since 1962; partner, Rozran and Wigodzky Tree Farms, since 1950; att phys, Robert B Green Hosp, since 1951; lectr, dept of phys and internal med, U Tex Med Sch, since 1966, asso coord, reg med prog, since 1966; instr, physiol, Northwestern U, 1937-41; mem, profsl asso comm on atomic casualties, NRC, 1947-50; dir, San Antonio div, U Tex postgrad Sch of Med, 1955-60; cons, admn, Santa Rosa Med Cen, 1962-66. USAAF, 1941-47, res, 1939-41, and since 1947. Pres: J Soc Service Fed, 1954-56; Downtowners, 1958-60; mem, bd of trustees: St Mary's Hosp, 1960-64; Yorktown Coll, since 1966; mem: Amer Phys Soc; Soc for Experimental Biol and Med; NY Acad of Scis; AMA; Tex, and Bexar Co Med Assns; Amer Inst of Biol Scis; Amer, and Fla Forestry Assns; Soc for Visiting Scis, London; AAAS; AJComm. Asst ed: De Re Medica, 1946-47; contbr to: Amer People's Ency, 1946, med jours. Home: 300 Primera Dr, San Antonio, Tex. Office: 420 E Houston St, San Antonio, Tex.

WIJSENBEEK, Henricus, Isr, psychiatrist, educator, administrator; b. Rotterdam, Holland, 1916; s. Siegfried and Rosa (van den Bergh); in Isr since 1950; MD, Leyden U, 1941; PhD, Utrecht U, 1949; postgrad study: Minn U, 1947; Utrecht U, 1952; Rochester U, 1960; m. Henriette Wyler, 1942; c: Tirtsah Kenan, Arieh, Yigal. Prof, chmn, psycht sect, fac continuing med educ, Tel Aviv U, since 1968, head, psycht dept, Beilinson Med Cen, since 1956, mgr, The Gehah Psychiatric Hosp, since 1956. IDF, 1950-60. Mem: adv council, Kupat Holim, dist psycht comm; Dutch Neuropsycht Assn; guest mem, Isr Psychoanalytic Assn. Author: On Prefrontal Lobotomy, 1949; contbr to profsl jours. Home: 13 Ofakim St, Afeka, Isr. Office: POB 72, Petach Tikvah, Isr.

WIJSENBEEK, Louis J F, Netherlands, museum dir; b. Rotterdam, Apr 21, 1912; s. Siegfried and Rosa (van den Bergh); LLM, U Leyden, 1935; D Hist of Art, U Utrecht, 1942; m. Elisa Cremers, Aug 24, 1937; c: Siep, Constant, Florus, André, Frederik, Elisabeth. Dir, Dienst voor Schone Kunsten der Gemeente Den Haag, directorate, Munic Mus, since 1951; fmr: staff, Min of Educ and Fine Arts, The Hague, 1938-40; asst keeper, Munic Mus, 1940-42; with Bur of Recuperation Art Treasures from Ger, 1945-47; dir, Prinsenhof Mus and Lambert van Meerten Mus, Delft, 1947-51. Served, Netherlands resistance movement, 1940-43; in Ger concentration camps, 1943-45. Org exhbs: Monet, 1952; Vincent van Gogh, 1953: Etruscan Art, 1955; Japanese Art, 1956; Chinese Painting, 1958; Cézanne, 195.; Mexican Art, 1960; Ger Expressionist Painting, 1961; Persian Art, 1962; Kandinsky, 1963; Intl Pop Art, 1964; Mondrian, 1966; Chinese Art, 1968; Brancusi, 1969. Pres: State Commn for Contemporary Art; Icom Comm for Mus Architecture; vice-pres: bd trustees, Royal Acad Fine Arts; Netherlands Mus Assn; mem: De Witte Soc; State Commn for Exhbs; cons bd, Intl Council Mus; bd trustees: Netherlands Tourist Assn; Netherlands Pavilion, Brussels World Exhb, 1953-58; Soc voor Culturele Samenwerking; asst dir, UNESCO Sem on Art and Educ, NY, 1952; club, Arts, London. Author: Het Tijdperk van de Camera Obscura, 1940; Dutch Antique Furniture, 1949; Mij spreeket de Blomme een Tale, 1951; Pablo Picasso, 1953; Mondrian, 1962; Delfts Zilver, 1962; Mondrian, 1968; contbr to learned publs. Recipient: Royal House medal, 1966; cdr: Order of Merit, It; Order of the Right Hand of the Ghurka, Nepal; Order of the Mexican Eagle; off: Royal Netherlands Order of Orange-Nassau; Royal Victorian Order; Crown Order of Belgium; Royal Vasa Order of Swed; knight: Legion of Honor, Fr; Pius Order of Holy Sea; gold medal, It; hon citizen, City of Delft. Home: 74a Anna Paulownastraat, The Hague, Netherlands. Office: Gameentemuseum, 41 Stadhouderslaan, The Hague, Netherlands.

WIKLER, Samuel J, US, attorney; b. NYC, Sep 27, 1905; s. Joseph and Sarah (Roth); att, NYU; LLB, Bklyn Law Sch, 1927; m. Dorothy Strogoff, May 31, 1942; c: Joseph, Marvin. Mem, law firm, Wikler, Gottlieb, Taylor, Stewart & Long; fmr with: Wikler, Gottlieb & Wikler; Klein, Wikler & Gottlieb; fmr: chmn, Public Housing Auth, Mt Vernon, NY, 1953, 1959; acting judge, City Court, Mt Vernon, 1958-59. Mem, adv comm, local draft bd, WW II. Chmn: campaign comm, Dem party, 1962; finance comm, local Dem party; co-found, Heetwood Syn, chmn, bldg comm; vice-pres: Westchester Rel Inst; Downtown Syn; bd of V'aad haKashruth, Mt Vernon; treas, Cong Emanu-El, Mt Vernon; bd of trustees, Heb Inst of U Hgts, Bx; bd govs, Westchester Day Sch; mem: ZOA, Westchester; B'nai B'rith; Amer, NY State and NY Co Bar Assns; YMHA, Mt Vernon. Home: 580 Westchester Ave, Mt Vernon, NY. Office: 64 Wall St, New York, NY.

WILCHEK, Meir Asher, Isr, chemist, educator; b. Warsaw, Pol, Oct 17, 1935; s. Eliezer and Rachel (Zeidenberg); in Isr since 1949; BS, Bar Ilan U, 1960; PhD, Weizmann Inst, 1965; m. Esther Edlis, Mar 14, 1960; c: Eliezer, Yael. Sr sci, Weizmann Inst since 1969; sci mgr, Miles Yeda Co, since 1968; research asso, NIH, 1966-68. IAF, 1954-56. Mem: Amer Chem Soc; Isr Biochem Soc. Contbr to sci jours. Home: 24 Ben Yehuda St, Rehovot, Isr. Office: Weizmann Inst, Rehovot, Isr.

WILDER, Joseph, US, neuropsychiatrist, educator; b. Drohobycz, Aus, Feb 13, 1895; s. Isidor and Frieda (Lauterbach); in US since 1938; MD, U Vienna, 1919; m. Hedy Walter, May 22, 1930; c: Viola Breit, Diana Weinberg. Pvt practice since 1919; prof em, neur, NY Med Col, since 1968, staff mem since 1954; cons neuropsycht, Daughters of Isr Home and Hosp, since 1943; cons neuropsycht, Goldwater Mem Hosp, since 1944; asso neur, Metro Hosp, Bird S Coler Hosp, since 1954; att neur. Flower-Fifth Ave Hosp, since 1954; fmr: intern and res, Allgemeines Krankenhaus, 1920-23; res and acting dir, Rothschild Found, Maria-Theresien-Schloessel, 1923-29, dir; Rothschild Found, Rosenhuegel, 1931-38; asst prof, U Vienna, 1937, all of Vienna; staff mem: Montefiore Hosp, 1939-42, Med Center, 1942-47. Served US Selective

Service, 1941-46. Mem: Amer Psych Assn; Royal Soc of Med, London; Assn for the Advancement of Psychotherapy; Amer Psychosomatic Soc; NY Acad of Sci; AAAS; Pirquet Soc Med Circle; AJCong; Amer Friends of Heb U; corresp mem: Viennese Soc for Neuropsycht; Wiener Gesellschaft der Aerzte. Author: Narkolepsie, Bumke und Foerster, Handbuch der Neurologie, 1935; Klinik und Therapie der Zuckermangelkrankhiet, 1936; Stimulus and Response, The Law of Initial Value (Wilder's Law), 1960; co-author: Beitraege zum Ticproblem, 1927; Der Kopfschmerz, 1934; chaps: Progress in Psychotherapy, 1959; Handbuch der Psychoterapie, 1959; Results of Psychotherapy, 1968; Biokybernetik, 1967. Recipient: Congressional Selective Service medal, 1946; Gutheil Memorial medal, Assn for Advancement of Psychotherapy, 1966. Home and office: Main St, Tannersville, NY.

WILENSKY, Moshe, Isr, composer conductor; b. Warsaw, Pol, Apr 17, 1910; s. Zelig and Henia (Liebman); in Isr since 1932; att, Warsaw State Conservatory, 1928-32; m. Bertha Yakimovska, 1939. Dir, light music, Kol Isr Radio, since 1961; composer: for theaters: Mateneh, 1932-36; LiLaLo, 1944-51; Habima; Radio City Music Hall, NYC; children's theaters; films: Hatikva, Not a Word to Morgenstein, Pillar of Fire; musicals: Shulamit, Fishke the Lame; radio and TV: CBS, NYC; BBC, London; songs: art form and popular; orchestral and choral works; arrangements of oriental folklore for orch; arranged and directed recordings: Isr, Fr, Belgium, Swed,US; composer for Hed Arzi Record Mfg Co, 1949-51; toured Eur, N Amer, S Amer, Afr. Recipient: 1st prize, Monte Carlo Intl Radio Contest. Home: 42 Pinkas St, Tel Aviv, Isr. Office: Kol Isr Radio, Hakiriya, Tel Aviv, Isr.

WILENTZ, William C, US, physician; b. Perth Amboy, NJ, Mar 25,1900; s.Nathan and Bertha(Crane);MD, Jefferson Med Coll. 1923; m. Elsie Rosenzweig, Nov 27, 1930; c: Jack. Chief med examiner, Middlesex Co, since 1933; med dir, Natl Lead Co, Perth Amboy, since 1939; fmr: phys, NJ Port, 1927-32; chief of staff, Peth Amboy Gen Hosp, 1944-46. US Army, 1918. Vice-pres: Amer Acad of Compensation Med, mem, bd of govs; Amer Acad of Forensic Scis; f, Ind Med Assn; mem: Public Assistance Bd; AMA; NJ State and Middlesex Co Med Socs; Essex Co Path Soc; Amer Urol Assn; Elks; fmr: pres, Garden State Hospitalization Plan, 1967-69; mem, bd trustees, Med Soc of NJ. Home: 185 High St, Perth Amboy, NJ. Office: 188 Market St, Perth Amboy, NJ.

WILINSKY, Harriet, US, business exec; b. Boston, Mass; d. Charles and Jeanette (Isenberg); att: Wellesley Coll, 1923-24; AB, Barnard Coll, 1927; m. Sylvan Goodman, 1933. Vice-pres, sales promotion div, Wm Filene Sons' Co, since 1968, on staff since 1943; fmr: psychol, Judge Baker Guidance Cen, 1927-29; advt copywriter, R H White Co, 1930-31; advt mgr, E T Slattery Co, Boston, 1931-43. Dir: Boston BBB, since 1957, Boston C of C, 1951-54; Advt Club of Gtr Boston, 1961-63; chmn: Fashion Group of Boston, 1943-45; publicity dir group, Asso Merchandising Corp, 1954-55; bd dirs, Natl Retail Merchants Assn, NY, since 1968; asso in retailing, Simmons Coll, since 1964; mem: Retail Trade Bd, Boston; Fashion Group of NY; Altrusa; Phi Beta Kappa; club: Bus and Profsl Womens. Recipient: awards: bus-women-of-the-year, Boston, 1952; advt-woman-of-the-year, Boston, 1961, Home: 51 Deacon St, Boston, Mass. Office: Wm Filene Sons Co, 426 Washington St, Boston, Mass.

WILKES, Edward T, US, physician, educator; b. NYC, Mar 28, 1889; s. Morris and Rose (Ziporkes); BA, CCNY, 1918; MD, Cornell U, 1921; m. Matilda Schmerler (decd); m. 2nd, Lillian Genn, June 14, 1940; c: Daniel, Asso clinical prof, ped, NYU, since 1956, fac mem since 1953; asso instr, ped, Columbia U Postgrad Med Sch, 1934-46. US Army, 1917. F, AMA; dipl, Amer Bd of Peds; pres, NY Peds Soc, 1949; mem: Queens Co Med Soc; Acad Peds; Harvey Soc; men's club, Park Ave Syn. Author: Baby's Daily Exercise, 1927; Family Guide to Teenage Health, 1958; co-author: Mother's Guide When Sickness Comes, 1934; contbr to med jours and natl mags. Hobby: ice skating. Home: 2 Sutton Pl, S, New York, NY. Office: 4709 Skillman Ave, Long Island City, NY.

WILLEN, Joseph, US, social welfare exec; b. Kushnitza, Russ, June 22, 1897; s. Barnet and Sarah (Katch) Willencheck; in US since 1905; BA, CCNY, 1919; hon: DHum, Boston U, 1963; LLD, JTSA, 1964; m. Pearl Larner, Dec 29, 1925; c: Paul, Deborah Meier. Ret, exec cons, FJP, NY, since 1967, vice-pres, 1941-67, with FJP since 1919. Served US Army, WW I; mem, NY State finance comm, US Treasury: hon chmn, Victory Legion div, War Finance comm, both WW II. Vice-pres, AJComm, since 1951, mem, steering comm, public affairs comm, fiftieth anniversary planning comm; f, Brandeis U, since 1963; mem bd of overseers, Florence Heller Grad Sch for Advanced Studies in Social Wfr, since 1962; mem: bd dirs: CJFWF, since 1948; Natl JWB; NYC Wfr and Health Council; Amer Friends of Heb U; Technion, Haifa; Fountain House; bd of advs, Vocational Adv Service; natl council, JDC; exec comm: Natl Patrons Soc of JTSA; Amer J Tercentenary comm, 1952-61; JTSA; mem: Navy League, Wash, DC; Citizens Budget comm, 1949; Mayor's Comm on Unity, 1951; exec council, Amer J Hist Soc; fmr dir, Comty Council, Gtr NY, mem, cen planning bd; dir: J Educ comm; JTA; cons: ARC; Gtr NY Fund. Recipient: spec citations, ADL and AJComm, 1950. Home: 470 Park Ave, New York, NY. Office: 130 E 59 St, New York, NY.

WILLIAMS, Walter N, US, business exec; b. Russ, 1886; m. Gabriella Deutch; c: Gertrude Landy, Freda Pollard, Sadie Levy, Monica Bension. Chmn and mgn dir: Isr-Brit Bank (London) Ltd; Natl Ins and Guarantee Corp Ltd; Sentinel Ins Co Ltd; London City and Westcliff Properties Ltd; Atlas Securities, all London: chmn: Isr-Brit Bank, Isr; Zur Ins Co Ltd, Isr; treas, Heichal Shlomo, Jerusalem. Homes: Jerusalem; London.

WILLMAN, Felix Shraga, UK, administrator, rabbi; b. Cologne, Ger, Aug 2, 1925; s. David and Sara (Spanier) Wilman; in US since 1951; dipl, Sch of Law and Econ, Tel Aviv, 1946; ordained rabbi, Yeshivat Slonim, Isr, 1947; DD, PhD, Philathea Coll, 1969; m. Josephine Greiniman, 1949; c: Esther, Leah, David, Meyer, Shmuel. Exec-pres: Or-Hachaim Inc, since 1963; Natl Assn Adv Orthodox Judaism Inc; fmr, teaching and mgt, 1951-60. Pres: Amer Friends Kolel Chazon Isr; Amer Comm for Kolel Jagdil Torah, Isr; vice-pres, Inst Rabb Studies, Fr. Author: Roshei Prakim beEmunah, 1966; Tosfot haRosh Sanhedrin-Yumma, 1968; publ, ed-in-chief, J Guardian Monthly, NY, 1956-67; contbr to press. Recipient: gold medal and dipl, Eloy Elfaro Intl Found, 1966; gold medal, City of B'nai Brak, Isr, 1968. Home: 377 Montgomery St, Brooklyn, NY. Office: 132 Nassau St, New York, NY.

WILNER, Morton H, US, attorney; b. Baltimore, Md, May 28, 1908; s. Joseph and Ida (Berkow); BS, U of Pa, 1930; LLB, Georgetown U, 1934; m. Zelda Dunkelman, 1940; c: James, Thomas, Lawrence, Theodora. Partner, Wilner, Scheiner & Greeley; dir: Security Bank; Giant Food; gen counsel, Aerospace Ind Assn; Armed Forces Relief and Benefit Assn; dep dir, aircraft div, US War Produc Bd, 1944-45. Maj, USAF, WW II. Bd trustees: U of Pa; J Publ Soc; bd dirs, Wash J Comty Found; bd govs, St Albans Sch; pres, J Comty Cen of Wash, 1954-57; pres, Fed Bar Assn, 1969-70; clubs: Army and Navy; Woodmont Country. Contbr to profsl jours. Recipient: Legion of Merit, 1945; Central High Alumni award, 1961. Home: 2701 Chesapeake St, Washintgton, DC. Office: 1343 H St NW, Washington, DC.

WILSON, Sol, US, artist; b.Vilna, Pol, Aug 23, 1896; s. Herman and Ida (Volk); in US since 1911; att: Cooper Union, Coll, 1918-20; Beaux Arts, 1919; Natl Acad of Design, 1920-23, all NYC; studied with George Bellows, Robert Henri; m. Dora Pockriss, Sep 11, 1921; c: Jacqueline Arkin. Free-lance artist since 1922; instr: YMHA, New Haven, 1926-27; Amer Artists Sch, 1936-40; Sch of Art Studies, 1946-48; both NYC. One-man shows: since 1925; perm collections: Bklyn Coll; Bklyn Mus; Metrop Mus of Art; Whitney Mus of Amer Art; Living Art Found, Bd of Educ, all NYC; ARC; Lib of Cong, both Wash, DC; Newark Mus, NJ; Delgado Mus, New Orleans; Bulter Inst, O; Blandon Mus, Ia; Ball State Tchrs Coll, Ind; U Minn; Bezalel Mus, Jerusalem; Art Mus, Ein Harod, Isr; murals: Delmar PO, 1942; Westhampton PO, 1942; both NY; invited to natl exhbs: NY World's Fair; Carnegie Inst; Corcoran Gal; Pa Acad of Art; Chgo Art Inst; Natl Acad of Design; Va Mus; Critic's Choice, NYC; Whitney Mus; U of Ill; Metrop Mus; Amer Painters, Brussels, Belgium; traveling in Eur, Amer Contemporary Paintings. Mem: Artists Equity Assn; Provincetown Art Assn; Cape Cod Art Assn; Audubon Artists. Recipient: Purchase prize, ARC competition, 1942; 3rd prize, Artists for Victory, NYC, 1943; prize, Pepsi Cola contest, NYC, 1944, medal of hon, 1948; hon mention: Concoran biennial, Wash, DC, 1947; Carnegie annual, Pittsburgh, Pa, 1947; Marian S Bush Memorial award, Audubon Artists, 1947, prize, 1950, medal, 1959; grant, Amer Acad Arts and Letters, 1952; 1st prize, Cape Cod Art Assn, 1952, prizes, 1954, 1955; Child Hassan

Fund purchase, 1954; prizes: Soc of Painters in Casein,1955; Natl Acad of Design, 1958; Ranger Fund purchase prize 1958; Audubon medal of honor, 1959; prize, Audubon Artists, NYC, 1963, 1969; Andrew Carnegie prize, Natl Acad of Design. Home: 530 W 113 St, New York, NY. Studio: 200 W 72 St, New York, NY.

WINCELBERG, Shimon, US, author, playwright; b. Kiel, Ger, Sep 26, 1924; s. David and Hertha (Herzberg); in US since 1938; att, Providence Coll; dipl, Manhattan Tech Inst, 1947; m. Anita Marateck, July 4, 1954; c: Bryna Yached, David,Yakov. Playwright, short story, screen, and TV writer, since 1952; fmr lectr, Eng, med coll, Japan. Full-length plays: Kataki, 1958; The Windows of Heaven, 1969; The Travels of Benjamin IV; repr in: Best Short Plays of 1954-55; Best Amer Short Stories of 1953; Best Plays of 1958-59; contbr ofstories,criticismsto: Commentary; Harpers Bazaar: Punch; New Leader. US Army, 1943-46. Mem: Young Isr; Mizrachi: fmr: pres: Young Isr of LA; Hapoel Hamizrachi of Hollywood. Recipient: wrestling championship, Maccabi Athletic club, Berlin, 1935; year's best written script award, Writers Guild of Amer, 1957- 58, 1966-67; best sci film award, Edison, Found for Youth, 1956; Torah award, Bais Yaakov Sch, 1963; dist artist award, Isr Bonds, 1965, Chai award, 1966. Hobbies: sailing, theatre, antique Heb books, photography, judo. Office: 9169 Sunset Blvd, Los Angeles, Cal.

WIND, Leon, US, rabbi; b. Turka, Pol, Mar 1, 1914; s. Jehoshua and Hannah (Teichman); in US since 1938; att: U Lvov, 1933-38; Heb Tchrs Coll, Lvov, 1933-38; ordained rabbi, JTSA, 1943, DHL, 1958; m. Ruth Youngman, July 4, 1943; c: Joel, Joshua. Rabbi, Temple Beth Sholom, since 1945; fmr: instr, phil, U Hartford, 1959-60; rabbi, Knesset Isr Syn, Kan City, 1943-45. Mem: RA, fmr pres,Conn br; NY Bd of Rabbis; ZOA; JWF; Cmty Relations Council. Home: 241 Parker St, Manchester, Conn. Study: 400 Middle Turnpike E, Manchester, Conn.

WINDREICH, Meshullam, Isr, educator; b. Berlin, Ger, Sep 17, 1918; s. Josef and Selma (Kessler); in Isr since 1934; att Mizrachi Tchrs Coll, Jerusalem; MA, Heb U, 1954; PhD, Dropsie Coll, 1966; m. Pnina Margalit, 1951; c: Yigal. Lectr, Bible, Bar Ilan U, since 1966. Home: 36 Tshernichovski St, Jerusalem, Isr. Office: Bar Ilan U, Ramat Gan, Isr.

WINER, Frank, US, psychoanalyst, psychologist; b. NYC, Apr 4, 1917; s. Louis and Gussie (Steinhart); BA, U Conn, 1941; MSW, U Pittsburgh, 1947; cert psychan, Postgrad Cen for Mh, 1959; PhD, NYU, 1962; m. Roslyn Schwartz, July 6, 1941; c: Ellen Falk, Ethan. Pvt practice since 1959; cons, Norwalk Hosp, since 1958; sup, J Family and Child Service of Minneapolis, 1947-54; lectr, U Minn, 1951-53. Sgt, US Army, 1941-45. Bd dirs: Norwalk J Comty Cen, vice-pres, 1963-66; Norwalk Mh Assn, pres, 1965-66; delg, Norwalk J Comty Council, pres, 1963-64; chmn, Norwalk UJA, 1965; mem: Amer and Conn Psych Assns. Contbr to profsl jours. Hobby: volleyball. Home: Cavray Rd, E Norwalk, Conn. Office: 111 East Ave, Norwalk, Conn.

WINER, Louis H, US, dermatologist, educator; b. Superior, Wis, March 19, 1903; s. Israel and Celia (Milavetz); BS, MB, MD, U Minn, 1926; m. Helen Grouse, Dec 28, 1930; c: Barbara Levin, Marylee Silverman. Pvt practice since 1930; clinical prof, dermat and med, UCLA, since 1950; clinical asso prof, dermat: U Minn, 1930-45; U of S Cal, 1945-50. Draft bd examiner, WW II. Pres, Dermat Research Found of Cal, Inc, since 1955; mem, bd dirs, Amer Acad of Dermat, since 1961, vice-pres, 1963; mem, nominating comm, Pacific Dermat Assn, since 1961, pres, 1960; chmn, exec comm, LA Dermat Soc, since 1962, pres, 1952; chmn, med dir, Camp Hess Kramer, LA, 1950-62; med cons and bd mem, HUC-JIR, Cal, since 1962; hon mem: Israeli, Danish, Austrian Dermat Socs; Chgo Dermat Soc; Pan Amer Med Assn; corresp mem: Australasian, Fr, Brazilian Dermat Socs; mem: Amer Dermat Assn Inc, vice-pres, 1968-69; LA Acad of Med. Contbr to profsl jours. Recipient: prizes for med exhibits. Spec interests: photomicrography, histopathology. Home: 1036 Corsica Dr, Pacific Palisades, Cal. Office: 9915 Santa Monica Blvd, Beverly Hills, Cal.

WINER, Norman, US, attorney; b. Chattanooga, Tenn, Dec 5, 1910; s. Harry and Jennie (Abelson); AB, Harvard, 1929. LLB, Law Sch, 1932; m. Bertha Jacobi (decd); c: Joanne; m, 2nd, Elyse Thalheimer, Apr 24, 1969. Partner, Nathan, Mannheimer, Asche, Winer, & Friedman, since 1944; asso, Bondy & Schloss, 1932-43. NY State Natl Guard, 1942-45.

Vice-chmn, lawyers div, UJA; mem: ZOA; AJComm, Isr and Intl Org comms; Assn Bar of NYC; Amer Bar Assn; clubs: Harvard, NYC; Fairview Country, NY. Contbr to law jours. Hobbies: music, golf, bridge. Home: 11 Oakway, Scarsdale, NY. Office: 295 Madison Ave, New York, NY.

WINGATE, Arline, US, sculptor; b. NYC, Oct 18, 1906; d. Benjamin and Isabel (Roth) Shapiro; att, Smith Coll; m. Clifford Hollander, Aug 4, 1934; c: Richard. Sculptor since 1934; perm collections in muss: Natl of Stockholm; Newark, NJ; Ghent; Parish, Southampton; Easthampton Guild Hall; Syracuse U; Norfolk; Birmingham; Farnsworth; J Walter Thompson Co; exhb: Petit Palais, Paris; Burlington Gals; London; Metrop Mus; Whitney Mus, both NYC; Museo des Belles Artes, Buenos Aires; SF Mus; Wadsworth Atheneum Mus; Baltimore Mus; Pa Acad; Art Inst of Chgo; Bklyn Mus; Golden Gate and NY World's Fairs; Sculpture Intl, Fairmont Park; one-man shows: Midtown and Feingarten gals, both NYC. Mem: Fed of Modern Painters and Sculptors; Sculptors Guild; Natl Assn of Women Artists; Architectural League of NY. Recipient: three awards, Natl Assn of Women Artists; Amelia Peabody award, 1956; award, Easthampton Guild Hall, 1958. Home and studio: 23 E 74 St, New York, NY.

WINKELMAN, Stanley J, US, merchant; b. Saulte Ste Marie, Mich, Sep 23, 1922; s. Leon and Josephine (Rosenblum); BS, U Mich, 1943; m. Margaret Wallace, Mar 27, 1943; c: Andra Barr, Marjorie, Roger. Pres, Winkelman Stores Inc, since 1965, exec vice-pres, dir, predecessor firm, Winkelman Bros Apparel Inc, since 1957, with firm since 1948; fmr: research chem, OSRD projects, Cal Inst of Tech and U Cal, 1943-44. Lt, USN, 1944-46. Dir: JWF, vice-pres, and mem, exec comm; Natl Retail Merchants Assn, chmn, retailer-consumerrelations commn; United Found; Detroit convention bur; Wayne State U Press; Gtr Detroit bd of commerce; Detroit Round Table; mem: exec comm, JCC, pres, 1960-63; adv comm, AJComm; Detroit Comty Relations comm; New Detroit comm, chmn, Comty Services subcomm; Citizens comm for equal opportunity; Detroit HS study comm, chmn of comty relations subcommittee; Gov's Ethical and Moral Panel; Mich Fair Campaign Practices commn, advs council, Mich Wfr League, 1968-1971; fmr: pres, JCC, 1960-63; vice-pres, Temple Beth El; mem, commn on social action, UAHC; clubs: Franklin Hills Country, Standard City, Circumnavigators. Recipient: awards: St Cyprian, 1965; Amity, 1968; Liberty Bell, 1968; human relations, U Detroit, 1968; human rights, 1968. Home: 19420 Canterbury Dr, Detroit, Mich. Office: 25 Parsons, Detroit, Mich.

WINKELMAN, Stanton Ivan, US, communal leader; b. Bx, NY, June 20, 1947; s. Samuel and Lily (Nadel); att, Yeshiva U, 1964-68; Inst for Youth Leaders, Jerusalem, 1966-67. Chmn, natl exec, Betar, since 1967; political actions chmn, ZC, since 1967. Steering comm mem, N Amer J Youth Council; exec mem, Student Struggle for Soviet J. Home: 87-10 204 St, Jamaica, NY. Office: 116 Nassau St, New York, NY.

WINKELSTEIN, Asher, US, physician, gastroenterologist; b. Syracuse, NY, Oct 15, 1893; s. Myer and Ida (Marqusee); BS, Syracuse U, 1915; MD, 1917; postgrad studies: Berlin and Vienna, 1922-23; m. Celia Rose, Feb 28, 1925; c: Charles, Ellen. Clinical prof em, Mt Sinai Sch of Med, since 1968; cons, Mt Sinai Hosp, since 1937, chief, dept of gastroenterology, 1926-55, staff mem, since 1917; asst clinical prof, Columbia U; cons, VA. Prin contribs: described peptic esophagitis; devised peptic ulcer intragastric drip treatment. Mem: AMA; NY Acad Med; Harvey Soc; NY Co Med Soc; Amer Gastroenterological Assn; Amer Gastroscopia Soc; hon mem: Cuban Chilean, Arg, and Brazilian Gastroenterological Assns. Author: Outline of Gastro-intestinal Diseases; Modern Therapy of Peptic Ulcer; contbr to profsl jours. Home: 40 E 84 St, New York, NY. Office: 1185 Park Ave, New York, NY.

WINKELSTEIN, Warren, Jr, US, physician, educator; b. Syracuse, NY, July 1, 1922; BA, U of NC, 1943; MD, Syracuse U, 1947; MPH, Columbia U, 1950; m. Malce Fittz, 1947; c: Joshua, Malce, Rebecca Yamin. Prof, head of div, epidemiology, Sch of Public Health, U Cal, Berkeley, since 1968; fmr: dep commnr, Erie Co Health Dept, 1959-63; asst to prof, U Buffalo Sch of Med, 1963-68. US Army, 1944-46; USPHS: active res, 1951-53; inactive res, since 1953. Secy, epidemiology sect, Amer Public Health Assn; fmr pres, NY Acad Preventive Med. Contbr to profsl jours and books. Home: 1400 Westview Dr, Berkeley, Cal. Office: Sch of Public Health, U Cal, Berkeley, Cal.

WINKLER, Henry R, US, educator; administrator, historian; b. Waterbury, Conn, Oct 27, 1916; s. Jacob and Ethel (Reiger); BA, U Cincinnati, 1938, MA, 1940; PhD, U Chgo, 1947; m. Clare Sapadin, Aug 18, 1940; c: Allan, Karen. Vice-provost, Rutgers U, since 1968, dean, lib arts fac, since 1967, prof, hist, since 1958, dept chmn since 1960, fac mem since 1947; fmr: instr, Eur hist, U Cincinnati, 1938-40; asst prof, Eur hist, Roosevelt Coll, 1946-47; visiting prof, Bryn Mawr Coll, 1959-60. Info analyst, OWI, 1942-43; intelligence off, USN, 1943-46. Chmn, Herbert Baxter Adams prize comm, Amer Hist Assn, 1959-60; mem: AAUP; Amer Hist Assn; Conf on Brit Studies; Inst of Hist Research; Phi Beta Kappa; Tau Kappa Alpha; Highland Park Bd of Educ; Anshe Emeth Temple, New Brunswick. Author: The League of Nations Movement in Great Britain: 1914-19, pub 1953; mgn ed, Amer Hist Rev, 1964-68; co-ed, Great Problems of European Civilization, 1954; ed bd, The Historian, since 1957; contbr to hist jours. Recipient: Fulbright Research prof, LSE, 1953-54. Home: 354 N Fourth Ave, Highland Park, NJ. Office: Rutgers U, New Brunswick, NJ.

WINKLER, Manfred, Isr, archivist, poet; b. Bukovina, Rum, Oct 27, 1922; s. Emilian and Johanna (Wildholz); in Isr since 1959; BA, Heb U, 1963; m. Herma Levin, May 15, 1956; c. Anath. Archivist, Cent Zionist Archives, since 1964; fmr: technician, 1941-50; officer, 1950-54; free lance writer, 1954-59. Served, IDF. Council mem, Assn Heb Writers; mem, Isr Archivist Assn. Author: Tief Pflügt Das Leben, 1956; Kunterbunte Verse, 1957; Fritzchens Abenteuer, 1958; Shirim, 1965; ed, collected writings of Theodor Herzl, in Heb. Home: 9 Bolivar, Jerusalem, Isr. Office: One Ibn Gvirol Blvd, Jerusalem, Isr.

WINOCOUR, Jack Emanuel, Eng, barrister, editor, writer; b. Glasgow, Scotland, Apr 3, 1913; s. Percy and Martha (Jackson); in Eng since 1961; BA, Magdalen Coll, Oxford U, 1935; LLB, Inner Temple, London, 1935; m. Jerene Jones, July 25, 1964; c: Michael, Daniel, Miriam, Jonathan. Dir, info, WJC, since 1964; ed, World Jewry, since 1962; dir: Brit info service, Wash, DC, 1941-45; Amer info dept, Fgn Office, London, 1945-46; dep ed, Illustrated, London, 1946-49; war corresp in Isr, 1948-49; US corresp, Picture Post, 1951-57; dir of info, AZC, 1953-56; PR adv, Isr Emb, Wash, DC, 1955-61. Contbr to mags. Home: 42 Mornington Terr, London, Eng. Office: 55 New Cavendish St, London, Eng.

WINOGRAD, Leonard, US, rabbi, educator; b. Pittsburgh, Pa, Nov 14, 1922; s. Emil and Bessie (Horvitz); BS, U Pittsburgh, 1946; BHL, MHL, ordained rabbi, DHL, all HUC, 1953-58; m. Pescha Cooper, Mar 30, 1952; c: Emil, Harry, Michael, Ethan. Rabbi, Beth Zion Temple, since 1961; instr, psych, Mt Aloysius Women's Coll, since 1967; lectr, J hist and rabb lit: St Francis Sem, Loretto; Christ The Saviour Sem, Johnstown; chaplain, Somerset State Mental Hosp; fmr: gen mgr, Rochester Amusement Co, 1946-53; rabbi, Temple Beth Am, Framingham, Mass, 1958-61. Lt, navigator, USAF, 1943-45. Mem, natl exec, ZOA, since 1963; mem bd: Mh Assn; Multiple Sclerosis Soc; Cripped Children and Adults Soc; pres: Johnstown Teen Canteen, 1964-66; Tri-State reg, ZOA, 1965-67; chmn: UJA, Lower Beaver Valley, 1951-53; adult educ, B'nai B'rith, W Pa, 1963-65; Pa Human Relations Adv Council, 1965-67; State Police Workship, urban tension control, 1966; found: Johnstown Jr Judea; Sr Citizens Activity Cen; org, Johnstown Zionist dist, 1962; mem: Amer Psych Assn; Acad Council, Amer Coll of Jerusalem; CCAR; Masons; KP. Contbr to J jours. Spec interests: psych, civil rights, youth, Amer-J hist. Home: 1440 Mary Drive, Johnstown, Pa. Study: 700 Indiana St, Johnstown, Pa.

WINOGRAD, Yeshayahu Yehuda, Isr, engineer; b. Tel Aviv, Isr, Dec 3, 1938; s. Pinchus and Rachel (Makovsky); BS, Technion, 1962; MS, Brown U, 1952-66; m. Ruth Gnatek, Aug 8, 1960; c: Sigal, Alon. Sr lectr, mech engr, Technion, since 1961; research asso, MIT, 1966-67. Lt, IDF, 1956-58. Mem: Sigma Xi; Tau Beta Phi; Brown U; Amer Phys Soc; Amer Inst for Aeronautics and Astronautics. Contbr to profsl jours. Home: 42 Einstein St, Haifa, Isr. Office: Technion, Haifa, Isr.

WINOGRADOW, Daniel, Isr, accountant, banker; b. Lida, Pol, Apr 4, 1909; s. Samuel and Johanna (Tobias); in Isr since 1935; BA, cum laude, U Commerce, Cracow, 1931; qualified CPA, Isr, 1953; m. Eugenia Miller, Sep 10, 1929; c: Raya. Mgr, Haifa br, Bank of Isr, since 1955; fmr: Natl Comptroller of Ind Enterprises, Solel Boneh Ltd, 1947-52; asst mgr, S Afr Binyan Mortgage Bank Ltd, 1952-54; CPA, Adm-Gen, 1954-

55. Post cdr, Haganah. Mem: finance comm, Isr Mgmt Cen; Inst of CPAs in Isr; Isr Mgmt Cen, Haifa. Author: The Insurance of Commercial Credits, 1931; Survey of London and Paris Clearing Houses, 1962. Hobbies: archaeol, philately. Home: 64 Hatashbi Rd, Haifa, Isr. Office: 24 Haazmaut Rd, Haifa, Isr.

WINOGRADOW, Eugenia, Isr, jurist; b. Ozany, Lith, Nov 27, 1910; d. Eliyahu and Raisa (Jershansky) Miller; in Isr since 1935; ML, law fac, U Cracow; m. Daniel Wingradow, Sep 19, 1929; c: Raya. Judge, Dist Court, Haifa, since 1953; fmr: advocate, Tel Aviv, 1939-49; magistrate, Magistrate Court, Haifa, 1949-53, chief magistrate, 1953. First woman judge in Isr. Office: District Court, Haifa, Isr.

WINOKUR, Arnold, Isr, educator; b. Russ, Aug 13, 1915; s. Abraham and Ethel (Alperson); in Isr since 1957; BSc, Warsaw Polytech, 1939, MS, 1946; m. Maria Walas, July 11, 1948; c: Aleksander, Ewa. Prof, engr, Technion, since 1968, asso prof, 1958-68. Mem, Comite Zur du Beton; adv sci comm, Isr Standards Instn. Author: Design of Composite-Shaped Tanks, 1953; Plastic Design of Reinforced Concrete Elements, 2nd ed, 1958. Recipient: State Prize of Pol, 1952; prize, Pol Acad Sci, 1956. Home: 124 Hanasi Ave, Haifa, Isr. Office: Technion, Haifa, Isr.

WINSTEN, Louis, US, certified public acctnt; b. NYC, Dec 18, 1892; s. Isaac and Annie (Levinson) Weinstein; BCS, NYU, 1915; m. Libbie Feldman, June 16, 1920; c: Sybil Conrad, Irwin. Partner, Homes & Davis, CPA's, since 1920. Pvt, US Army, 1918. Dir, UJA, Gtr NY; mem: natl council, JDC; life, ZOA; natl gov council, AJCong; trustee, Cong Emanuel, Mt Vernon; vice-pres, Westchester Zionist reg; NY State Soc CPA's, past dir, vice-pres; Amer Inst CPA's; fmr: pres: YMHA; Zionist Dist; Cong Emanuel, all Mt Vernon; found, first pres, Menorah Soc, NYU; first pres, acctnts chap, AJCong; master, Mt Massada lodge, Masons; chmn, Isr Bonds, Mt Vernon. Recipient: guest of hon: Mt Vernon: Isr Bonds, 1956; JTSA, 1960; Yeshiva U, 1961; UJA, 1962; acctnts div, NYC: Isr Bonds, 1954; UJA, 1961; AJ Cong, 1967; designated Hatan Bereshit, Cong Emanuel, 1968. Contbr to profsl jours. Spec interests: Isr, Isr stamps. Home: 1200 Midland Ave, Bronxville, NY. Office: 521 Fifth Ave, New York, NY.

WINTER, Fritz Salomon, Uruguay, rabbi; b. Königsberg, Ger, Dec 11, 1914; s. Moritz and Ernestine (Abraham); in Uruguay since 1950; PhD, U Würzburg, 1936; ordained rabbi, Hochschule für Wissenschaft des Judentums, Berlin, 1938; m. Johanna Hahn, Nov 23, 1941; c: Alfredo, Herberto, Wolf. Chief rabbi, Neuva Congregacion Israelita, since 1964, rabbi, 1950-64; fmr: preacher, tchr, J comty, Berlin, 1935-39; rabbi: J comty, Cochbamba, Bolivia, 1939-50; Union of J comtys, Bolivia, 1942-47. Pres, co-found, J-Chr Interfaith Movement of Uruguay; fmr: pres, JWC, Uruguay sect, 1960-61; mem bd govs, CENTRA, Latin Amer Assn of Comtys and Orgs of Cen Eur Origin, 1956-68; pres, Montevideo lodge 2002, B'nai B'rith, 1956-58; mem: RA, NY; Union de Rabinos Latino Americanos, Santiago de Chile. Contbr to J jours. Home and study: Julio Herrera y Obes 1205, Montevideo, Uruguay.

WINTER, Ruth, US, artist; b. NYC, Jan 17, 1913; d. Benjamin and Yetta (Rosenberg) Cohen; BS, NYU, 1932, MA, 1933; att, Art Students League, 1955-59; m. Alexander Winter, Apr 4, 1941; c: James. Exhbs: City Cen, NY, 1956-60; Argent Gal, Silvermine, Conn, 1957-59; Amer Art at Mid-Cent, Orange, NJ, 1957; Art USA, 1958; Provincetown, Mass, 1958; Natl Assn of Women Artists, 1958, 1959, 1960, 1963; Natl Acad of Design, 1960; Bklyn Mus, 1960; Knickerbocker Art Assn, 1960; Pepsi Cola Bldg; Denker and Simon Art Gal, both NYC, 1964; Ethical Culture Soc auction, 1966; Lever House, 1967; Lever House and Acad of Design, Natl Assn of Women Artists, yearly show, 1968; group shows and one-man shows. Mem: Art Students League; Natl Assn of Women Artists; Mahopac Art League; chmn, vets comm, Gtr NY B'nai B'rith, 1941. Recipient: Marcia Brady Tucker prize, 1957; hon mention, Mahopac Art League, 1958, prize, 1959; Low award, 1959; hon mention, City Cen, 1960. Home and studio: 98-50 67 Ave, Forest Hills, NY.

WINTER, Ted, US, publisher, lithographer; b. Chgo, Ill, May 9, 1919; s. Irving and Florence (Regensteiner); att: U Mich, 1937-40; Loyola U, 1940-42; m. Joan Lee, July 1, 1941; c: John, Thomas. Pres, Regensteiner Publ Enterprises Inc, since 1960. Lt, US Army, 1942-46. Dir: Printing Ind of Ill; Graphic Arts Tech Found; W Cen Assn; fmr chmn, Graphic Arts

Council Found; chmn, Graphic Arts Crusade of Mercy, 1962; vice-chmn, Chgo AJComm, 1959; treas, Amer Vets Comm, 1948; mem, coop agcys bd, Ill Comm on Children and Youth, 1957; bd assos, Natl Coll of Educ; bd dirs: bd educ, Highland Park-Deerfield HSs; Highland Park Comty Fund, 1958; Henry Horner Boys Clubs, 1959; mem: urban renewal comm, Chgo Assn Commerce and Ind; Zeta Beta Tau; clubs: Standard; Northmoor Country. Spec interest: intergroup relations. Home: 223 Linden Park Pl, Highland Park, Ill. Office: 1224 W Van Buren St, Chicago, Ill.

WINTROBE, Maxwell M, US, physician, researcher, educator; b. Halifax, NS, Oct 27, 1901; s. Herman and Ethel (Zwerling); in US since 1927; BA, U Man, 1921, MD, 1926, BS, med, 1927, hon DS, 1958; PhD, Tulane U, 1929; hon DS, U of Utah, 1967; m. Becky Zanphir, 1928; c: Susan, Paul (decd). Prof, dept head, med, U of Utah Coll of Med, since 1943, dir, lab for study of hereditary and metabolic disorders, since 1945; spec cons, nutritional anemias, WHO, since 1961; chief cons, VA hosps; cons: FDA; USPHS; AEC; fmr: intern, Winnipeg Gen Hosp, 1925-26; Gordon Bell f, U Man, 1926-27; instr, Tulane U; asst visiting phys, Charity Hosp, both New Orleans, 1927-30; asso prof, Johns Hopkins U Med Sch, 1935-43, fac mem since 1930; phys i/c, clinic for nutritional, gastro-intestinal, and hemopoietic disorders, Johns Hopkins Hosp, 1941-43, hosp staff mem since 1935; phys-in-chief: Salt Lake Co Gen Hosp, 1943-65; U of Utah Med Cen, 1965-67. Research and devl command, Surg Gens Office, US Army, 1949. FACP; dipl, Amer Bd Internal Med; mem: AMA, vice-chmn, council on durgs; Salt Lake Co Med Assn; AAAS; Amer Soc for Clinical Inves; Amer Soc for Experimental Path; Amer, Fed, and W Socs for Clinical Research; Soc for Experimental Biol and Med; Intl, and Eur Socs of Hematology; Assn of Clinical Paths, London; Assn of Profs of Med; Leukemia Soc, chmn, natl med adv bd; Natl Adv Arthritis and Metabolic Diseases Council, USPHS, 1950-54, chmn, hematology study sect, 1956-59; Natl Adv Allergy and Infectious Disease Council, since 1967; Natl Acad of Sci; chmn, adv council, Life Ins Med Research Fund, 1949-53; dir, Amer Soc Hum Genetics, 1948; anti-anemia preparations adv bd, US Pharmacopeia, 1941-49, comm on revision, 1950-69; Assn Amer Phys, fmr pres, councillor; W Assn Phys, fmr pres; Sigma Xi; Sigma Alpha Mu; bd dirs, Utah Sym Orch; Pro-Utah Inc; hon mem: Harvey Soc; It Soc of Hematology; fgn f, La Asociacion Mexicana de Medicos Laboratoristas; club: Pacific Interurban Clinical. Author: Clinical Hematology, 1942, 6th ed, 1967; co-ed: Harrison's Principles of Internal Med, 1950, 5th ed, 1966; asso ed: Blood; Jour of Clinical Path, Gt Brit; Med; Cancer; adv ed, Tice Prac of Med, 1937-63; asso ed, Intl Med Digest, 1944-58; contbr to sci and med jours. Recipient: Modern Med award, 1958; Gold Headed Cane, U Cal, 1958; Premium Ferrata, Intl Soc of Hematology, Rome, 1958; lectureships: Hosp Gen, Mexico City, 1946; Fulbright Intl Exch prog, India, 1956; Pfizer, Austr and NZ, 1958; Thayer, Johns Hopkins U, 1967; Lilly, Royal Coll of Phys, London, 1968; Billings, AMA, 1969. Home: 5882 Brentwood Dr, Salt Lake City, Utah. Office: U of Uath College of Med, Salt Lake City, Utah.

WIRGUIN, Joseph, Isr, economist; b. Warsaw, Pol, Sep 20, 1913; s. Moshe and Nechama (Edelsberg); in Isr since 1948; BCom, Hochschule für Welthandel, Vienna, 1934; m. Carla Heitner, Nov 9, 1954; c: Itzhak. Econ adv, State Controller of Isr, since 1959; fmr: dep mgr, fgn exch dept, Bank Zachodni SA, Warsaw, 1935-39; dep dir, food import dept, Min of Trade and Ind, Isr, 1949-59. Lt, IDF, 1948-49. Author: The Doctrine of Perfect Capitalism, 1958. Home: 10 Mesilat Yesharim St, Jerusalem, Isr. Office: State Controllers Office, 60 Rashi St, Jerusalem, Isr.

WIRTH, Otto, US, educator; b. Gemünden, Ger, June 26, 1905; s. Joseph and Rosalie (Lorig); in US since 1932; BA, Cen YMCA Coll, 1935; MA, U Chgo, 1935, PhD, 1937; m. Magda Gmirek, Aug 31, 1934. Dean of facs, vice-pres for acad affairs, Roosevelt U, since 1967; dean, Coll of Arts and Sci, 1960-67, prof, modern lang, 1945-46, dept chmn since 1946; fmr: instr, George Williams Coll, 1935-36; f, U Chgo, 1936-37; lectr, Ind U ext div, Calumet Cen, 1937-42. Spec agt, Counter Intelligence Corps, 1943-45. Mem: bd trustees, Roosevelt U, since 1965; exec comm, ADL; AAUP; MLA; Amer Assn of Tchrs of Ger; Southeast Chgo Commn; Hyde Park-Kenwood Comty Conf; secy, Auditorium Theatre Council; fmr, mem, bd dirs, Adult Educ Council of Gtr Chgo, 1950-56. Contbr to profsl jours. Recipient: Bronze Star, 1945. Home: 1377 E 55 Pl, Chicago, Ill. Office: Roosevelt U, Chicago Ill.

WISAN, Joseph E, US, educator; b. NYC, Feb 26, 1901; s. Abraham and Mollie (Kamber); BS, cum laude, CCNY, 1922; PhD, Columbia U, 1934; m. m. Edith Fox, Feb 25, 1930. Prof em, CCNY, since 1966, prof, hist since 1950, dept chmn, 1949-66, prof, Grad Sch of Intl Relations, since 1955, fac mem since 1922. Dir, courses, Civil Defense Council, 1942-45. Juror, Bancroft prizes in Amer Hist, 1958; cons, Grad Record Examinations, 1946-47; mem: AAUP; Amer Hist Assn; Org of Amer Hists; Amer Acad of Political and Social Sci; Phi Beta Kappa, Pres, gamma of NY, 1958-59; Phi Alpha Theta. Author: The Cuban Crisis, 1934. Home: 25 Monroe Place, Brooklyn, NY. Office: CCNY, New York, NY.

WISBAUM, Franklin Courtland, US, attorney; b. Niagara Falls, NY, Jan 3, 1905; s. Louis and Ida (Boff); LLB, U Buffalo, 1926; m. Elizabeth Boff, Jan 5, 1930; c: Joyce Underberg, Wayne. Pvt law practice since 1930; pres: Wisbaum Realty Assn, since 1943; Cataract Realty Assn, since 1938; dir, Niagara Co Savings Bank; fmr, atty, Moore, Killian & Knowles, 1926-30; Found, hon pres, J Fed, since 1950, pres, 1935-50; pres, Coll Mens Assn; secy, Temple Beth Isr, since 1924; mem bd: Council Social Agcys; appeal revs bd, Niagara Falls Comty Chest; mem: Masons; Elks; Shriners; ZOA; fmr, pres, B'nai B'rith lodge, 1933. Recipient: citation, NCCJ, 1967. Home: 526 Jefferson Ave, Niagara Falls, NY. Office: 809 United Office Bldg, Niagara Falls, NY.

WISCHNITZER, Rachel, US, art historian, author, educator; b. Minsk, Russ; d. Wladimir and Sophie (Halpern) Bernstein; in US since 1940; architect's dipl, Sch of Architecture, Paris, 1907; postgrad studies, Us: Heidelberg; Munich; Berlin; MA, NYU, 1944; D, HC, Yeshiva U; m. Mark Wischnitzer, June 5, 1912 (decd); c: Leonard. Prof em, fine arts, Stern Coll, Yeshiva U, NYC; art ed: Rimon; Milgrom, both, 1922-24; Ency Judaica, 1928-34; curator, J Mus, 1933-38; all Berlin; art ed, Universal J Ency, 1942-44; research f, Amer Acad for J Research, 1940-43; lectr, Sch of Educ, NYU, 1949, all NYC; lectr, McGill U, 1953. Author: Symbole und Gestalten der Jüdischen Kunst, 1935; The Messianic Theme in the Paintings of the Dura Synagogue, 1948; Synagogue Architecture in the United States, 1955; The Architecture of the European Synagogue; co-author: History of the Jewish People, 1914; Sabbath, 1944; The Purim Anthology, 1949; The Jews, Their History, Culture and Religion, 1949; The Passover Anthology, 1961; contbr to: books; scholarly and J jours. Mem: Amer Oriental Soc; Soc Bibl Lit; Soc Architectural Hists; Amer J Hist Soc; Conf on J Social Studies; YIVO; ORT. Recipient: Akiba Eger medal, J Comty, Berlin, 1937. Home: 50 Overlook Terr, New York, NY. Office: Yeshiva U, New York, NY.

WISE, Aaron Medalie, US, rabbi; b. Cincinnati, O, Apr 5, 1913; s. Abraham and Esther (Medalie); att, Yeshiva Coll, 1930-32; BA, U Cincinnati, 1933; MHL, JTSA, 1938; DD, U of Judaism, 1967; m. Miriam Lipson, June 22, 1941; c: Tamar, Jonathan, Joel. Rabbi, Valley J Comty Cen and Temple, since 1947; fac mem, U of Judaism, since 1948; fmr: rabbi, Nott Terr Syn, 1938-47. Chmn, San Fernando Valley Bd Rabbis; bd govs, acad depts, U of Judaism; bd dirs, J Fed Council of Gtr LA, mem, comty planning dept; mem: Natl Council J Educ; LA Bur J Educ; fmr: pres, Bd of Rabbis, S Cal, 1955-56; inst, Brandeis Camp Inst, 1950-68. Ed, W states RA Bull, 1961-63; contbr of sermons to anthols. Spec interests: educ, politics, all religions, The State of Isr. Home: 5444 Ben Ave, N Hollywood, Cal. Study: 5540 Laurel Canyon Blvd, N Hollywood, Cal.

WISE, George S, administrator, educator; b. Pinsk, Pol, Apr 7, 1906; s. Noah and Chaya (Rabinowitz) Schneiweis; BS, Furman U, 1928; MA, Columbia U, 1930, PhD, 1950; m. Florence Rosenberg, Dec 8, 1933. Pres, Tel Aviv U, since 1963; pres, Inter-Amer Paper Corp, since 1940; chmn of bd, Isr-Latin Amer Development Co; bd dirs: Ind Devl Bank of Isr Ltd; The Isr Corp; Isr Chems Ltd; Isr Devl Corp; Isr Research and Devl Corp; fmr, lectr, sociol, Columbia U, 1951-52; Natl pres, Amer Friends of Heb U, 1951-55; chmn, bd govs, Heb U, 1953-62; club: Columbia U. Author: Caudillo, A Portrait of Antonio Guzman Bianco, 1951; El Mexico de Aleman, 1952. Recipient: Aguila Azteca, Govt of Mexico, 1946. Home: Tel Aviv, Isr. Offices: 41 E 42 St, New York, NY; Tel Aviv U, Ramat Aviv, Isr.

WISE, Henry, US, scientist, educator; b. Ciechanow, Pol, Jan 14, 1919; s. Herman and Belle (Hercberg); in US since 1936; att, U Louisville, 1938-40; BS, U Chicago, 1941; MS, 1943, PhD, 1947; m. 1st, Hadassah Shuster, June 13, 1943; c: Dav-

id, Daniel, Nina; m. 2nd, Tamar Roth, Nov 12, 1960; c: Daphna, Naomi, Michael. Chmn, chem dynamics dept, Stanford Research Inst, since 1955; lectr, Stanford U School of Engr, since 1962; fmr: sr sci, jet propulsion lab, Cal Inst of Tech, 1947-55; visiting prof, Technion, Haifa, 1965. Mem: Amer Phys Soc; Amer Chem Soc; Sigma Xi; B'nai B'rith; adv, Hillel Found, U Chicago, 1940-44; officer, Sigma Alpha Mu. Contbr to profsl jours. Spec interests: sci and chem knowledge of Biblical times. Hobbies: photography, sailing. Home: 735 Loma Court, Redwood City, Cal. Office: Stanford Research Inst, Menlo Park, Cal.

WISE, Louis E, US, forest chemist, educator; b. NYC, Jan 29, 1888; s. Isaac and Bertha (Jaros); BA, Columbia U, 1907; PhD, 1911; postgrad research, Pasteur Inst, Paris, 1926-27; hon MS, Lawrence U, 1966; m. 1st, Ethel Brand, Sep 1, 1913 (decd); c: Robert, Brenda; m. 2nd, Christine Balazs, 1940; c: Enika, Catherine. Ret; sr em research asso, Inst of Paper Chem, Lawrence Coll, 1941-66; fmr: instr: biochem, Columbia U, 1912-1913; chem, U of Mo, 1913-14; biochem, US Dept of Agric, 1914-18; chem, US War Dept, 1918-19; research chem, DuPont de Nemours Co, 1919; prof, forest chem, NY State Coll of Forestry, 1919-32, prof em, 1932; prof, organic chem, Rollins Coll, 1933-37. Mem: AAAS; Amer Chem Soc; Tech Assn of Pulp and Paper Ind; Wis Acad of Sci; Sigma Xi; Phi Beta Kappa. Co-author: Chemistry of Wood, 1926; Wood Chemistry, 1944, 2nd ed, 1952; contbr to sci jours. Recipient: gold medal, Tech Assn of Pulp and Paper Ind; first Anselme Payen award, Amer Chem Soc, 1962. Home: 108 N Green Bay St, Appleton Wis. Office: Inst of Paper Chem, Lawrence Coll, Appleton, Wis.

WISE, Richard Jacob, US insurance agt, b. Niederhochstadt, Ger, May 26, 1902; s. Adolf and Marie (Feibelman); in US since 1934; referendar, Djns, Us: Heidelberg, Munich, Berlin, Wurzburg, 1922-26; dipl, referendar, London, 1919; m. Trude Rheinheimer, July 17, 1932; c: Frank. Ins agt since 1935; lawyer, 1929-33; ins agt, 1933-34; factory worker, 1934-35. Co-found, Temple Sholom, vice-pres, 1963-64, fmr trustee; pres: Cincinnati Comm for Refugees, 1963-66; Gate Club, 1949-50; regional vice-chmn, United Appeal, 1959; trustee, Avon Temple Corp; bd dirs, JWF, 1963-66; mem: Alfred M Cohen lodge, B'nai B'rith; AJComm; Avon lodge, Masons; Scottish Rite; Shriners. Spec interest: adult educ. Home: 7338 Scottwood Ave, Cincinnati, O. Office: 2800 Carew Tower, Cincinnati O.

WISEMAN, Joseph, US, stage and film actor; b. Montreal, Can, May 15, 1918; s. Louis and Pearl (Rubin); in US since 1930; att CCNY, 1935-36; m. Pearl Lang, Nov 9, 1964; c: Martha. Actor: The Theater Group, UCLA; Repertory Theatre: Lincoln, Cen; ANTA-Wash Sq; Amer Shakespeare Festival. Prin roles: plays: Uncle Vanya; In the Matter of J Robert Oppenheimer; Abe Lincoln in Illinois; Candle in the Wind; The Three Sisters; Joan of Lorraine; Detective Story; King Lear; The Lark; Incident at Vichy; The Duchess of Malfi; Murder in the Cathedral; films: Dr No; Bye-Bye Braverman; The Night They Raided Minsky's; Stiletto; Detective Story; Viva Zapata; The Unforgiven. Recipient: Drama Desk award. Home: 382 Central Park W, New York, NY.

WISEMAN, Shlomo, Can, educator, editor; b. Ukraine, Russ, Mar 10, 1899; s. Shamai and Dvorah (Pomerantz); in Can since 1913; BA, McGill U, 1920, MA, 1923; m. Annie Potashner, Mar 27, 1920; c: Dvorah Marcuse, Gdalyah. Educ dir, J People's Schs, since 1969, sch prin, 1920-69; educ dir: J Tchrs Sem, 1946-48; Combined J Tchrs Sem, 1949-50; lectr, Heb, Sir George Williams Coll, 1953-55, 1954-56. Founded first modern J people's secondary sch, 1922. Mem: educ comm, Can J Cong; bd govs, YIVO Inst for J Research; educ comm, J Folk Schs, US, Can; J Natl Workers Alliance; Poale Zion Org; J Public Libr; fmr: mem, Conf of Can J Cong; secy, comm for establishment of a separate J sch panel for Que; secy, Vaad Ha'ir, Montreal. Ed: Dos Vort, anthol of Yiddish lit, 1931; Messaprim Americaiin, 1956; The Schlomie Wisemann book, 1961; co-ed: Letzte Lieder of I J Segal; contbr to lit and J mags. Recipient: awards: Cong for J Culture, NYC, 1961; Council of J Educ Instns, Can J Cong; I J Segal Found, 1969. Spec interests: research in Hellenistic J culture, integrated J educ, Heb lit, world lit, educ theory and practice. Home: 5826 Clanranald Ave, Montreal, Can. Office: 5170 Van Horne Ave, Montreal, Can,

WISENTHAL, Miles, Can, educator; b. Montreal, Can, Oct 29, 1913; s. Esidore and Bertha (Weiner); BA, Sir George Williams U, 1955; MA, McGill U, 1956; PhD, London U,

1964; m. Dorothy Rosenbloom, Sep, 1935; c: Jonathan, David. Asso dean, fac of arts and sci, McGill U, since 1969, asst to dir, Inst of Educ, 1958-69; dir, educ div, Dominion Bur of Stats; fmr: vice-pres, Stag Shoe Ltd, 1935-54. Capt, Royal Can Army, 1942-45. Chmn, research comm, Que Tchrs Assn; mem, bd trustees and educ div, Temple Emanu-El, Montreal; mem: Can Coll of Tchrs Educ Assn; U Tchrs Assn; Can Assn Profs of Educ; research adv bd, Can Tchrs Fed. Home: 72 Oxford Rd, Baie d'Urfe, Quebec, Can. Office: McGill U, Montreal, Can.

WISER, Nathan, Isr, physicist, educator; b. Zurich, Switz, Nov 7, 1935; s. Moses and Taube (Horowitz); in Isr since 1967; BS, Wayne U, 1957; MS, PhD, U Chgo, 1964; m. Dvora Bekker, Dec 17, 1961; c: David, Meir, Timna. Asso prof, physics, Bar Ilan U, since 1967; fmr: research asso, U of Ill, 1964-65; sr research physicist, IBM-Watson Research Cen, 1965-67. Fmr, regional, vice-pres, Orthodox J Sci Assn; mem: Amer Phys Soc: Isr Phys Soc. Ed, Quantum Fluids, 1969; contbr to profsl jours. Home: 117 Modiin St, Ramat Gan, Isr. Office: Bar Ilan U, Ramat Gan, Isr.

WISHENGRAD, Hyman, (HR Wishengrad); US, ed; b. Brest-Litovsk, Russ, Aug 28, 1903; s. Samuel and Augusta (Naidus), in US since 1907; att CCNY, 1920-21; BLitt, Columbia U, 1926; att, Sch of Journalism, 1922-24; m. 1st, Ruth Goldman, Oct 15, 1926 (decd); c: Paul, Kay Coltoff, Bette Cohen; m. 2nd, Eleanor Schoolman. Exec ed, Wash Star syndicate, since 1968; ed, JTA, 1935-41; ed, Overseas News Agcy, 1941-52; owner, eds Ed, Syndicate, 1952-59; exec ed, Bridgeport Sun Herald, 1959-62; mgn ed, Scarsdale Inquirer, 1963-65. Club: Natl Press, Wash, DC. Home: 630 W 246 St, New York, NY. Office: 444 Madison Ave, New York, NY.

WISHIK, Samuel M, US, administrator, physician, educator; b. NYC, Apr 7, 1905; s. Nathan and Antoinette (Pimsler); BA, Columbia Coll, 1926, MD, Coll of Phys and Surgs, 1929; MPH, Sch of Hygiene and Public Health, Johns Hopkins U, 1948; m. Caroline Sulzer, Nov 17, 1947, div, Oct, 1968; c: Ruth, Anton, Laura. Dir, div for prog devl and evaluation, Intl Inst of Hum Reproduction, Columbia U, since 1967; fmr: pvt practice, ped, Flushing, NY, 1934-42; asst att phys, Queensboro Hosp for Communicable Diseases, 1935-36; asst ped, St John's Hosp, LIC, 1937-38; lectr, NYU Coll of Med, 1936-39; chief att ped, children's allergy clinic, Flushing Hosp, 1941-42; asso att ped, Queens Gen Hosp, 1940-42; lectr, Tchrs Coll, Columbia U, 1942; sr asst surg, USPHS, 1942-43; med dir, Emergency Poliomyelitis Hosp, Honolulu, 1943-44; lectr, U Hawaii, 1943-46; dir, Burs of Crippled Children; and of Maternal and Child Health, Hawaii, 1943-46; chief, div for physically handicapped children, Dept of Health, NYC, 1946-47, dir, bur child health, 1949-51; chief, prog planning sect, asst dir, health services div, US children's bur, Wash, DC, 1948-49; lectr, Johns Hopkins U, 1949-50; prof, maternal and child health, Grad Sch of Public Health, U Pittsburgh, 1951-67. F: Amer Public Health Assn; NY Acad of Med; Amer Acad of Peds; licentiate, Amer Bd of Ped; dipl, Amer Bd of Preventive Med and Public Health; mem: Queens Co Med Soc; AMA; Amer Sch Health Assn; Assn for Childhood Educ; Soc for Research in Child Devl; Amer Acad for Cerebral Palsy; AHA; NY Heart Assn; Natl Conf of Social Work; Amer Ped Soc; Amer Orthopsycht Assn; Amer Phys Therapy Assn; Alpha Omega Alpha. Mem, ed bd, Pediatrics, 1956-68; contbr to profsl jours. Home: 345 W 58 St, New York, NY. Office: 45 Overlook Terr, New York, NY.

WISLICKI, Leo, Isr, physician; b. Kattowitz, Ger, Aug 12, 1901; s. Lazarus and Hedwig (Hirsch); in Isr since 1949; MD, Us: Berlin, Munich, Breslau, 1918-25; LRCP, LRCS, Royal Coll of Phys and Surgs, Glasgow-Edinburgh, 1934; m. Luise Hirsch, Apr 19, 1933. Clinical asso prof, pharm, since 1961; res med off, med dept, Urbankrankenhaus, Berlin, 1928-33; research worker, clinical lectr, 1949-57. Hon mem, Med Assn Sina, Teheran; chmn, poison control comm, IMA. Contbr to profsl books and jours. Spec interests: Biblical and Talmudic lit. Home: 29 Metudela St, Jerusalem, Isr. Office: Heb U-Hadassah Med Sch, Jerusalem, Isr.

WISOTZKY, Joel, US, dental educator; b. Chgo, Ill, Feb 17, 1923; s. Isadore and Rose (Sheveloff); BS, Cen YMCA Coll, 1943; DDS, Loyola Dent Sch, Chgo, 1947; PhD, U of Rochester, NY, 1955; m. Eleanor Pinsky, Feb 16, 1949; c: Sharen, Philip, Ira. Prof, oral biol, med, dir, grad training and research, dir, dent research, Sch of Dent, Case W Reserve U, Cleveland, O, since 1959; pvt practice, 1947-48; research asso, dent med div, Colgate Palmolive Co, 1956-59; hon asso research special-

ist, Rutgers U Bur of Biol Research, 1956-59. US Army, 1942-45; asst dent surg, USPHS, 1949-51. Mem: AAAS; Omicron Kappa Upsilon; Sigma Xi; Intl Assn for Dent Research; Amer Socs for Experimental Biol; Amer Soc for Experimental Path. Contbr to profsl jours. Recipient: U F, dent, U of Rochester, 1951-52; postdoc USPHS research f, 1952-56; career devl award, USPHS, 1959. Spec interest: electronics. Home: 3407 Blanche, Cleveland, O. Office: 2123 Abington, Cleveland, O.

WITKON, Alfred, Isr, judge; b. Berlin, Ger, Feb 23, 1910; in Isr since 1934; att Us: Berlin; Bonn; JD, U Freiburg, 1933; Middle Temple, London, 1936; m. Greta Philipsohn, Mar 6, 1936; c: Naomi Gash, Gideon. Supr Court Judge since 1954; pres, Dist Court, Jerusalem, 1948-54; lectr, Heb U, Tel Aviv, 1954-64. Author: Law and Society, 1954; Law and Politics, 1965; Laws of Taxation, 4th ed, 1969; contbr to profsl jours. Home: Shmaryahu Levin St, Kiryat Hayovel, Jerusalem, Isr. Office: Supr Court, Jerusalem, Isr.

WITTENBERG, Philip, US, attorney, author; b. Bklyn, NY, Apr 4, 1895; s. William and Elizabeth (Plesetzkaya); LLB, NYU, 1916; m. Ruth Budinoff, Nov 22, 1919; c: Susanna Berger, Jonathan. Mem, Wittenberg, Carrington & Farnsworth, since 1935; lectr, New Sch for Social Research, Columbia U, Cooper Union, NYC. Psych examiner, WW I. Author: Literary Property, 1938; Dangerous Words, 1947, Japanese, 1954; The Lamont Case, 1957; The Law of Literary Property, 1957; The Protection of Literary Property, 1968; contbr to Ency of Social Scis; law revs. Trustee: Amer Acad Dramatic Arts; Copyright Soc of US; counsel: Mystery Writers of Amer; Bill of Rights Fund; dir, Wash Sq Assn. Home: 35 W 10 St, New York, NY. Office: 15 W 44 St, New York, NY.

WITTKOWER, Eric David, Can, psychiatrist, educator; b. Berlin, Ger, Apr 4, 1899; s. Louis and Bertha (. ﹍'z); in Can since 1951; MD, Berlin U, 1924; m. Claire Weil, July 29, 1931; c: Andrew, Sylvia. Prof, psycht, McGill U, since 1963, asso prof, 1953-63, asst prof, 1951-53; hon cons psycht, hosps: Royal Victoria; Montreal Gen; Queen Elizabeth; Reddy Memorial, all Montreal; Halley Steward research f, Tavistock Clinic, 1935-41, cons psycht, 1948-51; psycht research f, Natl Assn for Prevention of TB, 1945-48, both London, Eng; cons psycht: Natl Sanatorium, Beneden, Eng, 1947-51; dermat dept, St Bartholomew's Hosp, London, 1948-51. M , Brit Army, War Off, 1941-45. Chmn, Comm on Transcultural Psycht, Can Psycht Assn; life gov, Montreal Gen Hosp; f: Amer Psycht Assn; Brit Psych Soc; Royal Soc Med, Eng; World Fed Mh; Acad of Psychan, fmr council mem; charter f, Amer Coll Psychts; mem: Intl Council, Inst Social Psycht, Lima, Peru; Quebec Psycht Assn; hon adv council, Can Assn Occupational Therapy, Que; profsl bd, Intl Inst for Mh Research; NY Acad Scis; hon mem: Arg Psychosomatic Soc; Hellenic Soc of Neur and Psycht, Athens, Greece; Soc de Medicos y Cirujanos, Caracas, Venezuela; Soc Venezolana de Psiquiatria y Neurologia; asso mem, Brit Psychan Soc; life mem: Can Psycht Assn; Pan Amer Med Assn; Can Psychan Soc; profsl affiliate, Intl Council Psychols; fmr pres: Can Psychan Soc; Amer Psychosomatic Soc. Author of several books; ed in chief, Transcultural Psycht Research Rev, McGill U; asso ed: Psychosomatic Medicine, US; Jour of Psychosomatic Research, Eng; asst ed, Intl Jour of Social Psycht Eng; contrib ed, Psychotherapy and Psychosomatics, Intl Fed for Med Psychotherapy; Can corresp, Medicina Psicosomatica, It; regional ed for Can, Social Sci and Med, Harvard Med Sch; mem ed bd, various profsl jours; contbr to profsl publs. Home: 363 Clarke Ave, Westmount, Que, Can. Office: 1266 Pine Ave W, Montreal, Can.

WITTKOWER, Rudolf J, US, historian; b. Berlin, Ger, June 22, 1901; s. Henry and Gertrude (Ansbach); in US since 1954; PhD, Berlin U, 1923; m. Margot Holzmann; c: Mario. Kress Found prof, Natl Gal, Wash, DC, 1969-70; asst, Bibliotheca Hertziana, Rome, 1923-28; mem, Warburg Inst, London, 1934-35; reader, U of London, 1945-49, prof, 1949-55; chmn, dept art hist and archaeol, Columbia U, 1955-68, Avalon Found prof, hum, 1968-69. F: Royal Inst Brit Architects; Academia Olimpica, Vicenza; Accademia delle Belle Arti, Venice; Accademia dei Lincei, Rome; Amer Acad Arts and Scis; Brit Acad; Max-Planck Gesellschaft, Goettingen; Warburg Inst, London. Author: Die Zeichnungen des G L Bernini, 1931; The Drawings of the Carracci, 1952; Architectural Principles in the Age of Humanism, 1952; G L Bernini, 1955; Art and Architecture in Italy, 1600-1750, 1958; co-author: Michelangelo-Bibliographie, 1928; British Art and the Mediterranean, 1948; Born Under Saturn, 1963. Home:25 Claremont Ave, New York, NY. Office: Columbia U, New York, NY.

WITTKOWER, Werner J, Isr, architect; b. Berlin, Ger, May 12, 1908; s. Henry and Gertrude (Ansbach); in Isr since 1933; att Us: Berlin; Heidelberg; dipl, engr, Stuttgart Tech Coll; m. Eva Fuerst, Sep 19, 1933. Pvt practice, Tel Aviv, since 1933; mem, town planning comm, Tel Aviv, 1946-54; asso with E W Baumann, architect, 1953-66. Designer: Accadia Hotel, Herzliya; Sheraton Hotel, Tel Aviv; Mus Haaretz, Tel Aviv; co-designer: Tel Aviv U; Tel Aviv Bus Terminal; Petah Tikva Munic Off and Civic Cen. Mem: exec comm, Tel Aviv Mus; Assn Engrs and Architects in Isr. Home: 26 Basel St, Herzliya Pituah, Isr. Office: 19 Dov Hoz St, Tel Aviv, Isr.

WITTLIN, Joseph, US, author, poet, translator; b. Dmytrow, Pol, Aug 17, 1896; s. Karol and Eliza (Rosenfeld); in US since 1941; att, U Vienna, 1914-16; U Lvov, 1918-19; m. Halina Handelsman, July 6, 1924; c: Elizabeth Lipton. Poet, author,trans,since 1919. Author: Hymns (poems), 1920, 1925, 1929; Essays and Travels, 4 vols, 1925, 1932, 1947, 1962; Salt of the Earth, 1935, trans into 13 langs, first Amer ed, 1941; Orpheus in the Hell of the 20th Century, collected essays, 1963; trans: Homer's Odyssey, into Pol hexameter, 1924, 3rd ed, 1957; over 20 vols of poetry, drama, and novels, into Pol. Recipient: awards: Pol PEN club, 1935; Pol Acad of the Independents, 1936; decoration, Pol Acad of Letters, 1937; grant, Amer Acad and Natl Inst of Arts and Letters, 1943; awards: Pol Writers Assn, London, 1957; Alfred Jurzykowski Found, 1966. Mem: Pol Inst of Arts and Sciences in Amer; PEN club; Amer br, PEN club-in-exile, chmn since 1961. Home: 5400 Fieldston Rd, New York, NY.

WITZ, Isaac Peter, Isr, scientist; b. Vienna, Aus, Nov 7, 1934; s. Herman and Frieda (Gerstman); in Isr since 1939; MSc, Heb U, Jerusalem, 1959, PhD, 1965; m. Eve Shnaidovitz, Apr 15, 1959; c: Maritte, Oded. Sr lectr, immunology, dept microbiol, Tel Aviv U, since 1968; sr cancer research sci, Roswell Pk Memorial Inst, Buffalo, NY, 1965-68. Lt, IDF, 1952-54. Mem: Isr Immunological Soc; Amer Assn Cancer Research; Intl Transplantation Soc. Contbr to profsl publs. Home: 89 University Rd, Ramat Aviv, Isr. Office: Tel Aviv U, Ramat Aviv, Isr.

WIZNITZER, Arnold Aharon, US, educator; b. Aus, Dec 20, 1899; s. Israel and Charlotte (Friedmann); PhD, U of Vienna, 1920; DHL, JTSA; m. Deborah Safier, July 7, 1921 (decd). Em research prof, U of Judaism, LA. Author: The Records of the Earliest Jewish Community in the World, 1954; Jews in Colonial Brazil, 1960; contbr to hist jours in US and Brazil. Fmr pres, Brazilian-J Inst of Hist Research. Home and office: 160 S Gramercy Pl, Los Angeles, Cal.

WODAK, Ernst Felix, Isr, business exec; b. Vienna, Aus, Feb 26, 1918; s. Karl and Helen (Bruzt); in Isr since 1938; att U of Vienna, 1936-38; Sch of Textile Tech, Vienna, 1936-37; m. Suzanne Perutz, Jan 19, 1943; c: Naomi, Jonathan. Dir, shareholder: Adereth Co Ltd; Orna Textile Dye Works; Syntex; Afuda Knitting Mill; Amer Products Co, since 1946. Intelligence, Brit Army, 1942-44; cpl, IDF, 1948. Chmn, Man-Power Comm of Textile Ind; mem bd: Isr Export Inst; Wool and Synthetics Equalisation Fund; mem: B'nai B'rith, Theodor Herzl Lodge; Isr Mfrs Assn; Rotary. Recipient: King's Medal; campaign stars. Hobby: riding. Home: Herzliya B, Isr. Office: Adereth Group of Textile Enterprises, Herzliya, Isr.

WOHL, Amiel, US, rabbi; b. Cincinnati, O, June 29, 1930; s. Samuel and Belle (Myers); BA, U of Cincinnati, 1953; BHL, MHL, ordained rabbi, HUC, 1957; m. Rita Murstein, June 27, 1954; c: Susan, Dewey. Rabbi: Temple B'nai Isr, since 1968; fmr: Baltimore Heb Cong; Rodef Sholom, Waco, Tex; World exec comm, Kfar Silver, Isr; delg, World Union for Progressive Judaism; mem: Natl Commn Social Action, UAHC; Nominating, Justice and Peace Comms, Natl CCAR; life, Natl Fed Temple Youth; found, Waco Clergymen's Counseling Service; mem: AJCong; ZOA; AJComm. Hobbies: folk music, tennis. Home: 4805 S Land Park Dr, Sacramento, Cal. Study: 3600 Riverside Blvd, Sacramento, Cal.

WOHL, Michael G, US, physician, educator; b. Russ, Apr 22, 1889; s. Gershon and Sarah (Block); in US since 1908; MD, Medico-Chirurgical Coll, Phila, Pa, 1912; postgrad work: Columbia U, 1923; U Vienna, Aus, 1927-28; m. Rose Hillerson,1915; c: George, Joseph, Milton. Pvt practice, since 1929; chief, nutrition clinic, Phila Gen Hosp, since 1949; cons phys,

Albert Einstein Med Cen, since 1956, sr att phys, 1933-56; prof, path and bact, Temple U Sch of Med, 1915-16, clinical prof, med, chief endocrine clinic, 1932-55; i/c diagnostic labs, dept of diseases of metabolism, Nicholas Senn Hosp, Omaha, Neb, 1916-18; asso prof, Creighton Med Sch; chief of staff, Paxton Memorial Hosp, Omaha; chief, dept metabolic diseases and diagnostic labs, Mercy Hosp, Council Bluffs, Ia, 1917-28; asso prof, oral med, Sch of Dent, U Pa, 1951-55. FACS; f: NY Acad Scis; Amer Inst Nutrition; Phila Coll Phys; chmn: comm on nutrition, metabolism and endocrinology, Phila Co Med Soc; exec bd, Amer Friends of Heb U, phys div; dir, J Phys Comm, since 1948; mem: AMA; Amer Diabetes Soc; Phi Delta Epsilon; hon mem: Del, Bx, NY Acads of Gen Practice; fmr chmn, Solomon Solis-Cohen Med Lit Soc; club,Phila. Med. Author: Bedside Interpretations of Laboratory Findings, 1930; Dietotherapy, 1945; Long Term Illness, 1959; co-author: Internal Medicine, 1951; Modern Nutrition in Health and Disease, 4th ed, 1968; contbr to med jours; Cyclopedia of Med. Recipient: awards: NJ Acad of Gen Practice; Alumni, Medico-Chirurgical Coll; annual Michael G Wohl lectureship, Comm on Nutrition and Metabolism, Phila Co Med Soc. Hobbies: music, fishing. Home and office: 1727 Pine St, Philadelphia, Pa.

WOHL, Samuel, US, rabbi; b. Novaya-Ushitza, Russ, June 21, 1895; s. Mordecai and Rachel (Dolberg); in US since 1913; BA, U of Cincinnati, 1927; ordained rabbi, HUC, Cincinnati, 1927; DD, U of Chgo Divinity Sch, 1946; m. Belle Myers, June 26, 1921; c: Theodore, Amiel. Rabbi: Isaac M Wise Temple, Cincinnati, since 1927, fmr Reading Rd Temple; prin, B'nai Jeshurun Rel Sch, Cleveland, 1919-22. Fmr vice-pres, LZOA; mem, bd dirs, Isr Histadrut; mem bd: Amer Cancer Soc; UAHC; UJA; JDC; mem: Conf of Amer Rabbis; HUC Alumni Assn. Recipient: scrolls, LZOA, Isr Histadrut Campaign; JNF Forest in his name. Hobby: travel. Home: 3896 Reading Rd, Cincinnati, O. Study: Reading Rd and N Crescent, Cincinnati, O.

WOHLGELERNTER, Maurice, US, rabbi, educator; b. Pol, Feb 13, 1921; s. Jacob and Deborah (Yagoda); in US since 1936; BA, Yeshiva U, 1941; ordained rabbi, Rabbi Isaac Elchanan Theol Sem, 1944; MA, Columbua U, 1946, PhD, 1960; m. Esther Feinerman, Feb 1, 1948; c: Debra, Elli, Beth. Rabbi, Inwood J Cen, NY, since 1946; asso prof, Eng, Yeshiva U, mem fac, since 1955; visiting prof: CCNY; Bar Ilan U, Isr; New Sch for Social Research, NY. Mem: RabCA; MLA; Natl Council Tchrs of Eng. Author: Israel Zangwill; A Study; ed, The King of Schnorrers, by Israel Zangwill. contbr to jours. Home: 62 Park Terrace W, New York, NY. Study: 12 Ellwood St, New York, NY.

WOLBERG, John Robert, Isr, educator; b. NYC, May 23, 1936; s. Sidney and Beatrice (Bernstein); in Isr since 1962; BME, Cornell U, NY, 1958; PhD, MIT, 1962; m. Laurie Holbreich, June 14, 1959; c: Beth, David, Daniel. Asso prof, mech engr dept, Technion, Haifa, since 1969, lectr, 1962-65, sr lectr, 1965-69. IDF, 1969. Mem, Amer Nuclear Soc. Author: Prediction Analysis, 1967; contbr to sci jours. Home: 6 Havradim St, Haifa, Isr. Office: Technion, Haifa, Isr.

WOLCHOK, Sidney S, US, attorney; b. NYC, Sep 17, 1920; s. Samuel and Bella (Delman); BSS, CCNY, 1941; JD, Columbia Law Sch, 1944; m. Silkaly Moskowitz, Oct 16, 1949; c: Carol, James, Robert. Sr partner, Katz & Wolchok, since 1944; dir, Andy Gard Corp, 1964-67. Mem: Yeshiva U, lab mgmt comm; Amer Bar Assn, lab law comm; NY Co Lawyers Assn, lab comm; candidate for NY State Leg, 1949; club, Town, Scarsdale, NY. Contbr: chap, Union Activity in Mass Merchandizing, 1970; to law jours. Hobbies: art, travel. Home: 20 Mamaroneck Rd, Scarsdale, NY. Office: 360 Lexington Ave, New York, NY.

WOLDMAN, Albert A, US, jurist; b. Russ, Jan 1, 1897; s. Isaac and Gertrude (Kydush); in US since 1898; BA, W Reserve U, 1917, att Law Sch, 1918; LLB, O Northern U Law Sch, 1919; hon LLD, Monrovia U, 1956; m. Lydia Levin, July 3, 1921; c: Robert, Phyllis Klein, Stuart. Judge, Juvenile Court, Cuyahoga Co, O, since 1953; pvt practice, Cleveland, since 1919; reporter, Cleveland Press, 1917; asst state ed, Cleveland Plain Dealer, 1918; instr, legal hist and constitutional law, John Marshall Law Sch, 1936; asst dir, law, City of Cleveland, 1941-45; chmn, Unemployment Compensation Bd of Rev, State of O, 1945-49; dir, Dept of Ind Relations, State of O, 1949-53. Pres, Abraham Lincoln Assn of O, since 1958; vice-chmn, Abraham Lincoln Sesquicentennial Commn, O, 1959; natl commn, B'nai B'rith Hillel Commn, since 1959; pres,

B'nai B'rith Grand Lodge, 1945-46; trustee, Cleveland Wfr Fed, since 1960; trustee, chmn, planning comm, Cleveland J Comty Fed 1955-58; mem: O, Cuyahoga Co and Cleveland Bar Assns; Miss Valley Hist Assn; Chgo Civil War Round Table; Intl Mark Twain Soc; Tau Epsilon Rho. Author: Lawyer Lincoln, 1936; Lincoln and the Russians, 1952; co-author: The Governors of Ohio, 1954; Lincoln for the Ages, 1959; contbr to mags. Hobby: Lincolniana. Home: 24260 Deptford Dr, Beachwood Village, Cleveland, O.

WOLF, Alfred, US, rabbi; b. Eberbach, Ger, Oct 7, 1915; s. Hermann and Regine (Levy); in US since 1935; BA, U Cincinnati, O, 1937; ordained rabbi, MHL, HUC, 1941; PhD, U of S Cal, 1960; DD, HUC-JIR, 1966; m. Miriam Office, June 16, 1940; c: David, Judy, Dan. Rabbi Wilshire Blvd Temple, LA, since 1949; lectr, rel, U of S Cal, since 1955; adj prof, theol, Loyola U, since 1968; rabbi, Temple Emanuel, Dothan, Ala, 1941-46; part-time regional dir, SE, UAHC, 1944-46; regional dir, W area, 1946-49; visiting prof, Chapman Coll, 1967. Civilian chaplain, US Army Camps, WW II. Mem: Pacific Assn of Reform Rabbis, fmr: chmn, youth conf, treas, vice pres, pres; S Cal Assn of Lib Rabbis, fmr secy-treas, vice-pres, pres; AJComm; Nathan Strauss Isr Soc; LA Co Commn on Hum Relations, fmr chmn; Amer J Hist Soc; Comty Relations Comm of J Fed Council; fmr: CCAR exec bd; pres, secy, Bd of Rabbis of S Cal; mem bd, LA Bur of J Educ; steering comm, United JWF. Co-author: Our Jewish Heritage, 1957. Hobby: photography. Home: 3389 Ley Dr, Los Angeles, Cal. Study: 3663 Wilshire Blvd, Los Angeles, Cal.

WOLF, Bernard S, US, physician, educator; b. NYC, Sep 8, 1912; s. Alex and Mildred (Levy); BS, NYU, 1932, MD, 1936; m. Isabel Masket, May 4, 1939; c: Ellen, Susan. Chmn, dept radiology, Mt Sinai Sch of Med, since 1966, on staff since 1947; served on Manhattan dist atom bomb project, 1944-47; med dir, NY off, AEC, 1947-49; adv comm for atomic defense, Dept of Health, NYC, 1950. F, Amer Bd Radiology; mem: Amer Roentgen Ray Soc; State, Co Med Socs; AMA; NY Acad Med; NY Roentgen Ray Soc; Amer Gastroenterological Soc; Mayor's Adv Comm on Radiation Protection, NYC; Radiological Soc of N Amer; Amer Soc Neuroradiologists. Contbr to sci and med jours. Home: 1215 Fifth Ave, New York, NY. Office: 11 E 100 St, New York, NY.

WOLF, David, Isr, chemical engr; b. Rum, Jan 21, 1932; s. Chaim and Nehama (Fredman); in Isr since 1948; BSc, cum laude, Technion, Haifa, 1957, MSc, 1959, DSc, 1963; m. Yael Dunsky, Aug 20, 1957; c: Ronith, Yoram, Eran. Asso prof, chem engr, head, isotope separation plant, U of Beersheva, since 1966; head, chem engr dept, Jr Tech Coll, Technion, Haifa, 1961-63; postdoc f, Carnegie Inst of Tech, Pittsburgh, Pa 1963-64; asst prof, chem engr dept, McGill U, Montreal, Can, 1964-66. Lt, IDF, 1950-52. Prin contribs: co-found, chem engr dept, Jr Coll, Technion, Haifa; chem engr dept, U of Beersheva. Mem: comm, Isr Inst Chem Engr, local br; adv council, Isr Chem Soc; Chem Inst of Can; Can Soc for Chem Engr; Amer Inst Chem Engr; Isr Inst Chem Engr; Isr Soc for Vacuum Tech. Contbr to profsl jours. Spec interest: educ of youth. Home and office: Weizmann Inst of Sci, Rehovot, Isr.

WOLF, Edwin, II, US, librarian, author; b. Phila, Pa, Dec 6, 1911; s. Morris and Pauline (Binswanger); educated in Eng; m. Margaret Gimbel Dannenbaum, July 2, 1934 (decd); c: Ellen Schrecker, Anthony, Mary Hurtig, Sandra, Barbara, Ann; m. 2nd, Mary Paxson Matthews, Nov 16, 1965. Libr, Libr Co of Phila, since 1953; cataloguer, bibliographer, mgr, Rosenbach Co, rare books, 1930-52; lectr, bibliography, Bryn Mawr Coll, 1940-42; research f, Winterthur Mus, Council, Inst of Early Amer Studies, Williamsburg, 1966-68; Rosenbach f, bibliography, Athenaeum, Phila, 1965. Spec agt, Counter Intelligence Corps, US Army, 1943-45. Pres: J Publ Soc of Amer, 1955-59, presently chmn, publ comm; Fed of J Charities of Phila, since 1959; Friends of U of Pa Libr, 1947-52; fmr pres: Natl Found for J Culture; Fed of JAs of Gtr Phila; Amer J Hist Soc; Bibliographical Soc of Amer; vice-pres, J Ys and Cens of Phila; asso trustee, U of Pa, 1947-60, and since 1968; dir: JWB; J Exponent of Phila; mem: Amer Antiquarian Soc; Hist Soc of Pa; MLA; Amer Hist Assn; Amer Libr Assn; clubs: Franklin Inn; Art Alliance; Locust-Midcity; Grolier, NY. Author: European Manuscripts in the John Lewis Collection, 1937; Doctrine Christiana, 1947; Franklin's Way to Wealth as a Printer, 1951; American Song Sheets, 1850-1870, 1963; Bibliothesauri: Jewels from the Shelves of the Library Company, 1966; Negro History, 1553-

1903, 1969; co-author: William Blake's Illuminated Books, 1953; A History of the Jews of Philadelphia, 1957; Rosenbach: A Biography, 1960; contbr to mags. Recipient: Guggenheim f, 1961; lit award, Athenaeum of Phila, 1961. Home: 10 Curtis Park Dr, Wyncote, Pa. Office: The Library Co of Phila, Broad and Christian Sts, Philadelphia, Pa.

WOLF, Franz Benjamin, US, economist; b. Stuttgart, Ger, June 15, 1900; s. Salomon and Lina (Halle); in US since 1936; att U of Heidelberg, 1918-19; DRerPol, U of Freiburg, 1922; m. Ile Nathan, Dec 30, 1924; c: Dorothy Ettlinger, Hans, Robert. Vive-pres, Robert R Nathan Assos, Inc, Wash, DC, since 1954; asst to exec secy, Württ Städtetag, 1922; econ, Dresdner Bank, Stuttgart, 1923-25; asst and asso ed, Frankfurter Zeitung, 1925-36; econ, stat, Bear, Strearns & Co, 1936-41; commodity and war controls ed, The Jour of Commerce, 1941-43; exec ed, Research Inst of Amer, 1943-50; dir, research, stat, Off of Price Stabilization, dep econ adv, 1951-53. Fmr mem: Ger br, JA; exec bd, J Comty, Frankfurt. Contbr to profsl publs. Home: 5420 Connecticut Ave, Washington, DC. Office: 1218 16 St, NW, Washington, DC.

WOLF, J Jay, US, computer programming mgr; b. Wash, DC, Nov 3, 1928; s. David and Minnie (Witkin); MA, George Wash U, 1950; computer tech: Amr U, 1951-54; U of Pa, 1957-60; m. Adele Solomon, Mar 21, 1956; c: Judith, Aron. Programming activity mgr, Burroughs Corp, since 1969, staff mem since 1956; project dir, Applied Psych Services, since 1958; tech dir, digital computers, George Wash U, 1950-54. US Army, 1954-56. Prin contribs: to test, design and programming of Atlas missile guidance computer; elec digital computer applications to logistics and man-machine simulation. Chmn, stat comm, United Syn of Amer, Phila br; pres, Cong Beth El, 1966-67; mem: Assn for Computing Machinery; Research Soc of Amer; Phi Beta Kappa, hon. Author: Man Machine Simulation Models, 1969. Hobbies: numismatics, sculpture, violin. Home: 345 Robinson Dr, Broomall, Pa. Office: Burroughs Corp, Paoli, Pa.

WOLF, Seymour D, US, business executive, engr; b. Fallsburg, NY, July 26, 1921; s. Abraham and Dora (Herzer); BS, U of Md, 1942; MBA, Amer U, 1964; att Georgetown U, 1949-50; m. Barbara Krupsaw; c: Douglas, Beth, Deborah. Pres, Amer Wholesalers, Inc, and subsidiaries, since 1960, div mgr, 1951-60, ind engr, plant mgr, 1946-51; vice-pres, Reconstruction and Devl Corp, DC, since 1968; chem engr, Bur of Mines, US Dept Interior, 1942-43. Lt, USNR, 1943-46. Pres: Natl Assn Bedding Mfrs, 1958; BBB of Metrop Wash, 1966-68; JCC, Gtr Wash, since 1969; Engr Alumni, U of Md, 1965-65; Seaboard Region, United Syn of Amer, 1963-65; Cong Beth El, Bethesda, Md, 1953-55; mem, bd: UJA, Gtr Wash; Interracial Council for Bus Opportunity; NCCJ, Wash, DC; Metrop Wash Housing Opportunity Council; mem: AJCong; Metrop Wash Bd of Trade; Amer Zionist Org; Pi Sigma Epsilon; club, Sales Execs, Wash, DC, pres, 1958. Contrib author: Plant Engineering Practice, 1958. Recipient: Potomacland Ambass, Wash Bd of Trade, 1960; Man of the Decalogue, annual award of Solomon Schechter Day Sch, Gtr Wash, 1967; Stephen S Wise Medallion award, 1967; award for dist service, Natl Assn of Bedding Mfrs, 1968. Spec interests: comty service, fishing, golf, collecting commemorative medals, reading. Home: 3215 Brooklawn Terr, Chevy Chase, Md. Office: 8415 Ardmore Rd, Landover, Md.

WOLFBEIN, Seymour L, US, economist, educator; b. Bklyn, NY, Nov 8, 1915; s. Samuel and Fanny (Katz); BA, Bklyn Coll, 1936; MA, Columbia U, 1937, PhD, 1941; m. Mae Lachterman, Mar 1, 1941; c: Susan, Deeva. Dean, Sch of Bus Admn, Temple U, since 1967; dep manpower admnr, dir, Off of Manpower Automation and Training, Lab Dept, since 1961, with dept since 1946; adj prof, econ, Amer U, since 1950. US Army, 1944-45. F, chmn, social stat sect, Amer Stat Assn; pres, Wash Stat Soc; f, AAAS; bd dirs: J Employment and Vocational Service; mem, Bannockburn, Md Civic Assn. Author: Decline of a Cotton Textile City, 1944; World of Work, 1951, 2nd ed, 1961; Employment, Unemployment in US, 1964; Employment, Unemployment and Public Policy, 1965; Education and Training for Full Employment, 1966; Occupational Information, 1967; contbr to profsl jours. Recipient: Alumni Honor Award, 1954; dist service award, Lab Dept, 1955, 1961. Home: 6305 Crathie Lane, Washington, DC. Office: Sch of Bus, Temple U, Philadelphia, Pa.

WOLFE, Bertram D, US, author, educator; b. Bklyn, NY, Jan 19, 1896; s. William and Rachel (Samter); BA, CCNY, 1916;

MA, U of Mexico, 1924; MA, Columbia U, 1930; LLD, HC, U of Cal, 1962; m. Ella Goldberg, Apr 17, 1917. Author: Portrait of America, 1934; Portrait of Mexico, 1937; Diego Rivera, His Life and Times, 1939; Three Who Made a Revolution: Lenin, Trotsky, Stalin, 1948; Six Keys to the Soviet System, 1956; Kruschev and Stalin's Ghost, 1957; Communist Totalitarianism, 1962; The Fabulous Life of Diego Rivera, 1963; Marxism, 100 Years in the Life of a Doctrine, 1965; The Bridge and the Abyss, The Troubled Friendship of Maxim Gorky and V I Lenin, 1967; An Ideology in Power, Reflections on the Russian Revolution, 1969. Sr research f, Hoover Inst, Stanford, since 1966; tchr, Eng lit, Boys HS, Bklyn, 1916-17; head, dept of fgn langs, Escuela Superior Miguel Lerdo, Mexico City, 1922-25; dir, Workers Sch, 1925-28; tchr, Eron Prep Sch, NYC, 1929-34; dir, ideological adv sect, State Dept and Voice of Amer, 1950-54; Guggenheim f, 1949, 1950, 1954; Hoover Libr sr f, Slavic studies, Stanford U, Cal, 1951; Russian Inst, Columbia U, 1951-55; visiting prof, Russ hist, U of Cal, Davis, 1961-62. Mem: Phi Beta Kappa; Authors Guild; Amer Hist Assn; PEN club. Hobbies: research, hiking. Home: 2030 Sand Hill Rd, Menlo, Cal. Office: Hoover Inst, Stanford U, Cal.

WOLFERT, Helen, US, author; b. NYC; d. Alexander and Rosa (Granzfried) Herschdorfer; BA, Hunter Coll; m. Ira Wolfert; c: Ruth, Michael. Author: Nothing is a Wonderful Thing, poem, 1946; The Music, Poems, 1965; contbr poems, short stories, articles to newspapers and mags; poetry readings; fmr: reviewer, poetry, PM, NYC newspaper; tchr, NYC Schs. Mem: Hadassah; Woodstock Art Assn; Poetry Soc, Amer; Authors League, Amer. Spec interest: hist research. Home: Lake Hill, NY.

WOLFERT, Ira, US, author, journalist; b. NYC, Nov 1, 1908; s. Moses and Sophie (Seidel); BLitt, Columbia U, 1930; m. Helen Herschdorfer, Feb 18, 1928; c: Ruth, Michael. Freelance since 1945; staff writer, Readers Digest, since 1954; reporter, fgn corresp, drama reviewer, war corresp, Pacific and Eur theaters, N Amer Newspaper Alliance, 1932-45. Author: novels: Tucker's People, 1943; An Act of Love, 1948, 1954; Married Men, 1953; non-fiction: Battle for the Solomons, 1943; Torpedo 8, 1943; American Guerilla in the Philippines, 1945; An Epidemic of Genius, 1960; co-author: One-Man Air Force, 1944; Let us Begin, 1961; author of two motion picture scenarios; contbr, short stories and mag articles to publs. Recipient: Pulitzer Prize for war dispatches from Guadalcanal, 1943; commendation for war corresp, USN and Army, 1945. Home and office: Lake Hill, New York, NY.

WOLFF, Benno F, US, attorney; b. St Paul, Minn, Jan 10, 1905; s. Otto and Elise (Bach); BA, U of Minn, 1925, LLB, 1927; m. Gertrude Brody, Sep 25, 1934; c: Robert. Partner, Oppenheimer, Hodgson, Brown, Wolff & Leach, St Paul, since 1942, with firm since 1927; mem, bd: Northwestern Natl Bank of St Paul; US Bedding Co; Sterling Plastics Corp. Chmn, bldgs, youth allocations comm, Gtr St Paul United Fund, fmr vice-pres, mem, bd dirs, since 1961; treas, mem, bd dirs, Capital Comty Services; mem bd: St Paul Comty Chest and Council, fmr chmn, social planning and children's study comms; United J Fund and Council, St Paul; J Comty Cen, St Paul, since 1962; mem: bd trustees, secy: Mt Zion Cemetery, since 1931; Harris Found, since 1947; bd trustees, Mt Zion Heb Cong, St Paul, fmr pres; Minn chap, Amer Friends Heb U; bd trustees, exec comm, Children's Hosp, St Paul, since 1961; Amer, Minn State, Ramsey Co Bar Assns; natl bd delgs, AJComm; B'nai B'rith; Hai Resh; fmr: pres, J Comty Relations Council, Minn; co-chmn, St Paul Round Table, NCCJ; mem: bd dirs, Minn J Council; budget comm, St Paul Council Arts and Scis; club, St Paul Athletic. Ed, Minn Law Review, 1925-27. Recipient: Order of the Coif, Minn. Hobbies: music, fishing. Home: 1935 Sargent Ave, St Paul, Minn. Office: 1781 First Natl Bank Bldg, St Paul, Minn.

WOLFF, Ernst, US, pediatrician, educator; b. Berlin, Ger, Feb 2, 1892; s. Sally and Fenny (Cohn); in US since 1925; MD, U of Freiburg, 1918; m. Leona Mayer, 1932; c: Ursula, Frank, Carla, Thomas. Ped coord, service for developmentally handicapped children, Pacific Med Cen, since 1965; first sch phys, Hadassah Med Org, Tel Aviv, 1923-24; pvt ped practice, Jerusalem, 1924-25; instr, asst clinical prof, ped, U of Cal, 1926-50, lectr, dent, 1940-50; med adv, Presidio Air Sch, 1930-45; dir, child guidance clinic, Fed J Charities, 1935-38; chmn, ped dept, French Hosp, 1945-50; dir, Inst for Developmentally Handicapped Children, Mt Zion Hosp, 1952-55; on staff since 1927. Licentiate, Amer Bd Ped; f: AMA; Ortho-

psycht Assn; fmr pres, N Cal Mh Soc; mem: Acad of Ped; SF Psychosomatic Soc; asso mem, SF Psychan Soc. Contbr to med jours. Home: 2535 Vallejo St, San Francisco, Cal. Office: 2340 Clay St, San Francisco, Cal.

WOLFF, Hans Anton, Isr, business exec; b. Frankfurt, Ger, Dec 1, 1906; s. Yaacov and Martha (Loewenthal); in Isr since 1933; PhD, DCh, U of Berlin; m. Suzanna Meseritz, Dec 31, 1936; c: Benjamin. Gen mgr, Serafon Resinous Chem Corp, Rehovot, since 1954. Home: 4 Leviathan St, Tel Aviv, Isr. Office: Serafon, Rehovot, Isr.

WOLFF, Harold I, US, chemical engr; b. SF, Cal, Aug 4, 1908; s. William and Hattie; BS, U of Cal, 1930; m. Esther Barak, July 11, 1930; c: Babette, Billie, Barak. Tech secy, Shell Engr Council, since 1969; mgr, engr tech, Shell Chem Corp, 1952-68, asst mgr, cen engr dept, 1959-62; chem, Shell Devl Co, 1934-36, chem engr, 1937-43, chief tech, Cal, 1943-47, chief tech, Tex, 1947-50, head, process engr sect, devl dept, Shell Chem Corp, 1951-55, asst mgr, mfg and devl dept, 1959-62; petroleum tech, Standard Oil Co, Cal, 1930-34. F: AAAS; Amer Inst Chems; NY Acad Sci; mem: Amer Chem Soc; Amer Inst Chem Engrs. Contbr to profsl jours; holder, patents in petro-chems. Home: 6666 Chetwood, Houston, Tex. Office: 2525 Murworth, Houston, Tex.

WOLFF, Herbert Alfred, US, attorney; b. NYC, July 20, 1889; s. Alfred and Martha (Stettheimer); AB, Dartmouth Coll, 1910; LLB, Columbia U Law Sch, 1913; m. Daisy Kempner, Apr 6, 1916; c: Alfred, Helen Vogel, Herbert, John, Richard. Sr partner, Greenbaum, Wolff & Ernst, since 1915. Fmr vice-chmn, NY State Bd of Social Wfr; hon trustee, Soc for Ethical Culture, fmr pres; hon gov, Ethical Culture Schs, fmr chmn, bd govs; mem, bd dir, Comty Research Asso, Inc; mem: NY State Bar Assn; Assn of Bar, NYC; NY Co Lawyers Assn, fmr mem, comm on profsl ethics; Westchester Co Bar Assn; Phi Beta Kappa; club, Fairview Country, fmr pres. Recipient: Selective Service Medal, USA. Home: Hotel Gramatan, Bronxville, NY. Office: 437 Madison Ave, New York, NY.

WOLFF, Irving, US, physicist; b. NYC, July 6, 1894; s. Max and Julie (Gutman); BS, Dartmouth Coll, 1916; PhD, Cornell U, 1923; m. Consuelo Hughes, July 30, 1941; c: Margaret. Ret; chmn, educ comm, RCA, 1959-62, with firm since 1945; instr, physics: Ia State Coll, 1919-20; Cornell U, 1920-23; research, elec, RCA, NYC, Camden, Princeton, NJ, from 1924; adv comm, physics dept, Princeton U; cons, elec engr, Manhattan Coll. F: Inst Radio Engrs; AAAS; Acoustical Soc of Amer; Phys Soc of Amer; mem: Sigma Xi; Phi Kappa Phi; clubs: Nassau; Old Guard; Mt Shadows CC. Recipient: modern pioneer award, NAM, 1937; dist public service award, USN, 1948; Cresson medal, Franklyn Inst, 1960. Home: Le Chamonix, Aspen, Colo.

WOLFF, Kurt H, US, sociologist, educator; b. Darmstadt, Ger, May 20, 1912; s. Oscar and Ida (Kohn); in US since 1939; att Us of Frankfurt, Munich, 1930-33; D, U of Florence, 1935; m. Carla Bruck, June 11, 1936; c: Carlo. Yellen prof, social relations, Brandeis U, since 1969, prof, sociol, since 1959; Schule am Mittelmeer, Recco, It, 1934-36; Mare-Monto, Ruta and Pontedilegno, It, 1936-38; research asst, S Methodist U, Dallas, Tex, 1939-43; researcher: Dallas, 1939-40; NM, 1942, 1944, 1948; asst prof: Earlham Coll, Richmond, Ind, 1944-45; Coll of Pacific, 1948; New Sch for Social Research, 1950; mem, Social Sci Research Council, inter-U summer sem, Northwestern U, 1952; US specialist, State Dept, Inst für Sozialforschung, Frankfurt U, 1952, 1953; asso prof, sociol, O State U, 1952-59, asst prof, 1945-52; cons, Inst for Social Research, Oslo, 1959; Fulbright sr lectr, Rome U, 1963-64; visiting prof: U of Freiburg, Ger, 1966; Frankfurt, 1966-67; Nanterre, Fr, 1967. Chmn, Research Comm on Sociol of Knowledge, Intl Sociol Assn; f, Social Sci Research Council, 1943-44; mem: Amer Sociol Assn. Author: Versuch zu einer Wissenssoziologie, 1968; Hingebung und Begriff, 1968; ed and trans, The Sociology of Georg Simmel, 1950; ed: Georg Simmel, 1858-1918, publ 1959; Emile Durkheim, 1858-1917, publ 1960; contbr to sci and lit jours. Recipient: grant: Viking Fund, 1947-48, 1949, for write-up of New Mexican research; Social Sci Research Council, 1966-67, for write-up of study of sociol of knowledge in US. Home: 58 Lombard St, Newton, Mass. Office: Brandeis U, Waltham, Mass.

WOLFF, Max, US, educator, community cons; b. Metz, Fr, Mar 14, 1905; s. Julius and Hulda (Kahn); in US since 1939; att U of Cologne, 1927; PhD, U of Geneva, 1928; att: U of Berlin,

1933; Sorbonne, Paris, 1936; m. Lieselotte Katz, July 6, 1941; c: Richard, Karen. Project dir, Cen for Urban Educ, NYC, since 1965; cons on comty research; dir, research, migration div, Commonwealth of Puerto Rico; vice-pres, Rice & Wolff, Inc, since 1959; fmr asso prof, NYU; adj prof, sociol, Pace Coll, 1962. Mem: Amer Sociol Soc; Soc for Study of Social Problems. Contbr to sociol jours. Recipient: grants from: Columbia U Social Research Council; Sears Roebuck Found; Necchi Found; Rabinowitz Found. Home: 179 Woodlawn Ave, New Rochelle, NY. Office: 105 Madison Ave, New York, NY.

WOLFF, Robert I, US, educator; b. Bklyn, NY, Apr 27, 1903; s. Barnet and Ella (Nislowsky); BS, CCNY, 1924; MA, Columbia U, 1926; PhD, Yale U, 1935; m. Rose Rosenberg, 1928; c: Barnet. Prof, physics, CCNY. Fac adv, Hillel, CCNY; vice-pres, fac chap, AJCong; mem, Phi Beta Kappa. Home: 2448 Bronx Park E, New York, NY. Office: CCNY, New York, NY.

WOLFOWITZ, Jacob, US, mathematician, educator; b. Warsaw, Pol, Mar 19, 1910; s. Samuel and Helen (Perlman); in US since 1920; BS, CCNY, 1931; PhD, NYU, 1942; m. Lillian Dundes, 1934; c: Laura, Paula. Prof, math, Cornell U, since 1951; asso prof, math, stat: U of NC, 1945-46; Columbia U, 1946-49, prof, 1949-51; visiting prof, math: U of Cal, LA, 1952-53; U of Ill, 1953; Technion, Isr, 1957, 1967; U of Paris, 1967; U of Heidelberg, 1969. F, Inst Math, Stat; mem: Amer Math Soc; Econometric Soc; Inst Elec and Electronic Engrs. Contbr in fields of math stat, probability and info theory. Home: 241 Valley Rd, Ithaca, NY. Office: Cornell U, Ithaca, NY.

WOLFSON, Harry A, US, educator, author; b. Austryn, Russ, Nov 2, 1887; s. Mendl and Sarah (Savitsky); in US since 1903; AB, Harvard U, 1912, AM, 1912, PhD, 1915; hon: DHL: JIR, 1935; JTSA, 1937; HUC, 1945; LHD, Yeshiva U, 1950; DLitt, Dropsie Coll, 1952; LHD, Chgo U, 1953; DLitt, Harvard U, 1956; DHL, Brandeis U, 1958. Nathan Littauer prof em, Heb lit and phil, Harvard U, since 1958, fac mem since 1915. US Army, 1918-19. Pres: Amer Acad for J Research, 1935-37; Amer Oriental Soc, 1957-58; mem: Amer Phil Soc; Amer Acad Arts and Scis; Medieval Acad of Amer; Intl Soc for Hist of Ideas; Pol Inst Arts and Scis in Amer; J Acad Arts and Scis; Amer Phil Assn; Soc of Bibl Lit and Exegesis; Amer Hist Assn; Hist of Sci Soc. Author: Crescas' Critique of Aristotle, 1929; The Philosophy of Spinoza, 1934; Philo, 1947; The Philosophy of the Church Fathers, Vol 1, 1956; Religious Philosophy, 1961. Recipient: award, JBCA, 1948; Stephen Wise award, AJCong, 1950; Annual Natl Service award, Phi Epsilon Pi Frat, 1953; citation, NCCJ, 1956; fac prize, Harvard U Press, 1956; prize, Amer Council of Learned Socs, 1958; Franklin L Weil award, JWB, 1961; Tarbuth Found Scroll of Honor, 1962; B'nai B'rith Hillel Found acad award, 1963; JTSA 80th Anniversary medal, 1965. Office: Widener Libr, Harvard U, Cambridge, Mass.

WOLFSON, Harry L, Can, economist; b. Toronto, Can, Sep 17, 1910; s. Hyman and Rebecca (Trambitskoy); BCom, Toronto U, 1932; research f, King's Coll, Cambridge, 1932-34; m. Rose Chrom, Jan 16, 1942; c: Sheila, Alan, Judith, Lawrence. Bus cons, dir, various corps since 1955; research asst, Ont Unemployment Research, Commn, 1931; sr lectr, U of Liverpool, 1934; gen mgr, PICA, Pal, 1934-50; controller of salvage, Brit Admn in Pal, 1942-47; exec dir, econ stabilization commn, 1943-47; asso econ coord, Isr Govt, 1948-50; financial counsellor, Can Emb, Wash, 1951-52; alternate exec dir: Intl Monetary Fund, 1951-52; Intl Bank for Reconstruction and Devl, 1951-52; vice-pres, dir, Canadera Ltd, Toronto, 1952-54. Pres, Social Planning Council of Metrop Toronto; vice-pres: United JWF; Can Inst on Public Affairs; mem: admn comm, Can J Cong; Bd J Educ; Bd J Home for Aged; Jt Comty Relations Comm; bd, Baycrest Hosp. Home: 318 Vesta Dr, Toronto, Can.

WOLFSON, Henry, US, business exec; b. Vaslui, Rum, Sep 19, 1889; s. User and Clara (Poppersdorf); in US since 1901; BA, U of Nev, 1914, Coll of Educ, 1915; m. Margaret Neuman, Feb 22, 1923. Ret; vice-pres, dir, H L Green Co, Inc, 1933-59; real estate expert since 1921; lectr, natl, city and state Real Estate Bds. Capt, US Army, 1917-19, maj, 1942-45. Mem: Freedom House; Amer Acad Social Scis; Fgn Policy Assn; Conf on J Relations; Masons; Amer Legion; Retired Offs Assn. Home: 2016 Bay Drive, Miami Beach, Fla.

WOLFSON, Sir Isaac, 1st baronet, Eng, business exec, communal leader; b. Glasgow, Sep 17, 1897; s. Solomon; hon:

LLD, London, 1959; FRCP, 1959; DCL, Oxford 1963; LLD, Glasgow, 1963; hon f, Weizmann Inst of Sci, Isr; hon f, St Edmund Hall, Oxford; f, Royal Soc; m. Edith Specterman, 1926; c: Leonard. Chmn, The Great Universal Stores, Ltd, since 1946, mgn dir since 1934, joined firm, 1932. Mem, Worshipful Company of Patternmakers; mem, Grand council, Brit Empire Cancer Campaign; hon treas, Victoria League for Commonwealth Friendship; patron, Royal Coll Surg; found, trustee, Wolfson Found, created in 1955, mainly for the advancement of health, educ and youth activities in UK and Commonwealth; hon pres, Weizmann Inst of Sci Found; trustee, Rel Cen, Jerusalem; club: Reform. Hobby: golf. Home: 74 Portland Place, London, W1, Eng.

WOLFSON, James J, US, engineering exec; b. Boston, Mass, Apr 3, 1899; s. Jacob and Annie (Fine); BS, MIT, 1920; m. Gertrude Ednas, Dec 24, 1924; c: George, Stephen, Daniel. Sr vice-pres, Tishman Construction Corp, since 1960, vice-pres, 1956-60; first vice-pres, M Shapiro & Son Construction Co, 1926-55. Dir, Peninsula Gen Hosp; mem: Profsl Engr Soc, NY; Equality Lodge, B'nai B'rith; fmr pres, Temple Beth El, Rockaway Pk, NY; club, Tech, NY. Home: 342 Beach 142 St, Neponsit, NY. Office: 666 Fifth Ave, New York, NY.

WOLFSON, Louis E, US, industrialist; b. St Louis, Mo, Jan 28, 1912; s. Morris and Sarah (Goldberg); att U of Ga, 1930-33; m. Florence Monsky, 1926 (decd); c: Marcia Rechtschaffen, Stephen, Gary, Martin. Chmn, bd dirs: Merritt-Chapman and Scott Corp, NYC, since 1951, pres, 1953-59; NY Shipbuilding Corp, Camden, NJ, 1953-61, chmn, exec comm, since 1961; dir, Revday Inds, Inc, 1964-68; owner, Harbor View Farm, racing and breeding stable, Ocala, Fla, since 1958; dir, Fla Pipe and Supply Co, Inc, Jacksonville, Fla, 1934-49; off, ML and S Corp, real estate and inves, 1946-56; pres, S Pipe and Supply Co, Orlando, Fla, 1948-57; controlling stockholder, Tampa, Fla, Shipbuilding Co, Inc, 1945-48; chmn, bd: Capital Transit Co, Wash, DC, 1951-56; Newport Steel Corp, Ky, 1954-56; dir, Montgomery Ward and Co, 1955-56. Mem, bd trustees: Ga Student Educ Fund, Inc; Wolfson Family Found, Inc; bd govs, Eleanor Roosevelt Cancer Found; adv bd, Boys Estate; mem: Comm to Advance the World Fight Against Cancer; Amer Cancer Soc; Natl Spec Gifts Comm; NCCJ; natl adv council, Syn Council of Amer; Acad of Political Sci; Thoroughbred Owners and Breeders Assn; Natl Steeplechase and Hunt Assn; Phi Epsilon Pi; Masons; clubs: Standard, Miami; Golden Hills Turf and Country, Ocala, Fla; Econ, NY. Recipient: Charter Day award, Fla chap, Yeshiva U, 1958. Home: 6466 N Ray Rd, Miami Beach, Fla. Office: POB 4, Jacksonville, Fla.

WOLFSON, Phillip John, US, certified public acctnt; b. Richland Cen, Wis, July 28, 1921; s. Aaron and Libby (Klitsner); BBA, U of Wis, 1947; m. Violet Moss, Mar 17, 1950; c: Alan, Susan. Dir, Bycosin NSA, Inc; vice-pres, treas, Allied Bus Counselors; partner, Wolfson, Weiner & Co, CPAs, since 1950; secy-treas, Wolfson Bros Realty Co, since 1950; vice-pres, dir: Nan Goodman Inc, since 1954; US Realty Co, since 1958; dir, Vacuum Plate Corp, since 1958. USAAC, WW II. Mem: Cal Soc CPAs; Amer Inst CPAs; Natl Assn Real Estate Bds; Cal Real Estate Assn; LA Realty Bd; Beverly Hills Realty Bd; JWV; B'nai B'rith; Alpha Epsilon Pi. Co-author: Wage Earner's Tax Guide, 1959. Home: 805 N Camden Dr, Beverly Hills, Cal. Office: 8899 Beverly Blvd, Los Angeles, Cal.

WOLFSON, Richard Frederick, US, business exec, attorney; b. NYC, Jan 7, 1923; s. William and Gertrude (Quitman); BS, Harvard Coll, 1942; LLB, Yale Law Sch, 1944; m. Elaine Reinherz, June 6, 1954; c: Liza, Paul. Sr vice-pres, Wometco Enterprises, Inc, since 1959; dir, City Natl Bank of Coral Gables; law secy: Judge Thomas Swan, US Court of Appeals, 1944-45; Justice Rutledge, US Supr Court, 1945-47. Dir: Variety Childrens Hosp; Dade Co chap, ARC; vice-pres, Miami Philharmonic Soc; trustee, Everglades Sch for Girls; bd dirs, NCCJ. Co-author: Jurisdiction of the Supreme Court of the United States; contbr to legal jours. Recipient: Guggenheim, f, 1949-50. Home: 630 University Dr, Coral Gables, Fla. Office: 306 N Miami Ave, Miami, Fla.

WOLFSON, Victor, US, author, playwright; b. NYC, Mar 8, 1910; s. Adolph and Rebecca (Hochstein); BA, U Wis, 1931; m. Alice Dodge, Mar 21, 1942; c: Martin, Nicholas, John (decd), Thomas. Author of plays, novels, short stories, TV and movie scripts; asst stage mgr, Counselor at Law, 1932-33; dir, The Mother, 1934; adapter, produc, dir, Crime and Punishment, 1936; author: plays produc: Bitter Stream, 1935;

Excursion, 1937; Pastoral, 1938; The Family, 1943; Love in the City, 1947; Pride's Crossing, 1950; A Murder in the Family, 1952; American Gothic, 1953; Seventh Heaven, 1955; novels: The Lonely Steeple,1945; The Eagle on the Plain,1947; My Prince, My King, 1962; Midsummer Madness, 1967; hist study, The Mayerling Murder, 1969; biography of Harry S Turman, The Man Who Cared, 1966; contbr of short stories to mags; recording, The Joy of Wine, 1968. Arbitrator, Amer Arbitration Assn, since 1943; mem council, Dramatists Guild, since 1938, fmr secy; fmr: bd mem: Theater Union; Experimental Theater; Amer Natl Theater and Acad; secy, Author's League of Amer; clubs: PEN, Beachcombers. Recipient: Emmy Award, Natl Acad of TV Arts and Scis, 1961. Home: 549 E 86 St, New York, NY.

WOLICKI, Jerome Bernard, US, rabbi; b. Bklyn, NY, Mar 17, 1939; s. Paul and Miriam (Goldstein); BA, Yeshiva U, 1960; att Yeshivat Kerem B'Yavneh, Isr, 1960-61; ordained rabbi, MHL, Yeshiva U, 1964; m. Marsha Dubow, Oct 29, 1961; c: David, Zvi, Eliav, Benjamin. Rabbi: Beth Tephilath Moses Cong, since 1966; Beth Isr Syn, Wallingford, Conn, 1964-66. Exec bd, JCC, Mt Clemens, Mich; coord, youth activities, Mich-Ont orthodox syns, sems for Yeshiva U; secy, Rabb Council, Conn, 1965-66; mem: RabCA, Detroit; Council of Orthodox Rabbis; B'nai B'rith. Spec interest: J hist. Home: 90 Moross, Mt Clemens, Mich. Office: 53 South Ave, Mt Clemens, Mich.

WOLIN, Donald, US, editor; b. Rochester, NY, Dec 30, 1926; BA, Syracuse U, 1951; div; c: Donna, Steven, Wendi. Ed, J Ledger, weekly, Rochester, NY. Served US Army. Home: 201 Butler Dr, Pittsford, NY. Office: 721 Monroe Ave, Rochester, NY.

WOLL, Harry L, US, educational exec; b. Gomel, Russ, Sep 26, 1898; s. Benzion and Frieda (Levitsky); in US since 1921; att: U of Omaha, 1925-27; NYU, 1927; m. Rivka Seldin, July 1, 1921; c: Libbie Soifer, Yael. Dir, dept for tchrs and prins, J Educ Comm, NY, since 1949; exec dir: Bd of License for Heb tchrs, NY, since 1955; Bd of Rev, since 1955; chmn, Bd Examiners, Natl Bd of License, since 1958. Pres: Natl Council for J Educ, 1959-60; educs council, JNF; Heb Prins Assn, 1955-57; mem: exec, admn comms, AJCong, 1956-61; admn comm, World J Cultural Cong; Poal Zion, Lab Zionist Org; natl exec comm: Histadrut campaign; Conf of J Communal Workers; Folk Shulen of Amer; exec comm, educ council, FJP, 1958-60; Heb Tchrs Wfr Fund; Histadruth Ivrith; bd, Hadoar; comm on book publs, United Syn of Amer; delg, ZC, 1960. Contbr to educ jours and newspapers. Home: 280 Ninth Ave, New York, NY. Office: 426 W 58 St, New York, NY.

WOLLSTEIN, Shlomoh, Isr, psychiatrist; b. Berlin, Ger, Apr 27, 1929; s. Herman and Minna (Brody); MD, Med Sch, Zurich, 1955; MPH, Med Sch, Jerusalem, 1965; m. Malvine Trau, Sep 2, 1952; c: Ilana, Irith, Gad. Med dir, Tarnowski Psychiatric Hosp, since 1966; psycht: Natl Ins Inst, since 1967; Min of Defense, since 1966; dir, Marriage Guidance Clinic, Acad of Med, Jerusalem, since 1968. Lt, IDF. Mem, Neuropsycht Assn, Jerusalem. Contbr to profsl jours. Home and office: 3 Bartenura St, Jerusalem, Isr.

WOLMAN, Abel, US, sanitary engr, educator; b. Baltimore, Md, June 10, 1892; s. Morris and Rose (Wachsman); AB, Johns Hopkins U, 1913, BSE, 1915, hon DEngr, 1937; hon DS, Drexel Inst; LHD, Maryland Inst, Baltimore, 1969; LLD, Johns Hopkins U, 1969; m. Anne Gordon, 1920; c: Markley Gordon. Prof em, sanitary engr, Johns Hopkins U, since 1959, prof, 1937-59; engr, research, USPHS, 1913; construction engr, Md State Dept of Health, 1914; lectr, sanitary engr: Sch of Hygiene and Public Health, Johns Hopkins U, 1921-27, 1936-37; Princeton U, 1925, 1929; U of Chgo, 1929; cons sanitary expert, State of NJ, 1929-30; arbitrator, Baltimore City and Co Metrop Dist, 1930; cons engr: Baltimore City Dept of Public Works, since 1931; PWA, Md, 1933-34; USPHS, US Engr Corps, 1937-44; Water and Power Resources Bd, Dept of Health, State of Pa, 1937; Wash Suburban Sanitary Commn, 1938-39, 1945, 1948, 1956-57; Portland, Ore, 1939-41; Richmond, Va, 1939-40, 1943; TVA, since 1939; Bethlehem Steel Co, since 1940; Seattle, Wash, 1944-47; Kan River Basin Study; Jacksonsville and Sanford, Fla, 1953; W Va Pulp and Paper Co, 1954; state engr, FEA Public Works, Md, 1933-34, acting state dir, Md and Del, 1934-37; chmn, bd cons: Jordan River Project, 1945-46; Middlesex Co Sewerage Auth, NJ, 1953-56, 1967; Calcutta Water Supply, WHO, 1959; chmn, Interdepartmental Bd for Sanitary Control and Protection of Public Water Supply, NYC, 1943-46; hon cons, USN Dept, 1944-46; cons dir, sanitation research, Assn of Amer RR, Baltimore, Md, 1946-56; mem, reactor safeguard comm, safety and ind health adv bd, chmn, stack gas working group, AEC, 1947-60; Md State Rds Prog and Policy, 1951-57; cons: USPHS, 1939-45; Natl Resources Planning Bd, 1941-43; War Produc Bd, 1942-45; US Dispersal of Fed Bldgs, 1950-51; Natl Sci Found, 1955; Govt of Ceylon, 1955; Intl Coop Admn, 1957; Isr Water Supply, since 1946; NYC Water Supply, 1950-51; Detroit Metrop Region, 1956-57; Miami Conservancy Dist, since 1956; Indianapolis Water Co, 1957; mem: Mission to S Amer, WHO, 1956; Geneva Conf, Peaceful Uses of Atomic Energy, 1958; Intl Mission, Org of Govt of Arg, 1956-57; Mission to S Amer, Intl Coop Admn, 1959; chmn: Johns Hopkins U Team, Intl Coop Admn, 1960; Mission to Taiwan, Comty Water Supply, WHO, 1961; Panel on Water Resources, Agcy for Intl Devl, 1962-66; Comm to Study Dept of Public Works, Baltimore, 1963-67; bd cons, Metrop Wash, DC Council of Govts, since 1964; cons: US Sen Select Comm on Water Resources, 1959-61; Comm on Sci and Astronautics, US House of Reprs, 1965-68; Devl Comm for Gtr Columbus, O, since 1966; Natl Water Commn, Wash, DC, 1969; Natl Council on Marine Resources and Engr Devl, Wash, DC, since 1966; mem, Atomic Safety and Licensing Bd Panel, US AEC, since 1960. Co-author: The Significance of Waterborne Typhoid Fever Outbreaks; ed, Solving Sewage Problems; ed in chief: Jour of Amer Water Works Assn, 1921-37; Water Works Practice, 1924; Munic Sanitation, 1929-35; Amer Jour of Public Health, 1955; contbr to periodicals. Mem: Amer Public Health Assn; Amer Water Works Assn; Amer Stat Assn; Amer Soc of Munic Improvements; Fed of Sewage Works Assns; Amer Public Works Assn; Royal Inst Public Health, Eng; Farady Soc, Eng; Natl Conf on City Planning; Amer Econ Assn; NE Water Works Assn; Amer Soc CEs; AAAS; Inst Mgrs Sewage Works, Eng; Amer Geog Soc; NJ Assn of Profsl Engrs and Land Surveyors; hon, Franklin Inst, Phila, Pa; Md-Del Water and Sewerage Assn; Soc for Promotion of Engr Educ; hon, Inst of Engrs of Chile; Amer Soc Mil Engrs; Amer Geophys Union; Natl Research Council; Amer Soc Tropical Hygiene and Med; Natl Acad Scis; Natl Acad Engrs; Phi Beta Kappa; Tau Beta Pi; Delta Omega Soc; Sigma Xi; Omicron Delta Kappa. Recipient: War-Navy Cert, 1948; spec award, Lasker Found, Amer Public Health Assn, 1960; Hemisphere Award, Inter-Amer Assn of Sanitary Engrs, 1962; William Procter prize, Sci Research Soc of Amer, 1967; Lewis L Dollinger pure environment award, Franklin Inst, 1968. Home: 3213 N Charles St, Batlimore, Md. Office: 209 Ames Hall, Johns Hopkins U, Baltimore, Md.

WOLMAN, Basil, Eng, physician, communal leader; b. Colwyn Bay, Wales, Mar 17, 1918; s. Mark and Sophie (Rose); MB, ChB, MD, MRCP, DCh, U of Manchester; m. Helena Novis, June 10, 1945; c: John, Amy. Cons ped, since 1951; lectr, ped, since 1947; research f, tutor, McGill U, Montreal, 1949-50. Found, chmn, Cen for Mentally Handicapped Children, Bury, Lancs, Rochdale; pres, Manchester J Social Services; chmn, Manchester J Wfr Coord Comm; hon treas, Council of Manchester and Salford J; pres, Friends of Heb U, med br, 1959-60, 1964-65; mem: Brit Ped Assn; BMA. Contbr to med jours. Home: 12 Sheepfoot Lane, Prestwich, Eng. Office: 14 St John St, Manchester, Eng.

WOLMAN, Benjamin B, US, psychologist, psychoanalyst; b. Warsaw, Pol, Oct 27, 1908; s. Jehuda and Lea (Cukier); in US since 1948; MA, U of Warsaw, 1932, PhD, 1935; m. Roma Jastrzebska, 1932 (div); c: Danielle. Pvt practice, psychan and psychotherapy, since 1939; prof, doctoral prog, psych, and dean, fac, Inst of Applied Psychan, LIU, since 1965; clinical psychol, asst dir, Centos Inst, 1930-32; chief psychol, dir, Mh Clinic, Tel Aviv, Isr, 1935-42; dir, Educ Services for J Servicemen's Families, 1942-45; lectr: psych, Tchrs Coll, Tel Aviv, 1945-48; Columbia U, 1949-53; asso prof, psych, Yeshiva U, 1953- 57; clinical lectr, psycht, postdoc prog, Albert Einstein Coll of Med, 1959-62; clinical prof, psych, postdoc prog, Adelphi U, 1963-65. Author of numerous sci papers and books in psych and related fields, including: Freedom and Discipline in Education, Heb, 1948; Contemporary Theories and Systems in Psychology, 1960; Vectoriasis Praecox, 1966; Unconscious Mind, 1967; Principles of Abnormal Psychology, 1969; Children without Childhood: A Study in Childhood Schizophrenia, 1969; Adolescence in a Changing Society, 1969; ed: Sci Psychology, 1965; Handbook of Clinical Psychology, 1965; Historical Roots of Contemporary Psychology, 1967; Psychological Techniques, 1967; Psychotherapy in Transition, 1969; Manual of Child Psychopathology, 1969; ed in chief, Ency of Neur, Psycht and Psych; co-ed,

Ency Hebraica. F: Amer Psych Assn; Amer Sociol Assn; Assn for Advancement of Psychotherapy; chmn, comm on fac, Assn for Applied Psychan; mem, Council of Reprs, Amer Psych Assn. Home: 295 Central Park W, New York, NY. Office: 12 W 96 St, New York, NY.

WOLMAN, Irving J, US, pediatrician; educator; b. Holyoke, Mass, Feb 5, 1905; s. Benjamin and Pauline (Resnick); BA, Amherst Coll, 1925; MD, Johns Hopkins U, 1929; m. Roslyn Stone, Apr 12, 1935; c: Carol, James. Dir, clinical labs, hematologist, Children's Hosp of Phila, since 1947; prof, ped, head, grad ped div, Sch of Med, U of Pa. USPHS, Res Corps, 1942-46. Chmn, Phila Med Milk Commn; dipl: Amer Bd Ped; Amer Bd Path; bd dirs, Cong Rodeph Shalom, Phila; mem: AMA; Phila Coll Phys and Surgs; Phila Co Med Soc; Phila Ped Soc; Coll Amer Paths; Amer Acad Ped; Soc Ped Research; Amer Ped Soc; Phi Beta Kappa; Alpha Omega Alpha; Sigma Xi. Author: Laboratory Applications in Clinical Pediatrics, 1957; ed, Clinical Pediatrics. Home: 7607 Woodlawn Ave, Melrose Park, Philadelphia, Pa. Office: Children's Hosp of Phila, Philadelphia, Pa.

WOLMAN, Moshe, Isr, pathologist; b. Warsaw, Pol, Oct 19, 1914; s. Yehuda and Leah (Cukier); att U of Florence, It, 1932-35; MD, U of Rome, 1938; m. Brigitte Koebbel, Jan 25, 1939; c: Dan, Ruth Manor, Naomi, Amnon. Prof path, chmn dept, Tel Aviv U Med Sch since 1964; head, dept path, Govt Hosp Tel Hashomer, since 1959; res, chief phys, Hadassah U Hosp, Jerusalem, 1939-59; asst, asso prof, path, Heb U Hadassah Med Sch, 1949-59. Capt, RAMC, 1941-46; pvt, IDF, sci corps, 1948. Prin contribs: new techniques and procedures, new approaches to study of lipidoses, myelin sheath and cell membranes. Mem: several natl, intl profsl orgs, acads, ed and adv bds. Author: Histochemistry of Lipids in Pathology, 1964; ed, Pigments in Pathology, 1969. Spec interest: med educ. Home: 15 Ido St, Ramat Gan, Isr. Office: Tel Hashomer Govt Hosp, Isr.

WOLMAN, Paul C, Jr, US, attorney; b. Baltimore, Md, Aug 21, 1926; s. Paul and Jeanette (Rosner); BS, Wharton Sch Finance and Commerce, U of Pa, 1948; LLB, Harvard Law Sch, 1951; m. Susan Askin, June 24, 1954; c: Paul, Peter, Margot. Partner, Blades & Rosenfeld, since 1956, with firm since 1954; law clerk, US Circuit Judge Morris Soper, US Court of Appeals, 1951-52; esst, US Atty, Dist of Md, 1952-54. US Army, 1945. Pres, bd trustees, Happy Hills Hosp Inc; trustee, mem exed comm, Comty Chest of Baltimore; bd dirs: AJComm, Baltimore; Cen Scholarship Bur, Inc; secy-treas, Harvard Law Sch Assn of Md; mem: Md Gov's Commn on Children and Youth; Md Gov's Commn on Employment Problems; Amer, Fed, Baltimore, Md State Bar Assns; Phi Epsilon Pi; B'nai B'rith; Baltimore Heb Cong; clubs: Suburban; Cen. Home: 1817 Greenberry Rd, Baltimore, Md. Office: 912 Fidelity Bldg, Baltimore, Md.

WOLOVSKY, Reuven, Isr, scientist, educator; b. Krakow, Pol, Mar 24, 1924; s. Yechiel and Bluma (Alster); in Isr since 1933; MS, Heb U, 1952, PhD, 1955; m. Haya Peltz, Dec 20, 1951; c: Tal, Ofer. Sr sci, Weizmann Inst of Sci, since 1956; visiting sci: Harvard U, 1965-66; Bell Telephone Labs, 1966-67; visiting prof, Yeshiva U, 1966-67. IDF, 1947-49. Contbr to sci jours. Recipient: Daniel Bukstein award, Heb U, 1951. Home: 6 Arnon St, Tel Aviv, Isr. Office: Weizmann Inst of Sci, Rehovot, Isr.

WOLPE, Claire F, US, communal worker; b. NYC, June 24, 1909; d. David and Pauline (Hirsch) Fox; BA, Mills Coll, 1930; att Smith Coll, Sch of Social Work, 1931; MA, U of S Cal, 1936; m. Arthur Wolpe, 1932; c: Ruth Rose, Selma Langer. Comty org work since 1940; adv to J students, U Rel Conf, Hillel Found, UCLA, 1931-32; med social worker: LA Co Hosp, 1934-38; USPHS, 1938. Pres: Sisterhood of Temple Isr, Hollywood, 1940-41; Personal Service Assos, 1943-45; Conf J Women's Orgs of LA, 1948-50; Beverly Hills B'nai B'rith Women, 1952-53; chmn: J Youth Council of LA, 1953-57; adult educ prog, B'nai B'rith Women, Dist No 4, 1955-58; J Youth Org, 1954-58; social action comm, 1960-63, constitutional rev comm, 1962-63, both Temple Isr Sisterhood; mem, bd: S Cal Mental Hygiene Soc, 1951-54; LA J Comty Council, 1951-57; NCCJ, 1952-55; B'nai B'rith Youth Org; mem: family educ comm, 1949-50; Comty Relations Comm, 1952-59; Gov Warren's Conf on Childhood and Youth; Gov Warren's Conf on Problems of the Aging; Gov Warren's Conf on Mh; Hadassah; Natl Council of J Women; PTA. Recipient: Woman of the Year award, LA Times, 1950; S service award, JWF; NCCJ; comty service award, AJ

Cong. Hobbies: swimming, painting. Home: 234 S Orange Dr, Los Angeles, Cal.

WOLPE, Donald Elliott, US, banker; b. Wash, DC, May 15, 1925; s. Julius and Anna (Cooper); BCS, Benjamin Franklin U, 1948; m. Paula Bellmore, Mar 20, 1949; c: Bruce, Jeffrey, Beth. Chmn bd, U Natl Bank, since 1964; secy-treas, Julius H Wolpe Inc, Jewelers, 1946-64. Tech sgt, US Army, 1943-46. Dir: J Comty Cen, Gtr Wash; B'nai B'rith Hillel Bldg Corp, U of Md; vice-pres: Adas Isr Cong; JNF Council, Gtr Wash; bd trustees, United Isr Appeal; natl exec comm, ZOA; pres: Coll Park Bd of Trade, 1960-61; Gtr Wash Retail Jewelers Assn, 1959; Md, Del, DC Jewelers Assn, 1962; Louis Brandeis Zionist Dist, 1964; Columbia Hgts Bus Mens Assn, 1949; chmn, Inst Purchases Comm, Isr Bonds, 1968; exec comm, UJA, Gtr Wash, 1950-68; clubs: Woodmount Country; Amity, Wash, DC, pres, 1967; Coll Park Lions, pres, 1954-55. Home: 4701 Willard Ave, Chevy Chase, Md. Office: 4321 Hartwick Rd, College Park, Md.

WOLPERT, Stanley A, US, educator, author; b. Bklyn, NY, Dec, 23, 1927; s. Nathan and Frances (Gittelson); BA, CCNY, 1953; AM, U of Pa, 1955, PhD, 1959; m. Dorothy Guberman, June 12, 1953; c: Daniel, Adam. Prof, chmn, dept of hist, UCLA, since 1958. Lt, jg, USNR. Author: Aboard the Flying Swan, 1954; Tilak and Gokhale, 1962; Nine Hours to Rama, 1962; India, 1965; Morley and India, 1906-1910, 1967; The Expedition, 1968; An Error of Judgment, 1970. Mem: Amer Hist Assn; Amer Asiatic Soc; Amer Oriental Soc; Asia Soc; AAUP; Phi Alpha Theta; Phi Beta Kappa. Recipient: Watumull prize in Indian hist, 1962. Home: 811 Thayer Ave, Los Angeles, Cal. Office: U of Cal, Los Angeles, Cal.

WOLSKY, Milton, L, US, artist; b. Omaha, Neb, Jan 23, 1916; s. Samuel and Agnes (Horwich); att: U of Omaha, 1932-34; Art Inst of Chgo, 1934-38. Independent artist and illus since 1954; illus, series, Cities of the N Plains in Time Mag, since 1956; mag illus, NY, 1946-54; instr, painting, Joslyn Art Mus, 1958-62; one-man show, 1961. US Army, 1942-46. Mem: Cen Area chap, Artists Equity Assn; Natl Soc Art Dirs; Soc of Illus, NY; Intl Inst Art and Letters; Amer Watercolor Soc. Recipient: first gov's award to an artist, Neb,1962. Home and studio: 5804 Leavenworth St,Omaha,Neb.

WOOLFSON, Edward, Scotland, business exec; b. Glasgow, May 20, 1903; s. Philip and Clara (Gerber); m. Adela Gottlieb, May 24, 1932; c: Judith Tankel, Michael. Chmn, mgn dir, Clyde Factors Ltd, radio, TV & elec distributors, since 1964; dir, Philip Woolfson Ltd, 1924-63. Hon vice-pres, ZF, Gt Brit; co-chmn, bd govs, Calderwood Lodge J Primary Day Sch; vice-chmn, Elec Wholesale Fed, Scottish sect; natl vice-pres: JPA; WJC, Brit sect; Fed Zionist Youth; pres, Zionist Org; chmn, bd govs, Habonim Youth Cen; found, hon life pres, Young Zionist Org, all Glasgow; JP, Co of City of Glasgow; fmr: pres, J Repr Council; hon pres, J Students' Soc; hon secy, trustee, JNF; mem: Jt Comm Church of Scotland and Glasgow, J Repr Council for Chr-J Relations; J Bd of Shechita; J Bd of Guardians, all Glasgow; mem, bd deps, British J; delg, 23rd, 24th, 25th ZCs, Jerusalem; mem: Inst of Dirs, Lodge Montefiore 753; club, Radio Ind, fmr pres. Spec interests: communal, charitable, Zionist, youth, Isr. Home: 399 Albert Dr, Glasgow S1, Scotland. Office: 25-35 Cadogan St, Glasgow C2, Scotland.

WOOLFSON, Mordekai, Isr, government official; b. Jaffa, Pal, Jan 1, 1900; s. Yehoshua and Sime (Königsberg) Wolfinson; att: Tchrs Sem, Jerusalem; Sch of Law and Econ, Tel Aviv; local govt course, Eng; m. Ray Cinamon, Apr 8, 1935; c: Yehoshua Zohar. Ret since 1966; fmr: town clerk, chief, munic corp, mem local council, all Petah Tikva. Pal Police Force, 1918-20; Haganah. Mem: Free Masons; fmr: hon secy, treas, Maccabi Sports Org, Petah Tikva; hon secy: Magen David Adom, Petah Tikva; Brit War Comfort; mem, Inst of Cert Bookkeepers, S Afr; clubs: Soldiers, Petah Tikva; Ex-Policemen's, Tel Aviv; Pensioner's, mem council. Hobbies: reading, bridge. Home: 4 93 St, Petah Tikva, Isr.

WOOLMAN, Samuel, US, business exec; b. Kiev, Russ, July 15, 1890; s. Louis and Chuva (Chernoff) Vool; in US since 1911; m. Bertha Dubester, Apr 4, 1925; c: Eleanor Schor, Leatrice Karlin. Pres: S Woolman, Inc, since 1927; Woolman & Mirvis, since 1949. Pvt, US Army, 1917. Mem, KP; fmr trustee, Ocean Parkway J Cen. Hobbies: swimming, sports, card playing. Home: 70-20 108 St, Forest Hills, NY. Office: 400 Broadway, New York, NY.

WORMANN, Curt, Isr, librarian; b. Berlin, Ger, Jan 5, 1900; s. David and Sophie (Friedländer); in Isr since 1933; att U Berlin, 1918-20; PhD, U Freiburg, 1923; m. Carola Gottheil, 1931. Dir em, J Natl and U Libr and Grad Libr Sch, Heb U, Jerusalem, since 1968, dir since 1947; asst chief, dept for adult educ, Kreuzberg dist, Berlin Munic, 1923-26; chief of dept, 1926-33; dir, Public Librs, Kreuzberg dist, 1926-33; lectr: lit, Inst for Adult Educ, 1923-33; adult educ, Sch for Public Admn and Political Sci, 1929-33; libr sci and gen lit, Libr Sch, 1930-33, all Berlin; gen lit, sems for adult educ, Pal, 1934-37; head, Heb Sem Assn of Cen Eur settlers, Tel Aviv, 1939-47; academic libr, chief, fgn lang sect, Munic Libr, Tel Aviv, 1937-47; visiting prof, Columbia U, NY, 1965 and 1969. Corresp mem, UNESCO Commn on Intl Bibliography, 1953; mem bd, Leo Baeck Inst, Jerusalem. Author: Der Deutsche Bauernroman, 1923; Die Russische Literatur der Gegenwart, 1931; Autorität und Familie in der Deutschen Belletristik nach dem Weltkrieg, 1936; Gustav Landauer, A Teacher of Literature and Life, Heb, 1939; Library Problems in Israel, Heb, 1950; Goethe, Ency Hebraica, 1957; Contemporary Problems in Libraries and Librarianship, Heb, 1958; National Libraries in Our Time, 1959; Two International Library Conferences, Heb, 1962; Kulturelle Probleme und Aufgaben der Juden aus Deutschland in Israel seit 1933, pub 1962; Education for Librarianship in Israel, 1963; Cooperation of National Libraries With Other Libraries in the Same Country and in Other Countries, 1964; Aspects of International Library Cooperation—Historical and Contemporary, 1968; co-author: Hinukh, Führer durch das Palästinensische Erziehungswesen, 1937; asso ed, Libri, Intl Libr Rev, Copenhagen, Den; contbr to UNESCO publs and press. Home: 6 Ben Lavrat St, Jerusalem, Isr. Office: POB 503, Jerusalem, Isr.

WORMSER, André A F, Fr, banker; b. Paris, Jan 21, 1926; s. Georges and Lucie (Beleys); diplomé d'Etudes Supérieures de Lettres Classiques; licencié en Philosophie; both Sorbonne, Paris. Pres, dir gen, Banque Wormser Frères, Paris. Mem, cen comm, Alliance Israélite Universelle. Home: 30 rue Spontini, Paris 16, Fr.

WOTIZ, Herbert H, US, biochemist, educator; b. Vienna, Aus, Oct 8, 1922; s. Edward and Irene (Politzer); in US since 1938; BS, Providence Coll, 1944; PhD, Yale U, 1951; m. Miriam Rose, June 15, 1947; c: Harriet, Robert, Richard. Prof, biochem, Boston U Med Sch, since 1963, fac mem since 1951. F, Amer Inst Chems; mem: Soc Experimental Med and Biol; Amer Chem Soc; Amer Soc Biol Chems; Amer Assn for Cancer Research; Endocrine Soc; Sigma Xi. Ed bd: Steroids; Jour Chromatography; Jour Chromatographic Sci. Home: 9 Cape Cod Lane, Milton, Mass. Office: Boston U Sch of Med, 80 E Concord St, Boston, Mass.

WOUK, Herman, US, author; b. NYC, May 27, 1915; s. Abraham and Esther (Levine); AB, hons Columbia Coll, 1934; hon LHD, Yeshiva U, 1954; hon LLD, Clark U, 1960; m. Betty Brown, Dec 9, 1945; c: Abraham (decd), Nathaniel, Joseph. Visiting prof, Yeshiva U, 1953-58. Author: novels: Aurora Dawn, 1947; The City Boy, 1948; The Caine Mutiny, 1951; Marjorie Morningstar, 1955; Youngblood Hawke, 1962; Don't Stop The Carnival, 1965; plays: The Traitor, 1949; The Caine Mutiny Court-Martial, 1953; Nature's Way, 1957; non-fiction: This is My God, 1959. USN, 1942-46. Co-found: Fifth Ave Syn; Fire I Syn; Gt Neck Syn; trustee: Coll of VI; Georgetown Syn; Wash Natl Sym Orch Assn; mem, Authors Guild Council; clubs: Cosmos; Metrop, Wash; Bohemian, SF. Recipient: Pulitzer Prize, 1952; Columbia U medal, 1952. Office: c/o Harold Matson Co, 22 E 40 St, New York, NY.

WRESCHNER, Walter, Switz, attorney; b. Oct 22, 1904; s. Arthur and Bella (Mamelok); DJur, U of Zurich; m. Marianne Sigaloff, 1937. Pvt law practice since 1929. Pres, Israelitische Kultusgemeinde, Zurich, since1955; mem: Bus Mgmt of Switz; Isr Comty League; delg, WJC; fmr pres, KH, Switz. Home: Röslistrasse 54, Zurich, Switz. Office: 43 Löwenplatz, Zurich, Switz.

WRONKOW, Ludwig, US, journalist-cartoonist; b. Berlin, Ger, Dec 3, 1900; s. Hugo and Bertha (Ephraim); in US since 1938; m. Ursula Meyer, Feb 17, 1951. Staff mem: Aufbau, since 1938, exec ed, since 1966; Solidarity, since 1957; writer, cartoonist, art dir: Rudolf Mosse, Berlin, 1921-33; Fr Presse, Paris, 1933-35; Prager Tagblatt, Prague, 1935-38. Prussian Army, 1918. Hobby: photography. Home: 2 Washington Sq Village, New York, NY. Office: 2121 Broadway, New York, NY.

WUERZBURGER, Uri Shraga, Isr, geologist, educator; b. Ger, June 26, 1932; s. Sigmund and Mira (Mayer); in Isr since 1938; MSc, Heb U, Jerusalem, 1958; MSc, DIC, Imperial Coll, London, 1967; m. Michal Goldschmidt, Dec 18, 1957; c: Yael, Rachel, Efrat, Itschak. Head, Mineral Resources Div, GSI, since 1961; lectr, mineralogy, Bar Ilan U, since 1961; geologist, Isr Mining Ind, 1954-58. IDF, 1950-52. Pres, Geological Soc of Isr; mem: Inst of Mining and Metallurgy, London; Intl Comm, Genesis of Ore Deposits. Contbr to profsl jours. Home: 2 Ben Zion St, Jerusalem, Isr.

WULKAN, Paul, US, chemist; b. Sobotiste, Czech, Mar 2, 1897; s. Bernard and Ida (Bellak); MS, U Vienna, 1921; m. Eva Falk, June 3, 1930. Reaearch chem, Enterprise Paint Mfg Co, Chgo since 1942; chief chem, tech dir, Vienna, Aus, 1925-38. Mem: Amer Chem Soc; Chgo Soc for Paint Tech. Contbr to trade jours; patents on sulphite waste liquor, adhesives. Home: 4880 Marine Dr, Chicago, Ill. Office: 2841 S Ashland Ave, Chicago, Ill.

WUNSH, Israel E, S Afr, business exec; b. Johannesburg, Feb 11, 1912; s. Sebia and Rachel (Jacobs); c: Anthony, Richard. Mgn dir, Dugson Clothing Mfgs, Ltd, since 1946; asso with clothing ind since 1928; commn of oaths, Johannesburg, since 1952. Sgt, S Afr Air Force, 1941-43. Pres, Transvaal Clothing Mfgs, 1952-53, 1953-54; mem, exec council, S Afr Federated Chamber of Inds, natl coord council clothing ind, 1953-54; master, Travelers Lodge, 1952-53; mem, Freemasons; clubs: Wanderers; Balfour Park; Beaconsfield; Transvaal Automobile. Home: 64 Westcliff Dr, Johannesburg, S Afr. Office: POB 3561, Johannesburg, S Afr.

WURM, Shalom, Isr, editor, translator, farmer; b. Yanov, Galicia; s. Aron and Michal; in Isr since 1920. Farmer, Kibbutz Ramat Yochanan, since 1940; trans, Am Oved Pub House: fmr: co-found, Kibbutz Bet Alpha; i/c training of youth from Eng speaking countries; delg, Gen Fed of Lab to Hecalutz, Ger, US. Author: Communal Societies and their Way of Life; ed: Giora Yoseftal, Life and Work; Joseph Russel, Life and Work, 1960; An Anthology of Socialist Thought, 3 vols, 1962, 1965, 1967; Anthology of Zionist Thought; fmr: mem, ed bd, Ichud Hakvutzot vehakibbutzim. Recipient: Bareli Fund award. Home: Kibbutz Ramat Yochanan, Isr.

WURZBURGER, Walter S, US, rabbi, educator; b. Munich, Ger, Mar 29, 1920; s. Adolph and Hedwig (Tannenwald); in US since 1938; BA, magna cum laude, Yeshiva U, NY, 1943; ordained rabbi, Rabbi Isaac Elchanan Theol Sem, NY, 1944; MA, Harvard U, 1946, PhD, 1951; m. Naomi Rabinovitz, Aug 18, 1947; c: Benjamin, Myron, Joshua. Rabbi, Cong Shaarei Tefilah and J Cen, Far Rockaway, since 1967; visiting asso prof, phil, Yeshiva U, since 1967; rabbi: Cong Chai Odom, Boston, 1944-53; Cong Shaarei Shomayim, Toronto, Can, 1953-67; columnist, Toronto, Telegram, 1957-67. Mem: exec comm, RabCA, bd, Beth Din; FJP; Amer Phil Assn; Amer Acad Rel; Conf on J Phil; asso, Rogozin Inst for J Ethics and Hum Values of Yeshiva U; fmr: pres, Rabb Council of Can; co-chmn, Toronto Rabb F for Comty Affairs; mem: exec comm, United JWF of Toronto; interfaith comm, United Comty Fund of Toronto; exec comm, Can J Cong; UJA; Unipres, Orthodox Rabb Council, Gtr Boston. Ed, A Treasury of Tradition, 1967; contbr to books: Guardians of Our Heritage; Condition of Jewish Belief; Leo Jan, Jubilee Vol; ed, Tradition, Jour of Orthodox J Thought, since 1961; mem, ed bd, MIT, Isr; contbr to gen, rel and scholarly publs. Home: 1152 Sage St, Far Rockaway, NY. Study: 1295 Central Ave, Far Rockaway, NY.

WURZEL, Leonard, US, business exec, b. Phila, Pa, Feb 4, 1918; s. Maurice and Dora (Goldberg); BS, Wash and Jefferson Coll, 1939; MBA, Harvard U, 1941; m. Elaine Cohen, Aug 18, 1949; c: Mark, Lawrence. Pres: Calico Cottage Candies, Inc, since 1964; Loft Candy Corp, 1957-64, with firm since 1948. Capt, US Army, 1941-46. Chmn, Assn Mfrs Confectionery and Chocolate, NY; treas, Candy, Chocolate and Confectionery Inst, since 1960; fmr: pres, Asso Retail Confectioners, N Amer; trustee, Comty Syn, Port Wash, NY. Recipient: Bronze Star Medal. Home: 18 Sycamore Dr, Sands Point, NY. Office: 1163 Broadway, Hewlett, NY.

WYDRA, Heinz Naftali, Isr, organization exec; b. Leipzig, Oct 24, 1909; s. Simon and Rebecca (Epstein); in Isr since 1933; LLB, U of Leipzig, 1933; att: U of Heidelberg, U of Berlin; m. Joheved Kaplan, Sep 18, 1933; c: Jael, Reuben. Dir, Isr Shipping Research Inst, since 1969; chmn, Isr Port Auth, since 1969; mgr, shipping agcy, Haifa, 1933- 36; mgr, maritime dept, JA, Jerusalem, 1936-46; mgn dir: Zim, Isr Navigation Co, Ltd; Isr-Amer Shipping Co; Shoham Sherutey Hayam Ltd, all 1947-66. Club, Rotary, Haifa. Home: 8 Lakhish, Haifa, Isr. Office: Isr Shipping Research Inst, Haifa, Isr.

WYGNANSKI, Israel Jerzy, US, scientist; b. Warsaw, Pol, June 3, 1935; s. Zvi and Deborah; in US since 1965; MEngr, McGill U, Montreal, Can, 1962, PhD, 1964; m. Renate; c: Tamara, Dorit. Research sci, Boeing Sci Research Labs, Wash, since 1965; asso prof, Technion, Haifa, since 1968; asst prof, U of BC, 1964-65. IAF, 1954-57. Mem, Amer Inst Physics. Contbr to sci jours. Recipient: Brit Assn Medal, McGill U, 1961. Hobbies: sailing, flying. Home: 9705 NE 13 St, Bellevue, Wash. Office: Boeing Sci Research Labs, Seattle, Wash.

WYGODSKI, Stanislaw, Isr, author; b. Bendzin, Pol, Jan 13, 1907; s. Izak and Riwa (Werdiger); in Isr since 1968; m. Irena Bajtner, Mar 13, 1946; c: Adam, Ewa. Author: Challenge, 1933; Arrested for Further Investigation, 1969; and numerous books; trans various works. Pres, Writers Assn, Warsaw; mem, Eur Cultural Assn; club, PEN, Warsaw. Recipient: Writers Assn award, Pol, 1948; Nowa Kultura award, 1960. Home: 12 Mishmar Hayarden St, Givatayim, Isr.

WYKANSKY, Benjamin B, US, rabbi; b. Hull, Eng, Aug 27, 1907; s. Simon and Rose (Greenfield); att: Aria Rabb Coll, 1920-26; Portsmouth U Coll, 1924-26; London U, 1926-27, all Eng; m. Freda Lichtman, June 17, 1933; c: Genicia. Rabbi, Temple Emanu-El, Staten I, NY, since 1951; min and spiritual leader: Hendon Syn, London, Eng, 1928-31; Finchley Syn, 1932-37; Brondesbury Syn, 1938-50; vice-pres, NW London J Day Sch, 1948-50. Brit Army, 1941-45. Chaplain: Masonic Lodge, Staten I, since 1952; grand chaplain, Grand Lodge of Masons, NY State, since 1964; Willesden J Ex-Servicemen's Assn, London, 1950. Home and study: 83 Palmer Ave, Staten Island, NY.

WYLER, Berthold, Switz, editor, pulisher; b. Baden, Switz, Oct 26, 1913; s. Louis and Rose (Kahn); LLD, U of Berne, 1940; m. Marion Frank, 1942; c: Michel. Publisher, Universum Press, Switz, publishers of econ periodicals, since 1939. Chmn, Assn Swiss Friends of Midrasha in Sdeh-Boker; mem: exec comm, World ORT Union; bd govs, Swiss Fed J Comtys. Homes: 75 Chemin des Eidguenots, Geneva, Switz; Yemin Moshe, Jerusalem, Isr.

WYLER, Hugo, Switz, attorney; b. Zurich, Switz, Aug 2, 1896; s. Joseph and Melanie Wyler-Bernheim; DJ, U of Zurich, 1921; m. Trudy Bloch, Oct 19, 1925; c: Marianne, Erika. Pvt practice, specializing in commercial, financial and admn matters, since 1925; hon consul, Monaco, since 1936; mem, staff of bank, Florence, It, 1924-25. Served Swiss Army. Mem: State Commn for Taxes; comm, J Old Age Home, Lengnau AG; comm, Haffkine Found; fmr pres, B'nai B'rith, Zurich. Author: Die Amortisationshypothek; contbr to profsl jours, periodicals. Recipient: Chevalier de l'Ordre Saint Charles. Home: Klosbachstr 109, Zurich 7/32, Switz. Office: Tödistr 60, Zurich 2, Switz.

WYLER, Veit, Switz, attorney, editor; b. Baden, Switz, Aug 28, 1908; s. Louis and Rosa (Kahn); att Us: Zurich; Vienna; Hamburg, 1927-30; DJ, U Leipzig, 1930; m. Anna Salten, Dec 14, 1944; c: Judith, Lea. Pvt practice, Zurich, since 1932; found, ed, Das Neue Isr, monthly official organ of Swiss Zionist Fed, 1948. Mem: Swiss Assn of Authors Rights; chmn, KH ; fmr: pres, ZF, Switz; mem, comm, J Comty of

Zurich. Home: Boeklinstr 27, Zurich, Switz. Office: Stamp, fenbachstr 7, Zurich, Switz.

WYLER, Wilfred, US, certified public acctnt; b. NYC, Feb 24, 1908; s. Sigmund and Fanny (Rosenfield); BS, Harvard U, 1928; MBA,NYU,1934; att Columbia U, 1935-38; m. Marjorie Goldwasser, June 23, 1938; c: Ruth Messinger, Barbara Gold. Sr partner, Wilfred Wyler and Co, CPAs, since 1937; security analyst, Wall St, 1928-32; public acctnt, 1933-36; vice-pres, treas, Jones and Larson Corp, 1941-58. Chmn: budget comm, J Home and Hosp for Aged, 1950-58; J Retirement Bd, 1959-66, mem, bd trustees, since 1959, vice-chmn, since 1966; co-chmn, Manhattan War Records Comm, Natl JWB, 1941-43; pres, Fan and Sig Wyler Found, since 1947; hon trustee, Phil Educ Soc; mem, bd overseers, JTSA, since 1956; mem: NY State Soc of CPAs; club, Harmonie. Homes: 333 Central Park W, New York, NY; 18 Danbury Ave, Westport, Conn. Office: 200 Park Ave, New York, NY.

WYSENBEEK, Henricus, Isr, physician, educator; b. Rotterdam, Holland, May 28, 1916; s. Siegfried and Rosa (van den Bergh); in Isr since 1950; MD, Med Sch, Leuden, 1941; PhD, Utrecht, 1950; postgrad: Minn, 1947; Rochester, NY, 1960; m. Henriette Wijler, Dec 17, 1942; c: Tirtsah, Arjeh, Yigal. Head dept, dir, Tel Aviv U, postgrad fac, since 1956; chmn, sect psycht, since 1968; asst dir, Shalwatha Hosp, 1955-56. Mem: Isr and Dutch Bds Psycht and Neur; Govt Regional Psycht Comm; fmr mem: Natl Adv Council; Cen Bd Isr Neuro-Psych Assn. Contbr to profsl jours. Recipient: Histadrut yearly award, 1966. Home: 13 Ofakim St, Afeka, Tel Aviv, Isr. Office: POB 72, Petah Tikva, Isr.

WYZANSKI, Charles Edward, Jr, US, judge; b. Boston, Mass, May 27, 1906; s. Charles and Maude (Joseph); AB, Harvard, 1927, LLB, 1930, hon LLD, 1958; hon LLD: U Pa, 1953; Carleton Coll, 1953; Tufts Coll, 1953; Swarthmore Coll, 1956; Brandeis U, 1956; Clark U, 1963; m. Gisela Warburg, July 23, 1943; c: Charles, Anita Robboy. Chief judge, US Dist Court, Mass, since 1966, on court since 1941; asso with Ropes, Gray, Borden & Perkins, 1930-33; law secy: US Circuit Judge Augustus Hand, 1930-31; US Circuit Judge Learned Hand, 1932; solicitor, US Lab Dept, Wash DC, 1933-35; US repr, 71st, 72nd sessions, governing body, ILO, Geneva, Switz, 1935; substitute delg, govt adv, 19th session, Intl Lab Conf, Geneva, 1935; spec asst to US atty gen, solicitor gen's staff, Justice Dept, 1935-37; partner, Ropes, Gray, Boyden & Perkins, later, Ropes, Gray, Best, Coolidge & Rugg, 1938-41; mem, Natl Defense Mediation Bd, 1941; lectr, govt, Harvard Coll, 1942-43, 1949-50; visiting prof, MIT, 1948-50; copyright expert, UNESCO, Paris, 1949, Wash, 1950. Sr f, Soc Fs, Harvard U; trustee, Ford Found; mem, Council Amer Law Inst; fmr: mem, ILO Comm on Application Convs; f, Amer Acad Arts and Scis. Author: A Trial Judge's Freedom and Responsibility, 1952; Whereas—A Judge's Premises, 1956. Home: 39 Fayerweather St, Cambridge, Mass. Office: US Dist Court, Boston, Mass.

WYZANSKI, Gisela W, US, civic worker; b. Hamburg, Ger, May 5, 1912; d. Max and Alice (Magnus) Warburg; in US since 1939; att: U of Hamburg, 1930-31; LSE, 1932; Oxford U, 1932; m. Charles Wyzanski, July 23, 1943; c: Charles, Anita. Natl Asso, Hadassah, Youth Aliyah chmn, NE region, Natl Youth Aliyah chmn, 1941-45; mem, bd, Combined J Philanthropies of Boston; mem, exec: F in Isr for Arab J Youth, Inc; The Window Shop; dir, World Affairs Council, Boston; co-dir, Jüdische Jugendhilfe, Berlin, Ger, 1935-38; active, Youth Aliyah, Gt Brit, 1938-39; bd mem, Boston council, Girl Scouts, 1947-52; chmn, volunteers for UNICEF, Cambridge, 1966, 1967, Boston, 1968, 1969. Home: 38 Fayerweather St, Cambridge, Mass.

Y

YAACOBI, Gad, Isr, economist, Government official; b. Kfar Vitkin, Isr, Jan 18 1935; s. Alexander and Sara (Gorin); MSc, Sch of Law and Econ, Tel Aviv, 1959; m. Tova, Nov, 1957; c: Yariv, Yechiam, Yoav. Dep min, Min of Transp, since 1970; mem: Histadrut Exec Bur, since 1966; Lab Party Exec Bur, since 1969; spokesman, Min of Agric, 1960-62, asst to Min, 1962-64, head, planning, devl auth, 1964-66. Lt, Intelligence br, IDF, 1953-56. Prin contribs: five year plan, Isr agric; reform plans, Isr econ. Fmr chmn, econ comm, Rafi Party. Home: 13 Shivtei Israel St, Ramat Hasharon, Isr. Office: Arlosoroff St, Tel Aviv, Isr.

YAARI, Shmuel, Isr, government official; b. Pol, Feb 17, 1925; s. Asher and Rivka; in Isr since 1935; MA, Heb U, Jerusalem, 1949; m. Hanna Jurovics, 1961; c: Ada, Itzhak, Avinoam. Consul gen, Amsterdam, since 1968; first secy, Isr Emb, Wash, 1957-60; dep dir, Intl Org Dept, Fgn Min, 1961-64; counselor, Isr Emb, The Hague, 1964-68. Contbr articles to jours. Office: Consulate Gen of Isr, 26 Vermeer St, Amsterdam, Netherlands.

YACOEL, David Asseo, Uruguay, engineer, educator; b. Izmir, Turkey, Jan 16, 1915; s. Abraham and Ana (Asseo); in Uruguay since 1923; CE, U Montevideo, 1944; MSc, MPH, U of NC, Chapel Hill, 1945; m. Sara Mizratti Dec 6, 1947; c: Ana Choroszucha, Victor, Enrique, Victoria. Owner, Ingeniero-Emp Constructora, since 1946; prof, Joaquin Suarez HS, since 1948; bd tchrs, selection of candidates for professorship, math, astronomy, since 1950; prof, tchrs training, since 1950; sanitary engr, Min Public Works, 1945-49; fmr, prof math, various HSs and insts. Prin contribs, research: reduction of hardness in water supply of San Ramon; reform of Fr teaching, 1967-68. Mem: J Cen Comm; KH; B'nai B'rith, lodge 1229; Engrs Assn; Tchrs Assn. Home: Juan Benito Blanco 1239, Montevideo, Uruguay. Office: Ejido 1363, Montevideo, Uruguay.

YADIN, Yigael, Isr, archaeologist, army off; b. Jerusalem, Mar 21, 1917; s. Elazar and Chassia (Feinsod) Sukenik; MA, Heb U, 1945, PhD, 1955; m. Carmella Ruppin, Dec 22, 1941; c: Orly, Littal. Prof, archaeol, Heb U, since 1959; dir: James de Rothschild expedition to Hazor, 1955-58; excavations in cave, Judean Desert, 1960-61; Massada, 1963-65. Mem, Haganah, 1932-48, instr, small arms, 1937, instr, offs training sch, 1940-41, adj to chief of staff, 1941-45, chief, planning sect, hqrs, 1945-47, chief oprs, 1947-48; chief oprs, IDF, 1948-49; delg, Isr-Arab armistice negotiations, Rhodes, 1949; chief, Gen Staff, IDF, 1949, maj gen, Chief of Staff, 1949-52. Author: The Message of the Scrolls, 1956; Hazor, 3 vols, 1957-62; Genesis Apocryphon, 1957; The Art of Warfare in Biblical Lands in the Light of Archaeological Discovery, 1963; The Finds from the Cave of Bar Kochba, 1963; Massada-Herod's Fortress and the Zealots' Last Stand, 1966. Home: 47 Rambam Rd, Jerusalem, Isr. Office: Heb U, Jerusalem, Isr.

YADLIN, Aharon, Isr, government official; b. Tel Aviv, Isr, April 17, 1926; s. Haim and Zippora (Pollak); BA, Heb U, Jerusalem, 1955, MA, 1964; m. Ada Hacohen; c: Amos, Yoram, Amir. Dep Min, Educ and Culture, since 1964; MK since 1960; mem, exec comm: scout movement, 1949-50; Gen Fed of Lab, Histadrut, 1950-52; lectr, dir, Beth Berel Inst, 1956-58; fmr: agric worker, teacher. Cpl, Haganah, Palmach, 1947-49. Chmn, Sci Teaching Cen; mem: cen comm, Kibbutz Movement; chmn, youth movement's council, 1962-69; secy, Kibbutz Hatzerim, 1951-58. Author: Hakarat Hahevrah; contbr to publs. Hobbies: philately, books. Recipient, decorations: Haganah; War of Independence; Sinai Campaign. Home: Kibbutz Hatzerim, Mobile Post, Negev, Isr. Office: Min of Educ, 34 Shivtey Yisrael St, Jerusalem, Isr.

YADLIN, Asher, Isr, economist, coop exec; b. Jerusalem, Mar 1, 1923; s. Naftali and Rachel (Lerner); att UCLA, 1950; BA, New Sch for Social Research, 1953; MA, CCNY, 1958; m. Dalia Golomb, June 25, 1948; c: Anat, Omer. Gen secy, Coop Assn, Isr, since 1966; dir, El Al, Isr Airline; secy, Civil Service Union, Isr, 1958-62; dir, Kupat Cholim Med Org, 1962-66. Mem, exec and central comm, Lab Party.

Contbr to profsl jours. Home: 100 Bnei Dan, Tel Aviv, Isr. Office: 93 Arlosorov, Tel Aviv, Isr.

YAELI, Joseph Michael, Isr, physicist, educator; b. Haifa, Isr, Sep 29, 1941; s. Abraham and Rivka (Blanc); BS, Technion, 1963, MSc, 1967; m. Ruth Degani. Physicist since 1967; tchr: Bosmat Sch, 1962-63; Reali Sch, 1963-65. Cpl, IDF, 1963-66. Mem, bd govs, Technion. Spec interest: educ. Home: 10 Edmond Fleg St, Haifa, Isr. Office: Technion, Haifa, Isr.

YAFEH, Aviad, Isr, civil servant; b. Rehovot, Isr, Sep 21, 1923; s. Yitshak and Bilha; tchr, Heb U, Jerusalem, 1945; m. Ora Sasson, July 26, 1950; c: Doritte, Revital. Head, Bur, political secy for PM, since 1965; tchr, secondary sch, Jerusalem, 1946; consul, dir, info services, Fgn Min, 1958-62, dir, 1963-64. IDF, 1948-50. Mem: Lab Party, Jerusalem; fmr: natl leader, Young Maccabi, Isr; mem, Jr Chamber Intl. Contbr to newspapers. Hobbies: bridge, basketball, chess. Home: 5 Hechalutz St, Jerusalem, Isr. Office: PM Off, Jerusalem, Isr.

YAFEH, Hava Lazarus, Isr, educator; b. Wiesbaden, Ger, May 6, 1930; d. Paul and Jadwiga (Walfisch) Lazarus; in Isr since 1939; BA, Heb U, 1953, MA, 1959, PhD, summa cum laude, 1966; m. Immanuel Yafeh, 1954; c: Yishay. Sr lectr, Islamic civilization, Inst for Asian and Afr Studies, Heb U, since 1966, on fac since 1960; tchr, secondary sch, Haifa, Jerusalem, 1954-56, 1958-60. Vice-pres, youth sect, World Union for Progressive Judaism, 1952-55. Ed, Studies in the History of the Arabs and Islam, 1967-68; trans, The Deliverer from Error, by Al-Ghazzali, 1965; ed bd, Petahim; contbr of articles and trans. Home: 11 Ben-Lavrat St, Jeusalem, Isr. Office: Heb U, Jerusalem, Isr.

YAFFE, Leo, Can, researcher, educator; b. Devil's Lake, ND, July 6, 1916; s. Samuel and Mary (Cohen); in Can since 1920; BSc, hons, U of Man, Winnipeg, 1940, MSc, 1941; PhD, McGill U, Montreal, 1943; m. Betty Workman, Mar 18, 1945; c: Carla, Mark. Chmn, dept of chem, McGill U, since 1965, Macdonald Prof, chem, since 1958, prof, 1952-58, on leave of absence, 1963-65, as dir, research and labs, Intl Atomic Energy Agcy, Vienna, project leader, nuclear chem and tracer research Atomic Energy of Can, Ltd, 1943-52. F: Royal Soc, Can; Chem Inst of Can; Amer Phys Soc; mem, Sigma Xi. Contbr to sci jours. Home: 5777 McAlear Ave, Montreal, Can. Office: McGill U, Montreal, Can.

YAFFE, Richard, US, journalist; b. Reading, Pa, June 10, 1903; s. Elchanan and Elka (Pearlman); m. Sara Mishler, June 10, 1928; c: Marc. US and UN corresp: J Chronicle, London; Al Hamishmar, Tel Aviv, since 1955; staff mem: Phila Inquirer, 1929-35; NY Post, 1935-38; NY Journal-Amer, 1938-41; fgn ed, PM, NYC, 1941-48; news ed, NY Star, 1948-49; spec E Eur corresp, CBS, 1949. Natl vice-chmn, Amers for Progressive Isr, since 1955; mem: exec comm, Fgn Press Assn, since 1961, fmr pres; UN Corresps Assn; club, Overseas Press. Author: A Short History of the American. Jews, 1963; ed, Isr Horizons, since 1952; contbr to mags. Home: 301 W 108 St, New York, NY. Office: 507 Fifth Ave, New York, NY.

YAGIL, Shimon, Isr, mathematician; b. Berlin, Ger, June 4, 1931; s. Franz and Kaete (Weiss) Stiassny; in Isr since 1933; BS, U of Cal, Davis, 1954, MA, Berkeley, 1958; m. Varda Arditi, May 8, 1966; c: Ariel. Mgr, Sci Marketing Support, since 1965; stat, IBM Research, NY, 1958-59; sr analyst, Isr Min of Defense, 1960-62; sci sys analyst, IBM, Isr, Ltd, 1962-65, guest lectr: Heb U, Tel Aviv U. Cpl, IDF, 1950-52. Mem: Phi Beta Kappa; Assn for Computing Machinery; Opr Research Soc; Info Processing Assn; Inst Mgmt Sci, all Isr; Opr Research Soc of Amer. Contbr to profsl jours. Home: 38 Hama'agal St, Kiryat Ono, Isr. Office: 15 Lincoln St, Tel Aviv, Isr.

YAHIL, Leni, Isr, historian; b. Düsseldorf, Ger; d. Ernst and Helene (Simon) Westphal; in Isr since 1934; MA, Heb U, Jerusalem, 1940, PhD 1965; m. Chaim Yahil, 1942; c: Amos, Jonathan (decd). Lectr, Heb U, since 1966; journalist, Omer,

Heb daily, 1949-52; secy, Inst for Holocaust Research, 1961-63; lectr, Technion, Haifa, 1965-67. Mem: bd, Friendship Assn, Isr-Den; Hist Soc of Isr; fmr mem, cultural dept: Women's Pioneer Org; Histadrut. Author: Rescue of Danish Jews, Test of A Democracy, 1966, 1969, Danish, 1967; contbr to jours. Home: 4 Hamapilim St, Jerusalem, Isr. Office: Heb U, Jerusalem, Isr.

YALAN-STEKELIS, Miriam, Isr, poet, librarian; b. Kremenchug, Russ, Aug 26, 1900; d. Yehuda and Hoda (Lifshitz) Vilensky; in Isr since 1920; att: U Kharkov, 1917-19; Coll of Judaic Studies, Berlin, 1924-25; Sch of Libr Sci, Paris, 1928-29. Ret; fmr libr, Slavonic dept, Heb U Libr, Jerusalem, 1926-56. Author: Atzu-Ratzu Gamadim, 1939; Sefer Dani, 1943; Gveret im Klavlav, 1943; Geshem, 1944; Tol-Tol Baal-Hol, 1944; Hamasa el Ha'i Ulay, 1944; Maase beYalda Milik uve-Doda Pilik, 1945; Maase beYalda, 1947; Shiri li Mirili, 1947; Bimi, 1952; Maase bePharohet, 1952; Galgalim, 1955; Shir haGedi, 1956; Yom Huledet, 1961; Yeshli Sod, 1963; Bahalomi, 1963; Vetvi, poems and stories, in Russ, 1966; Sheker?, 1967; trans: into Ger, Tagebücher und Briefe, by Joseph Trumpeldor, 1925; into Heb: Perach haShani, Russ folk tales, 1951; A Baby is Born, by M I Levin and J H Seligman, 1957; Die Konferenz der Tiere, by Erich Kaestner, 1958; Stories by Anne Frank, 1962; Hey, Yahad, folk songs from far and near, with music, 1964; Walt Disney's Mary Poppins, 1966; Prokim fun mayn effentlihn lebn, by Dr Y L N Vilensky, trans and ed with biography, 1968; contbr: poems, essays, trans to Heb press; poems in Yiddish and Russ; children's poems with music by Isr composers. Recipient: Hadassah Lanoar Prize, 1951; Isr Prize for children's lit, 1956; title of honor, Yakirat, Yerushalaim. 1968. Home: 31 Abarbanel St, Jerusalem, Isr.

YALIN-MOR, Nathan, Isr, journalist; b. Grodno, Russ, June 28, 1913; s. Eliyahu and Hanna (Feingold) Friedman-Yellin; in Isr since 1941; att: Gymnasium Tarbut, Grodno, 1925-32; Poly, Warsaw, 1936-39; m. Efrath Morein, Sep 5, 1939; c: Dorith, Elisha. Journalist, daily newspaper, Ha'Aretz; mem-Betar and Revisionist Party, 1933; Betar Command, Pol; Re: visionist Cen Comm, 1936-37; joined IZL, 1937; org, Aliya B; ed, Di Tat, organ of IZL, 1938-39; joined LHI under Abraham Stern, 1941, known as Ster Group; ed, underground monthly, Ba-Machteret; LHI mission, Balkan countries to have J youth move to Pal for political activity, 1941; arrested in Syria by Brit Security Mission, 1942; detention camp: Mazra'a; Latrun, 1942-43; escaped Latrun with other LHI fighters, 1943; mem, three-man LHI High Command, 1943-45, head, political activities; ed, underground jours: He-Hazit; Ha-Ma'as; head, LHI, 1946-48; after assassination of Count Bernadotte arrested by Isr auth and sentenced to 8 years prison on accusation of heading a terrorist org, 1948; released after gen amnesty law; mem, 1st Knesset; farm mgr, 1954-65. Found, Semitic Action Movement, 1960-67; ed, political bi-weekly, Ethgar; org, Movement for a Fed Isr-Pal, 1967; mem, movement for Peace and Security. Home: 75 Rehov Einstein, Tel Aviv, Isr.

YALON, Reuven, US, educator; b. Tel Aviv, Isr, Mar 7, 1935; s. Joseph and Polly (Green); in US since 1955; BA, CCNY, 1961; MA, Amer U, 1965; m. Norma Goldstein, June 7, 1964; c: Donna, Noam, Zach. Dir, experimental educ and sup, BJE, Cleveland, Ohio, since 1968; youth dir, lang cons, tchr, Adas Isr Cong, 1962-67; tchr training, US, Can, EMC Corp, 1967-68. Sgt, IDF, 1953-55. Prin contrib: devl, B'Yad Halashon materials, tchr training courses and TV prog, in Heb as a second lang. Exec comm, Isr Students Org, 1958-59; mem: Amer Council on Teaching Fgn Langs; Ling Soc Amer; Phi Kappa Phi; Natl Council of J Educ. Spec interest: dramatics. Home: 2265 S Green Rd, Cleveland, O. Office: 2030 S Taylor Rd, Cleveland, O.

YALOW, Samuel, US, rabbi; b. Rakiskis, Lith, Oct 10, 1892; s. Moses and Rachel (Stern) Yalowetsky; in US since 1913; att Rabbi Isaac Elchanan Theol Sem, 1913-17; ordained rabbi, 1917; att Syracuse U, 1921, 1925; m. Esther Marcus, Aug 9, 1918; c: Aaron, Ethel Lerner. Rabbi, Cong Ahavath Achim, since 1919; chaplain: Syracuse Psycht Hosp, since 1932; Onondaga Sanatorium since 1945; Onondaga Home and Hosp, since 1958; Rome State Sch, 1930-40; VA, 1934-50. Pres, J Educ Comm and Heb Sch; mem: natl bd, Mizrachi Org of Amer; Union of Orthodox Rabbis. Author: Minchat Schmuel; Shalmei Schmuel, both on the Talmud; contbr to periodicals. Home: c/o Lerner, 1646 54 St, Brooklyn, NY.

YAMNIK, Elchanan Dov, Isr, educational admnr; b. Tel Aviv, Feb 22, 1947; s. Synai and Esther Stynsneider; att Yeshivat:

Rabbi Chaim Berlin, Bklyn, NY; Rabbi Amiel-Yeshuv Hachadash; Talmudical Acad, Bat Yam; Coll for Rabbis, Tel Aviv; m. Rachel Rosenblum, Mar 28, 1967; c: Naava, Chaim. Dean, exec dir, Yeshivat Or Meir, since 1967. Secy gen, Union of Rel Intellectuals, since 1967; mem: Cen World Comm, Mishna and Halacha Yomit, since 1968; adv council: Assn of Rel Councils of Isr; Union of Agudath Isr Tchrs. Author: Otzar Hamelech, 1968. Spec interests: educ problems, Halacha-Oral law. Home: 84 Bograchov St, Tel Aviv, Isr. Office: POB 29226, Tel Aviv, Isr.

YAMPOLSKY, Joseph, US, physician, educator; b. Nemirow, Russ, Sep 9, 1892; s. Samuel and Mary (Dechovitz); in US since 1906; BA, U of Ga, 1913; MD, Columbia U, 1917; m. Pauline Rosen, Aug 8, 1918; c: Gertrude Brown. Asso prof, peds, Emory U Sch of Med, since 1920; chief, dept peds, Ga Baptist Hosp, since 1953. Lt, US Army, 1918. F, Amer Coll Phys; bd dirs, J Children's Service; mem: Fulton Co Med Soc, fmr ed, bull; Amer Acad Peds; AMA; S Med Assn; Med Assn of Ga; Ga Ped Soc, fmr pres; Fulton Co Ped Soc, fmr pres; AAAS; B'nai B'rith, fmr lodge pres; club, Mayfair Social. Author: chaps in: Litchfield and Dembo's, Therapeutics of Infancy and Childhood, 1947; Grulee and Eley's, The Child in Health and Disease, 1952; contbr to med publs. Home: 150 Robin Hood Rd, NE, Atlanta, Ga.

YANAI, Reuben, Isr, editor; b. Pol, Mar 8, 1922; s. Shlomo and Yetta (Segal) Januar; in Isr since 1935; MA, Heb U, Jerusalem, 1947; m. Avigail Wertheim; c: Orna, Eyal. Ed, found: Ma'ariv laNo'ar, since 1957; beMahane Gadna, 1948-56. Sgt, J Brig, Brit Army, 1942-46; maj, IDF, 1948-56. Author: beMahane Gadna, 1952; miHaham veYeida, 1954; contbr short stories to newspapers. Recipient: 1939-45 medal; Africa Star; It Star; Independence, Sinai medals. Home: 10 Barak St, Zahala, Tel Aviv, Isr. Office: 2 Carlebach St, Tel Aviv, Isr.

YANIV, Azriel Edward, Isr, chemist, metallurgist; b. Czortkow, Pol, Nov 9, 1922; s. Eliezer and Malka (Kassierer) Weinraub; in Isr since 1944; BSc, engr, Technion, Haifa, 1949; postgrad dipl, Battersea Coll of Tech, London, 1958; PhD, Sir John Cass Coll, London, 1965; m. Blanka Liebergall; c: Amir, Ran. Sr research chem, sci dept, Min Defense, since 1948. Capt, IDF, 1948-57. Mem: Isr Chem Soc; Corrosion and Protection Assn. Contbr to profsl jours. Recipient: Independence; Sinai; Six Days War decorations. Hobbies: bridge, philately. Home: 14 Mapu Ave, Haifa, Isr. Office: POB 7063, Tel Aviv, Isr.

YANKAUER, Walter D, US, business exec; b. NYC, Mar 14, 1899; s. Max and Emma (Strauss); BA, Columbia U, 1919, LLB, 1920, MA, 1920; m. Josephine Sperry, Nov 30, 1925; c: Susan Maier, Judith Astrove. Chmn, Mill Factors Corp; partner, Sperry & Yankauer, 1923-42. US Army, WW I. Vice-pres, trustee: Hillside Hosp; Irvington House; mem: Assn of Bar, NYC; Amer, NY State Bar Assns; clubs: Harmonie; Sunningdale Country. Home: 111 E 48 St, New York, NY. Office: 380 Park Ave S, New York, NY.

YANOFSKY, Daniel Abraham, Can, attorney; b Brody, Pol, Mar 26, 1925; s. Abba and Mania (Lukatzki); in Can since 1925; BS, U Man, 1944, LLB, Law Sch, 1951; B Civil Law, Oxford U, Eng, 1953; m Hilda Gutnik, July 8, 1951; c: Rochelle, Heather, Michael. Sr partner, Yanofsky, Pollack & Assos, since 1953. Can Navy, 1944-46. Mem, B'nai B'rith; fmr, dep mayor, City of W Kildonan. Author: Chess the Hard Way, 1954; Winning Chess Endings, 1955 Recipient: Intl Chess Grandmaster, Intl Chess Fed, 1964. Home: 62 Ashbury Bay, Winnipeg, Can. Office: 457 Main St, Winnipeg, Can.

YANOWITZ, Bernard, US, dentist; b. Malone, NY, Feb 19, 1926; s. Paul and Bertha (Jebrock); att St Lawrence U, 1943-45; DDS, Columbia U, 1949; m Helen Nanchu, Dec 16, 1951; c: Melissa, John, Julie, Mark, Beth. Pvt practice. Lt, USN, 1950-52. Chmn, dent div, UJA; vice-pres, WHC Brotherhood; mem: bd mgrs, Wash, DC Heb Cong; dent staff, Heb Home for Aged; exec comm, DC Dent Soc; Amer Acad Gen Dent; Omega Kappa Upsilon; fmr pres: Maimonides Soc; Wash, DC Council of Temple Brotherhoods; club, Dent Sci. Hobby: tennis. Home: 5807 Surrey St, Chevy Chase, Md. Office: 4201 Massachusetts Ave, NW, Washington, DC.

YAOS-KEST, Itamar, Isr, poet, author; b. Hung, Aug 3, 1934; s. Bella and Hanna (Öze); in Isr since 1951; BA, Tel Aviv U; m. Hanna Mercasy, Aug 21, 1958; c: Shilhav, Erel. Ed, dir, Eked Pub House, since 1958. Author: poetry: Mal'ach leLo Knafaim 1959; Nof beAshan, 1961; Yerushat Einaim, 1965;

Shirim, 1966; leMorad Beita, 1969; plays: Or haNehshach, 1963; Gidrei Laila; trans: Shika, Japanese poems, 1958; Mivhar haShira haYehudit beHungaria veToldoteha, 1960; Horatius, selected poems, 1965; Ktav beGavish, 1968. Sgt, IDF, 1953-56 Recipient: Nordau award, 1963; Talpir award, 1967. Home: 51 Nahmani St, Tel Aviv, Isr. Office: 29 Bar Kochba St, Tel Aviv, Isr.

YARDENY-YAFFE, Tamar, Isr, music tchr; b. Rovna, Russ, Feb 13, 1918; d. Yaacob and Devora (Brin); in Isr since 1921; att Music Tchrs Sem, Tel Aviv; Music Conservatory, Jerusalem; m. Uri Yaffe, 1940; c: Amir, Osnat, Arnon, Yehiam, Efrat, Eyal. Dir, Music Sch, Bet Shean Valley, since 1959; tchr, Kibbutz Maoz Haim Sch, 1941-59. Author: Musical Instruments Out of Plants; The Story of the Flute-String and Wind. Hobbies: music therapy, creating musical instruments. Home: Kibbutz Maoz Haim, Bet Shean Valley, Isr.

YARIV, Aharon, Isr, army off; b Latvia, 1920; in Isr since 1935; att: course, Political Dept, JA; Agric Sch; Fr Staff Offs Sch; m; one c. Chief, Intelligence Br, IDF, since 1964; fmr: mem, Haganah; capt, Brit Army, Heb Units in: Eur, ME, N Afr; took part in rescuing survivors of the Holocaust; Haganah instr, Jerusalem; adj to Haganah Chief of Staff Yaacov Dori; Oprs Dept, Haganah Gen Staff; dep battalion cdr, Alexandroni Brig; battalion cdr, Carmeli Brig, took part in conquest of Nazareth; grad, instr, Battalion Cdrs Course; co-found, cdr, IDF Command and Staff Coll; Cen Command Chief of Staff; IDF Mil Attaché to US, Can; Infantry Brig Cdr; rank of maj gen, 1964. Office: IDF, Isr.

YARMOLINSKY, Adam, US, lawyer, educator; b NYC, Nov 17, 1922; s. Avraham and Babette (Deutsch); AB, Harvard, 1943; LLB, Yale Law Sch, 1948; m. Harriet Rypins, 1945; c: Sarah Franklin, Tobias, Benjamin, Matthew. Chief exec off, Wfr I Devl Corp, NYC, cince 1970; prof, law, Harvard Law Sch; mem, Inst of Politics, John F Kennedy Sch of Govt, Harvard, both since 1966; law clerk: Judge Charles Clark, US 2nd Circuit Court Appeals, 1948-49; Justice Reed, US Supr Court, 1950-51; pvt practice: Root, Ballantine, Harlan, Bushby & Palmer, NYC, 1949-50; Cleary, Gottlieb, Friendly & Ball, Wash, DC, 1951-55; secy, Fund for Rep, 1955-57; public affairs ed, Doubleday & Co, 1957-59; cons, philanthropic founds, 1959-61; spec asst to US Secy of Defense, 1961-64; dep dir, Pres' Task Force on War Against Poverty, 1964; chief, US emergency relief mission, Dominican Rep, 1965; dep asst Defense Secy, 1965-66; lectr: Amer U Law Sch, 1951-56; Yale Law Sch, 1958-59. USAAF, 1943-46. Trustee: Robert Kennedy Memorial; Vera Inst of Justice; f: Amer Acad Arts and Scis; Ezra Stiles Coll, Yale; mem: Assn Bar, NYC; Amer Bar Assn; Amer Law Inst; Council on Fgn Relations; Cen for Inter-Amer Relations; Inst for Strategic Studies; Inst Med, Natl Acad of Sci. Author: Recognition of Excellence, 1960; The Military Establishment, 1971; ed, Case Studies in Personnel Security, 1955; contbr to periodicals. Recipient: Dist Public Service Medal, Defense Dept, 1966. Home: 281 Henry St, Brooklyn Heights, NY. Office: 1345 Sixth Ave, New York, NY.

YARMOLINSKY, Avrahm, US, author, librarian; b. Haisin, Russ, Jan 1, 1890; s. Bezaleel and Malka (Nemoy); in US since 1913; att U of Neuchâtel, Switz, 1912-13; BA, CCNY, 1916; PhD, Columbia U, 1921; m Babette Deutsch, Apr 28, 1921; c: Adam, Michael. Ret; fmr chief, Slavonic div, NY Public Libr, 1918-55; instr: Russ, CCNY, 1917-23; Russ lang and lit, Columbia U, 1919-20. Author: Turgenev, 1926, 1959; The Jews and Other Minor Nationalities Under the Soviets, 1928; Picturesque United States of America, 1930; Russian Literature, 1931; Dostoevsky, 1934, 1957; Early Polish Americana, 1937; Russian Americana, 1943; The Road to Revolution, 1957, 1959, 1962, Ger, 1968; Literature Under Communism, 1960; A Russian's American Dream, A Memoir of William Frey, 1965; The Russian Literary Imagination, 1969; ed: Brothers Karamazov, 1933; The Possessed, 1936; Crime and Punishment, 1951; The Idiot, 1956, all by Dostoevsky; The Works of Alexander Pushkin, 1936; Eugene Onegin, by Alexander Pushkin, 1943, 1964; A Treasury of Great Russian Short Stories, 1944; Chichikov's Journeys, by Gogol, 1944; Portable Chekhov, 1947; A Treasury of Russian Verse, 1949; The Borzoi Turgenev, 1950; The Unknown Chekhov, 1954; Soviet Short Stories, 1960; An Anthology of Russian Verse, 1812-1960, publ 1962; Russia: Then and Now, 1963; Two Centuries of Russian Verse, an Anthology, 1966; co-ed: A Book of Short Stories by Maxim Gorki, 1939; The Heritage of European Literature, 2 vols, 1948-49; trans: The Russian School of Painting, by Alexander Benois, 1916; A Family of

Noblemen, by Saltykov, 1917; The Shield, 1917; Memoirs of Count Witte, 1921; co-trans: Modern Russian Poetry, 1921; Contemporary German Poetry, 1923; Russian Poetry, 1927; The Twelve, 1931. Mem: Amer Friends of Heb U; YIVO; Phi Beta Kappa. Recipient: Townsend Harris Medal, 1939. Home: 300 W 108 St, New York, NY.

YARMON, Morton, US, author, editor, public relations exec; b. NYC, Mar 8, 1916; s Jacob and Mary (Berman); BSS, CCNY, 1934; BS, Columbia Sch of Journalism, 1935; m. Betty Gross, Nov 7, 1948. Dir, PR, AJComm, since 1963; gen mgr: Civil Service Leader, 1939-54; Natl Antiques Show, 1946-54; asst to ed, Eur ed, NY Herald Tribune, 1945-46; mem, fgn desk, NY Times, 1948-56; lectr, Eng, CCNY, 1954-55; dir, creative services, Ruder & Finn, Inc, 1956-59; asso mgn ed, Parade Mag, 1959-63; cons, Commerce Dept, 1961-62. Capt, US Army, 1942-45. Author: Opportunities in the Armed Forces, 1942; Complete Guide to Your Civil Service Job, 1949; Every Woman's Guide to Spare-Time Income, 1950; Early American Antique Furniture, 1952; Put Your Money to Work for You, 1954; Jobs After Retirement, 1954; The Art of Writing Made Simple, 1956; Invest Smartly, 1961; weekly columnist, Women's News Service; occasional columnist, NY Times; contbr to natl mags. Mem: Soc of Mag Writers; club, Overseas Press. Home: 35 Sutton Pl, New York, NY. Office: 165 E 56 St, New York, NY.

YARNITSKY, Yeshaya, Isr, educator; b. Haifa, Feb 8, 1928; s. Dov and Tcharna (Kagan); BSc, summa cum laude, Technion, 1953, PhD, 1961; m. Ester Solomon, Nov 15, 1955; c: David, Daphna, Ariel. Sr lectr, head, Diamond Research Lab, Haifa; head, Experimental Diamond Polishing Pilot Plant, Tel Aviv; staff, research and devl, Min of Defense, 1953-58. Off, IDF. Chmn, Educ Comm, Histadrut, Hapoel Hamizrachi, Haifa; youth leader, Hanoar Hamizrachi, 1945-48; mem, Hamishmeret Hatzehira, Hapoel Hamizrachi. Author: atlases of machine tools and processes; contbr to jours. Spec interests: educ, gemology. Home: 89 Herzl St, Haifa, Isr. Office: Technion, Haifa, Isr.

YARON, Arieh, Isr, scientist; b. Cadca, Czech, Oct 3, 1927; s. Chanoch and Tziporah (Freller) Vesely; in Isr since 1949; MSc, Heb U, Jerusalem, 1956, PhD, 1956; m. Esther Krausz, June 26, 1950; c: Amir, Dan. Sr sci, Weizmann Inst of Sci, since 1969, research asso, 1965-68. Mem: Isr Biochem Soc; Isr Immunological Soc. Contbr to biochem publs. Home: Shikun Ovdei Hamahon 10, Rehovot, Isr. Office: Weizmann Inst, Rehovot, Isr.

YARON, Izhar, Isr, educator; b. Tel Aviv, July 8, 1910; s. Nachum and Fania (Itin) Papper; att, Technion, Haifa, 1929-31; BA, Tel Aviv U, 1969; m. Sima Kremenchugski, 1940; c: Nachum, Merav. Dir, music sch; lectr, Tchrs Sem. Sgt maj, Isr Navy, 1948-49. Mem: ACUM; Composers Union; Musicologists Union; four chmn, music div, Kibbutz Arzi. Author: The Human Voice, 1963; Rinot, 1965. Home: Kibbutz Ein HaShofet. Isr.

YARON, Reuven, Isr, educator; b. Vienna, Aus, Sep 6, 1924; s. Josef and Fanny (Weinberger); in Isr since 1939; MJur, Heb U, Jerusalem, 1953; att U of Aberdeen, 1954-55; PhD, Oxford U, 1956; m. Shoshana Cohen, Aug 23, 1953. Prof, Roman and ancient Near E law, Heb U, Jerusalem, since 1968, lectr, 1957-1963, asso prof, 1963-68; visiting prof, Aberden U, 1965-66. Author: Gifts in Contemplation of Death in Jewish and Roman Law, 1960; The Law of the Aramaic Papyri, 1961; The Laws of Eshnunna, 1969. Home: 6 Magnes Sq, Jerusalem, Isr. Office: Heb U, Jerusalem, Isr.

YASCHIK, Henry, US, business exec; b. Tucuman, Arg, Dec 3, 1910; s. Nathan and Elka (Lipchensky); in US since 1914; att U of SC, 1941; m. Sylvia Vlosky, Feb 11, 1940; c: Anne Silverman, Marsha, Bonnie. Owner, Henry Yaschik Agcy; pres: Yaschik Mortgage Co; Yaschik Construction Co; Charleston Capital Corp. Pres, exec comm, S regional ADL, since 1952; mem: Charleston Real Estate Bd; Charleston Bd Ins Underwriters; SC Real Estate Bd; SC bd, Ins Assn; natl bd, Assn Ins Underwriters; Natl Real Estate Bd, Charleston C of C; US C of C; Natl Assn Small Bus Inves Co; Charleston Devl Bd; Charleston Mus; Home Bldrs, Gtr Charleston; Natl Assn Home Bldrs; Carolina Mortgage Bank Assn; AJ Comm; exec comm, J Children's Service of Atlanta, Ga, since 1955; educ comm, Trident C of C; dir, Charleston J Comty Cen; fmr: pres: Charleston JWF; State Assn of B'nai B'rith Lodges; Heb Benevolent Soc; chmn, Isr Bond Drive; treas, Beth Isr Syn; co-chmn, ticket comm, Bi-Centennial Celebration of Charleston Jewry; mem, adv budget comm, Charleston United Fund; treas, Charleston chap, ZOA; mem: Charleston chap, B'nai B'rith; Master, Friendship Lodge, Masons. Home: 27 Devereaux Ave, Charleston, SC. Office: 19 Broad St, Charleston, SC.

YASSER, Joseph, US, musicologist; b. Lodz, Pol, Apr 16, 1893; s. Samuel and Clara (Newmark); in US since 1923; MA, State Conservatory, Moscow, 1917; hon DMus, Musical Arts Conservatory, W Texas, 1950; m. Marie Lourie, Nov 11, 1918. Choirmaster, organist, Temple Rodeph Sholom, NYC, 1929-60; fac mem, Cantors Inst, JTSA, 1952-60; organ prof, State Conservatory, Moscow, 1918-20; chief organist, State Grand Opera, Bolshoi, 1919-20; music commentator, Siberian Bd Educ, 1920-21; conductor, Shanghai Songsters Choral Soc, 1921-22. Pres, Gtr NY Chap, Amer Musicological Soc, 1935-37; vice-pres, Amer Libr Musicology, 1932-41; pres, J Music Forum, 1945-58. Mem: Amer Musicological Soc; Music Libr Assn; J Music Council of Amer. Author: A Theory of Evolving Tonality, 1932; Medieval Quartal Harmony, 1938; contbr to profsl periodicals. Hobbies: phil and rel lit, painting. Home: 905 West End Ave, New York, NY.

YASUNA, Alvin D, US, proctologist; b. NYC, Oct 21, 1908; s. Isidore and May (Rubin); BA, Cornell U, 1929; MD, NYU-Bellevue Med Sch, 1933; m. Myrtis Woods, May 26, 1950; c: Susan, Debra. Asst clinical prof, proctology, NY Med Coll, since 1926; pvt practice, NYC, since 1935; med dir, chief, proctology, Mt Eden Gen Hosp, secy, med bd and med staff; asso, surg, chief, proctology, Bx Lebanon Hosp Cen; chief, proctology, vice-pres, med bd, Hosp of Daughters of Jacob; asso visiting proctologist, Metrop Hosp Cen; asst att proctologist, Flower and Fifth Ave Hosp; asso visiting proctologist, Bird S Coler Hosp; fmr: chief proctologist, VA Hosp, Biloxi, Miss; att proctologist, Hosp of Daughters of Isr; visiting proctologist, Seton Hosp, asso visiting surg, Morrisania City Hosp; cons proctologist: Royal Hosp; Prospect Hosp; VA Hosp, Miss; Consolidated Edison Co of NY; NY Police Dept, Fire Dept, Telephone Co, PO. Maj, US Army, qualified flight surg; CO, USAF Hosp, Birmingham, Ala; regional flight surg, Dale Mabry Field, Tallahassee, Fla; chief, proctology, 217th and 48th Gen Hosps, ETO, Fr; CO, POW Hosp, Bad Andernach, Ger. F: AMA; Amer Coll Gastroenterology; Amer Geriatrics Soc; Intl Coll Surgs; NY Acad Med; NY Soc Colon and Rectal Surgs; Jerusalem Acad Med; NY Acad Gastroenterology; secy, Bx Co Med Soc; med cons, Bx Co Borough Pres; dipl: Amer Bd Proctology, 1950; Amer Bd Colon and Rectal Surg, 1950; Intl Coll Surgs, 1954; Pan Amer Med Assn, 1955; vice-pres, bd health, Englewood Cliffs, NJ; mem: State of NY Med Soc; Bx Co Med Soc; Assn Mil Surgs, US; IMA; Amer Proctology Soc; NY Workmen's Compensation Bd; bd trustees, CBA, NJ; Congs: Temple Isr, New Rochelle; Temple Sinai, Tenafly, NJ; Morrisania Hosp Clinical Soc; Leb Hosp Alumni Soc; Phi Lambda Kappa; Amer Philatelic Soc, fmr pres; Masons; KP; fmr, pres, Adv Council to Commn of Hosps of NYC; clubs: Phys Sq; Hippocrates; Cornell, NY; Cornell, Bergen Co, NJ. Asst review ed, Amer Jour of Gastroenterology; contbr to med jours. Recipient: citation, for ed proficiency in proctology, Jour of Proctology, 1950. Hobbies: philately, hi-fi, reading. Home: 6 Samford Dr, Englewood Cliffs, NJ. Office: 1700 Grand Concourse, Bronx, NY.

YATES, Sydney R, US, attorney, legislator; b. Chgo, Ill, Aug 27, 1909; s. Louis and Ida (Siegel); PhB, U of Chgo, 1931, JD, Law Sch, 1933; m. Adeline Holleb, June 24, 1935; c: Stephen. Repr of 9th Dist, Ill, 81st through 87th US Congress, re-elected, 89th through present; delg, UN Trusteeship Council, 1963-64. Lt, USN, WW II. Mem: Amer, Ill, Chgo Bar Assns; Decalogue Soc of Lawyers, ed, bull, 1947; Chgo Council on Fgn Relations; Amer Vets Comm; clubs: City; Bryn Mawr Country. Home: 3500 Lake Shore Dr, Chicago, Ill. Office: 219 S Dearborn, Chicago, Ill.

YATSIV, Shaul, Isr, educator; b. Rehovot, Nov 8, 1927; s. Avner and Slava (Brostein); MS Heb U, Jerusalem, 1952, PhD, 1956; m. Ora Zeldes, 1952; c: Ido, Avner, Michal. Asso prof, physics, Heb U; research asso, Stanford U, Cal, 1956-58; sr physicist, sci staff, Hughs Research Lab, Malibou, Cal, 1964-65. Prin contribs: discovery of: resonance to photon absorption and of Raman effects in free atoms; stimulated two-photon emission. Org, Isr Phys Soc; mem, Amer Phys Soc. Home: 5 Hehalutz St, Jerusalem, Isr. Office: Heb U, Jerusalem, Isr.

YAVETZ, Zvi, Isr, educator; b. Cernovitz. Rum, Apr 26, 1925; s. Arie and Amalia; in Isr since 1944; MA, PhD, Jerusalem, 1950; research f, Oxford; m. Dvorah Markus Lwow. Chmn,

dept hist, Tel Aviv U, since 1958, dean, hums, 1966; visiting prof, Cornell U, 1966-67; dean, hums, U of Ethiopia, 1964. Capt, IDF. Author: Spartacus, 1958; Abolition of Debts in Antiquity, 1958; Urban Crowds in Roman Politics, 1966; Plebs and Princeps, 1969. Home: 89 University Ave, Tel Aviv, Isr. Office: Tel Aviv U, Tel Aviv, Isr.

YAVIN, Avivi Israel, Isr, physicist, educator; b. Isr, June 20, 1928; s. David and Yemima (Brauner) Mondjak; MSc, Heb U, Jerusalem, 1954; PhD, U of Wash, Seattle, 1958; m. Rivka Krimsky, July 18, 1951; c: Talma, David, Ayellet. Prof, physics: Tel Aviv U, since 1967; U of Ill, 1958-67. Lt, IDF, 1948-49. F, Amer Phys Soc; mem, Sigma Xi. Contbr to sci jours. Home: 4 Levitan St, Ramat Aviv, Isr. Office: Tel Aviv U, Tel Aviv, Isr.

YEDIDIAH, Shalom, Isr, journalist; b. Kamionka, Pol, June 29, 1902; s. Jacob and Henia (Sztolzberg) Gottlieb; in Isr since 1940; att: Tchrs Sem, Lwow; U of Lwow, Pol; m. Miriam Rap, Aug 18, 1948. Ed in chief, Nowiny Kurier, Pol lang daily, since 1956; ed, Hayei Sha'a, weekly, since 1953; mem, ed staff, Moment, Yiddish daily, Warsaw, 1930-39; ed, Warshaver Radio, 1935-39; mem, ed staff, Haaretz, daily, Tel Aviv, 1942-52. Author: Zwischen Sinai und Zanzibar, Yiddish, 1938. Home: 14 Bloch St, Tel Aviv, Isr. Office: 52 Harakevet St, Tel Aviv, Isr.

YEHOSHUA, Abraham B, Isr, author, educator; b. Jerusalem, Dec 9, 1936; s. Yakov and Malka (Rosilio); BA, Heb U, Jerusalem, 1962; m. Rivka Kirsninski; c: Sivan. Dean of students, Haifa U Coll, since 1967; tchr, HS, Jerusalem, 1962-63; dir, Isr Sch, Paris, 1963-64; gen secy, World Union J Students, Paris, 1964-67. Author: Mot haZaken, 1963; Mul haYe'arot, 1968; Laila beMai, play, 1969. Cpl, IDF, 1954-57. Recipient: Acum Award, 1962; Ramat Gan Award, Ramat Gan Munic, 1968. Home: 63 Shoshanat Hacarmel St, Haifa, Isr. Office: Haifa U Coll, Haifa, Isr.

YEHOSHUA, Jacob, Isr, government official; b. Jerusalem, July 1, 1905; s. Hanania and Rahel; MA Heb U, Jerusalem, 1935; m. Malka, Oct 23, 1932; c: Avraham, Zilla. Dir, Muslim and Druze Dept, Min Rel Affairs, since 1959; Pal Mandatory Govt Official, 1929-48. Hon secy, Isr Oriental Soc. Author: Childhood in the Old City of Jerusalem, 3 vols; ed, Muslim, Druze bulls, pub by Muslim and Druze dept, Min for Rel Affairs; contbr to press. Home: 4 Disraeli St, Jerusalem, Isr. Office: Min of Rel Affairs, Jerusalem, Isr.

YEIVIN, Esther, Isr, teacher; b. Odessa, Russ, Feb 2, 1877; d. Shlomo and Feige (Lifshitz) Yonis; in Isr since 1905; m. Ison Yelvin; two c. Fmr: tchr, sch for abandoned children, illiterate adults, Russia; mem, Haifa Comty Council; appeared before Rabb Courts; elected to Heb Magistrates Court, Tel Aviv, Haifa; exec comm, Heb Magistrates Court, Haifa. Fmr mem: JNF; KH; fought for women's equal rights, elected to 1st, 2nd assembly; natl comm. Home: 32 Kadimah Rd, Haifa, Isr.

YEIVIN, Shemuel, Isr, archaeologist, educator; b. Odessa, Russ, Sep 2, 1896; s. Nissan and Esther (Yonis); in Isr since 1905; BA, hons, Egyptology, U Coll, 1923, MA, 1928, dipl, Arabic, Sch of Oriental Studies, 1923, all U of London; postgrad study, U of Berlin, 1928-29; m. Bathia Stern, Sep, 1920; c: Yehuda, Ephrath-Tirza. Head, dept, Ancient and ME studies, Tel Aviv U, since dept was established, 1961, prof, ME hist and archaeol, 1959-69, em external lectr, 1955-59; sr archaeol adv, dep dir, dir, expeditions: Pal, Egypt, Iraq, 1923-24, 1929-33, 1936-37, 1938-39; research secy, Heb Lang Comm, Tel Aviv, 1935-42; gen secy, Ency Biblica, Jerusalem, 1942-44; chief Heb trans, Pal Govt, 1944-48; dir, Isr Govt Dept of Antiquities, 1948-59. Lt, Turkish Army, 1916-18; capt, Air Raid Precautions, Tel Aviv, 1938-42; mem, Civic Guard, Jerusalem, 1947-48. Mem: Heb Lang Acad, chmn, admn comm, mem, exec comm and comm on terminology, all since 1953; govt comm on geog names, since 1949, chmn, sub-comm on hist identifications; exec: Isr Soc for Bible Research; Heb Lang Council, 1946-53; Isr Exploration Soc, since 1930, chmn, 1944-46, 1949-50; 1st UNESCO Comm, 1952-59, corresp mem for Isr on hist documents and archaeol excavations, 1953-61; Isr repr, perm council, Intl Congs of Anthropological and Ethnological Scis, since 1957. Author: Megillat Sanehat, 1930, 4 eds; Massa Wen-Amon, 1930, 4 eds; Toledot kak-Kebav ha-Ivri, 1939; Melhemet Bar-Kokhba, 1946, 3 eds; Archaeological Activities in Israel, 1948-55, Heb, Eng, 1956; Mehqarim be Toledot Yisrael veArzo, 1960; A Decade of Archaeology in Israel, 1961; Preliminary Report on Tel Gat, Heb, Eng, 1961; Taba-at Chronologist le-Toledot Yisrael beTequfat ham-Melakhim, 1962;

co-author: Palestine Guide for Army, Navy and Air Force, 1940; Qadmoniot Arzenu, 1955; fmr ed: Bull of Isr Exploration Soc, 1945-49, co-ed, 1933-45; Atikot, Heb, Eng, 1955-58; Libr of Palestinology; archaeol sect, Ency Biblica, 1944-62, co-ed, hist sect, mem, ed bd, since 1944; contbr: Heb Ency; Enciclopedia de la Biblia, Barcelona; World History of the Jews; newspapers and periodicals. Recipient: Turkish Mil Medal, 1918; Ger War Decoration, 1918, returned in protest to Ger in 1933; Bialik Prize, for Qadmoniot Arzenu, 1955; Pras Israel, 1968. Home: 24 Ibn Ezra St, Jerusalem, Isr.

YEIVIN, Yehuda, Isr, physicist; b. London, Eng, Jan 15, 1924; s. Shmuel and Bathya (Stern); in Isr since 1926; MSc, Heb U, Jerusalem, 1952; PhD Weizmann Inst, Rehovot, 1956; m. Rina Kushnir, Feb 1, 1949. Asso prof, physics, Tel Aviv U, since 1967, acting head, dept phys, 1964-65; chief phys, ind div, Isr AEC, 1957-61. J Brig, Brit Army, 1942-46; IDF, 1947-49. Prin contribs: theory of positive excess of cosmic ray muons; extension of Fermi's model of multiple particle produc; energy dependent transp approximation of Boltzmann Equation; neutron cross-sect evaluation by integral data. Mem, council: Isr Phys Soc, fmr vice-pres, pres; Eur Phys Soc; mem, Isr Natl Comm on Nuclear Safety. Author: Electromagnetic Theory, Heb, 1965; contbr to sci jours. Home: 12 Shamai St, Jerusalem, Isr. Office: Tel Aviv U, Ramat Aviv, Isr.

YEKUTIELI, Baruch, Isr, business exec; b. Tel Aviv, Jan 23, 1926; s. Israel and Shulamith; ML, Heb U, Jerusalem; m. Naomi Torok. Asst gen mgr, Bank Leumi, head off; dep controller, fgn exch, Min of Finance, 1958-61. Home: 55 David Hamelech St, Tel Aviv, Isr. Office: POB 2, Tel Aviv, Isr.

YELLEN, Samuel, US, educator, author; b. Vilna, Lith, July 7, 1906; s. Sidney and Rebecca (Epstein); in US since 1907; BA, W Reserve U, 1926; MA, Oberlin Coll, 1931; m. Miriam Friend, June 11, 1931 (decd); m. 2nd, Edna Bard, June 26, 1966. Prof, Eng, Ind U, since 1963, on fac since 1929. Author: American Labor Struggles, 1936; In The House and Out, and Other Poems, 1952; The Passionate Shepherd: A Book of Stories, 1957; The Wedding Band, 1961; New and Selected Poems, 1964. Mem: AAUP; MLA; PEN club. Home: 922 E University St, Bloomington, Ind. Office: Ind U, Bloomington, Ind.

YELLIN, Reuven, Isr, organization exec; b. Grodno, Pol, July 26, 1915; s. Dover and Mita (Strelez); in Isr since 1936; att Heb U, Jerusalem, 1963-66; m Shoshana Braude, Sep 16, 1938; c: Ariela Atzmon, Benjamin. Pres, Midar Jabotinsky, since 1965; mgr, Kupat Holim Leumit, Tel Aviv, since 1954. Off, Irgun Zvai Leumi, 1936-48. Mem mgmt, Social Ins Fund for Natl Workers; official arbitrator for work disputes, Min of Lab; mem: Jabotinsky Order, Rishon Lejehuda Lodge; B'nai B'rith, Jacob Frand Lodge; fmr mem, cen comm, Tnuath Hacherut; mgmt, Shelah, rehab fund. Author: Public Health Insurance, 1963; contbr to press. Recipient: Ot Hashevy, Aleh; Golden Menorah Award, Jabotinsky Order, 1968. Home: 1 Ankorim St, Ramat Gan, Isr. Office: 4 Heftman St, Tel Aviv, Isr.

YELLIN, Richard M, US, rabbi; b. Phila, Pa, Nov 24, 1942; s. Carl and Sue (Axelman); BS, Columbia, 1964; MHL, JTSA, 1966; att Heb U, Jerusalem, 1964-65; ordained rabbi, JTSA, 1969; m. Judith Lipton, June 14, 1964; c: Aliza, Ariel. J chaplain, Ft Knox, Ky, since 1969; asst dir, Camp Ramah, Palmer, Mass, 1968; tchr, J Educ Assn, Essex Co, 1968-69. Capt, US Army, since 1969. Mem, RA, Conservative Judaism. Hobbies: bowling, photography. Home: 4098 Farragut St, Ft Knox, Ky. Study: Chaplain-USAARMC, Ft Knox, Ky.

YELLIN, Solomon, S Afr, business exec; b. Vilna, Pol, Oct 22, 1911; in S Afr since 1930; m. Zipora Entin, 1947; two c. Chmn, Anchor Mining Corp Ltd, since 1947. Chmn: Friends of Isr Philharmonic Orch and Habima, 1948-54; United Comty Fund, 5th campaign, 1957-59, vice-pres, 6th campaign, 1959-61; Bd J Educ, 1953-67; mem, Zionist Exec, since 1967; clubs: Zionist Luncheon; Balfour Park, Beaconsfield. Hobbies: tennis, soccer. Home: 303 Northdene, Princes Pl, Parktown, Johannesburg, S Afr. Office: 1000 Winchester House, Loveday St, Johannesburg, S Afr.

YENISH, Joseph, US, librarian; b. May 9, 1908; s. Leon and Bessie (Sucher); BS, Temple U, 1937, MA, 1942; BS, libr service, Columbia U, 1948; BHL, Gratz Coll, 1957; m. Pearl Slot, Aug 19, 1941. Libr, Gratz Coll, since 1965; social worker, Pa Dept Public Assistance, 1938-43; field repr, Lab Dept,

1943-46; personnel mgr, Amer Vending Corp, 1946-47; f, educ libr, CCNY, 1947-48; libr: Grad Libr, Yeshiva U, 1948-49; Comty Coll, Temple U, 1949-65. Vice-pres, Assn J Librs, since 1962; mem: cen comm, LZOA, since 1958; Amer Libr Assn; Assn Coll and Research Librs; fmr pres, J Libr Assn; Gtr Phila. Contbr to profsl jours. Home: 8403 Williams Ave, Philadelphia, Pa. Office: 10 St and Tabor Rd, Philadelphia, Pa.

YENKIN, Fred, US, business exec; b. Logan, O, June 20, 1911; s. Jacob and Mary (Maggied); MChemE, O State U, 1934; m. Mildred; c: Judith, Cynthia. Vice-pres: The Yenkin Majestic Paint Corp; Majestic Paint Cens. Pres: Columbus United J Fund and Council; Columbus JCC; O Valley Zionist Dist; bd dir: Planned Parenthood Assn; mem: Amer Chem Soc; Amer Inst ChemEs; Soc Paint Tech; O State Bd Profsl Engrs and Surveyors; Fgn Policy Assn; Fgn Trade Assn; Masons; clubs: Intl Assn Lions; Winding Hollow Country. Home: 201 S Drexel, Columbus, O. Office: 1920 Leonard Ave, Columbus, O.

YERUSHALMY, Jacob, US, biostatistician, educator; b. Vienna, Aus, Aug 5, 1904; s. Zeev and Anna (Ziev); in US since 1924; BA, Johns Hopkins U, 1927, MA, 1929, PhD, 1930. Prof, biostat, U of Cal, Berkeley, since 1948; stat, NIH, 1938-41; dir, stat research, Children's Bur, 1941-43; prin stat, USPHS, 1943-48. Mem: natl adv neur diseases and blindness council, NIH; Amer Public Health Assn; Amer Stat Assn; Phi Beta Kappa. Contbr to sci jours. Home: 526 Santa Barbara Rd, Berkeley, Cal. Office: Sch of Public Health, U of Cal, Berkeley, Cal.

YESHURUN, Avot, Isr, author; b. Niskhish, Pol, Sep, 1904; s. Barukh and Rikl (Shapira) Perlmuter; in Isr since 1925; m. Pessia Yustman, June 15, 1934; c: Helit Mory-Katmor. Author: Al Hahmot Derahim, 1942; Re'em, 1960; Shloshim Amud, 1964; Brenner, 1967. Hagana, IDF, 1929-49. Home: 8 Berditchevski St, Tel Aviv, Isr.

YETWIN, I Jacques, US, physician, educator; b. Lachowicze, Pol, July 19, 1908; s. Harry and Anna (Zajc); in US since 1912; BS, Rutgers U, 1929; MS, U of Chgo, 1932; MD, Middlesex U, 1940; grad: Walter Reed Army Med Sch; Armed Forces Inst of Path; m. Ruth Horowitz, Dec 21, 1941; c: Barbara, Richard, Neil. Phys, surg, pvt practice, since 1940; sci instr, public sch, Elizabeth, NJ, 1932-34; chmn, biol dept, Union Co Jr Coll, NJ, 1934-36; med tech, Amer Soc Clinical Path, Muncie, Ind, 1935; research histologist, Hartford Hosp, Conn, 1936; instr, parasitology and tropical med, Middlesex U Sch of Med, 1936-40, asst prof, 1940-42, asso prof, 1942-44; bact, Waltham, Mass Water Dept, 1940-44; lectr: Amer Intl Coll, Springfield, Mass, 1949-51; parasitology, 1951-54; instr, Adult Educ Prog, Public Sch, Springfield, Mass, 1961-69; mil aide de camp, Gov Endicott Peabody, 1963-65. Lt, US Army, MC, 1944; lt col, Natl G uard, 1955, ret 1967. F, Springfield Acad Med; chmn, org and ext comm, NE dist, Boy Scouts of Amer, 1953; mem: bd dirs, Kodimoh Syn, Springfield, 1955-56; Mayor's Comm on Alcoholism 1959; mil aide de camp, Gov Foster Furcolo, Mass, 1957; delg, sch repr, Rutgers U, 1958; mem: Royal Soc Health, Gt Brit, 1957, f, 1967; AAAS; Amer Soc Clinical Path; Amer, Mass Heart Assns; Amer Public Health Assn; Natl Guard Assn, Mass; Assn Mil Surgs; IMA; Springfield Acad Med; Amer Philatelic Soc; B'nai B'rith; accredited judge, Eur and Topicals, Amer Phil Soc. Contbr to jours. Recipient: 10 Year Reserve Medal, 1957; 9 Year Natl Guard Service Medal. Hobbies: philately, microphotography. Home: 22 Bronson Terr, Springfield, Mass. Office: 525½ Belmont Ave, Springfield, Mass.

YINNON, Moshe, US, journalist; b. Pol, Mar 11, 1895; s. Josef and Alta (Berwikunkin) Indelman; in US since 1957; att Berlin U, Ger, 1923-26; m. Helene Lande, Dec 13, 1959; c: Miriam Kreiter. Ed, Hadoar, Heb weekly, since 1959; mgn ed, Haolam, Berlin, 1922-25; parliamentary reporter, Haint Daily, Warsaw, 1925-29; ed, Bialik Inst, Jerusalem, 1940-56. Fmr, chmn, Syndicate J Journalists, Warsaw. Home: 240 W 98 St, New York, NY. Office: 150 Fifth Ave, New York, NY.

YINON, Yaacov Avraham, Isr, attorney, diplomat; b. Warsaw, Pol, Nov 6, 1914; s. Israel and Feiga (Liberson) Blumberg; in Isr since 1934; att Rabb Sem, Warsaw, 1927-31; law fac, U of Warsaw, 1934; law dipl, Govt Law Sch, Jerusalem, 1942; m. Devora Mowszowicz, May 3, 1935; c: Yoel, Micha Yoef. Isr Ambass to Uruguay, since 1968; secy gen, Min of Immigration, 1948-50; secy, finance dept, JA for Pal, Jerusalem; atty, Caspi and Co, 1952-68; Isr Ambass to Colombia, 1963-65. Cdr, Haganah, lt, IDF, 1937-62. Mem, cong court, World Zionist Org; mem: B'nai B'rith, Montevideo; Isr Fgn Policy Assn; fmr, mem cen comm: Isr Bar; Isr Lawyers Assn; Mizrachi Hapoel Hamizrachi; Isr Inst for Intl Problems. Hobbies: writing, public activity. Home: 8 Ekron St, Tel Aviv, Isr. Office: 1585 Bulevar Artigas, Montevideo, Uruguay.

YOCHIM, Louise D, US, artist, teacher; b. Jitomir, Russ, July 18, 1909; d. Solomon and Gitel (Milstein) Dunn; in US since 1924; att Art Inst, 1929-32; BAE, U of Chgo, 1942, MAE, 1952, postgrad studies, 1956; m. Maurice Yochim, 1932; c: Jerome. Sup, art, Chgo Public Schs, since 1950, tchr, art, 1934-50; six one-man shows, Chgo; exhbs: Ill State Mus, Springfield; Northwestern U, Evanston; U of Chgo; Fine Arts Gal; Art Inst; Asso Artists Gal; Marshall Field Gals; First Fed Gal; Contemporary Art Gal, all Chgo; Libr of Cong; Asso Artists Gal, both Wash, DC; A Werbe Gal, Detroit; Mus of Art, Detroit; Riverside Mus, NY; Terry Mus of Art, Fla; Omaha Mus of Art, Neb; Kan City Art Gal, Mo; Ia Art Cen; Rapid City Art Gal; Mus of Art, Sioux City; Butler Mus, Cleveland; Spearfish Mus, ND; repr in pvt collections. F: Intl Inst Arts and Letters; pres, Amer J Art Club, since 1961; mem: Natl Educ Assn; Natl Art Educ Assn; W and E Art Educ Assns; Natl Comm on Art Educ; Chgo Soc Artists; Renaissance Soc Art; Artists Equity; Chgo Art Educ Assn; Delta Kappa Gamma. Author: Building Human Relationships Through Art, 1954; Perceptual Growth in Creativity, 1967; chap on art in History of Chicago Jewry, 1961; ed, Art in Action, 1969; contbr to mags. Recipient: Chgo Soc of Artists award, 1953; awards from Amer J Arts Club; awards for painting: 1948, 1953, 1955, 1958, 1959, 1961. Home: 9545 Drake, Evanston, Ill. Office: 228 N La Salle, Chicago, Ill.

YOËL, Marcel-Meir M, Greece, public relations exec and cons; b. Athens, Greece, July 13, 1931; s. Maurice and Linda (Barki); BA, Pandios U, Athens, 1959; m. Rosella Levy, Dec 6, 1959. PR cons since 1958; gen mgr, Interpress PR and Advt Agcy; info, press and cultural attaché, dept org, Emb of Isr, Athens, 1955-59. Info off, IDF, 1952-54. Mem: bd, hon treas, Intl PR Assn; Greek, Fr, Brit, It PR Assns; J Home of Athens, since 1960; B'nai B'rith; gen secy, cultural comm, Cen Bd J Comtys of Greece, since 1960. Ed, mgn dir: Hellas-Isr, monthly rev of Greek-Isr relations; Epitheorissis, fortnightly organ of Greek Jewry; contbr to press. Home: 23 Amerikis St, Athens, Greece. Office: 1 Demokritou St, Atnehs, Greece.

YOELI, Pinhas, Isr, educator; b. Bayreuth, Ger, July 1, 1920; s. Julius and Edith (Schindler) Aptekmann; in Isr since 1936; dipl ing, Zürich, 1956; m. Agi Izakowa, 1949; c: Dan, Raphael. Asso prof, Technion, since 1967; dep dir, Survey of Isr, 1948-52. Head, mil topography dept, Haganah, 1942-48, IDF, 1948-52, Intelligence Br, lt col, 1948-57. Prin contrib: devl of modern cartographic methods. Contbr to profsl jours. Recipient: Ot Hahaganah; Ot Hamishmar; Ot Hakomemiuth. Hobby: painting. Home: 113 Hatishbi St, Haifa, Isr. Office: Technion, Haifa, Isr.

YOFFE, Abraham, Isr, army officer, government official; b. Pal, Sep 15, 1913; s. Haim and Miriam (Kevashny); m. Aviva Shlosberg, Mar 1, 1946; c: Dan, Ruth, Ronit. Dir, Nature Res Auth, since 1964, Brig gen, commanding S command, IDF, 1958-62, N command, 1962-64; Brit Army, 1940-46; trained units of Gen Orde Wingate's Raiders. Hobbies: hunting, fishing, archaeol, skin diving, gardening, nature stamps. Office: 110 Har Zion Blvd, Tel Aviv, Isr.

YOFFE, Abraham B, Isr, author, editor; b. Bessarabia, Rum, Mar 14, 1924; s. Rachmiel and Haia (Yoffe); in Isr since 1940; att Heb U, Jerusalem, 1942-44; m. Judith Oberländer, July 9, 1952; c: Amital, Haggai. Lit ed, Al Hamishmar, daily, Tel Aviv, since 1951. IDF, 1948-50. Author: Poetry and Reality, 1950; Charlie Chaplin, a biography, 1953; French Dialogue, 1958; Major Events in World Literature, 1960; Hemingway, the Writer and His Work, 1966; A Shlonsky, His Life and Work, 1966. Mem: cen comm, Heb Writers Assn; Isr Journalists Assn. Home: 21 Veidath Katowicz St, Tel Aviv, Isr. Office: Al Hamishmar, Hamasger St, Tel Aviv, Isr.

YOFFE, Shlomo, Isr, composer; b. Warsaw, Pol, 1909; s. Moshe and Shaina (Epstein); in Isr since 1930; att: Tchrs Sem, Pol, 1924-29; Agric Sch, Czech; Music Acad, Tel Aviv,

Jerusalem; studied under A Boscovitz; m. Shulamit Desau; c: Avner, Amir. Dir, Beisan Valley Conservatory; mem, Kibbutz Beit Alpha. Recipient: Min of Educ Prize for Alilot Gilboa cantata, 1955; Nissimow Prize for 10 choir songs, 1955; Tel Aviv Munic Engel Prize for Concert for Violin and Orch, 1956; Kol Israel Prize for Quarter for Two Flutes, Cello and Piano, 1958. Home: Kibbutz Beit Alpha, Isr.

YOFFEY, Joseph Mendel, Isr, physician; b. Manchester, Eng, July 10, 1902; s. Israel and Pere (Jaffe); MD, Manchester U, 1928, DSc, 1940; FRCS, Eng, 1932; m. Betty Gillis, July 28, 1940; c: Naomi Tsur, Judith Boxer, Deborah Freeman. Prof em, anat, U of Bristol, Eng, since 1967; visiting prof, Heb U, Jerusalem, since 1969; fmr: Hunterian prof, Royal Coll of Surgs, Eng; visiting prof: U of Wash, Seattle; U of SF, Cal; John Curtin Sch of Med Research, Austr Natl U. Vice-pres, ZF, Gt Brit and Ir; pres, Bristol Heb Cong. Author: Quantitative Cellular Haematology, 1960; co-author: Lymphatics, Lymph and Lymphoid Tissue, 1940. Recipient: Knight of Dannebrog, first grade, 1961; John Hunter Triennial Medal, Royal Coll of Surgs, Eng, 1967. Home: 1 Rehov Degania, Jerusalem, Isr. Office: Heb U, Jerusalem, Isr.

YOGEV, Samuel, Isr, psychologist; b. Krakow, Pol, Mar 5, 1915; s. Peretz and Ernestine (Körner) Jungerwirth; in Isr since 1935; dipl, psych, Acad for Applied Psych, Zurich, 1962; dipl, graphology, Graphology Sem, Bern, 1963; m. Jenny Propper; c: Ram, Orna. Lectr, Bar Ilan U, Ramat Gan, sonce 1964; col, asst commn of prisons, since 1965. Mem: Intl Police Offs Assn; Swiss Psych Assn; Swiss Graphologists Assn; Sci Council, Acad of Applied Psych. Recipient: Independence, Sinai, Isr Fighters', Six Days War Decorations. Home: 25 Oded St, Ramat Chen, Isr. Office: 8 Het St, Tel Aviv, Isr.

YOLLES, Ephraim Eliezer, US, rabbi; b. Sambor, Aus, Jan 14, 1894; s. Sholom and Esther (Luria-Teicher); in US since 1921; ordained rabbi: Chief Rabbi David Horowitz, Stanislav, Pol, 1912; Chief Rabbi Kopel Reich, Budapest, 1915; m. Betty Wolkenfeld, June, 1912 (decd); c: Sara; m. 2nd, Pepi Pollak, Aug 12, 1932; c: Esther, Shoshanna. Head, Orthodox Rabbinate, Beth Din, Phila, since 1949; rabbi, Kerem Isr Syn, since 1921; asst rabbi, instr, Talmudic law, J Comty of Stryi, Pol, 1916-21; rabbi, co-org, JCC, 1928-32; United Orthodox Congs, 1935-38; Mizrachi Org, since 1938, all Phila, Pa. Hon pres: Union Orthodox Rabbis of US and Can, since 1965; Mizrachi Org, Phila, since 1940; chmn, exec bd, United Orthodox Rabbinate, Phila, since 1935. Author: Kiswei Achiezer, 1933; K'tzei Hahor, Horei B'somim, 1965; contbr to Talmudical publs. Home and study: 5601 Woodcrest Ave, Philadelphia, Pa.

YOLLES, Stanley Fausst, US, government official; b. NYC, Apr 19, 1919; s. Louis and Rose (Fausst); AB, Bklyn Coll, 1939; AM, Harvard U, 1940; MD, NYU, 1950; MPH, Johns Hopkins U, 1957; m. Tamaratk Knigin, Oct 10, 1942; c: Melanie, Jennifer. Dir, Natl Inst of Mh, since 1964; acting dir, 1964, dep dir, 1963-64, asso dir, extramural progs, 1960-63, dir, Mh Study Cen, Comty Services Br, 1957-60, asso dir, 1955-57, staff psycht, 1954; clinical prof, psycht, George Wash U, since 1967; parasitologist: Army Med Sch, Wash, DC, 1940-41; US Army Engr Dept, Brit Guiana, S Amer, 1941; US Army, sector epidemiological lab, Trinidad, 1941-43, asso dir, 1943-45, CO, 1945-46; guest lectr, tropical med, NYU, Coll of Med, postgrad courses, 1947-48; commissioned, USPHS, 1950; Porter Award lectr, Assn of Mil Surgs of US, 1966; dist alumni lectr, NYU Sch of Med, 1966; George Kirby Collier lectr, U Rochester Med Sch, 1967; Herman Goldman intl lectr, NY Med Coll, NY, 1968; visiting lectr, Harvard U, dept of psycht, since 1963; visiting lectr: Sch of Hygiene and Public Health, Johns Hopkins U, 1964-68; U of Colo Med Cen, dept psycht, 1969. Lt, USN, 1944-46; rear admiral, 1964, in USPHS since 1950. F: Amer Coll Psychts; Amer Psycht Assn; Amer Public Health Assn; Amer Assn of Suicidology; mem: AAAS; AMA, Mh council; Amer Psychopath Assn; Amer Soc Parasitologists; Group for Advancement of Psycht; Md Public Health Assn; NY Acad Scis; Pan Amer Med Assn; Wash Psycht Soc; Woeld Fed for Mh; Med Soc of St Elizabeth Hosp; Alpha Omega Alpha; Intl Narcotic Enforcement Offs Assn; psycht, neur, and psych service, VA adv comm; Profsl Adv Bd, Daytop Village, Inc; spec adv, Bd Educ, NYC; bd trustees, NY Sch Psycht; Fed Panel on Early Childhood; profsl adv bd, Intl Comm against Mental Illness; WHO expert adv panel on Mh; White House Ad Hoc Comm Drug Abuse Research and Educ; fmr: chmn:

Public Health Service Inter-Bur Comm on Narcotic Drug Addiction; Hofheimer Prize Bd, Amer Psycht Assn; Comm on Fed Govt Health Agcys; Interdepartmental Comm on Narcotics. Asso ed bd, jour, Diseases of the Nervous System, since 1968; ed adv bd, Medical Insight, since 1969; bd eds, Psychiatry Digest, since 1965; contbr to: sci jours and mags; Ency Britannica. Recipient: Meritorious Service Medal, HEW, USPHS, 1966; Dist Alumnus Award, Bklyn Coll, CUNY, 1966; Porter Award, Assn of Mil Surgs, US, Wash, DC, 1966; Dist Service Medal, HEW, USPHS, 1969. Spec interests: photography, Egyptology, archaeol, model RRs, philately. Home: 5206 Locust Ave, Bethesda, Md. Office: 5454 Wisconsin Ave, Chevy Chase, Md.

YONATHAN, Nathan, Isr, teacher, author; b. Kiev, Russ, Sep 20, 1923; s. Yona and Lea (Buchman) Klein; in Isr since 1925; tchr, Sem Hakibbutzim, Tel Aviv, 1948; att Heb U, Jerusalem, 1956-57; m. Tsfira, 1950; c: Lior, Ziv. Tchr, Sem Hakibbutzim; head, Educ Dept, Hashomer Hatzair Org. Author: Shvilei Afar, 1951; El haNirim, 1954; Asher Ahavnu, 1957; Bein Aviv leAnan, 1959; Shirim leOrech haHof, 1962; Lilach miKvutzat Ilanot, 1963; Shirei Afar veRuah, 1965; Ad Sof haKaitz, 1968. Sgt, IDF. Delg, Youth Org, Hashomer hatzair, NY, 1963, 1966. Recipient: Lamdan Award, Ramat Gan Munic, 1960; Azmaut Award, Emek Yezreel Zone, 1962. Home: Kibbutz Sarid, Isr.

YOOD, Bertram, US, educator; b. Bayonne, NJ, Jan 6, 1917; s. Benjamin and Fannie (Kowal); BS, Yale U, 1938; MS, Cal Inst Tech, 1939; att Brown U, 1939-41; PhD, Yale U, 1947; m. Shirley Saffran, Jan 25, 1944; c: Robert, Janet, Arthur. Prof, math, U of Ore, since 1960, on fac since 1953; visiting prof, U of Edinburgh, 1969-70; asst prof, Cornell U, 1949-53; visiting asso prof, U Cal, Berkeley, 1956-57; research asso, Yale U, 1958-59; mem, Inst for Advanced Study, Princeton, 1961-62. Lt, USNR, 1941-45. Mem: Amer Math Soc; Sigma Xi; Phi Beta Kappa. Contbr to profsl jours. Home: 70 W 35 Place, Eugene, Ore. Office: U of Oregon, Eugene, Ore.

YORAN, Shalom, Isr, business exec; b. Warsaw, Pol, Mar 23, 1923; s. Shmuel and Hanna (Reichert) Sznycer; in Isr since 1946; att Tech Inst, Tel Aviv; flight engr, Spartan Sch of Aeronautics, 1951; aeronautical engr, London, 1968; m. Varda Granevsky, June 29, 1954; c: Yael, Daphna. Vice-pres, Isr Aircraft Ind, since 1964, gen mgr, Bedek Aviation Div, since 1968, dir, aircraft maintenance, 1964-68, asst dir, 1958-60; training off, 1954-58, all Isr Aircraft Ind. Off, IAF, 1948-54. Asso f, Royal Aeronautical Soc, London. Hobbies: photography, politics. Home: 91 University St, Ramat Aviv, Isr. Office: Lod Airport, Isr.

YOSHA, Aveshalom, Isr, business exec; b. Tel Aviv, Feb 29, 1916; s. Teodor and Beia; m. Miriam Gordon, Sep 24, 1940; c: Matityahu, Dafna. Dep mgr, Kupat Am Bank; vice-chmn, Isr Chess Fed. Author: Know How to Play Chess, 1967; The Israel Chess Guide, 1967. Home: 5 Epstein St, Tel Aviv, Isr. Office: Kupat Am Bank, Tel Aviv, Isr.

YOSHOR, Moses M, US, rabbi; b. Pol, Nov 23, 1896; s. David and Sarah (Bergstein); in US since 1921; att: Yeshivoth in Pol; Rabbi Isaac Elchanan Theol Sem; CCNY; m. Susanna Weizman, Dec 13, 1927; c: Joshua, Debora. Rabbi: New Brighton J Cen, since 1934; Cong Adath Wolkowisk, NY, 1921-22; Cong Ahavath Achim, Staten I, NY, 1922-25; Cong Tifereth Torah, Bensonhurst, NY, 1925-34. Vice-pres, Rabb Bd Gtr NY; pres: Rabb Org, Shore Front; Amer comm, Yeshiva Petach Tikva, Isr. Author: Dos Leben un Shafen for Hafetz Hayim, 2 vols, 1937; Saint and Sage, 1937; Israel in the Ranks, 1940; Hahafetz Hayim Hayov Upoolev, 3 vols, 1958-60; contbr of biographies, lit sketches and scholarly essays. Home: 711 Brightwater Court, Brooklyn, NY. Study: 184 Brighton 11 St, Brooklyn, NY.

YOUDOVIN, Ira S, US, rabbi; b. NYC, Apr 10, 1941; s. Julius and Ann (Goldberg); BA, Columbia, 1962; BHL, MA, ordained rabbi, HUC-JIR, 1968; m. Susan Welber, Aug 26, 1926; c: Julie. J chaplain, USAF, since 1968; rabbi, Temple Isaiah, Stony Brook, NY, 1965-68. Home and study: 824 CSG (BCH) APO San Francisco, 96239.

YOUNG, Harold E, US, forester, educator; b. Arlington, Mass, Sep 4, 1917; s. Harry and Rosa (Caplan); BS, U of Me, 1937; MF, Duke U, 1946, PhD, 1948; m. Audrey London, Feb 20, 1943; c: Marjorie, Susan, Emily, Michael. Prof, Sch of Forestry, U of Me, ince 1961, fac mem since 1948; with US Forest Service, 1937-40; asst, asso forester, Me Agric Experiment

Station, 1953-61; Fulbright research scholar, Norway, 1963-64; visiting lectr, Austr Natl U, Canberra, 1968-69. US Army, 1942-46. F, AAAS; mem: Soc Amer Foresters, chmn, div educ, 1963, div forest mensuration, 1964; Amer Soc Plant Phys; Soil Sci Soc of Amer; Ecology Soc; Amer Soc Photogrammetry; Amer Stat Assn; Biometrics Soc; Sigma Xi; Xi Sigma Pi. Contbr to profsl jours. Home: 77 Forest Ave, Orono, Me. Office: U of Me, Orono, Me.

YOUNG, Joseph L, US, artist, author, educator; b. Pittsburgh, Pa, Nov 27, 1919; s. Louis and Jennie (Eger); AB, Westminster Coll, New Wilmington, Pa, 1941, hon DLitt, 1959; grad, Boston Mus Sch of Fine Arts, Mass, 1951; grad studies: Carnegie and Mass Inst of Tech; Art Students League, NY; Cranbrook Acad of Art; Amer Acad, Rome; m. Millicent Goldstein, June 19, 1949; c: Leslie, Cecily. Found chmn, Dept Architectural Arts, Brooks Inst Sch Fine Arts, Santa Barbara, Cal; chmn, dept visual arts, U of Judaism, LA, since 1962; found, dir, Joseph Young Mosaic Workshop, LA, since 1952; W Coast cons, Reinhold Pub Co, since 1960; asso ed, Creative Crafts mag; one-man shows: Architectural League, NY; City of Pittsburgh Arts & Crafts Cen, Pa; Falk-Raboff Gal, LA; Desert Mus, Palm Springs; exhbs: Boston Mus Fine Arts; Carnegie Mus Fine Arts; LA Co Mus; Natl Gal, Wash; Butler Art Inst; Oakland Art Mus; Sacramento State Fair; Amer Inst Architecture Arts; Idyllwild Arts Found; Brandeis Camp Inst; prin commns: cantilevered mural, City of LA Police Bldg; foyer murals, Temple Emanuel, Beverly Hills, Cal; outdoor mural, Don Bosco HS, San Gabriel, Cal; murals, Southland Shopping Cen, Minneapolis; Chapel, Our Lady of Lourdes, E LA; plastic mural, model home, Home Show, LA; Memorial Gate, Eden Memorial Park, San Fernando, Cal; granite sculptured plaque, Sinai Temple, Westwood, Cal; Co of LA Hall of Records, LA; Memorial panels, Shalom Memorial Park, Palatine, Ill; murals for presentation, BVM Church, Midland, Pa; bas-relief murals and art work, Temple Beth Emet, Anaheim, Cal; War Memorial fresco, Boston Mus Sch Fine Arts; metal sculpture and art work, Sinai Temple, Glendale, Cal; ourdoor mural panel, Courtyard Silversmiths, Boston, Mass; mosaic mural, Hollenbeck Police Sta, LA; mosaic mural, Loyola Coll, LA; mosaics for educ instns: Westminster Coll, New Wilmington, Pa; Ceres Union HS, Ceres, Cal; Brandeis Inst, Santa Susanna, Cal; Fresno HS, Fresno, Cal; 14 panel mosaic mural, Math Sci Bldg, UCLA; mosaics for commercial structures: Texaco Oil Bldg, LA; Merlin Med Cen, Santa Barbara; Cornhusker Hotel, Lincoln, Neb; Searson & Hammill Stock Exch, Santa Barbara; Horseshoe Club, Gardena, Cal; works in pvt collections. Reporter, United Press, 1941-43; lectr, Tufts Coll, 1949; mem fac, Boston Mus Sch, 1950; survey, govt sponsored art progs, Min of Educ, Isr; lectr, It Govt, Venice, Florence, Rome, 1959. USAAC, 1943-46. F: Intl Inst of Arts and Letters; Amer Acad of Rome, It; mem: Natl Soc Mural Painters; Amer Craftsmen's Council; Artists Equity Assn, natl vice-pres, 1961-62, chmn, S Cal chap, 1959-61; S Cal Designer Craftsmen; Architectural Guild; Shaw Soc, S Cal; Asso Artists, Pittsburgh; Westwood Village Art Assn; Watt's Towers Comm; Pi Delta Epsilon; Sphinx; Kappa Phi Lambda of Sigma Nu. Author: A Course in Making Mosaics, 1957; Principles and Practices, 1963; work represented in: documentary film, The World of Mosaic; Graphis Annual; Landscape for You, 1955; Dialogues in Art, on KNBC/TV, 1968; designed set, commemoration coins, 12 tribes of Isr; contbr to art publs. Recipient: Army Arts Contest Award, 1944; Edwin Austin Abbey Scholarship, 1949; Albert H Whitin f, 1951; Huntington Hartford Found f, 1953; award of merit, Amer Inst of Architects, for film The World of Mosaic, 1958; award of merit, Cal State Fair, 1959. Home: 7917 ½ W Norton Ave, Los Angeles, Cal. Studio: 8426 Melrose Ave, Los Angeles, Cal.

YOUNG, Milton, US, attorney, educator; b. NYC, May 11, 1910; s. Louis and Yetta (Karpman) Yanowich; LLB, Fordham U, 1931; m. Marion Peterfreund, Jan 29, 1933; c: Judith Mallin, Lois Erlichman. Partner, Young, Kaplan & Edelstein, since 1948; lectr: Practising Law Inst, since 1946; NYU Sch of Law, 1949-53. Asst tax counsel, Off of US Alien Property Custodian, 1942-45; adv bd, NYU Tax Inst, 1954-63; mem, Adv Group to Commn of Internal Revenue, 1964. Contbr to legal jours. Home: 60 Burkewood Rd, Mt Vernon, NY. Office: 277 Park Ave, New York, NY.

YOUNGMAN, Moshe, Isr, author, school insp; b. Hodorov, Pol, Jan 4, 1922; s. Itzhak and Rachel (Landman); in Isr since 1941; m. Miriam Slonimchik, Apr 2, 1946; c: Itzhak, Shulamit. Sch insp since 1967; prin, Shalom Aleichem Elem Sch, 1950-67. Author: In Hinerplet, 1946; In Shotn Fun Moiled, 1954; Voise Toiern, 1964, all Yiddish poems; Stories of Warsaw, 1966; Schmejhlen fun Eretz-Hakodesh, 1969; contbr of poems, trans, essays to Yiddish mag. Recipient: prizes: DP org, Rome; Acad of J Lit, Paris, WJC; J PEN Club, US, 1966; "Opatoshu", WJC, Paris, 1967. Home: 28 Hatzipornaim St, Tivon, Isr. Office: Nazareth, Isr.

YSHANI, Dan Iesanu, Isr, organization exec; b. Bucharest, Rum, Sep 25, 1905; s. Max and Bela (Starck) Ieşanu; in Isr since 1957; BEcon, Econ HS, Bucharest; m. Clara Abramovici. Chief, fgn press dept, Lab Archives of Histadrut; fmr, mgr, Shell repr, Rum. Mem, mgn bd: Rum sect, Isr Lab Party; Union of Rum J in Isr; mem exec, Brith Asserei Zion; fmr: gen secy: Young Zionist Assn, Rum; Ihud Poalei Zion-Zeirei Zion, Rum; vice-pres, Zionist Org, Rum, repr, Rum Joint Distribution Comm Exec; delg to WZCs; arrested and imprisoned for illegal Zionist activities, Rum; mem: cen comm, Mapai. Contbr ro press. Home: 3 Salvador St, Ramat Aviv, Isr. Office: 3 Weizmann St, Tel Aviv, Isr.

YUDKIN, John, Eng, nutritionist; b. London, Eng, Aug 8, 1910; s. Louis and Sarah (Itkin); BSc, London U, 1931; MA, Cambridge U, 1938; PhD, MD; m. Emily Himmelweit, Dec 17, 1933; c: Michael, Jonathan, Jeremy. Prof, head, dept of nutrition, Queen Elizabeth Coll, London U, since 1954; dir, med studies, Christ Coll, Cambridge, 1941-43; prof, phys, London U, 1945-54. Capt, Brit Army MC, 1943-45. Author: This Slimming Business, 1958; The Slimmer's Cook Book,

1960. Pres, W London JPA; vice-chmn, Brit OSE. Hobby: collecting modern paintings, med and sci books. Home: 16 Holly Walk, London NW3, Eng. Office: Queen Elizabeth College, London U, London W8, Eng.

YUTAR, Percy, S Afr, attorney, government official; b. Cape Town, July 19, 1911; s. David and Rose (Promnick); BA, U of Cape Town, 1931, LLB, 1933, LLM, 1935, LLD, 1938; m. Cecilia Fainsinger, Mar 30, 1948; c: David. Atty gen, Orange Free State, since 1968, with Justice Dept since 1939. Fmr pres, United Heb Cong, Johannesburg; mem, sch comm, Parktown Boys HS; fmr, mem council: United Heb Schs, Johannesburg; S Afr Bd J Educ; Fed of Syns. Recipient: Queens Medal; Sr Counsel award. Hobbies: music, soccer, cricket. Home: 7 Riviera Rd, Killarney, Johannesburg, S Afr. Office: 64 Supreme Court, Bloemfontein, S Afr.

YUVAL, Moshe, Isr, government official; b. Dwinsk, Latvia, Sep 24, 1913; s. Zalman and Chava (Berger) Zimbel; in Isr since 1932; att Heb U, Jerusalem, 1932-37; m. Tamar Roos, Mar 30, 1952; c: Naomi, Boaz. Ambass of Isr: Peru, since 1967; Bolivia, since 1968; various appointments, Min Fgn Affairs, since 1948; liaison off, JA for Pal, 1936-48; personal asst to Moshe Sharett, 1940-43. Mem, JA delg to UN, 1947-68; fmr, secy gen, Students Fed; mem: Histadrut; Isr Lab Party; B'nai B'rith. Recipient: Haganah, Hitnadvut, Isr Fighters' Medals. Home: 7 Aza St, Jerusalem, Isr. Office: Min of Fgn Affairs, Jerusalem, Isr.

Z

ZABARSKY, Abraham, Isr, economist, business exec; b. Fastov, Russ, Mar 29, 1897; s. Zalman and Henya; in Isr since 1924; JD, U Kharkov, 1920; m. Sara Sragovitz, 1920; c: Haviva. Mgr: Bank Hapoalim Ltd, since 1949; Isr Amer Ind Devl Bank, since 1956; chmn, Housing Mortgage Bank; mem bd, Bank of Isr, since 1954; vice-chmn, Isr Ind Bank, since 1957; mem, bd dirs, Ampal—Isr Trading Corp, NY; chmn: Hasneh Ins Corp, since 1956; Delek Petroleum Corp; mgr: Coop Banks Union, Lith, 1921-24; Hamashbir, 1924; Kupat Milve Bank, 1925-49; secy, Coops Cen, 1925-45, all Tel Aviv. Mem: Histadrut Council; gen council, Mapai; bd, Intl Coop Bank, Basel; fmr: Tel Aviv City Council; cen comm, Intl Alliance of Coops. Author: The Jewish Cooperative Movement in Palestine; mem, ed bd, Econ Quarterly, Tel Aviv. Home: 11 Keren Kayemet Blvd, Tel Aviv, Isr. Office: 50 Rothschild Blvd, Tel Aviv, Isr.

ZADEK, Isidore, US, surgeon; b. Montgomery, Ala, Dec 15, 1890; s. Sigmund and Kate (Fraleigh); BS, Ala Poly Inst, 1910; MD, Johns Hopkins U Med Sch, 1914; m. Kate Engle, Sep 21, 1922; m. 2nd, Janet Wolf, Oct 14, 1944; c: Robert, David. Ret, 1969; cons, Mt Vernon Hosp; fmr: chief orthopedic surg, Mt Vernon Hosp; cons, Hosp for Jt Diseases, NYC. Mem: Alpha Omega Alpha; AMA; Amer Orthopedic Assn; Acad Orthopedic Surgs; f: Amer Acad Surgs; NY Acad Med; Soc Intl de Chirurgie Orthopedique et de Traumatologie. Contbr to med jours. Home: 1200 Midland Ave, Bronxville, NY.

ZADOK, Haim Joseph, Isr, legislator, attorney; b. Wolka-Tanewska, Pol, Oct 2, 1913; s. Abraham and Malka; in Isr since 1935; att Warsaw U, Pol, 1934-35; dipl, Govt Law Sch, Jerusalem, 1942; m. Esther Berger, 1941; c: Ruth, Ophra. MK since 1959, chmn, Kenesset Constitutional Comm, mem, defense and fgn affairs comm; Isr observer to Consultative Assembly of Council of Eur; in pvt law practice; fmr: bldg laborer; dep atty gen, Min of Justice, 1949-52; lectr, Tel Aviv U, 1954-59; Min of Commerce and Ind, 1965-66. Off, Haganah, J Settlement Police; IDF, 1948-49; maj, res, Judge of Appeal Court Martial. Mem: perm comm, Heb U; Isr Bar. Home: Hamitnadev St, Afeka, Isr. Office: 33 Lilienblum St, Tel Aviv, Isr.

ZAFREN, Herbert C, US, librarian; b. Baltimore, Md, Aug 25, 1925; s. Morris and Sadie (Edlavitch); BA, Johns Hopkins U, 1944; dipl, Baltimore Heb Coll, 1944, hon LHD, 1969; AM, U of Mich, 1950; m. Miriam Koenigsberg, Feb 11, 1951; c: Victor, Edith. Dir of librs, HUC-JIR, since 1966, prof, J bibliography, since 1968, libr since 1950; exec dir, Amer J Periodical Cen, since 1956; ed, Studies in Bibliography and Booklore, since 1953. USN, 1944-46. Mem: Amer Libr Assn; Amer Hist Assn; Amer J Hist Soc; Amer Acad for J Research; Medieval Acad of Amer; AAUP; Assn of J Librs; Phi Beta Kappa; club, Grolier. Contbr to profsl jours. Home: 7320 Eastlawn Dr, Cincinnati, O. Office: 3101 Clifton Ave, Cincinnati, O.

ZAGAT, Eugene H, US, realtor; b. NYC, Oct 9, 1909; s. Paul and Anna (Klatzkin); BA, cum laude, Dartmouth Coll, 1930; att: Oxford U, 1929; Sorbonne, 1930; Harvard Law Sch, 1931; Columbia U, 1932; m. Cornelia Ernst, June 12, 1935 (div); c: Eugene, Cornelia; m. 2nd, Elizabeth McNichol. Real estate bus since 1935; pres, treas: Algonquin Realty Corp; Progressive Income Corp; Donmar Realty Corp; Paul H Zagat and Co; Phoenix Realty Corp; fmr: Cumulative Holding Corp; Devl Revenue Corp; Intercontinental Realty Corp; asso with NY Times, 1931-35; lectr, real estate, CCNY. Dir: Amer Council for Nationalities Service; Broadway Assn; 34 St Midtown Assn; mem: comm on bd mem for cens, NY FJP; Friends of Philharmonic; exec comm: League of W Side Orgs; Real Estate Bd of NY; advance gifts comm, March of Dimes Natl Found; convener, Planned Parenthood Assn of Amer; co-chmn, hon mem, chmn, real estate div, NY div, Assn for Mentally Retarded Children; fmr: vice-pres, trustee, Educ Alliance; dir: NY div, JWB; Surprise Lake Camp; area chmn, 4th War Loan, NYC; pres: Pi Lambda Phi; Alpha

Delta Sigma; Delta Omicron Gamma, Dartmouth chaps; club, Dartmouth Coll. Home: 799 Park Ave, New York, NY.

ZAHAVI, Yacov, Isr, transportation and traffic engr; b. Petah Tikva, Isr, July 13, 1926; s. Israel and Shoshana (Oransky); dipl, CE, Technion, 1950; m. Dahlia Gutmann, May 26, 1953; c: Mina, Ron. Partner, Kolin and Zahavi, transp and traffic engrs, since 1954; dep chief traffic engr: Munic of Tel Aviv-Jaffa, 1951-52; Min of Transp, 1953-54; lectr, Technion. Served IAF. Prin contribs: found: first transp and traffic engr off in Isr, 1954; first factory in Isr for elec traffic signals, 1960. Mem: Tech Council, Assn of Engrs and Archs in Isr; AM Inst of Traffic Engrs, US; SM Highway Research Bd, US; intl corresp, Intl Commn on Illumination; gen secy, Isr Chess Fed, 1954-58. Ed, haMatos, aviation monthly, since 1954; contbr to: Traffic Engr, US; Sixth Intl Study Week in Traffic, Traffic Engr and Control, Eng. Hobbies: aviation, chess. Home: 2 Hamelitz St, Tel Aviv, Isr. Office: 4 Herzl St, Tel Aviv, Isr.

ZAHAVY, Zev, US, rabbi, author; b. NYC, Sep 8, 1920; s. David and Anna (Epstein); BA, Yeshiva U, 1939, MHL, 1948, PhD, 1959; ordained rabbi, Rabbi Isaac Elchanan Theol Sem, 1942; MA, Columbia U, 1959; m. Edith Medine, July 1, 1947; c: Tzvee, Reuvain, Miryam. Prof, Eng and lit, CUNY, since 1964; pres, dir, Limud Soc-Intl Soc for J Knowledge, since 1962; counselor, B'nai B'rith Hillel, since 1966; asst rabbi, W Side Institutional Syn, 1943-45; asso rabbi, Cong Ohab Zedek, 1945-52; rabbi, Cong Zichron Ephraim, 1952-61; prin, Park E Day Sch, 1954-59; fac mem, Grad Sch of Educ, Yeshiva U, 1959-61. natl dir, dept of comty consultation, Amer Assn J Educ, 1961-62. Hon vice-pres, Manhattan div, AJCong; vice-pres, NY region, RabCA, 1956-57; chmn, J Orthodox div, UN Appeal for Children, 1948; mem, exec bd: Rabb Alumni Assn; NY Bd of Rabbis, 1950-55; chief chaplain, Manhattan Civil Defense Admn, mem chaplains adv bd, NY State Civil Defense Admn, 1953; mem: Mizrachi Org Amer; Agudath Isr; Yorkville Wfr Council; Lenox Hill Wfr Assn; ZOA; AAUP; Natl Council Tchrs of Eng; MLA; Leg Conf, NY. Author: The Halacha in the Book of Jubilees, 1948; Independence and Modernity, 1953; A History and Evaluation of Jewish Religious Broadcasting, 1959; Dynamic Judaism 1960; The Life and Responsa of Rabbi Joseph Kolon, 1961; Hearken, Ye Heavens, 1963. Home: 210 E 68 St, New York, NY.

ZAHN, Louis, US business exec; b. Koenigsberg, Ger, Sep 24, 1909; s. Abraham and Bella (Bobtelsky); in US since 1910; m. Frieda Kaplan, Aug 12, 1934; c: Melvyn, Barbara Gunther. Pres, Louis Zahn Drug Co, since 1932. Bd trustees, Shimer Coll; bd govs, Gottlieb Memorial Hosp; bd dirs: Sears Bank & Trust Co; Exec House; natl chmn, Karyn Kupcinet Playhouse, Shimer Coll; chmn: Gtr Chgo Isr Bond Drive, 1960-62; bd govs, Isr Bond Drive, 1962; mem, Shriners; clubs: Covenant; Standard; Bryn Mawr Country. Recipient: Horatio Alger Award, 1957; John F Kennedy Peace Award, 1964. Home: 1140 NE Ave, Oak Park, Ill. Office: 1930 George St, Melrose Park, Ill.

ZAHN, Shammai, Eng, rabbi; b. Nuremberg, Ger, July 6, 1920; s. Siegmund and Pessel (Krischer); in Eng since 1939; ordained rabbi, Inst for Higher Rabb Studies, Gateshead, 1946; m. Lotte Bergmann, May 1, 1945; c: Rutleah Ehrentreu, Abraham, Michael, David. Prin, Sunderland Talmudical Coll, since 1946. Home: 11 The Oaks East, Sunderland, Eng. Office: 1-2 The Cedars, Sunderland, Eng.

ZAHTZ, Hyman, US, physician; b. St Louis, Mo, Aug 6, 1921; s. Haskel and Rose (Roitman); BS, St Louis U, 1942, MD, 1946; m. Masha Borvick, Dec 14, 1947; c: Merrill, Alan, Gerald, Joyce. Pvt practice, ped and ped card, since 1952; att staff: LI J Hosp, ped and ped card, since 1954; chief, ped cardiac clinic, Queens Gen Hosp, since 1954; chief, ped cardiac clinic, Jamaica Hosp, since 1960; cons, Queensborough Card, Bur of Handicapped Children, Dept of Health, since 1964. Capt, US Army MC, 1947-48. Cert ped, Amer

Acad Peds, 1954; f: Amer Acad Peds; Amer Coll Card; Amer Coll Chest Phys; pres: Yeshiva HS, Queens, since 1967; Young Isr, Kew Gardens Hills, 1964-66; mem, bd dirs, Yeshiva Rabbi Dov Revel, since 1956, fmr vice-pres; mem: exec comm, Commn on Syn Relations, FJP, since 1960; AMA; Queens Co Med Soc; Queens Ped Soc; AHA; NY Heart Assn; Queensborough Soc for Arts and Crafts; life, Phi Delta Epsilon; Amer Orthodox J Scis; Hapoel Hamizrachi. Contbr, health column, The J Parent Mag. Recipient: Award of Honor, FJP, 1959; Citation of Honor, Talmud Torah of Queens, 1966; Guest of Honor, Young Isr of Kew Gardens Hills, 1968; Shofer award, Natl Council of Young Isr, 1969. Hobby: oil and water color painting. Home and office: 147-15 70 Rd, Flushing, NY.

ZAICHYK, Baruch, S Afr, rabbi; b. Bklyn, NY, May 5, 1938; s. Chaim and Gita (Koschevsky); in S Afr since 1967; ordained rabbi, Tifereth Jerusalem, NY, 1961; DD, Philathea, Ontario, Can, 1965; m. Phoebe Berger, May 26, 1960; c: Miriam, Rachel, Sarah. Rabbi: Emmarentia Heb Cong, Johannesburg, since 1967; Beth Isr Cong, Richmond, Va, 1962-67. Council mem: Rabbis' Org; Fed of Syns; Yeshiva Coll of Johannesburg, all S Afr; fmr: educ dir, B'nai B'rith of New Eng; bd dir, J Comty Cen, Richmond. Contbr to press. Home: 37 Buffalo Rd, Emmarentia, Johannesburg, S Afr. Study: 129 Barry Hertzog Ave, Johannesburg, S Afr.

ZAIDENS, Sadie H, US, psychiatrist; b. NYC, Apr 22, 1910; d. Nathan and Sterra (Levine); MD, George Wash U, 1933; m. Morris Brand, June 2, 1933; c: Debra. Pvt practice, psycht and dermat, since 1933; clinical prof, psycht, Mt Sinai Sch of Med, liaison, dept dermat. Mem: Acad Dermat; Acad Psychan; Soc Psychoanalytic Phys. Contbr to med jours. Hobbies: music, theater, painting, sculpture. Office: 333 W 56 St, New York, NY.

ZAITSCHEK, Elazar Alois, Isr, educator; b. Brno, Czech, Sep 5, 1899; s. Heinrich and Katharina (Strauss); in Isr since 1939; Ing Agron, Hochschule für Bodenkultur, Vienna, 1924; PhD, Heb U, Jerusalem, 1961; m. Berta Frischer; c: Gershom. Lectr, Bar Ilan U, Ramat Gan, since 1961; tchr: secondary sch, Czech, 1925-39; Kibbutz Geva, 1940-41; admn off, Heb U, Jerusalem, 1946-64. Served WWI, WWII, War of Independence. Contbr to profsl publs. Home: 37 Yehoshua Ben Jerusalem, Isr. Office: Bar Ilan U, Ramat Gan, Isr.

ZAJICEK, Gershom, Isr, physician; b. Brno, Czech, July 4, 1929; s. Elazar and Bilha (Frischer); in Isr since 1939; att premed sch, Bern, Switz, 1950-52; MD, Heb U, Med Sch, Jerusalem, 1956; m. Zipora Zelikowitz, Oct 4, 1956; c: Irit, Ofer, Uri, Ram. Sr lectr, experimental med, cancer research, Heb U Hadassah Med Sch, Jerusalem, since 1969, jr path, 1956-57, asst, 1957-60, lectr, 1960-69. Palmach, War of Independence. Mem: IMA; Eur Soc for Clinical Inves; Isr Soc Phys and Pharm. Contbr to med and sci jours. Spec interest: biomed applications of computer. Home: 30 Yehoshua Ben Nun St, Jerusalem, Isr. Office: Hadassah Med Sch, Jerusalem, Isr.

ZAJICEK, Zipora, Isr, physician; b. Baranovitz, Pol, Aug 7, 1933; d. Zvi and Rivka (Berkovitz) Zelikovitz; in Isr since 1933; MD, Heb U Med Sch, Jerusalem, 1957; m. Gershom, Oct 4, 1956; c: Irit, Ofer, Uri, Ram. Phys since 1959; with Kupat Holim, Prozinin Br, since 1961. Home: 30 Yeshoshua Ben Nun St, Jerusalem, Isr. Office: Kupat Holim Prozinin, Jerusalem, Isr.

ZAK, David Zvi, Isr, artist; b. Warsaw, Pol, May 1, 1904; s. Eliahu and Pauline (Frendzel); in Isr ince 1920; att Bezalel Art Sch, Jerusalem; m. Judith Berkowitz, Sep 15, 1942; c: Eyra. One-man shows: Cairo; Isr; S Afr; J Mus, NY; repr in various pvt collections and instns; found, Artists House, Jerusalem; fmr: railwayman, commercial artist. Camouflage expert, RAF, WW II. Fmr mem: cen comm: Railway Workers; Isr Artists and Sculptors Soc. Pub: album, Jerusalem, 1965. Home and studio: 4 Itzhak Kaznelson St, Jerusalem, Isr.

ZAK, Moshe I, Isr, editor; b. Pol, July 10, 1918; s. Chaim, and Rachel (Kaplan); in Isr since 1936; att Heb U, Jerusalem, 1936-40; m. Sara Barsky, Mar 24, 1957; c: Issar, Rachel Zeev. Ed, Maariv, Heb daily, weekend supplements, since 1961; mgn ed, Maariv evening paper, since 1956, fgn affairs corresp, 1948-56; mgr, Jerusalem Off, 1953. Dep chmn, Isr Press Council; mem comm, Isr Fgn Policy Assn, since 1952. Author: Contemporary Israeli Press, 1961. Home: 9 Struck St, Tel Aviv, Isr. Office: 2 Carlebach St, Tel Aviv, Isr.

ZAK, Shalom, Isr, banker; b. Berdiszev, Russ, 1901; s. Aharon and Bella (Rotblatt); in Isr since 1925; m. Penina Spreiser, 1923; c: Aviva Shulman, Ram. Mgr, Bank Hapoalim,Tel Aviv, since 1950; mem, bd mgmt: Gmul; Kupat Holim; Ind Devl Bank of Isr Ltd; Isr-Amer Ind Devl Bank; Isr Fuel Corp; Nir; Keren Gimlauth; mem, Kibbutz Givat Hashlosha. Prin contribs: one of first econs of settlement movement; found, Keren Hakibbutz Hameuhad; initiator of econ financial prog of settlement movement. Fmr mem, Munic Council, Petah Tikva; delg to 20th WZC. Contbr to daily press. Home: Kibbutz Givat Hashlosha, Isr. Office: 50 Rothschild Blvd, Tel Aviv, Isr.

ZAKAI, Moshe, Isr, electrical engr, educator; b. Sokolka, Pol, Dec 22, 1926; s. Eliezer and Rachel (Stavorovsky) Zakheim; in Isr since 1936; BSc, Technion, Haifa, 1951; PhD, U of Ill, Urbana, 1958; m. Shulamit Briskman, Dec 23, 1952; c: Tamar, Michal, Avinoam. Prof, elec engr, Technion, Haifa, since 1969, asso prof, 1965-69; sr sci, sci dept, Min of Defense, 1965. Pvt, IDF, 1948. Mem, Isr Natl Comm, Intl Radio Research Union. Contbr to sci jours. Home: 11 Adam Hacohen St, Haifa, Isr. Office: Technion, Haifa, Isr.

ZAKAY, David, Isr, journalist, editor; b. Ostroshitski-Gorodok, Russ, Oct 10, 1886; s. Itzchak and Hodah; in Isr since 1909; m. Rachel Aharonson; c: Yaakov, Hannah Zur, Avraham. Asso ed, Davar daily, since 1925; lectr, astronomy, Kol Isr; corresp, Zurich Observatory; tchr, Beer Tuvia and Gedera, until WW I; mem, cultural dept, Ahdut Haavoda, 1920-25; secy, Histadrut Haovdim, 1921-25. Fmr mem: cen comm, Tchrs Assn; Educ Council; Second Electoral Assembly; Brit Astronomical Assn; delg to 19th WZC. Contbr to press. Home: 9/3 Maoz Aviv, Tel Aviv, Isr. Office: 45 Shenkin St, Tel Aviv, Isr.

ZAKHEIM, Schlomo, Isr, attorney; b. Russ, Sep 1, 1899; s. Haim Nachman and Anna (Kagan); in Isr since 1920; grad: Commercial Inst, Kiev; Jerusalem Law Classes, 1932. Pvt practice since 1932; mem: Isr Peoples Supr Court, 1948; legal council, Isr, 1956-62. Mem, gen council, Isr Bar Assn, since 1962. Hobbies: paintings, music. Home: 16 Abraham Blvd, Ramat Gan, Isr. Office: 13 Dubnov St, Tel Aviv, Isr.

ZAKIN, Jacques Louis, US, educator; b. NYC, Jan 28, 1927; s. Mordecai and Ada (Fishbein); ChE, Cornell U, NY, 1949; MSc, Columbia U, NY, 1950; DEng, NYU, 1959; m. Laura Pienkny, June 11, 1950; c: Richard, David, Barbara, Emily, Susan. Prof, chem engr, U of Mo, since 1965; chem engr, Flintkote Research Labs, 1950-51; supt technologist, Socony Mobil Research Labs, 1951-62; visiting prof, chem engr, Technion, Haifa, 1968-69. USN, 1945-46. Prin contribs: research on turbulent drag reducing flows; structure of turbulence. Mem: bd, Rolla Comty Concert Assn; Amer Inst Chem Engrs; Soc Rheology; Amer Chen Soc; Sigma Xi; Phi Lambda Upsilon; Alpha Chi Sigma; fmr pres, secy, Rolla chap, AAUP. Contbr to sci jours. Hobbies: reading, tennis, J hist, archaeol. Home: Route 4, Rolla, Mo. Office: U of Mo, Rolla, Mo.

ZAKON, Samuel J, US, dermatologist, educator; b. Kiev, Russ, Dec 28, 1898; s. Joseph and Feiga (Sagalov); in US since 1913; AA, Lewis Inst, Chgo, Ill, 1920; MD, Eclectic Med Coll, Cinn, O, 1925; m. Dorothy Gavlin, Mar 11, 1934; c: Daniel, Diane. Prof em, dermat, Northwestern U Med Sch; hist, Amer Acad Dermat, since 1955; cons, Rest Haven; Park View Home; Orthodox J Home for Aged, since 1943. Pres: Mt Sinai Hosp med staff, Chgo, 1943-55; Chgo Dermat Soc, 1953-54; preceptor, Amer Bd Dermat; mem: Chgo Med Soc; Ill State Med Soc; AMA; Amer Acad Dermat and Syphilology; Soc for Inves Dermat; Amer Assn of Hist of Med; Assn of Amer Med Colls; Chgo Soc Med Hist; Phi Delta Epsilon, hon life; ZOA; AJCong; HIAS; B'nai B'rith. Contbr to sci jours. Spec interest: hist of med. Home: 5840 W Adams Blvd, Chicago, Ill. Office: 25 E Washington St, Chicago, Ill.

ZALEON, Isaac, US, jurist; b. Utica, NY, June 27, 1914; s. Joseph and Fanny (Berkowitz); AB, Syracuse U, 1935; att Albany Law Sch, 1938; m. Rae Gordon, Aug 18, 1940; c: Donna, Beverly. Family Court Judge, since 1964; clerk, NY State Assembly, 1936-50; clerk, Comm on Taxation, NY State Assembly, 1958; city judge, Gloversville, NY, 1959-64, asst city judge, 1956-59. US Army, 1943-45. Pres: B'nai B'rith Lodge; J Comty Cen; NY State sect, JWB, 1963-65; dir: Fulton Co TB and Heart Assn; Knesseth Isr Syn; fmr: commn, Glove Cities Post No 402; chmn, Fulton Co Vets Council; mem: Amer Legion; VFW; 69th Infantry Div Assn;

Fulton Co Bar Assn; NY State Bar Assn; Natl Comm on Syn Cen Relations; lawyer's comm, JNF; Fulton Co chap, Disabled Amer Vets Assn; Young Men's Rep Club of Fulton Co; Assn Family Court Judges; NY State Magistrates Assn; Natl Assn Juvenile Court Judges. Recipient: medals: Good Conduct; ETO; Victory; Conspicuous Services Cross of NY State. Home: 138 Fifth Ave, Gloversville, NY. Office: Co Bldg, Johnstown, NY.

ZALESKY, Moses, US, organization exec; b. Krynki, Pol, Jan 1, 1905; s. Jacob and Malka (Levitan); BS, U Chgo, 1931, PhD, 1934; m. Genia Oko, Nov 3, 1940; c: Hanita Schreiber, Malka. Exec dir, Bur of J Educ, Cinn, O, since 1946; lectr, Heb, U of Cinn, since 1951; educ dir, B'nai Zion Schs, Chgo, 1929-46. Bd mem: J Comty Cen; J Comty Relations Comm; Cinn Comty Heb Schs; dir: Friends of Heb Culture; Ivriah Soc; J Culture and Art Comm, all Cinn; fmr pres: Chgo Heb Tchrs Assn, 1941-44; midwest region, Natl Council for J Educ, 1958-60; secy, Natl Fed Heb Tchrs, 1939-41; mem: Cong Adath Isr; B'nai B'rith; NCJE; Histadruth Ivrith of Amer; Phi Beta Kappa; Sigma Xi. Author: Am V'Giborav, Heb textbook, 1949; contbr to jours; collaborator on Eng trans of On Ben Pele, by Shin Shalom, 1963. Home: 7750 Greenland Pl, Cincinnati, O. Office: 1580 Summit Rd, Cincinnati, O.

ZALIOUK, Yuval, Isr, conductor; b. Haifa, Isr, Feb 10, 1939; s. Israel and Ahuda (Nathanson); in Eng since 1965; LLB, Heb U, Jerusalem, 1963; att: Acad of Music, Jerusalem, 1962-63; Guildhall Sch of Music, London, 1965-66; m. Adina Gitter, Sep 13, 1964; c: Eyal. Conductor, Royal Opera House, Covent Garden, London, since 1966; perm conductor of Royal Ballet, Covent Garden; guest conductor: Eng; Isr; Fr; toured with Royal Ballet, Covent Garden, with Fonteyn and Nureyev in Eur, including: Orquesta Nacional, Madrid; Lux Radio Orch; Orch of Monte Carlo; Wiesbaden Opera Houses; Lisbon Radio Orch; debut in US with Detroit Sym Orch. Served IDF. Recipient: first prize: Amer-Isr Cultural Found Conducting Competition, 1965; Intl Competition, Profsl Sect, Besançon, Fr, 1967. Home: 63 Haazmaut Ave, Haifa, Isr. Office: Royal Opera House, Covent Garden, London, Eng.

ZALLEA, Sol, US, business exec; b. Phila, Pa, Mar 5, 1910; s. Morris and Fannie (Kopperman); m. Tanya Rabinowitz, Nov 13, 1938; c: Marilyn, Barbara. Pres: Zallea Bros, Inc, since 1962, partner since 1931; Expansion Joint Mfrs Assn, 1968-69; sports writer, Phila Record, 1927-29. Mem, bd dirs: J Fed, Del, since 1951, pres, 1958-61; Kutz Home for Aged, since 1960; Temple Beth Shalom, since 1941; mem, exec comm, Unity Comty Fund of N Del, 1961-63. Recipient: comty service award, J Fed, Del, 1961. Home: 2401 Penna Ave, Wilmington, Del. Office: Taylor & Locust Sts, Wilmington, Del.

ZAMBROWSKY, Zemach Menachem, Isr, communal leader; b. Warsaw, Pol, Apr 15, 1911; s. Yehoshua and Rivka (Gewelbe); in Isr since 1968; att: Orthodox Rabb Sems: New Haven, Conn; Cleveland, O; m. Belle Lifshetz, Mar 3, 1934; c: Rena Bender, Joshua. Chmn, Mizrachi-Hapoel Hamizrachi World Org; natl chmn, Mizrachi-Hapoel Hamizrachi of Can; rabbi: Hgts I Cen, Cleveland, O; Cong Shevet Achim, Montreal. Official repr, Can J, ecclesiastical affairs, to Can Govt; natl chmn, Rel Affairs Comm, Can J Cong; fmr: pres, Bd J Mins, Gtr Montreal; delg, JWF Conf; mem, Social Planning Comm, J Fed; vice-chmn, bd trustees, Bar Ilan U; bd dirs, Bank Hamizrachi, both Isr; mem: presidium: Vets, Zionist Gen Council, World Zionist Org; bd govs, Intl Org for Isr Bonds, United Isr Appeal; J Writers Assn; co-found, De Sola Club, both Montreal. Home: 16 Achad Haam St, Jerusalem, Isr. Office: 54 King George St, Jerusalem, Isr.

ZAOUI, André C, Isr, rabbi; b. Oran, Algeria, June 4, 1916; s. Leon and Tamar (Corsia); att Sorbonne, Paris, 1935-39; rabb deg, l'Ecole Rabb de Fr, 1946; m. Sophie Sorin, 1939; c: Daniel, Michael, Ariel. Rabbi: Har El Syn, World Union for Progressive Judaism, Jerusalem, since 1969; fmr, L'Union Libérale Isr de Paris. Chaplain, Fr Army, 1943-46. Mem: exec comm, gov body, World Union for Progressive Judaism; Soc of J-Chr Friendship; found, pres, Intl Inst Heb Studies, Paris; fmr: dir: La Revue de la Pensée Juive; Le Rayon; rabbi delg, Progressive Syn, Jerusalem. Recipient: Croix de Guerre, 1944. Study: 16 Shmuel Hanagid St, Jerusalem, Isr.

ZARAI, Yohanan, Isr, composer; b. Budapest, Hung, Feb 14, 1929; s. Samuel and Ilonka (Weisz); in Isr since 1950; att Acads of Music: Budapest; Vienna; Graz; Salzburg; m. 2nd,

Yael Gilboa; c: Yael. Free-lance composer; tchr, Jerusalem Acad of Music, 1950-52. Maj film scores: Eldorado; Sallah Shabati; The Six Day War; Matzor; The Miracle; maj songs: haSela haAdom; haKatar; Habibibi; vaYiven Uziyahu; Mi haHolem; music for theater: Hamesh Hamesh; Ish Hassid Haya; haBetula miRoma; Mashehu Lo Normali; two one-act plays by Lorca; music for army groups. Contbr to press. Home: 7 Schatz St, Tel Aviv, Isr.

ZARCHIN, Alexander Moshe, Isr, engineer, technological adv; b. Zolotonosha, Russ, Jan 2, 1897; s. Moshe and Bluma (Lopata); in Isr since 1947; engr, Leningrad Tech Inst, 1931, electrochemist, 1931; m. Sara Slonimsky, 1943. Cons engr, since 1954; mgr, steam mill, Brechinsky, 1918-24; mem, sci staff, Leningrad Tech Inst, 1930-34; mgr lab, asphalt mine, 1935-39, all Russ; mem, sci staff, Weizmann Inst, 1950-52; tech adv, Isr Min of Devl, 1956-60. Prin contribs: invention of process for demineralization of sea water; holder, numerous patents for chem, phys and mechanical processes. Mem: Isr Assn Engrs. Spec interest: Talmud. Home: 10A Ruppin St, Tel Aviv, Isr. Office: POB 18041, Tel Aviv, Isr.

ZARCHIN, Joseph, Isr, industrialist; b. Moscow, Russ, Apr 2, 1917; s. Samuel and Fanja (Gurwitch); in Isr since 1939; att Heb U, Jerusalem, 1939-41; m. Emmy Perutz, Mar 26, 1947; c: Samuel Michael, Sarit. Co-owner, dir, Adereth Group of Textile Enterprises, since 1948; vice-pres, mem presidium, Mfrs Assn of Isr, since 1965; fmr: head: export dept, Min of Trade and Ind, 1951-52; trade delg to S Afr, 1953; mem, missions to China, Far E, 1955, US, 1957. Capt, Brit Army, 1941-46; maj, IDF, 1948-49. Mem, exec comm, Jerusalem Econ Conf, 1968. Contbr to newspapers. Home: 7 Hateena St, Tel Aviv, Isr. Office: Ind Cen, Herzliya, Isr.

ZARETSKY, Hinde, US, author; b. Petrikow, Russ, July 14, 1899; d. Menachem and Leah (Reider); Hyim; in US since 1914; att: Bernard Coll, 1928-30; Art Workshop, NYC, 1930-32; m. Nelson Zaretsky, July 14, 1932. Author: Crotona Park Bridge, 1949; The Fourth Melody, 1960; And So He Sang, 1968; contbr to mags and press. Mem: Pioneer Women; Farband Lab Zionist. Home: 2418 Olinville Ave, Bronx, NY.

ZARISKI, Oscar, US, educator, mathematician; b. Korbin, Russ, Apr 24, 1889; s. Bezalel and Anna (Tennenbaum); in US since 1927; DMath, Rome U, 1923; hon: MA, Harvard U, 1947; DSc, Coll of Holy Cross, 1959; Brandeis U, 1965; m. Yole Cagli, Sep 11, 1924; c: Raffael, Vera. Dwight Parker Robinson prof, math, Harvard U, since 1960, fac mem since 1947; f, Intl Educ Bd, 1924-26; visiting lectr: U of Chgo, 1931; Moscow U, 1935; visiting mem, Inst Advanced Study, 1935-36, 1939, 1960-61; prof, Johns Hopkins U, 1937-45; visiting prof: U of Sao Paulo, 1945; U of Cal, Berkeley, 1948, 1968, 1969; Inst Hautes Études Scientifique, Paris, 1961, 1967; research prof, U of Ill, 1946-47. Pres, Amer Math Soc, 1969; mem: hon, London Math Soc; Math Assn Amer; Natl Acad Scis; Amer Phil Soc; Peru Acad Sci; Instituto Lombardo delle Scienze; Soc Math, Fr; fgn mem: Accademia Nazionale dei Lincei, It; Brazilian Acad Sci. Author: annotated It trans of Dedekind's: Was Sind und Was Sollen die Zahlen; Stetigkeit und Irrazionale Zahlen, both 1926; Comitative, Algebra, 2 vols, 1958, 1961; co-author, Algebraic Surfaces, 1935; ed: Amer Jour of Math, 1934-42; Transactions of the Amer Math Soc, 1942-47; asso ed, Annals of Math, 1934-52; mem, ed bd, The U Series of Higher Maths, 1946-62; contbr to math mags. Recipient: Cole prize, algebra, Amer Math Soc, 1944; Natl Medal of Sci, Wash, 1966. Home: 27 Lancaster St, Cambridge, Mass. Office: Harvard U, Cambridge, Mass.

ZARROW, Eva, US, physician; b. Paterson, NJ, Feb 14, 1904; d. Harry and Zelda (Pollack); BS, Jackson Coll, Tufts U, 1925, MD, Med Coll, 1929; div; c: Ruth Spero, Brenalea Feldman. Pvt practice since 1933; adjunct att med, Andrus Pavilion, St John's Riverside Hosp, Yonkers, NY and its gyn clinic; dir, casualty sta, Neppera Park, Yonkers, 1943-46. Mem: bd govs, Yonkers Acad Med, since 1961, recording secy, 1963, vice-pres, 1964-65, pres elect, 1965-66, pres, 1966-67; med adv bd, TB and Heart Assn, Yonkers; exec bd: Westchester div, AJComm; Yonkers chap, UN-USA; Westchester div, Amer Cancer Soc, pres, 1963; Westchester div, Public Educ; Commn on Human Rights, Yonkers, chmn, educ; perm secy, class 1929, Tufts Med Sch; vice-chmn, venture adv comm, N Atlantic region, Soroptimist Fed of Amer, since 1962; fmr pres: Westchester Women's Med Assn; Zeta Phi chap, Tufts Med Coll; mem: Westchester Med Soc; Westchester Acad Med; NY State Med Soc; AMA; NY State Women's Med Assn; Amer Women's Med Assn; Amer

Geriatric Soc; Jackson Alumnae Assn; Tufts Alumni Assn; Tufts Med Alumni Assn; Intl Platfrom Assn; C of C, Yonkers; fmr mem: exec bd, Natl Council J Women; Sisterhood exec bd, Temple Emanu-El; women's auxiliary, St John's Riverside Hosp; B'nai B'rith; Family Service Soc, Yonkers; J Comty Cen; Natl Council Negro Women; Nepperhan Comty Cen; Yonkers chap, Natl Assn, UN; Civil Defense Council, Yonkers; clubs: Yonkers Bus and Profsl Women's; Westchester Tufts; NY Tufts; Yonkers Soroptimist, charter mem, fmr pres, vice-pres. Recipient: Outstanding Civic Leaders of Amer, 1968. Hobbies: cooking, antiques. Home and office: 522 Park Ave, Yonkers, NY.

ZARROW, Meyer, US, educator; b. Worcester, Mass, Nov 1, 1913; s. Max and Ida (Medlinsky); AB, Clark, U, Worcester, 1934, MS, 1936; PhD, Harvard U, 1947; m. Irma Gue, Apr 5, 1946; c: Peter. Prof, U Conn, since 1969; prof, zool, Purdue U, 1956-69, asso prof, 1949-56; asst pharm, Hoffman-LaRoche, 1937-47; research asst, instr, Yale U, 1947-48; instr, Harvard U, 1948-49. Lt, Sanitary Corps, US Army, 1942-46. Prin contribs: research in endocrinology, reproduction, maternal behavior. F: AAAS; NY Acad Scis; mem: Amer Phys Soc; Amer Endocrine Soc; Amer Soc Zools; Amer Soc Anats; Soc Experimental Biol and Med; fmr mem: comm on hormone assay, cancer chemotherapy, natl service comm, HEW; comm on role of hormones in livestock produc, div of biol and agric, Natl Acad of Sci-NRC. Contbr: chap on gestation, Sex and Internal Secretions; to profsl jours. Home: 2213 Indian Trail, Dr, W Lafayette, Ind. Office: U of Connecticut, Storrs, Conn.

ZASLAVSKY, Aron, Isr, engineer, educator; b. Riga, Latvia, Feb 11, 1915; s. Menahem and Marie (Tumarkin); in Isr since 1934; dipl engr, Technion, Haifa, 1937; m. Genia Richter, 1943; c: Menahem. Ron. Asso prof, civil engr, Technion, Haifa, since 1960, head, dept mechanics, 1960-62; civil engr, housing corp, 1947-48; Brit Army, 1943-46; maj, IDF, 1948-51. Mem, Assn Architects and Engrs in Isr. Author: Strength of Materials, 1954; Limit Design of Steel and Reinforced Concrete, 1961; Limit Design of Steel Structures, 1964; Yield Line Analysis of Reinforced Concrete Slabs, 1967; contbr to sci jours. Home: 17 Wingate Ave, Haifa, Isr. Office: Technion, Haifa, Isr.

ZASLAVSKY, Dan, Isr, engineer; b. Tel Aviv, Isr, May 12, 1931; BSc, Technion, Haifa, 1954; dipl engr, 1955; MSc, 1957; PhD, Iowa State U, 1960; m. Aviva Rabinovitz; c: Amos, Michal. Asso prof, facs agric engr and civil engr, Technion, Haifa, since 1966; spec cons, Agric Research Service, US Dept Agric, 1967-68; asst fluid mech, descriptive geometry, Technion, 1953-56; surveyor, sup field engr, design of roads, 1950-54; cons engr, Tahal Inc, 1961-66; cons on drainage, master plans, cities: Ashdod, Arad, Kiryat Gat; N Tel Aviv, 1964-67; drainage and soil amelioration design in Adana Plain, Turkey, 1965. Prin contribs: research in: saturated and unsaturated flow through porous media; transfer processes; thermodynamics of soil water; soil structure. Mem: Geophys Union, US; Isr Geophys Soc; Isr Clay Soc; Intl Soil Sci Soc; Sigma Xi; Agric Engr Soc of Isr. Contbr to profsl publs. Home: 22 Nehemya St, Haifa, Isr. Office: Technion, Haifa, Isr.

ZASLOW, Jerry, US, surgeon; b. Phila, Pa, Mar 29, 1918; s. Samuel and Bella (Segal); BS, Temple U, 1937; MD, 1940; MS, U of Minn, Mayo Clinic, 1947; m. Rose Paul, June 8, 1941; c: Richard (decd); Teresa. Chief surg; John F Kennedy Memorial Hosp; Rolling Hill Hosp; asso surg: Einstein Med Cen, since 1948; asst prof, surg, Temple U Med Cen, since 1953. F, Amer Soc Abdominal Surg; mem: AMA; Phila Co Med Soc; Phila Acad Surg; Amer Coll Surgs; Intl Coll Surgs; Amer Med Writers Assn; AAAS; Amer Bd Surg; Allied J Appeal; Amer Friends of Heb U. Contbr to surg and allied sci publs. Recipient: Sigma Xi Hon Soc award. Home: 1420 Academy Lane, Melrose Park, Pa. Office: 1301 W Tabor Rd, Philadelphia, Pa.

ZAVIN, Theodora, US, attorney; b. NYC, Jan 29, 1922; d. Isidore and Lillian (Meyers) Itkowitz; AB, Hunter Coll, 1941; LLB, Columbia U, 1943; m. Benjamin Zavin, June 17, 1945; c: Jonathan, Daniel. Sr vice-pres, Bc Music, Inc, since 1968, res counsel, 1952-58, asst vice-pres, 1958-64, vice-pres, 1964-68; staff atty: Hon Geo Z Medalie, 1943-44; Greenbaum, Wolff & Ernst, 1944 50. Dir at large, Amer Women in Radio and TV, Inc, chmn, bylaws comm, 1957-61; trustee, Copyright Soc of US; mem: Amer, NYC Bar Assns; Intl Radio and TV Soc. Co-author: Your Marriage and The Law, 1952; Rights and Writers, 1961; The Working Wives' Cookbook,

1963. Home: 79 W 12 St, New York, NY. Office: 589 Fifth Ave, New York, NY.

ZEEVY, Rechavam, Isr, army off; b. Jerusalem, Isr, June 20, 1926; s. Shlomo and Mina (Zubak); att Agric HS; Command and Gen Staff Coll, US; m. Yael Sela, Aug 29, 1950; c: Yiftach Palmach, Sayar Benjamin, Masada, Tséla, Arava. Maj gen, commanding gen off, Cen Command, IDF, since 1968; fmr: Palmach, Yiftach Brig, War of Independence; brig intelligence off; N Front oprs off; S Command intelligence off; battalion cdr, Golani Brig; chief, oprs sect, Gen Staff; gen staff off, chief of staff, S Command, Sinai Campaign; chief, Dept of Staff Functions, Gen Staff; chief, Staff Cen Command; asst to Chief of Staff, Gen Br. Office: IDF, Isr.

ZEHAWI, Jekutiel Zwi, Isr, author; b. Hung, Feb 20, 1902; s. Abraham and Esther (Kain) Goldstein; in Isr since 1925; dipl, Tchrs Sem, Jerusalem, 1929; MA, Heb U, Jerusalem, 1936, PhD, 1943; m. Eva Beregi, July 1, 1948. Mem: Govt Council for State Rel Educ, since 1956; Council of Tchrs Org in Isr, since 1948; sch master: Yavne, evening sch, 1932-35; Pinkas sch, Tel Aviv, 1944-65. Pres, Megurim Syn; dir, Archives of J Educ, both Tel Aviv; fmr pres: Cen Comm of Rel Tchrs Org in Isr; Hillel Lodge, B'nai B'rith, mem, B'nai B'rith Order, Tel Aviv. Author: The Problem of Jewish Assimilation, 1941; Thoughts and Ethics in Judaism, 1954; From Chatam Sofer until Herzl, 1967. Recipient: Churgin prize, Heb U, Jerusalem, 1941; Nordau prize, 1967; Ben Zvi prize, 1968. Home: 23 Haifa St, Tel Aviv, Isr.

ZEICHNER, Irving B, US, jurist, editor; b. NYC, Mar 27, 1919; s. Bernard and Gertrude (Reiter); AB, NYU, 1939; LLB, Fordham Law Sch, 1941, JD, 1968. Chief, legal research, Admn Off of Courts, NJ, since 1969; judge, Atlantic Highlands Munic Court, 1951-69. USAAC, 1942-46. Pres, Monmouth Lodge, B'nai B'rith, 1964-65; bd dirs, Air Force Assn, 1949-50; secy, NJ State Jr C of C, 1950-51; bd delgs, AJComm, since 1956; mem: Amer Bar Assn; NJ State Bar Assn; Monmouth Co Bar Assn. Ed: Law and Order, 1954-69; Mayor and Manager, 1957-69; contr to legal jours. Recipient: Lasker F in Civil Rights and Civil Liberties, Brandeis U, 1960. Spec interest: lecturing on police-comty relations. Home: 1 Highgate Dr, Trenton, NJ. Office: State House Annex, Trenton, NJ.

ZEICHNER, Oscar, US, educator, historian; b. NYC, Jan 2, 1916; s. Joseph and Lena (Shaeffer); BA, CCNY, 1936; MA, Columbia U, 1938, PhD, 1946; m. Florence Koenigsberg, June 27, 1942; c: Barbara, Carolyn. Dean, grad studies, Coll of Lib Arts and Sci, CCNY, since 1968, fac mem since 1936. Pres, CCNY chap, AAUP, 1952-53; mem: Amer Hist Assn; Phi Beta Kappa. Author: Connecticut's Years of Controversy, 1750-1776, pub 1949; contbr to scholarly jours. Home: 5500 Fieldston Rd, New York, NY. Office: CCNY, Convent Ave and 139 St, New York, NY.

ZEIFERT, Mark, US, neuropsychiatrist, educator; b. Russ, Mar Mar 20, 1907; s. Joseph and Sarah (Zak); in US since 1911; att: NYU; Columbia U; CCNY, 1925-29; BS, St Louis U, 1931, MD, Sch of Med, 1933; MS, neur, U of Mich, 1947; m. Peggy Donnelly, Apr 14, 1941; c: Leslie, Joan, Roberta, Penelope, Pamela. Pvt practice since 1949; prof, psych, Fresno State Coll, mem staff since 1955; asso clinical prof, psycht, U of S Cal Med Sch, since 1957, mem staff since 1955; att neur, Pacific Med Cen, SF, since 1960; research asso, encephalitis studies, Cal State Dept of Health and Stanford Med Sch, since 1953; cons: Natl Comm on Alcohol Hygiene, since, 1954; USIA, since 1959; Fresno VA Hosp; Dearborn Hosp; Madera Hosp; Sanger Hosp; Exeter Memorial Hosp; Tulare Dist Hosp; Coalinga Dist Hosp; Merced Co Hosp; sr staff: Fresno Comty Hosp, since 1949, fmr chief of staff; Valley Children's Hosp, since 1949; staff, St Agnes Hosp, Fresno, since 1949; att neur and psycht, Fresno Co Hosp; lectr, psycht: Bklyn State Hosp, 1936-41; LI Coll Med Sch; 1936-41; asst psycht, NY State Dept Mental Hygiene, 1938-46; phys, i/c shock therapy research, Bklyn State Hosp, 1938-41; research asso, neurophys, Albany Med Coll, 1940-41; instr, neur, U of Mich, 1946-48; chief of instr, VA med teaching group, Memphis, Tenn, 1948; asso prof, dir, dept neur, U of Ark Med Sch, 1948-49; psycht, outpatient dept: Bklyn Hosp, 1937-41; LI Coll Hosp, 1937-41; chief: mental hygiene clinic and hosp neuropsych service: Camp Blanding, Fla, 1941-42; Hammond Gen Hosp, 1942-46; neur service, VA Hosp, Memphis, 1948; VA Hosp, N Little Rock, 1948-49; neur: U Hosp, Ann Arbor, Mich, 1947-48; U of Ark Hosp, 1948-49; psycht, dir, Fresno State Mental Hygiene Clinic, 1953-56; mem, Gov's

Adv Comm for Mh, 1953-59. US Army, 1941-46. F: Amer Psycht Assn; Amer Acad Neur; Amer Acad Forensic Scis; mem: AMA; Cal Med Assn; Assn for Research in Nervous and Mental Diseases; Natl Epilepsy Assn; Amer League Against Epilepsy; NY Soc for Clinical Psycht; W Electroencephalographic Assn; Fresno Co Med Soc; asst examiner, Amer Bd Psycht and Neur; found: Fresno Psycht Soc; Cen Cal dist br, Amer Psycht Assn, first and second pres; bd dirs, Crippled Children's Soc, fmr pres. Contbr to profsl jours. Home: 72 E Terrace, Fresno, Cal. Office: 1065 S St, Fresno, Cal

ZEIGER, Bernard, US, rabbi, educational adv; b. Canton, O, July 5, 1900; s. Louis and Sarah (Goldstein); BA, U of Mich, 1922; rabbi, HUC, 1929; m. Ethel Nachamson, Aug 28, 1938; c: Judith. Counselor, Amer Inst of Family Relations, since 1969; counselor on dean's staff, U of Cal, Riverside; rabbi: Beth El, Mich, 1929-36; lectr, Flint Coll, 1929-36; dir, Hillel Found, U of NC, 1936-40; rabbi: Cong Emanuel, Roanoke, Va, 1940-47; Temple Beth El, Riverside, 1947-59. Mem: CCAR; club, Rotary. Home: 4228 Brentwood Ave, Riverside, Cal.

ZEIGERMAN, Joseph H, US, physician; b. Berezdow, Russ, Apr 15, 1906; s. Harry and Jennie (Pogach); in US since 1921; att Temple U, 1926; BA, LaSalle Coll, 1931; MD, U Vienna, 1936; MD, U Bern, 1938; MS, U Pa, 1942; m. Molly Blecher, Sep 17, 1933 (div); m. 2nd, Harriett Goldstein, Nov 15, 1958; c: Gerald, Louise, Debbie. Asst prof, U of Pa Grad Sch of Med, since 1954; chief, gyn, St Agnes Hosp, Phila, Pa, 1950; asso prof, Hahnemann Med Coll, 1951; asst, Phila Lying-In Hosp, 1953; asso, gyn, U of Pa Grad Hosp, 1954; chief, obstets, gyn, Wills Eye Hosp, Phila, 1954. F: Amer Coll Surgs; Intl Coll Surgs; Phila Coll Phys, AMA; found f, Amer Coll Obstets and Gyns; cert, Amer Bd Obstets and Gyn, 1945; mem: Phila Obstet Soc; AAUP. Home and office: 2105 Spruce St, Philadelphia, Pa.

ZEITLEN, Joseph G, Isr, educator; b. Boston, Mass, Oct 31, 1916; s. Benjamin and Ida (Shulatzky); in Isr since 1953; BSc, MIT, 1939, MSc, 1946; m. Frances Dunn, Oct 9, 1937; c: Eleanor Relis, Steven, Lorraine, Joanne. Prof, soil engr, Technion, Haifa, since 1958; sr dir, Soil Engr, Ltd, cons engrs; asst safety engr, Liberty Mutual Ins Co, US, 1939; soils research engr, MIT, 1940; soil mech expert, Tech Asst Admn, UN, 1953-58; dean, fac civil engr, Technion, 1958-61, 1966-67; visiting prof, UCLA, 1961-62. Civil engr and soil engr, Corps of Engrs, US Army, 1940-42, 1946-53. Prin contribs: established soil labs, teaching and research prog. Pres, Isr Soc Soil Mech and Found Engr, since 1958; vicepres, Asia, Intl Soc Soil Mechs and Found Engrs; f, Amer Soc Civil Engrs; bd dirs, Isr Inst for Petroleum and Geophys Research; mem: Highway Research Bd; Amer Soc for Testing and Materials; Soc of Amer Mil Engrs; Chi Epsilon; Sigma Xi; Intl Union of Testing and Research Labs for Materials and Structures; club, MIT, Isr, pres. Contbr to sci jours. Recipient: Bronze Star, 1946. Hobbies: music, photography. Home: 46 Sea Rd, Mt Carmel, Haifa, Isr. Office: Technion, Haifa, Isr.

ZEITLIN, Aaron Eliezer, US, author; b. Uvarovich, Russ, May 22, 1898; s. Hillel and Esther (Kunin); in US since 1940; m. Rachel Abramovich; hon DHL, JTSA. Staff writer, The Day-Morning Jour, NYC, since 1940; fmr tchr, prof, Heb lit, Tchrs Inst, JTSA. Author: Gesamelte Lider, collected Yiddish poems, 3 vols; Brenedige Erd, novel; Shotens Oifen Shnei; I H Brenner, drama; plays: Helemer Hachomin and Estherke, both produced on stage by Maurice Schwartz, Jacob Frank, Jacob Jacobson; Yidn-Shtot, staged by Wilner Trope; Bein haEsh veHayesha, Heb; Shitim Upoemot, Heb; Shirav haYiddim shel Bialik, Heb; Min HaAdam Vamaala, 2 dramatic poems, Heb; Medina VaHazon Medina, phil; HaMetziut HoAhereth, on psychic phenomena, all Heb; Alle Lider un Poemes, Vol 1, inclusive ed of Yiddish poetry; plays, poems and essays in Heb and Yiddish. Pres, Heb PEN Club, NY, fmr pres, Yiddish PEN Club, Warsaw. Recipient: lit awards, including: Ussishkin Prize, for Bein haEsh veHayesha; LaMed Prize, three times. Home: 920 Riverside Dr, New York, NY. Office: 183 E Broadway, New York, NY.

ZEITLIN, Joseph, US, rabbi, educator; b. Bklyn, NY, May 18, 1906; s. Isaac and Esther (Lewinson); BA, CCNY, 1926; MA, Columbia U, 1940, PhD, 1943; ordained rabbi, MHL, JTSA, 1930; m. Helene Rich, 1940; c: Judith. Prof, U Bridgeport, since 1965; fmr: rabbi: Temple Anshe Chesed, NYC; em, Riverside Syn, NYC; conducted High Holy Days Services for Armed Forces, Ft Eustis. Fmr: grand chaplain,

Free Sons of Isr; chmn: Comm on Church and State, NY Bd of Rabbis; speakers bur, United Syn of Amer; mem: exec comm, RA; UJA; FJP; ZOA; club, Town, NYC. Author: Disciples of the Wise, 1945, 1947; Speech Power; co-author, Hebrew Made Easy. Recipient: cited for outstanding contrib to contemporary lit, Natl Assn Authors and Journalists, 1945; Elroy Alfaro Grand Medal of Honor, Rep of Panama; medal, NYC Police Dept; award, JWB; plaques: UJA; FJP; ZOA. Hobbies: tennis, table tennis, swimming. Home: 7 E 86 St, New York, NY. Office: U of Bridgeport, Conn.

ZEITLIN, Maurice, US, educator, author; b. Detroit, Mich, Feb 24, 1935; s. Albert and Rose (Goldberg); BA, cum laude, Wayne State U, 1957; MA, PhD, U of Cal, Berkeley; m. Marilyn Geller, Mar 1, 1959; c: Michelle, Carla, Erica. Asso prof, sociol, U of Wis, since 1967, asst prof, 1964-67; instr, Princeton U, 1961-64. Chmn, Madison Citizen's Comm for a Vote on Vietnam; mem, exec comm, U of Wis Fac for Peace; original signer, Call to Resist Illegitimate Auth; mem: Amer Sociol Assn; Amer Hist Assn; ACLU; AAUP; AFT, local 223. Author: Revolutionary Politics and the Cuban Working Class, 1967; co-author: Cuba: Tragedy in Our Hemisphere, 1963; Latin America: Reform or Revolution, 1968; asso ed, Amer Sociol; contrib ed, Ramparts Mag; contbr to mags and jours. Recipient: Woodrow Wilson f, 1959-61; Ford Found f, 1965-66. Hobby: folk dance. Home: 2115 Chadbourne Ave, Madison, Wis. Office: U of Wis, Madison, Wis.

ZEITLIN, Shneor Zalman, Isr, physician; b. Dobrova, Russ, 1892; s. Shimeon and Batia; in Isr since 1924; MD, U of Moscow, 1923; widower; s: Shimeon, Anava Kantor. Surg, phys, Hadassah Hosp, Tel Aviv, since 1967; Ichilov Hosp, since 1961; Nesher, Haifa, 1926-60. Fmr, active: Jabotinsky Movement; Zionist orgs. Author: Mapat Eretz Israel Lefi Brit Ben Habetarim, 1957; contbr to jours. Home: 7 Amsterdam St, Tel Aviv, Isr. Office: Balfour St, Tel Aviv, Isr.

ZEITLIN, Zvi, Isr, musician; b. Dubrowna, Russ, Feb 21, 1923; s. Zalman and Rivka; att: Juilliard Sch of Music, NYC, postgrad work, honor dipl, 1947-49; Talmudical Acad of Yeshiva U, NY, 1933-39; Heb U, Jerusalem, 1941-43; m. Marianne Langner, May 5, 1951; c: Hillel, Leora. Concert violinist; prof, Eastman Sch of Music, U of Rochester, NY, since 1967; fmr: artist in res, Ind U; chamber music fac, Berkshire Music Cen; regular concert tours in recital and as soloist with maj sym orchs in: US; Eur; Isr; S Amer; Austr; NZ; introduced many new works; promotion Isr, J composers; premiered: violin concerto by Ben Haim, Isr, Austr, NZ; Stravinsky violin concerto with NY Philharmonic; Schönberg violin concerto with Leonard Bernstein and NY Philharmonic. Ed, newly discovered concerti by Nardini, 1969. Recipient: Amer-Isr Soc Award, 1957. Home: 204 Warren Ave, Rochester, NY. Office: U of Rochester, NY.

ZELDIN, Isaiah, US, rabbi; b. Bklyn, NY, July 11, 1920; s. Morris and Esther (Freedman); BA; Bklyn Coll, 1941; ordained rabbi, HUC, 1946; m. Florence Karp, July 4, 1943; c: Joel, Michael. Rabbi: Stephen S Wise Temple, since 1964; Temple Beth Sholom, Flushing, 1950-53; Temple Emanuel, Beverly Hills, 1958-64; asst dean, Heb Union Sch of Educ & Sacred Music, NY, 1948-53; dean, LA Coll J Studies, 1953-58. Dir, W Coast region, UAHC, since 1953; chmn, S Cal region, AZC; vice-pres, mem, exec comm, W Assn Reform Rabbis; fmr pres: S Cal Assn Liberal Rabbis; Essex Co Bd Rabbis; mem: bd, LA council, J Fed; Natl Council for J Educ; comm on Amer J hist, CCAR. Contbr to J pubs. Home: 1107 Maybrook Dr, Beverly Hills, Cal. Study: 15500 Stephen S Wise Dr, Los Angeles, Cal.

ZELDNER, Max, US, educator; b. Brest-Litovsk, Pol, Aug 25, 1907; s. Aaron and Toibe (Leff); in US since 1921; grad, Tchrs Inst, Yeshiva U, 1927; BS, NYU, 1931; MA, Columbia U, 1933; m. Fannie Brody, 1933; c: Adina Nadelhaft, Miriam Klipper. Head, dept fgn langs, William Howard Taft HS, since 1961; instr: Tchrs Inst, Yeshiva U, 1934-35; Yeshiva Coll, 1935-37; tchr: Wash Irving HS, 1937-39; Day HSs, NYC, 1939-58; Herzliah Tchrs Inst, 1949-58; Queens Coll Adult Educ, 1949-50; visiting asst prof, Stern Coll, 1958; Hunter Coll, 1960-61; fac mem, Yeshiva U, Grad Sch Educ, 1948-64; head, dept fgn langs, Ft Hamilton HS, Bklyn, 1958-61. Mem: Assn Chmns in NYC HSs; Standing Commn Fgn Lang Chmns; evaluation comm, MLA. Author: A Bibliography of Methods and Materials of Teaching Hebrew in the Light of Modern Language Methodology, 1951; Bible Teaching: A Bibliography of Methods, Materials and Model

Lessons, 1960; co-author, Modern Hebrew Literature; contbr to Heb, educ, Anglo-J jours. Home: 35 W 82 St, New York, NY. Office: William Howard Taft HS, Bronx, NY.

ZELENKA, Carlos Luis, Panama, business exec; b. Vienna, Aus, July 8, 1918; s. Max and Clara (Abeles); att HS for World Trade, Vienna, 1932-35; m. Lotte Lewie, Feb 2, 1946; c: George, Rodney, Yvonne. Pres, several bus, since 1951; mgr, Lewis Service, 1946-51. Secy gen, B'nai B'rith, dist grand lodge XXIII, fmr pres; mem, Masons; fmr: pres, Albert Einstein Sch Bd; Kol Shearith Isr Cong; dir, Cen J Council; secy, J Benevolent Soc; club, Rotary, Panama chap. Spec interests: comty work, bridge. Home: POB 6528, Panama. Office: POB 1634, Panama.

ZELERMYER, William, US, educator; b. Chelsea, Mass, Jan 7, 1914; s. Louis and Eva (Solomon); AB, Williams Coll, 1935; LLB, Harvard Law Sch, 1939; m. Herma Zetterbaum, June 30, 1940; c: Benjamin, Milton. Prof, bus law, Syracuse U, NY, since 1948; pvt practice, Buffalo, NY, 1945-46; asst prof, bus law, Rider Coll, 1946-48. Pres, Syracuse U chap, AAUP, 1962-63; pres, Amer Bus Law Assn, 1959-60, co-ed, bull, 1954-62; mem: Amer Bar Assn; Beta Gamma Sigma. Author: Invasion of Privacy, 1959; Legal Reasoning, 1960; The Process of Legal Reasoning, 1963; Introduction to Business Law, 1964; Business Law, 1967. contbr to legal periodicals. Home: 105 Wilson Pl, Syracuse, NY. Office: Syracuse U, Syracuse, NY.

ZELIG, Ernest, US, business exec; b. Dej, Rum, May 28, 1921; s. Joseph and Theresia (Jaray); in US since 1949; att: Gymnasium, Dej, Rum, 1931-37; Rabbinical Yeshivah: Dej, Rum, 1931-37; Secuieni, Rum, 1937-38; Ujoara, 1939-41; m. Elizabeth Solomon, Nov 27, 1945; c: Beatrice Sparber, Vivian Fischer. Pres: Jay Plastics, Inc, since 1954; Sayville Film, Inc, since 1959. Labor Camps, 1942-44. Pres, Manhattan region, B'nai Zion, exec bd, natl, Transylvania Lodge 96, fmr pres of lodge; mem: B'nai B'rith, Colossus lodge; fmr: vicepres, Beth Sholom Cen, Amityville, NY; secy treas, J Comm, Dej, Rum. Spec interest: Isr coins and medals. Home: 106 Harbour View Dr, Massapequa, NY. Office: 1515 Fifth Industrial Ct, Bayshore, NY.

ZELIGMAN, Israel, US, dermatologist, educator; b. Baltimore, Md, July 24, 1913; s. Bernard and Rebecca (Kamenson); BA, Johns Hopkins U, 1933; MD, U of Md, 1937; MedScD, Columbia U, 1942; m. Tess Koppelman, Sep 22, 1934; c: Bernard, Sandra, Rebecca, Marilyn. Asso prof, dermat, Johns Hopkins U, since 1963, on staff since 1955; head, dermat, Sinai Hosp, since 1963, on staff since 1948; att dermat, Lutheran Hosp of Md, since 1947; dermat, Johns Hopkins Hosp, since 1950; cons dermat: Rosewood State Hosp, since 1951; Baltimore Eye, Ear & Throat Hosp, since 1951; att dermat, Vet Hosp, Ft Howard, Md, 1946-52; dermat, U of Md Hosp, 1947-56; asst prof, dermat, U of Md, 1952-56. Lt cdr, USN, 1942-46. Mem: Baltimore City Med and Dermat Assns; Amer Acad Dermat. Contbr to med jours. Home: 2310 South Rd, Baltimore, Md. Office: Med Arts Bldg, Baltimore, Md.

ZELIZER, Gerald Lee, US, rabbi; b. Columbus, O, Dec 14, 1938; s. Nathan and Florence (Handler); BA, Capital U, Columbus, O, 1960; MHL, ordained rabbi, JTSA; 1964; m. Viviana Rotman. Rabbi: Temple Isr, since 1966; Cong Beth-El, Buenos Aires, Arg, 1946-66; Mishna tchr, Rabb Sem, Buenos Aires. Fmr pres, United Syn Youth; fmr dir, Leaders Training F. Contbr to J jours. Home: C-10 Girard St, Union, NJ. Study: 2372 Morris Ave, Union, NJ.

ZELIZER, Nathan, US, rabbi; b. Stavysk, Pol, Sep 22, 1907; s. Henry and Rose (Kaddish); in US since 1919; BS, NYU, 1929; MA, Columbia U, 1931; ordained rabbi, JTSA, 1931, hon DD, 1964; m. Florence Handler, Oct 31, 1947; c: Gerald, Deborah. Rabbi, Tifereth Isr Cong, since 1931; chaplain: mental and penal instns for wfr dept, O State, since 1947; VA, Vet Hosp, Chillicothe, O, since 1947; Amer Legion, dept of O. US Army, 1944-46. Chmn, Columbus Park Comm; fmr pres, City Recreation Comm; bd mem, Franklin Co Council of Churches and Ministers Assn; exec bd, O Wfr Citizens Comm; mem: RA; JWV; ZOA; B'nai B'rith. Author: The History of Higher Jewish Education in America, 1931. Home: 166 N Cassady Ave, Columbus, O. Study 1354 E Broad St, Columbus, O.

ZELLER, Belle, US, educator; b. NYC, Apr 8, 1903; d. Davis and Celia (Davidson); BA, Hunter Coll, 1924; MA, Columbia U, 1926, PhD, 1937. Prof, political sci, Bklyn Coll, since 1952, fac mem since 1930; visiting prof, grad fac, New Sch for Social Research, since 1960; research cons, house select comm in lobbying activities, US Cong, 1949-50. Chmn: Leg Conf of CUNY, since 1944; comm on Amer leg, Amer Political Sci Assn, 1948-53, mem, exec council, 1947-49; Higher Educ Comm, Citizens Union; bd dirs, Public Affairs Comm, since 1966; bd ed, NY Leg Service, since 1938; mem: NY State Temporary Comm; Acad of Political and Social Sci; Amer Soc for Public Admn; Natl Munic League; Leg Service Conf, Chgo; Amer Assn for Public Opinion Research; AAUP; Amer Assn U Women; AJCong; Hadassah; Phi Beta Kappa. Author: Pressure Politics in NY, 1937, 1967; The Federal Regulation of Lobbying Act, 1948; co-author, ed, American State Legislatures, 1954. Home: 25 Central Park W, New York, NY. Office: Bklyn College, Brooklyn, NY.

ZELLERBACH, Harold L, US, industrialist; b. SF, Cal, Mar 25, 1894; s. Isadore and Jennie (Baruh); att U of Cal, 1913-15; BS, U of Pa, 1917; m. Doris Joseph, Apr 19, 1917; c: Rolinde, William, Stephen. Cons, dir, Crown Zellerbach Corp; personnel mgr, Zellerbach Paper Co, 1917-28, pres, dir, 1928-5/. Pres: SF Art Commn; Newhouse Found; trustee, U of Pa; mem, Cal State Park Commn; fmr pres: Natl Paper Trade Assn; Temple Emanu-El, SF; mem, Masons; clubs: Stock Exch; SF Commercial; St Francis Yacht; Concordia; Press; Commonwealth, all SF; Fifth Ave, NYC. Home: 2288 Broadway, San Francisco, Cal. Office: 1 Bush St, San Francisco, Cal.

ZELMAN, Morris, US, surgeon; b. Springfield, Mass, Dec·8, 1914; s. Abraham and Ida (Kobrinsky); AB, Johns Hopkins U, 1938; MD, NY Med Coll, 1942; m. Irma Stein, Dec 25, 1945; c: Steven, Sandra, Caryl. Chief, surg, Mt Vernon State TB Sanitarium, since 1951. US Army, 1944-46. F: Amer Coll Chest Phys; Amer Coll Surgs; Intl Coll Surgs; mem: AMA; Jefferson-Hamilton Co Med Soc; sixth dist, med dir, State bd, Amer Cancer Soc. Contbr to profsl publs. Home: Richview Road, Mt Vernon, Ill. Office: 117 N Tenth St, Mt Vernon, Ill.

ZELSON, Carl, US, physician, educator; b. Phila, Pa, Sep 29, 1905; s. Joseph and Mary (Lachman); BS, U of Wis, 1928; MD, Wash U Med Sch, 1930; m. Annette Gitenstein, Jan 28, 1934; c: Julia Rosenblum, Joseph. Prof, peds, NY Med Coll, since 1966; cons ped, premature infant prog, NYC Dept of Health, since 1950; visiting ped, Flower Fifth Ave Hosp, since 1966; att ped, Metrop Hosp, dir, newborn services, since 1966. USCG, 1943-46. F, Amer Acad Ped; mem: Sigma Sigma, U of Wis; Phi Lambda Kappa. Contbr to ped jours. Home: 200 W 86 St, New York, NY. Office: 1249 Fifth Ave, New York, NY.

ZELTNER, Wladimir Z, Isr, jurist; b. Kiev, Russ, Jan 19, 1909; s. Josef and Elisabeth (Zeitlin); in Isr since 1936; att Us: Berlin; Leipzig; Heidelberg; Sorbonne; m. Elfriede Süsskind; c: Michael, Ariella Gonen. Pres, Dist Court of Tel Aviv, since 1966, relieving pres since 1953; asso prof, Heb U, since 1964; prof, Tel Aviv U, since 1970; jr barrister, Berlin, 1930-33; tchr, Tel Aviv, 1936-39; partner, law firm, Sommerfeld and Zeltner, 1940-49. Chmn: Restrictive Trade Practices Tribunal; Comm on Secondary Educ; Comm on Co Law; mem, UNO Commn for Hum Rights, Expert Commn; gov, Rotary Intl, district 199, fmr pres, Tel Aviv-Jaffa. Author: Die Entwicklung des Sozialismus von der Wissenschaft zur Utopie, 1929; chief ed, Hapraklit, 1951-62; ed: Law and Econ, 1955-59; Psakim, 1950-61; Contracts, 3 Vols, 1960-70. Recipient: Ruppin prize, Haifa Munic, 1961; State of Isr prize, 1971. Spec interests: music, art, hist. Home: 39 Hashoftim St, Tel Aviv, Isr. Office: 1 Weizmann St, Tel Aviv, Isr.

ZELTZER, George Meyer, US, business exec; b. Detroit, Mich, May 18, 1922; s. Joseph and Fannie (Chover); LLB, Wayne State U, 1946; JD, U of Mich, 1949; m. Pearl Melnick, Sep 12, 1948; c: David, Gary, Elliot, Jeremy. Pres: Amer Savings Assn, since 1969; Citizens Family Assurance Co, since 1965. Sgt, USAAC, 1942-46. Chmn, educ div, JWF; vice-pres, JCC; pres: Sholem Aleichem Inst; United Heb Schs, 1965-68; fmr chmn: Real Estate Div, Allied J Campaign; pres; Mich Savings & Loan League. Home: 23861 Rensselaer, Oak Park, Mich. Office: 600 Woodward, Detroit, Mich.

ZEMACH, Ada, Isr, literary critic, editor; b. Odessa, Russ, July 7, 1919; d. Shlomo and Hana (Smiliansky); MA, Heb U, Jerusalem; m. Meir Vereté; three c. Lit critic and ed, Orot, bilingual lit quarterly, Heb-Eng, Heb-Span. Haganah, ATS,

WW II. Trans from Fr into Heb: Tocqueville's L'ancien Régime et la Révolution; Courtant's Adlophe; texts of Voltaire. Mem, Isr Writers Org. Recipient: Afr Star; Tchernichovsky Prize for trans. Home: 13 Abarbanel St, Jerusalem, Isr. Office: POB 92, Jerusalem, Isr.

ZEMANSKY, Mark W, US, physicist, educator; b. NYC, May 5, 1900; s. Abraham and Rebbecah (Cohen); BS, CCNY, 1921; AM, Columbia U, 1922, PhD, 1927; m. Adele Cohen, Sep 25, 1932; c: Philip, Herbert. Exec secy, Amer Assn Physics Tchrs; NRC f, physics: Princeton U, 1928-30; Kaiser Wilhelm Inst, Berlin, 1930-31; prof, physics, CCNY, since 1933. Student Army Training Corps, 1918. Mem: Amer Phys Soc; Zeta Beta Tau; Phi Beta Kappa; Sigma Xi; Sigma Pi Sigma. Author: Heat and Thermodynamics, 1937; Low and High Temperatures, 1963; co-author: Resonance Radiation and Excited Atoms, 1934; College Physics, 1947; University Physics, 1949; ed, sect on heat in Amer Inst of Physics Handbook; contbr to profsl jours. Recipient: Oersted medal, Amer Assn Physics Tchrs, 1956; Townsend Harris medal, CCNY Asso Alumni, 1960. Home: 736 Rutland Ave, Teaneck, NJ. Office: 335 E 45 St, New York, NY.

ZENOWITZ, Allan Ralph, US, business cons; b. Queens Village, NY, Apr 18, 1928; s. Ralph and Ann (Brickman); att Trinity Coll, Hartford, Conn, 1947-49; BA, U of Conn, 1960; JD, NE Sch of Law, 1964; spec studies: Yale U; Harvard U; U of Va; US Army Command and Gen Staff Coll. Bus cons since 1953; aide, Gov of Mass, 1961-62; Mass Rep State committeeman, 1964-65. Cavalry off, US Army, 1950-52, brig gen, military aide, Gov of Mass, since 1968; col, US Army Res; ex-seaman, USNR. Mem: Amer Soc Intl Law; Amer Acad Political Sci; Vets of 7th Regiment, NY; Amer Legion; NE regional bd, AJComm, since 1961; adv council, Mass Commn against Discrimination, since 1963; Mass Flood Relief Bd; World Affairs Council of Boston; Mass Emergency Communications Commn; Mass Radiological Adv Protection Comm; Mass Gov's Water Emergency Adv Comm; Soc Amer Mil Engrs; adv, lectr, cons, US Govt; volunteer, disaster planning cons, ARC; natl strategy participant, US Natl, Army, Naval and Air War Colls; state dir, Mass off of Civil Defense and Emergency Preparedness; fmr: pres, Natl Assn of State Civil Defense Dirs; planning cons, Cal State Colls in Eur; club, Rep Mass dir. Recipient: Army Commendation Medal; mil service medals; White House citation for outstanding public service, 1967. Home: Berkshire Hgts Rd, Great Barrington, Mass. Office: 37 Beacon St, Boston, Mass.

ZER-KAWOD, Mordechay, Isr, educator; b. Aus, July 4, 1901; s. Abraham and Doba (Sommer) Ehrenkranz; in Isr since 1937; tchrs dipl, Heb Paedagium, Vienna, 1923; MA, PhD, U of Berlin; m. Batya Bickel, Aug 16, 1938; c: Nizsa Glazner, Moshe Glazner, Menahem. Asso prof, Bible, Bar Ilan U, since 1964; head sup, youth movement, Vienna, 1924-25; dir, Heb schs: Czech, 1926-29; Munich, 1935-37. Info off, Civil Defense Service, IDF, 1947-48. Prin contribs: research in methods of teaching Bible and Talmud. Chmn, Soc for Bible Research, Haifa br; mem: comm, Libr of J Studies, Haifa; Assn Secondary Sch Tchrs; Isr Numismatic Soc; fmr: pres, Cen Syn, Ahuza, Haifa; mem, Haifa Rel Council. Author: Commentary on Daniel, Ezra-Nehemia; Commentary on Qoheleth; contbr to various books and jours. Recipient: recognition of scholarship, Mosad Harav Kook, 1949; Zer-Kawod Vol, Isr Soc for Bible Research, 1968. Hobbies: numismatics, antiquities, plastic art. Home: 10 Mapu Ave, Haifa, Isr. Office: Bar Ilan U, Ramat Gan, Isr.

ZERNIK, Rafael Robert, Isr, engineer; b. Berlin, Ger, Aug 9, 1927; s. Felix and Irene (Shimek); in Isr since 1936; BSc, engr, Technion, Haifa, 1951; m. Rivka Shamir, Apr 15, 1971; c: Uri, Joseph, Dror. Asst dir, R & D Found, Technion, Haifa, since 1962; engr: Rassco Co, Jerusalem, 1951-54; Solel Boneh Bldg Co, 1954-59; chief supt, Min of Defense, 1959-62. Sgt, IDF, 1947-49. Home: 2 Kidron St, Haifa, Isr. Office: Technion, Haifa, Isr.

ZEWI, Moses, Finland, physician; b. Mena, Russ, Mar 1, 1909; s. Israel and Golde (Schapira); in Finland since 1921; MD, U of Helsingfors, 1939; m. Hanna Linder, Dec 20, 1936; c: Josef, Haim. Dozent, Ophthal Clinic, U of Turku, Abo, since 1956. Capt, MC, 1939-44. Author, med papers: Das Lactoflavin, Vitiman B-2, der Netzhaut bei verschieden Adaptionszuständen, 1937; Mode of Action of Visual Purple, 1938; The Relation Between Concentration of Visual Purple and Retinal Sensitivity to Light During Dark Adaptation, 1939; On the Regeneration of Visual Purple, 1939; Evidence

for Two Phases in the Regeneration of Visual Purple, 1940; Morbus Reiteri, 1947; Rubella in Pregnancy and Congenital Deformities in the Child, 1948; Xerophthalmia in Sick Infants Due to Deficient Absorption of Vitiman A, 1953; The Syndrome of Glaucomatocyclitic Crises, 1954; Quinine Amblyopia and the Electroretinogram, 1954; The Effect of Vasodilation on the Electro-retinogram, 1955; On the Electro-retinogram, 1955; Flickerelectroretinography in Six Cases of Total Color Blindness, 1958; Eye Changes in Patients Treated at Tuberculosis Sanatoria, 1957; Ureteral Colic Following Azetazolamide, Diamox, Therapy, 1961; Testing of Color Vision, 1965; On Screening Tests of Color Vision, 1965. Mem: bd, J Cong of Turku, since 1946; Med Assn of Finland; Ophthal Assn of Finland, Fmr vice-chmn; IMA; fmr chmn, Med Soc, Turku. Home and office: Mariegatan 3, Abo, Finland.

ZFATI, Amnon, Isr, technical engr; b. Tel Aviv, Oct 16, 1933; s. Emanuel and Paya (Gepstein); BSc, Techinon, Haifa, 1955, engr, 1956; m. Yael Zeelig, Apr 5, 1959; c: Yehuda, Irit, Amit. Tech mgr, Isr Desalination Ltd, since 1968, mgr, application, since 1965, research engr since 1960; design engr, Merkavim Ltd, 1959-60; sup, erection, sea water desalination plant, Eilat. Lt, tech, IAF, 1955-59. Home: 20 Aluf David St, Ramat Chen, Isr. Office: POB 18041, Tel Aviv, Isr.

ZICHRONY, Amnon, Isr, attorney; b. Tel Aviv, Sep 22, 1935; s. Tobias and Masha (Wasserman); LLB, Tel Aviv U, 1962; m. Miriam Mandelberger, Sep 1, 1959; c: Tivona, Sharon. Atty, appeared in political law cases which set precedent; co-found, adv, Haolam Hazeh, New Force, Political Party. Co-org, Tel Aviv Youngsters for Volunteer Work in Maabarot; active mem, various orgs for rights of Arab population in Isr; fmr: secy, Comm for Recognition of Civil Marriage; mem: exec, League for Hum Rights; Intl War Resistors. Author: several works and research papers; book on Party activities in Knesset. Home: 12 Weizmann St, Givatayim, Isr. Office: 4 Hagilboa St, Tel Aviv, Isr.

ZIEF, Morris, US, chemist; b. Boston, Mass, Aug 8, 1914; s. Eli and Rose (Shulman); BA, Harvard Coll, 1937; MA, Boston U, 1938, PhD, 1941; m. Hazel Zislin, Jan 4, 1948; c: Donald, Joel. Sr research chem, JT Baker Chem Co, since 1951; project dir, Sugar Research Found, 1946-51, staff mem from 1942. Prin contribs: research on antibiotics, blood expanders, purification of chem, polymers. Vice-pres, Temple Convenant of Peace, 1961-62; mem: Amer Chem Soc; B'nai B'rith Lodge 30, Easton, Pa, fmr pres. Ed: Fractional Solidification, since 1967; Purification of Inorganic and Organic Materials, since 1969. Hobbies: sailing, squash. Home: 2820 Hermitage Ave, Easton, Pa. Office: N Broad St, Phillipsburg, NJ.

ZIEGLER, Siegfried, US, artists; b. Munich, Ger, Mar 23, 1894; s. Wilhelm and Anna (Goldfarb); in US since 1938; att Acad of Fine Arts, Munich, 1914-17, 1924-26; m. Lee Marxsohn, May 26, 1940; c: Henry. One-man shows: Soc for Advancement of Judaism; Wash Heb Cong; repr in collections: Truman Libr; Newcomen Soc of Eng; Staatsgallerie, Munich; Lafayette Mus, Paris; Heb U, Jerusalem; Franklin Inst, Phila; art dir, Abbe Inst, NYC, 1939-41; conducted art classes, Adult Educ Prog, Stephen Wise Free Syn, NY, 1955-57. F, Royal Soc of Art; mem, Audubon Artists. Recipient: grand govt prize Prix de Rome, 1915; Grumbacher award, 1959; Dorothy M Armbruster award, 1961. Home and studio: 143 Garth Rd, Scarsdale, NY.

ZIEGLER, Zvi, Isr, mathematician, educator; b. Lvov, Pol, Feb 7, 1939; s. Rubin and Malka (Lehrer); in Isr since 1946; BSc, Technion, Haifa, 1960, MSc, 1961; PhD, Stanford U, Cal, 1965; m. Ilana Roll; c: Karni, Naama. Sr lectr, dept of math, Technion, Haifa, since 1967; research asso, Stanford U, Cal, 1967; visiting asso prof, U of Wis, 1968-69. Lt, IDF, 1960-62. Mem: Amer Math Soc; Isr Math Soc; Soc for Ind and Applied Math. Contbr to profsl jours. Home: 28 Einstein St, Haifa, Isr. Office: Technion, Haifa, Isr.

ZIELONKA, David L, US, rabbi; b. El Paso, Tex, Oct 21, 1904; s. Martin and Dora (Schatzky); AB, U Cinn, 1926; BHL, HUC, 1925, ordained rabbi, 1929, hon DD; hon DHum, U Tampa, 1945; m. Carol Ciener, Aug 17, 1930; c: David, Carl. Rabbi, Cong Schaarai Zedek, since 1930; prof, rel, U Tampa. Life mem bd, Family Service Assn of Tampa; mem bd: Tampa chap, ARC; CCAR; Hillsborough Polio Found; HUC-JIR; J Comty Cen; Tampa chap, B'nai B'rith;

Hillsborough TB and Health Assn; Travelers Aid Assn; club, Rotary, Tampa. Home: 819 S Edison Ave, Tampa, Fla.

ZIENTS, Bernard B, US, business exec; b. Newark, NJ, Oct 20, 1912; s. Harry and Rose (Coopersmith); BS, Rutgers U, 1933; MBA, Harvard Grad Sch Bus Admn, 1935; m. Blanche Chapp, Dec 27, 1936; c: Jeffery, Bonnie Forgash. Pres, Gimbels, NY, since 1968; buyer, Abraham & Straus, 1936-39; divisional merchandise mgr, Asso Merchandising Corp, 1939-47; vice-pres, mem bd dirs, gen merchandise mgr, City Stores Mercantile Corp, 1947-55; vice-pres, head, Gimbels Corporate Buying Off, 1955-62; exec head, Gimbels NY Stores, 1962-68. Mem: bd trustees, Temple B'nai Jeshurun, since 1953; bd dirs, NJ Soc for Crippled Children and Adults, since 1960; club, Harvard, NY. Home: 166 Windsor Way, Hillside, NJ. Office: 1272 Broadway, New York, NY.

ZIERING, Sigi, US, business exec; b. Kassel, Ger, Mar 20, 1928; s. Isaac and Cilly (Frisch); in US since 1949; BS, Bklyn Coll, 1953; MA, Syracuse U, NY, 1955, PhD, 1957; m. Marilyn Brisman, June 14, 1953; c: Michael, Ira, Amy, Rosanne. Vice-pres, Dynasciences Corp, LA, Cal, since 1969; research staff mem, Raytheon Co, 1957-59; mgr, physics dept, Allied Research Assos, 1959-61; pres, Space Sciences, 1961-67; corp dir, research, Whittaker Corp, 1968-69. Prin contrib: with Prof E P Gross introduced method of half-range distribution functions into kinetic theory. Asso, f, Amer Inst Aeronautics and Astronautics; mem: AAAS; Amer Inst Phys; Amer Geophys Union; NY Acad Scis; org, Woods Hole Conf on transport theory, jt sponsorship of Air Force Off of Sci Research and Natl Acad Scis. Contbr to phys and engr sci jours. Home: 720 N Walden, Los Angeles, Cal. Office: 11661 San Vicente, Los Angeles, Cal.

ZIFFER, Moshe, Isr, sculptor; b. Przemysl, Pol, Apr 26, 1902; s. Menahem and Henia (Sommer); in Isr since 1919; att Kunstgewerbschule, Vienna, 1924-28; MA, Acad of Art, Berlin, 1933; att Acad of Art, Paris, 1937-39; m. Rachel Melzer. Art tchr, WIZO Sch, 1957-68. Maj works: Albert Einstein; Chaim Weizmann; Ben Gurion; Lot's Wife, at Brussels World Fair; garden figure in stone, Technion; figure and relief, Jerusalem U; monument in honor of battle of Jerusalem; garden sculpture, Weizmann Inst, Rehovot; exhbs: Intl World Exhb, Paris, 1925; Holbein Gal, Vienna, 1928; Berlin, 1932; Paris, 1938; NY World Fair, 1938. Mem, cen comm, Painters & Sculptors Assn, Isr. Recipient: Dizengoff Art Prize, Tel Aviv Mus, 1941, 1943, 1947; 1st prize, War Memorial, Netanya Munic, 1957; 1st prize, wall decor, Haganah, House, Tel Aviv, 1960. Home: 1 Harav Friedman, Tel Aviv, Isr.

ZIFFREN, Chaim J, US, business exec; b. Rock Island, Ill, Nov 4, 1907; s. David and Rose (Frankel); BS, U of Ill, 1930; m. Adele Zimel, Dec 31, 1939; c: Deborah, Harold. Owner: Ziffren Loan Co, since 1939; Ziffren Realty Co, since 1940. Pres, Beth Isr Cong, 1940-50; hon life co-chmn, Rel Comm, Tri-City J Cen; hon life dir, Tri-City Cemetry Assn; found, Vaad Hakashrut; secy, treas, Hatikvah Credit Union, Gemeelos Chesed, 1930-45; co-chmn, UJA drive, 1946; bd mem: JDC; Rock I J Charities; mem: AJComm; B'nai B'rith; Davenport C of C. Home: 14 Hillcrest Court, Rock Island, Ill. Office: 124 E 3 St, Davenport, Ia.

ZIFFREN, Paul, US, attorney; b. Davenport, Ia, July 18, 1913; s. Jacob and Belle (Rothenberg); BS, Northwestern U, 1935, JD, Sch of Law, 1938; m. Muriel Averett, May 20,1948; c: John, Kenneth, Abbie. Sr partner, Ziffren & Ziffren, since 1950; lectr, fed taxation, Northwestern U Sch of Law, 1939-41; spec asst to chief counsel, Bur of Internal Revenue, Chgo, Ill, 1939-40; asst US atty, chief of tax div, Chgo, 1941-42. Mem: bd trustees, Citizen's Research Found, Princeton, NJ; cabinet, Music Cen Arts and Educ Fund; bd govs, Cedars Sinai Med Cen; LA World Affairs Council; exec comm, bd dirs, Cen Theater Group of LA, Music Cen; fmr: vice-pres, Temple Isr, Hollywood, Cal; Dem natl committeeman, Cal; chmn, Cal conv comm, Dem Natl Conv, 1960; Order of Coif; Sigma Delta Chi; clubs: LA; Hillcrest Country; LA Press; Friars. Fmr mem, ed bd, Ill Law Rev. Home: 23920 Malibu Rd, Malibu Cal. Office: 10889 Wilshire Blvd, Los Angeles, Cal.

ZIFFREN, Sidney E, US, surgeon, educator; b. Rock Island, Ill, Aug 30, 1912; s. David and Rose (Frankel); att: Augustana Coll, 1930; U of Neb, 1931; St Ambrose Coll, 1932; BS, MD, U of Ill, 1936. Prof, surg, U of Ia, since 1953, asst prof, 1949-51, asso prof, 1951-53. US Army MC. Mem: Amer Bd

Surg; Amer Coll Surgs; Amer Surg Assn; Cen Surg Assn; W Surg Assn; Cen Soc for Clinical Research; Soc for Experimental Biol and Med; Soc of U Surgs; Amer Geriatrics-Soc; Soc of Nuclear Med; Amer Assn for Surg and Trauma. Author: The Management of the Aged Surgical Patient.,1960. Home: 928 Crest, Iowa City, Ia. Office: U Hosp, Iowa City, Ia.

ZIFRONI, Abraham, Isr, physician; b. Bialystock, Pol, Aug 10, 1907; in Isr since 1934; att U Basel, Switz; m. Fanny Pewsner, June 17, 1934; c: Yael Galon, Anat Rosental. TB and lung diseases specialist since 1935; dir, Hadassah Hosp, Safad, 1948-57; sr, lung dept, Hadassah Hosp, Jerusalem, 1957-62. Vice-pres, Swiss-Isr comm; f: Amer Coll Chest Phys; Isr Coll Chest Phys; fmr: pres; B'nai B'rith, Safad; Rotary, Safad; and found, Magen David Adom, Safad. Author: Pulmonary Tuberculosis. Home: 6 Haray Maymon St, Jerusalem, Isr. Office: 5 Sarey Israel St, Jerusalem, Isr.

ZILKHA, Ezra K, US, banker; b. Baghdad, July 31, 1925; s. Khedoury and Louise (Bashi); in US since 1941; BA, Wesleyan U, Conn, 1946; m. Cecile Iny, Feb 5, 1950; c: Donald, Donna, Bettina. Pres, Zilkha & Sons, Inc, NY, since 1956; chmn bd, chief exec off, Amer Intl Bank, NY, since 1968; dir, vice-chmn bd, chmn exec comm, Hudson Leasing Corp, NY; dir, chmn exec comm, Federal's Inc, Detroit; dir: Handy & Harman, NY; Ins Co of N Amer, Phila; Banque Européenne de Finalement, Paris; Henry Ansbacher & Co, Ltd, London; Speech Rehab Inst, NY; Alliance Française, NY; INA Corp, Phila; French C of C, US. Trustee: Lycée Français de New York; Wesleyan U, Middletown, Conn, clubs: Bankers of Amer, NYC; St James' London; Polo, Paris; U, NY, Home: 927 Fifth Ave, New York, NY. Office: 120 Broadway, New York, NY.

ZILZER, Gyula, US, artist, film production designer; b. Budapest, Hung, Feb 4, 1898; s. Rudolf and Berta (Kaiser); in US since 1932; grad: Royal Acad Art ,Budapest; Acad Art, Munich; Royal Hungarian Coll; Royal Joseph Poly U, Budapest; Hans Hoffman Acad, Munich, 1923; Colarossi Acad, Paris; m; c: Vera; m. 2nd, Mary Fuchs, Feb 10, 1953. Free-lance art dir, produc designer, 1 quality control specialist; art dir, color TV films; designer, produc asst, motion pictures: Fr; Hollywood; prin films: Know Your Enemy; Life of Jack London; Portrait of Dorian Gray; Sahara; Counter Attack; The Macomber Affair; The Miracle of the Bells; The Eighth Day, the story of atomic energy for peace; designer, stage settings: A Bell for Adano; Androcles and the Lion; quality control specialist, NBC, TV, 1941-52; with art dept, Universal Intl, Hollywood, 1953. Prin works: Kaleidoscope, lithography album, 1924; The Black Cat, illustrations for Edgar Allan Poe, 1927; Gas Attack, lithographs, 1932; The Mechanical Man, illustrations for book, 1959; numerous one-man shows and exhbs: US; Moscow; Amsterdam; London; Budapest; perm collections: Luxembourg; Paris; Munich; Moscow; Budapest; NY Public Libr; Mus of Modern Art, NY; Metrop Mus of Art; Bezalel Natl Mus, Jerusalem. Recipient: hon dipl, Intl Exhb, Bordeaux, 1927; Off of Legion of Merit-Humain, Zurich, 1933. Home: 27 W 96 St, New York, NY.

ZIMERING, Max, US, certified public acctnt, educator; b. Aus, Mar 4, 1907; s. Shalom and Chaya (Gross); in US since 1921; BBA, magna cum laude, CCNY, 1933; CPA, NY State, 1936; MBA, NYU, 1942; m. Anne Goldberg, June 12, 1937; c: Seth, Charles. Asso prof, acctnt, Baruch Sch of Bus and Public Admn, CCNY, since 1957, instr, 1934-47, asst prof, 1947-57; cost dept, Consolidated Laundries Corp, 1933-35; auditor, NYC Comptroller's Off, 1935-38; partner: Zimering & Misthal, 1938-53; Zimering, Misthal & Co, 1953-59; pvt practice, CPA, since 1959. Life mem, ZOA, pres, dist 34 Manhattan Beach; mem: Acctnt Assn; Amer Inst CPAs; Soc of Munic Acctnts, Inc; AJCong; Masons; Beta Gamma Sigma; Beta Alpha Psi; Delta Sigma Tau; fmr: pres, Baruch Alumni Soc; financial secy, Manhattan Beach J Cen, recording secy, 2nd vice-pres, secy, bd educ; treas, Sch of Bus Alumni, CCNY, 3rd vice-pres, bd dirs, chmn, comms; auditor-asso, Alumni of CCNY; delg: Bklyn JCC; Heb U; admissions comm, NY State Soc of CPAs; participant in Conf of US Cen Off, Wash, DC. Author: Auditing Laboratory Manual to Accompany Jackson's Auditing Text, 1936; Auditing Questions and Problems, 1937; Advanced Accounting Simplified, 1940; co-author: Advanced Accounting Theory and Problems, Parts I and II, 1950, 1953; Advanced Accounting Problems-Theory and Practice, 1958. Recipient: citation,Treasury Dept, 1945; award of merit, UJA, 1953; service award, Sch of Bus. evening div, 1954; Alumni service award, 1955; Saxe House plan award, 1955; Outstanding Alumnus award, 1962; Award of Appreciation from Alumni, 1966. Home: 144 Pembroke St, Brooklyn, NY. Offices: 17 Lexington Ave, New York, NY; 507 Fifth Ave, New York, NY.

ZIMET, Erwin, US, rabbi; b. Berlin, Ger, Mar 27, 1912; s. Hermann and Anna (Dingenthal); in US since 1939; att U of Berlin, 1930-33; ordained rabbi, Hochschule für die Wissenschaft des Judentums, 1938; m. Lilli Gehr, Nov 3, 1940; c: Miriam, Michael, Jonathan. Rabbi, Temple Beth-El, since 1946; chaplain, Green Haven Prison, Stormville, NY, since 1950; counselor, Vassar Coll Hillel Found, since 1950; asst rabbi, Park Ave Syn, NYC, 1939-46. Pres: Amer Correctional Chaplains Assn, 1965-66; Dutchess Co Ministerial Assn, 1963-64; ZOA, Poughkeepsie chap, 1957-58; mem: RA; NY Bd Rabbis; B'nai B'rith; City of Poughkeepsie, N Commn on Human Relations, 1964-66. Home: 39 Thornwood Dr, Poughkeepsie, NY. Study: 118 Grand Ave, Poughkeepsie, NY.

ZIMMER, Alex, US, cantor; b. Bklyn, NY, Aug 21, 1922; s. Hyman and Hannah (Singer); MA, NYU, 1951; BSM, HUC-JIR, 1954; m. Doris Dukaten, Dec 8, 1945; c: William, Michael, Wendy, Lisa. Cantor, dir of music, since 1955; co mgr, soloist, Robert Shaw Chorale, 1949-53; cantor, prin, Cen Syn of Nassau Co, 1953-54. Lt, USAAF, 1942-45. Pres, Amer Conf Cantors; found, NE J Music Forum, 1958-66; exec bd, Natl J Music Council, JWB; mem, JWV. Contbr to J publs. Spec interests: youth work, carpentry. Home: 6 Valley Spring Rd, Newton, Mass. Office: 1187 Beacon St, Brookline, Mass.

ZIMMERMAN, Charles S, US, labor union exec; b. Kiev, Russ, Nov 27, 1897; s. Ben Zion and Leah; in US since 1913; m. Rose Prepstein, Nov 25, 1925; c: Paul. Vice-pres, ILGWU, since 1934; gen mgr, Jt Bd Dress and Waistmakers Union, ILGWU, since 1958; factory worker, 1916-33; secy-mgr, Local 22, ILGWU, 1933-58. Pres, J Lab Comm, chmn, Natl Trade Council for Hum Rights; chmn: natl bd dirs, Natl Comm for Lab Isr; commn, NYC Commn on Intergroup Relations, 1955-62; exec chmn, Lab Comm, City of Hope; lab mem of commn, Fed Minimum Wage Comm, Puerto Rico, 1956-62; mem, bd dirs: NYC Cen Lab Council; AFL-CIO Ind Union Dept; Asso Hosp Service of NY, Blue Cross; Health Ins Plan; United Housing Found; Natl Comm Against Discrimination in Housing; City of Hope, Duarte, Cal; NYC Commercial Devl Corp; Educ Found for Fashion Inds; Intl Rescue Comm; ORT; League for Ind Democracy: mem: exec comm, Intl Textile and Garment Workers Fed; exec comm, Inter-Amer Fed of Textile and Garment Workers; AFL-CIO Civil Rights Comm, fmr chmn; natl adv comm, Planned Comtys, Inc; Trade Union Adv Comm; Lab Educ Advancement Prog of Natl Urban League; Mayor's Task Force Study Panel; admn comm, HIAS. Recipient: dist services award, NYC Cen Lab Council, 1965. Home: 240 Cabrini Blvd, New York, NY. Office: 218 W 40 St, New York, NY.

ZIMMERMAN, Harry M, US, pathologist, educator; b. Vilna, Russ, Sep 28, 1901; s. Jacob and Anna (Kaplan); in US since 1909; BS, Yale U, 1924, MD, 1927; att Deutsche Forschungsanstalt für Psychiatrie, Munich, 1929; hon LHD, Yeshiva U, 1957; m. Miriam Gordon, Sep 2, 1930. Prof, Coll Phys and Surgs, Columbia U, since 1947; chief, lab div, Montefiore Hosp, since 1946; sr cons, path Bx VA Hosp, since 1947; asso prof, Yale U, 1930-43; cons, neuropath, Armed Forces Inst Path, 1948-67. Cdr, USN, MC, 1944-46. Adv bd, Tel Aviv U Sch Med, since 1965; dir, Albert Einstein Coll of Med, Yeshiva U, 1953-55; f: NY Acad Med; Amer Neur Assn; Amer Assn Path and Bact. Co-author: Atlas of Tumors of the Nervous System, 1956; Neuroradiology Workshop, 1961; ed, Infections of the Nervous System, 1968; contbr to med jours. Home: 200 Cabrini Blvd, New York, NY. Office: Montefiore Hosp, New York, NY.

ZIMMERMAN, Hyman J, US, physician, educator; b. Rochester, NY, July 19, 1914; s. Philip and Rachel(Marine); AB, U Rochester, 1936; MA, Stanford U, 1938, MD, Sch of Med, 1942; m. Kathrin Jones, Feb 28, 1943; c: Philip, David, Robert, Diane. Chief, med service, VA Hosp, Boston; prof, med, Boston U Sch of Med; both since 1968; asst res, med, George Wash U Med Div, Gallinger Munic Hosp, 1946-47, chief res, 1947-48; clinical instr, med, George Wash Sch Med, 1948-51; asst chief, med service, VA Hosp, Wash, DC, 1949-51; asst prof, med, U Neb Coll Med, 1951-53; clinical prof, med, U Ill Coll Med, Chgo, 1953-57; chief, med service, VA W Side Hosp, Chgo, 1953-57; prof, med, George Wash U Sch Med, 1965-68; prof, chmn dept med, Chgo Med Sch, 1957-

68; chmn, dept med, Mt Sinai Hosp, 1957-68. US Army, 1943-46. Mem: Amer Fed for Clinical Research; Endocrine Soc; Amer Diabetes Assn; Assn for Study of Liver Disease; Amer Soc Clinical Inves; FACP; NY Acad Sci; Cen Soc for Clinical Research; AMA; Soc for Experimental Biol and Med; AAAS; Chgo Med Soc; Assn of Profs Med; Sigma Xi; Alpha Omega Alpha. Contbr to med jours. Office: 150 S Huntington Ave, Boston, Mass.

ZIMMERMAN, Joseph, US, metal consultant, editor; b. Aus, Sep 21, 1891; s. Louis and Bessie (Weintraub); in US since 1899; BA, CCNY, 1915; MA, Columbia U, 1916; JD, NYU, 1931; m. Anna Cohen, Mar 9, 1918; c: Phyllis Seton, Mimi Gordon. Vice-pres, Miles Metal Co; metal cons and market analyst; fmr: ed in chief, Daily Metal Reporter; instr, educ, asst dir, educ clinic and examining psychol, CCNY. Mem comm: UJA; B'nai B'rith; mem: Phi Beta Kappa; Amer Inst Mining and Metallurgical Engrs; Acad Political Sci; Mining and Metallurgical Soc of Amer; Amer Technion Soc of Amer; AAAS; club, Mining. Author: Comparative Study of Binet-Simon Test and Yerkes Point Scale Test, 1916. Recipient: Ward and Pell medals, CCNY; citation, ADL. Home: Stonybrook, Westport, Conn. Office: 1 Chase Manhattan Plaza, New York, NY.

ZIMMERMAN, Leo M, US, surgeon, educator; b. Toluca, Ill, Oct 27, 1898; s. Louis and Sara (Kahan); AB, U of Ind, 1919; MD, Rush Med Coll, 1922; m. Sara Radoff, Apr 10, 1928; c: David, Judith. Pvt practice since 1927; prof, chmn, dept of hist and phil of med, Chgo Med Sch, since 1968; fac mem since 1948; att surg: Michael Reese, Cook Co Hosps, both since 1930; prof, surg, Cook Co Grad Sch of Med, since 1950; asst prof, surg, Northwestern U Med Sch, 1924-48. Cdr, USN, WW II. Pres, Soc Med Hist of Chgo; regional dir, Amer Phys Art Assn; f: AMA; Amer Coll Surgs; mem: Ill Med Soc; Chgo Med Soc; Chgo Surg Soc; Amer Goiter Assn; Intl Coll Surgs; Amer Assn for Hist of Med; f: Alpha Omega Alpha; Sigma Xi. Author: Anatomy and Surgery of Hermia, 1953; Physiologic Principles of Surgery, 1957; Principles of Surgical Practice, 1960; Great Ideas in Surgery, 1961; ed: The Surgical Clinics of N America, 1962; Hernioplasty, film, 1953; contbr to med jours. Home: 5000 E End Ave, Chicago, Ill. Office: 55 E Washington St, Chicago, Ill.

ZIMMERMAN, Michael B, Can, business exec; b. Bessarabia, Rum, Dec 22, 1922; s. Baruch and Vitea (Eisenstein); in Can since 1951; att Loyola Coll, Montreal, 1964-68; div; c: Jack. Secy-treas: Zimmco Co; Tanaco Ltd, both since 1951; Ramsay Ind, Ltd, since 1960; Bell Aluminum, since 1964; Artmetwork Co, since 1968; dir: Modern Aluminium, Eng, since 1967; Zimcor, Isr, since 1966; Alubin Ltd, since 1966. Mem: B'nai B'rith; J Peretz Sch; YM-YWHA; J People's Sch. Spec interests: political sci, political phil, chess. Home: 39 Roxton Circle, Montreal W, Can. Office: 2100 Remembrance, Lachine, Que, Can.

ZIMMERMAN-GRIES, Sara, Isr, agronomist; b. Tiberias, Isr, Sep 20, 1913; d. Chaim and Chaya (Lieberman); att fac agric, Portici, Napoli, It; PhD, agric sci, U of Milano, It, 1937; m. Max Gries-Honig, Apr, 1943; c: Ada Naamoni, Zeev, Dvorah, Glilya, Chaim. Sr research worker, potato expert, since 1967, potato adv, seed dept, Volcani Inst, since 1959; potato research, Agric Experimental Sta, Rehovot, 1937-42; potato research, Rehovot, 1943-50; specialist, virus diseases of potatoes, U of Wis, 1950; chief specialist, seed potatoes: JA Agric Settlement Dept; Isr Min of Agric, 1950-58. Cpl, Brit Army, ATS, 1942-43. Town councilor, City of Rehovot; mem jury, Haklait, Zimmerman Prize Comm, for research, services, devl of cattle ind in Isr; delg, Fed of Agric Workers, Isr; mem: Adv Comm for Potato Field Inspection; Mediterranean Phytopath. Contbr to jours. Spec interests: lit, art, growing flowers, canning fruits and vegetables. Home: 9 Beeri St, Rehovot, Isr. Office: Volcani Inst of Agric Research, Isr.

ZINDER, Hemdah, Isr, government official; b. Jerusalem, June 23, 1916; d. Aryeh and Rahel (Meyouhas) Feigenbaum; att Pratt Inst, Bklyn, NY; m. Harry Zinder, Feb 24, 1939; c: Oren, David. Secy, Isr Natl Commn for UNESCO, since 1956; broadcaster, Pal Bc Service, 1936-38, org, children's hour, dramatic producs, 1938-40; dir, bur, Min of Educ and Culture, 1955-56. Hobbies: music, art, archaeol. Home: 31 Ben Maimon St, Jerusalem, Isr. Office: 34 Shivtey Yisrael St, Jerusalem, Isr.

ZINDER, Zvi Harry, Isr, government official, public relations exec; b. Monongahela, Pa, Aug 26, 1909; s. Mathias and Esther

(Federhar); in Isr since 1934; BA, Northwestern U, 1932; m. Hemda Feigenbaum, Feb 24, 1939; c: Oren, David. Admnr, Harry S Truman Cen for Advancement of Peace, Heb U, Jerusalem; dir, Isr Cen Off of Info, MP's Off, since 1960; free-lance journalist, Balkans, ME, 1933-34; staff mem, Pal Post, 1935-37; corresp, Asso Press, Pal, Syria, Leb, 1937-41; staff corresp, Time and Life mags, attached to ME Forces, 1941-44, war corresp: Burma and China, 1944, Eur Theater of oprs, 1945, acting bur chief, Paris off, 1945, bureau chief, ME area, 1946-48; staff mem, JA offs, Wash, DC, 1948-50; dir, press relations: Isr Off of Info, NYC, 1951-54; Isr delg to UN, 1951-54; dir, Isr Bc Service, Jerusalem, 1954-60. Contbr to newspapers and mags. Recipient: N Afr Medal; Eur Theater Medal; China, Burma, India Theater Medal, 1945. Home: 31 Ben Maimon Rd, Jerusalem, Isr. Office: PM Off, Jerusalem, Isr.

ZINGER, Zvi Salomon, Isr, educator, author; b. Pol, Dec 23, 1921; in Isr since 1950; grad: Yeshivot, Belgium, Eng; Heb U, Jerusalem; m. Karla Bernhard-Rath, 1946; c: Shoshana, Ira. Dir, Press and PR Bur, JA, Jerusalem; ed, daily Bible reading and commentary, Isr Bc Services; fmr: co-found, Kibbutz Lavi, dir, Hodayot, settlement's Youth Aliyah instn; dir, cultural div, Hakkibutz Hadati, found, ed, Amudim, monthly; dir, rel sect, youth and chalutz dept, JA, Jerusalem; lectr tour, US, on behalf Isr Fgn Min. Author: book on philosophy of Rabbi Kook, Heb, 1970; contbr to lit, jours; educ materials. Fmr, leader, Zionist youth, dir, Brit Chalutzim Datiim, cultural cen, Gt Brit. Home: 54 Hapisga St, Jerusalem, Isr.

ZINMAN, Philip, US, business exec; b. Phila, Pa, July 18, 1904; s. Robert and Esther (Stambler); att Temple U Law Sch, 1925-29; BS, econ, U of Pa, Wharton Sch, 1925; m. Zola Nelson, June 24, 1932; c: Sally, Anne Lorch. Chmn bd: Philip Zinman & Co, since 1967, pres, 1925-67; Asso Mortgage Cos, since 1962; S Jersey Mortgage Co, since 1959, pres, 1943-59. Fmr pres: NJ Mortgage Bankers Assn Educ Found, 1962; NJ Mortgage Bankers Assn, 1957; NJ chap, Amer Inst of Real Estate Appraisers, 1941; Camden Co Real Estate Bd, 1947; Camden NJ chap, Soc Residential Appraisers, 1941; vice-pres, bd mem, Amer Friends Heb U; mem, bd dirs, Phila Friends Heb U, fmr pres; bd mem, Fed of J Charities, Phila, 1966-68; gen chmn, Camden Co Allied J Appeal, 1948, 1959; bd mem, Phila Friends Amer Technion Soc; gen chmn: Camden Co Isr Bond Comm, 1952-53; NJ State of Isr Bonds, 1952-53; natl bd, Bonds for Isr, mem, exec comm, Phila, 1957-58; vice-chmn, Camden Co Comm Fund, 1952; natl chmn, UJA, co-found, Isr Inves Corp; club; Ashbourne Country, pres, 1954-55. Home: Elkins Park House, Elkins Park, Pa. Office: 500 Market St, Camden, NJ.

ZIONS, Aba, US, rabbi; b. Brest-Litovsk, Aug 15, 1911; s. Chaim and Tauba-Basheva (Syrkin); in US since 1946; ordained rabbi: Brisk Yeshiva, 1932; Slobodka-Kamenetz Yeshiva, 1939; Mir Yeshiva, 1943; MEd, Yeshiva U, 1962, PhD, 1963; m. Riva Tellem, 1948; c: Tova, Chaim, Pinchas, Mordechai, Zev. Rabbi: Cong Knesseth Isr, Bx, NY, since 1946; org, prin, Darkei Noah; rabbi, Cong Zivchei Zedek, both Brest-Litowsk, 1932-39; rabbi, Minian Hazedek, Shaghai, China, 1942-46. Vice-pres, Rabb Bd, Bx, 1955-62; secy, Mikvah Isr, Bx; mem: Union Orthodox Rabbis, US and Can; Agudath Isr, Amer; fmr: secy, Poalei Agudath Isr, Pol; gen secy, org, Yahaduth movement, Pol, later Isr. Author: Der Ruf zu Yung und Alt, 1937; Droshat Harapam, 1949. Contbr to J periodicals. Home: 735 Walton Ave, Bronx, NY. Study: 844 Gerard Ave, Bronx, NY.

ZIPKIN, Isadore, US, educator; b. Rochester, NY, Oct 30, 1914; s. Abraham and Bluma (Yavker); AB, U of Rochester, 1937; MS, Pa State U, 1940, PhD, 1942; postgrad studies, Stanford U, Cal, 1958; m. Lillian Furman, Jan 30, 1943; c: Richard, Michael. Prof, biochem, Sch of Dent, U of Cal, SF, since 1968; sci dir, asso chief, biochem lab, Natl Inst Dent Research, NIH, Bethesda, Md, 1967-68, with NIH since 1946; guest lectr in US and abroad. Capt, US Army, 1942-46. F: Amer Inst Nutrition; Amer Soc Biol Chems; Amer Coll Dents; mem: Amer Chem Soc; Gamma Sigma Delta; Phi Lambda Upsilon; Sigma Xi; AAAS; Intl Assn Dent Research, fmr, chmn, Wash sect; Soc for Experimental Biol and Med; Biochem Soc, London; fmr, chmn, Gordon Research Conf on Chem, Phys and Structure of Bones and Teeth. Contbr to sci publs. Recipient, travel grants: Amer Inst Nutrition, 1966; 7th Intl Cong of Nutrition, 1966; 8th Intl Cong of Nutrition, Amer Inst of Nutrition, 1969. Hobbies:

sport, theater. Home: 310 Arballo Dr, San Francisco, Cal. Office: U of Cal, Sch of Dent, San Francisco, Cal.

ZIPMAN, Chaja, Isr, organization exec; b. Ukraine, Feb 10, 1907; d. Ben Zion and Sara (Barstein) Sternfeld; in Isr since 1926; m. Shlomo Zipman, 1928; c: Zafrira Vishnievski, Drora. Head, vocational training dept, mem active, secretariat, Moetzet Hapoalot; fmr: mem, Zionist Youth Group, Hecalutz, Russ; agric, road bldg worker, Nes Ziona; absorption work, Yemenite Aliyah; secy, Irgun Imahot Ovdot; absorption work, Aliyah Bet; with cen off, Moetzet Hapoalot. Mem: Kfar Hess Mgn Council; Ramat Gan Workers' Council Secretariat; local council, Givatayim; Ramat Gan Munic Council; natl secretariat, Women's Workers Council. Contbr to press. Home: 29A Arlosoroff St, Tel Aviv, Isr.

ZIPORYN, Marvin, US, psychiatrist, musician; b. NYC, Sep 26, 1923; s. Isidore and Anna (Markovich); BS, Northwestern U, 1942; BM, Chgo Med Sch, 1946, MD, 1948; m. Charlotte Weinberg, Mar 25, 1956; c: Terra, Evan, Brook. Chief psycht, Ill State Training Sch for Boys, St Charles, Ill; cons, Chgo Bd Educ, USPHS, 1948-51; asso, psycht, Chgo Med Sch, 1958-62; cons, Ill Dept Mh, 1961-62; staff psycht: Munic Court, Chgo, 1958-59; Cook Co Hosp, 1961-67; fmr asst prof, psycht, U of Ill Coll of Med. Concert violinist; toured Far East; concerts in US. Mem, Amer Psycht Assn. Coauthor: Born to Raise Hell, The Untold Story of Richard Speck, 1967; contbr to med jours. Home: 8922 Ewing, Evanston, Ill. Office: 410 S Michigan, Chicago, Ill.

ZIPPER, Yakov I, Can, educator; b. Tyshowietz, Pol, Oct 10, 1900; s. Abraham and Gitel (Zimmerman); in Can since 1925; m. Sarah Pofelis, Sep, 1925; c: Oda, Chana. Prin, J Peretz Schs, Montreal, since 1928. Mem: cen comm, Yiddish Folkshulen; natl educ comm, Can J Cong; Assn of J Schs of Can. Author: Geven is a Mensch, the story of the Baalshem, trans into Heb, 1940; Oif Jener Sait Bug, 1946; Zwishn Taichn un Wassern, 1961, trans into Heb, poem in book form, Ich Bin Vider in mine Chorever Haim Gekumen, 1967; contbr to Yiddish and Heb periodicals. Home: 5786 McAlear Ave, Montreal, Can. Office: 7950 Wavell Rd, Cote St Luc, Montreal, Can.

ZIPRIN, Nathan, US, editor; b. Chmelnik, Russ, June 5, 1898; in US since 1909; LLB, NYU, 1922. Ret; Seven Arts Feature Syndicate, NYC, 1941-68; free-lance writer since 1930. Club: Farband. Home: 181 E 161 St, New York, NY.

ZIPRKOWSKI, Leo, Isr, physician; b. Grajewo, Russ, Mar 27, 1909; s. Jacob and Rosa (Kianowski); att U of Berlin, 1930-33; MD, U of Basel, 1939; m. Ilse Jacobowitz, Apr 28, 1941; c: Varda Farchi, Micha, Ruth. Prof, head dept dermat, Tel Hashomer Hosp, since 1948; prof, chmn, dermat sect, Postgrad Med Sch, Tel Aviv U, since 1968. Maj, RAMC, 1939-46; lt col, IDF, 1948-65. Pres, Dermat Soc of IMA, Tel Aviv br; corresp mem, Soc Fr de Dermat et de Syphiligraphie; mem: Intl Tropical Dermat Soc; B'nai B'rith; KJV. Contbr to dermat jours. Hobbies: music, art. Home: 5 Hashoshanim St, Tel Aviv, Isr. Office: Tel Hashomer Govt Hosp, Tel Hashomer, Isr.

ZIRINSKY, Julius, US, artist; b. Libau, Latvia, Jan 12, 1898; s. Isaiah and Goldie (Rabinowitz); in US since 1920; att: Acad of Fine Arts, Dresden, Ger, 1919-20; Natl Acad of Design, NY, 1926-27; m. Helen Feldstein, Sep 25, 1947. Portrait painter; prin portraits include: Albert Einstein; Judge Cardozo; Theodore Dreiser; Judge Felix Frankfurter; stage personalities: Gertrude Lawrence; Otts Skinner; Misha Elman; repr in perm collections: Whitney Gal; J Mus; Ein Harod Mus, Isr; Brandeis U; NY Bar Assn Bldg. Mem: Artists Equity Assn. Hobbies: music, singing. Home and studio: 300 E 57 St, New York, NY.

ZIRINSKY, Victor J, Hong Kong, business exec; b. Vladivostok, USSR, Oct 23, 1920; s. Jacob and Sophia (Radomishelsky); in Hong Kong since 1948; BSc, St John's U, Shanghai, 1942; MSc, McGill U, Montreal, 1948; m. Joan Saphiere, Mar 26, 1953; c: Sonia, Linda, Jacob. Dir: United Paper Co Ltd since 1948; United Agcys Ltd; Hon Consul Gen for Isr. Repr in Hong Kong for: United HIAS Service, since 1955; JA, since 1955; vice-chmn, Hong Kong Contract Bridge Assn; treas, Far East Contract Bridge Assn; trustee, Syn Ohel Leah; clubs: J Recreation; Hong Kong Country. Home: 5A Repulse Bay Mansions, Hong Kong. Office: 425 Alexandra House, Hong Kong.

ZIRKIN, Nathan Leonard, US, accountant, comptroller; b. Tcherske, Russ, Oct 11, 1910; s. Samuel and Rachel; BA, LIU, 1932; m. Nora Shapiro, Oct 15, 1939; c: Barry, Stanley, Regina. Comptroller, Retail, Wholesale & Dept Store Union AFL-CIO: CLC, since 1938. Pres, Herbert Shapiro Menorah, Chap 18, B'nai Zion, mem, exec bd; treas, Bay Terr Corp, sect 2, Inc; mem, KP. Home: 212-23 15 Ave, Bayside, NY. Office: 101 W 31 St, New York, NY.

ZIV, Daniel, Isr, agronomist; b. Lodz, Pol, Jan 25, 1902; s. Akiva and Chava (Shmigelski) Weiss; in Isr since 1906; att Herzliya Gymnasium; m. Chaya Barash, May, 1925; c: Chana Niv. Agric research specialist, Jordan Valley Experimental Comm, since 1939; agron, Degania Bet, since 1921. Author: Growing Alfalfa, 1946; Yedidai HaKtanim, children's songs, 1950; Irrigation, 1955; Investigations in Banana and Irrigated Crops, 1962; Lashon VeTeva, 1969. Hobby: Heb philol. Home and office: Degania Bet, Isr.

ZIV, Michael, Isr, educator; b. Boryslaw, Pol, Nov 5, 1902; s. Holzman and (Weisinger); PhD, U of Cracov, 1928; m. Hanna Graf; c: Rut Brandes, Zeev. Lectr, modern hist: U of Tel Aviv; U of Beersheva; prin, secondary sch, U of Jerusalem, 1947-50; insp, secondary schs, Min of Educ, 1950-51, dir, dept on secondary educ, 1951-67. Author of handbooks on hist for secondary schs, hist atlas, anthol. Home: Shikun Kiryat Moshe, Ben Zion Gat, Jerusalem, Isr.

ZIV, Yoram, Isr, government official; b. Tel Aviv, Mar 30, 1937; s. Yechiel and Esther (Gelander) Wiesen; BA, Heb U, Jerusalem, 1961; m. Tamar Gurman, June 22, 1961; c: Daphna, Nourith. Econ adv, Min Commerce and Ind, since 1968; with Min for Fgn Affairs since 1962; commercial attaché: Emb of Isr, Brussels, 1962-65; Paris, 1965-68. Home: 23 Guatemala St, Jerusalem, Isr. Office: Min of Commerce and Ind, Jerusalem, Isr.

ZIV-AV, Izchak, Isr, organization exec, author; b. Smolensk, Russ, June 4, 1907; s. Avraham and Miriam (Luitin); in Isr since 1926; att Fac of Educ, Smolensk, 1923-26; m. Deborah Kobrinsky, Nov 8, 1934; c: Avraham, Aharon. Contbr ed, Hayom, Heb daily, since 1967; gen dir, Farmers Fed of Isr, 1952-65, on staff since 1934; farmer, Magdiel, 1926-34; mgr, Magdiel Local Council, 1930-33; mgn ed, Haboker, Heb daily, 1935-48; mem, supr court, Yishuv Defence Mobilization, 1947; first mil corresp, with IDF, War of Independence, 1948; dir, PR dept, Isr Min of Defence, 1948-52. Mem, bd dirs: JNF, since 1960; Land Dept of Isr, since 1960; Coop Soc of Min of Lab, 1963-65; ZOA House, Tel Aviv, since 1953; mem: adv bd, Kol Isr, Isr radio, 1962-65; hon court, Journalists Assn, 1949; cen comm, Gen Zionist Party, 1952; Lib Party, since 1968; delg: World Cong of Farmers, India, 1959; Yugo, 1961; NZ, 1965; mem, mission to Iran and Aden, The Magic Carpet, 1950-51. Author: Unknown Land, 1943; I Seek My Brethren, 1946; Good Morning, Uncle Spring; Animals Holiday, both children's books, 1947; The Price of Freedom, 1950; Travels, 1951; Forever Ours, 1956; A World to Live In, 1962; Another World, 1966; all Heb; contbr to local press and radio. Recipient: Ramat Gan Lit Prize for Unknown Land, 1945; KH Jubilee Prize for parts of Unknown Land, 1945; Ussishkin Lit Prize for Forever Ours, 1957. Home: 3 Samuely St, Ramat Gan, Isr. Office: POB 209, Tel Aviv, Isr.

ZLOTNICK, Avinoam, Isr, physician; b. Minsk, Russ, Apr 27, 1919; s. Yaacov and Tova (Feigin); in Isr since 1930; MSc, Heb U, Jerusalem, 1946; MD, U of Geneva, Switz, 1951; m. Hanna Mendelowitsch, June 9, 1949; c: Odeda, Aviad, Amnon. Chief phys, dept A, Hadassah U Hosp, Jerusalem, since 1962, head, research lab, auto-immune diseases, since 1965; asso prof, med, Heb U-Hadassah Med Sch, since 1965. Lt, IDF, MC, 1949-69. Prin contrib: described for first time amyloid-producing cell in human being. Affiliate mem, Royal Soc Med, London; mem: Intl Soc Hematology; Soc Internal Med; Immunological Soc, both Isr. Contbr to profsl jours. Recipient: Baque Med Fac Prize, 1964. Hobby: photography. Home: 23 Metudela St, Jerusalem, Isr. Office: Heb U-Hadassah Hosp, Jerusalem, Isr.

ZLOTNICK, Dov, US, educator; b. Pol, Mar 18, 1925; s. William and Rebecca (Berman); in US since 1927; BA, Bklyn Coll, 1948; MA, Columbia U, 1950; MHL, JTSA, 1954, DHL, 1962; m. Alice Aaronson, June 9, 1953; c: Cindy, Karen, Tamar, Dena. Asso prof, Talmud, JTSA, since 1959; rabbi, Temple Sinai, Swampscott and Warkleed, 1955-57. US Army, 1943-46. Cdr, JWV Post 571, 1946-47. Author:

The Tractate Mourning, 1966; Today's Met Mitsvah, in Best Jewish Sermons, 1968. Home: 4695 Arlington Ave, New York, NY. Office: 3080 Broadway, New York, NY.

ZMORA, Israel, Isr, author, publisher; b. Russ, May 7, 1899; s. Ahron and Nehama (Wolfenson); in Isr since 1925; m. Ada Kremiansky, Dec 30, 1918; c: Zvi, Ohad. Author: R M Rilke; Abraham Shlonsky; Sifrut Al Phrashot Dorot, 3 vols; Shnei Mesaprim; Neviim Aharonim; U N Gnessin; trans from: Paul Valery, Marcel Proust; Tolstoy; Chekov; Gogol; Kleist; R M Rilke; ed: Moznaim 1958; Mahbarot leSifrut, 1940-45; lit ed, Kol Isr Radio, 1953-56. Mem: Heb Authors Assn; Inst for Trans of Heb Lit; fmr: delg, KH; secy, Tel Aviv Devl Co. Recipient: Phichman Award, 1967. Spec interests: children's books, bibliography. Home: 5 Gnessin St, Tel Aviv, Isr.

ZMORA, Ohad, Isr, journalist; b. Tel Aviv, July 23, 1933; s. Israel and Ada (Kremianski); att Heb U, Jerusalem, 1953-55; m. Zohara Poznanski, Sep 9, 1952; c: Eran, Shahar, Heali. Ed in chief, Dvar haShavua, since 1964. Ed: Mission Survival; The Victory; Days of Ben Gurion. Home: 7 Kaplan St, Tel Aviv, Isr. Office: 45 Sheinkin St, Tel Aviv, Isr.

ZOBER, Martin, US, business cons, educator; b. Pittsburgh, Pa, June 12, 1918; s. Morris and Fanny (Chasinoff); BA, U of Pittsburgh, 1940; ML, 1943, PhD, 1950; m. Edith Swartz, Dec 21, 1940; c: Norman, Janet. Bus cons since 1951; prof, marketing, Ia State U, since 1957; asst prof, Upper Ia U, 1947-51; asso prof, Drake U, 1951-57. US Army, 1943-45. Cons: Des Moines C of C; Park Fair Shopping Cen; Meredith Pub Co; Maytag Co; Thriftway; Northland Milk Co; expert witness for: Lab Dept; Boone Merchants; Prairie Queen Co; vice-pres, prog, Ia chap, Amer Marketing Assn, since 1953; mem: Beta Gamma Sigma; Alpha Kappa Psi. Author: Marketing Management, 1963; Principles of Marketing, 1969. Home: 615 Carr Drive, Ames, Ia. Office: 101 Industrial Arts Bldg, Ames, Ia.

ZOHAR, Haim, Isr, government exec; b. Sasow, Pol, Sep 15, 1925; s. Simha and Thila (Werfel) Lauterstein; in Isr since 1935; tchrs dipl, Tchrs Sem, 1942; MA, Heb U, 1950; m. Bella Boitman, Aug 2, 1953; c: Ron, Iris. Head, students auth, Min Immigrant Absorption, since 1968; corresp, Hatzofe, Yediot Aharonot, 1950-54; dir, Govt Press Off, Jerusalem, 1954-62; Counsel of Isr, NY, 1962-68. Signal Corps, IDF, 1948-49. Contbr to periodicals. Home: 2 Oliphant, Jerusalem, Isr. Office: 14 Hillel, Jerusalem, Isr.

ZOHARY, Michael, Isr, botanist, educator; b. Bobrka, Pol, Apr 9, 1898; s. Zeev and Rivka (Widrich) Schein; in Isr since 1920; att Heb Tchrs Sem, Jerusalem, 1922-25; DRerNat, Ger U, Prague, 1936; m. Leah Simirovska, Dec, 1925; c: Daniel, Erela Meiri. Prof, botany, Heb U, Jerusalem, since 1952, on staff since 1928. Mem: Botanical Soc, Isr; Brit Ecological Soc; Société Botanique de France; Intl Soc of Plant Morphologists; Intl Assn of Plant Taxonomists. Author: Introduction to the Geobotany of Palestine, 1948; Botany-A Textbook for Secondary Schools, 1935; The Flora of Iraq and Its Plantgeographical Affinities, 1950; Plant World-A Manual of Taxonomic Botany, 1954; Geobotany, 1955; Plant Life of Palestine-Israel and Jordan, 1962; co-author: The Plants of Palestine-Analytical Key, 1931, Analytical Flora of Palestine, 1948; Iconographia Florae Terrae Israelis, 1949, 1952, 1958; The Cultivated Plants of Israel, 1957; Flora Palestina in 4 parts, vol 1 and 2, 1967-69; contbr to profsl jours; botanical congresses: Atlas Isr; Geog Atlas; Heb Ency; Biblical Ency; mem, ed bd: Vegetatio, since 1948; Bull of Research Council of Isr, sect D, Botany, since 1955; Pal Jour of Botany, Jerusalem, series 1948-54. Recipient: Isr prize for natural scis, 1954; Weizmann prize for sci, 1956. Home: 18 Ben Maimon Blvd, Jerusalem, Isr. Office: Heb U, Jerusalem, Isr.

ZOHN, Baruch, Isr, engr; b. Lvov, Pol, Feb 6, 1913; s. Jonathan and Sara (Schtachel); in Isr since 1936; CE, U of Lvov, 1936; m. Lea Remen, Mar 13, 1938; c: Jonathan. Devl engr since 1956; project mgr, Water Planning for Isr, 1954-56; div engr, Rassco, Ltd, 1946-53; Engr corps, Brit Army, IDF, 1940-49. Mem: educ comm, Engrs Org; safety comm, Isr Petroleum Inst; Isr Assn Engrs and Architects; Soc of Petroleum Engrs, US. Hobbies: photography, bridge. Home: 20 Harimon St, Tel Aviv, Isr.

ZOLOTOW, Maurice, US, author; b. NYC, Nov 23, 1913; s. Harry and Paula (Edelstein); BA, U of Wis, 1936; m. Charlotte

Shapiro, Apr 14, 1938; c: Stephen, Ellen. Author: Never Whistle in a Dressing Room, 1944; The Great Balsamo, 1946; No People Like Show People, 1951; It Takes All Kinds, 1952; Oh Careless Love, 1959; Marilyn Monroe: a Biography, 1960; Stagestruck: The Romance of Alfred Lunt and Lynn Fontanne, 1965; co-author: A Gift of Laughter, 1966; ed staff, Billboard Mag, 1936-37; actors publicity agt, 1937-39; contbr articles and short stories to mags. Found, first pres, Soc of Mag Writers, 1948. Home and office: 310 E 44 St, New York, NY.

ZON, Yoel, Isr, agronomist, b. Kovno, Lith, Oct 22, 1908; s. Zeev and Miriam; in Isr since 1933; engr dipl, Nancy U, Fr, 1930; m. Haviva Shapira, 1933; c: Shulamit Troyherz, Rachel Cohen, Miriam. Bank mgr, Halvaa Ve'hisachon, Rehovot br, since 1968; surveyor, citrus groves mgr, 1933-40; mgr, Coop Credit Orgs, Rehovot, 1940-48; financial mgr, Volcani Agric Inst, Rehovot, 1948-54; reporter, Haaretz, Heb daily, 1940-50. Contbr to jours. Home: 62 Beeri St, Rehovot, Isr.

ZOREA, Meir, Isr, army off; b. Rum, 1923. Maj gen, chief N Command, IDF, 1959-62; mem, Kibbutz Maagan Michael; fmr: Haganah, mem perm staff, Zevulun dist; mem, J settlement police; J Brig, Brit Army; co, Haganah cdrs, course, 1947-48; battalion cdr, IDF, 1950-52; cdr, 9th Brigade, 1954-55; asst, head, opr br, Gen Hqrs,1956; 2nd in command, S front, Sinai Campaign, 1956; head training sect, gen hqrs; cdr, armored forces; head opr bd, GHO. Recipient: Mil Cross, Eng. Office: IDF, Isr.

ZSOLDOS, Jenö, Hung, author, educator; b. Budapest, Apr 2, 1896; s. Ferenc and Rósa (Blau) Stern; deg, U of Budapest, 1920. Prin, J Comty HS, Budapest, since 1939; org, J Girls Ind Elem Sch, upper level, 1939. Hung Army, WW I; forced lab, WW II. Author, in Hung: Hungarian Literature and Jewry, 1943; 1848-49 in the Life of Hungarian Jewry, 1948; Hungarian Grammar, 1953; Letters by John Vajda to I Milko, 1958; Letters by Mikorath, 1969; co-ed, Libanon, J learned periodical, 1936-43; contbr to learned jours. Mem: Hung Lang Assn; Natl J Tchrs Soc; Hung J Lit Soc; fmr: bd dirs, Hung J Mus Soc; vice-pres, Natl Folklore Soc; Hung sect, WJC. Home: Cházár András utca 8, Budapest, Hung.

ZUBIN, Joseph, US, psychologist; b. Raseinaii, Lith, Oct 9, 1900; s. Jacob and Rachel (Brody); in US since 1909; AB, Johns Hopkins U, 1921; PhD, Columbia U, 1932; m. Winifred Anderson, Oct 12, 1934; c: Winifred, Jonathan, David. Chief, psychiatric research, biometrics, NY State Dept Mental Hygiene, since1960, on staff since 1956; prof em, psych, spec lectr, psych, psycht, Columbia U, since 1970, on fac since 1939; adj prof, Queens Coll, since 1970; f, UAHC, 1929-32; asst, educ psych, Tchrs Coll, Columbia U, 1930-31; instr, psychometrics, Coll Phys and Surgs, 1931-32; instr, educ psych, CCNY, 1934-36; asst psychol, Mental Hosp Survey Comm, Natl Comm for Mental Hygiene, 1936-38; asso research psychol, NY State Psychiatric Inst and Hosp, 1938-56; visiting prof: U Wis, 1948; U Cal, LA, 1951; Hawaii, 1961; instr, postdoc inst, Div Clinical and Abnormal Psych, Amer Psych Assn, 1950, 1953, 1955, 1956, 1960, 1961, 1964, 1965, 1967. Lt cdr, USPHS, WW II. Mem: Amer Psych Assn; Amer Assn on Mental Deficiency; Amer Stat Assn; Amer Psychopath Assn, fmr pres; Amer Bd Examiners; Psychometric Soc; Harvey Soc; NY Acad Med; NY Acad Sci; Assn for Research in Nervous and Mental Diseases; Sigma Xi; Amer Genet Soc; study sect, psychopharm, NIMH, 1962-65; bd profsl affairs, Amer Psych Assn, 1967-70; pres, Amer Coll Neuropsychopharm, 1971. Co-author: Sorting Tests in Relation to Drug Therapy in Schizophrenia, 1947; Analysis of Handwriting, 1943; co-ed: Comparative Psychopathology; Animal and Human, 1967; Psychopathology of Mental Development, 1967; Social Psychiatry, 1968; The Psychopathology of Adolescence, 1970; asso ed: Jour of Applied Psych, 1942-48; Jour of Experimental Psych, 1947-50; Psychological Monographs, 1951-58; Jour of Personality, since 1948; Comprehensive Psycht, since 1963; Jour of Abnormal Psych, since 1965; Jour of Gen Psych, since 1964; Jour of Psych, since 1964; contbr to sci publs. Recipient: cert merit, Amer Psych Assn, 1968; dist service citation, for research, NY State Dept Mental Hygiene, 1968; Paul H Hoch Memorial Award, Amer Psychopathological Assn, 1968. Home: 190 Highwood Ave, Leonia, NJ. Office: 722 W 168 St, New York, NY.

ZUCKER, Henry L, US, social worker; b. Cleveland, O, Mar 11, 1910; s. Morris and Rose (Edelman); AB, Case W Reserve U, 1932; MSS, Sch Applied Social Sci, 1935; m. Harriet Weiner, Mar 30, 1941; c: John, Constance. Exec vice-pres, J Comty

Fed of Cleveland, on staff since 1946; dir, social surveys, New Orleans, LA, St Louis; cons, Overseas Comty Org and Fund Raising, JDC; secy, casework, children's councils, Wfr Fed of Cleveland, 1936-46. Chmn, Sch Applied Social Sci; bd overseers, Case W Reserve U; bd trustees, Baldwin Wallace Coll; bd dirs, Natl JWB; found, 1st treas, Amer Assn for Study of Comty Org, 1938; mem: Natl Assn Social Workers; Amer Acad Political and Social Sci. Home: 20699 University Blvd, Shaker Heights, O. Office: 1750 Euclid Ave, Cleveland, O.

ZUCKER, Jacques, US, artist; b. Radom, Pol, June 15, 1900; s. Isaac and Sarah (Handelsman); in US since 1922; att: Bezalel Art Sch, Jerusalem; art acads, Paris; m. Nina Wohlman, Feb 4, 1926; c: Inez, John. Artist, painter; numerous one-man shows in US and abroad; participant in group shows and mus exhbs; repr in: Paris Mus of Modern Art; Bezalel Mus, Jerusalem; Tel Aviv Mus; notable pvt collections world over. Gdud Haivri, Pal. Mem, Artists Equity. Contbr monographs, articles to press. Recipient: two Brit medals for valor, WW I. Home and studio: 44 W 77 St, New York, NY.

ZUCKER, John J, US, rabbi; b. Lossen, Ger, May 14, 1909; s. Bruno and Erna (Bernhardt); in US since 1939; PhD, U Berlin, Ger, 1936; ordained rabbi, Lehranstalt für die Wissenschaft des Judentums, Berlin, 1939; m. Lillian Straus, Aug 11, 1938; c: Miriam, David, Daniel. Rabbi: Temple Beth Sholom, San Leandro, Cal, since 1947; Heidelberg, Ger, 1938-39; asst rabbi, The Temple, Cleveland, O, 1939-42; rabbi, Temple Beth Or, Reno, Nev, 1942-46. Chmn: J Family Service, Oakland, Cal, 1952-53; Bay Council of Rabbis, 1956-64; Bd of Rabbis, N Cal, 1965-67; club, Rotary Intl. Author: Studien Zur Jüdischen Selbstverwaltung im Altertum, 1936. Home: 795 Cary Dr, San Leandro, Cal. Study: 642 Dolores Ave, San Leandro, Cal.

ZUCKER, Louis C, US, educator; b. Phila, Pa, Apr 10, 1895; s. Hyman and Helen (Friedenberg); MA, U of Pa, 1921; PhD, U of Wis, 1928; m. Ethel Kaplan, June 6, 1920; d: Anatole. Tchr, Judaics, U of Utah, since 1967, prof em, Eng, since 1963, fac mem since 1928; instr, U of Wis, 1920-28. Pres: Salt Lake dist, ZOA, since 1948; Folklore Soc of Utah, 1958-60; secy, Salt Lake chap, Amer Friends Heb U, since 1953; bd dirs: Salt Lake Civic Music Assn; Temple B'nai Isr; Friends of Public Libr; ACLU, Utah; mem: MLA; AAUP; Soc Bibl Lit and Exegesis. Co-author: A History of the Jews in Utah and Idaho; contbr: Ency Judaica; profsl jours. Hobbies: fine arts, mt hiking. Home: 1138 E 27 S, Salt Lake City, Utah. Office: U of Utah, Salt Lake City, Utah.

ZUCKER, Max, US, rabbi; b. NYC, June 12, 1898; s. Aaron and Bessie (Siegelshiffer); BA, NYU, 1919; MA, Columbia U, 1922; MHL, ordained rabbi, JTSA, 1925, DD, 1959; m. Lee Fischman, Aug 6, 1933; c: Samuel. Rabbi em, Temple Emanuel, Passaic, NJ, rabbi since 1925. Chaplain, US Army, 1943-46. Found, JCC, Passaic and vicinity, 1933; mem: NJ Bar; Neighborhood Comty Chest; NCCJ; Bd of Educ, Passaic, 1941-43. Author: The Philosophy of Zionism, 1919; Social and Political History of the Jews During the Time of the Talmud, 1922. Recipient: plaque as First Citizen of Passaic J Comty, 1947. Home: 1200 West Ave, Miami Beach, Fla.

ZUCKER, Moses, US, educator; b. Kopeczowka, Pol, Feb 26, 1902; s. Mordecai and Feiga (Frisher); in US since 1938; ordained rabbi, Theol Sem, Vienna; PhD, Dropsie Coll; m. Mania Kiperwasser, May 14, 1932. Prof, Talmud, Bibl Exegesis, JTSA, since 1947; fmr rabbi: Bangor, Me; Bklyn; Vienna. F, Amer Acad J Research. Author: Saadia Gaon's Translation of the Torah; Mubashirs Critique of Saadia Gaon; Scientific Edition of Saadia's Commentaries on the Pentateuch; contbr to periodicals. Spec interest: liturgical music. Home: 70 La Salle St, New York, NY. Office: 3080 Broadway, New York, NY.

ZUCKER, Paul, US, art historian, educator; b. Berlin, Ger, Aug 14, 1888; s. Julius and Anna (Samter); in US since 1937; att Inst of Tech, Berlin and Munich; PhD, U Berlin, 1913; m. Rose Walter, Sep 16, 1916 (decd). Lectr: New Sch for Social Research, since 1937; State Acad of Arts, Berlin, 1928-33; Lessing Hochschule, 1917-35; practicing architect, Berlin, 1920-37; adj prof, Cooper Union Art Sch, 1948-65; visiting lectr, 1969. Fmr pres: Amer Soc Aesthetics, NY chap; Soc Architectural Hist, NY chap; mem, Coll Art Assn Amer. Author: Space and Architecture in Paintings of the Florentine Quattrocento, 1913; The Bridge-Typology and History of its Artistic Form, 1921; Stage Setting at the Time of the Baroque, 1925; Stage Setting at the Time of Classicism, 1925; Theatres and Motion Picture Houses, 1926; Architecture in Italy at the Time of the Renaissance, in Handbuch der Kuntswissenschaft, 1927; The Development of the City, 1929; American Bridges and Dams, 1941; Styles in Painting, 1950, 2nd ed, 1962; Town and Square—From the Agora to the Village Green, 1959, 1966; Fascination of Decay, 1968; ed, New Architecture and City Planning, 1944. Recipient: 1st and 2nd prizes in architectural competitions, Berlin, 1913-33; Brunner Scholarship Award, Amer Inst Architects, 1953; Rossi Prize, 1969. Home: 227 E 57 St, New York, NY.

ZUCKERMAN, Arthur J, US, rabbi; b. Bklyn, NY, Dec 16, 1907; s. Charles and Mollie (Hittner); BA, CCNY, 1928; ordained rabbi, HUC, 1931; PhD, Columbia U, 1963; hon DD, HUC-JIR, 1957; m. Janet Crohn, Apr 28, 1968; c: Anne, Judith, Sharon. Dir, B'nai B'rith Hillel Found, CCNY, since 1945; fac mem, CCNY, since 1946; instr, J hist and rel, HUC Sch Educ and Sacred Music, since 1952; rabbi: Winston-Salem, 1936-38; Lansing, 1938-40; found, dir, Hillel Found, Seattle, 1940-45; visiting prof, J hist, Inst Intl d'Etudes Hébraiques, Paris, 1956. Pres, Natl Assn Hillel Dirs, 1955-57; chmn, NY chap, Rel Educ Assn, 1958-60; mem, CCAR. Author: A Vassal Jewish Principate in Carolingian France, 1970; contbr articles on Judaica and hist. Home: 375 Riverside Dr, New York, NY. Office: Hillel Found, CCNY, 475 W 140 St, New York, NY.

ZUCKERMAN, Herzl, Isr, business exec; b. Cape Town, S Afr, Nov 3, 1911; s. Moses and Rebecca (Glaser); in Isr since 1934; m. Judith Mosseri, 1937. Mgn dir, The Isr Bd of Executors and Trust Co, Ltd, since 1956; secy, jt mgr, Marine Trust, Tel Aviv Harbor, 1936-46; mgr, Anglo-Saxon dept, Fgn Trade Inst, 1947-48; dir, econ dept, info bur, JA for Isr, 1949-50; gen mgr, Rock Products Corp, 1951-54; took first Pal ind exhb to S Afr, 1947-48. Gen secy, Anglo-Isr C of C; exec dir, Assn of Bi-Natl C of C in Isr; fmr leader, S Afr Zionist Youth Movement. Recipient: OBE. Home: 9 Struck St, Tel Aviv, Isr. Office: 82 Allenby Rd, Tel Aviv, Isr.

ZUCKERMAN, Jacob, US, insurance agt; b. NYC, Nov 28, 1892; s. Eli and Sarah; m. Rebecca Wice, Sep 6, 1922; c: Ellis. Ret; fmr owner, J Zuckerman and Co, ins agcy, Petersburg, Va; asso with gen ins agcys in: Durham, NC; Norfolk; Newport News, both Va; Petersburg. Mem, exec bd, Robert E Lee Council, Boy Scouts of Amer, Richmond, Va, since 1941, fmr vice-pres; mem, Amer Cancer Soc, fmr pres, campaign chmn, Petersburg unit; fmr: 4th dist chmn, Amer Legion Oratorical Contest; chef de gare, Voiture 977; pres, campaign chmn, J Comty Fund, Petersburg; pres, B'nai B'rith; cdr, Amer Legion Post, Petersburg; first chmn, JWB; pres, Temple Rodof Sholom; mem, State of Va Finance Comm. Recipient: Green Silver Beaver award, Robert E Lee Council, Boy Scouts of Amer, 1957. Home: 1760 Fairfax St, Petersburg, Va. Office: 202 Union Trust Bldg, Petersburg, Va.

ZUCKERMAN, Leon, Switz, maufacturer; b. Moscow, June 24, 1891; s. Wolf and Esther (Reinin); in Switz since 1919; DJ, U of Warsaw, 1914; m. Cecile Reinin, Jan 26, 1926; c: Boris. Owner, Benedict Watch factory. Co-found: Zionist Soc, Yardenia, Warsaw; Assn Suisse-Israel, Neuchâtel; mem: exec, J comty, La Chaux-de-Fonds; exec, Fed Swiss Zionists; econ council, JA, Switz; Swiss comm, Weizmann Inst of Sci. Home: 83 rue Léopold Robert, La Chaux-de-Fonds, Switz. Office: 81 rue Léopold Robert, La Chaux-de-Fonds, Switz.

ZUCKERMAN, Narkis, Isr, executive engr; b. Izmir, Turkey, Feb 4, 1915; s. Benjamin and Rosa (Schahevits); in Isr since 1925; BSc, 1st class hons, ACGI, City and Guilds Imperial Coll, London, 1938; m. Dvora Fruchter, July 3, 1941; c: Nitsa Shelef, Elda. Chief engr, mem mgnt comm, Isr Elec Corp Ltd, since 1969, mgr, opr, 1964-68, mgr, power plants, 1960-64, Reading Power Plant sup, 1952-60. IDF, Res, 1948-64. Mem: Isr AEC; Inst of EE, London; Assn Engrs and Architects, Isr. Author: Eilat Desalination Plant, Operating Experience, 1968, 1969. Home: 5 Rachel St, Haifa, Isr. Office: POB 10, Haifa, Isr.

ZUCROW, Maurice J, US, mechanical engr, educator, jet propulsion expert; b. Kiev, Russ, Dec 5, 1899; s. Solomon and Dora (Smarskin); in US since 1914; BS, Harvard U, 1922, MS, 1923; PhD, Purdue U, 1928; m. Lillian Feinstein, Aug 1, 1925; c: Barbara Cohen. Cons engr since 1946; prof em, mech engr, Purdue U, since 1966, Atkins prof, engr, 1959-65, prof, gas turbines and jet propulsion, 1946-59, dir, Jet Propulsion Cen, 1948-65; fmr: vice-pres i/c engr, Paragon Vaporizer Corp, Chgo, 1929-34; partner, Hubbard Engr Co,

1937-40; vice-pres, gen mgr, Ring Balance Instrument Co, Chgo, 1940-41; research and devl engr, Elliott Co, Jeannette, Pa, 1941-42; tech asst to exec vice-pres, Aerojet Engr Corp, Azusa, Cal, 1942-46. Mem: comm on guided missiles, Research and Devl Bd, Natl Mil Establishment, chmn, panel on propulsion and fuels, 1947-52, tech cons group, 1951-53, cons, aeronautics panel, Off of Asst Secy of Defense for Research and Development, 1953-57; mem, Ordnance Sci Adv comm, US Army Dept, 1950-62; Natl Adv Comm on Aeronautics, subcomm on propulsion sys analyses, 1947-50, chmn, subcomm on rocket engines, 1950-53, 1953-58; adv comm on chem energy sys, NASA, 1960-62; mem, Sci and Engr comm, sect of automative engrs, 1959-62; mem, Research Adv comm, air breathing engines, since 1962; mem, Panel on Sci and Tech, Sci and Astronautics comm, US House of Reprs, since 1960; fmr: bd dirs, Amer Rocket Soc; mem, bd dirs, AIAA; mem: Missile Adv Group, AMICOM, Redstone Arsenal, since 1962. F: Amer Soc Mech Engrs; Amer Rocket Soc; Amer Inst Aeronautics and Astronautics; mem: Intl Acad Astronautics; Amer Soc Engr Educ; Amer Sigma Xi; Tau Beta Pi; Pi Tau Sigma; Gamma Alpha Rho; Sigma Alpha Mu. Author: Principles of Jet Propulsion and Gas Turbines, 1948; Aircraft and Missile Propulsion, 2 vols, 1958; co-author: Principles of Guided Missile Design, vol II; contbr to tech publs. Recipient: awards: US Army Dept, 1967; Pendray, Amer Rocket Soc, 1952; Vincent Bendix, Amer Soc Engr Educ, 1960. Home: 801 Arguello St, Santa Barbara, Cal.

ZUGER, Bernard, US, psychiatrist, educator; b. Ludmir, Russ, Sep 20, 1905; s. Mendel and Adele (Kubernik); in US since 1913; AB, Columbia Coll, 1927; MD, Coll Phys and Surgs, Columbia U, 1931; m. Miriam Troop, Jan 29, 1954; c: Abbie. Pvt psycht practice since 1947; asst clinical prof, neuropsycht, NYU Med Sch, since 1961; dir, children's psycht clinic, Greenwich Hosp, since 1951; asst att neuropsycht: Bellevue Hosp, since 1959; U Hosp, since 1962; att psycht, Bklyn J Chronic Diseases Hosp, since 1958; research in epidemiology, Yale U Sch of Med, 1933-34; res, ped, J Hosp of Bklyn, 1934-36, research in immunology, 1936-38; field epidemiologist, NYC Dept Health, 1938-42; pvt ped practice, Bklyn, 1938-42. Maj, USPHS, 1943-45. Dipl: Amer Bd Ped; Amer Bd Psycht and Neur; Amer Bd Child Psycht; mem: Amer Psycht Assn; Amer Psychosomatic Soc; Amer Orthopsycht Assn; Amer Acad Psychan; Amer Acad Ped; NY Ped Soc; Assn for Advancement of Psychan. Contbr to med jours. Home and office: 1148 Fifth Ave, New York, NY.

ZUKERKORN, James, US, business exec; b. Warsaw, Pol, Oct 12, 1898; s. Jacob and Marga (Olivenstein); in US since 1918; m. Sally Nalewansky, May 24, 1925; c: Jack, Herbert, Morton. Pres: Kapiolani Motors, Ltd, Pontiac distributor on Oahu, Hawaii, since 1938; Wahiawa Motors; Fed Transp Co. US Army Air Service, 1922-27; col, USAAC, 1941-45. State of Hawaii dir, Natl Automobile Dealers Assn; dir, Hawaii JWF, fmr pres; mem, Hawaii State Highway Safety Council; pres, Temple Emanu-El, Honolulu; mem: bd trustees, UAHC, exec comm, N Cal region; bd govs, Camp Saratoga Union Inst; chmn, bd trustees, James and Sally Zukerkorn Found; chmn, adv council, Hawaii, Pacific region, natl JWB, armed forces div; sub-comm on transp, State of Hawaii, Gov Emergency Ind Comm, since 1962; sponsored first Motor Vehicle Dealers licensing law, Territory of Hawaii, 1935; Honolulu C of C; Air Force Assn, US; Res Offs Assn, US; Masons; Shriners; clubs: Propeller, US; Outrigger Canoe, Honolulu. Recipient: Bronze Star. Home: 1314 Kapiolani Blvd, Honolulu, Hawaii.

ZUKERMAN, Jacob T, US, jurist, social work exec, attorney; b. Bklyn, May 31, 1907; s. Joseph and Lena (Shapiro); BS, NYU, 1928, LLB, 1929; att: NY Sch of Social Work, Columbia U, 1938-39; NYU Grad Sch for Training and Public Service, 1941-42; Acad of Cert Social Workers, 1961; m. Sadie Garber, Sep 11, 1928; c: Karl. Judge, Family Court, State of NY, since 1965; exec dir, Emergency Wfr div, NYC, 1942-44; asst to commn, Wfr dept, NYC, 1944-46; exec dir, chief counsel Family Location Service, 1948-65, asst dir, 1946-48. Fmr: natl pres, Workmens Circle, 1954-58, 1962-66; co-chmn, Natl Conf Lawyers and Social Workers, 1962-66; chmn: Social Policy and Action Comm; Natl Assn Social Workers, NYC, 1959-61; family law sect, Amer Bar Assn, 1967-68, council mem since 1961; pres, Natl Conf J Communal Service, 1963-64, exec since 1959; 1st vice-pres: J Lab comm; Domestic Relations comm, NY Co Lawyers Assn, since 1958; pres, Forward Assn since 1969; secy, Citizens Comm for Domestic Relations Court, NYC, 1960-66; mem, bd dirs: United HIAS Service; Amer ORT Fed; YIVO Inst for J Research; Natl Comty Relations Adv Council; J Daily Forward; Seward

Park Housing Corp; bd, J Family Service; Natl Found for J Culture; FJP, NY, fmr chmn, social service div; mem: ADA; People's Educ Soc; Worker's Defense League; Natl Assn Social Workers; Acad Cert Social Workers. Author: The Problem of Family Desertion, 1949; Sociol-Legal Approach to Family Desertion, 1950; Woman in Chains—The Agunah, 1951; The Social Workers Role in Non-Support Cases, 1955; Role of Public Agency with the Deserted Family, 1957; Role of Lawyer in Family Court, 1964; Family Court, Solution for Families in Distress? 1967; contbr to profsl jours. Recipient: Mayor's scholarship, 1941; citation, B'nai B'rith, 1955. Home: 815 Ave J, Brooklyn, NY. Office: 283 Adams St, Brooklyn, NY.

ZUMOFF, Barnett, US, physician, medical researcher; b. Bklyn, NY, June 1, 1926; s. Abraham and Stella (Zumoff); AB, Columbia U, 1945; MD, LI Coll of Med, 1949; m. Selma Silver, Nov 11, 1951; c: Janine, Francine, Linda. Att phys, asst chief, dept oncology, asst dir, Cinical Research Cen, Montefiore Hosp, all since 1961; asst prof, med, Albert Einstein Coll of Med, since 1965; clinical instr, SUNY Coll of Med, 1957-62; instr, med, Cornell U Coll of Med, 1958-62; asst, sect clinical biophysics, Sloan-Kettering Inst for Cancer Research, 1957-60, asso, 1960-61. USAF, 1951-53, col, USAF Res. Chmn, sch bd, Midwood I L Peretz J Sch, Workman's Circle, since 1960; mem: Endocrine Soc; AAAS; Amer Fed Clinical Research; Aerospace Med Assn; Assn Mil Surgs; Amer Physiological Soc; Council on Arteriosclerosis, AHA; Soc USAF Flight Surgs; med policy council, Air Force Assn, since 1965; Res Off Assn, natl surg, 1964-65. Contbr to profsl jours. Recipient: Natl Defense medal; Armed Forces Res medal. Home: 3710 Bedford Ave, Brooklyn, NY. Office: Montefiore Hosp, Bronx, NY.

ZUNSER, Charles, US, attorney, social worker; b. Minsk, Russ, June 17,1881; s. Eliakum and Fanny (Katzewich); in US since 1890; att NYU Law Sch, 1905; m. Miriam Shomer, Dec, 26, 1905; c: Helen Wortis, Shomer, Florence Saltz; m. 2nd, Rosalind London, Mar 31, 1954. Ret; fmr: secy, Comm for Deserted Women and Children, 1904-06; pvt law practice, 1907-12; chief counsel, Natl Desertion Bur, 1911-48. Pres, Natl Conf of J Communal Services, 1950-51; secy, Family Location Service, NY, since 1948; mem, exec comm, YIVO, since 1955; chmn: comm on domestic relations courts, Wfr Council of NY, 1931-34; comm, Central J Archives,1946-54; dir, comm on War Orphans, 1920; Mem: Amer Assn Social Workers; Amer Acad Social and Political Sci; Natl Conf J Social Wfr; club, J, pres, 1950-52. Contbr to profsl publs. Home: 155 W 68 St, New York, NY.

ZURR, Zwi, Isr, chemical engr; b. Pol, May 5, 1919; s. Zeev and Anna (Zucerberg); in Isr since 1937; MSc, Heb U, Jerusalem, 1943, postgrad studies, 1944; m. Miriam Gurevitz, 1940; c: Daniel, Zeev, Ofra. Gen mgr, Makheshim Chem Works Ltd, Beersheva, since 1952; chem, produc mgr, Agan Mfrs, 1944-52. Lt, IDF, 1948-50. Mem directorate, Negev U, Beersheva; club, Desert Inn, Beersheva. Home: 21 Hakotel Hamaaravi: St, Beersheva, Isr. Office: Ind Zone, Beersheva, Isr.

ZUSSMAN, Lesser, US, organization exec; b. Rochester, NY, May 1, 1908; s. Simon and Yetta (Sarachan); BS, U of Pa, 1931, MSW, Sch of Social Work, 1939; att Heb U, Jerusalem, 1933-34; m. Beatrice Barris, Dec 24, 1931. Exec dir, J Publ Soc of Amer, since 1950; social case worker, 1934-38; case work and child wfr sup, Pa and Md, 1939-42; admn secy, Phila Allied J Appeal, 1946-50. US Army, 1942-46, res off, 1946-62. Mem: bd dirs, Phila Amer Friends Heb U, 1952; bd govs, Har Zion Syn Cen, Phila, 1953; Amer Assn Social Workers; Ret Offs Assn; B'nai B'rith. Recipient: Army Commendation Medal, 1946. Home: 50 Belmont Ave, Bala Cynwyd, Pa. Office: 222 N 15 St, Philadelphia, Pa.

ZWEIG, Joseph P, Can, educator; b. Montreal, Can, July 12, 1914; s. Samuel and Anna (Goldberg); BCom, Sir George Williams Coll, 1944, BSc, 1944; MA, McGill U, 1952; PhD, Columbia U, 1964. Asso prof, psych, Sir George Williams U, Montreal, since 1960, secy, social scis div, 1961-63, mem fac since 1949; research cons, Cen for Hum Relations and Comty Studies,since 1965; insp, Dept of Trade and Commerce, Govt of Can, 1940-42; sr research asst, NRC, 1942-46; lectr, McGill U, 1946-47; prin, secular dept, Rabb Coll of Can, 1950-62; spec lectr, McGill Sch of Social Work, 1962-64.

Mem: Intl Assn Applied Psych; Amer Psych Assn; Can Psych Assn; Inter-Amer Soc Psych; Corp Psychs, Province of Que; Can Assn U Tchrs. Home: 7944 Querbes Ave, Montreal, Can. Office: 1435 Drummond St, Montreal, Can.

ZWEIG, Felix, US, educator; b. Fort Wayne, Ind, Sep 25, 1916; s. Samuel and Celia (Schwartz); BE, Yale Sch of Engr, 1938, PhD, 1941; m. Jeanne Travers, Dec 23, 1945; c: Jonathan, Richard, David. Prof, engr and applied sci, Yale Sch of Engr, since 1966, chmn dept, prof elec engr, 1955-61, dean, 1961-66; research asso, MIT, 1946; engr specialist, N Amer Aviation, 1961; Mem: sch bd, Hamden, Conn; bd dirs, New Haven Coll; Inst Radio Engrs; Amer Inst Elec Engrs; Amer Soc Elec Engrs. Contbr to tech jours. Recipient: Yale Engr Assn Award. Home: 75 Hall St, Hamden, Conn. Office: 214 Dunham Lab, Yale Sta, New Haven, Conn.

ZWEIG, Max, Isr, author; b. Prossnitz, June 22, 1892; s. Gustav and Helene (Rottberger); in Isr since 1938; att: U of Vienna, 1910-14; U of Prague, 1919-20; m. Margarete Bauer, Mar 16, 1932. Author: Ragen, 1925; Die Marranen, 1938; Saul, Heb, 1951; Dramen, 1961, Dramen II, 1963. Plays performed in: Isr; Paris; Ger; Finland; Austr; Arg. Mem, PEN-Zentrum Deutschsprachiger Autoren im Ausland. Recipient: 2nd prize, intl drama competition, Bregenz, Aus, 1957. Home: 90 Achad Haam St, Tel Aviv, Isr.

ZWERDLING, Osias, US, business exec, communal leader; b. Brody, Aus, Oct 27, 1878; s. Moses and Leah (Richter); in US since 1901; m. Hannah Kaufman, Dec 25, 1907 (decd); c: Morris, Joseph, Abraham. Ret since 1943; owner, Zwerdling's Fur Shop, 1904-1943. Chmn: United Fund; USO; UJA; pres: Jones Sch, PTA; Mich Syn Council, 1941-46; em, Mich B'nai B'rith Hillel Found; Beth Isr Cong; treas, Family Service Agcy, 1921-38; mem, bd: Ann Arbor Fed Savings and Loan Bank, since 1921; mem: YM-YWCA; Boy Scouts of Amer; Kiwanis; Masons; NCCJ; chaplain, B'nai B'rith. Recipient: Jr C of C Hum Relations Award, 1956; Sr Citizen Award, 1967. Home: 1056 Baldwin St, Ann Arbor, Mich.

ZWERGBAUM, Aaron, Isr, attorney, organization exec; b. Brno, Czech, Oct 8, 1913; s. William and Gertrud (Feitler); in Isr since 1945; LLD, U of Brno,1937; admitted to Isr bar,1954; m. Regina Kroj, Sep 4, 1942; c: Naphtali Regev, Leah. Legal adv, WZO, since 1964, dir, Cen Eur Desk, org dept, secy, comm for vet Zionist leaders, since 1945, fmr dir, Shekel dept. Sgt, Czech Army, 1937-39; IDF, 1948-60. Chmn, Histadrut Olei Czech; fmr: secy, Zionist Assn, Mauritius; vice-chmn, Maccabi, Brno; chmn, Assn of Zionist Students, Brno. Author: Exile in Mauritius, 1960; contbr to Zionist publs, encys. Spec interests: J and Zionist hist, langs. Home: 58 Tchernichovsky St, Jerusalem, Isr. Office: POB 92, Jerusalem, Isr.

ZWERLING, Israel, US, psychiatrist, educator; b. NYC, June 12, 1917; s. Maz ans Ann (Greidinger); BS, CCNY, 1937, MS, 1938; PhD, Columbia U, 1947; MD, SUNY, Downstate Med Cen Coll of Med, 1950; cert in pysychoanalytic med, Coll of Phys and Surgs, 1960; m. Florence Erdtrachter, 1940; c: Matthew, Sara. Dir, Bx State Hosp; prof, psycht, Albert Einstein Coll of Med, both since 1955, dir, div social and comty psycht, since 1959; instr: biol, gen sci, Roosevelt HS, 1939-42; dept psych, City and Hunter Colls, 1947-50; dir, State U Alcohol Clinic, Downtown Med Cen, 1954-56. Maj, USAAC, W W II. Dipl, Amer Bd Neur and Psycht; mem: Amer Psych Assn; Amer Psycht Assn; AMA; Amer Psychosomatic Soc; Amer Psychoanalytic Assn; Sigma Xi; Alpa Omega Alpha. Contbr, chaps in: Amer Handbook of Psycht, 1959; Current Psycht Therapies, 1962; articles to psycht, psych jours. Recipient: Bronze Star, 1946; Stecker award, Inst of Pa Hosp, 1965. Home: 1500 Waters Pl, Bronx, NY. Office: Albert Einstein Coll of Med, New York, NY.

ZWIBAK, Jacques, US, author, editor; b. Feodosia, Russ, Aug 14, 1902; s. Moses and Sophie (Rubin); in US since 1942; att Sch of Political Sci, Paris, 1923-26; m. Eugenie Lipovsky, May 14, 1932. Mgn ed, Novoye Russkoye Slovo, since 1967, city ed, 1942-67; parl corresp, Dernieres Nouvelles, Paris, 1924-40. Author: This Land of Israel, 1968; Jerusalem, Joyful Name, in Russ, 1969; short stories, essays, books on hist and travel; contbr to jours. Chmn, Amer and Eur Friends of ORT; bd dirs, exec comm, Amer ORT Fed; vice-pres, Lit Found for Russ Writers Abroad; club, PEN, Writers in Exile chap. Recipient: Man of Year, Amer ORT Fed, 1968.

Home: 114 W 70 St, New York, NY. Office: 243 W 56 St, New York, NY.

ZWICK, Abraham, Isr, engineer; b. Vienna, Aus, Dec 25, 1919; s. Israel and Sarah (Weizenblum); in Isr since 1938; att Technion, Haifa, 1939-43; U of Pa, Phila, 1960; m. Judith Halevy, May 17, 1949; c: Hanan, Rami, Uri. Gen mgr, Isr RR, since 1964; civil engr, Haifa Munic, 1943-46; planning engr, Nesher Cement Factory, 1946-56. Maj, Engr Corps, IDF, 1948-49. Mem: Engrs and Architects Assn, Isr; club, Rotary, Haifa. Home: 2 Haoranim St, Kiryat Tivon, Isr. Office: Isr RR, Plumer Sq, Haifa, Isr.

ZWICK, Leon, US, merchant; b. Herrin, Ill, Apr 27, 1905; s. Morris and Lizzie (Landau); BS, Wash U, 1925; m. Lillie Hart, June 11, 1933; c: Jack, Burton, Malcolm, Marilyn. Mgr, Zwick Store, since 1967; partner, gen mgr, M P Zwick and Sons, 1929-67; bd dirs, Bank of Herrin, since 1935. Chmn, OPA Ration Bd, 1941-43; pres: Merchants Assn, 1939-69; Herrin C of C, 1960-61; B'nai B'rith lodge, 1936; vice-pres, S Ill chap, JWB, 1952; exec bd, S Ill chap, Boy Scouts Council, since 1952; mem: Elks; Eagles; Sigma Alpha Mu; club, Herrin Rotary, pres, 1933. Home: 512 S 16 St, Herrin, Ill. Office: 120 North Park, Herrin, Ill.

ZYCHLINSKA, Rajzel, US, poet; b. Gombin, Pol, July 27, 1910; d. Mordecai and Deborah (Appel); m. Izaak Kanter, 1941; c: Mark. Author: Lieder, 1936; Der Regen Zingt, 1939; Zu Loitere Bregen, 1948; Shvaygendike Teern, 1962; Autumn Squares. Club, Yiddish PEN. Recipient: Pioneer Women Award, 1963. Home: 235 W 102 St, New York, NY. Office: POB 331, Cathedral Station, 215 W 104 St, New York, NY.